COLLINS COBUILD

COLLINS Birmingham University International Language Database

Essential
English
Dictionary

**COLLINS
PUBLISHERS**

**THE UNIVERSITY
OF BIRMINGHAM**

**Collins
London and Glasgow**

Collins ELT
8 Grafton Street
London W1X 3LA

COBUILD is a trademark of William Collins Sons & Co Ltd

© William Collins Sons & Co Ltd 1988
First published 1988

Reprinted 1988, 1989

10 9 8 7 6 5 4 3

ISBN 0 00 370261 8 Paperback
ISBN 0 00 375022 1 Cased

Computer typeset by C R Barber & Partners
Wrotham, England.

Printed and bound in Great Britain by
William Collins Sons & Co Ltd, Glasgow

輸入　日本総代理店
株式会社　秀文インターーナショナル
東京都豊島区駒込 4 −12− 7
◆原著作権者の書面による許諾なく，無断引用，転載，複製などは禁じます．

Contents

EDITORIAL TEAM

EDITOR IN CHIEF
John Sinclair

MANAGING EDITOR
Patrick Hanks

EDITOR
Gwyneth Fox

SENIOR COMPILERS
Sheila Dignen
Ramesh Krishnamurthy

EXTRA COLUMN
Stephen Bullon
Rosamund Moon

COMPILERS
Deborah Kirby
Helen Liebeck
Elizabeth Manning
John Todd

COMPUTER OFFICER
Tim Lane

PRONUNCIATION REVISION
Martin Hewings
Tim Lane

CLERICAL STAFF
Sue Smith
Debbie Morris

COLLINS PUBLISHERS
Annette Capel
Lorna Heaslip
Douglas Williamson

Illustrated by **Jerry Collins**

We would also like to thank all the people who worked on the *Collins COBUILD English Language Dictionary*, whose original work provided the impetus for this book.

Preface

Collins COBUILD Essential English Dictionary is the second *COBUILD* dictionary. The first one, *Collins COBUILD English Language Dictionary,* was published in 1987 and offers learners a great deal of new information which they can use to help them learn the language. However, it was clear from the start that a smaller dictionary was also needed for everyday use. The *Essential* is that dictionary.

The *Essential* keeps all the main features of the original *COBUILD* dictionary, but it concentrates them into a smaller space. Also, we have added some new features that are designed to make the dictionary both more useful and more enjoyable to use.

The most important feature about *COBUILD* is that it is a completely new description of the English of today. The information in the entries comes from a study of about twenty million words of text. It is reliable and up-to-date, and has been made possible by using the latest computer techniques.

Because of this method of work, the examples given in the dictionary are from actual texts, and show the word or phrase as it has been used in these texts. The examples are not meant to show just the meaning of the word. The explanation does that. The examples are there to show you how to use it.

COBUILD is already famous for the way in which it sets out the explanations. They are in sentences, and the actual way they are written can help you use the words.

Here is the entry for **inside**:

inside /ɪnsaɪd/, **insides.** 1 Something or someone that is **inside** a place, container, or object is surrounded by its sides. EG *Two minutes later we were inside the taxi... You left your lighter inside... It is a fruit with a seed inside.* ▸ used as an adjective. EG *The door had no inside bolt.* `PREP OR ADV` `▸ADJ CLASSIF: ATTRIB`
2 The **inside** of something is the part or area that its sides surround or contain. EG *The inside of my mouth was dry... ...the inside of the castle.* `N COUNT`
3 You can also say that someone is **inside** when they are in prison. `ADV Informal`
4 On a wide road, the **inside** lanes are the ones which are closest to the edge of the road. `ADJ CLASSIF: ATTRIB`
5 **Inside** information is obtained from someone who is involved in a situation and therefore knows a lot about it. `ADJ CLASSIF: ATTRIB`
6 If you are **inside** an organization, you belong to it. EG *Nobody inside the company will be surprised.* `PREP`
7 If you say that someone has a feeling **inside** them, you mean that they have not expressed this feeling. EG *His true feelings keep surging up inside him... I always felt inside that I wanted to write.* `PREP OR ADV`
8 If something such as a piece of clothing is **inside out,** the inside part has been turned so that it faces outwards. `PHRASE`
9 Your **insides** are your internal organs, especially your stomach. EG *What we all need is a bit of food in our insides.* `N PLURAL: USU+POSS Informal`

Notice that paragraph 1 starts 'Something or someone . . . ', while paragraph 2 has only 'something' and paragraph 3 has only 'someone'. This means that the kind of meaning in paragraph 2 applies to things, and not to people; and in paragraph 3 people, not things, are sent to prison.

In paragraph 4, this meaning of **inside** applies only to traffic lanes on a main road. Paragraph 5 is about a kind of information, and so on. As you can see, you can learn a lot by reading the explanations carefully.

A special feature of *COBUILD* is the extra column of information about the grammar and usage. There is a lot of very useful information in this column, and it is worthwhile making sure you understand the simple terms that are used: v = verb, ADJ = adjective, and so on. If you are not sure of any of the words or abbreviations in the Extra Column, you can look them up in their alphabetical place in the dictionary. So you will find ATTRIB on page 45 and ADJ PRED on page 12. Each one is in a box to make it easier to find. A list of everything used in the Extra Column is given on page vii.

You will also find helpful labels such as *Informal* and *American* in the Extra Column. These give you more information about the word and tell you when you can use it.

The Extra Column can also help you to find the meaning you want in a long entry. For example if you read 'The doctors had worked without a break', and you do not know the meaning of **break,** you can at least tell that it is a noun. So you can run your finger down the **break** entry, past the verbs until you find the nouns, starting at the end of paragraph 6, with the meaning you want in paragraph 10. You thus only need to read the noun meanings.

All the headwords are written in a phonetic transcription which shows you how to pronounce a word. A key to the symbols is given on page ix – they are all symbols of the International Phonetics Association. We have added some information on what happens to a word in connected speech, because many words can vary in pronunciation. This information is in tiny numbers above vowel letters, and you can ignore it if you want to say just one word out loud.

These are all features of the original dictionary. The *Essential* has some new features, which we hope will make the dictionary easier and more interesting to use. For example, the illustrations have been specially drawn for this book, to help where an object is not easy to describe, but is easy to recognize.

The grammar notes have been written specially for use by students. In addition to the short explanations, we have taken a whole page for each of seventeen major points of grammar. The list is on page viii, and the page-long entries are as near as possible to their alphabetical places. In these entries we have gathered together a lot of information and examples about the main categories of English grammar.

We have also added over 400 language activities, called *Checkpoints.* You will find one at the bottom of the right-hand column on each left-hand page. They are puzzles or points for discussion, and all the information you need is somewhere on the two pages that will be open around the *Checkpoint.* A key to these activities is given on pages 945-948.

These activities can be used to make you think a bit about words and to extend your vocabulary range. They can also be used during a class lesson, and should help to make the dictionary a regular tool for language learning. I hope that you, the user, will enjoy these activities. They won't interfere with using the dictionary in the normal way, but they should add some interest to your learning of English.

On pages 938-944 we have included a list of the words that we have found useful in explaining the meanings and uses of English. Teachers may also find this list useful as the basis of a syllabus, to develop students' dictionary skills. The language we have used has been kept as simple as possible but we have avoided the restrictions and awkwardness of a fixed defining vocabulary. In this book only about 2000 words have been used ten times or more, and there are only a total of 3000 different forms in the Wordlist.

These new features are part of *COBUILD's* general policy of trying out new ways to present information about the English Language. I would be glad to hear what things you find easy or difficult, useful or useless. I have had a lot of valuable criticism from users of the first *COBUILD* dictionary, and some of the points made have already been used to improve this new one.

John Sinclair
Editor in Chief

A Guide to the Use of the Dictionary

1 Finding words

1.1 Main entries

The order of entries is alphabetical, with no notice being taken of capital letters, hyphens, or spaces between words. So the order of words in a small section of 'B' is:

backbiting
backbone
back-breaking
backdate
backdoor
backer
backfire
backgammon
background

1.2 Phrasal verbs

Phrasal verbs are put in paragraphs immediately after the simple verb. So you will find **close down** and **close in** at the end of the entry for **close** and before the entry for **close-cropped,** so that the dictionary headword list reads:

close
   close down
   close in
closed

1.3 Phrases

Phrases are fixed combinations of words which have their own special meanings, so that you cannot normally guess the meaning from the individual words.

Phrases are printed in bold type in the entry for the most important word in the phrase. When the phrase is close in meaning to another meaning of the word, the phrase will be found in the same paragraph as that meaning, but will be introduced by a •. For example:

If a part of your body is **bare**, it is not covered by any clothing. • If someone does something **with** their **bare hands**, they do it without using any weapons or tools.

Other phrases are put in separate paragraphs or sometimes a number of phrases are put in one paragraph. For example:

12 **Back** is also used in these phrases. 12.1 If you PHRASES are wearing something **back to front**, you are wearing it incorrectly, with the back of it on the front of your body. 12.2 If you do something **behind** someone's **back**, you do it without them knowing about it.

1.4 Cross-references

If you cannot find the explanation of a phrase, expression, or compound at the word you have looked up, you will often find a note telling you which entry has the explanation. For example, at the entry for **bag**, **bag 6** reads:

6 a **bag of bones**: see **bone**.

Similarly, **face 9.14** reads:

9.14 at **face value**: see **value**.

At the end of **cover up 2** you will find:

● See also **cover-up**.

1.5 Words which are defined together

The dictionary tells you how to use all the important members of a word family, such as adjectives, adverbs, and nouns. Where the meaning of the words is similar, the meaning is only given for the headword. The other words in the family are printed at the end of a paragraph dealing with that meaning. Each word of this kind is introduced by a ◊, to show that you have a word with a new word class but with very little change of meaning.

The different endings that can be added to form the new words are all explained in alphabetical order in the text of the dictionary. So there are entries for **-ly, -ness, -ation,** and so on.

Even though these words are not defined separately, they always have grammatical information in the Extra Column and an example in the main text to show how they have been used.

eager /íːgə/. If you are **eager** to do something, you ADJ QUALIT: want to do it very much. EG *The majority were* OFT+to-INF OR *eager to express their opinions... ...people eager for* for *a quick cure.* ◊ **eagerly**. EG *They began to talk* ◊ ADV *eagerly.* ◊ **eagerness**. EG *...my eagerness to learn...* ◊ N UNCOUNT *...an eagerness for total freedom.*

Words which belong to the same family but which have differences in meaning are treated as separate headwords and will be found in their correct alphabetical place. So there are different entries for words such as **hopeful** and **hopefully,** and **sure** and **surely.**

There is sometimes very little difference in meaning between words with different grammatical functions. When this is the case, one word is defined, and the other is treated in the same paragraph, preceded by a ►. For example:

When you **amble,** you walk slowly and in a relaxed V :USU+A manner. EG *I ambled home through the village.* ► *used as a noun.* EG *He slowed down to his usual* ► N SING *steady amble.*

2 Forms and spelling

The spelling for each form of word is given in bold letters at the beginning of an entry. For example:

earthquake /ɜ́ːθkweɪk/, **earthquakes**.

echo /ɛ́kəʊ/, **echoes, echoing, echoed**.

easy /iːzi¹/, **easier, easiest**.

light /laɪt/, **lights, lighting, lighted, lit** /lɪt/; **lighter, lightest**.

If there is anything unusual about the use of the forms, this is explained in a note immediately after they are given. for example:

burst /bɜːst/, **bursts, bursting**. The form **burst** is used in the present tense and is the past tense and past participle of the verb.

If the word is spelled differently in American English, this is explained in a note immediately after the forms, for example:

fuel /fjʊəl/, **fuels, fuelling, fuelled**; also spelled **fueling, fueled** in American English.

3 Pronunciation

The pronunciation is normally given after the first form of the word. For example:

key /kiː/, **keys**.

But if the word is pronounced in different ways, this is explained after all the forms. For example:

bow, bows, bowing, bowed; pronounced /baʊ/ for paragraphs 1 to 4 and for the phrasal verbs, and /bəʊ/ for paragraphs 5, 6 and 7.

When the pronunciation of one of the forms is very different from the first form given, then its pronunciation is also given immediately after it. For example:

give /ɡɪv/, **gives, giving, gave** /ɡeɪv/, **given**.

For further information about pronunciation and a key to symbols used see pages viii-ix.

4 Explanations

Words are explained in simple English, easy to understand, and with a lot of information about their uses. If you read the explanations carefully, you should be able to use the word yourself in good, natural English.

5 Examples

The dictionary contains a large number of examples, showing how the words have been used by English writers and speakers. The examples have been chosen to show the most typical grammatical patterns in which the words are used, and also to show the situations in which you are most likely to find each word used. Examples are printed in italic type after the explanation of meaning. For example:

When you **leave** a place, you go away from it. EG *They left the house to go for a walk after tea.*

6 Grammar

All the words that are explained in the dictionary have grammatical information given about them in the Extra Column. Explanations of the labels used in the Extra Column are in the main dictionary text, in alphabetical order but inside a box, to show that we are talking about the language used in the dictionary. For example:

> **COMPAR** stands for **comparative**
> Adjectives which have the label COMPAR in the Extra Column are in the comparative form. A few adverbs are also labelled COMPAR.
> See the entry headed ADJECTIVES for more information.

Here is a list of the grammatical labels used in the Extra Column, all of which have special entries in the dictionary text:

A	MODAL	PRON REL
ADJ	N	QUANTIF
ADJ AFTER N	N COLL	QUOTE
ADJ CLASSIF	N COUNT	RECIP
ADJ COLOUR	N ING	REPORT
ADJ PRED	N MASS	SUBMOD
ADJ QUALIT	N MOD	SUFFIX
ADV	N PART	SUPERL
ADV SEN	N PLURAL	SUPP
ADV AFTER VB	N PROPER	USU
ADV BRD NEG	N SING	V
ATTRIB	N UNCOUNT	V+A
AUX	NEG	V+C
BROAD NEG	NUMBER	V+O
C	O	V+O+A
COMPAR	ORDINAL	V+O+C
CONJ	POSS	V+O+O
CONT	PREDET	V−ERG
DET	PREFIX	V−PASS
DET POSS	PREP	V−REFL
EXCLAM	PRON	V−SPEECH
IMPER	PRON INDEF	VB
INF	PRON POSS	VOCATIVE
-ING	PRON REFL	WH

The following punctuation marks are used in the Extra Column.

, A comma comes between basic word classes if more than two are mentioned – for example V+O, V+O+O, or V+O+A. Commas also come between pieces of extra information that follow a basic word class. For example, ADJ PRED+*to*-INF, REPORT, OR *for*.

: A colon comes after a basic word class and introduces extra information about the way the word works. For example, ADJ CLASSIF: ATTRIB.

/ Sometimes, the Extra Column tells you what preposition is likely to come after a particular verb, adjective, or noun. If more than one preposition is likely, they are separated by a slash. For example, V+*for/of*.

+ A plus sign introduces information about whether a verb has an object (V+O), a complement (V+C), a quote structure (V+QUOTE), and so on. Plus signs are also used with other word classes to introduce the sort of words or structures that typically occur with the word being explained. For example, N COUNT+POSS.

7 Style and Usage

In addition to the grammar codes, the Extra Column also has information about how and when you should use a word. It tells you, for example, whether a word is formal or informal, whether it is British or American, or whether it is used mainly in technical or literary writing. For example:

ignominious /ɪgnə⁶mɪniəs/. **Ignominious** behaviour is considered shameful or morally unacceptable.   ADJ QUALIT / Formal

inferno /ɪnfɜːnəʊ/, **infernos**. You can refer to a very large, dangerous fire as an **inferno**.   N COUNT / Literary

The explanations for many words tell you the situations in which you would be likely to use the word or hear it used. So, if a word is used mainly by someone who is angry or worried or frightened, then the explanation says so. For example, in the entry for **help**, you find:

10 You shout **'Help!'** when you are in danger, in order to attract someone's attention.

There is a lot of information of this kind in the explanations in this dictionary. It is there in order to help you to use the right language for each particular situation.

8 Study Pages

As well as having grammar explanations in the main dictionary text, more detailed information is given on Study Pages, where the main grammatical categories, such as adjectives, phrasal verbs, and pronouns, are dealt with. Here is a list of the topics covered in the Study Pages:

ADJECTIVES	NUMBER
ADJUNCTS	PHRASAL VERBS
ADVERBS	PHRASES
COMPLEMENTS	PRONOUNS
CONJUNCTIONS	QUANTIFIERS
CONVENTIONS	SEMI-MODALS
DETERMINERS	SUBMODIFIERS
MODAL VERBS	VERBS
NOUNS	

The verbs BE and HAVE are also explained on full pages, rather than in the main text.

There are also special entries for AGE, DATE, MEASUREMENT, MONEY, and TIME, where examples are given of the different ways in which these can be expressed.

Pronunciation

In this dictionary a guide is given to the pronunciation of English words using the International Phonetic Alphabet. The accent represented is Received Pronunciation, or RP for short, which is an accent used by many speakers of Southern British English. There are several other accents of English, but RP is perhaps the most widely used as a norm for teaching purposes.

Two kinds of information are needed if a word is to be appropriately pronounced. We need to know about each of the sounds that make up the word, and we need to know about stress. In each of the pronunciations shown in this dictionary, at least one vowel symbol is in heavier type and underlined. Sometimes more than one vowel is in heavier type and underlined:

result /rɪzʌlt/

disappointing /dɪsəpɔɪntɪŋ/

Heavy type and underlining give important information both about stress and the sounds that make up a word.

When a word is spoken in isolation, stress falls on all the syllables that contain vowels that are in heavier type and underlined. When two syllables are marked in this way, the second syllable has primary stress while the first has secondary stress; if only one is marked, it has primary stress. A word spoken in isolation is called the citation form.

When a word is used in context, either or both of the stresses found in the citation form may be absent. The one-stress or two-stress patterns of English speech are associated not with individual words but with the information units that a speaker constructs:

The result was disappointing
/ðə rɪzʌlt wəz dɪsəpɔɪntɪŋ/

A disappointing result
/ə dɪsəpɔɪntɪŋ rɪzʌlt/

Very disappointing indeed
/verɪ¹ dɪsəpɔɪntɪŋ ɪndiːd/

Because stress patterns are associated with linguistic units larger than the word, a dictionary cannot state in advance which of the stresses present in a citation form will be absent when a word is used in context.

Vowels that are in heavier type and underlined are called protected vowels. This means that, irrespective of whether a vowel is stressed or unstressed in a particular context, there is very little variation in the way a speaker pronounces it. Unprotected vowels, conversely, which are always unstressed, may show considerable variation in the way they are pronounced.

In this dictionary, the range of possible variation is shown by the tiny superscript numbers printed just above and to the right of the vowel symbol. In the word /sɪti¹/ (city), for example, the protected vowel is always pronounced /ɪ/, irrespective of whether it is stressed or not. Conversely, the key at the foot of this page shows that the pronunciation of the unprotected vowel may be made in the range between /iː/ and /ɪ/. In the word /juːslɪ²s/

(useless) the protected vowel is always pronounced /uː/, irrespective of whether it is stressed or not, while the pronunciation of the unprotected vowel may be made in the range between /ɪ/ and /ɛ/.

Some unprotected vowels are pronounced in only one way. For example, the second vowel in /hɔːlmaːk/ (hallmark) is stressed neither in its citation form nor when the word is used in context, but there is still very little variation in the way it is pronounced.

Some sounds, both vowels and consonants, are heard only in rather slow and careful speech. /juːʒʊəl/ (usual) and /kɒləmnɪst/ (columnist) are often heard as /juːʒəl/ and /kɒləmɪst/. In such cases, the superscript ° indicates that the sound in question is often omitted:

usual /juːʒʊ°əl/
columnist /kɒləmn°ɪst/

All superscripts and the variations they stand for are given in the key below.

Pronunciation Key

Vowels		Consonants				Superscripts			
aː	heart, start, calm.	b	bed	t	talk	ə⁰ (ə ↔ 0)		ɪ⁰ (ɪ ↔ 0)	
æ	act, mass, lap.	d	done	v	van	ə¹ (ə ↔ ɪ)		ɪ¹ (ɪ ↔ ə)	
aɪ	dive, cry, mind.	f	fit	w	win	ə² (ə ↔ ɛ)		ɪ² (ɪ ↔ ɛ)	
aɪə	fire, tyre, buyer.	g	good	x	loch	ə³ (ə ↔ æ)		ɪ³ (ɪ ↔ eɪ)	
aʊ	out, down, loud.	h	hat	z	zoo	ə⁴ (ə ↔ ʊ)		ɪ⁵ (ɪ ↔ aɪ)	
aʊə	flour, tower, sour.	j	yellow	ʃ	ship	ə⁵ (ə ↔ ɜː)		iˡ (ɪ ↔ iː)	
ɛ	met, lend, pen.	k	king	ʒ	measure	ə⁶ (ə ↔ əʊ)		ɛˡ (ɛ ↔ ɪ)	
eɪ	say, main, weight.	l	lip	ŋ	sing	ə⁷ (ə ↔ ɒ)		u⁴ (uː ↔ ʊ)	
ɛə	fair, care, wear.	m	mat	tʃ	cheap	ə⁸ (ə ↔ ɔː)		m¹ (m ↔ n)	
ɪ	fit, win, list.	n	nine	θ	thin	ə⁹ (ə ↔ ʌ)		ŋ¹ (ŋ ↔ n)	
iː	feed, me, beat.	p	pay	ð	then				
ɪə	near, beard, clear.	r	run	dʒ	joy				
ɒ	lot, lost, spot.	s	soon						
əʊ	note, phone, coat.								
ɔː	more, cord, claw.								
ɔɪ	boy, coin, joint.								
ʊ	could, stood, hood.								
uː	you, use, choose.								
ʊə	sure, pure, cure.								
ɜː	Turn, third, word.								
ʌ	but, fund, must.								
ə	the weak vowel in butter, about, forgotten.								

° after a consonant symbol indicates probable omission; kº, tº, hº, etc

Corpus Acknowledgements

We wish to thank the following, who have kindly given permission for the use of copyright material in the the Birmingham Collection of English Texts.

Associated Business Programmes Ltd for: *The Next 200 Years* by Herman Kahn with William Brown and Leon Martel first published in Great Britain by Associated Business Programmes Ltd 1977 © Hudson Institute 1976. David Attenborough and William Collins Sons & Co Ltd for: *Life on Earth* by David Attenborough first published by William Collins Sons & Co Ltd 1979 © David Attenborough Productions LTD 1979. James Baldwin for: *The Fire Next Time* by James Baldwin Published in Great Britain by Michael Joseph Ltd 1963 © James Baldwin 1963. B T Batsford Ltd for: *Witchcraft in England* by Christina Hole first published by B T Batsford Ltd 1945 © Christina Hole 1945. Michael Billington for: 'Lust at First Sight' by Michael Billington in the *Illustrated London News* July 1981 and 'Truffaut's Tolerance' by Michael Billington in the *Illustrated London News* August 1981. Birmingham International Council For Overseas Students' Aid for: BICOSA Information Leaflets 1981. Basil Blackwell Publishers Ltd for: *Breaking the Mould? The Birth and Prospects of the Social Democratic Party* by Ian Bradley first Published by Martin Robertson & Co Ltd 1981 © Ian Bradley 1981. *Seeing Green (The Politics of Ecology Explained)* by Jonathon Porritt first published by Basil Blackwell Publisher Ltd 1984 © Jonathon Porritt 1984. Blond & Briggs Ltd for: *Small is Beautiful* by E F Schumacher first published in Great Britain by Blond & Briggs Ltd 1973 © E F Schumacher 1973. The Bodley Head Ltd for: *The Americans (Letters from America 1969-1979)* by Alistair Cooke first published by Bodley Head Ltd 1979 © Alistair Cooke 1979. *Baby and Child Care* by Dr Benjamin Spock published in Great Britain by The Bodley Head Ltd 1955 © Benjamin Spock MD 1945, 1946, 1957, 1968, 1976, 1979. *What's Wrong With The Modern World?* by Michael Shanks first published by The Bodley Head Ltd 1978 © Michael Shanks 1978. *Future Shock* by Alvin Toffler first published in Great Britain by The Bodley Head Ltd 1970 © Alvin Toffler 1970. *Zen and the Art of Motorcycle Maintenance* by Robert M Pirsig first published in Great Britain by The Bodley Head Ltd 1974 © Robert M Pirsig 1974. *Marnie* by Winston Graham first published by the Bodley Head Ltd 1961 © Winston Graham 1961. *You Can Get There From Here* by Shirley MacLaine first published in Great Britain by The Bodley Head Ltd 1975 © Shirley MacLaine 1975. *It's An Odd Thing, But ...* by Paul Jennings first published by Max Reinhardt Ltd 1971 © Paul Jennings 1971. *King of the Castle (Choice and Responsibility in the Modern World)* by Gai Eaton first published by the Bodley Head Ltd 1977 © Gai Eaton 1977. *Revolutionaries in Modern Britain* by Peter Shipley first published by The Bodley Head Ltd 1976 © Peter Shipley 1976. *The Prerogative of the Harlot (Press Barons and Power)* by Hugh Cudlipp first published by The Bodley Head Ltd 1980 © Hugh Cudlipp 1980. *But What About The Children (A Working Parents' Guide to Child Care)* by Judith Hann first published by The Bodley Head Ltd 1976 © Judith Hann 1976. *Learning to Read* by Margaret Meek first published by The Bodley Head Ltd 1982 © Margaret Meek 1982. Bolt & Watson for: *Two is Lonely* by Lynne Reid Banks first published by Chatto & Windus 1974 © Lynne Reid Banks 1974. The British and Foreign Bible Society with William Collins Sons & Co Ltd for: *Good News Bible (with Deuterocanonical Books/Apocrypha)* first published by The British and Foreign Bible Society with William Collins Sons & Co Ltd 1979 © American Bible Society: Old Testament 1976, Deuterocanonical Books/Apocrypha 1979, New Testament 1966, 1971, 1976, © Maps, British and Foreign Bible Society 1976, 1979. The British Council for: *How to Live in Britain (The British Council's Guide for Overseas Students and Visitors)* first published by The British Council 1952 © The British Council 1984. Mrs R Bronowski for: *The Ascent of Man* by J Bronowski published by Book Club Associates by arrangement with The British Broadcasting Corporation 1977 © J Bronowski 1973. Alison Busby for: *The Death of Trees* by Nigel Dudley first published by Pluto Press Ltd 1985 © Nigel Dudley 1985. Tony Buzan for: *Make The Most of your Mind* by Tony Buzan first published by Colt Books Ltd 1977 © Tony Buzan 1977. Campbell Thomson & McLaughlin Ltd for: *Ring of Bright Water* by Gavin Maxwell first published by Longmans Green & Co 1960, published in Penguin Books Ltd 1976 © The Estate of Gavin Maxwell 1960. Jonathan Cape Ltd for: *Manwatching (A Field Guide to Human Behaviour)* by Desmond Morris first published in Great Britain by Jonathan Cape Ltd 1977 © Text, Desmond Morris 1977 © Compilation, Elsevier Publishing Projects SA, Lausanne, and Jonathan Cape Ltd, London 1977. *Tracks* by Robyn Davidson first published by Jonathan Cape Ltd 1980 © Robyn Davidson 1980. *In the Name of Love* by Jill Tweedie first published by Jonathan Cape Ltd 1979 © Jill Tweedie 1979. *The Use of Lateral Thinking* by Edward de Bono first published by Jonathan Cape 1967 © Edward de Bono 1967. *Trout Fishing in America* by Richard Brautigan first published in Great Britain by Jonathan Cape Ltd 1970 © Richard Brautigan 1967. *The Pendulum Years: Britain and the Sixties* by Bernard Levin first published by Jonathan Cape Ltd 1970 © Bernard Levin 1970. *The Summer Before The Dark* by Doris Lessing first published in Great Britain by Jonathan Cape Ltd 1973 © Doris Lessing 1973. *The Boston Strangler* by Gerold Frank first published in Great Britain by Jonathan Cape Ltd 1967 © Gerold Frank 1966. *I'm OK - You're OK* by Thomas A Harris MD first published in Great Britain as The Book of Choice by Jonathan Cape Ltd 1970 © Thomas A Harris MD, 1967, 1968, 1969. *The Vivisector* by Patrick White first published by Jonathan Cape Ltd 1970 © Patrick White 1970. *The Future of Socialism* by Anthony Crosland first published by Jonathan Cape Ltd 1956 © C A R Crosland 1963. *Funeral in Berlin* by Len Deighton first published by Jonathan Cape Ltd 1964 © Len Deighton 1964. Chatto & Windus Ltd for: *A Postillion Struck by Lightning* by Dirk Bogarde first published by Chatto & Windus Ltd 1977 © Dirk Bogarde 1977. *Nuns and Soldiers* by Iris Murdoch published by Chatto & Windus Ltd 1980 © Iris Murdoch 1980. *Wounded Knee (An Indian History of the American West)* by Dee Brown published by Chatto & Windus Ltd 1978 © Dee Brown 1970. *The Virgin in the Garden* by A S Byatt published by Chatto & Windus Ltd 1978 © A S Byatt 1978. *A Story Like The Wind* by Laurens van der Post published by Clarke Irwin & Co Ltd in association with The Hogarth Press Ltd 1972 © Laurens van der Post 1972. *Brave New World* by Aldous Huxley

published by Chatto & Windus Ltd 1932 © Aldous Huxley and Mrs Laura Hux
1932, 1960. *The Reivers* By William Faulkner first published by Chatto & Win
Ltd 1962 © William Faulkner 1962. *Cider With Rosie* by Laurie Lee published
The Hogarth Press 1959 © Laurie Lee 1959 *The Tenants* by Bernard Malar
first published in Great Britain by Chatto & Windus Ltd 1972 © Bern
Malamud 1971. *Kinflicks* by Lisa Alther first published in Great Britain by Cha
& Windus Ltd 1976 © Lisa Alther 1975. William Collins Sons & Co Ltd for:
Companion Guide to London by David Piper published by William Collins S
& Co Ltd 1964 © David Piper 1964. *The Bedside Guardian 29* edited by W L W
published by William Collins & Sons Ltd 1980 © Guardian Newspapers Ltd 1
Bear Island by Alistair MacLean first published by William Collins Sons Co
1971 © Alistair MacLean 1971. *Inequality in Britain: Freedom, Welfare and*
State By Frank Field first published by Fontana Paperbacks 1981 © Frank Fi
1981. *Social Mobility* by Anthony Heath first published by Fontana Paperba
1981 © Anthony Heath 1981. *Yours Faithfully* by Gerald Priestland first publis
by Fount Paperbacks 1979 © British Broadcasting Corporation 1977, 1978. *Po*
Without Responsibility: The Press and Broadcasting in Britain by Jar
Curran and Jean Seaton first published by Fontana Paperbacks 1981 © Jar
Curran and Jean Seaton 1981. *The Times Cookery Book* by Katie Stewart f
published by William Collins Sons & Co Ltd 1972 © Times Newspapers
Friends from the Forest by Joy Adamson by Collins and Harvill Press 198
Elsa Limited 1981. *The Media Mob* by Barry Fantoni and George Melly f
published by William Collins Sons & Co Ltd 1980 © Text, George Melly 198
Illustrations, Barry Fantoni 1980. *Shalom (a collection of Australian and Jew*
Stories) compiled by Nancy Keesing first published by William Col
Publishers Pty Ltd 1978 © William Collins Sons &Co Ltd 1978. *The Beds*
Guardian 31 edited by W L Webb first published by William Collins Sons &
Ltd 1982 © Guardian Newspapers Ltd 1982. *The Bedside Guardian 32* edited
W L Webb first published by William Collins Sons & Co Ltd 1983 © Guard
Newspapers Ltd 1983. *Design for the Real World* by Victor Papanek f
published in Great Britain by Thames & Hudson Ltd 1972 © Victor Papanek 1
Food For Free by Richard Mabey first published by William Collins Sons &
Ltd 1972 © Richard Mabey 1972. *Unended Quest* by Karl Popper (first publis
as Autobiography of Karl Popper in The Philosophy of Karl Popper in
Library of Philosophers edited by Paul Arthur Schlipp by the Open Co
Publishing Co 1974) published by Fontana Paperbacks 1976 © The Library
Living Philosophers Inc 1974 © Karl R Popper 1976. *My Mother My Self*
Nancy Friday first published in Great Britain by Fontana Paperbacks 197
Nancy Friday 1977. *The Captain's Diary* by Bob Willis first published by Wil
Books/William Collins Sons & Co Ltd 1984 © Bob Willis and Alan Lee 1984 © N
Zealand Scorecards, Bill Frindall 1984. *The Bodywork Book by Es*
Newton-Dunn first published in Great Britain by Willow Books/William Col
Sons & Co Ltd 1982 © TVS Ltd/Esme Newton-Dunn 1982. *Collins' Encyclopae*
of Fishing in The British Isles edited by Michael Prichard first published
William Collins Sons & Co Ltd 1976 © William Collins Sons & Co Ltd 1976.
AAA Runner's Guide edited by Heather Thomas first published by Willi
Collins Sons & Co Ltd 1983 © Sackville Design Group Ltd 1983. *Heroes*
Contemporaries by David Gower with Derek Hodgson first published
William Collins Sons & Co Ltd 1983 © David Gower Promotions Ltd 1983.
Berlin Memorandum by Adam Hall first published by William Collins Sons &
Ltd 1965 © Jonquil Trevor 1965. *Arlott on Cricket: His Writings on the Ga*
edited by David Rayvern Allen first published by William Collins (Willow Boo
1984 © John Arlott 1984. *A Woman in Custody* by Audrey Peckham f
published by Fontana Paperbacks 1985 © Audrey Peckham 1985. *Play Golf w*
Peter Alliss by Peter Alliss published by the British Broadcasting Corporat
1977 © Peter Alliss and Renton Laidlaw 1977. Curtis Brown Ltd for: *The Pearl*
John Steinbeck first published by William Heinemann Ltd 1948 © John Steinbe
1948. *An Unfinished History of the World* by Hugh Thomas first published
Great Britain by Hamish Hamilton Ltd 1979 © Hugh Thomas 1979, 1981.
Winter of our Discontent by John Steinbeck first published in Great Britain
William Heinemann Ltd 1961 © John Steinbeck 1961. *Burr* by Gore Vidal f
published in Great Britain by William Heinemann Ltd 1974 © Gore Vidal 19
Doctor on the Job by Richard Gordon first published by William Heinemann
1976 © Richard Gordon Ltd 1976. Andre Deutsch Ltd for: *How to be an Alien*
George Mikes first published by Andre Deutsch Ltd 1946 © George Mikes a
Nicholas Bentley 1946. *Jaws* by Peter Benchley first published in Great Brit
by Andre Deutsch Ltd 1974 © Peter Benchley 1974. *A Bend in the River* by
Naipaul first published by Andre Deutsch Ltd 1979 © V S Naipaul 1979. *Coup*
by John Updike first published by Andre Deutsch Ltd 1968 © John Updike 19
Games People Play by Eric Berne published in Great Britain by Andre Deuts
Ltd 1966 © Eric Berne 1964. *The Age of Uncertainty* by John Kenneth Galbra
first published by The British Broadcasting Corporation and Andre Deutsche
1977 © John Kenneth Galbraith 1977. The Economist Newspaper Ltd for:
Economist (9-15 May 1981 and 22-28 August 1981) © published by The Econom
Newspaper Ltd 1981. Faber & Faber Ltd for: *Lord of the Flies* by Willi
Golding first published by Faber & Faber Ltd 1954 © William Golding 1954.
Complete Book of Self-Sufficiency by John Seymour first published in Gr
Britain by Faber & Faber Ltd 1976 © Text, John Seymour 1976, 1977 © Dorli
Kindersley Ltd 1976, 1977. *Conversations with Igor Stravinsky* by Ig
Stravinsky and Robert Craft first published by Faber & Faber Ltd 1959 © Ig
Stravinsky 1958,1959. John Farquharson Ltd for: *The Moon's A Balloon* by Da
Niven published in Great Britain by Hamish Hamilton Ltd 1971 © David Niv
1971. John Gaselee for: 'Going it Alone' by John Gaselee in the *Illustra*
London News July 1981 and 'The Other Car's Fault' by John Gaselee in
Illustrated London News August 1981. Glidrose Publications Ltd for: *The M*
with the Golden Gun by Ian Fleming first published by Jonathan Cape Ltd
Glidrose Productions Ltd 1965. Victor Gollancz Ltd for: *The Next Horizon*

ıris Bonnington published by Victor Gollancz Ltd 1976 © Chris Bonnington 73. *Summerhill: A Radical Approach to Education* by A S Neill first published · Victor Gollancz Ltd 1962 © A S Neill 1926, 1932, 1937, 1953, 1961 (US ·rmission by Hart Publishing Inc). *Lucky Jim* by Kingsley Amis first published · Victor Gollancz Ltd 1954 © Kingsley Amis 1953. *The Mighty Micro (The ıpact of the Computer Revolution)* by Christopher Evans first published by ctor Gollancz Ltd 1979 © Christopher Evans 1979. *The Longest Day* by ·rnelius Ryan published by Victor Gollancz Ltd 1960 © Cornelius Ryan 1959. *king for Trouble (Autobiography of a Banned Journalist)* by Donald Woods ıblished by Victor Gollancz Ltd 1980 © Donald Woods 1980. *The Turin Shroud* · Ian Wilson first published in Great Britain by Victor Gollancz Ltd 1978 © Ian ılson 1978. *Murdo and Other Stories* by Iain Crichton Smith published by ctor Gollancz Ltd 1981 © Iain Crichton Smith 1981. *The Class Struggle in ırliament* by Eric S Heffer published by Victor Gollancz Ltd 1973 © Eric S ·ffer 1973. *A Presumption of Innocence (The Amazing Case of Patrick ·eehan)* by Ludovic Kennedy published by Victor Gollancz Ltd 1976 © Ludovic ·nnedy 1976. *The Treasure of Sainte Foy* by MacDonald Harris published by ctor Gollancz Ltd 1980 © MacDonald Harris 1980. *A Long Way to Shiloh* by ·nel Davidson first published by Victor Gollancz Ltd 1966 © Lionel Davidson 66. *Education After School* by Tyrrell Burgess first published by Victor ·llancz Ltd 1977 © Tyrrell Burgess 1977. *The View From Serendip* by Arthur C ·arke published by Victor Gollancz Ltd 1978 © Arthur C Clarke 1967, 1968, 1970, 72, 1974, 1976, 1977. *On Wings of Song* by Thomas M Disch published by Victor ·llancz Ltd 1979 © Thomas M Disch 1979. *The World of Violence* by Colin ·lson published by Victor Gollancz Ltd 1963 © Colin Wilson 1963. *The Lightning ·ee* by Joan Aiken published by Victor Gollancz Ltd 1980 © Joan Aiken ·terprises 1980. *Russia's Political Hospitals* by Sidney Bloch and Peter ·ddaway published by Victor Gollancz Ltd 1977 © Sidney Bloch and Peter ·ddaway 1977. *Unholy Loves* by Joyce Carol Oates first published in Great ·itain by Victor Gollancz Ltd 1980 © Joyce Carol Oates 1979. *Consenting Adults · The Duchess will be Furious)* by Peter De Vries published by Victor Gollancz ·d 1981 © Peter De Vries 1980. *The Passion of New Eve* by Angela Carter ·blished by Victor Gollancz Ltd 1977 © Angela Carter 1977. Gower Publishing · Ltd for: *Solar Prospects (The Potential for Renewable Energy)* by Michael ·ood first published in Great Britain by Wildwood House Ltd in association with ·iends of the Earth Ltd 1983 © Michael Flood. *Voiceless Victims* by Rebecca ·ll first published in Great Britain by Wildwood House Ltd 1984 © Rebecca Hall 84. Graham Greene and Laurence Pollinger Ltd for: *The Human Factor* by ·aham Greene first published by The Bodley Head Ltd 1978 © Graham Greene 78. Syndication Manager, The Guardian, for: *The Guardian* (12 May 1981, 7 ·ptember 1981 and 15 September 1981) © published by Guardian Newspapers ·d 1981. Hamlyn for: *How to Play Rugby* by David Norrie published by The ·mlyn Publishing Group Ltd 1981 © The Hamlyn Publishing Group Ltd 1981. ·w *to Play Badminton* by Pat Davies first published by The Hamlyn ·blishing Group Ltd 1979 © The Hamlyn Publishing Group Ltd 1979. Margaret ·nbury for: *Crisis and Conservation: Conflict in the British Countryside* by ·arlie Pye-Smith and Chris Rose first published by Pelican/Penguin Books Ltd 84 © Charlie Pye-Smith and Chris Rose 1984. Paul Harrison for: *Inside the ·ird World* by Paul Harrison first published in Great Britain by The Harvester ·ess Ltd 1980 © Paul Harrison 1979. A M Heath & Co Ltd for: *Rembrandt's Hat* · Bernard Malamud published by Chatto & Windus Ltd 1982 © Bernard ·alamud 1968, 1972, 1973. William Heinemann Ltd for: *It's an Old Country* by J ·Priestley first published in Great Britain by William Heinemann Ltd 1967 © J ·Priestley 1967. Heinemann Educational Books Ltd and Gower Publishing Co ·d for: *The Environmental Crisis (A Handbook for all Friends of the Earth)* ·ted by Des Wilson first published by Heinemann Educational Books Ltd 1984 · Foreword, David Bellamy 1984 © Individual Chapters, the Author of the ·apter 1984 © In the selection and all other matters Des Wilson 1984. The ·ntroller, Her Majesty's Stationery Office, for: Department of Health and Social ·curity leaflets published by Her Majesty's Stationery Office 1981 © The Crown. ·vid Higham Associates Ltd for: 'Two Peruvian Projects' by E R Chamberlain · the *Illustrated London News* September 1981. *Akenfield: Portrait of an ·glish Village* by Ronald Blythe first published by Allen Lane, Penguin Books ·d 1969 © Ronald Blythe1969. *The Far Pavillions* by M M Kaye first published · Allen Lane/Penguin Books Ltd 1978 © M M Kaye 1978. *Staying On* by Paul ·ott first published by William Heinemann Ltd 1977 © Paul Scott 1977. *Let ·eping Vets Lie* by James Herriot first published by Michael Joseph Ltd 1973 © ·mes Herriot 1973. *The Midwich Cuckoos* by John Wyndham first published in ·eat Britain by Michael Joseph Ltd 1957 © The Estate of John Wyndham 1957. ·e *Girl in a Swing* by Richard Adams first published in Great Britain by Allen ·ne in Penguin Books Ltd 1980 © Richard Adams 1980. Dr K B Hindley for: 'Hot ·ots of the Deep' by Dr K B Hindley in the *Illustrated London News July* 1981. ·dder and Stoughton Ltd for: *Supernature* by Lyall Watson first published by ·dder & Stoughton Ltd 1973 © Lyall Watson 1973. *Tinker Tailor Soldier Spy* by ·n Le Carre first published by Hodder & Stoughton Ltd 1974 © Le Carre ·oductions 1974. The Editor, Homes and Gardens, for: *Homes and Gardens* ·ctober 1981) (Number 4 Volume 63) © published by IPC Magazines Ltd 1981. ·ghes Massie Ltd for: *Elephants Can Remember* by Agatha Christie first ·blished by William Collins Sons & Co Ltd 1972 © Agatha Christie Mallowan. ·tchinson Publishing Group Ltd for: *An Autobiography* by Angela Davis ·blished in Great Britain by Hutchinson & Co Publishers Ltd by arrangement ·h Bantam Books Inc 1975 © Angela Davis 1974. *The Day of the Jackal* by ·ederick Forsyth published in Great Britian by Hutchinson & Co Publishers Ltd ·1 © Frederick Forsyth 1971. *Roots* by Alex Haley first published in Great ·itain by Hutchinson & Co Publishers Ltd 1977 © Alex Haley 1976. *The Climate ·Treason* by Andrew Boyle first published by Hutchinson & Co Publishers Ltd ·9 © Andrew Boyle 1979. *The Collapsing Universe: The Story of Black Holes* · Isaac Asimov first published by Hutchinson & Co Publishers Ltd 1977 © Isaac ·mov. *XPD* by Len Deighton published by Book Club Associates by ·angement with Hutchinson & Co Publishers Ltd 1981 © Len Deighton 1981. ·w *Jumping with Harvey Smith* by Harvey Smith first published by Stanley ·ul & Co Ltd 1979 © Tyne-Tees Television Ltd, A Member of the Trident Group ·9. *2001: A Space Odyssey* by Arthur C Clarke first published by Hutchinson & · Publishers Ltd 1968 © Arthur C Clarke and Polaris Productions Inc 1968 © ·logue material, Serendip BV 1982, 1983. The Illustrated London News and Sketch Ltd for: *The Illustrated London News* (July 1981, August 1981 and September 1981) © published by the Illustrated London News and Sketch Ltd 1981. The Editor, International Herald Tribune, for: *International Herald Tribune* (25-26 July 1981) © published by International Herald Tribune with The New York Times and The Washington Post 1981. Michael Joseph Ltd for: *Chronicles of Fairacre: Village School* by Miss Read first published in Great Britain by Michael Joseph Ltd 1964 © Miss Read 1955, 1964. *Fire Fox* by Craig Thomas first published in Great Britain by Michael Joseph Ltd 1977 © Craig Thomas 1977. William Kimber & Co Ltd for: *Exodus* by Leon Uris originally published in Great Britain by Alan Wingate Ltd 1959 © Leon Uris 1958. Kogan Page Ltd for: *How to Save the World (Strategy for World Conservation)* by Robert Allen first published by Kogan Page Ltd 1980 © IUCN-UNEP-WWF 1980. Marketing Department, Lloyds Bank PLC, for: *Lloyds Bank Leaflets* (1981) © published by Lloyds Bank PLC 1981. Macmillan Publishers Ltd for: *Appropriate Technology: Technology with a Human Face* by P D Dunn first published by the Macmillan Press Ltd 1978 © P D Dunn 1978. John Murray Publishers Ltd for: *A Backward Place* by Ruth Prawer Jhabvala first published by John Murray Publishers Ltd 1965 © R Prawer Jhabvala 1965. *Food For All The Family* by Magnus Pyke first published by John Murray Publishers Ltd 1980 © Magnus Pyke 1980. *Simple Movement* by Laura Mitchell and Barbara Dale first published by John Murray Publishers Ltd 1980 © Laura Mitchell and Barbara Dale 1980. *Civilisation: A Personal View* by Kenneth Clark first published by the British Broadcasting Corporation and John Murray Publishers Ltd 1969 © Kenneth Clark 1969. The Editor, National Geographic, for: *National Geographic* January, February and March (1980) © published by The National Geographic Society 1979, 1980. The National Magazine Co Ltd for: *Cosmopolitan* (May 1981 and July 1981) © published by the National Magazine Co Ltd 1981. Neilson Leisure Group Ltd for: *NAT Holidays' 'Caravans and Tents in the Sun'* (Summer 1983) holiday brochure. Newsweek Inc for: *Newsweek* (11 May 1981, 27 July 1981 and August 1981) © published by Newsweek Inc 1981. The Associate Editor, Now!, for: *Now!* (14-20 November 1980) © published by Cavenham Communications Ltd 1980. Harold Ober Associates Inc for: *The Boys from Brazil* by Ira Levin first published by Michael Joseph Ltd 1976 © Ira Levin 1976. Edna O'Brien and A M Heath & Co Ltd for: *August is a Wicked Month* by Edna O'Brien first published by Jonathan Cape Ltd 1965 © Edna O'Brien 1965. Pan Books Ltd for: *Dispatches* by Michael Herr first published in Great Britain by Pan Books Ltd 1978 © Michael Herr 1968, 1969, 1970, 1977. *Health and Safety at Work* by Dave Eva and Ron Oswald first published by Pan Books Ltd 1981 © Dave Eva, Ron Oswald and the Workers' Educational Association 1981. *Democracy at Work* by Patrick Burns and Mel Doyle first published by Pan Books Ltd 1981 © Patrick Burns,Mel Doyle and the Workers' Educational Association 1981. *Diet for Life (A Cookbook for Arthritics)* by Mary Laver and Margaret Smith first published by Pan Books Ltd 1981 © Mary Laver and Margaret Smith 1981. Penguin Books Ltd for: *Inside the Company: CIA Diary* by Philip Agee first published in Allen Lane/Penguin Books Ltd 1975 © Philip Agee 1975. Penguin Books Ltd and Spare Ribs Ltd for: *Spare Rib Reader* edited by Marsha Rowe first published in Penguin Books Ltd 1982 © Spare Ribs Ltd 1982. A D Peters & Co Ltd for: 'The Dark Side of Israel' by Norman Moss in Illustrated London News July 1981, 'Aftermath of Osirak' by Norman Moss in the *Illustrated London News* August 1981 and 'Turning Point for Poland' by Norman Moss in the *Illustrated London News* September 1981. 'Recent Fiction' by Sally Emerson in the *Illustrated London News* July 1981, August 1981 and September 1981. *The Complete Upmanship* by Stephen Potter first published in Great Britain by Rupert Hart-Davis Ltd 1970 © Stephen Potter. Elaine Pollard for: Personal Letters 1981 donated by Elaine Pollard. Laurence Pollinger Ltd for: *A Glastonbury Romance* by John Cowper Powys first published by MacDonald & Co Ltd 1933. Murray Pollinger for: *Kiss Kiss* by Roald Dahl published in Great Britain by Michael Joseph Ltd 1960 © Roald Dahl 1962. *Can You Avoid Cancer?* by Peter Goodwin first published by the British Broadcasting Corporation 1984 © Peter Goodwin 1984. Preston Travel Ltd for: Preston Sunroutes 'Camping and Self-Catering' (April to October 1983) holiday brochure. Punch Publications Ltd for: *Punch* (6 May 1981, 29 July 1981, 12 August 1981, 26 August 1981 and 9 September 1981) © published by Punch Publications Ltd 1981. Radala and associates for: *The Naked Civil Servant* by Quentin Crisp first published by Jonathan Cape Ltd 1968 © Quentin Crisp 1968. The Rainbird Publishing Group Ltd for: *The Making of Mankind* by Richard E Leakey first published in Great Britain by Michael Joseph Ltd 1981 © Sherma BV 1981. Robson Books Ltd for: *The Punch Book of Short Stories 3* selected by Alan Coren first published in Great Britain by Robson Books Ltd in association with Punch Publications Ltd 1981 © Robson Books Ltd 1981.*The Best of Robert Morley* by Robert Morley first published in Great Britain by Robson Books Ltd 1981 © Robert Morley 1981. Deborah Rogers Ltd for: 'Picasso's Late Works' by Edward Lucie-Smith in the *Illustrated London News* July 1981, 'David Jones at the Tate' by Edward Lucie-Smith in the *Illustrated London News* August 1981 and 'Further Light on Spanish Painting' by Edward Lucie-Smith in the *Illustrated London News* September 1981. *The Godfather* by Mario Puzo first published in Great Britain by William Heinemann Ltd 1969 © Mario Puzo 1969. Routledge & Kegan Paul Ltd for: *How To Pass Examinations* by John Erasmus first published by Oriel Press Ltd 1967 © Oriel Press Ltd 1980. *Daisy, Daisy* by Christian Miller first published by Routledge & Kegan Paul Ltd 1980 © Christian Miller 1980. *The National Front* by Nigel Fielding first published by Routledge & Kegan Paul Ltd 1981 © Nigel Fielding 1981. *The Myth of Home Ownership* by Jim Kemeny first published by Routledge & Kegan Paul Ltd 1980 © J Kemeny 1981. *Absent With Cause (Lessons of Truancy)* by Roger White first published by Routledge & Kegan Paul Ltd 1980 © Roger White 1980. *The Powers of Evil (in Western Religion, Magic and Folk Belief)* by Richard Cavendish first published by Routledge & Kegan Paul Ltd 1975 © Richard Cavendish 1975. *Crime and Personality* by H J Eysenck first published by Routledge & Kegan Paul Ltd 1964 © H J Eysenck 1964, 1977. Martin Secker & Warburg Ltd for: *Changing Places* by David Lodge first published in England by Martin Secker & Warburg Ltd 1975 © David Lodge 1975. *The History Man* by Malcolm Bradbury first published by Martin Secker & Warburg 1975 © Malcolm Bradbury 1975. *Humboldt's Gift* by Saul Bellow first published in England by The Alison Press/Martin Secker & Warburg Ltd 1975 © Saul Bellow 1973, 1974, 1975. *Wilt* by Tom Sharpe first published in England by Martin Secker & Warburg Ltd 1976 © Tom Sharpe 1976. *The Last Days of*

America by Paul E Erdman first published in England by Martin Secker & Warburg Ltd 1981 © Paul E Erdman 1981. *Autumn Manoeuvres* by Melvyn Bragg first published in England by Martin Secker & Warburg Ltd 1978 © Melvyn Bragg 1978. *The Act of Being* by Charles Marowitz first published in England by Martin Secker & Warburg Ltd 1978 © Charles Marowitz 1978. *As If By Magic* by Angus Wilson first published in England by Martin Secker & Warburg Ltd 1973 © Angus Wilson 1973. *All the President's Men* by Carl Bernstein and Bob Woodward first published in England by Martin Secker & Warburg Ltd 1974 © Carl Bernstein and Bob Woodward 1974. *The Myth of the Nation and the Vision of Revolution* by J L Talmon first published by Martin Secker & Warburg Ltd 1981 © J L Talmon 1980. *Animal Farm* by George Orwell first published by Martin Secker & Warburg 1945 © Eric Blair 1945. Anthony Sheil Associates Ltd for: *Daniel Martin* by John Fowles first published in Great Britain by Jonathan Cape Ltd 1977 © J R Fowles Ltd 1977. *Love Story* by Erich Segal published by Hodder & Stoughton Ltd 1970 © Erich Segal 1970. Sidgwick & Jackson Ltd for: *The Third World War* by General Sir John Hackett and others first published in Great Britain by Sidgwick & Jackson Ltd 1978 © General Sir John Hackett 1978. *Superwoman* by Shirley Conran first published by Sidgwick & Jackson Ltd 1975 © Shirley Conran 1975, 1977. *An Actor and His Time* by John Gielgud first published in Great Britain by Sidgwick & Jackson Ltd 1979 © John Gielgud, John Miller and John Powell 1979 © Biographical Notes, John Miller 1979. Simon & Schuster for: *Our Bodies Ourselves (A Health Book by and for Women)* by the Boston Women's Health Book Collective (British Edition by Angela Phillips and Jill Rakusen) published in Allen Lane and Penguin Books Ltd 1978 © The Boston Women's Health Collective Inc 1971, 1973, 1976 © Material for British Edition, Angela Phillips and Jill Rakusen 1978. Souvenir Press Ltd for: *The Bermuda Triangle* by Charles Berlitz (An Incredible Saga of Unexplained Disappearances) first published in Great Britain by Souvenir Press Ltd 1975 © Charles Berlitz 1974. Souvenir Press Ltd and Michael Joseph Ltd for: *Airport* by Arthur Hailey first published in Great Britain by Michael Joseph Ltd in association with Souvenir Press Ltd 1968 © Arthur Hailey Ltd 1968. Sunmed Holidays Ltd for: 'Go Greek' (Summer 1983) holiday brochure. Maurice Temple Smith Ltd for: *Friends of the Earth Pollution Guide* by Brian Price published by Maurice Temple Smith Ltd 1983 © Brian Price 1983. Maurice Temple Smith and Gower Publishing Co Ltd for: *Working the Land (A New Plan for a Healthy Agriculture)* by Charlie Pye-Smith and Richard North first published by Maurice Temple Smith Ltd 1984© Charlie Pye-Smith and Richard North 1984. Times Newspapers Ltd for: *The Sunday Times Magazine* (13 January 1980, 20 January 1980 and 11 May 1980) © published by Times Newspapers Ltd 1981. *The Times* (7 September 1981) © published by Times Newspapers Ltd 1981. Twenty's Holidays for: 'The Best 18-33 Holidays' (Winter 1982/83) holiday brochure. University of Birmingham for: Living in Birmingham (1984) © published by The University of Birmingham 1984. Birmingham University Overseas Student Guide © The University of Birmingham. Working with Industry and Commerce © published by The University of Birmingham 1984. University of Birmingham Prospectus (June 1985) © published by The University of Birmingham 1985. University of Birmingham Library Guide © published by The University of Birmingham. University of Birmingham Institute of Research and Development (1984) © published by the University of Birmingham 1984. Biological Sciences at The University of Birmingham (1985) © published by The University of Birmingham 1985. History at the University of Birmingham (1985) © published by The University of Birmingham 1985. Faculty of Arts Handbook (1984-85) © published by The University of Birmingham 1984. Virago Press Ltd for: *Benefits* by Zoe Fairbairns published by Virago Press Ltd 1979 © Zoe Fairbairns 1979. *Simple Steps to Public Life* by Pamela Anderson, Mary Stott and Fay Weldon published in Great Britain by Virago Press Ltd 1980 © Action Opportunities 1980. *Tell Me A Riddle* by Tillie Olsen published by Virago Press Ltd 1980 © this edition Tillie Olsen 1980. A P Watt (& Sons) Ltd for: *The Glittering Prizes* by Frederic Raphael first published in Great Britain by Penguin Books Ltd 1976 © Volatic Ltd 1976. *Then and Now* by W Somerset Maugham first published by William Heinemann Ltd 1946 © W Somerset Maugham 1946. *The Language of Clothes* by Alison Lurie published by William Heinemann Ltd 1981 © Alison Lurie 1981. 'Herschel Commemorative' by Patrick Moore in the *Illustrated London News* July 1981. 'The Outermost Giant' by Patrick Moore in the *Illustrated London News* August 1981. 'Cosmic Bombardment' by Patrick Moore in the *Illustrated London News* September 1981. Weidenfeld & Nicolson Ltd for: 'The Miraculous Toy' by Susan Briggs in the *Illustrated London News* August 1981. *The Needle's Eye* by Margaret Drabble first published by Weidenfeld & Nicolson Ltd 1972 © Margaret Drabble 1972. *Success Without Tears: A Woman's Guide to the Top* by Rachel Nelson first published in Great Britain by Weidenfeld & Nicolson Ltd 1979 © Rachel Nelson 1979. *Education in the Modern World* by John Vaizey published by Weidenfeld & Nicolson Ltd 1967 © John Vaizey 1967. *Rich Man, Poor Man* by Irwin Shaw first published by Weidenfeld & Nicolson Ltd 197 Irwin Shaw 1969,1970. *Lolita* by Vladimir Nabokov first published in Gr Britain by Weidenfeld & Nicolson Ltd 1959 © Vladimir Nabokov 1955, 1959, 19 © G P Putnam's Sons 1963 © McGraw-Hill International Inc 1971. *The Th World* by Peter Worsley first published by Weidenfeld & Nicolson Ltd 1964 Peter Worsley 1964, 1967. *Portrait of a Marriage* by Nigel Nicolson published Weidenfeld & Nicolson Ltd 1973 © Nigel Nicolson 1973. *The Dogs Bark: Pu People and Private Places* by Truman Capote first published in Great Britain Weidenfeld & Nicolson Ltd 1974 © Truman Capote 1974. *Great Plann Disasters* by Peter Hall first published in Great Britain by George Weidenfel Nicolson Ltd 1980 © Peter Hall 1980. The Writers and Readers Publish Co-operative Ltd for: *Working with Words, Literacy Beyond School* by Ja Mace published by The Writers and Readers Publishing Co-operative Ltd 197 Jane Mace 1979. *The Alienated: Growing Old Today* by Gladys Elder O. published by The Writers and Readers Publishing Co-operative Ltd 1977 © Te The Estate of Gladys Elder 1977 © Photographs, Mike Abrahams 1977. *Beyc the Crisis in Art* by Peter Fuller published by The Writers and Read Publishing Co-operative Ltd 1980 © Peter Fuller 1980. *The War and Peace Bc* by Dave Noble published by The Writers and Readers Publishing Co-operat Ltd 1977 © Dave Noble 1977. *Tony Benn: A Political Biography* by Rob Jenkins first published by The Writers and Readers Publishing Co-operative 1980 © Robert Jenkins 1980. *Nuclear Power for Beginners* by Stephen Croall a Kaianders Sempler first published by The Writers and Readers Publish Co-operative Ltd 1978 © Text, Stephen Croall 1978,1980 © Illustrations Kaiand Sempler 1978, 1980. Yale University Press for: *Life in the English Coun House: A Social and Architectural History* by Mark Girouard published by Y University Press Ltd, London 1978 © Yale University 1978. The Bri Broadcasting Corporation for transcripts of radio transmissions 'Kaleidoscope', 'Any Questions', 'Money Box' and 'Arts and Africa' 1981 and 19 The British Broadcasting Corporation and Mrs Shirley Williams for transcri of television interviews with Mrs Shirley Williams 1979. Dr B L Smith, Schoo Mathematics and Physical Sciences, University of Sussex for programmes Current Affairs, Science and The Arts originally broadcast on Radio Sussex ▶ and 1980 © B L Smith. The following people in the University of Birmingh: Professor J McH Sinclair, Department of English, for his tapes of inforn conversation (personal collection). Mr R Wallace, formerly Department Accounting and Finance, and Ms D Houghton, Department of English, transcripts of his accountancy lectures. Dr B K Gazey, Department of Electri Engineering and Dr M Montgomery, University of Strathclyde, Departmen English, for a transcript of Dr Gazey's lecture. Dr L W Poel, Departmen Plant Biology, and Dr M Montgomery, University of Strathclyde, Departmen English, for a transcript of Dr Poel's lecture. Professor J G Hawkes, forme Department of Plant Biology, for recordings of his lectures. Dr M S Sna Department of Transportation for recordings of his lectures. Dr M P H(Department of English, and Dr M Cooper, The British Council, for a recordin their discussion on discourse analysis. Ms A Renouf, Department of English, recordings of job and academic interviews 1977. Mr R H Hubbard, formerly Phil (Ed) student, Faculty of Education, for his research recordings expressions of uncertainty 1978-79. Mr A E Hare, formerly a B Phil (Ed) stu Faculty of Education, for his transcripts of telephone conversations 1978. D Tsui, formerly Department of English, for her recordings of inforn conversation. Mr J Couperthwaite, formerly Department of English, fo recording of informal conversation 1981. Ms C Emmott, M Litt stud Department of English, for a recording of informal conversation 1981. Mrs Atkins for the transcript of an account of a dream 1981. The British Council 'Authentic Materials Numbers 1-28' 1981. Professor M Hammerton and M Coghill, Department of Psychology, University of Newcastle-upon-Tyne, for ↑ recordings of their lectures 1981. Mr G P Graveson, formerly research stud University of Newcastle, for his recordings of teacher discussion 1977. Mr V Jones, formerly research student, University of Southampton, for his record of classroom talk. Mr Ian Fisher, formerly BA student, Newcastle Polytech for his transcripts of interviews on local history 1981. Dr N Coupland, form PhD student, Department of English, UWIST, for his transcripts of travel age talk 1981. Professor D B Bromley, Department of Psychology, University Liverpool, for his transcript of a research recording. Mr Brian Lawre formerly of Saffron Walden County High School, for a tape of his talk on ' British Education System' 1979.

Every effort has been made to trace the copyright holders, but if any have b inadvertently overlooked the publishers will be pleased to make the necess acknowledgments at the first opportunity.

A a

A, a /eɪ/, **A's, a's. A** is the first letter of the English N COUNT
alphabet.

A stands for adjunct
Verbs which have the label +A in the Extra Column need an adjunct to complete their meaning.
See the entry headed ADJUNCTS for more information.

---

a /eɪ/ or /ə/, **an** /æn/ or /ən/.
1 You use **a** or **an** at the beginning of noun groups DET
when you are referring to someone or something
and you do not want to say which particular person
or thing you mean. EG *Tom could see a hallway...
She wanted to be an actress.*
2 You can use **a** or **an** instead of the number 'one'. DET
EG *...a year or two ago... ...in an hour's time.*
3 When you express rates, prices, and measure- DET
ments, you can use **a** to say how many units
apply to each of the items being measured. EG *He
charges 100 dollars an hour.*
4 You can use **a** or **an** in front of uncount nouns DET
when they are preceded by adjectives or followed
by words that describe the uncount noun more
fully. EG *...a happiness that he couldn't quite hide.*
5 You use **a** or **an** in front of the names of people DET
when you are referring to someone who you do not
know personally. EG *You don't know a Mrs Burton,
do you?*

aback /əbæk/. See **take aback**.

abacus /æbəkəs/, **abacuses. An abacus** is a N COUNT
frame used for counting. It has rods with sliding
beads on them.

abandon /əbændən/, **abandons, abandoning,
abandoned. 1** If you **abandon** a place, thing, or V+O
person, you leave it permanently or for a long
time. EG *You're not supposed to abandon your car
on the motorway.*
2 If you **abandon** a plan, activity, or piece of work, V+O
you stop doing it before it is finished. EG *I abandoned the search.*
3 If you **abandon** an idea or way of thinking, you V+O
stop thinking in that way. EG *I have abandoned the
idea of consistency.*
4 If you **abandon** yourself to an emotion, you think V-REFL+to
about it a lot and feel it strongly. EG *She abandoned
herself to grief.*
5 If you do something with **abandon**, you do it in a N UNCOUNT
carefree way. EG *The food was consumed with
joyous abandon.*

abandoned /əbændənd/. An **abandoned** place or ADJ CLASSIF
building is no longer used or occupied.

abandonment /əbændənmənt/. **1** The **abandon-** N UNCOUNT:
ment of a place, thing, or person is the act of USU+of
leaving it permanently or for a long time. EG *...the
abandonment of the farms.*
2 The **abandonment** of a piece of work or a plan is N UNCOUNT:
the act of stopping doing it before it is finished. USU+of

abashed /əbæʃt/. If you are **abashed**, you feel ADJ PRED
embarrassed and ashamed. EG *The students looked
guilty and abashed.*

abate /əbeɪt/, **abates, abating, abated.** When V
something **abates**, it becomes much less strong or Formal
widespread. EG *My terror abated a little.*

abattoir /æbətwɑː/, **abattoirs. An abattoir** is a N COUNT
place where animals are killed for meat.

abbess /æbɪˀs/, **abbesses. An abbess** is a nun N COUNT
who is in charge of the other nuns in a convent.

abbey /æbiˡ/, **abbeys. An abbey** is a church with N COUNT
buildings attached to it in which monks or nuns live
or used to live. EG *...Westminster Abbey.*

abbot /æbət/, **abbots. An abbot** is a monk who is N COUNT
in charge of the other monks in a monastery or
abbey.

abbreviate /əˈbriːvɪeɪt/, **abbreviates,
abbreviating, abbreviated. 1** If you **abbreviate** V+O
a piece of writing or a speech you make it shorter.
◇ **abbreviated.** EG *...an abbreviated version of a* ◇ ADJ CLASSIF
talk.
2 A word or phrase that **is abbreviated** is made V+O : USU PASS
shorter by leaving out some of the letters or by
using only the first letters of each word. EG *...the
Ultra-Intelligent Machine (or UIM as it is abbreviated).*

abbreviation /əˌbriːvɪeɪʃəˀn/, **abbreviations. An** N COUNT
abbreviation is a short form of a word or phrase,
made by leaving out some of the letters or by using
only the first letters of each word.

abdicate /æbdɪkeɪt/, **abdicates, abdicating, abdicated. 1** If a king or queen **abdicates**, he or she V
resigns. ◇ **abdication** /æbdɪkeɪʃəˀn/. EG *...the* ◇ N UNCOUNT
abdication crisis of 1936.
2 If you **abdicate** your responsibility for some- V+O
thing, you refuse to accept the responsibility for it
any longer. ◇ **abdication.** EG *...an abdication of* ◇ N UNCOUNT
political responsibility. +SUPP

abdomen /æbdəˀmən/, **abdomens.** Your **abdo-** N COUNT
men is the part of your body below your chest
where your stomach and intestines are.
◇ **abdominal** /əˈbdɒmɪˀnəˀl/. EG *...a patient suffer-* ◇ ADJ CLASSIF
ing from abdominal pains.

abduct /əˀbdʌkt/, **abducts, abducting, ab-** V+O
ducted. If someone **abducts** another person, they
take the person away, using force. ◇ **abduction** ◇ N UNCOUNT
/əˀbdʌkʃəˀn/. EG *...the recent abduction of his son.*

aberration /æbəreɪʃəˀn/, **aberrations. An aber-** N COUNT
ration is an action or way of behaving that is not
normal. EG *This is a temporary aberration and will
soon be put right.*

abet /əbet/, **abets, abetting, abetted.** If you **abet** V+O
someone, you help them to do something wrong. EG
...aiding and abetting the enemy.

abhor /əˀbhɔː/, **abhors, abhorring, abhorred.** If V+O
you **abhor** something, you hate it very much. EG
She abhors any form of cruelty.

abhorrent /əˀbhɒrənt/. If something is **abhor-** ADJ QUALIT
rent to you, you hate it very much or consider it
completely unacceptable. EG *...a ruthless and utterly abhorrent system.* ◇ **abhorrence** /əˀbhɒrəns/. ◇ N UNCOUNT
EG *...an abhorrence of war.*

abide /əbaɪd/, **abides, abiding, abided. 1** If you PHRASE
can't abide something, you dislike it very much. EG
He likes you but he can't abide Dennis.
2 If something **abides**, it continues to happen or V
exist for a long time. ◇ **abiding.** EG *...a constant* ◇ ADJ CLASSIF :
and abiding joy. ATTRIB

abide by. If you **abide by** a law, agreement, or PHRASAL VB :
decision, you do what it says you should do. EG *Both* V+PREP
parties must agree to abide by the court's decision.

ability /əbɪləˀtiˡ/, **abilities.** Your **ability** to do N COUNT OR
something is the quality or skill that you have N UNCOUNT
which makes it possible for you to do it. EG *...the
ability to see... ...his ability as a journalist.* ● If you ● PHRASE
do something **to the best of** your **ability** or **to the
best of** your **abilities**, you do it as well as you
possibly can.

-ability is added in place of '-able' at the end of SUFFIX
adjectives to form nouns. These nouns are often
not defined in this dictionary, but are treated with

the related adjectives. EG ...*the suitability of particular courses... ...their vulnerability to criticism.*

abject /ˈæbdʒɛkt/. 1 You use **abject** to emphasize that a situation or quality is shameful or depressing. EG ...*abject poverty.* ADJ CLASSIF : ATTRIB

2 Someone who is **abject** shows no self-respect or courage. EG *Even the most abject slaves joined in the revolt.* ADJ QUALIT

ablaze /əˈbleɪz/. 1 Something that is **ablaze** is burning fiercely. EG *In a moment the tents were ablaze.* ADJ PRED

2 If a place is **ablaze** with lights or colours, it is very bright because of them. ADJ PRED + with

able /ˈeɪbəl/, **abler, ablest.** 1 If someone or something is **able** to do something, 1.1 they have the physical skill or the knowledge to do it. EG *The frog is able to jump three metres... I wasn't able to do these quizzes.* 1.2 they have enough freedom, power, time, or money to do it. EG *I thought I wouldn't be able to visit you this week... I was able to buy a caravan after a long search.* ADJ PRED + to-INF

2 Someone who is **able** is very clever or very good at doing something. EG *He was an unusually able detective.* ADJ QUALIT

-able is added to some verbs to form adjectives. These adjectives describe someone or something as able to have the thing done to them described by the verb. For example, something that is identifiable can be identified. EG *They are both immediately recognizable... Only the titles were readable.* SUFFIX

able-bodied /ˌeɪbəl ˈbɒdɪd/. An **able-bodied** person is physically strong and healthy. ADJ CLASSIF

ably /ˈeɪblɪ/ means skilfully and successfully. EG *They were ably supported by the Party members.* ADV

abnormal /æbˈnɔːməl/. Someone or something that is **abnormal** is unusual, especially in a way that is worrying. EG *Maybe my child is abnormal... ...an abnormal interest in food.* ◊ **abnormality** /ˌæbnəˈmælɪtɪ/, **abnormalities.** EG ...*an abnormality in the blood.* ADJ CLASSIF

◊ N COUNT OR N UNCOUNT

abnormally /æbˈnɔːməlɪ/ means 1 to a much greater extent than usual. EG ...*the abnormally warm day.* 2 in an unusual, often worrying way. EG ...*people who are behaving abnormally.* SUBMOD

ADV

aboard /əˈbɔːd/. If you are **aboard** a ship or plane, you are on or in it. EG *The plane crashed, killing all 271 aboard.* PREP OR ADV

abode /əˈbəʊd/, **abodes.** Your **abode** is the place where you live. EG *He took his new bride directly to their new abode.* N COUNT : OFT + POSS Formal

abolish /əˈbɒlɪʃ/, **abolishes, abolishing, abolished.** If you **abolish** a system or practice, you formally put an end to it. EG *They believed the death penalty should be abolished.* ◊ **abolition** /ˌæbəˈlɪʃən/. EG ...*the abolition of slavery.* V + O

◊ N UNCOUNT + SUPP

abominable /əˈbɒmɪnəbəl/. Something that is **abominable** is very unpleasant or very bad. EG *They work in abominable conditions.* ◊ **abominably.** EG *She had been treated abominably.* ADJ QUALIT

◊ ADV

abort /əˈbɔːt/, **aborts, aborting, aborted.** 1 If a woman's pregnancy **is aborted** or if she **aborts,** her pregnancy is ended deliberately and the baby dies. V + O : USU PASS; ALSO V

2 If you **abort** a process, plan, or activity, or if it **aborts,** you stop it before it has been completed. EG *Harris tried to abort the operation half-way through.* V-ERG

abortion /əˈbɔːʃən/, **abortions.** If a woman has an **abortion,** she ends her pregnancy deliberately and the baby dies. N COUNT OR N UNCOUNT

abortive /əˈbɔːtɪv/. An **abortive** attempt or action is unsuccessful. EG ...*a year of demonstrations and abortive revolts.* ADJ CLASSIF : ATTRIB

abound /əˈbaʊnd/, **abounds, abounding, abounded.** If things **abound,** or if a place **abounds** with things, there are very large numbers of them. EG *Rumours abounded... Its hills abound with waterfalls.* V OR V + with/in Formal

about /əˈbaʊt/. 1 If you talk, write, or think **about** a particular thing, it is the subject of what you are saying, writing, or thinking. EG *I'll have to think about that... He had to talk about his profession... This is a book about India.* PREP

2 If you do something **about** a problem, you take action in order to solve it. EG *They knew they had to do something about their mother's unhappiness.* PREP

3 When you say that there is a particular quality **about** someone or something, you mean that they have this quality. EG *There's something peculiar about him.* PREP

4 **About** in front of a number means that the number is approximate, not exact. EG *We went about forty miles.* ADV

5 If someone or something moves **about,** they keep moving in different directions. EG *We saw them walking about... I stood waving my arms about.* ADV AFTER

6 **About** is used in phrasal verbs such as 'sit about' or 'mess about' to indicate that someone is not achieving very much. ADV AFTER

7 If someone or something is **about,** they are present or available. EG *There was no money about.* ADJ PRED

8 If you **are about to** do something, you are going to do it very soon. EG *Her father is about to retire.* PHRASE

about-turn, about-turns. An **about-turn** or an **about-face** is a complete change of attitude or opinion. EG *The Conservatives performed a swift about-turn.* N COUNT

above /əˈbʌv/. 1 If one thing is **above** another one, it is directly over it or higher than it. EG ...*the branches above their heads... A noise was coming from the bedroom above.* PREP OR A

2 You use **above** in writing to refer to something that has already been mentioned. EG *All the above items can be obtained from Selfridges... The meanings of the terms used above are given in leaflet NI 12.* ADJ, ADV, OR the + N

3 If an amount or measurement is **above** a particular level, it is greater than that level. EG ...*children above the age of 5... ...aged 15 and above.* PREP OR A

4 If someone is **above** you, they are in a position of authority over you. EG *He will have an executive above him to whom he reports.* PREP

5 If someone thinks that they are **above** a particular activity, they do not want to get involved in it because they do not approve of it. EG *They consider themselves above such mercenary transactions.* PREP

6 If someone is **above** criticism or suspicion, they cannot be criticized or suspected because of their good qualities or their position. PREP

above board. If an arrangement or deal is **above board,** it is completely honest. ADJ PRED

abrasion /əˈbreɪʒən/, **abrasions.** An **abrasion** is an area on a person's body where the skin has been scraped. EG ...*abrasions to the side of the neck.* N COUNT Formal

abrasive /əˈbreɪsɪv/. 1 Someone who is **abrasive** is unkind and rude. EG *He could be abrasive and insensitive... ...an abrasive manner.* ADJ QUALIT

2 An **abrasive** substance is rough and can be used to clean hard surfaces. EG ...*an abrasive cleaner.* ADJ CLASSIF

abreast /əˈbrest/. 1 If people or things walk or move **abreast,** they are next to each other, side by side. EG ...*carts pulled by donkeys three abreast.* ADV

2 If you keep **abreast of** a subject, you know all the most recent facts about it. EG *The press kept abreast of each development.* PREP

abridged /əˈbrɪdʒd/. A book or play that is **abridged** has been made shorter by removing some parts of it. EG ...*an abridged version of the novel.* ADJ CLASSIF

abroad /əˈbrɔːd/. 1 If you go **abroad,** you go to a foreign country. EG ...*a holiday abroad... I just got back from abroad.* ADV

If someone told you something in absolute secrecy, would you tell other people?

2 If a story or feeling is **abroad**, people generally ADV
know about it or feel it.

abrupt /əbrʌpt/. 1 If an action is **abrupt**, it is very ADJ QUALIT
sudden and often unpleasant. EG *It came to an*
abrupt end... ...an abrupt movement. ◊ **abruptly**. ◊ ADV
EG *I had to apply the brakes abruptly.*

2 Someone who is **abrupt** is rather rude and ADJ QUALIT
unfriendly. EG *...David's abrupt and bullying man-*
ner. ◊ **abruptly**. EG *I wouldn't have spoken so* ◊ ADV
abruptly if I'd realized you were ill.

abscess /æbsɪs/, **abscesses**. An **abscess** is a N COUNT
painful swelling on your skin, containing pus.

abscond /əbskɒnd/, **absconds**, **absconding**, **ab-**
sconded. 1 If someone **absconds** with something, V+with
they run away with it. EG *He absconded with* Formal
everyone's wages.

2 If someone **absconds** from somewhere such as a V:OFT+from
prison, they run away from it.

absence /æbsəns/, **absences**. 1 Someone's **ab-** N UNCOUNT
sence from a place is the fact of their not being OR N COUNT:
there. EG *They remained in their seats during my* +SUPP
absence... ...frequent absences from school.

2 The **absence** of something is the fact that it is N SING+SUPP
not there. EG *The absence of electricity made*
matters worse.

absent /æbsənt/. 1 If someone or something is ADJ CLASSIF:
absent from a place or situation, they are not OFT+from
there. EG *You have been absent twenty minutes...*
...something which is still absent from your work.

2 If someone appears **absent**, they are not paying ADJ CLASSIF
attention because they are thinking about some-
thing else. EG *...an absent stare.* ◊ **absently**. EG *'Did* ◊ ADV
you?' Boylan said absently.

absentee /æbsəntiː/, **absentees**. An **absentee** is N COUNT
a person who should be in a particular place but
who is not there. EG *...absentees from school.*

absent-minded. Someone who is **absent-** ADJ QUALIT
minded often forgets things. ◊ **absent-mindedly**. ◊ ADV
EG *...if you absent-mindedly drop a diamond ring*
down the sink.

absolute /æbsəluːt/, **absolutes**. 1 **Absolute** ADJ CLASSIF:
means total and complete. EG *...the necessity for* ATTRIB
absolute secrecy.

2 You use **absolute** to emphasize something that ADJ CLASSIF:
you are saying. EG *The script is an absolute mess.* ATTRIB

3 An **absolute** ruler has complete power and ADJ CLASSIF
authority over his or her country.

4 **Absolute** rules and principles are believed to be ADJ CLASSIF:
true or right for all situations. ATTRIB

5 An **absolute** is a rule or principle that is believed N COUNT
to be true or right in all situations. EG *...rigid*
absolutes, such as 'divorce is always wrong'.

absolutely /æbsəluːtliː/. 1 **Absolutely** means ADV OR SUBMOD
totally and completely. EG *That's an absolutely*
fascinating piece of work.

2 You say **absolutely** as an emphatic way of CONVENTION
saying yes or agreeing with someone. EG *'She's*
excellent though.' – 'Absolutely.'

absolution /æbsəluːʃən/. If someone is given N UNCOUNT
absolution, they are forgiven for something wrong Formal
that they have done.

absolve /əbzɒlv/, **absolves**, **absolving**, **ab-** V+O:USU PASS
solved. If someone **is absolved** from blame or +from/of
responsibility, a formal statement is made that
they are not guilty or are not to blame. EG *The*
captain is absolved from all blame and responsibil-
ity for the shipwreck... Before you die you're
absolved of your sins.

absorb /əbzɔːb/, **absorbs**, **absorbing**, **ab-**
sorbed. 1 If something **absorbs** a liquid, gas, light, V+O
or heat, it soaks it up or takes it in. EG *Frogs absorb*
water through their skins.

2 If a group **is absorbed** into a larger group, it V+O:
becomes part of the larger group and loses its OFT+into
individuality. EG *Small businesses are absorbed by*
larger ones.

3 If a system or society **absorbs** changes or V+O
effects, it is able to deal with them without being
badly affected.

4 If you **absorb** information, you learn and under- V+O
stand it.

5 If something **absorbs** you, it interests you very V+O
much and you pay a lot of attention to it.
◊ **absorbed**. EG *I was utterly absorbed in what I* ◊ ADJ QUALIT
was doing. ◊ **absorbing**. EG *The work is absorbing.* ◊ ADJ QUALIT

absorbent /əbzɔːbənt, -zɔː-/. **Absorbent** material ADJ QUALIT
soaks up liquid easily.

absorption /əbzɔːpʃən, -zɔːp-/. 1 If you have an N SING+SUPP
absorption in something, you are very interested
in it. EG *...her growing absorption in the study of*
natural history.

2 **Absorption** is the action of absorbing something. N UNCOUNT
EG *...the absorption of foreign minorities.* +SUPP

abstain /əbsteɪn/, **abstains**, **abstaining**, **ab-**
stained. 1 If you **abstain** from doing something V:OFT+from
enjoyable, you deliberately do not do it. EG *He*
abstained from eating for six days.

2 If you **abstain** during a vote, you do not vote. V

abstemious /əbstiːmɪəs/. Someone who is **abste-** ADJ QUALIT
mious avoids doing too much of something enjoy- Formal
able such as eating or drinking.

abstention /əbstenʃən/, **abstentions**. An **ab-** N COUNT OR
stention is a formal act of not voting either for or N UNCOUNT
against a proposal. EG *There were 4 abstentions.*

abstinence /æbstɪnəns/ is the practice of ab- N UNCOUNT
staining from something that you enjoy doing,
especially from drinking alcoholic drinks. EG *He*
practised total abstinence for a month.

abstract, abstracts, abstracting, abstracted;
pronounced /æbstrækt/ when it is an adjective or a
noun, and /əbstrækt/ when it is a verb.

1 An idea or argument that is **abstract** is based on ADJ QUALIT
general ideas rather than on particular things and
events. EG *...our capacity for abstract reasoning...*
...an abstract principle.

2 **Abstract** art is a style of art which uses shapes ADJ CLASSIF:
and patterns rather than representing people or ATTRIB
things. EG *...abstract sculptures.*

3 An **abstract** noun is a noun that describes a ADJ CLASSIF:
quality or idea rather than a physical object. ATTRIB

4 An **abstract** of an article or speech is a short N COUNT
piece of writing that summarizes the main points
of it.

5 If you **abstract** information from an article or V+O
other piece of writing, you make a summary of the
main points in it.

abstracted /əbstræktɪd/. Someone whose be- ADJ QUALIT
haviour is **abstracted** is thinking so deeply that
they do not notice what is happening around them.
EG *...a dreamy, abstracted stare.*

abstraction /əbstrækʃən/, **abstractions**. 1 An N COUNT
abstraction is a general idea rather than one
relating to a particular object, person, or situation.
EG *...abstractions of philosophy and religion.*

2 **Abstraction** is the state of being very deep in N UNCOUNT
thought.

absurd /əbsɜːd/. Something that is **absurd** is ADJ QUALIT
ridiculous. EG *It seemed absurd to try to carry a*
twenty-five-pound camera about. ◊ **absurdity** ◊ N COUNT OR
/əbsɜːdɪtɪ/, **absurdities**. EG *...the oddities and* N UNCOUNT
absurdities of the language. ◊ **absurdly**. EG *...an* ◊ ADV OR
absurdly low rent. SUBMOD

abundance /əbʌndəns/. 1 An **abundance** of N PART:SING
something is a large quantity of it. EG *...an abun-*
dance of evidence.

2 If something is **in abundance**, there is a lot of it. PHRASE
EG *There was grass in abundance.*

abundant /əbʌndənt/. Something that is **abun-** ADJ QUALIT
dant is present in large quantities. EG *...an abun-*
dant supply of food.

abundantly /əbʌndəntliː/. 1 If something is SUBMOD
abundantly obvious, it is extremely obvious. EG *It*
has become abundantly clear that there is no time
to lose.

2 Something that occurs **abundantly** is present in ADV
large quantities. EG *...a plant growing abundantly at*
the edges of a road.

abuse, abuses, abusing, abused; pronounced /ə³bjuːs/ when it is a noun and /ə³bjuːz/ when it is a verb.

1 Abuse is rude and unkind things that people say when they are angry. EG *The girls shrieked abuse at the lawyers.* N UNCOUNT

2 Abuse of someone is cruel and violent treatment of them. EG *...found guilty of gross neglect and abuse.* N UNCOUNT +SUPP

3 Abuse of something is the use of it in a wrong way or for a bad purpose. EG *...the uses and abuses of power... ...drug abuse.* N UNCOUNT OR N COUNT : +SUPP

4 If you **abuse** something, you use it in a wrong way or for a bad purpose. V+O

5 If someone **abuses** you, **5.1** they say rude or unkind things to you. EG *He did not like to hear Elaine abused or criticized.* **5.2** they treat you cruelly and violently. EG *The patients were often physically abused.* V+O

abusive /ə³bjuːsɪv/. Someone who is **abusive** says or writes rude or unkind things. EG *...abusive language.* ADJ QUALIT

abysmal /əbɪzmə⁰l/ means very bad or poor in quality. EG *...abysmal wages... ...an abysmal failure.* ADJ QUALIT

◊ **abysmally**. EG *He failed abysmally.* ◊ ADV

abyss /ə³bɪs/, **abysses. 1** An **abyss** is a very deep hole in the ground. EG *We looked down into the abyss.* N COUNT

2 A very frightening or threatening situation can be referred to as an **abyss**. EG *The world was teetering on the edge of the abyss of World War III.* N COUNT+SUPP Literary

AC is used to refer to an electric current that continually changes direction as it flows. **AC** is an abbreviation for 'alternating current'.

academic /ækə⁰demɪk/, **academics. 1 Academic** work is work which is done in schools, colleges, and universities. EG *...the academic system.* ADJ CLASSIF : ATTRIB

◊ **academically**. EG *...people who are well qualified academically.* ◊ ADV

2 Someone who is **academic** is good at studying. ADJ QUALIT

3 An **academic** is a member of a university or college who teaches or does research. N COUNT

4 You also use **academic** to say that you think a particular point has no real effect on or relevance to what is happening. EG *It was all academic, because there were never any profits to share out.* ADJ QUALIT

academy /ə³kædə³miː/, **academies.** Some schools or colleges are called **academies**, especially ones that specialize in a particular subject. EG *...the Royal Academy of Dramatic Art.* N COUNT

accede /ə³ksiːd/, **accedes, acceding, acceded.** If you **accede** to someone's request or opinion, you allow it or agree with it. V : USU+*to* Formal

accelerate /ə³kseləreɪt/, **accelerates, accelerating, accelerated. 1** When a process or the rate of something **accelerates**, it gets faster and faster. EG *Inflation rates began to accelerate.* V-ERG

◊ **acceleration** /ə³kseləreɪ⁰ʃə⁰n/. EG *...the acceleration of economic growth.* ◊ N UNCOUNT

2 When moving vehicles **accelerate**, they go faster and faster. ◊ **acceleration**. EG *The acceleration of this car is very impressive.* V ◊ N UNCOUNT

accelerator /ə³kseləreɪtə/, **accelerators.** The **accelerator** in a car or other vehicle is the pedal which you press with your foot in order to make the vehicle go faster. See picture at CAR. N COUNT

accent, accents, accenting, accented; pronounced /æksə²nt/ when it is a noun and /æksent/ when it is a verb.

1 Someone who speaks with a particular **accent** pronounces the words of a language in a distinctive way that shows which country, region, or social class they come from. EG *She has a strong Irish accent.* N COUNT : USU+SUPP

2 An **accent** is also a short line or other mark which is written above certain letters in some languages and which affects the way those letters are pronounced. N COUNT

3 If you say that the **accent** is on a particular N SING

feature of something, you mean that this feature is especially important. EG *The accent is on presentation in this contest.*

4 If you **accent** a word or a musical note, you emphasize it, for example by making it louder. V+O

accentuate /ə³ksentʃueɪt/, **accentuates, accentuating, accentuated.** To **accentuate** something means to emphasize it or make it more noticeable. EG *These laws accentuate inequality and exploitation.* V+O

accept /ə³ksept/, **accepts, accepting, accepted.**

1 If you **accept** something that you have been offered, you say yes to it or agree to take it. EG *He accepted our invitation... Her article has been accepted for publication.* V+O OR V

2 If you **accept** someone's advice or suggestion, you agree to do what they say. EG *I knew that they would accept my proposal.* V+O

3 If you **accept** a story or statement, you believe it. EG *The panel accepted her version of the story... The majority do not accept that there has been any discrimination.* V+O; ALSO V+REPORT : ONLY *that*

4 If you **accept** a difficult or unpleasant situation, you get used to it and recognize that it cannot be changed. EG *...unwillingness to accept bad working conditions... The astronaut accepts danger as being part of the job.* V+O

5 If you **accept** the blame or responsibility for something, you admit that you are responsible for it. V+O

6 When an institution or organization **accepts** someone, they give them a job or allow them to join. EG *I was accepted by the Open University.* V+O

7 If a group **accepts** you, they begin to think of you as part of the group. EG *The children gradually begin to accept her.* V+O

8 If a machine **accepts** a particular kind of thing, it is designed to take it and deal with it. EG *The ticket machine won't accept 20p pieces.* V+O

9 See also **accepted**.

acceptable /ə³kseptəbə⁰l/. **1** If something is **acceptable**, people generally approve of it or allow it to happen. EG *In war killing is acceptable.* ADJ QUALIT

◊ **acceptability** /əkseptə³bɪlɪ³tiː/. EG *The proof of a doctrine is its acceptability to the man in the street.* ◊ **acceptably**. EG *...an acceptably low heat loss.* ◊ N UNCOUNT ◊ ADV

2 If you think that something is **acceptable**, you consider it to be good enough. EG *To my relief he found the article acceptable.* ADJ CLASSIF

acceptance /ə³kseptə⁰ns/, **acceptances. 1 Acceptance** of something that has been offered to you is the act of taking it or agreeing to use it. EG *...the acceptance of foreign aid.* N UNCOUNT

2 If you receive an **acceptance** for a job or membership that you have applied for, you are offered the job or membership. EG *Within two days I had a letter of acceptance from the manager.* N COUNT OR N UNCOUNT

3 Acceptance of someone into a group is the act of beginning to think of them as part of the group, treating them in the same way as other members of it. N UNCOUNT

4 Acceptance of an idea is a general belief or agreement that it is true. EG *...their acceptance of his right to rule.* N UNCOUNT

5 Your **acceptance** of an unpleasant or difficult situation is your getting used to it and recognizing that you cannot change it. EG *...their acceptance of their plight.* N UNCOUNT

accepted /ə³kseptɪ²d/. **Accepted** ideas are generally agreed to be correct. EG *...the accepted wisdom about old age.* ADJ CLASSIF ATTRIB

access /ækses/, **accesses, accessing, accessed.**

1 If you gain **access** to a building or other place, N UNCOUNT :

you succeed in getting into it. EG *The entrance door* OFT+*to*
gives access to a living room.   Formal
2 Access is also the opportunity or right to use or N UNCOUNT:
see something or someone. EG *I demanded access* OFT+*to*
to a telephone... Has Donald got access to the
child?
3 If you **access** information from a computer, you V+O
get it.

accessible /ə³ksɛsə¹bᵊl/. **1** If a place is **acces-** ADJ QUALIT
sible, you are able to reach it. EG *The hidden room*
was accessible only through a secret back en-
trance. ◊ **accessibility** /əksɛsə¹bɪlɪ¹tɪ¹/. EG *The* ◊ N UNCOUNT
site was picked because of its accessibility by rail.
2 If something is **accessible** to people, they are ADJ PRED+*to*
able to use it or buy it. EG *...computers cheap*
enough to be accessible to virtually everyone.
3 If a book, painting, or other work of art is ADJ PRED
accessible to people, they are able to understand
it and appreciate it.

accession /ə³ksɛʃə³n/ is the act of taking up a N UNCOUNT
position as the ruler of a country. EG *...Queen*
Victoria's accession in 1837.

accessory /ə³ksɛsəri¹/, **accessories. 1 Accesso-** N COUNT:
ries are **1.1** extra parts added to a machine or tool USU PLURAL
in order to make it more efficient or able to
perform extra jobs. EG *The car has an attractive*
range of extra accessories such as built-in tape
decks and radios. **1.2** articles, such as belts and
handbags, which you wear or carry but which are
not part of your main clothing. EG *...a grey silk suit*
and accessories to match.
2 A person who is an **accessory** to a crime knows N COUNT
that someone has committed the crime but does Legal
not tell the police. EG *They are all accessories to*
murder.

accident /æksɪdə³nt/, **accidents. 1** An **accident** N COUNT
is **1.1** an event which happens completely by
chance. EG *The fact that there is a university here*
is due to a historic accident. **1.2** something unpleasant and unfortunate that happens and that often
leads to injury or death. EG *He had an accident on*
his way home... She was killed in a motor accident.
2 If something happens **by accident**, it happens PHRASE
completely by chance. EG *I only came to Liverpool*
by accident.

accidental /æksɪdɛntə³l/. Something that is **acci-** ADJ CLASSIF
dental happens by chance. EG *The evidence doesn't*
suggest accidental death. ◊ **accidentally**. EG *We* ◊ ADV
accidentally found an ideal solution.

accident-prone. Someone who is **accident-** ADJ QUALIT
prone keeps having accidents.

acclaim /əkleɪm/, **acclaims, acclaiming, ac-**
claimed. 1 If someone or something **is ac-** V+O: USU PASS
claimed, they are praised enthusiastically. EG *He* Formal
has been widely acclaimed for his paintings.
2 Acclaim is praise for someone or something. EG N UNCOUNT
His book was published in 1919 and met with Formal
unusual acclaim.

acclimatize /əklaɪmətaɪz/, **acclimatizes, accli-** V OR V-REFL
matizing, acclimatized; also spelled **acclima-**
tise. When you **acclimatize** to something or **ac-**
climatize yourself to it, you become used to it. EG
Once you've acclimatized to the heat you won't feel
so tired.

accolade /æko⁶leɪd/, **accolades.** An **accolade** is N COUNT+SUPP
praise or an award that is given publicly to some- Formal
one who is greatly admired. EG *This was the highest*
accolade he could receive.

accommodate /əkɒmədeɪt/, **accommodates,**
accommodating, accommodated. 1 If you **ac-**
commodate someone, **1.1** you provide them with a V+O: USU+A
place where they can stay, live, or work. EG *She*
can't accommodate guests at the moment. **1.2** you V+O
do something to help them. EG *The bank is accom-*
modating its customers more than it used to.
2 If a place or building can **accommodate** a V+O
number of people or things, it has enough room for
them. EG *The cottage could accommodate up to five*
people.

accommodating /əkɒmədeɪtɪŋ/. Someone who ADJ QUALIT
is **accommodating** is very willing to help you. EG
The warder was always accommodating in allow-
ing visitors in.

accommodation /əkɒmədeɪʃə³n/ is a room or N UNCOUNT
building to stay in, work in, or live in. EG *There is a*
shortage of accommodation.

accompaniment /əkʌmpə³nɪmə³nt/, **accompa-**
niments. 1 The **accompaniment** to a song or N UNCOUNT:
tune is the music that is played at the same time USU+SUPP
and that forms a background to it. EG *...a guitar*
accompaniment.
2 An **accompaniment** to something is something N COUNT:
else that happens or exists at the same time. EG OFT+*to/of*
This sauce is often served as an accompaniment to
fish.

accompanist /əkʌmpə³nɪst/, **accompanists.** An N COUNT+SUPP
accompanist is a musician, especially a pianist,
who plays one part of a piece of music while
someone else sings or plays the main tune.

accompany /əkʌmpə³ni¹/, **accompanies, ac-**
companying, accompanied. 1 If you **accompany** V+O: USU+A
someone, you go somewhere with them. EG *She*
asked me to accompany her to the church.
2 If something **accompanies** something else, it V+O
happens or exists at the same time or as a result of
it. EG *A high fever often accompanies a mild*
infection.
3 When you **accompany** a singer or a musician, V+O OR V-REFL
you play one part of a piece of music while they
sing or play the main tune. EG *Sarah sings and Bill*
accompanies her on the guitar.

accomplice /əkɒmplɪs, əkʌm-/, **accomplices.** N COUNT
Someone's **accomplice** is a person who helps
them to commit a crime.

accomplish /əkɒmplɪʃ, əkʌm-/, **accomplishes,** V+O
accomplishing, accomplished. If you **accom-**
plish something, you succeed in doing it. EG *I never*
seem to accomplish anything.

accomplished /əkɒmplɪʃt, əkʌm-/. If someone is ADJ QUALIT
accomplished at something, they are very good at
it. EG *...an accomplished cook.*

accomplishment /əkɒmplɪʃmə³nt, əkʌm-/, **ac-**
complishments. 1 A person of **accomplishment** N UNCOUNT
has knowledge or skill to be able to do something
well. EG *...actors of similar experience and accom-*
plishment.
2 The **accomplishment** of something is the fact of N UNCOUNT
achieving or finishing it. EG *The accomplishment of* +SUPP
this task filled him with satisfaction.
3 Your **accomplishments** are the things that you N COUNT
can do well. EG *One of her few accomplishments*
was the ability to do cartwheels.
4 An **accomplishment** is something remarkable N COUNT+SUPP
that has been done or achieved. EG *This is no small*
accomplishment.

accord /ə³kɔːd/, **accords, according, accorded.**
1 When you do something **of** your **own accord,** PHRASE
you do it freely and because you want to. EG *She*
knew they would leave of their own accord.
2 If people are in **accord**, they agree about some- N UNCOUNT
thing. EG *There are few issues on which the two are*
in perfect accord.
3 If you **accord** someone a particular kind of V+O+O OR
treatment, you treat them in that way. EG *Newsmen* V+O+*to*
accorded her the kind of coverage normally re-
served for film stars.
4 If an idea, policy, or situation **accords** with V+*with*
something else, it fits in with it. EG *I rewrote the* Formal
article because it didn't accord with our policy.

accordance /ə³kɔːdə³ns/. If something is done **in** PREP
accordance with a particular rule or system, it is
done in the way that the rule or system says that it
should be done. EG *...in accordance with Islamic*
law.

accordingly /ə³kɔːdɪŋli¹/. You use **accordingly** ADV
when you are saying that something happened as
the result of something else. EG *Sometimes the*
press went too far, and suffered accordingly.

according to. 1 If you say that something is true PREP
according to a particular person, book, or document, you mean that you got the information from
that person, book, or document. EG *According to Dr
Santos, the cause of death was drowning... The road
was some forty miles long according to my map.*
2 If something is done **according to** a particular PREP
principle or condition, this principle or condition is
used as the basis for the way it has been done. EG
*Each person was given tasks according to their
skills... There are six classes organized according
to age.*
3 If something happens **according to** a particular PREP
plan or system, it happens in the way that the plan
or system says that it should be done. EG *Everything went according to plan.*

accordion /ɔˈkɔːdɪən/, **accordions.** An accordi- N COUNT
on is a box-shaped musical instrument. You play it
by pressing keys or buttons on either side while
moving the two sides together and apart.

accost /ɔˈkɒst/, **accosts, accosting, accosted.** If V+O
you **accost** someone, especially a stranger, you
stop them or go up to them and speak to them. EG
In the hall he was accosted by two men.

account /ɔˈkaʊnt/, **accounts, accounting, ac-
counted.** 1 An **account** is a written or spoken N COUNT :
report of something that has happened. EG *There OFT+of
were accounts of the incident in the paper.*
2 **Accounts** are detailed records of all the money N COUNT :
that a person or business receives and spends. EG USU PLURAL
He had to submit accounts of his expenditure.
3 If you have an **account** with a bank, you leave N COUNT
money with it and withdraw it when you need it. EG
I would like to open an account.
4 If you have an **account** with a shop or company, N COUNT
you can get goods or services from the shop or
company and pay for them at a later date, usually
once a month.
5 **Account** is also used in these phrases. 5.1 If you PHRASES
take something **into account** or **take account of**
it, you include it when you are thinking about a
situation. EG *We'll certainly take your feelings into
account.* 5.2 If you do something **on account of**
something or someone, you do it because of that
thing or person. EG *'Auntie told me not to run,' he
explained, 'on account of my asthma.'... Don't abstain from smoking on my account.* 5.3 If you say
that something should **on no account** be done, you
mean that it should not be done under any circumstances. EG *On no account must strangers be let in.*
5.4 If something is **of no account**, it does not
matter at all. EG *It's of no account to me whether
you go or stay.* 5.5 If you **give a good account of**
yourself, you behave in a way which brings you
praise and respect from other people. EG *Your son
gave a very good account of himself last night.*

account for. 1 If you **account for** something PHRASAL VB :
that has happened, you explain how it happened. EG V+PREP
How do you account for the dent in the car? 2 If V+PREP
something **accounts for** a part or proportion of
something, it is what that part or proportion consists of. EG *Computer software accounts for some 70
per cent of our range of products.*

accountable /ɔˈkaʊntəbəl/. If you are **account-** ADJ PRED
able to someone for something that you do, you
are responsible for it and must be prepared to
justify your actions to that person. EG *They cannot
be held accountable for what they did... ...a public
corporation fully accountable to Parliament.*
◊ **accountability.** EG *...the need for greater ac-* ◊ N UNCOUNT
countability of the police.

accountancy /ɔˈkaʊntənsɪ/ is the work of keep- N UNCOUNT
ing financial accounts. EG *...a career in accountancy.*

accountant /ɔˈkaʊntənt/, **accountants.** An ac- N COUNT
countant is a person whose job is to keep financial
accounts.

accredit /ɔˈkrɛdɪt/, **accredits, accrediting, ac-** V+O : USU PASS
credited. If someone **is accredited** in a particular

position or job, it is officially recognized that they
have that position or job. EG *...an accredited shop
steward.*

accumulate /ɔˈkjuːmjəˈleɪt/, **accumulates, ac-** V-ERG
cumulating, accumulated. When you **accumu-**
late things or when they **accumulate**, they collect
or gather over a period of time. EG *...the things I
had accumulated over the last four years.*

accumulation /ɔˈkjuːmjəˈleɪʃən/, **accumula-**
tions. 1 An **accumulation** is a large number of N COUNT+SUPP
things which have been gathered together over a
period of time. EG *...an accumulation of facts.*
2 **Accumulation** is the collecting together of N UNCOUNT
things over a period of time. EG *...the accumulation +SUPP
of wealth.*

accuracy /ˈækjɔˈrəsɪ/ is 1 the ability to perform a N UNCOUNT
task without making a mistake. EG *...the speed and
accuracy with which she typed.* 2 the quality of
being true or correct. EG *...the reputation of The
Times for accuracy.*

accurate /ˈækjɔˈrət/. 1 An account or description ADJ QUALIT
that is **accurate** gives a true idea of what someone
or something is like. EG *...an accurate picture of
social history.* ◊ **accurately.** EG *The story is* ◊ ADV
accurately told.
2 A person, device, or machine that is **accurate** is ADJ QUALIT
able to perform a task precisely and without
making a mistake. EG *Missiles are becoming more
accurate... She is accurate in punctuation and
spelling.* ◊ **accurately.** EG *I have not drawn it* ◊ ADV
accurately enough.

accusation /ˈækjɔˈzeɪʃən/, **accusations.** 1 An N COUNT
accusation is a statement that someone has done
something wrong or has committed a crime. EG
*...accusations of cheating... He should defend him-
self against false accusations.*
2 **Accusation** is the quality of showing by your N UNCOUNT
voice or behaviour that you think that someone has
done something wrong. EG *Her eyes were full of
accusation.*

accuse /ɔˈkjuːz/, **accuses, accusing, accused.** 1 V+O : OFT+
If you **accuse** someone of something, you say that
they have done something wrong. EG *He was accused of incompetence.*
2 If someone **is accused** of a crime, they have V+O : USU
been charged with the crime and are on trial for it. PASS+of
EG *He is accused of killing ten young women.*

accused /ɔˈkjuːzd/. **Accused** is both the singular N COUNT :
and the plural. the+N
The **accused** refers to the person or group of
people being tried in a court for a crime. EG *Will
the accused please stand.*

accusing /ɔˈkjuːzɪŋ/. If your expression or tone of ADJ QUALIT
voice is **accusing**, it indicates that you think that
someone has done something wrong. EG *She gave
him an accusing look.* ◊ **accusingly.** EG *'You liked* ◊ ADV
him,' he said accusingly.

accustom /ɔˈkʌstəm/, **accustoms, accustom-** V-REFL+to
ing, accustomed. If you **accustom** yourself or OR V+O+to
someone else to something different, you make
yourself or them used to it. EG *He sat very still,
trying to accustom himself to the darkness.*

accustomed /ɔˈkʌstəmd/. 1 If you are **accus-** ADJ PRED+to
tomed to something, you are used to it or familiar
with it. EG *I am not accustomed to being interrupted... My eyes became accustomed to the dim
lighting.*
2 **Accustomed** means usual. EG *He drove with his* ADJ CLASSIF
accustomed, casual ease. ATTRIB

ace /eɪs/, **aces.** 1 An **ace** is a playing card which N COUNT
has a single symbol on it. EG *...the ace of spades.*
2 A person who is **ace** at something is extremely ADJ CLASSIF
good at it. EG *...an ace marksman.* Informal

ache /eɪk/, **aches, aching, ached.** 1 If you **ache** V
or if a part of your body **aches**, you feel a dull

Does an accountant have to be accurate?

steady pain. EG *I was tired, aching, and miserable...*
His leg ached.

2 If you **ache** for something or **ache** to do some- V+for/with
thing, you want it very much. EG *She was aching for* OR to-INF
a cigarette... I was aching to tell you all my news.

3 An **ache** is a dull steady pain in a part of your N COUNT
body. EG *my usual aches and pains.*

achieve /ɔˈtʃiːv/, **achieves**, **achieving**, V+O
achieved. If you **achieve** a particular aim or
effect, you succeed in doing it or causing it to
happen, usually after a lot of effort. EG *He will do
anything in order to achieve his aim... The riots
achieved nothing.*

achievement /ɔˈtʃiːvmɔnt/, **achievements**. **1** N COUNT+SUPP
An **achievement** is something which someone has
succeeded in doing, especially after a lot of effort.
EG *It was an astonishing achievement.*

2 Achievement is the process of achieving some- N UNCOUNT
thing. EG *This fact did not lessen her sense of
achievement.*

acid /ˈæsɪd/, **acids**. **1** An **acid** is a liquid with a pH N MASS
value of less than 7. Strong acids can burn your
skin and make holes in your clothes.

2 An **acid** substance or liquid has a pH value of less ADJ CLASSIF
than 7. EG *an acid soil.* ◊ **acidity** /ɔˈsɪdɪˈtiɪ/. EG ◊ N UNCOUNT
the acidity of the wine.

3 An **acid** fruit or drink has a sour or sharp taste. ADJ QUALIT
EG *These oranges are very acid.*

4 An **acid** remark is very unkind or critical. EG ADJ QUALIT
her acid wit. ◊ **acidity**. EG *I noticed a certain* ◊ N UNCOUNT
acidity in his comments.

5 If you say that something is **an acid test**, you PHRASE
mean that it is a way of proving whether some-
thing is true or not, or of good quality or not. EG
This venture is seen as an acid test of the alliance.

6 Acid is also the drug LSD. EG *One speaker was* N UNCOUNT
high on acid. Informal

acidic /ɔˈsɪdɪk/. Something that is **acidic** contains ADJ CLASSIF
acid or has a pH value of less than 7.

acknowledge /ɔˈknɒlɪdʒ/, **acknowledges**, **ac-**
knowledging, **acknowledged**. **1** If you **acknowl-** V+O; ALSO
edge a fact or a situation, you accept or admit that V+REPORT:
it is true or that it exists. EG *Most people will now* ONLY that
*acknowledge that there is a crisis... He was ac-
knowledged as America's finest writer.*

2 If you **acknowledge** someone, for example with V+O:
a nod or a smile, you show that you have seen and OFT+with
recognized them.

3 If you **acknowledge** a message, letter, or parcel, V+O; ALSO
you tell the person who sent it that you have V+REPORT:
received it. EG *You have to sign here and acknowl-* ONLY that
edge receipt.

4 If you **acknowledge** applause, compliments, or V+O
something which is done for you, you show your
appreciation. EG *The president stood up to acknowledge the cheers of the crowd.*

acknowledgement /ɔˈknɒlɪdʒmɔnt/, **acknowl-**
edgements; also spelled **acknowledgment**. **1 Ac-** N UNCOUNT
knowledgement of something is **1.1** accepting or OR N COUNT:
admitting that it is true. EG *his acknowledgement* USU+SUPP
of his guilt. **1.2** expressing your gratitude for it or
appreciation of it. EG *her acknowledgement of
their offerings.*

2 Acknowledgement of someone is showing that N UNCOUNT
you have seen and recognized them. EG *One of the
men raised an arm in acknowledgment.*

3 Acknowledgement of a message, letter, or N UNCOUNT:
parcel is telling the sender that you have received OFT+of
it. EG *in acknowledgement of telephone orders.*

4 An **acknowledgement** is a letter or message N COUNT
telling the sender of a letter, message, or parcel
that it has arrived.

5 The **acknowledgements** at the beginning or end N PLURAL
of a book are the short piece of writing in which
the author thanks all the people who have helped
him or her.

acne /ˈækniɪ/. If someone has **acne**, they have a lot N UNCOUNT
of spots on their face and neck. Acne is common
among teenagers.

acorn /ˈeɪkɔːn/, **acorns**. An **acorn** is a pale oval N COUNT
nut that is the fruit of an oak tree.

acoustic /ɔˈkuːstɪk/, **acoustics**. **1 Acoustic** means ADJ CLASSIF:
relating to sound or hearing. EG *Acoustic contact* ATTRIB
had been made.

2 The **acoustics** of a room are the structural N PLURAL
features which determine how well you can hear
music or speeches in it. EG *The theatre was large,
with good acoustics.*

acquaint /ɔˈkweɪnt/, **acquaints**, **acquainting**, V+O+with
acquainted. If you **acquaint** someone with some- Formal
thing, you tell them about it or make them familiar
with it. EG *I will acquaint you with the facts... They
were well acquainted with modern farming methods.*

acquaintance /ɔˈkweɪntɔns/, **acquaintances**. **1** N COUNT:
An **acquaintance** is someone who you have met USU+SUPP
but do not know well. EG *My cousin is an acquaintance of Lord Northcliffe.*

2 If something is **of** your **acquaintance**, you know PHRASE
them slightly, but not well. EG *doctors of my
acquaintance.*

3 When you **make** someone's **acquaintance**, you PHRASE
meet them for the first time and get to know them
a little.

4 Your **acquaintance** with a subject is your knowl- N SING+SUPP
edge or experience of it. EG *her acquaintance with
modern art.*

5 If you have a **nodding** or **passing acquaint-** PHRASE
ance with someone, you know them slightly but
not very well.

acquainted /ɔˈkweɪntɪd/. If you are **acquainted** ADJ PRED:
with someone, you know them slightly but they are OFT+with
not a close friend. EG *Mrs Oliver is acquainted with
my mother... The families were acquainted.*

acquiesce /ˌækwiˈes/, **acquiesces**, **acquiescing**, V:OFT+to/in
acquiesced. If you **acquiesce** to something, you Formal
agree to do what someone wants or to accept what
they do. EG *He acquiesced to the demand.*

◊ **acquiescence** /ˌækwiˈesɔns/. EG *passive acqui-* ◊ N UNCOUNT:
escence to the new arrangements. OFT+to/in

acquire /ɔˈkwaɪɔ/, **acquires**, **acquiring**, **ac-**
quired. **1** If you **acquire** something, you get it or V+O
buy it for yourself, or you are given it. EG *I tried to
acquire the information I needed.* ◊ **acquired**. EG ◊ ADJ CLASSIF
acquired wealth.

2 If you **acquire** a skill or habit, you learn it or V+O
develop it as you live your daily life or grow up. EG
It is a habit well worth acquiring. ◊ **acquired**. EG ◊ ADJ CLASSIF
hereditary and acquired characteristics.

acquisition /ˌækwɪˈzɪʃɔn/, **acquisitions**. **1** An N COUNT
acquisition is something that you have obtained.
EG *He invited me to inspect his latest acquisition.*

2 Acquisition of something is getting it or being N UNCOUNT
given it. EG *the acquisition of land.* +SUPP

3 The **acquisition** of a skill or habit is the process N UNCOUNT
of learning it or developing it. EG *the acquisition* +SUPP
of knowledge.

acquit /ɔˈkwɪt/, **acquits**, **acquitting**, **acquitted**. **1** V+O:USU PASS
If someone **is acquitted** of a crime in a court of
law, it is formally declared that they did not
commit the crime. EG *The jury acquitted her of
theft... Campbell was acquitted on all charges.*

2 If you **acquit** yourself in a particular way, other V-REFL
people feel that you behave in that way. EG *She* Formal
acquitted herself well.

acquittal /ɔˈkwɪtɔl/, **acquittals. Acquittal** is a N UNCOUNT
formal declaration in a court of law that someone OR N COUNT
who has been accused of a crime is innocent.

acre /ˈeɪkɔ/, **acres**. An **acre** is an area of land N PART
measuring 4840 square yards or 4047 square me-
tres. EG *an acre of orchard.*

acrid /ˈækrɪd/. **1** An **acrid** smell or taste is strong ADJ QUALIT
and sharp, and usually unpleasant. EG *The room
was filling with acrid smoke.*

2 Acrid words or remarks are bitter and angry. EG ADJ QUALIT
an acrid attack on capitalism.

acrimonious /ˌækrɪ'məʊnɪəs/. **Acrimonious** ADJ QUALIT Formal words or quarrels are bitter and angry. EG *An acrimonious dispute broke out.*

acrimony /'ækrɪməniˈ/ is bitterness and anger N UNCOUNT about something. EG *...acrimony over the involve-* Formal *ment of the police.*

acrobat /'ækrəʊbæt/, **acrobats.** An **acrobat** is an N COUNT entertainer who performs difficult jumps, somersaults, and balancing acts.

acrobatic /ˌækrəʊ'bætɪk/, **acrobatics. 1** An **acro-** ADJ QUALIT **batic** movement or display involves difficult jumps, somersaults, and balancing acts.
2 Acrobatics are acrobatic movements. EG *He can* N PLURAL *do the most amazing acrobatics.*

acronym /'ækrəʊnɪm/, **acronyms.** An **acronym** is N COUNT a word composed of the initial letters of the words in a phrase, especially when this is the name of something. An example of an acronym is AIDS.

across /ə'krɒs/. **1** If you go or look **across** a room PREP, OR ADV or other place, you go or look from one side of it to AFTER VB the other. EG *We ran across the bridge... He turned his head and looked across at me... He wandered across Hyde Park.*
2 Something that is situated or stretched **across** PREP something else is situated or stretched from one side of it to the other. EG *...a banner stretched across the street... A straight line was ruled across the map.*
3 Something that is situated **across** a street or PREP river is on the other side of it. EG *He stared at the houses across the street.*
4 Across is used to show the width of something. ADV EG *The bomb blasted a hole 200 kilometres across.*

acrylic /ə'krɪlɪk/. **Acrylic** material is man-made, ADJ CLASSIF : manufactured by a chemical process. EG *...acrylic* ATTRIB *blankets.*

act /ækt/, **acts, acting, acted. 1** When you **act**, V : USU+A you do something for a particular purpose. EG *We have to act quickly... He acted alone in the shooting.*
2 If someone **acts** in a particular way, they behave V+A in that way. EG *We acted as if we had never seen each other before... You're acting like a lunatic.*
3 If one thing **acts** as another, it functions as that V+as/like other thing. EG *The shark can twist its fins to act as brakes.*
4 If you **act**, or **act** a part, in a play or film, you V OR V+O have a part in it.
5 An **act** is a single thing that someone does. EG N COUNT+SUPP *...an act of aggression... Sometimes the act of writing down the problems straightens out your thinking.*
6 If you say that someone's behaviour is an **act**, N SING you mean that it does not express their real feelings. EG *She appeared calm and confident but it was just an act.*
7 An **Act** is a law passed by the government. EG N COUNT *...the 1944 Education Act.*
8 An **act** in a play, opera, or ballet is one of the N COUNT main parts into which it is divided.
9 An **act** in a show is a short performance which is N COUNT one of several in the show. EG *...comedy acts.*
10 If you are in the **act of** doing something, you PHRASE are doing it. EG *He saw Jones in the act of snatching a gun.*

act up. 1 If something **is acting up**, it is not PHRASAL VB : working properly. EG *Her car has started acting up* V+ADV *again.* **2** If a child **is acting up**, he or she is V+ADV behaving badly.

acting /'æktɪŋ/. **1 Acting** is the activity or profes- N UNCOUNT sion of performing in plays or films. EG *...the brilliant acting of Hawtrey.*
2 You use **acting** before the title of a job to ADJ CLASSIF : indicate that someone is only doing that job tempo- ATTRIB rarily. EG *...Yassin, acting Director of Education.*

action /'ækʃ⁰n/, **actions. 1 Action** is doing some- N UNCOUNT thing for a particular purpose. EG *The government was already taking action.*
2 An **action** is something that you do on a particu- N COUNT

lar occasion. EG *Surely resigning was rather a rash action?*
3 The **action** is all the important and exciting N SING things that are happening in a situation. EG *They want to be where the action is... The whole action of the book takes place in one day.*
4 Action is also fighting which takes place in a N UNCOUNT war. EG *...reports of military action... Henry had been killed in action.*
5 If you **put** an idea or policy **into action**, you PHRASE begin to use it or cause it to operate.
6 If something is **out of action**, it is damaged and PHRASE cannot work or be used. EG *The trucks were out of action for three months.*

activate /'æktɪveɪt/, **activates, activating, acti-** V+O **vated.** To **activate** something means to cause it to start working. EG *...a device that activates a loud bell... The system is activated by computer.*

active /'æktɪv/. **1** An **active** person or animal is ADJ QUALIT energetic and always busy or moving about. EG *...active and noisy children.*
2 If someone is **active** in an organization or cause, ADJ QUALIT they are involved in it and work for it. EG *He was active in drawing public attention to our problems.*
◊ **actively.** EG *He had not actively participated in* ◊ ADV *politics during his stay.*
3 You use **active** to emphasize the energy or ADJ CLASSIF enthusiasm with which something is done. EG *The* ATTRIB *proposal is under active discussion.* ◊ **actively.** EG ◊ *Such qualities were actively discouraged.*
4 If a volcano is **active**, it has erupted quite ADJ CLASSIF recently or is expected to erupt quite soon.

activist /'æktɪvɪst/, **activists.** An **activist** is a N COUNT person who works to bring about political or social changes. EG *...a vigorous civil rights activist.*

activity /æk'tɪvɪˈtiˈ/, **activities. 1 Activity** is a N UNCOUNT situation in which a lot of things are happening or being done. EG *There was a flurry of activity in the hall... ...periods of high economic activity.*
2 An **activity** is something that you spend time N COUNT doing. EG *I find tennis a very enjoyable activity.*
3 The **activities** of a group are the things that they N PLURAL do in order to achieve their aims. EG *...the activities* +SUPP *of trade unions.*

actor /'æktə/, **actors.** An **actor** is someone whose N COUNT job is acting in plays or films. 'Actor' in the singular usually refers to a man. EG *He was a fine actor.*

actress /'æktrɪˈs/, **actresses.** An **actress** is a N COUNT woman whose job is acting in plays or films.

actual /'æktʃʊəl/. **1** When you are emphasizing ADJ CLASSIF : that a place, object, or person is real and not ATTRIB imaginary, you can say that it is an **actual** place, object, or person. EG *The predicted results and the actual results are very different.*
2 When you want to emphasize that you are ADJ CLASSIF : referring only to the specific thing mentioned and ATTRIB not to other things associated with it, you can talk about the **actual** thing. EG *The actual wedding procession starts at 10 a.m.*

actuality /ˌæktʃʊˈælɪˈtiˈ/. When you want to em- PHRASE phasize that what you are saying is true, although it may be surprising, you can say that it is true **in actuality.** EG *The party in actuality contains only a small minority of extremists.*

actually /'æktʃʊəliˈ/. **1** You use **actually** to indi- ADV cate **1.1** that a situation exists in real life and not just in theory or in people's imaginations. EG *No one actually saw this shark.* **1.2** that you are giving correct or true details about a situation. EG *He actually died in exile, didn't he?* **1.3** that something is surprising or slightly shocking. EG *I was actually cruel sometimes.*
2 You also use **actually** to introduce a new topic ADV SEN into a conversation. EG *Actually, Dan, before I forget, she asked me to give you this.*

Would an acting treasurer appear in a film or play?

3 You also use **actually** as a way of expressing ADV SEN things more politely **3.1** when you are stating an opinion. EG *I think that's pretty cheap actually.* **3.2** when you are correcting or contradicting someone. EG *I didn't mean it that way actually... Actually, it was more complicated than that.* **3.3** when you are giving instructions or advice. EG *Actually it might be a good idea to stop recording now.*

acumen /ǽkjʊmɛn/ is the ability to make good N UNCOUNT judgements and quick decisions. EG *...a man with big ideas and keen business acumen.*

acupuncture /ǽkjʊpʌŋktʃə/ is the treatment of a N UNCOUNT person's illness or pain by sticking small needles into their body.

acute /əˈkjuːt/. **1** An **acute** situation, feeling, or ADJ QUALIT illness is very severe or intense. EG *...acute staff shortages... ...acute anxiety... These problems have become more acute.*

2 If your sight, hearing, or sense of smell is **acute**, ADJ QUALIT it is sensitive and powerful.

3 In geometry, an **acute** angle is less than 90°. ADJ CLASSIF

acutely /əˈkjuːtliˈ/. **1** If you feel something **acute-** ADV **ly**, you feel it very strongly. EG *They were acutely aware of the difficulties.*

2 If a feeling or quality is **acutely** unpleasant, it is ADV extremely unpleasant. EG *It was acutely embarrassing.*

ad /æd/, **ads**. An **ad** is an advertisement. EG *...a* N COUNT *newspaper ad.* Informal

AD /eɪ diː/. You use **AD** in dates to indicate a number of years or centuries since the year in which Jesus Christ is believed to have been born. EG *...as early as AD 1200... ...2000 AD.*

adamant /ǽdəmənt/. If you are **adamant** about ADJ CLASSIF something, you are determined not to change your mind about it. EG *He is adamant that we must put less emphasis on nationalism.* ◊ **adamantly.** EG *He* ◊ ADV *adamantly refused to be moved to a hospital.*

Adam's apple /ǽdəmz ǽpᵊlˈ/, **Adam's apples.** N COUNT Your **Adam's apple** is the lump that sticks out of the front of your neck below your throat.

adapt /əˈdæpt/, **adapts, adapting, adapted. 1** If V OR V-REFL : you **adapt** to a new situation or **adapt** yourself to OFT+*to* it, you change your ideas or behaviour in order to deal with it successfully. EG *This book is about change and how we adapt to it... He cannot adapt himself to being free.*

2 If you **adapt** something, you change it to make it V+O : OFT+*to* suitable for a new purpose or situation. EG *Reformers attempted to adapt traditional religion.*

3 If you **adapt** a book or play, you change it so that V+O it can be made into a film or a television programme. EG *Mortimer is adapting the novel for television.*

4 See also **adapted**.

adaptable /əˈdæptəbᵊl/. Someone who is **adapt-** ADJ QUALIT **able** is able to change their ideas or behaviour in order to deal with new situations. ◊ **adaptability** ◊ N UNCOUNT /əˈdæptəbɪlˈtiˈ/. EG *...adaptability to his environment.*

adaptation /ædəˈpteɪʃᵊnˈ/, **adaptations. 1** An N COUNT : **adaptation** of a story or novel is a play or film that OFT+*of* is based on it. EG *...a new television adaptation of 'A Tale of Two Cities'.*

2 **Adaptation** is the act of changing something to N UNCOUNT make it suitable for a new purpose or situation. EG *This windmill was designed for adaptation to different local requirements.*

adapted /əˈdæptɪdˈ/. If something is **adapted** to a ADJ PRED new situation or for a different purpose, it is +*for/to* especially suitable for it. EG *The cleaner is well adapted for use in the home and car.*

adaptor /əˈdæptə/, **adaptors;** also spelled **adapt-** N COUNT **er.** An **adaptor** is a device for connecting two or more electrical plugs to the same socket.

add /æd/, **adds, adding, added. 1** If you **add** one V+O : OFT+*to* thing to another, you put it in the same place as the other thing. EG *She added a tree to the picture.*

2 If you **add** numbers or amounts together, you V+O OR V calculate their total.

3 If one thing **adds** to another, it makes the other V+*to* OR thing greater in degree or amount. EG *He is given* V+O+*to* *answers that only add to his confusion... This process can add £3 a barrel to the cost.* ◊ **added.** ◊ ADJ CLASSIF : EG *There are added complications... This gave her* ATTRIB *an added charm.*

4 If you **add** something when you are speaking, you V-SPEECH say something more. EG *'Sorry,' he added... He added that the fee would be £100.*

add up. 1 If you **add up** several numbers, you PHRASAL VB : calculate their total. EG *What's the total when we* V+O+ADV *add all the marks up?* **2** If facts or events **add up**, V+ADV they make you realize or understand the true nature of the situation. EG *It all added up. I became aware that Halliday was the thief.*

add up to. If amounts **add up to** a particular PHRASAL VB : total, they result in that total when they are put V+ADV+PREP together. EG *This adds up to 75,000 miles of new streets.*

adder /ǽdə/, **adders.** An **adder** is a small poison- N COUNT ous snake.

addict /ǽdɪkt/, **addicts.** An **addict** is **1** someone N COUNT who takes harmful drugs and cannot stop taking them. **2** someone who is very fond of something or N COUNT+SUPP very interested in it. EG *He was a radio addict.*

addicted /əˈdɪktɪˈdˈ/. **1** Someone who is **addicted** ADJ PRED : to a harmful drug cannot stop taking it. EG *He* OFT+*to* *became addicted to drink.*

2 If you are **addicted** to something, you like it very ADJ PRED : much and want it a lot. EG *He was addicted to* OFT+*to* *chocolate.*

addiction /əˈdɪkʃᵊnˈ/, **addictions. 1** Addiction is N UNCOUNT the condition of taking harmful drugs and being OFT+*to* unable to stop taking them. EG *...heroin addiction.*

2 An **addiction** to something is a very strong N SING : desire for it. EG *...an addiction to sweets.* OFT+*to*

addictive /əˈdɪktɪv/. If a drug is **addictive**, people ADJ QUALIT who take it cannot stop taking it.

addition /əˈdɪʃᵊnˈ/, **additions. 1** You use **in addi-** PHRASE **tion** when you want to add something to what you have already said. EG *In addition, there were meetings with trade unionists.*

2 An **addition** to something is a thing which is N COUNT+SUPP added to it. EG *They can also award a weekly addition for extra heating.*

3 The **addition** of something is the fact that it is N UNCOUNT added as an extra. EG *These houses have been* +SUPP *improved by the addition of bathrooms.*

4 **Addition** is the process of calculating the total of N UNCOUNT two or more numbers.

additional /əˈdɪʃᵊnəl, -ʃənᵊlˈ/. **Additional** things ADJ CLASSIF : are extra things apart from the ones already OFT ATTRIB present. EG *Additional troops were needed.*

additionally /əˈdɪʃᵊnəliˈ, -ʃənᵊliˈ/. **1** You use ADV SEN **additionally** to introduce an extra fact. EG *Additionally, there was a substantial bill.*

2 If something happens **additionally**, it happens to ADV a greater extent than before. EG *There was no point in additionally burdening her with this painful news.*

additive /ǽdɪtɪv/, **additives.** An **additive** is a N COUNT substance which is added to foods or other substances in order to improve them.

address /əˈdrɛs/, **addresses, addressing, ad-** **dressed. 1** Your **address** is the number of the N COUNT : house, the name of the street, and the town where OFT+POSS you live or work. EG *The address is 70 Brompton Road, London SW1... He wrote down his name and address.*

2 If a letter, envelope, or parcel **is addressed** to V+O : USU PASS you, your name and address has been written on it.

3 An **address** is also a formal speech. EG *He gave* N COUNT *an address to the Psychological Association.*

4 If you **address** a group of people, you give a V+O speech to them. EG *He addressed a meeting in Bristol.*

ADJECTIVES

An adjective (ADJ) tells you something about a noun – anything about it that is relevant. This includes its size, quality, colour, and type. For example, in the group of words *pretty blue dresses,* the word 'dresses' is a noun and 'pretty' and 'blue' are adjectives which tell you what kind of dresses they are.

There are two main things to notice about adjectives:

1 Their position
Most adjectives can have two positions in a clause. They can come before a noun, as in *the pretty blue dresses.* Or they can come after a verb such as **be, seem,** or **look,** as in *These dresses are expensive . . . She looks happy.*

A few adjectives occur in only one of these positions. Adjectives which only come before a noun are labelled ATTRIB (meaning 'attributive'), and adjectives which only come after a verb are labelled PRED (meaning 'predicative').

For example, 'classical', 'musical', and 'prospective' are examples of adjectives labelled ATTRIB, as in *Greek is a classical language . . . . . . a musical career . . . . . . 500 prospective students.*

On the other hand, 'alike', 'alive', and some meanings of 'dead' are examples of adjectives labelled PRED, as in *The twins are alike . . . My father is still alive . . . My foot has gone dead.*

2 Their meaning
There are two ways in which adjectives state the features that describe a noun. In some cases, it is possible to have more or less of the feature, and words such as **very** and **rather** are used to say how much. Adjectives of this kind are labelled QUALIT (meaning 'qualitative'). For example, *a very funny film . . . . . . a rather deep pool.*

Adjectives labelled QUALIT have comparative and superlative forms, which are formed either by adding the endings **-er** and **-est** to the word or by using **more** and **most** in front of it. Where an adjective has forms ending in **-er** and **-est,** these are given in the dictionary. For example, *small, smaller, smallest.*

If an adjective is labelled ADJ QUALIT, but no different forms are given, this means that you use **more** and **most.** For example, *important, more important, most important.* A few adjectives have forms which do not end in **-er** and **-est,** such as **good, better, best.** All three forms are given in the dictionary.

The second main way in which an adjective states a feature is to classify the noun as being of a particular type. Adjectives of this kind are labelled CLASSIF (meaning 'classifying'). For example, *. . . a French girl . . . . . . a wooden gate.*
Adjectives of this kind do not have comparative and superlative forms.

A very few adjectives are normally only used immediately following a noun (ADJ AFTER N). For example, **elect** is used after a noun, as in *. . . the President elect.*

Adjectives which are labelled COLOUR, such as **blue, red,** or **green,** can come either before a noun or after a verb, so you can say *Her father had a red beard . . . Roses are red.*

If there is more than one adjective in front of a noun, a qualitative adjective comes before a colour adjective, and a colour adjective comes before a classifying adjective, which comes nearest to the noun. So you could have a groups of words such as *. . . a small brown wooden gate,* although long strings of adjectives are not very common, especially in speech.

ADJUNCTS

An adjunct (A) is one of the main elements of a clause. It expresses ideas such as those of time, place, manner, and possibility. An adjunct tells you, for example, the time that something happens, the place where it happens, the way in which it happens, or how likely it is that it will happen. When A is used in the Extra Column, it shows that the structure of the word being explained is not complete without an adjunct.

V+A

There are a number of verbs which need an adjunct to complete their meaning. For example, the verbs **behave** and **belong** are nearly always followed by an adjunct. You say that someone 'behaves well', 'behaves badly', 'behaves in a strange way', but you hardly ever just say that they 'behave'. In the same way, you say that something 'belongs to someone'; you do not just say that it 'belongs'.

V+O+A

Some other verbs need both an object and an adjunct, see for example **put 1** and **empty 5**. This means that you can say that you 'put the book down', or that you 'put the book on the shelf', but you cannot just say 'put the book'. In the same way you say that you empty water out of a container; you do not say that you empty water.

Phrasal verbs

There are other associations between verbs and adjuncts. For example, in *he came to a decision,* the words 'to a decision' are closely associated with the particular meaning of 'came' and the whole clause means more or less the same as 'he decided'. Other examples of this can be found in the entry on PHRASAL VERBS.

Types of adjunct

A wide variety of words and phrases are used as adjuncts. Some of these are single words, for example adverbs such as **sadly**, **quickly**, **then**, and **down**. Some adjuncts are noun groups, such as **last night** and **yesterday morning**. Many other adjuncts are prepositional phrases, such as **in the evening**, **at school**, and **round the corner**.

Adjuncts can also be added to a clause in order to give extra information, even though the structure does not actually require them. For example, the sentence *The children sang* gives you one piece of information, but you can also say when they sang: *This morning the children sang*. You can say how they sang: *The children sang beautifully.* You can say where they sang: *The children sang at the school concert.* It is possible to have more than one adjunct in a sentence, and so you can combine these adjuncts to make the sentence: *This morning the children sang beautifully at the school concert.*

Sentence adverbs

There is another type of adjunct which shows how one clause or sentence is linked or joined to another. These are words like **therefore** and **however**. Words or phrases of this kind are called ADV SEN in this dictionary. See the entry for ADVERBS for more information about these words.

5 If you **address** a remark to someone, you say it to them. `v+o+to`

6 If you **address** a problem or task or if you **address** yourself to it, you try to understand it or deal with it. EG *He has not addressed the issue of the strike... We should address ourselves directly to this question.* `v+o OR V.REFL+to`

address book, address books. An **address book** is a book in which you write people's names and addresses. `N COUNT`

adept /ə³dɛpt/. Someone who is **adept** at something can do it skilfully. EG *They have become adept at filling in forms... ...an adept swimmer.* `ADJ QUALIT: OFT+at/in`

adequate /ædɪ¹kwə¹t/. **1** If the amount of something is **adequate**, there is just enough of it. EG *The pay was adequate... ...a country with adequate rainfall.* ◇ **adequately.** EG *The children are not being adequately fed.* ◇ **adequacy** /ædɪ¹kwəsi¹/. EG *...the adequacy of resources.* `ADJ CLASSIF` ◇ `ADV` ◇ `N UNCOUNT`

2 If something is **adequate**, it is good enough to be used or accepted. EG *She could not think of an adequate answer.* ◇ **adequately.** EG *This has never been adequately explained.* ◇ **adequacy.** EG *...his belief in the adequacy of Mr Hope's methods.* `ADJ QUALIT` ◇ `ADV` ◇ `N UNCOUNT`

adhere /ə³dhɪə/, **adheres, adhering, adhered. 1** If something **adheres** to something else, it sticks firmly to it. EG *This helps the plaster to adhere to the wall.* `v+to`

2 If you **adhere** to a rule or agreement, you act in the way that it says you should. EG *The fire regulations have been adhered to.* ◇ **adherence** /ə³dhɪə²ns/. EG *Do they question our adherence to the treaty?* `v+to` ◇ `N UNCOUNT +to`

3 If you **adhere** to an opinion or belief, you support or hold it. EG *She has adhered to the view that it is my responsibility.* ◇ **adherence.** EG *...their adherence to democratic systems.* `v+to` ◇ `N UNCOUNT +to`

adhesive /ə³dhiːsɪv/, **adhesives. 1** An **adhesive** is a substance, such as glue, which is used to make things stick firmly together. EG *Make sure you stick them on with the correct adhesive.* `N MASS`

2 Something that is **adhesive** is able to stick firmly to something else. EG *...adhesive tape... ...adhesive plasters.* `ADJ CLASSIF`

ad hoc /æd hɒk/. An **ad hoc** activity or organization is done or formed only because a situation has made it necessary and was not planned in advance. EG *Rescue work continued on an ad hoc basis... The men agreed to set up an ad hoc committee.* `ADJ CLASSIF: ATTRIB`

ADJ stands for **adjective**
Words which have the label ADJ in the Extra Column are adjectives.
For information about the different kinds of adjectives in English, see the entry headed ADJECTIVES.

---

adjacent /ə³dʒeɪsə⁰nt/. If one thing is **adjacent** to another, the two things are next to each other. EG *The bench was adjacent to the court... ...the adjacent room.* `ADJ CLASSIF: OFT+to`

ADJ AFTER N stands for **adjective after noun**
Adjectives which have the label ADJ AFTER N in the Extra Column are normally only used immediately following a noun.
See the entry headed ADJECTIVES for more information.

ADJ CLASSIF stands for **classifying adjective**
Adjectives which have the label ADJ CLASSIF in the Extra Column classify a noun as being of a particular type. Classifying adjectives do not have com-

parative and superlative forms, and do not have words like 'very', 'more', or 'rather' in front of them.
See the entry headed ADJECTIVES for more information.

ADJ COLOUR stands for **colour adjective**
Words which have the label ADJ COLOUR in the Extra Column show that the word describes a colour such as 'red', 'blue', and 'purple'.
Colour adjectives can be used before a noun or after a verb. EG *Her father had a **red** beard... Roses are often **red**.*
Colour adjectives can have other adjectives in front of them that describe the colour more accurately. EG *...**bright** yellow... ...**pale** green... ...**dark** blue.*
Words which have the label ADJ COLOUR can also be used as nouns. EG *...a **blue** dress... ...a pretty shade of **blue**.*
See the entry headed ADJECTIVES for more information about other kinds of adjectives.

---

adjective /ædʒɔktɪv/, **adjectives.** An **adjective** is a word that describes a noun by telling you about its colour, size, or other qualities. See the entry headed ADJECTIVES for more information. `N COUNT`

adjoin /ə³dʒɔɪn/, **adjoins, adjoining, adjoined.** If one room, place, or object **adjoins** another, they are next to each other. EG *Her bedroom adjoined Guy's room.* ◇ **adjoining.** EG *The adjoining room is the office of Professor Marvin.* `v+o Formal` ◇ `ADJ CLASSI ATTRIB`

adjourn /ə³dʒɜːn/, **adjourns, adjourning, adjourned.** If a meeting or trial **adjourns**, it is stopped for a short time. EG *He announced that the trial would be adjourned until the next morning.* ◇ **adjournment** /ə³dʒɜːnmə²nt/, **adjournments.** EG *An adjournment was called.* `V-ERG` ◇ `N COUNT`

ADJ PRED stands for **predicative adjective**
Adjectives which have the label ADJ PRED in the Extra Column are normally only used after a verb such as 'be', 'become', 'feel', and 'seem'.
See the entry headed ADJECTIVES for more information.

ADJ QUALIT stands for **qualitative adjective**
Adjectives which have the label ADJ QUALIT in the Extra Column describe features of a noun that can vary in amount or intensity, so that you can have more or less of the feature described. They can show this by comparative and superlative forms, or by words like 'very', 'more', and 'most'.
See the entry headed ADJECTIVES for more information.

---

adjudged /ə³dʒʌdʒd/. You use **adjudged** to say what someone is considered to be. For example, if someone **is adjudged** a criminal, they are considered to be a criminal. `V-PASS+C OR to-INF Formal`

---

adjudicate /əˈdʒuːdɪkeɪt/, **adjudicates, adjudi-** v:OFT+*on* **cating, adjudicated.** If you **adjudicate** on a dis- OR v+O pute or problem, you make an official judgement or decision about it. EG *The boards adjudicate on the punishment of prisoners.*

adjunct /ˈædʒʌŋkt/, **adjuncts. 1** An **adjunct** is N COUNT+*to/of* something that is connected with a larger or more important thing. EG *Duncan's survey was an adjunct to the current population survey.*

2 In grammar, an **adjunct** is one of the main N COUNT elements of a clause. See the entry headed ADJUNCTS for more information.

adjust /əˈdʒʌst/, **adjusts, adjusting, adjusted. 1** v:OFT+*to* When you **adjust** to a new situation, you get used to it by changing your behaviour or your ideas. EG *Couples do not give themselves time to adjust to marriage before a baby arrives.* ● See also **adjusted.**

2 If you **adjust** your clothing, a machine, or a v+O device, you correct or alter its position or setting. EG *He spent several minutes adjusting his tie... I went to adjust the television set.*

adjustable /əˈdʒʌstəbəl/. If something is **adjust-** ADJ CLASSIF **able**, it can be changed to different positions. EG *...an adjustable spanner.*

adjusted /əˈdʒʌstɪd/. A well **adjusted** person can ADJ QUALIT control their behaviour and emotions and deal with the problems of life. A badly **adjusted** person cannot. EG *They grow up happy and well adjusted.*

adjustment /əˈdʒʌstmənt/, **adjustments.** An N COUNT OR **adjustment** is **1** an alteration or correction made N UNCOUNT: to something such as a machine. EG *He spent weeks making repairs and adjustments.* **2** a change in a person's behaviour or thinking. EG *Foreign students have problems of adjustment to living in Britain.*

ad-lib /ˈædlɪb/, **ad-libs, ad-libbing, ad-libbed. 1** If v OR v+O you **ad-lib** something in a play or a speech, you say something which has not been planned or prepared beforehand. EG *The commentator decided to ad-lib his way into the report.*

2 If you say something **ad lib**, you have not ADV planned or prepared it beforehand. EG *We discussed the result ad lib.*

administer /ədˈmɪnɪstə/, **administers, adminis-tering, administered. 1** To **administer** a coun- v+O try, company, or institution means to be respon-sible for organizing and supervising it. EG *She had a huge department to administer.*

2 If you **administer** the law, a punishment, or a v+O test, you organize it and make sure everything is done correctly. EG *Experts administer the tests and publish the results.*

3 If you **administer** a drug to someone, you give it v+O to them to swallow. EG *The prison officers helped to* Formal *administer a sedative to him.*

administration /ədˌmɪnɪˈstreɪʃən/. **1 Adminis-** N UNCOUNT **tration** is the range of activities connected with organizing and supervising the way that a country, company, or institution functions. EG *They need to spend less on administration.*

2 The **administration** of something is the process N UNCOUNT: of administering something. EG *...the administration* OFT+*of* *of justice.*

3 The **administration** of a company or institution N SING+SUPP is the group of people who organize and supervise it. EG *...the University administration.*

4 The **Administration** of a country, especially the N SING:the+N United States, is its government. EG *...the Reagan Administration.*

administrative /ədˈmɪnɪstrətɪv/. **Administra-** ADJ CLASSIF: **tive** work involves organizing and supervising a USU ATTRIB country, company, or institution. EG *...the adminis-trative head of the country.*

administrator /ədˈmɪnɪstreɪtə/, **administra-** N COUNT **tors.** An **administrator** is a person whose job involves helping to organize and supervise the way that a country, company, or institution functions.

admirable /ˈædmərəbəl/. A quality or action that ADJ QUALIT is **admirable** deserves to be praised and admired.

EG *The trains ran with admirable precision.*

◊ **admirably.** EG *It fulfils its purpose admirably.* ◊ ADV

admiral /ˈædmərəl/, **admirals.** An **admiral** is a N COUNT very senior officer who commands a navy or fleet of ships.

admiration /ˌædməˈreɪʃən/ is a feeling of great N UNCOUNT: liking and respect for a person or thing. EG *Benson* OFT+*for/of* *had enormous admiration for them all.*

admire /ədˈmaɪə/, **admires, admiring, ad-** v+O **mired.** If you **admire** someone or something, **1** you like and respect them very much. EG *I admire courage... They had been admired for their disci-pline.* **2** you look with pleasure at them. EG *He went along the lane admiring the crocuses.*

admirer /ədˈmaɪərə/, **admirers. 1** A woman's N COUNT+POSS **admirers** are the men who are attracted to her.

2 If you are an **admirer** of someone, you like and N COUNT+POSS respect them or their work very much. EG *I am not myself an admirer of Hogarth.*

admiring /ədˈmaɪərɪŋ/. An **admiring** expression ADJ QUALIT indicates a person's liking and respect for someone or something. EG *She gave me one of her rare admiring looks.* ◊ **admiringly.** EG *Ralph glanced* ◊ ADV *at them admiringly.*

admission /ədˈmɪʃən/, **admissions. 1 Admis-sion** is **1.1** permission given to a person to enter a N UNCOUNT place or country. EG *No admission allowed after 10* OR N COUNT *pm... His Act tightened up the admission of immi-grants into Britain.* **1.2** permission given to a N UNCOUNT: person or a country to join an organization. EG *...the* OFT+*of/to* *admission of China to the United Nations.*

2 The **admission** fee at a park, museum, or other N UNCOUNT place is the amount of money that you pay to enter it. EG *They charge fifty cents admission.*

3 An **admission** is a statement that something bad, N COUNT: unpleasant, or embarrassing is true. EG *He submit-* OFT+*of* OR *ted his resignation, together with an admission of* REPORT *his guilt.*

admit /ədˈmɪt/, **admits, admitting, admitted. 1** V:SPEECH, If you **admit** something bad, unpleasant, or embar- V+ING, rassing, you agree, often reluctantly, that it is true. OR V+O EG *'I don't know,' he admitted... The President admitted taking bribes... He admitted that he had been disappointed by the failure.*

2 If you **admit** defeat, you accept that you cannot PHRASE complete something which you have started.

3 If someone or something **is admitted** to a place, V+O:OFT PASS they are allowed to enter it. EG *Junior members of staff are not admitted.*

4 If someone **is admitted** to hospital, they are kept V+O:USU there until they are well enough to go home. EG *He* PASS+*to* *was admitted to hospital with an ulcerated leg.*

5 If someone **is admitted** to an organization or V+O:OFT group, they are allowed to join it. EG *He was* PASS+*to/into* *admitted to full membership of the academy.*

admittance /ədˈmɪtəns/ is the act of entering a N UNCOUNT place or the right to enter it. EG *How was he to gain admittance?*

admittedly /ədˈmɪtɪdli/. You use **admittedly** ADV SEN when you are saying something which weakens your previous statement or claim. EG *Admittedly, economists often disagree among each other.*

admonish /ədˈmɒnɪʃ/, **admonishes, admonish-** v+O **ing, admonished.** If you **admonish** someone, you Formal tell them sternly that they have done something wrong. EG *They are frequently admonished for their failure to act quickly.*

ado /əˈduː/. If you do something **without further** PHRASE **ado** or **without more ado**, you do it at once and do Outdated not discuss or delay it any longer. EG *So, without more ado, let me introduce tonight's guests.*

adolescence /ˌædəˈlesəns/ is the period of your N UNCOUNT life in which you develop from being a child into being an adult. EG *His adolescence was not a happy time for him.*

adolescent /ˌædəˈlesənt/, **adolescents.** An ado- N COUNT **lescent** is a young person who is no longer a child but who has not yet become an adult. ▸ used as an ▸ ADJ CLASSIF: adjective. EG *...a father with an adolescent son.* ATTRIB

adopt /ədɒpt/, **adopts, adopting, adopted. 1** If you **adopt** someone else's child, you take it into your own family and make it legally your son or daughter. ◊ **adopted.** EG ...the parents of adopted children. ◊ **adoption** /ədɒpʃəⁿn/, **adoptions.** EG ...the shortage of children available for adoption. — *V+O; ◊ ADJ CLASSIF; ◊ N UNCOUNT OR N COUNT*

2 If you **adopt** a new attitude, plan, or way of behaving, you begin to have it. EG I had to adopt other methods of persuasion. EG That led to Labour's adoption of a radical foreign policy. — *V+O; ◊ N UNCOUNT +of*

3 If you **adopt** a physical position, you move yourself into it. EG Green adopts a golfing stance, his weight forward. — *V+O; Formal*

adorable /ədɔːrəbəⁿl/. If you say that a child or animal is **adorable**, you think that it is very attractive and you feel great affection for it. — *ADJ QUALIT*

adoration /ædəⁿreɪʃəⁿn/ is a feeling of great admiration and love for someone or something. EG He did not tell anyone of his adoration for her. — *N UNCOUNT*

adore /ədɔː/, **adores, adoring, adored. 1** If you **adore** someone, you feel great admiration and love for them. EG She adored her sister. ◊ **adoring.** EG ...listening with adoring concentration. — *V+O : NO CONT; ◊ ADJ QUALIT : ATTRIB*

2 If you **adore** something, you like it very much. EG People will adore this film. — *V+O : NO CONT; Informal*

adorn /ədɔːn/, **adorns, adorning, adorned.** To **adorn** something means to add things to it in order to make it more beautiful. EG Oil paintings adorned the walls... ...stalls adorned with candles. — *V+O; Literary*

adornment /ədɔːnməⁿnt/, **adornments. 1** An **adornment** is something that is used to make someone or something more beautiful. EG ...adornments such as make-up and jewellery. — *N COUNT*

2 Adornment is making something more beautiful by adding something to it. EG Styles of adornment have changed over the centuries. — *N UNCOUNT*

adrenalin /ədrenəlɪn/; also spelled **adrenaline. Adrenalin** is a substance which your body produces when you are angry, scared, or excited. It makes your heart beat faster and gives you more energy. EG He felt the surge of adrenalin in his system. — *N UNCOUNT*

adrift /ədrɪft/. If a boat is **adrift**, it is floating on the water and is not tied to anything or controlled by anyone. EG The pirates would cut ships adrift at night. — *ADJ PRED*

adroit /ədrɔɪt/. Someone who is **adroit** is quick and skilful in their thoughts, behaviour, or actions. EG Jamie was adroit at flattering others. ◊ **adroitly.** EG The young men picked the papers up adroitly. — *ADJ QUALIT; Formal; ◊ ADV*

adulation /ædjʊleɪʃəⁿn/ is very great and uncritical admiration and praise. EG He was greeted with adulation. — *N UNCOUNT*

adult /ædʌlt, ədʌlt/, **adults. 1** An **adult** is a mature, fully developed person or animal. EG A happy home is one in which children and adults have equal rights... I spent all my adult life in England. — *N COUNT*

2 An **adult** person or animal is fully developed and mature. EG ...adult insects. — *ADJ CLASSIF : ATTRIB*

3 Something that is **adult** is suitable for, or typical of, adult people. EG Children can assist in adult work at an early age. — *ADJ CLASSIF*

adulterate /ədʌltəreɪt/, **adulterates, adulterating, adulterated.** If you **adulterate** drink or food, you make its quality worse by adding water or cheaper products to it. EG The champagne had been adulterated. — *V+O*

adultery /ədʌltəⁿri/. If a married person commits **adultery**, they have sex with someone that they are not married to. EG Adultery was a ground for divorce. — *N UNCOUNT*

adulthood /ædʌlthʊd/ is the state of being an adult. EG ...young Russians maturing to adulthood... There is no reason why she shouldn't survive into healthy adulthood. — *N UNCOUNT*

ADV stands for **adverb**

Words which have only the label ADV in the Extra Column are of two kinds:

1. Some can be used with verbs, or adjectives, or other adverbs.

2. Some can only be used with verbs, but they can come before or after the verb.

The examples given for these adverbs will show you how they should be used.

See the entry headed ADVERBS for more information about these and about the other kinds of adverb noted in this dictionary as ADV AFTER VB, ADV BRD NEG, and ADV SEN.

ADV AFTER VB stands for **adverb used after verb**

Words which have the label ADV AFTER VB in the Extra Column are adverbs that can only be used after verbs.

See the entry headed ADVERBS for more information.

---

advance /ədvɑːns/, **advances, advancing, advanced. 1** To **advance** means **1.1** to move forward, often in order to attack someone. EG She advanced on him, shouting and waving her ticket. ◊ **advancing.** EG ...rows of advancing enemy tanks. **1.2** to make progress, especially in your knowledge of something. EG This student has advanced in reading and writing. ● See also **advanced.** — *V; ◊ ADJ CLASSIF; V*

2 If you **advance** someone a sum of money, you lend it to them, or pay it to them earlier than arranged. EG Axel advanced him the money for a suit. — *V+O+O*

3 An **advance** is money which is lent to someone or paid to them before they are due to receive it. — *N COUNT*

4 If you make **advances** to someone, you try to start a sexual relationship with them. — *N PLURAL; Outdated*

5 Advance in a particular subject or activity is progress in understanding it or in doing it well. EG ...radical advances in computer design. — *N COUNT OR N UNCOUNT*

6 Advance booking, notice, or warning is done or given before an event happens. EG There was no advance warning of the President's departure. — *ADJ CLASSIF : ATTRIB*

7 If an idea or product is **in advance** of another one, it is more highly developed. EG Their facilities were far in advance of anything in Europe. — *PHRASE*

8 If you do something **in advance**, you do it before a particular date or event. EG You should book well in advance, preferably six weeks before. — *PHRASE*

advanced /ədvɑːnst/. **1** An **advanced** student has already learned the basic facts of a subject and is doing more difficult work. — *ADJ QUALIT*

2 A country that is **advanced** has reached a high level of industrial or technological development. EG Japan is becoming the most advanced country technologically. — *ADJ QUALIT*

advancement /ədvɑːnsməⁿnt/. **1 Advancement** is promotion in your job, or to a higher social class. EG ...opportunity for personal advancement. — *N UNCOUNT*

2 The **advancement** of something is the process of helping it to progress. EG ...the advancement of knowledge. — *N UNCOUNT +SUPP*

advantage /ədvɑːntɪdʒ/, **advantages. 1** An **advantage** is **1.1** something that puts you in a better position than other people. EG As a scientist I have — *N COUNT*

What can you be advanced?

ADVERBS

An adverb is a word which gives more information about a verb, an adjective, or another adverb. There are several different kinds of adverbs.

1 Many adverbs (ADV) can be used with either a verb or an adjective. For example, in the sentence *Smoking can **seriously** damage your health,* the adverb 'seriously' tells you how much damage can be done. In *She was **seriously** ill,* the adverb tells you how ill she was. Occasionally, an adverb of this kind is used with another adverb, as in *I did not feel I knew her **sufficiently well**.*

2 Many adverbs (also ADV) can only be used with verbs. They can come either before or after the verb. So you can say *She grinned **happily** at him* and *He **happily** handed over ten pounds . . .   They smiled **cheerfully** at each other* and *They **cheerfully** agreed to help.*

3 Many other adverbs (ADV AFTER VB) are used with verbs, but they can only come after the verb. These fall into two main groups.

The first group consists of some of the commonest adverbs in English, such as **back**, **up**, and **down**, and are used when you are describing, for example, where something happens and what direction something is going in. For example, *She nodded and looked down.* Very often adverbs of this kind are used with phrasal verbs. For more information about how they behave see the entry headed PHRASAL VERBS.

The second group consists of less common words which have a much more specific meaning, such as 'cross-legged', 'counter-clockwise', and 'barefoot'. For example, *She ran **barefoot** through the field.*

4 All of the groups of adverbs already mentioned can come after verbs. There is one group that cannot, and there are special rules about how these adverbs are used. This is a small group of adverbs which have a meaning close to the word 'not', but which are not quite negative (ADV BRD NEG). These are **hardly**, **scarcely**, **barely**, **rarely**, **seldom**, and **little**. So *He was hardly awake* means 'he was almost asleep'.

These adverbs can all be used as the first word in a clause, in order to emphasize their importance. So you can say *Hardly had I got into the house than the phone rang . . . Seldom did a week pass without a request for information . . .   Rarely has so much time been wasted.* When one of these words begins a clause, notice that the rest of the clause has a word order that is similar to a question.

5 There is another kind of adverb (ADV SEN) that is used to comment on the whole sentence rather than just on part of it.

There are a number of words like **however**, **thus**, and **nevertheless** which help you to order and explain the argument you are putting forward in your statements. Here are some examples: *Most people think that David is nice. Not me, **however** . . . The new car is smaller and **therefore** cheaper . . .   Life now is much less elaborate and, **consequently**, much less interesting than it used to be.* ·

6 The words that are labelled SUBMOD in this dictionary are often called adverbs. These are words like **very**, **rather** and **extremely**. See the entry headed SUBMOD for more information about these words.

a slight advantage over him. **1.2** a benefit or improvement that is likely to result from something. EG *The advantages of electricity are the lack of fumes and the ease of distribution.*

2 Advantage is used in these phrases. **2.1** If PHRASES something is **to your advantage**, it will be useful for you or will benefit you. EG *It is to your advantage to keep him as happy as possible.* **2.2** If you **take advantage of** someone, you treat them unfairly for your own benefit. **2.3** If you **take advantage of** something, you make good use of it while you can. EG *Companies took advantage of favourable interest rates... You should take advantage of his generosity.*

advantageous /ædvə³nteɪdʒəs/. Something that ADJ QUALIT is **advantageous** to you is likely to benefit you. EG *Economic growth is inevitable and advantageous.*

ADV BRD NEG stands for **broad negative adverb**

Words which have the label ADV BRD NEG in the Extra Column are used to make the sentence almost, but not quite, negative. Six words are labelled in this way: *hardly, scarcely, rarely, barely, seldom, little.*

See the entry headed ADVERBS for more information.

---

advent /ædvə³nt/. The **advent** of something im- N SING+POSS portant is the fact of it starting or coming into Formal existence. EG *...the advent of computers.*

adventure /ə³dvɛntʃə/, **adventures**. An **adven-** N COUNT OR **ture** is a series of events that you become involved N UNCOUNT in that are unusual, exciting, and rather dangerous. EG *...my Arctic adventures... They were bored, and looking for adventure.*

adventurer /ə³dvɛntʃərə/, **adventurers**. An **ad-** N COUNT **venturer** is a person who enjoys adventure. EG *...a daring band of adventurers.*

adventurous /ə³dvɛntʃərəs/. Someone who is **ad-** ADJ QUALIT **venturous** is **1** willing to take risks and to try new methods. EG *I wish that he had been a bit more adventurous in his investigation.* **2** eager to visit new places and have new experiences. EG *The romance of the East had appealed to his adventurous spirit.*

adverb /ædvɜ:b/, **adverbs**. In grammar, an **ad-** N COUNT **verb** is a word that adds information about a verb, about a following adjective or adverb, or about a following prepositional group. See the entry headed ADVERBS for more information.

adversary /ædvəsə³ri¹/, **adversaries**. Your **ad-** N COUNT+SUPP **versary** is someone you are competing with, or arguing or fighting against. EG *She had two potential political adversaries.*

adverse /ædvɜ:s/. **Adverse** decisions, conditions, ADJ QUALIT : or effects are unfavourable to you. EG *Falling prices* ATTRIB *had an adverse effect on business... ...adverse weather conditions.* ◊ **adversely**. EG *The majority* ◊ ADV *of children are adversely affected.*

adversity /ə³dvɜ:sɪ¹tɪ¹/ is a very difficult or unfa- N UNCOUNT vourable situation. EG *They continue to fight in the face of adversity.*

advert /ædvɜ:t/, **adverts**. An **advert** is the same N COUNT as an advertisement. Informal

advertise /ædvətaɪz/, **advertises, advertising, advertised**. **1** If you **advertise** something such as v+O a product, an event, or a job, you tell people about it in newspapers, on television, or on posters in order to encourage them to buy the product, go to the event, or apply for the job. EG *...deodorants she had seen advertised on television... ...a leaflet advertising a fishing competition.*

2 If you **advertise** for something or for someone to V :OFT+*for* do a job, you announce in a newspaper, on television, or on a notice board that you want that thing

or want a person to do that job. EG *The Council advertised for accountants.*

advertisement /ə³dvɜ:tɪsmə²nt/, **advertise-** N COUNT **ments**. An **advertisement** is an announcement in a newspaper, on television, or on a poster about something such as a product, event, or job vacancy. EG *...an advertisement for Adler shoes... ...an advertisement for an assistant cashier.*

advertiser /ædvətaɪzə/, **advertisers**. An **adver-** N COUNT **tiser** is a person or company that pays for a product, event, or job vacancy to be advertised on television, in a newspaper, or on posters.

advertising /ædvətaɪzɪŋ/ is the activity of telling N UNCOUNT people about products, events, or job vacancies, and making people want to buy the products, go to the events, or apply for the jobs. EG *Retailers spend a lot of money on advertising... ...an advertising agency.*

advice /ə³dvaɪs/. If you give someone **advice**, you N UNCOUNT : tell them what you think they should do in a USU+SUPP particular situation. EG *She promised to follow his advice... They want advice on how to do it.*

advisable /ə³dvaɪzəbə⁰l/. If a course of action is ADJ QUALIT **advisable**, it is sensible or is likely to achieve the result you want. EG *It's advisable to ring up first to make an appointment.*

advise /ə³dvaɪz/, **advises, advising, advised**. **1** If V+O+*to*-INF you **advise** someone to do something, you tell REPORT, them what you think they should do. EG *He advised* OR *against* *me not to buy it... Their job involves advising people how to avoid this disease... I would strongly advise you against it.*

2 If you **advise** people on a particular subject, you V OR V+O :O¹ give them help and information on the subject. EG *A* +*on* *panel of bishops has been appointed to advise on matters of religious policy.*

advocate, advocates, advocating, advocated; pronounced /ædvə⁶keɪt/ when it is a verb and /ædvə⁶kət/ when it is a noun.

1 If you **advocate** a particular action or plan, you v+O OR support it publicly. EG *He advocated the creation of* V+REPORT: *a permanent United Nations... He advocated that* ONLY *that* *Britain should join the alliance.*

2 An **advocate** of a particular action or plan is N COUNT+*of* someone who supports it publicly. EG *...the advocates of women's rights... ...a strong advocate of nuclear power.*

3 An **advocate** is a lawyer who speaks in favour of N COUNT someone or defends them in a court of law. Legal

---

ADV SEN stands for **sentence adverb**

Words and phrases which have the label ADV SEN in the Extra Column are used to comment on the whole sentence rather than on individual parts.

See the entry headed ADVERBS for more information.

---

aerial /ɛərɪəl/, **aerials**. **1** You use **aerial** to ADJ CLASSIF : describe things that are fixed above the level of the ATTRIB ground or that happen in the air. EG *An aerial railway had been erected... ...aerial warfare.*

2 Aerial photographs are photographs taken from ADJ CLASSIF : aeroplanes of things on the ground. ATTRIB

3 An **aerial** is a piece of wire that receives N COUNT television or radio signals. Aerials are often fixed British to buildings, cars, radios, and television sets. See picture at CAR.

aerodynamic /ɛərə⁶daɪnæmɪk/. **Aerodynamic** ADJ CLASSIF : effects and principles are concerned with the way ATTRIB in which objects move through the air. EG *...aerodynamic improvements in design.*

Is an adventurer likely to encounter adversity?

aeroplane /ˈɛərəˌpleɪn/, **aeroplanes**. An **aero-** N COUNT
plane is a vehicle with wings and one or more OR by+N
engines that enable it to fly through the air. British

aerosol /ˈɛərəˌsɒl/, **aerosols**. An **aerosol** is a N COUNT
small container in which a liquid such as paint or
deodorant is kept under pressure. When you press
a button, the liquid is forced out as a fine spray or
foam.

aesthetic /iˈsθetɪk; spelled **esthetic** in American ADJ CLASSIF
English. **Aesthetic** means involving beauty or art,
and people's appreciation of beautiful things. EG ...a
purely aesthetic appeal. ◊ **aesthetically.** EG ...aes- ◊ ADV
thetically pleasing products.

afar /əˈfɑː/. **From afar** means from a long way PHRASE
away. EG He saw me from afar. Literary

affable /ˈæfəbəl/. Someone who is **affable** is ADJ QUALIT
pleasant and friendly. EG Dominic was always af- Literary
fable with my friends.

affair /əˈfɛə/, **affairs. 1** You refer to an event or a N COUNT
situation as an **affair** when you are talking about it +SUPP:
very generally. EG The wedding was a quiet affair... USU SING
An enquiry will be conducted into the whole affair.

2 You can use **affairs** to refer to all the important N PLURAL
facts or activities that are connected with a par- +SUPP
ticular subject. EG ...a specialist in Eastern Euro- Formal
pean affairs... ...affairs of state. ● See also **current
affairs, state of affairs.**

3 Your **affairs** are all the things connected with N PLURAL
your life which you consider to be private and +POSS
nothing to do with other people. EG What had
induced her to meddle in his affairs?

4 If someone says that something is your **affair**, N SING+POSS
they mean that they do not wish to know about it
or become involved in it. EG What went on behind
that door was your own affair.

5 If two people who are not married to each other N COUNT
are having an **affair**, they have a sexual relationship.

affect /əˈfekt/, **affects, affecting, affected. 1** v+o
When something **affects** someone or something
else, it influences them or causes them to change
in some way. EG ...the ways in which computers can
affect our lives.

2 When a disease **affects** someone, it causes them v+o
to become ill. EG The disease primarily affected
Jane's lungs.

3 If you **affect** a particular characteristic or way v+o OR
of behaving, you pretend that it is natural for you. V+to-INF
EG She affected a lisp... He affected to despise every Formal
Briton he met.

affectation /ˌæfekˈteɪʃən/, **affectations**. An **af-** N COUNT OR
fectation is an attitude or type of behaviour that is N UNCOUNT
not genuine or natural, but which is intended to
impress other people. EG His film star affectations
had disappeared.

affected /əˈfektɪd/. Someone who is **affected** ADJ QUALIT
behaves in an unnatural way that is intended to
impress other people. EG He was affected and
conceited.

affection /əˈfekʃən/ is a feeling of fondness and N UNCOUNT
caring that you have for another person or for an
animal. EG She gazed with deep affection at him.

affectionate /əˈfekʃənət/. If you are **affection-** ADJ QUALIT
ate, you show your love or fondness for another
person in the way that you behave towards them.
EG They were an affectionate couple... His tone was
affectionate. ◊ **affectionately.** EG He stroked her ◊ ADV
affectionately.

affinity /əˈfɪnɪti/, **affinities. 1** If you have an N COUNT
affinity with someone or something, you feel that OR N UNCOUNT:
you are similar to them and understand them very OFT+with/for
well. EG I had this tremendous sense of affinity with
the place.

2 If people or things have an **affinity** with each N COUNT
other, they are similar in some ways. EG In anatomical structure, Prehistoric Man has close affinities with modern humans.

affirm /əˈfɜːm/, **affirms, affirming, affirmed. 1** V·SPEECH:
If you **affirm** a fact, you state that it is definitely ONLY that
true. EG I affirmed my innocence. Formal

2 If you **affirm** an idea or belief, you indicate v+o
clearly that you have this idea or belief. EG They Formal
affirm a policy of religious toleration.

affirmative /əˈfɜːmətɪv/. An **affirmative** word ADJ CLASSIF:
or gesture indicates that you agree with what ATTRIB
someone has said or that the answer to a question Formal
is 'yes'. EG ...the affirmative nodding of my head.
● If you reply to a question **in the affirmative**, ● PHRASE
you say 'yes' or make a gesture that means 'yes'.

afflict /əˈflɪkt/, **afflicts, afflicting, afflicted.** If v+o:OFT
pain, illness, or sorrow **afflicts** someone, it affects PASS+with/by
them and makes them suffer. EG Cameron had been
afflicted with blindness.

affliction /əˈflɪkʃən/, **afflictions**. An **affliction** N COUNT OR
is something which causes physical or mental N UNCOUNT
suffering. EG ...the horrors and afflictions of his time
in prison.

affluent /ˈæfluənt/. If you are **affluent**, you have a ADJ QUALIT
lot of money and a high standard of living. EG
...affluent young professionals. ◊ **affluence** ◊ N UNCOUNT
/ˈæfluəns/. EG ...the general affluence of a consumer Formal
society.

afford /əˈfɔːd/, **affords, affording, afforded. 1** If v+o OR
you can **afford** something, you have enough mon- V+to-INF
ey to pay for it. EG ...families who can afford cars... I
can't afford to rent this flat.

2 If you say that you cannot **afford** to do something v+o OR
or to allow it to happen, you mean that you must V+to-INF
not do it or must try to prevent it happening
because it would be harmful or embarrassing to
you. EG He could not afford to be associated with
them... We can't afford another scandal.

3 If something **affords** you support or an opportun- v+o+to
ity, it gives it to you. EG ...the protection afforded to OR V+o+o
the workers by the unions... They have been af- Formal
forded some assistance.

affront /əˈfrʌnt/, **affronts, affronting, affronted.**
1 If you **are affronted** by something, you feel v+o:USU PASS
insulted and hurt because of it. EG They were
deeply affronted by their abrupt dismissal.

2 If something is an **affront** to you, it is an obvious N COUNT:
insult to you. EG This is a serious affront to large OFT+to
numbers of citizens.

afield /əˈfiːld/. If someone comes from **far afield**, PHRASE
they come from a long way away. EG Groups from
as far afield as Scotland have sent deputations.

afloat /əˈfləʊt/. **1** When someone or something is ADJ PRED
afloat, they remain partly above the surface of
water and do not sink. EG By kicking constantly he
could stay afloat.

2 If you stay **afloat** or if you keep a business ADJ PRED
afloat, you have only just enough money to pay
your debts or to run the business. EG They have
kept Vickers afloat during the recession.

afoot /əˈfʊt/. If a plan or scheme is **afoot**, it is ADJ PRED
already happening or being planned, but you do not
know much about it. EG There was a plan afoot to
have her sent to a camp.

aforementioned /əˈfɔːˌmenʃənd/. When you refer ADJ CLASSIF:
to the **aforementioned** person or subject, you ATTRIB
mean the person or subject that has already been Formal
mentioned. EG ...the works of all the aforementioned writers.

aforesaid /əˈfɔːsed/ means the same as aforemen- ADJ CLASSIF:
tioned. ATTRIB

afraid /əˈfreɪd/. **1** If you are **afraid** of someone or ADJ PRED:
afraid to do something, you are frightened be- OFT+of
cause you think that something horrible is going to OR to-INF
happen. EG They were afraid of you... He was afraid
even to turn his head... She suddenly looked afraid.

2 If you are **afraid** that something unpleasant will ADJ PRED
happen, you are worried that it may happen and +REPORT, of,
you want to avoid it. EG She was afraid that I might OR to-INF
be embarrassed... He was terribly afraid of offending anyone... Don't be afraid to ask questions.

3 When you want to apologize to someone or to CONVENTION disagree with them in a polite way, you can begin by saying **I'm afraid**. EG *I'm afraid I can't agree... 'Can you come?' – 'I'm afraid not.'*

afresh /əfreʃ/. If you do something **afresh**, you do ADV it again in a different way. EG *I'm too old to start afresh.*

African /æfrɪkən/, **Africans. 1 African** means ADJ CLASSIF **1.1** belonging or relating to the continent of Africa, or to its countries or peoples. **1.2** belonging or relating to black people who come from Africa. EG *He impressed people by the way he presented the African case.*
2 An **African** is someone, usually black, who N COUNT comes from Africa. EG *...civic rights for Africans... ...the African population of Johannesburg.*

after /ɑːftə/. **1** If something happens **after** a PREP, ADV, OR particular date or event, it happens during the CONJ period of time that follows it. EG *She arrived just after breakfast... Soon after, Faraday began his research into electricity... He was ill after eating the meal.*
2 If you go **after** someone, you follow them. EG *She* PREP *ran after him into the courtyard.*
3 If someone is **after** you, they are chasing you or PREP searching for you. EG *The Germans were after him.*
4 If you are **after** something, you are trying to get PREP it for yourself. EG *Those youngsters are after my job.*
5 If you call or look **after** someone, you call or look PREP towards them when they are moving away from you. EG *'Hunter!' she called after him.*
6 If you clean up **after** someone, you clean up the PREP mess which they have made. EG *Why do you spend your life cleaning up after him?*
7 If something is written **after** something else on a PREP page, it is written following it or underneath it.
8 To be named **after** someone means to be given PREP the same name as them. EG *...a street named after my grandfather.*
9 Americans use **after** when they are telling the PREP time. If they say that it is, for example, ten **after** American six, the time is ten minutes past six. EG *They met at twenty after eight.*
10 If you do several things **one after the other** or PHRASE **one after another**, you do them immediately following each other in time. EG *He begins opening bottles, one after another.*
11 If something happens **day after day** or **year** PHRASE **after year**, it happens every day or every year. EG *Some jokes go round school year after year.*
12 After is also used in the phrasal verbs 'ask ADV OR PREP after', 'go after', 'look after', 'run after', and 'take after'.

after-effect, after-effects. The **after-effects** of N COUNT : an activity or event are the conditions which result USU PLURAL from it. EG *100,000 died from the after-effects of radiation over the next few decades.*

aftermath /ɑːftəmɑːθ, -mæθ/. The **aftermath** of N SING+POSS an important event is the situation that results from it. EG *In the immediate aftermath of the accident, no one knew who had been hurt... ...the aftermath of war.*

afternoon /ɑːftənuːn/, **afternoons.** The **after-** N COUNT OR **noon** is the part of each day which begins at N UNCOUNT lunchtime and ends at about six o'clock. EG *I'll do it this afternoon... ...my afternoon walk.*

after-shave /ɑːftəʃeɪv/ is a liquid with a pleasant N UNCOUNT smell that men sometimes put on their faces after they have shaved.

afterthought /ɑːftəθɔːt/, **afterthoughts.** If you N COUNT : do or say something as an **afterthought**, you do or USU SING say it after something else as an addition, but without careful thought. EG *After a while she said as an afterthought, 'I could do that.'*

afterwards /ɑːftəwədz/. The word **afterward** is ADV SEN also used, especially in American English.
If you do something or if something happens **afterwards**, you do it or it happens after a particular event or time that has already been described.

EG *Afterwards we all helped with the washing up... She died soon afterwards.*

again /əgen, əgeɪn/. **1** If you do something **again**, ADV you do it once more or on another occasion. EG *Try again in half an hour... Let's do it, I may never have the chance again.* ● If you do something **again** ● PHRASE **and again** or **time and again**, you do it many times or on many occasions. EG *This process is repeated again and again.*
2 When something is in a particular state or place ADV **again**, it has returned to the state or place that it used to be in. EG *At last the assembly was silent again.*
3 When you are asking someone to repeat some- ADV SEN thing that they have already told you, you can add **again** to the end of your question. EG *What's his name again?*
4 You can use **again** when you want to emphasize ADV SEN that there is a similarity between the subject that you are talking about now and a previous subject. EG *My last question is again a personal one.*
5 When you want to introduce a different point, ADV SEN often one that contradicts something that has just been said, you can say **'then again'**. EG *I don't think it should be an arts subject. But then again it's not really a science subject.*

against /əgenst, əgeɪnst/. **1** If something is lean- PREP ing or pressing **against** something else, it is touch- ing it and leaning or pressing on it. EG *Ralph leaned against a tree... She was pressing his nose against the window.*
2 If you compete **against** someone in a game or PREP other activity, you try to beat them or to do better than them. EG *He played in the first Test Match against Australia.*
3 If you do something **against** someone or some- PREP thing, you do something that might harm them. EG *They were not allowed to use arms against their enemies.*
4 If you are **against** an idea, policy, or system, you PREP OR ADV are opposed to it. EG *He was fanatically against American intervention in the war.*
5 If something is **against** the law, there is a law PREP which says that you must not do it.
6 If you take action **against** a possible future PREP event, you try to prevent it or to make its effects less serious. EG *He has taken certain precautions against burglary.*
7 If you are moving **against** a current, tide, or PREP wind, you are moving in the opposite direction to it.
8 The chances or odds **against** something happen- PREP OR ADV ing are the chances or odds that it will not happen.

age /eɪdʒ/, **ages, ageing** or **aging, aged. 1** Your N UNCOUNT **age** is the number of years that you have lived. EG +SUPP *He is eighty years of age... He died at the age of forty... She thought I was her own age.*
2 Someone who is **under age** is not legally old PHRASE enough to do something, for example to buy an alcoholic drink. EG *He had been under age when he joined the army.*
3 When someone **comes of age**, they become legally an adult. In Britain young people come of age when they are 18.
4 Age is the state of being old. EG *Her age and* N UNCOUNT *frailty are giving him cause for concern... ...medals stained with age.*
5 When someone **ages**, they become or seem V-ERG much older and less strong or less alert. EG *She was dismayed to see how much he had aged... The strain of looking after her had aged him.*
6 An **age** is a period in history. EG *...the great age of* N COUNT : *Greek sport... ...a detailed study of woman's role* IF SING, *throughout the ages.* THEN+SUPP
7 You can say **an age** or **ages** to mean a very long N SING : *an*+N

Are you named after anyone?

time. EG *I've known him for ages... She took an age* OR N PLURAL
to dress.   Informal
8 See also **aged**, **ageing**.

AGE

There are a number of different ways of talking
about age in English.

The following examples show how to ask a person's age and how to say how old they are. EG *How
old are you?... What age is she?... She is twenty-five
years old... She must be nearly eighty... ...a young
woman of sixteen... She died in 1816 at the age of
83... ...their three children, Andrea, aged 17, Julie,
aged 16, and Paul, aged 13... ...a forty-year-old
female... ...a class of 4-year-olds... ...nursery schools
for the fives and under... My mother died just
before my fourth birthday.*

If you say that someone is in their twenties, you
mean that they are between twenty and thirty
years old. If you say that someone is in their early
fifties, you mean that they are older than fifty, but
younger than fifty-five; if you say that someone is
in their late fifties, you mean that they are over
fifty-five, but less than sixty.

---

aged; pronounced /eɪdʒd/ for paragraph 1 and
/ˈeɪdʒɪd/ for paragraphs 2 and 3.
1 You use **aged** followed by a number to say how ADJ PRED
old someone is. EG *...men aged 60 and over.* ● See
also **middle-aged**.
2 Someone or something that is **aged** is very old. EG ADJ QUALIT
...his aged aunt.
3 You can refer to all people who are very old as N PLURAL :
the aged. EG *...the care of the aged.*   the+N
ageing /ˈeɪdʒɪŋ/; also spelled **aging. 1** Ageing ADJ CLASSIF
means becoming older and less attractive or efficient. EG *...an ageing film star.*
2 Ageing is the process of becoming old.   N UNCOUNT
ageless /ˈeɪdʒlɪs/. If you describe someone or ADJ CLASSIF
something as **ageless**, you mean that it is impossible to tell how old they are. EG *...an ageless ritual.*
agency /ˈeɪdʒənsɪ/, **agencies**. An **agency** is **1** a N COUNT
business which provides services for another busi-
ness. EG *...an advertising agency.* **2** an administrative organization run by a government. EG *...the
Central Intelligence Agency.*
agenda /əˈdʒɛndə/, **agendas**. An **agenda** is a list N COUNT
of the items that have to be discussed at a meeting.
EG *What is on the agenda today?*
agent /ˈeɪdʒənt/, **agents**. **1** An **agent** is **1.1** N COUNT
someone who arranges business for someone else,
especially someone who gets work for actors or
musicians. EG *I phoned my agent in London about
the job.* **1.2** someone who works for a country's
secret service. EG *...an enemy agent.*
2 If you refer to someone or something as the N COUNT+SUPP
agent of a particular effect, you mean that they
cause this effect. EG *...the agent of change.*
age-old. An **age-old** story, tradition, or connection ADJ CLASSIF :
has existed for longer than people can remember.   ATTRIB
aggravate /ˈæɡrəveɪt/, **aggravates**, **aggravat-**
ing, **aggravated. 1** If you **aggravate** a situation, v+o
you make it worse. EG *National poverty was aggravated by rapid population growth.*
2 If someone or something **aggravates** you, they v+o
make you annoyed. EG *It's the little things that* Informal
aggravate me.
aggregate /ˈæɡrɪɡət/, **aggregates**. An **aggre-** N COUNT :
gate is an amount that is made up of several OFT+*of*
smaller amounts. EG *He had spent an aggregate of
fifteen years in various jails.*
aggression /əˈɡrɛʃən/ is **1** a quality of anger and N UNCOUNT
determination that makes you ready to attack
other people. EG *Barbara defended herself with a*

sudden new aggression. **2** violent and attacking N UNCOUNT
behaviour. EG *...an act of aggression.*
aggressive /əˈɡrɛsɪv/. **1** Someone who is **aggres-** ADJ QUALIT
sive shows aggression. EG *Mrs Zapp was in a highly
aggressive mood.*
2 People who are **aggressive** in their work or ADJ QUALIT
other activities behave in a forceful way because
they are very eager to succeed. EG *...aggressive
businessmen.*
aggressor /əˈɡrɛsə/, **aggressors**. The **aggres-** N COUNT
sor is the person, group, or country that starts a
fight.
aggrieved /əˈɡriːvd/. If you feel **aggrieved**, you ADJ QUALIT
feel upset and angry because of the way in which
you have been treated.
aggro /ˈæɡrəʊ/ is aggressive or violent behaviour. N UNCOUNT
EG *There wasn't a hint of aggro.*   Informal
aghast /əˈɡɑːst/. If you are **aghast**, you are filled ADJ PRED
with horror and surprise. EG *What she had learned
had left her aghast.*
agile /ˈædʒaɪl/. **1** Someone who is **agile** can move ADJ QUALIT
with surprising ease and speed. EG *He was as agile
as a monkey.* ◊ **agility** /əˈdʒɪlɪtɪ/. EG *He leaped* ◊ N UNCOUNT
out of the car with surprising agility.
2 If you have an **agile** mind, you think quickly and ADJ QUALIT
intelligently. ◊ **agility**. EG *...tests of mental agility.* ◊ N UNCOUNT
aging /ˈeɪdʒɪŋ/. See **age**, **ageing**.
agitate /ˈædʒɪteɪt/, **agitates**, **agitating**, **agitated.**
1 If you **agitate** for something, you talk and v+*for/against*
campaign enthusiastically in an attempt to get it.
EG *...a group agitating against the use of chemical
fertilizers.* ◊ **agitation** /ˌædʒɪˈteɪʃən/. EG *...anti-* ◊ N UNCOUNT
imperialist agitation.
2 If something **agitates** you, it worries you and v+o
makes you unable to think clearly or calmly. EG *I
don't want to agitate him unduly.* ◊ **agitated** ◊ ADJ QUALIT
/ˈædʒɪteɪtɪd/. EG *He looked dishevelled and agitated.* ◊ **agitation**. EG *I saw Peter glancing at his* ◊ N UNCOUNT
watch in some agitation.
agitator /ˈædʒɪteɪtə/, **agitators**. An **agitator** is N COUNT
someone who tries to bring about political or social
change by making speeches and campaigning in
public. EG *...political agitators.*
agnostic /æɡˈnɒstɪk/, **agnostics**. An **agnostic** N COUNT
believes that it is not possible to know whether God
exists or not. ▸ used as an adjective. EG *She* ▸ ADJ CLASSIF
remained agnostic.
ago /əˈɡəʊ/. You use **ago** to refer to past time. For ADV
example, if something happened one year **ago**, it is
one year since it happened. If it happened a long
time **ago**, it is a long time since it happened. EG
*Five years ago, I went to the tropics... How long
ago was that?*
agog /əˈɡɒɡ/. If you are **agog**, you are excited by ADJ PRED
something, and eager to know more about it.
agonize /ˈæɡəˌnaɪz/, **agonizes**, **agonizing**, **ago-** v
nized; also spelled **agonise**. If you **agonize** over
something, you feel very anxious about it and
spend a long time thinking about it. EG *He is
agonizing over how to reply to the letter.*
agonized /ˈæɡəˌnaɪzd/; also spelled **agonised**. ADJ CLASSIF
Agonized describes something that you say or do
when you are in great physical or mental pain. EG
He could hear the prisoner's agonized moans.
agonizing /ˈæɡəˌnaɪzɪŋ/; also spelled **agonising.**
1 Something that is **agonizing** causes you to feel ADJ QUALIT
great physical or mental pain. EG *...agonizing feelings of shame and guilt.* ◊ **agonizingly**. EG *The* ◊ ADV
sound was agonisingly painful.
2 Agonizing decisions and choices are very diffi- ADJ QUALIT
cult to make.
agony /ˈæɡənɪ/, **agonies**. Agony is great physical N UNCOUNT
or mental pain. EG *The blow made him scream in* OR N PLURAL
agony.
agree /əˈɡriː/, **agrees**, **agreeing**, **agreed. 1** If V OR V+*with* :
people **agree** with one another about something, RECIP
they have the same opinion about it. EG *Do you
agree with him about this?... People agree that the
law is behind the times.*

2 If you **agree** to do something, you say that you will do it. EG *She agreed to let us use her flat while she was away.* V:OFT+*to*-INF OR *to*

3 If people are **agreed** about something, they agree about it. EG *Are we agreed, gentlemen?* ADJ PRED

4 If you **agree** with an action or a suggestion, you approve of it. EG *I agree with what they are doing.* V+*with*

5 If two stories, accounts, or totals **agree**, they are the same as each other. EG *My theories and his do not always agree.* V

6 If food that you eat does not **agree** with you, it makes you feel ill. V+*with*

agreeable /əgriːəbəˀl/. **1** If something is agreeable, it is pleasant and you enjoy it. EG *...an agreeable sensation.* ADJ QUALIT

2 If someone is **agreeable**, they are pleasant and try to please people. EG *She always made a point of being agreeable to them.* ADJ QUALIT: OFT+*to*

3 If you are **agreeable** to something or if it is agreeable to you, you are willing to do it or to allow it to happen. EG *Get your secretary to do it if she is agreeable.* ADJ PRED: OFT+*to*

agreement /əgriːməˀnt/, **agreements**. **1** An agreement is a decision that two or more people have reached together. EG *Half of the land was given away under the same agreement.* N COUNT

2 Agreement is **2.1** the act of reaching a decision that is acceptable to everyone involved. EG *There was no general agreement on the timing.* **2.2** the act of saying or indicating that you will accept something or believe something. EG *They nodded agreement.* N UNCOUNT OFT+*on/about* N UNCOUNT

3 If you are **in agreement** with someone, you have the same opinion as they have. EG *They were in complete agreement.* PHRASE

agriculture /ægrɪkʌltʃə/ is farming and the methods that are used to raise and look after crops and animals. EG *...areas that are unsuitable for agriculture.* ◇ **agricultural** /ægrɪkʌltʃəˀrəl/. EG *...modern agricultural methods.* N UNCOUNT ◇ ADJ CLASSIF

aground /əgraʊnd/. If a ship runs **aground**, it touches the ground in a shallow part of a river, lake, or the sea. ADJ PRED

ah /ɑː/. When you want to express agreement, surprise, pleasure, or sympathy, you can say **'ah'**. EG *Ah, you poor fellow... Ah, Howard. Come in.*

aha /ɑːhɑː/. When you want to indicate that you understand, know, or have found something, you can say **'aha'**, especially when you are pleased about it. EG *I had a report here somewhere. Aha, here we are.*

ahead /əhɛd/. **1** If something is **ahead**, it is in front of you. EG *The road ahead is foggy... She stared ahead.* ADV

2 If you are **ahead** of someone in your work or achievements, you have made more progress than they have. EG *He is ten years ahead of the rest.* ADV:OFT+*of*

3 If a person or a team is **ahead** in a competition, they are winning. EG *Another goal put United ahead.* ADJ PRED

4 If someone goes **on ahead** or is sent **on ahead**, they leave for a place before other people or things. EG *Our parents had gone on ahead in father's car.* PHRASE

5 If someone arrives somewhere **ahead** of you, they arrive before you. ADV+*of*

6 If someone is **ahead** of you in a queue, they are in front of you. ADV+*of*

7 Ahead also means in the future. EG *I haven't had time to think far ahead.* ADV

8 See also **go ahead**.

aid /eɪd/, **aids, aiding, aided. 1 Aid** is money, equipment, or services that are provided for people in need. EG *...overseas aid for the less developed countries... ...food and medical aid.* N UNCOUNT +SUPP

2 An **aid** is something that makes things easier to do. EG *...a valuable aid to digestion.* N COUNT

3 If you **aid** a person or an organization, you help them by providing them with something they V+O

need. EG *He crossed the border aided by a priest... ...state intervention to aid private industry.*

4 Aid is also used in these phrases. **4.1** If an activity or event is **in aid of** a particular cause, it raises money for that cause. EG *...a cricket match in aid of cancer relief.* **4.2** If you do something **with the aid of** someone or something, they help you to do it. EG *The programmes had been prepared with the aid of various broadcasters.* **4.3** If you go **to the aid of** someone, you try to help them when they are in danger or difficulty. EG *They had rushed to her aid.* PREP PREP PHRASE

aide /eɪd/, **aides**. An **aide** is an assistant to someone who has an important job, especially in government or in the armed forces. N COUNT

AIDS /eɪdz/ is an illness which destroys the natural system of protection that the body has against disease. **AIDS** is an abbreviation for 'acquired immune deficiency syndrome'. N UNCOUNT

ailing /eɪlɪŋ/. **1** If someone is **ailing**, they are ill and are not getting better. EG *...his ailing wife.* ADJ CLASSIF

2 If an organization or society is **ailing**, it is in difficulty and is becoming weaker. ADJ CLASSIF

ailment /eɪlməˀnt/, **ailments**. An **ailment** is an illness, especially one that is not very serious. EG *The crew began suffering a variety of ailments.* N COUNT

aim /eɪm/, **aims, aiming, aimed. 1** If you **aim** a weapon or object at something, you point it in the direction of the thing. EG *Roger picked up a stone, aimed it, and threw it at Henry... He lunged toward me as if he expected me to aim a gun at him.* V+O OR V:OF +*at*

▶ used as a noun. EG *He leaned against a tree to steady his aim.* ▶ N UNCOUNT +SUPP

2 If you **take aim** at someone or something, you point a weapon or object at them, ready to shoot or throw. EG *He took careful aim at the centre and fired.* PHRASE

3 If you **aim** at something or **aim** to do something, you plan or hope to achieve it. EG *We are aiming at a higher production level... A good solid job is the thing to aim for.* V+*at/for* OR *to*-INF

4 If an action or plan **is aimed** at achieving something, it is intended to achieve it. EG *...policies aimed at securing mass support.* V-PASS+*at*

5 An **aim** is the thing that an action or plan is intended to achieve. EG *It is our aim to set up a workshop.* N COUNT+SUPP +SUPP

6 If you **aim** an action at a particular person or group, you intend that they should notice it and be influenced by it. EG *This anti-smoking campaign is mainly aimed at young teenagers.* V+O+*at*: USU PASS

aimless /eɪmlɪ²s/. A person or activity that is aimless has no clear purpose or plan. EG *...drawing aimless doodles in the sand.* ◇ **aimlessly**. EG *She wandered aimlessly along the beach.* ADJ QUALIT ◇ ADV

ain't /eɪnt/ is used in nonstandard spoken English instead of 'am not', 'aren't', or 'isn't'.

air /eə/, **airs, airing, aired. 1 Air** is the mixture of gases which forms the earth's atmosphere and which we breathe. EG *She took a gulp of air... The air temperature was below freezing.* N UNCOUNT

2 The **air** is the space around things that is above the ground. EG *My dog was lying on the floor with its feet in the air... The smell of cooking filled the air.* N SING: the+N

3 Air is used to refer to travel in aircraft. EG *The fare by air from London to Luxembourg is £145 return... Philip was unaccustomed to air travel.* N UNCOUNT by+N

4 If you say that someone or something has a particular **air**, you mean that they give this general impression. EG *He has a faintly old-fashioned air.* N SING+SUPP

5 If you **air** your opinions, you make them known to people. EG *He spoke on the radio, airing his views to the nation.* V+O

Can an aircraft run aground?

6 If you **air** a room or building, you let fresh air v+o into it.

7 If you **air** clothing or bedding, you put it some- v-erg where warm in order to make sure that it is completely dry.

8 Air is also used in these phrases. **8.1** If someone phrases or something disappears **into thin air**, they disappear completely. **8.2** If someone or something appears **out of thin air**, they appear suddenly and mysteriously. eg *I can't simply conjure up the money out of thin air.* **8.3** If someone is **on the air**, they are broadcasting on radio or television. eg *The president went on the air to make a public statement.*

9 See also **airing**.

airborne /ˈɛəbɔːn/. If something is **airborne**, it is adj classif in the air or it comes from the air. eg *...airborne attacks.*

air-conditioned. If a room is **air-conditioned**, adj classif the air in it is kept cool and dry by means of a special machine.

aircraft /ˈɛəkrɑːft/. **Aircraft** is both the singular n count and the plural. An **aircraft** is a vehicle which can or by+n fly, for example an aeroplane or a helicopter.

aircraft carrier, aircraft carriers. An **air-** n count **craft carrier** is a warship with a long, flat deck where aircraft can take off and land.

airfield /ˈɛəfiːld/, **airfields.** An **airfield** is an area n count of ground where aircraft take off and land. It is smaller than an airport.

air force, air forces. An **air force** is the part of a n count country's military organization that is concerned with fighting in the air.

air hostess, air hostesses. An **air hostess** is a n count woman whose job is to look after the passengers in an aircraft.

airing /ˈɛərɪŋ/. **1** If you give a room an **airing**, you n sing : an+n let fresh air into it, often in order to remove unpleasant smells.

2 If you give bedding or clothing an **airing**, you put n sing : an+n it somewhere warm in order to make sure that it is completely dry.

3 If you give your opinions an **airing**, you make n sing : an+n them known to people. eg *Her views on sex and death regularly get an airing on television.*

airless /ˈɛəlɪs/. If a room is **airless**, there is no adj classif fresh air in it. eg *...a small airless theatre crammed with children.*

airline /ˈɛəlaɪn/, **airlines.** An **airline** is a compa- n count ny which provides regular services carrying peo- ple or goods in aeroplanes. eg *There were no other airlines doing a direct flight to London.*

airliner /ˈɛəlaɪnə/, **airliners.** An **airliner** is a n count large aeroplane that is used for carrying passen- gers.

airmail /ˈɛəmeɪl/ is the system of sending letters, n uncount parcels, and goods by air. eg *She gave him a letter to post by airmail... ...an airmail envelope.*

airplane /ˈɛəpleɪn/, **airplanes.** An **airplane** is a n count vehicle with wings and one or more engines that American enable it to fly through the air.

airport /ˈɛəpɔːt/, **airports.** An **airport** is a place n count where aircraft land and take off, usually with a lot of buildings and facilities.

air raid, air raids. An **air raid** is an attack by n count enemy aircraft in which bombs are dropped.

airship /ˈɛəʃɪp/, **airships.** An **airship** was an n count aircraft that was supported in the air by a large balloon filled with gas. Passengers sat in a com- partment underneath the balloon.

airsick /ˈɛəsɪk/. If you are **airsick**, the effects of adj qualit flying in an aeroplane make you sick.

airspace /ˈɛəspeɪs/. A country's **airspace** is the n uncount part of the sky that is over that country and is considered to belong to the country. eg *The plane crashed just after entering British airspace.*

air terminal, air terminals. An **air terminal** is n count a building in which passengers wait before they get on to their aeroplane.

airtight /ˈɛətaɪt/. If a container is **airtight**, its lid adj classif fits so tightly that no air can get in or out.

air-traffic control is the group of people who n uncount organize routes for aircraft and who give instruc- tions to pilots by radio about their routes.

airwaves /ˈɛəweɪvz/ are the radio waves which n plural are used in radio and television broadcasting.

airy /ˈɛəri/, **airier, airiest. 1** If a building is **airy**, adj qualit it is large and has plenty of fresh air inside. eg *The church was airy and light inside.*

2 You can use **airy** to describe someone who is adj qualit light-hearted and casual about things which should be taken seriously. eg *He applied in an airy way for the job of assistant manager.* ◊ **airily.** eg *People's* ◊ adv *jobs matter, yet you're talking airily of closing our company.*

aisle /aɪl/, **aisles.** An **aisle** is a long narrow gap n count that people can walk along between rows of seats in a public building or between rows of shelves in a supermarket.

ajar /əˈdʒɑː/. If a door is **ajar**, it is slightly open. adj pred

akin /əˈkɪn/. If one thing is **akin** to another, it is adj pred+to similar to it in some way. eg *She had answered with* Formal *something akin to anger.*

-al is added to nouns to form adjectives. For suffix example, 'agricultural' means related to agricul- ture and 'departmental' means related to the work of a department. Adjectives like these are often not defined in this dictionary, but are treated with the related nouns. eg *There she stood in her bridal gown... They were still arguing about doctrinal matters.*

alacrity /əˈlækrɪti/. If you do something with n uncount **alacrity**, you do it quickly and eagerly. eg *He rose* Formal *with alacrity to welcome her.*

alarm /əˈlɑːm/, **alarms, alarming, alarmed. 1** n uncount **Alarm** is a sudden feeling of fear or anxiety. eg *She looked round in alarm.*

2 An **alarm** is an automatic device that warns you n count of danger, for example by ringing a bell. eg *The alarm went off... ...a burglar alarm.*

3 If you **sound** or **raise the alarm**, you warn phrase people of danger.

4 If something **alarms** you, it makes you suddenly v+o afraid or anxious. eg *The sight of the school alarmed her... Even little things alarm them.* ◊ **alarmed.** eg *She looked alarmed.* ◊ adj qualit

alarm clock, alarm clocks. An **alarm clock** is a n count clock that you can set to make a noise so that it wakes you up at a particular time.

alarming /əˈlɑːmɪŋ/. Something that is **alarming** adj qualit makes you worried or concerned. eg *The world's forests are shrinking at an alarming rate.* ◊ **alarmingly.** eg *McPherson's sight had begun to* ◊ adv or *deteriorate alarmingly.* adv sen

alarmist /əˈlɑːmɪst/, **alarmists.** Someone or adj qualit something that is **alarmist** causes unnecessary alarm. eg *Don't be too alarmist.*

alas /əˈlæs/. You use **alas** to say that you think adv sen that the facts you are talking about are sad, Formal unfortunate, or regrettable. eg *There was, alas, no shortage of assassinations.*

albatross /ˈælbətrɒs/, **albatrosses.** An **albatross** n count is a very large white seabird.

albeit /ɔːlˈbiːɪt/. When you want to introduce a fact conj or a comment which contrasts with something that Formal you have just said, you can use **albeit**. eg *It continues to publish, albeit irregularly, two jour- nals.*

albino /ælˈbiːnəʊ/, **albinos.** An **albino** is a person n count or animal with very white skin, white hair, and pink eyes. ▶ used as an adjective. eg *...an albino* ▶ adj classif *monkey.*

album /ˈælbəm/, **albums.** An **album** is **1** a record n count with about 25 minutes of music or speech on each side. eg *...an album sleeve.* **2** a special book in n count+supp which you keep things such as photographs or stamps that you have collected.

alcohol /ˈælkəˌhɒl/ is **1** drink such as beer, wine, N UNCOUNT
and whisky that can make people drunk. EG *I never
touch alcohol in any form.* **2** a colourless liquid that
is found in drinks such as beer, wine, and whisky. It
is also used as a solvent.

alcoholic /ˌælkəˈhɒlɪk/, **alcoholics. 1** An **alcohol-** ADJ QUALIT
ic drink contains alcohol.

2 Someone who is an **alcoholic** is addicted to N COUNT
alcohol and continues drinking even though it
makes them ill.

alcoholism /ˈælkəhɒlɪzəm/ is a kind of poisoning N UNCOUNT
caused by drinking too much alcohol over a long
period of time.

alcove /ˈælkəʊv/, **alcoves.** An **alcove** is a small N COUNT
area of a room which is formed by one part of a
wall being built further back than the rest of the
wall.

ale /eɪl/ is a kind of beer. N MASS

alert /əˈlɜːt/, **alerts, alerting, alerted. 1** If you ADJ QUALIT
are **alert**, you are paying full attention to what is
happening. EG *We have to be alert all the time and
look for our opportunity.* ◊ **alertly.** EG *We were all* ◊ ADV
watching Dixon alertly. ◊ **alertness.** EG *The job* ◊ N UNCOUNT
requires constant alertness and vigilance.

2 If you are **on the alert**, you are ready to deal PHRASE
with anything that might happen.

3 If you are **alert** to something, you are fully aware ADJ PRED
of it. EG *They were both alert to the dangers in the* OFT+to
grim business.

4 An **alert** is a situation in which people prepare N COUNT
themselves for something dangerous that might
happen. EG *The city centre was on a nuclear alert.*

5 If you **alert** someone, you warn them of danger V+O
or trouble.

A level, A levels. An **A level** is an educational N COUNT
qualification in England, Wales, and Northern Ireland. Schoolchildren take A level examinations
when they are seventeen or eighteen years old.
People usually need A levels if they want to go to
university in Britain.

algebra /ˈældʒɪbrə/ is a type of mathematics in N UNCOUNT
which letters are used to represent possible quantities.

alias /ˈeɪlɪəs/, **aliases. 1** An **alias** is a false name, N COUNT
especially one used by a criminal.

2 You use **alias** when you mention someone's false PREP
name. EG *Peter Lewis, alias John Lord, was convicted of fraud.*

alibi /ˈælɪbaɪ/, **alibis.** If you have an **alibi**, you can N COUNT:
prove that you were somewhere else when a crime OFT+for
was committed. EG *...his alibi for the night of the
murder.*

alien /ˈeɪlɪən, ˈeɪliən/, **aliens. 1** Something that is ADJ CLASSIF:
alien belongs to a different country, race, or ATTRIB
group. EG *...alien rulers... ...adjusting to an alien
society.*

2 If you describe something as **alien**, you mean ADJ QUALIT
that it seems strange and perhaps frightening,
because it is not part of your normal experience. EG
...a totally alien and threatening environment.

3 If something is **alien** to your normal feelings or ADJ CLASSIF:
behaviour, it is not the way you would normally OFT+to
feel or behave. EG *Their system of parental care
seems alien to us today.*

4 An **alien** is **4.1** someone who is not a legal citizen N COUNT
of the country in which they live. **4.2** a creature
from outer space. EG *...an alien spacecraft.*

alienate /ˈeɪlɪəneɪt, ˈeɪliə-/, **alienates, alienating,
alienated. 1** If you **alienate** someone, you make V+O
them become unfriendly or unsympathetic towards
you. EG *I managed to alienate Dennis, who earlier
on had been so very friendly.* ◊ **alienation** ◊ N UNCOUNT
/ˌeɪlɪəˈneɪʃən, ˌeɪliə-/. EG *...alienation on the part of
many workers.*

2 If someone **is alienated** from something that V+O:USU PASS
they are normally linked with, they are emotional-
ly or intellectually separated from it. EG *People
have been alienated from their roots.*

◊ **alienation.** EG *...a growing feeling of despair and* ◊ N UNCOUNT
alienation.

alight /əˈlaɪt/, **alights, alighting, alighted. 1** If
something is **alight**, **1.1** it is burning. EG *...paraffin* ADJ PRED
that has been set alight. **1.2** it is very bright and ADJ PRED:
colourful. EG *... bushes alight with glow-worms and* OFT+with
fireflies.

2 If you describe someone's face or expression as ADJ PRED
alight, you mean they look excited. EG *She was
looking at him, her eyes alight.*

3 If a bird or insect **alights** somewhere, it lands V:USU+A
there. EG *It flew across to the tree and alighted on a
branch.*

4 When you **alight** from a train or bus, you get out V:OFT+from
of it after a journey. EG *He was photographed* Formal
alighting from his private plane.

align /əˈlaɪn/, **aligns, aligning, aligned. 1** If you V-REFL OR
align yourself with a particular group or are V-PASS:
aligned with them, you support them in the same OFT+with
political aim. EG *They have avoided aligning them-* /against
selves with any one political party... The Soviet
Union was aligned with the Western powers
against the Nazis.* ◊ **alignment** /əˈlaɪnmənt/, ◊ N COUNT
alignments. EG *...political alignments with foreign
powers.*

2 If you **align** something, you place it in a certain V+O
position in relation to something else, usually parallel to it. EG *He aligned his papers in geometrical
patterns on his desk.* ◊ **alignment.** EG *Something* ◊ N UNCOUNT
had slipped out of alignment.

alike /əˈlaɪk/. **1** If two or more things are **alike**, ADJ PRED
they are similar. EG *They all look alike to me.*

2 Alike also means in a similar way. EG *The* ADV
*children are all treated alike... They did everything
alike.*

3 When you want to emphasize that you are ADV
referring to all of a group of people or things, you
can use **alike** after you mention them. EG *The
strike is damaging to managers and workers alike.*

alimony /ˈælɪmənɪ/ is money that someone has to N UNCOUNT
pay regularly to their former wife or husband after
they have been divorced.

alive /əˈlaɪv/. **1** If people or animals are **alive**, they ADJ PRED
have life. EG *I think his father is still alive.*

2 If you describe someone as **alive**, you mean that ADJ PRED
they are very lively and enjoy everything that they
do. EG *Young people are so alive and exciting.*

3 If an activity, organization, or situation is **alive**, it ADJ PRED
continues to exist or function. EG *Theatre outside
London is very much alive.*

4 If a place is **alive** with something, a lot of people ADJ PRED
or things are there and it seems busy or exciting. +with
EG *The ditches beside the fields were alive with
frogs... The church hall was alive with song.*

5 If you are **alive** to a problem or situation, you are ADJ PRED+to
aware of it and realize how important it is. EG *They
were fully alive to the danger.*

6 If a story or description **comes alive**, it becomes PHRASE
interesting, lively, or realistic. EG *None of his
characters actually comes alive.*

7 If people or places **come alive**, they start to be PHRASE
active or lively again after a quiet or dull period. EG
The house had come alive.

alkali /ˈælkəlaɪ/, **alkalis.** An **alkali** is a substance N MASS
with a pH value of more than 7. Alkalis form
chemical salts when they are combined with acids.

all /ɔːl/. **1** You use **all** to refer to the whole of a PREDET
particular group or thing. EG *All the girls think it's* OR PRON
*great... They carried all the stuff into the hall... All
of the defendants were proved guilty... They all live
together in the same house... All was quiet in the
gaol.*

2 You also use **all 2.1** to emphasize that a quality is DET
complete and total. EG *I say this in all seriousness.*
2.2 to emphasize that something happens or is true ADV

to a very great extent. EG *He spilled coffee all over himself... I forgot all about him... I'm all alone.*

3 You can use **all** when you are emphasizing that PRON something is the only thing that is important. EG *All you do is add water... Look, give me a chance. That's all I want.*

4 You use **all** when you are talking about an equal ADV : score in a game. For example, if the score is three NUMBER+ADV **all**, both players or teams have three points.

5 All the more or **all** the better mean even more PREDET or even better than before. EG *You must work all the more quickly now.*

6 You say **above all** to emphasize that a particular ADV SEN thing is more important than other things. EG *Relax, and above all don't panic.*

7 You use **after all 7.1** when you want to ADV SEN emphasize something that other people might have forgotten. EG *It had to be recognized, after all, that I was still a schoolboy.* **7.2** when you are saying that something that you thought was not true is in fact true. EG *Could it be true, after all, that money did not bring happiness?*

8 You use **all in all** to introduce a summary or ADV SEN generalization. EG *All in all, I'm not in favour.*

9 If you say that something is not **all that** good or PHRASE not **all** that important, you mean that it is not very Spoken good or not very important. EG *I don't know him all that well.*

10 If you say that something is **all very well**, you PHRASE are suggesting that you do not really approve of it. EG *Look, it's all very well, but he scared the life out of me.*

11 You use **at all** to emphasize a negative state- PHRASE ment. EG *We didn't go there at all... Haven't you got any at all?*

12 You use **for all 12.1** to say that a particular fact PHRASE does not affect or contradict what you are saying, although you know that it may seem to do so. EG *For all her sensitivity, she's extremely tough.* **12.2** in phrases such as 'for all I know', and 'for all he cares', to emphasize that something does not really matter. EG *It might have been tomato soup for all we knew.*

13 In all means in total. EG *There were nine in all.* PHRASE

14 You use **of all** to emphasize the words 'first' or PHRASE 'last', or a superlative adjective or adverb. EG *I asked them first of all if they were Welsh... This view is the best of all.*

Allah /ˈælə/ is the name of God in Islam. N PROPER

allay /əˈleɪ/, **allays, allaying, allayed.** To **allay** V+O an emotion means to cause it to be felt less Formal strongly. EG *His efforts to allay her fears met with little success.*

all clear. The **all clear** is a signal that a danger- N SING ous situation has ended. EG *They eventually went back in after the all clear was sounded.*

allegation /ˌæliˈgeɪʃən/, **allegations.** An allega- N COUNT tion is a statement suggesting that someone has done something wrong. EG *...allegations of improper business dealings.*

allege /əˈlɛdʒ/, **alleges, alleging, alleged.** If you V+REPORT : **allege** that something is true, you say it but do not ONLY that, prove it. EG *The reports alleged that the motive was* OR V-PASS financial. +to-INF

alleged /əˈlɛdʒd/. An **alleged** fact has been stated ADJ CLASSIF : but has not been proved to be true. EG *...alleged* ATTRIB *police brutality.* ◇ **allegedly** EG *...the crimes he* ◇ ADV *had allegedly committed.*

allegiance /əˈliːdʒəns/, **allegiances.** Your alle- N UNCOUNT **giance** is your support and loyalty to a particu- OR N COUNT : lar group, person, or belief. EG *...an oath of alle-* OFT+to *giance to his country... How can we win the allegiance of the masses?*

allegorical /ˌæliˈgɒrɪkəl/. An **allegorical** story, ADJ CLASSIF poem, or painting uses allegory.

allegory /ˈæliɡəri/, **allegorics.** An **allegory** is a N COUNT OR story, poem, or painting in which the characters N UNCOUNT and events are symbols of something else. Allego- ries are often moral, religious, or political.

alleluia /ˌæliˈluːjə/. See **hallelujah.**

allergic /əˈlɜːdʒɪk/. If you are **allergic** to some- ADJ PRED+to thing, you become ill or get a rash when you eat it, OR ADJ smell it, or touch it. EG *Are you allergic to dogs?...* CLASSIF : *...an allergic rash.* ATTRIB

allergy /ˈælədʒi/, **allergies.** An **allergy** is an N COUNT OR illness that you have when you eat, smell, or touch N UNCOUNT : a substance which does not normally make people OFT+to ill. EG *He had an allergy to milk.*

alleviate /əˈliːvieɪt/, **alleviates, alleviating, al-** V+O **leviated.** If something **alleviates** pain or suffer- ing, it makes it less intense or severe. EG *We want to help alleviate the national food shortage.*
◇ **alleviation** /əˌliːviˈeɪʃən/. EG *...the alleviation of* ◇ N UNCOUNT *pain.* OFT+of

alley /ˈæli/, **alleys.** An **alley** or an **alleyway** is a N COUNT narrow path or street.

alliance /əˈlaɪəns/, **alliances.** An **alliance** is a N COUNT relationship in which two or more people or groups work together for some purpose. EG *We met to discuss the strategies of a military alliance... This pleasant alliance between Mrs Bixby and the Colo- nel continued.*

allied /ˈælaɪd/. **1 Allied** countries, political parties, ADJ CLASSIF : or other groups are united by a political or military ATTRIB agreement. EG *...allied leaders.*
2 Allied describes things that are related to other ADJ CLASSIF : things because they have particular qualities or ATTRIB characteristics in common. EG *The aircraft and allied industries were nationalized.*
3 See also **ally.**

alligator /ˈæliɡeɪtə/, **alligators.** An **alligator** is a N COUNT large animal, chiefly of the southern United States, similar to a crocodile.

allocate /ˈæləkeɪt/, **allocates, allocating, allo-** V+O : **cated.** If something **is allocated** to a particular OFT PASS+to person or for a particular purpose, it is given to that person to use or is used for that purpose. EG *...money allocated to books and stationery... You've been allocated room 426.* ◇ **allocation** ◇ N UNCOUNT /ˌæləˈkeɪʃən/. EG *...the allocation of responsibilities.*

allot /əˈlɒt/, **allots, allotting, allotted.** If some- V+O : thing **is allotted** to someone, it is given to them as OFT PASS+to their share. EG *She would be content to sleep in any corner that was allotted to her.* ◇ **allotted.** EG *We* ◇ ADJ CLASSIF *will spend our allotted sum of money on a larger* ATTRIB *swimming pool.*

allotment /əˈlɒtmənt/, **allotments. 1** An **allot-** N COUNT **ment** is a small area of land in a town which a British person rents to grow vegetables on.
2 An **allotment** of something is a share or amount N SING+of of it that is given to someone.

all-out. You use **all-out** to describe aggressive ADJ CLASSIF : actions that are done in a very energetic and ATTRIB determined way. EG *...an all-out attack on trade unions.*

allow /əˈlaʊ/, **allows, allowing, allowed. 1** If you V+O+to-INF **are allowed** to do something, it is all right for you OR V+A : to do it and you will not get into trouble. EG *No one* USU PASS *is allowed here... He agreed to allow me to take the course.*
2 If you **are allowed** something, you are given V+O+O : permission to have it. EG *Sometimes, we were* USU PASS *allowed a special treat.*
3 If you **allow** something to happen, you do not V+O+to-INF prevent it. EG *The further this process is allowed to* OR V-REFL *go, the more difficult it will be to reverse it... You* +to-INF *must not allow yourself to be upset.*
4 If something **allows** something to happen, it V+O+to-INF gives the opportunity for it to happen. EG *The creatures had warm blood, which allowed them to be active at night.*
5 When you are politely offering to do something CONVENTION for someone, you can say 'allow me'. EG *Mr Smith jumped up and said, 'Allow me.'*
6 If you **allow** that something is true, you admit or V+REPORT : agree that it is true. EG *He allowed that even world* ONLY that *leaders could make mistakes.*
allow for. If you **allow for** certain problems or PHRASAL VB : V+PREP

expenses, you include some extra time or money in your planning so that you can deal with them if they occur.

allowable /əlauəbəl/. If people decide that something is **allowable**, they let it happen without trying to stop it. EG ...*allowable departures from the norms of behaviour*. ADJ CLASSIF

allowance /əlauəns/, **allowances**. 1 An **allowance** is money that is given regularly to someone, in order to help them pay for the things that they need. EG ...*a maternity allowance*. N COUNT+SUPP

2 If you **make allowances** for something, you take it into account in your plans or actions. EG *They make no allowances for a child's age*. PHRASE

all-powerful. Someone or something that is **all-powerful** has a great deal of power or influence. ADJ CLASSIF

all right; also spelled **alright**. 1 If you say that someone or something is **all right**, you mean that you find them satisfactory or acceptable. EG '*Do you like this champagne?*' – '*It's all right.*'... *Is everything all right?*... *He's getting on all right*. ADJ PRED OR ADV

2 If someone or something is **all right**, they are well or safe. EG *Someone should see if she's all right*. ADJ PRED

3 You say '**all right**' when you are agreeing to something. EG '*Can you help?*' – '*All right. What do you want me to do?*' CONVENTION

4 If you say '**all right?**' to someone, you are checking that they have understood what you have just said. EG *If you feel dizzy again put your head in your hands, all right?* ADV SEN

5 Teachers and parents often say '**all right**' to indicate that they want you to end one activity and start another. EG *Alright team, let's move on to another question*. ADV SEN

all-rounder, **all-rounders**. Someone who is an **all-rounder** is good at a lot of different skills, academic subjects, or sports. N COUNT British

allude /əˈljuːd/, **alludes**, **alluding**, **alluded**. If you **allude** to something, you mention it in an indirect way. V+to Formal

allure /əˈljʊə/. The **allure** of something is the pleasing or exciting quality that it has. EG ...*the allure of money*. N SING

alluring /əˈljʊərɪŋ/. Someone or something that is **alluring** is very attractive. EG ...*alluring dark eyelashes*. ADJ QUALIT

allusion /əˈljuːʒəⁿn/, **allusions**. An **allusion** is a reference to someone or something in which they are not mentioned directly or in detail. EG *English literature is full of allusions to Latin and Greek authors*. N COUNT OR N UNCOUNT : OFT+to

ally, **allies**, **allying**, **allied**; pronounced /ælaɪ/ when it is a noun and /əˈlaɪ/ when it is a verb.

1 A country's **ally** is another country that has an agreement to support it, especially in war. EG ...*our European allies*. N COUNT : OFT+POSS

2 Someone who is your **ally** helps and supports you, especially when other people are opposing you. EG *She wanted an ally so badly*. N COUNT : OFT+POSS

3 If you **ally** yourself with someone, you support them. EG ...*countries who do not ally themselves with the super powers*. V-REFL+with

4 See also **allied**.

almighty /ɔːlmaɪti/. 1 The **Almighty** is another name for God. EG ...*the mercy of the Almighty*. N PROPER : the+N
▸ used as an adjective. EG *Almighty God appeared to Jacob in the land of Canaan*. ▸ ADJ CLASSIF : ATTRIB

2 An **almighty** row, problem, or mistake is a very great or serious one. EG *She made the most almighty fuss*. ADJ CLASSIF : ATTRIB Informal

almond /ɑːmənd/, **almonds**. An **almond** is a kind of pale oval nut. N COUNT

almost /ɔːlməʊst/ means very nearly. You can use it before nouns, adjectives, verbs, and adverbs, and before words such as 'anyone' and 'anything'. EG *I spent almost a month in China*... *He is almost blind*... *I had almost forgotten about the trip*... *The door opened almost before Brody had finished* ADV

knocking... *In Oxford Street, you can buy almost anything*.

aloft /əˈlɒft/. Something that is **aloft** is in the air or off the ground. EG *Simon held his hands aloft*. ADV AFTER VB Literary

alone /əˈləʊn/. 1 When you are **alone**, 1.1 you are not with any other people. EG *I wanted to be alone*... *Barbara spent most of her time alone in the flat*. 1.2 you are amongst people who you do not know. EG *She was going all alone to Paris*. 1.3 you have no family or friends. EG *I had never felt so alone and without hope in my life*. ADJ PRED

2 If one person is **alone** with another person, or if two people are **alone**, they are together, without anyone else present. EG *I was alone with the attendant*... *We'd never spent such a long time alone together*. ADJ PRED

3 If you do something **alone**, you do it without help from other people. EG *I was left to bring up my two children alone*. ● When someone **goes it alone**, they do something without any help from other people. EG *He aimed to 'go it alone' politically*. ADV AFTER VB ● PHRASE Informal

4 If you **alone** do something, you are the only person who does it. EG *Simon alone knew the truth*. ADJ AFTER N

5 If something consists of one idea or feature **alone**, nothing else is involved. EG *Pride alone prevented her from giving up*. ADJ AFTER N

along /əˈlɒŋ/. 1 If you move or look **along** something such as a road, you move or look towards one end of it. EG *He was driving along a lane*... *She glanced along the corridor*. PREP

2 If something is situated **along** a road, river, or corridor, it is situated in it or beside it. EG ...*an old house along the Lanark Road*... *Room 64 was half way along on the right*. PREP OR ADV

3 When someone or something moves **along**, they keep moving steadily and continuously. EG *I put my arm around him as we walked along*. ADV AFTER VB

4 If you say that something is going **along** in a particular way, you mean that it is progressing in that way. EG *It was going along nicely*... *His divorce is dragging along*. ADV AFTER VB

5 If you take someone **along** when you go somewhere, you take them with you. EG *He liked taking her along to parties*... *Why don't you come along too?* ADV AFTER VB

6 If something has existed or been true **all along**, it has existed or been true throughout a period of time. EG *Perhaps they had been mistaken all along*. PHRASE

7 If you do something **along with** someone else, you both do it. If you take one thing **along with** another, you take both things. EG *Along with thousands of others, he fled the country*... *The eggs were delivered along with the milk*. PREP

alongside /əlɒŋsaɪd/. 1 If something is **alongside** something else, it is next to it. EG *There was a butcher's shop alongside the theatre*... *A car drew up alongside*. PREP OR ADV

2 If several people are working **alongside** other people, they are working in the same place and are co-operating with each other. EG *The idea is to get them working on simple things alongside other people*. PREP

3 When you talk about one system or attitude existing **alongside** another one, you are comparing them and considering whether they can exist well or properly together. EG *I cannot imagine two political systems less likely to live at peace alongside each other*. PREP

aloof /əˈluːf/. 1 Someone who is **aloof** likes to be alone and does not talk much to other people. ADJ QUALIT

2 If someone stays **aloof** from something, they do not become involved in it. EG *The Emperor kept aloof from all political parties*. ADJ PRED : OFT+from

If you are not altogether aloof, do you talk much to other people?

aloud /əlaʊd/. When you speak or read **aloud**, you ADV AFTER VB
speak so that other people can hear you. EG *She
read aloud to us from the newspaper.*

alphabet /ælfəbet/, **alphabets**. The **alphabet** is N COUNT
the set of letters arranged in a fixed order which is
used for writing the words of a language.

alphabetical /ælfəbetɪkəºl/ means arranged ac- ADJ CLASSIF:
cording to the normal order of the letters in the ATTRIB
alphabet. EG *...an alphabetical list.*
◊ **alphabetically.** EG *Books are catalogued alpha-* ◊ ADV
betically by author.

alpine /ælpaɪn/ means existing in or relating to ADJ CLASSIF:
mountains. EG *...alpine meadows.* ATTRIB

already /ɔːlredɪ¹/. If something has **already** hap- ADV
pened, it has happened before the present time,
and therefore does not need to happen again. EG
I've had tea already, thank you. 2 it has happened
earlier than you expected. EG *By the time he got
home, Julie was already in bed.*

alright /ɔːlraɪt/. See **all right**.

also /ɔːlsəʊ/. You use **also** 1 when you are giving ADV
more information about a person or thing, or
adding another relevant fact. EG *Tony Nuttall is
Vice-Chancellor and also a Professor of English at
Sussex... ...also available in blue and green.* 2 to say
that the same fact applies to someone or something else. EG *His first wife was also called
Margaret.*

altar /ɒltə/, **altars**. An **altar** is a holy table in a N COUNT:
church or temple. USU the+N

alter /ɒltə/, **alters, altering, altered**. If some- V-ERG
thing **alters** or if you **alter** it, it changes. EG *The
weather could alter violently... America must radically alter its economic policy.* ◊ **alteration** ◊ N COUNT:
/ɒltəreɪʃəºn/, **alterations**. EG *It is not possible to* USU+SUPP
make major alterations to existing arrangements.

altercation /ɒltəkeɪʃəºn/, **altercations**. An **al-** N COUNT
tercation is a noisy argument. Formal

alternate, alternates, alternating, alternated;
pronounced /ɒltəneɪt/ when it is a verb and
/ɒltɜːnət/ when it is an adjective.
1 When you **alternate** between two things, you V+between
regularly do or use one thing and then the other. EG
*They alternated between patronising us and ignor-
ing us.*
2 When one thing **alternates** with another, the two V+with
things regularly occur after each other. EG *The
Third World suffers from an annual cycle of
drought alternating with flood.* ◊ **alternation** ◊ N UNCOUNT:
/ɒltəneɪʃəºn/. EG *...an alternation of right-wing and* USU+SUPP
left-wing governments.
3 **Alternate** actions, events, or processes regularly ADJ CLASSIF:
occur after each other. EG *...the alternate contrac-* ATTRIB
tion and relaxation of muscles. ◊ **alternately.** EG ◊ ADV
*Each piece of material is washed alternately in
soft water and coconut oil.*
4 If something happens on **alternate** days, it ADJ CLASSIF:
happens on one day, then does not happen on the ATTRIB
next day, then happens again on the day after it,
and so on. In the same way, something can happen
in **alternate** weeks, years, or other periods of
time. EG *We saw each other on alternate Sunday
nights.*

alternative /ɒltɜːnətɪv/, **alternatives**. 1 An **al-** N COUNT:
ternative is something that can exist instead of OFT+to
something else or that you can do instead of
something else. EG *Are there alternatives to prison?*
▸ used as an adjective. EG *But still people try to find* ▸ ADJ CLASSIF:
alternative explanations. ATTRIB
2 **Alternative** is also used to describe something ADJ CLASSIF:
that is very different from the usual things of its ATTRIB
kind, especially when it is simpler or more natural
than normal. EG *...sources of alternative energy...
...alternative newspapers.*

alternatively /ɒltɜːnətɪvlɪ¹/. You use **alterna-** ADV SEN
tively to suggest or mention something different
from what has just been mentioned. EG *Alternatively, you can use household bleach.*

although /ɔːlðəʊ/. You use **although** to introduce CONJ
subordinate clauses. It introduces 1 a clause which
contains a statement that makes the main clause
of the sentence seem surprising. EG *Although he
was late he stopped to buy a sandwich... Gretchen
kept her coat on, although it was warm in the
room.* 2 a clause, often one that contains 'not', that
modifies the main clause and corrects a wrong
impression that someone might get from it. EG *I
have a lot of my grandfather's features, although
I'm not so tall as he was.*

altitude /æltɪtjuːd/, **altitudes**. If something is at a N UNCOUNT
particular **altitude**, it is at that height above sea OR N COUNT
level. EG *The valley lies at an altitude of about 8,000
ft... ...an airliner flying at high altitude.*

alto /æltəʊ/, **altos**. 1 An **alto** is a woman with a N COUNT
low singing voice.
2 An **alto** musical instrument has a range of ADJ CLASSIF:
musical notes of medium pitch. EG *...an alto sax.* ATTRIB

altogether /ɔːltəgeðə/. 1 If something stops **alto-** ADV AFTER VB
gether, it stops completely. EG *The noise had
stopped altogether... He abandoned his work altogether.*
2 If one thing is **altogether** different from another, ADV
the two things are completely different. EG *...an
altogether different kind of support.*
3 If you say that you do **not altogether** trust PHRASE
someone, you mean that you do not trust them
completely.
4 If you say that something is **not altogether** true PHRASE
or **not altogether** satisfactory, you mean that it is
not completely true or not completely satisfactory.
5 You can use **altogether** to summarize something ADV SEN
you have been saying. EG *Yes, it's quite a pleasant
place altogether.*
6 If several amounts add up to a particular amount ADV SEN
altogether, that amount is their total. EG *You will
get £340 a week altogether... Altogether, he played
in 44 matches.*

altruism /æltruːɪzəºm/ is unselfish concern for N UNCOUNT
other people's happiness and welfare. ◊ **altruistic** ◊ ADJ QUALIT
/æltruːɪstɪk/. EG *My invitation was not completely
altruistic.*

aluminium /æljuºmɪnɪəm/; spelled **aluminum** N UNCOUNT
/əluːmɪnəm/ in American English. **Aluminium** is a
lightweight metal used for making cooking equipment and aircraft parts. EG *...an aluminium frying
pan.*

always /ɔːlwɪ¹z/. 1 If you **always** do a particular ADV
thing, you do it all the time or on every possible
occasion. EG *I shall always love you... You're always
looking for faults... She always arrived before
Watson.*
2 If something is **always** the case, it is the case all ADV
the time. EG *I had always been poor... It's always
raining.*
3 If you say that someone can **always** take a ADV
particular course of action, you mean that they can
try it if all other methods are unsuccessful or
undesirable. EG *Oh well, I can always come back
later.*

am /æm/ is the first person singular of the present
tense of **be**.

a.m. /eɪ em/ after a number refers to a particular ADV
time between midnight and noon. EG *85 students
were still in the hall at 2 a.m.*

amalgamate /əˈmælgəmeɪt/, **amalgamates,** V OR V+with:
amalgamating, amalgamated. When two or RECIP
more organizations **amalgamate** or **are amalgamated**, they become one large organization. EG
*...the Variety Artistes Federation, which has since
amalgamated with Equity.* ◊ **amalgamation** ◊ N UNCOUNT
/əˈmælgəmeɪʃəºn/, **amalgamations**. EG *...the amal-* OR N COUNT
gamation of several large businesses.

amass /əmæs/, **amasses, amassing, amassed**. If V+O
you **amass** something such as money or information, you gradually get a lot of it. EG *They had
amassed enough money to start a business.*

amateur /ˈæmətjʊˈʊˈə, -tʃə/, **amateurs. 1** An ama- N COUNT
teur is someone who does something as a hobby
and not as a job. EG *It's a business for professionals
not amateurs... ...a good amateur viola player.*

2 Amateur can also mean the same as amateur- ADJ QUALIT
ish.

amateurish /ˌæmətjʊˈʊˈərɪʃ/. If you describe some- ADJ QUALIT
thing as **amateurish**, you mean that it is not
skilfully made or done. EG *Their publications were
amateurish and inadequately researched.*

amaze /əˈmeɪz/, **amazes, amazing, amazed.** If v+o
something **amazes** you, it surprises you very
much. EG *She was amazed that I was only twenty...
He was amazed by the response... It amazed them
to learn that I was here.* ◊ **amazed.** EG *I saw her* ◊ ADJ QUALIT
amazed look.

amazement /əˈmeɪzməˈnt/ is what you feel when N UNCOUNT
something surprises you very much. EG *Her eyes
were wide with amazement... To my amazement,
he burst out laughing.*

amazing /əˈmeɪzɪŋ/. You say that something is ADJ QUALIT
amazing when it is very surprising and makes you
feel pleasure, approval, or admiration. EG *New
York is an amazing city... It's amazing how useful
they are... Her general knowledge is amazing.*
◊ **amazingly.** EG *Our holiday was amazingly* ◊ SUBMOD
cheap.

ambassador /æmˈbæsədə/, **ambassadors.** An N COUNT
ambassador is an important official who lives in a
foreign country and represents his or her own
country's interests there. EG *...the British Ambassador to Turkey.*

amber /ˈæmbə/. **1 Amber** is a hard yellowish- N UNCOUNT
brown substance used for making jewellery. EG *...a
dark amber necklace.*

2 Something that is **amber** is of an orange or ADJ COLOUR
yellowish-brown colour. EG *...clusters of amber berries... The lights constantly switch from red to
amber and green.*

ambience /ˈæmbɪˈəns/; also spelled **ambiance.** N SING
The **ambience** of a place is the character and Literary
atmosphere that it seems to have. EG *...the 'liberal'
ambience of the average university.*

ambiguity /ˌæmbɪˈgjuːˈɪˈtɪˈ/, **ambiguities.** You say N UNCOUNT
that there is **ambiguity** when something can be OR N COUNT
understood in more than one way. EG *...a speech
which was a masterpiece of ambiguity.*

ambiguous /æmˈbɪgjuːˈəs/. Something that is **am-** ADJ QUALIT
biguous can be understood in more than one way.
EG *There was nothing ambiguous in the message.*
◊ **ambiguously.** EG *The announcement was am-* ◊ ADV
biguously worded.

ambition /æmˈbɪʃəˈn/, **ambitions. 1** If you have N COUNT
an **ambition** to do or achieve something, you want
very much to do it or achieve it in your life. EG *Her
ambition was to be a teacher.*

2 If someone has **ambition** or **ambitions**, they N UNCOUNT
want to be successful, rich, or powerful. EG *...men of* OR N PLURAL
enterprise, energy, and ambition.

ambitious /æmˈbɪʃəs/. **1** Someone who is **ambi-** ADJ QUALIT
tious wants to be successful, rich, or powerful. EG
...the President's ambitious wife.

2 An **ambitious** idea or plan is on a large scale and ADJ QUALIT
needs a lot of work to be carried out successfully.
EG *She then attempted something more ambitious,
a novel of 120,000 words.*

ambivalent /æmˈbɪvələnt/. If you are **ambiva-** ADJ QUALIT
lent about something, you have, or seem to have,
opposite feelings about it. EG *...an ambivalent attitude towards women.* ◊ **ambivalence** ◊ N UNCOUNT
/æmˈbɪvələns/. EG *She was in a state of ambivalence
about having children.*

amble /ˈæmbəˈl/, **ambles, ambling, ambled.** V : USU+A
When you **amble**, you walk slowly and in a relaxed
manner. EG *I ambled home through the village.*
▸ used as a noun. EG *He slowed down to his usual* ▸ N SING
steady amble.

ambulance /ˈæmbjəˈləns/, **ambulances.** An am- N COUNT
bulance is a vehicle for taking people to and from
hospital.

ambush /ˈæmbʊʃ/, **ambushes, ambushing, am-** V+O
bushed. If a group of people **ambush** a group of
their enemies, they attack them after hiding and
waiting for them. EG *Weyler's troops successfully
ambushed a rebel force.* ▸ used as a noun. EG *A* ▸ N COUNT OR
whole battalion got caught in an ambush. N UNCOUNT

amen /eɪˈmɛn, ɑːˈmɛn/ is said or sung by Christians CONVENTION
at the end of a prayer. EG *This we ask in the name
of Thy Son Jesus Christ, Amen.*

amenable /əˈmiːnəbəˈl/. If you are **amenable** to ADJ QUALIT
something, you are willing to do it or accept it. EG
She was amenable to whatever I suggested.

amend /əˈmɛnd/, **amends, amending, amended.**
1 If you **amend** something that has been written or V+O
said, you change it. EG *Last year the regulations
were amended to allow other awards to be made.*

2 If you **make amends** when you have harmed PHRASE
someone, you show that you are sorry by doing
something to please them. EG *He wanted to make
amends for his former unkindness.*

amendment /əˈmɛndməˈnt/, **amendments.** An
amendment is **1** a section that is added to a law or N COUNT OR
rule in order to change it. EG *...amendments to the* N UNCOUNT
Industrial Relations Bill. **2** a correction to a piece N COUNT
of writing.

amenity /əˈmiːnɪˈtɪˈ/, **amenities.** An **amenity** is N COUNT
something such as a shopping centre or sports
facility that is provided for people's convenience or
enjoyment. EG *When you are young you want the
amenities of the town... ...first class hotels with
every amenity.*

American /əˈmɛrɪkən/, **Americans. 1** An **Ameri-** ADJ CLASSIF
can person or thing belongs to or comes from the
United States of America. EG *...an American accent... ...the American economy.*

2 An **American** is a person who comes from the N COUNT
United States of America.

Americanism /əˈmɛrɪkənɪzəˈm/, **American-** N COUNT
isms. An **Americanism** is an expression or custom that is typical of people living in the United
States of America.

amiable /ˈeɪmɪəbəˈl/. Someone who is **amiable** is ADJ QUALIT
friendly and pleasant to be with. EG *...her amiable
manner.* ◊ **amiably.** EG *He chatted amiably with* ◊ ADV
Dorothy.

amicable /ˈæmɪkəbəˈl/. When people have an ADJ QUALIT
amicable relationship, they are pleasant to each
other and solve their problems without quarrelling.
EG *We hope to settle the dispute in an amicable
way.* ◊ **amicably.** EG *They parted amicably.* ◊ ADV

amid /əˈmɪd/. **1** If something happens **amid** other PREP
things, it happens while the other things are happening. EG *Suddenly, amid the cries, I heard some
words.*

2 If something is **amid** other things, it is surround- PREP
ed by them. EG *Tombstones stood amid the swaying* Literary
grass.

amidst /əˈmɪdst/ means the same as amid.

amiss /əˈmɪs/. **1** If you say that something is ADJ PRED
amiss, you mean that there is something wrong. EG
I immediately sensed something amiss.

2 If someone **takes** something **amiss**, they are PHRASE
offended and upset by it. EG *You mustn't take
anything I say amiss.*

3 If you say that something would **not come** PHRASE
amiss, you mean that it would be welcome and
useful. EG *A little calm wouldn't come amiss.*

ammonia /əˈməʊnɪə, -njə/ is a colourless liquid or N UNCOUNT
gas with a strong, sharp smell. It is used in making
household cleaning substances.

Would you need an anaesthetic for an
amputation?

ammunition /æmjə⁴nɪʃə⁰n/. **1 Ammunition** is bullets and rockets that are made to be fired from guns. N UNCOUNT

2 You can also use **ammunition** to mean information that you can use against someone. EG *The letters might be used as ammunition by reactionary groups.* N UNCOUNT

amnesia /æmniːzɪə/ is a person's loss of memory. N UNCOUNT

amnesty /æmnɪ²sti¹/, **amnesties.** An **amnesty** is **1** an official pardon granted to a prisoner by the state. **2** a period of time during which people can confess to a crime or give up weapons without being punished. N COUNT

among /əmʌŋ/; the form **amongst** is also used.

1 A person or thing that is **among** a group of people or things is surrounded by them. EG *James wandered among his guests... We stood there among piles of wooden boxes... Among his baggage was a medicine chest.* PREP

2 If you are **among** a group of people, you are in their company. EG *I was among friends.* PREP

3 If you say that one person **among** others did something, you are saying that other people did it, and not just that one person. EG *Bluestone, among other union leaders, argued against a strike.* PREP

4 If an opinion, feeling, or state exists **among** a group of people, they have it or experience it. EG *He has always been popular among MPs... Unemployment amongst married women reached a peak.* PREP

5 If something is divided **among** three or more people, they all get a part of it. EG *The estate was divided among his brothers and sisters.* PREP

amongst /əmʌŋst/ means the same as among.

amoral /æmɒrəl, eɪ-/. Someone who is **amoral** does not care whether what they do is considered to be right or wrong; used showing disapproval. ADJ QUALIT

amorous /æmə⁸rəs/. **Amorous** feelings and behaviour involve sexual desire. EG *...amorous affairs.* ADJ CLASSIF Literary

amorphous /əmɔːfəs/. Something that is **amorphous** has no clear shape or structure. EG *...an amorphous cloud... ...an amorphous society.* ADJ CLASSIF

amount /əmaʊnt/, **amounts, amounting, amounted. 1** The **amount** of something that you have, need, or get is how much of it you have, need, or get. EG *...the amount of potatoes that people buy... I was horrified by the amount of work I had to do.* N PART

2 If something **amounts** to a particular total, all the parts of it add up to that total. EG *...very high fees which amount to £2,000.* V+*to*

3 If an idea or feeling **amounts** to something else, it is almost the same as this other thing. EG *His attitude towards her amounted to loathing.* V+*to*

4 If something **amounts** to little, it is unimportant. If it **amounts** to a lot, it is important. EG *It is unlikely that the talks will amount to much.* V+*to*

amphibian /æmfɪbɪən/, **amphibians.** An **amphibian** is an animal such as a frog that can live both on land and in water. N COUNT

amphibious /æmfɪbɪəs/. An **amphibious** animal can live both on land and in water. ADJ CLASSIF

amphitheatre /æmfɪθɪətə/, **amphitheatres;** spelled **amphitheater** in American English. An **amphitheatre** is a large open area surrounded by rows of seats sloping upwards, and often used for performances of plays. N COUNT

ample /æmpə⁰l/. **1** If there is an **ample** amount of something, there is enough of it and some extra. EG *This leaves her ample time to prepare... ...ample supplies of goods.* ◊ **amply.** EG *This has been amply demonstrated over the past few years.* ADJ QUALIT ◊ ADV

2 Ample also means large. EG *There was provision for an ample lawn.* ADJ QUALIT : ATTRIB

amplifier /æmplɪfaɪə/, **amplifiers.** An **amplifier** is an electronic device in a radio or stereo system, which causes sounds or signals to become louder. N COUNT

amplify /æmplɪfaɪ/, **amplifies, amplifying, amplified. 1** If you **amplify** a sound, you make it louder. EG *These signals are then amplified.* ◊ **amplified.** EG *...an amplified electric guitar.* V+O ◊ ADJ CLASSIF

2 If you **amplify** an idea, statement, or piece of writing, you explain it more fully. EG *They are simply rough ideas. They need amplifying, of course.* ◊ **amplification** /æmplɪfɪkeɪʃə⁰n/. EG *His story needed confirmation and amplification.* V+O ◊ N UNCOUNT

amputate /æmpjə⁴teɪt/, **amputates, amputating, amputated.** If a surgeon **amputates** someone's arm or leg, he or she cuts part or all of it off. ◊ **amputation** /æmpjə⁴teɪʃə⁰n/. EG *Punishment for a thief was amputation of a hand.* V+O ◊ N UNCOUNT

amuse /ə³mjuːz/, **amuses, amusing, amused. 1** If something **amuses** you, it makes you want to laugh or smile. EG *He laughed as if the idea amused him.* V+O

2 If you **amuse** yourself, you do something in order to pass the time and not become bored. EG *Sam amused himself by throwing branches into the fire.* V-REFL OR V+O

amused /ə³mjuːzd/. **1** If you are **amused** at or by something, it makes you want to laugh or smile. EG *I was highly amused by a comment Shaw made... ...an amused stare.* ADJ QUALIT

2 If you **keep** yourself **amused**, you find things to do which stop you from being bored. PHRASE

amusement /ə³mjuːzmə²nt/, **amusements. 1 Amusement** is **1.1** the feeling that you have when you think that something is funny. EG *She smiled in amusement.* **1.2** the pleasure that you get from being entertained or from doing something interesting. EG *Every kind of facility was laid on for their amusement.* N UNCOUNT

2 Amusements are **2.1** ways of passing the time pleasantly. EG *What amusements have you found to keep a young boy out of mischief?* **2.2** the games, rides on roundabouts, and other things that you can enjoy at a fairground or holiday resort. N COUNT : USU PLURAL; N PLURAL

amusing /ə³mjuːzɪŋ/. Someone or something that is **amusing** makes you laugh or smile. EG *Francis was such a witty chap, so amusing... There was an amusing story in the paper.* ◊ **amusingly.** EG *He talked lightly and amusingly.* ADJ QUALIT ◊ ADV

an /æn/ or /ən/. **An** is used instead of 'a', the indefinite article, in front of words that begin with vowel sounds: see **a.** DET

anachronism /ə³nækrə⁷nɪzə⁰m/, **anachronisms.** You say that something is an **anachronism** when you think that it is out of date or old-fashioned. EG *The English public schools are an anachronism.* N COUNT

anachronistic /ə³nækrə⁷nɪstɪk/. You say that something is **anachronistic** when you think that it is out of date or old-fashioned. EG *...a peculiarly anachronistic view of communism.* ADJ QUALIT

anaemia /ə³niːmɪə/; also spelled **anemia.** If you have **anaemia**, you have too few red cells in your blood, so that you feel tired and look pale. N UNCOUNT

anaemic /ə³niːmɪk/; also spelled **anemic. 1** Someone who is **anaemic** suffers from anaemia. ADJ CLASSIF

2 If you describe something as **anaemic**, you mean that it is pale in an unpleasant or unhealthy way. EG *...pale, anaemic flowers.* ADJ QUALIT

anaesthesia /ænəsθiːzɪə/; also spelled **anesthesia. Anaesthesia** is **1** the use of anaesthetics in medicine and surgery. **2** a state in which you cannot feel anything in your body or in a part of your body. N UNCOUNT Technical

anaesthetic /ænəsθetɪk/, **anaesthetics;** also spelled **anesthetic.** An **anaesthetic** is a substance that stops you feeling pain, either in the whole of your body when you are unconscious, or in a part of your body when you are awake. EG *He was operated on without an anaesthetic.* N COUNT

anaesthetist /ə³niːsθətɪst/, **anaesthetists;** also spelled **anesthetist.** An **anaesthetist** is a doctor who specializes in giving anaesthetics to patients. N COUNT

anaesthetize /ə³niːsθətaɪz/, **anaesthetizes, anaesthetizing, anaesthetized;** also spelled **anaesthetise** or **anesthetize.** To **anaesthetize** someone means to make them unconscious by V+O giving them an anaesthetic. EG *The animals were anaesthetized for the experiment.*

anagram /ˈænəgræm/, **anagrams.** An **anagram** N COUNT is a word or phrase that is formed by changing the order of the letters in another word or phrase. For example, 'triangle' is an anagram of 'integral'.

anal /ˈeɪnə⁰l/ means relating to the anus of a ADJ CLASSIF: person or animal. ATTRIB

analogous /əˈnæləⁿgəs/. If something is **analo-** ADJ CLASSIF: **gous** to something else, the two things are similar OFT+*to* in some way.

analogy /əˈnæləⁿdʒiˈ/, **analogies. 1** If you make or N COUNT draw an **analogy** between two things, you show that they are alike in some way. EG *He made an analogy between parental and judicial discipline.* **2** If you explain something **by analogy**, you ex- PHRASE plain it by describing something that is similar to it in some way. EG *The models are meant to show, by analogy, how matter is built up.*

analyse /ˈænəlaɪz/, **analyses, analysing, ana-** V+O **lysed;** also spelled **analyze.** If you **analyse** something, you consider it or examine it in order to understand it or to find out what it consists of. EG *Specialists may analyse a situation and suggest solutions... He analysed the chemical structure of the molecules.*

analysis /əˈnæliˈsɪs/, **analyses** /əˈnæliˈsiːz/. **1** N UNCOUNT **Analysis** is the process of considering something OR N COUNT in order to understand it or to find out what it consists of. EG *...linguistic analysis... ...a chemical analysis of the poison.* **2** An **analysis** is also an explanation or description N COUNT that is the result of considering something. EG *He offers a calm analysis of the situation.* **3** You use the expression **in the final analysis** or PHRASE **in the last analysis** to indicate that the statement you are making is about the basic facts of a situation. EG *In the final analysis power rested in the hands of one man.*

analyst /ˈænəlɪst/, **analysts.** An **analyst** is **1** a N COUNT person whose job is to analyse a subject and give opinions about it. EG *...political analysts.* **2** someone who examines and treats people who are emotionally disturbed.

analytic /ˌænəlɪtɪk/ or **analytical** /ˌænəlɪtɪkə⁰l/ ADJ QUALIT means using logical reasoning. EG *...her acute analytical powers.*

analyze /ˈænəlaɪz/. See **analyse.**

anarchic /æˈnɑːkɪk/ means without rules or laws. ADJ CLASSIF EG *The system is economically inefficient and politically anarchic.*

anarchism /ˈænəkɪzə⁰m/ is the belief that the N UNCOUNT laws and power of governments should be replaced by people working together freely. ◊ **anarchist** ◊ N COUNT /ˈænəkɪst/, **anarchists.** EG *Anarchists oppose the organised violence of war.*

anarchy /ˈænəkiˈ/ is a situation where nobody N UNCOUNT seems to pay attention to rules or laws; used showing disapproval. EG *...his will to reverse the drift into anarchy and economic chaos.*

anathema /əˈnæθəmə/. If something is **anath-** N UNCOUNT: **ema** to you, you dislike it strongly. EG *The idea of* OFT+*to* *taking an exam was anathema to him.*

anatomical /ˌænəˈtɒmɪkə⁰l/ means relating to the ADJ CLASSIF: structure of the bodies of people and animals. EG ATTRIB *...the anatomical features that animals have in common.*

anatomy /əˈnætəⁿmiˈ/, **anatomies. 1 Anatomy** is N UNCOUNT the study of the structure of the bodies of people or animals. **2** An animal's **anatomy** is the structure of its body. N COUNT EG *...the anatomy of a fish.*

-ance. -ance and **-ancy** are added to adjectives, SUFFIX usually in place of -ant, to form nouns. These nouns often refer to a quality or state. For example, 'brilliance' refers to the quality of being brilliant and 'buoyancy' refers to the state of being buoyant. Nouns like these are often not defined in this dictionary, but are treated with the related adjec-

tives. EG *His arrogance was intolerable... We must maintain the constancy of family life.*

ancestor /ˈænsestə/, **ancestors. 1** Your **ances-** N COUNT **tors** are the people from whom you are descended. EG *The firm was founded by their ancestor, James Worthington.* **2** An **ancestor** of something modern is an earlier N COUNT thing from which it developed. EG *These creatures are the ancestors of modern man.*

ancestral /ænˈsestrəl/ means relating to your ADJ CLASSIF: family in former times. EG *...Gladstone's ancestral* ATTRIB *home at Hawarden.*

ancestry /ˈænsestriˈ/, **ancestries.** Your **ancestry** N COUNT is the people from whom you are descended. EG *...American citizens of Japanese ancestry.*

anchor /ˈæŋkə/, **anchors, anchoring, anchored. 1** An **anchor** is a heavy hooked object that is N COUNT dropped from a boat into the water at the end of a chain in order to make the boat stay in one place.

anchor

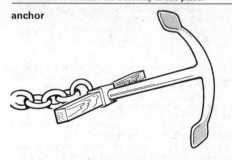

2 When a boat **anchors** or when you **anchor** it, its V-ERG anchor is dropped into the water in order to make it stay in one place. **3** If you **anchor** an object, you prevent it from V+O: OFT+*to* moving. EG *We anchored his wheelchair to a huge stone.*

ancient /ˈeɪnʃənt/. You use **ancient** to describe ADJ QUALIT things **1** that belong to the distant past. EG *...ancient Greece and Rome... ...ancient monuments.* **2** that have existed for a long time. EG *He came from an ancient Catholic family.* **3** that are very old. EG *...old men with ancient faces.*

ancillary /ænˈsɪləriˈ/. **1** The **ancillary** workers in ADJ CLASSIF: an institution are the people such as the cleaners ATTRIB and cooks, whose work supports the main work of the institution. EG *...hospital ancillary workers.* **2** Something that is **ancillary** to something else is ADJ CLASSIF additional to it. EG *Local resources were ancillary* Formal *to a wider system of control.*

-ancy. See **-ance.**

and /əⁿnd/. **1** You use **and 1.1** to link two or more CONJ words, groups, or clauses. EG *...my mother and father... I came here in 1972 and I have lived here ever since... He opened the car door and got out.* **1.2** to link two identical words or phrases in order to emphasize the degree of something or to suggest that something continues or increases over a period of time. EG *He became more and more annoyed... When Bill was happy, he laughed and laughed.* **1.3** to indicate that two numbers are to be added together. EG *Two and two is four.* **2** You also use **and** to interrupt yourself in order to CONJ make a comment on what you are saying. EG *Finally – and I really ought to stop in a minute – I wish to tell a little story.* **3** You use **and** in some numbers, especially when CONJ you say them. See the entry headed NUMBER. EG *...three hundred and fifty people... ...two and a half years.*

Could an animated conversation include anecdotes?

anecdotal /ænɪˈkdəʊtəl/. Anecdotal speech or ADJ CLASSIF writing is full of anecdotes or is based on anecdotes. EG ...anecdotal evidence.

anecdote /ˈænɪˈkdəʊt/, anecdotes. An anecdote N COUNT is a short, entertaining account of something that has happened. EG She told him anecdotes about the hospital and the patients.

anemia /əˈniːmɪə/. See anaemia.

anemic /əˈniːmɪk/. See anaemic.

anemone /əˈnemənɪ/, anemones. An anemone N COUNT is a garden plant with red, purple, or white flowers.

anesthesia /ænəsˈθiːzɪə/. See anaesthesia.

anesthetic /ænəsˈθetɪk/. See anaesthetic.

anesthetist /əˈniːsθətɪst/. See anaesthetist.

anesthetize /əˈniːθətaɪz/. See anaesthetize.

anew /əˈnjuː/. If you do something anew, you do it ADV AFTER VB again, often in a different way from before. EG Literary ...starting life anew in a fresh place.

angel /ˈeɪndʒəl/, angels. 1 Angels are spiritual N COUNT beings that some people believe are God's messengers and servants in heaven.

2 You can call someone an angel when they have N COUNT been very kind to you, or when you are very fond of them. EG Thank you, you're an angel.

angelic /ænˈdʒelɪk/. You can describe someone as ADJ QUALIT angelic when they are, or seem to be, very good, kind, and gentle.

anger /ˈæŋgə/, angers, angering, angered. 1 N UNCOUNT Anger is the strong emotion that you feel when you think that someone has behaved in an unfair, cruel, or insulting way. EG There was anger at the sufferings inflicted by the bombing... 'You're a fool.' – 'Am I?' he said, red with anger.

2 If something angers you, it makes you feel V+O angry. EG His hostile attitude angered her.

angle /ˈæŋgəl/, angles, angling, angled. 1 An N COUNT angle is 1.1 the difference in direction between two lines or surfaces. Angles are measured in degrees. EG The base angles of an isosceles triangle are equal... Oxford Road joins the High Street at an angle of ninety degrees. ● See also right angle. 1.2 the shape that is created where two lines or surfaces join together. EG He lay in the boat with his head against the angle of its bow. 1.3 the direction from which you look at something. EG He held the vase close to his face, peering at it from all angles.

2 If something is at an angle, it is not in a vertical PHRASE or horizontal position. EG ...an old table leaning at an angle.

3 You can refer to a way of presenting something, N COUNT+SUPP for example in a play or a newspaper, as a particular angle. EG The play's pacifist angle had a great appeal.

4 If you angle for something, you try to make V+for someone offer it to you without asking for it directly. EG He got the invitation to Washington he had been angling for.

5 If you angle something in a particular way, you V+O:OFT consider or present it in that way. EG The whole +towards/to thing was angled towards flirtation and amusement.

6 See also angling.

angler /ˈæŋglə/, anglers. An angler is someone N COUNT who fishes with a fishing rod as a hobby.

angling /ˈæŋglɪŋ/ is the activity of fishing with a N ING fishing rod.

Anglo- forms adjectives which describe something PREFIX connected with relations between Britain and another country. EG ...the 1921 Anglo-Irish treaty... ...Anglo-German friendship.

angry /ˈæŋgrɪ/, angrier, angriest. When you are ADJ QUALIT angry, you feel or show strong emotion about something that you consider unfair, cruel, or insulting. EG Are you angry with me?... He was angry at Sally for accusing him... She was always sending angry letters to the newspapers. ◊ **angrily**. EG The ◊ ADV story was angrily denied by the dead man's family.

anguish /ˈæŋgwɪʃ/ is great mental suffering or N UNCOUNT physical pain. EG ...a quarrel which caused her intense unhappiness and anguish.

anguished /ˈæŋgwɪʃt/ means showing great men- ADJ QUALIT tal suffering or physical pain. EG The anguished cries continued.

angular /ˈæŋgjələ/. Angular things have shapes ADJ CLASSIF: that seem to contain a lot of straight lines and ATTRIB sharp points. EG ...his angular face... ...angular hats.

animal /ˈænɪməl/, animals. 1 An animal is 1.1 a N COUNT living creature such as a dog, lion, or rabbit, rather than a bird, fish, reptile, insect, or human being. EG They used to hunt wild animals... ...domestic animals such as dogs and cats. 1.2 any living thing that is not a plant, including people. EG Man is a very weak animal... ...the animal kingdom.

2 If you refer to someone as an animal, you mean N COUNT that their behaviour is unpleasant or disgusting. EG Her husband was an animal.

3 Animal qualities, feelings, or abilities relate to ADJ CLASSIF: someone's physical nature and instincts rather ATTRIB than to their mind. EG Animal instinct warned me to tread carefully.

animate /ˈænɪmət/. Something that is animate ADJ CLASSIF has life, in contrast to things like stones and machines which do not have life.

animated /ˈænɪmeɪtɪd/. 1 Someone or something ADJ QUALIT that is animated is lively and interesting. EG The conversation was animated... He had an expressive, animated face.

2 An animated film has been filmed by means of ADJ CLASSIF animation. EG ...an animated cartoon.

animation /ænɪˈmeɪʃən/. 1 Animation is the N UNCOUNT process of making films in which drawings or puppets appear to move.

2 Someone with animation shows liveliness in the way that they speak, look, or behave. EG She seemed to talk with animation.

animosity /ænɪˈmɒsɪtɪ/, animosities. Animos- N UNCOUNT ity is a feeling of strong dislike and anger. EG Local OR N COUNT animosities were forgotten in the face of this danger.

ankle /ˈæŋkəl/, ankles. Your ankle is the joint N COUNT where your foot joins your leg. See picture at THE HUMAN BODY. EG Rosa fell and sprained her ankle.

annals /ˈænəlz/. If something is in the annals of a N PLURAL nation or society, it is recorded as part of its +SUPP history. EG ...the most improbable soldiers in the annals of military history.

annex /ˈæneks/, annexes, annexing, annexed; also spelled annexe.

1 An annex is a building which is joined to or next N COUNT to a larger main building. EG ...the annexe to the Town Hall.

2 If a country annexes another country or an area V+O of land, it seizes it and takes control of it. EG The State was conquered and annexed in 1832. ◊ **annexation** /ænekˈseɪʃən/. EG ...the annexation ◊ N UNCOUNT of Hawaii.

annihilate /əˈnaɪəleɪt/, annihilates, annihilat- ing, annihilated. 1 If something is annihilated, it V+O:USU PASS is destroyed completely. EG What would happen if the human race should be annihilated? ◊ **annihilation** /ənaɪəˈleɪʃən/. EG ...threatening the ◊ N UNCOUNT total annihilation of the planet.

2 If you annihilate someone in a contest or V+O argument, you defeat them completely. EG The new party was annihilated in the 1931 election.

anniversary /ænɪˈvɜːsərɪ/, anniversaries. An N COUNT anniversary is a date which is remembered or celebrated because a special event happened on that date in a previous year. EG ...the fiftieth anniversary of the Russian Revolution... It was his wedding anniversary.

announce /əˈnaʊns/, announces, announcing, V SPEECH announced. If you announce something, 1 you tell people about it publicly or officially. EG It was announced that the Prime Minister would speak on television... Mr Heath announced his decision. 2

you say it in a deliberate and rather aggressive way. EG '*I am Mrs Jones,*' *she announced... He announced to his wife that he was leaving.*

announcement /ə'naʊnsmənt/, **announcements. 1** An **announcement** is a public statement N COUNT which gives information about something that has happened or that will happen. EG *The Government announcement gave details of small increases in taxes.*
2 The **announcement** of something is the act of N SING telling people about it. EG *...the events which follow the announcement of your resignation.*

announcer /ə'naʊnsə/, **announcers.** An an- N COUNT **nouncer** is someone who introduces programmes on radio or television.

annoy /ə'nɔɪ/, **annoys, annoying, annoyed.** If V+O someone **annoys** you, they make you fairly angry. EG *You're just saying that to annoy me.*

annoyance /ə'nɔɪəns/ is the feeling that you get N UNCOUNT when someone annoys you. EG *The Englishman showed no signs of his annoyance.*

annoyed /ə'nɔɪd/. If you are **annoyed**, you are ADJ PRED fairly angry about something. EG *I got really annoyed because my father kept interrupting... She shook her head, annoyed with herself for forgetting.*

annoying /ə'nɔɪɪŋ/. An **annoying** person or ac- ADJ QUALIT tion makes you feel fairly angry and impatient. EG *It was annoying to be corrected by him all the time... ...her annoying habits.*

annual /'ænjuəl/, **annuals. 1** Annual means **1.1** ADJ CLASSIF : happening or done once every year. EG *...the annual* ATTRIB *meeting of the Association... ...her annual holiday.* ◊ **annually.** EG *Independence day is celebrated* ◊ ADV *annually.* **1.2** calculated over a period of one year. ADJ CLASSIF : EG *...an annual income of twelve thousand dollars.* ATTRIB ◊ **annually.** EG *They import 500 million tonnes of* ◊ ADV *crude oil annually.*
2 An **annual** is **2.1** a book or magazine that is N COUNT published once a year. **2.2** a plant that grows and dies within one year.

annul /ə'nʌl/, **annuls, annulling, annulled.** If a V+O : USU PASS contract or marriage **is annulled**, it is declared invalid, so that legally it is considered never to have existed.

annum /'ænəm/. See **per annum**.

anomalous /ə'nɒmələs/. Something that is ADJ CLASSIF **anomalous** is different from what is normal or Formal usual. EG *These calculations have given anomalous results.*

anomaly /ə'nɒməli'/, **anomalies.** If a rule or N COUNT practice is an **anomaly**, it is different from what is Formal normal or usual. EG *We must correct these injustices and anomalies.*

anon. means anonymous; often written after poems or other writing whose author is not known.

anonymity /ænə'nɪmɪti'/. **1** Anonymity is the N UNCOUNT state of not having your name or identity known. EG *...a benefactor who insisted on anonymity.*
2 The **anonymity** of something is **2.1** the fact that N UNCOUNT it hides your identity. EG *...the anonymity of a* +SUPP *typewritten letter... ...the anonymity of life in big cities.* **2.2** its lack of unusual or interesting features. EG *...the anonymity of a hotel room.*

anonymous /ə'nɒnɪməs/. **1** If you remain anony- ADJ CLASSIF **mous** when you do something, you do not let people know that you were the person who did it. EG *The donor prefers to remain anonymous... ...anonymous letters.* ◊ **anonymously.** EG *Anyone* ◊ ADV *who wanted to make a complaint could do so anonymously.*
2 Something that is **anonymous** **2.1** does not ADJ CLASSIF reveal who you are. EG *A taxi is anonymous. Nobody knows who's inside.* **2.2** has no unusual or interesting features. EG *...an anonymous little town.*

anorak /'ænə'ræk/, **anoraks.** An **anorak** is a N COUNT warm waterproof jacket, usually with a hood.

another /ə'nʌðə/. **1** Another thing or person means **1.1** an additional thing or person. EG *She* DET OR PRON : SING

finished her cigarette, then lit another one... We walked another hundred metres... ...a tin of pink paint and another of brown.* **1.2** a different thing or DET OR PRON person. EG *They made it a crime to marry a person of another race... Parents say one thing and do another.*
2 You use **one another** to indicate that each PHRASE member of a group does something to or for the other members. EG *They didn't dare to look at one another... Members usually meet in one another's homes.*
3 If you talk about **one** thing **after another**, you PHRASE are referring to a series of repeated or continuous events. EG *She found one excuse after another to postpone it.*

answer /'ɑːnsə/, **answers, answering, an-** **swered. 1** When you **answer** someone who has V:SPEECH : asked you something, you say something back to ONLY *that;* them. EG '*Did he win?*' – '*No,*' *I answered... I tried* ALSO V *my best to answer her questions... He answered that the price would be three pounds... 'What's up?' said Sue. He didn't answer.*
2 If you **answer** a letter or advertisement, you V+O OR V write to the person who wrote it. EG *She hadn't answered his letters.*
3 An **answer** is something that you say or write N COUNT when you answer someone. EG *The answer to your question is no!... I got their answer to my letter.*
4 When you **answer** the telephone, you pick it up V+O OR V when it rings. When you **answer** the door, you open it when you hear a knock or the bell. EG *A girl he didn't know answered the doorbell.* ▸ used as a ▸ N COUNT noun. EG *I rang the doorbell, but there was no answer.*
5 An **answer** to a problem is a possible solution to N COUNT : it. EG *There is no easy answer to the problem of* OFT+*to* *pollution.*
6 The **answer** to a question in a test is something N COUNT : that a student writes or says in an attempt to give OFT+*to* the facts that are asked for. EG *I think the answer to No. 5 is fourteen.* ▸ used as a verb. EG *You have to* ▸ V+O *answer four questions.*
7 If you say or do something **in answer** to some- PHRASE thing that someone else has said or done, you say it or do it as a response to what they have said or done. *She gave him a dreamy stare in answer.*

answer back. If someone, especially a child, PHRASAL VB : **answers** you **back** or **answers back**, they speak V+O+ADV rudely to you when you speak to them. OR V+ADV

answer for. 1 If you say that someone **has a lot** PHRASE **to answer for**, you mean that their actions have had a lot of bad results. **2** If you say that you can or PHRASAL VB : will **answer for** someone or for their qualities, you V+PREP mean that you are sure that they will do what is wanted. EG *I can answer for his loyalty.*

answerable /'ɑːnsə'rəbə'l/. **1** If you are **answer-** ADJ PRED+*to* **able** to someone, you have to report and explain your actions to them. EG *These three are answerable to the whole group.*
2 If you are **answerable** for your actions or for ADJ PRED+*for* someone else's actions, you are considered to be responsible for them.

ant /ænt/, **ants.** Ants are small crawling insects N COUNT that live in large groups.

antagonism /æn'tægənɪzəm/ is hatred or hostil- N UNCOUNT ity. EG *...a mother who feels antagonism towards* OFT+*towards* *her children.*

antagonist /æn'tægənɪst/, **antagonists.** Your an- N COUNT **tagonist** is your opponent or enemy.

antagonistic /æntægə'nɪstɪk/. Someone who is ADJ QUALIT **antagonistic** shows hatred or hostility towards OFT+ you. EG *Many of them are antagonistic towards the* *towards/to* *President.*

antagonize /æn'tægənaɪz/, **antagonizes, antago-** V+O **nizing, antagonized;** also spelled **antagonise.** If

Is it polite to answer back?

you **antagonize** someone, you make them feel angry or hostile towards you. EG *He had antagonized local tribesmen.*

antecedent /æntɪsiːdənt/, **antecedents. 1** An **antecedent** of something is something else that happened or existed before it and that was similar to it in some way. EG *...the prehistoric antecedents of the horse.*   N COUNT: OFT+POSS

2 Your **antecedents** are your ancestors.   N PLURAL

antelope /æntɪləup/, **antelopes.** The form **antelope** can also be used for the plural.   N COUNT
An **antelope** is an animal with long legs and horns that looks like a deer.

antenna /æntenə/, **antennae** /æntenaɪ/ or **antennas.** For paragraph 2 the plural is usually **antennas.**

1 The **antennae** of something such as an insect or lobster are the two long, thin parts attached to its head that it uses to feel things with.   N COUNT: USU PLURAL

2 An **antenna** is also a piece of wire that receives television or radio signals. Antennas are often fixed to buildings, cars, radios, and television sets.   N COUNT American

anthem /ænθəm/, **anthems.** An **anthem** is a song or hymn written for a special occasion. ● See also **national anthem.**   N COUNT

anthology /ænθɒlədʒiː/, **anthologies.** An **anthology** is a collection of writings by different writers published together in one book. EG *...an anthology of English poetry.*   N COUNT

anthropology /ænθrəpɒlədʒiː/ is the scientific study of people, society, and culture.   N UNCOUNT
◊ **anthropologist, anthropologists.** EG *...an English anthropologist, Colin Turnbull.*   ◊ N COUNT
◊ **anthropological.** EG *...anthropological research.*   ◊ ADJ CLASSIF

anti- is used to form words that mean 1 opposed to a particular system, practice, or group of people. EG *...the anti-apartheid movement... ...anti-abortion campaigns... ...anti-American feelings.* **2** intended to prevent something from happening or to destroy something harmful. EG *...anti-freeze... ...anti-aircraft guns.*   PREFIX   PREFIX

antibiotic /æntɪbaɪɒtɪk/, **antibiotics.** Antibiotics are chemicals or drugs that are used in medicine to kill bacteria and to cure infections.   N COUNT: USU PLURAL

anticipate /æntɪsɪpeɪt/, **anticipates, anticipating, anticipated. 1** If you **anticipate** an event, you realize in advance that it may happen and you are prepared for it. EG *The Secretary had anticipated the question... Incomes rose faster than anticipated... Some scientists anticipate that more food will be taken from the oceans.* ◊ **anticipation** /æntɪsɪpeɪʃəⁿn/. EG *Petrol coupons were issued in anticipation of rationing.*   V+O OR V+REPORT   ◊ N UNCOUNT

2 If you **anticipate** something pleasant or exciting that is going to happen, you look forward to it with pleasure. EG *She had often pleasurably anticipated the moment when she would hand in her resignation.* ◊ **anticipation.** EG *'Please!' the children cried, jumping up and down in anticipation.*   V+O   ◊ N UNCOUNT

anticlimax /æntiˈklaɪmæks/, **anticlimaxes.** If something is an **anticlimax,** it disappoints you because it is not as exciting as you expected, or because it happens after something that was very exciting. EG *Polling day was a bit of an anticlimax... ...a sense of anticlimax.*   N COUNT OR N UNCOUNT

anti-clockwise /æntiˈklɒkwaɪz/. When something moves **anti-clockwise,** it moves in a circle in the opposite direction to the hands of a clock. EG *I gave it a sharp turn anti-clockwise.*   ADV AFTER VB OR ADJ CLASSIF: ATTRIB British

antics /æntɪks/ are 1 funny and unusual ways of behaving. EG *She was smiling at the antics of the squirrels.* **2** actions which seem silly. EG *...the antics of the main political parties.*   N PLURAL

antidote /æntiˈdəʊt/, **antidotes. 1** An **antidote** is a chemical substance that stops or controls the effect of a poison.   N COUNT

2 An **antidote** to a difficult or unpleasant situation is something that helps you to overcome the situation. EG *Work is a wonderful antidote to misery.*   N COUNT: OFT+to

antipathy /æntɪpəθiː/ is a strong feeling of dislike or hostility. EG *...political antipathy to student radicalism.*   N UNCOUNT: OFT+to

antiquarian /æntɪkweərɪən/ means concerned with old and rare objects. EG *...antiquarian bookshops.*   ADJ CLASSIF: ATTRIB

antiquated /æntɪkweɪtⁱd/. You describe something as **antiquated** when it is very old or old-fashioned. EG *...the clatter of the antiquated air-conditioning machine.*   ADJ QUALIT

antique /ænti:k/, **antiques.** An **antique** is an old object, for example a piece of china or furniture, which is valuable because of its beauty or rarity. EG *His house was filled with antiques... ...antique furniture.*   N COUNT

antiquity /æntɪkwɪˈtiː/, **antiquities. 1** Antiquity is the distant past, especially the time of the ancient Egyptians, Greeks, and Romans. EG *...the great lost paintings of antiquity.*   N UNCOUNT

2 Antiquities are interesting old buildings, statues, or other things that you can go and see.   N COUNT: USU PLURAL

3 The **antiquity** of something is its great age. EG *...a famous landmark of great antiquity.*   N UNCOUNT

anti-Semitism /æntiˈsemiˈtɪzəⁿm/ is dislike for and prejudice against Jewish people.   N UNCOUNT

antiseptic /æntiˈseptɪk/ is a substance that kills germs and harmful bacteria. EG *I washed out the wound with antiseptic.*   N MASS

anti-social. 1 Someone who is **anti-social** is unwilling to meet and be friendly with other people.   ADJ QUALIT

2 Anti-social behaviour is annoying or upsetting to other people. EG *I don't like people phoning at this hour – it's anti-social.*   ADJ QUALIT

antithesis /æntɪθəˈsɪs/, **antitheses** /æntɪθəˈsiːz/. The **antithesis** of something is its exact opposite. EG *That is the antithesis of what he believes.*   N COUNT Formal

antler /æntlə/, **antlers.** A male deer's **antlers** are the branched horns on its head.   N COUNT: USU PLURAL

anus /eɪnəs/, **anuses.** A person's **anus** is the hole between their buttocks, from which faeces leave their body.   N COUNT Medical

anvil /ænvɪl/, **anvils.** An **anvil** is a heavy iron block on which hot metals are beaten into shape.   N COUNT

anxiety /æŋzaɪⁱtiː/, **anxieties. 1** Anxiety is a feeling of nervousness or worry. EG *'What do you think?' asked the Belgian with a touch of anxiety... ...their anxiety over what was to be done.*   N UNCOUNT

2 An **anxiety** is something which causes you to feel nervous or worried. EG *...major financial anxieties.*   N COUNT

anxious /æŋkˈʃəs/. **1** If you are **anxious,** you are nervous or worried about something. EG *It's time to be going home, your mother will be anxious... She was anxious about her job.* ◊ **anxiously.** EG *'I'm not boring you?' she asked anxiously.*   ADJ QUALIT   ◊ ADV

2 An **anxious** time or situation is one during which you feel nervous and worried. EG *You must have had an anxious day.*   ADJ QUALIT ATTRIB

3 If you are **anxious** to do something or **anxious** that something should happen, you very much want to do it or very much want it to happen. EG *...civil servants anxious for promotion... She's anxious to go abroad.*   ADJ PRED +to-INF, REPORT, OR for

any /eniː/. **1** You use **any** in negative statements, for example with 'not' or 'never', to mean none of a particular thing. EG *I hadn't had any breakfast and I was getting hungry... It won't do any good... I don't like any of this.*   DET OR PRON

2 You use **any** in questions and conditional clauses to ask if there is some of a particular thing or to suggest that there might be. EG *Were you in any danger?... They will retaliate if any of their ships are attacked.*   DET OR PRON

3 You use **any** in positive statements when you are referring to something or someone without saying exactly what, who, or which kind you mean. EG *Any big tin container will do... ...things that any man*   DET OR PRON might do under pressure... The meeting was different from any that had gone before.

4 You can also use **any** to emphasize a compara- ADV WITH NEG
tive adjective or adverb in a negative statement. EG
I couldn't stand it any longer... He didn't want to
express himself any more strongly than he had to.

anybody /ɛnɪbɔˀdiˀ/. See **anyone**.

anyhow /ɛnɪhaʊ/. **1 Anyhow** means the same as
anyway.

2 If you do something **anyhow**, you do it in a ADV
careless or untidy way. EG They were all shoved in
anyhow.

anyone /ɛnɪwəˀn/. The form **anybody** is also
used.

1 You use **anyone** or **anybody** in negative state- PRON INDEF
ments, for example with 'not' or 'never', to say that
nobody is present or involved in an action. EG There
wasn't anyone there.

2 You use **anyone** or **anybody** in questions and PRON INDEF
conditional clauses to ask or talk about whether
someone is present or doing something. EG Was
there anyone behind you?... If anyone asks where
you are I'll say you've just gone out.

3 You also use **anyone** and **anybody** to refer to a PRON INDEF
person or to people in general, when you do not
want to say which particular person or people you
are referring to. EG Their laughter woke anyone
who was not already up... He took longer than
anybody else.

anything /ɛnɪθɪŋ/. **1** You use **anything** in nega- PRON INDEF
tive statements, for example with 'not' or 'never',
to say that nothing is present or an action or event
does not happen. EG I did not say anything... They
couldn't afford anything better.

2 You use **anything** in questions and conditional PRON INDEF
clauses to ask or talk about whether something is
present or happening. EG I've told her to come to
you if she wants anything.

3 You can use **anything** to refer to a thing, an PRON INDEF
event, or an idea without saying exactly which one
you mean. EG The situation was very tense; anything might happen... Lemon gives a fresh flavour
to almost anything.

4 You can use **anything** for emphasis, when you ADV+like/
are saying that something is not at all like some- near
thing else. EG It didn't taste anything like soup.

5 You use **anything but** to emphasize that something is not the case. For example, if you say that
someone or something is **anything but** attractive,
you mean that they are not at all attractive. EG The
operation was anything but funny.

anyway /ɛnɪweɪ/. The form **anyhow** is also used. ADV SEN
You use **anyway** or **anyhow 1** to indicate that a
statement explains or supports a previous point. EG
We ought to spend less on the defence missiles,
which I reckon are pretty useless anyway. **2** to
suggest that a statement is true or relevant in spite
of other things that have been said. EG 'I can give
you a lift.' – 'No, I'll walk. Thanks, anyway.' **3** to
correct or modify a statement, for example to limit
it to what you definitely know to be true. EG 'All of
them?' I asked. 'Some, anyway.' **4** to change the
topic or return to a previous topic. EG What are you
phoning for, anyway?... Anyway, I'll see you later.

anywhere /ɛnɪwɛə/. **1** You can use **anywhere** in ADV
negative statements, questions, and conditional
clauses to refer to a place without saying exactly
where you mean, for example because it does not
matter about being exact. EG I changed my mind
and decided not to go anywhere... Is there an
ashtray anywhere?

2 You can also use **anywhere** in positive statements **2.1** for emphasis with an expression that ADV:
refers to a place or area. EG They are the oldest OFT+PREP
rock paintings anywhere in North America... It is
better in the kitchen than anywhere else. **2.2** to ADV+from/
refer to a point within a stated range when you do between
not know what the point is. EG ...a time anywhere
from zero to fifteen years from now.

apart /əpɑ:t/. **1** When something is **apart** from ADV+from
something else, there is a space between them. EG I
was sitting apart from the rest.

2 If two things are a particular distance **apart**, ADJ PRED
they are that distance from each other. EG Their
faces were a couple of inches apart.

3 If two things move **apart** or are pulled **apart**, ADV AFTER VB
they move away from each other. EG I tried to pull
the dogs apart.

4 If two people are **apart**, they are no longer living ADJ PRED
together or spending time together. EG They could
not bear to be apart.

5 If you take something **apart**, you separate it into ADV AFTER VB
the pieces that it is made of. If it comes or falls
apart, its parts separate from each other.

6 If something such as an organization or relation- ADV AFTER VB
ship falls **apart**, it can no longer continue because
it has serious difficulties. EG Their marriage began
to fall apart.

7 If you **can't tell** two people or things **apart**, they PHRASE
look exactly the same to you. EG He couldn't tell the
boys apart.

8 You use **apart from 8.1** when you are giving an PREP
exception to a general statement that you are
making. EG Apart from Ann, the car was empty...
She had no money, apart from the five pounds that
Christopher had given her. **8.2** to say that you want
to ignore one aspect of a situation so that you can
talk about another aspect. EG Quite apart from the
expense, I don't think I would want to fly anyway.

apartheid /əpɑ:th⁰aɪt, -h⁰eɪt/ is a political system N UNCOUNT
in South Africa in which people of different races
are kept apart by law.

apartment /əpɑ:tmɔˀnt/, **apartments**. An **apart-** N COUNT
ment is **1** a set of rooms for living in, usually on
one floor of a large building. EG They pay 2,000
dollars a month for their three-bedroomed apartment. **2** one of a set of large rooms used by an
important person such as a king, queen, or president. EG ...splendid apartments of state.

apathetic /æpəθetɪk/. Someone who is **apathetic** ADJ QUALIT
is not interested in anything. EG ...bored, apathetic
youngsters. ◇ **apathetically**. EG The onlookers ◇ ADV
applauded apathetically.

apathy /æpəθiˀ/ is a state of mind in which you N UNCOUNT
are not interested in or enthusiastic about anything. EG He began to lose his apathy and take a
keen interest in sport.

ape /eɪp/, **apes**, **aping**, **aped**. **1** Apes are animals N COUNT
such as chimpanzees or gorillas.

2 If you **ape** someone's speech or behaviour, you V+O
imitate it. EG ...aging television personalities who
aped the fashions of the young.

aperitif /ə³peɪriˀtiˀf/, **aperitifs**. An **aperitif** is an N COUNT
alcoholic drink that you have before a meal.

aperture /æpətʃə/, **apertures**. An **aperture** is a N COUNT
narrow hole or gap, for example the opening in a
camera through which light passes into it. EG Into
this aperture a drop of mercury was poured.

apex /eɪpɛks/, **apexes**. The **apex** of something is N COUNT:
its pointed top or end. EG ...the apex of the pyramid. OFT+of

aphorism /æfɔˀrɪzɔˀm/, **aphorisms**. An **apho-** N COUNT
rism is a short, clever sentence which expresses a
general truth.

aphrodisiac /æfrɔˀdɪziæk/, **aphrodisiacs**. An N COUNT
aphrodisiac is a food, drink, or drug which makes
people want to have sex.

apiece /əpi:s/. If people have a particular number ADV
of things **apiece**, they have that number each. EG
He gave his daughters £200 apiece.

aplomb /əplɒm/. If you do something with N UNCOUNT
aplomb, you do it with great confidence. EG She
spoke with great aplomb.

apolitical /eɪpəlɪtɪkɔˀl/. Someone who is **apoliti-** ADJ QUALIT
cal is not interested in politics.

Does something that is appalling appeal to you?

apologetic /ɒpɒlədʒetɪk/. If you are **apologetic**, ADJ QUALIT
you show or say that you are sorry that you have
hurt someone or caused trouble for them. EG 'Oh,
I'm sorry,' said the girl, immediately apologetic...
He was apologetic about his behaviour at dinner.
◊ **apologetically.** EG He smiled apologetically. ◊ ADV

apologize /ɒpɒlədʒaɪz/, **apologizes, apologizing,** V : OFT+to/for
apologized; also spelled **apologise.** When you OR V+QUOTE
apologize to someone, you say that you are sorry
that you have hurt them or caused trouble for
them. EG I apologise for my late arrival... 'Sorry I
haven't called you yet,' he apologized.

apology /ɒpɒlədʒi/, **apologies.** An **apology** is N COUNT OR
something that you say or write in order to tell N UNCOUNT
someone that you are sorry that you have hurt
them or caused trouble for them. EG He sent a
letter of apology to the publisher... He phoned and
was full of apologies.

apostrophe /ɒpɒstrɒfi/, **apostrophes.** An **apos-** N COUNT
trophe is a mark written to indicate that one or
more other letters have been omitted from a word,
as in can't and he'll. An apostrophe is also written
before or after an 's' at the end of a word to
indicate that what follows belongs or relates to the
word, as in the cat's whiskers and the players'
entrance.

appal /əpɔːl/, **appals, appalling, appalled;** V+O : USU PASS
spelled **appall** and **appalls** in American English. If
something **appals** you, it shocks and disgusts you
because it is so bad. EG The architecture appalled
her. ◊ **appalled.** EG I was absolutely appalled at ◊ ADJ QUALIT :
the quality of the reporting. OFT+at/by

appalling /əpɔːlɪŋ/. 1 Something that is **appalling** ADJ QUALIT
is so bad or unpleasant that it shocks and disgusts
you. EG These people live in appalling conditions.
◊ **appallingly.** EG He had behaved appallingly. ◊ ADV
2 You can use **appalling** to emphasize that some- ADJ QUALIT :
thing is extremely bad. EG I had the most appalling ATTRIB
depression.

apparatus /æpəreɪtəs/. 1 **Apparatus** is the N UNCOUNT
equipment, such as tools and machines, which is
used to do a particular job or activity. EG ...large
apparatus like slides and climbing frames.
2 The **apparatus** of an organization or system is N UNCOUNT
its structure and method of operation. EG ...the +SUPP
whole apparatus of the welfare state.

apparent /əpærənt/. 1 An **apparent** situation, ADJ CLASSIF :
quality, or feeling seems to exist, although you ATTRIB
cannot be certain that it does exist. EG ...the apparent success of their marriage.
2 If something is **apparent** to you, it is clear and ADJ PRED :
obvious to you. EG It was becoming increasingly OFT+to OR
apparent to me that he disliked me... Everyone ran REPORT
out for no apparent reason.

apparently /əpærəntli/. You use **apparently** 1 ADV SEN
to indicate that the information that you are giving
is something that you have heard but you are not
certain that it is true. EG Apparently she's living
with them. 2 to refer to something that seems to be ADV
the case although it may not be. EG She was
standing by the window, apparently quite calm and
relaxed.

apparition /æpərɪʃən/, **apparitions.** An **appari-** N COUNT
tion is something that you think you see but that is
not really there. EG He was visited by an apparition,
a girl resembling his dead daughter.

appeal /əpiːl/, **appeals, appealing, appealed.** 1 V+for OR
If you **appeal** for something that you need such as V+QUOTE
money or help, you make a serious and often
urgent request for it. EG He was appealing for funds
to build a new school. ▸ used as a noun. EG A radio ▸ N COUNT
appeal she made, asking for money for cancer
research, raised £75,000.
2 If you **appeal** to someone's honour, reason, or V+to
sense, you suggest that they should do what you ask
if they want to seem honourable, reasonable, or
sensible. EG They are confident they can appeal to
her sense of duty. ▸ used as a noun. EG ...an appeal ▸ N COUNT+to
to her maternal feelings.

3 If you **appeal** to someone in authority against a V+to/against
decision, you formally ask them to change it. EG He
successfully appealed against his conviction.
▸ used as a noun. EG The Supreme Court turned ▸ N COUNT
down our appeal.
4 If something **appeals** to you, you find it attrac- V+to
tive or interesting. EG These books are designed to
appeal to children... The idea appealed to him.
◊ **appealing.** EG He has an appealing sense of ◊ ADJ QUALIT
humour.
5 The **appeal** of something is a quality that it has N UNCOUNT
which people find attractive or interesting. EG What +SUPP
is the main appeal of these cars?

appear /əpɪə/, **appears, appearing, appeared.** 1 V : USU+A
When something which you could not see before
appears, it moves into a position where you can
see it. EG A glow of light appeared over the sea...
Two men suddenly appeared.
2 When something new **appears**, it begins to exist V : USU+A
or becomes available. EG ...the newest political
party to appear in Britain... His second novel
appeared under the title 'Getting By'.
3 When someone **appears** in a play or show, they V+in
take part in it. EG He is currently appearing in the
TV series 'Funny Man'.
4 When someone **appears** before a court of law, V : USU+A
they go there in order to answer charges or to give
information as a witness.
5 If you say that something **appears** to be the way V+to-INF
that you describe it, you mean that you believe it to OR C; ALSO
be that way. EG Their offer appears to be the most V+REPORT
attractive... He appears confident... It appears that ONLY that
he followed my advice.

appearance /əpɪərəns/, **appearances.** 1 The ap- N SING+SUPP
pearance of someone in a place is their arrival
there, especially when it is unexpected. EG The
fight was soon stopped, thanks to the prompt
appearance of the police.
2 If you talk about the **appearance** of something N SING+SUPP
new, you are referring to the fact that it has begun
to exist. EG With the appearance of credit cards
more people got into debt.
3 When you make an **appearance** in a play or N COUNT
show, you take part in it. EG She has made several
television appearances recently.
4 If you **put in an appearance** at an event, you go PHRASE
to it for a short time but do not stay.
5 Someone or something's **appearance** is the way N UNCOUNT
that they look to other people. EG I had ceased to
worry about my appearance... The building has
changed the appearance of the whole area... The
sisters were alike in appearance.
6 If something is true **to all appearances** or **by** PHRASE
all appearances, it seems from what you know
about it that it is true. EG To all appearances he
doesn't work hard.

appease /əpiːz/, **appeases, appeasing, ap-** V+O
peased. If you try to **appease** someone, you try to Formal
stop them being angry by giving them what they
want. EG He had ample funds to appease the king's
anger. ◊ **appeasement.** EG ...a gift of appease- ◊ N UNCOUNT
ment.

appendicitis /əpendɪsaɪtɪs/ is an illness in N UNCOUNT
which your appendix is infected and painful.

appendix /əpendɪks/, **appendices** /əpendɪsiːz/
or **appendixes.** 1 Your **appendix** is a small closed N COUNT
tube inside your body at the end of your digestive
system. It has no particular function.
2 An **appendix** to a book is extra information that N COUNT
is placed after the end of the main text. EG A list of
hotels is given in the Appendix.

appetite /æpɪtaɪt/, **appetites.** 1 Your **appetite** N COUNT OR
is your desire to eat and your feeling about how N UNCOUNT
much you want to eat. EG All that work has given
me an appetite.
2 If you have an **appetite** for something, you have N COUNT :
a strong desire for it. EG ...a repressed appetite for OFT+for
sensual pleasure.

appetizing /ˈæpəˈtaɪzɪŋ/; also spelled **appetising.** ADJ QUALIT
Food that is **appetizing** looks and smells nice, and makes you want to eat it.

applaud /əˈplɔːd/, **applauds, applauding, applauded. 1** When a group of people **applaud**, they V OR V+O clap their hands in order to show approval, for example when they have enjoyed a play or concert. EG *The whole assembly applauded him.*
2 When an action or attitude **is applauded**, people V+O : USU PASS praise it. EG *These changes will be applauded.*

applause /əˈplɔːz/ is an expression of praise or N UNCOUNT appreciation by a group of people, in which they clap their hands. EG *The delegates burst into loud applause.*

apple /ˈæpəl/, **apples.** An **apple** is a round fruit N COUNT OR with a smooth skin and firm white flesh. EG *...apple* N UNCOUNT *pie... ...the apple tree.*

appliance /əˈplaɪəns/, **appliances.** An **appliance** N COUNT is a device or machine that does a particular job in your home. EG *...heating appliances.*

applicable /ˈæplɪkəbəl, əˈplɪkə-/. Something that is ADJ QUALIT : **applicable** to a particular situation is relevant to OFT+*to* it. EG *...a rule applicable to all cases... The following special regulations are applicable to overseas students.*

applicant /ˈæplɪkənt/, **applicants.** An **applicant** N COUNT for a job or a place at a college is someone who formally asks to be given it.

application /ˌæplɪˈkeɪʃən/, **applications. 1** An N COUNT OR **application** for a job or a place at a college is a N UNCOUNT formal written request to be given it. EG *The school receives up to 3,300 applications each year.*
2 The **application** of a rule or piece of knowledge N UNCOUNT is the use of it in a particular situation. EG *Do the* OR N COUNT *results have any practical application?*
3 Application is hard work and concentration on N UNCOUNT what you are doing over a period of time.

applied /əˈplaɪd/. An **applied** subject of study has ADJ CLASSIF : a practical use. EG *...applied psychology.* ATTRIB

apply /əˈplaɪ/, **applies, applying, applied. 1** If V : OFT+*for* you **apply** to have something or to do something, you write asking formally to be allowed to have it or do it. EG *I've applied for another job.*
2 If you **apply** yourself to something, you concen- V REFL trate hard on it. EG *He applied himself energetically* OR V+O : *to looking for work... He tried to apply his mind to* OFT+*to* *Rose's problems.*
3 If something **applies** to a person or a situation, it V : USU+*to* is relevant to the person or the situation. EG *The leaflet explains how the system will apply to you.*
4 If you **apply** a rule, system, or skill, you use it in V+O a situation or activity. EG *...countries which have been the first to apply the death penalty... ...the capacity to develop and apply technology.*
5 If you **apply** a name to someone or something, V+O : USU PASS you refer to them by that name. EG *The label 'cold-blooded', so often applied to reptiles, is a very misleading one.*
6 If you **apply** something to a surface, you put it or V+O rub it on to the surface. EG *Apply a little wax polish.*
7 See also **applied.**

appoint /əˈpɔɪnt/, **appoints, appointing, appointed. 1** If you **appoint** someone to a job or post, V+O : USU+A you formally choose them for it. EG *Ramsay* OR V+O+C *MacDonald appointed him Secretary of State for India.*
2 If you **appoint** a time or place for something to V+O happen, you decide when or where it will happen. Formal
◊ **appointed.** EG *I arrived at precisely the appoint-* ◊ ADJ CLASSIF : *ed time.* ATTRIB

appointment /əˈpɔɪntməˈnt/, **appointments. 1** N UNCOUNT : The **appointment** of a person to do a particular OFT+*of* job is the choice of that person to do it. EG *Their duties include the appointment of all the staff.*
2 An **appointment** is a job or position of respon- N COUNT sibility. EG *She applied for and got the appointment.*
3 If you have an **appointment** with someone, you N COUNT have arranged to see them at a particular time, usually in connection with their job. EG *I had an*

appointment with the editor of the Arkansas Gazette... The doctor's appointment was for 11 am.
4 If you do something **by appointment**, you ar- PHRASE range in advance to do it at a particular time. EG *They allow people to visit by appointment during the weekend.*

appraisal /əˈpreɪzəl/, **appraisals.** If you make an N COUNT OR **appraisal** of something, you consider it carefully N UNCOUNT and form an opinion about it. OFT+*of*

appraise /əˈpreɪz/, **appraises, appraising, ap-** V+O **praised.** If you **appraise** something, you consider it carefully and form an opinion about it. EG *Harris stood back and appraised his work.*

appreciable /əˈpriːʃəbəl, -sɪ-/. An **appreciable** ADJ CLASSIF : amount or effect is large enough to be important or ATTRIB clearly noticed. EG *...an appreciable percentage of the university's expenditure.* ◊ **appreciably.** EG ◊ SUBMOD *The following week it was appreciably colder.*

appreciate /əˈpriːʃɪeɪt, -sɪ-/, **appreciates, appre-** **ciating, appreciated. 1** If you **appreciate** some- V+O thing, you like it because you recognize its good qualities. EG *He appreciated beautiful things.*
2 If you **appreciate** a situation or problem, you V+O; ALSO understand it and know what it involves. EG *I* V+REPORT: *appreciate the reasons for your anxiety... I appreci-* ONLY *that* *ate that this is not a fair comparison.*
3 If you say that you **appreciate** something that V+O someone has done for you, you mean that you are grateful to them for it. EG *We would much appreci-ate guidance from an expert.*
4 If something **appreciates** over a period of time, V its value increases. EG *These diamonds should ap-preciate in value.*

appreciation /əˌpriːʃɪˈeɪʃən, -sɪ-/, **appreciations. 1 Appreciation** of something is recognition and N UNCOUNT : enjoyment of its good qualities. EG *He had little* OFT+*of* *appreciation of great plays.*
2 Your **appreciation** for something that someone N UNCOUNT : has done for you is your gratitude for it. EG *...some-* OFT+*of* *thing to show their appreciation of his services.*
3 An **appreciation** of a situation or problem is an N UNCOUNT understanding of what it involves. EG *...a full appre-ciation of the implications.*
4 Appreciation in the value of something is the N UNCOUNT increase in its value over a period of time.
5 An **appreciation** of a person or a work of art is a N COUNT : discussion and evaluation of them. EG *...an apprecia-* OFT+*of* *tion of the life and work of Dame Flora Robson.*

appreciative /əˈpriːʃɪˈeɪtɪv/. **1** An **appreciative** ADJ QUALIT reaction, comment, or expression shows the pleas-ure that you are getting from something. EG *...ap-preciative laughter.*
2 If you are **appreciative** of something, you are ADJ QUALIT grateful for it. EG *She won't be appreciative of his efforts.* ◊ **appreciatively.** EG *'Want a lift?' she* ◊ ADV *asked. I nodded appreciatively.*

apprehension /ˌæprɪˈhenʃən/, **apprehensions.** N UNCOUNT **Apprehension** is a feeling of fear that something OR N COUNT terrible may happen. EG *His mother trembled with* Formal *apprehension.*

apprehensive /ˌæprɪˈhensɪv/. Someone who is ap- ADJ QUALIT **prehensive** is afraid that something terrible may OFT+*about* happen. EG *I felt apprehensive about the whole operation.* ◊ **apprehensively.** EG *She looked up* ◊ ADV *apprehensively.*

apprentice /əˈprentɪs/, **apprentices.** An ap- N COUNT **prentice** is a young person who works with some-one in order to learn their skill. EG *...an apprentice instrument maker.*

apprenticeship /əˈprentɪsˈʃɪp/, **apprentice-** N COUNT OR **ships.** Someone who has an **apprenticeship** N UNCOUNT works for a fixed period of time with a person who has a particular skill in order to learn the skill. EG *On leaving school he had an apprenticeship with his brother in leatherwork.*

Is a valuable painting likely to appreciate?

approach /əprəʊtʃ/, **approaches, approaching, approached. 1** When someone **approaches** you, v+o or v they come nearer to you. eg *He opened the door for her as she approached.* ▸ used as a noun. eg *The* ▸ N COUNT *dogs began to bark as if aware of our approach.* +SUPP
2 If you **approach** someone about something, you v+o : OFT+A speak to them about it for the first time, often making a request or offer. eg *They had approached us about working with their party.* ▸ used as a ▸ N COUNT noun. eg *I had an approach to join the staff of the Daily Mail.*
3 When you **approach** a situation or problem in a v+o+A particular way, you think about it or deal with it in that way. eg *Governments must approach the subject of disarmament in a new spirit.*
4 When a future event or date **approaches** or v-ERG when you **approach** it, it gradually becomes nearer as time passes. eg *As the end of the month approached, I was eating less and less... We are approaching the day of the race.* ▸ used as a noun. ▸ N SING+SUPP eg *...the approach of winter.*
5 If something **approaches** a particular level or v+o state, it almost reaches that level or state. eg *These rocket planes approached speeds of 4000 mph.*
◊ **approaching.** eg *...bills of approaching a million* ◊ ADV *pounds.*
6 An **approach** to a place is a road or path that N COUNT : leads to it. OFT+*to*
7 An **approach** to a situation or problem is a way N COUNT : of thinking about it or of dealing with it. eg *We need* OFT+*to* *a new approach to this problem.*

approachable /əprəʊtʃəbəl/. **1** Someone who is ADJ QUALIT **approachable** is friendly and easy to talk to. eg *...a hotel with approachable staff.*
2 A place which is **approachable** by a particular ADJ PRED route can be reached by that route. eg *The statue is* +*by/from* *approachable by steps inside the column.*

appropriate, appropriates, appropriating, appropriated; pronounced /əprəʊprɪət/ when it is an adjective and /əprəʊprɪeɪt/ when it is a verb.
1 Something that is **appropriate** is suitable or ADJ QUALIT : acceptable for a particular situation. eg *...the insti-* OFT+*to/for* *tutional structure appropriate to each country... It* OR *to*-INF *seemed appropriate to end with a joke.*
2 If you **appropriate** something which does not v+o belong to you, you take it for yourself. eg *The* Formal *materials are exported and other countries appropriate the profits.*

approval /əpruːvəl/ is **1** agreement which is N UNCOUNT given to a plan or request. eg *The decision met with* +SUPP *the committee's approval... He required his father's approval.* **2** admiration for someone. eg *Oliver* N UNCOUNT *looked at Simon with approval.*

approve /əpruːv/, **approves, approving, approved. 1** If you **approve** of an action, event, or v : USU+*of* suggestion, you are pleased about it. eg *My grandfather did not approve of my father's marriage.*
2 If you **approve** of someone or something, you v : USU+*of* like and admire them. eg *He did not approve of my pictures.*
3 If someone in a position of authority **approves** a v+o plan or idea, they formally agree to it and say that it can happen. eg *The firm's directors quickly approved the new deal.*

approved /əpruːvd/. **1** An **approved** method or ADJ QUALIT course of action is generally or officially accepted as appropriate in a particular situation.
2 Someone who is **approved** in a particular posi- ADJ CLASSIF tion has been formally accepted in that position by people in authority. eg *...lists of approved candidates.*

approving /əpruːvɪŋ/. An **approving** reaction or ADJ QUALIT expression shows support for something, or satisfaction with it. eg *Cameron gave Scylla an approving nod.* ◊ **approvingly.** eg *His wife watched* ◊ ADV *approvingly.*

approximate, approximates, approximating, approximated; pronounced /əprɒksɪmət/ when it is an adjective and /əprɒksɪmeɪt/ when it is a verb.
1 An **approximate** number, time, or position is ADJ QUALIT close to the correct number, time, or position but not exact. eg *...the approximate value of the property.* ◊ **approximately.** eg *We have approximately* ◊ ADV *40 pupils.*
2 An idea or description that is **approximate** is not ADJ QUALIT intended to be precise or accurate.
3 If something **approximates** to a particular num- v+*to* ber or size, it is close to it.
4 If something **approximates** to something else, it v+*to* OR v+o is similar to it but not exactly the same. eg *Worsening social conditions approximate to those of the early thirties.*

approximation /əprɒksɪmeɪʃən/, **approxima-** N COUNT : **tions.** An **approximation** is **1** a fact, object, or OFT+*to/of* description which is similar to something else but which does not have all its features. eg *...an approximation to the truth.* **2** a number, calculation, or position that is not exact. eg *...a rough approximation of the proportions.*

apricot /eɪprɪkɒt/, **apricots.** An **apricot** is a N COUNT small, soft, round fruit with yellowish-orange flesh and a stone inside.

April /eɪprəl/ is the fourth month of the year in N UNCOUNT the Western calendar. eg *He will be seven next April... The Treaty was signed on 4 April 1949.*

apron /eɪprən/, **aprons.** An **apron** is a piece of N COUNT clothing that you put on over the front of your normal clothes and tie round your waist, especially when you are cooking, in order to prevent your clothes from getting dirty.

apt /æpt/. **1** Something that is **apt** is suitable. eg *...a* ADJ QUALIT *very apt description.* ◊ **aptly.** eg *...as Dr Hochstadt* ◊ ADV *so aptly remarked to his wife.*
2 If someone is **apt** to behave in a particular way, ADJ PRED they usually behave in that way. eg *I was apt to* +*to*-INF *fidget during a long performance.*

aptitude /æptɪtjuːd/, **aptitudes.** Someone's **apti-** N COUNT : **tude** for a skill is their ability to learn it quickly OFT+*for* and to do it well. eg *He had an aptitude for journalism.*

aquarium /əkwɛərɪəm/, **aquaria** /əkwɛərɪə/ or N COUNT **aquariums.** An **aquarium** is **1** a glass tank filled with water, in which people keep fish. **2** a building, often in a zoo, where fish and underwater animals are kept.

aquatic /əkwætɪk/. **1** An **aquatic** animal or plant ADJ CLASSIF : lives or grows in water. ATTRIB
2 **Aquatic** also means relating to water. eg *...aquat-* ADJ CLASSIF : *ic sports.* ATTRIB

aqueduct /ækwɪdʌkt/, **aqueducts.** An **aqueduct** N COUNT is a long bridge with many arches, which carries a water supply or a canal over a valley.

Arab /ærəb/, **Arabs.** An **Arab** is a member of a N COUNT people who live in the Middle East and North Africa. ▸ used as an adjective. eg *The Ambassadors* ▸ ADJ CLASSIF *of several Arab countries were invited.*

Arabian /əreɪbɪən/ means belonging or relating ADJ CLASSIF : to Arabia, especially to Saudi Arabia. eg *...the* ATTRIB *Arabian peninsula.*

Arabic /ærəbɪk/. **1** **Arabic** is a language that is N UNCOUNT spoken in the Middle East and in parts of North Africa.
2 Something that is **Arabic** belongs or relates to ADJ CLASSIF the language, writing, or culture of the Arabs.
3 An **Arabic** numeral is one of the written figures, ADJ CLASSIF : such as 1, 2, 3, or 4. ATTRIB

arable /ærəbəl/ is used to describe things relating ADJ CLASSIF to growing crops. eg *...arable farming... ...arable land... ...arable crops.*

arbiter /ɑːbɪtə/, **arbiters.** An **arbiter** is a person N COUNT or institution that judges and settles a quarrel Formal between two other people or groups. eg *The Court was an arbiter between the States and the Federal government... The state is the final arbiter of morality in these cases.*

arbitrary /ɑːbɪtrərɪ, ɑːbɪtrɪ/. An **arbitrary** deci- ADJ QUALIT sion or action is taken without considering all its

probable effects. EG ...*the brutal and arbitrary expulsion of immigrants... It is difficult to discern the motive of this seemingly arbitrary attack.*
◊ **arbitrarily.** EG *The items are selected arbitrarily... ...laws that empowered them to close down any newspaper arbitrarily.* ◊ ADV

arbitrate /ˈɑːbɪtreɪt/, **arbitrates, arbitrating, arbitrated.** When someone **arbitrates** between two people who are in dispute, they consider all the facts and decide who is right. V OR V+O

arbitration /ɑːbɪˈtreɪʃən/ is the judging of a dispute between people or groups by someone who is not involved. EG ...*arbitration between employers and unions.* N UNCOUNT

arc /ɑːk/, **arcs.** An **arc** is 1 a smoothly curving shape or line of movement. EG *The ball rose in an arc and landed about 150 yards away.* 2 a section of the line that forms the outside of a circle. N COUNT / Technical

arcade /ɑːkeɪd/, **arcades.** An **arcade** is a covered passageway where there are shops or market stalls. EG ...*a shopping arcade.* N COUNT

arches

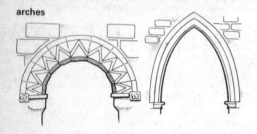

arch /ɑːtʃ/, **arches, arching, arched.** 1 An **arch** is a structure that has a curved roof or top supported on either side by a pillar or wall, sometimes part of a bridge carrying a road or railway, or a doorway in a building. EG ...*a house beneath the railway arches... We walked through an arch and into a huge square.* N COUNT
2 When something **arches**, it forms a curved shape or line. EG *She looked at him and her eyebrows arched... He arched his back.* V-ERG
3 An **arch** look is mysterious and mischievous. EG *She giggled and gave me an arch look.* ADJ QUALIT : ATTRIB
4 See also **arched.**

archaeology /ɑːkiˈɒlədʒiˈ/; also spelled **archeology,** especially in American English. N UNCOUNT
Archaeology is the study of the societies and peoples of the past, by examining the remains of their buildings, tools, and other things.
◊ **archaeologist, archaeologists.** EG *Archaeologists date the fragment between 4650 and 4500 BC.* ◊ N COUNT
◊ **archaeological.** EG ...*dramatic archaeological discoveries.* ◊ ADJ CLASSIF

archaic /ɑːkeɪɪk/. Things that are **archaic** are very old or very old-fashioned. EG ...*the archaic stove in the kitchen... ...archaic language.* ADJ QUALIT

archbishop /ɑːtʃbɪʃəp/, **archbishops.** An **archbishop** is a bishop of the highest rank, who is in charge of all the bishops and priests in a particular country or region. N COUNT

arched /ɑːtʃt/. 1 A roof, window, or doorway that is **arched** has a curved roof or top that is supported on either side by a pillar or wall. EG ...*the arched roof over the staircase.* ADJ CLASSIF
2 Something that is **arched** curves upwards in the middle. EG ...*his arched black eyebrows.* ADJ CLASSIF

archeology /ɑːkɪɒlədʒiˈ/. See **archaeology.**

archer /ɑːtʃə/, **archers.** An **archer** is someone who shoots with a bow and arrow. N COUNT

archery /ɑːtʃəriˈ/ is a sport in which people shoot at a target with a bow and arrow. N UNCOUNT

archetype /ɑːkiˈtaɪp/, **archetypes.** An **archetype** is something that is considered to be a N COUNT : OFT+*of*

perfect example of a particular kind of person or thing, because it has all their most important characteristics. EG *He is said to be the archetype of the modern journalist.* ◊ **archetypal.** EG ...*the archetypal Romantic heroes.* ◊ ADJ CLASSIF ATTRIB

archipelago /ɑːkɪpeləgəʊ/, **archipelagos.** An **archipelago** is a group of small islands. EG ...*the Philippine archipelago.* N COUNT

architect /ɑːkɪtekt/, **architects.** 1 An **architect** is a person who designs buildings. N COUNT
2 The **architect** of an idea or event is the person who invented it or made it happen. EG *He was the real architect of the country's independence.* N COUNT : OFT+*of*

architectural /ɑːkɪtektʃərəˈl/ means relating to the design and construction of buildings. EG ...*the architectural style suitable for government buildings.* ADJ CLASSIF : ATTRIB

architecture /ɑːkɪtektʃə/. 1 **Architecture** is the art of planning, designing, and constructing buildings. N UNCOUNT
2 The **architecture** of a building is the style in which it is designed and constructed. EG ...*the Late Victorian architecture of the Chapel.* N UNCOUNT +SUPP

archive /ɑːkaɪv/, **archives.** An **archive** or **archives** are a collection of documents and records that contain information about the history of a family, organization, or other group of people. EG ...*the national archive of wills.* N COUNT OR N PLURAL

ardent /ɑːdəˈnt/. Someone who is **ardent** about something has very enthusiastic or passionate feelings about it. EG ...*an ardent religious faith... ...an ardent love-letter.* ◊ **ardently.** EG *This is what he so ardently seeks.* ◊ ADV ADJ QUALIT

ardour /ɑːdə/; spelled **ardor** in American English. **Ardour** is an intense and passionate feeling of love or enthusiasm for something. EG ...*revolutionary ardour.* N UNCOUNT

arduous /ɑːdjuːəs/. Something that is **arduous** is tiring and involves a lot of effort. EG ...*a long and arduous journey.* ADJ QUALIT

are /ɑː/ is the plural and the second person (singular and plural) of the present tense of the verb **be.**

area /ɛəriə/, **areas.** 1 An **area** is 1.1 a particular part of a city, a country, or the world. EG ...*a dry area that gets only a few months rain a year... ...all areas of Great Britain... ...the Brighton area.* 1.2 a part of a surface that looks different from its surroundings. EG ...*a pink area on the front of his thighs.* N COUNT : USU +SUPP / N COUNT+SUP
2 A particular **area** of a room, building, or other place is a part of it that is used for a particular activity. EG ...*an outdoor play area... ...a communal washing area.* N COUNT+SUPP
3 The **area** of a piece of land is the amount of ground that it covers, measured in a measurement such as square feet or square metres. EG *The farm was about 50 square kilometres in area.* N COUNT
4 An **area** of knowledge, interest, or activity is a particular kind of subject or activity. EG *His special interest lies in the area of literature.* N COUNT+SUP

arena /əriːnə/, **arenas.** 1 An **arena** is a place where sports and other public events take place, with seats around it where the public can sit and watch. N COUNT
2 A particular **arena** is the centre of attention in a particular situation. EG *He had come to the political arena late in life.* N COUNT+SUP

aren't /ɑːnt/ is 1 the usual spoken form of 'are not'. EG *We aren't ready... They are coming, aren't they?* 2 the form that is usually used instead of 'am' in negative questions. EG *I'm right, aren't I?*

arguable /ɑːgjʊəbəˈl/. 1 An idea, point, or comment that is **arguable** is not obviously true or correct and should be questioned. EG *Whether he was right or not is arguable.* ADJ CLASSIF

Is an archer armed?

2 If you say that it is **arguable** that something is true, you mean that it can be supported by evidence and is probably true. EG *It is arguable that the real damage will be seen much later.* ◊ **arguably.** EG *Deforestation is arguably the most serious environmental issue of our time.* `ADJ CLASSIF: USU PRED` `◊ ADV SEN`

argue /ɑ:gju:/, **argues, arguing, argued. 1** If you **argue** with someone about something, you say things which show that you disagree with them about it, sometimes speaking angrily. EG *Don't argue with me, George, just do as you're told... They were arguing about who should sit in front.* `V OR V+with: RECIP`

2 If you **argue** that something is the case, you say that you think it is the case and give reasons why. EG *There are those who argue that the existence of nuclear weapons has helped to maintain peace... Bradbury argued the case for the opposition.* `V+REPORT: ALSO V+O`

3 If you **argue** for or **argue** against something, you give reasons why it should or should not happen and try to convince people that you are right. EG *Some politicians argued against giving women the vote.* `V+for/against`

4 If you **argue** someone **out of** doing something, you persuade them not to do it by talking to them. EG *He argued the man out of suicide.* `PHRASE`

argument /ɑ:gjɔ⁴mɔ²nt/, **arguments. 1** An **argument** is a disagreement between two or more people, sometimes resulting in them shouting angrily at each other. EG *I said no and we got into a big argument over it... We accepted it without argument.* `N COUNT OR N UNCOUNT`

2 An **argument** is also a set of statements that you use in order to try to convince people that your opinion about something is correct. EG *There are strong arguments against these measures.* `N COUNT: OFT+for/ against OR REPORT`

argumentative /ɑ:gjɔ⁴mɛntə²tɪv/. Someone who is **argumentative** is always ready to disagree with you. EG *'What did you mean by that?' he said in an argumentative tone.* `ADJ QUALIT`

aria /ɑ:rɪə/, **arias.** An **aria** is a song for one of the leading singers in an opera or choral work. `N COUNT`

arid /ærɪd/. **1** Land that is **arid** is so dry that very few plants can grow on it. `ADJ QUALIT`

2 A subject or piece of writing that is **arid** is dull and uninteresting. `ADJ QUALIT`

arise /əraɪz/, **arises, arising, arose** /ərəʊz/, **arisen** /ərɪzə⁰n/. When something such as an opportunity, problem, or new state of affairs **arises**, it begins to exist. EG *A serious problem has arisen... He promised to help if the occasion arose... A whole community now arose.* `V`

aristocracy /ærɪ'stɒkrəsɪ/, **aristocracies.** The **aristocracy** is a class of people in some countries who have a high social rank and special titles. `N COLL`

aristocrat /ærɪstə⁶kræt/, **aristocrats.** An **aristocrat** is someone whose family has a high social rank, especially someone who has a title. `N COUNT`

aristocratic /ærɪstə⁶krætɪk/. **1** Someone who is **aristocratic** belongs to the aristocracy. `ADJ CLASSIF`

2 Something that is **aristocratic** has characteristics which are considered to be typical of people of high social rank. EG *...his aristocratic features.* `ADJ QUALIT`

arithmetic /ə³rɪθmə²tɪk/ is the part of mathematics that is concerned with the addition, subtraction, multiplication, and division of numbers. EG *I blame the school for not making him learn arithmetic... ...simple arithmetic problems.* `N UNCOUNT`

arm /ɑ:m/, **arms. 1** Your **arms** are the two long parts of your body that are attached to your shoulders and that have your hands at the end. See picture at THE HUMAN BODY. EG *She put her arm around his neck and kissed him.* `N COUNT`

2 The **arm** of a piece of clothing is the part of it that covers your arm. `N COUNT`

3 The **arm** of a chair is the part of it on which you rest your arm when you are sitting down. `N COUNT`

4 An **arm** of an organization is a section of it. EG *...the political arm of a trade union movement.* `N COUNT+SUPP`

5 Arms are weapons that are used in a war. `N PLURAL`

6 Arm is used in these phrases. **6.1** If you are walking **arm in arm** with someone, you are walking with your arm linked through their arm. **6.2** If you welcome someone **with open arms**, you hold your arms stretched out and apart, ready to hug them. **6.3** If you welcome an event or change **with open arms**, you are very pleased about it. **6.4** If you hold something **at arm's length**, you hold it at a distance from your body. EG *...holding the paper at arm's length to read it.* **6.5** If you **keep** someone **at arm's length**, you avoid becoming too friendly or involved with them. **6.6** If someone is **up in arms** about something, they are very angry about it and are protesting strongly. EG *Feminists are now up in arms over the new laws.* `PHRASES`

7 See also **armed.**

armada /ɑ:mɑ:də/, **armadas.** An **armada** is a large fleet of warships. `N COUNT`

armament /ɑ:məmə²nt/, **armaments. 1 Armaments** are weapons and military equipment belonging to an army or country. `N PLURAL`

2 Armament is the increase by a country in the number and effectiveness of its weapons. `N UNCOUNT`

armchair /ɑ:mtʃɛə/, **armchairs.** An **armchair** is a comfortable chair which has a support on each side for your arms. See picture at CHAIRS. `N COUNT`

armed /ɑ:md/. **1** Someone who is **armed** is carrying a weapon, usually a gun. `ADJ CLASSIF`

2 An **armed** attack or conflict involves people fighting with guns. EG *...armed assaults on homes.* `ADJ CLASSIF: ATTRIB`

3 If you are **armed** with something useful such as information or a skill, you have it. EG *Armed with secretarial skills, she will easily find a job.* `ADJ PRED +with`

armed forces. The **armed forces** of a country are its military forces, usually the army, navy, and air force. `N PLURAL`

armful /ɑ:mfʊl/, **armfuls.** An **armful** of something is the amount of it that you can carry in one or both of your arms. EG *She came back with an armful of paperbacks.* `N PART`

armistice /ɑ:mɪ'stɪs/, **armistices.** An **armistice** is an agreement between countries who are at war with one another to stop fighting and to discuss ways of making a peaceful settlement. `N COUNT OR N UNCOUNT`

armour /ɑ:mə/; spelled **armor** in American English. **1 Armour** is special metal clothing that soldiers used to wear for protection in battle. EG *...knights in armour.* `N UNCOUNT`

2 The **armour** of something is a hard covering that protects it against attack. EG *...the steel armour of a tank... The animal has an armour of horny scales.* `N SING+SUPP`

armoured /ɑ:məd/; spelled **armored** in American English. An **armoured** vehicle is fitted with a hard metal covering in order to protect it from gunfire and other missiles. EG *...armoured cars.* `ADJ CLASSIF`

armpit /ɑ:mpɪt/, **armpits.** Your **armpit** is the area of your body that is under your arm where your arm joins your shoulder. `N COUNT`

army /ɑ:mɪ/, **armies. 1** An **army** is a large organized group of people who are armed and trained to fight on land in a war. EG *Both armies suffered thousands of wounded.* `N COLL`

2 An **army** of people, animals, or things is a large number of them, especially when they are regarded as a force of some kind. EG *...an army of ants.* `N PART`

aroma /ərəʊmə/, **aromas.** An **aroma** is a strong, pleasant smell. EG *The house was filled with the aroma of coffee.* `N COUNT+SUPP`

aromatic /ærə⁶mætɪk/. A plant or food that is **aromatic** has a strong, pleasant smell of spice or herbs. `ADJ QUALIT`

arose /ərəʊz/ is the past tense of **arise.**

around /əraʊnd/. **1 Around** can be an adverb or preposition, and is often used instead of **round** as the second part of a phrasal verb. Examples of these uses of **around** are explained at **round.** `ADV AFTER VB, OR PREP`

2 If someone or something **is around**, they are present or available. EG *He went back to see who* `PHRASE` was around... *It's a gadget which has been around for years.*

3 If someone **has been around**, they have had a lot of experience of different people and situations. EG *I've been around and I know how to handle people like him.*   PHRASE Informal

4 Around also means approximately. EG *He owns around 200 acres.*   ADV

arousal /ərɑʊzəºl/. If something causes the **arousal** of a feeling, it causes you to begin to have this feeling. EG *...the arousal of interest... ...feelings of sexual arousal.*   N UNCOUNT +SUPP

arouse /ərɑʊz/, arouses, arousing, aroused. **1** If something **arouses** a feeling in you, it causes you to begin to have this feeling. EG *It may arouse his interest in the subject... ...a move that would arouse opposition.*   V+O

2 If something **arouses** people, it makes them feel angry.   V+O

3 When people or things **arouse** you from sleep, they wake you up.   V+O Literary

arr. is an abbreviation for 'arrives'. It is used on timetables to indicate what time a bus, train, or plane will reach a place.

arrange /ə³reɪndʒ/, arranges, arranging, arranged. **1** If you **arrange** an event or meeting, you make plans for it to happen. EG *Progressive Tours arrange holidays in Eastern Europe.*   V+O

2 If you **arrange** with someone to do something, you make plans with them to do it. EG *We've arranged with somebody else to go to the cinema this evening... We had arranged to meet in the street outside... It was suddenly arranged that Celia should come to Switzerland.*   V+with OR REPORT: ONLY that

3 If you **arrange** something for someone, you make it possible for them to have it or to do it. EG *We can arrange loans... I asked if it could be arranged for me to meet one of the leaders.*   V+O OR V+to-INF: OFT+for

4 If you **arrange** things, such as flowers in a vase or books on a shelf, you put them in a particular position, usually in order to make them look attractive or tidy. EG *...four chairs arranged around the table.*   V+O+A

arranged /ə³reɪndʒd/. An **arranged** marriage is a marriage in which the parents choose the person who their son or daughter will marry.   ADJ CLASSIF

arrangement /ə³reɪnʒməºnt/, arrangements. **1** Arrangements are plans and preparations which you make so that something will happen or be possible. EG *I've made all the arrangements for the conference.*   N PLURAL OFT+for

2 An **arrangement** is **2.1** an agreement that you make with someone to do something. EG *He made an arrangement to rent the property.* **2.2** a plan for doing something. EG *What are the sleeping and eating arrangements?*   N COUNT

3 An **arrangement** of things, for example flowers or furniture, is a group of them that have been set out in a particular position. EG *There was an arrangement of books in the window.*   N COUNT+SUPP

array /əreɪ/, arrays, arrayed. **1** An **array** of different things is a large number of them, especially when they are impressive. EG *They looked in the window at the array of cakes.*   N COUNT: OFT+of

2 If things are **arrayed** somewhere, they are displayed there attractively. EG *Daggers and pistols were arrayed on the walls.*   V-PASS+A Formal

arrears /ərɪəz/. **1 Arrears** are amounts of money that you owe. EG *He vanished leaving massive arrears.*   N PLURAL

2 If someone is **in arrears** with their payments, they have not paid the regular amounts of money that they should have paid. EG *The council complained that his rent was in arrears.*   PHRASE

3 If you are paid **in arrears**, your wages are paid to you at the end of the period of time in which you earned them.   PHRASE

arrest /ərest/, arrests, arresting, arrested. **1** If the police **arrest** someone, they catch them and   V+O: OFT+for

take them somewhere in order to decide whether they should be charged with an offence. EG *A friend had been arrested for possession of explosives.*

▶ used as a noun. EG *The riots led to the arrest of many union leaders... A number of arrests were made.* ● If someone is **under arrest**, they have been caught by the police and are not allowed to go free.   ▶ N UNCOUNT OR N COUNT   ● PHRASE

2 If you **arrest** something, you stop it happening. EG *He tried to arrest the course of destruction.*   V+O Formal

3 If something **arrests** your attention, it interests or surprises you so that you look at it or listen to it carefully. ◊ **arresting.** EG *...an arresting drawing of people turning into animals.*   V+O ◊ ADJ QUALIT

arrival /ərɑɪvəºl/, arrivals. **1** Your **arrival** at a place is the act of arriving there. EG *I apologize for my late arrival.*   N UNCOUNT: USU+A

2 If you talk about the **arrival** of something new, you are referring to the fact that it has begun to exist or happen. EG *Industry has been revolutionized by the arrival of the computer.*   N SING

3 The **arrival** of a baby is its birth.   N SING

4 An **arrival** is someone who has just arrived at a place. EG *One of the new arrivals at the college was an old friend.*   N COUNT

arrive /ərɑɪv/, arrives, arriving, arrived. **1** When you **arrive** at a place, **1.1** you reach it at the end of a journey. EG *He arrived back at his hotel after midnight.* **1.2** you come to it for the first time in order to stay there or live there. EG *Since arriving in England in 1979, she has established herself as a major writer... ...newly arrived students.*   V: USU+A

2 When a letter or piece of news **arrives**, it is brought or delivered to you. EG *Your card arrived on Monday... News arrived of an invasion in the south.*   V: USU+A

3 When you **arrive** at an idea, decision, or conclusion, you reach it, make it, or decide on it. EG *It took us hours to arrive at a decision.*   V+at

4 When a baby **arrives**, it is born.   V: USU+A

5 When a moment, event, or new thing **arrives**, it begins to happen or exist. EG *Her wedding day arrived.*   V

arrogant /ærəgəºnt/. Someone who is **arrogant** behaves in a proud, unpleasant way towards other people because they believe that they are more important than others. EG *I think it would be arrogant if I tried to give any advice.* ◊ **arrogantly.** EG *The group had arrogantly assumed themselves to be in command.* ◊ **arrogance** /ærəgəºns/. EG *He had a reputation for arrogance.*   ADJ QUALIT ◊ ADV ◊ N UNCOUNT

arrow /ærəʊ/, arrows. **1** An **arrow** is a long thin weapon which is sharp and pointed at one end. An arrow is shot from a bow.   N COUNT

2 An **arrow** is also a written sign that consists of a straight line with another line bent at a sharp angle at one end. The arrow points in a particular direction to indicate where something is. EG *The exit sign is marked with an arrow.*   N COUNT

arsenic /ɑːsəºnɪk/ is a very strong poison which can kill people.   N UNCOUNT

arson /ɑːsəºn/ is the crime of deliberately setting fire to a building.   N UNCOUNT

art /ɑːt/, arts. **1 Art** is **1.1** the creation of drawings, paintings, and sculpture, when these things are considered to be beautiful or to express a particular idea. EG *...the study of contemporary art.* **1.2** objects, such as paintings or pieces of sculpture, which are considered to be beautiful and which are part of a society's culture. EG *...sales of oriental art... ...an art collection.*   N UNCOUNT

2 An **art** is an activity such as drama, poetry, or sculpture in which people try to create something   N COUNT

What is the difference between 'artistic' and 'arty'?

beautiful or to express a particular idea. EG *The strongest 20th century art is film... ...the visual arts.*

3 The **arts** refers to the creation or performance N PLURAL of drama, music, poetry, or painting, especially in a particular country or region. EG *How much will they spend on sport, how much on the arts?*

4 Arts is used to refer to subjects such as history N PLURAL or languages in contrast to scientific subjects. EG *...an arts degree.*

5 You describe an activity as an **art** when it N SING requires a lot of skill. EG *...the art of camouflage.*

● If you **get** something **down to a fine art**, you are ● PHRASE able to do it in a very skilled way because you have had a lot of experience of doing it.

artefact /ɑːtɪˈfækt/, **artefacts**; also spelled **arti-** N COUNT **fact**. An **artefact** is an ornament, tool, or other object that is made by a human being.

artery /ɑːtəriˈ/, **arteries**. Your **arteries** are the N COUNT tubes in your body that carry blood from your heart to the rest of your body.

artful /ɑːtfʊl/. Someone who is **artful** is clever ADJ QUALIT and skilful, often in a cunning way. EG *...the artful schemer.* ◇ **artfully.** EG *The lighting was artfully* ◇ ADV *arranged to flatter people's faces.*

arthritic /ɑːˈθrɪtɪk/. A person who is **arthritic** has ADJ QUALIT swollen and painful joints in their body.

arthritis /ɑːˈθraɪtɪs/ is a condition in which the N UNCOUNT joints in someone's body are swollen and painful.

artichoke /ɑːtɪtʃəʊk/, **artichokes**. **1** An **arti-** N COUNT **choke** or a **globe artichoke** is a round, green vegetable that has a cluster of fleshy leaves, of which you can eat the bottom part.

2 An **artichoke** or a **Jerusalem artichoke** is a N COUNT small, yellowish-white vegetable that grows underground and looks like a potato.

article /ɑːtɪkəlˈ/, **articles**. **1** An **article** is **1.1** a N COUNT piece of writing that has been written for publication in a newspaper or magazine. EG *...an article by J B Priestley in the New Statesman.* **1.2** a particu- N PART lar object or item. EG *He was ordered to pay for the articles he had stolen... ...an article of furniture.*

2 An **article** of a formal agreement or document is N COUNT a section of it which deals with a particular point. EG *The invasion contravened article 51 of the UN charter.*

3 In grammar, the words 'a' and 'an' are sometimes N COUNT called 'indefinite articles' and the word 'the' is called the 'definite article'. In this dictionary these words are called determiners (DET). See the entry headed DETERMINERS for more information about determiners in English.

articulate, **articulates**, **articulating**, **articulat- ed**; pronounced /ɑːtɪkjəˈlət/ when it is an adjective and /ɑːtɪkjəˈleɪt/ when it is a verb.

1 If you are **articulate**, you are able to express ADJ QUALIT yourself well. EG *He was the most articulate speaker.*

2 When you **articulate** your ideas or feelings, you V+O say in words what you think or how you feel. EG *I* Formal *could not define or articulate the dissatisfaction I felt.*

articulated /ɑːtɪkjəˈleɪtɪˈd/. An **articulated** lorry ADJ CLASSIF : is made in two sections which are joined together ATTRIB by a metal bar, so that the lorry can turn corners more easily.

articulation /ɑːtɪkjəˈleɪʃəˈn/. **1** The **articulation** N UNCOUNT of an idea or feeling is the expression of it, OFT+*of* especially in words. Formal

2 The **articulation** of a sound or word is the way N UNCOUNT in which it is produced or spoken.

artifact /ɑːtɪfækt/. See **artefact**.

artificial /ɑːtɪfɪʃəl/. **1** An **artificial** state or situa- ADJ QUALIT tion is not natural and exists or happens because people have created it. EG *These results appear only in very artificial conditions.* ◇ **artificially.** EG ◇ ADV *The government keeps prices artificially high.*

◇ **artificiality** /ɑːtɪfɪʃiˈælɪti/. EG *...the artificiality* ◇ N UNCOUNT *of a three hour written examination.*

2 Artificial objects or materials do not occur ADJ CLASSIF

naturally and are created by people. EG *...artificial fibres... ...artificial flowers.*

3 An **artificial** arm or leg is made of metal or ADJ CLASSIF : plastic and is fitted to someone's body when their ATTRIB own arm or leg has been removed.

4 Someone who is **artificial** pretends to have ADJ QUALIT attitudes and feelings which other people realize are not real. EG *They jumped at the suggestion with artificial enthusiasm.*

artillery /ɑːtɪləriˈ/ consists of large, powerful N UNCOUNT guns which are transported on wheels and used by an army. EG *Artillery fire caused heavy losses.*

artist /ɑːtɪst/, **artists**. An **artist** is **1** someone who N COUNT draws, paints, or produces other works of art as a job or a hobby. EG *This abstract picture was painted by John Hoyland, an artist who emerged in the 1960's.* **2** someone who is very skilled at a particular activity. EG *He knew that he was good, that he was an artist.* **3** a performer such as a musician, actor, or dancer. EG *She has acted with great artists like Edith Evans.*

artiste /ɑːtiːst/, **artistes**. An **artiste** is a profes- N COUNT sional entertainer, for example a singer or a dancer.

artistic /ɑːtɪstɪk/. **1** Someone who is **artistic** is ADJ QUALIT able to create good paintings, sculpture, or other works of art. EG *I talked to many artistic people: writers, dancers, and film makers.* ◇ **artistically.** ◇ ADV EG *She is artistically gifted, especially in dance.*

2 Artistic means relating to art or artists. EG ADJ CLASSIF *...artistic freedom... ...mediums of artistic expression.*

3 A design or arrangement that is **artistic** is ADJ QUALIT attractive. EG *These are very artistic images.*

artistry /ɑːtɪstriˈ/ is the creative skill of an artist, N UNCOUNT writer, actor, or musician. EG *He acted the final scenes with superb artistry.*

arty /ɑːtiˈ/. Someone who is **arty** seems to be very ADJ QUALIT interested in painting, sculpture, and other works of art.

as /əˈz/. **1** If something happens **as** something else CONJ happens, it happens when the other thing happens. EG *She wept bitterly as she told her story... Parts are replaced as they grow old.*

2 You use the structure **as...as** when you are comparing things or saying that they are similar. EG *I'm as good a cook as she is... Treat the patient as soon as possible.*

3 You use **as** when you are describing someone's PREP attitude or reaction to situations, people, or events. EG *You regard the whole thing as a joke... The sudden change had come as a shock to Castle.*

4 You use **as** when you are specifying a feature or PREP function that something or someone has. EG *He established his reputation as a radical with his very first speech... Over the summer she worked as a waitress... ...a story she had heard many times as a girl.*

5 You use **as** when you are mentioning the way CONJ that something happens or is done. EG *I like the freedom to organise my day as I want to... He looked over his shoulder as Jack had done.*

6 You use **as** to introduce a comment that you are PREP making. EG *As usual at the weekend, the club was* OR CONJ *almost empty... As you can see, we've got a problem with the engine.*

7 You use **as** when you are explaining the reason CONJ for something. EG *She bought herself an iron, as she felt she couldn't keep borrowing Anne's.*

8 You use **as if** and **as though** when you are CONJ giving a possible explanation for something. EG *The furniture looked as though it had come out of somebody's attic... He looked at me as if I were mad.*

9 You use **as for** and **as to** at the beginning of a PREP sentence in order to introduce a slightly different subject that is still connected to the previous one. EG *That's the answer. As for the cause, how do I know?*

10 You also use **as to** to specify the particular PREP subject that you are talking about. EG *John had* British *been given no directions as to what to write.*

11 If you say that something will happen **as of** or PREP **as from** a particular date or time, you mean that it will happen from that time onwards. EG *As of next week I'll be working at home.*

12 You say **as it were** in order to make what you ADV SEN are saying sound less definite. EG *That was as it were part of the job.*

13 You use expressions such as **as it is**, **as it turns** ADV SEN **out**, and **as things stand** when you are making a contrast between a possible situation and what actually happened or is the case. EG *He could have been killed. As it was, he suffered severe back injuries.*

asbestos /æsbɛstɒs/ is a grey material which N UNCOUNT does not burn. EG *...an asbestos mat.*

ascend /əsɛnd/, **ascends, ascending, ascended.**

1 If something **ascends**, it moves or leads up- V : USU+A wards. EG *The sound ascended to the room above...* Literary *...tiers of seats ascending to the roof.*

2 If you **ascend** a hill or a staircase, you go up it. EG V+O *He ascended the flight of narrow stairs to his* Literary *bedroom.*

3 When someone **ascends the throne**, they be- PHRASE come king or queen. EG *Queen Victoria ascended the throne in 1837.*

4 See also **ascending**.

ascendancy /əsɛndənsi/. If one group has **as-** N UNCOUNT : **cendancy** over another group, it has more power OFT+over or influence than the other group. EG *...Unionist* Formal *ascendancy over the Catholic minority.*

ascendant /əsɛndənt/. Someone or something PHRASE that is **in the ascendant** is increasing in power, influence, or popularity. EG *His party was now in the ascendant.*

ascending /əsɛndɪŋ/. When a group of things is ADJ CLASSIF : arranged in **ascending** order, each thing is higher ATTRIB in position or greater in amount or importance than the thing before it. EG *Arrange the four digits in ascending order... ...houses built on ascending levels on the slopes of hills.*

ascent /əsɛnt/, **ascents. 1** An **ascent** is **1.1** an N COUNT upward journey, for example when you climb a mountain. EG *The final ascent took an hour.* **1.2** an upward slope, especially one that you are walking up. EG *John toiled up the dusty ascent.*

2 Someone's **ascent** is a process by which they N UNCOUNT become more important or advanced than before. +SUPP EG *Nick and he had both succeeded, though Nick's* Formal *ascent had been more honourable.*

ascertain /æsəteɪn/, **ascertains, ascertaining,** V+REPORT **ascertained.** If you **ascertain** that something is OR V+O the case, you find out that it is the case. EG *I* Formal *ascertained that Lo was still sound asleep.*

ascetic /əsɛtɪk/, **ascetics.** People who are **ascet-** ADJ QUALIT **ic** have a way of life that is simple and strict, usually because of their religious beliefs. EG *He subjected himself to a strenuous ascetic discipline.*
▸ used as a noun. EG *...a religious ascetic.* ▸ N COUNT

ascribe /əˈskraɪb/, **ascribes, ascribing, as-** **cribed. 1** If you **ascribe** an event or state of V+O+to affairs to a particular factor, you consider that it is caused by that factor. EG *It is wrong to ascribe all that has happened simply to the war... ...headaches which may be ascribed to stress.*

2 If you **ascribe** a quality to someone, you consider V+O+to that they possess it. EG *Husbands are often mistaken in the virtues they ascribe to their wives.*

3 If you **ascribe** a work of art to someone, you say V+O+to that they created it. EG *...a magnificent painted ceiling, doubtfully ascribed to Holbein.*

asexual /eɪsɛksjuˀəl/. Something that is **asexual** ADJ CLASSIF has no sex or involves no sexual activity. EG *...two methods of reproduction, sexual and asexual.*

ash /æʃ/, **ashes. 1 Ash** is the grey or black N UNCOUNT powdery substance that is left after something is OR N PLURAL burnt. EG *...cigarette ash... Ashes blew into Ralph's face from the dead fire.*

2 An **ash** is a kind of tree. N COUNT

ashamed /əʃeɪmd/. **1** If someone is **ashamed,** ADJ PRED : they feel embarrassed or guilty because of some- OFT+of thing that they have done. EG *She was ashamed of her tears... It's nothing to be ashamed of... You should be ashamed of yourself.*

2 If someone is **ashamed** to do something, they do ADJ PRED not want to do it because they feel embarrassed +to-INF about it. EG *I bet that's what happened, only you're ashamed to admit it.*

3 If you are **ashamed** of someone, you feel embar- ADJ PRED+O rassed to be connected with them. EG *He was ashamed of her for writing such lies.*

ashore /əʃɔː/. Something that comes **ashore** ADV AFTER V comes from the sea onto the shore. EG *He managed to swim ashore.*

ashtray /æʃtreɪ/, **ashtrays.** An **ashtray** is a small N COUNT dish in which people can put the ash from their cigarettes and cigars.

Asian /eɪʃən, eɪʒən/, **Asians. 1** Someone or some- ADJ CLASSIF thing that is **Asian** comes from Asia. EG *His philosophy is a mixture of both Western and Asian thought.*

2 An **Asian** is a person who comes from a country N COUNT or region in Asia.

aside /əsaɪd/, **asides. 1** If you move something ADV AFTER V **aside**, you move it to one side of you. EG *He threw the manuscript aside.*

2 If you take or draw someone **aside**, you take ADV AFTER V them a little way away from a group of people in order to talk to them in private.

3 If you move **aside**, you get out of someone's way. ADV AFTER V EG *She stepped aside, holding the door wide open.*

4 If you brush or sweep a feeling or suggestion ADV AFTER V **aside**, you reject it. EG *She brushed his protests aside.*

5 You use **aside** to indicate that you have finished ADV AFTER N talking about something, or that you are leaving it out of your discussion, and that you are about to talk about something else. EG *High technology aside, New England's economy is still largely based on fishing.*

6 An **aside** is **6.1** a comment that a character in a N COUNT play makes to the audience, which the other characters are supposed not to be able to hear. **6.2** something that you say that is not directly connected with what you are talking about. EG *In an aside he said to his servant, 'See that man gets something to eat.'*

ask /ɑːsk/, **asks, asking, asked. 1** If you **ask** V+O+O someone something, you say something to them in V+O+QUOTE the form of a question because you want to know ALSO something. EG *I asked him what he wanted... 'Why?'* V+O+REPORT *he asked... He started asking questions... Five or six* ONLY WH *years ago her sister asked me if I would paint her.*

2 If you **ask** someone to do something, you say to V+O: them that you want them to do it. EG *He asked her* USU+to-INF *to marry him... He was asked to leave.*

3 If you **ask** someone's permission or forgiveness, V+O OR V you try to obtain it by putting a question to them. EG *I asked permission to leave.*

4 If you **ask** someone somewhere, you invite them V+O+A there. EG *I asked her to the party... She asked me in.*

5 If something is yours **for the asking**, you can PHRASE have it simply by saying that you would like it.

6 You can say '**if you ask me**' to emphasize that ADV SEN you are stating your personal opinion. EG *The whole thing's stupid if you ask me.*

ask after. If you **ask after** someone, you ask PHRASAL VB how they are. EG *He asks after you a lot.* V+PREP

ask for. 1 If you **ask for** someone, you say that PHRASAL VB you would like to speak to them. EG *He rang the* V+PREP *office and asked for Cynthia.* **2** If you **ask for** V+PREP

If you ascribe a picture to Leonardo da Vinci, did he definitely paint it?

something, you say that you would like it. EG *She
asked for a drink of water.* 3 If you say that   v+PREP,
someone **is asking for** trouble, you mean that   USU CONT
they are behaving in a way that makes it very
likely that they will get into trouble.

askew /əˈskjuː/. Something that is **askew** is not   ADJ PRED
straight or level. EG *His tie was askew.*

asleep /əˈsliːp/. 1 Someone who is **asleep** is sleep-   ADJ PRED
ing.

2 When you **fall asleep**, you start sleeping.   PHRASE

3 Someone who is **fast asleep** or **sound asleep** is   PHRASE
sleeping deeply.

asparagus /əˈspærəgəs/ is a vegetable with green   N UNCOUNT
shoots that you can cook and eat when they are
young.

aspect /ˈæspekt/, **aspects.** 1 An **aspect** of some-   N COUNT+SUPP
thing is one of the parts of its character or nature.
EG *The most terrifying aspect of nuclear bombing is
radiation... ...the influence which America had on
many aspects of British cultural life.*

2 The **aspect** of a building or a window is the   N COUNT+SUPP
direction in which it faces. EG *...an office with a*   Formal
south-west aspect.

3 If something acquires a new **aspect**, it acquires a   N COUNT+SUPP
new appearance or quality. EG *The whole scheme
began to take on a more practical aspect.*

aspersions /əˈspɜːʃənz/. If you **cast aspersions**   PHRASE
on someone or something, you suggest that they   Formal
are not very good in some way.

asphalt /ˈæsfælt, -fɔːlt/ is a black substance used to   N UNCOUNT
make surfaces on things such as roads and play-
grounds.

asphyxiate /æsˈfɪksɪeɪt/, **asphyxiates, asphyxi-**   v+o
ating, asphyxiated. If someone is **asphyxiated**
by smoke or a poisonous gas, they breathe it in and
die.

aspirant /ˈæspərənt, əˈspaɪərənt/, **aspirants.**   N COUNT
Someone who is an **aspirant** to political power or   Formal
to an important job has a strong desire to achieve
it.

aspiration /æspəˈreɪʃən/, **aspirations.** Some-   N COUNT OR
one's **aspirations** are their ambitions to achieve   N UNCOUNT
something. EG *Educational standards and aspirations have risen in recent years.*

aspire /əˈspaɪə/, **aspires, aspiring, aspired.** If   v+to OR to-INF
you **aspire** to something such as an important job,
you have an ambition to achieve it. EG *She has
always aspired to leadership.* ◊ **aspiring.** EG *...an*   ◊ ADJ CLASSIF :
aspiring concert pianist.   ATTRIB

aspirin /ˈæsprɪn/, **aspirins. Aspirin** is a mild   N UNCOUNT
drug in the form of tablets which reduces pain and   OR N COUNT
fever. EG *She gave me an aspirin for my headache.*

ass /æs/, **asses.** 1 An **ass** is an animal related to a   N COUNT
horse but smaller and with long ears.

2 If you say that someone is an **ass**, you mean that   N COUNT
they say or do silly things.   Informal

assail /əˈseɪl/, **assails, assailing, assailed.** 1 If   v+o
you **assail** someone, you criticize them strongly. EG   Literary
He was assailed in the Press.

2 If you **are assailed** by unpleasant thoughts or   v+o : USU PASS
problems, you are greatly troubled or bothered by   Literary
a large number of them. EG *They are assailed by
doubts.*

assailant /əˈseɪlənt/, **assailants.** Someone's as-   N COUNT
sailant is the person who physically attacks them.   Formal
EG *He dared not take his eyes off his assailant for a
second.*

assassin /əˈsæsɪn/, **assassins.** An **assassin** is a   N COUNT
person who assassinates someone.

assassinate /əˈsæsɪneɪt/, **assassinates,**   v+o
assassinating, assassinated. When someone important **is assassinated**, they are murdered.
◊ **assassination** /əˌsæsɪˈneɪʃən/, **assassinations.**   ◊ N UNCOUNT
EG *...an assassination attempt.*   OR N COUNT

assault /əˈsɔːlt/, **assaults, assaulting, assaulted.**

1 An **assault** by an army is a strong attack that is   N COUNT : OFT
made on an area held by the enemy. EG *They*   +against/on
responded with assaults against the enemy's bases.

2 An **assault** on a person is a physical attack on   N COUNT OR
   N UNCOUNT

them. EG *He was threatened with assault in the
street.* ▸ used as a verb. EG *She was found guilty of*   ▸ v+o
assaulting a police officer.

3 An **assault** on someone's beliefs is a strong   N COUNT
criticism of them. EG *...an all-out assault on racism.*

assemble /əˈsembəl/, **assembles, assembling,**
assembled. 1 When people or things **assemble** or   v-ERG
are assembled, they gather together in a group,
usually for a particular purpose. EG *The leaders
assembled in Paris for a meeting... His job was to
assemble the facts and evaluate them.*
◊ **assembled.** EG *She announced to the assembled*   ◊ ADJ CLASSIF
relatives that she intended to move abroad.

2 To **assemble** something means to fit the parts of   v+o
it together. EG *...a vast range of products that were
assembled locally.*

assembly /əˈsembli/, **assemblies.** 1 An **assem-**   N COUNT
bly is 1.1 a gathering of people or things. EG *...a
great assembly of senators.* 1.2 a group of people
who meet regularly to make laws for a region or
country.

2 **Assembly** is the gathering together of people for   N UNCOUNT
a particular purpose. EG *They are demanding rights
of assembly.*

3 The **assembly** of the parts of a machine or   N UNCOUNT
device is the process of fitting them together. EG
...instructions for assembly of an outdoor barbecue.

assembly line, assembly lines. An **assembly**   N COUNT
line is an arrangement of workers and machines
in a factory where the product passes from one
worker to another until it is finished.

assent /əˈsent/, **assents, assenting, assented.** If   N UNCOUNT
someone gives their **assent** to something that has
been suggested, they agree to it. EG *Haldane acted
with the full assent of the Foreign Office.* ▸ used as   ▸ v+to OR
a verb. EG *They all assented to the proposition.*   V+QUOTE

assert /əˈsɜːt/, **asserts, asserting, asserted.** 1 If   V-SPEECH :
someone **asserts** a fact or belief, they state it   ONLY that
firmly. EG *The protesters asserted their right to be
heard.* ◊ **assertion** /əˈsɜːʃən/, **assertions.** EG *I*   ◊ N COUNT OR
challenge that assertion.   N UNCOUNT

2 If you **assert** your authority, you make it clear   v+o
by your behaviour that you have authority. EG *He
wished to assert his authority in his own house.*
◊ **assertion.** EG *...an assertion of power.*   ◊ N UNCOUNT

3 If you **assert** yourself, you speak and act in a   V-REFL
forceful way so that people take notice of you. EG
She had begun to assert herself strongly.

assertive /əˈsɜːtɪv/. Someone who is **assertive**   ADJ QUALIT
speaks and acts in a forceful way so that people
take notice of them.

assess /əˈses/, **assesses, assessing, assessed.** 1   v+o; ALSO
When you **assess** a person, feeling, or situation,   V+REPORT :
you consider them and make a judgement about   ONLY WH
them. EG *They meet monthly to assess the current
political situation... Ellen tried to assess how she
felt.*

2 When you **assess** the amount of money that   v+o
something is worth or that should be paid, you
calculate or estimate it. EG *She looked the house
over and assessed its rough market value.*

assessment /əˈsesmənt/, **assessments.** 1 An   N COUNT+SUPP
assessment is a consideration of someone or
something and a judgement about them. EG *There
has to be a clear assessment of the country's social
needs... ...the assessment of his academic progress.*

2 An **assessment** of the amount of money that   N COUNT
something is worth or that should be paid is a
calculation or estimate of the amount.

asset /ˈæset/, **assets.** 1 An **asset** is someone or   N COUNT :
something that is considered useful or that helps a   OFT+to
person or organization to be successful. EG *He was
a great asset to the committee... Her only asset was
a gentle nature.*

2 The **assets** of a company or a person are all the   N PLURAL
things that they own.

assiduous /əˈsɪdjuːəs/. Someone who is **assiduous**   ADJ QUALIT
works hard at a particular task. EG *...an assiduous*

student. ◊ **assiduously.** EG *Throughout 1954 he* ◊ ADV
assiduously studied law.

assign /əsaɪn/, **assigns, assigning, assigned. 1** V+O+O
If you **assign** a piece of work to someone, you give OR *to*-INF;
them the work to do. EG *She kept calling him up to* ALSO V+O+O
*assign some new task to him... She had been
assigned to work in the fields.*

2 If you **assign** something to someone, you say that V+O+*to*
it is for their use. EG *The bed which I'd been* OR V+O+O
assigned was in Dormitory 2.

3 If someone **is assigned** to a particular place, V+O:
group, or person, they are sent there, usually in USU PASS+*to*
order to work there or for that person. EG *She was
assigned to the men's wards.*

4 If you **assign** a particular function or value to V+O+*to*
someone or something, you give it to them. EG OR V+O+O
*Mother and father play out the roles assigned to
them.*

assignation /æsɪgneɪʃəⁿn/, **assignations.** An **as-** N COUNT
signation is a secret meeting with someone, espe- Formal
cially with a lover.

assignment /əsaɪnməⁿnt/, **assignments. 1** An N COUNT
assignment is a task or piece of work that you are
given to do, especially as part of your job or
studies. EG *My first major assignment was to cover
a large-scale riot.*

2 You can refer to someone being given a particu- N UNCOUNT
lar task or job as their **assignment** to the task or +POSS
job. EG *...the uproar about his assignment to the
case.*

assimilate /əsɪmɪleɪt/, **assimilates, assimilat-**
ing, assimilated. 1 If you **assimilate** ideas, cus- V+O
toms, or techniques, you learn them and make use
of them. EG *He was quick to assimilate new ideas.*
◊ **assimilation** /əsɪmɪleɪʃəⁿn/. EG *...the rapid as-* ◊ N UNCOUNT
similation of new techniques in industry.

2 When people such as immigrants **assimilate** or V-ERG:
are assimilated into a community, they become OFT+*into*
an accepted part of it. ◊ **assimilation.** EG *...the* ◊ N UNCOUNT
assimilation of the new arrivals.

assist /əsɪst/, **assists, assisting, assisted. 1** If V+O OR V:
you **assist** someone, **1.1** you help them do some- OFT+*with/in*
thing. EG *He was asked to assist in keeping the hotel
under surveillance.* **1.2** you give them information,
advice, or money. EG *We may be able to assist with
the tuition fees.*

2 If something **assists** you with a task, it makes it V+O OR V:
easier for you. EG *With these clues to assist us, we* OFT+*with/in*
can begin to identify the parents.

assistance /əsɪstəns/. **1** If you give someone N UNCOUNT
assistance, 1.1 you help them do something. EG *He
thanked me for my assistance... They could not
walk without assistance.* **1.2** you give them information, advice, or money. EG *The department provides special assistance to those with large families.*

2 Someone or something that is **of assistance** to PHRASE
you is helpful or useful to you. EG *I would be of little
assistance in that kind of work.*

assistant /əsɪstənt/, **assistants. 1 Assistant** is ADJ CLASSIF:
used in front of titles or jobs to indicate a slightly ATTRIB
lower rank or title. For example, an **assistant**
director is one rank lower than a director in an
organization.

2 Someone's **assistant** is a person who helps them N COUNT+POSS
in their work.

3 An **assistant** or a **shop assistant** is a person N COUNT
who works in a shop selling things to customers.

associate, associates, associating, associated;
pronounced /əsoʊsieɪt/ when it is a verb and
/əsoʊsiⁱət/ when it is a noun or adjective.

1 If you **associate** one thing with another, the two V+O+*with*
things are connected in your mind. EG *Dignity is the
quality which I associate mostly with her... The
smoking of pipes is often associated with old-
fashioned 'masculine' values.*

2 If one thing **is associated** with another, the two V+O: USU
things are connected with each other. EG *Zuse* PASS+*with*
worked on problems associated with aircraft de-

sign... ...the Executive and its associated committees.

3 If you **are associated** with a particular organiza- V+O+*with* OR
tion, cause, or point of view, or if you **associate** V-REFL+*with*
yourself with it, you support it publicly. EG *They
became closely associated with the International
Socialists.*

4 If you **associate** with a particular group of V+*with*
people, you spend a lot of time in their company;
often used showing disapproval. EG *She spent her
adolescence associating with criminals.*

5 Your **associates** are your business colleagues. EG N COUNT
*The series is directed by my old associate Jack
Good.*

6 Associate is used before a rank or title to ADJ CLASSIF:
indicate a slightly different or lower rank or title. ATTRIB
EG *Non-professional people could only be Associate
Members.*

association /əsoʊsieɪʃəⁿn, -ʃiⁱ-/, **associations. 1** N COUNT
An **association** is an official group of people with
a common occupation, aim, or interest. EG *...the
President of the British Medical Association.*

2 Your **association** with a person, group, or or- N UNCOUNT
ganization is the connection that you have with +SUPP
them. EG *We shall do what we can while our
business association lasts.* ● If someone does ● PREP
something **in association with** someone else, they
do it together. EG *The programme was made in
association with Radio Brighton.*

3 If something has a particular **association** for N COUNT+SUPP
you, it is connected in your mind with a particular
memory or feeling. EG *A number of tunes have a
really strong association for individuals.*

assorted /əsɔːtɪ²d/. A group of **assorted** things or ADJ CLASSIF:
people is a group of similar things that have ATTRIB
different sizes, colours, or other qualities. EG *...a
bunch of assorted wild flowers.*

assortment /əsɔːtməⁿnt/, **assortments.** An **as-** N COUNT:
sortment is a group of similar things that have OFT+*of*
different sizes, colours, or other qualities. EG *...an
assortment of plastic bags.*

assume /əsjuːm/, **assumes, assuming, as-**
sumed. 1 If you **assume** that something is true, V+REPORT:
you imagine that it is true, sometimes wrongly. EG *I* ONLY *that* OR
assume you don't drive... I was mistakenly assumed V+O+*to*-INF
to be a Welshman because of my surname.

2 If someone **assumes** power or responsibility, V+O
they take power or responsibility. EG *Hitler assumed power in 1933.*

3 If you **assume** a particular expression, quality, V+O
or way of behaving, you start to look or behave in
this way. EG *He assumed an expression of resignation... Her eyes assumed a strange, indifferent look.*

assuming /əsjuːmɪŋ/. You use **assuming** or **as-** CONJ
suming that when you are imagining that something is true, so that you can think about what the
consequences would be. EG *Keep your goods (assuming that you have any) separate from those of
your husband.*

assumption /əsʌmpʃəⁿn/, **assumptions. 1** If N COUNT
you make an **assumption**, you imagine that something is true, sometimes wrongly. EG *His suggestions are based on an assumption that the system is
out of date.*

2 Someone's **assumption** of power or responsibil- N UNCOUNT+*of*
ity is their taking of it.

assurance /əʃʊərəns/, **assurances. 1** If you give N COUNT OR
someone an **assurance** that something is true or N UNCOUNT
will happen, you say that it is definitely true or will
definitely happen, in order to make them less
worried. EG *One must be content with assurances
that progress is being made... ...the assurance of
full employment.*

2 If you do something with **assurance**, you do it N UNCOUNT

What is the difference between an astrologer and
an astronomer?

with a feeling of confidence and certainty. EG *'She'll like that,'* said Lally with assurance.

3 Assurance is also insurance that provides for certain events such as death. N UNCOUNT

assure /əˈʃuə/, **assures, assuring, assured. 1** If you **assure** someone that something is true or will happen, you tell them that it is definitely true or will definitely happen, often in order to make them less worried. EG *Kurt assured me that he was an excellent climber... I can assure you that this feeling will soon pass... Once assured of his daughter's safety, he was casual and relaxed.* V+O+QUOTE OR REPORT: ONLY *that*

2 If you **are assured** of something, it is certain that you will get it. EG *This film had assured him a place in movie history.* V+O+of OR V+O+O

3 You say **'rest assured'** when you want to reassure someone about something. EG *You can rest assured your son didn't die in vain.* PHRASE

assured /əˈʃuəd/. Someone who is **assured** is very confident and feels at ease. ADJ QUALIT

assuredly /əˈʃuərəˈdli¹/. If something is **assuredly** true, it is definitely true. EG *She would assuredly be back.* ADV OR ADV SEN

asterisk /ˈæstə⁰rɪsk/, **asterisks**. An **asterisk** is the sign *. It is used, for example, to indicate that there is a comment at the bottom of the page. N COUNT

asthma /ˈæsmə/ is a chest disease which makes breathing difficult. N UNCOUNT

asthmatic /æsˈmætɪk/. Someone who is **asthmatic** suffers from asthma. ADJ CLASSIF

astonish /əˈstɒnɪʃ/, **astonishes, astonishing, astonished.** If something or someone **astonishes** you, they surprise you very much. EG *You never cease to astonish me.* V+O

astonished /əˈstɒnɪʃt/. If you are **astonished**, you are very surprised about something. EG *They were astonished at the extraordinary beauty of the picture... ...groups of astonished customers.* ADJ QUALIT: USU PRED

astonishing /əˈstɒnɪʃɪŋ/. Something that is **astonishing** is very surprising. EG *The shape of their bodies changes with astonishing speed.* ◇ **astonishingly.** EG *Birth rates there are astonishingly high.* ADJ QUALIT ◇ SUBMOD OR ADV SEN

astonishment /əˈstɒnɪʃmə⁰nt/ is a feeling of great surprise. EG *John stared at him in astonishment... To the astonishment of his friends, he took off his shoes.* N UNCOUNT

astound /əˈstaʊnd/, **astounds, astounding, astounded.** If something **astounds** you, you are amazed and perhaps shocked by it. EG *What newspapers will do for a story never fails to astound me.* ◇ **astounded.** EG *Visitors to Sweden were astounded by its cleanliness... Everyone was astounded when Ruth quit.* ◇ **astounding.** EG *It seemed an astounding decision.* V+O ◇ ADJ QUALIT: USU PRED ◇ ADJ QUALIT

astray /əˈstreɪ/. **1** If you **lead** someone **astray**, you make them behave in a bad or foolish way. PHRASE

2 If something **goes astray**, it gets lost while it is being taken or sent somewhere. PHRASE

astride /əˈstraɪd/. If you sit or stand **astride** something, you sit or stand with one leg on each side of it. EG *Karen sat astride a large white horse.* PREP

astringent /əˈstrɪndʒə⁰nt/, **astringents. 1** An **astringent** is a substance that makes your skin less greasy or that stops it bleeding. ▶ used as an adjective. EG *...an astringent lotion.* N COUNT OR N UNCOUNT ▶ ADJ CLASSIF

2 Astringent comments are forceful and critical. EG *...fierce and astringent attacks on the government.* ADJ QUALIT

astrologer /əˈstrɒlədʒə/, **astrologers.** An **astrologer** is a person who uses astrology in order to tell you things about your character and your future. N COUNT

astrology /əˈstrɒlədʒi¹/ is the study of the movements of the planets, sun, moon, and stars in the belief that these movements can influence people's lives. ◇ **astrological.** EG *...astrological predictions.* N UNCOUNT ◇ ADJ CLASSIF

astronaut /ˈæstrəˈnɔːt/, **astronauts.** An **astronaut** is a person who is trained to fly in a spacecraft. N COUNT

astronomer /əˈstrɒnəmə/, **astronomers.** An **astronomer** is a scientist who studies the stars, planets, and other natural objects in space. N COUNT

astronomical /æstrəˈnɒmɪkə⁰l/. **1** If you describe a value, price, or amount as **astronomical**, you mean that it is very large indeed. EG *He was trying to sell the ranch at an astronomical price.* ADJ CLASSIF

2 Astronomical also means relating to astronomy. EG *...The Royal Astronomical Society.* ADJ CLASSIF

astronomy /əˈstrɒnəmi¹/ is the scientific study of the stars, planets, and other natural objects in space. N UNCOUNT

astute /əˈstjuːt/. Someone who is **astute** is clever and skilful at understanding behaviour and situations. EG *...an astute politician.* ADJ QUALIT

asylum /əˈsaɪləm/, **asylums. 1** An **asylum** is a mental hospital. EG *They put him into an asylum.* N COUNT

2 Asylum is protection that is given by a government to foreigners who leave their own country for political reasons. N UNCOUNT

asymmetrical /eɪsɪmeˈtrɪkə⁰l/. Something that is **asymmetrical** has two sides or halves that are different. EG *...an asymmetrical pattern.* ADJ CLASSIF

at /əˈt/. **1** If something happens or is situated **at** a place, that is the place where it happens or is situated. EG *The play takes place at a beach club... They've been away at a boarding school... There was a knock at his door.* PREP

2 If you look **at** someone or something or if you direct something **at** them, you look towards them or you direct the thing towards them. EG *They were staring at a garage roof... He grinned at Gretchen... Supporters threw petals at his car.* PREP

3 If something is **at** a distance from something else, or **at** an angle to something else, it is in that place in relation to it. EG *Place it at right angles to the door.* PREP

4 If something happens **at** a particular time, that is the time when it happens. EG *She leaves her house every day at 11 a.m... She had come in at dawn... You can come back at a later stage.* PREP

5 If something happens **at** a particular rate, that is how quickly or regularly it happens. EG *The high technology companies have grown at an astonishing rate... He hurtles through the air at 600 miles per hour.* PREP

6 If you buy or sell something **at** a particular price, you buy it or sell it for that price. EG *The book is published at $7.95.* PREP

7 If you are **at** lunch, dinner, or any other meal, you are eating in. PREP

8 If you are working or aiming **at** something, you are trying to do it or achieve it. EG *It means working harder at your thesis.* PREP

9 If something is done **at** someone's command or invitation, it is done as a result of it. EG *At the director's command, the people all left.* PREP

10 You also use **at. 10.1** to say that someone or something is in a particular state or condition. EG *He remains at liberty... The two nations are at war.* **10.2** to say how something is being done. EG *He seemed to read at random... Guardsmen herded them back at gun point.* **10.3** to show that someone is doing something in a tentative way. EG *Rudolph sipped at his drink.* PREP

11 If you are good **at** something, you do it well. If you are bad **at** something, you do it badly. EG *They seemed to be very good at reading.* PREP

12 If you are delighted, pleased, or appalled **at** something, that is the effect it has on you. EG *I was appalled at the quality of the reporting.* PREP

ate /eɪt, ɛt/ is the past tense of **eat.**

atheism /ˈeɪθiˈɪzə⁰m/ is the belief that there is no God. ◇ **atheist** /ˈeɪθiˈɪst/, **atheists.** EG *He is a convinced atheist.* N UNCOUNT ◇ N COUNT

athlete /ˈæθliːt/, **athletes**. An **athlete** is a person N COUNT
who takes part in athletics competitions.

athletic /æθˈletɪk/, **athletics**. 1 **Athletics** consists N UNCOUNT
of sports such as running, the high jump, and the
javelin. EG ...an athletics meeting... He has retired
from active athletics.

2 Athletic means relating to athletes and athletics. ADJ CLASSIF:
EG ...athletic excellence. ATTRIB

3 An **athletic** person is fit, healthy, and active. EG ADJ QUALIT
...athletic young men... ...his lean, athletic build.

-ation, -ations. -ation, -tion, and **-ion** are added SUFFIX
to verbs to form nouns. These nouns usually refer
to an action or to the result of an action. For
example, 'alteration' can refer to the altering of
something or to the result of altering something.
Nouns like these are often not defined in this
dictionary, but are treated with the related verbs.
EG He was annoyed by the cancellation of the visit...
The majority of adoptions are highly successful.

atlas /ˈætləs/, **atlases**. An **atlas** is a book of maps. N COUNT

atmosphere /ˈætməsfɪə/, **atmospheres**. 1 A plan- N COUNT:
et's **atmosphere** is the layer of air or other gas USU the+N
around it. EG ...the testing of nuclear weapons in the
atmosphere.   ◇ **atmospheric** /ætməsˈferɪk/. ◇ ADJ CLASSIF:
...atmospheric pollution. ATTRIB

2 The **atmosphere** of a place is **2.1** the air that you N SING
breathe there. EG ...the polluted atmosphere of
towns and cities.   **2.2** the general impression that N SING+SUPP
you get of the place. EG It's got such a friendly
atmosphere.

3 If a place has **atmosphere**, it is interesting. EG N UNCOUNT
The place has no character, no atmosphere.

atom /ˈætəm/, **atoms**. 1 An **atom** is the smallest N COUNT
amount of a substance that can take part in a Technical
chemical reaction. EG ...an atom of hydrogen... ...the
nucleus of an atom.

2 You can refer to a very small amount of some- N PART
thing as an **atom** of it. EG There's not one atom of
romance in her.

atom bomb, atom bombs. An **atom bomb** or an N COUNT
atomic bomb is a bomb that causes an explosion
by a sudden release of energy that results from
splitting atoms.

atomic /əˈtɒmɪk/ means **1** relating to power that ADJ CLASSIF:
is produced from the energy released by splitting ATTRIB
atoms. EG ...atomic energy... ...atomic weapons. **2**
relating to the atoms of substances.

atone /əˈtəʊn/, **atones, atoning, atoned**. If you V+for
atone for something that you have done, you do Formal
something to show that you are sorry you did it. EG
He has to atone for his sins.

atrocious /əˈtrəʊʃəs/. Something that is **atrocious** ADJ QUALIT
is extremely bad. EG ...speaking French with an
atrocious accent.   ◇ **atrociously**. EG The farm ◇ ADV
animals are treated atrociously.

atrocity /əˈtrɒsɪti/, **atrocities**. An **atrocity** is a N COUNT OR
very cruel, shocking action. EG They were guilty of N UNCOUNT
barbarous atrocities.

attach /əˈtætʃ/, **attaches, attaching, attached**. **1** V+O: OFT+to
If you **attach** something to an object, you join it or
fasten it to the object. EG He attached some string
to the can... Attached to the letter was a list of
hotels.

2 If someone **is attached** to an organization or V+O:
group of people, they are working with them, often USU PASS+to
only for a short time. EG Hospital officers would be
temporarily attached to NHS hospitals.

3 If one organization **is attached** to a larger one, it V+O:
is part of the larger one and is controlled and USU PASS+to
administered by it.

4 If you **attach** a quality to someone or something, V-ERG+to
or if it **attaches** to them, you consider that they
have that quality. EG Don't attach too much importance to what he said... No blame attaches to him.

5 See also **attached**.

attaché /æˈtæʃeɪ/, **attachés**. An **attaché** is a N COUNT
member of staff in an embassy.

attaché case, attaché cases. An **attaché case** N COUNT
is a briefcase.

attached /əˈtætʃt/. If you are **attached** to some- ADJ PRED+to
one or something, you are very fond of them. EG He
had become attached to a student called Hilary.

attachment /əˈtætʃmənt/, **attachments**. **1** If you N COUNT:
have an **attachment** to someone or something, OFT+to
you are fond of them. EG ...a romantic attachment...
...their attachment to Western ways.

2 An **attachment** is a device that can be fixed onto N COUNT
a machine in order to enable it to do different jobs.
EG It has a special attachment for cleaning upholstery.

attack /əˈtæk/, **attacks, attacking, attacked**. **1** If V+O OR V
you **attack** someone, you try to hurt them or to get
them in your power using physical violence. EG He
attacked and mutilated two women... She was
attacked by a shark. ▶ used as a noun. EG There ▶ N COUNT OR
were more attacks on women going alone on the N UNCOUNT
street... There were no defences against nuclear
attack.

2 If you **attack** a person, belief, or idea, you V+O
criticize them strongly. EG The senator attacked the
press for misleading the public. ▶ used as a noun. ▶ N COUNT OR
EG ...attacks on apartheid... Burt's work came under N UNCOUNT
violent attack.

3 If something such as a disease, a chemical, or an V+O
insect **attacks** something, it harms it or spoils it. EG
The venom attacks the nervous system.

4 If you **attack** a job or a problem, you start to deal V+O
with it with energy and enthusiasm. EG He attacked
his task with determination.

5 When players **attack** in a game such as football V
or hockey, they try to score a goal.

6 An **attack** of an illness is a short period in which N COUNT:
you suffer badly from it. EG ...an attack of smallpox. OFT+of

attacker /əˈtækə/, **attackers**. Someone's **attack-** N COUNT
er is the person who attacks them. EG He described
his attacker to the police.

attain /əˈteɪn/, **attains, attaining, attained**. If V+O
you **attain** something, you gain it or achieve it,
often after a lot of effort. EG ...the qualities which
enabled him to attain his ambitions... From 1976 to
1978 the party attained a position of prominence.

attainable /əˈteɪnəbəl/. Something that is **attain-** ADJ CLASSIF
able can be achieved. EG This kind of accuracy is
attainable by modern techniques.

attainment /əˈteɪnmənt/, **attainments**. **1** The N UNCOUNT:
attainment of an aim is the achieving of it. EG +SUPP
...the attainment of independence. Formal

2 An **attainment** is a skill you have learnt or an N COUNT
achievement you have made. EG ...your literary Formal
attainments.

attempt /əˈtempt/, **attempts, attempting, at-**
tempted. **1** If you **attempt** something or **attempt** V+O OR
to do something, especially something difficult, you V+to-INF
try to do it. EG A long time had elapsed since I had
attempted any serious study... Some of the crowd
attempted to break through police cordons.

2 If you make an **attempt** at something, you try to N COUNT:
do it, often without success. EG ...an attempt at a OFT+to-INF
joke... ...in a vain attempt to have the report OR at
suppressed... The young birds manage to fly several kilometres at their first attempt.

3 An **attempt on** someone's **life** is an attempt to PHRASE
kill them.

attempted /əˈtemptɪd/. An **attempted** crime or ADJ CLASSIF:
other action is an unsuccessful effort to commit the ATTRIB
crime. EG He was charged with attempted murder.

attend /əˈtend/, **attends, attending, attended**. **1** V+O
If you **attend** a meeting or other event, you are
present at it. EG I stopped off in London to attend a
conference... The plays here are always well attended.

2. If you **attend** an institution such as a school, V+O
college, or church, you go to it regularly.

What is an attaché attached to?

3 If you **attend** to something, you deal with it. EG *I* v+*to* *had two items of business to attend to.*

4 If you **attend** to something, you pay attention to v : OFT+*to* it. EG *She was attending closely to the music.* Formal

attendance /ə'tɛndəns/, **attendances. 1** The at- N COUNT OR **tendance** at a meeting is the number of people N UNCOUNT who are present at it. EG *At Easter, attendances at churches rose.*

2 Someone's **attendance** at an event or an institu- N UNCOUNT : tion is the fact that they are present at the event or OFT+*at* go regularly to the institution. EG *She was allowed to resume her attendance at the High School.*

attendant /ə'tɛndənt/, **attendants. 1** An **attend-** N COUNT **ant** is someone whose job is to serve people in a place such as a petrol station or a museum.

2 You use **attendant** to describe something that ADJ CLASSIF : results from a thing already mentioned or that is ATTRIB connected with it. EG *...nuclear energy and its* Formal *attendant dangers.*

attention /ə'tɛnʃəⁿn/, **attentions. 1** If you give N UNCOUNT something your **attention**, you look at it, listen to it, or think about it carefully. EG *When he felt he had their attention, he began... He switched his attention back to the magazine... They were listen- ing with close attention... She was the centre of attention.*

2 If someone brings something important or inter- N UNCOUNT esting to your **attention** or draws your **attention** to it, they point it out to you. EG *I feel it is my duty to bring to your attention the following facts.*

3 If something **attracts** your **attention** or **catches** PHRASE your **attention**, you suddenly notice it. EG *How can I attract the captain's attention?*

4 Attention to something is dealing with it or N UNCOUNT caring for it. EG *They needed medical attention.*

5 If you **pay attention** to someone or something, PHRASE **5.1** you watch them or listen to them carefully. EG *You must pay attention to his eyes.* **5.2** you show great interest in them and take notice of them. EG *There's far too much attention being paid to these hooligans.*

6 If you **pay no attention** to someone or some- PHRASE thing, you behave as if you are not aware of them or as if they do not matter. EG *We didn't pay any attention to him.*

7 Attentions that you pay to someone are things N PLURAL that you do to help them and to show your affec- tion.

8 When soldiers or policemen **stand to attention**, PHRASE they stand up straight with their feet together and their arms at their sides. ▸ **Attention!** is used as a ▸ CONVENTION command to stand in this way.

attentive /ə'tɛntɪv/. Someone who is **attentive 1** ADJ QUALIT pays close attention to the person or thing that they are listening to or looking at. EG *...an attentive audience.* ◊ **attentively.** EG *He was listening* ◊ ADV *attentively.* **2** is very helpful and polite to someone ADJ QUALIT else, often because they like them very much. EG *He was unfailingly attentive.*

attest /ə'tɛst/, **attests, attesting, attested.** To v+o OR v+*to* **attest** something or **attest** to something means Formal to show or prove that it is true. EG *The perfection of their design is attested by the fact that they survived for thousands of years.*

attic /'ætɪk/, **attics.** An **attic** is a room at the top N COUNT of a house just below the roof.

attire /ə'taɪə/ is clothing. EG *Her whole attire was* N UNCOUNT *rich in appearance.* Formal

attired /ə'taɪəd/. Someone who is **attired** in a ADJ CLASSIF : particular way is dressed that way. EG *He was* OFT+*in* *elegantly attired in a cashmere coat.* Formal

attitude /'ætɪtjuːd/, **attitudes. 1** Your **attitude** to N COUNT+SUPP something is the way that you think and feel about it. EG *They are adopting our attitude to life... She took the attitude that acting was a recreation.*

2 Your **attitude** to someone is the way that you N COUNT+POSS behave when you are dealing with them. EG *I resented his attitude.*

3 A particular **attitude** is a particular position in N COUNT+SUPP

which you hold your body. EG *...with her arms flung out in an attitude of surrender.*

attorney /ə'tɜːni¹/, **attorneys.** An **attorney** is a N COUNT lawyer. American

attract /ə'trækt/, **attracts, attracting, attract- ed. 1** If something **attracts** people or animals, it v+o : OFT+*to* has features that cause them to come to it. EG *The show attracted large crowds this year... Moths are attracted to lights.*

2 If someone or something **attracts** you, they have v+o particular qualities which cause you to like or admire them. EG *She didn't attract me physically.*

3 If a particular quality **attracts** you to a person or v+o : OFT+*to* thing, it is the reason why you like them. EG *What attracted me to Valeria was her sense of humour.*

4 If something **attracts** support or publicity, it v+o receives support or publicity. EG *The women's movement has attracted a lot of publicity in the last decade.*

5 If something **attracts** your attention, it makes v+o you notice it.

6 If something magnetic **attracts** an object, it v+o causes the object to move towards it.

attracted /ə'træktɪ¹d/. If you are **attracted** to ADJ PRED+*to* someone or something, you like them and are interested in them. EG *I was becoming attracted to a girl from the next office... I'm not attracted to sociology.*

attraction /ə'trækʃəⁿn/, **attractions. 1 Attrac- tion** is **1.1** a feeling of liking someone, and often of N UNCOUNT : being sexually interested in them. EG *He couldn't* OFT+*to* *explain his attraction to her.* **1.2** a quality that N SING+SUPP something has of being interesting or desirable. EG *The attraction of the house lay in its simplicity.*

2 An **attraction** is **2.1** a feature which makes a N COUNT thing or person interesting or desirable. EG *One of the main attractions of the city was its superb transport system.* **2.2** something that people can go to for interest or enjoyment, for example a famous building. EG *...to visit the tourist attractions.*

attractive /ə'træktɪv/. **1** A person who is **attrac-** ADJ QUALIT **tive** is pretty or handsome. EG *...a remarkably attractive girl.* ◊ **attractiveness.** EG *...one's physi-* ◊ N UNCOUNT *cal attractiveness.*

2 Something that is **attractive 2.1** has a pleasant ADJ QUALIT appearance or sound. EG *...attractive illustrations... ...an attractive name.* **2.2** seems good to have or choose. EG *The company offers more time off and attractive pay.*

> **ATTRIB** stands for **attributive adjective**
> Adjectives which are labelled ATTRIB in the Extra Column are normally only used in front of a noun. See the entry headed ADJECTIVES for more infor- mation.

attribute, attributes, attributing, attributed; pronounced /ə'trɪbjuːt/ when it is a verb and /'ætrɪbjuːt/ when it is a noun.

1 If you **attribute** something to an event or v+o+*to* situation, you think that it was caused by that event or situation. EG *Economists attributed the lack of progress to poor cooperation.*

2 If you **attribute** a remark, a piece of writing, or v+o+*to* a work of art to someone, you say that they said it, wrote it, or created it. EG *...a remark that was later attributed to Haldane.*

3 If you **attribute** a particular quality or feature to v+o+*to* someone or something, you think that they have got it. EG *Here we are attributing human feelings to animals.* ◊ **attribution** /ætrɪbjuː'ʃəⁿn/. EG *...the* ◊ N UNCOUNT *attribution of mysterious powers to these men.*

4 An **attribute** is a quality or feature. EG *They* N COUNT appeared to possess all the attributes of a ruling class... ...her physical attributes.*

attuned /ə'tjuːnd/. **1** If you are **attuned** to some- ADJ PRED+to thing, you can understand and appreciate it. EG *The public is not quite attuned to this kind of art.*
2 If your ears are **attuned** to a sound, you can hear ADJ PRED+to it and recognize it quickly. EG *Her ears were sharply attuned to any noise from the bedroom.*

aubergine /'əʊbəʳʒiːn/, **aubergines.** An auber- N COUNT OR gine is a vegetable with a smooth, dark purple N UNCOUNT skin. British

auburn /'ɔːbəʳn/. **Auburn** hair is reddish brown. ADJ COLOUR

auction /'ɔːkʃəʳn/, **auctions, auctioning, auc- tioned. 1** An **auction** is a public sale of goods N COUNT where the goods are sold to the person who offers the highest price. ● If something is sold **by** PHRASE **auction** or **at auction**, it is sold at an auction to the person who offers the highest price. EG *The big house was sold by auction.*
2 If you **auction** something, you sell it in an V+O auction. EG *Her car is going to be auctioned.*
auction off. If you **auction off** a number of PHRASAL VB: things, you get rid of them all by selling them at an V+O+ADV auction.

auctioneer /ɔːkʃəˈnɪə/, **auctioneers.** An auction- N COUNT eer is a person in charge of an auction.

audacious /ɔːˈdeɪʃəs/. **Audacious** behaviour is ADJ QUALIT bold and sometimes cheeky. EG *...a series of auda- cious ventures.* ◊ **audacity** /ɔːˈdæsɪˈtiʲ/. EG *He had* ◊ N UNCOUNT *the audacity to blame Baldwin for their failure.*

audible /'ɔːdɪ'bəʳl/. A sound that is **audible** is loud ADJ QUALIT enough to be heard. EG *He spoke in a scarcely audible voice.* ◊ **audibly.** EG *The clock ticked* ◊ ADV *audibly.*

audience /'ɔːdɪəns/, **audiences. 1** An **audience** is N COLL **1.1** the group of people who are watching or listening to something such as a play, concert, or film. EG *Someone in the audience began to laugh... She spoke before an audience of schoolchildren.* **1.2** all the people who watch television or listen to the radio. EG *the people who read the books of a writer or hear about the ideas of a thinker.* EG *...the need for intellectuals to communicate their ideas to a wider audience.*
2 If you have an **audience** with someone impor- N COUNT tant, you have a formal meeting with them. EG *He stood up to show that the audience was over.*

audio /'ɔːdɪəʊ/. **Audio** equipment is used for re- ADJ CLASSIF: cording and reproducing sound. ATTRIB

audio-typist, audio-typists. An **audio-typist** is a N COUNT typist who types letters and reports that have been dictated into a tape-recorder.

audio-visual. Audio-visual teaching aids involve ADJ CLASSIF: both recorded sound and pictures. ATTRIB

audit /'ɔːdɪt/, **audits, auditing, audited.** If an V+O accountant **audits** an organization's accounts, he or she examines the accounts officially in order to make sure that they have been done correctly.
► used as a noun. EG *We're going to conduct a full* ► N COUNT *audit.*

audition /ɔːˈdɪʃəʳn/, **auditions, auditioning, audi- tioned. 1** An **audition** is a short performance that N COUNT someone gives so that a director can decide if they are good enough to be in a play, film, or orchestra.
2 If you **audition** or if someone **auditions** you, you V-ERG: perform an audition. EG *Are you going to audition* OFT+for *for 'Stars of a Summer Night'?*

auditor /'ɔːdɪtə/, **auditors.** An **auditor** is an ac- N COUNT countant who officially examines the accounts of organizations.

auditorium /ɔːdɪˈtɔːrɪəm/, **auditoriums** or audi- N COUNT **toria** /ɔːdɪˈtɔːrɪə/. An **auditorium** is **1** the part of a theatre or concert hall where the audience sits. **2** a Formal large building which is used for events such as public meetings and concerts.

augment /ɔːgˈment/, **augments, augmenting,** V+O **augmented.** To **augment** something means to Formal make it larger by adding something to it. EG *They hit upon another idea to augment their income.*

augur /'ɔːgə/, **augurs, auguring, augured.** If V+A : OFT+for something **augurs** well or badly for someone, it is Formal a sign that things will go well or badly for them. EG *The start could not have augured better for suc- cess.*

august; pronounced /'ɔːgəst/ when it is a noun and /ɔːˈgʌst/ when it is an adjective. It is spelled with a capital letter for paragraph 1.
1 August is the eighth month of the year in the N UNCOUNT Western calendar. EG *War broke out on August 4th... You start your new job in August.*
2 Someone or something that is **august** is dignified ADJ QUALIT and impressive. EG *He was probably the most* Literary *august figure in the House of Lords.*

aunt /ɑːnt/, **aunts.** Your **aunt** is the sister of your N COUNT mother or father, or the wife of your uncle. EG *...Aunt Alice.*

auntie /'ɑːntiʲ/, **aunties;** also spelled **aunty.** Your N COUNT **auntie** is your aunt. Informal

au pair /əʊpeə/, **au pairs.** An **au pair** is a young N COUNT foreigner, usually a woman, who lives for a time with a family in order to learn the language and to help with the children and housework.

aura /'ɔːrə/, **auras.** An **aura** is a quality or feeling N COUNT : that seems to surround a person or place or to OFT+of come from them. EG *European things acquired an aura of glamour and prestige.*

aural /'ɔːrəl/ means related to the sense of hear- ADJ CLASSIF ing. EG *I have used written and aural material.*

auspices /'ɔːspɪsɪz/. If something is done **under** PREP **the auspices of** a particular person or organiza- Formal tion, it is done with their support and approval.

auspicious /ɔːˈspɪʃəs/. Something that is **auspi-** ADJ QUALIT **cious** indicates that success is likely. EG *It was an* Formal *auspicious start.*

austere /ɒsˈtɪə/. **1** Something that is **austere** is ADJ QUALIT plain and not decorated. EG *The interior of the church is sober and austere.* ◊ **austerity** ◊ N UNCOUNT /ɒsˈterɪˈtiʲ/. EG *...the elegant austerity of her room.*
2 An **austere** person is strict and serious. EG *She* ADJ QUALIT *was an austere religious woman.*
3 An **austere** way of life is one that is simple and ADJ QUALIT without luxuries. EG *In these austere times, we are all having to cut back.* ◊ **austerity.** EG *...post-war* ◊ N UNCOUNT *austerity.*

Australian /ɒsˈtreɪlɪən/, **Australians. 1** Some- ADJ CLASSIF thing that is **Australian** belongs or relates to Australia, or to its people. EG *...the Australian novelist Patrick White.*
2 An **Australian** is someone who comes from N COUNT Australia.

authentic /ɔːˈθentɪk/. **1** If something such as a ADJ CLASSIF painting or piece of writing is **authentic**, it is genuine rather than being an imitation. ◊ **authenticity** /ɔːθenˈtɪsɪˈtiʲ/. EG *...paintings of* ◊ N UNCOUNT *doubtful authenticity.*
2 If information or an account is **authentic**, it is ADJ QUALIT reliable and accurate. EG *The book gives an authen- tic account of the war.* ◊ **authenticity.** EG *...the* ◊ N UNCOUNT *authenticity of Haldane's account.*

authenticate /ɔːˈθentɪkeɪt/, **authenticates,** V+O **authenticating, authenticated.** If you **authenti- cate** something, **1** you state officially that it is genuine after examining it. EG *He was responsible for authenticating the photographs.* **2** you prove or confirm that it is true. EG *These stories seem to be well authenticated.*

author /'ɔːθə/, **authors. 1** The **author** of a piece of N COUNT : writing is the person who wrote it. EG *...Bill Davies,* OFT+of *author of a new book on money.*
2 An **author** is a person whose occupation is N COUNT writing books. EG *...Simone de Beauvoir, the French author.*

authorise /'ɔːθəʳraɪz/. See **authorize.**

authoritarian /ɔːθɒrəˈteərɪən/, **authoritarians.** ADJ QUALIT Someone who is **authoritarian** wants to control other people rather than letting them decide things

Is an autobiography likely to be an authentic account of someone's life?

themselves; used showing disapproval. EG ...*authoritarian parents... ...an authoritarian regime.* ▸ used as a noun. EG *The old rulers were authoritarians.* ▸ N COUNT

authoritative /ɔːˈθɒrəˈtətɪv/. **1** Someone or something that is **authoritative** gives an impression of power and importance and is likely to be obeyed. EG ...*a deep authoritative male voice.* ADJ QUALIT
◊ **authoritatively.** EG *'Don't do that,' he said authoritatively.* ◊ ADV

2 Someone or something that is **authoritative** has a lot of knowledge of a particular subject. EG ...*in his authoritative study of the Commonwealth.* ADJ QUALIT

authority /ɔːˈθɒrəˈtiˈ/, **authorities. 1** The **authorities** are the people who have the power to make decisions, especially the government. EG *The authorities have got to clamp down on people like this.* N PLURAL : *the*+N

2 An **authority** is an official organization or government department that has the power to make decisions. EG *She sold the house to the local authority... ...the Regional Health Authorities.* N COUNT+SUPP

3 Authority is **3.1** the right to command and control other people. EG *He would be reported to those in authority... He made efforts to reassert his authority over them.* **3.2** a quality that someone has which makes other people take notice of what they say. EG *Her voice carried a note of authority.* **3.3** official permission to do something. EG *Have you been ordering taxis without signed authority?* N UNCOUNT : OFT+*over* / N UNCOUNT / N UNCOUNT

4 Someone who is an **authority** on a particular subject knows a lot about it. EG *He is an authority on India.* N COUNT : OFT+*on*

5 If you **have it on good authority** that something is true, you are fairly certain that it is true because you trust the person who told you about it. PHRASE

authorize /ˈɔːθəraɪz/, **authorizes, authorizing, authorized;** also spelled **authorise.** If someone in a position of authority **authorizes** something, they give their official permission for it to happen. EG *The president authorized the bombings... I am not authorized to approve payments.* ◊ **authorization** /ˌɔːθəraɪzeɪˈʃⁿn/. EG *They will have to phone your branch for authorization.* V+O : OFT+*to*-INF / ◊ N UNCOUNT

auto /ˈɔːtəʊ/, **autos.** An **auto** is a car. EG ...*the U.S. auto industry.* N COUNT American

autobiographical /ˌɔːtəˈbaɪəgræfɪkəⁿl/. A piece of writing that is **autobiographical** relates to events in the life of the person who has written it. ADJ CLASSIF

autobiography /ˌɔːtəˈbaɪɒgrəfiˈ/, **autobiographies.** Your **autobiography** is an account of your own life, which you write yourself. EG *She describes in her autobiography a visit to Russia in 1909.* N COUNT OR N UNCOUNT

autocracy /ɔːˈtɒkrəsiˈ/ is government or management by one person who has complete power. N UNCOUNT

autocrat /ˈɔːtəˈkræt/, **autocrats.** An **autocrat** is a person in authority who has complete power. N COUNT

autocratic /ˌɔːtəˈkrætɪk/. Someone who is **autocratic** has complete power and makes decisions without asking anyone else's advice. ADJ QUALIT

autograph /ˈɔːtəˈgrɑːf/, **autographs, autographing, autographed. 1** An **autograph** is the signature of someone famous; used especially when you have asked the person to write it for you. EG ...*boys queueing to get his autograph.* N COUNT : USU+POSS

2 If someone famous **autographs** something, they put their signature on it. ◊ **autographed.** EG *He gave me an autographed copy of his book.* V+O / ◊ ADJ CLASSIF

automate /ˈɔːtəˈmeɪt/, **automates, automating, automated.** To **automate** a factory, office, or industrial process means to install machines which can do the work instead of people. ◊ **automation** /ˌɔːtəˈmeɪʃⁿn/. EG ...*an age of high technology and automation.* V+O / ◊ N UNCOUNT

automatic /ˌɔːtəˈmætɪk/, **automatics. 1** An **automatic** machine is one which can perform a task without needing to be operated by a person. EG ...*automatic washing machines... ...automatic data processing.* ◊ **automatically.** EG *The lights come on automatically.* ADJ CLASSIF / ◊ ADV

2 A gun, car, or washing machine that is automatic or partly automatic can be called an **automatic**. N COUNT

3 An **automatic** action is one that you do without thinking about it because it has become a habit. EG ...*an automatic gesture.* ◊ **automatically.** EG *Billy found himself automatically walking up to the house.* ADJ QUALIT / ◊ ADV

4 If something such as an action or a punishment is **automatic**, it always happens as the normal result of something else. EG *These offences carry automatic fines.* ◊ **automatically.** EG *Once people retire they automatically cease to be union members.* ADJ CLASSIF / ◊ ADV

automaton /ɔːˈtɒmətən/, **automatons** or **automata** /ɔːˈtɒmətə/. If you say that someone is an **automaton**, you mean that they are so tired or bored that they act without thinking. N COUNT

automobile /ˈɔːtəməˈbiːl/, **automobiles.** An **automobile** is a car. N COUNT American

autonomous /ɔːˈtɒnəməs/. A country, organization, or group that is **autonomous** governs or controls itself rather than being controlled by anyone else. ◊ **autonomy** /ɔːˈtɒnəmiˈ/. EG *They wanted more autonomy.* ADJ QUALIT / ◊ N UNCOUNT

autopsy /ˈɔːtɒpsiˈ, ˈɔːtəˈp-/, **autopsies.** An **autopsy** is an examination of a dead body by a doctor who cuts it open in order to try to discover the cause of death. N COUNT

autumn /ˈɔːtəm/, **autumns. Autumn** is the season between summer and winter. In the autumn the weather becomes cooler. N UNCOUNT OR N COUNT

autumnal /ɔːˈtʌmnəⁿl/. Something that is **autumnal** has features that are characteristic of autumn. EG ...*autumnal browns and golds.* ADJ CLASSIF

AUX stands for **auxiliary verb**

English has three verbs which are used as auxiliaries: the verbs 'be', 'have', and 'do'.
Auxiliaries are used before a main verb to show, for example, whether it is continuous or passive. They are also used in negative clauses, and are one of the ways of forming questions. So in the sentence *She **was** eating an apple*, 'was' is an auxiliary helping to form the past continuous tense. In *He **has** never been to London*, 'has' is an auxiliary forming the present perfect tense. In *I **don't** like him*, 'do' is an auxiliary being used to form a negative clause, and in *Do you like Rome?* it is forming a question.
AUX is used in the Extra Column in the entries for 'be', 'have', and 'do' to show you where the auxiliary uses are being explained.
The modal verbs in English are also often called auxiliaries. In this dictionary we call them modal verbs, and their uses are explained in the entry headed MODAL VERBS.

---

auxiliary /ɔːɡˈzɪljəriˈ, -ləⁿriˈ/, **auxiliaries. 1** An **auxiliary** is a person who is employed to help other people. Auxiliaries are often medical workers or members of the armed forces. EG ...*nursing auxiliaries.* ▸ used as an adjective. EG ...*six auxiliary squadrons.* N COUNT / ▸ ADJ CLASSIF : ATTRIB

2 Auxiliary equipment is extra equipment that is used when necessary. EG ...*auxiliary scaffolding.* ADJ CLASSIF : ATTRIB

avail /əˈveɪl/, **avails, availing, availed. 1** If something that you do is **of no avail** or is done to little **avail**, it does not enable you to achieve what you want. EG *They were fighting to no avail... Speeches and protests were of no avail.* PHRASE

2 If you **avail** yourself of an offer or an opportunity, you accept the offer or make use of the opportunity. V-REFL+*of* Formal

available /əveɪləbəºl/. **1** If something is avail- ADJ CLASSIF
able, you are able to use it or obtain it. EG ...*the*
amount of money available for spending... Will
your accommodation be available next October?
◊ **availability** /əveɪləbɪlˈtiˈ/. EG *Laws still con-* ◊ N UNCOUNT
trolled the availability of contraceptives. OFT+*of/for*
2 Someone who is **available** is not busy and is ADJ CLASSIF
therefore free for you to talk to. EG *The MP was not*
available for comment yesterday.
avalanche /ævəlɑːntʃ/, **avalanches**. **1** An ava- N COUNT
lanche is a large mass of snow that falls down the
side of a mountain.
2 You can refer to a very large quantity of things N COUNT+SUPP
that all arrive or happen at the same time as an
avalanche of them. EG ...*an avalanche of tourists.*
avant-garde /ævɒŋɡɑːd/. **Avant-garde** art, thea- ADJ QUALIT
tre, and writing is very modern and experimental.
avarice /ævərɪs/ is extreme greed for money. N UNCOUNT
avaricious /ævərɪʃəs/. Someone who is **avari-** ADJ QUALIT
cious is very greedy for money.
avenge /əvɛndʒ/, **avenges**, **avenging**, **avenged**. V+O OR V-REFL
If you **avenge** a wrong or harmful act, you hurt or
punish the person who has done it. EG *He was*
determined to avenge his father's death... ...a desire
to avenge himself on all humanity.
avenue /ævɪˈnjuː/, **avenues**. **1 Avenue** is used in
the names of some streets. EG ...*Madison Avenue.*
2 An **avenue** is a wide road with trees on either N COUNT
side.
3 You can also use **avenue** to mean a way of N COUNT
getting something done. EG *We are exploring a*
number of avenues.
average /ævəˈrɪdʒ/, **averages**, **averaging**, **aver-**
aged. **1** An **average** is the result that you get when N COUNT
you add two or more numbers together and divide
the total by the number of numbers you added
together. EG *These pupils were examined in 39*
subjects, an average of 6.5 subjects for each pupil.
▸ used as an adjective. EG *The average age of the* ▸ ADJ CLASSIF :
group was thirty-nine years. ATTRIB
2 You use **average** to describe a person or thing in ADJ CLASSIF :
order to indicate that they are typical or normal. ATTRIB
EG *Today the average American car driver drives*
10,000 miles per year... ...a sheet of paper of aver-
age thickness.
3 An amount or quality that is the **average** is the N SING
normal amount or quality for a particular group of
things or people. EG *They have long working hours*
– 50 a week is about the average... Their language
development is below average. ▸ used as an ▸ ADJ CLASSIF
adjective. EG ...*above average inflation.*
4 Something that is **average** is neither very good ADJ QUALIT
nor very bad. EG ...*an average piece of work.*
◊ **averagely**. EG ...*an averagely attractive woman.* ◊ ADV
5 To **average** a particular amount means to do, V+C
get, or produce that amount as an average over a
period of time. EG *Price increases during these*
years averaged around 20%.
6 You say **on average** or **on an average** to ADV SEN
indicate that a number is the average of several
numbers. EG *We can discover how many words, on*
average, a person reads in a minute.
average out. When you **average out** a set of PHRASAL VB :
numbers or when it **averages out** at a particular V+ADV OR
figure, you work out the average. V+O+ADV
averse /əˈvɜːs/. If you say that you are not **averse** ADJ PRED+*to*
to something, you mean that you quite like it or Formal
quite want to do it. EG *They were not averse to*
making a little extra money.
aversion /əˈvɜːʃəºn/, **aversions**. **1** If you have an N COUNT :
aversion to someone or something, you dislike USU SING+*to*
them very much. EG *She had a great aversion to*
children.
2 An **aversion** is also something that you strongly N COUNT :
dislike. EG *His current aversion is pop music.* USU+POSS
avert /əˈvɜːt/, **averts**, **averting**, **averted**. **1** If you V+O
avert something unpleasant, you prevent it from
happening. EG *There must be immediate action if*
total chaos is to be averted.

2 If you **avert** your eyes or gaze from someone or V+O :
something, you look away from them. EG *Winifred* OFT+*from*
averted her eyes from the figure in the bed.
aviary /eɪvjəriˈ/, **aviaries**. An **aviary** is a large N COUNT
cage or covered area in which birds are kept.
aviation /eɪviɛɪʃəºn/ is the operation and produc- N UNCOUNT
tion of aircraft. EG ...*in the early days of aviation.*
avid /ævɪd/. **1** You use **avid** to describe someone ADJ QUALIT :
who is very keen and enthusiastic about something. ATTRIB
EG ...*an avid reader of movie magazines.* ◊ **avidly**. ◊ ADV
EG *Sheila reads avidly... They listened avidly.*
2 Someone who is **avid** for something is eager to ADJ PRED+*f*
get it. EG *The girls were avid for information.*
avocado /ævəˈkɑːdəʊ/, **avocados**. An **avocado** or N COUNT OR
an **avocado pear** is a tropical fruit in the shape of N UNCOUNT
a pear with a dark green skin and a large stone
inside it.
avoid /əvɔɪd/, **avoids**, **avoiding**, **avoided**. **1** If you V+O
avoid something, you take action in order to
prevent it from happening. EG ...*a book on how to*
avoid a heart attack.
2 If you **avoid** doing something, you make a V+-ING
deliberate effort not to do it. EG *Thomas turned his*
head, trying to avoid breathing in the smoke.
3 If you **avoid** someone or something, you keep V+O
away from them. EG *Joy tried to avoid her... They*
drive through the towns to avoid the motorway.
avoidable /əˈvɔɪdəbəºl/. Something that is **avoid-** ADJ CLASSIF
able can be prevented from happening. EG *Any*
avoidable risk should be avoided.
avoidance /əvɔɪdəns/. **Avoidance** of someone or N UNCOUNT
something is the act of avoiding them. EG ...*the* +SUPP
avoidance of responsibilities.
avowal /əvaʊəºl/, **avowals**. An **avowal** of some- N COUNT OR
thing is an admission or declaration of it. EG *He* N UNCOUNT
made a shy avowal of love. Formal
avowed /əvaʊd/. **1** If you are an **avowed** support- ADJ CLASSIF :
er or opponent of something, you have declared ATTRIB
that you support it or oppose it. EG *They were* Formal
avowed enemies of the British.
2 An **avowed** belief or aim is one that you hold ADJ CLASSIF :
very strongly. EG *The avowed aim of revolution-* ATTRIB
aries is to disrupt society.
avuncular /əvʌŋkjəˈlə/. A man who is **avuncular** ADJ QUALIT
acts in a friendly and helpful way towards someone Formal
younger. EG *In my best avuncular fashion I put my*
arm round her shoulder.
await /əweɪt/, **awaits**, **awaiting**, **awaited**. **1** If V+O
you **await** someone or something, you wait for
them. EG *I returned to the States to find the FBI*
awaiting me... Huey was awaiting trial for murder.
2 Something that **awaits** you is going to happen or V+O
come to you in the future. EG ...*the adventures that*
awaited him.
awake /əweɪk/, **awakes**, **awaking**, **awoke**
/əwəʊk/, **awoken** /əwəʊkəºn/. **1** Someone who is ADJ PRED
awake is not sleeping. EG *He lay awake all night.*
● Someone who is **wide awake** is fully awake. ● PHRASE
2 When you **awake** or when something **awakes** V-ERG
you, you wake up. EG *I awoke from a deep sleep.* Literary
awaken /əweɪkəºn/, **awakens**, **awakening**,
awakened. **1** To **awaken** a feeling in a person V+O
means to cause them to have this feeling. EG *My* Literary
first visit to a theatre awakened an interest which
never left me.
2 When you **awaken** to a fact or when someone V-ERG+*to*
awakens you to it, you become aware of it. EG Literary
Gradually people are awakening to their respon-
sibilities.
3 When you **awaken** or when something **awakens** V-ERG
you, you wake up. EG *He was awakened by the* Literary
sound of singing.
awakening /əweɪkəºnɪŋ/. **1** The **awakening** of a N SING :
particular feeling or realization in someone is the USU+SUPP

Are women usually described as avuncular?

start of this feeling or realization in them. EG ...*the awakening of love for another person.*

2 If you have a **rude awakening**, you are suddenly PHRASE made aware of an unpleasant fact.

award /əwˈɔːd/, **awards, awarding, awarded. 1** N COUNT An **award** is **1.1** a prize or certificate that a person is given for doing something well. EG *He won the Current Affairs Award for his radio reporting.* **1.2** a sum of money that a court of law decides should be given to someone.

2 To **award** someone something such as a prize or V+O+O a mark means to give it to them. EG *This year's* OR V+O+to *board awarded the top prize to reporter Carol Clay.*

3 If someone such as a judge or referee **awards** V+O+to, something to a person, they decide that the person V+O+O, will be given it. EG *It was the biggest libel settle-* OR V+O *ment awarded up to that time.*

aware /əwˈeə/. **1** If you are **aware** of a fact, you ADJ PRED: know about it. EG *He was aware that he had drunk* OFT+of OR *too much whisky... I was quite aware of this before* REPORT *we married... As far as I am aware, that's correct.*

◊ **awareness.** EG ...*the present public awareness of* ◊ N UNCOUNT *the need for conservation... ...an awareness that* +of OR REPORT *there was a problem.*

2 If you are **aware** of something, you realize that it ADJ PRED+of is present or is happening because you hear it, see OR REPORT it, smell it, or feel it. EG *Ralph was aware of the heat for the first time that day.*

3 Someone who is **aware** notices what is happen- ADJ QUALIT: ing around them. EG *Some people are more politi-* USU PRED *cally aware than others.* ◊ **awareness.** EG ...*the* ◊ N UNCOUNT *students' political awareness.*

away /əwˈeɪ/. **1** If you move **away** from a place, ADV AFTER VB you move so that you are no longer there. EG *He rose and walked away... I kissed her goodbye and drove away.*

2 If you look or turn **away** from something, you ADV AFTER VB move your head so that you are no longer looking at it. EG *He turned away from the window.*

3 If something is **away** from a person or place, it is ADV: at a distance from that person or place. EG ...*a* OFT+from *pleasant picnic spot away from the city... I was only four hours away from Oslo.*

4 If you put something **away**, you put it in a safe ADV AFTER VB place. EG *Tom put the book away... This work is ready to be filed away in the archives.*

5 If you are **away**, you are not in the place, such as ADV AFTER VB your home or office, where people expect you to be. EG *Is he at home or has he gone away?*

6 You also use **away** to talk about future events. ADV For example, if an event is a week **away**, it will happen in a week. EG *The debate on the Afghan crisis is only a fortnight away.*

7 If you give something **away** or if someone takes ADV AFTER VB it **away** from you, you no longer have it. EG *She gave a fortune away.*

8 When a sports team plays an **away** game, it ADJ CLASSIF: plays on its opponents' ground. ATTRIB

9 You can use **away** to say that something slowly ADV disappears, becomes less significant, or changes so that it is no longer the same. EG *The snow had all melted away... A murmur rose among the boys and died away... ...the shift away from crimes of theft.*

10 You can also use **away** to emphasize a continu- ADV AFTER VB ous or repeated action. EG *Howard was still working away in the university library... She was coughing away.*

awe /ɔː/, **awes, awed. 1 Awe** is the feeling of N UNCOUNT respect and amazement that you have when you are faced with something wonderful and often rather frightening. EG *The child stared at him in silent awe.*

2 If you **are in awe of** someone or if you **stand in** PHRASE **awe of** them, you have a lot of respect for them and are slightly afraid of them.

3 If you **are awed** by someone or something, they V+O: USU PASS make you feel amazed and often rather frightened.

◊ **awed.** EG ...*talking in an awed whisper... He took* ◊ ADJ CLASSIF: *it reluctantly, awed by the value of the gift.* OFT+by

awe-inspiring. Someone or something that is ADJ QUALIT **awe-inspiring** is amazing and rather frightening. EG *It was an awe-inspiring sight.*

awesome /ɔːsəm/. Something that is **awesome** is ADJ QUALIT very impressive and frightening. EG ...*an awesome responsibility... ...an awesome weapon.*

awe-struck. If someone is **awe-struck**, they are ADJ QUALIT very impressed and amazed by something. EG Formal ...*watching with awestruck interest.*

awful /ˈɔːfəl/. **1** If you say that something is **awful**, ADJ QUALIT you mean that it is **1.1** not very good or not very nice. EG *Isn't the weather awful?* **1.2** very unpleas- ant, shocking, or bad. EG ...*that awful war.*

2 If you look or feel **awful**, you look or feel ill. ADJ PRED

3 You can use **awful** to emphasize how large an ADJ CLASSIF: amount is. EG *It must have taken an awful lot of* ATTRIB *courage.* ◊ **awfully.** EG *She was awfully nice... I'm* ◊ SUBMOD *awfully sorry.*

awhile /əwˈaɪl/ means for a short time. EG *Can't* ADV *you just wait awhile?* Literary

awkward /ˈɔːkwəd/. **1** An **awkward** movement or ADJ QUALIT position is uncomfortable or clumsy. EG ...*an awk- ward gesture.* ◊ **awkwardly.** EG *He fell and lay* ◊ ADV *awkwardly, covered in mud.*

2 Someone who is **awkward 2.1** behaves in a shy ADJ QUALIT or embarrassed way. EG *I hated the big formal dances and felt very awkward.* ◊ **awkwardly.** EG ◊ ADV *Sonia patted her shoulder awkwardly.* ◊ **awkwardness.** EG *There was no awkwardness* ◊ N UNCOUNT *between them.* **2.2** is unreasonable and difficult to ADJ QUALIT live with or deal with.

3 A tool or machine that is **awkward** is difficult to ADJ QUALIT use. A job that is **awkward** is difficult to do. EG *It is awkward to make this recipe.*

4 A situation that is **awkward** is embarrassing and ADJ QUALIT difficult to deal with. EG *The press conference came at an awkward time for me... He asked a lot of awkward questions... McPherson started making things awkward for him.*

awning /ˈɔːnɪŋ/, **awnings.** An **awning** is a piece of N COUNT material attached to a caravan or building which provides shelter from the rain or sun.

awoke /əwˈəʊk/ is the past tense of **awake.**

awoken /əwˈəʊkən/ is the past participle of **awake.**

awry /əraɪ/. **1** If something is **awry**, it is not in its ADJ PRED normal or proper position. EG *His tie was awry.*

2 If something goes **awry**, it does not happen in the ADJ PRED way it was planned and it goes wrong. EG *Here the plan began to go awry.*

axe /æks/, **axes, axing, axed. 1** An **axe** is a tool N COUNT used for cutting wood. It consists of a blade at- tached to the end of a long handle, at the side.

2 If the government or a company **axes** something, V+O it suddenly ends it or reduces it greatly. EG *After six months the project was axed.*

axiom /ˈæksɪəm/, **axioms.** An **axiom** is a state- N COUNT ment or idea which people accept as being true. Formal

axiomatic /ˌæksɪəmˈætɪk/. If something is **axio-** ADJ PRED **matic**, it seems to be obviously true. EG *It has come* Formal *to be regarded as axiomatic that good nutrition must always imply eating expensively.*

axis /ˈæksɪs/, **axes** /ˈæksiːz/. **1** An **axis** is an N COUNT imaginary line through the middle of something. EG *The earth's axis is tilted at an angle of about 23°.*

2 An **axis** of a graph is one of the two lines on N COUNT which the scales of measurement are marked.

axle /ˈæksəl/, **axles.** An **axle** is a rod connecting a N COUNT pair of wheels on a car or other vehicle.

aye /aɪ/; also spelled **ay. 1 Aye** means yes. EG CONVENTION *'Surely that would help?' – 'Aye, we could do that.'* Scottish

2 If you vote **aye**, you vote in favour of something. ADV

azure /ˈæʒʊə, eɪ-/. Something that is **azure** is ADJ COLOUR bright blue. EG ...*the pure azure of the sky.* Literary

B b

B, b /biː/, **Bs, b's. B** is the second letter of the N COUNT
English alphabet.

B.A. /biː eɪ/, **B.A.s.** A **B.A.** is a degree in arts or N COUNT
social sciences. **B.A.** is an abbreviation for 'Bachelor of Arts'. EG *She took a B.A. in French... ...John
Adams B.A.*

babble /bæbəˀl/, **babbles, babbling, babbled. 1** V : USU + A
If you **babble**, you talk in a confused or excited OR V + QUOTE
way. EG *He babbled on about old enemies... She
babbled, 'Sonny, just send a car to bring me home.'*
▸ used as a noun. EG *...the babble of women's voices.* ▸ N SING
2 When a stream **babbles**, it makes a low, bubbling V : USU + A
sound. Literary

babe /beɪb/, **babes. 1** A **babe** is the same as a N COUNT
baby. Outdated
2 Some people use **babe** as an affectionate way of VOCATIVE
addressing someone. EG *Take it easy, babe, be* Informal
calm, she'll be all right. American

baboon /bəbuːn/, **baboons.** A **baboon** is a type of N COUNT
monkey that lives in Africa.

baby /beɪbiˀ/, **babies. 1** A **baby** is a very young N COUNT
child, especially one that cannot yet walk or talk.
2 Some people use **baby** as an affectionate way of VOCATIVE
addressing someone. EG *Con said, 'Don't worry,* Informal
baby, I'll think of something.' American

babyhood /beɪbiˀhʊd/. Your **babyhood** is the N UNCOUNT
period of your life when you were a baby.

babyish /beɪbiˀɪʃ/. Something that is **babyish** is ADJ QUALIT
suitable for a baby, or typical of a baby. EG *Don't
think that a picture book is too babyish.*

baby-sit, baby-sits, baby-sitting, baby-sat. If V
you **baby-sit** for someone, you look after their
children while they are out. EG *Students occasional-
ly baby-sit in the evenings.* ◊ **baby-sitter.** EG *Can't* ◊ N COUNT
you find a baby-sitter? ◊ **baby-sitting.** EG *Grand-* ◊ N UNCOUNT
mother helps with washing and baby-sitting.

bachelor /bætʃəˀlə/, **bachelors.** A **bachelor** is a N COUNT
man who has never married.

Bachelor of Arts, Bachelors of Arts. A **Bach-** N COUNT
elor of Arts is a person with a first degree, usually
in an arts or social science subject.

Bachelor of Science, Bachelors of Science. A N COUNT
Bachelor of Science is a person with a first
degree in a science subject.

back /bæk/, **backs, backing, backed. 1** If some- ADV AFTER VB
one moves **back**, they move in the opposite direction to the one in which they are facing or in which
they were moving before. EG *The child stepped
back nervously... She pushed back her chair... Her
head jerked back.* ● If someone moves **back and** ● PHRASE
forth, they repeatedly move in one direction and
then in the opposite direction. EG *Someone was
pacing back and forth behind the curtains.*
2 If someone or something goes **back** or is put ADV AFTER VB
back, they return to the place where they were
before. EG *I went back to the kitchen... She put it
back on the shelf.*
3 If someone or something is **back** in a particular ADV AFTER VB
state, they were in that state before and are now in
it again. EG *He went back to sleep... Things will soon
get back to normal.*
4 If you get something **back**, you get it again after ADV AFTER VB
not having it for a while. EG *You'll get the money
back... They wanted their children back.*
5 You use **back** after verbs such as 'write', 'look', ADV AFTER VB
and 'phone' to say that you write to, look at, or
phone someone after they have done the same
thing to you. EG *He looked at her, and the girl
stared back... I shall make some enquiries and call
you back.*
6 If someone or something is kept or situated **back** ADV AFTER VB
from a place, they are at a distance away from it.

EG *Police struggled to keep the crowd back... Stay
back... The house is set back from the road.*
7 If you talk or think about something that hap- ADV AFTER VB
pened **back** in the past, you are talking or thinking
about something that happened in the past. EG *I
invested in the company way back in 1971... ...a law
that goes back to the fifteenth century... Think
back to what we've said.*
8 Your **back** is the part of your body that is behind N COUNT :
you, from your neck to the top of your legs. EG *We* USU + POSS
lay on our backs under the tree.
9 The **back** of something is the side or part of it N COUNT + SUPP
that is towards the rear or farthest from the front.
The back of something is normally not used or
seen as much as the front. EG *...the back of her
hand... Sign on the back of the prescription form...
He went to the small counter at the back of the
store.* ▸ used as an adjective. EG *The back wheels* ▸ ADJ CLASSIF :
were spinning in the mud. ATTRIB
10 The **back** of a chair is the part that you lean N COUNT + SUPP
against when you sit on it.
11 A **back** road is small and has very little traffic ADJ CLASSIF :
on it. EG *...driving through back streets towards the* ATTRIB
outskirts of town.
12 Back is also used in these phrases. **12.1** If you PHRASES
are wearing something **back to front**, you are
wearing it incorrectly, with the back of it on the
front of your body. **12.2** If you do something **behind**
someone's **back**, you do it without them knowing
about it. EG *People used to laugh at him behind his
back.* **12.3** If you tell someone to **get off** your **back**, Informal
you are telling them to stop criticizing you or
putting pressure on you. EG *Just get off my back,
will you?* **12.4** If you **put** someone's **back up**, you Informal
annoy them. **12.5** If you say that you will be glad to
see the back of someone, you mean that you want
them to leave. **12.6** If you **turn** your **back on**
someone or something, you ignore them or refuse
to help them. EG *We have turned our backs on the
very principles we were elected to uphold.*
13 If a building **backs** onto something, the back of V + onto
it faces in that direction. EG *...the houses backing
onto the park.*
14 When a car **backs** or when you **back** a car, it V-ERG : USU + A
moves backwards. EG *She backed out of the drive-
way.*
15 If you **back** someone, you give them support or V + O
money. EG *The organization is backed by the U.N.*
16 If you **back** a particular person, team, or horse V + O
in a competition, you bet money that they will win.
17 See also **backing**.

back away. If you **back away**, you move away PHRASAL VB :
because you are nervous or frightened. V + ADV

back down. If you **back down**, you withdraw a PHRASAL VB :
claim or demand that you made earlier. EG *They* V + ADV
refused to back down.

back off. If you **back off**, you move away in PHRASAL VB :
order to avoid problems or a fight. V + ADV

back out. If you **back out**, you decide not to do PHRASAL VB :
something that you previously agreed to do. V + ADV

back up. 1 If you **back up** a statement, you PHRASAL VB :
supply evidence to show it is true. EG *This claim is* V + O + ADV
*backed up by the fact that every year more and
more money is being spent on arms.* **2** If you **back** V + O + ADV
someone **up, 2.1** you help and support them. **2.2** V + O + ADV
you confirm that what they are saying is true. EG
He had loyally backed up his boss. **3** See also **back-
up.**

backache /bækeɪk/ is a dull pain in your back. N UNCOUNT
backbencher /bækbentʃə/, **backbenchers.** A N COUNT
backbencher is an MP who is not a minister and British
who does not hold an official position in any party.

ackbiting /bækbaɪtɪŋ/ is the saying of unpleasant or unkind things about someone who is not present. N UNCOUNT

ackbone /bækbəʊn/, **backbones**. 1 Your backbone is the column of small linked bones along the middle of your back. N COUNT
2 The **backbone** of an organization or system is the part of it that gives it its main strength or unity. EG *Business people are the backbone of the nation.* N SING+SUPP

back-breaking work involves a lot of hard physical effort. ADJ QUALIT

ackdate /bækdeɪt/, **backdates, backdating, backdated**. If an arrangement or document is **backdated**, it is valid from a date before the date when it is completed or signed. EG ...*a 4% increase in basic pay backdated to last April.* V+O : USU PASS

ackdoor /bækdɔː/. You use **backdoor** to describe something that is done or achieved in a secret, indirect, or dishonest way. EG ...*charges of backdoor nationalization.* ADJ CLASSIF : ATTRIB

acker /bækə/, **backers**. A **backer** is someone who gives support or financial help to a person or project. EG ...*the party's chief financial backers.* N COUNT+SUPP

ackfire /bækfaɪə/, **backfires, backfiring, backfired**. 1 If a plan or project **backfires**, it has the opposite result to the one that was intended. V
2 When a motor vehicle or its engine **backfires**, it produces an explosion in the exhaust pipe. V

ackgammon /bækgæmən/ is a game for two people. You throw dice and move pieces of wood or plastic around a board marked with long triangles. N UNCOUNT

ackground /bækgraʊnd/, **backgrounds**. 1 Your background is the kind of family you come from and the kind of education you have had. EG ...*people from working-class backgrounds.* N COUNT+SUPP
2 The **background** to an event or situation consists of the facts that explain what caused it. EG ...*against a background of poor housing conditions... ...background information.* N SING+SUPP
3 The **background** also refers to 3.1 the things, shapes, or colours in a picture or scene that are less noticeable or less important and are often partly hidden by the main things or people in it. EG *In the background is a tall cypress tree... ...blue flowers on a grey background.* 3.2 sounds, such as music, which you can hear but which you are not listening to with your full attention. EG *The TV set was blaring in the background... ...background music.* N SING

ackhand /bækhænd/, **backhands**. A **backhand** is a shot in tennis or squash, which you make with your arm across your body. EG ...*a backhand return.* N COUNT

acking /bækɪŋ/, **backings**. 1 If someone or something has the **backing** of an organization or an important person, they receive support or money from that organization or person in order to do something. EG *The bid has the backing of the directors... ...secret Government backing.* N UNCOUNT +SUPP
2 A **backing** is a layer of something such as cloth, that is put onto the back of something in order to strengthen or protect it. N COUNT OR N UNCOUNT
3 The **backing** of a popular song is the music which is sung or played to accompany the main tune. N SING

acklash /bæklæʃ/. A **backlash** is a sudden, strong reaction against a tendency or recent development in society or politics. EG ...*a backlash against the Thatcher government.* N SING

acklog /bæklɒg/, **backlogs**. A **backlog** is a number of things which have not yet been done, but which need to be done. EG *There is a large backlog of cases to hear.* N COUNT : USU+*of*

ackpack /bækpæk/, **backpacks**. A **backpack** is a rucksack. N COUNT American

back pay is money which an employer owes an employee for work that he or she did in the past. N UNCOUNT

back-seat driver, **back-seat drivers**. A **back-seat driver** is a passenger in a car who repeatedly N COUNT gives advice to the driver without being asked for it.

backside /bæksaɪd/, **backsides**. Your **backside** is the part of your body that you sit on. N COUNT Informal

backstage /bæksteɪdʒ/. In a theatre, **backstage** refers to the dressing rooms and other areas behind the stage. ▸ used as an adverb. EG *He went backstage.* N UNCOUNT ▸ ADV AFTER VB

backstreet /bækstriːt/. **Backstreet** activities are carried out unofficially, secretly, and often illegally. EG ...*backstreet abortions.* ADJ CLASSIF : ATTRIB

backstroke /bækstrəʊk/ is a kind of swimming stroke that you do lying on your back. See picture at SWIMMING. N SING

back-up. 1 **Back-up** is extra help or support from people or machines which you need in order to be able to achieve what you want. EG ...*the computer back-up which each mission required.* N UNCOUNT
2 If you have something such as a second piece of equipment or set of plans as **back-up**, you have arranged for them to be available for use in case the first one does not work. EG *You can use a conventional heating system as back-up.* N UNCOUNT

backward /bækwəd/, **backwards**. When it is an adverb, the form **backwards** is normally used in British English and **backward** in American English or formal British English.
1 If you move or look **backwards**, you move or look in the direction that your back is facing. EG *He overbalanced and stepped backwards onto a coffee cup.* ▸ used as an adjective. EG ...*a backward jerk of her head... Without a backward glance, he walked away.* ADV AFTER VB ▸ ADJ CLASSIF : ATTRIB
2 If someone moves **backwards and forwards**, they repeatedly move in one direction and then in the opposite direction. EG *He ran backwards and forwards along the cliff.* PHRASE
3 If you do something **backwards**, you do it in the opposite way to the usual way. EG *Listen to the tape backwards.* ADV AFTER VB
4 If you **know** something **backwards**, you know it very well. EG *He knew their history backwards.* PHRASE
5 A **backward** country or society does not have modern industries and machines. EG ...*the backward regions of Africa and Asia.* ADJ QUALIT
6 A **backward** child has difficulty in learning. EG *I cannot make up my mind whether your son is backward or just lazy.* ADJ QUALIT

backward-looking attitudes, ideas, or actions are based on old-fashioned opinions or methods; used showing disapproval. EG ...*their backward-looking suspicion of gadgets.* ADJ QUALIT

backwater /bækwɔːtə/, **backwaters**. A **backwater** is a place or an institution that is isolated from modern ideas or influences; often used showing disapproval. EG ...*a cultural backwater.* N COUNT

backwoods /bækwʊdz/. Someone who lives in the **backwoods** lives a long way from large towns, and is isolated from modern life and modern ideas. EG ...*his great familiarity with life in the backwoods.* ▸ used as an adjective. EG ...*this tiny backwoods community.* N PLURAL ▸ ADJ CLASSIF : ATTRIB

back yard, **back yards**. A **back yard** is a small area of ground behind a house. N COUNT

bacon /beɪkən/ is salted or smoked meat which comes from the back or sides of a pig. EG ...*bacon and eggs.* N UNCOUNT

bacteria /bæktɪərɪə/ are very small organisms. Some bacteria can cause disease. N PLURAL

bacteriology /bæktɪərɪɒlədʒi/ is the science and study of bacteria. ◇ **bacteriological**. EG ...*chemical and bacteriological warfare... ...the Bacteriological Research Institute.* N UNCOUNT ◇ ADJ CLASSIF : ATTRIB

bad /bæd/, **worse** /wɜːs/, **worst** /wɜːst/. 1 Something that is **bad** is 1.1 unpleasant, harmful, or undesirable. EG *I have some very bad news... Candy is bad for your teeth... The weather was bad.* 1.2 severe or great in degree. EG *Is the pain bad?* 1.3 of an unacceptably low standard, quality, or amount. ADJ QUALIT

EG *His flat is in bad condition... ...bad management... ...bad behaviour... The light's bad.*

2 Someone who is **bad** at doing something **2.1** is not ADJ QUALIT very skilful at it. EG *I was bad at sports... ...a bad actor.* **2.2** fails to do it when they should do it. EG ADJ PRED+*at* *Students are very bad at turning up for lectures.*

3 Food that has gone **bad** has started to decay. EG ADJ PRED *The milk's gone bad.*

4 If you have a **bad** leg, heart, or eye, it is injured ADJ CLASSIF · or there is something wrong with it.

5 If you call a child a **bad** boy or a **bad** girl, you ADJ QUALIT : mean that he or she is naughty and disobedient. ATTRIB

6 If you are in a **bad** mood, you are cross and ADJ QUALIT behave unpleasantly to people. EG *The children were tired and bad-tempered.*

7 If you say that something is **not bad**, you mean ADJ PRED that it is quite good or acceptable. EG *It was an awful job, but the money wasn't bad.*

8 If you **feel bad** about something, you feel rather PHRASE sorry and sad about it.

9 If you say **'too bad'**, you are indicating in a CONVENTION rather harsh way that nothing can be done to change the situation. EG *'I want to speak to the director.' – 'Too bad,' Castle said. 'You can't.'*

10 If a situation **goes from bad to worse**, it PHRASE becomes even more unpleasant or unsatisfactory.

11 bad blood: see **blood**. ● **bad luck**: see **luck**.
● See also **worse, worst**.

bade /bæd, beɪd/ is a form of the past tense of **bid.**

badge /bædʒ/, **badges. 1** A **badge** is a small piece N COUNT of metal or cloth which you attach to your clothes. Badges often have messages or designs on them. EG *...a shirt with a company badge on the pocket.*

2 Any feature which is regarded as a sign of a N COUNT : particular quality can be referred to as a **badge of** USU+*of* that quality. EG *Wisdom is the badge of maturity.*

badger /bædʒə/, **badgers, badgering, badgered.** **1** A **badger** is a wild animal which has a white N COUNT head with two wide black stripes on it. Badgers live underground and usually come up to feed at night.

2 If you **badger** someone, you repeatedly tell them v+o to do something or repeatedly ask them questions. EG *They badgered me to take them to the circus.*

badly /bædliⁱ/, **worse** /wɜːs/, **worst** /wɜːst/. **1** If ADV something is done **badly**, it is done with very little success or effect. EG *The party did badly in the election... The room was so badly lit I couldn't see what I was doing.*

2 If someone or something is **badly** hurt or **badly** ADV affected, they are severely hurt or affected. EG *The house was badly damaged... I cut myself badly.*

3 If you need or want something **badly**, you need ADV or want it very much. EG *We need the money badly... I am badly in need of advice.*

4 You can use **badly** to say that something harms ADV the reputation of someone or something. EG *The story reflected badly on Amity.*

5 See also **worse, worst.**

badly off, worse off, worst off. 1 If you are ADJ PRED : **badly off** for something, you do not have enough USU+*for* of it.

2 If you are **badly off**, you do not have much ADJ PRED money. EG *In the cities, the poor are as badly off as they were in the villages.*

badminton /bædmɪntən/ is a game in which you N UNCOUNT use a racket to hit a small, feathered object called a shuttlecock over a high net to your opponent.

baffle /bæfəⁿl/, **baffles, baffling, baffled.** If you v+o : USU PASS are **baffled** by something, you cannot understand it or explain it. EG *I was baffled by his refusal... The TV reporters looked slightly baffled.* ◇ **baffling.** ◇ ADJ QUALIT EG *Some of these methods must be very baffling to a simple villager.*

bag /bæg/, **bags. 1** A **bag** is **1.1** a container made N COUNT of thin paper or plastic. EG *...a paper bag.* **1.2** a strong container with a handle or handles, used to carry things in. EG *He packed his bags and drove to the airport.* **1.3** a handbag. EG *She opened her bag and took out a handkerchief.*

bags

shopping bag

handbag

shoulder bag

2 A **bag** of something can refer to either the bag N PART and its contents or just to the contents. EG *Mrs Wilkins dropped her bag of plums... He ate a whole bag of sweets.*

3 If you have **bags** under your eyes, you have folds N PLURAL of skin there, usually because you have not had enough sleep.

4 If you say there is **bags** of something, you mean N PART that there is a large amount of it. If you say that Informal there are **bags** of things, you mean that there are a British large number of them. EG *There's bags of room... We've got bags of things to do before we leave.*

5 If you say that something is **in the bag**, you PHRASE mean that you are certain that you will get it or Informal achieve it.

6 a **bag of bones**: see **bone**. ● See also **mixed bag**.

baggage /bægɪdʒ/. Your **baggage** consists of the N UNCOUNT suitcases and bags that you take with you when you travel. EG *...a passenger who has lost his baggage.*

baggy /bægiⁱ/, **baggier, baggiest.** If a piece of ADJ QUALIT clothing is **baggy**, it hangs loosely on your body. EG *...a pair of baggy trousers.*

bagpipes /bægpaɪps/ are a musical instrument N PLURAL which you play by blowing air through a pipe into a leather bag, and then squeezing the bag to force the air out through other pipes. EG *...the sound of bagpipes... He played a few tunes on the bagpipes.*

bail /beɪl/, **bails, bailing, bailed;** also spelled **bale, bales, baling, baled** for paragraph 2 and for **bail out** 1.2 and 2.

1 Bail is **1.1** money that must be given to a law N UNCOUNT court before an arrested person can be released while they are waiting for their trial. EG *She was released on $2,500 bail.* **1.2** permission for an arrested person to be released after bail has been paid. EG *The judge refused to grant bail.*

2 If you **bail** water from a boat, you remove it v+o OR v : using a container. USU+A

bail out. 1 If you **bail** someone **out, 1.1** you pay PHRASAL VB bail on their behalf. **1.2** you help them out of a v+o+ADV difficult situation. **2** If you **bail out** of an aircraft, v+ADV you jump out of it with a parachute because the aircraft is likely to crash.

bailiff /beɪlɪf/, **bailiffs.** A **bailiff** is **1** a law officer N COUNT who makes sure that the decisions of a court are British obeyed. EG *The bailiffs had arrived.* **2** a person who

Should you drive a car if the tyres are bald?

is employed to look after land or property for the owner.

bait /beɪt/, **baits, baiting, baited. 1 Bait** is food N UNCOUNT
which you put on a hook or in a trap in order to
catch fish or animals.

2 When you **bait** a hook or trap, you put bait on it V+O
or in it.

3 A person or thing that is being used as **bait** is N SING
being used to tempt or encourage someone to do
something. EG *He's using my papers as a bait.*

4 If you **bait** someone, you deliberately try to make V+O
them angry by teasing them. EG *Lucy seemed to
take a delight in baiting him.*

5 If you **rise to the bait** or **take the bait**, you PHRASE
react angrily to someone who is teasing you. EG *I
knew that she, if anyone, would rise to the bait and
argue.*

baize /beɪz/ is a thick, green, woollen material N UNCOUNT
used for covering snooker tables and card tables.

bake /beɪk/, **bakes, baking, baked. 1** When you V OR V-ERG
bake food or when it **bakes**, you cook it in an oven
without using extra liquid or fat. EG *She said she
would bake a cake... Mrs Burns was baking: it was
Lionel's day off... ...while the souffle was baking.*

◊ **baked.** EG *...baked potatoes.* ◊ ADJ CLASSIF

2 When earth or clay **bakes**, it becomes hard and V-ERG
dry because of the heat of the sun. EG *The ground
was baked hard.*

3 See also **baking.**

baked beans are haricot beans cooked in tomato N PLURAL
sauce. They are usually sold in tins.

baker /beɪkə/, **bakers. 1** A **baker** is a person N COUNT
whose job is to bake and sell bread, rolls, and
cakes.

2 You can refer to a shop where bread and cakes N SING
are sold as the **baker** or the **baker's.** EG *I saw her
at the baker's yesterday.*

bakery /beɪkə⁰riː/, **bakeries.** A **bakery** is a build- N COUNT
ing where bread, rolls, and cakes are baked.

baking /beɪkɪŋ/. **1 Baking** is the activity of mak- N UNCOUNT
ing bread, rolls, and cakes.

2 If you say that a place is **baking**, you mean that ADJ CLASSIF
it is very hot indeed. EG *He stared out across the* Informal
baking roofs of Rome.

balance /bæləns/, **balances, balancing, balanced. 1** If a person or thing **balances** or **is** V-ERG:
balanced, they are steady and do not fall over. EG OFT+*on*
*An ashtray was balanced on the arm of her chair...
Balancing on one leg is an excellent exercise.*

2 Balance is **2.1** the steadiness that someone or N UNCOUNT
something has when they are balanced on some-
thing. EG *She lost her balance.* **2.2** a situation in N SING+SUPP
which all the different things involved are equal or
correct in size, strength, or importance. EG *...the
ecological balance of the lake... They had given the
country a unique balance of freedom and order.*

3 If you **balance** one thing with another or if V+O OR
several things **balance** each other, each of the V+O+*with*:
things has the same weight, strength, or impor- RECIP
tance. EG *Any escapism in the magazine is balanced
by more practical items.*

4 In a game or contest, if the **balance** swings in N SING: *the*+N
your favour, you start winning. EG *Competition was
keen, and the balance swung this way and that.*

5 To **balance** a budget or **balance** the books V-ERG
means to make sure that the amount of money that
is spent is not greater than the amount that is
received. EG *I just couldn't get the books to balance.*

6 The **balance** in your bank account is the amount N COUNT
of money you have in it.

7 Balance is also used in these phrases. **7.1** If you PHRASES
are **off balance**, you are in an unsteady position
and about to fall. EG *I pulled her off balance and she
slipped down.* **7.2** If a person or group **holds the
balance of power** in a situation, that person or
group will be able to win. **7.3** If something is **in the
balance**, it is uncertain whether it will happen or
continue. EG *The destiny of our race lies in the
balance.* **7.4** You can say **on balance** to indicate

that you are stating an opinion only after considering all the relevant facts or arguments. EG *On
balance, he felt he had at least a month.*

balanced /bælənst/. **1** A **balanced** account or ADJ QUALIT
report presents information in a fair and reason-
able way. EG *...a balanced summary of the debate.*

2 Something that is **balanced** is pleasing or benefi- ADJ QUALIT
cial because its parts have been used or arranged
skilfully and in the correct proportions. EG *...a
beautifully balanced play... ...a balanced diet.*

balcony

balcony /bælkəniː/, **balconies. 1** A **balcony** is a N COUNT
platform which is on the outside of a building and
has a wall or railing around it. EG *The Queen
appeared on the balcony.*

2 The **balcony** in a theatre or cinema is an area of N COUNT
seats upstairs.

bald /bɔːld/, **balder, baldest. 1** Someone who is ADJ QUALIT
bald has little or no hair on the top of their head.
EG *You're going bald... He has a large bald patch.*

◊ **baldness.** EG *I think you'll suffer from early* ◊ N UNCOUNT
baldness.

2 A tyre that is **bald** has become very smooth and ADJ QUALIT
is no longer safe to use.

3 A **bald** statement, question, or account has no ADJ QUALIT:
unnecessary words in it. EG *The bald fact is that the* ATTRIB
first ten years were wasted. ◊ **baldly.** EG *Stated* ◊ ADV
*baldly like this, these comments seem rather obvi-
ous.*

balding /bɔːldɪŋ/. Someone who is **balding** is ADJ CLASSIF
becoming bald. EG *...a trim, balding man in his early
60's.*

bale /beɪl/, **bales, baling, baled. 1** A **bale** is a N COUNT
large quantity of something such as cloth, paper, or OR N PART
hay, tied into a tight bundle. EG *...bales of old
newspaper.*

2 Bale can be used as a verb: see **bail.**

baleful /beɪlfʊl/. Something that is **baleful** is ADJ CLASSIF
likely to have harmful effects, or expresses some- Literary
one's harmful intentions. EG *We saw his baleful eye
fixed on us.* ◊ **balefully.** EG *He glared at me* ◊ ADV
balefully as I entered.

balk /bɔːlᵏk/, **balks, balking, balked;** also spelled V: OFT+*at*
baulk. If you **balk** at something, you are very
reluctant to do it or to let it happen. EG *I balked at
cleaning the lavatory.*

ball /bɔːl/, **balls. 1** A **ball** is **1.1** a round object that N COUNT
is used in games such as tennis, cricket, and
football. EG *...a golf ball.* **1.2** something that has a N COUNT
round shape. EG *...a ball of wool... He rolled the* OR N PART
socks into a ball.

2 The **ball** of your foot or the **ball** of your thumb is N COUNT+*of*
the rounded part where your toes join your foot or
where your thumb joins your hand.

3 A **ball** is also a large, formal, social event at N COUNT
which people dance.

4 Ball is used in these phrases. **4.1** If you **are** PHRASES
having a ball, you are having a very enjoyable Informal

time. **4.2** If someone is **on the ball**, they are very alert and aware of what is happening. **4.3** If you are willing to **play ball** with someone, you are willing to do what they want you to do. **4.4** If you **start the ball rolling**, **set the ball rolling**, or **keep the ball rolling**, you start something happening or make sure that it keeps happening. EG *The banks set the ball rolling when they reduced their lending rates.*

ballad /bæləd/, **ballads.** A **ballad** is a long song or N COUNT poem which tells a story in simple language.

ballast /bæləst/ consists of a substance such as N UNCOUNT sand, iron, or water when it is used in ships or hot-air balloons to make them heavier and more stable.

ball bearing, ball bearings. Ball bearings are N COUNT small metal balls placed between the moving parts of a machine to make the parts move smoothly.

ballerina /bæləriːnə/, **ballerinas.** A **ballerina** is N COUNT a woman ballet dancer.

ballet /bæleɪ, bæleɪ/, **ballets. 1 Ballet** is a type of N UNCOUNT very skilled and artistic dancing with carefully planned movements. EG *...a ballet dancer.*
2 A **ballet** is an artistic work that is performed by N COUNT ballet dancers. EG *...a ballet by Michel Fokine.*

ball game, ball games. 1 A **ball game** is a N COUNT baseball match. American
2 If you say that a situation is **a whole new ball** PHRASE **game**, you mean that it is completely different Informal from the previous one or from any that you have ever experienced before.

ballistics /bəlɪstɪks/. **Ballistics** is the study of N UNCOUNT the movement of objects that are shot or thrown through the air.

balloon /bəluːn/, **balloons, ballooning, bal-** N COUNT **looned. 1** A **balloon** is **1.1** a small, thin, rubber bag that you blow air into so that it becomes larger and rounder or longer. Balloons are used as toys or decorations. **1.2** a large, strong bag filled with gas or hot air, which can carry passengers in a basket or compartment underneath it.
2 When something **balloons**, it quickly becomes V bigger in size and rounder in shape. EG *She crossed the park, her skirt ballooning in the wind.*

ballot /bælət/, **ballots, balloting, balloted. 1** A N COUNT **ballot** is a secret vote in which people select a candidate in an election, or express their opinion about something. ● If someone is elected **by** ● PHRASE **ballot**, they are chosen by the people voting in a ballot. EG *Committee members were picked by ballot.*
2 If you **ballot** a group of people, you find out what V+O they think about a subject by organizing a secret vote. ◊ **balloting.** EG *Balloting takes place next* ◊ N UNCOUNT *month.*

ballot box, ballot boxes. 1 A **ballot box** is the N COUNT box into which ballot papers are put after people have voted.
2 You can also refer to the system of democratic N SING : the+N elections as the **ballot box.** EG *Social change can be achieved through the ballot-box.*

ballot paper, ballot papers. A **ballot paper** is a N COUNT piece of paper on which you indicate your choice or opinion on a ballot.

ballpoint /bɔːlpɔɪnt/, **ballpoints.** A **ballpoint** or a N COUNT **ballpoint pen** is a pen with a small metal ball at the end which transfers the ink from the pen onto a surface.

ballroom /bɔːlruːm/, **ballrooms.** A **ballroom** is a N COUNT very large room that is used for dancing or for formal balls.

ballroom dancing is a type of dancing in which N UNCOUNT a man and a woman dance together, using fixed sequences of steps and movements.

balustrade /bæləstreɪd/, **balustrades.** A **balus-** N COUNT **trade** is a railing or wall on a balcony or staircase.

bamboo /bæmbuː/, **bamboos. 1 Bamboo** is a tall N UNCOUNT tropical plant with hard, hollow stems. The young OR N COUNT shoots of the plant can be eaten.

2 Bamboo also refers to the stems of the plant, N UNCOUNT which are used for making furniture and other things. EG *...a bamboo fence.*

bamboozle /bæmbuːzəl/, **bamboozles, bamboo-** V+O : OFT+A **zling, bamboozled.** If you **bamboozle** someone, Informal you confuse them and often trick them. EG *Their sermons were intended to bamboozle the workers into obedience.*

ban /bæn/, **bans, banning, banned. 1** If some- V+O : USU PA thing is **banned**, it is not allowed to be done, shown, or used. EG *His play was banned by the BBC... The treaty bans all nuclear tests.* ▶ used as a ▶ N COUNT : noun. EG *There was no ban on smoking.* OFT+on
2 If you **are banned** from doing something, you V+O : USU are officially prevented from doing it. EG *He was* PASS+from *banned from driving.*

banal /bənɑːl/. Something that is **banal** is so ADJ QUALIT ordinary that it is not at all effective or interesting. EG *Janis could make the most banal songs sound intensely personal.* ◊ **banality** /bənælɪtiˀ/. EG ◊ N UNCOUN *Throughout the film, there are moments of banal-ity.*

banana /bənɑːnə/, **bananas. 1** A **banana** is a long N COUNT OR curved fruit with a yellow skin and cream-coloured N UNCOUNT flesh. EG *...a bunch of bananas.*
2 If you say that someone is **bananas**, you mean ADJ PRED that they are silly or mad. EG *You didn't save any of* Informal *it? You must be bananas.*

band /bænd/, **bands, banding, banded. 1** A **band** N COUNT is **1.1** a group of musicians who play jazz, rock, or pop music. EG *...a rock band.* **1.2** a group of musi-cians who play brass or percussion instruments. EG *He played the cornet in the school band.* **1.3** a group of people who have joined together because they share an interest or belief. EG *...a small band of revolutionaries.*
2 A **band** is also **2.1** a flat, narrow strip of cloth N COUNT which you wear round your head or wrists, or which forms part of a piece of clothing. EG *...a panama hat with a red band.* **2.2** a strip of N COUNT+SU something such as colour or light which contrasts with the areas on either side of it. EG *...a band of sunlight.* **2.3** a range of numbers or values within a N COUNT+SU system of measurement. EG *...a very wide band of radio frequencies.*

band together. If people **band together**, they PHRASAL VB meet and act as a group in order to try and achieve V-ERG+ADV something. EG *Everywhere women banded together to talk about liberation.*

bandage /bændɪdʒ/, **bandages, bandaging, bandaged. 1** A **bandage** is a long strip of cloth N COUNT which is wrapped around a wounded part of some-one's body to protect it. EG *She was wearing a bandage round her head.*
2 If you **bandage** a wound or part of someone's V+O body, you tie a bandage around it. ◊ **bandaged.** EG ADJ CLASSIF *...a man with a bandaged arm.*

bandit /bændɪt/, **bandits.** A **bandit** is an armed N COUNT robber. Outdated

bandstand /bændstænd/, **bandstands.** A **band-** N COUNT **stand** is a platform with a roof where a military band or a brass band can play in the open air.

bandwagon /bændwægən/. If you say that some- PHRASE one has **jumped on the bandwagon**, you mean that they have become involved in an activity or cause because it has become fashionable and they hope to gain some advantage from it.

bandy /bændiˀ/, **bandies, bandying, bandied.** If V+O+A : ideas or words **are bandied** about or around, they OFT PASS are mentioned or used by a lot of people. EG *Various suggestions were bandied around... The words dedication and loyalty are bandied about.*

bandy-legged Someone who is **bandy-legged** ADJ QUALIT has legs which curve outwards at the knees.

If you have done everything bar the ironing, have you anything still to do?

bang /bæŋ/, **bangs, banging, banged. 1** A **bang** N COUNT
is a loud noise such as the noise of an explosion. EG
*Walking across the street, we heard a bang... She
slammed the drawer shut with a bang.* ● **Bang** is CONVENTION
used in speech and writing to represent a loud
noise. EG *Bang! There's an explosion behind us...
Bang! Bang! go the guns.*
2 If you **bang** a door or if it **bangs**, it closes V-ERG : OFT+A
violently with a loud noise. EG *She banged the door
hard behind her... The door of the cafe banged
shut.*
3 If you **bang** on something or if you **bang** it, you V+A OR
hit it so that it makes a loud noise. EG *He banged on* V+O+A
the door angrily... I banged the desk with my fist.
4 If you **bang** part of your body against something, V-ERG : USU+A
you accidentally knock into it and hurt yourself. EG
I bang my head against it every time. ▸ used as a ▸ N COUNT
noun. EG *Did you suffer any bangs or bumps?*
5 Bang is also used in these phrases. **5.1** If PHRASES
something goes **with a bang**, it is very successful. Informal
5.2 If you say **bang goes** something, you mean that
it is now obvious that it cannot succeed or be
achieved. EG *Bang goes the Massachusetts vote!*
6 If you say that something is **bang** in a particular ADV+PREP
position, you mean that it is in exactly that posi- Informal
tion. EG *Emory University is bang in the middle of
Atlanta.*
bang down. If you **bang** something **down**, you PHRASAL VB :
put it down violently so that it makes a loud noise. V+O+ADV
EG *He banged down the phone... I heard Marvin
bang his files down hard onto the desk.*
banger /bæŋə/, **bangers.** A **banger** is **1** a N COUNT
sausage. EG *...bangers and mash.* **2** an old car that is Informal
in bad condition. **3** a small firework that makes a British
loud noise.
bangle /bæŋgəl/, **bangles.** A **bangle** is a decorat- N COUNT
ed bracelet or band that you can wear round your
wrist or ankle.
banish /bænɪʃ/, **banishes, banishing, banished.**
1 If someone **is banished**, they are punished by V+O : USU PASS
being sent away from the country where they live.
◇ **banishment** /bænɪʃmənt/. EG *They ordered the* ◇ N UNCOUNT
banishment of political and tribal leaders.
2 If someone or something **is banished** from a V+O+A :
place or situation, they are got rid of or are USU PASS
prevented from remaining in it. EG *The secretaries
were banished to another room... Tobacco had
been banished from polite society... Ignorance can
be banished only by communication.*
3 If you **banish** something from your thoughts, you V+O
stop thinking or worrying about it. EG *He could not
banish his anxieties.*
banister /bænɪstə/, **banisters;** also spelled **ban-** N COUNT
nister. A **banister** is a rail supported by posts and
fixed along the side of a staircase.
banjo /bænd͡ʒəʊ/, **banjos** or **banjoes.** A **banjo** is a N COUNT
musical instrument with a circular body and four
or more strings.
bank /bæŋk/, **banks, banking, banked. 1** A **bank** N COUNT
is a place where you can keep your money in an
account. EG *You should ask your bank for a loan.*
2 You use **bank** to mean a store of something. For N COUNT+SUPP
example, a blood **bank** or a data **bank** is a store of
blood or a store of data that is kept ready for use.
3 A **bank** is also **3.1** the raised ground along the N COUNT
edge of a river or lake. EG *...the river bank.* **3.2** a N COUNT+SUPP
long high row or mass of something. EG *...a bank of
fog.*
bank on. If you **bank on** something happening, PHRASAL VB :
you expect it to happen and rely on it happening. V+PREP
EG *He may come, but I'm not banking on it.*
bank account, bank accounts. A **bank account** N COUNT
is an arrangement with a bank which allows you to
keep your money in the bank and to withdraw it
when you need it.
banker /bæŋkə/, **bankers.** A **banker** is someone N COUNT
involved in banking at a senior level.
bank holiday, bank holidays. A **bank holiday** is N COUNT
a public holiday. EG *...August Bank Holiday.* British

banking /bæŋkɪŋ/ is the business activity of banks N UNCOUNT
and similar institutions.
banknote /bæŋknəʊt/, **banknotes.** A **banknote** is N COUNT
a piece of paper money. EG *...a roll of banknotes.*
bankrupt /bæŋkrəᵖpt/, **bankrupts, bank-
rupting, bankrupted. 1** People or organizations ADJ CLASSIF
that are **bankrupt** do not have enough money to
pay their debts. EG *The company has gone bank-
rupt.* ◇ **bankruptcy** /bæŋkrəᵖptsiː/. EG *A really* ◇ N UNCOUNT
big strike will throw the firm into bankruptcy.
2 To **bankrupt** a person or organization means to V+O
make them go bankrupt. EG *...contracts which
would bankrupt the company.*
3 A **bankrupt** is a person who has been legally N COUNT
declared bankrupt and is not allowed to take part
in some kinds of business activities.
4 Something that is **bankrupt** is completely lack- ADJ CLASSIF
ing in a particular quality. EG *...the mindless, intellectually bankrupt leadership.* ◇ **bankruptcy.** EG ◇ N UNCOUNT :
...the moral bankruptcy of our industrial economy. USU+SUPP
bank statement, bank statements. A **bank** N COUNT
statement is a list of all the money transactions
into and out of a bank account.
banner /bænə/, **banners.** A **banner** is a long strip N COUNT
of cloth with a message or slogan on it. Banners
can be carried by people or stretched across a
street. EG *Crowds filled the streets carrying banners.*
bannister /bænɪstə/. See **banister.**
banquet /bæŋkwɪt/, **banquets.** A **banquet** is a N COUNT
grand formal dinner.
banter /bæntə/ is teasing or joking talk that is N UNCOUNT
amusing and friendly.
baptism /bæptɪzəᵐm/, **baptisms.** A **baptism** is a N COUNT OR
Christian ceremony in which a person is baptized. N UNCOUNT
baptize /bæptaɪz/, **baptizes, baptizing, bap-** V+O : USU PASS
tized; also spelled **baptise.** When someone **is
baptized**, water is sprinkled on them or they are
immersed in water as a sign that they have become a member of a Christian Church.
bar /bɑː/, **bars, barring, barred. 1** A **bar** is **1.1** N COUNT
especially in America, a place where you can buy
and drink alcoholic drinks. EG *Norris was drinking
at a bar in San Francisco.* **1.2** especially in Britain, N COUNT :
a room in a pub or hotel where alcoholic drinks are USU the+N
served. EG *He called for the menu and ordered in
the bar while they were finishing their drinks.* **1.3** N COUNT :
a counter on which alcoholic drinks are served. EG USU the+N
Sally serves behind the bar.
2 A **bar** is also **2.1** a long, straight, rigid piece of N COUNT
metal. EG *...an iron bar... We beat on the bars of our
cells.* **2.2** a roughly rectangular piece of something. N COUNT+SUPP
EG *...a bar of chocolate... ...a bar of soap.*
3 If you say that someone is **behind bars**, you PHRASE
mean that they are in prison. Informal
4 If you **bar** someone's way, you prevent them V+O
from going somewhere or entering a place, by
blocking their path. EG *I turned to go. Stryker
barred my way... Once inside, we barred the door.*
5 If you **bar** someone from a place or from doing V+O :
something, you officially forbid them to go there or OFT+*from*
to do it. EG *Demands were made for the leader of
the sect to be barred from Britain... ...restrictions
barring the use of US-supplied weapons.*
6 If something is a **bar** to doing a particular thing, N COUNT+SUPP
it prevents someone from doing it. EG *This need not
be a bar to success.*
7 You can use **bar** when you mean 'except'. For PREP
example, all the work **bar** the washing means all Formal
the work except the washing. EG *Every woman, bar
the very young, can produce tales of this sort.*
8 In music, a **bar** is one of the several short parts N COUNT
of the same length into which a piece of music is
divided.
9 See also **barring.**
barb /bɑːb/, **barbs.** A **barb** is **1** a sharp curved N COUNT
point on the end of an arrow or fish-hook. **2** an N COUNT :
unkind remark. USU+SUPP

barbarian /bɑːbeərɪən/, **barbarians**. **Barbar- N COUNT
ians** were members of wild and violent tribes in
former times.

barbaric /bɑːbærɪk/. If you describe a person or ADJ QUALIT
their behaviour as **barbaric**, you mean that they
are extremely cruel. EG ...*the barbaric sport of
hunting.*

barbarism /bɑːbərɪzə⁰m/ is behaviour which is N UNCOUNT
extremely rough or cruel. EG *War is barbarism.*

barbarous /bɑːbərəs/. Something that is **barba- ADJ QUALIT
rous** is **1** rough and uncivilized. EG *Everything
looked primitive and barbarous.* **2** extremely cruel.
EG ...*the most barbarous atrocities.*

barbecue /bɑːbɪkjuː/, **barbecues**. A **barbecue** is N COUNT
1 a grill that you use to cook food outdoors. **2** an
outdoor party at which people eat food cooked on a
barbecue.

barbed /bɑːbd/. A **barbed** remark or joke seems ADJ QUALIT
humorous or polite, but contains a cleverly hidden
criticism. EG ...*a barbed compliment.*

barbed wire

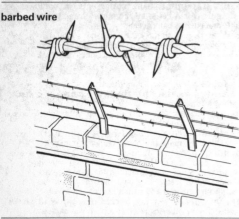

barbed wire is strong wire with sharp points N UNCOUNT
sticking out of it, which is used to make fences. EG
*This fence had barbed wire along the top and
carried a metal notice.*

barber /bɑːbə/, **barbers**. **1** A **barber** is a man N COUNT
who cuts men's hair.

2 You can refer to the shop or place where a N SING
barber works as the **barber's**. EG *He went to the
barber's to please his mother.*

bare /beə/, **barer, barest; bares, baring, bared.**

1 If a part of your body is **bare**, it is not covered by ADJ CLASSIF
any clothing. EG ...*her bare feet.* ● If someone does ● PHRASE
something **with** their **bare hands**, they do it
without using any weapons or tools. EG *He killed
those two men with his bare hands.*

2 If a surface is **bare**, it is not covered or decorated ADJ CLASSIF
with anything. EG *The doctor stood uneasily on the
bare floor... The walls were bare.*

3 If a tree or a branch is **bare**, it has no leaves on ADJ CLASSIF
it. EG *The trees were almost bare.*

4 If a room, cupboard, or shelf is **bare**, it is empty. ADJ QUALIT
EG *Inside the dairy, the counters and shelves were
bare.*

5 If you talk about the **bare** minimum or the **bare** ADJ QUALIT :
essentials, you mean the very least that is neces- ATTRIB
sary. EG *She packed the barest minimum of clothing.*

6 If you **bare** something, you uncover it. EG *She* V+O
bared her teeth.

bareback /beəbæk/. If you ride **bareback**, you ADV AFTER VB
ride a horse without a saddle. EG *She galloped
bareback down the road towards the village.*

barefoot /beəfʊt/. Someone who is **barefoot** or ADJ CLASSIF
barefooted is not wearing anything on their feet.
EG ...*a thin, barefooted boy with straw-coloured*

hair. ► used as an adverb. EG *She ran barefoot* ► ADV AFTER
through the field. VB

barely /beəli¹/. If something is **barely** true or ADV BRD NEG
possible, it is only just true or possible. EG *He was so
drunk that he could barely stand... It was barely
two months old.*

bargain /bɑːgɪn/, **bargains, bargaining, bargained. 1** A **bargain** is a business agreement in N COUNT
which two people or groups agree what each of
them will do, pay, or receive. EG *We shook hands on
the bargain.*

2 When people **bargain** with each other, they V : OFT
discuss what each of them will do, pay, or receive. + with/for
EG *Trade unions bargain with employers for better
conditions.* ◊ **bargaining**. EG ...*the kind of bargain-* ◊ N UNCOUNT
ing that goes on in industry.

3 A **bargain** is also something which is sold at a N COUNT
low price and which you think is good value for the
money. EG *He couldn't resist a bargain... ...bargain
prices.*

4 When you are adding an extra piece of informa- PHRASE
tion to a statement and you want to emphasize it,
you can say **into the bargain**. EG *She was an
exceptional mathematician and an unusually beautiful one into the bargain.*

bargain for. If you say that someone had not PHRASAL VB :
bargained for something, you mean that they did V+PREP,
not expect it to happen. EG *They had not bargained* HAS PASS
for such opposition.

barge /bɑːdʒ/, **barges, barging, barged. 1** If you V+A OR
barge into a place, you rush or push into it in a V+O+A
rough and rude way. EG *Arthur barged into the* Informal
garden... ...barging his way through the crowd.

2 If you **barge** into someone, you bump against V+*into*
them roughly and rudely while you are walking. Informal

3 A **barge** is a boat with a flat bottom. Barges are N COUNT
used for carrying heavy loads, especially on canals.

barge in. If you **barge in**, you rudely interrupt PHRASAL VB :
what someone else is doing or saying. EG *I'm sorry* V+ADV
to barge in on you like this. Informal

barge pole. If you say that you **wouldn't touch** PHRASE
someone or something **with a barge pole**, you Informal
mean that you do not want to have anything to do British
with them because you think that they are untrustworthy or unreliable.

baritone /bærɪtəʊn/, **baritones**. A **baritone** is a N COUNT
man with a fairly deep singing voice.

bark /bɑːk/, **barks, barking, barked. 1** When a V
dog **barks**, it makes a short, loud noise, once or
several times. EG *The dogs began to bark.* ► used as ► N COUNT
a noun. EG *His spaniel gave a sudden bark.*

2 If you **bark** at someone, you shout at them in a V OR V+O
loud, rough voice. EG *He barked an order at us...* OFT +at;
'Shut up!' Caldwell barked. ALSO V+QUOTE

3 Bark is the tough material that covers the N UNCOUNT
outside of a tree.

4 If you say that someone **is barking up the** PHRASE
wrong tree, you mean that they will not succeed Informal
in what they are trying to do.

5 If you say that someone's **bark is worse than** PHRASE
their **bite**, you mean that they are not as unpleas- Informal
ant or as hostile as they seem to be.

barley /bɑːli¹/ is **1** a tall, grass-like plant that is N UNCOUNT
grown for food and for the production of beer and
whisky. **2** the grain produced by this plant.

barmaid /bɑːmeɪd/, **barmaids**. A **barmaid** is a N COUNT
woman who serves drinks in a bar or pub.

barman /bɑːmə³n/, **barmen**. A **barman** is a man N COUNT
who serves drinks in a bar or pub.

barmy /bɑːmi¹/, **barmier, barmiest**. Someone or ADJ QUALIT
something that is **barmy** is slightly mad or very Informal
foolish. EG *The old woman's very rich and quite* British
barmy... The whole scheme seems barmy to me.

barn /bɑːn/, **barns**. A **barn** is a large building on a N COUNT
farm in which crops or animal food can be kept.

> If your fridge is bare, what have you got in it?

barnacle /bɑːnəkəl/, **barnacles. Barnacles** are small shellfish that fix themselves tightly to rocks and the bottoms of boats. N COUNT

barometer /bərɒmɪtə/, **barometers. 1** A barometer is an instrument that measures air pressure and shows when the weather is changing. N COUNT

2 When something indicates what people's feelings are about a situation, you can describe it as a **barometer** of their feelings. EG *The recent press statements have been the most telling barometer of the government's anxiety.* N COUNT+SUPP

baron /bærən/, **barons. 1** A baron is a man who is a member of the nobility. N COUNT

2 You can use **baron** to refer to someone who controls a large amount of a particular industry and who is therefore extremely powerful. EG *...the press barons... ...oil and wheat barons.* N COUNT+SUPP

baroness /bærənɪs/, **baronesses.** A baroness is a woman who has the same rank as a baron, or who is the wife of a baron. N COUNT

baronet /bærənɪt/, **baronets.** A baronet is a man who is given the honorary British title 'baronet' by the King or Queen, and can pass the title on to his son. N COUNT

baronial /bərəʊnɪəl/ means belonging or relating to a baron or barons. ADJ CLASSIF

baroque /bərɒk, bərəʊk/. **1 Baroque** art is an elaborate style of art that was used in Europe from the late 16th to the early 18th century. ADJ CLASSIF: ATTRIB

2 Baroque music is a style of European music that was written in the 18th century. ADJ CLASSIF: ATTRIB

barrack /bærək/, **barracks, barracking, barracked. 1** If you **barrack** someone, you shout loudly in order to interrupt them when they are making a speech. ◊ **barracking.** EG *The barracking was led by a bearded man in jeans.* V OR V+O ◊ N UNCOUNT

2 A **barracks** is a building or group of buildings where soldiers or other members of the armed forces live and work. The plural form is also **barracks.** EG *...soldiers from the nearby barracks.* N COUNT

barrage /bærɑːʒ/, **barrages.** If you get a lot of questions or complaints about something, you can say that you are getting a **barrage** of them. EG *His comments provoked a barrage of criticism... She faced a barrage of queries and complaints.* N COUNT+SUPP

barred /bɑːd/. **1 Barred** is the past tense and past participle of **bar.**

2 A **barred** window or door has bars on it to prevent people from getting into or out of a room. ADJ CLASSIF

barrel /bærəl/, **barrels. 1** A barrel is a round container for liquids. Barrels are wider in the middle than at the top and bottom and are usually made of wood. EG *...a wine barrel.* N COUNT

2 You can use **barrel** to refer to the contents of a barrel. EG *...a barrel of beer.* N PART

3 If you say that you are **scraping the barrel**, you mean that you are having to use people or things of the poorest quality because all the better ones have already been used. PHRASE Informal

4 The **barrel** of a gun is the long, cylindrical part through which the bullet moves when the gun is fired. N COUNT

5 lock, stock, and barrel: see **lock.**

barren /bærən/. **1 Barren** land has soil of such poor quality that plants cannot grow on it. ADJ CLASSIF

2 A **barren** woman is unable to have babies. EG *After twenty years of marriage, she remained barren.* ADJ CLASSIF Outdated

barricade /bærɪkeɪd/, **barricades, barricading, barricaded. 1** A barricade is a line of vehicles or other objects placed across a road or passage to stop people getting past. EG *They refused to man the barricades during the uprising.* ▸ used as a verb. EG *They were barricading the house... ...barricaded roads.* N COUNT ▸ V+O

2 If you **barricade** yourself inside a room or building, you put something heavy against the door so that other people cannot get in. EG *We rushed* V-REFL+A OR V+O+A

into the bedroom and barricaded ourselves in... They barricaded themselves behind concrete slabs.

barrier /bærɪə/, **barriers. 1** A barrier is a fence or wall that prevents people or things from moving from one area to another. EG *They were on different sides of a high barrier... Show your tickets at the barrier, please.* N COUNT

2 A **barrier** is also a problem that prevents two people or groups from agreeing or communicating with each other. EG *They have helped to break down the old barriers between the two parties.* N COUNT

3 A **barrier** to the happening or achievement of something is something that makes it difficult or impossible for it to happen or to be achieved. EG *Pollution is not a barrier to future economic growth.* N COUNT: OFT+to

barring /bɑːrɪŋ/. You use **barring** to indicate that the person, thing, or event that you are mentioning is an exception to your general statement. EG *It is hard to imagine anyone, barring a lunatic, starting a war.* PREP

barrister /bærɪstə/, **barristers.** A barrister is a lawyer who speaks in the higher courts of law on behalf of either the defence or the prosecution. N COUNT British

barrow /bærəʊ/, **barrows.** A barrow is **1** a wheelbarrow. **2** a cart from which fruit or other goods are sold in the street. N COUNT

bartender /bɑːtendə/, **bartenders.** A bartender is a person who serves drinks in a bar. N COUNT American

barter /bɑːtə/, **barters, bartering, bartered.** If you **barter** goods, you exchange them for other goods, rather than selling them for money. EG *They bring meat, grain, and vegetables to sell or barter.* ▸ used as a noun. EG *They send the fish for barter to the next village... Metal discs and chains were used for barter.* V+O OR V ▸ N UNCOUNT

base /beɪs/, **bases, basing, based. 1** The **base** of something is **1.1** its lowest edge or part. EG *...at the base of a cliff. ...the switch on the lamp base.* **1.2** the part at which it is attached to something else. EG *...the scar at the base of his thumb... These birds have a large white mark near the base of the tail.* N COUNT: USU+SUPP

2 A position or thing that is a **base** for something is one from which that thing can be developed or achieved. EG *This innovation was regarded as a sensible base for teaching and research... The League had no real power base on which it could build.* N COUNT: OFT+SUPP

3 If you **base** one thing on another, you develop it from that thing. EG *The new agreement is based on the original United Nations proposal... ...movies based on British life.* V+O+on/upon

4 If you **are based** in a particular place, that is the place where you live or do most of your work. EG *I was based in London.* V+O+A: USU PASS

5 A military **base** is a place which part of an army, navy, or air force works from. EG *...the new air base at Buzaruto... The submarines abandoned the chase and returned to base.* N COUNT OR N UNCOUNT

6 Your **base** is the main place where you work, stay, or live. EG *The company made Luxembourg city their base... The best base for the visitor to London must be the West End.* N COUNT

baseball /beɪsbɔːl/ is a game played by two teams of nine players. Each player from one team hits a ball with a bat and then tries to run round all four bases before the other team can get the ball back. N UNCOUNT

baseless /beɪslɪs/. A story or belief that is **baseless** is not true and is not based on facts. EG *...baseless gossip.* ADJ CLASSIF

basement /beɪsmənt/, **basements.** The **basement** of a building is a floor built partly or wholly below ground level. EG *They took the lift down to the basement of the hotel... It was horrible. There were rats in the basement!... ...a small basement flat.* N COUNT

bases is **1** the plural of **base,** pronounced /beɪsɪz/. **2** the plural of **basis,** pronounced /beɪsiːz/.

bash /bæʃ/, **bashes, bashing, bashed. 1** If you [V+O:USU+A] [Informal] **bash** someone or something, you deliberately hit them hard. EG *She was bashing him over the head with a saucepan.*

2 If you **bash** into something or against something, [V+A] [Informal] you hit it or bump into it accidentally with a lot of force. EG *He bashed into a tree... The cradle swayed and bashed against the walls.* ▸ used as a noun. EG [▸ N COUNT] *...a bash on the nose.*

3 If you **have a bash** at something or if you **give it** [PHRASE] [Informal] **a bash**, you try to do it. EG *She was going to have a bash at swimming the Channel... Why don't you go and fetch the tools and we'll give it a bash.*

bashful /bæʃful/. Someone who is **bashful** is shy [ADJ QUALIT] and easily embarrassed. EG *Most new parents are bashful about asking questions.* ◊ **bashfully.** EG *He* [◊ ADV] *smiled bashfully when she said, 'You look lovely.'*

basic /beɪsɪk/, **basics. 1** You use **basic** to de- [ADJ CLASSIF: ATTRIB] scribe things which are the most important or the simplest parts of something. EG *The basic theme of these stories never varies... We never seem to solve the basic economic problems... ...people with only a basic education... We have taken this basic arrangement and elaborated it.*

2 Something that is **basic** to the achievement or [ADJ PRED: OFT+to] success of something else is necessary for it. EG *There are certain things that are absolutely basic to a good relationship.*

3 You describe something as **basic** when it has [ADJ QUALIT] only the most important features and no luxuries. EG *The people are having to move from luxury homes to basic two-roomed flats... The facilities are terribly basic.*

4 The **basics** of a subject or activity are the [N PLURAL] simplest and most important aspects of it. EG *For a year I learnt the basics of journalism.*

basically /beɪsɪkᵊli/. You use **basically** when [ADV SEN] you are indicating what the most important feature of something is or when you are giving a general description of something complicated. EG *This was basically a political row... There are basically three types of vacuum cleaner... This is basically where we differ... Basically, I think Britain shouldn't have gone into the Common Market... To answer your question, I would say, basically, yes.*

basin /beɪsᵊn/, **basins. 1** A **basin** is **1.1** a deep [N COUNT] bowl that you use for mixing or storing food. EG *Cover the basin with a clean cloth.* **1.2** a washbasin.

2 The **basin** of a large river or lake is the area of [N COUNT] land around it from which water and streams run down into it. EG *...the Amazon basin.*

basis /beɪsɪs/, **bases** /beɪsiːz/. **1** The **basis** of [N COUNT: USU+SUPP] something is the central and most important part of it, from which it can be further developed. EG *Many of the old actors used a script merely as a basis for improvization... This was the basis of the final design... Such dreams are the basis on which you later structure your life.*

2 The **basis** for something is the thing that pro- [N COUNT: USU+SUPP] vides a reason for it. EG *There is no basis for this belief... ...arguments which had no logical basis.*

3 If you make a decision **on the basis of** some- [PHRASE] thing, it provides the reason for making that deci- sion. EG *I shall make up my own mind on the basis of the advice I've been given... The choice might have been made on the basis of convenience.*

4 If something happens or is done **on a** particular [PHRASE] **basis**, it happens or is done in that way or using that method. EG *We run the service on a voluntary basis... The results are checked on a daily basis... All the teachers work on a temporary basis at first.*

bask /bɑːsk/, **basks, basking, basked. 1** If you [V:OFT+in] **bask** in the sunshine, you lie in it and enjoy its warmth. EG *I want to spend the whole holiday just basking in the sun.*

2 If you **bask** in someone's approval or favour, you [V+in] get it and enjoy it. EG *The two journalists basked in the gratitude of the new rulers.*

baskets

shopping basket

dog basket

wastepaper basket

basket /bɑːskɪt/, **baskets.** A **basket** is a contain- [N COUNT: USU+SUPP] er made of thin strips of cane woven together. EG *...a shopping basket... ...a basket of washing.*

basketball /bɑːskɪtbɔːl/ is a game in which two [N UNCOUNT] teams of five players each try to score goals by throwing a large ball through a circular net fixed to a metal ring at each end of the court.

bass /beɪs/, **basses. 1** A **bass** is a man with a very [N COUNT] deep singing voice.

2 A **bass** drum, guitar, or other musical instrument [ADJ CLASSIF: ATTRIB] is one that produces a very deep sound.

3 In popular music, a **bass** is a bass guitar or a [N COUNT OR N UNCOUNT] double bass. EG *...with himself on trumpet and Kessler on bass... ...a new bass player.*

bassoon /bəsuːn/, **bassoons.** A **bassoon** is a [N COUNT] woodwind musical instrument which can produce a very deep sound.

bastard /bɑːstəd, bæs-/, **bastards. 1** A **bastard** is [N COUNT] [Outdated] someone whose parents were not married to each other at the time that he or she was born. EG *...the bastard son of the Marquis.*

2 If you call someone a **bastard**, you are insulting [N COUNT OR VOCATIVE] them; an offensive use.

bastion /bæstɪən/, **bastions.** A **bastion** is some- [N COUNT+SUPP] [Literary] thing that protects a system or way of life from something that is likely to harm it. EG *They regard the wealth-producing system as a bastion of capi- talistic privilege... Love is a bastion against loneli- ness.*

bat /bæt/, **bats, batting, batted. 1** A **bat** is a [N COUNT] specially shaped piece of wood that is used for hitting the ball in cricket, baseball, rounders, or table-tennis. EG *...a cricket bat.*

2 When you **bat**, you have a turn at hitting the ball [V] with a bat in cricket, baseball, or rounders.

3 A **bat** is also a small flying animal that looks like [N COUNT] a mouse with leathery wings. Bats fly at night.

4 If someone does something **off** their **own bat**, [PHRASE] they do it without anyone else suggesting it.

5 If you say that someone did **not bat an eyelid**, [PHRASE] you mean that they showed no sign of surprise.

batch /bætʃ/, **batches.** A **batch** of things or [N PART] people is a group of things or people of the same kind, especially a group that is dealt with at the same time. EG *Another batch of letters came in... ...the next batch of trainees.*

bated /beɪtɪᵈd/. If you wait for something **with** [PHRASE] [Literary] **bated breath**, you are very anxious about it.

Find two words on these pages which have exactly the same meaning.

bath /bɑːθ/, baths, bathing, bathed. 1 A bath is a N COUNT long, rectangular container which you fill with water and sit in while you wash your body.

2 When you have a **bath** or take a **bath**, you wash N COUNT : your body while sitting in a bath filled with water. USU SING EG *I must have a bath before we go.*

3 If you **bath** someone, you wash them in a bath. EG V+O *She will show you how to bath the baby.*

4 A public swimming pool is sometimes called the N PLURAL **baths**. EG *I take my older children to the baths once a week.*

bathe /beɪð/, bathes, bathing, bathed. 1 When V : OFT+*in* you **bathe**, you swim or play in a sea, river, or lake. EG *It is dangerous to bathe in the sea here.* ▸ used ▸ N SING : a+N as a noun. EG *Let's go for a bathe.* ◊ **bathing**. EG *I* ◊ N UNCOUNT *know a place where we can go bathing.*

2 When you **bathe**, you have a bath. EG *After golf I* V *would return to the flat to bathe and change.* American

3 When you **bathe** a wound, you wash it gently. V+O

4 If a place **is bathed** in light, it is covered with V+O : light. EG *The room was bathed in sunlight.* USU PASS+*in*

bather /beɪðə/, bathers. A **bather** is a person N COUNT who is swimming or playing in the sea, a river, or a lake.

bathing costume /beɪðɪŋ kɒstjuːm/, bathing N COUNT costumes. A **bathing costume** is the same as a British bathing suit.

bathing suit /beɪðɪŋ sjuːt/, bathing suits. A N COUNT **bathing suit** is a tight-fitting garment which a American woman wears when she goes swimming.

bathing trunks /beɪðɪŋ trʌŋks/. **Bathing** N PLURAL **trunks** are the shorts that a man wears when he British goes swimming.

bathrobe /bɑːθrəʊb/, bathrobes. A **bathrobe** is 1 N COUNT a loose piece of clothing made of towelling which you wear before or after you have a bath or a swim. **2** a dressing gown. American

bathroom /bɑːθruːm/, bathrooms. 1 A **bath-** N COUNT **room** is a room in a house that contains a bath or shower, a washbasin, and sometimes a toilet. See picture at HOUSE. EG *She went into the bathroom and took a shower.*

2 People sometimes refer to a toilet as the **bath-** N SING : **room**. EG *Can I go to the bathroom, please?* USU the+N

bathtub /bɑːθtʌb/, bathtubs. A **bathtub** is a N COUNT large, long container which you fill with water and Outdated sit in while you wash your body.

baton /bætɒn/, batons. A **baton** is 1 a light, thin N COUNT stick used by a conductor to direct an orchestra or a choir. 2 a short stick that is passed from one runner to another in a relay race. 3 a short heavy stick used as a weapon by a policeman.

baton charge, baton charges. A **baton charge** N COUNT is an attacking forward movement made by a large group of policemen carrying batons.

battalion /bətælɪən/, battalions. A **battalion** is N COUNT a large group of soldiers that consists of three or more companies.

batter /bætə/, batters, battering, battered. 1 If V+O someone **batters** a child or a woman, they injure them by hitting them many times. EG *Such parents have been known to batter their children.* ◊ **battered**. EG *Battered women may be protected* ◊ ADJ CLASSIF *one day.*

2 To **batter** something means to hit it many times. V+O OR V+O EG *The ship was being battered by the waves... He was battering on the front door.*

3 **Batter** is a mixture of flour, eggs, and milk which N UNCOUNT you use to make things such as pancakes.

batter down. If you **batter down** a door, you hit PHRASAL VB : it so hard that it breaks and falls down. V+O+ADV

battered /bætəd/. Something that is **battered** is ADJ QUALIT old, worn, and damaged as a result of being used a lot. EG *...a battered old hat.* ● See also **batter**.

battering /bætərɪŋ/, batterings. A **battering** is N COUNT an experience in which someone suffers badly through being attacked. EG *The Eighth Army had taken the worst battering.*

battery /bætərɪ/, batteries. 1 A **battery** is a N COUNT device that produces the electricity in something such as a torch or radio.

2 A **battery** of things, people, or events is a large N PART number of them. EG *Batteries of cameras were set to record the event... We would undergo a battery of tests.*

3 **Battery** hens are kept in small cages and made ADJ CLASSIF : to produce large numbers of eggs. ATTRIB

battle /bætəl/, battles, battling, battled. 1 In a N COUNT OR war, a **battle** is a fight between armies or between N UNCOUNT groups of ships or planes. EG *...the Battle of Balaclava... The general was killed in battle.*

2 A **battle** is also 2.1 a process in which two people N COUNT : USU or two groups of people compete for power or try +between/for to achieve opposite things. EG *...the battle between the sexes... ...his battle for control of the adminis- tration.* 2.2 an attempt by a group of people to N COUNT : USU achieve something that is difficult and that can +for/against only be achieved slowly. EG *...the battle for women's liberation... ...the battle against inflation.*

3 **Battle** is used in these phrases. 3.1 When there PHRASES is a **battle of wits**, people with opposing aims compete with each other using their intelligence. 3.2 If you say that something is **half the battle**, you mean that it is the most important step to- wards achieving something. 3.3 If you are **fighting a losing battle**, you are trying to achieve some- thing but are not going to be successful.

4 To **battle** means to fight very hard. EG *The males* V+A settle their problems by battling between them- selves... Dad was soon battling for his life.*

battlefield /bætəlfiːld/, battlefields. A **battle-** N COUNT **field** is a place where a battle is fought. EG *...First World War battlefields.*

battleground /bætəlgraʊnd/, battlegrounds. 1 N COUNT A **battleground** is a battlefield.

2 You can also refer to a subject over which people N COUNT disagree or compete as a **battleground**. EG *The theory of evolution is no longer a battleground.*

battlements /bætəlmənts/. The **battlements** of N PLURAL a castle or fortress consist of a wall built round the top, with gaps through which guns or arrows can be fired.

battleship /bætəlʃɪp/, battleships. A **battleship** N COUNT is a very large, heavily armoured warship.

batty /bætɪ/, battier, battiest. If you say that ADJ QUALIT someone is **batty**, you think that they are rather Informal strange or slightly mad. EG *She must be going batty.*

bauble /bɔːbəl/, baubles. A **bauble** is a small, N COUNT cheap ornament or piece of jewellery. EG *...Christ- mas tree baubles.*

baulk /bɔːlk/. See balk.

bawdy /bɔːdɪ/, bawdier, bawdiest. A **bawdy** ADJ QUALIT story or joke contains humorous references to sex. Outdated EG *...bawdy songs.*

bawl /bɔːl/, bawls, bawling, bawled. 1 If you V : OFT+A **bawl**, you shout or sing something loudly and OR V+QUOTE harshly. EG *They bawl down the telephone at me... 'Truman,' he bawled, 'has been shot!'*

2 If a child **bawls**, it cries loudly. EG *Josephine* V *started bawling.*

bawl out. 1 If someone **bawls** you **out**, they scold PHRASAL VB : you angrily for doing something wrong. EG *I was* V+O+ADV *regularly bawled out at school for not doing home-* Informal *work.* 2 If you **bawl** something **out**, you shout it or V-SPEECH+ADV sing it very loudly. EG *...people bawling out, 'What about pensions?'*

bay /beɪ/, bays, baying, bayed. 1 A **bay** is a part N COUNT of a coastline where the land curves inwards. EG *Hearst sailed from San Francisco across the bay to Oakland.*

2 A **bay** is also a space or area that is used for a N COUNT : particular purpose. EG *...the corridor beyond the* USU+SUPP *loading bay.*

3 If you **keep** something that frightens or upsets PHRASE you **at bay**, you prevent it from reaching you. EG *...lighting a fire to keep dangerous animals at bay.*

BE

be /biː/ **am, are, is; was, were; being, been**.

There is a separate entry in this dictionary for each of the forms of **be** which will help you identify their shortened and negative forms.

'Be' as an auxiliary

1 In front of a present participle, it makes the continuous tense of verbs. For example: *... a problem which is getting worse and worse.*

2 In front of a past participle, it makes the passive voice of verbs. For example: *You have been warned.*

3 In front of an infinitive, it says something definite about a later event. For example: *You are to come back home by ten o'clock ...   The President is to appear on TV.*

'Be' with a complement

4 In front of a proper noun, it names a person or place. For example: *The head of the corporation is Sir Paul Simpson ...   This is London.*

'Be' with a complement or adjunct

5 In front of an adjective, a noun, or a prepositional phrase, it gives information about the subject, telling you about its features or qualities, or about things such as the identity of the subject or how old it is or where it is. For example: *The house was big and old ...   Rose Gibson is twenty-seven ...   The iron was in her left hand.*

'Be' with 'it' and 'there'

6 The subject of **be** can be 'it' or 'there'. These words do not refer to anything outside the sentence. The focus of the sentence is always on what follows **be**, and these words are just present to alert you to what follows.

6.1 With 'it' as subject, a feature or quality can be stated without any mention of what 'it' refers to. For example: *It's a pity ...   It's a lovely day ...   It was about four o'clock.*

6.2 With 'it' as subject, a statement like 'John bought the car yesterday' can be varied in emphasis by changing it to 'It was John who bought the car yesterday', or 'It was yesterday that John bought the car'.

In the same way, the statement can be introduced by a comment, as in: 'It was true that John bought the car', or 'It's unfortunate that John bought the car'.

6.3 With 'there' as subject, a noun or noun group can be stated without saying anything else about it. For example: *There was a rustling of papers.*

'Be' on its own

7 A form of **be** can be used without anything after it. This occurs in co-ordination and various kinds of responses and tags. For example:
Co-ordination: *She wasn't enjoying it but the children were.*
Response: *'Was she at the same hotel?' – 'No, she wasn't.'*
Tag: *'She's Welsh, isn't she?'*

4 When a dog or wolf **bays**, it makes a howling v noise.

bayonet /ˈbeɪənət/, **bayonets**. A **bayonet** is a N COUNT long, sharp blade that can be fixed to the end of a rifle and used as a weapon.

bay window, bay windows. A **bay window** is a N COUNT window that sticks out from the outside wall of a house. See picture at HOUSE.

bazaar /bəˈzɑː/, **bazaars**. **1** A **bazaar** is an area N COUNT where there are many small shops and stalls, especially in the Middle East and India. EG ...the bazaars of old Delhi.
2 A **bazaar** is also a sale to raise money for N COUNT charity. EG Our local church is having a Christmas bazaar.

BC /biː siː/. You use **BC** in dates to indicate a number of years or centuries before the year in which Jesus Christ is believed to have been born. EG ...1600 BC... ...the fifth century BC.

be. See the panel on the opposite page.

beach /biːtʃ/, **beaches**. A **beach** is an area of sand N COUNT or pebbles beside the sea. Tourists go there to walk on the beach.

beacon /ˈbiːkən/, **beacons**. A **beacon** is a light or a N COUNT fire on a hill or tower, which acts as a signal or a warning.

bead /biːd/, **beads**. **1** **Beads** are small pieces of N COUNT : coloured glass, wood, or plastic with a hole through USU PLURAL the middle. Beads are often put together on a piece of string or wire to make necklaces, bracelets, and other jewellery. EG ...strings of beads.
2 A **bead** of liquid or moisture is a small drop of it. N PART EG Beads of perspiration began to form on his brow.

beady /ˈbiːdiˈ/, **beadier, beadiest. Beady** eyes are ADJ QUALIT small, round, and bright.

beak /biːk/, **beaks**. A bird's **beak** is the hard N COUNT : curved or pointed part of its mouth. USU+POSS

beaker /ˈbiːkə/, **beakers**. A **beaker** is a plastic cup N COUNT used for drinking, usually one with no handle.

beam /biːm/, **beams, beaming, beamed. 1** If you v : OFT+at **beam**, you smile because you are happy. EG He beamed at Ralph... ...beaming faces. ▸ used as a ▸ N COUNT noun. EG ...a beam of satisfaction.
2 A **beam** of light is a line of light that shines from N COUNT+SUPP an object such as a torch or the sun. EG I could see the beam of his flashlight waving around in the dark.
3 If you **beam** a signal or information to a place, v+o+A you send it by means of radio waves. EG We were able to beam pictures of the riots out to Denmark.
4 A **beam** is also a long thick bar of wood, metal, N COUNT or concrete, especially one which is used to support the roof of a building. EG ...the low oak beams.

bean /biːn/, **beans**. **1** Beans are **1.1** the pods of a N COUNT : climbing plant, or the seeds that the pods contain, USU PLURAL which are eaten as a vegetable. EG ...pork and beans... ...a garden where they grow beans. **1.2** the seeds of various plants which are used for different purposes, for example to make drinks such as coffee or cocoa, or to produce oil. EG ...coffee beans.
2 If someone is **full of beans**, they are very lively PHRASE and full of energy and enthusiasm. Informal
3 If you **spill the beans**, you tell someone some- PHRASE thing that people have been trying to keep secret. Informal

beansprouts /ˈbiːnsprauts/ or **beanshoots** are N COUNT : small shoots grown from beans. You can eat them USU PLURAL raw or lightly cooked.

bear /beə/, **bears, bearing, bore** /bɔː/, **borne** /bɔːn/. **1** A **bear** is a large, strong wild animal with N COUNT thick fur and sharp claws. ● See also **polar bear**.
● **teddy bear**: see **teddy**.
2 If you **bear** something somewhere, you carry it v+o : USU+A there or take it there. EG Camels and donkeys bear Formal those goods inland... She arrived bearing a large bunch of grapes.
3 If something **bears** the weight of something else, v+o it supports the weight of that thing. EG His ankle now felt strong enough to bear his weight.
4 If something **bears** a particular mark or charac- v+o

teristic, it has that mark or characteristic. EG ...a petition bearing nearly half a million signatures... The scene bore all the marks of a country wedding... The interpretation bore no relation to the actual words spoken.
5 If you **bear** something difficult, you accept it and v+o are able to deal with it. EG It was painful of course but I bore it... Their policies are putting a greater strain on the economic system than it can bear.
● to **grin and bear it**: see **grin**.
6 If you **can't bear** someone or something, you PHRASE dislike them very much. EG I can't bear weddings.
7 If you **bear** the responsibility for something, you v+o accept responsibility for it. EG It would be unjust for him to bear personally the great expenses involved.
8 When a plant or tree **bears** flowers, fruit, or v+o leaves, it produces them.
9 If you **bear** someone a feeling such as love or v+o+o hate, you feel that emotion towards them. EG He Formal bore his children no malice.
10 If you **bring** pressure or influence **to bear** on PHRASE someone, you use it to try and persuade them to do something.
11 If you **bear** left or **bear** right when you are v+A driving or walking along, you turn slightly in that direction. EG Bear right down the south side of the church.

bear down. If something large **bears down** on PHRASAL VB : you, it moves quickly towards you in a threatening V+ADV, way. EG We struggled to turn the boat as the wave USU+on/upon bore down on us.
bear out. If someone or something **bears** a PHRASAL VB : person **out** or **bears out** what that person is V+O+ADV saying, they support what that person is saying. EG The claims are not borne out by the evidence.
bear up. If you **bear up** when experiencing PHRASAL VB : problems, you remain cheerful and show courage V+ADV in spite of them. EG You have to bear up under the strain.
bear with. If you ask someone to **bear with** you, PHRASAL VB : you are asking them to be patient. EG I hope you'll V+PREP bear with me as I explain.

bearable /ˈbeərəbəˈl/. If something is **bearable**, ADJ QUALIT you feel that you can accept it or deal with it. EG The heat was just bearable... He hoped for some news that would make life more bearable.

beard /bɪəd/, **beards**. A man's **beard** is the hair N COUNT that grows on his chin and cheeks. EG He had a long grey beard. ◊ **bearded** /ˈbɪədɪˈd/. EG ...a bearded ◊ ADJ CLASSIF man.

bearer /ˈbeərə/, **bearers**. **1** A **bearer** is a person N COUNT who carries a stretcher or coffin. EG The four bearers lifted the coffin slowly.
2 The **bearer** of something such as a letter or a N COUNT : piece of news is the person who brings it to you. EG OFT+of ...the bearer of the invitation.
3 The **bearer** of a document is the person who has N COUNT it in their possession and who has the authority or Formal right to possess it. EG The identification document contains the bearer's fingerprints.
4 The **bearer** of a name or title is the person who N COUNT has it.

bearing /ˈbeərɪŋ/, **bearings**. **1** If something **has a** PHRASE **bearing on** a situation or event, it is relevant to it. EG That is all in the past. It has no bearing on what is happening today.
2 Someone's **bearing** is the way in which they N SING : move or stand. EG Because of her bearing I realized USU POSS+N that she was someone important. Formal
3 If you **get** or **find** your **bearings**, you find out PHRASE where you are or what you should do next. If you **lose** your **bearings**, you do not know where you are or what you should do next. EG They stopped to get their bearings... After a week in the job, she had got her bearings.

beast /biːst/, **beasts**. **1** A **beast** is an animal, N COUNT especially a large one. EG ...that most dangerous of all beasts – a maddened buffalo.

2 If you call someone a **beast**, you mean that they behave in a selfish, cruel, or unpleasant way.   N COUNT   Outdated

beastly /biːstliˈ/, **beastlier, beastliest. 1** Something that is **beastly** is very unpleasant. EG ...*a beastly smell... It's so beastly there.*   ADJ QUALIT   Outdated

2 Someone who is **beastly** is unkind, mean, and spiteful. EG *He was so beastly, you've no idea.*   ADJ QUALIT   Outdated

beat /biːt/, **beats, beating, beaten.** The form **beat** is used in the present tense and is the past tense of the verb.

1 If you **beat** someone or something, you hit them very hard. EG *His stepfather used to beat him... The rain beat against the window.*   V+O OR V : OFT+A

2 When a bird or insect **beats** its wings or when its wings **beat**, its wings move up and down. EG *It was trying to escape, frantically beating its wings.*   V-ERG
▶ used as a noun. EG *Flies can move their wings at 1000 beats per second.*   ▶ N COUNT

3 When your heart or pulse **is beating**, it is continually making movements with a regular rhythm. EG *His heart beat faster.* ▶ used as a noun. EG *He could feel the beat of her heart.*   V   ▶ N COUNT : USU+SUPP

4 The **beat** of a piece of music is the main rhythm that it has.   N SING : the+N

5 If you **beat time** to a piece of music, you move your hand or foot up and down in time with the music.   PHRASE

6 If you **beat** eggs, cream, or butter, you mix them thoroughly using a fork or whisk.   V+O

7 If you **beat** someone in a game, race, or competition, you defeat them. EG *He's going to be a tough candidate to beat.*   V+O

8 If someone or something **beats** a particular thing, they do better than it or are better than it. EG *He'll be trying to beat the world record... To my mind nothing beats a bowl of natural yogurt.*   V+O

9 If you intend to do something but someone **beats** you **to it**, they do it before you do. EG *The Italians beat them to it by about 36 hours.*   PHRASE

10 You use **beat** in expressions such as '**It beats me**' to indicate that you cannot understand or explain something. EG *What beats me is where they get the money from.*   PHRASE   Informal

11 A police officer **on the beat** is on duty, walking around the area for which he or she is responsible.   PHRASE

12 If you tell someone to **beat it**, you are telling them to go away.   CONVENTION   Informal

13 to **beat about the bush**: see **bush**. ● to **beat a retreat**: see **retreat**. ● See also **beating.**

beat down. 1 When the sun **beats down**, it is very hot and bright. EG ...*feeling the hot Alabama sun beat down.* **2** When the rain **beats down**, it rains very hard. EG *The soil absorbs only a fraction of the rain that beats down.* **3** When you **beat** a person who is selling you something, you force them to accept a lower price for it.   PHRASAL VB : V+ADV   V+ADV   V+O+ADV

beat up. If someone **beats** a person **up**, they hit or kick the person many times. EG *He told us that he had been beaten up by the police.*   PHRASAL VB : V+O+ADV

beating /biːtɪŋ/, **beatings. 1** If you are given a **beating**, you are hit hard many times, especially with something such as a stick. EG *She had left home after a savage beating.*   N COUNT

2 If a team takes a **beating**, it is defeated by a large amount in a game or contest.   N SING : a+N

3 If you say that something will **take some beating**, you mean that it is very good and it is unlikely that anything better will be done or made.   PHRASE   Informal

beating up, beatings up. A **beating up** is an attack on someone in which they are hit and kicked so that they are very badly hurt. EG *They gave him an awful beating up.*   N COUNT

beatnik /biːtnɪk/, **beatniks. Beatniks** were young people in the late 1950's who wore strange clothes and had unconventional beliefs.   N COUNT

beautician /bjuːtɪʃəˈn/, **beauticians.** A **beautician** is a person whose job is giving people beauty treatments such as cutting and polishing their

nails, treating their skin, and putting on their make-up.

beautiful /bjuːtɪfʊl/. **1** A **beautiful** woman is very attractive to look at. EG ...*a very beautiful girl.*   ADJ QUALIT

2 You say that something is **beautiful** when you find it very attractive or pleasant. EG ...*beautiful music... a beautiful house... It's such a beautiful day.* ◊ **beautifully.** EG ...*beautifully dressed young men.*   ADJ QUALIT   ◊ ADV

3 You can describe something that someone does as **beautiful** when they do it very skilfully. EG *It was a beautiful shot.* ◊ **beautifully.** EG *Doesn't he play the piano beautifully?*   ADJ QUALIT   ◊ ADV

beautify /bjuːtɪfaɪ/, **beautifies, beautifying, beautified.** If you **beautify** something, you make it look more beautiful. EG *Charlotte went on beautifying her home.*   V+O   Formal

beauty /bjuːtiˈ/, **beauties. 1 Beauty** is the state or quality of being beautiful. EG *Her beauty grew in her old age... ...the beauty of Kreisler's violin playing... She learned to appreciate beauty.*   N UNCOUNT

2 A **beauty** is a beautiful woman. EG *Vita had turned into a beauty.*   N COUNT

3 You can say that something is a **beauty** when you think it is very good. EG *My bike's a real beauty.*   N COUNT   Informal

4 The **beauties** of something are its attractive qualities or features. EG ...*the beauties of nature... With him, I explored all the beauties of pre-war Warsaw.*   N COUNT : +SUPP : USU PLURAL

5 If you say that a particular feature is the **beauty** of something, you mean that this feature is what makes the thing so good. EG *That's the beauty of the plan – it's so simple.*   N SING : the+N+of

6 Beauty is used to describe people, products, and activities that are concerned with making women look beautiful. EG ...*beauty products... ...the magazine's beauty editor.*   N MOD

beauty spot, beauty spots. A **beauty spot** is a place that is popular because of its beautiful countryside. EG ...*Ashness Bridge, a popular beauty spot.*   N COUNT

beaver /biːvəˈ/, **beavers, beavering, beavered.** A **beaver** is a furry animal like a large rat with a big flat tail. Beavers build dams in streams.   N COUNT

beaver away. If you **are beavering away** at something, you are working very hard at it.   PHRASAL VB : V+ADV

became /bɪˈkeɪm/ is the past tense of **become.**

because /bɪˈkɒz/. **1** You use **because** when stating the reason for something. EG *I couldn't see Helen's expression, because her head was turned... 'Why shouldn't I come?' – 'Because you're too busy.'*   CONJ

2 You also use **because of** when stating the reason for something. EG *He retired last month because of illness.*   PREP

beck /bɛk/. If someone wants you to be **at** their **beck and call**, they want you to be constantly available and ready to do what they ask.   PHRASE

beckon /bɛkəˈn/, **beckons, beckoning, beckoned. 1** If you **beckon** to someone, you signal to them to come to you. EG *Claus beckoned to him excitedly... He beckoned and the girl came over... He beckoned me to follow him.*   V : OFT+to OR V+O+to-INF

2 If something **beckons**, it is so attractive to someone that they feel they must become involved in it. EG *Vast countries beckon to young men in search of adventure... No restaurants beckoned late diners into the area.*   V : OFT+to OR V+O

become /bɪˈkʌm/, **becomes, becoming, became** /bɪˈkeɪm/. The form **become** is used in the present tense and is also the past participle.

1 If something **becomes** a particular thing, it starts being that thing. EG *The smell became stronger and stronger... It became clear that the Conservatives*   V+C were not going to win... We became good friends at once.

2 If you wonder **what has become of** someone, PHRASE you wonder where they are and what has happened to them. EG He was an odd chap, Boon. I wonder what became of him.

becoming /bɪ'kʌmɪŋ/. A piece of clothing, a col- ADJ QUALIT our, or a hairstyle that is **becoming** makes the Outdated person who is wearing it look attractive. EG She was dressed in an extremely becoming trouser suit.

bed /bɛd/, **beds, bedding, bedded. 1** A **bed** is a N COUNT OR piece of furniture that you lie on when you sleep. EG N UNCOUNT He sat down on the bed... He went to bed at ten... She had just got out of bed. ● When you **make** the ● PHRASE **bed**, you neatly arrange the sheets and covers of a bed.

2 If you **go to bed with** someone, you have sex PHRASE with them.

3 A flower **bed** is an area of earth in which you N COUNT+SUPP grow plants. EG ...beds of marigolds. ● **not a bed of roses**: see **rose**.

4 The sea **bed** or a river **bed** is the ground at the N COUNT+SUPP bottom of the sea or of a river.

5 See also **bedding**.

bed down. If you **bed down** somewhere, you PHRASAL VB : sleep there for the night, not in your own bed. V+ADV+A

bed and breakfast is a system of accommoda- N UNCOUNT tion in a hotel or guest house in which you pay for a room for the night and for breakfast the following morning. EG ...£15.50 a night for bed and breakfast.

bedclothes /bɛdkləʊðz/ are the sheets and covers N PLURAL which you put over you when you get into bed. EG Jamie pulled back the bedclothes and got into bed.

bedding /bɛdɪŋ/ is sheets, blankets, and other N UNCOUNT covers that are used on beds. EG She changed the bedding.

bedevil /bɪ'dɛvəl/, **bedevils, bedevilling, be-** V+O : USU PASS **devilled;** spelled **bedeviling, bedeviled** in Ameri- Formal can English. If you **are bedevilled** by something unpleasant, it causes you a lot of problems. EG He has been bedevilled by injuries.

bedfellow /bɛdfɛləʊ/, **bedfellows.** You refer to N COUNT two things or people as **bedfellows** when they have become associated or related in some way. EG The oddest of enemies might become bedfellows.

bedlam /bɛdləm/. If you say that a place or N UNCOUNT situation is **bedlam**, you mean that it is very noisy and disorderly.

bedraggled /bɪ'drægəld/. Someone or something ADJ QUALIT that is **bedraggled** is untidy and disorderly, because they have got wet or dirty. EG She came in looking grubby and bedraggled.

bedridden /bɛdrɪdəⁿn/. Someone who is **bedrid-** ADJ CLASSIF **den** is so ill or disabled that they cannot get out of bed.

bedrock /bɛdrɒk/. The **bedrock** of something N UNCOUNT : refers to all the principles, ideas, or facts on which USU+SUPP it is based. EG The Act reaffirmed family values as Formal the moral bedrock of the nation.

bedroom /bɛdru⁴m/, **bedrooms.** A **bedroom** is a N COUNT room which is used for sleeping in. See picture at HOUSE. EG ...a hotel bedroom... The bedroom door was closed.

bedside /bɛdsaɪd/. Your **bedside** is the area N SING beside your bed. EG An excellent breakfast had been left on the tray by his bedside... ...a bedside light.

bedsitter /bɛdsɪtə/, **bedsitters.** A **bedsitter** or N COUNT **bedsit** is a single furnished room in a house, which British you pay rent for and in which you live and sleep. Some bedsitters also have a washbasin and a small cooker. EG A lot of students live off campus in flats, houses, and bedsitters.

bedspread /bɛdsprɛd/, **bedspreads.** A **bed-** N COUNT **spread** is a decorative cover which is put over a bed, on top of the sheets and blankets.

bedtime /bɛdtaɪm/. Your **bedtime** is the time N UNCOUNT when you usually go to bed. EG It's long past bedtime.

bee /biː/, **bees. 1** A **bee** is an insect that makes a N COUNT buzzing noise as it flies and usually has a yellow-and-black striped body. Bees make honey, and live in large groups.

2 If you **have a bee in** your **bonnet** about some- PHRASE thing, you are so enthusiastic or worried about it that you keep mentioning it or thinking about it.

beech /biːtʃ/, **beeches.** A **beech** is a tree with a N COUNT OR smooth grey trunk. EG ...under the shade of a huge N UNCOUNT beech... ...forests of ash, elm, and beech.

beef /biːf/ is the meat of a cow, bull, or ox. EG ...a N UNCOUNT joint of roast beef... ...beef sandwiches.

beefy /biːfɪ/, **beefier, beefiest.** Someone, espe- ADJ QUALIT cially a man, who is **beefy** is strong and muscular. Informal EG Ronald was big, beefy, and aggressive.

beehive /biːhaɪv/, **beehives.** A **beehive** is a struc- N COUNT ture in which bees are kept, which is designed so that the keeper can collect the honey that they produce.

beeline /biːlaɪn/. If you **make a beeline for** a PHRASE place, you go to it as quickly and directly as Informal possible. EG Three of them made a beeline for the pub.

been /biːn, bɪn/. **1 Been** is the past participle of be.

2 You use **been** after the auxiliaries 'has', 'have', and 'had' in these ways. **2.1** If you **have been** to a place, you have gone to it or visited it. EG She has not been to church for almost twenty years... I haven't been to Birmingham. **2.2** If someone such as a postman or milkman **has been**, they have called at your house. EG Has the milkman been yet?

3 If you say that someone **has been and** done PHRASE something, you are expressing surprise or horror Informal at something that they have done. EG Now you've been and set the whole box on fire!

beer /bɪə/, **beers. 1 Beer** is a bitter alcoholic N MASS drink made from grain. EG We drank a few pints of beer.

2 A **beer** is a glass, bottle, or can containing beer. N COUNT EG He'd had two beers.

beet /biːt/ is a root vegetable that is used as food N UNCOUNT for animals, especially for cows.

beetle /biːtəⁿl/, **beetles.** A **beetle** is an insect with N COUNT a hard covering to its body.

beetroot /biːtruːt/, **beetroots.** Beetroot is a dark N UNCOUNT red root vegetable which can be cooked or pickled, OR N COUNT and eaten in salads.

befall /bɪ'fɔːl/, **befalls, befalling, befell** /bɪ'fɛl/, V+O **befallen.** If something bad or unlucky **befalls** you, Literary it happens to you. EG She knew no harm would ever befall her... A similar fate befell the British.

befit /bɪ'fɪt/, **befits, befitting, befitted.** If some- V+O thing **befits** a person or thing, it is suitable for Formal them or is expected of them. EG He was courteous, as befitted a young man speaking to an older man.

before /bɪ'fɔː/. **1** If something happens **before** a PREP OR CONJ time or event, it happens earlier than that time or event. EG We arrived just before two o'clock... Can I see you before you go, Helen?... A dozen ideas were considered before he decided on this plan.

2 you use **before** when you are talking about time. ADJ AFTER N For example, if something happened the day **be-fore** or the weekend **before**, it happened during the previous day or during the previous weekend. EG It had rained the night before.

3 If someone has done something **before**, they ADV have done it on a previous occasion. EG Have you been to Greece before?

4 If someone is **before** something, they are in front PREP of it. EG He stood before the door to the cellar... He Formal will appear before the magistrate.

5 When you have a task or difficult situation PREP+PRON **before** you, you have to deal with it. EG Let's get started. I have a difficult job before me.

beforehand /bɪˈfɔːhænd/. If you do something ADV
beforehand, you do it earlier than a particular
event. EG *Kathleen got married without telling
anyone beforehand.*

befriend /bɪˈfrɛnd/, **befriends, befriending, be-** V+O
friended. If you **befriend** someone, you make
friends with them. EG *I befriended a lonely little boy
in the village.*

befuddle /bɪˈfʌdəˀl/, **befuddles, befuddling, be-** V+O
fuddled. If something **befuddles** you, it confuses
you. EG *His words were sufficient to befuddle the
girls.*

beg /bɛg/, **begs, begging, begged. 1** If you **beg** V+O:
someone to do something, you ask them very OFT+to-INF,
anxiously or eagerly. EG *I begged him to stay, but* V+for,
he wouldn't... He begged for help... 'Tell me all the OR V+QUOTE
news,' I begged.
2 When someone **begs**, they ask people to give V:OFT+for,
them food or money because they are very poor. EG OR V+O:
...children in the streets begging for money... Kids OFT+for/from
were begging milk from the governor.
3 I beg your pardon: see **pardon.**

began /bɪˈgæn/ is the past tense of **begin.**

beget /bɪˈgɛt/, **begets, begetting, begot** /bɪˈgɒt/, V+O
begotten /bɪˈgɒtəˀn/. To **beget** something means Formal
to cause it to happen or be created. EG *Malnutrition
begets disease.*

beggar /bɛgə/, **beggars.** A **beggar** is someone N COUNT
who lives by asking people for money or food.

begin /bɪˈgɪn/, **begins, beginning, began**
/bɪˈgæn/, **begun** /bɪˈgʌn/. **1** If you **begin** to do V+to-INF
something, you start doing it. EG *The actors began* OR V+-ING
to rehearse a scene... I began eating the grapes.
2 When something **begins** or when you **begin** it, it V-ERG OR V:
takes place from a particular time onwards. EG *The* OFT+A
*concerts begin at 8 pm... Malcolm began his
speech... They decided to begin by looking at the
problems.*
3 You use the phrase **to begin with 3.1** when you PHRASE
are talking about the first event or stage in a
process. EG *To begin with, they just take your name
and address.* **3.2** to introduce the first of several
things that you want to say. EG *To begin with, the
invitation for eight really means eight-thirty.*
4 When you want to emphasize that it is difficult V+to-INF
for you to do something, you can say that you
cannot **begin** to do it. EG *He could not begin to
explain his feelings.*
5 If you say that a place or region **begins** some- V+A
where, you are talking about or pointing to one of
its edges. EG *The ocean begins here.*

beginner /bɪˈgɪnə/, **beginners.** A **beginner** is N COUNT
someone who has just started learning to do something and cannot do it very well yet. EG *This is the
sort of thing that beginners write.*

beginning /bɪˈgɪnɪŋ/, **beginnings. 1** If you refer N COUNT:
to the **beginning** or the **beginnings** of something, the+N
you mean the first part of it. EG *I say this at the
beginning of my book... ...the beginnings of a new
relationship.*
2 The **beginning** of a period of time is when it N SING:the+N
starts. EG *I came back at the beginning of the
term... The number had increased by the beginning
of the following year.*

begot /bɪˈgɒt/ is the past tense of **beget.**

begotten /bɪˈgɒtəˀn/ is the past participle of **beget.**

begrudge /bɪˈgrʌdʒ/ **begrudges, begrudging,** V+O+O
begrudged. If you say that you do not **begrudge**
someone something, you mean that you do not feel
angry, upset, or jealous that they have got it. EG *I do
not begrudge her that happiness... Let us not
begrudge Shirley her victory.*

beguiling /bɪˈgaɪlɪŋ/. Something that is **beguiling** ADJ QUALIT
seems attractive, but may be dangerous or harm-
ful. EG *...this beguiling idea... The fruit is a beguiling
red berry.*

begun /bɪˈgʌn/ is the past participle of **begin.**

behalf /bɪˈhɑːf/. If someone does something **on** PHRASE
your **behalf**, they do it for you and as your
representative. EG *Wilkins spoke on behalf of the
Labour Party.*

behave /bɪˈheɪv/, **behaves, behaving, behaved.
1** If you **behave** in a particular way, you act in that V+A
way. EG *In New York, he had behaved in a very
strange way... You are behaving like a silly child.*
2 If you **behave** yourself, you act in the way that V OR V-REFL
people think is correct and proper. EG *Their star-
tled boyfriends got warnings to behave... He's old
enough to behave himself.*

behaviour /bɪˈheɪvjə/; spelled **behavior** in
American English. **1** A person's **behaviour** is the N UNCOUNT:
way they behave. EG *I had been puzzled by his* OFT+SUPP
*behaviour... ...the obstinate behaviour of a small
child.*
2 The **behaviour** of something is the way in which N UNCOUNT:
it acts, functions, or changes. EG *...the behaviour of* USU+SUPP
the metal as we heat it.

behead /bɪˈhɛd/, **beheads, beheading, behead-** V+O:USU PASS
ed. If someone **is beheaded**, their head is cut off.
EG *Lady Jane Grey was beheaded in 1554.*

beheld /bɪˈhɛld/ is the past tense of **behold.**

behind /bɪˈhaɪnd/, **behinds. 1** If something is PREP OR ADV
behind a thing or person, the back of that thing or
person is facing it. EG *There were two boys sitting
behind me... The sun went behind a cloud... Joe was
limping along behind his wife... He followed a few
paces behind.*
2 The reason or person **behind** something caused PREP
that thing or is responsible for it. EG *These were the
reasons behind Macleod's statement... ...the man
behind the modernizing of the station.*
3 If you are **behind** someone, you support them. EG PREP
The country was behind the President.
4 You say that you are **behind** when you have ADV OR PREP
done less work than you should have done, or when
you have been less successful than someone else.
EG *I got more and more behind... The bus was badly
behind schedule... In the Championship, he finished
11 strokes behind Watson.*
5 If an experience is **behind** you, it is finished. EG PREP OR ADV
*...now that the war is behind us... We must leave
adolescence behind and grow up.*
6 If you stay **behind**, you remain in a place after ADV AFTER VB
other people have gone. EG *Susan asked me to stay
behind.*
7 If you leave something **behind**, you do not take it ADV AFTER VB
with you when you go. EG *Millie had left her cloak
behind.*
8 Your **behind** is the part of your body that you sit N COUNT
on.

behold /bɪˈhəʊld/, **beholds, beholding, beheld**
/bɪˈhɛld/. **1** If you **behold** someone or something, V+O
you notice them or look at them. EG *She was a* Literary
*terrible sight to behold... I beheld with sorrow an
old woman in tears.*
2 People sometimes say **'Behold'** to draw your V:ONLY IMPER
attention to something important or surprising that Literary
they are about to tell you or show you. EG *'Behold, I
show you a mystery,' the Vicar read... And, behold,
the Pentagon gave in.*

beholder /bɪhəʊldə/, **beholders.** The **beholder** of N COUNT
something is the person who is looking at it. EG *The* Outdated
*picture was very pleasing to beholders... Beauty is
in the eye of the beholder.*

beige /beɪʒ/. Something that is **beige** is a very ADJ COLOUR
pale brown colour. EG *...his pale beige summer coat.*

being /biːɪŋ/, **beings. 1 Being** is the present
participle of **be.** EG *Julie, you're being unreasonable.*
2 Something that is **in being** exists. EG *...laws* PHRASE
*already in being... The Polytechnic came into
being in 1971.*

Do you apologize if you give someone a belated
birthday present?

3 You can refer to any real or imaginary creature as a **being**. EG *Man is a rational being... ...the sight of these alien beings gliding down.* ● See also **human being**. N COUNT : USU+SUPP Literary

belated /bɪˈleɪtɪ²d/. A **belated** action happens later than it should have done. EG *Please accept my belated thanks for your kind gift... The Government is making a belated attempt to stop profiteering.* ◊ **belatedly.** EG *Bill belatedly agreed to call in the police.* ADJ QUALIT : ATTRIB Formal ◊ ADV

belch /beltʃ/, **belches, belching, belched. 1** If someone **belches**, they make a sudden noise in their throat because air has risen up from their stomach. EG *The baby drank his milk and belched.* V
▸ used as a noun. EG *'Amazing,' said Brody, stifling a belch.* ▸ N COUNT

2 If something **belches** smoke, fire, or loud sounds, it gives them out in large amounts. EG *Loudspeakers belched out deafening pop music... Smoke belched from the engine.* ▸ used as a noun. EG *...a belch of flame.* V+O OR V+A Literary ▸ N COUNT +SUPP

beleaguered /bɪˈliːgəd/. **1** A **beleaguered** person is experiencing a lot of difficulties, opposition, or criticism. EG *The beleaguered prime minister explained this to an angry crowd.* ADJ CLASSIF : ATTRIB Formal

2 A **beleaguered** place or army is surrounded by its enemies. EG *...the distressed defenders of a beleaguered city.* ADJ CLASSIF : ATTRIB Formal

belfry /ˈbelfriː/, **belfries.** The **belfry** of a church is the top part of its tower or steeple, where the bells are. N COUNT

belie /bɪˈlaɪ/, **belies, belying, belied.** If one thing **belies** another, **1** it makes the other thing seem very surprising. EG *The young face belied the grey hair above it.* **2** it proves that the other thing is not genuine or true. EG *Their social attitudes belie their words.* V+O Formal

belief /bɪˈliːf/, **beliefs. 1 Belief** is a feeling of certainty that something exists, is true, or is good. EG *...belief in God... It is my belief that more people could have been helped... ...the religious beliefs of her parents.* N COUNT OR N UNCOUNT : USU+SUPP

2 If you do something **in the belief that** something is true or will happen, you do it because you think this. EG *They put more and more demands on the system in the belief that it was indestructible.* PHRASE

3 You use **beyond belief** to emphasize that something is true to a very great degree. EG *They are generous beyond belief.* PHRASE

believable /bɪˈliːvəbə²l/. Something that is **believable** makes you think that it could be true or real. EG *...the only believable explanation for the disappearance of the plane.* ADJ CLASSIF

believe /bɪˈliːv/, **believes, believing, believed. 1** If you **believe** that something is true, you think that it is true. EG *It is believed that two prisoners have escaped... I couldn't believe what I had heard... We believed him dead... I believed him to be right.* V+REPORT; V+O+C, OR V+O+to-INF

2 You can say **I believe** to indicate that you are not sure that what you are saying is correct. EG *He's very well known, I believe, in Germany.* PHRASE

3 If you **believe** someone, you accept that they are telling the truth. EG *He knew I didn't believe him... Don't believe a word he says.* V+O : NO CONT

4 You can say **'believe me'** to emphasize that what you are saying is true. EG *Believe me, it's important.* CONVENTION

5 You say **'believe it or not'** when you think that someone is going to be surprised by what you are saying. EG *Believe it or not, I'm feeling quite homesick.* ADV SEN

6 If you **believe** in things such as God, fairies, or miracles, you are sure that they exist or happen. EG *I don't believe in ghosts.* V+in

7 If you **believe** in something, you are in favour of it because you think it is good or right. EG *...all those who believe in democracy... He did not believe in educating women.* V+in

believer /bɪˈliːvə/, **believers. 1** If you are a **believer** in something, you think that it is good, right, or beneficial. EG *...the true believer in democracy... Bob is a great believer in jogging.* N COUNT+in

2 A **believer** is someone who is sure that God exists or that their religion is true. EG *Of course you, as a believer, try to convert others?... We want to unite believers of all religions.* N COUNT

belittle /bɪˈlɪtə²l/, **belittles, belittling, belittled.** If you **belittle** someone or something, you make them seem unimportant or not very good. EG *The press gave the election no publicity and belittled its significance... Don't think I'm trying to belittle Turner. He was a genius.* V+O

bell

bell /bel/, **bells. 1** A **bell** is **1.1** a device that makes a ringing sound and is used to give a signal or to attract people's attention. EG *He approached the front door and rang the bell.* **1.2** a hollow metal object shaped like a cup which has a piece hanging inside it that hits the sides and makes a sound. EG *In the distance a church bell was ringing.* N COUNT

2 If you say that something **rings a bell**, you mean that it reminds you of something else, but you cannot remember exactly what it is. EG *The name rings a bell.* PHRASE Informal

belligerent /bɪˈlɪdʒə³rənt/. If you are **belligerent**, you are eager to defend yourself or your opinions when you know that other people are likely to oppose you. EG *Not even the belligerent Leggett was willing to face that mob... The women were belligerent about their freedom not to have babies.* ◊ **belligerently.** EG *Mr Kidley looked at him belligerently.* ◊ **belligerence** /bɪˈlɪdʒə³rəns/. EG *'I wanted to teach him a lesson,' she said with sudden belligerence.* ADJ QUALIT ◊ ADV ◊ N UNCOUNT

bellow /ˈbeləʊ/, **bellows, bellowing, bellowed. 1** If someone **bellows**, they shout in a loud, deep voice. EG *The president bellowed with laughter... 'Thirty-two!' bellowed Mrs Pringle... Lionel bellowed his contribution from across the room.* ▸ used as a noun. EG *He raised his voice to a bellow.* V : OFT+QUOTE OR V+O ▸ N COUNT

2 When an animal **bellows**, it makes a loud, deep sound. EG *The cow charged across the farmyard with the bull bellowing afte.* V

3 A **bellows** is a device used for blowing air into a fire in order to make it burn more fiercely. The plural form is also **bellows**. EG *The blast can be provided by a bellows worked by hand, or by an electric air pump.* N COUNT

belly /ˈbeliː/, **bellies. 1** Your **belly** is your stomach. EG *Their bellies were now filled with food... John was rather jolly, with a big belly and a pipe.* N COUNT Informal British

2 The **belly** of an animal is the lower part of its body. EG *...lions creeping on their bellies... ...fish with grey backs and white bellies.* N COUNT

belong /bɪˈlɒŋ/, **belongs, belonging, belonged. 1** If something **belongs** to you, you own it or it is V+to yours. EG *The land belongs to a big family... ...a myth belonging to some tribe in Western Australia.*

2 If someone or something **belongs** to a particular group, they are a member of that group. EG *She belongs to the Labour Party... ...bats belonging to eight different species.* v+to

3 If a person or thing **belongs** in a particular place, that is the place where they should be. EG *I don't belong here, mother, I am not like you... The plates don't belong in that cupboard.* v:OFT+A

belongings /bɪˈlɒŋɪŋz/. Your **belongings** are the things that you own and that you have with you or in your house. EG *She was tidying up her belongings... We packed the few belongings we had and left.* N PLURAL

beloved /bɪˈlʌvɪ²d/; also pronounced /bɪˈlʌvd/ when used after a noun or after the verb 'be'. A **beloved** person, thing, or place is one that you feel great affection for. EG *He withdrew to his beloved Kent... ...Marilyn Monroe, beloved of men in their millions.* ADJ CLASSIF : ATTRIB OR ADJ PRED+of

below /bɪˈləʊ/. **1** If something is **below** something else, it is in a lower position. EG *The sun had just sunk below the horizon... ...a mile below the surface of the ocean... Their office is on the floor below... The fish attacked from below.* ● **Below ground** or **below the ground** means in the ground. EG *They spend their lives below ground.* PREP OR ADV ● PHRASE

2 You use **below** in a piece of writing to refer to something that is mentioned further on in it. EG *Get legal advice on how to do this (see below).* ADV

3 If something is **below** a particular amount, rate, or level, it is less than that amount, rate, or level. EG *The temperature was below freezing... Their reading ability is below average.* PREP

4 If someone is **below** you in an organization, they are lower in rank. EG *Below him are 14 Regional Health Authorities... Problems occur at the departmental level or below.* PREP OR ADV

belt /bɛlt/, **belts, belting, belted. 1** A **belt** is a strip of leather or cloth that you fasten round your waist. EG *From his belt there dangled a large ring of keys.* ● See also **safety belt, seat-belt.** N COUNT

2 A **belt** is also a circular strip of rubber that is used in machines to drive moving parts or to move objects along. EG *A belt snapped in the vacuum cleaner.* ● See also **conveyor belt.** N COUNT

3 A **belt** of land or sea is a long, narrow area of it that has some special feature. EG *...the cotton belt of the USA.* N COUNT+SUPP

4 If someone **belts** you, they hit you very hard. EG *Her Dad belted her when she got home late.* v+o Informal

5 If you **belt** somewhere, you move or travel there very fast. EG *I came belting out of the woods.* v+A Informal

6 Belt is used in these phrases. **6.1** A comment or remark that is **below the belt** is cruel and unfair. **6.2** If you have something **under** your belt, you have already achieved it or done it. EG *You already had one university degree under your belt.* **6.3** When you **tighten** your belt, you have less money to spend than you used to. EG *We've all got to tighten our belts, you know.* PHRASES Informal

bemoan /bɪˈməʊn/, **bemoans, bemoaning, bemoaned.** If you **bemoan** something, you express sorrow or dissatisfaction about it. EG *The farmer bemoaned his loss... They were weeping and bemoaning their fate.* v+o Formal

bemused /bɪˈmjuːzd/. If you are **bemused,** you are puzzled or confused. ADJ QUALIT

bench /bɛntʃ/, **benches. 1** A **bench** is **1.1** a long seat of wood or metal that two or more people can sit on. EG *Rudolf sat on the bench and waited... ...a park bench.* **1.2** a long, narrow table in a factory or laboratory. EG *...the carpenter's bench... ...a work bench.* N COUNT

2 In Parliament, different groups sit on different **benches**. For example, the government sits on the government **benches**. N PLURAL

bend /bɛnd/, **bends, bending, bent** /bɛnt/. **1** When someone **bends**, they move the top part of their body towards the ground. EG *He bent down and undid his shoelaces... He was bending over the basin.* ◊ **bent.** EG *Dan is bent over the fireplace.* v:USU+A ◊ ADJ PRED

2 When you **bend** a part of your body such as your arm or leg, you change its position so that it is no longer straight. ◊ **bent.** EG *Keep your knees bent.* v-ERG ◊ ADJ CLASSIF

3 When you **bend** something that is flat or straight, you use force to make it curved or angular. EG *...pliers for bending wire.* ◊ **bent.** EG *...two bent pipes.* v-ERG ◊ ADJ CLASSIF

4 A **bend** in a road, river, or pipe is a curved part of it. EG *When I reached the first bend, I ran.* N COUNT

5 If you say that someone **is bending over backwards,** you mean that they are trying very hard to be helpful or kind. EG *We bend over backwards to keep young people out of prison.* PHRASE

6 If you say that someone or something is driving you **round the bend,** you mean that they are annoying you or upsetting you very much. PHRASE Informal

7 If you **bend the rules,** you interpret them in a way that allows you to do something that they really forbid. PHRASE

8 to **bend double** or to **be bent double:** see **double.** ● See also **bent.**

beneath /bɪˈniːθ/. **1** Something that is **beneath** another thing is under the other thing. EG *She concealed the bottle beneath her mattress... ...the soft ground beneath his feet... A trickle of sweat ran down his spine, beneath the loose cotton shirt.* PREP

2 If you talk about what is **beneath** the surface of something, you are talking about the aspects of it which are hidden or not obvious. EG *Beneath the veneer of civilization, he was a very vulgar man.* PREP

benefactor /ˈbɛnɪ²fæktə/, **benefactors.** A **benefactor** is a person who helps someone by giving them money. EG *He went to Long Beach to thank his benefactor.* N COUNT : OFT+POSS

beneficial /ˌbɛnɪˈfɪʃ³l/. Something that is **beneficial** helps people or improves their lives. EG *...the beneficial effects of exercise... Such a system will be beneficial to society.* ADJ QUALIT OFT+to

beneficiary /ˌbɛnɪˈfɪʃə³riˈ/, **beneficiaries. 1** A **beneficiary** of something is someone who is helped by it. EG *Who are the main beneficiaries of the changes?* A N COUNT: OFT+POSS

2 The **beneficiaries** of a will legally receive money or property from someone when they die. EG *He wrote a will naming his children as beneficiaries.* N COUNT

benefit /ˈbɛnɪ²fɪt/, **benefits, benefiting, benefited. 1** A **benefit** is something that helps you or improves your life. EG *The industrial age has brought innumerable benefits... ...the benefits of modern technology.* N COUNT

2 If something is to your **benefit** or is of **benefit** to you, it helps you or improves your life. EG *This will be of benefit to the country as a whole.* N UNCOUNT

3 If you do something **for the benefit of** someone, you do it specially for them. EG *He smiled for the benefit of the reporters... They explained, for the benefit of the members, what they had done.* PHRASE

4 If something **benefits** you or if you **benefit** from it, it helps you or improves your life. EG *...a medical service which will benefit rich and poor... The firm benefited from his ingenuity.* v-ERG IF V, THEN +from/by

5 If you have the **benefit** of something, it gives you an advantage. EG *I had the benefit of a good education.* N SING the+N+of

6 If you **give** someone **the benefit of the doubt,** you accept what they say as true, because you cannot prove that it is not true. PHRASE

7 Benefit is money that is given by the govern- N UNCOUNT

> What is the difference between a bend and a bent?

ment to people who are poor, ill, or unemployed. EG *You are entitled to child benefit... He is unemployed and receiving benefit.*

benevolent /bɪˈnevələnt/. Someone who is benevolent is kind, helpful, and tolerant. EG *My aunt and uncle were looking benevolent and prepared to forgive me... We live under a benevolent government.* ◊ **benevolently.** EG *He smiled benevolently.* ◊ ADV ◊ **benevolence** /bɪˈnevələns/. EG *...the benevolence of the Vicar's smile.* ◊ N UNCOUNT

benign /bɪˈnaɪn/. 1 Someone who is benign is ADJ QUALIT kind, gentle, and harmless. EG *They are among the most benign people on earth... His face was calm and benign.* ◊ **benignly.** EG *The vicar smiled* ◊ ADV *benignly.*

2 A **benign** disease or substance will not cause ADJ CLASSIF death or serious harm. EG *...women with benign* Technical *breast disease.*

bent /bent/. 1 Bent is the past participle and past tense of **bend.**

2 If an object is **bent**, it is damaged and no longer ADJ QUALIT has its correct shape. EG *...bent saucepans.*

3 If a person is **bent**, their body has become curved ADJ QUALIT because of old age or disease. EG *He was bent with arthritis... ...old Mr Halliday, bent and white-haired.*

4 If you are **bent** on doing something, you are ADJ PRED determined to do it. EG *They are bent on improving* +on/upon *existing weapon systems.*

5 If you have a **bent** for something, you have a N SING+SUPP natural interest in it or a natural ability to do it. EG *...a boy with a mechanical bent.*

bequeath /bɪˈkwiːð/, **bequeaths, bequeathing, bequeathed.** 1 If you **bequeath** your money or V+O+to OR property to someone, you legally state that they V+O+O should have it when you die. EG *He bequeathed his* Formal *collection to the nation... ...bequeathing me an annual income of a thousand pounds.*

2 If you **bequeath** an idea or system, you leave it V+O+O OR for other people to use or develop. EG *...the country* V+O+to *your generation has bequeathed us... ...the econo-* Literary *my bequeathed to the new President.*

bequest /bɪˈkwest/, **bequests.** A **bequest** is mon- N COUNT ey or property which you legally leave to someone Formal when you die. EG *Except for a few small bequests to relatives, he left all his property to charity.*

bereaved /bɪˈriːvd/. A **bereaved** person is one ADJ CLASSIF: who had a relative or close friend who has recently USU ATTRIB died. EG *His personal effects would be returned to* Formal *the bereaved family.*

bereavement /bɪˈriːvmənt/, **bereavements.** N UNCOUNT **Bereavement** is the experience you have or the OR N COUNT state you are in when a relative or close friend Formal dies. EG *...bereavement in old age... ...planning for the future after a bereavement.*

bereft /bɪˈreft/. If a person or thing is **bereft** of ADJ PRED+of something, they no longer have it. EG *They were* Literary *bereft of speech... Her cheeks were bereft of colour... ...crumbling slums bereft of basic amenities.*

beret /ˈbereɪ/, **berets.** A **beret** is a circular, flat N COUNT hat that is made of soft material and has no brim.

berry /ˈberiˈ/, **berries.** A **berry** is a small, round N COUNT: fruit that grows on a bush or a tree. You can eat USU PLURAL some berries.

berserk /bəˈzɜːk, -sɜːk/. If someone goes **berserk**, ADJ PRED they lose control of themselves and become very violent. EG *One night she went berserk and wrecked her room.*

berth /bɜːθ/, **berths.** 1 If you **give** someone or PHRASE something **a wide berth**, you avoid them because they are unpleasant or dangerous. EG *One gives a wide berth to drunkards lying on the pavement.*

2 A **berth** is 2.1 a space in a harbour where a ship N COUNT stays for a period of time. 2.2 a bed in a boat, train, or caravan. EG *...berths on the boat from Harwich... ...a twelve berth caravan.*

beseech /bɪˈsiːtʃ/, **beseeches, beseeching, be-** V+O+to-INF **sought** /bɪˈsɔːt/. The form **beseeched** is some- OR QUOTE times used for the past tense and past participle. Literary

If you **beseech** someone to do something, you ask them very insistently and desperately. EG *I beseech you to tell me... 'Cal, Cal!' his sister besought him, 'Remember your promise!'* ◊ **beseeching.** EG *She* ADJ CLASSIF: *was staring at me with great beseeching eyes...* USU ATTRIB *Mary put a beseeching hand on my arm.* ◊ **beseechingly.** EG *Larsen looked beseechingly at* ◊ ADV *Rudolph.*

beset /bɪˈset/, **besets, besetting.** The form **beset** V+O: USU PASS is used in the present tense and is also the past +by/with tense and past participle. Formal

If someone or something **is beset** by problems or fears, they have many problems or fears which affect them severely. EG *She had been beset by doubts... The policy is beset with problems... ...the difficulties that beset the Africans.*

beside /bɪˈsaɪd/. 1 Something that is **beside** some- PREP thing else is at the side of it or next to it. EG *I sat down beside my wife... There right beside the road is a large grey house.*

2 If you are **beside yourself** with anger or excite- PHRASE ment, you are extremely angry or excited.

3 See also paragraph 1 of **besides. ● beside the point:** see **point.**

besides /bɪˈsaɪdz/. The form **beside** can be used for paragraph 1.

1 **Besides** something or **beside** it means in addi- PREP OR ADV tion to it. EG *What languages do you know besides English?... He needed so much else besides.*

2 You can use **besides** when you are making an ADV SEN additional point or giving an additional reason for something. EG *Would these figures prove anything? And besides, who keeps such statistics?*

besiege /bɪˈsiːdʒ/, **besieges, besieging, be-** **sieged.** 1 If you **are besieged** by people, many V+O: USU PASS people want something from you and continually +by/with bother you. EG *I am besieged with visitors from abroad.*

2 If soldiers **besiege** a place, they surround it and V+O: USU PASS wait for the people in it to surrender.

besought /bɪˈsɔːt/ is the past tense and past participle of **beseech.**

best /best/. 1 Best is 1.1 the superlative of good. ADJ QUALIT: EG *That was one of the best films I've seen... ...my* SUPERL *best friend... I'm doing what is best for you... It's best to be as clear as possible... They told me it was best that I stay in New York... There were hills and trees and, best of all, a lake... I want her to have the very best. Private room. Special nurses. Everything.* **1.2** the superlative of well. EG *I think mine* ADV: SUPERL *would suit her best.*

2 Your **best** is the greatest effort or the highest N SING achievement that you are capable of. EG *They are trying their best to discourage them... The way to get the best out of a diesel is to drive it smoothly.*

3 If you like something **best** or like it the **best**, you ADV OR ADJ: prefer it. EG *Which did you like best – the Vivaldi or* SUPERL *the Schumann?*

4 **Best** is also used in these phrases. **4.1** You use **at** PHRASE **best** to indicate that even if you describe something as favourably as possible, it is still not very good. EG *At best the proposal was a lame compromise.* **4.2** If you **make the best of** an unsatisfac- PHRASE tory situation, you accept it and try to be cheerful about it. EG *There is nowhere else to go, so make the best of it.* **4.3** If someone does something **as** PHRASE **best** they **can**, they try as hard as they can to succeed in doing it. EG *I kept out of trouble as best I could.* **4.4** You can say **'All the best'** when you are CONVENTION saying goodbye to someone, or at the end of a letter.

5 **Best** is also used to form the superlative of compound adjectives beginning with 'good' and 'well'. EG *...the best-looking women... ...the best-known author of books for children.*

6 to **do** your **best:** see **do. ●** to **know best:** see **know. ● the best part** of something: see **part. ●** to **think the best of** someone: see **think. ● the best**

of both worlds: see **world**. ● See also **second-best**.

bestial /bestɪəl/. You describe behaviour as **bestial** when it is very unpleasant or disgusting. EG *His habits are bestial... ...bestial violence.*   ADJ CLASSIF Literary

bestow /bi'stəʊ/, **bestows, bestowing, bestowed.** If you **bestow** something on someone, you give it to them. EG *The Duke bestowed this property on him... ...the attention bestowed upon her son.*   V+O: OFT+on/upon Formal

best-seller, best-sellers. You say that a book is a **best-seller** when a large number of copies of it have been sold. EG *It was soon a best-seller in Los Angeles.*   N COUNT

bet /bet/, **bets, betting.** The form **bet** is used in the present tense and is the past tense and past participle of the verb.
1 If you **bet** on a future event, you make an agreement with someone that if what you say will happen does happen, they will give you a sum of money, and if you are wrong you will give them a sum of money. EG *I told him which horse to bet on... He bet me a hundred pounds that I wouldn't get through.* ◊ **betting.** EG *They spend their money on betting.*   V+on, V+O:OFT+on, OR V+O+O / ◊ N UNCOUNT
2 A **bet** is the act of betting on something, or the amount of money that you agree to give. EG *I didn't put a bet on.*   N COUNT: OFT+on
3 You use **bet** in expressions such as 'I bet', 'I'll bet', and 'my bet is', to say that you are sure that something is true or will happen. EG *I bet nobody's been here before... My bet is he'll be right back.*   PHRASE Informal
4 You say **'You bet'** as an emphatic way of saying 'yes' or of emphasizing a statement. EG *'Are you coming?' – 'You bet!'... You bet I'm getting out.*   CONVENTION Informal
5 If you tell someone that something is **a good bet** or is their **best bet**, you are suggesting that it is the thing or course of action they should choose. EG *Your best bet is to go to Thomas Cook in the High Street.*   PHRASE

betray /bi'treɪ/, **betrays, betraying, betrayed.** 1 If you **betray** someone who thinks you support or love them, you do something which harms them, often by helping their enemies or opponents. EG *His best friend betrayed him... Daintry felt betrayed.*   V+O
2 If you **betray** something such as a person's trust, you behave badly towards them when they trust you. EG *He would be betraying their trust if he ignored their wishes now.*   V+O
3 If you **betray** a secret, you tell it to people who you should not tell it to. EG *The name was strictly private, never to be betrayed to a stranger.*   V+O
4 If you **betray** a feeling or quality, you show it without intending to. EG *People learned never to betray their anger.*   V+O

betrayal /bi'treɪəl/, **betrayals.** If a person betrays something or someone, you refer to their action as a **betrayal**. EG *...the betrayal of socialist principles... Alex was filled with anger at Ned's betrayal of their secret sign.*   N COUNT OR UNCOUNT: OFT+of

betrothed /bi'trəʊðd/. If you are **betrothed** to someone, you are engaged to be married to them.   ADJ CLASSIF Outdated

better /betə/. 1 **Better** is 1.1 the comparative form of **good**. EG *The results were better than expected... I was better at mathematics than other subjects... Milk is much better for you than lemonade... It was better than nothing.* 1.2 the comparative of **well**. EG *Some people can ski better than others... We are better housed than ever before.*   ADJ QUALIT: COMPAR / ADV : COMPAR
2 If you like one thing **better** than another, you like it more. EG *I love this place better than anywhere else.*   ADV : COMPAR
3 If you say that someone **had better** do something, you mean that they ought to do it. EG *I'd better go.*   PHRASE
4 If someone **is better off**, they are in a pleasanter situation than before, often because they have more money than they had before. EG *They are much better off than they were two years ago... She will be better off in hospital... I'd be better off dead.*   PHRASE

5 If something changes **for the better**, it improves. EG *The weather had changed for the better.*   PHRASE
6 If something **gets the better of** you, you are unable to resist it. EG *My curiosity got the better of me.*   PHRASE
7 If you are **better** after an illness or injury, you are feeling less ill. EG *Her cold was better.*   ADJ PRED: COMPAR
8 You use **better** to form the comparative of compound adjectives beginning with 'good' or 'well.' EG *My husband was better-looking than that... She's much better known in Europe.*
9 **to know better**: see **know**. ● **the better part of**: see **part**. ● **to think better of it**: see **think**.

between /bi'twiːn/. 1 If something is **between** two things or is **in between** them, it has one of the things on one side of it and the other thing on the other side. EG *The island is midway between Sao Paolo and Porto Alegre... She put the cigarette between her lips and lit it... ...Penn Close, Court Road, and all the little side streets in between.*   PREP OR ADV
2 If people or things are moving **between** two places, they are moving regularly from one place to the other and back again. EG *I have spent a lifetime commuting between Britain and the United States.*   PREP
3 A relationship, discussion, or difference **between** two people, groups, or things is one that involves them both or relates to them both. EG *...marriages between Dutch men and African women... ...negotiations between Britain and Germany... ...a clash between the two gangs... I asked whether there was much difference between British and European law.*   PREP
4 If something stands **between** you and what you want, it prevents you from having it. EG *These men stand between you and the top jobs.*   PREP
5 If something is **between** or **in between** two amounts or ages, it is greater or older than the first one and smaller or younger than the second one. EG *...at temperatures between 36 and 39°C... ...a man aged between 20 and 25.*   PREP
6 If something happens **between** or **in between** two times or events, it happens after the first time or event and before the second one. EG *The house was built between 1840 and 1852... Between sessions I spent my time with my husband.*   PREP
7 If you must choose **between** two things, you must choose one thing or the other one. EG *The choice is between defeat or survival.*   PREP
8 If people have a particular amount of something **between** them, this is the total amount that they have. EG *They have both been married before and have five children between them.*   PREP
9 When something is divided or shared **between** people, they each have a share of it. EG *The land was divided equally between them.*   PREP

beverage /bevəʳrɪdʒ/, **beverages.** A **beverage** is a drink.   N COUNT Formal

bevy /bevi/. A **bevy** of people or things is a group of them. EG *...a bevy of village girls... There are a whole bevy of reasons for this.*   N PART : SING

beware /bi'weə/. If you tell someone to **beware** of a person or thing, you are warning them that the person or thing may harm them. EG *Beware of the dog!... I would beware of companies which depend on one product only.*   V : USU IMPER

bewildered /bi'wɪldəd/. If you are **bewildered**, you are very confused and cannot understand something or decide what you should do. EG *His wife watched him, bewildered... I was bewildered by the volume of noise... ...bewildered and embarrassed tourists.*   ADJ CLASSIF

bewildering /bi'wɪldərɪŋ/. Something that is **bewildering** is very confusing and difficult to understand or to make a decision about. EG *There is a*

How many people do you know who are betrothed?

bicycle

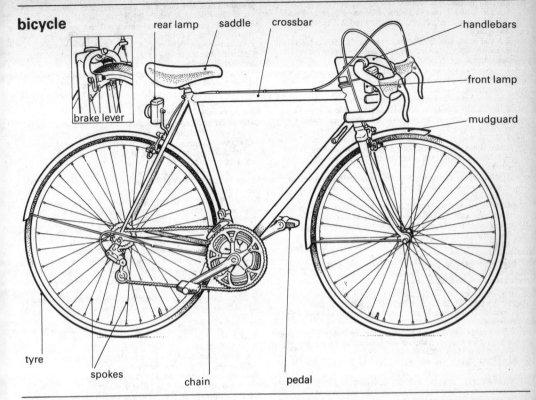

rear lamp   saddle   crossbar   handlebars   front lamp   mudguard   brake lever   tyre   spokes   chain   pedal

bewildering variety of activities... It was a bewildering and upsetting experience.

bewilderment /bɪˈwɪldəməⁿnt/ is the feeling of N UNCOUNT being bewildered. EG *'But I just rented it,' Morris protested in bewilderment... To my complete bewilderment, she rang and offered to buy the place.*

bewitch /bɪˈwɪtʃ/, **bewitches, bewitching, be-** V+O **witched.** If someone or something **bewitches** you, you find them so attractive that you cannot think about anything else. EG *She had been bewitching the audience with her singing.* ◊ **bewitching.** EG ◊ ADJ QUALIT *...a bewitching smile... ...the bewitching Mrs Paget.*

beyond /bɪˈjɒnd/. **1** If something is **beyond** a PREP OR ADV place, it is on the other side of it. EG *...a farm beyond Barnham... He indicated the street beyond.*

2 If something extends, continues, or progresses PREP **beyond** a particular thing or point, it extends, continues, or progresses further than that thing or point. EG *My responsibilities go beyond computers... Few children remain in the school beyond the age of 16... She was there for twenty years without progressing beyond her secretarial status.*

3 If someone or something is **beyond** understand- PREP ing, control, or help, they have become impossible to understand, control, or help. EG *The situation has changed beyond recognition.*

4 If you say that something is **beyond** you, you PREP mean that you cannot understand it. EG *How he managed to find us is beyond me.*

bias /ˈbaɪəs/, **biases.** Someone who shows **bias** is N UNCOUNT unfair in their judgements or decisions, because OR N COUNT they allow themselves to be influenced by their own opinions, rather than considering the facts. EG *You're accusing me of bias in my marking... There's an intense bias against women.*

biased /ˈbaɪəst/. **1** Someone who is **biased** shows ADJ QUALIT bias in their judgements or decisions. EG *I am biased in favour of Eisenhower.*

2 If something is **biased** towards one thing, it is ADJ PRED : USU more concerned with it than with other things. EG +*towards The university is biased towards the sciences.*

bib /bɪb/, **bibs.** A **bib** is a piece of cloth or plastic N COUNT which is worn by very young children while they are eating, to protect their clothes.

bible /ˈbaɪbəl/, **bibles. 1** The **Bible** is the sacred N PROPER : book on which the Jewish and Christian religions *the+N* are based. EG *...a new translation of the Bible.* ◊ **biblical** /ˈbɪblɪkəl/. EG *...the biblical account of* ◊ ADJ CLASSIF : *creation.* ATTRIB

2 A **bible** is a copy of the Bible. EG *He took a bible* N COUNT *from his pack and began reading.*

bibliography /ˌbɪbliˈɒɡrəfiⁱ/, **bibliographies.** A N COUNT **bibliography** is **1** a list of books on a particular subject. EG *...a bibliography of basic works in philosophy.* **2** a list of the books and articles that are referred to in a particular book.

biceps /ˈbaɪsɛps/. Your **biceps** are the large mus- N COUNT cles at the front of the upper part of your arms. **Biceps** is both the singular and the plural form.

bicker /ˈbɪkə/, **bickers, bickering, bickered.** V : USU+A When people **bicker**, they argue or quarrel about unimportant things. EG *The girls were bickering over a packet of felt pens.* ◊ **bickering.** EG *...after* ◊ N UNCOUNT *months of bickering and confusion.*

bicycle /ˈbaɪsɪkəl/, **bicycles.** A **bicycle** is a vehi- N COUNT cle with two wheels which you ride by sitting on it and pushing two pedals with your feet.

bid /bɪd/, **bids, bidding; bade** /bæd, beɪd/, **bid-** **den.** The form **bid** is used in the present tense for all the verbs, and is also the past tense and past participle for the verb in paragraph 3. The past tense of the verb in paragraphs 4 and 5 is **bade** and the past participle is **bidden**.

1 A **bid** is an attempt to obtain or do something. EG N COUNT :
He made a bid for power... Brandt failed in a bid to OFT+*for*
see Reagan. OR *to*-INF

2 A **bid** is also an offer to pay a particular amount N COUNT :
of money to buy something. EG *...bids for other oil* OFT+*for*
companies.

3 If you **bid** for something that is being sold, you V OR V+O :
offer to pay a particular amount of money for it. EG OFT+*for*
...companies that want to bid for Conoco... He bid a
quarter of a million pounds for the portrait.

4 If you **bid** someone good morning or **bid** them V+O+O
farewell, you say hello or goodbye to them. EG *I bid* OR V+O+to
you good night, young man... We bade her farewell. Formal

5 If you **bid** someone do something, you ask or V+O+INF
invite them to do it. EG *The holy man bade them* Literary
rise from their knees... As bidden, Mrs Oliver sat
down.

bidder /bɪdə/. If you sell something to the **highest** PHRASE
bidder, you sell it to the person who offers most
money for it.

bide /baɪd/, **bides, biding, bided.** If you **bide** your PHRASE
time, you wait for a good opportunity before doing
something. EG *He never showed this anger but*
bided his time.

bidet /biːdeɪ/, **bidets.** A **bidet** is a low basin in a N COUNT
bathroom which you wash your bottom in.

big /bɪg/, **bigger, biggest. 1** Something that is **big** ADJ QUALIT
is **1.1** large in size. EG *He was holding a big black*
umbrella... A big crowd had gathered. **1.2** great in
degree, extent, or importance. EG *I have noticed a*
big change in Sue... The biggest problem at the
moment is unemployment... You're making a big
mistake.

2 You can refer to your older brother or sister as ADJ CLASSIF :
your **big** brother or sister. EG *He hoped that his big* ATTRIB
brother would take him out again. Informal

biggish /bɪgɪʃ/ means fairly big. EG *He was a* ADJ QUALIT :
biggish fellow... ...a biggish town. USU ATTRIB

bigot /bɪgət/, **bigots.** A **bigot** is someone who is N COUNT
bigoted. EG *...the religious bigots who put him on*
trial.

bigoted /bɪgətᵻd/. Someone who is **bigoted** has ADJ QUALIT
strong and often unreasonable opinions and will
not change them, even when they are proved to be
wrong. EG *He was a bigoted, narrow-minded fanat-*
ic.

bigotry /bɪgətrɪ/ is the possession or expression N UNCOUNT
of strong and often unreasonable opinions. EG
...campaigns against bigotry and racism.

bigwig /bɪgwɪg/, **bigwigs.** You can refer to an N COUNT
important person as a **bigwig**. EG *The bigwigs in* Informal
Paris wanted to have a look at it.

bijou /biːʒuː/. Small houses are sometimes de- ADJ CLASSIF :
scribed as **bijou** houses in order to make them ATTRIB
sound attractive or fashionable. EG *...a bijou resi-*
dence.

bike /baɪk/, **bikes.** A **bike** is a bicycle or a N COUNT
motorcycle. Informal

bikini /bɪkiːnɪ/, **bikinis.** A **bikini** is a two-piece N COUNT
swimming costume worn by women.

bile /baɪl/ is a liquid produced by your liver which N UNCOUNT
helps you to digest fat.

bilingual /baɪlɪŋgwəl/. **1 Bilingual** means involv- ADJ CLASSIF
ing or using two languages. EG *...bilingual diction-*
aries... ...bilingual street signs.

2 Someone who is **bilingual** can speak two lan- ADJ CLASSIF
guages. EG *...a bilingual local farmer.*

bilious /bɪlɪəs/. **1 Bilious** means unpleasant and ADJ CLASSIF
rather disgusting. EG *...a rather bilious green.*

2 If you feel **bilious**, you feel sick and have a ADJ CLASSIF
headache. EG *...bilious attacks.*

bill /bɪl/, **bills, billing, billed. 1** A **bill** is a written N COUNT :
statement of money that you owe for goods or USU+SUPP
services. EG *...an enormous electricity bill.*

2 A **bill** is also a piece of paper money. EG *...a dollar* N COUNT
bill. American

3 In parliament, a **bill** is a formal statement of a N COUNT

proposed new law that is discussed and then voted
on. EG *The Bill was defeated by 238 votes to 145.*

4 The **bill** of a show or concert is **4.1** the people N SING : *the*+N
who are going to appear in it. EG *There were some*
famous names on the bill. **4.2** the items of enter- N SING
tainment that it consists of. EG *The Chamber Opera*
is offering a double bill of Mozart and Haydn.

5 If someone **is billed** to appear at a particular V+O : USU PASS
show, it has been advertised that they are going to
be in it. ◇ **billing.** EG *She was booked for two* ◇ N UNCOUNT
weeks at the Coliseum with top billing.

6 A bird's **bill** is its beak. N COUNT

billboard /bɪlbɔːd/, **billboards.** A **billboard** is a N COUNT
very large board on which posters are displayed.

billiards /bɪlɪədz/. The form **billiard** is used N UNCOUNT
before another noun. **Billiards** is a game played
on a large table, in which you use a long stick
called a cue to hit small heavy balls against each
other or into pockets around the sides of the table.
EG *...a game of billiards... ...a billiard table.*

billion /bɪljən/, **billions. 1** A **billion** is a thousand NUMBER
million. See the entry headed NUMBER. EG *...4.5*
billion years ago... ...a £1 billion contract.

2 You can also use **billions** and **billion** to mean an N PART
extremely large amount. EG *...billions of tons of*
ice... They printed the papers off by the billion.

billow /bɪləʊ/, **billows, billowing, billowed. 1** V
When something made of cloth **billows**, it swells
out and flaps slowly in the wind. EG *Hundreds of*
flags billowed in the breeze.

2 When smoke or cloud **billows**, it moves slowly V : USU+A
upwards or across the sky. EG *Clouds of white dust*
billowed out.

3 A **billow** of smoke is a large mass of it rising N COUNT+SUPP
slowly into the air. EG *The flames illuminated*
billows of smoke.

bin /bɪn/, **bins.** A **bin** is **1** a container that you put N COUNT
rubbish in. EG *She threw both letters in the bin.* **2** a
container that you keep or store things in. EG *...the*
computer storage bin. ● See also **litter bin**.

binary /baɪnəˈriˈ/. The **binary** system expresses ADJ CLASSIF :
numbers using only the two digits 0 and 1. It is used ATTRIB
especially in computing.

bind /baɪnd/, **binds, binding, bound** /baʊnd/. **1** If V+O : USU+A
you **bind** something, you tie a piece of string or
rope tightly round it so that it is held firmly. EG *His*
hands were bound behind the post.

2 If something **binds** people, it unites them. EG *We* V+O : USU+A
were bound together by our common grief... ...the Literary
ideology which binds members to the group.

3 If a duty or legal order **binds** you to a course of V+O : USU+A
action, it forces you to do it. EG *This oath binds you*
to secrecy.

4 When a book **is bound**, the pages are joined V+O : USU PASS
together and the cover is put on.

5 If you say that something is a **bind**, you mean N SING : *a*+N
that it is unpleasant and boring to do. EG *It's a* Informal
terrible bind to have to cook your own meals.

6 See also **binding, bound**.

binder /baɪndə/, **binders.** A **binder** is a hard N COUNT
cover with metal rings inside, which is used to hold
loose pieces of paper.

binding /baɪndɪŋ/, **bindings. 1** If a promise or ADJ CLASSIF
agreement is **binding**, it must be obeyed or carried out. EG *...a Spanish law that is still binding in*
California.

2 The **binding** of a book is its cover. EG *...books in* N COUNT OR
ugly economy bindings... ...durable leather binding. N UNCOUNT

3 Binding is a strip of material that you put round N UNCOUNT OR
the edge of a piece of cloth or an object, in order to N COUNT
strengthen it or decorate it.

binge /bɪndʒ/, **binges.** If you go on a **binge**, you N COUNT
go somewhere and drink a lot of alcohol. EG *Barber* Informal
had gone on a monumental binge the night before.

bingo /bɪŋgəʊ/ is a game in which each player has N UNCOUNT a card with numbers on. Someone calls out numbers and if you are the first person to have all your numbers called out, you win the game.

binoculars

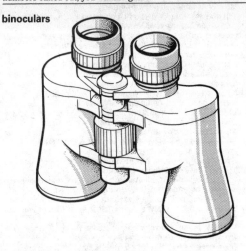

binoculars /bɪˈnɒkjəˈləz/ consist of two small N PLURAL telescopes joined together side by side, which you look through in order to see things that are a long way away. EG *He studied the house through his binoculars... ...a pair of binoculars.*

biochemistry /baɪəˈkemɪstriˈ/ is the study of the N UNCOUNT chemistry of living things.

biographer /baɪɒgrəfə/, **biographers.** Someone's **biographer** is a person who writes an account of their life. N COUNT

biographical /baɪəˈgræfɪkəˈl/. You use **biographical** to describe something which gives information about someone's life. EG *...a brief biographical sketch.* ADJ CLASSIF

biography /baɪɒgrəfiˈ/, **biographies. 1** A **biography** of someone is an account of their life, written by someone else. EG *...a biography of Dylan Thomas... I'm having my biography written.* N COUNT

2 Biography is the branch of literature which N UNCOUNT deals with accounts of people's lives.

biological /baɪəlɒdʒɪkəˈl/. **1** A **biological** process, system, or product is connected with or produced by natural processes in plants, animals, and other living things. EG *...the effect of heat on biological activity.* ◊ **biologically.** EG *These beings* ◊ ADV *were biologically different from man.* ADJ CLASSIF

2 Biological studies and discoveries are connected ADJ CLASSIF : with research in biology. EG *...recent biological* ATTRIB *breakthroughs.*

3 Biological weapons and **biological** warfare ADJ CLASSIF : involve the use of organisms which damage living ATTRIB things. EG *...the stockpiling of biological weapons.*

biology /baɪɒlədʒɪ/ is the science which is con- N UNCOUNT cerned with the study of living things. ◊ **biologist** ◊ N COUNT /baɪɒlədʒɪst/, **biologists.** EG *This has puzzled biologists for a long time.*

birch /bɜːtʃ/, **birches. 1** A **birch** or a **birch tree** N COUNT OR is a tall tree with thin branches. EG *...forests of pine* N UNCOUNT *and birch.*

2 The **birch** is a punishment in which someone is N SING : the+N hit with a wooden cane. EG *Some MPs think we should bring back the birch.*

bird /bɜːd/, **birds. 1** A **bird** is a creature with N COUNT feathers and wings. Female birds lay eggs. Most birds can fly.

2 If you say that **a bird in the hand is worth two** PHRASE **in the bush**, you mean that it is better to keep

what you already have than to risk losing it by trying to achieve something else.

3 If you say that something will **kill two birds** PHRASE **with one stone**, you mean that it will have two good results, and not just one.

4 Some men refer to young women as **birds**. Many N COUNT women think that this is insulting. EG *There were* Informal *some smashing birds there.*

birdcage /bɜːdkeɪdʒ/, **birdcages.** A **birdcage** is N COUNT a cage in which a bird is kept.

bird of prey, birds of prey. A **bird of prey** is a N COUNT bird, such as an eagle or a hawk, that kills and eats other birds and animals.

Biro /baɪrəʊ/, **Biros.** A **Biro** is a pen with a small N COUNT metal ball at its tip which transfers the ink onto the Trademark paper. EG *Keep a notebook and a Biro handy.*

birth /bɜːθ/, **births. 1** When a baby is born, you N UNCOUNT refer to this event as its **birth.** EG *...the birth of her* OR N COUNT *first child... ...a girl deaf from birth... ...a birth certificate.* ● When a woman **gives birth**, she ● PHRASE produces a baby from her body. EG *Betta gave birth to our third child.* ● See also **date of birth.**

2 If you are French **by birth**, you are French PHRASE because your parents are French, or because you were born in France. EG *Dr Cort's father is a Russian by birth.*

3 The country, town, or village **of** your **birth** is the PHRASE place where you were born.

4 You can refer to the beginning or origin of N SING+SUPP something as its **birth.** EG *...the birth of the Indonesian Republic... ...the birth of television.*

birth control is the same as contraception. N UNCOUNT

birthday /bɜːθdeɪ/, **birthdays.** Your **birthday** is N COUNT the anniversary of the date on which you were born. EG *Happy birthday!... ...a birthday party.*

birthplace /bɜːθpleɪs/, **birthplaces. 1** Your N COUNT+POSS **birthplace** is the place where you were born.

2 The **birthplace** of something is the place where N SING+POSS it began or originated. EG *...the birthplace of the Renaissance.*

birth rate, birth rates. The **birth rate** in a place N COUNT is the number of babies born there for every 1000 people during a particular period of time.

biscuit /bɪskɪt/, **biscuits.** A **biscuit** is a small, flat N COUNT cake that is crisp and usually sweet. EG *Do you want* British *a biscuit?... Have a chocolate biscuit.*

bisect /baɪsekt/, **bisects, bisecting, bisected.** If V+O something long and thin **bisects** an area or line, it divides the area or line in half. EG *The main north-south road bisects the town.*

bishop /bɪʃəp/, **bishops. 1** A **bishop** is a clergy- N COUNT man of high rank, especially in the Roman Catholic, Anglican, and Orthodox churches. EG *...the Bishop of Exeter.*

2 In chess, a **bishop** is a piece that is moved N COUNT diagonally across the board.

bistro /biːstrəʊ/, **bistros.** A **bistro** is a small N COUNT restaurant or bar.

bit /bɪt/, **bits. 1** A **bit** of something is a small N PART amount or piece of it. EG *There'll be a bit of* Informal *sunshine... I was doing a bit of shopping... ...a little bit of cheese... I really enjoyed your letter, especially the bits about Dr O'Shea.*

2 Quite a bit of something is quite a lot of it. EG *...a* PHRASE *rich Irishman who's made quite a bit of money.* Informal

3 A **bit** is also an item or thing of a particular kind. N PART EG *They charge for every bit of work... ...a bit of* Informal *furniture.*

4 A **bit** means to a small extent or degree. EG *He* PHRASE *was a bit deaf... You're a bit late, aren't you?* Informal

5 You can also use **a bit** in these ways. **5.1** You can PHRASES use **a bit of** to make a statement less extreme. For Informal example, the statement 'It's a bit of a nuisance' is less extreme than 'It's a nuisance'. EG *Our room was a bit of a mess... This has all come as a bit of a shock.* **5.2** You use **not a bit** when you want to Informal make a strong negative statement. EG *It was all very clean and tidy, not a bit like his back garden... You haven't changed a bit.* **5.3** If you do something Informal

for a bit, you do it for a short period of time. EG *Why can't we stay here for a bit?* **5.4** You can say Informal that someone's behaviour is **a bit much** when you are annoyed about it. EG *It's asking a bit much to expect a lift.*

6 You say that something is **every bit as** good, PHRASE interesting, or worthwhile as something else to emphasize that it is just as good, interesting, or worthwhile. EG *She wanted to prove to them that she was every bit as clever as they were.*

7 If something is smashed or taken **to bits** or falls PHRASE **to bits**, it is broken or comes apart so that it is in several pieces. EG *The dog was pulling the Christmas tree to bits.*

8 You can refer to a collection of different things PHRASE as **bits and pieces**. EG *I saw her gathering up her bits and pieces for the move to the cabin.*

9 If you do something **bit by bit**, you do it in stages. PHRASE EG *We eased the lid off, bit by bit.*

10 If you do something that, to a **bit**, you do PHRASE small or limited extent, helps to achieve something. EG *...having done his bit for king and country.*

11 In computing, a **bit** is the smallest unit of N COUNT information that is held in a computer's memory. It is either 1 or 0. Several bits form a byte.

12 Bit is also the past tense of **bite**.

bitch /bɪtʃ/, **bitches, bitching, bitched.** **1** If you N COUNT call a woman a **bitch**, you mean that she behaves in a very unpleasant way; a rude and offensive use.

2 If someone **bitches**, they complain about some- V thing in a nasty way. EG *You haven't done a thing* Informal *except bitch ever since we got here.*

3 A **bitch** is also a female dog. N COUNT

bite /baɪt/, **bites, biting, bit** /bɪt/, **bitten** /bɪtəⁿn/.
1 When a person or animal **bites** something, they V+O OR V+A use their teeth to cut into it or through it. EG *My dog bit me... She bit into her cake... I have a habit of biting my nails.* ▶ used as a noun. EG *Madeleine* ▶ N COUNT *took a bite. 'It's delicious.'*

2 When an insect or a snake **bites** you, it pierces V+O your skin and causes an area of your skin to be itchy or painful. EG *...what to do if someone is bitten by a viper.* ▶ used as a noun. EG *My hands are* ▶ N COUNT *covered with mosquito bites.*

3 When an action or policy begins to **bite**, it begins V to have a significant or harmful effect. EG *The sanctions are beginning to bite.*

4 If you have a **bite** to eat, you have a small meal N SING : a+N or a snack. Informal

biting /baɪtɪŋ/. **1** A **biting** wind is extremely cold. ADJ QUALIT EG *...a biting east wind... ...a biting cold day.*

2 Biting speech or writing is sharp and clever in a ADJ QUALIT way that makes people feel uncomfortable. EG *...biting sarcasm... ...a writer with a biting wit.*

bitten /bɪtəⁿn/ is the past participle of **bite.**

bitter /bɪtə/, **bitterest; bitters.** **1** If someone is ADJ QUALIT **bitter**, they feel angry and resentful. EG *He was a jealous, slightly bitter man.* ◊ **bitterly.** EG *'I'm glad* ◊ ADV *somebody's happy,' he said bitterly.* ◊ **bitterness.** ◊ N UNCOUNT EG *He remembers with bitterness how his father was cheated.*

2 If you have a **bitter** disappointment or experi- ADJ QUALIT : ence, you feel angry or unhappy for a long time ATTRIB afterwards. EG *I have had long and bitter experience of dealing with people like that.* ● If you ● PHRASE continue doing something difficult or unpleasant **to the bitter end**, you continue doing it until it is completely finished. EG *We have pursued everything to the bitter end.*

3 In a **bitter** argument, war, or struggle, people ADJ QUALIT argue or fight fiercely and angrily. EG *...a bitter struggle for supremacy.*

4 A **bitter** wind or **bitter** weather is extremely ADJ QUALIT cold. EG *I had never known such bitter cold.*

5 Something that tastes **bitter** has a sharp, un- ADJ QUALIT pleasant taste. EG *It tasted faintly of bitter almonds.*

6 Bitter is a kind of British beer with a slightly N MASS bitter taste. EG *...two pints of bitter.*

bitterly /bɪtəli/. **1 Bitterly** means strongly and ADV intensely. You use it to describe strong emotions such as anger, hatred, or shame. EG *No man could have hated the old order more bitterly... He was bitterly ashamed... She wept bitterly.*

2 If the weather is **bitterly** cold, it is extremely ADV+ADJ cold. EG *...a bitterly cold New Year's Day.*

bizarre /bɪˈzɑː/. Something that is **bizarre** is very ADJ QUALIT odd and strange. EG *He had some bizarre conversations with his landlady... ...bizarre gadgets.*

black /blæk/, **blacker, blackest; blacks, blacking, blacked.** **1** Something that is **black** is of the ADJ COLOUR darkest colour that there is, the colour of the sky at night when there is no light at all. EG *...a black leather coat... ...a woman dressed in black.*

2 Someone who is **black** belongs to a race of ADJ CLASSIF people with dark skins, especially a race from Africa. EG *...black musicians.* ▶ used as a noun. EG ▶ N COUNT *He was the first black to be elected to the Congress.*

3 Black coffee or tea has no milk or cream added ADJ CLASSIF to it. EG *...cups of strong black coffee.*

4 If you describe a situation as **black**, you mean ADJ QUALIT that it is bad and not likely to improve. EG *I don't think the future is as black as that.*

5 Black magic involves communicating with evil ADJ CLASSIF : spirits. EG *...the black arts.* ATTRIB

6 Black humour involves jokes about things that ADJ QUALIT : are sad or unpleasant. EG *...a black comedy.* ATTRIB

7 Someone who is **black and blue** is badly bruised. PHRASE EG *He used to beat me black and blue.*

8 When a group **blacks** particular goods or people, V+O it refuses to handle the goods or to have dealings with the people. EG *Their members had blacked these goods at the London Docks.*

black out. If you **black out**, you lose conscious- PHRASAL VB : ness for a short time. ● See also **blackout.** V+ADV

black and white. **1** In a **black and white** photo- ADJ COLOUR graph or film, everything is shown in black, white, and grey. EG *...black-and-white horror movies.*

2 You say that something is **in black and white** PHRASE when it has been written or printed, and not just spoken. EG *He was surprised to see his conversation in black and white.*

blackberry /blækbəri/, **blackberries.** A **black-** N COUNT **berry** is a small black or dark purple fruit.

blackbird /blækbɜːd/, **blackbirds.** A **blackbird** N COUNT is a common European bird with black or brown feathers.

blackboard /blækbɔːd/, **blackboards.** A **black-** N COUNT **board** is a dark-coloured board in a classroom, which teachers write on with chalk.

blackcurrant /blækˈkʌrənt/, **blackcurrants.** A N COUNT **blackcurrant** is a very small dark purple fruit that grows in bunches.

blacken /blækən/, **blackens, blackening, blackened.** **1** To **blacken** something means to make it V+O black or very dark in colour. EG *His face was blackened with charcoal.*

2 If someone **blackens** your reputation, they make V+O other people believe that you are a bad person.

black eye, black eyes. If you have a **black eye,** N COUNT you have a dark-coloured bruise around your eye.

blackish /blækɪʃ/. Something that is **blackish** is ADJ COLOUR very dark in colour.

blackmail /blækmeɪl/, **blackmails, blackmail-** N UNCOUNT **ing, blackmailed. Blackmail** is the action of threatening to do something unpleasant to someone, for example to reveal a secret about them, unless they give you money or behave in the way you want them to. EG *The statements amounted to blackmail.* ▶ used as a verb. EG *He tried to* ▶ V+O *blackmail me.* ◊ **blackmailer** /blækmeɪlə/, ◊ N COUNT **blackmailers.** EG *...the blackmailer's cruelty to his victim.*

Can a blackbird be a brown bird?

black market, black markets. The **black mar-** N COUNT
ket is a system of buying and selling goods which is
not legal. EG *He whispered that he could change
money on the black market.*

blackout /blǽkaʊt/, **blackouts. 1** A **blackout** is a N COUNT
period of time during a war in which a place is
made dark for safety reasons. EG *We couldn't get
home before the blackout.*

2 If you have a **blackout**, you temporarily lose N COUNT
consciousness.

black sheep. If you refer to someone as the N SING
black sheep of a group, you mean that everyone
else in the group is good, but that person is bad.

blacksmith /blǽksmɪθ/, **blacksmiths.** A **black-** N COUNT
smith is someone whose job is making things out
of metal, for example horseshoes or farm tools. EG
...the village blacksmith.

bladder /blǽdə/, **bladders.** Your **bladder** is the N COUNT
part of your body where urine is held until it leaves
your body. ● See also **gall bladder.**

blade /bleɪd/, **blades. 1** The **blade** of a knife, axe, N COUNT
or saw is the sharp part.

2 The **blades** of a propeller are the parts that turn N COUNT
round.

3 The **blade** of an oar is the thin, flat part that you N COUNT
put into the water.

4 A **blade** of grass is a single piece of grass. N COUNT

5 See also **razor blade, shoulder blade.**

blame /bleɪm/, **blames, blaming, blamed. 1** If V+O:OFT+for
you **blame** a person or thing for something bad,
you think or say that they are responsible for it. EG *I
was blamed for the theft... Violence at school is
blamed on immigrants.* ▸ used as a noun. EG *You* ▸ N UNCOUNT
haven't said a word of blame.

2 The **blame** for something bad that has happened N UNCOUNT
is the responsibility for causing it or letting it
happen. EG *He had to take the blame for everything.* ● If you are **to blame** for something bad ● PHRASE
that has happened, you are responsible for it.

3 If you say that you do not **blame** someone for V+O:WITH
doing something, you mean that it was a reason- BROAD NEG
able thing to do in the circumstances. EG *I can't
really blame him for wanting to make me suffer.*

blameless /bleɪmlɪs/. Someone who is **blame-** ADJ QUALIT
less has not done anything wrong. EG *On that score,
he was blameless... ...a blameless career.*

blanch /blɑːntʃ/, **blanches, blanching,** V
blanched. If you **blanch**, you suddenly become
very pale. EG *Eddie blanched and clutched my arm.*

bland /blænd/, **blander, blandest. 1** Someone ADJ QUALIT
who is **bland** is calm, unexcited, and polite. EG
Manfred smiled his bland smile. ◊ **blandly.** EG *Mr* ◊ ADV
Jones blandly dismissed their arguments.

2 Food that is **bland** has very little flavour. EG ADJ QUALIT
*...bland cheeses... The food was bland and unattrac-
tive.*

3 You can describe something such as music or ADJ QUALIT
architecture as **bland** when it is dull and uninteresting. EG *...the bland facades of Belgravia.*

blandishments /blǽndɪʃmənts/ are pleasant N PLURAL
things that you say to someone in order to per- Formal
suade them to do something. EG *He remained
impervious to all Nell's blandishments.*

blank /blæŋk/, **blanker, blankest. 1** Something ADJ QUALIT
that is **blank** has nothing on it. EG *...a blank sheet of
paper... ...a blank wall.* ● See also **point-blank.**

2 If you look **blank**, your face shows no feeling, ADJ QUALIT
understanding, or interest. EG *Her face went blank.*
◊ **blankly.** EG *I sat quietly, staring blankly ahead.* ◊ ADV

3 If your mind or memory is a **blank**, you cannot N SING:a+N
think of anything or remember anything.

4 If you **draw a blank** when you are looking for PHRASE
someone or something, you fail to find them. Informal

blanket /blǽŋkɪt/, **blankets, blanketing, blan-**
keted. 1 A **blanket** is a large square or rectangu- N COUNT
lar piece of thick cloth, especially one which you
put on a bed to keep you warm. ● See also **wet
blanket.**

2 If something such as snow **blankets** an area, it V+O

covers it. EG *The streets were blanketed in a thin
mist... Snow blanketed the plains.* ▸ used as a noun. ▸ N PART
EG *...a blanket of cloud.*

3 You use **blanket** to describe something which ADJ CLASSIF:
affects or refers to every person or thing in a ATTRIB
group, without any exceptions. EG *...our blanket
acceptance of everything they say.*

blare /bleə/, **blares, blaring, blared.** When V
something such as a siren or radio **blares**, it makes
a loud, unpleasant noise. EG *The TV set was blaring
in the background.* ▸ used as a noun. EG *...the blare* ▸ N SING:
of conversation. OFT+of

blare out. When a radio or record player **blares** PHRASAL VB:
out loud noise or when loud noise **blares out** of it, V-ERG+ADV
it produces this noise. EG *A radio was blaring out
the news... Indian music had been blaring out all
evening.*

blasé /blɑːzeɪ/. If you are **blasé** about something ADJ QUALIT
which other people find exciting, you show no
excitement in it, because you have experienced it
before. EG *You sound very blasé about it... He
watched everything with a blasé air.*

blaspheme /blæsfíːm/, **blasphemes, blasphem-** V OR V+QUOTE
ing, blasphemed. If someone **blasphemes**, they
say rude or disrespectful things about God, or they
use God's name as a swear word. EG *He no longer
felt afraid of blaspheming.*

blasphemous /blǽsfəməs/. If someone says or ADJ QUALIT
does something that shows disrespect for God, you
can say that they are being **blasphemous** or that
what they are saying or doing is **blasphemous.** EG
*She was foul-mouthed and blasphemous... ...a blas-
phemous poem.*

blasphemy /blǽsfəmɪ/, **blasphemies.** If some- N UNCOUNT
one says or does something that shows disrespect OR N COUNT
for God, you can say that what they are saying or
doing is **blasphemy.** EG *Any attempt to violate that
image is blasphemy.*

blast /blɑːst/, **blasts, blasting, blasted. 1** A **blast** N COUNT
is a big explosion, especially one caused by a bomb.
EG *Nobody had been hurt in the blast.*

2 If you **blast** a hole in something, you make a hole V+O
in it with an explosion. EG *Tunnels have been
blasted through bedrock beneath the city.*

3 A **blast** is also **3.1** a sudden strong rush of air or N COUNT:
wind. EG *...icy blasts.* **3.2** a short loud sound made by USU+SUPP
a whistle or a wind instrument. EG *Ralph blew a
series of short blasts.*

4 If a machine is on **at full blast**, it is producing as PHRASE
much sound or heat as it is able to. EG *She insists on
having the radio on at full blast.*

5 Blast is a mild swear word that people use when EXCLAM
they are irritated or annoyed about something.

blast off. When a space rocket **blasts off**, it PHRASAL VB:
leaves the ground at the start of its journey. ● See V+ADV
also **blast-off.**

blasted /blɑːstɪd/. You can use **blasted** to indi- ADJ CLASSIF:
cate that you are annoyed or irritated with some- ATTRIB
one or something. EG *...that blasted bank manager.*

blast-off is the moment when a rocket or space N UNCOUNT
shuttle leaves the ground and rises into the air.

blatant /bleɪtənt/ is used to describe something ADJ QUALIT
bad which is very obvious and not concealed in any
way. EG *...blatant discrimination... I wasn't quite as
blatant as that.* ◊ **blatantly.** EG *They blatantly* ◊ ADV
ignored the truce agreement.

blaze /bleɪz/, **blazes, blazing, blazed. 1** When a V
fire **blazes**, it burns strongly and brightly.

2 A **blaze** is a large fire in which things are N COUNT
damaged. EG *You never saw such a blaze.*

3 If something **blazes** with light or colour, it is V:OFT+with
extremely bright. EG *The flower beds blazed with
colour.* ▸ used as a noun. EG *...a blaze of sunlight...* ▸ N COUNT
...the blaze of electric lights. +SUPP

4 If your eyes **are blazing**, they look very bright, V
because you are angry. EG *She turned and faced* Literary
him, her eyes blazing.

5 A **blaze** of publicity or attention is a great N SING+of
amount of it. EG *The School opened in a blaze of*

publicity... She eventually retired in a blaze of glory.

blazer /bleɪzə/, **blazers.** A **blazer** is a kind of N COUNT jacket, especially one worn by schoolchildren or members of a sports team.

blazing /bleɪzɪŋ/. 1 You use **blazing** to describe ADJ CLASSIF: the weather or a place when it is very hot and ATTRIB sunny. EG ...*the blazing beach*... ...*the blazing heat of the plain.* ● **Blazing hot** means very hot indeed. EG ● PHRASE *Already the square was blazing hot.*

2 When people have a **blazing** row, they quarrel in ADJ CLASSIF: a noisy and excited way. EG *She had a blazing row* ATTRIB *with her boss.*

bleach /bliːtʃ/, **bleaches, bleaching, bleached.** 1 V-ERG To **bleach** material or hair means to make it white or pale in colour, either with a chemical or by leaving it in the sunlight. EG *He bleaches his hair...* ...*a pair of bleached jeans... I left the cloth in the sun to bleach.*

2 **Bleach** is a chemical that is used to make cloth N UNCOUNT white, or to clean things thoroughly and kill germs. EG ...*a strong household bleach.*

bleak /bliːk/, **bleaker, bleakest.** 1 If a situation is ADJ QUALIT **bleak**, it is bad, and seems unlikely to improve. EG *The future looked bleak.* ◊ **bleakness.** EG ...*the* ◊ N UNCOUNT *bleakness of the post war years.*

2 If a place is **bleak**, it looks cold, bare, and ADJ QUALIT unattractive. EG ...*the bleak coastline.*

3 When the weather is **bleak**, it is cold, dull, and ADJ QUALIT unpleasant. EG ...*the bleak winters.*

4 If someone looks or sounds **bleak**, they seem ADJ QUALIT depressed, hopeless, or unfriendly. EG ...*his bleak features.* ◊ **bleakly.** EG *He stared bleakly ahead...* ◊ ADV *'What,' he asked bleakly, 'are these?'*

bleary /blɪəri¹/, **blearier, bleariest.** If your eyes ADJ QUALIT are **bleary**, they are red and watery, usually because you are tired. EG *We watched with bleary eyes.* ◊ **blearily.** EG *He looked up blearily at Tom.* ◊ ADV

bleat /bliːt/, **bleats, bleating, bleated.** 1 When a V sheep or goat **bleats**, it makes the sound that sheep and goats usually make. ▶ used as a noun. EG ▶ N COUNT ...*the bleat of a goat.*

2 When people **bleat**, they speak in a weak, high, V OR V+QUOTE complaining voice. EG *'Now?' Dixon bleated.*

bled /bled/ is the past tense and past participle of **bleed.**

bleed /bliːd/, **bleeds, bleeding, bled.** When you V **bleed**, you lose blood from your body as a result of injury or illness. EG *His feet had begun to bleed... He was bleeding heavily.* ◊ **bleeding.** EG *Has the* ◊ N UNCOUNT *bleeding stopped?* ● See also **nosebleed.**

blemish /blemɪʃ/, **blemishes, blemishing, blemished.** 1 A **blemish** is a mark that spoils the N COUNT appearance of something. EG *There wasn't a blemish on his body.*

2 If something **blemishes** your reputation, it spoils V+O it. EG *I shall never teach again. My good character is blemished.*

blend /blend/, **blends, blending, blended.**

1 When you **blend** substances together, you mix V+O OR them together so that they become one substance. V+O+with: EG *Blend the cornflour with a little cold water.* RECIP ▶ used as a noun. EG ...*a blend of different oils.* ▶ N COUNT

2 If someone or something shows a **blend** of N COUNT+SUPP qualities, these qualities are combined together so that they produce a new effect. EG ...*the company's blend of modern and classical dance.*

3 When colours or sounds **blend**, they come togeth- V OR V+with: er or are combined in a pleasing way. EG ...*their* RECIP *voices blending marvellously as they sing in harmony.*

blend into. If something **blends into** the back- PHRASAL VB: ground or **blends in**, it is so similar to the back- V+ADV OR ground in appearance or sound that it is difficult to V+PREP see or hear it separately. EG *Tree snakes blend well into foliage.*

blender /blendə/, **blenders.** A **blender** is a ma- N COUNT chine used in the kitchen for mixing liquids and soft foods together at high speed.

bless /bles/, **blesses, blessing, blessed, blest.** **Blessed** and **blest** are both used as the past tense and past participle.

1 When a priest **blesses** people or things, he asks V+O for God's favour and protection for them. EG ...*bringing baskets of food to the church to be blessed.*

2 If someone is **blessed with** a particular good PHRASE quality or skill, they have it. EG *She is blessed with immense talent and boundless energy.*

3 When people say **God bless** or **bless you** to CONVENTION someone, they are expressing their affection, thanks, or good wishes. EG *Bless you, it's terribly good of you to come.*

4 You can say **bless you** to someone who has just CONVENTION sneezed.

blessed /blesɪ²d, blest/. You use **blessed** to de- ADJ CLASSIF: scribe something that you think is wonderful, and ATTRIB that you are thankful for or relieved about. EG ...*blessed freedom.* ◊ **blessedly.** EG ...*the blessedly* ◊ SUBMOD *cool oasis of the airport.*

blessing /blesɪŋ/, **blessings.** 1 A **blessing** is N COUNT something good that you are thankful for. EG *Health is a blessing that money cannot buy.*

2 If something is done with someone's **blessing**, N COUNT+POSS they approve of it and support it. EG *She did it with the full blessing of her parents.*

3 If you say that something was **a blessing in** PHRASE **disguise**, you mean that it caused problems and difficulties at first but later you realized that it was the best thing that could have happened.

4 If you tell someone to **count** their **blessings**, you PHRASE are saying that they should think about how lucky they are instead of complaining.

5 If you say that a situation is a **mixed blessing**, PHRASE you mean that it has disadvantages as well as advantages.

blew /bluː/ is the past tense of **blow.**

blight /blaɪt/, **blights, blighting, blighted.** You N COUNT: can refer to something as a **blight** when it causes USU SING great difficulties, and damages or spoils other things. EG *We think of pollution as a modern blight, but it is not.* ▶ used as a verb. EG *Her career has* ▶ V+O: *been blighted by clashes with the authorities.* USU PASS

blind /blaɪnd/, **blinds, blinding, blinded.** 1 Some- ADJ CLASSIF one who is **blind** is unable to see because their eyes are damaged. ◊ **blindness.** EG *Eye damage* ◊ N UNCOUNT *can result in temporary or permanent blindness.* ● See also **colour blind.**

2 You can refer to people who are blind as the N PLURAL: **blind.** EG ...*the help that's given to the blind.* the+N

3 If something **blinds** you, you become unable to V+O see, either for a short time or permanently. EG *My eyes were momentarily blinded by flash bulbs.*

4 If you are **blind** to a fact or situation, you take no ADJ PRED+to notice of it or are unaware of it. EG *He was blind to everything except his immediate needs.*

5 If something **blinds** you to a fact or situation, it V+O+to prevents you from realizing that it exists. EG *We have to beware that missionary zeal doesn't blind us to the realities here.*

6 You describe someone's beliefs or actions as ADJ CLASSIF: **blind** when they take no notice of the facts or ATTRIB behave in an unreasonable way. EG ...*her blind faith in the wisdom of her Church... ...their blind pursuit of their plans... She had driven him into a blind rage.*

7 If you **turn a blind eye** to something that PHRASE someone is doing, you pretend not to notice it. EG *He had often turned a blind eye to Barber's drinking sessions.*

8 A **blind** corner is one that you cannot see round ADJ CLASSIF because something is blocking your view.

9 If you say that someone **is not taking a blind** PHRASE

What could you make if you used a blender?

bit of notice, you are emphasizing that they are Informal taking no notice at all.

10 A **blind** is a roll of cloth or paper which you can N COUNT pull down over a window in order to keep out the light. ● See also **Venetian blind**.

11 See also **blinding**, **blindly**.

blind alley, blind alleys. If you go up a **blind** N COUNT **alley** when you are trying to achieve something, you do something which fails to help you to achieve it.

blind date, blind dates. A **blind date** is an N COUNT arrangement made for you to spend an evening with someone of the opposite sex who you have never met before. EG *We met on a blind date.*

blindfold /ˈblaɪndfəʊld/, **blindfolds, blindfolding, blindfolded.** **1** A **blindfold** is a strip of cloth that is N COUNT tied over someone's eyes so that they cannot see. EG *They pulled off his blindfold.*

2 If you **blindfold** someone, you tie a blindfold V+O over their eyes. ◊ **blindfolded.** EG *He was shoved* ◊ ADJ CLASSIF *down into a canoe, still blindfolded.*

blinding /ˈblaɪndɪŋ/. **1** A **blinding** light is ex- ADJ CLASSIF tremely bright. EG *There came a blinding flash.*

2 You use **blinding** to emphasize that something is ADJ CLASSIF: very obvious. EG *...the blinding obviousness of the* ATTRIB *advantage.* ◊ **blindingly.** EG *Isn't it blindingly* ◊ SUBMOD *obvious?*

blindly /ˈblaɪndlɪ/. If you do something **blindly**, **1** ADV you do it when you are unable to see properly. EG *He ran blindly across the clearing.* **2** you do it without having much information, or without thinking much about it. EG *With the information we have now, we can only speculate blindly.*

blind spot, blind spots. **1** If you have a **blind** N COUNT **spot** about something, you are unable to understand it. EG *Ford always had a terrible blind spot about these things.*

2 A **blind spot** is a part of something that you N COUNT cannot see properly, for example a part of the road when you are driving a car.

blink /blɪŋk/, **blinks, blinking, blinked.**

1 When you **blink** or when you **blink** your eyes, V OR V-ERG you shut your eyes and very quickly open them again. EG *They looked at him without blinking... The girl blinked her eyes several times.* ▸ used as a ▸ N COUNT noun. EG *It was his guilty blink that gave him away.*

2 When a light **blinks**, it flashes on and off. EG *An* V *amber light blinked down through the clouds.* ▸ used as a noun. EG *There was a blink of bright* ▸ N COUNT *light beyond the forest.*

3 If a machine goes **on the blink**, it stops working PHRASE properly. EG *The Hoover is on the blink.* Informal

blinkered /ˈblɪŋkəd/. A **blinkered** view, attitude, ADJ CLASSIF or approach considers only a narrow point of view British and does not take into account other people's opinions. EG *...blinkered self-interest.*

blinkers /ˈblɪŋkəz/. **1** Blinkers are two pieces of N PLURAL leather which are placed at the side of a horse's British eyes so that it can only see straight ahead.

2 If you describe someone as wearing **blinkers**, N PLURAL you mean that they are considering only a narrow British point of view and are not taking into account other people's opinions.

bliss /blɪs/ is a state of complete happiness, or a N UNCOUNT time or situation in which you are very happy. EG *For a couple of months, weekends were bliss.*

blissful /ˈblɪsfʊl/. **1** A **blissful** situation or period ADJ QUALIT of time is one in which you are extremely happy. EG *They sat there together in blissful silence... ...those blissful afternoons on the beach.* ◊ **blissfully.** EG *His eyes shut blissfully and he* ◊ ADV *smiled.*

2 If someone is in **blissful** ignorance of something ADJ CLASSIF: unpleasant or serious, they are totally unaware of ATTRIB it. ◊ **blissfully.** EG *Most people remain blissfully* ◊ ADV+ADJ *unaware of the problem.*

blister /ˈblɪstə/, **blisters, blistering, blistered.** **1** N COUNT A **blister** is a painful swelling containing clear liquid on the surface of your skin.

2 When your skin **blisters** or **is blistered**, blisters V-ERG appear on it as a result of burning or rubbing. EG *My feet were blistered and aching.*

3 When paint or rubber **blisters**, small bumps V-ERG appear on its surface.

blistering /ˈblɪstəʳrɪŋ/. **1** When the weather or the ADJ QUALIT sun is **blistering**, it is extremely hot. EG *...the blistering days of midsummer.*

2 A **blistering** remark or reply expresses great ADJ CLASSIF anger or sarcasm. EG *He wrote a blistering reply.*

blithe /blaɪð/. **1** You use **blithe** to indicate that ADJ QUALIT something is done casually, without serious or careful thought. EG *I made a blithe comment about the fine weather.* ◊ **blithely.** EG *...the blessing of* ◊ ADV *good health which we blithely take for granted.*

2 Someone who is **blithe** is carefree and cheerful. ADJ QUALIT EG *I was feeling unusually blithe that day.* Outdated

blizzard /ˈblɪzəd/, **blizzards.** A **blizzard** is a very N COUNT bad snowstorm with strong winds.

bloated /ˈbləʊtɪd/. **1** Something that is **bloated** is ADJ QUALIT much larger than normal because it has a lot of liquid or gas inside it. EG *...bloated corpses.*

2 If you feel **bloated** after eating a large meal, you ADJ QUALIT feel very full and uncomfortable. Informal

blob /blɒb/, **blobs.** **1** A **blob** of thick or sticky N PART liquid is a small amount of it. EG *...a blob of melted wax... ...the blob of blood on her wrist.*

2 You describe something that you cannot see very N COUNT clearly, for example because it is in the distance, as a **blob**. EG *He saw a white blob crossing the street... You see a blob of grey in the distance.*

bloc /blɒk/, **blocs.** **1** A **bloc** is a group of countries N COUNT+SUPP with similar political aims and interests acting together. EG *...an Eastern bloc country.*

2 See also **en bloc**.

block /blɒk/, **blocks, blocking, blocked.** **1** A N COUNT **block** of flats or offices is a large building containing them. EG *...a large office block.*

2 A **block** in a town is an area of land with streets N COUNT on all its sides. EG *The store was three blocks away.*

3 A **block** of a substance is a large rectangular N PART piece of it. EG *...a block of ice... ...blocks of stone.*

4 To **block** a road, channel, or pipe means to put V+O an object across it or in it so that nothing can get through. EG *They had blocked the land routes.* ◊ **blocked.** EG *The road was completely blocked.* ◊ ADJ CLASSIF

5 If something **blocks** your view, it prevents you V+O from seeing something by being between you and that thing. EG *The driver blocked his view.*

6 If you **block** something that is being arranged, V+O you prevent it from being done. EG *He couldn't block the deal... The Council blocked his plans.*

7 If you have a mental **block** for a short period, N COUNT you are unable to do something that you can normally do which involves using your brain or memory. EG *I must have had a block.*

block out. 1 If someone **blocks** out a thought, PHRASAL VB: they try not to think about it. EG *They attempt to* V+O+ADV *withdraw from the world, to block it out.* **2** V+O+ADV Something that **blocks out** light prevents it from reaching a place. EG *...tall buildings that block out sunlight.*

block up. If you **block** something **up** or if it PHRASAL VB: **blocks up**, it becomes completely blocked so that V-ERG+ADV nothing can get through it. EG *Never block up ventilators... The sink keeps blocking up.*

blockade /blɒˈkeɪd/, **blockades, blockading,** N COUNT **blockaded.** A **blockade** is an action that is taken to prevent goods from reaching a place. EG *...the blockade of Berlin.* ▸ used as a verb. EG *The* ▸ V+O *Atlantic Squadron promptly blockaded Santiago.*

blockage /ˈblɒkɪdʒ/, **blockages.** A **blockage** in a N COUNT OR pipe, tube, or tunnel is something that is blocking N UNCOUNT it. EG *Perhaps there was a blockage in the fuel line.*

block capitals or **block letters** are simple capi- N PLURAL tal letters that are not decorated in any way.

bloke /bləʊk/, **blokes.** A **bloke** is a man. EG *I'm* N COUNT *only an ordinary bloke... He's a good bloke... ...the* Informal *bloke next door... ...a bloke called Robertson.* British

blonde /blɒnd/, **blondes;** also spelled **blond. 1** A **blonde** person has pale yellow-coloured hair. EG *...a tall, blond Englishman... ...her long blonde hair.* ADJ QUALIT

2 A **blonde** is a person, especially a woman, who has blonde hair. EG *...a plump blonde of about thirty.* N COUNT

blood /blʌd/. **1 Blood** is the red liquid that flows inside your body. EG *...the circulation of the blood... Her hand was covered with blood.* N UNCOUNT

2 If something **makes** your **blood boil**, it makes you very angry. PHRASE

3 Bad blood refers to feelings of hate and anger. EG *The rebels hoped to create bad blood between Spain and the United States.* PHRASE

4 If something violent and cruel is done **in cold blood**, it is done deliberately and in an unemotional way. EG *People were murdered in cold blood.* PHRASE

5 If something **makes** your **blood run cold**, it makes you feel very frightened. PHRASE

6 You can use **blood** to refer to the race or social class of someone's parents or ancestors. EG *There was eastern blood on her mother's side.* N UNCOUNT +SUPP

7 If a quality or talent is **in** your **blood**, it is part of your nature, and other members of your family have it too. EG *Music is in her blood.* PHRASE

8 New people who are introduced into an organization and whose fresh ideas are likely to improve it are referred to as **new blood**, **fresh blood**, or **young blood**. PHRASE

bloodbath /blʌdbɑːθ/, **bloodbaths.** If you describe an event as a **bloodbath**, you mean that a lot of people were killed very violently. N COUNT

bloodcurdling /blʌdkɜːdlɪŋ/. A **bloodcurdling** sound or story is very frightening and horrible. EG *...a bloodcurdling shriek.* ADJ CLASSIF : ATTRIB

blood donor, blood donors. Blood donors give blood from their bodies so that it can be used for transfusions or operations. N COUNT

bloodless /blʌdlɪ²s/. **1** If you describe someone's face or skin as **bloodless**, you mean that it is very pale. EG *Lily wiped her bloodless lips.* ADJ CLASSIF

2 A **bloodless** coup or victory is one in which nobody is killed. ADJ CLASSIF

blood poisoning is a serious illness resulting from an infection in your blood. N UNCOUNT

blood pressure. Your **blood pressure** is a measure of the amount of force with which your blood flows around your body. EG *I have high blood pressure and heart trouble.* N UNCOUNT

bloodshed /blʌdʃɛd/ is violence in which people are killed or wounded. EG *There was no evidence of bloodshed or attack.* N UNCOUNT

bloodshot /blʌdʃɒt/. If your eyes are **bloodshot**, the parts that are usually white are red or pink. ADJ QUALIT

blood sport, blood sports. Blood sports are sports such as hunting in which animals are killed. N COUNT

bloodstained /blʌdsteɪnd/. Something that is **bloodstained** is covered with blood. EG *...bloodstained clothing.* ADJ CLASSIF

bloodstream /blʌdstriːm/, **bloodstreams.** Your **bloodstream** is your blood as it flows around your body. EG *...a drug that dissolves in the bloodstream.* N COUNT

bloodthirsty /blʌdθɜːsti¹/. Someone who is **bloodthirsty** is extremely eager to use violence or to see other people use violence. ADJ QUALIT

blood vessel, blood vessels. Blood vessels are the narrow tubes through which your blood flows. N COUNT

bloody /blʌdi¹/, **bloodier, bloodiest. 1 Bloody** is a swear word. You use 'bloody' to emphasize how annoyed or angry you are. EG *Bloody students!* ADJ CLASSIF : ATTRIB OR ADV British

2 A situation or event that is **bloody** is one in which there is a lot of violence and a lot of people are killed. EG *The effects will be violent, disruptive, and probably bloody.* ◊ **bloodily.** EG *Helen was most horribly, most bloodily, killed.* ADJ QUALIT ◊ ADV

3 Something that is **bloody** has a lot of blood on it. EG *...hands that were black and bloody.* ADJ QUALIT

bloody-minded. Someone who is being **bloody-minded** is deliberately making difficulties instead of being helpful. EG *You're just being bloody-minded.* ◊ **bloody-mindedness.** EG *It's sheer bloody-mindedness on their part.* ADJ QUALIT ◊ N UNCOUNT

bloom /bluːm/, **blooms, blooming, bloomed. 1** A **bloom** is the flower on a plant. EG *...great scarlet hibiscus blooms.* ● A plant or tree that is **in bloom** has flowers on it. EG *...lovely almond trees in bloom.* N COUNT ● PHRASE

2 When a plant or tree **blooms**, it produces flowers. When a flower **blooms**, the flower bud opens. EG *It has a beautiful orange flower which blooms in November.* V : USU+A

blossom /blɒsəᵒm/, **blossoms, blossoming, blossomed. 1 Blossom** is the flowers that appear on a tree before the fruit. EG *The trees along the road were heavy with yellow blossoms.* ● A tree that is **in blossom** has blossom on it. EG *...a cherry-tree in blossom.* N UNCOUNT OR N COUNT ● PHRASE

2 When a tree **blossoms**, it produces blossom. V

3 You say that a person **blossoms** when they develop attractive qualities or abilities. EG *She had blossomed into a real beauty... Harold had suddenly blossomed at university.* V

blot /blɒt/, **blots, blotting, blotted. 1** A **blot** is a drop of liquid, especially ink, that has been spilled on a surface and has dried. N COUNT

2 If something is a **blot** on someone's reputation, it spoils their reputation. EG *...a blot on his career.* N SING+*on*

3 If you **blot** a surface, you remove liquid from it by pressing a piece of soft paper or cloth onto it. V+O

blot out. 1 If one thing **blots out** another thing, it is in front of the other thing and prevents it from being seen. EG *The resulting dust cloud blotted out the sun.* **2** If one thought or memory **blots out** other thoughts or memories, it becomes the only one that you can think about. If you try to **blot out** a memory, you try to forget it. PHRASAL VB : V+O+ADV; V+O+ADV

blotch /blɒtʃ/, **blotches.** A **blotch** is a small area of colour, for example on someone's skin. EG *There were purple blotches around her eyes.* N COUNT : USU PLURAL

blotchy /blɒtʃi¹/. Something that is **blotchy** has blotches on it. EG *His skin was blotchy.* ADJ QUALIT

blotting paper is thick soft paper that you use for soaking up and drying ink on a piece of paper. N UNCOUNT

blouse /blaʊz/, **blouses.** A **blouse** is a kind of shirt worn by a girl or woman. See picture at CLOTHES. N COUNT

blow /bləʊ/, **blows, blowing, blew** /bluː/, **blown** /bləʊn/. **1** When a wind or breeze **blows**, the air moves. EG *The winds had been blowing from the west.* V : OFT+A

2 If something **blows** somewhere or if the wind **blows** it there, it is moved there by the wind. EG *The dust blew all over the decks... The wind blew his papers away.* V-ERG : USU+A

3 If you **blow**, you send out a stream of air from your mouth. EG *Eric put his lips close to the hole and blew softly.* V : USU+A

4 If you **blow** bubbles, you make them by blowing air out of your mouth through liquid. V+O

5 When you **blow** a whistle or a horn, you make a sound by blowing into it. EG *The conductor blew his whistle and the tram stopped.* V+O

6 When you **blow** your nose, you force air out of it through your nostrils in order to clear it. V+O

7 If you give someone a **blow**, you hit them. EG *He knocked Thomas unconscious with one blow of his fist... ...a blow on the back of the neck.* ● If two people or groups **come to blows**, they start fighting. N COUNT : USU+SUPP ● PHRASE

8 A **blow** is also something that happens which makes you very disappointed or unhappy. EG *It must have been a fearful blow to him.* ● Something that **softens the blow** or **cushions the blow** makes an unpleasant piece of news easier to accept. N COUNT : OFT+*to* ● PHRASE

9 A **blow** for a particular cause or principle is an N COUNT :

What is the difference between a blot and a blotch?

action that makes it more likely to succeed. A USU+for/
blow against it makes it less likely to succeed. EG against
He struck a blow for liberty.
10 If you **blow** something off, you violently remove V+O+A
or destroy it with an explosion. EG *He would have*
blown his hand off if he'd fired the gun... It blew a
hole in the roof.
11 If you **blow** a large amount of money, you spend V+O
it quickly on things that you do not really need. Informal
12 If you say '**Blow him**' or '**Blow the expense**', PHRASE
you mean that you do not care about what some- Informal
one thinks or how much something costs. Outdated
blow out. If you **blow out** a flame or a candle, PHRASAL VB:
you blow at it so that it stops burning. EG *Rudolph* V-ERG+ADV
blew out the candles... The pilot light had blown
out.
blow over. If something such as trouble or an PHRASAL VB:
argument **blows over**, it comes to an end. V+ADV
blow up. 1 If you **blow** something **up** or if it PHRASAL VB:
blows up, it is destroyed by an explosion. EG *He* V-ERG+ADV
was going to blow the place up... One of the
submarines blew up. **2** If you **blow up** something V+O+ADV
such as a balloon or a tyre, you fill it with air.
blow-by-blow. A **blow-by-blow** account of an ADJ CLASSIF:
event describes every stage of it in detail. EG *...a* ATTRIB
blow-by-blow description of the trial.
blower /bləʊə/. The **blower** is the telephone. EG N SING:the+N
Miss Callaghan was on the blower to Atkinson. Outdated
blown /bləʊn/ is the past participle of **blow**.
bludgeon /blʌdʒəⁿn/, **bludgeons, bludgeoning,**
bludgeoned. 1 If someone **bludgeons** you, they hit V+O
you several times with a heavy object. Formal
2 If someone **bludgeons** you into doing something, V+O+into
they make you do it by bullying or threatening you.
blue /bluː/, **bluer, bluest; blues. 1** Something that ADJ COLOUR
is **blue** is the colour of the sky on a sunny day. EG
She had bright blue eyes.
2 Something that happens **out of the blue** happens PHRASE
suddenly and unexpectedly. EG *She suddenly wrote*
out of the blue and asked me to go on holiday with
her.
3 The **blues** is a type of music which is similar to N UNCOUNT
jazz, but is always slow and sad.
4 Blue films, stories, or jokes are mainly about sex. ADJ QUALIT
bluebell /bluːbel/, **bluebells. Bluebells** are N COUNT
plants that have blue bell-shaped flowers on thin
upright stems.
blue-black. Something that is **blue-black** is very ADJ COLOUR
dark blue in colour.
bluebottle /bluːbɒtəⁿl/, **bluebottles.** A **bluebottle** N COUNT
is a large fly with a shiny dark-blue body.
blue-collar. Blue-collar workers work in indus- ADJ CLASSIF
try, doing physical work, rather than in offices.
blueish /bluːɪʃ/. See **bluish**.
blueprint /bluːprɪnt/, **blueprints.** A **blueprint** N COUNT:
for something is an original plan or description of OFT+of/for
how it is expected to work. EG *...a blueprint for a*
better world.
bluff /blʌf/, **bluffs, bluffing, bluffed. 1** A **bluff** is N COUNT OR
an attempt to make someone believe that you will N UNCOUNT
do something when you do not really intend to do
it. EG *The soldiers thought it was a bluff... His*
threats are merely bluff. ● If you **call** someone's ● PHRASE
bluff, you tell them to do what they have been
threatening to do, because you are sure that they
will not really do it. EG *It is time to call their bluff.*
2 If you **bluff** or if you **bluff** someone, you make V OR V+O
them believe that you will do something when you
do not really intend to do it. EG *I was sure he was*
bluffing again.
bluish /bluːɪʃ/; also spelled **blueish.** Something ADJ COLOUR
that is **bluish** is slightly blue in colour. EG *...bluish-*
grey water.
blunder /blʌndə/, **blunders, blundering, blun-**
dered. 1 If you **blunder**, you make a stupid or V
careless mistake. EG *Clearly, Alec had blundered*
badly. ► used as a noun. EG *I might have committed* ► N COUNT
some dreadful blunder.
2 If you **blunder** somewhere, you move in a V+A

clumsy and careless way. EG *She blundered into a*
tree.
blunt /blʌnt/, **blunter, bluntest; blunts, blunt-**
ing, blunted. 1 If you are **blunt**, you say exactly ADJ QUALIT
what you think without trying to be polite. EG *Let*
me ask a blunt question... To be blunt, you are no
longer needed here. ◊ **bluntly.** EG *He told them* ◊ ADV
bluntly what was acceptable. ◊ **bluntness.** EG ◊ N UNCOUNT
Other leaders have stated their views with equal
bluntness.
2 A **blunt** object has a rounded or flat end rather ADJ QUALIT
than a sharp one. EG *...a wooden spoon or similar*
blunt instrument.
3 A **blunt** knife is no longer sharp and does not cut ADJ QUALIT
well.
4 If something **blunts** an emotion or feeling, it V+O
weakens it. EG *This side of his personality has been*
blunted by toil.
blur /blɜː/, **blurs, blurring, blurred. 1** A **blur** is a N COUNT:
shape or area which you cannot see clearly be- USU SING
cause it has no distinct outline or because it is
moving very fast. EG *Everything becomes a blur*
when you travel beyond a certain speed.
2 When a thing **blurs** or when something **blurs** it, V-ERG
you cannot see it clearly because its edges are no
longer distinct. ◊ **blurred.** EG *...a blurred snapshot.* ◊ ADJ QUALIT
3 If an idea or a concept **blurs** or if something V-ERG
blurs it, it no longer seems clear. EG *...a determina-*
tion to blur the line between art and reality.
◊ **blurred.** EG *The distinction between reform and* ◊ ADJ QUALIT
revolution had become blurred in his mind.
blurt /blɜːt/, **blurts, blurting, blurted.** If you PHRASAL VB:
blurt something **out**, you say it suddenly, after V-SPEECH+ADV
trying hard to keep quiet or to keep it secret. EG *She*
suddenly blurted out, 'I'm not going.'
blush /blʌʃ/, **blushes, blushing, blushed.** When V
you **blush**, your face becomes redder than usual
because you are ashamed or embarrassed. EG
Philip blushed and laughed uneasily... I felt myself
blushing. ► used as a noun. EG *'I made it myself,' Mr* ► N COUNT:
Solomon informed them with a modest blush. USU SING
bluster /blʌstə/, **blusters, blustering, blus-** V
tered. When someone **blusters**, they speak angrily and aggressively because they are angry or
offended. EG *They blustered and swore that the*
pictures were fakes. ► used as a noun. EG *She* ► N UNCOUNT
simply ignored his bluster.
blustery /blʌstəriⁱ/. **Blustery** weather is rough ADJ QUALIT
and windy.
boa /bəʊə/, **boas.** A **boa** is a large snake that kills N COUNT
animals by squeezing them.
boa constrictor /bəʊə kənstrɪktə/, **boa con-** N COUNT
strictors. A **boa constrictor** is the same as a boa.
boar /bɔː/, **boars. 1** A **boar** is a male pig. N COUNT
2 A **boar** or a **wild boar** is a wild pig. The plural N COUNT
can be 'boar' or 'boars'.
board /bɔːd/, **boards, boarding, boarded. 1** A N COUNT
board is **1.1** a rectangular piece of wood on which
something can be put, spread out, or cut. EG *He took*
a knife from a magnetic board on the wall... a
chopping board. **1.2** a square piece of wood or stiff
cardboard that you use for playing games such as
chess. **1.3** a long flat piece of wood which is used to
make a floor, wall, or shelf.
2 You can also refer to a blackboard, diving board, N COUNT
or notice board as a **board**. EG *I'll write the sum up*
on the board.
3 The **board** of a company or organization is the N COUNT:
group of people who control it. EG *He was on the* OFT the+N
board of directors... ...board meetings.
4 If you **board** a train, ship, or aircraft, you get on V+O
it in order to travel somewhere. Formal
5 When you are **on board** a train, ship, or aircraft, PHRASE
you are on it or in it.
6 Board is the food which is provided when you N UNCOUNT
stay somewhere, for example in a hotel. EG *...the*
low price that my hostess was asking for board and
bed.

7 An arrangement or deal that is **above board** is PHRASE legal and is being carried out honestly and openly.

8 If a policy or a situation applies **across the** PHRASE **board**, it affects everything or everyone in a particular group. EG *We're aiming for a 20% reduction across the board.*

9 If an arrangement or plan **goes by the board** PHRASE when something unexpected happens, it is not used or does not happen.

10 If someone **sweeps the board** in a competition, PHRASE they win everything.

board up. If you **board up** a door or window, you PHRASAL VB: fix pieces of wood over it so that it is covered up. V+O+ADV

boarding house, boarding houses. A **boarding** N COUNT **house** is a house where people pay to stay for a short time.

boarding school, boarding schools. A **board-** N COUNT **ing school** is a school where the pupils live during the term.

boardroom /bɔːdruːm, -rʊm/, **boardrooms.** The **boardroom** is 1 a room where the board of a N COUNT company meets. EG *I got a summons to the boardroom on the top floor.* **2** the people at the highest N SING : the+N level of management in a company. EG *...the devolution of power from the boardroom to the shop floor.*

boast /bəʊst/, **boasts, boasting, boasted.** If you V+OFT+A **boast** about something that you have done or that QUOTE, OR you own, you talk about it in a way that shows that REPORT: you are proud of it. EG *Williams boasted of his* ONLY that *influence over the Prime Minister... British Rail can boast about their safety record... He's not all that exciting – even if he likes to boast that he is.*
▶ used as a noun. EG *It is his boast that he has read* ▶ N COUNT: *the entire works of Trollope.* OFT+REPORT

boastful /bəʊstfʊl/. If someone is **boastful**, they ADJ QUALIT talk too proudly about something that they have done or that they own. EG *They are rather boastful about their equipment... ...his boastful laughter.*

boat /bəʊt/, **boats.** **1** A **boat** is a small vehicle N COUNT which is used for travelling across water. EG *John* OR by+N *took me down the river in the old boat... We are going by boat... ...a fishing boat.*

2 You can refer to a passenger ship as a **boat**. EG N COUNT *She was intending to take the boat to Stockholm.* Informal

3 Boat is used in these phrases. **3.1** If you say that PHRASES someone is **rocking the boat**, you mean that they Informal are upsetting a calm situation and causing trouble. **3.2** If two or more people are **in the same boat**, they are in the same unpleasant situation. EG *We are all in the same boat.*

boating /bəʊtɪŋ/ is travelling on a lake or river in N ING a small boat for pleasure. EG *Uncle Jack once took me out boating... ...a number of boating accidents.*

bob /bɒb/, **bobs, bobbing, bobbed.** **1** If something V+A **bobs**, it moves up and down, like something does when it is floating on water. EG *The toy boat bobbed gently on the ripples.*

2 If you **bob** somewhere, you move there quickly. V+A EG *The receptionist bobbed back into the rear office.*

3 People used to refer to a shilling as a **bob**. The N COUNT plural form was also **bob**. EG *They used to get four* Informal *bob an hour.*

4 A **bob** is also a hair style in which a woman's hair N COUNT is cut level with her chin.

bobbed /bɒbd/. If a woman's hair is **bobbed**, it is ADJ CLASSIF cut in a bob. EG *...a girl with blonde bobbed hair.*

bode /bəʊd/, **bodes, boding, boded.** If something PHRASE **bodes ill, bodes no good**, or **does not bode well**, Literary it makes you think that something bad will happen. EG *This does not bode well for his chances against the champion... Her expression boded ill for somebody.*

bodice /bɒdɪs/, **bodices.** The **bodice** of a dress is N COUNT the part above the waist.

bodily /bɒdɪli/. **1** Your **bodily** needs and func- ADJ CLASSIF : tions are the needs and functions of your body. EG ATTRIB

They have no interests beyond their bodily needs... ...a general slowing up of the bodily functions.

2 You use **bodily** to refer to actions that involve ADV the whole of someone's body. EG *He carried her bodily past the rows of empty seats... He hurled himself bodily at the Prince.*

body /bɒdi/, **bodies.** **1** Someone's **body** is all their N COUNT physical parts, or the main part and not their head, OFT+POSS arms, and legs. EG *His whole body felt as if it were on fire... They respond with slow movements of their arms, legs, and bodies.*

2 You can refer to a person's dead body as a **body**. N COUNT EG *His body has not been found.* ● **over my dead body**: see **dead**.

3 A **body** is also an organized group of people who N COUNT : deal with something officially. EG *...a unique body* USU+SUPP *called the Inner London Education Authority... ...local voluntary bodies.*

4 The **body** of a car or aeroplane is the main part N COUNT : of it, not including its engine, wheels, or wings. USU+SUPP

bodyguard /bɒdɪɡɑːd/, **bodyguards.** A **body-** N COUNT **guard** is **1** a person who is employed to protect someone. EG *He came striding into the room followed by his two bodyguards.* **2** a group of people who are employed to protect someone. EG *...one of the Rajah's personal bodyguard.*

bodywork /bɒdɪwɜːk/. The **bodywork** of a motor N UNCOUNT vehicle is the outside part of it.

bog /bɒɡ/, **bogs.** A **bog** is an area of land which is N COUNT very wet and muddy.

bogged down /bɒɡd daʊn/. **1** If you are **bogged** ADJ PRED **down** in something, it prevents you from making progress or getting something done. EG *Don't get bogged down in details... We had been bogged down in red tape.*

2 If a vehicle is **bogged down** in mud or snow, it is ADJ PRED stuck and cannot move.

boggle /bɒɡəl/, **boggles, boggling, boggled.** If V-ERG your mind **boggles** at something or if something **boggles** your mind, you find it difficult to imagine or understand. EG *The questions raised by the new biology simply boggle the mind.*

boggy /bɒɡi/. **Boggy** land is very wet and muddy. ADJ QUALIT

bogus /bəʊɡəs/. You say that something is **bogus** ADJ CLASSIF when someone is pretending that it is genuine and you know that it is not. EG *...bogus names... She was speaking with a terrible bogus accent.*

bohemian /bəʊhiːmɪən/, **bohemians.** A **bohe-** N COUNT **mian** is someone who lives and dresses in a casual Outdated way that many people do not approve of. Bohemians are often connected with art, literature, or music. EG *Brian saw Tim as a romantic Bohemian.*
▶ used as an adjective. EG *My parents disapproved* ▶ ADJ QUALIT *of the bohemian life I led.*

boil /bɔɪl/, **boils, boiling, boiled.** **1** When a hot V-ERG liquid **boils** or when you **boil** it, bubbles appear in it and it starts to change into steam or vapour. EG *When the water has boiled let it cool... Fill the teapot with boiling water.*

2 When you **bring** a liquid **to the boil**, you heat it PHRASE until it boils. When it **comes to the boil**, it begins to boil.

3 When you **boil** a kettle, you heat it until the V-ERG water inside it boils. When a kettle **is boiling**, the water inside it is boiling. EG *He boiled the kettle and made the tea.*

4 When you **boil** food, you cook it in boiling water. V+O EG *She didn't know how to boil an egg... ...boiled potatoes.*

5 If something is **boiling** or **boiling** hot, it is very ADJ CLASSIF hot. EG *I immersed my boiling body in a cool pool.*

6 If you **are boiling** with anger, you are very V : USU+with angry.

7 A **boil** is a red, painful swelling on your skin. N COUNT

Would you be annoyed if someone was rocking the boat?

boil away. When a liquid **boils away**, all of it PHRASAL VB: V+ADV
changes into steam or vapour.

boil down to. If you say that a situation or PHRASAL VB: V+ADV+PREP
problem **boils down to** a particular thing, you
mean that this is the most important aspect of it. EG
What it all seemed to boil down to was money...
The question boils down to one of social priorities.

boil over. 1 When a liquid that is being heated PHRASAL VB: V+ADV
boils over, it rises and flows over the edge of the
container. EG *The milk's boiling over.* 2 When V+ADV
someone's feelings **boil over**, they lose their temper or become violent. EG *George's temper prompt-*
ly boiled over again.

boiler /bɔɪlə/, **boilers. A boiler** is a device which N COUNT
burns gas, oil, electricity, or coal in order to
provide hot water, especially for the central heating in a building.

boisterous /bɔɪstə'rəs/. Someone who is **boister-** ADJ QUALIT
ous is noisy, lively, and full of energy.

bold /bəʊld/, **bolder, boldest. 1** Someone who is ADJ QUALIT
bold is 1.1 not afraid to do things which involve
risk or danger. EG *...the most ambitious, bold, and*
imaginative of Europe's citizens... ...a bold action.
◊ **boldly.** EG *...boldly going where no man had gone* ◊ ADV
before. ◊ **boldness.** EG *For any success, boldness* ◊ N UNCOUNT
is required. **1.2** not shy or embarrassed in the ADJ QUALIT
company of other people. EG *Mary was surprisingly*
bold for a girl who seemed so young... She had bold
brown eyes. ◊ **boldly.** EG *He returned her gaze* ◊ ADV
boldly.
2 Bold lines or designs are painted or drawn in a ADJ QUALIT
clear, strong way. EG *...bold handwriting... She be-*
gan to paint her lips with bold, defiant strokes.
3 A **bold** colour or pattern is very bright and ADJ QUALIT
noticeable. EG *...his bold black-and-white striped*
shirt.
4 If printed letters are in **bold** print or **bold** ADJ CLASSIF:
typeface, they are thicker and look blacker than ATTRIB
ordinary printed letters. **This sentence is in bold**
type.

bollard /bɒlɑːd, bɒləd/, **bollards. Bollards** are N COUNT
short thick posts that are used to prevent cars from
going on to someone's land or on to part of a road.

bolster /bəʊlstə/, **bolsters, bolstering, bol-** V+O
stered. If you **bolster** someone's confidence or
courage, you make them more confident or more
courageous. EG *We arranged a daily routine that*
would bolster her sense of security.

bolster up. If you **bolster** something **up**, you PHRASAL VB:
help it or support it in order to make it stronger. EG V+O+ADV
The industries provided the work that bolstered up
the system... To bolster up their case, they quoted a
speech by Ray Gunter.

bolt /bəʊlt/, **bolts, bolting, bolted. 1** A **bolt** is a N COUNT
long metal object which screws into a nut and is
used to fasten things together. EG *The bolts are all*
tight enough.
2 When you **bolt** one thing to another, you fasten V+O: USU+A
them firmly together, using a bolt. EG *...an iron cot*
bolted to the floor.
3 A **bolt** on a door or window is a metal bar that N COUNT
you can slide across in order to fasten the door or
window.
4 When you **bolt** a door or window, you slide the V+O
bolt across to fasten it.
5 If a person or animal **bolts**, they suddenly start to V
run very fast, often because something has frightened them.
6 If you **bolt** your food or **bolt** it down, you eat it so V+O OR
quickly that you hardly chew it or taste it. EG *Daniel* V+O+A
bolted one slice of his mother's cake and rushed
out.
7 If someone is sitting or standing **bolt upright**, PHRASE
they are sitting or standing very straight.

bomb /bɒm/, **bombs, bombing, bombed. 1** A N COUNT
bomb is a device which explodes and damages or
destroys a large area. EG *...the bombs which de-*
stroyed these cities... They had planted the bomb
beneath the house.

2 Nuclear weapons are sometimes referred to as N SING: the+N
the **bomb**. EG *Ban the bomb!*
3 When people **bomb** a place, they attack it with V+O
bombs. EG *They bombed the airports in three*
cities... The premises were bombed in the Second
World War. ◊ **bombing, bombings.** EG *It replaced* ◊ N UNCOUNT
the building destroyed by bombing in 1940... ...the OR N COUNT
current wave of bombings.

bomb out. If a building **is bombed out**, it is PHRASAL VB:
destroyed by a bomb. If people **are bombed out**, V-PASS+ADV
their houses are destroyed by bombs. EG *Their*
factories were bombed out... These were people
bombed out by the Allies.

bombard /bɒmbɑːd/, **bombards, bombarding,**
bombarded. 1 If you **bombard** someone with V+O:
questions or criticism, you keep asking them a lot OFT+with
of questions or you keep criticizing them.
2 When soldiers **bombard** a place, they attack it V+O
with continuous heavy gunfire or bombs.
◊ **bombardment** /bɒmbɑːdmə'nt/, **bombard-** ◊ N COUNT OR
ments. EG *...increasingly heavy artillery bombard-* N UNCOUNT
ment.

bombastic /bɒmbæstɪk/. **Bombastic** statements ADJ QUALIT
or threats contain long and important sounding
words, chosen to impress people rather than to
express meaning clearly. EG *...bombastic threats of*
retaliation.

bomber /bɒmə/, **bombers. A bomber** is 1 an N COUNT
aircraft which drops bombs. **2** a person who causes
a bomb to explode in a public place.

bombshell /bɒmʃel/, **bombshells. A bombshell** N COUNT
is a sudden piece of bad or unexpected news. EG *She*
dropped her bombshell. 'I'm pregnant.'

bona fide /bəʊnəfaɪdɪ'/, **bona fides. 1** If some- ADJ CLASSIF:
thing is **bona fide**, it is genuine or real. EG *...bona* ATTRIB
fide applications to join the Service. Formal
2 Your **bona fides** are your good or sincere N PLURAL
intentions. EG *He wanted to check on my bona* Formal
fides... They may have difficulty in establishing
their bona fides.

bonanza /bənænzə/, **bonanzas.** You can refer to N COUNT
a time or situation when people suddenly become
much richer as a **bonanza**. EG *...an oil bonanza.*

bond /bɒnd/, **bonds, bonding, bonded. 1** A **bond** N COUNT:
between people is **1.1** a strong feeling of friend- OFT+SUPP
ship, love, or shared beliefs that unites them. EG
...the bond between mother and child... ...bonds of
friendship. **1.2** a close connection that they have
with each other as a result of an agreement. EG
Many people see marriage as a permanent bond.
2 When people or animals **bond** or **are bonded**, V OR V-PASS
they unite to help and protect each other. EG
Societies have always been bonded together by a
threat from outside.
3 A **bond** is a certificate issued by a government or N COUNT
company which shows that you have lent them
money and that they will pay you interest. EG
Investors would refuse to buy the bonds at the low
interest rate offered.
4 Bonds are feelings, duties, or customs that force N PLURAL
you to behave in a particular way. EG *...the bonds of* +SUPP
party discipline.
5 When you **bond** two things, you stick them V+O: OFT
together using glue. +to/together

bondage /bɒndɪdʒ/ is the condition of belonging N UNCOUNT
to someone as their slave. EG *They were kept in* Literary
bondage.

bone /bəʊn/, **bones, boning, boned. 1** Your N COUNT OR
bones are the hard parts inside your body which N UNCOUNT
together form your skeleton. EG *...hip bones... Mary*
broke a bone in her back... Its eye sockets are
encircled by bone.
2 If you **bone** a piece of meat or fish, you remove V+O
the bones from it before cooking it. EG *...boned*
sirloins of beef.
3 A **bone** tool or ornament is made of bone. EG ADJ CLASSIF
They fished with bone harpoons.
4 Bone is used in these phrases. **4.1** If you **feel** or PHRASES
know something **in** your **bones**, you are certain Informal

about it, although you cannot explain why. EG *He felt in his bones he could do it... James knew in his bones that she was the right girl for him.* **4.2** If you **make no bones** about doing something unpleasant or difficult, you do it without hesitation. EG *They made no bones about acknowledging their debt to him.* **4.3** When someone is very thin, you can say that they are **a bag of bones** or **all skin and bone**.

bonfire /bɒnfaɪə/, **bonfires.** A **bonfire** is a fire N COUNT that is made outdoors, especially in order to burn rubbish from a garden.

bonhomie /bɒnəmɪ¹/ is happy, jolly friendliness. N UNCOUNT EG *...the grin of bonhomie on his face.* Literary

bonnet /bɒnɪt/, **bonnets. 1** The **bonnet** of a car is N COUNT the metal cover over the engine at the front. See British picture at CAR.
2 A baby's or woman's **bonnet** is a hat tied under N COUNT their chin.

bonny /bɒni¹/; also spelled **bonnie.** Someone or ADJ QUALIT something that is **bonny** is nice to look at. EG *She* Scottish *had a big bonny boy with fair hair.*

bonus /bəʊnəs/, **bonuses.** A **bonus** is **1** an N COUNT amount of money that is added to your usual pay, especially because you have worked very hard. EG *The farmer gave his men a five pound bonus.* **2** something good that you get in addition to something else. EG *Any sort of party after work was a bonus.*

bony /bəʊni¹/. A **bony** person is very thin. EG *He* ADJ QUALIT *was tall, thin, and bony... ...his long bony fingers.*

boo /buː/, **boos, booing, booed.** If you **boo** a V+O OR V speaker or performer, you shout 'boo' to indicate that you do not like them, their opinions, or their performance. EG *By now most of the audience was booing.* ▸ used as a noun. EG *There were loud boos* ▸ N COUNT *from the fans.*

boob /buːb/, **boobs.** A woman's **boobs** are her N COUNT : breasts; a rude word. USU PLURAL

booby prize /buːbi¹ praɪz/, **booby prizes.** The N COUNT **booby prize** is a prize given to the person who comes last in a competition. EG *It looks as if you've got the booby prize.*

booby-trap, /buːbi¹ træp/, **booby-traps, booby-trapping, booby-trapped. 1** A **booby-trap** is N COUNT something such as a bomb which is hidden or disguised and which causes death or injury when it is touched. EG *They searched the ground for booby traps.*
2 If something **is booby-trapped**, a booby-trap is V+O : USU PASS placed in it or on it. EG *How do you know the building's not booby-trapped?*

book /bʊk/, **books, booking, booked. 1** A **book** is N COUNT a number of pieces of paper, usually with words printed on them, which are fastened together and fixed inside a cover of stronger paper or cardboard. Books contain information, stories, or poetry, for example. EG *...a book by John Fisher about Emily Hobhouse... ...a book on hypnotism... She opened the book and put the envelope between the pages.*
2 A **book** of something such as stamps, matches, or N PART tickets is a small number of them fastened together between thin cardboard or plastic covers.
3 When you **book** something such as a hotel room V+O : OFT+*for* or a ticket, you arrange to have it or use it at a OR V+O+O particular time. EG *I'd like to book a table for four* British *for tomorrow night.* ● See also **booking.**
4 If a hotel, restaurant, or theatre is **booked up** or PHRASE is **fully booked**, it has no rooms, tables, or tickets left for a particular time or date.
5 A company's or organization's **books** are its N PLURAL records of money that has been spent and earned or of the names of people who belong to it. EG *He's going to help me go over my books and check the totals... His name is no longer on our books.*
6 If you are **in** someone's **bad books**, they are PHRASE annoyed with you. If you are **in** their **good books**, they are pleased with you.

book in or **book into.** When you **book into** a PHRASAL VB : hotel or when you **book in**, you officially state that V+PREP you have arrived to stay there, usually by signing OR V+ADV your name in a register. EG *He booked in at the* British *Hotel d'Angleterre.*

bookcase /bʊkkeɪs/, **bookcases.** A **bookcase** is a N COUNT piece of furniture with shelves that you keep books on.

booking /bʊkɪŋ/, **bookings.** A **booking** is the N COUNT arrangement that you make when you book something such as a theatre seat or a hotel room.

bookish /bʊkɪʃ/. Someone who is **bookish** spends ADJ QUALIT a lot of time reading serious books.

bookkeeping /bʊkkiːpɪŋ/ is the job of keeping an N UNCOUNT accurate record of the money that is spent and received by a business or other organization.

booklet /bʊklɪ¹t/, **booklets.** A **booklet** is a small N COUNT book with a paper cover that gives you information about something.

bookmaker /bʊkmeɪkə/, **bookmakers.** A **book-** N COUNT **maker** is a person whose job is to take your money when you bet and to pay you money if you win.

bookmark /bʊkmaːk/, **bookmarks.** A **bookmark** N COUNT is a narrow piece of card or leather that you put between the pages of a book so that you can find a particular page easily.

bookseller /bʊksɛlə/, **booksellers.** A **bookseller** N COUNT is a person who sells books.

bookshelf /bʊkʃɛlf/, **bookshelves.** A **bookshelf** is N COUNT **1** a shelf on which you keep books. **2** a bookcase.

bookshop /bʊkʃɒp/, **bookshops.** A **bookshop** is a N COUNT shop where books are sold. British

bookstall /bʊkstɔːl/, **bookstalls.** A **bookstall** is a N COUNT small shop with an open front where books and magazines are sold.

bookstore /bʊkstɔː/, **bookstores.** A **bookstore** is N COUNT the same as a bookshop. American

boom /buːm/, **booms, booming, boomed. 1** If N COUNT+SUPP there is a **boom** in something, there is a fast increase or development in it. EG *We must take advantage of the boom in world shipping... ...the population boom.* ▸ used as a verb. EG *The garden-* ▸ V *ing industry is booming.*
2 When something such as a big drum, a cannon, or V OR V+QUOTE someone's voice **booms**, it makes a loud, deep, echoing sound. EG *The cannon boomed again... He had a booming voice... 'Nonsense!' boomed Mrs Pringle.* ▸ used as a noun. EG *The boom of the drum* ▸ N COUNT *echoed along the street.*

boom out. When someone **booms out** a greeting PHRASAL VB : or command, or when their voice **booms out**, they V+O+ADV speak in a very loud, deep voice. EG *He boomed out:* OR V+ADV *'Good evening ladies and gentlemen!'... Hogan's voice boomed out of the telephone receiver.*

boomerang /buːməræŋ/, **boomerangs.** A **boom-** N COUNT **erang** is a curved piece of wood which comes back to you if you throw it the correct way. Boomerangs were first used by Australian natives as weapons.

boon /buːn/, **boons.** You say that something is a N COUNT **boon** when it makes life better or easier for someone. EG *The bus service is a great boon to old people.*

boor /bʊə/, **boors.** A **boor** is a boorish person. EG N COUNT *...drunken boors.* Outdated

boorish /bʊərɪʃ/. Someone who is **boorish** be- ADJ QUALIT haves in a rough, impolite, clumsy way.

boost /buːst/, **boosts, boosting, boosted. 1** If one V+O thing **boosts** another, it causes it to increase. EG *This new technology will boost food production... ...an auxiliary motor capable of boosting our speed to fifteen knots.* ▸ used as a noun. EG *This will be a* ▸ N COUNT *great boost to the economy.*
2 If something **boosts** your confidence or morale, V+O it improves it. EG *There is nothing like winning to*

boost the morale of players. ▸ used as a noun. EG ...a ▸ N COUNT
boost to self-confidence.

3 If you **boost** someone or **boost** something that V+O
they have done, you praise them or publicize them
in order to make them more popular. EG Her books
have been boosted in the Observer recently.

boot /buːt/, **boots, booting, booted. 1** Boots are N COUNT:
1.1 shoes that cover your whole foot and the lower USU PLURAL
part of your leg. See picture at SHOES. EG I put on my
fur coat and boots. **1.2** strong, heavy shoes which
cover your ankle and which have thick soles. EG I
haven't got any climbing boots.

2 If you **boot** something such as a ball, you kick it V+O : USU+A
hard. EG She booted the ball back onto the pitch. Informal

3 The **boot** of a car is a covered space at the back N COUNT
or front, in which you carry things such as luggage British
and shopping. See picture at CAR.

4 If someone **puts the boot in, 4.1** they repeatedly PHRASE
kick someone who is lying on the ground. **4.2** they Informal
say something cruel to someone who is already
feeling weak or upset.

5 If someone says that you **are getting too big for** PHRASE
your **boots**, they mean that you are becoming too Informal
proud and pleased with yourself.

6 If you **get the boot** or **are given the boot**, you PHRASE
are dismissed from your job. Informal

7 You can say **to boot** when you have just added a PHRASE
further comment to something that you have said. Literary
EG She was an unaccompanied female, and a foreigner to boot.

boot out. If you **are booted out** of a job, organi- PHRASAL VB :
zation, or place, you are forced to leave it. EG I was V+O+ADV
a drunken swine. No wonder Gertrude booted me Informal
out.

booth /buːð/, **booths.** A **booth** is **1** a small area N COUNT
separated from a larger public area by screens or
thin walls where, for example, you can make a
telephone call. EG He went into the booth and
dialled the number. **2** a small tent or stall, usually
at a fair, in which you can buy goods or watch
some form of entertainment.

booty /buːtiˈ/ is a collection of valuable things N UNCOUNT
taken from a place, especially by soldiers after a Literary
battle. EG The victorious forces were laden with
enemy booty.

booze /buːz/, **boozes, boozing, boozed. 1** Booze is N UNCOUNT
alcoholic drink. EG You could smell the booze on his Informal
breath.

2 When people **booze**, they drink alcohol. EG All V
these lads do is sit about and booze. Informal

boozer /buːzə/, **boozers. 1** A **boozer** is a person N COUNT
who drinks a lot of alcohol. Informal

2 The **boozer** is a pub near to where you live or N COUNT
work. Informal

boozy /buːziˈ/. A **boozy** person drinks a lot of ADJ CLASSIF
alcohol. EG ...his boozy companions... ...boozy sing- Informal
ing.

bop /bɒp/, **bops, bopping, bopped.** A **bop** is a N COUNT
dance. ▸ used as a verb. EG There we were, bopping ▸ V : USU+A
away till the small hours. Informal

border /bɔːdə/, **borders, bordering, bordered. 1** N COUNT
The **border** between two countries or regions is
the dividing line between them. Sometimes the
border also refers to the land close to this line. EG
He lives in the French Alps near the Swiss border...
They crossed the border into Mexico.

2 If a country **borders** another country or **borders** V+O OR V+on
on it, it is next to it.

3 A **border** is also **3.1** a strip or band around the N COUNT
edge of something. EG It's painted in white with a
gold border. **3.2** a strip of ground planted with
flowers along the edge of a lawn.

4 If something **borders** something else, it forms a V+O
line along the edge of it. EG Huge elm trees
bordered the road.

border on. When you say that something **bor-** PHRASAL VB :
ders on a particular state, you mean that it has V+PREP
almost reached that state. EG I was in a state of

excitement bordering on insanity... Their treatment of each other bordered on brutality.

borderline /bɔːdəlaɪn/. **1** Something that is ADJ CLASSIF
borderline is only just acceptable as a member of
a class or group. EG He is a borderline candidate for
a special school... ...borderline cases.

2 The **borderline** between two conditions or qual- N SING
ities is the division between them. EG ...the narrow
borderline between laughter and tears.

bore /bɔː/, **bores, boring, bored. 1** If something V+O :
bores you, you find it dull and uninteresting. EG OFT+with
Most of the book had bored him... I won't bore you
with the details. ● If something **bores** you **to** ● PHRASE
tears, bores you **to death**, or **bores** you **stiff**, it Informal
bores you very much indeed.

2 You describe someone as a **bore** when you think N COUNT
that they talk in a very uninteresting way. EG Steve
is the most frightful bore.

3 You can describe a situation as a **bore** when you N SING : a+N
find it annoying or a nuisance.

4 If you **bore** a hole in something, you make a deep V+O : USU+A
round hole in it using a special tool. EG They were
shown how to bore rivet holes in the sides of ships.

5 If someone's eyes **bore** into you, they stare V+into
intensely at you.

6 Bore is also the past tense of **bear.**

7 See also **bored, boring.**

bored /bɔːd/. When you are **bored**, you feel tired ADJ QUALIT :
and impatient because you have lost interest in OFT+with
something or because you have nothing to do. EG
Tom was bored with the film... There is no chance
of getting bored.

boredom /bɔːdəm/ is the state of being bored. EG N UNCOUNT
Many of the audience walked out through sheer
boredom.

boring /bɔːrɪŋ/. Something that is **boring 1** is so ADJ QUALIT
dull and uninteresting that it makes people tired
and impatient. EG ...a boring journey... Are all your
meetings so boring? **2** has been made in an uninteresting and unimaginative way. EG The gardens
were a bit boring.

born /bɔːn/. **1** When a baby **is born**, it comes out V-PASS :
of its mother's body at the beginning of its life. EG OFT+A OR C
Mary was born in Glasgow in 1899... ...the village
where she was born... It is a tragedy when a baby is
born abnormal.

2 You use **born** to talk about something that ADJ CLASSIF :
people can do very well and easily. For example, if ATTRIB
you are a **born** cook, you have a natural ability to
cook well. EG ...the curiosity and perception of the
born reporter.

3 When a thought, idea, or organization **is born**, it V-PASS
comes into existence. EG At that moment the con-
cept of the computer was born.

-born combines with the name of a place or
nationality to indicate where a person was born. EG
...South African-born Gus Calderwood.

borne /bɔːn/ is the past participle of **bear.**

borough /bʌrə/, **boroughs.** A **borough** is a town, N COUNT
or a district within a large town, which has its own
council. EG ...the London Borough of Lewisham.

borrow /bɒrəʊ/, **borrows, borrowing, bor-** V+O : OFT
rowed. If you **borrow** something that belongs to +from/off
someone else, they allow you to have it or use it for
a period of time. EG Could I borrow your car?... I
need to borrow five thousand pounds.

borrower /bɒrəʊə/, **borrowers.** A **borrower** is a N COUNT
person or organization that borrows money. EG
They increased the surcharge for big borrowers.

borrowing /bɒrəʊɪŋ/, **borrowings. Borrowing** N UNCOUNT
is the activity of borrowing money by people or
organizations. EG Lowering interest rates will make
borrowing cheaper.

borstal /bɔːstəl/, **borstals.** In Britain, a **borstal** N COUNT OR
is a prison for young criminals. EG Most of the boys N UNCOUNT
in borstals are from bad backgrounds... He was
sent to borstal.

bosom /bʊzəm/, **bosoms. 1** A woman's breasts N COUNT
are sometimes referred to as her **bosom**. EG She Outdated

had a very large bosom... ...hugging the cat to her bosom.

2 If you are in the **bosom** of your family or of a community, you are among people who love, accept, and protect you. EG *...torn from the bosom of his own family... ...acceptance into the bosom of the Establishment.* ● If you **take** someone to your **bosom**, you accept them and treat them with great affection.   N SING+SUPP Literary   ● PHRASE Literary

3 Strong feelings are sometimes described as being in your **bosom**. EG *...some dark, sinful passion you're nursing in your bosom.*   N COUNT+POSS Literary

4 A **bosom** friend is a friend who you know and like very much indeed. EG *...the son of her bosom friend Klara.*   N MOD

boss /bɒs/, **bosses, bossing, bossed. 1** Your **boss** is the person in charge of the organization where you work. EG *I met his boss at a dinner party... The crisis occurred while the boss was away.*   N COUNT

2 If you are the **boss** in a group or relationship, you are the person who makes all the decisions. EG *You're not the boss around here.*   N COUNT: USU the+N Informal

3 If you **are** your **own boss**, you work for yourself or do not have to ask other people for permission to do something. EG *I'm my own boss now, thank God.*   PHRASE

4 If someone **bosses** you, **bosses** you around, or **bosses** you about, they keep telling you what to do as if they had authority over you. EG *They've bossed us around enough... Some people like to be bossed and bullied.*   V+O:OFT +around/ about

bossy /bɒsɪ¹/. A **bossy** person enjoys telling other people what to do; used showing disapproval. EG *...one of those large, bossy women.* ◊ **bossiness.** EG *His bossiness didn't worry her unduly.*   ADJ QUALIT ◊ N UNCOUNT

botanic /bə²tænɪk/ means the same as botanical.

botanical /bə²tænɪkə¹l/. **Botanical** books, research, and activities relate to the scientific study of plants. EG *...botanical drawings... ...botanical gardens.*   ADJ CLASSIF: ATTRIB

botanist /bɒtənɪst/, **botanists**. A **botanist** is a scientist who studies plants.   N COUNT

botany /bɒtəni¹/ is the scientific study of plants.   N UNCOUNT

botch /bɒtʃ/, **botches, botching, botched.** If you **botch** a piece of work or **botch** it up, you do it badly or clumsily. EG *I hope I don't do something stupid and botch it... ...a botched job.* ▸ used as a noun. EG *She's made a botch of it again.*   V+O:OFT+up Informal ▸ N COUNT

both /bəʊθ/. **1** You use **both** when you are referring to two people or things and saying that something is true about each of them. EG *Both her parents were dead... Both policies make good sense.* ▸ used as a pronoun. EG *Most of them speak either English or German or both... He got angry with both of them... He's fond of you both... We were both young.*   PREDET OR QUANTIF ▸ PRON: OFT+of

2 You use the structure **both...and** when you are giving two facts or alternatives and emphasizing that each of them is true or possible. EG *These are dangers that threaten both men and women... The prospects both excited and worried me.*

bother /bɒðə/, **bothers, bothering, bothered. 1** If you do not **bother** to do something, you do not do it, because you think it is unnecessary or would involve too much effort. EG *I never bother to iron my shirts... Why bother learning all those facts?... Don't bother with the washing-up... Don't bother about the rug.*   V:OFT +to-INF, -ING, OR with/about

2 If you say that you **can't be bothered** to do something, you mean that you are not going to do it because you think it is unnecessary or would involve too much effort. EG *I can't be bothered to cook for myself.*   PHRASE

3 **Bother** is trouble, fuss, or difficulty. EG *We found the address without any bother.*   N UNCOUNT

4 If a task or a person is a **bother**, they are boring or irritating. EG *Sorry to be a bother, but could you sign this for me?*   N SING:a+N Informal

5 If something **bothers** you or if you **bother** about   V+O OR V+about

it, you are worried, concerned, or upset about it. EG *Is something bothering you?... You can come along too, if you like – it doesn't bother me... I didn't bother about what I looked like.* ◊ **bothered.** EG *She was bothered about Olive.*   ◊ ADJ PRED

6 If you **bother** someone, you talk to them or interrupt them when they are busy. EG *I didn't want to bother him while he was working... Don't bother me with little things like that.*   V+O: OFT+with

7 Some people say '**Bother**' when they are annoyed about something.   EXCLAM British

bottle /bɒtə¹l/, **bottles, bottling, bottled. 1** A **bottle** is a container for keeping liquids in. Bottles are usually made of glass or plastic and are shaped like a cylinder with a narrow top. EG *She was screwing the top back on to her scent bottle.*   N COUNT

2 You can also use **bottle** to refer to a full bottle and its contents, or to the contents only. EG *She drank half a bottle of whisky a day.*   N PART

3 When people **bottle** wine or beer, they put it into bottles after it has been made.   V+O

4 A **bottle** is also a drinking container used by babies. It has a special rubber part at the top through which they can suck their drink. EG *The baby went on sucking the bottle.*   N COUNT

bottle up. If you **bottle up** strong feelings, you do not express them or show them. EG *...all the rage that had been bottled up in him for so long.*   PHRASAL VB V+O+ADV

bottled /bɒtə¹ld/. **Bottled** drinks are sold in bottles. EG *...bottled beer... ...bottled water.*   ADJ CLASSIF

bottom /bɒtə¹m/, **bottoms, bottoming, bottomed. 1** The **bottom** of something is the lowest part of it. EG *I stood there at the bottom of the steps... It sank to the bottom of the lake.*   N COUNT: USU SING

2 The **bottom** thing or layer in a series of things or layers is the lowest one. EG *...the bottom button of my waistcoat.*   ADJ CLASSIF: ATTRIB

3 The **bottom** of a place such as a street or garden is the end of it that is farthest away from the entrance. EG *...down at the bottom of the meadow.*   N COUNT

4 The **bottom** of an organization or scale is the least powerful or important level in it or the lowest point on it. EG *Officials at the top make the decisions; men at the bottom carry them out.*   N SING:the+N

5 If you are **bottom** of the class or come **bottom** in a test, you are the worst student in the class or get the lowest marks in the test.   ADJ PRED

6 If you **get to the bottom of** something, you discover the real truth about it or the real cause of it. EG *I'm going to get to the bottom of this, once and for all.*   PHRASE

7 The thing that is **at the bottom of** something is the real cause of it. EG *Greed lies at the bottom of our ecological predicament.*   PHRASE

8 Your **bottom** is the part of your body that you sit on. See picture at THE HUMAN BODY.   N COUNT

bottom out. When something that has been getting worse or lower **bottoms out**, it stops getting worse or lower, and remains at a particular level or amount. EG *Even if the recession has bottomed out, it will not help the unemployed.*   PHRASAL VB V+ADV

bottomless /bɒtəmlɪ¹s/. If you describe a supply of something as **bottomless**, you mean that it seems so large that it will never run out. EG *...American millionaires with bottomless purses.*   ADJ CLASSIF

bough /baʊ/, **boughs**. A **bough** is a large branch of a tree. EG *...leafy boughs.*   N COUNT Literary

bought /bɔːt/ is the past tense and past participle of **buy**.

boulder /bəʊldə/, **boulders**. A **boulder** is a large rounded rock. EG *...huge granite boulders.*   N COUNT

boulevard /buːlə⁰vɑːd⁰/, **boulevards**. A **boulevard** is a wide street in a city, usually with trees along each side.   N COUNT

What is the connection between a bouquet and a botanist?

bounce /bauns/, **bounces, bouncing, bounced. 1** V:OFT+A
When an object such as a ball **bounces**, it moves
upwards or away immediately after hitting something. EG *Enormous hailstones bounced off the*
pavements. ▸ used as a noun. EG *She had not* ▸N COUNT
reached the ball before its second bounce.

2 When you **bounce** a ball, you throw it hard V+O
against a surface so that it immediately moves
away. EG *She bounced the ball twice before serving.*

3 If sound or light **bounces** off a surface, it reaches V:OFT+A
the surface and is reflected back. EG *Its flickering*
light bounced off the walls.

4 You can say that something **bounces** when it V
swings or moves up and down. EG *The rucksack*
bounced and jingled on my shoulders.

5 If you **bounce** on something, you jump up and V+A
down on it repeatedly. EG *...bouncing on a trampo-*
line.

6 If someone **bounces** somewhere, they move in V+A
an energetic way, because they are feeling happy.
EG *He came bouncing in, grinning.*

7 If a cheque **bounces** or if a bank **bounces** it, the V-ERG
bank refuses to accept it and pay out the money,
because there is not enough money in the account.

bounce back. If you **bounce back** after a bad PHRASAL VB:
experience, you return quickly to your previous V+ADV
level of activity, enthusiasm, or success. EG *You*
always bounce back.

bouncer /baunsə/, **bouncers. A bouncer** is a N COUNT
man who is employed to stand at the door of a club, Informal
in order to prevent unwanted people from coming
in and to throw people out if they cause trouble.

bouncy /baunsi¹/. Someone who is **bouncy** is very ADJ QUALIT
lively and enthusiastic. EG *...a bouncy little man.*

bound /baund/, **bounds, bounding, bounded. 1** If ADJ PRED
something is **bound** to happen, it is certain to +to-INF
happen. EG *We are bound to win.*

2 If you are **bound** by an agreement or law, you ADJ PRED:
have a duty to obey it. EG *We are bound by the* USU+by
government's pay policy.

3 You can say **'I am bound to say'** or **'I am** ADV SEN
bound to admit' when mentioning a fact which
you regret. EG *Sometimes, I'm bound to say, they*
are a hopeless muddle.

4 If one thing is **bound up with** another, it is PHRASE
closely connected with the other thing. EG *All this*
was bound up with what was happening in Egypt.

5 If a vehicle is **bound** for a particular place, it is ADJ PRED+for
travelling towards it. EG *He put her aboard the*
steamer bound for New York.

6 Bounds are limits which restrict what can be N PLURAL
done. EG *It is not outside the bounds of possibility.*

7 If a place is **out of bounds**, people are forbidden PHRASE
to go there. EG *The staff room at school was out of*
bounds.

8 If an area of land **is bounded** by something, that V+O:USU PASS
thing is situated around its edge. EG *The plantation*
was bounded by marsh.

9 When animals or people **bound**, they move V:USU+A
quickly with large leaps. EG *Goats were bounding*
off in all directions. ▸ used as a noun. EG *He* ▸N COUNT
advanced towards Alexandra with great bounds.

10 Bound is also the past tense and past participle
of **bind**.

boundary /baundə⁰ri¹/, **boundaries. 1** The N COUNT:
boundary of an area of land is an imaginary line USU+SUPP
that separates it from other areas. EG *...the bounda-*
ry of the Snowdonia National Park... You have to
stay within your county boundary.

2 The **boundaries** of something such as a subject N COUNT+SUPP
or activity are the limits that people think that it
has. EG *The old boundaries between subjects are*
collapsing.

boundless /baundlɪ²s/. If you describe something ADJ CLASSIF
as **boundless**, you mean that there seems to be no
end or limit to it. EG *...her boundless energies.*

bountiful /bauntɪful/. Something that is **bountiful** ADJ QUALIT
is provided in large amounts. EG *...a bountiful supply* Literary
of Madame's favourite cigarettes.

bounty /baunti¹/. **1** Someone's **bounty** is their N SING+POSS
generosity in giving something. EG *They must ac-* Literary
cept the colonel's bounty.

2 You can refer to something that is provided in N UNCOUNT
large amounts as **bounty**. EG *...potatoes and peas,* Literary
ducks and turkeys, all the bounty of the freezer.

bouquet /bəʊkeɪ, buː-/, **bouquets. A bouquet** is a N COUNT
bunch of flowers which is attractively arranged,
especially one which is given as a present. EG *...a*
bouquet of roses.

bourbon /bɜːbə⁰n/, **bourbons. Bourbon** is a type N MASS
of whisky that is made mainly in America.

bourgeois /bʊəʒwɑː/. **1** If you describe things, for ADJ QUALIT
example people's attitudes, as **bourgeois**, you
mean that you consider them typical of fairly rich
middle-class people; used showing disapproval. EG
They're the most conventional, dull, bourgeois peo-
ple you've ever met.

2 Marxists use **bourgeois** when referring to the ADJ CLASSIF
capitalist system and to the social class who own
most of the wealth in that system. EG *She condemns*
modern bourgeois society.

bourgeoisie /bʊəʒwɑːziː/. In Marxist theory, the N COLL
bourgeoisie are the middle-class people who own
most of the wealth in a capitalist system.

bout /baut/, **bouts. 1** If you have a **bout** of N COUNT:
something such as an illness, you have it for a short OFT+of
period. EG *...a bout of malaria.*

2 A **bout** of activity is a short time during which N COUNT:
you put a lot of effort into doing something. EG OFT+of
...frenzied bouts of writing.

3 A **bout** is also a boxing or wrestling match. N COUNT

boutique /buːtiːk/, **boutiques. A boutique** is a N COUNT
small shop that sells fashionable clothes, shoes, or
jewellery.

bow, bows, bowing, bowed; pronounced /baʊ/ for
paragraphs 1 to 4 and for the phrasal verbs, and
/bəʊ/ for paragraphs 5, 6, and 7.

1 When you **bow** to someone, you briefly bend your V:OFT+to
body towards them as a formal way of greeting
them or showing respect. EG *'Goodbye, Miss Drew,'*
he said, bowing to her. ▸ used as a noun. EG *He* ▸N COUNT
opened the door with a bow.

2 If you **bow** your head, you bend it downwards so V+O
that you are looking towards the ground.

3 If you **bow** to someone's wishes or **bow** to V+to
pressure, you agree to do what someone wants you Formal
to do. EG *They bow to all her wishes regardless of*
their own.

4 The **bow** of a ship is the front part of it. EG *...the* N COUNT
spray about her bows.

bow

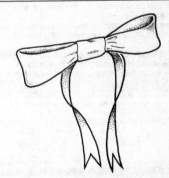

5 A **bow** is a knot with two loops and two loose N COUNT
ends that is used in tying shoelaces and ribbons.

6 A **bow** is also a weapon for shooting arrows, N COUNT
consisting of a long piece of wood bent into a curve
by a string attached to both its ends.

7 The **bow** of a violin or other stringed instrument N COUNT
is a long thin piece of wood with horsehair

stretched along it, which you move across the strings of the instrument in order to play it.

bow down. If you **bow down**, you bow very low in order to show great respect. EG *Their people bowed down before them.* PHRASAL VB: V+ADV

bow out. If you **bow out** of something, you stop taking part in it. EG *We may do one more perfor-mance before we bow out.* PHRASAL VB: V+ADV

bowed; pronounced /bəʊd/ for paragraph 1 and /baʊd/ for paragraph 2.

1 Something that is **bowed** is curved. EG *He had slightly bowed legs.* ADJ QUALIT

2 If a person's body is **bowed**, it is bent forward. EG *...a man bent and bowed, walking slowly along.* ADJ QUALIT

bowel /baʊəl/, **bowels. 1** Your **bowels** are the tubes in your body through which digested food passes from your stomach to your anus. N PLURAL OR N SING: the+N

2 You can refer to the parts deep inside something as the **bowels** of that thing. EG *...deep in the bowels of the earth.* N PLURAL +SUPP

bowl /bəʊl/, **bowls, bowling, bowled. 1** A **bowl** is a circular container with a wide, uncovered top. Bowls are used, for example, for serving food or mixing ingredients when cooking. N COUNT

2 You can also use **bowl** to refer to a bowl and its contents, or to the contents only. EG *...a bowl of water... I ate a big bowl of porridge.* N PART

3 The **bowl** of a lavatory, a tobacco pipe, or a spoon is the hollow, rounded part of it. N COUNT: USU+SUPP

4 When someone playing cricket **bowls** a ball, they throw it down the pitch towards the batsman. V+O OR V

5 **Bowls** is a game in which the players try to roll large wooden balls as near as possible to a small ball. N UNCOUNT

6 See **bowling**.

bowl over. 1 If you **bowl** someone **over**, you knock them down by accidentally hitting them when you are moving very quickly. EG *They leapt aside to avoid being bowled over by three boys as they raced past.* **2** If you **are bowled over** by something, you are very impressed or surprised by it. EG *I was bowled over by the beauty of Malawi.* PHRASAL VB: V+O+ADV / V+O+ADV, USU PASS

bow-legged /bəʊ lɛɡɪd/. Someone who is **bow-legged** has legs that curve apart at the knees. ADJ CLASSIF

bowler /bəʊlə/, **bowlers. 1** The **bowler** in a game of cricket is the person who is bowling the ball. N COUNT

2 A **bowler** or a **bowler hat** is a round, stiff hat with a narrow curved brim. N COUNT

bowling /bəʊlɪŋ/ is **1** a game in which you roll a heavy ball down a long narrow track towards a group of wooden objects and try to knock down as many of them as possible. **2** the action or activity of bowling the ball in cricket. EG *His bowling was generally disappointing.* N ING / N UNCOUNT

bow tie /bəʊ taɪ/, **bow ties.** A **bow tie** is a man's tie in the form of a bow, worn especially for formal occasions. N COUNT

box /bɒks/, **boxes, boxing, boxed. 1** A **box** is a square or rectangular container which sometimes has a lid. EG *...a cardboard box... ...boxes filled with old clothes... ...your tool box.* N COUNT

2 You can also use **box** to refer to a box and its contents, or to the contents only. EG *...a box of matches... ...a box of chocolates.* N PART

3 A **box** on a form that you fill in is a square or rectangular space in which you have to write something. EG *If you agree, put a tick in the box marked 'yes'.* N COUNT

4 A **box** in a theatre is a separate area like a little room where a small number of people can sit to watch the performance. EG *...the Royal Box.* N COUNT

5 You can refer to television as the **box**. EG *...eating, drinking, and watching the box... David Owen was on the box the other night.* N SING: the+N Informal

6 To **box** means to fight someone according to the rules of the sport of boxing. EG *He used to box, run, and swim for the county.* V

box in. If you **are boxed in**, you are unable to move from a particular place because you are PHRASAL VB: V+O+ADV

surrounded by other people or cars. EG *Two other drivers boxed me in.*

boxer /bɒksə/, **boxers.** A **boxer** is a sportsman whose sport is boxing. N COUNT

boxing /bɒksɪŋ/ is a sport in which two men wearing large padded gloves fight according to special rules, by punching each other. N UNCOUNT

Boxing Day is the twenty-sixth of December, the day after Christmas Day. N UNCOUNT British

box office, box offices. 1 The **box office** in a theatre, cinema, or concert hall is the place where the tickets are sold. N COUNT

2 The **box office** is also used when referring to the degree of success of a film, play, or actor in terms of the number of people who go to watch it or them. EG *She was a very hot box office attraction indeed.* N SING: the+N OR N MOD

boy /bɔɪ/, **boys. 1** A **boy** is a male child. EG *There were hundreds of boys and girls on the lawn.* N COUNT

2 You can also refer to a young man as a **boy**. EG *...the boy you were going to marry... 'Poor boy,' said Molly.* N COUNT Informal

3 You can also refer to a group of men as **boys**. EG *We may need the help of the science boys... Take him away, boys.* N PLURAL Informal

4 Some people say **'Boy'** or **'Oh boy'** in order to express strong feelings such as excitement or admiration. EG *Boy oh boy, was that some party!* EXCLAM American

boycott /bɔɪkɒt/, **boycotts, boycotting, boy-cotted.** A **boycott** is a refusal to be involved with a country, organization, or event that you strongly disapprove of. EG *...an Olympic boycott... The boy-cott of British goods began in 1906.* ▶ used as a verb. EG *He urged all citizens to boycott the polls.* N COUNT: OFT+SUPP / ▶V+O

boyfriend /bɔɪfrɛnd/, **boyfriends.** Someone's **boyfriend** is a man or boy with whom they are having a romantic or sexual relationship. EG *This is my boyfriend Oliver... She had lots of boyfriends.* N COUNT: USU+POSS

boyhood /bɔɪhʊd/ is the period of a male person's life during which he is a boy. EG *He began to talk about his boyhood in London.* N UNCOUNT USU+POSS

boyish /bɔɪɪʃ/. **1** If you say that a man is **boyish**, you mean that he is like a boy in his appearance or behaviour. EG *...a boyish smile... This incident was not a boyish prank.* ◊ **boyishly.** EG *He grinned boyishly.* ADJ QUALIT / ◊ ADV

2 If you say that a girl or woman is **boyish**, you mean that she looks or behaves like a boy, for example because she has short hair and small breasts. EG *...her boyish clothes.* ADJ QUALIT

bra /brɑː/, **bras.** A **bra** is a piece of underwear that women wear to support their breasts. N COUNT

brace /breɪs/, **braces, bracing, braced. 1** If you **brace** yourself for something unpleasant or diffi-cult, you prepare yourself for it. EG *He braced himself for the task... She had braced herself to read the letter.* V-REFL: OFT+for OR to-INF

2 If you **brace** your body against something, you press against it in order to steady your body or to avoid falling. EG *The taxi swung round a bend and he braced himself with his foot.* V+O OR V-REFL

3 If you **brace** your shoulders or legs, you keep them stiffly in a particular position. EG *He stood to attention, his shoulders braced.* V+O

4 A **brace** is **4.1** a metal device that is sometimes fastened to a child's teeth in order to help them grow straight. **4.2** a device attached to a part of a person's body, for example to a weak leg, in order to strengthen or support it. N COUNT

5 **Braces** are a pair of straps that you can wear instead of a belt to prevent your trousers from falling down. The straps pass over your shoulders and are fastened to your trousers at the front and back. N PLURAL British

6 You can refer to two things of the same kind as a N PART

On these pages, how many things can you wear?

brace, especially two wild birds that have been killed for sport or food. The plural form is also **brace**. EG ...a brace of pheasants.

bracelet /breɪslɪ²t/, **bracelets**. A **bracelet** is a N COUNT chain or band, usually made of metal, which you wear around your wrist as jewellery. See picture at JEWELLERY.

bracing /breɪsɪŋ/. If you describe a place, cli- ADJ QUALIT mate, or activity as **bracing**, you mean that it makes you feel fit and full of energy. EG ...mountain air, bracing and heady.

bracken /bræk³n/ is a plant like a large fern that N UNCOUNT grows on hills and in woods.

bracket /brækɪ²t/, **brackets, bracketing, brack-** N COUNT : **eted.** 1 **Brackets** are 1.1 a pair of written marks USU PLURAL such as ( ) that you place round a word, expression, or sentence in order to indicate that you are giving extra information. EG The comments in brackets are the author's. 1.2 a pair of marks that are placed around a series of symbols in a mathematical expression to indicate that the series functions as one item within the expression.

2 If you **bracket** a word, expression, or sentence, V+O you put brackets round it. EG ...a bracketed question mark.

3 If you say that someone or something is in a N COUNT+SUPP particular **bracket**, you mean that they come within a particular range, for example a range of incomes, ages, or prices. EG ...a professional in a high income bracket... ...the 14-16 age bracket.

4 When you **bracket** two or more things or people V+O+ together, you consider them as being similar or together/with related in some way. EG Should current affairs be bracketed with documentary?

5 A **bracket** is also a piece of metal, wood, or N COUNT plastic that is fastened to a wall to support something such as a shelf.

brag /bræg/, **brags, bragging, bragged.** If you V : OFT+A, **brag**, you say in a very proud way that you have QUOTE, OR something or have done something; used showing REPORT : disapproval. EG I didn't brag about the salary... He ONLY that bragged to two nurses that he had killed a man.

braid /breɪd/, **braids, braiding, braided.** 1 **Braid** N UNCOUNT is a narrow piece of decorated cloth or twisted threads, which is used to decorate clothes or curtains. EG ...a cap with gold braid on it.

2 If you **braid** hair or a group of threads, you plait V+O it. EG They wore their hair braided in long pigtails. American

3 A **braid** is a length of hair which has been plaited N COUNT and tied. EG Carole was plump, with long braids. American

Braille /breɪl/ is a system of printing for blind N UNCOUNT people. The letters are printed as groups of raised dots that you can feel with your fingers.

brain /breɪn/, **brains.** 1 Your **brain** is 1.1 the N COUNT organ inside your head that enables you to think and to feel things such as heat and pain. EG ...how the brain functions... ...brain damage. 1.2 your mind and the way that you think. EG He had one clear wish in his confused brain. ● If someone **has** ● PHRASE something **on the brain**, they keep thinking about Informal it.

2 If you say that someone has **brains** or a good N COUNT **brain**, you mean that they have the ability to learn and understand things quickly, to solve problems, and to make good decisions. EG He'd got brains but wouldn't use them... She has a very capable business brain.

3 If you **pick** someone's **brains**, you ask them to PHRASE help you with a problem because they know a lot Informal about the subject involved.

4 Very clever people are sometimes referred to as N COUNT **brains**. EG Not even the great brains of Cambridge Informal can solve his problem.

5 The person who plans the activities of an organi- N SING : the+N zation can be referred to as the **brains** of that Informal organization. EG She was the brains of the company.

6 to **rack** your **brains**: see **rack**.

brainchild /breɪntʃaɪld/. Someone's **brainchild** is N SING+POSS an idea or invention that they have thought up or

created. EG The project was the brainchild of Max Nicholson.

brain drain. When people talk about a **brain** N SING **drain**, they are referring to the movement of a large number of scientists or academics away from their own country to other countries where the conditions and salaries are better.

brainless /breɪnlɪ²s/. If you say that someone is ADJ QUALIT **brainless**, you mean that they are very silly.

brainstorm /breɪnstɔːm/, **brainstorms.** If you N COUNT have a **brainstorm**, you suddenly become unable British to think sensibly. EG I must have had a brainstorm.

brainwash /breɪnwɒʃ/, **brainwashes, brain-** V+O : **washing, brainwashed.** If you **brainwash** some- OFT+into one, you force them to believe something by continually telling them that it is true, and preventing them from thinking about it properly. EG The public continues to be brainwashed into believing that a nuclear war could be survived.

brainwave /breɪnweɪv/, **brainwaves.** A N COUNT **brainwave** is a clever idea that you suddenly think of. EG Then he had a brainwave.

brainy /breɪni¹/, **brainier, brainiest.** Someone ADJ QUALIT who is **brainy** is clever and good at learning. Informal

brake /breɪk/, **brakes, braking, braked.** 1 The N COUNT : **brakes** of a vehicle are devices in it or on it that USU PLURAL are used to make it go slower or stop. See picture at CAR. EG There was a sudden screech of brakes... He took his foot off the brake.

2 When a vehicle **brakes**, the driver makes it slow V down or stop by using the brakes. EG Try to avoid sudden braking.

3 A **brake** is also something that slows down or N COUNT stops action or progress. EG Restrictive practices were putting a savage brake on enterprise.

bramble /bræmbɔ¹l/, **brambles. Brambles** are N COUNT : wild, thorny bushes that produce blackberries. EG USU PLURAL ...a large house, all overgrown with brambles.

bran /bræn/ is the small brown flakes that are left N UNCOUNT when wheat grains have been used to make white flour. EG ...breakfast cereals containing bran.

branch /brɑːntʃ/, **branches, branching,** **branched.** 1 The **branches** of a tree are the parts N COUNT that grow out from its trunk and that have leaves, flowers, or fruit growing on them. EG A bird flew across to the tree and alighted on a branch.

2 A **branch** of a business or other organization is N COUNT+SUPP one of the offices, shops, or local groups which belong to it. EG ...the Ipswich branch of Marks and Spencer... All the organizations in this list have local branches.

3 A **branch** of a subject is a part or type of it. EG N COUNT+SUPP ...specialists in particular branches of medicine.

4 A **branch** of government is a part or department N COUNT+SUPP with a particular function. EG ...the executive branch of government.

branch off. A road or path that **branches off** PHRASAL VB : from another one starts from it and goes in a V+ADV/PREP slightly different direction. EG A dirt path branched off the main road.

branch out. If you **branch out**, you do some- PHRASAL VB : thing different from your normal activities or V+ADV work, especially something unusual or risky. EG She decided to branch out alone and launch a campaign.

brand /brænd/, **brands, branding, branded.** 1 A N COUNT **brand** of a product is the version of it that is made OFT+SUPP by one particular manufacturer. EG ...a preference for one brand of soft drink rather than another.

2 You can refer to a particular kind of thought, N COUNT+of behaviour, or writing as a particular **brand** of it. EG ...their brand of politics... ...a new brand of humour.

3 If you **are branded** as something bad, people V+O+as decide and say that you are that thing. EG His OR V+O+C :OFT political supporters had been branded traitors... OFT PASS Hamburgers have been branded as junk food.

4 When an animal **is branded**, a permanent mark V+O is burned on its skin, in order to indicate who it belongs to.

brandish /brændɪʃ/, **brandishes, brandishing,** v+o
brandished. If you **brandish** something, especially a weapon, you wave it vigorously as a sign of
aggression or triumph. EG *They sprang high into
the air brandishing their spears.*

brand name, brand names. The **brand name** of N COUNT
a product made by a particular manufacturer is
the name that appears on it.

brand-new. Something that is **brand-new** is com- ADJ CLASSIF
pletely new. EG *...a brand new religion.*

brandy /brændi¹/, **brandies. Brandy** is a strong N MASS
alcoholic drink, usually made from wine.

brash /bræʃ/, **brasher, brashest.** If someone's ADJ QUALIT
behaviour is **brash**, they are being too confident
and aggressive. EG *Jenny was alarmed by these
brash children.*

brass /brɑːs/, **brasses. 1 Brass** is a yellow- N UNCOUNT
coloured metal made from copper and zinc. It is
used especially for making ornaments and musical
instruments. EG *...brass buttons.*
2 Brasses are flat pieces of brass with writing or a N COUNT
picture cut into them, which are found in churches.
3 The section of an orchestra which consists of N PLURAL :
brass wind instruments such as trumpets and horns the+N
is called the **brass**. See picture at MUSICAL INSTRU-
MENTS.
4 If you **get down to brass tacks**, you discuss the PHRASE
basic, most important facts of a situation.

brassiere /bræsɪə, bræz-/, **brassieres.** A bras- N COUNT
siere is the same as a **bra**. Formal

brat /bræt/, **brats.** If you call a child a **brat**, you N COUNT
mean that he or she behaves badly or annoys you. Informal
EG *He's a spoilt brat.*

bravado /brəvɑːdəʊ/ is an appearance of courage N UNCOUNT
that someone shows in order to impress other
people. EG *...some mad, defiant act of bravado.*

brave /breɪv/, **braver, bravest; braves, brav-
ing, braved. 1** Someone who is **brave** is willing to ADJ QUALIT
do things which are dangerous, and does not show
fear in difficult or dangerous situations. EG *...the
brave soldiers of your country... I think you were
brave to defy convention.* ◊ **bravely.** EG *He fought* ◊ ADV
bravely at the Battle of Waterloo.
2 If you say that someone is **putting a brave face** PHRASE
on a difficult situation, you mean that they are
pretending that they are happy or that they can
deal with the situation easily.
3 If you **brave** a difficult or dangerous situation, v+o
you deliberately experience it, in order to achieve Literary
something. EG *Farmers braved wintry conditions to
rescue the sheep.*

bravery /breɪvə⁰ri¹/ is brave behaviour or the N UNCOUNT
quality of being brave. EG *Being a nurse requires
infinite patience and bravery.*

bravo /brɑːvəʊ/. Some people say **'Bravo'** to EXCLAM
express appreciation when someone has done Outdated
something well. EG *Kate applauded with the rest
and shouted out 'Bravo!'*

brawl /brɔːl/, **brawls, brawling, brawled.** A N COUNT
brawl is a rough fight or struggle. EG *His front
teeth were knocked out in a brawl.* ▶ used as a ▶ V
verb. EG *They were brawling in the street.*

brawny /brɔːni¹/. Someone who is **brawny** is ADJ QUALIT
strong and muscular. EG *...a brawny worker.*

bray /breɪ/, **brays, braying, brayed. 1** When a V
donkey **brays**, it makes the loud, harsh sound that
donkeys typically make. ▶ used as a noun. EG *...the* ▶ N COUNT
bray of a donkey.
2 If you say that someone **brays**, you mean that V
they make a loud harsh sound or talk in a loud Literary
harsh way. EG *...her dreadful braying laughter.*

brazen /breɪzə⁰n/, **brazens, brazening, bra-** ADJ QUALIT
zened. If you describe someone as **brazen**, you
mean that they are very bold and do not care if
other people think that they are behaving wrongly.
EG *...a brazen whore... ...brazen claims.* ◊ **brazenly.** ◊ ADV
EG *No industry is more brazenly orientated towards
quick, easy profits.*

brazen out. If you have done something wrong PHRASAL VB :
V+O+ADV

and you **brazen** it **out**, you behave confidently in
order not to appear ashamed. EG *However, I had to
brazen it out now, so I went up to him.*

brazier /breɪzɪə/, **braziers.** A **brazier** is a large N COUNT
metal container in which coal or charcoal is
burned to keep people warm when they are outside
in cold weather.

breach /briːtʃ/, **breaches, breaching, breached.**
1 If you **breach** an agreement or law, you do v+o
something that disobeys it. EG *...the ethical ques-* Formal
*tions involved in breaching the confidentiality of
patients.* ▶ used as a noun. EG *Does refusal to work* ▶ N COUNT O
on rest days constitute a breach of contract? N UNCOUNT
2 A **breach** in a relationship is a serious disagree- N COUNT
ment which often results in the relationship end- Formal
ing. EG *This was the most profound breach in our
marriage.*
3 If you **step into the breach**, you do a job or task PHRASE
which someone else was supposed to do, because
they are suddenly unable to do it. EG *Cooper loyally
stepped into the breach as official Tory candidate.*
4 A **breach** in a barrier is a gap or crack in it. EG N COUNT
They rush to defend any breach in the walls. Formal
5 If you **breach** a barrier, you deliberately make a v+o
gap in it, especially in order to let someone Formal
through. EG *He breached the enemy barbed wire.*

bread /bred/ is a very common food made from N UNCOUNT
flour, water, and often yeast. The mixture is made
into a soft dough and baked in an oven. EG *...some
bread and cheese... ...a loaf of bread... ...three slices
of bread.*

breadcrumb /bredkrʌm/, **breadcrumbs.** N COUNT :
Breadcrumbs are tiny pieces of bread. USU PLURAL

breadline /bredlaɪn/. Someone who is on or near N SING : the-
the **breadline** is very poor indeed. EG *One family in
four was on the breadline.*

breadth /bredθ/. **1** The **breadth** of something is N UNCOUNT
the distance between its two sides. EG *...six yards in
breadth and fifty yards long.*
2 The **breadth** of something is also its quality of N UNCOUNT
consisting of or involving many different things. EG +SUPP
*The very breadth of the subject gives it an added
interest... ...his breadth of vision.*
3 the **length and breadth** of somewhere: see
length. ● See also **hair's breadth.**

breadwinner /bredwɪnə/, **breadwinners.** The N COUNT
breadwinner in a family is the person in it who
earns the money that the family needs.

break /breɪk/, **breaks, breaking, broke** /brəʊk/,
broken /brəʊkə⁰n/. **1** When an object **breaks** or V-ERG
when you **break** it, it suddenly separates into two
or more pieces, often because it has been hit or
dropped. EG *He has broken a window with a ball...
She stepped backwards onto a cup, which broke
into several pieces... The string broke... She's broken her ankle.* ▶ used as a noun, usually of bones. ▶ N COUNT
EG *That looks like a nasty break.*
2 When a tool or piece of machinery **breaks** or V-ERG
when you **break** it, it is damaged and no longer
works.
3 If you **break** a rule, promise, or agreement, you v+o
do something that disobeys the law. EG *We're not breaking the law.*
4 If you **break free** or **break** someone's **hold**, you PHRASE
free yourself by force from someone or something
that is holding you. EG *He was thrashing to break
free... I broke away from her and raced for the
door... He had my hands behind my back in a hold
that was impossible to break.*
5 To **break** a connection or situation that has v+o
existed for some time means to end it suddenly.
EG *Radio contact was broken... Everything you've
tried has failed to break the deadlock... The stillness was broken by the barking of a dog... They
cannot break the habit.*

What is the difference between 'bravery' and
'bravado'?

6 If you **break** with a group of people or a way of v+A
doing things, you stop being involved with that
group or stop doing things in that way. EG *The
Chinese church broke with Rome in 1957... Two
United Party senators broke away to form the
Federal Party... He broke with precedent by making his maiden speech on a controversial subject.*
▸ used as a noun. EG *...their break with the Labour* ▸ N COUNT
Party in 1968.

7 If you **break** someone of a habit, you cause them v+O+*of*
to lose the habit. EG *...breaking a child of its bad
habits.*

8 To **break** someone means to destroy their suc- v+O
cess or their career. EG *...a prestigious competition
which could make or break his career.*

9 A **break** in a line, sound, or process is a gap or N COUNT
interruption in it. EG *...a break in routine.* ▸ used as ▸ v+O
a verb. EG *The blue horizon encircled them, broken
only by the mountain-top.*

10 A **break** is also a short period of time when you N COUNT
have a rest or a change from what you are doing.
EG *We all met in the pub during the lunch break...
The doctors had worked without a break.* ▸ used as ▸ v : OFT+*for*
a verb. EG *We broke for tea for an hour.*

11 To **break** the force of something such as a blow v+O
or fall means to weaken its effect. EG *Fortunately,
the tree broke her fall.*

12 When someone **breaks** a piece of news or when v-ERG
a piece of news **breaks**, the news is told to people.
EG *It was Ted who broke the news to me.*

13 A **break** is also a lucky opportunity that some- N COUNT
one gets to achieve something. EG *He has been* Informal
*running for 12 years, but his main break came last
spring in Australia.*

14 If you **break** a record, you beat the previous v+O
record for a particular achievement. EG *Oliver
Barrett was out to break his New York-Boston
speed record.*

15 When day **breaks**, it starts to grow light after v
the night has ended.

16 When a wave **breaks**, the water at the top of it v
falls down, for example when it reaches the shore.

17 When a company **breaks even**, it makes nei- PHRASE
ther a profit nor a loss.

18 If you **break** a secret code, you work out how to v+O
read it.

19 When a boy's voice **breaks**, it becomes perma- v
nently deeper.

20 In tennis, if you **break** your opponent's serve, v+O
you win a game in which your opponent is serving.
▸ used as a noun. EG *Gomer is one break of serve* ▸ N COUNT
up.

21 See also **broke, broken.**

break down. 1 When a machine or a vehicle PHRASAL VB :
breaks down, it stops working. EG *The car broke* v+ADV
down three miles outside Winchester. **2** When a v+ADV
system, plan, or discussion **breaks down**, it fails
because of a problem or disagreement. EG *This
efficient communication system started to break
down... The talks broke down over differences on
doctrine.* **3** When a substance **breaks down** or v-ERG+ADV
when something **breaks** it **down**, it changes into a
different form because of a chemical process. EG
Enzymes break down proteins by chemical action.
4 If someone **breaks down**, they start crying or v+ADV
laughing uncontrollably. EG *He had broken down
and cried... They often broke down in chuckles.* **5** If v+O+ADV
you **break down** a door or barrier, you hit it so
hard that it falls to the ground. **6** See also **breakdown.**

break in. 1 If someone **breaks in**, they get into a PHRASAL VB :
building by force. EG *They had broken in through* v+ADV
the back. **2** If you **break in** on someone's conver- v+ADV
sation or activity, you interrupt them. EG *'Don't look
at me,' Etta broke in brusquely.* **3** If you **break** v+O+ADV
someone **in**, you get them used to a new job or
situation. EG *Chief Brody liked to break in his young
men slowly.* **4** See also **break-in.**

break into. 1 If someone **breaks into** a building, PHRASAL VB :
v+PREP

they get into it by force. EG *He broke into a shop
one night.* **2** You can indicate that someone v+PREP
suddenly starts doing something by saying that
they **break into** laughter or **break into** a run, for
example. EG *When Rudolph saw her, he broke into
a run... The boys broke into applause.* **3** If you v+PREP,
break into a new area of activity, especially an HAS PASS
area of business, you become involved in it. EG
...women wanting to break into the labour market.

break off. 1 When part of something **breaks off** PHRASAL VB :
or when you **break** it **off**, it comes off or is v-ERG+ADV
removed by being snapped off or torn away. EG *A
little bit has broken off the left hand corner.
Garroway broke off another piece of bread.* **2** If v+ADV OR
you **break off** when you are doing or saying v+O+ADV
something, you suddenly stop doing it or saying it.
EG *He would break off the rehearsal... 'I thought – '
He broke off, then smiled. 'Sorry, not my business.'*
3 If someone **breaks off** a relationship, they end it. v+O+ADV
EG *She broke off her engagement.*

break out. 1 If something such as a fight or PHRASAL VB :
disease **breaks out**, it begins suddenly. EG *Fierce* v+ADV
fighting broke out between rival groups. **2** If you v+ADV, OFT+A
break out in a rash or a sweat or if it **breaks out**
on your body, it appears on your skin. EG *She felt
the sweat break out on her forehead.*

break through. 1 If you **break through** a PHRASAL VB :
barrier, you succeed in forcing your way through v+PREP
it. EG *I broke through the bushes.* **2** When some- v+ADV/PREP
thing that was previously hidden or unseen **breaks
through**, it appears. EG *Sometimes these impulses
break through in your work... The sun managed to
break through the clouds for a while.* **3** See also
breakthrough.

break up. 1 When something **breaks up** or when PHRASAL VB :
you **break** it **up**, it separates or is divided into v-ERG+ADV
several smaller parts. EG *The wood was so rotten
that, when they pulled, it broke up into a shower of
fragments.* **2** If you **break up** with your wife, v+ADV OR
husband, girlfriend, or boyfriend, your relationship v+ADV+*with* :
with that person ends. EG *Tim and I broke up...* RECIP
Their marriage is breaking up. **3** If an activity v-ERG+ADV
breaks up or if you **break** it **up**, it is brought to an
end. EG *The long drunken party had just broken
up... The policemen broke the fight up.* **4** When v+ADV
schools or the pupils in them **break up**, the school
term ends and the pupils start their holidays. EG *We
break up on Friday.* **5** See also **break-up.**

breakable /breɪkəbəʳl/. Breakable objects are ADJ CLASSIF
easy to break by accident. EG *My wife let her play
with breakable ornaments.*

breakage /breɪkɪdʒ/, **breakages. Breakage** is N UNCOUNT
the act or result of breaking something. EG *Acciden-* OR N COUNT
tal breakage of your household glass will be cov- Formal
ered by the policy... ...the cost of breakages.

breakaway /breɪkəweɪ/. A **breakaway** group is ADJ CLASSIF:
a group of people who have separated from a ATTRIB
larger group. EG *...a breakaway party.*

breakdown /breɪkdaʊn/, **breakdowns. 1** The N COUNT OR
breakdown of a system, plan, or discussion is its N UNCOUNT
failure or ending. EG *There was a serious break-* +SUPP
*down of communications... ...the threat of social
breakdown.*
2 If you suffer a **breakdown**, you become so N COUNT
depressed that you are unable to cope with your
life. EG *I shall probably have another breakdown if I
stay any longer in this house.*
3 If you have a **breakdown** when travelling some- N COUNT
where by car, your car stops working.
4 A **breakdown** of something is a list of its N COUNT
separate parts. EG *I forget what the breakdown of
hours is.*

breaker /breɪkə/, **breakers. Breakers** are big N COUNT :
sea waves. EG *...the roar of the breakers on the reef.* USU PLURAL

breakfast /brekfəst/, **breakfasts, breakfasting,
breakfasted. 1 Breakfast** is the first meal of the N UNCOUNT
day, which is usually eaten early in the morning. EG OR N COUNT
*I would get up early and eat my breakfast... ...men
who hurry their breakfasts.*

2 When you **breakfast**, you have breakfast. EG *She dressed early, and breakfasted.* · v · Formal

break-in, break-ins. When there is a **break-in**, someone gets into a building by force. EG *...the break-in at Blackburn Place.* · N COUNT

breakneck /breɪknɛk/. Something that happens or travels at **breakneck** speed happens or travels very fast indeed. EG *The construction of other hotels proceeded at breakneck speed.* · ADJ CLASSIF : ATTRIB

breakthrough /breɪkθruː/, **breakthroughs.** A **breakthrough** is an important development or achievement. EG *Scientists are hovering on the brink of a major breakthrough... ...a breakthrough in government-industry relations.* · N COUNT

break-up, break-ups. When the **break-up** of a group, relationship, or system occurs, it comes to an end. EG *This caused the break-up of the coalition... All marriage break-ups are traumatic.* · N UNCOUNT OR N COUNT

breakwater /breɪkwɔːtə/, **breakwaters.** A **breakwater** is a wooden or stone wall that extends from the shore into the sea and is built in order to protect a harbour or beach from the force of the waves. · N COUNT

breast /brɛst/, **breasts. 1** A woman's **breasts** are the two soft, round pieces of flesh on her chest that can produce milk to feed a baby. · N COUNT

2 A person's **breast** is the upper part of his or her chest. EG *The bullet pierced Joel's breast.* · N COUNT · Literary

3 The **breast** is often considered to be the part of your body where your emotions are. EG *...the creation of national pride in the breasts of Frenchmen.* · N COUNT+SUPP · Literary

4 A bird's **breast** is the front part of its body. · N COUNT

5 If you **make a clean breast of it**, you tell someone the truth about yourself or about something wrong that you have done. · PHRASE

breastbone /brɛstbəʊn/, **breastbones.** Your **breastbone** is the long vertical bone in the centre of your chest. · N COUNT

breast-feed, breast-feeds, breast-feeding, breast-fed. When a woman **breast-feeds** her baby, she feeds it with milk from her breasts, rather than from a bottle. ◊ **breast-feeding.** EG *A big advantage of breast-feeding is that the milk is always pure.* · V+O OR V · ◊ N UNCOUNT

breaststroke /brɛststrəʊk/ is a kind of swimming stroke which you do lying on your front, moving your arms and legs horizontally. See picture at SWIMMING. · N UNCOUNT

breath /brɛθ/, **breaths. 1** Your **breath** is the air which you take into and let out of your lungs when you breathe. EG *You could smell the whisky on his breath... Jenny paused for breath.* · N COUNT OR N UNCOUNT

2 When you take a **breath**, you breathe in. EG *He took a deep breath and blew into the bag.* · N COUNT

3 When you are **out of breath**, you breathe very quickly and with difficulty because you have been doing something energetic. · PHRASE

4 When you **get** your **breath** back after doing something energetic, you start breathing normally again. · PHRASE

5 If you **hold** your **breath**, you stop breathing for a short while. EG *We all held our breaths till the bomb burst.* · PHRASE

6 If you say that something **takes** your **breath away**, you mean that it is extremely beautiful or amazing. · PHRASE

7 If you say something **under** your **breath**, you say it in a very quiet voice. EG *I was cursing him under my breath.* · PHRASE

8 If you tell someone to **save** their **breath** or say that they are **wasting** their **breath**, you mean that the person they are planning to say something to will not take any notice of them. · PHRASE

9 If you go outside for a **breath of fresh air**, you go outside because it is stuffy indoors. · PHRASE

breathalyze /brɛθəlaɪz/, **breathalyzes, breathalyzing, breathalyzed;** also spelled **breathalyse.** When the police **breathalyze** the driver of a car, they ask the driver to breathe into · V+O

a special bag in order to see if he or she has drunk too much alcohol.

breathe /briːð/, **breathes, breathing, breathed.**
1 When people or animals **breathe**, they take air into their lungs and let it out again. EG *I breathed deeply... When we breathed the air, it smelt sweet.* ◊ **breathing.** EG *He could hear her deep, regular breathing.* · V OR V+O · ◊ N UNCOUNT

2 If you **breathe** smoke or fumes over someone, you send smoke or fumes out of your mouth towards them. EG *...breathing whisky fumes all over my face.* · V+O+A

3 When someone **breathes again** or **breathes more easily** after a frightening experience, they relax because the danger is over. EG *He breathed easier; he had made it.* · PHRASE

4 If you say that someone **is breathing down** your **neck**, you mean that they are paying such careful attention to everything you do that you feel uncomfortable and unable to act freely. · PHRASE

5 If someone says something very quietly, you can say that they **breathe** it. EG *'Frank,' she breathed. 'Help me, please.'* · V+O OR V+QUOTE · Literary

6 Someone who **breathes** life, confidence, or excitement into something gives this quality to it. EG *A teacher should try to breathe life into her subject.* · V+O : OFT+into · Literary

breathe in. When you **breathe in**, you take some air into your lungs. EG *Don't pant, breathe in slowly... He breathed in the cool crisp air.* · PHRASAL VB : V+ADV OR V+O+ADV

breathe out. When you **breathe out**, you send air out of your lungs through your nose or mouth. EG *She breathed out through parted lips.* · PHRASAL VB : V+ADV OR V+O+ADV

breather /briːðə/, **breathers.** If you take or have a **breather**, you stop what you are doing for a short time and have a rest. EG *I stopped and had another breather.* · N COUNT · Informal

breathing space. A **breathing space** is a short period of time between two activities in which you can recover from the first activity and prepare for the second one. · N SING OR N UNCOUNT

breathless /brɛθlɪs/. If you are **breathless, 1** you have difficulty in breathing properly, for example because you have been running. EG *She opened the door, a little breathless from climbing the stairs.* ◊ **breathlessly.** EG *'Miss Crabbe's on the telephone,' I said breathlessly.* ◊ **breathlessness.** EG *Obesity causes breathlessness.* **2** you are hardly able to breathe because you are so excited or afraid. EG *They followed the match with breathless interest.* ◊ **breathlessly.** EG *...waiting breathlessly for news.* · ADJ QUALIT · ◊ ADV · ◊ N UNCOUNT · ADJ CLASSIF · ◊ ADV

breathtaking /brɛθteɪkɪŋ/. If you say that something is **breathtaking**, you mean that it is extremely beautiful or amazing. EG *...breathtaking scenery... We were travelling at breathtaking speed.* ◊ **breathtakingly.** EG *Fashion magazines display breathtakingly beautiful gowns.* · ADJ QUALIT · ◊ SUBMOD

bred /brɛd/ is the past tense and past participle of **breed.**

breeches /brɪtʃɪz/ are trousers which reach your knees. EG *...riding breeches.* · N PLURAL

breed /briːd/, **breeds, breeding, bred** /brɛd/. **1** A **breed** of a pet animal or farm animal is a particular type of it. For example, terriers are a breed of dog. EG *Different breeds of sheep give wool of varying lengths.* · N COUNT

2 If you **breed** animals or plants, you keep them for the purpose of producing more animals or plants with particular qualities, in a controlled way. EG *Strains of the plant have been bred that resist more diseases.* ◊ **breeding.** EG *We retain a small proportion of bulls for breeding purposes.* · V+O · ◊ N UNCOUNT

3 When animals **breed**, they mate and produce · v

How many people are there on these pages?

offspring. ◊ **breeding.** EG *The breeding season is a* ◊ N UNCOUNT
very long one.

4 If something **breeds** a particular situation or V+O
feeling, it causes it to develop. EG *Success breeds
success, failure breeds failure... The rumours bred
hope.*

5 If someone **is bred** to do something, they are V+O+*to*-INF
trained or taught to do it as they grow up. EG *They* OR *for* :
were bred to rule... Danny was bred for the sea. USU PASS
                                                  Formal

6 Someone who was **born and bred** in a particular PHRASE
place was born there and spent their childhood
there. EG *I was born and bred in Edinburgh.*

7 A particular **breed** of person is a particular type N COUNT+SUPP
of person, with special qualities or skills. EG *This
required a special skill and a whole new breed of
actors.*

breeding /bri:dɪŋ/. Someone who has **breeding** N UNCOUNT
has been taught how to behave correctly and with
good manners, and is often upper-class. EG *She
certainly lacked breeding.* ● See also **breed**.

breeding ground, breeding grounds. 1 A place N COUNT+SUPP
that is a **breeding ground** for a particular situation or activity is a place where it is very likely to
develop. EG *...breeding grounds for passport forgery.*

2 A **breeding ground** of a particular type of N COUNT
animal is a place where this animal goes to breed.
EG *Those cliffs are the finest bird breeding grounds
in the Northern Hemisphere.*

breeze /bri:z/, **breezes, breezing, breezed.** 1 A N COUNT
breeze is a gentle wind. EG *...a cool breeze.*

2 If you **breeze** into a place, you enter it suddenly, V+A
in a very casual manner. EG *I just breezed into her
room, flinging the door wide.*

breezy /bri:zɪ¹/. 1 Someone who is **breezy** be- ADJ QUALIT
haves in a brisk, casual, cheerful, and confident
manner.

2 When the weather is **breezy**, there is a fairly ADJ QUALIT
strong but pleasant wind blowing.

brethren /breðrɪ²n/ is an old-fashioned plural
form of **brother.**

brevity /brevɪ¹tɪ¹/. 1 The **brevity** of something is N UNCOUNT
the fact that it lasts for only a short time. EG *...the* Formal
brevity and frailty of human existence.

2 **Brevity** is the fact of saying something in only a N UNCOUNT
few words. EG *Daniel delivered his message with* Formal
telegraphic brevity.

brew /bru:/, **brews, brewing, brewed.** 1 When V+O
you **brew** tea or coffee, you make it by pouring hot
water over tea leaves or ground coffee.

2 A **brew** is a drink made by mixing something N COUNT
such as tea with hot water. EG *...herbal brews.*

3 When people **brew** beer, they make it. V+O

4 If an unpleasant situation **is brewing**, it is V : USU CONT
starting to develop. EG *A crisis was brewing.*

brewer /bru:ə/, **brewers.** A **brewer** is a person N COUNT
who makes beer or who owns a place where beer
is made.

brewery /bruərɪ¹/, **breweries.** A **brewery** is a N COUNT
company which makes beer, or a place where beer
is made.

briar /braɪə/, **briars.** A **briar** is a wild rose with N COUNT
long, thorny stems.

bribe /braɪb/, **bribes, bribing, bribed.** 1 A **bribe** N COUNT
is a sum of money or something valuable that
someone gives to an official in order to persuade
the official to do something. EG *The Vice President
admitted taking bribes.*

2 If someone **bribes** an official, they give the V+O
official a bribe. EG *The attempt to bribe the clerk
had failed.* ◊ **bribery** /braɪbə⁰rɪ¹/. EG *The court* ◊ N UNCOUNT
found Williams guilty of bribery.

bric-a-brac /brɪkəbræk/ consists of small orna- N UNCOUNT
mental objects of no great value.

brick /brɪk/, **bricks, bricking, bricked. Bricks** N COUNT OR
are rectangular blocks of baked clay used for N UNCOUNT
building walls. EG *...a brick wall.*

brick up. If you **brick up** a hole, you close it with PHRASAL VB :
                                                      V+O+ADV

a wall of bricks. EG *Two workmen bricked up the
window.*

bricklayer /brɪkleɪə/, **bricklayers.** A **brick-** N COUNT
layer is a person whose job is to build walls using
bricks.

brickwork /brɪkwɜːk/. You can refer to the N UNCOUNT
bricks in the walls of a building as the **brickwork**.

bride /braɪd/, **brides.** A **bride** is a woman who is N COUNT
getting married or who has just got married.

◊ **bridal** /braɪdə⁰l/. EG *She was still wearing her* ◊ ADJ CLASSIF :
bridal costume.   ATTRIB

bridegroom /braɪdgruː⁴m/, **bridegrooms.** A N COUNT
bridegroom is a man who is getting married.

bridesmaid /braɪdzmeɪd/, **bridesmaids.** A N COUNT
bridesmaid is a woman or a girl who helps and
accompanies a bride on her wedding day.

bridge

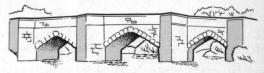

bridge /brɪdʒ/, **bridges, bridging, bridged.** 1 A N COUNT
bridge is a structure that is built over a river, road,
or railway so that people or vehicles can cross
from one side to the other. EG *We walked across the
railway bridge.*

2 Something that is a **bridge** between two groups N COUNT
or things makes it easier for the differences between them to be overcome. EG *We need to build a
bridge between East and West.*

3 Something that **bridges** the gap between two V+O
groups or things makes it easier for the differences
between them to be overcome. EG *...bridging the
gap between what society needs and what the
government can provide.*

4 If someone mentions a possible problem and you PHRASE
say that you will **cross that bridge when** you
come to it, you mean that you do not intend to
think about it until it arises.

5 The **bridge** of a ship is the high part from which N COUNT
the ship is steered.

6 **Bridge** is a card game for four players. N UNCOUNT

bridle /braɪdə⁰l/, **bridles, bridling, bridled.** 1 A N COUNT
bridle is a set of straps that is put around a horse's
head and mouth so that the person riding or
driving the horse can control it.

2 When you **bridle** a horse, you put a bridle on it. V+O

3 If you **bridle**, you show that you are angry or V : OFT+*at*
displeased by moving your head and body upwards
in a proud way. EG *Mrs Pringle bridled at the
memory.*

brief /briːf/, **briefer, briefest; briefs, briefing,
briefed.** 1 Something that is **brief** lasts for only a ADJ QUALIT
short time. EG *There was a brief scuffle... They
started with a brief description of their work... As
they talk, they exchange only the briefest of
glances.* ● See also **briefly**.

2 If you are **brief**, you say what you want to say in ADJ PRED
as few words as possible. EG *I shall have to be brief.*

3 A **brief** skirt or pair of shorts is very short. ADJ QUALIT

4 **Briefs** are pants or knickers. N PLURAL

5 When you **brief** someone, you give them infor- V+O
mation that they need before they do something. EG
*They had been well briefed about the political
situation.*

6 If someone gives you a **brief**, they officially give N COUNT
you the responsibility for dealing with a particular
thing. EG *I was appointed and given the brief of
developing local history research.*

briefcase

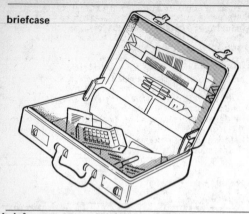

briefcase /briːfkeɪs/, **briefcases**. A **briefcase** is N COUNT a case used for carrying documents in.

briefing /briːfɪŋ/, **briefings**. A **briefing** is 1 a N COUNT OR meeting at which information or instructions are N UNCOUNT given to people, especially before they do something. EG *We had a special briefing on what lies ahead.* 2 the information or instructions that you N COUNT get at a meeting.

briefly /briːflɪ/. 1 Something that happens or is ADV done **briefly** happens or is done for a very short period of time. EG *He smiled briefly.*
2 If you say something **briefly**, you use very few ADV words or give very few details. EG *She told them briefly what had happened.*
3 You can say **briefly** to indicate that you are ADV SEN about to say something in as few words as possible. EG *The facts, briefly, are these.*

brigade /brɪgeɪd/, **brigades**. A **brigade** is one of N COLL the groups which an army is divided into. ● See also **fire brigade**.

brigadier /brɪgədɪə/, **brigadiers**. A **brigadier** is N COUNT a senior officer in the army.

bright /braɪt/, **brighter**, **brightest**. 1 A **bright** ADJ QUALIT colour is strong and noticeable, and not dark. EG *Her eyes were bright blue.* ◇ **brightly.** EG *...bright-* ◇ ADV *ly coloured silk blouses.*
2 A **bright** light, object, or place is shining strongly ADJ QUALIT or is full of light. EG *The sun was bright and hot... ...a bright, sunlit room.* ◇ **brightly.** EG *The sun shone* ◇ ADV *brightly... ...the brightly lit room.* ◇ **brightness.** EG ◇ N UNCOUNT *The stars were losing their brightness.*
3 Someone who is **bright** is quick at learning ADJ QUALIT things. EG *They were the brightest girls in the school.*
4. A **bright** idea is clever and original. EG *Then he* ADJ QUALIT : *had the bright idea of putting the engine at the* ATTRIB *back.*
5 If someone looks or sounds **bright**, they look or ADJ PRED sound cheerful. EG *'Good,' said Henry, looking brighter.* ◇ **brightly.** EG *'Fine!' I said brightly.* ◇ ADV
6 If the future is **bright**, it is likely to be pleasant ADJ QUALIT and successful. EG *The economic outlook is bright.*
7 If you do something **bright and early**, you do it PHRASE very early in the morning. EG *I was up bright and early, eager to be off.*

brighten /braɪtən/, **brightens**, **brightening**, **brightened**. 1 If you **brighten**, you suddenly look v happier. EG *Her face brightened. 'Oh, hi! It's you.'*
2 If your eyes **brighten**, you suddenly look interest- v ed or excited.
3 If someone or something **brightens** a situation, v+o they make it more pleasant and enjoyable. EG *You girls brighten our Sundays.*
4 When a light **brightens** a place or when a place v-ERG **brightens**, it becomes brighter or lighter. EG *Stars brighten the night sky.*
brighten up. 1 If you **brighten up**, you look PHRASAL VB : V+ADV

happier. EG *She seemed to brighten up a bit at this.*
2 If you **brighten up** a place, you make it more v+o+ADV colourful and attractive. EG *These flowers will brighten up your garden.* 3 Someone or something v+o+ADV that **brightens up** a situation makes it more pleasant and enjoyable. EG *The music brightened things up a little.*

brilliant /brɪljənt/. 1 If you describe people or ADJ QUALIT ideas as **brilliant**, you mean that they are extremely clever. EG *...a brilliant young engineer... It was a brilliant idea.* ◇ **brilliantly.** EG *He acted* ◇ ADV *brilliantly in a wide range of parts.* ◇ **brilliance** ◇ N UNCOUNT /brɪljəns/. EG *...a writer of tremendous brilliance.*
2 You can say that something is **brilliant** when ADJ QUALIT you are very pleased about it or think that it is very Informal good. EG *'Did you enjoy your holiday?' – 'Yes, it was* British *brilliant!'*
3 A **brilliant** career or future is very successful. EG ADJ CLASSIF : *He predicted a brilliant future for the child.* ATTRIB ◇ **brilliantly.** EG *Sotheby's publicity stunt came off* ◇ ADV *brilliantly.*
4 A **brilliant** colour is extremely bright. EG *...a* ADJ QUALIT : *brilliant yellow flame... ...brilliant white marble.* ATTRIB ◇ **brilliantly.** EG *Many of them are brilliantly* ◇ ADV *coloured.* ◇ **brilliance.** EG *The painting has been* ◇ N UNCOUNT *restored to its former brilliance.*
5 You describe light, or something that reflects ADJ QUALIT light, as **brilliant** when it shines very brightly. EG *The sea sparkled in the brilliant sunlight.* ◇ **brilliantly.** EG *A downstairs window was bril-* ◇ ADV *liantly illuminated.* ◇ **brilliance.** EG *...the bril-* ◇ N UNCOUNT *liance of the lagoon.*

brim /brɪm/, **brims**, **brimming**, **brimmed**. 1 The N COUNT **brim** of a hat is the wide part that sticks outwards at the bottom.
2 If a container is filled **to the brim** with some- PHRASE thing, it is filled right up to the top. EG *The pool was full to the brim with brown water.*
3 Someone or something that **is brimming** with v :OFT+with things of a particular kind is full of them. EG *...a group of youngsters, all brimming with ideas... Her eyes brimmed with tears.*

brim over. 1 When a container or the liquid in it PHRASAL VB : **brims over**, the liquid spills out. EG *He poured wine* V+ADV *into Daniel's glass until it brimmed over.* 2 If you v+ADV **are brimming over** with a pleasant feeling, you behave in a way that shows how pleased you are. EG *She rushed to her mother, brimming over with joy and pride.*

brine /braɪn/ is salty water, especially when it is N UNCOUNT used for preserving food.

bring /brɪŋ/, **brings**, **bringing**, **brought** /brɔːt/. 1 v+o : USU+A If you **bring** someone or something with you when you come to a place, they come with you or you have them with you. EG *He would have to bring Judy with him... Please bring your calculator to every lesson.*
2 If you **bring** something somewhere, you move it v+o+A somewhere. EG *He opened the case and brought out* OR V+O+O *a pair of glasses... Bring me a glass of wine... Sheldon brought his right hand to his head.*
3 To **bring** someone or something to a place v+o+A means to cause them to come to the place. EG *The festival brings a great many people to Glastonbury... They were responsible for bringing jazz to Europe.*
4 To **bring** someone or something into a particular v+o+A state or condition means to cause them to be in that state or condition. EG *These ideas had brought him into conflict with Stalin... Printing brought the cost of books down... The wind had brought several trees down... He brought the car to a stop.*
5 If something **brings** a particular feeling, situa- v+o :OFT+A tion, or quality, it makes you experience it or have it. EG *Could it be true that money did not bring*

Give an example of something that you might bristle at.

happiness?... It will bring shame on the family...
This generosity brought applause from the boys...
The biting wind brought tears to her eyes.

6 If you cannot **bring** yourself to do something, you v·REFL+ cannot make yourself do it. EG *I could not bring* to·INF : WITH BROAD NEG *myself to touch him.*

7 If you **bring** a legal action against someone, you v+o : officially accuse them of doing something unlawful. OFT+*against* EG *...a list of criminal charges brought against him by the government.*

bring about. To **bring** something **about** means PHRASAL VB : to cause it to happen. EG *The Administration helped* V+O+ADV *bring about a peaceful settlement.*

bring along. If you **bring** someone or something PHRASAL VB : **along**, you bring them with you when you come to V+O+ADV a place. EG *Bring your friends along.*

bring back. 1 Something that **brings back** a PHRASAL VB : memory makes you think about it. EG *Losing a* V+O+ADV *husband can bring back memories of childhood loss.* **2** When people **bring back** a fashion or V+O+ADV practice that existed at an earlier time, they introduce it again. EG *Many of the students appear to be trying to bring back the crew cut.*

bring down. When people **bring down** a gov- PHRASAL VB : ernment or ruler, they cause the government or V+O+ADV ruler to lose power. EG *A national strike would bring the government down.*

bring forward. 1 If you **bring forward** a PHRASAL VB : meeting or lecture, you arrange for it to take place V+O+ADV at an earlier date or time than had been planned. **2** V+O+ADV If you **bring forward** an argument or proposal, you state it so that people can consider it. EG *He brought forward some very cogent arguments.*

bring in. 1 When a government or organization PHRASAL VB : **brings in** a new law or system, they introduce it. V+O+ADV EG *Both Labour and Conservative administrations intend to bring in legislation to control their activities.* **2** Someone or something that **brings in** V+O+ADV money makes it or earns it. EG *Tourism is a big industry, bringing in £7 billion a year.* **3** If you V+O+ADV **bring in** someone, you invite them to take part in an activity. EG *It would be fatal to bring in an outsider.*

bring off. If you **bring off** something difficult, PHRASAL VB : you do it successfully. EG *The most brilliant ma-* V+O+ADV *noeuvre was brought off by Japan.* Informal

bring out. 1 When a person or company **brings** PHRASAL VB : **out** a new product, especially a new book or V+O+ADV record, they produce it and sell it. EG *I've just brought out a book on Dostoevski.* **2** Something V+O+ADV that **brings out** a particular kind of behaviour or feeling in you causes you to show it although you do not normally show it. EG *These dreadful circumstances bring out the worst in everybody.*

bring round or **bring** to. If you **bring round** PHRASAL VB : someone who is unconscious or **bring** them **to**, you V+O+ADV make them become conscious again.

bring up. 1 When someone **brings up** a child, PHRASAL VB : they look after it until it is grown up, and try to V+O+ADV give it particular attitudes. EG *Fathers are beginning to play a bigger role in bringing up their children... Tony was brought up strictly.* ● You ● PHRASE describe someone young as **well brought up** when you think that they behave well. **2** If you **bring up** V+O+ADV a particular subject, you introduce it into a discussion or conversation. EG *I advised her to bring the matter up at the next meeting.* **3** If you **bring up** V+O+ADV food, you vomit. EG *I felt sick, coughed, and then brought up most of my dinner.*

brink /brɪŋk/. If you are on the **brink** of some- N SING : the+N thing, usually something important, terrible, or exciting, you are just about to do it or experience it. EG *The country was on the brink of civil war... I was on the brink of losing my temper.*

brisk /brɪsk/, **brisker, briskest. 1** Someone who ADJ QUALIT is **brisk** behaves in a busy, confident way which shows that they want to get things done quickly. EG *Lynn's tone was brisk.* ◊ **briskly.** EG *'We've been* ◊ ADV

into that,' said Posy briskly. ◊ **briskness.** EG *She* ◊ N UNCOUNT adopted her usual briskness with him.

2 A **brisk** action is done quickly and in an energet- ADJ QUALIT ic way. EG *I went for a brisk swim.* ◊ **briskly.** EG *He* ◊ ADV walked briskly down the street.* ◊ **briskness.** EG ◊ N UNCOUNT *He was walking with unusual briskness.*

3 If trade or business is **brisk**, things are being sold ADJ QUALIT very quickly and a lot of money is being made. EG *They are doing a brisk trade in cars.*

4 If the weather is **brisk**, it is cold and refreshing. ADJ QUALIT EG *It was one brisk April morning... ...brisk winds.*

bristle /brɪsəl/, **bristles, bristling, bristled. 1** N COUNT OR **Bristles** are **1.1** thick, strong animal hairs that are N UNCOUNT sometimes used to make brushes. **1.2** the short hairs that grow on a man's chin after he has shaved it.

2 The **bristles** of a brush are the thick hairs or N PLURAL hair-like pieces of plastic which are attached to the handle.

3 If the hair on your body **bristles**, it rises away v from your skin because you are cold, frightened, or angry. EG *I felt the hairs bristle along the back of my neck.*

4 If you **bristle** at something, you react to it v : OFT+*at* angrily, and show this in your expression or the way you move. EG *Eddie bristled at being called a 'girl'.*

bristle with. If a place **bristles with** objects or PHRASAL VB : people, there are a lot of them there. EG *The hill* V+PREP *bristled with fortifications... The hotel was bristling with policemen.*

bristly /brɪsliⁱ/. **1 Bristly** hair is rough, coarse, ADJ QUALIT and thick. EG *...a bristly moustache.*

2 If a man's chin is **bristly**, it is covered with ADJ QUALIT bristles because he has not shaved recently.

Brit /brɪt/, **Brits.** British people are sometimes N COUNT referred to as **Brits.** Informal

British /brɪtɪʃ/. **1** Someone or something that is ADJ CLASSIF **British** belongs or relates to Great Britain. EG *...my British friends... ...British textile companies.*

2 The **British** are the people who come from N PLURAL Great Britain. EG *The British are very good at sympathy.*

Britisher /brɪtɪʃə/, **Britishers.** Americans some- N COUNT times refer to British people as **Britishers.** American

Briton /brɪtəⁿn/, **Britons.** A **Briton** is a person N COUNT who comes from Great Britain. EG *The youth, a 17-year-old Briton, was searched and arrested.*

brittle /brɪtəl/, **brittler, brittlest. 1** An object or ADJ QUALIT substance that is **brittle** is hard but easily broken. EG *...dry sticks as brittle as candy.*

2 Someone who is **brittle** says things which are ADJ QUALIT likely to hurt other people's feelings. EG *...a brittle, humourless child.*

3 A **brittle** sound is short, loud, and sharp. ADJ QUALIT

broach /brəʊtʃ/, **broaches, broaching,** v+o **broached.** When you **broach** a subject, you mention it in order to start a discussion on it. EG *She first broached the idea of a partnership in 1985.*

broad /brɔːd/, **broader, broadest. 1** Something ADJ QUALIT that is **broad** is wide. EG *The streets of this town are broad... He was tall, with broad shoulders... ...a broad grin.*

2 You use **broad** to describe **2.1** something that ADJ QUALIT includes or concerns a large number of different things or people. EG *She had a broader range of interests than Jane... This syllabus is a broad one... ...'cultural' in the broadest sense of the word.* **2.2** ADJ QUALIT : something that is experienced by many people, or ATTRIB by people of many different kinds. EG *...a broad feeling that the West lacks direction... ...a youth organization with a broader appeal.*

3 A **broad** description or idea is general rather ADJ QUALIT : than detailed. EG *The book gives a broad introduc-* ATTRIB *tion to linguistics.*

4 You use **broad** to describe a hint or sarcastic ADJ QUALIT : remark and indicate that its meaning is very ATTRIB obvious. EG *Broad hints were aired that the paper should be closed down.*

5 A **broad** accent is strong and noticeable. EG *He has a broad Wiltshire accent.*   ADJ QUALIT

6 A crime that is done **in broad daylight** is done during the day, rather than at night. EG *Mugging in the streets, even in broad daylight, was common.*   PHRASE

7 See also **broadly**.

broad bean, broad beans. Broad beans are flat, light green beans.   N COUNT : USU PLURAL

broadcast /brɔːdkɑːst/, **broadcasts, broadcasting, broadcasted.** The past tense and past participle can be either **broadcasted** or **broadcast**.
1 A **broadcast** is something that you hear on the radio or see on television. EG *He was criticized for making these broadcasts.*   N COUNT
2 To **broadcast** a programme means to send it out by radio waves, so that it can be heard on the radio or seen on television. EG *Episode One was broadcast last night.*   V+O OR V

broadcaster /brɔːdkɑːstə/, **broadcasters.** A **broadcaster** is someone who gives talks or takes part in discussions on radio or television. EG *...Anthony Howard, the journalist and broadcaster.*   N COUNT

broadcasting /brɔːdkɑːstɪŋ/ is the making and sending out of television and radio programmes. EG *...the purpose of educational broadcasting.*   N UNCOUNT

broaden /brɔːdəⁿn/, **broadens, broadening, broadened. 1** When something **broadens**, it becomes wider. EG *As the stream descends it broadens... Her smile broadened a little.*   V
2 When you **broaden** something or when it **broadens, 2.1** it includes or concerns a larger number of things or people. EG *Some members wished to broaden the scope of the campaign.* **2.2** it is experienced by or affects more people. EG *He made another attempt to broaden his appeal.*   V-ERG
3 If an experience **broadens** your **mind**, it makes you more willing to accept other people's beliefs and customs. EG *Travel broadens the mind.*   PHRASE

broaden out. When you **broaden** something **out** or when it **broadens out**, it includes or concerns a larger number of things or people. EG *...broadening out our political awareness.*   PHRASAL VB : V-ERG+ADV

broadly /brɔːdliⁱ/. **1** You can say **broadly** or **broadly speaking** to mean that although there may be a few exceptions to what you are saying, it is true in almost all cases. EG *You can see that, broadly speaking, it is really quite straightforward.*   ADV SEN
2 You can also use **broadly** to say that something is true to a large extent. EG *I was broadly in favour of it.*   ADV+PREP
3 If someone smiles **broadly**, their mouth is stretched very wide because they are very pleased or amused.   ADV

broadly-based. Something that is **broadly-based** involves many different kinds of things or people. EG *He wants it to be a broadly-based movement.*   ADJ QUALIT

broadminded /brɔːdmaɪndɪ²d/. Someone who is **broadminded** does not disapprove of actions or attitudes that many other people disapprove of.   ADJ QUALIT

BROAD NEG stands for **broad negative**
Some words or phrases have the label WITH BROAD NEG in the Extra Column. This means that they are normally used in sentences which have a negative word such as 'not' or 'never' or which have the broad negative adverbs 'hardly', 'barely','scarcely', 'rarely', 'seldom', or 'little' in them.
For example, one meaning of the word 'bother' nearly always has one of these words: EG *I can't be bothered to write this... He never bothered to do his homework...She barely bothers to speak to me these days.*

---

brocade /brɒ⁶keɪd/ is a thick, expensive material, often made of silk, with a raised pattern on it. EG *She wore a dress of white brocade.*   N UNCOUNT

broccoli /brɒkəliⁱ/ is a vegetable with green stalks and green or purple flower buds.   N UNCOUNT

brochure /brəʊʃⁱʊ²ə/, **brochures. A brochure** is a magazine or booklet with pictures that gives you information about a product or service. EG *...travel brochures... ...a brochure about retirement homes.*   N COUNT

broil /brɔɪl/, **broils, broiling, broiled.** When you **broil** food, you grill it. EG *...trout broiled over charcoal.*   V+O American

broke /brəʊk/. **1 Broke** is the past tense of **break**.
2 If you are **broke**, you have no money. EG *He'd taken the job because he was broke.*   ADJ PRED Informal
3 If a company **goes broke**, it loses money and is unable to continue in business. EG *The paper was going broke and would cease publication.*   PHRASE Informal

broken /brəʊkəⁿn/. **1 Broken** is the past participle of **break**.
2 An object that is **broken** has split into pieces or cracked, for example because it has been hit or dropped. EG *He sweeps away the broken glass under the window... He was rushed to hospital with a broken back.*   ADJ CLASSIF
3 A tool or piece of machinery that is **broken** is damaged and no longer works. EG *...a broken television set... The telephone is broken.*   ADJ CLASSIF
4 A line, sound, or process that is **broken** is interrupted or disturbed rather than continuous. EG *...a broken curve... ...broken, irregular screaming.*   ADJ CLASSIF
5 A **broken** promise or contract has not been kept or obeyed.   ADJ CLASSIF
6 A **broken** marriage has ended in divorce. EG *I came to hear a little about her broken marriage.*   ADJ CLASSIF : ATTRIB
7 If someone talks in **broken** English, for example, or in **broken** French, they speak slowly and make a lot of mistakes because they do not know the language very well.   ADJ QUALIT : ATTRIB

broken-down. 1 A **broken-down** vehicle or machine no longer works because it has something wrong with it. EG *...two men pushing a broken-down car.*   ADJ CLASSIF
2 If a building is **broken-down**, it is in very bad condition or has partly fallen down.   ADJ CLASSIF

broken-hearted. Someone who is **broken-hearted** is very sad and upset because they have had a serious disappointment.   ADJ CLASSIF

broken home, broken homes. If you say that someone comes from a **broken home**, you mean that their family did not live together, because their parents were separated or divorced.   N COUNT

broker /brəʊkə/, **brokers. A broker** is a person whose job is to buy and sell shares, foreign money, or goods for other people. EG *...an insurance broker.*   N COUNT

brolly /brɒliⁱ/, **brollies. A brolly** is the same as an umbrella.   N COUNT British

bronchial tubes. Your **bronchial tubes** are the two tubes which connect your windpipe to your lungs.   N PLURAL Medical

bronchitis /brɒŋkaɪtɪ¹s/ is an illness like a very bad cough, in which your bronchial tubes become sore and infected.   N UNCOUNT

bronze /brɒnz/, **bronzes. 1 Bronze** is a yellowish-brown metal which is a mixture of copper and tin. EG *...a large bronze statue.*   N UNCOUNT
2 A **bronze** is **2.1** a statue or sculpture made of bronze. EG *...a modern bronze of Icarus.* **2.2** a bronze medal.   N COUNT
3 Something that is **bronze** is yellowish-brown in colour. EG *...bronze hair.*   ADJ COLOUR

bronzed /brɒnzd/. Someone who is **bronzed** is attractively sun-tanned.   ADJ QUALIT

bronze medal, bronze medals. If you win a **bronze medal**, you come third in a competition,   N COUNT

If you come from a broken home, does your house need rebuilding?

especially a sports contest, and are given a medal made of bronze as a prize.

brooch /brəʊtʃ/, **brooches.** A **brooch** is a small N COUNT piece of jewellery with a pin at the back. You attach a brooch to a dress or a blouse. See picture at JEWELLERY.

brood /bruːd/, **broods, brooding, brooded. 1** A N COLL **brood** is a group of baby birds that a female bird has produced. EG ...a brood of ducklings. **2** You can humorously refer to someone's children N COLL as their **brood**. EG ...a squabbling brood of children. **3** If someone **broods** about something, they think V : OFT+A about it a lot, seriously and often unhappily. EG I slunk away to my room to brood... He brooded on his failure... Don't brood over your problems.

brooding /bruːdɪŋ/. Something that is **brooding** is ADJ CLASSIF disturbing and threatening. EG The silent, brooding presence of the woman made him uncomfortable.

broody /bruːdiꜜ/. **1** You say that someone is ADJ QUALIT **broody** when they are thinking a lot about something in an unhappy way. **2** A **broody** hen is ready to lay or sit on eggs. ADJ CLASSIF

brook /brʊk/, **brooks.** A **brook** is a small stream. N COUNT EG ...a mountain brook.

broom /bruːm/, **brooms.** A **broom** is a kind of N COUNT brush with a long handle. You use a broom for sweeping the floor.

broomstick /bruːmstɪk/, **broomsticks.** A N COUNT **broomstick** is **1** the handle of a broom. **2** a broom which has a bundle of twigs at the end. Witches are said to fly on broomsticks.

broth /brɒθ/ is soup. EG ...chicken broth. N UNCOUNT

brothel /brɒθəˀl/, **brothels.** A **brothel** is a build- N COUNT ing where men pay to have sex with prostitutes.

brother /brʌðə/, **brothers;** the old-fashioned form **brethren** /breðrɪˀn/ is also used as the plural for paragraphs 2 and 3. **1** Your **brother** is a boy or a man who has the N COUNT same parents as you. EG I have two brothers and one sister... ...his brother Harold. ● See also **half-brother, stepbrother. 2** You might describe as your **brother** a man who N COUNT : belongs to the same race, religion, profession, or USU PLURAL trade union as you, or who has ideas that are similar to yours. EG All men are our brothers... Both he and his brother judges had been amused. **3 Brother** is a title given to a man who belongs to a religious institution such as a monastery. EG ...Brother Michael, one of the Anglican Chaplains... ...the Brethren of the Trinity.

brotherhood /brʌðəhʊd/, **brotherhoods. 1** N UNCOUNT **Brotherhood** is the affection and loyalty that you feel for people who you have something in common with. EG ...a deepening sense of brotherhood. **2** A **brotherhood** is an organization whose mem- N COUNT : bers all have the same political aims and beliefs or OFT+of the same job or profession.

brother-in-law, brothers-in-law. Your N COUNT **brother-in-law** is the brother of your husband or wife, or the man who is married to your sister or to your wife's or husband's sister.

brotherly /brʌðəliꜜ/. **Brotherly** feelings are feel- ADJ CLASSIF : ings of love and loyalty which you expect a brother ATTRIB to show. EG ...brotherly love.

brought /brɔːt/ is the past tense and past partici- ple of **bring.**

brow /braʊ/, **brows. 1** Your **brow** is your fore- N COUNT head. EG He mopped his sweating brow. **2** Your **brows** are your eyebrows. ● to knit your N COUNT **brows**: see **knit.** Formal **3** The **brow** of a hill is the top part of it. EG I saw N COUNT : him disappear over the brow of the hill. the+N+of

browbeat /braʊbiːt/, **browbeats, browbeating,** V+O **browbeaten.** The form **browbeat** is used in the present tense and is also the past tense. If you **browbeat** someone, you bully them and try to force them to do what you want. EG She browbeat her parents into letting her go. ◊ **browbeaten.** EG ◊ ADJ CLASSIF ...his browbeaten wife.

brown /braʊn/, **browner, brownest; browns, browning, browned. 1** Something that is **brown** is ADJ COLOUR the colour of earth or of wood. EG His brown eyes twinkled at them... ...long brown hair... I never wear brown. **2** People are described as **brown** when **2.1** their ADJ COLOUR skin is darker than usual because they have been in the sun. EG His body was golden brown... ...her long brown legs. **2.2** they belong to a race of ADJ CLASSIF people who have brown-coloured skins. **3** When something **browns** or when you **brown** it, V-ERG it becomes browner in colour. EG Her hands had been browned by the sun.

brownish /braʊnɪʃ/. Something that is **brownish** ADJ COLOUR is slightly brown in colour. EG ...a patch of brownish lawn... ...a brownish face.

browse /braʊz/, **browses, browsing, browsed. 1** V : USU+A If you **browse** through a book or magazine, you look through it in a casual way. EG He spent half an hour browsing through sections he had already read. **2** If you **browse** in a shop, you look at things in a V : USU+A casual way, in the hope that you might find something you want. ▶ used as a noun. EG I had a browse ▶ N COUNT in the children's picture book section. +SUPP **3** When animals **browse**, they feed on plants. V : USU+A

bruise /bruːz/, **bruises, bruising, bruised.** A N COUNT **bruise** is an injury produced when a part of your body is hit by something. Your skin is not broken but a purple mark appears on it. EG I'm okay; just a few cuts and bruises. ▶ used as a verb. EG They ▶ V-ERG were jostled, bruised, and scratched.

brunette /bruːnet/, **brunettes.** A **brunette** is a N COUNT white-skinned woman or girl with dark brown hair.

brunt /brʌnt/. If someone **bears the brunt** or PHRASE **takes the brunt** of something unpleasant, they suffer the main part or force of it. EG Indian troops bore the brunt of the Burma campaigns.

brush /brʌʃ/, **brushes, brushing, brushed. 1** A N COUNT **brush** is an object which has a large number of bristles fixed to it. You use brushes for cleaning things, for painting, and for tidying your hair. **2** If you **brush** something, you clean it or tidy it V+O using a brush. EG I'm going to brush my teeth... She began to brush her hair. ▶ used as a noun. EG Give ▶ N SING : a+N the carpet a hard brush. **3** If you **brush** something away, you remove it by V+O+A pushing it lightly with your hand. EG She brushed back the hair from her eyes. **4** To **brush** something or **brush** against it means V+O OR V+A to touch it lightly while passing it. EG Something brushed against the back of the shelter... The girl's hair brushed his cheek. **5** If you have a **brush** with someone, you have a N COUNT+with small argument or fight with them. EG His attitude has led to some brushes with authority.

brush aside. If you **brush aside** an idea, re- PHRASAL VB : mark, or feeling, you refuse to consider it because V+O+ADV you think it is not important. EG She brushed his protests aside.

brush up. If you **brush up** a subject or **brush up** PHRASAL VB : on it, you revise or improve your knowledge of it. V+O+ADV OR EG They need to brush up their French. V+ADV+PREP

brushwood /brʌʃwʊd/ consists of small branches N UNCOUNT and twigs that have broken off trees and bushes. EG ...a pile of brushwood and dead leaves.

brusque /bruːsk, ʌsk/. Someone who is **brusque** ADJ QUALIT wastes no time when dealing with things and does not show much consideration for other people. EG I made a brusque apology and left... She had a brusque manner. ◊ **brusquely.** EG 'Sorry - no time ◊ ADV to waste,' she said brusquely.

brussels sprout, brussels sprouts; also spelled N COUNT : **brussel sprout.** Brussels sprouts are vegetables USU PLURAL which look like very small cabbages.

brutal /bruːtəˀl/. **1** Someone who is **brutal** is cruel ADJ QUALIT and violent. EG ...the government's brutal treatment of political prisoners... ...a brutal killing. ◊ **brutally.** EG Richard II was brutally murdered.

brushes

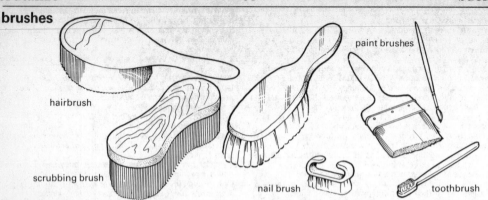

hairbrush

paint brushes

scrubbing brush

nail brush

toothbrush

◊ **brutality** /bruːˈtælɪtiˈ/, **brutalities.** EG *There is so much brutality shown on the television screen... I abhor the brutalities of the regime.* ◊ N UNCOUNT OR N COUNT

2 If someone expresses something with **brutal** honesty or frankness, they express it in an unpleasantly clear and accurate way. EG *He spelled out with brutal clarity what the consequences would be... ...explained with brutal frankness.* ◊ **brutally.** EG *The photographer was brutally honest.* ADJ QUALIT : ATTRIB ◊ ADV + ADJ

3 Brutal is used to emphasize an unpleasant or difficult quality. EG *...the brutal disenchantment of the people.* ◊ **brutally.** EG *We must ensure Britain's economic recovery in a brutally competitive world.* ADJ CLASSIF : ATTRIB ◊ ADV + ADJ

brutalize /bruːˈtəˈlaɪz/, **brutalizes, brutalizing, brutalized;** also spelled **brutalise.** If an unpleasant experience **brutalizes** someone, it makes them cruel, violent, or uncaring. EG *Her childhood was so awful, it's a wonder she was not brutalized by it.* V + O

brute /bruːt/, **brutes. 1** A **brute** is **1.1** a rough and insensitive man. EG *Go ahead and hit me, you big brute... He's an ugly brute.* **1.2** a large animal, especially one that you feel sorry for. EG *...the poor half-starved brutes.* N COUNT

2 When you refer to **brute** strength or force, you are contrasting it with gentler methods or qualities. EG *We will never yield to brute force... In the end, he had to use brute strength and wrench the lock off.* ADJ CLASSIF : ATTRIB

brutish /bruːtɪʃ/. If you describe human conditions or actions as **brutish**, you mean that they seem to be like an animal's; used showing disapproval. EG *Man's life is nasty, brutish and short... His expression was brutish and mocking.* ADJ QUALIT

B.Sc. /biː ɛs siː/, **B.Sc.s.** A **B.Sc.** is a science degree. **B.Sc.** is an abbreviation for 'Bachelor of Science'. EG *He's got a B.Sc... ...B.Sc. students... ...the final year of a B.Sc. course.* N COUNT

bubble /bʌbəˈl/, **bubbles, bubbling, bubbled. 1** A **bubble** is **1.1** a ball of air in a liquid. EG *Tiny bubbles were rising from the dissolving tablets... A bubble of air escaped from the drowned woman's mouth.* **1.2** a hollow, delicate ball of soapy liquid that is floating in the air or standing on a surface. EG *Her elbows were covered in bubbles... She knows how to blow bubbles with washing-up liquid.* N COUNT

2 When a liquid **bubbles**, bubbles form in it, because it is boiling, is fizzy, or is moving quickly. EG *Cook the mixture until it bubbles... The champagne bubbled in her glass.* V

3 When something **bubbles**, it makes a sound like water boiling. EG *On the table an electric coffee percolator bubbled... ...low, bubbling laughter.* V

4 If you are **bubbling** with excitement, enthusiasm, or liveliness, for example, you are full of it. EG *She was bubbling with confidence... At the end of the day I was bubbling with excitement.* V : USU + with

bubble gum is chewing gum that you can blow out of your mouth in the shape of a bubble. N UNCOUNT

bubbly /bʌbliˈ/, **bubblier, bubbliest. 1** A liquid that is **bubbly** is full of bubbles. EG *I like my mineral water bubbly rather than still.* ADJ QUALIT

2 Champagne is sometimes referred to as **bubbly**. EG *His wife opened a bottle of bubbly.* N UNCOUNT Informal

3 Someone who is **bubbly** is very lively and cheerful. EG *She's such a bubbly little girl.* ADJ QUALIT

buck /bʌk/, **bucks, bucking, bucked. 1** A **buck** is a US or Australian dollar. EG *It cost me four bucks for the taxi and ten bucks for the tickets.* N COUNT Informal

2 A **buck** is also the male of various animals, including the deer and rabbit. EG *The female deer attracts the buck with high-pitched sounds.* N COUNT

3 If an animal such as a horse **bucks**, it jumps into the air wildly with all four feet off the ground. EG *I fell off every time that stupid horse bucked.* V

4 When people **make a fast buck**, they make a lot of money quickly, especially by doing something dishonest. EG *Even some well-known politicians were making a fast buck at the expense of their innocent supporters.* PHRASE Informal

5 If you **pass the buck**, you refuse to accept responsibility for something, and say that someone else is responsible. EG *You're passing the buck! It was up to you to check!* PHRASE Informal

buck up. 1 If you **buck** someone **up** or if they **buck up**, they become more cheerful. EG *I need something to buck my spirits up today... He has bucked up the morale of the nation with his optimistic policies for social change.* **2** If you tell someone to **buck up**, you are telling them to hurry up. EG *Come on, Charlie, buck up or we'll be late!* PHRASAL VB : V-ERG + ADV / V + ADV Informal

bucket /bʌkɪt/, **buckets. 1** A **bucket** is a round metal or plastic container with a handle attached to its sides. Buckets are often used for holding and carrying water. EG *The hotel cleaner entered carrying a bucket and a mop.* N COUNT

2 You can use **bucket** to refer to a full bucket and its contents or just to the contents. EG *Dissolve the powder in a bucket of warm water.* N PART

3 You can use **buckets** to refer to large amounts of a liquid, especially rain. EG *We're going to get buckets of rain.* N PART : PLURAL Informal

bucketful /bʌkɪtˈfʊl/, **bucketfuls.** A **bucketful** is the amount contained in a bucket. EG *...a bucketful of cold water.* N PART

buckle /bʌkəˈl/, **buckles, buckling, buckled. 1** A **buckle** is a piece of metal or plastic attached to one end of a belt or strap, which is used to fasten it. EG *...shoes fastened with big metal buckles.* N COUNT

Find the animals on these pages.

buckles

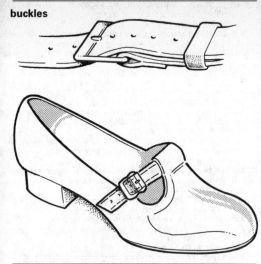

2 If you **buckle** a belt or strap, you fasten it. EG *The v+o cuffs of the raincoat are tightly buckled... He buckled on his revolver.*

3 If an object **buckles** or if something **buckles** it, v-ERG it becomes bent as a result of severe heat or force.

4 If your legs or knees **buckle**, they bend because v they have become very weak or tired. EG *My knees were buckling under me.*

buckle down. If you **buckle down** to something, PHRASAL VB : you start working seriously at it. EG *I'm going to* v+ADV *buckle down to the training course.* Informal

bud /bʌd/, **buds, budding, budded. 1** A **bud** is a N COUNT small pointed lump that appears on a tree or plant and develops into a leaf or flower. EG *...when the bud opens.* ● When a tree or plant is **in bud**, it has ● PHRASE buds on it.

2 When a tree or plant **buds**, buds appear on it. v

3 To **nip** something **in the bud** means to put an PHRASE end to it at an early stage. EG *This incident very* Informal *nearly nipped his political career in the bud.*

4 See also **budding**.

Buddhism /bʊdɪzəᵇm/ is a religion which teaches N UNCOUNT that the way to end suffering is by overcoming your desires.

Buddhist /bʊdɪst/, **Buddhists. 1** A **Buddhist** is a N COUNT person whose religion is Buddhism.

2 Buddhist means relating to Buddhism. EG *...Bud-* ADJ CLASSIF *dhist philosophy.*

budding /bʌdɪŋ/. A **budding** poet, artist, or musi- ADJ CLASSIF : cian is one who is just beginning to develop and be ATTRIB successful. EG *...a budding writer... ...budding doctors.*

buddy /bʌdiᵇ/, **buddies. 1** A **buddy** is a close N COUNT friend, especially a male friend of a man. EG *The* Informal *two of them have become great buddies.*

2 Men sometimes address other men as **buddy**. EG VOCATIVE *Keep going, buddy.* American

budge /bʌdʒ/, **budges, budging, budged. 1** If v : OFT someone will not **budge** on a matter, they refuse to +on/from change their mind or to compromise. EG *He refuses to budge on his design principles.*

2 If you cannot move something, you can say that it v-ERG will not **budge** or that you cannot **budge** it. EG *The screw just will not budge.*

budgerigar /bʌdʒəᵇrɪgɑː/, **budgerigars. Budg-** N COUNT **erigars** are small, brightly-coloured birds that people keep in their houses as pets.

budget /bʌdʒɪᵗt/, **budgets, budgeting, budgeted. 1** A **budget** is a plan showing how much money a N COUNT : person or organization has available and how it USU+SUPP

should be spent. EG *Work out a weekly budget... Education budgets have been cut.*

2 If you **budget**, you plan carefully how much you v : OFT+*for* are going to spend on each thing you want. EG *He could count on a regular salary and thus budget for the future.* ◊ **budgeting.** EG *Through careful* ◊ N UNCOUNT *budgeting they had equipped the entire school.*

3 Budget is used in advertising to suggest that ADJ CLASSIF something is being sold cheaply. EG *...budget* ATTRIB *prices... ...budget travel.*

budget for. If you **budget** for something, you PHRASAL VB : take account of it in your budget. EG *These ex-* v+PREP, *penses can all be budgeted for.* HAS PASS

budgetary /bʌdʒɪᵗtəᵇriː/. A **budgetary** matter or ADJ CLASSIF : policy is concerned with the amount of money that ATTRIB is available and how it is to be spent. EG *...disagree-* Formal *ments over budgetary policies.*

budgie /bʌdʒiᵇ/, **budgies.** A **budgie** is the same as N COUNT a budgerigar. Informal

buff /bʌf/, **buffs. 1** Something that is **buff** is pale ADJ COLOUR brown in colour. EG *...buff envelopes... ...She was wearing a buff uniform .*

2 You can use **buff** to talk about people who know N COUNT+SUPP a lot about a particular subject. For example, Informal someone who is a film **buff** knows a lot about films. EG *...chess buffs.*

buffalo /bʌfələʊ/, **buffaloes.** A **buffalo** is a wild N COUNT animal like a large cow with long curved horns. The plural of 'buffalo' is either 'buffaloes' or 'buffalo'.

buffer /bʌfə/, **buffers, buffering, buffered. 1** A N COUNT **buffer** is something that prevents something else from being harmed. EG *The world lacks the buffer of large international grain reserves... It acts as a buffer against harmful environmental change.*
▸ used as a verb. EG *When the fish bites, hold the* ▸ v+o *rod high to buffer any sudden shocks.*

2 The **buffers** on a train or at the end of a railway N COUNT : line are two metal discs on springs that reduce the USU PLURAL shock when they are hit.

buffet, buffets, buffeting, buffeted; pronounced /bʊfeɪ/ for paragraph 1, and /bʌfət/ for paragraphs 2 and 3.

1 A **buffet** is **1.1** a café in a station. **1.2** a meal of N COUNT cold food at a party or public occasion. Guests usually help themselves to the food and eat it standing up. EG *We found a huge buffet laid out... ...a buffet lunch.*

2 If the wind or the sea **buffets** something, it v+o pushes against it suddenly and violently. EG *The vessel was buffeted by huge waves.* ◊ **buffeting.** ◊ N UNCOUNT EG *...ships built to withstand the buffeting of the sea.*

3 If you have a lot of shocks or unpleasant experi- v+o : USU PASS ences, you can say that you **are buffeted** by them. Formal EG *He is severely buffeted by events and forces beyond his control.*

buffet car /bʊfeɪ kɑː/, **buffet cars.** A **buffet car** N COUNT is a carriage on a train where you can buy sandwiches, drinks, and other snacks.

buffoon /bʌfuːn/, **buffoons.** You call someone a N COUNT **buffoon** when they do silly things. ◊ **buffoonery** ◊ N UNCOUNT /bʌfuːnəᵇriː/. EG *...a harmless piece of buffoonery.* Outdated

bug /bʌg/, **bugs, bugging, bugged. 1** A **bug** is a N COUNT tiny insect, especially one that causes damage.

2 A **bug** is also a minor illness such as a cold that N COUNT people catch from each other. EG *There must be a* Informal *bug going around.*

3 If a place **is bugged**, tiny microphones are v+o : USU PASS hidden there to secretly record what people are saying. EG *Don't speak in the bedrooms; they are bugged... ...electronic bugging devices.*

4 If something **bugs** you, it worries or annoys you. v+o EG *That's what bugs me about the whole business.* Informal

5 You can say that someone **is bitten by** a **bug** PHRASE when they suddenly become very enthusiastic Informal about something. EG *She's been bitten by the skiing bug.*

bugle /bjuːgəᵇl/, **bugles.** A **bugle** is a simple brass N COUNT instrument that looks like a small trumpet.

build /bɪld/, **builds, building, built** /bɪlt/. **1** If you V+O,V+O+O, **build** a structure, you make it by joining things OR V+O+for together. EG *John had built a house facing the river... They were building a bridge.*
2 If people **build** an organization or a society, they V+O gradually form it. EG *They struggled to build a more democratic society.*
3 Your **build** is the shape that your bones and N UNCOUNT muscles give to your body. EG *She was in her early* +SUPP *thirties, with a lean, athletic build.*
4 See also **built**.

build into. 1 If you **build** something **into** a wall PHRASAL VB : or object, you make it in such a way that it is in the V+O+PREP wall or object, or is part of it. EG *There was a cupboard built into the whitewashed wall.* **2** If you V+O+PREP **build** something **into** a policy, system, or product, you make it a part of it. EG *...the inequalities built into our system of financing.*

build on or **build upon. 1** If you **build** an PHRASAL VB : organization, system, or product **on** or **upon** some- V+O+PREP thing, you base it on it. EG *...the principles on which these organizations are built... ...an economy built upon manufacturing industry.* **2** If you **build on** or V+PREP, **upon** the success of something, you take advan- HAS PASS tage of this success in order to make further progress. EG *We must try to build on the success of these growth industries.*

build up. 1 If an amount of something **builds up** PHRASAL VB : or if you **build** it **up**, it gradually gets bigger as a V-ERG+ADV result of more being added to it. EG *Mud builds up in the lake... We're trying to build up a collection of herbs and spices.* **2** If you **build up** someone's trust V+O+ADV or confidence, you gradually make them more trusting or more confident. EG *I found myself trying to reassure Ron, trying to build up his morale.* **3** To V+O+ADV **build** someone **up** means to cause them to be their normal weight again after they have been ill. EG *The patient badly needs building up.* **4** See also **build-up, built-up**.

build upon. See **build on**.

builder /bɪldə/, **builders**. A **builder** is a person N COUNT whose job is to build houses and other buildings. EG *Her father was a builder and decorator.*

building /bɪldɪŋ/, **buildings**. A **building** is a N COUNT structure that has a roof and walls, for example a house or a factory. EG *...a small farm building.*

building society, building societies. In Britain, N COUNT a **building society** is a business which will lend you money when you want to buy a house. You can also invest money in a building society, where it will earn interest.

build-up, build-ups. A **build-up** is a gradual N COUNT : increase in something. EG *...a massive build-up of* USU SING+of *nuclear weapons.*

built /bɪlt/. **1 Built** is the past tense and past participle of **build**.
2 If you say that someone is **built** in a particular ADJ CLASSIF way, you are describing the kind of body they have. EG *He didn't look as if he was built for this kind of work.* ● See also **well-built**.

built-in. Built-in devices or features are included ADJ CLASSIF : in something as an essential part of it. EG *...a* ATTRIB *dishwasher with a built-in waste disposal unit... ...built-in safeguards.*

built-up. A **built-up** area is an area where there ADJ QUALIT are many buildings. EG *Such vehicles could not be brought into built-up areas.*

bulb /bʌlb/, **bulbs**. **1** A **bulb** is the glass part of an N COUNT electric lamp, which gives out light when electric- ity passes through it. EG *The veranda was lit by a dim bulb... If it doesn't work it may need a new light bulb.*
2 A **bulb** is also **2.1** a root shaped like an onion that N COUNT grows into a flower or plant. EG *...tulip bulbs.* **2.2** something that has a round shape like a flower bulb. EG *...the bulb of the thermometer.*

bulbous /bʌlbəs/. Something that is **bulbous** is ADJ CLASSIF round and fat in a rather ugly way. EG *...people with great bulbous noses.*

bulge /bʌldʒ/, **bulges, bulging, bulged**. **1** If V :OFT+A something **bulges**, it sticks out from a surface. EG *Guns bulged on their hips.*
2 If something **is bulging** with things, it is very full V :OFT+with of them. EG *The shelves were bulging with knick- knacks.* ◊ **bulging**. EG *He arrived in the office with* ◊ ADJ CLASSIF a bulging briefcase.* ATTRIB
3 A **bulge** is a lump on a surface that is normally N COUNT flat. EG *'What's under there?' I asked, seeing the bulge at his waistline... He could see the bulge of the body against the side of the tent.*

bulk /bʌlk/, **bulks**. **1** A **bulk** is a large mass of N COUNT something. EG *Willie looked with loathing at the* USU SING *dark bulk of the building.*
2 The **bulk** of something is most of it. EG *The bulk* N PART :SING *of his days are spent quietly... ...the overwhelming bulk of the population.*
3 If you buy or sell something in **bulk**, you buy or PHRASE sell it in large quantities. EG *Goods can be very much cheaper if they're sold in bulk.*

bulky /bʌlki¹/, **bulkier, bulkiest**. Something that ADJ QUALIT is **bulky** is large and heavy, and therefore often difficult to move. EG *The equipment was so bulky that it had to be wheeled around on a large trolley... ...a bulky sweater.*

bull /bʊl/, **bulls**. A **bull** is **1** a male animal of the N COUNT cow family. **2** the male of some other animals, such as the elephant or the whale. EG *...a bull elephant.*

bulldog /bʊldɒg/, **bulldogs**. A **bulldog** is a dog N COUNT with a large square head and short hair.

bulldoze /bʊldəʊz/, **bulldozes, bulldozing, bull- dozed. 1** If people **bulldoze** something such as a V+O building, they knock it down using a bulldozer. EG *Settlements have been bulldozed out of the way.*
2 If people **bulldoze** earth, stone, or other heavy V+O material, they move it using a bulldozer.

bulldozer /bʊldəʊzə/, **bulldozers**. A **bulldozer** is N COUNT a large, powerful tractor with a broad metal blade at the front, which is used for knocking down buildings or moving large amounts of earth.

bullet /bʊlɪ¹t/, **bullets**. A **bullet** is a small piece of N COUNT metal with a pointed or rounded end, which is fired out of a gun. EG *...a bullet shot through the window... The car was covered with bullet holes.*

bulletin /bʊlɪ¹tɪn/, **bulletins**. A **bulletin** is **1** a N COUNT short news report on the radio or television. **2** a regular newspaper or leaflet that is produced by an organization or group such as a school or church. EG *The Institute publishes a fortnightly bulletin.*

bullet-proof. Something that is **bullet-proof** is ADJ CLASSIF made of a strong material that bullets cannot pass through. EG *...bullet-proof vests.*

bullfight /bʊlfaɪt/, **bullfights**. A **bullfight** is a N COUNT public entertainment in which a man makes a bull angry by sticking short spears in it before trying to kill it with a sword. Bullfights are especially popu- lar in Spain.

bullfighter /bʊlfaɪtə/, **bullfighters**. A **bull- N COUNT fighter** is the man who tries to kill the bull in a bullfight.

bullfighting /bʊlfaɪtɪŋ/ is the public entertain- N UNCOUNT ment in which men try to kill bulls in bullfights.

bullion /bʊlɪ⁸jən/ is gold or silver in the form of N UNCOUNT lumps or bars.

bullock /bʊlək/, **bullocks**. A **bullock** is a young N COUNT bull that has been castrated.

bull's-eye, bull's-eyes. 1 The **bull's-eye** is the N SING small circular area at the centre of a target. EG *He hit the bull's-eye and won the prize.*
2 A **bull's-eye** is a shot or throw of a dart that hits N COUNT the bull's-eyes.

bullshit /bʊlʃɪt/ is a swear word. If you say EXCLAM OR N 'bullshit!', you are telling someone that what they UNCOUNT have said is nonsense or completely untrue.

If you buy something in bulk, is it bulky?

bully /bʊli¹/, **bullies, bullying, bullied. 1** A **bully** N COUNT is someone who uses their strength or power to hurt or frighten other people. EG *There was a high proportion of sadists and bullies among the camp guards.*

2 If someone **bullies** you, they use their strength V+O or power to hurt or frighten you. EG *For the first month at my new school I was bullied constantly.*

◊ **bullying.** EG *All cases of bullying will be severely* ◊ N UNCOUNT *dealt with.*

3 If someone **bullies** you into doing something, V+O: they make you do it by using force or threats. EG *He* OFT+*into had been bullied into driving her home.*

bulrush /bʊlrʌʃ/, **bulrushes. Bulrushes** are tall, N COUNT : stiff reeds that grow on the edges of rivers. USU PLURAL

bulwark /bʊlwɔk/, **bulwarks.** A **bulwark** is N COUNT : something strong that protects you against un- OFT+*against* pleasant or dangerous situations. EG *The fund is a bulwark against your benefits being cut.*

bum /bʌm/, **bums. 1** A **bum** is a tramp. EG *If you* N COUNT *were a bum, you would be free to do whatever you* Informal *want.* American

2 You can say that someone is a **bum** when you N COUNT think that they are worthless or irresponsible. EG Informal *What an illiterate lot of bums you are!* American

3 Your **bum** is the part of your body which you sit N COUNT on. EG *...sitting down on their big fat bums.* Informal

bumble /bʌmbəˀl/, **bumbles, bumbling, bum-** V **bled.** When someone **bumbles,** they behave in a confused, disorganized way and make a lot of mistakes. ◊ **bumbling.** EG *Michael Hordern plays* ◊ ADJ CLASSIF : *the bumbling Englishman yet again.* ATTRIB

bumblebee /bʌmbəˀlbi:/, **bumblebees.** A N COUNT **bumblebee** is a large hairy bee.

bump /bʌmp/, **bumps, bumping, bumped. 1** If V+A OR V+O you **bump** into something, you accidentally hit it while you are moving. EG *He turned on the lamp so that he could find his way without bumping into anything.*

2 If a vehicle **bumps** over a surface, it travels in a V+A rough, bouncing way because the surface is very uneven. EG *The jeep was bumping over stony ground... ...bumping along the dirt road.*

3 If you have a **bump** while you are driving a car, N COUNT you have a minor accident in which you hit something. EG *Her car got three bad bumps while she was in London.*

4 If something makes a **bump** when it hits some- N COUNT thing, it makes a fairly gentle sound. EG *It slipped from his fingers and fell with a bump.*

5 A **bump** on a road is a raised, uneven part. EG *If* N COUNT *the motor cycle goes over a bump, the engine misfires.*

6 If you have a **bump** on your body, you have a N COUNT swollen shape there as a result of a blow. EG *You've got a bump on your forehead like an egg.*

bump into. If you **bump into** someone you PHRASAL VB : know, you meet them by chance. EG *I bumped into* V+PREP *Mary an hour ago... We occasionally bump into one* Informal *another.*

bump off. To **bump** someone **off** means to kill PHRASAL VB : them. V+O+ADV

bumper /bʌmpə/, **bumpers. 1 Bumpers** are bars N COUNT at the front and back of a vehicle which protect it British if it bumps into something. See picture at CAR. ● If ● PHRASE traffic is **bumper to bumper,** the vehicles are so British close to one another that they are almost touching and are moving very slowly.

2 A **bumper** crop or harvest is one that is larger ADJ CLASSIF : than usual. EG *We had a bumper crop of apples last* ATTRIB *year.*

bumptious /bʌmpʃəs/. You say that someone is ADJ QUALIT **bumptious** when they are continually expressing their own opinions and ideas in a self-important way. EG *I disliked these noisy bumptious types.*

bumpy /bʌmpi¹/, **bumpier, bumpiest. 1** A road ADJ QUALIT or path that is **bumpy** has a lot of bumps on it. EG *The track got bumpier and muddier the further we went.*

2 If a journey in a vehicle is **bumpy,** it is uncom- ADJ QUALIT fortable and rough, because you are travelling over an uneven surface. EG *The ride was a bit bumpy.*

bun /bʌn/, **buns. 1** A **bun** is a small cake or bread N COUNT roll, often containing currants or spices.

2 If a woman has her hair in a **bun,** it is fastened N COUNT into a round shape at the back of her head.

bunch /bʌntʃ/, **bunches, bunching, bunched. 1** A N PART **bunch** of people is a group of them. EG *They're a* Informal *bunch of tired old men... Ranchers are an inde- pendent bunch.*

2 A **bunch** of flowers is a number of them held or N PART tied together. EG *...a big bunch of poppies.*

3 A **bunch** of bananas, grapes, or other fruit is a N PART group of them growing on the same stem.

4 A **bunch** of similar things is a group of them N PART situated, held, or fastened closely together. EG *...a big bunch of keys... ...holding a bunch of balloons.*

5 If people **bunch** together or **bunch** up, they stay V : OFT close together in a group. +*together/up*

6 If you **bunch** things together or **bunch** them up, V+O : OFT+A you gather them together to make a tight bundle. OR V+A EG *She was holding her skirts bunched up over one arm.*

bundle /bʌndəˀl/, **bundles, bundling, bundled. 1** N COUNT A **bundle** is a number of things tied together or OR N PART wrapped in a cloth so that they can be carried or stored. EG *He tied the wood into a bundle... He had his bundle of personal belongings under his arm.*

2 If you **bundle** someone or something some- V+O+A where, you push them there in a rough and hurried OR V+A way. EG *He led her to the window and bundled her out... They bundled him into the ambulance.*

bundle off. If you **bundle** someone **off** some- PHRASAL VB : where, you send them there in a hurry. EG *Jack was* V+O+ADV, *bundled off to Ely to stay with friends.* OFT+*to*

bundle up. If you **bundle up** a mass of things, PHRASAL VB : you make them into a bundle by gathering or tying V+O+ADV them together. EG *My mother bundled up all my comics and threw them out.*

bung /bʌŋ/, **bungs, bunging, bunged. 1** A **bung** N COUNT is a round piece of wood, cork, or rubber which you use to close the hole in a container such as a barrel or flask.

2 If you **bung** something somewhere, you put it V+O+A there in a quick and careless way. EG *Just bung it in* Informal *the oven... I bunged the books on the shelf.*

3 See also **bunged up.**

bungalow /bʌŋgəˀləʊ/, **bungalows.** A **bungalow** N COUNT is a house which has only one storey.

bunged up. If a hole is **bunged up,** it is blocked. ADJ PRED EG *The sink's bunged up... ...a bunged-up nose.* Informal

bungle /bʌŋgəˀl/, **bungles, bungling, bungled.** If V OR V+O you **bungle** something, you fail to do it properly, because you make mistakes or are clumsy. EG *They bungled the whole operation.* ◊ **bungled.** EG *...the* ◊ ADJ CLASSIF *bungled murder of Bernard Lustig.* ◊ **bungling.** EG ◊ ADJ CLASSIF *...this bungling administration.*

bunion /bʌnjən/, **bunions.** A **bunion** is a large N COUNT painful lump on the first joint of a person's big toe.

bunk /bʌŋk/, **bunks. 1** A **bunk** is a bed fixed to a N COUNT wall, especially in a ship or caravan. EG *I ran to my cabin and threw myself on the bunk... Thomas was lying in the lower bunk.*

2 If you describe something that someone has said N UNCOUNT or written as **bunk,** you mean that it is foolish or Informal untrue. EG *That's all bunk – there can't be equality.*

3 If you **do a bunk,** you suddenly leave a place PHRASE without telling anyone. EG *The next thing I knew,* Informal *the whole family had done a bunk.*

bunker /bʌŋkə/, **bunkers.** A **bunker** is **1** a place, N COUNT usually underground, that has been built with strong walls to protect it against heavy gunfire and bombing. **2** a container for coal or other fuel.

bunny /bʌni¹/, **bunnies.** Small children call a N COUNT rabbit a **bunny** or a **bunny rabbit.**

bunting /bʌntiŋ/ consists of rows of small col- N UNCOUNT oured flags that are used to decorate streets and buildings on special occasions. EG *The street was decorated with red, white and blue bunting.*

buoy /bɔɪ/, **buoys, buoying, buoyed.** A **buoy** is a N COUNT floating object that shows ships and boats where they can go and that warns them of danger.

buoy up. If you **buoy** someone **up**, you keep PHRASAL VB : them cheerful in a situation in which they might V+O+ADV feel depressed. EG *He did his best to buoy her up.*

buoyant /ˈbɔɪənt/. **1** If you are **buoyant**, you feel ADJ QUALIT cheerful and behave in a lively way. EG *He suddenly smiled, feeling buoyant and at ease... His mood became buoyant.* ◇ **buoyancy** /ˈbɔɪənsiˈ/. EG *...a* ◇ N UNCOUNT *sensation of buoyancy and freedom.* ◇ **buoyantly.** ◇ ADV EG *'I hope she will,' said Pratt buoyantly.*
2 Something that is **buoyant** floats on a liquid or in ADJ QUALIT the air. EG *...a row of buoyant cylinders.* ◇ **buoyancy.** EG *New chambers were added to* ◇ N UNCOUNT *provide buoyancy.*
3 A **buoyant** economy is a successful one in which ADJ QUALIT there is a lot of trade and economic activity.

burble /ˈbɜːbəˈl/, **burbles, burbling, burbled.** If V something **burbles**, it makes a low continuous bubbling sound. EG *Hot mud burbled down from a side valley... Lucy was making burbling noises.*

burden /ˈbɜːdəˈn/, **burdens. 1** Something that is a N COUNT **burden** causes you a lot of worry or hard work. EG *He was weighed down by the burden of state secrets he carried with him... This would relieve the initial burden on hospital staff.*
2 A **burden** is also a heavy load that is difficult to N COUNT carry. EG *Men and women came bearing heavy* Formal *burdens of provisions.*

burdened /ˈbɜːdəˈnd/. If you are **burdened** with ADJ PRED something, it causes you a lot of worry or hard +with/by work. EG *He was burdened with endless paperwork.*

bureau /ˈbjʊərəʊ/, **bureaux** or **bureaus. 1** A **bu-** N COUNT **reau** is a writing desk with shelves and drawers British and a lid that opens to form the writing surface. EG *He was going through the drawers of the bureau.*
2 A **bureau** is also **2.1** an office, organization, or N COUNT government department that collects and distrib- American utes information. EG *The weather bureau promised a sunny weekend.* **2.2** an office of a company or American organization which has its headquarters in another town or country. EG *...the Washington bureau of a Midwestern newspaper.*

bureaucracy /bjʊəˈrɒkrəsiˈ/, **bureaucracies.** 1 A N COUNT **bureaucracy** is an administrative system operat- ed by a large number of officials following rules and procedures. EG *Each industry is guided by massive bureaucracies... ...an inefficient bureau- cracy.*
2 Bureaucracy is all the rules and procedures N UNCOUNT followed by government departments and similar organizations; often used showing disapproval. EG *One of the problems is the bureaucracy the claim- ant has to face.*

bureaucrat /ˈbjʊərəˈkræt/, **bureaucrats.** A **bu-** N COUNT **reaucrat** is an official who works in a bureaucra- cy, especially one who you think follows rules and procedures too strictly. EG *...endless paperwork dished out by bureaucrats.*

bureaucratic /ˌbjʊərəˈkrætɪk/. **Bureaucratic** ADJ QUALIT rules and procedures are complicated ones which can cause long delays.

bureaux /ˈbjʊərəʊz/ is a plural form of **bureau.**

burglar /ˈbɜːglə/, **burglars.** A **burglar** is a thief N COUNT who breaks into a house and steals things.

burglar alarm, burglar alarms. A **burglar** N COUNT **alarm** is an electric device that makes a bell ring loudly if someone tries to break into a building.

burglary /ˈbɜːgləriˈ/, **burglaries.** If someone car- N COUNT OR ries out a **burglary**, they break into a building and N UNCOUNT steal things. EG *Contact the police as soon as possible after a burglary... He was found guilty of burglary.*

burgle /ˈbɜːgəˈl/, **burgles, burgling, burgled.** If V+O someone **burgles** a building, they break into it and

steal things. EG *She thought they might be criminals come to burgle the house.*

burial /ˈberiˈəl/, **burials.** A **burial** is the ceremo- N COUNT OR ny that takes place when a dead body is put into a N UNCOUNT grave in the ground. EG *The bodies are brought home for burial... He read swiftly through the burial service.*

burly /ˈbɜːliˈ/, **burlier, burliest.** A **burly** man has ADJ QUALIT a broad body and strong muscles. EG *...two burly Irish workers... ...his tall, burly frame.*

burn /bɜːn/, **burns, burning, burned, burnt** /bɜːnt/. The past tense and past participle can be either **burned** or **burnt.**
1 If something **is burning**, it is on fire. EG *The* V *stubble was burning in the fields.* ◇ **burning.** EG ◇ N UNCOUNT *There was a smell of burning.* ◇ **burnt.** EG *...a* ◇ ADJ CLASSIF *charred bit of burnt wood.*
2 If you **burn** something, you destroy it with fire. EG V+O *We couldn't burn the rubbish because it was rain- ing.* ◇ **burning.** EG *...the burning of the Embassy* ◇ N UNCOUNT *during the riots.*
3 If you **burn** something that you are cooking or if V-ERG it **burns**, you spoil it by using too great a heat. EG *I burnt the milk.*
4 If you **burn** yourself, you are injured by fire or by V-REFL OR V+O something very hot. EG *'What's the matter with your hand?' - 'I burned it on my cigar.'* ▸ used as a ▸ N COUNT noun. EG *Many had serious burns over much of their bodies.*
5 If your face **is burning**, it is red because you are V : USU CONT embarrassed or upset.
6 If you **are burning** with an emotion such as V+with : anger, you feel very angry. EG *...letters burning with* USU CONT *indignation.*
7 If the sun **burns** your skin, it makes your skin V-ERG become red or brown. EG *Simon was burned by the sun to a deep tan... ...skin that usually burns in the sun.*
8 You can say that something **burns** when it gives V you a painful, hot feeling. EG *The whiskey he had drunk burned in his chest.*
9 If something is extremely hot, you can say that it ADJ CLASSIF : is **burning** or **burning hot.** EG *...burning deserts...* ATTRIB *...burning hot irons.*

burn down. If a building **burns down** or if PHRASAL VB : someone **burns** it **down**, it is completely destroyed V-ERG+ADV by fire. EG *My house was burnt down.*

burn out. 1 If a fire **burns** itself **out**, it stops PHRASAL VB : burning because there is nothing left to burn. EG *All* V-REFL+ADV *the fires had now burned themselves out.* **2** If you V-REFL+ADV **burn** yourself **out**, you make yourself exhausted or Informal ill by working too hard. **3** See also **burnt-out.**

burn up. 1 If something **burns up**, it is complete- PHRASAL VB : ly destroyed by fire or strong heat. EG *The satellite* V+ADV *had burned up on re-entering the atmosphere.* **2** If V+O+ADV you say that an engine **burns up** fuel, you mean that it uses a lot of fuel.

burned-out. See **burnt-out.**

burner /ˈbɜːnə/, **burners.** A **burner** is a device N COUNT which produces heat or a flame, especially as part of a cooker or heater.

burnish /ˈbɜːnɪʃ/, **burnishes, burnishing, bur-** V+O **nished.** When you **burnish** metal, you polish it so that it shines.

burnished /ˈbɜːnɪʃt/. You can describe something ADJ CLASSIF as **burnished** when it is bright or smooth. EG Literary *...burnished leaves... ...her burnished skin.*

burnt /bɜːnt/ is a past tense and past participle of **burn.**

burnt-out or **burned-out. Burnt-out** vehicles or ADJ QUALIT buildings have been very badly damaged by fire.

burp /bɜːp/, **burps, burping, burped.** When V someone **burps**, they make a noise because air from their stomach has been forced up through

Can you burgle your own house?

their throat. ▶ used as a noun. EG *A slight burp* ▶N COUNT
interrupted her flowing speech.

burrow /bʌrəʊ⁰/, **burrows, burrowing, bur-**
rowed. 1 A **burrow** is a tunnel or hole in the N COUNT
ground that is dug by an animal such as a rabbit.
2 When an animal **burrows**, it digs a tunnel or hole V OR V+O:
in the ground. EG *The fish burrows into the mud...* USU+A
*...earthworms burrowing their way through the
soil.*
3 When you **burrow** in a container or pile of V+A
things, you search there for something using your
hands. EG *She began burrowing underneath the
tissue paper.*

bursary /bɜːsə⁰ri¹/, **bursaries.** A **bursary** is a N COUNT
sum of money which is given to someone to allow
them to study in a college or university.

burst /bɜːst/, **bursts, bursting.** The form **burst** is
used in the present tense and is the past tense and
past participle of the verb.
1 When something **bursts** or when you **burst** it, it V-ERG
suddenly breaks open or splits open, and the air
inside or some other substance comes out. EG *As he
braked a tyre burst... She burst the balloon... ...a
burst water pipe.*
2 When a door or lid **bursts** open, it opens very V+open OR
suddenly and violently because there is great pres- V+O+open
sure behind it. EG *I was sure the door was going to
burst open any minute.*
3 If you **burst** into or through something, you V+A OR
suddenly go into it or through it with a lot of energy V+O+A
because you are in a great hurry. EG *O'Shea burst in
through the opposite door... A woman burst her
way through the guests at the buffet.*
4 If you say that someone is about to **burst** with an V:OFT+with
emotion such as pride or anger, you mean that
they feel very proud or very angry. EG *I could have
burst with pride... He felt himself about to burst
with rage.*
5 A **burst** of something is a sudden short period of N COUNT+of
it. EG *There was a burst of automatic rifle fire...
...capable of great bursts of speed.*

burst in on. If you **burst in on** someone, you PHRASAL VB:
suddenly and quickly enter the room that they are V+ADV+PREP
in. EG *He suddenly burst in on me without warning.*

burst into. 1 If you **burst into** tears or laughter, PHRASAL VB:
you suddenly begin to cry or laugh. EG *I keep V+PREP
bursting into tears... The whole room burst into
laughter.* **2** When plants **burst into** leaf, blossom, V+PREP
or flower, their leaves or flowers suddenly open. **3**
to **burst into flames**: see **flame.**

burst out. 1 If you **burst out** laughing or crying, PHRASAL VB:
you suddenly begin laughing or crying, usually V+ADV+-ING
loudly. **2** Writers use **burst out** to indicate that V+ADV+
someone says something suddenly and loudly. EG QUOTE
Then he burst out, 'Get into the car, Phil, can't Written
you?'

bursting /bɜːstɪŋ/. **1** If a place is **bursting** with ADJ PRED
people or things, it is full of them. EG *...parks* +with
bursting with flowers. ● If you say that a place is ● PHRASE
bursting at the seams, you mean that it is very Informal
full indeed. EG *The psychiatric wards are bursting
at the seams.*
2 Someone who is **bursting** with a feeling or ADJ PRED
quality is full of it. EG *Claud was bursting with pride* +with
and excitement... Jamie is bursting with energy.
3 Someone who is **bursting** to do something is ADJ PRED
very eager to do it. EG *I was bursting to tell* +to-INF
someone... All the children were bursting to take Informal
part.

bury /beri¹/, **buries, burying, buried. 1** When a V+O:USU+A
dead person **is buried**, their body is put into a
grave and covered with earth. EG *She will be buried
here in the churchyard.*
2 To **bury** something means to put it into a hole in V+O:USU+A
the ground and cover it up, often in order to hide it.
EG *Reptiles bury their eggs in holes... ...buried
treasure.*
3 If you **are buried** under something that falls on V+O:
top of you, you are completely covered and often USU PASS+A

cannot get out. EG *People were buried beneath
mountains of rubble.*
4 If you **bury** your face in something, you press V+O+A
your face against it, in order to hide your face. EG
*She buried her face in her hands... She turned
away, burying her face in the pillow.*
5 If you **bury** a feeling, you try not to show it. If V+O
you **bury** a memory, you try to forget it. EG *The
anger which had been buried inside me rose to the
surface... ...buried memories.*
6 If you **bury** yourself in something, you concen- V-REFL+in
trate hard on it. EG *He buried himself deep in the
wine list.*

bury away. If something **is buried away** some- PHRASAL VB:
where, you cannot easily find it or see it. EG *Buried* V+O+ADV,
away inside the paper, in a tiny paragraph, was an USU PASS
account of his visit.

bus /bʌs/, **buses.** A **bus** is a large motor vehicle N COUNT
which carries passengers from one place to anoth- OR by+N
er. EG *I'm waiting for the bus back to town... I could
go by bus... ...a bus driver.*

bus conductor, bus conductors. A **bus conduc-** N COUNT
tor is an official on a bus who sells passengers
their tickets.

bush /bʊʃ/, **bushes. 1** A **bush** is a large plant N COUNT
which is smaller than a tree and has a lot of
branches. EG *...a gorse bush... I peered through the
bushes.*
2 You can refer to the wild, uncultivated parts of N SING:the+N
some hot countries as the **bush.** EG *I went for a
walk in the bush... ...a bush fire.*
3 If you say to someone **'Don't beat about the** PHRASE
bush', you mean that you want them to tell you
something immediately and directly rather than
trying to avoid doing so.

bushy /bʊʃi¹/, **bushier, bushiest. Bushy** hair or ADJ QUALIT
fur grows very thickly. EG *...bushy eyebrows... ...a
fox with a bushy tail.*

busily /bɪzɪli¹/. If you do something **busily**, you do ADV
it in a very active way. EG *Some children were
busily catching crabs... I went on writing busily.*

business /bɪznɪs/, **businesses. 1 Business** is N UNCOUNT
work relating to the production, buying, and selling
of goods or services. EG *...firms that do business
with Britain... There are good profits to be made in
the hotel business... Are you in San Francisco for
business or pleasure?... He had a business appointment.*
2 A **business** is an organization which produces N COUNT
and sells goods or which provides a service. EG *He
set up a small travel business.*
3 If a shop or company goes **out of business**, it PHRASE
has to stop trading because it is not making enough
money. EG *Umbrella sellers went out of business.*
4 If you have some **business** to deal with, you have N UNCOUNT
something, especially something important, to deal
with. EG *She got on with the business of clearing
up... Let's get down to business now.*
5 If you say that something is your **business**, you N SING+POSS
mean that it concerns you personally and that
other people have no right to get involved in it. EG
*That's his business and no one else's... It's no
business of mine what you choose to read.*
6 If you say that someone **has no business** to do PHRASE
something, you mean that they have no right to do
it. EG *She had no business to publish his letters.*
7 If you say to someone **'Mind your own busi-** PHRASE
ness' or **'It's none of your business'**, you are Informal
telling them not to ask about something that does
not concern them. EG *'Where were you last night?'*
– 'That's none of your business.'
8 You use **business** to refer in a general way to an N SING+SUPP
event, situation, or activity that you are talking
about. EG *The whole business affected him profoundly... This assassination business has gone far
enough.*
9 If someone **means business**, they are serious PHRASE
and determined about what they are doing. Informal

businesslike /bɪznɪslaɪk/. Someone who is ADJ QUALIT businesslike deals with things in an efficient way without wasting time.

businessman /bɪznɪsməˀn/, **businessmen.** 1 A A N COUNT businessman is a man who works in business, for example by running a firm.

2 If you describe a man as a good **businessman** or N COUNT+SUPP a shrewd **businessman**, you mean that he knows how to deal with money and how to make good deals.

busker /bʌskə/, **buskers.** A **busker** is a person N COUNT who plays music or sings for money in city streets British or stations.

bus stop, bus stops. A **bus stop** is a place on a N COUNT road where buses stop to let passengers on and off. EG There were long queues at all the bus stops.

bust /bʌst/, **busts, busting, busted.** The form **bust** can be used as the past tense and past participle of the verb as well as the present tense.

1 When you **bust** something, you damage it so V+O badly that it cannot be used. EG She was furious Informal about Jack busting the double bass.

2 If something is **bust**, it is broken or very badly ADJ PRED damaged. EG The television's bust. Informal

3 If a company **goes bust**, it loses so much money PHRASE that it is forced to close down. EG The oil companies Informal went bust.

4 A **bust** is a statue of the head and shoulders of a N COUNT person. EG ...a bust of Shakespeare.

5 A woman's **bust** is her breasts. N COUNT

bustle /bʌsəˀl/, **bustles, bustling, bustled.** 1 If V+A someone **bustles** somewhere, they move there in a hurried and determined way, often because they are very busy. EG I watched housewives bustle in and out of a supermarket... He was bustling around the kitchen cooking up a huge pot of stew.

◊ **bustling.** ...the bustling curator of the mu- ◊ ADJ CLASSIF: seum. ATTRIB

2 A place that **is bustling** is full of people and very ADJ CLASSIF busy and lively. EG The station was bustling with activity... Fraserburgh is a bustling fishing town.

3 **Bustle** is busy, noisy activity. EG ...the bustle of N UNCOUNT the airport.

busy /bɪzɪˀ/, **busier, busiest; busies, busying, busied.** 1 When you are **busy**, you are working ADJ QUALIT hard or concentrating on a task, so that you are not free to do anything else. EG She's going to be busy till Friday... Not now, Jo, I'm busy.

2 A **busy** time is a period of time during which you ADJ QUALIT have a lot of things to do. EG I've had a busy day.

3 If you are **busy** doing something, it is taking all ADJ PRED+-ING your attention. EG She is too busy chasing after money to care about such things... Her assistant was busy putting the instruments away.

4 If you **busy** yourself with something, you occupy V-REFL : USU+A yourself by dealing with it. EG I decided to busy myself with our untidy lawn.

5 A **busy** place is full of people who are doing ADJ QUALIT things or moving about. EG ...a busy office... Curzon Street is usually very busy.

busybody /bɪzɪˀbɒdiˀ/, **busybodies.** If you call N COUNT someone a **busybody**, you mean that they inter- Informal fere in other people's affairs. EG ...a detective whom some busybody had hired to see what I was up to.

but /bʌt, bət/. 1 You use **but** to introduce a CONJ statement which contrasts with what you have just said. EG We'll have a meeting. But not today... It was a long walk but it was worth it... ...a cheap but incredibly effective carpet cleaner.

2 You also use **but** when you are about to add CONJ something further in a discussion or to change the subject. EG Later I'll be discussing this with Dr Peter Unsworth. But first let me remind you of some of the issues.

3 You also use **but** after you have made an excuse CONJ or apology for what you are just about to say. EG I'm sorry, but she's not in at the moment... Forgive my ignorance, but just what is Arista?

4 You use **but then** 4.1 before a remark which ADV SEN slightly contradicts what you have just said. EG Iron would do the job better. But then you can't bend iron so easily. 4.2 before a remark which suggests that what you have just said should not be regarded as surprising. EG They're very close. But then, they've known each other for years and years.

5 **But** also means 5.1 except. EG It hurt nobody but PREP himself... It could do everything but stop. 5.2 only. EG Low cost and high speed are but two of the Formal advantages of electronic data handling... When I first met her she had but recently divorced.

6 You use **but for** to introduce the only factor that CONJ causes a particular thing not to happen or not to be completely true. EG But for his ice-blue eyes, he looked like a bearded, wiry Moor.

7 **anything but**: see **anything**.

butch /bʊtʃ/. If you describe a woman as **butch**, ADJ QUALIT you mean that she behaves or dresses in a mascu- line way; an offensive word.

butcher /bʊtʃə/, **butchers, butchering, butch- ered.** 1 A **butcher** is a shopkeeper who sells meat. N COUNT

2 You can refer to a shop where meat is sold as a N COUNT **butcher** or a **butcher's**. EG There's a family butch- er at the end of our road.

3 To **butcher** a lot of people means to kill them in V+O a cruel way. EG He butchered tens of thousands of people. ◊ **butchery** /bʊtʃəriˀ/. EG ...the butchery of ◊ N UNCOUNT two hundred innocent citizens.

butler /bʌtlə/, **butlers.** A **butler** is the most N COUNT important male servant in a house.

butt /bʌt/, **butts, butting, butted.** 1 The **butt** of a N COUNT weapon is the thick end of its handle. EG ...the padded butt of the rifle... ...the butt end of a spear.

2 The **butt** of a cigarette or cigar is the small part N COUNT of it that is left when you have finished smoking it.

3 A **butt** is a large barrel used for collecting or N COUNT storing liquid. EG ...a water butt.

4 If you are the **butt** of teasing or criticism, people N SING : the+N keep teasing you or criticizing you. EG They made him the butt of endless practical jokes.

5 If you **butt** something, you hit it with your head. V+O EG He butted Stuart in the chest.

butt in. If you **butt in**, you rudely join in a private PHRASAL VB : conversation or activity without being asked to. EG V+ADV You can't just butt in on someone else's discussion.

butter /bʌtə/, **butters, buttering, buttered.** 1 N UNCOUNT **Butter** is a yellowish substance made from cream which you spread on bread or use in cooking. EG ...bread and butter... ...a shelf where the butter and cheese were kept.

2 When you **butter** bread or toast, you spread V+O OR butter on it. EG She buttered herself a piece of V-REFL+O bread.

3 If you say that **butter wouldn't melt in** some- PHRASE one's **mouth**, you mean that they look very inno- cent but you know that they have done something wrong or they are intending to.

butter up. If you **butter** someone **up**, you praise PHRASAL VB : them or try to please them, because you want to V+O+ADV ask them a favour. Informal

buttercup /bʌtəkʌp/, **buttercups.** A **buttercup** N COUNT is a small plant with bright yellow flowers.

butterfly /bʌtəflaɪ/, **butterflies.** 1 A **butterfly** is N COUNT a type of insect with large colourful wings and a thin body.

2 If you have **butterflies in** your **stomach**, you PHRASE are very nervous about something. EG I could feel Informal the butterflies in my stomach as I waited.

3 **Butterfly** is a kind of swimming stroke which N UNCOUNT you do lying on your front, bringing your arms over your head together. See picture at SWIMMING.

buttock /bʌtəˀk/, **buttocks.** Your **buttocks** are N COUNT : the part of your body that you sit on. USU PLURAL

button /bʌtəˀn/, **buttons, buttoning, buttoned.** 1 N COUNT **Buttons** are small hard objects sewn on to shirts,

Find words on these pages which apply only to men or only to women.

coats, or other pieces of clothing. You fasten the clothing by pushing the buttons through holes called buttonholes. EG *She opened the top two buttons of her dress.*

2 If you **button** a shirt, coat, or other piece of v+o clothing, you fasten it by pushing its buttons through the buttonholes.

3 A **button** is also a small object on a machine or N COUNT electrical device that you press in order to operate the machine or device. EG *I couldn't remember which button turns it off... The gate slid open at the push of a button.*

button up. If you **button up** a shirt, coat, or PHRASAL VB : other piece of clothing, you fasten it completely by V+O+ADV pushing all its buttons through the buttonholes.

buttonhole /bʌtəᵊnhəʊl/, **buttonholes, button- holing, buttonholed.** **1** A **buttonhole** is **1.1** a hole N COUNT that you push a button through in order to fasten a shirt, coat, or other piece of clothing. **1.2** a flower British that you wear on the collar or lapel of your jacket.

2 If you **buttonhole** someone, you stop them and v+o make them listen to you. EG *I was just on my way out and he buttonholed me.*

buttress /bʌtrɪs/, **buttresses, buttressing, but- tressed. 1** **Buttresses** are supports, usually made N COUNT of stone or brick, that support a wall.

2 To **buttress** a wall means to support it with v+o buttresses.

3 To **buttress** an argument or system means to v+o give support and strength to it. EG *The present system serves to buttress the social structure in Britain.*

buxom /bʌksᵊm/. If you describe a woman as ADJ QUALIT **buxom**, you mean that she looks healthy and attractive and has a rather large body.

buy /baɪ/, **buys, buying, bought** /bɔːt/. **1** If you v+o, v+o+o, **buy** something, you obtain it by paying money for OR V+O+*for* it. EG *Let me buy you a drink.*

2 If something is a good **buy**, it is of good quality N COUNT : and you can buy it cheaply. EG *Other good buys* MOD+N *include cameras and toys.*

buy out. If you **buy** someone **out**, you buy their PHRASAL VB : share of something that you previously owned V+O+ADV together. EG *He sold off the shops to buy out his partner.*

buy up. If you **buy up** land or property, you buy PHRASAL VB : large quantities of it, or all that is available. V+O+ADV

buyer /baɪə/, **buyers. 1** A **buyer** is a person who N COUNT is buying something or who intends to buy it. EG *I have a buyer for the house.*

2 A **buyer** who works in a large store decides what N COUNT goods are bought from manufacturers to be sold in the store. EG *She is the chief fashion buyer for Sparks & Spencer.*

buzz /bʌz/, **buzzes, buzzing, buzzed. 1** A **buzz** is N COUNT a continuous sound, like the sound of a bee when it is flying. EG *...the buzz of an insect.* ▶ used as a verb. ▶ v EG *Bees buzzed outside.*

2 If thoughts **are buzzing** round your head, you v+A are thinking about a lot of things, usually in a confused way. EG *Anne's head buzzed with angry, crazy thoughts.*

3 If a place **is buzzing** with conversation, it is v : OFT+*with* filled with the sound of a lot of people talking. EG *The room buzzed with excited questions.* ▶ used as ▶ N SING : a noun. EG *...the buzz of conversation around her.* USU+SUPP

buzz off. If you say **'buzz off'** to someone, you V+ADV are telling them rudely to go away. Informal

buzzard /bʌzəd/, **buzzards.** A **buzzard** is a large N COUNT bird of prey.

buzzer /bʌzə/, **buzzers.** A **buzzer** is a device that N COUNT makes a buzzing sound and that is used, for exam- ple, in alarm clocks and office telephones. EG *Press the buzzer... The intercom buzzer sounded.*

by /baɪ/. **1** If something is done **by** a person or PREP thing, that person or thing does it or causes it. EG *He was brought up by an aunt... I was startled by his anger... ...the use of pocket calculators by schoolchildren.*

2 If you achieve one thing **by** doing another thing, PREP+-ING your action enables you to achieve the first thing. EG *By bribing a nurse I was able to see some files... They were making a living by selling souvenirs to the tourists.*

3 If you do something **by** a particular thing, you do PREP it using that thing. EG *The money will be paid by cheque... We heard from them by phone... I always go home by bus.*

4 If something happens **by** chance or **by** accident, PREP it happens although you did not intend it. EG *They had met by chance.*

5 If you say what someone means **by** a particular PREP word or expression, you are saying what they intend the word or expression to refer to. EG *By 'John' I assumed he meant John Fletcher.*

6 If you say that something such as a book, a piece PREP of music, or a painting is **by** a particular person, you mean that this person wrote it or created it. EG *...three books by a great Australian writer.*

7 Someone or something that is **by** something else PREP is beside it and close to it. EG *I sat by her bed.*

8 When a person or vehicle passes **by** you, they PREP, OR move past you without stopping. EG *People rushed* ADV AFTER VB *by us... They watched the cars whizzing by.*

9 If something happens **by** a particular time, it PREP happens at or before that time. EG *He can be out by seven... By 1940 the number had grown to 185 millions.*

10 If you do something **by** day, you do it during the PREP day. If you do it **by** night, you do it during the night.

11 If something happens **by** law, it happens accord- PREP ing to the law. If something is the case **by** particu- lar standards, it is the case according to the standards. EG *Each year, by law, state pensions must be reviewed... He is rich by Chinese stand- ards.*

12 If you are **by yourself**, you are alone. EG *He was* PHRASE *standing by himself in a corner of the room.*

13 If you do something **by yourself**, you succeed in PHRASE doing it without anyone helping you. EG *She did not think she could manage by herself.*

14 In arithmetic, you use **by** before the second PREP number in a multiplication or division sum. EG *Twelve divided by three is four... Multiply it by three.*

15 You use **by** to talk about measurements of area. PREP For example, if a room is twenty feet **by** fourteen feet, it measures twenty feet in one direction and fourteen feet in the other direction.

16 Things that are made or sold **by** the million or PREP **by** the dozen are made or sold in those quantities. EG *Books can be mailed by the dozen.*

17 You use **by** to talk about things that happen PREP gradually, not all at once. EG *The university gets bigger year by year... The children had one by one fallen asleep.*

18 If something increases or decreases **by** a par- PREP ticular amount, that amount is gained or lost. EG *Its grant is to be cut by more than 40 per cent.*

19 If you hold someone or something **by** a particu- PREP lar part of them, you hold that part. EG *My mother took me firmly by the hand and led me downstairs.*

20 If someone is a particular type of person **by** PREP nature or **by** profession, they are that type of person because of their nature or their profession. EG *By trade he was a dealer in antique furniture.*

bye /baɪ/. **'Bye'** and **'bye-bye'** are informal ways CONVENTION of saying goodbye.

bye-law /baɪlɔː/. See **by-law.**

by-election, by-elections. A **by-election** is an N COUNT election that is held to choose a new member of parliament when a member has resigned or died.

bygone /baɪgɒn/, **bygones. 1** **Bygone** means hap- ADJ CLASSIF : pening or existing a very long time ago. EG *...em-* ATTRIB *pires established in bygone centuries.*

2 If you say to someone **'let bygones be bygones'**, PHRASE you are suggesting that you should both forget

about unpleasant things that have happened between you in the past.

by-law, by-laws; also spelled **bye-law. A by-law** N COUNT
is a law which is made by a local authority and
which applies only in their area.

bypass /ˈbaɪpɑːs/, **bypasses, bypassing, by-**
passed. 1 If you **bypass** someone in authority, you V+O
avoid asking their permission to do something. EG
*This is what happens when the worker by-passes
his foreman.*
2 If you **bypass** a difficulty, you avoid discussing it V+O
or getting involved in it. EG *It's no good trying to
bypass the issue.*
3 A **bypass** is a main road which takes traffic N COUNT
round the edge of a town rather than through its
centre. EG ...*the Oxford bypass.*
4 If you **bypass** a place, you go round it rather V+O
than through it. EG *We drove through Kilmarnock
but bypassed Ayr.*
5 A **bypass** operation is a surgical heart operation N MOD
in which the flow of blood is redirected so that it
does not flow through a part of the heart which is
diseased or blocked.

by-product, by-products. 1 A **by-product** is N COUNT :
something which is made during the manufacture USU+SUPP

or processing of another product. EG *Oxygen is
released as a by-product of the photosynthesis.*
2 A **by-product** of an event or situation is some- N COUNT :
thing that happens as a result of it, especially USU+SUPP
something that was not expected or planned. EG
*They see truancy as a by-product of compulsory
education.*

bystander /ˈbaɪstændə/, **bystanders.** A **by-** N COUNT
stander is a person who is present when something happens and who sees it but does not take
part in it. EG ...*curious bystanders watching from a
distance.*

byte /baɪt/, **bytes.** A **byte** is a unit of storage in a N COUNT
computer. Technical

byway /ˈbaɪweɪ/, **byways.** A **byway** is a small N COUNT :
road which is not used by many cars or people. USU PLURAL

byword /ˈbaɪwɜːd/, **bywords. 1** Someone or some- N COUNT+*for*
thing that is a **byword** for a particular quality is
well known for having that quality. EG *The department had become a byword for ignorance, obstinacy and brutality.*
2 A **byword** is a word or phrase which people N COUNT
often use. EG *Internal redesign has become a byword in Washington.*

C c

C, c /siː/, **C's, c's. 1** C is the third letter of the N COUNT
English alphabet.
2 C is an abbreviation for 'century' or 'centuries'.
You put 'C' before or after a number which refers
to a particular century. EG ...*living in the C14... ...the
14th C.*
3 c. is written in front of a date or number to
indicate that it is approximate. EG *He was born c.
834 A.D.*
4 C is also an abbreviation for 'centigrade'.

C stands for **complement**
Verbs which have the label +C in the Extra Column
are verbs which have a complement.
See the entry headed COMPLEMENTS for more information.

---

cab /kæb/, **cabs. 1** A **cab** is a taxi. EG *Morris* N COUNT
hurried off eagerly to get a cab. OR *by*+N
2 The **cab** of a lorry is the front part in which the N COUNT
driver sits.

cabaret /ˈkæbəreɪ/, **cabarets.** A **cabaret** is a N COUNT OR N
show that is performed in a restaurant or night- UNCOUNT
club, and that consists of dancing, singing, or
comedy acts. EG *The cabaret was just finishing... ...a
cabaret artiste.*

cabbage /ˈkæbɪdʒ/, **cabbages.** A **cabbage** is a N COUNT OR
vegetable which looks like a large ball of green N UNCOUNT
leaves.

cabin /ˈkæbɪn/, **cabins.** A **cabin** is **1** a small room N COUNT
in a ship or boat. **2** one of the areas inside a plane.
EG ...*the First Class cabin.* **3** a small wooden house.

cabinet /ˈkæbɪˈnɪt/, **cabinets. 1** A **cabinet** is a N COUNT
cupboard used for storing things such as medicine
or alcoholic drinks. EG ...*a cocktail cabinet... ...a
glass cabinet with Chinese things in it.* ● See also
filing cabinet.
2 The **Cabinet** is a group of the most senior N COLL:*the*+N
ministers in a government, who meet regularly to
decide policies. EG ...*a former cabinet minister.*

cable /ˈkeɪbəl/, **cables.** A **cable** is **1** a very strong, N COUNT
thick rope. EG ...*the suspension cables of the bridge.*
2 a bundle of wires inside a rubber or plastic N UNCOUNT
OR N COUNT

covering, along which electricity flows. EG ...*ten
metres of electrical cable.*

cable car, cable cars. A **cable car** is a cabin N COUNT
suspended from a wire, pulled by a moving cable. OR *by*+N
It is used to take passengers up mountains.

cable television is a television system in which N UNCOUNT
signals are sent along wires, rather than by radio
waves.

cache /kæʃ/, **caches.** A **cache** is a quantity of N COUNT
things, for example weapons or drugs, that have
been hidden. EG ...*an arms cache.*

cackle /ˈkækəl/, **cackles, cackling, cackled.** If V OR V+QUOT
you **cackle**, you laugh in a loud unpleasant way. EG
She cackled with delight... 'Fools!' she cackled.
▶ used as a noun. EG *He gave a malicious cackle.* ▶ N COUNT

cacophony /kəˈkɒfənɪ/. A **cacophony** is a loud, N SING
unpleasant noise that consists of a lot of different Formal
sounds together. EG ...*a cacophony of squeaks and
rattles.*

cactus /ˈkæktəs/, **cactuses** or **cacti** /ˈkæktaɪ/. A N COUNT
cactus is a thick fleshy plant that grows in deserts.
Cacti have no leaves and many of them are covered in spikes.

cadaverous /kəˈdævəˈrəs/. Someone who is ca- ADJ QUALIT
daverous is extremely thin and pale. EG *He was Formal
tall and spare, with a cadaverous face.*

cadence /ˈkeɪdəˈns/, **cadences.** A **cadence** is the N COUNT
way your voice gets higher and lower as you speak. Formal
EG *His voice had an unfamiliar cadence.*

cadet /kəˈdet/, **cadets.** A **cadet** is a young man or N COUNT
woman who is being trained in the army, navy, air
force, or police.

cadge /kædʒ/, **cadges, cadging, cadged.** If you V OR V+O :
cadge food, money, or help from someone, you ask +*from/off*
them for it and succeed in getting it. EG *He only Informal
came to cadge free drinks... ...living by cadging off British
relatives and doing odd jobs.*

Caesarean /sɪˈzeəriən/, **Caesareans.** A **Caesar-** N COUNT
ean or a **Caesarean section** is an operation in
which a baby is lifted out of a woman's womb
through an opening cut in her abdomen.

café /ˈkæfeɪ/, **cafés.** A **café** is a place where you N COUNT
can buy drinks and light meals or snacks. In
Britain cafés do not serve alcoholic drinks.

cafeteria /ˌkæfɪˈtɪərɪə/, **cafeterias.** A **cafeteria** N COUNT
is a restaurant where you choose your food from a

counter and carry it to your table yourself after paying for it.

caffeine /kæfi:n/; also spelled **caffein. Caffeine** N UNCOUNT is a chemical substance found in coffee, tea, and cocoa, which makes your brain and body more active.

cage /keɪdʒ/, **cages.** A **cage** is a structure of wire N COUNT or metal bars in which birds or animals are kept.

caged /keɪdʒd/. A **caged** bird or animal is inside a ADJ CLASSIF cage.

cagey /keɪdʒiˈ/. When people are being **cagey,** ADJ QUALIT they are being careful not to give much information. EG *They were so cagey about Lucy and her new job.*

cagoule /kəgu:l/, **cagoules.** A **cagoule** is a water- N COUNT proof jacket that you wear over other clothes to prevent them getting wet.

cahoots /kəhu:ts/. If someone is **in cahoots with** PHRASE someone else, they are planning something with them; used showing disapproval. EG *Halliday was in cahoots with the person who was so handy with poison.*

cajole /kədʒəʊl/, **cajoles, cajoling, cajoled.** If V+O : USU+A you **cajole** someone into doing something, you Formal persuade them to do it by flattering or praising them. EG *McKinley and Sherman were cajoled into coming with us.*

cake /keɪk/, **cakes. 1** A **cake** is **1.1** a sweet food N COUNT OR N made by baking a mixture of flour, eggs, sugar, and UNCOUNT fat in an oven. EG *She cut the cake and gave me a piece... ...a slice of cake.* **1.2** a food that is formed N COUNT+SUPP into a flat, round shape before it is cooked. EG *...fish cakes.*

2 A **cake** of something such as soap or wax is a N PART OR small block of it. N COUNT

3 Cake is used in these phrases. **3.1** If you say that PHRASES something is **a piece of cake,** you mean that it is Informal very easy to do. **3.2** If things are **selling like hot cakes,** people are buying a lot of them. **3.3** If someone says that **you can't have your cake and eat it,** they mean that people cannot have both alternatives that are available, but will have to choose only one. **3.4 the icing on the cake:** see **icing.**

caked /keɪkt/. **1** If something is **caked,** it has ADJ CLASSIF changed from a thick liquid into a dry layer or lump. EG *He sat slumped forward, with dried blood caked in his hair.*

2 If a surface is **caked** with something such as ADJ PRED mud, it is covered with it. EG *...heavy farm shoes caked with mud.*

calamitous /kəlæmɪˈtəs/. Something that is **ca-** ADJ CLASSIF **lamitous** is very unfortunate indeed. EG *I'm always* Formal *expecting calamitous to happen.*

calamity /kəlæmɪˈtiˈ/, **calamities.** A **calamity** is N COUNT OR an event that causes a great deal of damage, N UNCOUNT destruction, or personal distress. EG *...the glee with* Formal *which the media report scientific calamities... ...the awareness of approaching calamity.*

calcium /kælsɪəm/ is a soft white element which N UNCOUNT is found in bones and teeth, and also in limestone, chalk, and marble.

calculate /kælkjəˈleɪt/, **calculates, calculating, calculated.** ̄I If you **calculate** a number or V+O OR V amount, you work it out by doing some arithmetic. EG *The number of votes cast will then be calculated... She was busy calculating.*

2 If you **calculate** the effects of something, you V+O OR think about its effects and form an opinion about V+REPORT them. EG *...actions whose consequences can in no way be calculated... She calculated that the risks were worth taking.*

3 If something **is calculated** to have a particular V-PASS+to-INF effect, it is specially done or arranged in order to have that effect. EG *I adopted a cool dignified attitude that was calculated to discourage familiarity.* ◊ **calculated.** EG *...the deliberate, calculated* ◊ ADJ QUALIT *use of violence.*

calculating /kælkjəˈleɪtɪŋ/. A person who is **cal-** ADJ QUALIT **culating** arranges situations and controls people in order to get what he or she wants; used showing disapproval. EG *...the most calculating and selfish men in the community.*

calculation /kælkjəˈleɪʃəˈn/, **calculations. 1** A N COUNT OR **calculation** is something that you think about and N UNCOUNT work out mathematically. EG *'How long will it take me?' I did a rapid calculation. 'About ten years,' I said... ...a technique for quick calculation.*

2 Calculation is behaviour in which someone N UNCOUNT thinks only of themselves and not of other people; Formal used showing disapproval. EG *His behaviour seems free of all calculation.*

calculator /kælkjəˈleɪtə/, **calculators.** A **calcu-** N COUNT **lator** is a small electronic device that you use for doing mathematical calculations.

calendar /kælɪˈndə/, **calendars. 1** A **calendar** is N COUNT a chart which shows a particular year divided up into months, weeks, and days, and shows what the date of each day is in that year. EG *He glanced up at the wall calendar – today was Thursday.*

2 A **calendar** month is one of the twelve named ADJ CLASSIF : periods of time that a year is divided into. A ATTRIB **calendar** year is a period of 365 days, or 366 days in a leap year. EG *It costs one hundred dollars per calendar month.*

3 A **calendar** is also **3.1** a system for dividing up N COUNT : time, which establishes year zero, numbers the USU SING+SUPP years, and arranges the days into months and years. EG *...the Muslim calendar.* **3.2** a list of dates within a particular year that are important for an organization or kind of activity. EG *...a major event in the theatrical calendar.*

calf /kɑ:f/, **calves** /kɑ:vz/. **1** A **calf** is a young N COUNT cow.

2 Some other young animals, including elephants, N COUNT giraffes, whales, and seals, are also called **calves.**

3 Your **calf** is the thick part at the back of your leg N COUNT between your ankle and your knee. See picture at THE HUMAN BODY.

calibre /kælɪbə/, **calibres;** spelled **caliber** in American English. **1** The **calibre** of a person is the N UNCOUNT quality or standard of their ability or intelligence, +SUPP especially when this is high. EG *...directors of the right calibre.*

2 The **calibre** of a gun is the width of the inside of N COUNT+SUPP its barrel. Technical

call /kɔ:l/, **calls, calling, called. 1** If someone or V+O+C something **is called** by a particular name, that is their name or title. EG *She had a boyfriend called David... ...a novel called 'Memoirs of a Survivor'... All his friends call him Jo.*

2 Call is used to refer to ways of describing things V+O+C or people by using a particular word or phrase. For example, if you call someone a liar, you say that they are a liar. EG *President Nixon called his opponents traitors... I wouldn't call it awful, but it wasn't very well written.*

3 If you **call** someone's name, you say it in a loud V+O, voice, because you are trying to attract their V+QUOTE, attention. EG *'Edward!' she called. 'Edward! Lunch* OR V+A *is ready!'... I could hear a voice calling my name... Children are as likely to call for their father as for their mother.*

4 If you **call** someone, **4.1** you telephone them. EG V+O OR V *He promised to call me soon... 'I want to speak to Mr Landy, please.' – 'Who is calling?'* **4.2** you ask V+O them to come to you by shouting to them or telephoning them. EG *The editor called me to his office to tell me the news... When Margaret collapsed, I called the doctor.*

5 When you make a phone **call,** you phone some- N COUNT one. EG *There have been two telephone calls for you.*

6 If you **call** something such as a meeting or a V+O rehearsal, you arrange for it to take place at a particular time. EG *He called a press conference to explain his proposals.*

7 If you **call** somewhere, you make a short visit v+A there. EG *We called at the Vicarage.*

8 If you pay a **call** on someone, you visit them N COUNT briefly. EG *We went to pay a call on some people I know... Doctors have no time these days to make regular calls.*

9 A **call** for something is a demand or desire for it N COUNT OR to be done or to be provided. EG *Labour MPs* N UNCOUNT *renewed their call for the abolition of the House of Lords... There is little call for his services.*

10 The **call** of a bird is the short sound that it N COUNT makes.

11 to **call** it a day: see **day**. ● to **call** a halt: see **halt**.

call for. 1 If you **call for** someone or something, PHRASAL VB : you go to the building where they are in order to V+PREP, collect them. EG *I'll call for you about eight... I* HAS PASS *called at the station for my luggage.* **2** If you **call** v+PREP, **for** something, you demand that it should happen. HAS PASS EG *The declaration called for an immediate cease-fire.* **3** If something **calls for** a particular action or v+PREP, quality, it needs it in order to be successful. EG HAS PASS *Controlling a class calls for all your skill as a teacher.*

call in. If you **call** someone **in**, you ask them to PHRASAL VB : come and help you or do something for you. EG *We* V+O+ADV *called in the police.*

call off. If you **call off** an event that has been PHRASAL VB : planned, you cancel it. EG *We had to decide wheth-* V+O+ADV *er classes should be called off.*

call on or **call upon. 1** If you **call on** someone to PHRASAL VB : do something or **call upon** them to do it, you V+PREP appeal to them to do it. EG *The Opposition called on the Prime Minister to stop the arms deal.* **2** If you v+PREP **call on** someone, you pay them a short visit.

call out. 1 If you **call** something **out**, you shout it. PHRASAL VB : EG *The driver didn't stop or even call out thank* V-SPEECH+ADV *you... 'Where shall I put them?' I called out... She* OR V+ADV *turned into the yard, calling out to the porter that she'd arrived.* **2** If you **call** someone **out**, you order v+O+ADV *them to come to help, especially in an emergency.* EG *The National Guard has been called out.*

call up. 1 If you **call** someone **up**, you telephone PHRASAL VB : them. EG *Many of my friends called me up to* V+O+ADV *congratulate me.* **2** If someone is **called up**, they v+O+ADV are ordered to join the army, navy, or air force. EG *I was lucky not to be called up at the time.*

call upon. See **call on**.

call box, call boxes. A **call box** is a telephone N COUNT box.

caller /kɔːlə/, **callers.** A **caller** is **1** a person who N COUNT comes to see you for a short visit. EG *I had a lot of callers when I came home from hospital.* **2** a person who is making a telephone call. EG *The telephone rang and the caller asked to speak to my mother.*

call girl, call girls. A **call girl** is a prostitute who N COUNT makes appointments by telephone.

calling /kɔːlɪŋ/, **callings.** A **calling** is a profes- N COUNT sion or career, especially one which involves help-ing other people. EG *Teaching is said to be a worthwhile calling.*

callous /kæləs/. Someone who is **callous** is very ADJ QUALIT cruel and shows no concern for other people's feelings. EG *She was selfish, arrogant and often callous... ...a shocking act of callous irresponsibility.*

calm /kɑːm/, **calmer, calmest; calms, calming, calmed. 1** Someone who is **calm** does not show ADJ QUALIT any worry or excitement. EG *Gary was a calm and reasonable man... Sit down and keep calm... Her voice was calm.* ◊ **calmly.** EG *She calmly wiped* ◊ ADV *the blood away with her hand.* ◊ **calmness.** EG A ◊ N UNCOUNT *great sense of calmness began to settle upon her.*

2 Calm is a state of quietness and peacefulness. EG N UNCOUNT *...the peace of the countryside, the calm of the vicarage.*

3 A sea or lake that is **calm** does not have any big ADJ QUALIT waves. EG *He was not afraid, for the water was calm.*

4 Weather that is **calm** is very still without any ADJ QUALIT wind. EG *It was a calm, sunny evening.*

5 If you **calm** someone or **calm** their fears, you do v+O OR V-REF something to make them less upset, less worried, or less excited. EG *Mitchell tried to calm her, but she didn't hear him... To calm himself he walked over to the window.*

calm down. If you **calm down** or if someone PHRASAL VB : **calms** you **down**, you become less upset, excited, V-ERG+ADV or lively. EG *'Please, Mrs Kinter,' said Brody. 'Calm down. Let me explain.'... An officer tried to calm them down but had no success.*

Calor gas /kælə gæs/ is gas that is sold in N UNCOUNT portable metal containers. You can use it for Trademark cooking and heating. EG *...a little Calor gas stove.*

calorie /kæləri/, **calories.** A **calorie** is a unit of N COUNT measurement for the energy value of food. EG *He was put on a diet of only 1,700 calories a day.*

calve /kɑːv/, **calves, calving, calved. 1** When a v cow **calves**, it gives birth to a calf.

2 Calves is the plural of **calf**.

camaraderie /kæmərɑːdəri/ is a feeling of trust N UNCOUNT and friendship among a group of people. EG *There was a camaraderie between the girls.*

came /keɪm/ is the past tense of **come**.

camel /kæməl/, **camels.** A **camel** is a large N COUNT animal that lives in deserts. Camels have long necks and one or two humps on their backs.

cameo /kæmɪəʊ/, **cameos. 1** A **cameo** is a short N COUNT description or piece of acting which expresses cleverly and neatly the nature of a situation, event, or person's character. EG *She has starred in several small but delightful cameo parts... He gave cameos of debates with exquisite touches of irony.*

2 A **cameo** is also a piece of jewellery, usually oval N COUNT in shape, consisting of a raised stone figure or design fixed on to a flat stone of another colour.

camera /kæmərə/, **cameras.** A **camera** is a N COUNT piece of equipment that is used for taking photo-graphs, making films, or producing television pic-tures. EG *I took a camera and photographed some of the buildings... The press and television cameras were gathered.*

cameraman /kæmərəmæn/, **cameramen.** A N COUNT **cameraman** is a person who operates a camera for television or film making.

camouflage /kæməflɑːʒ/, **camouflages, camou-flaging, camouflaged. 1 Camouflage** consists of N UNCOUNT things such as leaves, branches, or brown and green paint, which are used to make it difficult for an enemy to see military forces and equipment. ▸ used as a verb. EG *The gun crews were in* ▸ V+O *camouflaged bunkers at the end of the beach.*

2 Camouflage is also the way in which some N UNCOUNT animals are coloured and shaped to blend in with their natural surroundings. EG *The snake's skin has the colours and patterns necessary for perfect camouflage.*

camp /kæmp/, **camps, camping, camped. 1** A N COUNT OR **camp** is a place where people live in tents or stay N UNCOUNT in tents on holiday. EG *The camp had a beautiful view of the mountains... We set up camp near the bay.*

2 If you **camp** somewhere, you stay or live there v : USU+A for a short time in a tent or a caravan. EG *That night I camped in the hills.* ◊ **camping.** EG *I don't* ◊ N UNCOUNT *like camping at all... ...camping equipment.*

3 A **camp** is also a collection of huts and other N COUNT buildings that has been specially built for people such as soldiers, refugees, or prisoners. EG *Three fifths of the refugees in the camp were starving.*

4 You can also use **camp** to refer to a group of N COUNT+SUPP people who all support a particular idea, person, or belief. EG *The realignment produced two clear-cut camps, reformists and reactionaries.*

Name three callings.

cameras

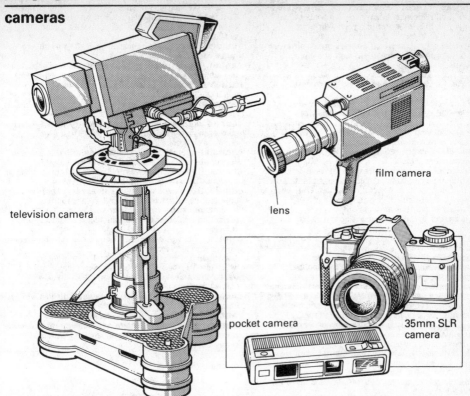

television camera

film camera

lens

pocket camera

35mm SLR camera

---

camp out. If you **camp out**, you sleep outdoors in a tent.   *PHRASAL VB : V+ADV*

campaign /kæmpeɪn/, **campaigns, campaigning, campaigned. 1** A **campaign** is a planned set of activities that people carry out over a period of time, in order to achieve something such as social or political change. *EG ...Labour's election campaign... ...the campaign against world hunger.* ▸ used as a verb. *EG He campaigned for political reform.* ◊ **campaigner, campaigners.** *EG ...anti-apartheid campaigners.*   *N COUNT*   *▸ V+A*   *◊ N COUNT*

2 In a war, a **campaign** is a series of planned movements carried out by armed forces. *EG ...bombing campaigns.*   *N COUNT*

camp bed, camp beds. A **camp bed** is a small bed that you can fold up.   *N COUNT*

camper /kæmpə/, **campers.** A **camper** is **1** a person who goes camping. *EG ...equipment for hunters, campers and fishermen.* **2** a van which is equipped with beds and cooking equipment so that you can live, cook, and sleep in it.   *N COUNT*

campsite /kæmpsaɪt/, **campsites.** A **campsite** is a place where people who are on holiday can stay in tents.   *N COUNT*

campus /kæmpəs/, **campuses.** A **campus** is the area of land that contains the main buildings of a university. *EG ...the university campus... How many students live on campus?*   *N COUNT OR N UNCOUNT*

can, cans, canning, canned. In paragraphs 1 to 5, **can** is pronounced /kæn/ or /kən/; in paragraphs 6 and 7, it is always pronounced /kæn/. The form **canned** is used as the past tense and past participle of the verb in paragraph 7. **Could** is sometimes considered to be the past form of the modal **can**, but in this dictionary the two words are dealt with separately. See **could.**

1 If you **can** do something, **1.1** it is possible for you *MODAL*

to do it. *EG Anybody can become a qualified teacher... Many elderly people cannot afford telephones... 'Will you stay for lunch?' – 'I can't,' the colonel said.* **1.2** you have the skill or ability to do it. *EG Some people can ski better than others... My wife can't sew.* **1.3** you are allowed to do it. Some speakers of English think that it is incorrect to use 'can' instead of 'may' with this meaning. *EG You can borrow that pen if you want to... Can I speak to Nicky please?*

2 You ask someone if they **can** do something as a polite way of asking them to do it. *EG Can you tell me the time?... Can you do me a favour?*   *MODAL*

3 You say that someone **cannot** do something as a way of saying that they should not do it. *EG We can't stop now. We've got to keep on struggling... A secretary can hardly be regarded as a status symbol.*   *MODAL WITH BROAD NEG*

4 If you say to someone **can't you** do something, you are suggesting that they do it or asking them to do it. *EG Can't we talk about it?... For goodness sake! Can't you keep your voice down?*   *MODAL+not*

5 If you say that something **cannot** be true or **cannot** happen, you mean that you feel sure that it is not true or will not happen. *EG This cannot be the whole story... The repression can't last... He can hardly have read the report with much care... He can't have said that. He just can't.*   *MODAL WITH BROAD NEG*

6 A **can** is a metal container in which something such as food, drink, or paint is put. The container is usually sealed to keep the contents fresh. *EG ...cans of beans... ...beer cans.*   *N COUNT*

7 When food or drink **is canned**, it is put into a metal container and sealed so that it will remain fresh. ◊ **canned.** *EG ...canned beer.*   *V+O*   *◊ ADJ CLASSIF*

8 See also **canned.**

canal /kənæl/, **canals.** A **canal** is a long, narrow N COUNT stretch of water that has been made for boats to travel along or to bring water to a particular area. EG ...the canals of Venice... ...irrigation canals.

canary /kəneəri¹/, **canaries. Canaries** are small N COUNT yellow birds which sing beautifully and are often kept as pets.

can-can /kæn kæn/. The **can-can** is a dance in N SING which women kick their legs in the air to fast music.

cancel /kænsəl/, **cancels, cancelling, can-celled;** spelled **canceling, canceled** in American English. **1** If you **cancel** something that has been V+O arranged, you stop it from happening. EG The performances were cancelled because the leading man was ill. ◊ **cancellation** /kænsə¹leɪʃə⁰n/. EG ◊ N UNCOUNT ...the cancellation of the tour.
2 If you **cancel** something such as a hotel room or V+O a seat at the theatre, you tell the management that you no longer want it. ◊ **cancellation, cancella-** ◊ N COUNT **tions.** EG ...a cancellation charge... I've had two cancellations already this morning.
3 If you **cancel** a cheque or a business arrange- V+O ment, you cause it to be no longer valid.

cancel out. If two things **cancel** each other **out,** PHRASAL VB : they have opposite effects, so that when they are V+O+ADV combined no real effect is produced. EG The one effect tends to cancel the other out... These politi-cal factions cancelled each other out.

cancer /kænsə/, **cancers. Cancer** is a serious N UNCOUNT disease in which cells in a person's body increase OR N COUNT rapidly in an uncontrolled way, producing abnor-mal growths. EG He had cancer of the throat... Nicholas was dying of lung cancer... Most cancers are preventable. ◊ **cancerous** /kænsərəs/. EG ◊ ADJ CLASSIF ...cancerous cells in the blood.

candid /kændɪd/. When you are **candid** with ADJ QUALIT someone, you speak honestly to them. EG I was entirely candid with him... ...a candid smile.
◊ **candidly.** EG Charlie got him to talk candidly ◊ ADV about his life.

candidacy /kændɪdəsi¹/. Someone's **candidacy** is N UNCOUNT their position of being a candidate in an election. EG +SUPP He had already formally announced his candidacy.

candidate /kændɪdeɪt, -də¹t/, **candidates.** A **can-** N COUNT **didate** is **1** someone who is being considered for a position, for example in an election or for a job. EG ...a parliamentary candidate... We're prepared to take candidates from any academic discipline. **2** someone who is taking an examination. EG Sixty per cent of the candidates failed their examinations. **3** a person or thing that is regarded as being suitable for a particular purpose. EG Small companies are likely candidates for take-over.

candle /kændə⁰l/, **candles.** A **candle** is a stick of N COUNT hard wax with a piece of string called a wick through the middle. You light the wick in order to give a steady flame that provides light. EG I blew out my candle and went to sleep.

candlelight /kændə⁰llaɪt/ is the light that a can- N UNCOUNT dle produces. EG She was reading by candlelight.

candlelit /kændə⁰llɪt/. A room or table that is ADJ CLASSIF **candlelit** is lit by the light of candles. EG ...a little candlelit restaurant.

candlestick /kændə⁰lstɪk/, **candlesticks.** A N COUNT **candlestick** is a narrow object with a hole at the top which holds a candle.

candour /kændə/; spelled **candor** in American N UNCOUNT English. **Candour** is the quality of speaking honest-ly and openly about things. EG They were talking of personal matters with unusual candour.

candy /kændi¹/, **candies.** A **candy** is a sweet. EG N COUNT OR There was a bowl of candies on his desk... You eat N UNCOUNT too much candy. It's bad for your teeth. American

cane /keɪn/, **canes, caning, caned. 1** Cane is **1.1** N UNCOUNT the long, hollow stems of a plant such as bamboo. EG ...sugar cane. **1.2** strips of cane that are used for weaving things such as baskets or chairs. EG ...cane chairs.

2 A **cane** is a long narrow stick. N COUNT
3 At school, when children used to be given the N SING : the+N **cane,** they were punished by being hit with a cane. EG I got the cane for smoking.
4 If a child **was caned** at school, he or she was hit V+O with a cane as a punishment.

canine /keɪnaɪn, kæn-/ means relating to dogs or ADJ CLASSIF : resembling a dog. ATTRIB

canister /kænɪstə/, **canisters.** A **canister** is a N COUNT metal container. EG ...a canister of shaving cream. OR N PART

cannabis /kænəbɪs/ is a drug which some people N UNCOUNT smoke. Cannabis is illegal in many countries.

canned /kænd/. **Canned** music, laughter, or ap- ADJ CLASSIF plause on a television or radio show has been recorded beforehand. ● See also **can.**

cannibal /kænɪbə⁰l/, **cannibals.** A **cannibal** is a N COUNT person who eats the flesh of other human beings.

cannibalism /kænɪbəlɪzə⁰m/. People who prac- N UNCOUNT tise **cannibalism** eat the flesh of other people.

cannibalize /kænɪbəlaɪz/, **cannibalizes, canni-** V+O **balizing, cannibalized;** also spelled **cannibalise.** If you **cannibalize** a machine or vehicle, you take parts from it in order to repair another machine or vehicle.

cannon /kænən/, **cannons. Cannon** can also be N COUNT used as the plural form.
A **cannon** is **1** a large gun, usually on wheels, which used to be used in battles. See picture at WEAPONS. **2** a heavy automatic gun, especially one that is fired from an aircraft.

cannon ball, cannon balls. A **cannon ball** is a N COUNT heavy metal ball that was fired from a cannon.

cannot /kænɒt, kænɒt/ means 'can not': see **can.**

canny /kæni¹/, **cannier, canniest.** Someone who ADJ QUALIT is **canny** is clever and able to think quickly. EG ...a canny smile.

canoe

canoe /kənuː/, **canoes.** A **canoe** is a small, narrow N COUNT boat that you row using a paddle.

canoeing /kənuːɪŋ/ is the sport of racing and N ING performing tests of skill in canoes. EG ...facilities for rock climbing, sailing, and canoeing.

canon /kænən/, **canons. 1** A **canon** is a member N COUNT of the clergy who is on the staff of a cathedral.
2 A **canon** is also a general rule or principle. EG N COUNT+SUPP ...the traditional canons of literary and artistic Formal judgement.

canonize /kænənaɪz/, **canonizes, canonizing,** V+O : USU PASS **canonized;** also spelled **canonise.** If a dead per-son **is canonized,** it is officially announced that he or she is a saint; used especially in the Catholic Church. EG Two years after his death the bishop was canonised.

canopy /kænəpi¹/, **canopies.** A **canopy** is **1** a N COUNT decorated cover, often made of cloth, which is placed above something such as a bed or a throne. EG There was a large bed with a silk canopy over it.
2 a layer of something that spreads out and covers N COUNT+SUPP

If you can can-can, what can you do?

an area, for example the branches and leaves that spread out at the top of trees in a forest. EG *The leaves created a dense canopy that cut out much of the light.*

can't /kɑːnt/ is the usual spoken form of 'cannot'.

cantankerous /kəˈntæŋkərəs/. Someone who is **cantankerous** is always finding things to argue or complain about. EG *Their boredom made them quarrelsome and cantankerous.* ADJ QUALIT Formal

canteen /kænˈtiːn/, **canteens**. A **canteen** is a place in a factory or other place of work where the people who work there can eat. EG *I had a cup of tea in the canteen.* N COUNT

canter /ˈkæntə/, **canters, cantering, cantered**. When a horse **canters**, it moves at a speed that is slower than a gallop but faster than a trot. ▶ used as a noun. EG *It broke into an easy canter.* V ▶ N COUNT

canvas /ˈkænvəs/, **canvases**. 1 **Canvas** is strong, heavy cloth. It is used for making things such as tents, sails, and bags. N UNCOUNT
2 If you are living and sleeping **under canvas**, you are living and sleeping in a tent. PHRASE
3 A **canvas** is 3.1 a piece of canvas or similar material on which an oil painting can be done. EG *...oil paintings on canvas.* 3.2 a painting that is done on canvas. EG *...the canvases of Hieronymus Bosch.* N COUNT OR N UNCOUNT / N COUNT

canvass /ˈkænvəs/, **canvasses, canvassing, canvassed**. 1 If you **canvass** for a particular person or political party, you go round an area trying to persuade people to vote for that person or party. EG *He had canvassed for Mr Foot in the leadership election.* ◇ **canvassing**. EG *...house-to-house canvassing.* V : USU + A ◇ N UNCOUNT
2 If you **canvass** public opinion, you find out how people feel about a particular subject by asking them. V + O

canyon /ˈkænjən/, **canyons**. A **canyon** is a long, narrow valley with very steep sides. EG *The cold wind sweeps down the canyon.* N COUNT

cap

cap /kæp/, **caps, capping, capped**. 1 A **cap** is 1.1 a soft, flat hat which is usually worn by men or boys. EG *On his head he wore a brown cloth cap.* 1.2 a special hat which is worn as part of a uniform. EG *...my school cap.* 1.3 a small flat lid on a bottle or container. EG *Brody grabbed the bottle, twisted off the cap, and sniffed.* 1.4 a contraceptive device consisting of a small round object that a woman places inside her vagina. N COUNT
2 If you go to someone **cap in hand**, you go to them very humbly, because you are asking them for something. EG *It's bad enough having to go cap in hand to ask for a rise.* PHRASE Informal
3 If you **cap** one thing with another, you put the second thing on top of the first thing. EG *...sweets coated with chocolate and capped with a cherry.* V + O + with
4 If you **cap** an action, you do something that is better or more exciting. EG *He capped his performance by telling the funniest joke I have ever heard.* V + O
5 A **cap** is also a small amount of explosive that is wrapped in paper. Caps are often used in toy guns. N COUNT

capability /ˌkeɪpəˈbɪlɪti/, **capabilities**. 1 If you have the **capability** or the **capabilities** to do N UNCOUNT + SUPP OR N COUNT

something, you have the ability or the qualities that are necessary to do it. EG *The work may be beyond his capability or endurance... She may worry about her capabilities as a parent.*
2 A country's military **capability** is its ability to fight in a war. EG *The French nuclear capability might never be used.* N UNCOUNT

capable /ˈkeɪpəbəl/. 1 If a person or thing is **capable** of doing something, they have the ability to do it. EG *...a man capable of killing the President... ...a mind capable of original ideas.* ADJ PRED + of
2 Someone who is **capable** has the skill or qualities necessary to do a particular thing well. EG *Basil proved a capable cricketer... She was extremely capable and dependable.* ◇ **capably**. EG *...a capably performed dance.* ADJ QUALIT ◇ ADV

capacious /kəˈpeɪʃəs/. Something that is **capacious** has a lot of space to put things in. EG *...her capacious pockets.* ADJ QUALIT

capacity /kəˈpæsɪti/, **capacities**. 1 The **capacity** of something is the largest amount that it can hold, produce, or carry. EG *The pipeline has a capacity of 1.2m barrels a day.* ● If something is filled **to capacity**, it is as full as it can possibly be. EG *The ship set sail with her hold filled to capacity.* N UNCOUNT + SUPP ● PHRASE
2 A **capacity** crowd or audience completely fills a theatre, sports ground, or other place. N MOD
3 The **capacity** of a person, society, or system is the power or ability that they have to do a particular thing. EG *This society demands of everyone the capacity to read and write... People have different capacities for learning.* N COUNT + SUPP
4 Someone's **capacity** for food or drink is the amount that they can eat or drink. EG *His capacity for brandy was phenomenal.* N UNCOUNT + SUPP
5 If you say that someone does something **in a** particular **capacity**, you mean that they do it as part of their duties. EG *I was involved in an advisory capacity.* PHRASE
6 **Capacity** in a factory or industry is the quantity of things that can be produced. EG *We need to raise productivity and expand capacity.* N UNCOUNT Technical

cape /keɪp/, **capes**. A **cape** is 1 a large piece of land that sticks out into the sea from the coast. EG *...Cape Horn.* 2 a short cloak. EG *Waving a red cape, Delgado provoked the bull to charge.* N COUNT

caper /ˈkeɪpə/, **capers, capering, capered**. 1 **Capers** are the flower buds of a type of bush, which are pickled and used to season food. EG *...wild duck in caper sauce.* N COUNT : USU PLURAL
2 If you **caper** about, you dance or leap about energetically. EG *The little girl capered towards Bill.* V : USU + A
3 A **caper** is a light-hearted practical joke or trick. N COUNT

capillary /kəˈpɪləri/, **capillaries**. Capillaries are tiny blood vessels in your body. N COUNT

capital /ˈkæpɪtəl/, **capitals**. 1 **Capital** is a large sum of money which you use to start or expand a business, or which you invest in order to make more money. EG *He gained overall control by putting up most of the capital.* N UNCOUNT
2 **Capital** investment or expenditure is money which is spent on equipment and buildings in a business or industry. EG *...substantial increases in capital expenditure on telephone exchanges.* N MOD
3 If you **make capital of** or **out of** a situation, you use the situation to gain some advantage for yourself. EG *At the time much political capital was made of the intention to increase top people's salaries.* PHRASE Formal
4 The **capital** of a country is the city or town where its government or parliament is. N COUNT
5 The **capital** of a particular industry, product, or activity is the place which is most famous for it. EG *...the peach capital of America... Rome was, I suppose, the capital of the art world.* N COUNT + SUPP
6 A **capital** or a **capital** letter is the written form of a letter which is used at the beginning of a sentence or a name. 'T', 'B', and 'F' are capital letters. N COUNT

car

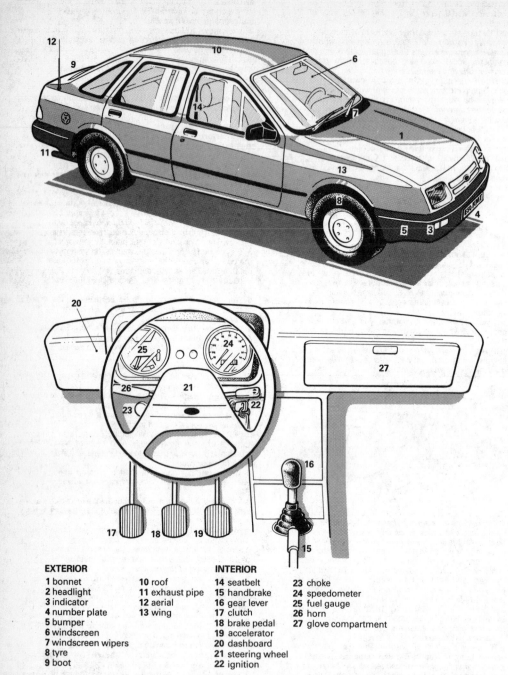

EXTERIOR

1 bonnet	**10** roof
2 headlight	**11** exhaust pipe
3 indicator	**12** aerial
4 number plate	**13** wing
5 bumper	
6 windscreen	
7 windscreen wipers	
8 tyre	
9 boot	

INTERIOR

14 seatbelt	**23** choke
15 handbrake	**24** speedometer
16 gear lever	**25** fuel gauge
17 clutch	**26** horn
18 brake pedal	**27** glove compartment
19 accelerator	
20 dashboard	
21 steering wheel	
22 ignition	

7 A **capital** offence is one that is so serious that the ADJ CLASSIF: person who commits it can be punished by death. ATTRIB EG ...the capital offence of murder.

capitalise /ˈkæpɪtəlaɪz/. See **capitalize**.

capitalism /ˈkæpɪtəlɪzm/ is an economic and po- N UNCOUNT litical system in which property, business, and industry are owned by private individuals and not by the state. EG ...modern industrial capitalism.

capitalist /ˈkæpɪtəlɪst/, **capitalists**. **1** A **capital-** ADJ CLASSIF **ist** country or society is one which supports capitalism. EG ...the enormous strength and influence of capitalist America... ...capitalist societies. **2** A **capitalist** system or economy is based on the ADJ CLASSIF principles of capitalism. EG Japan successfully built up a modern capitalist economy. **3** A **capitalist** is **3.1** someone who believes in and N COUNT supports the principles of capitalism. **3.2** someone who owns a business. EG Capitalists are encouraged to put their wealth into new industries.

capitalistic /ˌkæpɪtəlˈɪstɪk/ means supporting or ADJ CLASSIF based on the principles of capitalism; often used showing disapproval. EG ...the economic crisis in the capitalistic world.

capitalize /ˈkæpɪtəlaɪz/, **capitalizes**, **capitaliz-** V: OFT **ing**, **capitalized**; also spelled **capitalise**. If you +on/upon **capitalize** on a situation, you try to gain some advantage for yourself. EG Mr Healey has been capitalising on the anxiety expressed throughout the House.

capital punishment is punishment which in- N UNCOUNT volves the legal killing of a person who has committed a serious crime such as murder.

capitulate /kəˈpɪtjʊleɪt/, **capitulates**, **capitulat-** V: OFT+to **ing**, **capitulated**. If you **capitulate**, you stop resisting and do what someone else wants you to do. EG Economic pressures finally forced the Government to capitulate to our demands. ◊ **capitulation** /kəˌpɪtjʊˈleɪʃəⁿn/. EG ...the capitula- ◊ N UNCOUNT tion of the city without a struggle.

caprice /kəˈpriːs/, **caprices**. A **caprice** is an N COUNT OR unexpected action or decision which has no strong N UNCOUNT reason or purpose. EG Newspapers became subject Formal to the whims and caprices of their owners... His drawings could be hideous or comical according to caprice.

capricious /kəˈprɪʃəs/. **1** Someone who is **capri-** ADJ QUALIT **cious** often changes their mind unexpectedly. EG Authoritarian rulers are typically capricious. **2** Something that is **capricious** often changes ADJ QUALIT unexpectedly. EG ...a capricious postal system... ...a capricious summer breeze.

capsize /kæpˈsaɪz/, **capsizes**, **capsizing**, **cap-** V-ERG **sized**. If you **capsize** a boat or if it **capsizes**, it turns upside down in the water. EG Ships capsize when struck by these waves... ...a capsized boat.

capsule /ˈkæpsjuːl/, **capsules**. A **capsule** is **1** a N COUNT very small, round container with powdered medicine in it, which you swallow. **2** a small strong container used for storing or carrying things. **3** the part of a spacecraft in which people travel and in which they return to earth.

captain /ˈkæptɪn/, **captains**, **captaining**, **cap-** **tained**. **1** The **captain** of a ship is the officer in N COUNT charge of it. EG ...the captain of a battleship. **2** In the army, a **captain** is an officer of middle N COUNT rank. **3** The **captain** of an aeroplane is its pilot. N COUNT **4** The **captain** of a sports team is its leader. N COUNT **5** If you **captain** a group or team of people, you are V+O their leader. EG Willis is probably the best player to have captained England.

caption /ˈkæpʃəⁿn/, **captions**. A **caption** is the N COUNT words printed underneath a picture or cartoon which explain what it is about. EG Underneath was a caption that said: 'The greatest power on this earth'.

captivate /ˈkæptɪveɪt/, **captivates**, **captivating**, V+O **captivated**. If you **are captivated** by someone or something, you find them fascinating and attrac-

tive. EG At eighteen he had been captivated by a charming brunette. ◊ **captivating**. EG Roosevelt ◊ ADJ QUALIT was a captivating speaker.

captive /ˈkæptɪv/, **captives**. **1** A **captive** is a N COUNT prisoner. EG The troops took the women and chil- Literary dren as captives. ▶ used as an adjective. EG ...a ▶ ADJ CLASSIF wounded captive bird. **2** If you **take** someone **captive**, you take them as a PHRASE prisoner. EG Nine Indians were taken captive. **3** A **captive audience** is a group of people who PHRASE cannot leave a place and so have to watch or listen to someone. EG Give him a captive audience, and he can sell anything.

captivity /kæpˈtɪvɪtⁱ/ is the state of being kept as N UNCOUNT a captive. EG ...wild birds raised in captivity.

capture /ˈkæptʃəⁿ/, **captures**, **capturing**, **cap-** **tured**. **1** If you **capture** someone, you take them V+O prisoner, especially in a war or after a struggle. EG They had been captured and thrown in chains. ▶ used as a noun. EG He hadn't eaten anything since ▶ N UNCOUNT: the night before his capture. USU+POSS **2** When military forces **capture** a town or a V+O country, they take control of it by force. EG The city took 24 days to capture. ▶ used as a noun. EG ...the ▶ N UNCOUNT capture of the city. +SUPP **3** If you **capture** an animal, you catch it. V+O **4** To **capture** something also means to gain con- V+O trol of it. EG In August, overseas firms captured almost 41 per cent of the market. **5** If someone **captures** something such as the V+O atmosphere or quality of something, they represent it successfully in pictures, music, or words. EG With his camera he tried to capture changes as they took place before his eyes.

car /kɑː/, **cars**. **1** A **car** is a motor vehicle with N COUNT room for a small number of passengers. EG He OR by+N parked the car about a hundred yards from the gates... They usually go by car. **2** In America, a **car** is also a railway carriage. N COUNT **3** In Britain, railway carriages are called **cars** N COUNT+SUPP when they are used for a particular purpose. EG ...passengers in the dining car. **4** See also **cable car**.

carafe /kəˈræf, -ˈrɑːf/, **carafes**. A **carafe** is a glass N COUNT container in which you serve water or wine. EG ...a OR N PART carafe of house wine.

caramel /ˈkærəməⁿl, -meⁿl/, **caramels**. **1** A **cara-** N COUNT **mel** is a chewy sweet made from sugar, butter, and milk. **2 Caramel** is burnt sugar used for colouring and N UNCOUNT flavouring food.

carat /ˈkærət/, **carats**. A **carat** is **1** a unit for N COUNT measuring the weight of diamonds and other precious stones. It is equal to 0.2 grams. **2** a unit for measuring the purity of gold. The purest gold is 24-carat gold.

caravan /ˈkærəvæn/, **caravans**. A **caravan** is **1** a N COUNT vehicle with beds and other equipment inside, in which people live or spend their holidays. Caravans are usually pulled by a car. EG He went on a caravan holiday. **2** a group of people and animals who travel together in places such as deserts. EG Once we were part of a caravan of twelve thousand camels.

caravanning /ˈkærəvænɪŋ/ is the activity of hav- N ING ing a holiday in a caravan. EG We went caravanning in North Wales.

carbohydrate /ˌkɑːbəʊˈhaɪdreɪt/, **carbohydrates**. N UNCOUNT **Carbohydrate** is a substance found in food such as OR N COUNT sugar and bread, that gives you energy. EG Most fish are free from carbohydrate... ...our diet, with its high intake of carbohydrates and fat.

carbon /ˈkɑːbəⁿn/ is a chemical element that dia- N UNCOUNT monds and coal are made of. All living things contain carbon.

carbon copy, **carbon copies**. A **carbon copy** is N COUNT a copy of a piece of writing that is made using carbon paper. EG I kept a carbon copy of my letter.

carbon dioxide /kɑːbən daɪɒksaɪd/ is a gas. N UNCOUNT
Animals and people breathe out carbon dioxide.

carbon monoxide /kɑːbən məˈnɒksaɪd/ is a poi- N UNCOUNT
sonous gas that is produced especially by the
engines of vehicles.

carbon paper is thin paper with a dark substance N UNCOUNT
on one side. You use it to make copies of letters,
bills, and other papers.

carcass /kɑːkəs/, **carcasses**; also spelled **car-** N COUNT
case. A **carcass** is the body of a dead animal. EG
...*rotting carcasses of cattle*.

card /kɑːd/, **cards**. 1 A **card** is 1.1 a piece of stiff N COUNT OR
paper that you write information on. EG *Put all the* N UNCOUNT
details on the card... ...*report cards*. 1.2 a piece of N COUNT+SUPP
cardboard or plastic with your name, photograph,
or signature on it. EG ...*a membership card*... *Did*
you ask to see his card. 1.3 a piece of stiff paper N COUNT
with a picture and a message printed on it, which
you send to someone on a special occasion. EG ...*a*
Christmas card. 1.4 a postcard. EG *Send me a card* N COUNT
when you get there.
2 **Cards** are thin pieces of cardboard with numbers N COUNT :
or pictures printed on them which are used to play USU PLURAL
various games. EG *He shuffled the cards and dealt*
them.
3 If you are playing **cards**, you are playing a game N PLURAL
using cards.
4 You can use **card** to refer to something that N COUNT
gives you an advantage in a particular situation. EG
Her chief card was her perfect memory... *This*
placed all the cards in the hands of the landowners.

cardboard /kɑːdbɔːd/ is thick, stiff paper that is N UNCOUNT
used to make boxes and other containers. EG ...*a*
large cardboard box.

cardiac /kɑːdɪæk/ means relating to the heart. EG ADJ CLASSIF :
...*death caused by cardiac failure*... ...*a relaxation of* ATTRIB
the cardiac muscle. Medical

cardigan /kɑːdɪgən/, **cardigans**. A **cardigan** is a N COUNT
knitted woollen sweater that you fasten at the front
with buttons or a zip. See picture at CLOTHES.

cardinal /kɑːdɪnᵊl/, **cardinals**. 1 A **cardinal** is a N COUNT
priest of high rank in the Catholic church.
2 **Cardinal** means extremely important. EG ...*a* ADJ QUALIT :
cardinal part of the scheme... ...*a fact of cardinal* ATTRIB
importance. Formal

cardinal sin, cardinal sins. If you refer to an N COUNT
action as a **cardinal sin**, you are indicating in a
humorous way that some people strongly disapprove of it. EG *I had committed the cardinal sin of*
shutting the window.

card-index, card-indexes. A **card-index** is a set N COUNT
of cards with information on them. The cards are
arranged in alphabetical order. EG *The students*
were just names in the card index.

care /keə/, **cares, caring, cared**. 1 If you **care** V : USU+A
about something, you feel that it is important or
interesting and are concerned about it. EG ...*people*
who care about the environment.
2 If you do not **care** about something, it does not V, WITH
matter to you. EG *She couldn't care less what they* BROAD NEG
thought... *You can go with Roger for all I care*...
Who cares where she is?
3 If you **care** for someone or something, you look V+for
after them and keep them in a good state or
condition. EG *You must learn how to care for*
children. ▸ used as a noun. EG ...*the care of mental* ▸ N UNCOUNT
patients... *She needed a lot of care*... ...*the children*
in her care.
4 To **care** for someone also means to love them. EG V+for
Do you think she still cares for him? Outdated
5 If you say that you do not **care** for something, V+for, WITH
you mean that you do not like it. EG *I didn't much* BROAD NEG
care for the way he looked at me. Outdated
6 To **care** to do something means to want or V+to-INF
choose to do it. EG *It's wrong whichever way you* Formal
care to look at it... *It's not a problem I'd care to*
face myself.
7 If you do something with **care**, you do it with N UNCOUNT
great attention because you do not want to make

any mistakes or cause any damage. EG *He chose*
every word with care... *The label on the crate said*
'Glass. Handle with care.'
8 **Cares** are worries. EG ...*without a care in the* N COUNT
world.
9 Children who are **in care** are being looked after PHRASE
by the state, because their parents are dead or are
unable to look after them properly.
10 You use **take care** in these ways. 10.1 If you PHRASE
take care of something or someone, you look after
them and prevent them from being harmed or
damaged. EG *He takes good care of my goats*. 10.2 CONVENTION
You can say **'Take care'** when saying goodbye to Informal
someone or at the end of a letter. 10.3 If you **take** PHRASE
care to do something, you make sure that you do
it. EG *Take care not to spill the mixture*. 10.4 If you PHRASE
take care of a task or situation, you deal with it. EG
They can take care of their own breakfast.

career /kərɪə/, **careers, careering, careered**. 1 N COUNT :
A **career** is a type of job or profession that USU+SUPP
someone does for a long period of their life. EG ...*a*
career in accountancy... ...*careers like teaching*
and medicine... ...*a political career*.
2 Your **career** is the part of your life that you N COUNT :
spend working. EG *Her early career was not a great* USU+SUPP
success... *I did it for the sake of my husband's*
career.
3 **Careers** advisers give people information and N MOD
help them to decide what kind of work they want
to do.
4 If a person or vehicle **careers** somewhere, they V+A
move fast and in an uncontrolled way. EG *He*
careered into a wall.

carefree /keəfriː/. If someone is **carefree**, they ADJ QUALIT
have no problems, worries, or responsibilities. EG
She had been lively and carefree... ...*his normally*
carefree attitude.

careful /keəfʊl/. 1 If you say **'Be careful'** to CONVENTION
someone, you are warning them of a danger or a
problem. EG *Be careful or you'll fall!*... *Please be*
careful with the washing machine.
2 If you are **careful**, 2.1 you do something with a ADJ QUALIT
lot of attention and thought. EG *This law will*
encourage more careful driving... *He had to be*
careful about what he said. ◊ **carefully**. EG *He* ◊ ADV
walked carefully around the broken glass. 2.2 you ADJ QUALIT
do something thoroughly and make sure that all
the details are correct. EG *He made a careful copy*
of the notes... ...*careful preparation*. ◊ **carefully**. ◊ ADV
EG *Now listen carefully everybody*.

careless /keəlɪs/. 1 If you are **careless**, you do ADJ QUALIT
not pay enough attention to what you are doing,
and so you make mistakes or produce unsatisfactory results. EG *We are rather careless about the*
way we cook... *I had been careless and let him*
wander off on his own. ◊ **carelessly**. EG ...*a gate* ◊ ADV
left carelessly ajar. ◊ **carelessness**. EG *They* ◊ N UNCOUNT
severely criticized Crook for his carelessness.
2 You do something in a **careless** way when you ADJ CLASSIF
are relaxed or confident. EG ...*a careless laugh*...
...*her simplicity and careless grace*. ◊ **carelessly**. ◊ ADV
EG *'I'll give him a ring later,' Rudolph said, careless-*
ly. ◊ **carelessness**. EG *She handled it with the* ◊ N UNCOUNT
carelessness of an expert.

caress /kəres/, **caresses, caressing, caressed**. V OR V+O :
If you **caress** someone, you stroke them gently RECIP
and affectionately. EG *I caressed her hair and we*
kissed. ▸ used as a noun. EG ...*a loving caress*. ▸ N COUNT

caretaker /keəteɪkə/, **caretakers**. A **caretaker** N COUNT
is a person who looks after a large building such as
a school or a block of flats and deals with small
repairs to it.

cargo /kɑːgəʊ/, **cargoes**. The **cargo** of a ship or N COUNT OR
plane is the goods that it is carrying. EG ...*a cargo of* N UNCOUNT
wool... *The port is still handling cargo*.

Are you a carnivore?

caricature /kærɪkətjʊə/, **caricatures, caricaturing, caricatured. 1** A **caricature** of someone is a drawing or description of them that exaggerates their appearance or behaviour. EG ...a caricature of Max Beerbohm... He was a master of caricature. ▸ used as a verb. EG Lawson caricatured his boss in his cartoons.   N COUNT OR N UNCOUNT / ▸ V+O

2 If you describe something as a **caricature** of an event or situation, you mean that it is a very exaggerated account of it. EG ...an outrageous caricature of the truth.   N COUNT : OFT +of

caring /kɛərɪŋ/. **1** If someone is **caring**, they are affectionate, helpful, and sympathetic. EG ...a caring parent... We need a more caring society.   ADJ QUALIT

2 Caring is behaviour that is affectionate, helpful, and sympathetic. EG ...love and caring between a man and a woman.   N UNCOUNT

carnage /kɑːnɪdʒ/. When there is **carnage**, a lot of people are killed, especially in a war. EG Refugees crossed the border to escape the carnage.   N UNCOUNT Literary

carnal /kɑːnəl/ means involving sexual feelings or activity; used showing disapproval. EG ...carnal desires.   ADJ CLASSIF : ATTRIB Literary

carnation /kɑːneɪʃə⁰n/, **carnations.** A **carnation** is a plant with white, pink, or red flowers. EG ...a bouquet of pink carnations.   N COUNT

carnival /kɑːnɪvə⁰l/, **carnivals.** A **carnival** is a public festival during which people play music and sometimes dance in the streets.   N COUNT

carnivore /kɑːnɪvɔː/, **carnivores.** A **carnivore** is an animal that eats meat rather than plants.   N COUNT Formal
◊ **carnivorous** /kɑːnɪvə⁰rəs/. EG Snakes are carnivorous.   ◊ ADJ CLASSIF

carol /kærəl/, **carols. Carols** are Christian religious songs that are sung especially at Christmas. EG After the carols, presents were distributed.   N COUNT

carp /kɑːp/, **carps, carping, carped. 1** A **carp** is a kind of large fish that lives in lakes and rivers. The plural form is also **carp.**   N COUNT

2 If you **carp,** you keep criticizing or complaining about someone or something. EG To carp about his leadership seems almost churlish... There's no point in carping.   V : OFT +about/at Literary

car park, car parks. A **car park** is an area or building where people can leave their cars. EG ...the entrance to the multi-storey car park.   N COUNT British

carpenter /kɑːpɪntə/, **carpenters.** A **carpenter** is a person whose job is making and repairing wooden things.   N COUNT

carpentry /kɑːpɪntri¹/ is the skill or the work of a carpenter.   N UNCOUNT

carpet /kɑːpɪt/, **carpets. 1** A **carpet** is a thick, flat piece of cloth which is used to cover the floors and stairs in a building. EG ...an old brown carpet.   N COUNT
◊ **carpeted** /kɑːpɪtɪ²d/. EG The corridor was carpeted.   ◊ ADJ CLASSIF

2 A **carpet** of something is a layer of it which covers the ground. EG There was a carpet of snow everywhere. ◊ **carpeted.** EG The ground was carpeted with flowers.   N COUNT +SUPP / ◊ ADJ CLASSIF

carriage /kærɪdʒ/, **carriages.** A **carriage** is **1** one of the separate sections of a train that carries passengers. **2** an old-fashioned vehicle which is pulled by horses. EG ...a procession of eight carriages led by the Queen.   N COUNT British / N COUNT

carried away /kæri¹d əweɪ/. If you are **carried away,** you are so enthusiastic about something that you behave in a foolish way. EG She can get so carried away making the designs that she forgets the time.   ADJ PRED

carrier /kærɪə/, **carriers. 1** A **carrier** is a vehicle or device that is used for carrying things. EG ...a new luggage carrier for bicycles... ...a troop carrier. ● See also **aircraft carrier.**   N COUNT : USU +SUPP

2 A **carrier** is also someone who is infected with a disease and can make other people ill. EG ...mothers identified from blood tests as carriers.   N COUNT

carrier bag, carrier bags. A **carrier bag** is a bag made of paper or plastic which you carry shopping in.   N COUNT British

carrion /kærɪən/ is the decaying flesh of dead animals. EG These birds live by scavenging carrion.   N UNCOUNT

carrot /kærət/, **carrots. 1** A **carrot** is a long, thin, orange-coloured vegetable that grows under the ground. EG She served us beef with carrots and potatoes... ...carrot juice.   N COUNT OR N UNCOUNT

2 You use **carrot** to refer to something that is offered to people in order to persuade them to do something. The word 'stick' is used to refer to harsher methods of persuasion. EG The free cottage is the carrot which makes him accept his low wage... Their policy is all sticks and no carrots.   N COUNT

carry /kæri¹/, **carries, carrying, carried. 1** If you **carry** something, **1.1** you take it with you, holding it so that it does not touch the ground. EG He picked up his suitcase and carried it into the bedroom. **1.2** you have it with you wherever you go. EG I always carry a gun.   V+O : USU +A / V+O

2 If something **carries** a person or thing somewhere, it takes them there. EG A gentle current carried him slowly to the shore... ...trucks that carried casualties.   V+O : USU +A

3 If someone or something **carries** a disease, they are infected with it and can pass it on to people or animals. EG Rats carry very nasty diseases.   V+O

4 If an action or situation **carries** a particular quality or consequence, it has it or involves it. EG Any job carries with it daily periods of boredom... Adultery in those cultures carried the death penalty.   V+O : NO PASS, NO CONT

5 If you **carry** an idea or a method to a particular extent, you use or develop it to that extent. EG George carried this idea one step further.   V+O+A

6 If a newspaper or poster **carries** a picture or a piece of writing, it contains it or displays it. EG A poster carried a portrait of Churchill.   V+O

7 If a proposal or motion **is carried** in a debate, a majority of people vote in favour of it. EG The motion was carried by 259 votes to 162.   V+O : USU PASS

8 If a sound **carries,** it can be heard a long way away. EG Sound seems to carry better in the still evening air.   V

9 If a woman **is carrying** a child, she is pregnant.   V+O

10 If a person or their opinion **carries weight,** they are respected by other people and influence them. EG What I think doesn't carry much weight around here.   PHRASE

carry on. 1 If you **carry on** doing something, you continue to do it. EG I carried on without their support... The speaker carried on reading from his prepared manuscript. **2** If you **carry on** an activity, you take part in it. EG Our work is carried on in an informal atmosphere... She could not carry on a sensible conversation.   PHRASAL VB : V+ADV OR V+ADV+O / V+O+ADV

carry out. 1 If you **carry out** a task, you do it. EG They also have to carry out many administrative duties. **2** If you **carry out** an order, you do what you are told to do. EG He was simply carrying out the instructions he had received.   PHRASAL VB : V+O+ADV

carry over. If you **carry** something **over** from one situation to another, you make it continue to exist in the new situation. EG The habit of obedience is carried over from the war.   PHRASAL VB : V+O+ADV

carry through. If you **carry** a plan **through,** you put it into practice. EG ...the task of carrying through these reforms.   PHRASAL VB : V+O+ADV

carrycot /kæri¹kɒt/, **carrycots.** A **carrycot** is a cot for small babies which has handles for carrying it.   N COUNT British

cart /kɑːt/, **carts, carting, carted. 1** A **cart** is an old-fashioned wooden vehicle that is used for transporting goods or people. Some carts are pulled by animals. EG ...a cart loaded with hay... ...a donkey cart.   N COUNT

2 If you **cart** things or people somewhere, you   V+O+A Informal carry them or transport them there, often with difficulty. EG *It took several trips to cart it all back up the stairs... He was carted off to hospital.*

carte blanche /kɑːt blɑːntʃ/. If someone gives you **carte blanche**, they give you the authority to do whatever you think is right. EG *They gave him carte blanche to publish his proposals.* `N UNCOUNT Formal`

cartilage /kɑːtɪˀlɪdʒ/ is a strong, flexible substance in your body, especially around your joints. EG *...the cartilage on the inside of the kneecap.* `N UNCOUNT`

carton /kɑːtəˀn/, **cartons**. A **carton** is **1** a plastic or cardboard container in which food or drink is sold. EG *...a loaf of bread and a carton of milk.* **2** a large, strong cardboard box in which goods are packed for storage and transport. EG *He was putting metal bands round cartons.* `N COUNT OR N PART` `American`

cartoon /kɑːtuːn/, **cartoons**. A **cartoon** is **1** a humorous drawing or series of drawings in a newspaper or magazine. EG *The Telegraph had a very funny cartoon about the demonstration.* **2** a film in which all the characters and scenes are drawn rather than being real people or objects. `N COUNT`

cartoonist /kɑːtuːnɪst/, **cartoonists**. A **cartoonist** is a person whose job is to draw cartoons for newspapers and magazines. `N COUNT`

cartridge /kɑːtrɪdʒ/, **cartridges**. A **cartridge** is a metal or cardboard tube containing a bullet and an explosive substance. Cartridges are used in guns. `N COUNT`

cartwheel /kɑːtwiːl/, **cartwheels**. If you turn a **cartwheel**, you do a fast, circular movement with your body. You fall sideways, put your hands on the ground, swing your legs over, and return to a standing position. `N COUNT`

carve /kɑːv/, **carves**, **carving**, **carved**. **1** If you **carve** an object, you make it by cutting it out of stone or wood. EG *The statue was carved by John Gibson.* ◇ EG *Pat loved the carved Buddhas... ...a big, cracked mirror with little, carved Cupids in each corner.* `V+O : USU+A` `◇ ADJ CLASSIF : ATTRIB`
2 If you **carve** writing or a design on an object, you cut it into the surface of the object. EG *He begins to carve his initials on the tree.* `V+O OR V : USU+A`
3 If you **carve** a cooked piece of meat, you cut slices from it at a meal. EG *He knew how to carve a goose.* `V+O OR V`

carve out. If you **carve out** something for yourself, you create or obtain it, often with difficulty. EG *The company is carving out a huge slice of the electronics market.* `PHRASAL VB : V+O+ADV`

carve up. If you **carve** something **up**, you divide it into smaller areas or pieces. EG *They prepared to carve up the British Empire.* `PHRASAL VB : V+O+ADV`

carving /kɑːvɪŋ/, **carvings**. **1** A **carving** is an object that has been cut out of a substance such as stone or wood. EG *...a stone carving from central Europe.* `N COUNT`
2 **Carving** is the art of carving objects or carving designs on them. EG *Here you can see English carving at its best.* `N UNCOUNT`

carving knife, carving knives. A **carving knife** is a large, sharp knife that you use to cut cooked meat. `N COUNT`

cascade /kæskeɪd/, **cascades**, **cascading**, **cascaded**. **1** A **cascade** is a waterfall. EG *The river fell in a series of cascades down towards the Hudson.* `N COUNT` `Literary`
2 If you refer to a **cascade** of something, you mean a large amount or quantity of it. EG *Around her face fell cascades of curls.* `N PART` `Literary`
3 When water **cascades**, it pours downwards very fast and in large quantities. EG *The water is cascading through the air.* `V+A`
4 If people or things **cascade** somewhere, they move or arrive there in large quantities. EG *Telegrams of protest cascaded onto his desk... The crowd cascaded down a flight of stairs.* `V+A` `Literary`

case /keɪs/, **cases**. **1** A **case** is a particular situation or instance, or an event or situation of a particular kind. EG *In Catherine's case, it led to* `N COUNT+SUPP`

divorce... In some cases, they burst into flames... ...cases where both partners have been married before... All cases of bullying will be severely dealt with.
2 Case is also used in these phrases. **2.1** You say **in that case** or **in which case** to indicate that you are assuming that a previous statement is correct or true. EG *'The bar is closed,' the waiter said. 'In that case,' McFee said, 'I'll go to another hotel'.* **2.2** If you say that something **is the case**, you mean that it is true or correct. EG *Paul argued that this was the case.... ...if it is prohibited (as is the case in Britain).* **2.3** If you say that a job or task **is a case of** doing a particular thing, you mean that that is what it consists of. EG *There's very little work involved. It's just a case of drafting the summons.* **2.4** If you say that something **is a case in point**, you mean that it is a good example of a general statement you have just made. EG *Britain is a case in point. 75% of the population now have washing machines.* **2.5** You say **as the case may be** or **whatever the case may be** to indicate that the statement you are making applies equally to situations that are different in a minor way from the one first mentioned. EG *They say that the hat is red (or green, as the case may be).* `PHRASES`
3 You say **in any case** **3.1** when you are adding another reason for something you have said or done. EG *I couldn't ask him all the time, and in any case he wasn't always there.* **3.2** after talking about things that you are not sure about, to emphasize that you are sure about your next statement. EG *Perhaps he did nothing. In any case, there was a brief fight.* `ADV SEN`
4 You say **in case** to indicate that you have something or are doing something because a particular thing might happen or might have happened. EG *Do you want me to hold them just in case?... I've got the key in case we want to go inside... I have a phone number in case of emergency.* `CONJ OR PHRASE`
5 Doctors sometimes refer to a patient as a **case**. EG *...road accident cases.* `N COUNT : USU+SUPP`
6 Police and detectives refer to a crime or mystery that they are investigating as a **case**. EG *...one of Sherlock Holmes's cases.* `N COUNT`
7 In an argument or debate, the **case** for or against a plan or idea consists of the facts and reasons used to support it or oppose it. EG *...a book arguing the case for better adult education... He stated his case.* `N COUNT : USU SING +for/against`
8 In law, a **case** is a trial or other legal inquiry. EG *He had lost the case.* `N COUNT`
9 A **case** is also **9.1** a container that is specially designed to hold or protect something. EG *...scissors in a leather case.* **9.2** a suitcase. EG *They unload their trunks and cases.* `N COUNT`

case history, case histories. A person's **case history** is the record of past events or problems that have affected them. EG *They had no case history of illness... She was making out a case-history for each child.* `N COUNT` `Formal`

cash /kæʃ/, **cashes**, **cashing**, **cashed**. **1** **Cash** is money in the form of notes and coins rather than cheques. EG *How much cash do you have?... ...four hundred dollars in cash.* `N UNCOUNT`
2 If you **cash** a cheque, you exchange it at a bank for the amount of money that it is worth. EG *Cheques up to 50 pounds may be cashed at any of our branches.* `V+O`

cash in. If you **cash in** on a situation, you use it to gain an advantage, often in an unfair or dishonest way. EG *They cashed in on the public's growing suspicion.* `PHRASAL VB : V+ADV, OFT+on`

Would you do a carving with a carving knife?

cashier /kəˈʃɪə/, **cashiers.** A **cashier** is a person N COUNT
that customers pay money to or get money from in
a shop, bank, or garage.

cashmere /kæʃmɪə/ is a kind of very fine, soft N UNCOUNT
wool. EG ...*her cashmere shawl.*

casing /keɪsɪŋ/, **casings.** A **casing** is a substance N COUNT
or object that covers something and protects it. EG
...*the outer casing of a vacuum flask.*

casino /kəsiːnəʊ/, **casinos.** A **casino** is a building N COUNT
or room where people play gambling games such
as roulette.

cask /kɑːsk/, **casks.** A **cask** is a wooden barrel N COUNT
that is used for storing things, especially alcoholic
drink. EG ...*a four-gallon cask*... ...*a cask of beer.*

casket /kɑːskɪt/, **caskets.** A **casket** is **1** a small N COUNT
box in which you keep valuable things. EG ...*her
exquisite jewel casket.* **2** a coffin.   American

casserole /kæsərəʊl/, **casseroles.** A **casserole** is
1 a dish that you make by cooking food in liquid in N COUNT OR
an oven. EG *Use this stock in soups or casseroles*... N UNCOUNT
There's lamb casserole for dinner. **2** a large, heavy N COUNT
container with a lid which is used to cook food. EG
Cook this in a casserole for one and a half hours.

cassette /kəˈset/, **cassettes.** A **cassette** is a N COUNT
small, flat, rectangular plastic container with magnetic tape inside which is used for recording and
playing back sounds. EG *Some libraries have cassettes of stories*... ...*a cassette player.*

cassette recorder, cassette recorders. A **cas-** N COUNT
sette recorder is a machine that is used for
recording and listening to cassettes.

cast /kɑːst/, **casts, casting. Cast** is used in the
present tense and is the past tense and past
participle of the verb.
1 The **cast** of a play or film is all the people who N COLL
act in it. EG *Who was in the cast?*... *The whole cast
worked wonderfully together.*
2 To **cast** an actor in a play or film means to V+O:OFT+*as*
choose them to act a particular role in it. EG *I was
cast as the husband.*
3 If you **cast** your eyes or **cast** a look in a V+O+A
particular direction, you look in that direction. EG
He cast a quick glance at his friend.
4 If you **cast** your **mind back**, you think about PHRASE
things in the past or try to remember them. EG *He
cast his mind back over the day.*
5 If something **casts** light or shadows somewhere, V+O+A
it causes them to appear there. EG *The fire cast a* Literary
faint glow over the bed.
6 If you **cast** doubt or suspicion on something, you V+O:OFT
cause other people to be unsure about it. EG *He had* +*on/upon*
cast doubt on our traditional beliefs.
7 When you **cast** your vote in an election, you vote. V+O:OFT+A
EG *Will had cast his vote for the President.*
8 If you **cast** something somewhere, you throw it V+O:USU+A
there. EG *He casts his clothes on to the bench*... *She* Literary
cast her jewels into the lake.
9 To **cast** an object means to make it by pouring V+O
hot, liquid metal into a specially shaped container
and leaving it there until it becomes hard. EG ...*a
statue of Achilles, cast in bronze.*

cast about or **cast around.** If you **cast about** or PHRASAL VB:
cast around for something, you look for it. EG *I* V+ADV,
cast around for some place to hide.   OFT+*for*
   Literary

cast aside. If you **cast** someone or something PHRASAL VB:
aside, you get rid of them because you no longer V+O+ADV
need them; used showing disapproval. EG *His coun-* Formal
try cast him aside and disgraced him.

cast off. 1 If you **cast** something **off**, you get rid PHRASAL VB:
of it or no longer use it. EG *Organizations must cast* V+O+ADV
off old-fashioned practices in order to survive. Formal
● See also **cast-off. 2** If you are on a boat and you V+ADV OR
cast off, you untie the rope that is keeping the V+O+ADV
boat in a fixed position. EG *We cast off as quietly as* Technical
we could... *Hendricks cast off the bow line and
walked to the stern.*

caste /kɑːst/, **castes. 1** A **caste** is one of the social N COUNT
classes into which people in a society are divided,

especially in India. EG *Sushma came from a lower
caste.*
2 Caste is the system of dividing people in a N UNCOUNT
society into different social classes. EG *Duties were
determined by caste.*

caster /kɑːstə/. See **castor.**

castigate /kæstɪgeɪt/, **castigates, castigating,** V+O
castigated. If you **castigate** someone or some- Formal
thing, you scold them or criticize them severely. EG
He castigated me for my mistakes... *They castigated the report as inadequate.* ◇ **castigation** ◇ N UNCOUNT
/kæstɪgeɪʃəˀn/. EG ...*his castigation of their reckless
utterances.*

casting /kɑːstɪŋ/ is the activity or job of choosing N UNCOUNT
actors to play particular roles in films or plays. EG
...*people doing the casting for films*... ...*the casting
director.*

cast-iron. 1 Cast-iron objects are made of a ADJ CLASSIF:
special type of iron that contains carbon. EG ...*a* ATTRIB
cast-iron stove... ...*cast-iron gates.*
2 A **cast-iron** excuse, guarantee, or solution is one ADJ CLASSIF:
that is absolutely certain to be effective. EG *We* ATTRIB
offer no cast-iron solutions to the problems.

castle /kɑːsəˀl/, **castles. 1** A **castle** is a large N COUNT
building with thick, high walls. Castles were built
by kings, queens and other important people in
former times, especially for protection during wars
and battles. EG ...*Windsor Castle*... ...*a ruined castle.*
2 In chess, a **castle** is a piece that is moved N COUNT
forwards, backwards, or sideways.

cast-off, cast-offs. Cast-off things, especially ADJ CLASSIF:
clothes, are ones which you no longer use and ATTRIB
which you give to someone else or throw away. EG
They were wearing cast-off jackets. ► used as a ► N COUNT:
noun. EG *They dressed up in Winifred's cast-offs.* USU PLURAL

castor /kɑːstə/, **castors;** also spelled **caster. Cas-** N COUNT
tors are small wheels fitted to a piece of furniture
so that it can be moved more easily.

castrate /kæstreɪt/, **castrates, castrating, cas-** V+O
trated. To **castrate** a male animal means to Formal
remove its testicles so that it cannot reproduce. EG
The two bulls had to be castrated. ◇ **castration** ◇ N UNCOUNT
/kæstreɪʃəˀn/. EG *They used castration of men as a
form of punishment.*

casual /kæʒjʊəl/, **casuals. 1** If you are **casual,** ADJ QUALIT
you are relaxed and do things without great atten-
tion or concentration. EG *He tried to appear casual
as he asked her to dance*... ...*a casual glance.*
◇ **casually.** EG ...*saying goodbye as casually as I* ◇ ADV
could. ◇ **casualness.** EG ...*working with apparent* ◇ N UNCOUNT
casualness.
2 A **casual** event or situation happens by chance ADJ CLASSIF
or without planning. EG ...*a casual friendship*... *It is
not open to casual visitors.* ◇ **casually.** EG ...*any* ◇ ADV
casually assembled group of men.
3 Casual clothes are ones that you normally wear ADJ CLASSIF:
at home or on holiday, and not for work or formal ATTRIB
occasions. EG *She wears casual clothes in bright
colours.* ► used as a noun. EG ...*smart casuals.* ► N PLURAL
◇ **casually.** EG *The students dress casually, in jeans* ◇ ADV
and sweat shirts.
4 Casual work is done for short periods and not ADJ CLASSIF:
permanently or regularly. EG *He was doing casual* ATTRIB
jobs for two years... ...*a casual labourer.*

casualty /kæʒjʊəltiˀ/, **casualties. 1** A **casualty**
is **1.1** a person who is injured or killed in a war or N COUNT:
in an accident. EG *No casualties were reported*... USU PLURAL
There were heavy casualties on both sides. **1.2** a N COUNT:
person or a thing that has suffered badly as a result USU+*of*
of a particular event or situation. EG *She was one of
the casualties of the system.*
2 The **casualty** ward or department of a hospital is ADJ CLASSIF:
the place where people who have severe injuries ATTRIB
or sudden illness are taken for emergency treatment.

cat /kæt/, **cats. 1** A **cat** is **1.1** a small, furry animal N COUNT
with a tail, whiskers, and sharp claws, and is
often kept as a pet. EG *The cat was lying on the
sofa.* **1.2** a larger animal that is a type of cat, such

as a lion or tiger. EG *Lions will hunt as a team – the only cats that do so.*

2 If you talk about a **game of cat and mouse**, you PHRASE are referring to a situation in which someone uses their greater strength, skill, or authority to treat another person in an unfair or cruel way. EG *There followed a game of cat and mouse with my tormentor.*

cataclysm /kætəklɪsᵊm/, **cataclysms**. A cata- N COUNT **clysm** is an event that causes great change or Literary harm. EG *Europe is approaching a terrible cataclysm.* ◊ **cataclysmic** /kætəklɪsmɪk/. EG *...a cata-* ◊ ADJ QUALIT *clysmic effect on British politics.*

catalogue /kætəlɒg/, **catalogues, cataloguing, catalogued**; spelled **catalog** in American English.
1 A **catalogue** is a list of things such as the goods N COUNT you can buy from a particular company, the objects in a museum, or the books in a library. EG *...expensive illustrated catalogues... ...catalogues from publishers.* ▸ used as a verb. EG *Books are* ▸ V+O *catalogued on white cards filed alphabetically.*
2 A **catalogue** of similar things is a number of N COUNT+of them considered or discussed one after another. EG *Mrs Zapp recited a catalogue of her husband's sins.* ▸ used as a verb. EG *They had been cataloguing the* ▸ V+O *many discomforts of life in India.*

catalyst /kætəlɪst/, **catalysts**. A **catalyst** is **1** N COUNT something that causes a change or event to hap- Formal pen. EG *Nuclear power served as a catalyst for the emergence of the Greens as a political force.* **2** a Technical substance that causes a chemical reaction to take place more quickly.

cataract /kætərækt/, **cataracts**. **1** A **cataract** is N COUNT a layer that has grown over a person's eye because of old age or illness and that prevents them from seeing properly. EG *He had a cataract removed.*
2 A **cataract** is also a large waterfall. EG *The river* N COUNT *comes roaring down in a foaming cataract.* Literary

catastrophe /kətæstrɒfiˡ/, **catastrophes**. A ca- N COUNT OR **tastrophe** is an unexpected event that causes N UNCOUNT great suffering or damage. EG *Unemployment is a personal catastrophe... ...an overwhelming sense of catastrophe.*

catastrophic /kætəstrɒfɪk/ means extremely ADJ QUALIT bad or serious, often causing great suffering or damage. EG *The impact on Belgium has already been catastrophic... ...catastrophic mistakes.*

catcall /kætkɔːl/, **catcalls**. A **catcall** is a loud N COUNT noise that someone makes to show that they disapprove of something. EG *In the street, the whistles and cat-calls began.*

catch /kætʃ/, **catches, catching, caught** /kɔːt/. **1** V+O If you **catch** an animal or person, you capture them after pursuing them, or by using a trap, net, or other device. EG *I went fishing and caught a nice little trout... ...a wild otter caught in a trap... We can get six months in prison if they catch us.*
2 If you **catch** an object which is moving through V+O the air, you seize it with your hands. EG *Tom flipped a toffee in the air and Claude caught it.* ▸ used as a ▸ N COUNT noun. EG *...a magnificent catch.*
3 If you **catch** someone doing something wrong or V+O: doing something secretly, you notice them when USU+-ING OR A they are doing it. EG *A gardener was sacked if he was caught smoking... Don't let him catch you at it.*
4 If something **catches** something else, it hits it V+O: USU+A with a lot of force. EG *The wave caught the trawler on her bow.*
5 If something **catches** on an object or **is caught** V-ERG: USU+A between two things, it becomes attached to the object or becomes trapped. EG *There was a bit of rabbit's fur caught on the fence... He caught his fingers in the spokes of the wheel.*
6 If you **catch** a bus, train, or plane, you get on it in V+O order to travel somewhere. EG *She caught a train to Boston.*
7 If you **catch** something that someone has said, V+O you manage to hear it. EG *She whispered something he could not catch.*

8 If something **catches** your interest or your V+O imagination, you notice it or become interested in it. EG *A poster caught her attention.*
9 If you **catch sight** of someone or something, or PHRASE **catch** a glimpse of them, you suddenly notice them or get a quick look at them. EG *I walked slowly, hoping she would catch sight of me... I caught a glimpse of two men in uniform.*
10 If you **catch the post**, you succeed in putting a PHRASE letter or parcel in a post-box before it is emptied.
11 If you **are caught** in a storm or other unpleas- V-PASS+in ant situation, it happens when you cannot avoid its effects.
12 If you **catch** a cold or a disease, you become ill V+O with it.
13 To **catch** a liquid which falls from somewhere V+O: USU+A means to collect it in a container. EG *There were pots and bowls everywhere catching water-drops that fell from the ceiling.*
14 If something **catches** the light or if the light V+O **catches** it, it reflects the light and looks bright or shiny. EG *The grass is sparkling where the sunlight catches small drops from the rain.*
15 If the wind or water **catches** something, it V+O carries or pushes it along. EG *The wind caught her hat.*
16 A **catch** on a window or door is a device that N COUNT fastens it. EG *He put his hand through the hole in the glass and released the catch.*
17 A **catch** is also a hidden problem or difficulty in N SING a plan or course of action. EG *'There's a catch in this.' – 'There's no catch, Gordon. I swear it.'*
18 When people have been fishing, their **catch** is N COUNT the total number of fish that they have caught. EG *They won't be able to land their catches at the home port.*
19 **Catch** is **19.1** a game in which children throw a N UNCOUNT ball to each other and catch it. **19.2** a game in which one child chases other children and tries to touch or catch one of them.
20 to **catch** someone's **eye**: see **eye**. ● to **catch fire**: see **fire**.

catch at. If you **catch at** something, you quickly PHRASAL VB: take hold of it. EG *The children caught at my skirts* V+PREP *and tugged me back.*

catch on. **1** If you **catch on** to something, you PHRASAL VB: understand it, or realize that it is happening. EG *You* V+ADV, *were expected to catch on quick... They finally* OFT+to *caught on to our game.* **2** If something **catches on**, V+ADV it becomes popular. EG *Ballroom dancing caught on... If the machine had been cheaper, it might well have caught on.*

catch out. If you **catch** someone **out**, you make PHRASAL VB: them make a mistake, often by an unfair trick. EG V+O+ADV *Are you trying to catch me out?*

catch up. **1** If you **catch up** with someone who is PHRASAL VB: in front of you, you reach them by walking faster V+ADV, than they are walking. EG *Tim had just reached the* USU+with, *corner when Judy caught up with him... She stood* OR V+O+ADV *still, allowing him to catch her up.* **2** To **catch up** V+ADV, with someone also means to reach the same stand- OFT+with ard or level that they have reached. EG *Most leaders were obsessed with catching up with the West.* **3** If you **catch up** on an activity that you V+ADV, have not had much time to do, you spend time OFT+on/with doing it. EG *They went to the office to catch up on correspondence... I was catching up on my sleep.* **4** V-PASS If you **are caught up** in something, you are +ADV+in involved in it, usually unwillingly. EG *He was determined not to get caught up in any publicity nonsense.*

catch up with. **1** When people **catch up with** PHRASAL VB: someone who has done something wrong, they V+ADV+PREP succeed in finding them in order to arrest or punish them. EG *When Birmingham authorities*

Which words on these pages are spelled differently in British and American English?

finally *caught up with her, she had spent all the money.* **2** If something **catches up with** you, you   v+adv+prep
find yourself in an unpleasant situation which you have been able to avoid but which you are now forced to deal with. EG *I am sure that the truth will catch up with him.*

catchment area /ˈkætʃmənt ɛərɪə/, **catchment**   N COUNT
areas. The **catchment area** of a school or hospi-   British
tal is the area that it serves.

catch-phrase, catch-phrases. A **catch-phrase**   N COUNT
is a sentence or phrase which becomes popular or well-known for a while because it is often used by a famous person.

catchy /ˈkætʃɪ¹/, **catchier, catchiest.** If you de-   ADJ QUALIT
scribe a tune as **catchy**, you mean that it is easy to remember. EG *The songs are irresistibly catchy.*

categorical /ˌkætəˈgɒrɪkə⁰l/. If you are **categori-**   ADJ QUALIT
cal about something, you state your views with certainty and firmness. EG *I don't see how you can be so categorical.* ◊ **categorically.** *The propo-*   ◊ ADV
sals had been categorically rejected by Donovan.

categorize /ˈkætəˈgəraɪz/, **categorizes, catego-**   v+o : OFT+*as*
rizing, categorized; also spelled **categorise.** If you **categorize** people or things, you divide them into sets or you say which set they belong to. EG *Animals can be categorised according to the food they eat.* ◊ **categorization** /ˌkætɪgə⁰raɪzeɪʃə⁰n/,   ◊ N UNCOUNT
categorizations. EG *Today, this three-way catego-*   OR N COUNT
rization is no longer adequate.

category /ˈkætə¹gərɪ⁰/, **categories.** If people or   N COUNT
things are divided into **categories**, they are divid-ed into groups in such a way that the members of each group are similar to each other in some way. EG *They divided the nation into six social catego-ries... There are three categories of machine.*

cater /ˈkeɪtə/, **caters, catering, catered.** To **ca-**   v+*for/to*
ter for a person or group means to provide all the things that they need or want. EG *We can cater for all age groups... ...theatres catering to a white middle-class audience.*

caterer /ˈkeɪtərə/, **caterers.** A **caterer** is a per-   N COUNT
son or a company that provides food and drink for people in a particular place or on a special occa-sion. EG *...a hotel caterer.*

catering /ˈkeɪtə⁰rɪŋ/ is the activity or business of   N UNCOUNT
providing food and drink for people. EG *'Who did the catering?' – 'A firm in Arundel.'*

caterpillar /ˈkætəpɪlə/, **caterpillars.** A **caterpil-**   N COUNT
lar is a small, worm-like animal that feeds on plants and eventually develops into a butterfly or moth.

catharsis /kəˈθɑːsɪs/ is getting rid of strong emo-   N UNCOUNT
tions or unhappy memories by expressing them in   Literary
some way. EG *The catharsis of the confession had left her exhausted.*

cathedral /kəˈθiːdrə⁰l/, **cathedrals.** A **cathedral**   N COUNT
is a very large and important church which has a bishop in charge of it. EG *...Westminster Cathedral.*

cathode-ray tube, cathode-ray tubes. A   N COUNT
cathode-ray tube is a device used in televisions   Technical
and computer terminals which sends an image onto the screen.

Catholic /ˈkæθə⁰lɪk/, **Catholics.** A **Catholic** is   N COUNT
someone who belongs to the branch of the Chris-tian church which accepts the Pope as its leader. EG *She was a devout Catholic... ...the Catholic Church.*

Catholicism /kəˈθɒlɪsɪzə⁰m/ is the set of Christian   N UNCOUNT
beliefs that are held by Catholics.

cattle /ˈkætə⁰l/ are cows and bulls. EG *...herds of*   N PLURAL
cattle.

catty /ˈkætɪ¹/, **cattier, cattiest.** If you say that a   ADJ QUALIT
woman or girl is being **catty**, you mean she is being unpleasant and spiteful. EG *Miss Haynes was capable of being catty and jealous.*

caucus /ˈkɔːkəs/, **caucuses.** A **caucus** is a group   N COUNT :
of people within an organization who share similar   USU+SUPP
aims and interests or who have a lot of influence.   Formal

EG *...the California caucus at the National Conven-tion.*

caught /kɔːt/ is the past tense and past participle of **catch.**

cauldron /ˈkɔːldrən/, **cauldrons;** spelled **caldron**   N COUNT
in American English. A **cauldron** is a very large, round metal pot used for cooking over a fire. EG *...the cauldron in which she prepared the soup.*

cauliflower

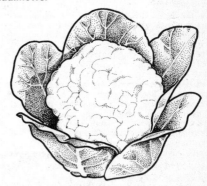

cauliflower /ˈkɒlɪflaʊə/, **cauliflowers.** A **cauli-**   N COUNT OR
flower is a vegetable with green leaves around a   N UNCOUNT
large white ball of flower buds.

causal /ˈkɔːzə⁰l/ means connected by a relation-   ADJ CLASSIF :
ship of cause and effect. EG *There may be no causal*   ATTRIB
link.

causality /kɔːˈzælɪ¹tɪ/ is the relationship of cause   N UNCOUNT
and effect. EG *...simple models of causality.*   Formal

causation /kɔːˈzeɪʃə⁰n/. The **causation** of some-   N UNCOUNT
thing is its cause or causes. EG *...a problem, the*   Formal
actual causation of which is unknown.

cause /kɔːz/, **causes, causing, caused. 1** The   N COUNT OR
cause of an event is the thing that makes it   N UNCOUNT :
happen. EG *Nobody knew the cause of the explo-*   USU+SUPP
sion... The argument seems to confuse cause and effect... The men died of natural causes.
2 If you have **cause** for a particular feeling or   N UNCOUNT
action, you have good reasons for feeling it or   +*for* OR *to*-INF
doing it. EG *Years of training gave him every cause for confidence... I have no cause to go back.*
3 To **cause** something means to make it happen.   v+o :
EG *...difficulties caused by price increases... What's*   OFT+*to*-INF
causing you so much concern?... The sound caused   OR v+o+o
her to step aside.
4 A **cause** is also an aim or principle which a   N COUNT :
group of people supports or is fighting for. EG *He is*   USU+SUPP
sympathetic to our cause... ...the cause of world peace.

causeway /ˈkɔːzweɪ/, **causeways.** A **causeway** is   N COUNT
a raised path or road that crosses water or marsh.

caustic /ˈkɔːstɪk/. **1 Caustic** chemical substances   ADJ CLASSIF
are very powerful and can dissolve other sub-stances. EG *Do not use a caustic cleaner on enamel.*
2 A **caustic** remark is extremely critical, cruel, or   ADJ QUALIT :
bitter. EG *...her caustic sense of humour.*   USU ATTRIB

caution /ˈkɔːʃə⁰n/, **cautions, cautioning, cau-**
tioned. 1 Caution is great care which you take in   N UNCOUNT
order to avoid possible danger. EG *You must pro-ceed with extreme caution.*
2 If someone **cautions** you, they warn you about   v+o OR
problems or danger. EG *I cautioned him not to*   v+QUOTE
reveal too much to anyone. ▸ used as a noun.   ▸ N UNCOUNT
...a word of caution.
3 When the police **caution** someone who they   v+o
have arrested, they warn them that anything that they say may be used as evidence in a trial. EG *He cautioned her, and read out the warrant.*

cautionary /kɔːʃənəᵊriː/. A **cautionary** story or ADJ CLASSIF: tale is intended to give a warning to people. ATTRIB

cautious /kɔːʃəs/. Someone who is **cautious** acts ADJ QUALIT very carefully in order to avoid possible danger. EG *Her husband is reserved and cautious.*
◊ **cautiously.** EG *We moved cautiously forward.* ◊ ADV

cavalier /kævəliːə/. Someone who is **cavalier** in ADJ QUALIT their behaviour does not consider other people's feelings or the seriousness of a situation. EG *Farmers were adopting a cavalier attitude to very dangerous substances.*

cavalry /kævəlriː/. The **cavalry** is **1** the part of N SING an army that uses fast armoured vehicles. **2** the group of soldiers in an army who ride horses. EG *...the Household Cavalry.*

cave /keɪv/, **caves, caving, caved.** A **cave** is a N COUNT large hole in the side of a cliff or hill, or under the ground. EG *The cliffs are riddled with caves.*

cave in. 1 When a roof or a ceiling **caves in,** it PHRASAL VB: collapses into the house or room. EG *In order to* V+ADV *prevent the sides caving in, it is lined with bricks.* **2** V+ADV If you **cave in,** you suddenly stop arguing or resisting, especially under pressure. EG *I more or less caved in, though I still defended my explanation.*

caveman /keɪvmæn/, **cavemen. Cavemen** were N COUNT people in prehistoric times who lived mainly in caves.

cavern /kævəᵊn/, **caverns.** A **cavern** is a large N COUNT deep cave.

cavernous /kævənəs/. A **cavernous** building is ADJ CLASSIF very large inside, so that it reminds you of a cave. EG *The engine noise boomed in the cavernous building.*

caviar /kæviɑː, kæviɑː/; also spelled **caviare.** N UNCOUNT **Caviar** is the salted eggs of a fish called the sturgeon.

cavity /kævəᵊtiː/, **cavities.** A **cavity** is **1** a space N COUNT or hole in something such as a solid object or a person's body. EG *...the nasal cavity.* **2** a hole in a tooth, caused by decay.

cavort /kəvɔːt/, **cavorts, cavorting, cavorted.** V When people **cavort,** they leap about in a noisy and excited way. EG *...children cavorting in an adventure playground.*

cc /siː siː/ is an abbreviation for 'cubic centimetres'. You use 'cc' when referring to the volume or capacity of something. EG *...500cc motorbikes.*

CD /siː diː/, **CDs. CD** is an abbreviation for 'compact disc'. EG *...a CD player.*

cease /siːs/, **ceases, ceasing, ceased. 1** If some- V thing **ceases,** it stops happening or existing. EG Formal *Hostilities must cease at once.*

2 If you **cease** to do something, you stop doing it. EG V+to-INF *Once people retire they automatically cease to be* OR-ING *union members... The vicar sighed as he ceased* Formal *speaking.*

3 If you **cease** something that you are producing or V+O providing, you stop producing or providing it. EG Formal *They threatened to cease financial support to the university... Existing units must cease production by 1991.*

ceasefire /siːsfaɪə/, **ceasefires.** A **ceasefire** is N COUNT an arrangement in which countries that are fighting each other agree to stop fighting. EG *...the cease-fire agreement.*

ceaseless /siːslⁱs/ means happening for a long ADJ CLASSIF: time without stopping or changing. EG *...his cease-* ATTRIB *less rebellion against discipline... ...the ceaseless* Formal *traffic.* ◊ **ceaselessly.** EG *Clarissa was talking* ◊ ADV *ceaselessly.*

cedar /siːdə/, **cedars.** A **cedar** is a kind of large N COUNT evergreen tree. EG *...cedar wood.*

cede /siːd/, **cedes, ceding, ceded.** If you **cede** V OR V+O: something to someone, you let them have it, often OFT+to as part of an official agreement. EG *The Louisiana* Formal *colony was ceded to Spain in 1762.*

ceiling /siːlɪŋ/, **ceilings. 1** A **ceiling** is the hori- N COUNT zontal surface that forms the top part inside a room. EG *...a large room with a high ceiling.*

2 You use **ceiling** to refer to an official upper limit N COUNT: on prices or wages. EG *...a ceiling on business rate* OFT+on *increases.*

celebrate /selⁱbreɪt/, **celebrates, celebrating, celebrated. 1** If you **celebrate** or if you cel- V OR V+O **ebrate** something, you do something enjoyable because of a special occasion or to honour someone's success. EG *We ought to celebrate; let's have a bottle of champagne... His victory was celebrated with music and dancing.* ◊ **celebration** ◊ N COUNT OR /selⁱbreɪʃᵊn/, **celebrations.** EG *We ought to have* N UNCOUNT *a little celebration... ...a time of celebration.*

2 If an organization or country is **celebrating** an V+O anniversary, it has existed for that length of time and is doing something special because of it. EG *The company was celebrating its fiftieth birthday.* ◊ **celebrations.** EG *...its tenth anniversary celebra-* ◊ N PLURAL *tions.*

3 When priests **celebrate** Holy Communion or V+O Mass, they officially perform the actions and ceremonies that are involved.

celebrated /selⁱbreɪtⁱd/. Someone or something ADJ QUALIT that is **celebrated** is famous. EG *Her mother was a celebrated actress... ...Churchill's celebrated remark.*

celebrity /sⁱlebrⁱtiː/, **celebrities.** A **celebrity** N COUNT is someone who is famous, especially in acting or show business. EG *Lots of celebrities have stayed here.*

celery /selⁱriː/ is a vegetable with long pale green N UNCOUNT stalks. It is often eaten raw in salads.

celestial /sⁱlestɪəl/ is used to describe things ADJ CLASSIF: connected with heaven. EG *They had no hope of* ATTRIB *admission to the celestial kingdom.* Formal

celibate /selⁱbⁱt/, **celibates.** Someone who is **celibate 1** does not marry or have sex, because of ADJ CLASSIF their religious beliefs. EG *The celibate life was* Formal *beginning to appeal to him.* ◊ **celibacy** ◊ N UNCOUNT /selⁱbəsiː/. EG *We are still required to take vows of poverty and celibacy and obedience.* **2** does not ADJ CLASSIF have sex during a particular period of their life. EG Formal *For once I had to spend a celibate night.*
◊ **celibacy.** EG *A month of enforced celibacy can't* ◊ N UNCOUNT *be good for anyone.*

cell /sel/, **cells. 1** A **cell** is the smallest part of an N COUNT animal or plant. Every animal or plant is made up of millions of cells. EG *...the cell walls of plants.*

2 A **cell** is also **2.1** a small room in which a N COUNT prisoner is locked. EG *There were four bunks in the cell.* **2.2** a small room in which a monk or nun lives.

3 You can refer to a small group of people within a N COUNT: larger organization as a **cell.** EG *...a Trotskyist cell* USU+SUPP *within the Labour organisation.*

cellar /selə/, **cellars.** A **cellar** is **1** a room in the N COUNT ground underneath a building, often used for storing things in. **2** a place where wine is stored. EG *He orders wine from the firm's cellars each week.*

cello /tʃeləʊ/, **cellos.** A **cello** is a musical instru- N COUNT ment that looks like a large violin. You hold it upright and play it sitting down.

cellophane /seləfeɪn/ is a thin, strong, transpar- N UNCOUNT ent material that is used to wrap things in. EG *...cheese and biscuits wrapped in cellophane.*

cellular /seljələ/. **1 Cellular** means relating to ADJ CLASSIF: the cells of animals or plants. EG *...basic cellular* ATTRIB *structures.*

2 Cellular blankets, clothes, or fabrics are very ADJ CLASSIF: loosely woven and keep you very warm. ATTRIB

celluloid /seljəlɔɪd/. **1 Celluloid** is a type of N UNCOUNT plastic. EG *He wore a celluloid collar.*

2 You can use **celluloid** to refer to films and the N UNCOUNT cinema. EG *...the celluloid world of Hollywood.* Literary

---

Find the one word after 'cavort' which does not begin with the sound /s/.

Celsius /sɛlsɪəs/ is a scale for measuring tempera- N UNCOUNT
ture, in which water freezes at 0 degrees and boils
at 100 degrees. It is represented by the symbol °C.

cement /sɪment/, **cements, cementing, ce-** N UNCOUNT
mented. 1 **Cement** is **1.1** a grey powder which is
mixed with sand and water in order to make
concrete. EG ...a sack of cement. **1.2** the same as
concrete. EG ...a little cement courtyard.
2 **Cement** is also a type of glue. EG ...a tube of N UNCOUNT
cement.
3 If you **cement** an area, you cover it with cement. V+O
EG The floor has been cemented over.
4 To **cement** something to something else means V+O
to stick or glue the two things together. EG The +to/together
lumps were cemented to the reef with coral... ...a
large heap of stones cemented together by lead.
5 If you **cement** a relationship, agreement, or V+O
position, you make it stronger or more official. EG
We would do the company some good by cementing relationships with business contacts.

cemetery /sɛmətriː/, **cemeteries.** A **cemetery** N COUNT
is a place where dead people are buried.

censor /sɛnsə/, **censors, censoring, censored.** 1 V+O
If someone **censors** letters or newspaper articles,
they officially examine them and cut out any
information that is regarded as secret. EG Believe it
or not they censor your letters here.
2 If someone **censors** a book, play, or film, they V+O
officially examine it and cut out any parts that are
considered to be immoral.
3 A **censor** is a person who has been officially N COUNT
appointed to examine plays, films, and books and
to cut out any parts that are considered to be
immoral. EG A film critic complained that the
censor was being too tolerant.

censorious /sɛnsɔːrɪəs/. When someone is **censo-** ADJ QUALIT
rious, they strongly criticize someone else's behav- Formal
iour. EG There is no need to be censorious about
such activities... She had had to put up with a
number of censorious comments.

censorship /sɛnsəʃɪp/. When there is **censor-** N UNCOUNT
ship, books, plays, and films are censored because
they are considered to be immoral, or letters and
newspaper reports are censored because they are
thought to reveal important secrets. EG ...the censorship of bad news in wartime.

censure /sɛnʃə/, **censures, censuring, cen-** V+O
sured. If you **censure** someone for something that Formal
they have done, you tell them that you strongly
disapprove of it. EG He had been censured for
showing cowardice in the battle. ▸ used as a noun. ▸ N UNCOUNT
EG The result exposed him to official censure...
Grimes seems to have escaped any severe censure.

census /sɛnsəs/, **censuses.** A **census** is an offi- N COUNT
cial survey of the population of a country that is
carried out in order to find out how many people
live there and to obtain details of such things as
people's ages and occupations.

cent /sɛnt/, **cents.** A **cent** is a small unit of money N COUNT
worth one hundredth of the main unit of money in
many countries. ● See also **per cent.**

centenary /sɛntiːnəriː/, **centenaries.** A **cente-** N COUNT
nary is a year in which people celebrate something important that happened exactly one hundred years earlier. EG 1928 was the centenary of
Ibsen's birth.

center /sɛntə/. See **centre.**

centigrade /sɛntɪɡreɪd/ is a scale for measuring N UNCOUNT
temperature, in which water freezes at 0 degrees
and boils at 100 degrees. It is represented by the
symbol °C.

centimetre /sɛntɪmiːtə/, **centimetres;** spelled N COUNT
centimeter in American English. A **centimetre** is
a unit of length in the metric system equal to ten
millimetres or one-hundredth of a metre.

centipede /sɛntɪpiːd/, **centipedes.** A **centipede** N COUNT
is a long, thin insect with a lot of legs.

central /sɛntrəl/. 1 Something that is **central** is in ADJ CLASSIF
the middle of a place or area. EG The houses are

arranged around a central courtyard... ...a film
about central Poland. ◊ **centrally.** EG The pin is ◊ ADV
centrally positioned on the circle.
2 A place that is **central** is easy to reach because ADJ QUALIT
it is in the centre of a city. ◊ **centrally.** EG ...a ◊ ADV
centrally located flat.
3 A **central** group or organization makes all the ADJ CLASSIF:
important decisions that are followed throughout a ATTRIB
larger organization or a country. EG Their activities
are strictly controlled by a central committee...
...local and central government. ◊ **centrally.** EG ◊ ADV
France has a centrally organized system.
4 The **central** person or thing in a particular ADJ CLASSIF:
situation is the most important one. EG The central OFT+to
character was played by William Hurt... These
statistics were central to the debate.

central heating is a heating system for build- N UNCOUNT
ings. Air or water is heated in one main tank and
travels round a building through pipes and radiators.

centralize /sɛntrəlaɪz/, **centralizes, centraliz-** V+O : USU PASS
ing, centralized; also spelled **centralise.** To **cen-**
tralize a country or state means to create a
system of government in which one central group
of people gives instructions to regional groups.
◊ **centralized.** EG We believe in a strong central- ◊ ADJ CLASSIF
ized state. ◊ **centralization** /sɛntrəlaɪzeɪʃ°n/. EG ◊ N UNCOUNT
Large-scale technology brings centralization.

centrally heated. A building that is **centrally** ADJ CLASSIF
heated has central heating.

centre /sɛntə/, **centres, centring, centred;**
spelled **center, centers, centering, centered** in
American English. 1 The **centre** of something is N COUNT :
the middle of it. EG He moved the table over to the OFT SING+of
centre of the room. ▸ used as an adjective. EG ...a ▸ ADJ CLASSIF :
black wig with a centre parting... The centre ATTRIB
section was coloured pink.
2 A **centre** is a building where people have N COUNT :
meetings, get help of some kind, or take part in a USU+SUPP
particular activity. EG ...a new arts centre... Treatment is available from the university's health
centre.
3 If an area or town is a **centre** for an industry or N COUNT+SUPP
activity, that industry or activity is very important
there. EG The region began as a centre for sheep-
farming.
4 The **centre** of an event or activity is the most N COUNT+SUPP
important thing involved. EG The Workers' move-
ment was at the centre of the 1972 strike... Smith
was right in the centre of the action.
5 If something is the **centre** of attention or inter- N COUNT+SUPP
est, people are giving it a lot of attention. EG The
television screen remained the centre of attention.
6 In politics, the **centre** refers to political groups N SING : the+N
and beliefs that are considered to be neither left-
wing nor right-wing. ▸ used as an adjective. EG In ▸ ADJ CLASSIF :
addition, there is one relatively small centre party ATTRIB
called the Free Democrats.
7 Someone or something that is **centred** in a ADJ CLASSIF :
particular place is based there. EG They were now OFT+in
centred in the new Royal Observatory at Greenwich.

centre around or **centre on.** If something PHRASAL VB :
centres around a person or thing or **centres on** V-ERG+PREP
them, that person or thing is the main feature or
subject of attention. EG The workers' demands
centred around pay and conditions... Attention was
for the moment centred on Michael Simpson.

century /sɛntʃəriː/, **centuries.** A **century** is 1 a N COUNT
period of a hundred years that is used when stating
a date. For example, the 19th century was the
period from 1801 to 1900. EG ...Italian paintings of
the fifteenth century. 2 any period of a hundred
years. EG ...a century of progress... ...a book written
centuries ago.

ceramic /sɪræmɪk/, **ceramics.** 1 **Ceramic** ob- ADJ CLASSIF :
jects are made of clay that has been heated to a ATTRIB
very high temperature. EG ...ceramic tiles.

2 Ceramics are ceramic objects. EG ...*Chinese* N COUNT : USU PLURAL
ceramics.

cereal /sɪərɪəl/, **cereals.** A **cereal** is **1** a plant N COUNT OR N UNCOUNT
such as wheat, maize, or rice that produces grain.
EG ...*cereal crops.* **2** a food made from grain, usually
mixed with milk and eaten for breakfast. EG ...*a box
of cereal.*

cerebral /serə'brəl/ means **1** relating to thought ADJ QUALIT
or reasoning rather than to emotions. EG ...*the* Formal
cerebral challenge of police work. **2** relating to the ADJ CLASSIF : ATTRIB
brain. EG *Her father died later of a cerebral hemor-* Technical
rhage.

ceremonial /serə'məʊnɪəl/, **ceremonials.** **1** ADJ CLASSIF
Something that is **ceremonial** is used in a ceremony or relates to a ceremony. EG ...*a ceremonial robe
from Africa.* ...*ceremonial dances.* ◊ **ceremo-** ◊ ADV
nially. EG *The bride is then ceremonially shown to
the crowd.*

2 Ceremonial consists of all the impressive things N UNCOUNT OR N COUNT :
that are done, said, and worn on very formal OFT+SUPP
occasions. EG ...*the splendid ceremonial of White-
hall on great occasions... As a child, he loved
parades and ceremonials.*

ceremonious /serə'məʊnɪəs/. You describe be- ADJ QUALIT
haviour as **ceremonious** when it is excessively
polite and formal. EG *He bid her an unusually
ceremonious farewell.* ◊ **ceremoniously.** EG *He* ◊ ADV
filled all their glasses ceremoniously.

ceremony /serə'mənɪ/, **ceremonies. 1** A **cer-**
emony is **1.1** a formal event such as a wedding or N COUNT
a coronation. EG ...*a coronation ceremony.* **1.2** an N COUNT :
action that is done in a very formal and polite way. USU SING
EG *The waiter gave them fresh glasses and there
was the ceremony of tasting the wine once more.*

2 Ceremony consists of **2.1** the special things that N UNCOUNT
are said and done on very formal occasions. **2.2**
very formal and polite behaviour. EG *At the BBC
she was received with respectful ceremony.*

3 If you do something **without ceremony**, you do PHRASE
it quickly and in a casual way. EG *He produced the
book, without ceremony, from under his bed.*

certain /sɜːtən/. **1** If you are **certain** about ADJ PRED :
something, you have no doubt about it. EG *He felt* USU+REPORT
*certain that she would disapprove... I'm absolutely
certain of that... We're not quite certain how much
there is.* ● If you know something **for certain**, you ● PHRASE
have no doubt at all about it. EG *It is not known for
certain where they are now.*

2 If something is **certain** to happen, it will definite- ADJ CLASSIF :
ly happen. EG *She's certain to be late... It is almost* OFT+*to*-INF
*certain that he will be elected... Such a vote would
mean the certain defeat of the government.*

3 Something that is **certain** is known to be true or ADJ CLASSIF
correct. EG *It was poison, that's certain...* ...*if you
want to get on with something in the certain
knowledge that you will not be interrupted.*

4 When you **make certain** that something hap- PHRASE
pens, you take action to ensure that it happens. EG
*We need to make certain that governments adhere
to disarmament agreements.*

5 You use **certain 5.1** to indicate that you are ADJ CLASSIF :
referring to one particular thing, person, or group, ATTRIB
although you are not saying exactly which it is. EG
*She arranged to meet him at three o'clock on a
certain afternoon... Certain areas in Sussex are
better than others for keeping bees.* ▸ used as a ▸ PRON+*of*
pronoun. EG *Certain of our judges have claimed that* Formal
this is the case. **5.2** before the name of a person in ADJ CLASSIF :
order to indicate that you do not know them. EG ...*a* ATTRIB
*certain Mrs Wendy Smith who worked for a large
company in Leeds.* **5.3** to suggest that a quality or ADJ CLASSIF :
condition is noticeable. EG *He wore a tweed over-* ATTRIB
coat which gave him a certain distinction.

6 If something is done or achieved **to a certain** PHRASE
extent, it is only partly done or achieved. EG *That
takes care of my anxieties to a certain extent.*

certainly /sɜːtənlɪ/. **1** You use **certainly** to
emphasize what you are saying **1.1** when you are ADV
making a statement. EG *If nothing is done there will*

certainly be an economic crisis... It certainly looks
wonderful, doesn't it?* **1.2** when you are agreeing ADV SEN OR
with what someone has said. EG *'Would you agree* CONVENTION
*that it is still a difficult world for women to live in?'
– 'Oh certainly.'* **1.3** when you are agreeing with a CONVENTION
proposal or suggestion. EG *He asked me if he could* OR ADV SEN
use my pen. I said, 'Certainly.'

2 You say **certainly not** when you want to say 'no' CONVENTION
in a strong way. EG *'Had you forgotten?' – 'Certainly
not.'*

certainty /sɜːtəntɪ/, **certainties. 1 Certainty** is N UNCOUNT
1.1 the state of having no doubts at all about
something. EG *Answers to such questions would
never be known with certainty.* **1.2** the fact of
something being certain to happen. EG ...*the certainty of death in battle.*

2 A **certainty** is something that nobody has any N COUNT
doubts about. EG *It's not a certainty that we'll win.*

certificate /sə'tɪfɪkət/, **certificates.** A **certifi-**
cate is **1** an official document stating that particu- N COUNT :
lar facts are true. EG ...*a medical certificate...* ...*your* USU+SUPP
birth certificate. **2** an official document that you N COUNT
receive when you have successfully completed a
course of study or training.

certify /sɜːtɪfaɪ/, **certifies, certifying, certified.**
1 To **certify** something means to declare formally V+O OR
that it is true. EG ...*a piece of paper certifying the* V+REPORT
payment of his taxes... ...*papers certifying that he
was a good friend of the United States.*

2 To **certify** someone means **2.1** to give them a V+O OR
certificate stating that they have successfully com- V+O+C
pleted a course of training. EG *The pilots are
certified by the navy.* **2.2** to officially declare that V+O+C
they are insane. EG *Her father was certified insane.* OR V+O+*as*

cessation /seseɪʃən/. The **cessation** of some- N UNCOUNT
thing is the stopping of it. EG ...*a cessation of* +SUPP
hostilities. Formal

chafe /tʃeɪf/, **chafes, chafing, chafed. 1** When V OR V-ERG
your skin **chafes** or **is chafed** by something, it
becomes sore as a result of something rubbing
against it. EG *Baby powder helps to avoid chafing.*

2 If you **chafe** at something such as a restriction, V+*at/under*
you feel annoyed about it. EG *He chafed at the* Formal
delay.

chaff /tʃæf/ consists of the outer parts of grain N UNCOUNT
such as wheat that are removed before the grain is
used as food.

chagrin /ʃægrɪn/ is a feeling of annoyance or N UNCOUNT
disappointment. EG *Thomas discovered to his great* Formal
chagrin that he was too late.

chain /tʃeɪn/, **chains, chaining, chained. 1** A N COUNT OR
chain consists of metal rings connected together N UNCOUNT
in a line. EG *She wore a silver chain around her
neck...* ...*a length of chain...* ...*bicycle chains.* See
picture at BICYCLE.

chain

Does a chambermaid clean chambers?

2 When you **chain** a person or thing to something, v+o:usu+a
you fasten them to it using a chain. EG *They*
chained themselves to the fence.

3 A **chain** of things is a group of them existing or N COUNT+SUPP
arranged in a line. EG *...the island chains of the*
Pacific.

4 A **chain** of shops or hotels is a number of them N COUNT+SUPP
owned by the same person or company. EG *...a*
chain of 970 food stores.

5 A **chain** of events is a series of them happening N COUNT+SUPP
one after another. EG *...the brief chain of events*
that led up to her death... ...a nuclear chain reac-
tion.

chain-smoke, chain-smokes, chain-smoking, V OR V+O
chain-smoked. Someone who **chain-smokes**
smokes cigarettes or cigars continuously.

chain store, chain stores. A **chain store** is one N COUNT
of several similar shops that are owned by the
same person or company.

---

chairs

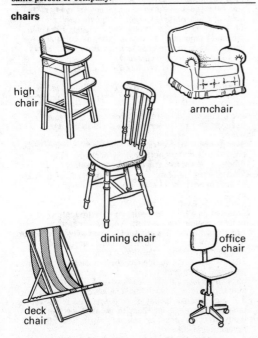

high
chair

armchair

dining chair

office
chair

deck
chair

---

chair /tʃeə/, **chairs, chairing, chaired. 1** A N COUNT
chair is a piece of furniture for one person to sit
on, with a back and four legs. EG *I sat in low chair*
by the fire, reading.

2 At a university, a **chair** is the post of professor. N COUNT
EG *He was extraordinarily young to get the Chair.*

3 If you **chair** a meeting, you are the chairman or v+o
chairwoman. EG *The commission was chaired by*
Professor Lunt.

chairman /tʃeəmə³n/, **chairmen. 1** The **chair-** N COUNT
man of a meeting or debate is the person in
charge, who decides when each person is allowed
to speak.

2 The **chairman** of a committee, organization, or N COUNT
company is the head of it. EG *...the Chairman of*
British Rail.

chairmanship /tʃeəmə³nʃɪp/. Someone's **chair-** N SING+POSS
manship is the fact that they are chairman, or the
period during which they are chairman. EG *...the*
efforts of the Spartacus League, under the chair-
manship of Peter Gowan.

chairperson /tʃeəpɜ:sə⁰n/, **chairpersons.** The N COUNT
chairperson of a meeting, committee, or organization is the person in charge of it.

chairwoman /tʃeəwumən/, **chairwomen.** The N COUNT
chairwoman of a meeting, committee, or organization is the woman in charge of it.

chalet /ʃæleɪ/, **chalets.** A **chalet** is a small wood- N COUNT
en house, especially in a mountain area or a
holiday camp.

chalk /tʃɔːk/, **chalks, chalking, chalked. 1** Chalk N UNCOUNT
is a soft white rock. You can use small pieces of it
for writing or drawing with. EG *...the chalk uplands*
of Wiltshire... He took a piece of chalk from his
pocket.

2 **Chalks** are small pieces of chalk used for writing N PLURAL
or drawing with.

3 If you **chalk** something, you draw or write it v+o or v+a
using a piece of chalk. EG *...a young man chalking*
on the blackboard.

chalk up. If you **chalk up** a success or victory, PHRASAL VB :
you achieve it. EG *The company has recently* V+O+ADV
chalked up its most outstanding success.

chalky /tʃɔːkiʲ/, **chalkier, chalkiest.** Something ADJ QUALIT
that is **chalky** contains chalk or is covered with
chalk. EG *...the white, chalky road.*

challenge /tʃælɪ³ndʒ/, **challenges, challenging,**
challenged. 1 A **challenge** is **1.1** something new N COUNT OR
and difficult which requires great effort and deter- N UNCOUNT
mination. EG *...the challenge of the unknown...*
Mount Everest presented a challenge to Hillary.
1.2 a suggestion from someone that you should N COUNT
compete or argue with them. EG *Her smile held a*
tiny hint of a challenge. **1.3** a questioning of the N COUNT OR
truth or value of something, or of a person's right N UNCOUNT
to do something. EG *...the challenge to authority...*
There will inevitably be challenges to the existing
order.

2 If you **challenge** someone, **2.1** you invite them to v+o:
fight or compete with you. EG *They had challenged* OFT+to-INF
and beaten the best teams in the world. **2.2** you OR to
question whether they have the right to do something, or whether what they are saying is true. EG
The idea has never been challenged... He chal-
lenged the minister to produce evidence.

challenger /tʃælɪ³ndʒə/, **challengers.** A **chal-** N COUNT
lenger is someone who competes with you for a
position or title that you already have, for example
a sports championship. EG *...a challenger to*
Mitterrand's leadership.

challenging /tʃælɪ³ndʒɪŋ/. **1** A **challenging** task ADJ QUALIT
or job requires great effort and determination. EG
Life as a housewife does not seem very challenging
to the highly educated girl.

2 If you do something in a **challenging** way, you ADJ QUALIT
seem to be inviting people to argue with you or
compete against you in some way. EG *...a suspicious*
challenging look. ◇ **challengingly.** EG *He looked* ◇ ADV
challengingly at the Doctor.

chamber /tʃeɪmbə/, **chambers. 1** A **chamber** is
1.1 a large room that is used for formal meetings. N COUNT
EG *...the Council Chamber... Labour MPs left the*
Chamber in protest. **1.2** a room designed and N COUNT+SUPP
equipped for a particular purpose. EG *...a built-in*
echo chamber... He led the way to the torture
chamber.

2 A **Chamber** of Commerce or **Chamber** of Trade N COUNT+of
is a group of business people who work together to
improve business in their town.

3 **Chambers** are rooms used by judges and barris- N PLURAL
ters. EG *All the barristers in Chambers seemed to*
be out.

chambermaid /tʃeɪmbəmeɪd/, **chambermaids.** N COUNT
A **chambermaid** is a woman who cleans and tidies
the bedrooms in a hotel.

chamber music is classical music written for a N UNCOUNT
small number of instruments.

chameleon /kəmiːliən/, **chameleons.** A **chame-** N COUNT
leon is a lizard whose skin changes colour to
match the colour of its surroundings.

chamois leather /ʃæmiʲ leðə/, **chamois leath-** N COUNT
ers. A **chamois leather** or a **chamois** is a soft
leather cloth used for cleaning and polishing.

champagne /ʃæmpeɪn/ is an expensive French white wine that has lots of bubbles in it. N UNCOUNT

champion /tʃæmpɪən/, **champions, championing, championed. 1** A **champion** is someone who has won the first prize in a competition, contest, or fight. EG ...the school tennis champion. N COUNT

2 If you are a **champion** of a person, a cause, or a principle, you support or defend them. EG ...a champion of liberty. ▶ used as a verb. EG He went on to champion the rights of accused criminals to have access to their lawyers. N COUNT+SUPP ▶ V+O

championship /tʃæmpɪənʃɪp/, **championships.** A **championship** is 1 a competition to find the best player or team in a particular sport. EG ...the first round of the U.S open golf championship. **2** the title or status of someone who has won a sports championship. EG ...the heavyweight championship of the world. N COUNT N COUNT+SUPP

chance /tʃɑːns/, **chances, chancing, chanced. 1** If there is a **chance** of something happening, it is possible. EG I think we've got a good chance of winning... There's little chance that the situation will improve... What are her chances of getting the job? ● If you say that someone doesn't **stand a chance** of achieving something, you mean that they cannot possible achieve it. N COUNT OR N UNCOUNT +SUPP ● PHRASE

2 If you have a **chance** to do something, you have the opportunity to do it. EG He gave me no chance to reply to this. N COUNT : USU+to-INF OR of

3 When you take a **chance**, you try to do something although there is a large risk of danger or failure. EG We may lose a lot of support, but that's a chance we'll have to take. N COUNT

4 Something that happens by **chance** was not planned by anyone. EG Almost by chance I found myself talking to him... ...a chance meeting... It was pure chance. N UNCOUNT

5 You can say **by any chance** when you are asking something politely or when you think the answer to your question will probably be 'no'. EG You aren't by any chance related to David Howe, are you? ADV SEN Formal

6 If you **chance** to do something, you do it although you had not planned or tried to do it. EG I chanced to overhear them. V+to-INF Formal

chandelier /ʃændə'lɪə/, **chandeliers.** A **chandelier** is a circular frame which holds light bulbs or candles and hangs from the ceiling. N COUNT

change /tʃeɪndʒ/, **changes, changing, changed. 1** If there is a **change** in something, it becomes different. EG ...a radical change in attitudes... ...the changes that had taken place since he had left China... There had been little change. N COUNT OR N UNCOUNT

2 If you say that an experience **makes a change**, you mean that it is enjoyable because it is different from what you are used to. EG Being out in the country made a refreshing change. PHRASE

3 If you say that something is happening **for a change**, you mean that it is different from what usually happens. EG They were glad to leave their cars and walk for a change... Its nice to see you with your books for a change. PHRASE

4 When something **changes** or when you **change** it, it becomes different. EG Her disdain changed to surprised respect... They can be used to change uranium into plutonium... A bird changes direction by dipping one wing and lifting the other. V-ERG

◇ **changed.** EG He returned to parliament a changed man... Their changed status is reflected in their clothes. ◇ **changing.** EG They are anachronisms in a changing world... ...a report on changing fashions in food. ◇ ADJ CLASSIF ◇ ADJ CLASSIF

5 To **change** something also means to replace it with something new or different. EG I changed the bulb... His doctor advised that he change his job. V+O

6 If there is a **change** of something, it is replaced. EG ...a change of government... That motorcycle needs a change of oil. N COUNT+SUPP

7 When you **change** your clothes, you take them off and put on different ones. EG I want to change my socks... She changed into her street clothes. V+O, OR V OFT+into/out of

8 A **change** of clothes is an extra set of clothes that you take with you when you go to stay somewhere. N COUNT+of

9 When you **change** a baby or **change** its nappy, you take off its dirty nappy and put on a clean one. V+O

10 When you **change** buses or trains, you get off one bus or train and get on to another in order to continue your journey. EG Don't forget to change at Crewe. V+O OR V

11 Your **change** is the money that you receive when you pay for something with more money than it costs because you do not have exactly the right amount of money. EG Morris handed Hooper his change. N UNCOUNT

12 Change is coins, rather than notes. EG We only had 80p in change. N UNCOUNT

13 If you have **change** for a note or a large coin, you have the same amount of money in smaller notes or coins. EG Have you got change for a fiver? N UNCOUNT+ for

14 When you **change** money, you exchange it for the same amount of money in different coins or notes. EG Can anyone change a ten pound note?... Do you change foreign currency? V+O

15 to **change hands**: see **hand.** ● to **change** your **mind**: see **mind.**

change over. If you **change over** from one thing to another, you stop being or doing one thing and start being or doing the other. EG They had been Liberal till several years ago, then they changed over to Conservative. ● See also **changeover.** PHRASAL VB : V+ADV, OFT+from/to

changeable /tʃeɪndʒəbəl/. Someone or something that is **changeable** is likely to change many times. EG He was as changeable as the weather. ADJ QUALIT

changeover /tʃeɪndʒəʊvə/, **changeovers.** A **changeover** is a change from one activity or system to another. EG The changeover had taken place in the Easter vacation. N COUNT

channel /tʃænəl/, **channels, channelling, channelled;** spelled **channeling** and **channeled** in American English. **1** A **channel** is a wavelength on which television or radio programmes are broadcast. EG He switched to the other channel. N COUNT

2 If you say that something has been done through particular **channels**, you are referring to the people who arranged for it to be done. EG I notified the authorities through the normal channels. N COUNT USU+SUPP

3 If you **channel** money or resources into something, you arrange for them to be used for that thing. EG ...the need to channel North Sea oil revenues into industry. V+O : USU+A

4 A **channel** is also **4.1** a passage along which water flows. EG ...irrigation channels. **4.2** a route used by boats. EG The main channels had been closed by enemy submarines. N COUNT

5 The **Channel** or the **English Channel** is the narrow area of water between England and France. N PROPER: the+N

chant /tʃɑːnt/, **chants, chanting, chanted. 1** A **chant** is **1.1** a word or group of words that is repeated over and over again. EG The assembly broke into a chant: 'What's your name? What's your name?' **1.2** a religious song or prayer that is sung on only a few notes. N COUNT

2 If you **chant** or if you **chant** something, **2.1** you repeat the same words over and over again. EG They marched to their coach chanting slogans... She chanted, 'Johnny never hurt me, Johnny never hurt me.' **2.2** you sing a religious song or prayer. V, V+O, OR V+QUOTE V+O OR V

chaos /keɪɒs/ is a state of complete disorder and confusion. EG Chaos began to develop on the roads... ...economic chaos. N UNCOUNT

If you do something that is out of character, is it characteristic of you?

chaotic /keɪɒtɪk/. Something that is **chaotic** is in ADJ QUALIT a state of complete disorder and confusion. EG ...a chaotic jumble of motor vehicles.

chap /tʃæp/, **chaps.** You can use **chap** to refer to N COUNT a man or boy. EG The chap she danced with was a Informal very good friend of mine.

chapel /tʃæpəᵒl/, **chapels.** A **chapel** is **1** a part of N COUNT a church which has its own altar and which is used for private prayer. **2** a small church attached to a school, hospital, or prison. **3** a building used for worship by members of some Protestant churches. EG ...a Methodist chapel.

chaperone /ʃæpərəʊn/, **chaperones, chaperoning, chaperoned;** also spelled **chaperon. 1** N COUNT Chaperones were women who used to accompany young unmarried women on social occasions, especially when men were present.

2 If you **chaperone** young people, you accompany V+O them, to make sure that they are safe and that they behave properly. EG We went to France with one of the mistresses to chaperone us.

chaplain /tʃæplɪn/, **chaplains.** A **chaplain** is a N COUNT member of the Christian clergy who does religious work in a hospital, school, or prison. EG ...a hospital chaplain.

chapped /tʃæpt/. If your skin is **chapped**, it is dry, ADJ QUALIT cracked, and sore. EG His lips were all chapped and rough.

chapter /tʃæptə/, **chapters. 1** A **chapter** is one of N COUNT OR the parts that a book is divided into. EG I'd nearly N+NUMBER finished chapter 8.

2 You can refer to a part of your life or a period in N COUNT+SUPP history as a **chapter** when it begins or ends with a Literary major event. EG A new chapter of my career as a journalist was about to commence.

character /kærəᵏktə/, **characters. 1** The **char-** N COUNT: **acter** of a person or place consists of all the USU+POSS qualities they have that make them distinct from other people or places. EG There was another side to his character... ...the character of New York.

2 If you say that what someone does is **in charac-** PHRASE **ter**, you mean that it is what you would expect them to do, knowing what kind of person they are. If what they do is **out of character**, it is not what you would expect them to do. EG It's quite in character for Carey to use a word like that... Her reading glasses had bright green frames, which seemed out of character.

3 If something has a particular **character**, it has a N UNCOUNT: particular quality. EG We need to emphasize the USU+SUPP radical character of our demands... Concessions are not always purely negative in character.

4 The **characters** in a film, book, or play are the N COUNT people that it is about. EG ...the tensions that develop between the two main characters.

5 You use **character** to say what kind of person N COUNT: someone is. EG He's a strange character, Evans... OFT ADJ+N Another colourful character regularly in the bar Informal was the local plumber.

6 If you say that someone is a **character**, you N COUNT: mean that they are interesting, unusual, or amus- OFT ADJ+N ing. EG She was a real character. Informal

7 A **character** is also a letter, number, or other N COUNT symbol that is written or printed. Technical

characteristic /kærəᵏtərɪstɪk/, **characteristics. 1** A **characteristic** is a quality or feature N COUNT: that is typical of someone or something and that OFT+SUPP makes that person or thing easy to recognize. EG Ambition is a characteristic of all successful businessmen.

2 Something that is **characteristic** of someone or ADJ QUALIT: something is typical of that person or thing. EG OFT+of ...those large brick tiles so characteristic of East Anglia. ◊ **characteristically.** EG He proposed a ◊ ADV characteristically brilliant solution.

characterize /kærəᵏktəraɪz/, **characterizes, characterizing, characterized;** also spelled **characterise. 1** If something **characterizes** a V+O period of history or a place, it is very typical of it.

EG ...the incessant demand for change that characterizes our time.

2 If you **characterize** someone or something, you V+O: OFT+as describe them by saying what their characteristics are. EG The revolutionaries characterize the seventies as an era of attack... How would you characterize a shanty town from that picture?

charade /ʃərɑːd/, **charades.** A **charade** is a N COUNT pretence which is so obvious that nobody is deceived by it. EG ...a charade of negotiations with the government.

charcoal /tʃɑːkəʊl/ is a black substance obtained N UNCOUNT by burning wood without much air. It can be burned as a fuel, and small sticks of it are used for drawing with. EG ...glowing charcoal fires... ...a charcoal drawing.

charge /tʃɑːdʒ/, **charges, charging, charged. 1** V+O+O If you **charge** someone an amount of money, you OR V+O: ask them to pay that amount for something that OFT+A you have sold to them or done for them. EG 'How much do you charge?' - '£6 a night.'... You can be sure he's going to charge you something for the service.

2 If you **charge** goods or services to a person or V+O+to organization, you tell the people providing the goods or services to send the bill to that person or organization.

3 A **charge** is the price that you have to pay for a N COUNT service or for something you buy. EG ...increases in postal and telephone charges... No charge is made for repairs. ● If something is **free of charge**, it ● PHRASE does not cost anything. EG They're happy to give their services free of charge.

4 A **charge** is also a formal accusation that N COUNT someone has committed a crime. EG The police arrested her on a charge of conspiracy to murder... ...a murder charge.

5 When the police **charge** someone, they formally V+O: accuse them of having done something illegal. EG OFT+with He was arrested and charged with a variety of offences.

6 If you have **charge** of something or someone, N UNCOUNT you have responsibility for them and control over +SUPP them. EG She intended to take charge of the boy herself. ● If you are **in charge** of something or ● PHRASE someone, you have responsibility for them and control over them. EG You had left me in charge, John... He was minister in charge of government business.

7 If you **charge** towards someone or something, V: USU+A you move quickly and aggressively towards them. EG Hendricks charged into the station house.

8 When you **charge** a battery, you pass an electri- V+O cal current through it in order to make it more powerful or to make it last longer.

charged /tʃɑːdʒd/ means filled with emotion and ADJ QUALIT: therefore very tense or excited. EG ...a highly OFT+with charged silence... His voice was charged with suppressed merriment.

chariot /tʃærɪət/, **chariots.** Chariots were fast- N COUNT moving vehicles with two wheels that were pulled by horses in ancient times.

charisma /kərɪzmə/. You say that someone has N UNCOUNT **charisma** when they can attract, influence, and inspire people by their personal qualities. ◊ **charismatic** /kærɪzmætɪk/. EG ...a charismatic ◊ ADJ CLASSIF politician.

charitable /tʃærɪtəbᵒl/. **1** Someone who is **chari-** ADJ QUALIT **table** is kind or tolerant towards other people. EG She was being unusually charitable to me... ...a charitable remark. ◊ **charitably.** EG He charitably ◊ ADV chose to ignore her impertinence.

2 A **charitable** organization or activity helps and ADJ CLASSIF supports people who are ill, handicapped, or very ATTRIB poor. EG ...charitable donations.

charity /tʃærɪˈtiᵀ/, **charities. 1** A **charity** is an N COUNT organization which raises money in order to help people who are ill, handicapped, or very poor. EG The proceeds will go to local charities.

2 Charity is **2.1** a kind, helpful and generous N UNCOUNT attitude towards other people. EG *She found the* Formal *charity in her heart to forgive them.* **2.2** money or gifts which are given to poor people. EG *He's far too proud to accept charity.*

charlatan /ˈʃɑːlətᵊn/, **charlatans.** A **charlatan** is N COUNT someone who pretends to have skills or knowledge Formal that he or she does not really possess. EG *The doctor was either a charlatan or a shrewd old rogue.*

charm /tʃɑːm/, **charms, charming, charmed.** 1 N UNCOUNT **Charm** is the quality of being attractive and pleas- OR N COUNT ant. EG *He bowed with infinite grace and charm...* *...the charms of the exotic.*

2 If you **charm** someone, you please them by being v+o charming. EG *I was charmed by his courtesy.*

3 A **charm** is **3.1** a small ornament that is fixed to N COUNT a bracelet or necklace. **3.2** an act, saying, or object that is believed to have magic powers.

charmer /ˈtʃɑːməᵊ/, **charmers.** You refer to some- N COUNT one as a **charmer** when they behave in a very charming but rather insincere way. EG *They're both tremendous charmers in their different ways.*

charming /ˈtʃɑːmɪŋ/. If someone or something is ADJ QUALIT **charming**, they are very pleasant and attractive. EG *Celia is a charming girl.* ◊ **charmingly.** EG *The* ◊ ADV *house has a charmingly medieval atmosphere.*

charred /tʃɑːd/. Something that is **charred** is ADJ QUALIT partly burnt and made black by fire.

chart /tʃɑːt/, **charts, charting, charted.** 1 A N COUNT **chart** is **1.1** a diagram, picture, or graph which makes information easy to understand. EG *...large charts illustrating world poverty.* **1.2** a map of the sea or stars.

2 The **charts** are the official lists that show which N PLURAL: pop records have sold the most copies each week. the+N

3 If you **chart** something, you observe it and v+o record it carefully. EG *We charted their move- ments.*

charter /ˈtʃɑːtəᵊ/, **charters, chartering, char- tered.** 1 A **charter** is a formal document describ- N COUNT: ing the rights, aims, or principles of an organiza- USU+SUPP tion or group of people. EG *...the Working Women's* Formal *Charter... It contravened article 51 of the UN charter.*

2 A **charter** plane or boat is hired for use by a ADJ CLASSIF: particular person or group. EG *He is travelling on a* ATTRIB *charter flight.*

3 If you **charter** a plane, boat, or other vehicle, v+o you hire it for your private use. EG *We plan to charter a special train for London.*

chartered /ˈtʃɑːtəd/ is used to describe people ADJ CLASSIF: who have formally qualified in their profession. EG ATTRIB *...a chartered accountant... ...the Royal Institute of Chartered Surveyors.*

chase /tʃeɪs/, **chases, chasing, chased.** 1 If you v+o OR· **chase** someone, you run after them or follow them v+after quickly in order to catch them. EG *Youngsters chase one another up trees... A dozen soldiers chased after the car.* ▸ used as a noun. EG *They* ▸ N COUNT *abandoned the chase and returned home.*

2 If you **chase** someone from a place, you force v+o+A them to leave by using threats or violence. EG *They were chased from the village.*

3 If you **chase** something such as work or money, v+o OR you spend a lot of time and effort trying to get it. EG v+after *We are getting more and more applicants chasing fewer and fewer jobs... Joe was away in Bombay, chasing after some film job.*

chasm /ˈkæzᵊm/, **chasms.** 1 A **chasm** is a very N COUNT deep crack in rock, earth, or ice.

2 If you say that there is a **chasm** between two N COUNT: OFT things or between two groups of people, you mean +between that there is a very large difference between them. EG *...the chasm between rich and poor... She be- came increasingly aware of the chasm between men and women that rigid sex roles create.*

chaste /tʃeɪst/. Someone who is **chaste** does not ADJ CLASSIF have sex with anyone, or only has sex with their Outdated

husband or wife; used showing approval.
◊ **chastity** /ˈtʃæstɪ¹tiː/. EG *A monk makes vows of* ◊ N UNCOUNT *poverty, chastity and obedience.*

chasten /ˈtʃeɪsᵊn/, **chastens, chastening, chas-** V+O: USU PASS **tened.** If you **are chastened** by something, it Formal makes you regret that you have behaved badly or foolishly. EG *I left the cafe secretly chastened.*

chastise /tʃæsˈtaɪz/, **chastises, chastising, chas-** v+o **tised.** If you **chastise** someone, **1** you scold them. Formal EG *He chastised members at the Conference for not taking things seriously enough.* **2** you punish them Outdated by beating them. EG *Dr O'Shea chastised his son with the end of his belt.*

chat /tʃæt/, **chats, chatting, chatted.** When peo- V : OFT+A ple **chat**, they talk in an informal and friendly way. EG *We sat by the fire and chatted all evening... She chatted amiably enough about the children.* ▸ used ▸ N COUNT OR as a noun. EG *We had a nice long chat about our* N UNCOUNT *schooldays... The chat goes on all day and night... ...popular subjects for lunchtime chat.*

chat up. If a man **chats** a woman **up**, he talks to PHRASAL VB : her in a friendly way because he is attracted to V+O+ADV her. EG *Hughie queued up for coffee and chatted up* British *the women serving it.*

château /ˈʃætəʊ/, **châteaux.** A **château** is a large N COUNT country house or castle in France.

chatter /ˈtʃætəᵊ/, **chatters, chattering, chat- tered.** 1 If you **chatter**, you talk quickly and v : OFT+A continuously, usually about things which are not important. EG *Off we set, with Bill chattering away all the time.* ▸ used as a noun. EG *At teatime there* ▸ N UNCOUNT *was much excited chatter.*

2 When birds and small animals **chatter**, they v make a series of short, quick, high-pitched noises. EG *The monkeys chattered high up in the trees.*
▸ used as a noun. EG *The wood was noisy with the* ▸ N UNCOUNT *song of birds and the chatter of squirrels.* +SUPP

3 You say that objects **chatter** when they make v : OFT+A repeated rattling or clicking sounds. EG *His teeth chattered uncontrollably because of the cold.*
▸ used as a noun. EG *...the chatter of the typewrit-* ▸ N UNCOUNT *ers... From the floor below came the continuous* +SUPP *whirr and chatter of machinery.*

chatterbox /ˈtʃætəbɒks/, **chatterboxes.** A N COUNT **chatterbox** is someone who talks a lot. Informal

chatty /ˈtʃæti¹/, **chattier, chattiest.** Someone who ADJ QUALIT is **chatty** talks a lot in a friendly, informal way. EG *The taxi driver was chatty and merry... ...a nice chatty letter.*

chauffeur /ˈʃəʊfə, ʃəʊˈfɜː/, **chauffeurs, chauf- feuring, chauffeured.** 1 The **chauffeur** of a rich N COUNT or important person is someone who is employed to look after their car and drive them around in it.

2 If you **chauffeur** someone somewhere, you drive v+o them there in a car, usually as part of your job. EG *You can't expect him to chauffeur you every- where... ...chauffeured limousines.*

chauvinism /ˈʃəʊvɪnɪzᵊm/ is a strong and unrea- N UNCOUNT sonable belief that your own country is more important and morally better than other people's.
◊ **chauvinist.** EG *...chauvinist pride.* ● See also ◊ N COUNT **male chauvinism.** OR N MOD

chauvinistic /ˌʃəʊvɪˈnɪstɪk/. Someone who is ADJ QUALIT **chauvinistic** believes that their own country is more important and morally better than other people's; used showing disapproval. EG *...chauvinis- tic nationalism and ethnic prejudice.*

cheap /tʃiːp/, **cheaper, cheapest.** 1 When goods ADJ QUALIT or services are **cheap**, they cost less money than usual. EG *...cheap plastic buckets... A solid fuel cooker is cheap to run.* ◊ **cheaply.** EG *He decorat-* ◊ ADV *ed my home cheaply and efficiently.*

2 If you do or buy something **on the cheap**, you PHRASE spend less money on it than you should; used Informal showing disapproval. EG ...*a clever way of running a college on the cheap.*

3 You describe a person's behaviour or remarks as **cheap** when they say unkind things about someone in an unnecessary way. EG *He could not resist making cheap jokes at their expense.* ADJ QUALIT

cheat /tʃiːt/, **cheats, cheating, cheated. 1** When someone **cheats**, they lie or behave dishonestly in order to get or achieve something. EG *We all used to cheat in exams.* ◇ **cheating.** EG ...*accusations of cheating.* V ◇ N UNCOUNT

2 If someone **cheats** you out of something, they get it from you by behaving dishonestly. EG *His father was cheated of his land... She cheated her sister out of some money.* V+O : OFT +of/out of

3 If you **feel cheated**, you feel that you have been treated wrongly or unfairly. EG *He will compare your life-style with his own and feel cheated.* PHRASE

4 If you call someone a **cheat**, you mean that they behave dishonestly in order to get what they want. N COUNT

check /tʃek/, **checks, checking, checked. 1** If you **check** something, you make sure that it is satisfactory, safe, or correct. EG *Did you check the engine?... Tony came in from time to time, to check on my progress... He needed a chance to check with Hooper to see if his theory was plausible... He checked that both rear doors were safely shut... Check when the bill will have to be paid.* ▸ used as a noun. EG *Checks on cars and televisions are thorough... ...security checks.* V+O, V+on/with, OR V+REPORT ▸ N COUNT : OFT+on

2 To **check** something also means to stop it from continuing or spreading. EG *The destruction of the bridge checked the enemy's advance.* V+O

3 If you **check** yourself or if something **checks** you, you suddenly stop what you are doing or saying. EG *He began to saunter off, then checked himself and turned back... Sudhir held up his hand to check him.* V-REFL OR V+O

4 If you keep something or someone **in check**, you keep them under control. EG *He had not conquered inflation but he had held it in check.* PHRASE

5 In a restaurant, your **check** is your bill. EG *The waiter brought him his check.* N COUNT American

6 A **check** is a pattern consisting of squares, usually of two colours. EG ...*the simplest of stripes and checks.* ▸ used as an adjective. EG ...*a tall fair-haired man in a check suit.* N UNCOUNT OR N COUNT ▸ ADJ CLASSIF

7 See also **cheque.**

check in or **check into. 1** When you **check** into a hotel or **check in**, you fill in the necessary forms before staying there. EG *He checked into a small boarding house... I checked in at the Gordon Hotel.* PHRASAL VB : V+ADV OR V+PREP

2 When you **check in** at an airport, you arrive and show your ticket before going on a flight. EG *He had already checked in for his return flight when the news reached him.* ● See also **check-in.** V+ADV

check out. 1 When you **check out** of the hotel where you have been staying, you pay the bill and leave. EG *The following morning he checked out of the hotel... Mr Leonard checked out this afternoon, Miss.* **2** If you **check** something **out**, you find out about it or examine it. EG *It might be difficult to transfer your money, so check it out with the manager.* **3** See also **checkout.** PHRASAL VB : V+ADV, OFT+of   V+O+ADV

check up. If you **check up** on someone or something, you obtain information about them, often secretly. EG *He had been asked to check up on a woman suspected of drug smuggling.* ● See also **check-up.** PHRASAL VB : V+ADV, OFT+on

checkered /tʃekəd/. See **chequered.**

check-in. At an airport, a **check-in** counter or desk is a place where you check in. ADJ CLASSIF

checkmate /tʃekmeɪt/. In chess, **checkmate** is a situation in which you cannot stop your king being captured and so you lose the game. N UNCOUNT

checkout /tʃekaut/, **checkouts.** In a supermarket, a **checkout** is a counter where you pay for the things that you have bought. N COUNT

checkpoint /tʃekpɔɪnt/, **checkpoints.** A **checkpoint** is **1** a place where traffic has to stop in order to be checked. **2** one of the items in a list of things that you can check, in order to make sure that you have done something correctly or completely. N COUNT

check-up, check-ups. A **check-up** is an examination by a doctor to see if your health is all right. N COUNT Informal

cheek /tʃiːk/, **cheeks, cheeking, cheeked. 1** Your **cheeks** are the sides of your face below your eyes. See picture at THE HUMAN BODY. EG *She kissed him on both cheeks.* N COUNT

2 You say that someone has **cheek** when you are annoyed about something unreasonable that they have done. EG *You've got a cheek, coming in here.* N UNCOUNT Informal

3 If you **cheek** someone, you are rude or disrespectful to them. EG *Charlie cheeked his dad today.* V+O Informal

cheekbone /tʃiːkbəʊn/, **cheekbones.** Your **cheekbones** are the two bones in your face just below your eyes. N COUNT

cheeky /tʃiːki¹/, **cheekier, cheekiest.** If someone is **cheeky**, they behave in a rude or disrespectful way. EG *They're such cheeky boys.* ADJ QUALIT

cheer /tʃɪə/, **cheers, cheering, cheered. 1** When you **cheer**, you make a loud noise with your voice to show your approval of something or to encourage someone who is taking part in a game. EG *The home crowd cheered their team enthusiastically... His speech was cheered.* ▸ used as a noun. EG *I heard a great cheer go up.* V OR V+O ▸ N COUNT

2 If you **are cheered** by something, it makes you happier or less worried. EG *We were cheered by her warmth and affection.* ◇ **cheering.** EG *It was very cheering to have her here.* V+O : USU PASS ◇ ADJ QUALIT

3 People say **'Cheers'** just before they drink an alcoholic drink. CONVENTION

cheer on. If you **cheer** someone **on**, you cheer loudly in order to encourage them. EG *Students stood on the roof, cheering the rioters on.* PHRASAL VB : V+O+ADV

cheer up. When you **cheer up** or when something **cheers** you **up**, you stop feeling depressed and become more cheerful. EG *She cheered up a little... Her friends tried to cheer her up.* PHRASAL VB : V-ERG+ADV

cheerful /tʃɪəfʊl/. **1** Someone who is **cheerful** is happy and joyful and shows this in their behaviour. EG *She remained cheerful throughout the trip.* ◇ **cheerfully.** EG *He smiled cheerfully at everybody.* ◇ **cheerfulness.** EG *They worked with great energy and cheerfulness.* ADJ QUALIT ◇ ADV ◇ N UNCOUNT

2 Something that is **cheerful** is pleasant and makes you feel happy. EG ...*literature of a more cheerful nature.* ADJ QUALIT

3 You describe someone's attitude as **cheerful** when they are not worried about something, and you think that they should be worried. EG ...*the cheerful conviction that no one will ever start a nuclear war.* ◇ **cheerfully.** EG *They live on irreplaceable capital, which they cheerfully treat as income.* ADJ QUALIT : ATTRIB ◇ ADV

cheerio /tʃɪəriəʊ/ is an informal way of saying 'goodbye'. CONVENTION

cheerless /tʃɪəlɪ²s/. Something that is **cheerless** is gloomy and depressing. EG *It was a cold, cheerless sort of morning.* ADJ QUALIT

cheery /tʃɪəri¹/, **cheerier, cheeriest.** If someone is **cheery**, they are cheerful and happy. EG *Mr Phillips was a cheery man... I wrote cheery letters home.* ◇ **cheerily.** EG *'Hello!' I shouted cheerily.* ADJ QUALIT Outdated ◇ ADV

cheese /tʃiːz/, **cheeses. Cheese** is a solid food made from milk. It is usually white or yellow. EG *You can't live on bread and cheese... I made a nice cheese omelette.* N MASS

cheesecake /tʃiːzkeɪk/, **cheesecakes. Cheesecake** is a dessert that consists of biscuit covered with a soft mixture containing cream cheese. EG *Have some more cheesecake... ...a delicious creamy cheesecake.* N UNCOUNT OR N COUNT

cheetah /tʃiːtə/, **cheetahs.** A **cheetah** is a wild animal that looks like a large cat with black spots on its body. Cheetahs can run very fast. N COUNT

chef /ʃef/, **chefs.** A **chef** is a cook in a restaurant N COUNT
or hotel.

chemical /kɛmɪkəˀl/, **chemicals.** 1 **Chemical** ADJ CLASSIF:
means concerned with chemistry or made by a ATTRIB
process in chemistry. EG *...the chemical composition of the atmosphere... ...chemical fertilizers.*
◊ **chemically.** EG *Chemically, this substance is* ◊ ADV OR
similar to cellulose. ADV SEN
2 A **chemical** is a substance that is used in a N COUNT
chemical process or made by a chemical process.

chemist /kɛmɪst/, **chemists.** 1 A **chemist** or a N SING
chemist's is a shop where you can buy medicine, British
cosmetics, and some household goods. EG *I found
her buying bottles of vitamin tablets at the chemist's.*
2 In Britain, a **chemist** is someone who is qualified N COUNT
to sell medicines prescribed by a doctor. British
3 A **chemist** is also a scientist who does research N COUNT
in chemistry.

chemistry /kɛmɪstri¹/. 1 **Chemistry** is the scien- N UNCOUNT
tific study of the characteristics and composition of
substances and of the way that they react with
other substances. EG *She did a degree in chemistry... ...a new chemistry lab.*
2 If you talk about the **chemistry** of a substance, N UNCOUNT+of
you are referring to its characteristics and composition and the way that it reacts with other substances.

cheque /tʃɛk/, **cheques;** spelled **check** in Ameri- N COUNT
can English. A **cheque** is a printed piece of paper
that you can use instead of money. You write on it
the name of the person you are paying and the
amount of money that you are paying them, and
then you sign it. ● If you **pay by cheque**, you give ● PHRASE
someone a cheque to pay for something, rather
than giving them cash.

chequebook /tʃɛkbʊk/, **chequebooks;** spelled N COUNT
checkbook in American English. A **chequebook**
is a book of cheques.

chequered /tʃɛkəd/; spelled **checkered** in ADJ QUALIT:
American English. If a person or organization has ATTRIB
had a **chequered** career or history, they have had
a varied past with both good and bad parts. EG *The
Journal was a paper with a chequered history.*

cherish /tʃɛrɪʃ/, **cherishes, cherishing, cherished.** 1 If you **cherish** something such as a hope v+o
or a memory, you keep it in your mind so that it
gives you happy feelings. EG *I cherish a hope that
one day we will be reunited.* ◊ **cherished.** EG ◊ ADJ QUALIT
...cherished memories.
2 If you **cherish** someone, you care for them v+o
lovingly and tenderly. EG *Comfort and cherish those
you love.*
3 If you **cherish** a right or a privilege, you regard v+o
it as important and try hard to keep it. EG *Can he
preserve the values he cherishes in his own culture?* ◊ **cherished.** EG *One of our cherished* ◊ ADJ QUALIT
privileges is the right of free speech.

cherry /tʃɛri¹/, **cherries.** 1 **Cherries** are small, N COUNT
round fruit with red or black skins.
2 A **cherry** or a **cherry tree** is a tree that cherries N COUNT
grow on. EG *...a cherry orchard.*

chess /tʃɛs/ is a game for two people, played on a N UNCOUNT
chessboard. Each player has 16 pieces, including a
king. The aim is to move your pieces so that your
opponent's king cannot escape being taken.

chessboard /tʃɛsbɔːd/, **chessboards.** A **chess-** N COUNT
board is a square board that you play chess on. It
is divided into 64 black and white squares.

chest /tʃɛst/, **chests.** 1 Your **chest** is the top part N COUNT
of the front of your body, where your ribs, lungs,
and heart are. See picture at THE HUMAN BODY. EG
*He folded his arms on his chest... She has severe
pains in her chest.*
2 A **chest** is a large, heavy box used for storing N COUNT
things. EG *...an oak chest... ...a medicine chest
stuffed with drugs.*
3 If you **get** something **off** your **chest**, you say PHRASE
what you have been worrying about. Informal

chestnut /tʃɛsnʌt/, **chestnuts.** 1 A **chestnut** is a N COUNT
type of reddish-brown nut.
2 A **chestnut** or a **chestnut tree** is a tree on N COUNT
which chestnuts grow.
3 Something that is **chestnut** or **chestnut-brown** ADJ COLOUR
is dark reddish-brown in colour. EG *He was riding a
chestnut mare.*

chest of drawers, chests of drawers. A **chest** N COUNT
of drawers is a piece of furniture with drawers.

chew /tʃuː/, **chews, chewing, chewed.** 1 When v+o; ALSO
you **chew** food, you use your teeth to break it up in V:OFT+at
your mouth, so that it becomes easier to swallow.
EG *He had started to chew a piece of meat... He
broke off another piece of bread and chewed at it.*
2 If you **chew** your fingernails, you keep biting v+o; ALSO
them because you are nervous. EG *He sat and* V:OFT+at
chewed his fingernails.
3 If an animal **chews** a hole in something, it makes v+o+A
a hole in it by biting it with its teeth. OR V+A
4 If you **chew** on or **chew** over a problem, you v+on/about
think carefully about it. EG *He chewed on this new* Informal
complication... We chew over problems and work
out possible solutions.
5 If you say that someone **has bitten off more** PHRASE
than they **can chew**, you mean that they are Informal
trying to do something which is too difficult for
them.

chewing gum is a kind of sweet which you chew N UNCOUNT
for a long time but do not swallow.

chic /ʃiːk, ʃɪk/. Something or someone that is **chic** ADJ QUALIT
is fashionable and sophisticated. EG *...a very chic
Art College.* ▶ used as a noun. EG *Vermont and New* ▶ N UNCOUNT
Hampshire have acquired a rural chic.

chick /tʃɪk/, **chicks.** A **chick** is a baby bird. N COUNT

chicken /tʃɪkɪn/, **chickens, chickening, chickened.** 1 **Chickens** are birds which are kept on a N COUNT
farm for their eggs and for their meat.
2 **Chicken** is the meat of a chicken. EG *There was* N UNCOUNT
fried chicken for dinner.
3 If you describe a situation as **a chicken and egg** PHRASE
situation, you mean that it is impossible to decide Informal
which of two things caused the other one.
4 You call someone a **chicken** when they are N COUNT
afraid to do something. EG *I was too much of a* Informal
chicken to fight.

chicken out. If you **chicken out** of something, PHRASAL VB:
you decide not to do it because you are afraid. EG *I* V+ADV
chickened out at the last moment. Informal

chickenpox /tʃɪkɪnpɒks/ is a disease which gives N UNCOUNT
you a high temperature and red spots that itch.

chicory /tʃɪkəri¹/ is a vegetable with crunchy, N UNCOUNT
sharp-tasting leaves.

chide /tʃaɪd/, **chides, chiding, chided.** If you v+o:OFT+for
chide someone, you scold them. EG *Maurice chided* OR V+QUOTE
him for his carelessness... 'Fusspot,' chided Outdated
Clarissa.

chief /tʃiːf/, **chiefs.** 1 The **chief** of an organization N COUNT
is the person who is in charge of it. EG *...the current
CIA chief... ...the chief of the Presidential Security
Corps.*
2 The **chief** of a tribe is its leader. EG *He was the* N COUNT
last of the Apache chiefs.
3 **Chief** is used to describe the most important ADJ CLASSIF:
worker of a particular kind in an organization. EG ATTRIB
Mr Zuckermann summoned his chief cashier.
4 The **chief** cause, part, or member of something ADJ CLASSIF:
is the most important one. EG *The 1902 Education* ATTRIB
Act was the chief cause of the Progressives' downfall... I was his chief opponent.

chiefly /tʃiːfli¹/. 1 You use **chiefly** to indicate the ADV OR
most important cause or feature of something. EG ADV SEN
*The experiment was not a success, chiefly because
the machine tools were of poor quality... They
were chiefly interested in making money.*
2 If something is done **chiefly** in a particular way ADV

In what way are 'chilli' and 'chilly' opposite in
meaning?

or place, it is done mainly in that way or place. EG *They lived chiefly by hunting... The film was made in Scotland, chiefly in Glasgow.*

chieftain /tʃiːftən/, **chieftains**. A **chieftain** is the leader of a tribe. N COUNT

chiffon /ʃɪfɒn, ʃɪfɒn/ is a kind of very thin silk or nylon cloth that you can see through. EG *...a green chiffon scarf.* N UNCOUNT

chilblain /tʃɪlbleɪn/, **chilblains**. **Chilblains** are painful red swellings which people get on their fingers or toes in cold weather. N COUNT

child /tʃaɪld/, **children** /tʃɪldrən/. 1 A **child** is a human being who is not yet an adult. EG *...a child of fourteen... ...a family with young children.* N COUNT

2 Someone's **children** are their sons and daughters of any age. EG *He has a wife and four children... Their children are all married.* N PLURAL

childbearing /tʃaɪldbɛərɪŋ/ is the process of giving birth to babies. EG *...muscles strained in childbearing... ...women of childbearing age.* N UNCOUNT

childbirth /tʃaɪldbɜːθ/ is the act of giving birth to a child. EG *His mother died in childbirth.* N UNCOUNT

childhood /tʃaɪldhʊd/. A person's **childhood** is the time when they are a child. EG *Her early childhood had been very happy... ...childhood games.* N UNCOUNT

childish /tʃaɪldɪʃ/. You describe someone as **childish** when you think that they behave in a silly and immature way. EG *I thought her nice but rather childish.* ◊ **childishly**. EG *'It's too hot here,' he complained childishly.* ◊ ADV

childless /tʃaɪldlɪs/. Someone who is **childless** has no children. EG *...childless couples.* ADJ CLASSIF

childlike /tʃaɪldlaɪk/. You describe someone as **childlike** when they seem like a child in their appearance or behaviour. EG *Her voice was fresh and childlike.* ADJ QUALIT

childminder /tʃaɪldmaɪndə/, **childminders**. A **childminder** is someone whose job is to look after other people's children when their parents are not at home. N COUNT

children /tʃɪldrən/ is the plural of **child**.

chili /tʃɪli/. See **chilli**.

chill /tʃɪl/, **chills**, **chilling**, **chilled**. 1 When you **chill** something, you lower its temperature so that it becomes colder but does not freeze. EG *White wine should be slightly chilled.* V-ERG

2 When something **chills** you, 2.1 it makes you feel very cold. EG *A bank clerk is more easily chilled outside than a farmer.* ◊ **chilling**. EG *A chilling wind swept round them... He was exhausted after a chilling swim in the lake.* 2.2 it frightens you very much. EG *She was chilled by his callousness.* ◊ **chilling**. EG *The thought was chilling... It was one of the most chilling articles I have ever read.* V+O: USU PASS ◊ ADJ QUALIT V+O ◊ ADJ QUALIT

3 A **chill** is 3.1 a mild illness which can give you a slight fever and headache. 3.2 a sudden feeling of anxiety. EG *The sound sent a chill down my spine.* N COUNT

4 **Chill** weather is cold and unpleasant. EG *It was a chill autumn day when I left London.* ▸ used as a noun. EG *Barnabas led the way home, feeling the chill of the night through his shirt.* ADJ QUALIT ▸ N UNCOUNT +SUPP

chilli /tʃɪli/, **chillies**; also spelled **chili**. **Chillies** are small red or green seed pods, which have a hot, spicy taste and are used in cooking. N COUNT OR N UNCOUNT

chilly /tʃɪli/, **chillier**, **chilliest**. 1 Something that is **chilly** is rather cold and unpleasant. EG *A draught of chilly air entered the room.* ADJ QUALIT

2 If you feel **chilly**, you feel cold. EG *Light the fire if you feel chilly.* ADJ PRED

chime /tʃaɪm/, **chimes**, **chiming**, **chimed**. When church bells or clocks **chime**, they make ringing sounds, especially to show what time it is. EG *The cathedral bells were chiming through the night... The clock chimed eight-thirty.* ▸ used as a noun. EG *...the silvery chime of the old stable clock.* V OR V+O ▸ N COUNT

chime in. If someone **chimes in**, they say something just after someone else has spoken. EG *Bill chimed in with 'This is an emergency situation.'* PHRASAL VB: V+ADV+ QUOTE, OFT+with

chimney /tʃɪmni/, **chimneys**. A **chimney** is a pipe through which smoke goes up into the air, usually through the roof of a building. See picture at HOUSE. EG *I sat watching the sparks fly up the chimney... ...factory chimneys.* N COUNT

chimney pot, **chimney pots**. A **chimney pot** is a short pipe on top of a chimney stack. N COUNT

chimney stack, **chimney stacks**. A **chimney stack** is the brick or stone part of a chimney that is above the roof of a building. N COUNT British

chimney sweep, **chimney sweeps**. A **chimney sweep** is a person whose job is to clean the soot out of chimneys. N COUNT

chimpanzee /tʃɪmpənziː/, **chimpanzees**. A **chimpanzee** is a kind of small African ape. N COUNT

chin /tʃɪn/, **chins**. Your **chin** is the part of your face that is below your mouth and above your neck. See picture at THE HUMAN BODY. N COUNT

china /tʃaɪnə/. 1 **China** or **china clay** is a kind of very thin clay from which cups, saucers, plates, and ornaments are made. EG *...china cups and saucers.* N UNCOUNT

2 Cups, saucers, plates, and ornaments made of china are referred to as **china**. EG *She laid out a small tray with the best china.* N UNCOUNT

chink /tʃɪŋk/, **chinks**, **chinking**, **chinked**. 1 A **chink** is a very narrow opening. EG *Through a chink she could see a bit of blue sky.* N COUNT

2 When objects **chink**, they touch each other, making a short, light, ringing sound. EG *Empty bottles chinked as the milkman put them into his crate.* ▸ used as a noun. EG *...the chink of money.* V ▸ N SING+of

chintz /tʃɪnts/ is a cotton fabric with bright patterns on it. EG *...chintz curtains.* N UNCOUNT

chip /tʃɪp/, **chips**, **chipping**, **chipped**. 1 In Britain, **chips** are long, thin pieces of potato fried in oil or fat. EG *...fish and chips.* N COUNT : USU PLURAL

2 In America, **chips** or **potato chips** are very thin slices of potato that have been fried until they are hard and crunchy. EG *...a packet of potato chips.* N COUNT : USU PLURAL

3 A **chip** is a very small piece of silicon with electric circuits on it which is part of a computer. EG *The entire contents of a book will be located on a single silicon chip.* N COUNT

4 When you **chip** something, you accidentally damage it by breaking a small piece off it. ◊ **chipped**. EG *...a chipped mug... Deirdre saw that the varnish was slightly chipped.* V+O ◊ ADJ QUALIT

5 A **chip** is also a small piece which has been broken off something. EG *...granite chips.* N COUNT

6 **Chips** are also plastic counters used in gambling to represent money. N COUNT : USU PLURAL

7 You use the expression **when the chips are down** to refer to a serious situation which must be dealt with, and which shows how well or badly someone or something is able to deal with it. EG *It's difficult to tell who is 'average' and who is not until the chips are down.* PHRASE Informal

8 If someone has **a chip on their shoulder**, they behave rudely and aggressively because they feel inferior or think that they have been treated unfairly. PHRASE Informal

chip in. 1 When a number of people **chip in**, each person gives some money so that they can pay for something together. EG *They all chipped in to pay the doctor's bill.* 2 If someone **chips in** during a conversation, they interrupt it in order to say something. EG *'Come on, back to work,' chipped in the supervisor.* PHRASAL VB : V+ADV Informal V+ADV, OFT+QUOTE Informal

chiropodist /kɪrɒpədɪst/, **chiropodists**. A **chiropodist** is a person whose job is to treat and care for people's feet. N COUNT

chirp /tʃɜːp/, **chirps**, **chirping**, **chirped**. When a bird or insect **chirps**, it makes short high-pitched sounds. EG *Birds had begun to chirp among the trees.* V

chisel /tʃɪzəl/, **chisels**, **chiselling**, **chiselled**; spelled **chiseling**, **chiseled** in American English. 1 A **chisel** is a tool that has a long metal blade with N COUNT

a sharp edge at the end. It is used for cutting and shaping wood and stone.
2 If you **chisel** wood or stone, you cut and shape it using a chisel. EG *The men chisel the blocks out of solid rock.* v+o:OFT+A

chivalrous /ʃɪvəlrəs/. A man who is **chivalrous** is polite, kind, and unselfish, especially towards women. EG *They were treated with chivalrous consideration.* ◊ **chivalrously.** EG *'A pleasure,' said Colonel Cameron chivalrously.* ADJ QUALIT ◊ ADV

chivalry /ʃɪvəlri¹/ is polite, kind, and unselfish behaviour, especially by men towards women. N UNCOUNT

chlorine /klɔːriːn/ is a strong-smelling gas that is used to disinfect water and to make cleaning products. N UNCOUNT

chlorophyll /klɒrəfɪl/ is a green substance in plants which enables them to use the energy from sunlight in order to grow. N UNCOUNT

chocolate /tʃɒkə⁰lə¹t/, **chocolates**. 1 Chocolate is 1.1 a sweet, hard, brown food made from cocoa beans, which is eaten as a sweet. EG *...a bar of chocolate... ...chocolate cake.* 1.2 a hot drink made from a powder containing chocolate. N UNCOUNT
2 A **chocolate** is a sweet or nut covered with a layer of chocolate. EG *...a box of chocolates.* N COUNT

choice /tʃɔɪs/, **choices; choicer, choicest.** 1 If there is a **choice** of things, there are several of them and you can choose the one you want. EG *There's a choice of eleven sports... The choice was very limited... ...the choice between peace and war.* N COUNT: USU SING
2 Your **choice** is the thing or things that you choose from a range of things. EG *He congratulated the chef on his choice of dishes.* N COUNT
3 The thing or person **of your choice** is the one that you choose. EG *They could attend the church of their choice... She was prevented from marrying the man of her choice.* PHRASE
4 If you **have no choice** but to do something, you cannot avoid doing it. EG *The President had no choice but to agree.* PHRASE
5 You use **choice** to describe things that are of high quality. EG *...choice cuts of meat.* ADJ QUALIT: ATTRIB

choir /kwaɪə/, **choirs.** A **choir** is a group of people who sing together, for example in a church. N COUNT

choirboy /kwaɪəbɔɪ/, **choirboys.** A **choirboy** is a boy who sings in a church choir. N COUNT

choke /tʃəʊk/, **chokes, choking, choked.** 1 When you **choke** or when something **chokes** you, you cannot breathe properly because you cannot get enough air into your lungs. EG *Philip choked on his drink... The pungent smell of sulphur choked him.* ◊ **choking.** EG *They were enveloped in a cloud of choking dust.* V-ERG : IF V, OFT+on ◊ ADJ QUALIT
2 If someone **chokes** someone else, they squeeze their neck until they are dead. EG *An old woman was found choked to death.* V+O
3 If a place **is choked** with things or people, it is full of them and they prevent movement in it. EG *The centre of the city was choked with cars.* V+O:USU PASS+with
4 The **choke** in a car, lorry, or other vehicle is a device that reduces the amount of air going into the engine and makes it easier to start; also used of the button on the dashboard which operates the device. See picture at CAR. N COUNT

choke back. If you **choke back** a strong emotion, you force yourself not to show it. EG *I choked back my sobs.* PHRASAL VB : V+O+ADV

choked /tʃəʊkt/. If you say something in a **choked** voice, your voice does not have its full sound, because you are upset or afraid. EG *He let out a choked scream.* ADJ QUALIT : ATTRIB

cholera /kɒlərə/ is a serious disease that affects your digestive organs. EG *His parents died of cholera.* N UNCOUNT

choose /tʃuːz/, **chooses, choosing, chose** /tʃəʊz/, **chosen** /tʃəʊzə⁰n/. 1 If you **choose** something from several things that are available, you decide to have it. EG *I chose a yellow dress... They were choosing sweets from one of the stalls... I had been* V+O: OFT+A OR to-INF

chosen to be trained as editor. ◊ **chosen.** EG *They undergo training in their chosen professions... He met them at a chosen rendezvous on the Common.* ◊ ADJ CLASSIF : ATTRIB
2 If you **choose** to do something, you do it because you want to or because you feel that it is right. EG *He chose to ignore her impertinence... They could fire employees whenever they chose.* V : USU+to-INF
3 If there is **little to choose between** things or **not much to choose between** them, it is difficult to decide which is better or more suitable. EG *There's nothing to choose between the two countries.* PHRASE

choosy /tʃuːzi¹/. You say that someone is **choosy** when they are difficult to please, because they will only accept something if it is exactly what they want or if it is of very high quality. EG *I'm very choosy about my whisky... It's not like you to be so choosy.* ADJ QUALIT

chop /tʃɒp/, **chops, chopping, chopped.** 1 If you **chop** something, you cut it into pieces by hitting it with an axe or a knife. EG *I don't like chopping wood... Peel, slice, and chop the apple.* V+O : USU+A
2 A **chop** is a small piece of meat cut from the ribs of a sheep or pig. EG *...lamb chops.* N COUNT
3 If something is **for the chop**, it is going to be stopped or closed. EG *The small theatres will be first for the chop.* PHRASE Informal British
4 When people **chop and change**, they keep changing their minds about what to do or how to act. PHRASE Informal

chop down. If you **chop down** a tree, you cut through its trunk with an axe so that it falls to the ground. PHRASAL VB : V+O+ADV

chop up. If you **chop** something **up** you chop it into small pieces. EG *Chop up some tomatoes and add them to the onion.* PHRASAL VB : V+O+ADV

chopper /tʃɒpə/, **choppers.** A **chopper** is 1 a helicopter. EG *Above the house a chopper buzzed and circled... These days we usually go by chopper.* N COUNT Informal
2 an axe. EG *We broke open the crate with a blow from the chopper.* Informal

choppy /tʃɒpi¹/, **choppier, choppiest.** When water is **choppy**, there are a lot of small waves on it. EG *The sea suddenly turned from smooth to choppy.* ADJ QUALIT

chopstick /tʃɒpstɪk/, **chopsticks. Chopsticks** are a pair of thin sticks which people in China and the Far East use to eat their food with. N COUNT

choral /kɔːrəl/. **Choral** music is sung by a choir. EG *...the pleasures of choral singing.* ADJ CLASSIF : ATTRIB

chord /kɔːd/, **chords.** 1 A **chord** is a number of musical notes played or sung at the same time with a pleasing or satisfying effect. EG *He played some random chords.* N COUNT
2 If something **strikes a chord** with you, it makes you feel sympathy or enthusiasm. EG *The idea struck a chord... Her story may strike a chord for other women in the same situation.* PHRASE

chore /tʃɔː/, **chores.** A **chore** is a task that you find unpleasant or boring. EG *Does your husband do his fair share of the household chores?* N COUNT : USU PLURAL

choreograph /kɒriəgræf/, **choreographs, choreographing, choreographed.** When someone **choreographs** a ballet or other dance, they invent the steps and movements and tell the dancers how to perform them. ◊ **choreographer** /kɒriɒgrəfə/, **choreographers.** EG *He joined the company as a choreographer in 1975.* V+O ◊ N COUNT

choreography /kɒriɒgrəfi¹/ is the art of inventing the steps and movements of ballets or other dances. EG *Our studies include choreography.* N UNCOUNT

chortle /tʃɔːtə⁰l/, **chortles, chortling, chortled.** When someone **chortles**, they laugh with pleasure or amusement. EG *She chortled with delight.* V OR V+QUOTE

chorus /kɔːrəs/, **choruses, chorusing, chorused.** 1 A **chorus** is 1.1 a large group of people who sing N COUNT

Find two words on these pages which mean 'laugh'.

together. **1.2** a piece of music written to be sung by a large group of people. EG ...the Soldiers' Chorus from Faust. **1.3** a part of a song which is repeated after each verse. **1.4** a group of singers or dancers who perform together in a show, in contrast to the soloists. EG ...the girls who danced in the chorus.

2 You can use **chorus** to talk about attitudes N COUNT: expressed by a lot of people at the same time. For USU+of example, you can talk about a **chorus** of disapproval or a **chorus** of satisfaction. EG In recent weeks the chorus of complaint has been growing.

3 When people **chorus** something, they say it or V+O OR sing it together. EG 'Shall I tell you a story?' – V+QUOTE 'Please!' the children would chorus. Literary

chose /tʃəʊz/ is the past tense of **choose**.

chosen /tʃəʊzəⁿn/ is the past participle of **choose**.

christen /krɪsəⁿn/, **christens, christening, christened. 1** When a baby **is christened**, he or V+O OR she is given a name during the Christian ceremony V+O+C: of baptism. EG She was christened Victoria Mary... USU PASS Charles II was christened in this church.

2 To **christen** a place or an object means to V+O+C choose a name for it and to start calling it by that Informal name. EG The crew christened the hot geysers the 'black smokers'.

christening /krɪsəⁿnɪŋ/, **christenings.** A chris- N COUNT **tening** is a Christian ceremony in which a baby is made a member of the Christian church and is officially given his or her name.

Christian /krɪstʃən/, **Christians. 1** A **Christian** is N COUNT a person who believes in Jesus Christ and follows his teachings. ▸ used as an adjective. EG ...a ▸ ADJ CLASSIF Christian missionary... Charity is the greatest of Christian virtues.

2 People are sometimes described as **Christian** ADJ QUALIT: when they are very good and kind. EG She was a ATTRIB really Christian woman... I wouldn't call that a very Christian attitude.

Christianity /krɪstɪænɪˈtiⁱ/ is a religion that is N UNCOUNT based on the teachings of Jesus Christ and the belief that he was the son of God.

Christian name, Christian names. A person's N COUNT **Christian name** is a name that is given to them when they are born or when they are christened. EG Do all your students call you by your Christian name?

Christmas /krɪsməs/, **Christmases.** Christmas N UNCOUNT is the Christian festival when the birth of Jesus OR N COUNT Christ on the 25th of December is celebrated. EG Merry Christmas and a Happy New Year!... ...the Christmas holidays... The past few Christmases have been very quiet.

Christmas Day is the 25th of December, when N UNCOUNT Christmas is celebrated.

Christmas Eve is the 24th of December, the day N UNCOUNT before Christmas Day.

Christmas tree, Christmas trees. A Christ- N COUNT **mas tree** is a fir tree, or an artificial tree that looks like a fir tree, which people put in their houses at Christmas and decorate with coloured lights and balls.

chrome /krəʊm/ is a hard silver-coloured metal. N UNCOUNT EG ...chrome bath taps.

chromium /krəʊmɪəm/ is the same as chrome. N UNCOUNT

chromosome /krəʊməsəʊm/, **chromosomes.** A N COUNT **chromosome** is a part of a cell in an animal or Technical plant. It contains genes which determine what characteristics the animal or plant will have.

chronic /krɒnɪk/. **1** A **chronic** illness lasts for a ADJ CLASSIF: very long time. EG Her father was dying of chronic USU ATTRIB asthma. ◇ **chronically.** EG ...pensions for the ◇ ADV+ADJ chronically sick.

2 You describe someone's bad habits or behaviour ADJ CLASSIF: as **chronic** when they have behaved like that for a ATTRIB long time and do not seem to be able to stop themselves. EG ...chronic drunkenness.

3 A **chronic** situation or problem is very severe ADJ CLASSIF: and unpleasant. EG ...chronic food shortages. USU ATTRIB

◇ **chronically.** EG ...an education service that is ◇ SUBMOD chronically short of finance.

chronicle /krɒnɪkəⁿl/, **chronicles, chronicling, chronicled. 1** If you **chronicle** a series of events, V+O you write about them in the order in which they Formal happened. EG Xenophon chronicled the Persian Wars.

2 A **chronicle** is a formal account or record of a N COUNT series of events. Formal

chronological /krɒnəlɒdʒɪkəⁿl/. If you describe a ADJ CLASSIF series of events in **chronological** order, you describe them in the order in which they happened.

◇ **chronologically.** EG The collection is arranged ◇ ADV chronologically.

chrysalis /krɪsəlɪs/, **chrysalises.** A **chrysalis** is N COUNT **1** a butterfly or moth in the stage between being a larva and an adult. **2** the hard, protective covering that a chrysalis has.

chrysanthemum /krɪsænθəməm/, **chrysan-** N COUNT **themums.** A **chrysanthemum** is a large garden flower with many long, thin petals.

chubby /tʃʌbiⁱ/, **chubbier, chubbiest.** A **chubby** ADJ QUALIT child is rather fat and round. EG ...chubby little fingers.

chuck /tʃʌk/, **chucks, chucking, chucked. 1** V+O+A When you **chuck** something somewhere, you Informal throw it there in a casual or careless way. EG Chuck my tights across, please.

2 If you **chuck** someone out of a place, you force V+O+A them to leave. EG We were chucked out of the Informal meeting.

chuck away or **chuck out.** If you **chuck** some- PHRASAL VB: thing **away** or **chuck** it **out,** you throw it away, V+O+ADV because you do not need it or cannot use it. EG The Informal clock had to be chucked away because it didn't work.

chuckle /tʃʌkəⁿl/, **chuckles, chuckling, chuck-** V OR V+QUOTE **led.** When people **chuckle,** they laugh quietly. EG They were chuckling over the photographs. ▸ used ▸ N COUNT as a noun. EG He shook his head with a soft chuckle.

chug /tʃʌg/, **chugs, chugging, chugged.** When a V: OFT+A vehicle or engine **chugs,** it makes short thudding sounds. EG A small fishing boat comes chugging towards them.

chum /tʃʌm/, **chums. 1** Your **chum** is your friend. N COUNT EG I had my chum with me... In Dublin he met an Outdated old school chum. Informal

2 Men sometimes address each other as **chum,** VOCATIVE usually in a slightly aggressive or unfriendly way. Outdated EG You've had it, chum. Informal

chunk /tʃʌŋk/, **chunks. 1** A **chunk** of something N PART solid is a piece of it. EG ...a great chunk of meat.

2 A **chunk** is also a large amount or part of N PART something. EG Research and development now take Informal up a sizeable chunk of the military budget.

chunky /tʃʌŋkiⁱ/. **1** You describe people as ADJ QUALIT **chunky** when they are broad and heavy. EG A chunky waitress came waddling towards him.

2 A **chunky** object is large and thick. EG ...great ADJ QUALIT chunky cardigans.

church /tʃɜːtʃ/, **churches. 1** A **church** is a build- N COUNT OR ing in which Christians worship. EG There were no N UNCOUNT services that day, and the church was empty... His parents go to church now and then.

2 A **Church** is one of the groups of people within N COUNT the Christian religion, for example Catholics. EG Jane had been received into the Church a month previously.

churchman /tʃɜːtʃmə³n/, **churchmen.** A N COUNT **churchman** is the same as a clergyman. Formal

churchyard /tʃɜːtʃjɑːd/, **churchyards.** A N COUNT **churchyard** is an area of land around a church where people are buried.

churlish /tʃɜːlɪʃ/. **Churlish** behaviour is unfriend- ADJ QUALIT ly, bad-tempered, or impolite. EG It seemed churlish to send him away.

churn /tʃɜːn/, **churns, churning, churned. 1** A N COUNT **churn** is a container which is used for making milk or cream into butter.

2 When someone **churns** milk or cream, they stir v+o it vigorously in order to turn it into butter.

3 If something **churns** mud or water, it moves it v-erg about violently. eg *The bulldozers were churning the mud... He could see the water churning about under the propellers.*

4 If you say that your stomach **is churning**, you v mean that you feel sick. eg *My stomach churned* Informal *when I saw them together.*

churn out. To **churn** things **out** means to pro- phrasal vb : duce large numbers of them very quickly. eg *His* v+o+adv *organization began churning out tracts and post-* Informal *ers... My brain was churning out objections at an incredible speed.*

churn up. When something **churns up** mud or phrasal vb : water, it moves it about violently. eg *The wind* v+o+adv *churned up the water into a swirling foam.*

chute /ʃuːt/, **chutes.** A **chute** is a steep, narrow n count slope down which objects such as coal or parcels can slide so that they do not have to be carried.

chutney /tʃʌtnɪ¹/ is a strong-tasting mixture of n uncount fruit, vinegar, sugar, and spices which you eat with meat or cheese. eg *...mango chutney.*

cider /saɪdə/ is an alcoholic drink made from n uncount apples.

cigar /sɪgɑː/, **cigars. Cigars** are rolls of dried n count tobacco leaves which people smoke.

cigarette /sɪgə¹ret/, **cigarettes. Cigarettes** are n count small tubes of paper containing tobacco which people smoke. eg *Boylan lit a cigarette.*

cinch /sɪntʃ/. If you say that something **is a cinch**, phrase you mean that it is very easy to do. eg *Beating* Informal *Rangers should be a cinch.*

cinder /sɪndə/, **cinders. 1 Cinders** are the pieces n count : of material that are left after wood or coal has usu plural burned.

2 If you burn something **to a cinder**, you burn it phrase until it is black.

cinema /sɪnə¹mə/, **cinemas. 1** A **cinema** is a n count place where people go to watch films.

2 Cinema is the business and art of making films. n uncount eg *...one of the classic works of Hollywood cinema.*

cinematic /sɪnə¹mætɪk/ means relating to films adj classif : made for the cinema. attrib

cinnamon /sɪnəmən/ is a spice used for flavour- n uncount ing sweet food.

cipher /saɪfə/, **ciphers;** also spelled **cypher.** A n count or **cipher** is a secret system of writing that you use to in+n send messages. eg *The necessary codes and ciphers will be included in your orders... They had been corresponding with one another in cipher.*

circa /sɜːkə/ in front of a year means that this is prep the approximate date when something happened or was made. eg *...an old British newspaper, circa 1785.*

circle /sɜːkə¹l/, **circles, circling, circled. 1** A n count **circle** is a curved line completely surrounding an area. Every part of the line is the same distance from the centre of the area. See picture at shapes. eg *The students sit in a circle on the floor.*

2 A **circle** of something is a round, flat piece or n count : area of it. eg *Stand the paint tin on a circle of* usu+supp *aluminium foil.*

3 If a bird or aircraft **circles**, it moves round in a v :oft+a circle in the air. eg *Hawks circled overhead looking for prey.*

4 If something **circles** something else, it moves v+o round it. eg *Galileo saw four moons circling Jupiter in 1610.*

5 You can refer to a group of people as a **circle.** eg n count+supp *I have widened my circle of acquaintances... This proposal caused an uproar in parliamentary circles.*

6 The **circle** in a theatre or cinema is an area of n sing : the+n seats on the upper floor.

7 If you say that someone is **going round in** phrase **circles**, you mean that they are not achieving Informal anything because they keep coming back to the same point or problem.

8 If you say that something **has come full circle**, phrase you mean that after a long series of events or changes the same situation exists as at the beginning.

circuit /sɜːkɪt/, **circuits. 1** An electrical **circuit** n count is a complete route which an electric current can flow around.

2 A **circuit** is also a series of places that are n count+supp visited regularly by a person or group. eg *...the American college lecture circuit.*

3 A racing **circuit** is a track on which cars, n count motorbikes, or cycles race.

circuitous /sə¹kjuːɪtəs/. A **circuitous** route or adj qualit : journey is long and complicated rather than simple usu attrib and direct. eg *After a long and circuitous journey* Formal *by train and boat, we finally arrived.*

circular /sɜːkjə¹lə/, **circulars. 1** Something that adj classif is **circular** is shaped like a circle. eg *...a circular pond.*

2 A **circular** journey or route is one in which you adj classif go to a place and return by a different route.

3 A **circular** argument or theory is not valid adj classif because it uses a statement to prove the conclusion Formal and the conclusion to prove the statement.
◇ **circularity** /sɜːkjə¹lærɪ¹ti¹/. eg *My argument* ◇ n uncount *suffered from circularity.*

4 A **circular** is an official letter or advertisement n count that is sent to a large number of people at the same time.

circulate /sɜːkjə¹leɪt/, **circulates, circulating, circulated. 1** When a piece of writing **circulates** v-erg : usu+a or **is circulated**, copies of it are passed round among a group of people. eg *The report was circulated to all the members... A union news paper was circulating at the congress.*

2 If something such as a joke or a rumour **circu-** v-erg : usu+a **lates** or **is circulated**, the people in a place tell it to each other. eg *Stories about him circulated at his club... A wicked rumour had been circulated that she was a secret drinker.*

3 If a substance **circulates** or **is circulated**, it v-erg : usu+a moves easily and freely within a closed place or system. eg *We are governed by the hormones that circulate around our bodies.*

4 If you **circulate** at a party, you move among the v guests and talk to different people.

circulation /sɜːkjə¹leɪʃə⁰n/, **circulations. 1 Cir-** n uncount **culation** refers to the process by which a piece of writing is passed round among a group of people. eg *...the circulation of illegal books.*

2 The **circulation** of a newspaper or magazine is n count+supp the number of copies that are sold each time it is produced. eg *The local paper had a circulation of only six thousand.*

3 The **circulation** of a substance is the process by n uncount which it moves freely within a place or system. eg *...the circulation of air.*

4 Your **circulation** is the movement of blood n sing : through your body. eg *He stamped his feet from* usu+supp *time to time to keep the circulation going.*

5 Money that is in **circulation** is being used by the n uncount public.

circumcise /sɜːkəmsaɪz/, **circumcises, circum-** v+o **cising, circumcised.** To **circumcise** a man or boy means to cut off the loose skin at the end of his penis for religious or medical reasons.
◇ **circumcision** /sɜːkəmsɪʒə⁰n/. eg *...the rite of* ◇ n uncount *circumcision.*

circumference /sə¹kʌmfə⁰rəns/, **circumfer-** n count+supp **ences.** The **circumference** of a circle, place, or round object is **1** its edge. eg *He went jogging around the circumference of the reservoir.* **2** the distance around its edge. eg *The area has a circumference of 54 miles.*

Could cider cause cirrhosis?

circumscribe /sɜːkəmskraɪb/, **circumscribes,** V+O : USU PASS **circumscribing, circumscribed.** If someone's Formal power or freedom **is circumscribed**, it is limited or restricted.

circumspect /sɜːkəmspɛkt/. If you are **circum-** ADJ QUALIT **spect**, you are cautious and avoid taking risks. EG Formal *Physicians are now more circumspect about making recommendations for surgery.* ◊ **circumspectly.** EG *He would have to behave* ◊ ADV *circumspectly.*

circumstance /sɜːkəmstəns/, **circumstances.** 1 **Circumstances** are the conditions which affect N PLURAL what will happen in a particular situation. EG *In* +SUPP *normal circumstances I would have resigned immediately... Under the circumstances Dolores had better stay away... the political and economic circumstances that exist in Ireland.*
2 You can emphasize that something must not or PHRASE will not happen by saying that it must not or will not happen **under any circumstances**. EG *Under no circumstances whatsoever will I support Mr Baldwin.*
3 If someone describes the **circumstances** of an N PLURAL event, they describe how it happened. EG *She died* +SUPP *without ever learning the circumstances of her grandfather's death.*
4 Your **circumstances** are the conditions of your N PLURAL life, especially the amount of money that you have. +POSS EG *...the change in George's circumstances.*
5 Events and situations which cannot be controlled N UNCOUNT are sometimes referred to as **circumstance**. EG *...a* Literary *victim of circumstance... Ambitions are thwarted by circumstance.*

circumstantial /sɜːkəmstænʃəl/. **Circumstan-** ADJ CLASSIF **tial** evidence makes it seem likely that something Formal happened, but does not prove it. EG *The circumstantial evidence is overwhelming.*

circus /sɜːkəs/, **circuses.** A **circus** is a show N COUNT performed in a large tent, with animals, clowns, and acrobats. EG *...the trainers from a nearby circus... We were going to take the children to the circus.*

cirrhosis /sɪrəʊsɪs/ is a serious disease which N UNCOUNT destroys a person's liver. It is often caused by Medical drinking too much alcohol.

cissy /sɪsiˈ/. See **sissy**.

cistern /sɪstən/, **cisterns.** A **cistern** is 1 a N COUNT container which holds the water that is used to flush a toilet. 2 a large tank in the roof of a house in which water is stored.

citadel /sɪtədəl/, **citadels.** A **citadel** is a strongly N COUNT fortified building in a city.

citation /saɪteɪʃən/, **citations.** A **citation** is 1 an N COUNT official document or speech which praises a person Formal for something brave or special that they have done. EG *The three policemen subsequently received citations.* 2 a quotation from a book or other Formal piece of writing.

cite /saɪt/, **cites, citing, cited.** 1 If you **cite** V+O something, you quote it from a written work or you Formal mention it, especially as an example or proof of what you are saying. EG *The most commonly cited example of a primitive device is the abacus.*
2 To **cite** someone or something in a legal action V+O means to officially name them. EG *...the woman* Formal *who was cited in his divorce action.*

citizen /sɪtɪzən/, **citizens.** 1 If someone is a N COUNT+SUPP **citizen** of a particular country, they are legally accepted as belonging to that country. EG *...a Swedish citizen.*
2 The **citizens** of a town or city are the people N COUNT+SUPP who live there. EG *...the citizens of Bristol.*
3 See also **senior citizen**.

citizenship /sɪtɪzənʃɪp/ refers to the country that N UNCOUNT you legally belong to. For example, if you have +SUPP Portuguese **citizenship**, you are legally accepted as belonging to Portugal.

citrus fruit /sɪtrəs fruːt/, **citrus fruits.** A citrus N COUNT OR fruit is a juicy, sharp-tasting fruit such as an N UNCOUNT orange, lemon, or grapefruit.

city /sɪtiˈ/, **cities.** 1 A **city** is a large town. EG N COUNT *...overcrowded cities... ...the city of Birmingham... ...a modern city centre.*
2 The **City** is the part of London where many N PROPER : important financial institutions have their main the+N offices. EG *...a City banker.*

civic /sɪvɪk/. You use **civic** to describe 1 people ADJ CLASSIF : or things that have an official status in a town or ATTRIB city. EG *...the civic centre... ...a civic leader from the local Pakistani community.* 2 the duties or feelings that people have because they belong to a particular community. EG *She was determined to carry out her civic responsibilities... ...civic pride.*

civil /sɪvəl/. 1 You use **civil** to describe 1.1 ADJ CLASSIF : events that happen within a country and that ATTRIB involve the different groups of people in it. EG *...a society in which wars or civil disturbances happen.* 1.2 people or things in a country that are not connected with its armed forces. EG *...the civil authorities... ...a supersonic civil airliner named the Concorde.* 1.3 the rights that people have within a society. EG *...the defence of civil liberties and human rights.*
2 Someone who is **civil** is polite. EG *He'd been* ADJ QUALIT *careful to be civil to everyone.* ◊ **civilly.** EG *He* ◊ ADV *was somewhat upset but he answered civilly enough.* ◊ **civility** /sɪvɪlˈtiˈ/. EG *She was treated* ◊ N UNCOUNT *with civility and consideration.*

civilian /sɪvɪljən/, **civilians.** A **civilian** is anyone N COUNT who is not a member of the armed forces. EG *They tried to avoid bombing civilians.*

civilise /sɪvɪlaɪz/. See **civilize**.

civilization /sɪvɪlaɪzeɪʃən/, **civilizations;** also N COUNT OR spelled **civilisation**. 1 A **civilization** is a human N UNCOUNT society which has its own highly developed social organization, culture, and way of life which makes it distinct from other societies. EG *...the entire history of Western civilisation.*
2 **Civilization** is the state of having a high level of N UNCOUNT social organization, culture, and a comfortable way of life. EG *The Romans brought civilization to much of Europe.*

civilize /sɪvɪlaɪz/, **civilizes, civilizing, civi-** V+O **lized;** also spelled **civilise**. To **civilize** a person or society means to educate them so that they can improve their social organization, culture, or way of life. EG *He treated them as savages to be tamed and civilised.*

civilized /sɪvɪlaɪzd/; also spelled **civilised**.
1 A society that is **civilized** has a highly developed ADJ QUALIT culture, technology, and system of government. EG *They aim to create an orderly and civilised society.*
2 If you describe a person as **civilized**, you mean ADJ QUALIT that they are polite and reasonable in their attitudes and behaviour. EG *...a civilized discussion.*

civil servant, civil servants. A **civil servant** is N COUNT a person who works in the Civil Service.

Civil Service. The **Civil Service** of a country N COLL : the+N consists of all the government departments and all the people who work in them.

civil war, civil wars. A **civil war** is a war which N COUNT OR is fought between different groups of people who N UNCOUNT live in the same country. EG *His brother was killed in the Spanish Civil War... There might be civil war again in this area.*

clad /klæd/. If you are **clad** in particular clothes, ADJ CLASSIF : you are wearing them. EG *...beggars clad in dirty* USU PRED+in *white rags.* Literary

claim /kleɪm/, **claims, claiming, claimed.** 1 You V+QUOTE, use **claim** to report what someone says when you REPORT want to indicate that you are not sure whether OR to-INF what they are saying is true or not. EG *He claimed that he found the money in the forest... They claimed to have shot down twenty-two planes... The marines were invited, it is claimed, by the government.*

2 If someone **claims** responsibility or credit for v+o
something, they say that they are responsible for it,
although they might not be telling the truth. EG *The
rebels claimed responsibility for the bombing.*

3 If you **claim** something, you ask for it because v+o or v+a
you have a right to it, or think that you have. EG
*Voluntary workers can claim travelling expenses...
Don't forget to claim for a first-class rail ticket to
London... ...claiming back land lost by his father.*

4 If you say that a fight or disaster **claims** some- v+o
one's life, you mean that they are killed in it. EG *The* Formal
*wave of bombings and street clashes is claiming
new lives every day.*

5 A **claim** is **5.1** something which someone says N COUNT:
which they cannot prove and which may be false. OFT+REPORT
EG *Forecasts do not support the government's
claim that the economy is picking up.* **5.2** a N COUNT
demand for something that you think you have a
right to. EG *...a pay claim... ...a claim for compensation.* **5.3** the right to have something. EG *They* N COUNT:
denied her rightful claim to the property... Henry OFT+to
*Cooper's chief claim to fame is that he knocked
down Mohammed Ali.*

6 If you have a **claim** on someone, you have the N COUNT
right to demand things from them. EG *She realized* +on/upon
that she had no claims on the man.

7 If you **lay claim to** something, you say that it is PHRASE
yours. EG *Both countries laid claim to the territory.* Formal

● **to stake a claim**: see **stake**.

claimant /kleɪmənt/, **claimants**. A **claimant** is N COUNT
someone who asks to be given something which
they think they are entitled to, especially money.
EG *It is not always clear whether a claimant is
entitled to benefit.*

clairvoyant /kleəˈvɔɪənt/, **clairvoyants**. Some- ADJ CLASSIF
one who is **clairvoyant** is believed to know about
future events or to be able to communicate with
dead people. ▸ used as a noun. EG *I'm like a* ▸ N COUNT
*clairvoyant receiving messages from another
world.* ◊ **clairvoyance** /kleəˈvɔɪəns/. EG *...the* ◊ N UNCOUNT
power of magic and clairvoyance.

clam /klæm/, **clams, clamming, clammed**. A N COUNT
clam is a kind of shellfish.

clam up. If someone **clams up**, they stop talking. PHRASAL VB:
EG *Then I clammed up and said nothing for the rest* V+ADV
of the meal. Informal

clamber /klæmbə/, **clambers, clambering**, v+a
clambered. If you **clamber** somewhere, you
climb there with difficulty, usually using your
hands as well as your feet. EG *We clambered up the
hill.*

clammy /klæmɪ¹/, **clammier, clammiest**. Some- ADJ QUALIT
thing that is **clammy** is unpleasantly damp and
sticky. EG *His handshake is cold and clammy.*

clamour /klæmə/, **clamours, clamouring,
clamoured**; spelled **clamor** in American English.

1 If people **clamour** for something, they demand it v+for
noisily or angrily. EG *...changes in the law for which* Formal
people are clamouring.

2 When large groups of people **clamour**, they all v
talk and shout together loudly. EG *The clamouring* Literary
crowd was spreading. ▸ used as a noun. EG *The* ▸ N UNCOUNT
clamour of voices from the living-room seemed +SUPP
louder than ever.

clamp /klæmp/, **clamps, clamping, clamped**. **1** N COUNT
A **clamp** is a device that holds two things firmly
together. EG *...containers which are sealed with
metal clamps.*

2 When you **clamp** one thing to another, you fasten v+o:OFT
the two things together with a clamp. EG *...trays* +to/together
that were clamped to the arm of a chair.

3 To **clamp** something in a particular place means v+o+a
to put it or hold it there firmly and tightly. EG *He
picked up his bowler hat and clamped it upon his
head... They clamped handcuffs around my wrists.*

clamp down. To **clamp down** on people or PHRASAL VB:
activities means to take strong official action to V+ADV,
stop or control them. EG *The authorities have got to* OFT+on
clamp down on these trouble-makers.

clan /klæn/, **clans**. A **clan** is a group of families N COLL
that are related to each other. EG *...a power struggle between two Somali clans.*

clandestine /klænˈdɛstɪⁿn/. Something that is ADJ CLASSIF:
clandestine is hidden or kept secret, often be- USU ATTRIB
cause it is illegal. EG *...a clandestine radio station...* Formal
*We had to ensure that no clandestine operations
were under way.*

clang /klæŋ/, **clangs, clanging, clanged**. When a V-ERG
large metal object **clangs**, it makes a loud, deep
noise. EG *...the sound of the bells clanging... She
clanged the gates behind her.* ▸ used as a noun. EG ▸ N COUNT:
The door opened with a heavy clang. USU SING

clank /klæŋk/, **clanks, clanking, clanked**. When v
metal objects **clank**, they make a loud noise because they are crashing together or against something hard. EG *All about him he heard chains
clanking.* ▸ used as a noun. EG *...the clank of metal* ▸ N COUNT:
upon stone. USU SING

clap /klæp/, **claps, clapping, clapped**. **1** When v
people **clap**, they hit their hands together several
times, usually in order to express appreciation. EG
*The audience clapped enthusiastically and called
for more.*

2 If you **clap** your hands, you hit your hands v+o
together once, usually in order to attract someone's attention. EG *The vicar clapped his hands for
silence.* ▸ used as a noun. EG *He called them to* ▸ N COUNT
order with a clap of his hands.

3 If you **clap** an object or your hand onto some- v+o+a
thing, you put it there quickly and firmly. EG *He
claps his hands to his head.*

4 If you **clap** someone on the back or on the v+o+a
shoulder, you hit their back or shoulder with your
hand in a friendly way. EG *He clapped her on the
back and laughed.* ● **to clap eyes on** someone: see
eye.

5 A **clap** of thunder is a sudden loud noise of N COUNT+of
thunder.

clapped-out. A machine that is **clapped-out** is ADJ QUALIT:
old and no longer working properly. EG *The last car* Informal
was a clapped-out old Ford. British

claptrap /klæptræp/. If you describe something N UNCOUNT
that someone says as **claptrap**, you mean that it is Informal
stupid or foolish. EG *A lot of claptrap is talked about
the 'dignity of labour'.*

claret /klærət/, **clarets**. **Claret** is a type of red N MASS
French wine.

clarify /klærɪfaɪ/, **clarifies, clarifying, clari-** v+o
fied. To **clarify** something means to make it
easier to understand. EG *If you don't understand,
ask the speaker to clarify the point.*
◊ **clarification** /klærɪfɪkeɪʃⁿn/. EG *We must wait* ◊ N UNCOUNT
for clarification of the situation.

clarinet /klærɪnɛt/, **clarinets**. A **clarinet** is a N COUNT
woodwind instrument with a straight tube and a
single reed in its mouthpiece. See picture at
MUSICAL INSTRUMENTS.

clarity /klærɪ¹tiⁱ/ is **1** the quality of being well N UNCOUNT
explained and easy to understand. EG *...the clarity* +SUPP
of her explanation. **2** the ability to think clearly. EG
*She was forcing me to think with more clarity
about what I had seen.*

clash /klæʃ/, **clashes, clashing, clashed**. **1** If V OR V+with:
someone **clashes** with someone else or if two RECIP
people **clash**, they fight, argue, or disagree with
each other. EG *Youths clashed with police in the
streets around the ground... The delegates clashed
from the first day of the congress.* ▸ used as a ▸ N COUNT
noun. EG *...the first public clash between the two
party leaders.*

2 Beliefs, ideas, or qualities that **clash** with each V OR V+with:
other are very different from each other and RECIP
therefore are opposed to each other. EG *This belief
clashes with all that we know about human psy-*

Which words on these pages can refer to
sounds?

chology... In a situation like this, moral values or principles may clash. ▶ used as a noun. EG ...a ▶ N COUNT personality clash.

3 If two events **clash**, they happen at the same V OR V+with : time so that you cannot attend both of them. EG A RECIP religious convention had clashed with a flower show.

4 When two or more colours or styles **clash**, they V OR V+with : look ugly together. EG She was wearing a pink RECIP jacket which clashed violently with the colour of her hair.

5 When metal objects **clash**, they make a lot of V noise by being hit together. ▶ used as a noun. EG ...a ▶ N COUNT clash of cymbals.

clasp /klɑːsp/, **clasps, clasping, clasped. 1** If you V+O **clasp** someone or something, you hold them tightly in your hands or arms. EG The woman was standing clasping the sleeping baby in her arms.

2 A **clasp** is a small device that fastens something. N COUNT EG ...a black bag with a silver clasp.

class /klɑːs/, **classes, classing, classed. 1** A **class** is **1.1** a group of pupils or students who are N COUNT taught together. EG If classes were smaller, children would learn more. **1.2** a short period of N COUNT teaching in a particular subject. EG Peggy took evening classes in French. ● If you do something ● PHRASE **in class**, you do it during a lesson in school. EG You're not supposed to eat in class.

2 Class is used to refer to the way that the people N COUNT OR in a society are divided into groups according to N UNCOUNT their social status. Each group is referred to as a particular **class**. EG ...the ruling class... ...other children of the same age and class... ...the British class system. ● See also **middle class, upper class, working class**.

3 A **class** of things is a group of them with similar N COUNT+SUPP characteristics. EG We can identify several classes of fern.

4 If you say that someone is **in a class of** their PHRASE **own**, you mean that they have more of a particular skill or quality than anyone else.

5 If you say that someone or something has **class**, N UNCOUNT you mean that they are elegant and sophisticated. Informal

6 If you **class** someone or something as a particu- V+O+as/with lar thing, you consider them as belonging to that group of things. EG At nineteen you're still classed as a teenager.

-class is added to words like 'first' and 'executive' to indicate that a service or product is of a particular official standard. EG I prefer to travel first class.

classic /klæsɪk/, **classics. 1** A **classic** example of ADJ CLASSIF : a thing or situation has all the features which you ATTRIB expect such a thing or situation to have. EG London is the classic example of the scattered city... This statement was a classic illustration of British politeness.

2 You use **classic** to describe something such as a ADJ CLASSIF : film or a piece of writing when it is of very high ATTRIB quality and has become a standard against which similar things are judged. EG ...one of the classic works of the Hollywood cinema.

3 A **classic** is a book which is well-known and N COUNT considered to be of a very high literary standard. EG ...a great classic of Brazilian literature.

4 Classics is the study of the ancient Greek and N UNCOUNT Roman civilizations, especially their languages, literature, and philosophy.

classical /klæsɪkⁿl/. You use **classical** to describe 1 something that is traditional in form, style, ADJ CLASSIF : or content. EG We offer tuition in classical ballet, USU ATTRIB modern ballet, and ballroom dancing... ...the classical Hindu scheme of values. **2** music that is ADJ CLASSIF : considered to be serious and of lasting value, as ATTRIB opposed to pop or jazz. EG ...classical pianists. **3** ADJ CLASSIF : something that relates to ancient Greek or Roman ATTRIB civilization. EG ...plays set in classical times.

classification /klæsɪfɪkeɪʃⁿn/, **classifications. 1** The **classification** of things is the activity or N UNCOUNT

process of classifying them into different types. EG The cataloguing and classification of the plants on the island took several months.

2 A **classification** is **2.1** a system of classifying N COUNT things. EG The broad outlines of most classifications are quite similar. **2.2** a division or category in a classifying system. EG Your insurance group classification changes when you buy a bigger car.

classified /klæsɪfaɪd/. Something that is **classi-** ADJ CLASSIF **fied** is officially secret. EG ...a man suspected of passing on classified information.

classify /klæsɪfaɪ/, **classifies, classifying, clas-** V+O : **sified.** To **classify** things such as animals, plants, USU PASS+as or books means to divide them into groups so that things with similar characteristics are in the same group. EG Pastimes may be classified in different ways... Twenty-two of these plants are now classified as rare... The books have been classified according to subject.

classless /klɑːslɪs/. A **classless** society is one in ADJ CLASSIF : which all people have the same social and econom- USU ATTRIB ic status.

classmate /klɑːsmeɪt/, **classmates.** Your **class-** N COUNT **mates** are students who are in the same class as you at school or college.

classroom /klɑːsruⁿm/, **classrooms.** A **class-** N COUNT **room** is a room in a school where lessons take place.

classy /klɑːsiⁱ/, **classier, classiest.** If you de- ADJ QUALIT scribe someone or something as **classy**, you mean Informal they are stylish and sophisticated. EG ...eating out in classy places.

clatter /klætə/, **clatters, clattering, clattered.** N COUNT : A **clatter** is a continuous series of short, loud USU SING+SUPP sounds made by hard things hitting each other. EG ...the clatter of dishes being washed. ▶ used as a ▶ V-ERG : verb. EG My sister was clattering the forks back USU+A into the drawer... The door clattered open.

clause /klɔːz/, **clauses. 1** A **clause** is a section of N COUNT a legal document. EG He included a clause in the contract that allowed him to buy the house back at the original price.

2 In grammar, a **clause** is a group of words N COUNT containing a verb. Sentences contain one or more clauses.

claustrophobia /klɒstrəˈfəʊbɪə, klɔːs-/. Someone N UNCOUNT who suffers from **claustrophobia** is afraid of being in small or enclosed places.

claustrophobic /klɒstrəˈfəʊbɪk, klɔː-/. **1** If you ADJ QUALIT feel **claustrophobic**, you feel uncomfortable or frightened when you are in a small or enclosed place. EG Leave the door open. I get very claustrophobic.

2 You describe a place or situation as **claustro-** ADJ QUALIT **phobic** when it makes you feel uncomfortable and unhappy because you are enclosed or restricted. EG ...a small claustrophobic restaurant... Life can seem claustrophobic.

claw /klɔː/, **claws, clawing, clawed. 1** The **claws** N COUNT of a bird or animal are the thin, hard, curved nails at the end of its feet. EG ...a cat sharpening its claws.

2 The **claws** of a lobster, crab, or scorpion are two N COUNT pointed parts at the end of one of its legs which are used for grasping things.

3 If an animal **claws** something, it scratches or V+O damages it with its claws. EG ...a tiger clawing the back of a water buffalo.

claw at. When people or animals **claw at** some- PHRASAL VB : thing, they try to get hold of it or damage it by V+PREP, using their nails or claws. EG His cats were clawing HAS PASS at his trousers.

clay /kleɪ/ is a substance in the ground that is soft N UNCOUNT when it is wet and hard when it is dry. Clay is used to make things such as pots. EG ...clay pots... ...modelling in clay.

clean /kliːn/, **cleaner, cleanest; cleans, clean-** **ing, cleaned. 1** Something that is **clean** is free ADJ QUALIT from dirt and unwanted substances or marks. EG

...clean white shirts... Knives should be wiped clean after use.

2 You say that people or animals are **clean** when they keep themselves or their surroundings clean. ADJ QUALIT

3 If you **clean** something, you make it free from dirt and unwanted substances or marks, for example by washing or wiping it. EG *Clean the bathroom and lavatory thoroughly... ...the industrial fluid used to clean grease from the hands.* ▸ used as a noun. EG *The windows could do with a clean.* V+O ▸ N SING : a+N

4 To **clean** means to make the inside of a house or other building and the furniture in it free from dirt and dust. ◊ **cleaning.** EG *We have a landlady who does our cooking and our cleaning.* V ◊ N UNCOUNT

5 If you describe humour as **clean**, you mean that it is morally acceptable and not offensive. EG *...clean jokes.* ADJ CLASSIF : ATTRIB

6 If someone's reputation or record is **clean**, they have never done anything illegal or wrong. EG *Applicants must have a clean driving licence.* ADJ CLASSIF

7 If you **come clean** about something that you have been keeping secret, you admit it. EG *She decided to come clean.* PHRASE Informal

8 Clean also means **8.1** smoothly and immediately. EG *The ninth shot went clean through the forehead.* ADV+PREP Informal **8.2** completely or thoroughly. EG *The thief got clean away... I'd clean forgotten.* ADV Informal

clean out. 1 If you **clean out** somewhere such as a cupboard, room, or house, you take everything out of it, often before cleaning it. EG *I was cleaning out my desk.* **2** If you **clean** someone **out**, you take all the money they have. If you **clean out** a place, you take everything of value that is in it. EG *Thomas thought idly of cleaning out the cash register.* PHRASAL VB : V+O+ADV

V+O+ADV Informal

clean up. If you **clean up** something or someone, you clean them, usually after they have just become dirty. EG *Clean up food spills at once... I cleaned up Allen as best I could.* PHRASAL VB : V+O+ADV

clean after. If you **clean up after** someone, you clean or tidy a place that they have made dirty or untidy. PHRASAL VB : V+ADV+PREP

clean-cut. Someone who is **clean-cut** has a neat, tidy appearance. EG *...a clean-cut American girl.* ADJ QUALIT

cleaner /kli:nə/, **cleaners. 1** A **cleaner** is **1.1** someone who is employed to clean the rooms and furniture inside a building. **1.2** someone whose job is to clean a particular type of thing. EG *...our window cleaner.* **1.3** a substance or device used for cleaning things. EG *...a spray oven cleaner... Never use lavatory cleaner in the bath.* ● See also **vacuum cleaner.** N COUNT N COUNT : USU+SUPP N COUNT OR N UNCOUNT

2 The **cleaner** or the **cleaner's** is a shop where things such as clothes and curtains are dry-cleaned. EG *She collected the curtains from the cleaner's.* N SING

cleanliness /klɛnlɪnəs/ is the habit of keeping yourself and your surroundings clean. N UNCOUNT

cleanly /kli:nli/. If something is done **cleanly**, it is done smoothly and completely, without making a mess. EG *The porcelain top of the ornament broke cleanly off.* ADV

cleanse /klɛnz/, **cleanses, cleansing, cleansed. 1** To **cleanse** a place or a person means to make them free from something dirty, unpleasant, or evil. EG *...his vow to cleanse Washington of subversives.* V+O : OFT+of/from Formal

2 If you **cleanse** your skin or a wound, you clean it, especially with disinfectant. V+O

cleanser /klɛnzə/, **cleansers.** A **cleanser** is a liquid that you use for cleaning something. EG *Use a gentle cleanser.* N MASS

clean-shaven. If a man is **clean-shaven**, he does not have a beard or a moustache. ADJ CLASSIF

clear /klɪə/, **clearer, clearest; clears, clearing, cleared. 1** Something that is **clear** is **1.1** easy to understand, see, or hear. EG *I gave a clear, frank account of the incident... The line of its footprints is still clear... ...a clear voice.* ◊ **clearly.** EG *They've got to clearly define their policies... Make sure that* ADJ QUALIT ◊ ADV

all your luggage is clearly labelled... I couldn't see him clearly. **1.2** obvious and impossible to be mistaken about. EG *They are faced with clear alternatives... It was clear from his letter that he was not interested.* ◊ **clearly.** EG *Whoever owned the house was clearly not expecting us... Clearly, it is very important for a solution to be found quickly.* ADJ QUALIT ◊ ADV OR ADV SEN

2 If you are **clear** about something, you understand it completely. EG *I'm not clear from what you said whether you support the idea or not.* ADJ PRED

3 If you **make** something **clear** or **make** yourself **clear**, you say something in a way that makes it impossible for there to be any doubt about your meaning, wishes, or intentions. EG *It is important to make clear your wishes about the funeral... All of them made it clear they would support my decision.* PHRASE

4 If your mind or your way of thinking is **clear**, you are able to think sensibly, reasonably, and logically. ◊ **clearly.** EG *Wait until you can think more clearly.* ADJ QUALIT ◊ ADV

5 If a substance is **clear**, you can see through it. EG *...a clear glue... ...a small creek with cold, clear water.* ADJ CLASSIF

6 If someone's eyes are **clear**, they are attractive and shining. EG *...clear brown eyes.* ADJ QUALIT

7 If a surface or place is **clear**, it is free of obstructions or unwanted objects. EG *The road was clear... ...a patch of floor that has been swept clear.* ADJ QUALIT

8 If it is a **clear** day or if the sky is **clear**, there is no mist, rain, or cloud. EG *On a clear day you can see the Welsh hills.* ADJ QUALIT

9 If your skin is **clear**, it is healthy and free from spots. ADJ QUALIT

10 If your conscience is **clear**, you do not feel guilty about anything. ADJ CLASSIF

11 If something is **clear** of something else, it is not touching it. EG *Raise the jack until the wheel is clear of the ground.* ADJ PRED : OFT+of

12 If you **stay clear** or **steer clear** of a person or place, you do not go near them. EG *He took special care to stay clear of any place where Sally might be.* PHRASE

13 If someone is **in the clear**, they are free from blame, suspicion, or danger. PHRASE Informal

14 When you **clear** an area or place, you remove things from it that you do not want to be there. EG *The children were helping me clear weeds from the pond... Will you clear the table when you've finished eating?... The princess's aides advanced before her to clear a passage.* V+O : OFT+A

15 To **clear** your mind or your head means to free it from confused thoughts or from the effects of alcohol. EG *He went for a walk to clear his mind.* V+O

16 If an animal or person **clears** a fence, wall, or hedge, they jump over it without touching it. V+O

17 When you **clear** your **throat**, you cough slightly in order to make it easier to speak. EG *He cleared his throat and spoke.* PHRASE

18 When fog or mist **clears**, it gradually disappears. EG *Outside the fog had cleared a little.* V

19 If a course of action **is cleared**, people in authority give permission for it to happen. V+O

20 If someone **is cleared**, they are proved to be not guilty of a crime or mistake. EG *The tribunal cleared all the people who had been accused.* V+O

21 the coast is clear: see **coast.** ● **loud and clear:** see **loud.** ● See also **clearing.**

clear away. When you **clear away**, you put away the things that you have been using. EG *We cleared away and helped with the washing-up... Brody began to clear away the soup bowls.* PHRASAL VB : V+ADV OR V+O+ADV

clear off. If you say 'clear off' to someone, you are telling them in a rude way to go away. EG *Clear off and leave me alone!* PHRASAL VB : V+ADV Informal

---

What is the word for a group of clients?

clear out. 1 If you **clear out** of a place or if you PHRASAL VB: **clear out**, you leave. EG *I've got to clear out of my* V+ADV, *place by next week... Just clear out and leave me in* OFT+*of* *peace!* **2** If you **clear out** a cupboard, room, or V+O+ADV *house*, you tidy it and throw away the things in it that you no longer want. EG *It's time I cleared out the kitchen cupboards.*

clear up. 1 When you **clear up** or **clear** a place PHRASAL VB: **up**, you tidy things and put them away. EG *I was too* V+ADV OR *exhausted to clear up properly... Go and clear up* V+O+ADV *your room.* **2** When a problem, disagreement, or V+O+ADV *misunderstanding* **is cleared up**, it is settled or a satisfactory explanation is given. EG *I'm assuming that the misunderstanding will be cleared up soon.* **3** When bad weather **clears up**, it stops raining or V+ADV *being cloudy.* EG *If it clears up tomorrow, why don't we do some walking?*

clearance /klɪərəns/. **1 Clearance** is the remov- N UNCOUNT *al of old buildings, trees, or other things that are not wanted from an area.* EG *He was responsible for slum clearance and rehousing programmes.* **2** If you get **clearance** for something, you get N UNCOUNT *official approval or permission for it.*

clear-cut. Something that is **clear-cut** is easy to ADJ QUALIT *understand and quite distinct from other things.* EG *It was a clear-cut decision... ...clear-cut economic groups.*

clear-headed. Someone who is **clear-headed** is ADJ QUALIT *sensible and thinks clearly, especially in a difficult situation.*

clearing /klɪərɪŋ/, **clearings.** A **clearing** is a N COUNT *small area of grass or bare ground in a wood or forest.* EG *They are alone in a clearing in the forest.*

clear-sighted. Someone who is **clear-sighted** is ADJ QUALIT *able to understand situations well and to make sensible judgements and decisions about them.* EG *He was too clear-sighted not to see what problems would follow.*

cleavage /kliːvɪdʒ/, **cleavages. 1** A woman's N COUNT: **cleavage** is the space between her breasts. USU+POSS **2** A **cleavage** between two people or things is a N COUNT: OFT *division or disagreement between them.* EG *There* +*between* *is no distinct cleavage between the classes.* Formal

clef /klef/, **clefs.** A **clef** is a symbol at the N COUNT *beginning of a line of a piece of music that indicates the range of the written notes.*

cleft /kleft/, **clefts.** A **cleft** in a rock or in the N COUNT: OFT *ground is a narrow opening in it.* EG *He could see* +*in/between* *the valley through a cleft in the rocks.* Literary

clemency /klemənsɪ/ is kind treatment that a N UNCOUNT *person receives, especially from someone who has* Formal *authority to punish them.* EG *...appeals for clemency by the lawyers of the condemned men.*

clench /klentʃ/, **clenches, clenching, clenched.** **1** When you **clench** your fist, you curl your fingers V+O *up tightly, usually because you are very angry.* **2** When you **clench** your teeth, you squeeze them V+O *together firmly, usually because you are angry or upset.* EG *She hissed through clenched teeth, 'Get out of here.'* **3** If you **clench** something in your hand or in your V+O:OFT+A *teeth, you hold it tightly with your hand or your teeth.* EG *There he sat, pipe clenched in his mouth, typing away.*

clergy /klɜːdʒɪ/. The **clergy** are the officially N PLURAL *appointed leaders of the religious activities of a particular church or temple.*

clergyman /klɜːdʒɪmən/, **clergymen.** A **clergy-** N COUNT **man** is a male member of the clergy.

cleric /klerɪk/, **clerics.** A **cleric** is a member of N COUNT *the clergy.* Outdated

clerical /klerɪkəl/. **1 Clerical** jobs, skills, and ADJ CLASSIF *workers are concerned with work that is done in an office.* EG *...clerical skills.* **2 Clerical** also means relating to the clergy. EG *...a* ADJ CLASSIF *priest in a clerical grey suit with a dog collar.* Formal

clerk /klɑːk/, **clerks.** A **clerk** is a person who N COUNT *works in an office, bank, or law court and whose job is to look after the records or accounts.*

clever /klevə/, **cleverer, cleverest. 1** Someone ADJ QUALIT *who is* **clever** *is intelligent and able to understand things easily or plan things well.* EG *My sister was very clever and passed all her exams at school... He's a clever rogue... How clever of you to know that.* ◊ **cleverly.** EG *They had gone about the* ◊ ADV *scheme cleverly... Mr White very cleverly ana- lyzed this game without any assistance.* ◊ **cleverness.** EG *Some men don't like cleverness* ◊ N UNCOUNT *in a woman.* **2** An idea, book, or invention that is **clever** is ADJ QUALIT *extremely effective and shows the skill of the people involved.* EG *This is a very clever way of running a college... It's such a clever gadget.*

cliché /kliːʃeɪ/, **clichés;** also spelled **cliche.** A N COUNT **cliché** is an idea or phrase which has been used so much that it is no longer original or effective. EG *...sentimental clichés about 'peace' and 'the open air'.*

click /klɪk/, **clicks, clicking, clicked. 1** When V-ERG *something* **clicks** *or when you* **click** *it, it makes a short, sharp sound.* EG *His camera was clicking away... He clicked the switch on the radio.* ▸ used ▸ N COUNT *as a noun.* EG *The lock opened with a click.* **2** When you suddenly understand something, you V *can say that it* **clicks.** Informal

client /klaɪənt/, **clients.** A **client** of a professional N COUNT *person or organization is a person or company that receives a service from them in return for pay- ment.* EG *...a solicitor and his client.*

clientele /kliːɒntel/. The **clientele** of a place or N COLL *organization are its customers or clients.* EG *...a restaurant with a predominantly upper-class clien- tele.*

cliff /klɪf/, **cliffs.** A **cliff** is a high area of land N COUNT *with a very steep side, especially one next to the sea.*

climactic /klaɪmæktɪk/. A **climactic** moment in ADJ CLASSIF *a situation is one in which a very exciting or* Formal *important event occurs.* EG *He keeps it secret from her until a climactic point in the story.*

climate /klaɪmət/, **climates. 1** The **climate** of a N COUNT OR *place is the general weather conditions that are* N UNCOUNT *typical of it.* EG *...the English climate... ...changes in climate... In very cold climates you cannot grow winter beans.* ◊ **climatic** /klaɪmætɪk/. EG *...favour-* ◊ ADJ CLASSIF: *able climatic conditions... The world was experien-* ATTRIB *cing tremendous climatic change.* **2** You can use **climate** to refer to people's atti- N COUNT+SUPP *tudes or opinions at a particular time.* EG *...this changing climate of public opinion... ...the prevail- ing political climate at Oxford.*

climax /klaɪmæks/, **climaxes.** The **climax** of a N COUNT: *process, book, or piece of music is the most excit-* USU+SUPP *ing or important moment in it, usually near the end.* EG *This proved to be the climax of his political career... The climax of the book happens in Egypt.*

climb /klaɪm/, **climbs, climbing, climbed. 1** If V+O, OR V: *you* **climb** *something tall such as a tree, mountain,* OFT+*to/up* *or ladder, you move towards the top of it, often with some effort or difficulty.* EG *We started to climb the hill... We climbed to the top of the mountain... I climbed up the ladder.* ▸ used as a ▸ N COUNT *noun.* EG *We were still out of breath from the climb.* **2** If you **climb** somewhere, you move there care- V+A OR V+O *fully, and often rather awkwardly, for example because you are moving into a small space or trying to avoid falling.* EG *She climbed into her car... Four men climbed down through the hatch.* **3** When something **climbs, 3.1** it moves gradually V:OFT+A *upwards to a higher position.* EG *The plane climbed steeply and banked.* **3.2** it increases in value or *amount.* EG *The cost has climbed to a staggering £35 billion.*

climber /klaɪmə/, **climbers. 1** A **climber** is N COUNT *someone who climbs rocks or mountains as a sport or a hobby.* EG *...a party of Swiss climbers en route to Everest.* **2** You use **climber** to say how good a person or N COUNT+SUPP animal is at climbing. For example, if you say that someone is a good **climber**, you mean that they are good at climbing. EG *He was an excellent climber... Chimpanzees are adept climbers.*

3 A **climber** is also a plant that grows upwards by N COUNT attaching itself to other plants or objects.

climbing /klaɪmɪŋ/ is the activity of climbing N ING rocks or mountains. EG *...a pair of climbing boots.*

clime /klaɪm/, **climes.** You use **clime** to refer to N COUNT+SUPP a place that has a particular kind of climate. For Literary example, a warm **clime** is a place with a warm climate. EG *He retreats to sunny climes, leaving the winter behind.*

clinch /klɪntʃ/, **clinches, clinching, clinched.** If v+o you **clinch** an agreement or an argument, you Informal settle it in a definite way. EG *The salesman was in Columbia trying to clinch a deal for his employer.*

cling /klɪŋ/, **clings, clinging, clung. 1** If you v:OFT+to/on **cling** to someone or something, you hold onto them tightly with your arms. EG *The human baby is too weak to cling to its mother for hours on end... I clung to the door to support myself.*

2 Clothes that **cling** to you stay pressed against v:OFT+A your body when you move, because they are wet or very tight. EG *The dress clung tight to Etta's waist.*

3 If you **cling** to someone you are fond of, you do v+to not allow them to have enough freedom or independence. EG *A working woman is not so likely to cling to her children when they leave home.*

◊ **clinging.** EG *There was something weak and* ◊ ADJ QUALIT *clinging in his nature.*

4 If you **cling** to an idea or way of behaving, you v+to continue to believe in its value or importance, even though it may no longer be valid or useful. EG *They cling to all the old, inefficient methods of doing things.*

clinic /klɪnɪk/, **clinics.** A **clinic** is a building N COUNT: where people go to receive medical advice or USU+SUPP treatment. EG *...dental clinics... the family planning clinic.*

clinical /klɪnɪkəl/. **1 Clinical** work, teaching, and ADJ CLASSIF: examination relates to the direct medical treat- ATTRIB ment of patients rather than to theoretical re- Medical search. EG *Doctors are hoping to start clinical tests next month.* ◊ **clinically.** EG *On examination she* ◊ ADV+ADJ *looked well and was not clinically anaemic.*

2 You use **clinical** to describe thought or behav- ADJ QUALIT iour which is very logical and detached and does not show any emotion or personal involvement; used showing disapproval. EG *She adopted an icy, impersonal, clinical attitude.*

3 A room or building that is **clinical** is designed to ADJ QUALIT look very plain, or is kept too neat and clean, so that people do not enjoy being in it. EG *...tiny offices painted clinical white.*

clink /klɪŋk/, **clinks, clinking, clinked.** When V-ERG objects made of glass, pottery, or metal **clink** or when you **clink** them, they touch each other and make a short, light sound. EG *The milk bottles clinked... She clinked her glass against Rudolph's.*

▶ used as a noun. EG *...the clink of glasses... There* ▶ N COUNT *was a clink as he put the cups into their saucers.*

clip /klɪp/, **clips, clipping, clipped. 1** A **clip** is a N COUNT small device, usually made of metal or plastic, that is specially shaped for holding things together. EG *He wore three pencils held by metal clips in his top pocket... ...hair clips.*

2 When something **clips** to something else or when V-ERG+A you **clip** it there, it fastens to it by means of one or more clips. EG *Keep the list clipped to that notebook.*

3 If you **clip** something, you cut small pieces from v+o it, especially in order to shape it. EG *Mr Willet had come to clip the hedges.*

4 A **clip** of a film or television programme is a N COUNT: short piece of it that is shown separately. EG USU+SUPP *Medical students were shown film clips depicting murders.*

5 See also **clipping, clipped.**

clipboard /klɪpbɔːd/, **clipboards.** A **clipboard** is N COUNT a board with a clip at the top. You use it to hold together pieces of paper that you need to carry around. It also provides a firm base so that you can write on the papers while you are standing.

clipped /klɪpt/. **1** If a man's hair or moustache is ADJ CLASSIF **clipped**, it is neatly trimmed. EG *...a handsome man with a clipped moustache.*

2 If you have a **clipped** way of speaking, you speak ADJ QUALIT with quick, short sounds. EG *He talked with a clipped, upper-class accent.*

clippers /klɪpəz/ are a tool used for cutting small N PLURAL amounts from something. EG *...a pair of nail clippers.*

clipping /klɪpɪŋ/, **clippings.** A **clipping** is an N COUNT: article, picture, or advertisement that has been cut OFT+SUPP from a newspaper or magazine. EG *Dawlish read the newspaper clipping I gave him.*

clique /kliːk, klɪk/, **cliques.** A **clique** is a small N COLL group of people who spend a lot of time together and are unfriendly towards other people. EG *They had made a small, superior, isolated clique.*

cloak /kləʊk/, **cloaks, cloaking, cloaked. 1** A N COUNT **cloak** is a wide, loose coat that fastens at the neck and does not have sleeves. See picture at CLOTHES.

2 You can refer to something that someone does or N COUNT+SUPP says as a **cloak** when it is intended to hide the truth. EG *He could be using the story as a cloak for more sinister activities.*

3 To **cloak** something means to cover it or hide it. v+o: EG *The hills were cloaked by thick mists.* USU PASS+in

cloakroom /kləʊkruːm/, **cloakrooms.** In a public N COUNT building, a **cloakroom** is **1** a place where you can leave your coat and hat. **2** a room containing toilets and washbasins.

clobber /klɒbə/, **clobbers, clobbering, clob- bered. 1** You can refer to someone's belongings as N UNCOUNT their **clobber**. EG *...bits of old army clobber.* Informal

2 If you **clobber** someone, you hit them. EG *If that* v+o *dog bites me I'll clobber it.* Informal

clock /klɒk/, **clocks, clocking, clocked. 1** A N COUNT **clock** is an instrument, for example in a room or on the outside of a building, that shows you what time of day it is. EG *...the ticking of the clock... The church clock struck eleven.*

2 If you work **round the clock**, you work all day PHRASE and all night without stopping.

3 To **put** or **turn the clock back** means to return PHRASE to ideas or situations that existed a long time ago; used showing disapproval. EG *This government seems to want to see the clock put back.*

4 A **clock** or a time **clock** on a machine or system N COUNT is a device that causes things to happen automatically at particular times. EG *Set the time clock on your central heating system to give heat only when it is needed.*

5 The **clock** in a car is an instrument that shows N COUNT the number of miles or kilometres that the car has travelled. EG *...a Mini with 5,000 miles on the clock.*

clock in. 1 When workers **clock in** at a factory PHRASAL VB: or office, they record the time that they arrive by V+ADV putting a special card into a device. EG *When they are late clocking in for factory work they may lose pay.* **2** If someone or something **clocks in** at a v+ADV: particular weight, they register that weight when OFT+at they are weighed. EG *The truck clocked in at about two thousand pounds.*

clock up. To **clock up** a large number or total PHRASAL VB: means to reach that total. EG *He has clocked up* V+ADV+O more than 171,750 miles in a lifetime of cycling.

clockwise /klɒkwaɪz/. When something moves in ADJ CLASSIF: a **clockwise** direction, it moves in a circle and in ATTRIB the same direction as the hands on a clock. EG *He* OR ADV *pushed the bolt back in and twisted it clockwise.*

What words for clothes are there on these pages?

clockwork /klɒkwɜːk/. **1 Clockwork** is the ma- N UNCOUNT chinery in some types of toys or models that makes them move or operate when they are wound up with a key.

2 If you say that something happens **like clock-** PHRASE **work**, you mean that it happens without any problems or delays. EG *That summer the work of the farm went like clockwork.*

clod /klɒd/, **clods.** A **clod** is a large lump of earth. N COUNT

clog /klɒg/, **clogs, clogging, clogged. 1** When V+O something **clogs** a hole, it blocks it so that nothing can pass through. ◊ **clogged.** EG *My nose and* ◊ ADJ CLASSIF *throat felt clogged... His rifle was clogged with sand.*

2 Clogs are heavy leather or wooden shoes with N COUNT : thick wooden soles. See picture at SHOES. USU PLURAL

clog up. When something **clogs up** or **is clogged** PHRASAL VB : **up**, it becomes blocked and no longer works prop- V-ERG+ADV, erly. EG *Their lungs may progressively clog up... If* OFT+with *the cooling unit gets clogged up with ice it can't do its job efficiently.*

cloister /klɔɪstə/, **cloisters.** A **cloister** is a paved N COUNT and covered area round a square in a monastery or a cathedral.

cloistered /klɔɪstəd/. If you have a **cloistered** ADJ QUALIT way of life, you live quietly and are not involved in the normal busy life of the world around you. EG *...cloistered academic solitude.*

clone /kləʊn/, **clones, cloning, cloned. 1** A **clone** N COUNT is an animal or plant that has been produced artificially, for example in a laboratory, from the cells of another animal or plant. A clone is identical to the original animal or plant.

2 To **clone** an animal or plant means to produce it V+O as a clone.

close, closes, closing, closed; closer, closest; pronounced /kləʊz/ when it is a verb and also in paragraph 4, and /kləʊs/ when it is an adjective or adverb and also in paragraphs 18 and 20.

1 When something **closes** as a door or a lid **closes** or V-ERG when you **close** it, it moves so that it covers or fills a hole or a gap. EG *He opened the door and closed it behind him... It took a bit of pressure to make the lid close.*

2 When a place **closes** or **is closed**, people cannot V-ERG use it, or all work stops there. EG *Many libraries close on Saturdays at 1 p.m... Shotton Steelworks was closed with the loss of nearly 8,000 jobs.*

3 To **close** a conversation, event, or matter means V+O to bring it to an end. EG *He spoke as though he wanted to close the conversation... The case is closed.*

4 The **close** of a period of time or an activity is the N SING : OFT+of end of it. EG *The view is best of all towards the close* Formal *of the day... The war in Europe drew to a close.*

5 If you **close** on someone or something that you V : OFT+on are following, you get nearer and nearer to them. EG *The shark closed on the woman... The boat was about 100 yards away from us but closing fast.*

6 Something that is **close** to something else is near ADJ PRED to it. EG *Their two heads were close together... I got close enough to see what the trouble was.* ▸ used as ▸ ADV an adverb. EG *He moved a bit closer... The children followed close behind them.* ◊ **closely.** EG *The* ◊ ADV *crowd moved in more closely around him.*

7 Something that is **close by** or **close at hand** is PHRASE near to you. EG *There was a small lamp on the table close by.*

8 If you look at something **close up** or **close to**, PHRASE you look at it when you are very near to it. EG *Close up, they should look even bigger... It was my first glimpse of him close to.*

9 You say that people are **close** to each other ADJ QUALIT when they like each other very much and know each other very well. EG *They felt very close to each other... Father and I are very close... Not even my closest friends had any idea that something was wrong.* ◊ **closeness.** EG *They felt a new* ◊ N UNCOUNT *closeness in relationships with their friends.*

10 Your **close** relatives are the members of your ADJ QUALIT : family who are most directly related to you, for ATTRIB example your parents and your brothers or sisters.

11 Close contact or co-operation involves seeing or ADJ QUALIT : communicating with someone often. EG *My sons* ATTRIB *have maintained extremely close ties with a college friend... ...his closest advisers.* ◊ **closely.** EG ◊ ADV *Every doctor works closely with the Child Health Service.*

12 If there is a **close** link or resemblance between ADJ QUALIT two things, they are strongly connected or are very similar. EG *...the close link between love and fear.* ◊ **closely.** EG *Status was closely linked with* ◊ ADV *wealth... ...a creature that closely resembles a newt.*

13 Close inspection or observation of something is ADJ QUALIT : careful and thorough. EG *These events deserve* ATTRIB *closer examination.* ◊ **closely.** EG *He studied the* ◊ ADV *photographs very closely.*

14 When a competition or election is **close**, it is ADJ QUALIT only won by a small amount. EG *The vote was close.*

15 If you are **close** to laughter or **close** to tears, ADJ PRED+to you are likely to laugh or cry soon.

16 If an event is **close**, it will happen soon. EG *An* ADJ PRED *agreement seems close.*

17 Something such as an opinion or emotion that is ADJ PRED+to **close** to something else is almost the same as it. EG *She regarded Lomax with something that was close to fear.*

18 If something is **close to** or **close on** a particular PREP amount or distance, it is slightly less than that amount or distance. EG *The Thompsons face a bill of close to £8,000 for a new roof... The pile of wood was close on ten feet in height.*

19 If the atmosphere is **close**, it is uncomfortably ADJ QUALIT warm with not enough air. EG *The room was hot* British *and close and full of smoke.*

20 Close is used in the names of some streets. EG *...7 Winchester Close.*

21 If you describe an event as **a close shave**, **a** PHRASE **close thing**, or **a close call**, you mean that an accident or a disaster very nearly happened. EG *It was a very close shave. The car only just missed me.*

22 See also **closed**, **closing**.

close down. If someone **closes down** a factory PHRASAL VB : or a business or if it **closes down**, all work or V-ERG+ADV activity stops there, usually for ever. EG *The mines had been closed down... The magazine was forced to close down.*

close in. If a group of people **close in** on a PHRASAL VB : person or place, they come nearer and nearer to V+ADV : them and gradually surround them. EG *As the* OFT+on/upon *enemy closed in, the resistance of the villagers shrank to nothing.*

closed /kləʊzd/. **1** If something such as a door or a ADJ CLASSIF lid is **closed**, it is covering or filling a hole or gap. EG *I fell asleep with my window closed tight... He was sitting in his wheelchair with closed eyes.*

2 If a shop or a public building is **closed**, people ADJ CLASSIF cannot use it. EG *It was Sunday and the garage was closed.*

3 A **closed** group of people is restricted to only a ADJ QUALIT : few people. EG *He had a fairly closed circle of* ATTRIB *friends... Britain dearly loves its little closed societies.*

4 If people do something **behind closed doors**, PHRASE they do it in secret. EG *On the whole these debates take place behind closed doors.*

closed-circuit television, closed-circuit tele- N UNCOUNT **visions. Closed-circuit television** is a television OR N COUNT system that is used inside a building, for example to film customers in a shop so that shoplifters can be identified.

closed shop, closed shops. A **closed shop** is a N COUNT factory, shop, or other business in which employees must be members of a particular trade union.

clothes

hat

shirt

tie

blouse

dungarees

waistcoat

pullover

jacket

scarf

skirt

trousers

gloves

tee-shirt

cardigan

tights

socks

coat

dress

shoes

shorts

close-knit /kləʊs nɪt/. If a group of people are ADJ QUALIT
close-knit, they are closely linked and share similar beliefs or activities. EG *It's a very close-knit
community.*

close-set /kləʊs set/. If someone's eyes are **close-** ADJ QUALIT
set, they are very near to each other.

closet /klɒzɪt/, **closets, closeting, closeted. 1** A N COUNT
closet is a cupboard.   American

2 If you **are closeted** with someone, you are V+O :
talking privately to them. EG *Judith is still closeted* USU PASS+with
with those two lawyers.

3 You use **closet** to describe beliefs, habits, or ADJ CLASSIF :
feelings that people keep private and secret, often ATTRIB
because they are embarrassed about them. EG
...closet fears... ...closet alcoholics.

close-up /kləʊs ʌp/, **close-ups.** A **close-up** is a N COUNT
photograph or film that shows a lot of detail
because it is taken very near to the subject. EG *The
team anxiously awaited close-ups of the moon.* ● If ● PHRASE
you see something **in close-up**, you see it in great
detail on a photograph or film which has been
taken very near to the subject. EG *...a portrait of the
chairman, huge and in close-up.*

closing /kləʊzɪŋ/. The **closing** part of an activity ADJ CLASSIF :
or period of time is the final part of it. EG *...the* ATTRIB
closing stages of the election campaign.

closure /kləʊʒə/, **closures. 1** The **closure** of a N UNCOUNT
business or factory is the permanent shutting of it. OR N COUNT
EG *...newspapers that are threatened with closure.*

2 The **closure** of a road or border is the blocking N UNCOUNT
of it in order to prevent people from using it. EG +SUPP
...the closure of the Suez Canal.

clot /klɒt/, **clots, clotting, clotted. 1** A **clot** is a N COUNT
sticky lump that forms when blood dries up and
becomes thicker. EG *...a blood clot.*

2 When blood **clots**, it becomes thick and forms a V-ERG
lump.

3 You call someone a **clot** when they have done or N COUNT OR
said something stupid. EG *That's what it's supposed* VOCATIVE
to look like, you clot.   Informal
     British

cloth /klɒθ/, **cloths. 1 Cloth** is fabric which is N MASS
made by weaving, knitting, or some other similar
process. Cloth is used especially for making
clothes. EG *...strips of cotton cloth.*

2 A **cloth** is a piece of cloth which you use for a N COUNT
particular purpose, such as cleaning. EG *Clean with
a soft cloth dipped in warm soapy water.*

clothe /kləʊð/, **clothes, clothing, clothed. 1** N PLURAL
Clothes are the things that people wear, such as
shirts, coats, trousers, and dresses. EG *I took off all
my clothes... They hadn't got any clothes on.*

2 If you **are clothed** in something, you are dressed V+O :
in it. EG *Mrs Travers was clothed in green.* USU PASS+in

3 To **clothe** someone means to provide them with V+O : USU PASS
clothes to wear. EG *Are we not better fed, better
clothed, and better housed than ever before?*

clothes line, clothes lines. A **clothes line** is a N COUNT
rope on which you hang washing so that it can dry.

clothes peg, clothes pegs. A **clothes peg** is a N COUNT
small wooden or plastic device which you use to
fasten clothes to a clothes line. See picture at PEGS.

clothing /kləʊðɪŋ/. **1 Clothing** is the clothes N UNCOUNT
people wear. EG *...loans to pay for food and clothing... ...waterproof clothing.*

2 You use **clothing** to describe something which is ADJ CLASSIF :
concerned with the business of designing, manufac- ATTRIB
turing, or selling clothes. EG *...a clothing factory.*

clotted cream is very thick cream that is made N UNCOUNT
mainly in the south-west of England.

cloud /klaʊd/, **clouds, clouding, clouded. 1** A N COUNT OR
cloud is a mass of water vapour that floats in the N UNCOUNT
sky. Clouds are usually white or grey. EG *There
were little white clouds high in the blue sky...
There will be heavy cloud over many areas.*

2 A **cloud** of smoke or dust is a mass of it floating N PART
in the air. EG *...billowing clouds of thick black
smoke.*

3 If something such as a room **clouds** or if you V-ERG

cloud it, it becomes less easy to see through. EG *He
lit a cigar and soon clouded the room in smoke.*

4 If one thing **clouds** another, **4.1** it confuses things V+O
so that you cannot understand a situation or judge
it properly. EG *His explanations clouded the issue.*
4.2 it makes a situation more unpleasant. EG *Insanity clouded the last years of his life.*

5 If you are **under a cloud**, you are in disgrace PHRASE
and people have a poor opinion of you. EG *I was* Informal
already under a cloud at the office.

cloud over. 1 If your face or eyes **cloud over**, PHRASAL VB :
you suddenly look sad or angry. EG *The vicar's face* V+ADV
clouded over and his mouth fell open. **2** If it **clouds** V+ADV
over, the sky becomes covered with clouds.

cloudless /klaʊdlɪˀs/. If the sky is **cloudless**, ADJ CLASSIF
there are no clouds in it.

cloudy /klaʊdiˀ/. **1** If it is **cloudy**, there are a lot of ADJ QUALIT
clouds in the sky. EG *It was a cloudy day.*

2 If a liquid is **cloudy**, it is less clear than it should ADJ QUALIT
be. EG *...cloudy water.*

3 Ideas or opinions that are **cloudy** are confused or ADJ QUALIT
uncertain. EG *Their policies seem fairly cloudy.*

clout /klaʊt/, **clouts, clouting, clouted. 1** If you V+O : OFT+A
clout someone, you hit them. EG *Then he clouted
me across the face.* ▸ used as a noun. EG *...a clout* ▸ N COUNT
on the head.

2 Someone who has **clout** has influence and power. N UNCOUNT
EG *The commission lacks the clout to force him to* Informal
resign... ...political clout.

clove /kləʊv/, **cloves. 1 Cloves** are small dried N COUNT :
flower buds which are used as a spice.   USU PLURAL

2 A **clove** of garlic is a small part of a garlic bulb. N COUNT

clover /kləʊvə/ is a small plant with pink or white N UNCOUNT
ball-shaped flowers.

clown /klaʊn/, **clowns, clowning, clowned. 1** A N COUNT
clown is a performer in a circus who wears funny
clothes and bright make-up, and does silly things in
order to make people laugh.

2 If you **clown**, you do silly things in order to make V
people laugh. EG *He clowned and joked with the
children.*

3 You can describe someone as a **clown** when you N COUNT
have no respect for them. EG *Any clown with a PhD* Informal
should be able to teach English.

cloying /klɔɪɪŋ/. You use **cloying** to describe ADJ QUALIT
something that you find unpleasant because it is
too sweet and sickly, or too sentimental. EG *...the
cloying scent of flowers... ...cloying sentimentality.*

club /klʌb/, **clubs, clubbing, clubbed. 1** A **club** is
1.1 an organization of people who are all interested N COUNT :
in a particular activity or subject. EG *Have you* USU+SUPP
joined the Swimming Club? **1.2** a place where the N COUNT
members of a club meet. EG *I'll see you at the club.*

2 A **club** is also **2.1** a thick heavy stick that can be N COUNT
used as a weapon. **2.2** a long thin stick which a
player uses to hit the ball in golf.

3 If you **club** someone, you hit them hard with V+O : OFT+A
something blunt and heavy. EG *They were going to
club him to death.*

clubs

4 Clubs is one of the four suits in a pack of playing N UNCOUNT
cards. Each card in the suit is marked with one or
more black symbols in the shape of a leaf with
three rounded parts.

5 A **club** is also one of the thirteen playing cards in N COUNT
the suit of clubs.

club together. If people **club together** for PHRASAL VB :
something, they all give money in order to share V+ADV,
     USU+to-INF

the cost of it. EG *We all clubbed together to buy her a present.*

cluck /klʌk/, **clucks, clucking, clucked. 1** When v a hen **clucks**, it makes the noise that hens typically make.
2 If you **cluck** over someone or something, you say v:OFT+over things in a disapproving or fussy way. EG *The women clucked disapprovingly over her hair.*

clue /klu:/, **clues. 1** A **clue** is **1.1** something that N COUNT provides information about a problem that you are OFT+SUPP trying to solve. EG *The clue to solving our energy problem lies in conservation... The police searched all the houses but found no clues.* **1.2** a short piece N COUNT of writing in a crossword or game, giving information which helps you to work out the answer to a question.
2 If you **haven't a clue** about something, for PHRASE example what it is or where it is, you do not know much about it. EG *I hadn't got a clue how to spell it.*

clump /klʌmp/, **clumps, clumping, clumped. 1** N COUNT+SUPP A **clump** of plants, people, or buildings is a small group of them growing or standing together. EG *...a clump of thistles... ...clumps of young fir trees.*
2 If someone **clumps** about, they walk with heavy v+A clumsy footsteps. EG *My sister came clumping back in her wellingtons.*

clumsy /klʌmzi¹/, **clumsier, clumsiest. 1** Some- ADJ QUALIT one who is **clumsy** moves or handles things in a careless, awkward way, often so that things are knocked over or broken. EG *I wanted to dance, but I felt stupid and clumsy and afraid to get up... I held the tweezers, but by fingers were too clumsy to handle them properly.* ◊ **clumsily.** EG *She stum-* ◊ ADV *bled clumsily, as though drunk, and sat down.* ◊ **clumsiness.** EG *The older boys would laugh* ◊ N UNCOUNT *loudly at his clumsiness.*
2 A **clumsy** action or statement is tactless and ADJ QUALIT likely to upset people. EG *Haldane's efforts at recon- ciliation were clumsy and naive.* ◊ **clumsily.** EG ◊ ADV *...a clumsily phrased apology.*
3 An object that is **clumsy** is not neat in design or ADJ QUALIT appearance, and is often awkward to use. EG *Me- chanical switches are often clumsy and unreli- able.... a clumsy weapon.* ◊ **clumsily.** EG *The* ◊ ADV *furniture was clumsily designed.*

clung /klʌŋ/ is the past tense and past participle of **cling**.

clunk /klʌŋk/, **clunks.** A **clunk** is a sound made N COUNT by heavy objects hitting against each other. EG *There was a metallic clunk as the gun struck the table.*

cluster /klʌstə/, **clusters, clustering, clustered.**
1 A **cluster** of people or things is a small group of N PART them close together. EG *There was a little cluster of admirers round the guest speaker... ...a cluster of cottages... ...clusters of white flowers.*
2 If people or things **cluster** together, they gather v:USU+A together or are found together in a small group. EG *Many of the guests immediately clustered around the table... ...a hill where the white buildings clus- tered together.* ◊ **clustered.** EG *They were clus-* ◊ ADJ PRED *tered round a radio.* +A

clutch /klʌtʃ/, **clutches, clutching, clutched. 1** v+O OR v+A If you **clutch** something, you hold it tightly, usually because you are afraid or anxious. EG *Myra came in, clutching her handbag... Her pony stumbled, and she clutched at the reins.* ● **to clutch at straws**: see **straw**.
2 If someone is in the **clutches** of another person, N PLURAL that person has captured them or has power over Informal them. EG *He escaped the clutches of the law.*
3 In a car, the **clutch** is the pedal that you press N COUNT before you change gear, and the mechanism that it operates. See picture at CAR.
4 A **clutch** is **4.1** a group of eggs laid by a bird at N PART one time. **4.2** a small group of people or things. EG Literary *Mrs Thatcher was there with a clutch of cabinet ministers.*

clutter /klʌtə/, **clutters, cluttering, cluttered. 1** N UNCOUNT **Clutter** is a lot of things in an untidy state, especially things that are not useful or necessary. EG *The rooms were full of clutter.*
2 If things **clutter** a place, they fill it untidily. EG v+O:OFT+up *Cluttering the table were papers, books, and ash- trays.* ◊ **cluttered.** EG *He glanced around the* ◊ ADJ QUALIT *small, cluttered room.*

cm is an abbreviation for 'centimetre'. EG *...two rolls of sterile bandage 5 cm wide.*

c/o. You write **c/o** before an address on an en- velope when you are sending it to someone who is staying or working at that address, often for only a short time. **c/o** is an abbreviation for 'care of'. EG *Mr A D Bright, c/o Sherman Ltd, 62 Burton Road, Bristol 8.*

co- /kəʊ/ is used to form words that refer **1** to PREFIX people sharing things or doing things together. EG *...co-ownership schemes... The two countries have continued to coexist peacefully.* **2** to people who share the same job. EG *...the co-author of a cookery book... He sat behind the pilot and co-pilot.*

Co. /kəʊ/. **1 Co.** is used as an abbreviation for 'company' in the names of companies. EG *...Morris, Marshall, Faulkner & Co.*
2 You can use **and co.** to refer to a group of people PHRASE associated with a particular person; used showing Informal disapproval. EG *The time may be coming for Mrs Thatcher and co. to redeem themselves.*

coach /kəʊtʃ/, **coaches, coaching, coached. 1** A **coach** is **1.1** a comfortable bus that carries passen- N COUNT gers on long journeys. EG *The coach leaves Cardiff* OR by+N *at twenty to eight... We usually go there by coach...* British *...a coach journey.* **1.2** one of the separate sections N COUNT of a train that carries passengers. **1.3** an enclosed N COUNT four-wheeled vehicle pulled by horses, in which OR by+N people used to travel. Coaches are still used for ceremonial events.
2 If you **coach** someone, you help them to become v+O OR v better at a particular sport or subject. EG *She had been coached by a former Wimbledon champion.*
3 A **coach** is also someone who coaches a person N COUNT or a sports team. EG *...a famous football coach.*

coachload /kəʊtʃləʊd/, **coachloads.** A **coachload** N PART of people is a group of people who travel some- where together in a coach. EG *...coachloads of tourists.*

coagulate /kəʊægjə¹leɪt/, **coagulates, coagulat-** V-ERG **ing, coagulated.** When a liquid such as paint or blood **coagulates**, it becomes very thick.

coal /kəʊl/, **coals. 1 Coal** is a hard black sub- N UNCOUNT stance that is taken from under the earth and burned as fuel. EG *...a lump of coal... ...coal, oil, and gas... ...the coal mining industry.*
2 Coals are burning pieces of coal. EG *...chestnuts* N COUNT: *roasting over glowing coals.* USU PLURAL

coalesce /kəʊələs/, **coalesces, coalescing, coa-** V OR V+with **lesced.** If two or more things **coalesce**, they come RECIP together and form a larger group or system. EG Formal *There is a tendency for industrial systems to coalesce into large units.*

coalface /kəʊlfeɪs/, **coalfaces.** In a coal mine, N COUNT the **coalface** is the part where the coal is being cut out of the rock.

coalfield /kəʊlfi:ld/, **coalfields.** A **coalfield** is a N COUNT region where there is coal under the ground.

coalition /kəʊəlɪʃə³n/, **coalitions.** A **coalition** is N COUNT **1** a government consisting of people from two or more political parties. EG *...the fall of Asquith's Coalition Government.* **2** a group consisting of people from different political or social groups who are cooperating to achieve a particular aim. EG *...a broad coalition of community groups in the area.*

coalman /kəʊlmə³n/, **coalmen.** A **coalman** is a N COUNT person who delivers coal to people's houses. British

coalminer /ˈkəʊlmaɪnə/, **coalminers.** A **coal-** N COUNT
miner is a person whose job is mining coal.
coal scuttle, coal scuttles. A **coal scuttle** is a N COUNT
special kind of bucket for keeping coal in.
coarse /kɔːs/, **coarser, coarsest. 1** Something ADJ QUALIT
that is **coarse** has a rough texture which consists
of thick strands or large pieces. EG *...coarse white
cloth... ...coarse black hair... ...coarse grass.*
2 Someone who is **coarse** talks and behaves in a ADJ QUALIT
rude and offensive way. EG *He objected to her
coarse remarks.* ◊ **coarsely.** EG *She speaks rather* ◊ ADV
coarsely. ◊ **coarseness.** EG *With deliberate* ◊ N UNCOUNT
*coarseness, he wiped his mouth with the back of
his hand.*
coarsen /ˈkɔːsəⁿn/, **coarsens, coarsening, coars-** V-ERG
ened. If someone **coarsens** or is **coarsened**, they
become less polite. EG *My whole nature had coarsened in a way that horrified me.*
coast /kəʊst/, **coasts, coasting, coasted. 1** The N COUNT :
coast is an area of land that is next to the sea. EG USU the+N
*...a trawler fishing off the coast of Portugal... We
had made up our minds to stay on the East Coast.*
2 If you say that **the coast is clear**, you mean that PHRASE
there is nobody around to see you or catch you.
coastal /ˈkəʊstəⁿl/ means in the sea or on the land ADJ CLASSIF :
near a coast. EG *Sea lions inhabit the coastal* ATTRIB
waters... ...the coastal plain.
coaster /ˈkəʊstə/, **coasters.** A **coaster** is a small N COUNT
mat that you put underneath a glass or mug.
coastguard /ˈkəʊstɡɑːd/, **coastguards. 1** A N COUNT
coastguard is an official who watches the sea
near a coast, in order to get help for sailors when
they need it, and to prevent smuggling.
2 The **coastguard** is the organization to which N SING : the+N
coastguards belong.
coastline /ˈkəʊstlaɪn/, **coastlines.** A country's N COUNT
coastline is the edge of its coast. EG *...a rocky and
treacherous coastline.*
coat /kəʊt/, **coats, coating, coated. 1** A **coat** is a N COUNT
piece of clothing with long sleeves which you wear
over your other clothes when you go outside. See
picture at CLOTHES.
2 An animal's **coat** is the fur or hair on its body. EG N COUNT :
It has a long shaggy coat.
3 If you **coat** something with a substance, you V+O : USU
cover it with a thin layer of the substance. EG *The* PASS+with
sweets are then coated with chocolate. ◊ **coated.** ◊ ADJ QUALIT
EG *My face was coated with dust.*
4 A **coat** of paint or varnish is a thin layer of it on a N COUNT
surface.

coat hanger

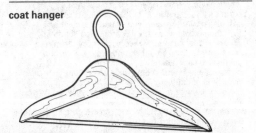

coat hanger, coat hangers. A **coat hanger** is a N COUNT
curved piece of wood, metal, or plastic that you
hang a piece of clothing on.
coating /ˈkəʊtɪŋ/, **coatings.** A **coating** of a sub- N COUNT+SUPP
stance is a thin layer of it spread over a surface. EG
...a coating of dust.
coat of arms, coats of arms. A **coat of arms** is N COUNT
a design in the form of a shield that is used as an
emblem by a family, a town, or an organization.
co-author, co-authors. The **co-authors** of a book N COUNT
are the people who have written it together.
coax /kəʊks/, **coaxes, coaxing, coaxed.** If you V+O : USU+A
coax someone to do something, you gently try to OR V+QUOTE

persuade them to do it. EG *You just coax them into
doing it... 'It won't hurt you,' Marsha coaxed.*
cobalt /ˈkəʊbɒlt, -bɔːlt/. **Cobalt** or **cobalt blue** is a ADJ COLOUR
deep blue colour. Literary
cobble /ˈkɒbəⁿl/, **cobbles, cobbling, cobbled.** N COUNT :
Cobbles are the same as cobblestones. USU PLURAL
cobble together. If you **cobble** something to- PHRASAL VB :
gether, you make it roughly or quickly; used V+O+ADV
showing disapproval. EG *Its author has cobbled
together a guide to the islands.*
cobbled /ˈkɒbəⁿld/. A **cobbled** street has a surface ADJ CLASSIF
made of cobblestones.
cobbler /ˈkɒblə/, **cobblers.** A **cobbler** is a person N COUNT
whose job is to make or mend shoes. Outdated
cobblestone /ˈkɒbəⁿlstəʊn/, **cobblestones.** N COUNT :
Cobblestones are stones with a rounded upper USU PLURAL
surface which were once used for making streets.
cobra /ˈkəʊbrə/, **cobras.** A **cobra** is a kind of N COUNT
poisonous snake.
cobweb /ˈkɒbwɛb/, **cobwebs.** A **cobweb** is the net N COUNT OR
which a spider makes for catching insects. N UNCOUNT
◊ **cobwebbed** /ˈkɒbwɛbd/. EG *...the dusty cob-* ◊ ADJ CLASSIF
webbed bulb.
cocaine /kəˈⁿkeɪn/ is a drug which people take for N UNCOUNT
pleasure, but which they can become addicted to.
In most countries it is illegal to take cocaine.
cock /kɒk/, **cocks, cocking, cocked. 1** A **cock** is N COUNT
an adult male chicken. EG *Cocks began to crow.* British
2 A **cock** bird is a male bird. EG *...a cock pheasant.* N COUNT
3 If you **cock** a part of your body in a particular V+O : USU+A
direction, you lift it or point it in that direction. EG
*He stepped back, his head cocked to one side, to
admire his work... A stray dog cocked his leg
against a lamp-post.*
4 If you **keep** your **ears cocked**, you listen very PHRASE
carefully for something. EG *She kept her ears
cocked for any mention of her name.*
cock up. If you **cock** something **up**, you ruin it by PHRASAL VB :
doing something wrong; a rude expression. EG *We* V+O+ADV
don't want to cock the whole thing up. ● See also Informal
cock-up. British
cockatoo /kɒkəˈtuː, ˈkɒkətuː/, **cockatoos.** A **cocka-** N COUNT
too is a kind of parrot which has a crest on its
head.
cockerel /ˈkɒkəⁿrəl/, **cockerels.** A **cockerel** is a N COUNT
young cock.
cockeyed /ˈkɒkaɪd/. If an idea or scheme is **cock-** ADJ QUALIT
eyed, it is stupid and very unlikely to succeed. EG
That sounds a cockeyed way of going about things.
cockle /ˈkɒkəⁿl/, **cockles. Cockles** are a kind of N COUNT :
small shellfish. USU PLURAL
cockney /ˈkɒkniⁱ/, **cockneys. 1** A **cockney** is a N COUNT
person who was born in the East End of London.
2 Cockney is the dialect and accent of the East N UNCOUNT
End of London. EG *...a cockney accent.*
cockpit /ˈkɒkpɪt/, **cockpits.** A **cockpit** is **1** the N COUNT
part of a small plane where the pilot sits. **2** the part
of a racing car where the driver sits.
cockroach /ˈkɒkrəʊtʃ/, **cockroaches.** A **cock-** N COUNT
roach is a large brown insect that is often found in
dirty rooms.
cocksure /kɒkˈʃʊə, -ˈʃɔː/. If someone is **cocksure**, ADJ QUALIT
they are too confident; used showing disapproval.
cocktail /ˈkɒkteɪl/, **cocktails.** A **cocktail** is **1** an N COUNT
alcoholic drink which contains several ingredients.
EG *...a champagne cocktail... ...a cocktail party.* **2** N COUNT+SUPP
something which is made by combining a number
of different things. EG *...a shrimp cocktail.*
cock-up /ˈkɒkʌp/, **cock-ups.** A **cock-up** is a mis- N COUNT
take that prevents something being done success- Informal
fully; a rude word. EG *There has been a series of* British
cock-ups.
cocky /ˈkɒkiⁱ/, **cockier, cockiest.** Someone who is ADJ QUALIT
cocky is very self-confident and rather cheeky. EG Informal
Don't be too cocky, you were only third.
cocoa /ˈkəʊkəʊ/ is **1** a brown powder made from N UNCOUNT
the seeds of a tropical tree, which is used in
making chocolate. **2** a hot drink made from cocoa
powder and milk or water. EG *...a cup of cocoa.*

coconut /ˈkəʊkənʌt/, **coconuts**. A **coconut** is a N COUNT very large nut with a hairy shell, which has white flesh and milky juice inside it.

cocoon /kəˈkuːn/, **cocoons**. 1 A **cocoon** is a cover- N COUNT ing of silky threads that the larvae of moths and other insects make for themselves before they grow into adults.

2 You can use **cocoon** to describe an environment N COUNT+SUPP in which someone feels protected and safe. EG *I lived in a cocoon of love and warmth.*

cocooned /kəˈkuːnd/. 1 If someone is **cocooned** in ADJ CLASSIF blankets or clothes, they are completely wrapped in them.

2 If you say that someone is **cocooned**, you mean ADJ CLASSIF that they are isolated and protected from everyday life and problems. EG *A historian cocooned in Oxford can easily lose touch with reality.*

cod /kɒd/. **Cod** is the singular and the plural form. N COUNT OR **Cod** is a kind of fish. EG *Their diet centres upon cod* N UNCOUNT *and fried chicken.*

coddle /ˈkɒdəᵊl/, **coddles**, **coddling**, **coddled**. If V+O you **coddle** someone, you treat them too kindly or you protect them too much. EG *Teachers shouldn't coddle their pupils.*

code /kəʊd/, **codes**, **coding**, **coded**. 1 A **code** is a N COUNT : set of rules about how people should behave. EG USU+SUPP *...accepted codes of behaviour... ...the IBA's code of advertising standards and practice.*

2 A **code** is also 2.1 a system of replacing the N COUNT OR letters or words in a message with other letters or N UNCOUNT words, so that nobody can understand it unless they know the system. EG *It is a code that even I can crack... The messages were typed in code.* 2.2 a N COUNT group of numbers or letters which is used to identify something, such as an educational course or a postal address. EG *My university course code is E5L21.* 2.3 any system of signs or symbols that has N COUNT a meaning. EG *We invented a code of telephone rings.*

3 If you **code** a message, 3.1 you replace the letters V+O or words in it with other letters or words, so that nobody can understand it unless they know the system. ◊ **coded**. EG *For several hours now coded* ◊ ADJ CLASSIF *messages had been going out by telephone.* 3.2 you V+O express it in a rather indirect way, because it would be dangerous or embarrassing to express it more plainly. ◊ **coded**. EG *The letters were full of* ◊ ADJ CLASSIF *coded threats.* 3.3 you identify it by a group of V+O numbers or letters.

code name, **code names**. A **code name** is a N COUNT name used for someone or something in order to keep their identity secret. EG *He is listed in the files by his code-name, the Jackal.*

code-named. If a police or military operation is ADJ PRED+N **code-named** a particular name, it is known by that name to the people involved in it. EG *It was code-named Operation Pegasus.*

codify /ˈkəʊdɪfaɪ, ˈkɒ-/, **codifies**, **codifying**, **codi-** V+O **fied**. If you **codify** a set of rules, you define them or present them in a clear and ordered way. ◊ **codified**. EG *...a codified system of criminal law.* ◊ ADJ CLASSIF

co-ed /kəʊˈɛd/. A **co-ed** school is the same as a co- ADJ CLASSIF : educational school. ATTRIB

co-educational /kəʊɛdjəˈkeɪʃəᵊnəl, -ʃənəᵊl/. A **co-** ADJ CLASSIF **educational** school is a school which is attended by both boys and girls.

coerce /kəʊˈɜːs/, **coerces**, **coercing**, **coerced**. If V+O : you **coerce** someone into doing something, you OFT+into make them do it, although they do not want to. EG Formal *They tried to coerce me into changing my appear-* *ance.* ◊ **coercion** /kəʊˈɜːʃəᵊn/. EG *No one was using* ◊ N UNCOUNT *coercion.*

coexist /ˌkəʊɪgˈzɪst/, **coexists**, **coexisting**, **coex-** V OR V+with : **isted**. If two or more things **coexist**, they exist RECIP together at the same time or in the same place. EG *Large numbers of species coexist here.* ◊ **coexistence** /ˌkəʊɪgˈzɪstəns/. EG *...the need for* ◊ N UNCOUNT *peaceful coexistence.*

coffee /ˈkɒfiᵊ/, **coffees**. 1 **Coffee** is 1.1 a hot N MASS brown drink that you make by pouring boiling water onto the roasted and ground seeds of a tropical tree, or onto a powder. EG *...a cup of coffee.* 1.2 the roasted seeds or powder from which the drink is made.

2 A **coffee** is a cup of coffee. N COUNT

coffee bar, **coffee bars**. A **coffee bar** is a small N COUNT café where drinks and snacks are sold.

coffee morning, **coffee mornings**. A **coffee** N COUNT **morning** is a social event that takes place in the morning in someone's house, and is usually intend- ed to raise money for charity.

coffee pot, **coffee pots**. A **coffee pot** is a tall N COUNT narrow container with a spout and a lid, in which coffee is made or served.

coffee table, **coffee tables**. A **coffee table** is a N COUNT small, low table in a living-room.

coffers /ˈkɒfəz/. When people refer to the **coffers** N PLURAL : of an organization, they are talking about the USU+SUPP amount of money it has. EG *...the flow of taxes into* Formal *the government's coffers.*

coffin /ˈkɒfɪn/, **coffins**. 1 A **coffin** is a box in N COUNT which a dead body is buried or cremated.

2 If one thing is **a nail in** another thing's **coffin**, it PHRASE will help bring about its end or failure. EG *Credit cards are the first nails in the coffin of traditional financial methods.*

cog /kɒg/, **cogs**. 1 A **cog** is a wheel with square or N COUNT triangular teeth around the edge, which is used in a machine to turn another wheel or part.

2 If you describe someone as **a cog in a machine**, PHRASE you mean that they have no importance or power within a large organization or group. EG *Workers on the production line feel that they are small cogs in the industrial machine.*

cogent /ˈkəʊdʒənt/. A reason, argument, or exam- ADJ QUALIT ple that is **cogent** has the power to make you Formal believe or accept it. EG *He put forward a cogent objection to our analysis.* ◊ **cogently**. EG *His* ◊ ADV *opinions were always cogently expressed.*

cognac /ˈkɒnjæk/, **cognacs**. **Cognac** is a kind of N MASS brandy.

cognitive /ˈkɒgnɪtɪv/ means relating to the mental ADJ CLASSIF : process of learning. EG *...a study of the cognitive* ATTRIB *functions in learning to read.* Technical

cohabit /kəʊˈhæbɪt/, **cohabits**, **cohabiting**, **co-** V OR V+with : **habited**. If two people **are cohabiting**, they are RECIP living together and have a sexual relationship, but Formal are not married. ◊ **cohabitation**. EG *We were* ◊ N UNCOUNT *thinking of marriage, or at least cohabitation.*

coherent /kəʊˈhɪərənt/. 1 If something is **coher-** ADJ QUALIT **ent**, its parts fit together well so that it is clear and easy to understand. EG *They can offer no coherent answer... ...a coherent theory.* ◊ **coherence** ◊ N UNCOUNT /kəʊˈhɪərəns/. EG *The theory possesses a certain intellectual coherence.*

2 If someone is **coherent**, they are talking in a ADJ QUALIT clear and calm way. EG *At last his sister was coherent enough to explain.* ◊ **coherently**. EG *Is* ◊ ADV *she able to talk coherently now?*

cohesion /kəʊˈhiːʒəᵊn/ is a state in which all the N UNCOUNT parts of something fit together well and form a united whole. EG *We lack a sense of national purpose and social cohesion.*

cohesive /kəʊˈhiːsɪv/. Something that is **cohesive** ADJ QUALIT consists of parts that fit together well and form a united whole. EG *The poor do not see themselves as a cohesive group.*

coil /kɔɪl/, **coils**, **coiling**, **coiled**. 1 A **coil** of rope N COUNT : or wire is a length of it that has been wound into a OFT+of series of loops.

2 A **coil** is a single loop that is one of a series into N COUNT which something has been wound. EG *Pythons kill*

Do you burn coke or drink it?

by tightening their coils so that their victim cannot breathe.

3 If you **coil** something or if it **coils**, it curves into a series of loops or into the shape of a ring. EG *Pythons coil themselves around their prey and kill it... Thick smoke coiled up over the fields.*   ◊ **coiled**. EG *The base is made of coiled springs.*   V-ERG : OFT+A   ◊ ADJ CLASSIF

coil up. If you **coil** something **up**, you wind it into a continuous series of loops. EG *He coiled up the hose.*   PHRASAL VB : V+O+ADV

coin /kɔɪn/, **coins, coining, coined. 1** A **coin** is a small piece of metal which is used as money. EG *...a 10p coin... ...notes and coins.*   N COUNT

2 If you **coin** a word or a phrase, you invent it. EG *Schumacher coined the slogan 'Small is beautiful'.*   V+O

● You say **'to coin a phrase'** when you realize that you have just used a cliché or are just about to use one. EG *It was, to coin a phrase, an offer I couldn't refuse.*   ● ADV SEN

3 If you say that two things are **two sides of the same coin**, you mean that they are two different aspects of the same situation.   PHRASE Formal

coinage /kɔɪnɪdʒ/ consists of the coins which are used in a country. EG *...decimal coinage.*   N UNCOUNT

coincide /kəʊɪnsaɪd/, **coincides, coinciding, coincided. 1** If two or more events **coincide**, they happen at about the same time. EG *Macmillan's departure coincided with Benn's return.*   V OR V+with : RECIP

2 If the opinions or ideas of two or more people **coincide**, they are the same. EG *On the whole their views coincided.*   V OR V+with : RECIP

3 If two or more lines or points **coincide**, they are in exactly the same place. EG *The boundary of the L.E.A. coincides with a county boundary.*   V OR V+with : RECIP

coincidence /kəʊɪnsɪdəns/, **coincidences.** A **coincidence** is what happens when two or more things occur at the same time by chance. EG *It was quite a coincidence that my sister was on the same train.*   N COUNT OR N UNCOUNT

coincidental /kəʊɪnsɪdentəl/. Something that is **coincidental** is the result of a coincidence and has not been deliberately arranged. EG *Any similarity to real people is purely coincidental.*   ADJ QUALIT   ◊ **coincidentally** /kəʊɪnsɪdentəliʲ/. EG *These players, coincidentally, are all left-handed.*   ◊ ADV SEN

coke /kəʊk/, **cokes. 1** **Coke** is a solid black substance that is produced from coal and is burned as a fuel.   N UNCOUNT

2 **Coke** is the name of a brown, fizzy, non-alcoholic drink.   N MASS Trademark

colander /kɒləndə, kʌl-/, **colanders.** A **colander** is a bowl-shaped container with holes in it which you wash or drain food in.   N COUNT

cold /kəʊld/, **colder, coldest; colds. 1** Something that is **cold** has a very low temperature or a lower temperature than is normal or acceptable. EG *Wash delicate fabrics in cold water... Your food is getting cold... This coffee's cold.*   ADJ QUALIT

2 If it is **cold**, the temperature of the air is very low. EG *It's bitterly cold... ...a cold winter's day... The building was cold and draughty.*   ADJ QUALIT

3 The **cold** is cold weather or a low temperature. EG *My fingers are so stiff from the cold.*   N SING : the+N

4 If you are **cold**, your body is at an unpleasantly low temperature. EG *Can I light the fire? I'm cold.*   ADJ PRED

5 Someone who is **cold** does not show much emotion, especially affection. EG *She seemed cold and uncaring.*   ◊ **coldly**. EG *'It's yours,' I said, politely, but coldly.*   ◊ **coldness.** EG *Kay was stunned by the coldness in his voice.*   ADJ QUALIT   ◊ ADV   ◊ N UNCOUNT

6 If something **leaves** you **cold**, it fails to excite or interest you. EG *Her performance left me cold.*   PHRASE

7 If you **have** or **get cold feet** about something that you were intending to do, you are now frightened of doing it.   PHRASE

8 A **cold** is a mild, very common illness which makes you sneeze a lot and gives you a sore throat or a cough. ● If you **catch cold**, you become ill with a cold.   N COUNT   ● PHRASE

9 in cold blood: see **blood.** ● to **make** your **blood run cold**: see **blood.** ● to **throw** or **pour cold water on** something: see **water.**

cold-blooded. Someone who is **cold-blooded** does not show any pity or emotion. EG *...a cold-blooded murderer.*   ADJ QUALIT

cold sweat. If you are in a **cold sweat**, you are sweating and feel cold, because you are very afraid or nervous. EG *He awoke trembling and in a cold sweat.*   N SING : a+N

cold war is a state of extreme political unfriendliness between two countries, although they are not actually fighting each other. EG *...the cold war years of the 1950s.*   N UNCOUNT, OR N SING : the+N

coleslaw /kəʊlslɔː/ is a salad of chopped cabbage, carrots, onions, and other vegetables, mixed together in mayonnaise.   N UNCOUNT

colic /kɒlɪk/. If a baby has **colic**, it has pain in its stomach and bowels.   N UNCOUNT

collaborate /kəlæbəreɪt/, **collaborates, collaborating, collaborated. 1** When people **collaborate**, they work together, especially on a book or on some research. EG *Antony and I are collaborating on a paper... The university hopes to collaborate with industry.*   ◊ **collaboration** /kəlæbəreɪʃən/. EG *...photographs published by Collins in collaboration with the Imperial War Museum.*   ◊ **collaborator** /kəlæbəreɪtə/, **collaborators.** EG *My collaborator Roy Lewis and I did a series of articles for Radio 4.*   V OR V+with : RECIP   ◊ N UNCOUNT   ◊ N COUNT

2 If someone **collaborates** with enemies who have taken control of their country by force, he or she helps them; used showing disapproval.   ◊ **collaborator**. EG *They committed treason as collaborators of the invaders.*   V OR V+with : RECIP   ◊ N COUNT

collaborative /kəlæbəʳrətɪv/. A **collaborative** piece of work is done by two or more people working together. EG *The project is a collaborative one.*   ADJ CLASSIF : ATTRIB Formal

collage /kəʳlɑːʒ, kɒlɑːʒ/, **collages.** A **collage** is a picture that has been made by sticking pieces of coloured paper and cloth onto paper.   N COUNT

collapse /kəlæps/, **collapses, collapsing, collapsed. 1** If a building **collapses**, it suddenly falls down. EG *These flimsy houses are liable to collapse in a heavy storm.* ▸ used as a noun. EG *The collapse of buildings trapped thousands of people.*   V   ▸ N UNCOUNT

2 If something **collapses**, it falls inwards and becomes smaller or flatter. EG *One of my lungs had collapsed.*   V

3 If a system or institution **collapses**, it fails completely and suddenly. EG *Their marriage had collapsed.* ▸ used as a noun. EG *...a company on the verge of collapse.*   V   ▸ N UNCOUNT

4 If you **collapse, 4.1** you suddenly fall down because you are very tired, weak, or ill. EG *As we walked into the hotel, Jane collapsed.* ▸ used as a noun. EG *Upon her collapse she was rushed to hospital.* **4.2** you sit down very suddenly, for example because you feel tired. EG *The music stopped and they collapsed onto cushions.*   V   ▸ N UNCOUNT   V : USU+A

collapsible /kəlæpsəʳbəl/. A **collapsible** object is designed to be folded flat when it is not being used. EG *...a collapsible bed.*   ADJ CLASSIF

collar /kɒlə/, **collars, collaring, collared. 1** The **collar** of a shirt or coat is the part which fits round the neck and is usually folded over.   N COUNT

2 A **collar** is also a leather band which is put round the neck of a dog or cat.   N COUNT

3 If someone **collars** you, they catch you. EG *I was collared by the police.*   V+O Informal

collarbone /kɒləbəʊn/, **collarbones.** Your **collarbone** is one of the two long bones which run from the base of your neck to your shoulder.   N COUNT

collate /kəʳleɪt/, **collates, collating, collated.** When you **collate** pieces of information, you gather them all together and examine them. EG *All the new evidence had been collated.*   V+O

collateral /kə'lætərəl/ is money or property N UNCOUNT which is used as a guarantee that someone will Formal repay a loan. EG *They have nothing to offer as collateral.*

colleague /'kɒli:g/, **colleagues**. Your **colleagues** N COUNT are the people you work with, especially in a professional job. EG *I talked to a colleague of yours recently.*

collect /kə'lekt/, **collects, collecting, collected.**
1 If you **collect** a number of things, you bring them v+o together from several places. EG *They're collecting wood for the fire.*
2 If you **collect** things, for example stamps or v+o books, as a hobby, you get a large number of them because you are interested in them. EG *Do you collect antiques?*
3 When you **collect** someone, you go and get them v+o: from a place where they are waiting for you. EG *I* OFT+from *have to collect the children from school.*
4 When things **collect** in a place, they gather there v+A over a period of time. EG *Damp leaves collect in gutters.*
5 If you **collect** for a charity or for a present for v OR v+o: someone, you ask people to give you money for it. OFT+for EG *How much have you collected so far?*
6 If you **collect** yourself or **collect** your thoughts, v-REFL OR v+o you make an effort to calm yourself or prepare yourself mentally. EG *I had five minutes in which to collect my thoughts before the interview.*

collect up. If you **collect up** things, you collect PHRASAL VB : them all together. EG *They collected up their gear.* v+o+ADV

collected /kə'lektɪ'd/. Someone's **collected** works ADJ CLASSIF or letters are all their works or letters published as one book or as a set of books. EG *...the collected works of Proust.*

collecting /kə'lektɪŋ/. 1 **Collecting** is the hobby N UNCOUNT : of collecting a particular type of thing. EG *...stamp* USU+SUPP *collecting... ...art collecting.*
2 A **collecting** tin or box is one that is used to ADJ CLASSIF : collect money for charity. ATTRIB

collection /kə'lekʃə'n/, **collections**. 1 A **collec-** N PART **tion** of things is 1.1 a group of things you have acquired over a period of time. EG *Davis had a large collection of pop records.* 1.2 a number of stories, poems or articles published in one book. EG *...a collection of Scott Fitzgerald's short stories.* 1.3 a group of things. EG *...a collection of old ruins.*
2 **Collection** is the act of collecting something N UNCOUNT from a place or from people. EG *...the collection of* OR N COUNT *national taxes... Your curtains are ready for collection.*
3 A **collection** is also 3.1 the organized collecting N COUNT OR of money from people for charity. EG *They organ-* N UNCOUNT *ized dances and collections which raised £450.* 3.2 N COUNT money that is given by people in church during some Christian services.

collective /kə'lektɪv/ means shared by or involv- ADJ CLASSIF : ing every member of a group of people. EG *It was a* ATTRIB *collective decision.*

collectively /kə'lektɪvli'/. 1 If people do some- ADV thing **collectively**, they do it together. EG *They were collectively responsible.*
2 You use **collectively** when you are referring to a ADV OR group of things as a whole. EG *...a small group of* ADV SEN *marsupials called, collectively, rat-kangaroos.*

collector /kə'lektə/, **collectors**. 1 A **collector** is a N COUNT+SUPP person who collects things of a particular type as a hobby. EG *...an art collector.*
2 You can also use **collector** to refer to someone N COUNT+SUPP whose job is to take something such as money or tickets from people. For example, a rent **collector** collects rent from tenants.

college /'kɒlɪdʒ/, **colleges.** 1 A **college** is 1.1 an N COUNT OR institution where students study after they have N UNCOUNT left school. EG *...the local technical college... What do you plan to do after college?* 1.2 one of the N COUNT institutions which some British universities are divided into. EG *Jesus College, Cambridge.*
2 **College** is 2.1 used in the titles of some second-

ary schools. EG *...Milton Ladies' College.* 2.2 used in the titles of some organized groups of people. EG *...the Royal College of Physicians.*

collide /kə'laɪd/, **collides, colliding, collided.** If a v OR v+with : moving person or object **collides** with something, RECIP they hit it. EG *The two vehicles collided.*

collie /'kɒli'/, **collies**. A **collie** or **collie** dog is a N COUNT dog used by farmers for controlling sheep.

colliery /'kɒljəri'/, **collieries**. A **colliery** is a coal N COUNT mine. British

collision /kə'lɪʒə'n/, **collisions**. 1 A **collision** N COUNT OR occurs when a moving object hits something. EG *...a* N UNCOUNT *mid-air collision... A meteor is on a collision course* OFT+with *with the Earth.*
2 A **collision** of cultures or ideas occurs when two N COUNT OR very different cultures or people meet and conflict. N UNCOUNT EG *...a collision of egos... This put them on a collision course with their elders.*

colloquial /kə'ləʊkwɪəl/. **Colloquial** words and ADJ QUALIT phrases are informal and are used especially in conversation. EG *...an intensive course in colloquial Greek.* ◊ **colloquially**. EG *This game is colloquially* ◊ ADV *known as 'Buzz off, Buster'.*

collude /kə'lu:d/, **colludes, colluding, colluded.** v OR v+with : If you **collude** with someone, you cooperate with RECIP them secretly or illegally; used showing disapprov- al. EG *Some groups have colluded with the unions in avoiding holding a ballot.* ◊ **collusion** /kə'lu:ʒə'n/. ◊ N UNCOUNT : EG *She was in collusion with Christopher for finan-* OFT+with/of *cial reasons.*

cologne /kə'ləʊn/ is a kind of weak perfume. N UNCOUNT

colon /'kəʊlə'n/, **colons**. 1 A **colon** is a punctua- N COUNT tion mark (:), which you can use in several ways. For example, you can put it before a list of things or before reported speech.
2 Your **colon** is the part of your intestine above N COUNT your rectum.

colonel /'kɜːnə'l/, **colonels**. A **colonel** is a senior N COUNT officer in an army or air force.

colonial /kə'ləʊnɪəl/ means relating to countries ADJ CLASSIF : that are colonies, or to colonialism. EG *...the libera-* ATTRIB *tion of oppressed peoples from colonial rule.*

colonialism /kə'ləʊnɪəlɪzə'm/ is the practice by N UNCOUNT which a powerful country directly controls less powerful countries. EG *The politics of the Third World had their origins in colonialism.*

colonialist /kə'ləʊnɪəlɪst/ means relating to colo- ADJ CLASSIF nialism. EG *Many people think of Northern Ireland as a colonialist situation.*

colonist /'kɒlə'nɪst/, **colonists**. A **colonist** is N COUNT someone who starts a colony. EG *...the Australian colonists.*

colonize /'kɒlə'naɪz/, **colonizes, colonizing, colonized**; also spelled **colonise**. 1 When people v+o **colonize** a foreign country, they go to live there and take control of it. EG *...the Europeans who colonized North America.*
2 When animals **colonize** a place, they move into v+o it and make it their home. EG *The plains of North America were colonised by ant-eaters and other species.*

colony /'kɒlə'ni'/, **colonies**. A **colony** is 1 a coun- N COUNT try which is controlled by a more powerful coun- try. EG *...the newly established colony of Australia.*
2 a place where a particular group of people lives. N COUNT EG *...a leper colony.* 3 a group of insects or animals N COUNT that live together. EG *...a colony of bees.*

color /'kʌlə/. See **colour**.

coloration /kʌlə'reɪʃə'n/. The **coloration** of an N UNCOUNT animal or a plant is the colours and patterns on it.

colossal /kə'lɒsə'l/. Something that is **colossal** is ADJ QUALIT very large. EG *...colossal sums of money.*

colour /'kʌlə/, **colours, colouring, coloured**; spelled **color** in American English. 1 The **colour** of N COUNT OR something is the appearance that it has as a result N UNCOUNT of reflecting light. Red, blue, and green are colours. EG *I don't know what colour her eyes are... All the rooms were painted different colours... His face was greyish in colour.*

2 Someone's **colour** is the normal colour of their skin, for example brown. EG *It was illegal to discriminate on the grounds of colour.* N UNCOUNT

3 A **colour** television, photograph, or picture is one that shows things in all their colours, and not just in black, white, and grey. EG *...marvellous colour illustrations.* ADJ CLASSIF: ATTRIB

4 If something such as a film or a television programme is **in colour**, it has been made in all colours, and not just in black, white, and grey. PHRASE

5 **Colour** is also a quality that makes something especially interesting or exciting. EG *The audiences liked the romance and colour of 'The Lady's Not for Burning'.* N UNCOUNT

6 If something **colours** your mind or opinion, it affects the way that you think about something. EG *Anger had coloured her judgement.* V+O

7 If you achieve something **with flying colours**, you achieve it in an extremely successful way. PHRASE

8 See also **coloured, colouring.**

colour in. If you **colour in** a drawing, you give it different colours using crayons. PHRASAL VB: V+O+ADV

colour blind. Someone who is **colour blind** cannot distinguish between colours, especially between red and green. ◊ **colour blindness.** EG *Colour blindness is a serious problem for pilots.* ADJ CLASSIF ◊ N UNCOUNT

coloured /kʌləd/, **coloureds**; spelled **colored** in American English. **1** Something that is **coloured** a particular colour has that colour. EG *The sky was mauve-coloured... The centre section was coloured pink... ...vividly coloured birds.* ADJ CLASSIF

2 Something that is **coloured** has a colour such as blue or red rather than being just white or black. EG *He drew patterns on the floor in coloured chalks.* ADJ CLASSIF

3 A person who is **coloured** belongs to a race of people who do not have white or pale skins. ADJ CLASSIF

colourful /kʌləful/; spelled **colorful** in American English. **1** Something that is **colourful** has bright colours. EG *...colourful posters of Paris and Venice.* ADJ QUALIT

2 A **colourful** story is full of exciting details. EG *Many colourful stories were told about him.* ADJ QUALIT

3 Someone who is described as **colourful** behaves in an interesting and amusing way; used showing approval. EG *He is one of the most colourful Parliamentary figures of his age.* ADJ QUALIT

colouring /kʌlərɪŋ/; **colourings**; spelled **coloring** in American English. **1** The **colouring** of something is the colours that it has. EG *...its rounded fins and distinctive green colouring.* N UNCOUNT

2 Someone's **colouring** is the colour of their hair, skin, and eyes. N SING+POSS

3 **Colouring** is a substance that is used to give colour to food. N MASS

colourless /kʌləlɪ²s/; spelled **colorless** in American English. Something that is **colourless 1** is dull and uninteresting. EG *He spoke in the same colourless, plodding voice.* **2** has no colour at all. EG *...a colourless and tasteless liquid.* ADJ QUALIT ADJ CLASSIF

colour supplement, colour supplements. In Britain, a **colour supplement** is a magazine that you get free when you buy a Sunday newspaper. N COUNT

colt /kɒlt/, **colts.** A **colt** is a young male horse. N COUNT

column /kɒləm/, **columns.** A **column** is **1.1** a tall solid cylinder, usually used to support or decorate part of a building. **1.2** something that has a tall narrow shape. EG *...columns of smoke.* **1.3** a group of people or animals which moves in a long line. EG *Behind the brass band came a column of workers.* N COUNT

2 In a newspaper or magazine, a **column** is a vertical section of writing, especially one that is always written by the same person or is always about the same topic. EG *Bill used to write a column for the Bristol Evening News.* N COUNT

columnist /kɒləmnⁿɪst/, **columnists.** A **columnist** is a journalist who writes a regular article in a newspaper or magazine. EG *...gossip columnists.* N COUNT

coma /kəumə/, **comas.** Someone who is in a **coma** is in a state of deep unconsciousness. N COUNT

comatose /kəumətəus, -təuz/. A person who is **comatose** is in a coma. ADJ CLASSIF Technical

comb /kəum/, **combs, combing, combed. 1** A **comb** is a flat piece of plastic or metal, which you use to tidy your hair. N COUNT

comb

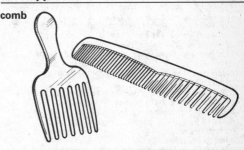

2 When you **comb** your hair, you tidy it using a comb. V+O

3 If you **comb** a place, you search everywhere in it in order to find someone or something. EG *It might amuse her to comb the town for antiques.* V+O: OFT+*for*

combat /kɒmbæt/, **combats, combating, combated. 1** **Combat** is fighting that takes place in a war. EG *He was awarded the Military Cross for gallantry in combat.* N UNCOUNT

2 A **combat** is a battle, or a fight between two people. EG *...the mighty combats between the West and the East.* N COUNT Formal

3 If people in authority **combat** something, they try to stop it happening. EG *The basic problem is that of combating poverty.* V+O

combatant /kɒmbətəⁿnt, kʌm-/, **combatants.** A **combatant** is someone who takes part in the fighting in a war. N COUNT

combination /kɒmbɪneɪʃəⁿn/, **combinations.** A **combination** is **1** a mixture of things. EG *All actors use a combination of these techniques... Perhaps it was a combination of all these reasons.* **2** a series of letters or numbers that is used to open a combination lock. EG *I can't remember the combination.* N COUNT OR N UNCOUNT / N COUNT

combination lock, combination locks. A **combination lock** is a lock which can only be opened by turning a dial according to a particular series of letters or numbers. N COUNT

combine, combines, combining, combined; pronounced /kəˈmbaɪn/ when it is a verb, and /kɒmbaɪn/ when it is a noun. **1** If you **combine** two or more things or if they **combine, 1.1** they exist together. EG *We would all prefer to combine liberty with order.* **1.2** they join together to make a single thing. EG *Later the two teams were combined.* V-ERG; ALSO V OR V+*with*: RECIP

2 A **combine** is a group of people or organizations that are working or acting together. EG *...a newspaper combine.* N COUNT

3 If someone or something **combines** two qualities or features, they have both those qualities or features at the same time. EG *Carbon fibre combines flexibility with immense strength.* V+O OR V+O+*with*: RECIP

4 If someone **combines** two activities, they do them both at the same time. EG *It's difficult to combine family life with a career.* V+O OR V+O+*with*: RECIP

combined /kəˈmbaɪnd/. **1** If someone or something has one quality or feature **combined** with another, they have both those qualities or features. EG *...a perfect example of professional expertise combined with personal charm... His eyes were wide with amazement and adoration combined.* ADJ PRED + *with*, OR ADJ AFTER N

2 A **combined** effort or attack is made by groups ADJ CLASSIF : of people at the same time. EG *The combined* ATTRIB *efforts of police and military were at last successful.*

combustion /kəmbʌstʃəᵇn/ is the act of burning N UNCOUNT something or the process of burning. EG *The ball of* Formal *paper was heated to combustion point.*

come /kʌm/, **comes, coming, came** /keɪm/. The form **come** is used in the present tense and is the past participle of the verb.

1 When a person or thing **comes** somewhere, V : OFT+A especially to where you are, they move there. EG OR to-INF *She looked up when they came into the room... Come and look... She came clambering over a pile of old junk... The waiter came to take the order... Can you and Myra come to a party next Saturday?... Are you ever coming back home?... You can come over tomorrow at four... Then this woman came up to me.*

2 If you **come** to a place, you reach it. EG *She* V+to *eventually came to the town of Pickering.*

3 If something **comes** up to a particular point or V+A down to it, it is tall enough, deep enough, or long enough to reach that point. EG *Her hair came right down to her waist.*

4 If something **comes** apart or **comes** to pieces, it V+A breaks into pieces. If something **comes** off or **comes** away, it becomes detached from something else. EG *It just came apart in my hands... All the wallpaper's coming off... Ordinary sticky tape comes unstuck.*

5 If someone or something **comes** to or into a V+to/into particular state, they enter or reach that state. EG *They had come to power ten years earlier... The elevator came to a stop... Christianity came into being in a hostile environment... Some people stared at me when I came into sight.*

6 If someone **comes** to do something, they gradual- V+to-INF ly start doing it over a period of time. EG *I have come to like him quite a lot.*

7 When a particular time or event **comes**, it V : USU+A arrives or happens. EG *The time has come for a full campaign against the government's spending cuts.*

8 **Come** is used in expressions such as 'come the PHRASE spring' and 'come the election' to mean when the time or event mentioned arrives or happens. EG *Come tomorrow you'll feel better about things.*

9 When you refer to a time **to come** or an event **to** PHRASE **come**, you are referring to a future time or event. EG *He hoped to play a significant role in the Parliamentary battle to come... Our income is going to be strictly limited for some time to come.*

10 If a memory, thought, or idea **comes** to you, you V+to suddenly remember or realize it. EG *The answer came to him just before noon... It came to me suddenly that what was wrong was that I was tired.*

11 You say **'Come to think of it'** to indicate that ADV SEN you have suddenly realized something, often something obvious. EG *Come to think of it, why should I apologize?*

12 If something **comes** to a particular number or V+to amount, it adds up to it. EG *My income now comes to £65 a week.*

13 If someone or something **comes** from a particu- V+from/ lar place or thing, it is their source or starting out of point. EG *'Where do you come from?' – 'India.'... Information coming out of the country was unreliable... This extract comes from a conversation I had with her recently... Did you know the word 'idea' comes from Greek?*

14 Something that **comes** from something else is V+from/of the result of it. EG *...the warm glow that comes from working co-operatively... You're always reading. No good will come of it, you'll see!*

15 If someone or something **comes** first, next, or V+C last, they are first, next, or last in a series, list, or competition. EG *What comes next then?... I was never in any race in which I didn't come last.*

16 If a type of thing **comes** in a particular range of V : USU+*in*

colours, styles, or sizes, it can have any of those colours, styles, or sizes. EG *The van came in two colours, medium brown or medium grey.*

17 The word **come** is also used in expressions such PHRASE as 'It came as a surprise', which indicate a person's reaction to something. EG *It comes as no surprise to discover that Americans usually love Britain.*

18 In a discussion, the next subject that you **come** V+to to is the one that you talk about next. EG *Now we come to the most important thing.*

19 If you say that you **do not know whether** you PHRASE **are coming or going**, you mean that you are so busy that you are rather confused.

20 See also **coming**.

come about. When you say how something PHRASAL VB **came about**, you say how it happened. EG *The* V+ADV *discovery of adrenalin came about through a mistake... How did the invitation come about?*

come across. 1 If you **come across** someone or PHRASAL VB : something, you meet them or find them by chance. V+PREP EG *I came across a letter from Brunel the other day.* **2** If someone who is speaking **comes across** V+ADV+A in a particular way, or if what they are saying **comes across** in that way, they make that impression on their audience. EG *He wasn't coming across as the idiot I had expected him to be.*

come along. 1 You say **'come along'** to some- PHRASE one **1.1** to encourage them to do something they do not really want to do. EG *Come along, now, drink this.* **1.2** to encourage them to hurry up. **2** When PHRASAL VB something **comes along**, it arrives or happens by V+ADV chance. EG *A new generation of planners came along who were much more scientifically based.* **3** V+ADV : If something **is coming along**, it is developing or ONLY CONT making progress. EG *There are even cookers which* Informal *tell you how the meat is coming along.*

come at. If a person or animal **comes at** you, PHRASAL VB : they move towards you in a threatening way and V+PREP attack you. EG *The bear came at me.*

come back. 1 If you **come back** to a topic or PHRASAL VB : point, you talk about it again later. EG *We'll come* V+ADV+to *back to that question a little later.* **2** If something V+ADV, that you had forgotten **comes back** to you, you USU+to remember it. EG *It was all coming back to him. It was the girl from the sweet shop.* **3** When some- V+ADV thing **comes back**, it becomes fashionable again. EG *She was pleased to see that mini skirts were coming back.* **4** See also **comeback.**

come by. To **come by** something means to find it PHRASAL VB : or obtain it. EG *Jobs were hard to come by... He had* V+PREP, *not come by these things through his own labour.* HAS PASS

come down. 1 If the cost, level, or amount of PHRASAL VB : something **comes down**, it becomes less than it V+ADV was before. EG *Inflation is starting to come down.* **2** If something **comes down**, it falls to the ground. EG *In the storm a tree came down.*

come down on. If you **come down on** someone, PHRASAL VB : you criticize them severely. EG *Social workers like* V+ADV+PREP *me come down harder on parents than on their children.*

come down to. If a problem, decision, or ques- PHRASAL VB : tion **comes down to** a particular thing, that thing V+ADV+PREP is the most important factor involved. EG *Your final choice of kitchen may well come down to cost.*

come down with. If you **come down with** an PHRASAL VB : illness, you get it. EG *She came down with pneumo-* V+ADV+PREP *nia and was taken to hospital.*

come for. If someone **comes for** you, they move PHRASAL VB : towards you quickly in a threatening way, in order V+PREP to attack you. EG *Jake was coming for me with a knife.*

come forward. If someone **comes forward**, PHRASAL VB : they offer to do what is required. EG *More coloured* V+ADV *men are now coming forward to join the police.*

come in. 1 If information or a report **comes in**, it PHRASAL VB :

What would you do if a lion came at you?

is received. EG *Reports are coming in from Mexico* v+ADV
of a major earthquake. **2** If you have some money v+ADV
coming in, you receive it regularly as your income. **3** If someone **comes in** on a discussion or v+ADV, USU+A
an arrangement, they join in. EG *He should come in
on the deal.* **4** If you ask where something or v+ADV
someone **comes in**, you are asking how they are
involved in a particular matter. EG *Where does your
husband come in?*

come in for. If someone or something **comes in** PHRASAL VB:
for criticism or blame, they receive it. EG *British* v+ADV+PREP
industry does come in for a great deal of criticism.

come into. **1** If someone **comes into** some PHRASAL VB:
money, some property, or a title, they inherit it. EG v+PREP
*She was going to come into some more money on
her mother's death.* **2** If someone **comes into** their PHRASE
own, they begin to perform or work really well
because the circumstances are just right. EG *Brooke
came into his own when he was appointed Home
Secretary.* **3** If you say that something **comes into** PHRASE
it, you mean that it is an important aspect of the
situation you are talking about. EG *Prestige comes
into it as much as other factors.*

come off. **1** If something **comes off**, it is success- PHRASAL VB:
ful or effective. EG *Sotheby's publicity stunt came* v+ADV
off brilliantly. **2** If you **come off** well when v+ADV+ADV
something happens, you are in a good position as a
result of it. If you **come off** badly, you are in a bad
position as a result of it. EG *They came off better
than the British.* **3** You say '**come off it**' to CONVENTION
someone to show them that you think what they Informal
are saying is untrue.

come on. **1** You say '**Come on**' to someone **1.1** to PHRASE
encourage them to do something they do not really
want to do. EG *Come on, Wendy, you say something.*
1.2 to encourage them to hurry up. **1.3** when you
think that what they are saying is silly or unreasonable. **2** If you have got a cold or a headache PHRASAL VB:
coming on, it is just starting. EG *I felt a cold coming* v+ADV
on. **3** If something **is coming on**, it is developing v+ADV
or making progress. EG *My new book is coming on
quite well.* **4** When something such as a machine v+ADV
or system **comes on**, it starts working or functioning. EG *The lights came on.*

come on to. When you **come on to** a particular PHRASAL VB:
topic, you start discussing it. EG *I want to come on* v+ADV+PREP
to the question of disease in a minute.

come out. **1** If a fact **comes out**, it becomes PHRASAL VB:
known to people. EG *All the facts came out after* v+ADV
*Seery's death... Something that comes out very
clearly in interviews is how predictable people's
answers are.* **2** When a new product **comes out**, it v+ADV
becomes available to the public. EG *Over the summer his book had come out and done well.* **3** To v+ADV,
come out in a particular way means to be in the USU+A OR C
position or state described at the end of a process
or event. EG *Who do you think will come out on
top?... The press was coming out of the affair very
badly.* **4** If you **come out** for something, you v+ADV+A
declare that you support it. If you **come out**
against something, you declare that you do not
support it. EG *He came out in support of the claim.*
5 If a photograph **comes out**, it is successful and v+ADV
all the details can be seen. **6** When the sun, moon, v+ADV
or stars **come out**, they appear in the sky.

come out in. If you **come out in** spots, you PHRASAL VB:
become covered with them. v+ADV+PREP

come over. If a feeling **comes over** you, it PHRASAL VB:
affects you. EG *I don't know what came over me.* v+PREP

come round. **1** If you **come round** to an idea, PHRASAL VB:
you eventually change your mind and accept it or v+ADV,
agree with it. EG *He knew I would have to come* USU+to
round to his way of thinking in the end. **2** When v+ADV
something **comes round**, it happens as a regular
or predictable event. EG *Don't wait for April to
come round before planning your vegetable garden.* **3** When someone who is unconscious **comes** v+ADV
round, they recover consciousness.

come through. **1** If you **come through** a dan- PHRASAL VB:
v+ADV/PREP

gerous or difficult situation, you survive it. EG *Most
of the troops came through the fighting unharmed.*
2 If something **comes through**, **2.1** it is clearly v+ADV
shown by what is said or done. EG *I think the
teacher's own personality has got to come through.*
2.2 it arrives, especially after some procedure has
been carried out. EG *Has my visa come through
yet?*

come to. When someone who is unconscious PHRASAL VB:
comes to, they recover consciousness. EG *That's* v+ADV
about all I remember, until I came to in a life-raft.

come under. **1** If something **comes under** a PHRASAL VB:
particular authority, it is managed or controlled by v+PREP
that authority. EG *Day Nurseries come under the
Department of Health and Social Security.* **2** If you
come under criticism or attack, you are criticized
or attacked. EG *The premier came under severe
criticism... British produce came under pressure
from foreign competition.* **3** If something **comes
under** a particular heading, it is in the category
mentioned. EG *Records and tapes come under published material.*

come up. **1** If something **comes up** in a conver- PHRASAL VB:
sation or meeting, it is mentioned or discussed. EG v+ADV
His name came up at a buffet lunch. **2** If something v+ADV
is coming up, it is about to happen or take place.
EG *There's a royal wedding coming up.* **3** If v+ADV
something **comes up**, it happens unexpectedly. EG *I
can't see you tonight. Something's come up.* **4** v+ADV,
When someone or something **comes up** for elec- USU+for
tion or review, the time arrives when they have to
be considered or dealt with. EG *A third of my
colleagues will come up for election next May.* **5** v+ADV
When the sun or moon **comes up**, it rises. EG *The
sun comes up in the East.* **6** In law, when a case v+ADV
comes up, it is heard in a court of law.

come up against. If you **come up against** a PHRASAL VB:
problem or difficulty, you are faced with it and v+ADV+PREP
have to deal with it. EG *Everyone comes up against
discrimination sooner or later.*

come upon. **1** If you **come upon** someone or PHRASAL VB:
something, you meet them or find them by chance. v+PREP
EG *They rounded a turn and came upon a family of
lions.* **2** If an attitude or feeling **comes upon** you, it Literary
begins to affect you. EG *His new outlook on life
had come upon him gradually.*

come up to. To be **coming up to** a time or state PHRASAL VB:
means to be getting near to it. EG *Some of them are* v+ADV+PREP
*coming up to retirement... It was just coming up to
ten o'clock.*

come up with. If you **come up with** a plan or PHRASAL VB:
idea, you think of it and suggest it. EG *I hope to* v+ADV+PREP
come up with some of the answers.

comeback /kʌmbæk/, **comebacks.** If something N COUNT
or someone makes a **comeback**, they become
popular or successful again. EG *Wigs and elaborate
hairstyles made a comeback.*

comedian /kəmiːdɪən/, **comedians.** A **comedian** N COUNT
is an entertainer whose job is to make people
laugh, especially by telling jokes or funny stories.

comedienne /kəmiːdɪɛn/, **comediennes.** A co- N COUNT
medienne is a female comedian.

comedy /kɒmədi¹/, **comedies.** **1** A **comedy** is an N COUNT
amusing play or film. EG *...a revival of Maugham's
comedy 'Caroline'.*
2 You can refer to amusing things in a play or film N UNCOUNT
as **comedy**. EG *The play had plenty of excitement
as well as comedy... ...her rare gift for comedy on
the stage.*

comely /kʌmli¹/, **comelier, comeliest.** A woman ADJ QUALIT
who is **comely** is attractive. Outdated

comet /kɒmɪ²t/, **comets.** A **comet** is an object N COUNT
that travels around the sun leaving a bright trail
behind it.

come-uppance /kʌmʌpəns/. When someone gets N SING+POSS
their **come-uppance**, they are justly punished for
something wrong that they have done. EG *It is
difficult not to be pleased at his come-uppance.*

comfort /kʌmfət/, **comforts, comforting, com-**   N UNCOUNT
forted. 1 Comfort is **1.1** the state of being
physically relaxed. EG *She longed to stretch out in
comfort... ...a hard narrow chair not made for
comfort.* **1.2** a pleasant style of life in which you
have everything you need. EG *She wanted a life of
reasonable comfort.* **1.3** a feeling of relief from
worries or unhappiness. EG *I found comfort in his
words.*

2 You can refer to a person, thing, or idea that   N COUNT
helps you to stop worrying as a **comfort**. EG *It will
be a comfort to know that you are standing by.*

3 You can use **comfort** in a phrase such as **too**   PHRASE
close for comfort to mean that you are worried
because something is closer than you would like it
to be. EG *Her comments were a little too revealing
for comfort.*

4 Comforts are things which make your life easier   N COUNT :
and more pleasant. EG *I longed for the comforts of*   USU PLURAL
home.

5 To **comfort** someone means to make them feel   V+O
less worried or unhappy. EG *Jeannie came to com-
fort him.* ◊ **comforting**. EG *It's a comforting*   ◊ ADJ QUALIT
thought that we have a few days before it starts.*

comfortable /kʌmfəˀtəbəˀl/. **1** Something that is   ADJ QUALIT
comfortable makes you feel physically relaxed
when you are using it. EG *That chair is quite
comfortable... The hotel was large and comfortable.*

2 If you are **comfortable**, or if you **make yourself**   ADJ QUALIT
comfortable, you are physically relaxed and at   OR PHRASE
ease. EG *Sit down and make yourself comfortable.*
◊ **comfortably**. EG *They were too cold to sleep*   ◊ ADV
comfortably.

3 If you say that someone is **comfortable**, you   ADJ QUALIT
mean that they have enough money to be able to   Outdated
live without financial problems. EG *She was comfortable, even wealthy by old standards.*
◊ **comfortably**. EG *She has been living quite com-*   ◊ ADV
fortably since her husband died.

4 If you feel **comfortable** in a particular situation,   ADJ QUALIT :
you feel confident and are not worried, afraid, or   USU PRED
embarrassed. EG *He did not feel comfortable with
strangers.*

5 When a person who has been ill or injured is said   ADJ PRED
to be **comfortable**, they are in a stable physical
condition.

6 A **comfortable** job or task is quite easy to do. EG   ADJ QUALIT
It's a comfortable two hours' walk from here.
◊ **comfortably**. EG *I can manage the work com-*   ◊ ADV
fortably.

7 A **comfortable** opinion or belief ignores the   ADJ QUALIT
difficult or unpleasant aspects of something; used
showing disapproval. EG *...the comfortable belief
that nothing is likely to go wrong.*

comic /kɒmɪk/, **comics. 1** Something that is **com-**   ADJ QUALIT
ic amuses you and makes you want to laugh. EG *...a
story rich in comic and dramatic detail.*

2 A **comic** is a person who tells jokes in order to   N COUNT
make people laugh. EG *When the comic comes on
they'll all laugh.*

3 A **comic** is also a magazine that contains stories   N COUNT
told in pictures. EG *He saw me reading a comic.*   British

comical /kɒmɪkəˀl/. Someone or something that is   ADJ QUALIT
comical makes you want to laugh. EG *There is
something slightly comical about him.*
◊ **comically**. EG *David looked comically aston-*   ◊ ADV
ished.

comic strip, comic strips. A **comic strip** is a   N COUNT
series of drawings that tell a story.

coming /kʌmɪŋ/, **comings. 1** A **coming** event or   ADJ CLASSIF :
time is an event or time that will happen soon. EG   ATTRIB
*The real struggle will take place in the coming
weeks.*

2 Comings and goings are the arrivals and depar-   PHRASE
tures of people at a particular place. EG *...the
comings and goings of the guests.*

comma /kɒmə/, **commas.** A **comma** is the punc-   N COUNT
tuation mark (,) which is used to separate parts of
a sentence or items in a list.

command /kəmɑːnd/, **commands, command-
ing, commanded. 1** If you **command** someone to   V+O+to-INF
do something, you order them to do it. EG *'Stay*   OR QUOTE;
here!' he commanded... She commanded me to lie   ALSO V
down and relax. ▸ used as a noun. EG *They waited*   ▸ N COUNT OR
for their master's command.   N UNCOUNT

2 If you **command** something, **2.1** you order it. EG   V+O
The king had commanded his presence at court.
2.2 you obtain it as a result of being popular or
important. EG *She was no longer in a position to
command obedience or admiration.*

3 An officer who **commands** part of an army,   V+O
navy, or air force is responsible for controlling and
organizing it. EG *He commanded a regiment of
cavalry in Algiers.* ▸ used as a noun. EG *He had*   ▸ N UNCOUNT
been in command of HMS Churchill for a year.

4 Someone who is **second in command** of an   PHRASE
organization or group is the second most important
person in charge of the organization or group.

5 Command is control over a particular situation.   N UNCOUNT
EG *Lady Sackville took command... He was looking
more relaxed and in command than ever before.*
● If you are **in command** of yourself, you are able   ● PHRASE
to react and behave in the way that you want to. EG
She felt happy and in command of herself.

6 Your **command** of something is your knowledge   N UNCOUNT+of
of it and your ability to use this knowledge. EG *...a
good command of spoken English.* ● If you have a   ● PHRASE
particular skill **at** your **command**, you have it and
can use it fully. EG *...a writer who has both elegance
and passion at his command.*

commandant /kɒməndænt/, **commandants.** A   N COUNT
commandant is an army officer in charge of a
particular place or group of people.

commandeer /kɒməndɪə/, **commandeers,
commandeering, commandeered. 1** If the army   V+O
commandeer a building or vehicle, they officially
take it from someone so that they can use it.

2 If you **commandeer** something, you take it from   V+O
someone who is less important or powerful than
you; used showing disapproval. EG *...a tiny office
that he has commandeered from a secretary.*

commander /kəmɑːndə/, **commanders.** A **com-**   N COUNT
mander is **1** an officer in charge of a military
operation or organization. EG *Montgomery was a
cautious commander who never took risks.* **2** an
officer in the Royal Navy.

commander-in-chief, commanders-in-chief.   N COUNT
A **commander-in-chief** is an officer in charge of
all the forces in a particular area.

commanding /kəmɑːndɪŋ/. **1** If you are in a   ADJ QUALIT :
commanding position or situation, you are able to   ATTRIB
control people and events. EG *Britain had lost her
commanding position in the world.*

2 If you have a **commanding** voice or manner,   ADJ QUALIT
you seem powerful and confident. EG *He gave
orders in a commanding voice.* ◊ **commandingly**.   ◊ ADV
EG *He speaks confidently and commandingly of his
views.*

3 A building that has a **commanding** position is   ADJ QUALIT :
high up and has good views of the surrounding   ATTRIB
area. EG *The University stands in a commanding
position overlooking the bay.*

commandment /kəmɑːndmətⁿt/, **command-**   N COUNT
ments. The Ten **Commandments** are the ten
rules of behaviour which, according to the Old
Testament of the Bible, God says that people
should obey.

commando /kəmɑːndəʊ/, **commandos.** A **com-**   N COUNT
mando is **1** a small group of specially trained
soldiers. EG *...the side road where the second commando of OAS men waited.* **2** a soldier who is a

member of a commando. EG *The commandos headed across the bridges.*

commemorate /kəmemərett/, **commemorates, commemorating, commemorated.** 1 An object v+o that **commemorates** a person or an event is intended to make people remember the person or event. EG *...a monument commemorating a great soldier.* ◇ **commemorative** /kəmemə'rətɪv/. EG ◇ ADJ CLASSIF: *...a commemorative plaque.* ATTRIB

2 If you **commemorate** an event, you do some- v+o thing special to show that you remember it. EG *...a Jewish holiday commemorating the destruction of the Temple.* ◇ **commemoration** ◇ N UNCOUNT: /kəmemərettʃə°n/. EG *...the commemoration of the* OFT+*of* *fiftieth anniversary of the revolution.*

commence /kəmens/, **commences, commenc-** v **ing, commenced.** 1 When something com- Formal **mences**, it begins. EG *He had been in prison for nine months when his trial commenced.* ◇ **commencement** /kəmensmə²nt/, **commence-** ◇ N UNCOUNT: **ments.** EG *...the commencement of the present* USU+SUPP *century.*

2 If you **commence** doing something, you begin v+-ING OR V+O doing it. EG *Laurie commenced running in his late* Formal *twenties... I commenced a round of visits.*

commend /kəmend/, **commends, commending, commended.** 1 If you **commend** someone, you v+o:OFT+*for* praise them formally. EG *I was commended for my reports.* ◇ **commendation** /kɒmendeɪʃə°n/, **com-** ◇ N UNCOUNT **mendations.** EG *His action earned the personal* OR N COUNT *commendation of the prime minister.*

2 If you **commend** something to someone, you tell v+o:OFT+*to* them that it is very good. EG *Rothermere commended Baldwin to his readers as a great man.*

3 If something **commends** itself to you, you ap- V-REFL+*to* prove of it. EG *The defence would scarcely commend itself even to other lawyers.*

commendable /kəmendəbə°l/. Behaviour that is ADJ QUALIT **commendable** is admired and praised. EG *The committee acted with commendable fairness and understanding.*

commensurate /kəmensərə¹t, -ʃə-/. If an amount ADJ PRED is **commensurate** with another amount, it is in +*with* proportion to the other amount. EG *The house* Formal *brings in a return commensurate with its current market value.*

comment /kɒment/, **comments, commenting, commented.** 1 If you **comment** on something, you v:USU+*on/* give your opinion about it or you give an explana- *upon*; ALSO tion for it. EG *Both girls commented on Chris's size...* V+QUOTE *'It needs washing,' she commented... Someone* ONLY *commented that Brian changes his mind every* *that* *day.*

2 A **comment** is something that you say which N COUNT OR expresses your opinion of something or which N UNCOUNT: gives an explanation of it. EG *People in the town* OFT+*on/upon* *started making rude comments... Well, this isn't a fair comment on the situation... He was not available for comment yesterday.*

3 People say **'no comment'** as a way of refusing to CONVENTION answer a question during an interview. EG *'Do you intend to keep them in prison?' – 'No comment.'*

commentary /kɒməntə°riː/, **commentaries.** 1 A N COUNT **commentary** is a description of an event that is broadcast on radio or television while the event is taking place. EG *We were gathered round a radio to hear the commentary.*

2 A **commentary** is also a book or article which N COUNT OR explains or discusses something. EG *...a series of* N UNCOUNT *political commentaries.*

commentator /kɒmənteɪtə/, **commentators.** 1 N COUNT A **commentator** is a broadcaster who gives a radio or television commentary on an event.

2 A **commentator** is also someone who often N COUNT+SUPP writes or broadcasts about a particular subject. EG *...Peter Jenkins, an experienced commentator on political affairs.*

commerce /kɒmɜːs/ is the activities and pro- N UNCOUNT cedures involved in buying and selling things. EG *...the world of industry and commerce.*

commercial /kəmɜːʃə°l/, **commercials.** 1 Com- ADJ CLASSIF: **mercial** means involving or relating to commerce ATTRIB and business. EG *...commercial and industrial organisations.*

2 A **commercial** activity involves producing goods ADJ CLASSIF: in large quantities in order to make a profit. EG ATTRIB *...commercial agriculture... ...a big commercial bakery.* ◇ **commercially.** EG *Slate was quarried* ◇ ADV *commercially here.*

3 **Commercial** television and radio are paid for by ADJ CLASSIF: the broadcasting of advertisements between pro- ATTRIB grammes.

4 A **commercial** is an advertisement that is broad- N COUNT cast on television or radio.

commercialized /kəmɜːʃəlaɪzd/; also spelled ADJ QUALIT **commercialised.** Something that is **commercial-** **ized** is mainly concerned with making money; used showing disapproval. EG *The ceremonies have degenerated into vulgar, commercialized specta-cles.*

commiserate /kəmɪzəreɪt/, **commiserates,** v:OFT+*with* **commiserating, commiserated.** If you **commis-** **erate** with someone, you show them pity or sympa- thy when something unpleasant has happened to them. EG *I commiserated with him over the recent news.* ◇ **commiseration** /kəmɪzəreɪʃə°n/. EG *She* ◇ N UNCOUNT *gave him a look of commiseration.*

commission /kəmɪʃə°n/, **commissions, com-** **missioning, commissioned.** 1 If you **commis-** v+o OR **sion** something or **commission** someone to do V+O+*to*-INF something, you formally arrange for someone to do a piece of work for you. EG *The Times commis-sioned a Public Opinion Poll... I was immediately commissioned to write another book.*

2 A **commission** is a piece of work that someone N COUNT is asked to do and is paid for. EG *Red House was Webb's first commission as an architect.*

3 **Commission** is a sum of money paid to a N UNCOUNT salesman for every sale that he or she makes. EG OR N COUNT *They get commission on top of their basic salary.*

4 A **commission** is also a group of people who N COLL have been appointed to find out about something or to control something. EG *A commission was appointed to investigate the assassination of the President.*

commissionaire /kəmɪʃə°neə/, **commission-** N COUNT **aires.** A **commissionaire** is a man employed by a hotel, theatre, or cinema to open doors and help customers. Commissionaires usually wear uniform.

commissioner /kəmɪʃə°nə/, **commissioners.** A N COUNT: **commissioner** is an important official in an or- USU+SUPP ganization. EG *...the Church Commissioners.*

commit /kəmɪt/, **commits, committing, com-** **mitted.** 1 If someone **commits** a crime or a sin, v+o they do it. EG *He has committed a criminal of-fence... Margaret had no intention of committing suicide.*

2 If you **commit** money or resources to something, v+o:OFT+*to* you decide to use them for a particular purpose. EG *Rolls Royce must commit its entire resources to the project.*

3 If you **commit** yourself to a course of action, you V-REFL: definitely decide that you will do it. EG *I really* OFT+*to* *wouldn't like to commit myself.*

4 If someone **is committed** to a hospital or prison, v+o: they are officially sent there for a time. EG *She was* USU PASS+*to* *committed to a nursing home.*

5 If you **commit** something **to memory**, you PHRASE memorize it. EG *You'll need these figures so often that you must commit them to memory.*

commitment /kəmɪtmə°nt/, **commitments.** 1 N UNCOUNT **Commitment** is a strong belief in an idea or system. EG *There is no doubting his enthusiasm or his commitment.*

2 A **commitment** is something which regularly N COUNT: USU PLURAL

takes up some of your time. EG *She's got family commitments.*

3 If you give a **commitment** to something, you N COUNT promise faithfully that you will do it. EG *He gave a* Formal *clear commitment to reopen disarmament talks.*

committal /kəmɪtəˀl/ is the process of officially N UNCOUNT sending someone to prison or to hospital. EG *One hundred and ten days may elapse between committal and trial.*

committee /kəmɪtiˀ/, **committees.** A commit- N COLL tee is a group of people who represent a larger group or organization and who make decisions or plans for that group or organization. EG *A special committee has been set up... The whole Committee are very grateful to you.*

commodious /kəməʊdiəs/. A room or house that ADJ QUALIT is **commodious** is large and has plenty of space. EG Formal *...a commodious building suitable for conversion.*

commodity /kəmɒdɪtiˀ/, **commodities.** A com- N COUNT modity is something that is sold for money. EG *He* Formal *dealt in all domestic commodities – clothes, hardware, and furniture.*

common /kɒmən/, **commoner, commonest; commons. 1** If something is **common**, it is found ADJ QUALIT in large numbers or it happens often. EG *Durand is a common name there... It was quite common for dogs to be poisoned this way.* ◊ **commonly.** EG *The* ◊ ADV *most commonly used argument is that clients do not like long delays.*

2 If something is **common** to two or more people, ADJ CLASSIF it is possessed, done, or used by them all. EG *We* IF PRED *shared a common language... It suppressed the* THEN + to *desire for freedom common to all people.*

3 If two or more things have something **in com-** PHRASE mon, they have the same characteristic or feature. EG *What have these names in common?... In common with many other companies, we advertise in the local press.* ● If two or more people have ● PHRASE something **in common**, they share the same interests or experiences. EG *You two have got a lot in common.*

4 Common is also used to indicate that something ADJ CLASSIF : is of the ordinary kind and not special in any way. ATTRIB EG *Sodium chloride is better known as common salt.*

5 If something is **common** knowledge or is the ADJ CLASSIF : common belief, it is known about or believed to be ATTRIB true by people in general. EG *It was common knowledge that he lived alone in the mansion.* ◊ **commonly.** EG *Chauffeurs, it is commonly* ◊ ADV *agreed, know more about what is going on than their employers think.*

6 Someone who is **common** behaves in a way that ADJ QUALIT shows lack of taste, education, and good manners; used showing disapproval.

7 A **common** is an area of grassy land in or near a N COUNT village where the public is allowed to go.

8 Common is also used in these phrases. **8.1** PHRASES **Common or garden** things are ordinary and not special in any way. EG *These are common or garden transistors.* **8.2** If something is done **for the common good**, it is done for the benefit of everyone in the community. **8.3 Common ground** is something which two or more people or groups agree about. EG *There is no common ground upon which dialogue can be based.*

commoner /kɒmənə/, **commoners.** A common- N COUNT er is a person who is not a member of the nobility.

common-law. A **common-law** relationship is ADJ CLASSIF : regarded as a marriage because it has lasted a long ATTRIB time, although no official marriage contract has been signed. EG *...common-law marriage... his common-law wife.*

Common Market. The **Common Market** is an N PROPER : organization of West European countries, including the + N the UK, who make decisions together about their trade, agriculture, and other policies.

commonplace /kɒmənpleɪs/. Something that is ADJ QUALIT **commonplace** is not surprising because it hap-

pens often or is often found. EG *Air travel has now become commonplace.*

common room, common rooms. A **common** N COUNT room is a room in a university or school where people can sit, talk, and relax.

common sense is a person's natural ability to N UNCOUNT make good judgements and to behave in a practical and sensible way. EG *Use your common sense... This precaution is simply common sense.* ▸ used as ▸ ADJ CLASSIF an adjective. EG *Take a few common-sense steps to* ATTRIB *help the situation.*

commotion /kəməʊʃəˀn/. A **commotion** is a lot N SING OR of noise, confusion, and excitement. EG *Suddenly* N UNCOUNT *there was a commotion at the other end of the bar.*

communal /kɒmjɔ̀ˀnəˀl/. Something that is com- ADJ CLASSIF munal is shared by a group of people. EG *...a communal dining-room... ...a communal style of life.* ◊ **communally.** EG *The mills are owned* ◊ ADV *communally.*

commune, communes, communing, com- muned; pronounced /kɒmjuːn/ when it is a noun, and /kəmjuːn/ when it is a verb.

1 A **commune** is a group of people who live N COLL together and share everything. EG *...a women's commune.*

2 If you **commune** with nature or some other V + with power or spirit, you feel that you have a very close Literary relationship with it. EG *...a beautiful spot where one communed with God and Nature.*

communicate /kəmjuːnɪkeɪt/, **communicates, communicating, communicated. 1** If you com- municate with another person or place, **1.1** you V OR V + with use signals such as speech, radio signals, or body RECIP; ALSO movements to give them information. EG *He com-* V + REPORT : municates with Miami by radio... Through signs* ONLY that *she communicated that she wanted a drink.* **1.2** V OR V + with you write a letter to them or you telephone them. RECIP EG *Anthony and I hadn't communicated for years.*

2 If you **communicate** an idea or a feeling to V + O : OFT + to someone, you make them aware of it. EG *...the failure of intellectuals to communicate their ideas to a wider audience.*

3 If people **communicate**, they can understand V OR V + with each other's feelings or attitudes. EG *Cliff talked to* RECIP *me a few times but we couldn't really communicate.*

communicating /kəmjuːnɪkeɪtɪŋ/. **Communi-** ADJ CLASSIF cating doors link one room directly to another. EG ATTRIB *The two rooms were next to each other, with a communicating door.*

communication /kəmjuːnɪkeɪʃəˀn/, **communi-** cations. 1 Communication is the activity or N UNCOUNT process of giving information to other people or to other living things. EG *Insects such as ants have a highly effective system of communication.*

2 Communications are the systems and processes N PLURAL that are used to communicate or broadcast information, especially by means of electricity or radio waves. EG *...large numbers of communications satellites.*

3 A **communication** is a letter or telephone call. N COUNT EG *...a secret communication from the Foreign* Formal *Minister.*

communicative /kəmjuːnɪkətɪv/. **1** Someone ADJ QUALIT who is **communicative** is able to talk to people easily. EG *He was as friendly and communicative as taxi-drivers commonly are.*

2 Communicative means relating to the ability to ADJ CLASSIF communicate. EG *...sounds whose communicative function can be understood.*

communion /kəmjuːnjəˀn/. **1 Communion** is the N UNCOUNT sharing of thoughts or feelings. EG *Society has lost* Literary *all communion with the elementary sources of life.*

2 Communion is also the Christian ceremony in N UNCOUNT which people eat bread and drink wine as a symbol

What is the difference between 'compact' and 'commodious'?

of Christ's death and sacrifice. EG *He started going to Communion.*

communiqué /kəmjuːˈnɪkeɪ/, **communiqués.** A N COUNT **communiqué** is an official statement or announcement. EG *On his desk were a dozen communiqués from various government departments.*

communism /ˈkɒmjəˌnɪzəᵐm/ is the political be- N UNCOUNT lief that the state should control the means of producing everything, and that there should be no private property. EG *But Communism still commands great respect in many countries.*

communist /ˈkɒmjəˌnɪst/, **communists.** A com- N COUNT **munist** is someone who believes in Communism. EG *...a young communist from Cleveland, Ohio.*
▸ used as an adjective. EG *I know you had some* ▸ ADJ CLASSIF *Communist friends.*

community /kəmjuːˈnɪtiˈ/, **communities. 1** A N COLL **community** is made up of the people who live in a particular area. EG *Members are drawn from all sections of the local community... ...community affairs.*
2 A particular **community** is a particular group of N COLL+SUPP people in society who are alike in some way. EG *...the black community in Britain.*

community service is unpaid work that crimi- N UNCOUNT nals sometimes do as a punishment instead of being sent to prison.

commute /kəmjuːt/, **commutes, commuting,** V : USU+A **commuted.** If you **commute,** you travel a long distance every day between your home and your place of work. EG *...the 120,000 workers who commute from nearby towns.* ◇ **commuter** ◇ N COUNT /kəmjuːtə/, **commuters.** EG *...a crowd of commuters on the London Underground.*

compact, compacts, compacting, compacted; pronounced /kɒmpækt/ or /kəˈmpækt/ when it is an adjective, /kəˈmpækt/ when it is a verb, and /kɒmpækt/ when it is a noun.
1 Something that is **compact** takes up very little ADJ QUALIT space. EG *The kitchen was small, compact, and immaculately clean... ...smaller, more compact computers.*
2 To **compact** something means to press it so that V+O it becomes more dense. EG *The tractor wheels* Formal *compact the soil to a damaging extent.*
◇ **compacted.** EG *...compacted soil.* ◇ ADJ CLASSIF
3 A **compact** is a small, flat, round case that N COUNT contains face-powder and a mirror.

compact disc /kɒmpækt dɪsk/, **compact discs.** N COUNT A **compact disc** is a type of record that has a very high quality of sound reproduction. Compact discs have to be played on a special machine.

companion /kəˈmpænjən/, **companions.** A com- N COUNT **panion** is someone who you spend time with or who you are travelling with. EG *He saw Vita as the companion of a lifetime.*

companionable /kəmpænjənəbəˈl/. A person ADJ QUALIT who is **companionable** is friendly and pleasant to be with.

companionship /kəmpænjənʃɪp/ is being with N UNCOUNT someone you know and like, rather than being on your own. EG *She missed her mother's companionship and love.*

company /ˈkʌmpəniˈ/, **companies. 1** A **company** N COLL is **1.1** a business organization that makes money by selling goods or services. EG *He is a geologist employed by an oil company.* **1.2** a group of actors, opera singers, or dancers who work together. EG *...the Royal Shakespeare Company.*
2 If you have **company,** you have a friend or N UNCOUNT visitor with you. EG *Are you expecting company?... She preferred his company to that of most people.*
3 If you **keep** someone **company,** you spend time PHRASE with them and stop them feeling lonely or bored.
4 If you **part company** with someone, you end PHRASE your association with them or disagree with them. EG *In 1911, Adler parted company with Freud... Even those who usually agree with the headmaster would part company with him on this point.*

---

comparable /ˈkɒmpərəbəˈl/. Something that is **comparable** to something else is **1** as good, as big, ADJ QUALIT or as important as the other thing. EG *At that* OFT+to/with *moment there seemed nothing in the world comparable to sleep... The sums of money involved were not, of course, comparable.* **2** similar to the other ADJ CLASSIF thing, and therefore able to be compared with it. EG OFT+to/with *They have much lower fuel consumption than comparable petrol-engined cars.*
◇ **comparability** /kɒmpərəbɪlɪtiˈ/. EG *There are* ◇ N UNCOUNT *problems over the comparability of data.*

comparative /kəˈmpærəˈtɪv/, **comparatives. 1** ADJ CLASSIF : You use **comparative** to say that you are judging ATTRIB something by the standards of what is normally the case. For example, **comparative** peace or silence is a state which is fairly peaceful or silent compared with what is normal. EG *He hoped they could spend the night in comparative safety.*
◇ **comparatively.** EG *There was comparatively* ◇ SUBMOD *little pressure for change.*
2 A **comparative** study is a study that involves the ADJ CLASSIF : comparison of two or more things of the same ATTRIB kind. EG *...a comparative study of Indian and Western food.*
3 In grammar, the **comparative** form of an adjec- ADJ CLASSIF tive or adverb is the form, usually ending in *-er,* OR N COUNT that indicates that there is an increase in quality, size, or amount. See the entry headed ADJECTIVES for more information.

compare /kəˈmpeə/, **compares, comparing, compared. 1** When you **compare** things, you V+O OR consider them and discover the differences or V+O+with/to : similarities between them. EG *It's interesting to* RECIP *compare the two prospectuses... ...studies comparing Russian children with those in Britain.*
◇ **compared.** EG *The fee is low, compared with* ◇ ADJ PRED *that at many other independent schools... Breast* +with/to *milk always looks thin, compared to cow's milk.*
2 If you **compare** one person or thing to another, V+O+to you say that they are like the other person or thing. EG *As an essayist he is compared frequently to Paine and Hazlitt.*
3 If one thing **compares favourably** with another, PHRASE it is better than the other thing. If it **compares unfavourably,** it is worse than the other thing. EG *Japanese children have an education which compares favourably with some other countries.*
4 If you say that something **does not compare** PHRASE with something else, you mean that it is much worse than it. EG *His intelligence doesn't compare with that of the average Londoner.*

comparison /kəˈmpærɪsən/, **comparisons. 1** N COUNT OR When you make a **comparison,** you consider two N UNCOUNT or more things and discover the differences between them. EG *Here, for comparison, is the French version... We have to find out more before we can make a proper comparison.*
2 If you say that something is large or small **in** PHRASE **comparison with** or **in comparison to** something else, you mean that it is larger or smaller than the other thing. EG *Their possessions were few in comparison to those of the older men.*
3 If something is large or small **in comparison** or ADV SEN **by comparison,** it is large or small when it is compared to something that has just been mentioned. EG *He made me look, in comparison, a good, calm, reasonable person.*

compartment /kə'mpɑ:tmə'nt/, **compartments.** N COUNT
A **compartment** is 1 one of the separate spaces
into which a railway carriage is divided. EG *I had a
first-class compartment to myself.* 2 one of the
separate parts of an object that is used for keeping
things in. EG *He tucked the ticket into the inner
compartment of his wallet.*

compartmentalize /kɒmpɑ:tmentəlaiz/, **com-** V+O
**partmentalizes, compartmentalizing, com-
partmentalized;** also spelled **compartmentalise.**
To **compartmentalize** something means to divide
it into separate sections. EG *I have found it best to
compartmentalize my contracts.*

compass /kʌmpəs/, **compasses.** 1 A **compass** is N COUNT
an instrument that you use for finding directions. It
has a dial and a magnetic needle that always points
to the north. EG *I set off clutching my map and
compass.*

compass

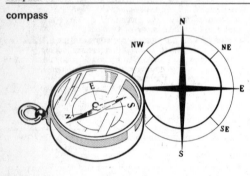

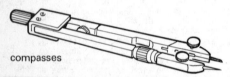

compasses

2 Compasses are a hinged V-shaped instrument N PLURAL
that you use for drawing circles.
3 The **compass** of something is the range over N COUNT+SUPP
which it can operate. EG *...reality beyond the mind's* Formal
normal compass.

compassion /kə'mpæʃə'n/ is a feeling of pity and N UNCOUNT
sympathy for someone who is suffering. EG *The
suffering of the Cubans aroused their compassion.*

compassionate /kə'mpæʃənə't/. Someone who is ADJ QUALIT
compassionate feels or shows pity and sympathy
for other people when they are suffering. EG *She
was among the most compassionate of women.*
◊ **compassionately.** EG *Liz looked at her compas-* ◊ ADV
sionately.

compatible /kə'mpætəbə'l/. If people or things ADJ QUALIT :
are **compatible**, they can live or exist together OFT+*with*
happily or safely. EG *These programs no longer
seem compatible with European society... We assumed that all these objectives were compatible.*
◊ **compatibility** /kə'mpætəbɪlɪti'/. EG *They failed* ◊ N UNCOUNT :
to achieve any compatibility of planning aims. OFT+SUPP

compatriot /kə'mpætrɪət/, **compatriots.** Your N COUNT
compatriots are people from your own country.

compel /kə'mpel/, **compels, compelling, compelled.** 1 If someone or something **compels** you to V+O+*to*-INF
do something, they force you to do it. EG *...illnesses
which compel people to change their diet... He felt
compelled to intervene in the dispute.*
2 To **compel** an attitude, feeling, or action means V+O
to make people have it or do it. EG *His appearance* Formal
was so bizarre that it compelled attention.

compelling /kə'mpelɪŋ/. An argument or reason ADJ QUALIT
that is **compelling** convinces you that something

is true or that something should be done. EG *I had
ended a man's life for no compelling reason.*

compensate /kɒmpə'nseit/, **compensates, com-** V OR V+O :
pensating, compensated. 1 To **compensate** OFT+*for*
someone for something means to pay them money
so that they can replace something that has been
lost, damaged, or destroyed. EG *The allowance
should be paid to compensate people for loss of
earnings.*
2 To **compensate** for the bad effect of something V :OFT+*for*
means to do something that cancels out this effect.
EG *Fish can compensate for the tiniest variation of
current by moving their fins.*

compensation /kɒmpə'nseiʃə'n/, **compensations.** 1 **Compensation** is money that you claim N UNCOUNT
from a person or organization that is responsible
for something unpleasant that has happened to
you. EG *If you were killed, your dependants could
get compensation.*
2 A **compensation** is **2.1** an action that cancels N COUNT OR
out another action that has had a bad effect. EG N UNCOUNT
*Look for some of the compensations your body has
to make.* **2.2** an event or fact that makes you feel
better in spite of something bad that has happened
to you. EG *Letters that began to arrive from Nell
were some compensation.*

compensatory /kɒmpə'nseitə'ri'/. Something ADJ CLASSIF :
that is **compensatory** 1 involves the payment of ATTRIB
compensation. EG *There must be compensatory
payments to the farmers.* 2 is designed to help
people who have special problems or disabilities.
EG *...compensatory education.*

compere /kɒmpeə/, **comperes, compering,** N COUNT
compered. A **compere** is the person on a radio or
television show who introduces the guests and
performers. ► used as a verb. EG *Esther Rantzen* ► V+O
agreed to compere the Miss World contest.

compete /kə'mpi:t/, **competes, competing,
competed.** 1 When one firm **competes** with an- V OR V+*with* /
other firm, it tries to get people to buy its own *against* : RECIP
goods in preference to the other firm's goods. EG
*This would enable British shipbuilders to compete
with foreign yards.*
2 If you **compete** with someone for something, you V OR V+*with* /
try to get it for yourself. EG *Senior members of staff against* : RECIP
*competed eagerly for the honour of representing
the company.*
3 If you **compete** in a contest or a game, you take V+A
part in it. EG *Dave Moorcroft has now competed in
two Olympics.*
4 If two statements or ideas **compete**, they cannot V OR V+*with* :
both be right, or cannot both be accepted. RECIP
◊ **competing.** EG *Various competing theories are* ◊ ADJ CLASSIF :
compared and discussed. ATTRIB

competent /kɒmpə'tənt/. Someone who is com- ADJ QUALIT
petent can do something in an efficient and effective way. EG *He was a competent amateur pilot... It
was a highly competent piece of work.*
◊ **competently.** EG *He carved the bird roughly, but* ◊ ADV
competently. ◊ **competence** /kɒmpə'təns/. EG *He* ◊ N UNCOUNT
*will be expected to show competence in the rel-
evant methods of research.*

competition /kɒmpə'tɪʃə'n/, **competitions.** 1 N UNCOUNT
Competition is **1.1** a situation in which two or
more people or groups are trying to get something
which not everyone can have. EG *Competition for
admission to the college is keen... The two parties
were not in competition with each other.* **1.2** an
activity involving two or more firms, in which each
firm tries to get people to buy its own goods in
preference to the other firms' goods. EG *Part of the
reason for the drop in sales is competition from
overseas suppliers.*
2 A **competition** is an event in which many people N COUNT
take part in order to find out who is best at a

If people are compatible, are they likely to
complement each other?

COMPLEMENTS

The complement (c) is one of the major elements in the structure of a clause. It takes the form of an adjective group or a noun group. It comes after a verb and gives information about the subject or object of the verb. For example, in the sentence *She is happy,* 'happy' is the complement. It is an adjective and it tells you something about the subject 'she'. In the sentence *She made him happy,* 'happy' is again the complement and tells you something about 'him', the object of the clause.

Where the complement is a noun, it refers to the same person or thing as the subject or object of the verb. In the sentence *Harold is a teacher,* 'a teacher' is the complement and gives you some information about the subject 'Harold'. Compare *Harold is a teacher* and *Harold met a teacher.* In the second example 'a teacher' is the object of the clause and is obviously not the same person as 'Harold'. In the sentence *We made Harold chairman,* 'chairman' is the complement and refers to the same person as the object 'Harold'.

A complement can occur with or without an object. For example, the verbs **be, seem,** and **look** have a complement but no object (v+c), as in *Her name is **Melanie** . . . He seemed **nice** . . . You look **very pale.*** Other verbs which have a complement are transitive and so they do have an object (v+o+c). Examples are **make, call,** and **leave,** as in *The women made her **welcome** . . . We called our son **Iain** . . . Who left the gates **open?***

particular activity. EG ...*the Segovia International Guitar Competition.*

competitive /kəˈmpetɪtɪv/. 1 Something that is ADJ QUALIT **competitive** involves people or firms competing with each other. EG ...*a highly competitive society.*

2 A person who is **competitive** is eager to be more ADJ QUALIT successful than other people. EG *I realize how awfully competitive I am.* ◇ **competitively.** EG *It's* ◇ ADV *running for fitness as opposed to running competitively.* ◇ **competitiveness.** EG *Why should we put* ◇ N UNCOUNT *such an emphasis on individualism and competitiveness?*

3 Goods that are **competitive** are likely to be ADJ QUALIT bought, because they are less expensive than other goods of the same kind. EG ...*a competitive car for the 1980s.* ◇ **competitively.** EG ...*competitively* ◇ ADV *priced newspapers.*

competitor /kəˈmpetɪtə/, **competitors.** 1 Some- N COUNT one who is your **competitor** is trying to sell goods or services to the same people as you are. EG ...*Austin-Rover's challenge to its foreign competitors.*

2 A **competitor** is also a person who takes part in N COUNT a competition or contest.

compilation /kɒmpɪˈleɪʃəᵇn/, **compilations.** 1 A N COUNT **compilation** is a book, record, or programme that contains many different parts that have been gathered together. EG ...*a compilation of Victorian poetry.*

2 Compilation is the act of compiling something. N UNCOUNT EG *One of the first steps was the compilation of a report.*

compile /kəmˈpaɪl/, **compiles, compiling, com-** v+o **piled.** When you **compile** a book, report, or film, you produce it by collecting and putting together many pieces of information. EG *The programme was compiled and presented by Dr Brian Smith.*

complacent /kəˈmpleɪsənt/. If you are **compla-** ADJ QUALIT: **cent,** you do not feel that you need to worry or do OFT+*about* anything about a situation; used showing disapprov-

al. EG *We cannot afford to be complacent about the energy problem.* ◇ **complacently.** EG *Her mother* ◇ ADV *smiled complacently.* ◇ **complacency** ◇ N UNCOUNT /kəˈmpleɪsənsɪ¹/. EG *No one has any cause for complacency.*

complain /kəˈmpleɪn/, **complains, complain-** **ing, complained.** If you **complain,** 1 you express v:OFT+A, the fact that you are not satisfied with a particular QUOTE, situation. EG *People had complained to Uncle* ONLY *that* OR REPORT: *Harold about his fights... Women complain of pressure on them to get jobs... 'He never told me, sir,' Watson complained... He complained that the office was not 'businesslike'.* **2** you say that you are v+*of* feeling pain or feeling ill. EG *He complained of pain* OR REPORT: *in the chest.* ONLY *that*

complaint /kəˈmpleɪnt/, **complaints.** 1 A com- **plaint** is 1.1 a statement in which you express your N COUNT OR dissatisfaction with a particular situation. EG *There* N UNCOUNT *were the usual complaints of violence... She wrote a letter of complaint to the manufacturer.* **1.2** a N COUNT reason for complaining. EG *As always, the main complaint is that people don't read the instructions.*

2 A **complaint** is also an illness, often one which is N COUNT not very serious. EG *It turned out to be a minor urinary complaint.*

complement /kɒmpləˈmənt/, **complements,** **complementing, complemented. 1** If one person v+o or thing **complements** another, they increase each other's good qualities when they are brought together. EG *Crisp pastry complements the juicy fruit of an apple pie.* ▶ used as a noun. EG *The* ▶ N COUNT: *exercises are an ideal complement to my usual* OFT+*to* *rehearsal methods.*

2 When you are talking about the number of people N COUNT you work with, you can refer to the **complement** +SUPP of them. EG *Forty four of the original complement* Formal *of 150 were dead... ...the ship's complement.*

3 The **full complement** of a group or set is every PHRASE item or person that it normally includes. EG *The birds all have their full complement of feathers.*

4 In grammar, a **complement** is one of the N COUNT
elements of clause structure. See the entry headed
COMPLEMENTS for more information.

complementary /kɒmpləˈmentəˁriˀ/. Two or ADJ CLASSIF :
more different things are **complementary** if they OFT+to
form a complete or better unit when they are
brought together. EG *These two approaches are
complementary... The roles of the sexes are complementary to one another.*

complete /kəˈpliːt/, **completes, completing,
completed**. **1** You use **complete** to emphasize ADJ QUALIT :
that something is as great in extent, degree, or USU ATTRIB
amount as it possibly can be. EG *You need a
complete change of diet... ...a complete break from
my children... They were in complete agreement.*
◊ **completely**. EG *He was completely bald.* ◊ ADV

2 If something is **complete**, **2.1** it has been fin- ADJ PRED
ished. EG *The harvesting was complete.* **2.2** it ADJ QUALIT
contains all the parts that it should contain. EG *This
is not a complete list... ...an almost complete skeleton of a dinosaur.*

3 If you **complete** something, you finish doing, V+O
making, or producing it. EG *The cathedral was
begun in 1240 and completed forty years later...
Give yourself plenty of time to complete a job.*

4 If something **completes** a group or set, it is the V+O
last item that is needed to make it a full group or
set. EG *A black silk tie completed the outfit.*

5 If you **complete** a form or questionnaire, you V+O
write down the answers to the questions on it.

6 Something that is **complete with** a particular PREP
thing has that thing as an extra part. EG *He bought
a lovely mansion, complete with swimming pool.*

completion /kəˈpliːʃəˁn/ is the finishing of a N UNCOUNT
piece of work. EG *The house was due for completion
in 1983.*

complex /kɒmpleks/, **complexes**. **1** Something ADJ QUALIT
that is **complex** has many different parts, and is
therefore often difficult to understand. EG *...com-
plex lace patterns... It is a complex problem.*

2 A **complex** is **2.1** a group or system of things N COUNT+SUPP
that are connected with each other in a complicat-
ed way. EG *...a complex of little roads... Conflicts
usually develop out of a complex of causes.* **2.2** a
group of buildings or a large building divided into
several areas. EG *...a splendid new sports and
leisure complex.*

3 If someone has a **complex**, they have a mental N COUNT :
or emotional problem because of an unpleasant OFT+about
experience in the past which continues to influence
them. EG *I am developing a guilt complex about it.*

complexion /kəˈmplekʃəˁn/, **complexions**. **1** N COUNT
Your **complexion** is the natural quality of the skin
on your face. EG *He said I had a good complexion.*

2 The **complexion** of something is its general N UNCOUNT
nature or character. EG *...the political complexion* +SUPP
of the press. Formal

complexity /kəˈmpleksiˀtiˀ/, **complexities**. **1** N UNCOUNT
Complexity is the state of having many different
parts connected or related to each other in a
complicated way. *...problems of varying complexity.*

2 The **complexities** of something are its many N PLURAL
connected parts, which make it difficult to understand or deal with. EG *...the complexities of tax law.*

compliance /kəˈmplaɪəns/ is the act of doing N UNCOUNT
what you have been asked to do. EG *I was surprised* Formal
by Melanie's compliance with these terms.

complicate /kɒmplɪkeɪt/, **complicates, compli-** V+O
cating, complicated. To **complicate** something
means to make it more difficult to understand or
deal with. EG *Just to complicate matters, I have to
be back by the end of the month.*

complicated /kɒmplɪkeɪtɪˀd/. Something that is ADJ QUALIT
complicated has so many parts or aspects that it
is difficult to understand or deal with. EG *I find the
British legal system extremely complicated... The
situation is much more complicated than that.*

complication /kɒmplɪkeɪʃəˁn/, **complications**. N COUNT
A **complication** is a circumstance that makes a
situation harder to deal with. EG *Finally, there is the
complication that wages help to determine the
level of inflation.*

complicity /kəˈmplɪsɪˀtiˀ/ is involvement with N UNCOUNT
other people in an illegal activity or plan. EG *She* Formal
suspected him of complicity in Ashok's escape.

compliment /kɒmpləˈməˀnt/, **compliments,
complimenting, complimented**. **1** A **compli-** N COUNT
ment is something that you say to someone to
show that you admire them. EG *He had just been
paid a great compliment.* ● If you **take** something ● PHRASE
that someone does or says **as a compliment**, you
regard it as an indication that they admire you. EG
She took his acceptance as a great compliment.

2 If you **compliment** someone, you tell them how V+O : OFT+
much you admire something that they own or on/for
something that they have done. EG *He complimented Morris on his new car... I was complimented for my opposition to the treaty.*

3 Compliments is used in some expressions when N PLURAL :
you want to formally express good wishes or USU+POSS
respect. EG *The Secretary of State presents his* Formal
*compliments and regrets that he is unable to
attend.*

complimentary /kɒmpləˈmentəˁriˀ/. **1** If you are ADJ QUALIT
complimentary about something, you express admiration for it. EG *In Russia a rhythmic slow
handclap can be highly complimentary.*

2 A **complimentary** seat, ticket, or book is given ADJ CLASSIF :
to you free. ATTRIB

comply /kəˈmplaɪ/, **complies, complying, com-** V : OFT+with
plied. If you **comply** with an order or set of rules,
you do what you are required or expected to do. EG
New vehicles must comply with certain standards.

component /kəˈmpəʊnənt/, **components**. The N COUNT
components of something are the parts that it is
made of. EG *The factory makes components for
cars... ...electronic components... ...the component
parts of the rifle.*

compose /kəˈmpəʊz/, **composes, composing,
composed**. **1** If something **is composed** of par- V-PASS+of
ticular things or people, it has those things or
people as its parts or members. EG *The book is
composed of essays written over the last twenty
years... The National Committee was composed of
22 manual workers and 6 white-collar workers.*

2 If a number of things **compose** something, they V+O
are the parts that it consists of. EG *...the elements* Formal
which compose his individuality.

3 When someone **composes** a piece of music, they V+O OR V
write it. EG *Mozart composed his first symphony in
1764.*

4 If you **compose** a letter, poem, or speech, you V+O
write it. EG *Mr Morris sat down to compose his
letter of resignation.*

5 If you **compose** yourself, you succeed in becom- V-REFL
ing calm after being angry, excited, or upset. EG *She
lay on her bed and cried and then she composed
herself and went downstairs.*

composed /kəˈmpəʊzd/. If someone is **com-** ADJ QUALIT
posed, they are calm and able to control their
feelings. EG *I felt calmer and more composed than I
had in a long time.*

composer /kəˈmpəʊzə/, **composers**. A **compos-** N COUNT
er is a person whose job is writing music, especially classical music.

composite /kɒmpəzɪt/, **composites**. You use ADJ CLASSIF :
composite to describe something that is made up ATTRIB
of several different things, parts, or substances. EG Formal
...the composite annual fee. ▶ used as a noun. EG *He* ▶ N COUNT
works in a composite of styles.

composition /kɒmpəˈzɪʃəˁn/, **compositions**. **1** N UNCOUNT
The **composition** of something is the things that it USU+SUPP

Should you comply with something compulsory?

consists of and the way in which these things are arranged. EG *...the chemical composition of the atmosphere.*

2 A **composition** is a piece of written work that you write at school. EG *The composition had to be at least three pages long.*   N COUNT

3 A composer's **compositions** are the pieces of music that he or she has written. EG *...another of his finer compositions – the B minor Sonata.*   N COUNT

4 Composition is also the act of composing something such as a piece of music or a poem. EG *He began by reading a poem of his own composition.*   N UNCOUNT

compost /kɒmpɒst/ is a mixture of decaying plants and manure, which is added to the soil to help plants grow. EG *...a compost heap.*   N UNCOUNT

composure /kəˈmpəʊʒə/. Someone's **composure** is their ability to stay calm and to control their feelings. EG *He had recovered his composure... She looked out over the auditorium with grave composure.*   N UNCOUNT   Formal

compound, compounds, compounding, compounded; pronounced /kɒmpaʊnd/ when it is a noun, and /kəˈmpaʊnd/ when it is a verb.

1 A **compound** is an enclosed area of land that is used for a particular purpose. EG *He led the men into the prison compound.*   N COUNT

2 In chemistry, a **compound** is a substance that consists of two or more elements.   N COUNT

3 If something is a **compound** of different things, it consists of those things. EG *The new threat was a compound of nationalism and social revolution.*   N COUNT

4 If something **is compounded** of different things, it is made by mixing those things together. EG *They specialize in local dishes compounded of fresh fish and vegetables.*   V-PASS : OFT + *of/from*   Formal

5 To **compound** a problem, difficulty, or mistake means to make it worse by adding to it. EG *Her uncertainty was now compounded by fear.*   V+O   Formal

comprehend /kɒmprɪhend/, **comprehends, comprehending, comprehended.** If you cannot **comprehend** something, you cannot fully understand or appreciate it. EG *...a failure to comprehend the huge power of computers... They did not comprehend how hard he had struggled.*   V+O, V+REPORT, OR V   Formal

comprehensible /kɒmprɪhensəˈbəl/. Something that is **comprehensible** can be easily understood. EG *The object is to make our research readable and comprehensible.*   ADJ QUALIT

comprehension /kɒmprɪhenʃəˈn/, **comprehensions. 1 Comprehension** is the ability to understand or appreciate something fully. EG *The problems of solar navigation seem beyond comprehension... Richard looked from face to face with dawning comprehension.*   N UNCOUNT

2 A **comprehension** is an exercise to find out how well you understand a piece of spoken or written language.   N COUNT

comprehensive /kɒmprɪhensɪv/, **comprehensives. 1** Something that is **comprehensive** includes everything that is needed or relevant. EG *...a comprehensive list of all the items in stock.*   ADJ CLASSIF

2 A **comprehensive** or a **comprehensive school** is a school in which children of all abilities are taught together.   N COUNT   British

compress /kəˈmpres/, **compresses, compressing, compressed. 1** When you **compress** something or when it **compresses**, it is pressed or squeezed so that it takes up less space. EG *I could feel my lips compress into a white line... ...compressed air.* ◊ **compression** /kəˈmpreʃəˈn/. EG *...the compression of air by the piston.*   V-ERG   ◊ N UNCOUNT

2 If you **compress** something such as a piece of writing or a description, you make it shorter. EG *I soon finished a paper, which I compressed to minimum length.* ◊ **compression.** EG *...the compression of information.*   V+O : USU PASS   ◊ N UNCOUNT

comprise /kəˈmpraɪz/, **comprises, comprising, comprised. 1** If something **comprises** a number of things or people, it has them as its parts or   V+C OR V-PASS   + *of*   Formal

members. EG *The Privy Council comprised 283 members... The fountain was comprised of three stone basins.*

2 If a number of things or people **comprise** something, they are the parts or members that it consists of. EG *Farmers comprise just 1.2 per cent of the country's population.*   V+C   Formal

compromise /kɒmprəmaɪz/, **compromises, compromising, compromised. 1** A **compromise** is an agreement between two people in which they both give up something that they originally wanted. EG *It was necessary for members to make compromises to ensure party unity... Delegates predict that some compromise will be reached.*   N COUNT OR N UNCOUNT

2 If you **compromise**, you reach an agreement with another person or group in which you both give up something that you originally wanted. EG *The best thing to do is to compromise.*   V

3 If you **compromise** yourself or your beliefs, you do something which causes people to doubt how sincere, moral, or honest you are. EG *The Government had compromised its principles... They claim he has already compromised himself.*   V-REFL OR V+O

◊ **compromising.** EG *There were photos and compromising letters.*   ◊ ADJ QUALIT

compulsion /kəˈmpʌlʃəˈn/, **compulsions. 1** A **compulsion** is a strong desire to do something, which you find difficult to control. EG *She feels a compulsion to tidy up all the time.*   N COUNT : OFT + *to*-INF

2 If someone uses **compulsion** in order to get you to do something, they force you to do it, for example by threatening to punish you if you do not do it. EG *We are not entitled to use compulsion... Pressed into rugby under compulsion, I began to enjoy the game.*   N UNCOUNT

compulsive /kəˈmpʌlsɪv/. **1** You use **compulsive** to describe people who keep doing something wrong or harmful and who cannot prevent themselves from doing it. For example, a **compulsive** liar is someone who cannot stop lying. EG *...a compulsive gambler.* ◊ **compulsively.** EG *He steals compulsively.*   ADJ CLASSIF   ◊ ADV

2 If a book or television programme is **compulsive**, it is so interesting that you do not want to stop reading or watching it. ◊ **compulsively.** EG *The book is compulsively readable.*   ADJ QUALIT   ◊ ADV + ADJ

compulsory /kəˈmpʌlsəˈrɪ/. If something is **compulsory**, you must do it. EG *In most schools, sports are compulsory... ...his compulsory retirement at the age of 60.*   ADJ CLASSIF

computation /kɒmpjəˈteɪʃəˈn/, **computations. Computation** is mathematical calculation. EG *There had been a sudden advance in the field of automatic computation... He sat over his adding machine making rapid computations.*   N UNCOUNT OR N COUNT

compute /kəˈmpjuːt/, **computes, computing, computed.** To **compute** a quantity or number means to calculate it. EG *It is difficult to compute the loss in revenue.* ● See also **computing.**   V+O

computer /kəˈmpjuːtə/, **computers.** A **computer** is an electronic machine that can quickly make calculations, store, rearrange, and retrieve information, or control another machine. EG *Portable computers can be plugged into TV sets... ...computer games.* ● If you do something **by computer**, you do it using a computer. EG *The entire process is done by computer.*   N COUNT   ● PHRASE

computerize /kəˈmpjuːtəraɪz/, **computerizes, computerizing, computerized**; also spelled **computerise. 1** To **computerize** a system, process, or type of work means to arrange for a lot of the work to be done by computers. EG *We are currently computerizing the Inland Revenue.* ◊ **computerized.** EG *He had just introduced a computerized filing system into the office.* ◊ **computerization** /kəˈmpjuːtəraɪzeɪʃəˈn/. EG *...the economic benefits of computerization.*   V+O   ◊ ADJ CLASSIF   ◊ N UNCOUNT

2 To **computerize** information means to store or process it in a computer.   V+O

computing /kəˈmpjuːtɪŋ/ is the activity of using a N UNCOUNT computer and writing programs for it. EG ...the impact of computing on routine office work.

comrade /ˈkɒmrɪˈd, -æd/, **comrades.** 1 Socialists VOCATIVE or communists call each other **comrade**, especially in meetings. EG This is what I propose, Comrades. 2 Someone's **comrades** are their friends or com- N COUNT panions. Outdated

con /kɒn/, **cons, conning, conned.** 1 If someone v+o: **cons** you, they persuade you to do something or OFT+into believe something by telling you things that are not Informal true. EG A lot of people are conned into thinking that they can't fight back. 2 A **con** is a trick in which someone deceives you N COUNT by telling you something that is not true. EG The Informal whole thing was a big con. 3 See also **mod cons.** ● **pros and cons:** see **pro.**

concave /kɒnˈkeɪv, kɒnˈkeɪv/. A surface that is ADJ QUALIT **concave** curves inwards in the middle. EG ...a concave valley.

conceal /kəˈnsiːl/, **conceals, concealing, concealed.** 1 If you **conceal** something, you cover it v+o or hide it carefully. EG She concealed the bottle beneath her mattress. 2 If you **conceal** a piece of information or a v+o: feeling, you do not let other people know about it. OFT+from EG He might be concealing a secret from me. 3 If something **conceals** an object, it covers it and v+o prevents it from being seen. EG The scarf concealed a revolver.

concealment /kəˈnsiːlməˈnt/ is the state of being N UNCOUNT hidden or the act of hiding something. EG The trees offered concealment and protection... ...the concealment of truth.

concede /kəˈnsiːd/, **concedes, conceding, conceded.** 1 If you **concede** something, you admit, V-SPEECH OR V often unwillingly, that it is true or correct. EG The +O+O company conceded that an error had been made... They reluctantly conceded the point... I'll concede you that. 2 If you **concede** defeat, you accept that you have V OR V+O lost a struggle. EG The government was forced to concede defeat.

conceit /kəˈnsiːt/ is very great pride in your N UNCOUNT abilities or achievements; used showing disapproval. EG His recent movies have shown signs of arrogance and conceit.

conceited /kəˈnsiːtɪˈd/. Someone who is **conceit-** ADJ QUALIT **ed** is very proud of their abilities or achievements; used showing disapproval. EG ...a conceited old fool.

conceivable /kəˈnsiːvəbəˈl/. If something is **con-** ADJ QUALIT **ceivable**, you can imagine it or believe it. EG Jenny learned every conceivable recipe for pasta... It is conceivable that he drowned. ◊ **conceivably.** EG ◊ ADV SEN She brought it because she thought it might conceivably be useful to me.

conceive /kəˈnsiːv/, **conceives, conceiving, conceived.** 1 If you can **conceive** of something, v+of OR you can imagine it or believe it. EG He could never REPORT conceive of such a thing happening to himself... We could not conceive where the energy came from. 2 If you **conceive** something as a particular thing, v+o:USU+as you consider it to be that thing. EG A politician conceives the world as a variety of conflicts. 3 If you **conceive** a plan or idea, you think of it and v+o work out how it can be done. EG A Prices and Incomes policy was boldly conceived. 4 When a child **is conceived** or when a woman v+o OR V **conceives**, the woman becomes pregnant. EG The boy had been conceived on their honeymoon.

concentrate /ˈkɒnsəˈntreɪt/, **concentrates, concentrating, concentrated.** 1 If you **concentrate** V:OFT+on on something, you give all your attention to it. EG Concentrate on your driving... He believed governments should concentrate more on education. 2 If something **concentrates the mind**, it makes PHRASE you think clearly and carefully. EG The prospect of death concentrates the mind wonderfully. 3 When an amount of something **is concentrated** v+o

in a small space, there is a lot of it there. EG Modern industry has been concentrated in a few large urban centres.

concentrated /ˈkɒnsəˈntreɪtɪˈd/. 1 A liquid that is ADJ CLASSIF **concentrated** has been increased in strength by having water removed from it. EG ...concentrated orange juice. 2 A **concentrated** activity is directed with great ADJ QUALIT intensity in one place. EG ...a heavily concentrated attack.

concentration /ˌkɒnsəˈntreɪʃəˈn/, **concentrations.** 1 **Concentration** on something is giving all N UNCOUNT your attention to it. EG It requires considerable OFT+on concentration... ...his concentration on civil rights. 2 A **concentration** of something is a large amount N COUNT OR of it or large numbers of it in a small area. EG ...the N UNCOUNT concentration of power in the hands of a single group.

concentration camp, concentration camps. N COUNT A **concentration camp** is a prison for political prisoners, especially in Germany during the Second World War.

concentric /kəˈnsentrɪk/. **Concentric** circles or ADJ CLASSIF: rings have the same centre. EG ...concentric circles ATTRIB of stones.

concept /ˈkɒnsept/, **concepts.** A **concept** is an N COUNT idea or abstract principle. EG ...the concept of trade unionism... Of course, it's a difficult concept.

conception /kəˈnsepʃəˈn/, **conceptions.** 1 A con- N COUNT **ception** is an idea that you have in your mind. EG He had a definite conception of how he wanted things arranged. 2 **Conception** is 2.1 the forming of an idea for N UNCOUNT something in your mind. EG The plan was very imaginative in conception. 2.2 the process in which a woman becomes pregnant. EG ...the nine months between conception and birth.

conceptual /kəˈnseptʃʊˈəl/ means related to ADJ CLASSIF: ideas and concepts formed in the mind. EG Most ATTRIB people have little conceptual understanding of Formal computers.

concern /kəˈnsɜːn/, **concerns, concerning, concerned.** 1 **Concern** is worry about a situation. EG N UNCOUNT ...the growing public concern over Britain's poor OR N COUNT economic performance... My concern is that many +SUPP of these cases are going unnoticed. 2 If something **concerns** you, it worries you. EG V+O One of the things that concerns me is the rise in vandalism. ◊ **concerned.** EG He was concerned ◊ ADJ QUALIT about the level of unemployment. 3 If you **concern** yourself with something, you give V-REFL OR V+ attention to it because you think that it is impor- O:OFT+with tant. EG I don't want you to concern yourself with it. ◊ **concerned.** EG We are more concerned with ◊ ADJ PRED efficiency than expansion. 4 If something is **of concern** to you, it is important PHRASE to you. EG This was of no concern to businessmen. 5 Your **concern** for someone is a feeling that you N UNCOUNT+ want them to be happy, safe, and well. EG She shows SUPP a true concern for others. 6 If a situation, event, or activity **concerns** you, it v+o affects or involves you. 7 If a situation or problem is your **concern**, it is N SING+POSS something that you have a duty to be involved with. EG That's your concern, I'm afraid... This quarrel is no concern of ours. 8 You say **as far as** something **is concerned** to PHRASE indicate the subject that you are talking about. EG We have rather a poor record as far as regional studies are concerned. 9 You say **'as far as I'm concerned'** to indicate PHRASE that you are giving your own opinion. EG This is all rubbish as far as I'm concerned. 10 The people **concerned** are the people who take ADJ AFTER N

Which meaning of 'concrete' is the opposite of 'conceptual'?

part in something or are affected by it. EG *It was a perfect arrangement for all concerned.*

11 If a book, speech, or piece of information V+O OR V-PASS **concerns** a particular subject or **is concerned** +with with it, it is about that subject. EG *This chapter is concerned with changes that are likely to take place.*

12 A **concern** is also a company or business. EG N COUNT *...the giant West German chemical concern,* Formal *Hoechst.*

concerning /kəˈnsɜːnɪŋ/. You use **concerning** to PREP indicate what a question, story or letter is about. EG *He refused to answer questions concerning his private life... I will now destroy some myths concerning these animals.*

concert /ˈkɒnsət/, **concerts. 1** A **concert** is a N COUNT performance of music given by musicians. EG *...pop concerts... ...a concert hall.* ● When pop groups are ● PHRASE **in concert**, they are giving a concert.

2 If a number of people do something **in concert,** PHRASE they do it together. EG *Sanctions will be more* Formal *effective if they are undertaken in concert by a group of countries.*

concerted /kəˈnsɜːtɪd/. A **concerted** action is ADJ CLASSIF: done by several people working together. EG *Every-* ATTRIB *one makes a concerted effort to help.*

concerto /kəˈntʃeətəʊ/, **concertos.** A **concerto** is N COUNT a piece of music written for a solo instrument and an orchestra.

concession /kəˈnseʃən/, **concessions.** A **con-** N COUNT **cession** is **1** something that you agree to let someone do or have, especially in order to end an argument. EG *The Prime Minister had been urged to make a concession by the government.* **2** a special right or privilege that is given to someone. EG *Foreign oil companies were granted concessions.*

conciliate /kəˈnsɪlɪeɪt/, **conciliates,** V OR V+O **conciliating, conciliated.** If you **conciliate,** you Formal try to end a disagreement with someone.
◊ **conciliation** /kənsɪlɪˈeɪʃən/. EG *Did you make* ◊ N UNCOUNT *any efforts at conciliation?*

conciliatory /kəˈnsɪlɪətrɪ/. When you are **con-** ADJ QUALIT **ciliatory**, you are willing to end a disagreement with someone. EG *She spoke in a conciliatory tone.*

concise /kəˈnsaɪs/. Something that is **concise** ADJ QUALIT says everything that is necessary without using any unnecessary words. EG *...a concise survey of English literature.* ◊ **concisely.** EG *Write clearly and* ◊ ADV *concisely.*

conclude /kəˈnkluːd/, **concludes, concluding, concluded. 1** If you **conclude** that something is V+REPORT: true, you decide that it is true because you know ONLY that, that other things are true. EG *Darwin concluded* OR V+from *that men were descended from apes... What do you conclude from all that?.*

2 When you **conclude,** you say the last thing that V+QUOTE you are going to say. EG *'That,' he concluded, 'is* Formal *why we're so poor.'* ◊ **concluding.** EG *...his con-* ◊ ADJ CLASSIF: *cluding remark.* ATTRIB

3 When you **conclude** something, you end it. EG *I* V-ERG *will conclude this chapter with a quotation from* Formal *Orwell.*

4 If you **conclude** a treaty or business deal, you V+O arrange or settle it finally. Formal

conclusion /kəˈnkluːʒən/, **conclusions. 1** A N COUNT: OFT **conclusion** is something that you decide is true +REPORT after you have thought about it carefully. EG *I came to the conclusion that I didn't really like civil engineering.* ● If you **jump to a conclusion,** you ● PHRASE decide too quickly that something is true, when you do not know all the facts. EG *Some people jumped rashly to the conclusion that something must be wrong.*

2 The **conclusion** of something is its ending. EG *We* N SING: *tried an experiment which had an interesting* USU+SUPP *conclusion.* ● You can describe something that ● PHRASE seems certain to happen as a **foregone conclusion.** EG *The result should be a foregone conclusion.*

3 The **conclusion** of a treaty or a business deal is N SING: its final settlement. USU+SUPP

conclusive /kəˈnkluːsɪv/. Facts or evidence that ADJ QUALIT are **conclusive** show that something is certainly true. EG *The evidence is not conclusive.* ◊ **conclusively.** EG *This has been difficult to prove* ◊ ADV *conclusively.*

concoct /kəˈnkɒkt/, **concocts, concocting, con-** cocted. **1** If you **concoct** an excuse or explanation, V+O you invent one. EG *He had to hastily concoct an excuse.*

2 If you **concoct** something, you make it by mixing V+O several things together. EG *Nancy had concocted a red wine sauce.*

concoction /kəˈnkɒkʃən/, **concoctions.** A **con-** N COUNT **coction** is something that has been made out of several things mixed together. EG *Chutney is a concoction of almost any fruit or vegetable you like.*

concomitant /kəˈnkɒmɪtənt/. Something that is ADJ CLASSIF: **concomitant** with another thing happens at the OFT+with same time and is connected with it. EG *...the growth* Formal *of bureaucracy, with its concomitant dangers of corruption.*

concord /ˈkɒnkɔːd/ is the state of living or work- N UNCOUNT ing together in peaceful agreement. EG *...this reli-* Formal *gion of peace and concord.*

concrete /ˈkɒnkriːt/, **concretes, concreting, concreted. 1 Concrete** is a substance used for N UNCOUNT building which is made by mixing together cement, sand, small stones, and water. EG *...a modern tower made of concrete and steel.*

2 When you **concrete** something such as a path, V+O you cover it with concrete.

3 You use **concrete** to describe something that is
3.1 definite and not general or vague. EG *There* ADJ QUALIT *were no specific, concrete proposals placed before the people.* **3.2** real and physical rather than ADJ CLASSIF abstract. EG *There were many concrete reminders of his existence.*

concur /kəˈnkɜː/, **concurs, concurring, con-** V: OFT+with curred. When you **concur,** you agree with some- OR REPORT: one or with their opinion. EG *The judge concurred* ONLY that *with earlier findings... Baghdad residents all con-* Formal *cur that food shortages are acute.*

concurrence /kəˈnkʌrəns/. **1** Someone's **con-** N UNCOUNT **currence** is their agreement to something. EG *The* +SUPP *French President gave his instant concurrence.* Formal

2 If there is a **concurrence** of two or more things, Formal they happen at the same time. EG *...a bizarre concurrence of events.*

concurrent /kəˈnkʌrənt/. If two things are **con-** ADJ CLASSIF: **current,** they happen at the same time. OFT+with ◊ **concurrently.** EG *Two subjects will be studied* ◊ ADV *concurrently.*

concussed /kəˈnkʌst/. If you are **concussed** by ADJ CLASSIF a blow to your head, it causes you to lose conscious- ness or to feel sick or confused.

concussion /kəˈnkʌʃən/. If you suffer **concus-** N UNCOUNT **sion** after a blow to your head, you lose conscious- ness or feel sick or confused. EG *She was in Newcas- tle Infirmary with concussion.*

condemn /kəˈndem/, **condemns, condemning, condemned. 1** If you **condemn** something, you V+O: OFT+ say that it is very bad and unacceptable. EG *He* for/as *condemned the report as partial and inadequate... I did not condemn him for what he had done.* ◊ **condemnation** /kɒndemˈneɪʃən/, **condemna-** ◊ N UNCOUNT **tions.** EG *...their strong condemnation of her con-* OR N COUNT *duct.*

2 If someone **is condemned** to a punishment, they V+O+to OR are given this punishment. EG *Susan was con-* to-INF *demned to death.*

3 If circumstances **condemn** you to an unpleasant V+O+to OR situation, they make it certain that you will suffer to-INF in that way. EG *Most of the applicants are con- demned to spend all morning waiting to be seen.*

4 If authorities **condemn** a building, they officially V+O decide that it is not safe and must be pulled down.

condemned /kəˈndemd/. A **condemned** man or woman is going to be executed. EG ...*the condemned prisoners.* `ADJ CLASSIF : ATTRIB`

condensation /kɒndɛnˈseɪʃəⁿn/ consists of small drops of water which form when warm water vapour or steam touches a cold surface such as a window. `N UNCOUNT`

condense /kəˈndɛns/, **condenses, condensing, condensed. 1** If you **condense** a piece of writing or speech, you make it shorter, usually by including only the most important parts. EG *I tried to condense every report into as few words as possible.* `V+O`
2 When a gas or vapour **condenses**, it changes into a liquid. `V-ERG`

condescend /kɒndɪˈsɛnd/, **condescends, condescending, condescended. 1** If you **condescend** to people, you behave in a way which shows them that you think you are superior to them. EG *He never condescended, never spoke down to me.* `V : OFT+to` `Formal`
◊ **condescending** /kɒndɪˈsɛndɪŋ/. EG *She addressed him with the same condescending tone.* `◊ ADJ QUALIT`
2 If you **condescend** to do something, you agree to do it, but in a way which shows that you think you are doing people a favour. EG *She did not condescend to have dinner with him.* `V+to-INF`

condescension /kɒndɪˈsɛnʃəⁿn/ is condescending behaviour or qualities. EG *He spoke to the labourers with no condescension.* `N UNCOUNT`

condition /kəˈndɪʃəⁿn/, **conditions, conditioning, conditioned. 1** The **condition** of someone or something is the state that they are in. EG *You can't go home in that condition... Families had only intervened when the condition of hunger strikers became critical... Keep your car exterior in good condition.* `N SING+SUPP`
2 The **conditions** in which people live or do things are the qualities or factors that affect their comfort, safety, or success. EG *These experiments were carried out under almost unimaginable conditions... ...adverse weather conditions... ...appalling living conditions.* `N PLURAL +SUPP`
3 A **condition** is something which must happen in order for something else to be possible. EG *You have to live there as a condition of your job.* `N COUNT : OFT+of/for`
4 When you agree to do something **on condition that** something else happens, you mean that you will only do it if this other thing happens or is agreed to first. EG *He has agreed to come on condition that there won't be any publicity.* `CONJ`
5 You can refer to an illness or other medical problem as a particular **condition**. EG *He has a heart condition.* `N COUNT+SUPP`
6 If someone is **out of condition**, they are unhealthy and unfit. `PHRASE`
7 If someone is **conditioned** by their upbringing or environment to do or think a particular thing, they are influenced by it over a period of time so that they do or think that thing. EG *Men had been conditioned to regard women as their inferiors.* `V+O : USU PASS +to-INF`
◊ **conditioning**. EG *It is very difficult to overcome your early conditioning.* `◊ N UNCOUNT`

conditional /kəˈndɪʃəⁿnəl, -ʃənəⁿl/. If a situation or agreement is **conditional** on something, it will only happen or be accepted if this thing happens. EG *Their support is conditional upon further reduction in public expenditure... ...conditional acceptance.* ◊ **conditionally**. EG *She said yes, conditionally.* `ADJ CLASSIF : OFT+on/upon` `◊ ADV SEN`

conditioner /kəˈndɪʃəⁿnə/, **conditioners**. A **conditioner** is **1** a substance which you can put on your hair after washing it in order to make it softer. **2** a thick liquid which you can use when you wash clothes in order to make them feel softer. `N MASS`

condolence /kəˈndəʊləns/, **condolences. Condolence** is sympathy that you express for someone when one of their friends or relatives has died. EG *...letters of condolence... She wished to offer her condolences.* `N UNCOUNT OR N PLURAL`

condom /ˈkɒndəⁿm/, **condoms**. A **condom** is a covering made of rubber which a man wears on his penis during sexual intercourse as a contraceptive. `N COUNT`

condone /kəˈndəʊn/, **condones, condoning, condoned**. If someone **condones** behaviour that is morally wrong, they accept it and allow it to happen. EG *We cannot condone the daily massacre of innocent people.* `V+O`

conducive /kəˈndjuːsɪv/. If one thing is **conducive** to another thing, it makes the other thing likely to happen. EG *Competition is not conducive to human happiness.* `ADJ PRED+to`

conduct, conducts, conducting, conducted; pronounced /kəˈndʌkt/ when it is a verb and /ˈkɒndʌkt/ when it is a noun.
1 When you **conduct** an activity or task, you organize it and carry it out. EG *We have been conducting a survey of the region.* ▸ used as a noun. EG *Secrets are essential to the conduct of a war.* `V+O` `▸ N UNCOUNT`
2 If you **conduct** yourself in a particular way, you behave in that way. EG *He instructed them in how to conduct themselves inside the mosque.* ▸ used as a noun. EG *The minister had several good reasons for his conduct.* `V-REFL+A` `Formal` `▸ N UNCOUNT : USU+POSS`
3 When someone **conducts** an orchestra or choir, they stand in front of it and direct its performance. `V+O OR V`
4 If something **conducts** heat or electricity, it allows heat or electricity to pass through it or along it. `V+O OR V`

conductor /kəˈndʌktə/, **conductors**. A **conductor** is **1** a person who sells tickets on a bus. **2** a person who stands in front of an orchestra or choir and conducts it. `N COUNT`

cone /kəʊn/, **cones**. A **cone** is **1** a shape with a circular base and smooth curved sides ending in a point at the top. See picture at SHAPES. EG *...a cone-shaped hill.* **2** the fruit of a tree such as a pine or fir which consists of a cluster of woody scales containing seeds. **3** an ice cream cornet. `N COUNT`

confectionery /kəˈnfɛkʃənəriː/. You can refer to sweets and chocolates as **confectionery**. `N UNCOUNT`

confederate /kəˈnfɛdərəⁱt/, **confederates**. Someone's **confederates** are the people they are working with in a secret activity. `N COUNT`

confederation /kəˌnfɛdəˈreɪʃəⁿn/, **confederations**. A **confederation** is an organization or alliance of groups of people for political or business purposes. EG *We are in favour of a loose confederation of states.* `N COUNT`

confer /kəˈnfɜː/, **confers, conferring, conferred. 1** When you **confer** with someone, you discuss something with them in order to make a decision. EG *He went home to confer with his wife.* `V OR V+with` `RECIP`
2 If something **confers** an advantage, it gives that advantage. EG *The system had conferred great benefits.* `V+O : OFT+on/upon` `Formal`

conference /ˈkɒnfərəⁿns/, **conferences. 1** A **conference** is a meeting at which formal discussions take place. EG *The Managing Director has daily conferences with the other staff members.* • If someone is **in conference**, they are having a formal meeting. EG *...the time he must spend in conference listening to reports.* `N COUNT` `• PHRASE`
2 A **conference** is also a meeting about a particular subject, often lasting a few days. EG *...a conference on nuclear disarmament in London.* `N COUNT`

confess /kəˈnfɛs/, **confesses, confessing, confessed. 1** If you **confess** something that you are ashamed of, you admit it. EG *Perhaps I shouldn't confess this, but I did on one occasion forge Tony's signature... I confess to a certain weakness for puddings.* `V-SPEECH, V+to, OR V-REFL+C`
2 You say **'I must confess'** to emphasize that you `PHRASE`

Would you tell a confidence to a confidante?

are being honest about something. EG *I must con-*
fess that I find him a bore.

3 If you **confess** to a crime, you admit that you   V:OFT+*to*
have committed that crime. EG *Bianchi had con-*   OR V+O
fessed to five of the murders... He had confessed
his guilt.

confessed /kəˈnfest/. You use **confessed** to de-   ADJ CLASSIF:
scribe someone who openly admits that they have   ATTRIB
a particular fault or weakness. EG *He was self-*
indulgent and cynical, a confessed failure.

confession /kəˈnfeʃəⁿn/, **confessions. 1** A con-   N COUNT
fession is a statement that you make in which you
admit that you have committed a crime or done
something wrong. EG *I have a confession to make...*
The moment you sign a confession, you can have
all the sleep you want.

2 Confession is **2.1** the act of confessing some-   N UNCOUNT
thing. EG *...a torrent of confession.* **2.2** a religious
act in which you tell a priest about your sins and
ask for forgiveness. EG *He had gone to confession.*

confetti /kəˈnfeti¹/ is small pieces of coloured   N UNCOUNT
paper that people throw over the bride and groom
at a wedding.

confidant /kɒnfɪdænt/, **confidants.** Someone's   N COUNT
confidant is a man who they discuss their private   Formal
problems with.

confidante /kɒnfɪdænt/, **confidantes.** Someone's   N COUNT
confidante is a woman who they discuss their   Formal
private problems with.

confide /kəˈnfaɪd/, **confides, confiding, confid-**   V-SPEECH:
ed. If you **confide** a secret to someone, you tell it   ONLY *that*, OFT
to them. EG *I never confided my fear to anyone...*   +*to*
He had confided to me that he wasn't an Irishman
at all. ◊ **confiding** /kəˈnfaɪdɪŋ/. EG *At first she was*   ◊ ADJ QUALIT
suspicious, then she became confiding.

confide in. If you **confide in** someone, you tell   PHRASAL VB:
them about a private problem or some other secret   V+PREP,
matter. EG *May I confide in you?*   HAS PASS

confidence /kɒnfɪdəns/, **confidences. 1** If you   N UNCOUNT
have **confidence** in someone, you feel that you
can trust them. EG *I have a lot of confidence in him.*

2 If you have **confidence**, you feel sure about your   N UNCOUNT
abilities, qualities, or ideas. EG *I was full of confi-*
dence.

3 Confidence is also a situation in which you tell   N UNCOUNT
someone a secret. EG *I'm telling you this in the*
strictest confidence... ...a breach of confidence.

4 If you **take** someone **into** your **confidence**, you   PHRASE
tell them a secret.

5 A **confidence** is a secret that you tell someone.   N COUNT
EG *Edith was used to receiving confidences.*

confident /kɒnfɪdənt/. **1** If you are **confident**   ADJ QUALIT
about something, you are certain that it will hap-
pen in the way you want it to. EG *He said he was*
very confident that the scheme would be success-
ful. ◊ **confidently.** EG *One could confidently rely*   ◊ ADV
on him.

2 People who are **confident** feel sure of their own   ADJ QUALIT
abilities, qualities, or ideas. EG *...a witty, young and*
confident lawyer. ◊ **confidently.** EG *I strode*   ◊ ADV
confidently up the hall.

confidential /kɒnfɪdenʃəⁿl/. **1** Information that is   ADJ QUALIT
confidential is meant to be kept secret. EG *This*
arrangement is to be kept strictly confidential.
◊ **confidentially.** EG *I wrote to you confidentially*   ◊ ADV
on 30th September 1987. ◊ **confidentiality**   ◊ N UNCOUNT
/kɒnfɪdenʃiˈæləⁱti¹/. EG *Please respect the confiden-*
tiality of this information.

2 If you talk to someone in a **confidential** way,   ADJ QUALIT
you talk to them quietly because what you are
saying is secret. EG *He became very confidential.*
◊ **confidentially.** EG *She leaned forward and whis-*   ◊ ADV
pered to him confidentially.

configuration /kəˈnfɪɡjə⁴reɪʃəⁿn/, **configura-**   N COUNT
tions. A **configuration** is an arrangement of a   Formal
group of things. EG *The blades collapse into an*
arrow-head configuration.

confine, confines, confining, confined; pronounced /kəˈnfaɪn/ when it is a verb and

/kɒnfaɪnz/ when it is a noun.

1 If something **is confined** to only one place,   V+O:
situation, or person, it only exists there or only   USU PASS+*to*
affects that person. EG *The problem appears to be*
confined to the tropics.

2 If you **confine** yourself to something, you do only   V-REFL+*to* OR
that thing and are involved with nothing else. EG   V+O+*to*
They confine themselves to discussing the weath-
er... Confine your messages to official business.

3 To **confine** someone means to keep them in   V+O:USU+A
prison or some other place which they cannot
leave. EG *William was confined to an institution for*
some years.

4 The **confines** of an area are the boundaries   N PLURAL
enclosing it. EG *...within the confines of the Gallery.*   Formal

confined /kəˈnfaɪnd/. A **confined** space or area is   ADJ CLASSIF
small and enclosed by walls.

confinement /kəˈnfaɪnməⁿnt/ is the state of be-   N UNCOUNT
ing forced to stay in a prison or another place
which you cannot leave. EG *...his many years in*
confinement.

confirm /kəˈnfɜːm/, **confirms, confirming, con-**
firmed. 1 If something **confirms** what you be-   V+O OR
lieve, it shows that it is definitely true. EG *My*   V+REPORT
suspicions were confirmed... He glanced round to
confirm that he was alone... They have confirmed
what I suspected long ago. ◊ **confirmation**   ◊ N UNCOUNT
/kɒnfəmeɪʃəⁿn/. EG *This discovery was a confirma-*
tion of Darwin's proposition.

2 If you **confirm** something, you say that it is true.   V+O OR
EG *She asked me if it was my car and I confirmed*   V+REPORT
that it was... There is no one to confirm whether
these memories are correct. ◊ **confirmation.** EG   ◊ N UNCOUNT
She turned to Jimmie for confirmation and he
nodded.

3 If you **confirm** an arrangement or appointment,   V+O OR
you say that it is definite, usually in a letter or on   V+REPORT
the telephone. EG *...a letter confirming that they*
expect you on the twelfth. ◊ **confirmation.** EG *All*   ◊ N UNCOUNT
times are approximate and subject to confirma-
tion.

4 When someone **is confirmed**, they are formally   V+O:USU PASS
accepted as a member of a Christian church.
◊ **confirmation, confirmations.** EG *...the confir-*   ◊ N UNCOUNT
mation service.   OR N COUNT

confirmed /kəˈnfɜːmd/. You use **confirmed** to   ADJ CLASSIF:
describe someone who has a particular habit or   ATTRIB
belief that they are very unlikely to change. EG *I am*
a confirmed non-smoker.

confiscate /kɒnfɪskeɪt/, **confiscates, confiscat-**   V+O
ing, confiscated. If you **confiscate** something
from someone, you take it away from them, often
as a punishment. EG *We had special instructions to*
confiscate all their cameras. ◊ **confiscation**   ◊ N UNCOUNT
/kɒnfɪskeɪʃəⁿn/. EG *I faced two years' jail plus the*
confiscation of the tapes.

conflagration /kɒnfləɡreɪʃəⁿn/, **conflagrations.**   N COUNT
A **conflagration** is a large fire.   Formal

conflict, conflicts, conflicting, conflicted; pronounced /kɒnflɪkt/ when it is a noun and
/kəˈnflɪkt/ when it is a verb.

1 Conflict is **1.1** serious disagreement and argu-   N UNCOUNT
ment about something important. EG *...the familiar*   OR N COUNT
conflict between government and opposition...
They often came into conflict with the islanders...
...a number of conflicts in the engineering industry.

1.2 a state of mind in which you find it impossible   N UNCOUNT
to make a decision. EG *Frequently he is in a state of*
conflict or indecision.

2 A **conflict** is **2.1** a serious difference between   N COUNT OR
two or more beliefs, ideas, or interests. EG *Conflicts*   N UNCOUNT
of loyalty arose. **2.2** fighting between countries or
groups of people. EG *A conventional conflict might*
escalate to a nuclear confrontation.

3 If ideas, interests, or accounts **conflict**, they are   V OR V+*with*:
very different from each other and it seems impos-   RECIP
sible for them to exist together or to both be true.
EG *There is some research that conflicts with this*
view. ◊ **conflicting.** EG *There are too many*   ◊ ADJ QUALIT

conflicting interests... The evidence seems to be conflicting.

conform /kə'nfɔːm/, **conforms, conforming, conformed.** 1 If you **conform**, you behave in the way that you are expected to behave. EG *You must be prepared to conform.*   v

2 If something **conforms to** a law, regulation, or wish, it is of the type or quality that is required or desired. EG *Such a change would not conform to the wishes of the great majority of people.*   v+to/with

conformist /kə'nfɔːmɪst/, **conformists.** A conformist is someone who behaves or thinks like everyone else rather than doing things that are original; often used showing disapproval. ▶ used as an adjective. EG *The school had grown more conformist and cautious.*   N COUNT   ▶ ADJ QUALIT

conformity /kə'nfɔːmɪ'tiː/ is behaviour, thought, or appearance that is the same as that of most other people. EG *All that seems to be required of us is conformity.*   N UNCOUNT

confound /kə'nfaʊnd/, **confounds, confounding, confounded.** If something **confounds** you, it makes you feel confused or surprised. EG *...speaking French to confound their friends.*   v+o

confront /kə'nfrʌnt/, **confronts, confronting, confronted.** 1 If you **are confronted** with a problem or task, you have to deal with it. EG *I was confronted with the task of designing the system... ...typical problems that confront Germans learning English... We will soon have to confront a fundamental question.*   v+o: OFT+with

2 If you **confront** someone, **2.1** you meet them face to face, especially when you are going to fight them. EG *The two men confronted each other... They were confronted by a line of guardsmen.* **2.2** you present facts or evidence to them in order to accuse them of something. EG *I decided to confront her with the charges of racism.*   v+o   v+o+with

confrontation /kɒnfrən'teɪʃəˈn/, **confrontations.** A **confrontation** is a dispute, fight, or battle between two groups of people. EG *Every now and then there is a confrontation between the pickets and police.*   N COUNT OR N UNCOUNT

confuse /kə'nfjuːz/, **confuses, confusing, confused.** 1 If you **confuse** two things, you get them mixed up, so that you think one of them is the other one. EG *You seem to confuse the words 'satire' and 'satyr' in your paper... You must be confusing me with someone else.*   v+o: OFT+with

2 To **confuse** someone means to make it difficult for them to know exactly what to do. EG *You're trying to confuse me.*   v+o

3 To **confuse** a situation means to make it complicated or difficult to understand. EG *To confuse matters further, her sister is married to her husband's uncle.*   v+o

confused /kə'nfjuːzd/. 1 Something that is **confused** does not have any order or pattern and is difficult to understand. EG *...a confused dream about the end of the world... My thoughts were confused.*   ADJ QUALIT

2 If you are **confused**, you do not understand what is happening or you do not know what to do. EG *She was bewildered and confused.*   ADJ QUALIT

confusing /kə'nfjuːzɪŋ/. Something that is **confusing** makes it difficult for people to know exactly what is happening. EG *The plot is fairly confusing.*   ADJ QUALIT

confusion /kə'nfjuːʒəˈn/, **confusions.** 1 Confusion is **1.1** making a mistake about a person or thing and thinking that they are another person or thing. EG *There is danger of confusion between them.* **1.2** a situation where it is not clear what is happening. EG *In all the confusion, both men managed to grab me.*   N UNCOUNT   N UNCOUNT OR N COUNT

2 If your mind is in a state of **confusion**, you do not know what to believe or what you should do. EG *Her answers to his questions have only added to his confusion.*   N UNCOUNT

congeal /kə'ndʒiːl/, **congeals, congealing, congealed.** When a liquid **congeals**, it becomes very   V-ERG

thick and sticky and almost solid. EG *The blood had already congealed.*

congenial /kə'ndʒiːnjəl, -nɪəl/. Someone or something that is **congenial** is pleasant. EG *A pub would be more congenial than a boarding house... ...congenial company.*   ADJ QUALIT Formal

congenital /kə'ndʒɛnɪtəˈl/. A **congenital** disease or medical condition is one that a person has had from birth, but not one that is inherited. EG *The brain damage was congenital.* ◊ **congenitally.** EG *She is congenitally disabled.*   ADJ CLASSIF Medical   ◊ ADV

congested /kə'ndʒɛstɪ²d/. A road or area that is **congested** is so crowded with traffic or people that normal movement there is impossible.   ADJ QUALIT

congestion /kə'ndʒɛstʃəˈn/. 1 If there is **congestion** in a place, the place is so crowded with traffic or people that normal movement is impossible. EG *...traffic congestion in urban areas.*   N UNCOUNT

2 **Congestion** in a part of the body is a medical condition in which the part becomes blocked. EG *...nasal congestion.*   N UNCOUNT +SUPP

conglomerate /kə'nglɒmərəˈt/, **conglomerates.** A **conglomerate** is a large business firm consisting of several different companies.   N COUNT

conglomeration /kə'nglɒmərˈeɪʃəˈn/, **conglomerations.** A **conglomeration** is a group of many different things. EG *...a conglomeration of white buildings.*   N COUNT +SUPP

congratulate /kə'ngrætjə'leɪt/, **congratulates, congratulating, congratulated.** 1 If you **congratulate** someone, you praise them for something that they have done. EG *Friends came to congratulate the parents and to see the baby... I must congratulate you on a successful interview.* ◊ **congratulation** /kə'ngrætjə'leɪʃəˈn/. EG *...a letter of congratulation.*   v+o: OFT+on   ◊ N UNCOUNT

2 If you **congratulate** yourself, you are pleased about something that you have done or that has happened to you. EG *I congratulated myself on not looking my age.*   V-REFL: OFT+on

congratulations /kə'ngrætjə'leɪʃəˈnz/. You say **'congratulations'** to someone in order to congratulate them. EG *'Congratulations,' the doctor said. 'You have a son.'... I offered him my heartiest congratulations.*   CONVENTION

congratulatory /kə'ngrætjə'lətriˈ/. Something that is **congratulatory** expresses congratulations. EG *...a congratulatory smile.*   ADJ CLASSIF

congregate /kɒngrɪ'geɪt/, **congregates, congregating, congregated.** When people **congregate**, they gather together and form a group. EG *The crowds congregated around the pavilion.*   V: USU+A

congregation /kɒngrɪ'geɪʃəˈn/, **congregations.** The people who attend a church service are referred to as the **congregation**. EG *There were only ten in the congregation.*   N COLL

congress /kɒŋgrɛs/, **congresses.** A **congress** is a large meeting that is held to discuss ideas and policies. EG *...the second Congress of Negro Writers and Artists.*   N COUNT

conical /kɒnɪkəˈl/. Something that is **conical** is shaped like a cone. EG *...a small conical shell.*   ADJ CLASSIF

conifer /kəʊnɪfə, kɒn-/, **conifers.** A **conifer** is a tree that has needle-like leaves and produces brown cones.   N COUNT

CONJ stands for **conjunction**

Words which have the label CONJ in the Extra Column are conjunctions, such as 'and' or 'although'.

See the entry headed CONJUNCTIONS for more information.

---

conjecture /kə'ndʒɛktʃə/, **conjectures. Conjecture** is the formation of ideas or opinions from   N UNCOUNT OR N COUNT Formal

CONJUNCTIONS

A conjunction is a word that joins together words, groups, or clauses. There are two main kinds of conjunction.

Coordinating conjunctions

There are a few words which we call coordinating conjunctions (CONJ). These are **and**, **but**, **yet**, **or**, and **nor**. They come between the two parts of a sentence, and these two parts are the same grammatical type. So they join words, as in *Jack **and** Jill*, groups of words, as in *We went to the Tower of London **and** Westminster Abbey,* and clauses, as in *I told them they should get on the bus outside the university **and** get off five stops later.*

As you can see from this last example, you do not need to repeat the subject of the second verb when it is the same as the first. You can also omit the second verb or part of it when it is the same as the first, as in the last example, where the word 'should' is omitted. Also in *Karen likes pop music but Liz doesn't,* where the form 'does' is used instead of 'likes'.

Here are some more examples of sentences with coordinating conjunctions in them: *John **and** Helen have just quarrelled ... We had a choice of home-made icecream **or** fresh fruit salad ... All the girls went swimming **but** none of the boys did ... She doesn't like school, **nor** do I.*

Subordinating conjunctions

There is a larger group of words which join subordinate clauses to main clauses. These are called subordinating conjunctions (also CONJ), and they are words such as **although**, **unless**, **if**, and **because**. A subordinating conjunction is usually the first word in the subordinate clause, although an adverb such as 'even' or 'especially' can sometimes be used in front of it.

Here are some examples of clauses joined by subordinating conjunctions: *He went to the party **although** he was very tired ... **Although** she is only fourteen, she thinks she is very grown-up ... I'll come for you at seven, **unless** you phone me before that ... **If** there's time, we could go to the cinema as well ... I like Americans **because** they are optimistic.*

incomplete or doubtful information. EG *The exact figure is a matter for conjecture.*

conjugal /ˈkɒndʒʊˈgəˀl/ means relating to marriage and the relationship between a husband and wife, especially their sexual relationship. EG *...conjugal happiness.*   ADJ CLASSIF : ATTRIB Formal

conjunction /kəˀndʒʌŋkˀʃəˀn/, **conjunctions.** 1 A **conjunction** of things, characteristics, or features is a combination of them. EG *The cause of suicide is a nasty conjunction of personal and social factors.*   N COUNT : OFT+of Formal

2 If two or more things are done **in conjunction**, they are done together rather than separately. EG *This course can only be taken in conjunction with course 234.*   PHRASE

3 In grammar, a **conjunction** is a word or a group of words that joins together words, groups, or clauses. See the entry headed CONJUNCTIONS for more information.   N COUNT

conjure /ˈkʌndʒəˀ/, **conjures, conjuring, conjured.** 1 If you **conjure** something into existence, you make it appear by magic or by a trick. EG *He appeared with a small bucket he'd apparently conjured from nowhere.*   V+O : USU+A

2 If you say that a particular name is **a name to conjure with**, you mean that it is a very important and influential name.   PHRASE

conjure up. If you **conjure up** a memory, picture, or idea, you create it in your mind. EG *To many people, the name Kalahari conjures up images of a desert of unrelenting aridity.*   PHRASAL VB : V+O+ADV

conjurer /ˈkʌndʒəˀrə/, **conjurers;** also spelled **conjuror.** A **conjurer** is a person who entertains people by doing magic tricks.   N COUNT

conjuring trick, conjuring tricks. A **conjuring trick** is a trick in which something is made to appear and disappear as if by magic.   N COUNT

conker /ˈkɒŋkə/, **conkers. Conkers** are round brown nuts which come from horse chestnut trees.   N COUNT

con-man, con-men. A **con-man** is a man who persuades people to give him their money or property by lying to them.   N COUNT

connect /kəˀnɛkt/, **connects, connecting, connected.** 1 To **connect** one thing to another means to join the two things to each other. EG *Connect the fishing line to the hook.*   V+O : OFT+to

2 If a piece of equipment **is connected**, it is joined by a wire or cable to an electricity supply or to another piece of equipment. EG *...a telephone line connected to their terminal.*   V+O : USU PASS+to

3 If a telephone operator **connects** you, he or she enables you to speak to another person by telephone. EG *I'm trying to connect you, sir.*   V+O

4 If a door or corridor **connects** two rooms or buildings, it joins them and makes it possible to walk between them. ◊ **connecting.** EG *The rooms had connecting doors between them.*   V+O ◊ ADJ CLASSIF : ATTRIB

5 If a train, plane, or bus **connects** with another form of transport, it arrives at a time which allows passengers to change to the other form of transport in order to continue their journey.   V : OFT+with

6 If you **connect** a person or thing with something, you realize that there is a relationship or link between them. EG *There is no evidence to connect Griffiths with the murder... Do you connect the two events?*   V+O : OFT+to/ with

connected /kəˀnɛktɪ²d/. If one thing is **connected** with another, there is a relationship or link between them. EG *There are serious questions connected with radioactive waste disposal.*   ADJ CLASSIF : USU PRED+ with

connection /kəˀnɛkʃəˀn/, **connections;** also spelled **connexion.** 1 A **connection** is a relationship between two things. EG *I do not think there is any logical connection between the two halves of the question.*   N COUNT : OFT +between/ with

2 If you talk or write to someone **in connection with** something, you talk or write to them about that thing. EG *The police wanted to interview him in connection with the murder.*   PREP

3 A **connection** is also the joint where two wires   N COUNT

or pipes are joined together. EG *There must be a loose connection.*

4 If you get a **connection** at a station or airport, you catch a train, bus, or plane after having got off another train, bus, or plane so that you can continue your journey. EG *I missed my connection.*   N COUNT

5 Your **connections** are the people who you know. EG *He's one of her husband's business connections.*   N COUNT : USU PLURAL

connive /kəˀnaɪv/, **connives, conniving, connived.** 1 If you **connive** at something, you allow it to happen even though you know that it is wrong. EG *He was assisted by his mother who connived at his laziness.* ◊ **connivance** /kəˀnaɪvəns/. EG *He kept out of jail with the connivance of corrupt police.*   V+at ◊ N UNCOUNT : USU+SUPP

2 If you **connive**, you secretly try to achieve something which is to your advantage. EG *He believes that Cal and Fanny connived together to do the deed.*   V OR V+with : RECIP

connoisseur /ˈkɒnəˀsɜː/, **connoisseurs.** A **connoisseur** is someone who knows a lot about the arts, food, drink, or some other subject. *...a connoisseur of Italian operatic music.*   N COUNT : OFT+of

connotation /ˌkɒnəˀteɪʃəˀn/, **connotations.** The **connotations** of a particular word or name are the ideas or qualities which it makes you think of. EG *'Intermediate' has connotations of the inferior and the second rate.*   N COUNT+SUPP

conquer /ˈkɒŋkə/, **conquers, conquering, conquered.** 1 If one country or group of people **conquers** another, they take complete control of their land. EG *...the white people who had conquered their land.* ◊ **conqueror** /ˈkɒŋkərə/, **conquerors.** EG *...the European conquerors of Mexico.*   V+O OR V ◊ N COUNT

2 If you **conquer** something difficult or dangerous, you succeed in destroying it or getting control of it. EG *...a tremendous international effort to conquer cancer.*   V+O

conquest /ˈkɒŋkwɛst/, **conquests.** 1 **Conquest** is the act of conquering a country or group of people. EG *Negotiations are preferable to conquest.*   N UNCOUNT

2 A **conquest** is land that has been conquered in war.   N COUNT

3 If you make a **conquest**, you succeed in winning the love or admiration of someone. EG *...stories of his conquests of bored housewives.*   N COUNT+SUPP

4 The **conquest** of something difficult or dangerous is success in getting control of it. EG *...the conquest of space.*   N SING : the+N+of

conscience /ˈkɒnʃəns/, **consciences.** 1 Your **conscience** is the part of your mind that tells you whether what you are doing is right or wrong. EG *My conscience told me to vote against the others... ...a matter which has been on my conscience for a long time.*   N COUNT

2 If you have a guilty **conscience**, you feel guilty because you have done something wrong. EG *When I got your letter it revived my guilty conscience.*   N UNCOUNT

3 **Conscience** is doing what you believe is right even though it might be unpopular, difficult, or dangerous. EG *In all conscience, I couldn't make things difficult for him.*   N UNCOUNT

conscience-stricken. Someone who is **conscience-stricken** feels very guilty about something wrong that they have done.   ADJ QUALIT

conscientious /ˌkɒnʃɪɛnʃəs/. Someone who is **conscientious** is very careful to do their work properly. ◊ **conscientiously.** EG *He'd been doing his job conscientiously for many years.*   ADJ QUALIT ◊ ADV

conscious /ˈkɒnʃəs/. 1 If you are **conscious** of something, **1.1** you notice or realize what is happening. EG *She became conscious of Rudolph looking at her... I was conscious that he had changed his tactics.* **1.2** you think about it a lot   ADJ PRED+of OR REPORT

Find two words on these pages which have the same pronunciation.

because of the special way in which it affects you.
EG *Tony was very conscious of his ancestry.*

2 Conscious is used in expressions such as 'social- ADJ QUALIT
ly conscious' and 'politically conscious' to describe
someone who believes that a particular aspect of
life is important. EG *Hundreds of women had become politically conscious.*

3 A **conscious** action or effort is done deliberately. ADJ CLASSIF:
EG *He made a conscious effort to look as though he* ATTRIB
was enjoying himself. ◊ **consciously.** EG *She* ◊ ADV
*couldn't believe that Mr Foster would ever con-
sciously torment her.*

4 Someone who is **conscious** is awake rather than ADJ PRED
asleep or unconscious. EG *The patient was fully
conscious during the operation.*

consciousness /kɒnʃəsnɪˀs/. **1** Your **conscious-** N UNCOUNT:
ness is your mind and your thoughts. EG *Doubts* USU+POSS
were starting to enter into my consciousness.

2 The **consciousness** of a group of people is all N UNCOUNT
the ideas, attitudes, and beliefs shared by the +SUPP
group. EG *This is a novel that has become imprinted
on the English consciousness.*

3 Consciousness is an interest in and knowledge N UNCOUNT
of a particular subject or idea. EG *...the awakening
political consciousness of Africans.*

4 If you lose **consciousness**, you are unconscious N UNCOUNT
rather than awake. If you have regained **consciousness**, you are awake again rather than
unconscious.

**conscript, conscripts, conscripting, conscript-
ed;** pronounced /kəˀnskrɪpt/ when it is a verb and
/kɒnskrɪpt/ when it is a noun.

1 If someone **is conscripted, 1.1** they are officially V+O : USU PASS
made to join the armed forces of a country. EG *Nine
countries decided to let women be conscripted.*
◊ **conscription** /kəˀnskrɪpʃəⁿn/. EG *The president* ◊ N UNCOUNT
has ended conscription. **1.2** they are officially V+O: USU PASS
forced to work for a country or group of people. EG
*Workers were conscripted into forced labour gangs
to build the railways.* ◊ **conscripted.** EG *...con-* ◊ ADJ CLASSIF
scripted labourers from Indo-China.

2 A **conscript** is a person who has been made to N COUNT
join the armed forces of a country.

consecrate /kɒnsɪˀkreɪt/, **consecrates, conse-** V+O
crating, consecrated. When a building, place, or
object **is consecrated,** it is officially declared to
be holy. EG *King Edward consecrated the original
church here in 1065.* ◊ **consecrated.** EG *He was* ◊ ADJ CLASSIF
refused burial in consecrated ground.
◊ **consecration** /kɒnsɪˀkreɪʃəⁿn/. EG *...the conse-* ◊ N UNCOUNT
cration of the church.

consecutive /kəˀnsekjʊˀtɪv/. Periods of time or ADJ CLASSIF
events that are **consecutive** happen one after the
other and are not interrupted. EG *I had been away
for forty-two consecutive days... ...three consecutive victories.*

consensus /kəˀnsensəs/ is general agreement N UNCOUNT
amongst a group of people. EG *There was some
consensus of opinion.*

consent /kəˀnsent/, **consents, consenting, consented. 1 Consent** is **1.1** permission given to N UNCOUNT :
someone to do something. EG *She had threatened to* USU+POSS
marry without her parents' consent. **1.2** agreement N UNCOUNT
about something between two or more people or +SUPP
groups. EG *By common consent they stopped.*

2 If you **consent** to something, you agree to do it or V : USU+*to* OR
to allow it to be done. EG *He consented to the* *to*-INF
removal of the flags.

consequence /kɒnsɪkwəns/, **consequences. 1** A N COUNT
consequence of a situation or event is a result or
effect of it. EG *...the economic consequences of the
computer revolution.*

2 If one thing happens and then another thing PHRASE
happens **in consequence,** the second thing happens as a result of the first. EG *These jobs are
considered suitable for females, and are usually
badly paid in consequence.*

3 Someone or something that is of **consequence** is N UNCOUNT
Formal

important or valuable. Someone or something that
is of little **consequence** is not important.

consequent /kɒnsɪkwənt/ means happening as a ADJ CLASSIF :
direct result of an event or situation. EG *...the non-* ATTRIB
publication of the report and the consequent ab- Formal
sence of public discussion. ◊ **consequently.** EG ◊ ADV SEN
*Absolute secrecy is essential. Consequently, the
fewer who are aware of the plan the better.*

consequential /kɒnsɪkwenʃəⁿl/ means happen- ADJ CLASSIF :
ing as a direct result of a particular event or ATTRIB
situation. EG *...overcrowding and the consequential* Formal
lack of privacy.

conservation /kɒnsəveɪʃəⁿn/ is the preservation N UNCOUNT
and protection of the environment. EG *...the present
public awareness of the need for conservation.*

conservationist /kɒnsəveɪʃənɪst/, **conserva-** N COUNT
tionists. A **conservationist** is someone who cares
greatly about conservation.

conservatism /kəˀnsɜːˀvətɪzəˀm/ is unwillingness N UNCOUNT
to accept changes and new ideas. EG *He has been
much criticized for his aesthetic conservatism.*

conservative /kəˀnsɜːˀvətɪv/, **conservatives. 1**
Someone who is **conservative 1.1** is unwilling to ADJ QUALIT
accept changes and new ideas. EG *Publishers in
Britain are more conservative than their continental counterparts.* ◊ **conservatively.** EG *He dresses* ◊ ADV
conservatively. **1.2** has right-wing views. EG *...a* ADJ QUALIT
conservative politician... ...conservative voters.
▸ used as a noun. EG *...leading conservatives in the* ▸ N COUNT
Senate.

2 A **conservative** estimate or guess is very cau- ADJ QUALIT
tious. EG *How long will it last? Three hundred years
at a fairly conservative estimate.*

conservatory /kəˀnsɜːˀvətrɪ/, **conservatories.** A N COUNT
conservatory is a room with glass walls and a
glass roof in which plants are kept and which is
usually attached to a house.

conserve /kəˀnsɜːˀv/, **conserves, conserving,
conserved. 1** If you **conserve** a supply of some- V+O
thing, you use it carefully so that it lasts for a long
time. EG *They made themselves wait quietly, conserving their strength.*

2 To **conserve** something means to keep it in its V+O
original form and protect it from harm, loss, or
change. EG *Such laws exist only to conserve the
privilege of this selfish minority.*

consider /kəˀnsɪdəˀ/, **considers, considering,
considered. 1** If you **consider** a person or thing to V+O+*to*-INF
be something, you have the opinion that this is OR as, V+O+C,
what they are. EG *They consider themselves to be* OR
very lucky... They do not consider a child as V+REPORT
*important... Some British generals considered the
attack a mistake... You always consider that I do
nothing.*

2 If you **consider** something, you think about it V+O
carefully. EG *He had no time to consider the matter... I had begun to consider the possibility of
joining a new company.*

3 You say **all things considered** to indicate that ADV SEN
you are making a judgement after taking all the
facts into account. EG *He's okay, all things considered.*

4 If you **consider** a person's needs, wishes, or V+O
feelings, you pay attention to them. EG *I've got a
family to consider.*

5 See also **consideration, considered, considering.**

considerable /kəˀnsɪdəˀrəbəⁿl/. Something that is ADJ QUALIT
considerable is great in amount or degree. EG *The
building suffered considerable damage.*
◊ **considerably.** EG *His work had improved consid-* ◊ ADV
*erably... Large windows make the car feel consid-
erably bigger.*

considerate /kəˀnsɪdəˀrəˀt/. Someone who is **con-** ADJ QUALIT
siderate pays attention to the needs, wishes, or
feelings of other people.

consideration /kəˀnsɪdəreɪʃəⁿn/, **considerations. 1 Consideration** is **1.1** careful thought N UNCOUNT
about something. EG *After careful consideration,*

her parents gave her permission. **1.2** attention that you pay to the needs, wishes, or feelings of other people. EG *He showed no consideration for his daughters.*

2 A **consideration** is something that should be thought about, especially when you are planning or deciding something. EG *An important consideration is the amount of time it will take.* N COUNT

3 If you **take** something **into consideration**, you think about it because it is relevant to what you are doing. EG *The first thing one has to take into consideration is the cost.* PHRASE

4 Something that is **under consideration** is being discussed. EG *The case was still under consideration.* PHRASE

considered /kə'nsɪdəd/. A **considered** opinion or way of behaving is one that you have as a result of careful thought. EG *...a considered change of mind.* ADJ CLASSIF: ATTRIB

considering /kə'nsɪdə'rɪŋ/. You use **considering** to indicate that you are taking a particular fact into account when making a judgement or giving an opinion. EG *Considering that he received no help, his results are very good... Considering her dislike of Martin, it was surprising that she invited him.* CONJ OR PREP

consign /kə'nsaɪn/, **consigns, consigning, consigned. 1** If you **consign** something to a particular place, you get rid of it by putting it there. EG *I discovered some wheels that had been consigned to the loft.* V+O+to Formal

2 If someone or something **is consigned** to a situation, they are put in that situation. EG *Such a policy would consign the poor to indefinite poverty.* V+O+to Formal

consignment /kə'nsaɪnməⁿnt/, **consignments.** A **consignment** of goods is a load that is being delivered to a place or person. EG *The shop announced the arrival of a new consignment of dress materials.* N COUNT: OFT+SUPP

consist /kə'nsɪst/, **consists, consisting, consisted. 1** Something that **consists** of particular things is formed from them. EG *The committee consists of scientists and engineers... Each convoy consisted of twelve ships.* V+of

2 Something that **consists** in something else has that thing as its main or only part. EG *Nineteenth-century trade consisted principally in luxuries such as silk, spices and ivory.* V+in

consistency /kə'nsɪstənsi¹/. **1 Consistency** is the condition of being consistent. EG *...consistency and continuity in government policy.* N UNCOUNT

2 The **consistency** of a substance is its degree of thickness or smoothness. EG *Small children dislike food with a sticky consistency.* N UNCOUNT

consistent /kə'nsɪstənt/. **1** Someone who is **consistent** never changes their behaviour or attitudes towards people or things. EG *Brook was Baldwin's most dangerous and consistent adversary.* ◇ **consistently.** EG *Hearst consistently opposed Roosevelt's policies.* ADJ QUALIT ◇ ADV

2 An idea or argument that is **consistent** is organized so that each part of it agrees with all the other parts. ADJ QUALIT: OFT+with

console, consoles, consoling, consoled; pronounced /kə'nsəʊl/ when it is a verb and /kɒnsəʊl/ when it is a noun.

1 If you **console** someone who is unhappy about something, you try to make them feel more cheerful. EG *She tried to console me by saying that I'd probably be happier in a new job.* ◇ **consoling.** EG *It is a consoling thought... Dad laid a consoling hand on his shoulder.* ◇ **consolation** /kɒnsəler¹əⁿn/, **consolations.** EG *...a few words of consolation... My only consolation is that nobody knows.* V+O: OFT+by/with ◇ ADJ QUALIT ◇ N UNCOUNT OR N COUNT

2 A **console** is a panel with a number of switches or knobs that you use to operate a machine. N COUNT

consolidate /kə'nsɒlɪdeɪt/, **consolidates, consolidating, consolidated. 1** If you **consolidate** power or a plan, you strengthen it so that it becomes more effective or secure. EG *The new* V+O OR V

middle class consolidated its wealth and power.

◇ **consolidation** /kə'nsɒlɪdeɪ¹əⁿn/. EG *...the long-term consolidation of party power.* ◇ N UNCOUNT

2 To **consolidate** a number of small groups or firms means to make them into one large organization. EG *British rule consolidated the states of the north into a unified Northern Region.* V-ERG

◇ **consolidation.** EG *...a dangerous trend toward consolidation that could destroy small businesses.* ◇ N UNCOUNT

consonant /kɒnsənənt/, **consonants.** A **consonant** is a sound such as 'p' or 'm' which you pronounce by stopping the air flowing freely through your mouth. Most words are pronounced with a combination of consonants and vowels. N COUNT

consort, consorts, consorting, consorted; pronounced /kə'nsɔːt/ when it is a verb and /kɒnsɔːt/ when it is a noun. **1** If someone **consorts** with a particular person or group, they spend a lot of time with them; often used showing disapproval. EG *Daddy would never approve of her consorting with drug addicts.* V+with Formal

2 A **consort** is the wife or husband of the ruling monarch. N COUNT

consortium /kə'nsɔːtɪəm/, **consortia** /kə'nsɔːtɪə/ or **consortiums.** A **consortium** is a group of people or firms who have agreed to work in cooperation with each other. EG *...a newly formed consortium of Rummidge businessmen.* N COLL

conspicuous /kə'nspɪkjʊəs/. If something is **conspicuous**, people can see or notice it very easily. EG *Her freckles were more conspicuous than usual... She felt conspicuous.* ◇ **conspicuously.** EG *He had been conspicuously successful.* ADJ QUALIT ◇ ADV

conspiracy /kə'nspɪrəsi¹/, **conspiracies.** **Conspiracy** is the secret planning by a group of people to do something illegal, usually for political reasons. EG *The police arrested her on a charge of conspiracy to murder... Very few people knew the details of the conspiracy.* N UNCOUNT OR N COUNT

conspirator /kə'nspɪrətə/, **conspirators.** A **conspirator** is a person who joins a conspiracy. N COUNT

conspiratorial /kə'nspɪrətɔːrɪəl/. **1** If you are **conspiratorial**, you behave as if you are sharing a secret with someone. EG *...a conspiratorial nod.* ADJ QUALIT

2 Something that is **conspiratorial** is secret and illegal, often with a political purpose. EG *...a conspiratorial group.* ADJ CLASSIF

conspire /kə'nspaɪə/, **conspires, conspiring, conspired. 1** If you **conspire**, you secretly agree with other people to do something illegal or harmful. EG *Anarchists were conspiring to kill the ruler... My enemies are conspiring against me.* V OR V+with: RECIP, USU+to-INF OR against

2 If events **conspire** towards a particular result, they seem to work together to cause this result. EG *Everything had conspired to make him happy.* V Literary

constable /kʌnstəbəˀl/, **constables.** A **constable** is a police officer of the lowest rank in Britain. N COUNT

constabulary /kɒnstæbjʊˀlərɪ/, **constabularies.** A **constabulary** is the police force of a particular area. EG *...the Wiltshire Constabulary.* N COUNT British

constant /kɒnstənt/. **1** Something that is **constant** happens all the time or is always there. EG *He was in constant pain... He is my constant companion.* ◇ **constantly.** EG *The world around us is constantly changing.* ADJ CLASSIF: USU ATTRIB ◇ ADV

2 An amount or level that is **constant** stays the same over a particular period of time. EG *...a constant voltage.* ◇ **constancy** /kɒnstənsi¹/. EG *...the constancy of the temperature.* ADJ CLASSIF ◇ N UNCOUNT

3 If you are **constant**, you are always faithful to a particular person or idea. EG *I might have known not to expect constancy from you.* ADJ CLASSIF ◇ N UNCOUNT

constellation /kɒnstəˀleɪˀʃəⁿn/, **constellations.** A **constellation** is a group of stars which form a pattern and have a name. N COUNT

If a speech sound is not a vowel, what is it likely to be?

consternation /kɒnstəneɪʃə⁰n/ is a feeling of anxiety or fear. EG *We looked at each other in consternation.* N UNCOUNT

constipated /kɒnstɪpeɪt²d/. Someone who is **constipated** is unable to defecate. ADJ QUALIT

constipation /kɒnstɪpeɪʃə⁰n/ is a medical condition which makes people unable to defecate. N UNCOUNT

constituency /kəˈnstɪtjuːənsɪ¹/, **constituencies**. A **constituency** is a town or area which is officially allowed to elect someone to represent them in parliament. EG *There were about 14,000 voters in the constituency.* N COUNT

constituent /kəˈnstɪtjuənt/, **constituents**. A **constituent** is 1 someone who lives in a particular constituency, especially someone who is able to vote in an election. EG *An MP is the servant of his constituents.* 2 one of the things that a mixture, substance, or system is made from. EG *Nitrogen is one of the essential constituents of living matter... What are the constituent parts of an atom?* N COUNT

constitute /kɒnstɪtjuːt/, **constitutes**, **constituting**, **constituted**. 1 If something **constitutes** a particular thing, it can be regarded as being that thing. EG *These questions constitute a challenge to established attitudes... Conifers constitute about a third of the world's forests.* 2 To **constitute** something means to form it from a number of parts or elements. EG *...the recently constituted board of directors.* V+C: NO CONT / V+O Formal

constitution /kɒnstɪtjuːʃə⁰n/, **constitutions**. 1 The **constitution** of a country or organization is the system of laws which formally states people's rights and duties. EG *...the US constitution.* 2 Your **constitution** is your health. EG *He has a strong constitution.* 3 The **constitution** of something is what it is made of, and how its parts are arranged. EG *Questions were asked concerning the constitution and scope of the proposed commission.* N COUNT / N COUNT / N SING: the+N+of

constitutional /kɒnstɪtjuːʃə⁰nəl, -ʃənə⁰l/ means relating to the constitution of a particular country or organization. EG *...a major constitutional change... ...constitutional privileges.* ADJ CLASSIF: USU ATTRIB

constrain /kəˈnstreɪn/, **constrains**, **constraining**, **constrained**. 1 If someone or something **constrains** you, they force you to act in a particular way. EG *Papa had told her that he would not constrain her in any way... ...the need to constrain groups to work together.* 2 To **constrain** something means to prevent it from developing freely. EG *The housing regulations constrain variety and diversity.* V+O: OFT+to-INF Formal / V+O Formal

constrained /kəˈnstreɪnd/. 1 If you feel **constrained** to do something, you feel forced or obliged to do it. EG *He felt constrained to apologize.* 2 If you feel **constrained** by the situation you are in, you feel that you are not able to behave in the way that you want to. EG *In the end, he felt constrained by the lack of privacy.* ADJ PRED: OFT +to-INF Formal / ADJ PRED: OFT +by Formal

constraint /kəˈnstreɪnt/, **constraints**. 1 A **constraint** is something that limits or controls the way you behave. EG *The constraint on most doctors is lack of time.* 2 **Constraint** is control over the way you behave which prevents you from doing what you want to do. EG *The list of instructions and guidelines brings with it a flavour of constraint.* N COUNT: OFT+on/of Formal / N UNCOUNT Formal

constrict /kəˈnstrɪkt/, **constricts**, **constricting**, **constricted**. 1 To **constrict** something, for example a part of the body, means to squeeze it tightly. EG *He rubbed his ankles where the bindings had constricted him.* ◊ **constricting**. EG *Her dress was too constricting.* ◊ **constriction** /kəˈnstrɪkʃə⁰n/. EG *Some snakes kill, not by constriction, but by poison.* 2 If something **constricts** you, it limits your actions so that you cannot do what you want to do. ◊ **constricting**. EG *...the constricting structure of* V+O / ◊ ADJ QUALIT / ◊ N UNCOUNT / V+O / ◊ ADJ QUALIT

schools. ◊ **constriction**, **constrictions**. EG *...the constrictions of family life.* ◊ N COUNT: USU PLURAL

construct, **constructs**, **constructing**, **constructed**; pronounced /kəˈnstrʌkt/ when it is a verb and /kɒnstrʌkt/ when it is a noun. 1 If you **construct** a building, vehicle, road, or machine, you build or make it. EG *We constructed a raft... ...a building constructed of brick.* 2 If you **construct** an idea, piece of writing, or system, you create it by putting different parts together. EG *It's a beautifully constructed book.* 3 A **construct** is 3.1 a complex idea. EG *...theoretical constructs.* 3.2 something that is built, made, or created. EG *These machines are vast constructs of cogs, screws, and wheels.* V+O / V+O / N COUNT / N COUNT Formal

construction /kəˈnstrʌkʃə⁰n/, **constructions**. 1 **Construction** is the building or creating of something. EG *...the construction of the Panama Canal... ...the careful construction of a theory by logical means.* 2 A **construction** is an object that has been made or built. EG *These wigs are complicated constructions of real and false hair.* 3 You use the word **construction** to talk about how things have been built. For example, if something is **of** simple **construction**, it is simply built. EG *The main walls of the building are of solid brick construction.* N UNCOUNT / N COUNT / PHRASE

constructive /kəˈnstrʌktɪv/. A piece of advice or criticism that is **constructive** is useful and helpful. EG *...constructive criticism... I did not have anything constructive to say.* ◊ **constructively**. EG *You must channel your anger constructively.* ADJ QUALIT / ◊ ADV

construe /kəˈnstruː/, **construes**, **construing**, **construed**. If you **construe** a situation, event, or statement in a particular way, you interpret its meaning in that way. EG *Any show of emotion would be construed as a weakness.* V+O: USU PASS+as Formal

consul /kɒnsə⁰l/, **consuls**. A **consul** is an official who is sent by his or her government to live in a foreign city in order to look after all the people there that belong to his or her own country. ◊ **consular** /kɒnsjʊ⁴lə/. EG *...the British Consular authorities in Barcelona.* N COUNT / ◊ ADJ CLASSIF: ATTRIB

consulate /kɒnsjʊ⁴lə¹t/, **consulates**. A **consulate** is the place where a consul works. N COUNT

consult /kəˈnsʌlt/, **consults**, **consulting**, **consulted**. 1 If you **consult** someone, you ask them for their opinion and advice. EG *If your baby is losing weight, you should consult your doctor promptly.* 2 If two or more people **consult** each other, they talk and exchange ideas and opinions. EG *We needed to consult each other nearly every day... They would have to consult with their allies.* 3 If you **consult** a book or a map, you refer to it for information. V+O / V+O OR V+with: RECIP / V+O

consultancy /kəˈnsʌltənsɪ¹/, **consultancies**. A **consultancy** is a group of people who set up a company to give expert advice on a particular subject. EG *You can start your own consultancy.* N COUNT

consultant /kəˈnsʌltə⁰nt/, **consultants**. A **consultant** is 1 an experienced doctor who specializes in one area of medicine. EG *I was the first woman consultant on the staff of Charing Cross Hospital.* 2 a person who gives expert advice to people who need professional help. EG *...a firm of public relations consultants.* N COUNT

consultation /kɒnsə⁰lteɪʃə⁰n/, **consultations**. 1 A **consultation** is a meeting which is held to discuss something. 2 **Consultation** is 2.1 discussion between people, especially when advice is being given. EG *This is a matter for the Prime Minister to decide in consultation with the Ministry of Defence.* 2.2 reference to a book or other source of information. EG *I keep my car handbook near me for frequent consultation.* N COUNT: OFT +about/with / N UNCOUNT OFT+with/about / N UNCOUNT

consultative /kə'nsʌltətɪv/. A **consultative** com- ADJ CLASSIF:
mittee or document is formed or written in order ATTRIB
to give advice about something. Formal

consulting room, consulting rooms. A **con-** N COUNT
sulting room is a room in which a doctor sees
patients.

consume /kə'nsj°u:m/, **consumes, consuming,**
consumed. 1 If you **consume** something, you eat v+o
or drink it. EG *They spend their evenings consum-* Formal
ing vodka.

2 To **consume** an amount of fuel, energy, or time v+o
means to use it up. EG *The ship consumed a great*
deal of fuel.

3 If a feeling or desire **consumes** you, it affects v+o
you very strongly indeed. EG *His hatred of them* Literary
consumed him.

consumer /kə'nsj°u:mə/, **consumers.** A **con-** N COUNT
sumer is a person who buys things or uses services. EG *The consumer is entitled to products that*
give value for money... ...consumer advice... ...gas
consumers.

consuming /kə'nsj°u:mɪŋ/. A **consuming** passion ADJ CLASSIF:
or interest is more important to you than anything ATTRIB
else. EG *Politics is the consuming passion of half the*
town.

consummate, consummates, consummating,
consummated; pronounced /kɒnsj°ə'meɪt/ when
it is a verb and /kɒnsj°ə'mət/ when it is an
adjective.

1 If two people **consummate** a marriage or rela- v+o
tionship, they make it complete by having sex. Formal
◇ **consummation.** EG *...the consummation of their* ◇ N UNCOUNT
marriage.

2 To **consummate** something means to do some- v+o
thing which makes it complete. EG *We need to* Formal
consummate what we have so far achieved.
◇ **consummation.** EG *This expedition was the* ◇ N UNCOUNT
consummation of what he regarded as his life's
work.

3 You use **consummate** 3.1 to describe someone ADJ CLASSIF:
who is extremely skilful. EG *He was a fighter of* ATTRIB
consummate skill. 3.2 to emphasize that something Formal
is a perfect or extreme example of a particular
thing. EG *We were both consummate snobs.*

consumption /kə'nsʌmpʃ°n/. 1 The **consump-** N UNCOUNT
tion of fuel or energy is 1.1 the amount of it that is +SUPP
used up. EG *Oil used to make up 10% of our total*
energy consumption. 1.2 the act of using it up. EG
...our consumption of energy.

2 **Consumption** is 2.1 the act of eating or drinking N UNCOUNT
something. EG *The water was unfit for consumption.* Formal
2.2 the act of buying and using things. EG *...new*
patterns of consumption.

3 If you say that information or a remark is **for** a PHRASE
particular person's **consumption**, you mean that it
is intended for that person. EG *That prim declara-*
tion was strictly for George's consumption.

CONT stands for **continuous tenses**

A few verbs have the label USU CONT in the Extra
Column. This means that they are normally only
used in continuous tenses. An example of a verb
that is labelled USU CONT is **burn 6.** You say *I am*
burning with indignation. You do not usually say 'I
burn with indignation'.

A few other verbs have the label NO CONT in the
Extra Column. This means that they are not normally used in continuous tenses. An example of a
verb that is labelled NO CONT is **know 1.** You say *I*
do not know her address. You do not usually say 'I
am not knowing her address'.

---

contact /kɒntækt/, **contacts, contacting, con-**
tacted. 1 If you are in **contact** with someone, you N UNCOUNT
regularly meet them, talk to them, or write to OR N COUNT
them, often as a part of your work. EG *I'm in*
contact with a number of schools... ...everyone who
came into contact with her... We have many con-
tacts with local people.

2 When people or things are in **contact**, they are N UNCOUNT
touching each other. EG *Close physical contact is*
important for a baby... My hand came into contact
with a small lump.

3 If you **make contact** with someone, you find out PHRASE
where they are and talk or write to them. EG *I*
finally made contact with my friend.

4 If you **lose contact** with someone you know, you PHRASE
no longer meet or write to each other.

5 If you **contact** someone, you telephone them or v+o
write to them. EG *As soon as we find out, we'll*
contact you.

6 A **contact** is a person in an organization or N COUNT
profession who you get special help or information
from, often unofficially. EG *He had contacts in*
America... ...business contacts.

contact lens, contact lenses. Contact lenses N COUNT
are two small pieces of plastic that you put on your
eyes to make you see better, instead of wearing
glasses.

contagious /kə'nteɪdʒəs/. 1 A **contagious** dis- ADJ QUALIT
ease is one that you can catch by touching people
or things that are infected with it. EG *It was as*
contagious as smallpox.

2 A feeling or attitude that is **contagious** spreads ADJ QUALIT
quickly among a group of people. EG *Quint's confi-*
dence was contagious.

contain /kə'nteɪn/, **contains, containing, con-**
tained. 1 If something such as a box or room v+o
contains things, those things are inside it. EG *...a*
basket containing groceries... The urban areas
contain several million people.

2 If a substance **contains** something, that thing is a v+o
part of it. EG *...chemical compounds containing*
mercury.

3 If writing, speech, or film **contains** particular v+o
information, ideas, or images, it includes them. EG
...the stories contained in the book.

4 If something **contains** a particular quality, it v+o
indicates or expresses it. EG *The letter contained an*
element of nastiness.

5 If you **contain** something, you control it and v+o
prevent it from increasing. EG *He could hardly* Formal
contain his eagerness to leave... ...measures to
contain population growth.

container /kə'nteɪnə/, **containers.** 1 A **contain-** N COUNT
er is something such as a box or bottle that is used
to hold or store things in. EG *...a soap container...*
...cheap plastic containers.

2 **Container** ships and lorries transport goods in N MOD
very large sealed metal boxes.

contaminate /kə'ntæmɪneɪt/, **contaminates,** v+o
contaminating, contaminated. If something **is**
contaminated by dirt, chemicals, or radiation, it
becomes impure, unhealthy, or harmful. EG *Many*
wells have been contaminated by chemicals...
...foods that are easily contaminated with poison-
ous bacteria. ◇ **contaminated.** EG *The men died* ◇ ADJ QUALIT
from drinking contaminated water.
◇ **contamination** /kə'ntæmɪneɪʃ°n/. EG *...infec-* ◇ N UNCOUNT
tions caused by the contamination of milk.

contemplate /kɒntə'mpleɪt/, **contemplates,**
contemplating, contemplated. 1 If you **contem-** v+o OR V+-ING
plate an action, you think about doing it. EG
Lawrence contemplated publishing the book.

2 If you **contemplate** an idea or subject, you think v+o OR
about it carefully and for a long time. EG *We have to* V+REPORT
pause and contemplate what we are talking about.
◇ **contemplation** /kɒntə'mpleɪʃ°n/. EG *...religious* ◇ N UNCOUNT
contemplation.

3 If you **contemplate** something, you look at it v+o OR v

What word do you use to describe a disease that
is spread by contact?

quietly for a long time. EG *They contemplated each other in silence.* ◊ **contemplation.** EG *She returned to the contemplation of the sunset.*

contemplative /kəˈntɛmplətɪv/. When you are **contemplative**, you think deeply in a serious and calm way. EG *...the contemplative civilizations of the Far East.* ADJ CLASSIF

contemporary /kəˈntɛmprəri[1]/, **contemporaries.** 1 **Contemporary** people or things 1.1 are alive or happening now. EG *...contemporary writers... ...life in contemporary America.* 1.2 were alive or happening in the past, at the same time as something else you are talking about. EG *...a contemporary account of the trial.* ADJ CLASSIF: ATTRIB

2 Someone's **contemporary** is a person who is or was alive at the same time as them. EG *...Darwin's contemporary, Sir James Simpson.* N COUNT: USU+POSS

contempt /kəˈntɛmpt/. 1 If you have **contempt** for someone or something, you have no respect for them or think that they are unimportant. EG *The women would often look at us with contempt... ...his contempt for the truth.* N UNCOUNT

2 If you **hold** someone or something **in contempt**, you feel contempt for them. EG *...the contempt in which he held professional politicians.* PHRASE

contemptible /kəˈntɛmptəbəl/. If you feel that someone or something is **contemptible**, you feel strong dislike and disrespect for them. EG *You are showing a contemptible lack of courage.* ADJ QUALIT

contemptuous /kəˈntɛmptjuəs/. If you are **contemptuous** of someone or something, you do not like or respect them at all. EG *Hamilton gave me a contemptuous look.* ◊ **contemptuously.** ◊ EG *He tossed the paper contemptuously on to the table.* ADJ QUALIT OFT+of Formal ◊ ADV

contend /kəˈntɛnd/, **contends, contending, contended.** 1 If you have to **contend** with a problem or difficulty, you have to deal with it or overcome it. EG *The girls had problems of their own at home to contend with.* V+with

2 If you **contend** that something is true, you state or argue that it is true. EG *She contended that the report was deficient.* V+REPORT: ONLY that Formal

3 If you **contend** with someone for something, you compete with them in order to get it. EG *Three parties are contending for power.* ◊ **contending.** EG *Those decisions were fought out between contending groups.* V OR V+with: RECIP ◊ ADJ CLASSIF: ATTRIB

contender /kəˈntɛndə/, **contenders.** A **contender** in a competition is someone who takes part in it. EG *...a contender in the Presidential election.* N COUNT

content, contents, contenting, contented; pronounced /ˈkɒntɛnt/ for paragraphs 1 to 4, and /kəˈntɛnt/ for paragraphs 5 to 8.

1 The **contents** of something such as a box or room are the things that are inside it. EG *He drank the contents of his glass in one gulp... ...pouring out the contents of the bag.* N PLURAL

2 The **contents** of something such as a document or tape are the things written in it or recorded on it. EG *He knew by heart the contents of the note.* N PLURAL

3 The **content** of a piece of writing, a speech, or a television programme is its main subject and the ideas and opinions expressed in it. EG *I was disturbed by the content of some of the speeches.* N UNCOUNT

4 You can use **content** to refer to the amount or proportion of something that a substance contains, for example its moisture **content** or its fibre **content**. EG *No other food has so high an iron content.* N SING+SUPP

5 If you are **content** to do something or if you are **content** with something, you are willing to do, have, or accept it. EG *A few teachers were content to pay the fines... Children are not content with glib explanations.* ADJ PRED +to-INF OR with

6 If you are **content**, you are fairly happy or satisfied. EG *However hard up they were, they stayed content.* ADJ PRED

7 If you **content** yourself with something, you are satisfied with doing or having that thing and do not V-REFL+with

try to do or have other things. EG *She didn't take part in the discussion, but contented herself with smoking cigarettes.*

8 to your **heart's content**: see **heart.**

contented /kəˈntɛntɪd/. If you are **contented**, you are happy and satisfied. EG *My father was the most contented man I ever met... ...firms with a loyal and contented labour force.* ◊ **contentedly.** EG *She plays contentedly by herself.* ADJ QUALIT ◊ ADV

contention /kəˈntɛnʃən/, **contentions.** 1 Someone's **contention** is the idea or opinion that they are expressing in an argument or discussion. EG *My main contention is that we must offer all our children the same opportunities.* N COUNT Formal

2 **Contention** is disagreement or argument about something. EG *This is an issue of great contention at the moment.* N UNCOUNT Formal

3 If you are **in contention** in a contest, you have a chance of winning it. EG *Rees was in contention to win the title.* PHRASE Formal

contentious /kəˈntɛnʃəs/. A subject or opinion that is **contentious** causes a lot of disagreement or arguments. EG *...his contentious view that mental illness is in fact a myth.* ADJ QUALIT Formal

contentment /kəˈntɛntmənt/ is a feeling of quiet happiness and satisfaction. EG *I sighed with contentment.* N UNCOUNT

contest, contests, contesting, contested; pronounced /ˈkɒntɛst/ when it is a noun and /kəˈntɛst/ when it is a verb.

1 A **contest** is 1.1 a competition or game in which people try to win. EG *...a fishing contest.* 1.2 a struggle to win power or control. EG *He won the contest for the deputy leadership.* N COUNT

2 If someone **contests** an election or competition they take part in it and try to win it. EG *There was an election contested by six candidates.* V+O

3 If you **contest** a statement or decision, you object to it formally because you think it is wrong or unreasonable. EG *We hotly contest the idea that any of them were ours.* V+O Formal

contestant /kəˈntɛstənt/, **contestants.** A **contestant** in a competition or quiz is a person who takes part in it. EG *...the contestants in the world championship.* N COUNT

context /ˈkɒntɛkst/, **contexts.** 1 The **context** of an idea or event is the general information about the time, place, and situation in which it occurred, which you need to know in order to understand it fully. EG *We need to place present events in some kind of historical context... ...the relevance of these ideas in the context of Britain.* N COUNT OR N UNCOUNT

2 The **context** of a word or sentence consists of the words or sentences before and after it which help to make its meaning clear. EG *What do we mean by 'growth' and 'power' in this context?... This remark was taken completely out of context.* N COUNT OR N UNCOUNT

continent /ˈkɒntɪnənt/, **continents.** 1 A **continent** is a very large area of land, such as Africa or Asia. EG *...the North American continent.* ◊ **continental** /kɒntɪˈnɛntəl/. EG *Defence should be organized on a continental scale.* N COUNT ◊ ADJ CLASSIF: ATTRIB

2 In Britain, the mainland of Europe is sometimes referred to as the **Continent**. EG *British artists are very well known on the Continent.* ◊ **Continental.** EG *...West Germany and other Continental countries... ...a Continental holiday.* N PROPER: the+N ◊ ADJ CLASSIF: ATTRIB

contingency /kəˈntɪndʒənsi/, **contingencies.** A **contingency** is something that might happen in the future. EG *He had anticipated all contingencies... ...contingency plans for nuclear attack.* N COUNT Formal

contingent /kəˈntɪndʒənt/, **contingents.** 1 A **contingent** is 1.1 a group of people representing a country or organization at a meeting or other event. EG *...a contingent of European scientists.* 1.2 a group of police, soldiers, or military vehicles. EG *Police contingents were ordered into the area.* N COUNT: USU+SUPP Formal

2 If something is **contingent** on something else, it ADJ PRED+on Formal

depends on it in order to happen or exist. EG *The raid was contingent on the weather.*

continual /kə'ntɪnjuəl/ means 1 happening all ADJ CLASSIF : the time without stopping. EG *...a continual move-* ATTRIB *ment of air... The figures show an almost continual increase.* ◊ **continually.** EG *We are continually* ◊ ADV *learning from experience.* 2 happening again and ADJ CLASSIF : again. EG *He ignored the continual warnings of his* ATTRIB *nurse.* ◊ **continually** EG *Tom was continually* ◊ ADV *asking me questions.*

continuance /kə'ntɪnjuəns/. The **continuance** of N UNCOUNT : something is its continuation. EG *...the continuance* USU+SUPP *of the war.* Formal

continuation /kə'ntɪnju:eɪʃəᵒn/, **continuations.** 1 N UNCOUNT : The **continuation** of something is the fact that it USU+SUPP continues to happen or exist. EG *People take for granted the continuation of economic growth.* 2 If something is a **continuation** of something else, N COUNT : it is situated next to it or happens after it and forms USU+SUPP an extra part of it. EG *The carpet seemed a continuation of the lawn.*

continue /kə'ntɪnju:/, **continues, continuing, continued.** 1 If you **continue** to do something, you V+*to*-INF keep doing it and do not stop. EG *The orchestra* OR -ING *continued to play... He continued talking.* 2 If something **continues** or if you **continue** it, 2.1 V OR V-ERG it does not stop happening. EG *If the trend con- tinues, the area will be ruined... They want to continue their education... The battle continued for an hour.* 2.2 It starts again after stopping for a V OR V-ERG period of time. EG *The next day the performance continued... He arrived in Norway, where he con- tinued his campaign.* 3 If you **continue** with something, you keep doing V+*with* it or using it. EG *The girls should continue with their mathematics.* 4 If you **continue**, you begin speaking again after a V OR V+QUOTE pause or interruption. EG *'May I continue?' – 'Go on.'... 'I mean Phil,' she continued, 'It's for him.'* 5 If you **continue** in a particular direction, you V+A keep walking or travelling in that direction. EG *I continued up the path... She continued on her way.*

continuity /kɒntɪnju:'ti¹/. The **continuity** of N UNCOUNT something is the fact that it is happening, existing, or developing without stopping or changing sud- denly. EG *...the importance of continuity in govern- ment policy... ...the continuity of this tradition.*

continuous /kə'ntɪnjuːəs/. 1 Something that is ADJ CLASSIF : **continuous** happens or exists without stopping. EG USU ATTRIB *...the continuous increase in their military capac- ity.* ◊ **continuously.** EG *The volcano had been* ◊ ADV *erupting continuously since March.* 2 A **continuous** line or surface has no gaps or ADJ CLASSIF : holes in it. ATTRIB 3 In English grammar, the **continuous** form of ADJ CLASSIF verbs is formed by the auxiliary 'be' and the present participle of a verb. When a verb typically occurs in the continuous or when it is rarely used in the continuous, this is mentioned in the Extra Column. See the entry headed CONT for more information.

continuum /kə'ntɪnjuəm/. A **continuum** is a N SING series of events that are considered as a single Formal thing or process. EG *...the continuum of the seasons.*

contort /kə'ntɔːt/, **contorts, contorting, con-** V-ERG **torted.** When something **contorts** or is **contort- ed**, it moves into an unnatural and unattractive shape or position. EG *His face contorted with ha- tred.* ◊ **contorted.** EG *...his mad contorted smile.* ◊ ADJ CLASSIF

contortion /kə'ntɔːʃəᵒn/, **contortions.** A **contor-** N COUNT OR **tion** is a movement of your body into an unusual N UNCOUNT shape or position. EG *...the child's ceaseless contor- tions.*

contour /kɒntuə/, **contours.** 1 The **contours** of N COUNT : something are its outer shape or outline. EG *Pain* USU PLURAL *altered the contours of his face.* Literary 2 A **contour** on a map is a line joining points of N COUNT : equal height and indicating hills, valleys, and the USU N MOD steepness of slopes. EG *...the 300ft contour line.*

contraband /kɒntrəbænd/ refers to goods that N UNCOUNT are taken into or out of a country illegally. EG *He might be carrying contraband.*

contraception /kɒntrəsɛpʃəᵒn/. The various N UNCOUNT methods of preventing pregnancy are called **contraception.** EG *...safe, easy methods of contra- ception.*

contraceptive /kɒntrəsɛptɪv/, **contraceptives.** N COUNT A **contraceptive** is a device or pill that prevents a woman from becoming pregnant during sexual intercourse. EG *There are clinics where women can be fitted with contraceptives... ...contraceptive pills.*

contract, contracts, contracting, contracted; pronounced /kɒntrækt/ when it is a noun, and /kə'ntrækt/ when it is a verb. 1 A **contract** is a written legal agreement between N COUNT people which usually involves buying something or doing work for a stated sum of money. EG *We won a contract to build fifty-eight planes... I did not sign a contract with them... ...a marriage contract.* 2 If you **contract** with someone to do something, V+*to*-INF you legally agree to do it. EG *They contracted to* Formal *supply us with horses.* 3 When something **contracts**, it becomes smaller V-ERG or shorter. EG *Metals expand with heat and con- tract with cold.* ◊ **contraction** /kə'ntrækʃəᵒn/, ◊ N COUNT OR **contractions.** EG *She first acted under the name of* N UNCOUNT *Terson (a contraction of Terry and Neilson).* 4 If you **contract** an illness, you become ill with it. V+O EG *She then contracted breast cancer.* Formal

contractor /kɒntræktə, kəntræk-/, **contractors.** N COUNT A **contractor** is a person or company that does work for other people or companies. EG *...houses built by private contractors.*

contractual /kə'ntræktjuᵒəl/. A **contractual** re- ADJ CLASSIF : lationship involves a legal agreement between ATTRIB people. EG *The union had a contractual agreement* Formal *with the company.*

contradict /kɒntrədɪkt/, **contradicts, contra-** **dicting, contradicted.** 1 If you **contradict** some- V+O OR one, you say that they are wrong and that the V+QUOTE opposite of what they have said is correct or true. EG *I took care not to contradict her... 'No,' contra- dicted her sister, 'it's because he doesn't care.'* 2 If one fact or statement **contradicts** another, it V+O suggests or indicates that the second one is wrong. EG *Research evidence contradicts this idea... Per- fectly reputable books may contradict each other.*

contradiction /kɒntrədɪkʃəᵒn/, **contradictions.** 1 If there is a **contradiction** in something, it has N COUNT OR features which are completely different from each N UNCOUNT other and so make it confused or difficult to understand. EG *There is a contradiction between the two laws... I hate to admit all these contradic- tions in myself... There is no contradiction in this approach.* 2 If you say that something is a **contradiction in** PHRASE **terms**, you mean that it is described as having a quality that it cannot have. EG *A rational religion is almost a contradiction in terms.*

contradictory /kɒntrədɪktəᵒri¹/. If two ideas, or ADJ QUALIT statements are **contradictory**, they say that oppo- site things are true. EG *The government had made two contradictory promises.*

contralto /kə'ntræltəʊ/, **contraltos.** A **contralto** N COUNT is a woman with a low singing voice.

contraption /kə'ntræpʃəᵒn/, **contraptions.** You N COUNT : can describe a device or machine as a **contrap-** USU+SUPP **tion**, especially when it looks strange or you do not know what it is used for. EG *Over his door was a contraption with a sliding shutter.*

contrary /kɒntrəri¹/. 1 You say **on the contrary** ADV SEN to emphasize that your next statement is true even though it contradicts what has just been said. EG

If you carry contraband, are you contravening the law?

*There was nothing ugly about her dress: on the
contrary, it had a certain elegance... 'You'll get
tired of it.' - 'On the contrary. I shall enjoy it.'*

2 Ideas, attitudes, or reactions that are **contrary** to ADJ CLASSIF:
each other are completely different from each OFT+ *to*
other. EG *They happily tolerated the existence of
opinions contrary to their own... ...contrary impulses.*

3 If you say that something is true **contrary to** PREP
other people's beliefs, you are emphasizing that it
is true and that they are wrong. EG *Contrary to
what is generally assumed, the adjustment is easily
made.*

4 If you talk about evidence **to the contrary**, you PHRASE
mean evidence that contradicts what you are say-
ing or what someone else has said. EG *This method,
despite statements to the contrary, has no damaging effects.*

contrast, contrasts, contrasting, contrasted;
pronounced /ˈkɒntrɑːst/ when it is a noun, and
/kəˈntrɑːst/ when it is a verb.

1 A **contrast** is a great difference between two or N COUNT : OFT
more things which is clear when you compare +*between/*
them. EG *...the contrast between his public image* *with*
and his private life.

2 You say **by contrast** or **in contrast** to empha- ADV SEN
size the difference between one thing and another
that you have already mentioned. EG *By contrast,
our use of oil has increased enormously... This
second movement, in contrast, reached a membership of 100,000 in two years.*

3 If one thing is **in contrast** to another, it is very PHRASE
different from it. EG *He thought of her idleness in
contrast to his own busy life.*

4 If something is a **contrast** to or with something N COUNT :
else, it is very different from it. EG *The atmosphere* OFT+ *to/with*
*of the Second War was a complete contrast to that
of the First.*

5 If you **contrast** things, you explain or emphasize V+O : OFT+
the differences between them. EG *The book con-* *with/to*
*trasts the methods used in America and Russia...
He contrasted America with the older European
countries.*

6 If one thing **contrasts** with another, it is very V OR V+*with* :
different from it. EG *This gesture contrasts oddly* RECIP
with her clothes. ◊ **contrasting.** EG *...their con-* ◊ ADJ CLASSIF :
trasting attitudes... ...contrasting colours. ATTRIB

contravene /ˌkɒntrəˈviːn/, **contravenes, contra-** V+O
vening, contravened. If someone **contravenes** a Formal
law or rule, they do something that is forbidden by
the law or rule. EG *They contravened the drug laws.*
◊ **contravention** /ˌkɒntrəˈvenʃəᵊn/, **contraven-** ◊ N UNCOUNT
tions. EG *The advert was in contravention of the* OR N COUNT
Race Relations Act.

contribute /kəˈntrɪbjuːt/, **contributes, contrib-**
uting, contributed. **1** If you **contribute** to something, **1.1** you do things to help to make it success- V OR V+O :
ful. EG *The elderly have much to contribute to the* OFT+ *to*
community. **1.2** you give money to help pay for V OR V+O:
something. EG *She persuaded friends to contribute* OFT+ *to*
$5,000 to the fund. ◊ **contributor** /kəˈntrɪbjəˈtə/, ◊ N COUNT :
contributors. EG *...contributors to a fund to save* OFT+ *to*
the house.

2 If something **contributes** to an event or situa- V+ *to/towards*
tion, it is one of the causes of it. EG *Soaring land
prices contribute to the high cost of housing.*

3 If you **contribute** to a magazine or book, you V OR V+O:
write things that are published in it. EG *Distin-* OFT+ *to*
guished writers had contributed to its pages.
◊ **contributor, contributors.** EG *...a contributor of* ◊ N COUNT :
short stories to a national weekly. OFT+ *to*

contribution /ˌkɒntrɪbjuːʃəᵊn/, **contributions. 1** If N COUNT :
you make a **contribution** to something, you do OFT+ *to*
something to help make it successful. EG *...the
BBC's contribution to the adult literacy campaign.*

2 A **contribution** is also **2.1** a sum of money that N COUNT :
you give in order to help pay for something. EG *The* OFT+ *to*
*United Kingdom had to make a contribution of
£1,000 million to the EEC budget.* **2.2** something N COUNT

*that you write which is published in a book or
magazine.* EG *...pamphlets with contributions from
trade unionists.*

contributory /kənˈtrɪbjəˈtəᵊri/. A **contributory** ADJ CLASSIF:
cause or factor of something is one of several USU ATTRIB
things which cause it to happen. EG *The inefficient* Formal
use of oil was a major contributory factor.

contrite /kəˈntraɪt, kɒnˈtraɪt/. If you are **contrite,** ADJ QUALIT
you are very ashamed and apologetic because you Literary
have done something wrong. EG *I tried to look
contrite.* ◊ **contrition** /kəˈntrɪʃəᵊn/. EG *They tell* ◊ N UNCOUNT
lies and show no sign of contrition.

contrivance /kəˈntraɪvəns/, **contrivances. 1** A N COUNT
contrivance is a device or machine that looks
strange and seems to have been quickly built. EG *...a
contrivance of wood and wire.*

2 A **contrivance** is also an unfair or dishonest N COUNT
scheme to gain an advantage for yourself. EG *...a
contrivance to raise prices.*

contrive /kəˈntraɪv/, **contrives, contriving,**
contrived. 1 If you **contrive** to do something V+ *to*-INF
difficult, you succeed in doing it. EG *I shall contrive* Formal
*to see you again... Mike contrived to grin without
taking his cigar out of his mouth.*

2 If you **contrive** an event or situation, you suc- V+O
ceed in making it happen, often by tricking some- Formal
one. EG *Confidential talks with professors were
contrived by reporters posing as students.*

contrived /kəˈntraɪvd/. **Contrived** behaviour is ADJ QUALIT
false and artificial. EG *Olivia displayed her contrived smile.*

control /kəˈntrəʊl/, **controls, controlling, con-**
trolled. 1 Control of a country or an organization N UNCOUNT :
is the power to make all the important decisions OFT+ *of/over*
about the way that it is run. EG *The bank took
control of a television station... ...political control
over colonies.*

2 If you have **control** of something, you are able to N UNCOUNT :
make it behave exactly as you want. EG *You should* OFT+ *of/over*
have control of your vehicle at all times.

3 If you show **control**, you are able to prevent N UNCOUNT
yourself behaving in an excited or emotional way.
EG *He told himself that he mustn't lose control if he
wanted to save his strength.*

4 Control is also used in these phrases. **4.1** If PHRASES
something is **beyond** your **control** or **outside** your
control, you do not have any power to affect it or
change it. EG *The service is being withdrawn for
reasons outside anyone's control.* **4.2** If you are **in
control** of something, you decide or influence the
way it develops. EG *Those who begin the revolution
rarely stay in control to complete the process.* **4.3**
If something is **out of control**, nobody has any
power over it. EG *Inflation got out of control.* **4.4** If
something harmful is **under control**, it is being
dealt with successfully and is unlikely to cause any
more harm. EG *The fever was brought under control.* **4.5** If something is **under** your **control**, you
have the power to decide what will happen to it. EG
...when a village is under enemy control.

5 The people who **control** a country or an organi- V+O
zation have the power to take all the important
decisions about the way that it is run. EG *The
Australians controlled the island.* ◊ **controlling.** ◊ ADJ CLASSIF :
EG *The family had a controlling interest in the firm.* ATTRIB

6 To **control** a machine, process, or system means V+O
to make it work in the way that is required. EG
Computer systems control the lighting and heating.
◊ **controlled.** EG *...the controlled release of water* ◊ ADJ QUALIT
from reservoirs.

7 When a government **controls** wages, prices, or V+O
the activities of a particular group, it uses its power
to restrict them. EG *...a law to control incomes.*

8 If you **control** yourself, you make yourself be- V-REFL OR V+O
have calmly when you are feeling angry, excited,
or upset.

9 To **control** something dangerous means to pre- V+O
vent it from becoming worse or from spreading. EG
...a way of controlling cancer.

CONVENTIONS

People often use ready-made phrases in conversation, and in this dictionary these are called CONVENTIONS. They are often used in situations where you are expected to say something, as for example when you meet someone for the first time. Here are some examples:

Meeting someone:	*Hello.*	Response:	*Hello.*
Leaving someone:	*Goodbye.*	Response:	*Goodbye. See you soon.*
Congratulating someone:	*Congratulations.*	Response:	*Thanks.*
Thanking someone:	*Thank you.*	Response:	*Oh, that's all right.*

You can of course often slightly vary the words that you use. The important thing is that there is a convention for you to use if you want to.

So, one important use of conventions is as the first utterance in a very common situation that you find yourself in. Another important use of conventions is that you can use them as responses to ordinary utterances. Here are some examples:

And this is your room, I suppose.	Response:	*Yes, it is.*
Would you like a coffee?	Response:	*Thanks very much.*
How about coming for a meal tomorrow?	Response:	*That'd be nice.*
I'll be back in the middle of August.	Response:	*See you then.*
Could you check this for me?	Response:	*No problem.*
I've got my French exam tomorrow.	Response:	*The best of luck.*

10 A **control** is a device which you use in order to operate a machine. EG *Just turn the volume control.* N COUNT

11 Controls are the methods that a government uses to restrict increases, for example in prices or wages. EG *...government price controls.* N PLURAL: USU+SUPP

controller /kə'ntrəʊlə/, **controllers**. A **controller** is a person who has responsibility for a particular task or for a section of an organization. EG *...an air traffic controller... ...the financial controller.* N COUNT: USU+SUPP

controversial /kɒntrəvɜːʃ⁰l/. Someone or something that is **controversial** causes a lot of discussion, argument, and strong feelings of anger or disapproval. EG *Many of the new taxes are controversial... He is a controversial politician.* ADJ QUALIT

controversy /kɒntrəvɜːsiˈ, kə'ntrɒvəsiˈ/, **controversies. Controversy** is a lot of discussion and argument about something, often involving strong feelings of anger or disapproval. EG *The government tried to avoid controversy... ...a violent controversy over a commercial treaty.* N UNCOUNT OR N COUNT

conundrum /kə'nʌndrəm/, **conundrums**. A **conundrum** is a difficult or confusing problem. EG *The belief in reincarnation poses some conundrums.* N COUNT Formal

conurbation /kɒnɜˈbeɪʃⁿn/, **conurbations**. A **conurbation** is a large urban area formed by several towns that have spread towards each other. EG *...major industrial conurbations.* N COUNT Formal

convalesce /kɒnvəles/, **convalesces, convalescing, convalesced.** If you **are convalescing**, you are resting and regaining your health after an illness or operation. EG *The fever is gone and the child is convalescing.* V

convalescence /kɒnvəlesⁿns/ is the period or process of becoming healthy and well again after an illness or operation. EG *Clem wasn't allowed to visit me during my convalescence.* N UNCOUNT

convalescent /kɒnvəlesⁿnt/ means relating to convalescence. EG *...a convalescent home in the country.* ADJ CLASSIF: ATTRIB

convene /kə'nviːn/, **convenes, convening, convened. 1** If you **convene** a meeting or conference, you arrange for it to take place. EG *Roland convened a small meeting to discuss the issue.* V+O Formal

2 If a group of people **convene**, they come together for a meeting. EG *The grand jury did not convene until February.* V Formal

convenience /kə'nviːnɪəns/, **conveniences. 1 Convenience** is the state or quality of being easy to use or making something easy to do. EG *We use frozen food for convenience.* N UNCOUNT

2 If something is done for your **convenience**, it is done in a way that is useful or suitable for you. EG *The entire event had been arranged for their convenience.* N UNCOUNT +POSS

3 If you describe something as a **convenience**, you mean that it is very useful. EG *It's a great convenience to have a separate room for the twins... ...a house with every modern convenience.* N COUNT

convenience food, convenience foods. Convenience food is frozen, dried, or tinned food that can be cooked quickly without any preparation. N MASS

convenient /kə'nviːnɪənt/. Something that is **convenient** is very useful or suitable for a particular purpose. EG *It will be more convenient to stick to a three-hour timetable... ...a convenient place to live.* ADJ QUALIT

◊ **conveniently**. EG *The amount of fuel is displayed conveniently on a gauge.* ◊ ADV

convent /kɒnvⁿnt/, **convents**. A **convent** is **1** a building in which a community of nuns live. **2** a school that is run by nuns. N COUNT

convention /kə'nvenʃⁿn/, **conventions. 1** A **convention** is **1.1** a way of behaving that is considered to be correct or polite by most people in a society. EG *...the everyday conventions and rules of behaviour... ...his arrogance and rejection* N COUNT OR N UNCOUNT

What is convenient about convenience food?

of convention. **1.2** a traditional method or style N COUNT
that is used in art or literature. EG *...the conventions
of the novel.*

2 A **convention** is also **2.1** an official agreement N COUNT
between countries or groups of people. EG *They
signed the convention in 1905.* **2.2** a large meeting
of an organization or political group. EG *He left New
York before the convention ended.*

conventional /kə'venʃə⁰nəl, -ʃənə⁰l/. **1** Someone ADJ QUALIT
who is **conventional** behaves in an ordinary and
normal way. EG *They're the most conventional, dull
people... ...the conventional housewife.*
◇ **conventionally.** EG *...a more conventionally* ◇ ADV
acceptable life.

2 A **conventional** method or product has been ADJ CLASSIF :
used or produced for a long time in the same way. ATTRIB
EG *...the abolition of conventional examinations...
...conventional fuels.* ◇ **conventionally.** EG *...con-* ◇ ADV
ventionally educated students.

3 Conventional wars and weapons do not involve ADJ CLASSIF :
nuclear explosives. ATTRIB

converge /kə'vɜːdʒ/, **converges, converging,
converged. 1** When roads or lines **converge**, they V : USU+A
meet or join at a particular place. EG *The paths
converge under the trees.*

2 When people or vehicles **converge** on a place or V : OFT
a person, they move towards them from different +on/upon
directions. EG *The guards converged on her and
flung her to the ground.*

3 When different ideas, forces, or societies **con-** V
verge, they gradually become similar to each Formal
other. EG *Two radically different types of society
were converging through economic evolution.*
◇ **convergence** /kə'vɜːdʒəns/. EG *There was* ◇ N UNCOUNT
some convergence of views.

conversant /kə'vɜːsə⁰nt/. If you are **conver-** ADJ PRED
sant with something, you are familiar with it and +with
able to deal with it. EG *The designer must be* Formal
conversant with all the aspects of the problem.

conversation /kɒnvəseɪʃə⁰n/, **conversations. 1** N COUNT OR
If you have a **conversation** with someone, you N UNCOUNT
talk to them. EG *Roger and I had a conversation
about the risks... He spent some hours in conversation with me.*

2 If you have to **make conversation**, you have to PHRASE
talk to someone in order to be polite and not
because you really want to. EG *He didn't like having
to make conversation.*

conversational /kɒnvəseɪʃə⁰nəl, -ʃənə⁰l/ means ADJ CLASSIF :
used in conversation or in casual and informal talk. ATTRIB
EG *...their brilliant conversational powers.*
◇ **conversationally.** EG *'Tell me,' she said conver-* ◇ ADV
sationally, 'does he bite?'

converse, converses, conversing, conversed;
pronounced /kə'vɜːs/ when it is a verb and
/kɒnvɜːs/ when it is a noun or an adjective.

1 If you **converse** with someone, you talk to them. V OR V+with :
EG *I consider it a privilege to have conversed with* RECIP
you. Formal

2 The **converse** of a statement is its opposite or N SING : the+N
reverse. EG *If you can do it, a machine can, at least
in theory, also do it. The converse, however, is not
true.* ▸ used as an adjective. EG *Political power is* ▸ ADJ CLASSIF :
used to win economic power. But the converse ATTRIB
process is just as common. Formal

conversely /kə'vɜːsli¹/. You say **conversely** to ADV SEN
indicate that the statement you are about to make
is the opposite or reverse of the one you have just
made. EG *You can use beer yeast for bread-making.
Conversely, you can use bread yeast in beer-
making.*

conversion /kə'vɜːʃə⁰n/, **conversions. 1** A **con-** N COUNT OR
version is the act or process of changing some- N UNCOUNT
thing into a different state or form. EG *...the conversion of coal into oil and gas.*

2 Someone's **conversion** is the process of chang- N COUNT OR
ing their religious or political beliefs. EG *...his* N UNCOUNT :
recent conversion to Christianity. OFT+to/from

convert, converts, converting, converted; pronounced /kə'nvɜːt/ when it is a verb, and /kɒnvɜːt/
when it is a noun.

1 To **convert** something into something else V-ERG :
means to change it into a different form. EG *A solar* OFT+into/to
cell takes radiation from the sun and converts it
into electricity... ...prams that convert into pushchairs... ...the formula for converting kilometres to
miles.*

2 If someone **converts** a building, they alter it in V+O : OFT+
order to use it for a different purpose. EG *The house* into/to OR
has been converted into two apartments. to-INF
◇ **converted.** EG *The theatre is a converted squash* ◇ ADJ CLASSIF :
court. ATTRIB

3 If you **convert** a vehicle or a system, you change V+O :
it so that it can use a different fuel. EG *They would* OFT+to/from
convert the entire country to coal gas.*

4 If someone **converts** you, they persuade you to V+O :
change your religious or political beliefs. EG *Birch* OFT+to/from
became converted to communism.

5 A **convert** is someone who has changed their N COUNT
religious or political beliefs. EG *...a Catholic convert... ...new converts to Trotskyism.*

convertible /kə'vɜːtəbə⁰l/, **convertibles. 1** A N COUNT
convertible is a car with a soft roof that can be
folded down or removed. EG *The red convertible
was following us.*

2 Money that is **convertible** can be easily ex- ADJ CLASSIF
changed for other forms of money. EG *The loan is
freely convertible into dollars.*

convex /kɒnveks, kɒnveks/. Something that is ADJ QUALIT
convex curves outwards at its centre. EG *...a con-* Technical
vex lens.

convey /kə'nveɪ/, **conveys, conveying, con-
veyed. 1** To **convey** information or feelings means V+O : OFT+to
to cause them to be known or understood by OR V+REPORT
someone. *Newspapers convey the impression that
the war is over... ...trying to convey that it did not
really matter.*

2 To **convey** someone or something to a place V+O : USU+A
means to carry or transport them there. EG *...the* Formal
truck conveying Daniel and the work crew.

conveyance /kə'nveɪəns/, **conveyances.** A **con-** N COUNT
veyance is a vehicle. EG *The conveyance had* Outdated
drawn up at her door.

conveyor belt /kə'nveɪə belt/, **conveyor belts.** N COUNT
A **conveyor belt** is a continuously moving strip of
rubber or metal which is used in factories for
moving objects along. EG *Slabs of toffee pass along
a conveyor belt.*

convict, convicts, convicting, convicted; pronounced /kə'nvɪkt/ when it is a verb, and
/kɒnvɪkt/ when it is a noun.

1 To **convict** someone of a crime means to find V+O : OFT+of
them guilty of it in a court of law. EG *He was
convicted of spying.* ◇ **convicted.** EG *...convicted* ◇ ADJ CLASSIF
criminals.

2 A **convict** is someone who is in prison. EG *...an* N COUNT
escaped convict. Outdated

conviction /kə'nvɪkʃə⁰n/, **convictions. 1** A **con-** N COUNT :
viction is a strong belief or opinion. EG *...his* USU+REPORT
conviction that he could run a newspaper.

2 If you have **conviction**, you have great confi- N UNCOUNT
dence and certainty in your beliefs or opinions. EG
'Yes,' I said without much conviction.

3 A **conviction** is also the act of finding someone N COUNT OR
guilty in a court of law. EG *...the trial and conviction* N UNCOUNT
of Ward... ...his record of previous convictions.

convince /kə'nvɪns/, **convinces, convincing,
convinced.** If someone or something **convinces**
you, **1** they make you believe that something is V+O : OFT
true or necessary. EG *It took them a few days to* + REPORT OR
convince me that it was possible... This had con- of/about
vinced her of the problems. **2** they persuade you to V+O+to-INF
do something. EG *You can convince people to buy
almost anything.*

convinced /kə'nvɪnst/. If you are **convinced** of ADJ PRED :
something, you are sure that it is true or genuine. OFT+of/about
REPORT

EG *He was convinced that her mother was innocent... I am convinced of your loyalty.*

convincing /kəˈnvɪnsɪŋ/. 1 Something that is ADJ QUALIT **convincing** causes you to believe that it is true, correct, or genuine. EG *...a more convincing explanation.*

2 Someone who is **convincing** is able to make you ADJ QUALIT believe that something is true. EG *He was a convincing liar.* ◊ **convincingly.** EG *She must speak more* ◊ ADV *convincingly.*

convivial /kəˈnvɪvɪəl/. 1 A social event that is ADJ QUALIT **convivial** is enjoyable and friendly. EG *The meal* Formal *was not a convivial one.*

2 **Convivial** people are friendly and pleasant to be ADJ QUALIT with. EG *...a happy and convivial group.*

convoluted /kɒnvəluːtɪˀd/. A **convoluted** sen- ADJ QUALIT tence or idea is complicated and difficult to under- Formal stand.

convoy /kɒnvɔɪ/, **convoys.** A **convoy** is a group N COUNT of vehicles or ships travelling together. EG *...a convoy of police cars.* ● If a group of vehicles or ● PHRASE ships are travelling **in convoy**, they are all travelling somewhere together. EG *...eight trucks moving in convoy.*

convulse /kəˈnvʌls/, **convulses, convulsing,** V-ERG **convulsed.** If someone **convulses** or if something Formal **convulses** them, their body moves suddenly in an uncontrolled way. EG *He convulsed in pain... A quiver convulsed his body.*

convulsion /kəˈnvʌlʃəˀn/, **convulsions.** If some- N COUNT OR one has a **convulsion** or **convulsions**, they suffer N UNCOUNT uncontrollable movements of their muscles. EG *Another convulsion shook him... Convulsions are rare after the first day of fever.*

convulsive /kəˈnvʌlsɪv/. A **convulsive** move- ADJ CLASSIF ment or action is sudden and cannot be controlled. EG *I gave his hand a sudden convulsive squeeze.* ◊ **convulsively.** EG *He shivered convulsively.* ◊ ADV

coo /kuː/, **coos, cooing, cooed.** 1 When a dove or v pigeon **coos**, it makes the soft sound that doves and pigeons typically make.

2 When someone **coos**, they speak in a very soft, V OR V+QUOTE quiet voice. EG *'Tell me all about it,' she cooed.*

cook /kʊk/, **cooks, cooking, cooked.** 1 When you V-ERG, V, **cook** food, you prepare it for eating and then heat V+O+O, it, for example in an oven or in a saucepan. EG *We* V+O+for, OR *cooked the pie in the oven... I could smell vegeta-* V+for *bles cooking in the kitchen... Mildred cooks remarkably well... Cook us a bit of supper... I cook for myself.*

2 A **cook** is a person who prepares and cooks food, N COUNT often as a job. EG *Are you a good cook?... Margaret employed a cook.*

3 See also **cooking.**

cook up. If someone **cooks up** a dishonest PHRASAL VB : scheme, they plan it. EG *They cook up all sorts of* V+O+ADV *little deals.* Informal

cooker /kʊkə/, **cookers.** A **cooker** is a large N COUNT metal box-shaped device for cooking food in the kitchen using gas or electricity. EG *The milk was warming in a saucepan on the cooker.*

cookery /kʊkəˀriː/ is the activity of preparing and N UNCOUNT cooking food. EG *...cookery demonstrations.*

cookie /kʊkiː/, **cookies.** A **cookie** is the same as a N COUNT biscuit. EG *...homemade oatmeal cookies.* American

cooking /kʊkɪŋ/ is 1 the activity of preparing and N UNCOUNT cooking food. EG *My mother was fond of cooking.* 2 N UNCOUNT cooked food. EG *She loves your cooking.* +SUPP

cool /kuːl/, **cooler, coolest; cools, cooling,** **cooled.** 1 Something that is **cool** has a tempera- ADJ QUALIT ture which is low but not cold. EG *The air was cool and fresh... ...a cool drink.* ◊ **coolness.** EG *...the* ◊ N UNCOUNT *coolness of the room.*

2 Clothing that is **cool** is made of thin material. EG ADJ QUALIT *I'll just change into a cooler frock.*

3 When something **cools** or when you **cool** it, it V-ERG becomes lower in temperature. EG *The water began to cool... Cool your feet in the stream.*

4 If someone's behaviour is **cool**, it is 4.1 calm and ADJ QUALIT

unemotional. EG *Keep cool and reasonable when complaining.* ◊ **coolly.** EG *He drove coolly and* ◊ ADV carefully. ◊ **coolness.** EG *I admired the coolness* ◊ N UNCOUNT *with which he dealt with a crisis.* **4.2** unfriendly or ADJ QUALIT unenthusiastic. EG *Should she be cool and withdrawn, or warm and welcoming?* ◊ **coolly.** EG *'I'm* ◊ ADV *not asking you,'* she informed him coolly. ◊ **coolness.** EG *Hagen was hurt by my coolness.* ◊ N UNCOUNT

5 When anger **cools**, it becomes less powerful. EG V-ERG *Their tempers had cooled.*

6 If you **play it cool**, you deliberately behave in a PHRASE calm and unemotional way. EG *They agreed to play* Informal *it cool if they saw the boys again.*

7 If you **keep** your **cool**, you control your temper PHRASE and remain calm. If you **lose** your **cool**, you Informal become angry or excited. EG *He struggled to keep his cool.*

cool down. 1 If something **cools down** or if you PHRASAL VB : **cool** it **down**, it becomes cooler and reaches the V-ERG+ADV temperature that you want it to be at. EG *The engine will take half an hour to cool down.*

2 If someone **cools down** or if you **cool** them V-ERG+ADV **down**, they become less angry. EG *I had great difficulty in cooling him down.*

cool off. If someone or something **cools off**, they PHRASAL VB : become cooler after having been hot. EG *We cooled* V-ERG+ADV *off with a refreshing swim.*

co-op /kəʊɒp/, **co-ops.** A **co-op** is a co-operative. N COUNT EG *I'm in the food co-op... ...a co-op house.* Informal

cooped up /kuːpt ʌp/. If someone is **cooped up** in ADJ PRED a place, they are kept in a place which is too small or which does not give them much freedom. EG *I hate being cooped up in the flat every day.*

co-operate /kəʊɒpəreɪt/, **co-operates, co- operating, co-operated. 1** If people **co-operate**, V OR V+with : they work or act together for a purpose. EG *The* RECIP *workers cooperated with the management and the police.* ◊ **co-operation** /kəʊɒpəreɪʃəˀn/. EG *...co-* ◊ N UNCOUNT *operation between staff and parents.*

2 If you **co-operate**, you do what someone asks v you to do. EG *You're not co-operating!* ◊ **co-** ◊ N UNCOUNT **operation.** EG *Thank you for your co-operation.*

co-operative /kəʊɒpəˀrətɪv/, **co-operatives. 1** A N COUNT **co-operative** is a business or organization run by the people who work for it, who share its benefits and profits. EG *...a food co-operative.*

2 A **co-operative** activity is done by people work- ADJ CLASSIF ing together. EG *...cooperative forms of ownership.* ◊ **co-operatively.** EG *The work is carried on co-* ◊ ADV *operatively.*

3 Someone who is **co-operative** does what you ask ADJ QUALIT them to. EG *Her children are considerate and co- operative.* ◊ **co-operatively.** EG *She pushed me,* ◊ ADV *and I rolled over cooperatively.*

co-opt /kəʊɒpt/, **co-opts, co-opting, co-opted.** If v+o the people in an official group **co-opt** you, they Formal make you a member of their group. EG *Committees can always co-opt members.*

co-ordinate, co-ordinates, co-ordinating, co- ordinated; pronounced /kəʊɔːdɪneɪt/ when it is a verb, and /kəʊɔːdɪnət/ when it is a noun.

1 If you **co-ordinate** an activity, you organize the v+o people and things involved in it. EG *They were asked to coordinate the election campaign.* ◊ **co-** ◊ ADJ QUALIT **ordinated.** EG *...an effective and co-ordinated attack.* ◊ **co-ordination** /kəʊɔːdɪneɪʃəˀn/. EG *...the* ◊ N UNCOUNT *co-ordination of public transport.* ◊ **co-ordinator** ◊ N COUNT : /kəʊɔːdɪneɪtə/, **co-ordinators.** EG *...the co-* USU+SUPP *ordinator of a project in Cornwall.*

2 If you **co-ordinate** the parts of your body, you v+o make them work together efficiently to perform particular movements. EG *The children could not*

If you cook up something with the cops and then
play it cool, what kind of language are you using?

co-ordinate their movements. ◊ **co-ordination.** EG ◊ N UNCOUNT
His arms moved in perfect co-ordination.

3 The **co-ordinates** of a point on a map or graph N COUNT :
are the two sets of numbers or letters that you USU PLURAL
need in order to find it. Technical

cop /kɒp/, **cops, copping, copped.** A cop is a N COUNT
policeman or policewoman. Informal

cop out. If someone **cops out,** they do not do PHRASAL VB :
what they should do; used showing disapproval. EG I V+ADV
simply and shamefully copped out. ● See also **cop-** Informal
out.

cope /kəʊp/, **copes, coping, coped. 1** If you **cope** V : USU+with
with a problem or task, you deal with it successful-
ly. EG John and Sally coped with all their problems
cheerfully... ...a computer capable of coping with
domestic requirements.

2 If you have to **cope** with an unpleasant situation, V : USU+with
you have to accept it or endure it. EG Poor families
have to cope with a lot of strain.

co-pilot, co-pilots. The **co-pilot** of an aeroplane N COUNT
is a pilot who assists the chief pilot.

copious /kəʊpɪəs/. Something that is **copious** ADJ QUALIT
exists or happens in large amounts or quantities. EG
Plants need copious sunshine... She made copious
notes. ◊ **copiously.** EG He cried copiously. ◊ ADV

cop-out, cop-outs. If you say that something is a N COUNT
cop-out, you think that someone is not doing what Informal
they should do. EG Such international co-operation
is often merely a cop-out.

copper /kɒpə/, **coppers. 1** Copper is a soft, N UNCOUNT
reddish brown metal. EG ...a copper mine... ...copper
wire.

2 A **copper** is a policeman or policewoman. EG N COUNT
Wait here till the coppers turn up. Informal

3 A **copper** is also a brown metal coin of low value. N COUNT
EG It only cost a few coppers. Informal

copse /kɒps/, **copses.** A copse is a small group of N COUNT
trees growing very close to each other. EG ...pretty
meadows and copses.

copulate /kɒpjʊˈleɪt/, **copulates, copulating,** V OR V+with :
copulated. When animals **copulate,** they have RECIP
sex. ◊ **copulation** /kɒpjʊˈleɪʃəⁿn/. EG ...the act of ◊ N UNCOUNT
copulation. Formal

copy /kɒpiⁱ/, **copies, copying, copied. 1** A **copy** N COUNT
is something that is made to look exactly the same
as something else. EG I will send you a copy of the
letter.

2 If you **copy** something that someone has written V+O
or said, you write it down exactly. EG ...a comment
she had copied from his notes.

3 If you **copy** a person or their ideas, you try to V+O
behave like them because you admire them. EG Our
scheme has been copied by other universities.

4 A **copy** of a book, newspaper, or record is one of N COUNT
the many identical ones that have been printed or
produced. EG Sixty thousand copies of the record
were sold.

copy down. If you **copy down** what someone PHRASAL VB :
has written or said, you write it down exactly. EG I V+O+ADV
shouldn't bother to copy these figures down.

copy out. If you **copy out** a piece of writing, you PHRASAL VB :
write it all down exactly. EG I remember copying V+O+ADV
out the whole play.

copyright /kɒpiⁱraɪt/, **copyrights.** The **copy-** N COUNT OR
right on a piece of writing or music is the legal N UNCOUNT
right of the writer or publisher to be asked for
permission and paid before anyone else can reproduce it or perform it. EG Who holds the copyright of
the song?

coral /kɒrəⁿl/, **corals. 1** Coral is a hard substance N UNCOUNT
formed from the skeletons of very small sea ani-
mals. It is often used to make jewellery. EG ...a coral
necklace.

2 A **coral** is a very small sea animal. EG ...primitive N COUNT
creatures like jellyfish and corals.

cord /kɔːd/, **cords. 1** Cord is **1.1** strong, thick N COUNT OR
string. EG She tied a cord around her box... ...a piece N UNCOUNT
of cord. **1.2** wire covered in rubber or plastic N COUNT
which connects electrical equipment to an electric-

ity supply. EG ...a small electric heater on a long
cord.

2 Cords are trousers made of corduroy. EG ...a pair N PLURAL
of grey cords.

cordial /kɔːdɪəl/, **cordials 1** Someone who is ADJ QUALIT
cordial is warm and friendly. EG Relations between Formal
the two men were far from cordial. ◊ **cordially.** ◊ ADV
EG She shook hands cordially with Charley.
◊ **cordiality** /kɔːdɪˈælɪˈtiⁱ/. EG They greeted me ◊ N UNCOUNT
with genuine cordiality.

2 Cordial is a sweet drink made from fruit juice. EG N MASS
...lime juice cordial.

cordon /kɔːdəⁿn/, **cordons, cordoning, cor-** N COUNT
doned. A **cordon** is a line or ring of police,
soldiers, or vehicles preventing people from entering or leaving an area. EG The crowd attempted to
break through the police cordons.

cordon off. If police or soldiers **cordon off** an PHRASAL VB :
area, they prevent people from entering or leaving V+O+ADV
it, usually by forming a line or ring. EG The area
surrounding the office had been cordoned off.

corduroy /kɔːdəˈrɔɪ, kɔːdəⁿrɔɪ/ is thick cotton N UNCOUNT
cloth with parallel raised lines on the outside. EG ...a
corduroy jacket.

core /kɔː/, **cores. 1** The **core** of a fruit is its hard N COUNT
central part which contains seeds or pips. EG ...the
core of an apple.

2 The **core** of an object, building, or city is its N COUNT :
central part. EG The planet probably has a molten USU+SUPP
core.

3 A **core** of people in an organization or system is N SING
an important group within it. EG ...a student body
led by a core of academics.

4 The **core** of a situation or problem is its most N SING :
important part. EG ...the core of industry's prob- USU+SUPP
lems. Formal

cork /kɔːk/, **corks. 1** Cork is a soft, light substance N UNCOUNT
which forms the bark of a type of Mediterranean
tree. It floats on water and is not easily damaged
by heat or liquids. EG ...cork table mats... ...a floor
covering such as cork.

2 A **cork** is a piece of cork or plastic that is pushed N COUNT
into the end of a bottle to close it. EG He removed
the cork from the wine bottle.

corkscrew

corkscrew /kɔːkskruː/, **corkscrews.** A **cork-** N COUNT
screw is a device for pulling corks out of bottles.

corn /kɔːn/, **corns. 1** Corn is used to refer to crops N UNCOUNT
such as wheat and barley, or the seeds from these British
plants. EG ...a field of corn... ...sacks of corn.

2 Corn is also the same as maize. EG ...corn bread. N UNCOUNT

3 A **corn** is a small, painful area of hard skin which N COUNT
can form on your foot, especially near your toes.

corned beef is beef which has been cooked and N UNCOUNT
preserved in salt water.

corner /kɔːnə/, **corners, cornering, cornered. 1** N COUNT :
A **corner** of something is a point or an area where OFT+SUPP
two or more of its edges, sides, or surfaces join. EG
He signed his name on the lower right-hand corner
of the drawing... There was a television set in the
corner of the room... Out of the corner of my eye I
caught a glimpse of two men in uniform.

2 A **corner** is also **2.1** a place where two streets N COUNT
join. EG There's a telephone box on the corner. **2.2** a

sharp bend in a road. EG *The lorry took the corner too fast.*

3 Places that are far away or difficult to get to are sometimes referred to as the **corners** of the world or of a country. EG *You have carried Britain's fame to the remotest corners of the earth.* N COUNT : USU PLURAL Literary

4 If you are in a **corner**, you are in a situation that is difficult to escape from or to deal with. EG *Laing talked himself into a corner.* N COUNT : USU a+N Informal

5 If you **corner** a person or animal, you get them into a place or situation which they cannot escape from. EG *The police pursued and cornered the wrong car.* ◊ **cornered.** EG *She had me cornered between the front porch and her car.* V+O ◊ ADJ CLASSIF

6 If you **corner** a market or some other area of activity, you gain control over it so that no one else can have any success in that area. EG *He had a crazy scheme to corner the champagne market.* V+O

7 If you **cut corners**, you do something quickly by doing it in a less thorough way than you should. PHRASE

cornerstone /kɔːnəstəun/, **cornerstones.** The **cornerstone** of something is the basic part which its existence, success, or truth depends on. EG *Mathematics is the cornerstone of scientific certainty... The trade union movement was the cornerstone of Labour's economic strategy.* N COUNT : USU+of Formal

cornet /kɔːnɪt/, **cornets. 1** A **cornet** is a small trumpet. N COUNT

2 An ice cream **cornet** is a soft thin biscuit shaped like a cone with ice cream in it. N COUNT

cornflakes /kɔːnfleɪks/ are a breakfast cereal made from maize. N PLURAL

cornflour /kɔːnflauə/ is a fine white flour made from maize. N UNCOUNT

cornucopia /kɔːnjukəupɪə/. A **cornucopia** of good things is a large number of them. N PART : SING Formal

corny /kɔːni/, **cornier, corniest.** Something that is **corny** is very obvious or sentimental and not at all subtle or original. EG *Ben loves corny old jokes.* ADJ QUALIT

corollary /kərɒləri/, **corollaries.** A **corollary** of something is an idea, argument, or fact which is the direct result of it. EG *This change is the inevitable corollary of the social revolution I have just described.* N COUNT : OFT+of/to Formal

coronary /kɒrənəri/, **coronaries.** If someone has a **coronary**, the flow of blood to their heart is blocked by a large blood clot and they suffer a lot of pain. EG *He died of a massive coronary.* N COUNT

coronation /kɒrəneɪʃən/, **coronations.** A **coronation** is the ceremony at which a king or queen is crowned. EG *...the coronation of Queen Elizabeth.* N COUNT

coroner /kɒrənə/, **coroners.** A **coroner** is an official who is responsible for investigating the deaths of people who have died in a sudden, violent, or unusual way. N COUNT

coronet /kɒrənɪt/, **coronets.** A **coronet** is a small crown. N COUNT

corporal /kɔːpərəl/, **corporals.** A **corporal** is an officer of low rank in the army. N COUNT

corporal punishment is the punishment of people by beating them. N UNCOUNT

corporate /kɔːpərət/ means owned or shared by all the members of a group or organization. EG *...a corporate identity.* ADJ CLASSIF : ATTRIB

corporation /kɔːpəreɪʃən/, **corporations.** A **corporation** is **1** a large business or company. **2** an organization that is responsible for running a particular town or city. EG *A petition was sent from the mayor and corporation.* N COUNT British

corps /kɔː/. **Corps** is both the singular and the plural.

A **corps** is **1** a part of the army which has special duties. EG *...the Royal Army Ordnance Corps.* **2** a small group of people who do a special job. EG *...the diplomatic corps.* N COUNT N COUNT+SUPP

corpse /kɔːps/, **corpses.** A **corpse** is a dead body, especially the body of a human being. N COUNT

corpulent /kɔːpjələnt/. Someone who is **corpulent** is fat. EG *...his corpulent figure.* ADJ QUALIT Formal

corpuscle /kɔːpʌsəl/, **corpuscles.** A **corpuscle** is a red or white blood cell. N COUNT

correct /kərekt/, **corrects, correcting, corrected. 1** Something that is **correct** is accurate and has no mistakes. EG *That's the correct answer.* ◊ **correctly.** EG *I hope I pronounced his name correctly.* ◊ **correctness.** EG *This confirmed the correctness of my decision.* ADJ CLASSIF ◊ ADV ◊ N UNCOUNT

2 If you are **correct**, what you have said or thought is true. EG *Jenkins is correct. We've got to change our strategy.* ADJ PRED

3 The **correct** thing is the thing that is required or is most suitable in a particular situation. EG *Make sure you ask for the correct fuse.* ◊ **correctly.** EG *Rice, correctly cooked and prepared, is delicious.* ADJ CLASSIF : ATTRIB ◊ ADV

4 If you **correct** a mistake, problem, or fault, you do something which puts it right. EG *I wish to correct a false impression which may have been created... They are studying ways of correcting the imbalance between the rich and poor countries.* V+O

5 If you **correct** someone, you say something which you think is more accurate or appropriate than what they have just said. EG *I suspect – though correct me if I'm wrong – that this is their view too... 'I'm a fighter like your dad is – or was,' Mr Cupples corrected himself.* V+O OR V-REFL OFT+QUOTE; ALSO V+QUOTE

6 When someone **corrects** a piece of writing, they look at it and mark the mistakes in it. EG *Miss Lennox was seated at her desk correcting papers.* V+O

7 Correct behaviour is considered to be morally or socially acceptable. EG *Charter's dealings with him have been wholly correct.* ◊ **correctly.** EG *We tried to behave correctly.* ◊ **correctness.** EG *Such a person should be treated with polite correctness.* ADJ QUALIT ◊ ADV ◊ N UNCOUNT

correction /kərekʃən/, **corrections. 1** A **correction** is something which puts right something that has been wrongly done, said, written, or believed. EG *We'll make the necessary corrections... A couple of mistakes need correction.* N COUNT OR N UNCOUNT

2 Correction is the changing of something so that it is no longer faulty or unsatisfactory. EG *Deaf children need speech correction.* N UNCOUNT OR N COUNT

corrective /kərektɪv/, **correctives. Corrective** measures or techniques are intended to put right something that is wrong. EG *...corrective surgery.* ADJ CLASSIF : USU ATTRIB

▶ used as a noun. EG *This analysis provides an important corrective to the traditional view.* ▶ N COUNT : OFT+to

correlate /kɒrəleɪt/, **correlates, correlating, correlated.** If two things **correlate** or if they are **correlated**, they always exist or happen together. EG *In Britain, class and region are strongly correlated.* ◊ **correlation** /kɒrəleɪʃən/, **correlations.** EG *There's no correlation between mental ability and physical strength.* V-ERG; ALSO V OR V+with : RECIP ◊ N UNCOUNT OR N COUNT

correspond /kɒrɪspɒnd/, **corresponds, corresponding, corresponded. 1** If one thing **corresponds** with or to another thing, it is similar to it. EG *His job in Moscow corresponds to your father's position here... ...a professional qualification corresponding to a first degree.* V OR V+with/to : RECIP

2 If two numbers or amounts **correspond**, they are the same. EG *The date of her birth corresponded with the date of her father's affair in Paris.* V OR V+with/to : RECIP

3 If two people **correspond**, they write letters to each other. EG *I've been corresponding with Tim Johns... Elizabeth and I corresponded regularly.* V OR V+with : RECIP

4 See also **corresponding.**

correspondence /kɒrɪspɒndəns/, **correspondences. 1** Correspondence is **1.1** the act of writing letters to someone. EG *The judges' decision is final and no correspondence will be entered into.* **1.2** the letters that someone receives. EG *The letter had been among his correspondence that morning.* N UNCOUNT OFT+with N UNCOUNT

2 If there is a **correspondence** between two things, there is a close relationship or similarity N UNCOUNT OR N COUNT

How valuable is costume jewellery?

between them. EG *In African languages there is a close correspondence between sounds and letters.*

correspondent /kɒrɪspɒndənt/, **correspond-** N COUNT : **ents.** A **correspondent** is a newspaper reporter USU+SUPP or television reporter. EG *...the Economics correspondent of the Guardian.*

corresponding /kɒrɪspɒndɪŋ/. You use **corre-** **sponding** 1 to describe a change which is the ADJ CLASSIF : result of a change in something else. EG *Any* ATTRIB *increase in complexity brings with it a correspond-* Formal *ing probability of error.* ◇ **correspondingly.** EG ◇ ADV SEN *The new edition is bigger and correspondingly more expensive.* 2 to describe something which is ADJ CLASSIF : similar to something else. EG *In France they study* ATTRIB *to the same standard and take the corresponding examinations.*

corridor /kɒrɪdɔː/, **corridors.** A **corridor** is a N COUNT long passage in a building or train, with doors and rooms on one or both sides.

corroborate /kərɒbəreɪt/, **corroborates, cor-** V+O **roborating, corroborated.** If someone or some- Formal thing **corroborates** an idea, account, or argument, they provide evidence or information that supports it. EG *Abrams and Rose corroborated this view in their influential study of the subject.* ◇ **corroboration** /kərɒbəreɪʃəᵒn/. EG *Evangelina's* ◇ N UNCOUNT *story was later published without corroboration.*

corrode /kərəʊd/, **corrodes, corroding, corrod-** V-ERG **ed.** When metal **corrodes,** it is gradually destroyed by a chemical or by rust. EG *Vinegar will corrode metal.* ◇ **corroded.** EG *The generator was badly* ◇ ADJ QUALIT *corroded.*

corrosion /kərəʊʒəᵒn/ is the damage that is N UNCOUNT caused when something is corroded. EG *Check that the terminals of the battery are free from dirt and corrosion.*

corrosive /kərəʊsɪv/. 1 A substance that is **corro-** ADJ QUALIT **sive** is able to destroy solid materials by a chemical reaction. EG *...a corrosive poison.*

2 Something that is **corrosive** has a harmful effect ADJ QUALIT over a period of time. EG *...the corrosive effects of* Literary *inflation.*

corrugated /kɒrəˈgeɪtɪd/. **Corrugated** metal or ADJ CLASSIF : cardboard has been folded into a series of small ATTRIB parallel folds to make it stronger. EG *...a corrugated iron roof.*

corrupt /kərʌpt/, **corrupts, corrupting, cor-** **rupted.** 1 Someone who is **corrupt** behaves in a ADJ QUALIT way that is morally wrong, especially by doing dishonest or illegal things in return for money or power. EG *...corrupt politicians... ...corrupt practices.*

2 To **corrupt** someone means 2.1 to cause them to V+O OR V become dishonest and unjust. EG *Power and wealth corrupted him... Young people in prison are corrupted by hardened criminals.* 2.2 to stop them from caring about moral standards. EG *I doubt that any film ever corrupted anyone.*

corruption /kərʌpʃəᵒn/. 1 **Corruption** is dishon- N UNCOUNT esty and illegal behaviour by people in positions of authority or power. EG *...police corruption.*

2 The **corruption** of someone is the process of N UNCOUNT making them behave in a way that is considered morally wrong. EG *His whole life seemed dedicated to the corruption of the young.*

corset /kɔːsɪt/, **corsets.** A **corset** is a stiff piece N COUNT of underwear worn by some women. It fits tightly around their hips and waist and makes them appear slimmer.

cos /kəz/ is a very informal way of saying 'be- CONJ cause'. EG *You'd better make a note of that, cos I* Spoken *haven't.*

cosmetic /kɒzmɛtɪk/, **cosmetics.** 1 **Cosmetics** N COUNT : are substances such as lipstick or powder, which USU PLURAL people put on their face to make themselves look more attractive.

2 **Cosmetic** measures or changes improve the ADJ CLASSIF appearance of something but do not change its

basic character. EG *It was a purely cosmetic measure.*

cosmetic surgery is surgery which is done to N UNCOUNT people in order to make them look more attractive.

cosmic /kɒzmɪk/ means belonging or relating to ADJ CLASSIF : the universe. EG *The other great cosmic reality is* ATTRIB *time.* Formal

cosmonaut /kɒzməˈnɔːt/, **cosmonauts.** A **cos-** N COUNT **monaut** is a Soviet astronaut.

cosmopolitan /kɒzməˈpɒlɪtəᵒn/. Something that ADJ QUALIT is **cosmopolitan** has been influenced by many different countries and cultures. EG *It remains a cosmopolitan street... ...his cosmopolitan wife.*

cosmos /kɒzmɒs/. You can refer to the universe N SING : the+N as the **cosmos.** EG *...the creation of the cosmos.*

cosset /kɒsɪt/, **cossets, cosseting, cosseted.** If V+O you **cosset** someone, you do everything possible for them and protect them from anything unpleasant. EG *We all yearn to be cosseted.*

cost /kɒst/, **costs, costing.** The form **cost** is used in the present tense and is the past tense and past participle of the verb.

1 The **cost** of something is the amount of money N COUNT that is needed in order to buy, do, or make it. EG *The total cost of the holiday was £300... The building was restored at a cost of £500,000... ...the huge increases in fuel costs.*

2 You use **cost** to talk about the amount of money V+O OR that you have to pay for things. For example, if V+O+O something **costs** £5, you have to pay £5 for it. EG *Those books cost £2.95 each... A two-day stay there cost me $125... A freezer doesn't cost much to run.*

3 The **cost** of something is also the loss, damage, N SING or injury that is involved in trying to achieve it. EG *The cost in human life had been enormous.*

4 If an event or mistake **costs** you something, you V+O+O lose that thing as the result of it. EG *A single error* OR V+O *here could cost you your life.*

5 If you say that something must be done **at all** PHRASE **costs,** you mean that it must definitely be done, even if it requires a lot of effort or money. EG *This right must be protected at all costs.*

co-star, co-stars, co-starring, co-starred. 1 An V OR V+with : actor or actress who **co-stars** in a film has one of RECIP the most important parts in it. EG *...Jackson Florentine, who co-starred in Gold-Diggers of 1984.*

2 An actor or actress who is a **co-star** of a film has N COUNT+SUPP one of the most important parts in it. EG *...a photograph of her with her co-star, Gerard Depardieu.*

cost-effective. Something that is **cost-effective** ADJ QUALIT saves or makes a lot of money in comparison with the costs involved. EG *We urgently need more cost-effective methods of production.*

costly /kɒstliᵈ/, **costlier, costliest.** Something ADJ QUALIT that is **costly** 1 is very expensive. EG *It proved a costly mistake.* 2 uses up a lot of time or effort. EG *That route will be too costly in time.*

cost of living. The **cost of living** is the average N SING : the+N amount of money that each person in a country needs to spend on food, housing, and clothing. EG *In Britain today the cost of living is still rising rapidly.*

costume /kɒstjuːm/, **costumes.** 1 A **costume** is a N COUNT set of clothes worn by an actor. EG *...theatrical costumes.*

2 The clothes worn by people at a particular time N UNCOUNT in history or in a particular country are referred to as a particular type of **costume.** EG *...17th-century costume.*

costume jewellery is jewellery made from N UNCOUNT cheap materials.

cosy /kəʊziᵈ/, **cosier, cosiest; cosies;** spelled **cozy** in American English.

1 A house or room that is **cosy** is comfortable and ADJ QUALIT warm. EG *They were beginning to miss the cosy flat in St John's Wood.*

2 If you are **cosy,** you are comfortable and warm. ADJ QUALIT EG *A hot water bottle will make you feel cosier.*

◊ **cosily.** EG *We were all sitting cosily in the* ◊ ADV
recreation room.

3 You use **cosy** to describe activities that are ADJ QUALIT
pleasant and friendly. EG *I had a cosy chat with
him... We had quite a few cosy evenings together.*
◊ **cosily.** EG *We spent the afternoon cosily gossip-* ◊ ADV
ing.

4 A **cosy** is a soft cover which you put over a N COUNT+SUPP
teapot to keep it warm. EG *...tea cosies.*

cot /kɒt/, **cots.** A **cot** is **1** a bed for a baby, with N COUNT
bars or panels round it so that the baby cannot fall British
out. **2** a small, narrow bed. American

cottage /kɒtɪdʒ/, **cottages.** A **cottage** is a small N COUNT
house in the country.

cottage cheese is soft white lumpy cheese made N UNCOUNT
from sour milk.

cotton /kɒtəⁿn/, **cottons, cottoning, cottoned. 1**
Cotton is **1.1** a natural cloth made from the soft N MASS
fibres that are produced by the cotton plant. EG *...a
cotton dress.* **1.2** a tall plant that is used to produce N UNCOUNT
this cloth. EG *...cotton fields.*

2 Cotton is also thread that is used for sewing. EG N MASS
...reels of cotton. British

cotton on. If you **cotton on** to something, you PHRASAL VB :
understand it or realize it, especially without peo- V+ADV,
ple telling you about it. EG *At long last he has* OFT+to
cottoned on to the fact that I don't want him!. Informal

cotton wool is soft, fluffy cotton, used especially N UNCOUNT
for applying liquids or creams to your skin.

couch /kautʃ/, **couches, couching, couched. 1** A N COUNT
couch is **1.1** a long piece of furniture which more
than one person can sit on. **1.2** a bed in a doctor's
consulting room, which patients lie on while they
are being examined or treated.

2 If you **couch** a statement in a particular style of V+O :
language, you express it in that style of language. USU PASS+in
EG *Here was a resolution couched in forthright* Formal
terms.

cough /kɒf/, **coughs, coughing, coughed. 1** V
When you **cough**, you force air out of your throat
with a sudden, harsh noise, often because you are
not well. EG *Mr Willet coughed nervously.* ▸ used as ▸ N COUNT
a noun. EG *There was a muffled cough outside the
study door.* ◊ **coughing.** EG *They suffered abdomi-* ◊ N UNCOUNT
nal pains and intense coughing.

2 If you **cough** blood or phlegm, you force it out of V+O
your throat with a sudden, harsh noise. EG *He
started coughing blood.*

3 A **cough** is also an illness in which you cough N COUNT
often and your chest or throat hurts. EG *I had a
terrible cough every winter.*

cough up. 1 If you **cough up** money, you give PHRASAL VB :
someone money. EG *They'll cough up the hundred* V+ADV OR
million... How can he persuade the authorities to V+O+ADV
cough up for the private education of his children? Informal

2 If you **cough up** blood or phlegm, you force it out V+O+ADV
of your throat with a sudden, harsh noise. EG *She
coughed up some phlegm.*

could /kud, kəd/. **Could** is sometimes considered
to be the past form of **can**, but in this dictionary
the two words are dealt with separately. See **can.**

1 If you **could** do something, you were able to do it. MODAL
EG *They complained that they couldn't sleep...
When I was young you could buy a packet for two
shillings... We just could not understand why he'd
failed.*

2 You use **could** in indirect speech to indicate that MODAL
someone has given permission for something or
that something is possible. EG *She said I could go... I
asked if we could somehow get a car.*

3 If you say that something **could** happen, **3.1** you MODAL
mean that it is possible that it will happen. EG *The
river could easily overflow, couldn't it?... It could
be disastrous.* **3.2** you mean that it is possible to do.
EG *We could do a great deal more in this country to
educate people.*

4 If you say that something **could** have happened, MODAL
you mean that it was possible although it did not

actually happen. EG *You were lucky. It could have
been awful.*

5 If you say that something **could** be the case, you MODAL
mean that it is possibly the case. If you say that
something **could** have been the case, you mean
that it was possibly the case. EG *It could be a
symbol, couldn't it?... It couldn't possibly be poison... It could have been an axe... He didn't carry a
dinghy, so he couldn't have rowed away.*

6 If you say that someone **could** do something, you MODAL
mean that it is possible for them to do it and that it
might be a good thing to do. EG *You could phone
her... Couldn't you just build more factories?... I
could ask her, I suppose.*

7 If you say that you **could** do something, you MODAL
mean that you would like to do it. If you say that
you **could** have done something, you mean that
you would have liked to do it. EG *I could kill you... I
could have screamed... I could have easily spent
the whole year on it.*

8 If you ask someone if they or you **could** do MODAL
something, you are politely asking them if they will
do it or allow it. EG *Could you just switch the
projector on behind you?... Could we put this fire
on?... Could I speak to Sue, please?*

9 If you say to someone that they **could** do MODAL
something, you mean that they ought to do it, and
you are angry with them because they have not. If
you say that they **could** have done something, you
mean that they should have done it, and you are
angry with them because they did not. EG *You could
at least apologize... You could have told me!*

10 You use **could** after 'if' when you are imagining MODAL
a situation or action, in order to consider what the
likely consequences might be. EG *If one could
measure this sort of thing, one might understand it
better.*

11 If you say that you **could not** do something, you MODAL+not
mean that you find it unacceptable or unreason-
able. EG *I couldn't let you do it on your own.*

couldn't /kudəⁿnt/ is the usual spoken form of
'could not'.

could've /kudəⁿv/ is the usual spoken form of
'could have', especially when 'have' is an auxiliary
verb.

council /kaunsəⁿl/, **councils. 1** A **council** is **1.1** a N COLL
group of people who are elected to run a town, British
borough, city, or county. EG *...Wiltshire County
Council... ...council meetings.* **1.2** a group of people
who give advice about a particular subject or who
run a particular organization. EG *...the Arts Council.*

2 A **council** house or flat is owned by the local ADJ CLASSIF :
council. You pay rent to live in it. EG *...council* ATTRIB
estates... ...a council tenant.

3 A **council** is also a specially organized meeting. N COUNT
EG *That afternoon a council of ministers and generals was held at No. 10.*

councillor /kaunsəⁿlə/, **councillors.** A **council-** N COUNT
lor is a member of a local council.

counsel /kaunsəl/, **counsels, counselling, counselled;** spelled **counseling** and **counseled** in
American English.

1 Counsel is serious or careful advice. EG *His voice* N UNCOUNT
had been heard before, giving counsel in times of Formal
stress.

2 If you **counsel** someone to do something, you V+O : OFT
advise them to do it. EG *'Ignore them,' Mrs Jones* + to-INF OR V
counselled... Some wanted to fight. Others coun- + QUOTE
selled caution. Formal

3 If you **counsel** people, you give them advice V+O
about their problems. EG *Part of her work is to
counsel families when problems arise.*
◊ **counselling.** EG *...psychiatric counselling.* ◊ N UNCOUNT

4 A **counsel** is a lawyer who gives advice on a N COUNT OR
legal case and fights the case in court. EG *...counsel* N UNCOUNT

Who is a count married to?

for the defence... You should take the advice of counsel.

counsellor /ˈkaʊnsələ⁰/, **counsellors**; spelled   N COUNT **counselor** in American English. A **counsellor** is a person whose job is to give advice to people who need it. EG *The hospital has trained counsellors who are used to dealing with depressed patients.*

count /kaʊnt/, **counts, counting, counted. 1**   V : OFT When you **count**, you say all the numbers one after   +*to/up to* another up to a particular number. EG *I'm going to*   OR V+O *count up to three... After counting sixty the rest set off in pursuit.*

2 If you **count** all the things in a group, you add   V+O them up in order to find how many there are. EG *He withdrew to his office to count the money.*

3 A **count** is a number that you get by counting a   N COUNT : particular set of things. EG *The official government*   USU SING *count has now risen to eight million.*

4 If you **keep count** of a number of things, you   PHRASE keep a record of how many have occurred. If you **lose count** of a number of things, you cannot remember how many have occurred. EG *Keep count of the unforeseen difficulties you encounter... I've lost count of the number of boyfriends she's had.*

5 The thing that **counts** in a particular situation is   V the thing that is most important in that situation. EG *What counts is how you feel about yourself.*

6 If you say that a particular thing **counts** for   V+*for* something, you mean that it is valuable or important. EG *I felt that all my years there counted for nothing.*

7 If something **counts** as a particular thing, it is   V-ERG : USU+*as* regarded as being that thing, especially in particular circumstances. EG *These benefits do not count as income for tax purposes... They can hardly be counted as friends.*

8 If you **count** something when you are making a   V+O calculation, you include it in that calculation. EG *We must count the infected trees as well as the healthy ones... ...36,600,000 Americans (not counting children less than one year old).*

9 You can also use **count** to refer to one or more   N COUNT : points that you are considering. For example, if   USU PLURAL something is wrong on two counts, it is wrong for two reasons. EG *The use of these tests is criticized on two counts.*

10 A **count** is also a European nobleman with the   N COUNT same rank as an English earl.

count against. If something **counts against**   PHRASAL VB : you, it may cause you to be punished or rejected. EG   V+PREP *It would count heavily against me if I got the Director into trouble.*

count on or **count upon. 1** If you **count on**   PHRASAL VB : something or **count upon** it, you expect it to   V+PREP happen and include it in your plans. EG *Doctors could now count on a regular salary.* **2** If you   V+PREP **count on** someone or **count upon** them, you rely on them to support you or help you. EG *You can count on me.*

count out. If you **count out** a sum of money, you   PHRASAL VB : count the notes or coins as you put them in a pile   V+O+ADV one by one.

count up. If you **count up** all the things in a   PHRASAL VB : group, you add them up in order to find out how   V+O+ADV many there are. EG *I counted up my years of teaching experience.*

count upon. See **count on**.

countable noun /ˈkaʊntə⁰bə⁰l naʊn/, **countable**   N COUNT **nouns**. A **countable noun** is the same as a count noun.

countdown /ˈkaʊntdaʊn/, **countdowns**. A **count-**   N COUNT **down** is the counting aloud of numbers in reverse order before something happens, especially before a spacecraft is launched.

countenance /ˈkaʊntɪ²nəns/, **countenances**.   N COUNT Someone's **countenance** is their face. EG *He saw*   Literary *the boyish countenance of Tom Barter before him.*

counter /ˈkaʊntə/, **counters, countering, coun-** **tered. 1** A **counter** is a long, narrow table or flat   N COUNT surface in a shop, where goods are displayed or sold. EG *There was a long queue at the medicine counter.*

2 If you **counter** something that is being done, you   V+O act in a way that makes it less effective. EG *He*   OFT+*by/with* *argued that Labour should counter this propaganda with a series of press statements.*

3 If you **counter** something that has just been said,   V+*by/with*; you say something in reaction to it or in opposition   ALSO to it. EG *I countered by enquiring whether she*   V-SPEECH : *actually knew this man.*   ONLY *that*   Formal

4 If one thing **runs counter** to another, it is in   PHRASE direct contrast with it. EG *The ideology of modern*   Formal *nationalism often runs counter to older ideology.*

5 A **counter** is also a small, flat, round object used   N COUNT in board games.

counteract /ˌkaʊntərˈækt/, **counteracts,**   V+O **counteracting, counteracted.** To **counteract** something means to reduce its effect by doing something that produces an opposite effect. EG *We added malt to counteract the bitterness of the taste.*

counter-attack, counter-attacks, counter-   V OR V+O **attacking, counter-attacked.** If you **counter-** **attack**, you attack someone who has attacked you.
▶ used as a noun. EG *...counter-attacks against*   ▶ N COUNT OR *enemy civilians.*   N UNCOUNT

counterbalance /ˌkaʊntəˈbæleⁱns/, **counterbal-**   V+O **ances, counterbalancing, counterbalanced.** To **counterbalance** something means to balance or correct it with an equal effect, force, or amount. EG *Political power counterbalances the other influences in society.*

counterclockwise /ˌkaʊntəˈklɒkwaɪz/ means the   ADV AFTER VB, same as anti-clockwise. EG *...a large counter-*   OR ADJ CLASSIF : *clockwise circulation of air.*   ATTRIB   American

counterfeit /ˈkaʊntəfiⁱt/, **counterfeits, counter-** **feiting, counterfeited. 1** Something that is   ADJ CLASSIF **counterfeit** is not genuine, but has been made to look exactly like something that is genuine, in order to deceive people. EG *...a counterfeit coin.*

2 To **counterfeit** something means to make an   V+O object that looks exactly like a genuine object, in order to deceive people.

counterfoil /ˈkaʊntəfɔɪl/, **counterfoils.** A   N COUNT **counterfoil** is the part of a cheque or receipt that you keep when you have paid for something.

countermand /ˌkaʊntəˈmɑːnd/, **countermands,**   V+O **countermanding, countermanded.** If you   Formal **countermand** an order, you cancel it, usually by giving a different order.

counterpane /ˈkaʊntəpeɪn/, **counterpanes.** A   N COUNT **counterpane** is a decorative cover on a bed.   Formal

counterpart /ˈkaʊntəpɑːt/, **counterparts.** The   N COUNT+POSS **counterpart** of a person or thing is another person or thing that has a similar function or position in a different place. EG *...the English merchant bank and its American counterpart, the Wall Street invest-* *ment bank.*

counter-productive. Something that is   ADJ QUALIT **counter-productive** achieves the opposite result from the one that you want to achieve.

countertenor /ˌkaʊntəˈtenə/, **countertenors.** A   N COUNT · **countertenor** is a man who sings with a high   Technical voice that is similar to a low female singing voice.

countess /ˈkaʊntɪ²s/, **countesses.** A **countess** is a   N COUNT woman who has the same rank as a count or earl, or who is married to a count or earl.

countless /ˈkaʊntlɪ²s/ means very many. EG *He*   ADJ CLASSIF : *sent countless letters to the newspapers.*   ATTRIB

count noun, count nouns. A **count noun** is a   N COUNT noun that has a singular and a plural form and is always used after a determiner in the singular. In this dictionary count nouns have N COUNT in the Extra Column. See the entry headed NOUNS for more information.

country /kʌntri¹/, **countries. 1** A **country** is one N COUNT
of the political areas which the world is divided
into. A **country** has its own government, people,
language, culture, and land. EG *The level of unem-*
ployment in this country is too high... Forests cover
about one third of the country... ...small East Euro-
pean countries, like Hungary.
2 You can also refer to the people who live in a N SING : the+N
particular country as the **country**. EG *The country*
was stunned.
3 The **country** is also land which is away from N SING : the+N
towns and cities. EG *We live in the country... There*
was a big move of people away from the country to
the towns. ▶ used as an adjective. EG *...lonely* ▶ ADJ CLASSIF :
country roads... I'm just a country boy. ATTRIB
4 A particular kind of **country** is an area of land N UNCOUNT
which has particular characteristics or is connect- +SUPP
ed with a particular person. EG *We were in moun-*
tain country... This is Max Ernst country.
5 Country music is the same as country and ADJ CLASSIF :
western music. ATTRIB

country and western is a style of popular N UNCOUNT
music from the USA.

country dancing is traditional dancing in which N UNCOUNT
people dance in rows or circles.

country house, country houses. A **country** N COUNT
house is a large, attractive house in the country,
owned by a rich or noble family.

countryman /kʌntrɪməᵊn/, **countrymen.** Your N COUNT :
countrymen are people from your own country. USU+POSS
EG *I hope this doesn't shock my fellow countrymen.*

countryside /kʌntrɪsaɪd/. The **countryside** is N SING : the+N
land which is away from towns and cities. EG *...the* OR N UNCOUNT
English countryside... It's very nice countryside
around there.

county /kaʊntɪ¹/, **counties.** A **county** is a region N COUNT
of Britain, Ireland, or the USA which has its own
local government. EG *I was a long way from home,*
on the other side of the county.

coup /kuː/, **coups.** A **coup** is **1** the same as a coup N COUNT
d'état. EG *A coup displaced the regime that had*
imprisoned him. **2** an achievement which is
thought to be especially brilliant because it was
very difficult. EG *Brooke went on to bigger things,*
his next notable coup being the case of Robert
Scott.

coup d'état /kuː deɪtɑː/, **coups d'état.** The plural N COUNT OR
is pronounced the same as the singular. N UNCOUNT
When there is a **coup d'état**, a group of people
seize power in a country. EG *Here governments are*
generally replaced by coups d'état.

couple /kʌpᵊl/, **couples, coupling, coupled. 1** A N COLL
couple is **1.1** two people who are married, living
together, or having a sexual relationship. EG *...mar-*
ried couples. **1.2** two people who you see together
on a particular occasion. EG *He watched a couple*
on the dance floor.
2 A **couple** of people or things means two people N PART
or things. EG *...a couple of Washington newspaper*
reporters... He met her a couple of years ago.
3 If one thing **is coupled** with another, the two V+O+with :
things are done or dealt with together. EG *Strong* USU PASS
protests were made, coupled with demands for an
international inquiry.

coupon /kuːpɒn/, **coupons.** A **coupon** is **1** a piece N COUNT
of printed paper which allows you to pay less
money than usual for something. EG *This coupon is*
worth five pounds. **2** a small form, for example in a
newspaper or magazine, which you send to an
organization to ask for information about their
products or services. **3** a form which you fill in in
order to enter a competition. EG *Every Thursday*
they fill in pools coupons.

courage /kʌrɪdʒ/. **1 Courage** is the quality shown N UNCOUNT
by someone who decides to do something difficult
or dangerous, even though they may be afraid;
used showing approval. EG *She would never have*
had the courage to defy him.

2 If you **have the courage of** your **convictions,** PHRASE
you have the confidence to do what you believe is
right, even though other people may not agree or
approve.
3 If you **take courage,** you begin to feel hopeful PHRASE
and confident about something. EG *I take courage*
from Robert Oppenheimer's vision.

courageous /kəreɪdʒəs/. Someone who is **coura-** ADJ QUALIT
geous shows courage. EG *...his courageous attempt*
to get the facts published. ◊ **courageously.** EG *She* ◊ ADV
fought courageously for her principles.

courgette /kʊəʒet/, **courgettes.** A **courgette** is a N COUNT
type of small vegetable marrow.

courier /kʊərɪə/, **couriers.** A **courier** is **1** a N COUNT
person employed by a travel company to look after
people who are on holiday. **2** a person who is paid
to take a special letter from one place to another.

course /kɔːs/, **courses, coursing, coursed. 1** ADV SEN
You say **of course 1.1** when you are saying
something that you expect other people already
realize or understand. EG *There is of course an*
element of truth in this argument. **1.2** when you
are talking about an event or situation that does
not surprise you. EG *He never writes to me, of*
course.
2 You also use **of course 2.1** as a polite way of CONVENTION
giving permission or agreeing with someone. EG
'Could I make a telephone call?' he said. 'Of
course,' Boylan said. **2.2** in order to emphasize a ADV SEN
statement that you are making, especially when
you are agreeing or disagreeing with someone. EG
'Do you love him, Dolly?' - 'Of course I do. He's
wonderful.'
3 Of course not is an emphatic way of saying no. CONVENTION
EG *'Do you think he was killed?' - 'No, no, of course*
not.'
4 A **course** is a series of lessons or lectures on a N COUNT
particular subject. It usually includes reading and
written work that a student has to do. EG *They have*
computer-science courses.
5 A **course** of medical treatment is a series of N COUNT+of
treatments that a doctor gives someone. EG *Anoth-*
er course of injections was prescribed.
6 A **course** in a meal is one of the sections of the N COUNT
meal. EG *...a three-course dinner... He didn't even*
finish his main course.
7 A **course** or a **course of action** is one of the N COUNT
things that you can do in a particular situation. EG OR PHRASE
The company has a choice of three courses of
action.
8 The **course** of a ship or aircraft is the route that N COUNT
it takes. EG *I set a course for the rock.* ● If a ship or ● PHRASE
aircraft is **on course**, it is travelling along the
correct route. If it is **off course**, it is no longer
travelling along the correct route. EG *He was at the*
wheel again, with the Morning Rose back on
course.
9 You can refer to the way that events develop as N SING :
the **course** of history, nature, or events. EG *It was* the+N+of
one of those ideas that change the course of
history.
10 If something happens **in the course of** a PREP
particular period of time, it happens during that
period of time. EG *I hope that in the course of the*
next two or three weeks they'll make up their
minds. ● **in due course**: see **due.**
11 If you do something **as a matter of course,** you PHRASE
do it as part of your normal work or way of life. EG
Harry now flies overseas as a matter of course.
12 If something **runs its course** or **takes its** PHRASE
course, it develops naturally and comes to a
natural end. EG *The illness was allowed to run its*
course.
13 If a liquid **courses** somewhere, it flows quickly. V : USU+A
EG *Tears coursed down my face.* Literary

Which words on these pages have a 'p' that is
not pronounced?

14 See also **golf course, racecourse**.

court /kɔːt/, **courts, courting, courted**. 1 A N COUNT
court is a place where legal matters are decided
by a judge and jury or by a magistrate. EG ...*divorce
courts*. ● If someone is **in court**, they are in a ● PHRASE
court while a trial is taking place. EG ...*evidence for
possible use in court*.

2 You can also refer to the people in a court, N COUNT:
especially the judge, jury, or magistrates, as the the+N
court. EG *The court dismissed the charges*.

3 If you **go to court** or **take** someone **to court**, PHRASE
you take legal action against them. EG *I told them I
could take them to court*.

4 A **court** is also an area in which you play a game N COUNT
such as tennis, badminton, or squash. EG ...*an indoor
court*. ● When tennis players are **on court**, they ● PHRASE
are playing tennis. When they are **off court**, they
are not playing.

5 The **court** of a king or queen is the place where N COUNT
he or she lives and carries out ceremonial or
administrative duties. ● When someone is **at** ● PHRASE
court, they are present at the king's or queen's
residence.

6 If a man and a woman **are courting**, they are v
spending a lot of time together, because they are Outdated
intending to marry each other.

courteous /kɜːtɪəs/. Someone who is **courteous** ADJ QUALIT
is polite, respectful, and considerate. EG *He was the
kindest, most courteous gentleman to work for.*
◇ **courteously**. EG *The jailer received me cour-* ◇ ADV
teously.

courtesy /kɜːtɪsɪ¹/, **courtesies**. 1 **Courtesy** is N UNCOUNT
behaviour that is polite, respectful, and consider-
ate. EG *He replied with promptness and courtesy.*

2 **Courtesies** are polite and respectful things that N PLURAL
you say or do. EG *There was a brief exchange of* Formal
courtesies with Elizabeth.

3 If something is done **by courtesy of** someone, PREP
they have given their permission for it to be done.
If something happens **by courtesy of** a situation, it
happens because the situation makes it possible for
it to happen. EG *He was Prime Minister by courtesy
of an uneasy alliance with the Liberals.*

courthouse /kɔːthaʊs/, **courthouses**. A **court-** N COUNT
house is a building in which a court of law meets. American

courtier /kɔːtɪə/, **courtiers**. **Courtiers** were N COUNT
noblemen and women who spent a lot of time at
the court of a king or queen.

court-martial,   court-martials,   court- V+O
martialling,   court-martialled. To **court-** Technical
martial a member of the armed forces means to
try them in a military court. ▸ used as a noun. EG ▸ N COUNT
*They arrested General Lee for disobedience, and
ordered a court-martial.*

court of appeal, courts of appeal. A **court of** N COUNT
appeal is a court which deals with appeals against
legal judgements.

court of inquiry, courts of inquiry. A **court of** N COUNT
inquiry is 1 an official investigation into a serious
accident or incident. 2 a group of people who are
officially appointed to investigate a serious accident or incident. EG *A court of inquiry sharply
criticized the local authority.*

courtroom /kɔːtruːm/, **courtrooms**. A **court-** N COUNT
room is a room in which a legal court meets.

courtship /kɔːtʃɪp/ is the activity of courting or N UNCOUNT
the time during which a man and a woman are Formal
courting. EG ...*the romance of courtship.*

court shoe, court shoes. **Court shoes** are ladies' N COUNT
shoes that have high heels and are made of plain
leather with no design. See picture at SHOES.

courtyard /kɔːtjɑːd/, **courtyards**. A **courtyard** is N COUNT
a flat open area of ground surrounded by buildings
or walls. It is often paved.

cousin /kʌzən/, **cousins**. Your **cousin** is the child N COUNT
of your uncle or aunt.

cove /kəʊv/, **coves**. A **cove** is a small bay on the N COUNT
coast. EG ...*Fisherman's Cove.*

covenant /kʌvənənt/, **covenants**. A **covenant** is N COUNT
a formal written promise to pay a sum of money
each year for a fixed period, especially to a charity.

cover /kʌvə/, **covers, covering, covered**. 1 If V+O:
you **cover** something, you place something else OFT+with
over it in order to protect it or hide it. EG *She
covered her face with her hands... The tray was
covered with a starched white cloth.*

2 If something **covers** something else, it forms a V+O
layer over it. EG *Her hand was covered with blood.*

3 If you **cover** a particular distance, you travel that V+O
distance. EG *I covered approximately twenty miles
a day.*

4 An insurance policy that **covers** a person or V+O
thing guarantees that money will be paid by the
insurance company in relation to that person or
thing. EG *Many people are covered by private
health insurance.*

5 If a law **covers** a particular set of people, things, V+O
or situations, it applies to them. EG *Workers in
factories are already covered by the Factories Act.*

6 If you **cover** a particular topic, you discuss it in a V+O
lecture, course, or book. EG *We've covered a wide
range of subjects today.*

7 If reporters, newspapers, or television companies V+O
cover an event, they report on it.

8 If a sum of money **covers** something, it is enough V+O
to pay for it. EG *I'll give you a cheque to cover the
cost of your journey.*

9 A **cover** is something which is put over an object, N COUNT
usually in order to protect it. EG *She put the cover
on her typewriter.*

10 Something that is a **cover** for secret or illegal N COUNT:
activities seems respectable or normal, but is OFT+SUPP
intended to hide the activities. EG ...*a cover for
murder.*

11 The **covers** on your bed are the sheet, blankets, N PLURAL:
and bedspread that you have on top of you. the+N

12 The **cover** of a book or a magazine is the N COUNT
outside part of it. EG *On the front cover was a
picture of a woman.*

13 **Cover** is trees, rocks, or other places where you N UNCOUNT
shelter from the weather or hide from someone. EG
*They crossed to the other side of the stream in
search of cover.*

14 Insurance **cover** is a guarantee from an insur- N UNCOUNT:
ance company that money will be paid by them if it OFT+for
is needed. EG *This policy gives unlimited cover for
hospital charges.*

15 **Cover** is also used in these phrases. 15.1 If you PHRASES
take cover, you shelter from the weather or from
gunfire. EG *I've got to put the car under cover.* 15.2 If you are **under cover**, you are
under something that protects you from the weath-
er. EG *I've got to put the car under cover.* 15.3 If you
do something **under cover of** a particular condition, you are able to do it without being noticed
because of this condition. EG *The attack usually
takes place under cover of darkness... Under cover
of the general panic, the assassin escaped.*

16 See also **covering**.

cover up. 1 If you **cover** something **up**, you put PHRASAL VB:
something else over it in order to protect it or hide V+O+ADV
it. EG *Cover yourself up with this sheet.* 2 If you V+O+ADV
cover up something that you do not want people to OR V+ADV
know about, you hide it from them. EG *There is a
great deal to cover up in this case... She tried to
cover up for Willie.* ● See also **cover-up**.

coverage /kʌvərɪdʒ/. The **coverage** of some- N UNCOUNT
thing in the news is the reporting of it. EG *They put
an immediate ban on all television coverage of
their operations.*

covering /kʌvərɪŋ/, **coverings**. A **covering** is a N COUNT OR
layer of something over something else. EG *Kitchen* N UNCOUNT
floor covering should be non-slip.

covering letter, covering letters. A **covering** N COUNT
letter is a letter that you send with a parcel or
with another letter in order to give extra information.

coverlet /kʌvəliʰt/, **coverlets**. A **coverlet** is a decorative cover which is put over a bed.   N COUNT   Formal

covert /kʌvət/. Something that is **covert** is secret or hidden, and not done or shown openly. EG ...*a covert involvement in activist politics.* ◊ **covertly**. EG *She watched Marina covertly.*   ADJ QUALIT   Formal   ◊ ADV

cover-up, cover-ups. A **cover-up** is an attempt to hide a crime or mistake. EG *He denied that he took any part in the cover-up.*   N COUNT

covet /kʌvəʰt/, **covets, coveting, coveted**. If you **covet** something, you strongly want to have it for yourself. EG *It was an honour he had long coveted.*   V+O   Formal

covetous /kʌvətəs/. **Covetous** feelings and actions involve a strong desire to possess something. EG *The United States Steel Corporation was casting covetous eyes at his company.*   ADJ QUALIT : ATTRIB   Formal

cow /kaʊ/, **cows, cowing, cowed**. 1 A **cow** is 1.1 a large female animal that is kept on farms for its milk. 1.2 any animal of this species, either male or female. You can refer to a number of these animals as 'cattle'. EG ...*a herd of cows.*   N COUNT

2 If you describe a woman as a **cow**, you mean that she is very unpleasant; an offensive use.   N COUNT   Informal

3 If someone **is cowed**, they are made afraid, or made to behave in a particular way because they have been frightened or oppressed. EG *People shouldn't allow themselves to be cowed into this.*   V+O : USU PASS   Formal

◊ **cowed**. EG ...*his tragically cowed and battered wife.*   ◊ ADJ QUALIT

coward /kaʊəd/, **cowards**. If you say that someone is a **coward**, you mean that they are easily frightened and avoid dangerous or difficult situations; used showing disapproval. EG *I was basically a dreadful coward.*   N COUNT

cowardice /kaʊədɪs/ is cowardly behaviour. EG *He despised them for their cowardice and ignorance.*   N UNCOUNT

cowardly /kaʊədliʰ/. If you describe someone as **cowardly**, you mean that they avoid doing dangerous or difficult things because they are afraid; used showing disapproval. EG ...*corrupt and cowardly generals... ...a cowardly refusal to face reality.*   ADJ QUALIT

cowboy /kaʊbɔɪ/, **cowboys**. 1 A **cowboy** is 1.1 a man employed to look after cattle in America. 1.2 a male character in a Western. EG ...*cowboy films.*   N COUNT

2 You can refer to someone who runs a business as a **cowboy** if they run it dishonestly or are not experienced, skilful, or careful in their work. EG ...*cowboy building contractors.*   N COUNT   British

cower /kaʊə/, **cowers, cowering, cowered**. If you **cower**, you bend forward and downwards or move back because you are very frightened. EG *Bernadette cowered in her seat.*   V : USU+A

cowshed /kaʊʃed/, **cowsheds**. A **cowshed** is a building where cows are kept or milked.   N COUNT

coy /kɔɪ/. If someone is **coy**, 1 they pretend to be shy and modest. ◊ *a coy little smile.* ◊ **coyly**. EG *They were looking at us coyly through their elegant lashes.* ◊ **coyness**. EG *There is no false modesty or coyness about her.* 2 they are unwilling to say something, in a way that people find slightly irritating. EG *Let us not be coy about the identity of this great man.*   ADJ QUALIT   ◊ ADV   ◊ N UNCOUNT   ADJ QUALIT

cozy /kəʊziʰ/. See **cosy**.

crab

crab /kræb/, **crabs**. A **crab** is a sea creature with a flat round body covered by a shell, and five pairs of legs with large claws on the front pair. Crabs usually move sideways.   N COUNT

crack /kræk/, **cracks, cracking, cracked**. 1 If something **cracks** or if you **crack** it, 1.1 it becomes slightly damaged, with lines appearing on its surface. EG *If you hold a glass under the hot tap, it may crack.* 1.2 it makes a sharp sound like the sound of a piece of wood breaking. EG *The whips began to crack over their heads.*   V-ERG

2 If someone **cracks**, they finally give in or have a nervous breakdown. EG *I thought I might crack if I didn't get away soon.*   V   Informal

3 If you **crack** a problem or a code, you solve it, especially after a lot of thought.   V+O

4 If you **crack** a joke, you tell it.   V+O

5 A **crack** is 5.1 a very narrow gap between two things. EG ...*the cracks between the boards of the ceiling... I felt a gust of wind through a crack in the wall... I opened the door a crack.* 5.2 a line that appears on the surface of something when it is slightly damaged. EG *She found a crack in one of the tea-cups.*   N COUNT : OFT +between/in   N COUNT : OFT+in

6 A **crack** is also a slightly rude or cruel joke. EG *There were the routine cracks about the Prime Minister.*   N COUNT

7 A **crack** soldier or sportsman is highly trained and very skilful. EG ...*a crack British regiment.*   ADJ CLASSIF: ATTRIB

8 If you do something **at the crack of dawn**, you do it very early in the morning. EG *He always got up at the crack of dawn.*   PHRASE

9 If you **have a crack at** something, you make an attempt to do it.   PHRASE   Informal

10 See also **cracked, cracking**.

crack down. If people in authority **crack down** on a group of people, they become stricter in making the group obey rules or laws. EG *Her first reaction to the riots was to crack down hard... They have cracked down on thieves and vandals.* ● See also **crackdown**.   PHRASAL VB : V+ADV, OFT+on

crack up. 1 If someone **cracks up**, they are under such a lot of emotional strain that they become mentally ill. EG *If I'd crack up if there wasn't someone I could talk to.* 2 If you say that something is **not all it's cracked up to be**, you mean that it is not as good as other people have said it is. EG *Marriage is not all it's cracked up to be.*   PHRASAL VB : V+ADV   Informal   PHRASE   Informal

crackdown /krækdaʊn/, **crackdowns**. A **crackdown** is strong official action that is taken to punish people who break laws. EG ...*a crackdown on criminals.*   N COUNT : OFT+on

cracked /krækt/. 1 An object that is **cracked** has lines on its surface because it has been damaged. EG ...*the big, cracked mirror.*   ADJ QUALIT

2 A voice or musical instrument that is **cracked** sounds rough and unsteady. EG ...*a high, cracked voice.*   ADJ QUALIT

cracker /krækə/, **crackers**. 1 A **cracker** is a thin, crisp biscuit which is often eaten with cheese.   N COUNT

2 A **cracker** is also a hollow cardboard tube covered with coloured paper. It can be pulled apart and usually contains a small toy and a paper hat. Children often pull crackers at parties.   N COUNT

cracking /krækɪŋ/. 1 If you tell someone to **get cracking**, you are telling them to start doing something immediately. EG *Get cracking or we'll never finish in time.*   PHRASE   Informal

2 If you walk at **a cracking pace**, you walk very quickly. EG *Gillian used to go at a cracking pace.*   PHRASE   Informal

crackle /krækəʰl/, **crackles, crackling, crackled**. If something **crackles**, it makes a rapid series of short, harsh noises. EG *The loudspeaker crackled.* ► used as a noun. EG ...*the crackle of the fire.*   V   ► N COUNT

◊ **crackling.** EG *The crackling became louder and louder.* ◊ N SING

crackpot /krækpɒt/, **crackpots.** You call someone a **crackpot** when you think that they have strange and crazy ideas. EG *Every crackpot in the world writes to him.* ▸ used as an adjective. EG *...a crackpot letter.* N COUNT Informal ▸ ADJ CLASSIF : ATTRIB

cradle /kreɪdᵊl/, **cradles, cradling, cradled.** 1 A **cradle** is a small box-shaped bed for a baby. N COUNT

2 A place that is referred to as the **cradle** of something is the place where it began. EG *New England saw itself as the cradle of American technology.* N SING : the+N+of Literary

3 If you **cradle** something in your arms or hands, you hold it carefully. EG *She cradled a child in her arms.* V+O

craft /krɑːft/, **crafts.** 1 A **craft** is 1.1 an activity such as weaving, carving, or pottery that involves making things skilfully with your hands. EG *...traditional crafts such as thatching and weaving... ...a craft festival.* 1.2 any activity or job that involves doing something skilfully. EG *He was still learning his journalistic craft.* N COUNT

2 You can refer to a boat, a spacecraft, or an aircraft as a **craft**. The plural form is also **craft**. EG *There were eight destroyers and fifty smaller craft... My little boat was too frail a craft to weather these storms.* N COUNT

craftsman /krɑːftsmən/, **craftsmen.** A **craftsman** is a man whose job is making things skilfully using his hands. EG *The equipment could be manufactured cheaply by local craftsmen.* N COUNT

craftsmanship /krɑːftsmənʃɪp/ is 1 the skill that someone uses when they make beautiful things with their hands. EG *...Bernini's great craftsmanship.* 2 the quality that something has when it is beautiful and has been very carefully made. EG *I bent down to examine the exquisite craftsmanship.* N UNCOUNT N UNCOUNT

crafty /krɑːftiⁱ/, **craftier, craftiest.** Someone who is **crafty** obtains or achieves things by deceiving people in a clever way. EG *...the crafty tactics of journalists... ...the craftiest of all politicians.* ADJ QUALIT

◊ **craftily.** EG *Several ploys are being craftily developed.* ◊ **craftiness.** EG *He shows the same craftiness as his brother.* ◊ ADV ◊ N UNCOUNT

crag /kræg/, **crags.** A **crag** is a steep, rocky cliff or part of a mountain. EG *...a 200 foot high crag.* N COUNT

craggy /krægiⁱ/. 1 A **craggy** mountain or cliff is steep and rocky. EG *...the craggy heights of Mount Rushmore.* ADJ QUALIT

2 A **craggy** face has large features and deep lines. ADJ QUALIT

cram /kræm/, **crams, cramming, crammed.** 1 If you **cram** people or things into a place, you put more of them into it than there is room for. EG *Thirty of us were crammed into a small dark room... He crammed the bank notes into his pockets.* V+O+A

2 If you **are cramming** for an examination, you are learning as much as possible in a short time just before you take the examination. V : OFT+for

crammed /kræmd/. If something is **crammed** with things or people, it is very full of them, so that there is hardly room for anything or anyone else. EG *The rooms were crammed with congressmen... ...a concrete bunker crammed full of radio equipment.* ADJ PRED+A

cramp /kræmp/, **cramps, cramping, cramped.** 1 If you have **cramp** or **cramps**, you feel a strong pain caused by a muscle suddenly contracting. EG *I had the most excruciating cramp in my leg... She had severe stomach cramps.* N UNCOUNT OR N PLURAL

2 If your behaviour **cramps** someone's **style**, it prevents them from impressing other people. EG *He was always butting in and saying the wrong thing and cramping her style.* PHRASE Informal

cramped /kræmpt/. A **cramped** room or building is not big enough for the people or things in it. EG *...bringing up children in cramped high-rise flats.* ADJ QUALIT

crane /kreɪn/, **cranes, craning, craned.** 1 A **crane** is a large machine that moves heavy things by lifting them in the air. N COUNT

2 A **crane** is also a kind of large bird with a long neck and long legs. N COUNT

3 If you **crane** your neck or head, you stretch your head in a particular direction in order to see or hear something better. EG *He craned his neck out of the window.* V OR V+O : USU+A

crank /kræŋk/, **cranks, cranking, cranked.** 1 If you call someone a **crank**, you mean that they have peculiar ideas and behave in a strange way. EG *I didn't want to be thought a crank.* N COUNT

2 A **crank** is also a device that you turn in order to make something move. EG *Brody began to turn the crank to reel in the fish.* N COUNT

3 If you **crank** something, you make it move by turning a handle. EG *She cranked down the window.* V+O : USU+A

cranky /kræŋkiⁱ/, **crankier, crankiest.** If you describe ideas or ways of behaving as **cranky**, you mean that they are strange and slightly mad. EG *...a bachelor of cranky habits... ...a cranky old woman.* ADJ QUALIT Informal

cranny /kræniⁱ/, **crannies.** A **cranny** is a very narrow opening in a wall or rock. EG *The fish have underwater crannies where they hide.* ● **every nook and cranny:** see **nook.** N COUNT

crash /kræʃ/, **crashes, crashing, crashed.** 1 A **crash** is an accident in which a moving car or other vehicle hits something and is badly damaged or destroyed. EG *Her mother was killed in a car crash.* N COUNT

2 If a moving car or other vehicle **crashes**, it hits something and is badly damaged or destroyed. EG *The plane crashed within seconds of taking off.* V OR V-ERG

3 If something **crashes** somewhere, it hits something else violently, making a loud noise. EG *The door crashed open.* V : USU+A

4 A **crash** is also a sudden, loud noise. EG *...a terrific crash of thunder.* N COUNT

5 The **crash** of a business or financial institution is its serious failure. EG *...one of the most spectacular financial crashes of the decade.* N COUNT : USU+SUPP

crash helmet, crash helmets. A **crash helmet** is a helmet that motor cyclists wear in order to protect their heads if they have an accident. N COUNT

crass /kræs/. Behaviour that is **crass** is stupid and insensitive. EG *I'm sorry I was so crass... Most Hollywood movies seemed crass and trivial.* ADJ QUALIT

crate /kreɪt/, **crates.** A **crate** is a large box used for transporting or storing things. EG *...a crate of oranges.... ...a crate of beer.* N COUNT OR N PART

crater /kreɪtə/, **craters.** A **crater** is a very large hole in the ground, which has been caused by something hitting it or by an explosion. EG *...bomb craters... ...the craters of the moon.* N COUNT

cravat /krəvæt/, **cravats.** A **cravat** is a piece of cloth which a man wears wrapped around his neck and tucked inside the collar of his shirt. N COUNT

crave /kreɪv/, **craves, craving, craved.** If you **crave** something or **crave** for it, you want to have it very much. EG *She craved luxury... ...finding the absolute security for which he had always craved.* V+O OR V+for

◊ **craving** /kreɪvɪŋ/, **cravings.** EG *Both the sisters had a craving for sweets... ...their powerful craving to succeed.* ◊ N COUNT : OFT+for OR to-INF

crawl /krɔːl/, **crawls, crawling, crawled.** 1 When you **crawl**, you move forward on your hands and knees. EG *Her baby is crawling about now.* V : USU+A

2 When an insect or a vehicle **crawls**, it moves very slowly. EG *A spider was crawling up my leg... The train crawled deeper into Russia.* V : USU+A

3 If you say that a place **is crawling** with people or things, you mean that it is full of them. EG *The forecourt was crawling with security men.* V : OFT+with; ONLY CONT

4 If something **makes** your **skin crawl**, it makes you feel horrified or revolted. EG *...a noise that made my skin crawl.* PHRASE Informal

5 If you **crawl** to someone, you try to please them in order to gain some advantage for yourself. V : OFT+to Informal

6 The **crawl** is a kind of swimming stroke which you do lying on your front, swinging one arm over your head, and then the other arm. See picture at SWIMMING. `N SING : the+N`

crayon /kreɪə⁷n/, **crayons**. A **crayon** is a pencil containing coloured wax or clay. EG ...a box of crayons... They wanted to draw in crayon. `N COUNT OR N UNCOUNT`

craze /kreɪz/, **crazes**. A **craze** is something that a lot of people show a strong interest in for a short time. EG ...the latest dance craze from America. `N COUNT : USU+SUPP`

crazed /kreɪzd/. **Crazed** behaviour is wild and uncontrolled. EG She fought with crazed ferocity. `ADJ QUALIT : ATTRIB`

crazy /kreɪzi¹/, **crazier, craziest**. **1** You say that someone is **crazy** when they talk or behave in a very strange or foolish way. EG ...a crazy American... My fellow students thought I was crazy... It's crazy to have a picnic in October. ◊ **crazily**. EG A man rushed past him shouting crazily. `ADJ QUALIT Informal` ◊ ADV

2 If you are **crazy** about something, you are very enthusiastic about it. EG They are crazy about football. `ADJ PRED +about OR ADJ AFTER N Informal`

3 If something makes you **crazy** or drives you **crazy**, it makes you extremely annoyed or upset. EG The tourists were beginning to drive me crazy. `ADJ PRED Informal`

creak /kri:k/, **creaks, creaking, creaked**. If something **creaks**, it makes a harsh sound when it moves. EG The door creaked... The lift creaks its way up the central tower. ▸ used as a noun. EG The creak of the mattress did not wake her. ◊ **creaking**. EG There was silence except for the creaking of the carriage. `V OR V+O+A` ▸ N COUNT +SUPP ◊ N UNCOUNT OR N COUNT

creaky /kri:ki¹/, **creakier, creakiest**. Something that is **creaky** creaks when it moves. EG He was careful on the creaky stairs. `ADJ QUALIT`

cream /kri:m/, **creams, creaming, creamed**. **1** **Cream** is a thick, yellowish-white liquid that is taken from milk. You can use it in cooking or pour it on fruit or puddings. EG ...strawberries and cream. `N UNCOUNT`

2 **Cream** is also **2.1** an artificial substance that looks and tastes like cream. EG ...chocolates with cream fillings. **2.2** a substance that you rub into your skin in order to make it soft. EG She wiped the cream off her face. `N UNCOUNT` N MASS

3 Something that is **cream** is of a yellowish-white colour. EG The shell was deep cream touched here and there with pink. `ADJ COLOUR`

4 You can refer to the best people or things in a group as the **cream** of the group. EG They were the cream of their generation. `N SING : the+N +SUPP`

cream off. If you **cream off** part of a group of people, you take them away and treat them in a special way, because you think that they are better than the others. EG The best pupils would be creamed off and given a superior training. `PHRASAL VB : V+O+ADV`

creamy /kri:mi¹/, **creamier, creamiest**. **1** Something that is **creamy** is of a yellowish-white colour. EG ...a house made of creamy limestone. `ADJ COLOUR`

2 Food or drink that is **creamy** contains a lot of cream. EG ...a nice cup of creamy coffee... ...rich creamy pastries. `ADJ QUALIT`

crease /kri:s/, **creases, creasing, creased**. **1** **Creases** are irregular lines that appear in cloth or paper when it has been crushed. EG She smoothed down the creases in her dress. `N COUNT : USU PLURAL`

2 If you **crease** cloth or paper or if it **creases**, lines appear in it because it has been crushed. ◊ **creased**. EG His suit had become creased. `V-ERG` ◊ ADJ QUALIT

3 If your face **creases** or if something **creases** it, lines appear on it because you are frowning. EG A wrinkle of doubt creased her forehead. ◊ **creased**. EG His face was creased in thought. `V-ERG` ◊ ADJ CLASSIF

create /kri:eɪt/, **creates, creating, created**. **1** To **create** something means to cause it to happen or exist. EG His work created enormous interest in England... They opened windows and doors to create a draught. `V+O`

2 When someone **creates** a new product or process, they invent it or design it. EG The industry responded by creating a new textile. `V+O`

3 If you say that something **creates** a thought or feeling, you mean that it gives you this thought or feeling. EG Your words create the most beautiful images. `V+O`

creation /kri:eɪʃə⁰n/, **creations**. **1** The **creation** of something is the act of bringing it into existence. EG They proposed the creation of Welsh and Scottish parliaments... ...a job creation scheme... ...the creation of visual images. `N UNCOUNT OFT+of`

2 In the Bible, the **Creation** is the making of the universe, earth, and creatures by God. `N PROPER : the+N`

3 People sometimes refer to the entire universe as **creation**. EG They look upon everything in creation as material for exploitation. `N UNCOUNT`

4 A **creation** is **4.1** something that has been made, especially a work of art. EG ...his ceramic creations. **4.2** a thought or image produced in your mind. EG ...the creations of a frightened imagination. `N COUNT Literary`

creative /kri:eɪtɪv/. **1** Someone who is **creative** has the ability to invent and develop original ideas, especially in art. **Creative** activities involve the inventing and developing of these ideas. EG He has more time to be creative... I'd like to get involved in something creative... ...creative writing. ◊ **creativity** /kri:eɪtɪvɪ¹ti¹/. EG ...adults who want to express their own creativity. `ADJ QUALIT` ◊ N UNCOUNT

2 If you use something in a **creative** way, you use it in a new way that produces interesting and unusual results. ◊ **creatively**. EG ...the desire to use mathematics creatively. `ADJ QUALIT` ◊ ADV

creator /kri:eɪtə/, **creators**. **1** The **creator** of something is the person who made it or invented it. EG The police were known as Peelers in honour of their creator, Sir Robert Peel... ...Kit Williams, the creator of the book 'Masquerade'. `N COUNT : USU+POSS`

2 God is sometimes referred to as the **Creator**. EG ...a song of praise to the Creator. `N PROPER : the+N`

creature /kri:tʃə/, **creatures**. **1** A **creature** is a living thing that can move about, such as an animal, a bird, or an insect. EG The opossum is a large rat-like creature... Worms are very simple creatures. `N COUNT`

2 You can also use **creature** to talk about people. For example, if you call someone a stupid **creature** or a spiteful **creature**, you are emphasizing that they are stupid or spiteful. EG She was a weak and helpless creature... ...a voluptuous creature with blonde bobbed hair. `N COUNT+SUPP`

crèche /kreʃ/, **crèches**. A **crèche** is a place where small children can be left and looked after while their parents are working. `N COUNT`

credence /kri:də⁰ns/. If something gives or lends **credence** to a theory or story, it makes it easier to believe. EG These latest discoveries give credence to Burke's ideas. `N UNCOUNT Formal`

credentials /krɪ²denʃə⁰lz/. Your **credentials** are **1** your previous achievements, training, and general background, which indicate that you are qualified to do something. EG I think he has established his credentials... His credentials as a journalist were beyond dispute. **2** a letter or certificate that proves your identity or qualifications. EG Didn't you ask for his credentials? `N PLURAL : USU+SUPP Formal` `N PLURAL Formal`

credibility /kredɪ¹bɪlɪ¹ti¹/. If someone or something has **credibility**, people believe in them and trust them. EG He felt that he had lost credibility... ...doubts about the credibility of the nuclear deterrent. `N UNCOUNT`

credible /kredɪ¹bə⁰l/. **1** Something that is **credible** can be believed. EG His latest statements are hardly credible. `ADJ QUALIT`

2 Someone who is **credible** is able to convince you that they can be trusted. EG No politicians seem credible these days. `ADJ QUALIT`

Do you think that a crematorium at night would be creepy?

credit /krɛdɪt/, **credits, crediting, credited. 1** If N UNCOUNT you are allowed **credit**, you are allowed to pay for goods or services several weeks or months after you have received them. EG ...the availability of cheap long-term credit... They sold grain on credit during times of famine.

2 If someone or their bank account is **in credit**, PHRASE their bank account has money in it.

3 If you get the **credit** for something, people praise N UNCOUNT : you for it. EG Some of the credit should go to Nick... OFT+for He deserves great credit for keeping them togeth-er.

4 Credit is also used in these phrases. **4.1** If you PHRASES say that something **does** someone **credit**, you mean that they should be respected or admired for it. EG Your concern for us all does you the greatest credit. **4.2** If someone says that something is **to** your **credit**, they mean that you deserve praise for it. EG Price, to his credit, denounced in private the brutalities of the regime. **4.3** If you already have one or more achievements **to** your **credit**, you have achieved them. EG She already had several London successes to her credit.

5 If you **are credited** with an achievement or if it V+O **is credited** to you, people believe that you were +with/to : responsible for it. EG ...the woman who is often USU PASS credited with originating the movement.

6 If you **give** someone **credit for** a good quality, PHRASE you believe that they have it. EG The public are more tolerant than they are often given credit for being.

7 If you cannot **credit** something, you cannot V+O : NO CONT believe that it is true. EG There must be many of Formal you who find this case hard to credit.

8 The list of people who helped to make a film, a N PLURAL record, or a television programme is called the **credits**.

creditable /krɛdɪtəbəl/. **1** Something that is ADJ QUALIT **creditable** is of a reasonably high standard. EG He polled a creditable 44.8 per cent.

2 If you describe someone's behaviour as **credit-able**, you mean that it should be respected or ADJ QUALIT admired. EG That, I think, was creditable on his part.

credit card, credit cards. A **credit card** is a N COUNT plastic card that you can use to allow you to buy goods on credit or to borrow money.

creditor /krɛdɪtə/, **creditors.** Your **creditors** N COUNT are the people who you owe money to.

credulity /krɪˈdjuːlɪtiˈ/ is a willingness to believe N UNCOUNT that something is real or true. EG Don't stretch my Formal credulity too far.

credulous /krɛdjəˈləs/. If you are **credulous**, you ADJ QUALIT are always ready to believe what people tell you, and are easily deceived. EG ...a well-meaning, credu-lous British officer.

creed /kriːd/, **creeds. 1** A **creed** is a set of beliefs, N COUNT principles, or opinions that strongly influence the way people live or work. EG They never embraced any particular creed... ...the free enterprise creed.

2 A **creed** is also a religion. EG ...the Christian N COUNT creed. Formal

creek /kriːk/, **creeks.** A **creek** is **1** a narrow inlet N COUNT where the sea comes a long way into the land. EG ...the muddy creeks of my home coast. **2** a small American stream or river. EG By early summer the creek was almost dry.

creep /kriːp/, **creeps, creeping, crept** /krɛpt/. **1** V+A When people or animals **creep** somewhere, they move quietly and slowly. EG I heard my landlady creeping stealthily up to my door.

2 If something **creeps** somewhere, it moves very V+A slowly, so that you hardly notice that it is moving. Literary EG Here and there, little breezes crept over the water.

3 If someone or something **gives** you the **creeps**, PHRASE they make you feel uncomfortable, or rather fright- Informal ened. EG The thought gives me the creeps.

4 If you call someone a **creep**, you mean that you N COUNT Informal

dislike them very much, especially because they flatter people. EG She's a cunning little creep.

creep in. If something such as a custom **creeps** PHRASAL VB : **in**, it gradually becomes used. EG New gestures do V+ADV occasionally manage to creep in.

creep up on. 1 If you **creep up on** someone, you PHRASAL VB : move slowly closer to them without being seen by V+ADV+PREP them. **2** If a feeling or state **creeps up on** you, you V+ADV+PREP hardly notice that you are about to experience it. EG Senility is creeping up on me, I guess.

creeper /kriːpə/, **creepers.** A **creeper** is a plant N COUNT with long stems that wind themselves around ob-jects. EG ...an impenetrable tangle of creepers and trees.

creepy /kriːpiˈ/, **creepier, creepiest.** Something ADJ QUALIT that is **creepy** gives you a strange, unpleasant Informal feeling of fear. EG It was very creepy in the woods... We've found a creepy caravan where a witch lives.

cremate /krɪˈmeɪt/, **cremates, cremating, cre-** V+O : USU PASS **mated.** When someone **is cremated**, their dead body is burned, usually as part of a funeral service. EG Her husband will be cremated.

cremation /krɪˈmeɪʃəˈn/, **cremations. 1** A **cre-** N COUNT **mation** is a funeral service during which a dead body is cremated.

2 Cremation is the process of burning a dead body N UNCOUNT at a funeral.

crematorium /krɛmətɔːriəm/, **crematoria** N COUNT /krɛmətɔːriə/ or **crematoriums.** A **crematorium** is a building in which the bodies of dead people are burned as part of a funeral service.

crepe /kreɪp/ is **1** a thin fabric made of cotton, N UNCOUNT silk, or wool with an uneven, ridged surface. EG ...a pink crepe evening gown. **2** a type of rubber with a rough surface. EG ...shoes with crepe soles.

crept /krɛpt/ is the past tense and past participle of **creep.**

crescendo /krɪˈʃɛndəʊ/, **crescendos.** A **crescen-** N COUNT **do** is **1** a noise that is getting louder or that is very loud. EG The ovation rose in a new crescendo... The noise reached a crescendo. **2** the time when some- Literary thing is at its most intense. EG The clamour in the press was reaching a crescendo.

crescent /krɛsəˈnt, -zəˈnt/, **crescents.** A **cres-** N COUNT **cent** is **1** a street or row of houses that is built in a curve. EG ...Grosvenor Crescent. **2** a curved shape that is wider in the middle than at its ends, like the shape of the moon during its first and last quarters. See picture at SHAPES. EG There was a scar on her right arm, a jagged crescent of white.

crest /krɛst/, **crests. 1** The **crest** of a hill or a N COUNT : wave is the highest part of it. EG We had reached USU+POSS the crest of the hill.

2 A **crest** on a bird is a tuft of feathers on the top of N COUNT its head. EG The birds' crests are raised.

3 A **crest** is also a small picture or design that is N COUNT the sign of a noble family, a town, or an organiza-tion.

crestfallen /krɛstfɔːlən/. Someone who looks ADJ PRED **crestfallen** looks sad and disappointed about something.

cretin /krɛtɪn/, **cretins.** If you call someone a N COUNT **cretin**, you mean that they are very stupid; an offensive word.

crevice /krɛvɪs/, **crevices.** A **crevice** is a narrow N COUNT crack or gap in a rock. EG Most of the year the insects are hidden in rock crevices.

crew /kruː/, **crews. 1** The people who work on N COLL and operate a ship, an aeroplane, or a spacecraft are called the **crew.** EG The Captain ordered his crew to prepare for action... The 'Maine' carried a crew of three hundred and fifty.

2 You also use **crew** to refer to people with special N COLL technical skills who work together on a task or project. EG The TV crews couldn't film at night.

crew cut, crew cuts. A **crew cut** is a man's N COUNT hairstyle in which his hair is cut very short. EG ...an ex-colonel with a bushy moustache and a crew cut.

crewman /kru:mə³n/, **crewmen**. A **crewman** is N COUNT a member of a crew. EG *One of the crewmen died...* *...TV crewmen.*

crib /krɪb/, **cribs, cribbing, cribbed.** 1 If you V OR V+O: **crib**, you copy something that someone else has OFT+*off/from* written and pretend that it is your own work. EG Informal *The teacher thought we'd cribbed off each other.*

2 A **crib** is written information that someone uses N COUNT dishonestly to help them in an examination. Outdated

3 A **crib** is also a baby's cot. EG *She used to throw* N COUNT *her toys out of her crib.* American

crick /krɪk/, **cricks, cricking, cricked.** 1 If you N COUNT: have a **crick** in your neck or in your back, you USU SING have a pain there caused by muscles becoming stiff.

2 If you **crick** your neck or back, you injure it so V+O that it becomes stiff and hurts.

cricket /krɪkɪt/, **crickets.** 1 **Cricket** is an outdoor N UNCOUNT game played between two teams. Players try to score points, called runs, by hitting a ball with a wooden bat. EG *I spent the afternoon watching cricket.*

2 A **cricket** is a small jumping insect that produces N COUNT sharp sounds by rubbing its wings together. EG *We lay in our tent listening to the crickets.*

cricketer /krɪkɪtə/, **cricketers.** A **cricketer** is a N COUNT person who plays cricket.

crime /kraɪm/, **crimes.** 1 A **crime** is an illegal N COUNT OR action for which a person can be punished by law. N UNCOUNT EG *A crime has been committed... ...the crime of murder... ...a life of crime.*

2 You can also refer to an action which is morally N COUNT: wrong as a **crime**. EG *To waste good food is a crime* OFT+*against* *against nature.*

criminal /krɪmɪnə³l/, **criminals.** 1 A **criminal** is N COUNT a person who has committed a crime. EG *...one of the country's ten most wanted criminals.*

2 Something that is **criminal** is **2.1** connected with ADJ CLASSIF crime. EG *He had done nothing criminal... ...a criminal offence.* ◊ **criminally.** EG *...the care of* ◊ SUBMOD *the criminally insane... ...criminally responsible for the loss of lives.* **2.2** morally wrong. EG *To refuse* ADJ QUALIT *medical aid would be criminal.* ◊ **criminally.** EG ◊ SUBMOD *The pay was criminally poor.*

criminology /krɪmɪnɒlədʒi¹/ is the scientific N UNCOUNT study of crime and criminals. ◊ **criminologist,** ◊ N COUNT **criminologists.** EG *Death was caused by what the criminologists call a solid object.*

crimson /krɪmzə³n/, **crimsons.** 1 Something that ADJ COLOUR is **crimson** is of a dark, purplish-red colour. EG *She was wearing a crimson dress.*

2 If a person goes **crimson**, their face becomes red ADJ PRED because they are angry or embarrassed.

cringe /krɪndʒ/, **cringes, cringing, cringed.** 1 If V : USU+A you **cringe**, you move away from someone or something because you are afraid of them. EG *She cringed against the wall.*

2 You also say that people **cringe** when they are V : USU+A very embarrassed. EG *Cringing under the stares of passers-by, I tried to read my newspaper.*

crinkle /krɪŋkə³l/, **crinkles, crinkling, crinkled.** 1 When something **crinkles** or when you **crinkle** V-ERG it, it becomes slightly creased or folded. EG *His face crinkled into a smile.* ◊ **crinkled.** EG *...brown* ◊ ADJ QUALIT *crinkled leaves.*

2 **Crinkles** are small creases or folds. EG *There* N COUNT: *were crinkles at the outer corners of his eyes.* USU PLURAL

crinkly /krɪŋkli¹/. Something that is **crinkly** has ADJ QUALIT many small creases or folds. EG *Her bodice was made of crinkly material.*

cripple /krɪpə³l/, **cripples, crippling, crippled.** 1 If someone is a **cripple**, they cannot move their N COUNT body properly because it is weak, injured, or affected by a disease.

2 If something **cripples** you, it seriously injures V+O you so that you can never move properly again.

3 If something **cripples** an organization or system, V+O it prevents it from working properly. EG *The gov-*

ernment had done much to cripple national enterprise.

crippled /krɪpə³ld/. Someone who is **crippled** ADJ CLASSIF cannot move their body properly because it is weak, injured, or affected by disease. EG *...his crippled mother... They will be crippled for life.*

crippling /krɪplɪŋ/. 1 A **crippling** illness or dis- ADJ QUALIT: ability severely damages your health or your body. ATTRIB EG *...the dread of crippling disablement.*

2 **Crippling** prices or taxes have a serious harmful ADJ QUALIT effect on a person's or country's financial situation.

crisis /kraɪsɪs/, **crises** /kraɪsi:z/. 1 A **crisis** is a N COUNT OR serious or dangerous situation which could cause N UNCOUNT death or hardship to many people. *I was in Munich* OFT+SUPP *during the 1938 crisis... They've still got an economic crisis on their hands.*

2 A **crisis** in someone's life is a time when they N COUNT OR have serious personal problems and are extremely N UNCOUNT: unhappy. EG *The anxiety of this personal crisis* OFT+SUPP *turned his hair white... Who can you turn to in time of crisis?*

crisp /krɪsp/, **crisper, crispest; crisps.** 1 Some- ADJ QUALIT thing that is **crisp** is hard or stiff, usually in a pleasant way. EG *...crisp bacon... ...crisp new bank notes... ...her crisp white blouse.*

2 **Crisps** are very thin slices of potato that have N COUNT: been fried until they are hard and crunchy. EG *...a* USU PLURAL *packet of crisps.* British

3 You describe the air or the weather as **crisp** ADJ QUALIT when it is pleasantly fresh, cold, and dry. EG *...a crisp October morning.*

4 You describe what someone says or writes as ADJ QUALIT **crisp** when they do not say unnecessary things and sound efficient and perhaps unfriendly. EG *He sent off two crisp telegrams.* ◊ **crisply.** EG *'What did* ◊ ADV *she want?' Etta said crisply. 'Money?'*

criss-cross /krɪskrɒs/, **criss-crosses, criss- crossing, criss-crossed.** 1 If things **criss-cross**, V OR V+O they make a pattern of crossed lines. EG *Dozens of searchlights criss-crossed to pick out possible tar- gets... ...the freeways that criss-cross the whole of Los Angeles.*

2 A **criss-cross** pattern or design has lines cross- ADJ CLASSIF: ing each other. EG *...light brown boots with criss-* ATTRIB *cross laces up the front.*

criterion /kraɪtɪərɪən/, **criteria** /kraɪtɪərɪə/. A N COUNT: **criterion** is a standard by which you judge or OFT+*for/of* decide something. EG *My own criterion of success is the ability to work joyfully... Little agreement exists on the criteria for defining mental illness.*

critic /krɪtɪk/, **critics.** 1 A **critic** is a person who N COUNT writes reviews and expresses opinions about books, films, music, and art. EG *What did the New York critics have to say about the production?... ...televi- sion critics.*

2 Someone who is a **critic** of a person or system N COUNT+SUPP disapproves of them and criticizes them publicly. EG *The Minister returned to London to face his parliamentary critics... ...critics of the Trade Union Movement.*

critical /krɪtɪkə³l/. 1 A **critical** time or situation is **1.1** extremely important. EG *This was a critical* ADJ QUALIT: *moment in his career... The twelve weeks of sum-* OFT+*to* *mer were critical to most of the restaurants and pubs.* ◊ **critically.** EG *The distribution of resources* ◊ ADV *is critically important.* **1.2** very serious and dan- ADJ CLASSIF gerous. EG *...the critical state of the economy.* ◊ **critically.** EG *He became critically ill.* ◊ ADV

2 If you are **critical**, **2.1** you criticize something or ADJ QUALIT: someone. EG *He had long been critical of Conserva-* OFT+*of* *tive policy... Whole groups of nations adopted a more critical attitude towards apartheid.* ◊ **critically.** EG *She had mentioned the book* ◊ ADV *critically to friends.* **2.2** you examine and judge ADJ QUALIT: something carefully. EG *...each player regarding the* ATTRIB

other with critical interest. ◊ **critically.** EG *Eva* ◊ ADV
looked at the picture critically... The problem
should be analysed more critically.

criticism /krɪtɪsɪzə⁰m/, **criticisms. 1 Criticism** N UNCOUNT
is the expression of disapproval of someone or
something. EG *The Government came in for severe*
criticism... Some fierce public criticism of the plan
had been voiced.

2 Criticism of a book, play, or other work of art is N UNCOUNT :
a serious examination and judgement of it. EG *She* OFT+SUPP
would write vivid and constructive criticism.

3 A **criticism** is a comment in which you say that N COUNT
someone or something has a particular fault. EG
One of the main criticisms against him is that he is
lazy... I don't mean this as a criticism.

criticize /krɪtɪsaɪz/, **criticizes, criticizing,** V+O : OFT+*for*
criticized; also spelled **criticise.** If you **criticize**
someone or something, you express your disap-
proval of them by saying what you think is wrong
with them. EG *Please don't get angry if I criticize*
you... I criticized the path the government was
taking... He was criticized for pursuing a policy of
conciliation.

critique /krɪtiːk/, **critiques.** A **critique** is a writ- N COUNT
ten examination and judgement of a situation or of Formal
a person's work or ideas. EG *...an intelligent and*
incisive critique of our society.

croak /krəʊk/, **croaks, croaking, croaked. 1** V
When animals or birds **croak**, they utter harsh, low
sounds. EG *A bullfrog was croaking in the distance.*
▶ used as a noun. EG *...the croak of a raven.* ▶ N COUNT

2 When someone **croaks** something, they say it in V, V+O, OR
a hoarse, rough voice. EG *'Brandy,' he croaked... He* V+QUOTE
croaked her name. ▶ used as a noun. EG *His voice* ▶ N COUNT
was a weak croak.

crochet /krəʊʃɪ³/, **crochets, crocheting, cro-** N UNCOUNT
cheted. Crochet is a way of making such things as
clothes out of thread by using a needle with a small
hook at the end. ▶ used as a verb. EG *She would* ▶ V+O OR V
patiently crochet complex patterns.

crock /krɒk/, **crocks.** A **crock** is an earthenware N COUNT
pot or jar. Outdated

crockery /krɒkə⁰ri¹/. The plates, cups, and sau- N UNCOUNT
cers that you use at mealtimes are referred to as
crockery. EG *...a sink overflowing with dirty crock-*
ery.

crocodile /krɒkədaɪl/, **crocodiles.** A **crocodile** is N COUNT
a large reptile with a long body. Crocodiles live in
rivers and eat meat.

crocus /krəʊkəs/, **crocuses. Crocuses** are small N COUNT
white, yellow, or purple flowers that are grown in
parks and gardens in the early spring.

croissant /krwʌsɒŋ/, **croissants.** A **croissant** is N COUNT
a type of small bread-like cake that is eaten for
breakfast.

crony /krəʊni¹/, **cronies.** Your **cronies** are the N COUNT :
friends who you spend a lot of time with. EG *He had* USU+POSS
a farewell drink with his cronies. Informal

crook /krʊk/, **crooks, crooking, crooked. 1** A N COUNT
crook is a criminal. Informal

2 If you call someone a **crook**, you mean that they N COUNT
are dishonest. EG *The accountants turned out to*
have been crooks... She called me a lousy crook.

3 The **crook** of your arm or leg is the soft inside N COUNT :
part where you bend your elbow or knee. EG *She* USU SING+*of*
buried her face in the crook of her arm.

4 If you **crook** your arm or finger, you bend it. V+O

5 A **crook** is also a long pole with a large hook at N COUNT
the end. EG *...a shepherd's crook.* Outdated

crooked /krʊkɪ²d/. **1** Something that is **crooked** is ADJ QUALIT
bent or twisted. EG *My back is so crooked and*
painful that I cannot stand upright.

2 A **crooked** smile or grin is uneven and bigger on ADJ QUALIT
one side than the other. EG *He showed his small*
pearly teeth in a crooked grin. ◊ **crookedly.** EG ◊ ADV
The grey-haired man smiled crookedly.

3 Someone who is **crooked** is dishonest or a ADJ QUALIT
criminal. EG *...a crooked cop.*

croon /kruːn/, **croons, crooning, crooned. 1** If V OR V+QUOTE
you **croon** something, you say it in a gentle voice.
EG *'You little charmer,' he crooned.*

2 To **croon** also means to sing or hum quietly and V OR V+O
gently.

crop /krɒp/, **crops, cropping, cropped. 1 Crops** N COUNT :
are plants such as wheat and potatoes that are USU PLURAL
grown in large quantities for food. EG *The popula-*
tion is dependent upon a simple crop, wheat...
...vast fields of crops.

2 The plants that are collected at harvest time are N COUNT :
referred to as a **crop.** EG *They get two crops of rice* OFT+*of*
a year.

3 You can also refer to a group of people or things N PART
that have appeared together as a **crop.** EG *What do* Informal
you think of the current crop of school-leavers?

4 If your hair **is cropped**, it is cut very short. EG V+O : USU PASS
Her grey hair was cropped close to her skull.
◊ **cropped.** EG *...a boy with closely cropped hair.* ◊ ADJ CLASSIF

5 When an animal such as a cow **crops** grass or V+O
leaves, it eats them. EG *Our goat was cropping the*
hedge.

crop up. If something **crops up**, it happens or PHRASAL VB :
appears unexpectedly. EG *I can come now, unless* V+ADV
any other problems crop up... Has anything Informal
cropped up that we should talk about?

cropper /krɒpə⁰/. If you say that someone has PHRASE
come a cropper, you mean that they have had an Informal
unexpected and embarrassing failure.

croquet /krəʊkɪ³/ is a game in which the players N UNCOUNT
use long-handled wooden mallets to hit balls
through metal arches stuck in a lawn.

cross /krɒs/, **crosses, crossing, crossed; cross-**
er, crossest. 1 If you **cross** something such as a V+O
room, a road, or an area of land, you move or
travel to the other side of it. EG *He crossed the*
room slowly... I wanted to prove that a woman
could cross a desert.

2 If you **cross** to a place, you go across an area of V : USU+A
land or water in order to reach the place. EG *He*
stood up at once and crossed to the door... Where
and how did you cross into Swaziland?

3 Lines or roads that **cross** meet and go across V+O OR V
each other.

4 If an expression **crosses** someone's face, it V+O
appears briefly on their face. EG *A flicker of* Literary
unconcealed distaste crossed his features.

5 If a thought **crosses** your **mind**, you think of it. PHRASE
EG *It had not crossed my mind to tell them I was*
leaving.

6 A **cross** is **6.1** a shape that consists of a vertical N COUNT
line with a shorter horizontal line across it. It is the
most important Christian symbol. EG *She wore a*
tiny golden cross. **6.2** a written mark in the shape
of an X. You can use it, for example, to indicate
that an answer to a question is wrong, or to mark
the position of something on a map. See picture at
SHAPES. EG *The reader has to indicate the answer*
with a cross or a tick.

7 If you **cross** your arms, legs, or fingers, you put V+O
one of them on top of the other. EG *She sat back and*
crossed her legs. ● If you say that you **are** ● PHRASE
crossing your **fingers** about something, you mean Informal
that you are hoping that everything will happen as
you want it to. EG *She just has to cross her fingers*
and hope.

8 Someone who is **cross** is rather angry. EG *He was* ADJ QUALIT :
looking very red and rather cross... We all get USU PRED
cross with our children. ◊ **crossly.** EG *'Don't ask* ◊ ADV
me,' the post office lady replied, crossly.

9 Something that is a **cross** between two things is N COUNT
neither one thing nor the other, but a mixture of +*between* :
both. EG *A Barbary duck is a cross between a wild* USU SING
duck and an ordinary duck.

cross off. If you **cross off** words on a list, you PHRASAL VB :
draw a line through them to indicate that they no V+O+ADV/
longer belong on the list. EG *...crossing off those* PREP
who were no longer interested.

cross out. If you **cross out** words on a page, you PHRASAL VB :
V+O+ADV

draw a line through them, usually because they are wrong. EG *She saw her name and crossed it out.*

crossbar /krɒsbaː/, **crossbars.** A **crossbar** is 1 a N COUNT horizontal piece of wood attached to two upright pieces, for example the top part of the goal in the game of football. 2 the horizontal metal bar between the handlebars and the saddle on a man's or boy's bicycle. See picture at BICYCLE.

cross-country. 1 If you go somewhere **cross-** ADJ CLASSIF : **country**, you use paths or less important roads or ATTRIB, OR railway lines, rather than the main routes. EG *...a* ADV AFTER VB *cross-country bicycle trip... He walked cross-country to the hospital.* 2 **Cross-country** is the sport of running across N UNCOUNT open countryside rather than along roads or around a running track. EG *He won a cup for cross-country in 1944... I'm in training for a cross-country run.*

cross-examine, cross-examines, cross- V+O **examining, cross-examined.** If you **cross-examine** someone during a trial in a court of law, you question them about the evidence that they have already given. ◊ **cross-examination, cross-** ◊ N UNCOUNT **examinations.** EG *Mr Fairbairn, in cross-* OR N COUNT *examination, took the matter further.*

cross-eyed. A person who is **cross-eyed** has eyes ADJ QUALIT that seem to look towards each other.

crossing /krɒsɪŋ/, **crossings.** 1 A **crossing** is a N COUNT journey by boat or ship to a place on the other side of a sea. EG *...the night ferry crossing to Esbjerg.* 2 A **crossing** is also the same as a pedestrian N COUNT crossing. EG *...light-controlled crossings.*

cross-legged /krɒslɛgɪ'd, krɒslɛgd/. If someone ADV AFTER VB, is sitting **cross-legged**, they are sitting on the floor OR ADJ CLASSIF with their legs bent so that their knees point outwards and their feet point inwards.

cross-purposes. If people are **at cross-** PHRASE **purposes,** there is a misunderstanding between them because they are talking about different things without realizing it. EG *They are bound to be at cross-purposes.*

cross-reference, cross-references. A **cross-** N COUNT **reference** is a note in a book which tells you that there is relevant or more detailed information in another part of the book.

crossroads /krɒsrəʊdz/. The plural form is also **crossroads.** 1 A **crossroads** is a place where two roads meet N COUNT and cross each other. EG *You could change buses at Polegate crossroads.* 2 If you say that something is **at a crossroads,** you PHRASE mean that it has reached a very important stage in its development. EG *Ecology stands at a cross-roads at present.*

cross-section, cross-sections. 1 A **cross-** N COUNT : **section** of something such as a group of people is a USU SING+of typical or representative sample. EG *It attracts a remarkable cross-section of the public.* 2 A **cross-section** of an object is what you would N COUNT+SUPP see if you could cut straight through the middle of it. EG *...a cross-section of a human brain.*

crossword /krɒswɜːd/, **crosswords.** A **cross-** N COUNT **word** or **crossword puzzle** is a word game in which you work out the answers to clues, and write the answers in the white squares of a pattern of small black and white squares. EG *I do the cross-word on the back page first.*

crotch /krɒtʃ/, **crotches.** 1 Your **crotch** is the N COUNT part of your body between the tops of your legs. EG *He is carrying a stack of books, which reach from the level of his crotch to just under his chin.* 2 The **crotch** of a pair of trousers or pants is the N COUNT : part that covers the area between the tops of your OFT+of legs. EG *There were grains of sand in the crotch of her swimming costume.*

crotchety /krɒtʃɪ'ti/. Someone who is **crotchety** ADJ QUALIT is grumpy and easily irritated. EG *...the most crotch-* Informal *ety judge in Cape Town.*

crouch /krautʃ/, **crouches, crouching,** **crouched.** 1 If you **are crouching,** your legs are V : USU+A bent under you so that you are close to the ground and leaning forward slightly. EG *He crouched down among the tangled foliage... There was an enormous cat crouching on the counter.* 2 If you **crouch** over something, you bend over it V : USU+A so that you are very near to it. EG *Her stout form crouched over a typewriter.*

crow /krəʊ/, **crows, crowing, crowed.** 1 A **crow** N COUNT is a kind of large black bird which makes a loud, harsh noise. 2 If you say that a place is a particular distance PHRASE away **as the crow flies,** you mean that it is that distance away measured in a straight line. EG *It was only about eight miles as the crow flies.* 3 When a cock **crows,** it utters a loud sound early V in the morning. EG *The cocks crowed again.* 4 If someone **crows** about something or **crows** V : USU over it, they keep telling people proudly about it; +about/over often used showing disapproval. EG *Now perhaps* Informal *that is something to crow about.*

crowbar /krəʊbaː/, **crowbars.** A **crowbar** is a N COUNT heavy iron bar which is used as a lever.

crowd /kraud/, **crowds, crowding, crowded.** 1 A **crowd** is 1.1 a large group of people who have N COUNT gathered together. EG *The crowd was silent... She* OR N PART *vanished into the crowd... ...crowds of tourists.* 1.2 N COUNT+SUPP a group of friends, or a set of people who share the Informal same interests or occupation. EG *They were mostly women, the usual crowd.* 2 When people **crowd** round someone or some- V+round thing, they gather closely together around them. EG *The boys crowded round him... We crowded round eagerly.* 3 If a group of people **crowd** a place or **crowd** into V+O OR it, they fill it completely. EG *Mobs of movie stars* V+in/into *were crowding the bar... The TV men crowded in, examining our equipment.* 4 If you **crowd** things into a place, you put them V+O+in/into into a space which is really too small for them. EG *He helped his dad crowd the animals into a truck.*

crowded /kraudɪ'd/. 1 If a place is **crowded,** 1.1 it ADJ QUALIT : is full of people. EG *The bar was very crowded...* OFT+with *...crowded pavements... The centre of Birmingham was crowded with shoppers.* 1.2 a lot of people live ADJ QUALIT there. EG *...crowded urban areas.* 2 If your mind is **crowded,** it is full of thoughts or ADJ QUALIT : memories. EG *His mind was crowded with memo-* OFT+with *ries of his mother.*

crown /kraun/, **crowns, crowning, crowned.** 1 N COUNT A **crown** is a circular ornament for the head, usually made of gold and precious jewels. Kings and queens wear crowns at official ceremonies. 2 The monarchy of a particular country is referred N PROPER : to as the **Crown** when it is regarded as an institu- the+N tion rather than as an individual king or queen. EG *...a senior Minister of the Crown.* 3 When someone **is crowned,** a crown is placed on V+O OR their head as part of a ceremony in which they are V+O+C : officially made king or queen. EG *The Emperor was* USU PASS *crowned by the Pope.* 4 If something **crowns** something else, it is on the V+O top of it. EG *...the shattered rocks that crowned the* Literary *hill.* 5 Your **crown** is the top part of your head, at the N COUNT : back. EG *The crown of his head is completely bald.* USU+POSS 6 An achievement, event, or quality that **crowns** V+O something is the most successful, exciting, or beautiful part of it. EG *The evening was crowned by a dazzling performance from Maria Ewing.* ◊ **crowning.** EG *...the crowning achievement of 16* ◊ ADJ CLASSIF : *years of research.* ATTRIB

crucial /kruːʃə⁰l/. Something that is **crucial** is ADJ QUALIT extremely important. EG *Success or failure here*

What cross-references are there on these pages?

would be crucial to his future prospects.
◊ **crucially.** EG The answer will depend crucially ◊ ADV
on the kind of data collected.

crucifix /ˈkruːsɪfɪks/, **crucifixes.** A **crucifix** is a N COUNT
cross with a figure of Christ on it.

crucifixion /ˌkruːsɪˈfɪkʃən/, **crucifixions. 1 Cru-** N UNCOUNT
cifixion is a way of killing people which was OR N COUNT
common in the Roman Empire, in which they
were tied or nailed to a cross and left there to die.

2 The **Crucifixion** was the death of Christ by this N PROPER:
method. the+N

crucify /ˈkruːsɪfaɪ/, **crucifies, crucifying, cruci-** V+O
fied. If someone **is crucified**, they are killed by
being tied or nailed to a cross and left there to die.

crude /kruːd/, **cruder, crudest. 1** Something that ADJ QUALIT
is **crude** is simple and unsophisticated. EG ...crude
methods of administration. ◊ **crudely.** EG ...crudely ◊ ADV
sewn shirts... The situation can be expressed,
crudely, by a mathematical equation. ◊ **crudity** ◊ N UNCOUNT
/ˈkruːdɪtiˈ/. EG ...the crudity of the draughtsmanship
in these sketches.

2 Someone who is **crude** speaks or behaves in a ADJ QUALIT
rude and often offensive way. EG Do you have to be
so crude?

crude oil is oil that is in a natural state and has N UNCOUNT
not yet been processed.

cruel /ˈkruːəl/, **crueller, cruellest. 1** Someone ADJ QUALIT:
who is **cruel** deliberately causes pain or distress to OFT+to
people or animals. EG He was cruel to her... She had
cruel parents. ◊ **cruelly.** EG They treated him ◊ ADV
cruelly.

2 A situation or action that is **cruel** is very harsh ADJ QUALIT
and causes people pain or distress. EG They don't
have the ability to survive in this cruel world.

cruelty /ˈkruːəltiˈ/, **cruelties. Cruelty** is behav- N UNCOUNT
iour that deliberately causes pain or distress to OR N PLURAL
people or animals. EG ...cruelty to animals... They
suffered beatings and other cruelties.

cruise /kruːz/, **cruises, cruising, cruised. 1** A N COUNT
cruise is a holiday during which you travel on a
ship and visit a number of places. ▸ used as a verb. ▸ V: USU+A
EG They spent the summer cruising in the Greek
islands.

2 If a car or ship **cruises**, it moves at a constant V: USU+A
speed that is comfortable and unhurried. EG The
taxi cruised off down the Cromwell Road.

cruise missile, cruise missiles. A **cruise mis-** N COUNT
sile is a missile which carries a nuclear warhead
and which is guided by a computer.

cruiser /ˈkruːzə/, **cruisers.** A **cruiser** is 1 a N COUNT
motor boat which has a cabin for people to live or
sleep in. **2** a large fast warship.

crumb /krʌm/, **crumbs. 1 Crumbs** are very N COUNT:
small pieces of bread, cake, or biscuit. USU PLURAL

2 A **crumb** of information or knowledge is a very N PART
small amount of it. EG They eagerly gathered each
crumb of information that he let drop.

crumble /ˈkrʌmbəˈl/, **crumbles, crumbling,**
crumbled. 1 If you **crumble** something soft or V-ERG
brittle or if it **crumbles**, it breaks into a lot of little
pieces. EG The bread crumbled in my fingers... The
flakes can be easily crumbled into small pieces.

2 When a building or cliff **crumbles**, it breaks into V
a lot of small pieces because it is old and is
decaying. EG The villages are crumbling into ruin.

3 When a society, organization, or relationship V
crumbles, it begins to fail or come to an end. EG
His first Labour Government crumbled.
◊ **crumbling.** EG We live in an age of crumbling ◊ ADJ CLASSIF
values.

crumbly /ˈkrʌmbliˈ/, **crumblier, crumbliest.** ADJ QUALIT
Something that is **crumbly** is easily broken into a
lot of little pieces. EG ...crumbly pastries.

crummy /ˈkrʌmiˈ/, **crummier, crummiest.** If ADJ QUALIT
you say that something is **crummy**, you mean that Informal
it is of very bad quality. EG ...a crummy little flat.

crumpet /ˈkrʌmpɪt/, **crumpets.** A **crumpet** is a N COUNT
round, flat, bread-like cake with holes in one side.

You toast crumpets and eat them with butter and
jam.

crumple /ˈkrʌmpəˈl/, **crumples, crumpling,**
crumpled. 1 If you **crumple** paper or cloth or if it V-ERG
crumples, it is squashed and becomes full of
untidy creases and folds. EG He took the letter and
crumpled it in his hand. ◊ **crumpled.** EG He was ◊ ADJ QUALIT
dressed in crumpled clothes.

2 If someone or something **crumples**, they col- V: USU+A
lapse suddenly in an untidy and helpless way. EG He
crumpled into a heap... Daddy's face crumpled
when she told him.

crumple up. If you **crumple up** a piece of PHRASAL VB:
paper, you crush it into a ball. EG She crumpled it V+O+ADV
up and threw it into the wastebasket.

crunch /krʌntʃ/, **crunches, crunching,**
crunched. 1 If you **crunch** something hard such V+O
as a sweet, you crush it noisily between your back
teeth. EG He put seven or eight pieces into his
mouth and began crunching them.

2 If you **crunch** gravel or glass or if it **crunches**, it V-ERG
makes a breaking or crushing noise when you step
on it. EG I crunched a wine glass underfoot. ▸ used ▸ N COUNT
as a noun. EG She could hear the crunch of footsteps +SUPP
on the gravel.

3 You can say **'if it comes to the crunch'** or PHRASE
'when the crunch comes', when you are considering what you would do if the situation became so
serious that you were forced to take action. EG
When the crunch comes, we can cope alone.

crunchy /ˈkrʌntʃiˈ/, **crunchier, crunchiest. 1** ADJ QUALIT
Food that is **crunchy** is hard or crisp so that it
makes a noise when you eat it. EG ...crunchy
vegetables.

2 Gravel or snow that is **crunchy** makes a noise ADJ QUALIT
when you step on it.

crusade /kruːˈseɪd/, **crusades, crusading, cru-** N COUNT+SUPP
saded. A **crusade** is a set of activities that you
carry out over a period of time in support of a
cause that you feel strongly about. EG ...the great
crusade to fight and conquer cancer. ▸ used as a ▸ V: USU+A
verb. EG We must crusade for better communication.

crusader /kruːˈseɪdə/, **crusaders.** A **crusader** is N COUNT+SUPP
someone who is involved in activities in support of
a cause that they feel strongly about. EG ...a communist crusader.

crush /krʌʃ/, **crushes, crushing, crushed. 1** If V+O
you **crush** something, **1.1** you press it very hard so
that you break it or destroy its shape. EG The jaws
snapped shut, crushing bones and flesh. **1.2** you
make it into a powder by pressing and grinding it.
EG To get the oil out you will have to crush the
seeds.

2 To **crush** an army or a political organization V+O
means to defeat it completely. EG The government
still think they can crush the unions. ◊ **crushing.** ◊ ADJ CLASSIF
EG It was a crushing result for the Labour Party. ATTRIB

3 If an event or a piece of news **crushes** someone, V+O
it shocks them or upsets them very much. EG He
has been crushed by the experience. ◊ **crushed.** ◊ ADJ CLASSIF
EG She saw that he was hurt and crushed.
◊ **crushing.** EG The lecture was interrupted by the ◊ ADJ CLASSIF:
crushing news of President Kennedy's death. ATTRIB

4 If you **are crushed** against other people or V+O: USU PASS
things, you are pushed or pressed against them. EG
Women were crushed up against men.

5 A **crush** is a dense crowd of people. EG A reporter N COUNT
made his way through the crush.

6 If you have a **crush** on someone, you have a N COUNT:
strong feeling of attraction for them that does not OFT+on
usually last very long. EG I had a crush on the violin Informal
master.

crust /krʌst/, **crusts. 1** The **crust** on a loaf of N COUNT OR
bread is the hard, crispy outside part of it. N UNCOUNT

2 A **crust** is also a hardened layer of something, N COUNT:
especially on top of a softer or wetter substance. EG USU SING
The snow had a fine crust on it.

3 The earth's **crust** is the outer layer of its surface. N COUNT+SUPP EG ...*movements of the earth's crust.*

crusted /krʌstɪ²d/. Something that is **crusted** with ADJ PRED: a substance is covered with a hard layer of it. EG OFT+*with* *The lane was crusted with cow dung.*

crusty /krʌstɪ¹/, **crustier, crustiest.** Something ADJ QUALIT that is **crusty** has a hard, crisp outside layer. EG ...*crusty bread.*

crutch /krʌtʃ/, **crutches. 1** A **crutch** is a support N COUNT like a stick, which you lean on in order to help you to walk when you have injured your foot or leg. EG *She came walking in on crutches, her foot still in a cast.*
2 If you refer to someone or something as a N COUNT **crutch**, you mean that they give you help or support. EG *The book was simply a crutch to my memory.*
3 A **crutch** is also the same as a crotch. N COUNT

crux /krʌks/. The **crux** of a problem or argument N SING: USU is the most important or difficult part of it which *the*+N+*of* affects everything else. EG *Here we come to the crux of the matter.*

cry /kraɪ/, **cries, crying, cried. 1** When you **cry**, **1.1** you produce tears in your eyes, usually because V you are unhappy or hurt. EG *Helen began to cry...* *'Oh don't cry,' said Florrie.* ▸ used as a noun. EG *I* ▸ N SING *think she had a good cry, for her eyes were rather red.* **1.2** you shout or say something loudly. EG V+QUOTE *'Come on!' he cried... 'Oh look!' she cried, seeing the ticket.*
2 A **cry** is **2.1** a loud, high sound that you make N COUNT: with your voice and that expresses a strong emo- OFT+*of* tion such as fear, pain, or pleasure. EG *Claud let out a cry of horror.* **2.2** a shout, usually made in order N COUNT+SUPP to attract someone's attention. EG ...*battle cries... I heard a cry for help.* **2.3** the sound that some birds N COUNT make. EG *A sea bird flapped upwards with a hoarse cry.*
3 Something that is a **far cry** from something else PHRASE is very different from it. EG *The tropical grasslands are a far cry from the lush green pastures of Ireland.*

cry off. If you **cry off**, you decide not to do PHRASAL VB: something that you had arranged to do. EG *I'm* V+ADV *afraid I cried off at the last moment.* Informal

cry out. If you **cry out**, **1** you call out loudly PHRASAL VB: because you are frightened, unhappy, or in pain. EG V+ADV *I heard Mary cry out in fright.* **2** you speak loudly. V+ADV, EG *'Father! You must stop that!' he suddenly cried* OFT+QUOTE *out.*

cry out for. If you say that one thing **is crying** PHRASAL VB: **out for** another, you mean that it needs that thing V+ADV+PREP very much. EG *There is a vast surplus of workers crying out for employment.*

crypt /krɪpt/, **crypts.** A **crypt** is an underground N COUNT room beneath a church or cathedral.

cryptic /krɪptɪk/. A **cryptic** remark or message ADJ QUALIT contains a hidden meaning or is difficult to under-stand. EG *I didn't ask what this cryptic remark was intended to convey.*

crystal /krɪstə⁰l/, **crystals. 1** A **crystal** is a N COUNT mineral that has formed naturally into a regular symmetrical shape. EG *Pure copper is made up of layers of crystals.*
2 Crystal is **2.1** a rock that is transparent like ice, N UNCOUNT often used in jewellery or ornaments. EG *The throne has a beautiful inlay of agate, onyx, and crystal.* **2.2** very high quality glass, usually with its surface cut so that it twinkles in the light. EG ...*a shimmering crystal chandelier.*

crystal clear. Something that is **crystal clear** is ADJ CLASSIF **1** absolutely clear and transparent like glass. EG ...*blue skies and crystal clear air.* **2** very easy to understand. EG *He challenged every point which he did not find crystal clear.*

crystallize /krɪstə⁰laɪz/, **crystallizes, crystal-lizing, crystallized;** also spelled **crystallise. 1** If V-ERG you **crystallize** an opinion or idea or if it **crystal-lizes**, it becomes fixed and definite in your mind.

EG *This involvement has helped me to crystallize my criticisms of the women's movement.*
◇ **crystallization** /krɪstə⁰laɪzeɪʃə⁰n/. EG ...*the crys-* ◇ N UNCOUNT *tallisation of our beliefs.*
2 If a substance **crystallizes**, it turns into crystals. V EG *Eventually the sugar crystallises.*

cub /kʌb/, **cubs.** A **cub** is a young wild animal N COUNT such as a lion, wolf, or bear. EG ...*a two-month-old leopard cub.*

cubby-hole /kʌbɪ hoʊl/, **cubby-holes.** A **cubby-** N COUNT **hole** is a very small room or space for storing Outdated things.

cube /kjuːb/, **cubes, cubing, cubed. 1** A **cube** is a N COUNT solid object with six square surfaces which are all the same size. See picture at SHAPES. EG ...*cubes of bread.*
2 The **cube** of a number is another number that is N COUNT: produced by multiplying the first number by itself USU *the*+N+*of* twice. For example, the cube of 2 is 8.
3 When a number **is cubed**, it is multiplied by itself V+O: USU PASS twice; for example, 3 cubed is 3 x 3 x 3, which is 27. 3 cubed is usually written as 3^3.

cubic /kjuːbɪk/. You use **cubic** in units of volume ADJ CLASSIF: to indicate that you are measuring length, width, ATTRIB and height. For example, a cubic metre is the equivalent of something a metre long, a metre high, and a metre wide.

cubicle /kjuːbɪkə⁰l/, **cubicles.** A **cubicle** is a N COUNT small enclosed area in a public building such as a sports centre, which people use for dressing and undressing.

cuckoo /kʊkuː/, **cuckoos.** A **cuckoo** is a grey bird N COUNT that has an easily recognizable call of two quick notes, and that lays its eggs in other birds' nests.

cucumber /kjuːkʌmbə/, **cucumbers.** A **cucum-** N COUNT **ber** is a long, thin vegetable, often used raw in salads, that has a green skin and is white and moist inside.

cud /kʌd/. When animals such as cows or sheep PHRASE **chew the cud**, they slowly chew their partly digested food over and over again in their mouth before finally swallowing it.

cuddle /kʌdə⁰l/, **cuddles, cuddling, cuddled.** If V OR V+O: you **cuddle** someone, you put your arms round RECIP them and hold them close as a way of showing your affection. EG *A baby must be cuddled a lot.* ▸ used ▸ N COUNT as a noun. EG *Give them a few cuddles and talk nicely to them.*

cuddle up. If you **cuddle up** to someone, you sit PHRASAL VB: or lie as near to them as possible and you hold V+ADV, USU+A them. EG *Jenny was cuddled up against me.* Informal

cuddly /kʌdlɪ¹/. People, animals, or toys that are ADJ CLASSIF **cuddly** are soft or furry so that you want to cuddle them. EG ...*cuddly toys.*

cudgel /kʌdʒə⁰l/, **cudgels. 1** A **cudgel** is a thick, N COUNT short stick used for hitting people. Outdated
2 If you **take up the cudgels** for someone or PHRASE• something, you speak or fight in support of them. EG *Brown took up the cudgels on his behalf.*

cue /kjuː/, **cues. 1** A **cue** is **1.1** something that is N COUNT+SUPP said or done by a performer that is a signal for another performer to begin speaking or doing something. EG *The violinist was late for her cue.* **1.2** anything that serves as a signal for some action. EG *The Director General stood up. It was Stuart's cue to depart.*
2 If you **take** your **cue** from someone, you use PHRASE their behaviour as an indication of what you should do in a particular situation. EG *Michael took his cue from the Duke's tone.*
3 If you say that something happened **on cue**, you PHRASE are emphasizing that it happened just when it was expected to happen. EG *Then, right on cue, the coach broke down.*
4 A **cue** that is used in games such as snooker, N COUNT

Is a culprit culpable?

billiards, and pool is a long, thin wooden stick with a leather tip at one end.

cuff /kʌf/, **cuffs, cuffing, cuffed. 1** A **cuff** is **1.1** N COUNT the end part of a sleeve which is thicker than the rest of the sleeve. **1.2** the bottom part of a trouser American leg, which is turned up.

2 If you are speaking **off the cuff**, you are PHRASE speaking spontaneously, without preparing what you are going to say. EG *I can't answer that question off the cuff.*

3 If you **cuff** someone, you hit them with your V+O hand, usually in a light, friendly way. EG *Sally cuffed my head lightly.* ▸ used as a noun. EG *...a cuff on the* ▸ N COUNT *head.* Informal

cufflink /kʌflɪŋk/, **cufflinks. Cufflinks** are small N COUNT : decorative objects used for holding together shirt USU PLURAL cuffs around the wrist.

cuisine /kwɪziːn/. **1** The **cuisine** of a country or N UNCOUNT district is the style of cooking which is characteris- +SUPP tic of that area. EG *...the delights of the Paris cuisine.*

2 The **cuisine** of a restaurant is the range of food N UNCOUNT that is served in it.

cul-de-sac /kʌldəsæk, kʊl-/, **cul-de-sacs.** A **cul-** N COUNT **de-sac** is a short road which is closed at one end.

culinary /kʌlɪnəˀriˀ/ means concerned with kitch- ADJ CLASSIF : ens or cooking. EG *...their culinary skills.* ATTRIB

cull /kʌl/, **culls, culling, culled. 1** If you **cull** V+O : ideas or information, you gather them together and OFT+*from* choose which of them you need. EG *...materials that I'd culled from all sorts of places.*

2 To **cull** animals means to kill the weaker ani- V+O mals in a group in order to reduce their numbers. EG *They start to cull the herds in dry years.* ▸ used ▸ N COUNT as a noun. EG *...a big elephant cull in Zimbabwe.*

culminate /kʌlmɪneɪt/, **culminates, culminat-** V+*in* **ing, culminated.** If a situation or process **culmi- nates** in something, this thing happens after the situation or process has gradually developed. EG *The struggle between King and Parliament had culminated in the Civil War.*

culmination /kʌlmɪneɪʃəˀn/. The **culmination** of N UNCOUNT : a situation or process is what happens as its final USU the+N+of result. EG *Marriage is seen as the culmination of a successful relationship.*

culpable /kʌlpəbəˀl/. If someone is **culpable**, they ADJ PRED are responsible for something wrong or unpleasant Formal that has happened. EG *Was Hearst culpable? To what extent?*

culprit /kʌlprɪt/, **culprits. 1** A **culprit** is someone N COUNT who has committed a crime or done something wrong. EG *The main culprits were caught and heavily sentenced.*

2 If you say that a particular thing is the **culprit**, N COUNT you mean that it is the cause of problems or trouble. EG *Fat is a major culprit in causing cancers of the bowel.*

cult /kʌlt/, **cults. 1** A **cult** is a religious group N COUNT : which worships a particular person or performs USU SING+*of* particular rituals, especially one which is consid- ered strange or unnatural. EG *The 'Moonies' cult gained adherents at an alarming rate.*

2 A particular person, object, or activity that is a N COUNT : **cult** has become very popular or fashionable. EG USU SING *The Beatles became the heroes of a world-wide cult.*

cultivate /kʌltɪveɪt/, **cultivates, cultivating, cultivated. 1** If you **cultivate** land, you prepare it V+O and grow crops on it. EG *He retired to his estate near Bordeaux to cultivate his vineyard.* ◊ **cultivated.** EG *Only 1 per cent of the cultivated* ◊ ADJ CLASSIF *area was under irrigation.* ◊ **cultivation** ◊ N UNCOUNT /kʌltɪveɪʃəˀn/. EG *Some extra land is being brought under cultivation in Asia.*

2 If you **cultivate** a feeling, idea, or attitude, you V+O try hard to develop it and make it stronger. EG *He was anxious to cultivate the trust of moderate Tories.* ◊ **cultivation.** EG *...the cultivation of good* ◊ N UNCOUNT *taste.* +of

3 If you **cultivate** someone, you try hard to V+O develop a friendship with them. EG *Their coopera- tion is vital, so cultivate them assiduously.*

cultivated /kʌltɪveɪtɪˀd/. **1** Someone who is **culti-** ADJ QUALIT **vated** has had a good education, and shows this in their behaviour. EG *...his cultivated Southern Eng- lish accent.*

2 Cultivated plants have been developed for grow- ADJ CLASSIF : ing on farms or in gardens. EG *...cultivated wheat...* ATTRIB *...cultivated mushrooms.*

cultural /kʌltʃəˀrəl/ means **1** relating to a particu- ADJ CLASSIF : lar society and its ideas, customs, and art. EG *...* ATTRIB *cultural traditions of great antiquity.* ◊ **culturally.** ◊ ADV EG *They had little in common culturally with us.* **2** ADJ CLASSIF : involving or concerning the arts. EG *...cultural ac-* ATTRIB *tivities such as plays, concerts, and poetry read- ings.* ◊ **culturally.** EG *...an elegant and culturally* ◊ ADV+ADJ *vital life.*

culture /kʌltʃəˀ/, **cultures. 1 Culture** consists of N UNCOUNT the ideas, customs, and art that are produced by a OFT+SUPP particular society. EG *He was specially interested in culture and history... ...African culture.*

2 A **culture** is a particular society or civilization, N COUNT+SUPP especially considered in relation to its ideas, art, or way of life. EG *We must respect the practices of cultures different from our own.*

3 In science, a **culture** is a group of bacteria or N COUNT : cells which are grown in a laboratory as part of an USU+SUPP experiment. EG *...blood cultures.*

cultured /kʌltʃəˀd/. Someone who is **cultured** has ADJ QUALIT good manners, is well educated, and knows a lot about the arts. EG *...a highly cultured man.*

culture shock is a feeling of anxiety, loneliness, N UNCOUNT and confusion that people sometimes experience when they first arrive in another country.

-cum- is placed between two words to form a compound noun describing something or someone as being partly one thing and partly another. EG *...a dining-cum-living room.*

cumbersome /kʌmbəsəm/. **1** Something that is ADJ QUALIT **cumbersome** is large and heavy and therefore difficult to carry, wear, or handle. EG *...a cumber- some piece of machinery.*

2 An activity, process, or system that is **cumber-** ADJ QUALIT **some** is very complicated and inefficient. EG *The process is cumbersome and inflexible.*

cumulative /kjuːmjəlɐtɪv/. Something that is **cu-** ADJ CLASSIF **mulative** keeps increasing steadily in quantity or degree. EG *It was an accelerating, cumulative pro- cess.*

cunning /kʌnɪŋ/. **1** Someone who is **cunning** has ADJ QUALIT the ability to plan things cleverly, often by deceiv- ing other people. EG *He knew nothing of the cun- ning means employed to get him out of his job.*

2 Someone who has **cunning** has the ability to plan N UNCOUNT things cleverly, often by deceiving other people. EG *They achieved their aim by stealth and cunning.*

cup /kʌp/, **cups, cupping, cupped. 1** A **cup** is a N COUNT small, round container, usually with a handle, from which you drink liquids such as tea and coffee. EG *...a china cup.*

2 You can use **cup** to refer to the contents of a cup, N PART as in a **cup** of tea or a **cup** of coffee. EG *I've just made some tea. Would you like a cup?... I had a cup of hot flavourless coffee.*

3 A **cup** is also **3.1** something which is small, round, N COUNT : and hollow in shape like a cup. EG *...an egg cup...* USU+SUPP *She tipped a pile of raisins into the cup of his hand.* **3.2** a prize of a large metal cup that is given to the N COUNT person or team that wins a game or competition. EG *...runner-up for the King's Cup.*

4 If you **cup** something in your hands, you hold it V-ERG : USU+A with your hands touching all round it. EG *....his hands were cupped around his lighter.*

cupboard /kʌbəd/, **cupboards.** A **cupboard** is a N COUNT piece of furniture which has one or two doors at the front and usually shelves inside it. It is used for keeping things in. EG *...a well-stocked kitchen cup- board.*

cupful /ˈkʌpful/, **cupfuls**. A **cupful** is the amount N PART which one cup can hold. EG ...*a cupful of rice.*

curable /ˈkjuərəbəl/. If a disease or illness is ADJ CLASSIF **curable**, it can be cured.

curate /ˈkjuərət/, **curates**. A **curate** is a clergy- N COUNT man in the Church of England who helps the vicar or rector of a parish.

curative /ˈkjuərətɪv/ is used to describe something ADJ CLASSIF that can cure people's illnesses or problems. EG ATTRIB ...*the curative power of herbal remedies.*

curator /kjuˈreɪtə/, **curators**. A **curator** is N COUNT : someone who is in charge of the objects or works OFT+*of* of art in a museum or art gallery.

curb /kɜːb/, **curbs**, **curbing**, **curbed**. 1 If you V+O **curb** something, you control it and keep it within fixed limits. EG ...*proposals to curb the powers of* the Home Secretary. ▸ used as a noun. EG *This* ▸ N COUNT : *requires a curb on public spending.* OFT+*on*

2 If you **curb** someone, you act firmly to control V+O them and make them behave properly. EG *Children whose instincts are to rebel often get curbed by their teachers.*

3 See also **kerb**.

curd /kɜːd/, **curds**. **Curds** are the thick white N COUNT : substance which is formed when milk turns sour. USU PLURAL

curdle /ˈkɜːdəl/, **curdles**, **curdling**, **curdled**. If V-ERG milk **curdles** or if something **curdles** it, it be- comes sour. ● See also **bloodcurdling**.

cure /kjuə/, **cures**, **curing**, **cured**. 1 If doctors or V+O medical treatments **cure** an illness or injury, they make it end or disappear. EG *There are few diseas- es that these modern drugs cannot cure.* ▸ used as ▸ N COUNT : a noun. EG *I'm interested in the cure of cancer.* OFT+*of*

2 If doctors or medical treatments **cure** a person, V+O they make the person well again after an illness or injury. EG *Her patients appear to be cured.*

3 A **cure** for an illness is a medicine or other N COUNT : treatment that cures people suffering from the OFT+*for* illness. EG *There's no known cure for a cold.*

4 If someone or something **cures** a problem, they V+O remove it. EG *The bishop had done nothing to cure the widespread lack of faith.* ▸ used as a noun. EG ▸ N COUNT : *The only cure for her unhappiness was to leave* OFT+*for* *home.*

5 If an action or event **cures** someone of a habit or V+O+*of* an attitude, it makes them give it up. EG *The shock of losing my purse cured me of my former care- lessness.*

6 If food, tobacco, or animal skin **is cured**, it is V-ERG treated by being dried, smoked, or salted so that it will last for a long time. EG ...*cured ham.* ◇ ADJ CLASSIF

cure-all, **cure-alls**. A **cure-all** is something that N COUNT people think will solve all their problems. EG *Low- ering of interest rates has been presented as the media as a kind of universal cure-all.*

curfew /ˈkɜːfjuː/, **curfews**. 1 A **curfew** is a law N COUNT stating that people must stay inside their houses after a particular time at night, for example during a war. EG *An emergency curfew was enforced.*

2 **Curfew** is the time after which you will be N UNCOUNT punished if you are found outside your house when OR N COUNT there is a curfew. EG *He had gone into a shop ten minutes after the curfew to buy some tobacco.*

curio /ˈkjuərɪəʊ/, **curios**. A **curio** is an object such N COUNT as a small ornament which is unusual and fairly rare.

curiosity /ˌkjuərɪˈɒsɪti/, **curiosities**. 1 **Curiosity** N UNCOUNT is a desire that someone has to know about things and to learn as much as possible about them. EG *She looked at me, eyes wide open and full of curiosity... She showed an insatiable curiosity for my past.*

2 A **curiosity** is something that is unusual, interest- N COUNT ing, and fairly rare. EG ...*old but natural curiosities like fossils... ...a little curiosity shop.*

curious /ˈkjuərɪəs/. 1 Someone who is **curious** is ADJ QUALIT interested in things and eager to learn as much as possible about them. EG *She was curious to see what would happen... He seemed awfully curious about*

Robertson's day-to-day routine. ◇ **curiously.** EG ◇ ADV *They stopped and looked at her curiously.*

2 Something that is **curious** is 2.1 unusual and ADJ QUALIT interesting. EG *Not long after our arrival, a curious thing happened.* ◇ **curiously.** EG *She had a curious-* ◇ ADV *ly husky voice.* 2.2 difficult to explain because you ADJ QUALIT cannot understand why it happens or what causes it. EG *It is curious how two such different problems can be solved so similarly.* ◇ **curiously.** EG *Curi-* ◇ ADV SEN *ously, Hearst worked energetically during his men- tal breakdown.*

curl /kɜːl/, **curls**, **curling**, **curled**. 1 **Curls** are N COUNT : lengths of hair that are shaped in tight curves and USU PLURAL circles. EG ...*a little girl with golden curls.*

2 Hair that has **curl** has waves or curls in it. EG *He* N UNCOUNT *now wore his hair shorter and it had lost its curl.*

3 A **curl** is a curved, spiral shape. EG ...*curls of* N COUNT : *smoke.* USU+SUPP

4 If something **curls** or if you **curl** it, it has tight V-ERG : OFT+A curves in it or it becomes tightly curved. EG *Her hair curled about her head like a child's... The bark was curling and falling away from the trunk... Her hands were curled around the cup.*

5 If something **curls** somewhere, it moves in V+A circles or spirals. EG *Smoke was curling out of kitchen chimneys.*

6 If an animal **curls** itself **into a ball**, it moves into PHRASE a position which makes a rounded shape.

curl up. 1 If you **curl up**, you lie down and bring PHRASAL VB : your arms, legs, and head in towards your stomach. V+ADV EG *He was lying curled up with his back to us.* 2 V+ADV When something flat such as a leaf or a piece of paper **curls up**, its edges bend up or towards the centre, usually because it is old.

curler /ˈkɜːlə/, **curlers**. **Curlers** are small plastic N COUNT : or metal tubes that women roll their hair round in USU PLURAL order to make it curly. EG *She took her curlers out.*

curly /ˈkɜːli/, **curlier**, **curliest**. 1 Hair that is ADJ QUALIT **curly** is full of curls.

2 Something that is **curly** is curved, circular, or ADJ QUALIT spiral in shape. EG *What are these curly bits of* Informal *paper for?*

currant /ˈkʌrənt/, **currants**. 1 **Currants** are N COUNT : small dried grapes, used especially in cakes. USU PLURAL

2 You use **currant** to refer to several different soft N COUNT fruits, such as blackcurrants or redcurrants. EG *The currant bushes were heavy with fruit.*

currency /ˈkʌrənsi/, **currencies**. 1 The **curren- cy** of a country is 1.1 the system of money that is N COUNT : used in it. EG *Sterling has once again become one of* USU+SUPP *the stronger currencies.* 1.2 the coins and bank- N UNCOUNT notes that are used in it. EG *Do you change foreign currency?*

2 If ideas, expressions, and customs have **curren- N UNCOUNT cy**, they are used and accepted by many people at Formal a particular time. EG *They have seen many of their basic ideas gain wide currency.*

current /ˈkʌrənt/, **currents**. 1 A **current** is 1.1 a N COUNT steady and continuous flowing movement of some of the water in a river, lake, or sea. EG *The child had been swept out to sea by the current.* 1.2 a N COUNT steady flowing movement of air.

2 An electric **current** is a flow of electricity N COUNT through a wire or circuit. EG *There was a powerful electric current running through the wires.*

3 A **current** of opinion or behaviour is a general N COUNT+SUPP tendency within a group of people to adopt a particular opinion or way of behaving. EG ...*the fickle currents of fashion.*

4 Something that is **current** is happening, being ADJ CLASSIF done, or being used at the present time. EG *Our current methods of production are too expensive... The conversation shifted onto what is current in art and music.* ◇ **currently.** EG ...*experiments* ◇ ADV *currently in progress.*

What currency is used in your country?

5 Ideas, expressions, and customs that are **current** ADJ CLASSIF are generally accepted and used by most people. EG *The words 'light pollution' are in current use only among astronomers.*

current account, current accounts. A **current** N COUNT **account** is a personal bank account which you can British take out money from at any time using your cheque book or cheque card.

current affairs are political and social events N PLURAL which are discussed in newspapers and on television and radio programmes. EG *...the BBC's current affairs programmes.*

curriculum /kərɪkjəˈləm/, **curriculums** or **cur-** N COUNT **ricula** /kərɪkjəˈlə/. A **curriculum** is **1** all the different courses of study that are taught in a school, college, or university. EG *Social studies have now been added to the curriculum.* **2** one particular course of study that is taught in a school, college, or university. EG *...our English curriculum.*

curriculum vitae /kərɪkjəˈləm viːtaɪ/. Your N SING : **curriculum vitae** is a brief written account of OFT + POSS your personal details, your education, and the jobs you have had. You are often asked to send a curriculum vitae when you are applying for a job.

curried /kʌrɪd/. **Curried** food has been flavoured ADJ CLASSIF : with hot spices. EG *...curried eggs.* ATTRIB

curry /kʌriˈ/, **curries. Curry** is an Indian dish N MASS made with hot spices. EG *...a vegetable curry.*

curse /kɜːs/, **curses, cursing, cursed. 1** If you v **curse,** you swear or say rude words because you are angry about something. EG *He missed the ball and cursed violently.* ▸ used as a noun. EG *With a* ▸ N COUNT *curse he disentangled his head from the netting.*
2 If you **curse** someone, you say insulting things to V+O : OFT+for them because you are angry with them. EG *I was cursing him under my breath for his carelessness.*
3 If you **curse** something, you complain angrily V+O about it, especially using rude language. EG *Cursing my plight, I tried to find shelter for the night.*
4 If you say that there is a **curse** on someone, you N COUNT : mean that there seems to be a supernatural power OFT + on/upon causing unpleasant things to happen to them. EG *There is a curse on this family.*
5 You can also refer to something or someone that N COUNT + SUPP causes a great deal of trouble or harm as a **curse.** EG *Loneliness in old age is the curse of modern society.*

cursed /kɜːsɪd, kɜːst/. **1** Someone who is **cursed** is ADJ CLASSIF suffering as the result of a curse. EG *The descendants of Ham were cursed for ever.*
2 If you are **cursed** with something, you are very ADJ PRED unlucky in having it. EG *...a land cursed with almost* + with *continuous rainfall.*

cursory /kɜːsəˈriˈ/. A **cursory** glance or examina- ADJ QUALIT : tion is a brief one in which you do not pay much USU ATTRIB attention to detail. EG *They signed with only a cursory glance at what I had written.*

curt /kɜːt/, **curter, curtest.** If someone is **curt,** ADJ QUALIT they speak in a brief and rather rude way. EG *He had been curt with Gertrude.* ◊ **curtly.** EG *Marsha* ◊ ADV *said curtly, 'You're supposed to be on watch.'*
◊ **curtness.** EG *His tone was characterised by* ◊ N UNCOUNT *curtness and dryness.*

curtail /kɜːˈteɪl/, **curtails, curtailing, curtailed.**
1 If you **curtail** something, you reduce it. EG V+O *Countries are under pressure to curtail public expenditure.*
2 If you **curtail** someone's power or freedom, you V+O restrict it. EG *...further legislation to curtail basic union rights.*

curtailment /kɜːˈteɪlməˈnt/. The **curtailment** of N UNCOUNT something is the act of reducing or restricting it. EG +SUPP *...the curtailment of military aid from the US.* Formal

curtain /kɜːtəˈn/, **curtains, curtaining, cur-** **tained. 1** A **curtain** is a piece of material which N COUNT : hangs from the top of a window. You pull it across USU PLURAL the window when you want to keep light out or prevent people from seeing you. EG *He drew the curtains.*

2 In a theatre, the **curtain** is the large piece of N SING : the+N material that hangs in front of the stage until a performance begins. EG *There was a burst of applause as the curtain went up.*
3 You can refer to something as a **curtain** when it N UNCOUNT hangs down thickly and is difficult to see through +SUPP or get past. EG *A dense curtain of reeds stretches across the water... ...an impenetrable curtain of blonde hair.*

curtain off. If you **curtain off** part of a room, PHRASAL VB : you separate it from the rest of the room by V+O+ADV hanging a curtain across the room.

curtained /kɜːtəˈnd/. A **curtained** window, door, ADJ CLASSIF or other opening has a curtain hanging across it. EG *The curtained stage was empty.*

curtsy /kɜːtsiˈ/, **curtsies, curtsying, curtsied;** V : OFT+ to also spelled **curtsey.** When a woman or a girl **curtsies,** she lowers her body briefly, bending her knees and holding her skirt with both hands, as a way of showing respect for an important person. EG *The ladies curtsied deeply to him.* ▸ used as a ▸ N COUNT noun. EG *I bobbed him a curtsy.*

curve /kɜːv/, **curves, curving, curved. 1** A N COUNT **curve** is a smooth, gradually bending line, for example part of the edge of a circle. EG *The beach stretched away before them in a gentle curve.*
2 When something **curves, 2.1** it has the shape of V+A a curve. EG *The lane curved round to the right.* **2.2** it moves in a curve, for example through the air. EG *The missile curved gracefully towards its target.*

curved /kɜːvd/. A **curved** object has the shape of ADJ QUALIT a curve. EG *...the curved tusks of a walrus.*

curvy /kɜːviˈ/ means the same as curved. EG *...a* ADJ QUALIT *settee with only one curvy end.*

cushion /kʊʃəˈn/, **cushions, cushioning, cush-** **ioned. 1** A **cushion** is **1.1** a fabric case filled with N COUNT soft material, which you put on a seat to make it more comfortable. **1.2** a soft pad or barrier, N COUNT+SUPP especially one that stops something hitting something else violently. EG *The device floats on a cushion of air.*
2 If objects **cushion** a collision, they are between V+O the things that hit each other and therefore make the collision less violent. EG *The pile of branches cushioned his fall.*
3 To **cushion** the effect of something unpleasant V+O means to reduce it. EG *A cut in income tax would cushion the blow of sharp price increases.* ▸ used ▸ N COUNT as a noun. EG *...that reassuring cushion of economic* +SUPP *growth.*

cushy /kʊʃiˈ/, **cushier, cushiest.** A **cushy** job or ADJ QUALIT task is very easy. EG *...that nice cushy job in the* Informal *bank.*

custard /kʌstəd/ is a sweet yellow sauce made N UNCOUNT from milk and eggs or from milk and a powder. You eat custard with fruit and puddings. EG *...jelly and custard.*

custodial /kʌstəʊdɪəl/ means relating to the cus- ADJ CLASSIF tody of people in prison. EG *...offences which called* Formal *for custodial sentences.*

custodian /kʌstəʊdɪən/, **custodians.** A **custo-** N COUNT **dian** is someone who is in charge of a building or the objects in a building such as a museum.

custody /kʌstədiˈ/. **1 Custody** is the legal right to N UNCOUNT keep and look after a child, especially the right given to the child's father or mother when they become divorced. EG *Divorce courts usually award custody to mothers.*
2 Someone who is **in custody** has been arrested PHRASE and is being kept in prison until they can be tried in a court. EG *...people who have been quite wrongly held in custody.*

custom /kʌstəˈm/, **customs. 1** A **custom** is **1.1** a N COUNT traditional activity or festivity. EG *My wife likes all the old English customs.* **1.2** something that the N COUNT OR people of a society always do in particular circum- N UNCOUNT stances because it is regarded as the right thing to do. EG *It is the custom to take chocolates or fruit when visiting a patient in hospital.* **1.3** something N COUNT : USU + POSS that someone usually does in a particular situation or at a particular time. EG *It is Howard's custom to take his class for coffee afterwards.*

2 Customs is the place at a border, airport, or harbour where people arriving from a foreign country have to declare goods that they bring with them. EG *At Kennedy airport I went through the customs... ...a customs officer.* N UNCOUNT OR N MOD

3 Custom is the practice of regularly buying things from a particular shop or tradesman. EG *Many local services depend on the University's custom.* N UNCOUNT Formal

customary /kʌstəməᵒriʲ/. **1** Something that is **customary** is usually done in a particular situation or at a particular time. EG *...the customary Christmas party.* ◇ **customarily.** EG *...the civil exchange of letters which customarily marks the departure of a minister.* ADJ CLASSIF
◇ ADV

2 Someone's **customary** behaviour is their usual behaviour. The **customary** way of doing something is the usual way of doing it. EG *Peter had never seen her so shaken out of her customary calm... She was rewarded in the customary way.* ADJ CLASSIF : ATTRIB

3 The **customary** time for something is the time at which it usually happens or is usually done. EG *At the customary hour the doctor knocked on my door.* ADJ CLASSIF : ATTRIB

customer /kʌstəmə/, **customers. 1** A **customer** is someone who buys something, especially from a shop. EG *She's one of our regular customers.* N COUNT

2 You can use **customer** when you are describing someone's behaviour. For example, if you describe someone as an awkward **customer**, you mean that you think they deliberately behave in a way which causes other people trouble. N COUNT : ADJ+N Informal

custom-made. Something that is **custom-made** is made for you according to your special requirements. EG *...custom-made cars.* ADJ CLASSIF

cut /kʌt/, **cuts, cutting.** The form **cut** is used in the present tense and is the past tense and past participle of the verb.

1 If you **cut** something, you push a knife or a similar tool into it in order to remove a piece of it or to mark it or damage it. EG *She cut the cake and gave me a piece... His wife killed herself by cutting her wrists.* ▶ used as an adjective. EG *...thinly cut rye bread.* ▶ used as a noun. EG *He made a deep cut in the wood.* V+O
▶ ADJ CLASSIF
▶ N COUNT

2 If you **cut** yourself, you accidentally injure yourself on a sharp object so that you bleed. EG *Robert cut his knee quite badly.* ▶ used as a noun. EG *I had some cuts and bruises but I'm OK.* V-REFL OR V+O
▶ N COUNT

3 To **cut** through something means to move or pass through it easily. EG *The big canoe was cutting through the water.* V+through

4 If you **cut** across or through a place, you go through it because it is the shortest route to another place. EG *I cut across country for the next hundred miles.* V+across/ through

5 If you **cut** the amount of something, you reduce it. EG *She cut her costs by half.* ▶ used as a noun. EG *...a tax cut... ...large cuts in government spending.* V+O
▶ N COUNT : USU+SUPP

6 If you **cut** part of something that someone has written, you do not print or broadcast it. EG *Her publishers insisted on cutting several stories out of her memoirs.* ▶ used as a noun. EG *He agreed to make a few minor changes and cuts in the play.* V+O : USU+A
▶ N COUNT : USU PLURAL

7 If you **cut** something, especially someone's hair, you shorten it using scissors or another tool. EG *Tell him to get his hair cut.* ▶ used as a noun. EG *He is having a cut and blow-dry.* V+O
▶ N COUNT

8 Well **cut** clothes have been well designed and well made. EG *He wears beautifully cut suits.* ADJ CLASSIF

9 If you **cut** a pack of playing cards, you divide it into two. V+O

10 A **cut** of meat is a large piece of meat which is ready for cooking. N COUNT

11 A person or thing that is **a cut above** other people or things of the same kind is better than PHRASE

them. EG *The meals they serve are a cut above most pub food.*

12 See also **cutting.**

cut across. If an issue or problem **cuts across** the division between two groups of people, it affects or matters to people in both groups. EG *Issues, however, tended to cut across party lines.* PHRASAL VB : V+PREP

cut back. If you **cut back** something such as expenditure or **cut back on** it, you reduce it. EG *Congress cut back the funds... Other countries have cut back on high-priced oil.* ● See also **cutback.** PHRASAL VB : V+O+ADV, V+ADV+PREP, OR V+ADV

cut down. 1 If you **cut down** on an activity, you do it less often. EG *She had cut down on smoking... Heavy drinkers must be prepared to cut down.* **2** If you **cut** a tree **down**, you cut through its trunk so that it falls to the ground. PHRASAL VB : V+ADV, OFT+ on V+O+ADV

cut in. If you **cut in** on someone, you interrupt them when they are speaking. EG *Mrs Travers began a reply, but Mrs Patel cut in again.* PHRASAL VB : V+ADV, OFT+QUOTE

cut off. 1 If you **cut** something **off**, you remove it by cutting it. EG *Lexington cut off a small piece of meat... ...egg sandwiches with the crusts cut off.* **2** To **cut** someone or something **off** means to separate them from things that they are normally connected with. EG *The town was cut off... We have cut ourselves off from the old ways of thinking.* PHRASAL VB : V+O+ADV
V+O+ADV, OFT+ from

▶ used as an adjective. EG *Mary feels cut off from the central life of the village... She is completely cut off from friends.* **3** If a supply of something **is cut off**, it stops being provided. EG *Gas supplies had now been cut off... They are threatening to cut off funds.* **4** If you **cut** someone **off** when they are having a telephone conversation, you disconnect them. **5** See also **cut-off.** ▶ ADJ PRED : OFT+ from
V+O+ADV
V+O+ADV

cut out. 1 If you **cut out** part of something, you remove it using a tool with a sharp edge. EG *Badly decayed timber should be cut out and replaced.* **2** If you **cut out** something that you are doing or saying, you stop doing or saying it. EG *Cut out waste... He's cut out the drinking altogether.* **3** If you **cut** someone **out** of an activity or event, you do not allow them to be involved in it. EG *I don't think I should be cut out of the trip.* **4** If an object **cuts out** the light, it is between you and the light so that you are in the dark. **5** If an engine **cuts out**, it suddenly stops working. EG *It keeps cutting out when I stop.* **6** If you are **cut out** for a particular type of work, you have the qualities that will make you able to do it. EG *I'm not really cut out for this job.* **7** See also **cut-out.** ● to **have your work cut out**: see **work.** PHRASAL VB : V+O+ADV
V+O+ADV
V+O+ADV, OFT+ of
V+O+ADV
V+ADV
PHRASE

cut up. If you **cut** something **up**, you cut it into several pieces. EG *She cut up her piece of cheese.* ● See also the separate entry **cut up.** PHRASAL VB : V+O+ADV

cut-and-dried. A **cut-and-dried** answer or solution is clear and obvious. EG *There is no cut-and-dried formula which can answer these questions.* ADJ QUALIT

cutback /kʌtbæk/, **cutbacks.** A **cutback** is a reduction in something, especially in the number of people that a firm or organization employs. EG *In the defence industries sudden cutbacks are common... ...the cutback in public services.* N COUNT : OFT+ in

cute /kjuːt/, **cuter, cutest.** If you describe someone or something as **cute**, you mean that you think they are very pretty or attractive. EG *What a cute little girl.* ADJ QUALIT American

cut glass is glass that has patterns cut into its surface. EG *...a cut-glass bowl.* N UNCOUNT OR N MOD

cutlery /kʌtləriʲ/. The knives, forks, and spoons that you eat your food with are referred to as **cutlery.** N UNCOUNT

cutlet /kʌtləᵒt/, **cutlets.** A **cutlet** is **1** a small piece of meat which is usually fried or grilled. EG *...veal cutlets.* **2** vegetables or nuts that are fried or grilled together in a small lump. EG *...a nut cutlet.* N COUNT

Would you be cut up by a cutting remark?

cut-off, cut-offs. A **cut-off** or a **cut-off** point is the level or limit at which you decide that something should stop happening. N COUNT OR N MOD

cut-out, cut-outs. 1 A **cut-out** is an automatic device that turns off a motor, for example because there is something wrong with it. EG ...*a cut-out to prevent the battery from overcharging.* N COUNT
2 A cardboard **cut-out** is a shape that has been cut from card. EG ...*a cut-out of a girl.* N COUNT

cut-price. You use **cut-price** to describe something that is for sale at a reduced price. EG *We enjoy going shopping and taking advantage of cut-price offers.* ADJ CLASSIF

cutter /kʌtə/, **cutters.** A **cutter** or a pair of **cutters** is a tool that you use for cutting through something. EG ...*a glass cutter*... ...*a pair of wire cutters.* N PLURAL OR N COUNT

cut-throat. You use **cut-throat** to describe situations in which people all want the same thing and do not care if they harm each other in getting it. EG ...*cut-throat competition*... ...*a cut-throat advertising battle.* ADJ QUALIT

cutting /kʌtɪŋ/, **cuttings. 1** A **cutting** is a piece of writing which has been cut from a newspaper or magazine. EG ...*press cuttings.* N COUNT
2 A **cutting** from a plant is a part of the plant, for example a leaf, that you cut and use in order to grow a new plant. EG *They are easy roses to grow from cuttings.* N COUNT
3 A **cutting** remark is unkind and likely to hurt someone's feelings. EG *Does this sound cutting? It's not meant to be.* ADJ QUALIT

cut up. If you are **cut up** about something that has happened, you are very unhappy because of it. EG *She's still terribly cut up about his death.* ● See also the phrasal verb **cut up** at the entry for **cut.** ADJ PRED Informal

CV /si: vi:/, **CV's. CV** is an abbreviation for 'curriculum vitae'.

cwt, cwts. cwt can also be used as the plural form. **cwt** is an abbreviation for 'hundredweight'. EG ...*75 cwt of wheat.*

cyanide /saɪənaɪd/ is a highly poisonous substance. N UNCOUNT

cycle /saɪkəl/, **cycles, cycling, cycled. 1** If you **cycle**, you ride a bicycle. EG *I decided to cycle into town.* ◊ **cycling.** EG *We recommend cycling as a good form of exercise.* V : USU+A ◊ N UNCOUNT
2 A **cycle** is **2.1** a bicycle. **2.2** a motorcycle. N COUNT
3 A **cycle** is also **3.1** a series of events or processes that is repeated again and again, always in the same order. EG ...*the endless cycle of the seasons.* **3.2** a single complete series of movements in an N COUNT+SUPP N COUNT

electrical, electronic, or mechanical process. EG ...*50 cycles per second.* **3.3** a series of songs or poems that are intended to be performed or read one after the other. N COUNT+SUPP

cyclic /saɪklɪk, sɪklɪk/ means the same as cyclical. EG ...*a cyclic process.* ADJ CLASSIF

cyclical /sɪklɪkəl/. A **cyclical** process happens again and again in cycles. EG ...*cyclical fluctuations in investment.* ADJ CLASSIF

cyclist /saɪklɪst/, **cyclists.** A **cyclist** is someone who rides a bicycle. N COUNT

cyclone /saɪkləʊn/, **cyclones.** A **cyclone** is a violent storm in which air circulates rapidly in a clockwise direction. N COUNT

cygnet /sɪgnət/, **cygnets.** A **cygnet** is a young swan. N COUNT

cylinder /sɪlɪndə/, **cylinders.** A **cylinder** is **1** a shape or an object with flat circular ends and long straight sides. See picture at SHAPES. **2** a piece of machinery with this shape, especially one in an engine in which a piston moves backwards and forwards. EG ...*a five cylinder engine.* N COUNT

cylindrical /sɪlɪndrɪkəl/. Something that is **cylindrical** is in the shape of a cylinder. EG ...*a cylindrical pipe.* ADJ CLASSIF

cymbal /sɪmbəl/, **cymbals.** A **cymbal** is a flat circular brass object that is used as a musical instrument. You hit it with a stick or hit two cymbals together, making a loud noise. See picture at MUSICAL INSTRUMENTS. EG ...*the clashing of the cymbals.* N COUNT : USU PLURAL

cynic /sɪnɪk/, **cynics.** A **cynic** is someone who believes that people always behave in a selfish way. EG *Pareto was a cynic, disillusioned by the society of his day.* N COUNT

cynical /sɪnɪkəl/. Someone who is **cynical** or who has **cynical** attitudes believes that people always behave in a selfish way. EG *You are taking a rather cynical view of marriage.* ◊ **cynically.** EG *Grant smiled cynically.* ADJ QUALIT ◊ ADV

cynicism /sɪnɪsɪzəm/ is an attitude towards people in which you always expect them to act in a selfish way. EG *The mood of political cynicism and despair deepened.* N UNCOUNT

cypher /saɪfə/. See cipher.

cypress /saɪprəs/, **cypresses.** A **cypress** is a type of evergreen tree. N COUNT

cyst /sɪst/, **cysts.** A **cyst** is a growth containing liquid that appears inside your body or under your skin. N COUNT

D d

D, d /di:/, **Ds, d's. 1 D** is the fourth letter of the English alphabet. N COUNT
2 d was a written form of 'penny' or 'pence' in Britain before decimal currency was introduced in 1971.

-'d. In spoken English and in informal written English, **-'d** is **1** a short form of 'would'. EG *She'd be sure to see it... I knew there'd be trouble.* **2** a short form of 'had', especially when 'had' is an auxiliary verb. EG *I'd heard it many times.*

dab /dæb/, **dabs, dabbing, dabbed. 1** If you **dab** a substance onto a surface, you put it there with quick, light, strokes. If you **dab** a substance from a surface, you remove it with quick, light strokes. EG *She dabbed some powder on her nose... He dabbed the cuts with disinfectant... He gently dabbed the sweat from Joe's upper lip.* V+O+A
2 A **dab** of something is a small amount of it that is put onto a surface. EG *She returned wearing a dab of rouge on each cheekbone.* N PART

3 If you are a **dab hand** at something, you are very good at doing it. EG *She is a dab hand at finding excuses for their mistakes.* PHRASE Informal British

dabble /dæbəl/, **dabbles, dabbling, dabbled.** If you **dabble** in an activity or subject, you take part in it or study it a bit, but not very seriously. EG *They dabble in politics.* V+in

dad /dæd/, **dads.** People often call their father **dad.** EG *Hey, Dad, what's for dinner?... My dad doesn't like her.* VOCATIVE OR N COUNT Informal

daddy /dædɪ/, **daddies.** Children often call their father **daddy.** EG *Daddy, why do we grow old?... My daddy is a policeman.* VOCATIVE OR N COUNT Informal

daffodil /dæfədɪl/, **daffodils.** A **daffodil** is a yellow trumpet-shaped flower that blooms in the spring. N COUNT

daft /dɑːft/, **dafter, daftest.** Someone or something that is **daft** is stupid or not sensible. EG *Don't be daft.* ADJ QUALIT Informal

dagger

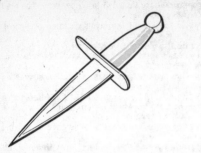

dagger /dægə/, **daggers**. A **dagger** is a weapon N COUNT
like a knife with two sharp edges.

daily /deɪli¹/, **dailies**. 1 If something happens ADV OR
daily, it happens every day. EG *He wrote to her* ADJ CLASSIF :
almost daily... Fights are a daily hazard... ATTRIB
...Margaret's daily visits.

2 Daily also means relating to a single day or to ADJ CLASSIF :
one day at a time. EG *Daily wage rates were around* ATTRIB
two dollars... ...the daily routine of the jail.

3 A **daily** newspaper or a **daily** is a newspaper ADJ CLASSIF :
that is published every day of the week except ATTRIB OR
Sunday. N COUNT

dainty /deɪnti¹/, **daintier**, **daintiest**. A **dainty** ADJ QUALIT
movement, person, or object is small, neat, or
pretty. EG *...walking with neat, dainty steps... ...a
dainty little girl... ...a dainty cup with flowers
painted on it.* ◊ **daintily**. EG *She raised a plump* ◊ ADV
arm, fingers daintily extended.

dairy /deəri¹/, **dairies**. 1 A **dairy** is **1.1** a shop or N COUNT
company that sells milk, butter, and cheese. **1.2** a
building on a farm where milk is kept or where
cream, butter, and cheese are made.

2 Dairy is used to refer to **2.1** foods such as butter N MOD
and cheese that are made from milk. EG *...dairy
products.* **2.2** the use of cattle to produce milk
rather than meat. EG *He owns a dairy herd of 105
cattle.*

dais /deɪɪs/. A **dais** is a raised platform in a hall. EG N SING
*As I stepped up on the dais, the Chief rose to greet
me.*

daisy /deɪzi¹/, **daisies**. A **daisy** is a small wild N COUNT
flower with a yellow centre and white petals.

dam /dæm/, **dams**, **damming**, **dammed**. 1 A N COUNT
dam is a wall that is built across a river in order to
stop the flow of the water and make a lake behind
it.

2 To **dam** a river means to build a dam across it. V+O

dam up. To **dam up** a river means to dam it or PHRASAL VB :
block it. V+O+ADV

damage /dæmɪdʒ/, **damages**, **damaging**, **damaged**. 1 To **damage** something means **1.1** to harm V+O
or spoil it physically, for example by breaking it. EG
A fire had severely damaged part of the school. **1.2** V+O
to have a harmful effect on it, for example by
making it weaker or less successful. EG *Unofficial
strikes were damaging the British economy.*
◊ **damaging**. EG *The incident was damaging to his* ◊ ADJ QUALIT :
career and reputation. OFT+*to/for*

2 Damage is **2.1** physical harm that is caused to N UNCOUNT :
something. EG *It can cause lethal damage to the* OFT+*to*
liver. **2.2** a harmful effect that something has on
something else. EG *He could not repair the damage
done to the party's standing and credibility.*

3 When a court of law awards **damages** to some- N PLURAL
one, it orders money to be paid to them by a person
who has harmed their reputation or property, or
who has injured them. EG *He finally got £4,000 in
damages.*

damask /dæməsk/ is a type of heavy cloth with a N UNCOUNT
pattern woven into it.

dame /deɪm/, **dames**. 1 A **dame** is a woman. EG N COUNT
The dame wore a veil... Remember, some of these Informal
dames are very powerful in movies, they can get American
you work.

2 In Britain, **Dame** is a title given to a woman as a
special honour because of important service or
work that she has done. EG *...Dame Flora Robson.*

dammit /dæmɪt/. See **damn**.

damn /dæm/. **1 Damn**, **damn it**, and **dammit** are EXCLAM
swear words which people sometimes use to ex-
press anger or annoyance.

2 The swear word **damn** is also used for emphasis. SUBMOD
EG *I knew damn well what he was going to say.*
▸ used as an adjective. EG *We kept tripping over* ▸ ADJ CLASSIF :
pieces of wood which some damn fool had left ATTRIB
lying about. Informal

3 If you say that someone does not **give a damn** or PHRASE
does not **care a damn** about something, you mean Informal
that they do not care about it at all.

damnation /dæmneɪʃⁿn/. According to some re- N UNCOUNT
ligions, if someone suffers **damnation**, they are
condemned to stay in hell for ever after death
because of their sins. EG *...eternal damnation.*

damned /dæmd/. **1 Damned** is a swear word that SUBMOD
some people use, especially when they are angry,
to emphasize what they are saying. EG *I don't know
what you're talking about, and I'm damned sure
you don't either.* ▸ used as an adjective. EG *He's a* ▸ ADJ CLASSIF :
damned nuisance. ATTRIB

2 If you say that you **are damned if** you are going PHRASE
to do something, you mean that you do not intend Informal
to do it and think it is unreasonable for someone to
expect you to do it.

3 You can say **I'll be damned** or **Well, I'm** EXCLAM
damned when you are expressing surprise at Informal
something.

4 According to some religions, the **damned** are N PLURAL
people who have been condemned to stay in hell *the*+N
for ever after they have died.

damning /dæmɪŋ/. Something that is **damning** ADJ QUALIT
suggests very strongly that someone is guilty of a
crime or error. EG *I was getting the type of
damning evidence I was looking for.*

damp /dæmp/, **damper**, **dampest**; **damps**,
damping, **damped**. **1** Something that is **damp** is ADJ QUALIT
slightly wet. EG *The building was cold and draughty
and damp... She wiped the table with a damp cloth.*
◊ **dampness**. EG *...the cold and dampness of win-* ◊ N UNCOUNT
ter.

2 Damp is slight wetness in the air or on the inside N UNCOUNT
walls of a house. EG *The paint had not fully covered
the damp on the walls.*

damp down. To **damp** something **down** means PHRASAL VB :
to reduce its liveliness, violence, or urgency. EG V+O+ADV
*Neighbouring countries had been of no help in
damping down the crisis.*

dampen /dæmpⁿn/, **dampens**, **dampening**,
dampened. **1** To **dampen** something means to V+O
reduce its energy, liveliness, or violence. EG *The
prospect of an election in no way dampened his
spirits.*

2 If you **dampen** something, you make it slightly V+O
wet. EG *He dampens his face, then dries it.*

damson /dæmzⁿn/, **damsons**. A **damson** is a N COUNT
small, sour purple plum.

dance /dɑːns/, **dances**, **dancing**, **danced**. 1 When V OR V+O
you **dance**, you move around in time to music. EG
*John danced with Julie... ...girls dancing the can-
can.* ◊ **dancing**. EG *The music and dancing lasted* ◊ N UNCOUNT
for hours.

2 A **dance** is **2.1** a series of steps and rhythmic N COUNT
movements which you do in time to music. EG
Before we knew it, we were doing this dance. **2.2** a

What is the difference between a place that is
damp and a place that is dank?

piece of music which people can dance to. **2.3** a social event where people can dance with each other. EG *I hated the big formal dances at college.*
● to make a **song and dance** about something: see **song**.

3 Dance is the activity of performing dances, N UNCOUNT especially as a public entertainment. EG *They are supreme artists of dance and theatre.*

4 If you **dance** from one place to another, you V+A jump and skip as you go along, usually because you are happy or excited. EG *Ralph danced out into the street.*

5 If you say that something **dances**, you mean that V : USU+A it moves about lightly and quickly. EG *The little metal boxes dance and vibrate.* ◊ **dancing.** EG *The* ◊ ADJ CLASSIF : *fires cast dancing shadows upon their faces.* ATTRIB

dancer /dɑːnsə/, **dancers. 1** A **dancer** is a person N COUNT who earns money by dancing, or a person who is dancing. EG *He always wanted to be a dancer.*

2 If someone is a good **dancer**, they dance well. N COUNT

dandelion /dændəˈlaɪən/, **dandelions.** A **dande-** N COUNT **lion** is a wild plant which has yellow flowers first, then fluffy balls of seeds.

dandruff /dændrəˀf/ refers to small white pieces N UNCOUNT of dead skin that are in someone's hair or that fall from their hair. EG *Miss Travers has dandruff.*

danger /deɪndʒə/, **dangers. 1 Danger** is the N UNCOUNT possibility that someone may be harmed or killed. EG *The child is too young to understand danger... My friends were round me. I was in no danger.*

2 A **danger** is something or someone that can hurt N COUNT or harm you. EG *Cigarette smoking is a danger to health... They warned us of the dangers of making assumptions.*

3 If there is a **danger** that something unpleasant N UNCOUNT will happen, it is possible that it will happen. EG +SUPP *There was a danger that she might marry the wrong man... There is no danger of fire.*

dangerous /deɪndʒəˀrəs/. Something that is **dan-** ADJ QUALIT **gerous** is able or likely to hurt or harm you. EG *...a dangerous animal... It is dangerous to drive with a dirty windscreen.* ◊ **dangerously.** EG *She was* ◊ ADV *dangerously close to the fire.*

dangle /dæŋgəˀl/, **dangles, dangling, dangled.** V-ERG When something **dangles** or when you **dangle** it, it hangs or swings loosely. EG *Huge wooden ear-rings dangled from her ears... Charlie was leaning across my desk dangling the long roll of paper.*

dank /dæŋk/, **danker, dankest.** A place that is ADJ QUALIT **dank** is unpleasantly damp and cold. EG *I slept in the dank basement room.*

dapper /dæpə/. A man who is **dapper** has a very ADJ QUALIT neat and clean appearance, and is small or slim.

dappled /dæpəˀld/. Something that is **dappled** has ADJ CLASSIF dark or light patches on it, or is made up of patches Literary of light and shade. EG *...dappled leafy sunlight.*

dare /deə/, **dares, daring, dared. Dare** is used both as a main verb and as a semi-modal. For information about semi-modals, see the entry head-ed SEMI-MODALS.

1 If you **dare** to do something, you have enough V+to-INF, OR courage to do it. EG *She did not dare to look at him...* SEMI-MODAL : *He dared not show that he was pleased... I can't do* USU WITH *that – I simply wouldn't dare.* BROAD NEG

2 If you say **don't you dare** do something, you are PHRASE angrily telling someone not to do it. EG *Don't you dare throw it away.*

3 You say **how dare you** when you are very PHRASE shocked and angry about something that someone has done. EG *How dare you speak to me like that!*

4 If you say **I dare say** or **I daresay**, you mean PHRASE that you think something is probably true. EG *I daresay you've spent all your money by now... It's worth a few pounds, I dare say, but no more.*

5 If you **dare** someone to do something dangerous V+O : or frightening, you suggest that they do it to show USU+to-INF how brave they are. EG *He looked round fiercely, daring them to contradict.*

6 A **dare** is a challenge which one person makes to N COUNT : USU SING

another to do something dangerous or frightening. EG *It was many years since James had accepted a dare.*

daren't /deənt/ is the usual spoken form of 'dare not'.

daresay /deəseɪ/. See paragraph 4 of **dare.**

daring /deərɪŋ/. **1** Someone who is **daring** does ADJ QUALIT things which might be dangerous or which might shock people. EG *He was the most daring of contemporary writers of fiction... ...a daring raid.* ◊ **daringly.** EG *One of the boys very daringly bent* ◊ ADV *down and touched it.*

2 Daring is the courage to do things which might N UNCOUNT be dangerous or which might shock people. EG *...the efficiency and daring shown by our armed forces.*

dark /dɑːk/, **darker, darkest. 1** When it is **dark,** ADJ QUALIT there is not enough light to see properly. EG *Luckily it was too dark for anyone to see me blushing... The room was dark and empty.* ◊ **darkness.** EG *The* ◊ N UNCOUNT *lights went out and the hall was plunged into darkness.*

2 The **dark** is the lack of light in a place. EG *He was* N SING : the+N *sitting in the dark at the back of the theatre.*

3 If you do something **before dark**, you do it PHRASE before the sun sets. If you do something **after dark**, you do it when night has begun. EG *I want to get there before dark.*

4 Something that is **dark** is a colour that is quite ADJ QUALIT near black. EG *...a man in an elegant dark suit... ...long dark hair. ...dark red curtains.*

5 Someone who is **dark** has brown or black hair, ADJ QUALIT and often brown skin as well. EG *He was a tall, dark, and undeniably handsome man.*

6 A **dark** period of time is unpleasant or frighten- ADJ QUALIT : ing. EG *...the dark days of high unemployment.* ATTRIB

7 Dark looks or remarks make you think that the ADJ QUALIT : person giving them wants to harm you or that ATTRIB something horrible is going to happen. ◊ **darkly.** ◊ ADV EG *Another of the men hinted darkly that there would be violence.*

8 If you are **in the dark** about something, you do PHRASE not know anything about it.

darken /dɑːkəˀn/, **darkens, darkening, dark-** **ened. 1** If a place or the sky **darkens** or **is** V-ERG **darkened**, it becomes darker, for example be-cause it is nearly night. EG *The autumn sky dark-ened.*

2 When you **darken** something or when it **dark-** V-ERG **ens,** it becomes darker in colour. EG *Rub in linseed oil to darken the wood... His hair was darkened by the rain.*

3 If someone's face **darkens**, they suddenly look V+O angry.

darkened /dɑːkəˀnd/. A **darkened** building has ADJ CLASSIF no lights on inside it.

dark glasses. Dark glasses are glasses which N PLURAL have dark-coloured lenses to protect your eyes in the sunshine.

darkish /dɑːkɪʃ/ means quite dark in colour. ADJ CLASSIF

darkroom /dɑːkruːm/, **darkrooms.** A **darkroom** N COUNT is a room which is lit only by red light, so that photographs can be developed there.

darling /dɑːlɪŋ/, **darlings. 1** You call someone VOCATIVE **darling** if you love them or like them very much. EG *You're looking marvellous, darling.*

2 In some parts of Britain, people call other people VOCATIVE **darling** as a sign of friendliness.

3 You can use **darling** to describe someone that ADJ CLASSIF : you love or like very much. EG *...her darling baby* ATTRIB *brother.*

4 You describe someone as a **darling** when you N COUNT are fond of them and think that they are nice. EG *The poor darling doesn't have a car.*

5 The **darling** of a group of people is someone who N COUNT+POSS is especially liked by that group. EG *She quickly became the darling of the crowds.*

darn /dɑːn/, **darns, darning, darned. 1** When you V+O OR V **darn** something made of cloth, you mend a hole in it by sewing stitches across the hole and then weaving stitches in and out of them. EG *I offered to darn Sean's socks... She started darning.*

2 A **darn** is a part of a piece of clothing that has N COUNT been darned. EG *Her jumper had a darn at the bottom.*

3 People sometimes use **darn** or **darned** to em- SUBMOD OR phasize what they are saying, often when they are ADJ CLASSIF : annoyed. EG *It's darned hot in here.* ATTRIB Informal

dart /dɑːt/, **darts, darting, darted. 1** If a person V : USU+A or animal **darts** somewhere, they move there suddenly and quickly. EG *...butterflies darting from one flower to another.*

2 If you **dart** a glance at someone or something, V+O+A you look at them very quickly.

3 A **dart** is a small, narrow object with a sharp N COUNT point which can be thrown or shot. EG *They killed the elephants with tiny poisoned darts.*

4 Darts is a game in which you throw darts at a N UNCOUNT round board which has numbers on it.

dash /dæʃ/, **dashes, dashing, dashed. 1** If you V+A **dash** somewhere, you run or go there quickly and suddenly. EG *People dashed out into the street to see what was happening.* ▶ used as a noun. EG *He* ▶ N COUNT *made a dash for the door.*

2 If you say that you **have to dash** or you **must** PHRASE **dash**, you mean that you are in a hurry and have to Informal leave.

3 A **dash** of a liquid is a small quantity of it which N PART you add when you are preparing food or mixing a drink. EG *Some soups are delicious served cold with a dash of cream.*

4 If you **dash** something somewhere, you throw it V+O+A or push it violently. EG *She picked up his photograph and dashed it to the ground.*

5 If your hopes **are dashed**, something happens V+O that makes it impossible for you to get what you hope for.

6 A **dash** is also a short horizontal line (–) that is N COUNT used in writing, for example before and after a sentence that occurs within another sentence.

dash off. If you **dash off** a letter or other piece PHRASAL VB : of writing, you write it very quickly and without V+O+ADV thinking about it very much.

dashboard /dæʃbɔːd/, **dashboards.** The **dash-** N COUNT **board** in a car is the panel facing the driver's seat where most of the instruments and switches are. See picture at CAR.

dashing /dæʃɪŋ/. Someone who is **dashing** or who ADJ QUALIT wears **dashing** clothes is very stylish and attractive. EG *She felt very dashing in her yellow suit.*

data /deɪtə, dɑːtə/ is information, usually in the N UNCOUNT form of facts or statistics that you can analyse. EG OR N PLURAL *The data was being processed at the Census Office... It isn't present in the data when they are received.*

database /deɪtəbeɪz/, **databases.** A **database** is a N COUNT collection of data that is stored in a computer and that can easily be used and added to.

date /deɪt/, **dates, dating, dated. 1** A **date** is a N COUNT particular day, for example 7th April 1988, or the year in which something happened or will happen, for example 1066. EG *No date was announced for the talks.*

2 When you **date** something, you give the date V+O when it began or when it was made. EG *How can we date these fossils?*

3 When you **date** something such as a letter or a V+O OR V+O+ cheque, you write the day's date on it. EG *The letter* O *was dated September 18 1952.*

4 At a particular **date** means at a particular time N SING or stage. EG *The matter may be worth pursuing at a later date.*

5 If something has happened or been true **to date**, PHRASE it has happened or been true until the present time. EG *Their effects to date have been limited.*

6 If something **dates**, it goes out of fashion. ● See V also **dated.**

7 A **date** is also an appointment to meet someone N COUNT : or to go out with them, especially someone of the OFT+*with*

opposite sex. EG *Sorry I can't come – I have a date with Jill.*

8 Your **date** is a person of the opposite sex that N COUNT : you have a date with. EG *Her date says that he* USU+POSS *doesn't know either.* American

9 If you **are dating** someone of the opposite sex, V+O you go out regularly with them. American

10 A **date** is also a small, sticky, dark brown fruit. N COUNT Dates grow on palm trees.

11 See also **out of date, up-to-date.**

date back. If something **dates back** to a particu- PHRASAL VB : lar time, it started or was made at that time. EG *The* V+ADV, *present city hall dates back to the 1880s.* USU+*to*

date from. If something **dates from** a particular PHRASAL VB : time, it started or was made at that time. EG *...a* V+PREP *manuscript dating from the eleventh century.*

DATE

This entry gives some of the ways in which you can express dates.

A date can be written as 'July 10', 'July 10th', '10 July' or '10th July', but is usually pronounced 'July the tenth' or 'the tenth of July'. However, 'July 10' is sometimes pronounced 'July ten' in American English. The year and the month are often left out of dates when it is clear which year or month you are referring to. The day of the week is usually mentioned before the rest of the date, and the year is usually mentioned after the day and month. EG *'What date is it?' – 'It's the 30th today.'... ...Tuesday May the thirteenth... ...Monday the fifth of April... They married on December 9, 1913... Labour was defeated in the General Election of 19 June 1970... The case was heard in the High Court in February 1910... Where were you on the night of February 4th?*

In British English, you can mention the month either after or before the day, but in American English it is more common to mention the month first. This is especially important when dates are written as a series of numbers, since a date such as 10/7/86 usually means July 10th 1986 in British English, but it means October 7th 1986 in American English.

In British English, you usually say that something happens **on** a particular day, for example 'It happened on Thursday', but in American English you can also leave out 'on' and say 'It happened Thursday'.

If you refer to the twenties, you are referring to the years between 1920 and 1929. If you refer to the 1840's, you are referring to the years between 1840 and 1849. The early sixties are the years between 1960 and 1965, and the late sixties are the years between 1965 and 1969. EG *...Stockholm in the thirties... I went on a computer training course in the nineteen fifties.*

In the following examples, the speaker is referring to things that usually happen on a particular day. EG *I'm terribly busy on Saturdays... On Monday nights, the pupils go to the local cinema... ...every Tuesday for the next few months... I've never worked on a Saturday.*

If you dash somewhere, do you dawdle on the way?

dated /deɪtɪ²d/. Something that is **dated** seems old- ADJ QUALIT fashioned, although it may once have been fashion- able. EG ...*dated clothes.*

date of birth, dates of birth. Your **date of birth** N COUNT : is the exact date on which you were born, including USU+POSS the year. EG *Give your name, age, and date of birth.*

daub /dɔːb/, **daubs, daubing, daubed.** When you V+O+A **daub** a substance such as mud or paint on some- thing, you carelessly spread it on the thing. EG *He had mud daubed on his boots... ...daubing walls with paint.*

daughter /dɔːtə/, **daughters.** Someone's **daugh-** N COUNT **ter** is their female child. EG *She is the daughter of a retired Army officer.*

daughter-in-law, daughters-in-law. Someone's N COUNT **daughter-in-law** is the wife of their son.

daunt /dɔːnt/, **daunts, daunting, daunted.** If V+O something **daunts** you, it makes you feel slightly afraid or worried about whether you can succeed in doing it. ◇ **daunting.** EG *It is a daunting prospect* ◇ ADJ QUALIT *for a party so recently formed.*

dawdle /dɔːdⁿl/, **dawdles, dawdling, dawdled.** V If you **dawdle**, you spend more time than is necessary doing something or going somewhere. EG *Billy dawdled behind her, balancing on the cracks in the pavement.*

dawn /dɔːn/, **dawns, dawning, dawned. 1 Dawn** N UNCOUNT is the time of day when light first appears in the OR N COUNT sky, before the sun rises. EG *Tom woke me at dawn... They worked from dawn till dusk.*

2 When a day **dawns**, the sky begins to grow light V after the night has ended. EG *The first day of the holidays* Written *dawned bright and fair.*

3 The **dawn** of a period of time or a situation is the N SING : beginning of it. EG *This marked the dawn of a new* the+N+of *era in human history.* Literary

4 If something **is dawning**, it is beginning to V develop or appear. EG *The age of the answering* Literary *machine is just dawning.* ◇ **dawning.** EG *She wrote* ◇ ADJ CLASSIF *of the dawning hopes of reconciliation in Western* ATTRIB *Europe.*

dawn on or **dawn upon.** If a fact or idea **dawns** PHRASAL VB : **on** you or **dawns upon** you, you realize it. EG *Then* V+PREP *it dawned on me that they were speaking Spanish.*

day /deɪ/, **days. 1** A **day** is **1.1** one of the seven N COUNT twenty-four hour periods of time in a week. EG *The attack occurred six days ago... Can you go any day of the week? What about Monday?* **1.2** the time N COUNT OR when it is light, or the time when you are awake N UNCOUNT and doing things. EG *They had waited three days and nights for this opportunity... They hunt by day... ...a typical working day.*

2 You can refer to a particular period in history as N COUNT+SUPP a particular **day.** EG *This is the main problem of the present day... ...in the early days of the republic... Are students interested in religion these days?*

3 If you **call it a day**, you decide to stop what you PHRASE are doing and you leave it to be finished later.

4 If something happens **day and night** or **night** PHRASE **and day**, it happens all the time without stopping. EG *The factories were working continuously day and night throughout the year.*

5 In this day and age means in modern times. EG PHRASE *Even in this day and age the old attitudes persist.*

6 If something **makes** your **day**, it makes you feel PHRASE very happy. EG *Her smile somehow makes my day.* Informal

7 One day or **some day** or **one of these days** PHRASE means at some future time. EG *We're all going to be old one day.*

8 If it is a month or a year **to the day** since a PHRASE particular thing happened, it is exactly a month or a year since it happened.

daybreak /deɪbreɪk/ is the time in the morning N UNCOUNT when light first appears. EG *They had to leave at daybreak.*

daydream /deɪdriːm/, **daydreams, daydream-** **ing, daydreamed. 1** A **daydream** is a series of N COUNT pleasant thoughts, especially about things that you

would like to happen. EG *He drifted off into another daydream.*

2 When you **daydream**, you think about pleasant V : OFT things for a period of time. EG *Boys and girls* +about/of *daydream about what they want to be.*

daylight /deɪlaɪt/ is **1** the light that there is N UNCOUNT during the day before it gets dark. EG *We've got at least two more hours of daylight... It looks different in daylight.* **2** the time of day when it begins to get light. EG *The ship sailed into harbour before day- light on 1 September 1942.* ● **in broad daylight**: see **broad.**

day off, days off. A **day off** is a day when you do N COUNT not have to go to work even though it is usually a working day. EG *'Where's Cynthia?' - 'It's her day off.'*

day return, day returns. A **day return** is a train N COUNT or bus ticket which allows you to go somewhere British and come back on the same day for a lower price than an ordinary return ticket.

daytime /deɪtaɪm/ is the part of a day between N UNCOUNT the time when it gets light and the time when it OR N SING : gets dark. EG *The forests were dark even in the* the+N *daytime... He held a daytime job as a shop assis- tant.*

day-to-day means happening every day as part of ADJ CLASSIF : ordinary life. EG *This is very much part of the day-* ATTRIB *to-day life of all human beings.*

daze /deɪz/, **dazed. 1** If someone is **in a daze**, they PHRASE are feeling very confused or upset. EG *I left the ranch in a daze.*

2 If someone **is dazed** by a sudden physical injury V-PASS or other unexpected event, they are unable to think clearly. EG *She was dazed by the news.* ◇ **dazed.** EG *He seemed dazed and bewildered.* ◇ ADJ QUALIT

dazzle /dæzⁿl/, **dazzles, dazzling, dazzled. 1** If V+O : USU PASS someone or something **dazzles** you, you are ex- tremely impressed by their skill, qualities, or beau- ty. EG *She had clearly been dazzled by the evening's performance.* ◇ **dazzling.** EG *She gave him a* ◇ ADJ QUALIT *dazzling smile... ...his dazzling political career.*

2 The **dazzle** of a light is its sudden brightness that N UNCOUNT makes it impossible for you to see properly for a short time. EG *They both blinked in the sudden dazzle.*

3 The **dazzle** of something is a quality it has, such N UNCOUNT as beauty or skill, which is impressive and attrac- tive. EG *...the dazzle of high technology.*

4 If a bright light **dazzles** you, it makes you unable V+O to see properly for a short time. ◇ **dazzling.** EG ◇ ADJ CLASSIF *Marsha shut her eyes against the dazzling sun.*

DC /diː siː/ is used to refer to an electric current that always flows in the same direction. **DC** is an abbreviation for 'direct current'.

DDT /diː diː tiː/ is a poisonous substance which is N UNCOUNT used for killing insects.

dead /ded/. **1** A person, animal, or plant that is ADJ CLASSIF **dead** is no longer living. EG *He was shot dead in a gunfight... Mary threw away the dead flowers.*

2 The **dead** are people who are dead. EG *I try to* N PLURAL : *forget the dead.* the+N

3 If a part of your body goes **dead**, you lose the ADJ PRED sense of feeling in it.

4 If a telephone or a piece of electrical equipment ADJ PRED is **dead**, it is not functioning. EG *The phone went dead.*

5 Dead can mean complete or absolute, especially ADJ CLASSIF : with the words 'silence', 'centre', and 'stop'. EG ATTRIB *There was dead silence... The table was placed in the dead centre of the room.*

6 Dead also means **6.1** precisely or exactly. EG *I* SUBMOD *was staring dead ahead.* **6.2** very or very much. EG Informal *It's dead easy... They were dead against the idea.*

7 If something stops **dead**, it stops quickly and ADV AFTER VB suddenly.

8 The **dead** of night is the middle part of it, when it N UNCOUNT+of is very dark and quiet. EG *They came at dead of night.*

9 If someone is **dead to the world**, they are sound asleep. `PHRASE Informal`

10 If you say **'Over my dead body'** when someone has just mentioned a future event, you mean that you feel very strongly that it should not happen, and that you will do everything you can to prevent it. EG *'Roger and I are going to get married.' – 'Over my dead body!'* `CONVENTION Informal`

11 If you say that you **wouldn't be seen dead** doing a particular thing, you mean that you would never do that thing because you think it is unfashionable or awful. EG *I wouldn't be seen dead in a skirt like that.* `PHRASE Informal`

deaden /dɛdəⁿn/, **deadens, deadening, deadened.** If something **deadens** a feeling or a sound, it makes it less strong so that you feel it less or hear it less. EG *Drugs deaden the pangs of hunger.* `V+O`

dead end, dead ends. 1 If a street is a **dead end**, there is no way out at one end of it. `N COUNT`

2 A job or course of action that is a **dead end** does not lead to further developments. EG *The investigation has reached a dead end... ...a dead-end job.* `N COUNT`

deadening /dɛdəⁿnɪŋ/. Something that is **deadening** destroys people's enthusiasm and creativity. EG *...degrading, deadening tasks.* `ADJ QUALIT`

dead heat, dead heats. If a race ends in a **dead heat**, two or more competitors reach the finishing line first at exactly the same time. `N COUNT`

deadline /dɛdlaɪn/, **deadlines.** A **deadline** is a time or date before which a particular task must be finished. EG *We must meet the deadline.* `N COUNT`

deadlock /dɛdlɒk/ is a state of affairs in an argument or dispute in which neither side is willing to give in at all and so no agreement can be reached. EG *The meeting between management and unions ended in deadlock.* `N UNCOUNT`

deadly /dɛdli¹/, **deadlier, deadliest. 1** Something that is **deadly** is likely or able to cause someone's death. EG *This is one of nature's deadliest poisons... ...deadly spiders.* `ADJ QUALIT`

2 You use **deadly** to emphasize the extent to which something has an unpleasant or serious quality. EG *The air was deadly cold... He was deadly serious.* `SUBMOD`

3 Deadly also means very great in degree and therefore very effective, especially at hurting someone. EG *This was the deadliest insult he could think of ....deadly accuracy.* `ADJ QUALIT`

deadpan /dɛdpæn/. If you do something **deadpan** or if you look **deadpan**, you appear to be serious and are hiding the fact that you are joking or teasing someone. EG *She looked at me deadpan.* `ADV`
▶ used as an adjective. EG *He speaks in a deadpan way.* `▶ ADJ CLASSIF`

dead weight, dead weights. A **dead weight** is a load which is surprisingly heavy and difficult to lift. `N COUNT`

deaf /dɛf/, **deafer, deafest. 1** Someone who is **deaf** is unable to hear anything or unable to hear very well. EG *...a school for deaf children... He was very deaf.* ◇ **deafness.** EG *They finally diagnosed her deafness when she was thirteen.* `ADJ QUALIT` ◇ `N UNCOUNT`

2 The **deaf** are people who are deaf. EG *The deaf know it perfectly well, but we choose to ignore that fact.* `N PLURAL: the+N`

3 If someone is **deaf** to something, they refuse to pay attention to it. EG *He was deaf to the public's complaints.* `ADJ PRED+to`

4 If you **turn a deaf ear** to something that someone says, you refuse to pay attention to it. EG *Young people sometimes seem to turn a deaf ear to the words of their anxious parents.* `PHRASE`

deafen /dɛfəⁿn/, **deafens, deafening, deafened.** If you **are deafened** by a noise, it is so loud that you cannot hear anything else at the same time. EG *She was momentarily deafened by the din.* `V+O: USU PASS`
◇ **deafening.** EG *The noise was deafening.* `◇ ADJ QUALIT`

deal /diːl/, **deals, dealing, dealt** /dɛlt/. **1 A good deal** or **a great deal** of something is a lot of it. EG *There was a great deal of concern about energy* `QUANTIF`

shortages... They talked a great deal... The teaching of the older children is a good deal better.

2 A **deal** is an agreement or arrangement that is made, especially in business. EG *He certainly hadn't done badly on the deal.* `N COUNT`

3 If someone has had a bad **deal**, they have been unfortunate or have been treated unfairly. `N COUNT: ADJ+N`

4 You can say **'Big deal'** when you are expressing scorn, because you are not impressed by what someone has just told you. EG *'I once knew all Keats's poems.' – 'Big deal.'* `EXCLAM Informal`

5 If you **deal** someone or something a blow, you inflict it or give it. EG *The growth of modern industry had dealt a heavy blow to their way of life... This woman dealt him an alarming series of blows.* `V+O+to OR V+O+O`

6 When you **deal** cards, you give them out to the players in a game of cards. EG *Deal seven cards to each player... You've dealt me eight cards!... Whose turn is it to deal?* `V+O: OFT+to, V+O+O, OR V`

7 See also **dealing** and **wheeling and dealing**.

deal in. To **deal in** a particular type of goods means to sell those goods. EG *The shop deals only in trousers.* `PHRASAL VB: V+PREP`

deal out. When you **deal out** cards, you give them out to the players in a game of cards. EG *Deal the cards out first, then I'll explain the points system.* `PHRASAL VB: V+O+ADV`

deal with. 1 When you **deal with** a situation or problem, you do what is necessary to achieve the result you want. EG *They learned to deal with any sort of emergency.* **2** If a book, speech, or film **deals with** a particular subject, it is concerned with it. EG *The film deals with a strange encounter between two soldiers.* `PHRASAL VB: V+PREP, HAS PASS` `V+PREP, HAS PASS`

dealer /diːlə/, **dealers.** A **dealer** is a person whose business involves buying and selling things. EG *...a dealer in antique furniture.* `N COUNT: USU+SUPP`

dealing /diːlɪŋ/, **dealings. 1** Your **dealings** with a person or organization are the relations that you have with them or the business that you do with them. EG *Ford insists that Carter's dealings with him have been totally correct... He was questioned about his past business dealings.* `N PLURAL: OFT+with`

2 You use **dealing** to talk about someone's job. For example, drug **dealing** is selling drugs and antique **dealing** is selling antiques. `N UNCOUNT`

dealt /dɛlt/ is the past tense and past participle of **deal**.

dean /diːn/, **deans.** A **dean** is **1** an important administrator at a university or college. **2** a priest who is the main administrator of a large church. `N COUNT`

dear /dɪə/, **dearer, dearest; dears. 1** You can call someone **dear** as a sign of affection. EG *How are you, dear?... Now, my dears, come with me.* `VOCATIVE`

2 You can use **dear** in expressions such as 'my **dear** fellow' or 'my **dear** Richard', to address someone that you are quite fond of. EG *My dear fellow, I really am sorry.* `ADJ CLASSIF: ATTRIB Outdated`

3 Dear is usually written at the beginning of a letter, followed by the name or title of the person you are writing to. EG *Dear Mum, I was glad to get your letter... Dear Sir, I regret to inform you that I cannot accept your kind invitation.* `ADJ CLASSIF: ATTRIB`

4 You use **dear** to describe someone or something that you feel affection for. EG *...dear old Aunt Elizabeth... ...a dear friend.* `ADJ QUALIT: ATTRIB`

5 If something is **dear** to you, you care very deeply about it. EG *Sussex was very dear to him... ...a cause that is very dear to her heart.* `ADJ PRED+to Formal`

6 You say **'Oh dear'** when you are sad or upset about something. EG *Oh dear, I'm late.* `EXCLAM`

7 Something that is **dear** costs a lot of money. EG *Firewood is getting dearer, as supplies dwindle.* `ADJ PRED Outdated`

If you are in someone's debt, do you owe them money?

dearest /dɪərɪ²st/. **1** You can call someone **dearest** when you are very fond of them. EG *It's too late now, my dearest.* VOCATIVE Outdated

2 You use **dearest** to describe something that is very important to you. EG *His dearest wish was to become a civil servant.* ADJ SUPERL Formal

dearly /dɪəli¹/. **1** If you love someone **dearly**, you love them very much. If you would **dearly** like to do or have something, you would very much like to do it or have it. EG *I loved him dearly... I dearly wish I had more money.* ADV Formal

2 If you **pay dearly** for doing something, you suffer a lot as a result. EG *He paid dearly for his mistake.* PHRASE Formal

dearth /dɜːθ/. If there is a **dearth** of something, there is not enough of it. EG *There is a dearth of good children's plays.* N SING : USU+of

death /deθ/, **deaths**. **1** Death is the end of the life of a person or animal. EG *...after the death of her parents... He bled to death... The two deaths could have been prevented.* N UNCOUNT OR N COUNT

2 If someone is **at death's door**, they are very ill indeed. PHRASE Informal

3 If something **frightens** or **worries** you **to death**, it frightens or worries you very much. EG *He was frightened to death of her.* PHRASE Informal

4 If you say that you are **sick to death** of something, you mean that you feel very angry about it. EG *The Town Council are sick to death of waiting for your report!* PHRASE Informal

5 If someone **is put to death**, they are executed. EG *Because she had loved a slave, she was put to death.* PHRASE Formal

deathbed /deθbed/, **deathbeds**. Someone's **deathbed** is the bed that they are lying in when they are about to die. EG *On his deathbed he asked her forgiveness.* N COUNT : USU+POSS

deathly /deθli¹/ is used to describe something that is characteristic of a dead person in some way, for example as cold, pale, or quiet as a dead person. EG *A deathly hush lay in the streets.* ▶ used as an adverb. EG *Her feet were deathly cold.* ADJ CLASSIF ATTRIB ▶ ADV+ADJ

death penalty. The **death penalty** is the punishment of death used in some countries for people who have committed very serious crimes. N SING : the+N

debacle /deɪbɑːkɔ⁰l, dɪ-/, **debacles**; also spelled **débâcle**. A **debacle** is an event or attempt that is a complete failure. EG *I couldn't afford to ask them again after the debacle of the TV series.* N COUNT

debar /dɪˈbɑː/, **debars**, **debarring**, **debarred**. If you **are debarred** from doing something, you are prevented from doing it by a law or rule. EG *He was debarred from attending the meetings.* V+O : OFT+from Formal

debase /dɪˈbeɪs/, **debases**, **debasing**, **debased**. If something **is debased**, its value or quality is reduced. EG *The quality of life can only be debased by such a system.* V+O : USU PASS Formal

debatable /dɪˈbeɪtəbɔ⁰l/. A statement or fact that is **debatable** is not definitely true or not definitely known. EG *'They won't notice it's gone.' – 'Well. That's debatable.'* ADJ QUALIT

debate /dɪˈbeɪt/, **debates**, **debating**, **debated**. **1** A **debate** is a discussion in which people express different opinions about a subject. EG *...a debate on education... There was a great deal of debate about the national health service.* N COUNT OR N UNCOUNT OFT+on/about

2 When people **debate** something, they discuss it fairly formally, putting forward different views. EG *These issues have been widely debated... They debated the motion that capital punishment should be re-introduced.* V+O OR V+REPORT

3 If you **debate** what to do, you think about possible courses of action before deciding what to do. EG *He turned round, debating whether to go back... He debated heating up the stew.* V+REPORT OR -ING

4 If something is **open to debate**, it has not been proved to be true. EG *Whether they actually are safer is open to debate.* PHRASE

debauchery /dɪˈbɔːtʃəri¹/ is excessive drunkenness or excessive sexual activity. N UNCOUNT Formal

debilitated /dɪˈbɪlɪteɪt²d/. A person, country, or organization that is **debilitated** has been made weak. EG *...the shabby and debilitated economy.* ADJ QUALIT Formal

debilitating /dɪˈbɪlɪteɪtɪŋ/. A **debilitating** illness, feeling, or action makes a person, country, or organization weak and unable to take action. EG *...the debilitating effects of the fast... ...economically debilitating situations.* ADJ QUALIT Formal

debility /dɪˈbɪlɪti¹/ is physical or mental weakness, especially weakness caused by an illness. EG *...the debility produced by old age.* N UNCOUNT : USU+SUPP

debit /debɪt/, **debits**, **debiting**, **debited**. **1** When your bank **debits** your account, money is taken from it, usually in order to pay for something. V+O

2 A **debit** is a record of the money which is taken out of your bank account, for example when you write a cheque. EG *...a statement showing all the credits and debits.* N COUNT

debonair /debəˈneə/. A man who is **debonair** is well-dressed, charming, and confident. ADJ QUALIT

debris /deɪbriː¹, debriː¹/ consists of pieces of things that have been destroyed, or rubbish that is lying around. EG *Two people were killed by flying debris... She began clearing up the debris.* N UNCOUNT

debt /det/, **debts**. **1** A **debt** is a sum of money that you owe someone. EG *You must spend less until your debts are paid off.* N COUNT

2 Debt is the state of owing money. EG *He began getting deeper and deeper into debt.* N UNCOUNT

3 A **debt** is also a feeling of gratitude towards someone for something that they have done for you, and a feeling that you owe them something. EG *...a debt that could never be repaid.* N COUNT+SUPP Formal

4 If you are **in** someone's **debt**, you are grateful to them for something that they have done for you, and you feel that you must do something for them in return. PHRASE Formal

debtor /detə/, **debtors**. A **debtor** is a person who owes money. N COUNT

debunk /diːbʌŋk/, **debunks**, **debunking**, **debunked**. If you **debunk** an idea or belief, you show that it is false or not important. V+O

debut /deɪbjuː, deɪbjuː/, **debuts**. The **debut** of a singer, musician, footballer, or other performer is his or her first public performance or recording. EG *She made her debut in this theatre.* N COUNT

decade /dekeɪd, dɪˈkeɪd/, **decades**. A **decade** is a period of ten years, especially one that begins with a year ending in 0, for example 1980 to 1989. EG *By the end of the decade he had acquired international fame.* N COUNT

decadent /dekədə²nt/. If you say that someone or something is **decadent**, you mean that they show low standards, especially low moral standards. EG *The gaudy casinos seemed even more decadent.* ◊ **decadence** /dekədə²ns/. EG *...moral decadence.* ADJ QUALIT ◊ N UNCOUNT

decaffeinated /diːˈkæfəneɪtɪ²d/. Coffee that is **decaffeinated** has had most of the caffeine removed from it. ADJ CLASSIF

decant /dɪˈkænt/, **decants**, **decanting**, **decanted**. If you **decant** port or sherry, you pour it slowly from its bottle into another container before serving it. V+O

decanter /dɪˈkæntə/, **decanters**. A **decanter** is a glass container that you use for serving port or sherry. N COUNT

decapitate /dɪˈkæpɪteɪt/, **decapitates**, **decapitating**, **decapitated**. To **decapitate** someone means to cut off their head. V+O : USU PASS Formal

decathlon /dɪˈkæθlə²n/, **decathlons**. A **decathlon** is a competition in which athletes compete in ten different sporting events. N COUNT

decay /dɪˈkeɪ/, **decays**, **decaying**, **decayed**. **1** When something such as a plant or a piece of meat **decays**, it rots and starts to fall apart. EG *The body had already started to decay.* ◊ **decayed**. EG *...black, decayed leaves... A decayed tooth may* V ◊ ADJ QUALIT cause pain. ◊ **decaying.** EG ...a smell of decaying meat. ◊ ADJ CLASSIF

2 If buildings **decay**, their condition becomes worse because they have not been looked after and repaired. EG The old palace decayed badly during Cromwell's time. ◊ **decayed.** EG ...slums and decayed factories... ...a decayed cloth-mill by the stream. ◊ **decaying.** EG ...decaying urban centres. ◊ ADJ QUALIT ◊ ADJ CLASSIF ◊ ADJ CLASSIF

3 If something such as a society or an institution **decays**, it gradually becomes weaker or more corrupt. EG Working class culture was decaying. ◊ **decaying.** EG ...a corrupt, decaying society... ...images of decaying imperial Rome. ◊ ADJ CLASSIF : ATTRIB

4 Decay refers to **4.1** the process or result of something such as a plant or a piece of meat rotting and falling apart. EG ...toothpaste that helps to prevent dental decay. **4.2** the process or result of buildings becoming worse in condition because they have not been looked after and repaired. EG ...saving houses from falling into decay. **4.3** the process or result of a society or institution gradually becoming weaker or more corrupt. EG ...a religion in the final stages of decay. N UNCOUNT

deceased /dɪˈsiːst/. **1** A person who has recently died can be referred to as the **deceased**. EG ...the property of the deceased. N SING : the+N Formal

2 A **deceased** person is one who has recently died. EG ...the relatives of the deceased couple. ADJ CLASSIF Formal

deceit /dɪˈsiːt/, **deceits. Deceit** is lying, or behaviour that is intended to make people believe something which is not true. EG ...marriages in which deceit was commonplace. N UNCOUNT OR N COUNT

deceitful /dɪˈsiːtfʊl/. Someone who is **deceitful** lies or tries to make other people believe things that are not true. ADJ QUALIT

deceive /dɪˈsiːv/, **deceives, deceiving, deceived.**
1 If you **deceive** someone, you deliberately make them believe something that is not true. EG He tried to deceive me... ...the man he had been deceived into calling 'father'. V+O: OFT+into

2 If you **deceive** yourself, you do not admit to yourself something that you know is true. EG They try to deceive themselves that everything is all right. V-REFL

3 If something **deceives** you, it causes you to believe something that is not true. EG His unkempt appearance deceived the staff into believing that he was a student. V+O: OFT+into

December /dɪˈsembə/ is the twelfth and last month of the year in the Western calendar. EG We gave a party early in December. N UNCOUNT

decency /ˈdiːsənsiɪ/ is **1** the quality of being sensible and following accepted moral standards. EG They tried to restore some sense and decency to the Administration. **2** behaviour that shows kindness towards people. EG Why hadn't they had the decency to ask him if he'd like to join in? N UNCOUNT

decent /ˈdiːsənt/. **1** You use **decent** to describe something which is **1.1** considered to be of an acceptable standard or quality. EG ...decent wages... It was several weeks before I got a decent night's rest. ◊ **decently.** EG The farm animals are decently treated and killed as humanely as possible. **1.2** morally correct or acceptable. EG He would marry her as soon as a decent amount of time had elapsed. ◊ **decently.** EG They only want the chance to live their lives decently. ADJ QUALIT ◊ ADV ADJ CLASSIF : ATTRIB ◊ ADV

2 Decent people are honest and respectable and behave morally. EG ...decent, hard-working citizens. ADJ QUALIT : ATTRIB

decentralize /diːˈsentrəlaɪz/, **decentralizes, decentralized;** also spelled **decentralise.** V+O
To **decentralize** a large organization means to move some departments of it away from the main administrative area, or to give more power to local departments. EG He accused the Minister of seeking to decentralise the Commission. ◊ **decentralized.** EG ...a decentralized health service. ◊ ADJ CLASSIF

◊ **decentralization** /diːˌsentrəlaɪzeɪʃəˈn/. EG ...the decentralization of government. ◊ N UNCOUNT

deception /dɪˈsepʃəˈn/, **deceptions. 1** A **deception** is something that you say or do which is intended to deceive someone. EG He would quickly have seen through Mary's deceptions. N COUNT

2 Deception is the act of deceiving someone or the state of being deceived by someone. EG ...his part in the deception of the British public... This made Tim sadder than his deception. N UNCOUNT

deceptive /dɪˈseptɪv/. If something is **deceptive**, it might cause you to believe something which is not true. EG Its fragile appearance was deceptive. ADJ QUALIT

◊ **deceptively.** EG It all looks deceptively simple... It was deceptively presented as a scientific study. ◊ SUBMOD OR ADV

decibel /ˈdesɪbel/, **decibels.** A **decibel** is a unit of measurement relating to how loud a sound is. EG He lowered his voice a few decibels. N COUNT

decide /dɪˈsaɪd/, **decides, deciding, decided. 1** If you **decide** to do something, you choose to do it, usually after you have thought carefully about the other possibilities. EG What made you decide to get married?... She decided that she would leave... He has a month to decide whether he's going to stay... I'm glad you decided against a career as a waiter. V+to-INF, REPORT, OR A

2 When something **is decided**, people choose what something should be like or what should be done. EG The case is to be decided by the International Court. V+O

3 If an event or fact **decides** something, it makes it certain that there will be a particular result or choice. EG It was this that decided the fate of the company. ◊ **deciding.** EG I suppose cost shouldn't be a deciding factor. V+O ◊ ADJ CLASSIF : ATTRIB

4 If you **decide** that something is the case, you form that opinion after considering the facts. EG He decided that the doorbell was broken... I couldn't decide whether she was joking or not. V+REPORT

decide on or **decide upon.** If you **decide on** something or **decide upon** it, you choose it from two or more possibilities. EG He decided on a career in the army. PHRASAL VB : V+PREP, HAS PASS

decided /dɪˈsaɪdɪd/ means clear and definite. EG This gave them a decided advantage over their opponents. ADJ QUALIT : ATTRIB

decidedly /dɪˈsaɪdɪdliɪ/. **1 Decidedly** means to a great extent and in a way that is very obvious. EG The men looked decidedly uncomfortable. SUBMOD

2 If you say something **decidedly**, you say it in a way that suggests that you are unlikely to change your mind. EG 'It's time things were altered,' said Mrs Moffat decidedly. ADV

deciduous /dɪˈsɪdjuːəs/. A tree that is **deciduous** loses its leaves in autumn every year. ADJ CLASSIF

decimal /ˈdesɪməˈl/, **decimals. 1** A **decimal** system involves counting in units of ten. EG ...the new decimal currency. ADJ CLASSIF : ATTRIB

2 A **decimal** is a fraction that is written in the form of a dot followed by one or more numbers which represent tenths, hundredths, and so on: for example .5, .51, .517. N COUNT

decimal point, decimal points. A **decimal point** is the dot that occurs before a fraction that is expressed as a decimal. N COUNT

decimate /ˈdesɪmeɪt/, **decimates, decimating, decimated.** To **decimate** a group of people or animals means to destroy a very large number of them. EG The soldiers would be decimated long before they reached the beaches. V+O

decipher /dɪˈsaɪfə/, **deciphers, deciphering, deciphered.** If you **decipher** a piece of writing, you work out what it says, even though it is very difficult to read or understand. EG Archaeologists labour to decipher clay tablets. V+O

In Britain, does a deciduous tree have leaves on it in December?

decision /dɪˈsɪʒəⁿn/, **decisions. 1** A **decision** is a N COUNT : choice that you make about what should be done or OFT+on/about about which is the best of various alternatives. EG *I think that I made the wrong decision... ...a decision on the issue might not be necessary... He has to make some difficult decisions about where he wants to go.*
2 Decision is **2.1** the act of deciding something. EG N UNCOUNT *Philip laced up his shoes slowly, delaying the moment of decision.* **2.2** the ability to decide quickly and definitely what to do. EG *...a man of decision and action.*

decisive /dɪˈsaɪsɪv/. **1** If a fact, action, or event is ADJ CLASSIF **decisive**, it makes it certain that there will be a particular result or that the result will be a definite one. EG *...a decisive battle... This promise was not a decisive factor in the election.* ◊ **decisively.** EG ◊ ADV *Thornton was decisively defeated.*
2 If someone is **decisive**, they have the ability to ADJ QUALIT make quick decisions. EG *...a decisive leader... How could a girl be so decisive?* ◊ **decisively.** EG *'Can I* ◊ ADV *see him?' Edgar shook his head decisively.*
◊ **decisiveness.** EG *The sight of the body had* ◊ N UNCOUNT *robbed her of her usual decisiveness.*

deck /dɛk/, **decks, decking, decked. 1** A **deck** on N COUNT a bus or ship is a downstairs or upstairs area on it. EG *They got on the bus and sat on the top deck.*
2 The **deck** of a ship is the top part of it that forms N SING : the+N, a floor in the open air which you can walk on. EG OR on+N *I'm going back up on deck. See picture at* YACHT.
3 A record **deck** is a piece of equipment on which N COUNT you play records.
4 A **deck** of cards is a pack of playing cards. N COUNT
5 If you **deck** something with pretty things, you V+O+with decorate it. EG *The graves are decked with flowers.* Written
deck out. If you **deck** someone or something **out,** PHRASAL VB : you decorate them or make them look attractive, V+O+ADV usually for a special occasion. EG *I decked myself* Written *out in a suit and tie.*

deckchair /dɛktʃeə/, **deckchairs.** A **deckchair** N COUNT is a simple folding chair which is used out of doors.

declaration /dɛkləreɪʃəⁿn/, **declarations.** A **declaration** is **1** a firm, emphatic statement. EG *He* N COUNT : *seemed embarrassed by her declaration of love...* OFT+of OR *...his earlier declarations that things were improv-* REPORT *ing.* **2** an official announcement or statement. EG N COUNT : *...the day after the declaration was signed... ...for-* OFT+SUPP *mal declarations of war.*

declare /dɪˈkleə/, **declares, declaring, declared. 1** If you **declare** that something is the V+QUOTE OR case, you say it in a firm, deliberate way. EG *'I like* REPORT : *it,' she declared... They were heard to declare that* ONLY that *they would never steal again.*
2 If you **declare** an attitude or intention or if you V+O OR **declare** yourself as having this attitude or inten- V-REFL+C tion, you make it known to people that you have it. EG *He declared his intention to fight... Mr Bell has declared his support... He declared himself strong- ly in favour of the project.* ◊ **declared.** EG *...his* ◊ ADJ CLASSIF : *declared intention to resign.* ATTRIB
3 If you **declare** something, you state it officially. V+O OR EG *...when the French declared war on England...* V+O+C *At his trial he was declared innocent.*
4 If you **declare** goods that you have bought V+O abroad or money that you have earned, you tell customs or tax officials about it so that you can pay tax on it.

decline /dɪˈklaɪn/, **declines, declining, declined. 1** If something **declines**, it becomes small- V er, weaker, or worse. EG *The number of congress members declined from 371 to 361... Since 1971 the party's influence has declined.* ◊ **declining.** EG ◊ ADJ CLASSIF : *...declining industries.* ATTRIB
2 If there is a **decline** in something, it becomes N COUNT OR smaller, weaker, or worse. EG *...a decline in stand-* N UNCOUNT *ards... ...the decline of the motor industry... The city's population is in decline.*
3 If something is **on the decline,** it is declining. EG PHRASE *Organized religion seems to be on the decline.*

4 If you **decline** something or **decline** to do V+O, something, you politely refuse to accept it or do it. V+to-INF, OR V EG *He has declined the invitation... Mr Santos* Formal *declined to comment on the news... On each occa- sion, he declined.*

decode /diːˈkəʊd/, **decodes, decoding, decoded.** V+O If you **decode** a message that has been written or spoken in code, you change it into ordinary lan- guage.

decompose /diːkəˈmpəʊz/, **decomposes, de-** V **composing, decomposed.** When something that has died **decomposes,** it changes chemically and begins to rot. EG *Shellfish decompose very quickly after death.* ◊ **decomposition** /diːkɒmpəzɪʃəⁿn/. ◊ N UNCOUNT EG *...the decomposition of organic matter.*

decor /deɪkɔː/. The **decor** of a house or room is N UNCOUNT : the style in which it is furnished and decorated. EG USU+SUPP *...the pine decor of the kitchen.*

decorate /dɛkəreɪt/, **decorates, decorating, decorated. 1** If you **decorate** something, you V+O make it look more attractive by adding things to it. EG *The walls were all decorated with posters.*
2 If you **decorate** a building or room, you put new V+O OR V paint or wallpaper on the walls, ceiling, and wood- work. ◊ **decorating.** EG *We said we would do the* ◊ N UNCOUNT *decorating.*

decoration /dɛkəˈreɪʃəⁿn/, **decorations. 1** Deco- N UNCOUNT **ration** is **1.1** something that is added to something OR N COUNT else in order to make it look more attractive. EG *...dresses that are white and plain, free of all decoration... ...Christmas decorations.* **1.2** the furni- ture, wallpaper, and ornaments of a room or building. EG *...the style of decoration typical of the 1920s... I like the interior decorations.*
2 A **decoration** is a medal which is given to N COUNT someone as an official honour.

decorative /dɛkəˈrətɪv/. Something that is **deco-** ADJ QUALIT **rative** is intended to look pretty or attractive. EG *...decorative objects.*

decorator /dɛkəreɪtə/, **decorators.** A **decorator** N COUNT is a person whose job is to paint houses or put wallpaper on the walls.

decorous /dɛkərəs/. Behaviour that is **decorous** ADJ QUALIT is polite and correct and does not offend people. EG Formal *He gave his wife a decorous kiss.* ◊ **decorously.** EG ◊ ADV *...teenage lovers strolling decorously.*

decorum /dɪˈkɔːrəm/ is behaviour that people N UNCOUNT consider to be correct and polite. EG *She was* Formal *expected to behave with decorum.*

decoy /diːkɔɪ/, **decoys, decoying, decoyed. 1** A N COUNT **decoy** is a person or object that you use to lead someone away from where they intended to go, especially so that you can catch them. EG *They chased the decoys down to the place of ambush.*
2 If you **decoy** someone, you lead them away from V+O+A where they intended to go, often by means of a trick. EG *Eight of the missiles were decoyed away from targets.*

decrease /dɪˈkriːs/, **decreases, decreasing, de-** V-ERG **creased. 1** When something **decreases** or is **decreased,** it becomes smaller or weaker. EG *Over a seven-year period the number of marriages has decreased by forty per cent... To save money, decrease the temperature.* ◊ **decreasing.** EG *...a* ◊ ADJ CLASSIF : *life of increasing labour and decreasing leisure.* ATTRIB
2 A **decrease** is a reduction in the quantity, size, or N COUNT : strength of something. EG *The decrease in size was* OFT+in/of *gradual.*

decree /dɪˈkriː/, **decrees, decreeing, decreed. 1** V+REPORT : If someone in authority **decrees** that something ONLY that must happen, they order this officially. EG *The minister decreed that there should be a full investi- gation.*
2 A **decree** is an official order, especially one N COUNT made by the ruler of a country.

decrepit /dɪˈkrɛpɪt/. Something that is **decrepit** ADJ CLASSIF is very old and in bad condition. EG *...decrepit houses.*

decry /dɪˈkraɪ/, **decries, decrying, decried.** If V+O you **decry** something, you say that it is bad. EG We Formal decry their absence of principle.

dedicate /ˈdedɪkeɪt/, **dedicates, dedicating, dedicated.** 1 If you **dedicate** yourself to some- V-REFL+to thing, you decide to devote a lot of time and effort to it because you think that it is important. EG ...a man who had dedicated himself to his work.

2 If you **dedicate** something such as a book or a V+O+to piece of music to someone, you say that the work is written for them, as a way of showing affection or respect. EG She dedicated her first book to her husband.

dedicated /ˈdedɪkeɪtɪ²d/. If you are **dedicated** to ADJ QUALIT something, you believe that it is right and worth- while, and give a lot of time and effort to it. EG ...people dedicated to social or political change... ...a dedicated surgeon.

dedication /ˌdedɪˈkeɪʃə⁰n/, **dedications.** 1 If you N UNCOUNT show **dedication** to something, you work hard at it, because you believe it is important or worth- while. EG I admired her dedication to her family.

2 A **dedication** is a message which is written at N COUNT the beginning of a book or said before a piece of music is performed, as a sign of affection or respect for someone.

deduce /dɪˈdjuːs/, **deduces, deducing, deduced.** V+REPORT If you **deduce** that something is true, you reach OR V+O that conclusion because of facts that you know to be true. EG Morris deduced that he was in the presence of the Head of Department... What do you deduce from all this?

deduct /dɪˈdʌkt/, **deducts, deducting, deducted.** V+O When you **deduct** an amount from a total, you reduce the total by that amount. EG Tax will be deducted automatically from your wages.

deduction /dɪˈdʌkʃə⁰n/, **deductions.** 1 A **deduc-** N COUNT OR **tion** is a conclusion that you reach about some- N UNCOUNT thing because of facts that you know to be true. EG That seems a reasonable deduction... If the battery is dead the horn will not work; that is deduction.

2 A **deduction** is also an amount that has been N COUNT OR subtracted from a total. EG ...tax and national N UNCOUNT insurance deductions.

deed /diːd/, **deeds.** 1 A **deed** is something that is N COUNT : done, especially something very good or very bad. USU+SUPP EG ...the brave deeds his son would do when he Literary grew up.

2 A **deed** is also a legal document containing an N COUNT+SUPP agreement or contract.

deem /diːm/, **deems, deeming, deemed.** If you V+O+to-INF **deem** something to be the case, you consider that OR V+O+C : it is the case. EG This was deemed to detract from USU PASS the dignity of the republic... He said he would take Formal what measures he deemed necessary.

deep /diːp/, **deeper, deepest.** 1 If something is ADJ QUALIT **deep**, it extends a long way down from the surface. OR ADV EG The sea is not very deep there... They dug deep down into the earth. ◊ **deeply.** EG His face was ◊ ADV deeply lined.

2 You use **deep** to talk about measurements. For ADJ AFTER N example, if something is two feet **deep**, it meas- ures two feet from the top to the bottom, or from the front to the back. EG ...a crater over 300 feet deep.

3 Something that is **deep** in an area is a long way ADJ CLASSIF inside it. EG ...deep in the forest... Guerrilla forces OR ADV were advancing deep into enemy territory.

4 You use **deep** to emphasize the degree or ADJ QUALIT : intensity of something. EG This was a matter of ATTRIB deep concern... Our hearts go out to you in deepest sympathy. ◊ **deeply.** EG ...deeply religious people. ◊ ADV+ADJ

5 If you feel something **deep down** or **deep inside** PHRASE you, you feel it very strongly although you may not show it. EG Deep down they're still frustrated adolescents.

6 If you are in a **deep** sleep, you are sleeping ADJ QUALIT : peacefully and it is difficult to wake you. ATTRIB

7 A **deep** breath or sigh uses the whole of your ADJ QUALIT : ATTRIB

lungs. EG He took a few deep breaths before jump- ing into the foaming water. ◊ **deeply.** EG She ◊ ADV sighed deeply.

8 A **deep** colour is strong and fairly dark. EG ...deep ADJ QUALIT blue eyes... The sky was a deep purple.

9 A **deep** sound is a low one. EG He sang in a deep ADJ QUALIT voice... ...fits of deep, hoarse coughing.

10 **Deep** thoughts are serious thoughts about im- ADJ QUALIT portant things.

11 **Deep** is also used in these phrases. 11.1 If you PHRASES are **deep in thought**, you are thinking very hard about something. 11.2 If you say that something **goes** or **runs deep**, you mean that it is very serious and hard to change. EG The crisis in the prisons goes deep. 11.3 If you **are thrown in at the deep end**, you are asked to do something new and difficult without being given any help.

deepen /ˈdiːpə⁰n/, **deepens, deepening, deep- ened.** 1 If people **deepen** something, they cause it V+O to become greater in measurement from the sur- face to the bottom. EG The authority wants to spend £7 million to widen and deepen the River Soar.

2 Where a river or a sea **deepens**, the bottom V begins to slope downwards and the water gets deeper.

3 If a situation or emotion **deepens** or is **deep-** V-ERG **ened**, it becomes stronger and more intense. EG The crisis deepened... The incident deepened my commitment to Richard.

4 If you **deepen** your knowledge of a subject, or if V-ERG your knowledge **deepens**, you learn more about it. EG Their object was to deepen man's understanding of the universe.

5 When a sound **deepens** or when you **deepen** it, it V-ERG becomes lower in tone.

deep freeze, deep freezes. A **deep freeze** is a N COUNT large container used for storing food. The tempera- ture inside it is always kept below freezing point.

deep-rooted. An idea or feeling that is **deep-** ADJ QUALIT **rooted** or **deeply rooted** is so firmly fixed in a person or a society that it is difficult to change or remove. EG ...a deep-rooted prejudice.

deep-sea. **Deep-sea** activities take place in areas ADJ CLASSIF of the sea that are a long way from the coast. EG ATTRIB ...deep-sea diving.

deep-seated. A **deep-seated** feeling or problem ADJ CLASSIF is very strong or basic, and is very difficult to change. EG ...deep-seated fears.

deer /dɪə/. **Deer** is both the singular and the N COUNT plural.

A **deer** is a large wild animal that eats grass and leaves. Male deer usually have large, branching horns.

deface /dɪˈfeɪs/, **defaces, defacing, defaced.** If V+O someone **defaces** something such as a wall or a notice, they deliberately spoil it by writing or drawing things on it. EG ...books with pages torn out or defaced with graffiti.

defamation /ˌdefəˈmeɪʃə⁰n/ is the damaging of N UNCOUNT someone's reputation by saying something bad and Formal untrue about them. EG ...defamation of character, Legal slander, and libel.

default /dɪˈfɔːlt/, **defaults, defaulting, de-** **faulted.** 1 If you **default**, you fail to do something V : OFT+on/in that you are legally supposed to do, such as make a payment that you owe. EG He said he had been right to default on that loan. ▸ used as a noun. EG ▸ N UNCOUNT ...default of payment.

2 If something happens **by default**, it happens only PHRASE because something else which might have pre- vented it has not happened. EG He is responsible either through bad design or by default.

defeat /dɪˈfiːt/, **defeats, defeating, defeated.** 1 If V+O you **defeat** someone, you win a victory over them in a battle, game, or contest. EG Arsenal were

Which word on these pages has the same form in the singular and the plural?

defeated on Saturday... Labour was defeated in the General Election of 19 June 1970.

2 If a proposal or a motion in a debate **is defeated**, v+o : USU PASS more people vote against it than vote for it. EG *The motion was defeated by 221 votes to 152.*

3 If a task or a problem **defeats** you, it is so v+o difficult that you cannot do it or solve it. EG *...a complex sum which defeats many adults as well as children.*

4 If someone or something **defeats** something else, v+o they cause it to fail. EG *Moral instruction thus defeats its own purpose... He would like to see the strike defeated.*

5 Defeat is **5.1** the state of being beaten in a N UNCOUNT battle, game, or contest. EG *The bad weather con-* OR N COUNT *tributed to the defeat of the navy... These defeats came as a setback for Thorne.* **5.2** failure to achieve something. EG *He would never admit de-feat... Her friend finally gave up in defeat.*

defeatism /dɪˈfiːtɪzəᵊm/ is a way of thinking or N UNCOUNT talking which suggests that you expect to be unsuc-cessful. EG *We were accused of defeatism.*
◊ **defeatist** /dɪˈfiːtɪst/, **defeatists**. EG *I was in a* ◊ N COUNT : *defeatist mood.* OFT N MOD

defecate /ˈdefəkeɪt/, **defecates**, **defecating**, **def-** v **ecated.** When you **defecate**, you get rid of waste Formal matter from your body through your anus.

defect, **defects**, **defecting**, **defected**; pronounced /ˈdiːfekt/ when it is a noun and /dɪˈfekt/ when it is a verb.

1 A **defect** is a fault or imperfection in a person or N COUNT : thing. EG *They were not blind to the defects of* OFT+of/in *Western society.*

2 If you **defect**, you leave your own country, v : OFT+to political party, or other group, and join an opposing one. EG *Several of the Labour MPs defected to the new party.* ◊ **defection** /dɪˈfekʃəᵊn/, **defections**. ◊ N COUNT OR EG *The number of defections has increased in* N UNCOUNT *recent years.* ◊ **defector**, **defectors**. EG *...defec-* ◊ N COUNT : *tors from the Liberal Party.* USU+SUPP

defective /dɪˈfektɪv/. If a piece of machinery is ADJ CLASSIF **defective**, there is something wrong with it and so it does not work properly. EG *One of the engines was found to be defective.*

defence /dɪˈfens/, **defences**; also spelled **defense** N UNCOUNT in American English. **1 Defence** is **1.1** action that is taken to protect someone or something against attack. EG *They carried sticks for defence rather than aggression... ...the defence of civil liberties.* **1.2** a country's armies and weapons, and their activi-ties. EG *...the Ministry of Defence... ...defence spend-ing... ...the defence forces.*

2 A **defence** is something that people or animals N COUNT : can use or do to protect themselves. EG *The jelly-* OFT+against *fish has had to develop this deadly poison as a defence... He had found coldness his only defence against despair.*

3 In a court of law, a person's **defence** is their N COUNT : denial of a charge against them. EG *He decided to* USU+SUPP *conduct his own defence.*

4 A **defence** is also something that you say in N COUNT support of ideas or actions that have been criti-cized. EG *His economists have drawn up a defence of his policy.* ● If you say something in **defence**, ● PHRASE you say it in order to support ideas or actions that have been criticized. EG *Brown, in defence, said that it was his boss who was violent.*

5 The **defence** is **5.1** the case that is presented by N SING : the+N a lawyer for the person in a trial who has been accused of a crime. EG *He gave evidence for the defence in the Hennessy case.* **5.2** the lawyers for this person.

6 The **defences** of a country or region are its N PLURAL armed forces and weapons.

7 In a sports team, the **defence** is the group of N COLL players who try to stop the opposing team scoring a goal or a point. EG *The English defence were weak.*

defenceless /dɪˈfensləs/; also spelled **defense-** ADJ QUALIT **less** in American English. If someone is **defence-less**, they are weak and unable to defend them-selves. EG *...attacks on defenceless civilians.*

defend /dɪˈfend/, **defends**, **defending**, **defended**.

1 If you **defend** someone or something, **1.1** you do V+O OR V-REFL something in order to protect them. EG *The village had to defend itself against raiders.* **1.2** you argue V+O OR V-REFL in support of them when they have been criticized. EG *The bank has defended its actions in these cases.*
◊ **defender**, **defenders**. EG *...a defender of right-* ◊ N COUNT : *wing views.* USU+SUPP

2 In a court of law, when a lawyer **defends** a v+o person who has been accused of a crime, he or she tries to prove that the charges are not true or that there was an excuse for the crime.

3 If a sports champion **defends** his or her title, he V+O OR V or she plays a match or a game against someone who will become the new champion if they win.

defendant /dɪˈfendənt/, **defendants**. The **de-** N COUNT **fendant** in a trial is the person who has been accused of a crime.

defense /dɪˈfens/. See **defence**.

defensible /dɪˈfensɪbəᵊl/. An opinion, system, or ADJ QUALIT action that is **defensible** is one that people can argue is right or good. EG *He gave a very defensible definition of socialism.*

defensive /dɪˈfensɪv/. **1** You use **defensive** to ADJ CLASSIF : describe things that are intended to protect some- ATTRIB one or something. EG *...defensive weapons... ...defen-sive measures... ...formidable defensive air cover.*

2 If you are **on the defensive**, you are trying to PHRASE protect yourself or your interests because you feel that you are being threatened.

3 Someone who is **defensive** is behaving in a way ADJ QUALIT that shows that they feel unsure or threatened. EG *I shuffled my feet and mumbled something defen-sive.* ◊ **defensively.** EG *'I'm in no hurry,' said* ◊ ADV *Rudolph defensively.*

defer /dɪˈfɜː/, **defers**, **deferring**, **deferred**. **1** If V+O OR V+-ING you **defer** an event or action, you arrange that it Formal will take place at a later date than was planned. EG *They offered to defer his appointment for a year.*

2 If you **defer** to someone, you accept their opinion V+to or you do what they want because you respect Formal them.

deference /ˈdefərəns/ is a polite and respectful N UNCOUNT : attitude to someone. EG *She is treated with defer-* OFT+to *ence... I refused to discuss the matter out of deference to my employer.*

deferential /ˌdefəˈrenʃəᵊl/. Someone who is **defer-** ADJ QUALIT **ential** is polite and respectful. EG *I made every effort to be pleasant and deferential to Mr Thoms.*
◊ **deferentially.** EG *'What work do you do, sir?' he* ◊ ADV *asked deferentially.*

defiance /dɪˈfaɪəns/. **1 Defiance** is behaviour N UNCOUNT which shows that you are not willing to obey someone or are not worried about their disapprov-al. EG *In a gesture of defiance, I wore a black mini-skirt.*

2 If you do something in **defiance of** a person or a PREP rule, you do it even though it has been forbidden. EG *The houses were erected in defiance of all building regulations.*

defiant /dɪˈfaɪənt/. If you are **defiant**, you refuse ADJ CLASSIF to obey someone or you ignore their disapproval of you. EG *The girl sat down with a defiant look at Judy.* ◊ **defiantly.** EG *She announced defiantly that* ◊ ADV *she intended to stay.*

deficient /dɪˈfɪʃənt/. **1** If someone or something is ADJ CLASSIF **deficient** in a particular thing, they do not have as USU PRED+in much of it as they need. EG *...old people deficient in vitamin C.* ◊ **deficiency** /dɪˈfɪʃənsi/, **deficien-** ◊ N COUNT OR **cies.** EG *...vitamin deficiency... Calcium deficiency* N UNCOUNT *causes acid soil.* +SUPP

2 Something that is **deficient** is not good enough. ADJ QUALIT EG *...increasingly deficient public services.* Formal
◊ **deficiency.** EG *The deficiency of the answers* ◊ N COUNT OR N UNCOUNT

was obvious to everybody... ...Lowell's deficiencies as an observer.

deficit /dɛfɪsɪt/, **deficits**. A **deficit** is the amount N COUNT by which the money received by a country or organization is less than the money it has spent. EG *The Post Office's deficit totalled 150m pounds.*

defile /dɪˈfaɪl/, **defiles, defiling, defiled**. If you V+O **defile** something precious, you spoil it or damage it. EG *...secret thoughts which defiled her purity.*

definable /dɪˈfaɪnəbəl/. Something that is **defin-** ADJ CLASSIF **able** can be described clearly. EG *The most important definable group is the community... The magic has gone, and for no definable reason.*

define /dɪˈfaɪn/, **defines, defining, defined**. If V+O you **define** something, you say exactly what it is. EG *Roland Buck asked Dr Kossou to define the problems discussed by the ministers... Each object had clearly defined functions... My dictionary defines 'crisis' as a 'turning point'.*

definite /dɛfɪnɪt/. 1 If something is **definite**, **1.1** ADJ QUALIT is firm and clear, and unlikely to be changed. EG *They have very definite views on this topic... There's a definite date for the wedding.* **1.2** it is true rather than being someone's opinion or guess. EG *There was no definite evidence.*

2 Someone who is **definite** behaves or talks in a ADJ QUALIT firm, confident way.

definite article, definite articles. In grammar, N COUNT the word 'the' is sometimes called the **definite article**. In this dictionary 'the' is called a determiner (DET). See the entry headed DETERMINERS for more information.

definitely /dɛfɪnɪtli[1]/. 1 You use **definitely** to ADV SEN emphasize that something is certainly the case. EG *They were definitely not for sale... Yes, we definitely need a car park.*

2 If something has **definitely** been decided, the ADV decision will not be changed. EG *I haven't definitely decided on going to law school.*

definition /dɛfɪnɪʃən/, **definitions**. 1 A **defini-** N COUNT **tion** is a statement giving the meaning of a word, especially in a dictionary. EG *There is no clear definition of schizophrenia.* ● If you say that ● PHRASE something has a particular quality **by definition**, you mean that it has this quality simply because of what it is. EG *Street life is, by definition, a life lived in public.*

2 **Definition** is the quality of being clear and N UNCOUNT distinct. EG *They lack definition and identity as a class.*

definitive /dəˈfɪnɪtɪv/. 1 Something that is **defini-** ADJ CLASSIF **tive** provides a firm conclusion that cannot be questioned. EG *...a definitive verdict.*
◊ **definitively.** EG *'Hearts of Darkness' will defini-* ◊ ADV *tively establish McCullin as a writer.*

2 A book or performance that is **definitive** is ADJ CLASSIF thought to be the best of its kind that has ever been done or that will ever be done. EG *He has written the definitive study of Hooker.*

deflate /dɪˈfleɪt/, **deflates, deflating, deflated**. 1 V+O If you **deflate** someone, you say or do something which makes them appear less important or makes them less confident. EG *...a mischievous desire to deflate the reputation of some contemporary.* ◊ **deflated.** EG *If that left us feeling deflated,* ◊ ADJ CLASSIF *worse was to come.*

2 When a tyre or balloon **deflates**, or when you V-ERG **deflate** it, all the air comes out of it.

deflation /dɪˈfleɪʃən/ is a reduction in economic N UNCOUNT activity in a country that leads to lower industrial output and lower prices.

deflect /dɪˈflɛkt/, **deflects, deflecting, deflect-ed**. 1 If you **deflect** something such as someone's V+O attention or criticism, you cause them to turn their attention to something else or to do something different. EG *Their main purpose was to deflect attention from the Government's proposals.*

2 When something moving **is deflected**, it starts V-ERG going in a slightly different direction from the way

it was going before, often because it has hit something. EG *The two streams of water are deflected.*

deform /dɪˈfɔːm/, **deforms, deforming, de-** V+O **formed**. If something **deforms** a person's body or an object, it causes it to have an unnatural shape or appearance. EG *Badly fitting shoes can deform the feet.* ◊ **deformed.** EG *The drug may have caused* ◊ ADJ QUALIT *deformed babies.*

deformity /dɪˈfɔːmɪti[1]/, **deformities**. 1 A de- N COUNT **formity** is a part of someone's body which is the wrong shape because of injury or illness.

2 **Deformity** is the condition of having a deform- N UNCOUNT ity.

defrost /diːˈfrɒst, diˈfrɒst/, **defrosts, defrosting, defrosted**. 1 When you **defrost** a fridge or freezer V-ERG or when it **defrosts**, you switch it off so that the ice inside it can melt.

2 When you **defrost** frozen food or when it de- V-ERG **frosts**, you allow it to become unfrozen so that you can eat it.

deft /dɛft/. A **deft** action is skilful and often quick. ADJ QUALIT EG *...cutting the edges away with deft movements of the knife... The deft fingers massaged his scalp.*
◊ **deftly.** EG *He deftly slit open the envelope.* ◊ ADV

defunct /dɪˈfʌŋkt/. If something is **defunct**, it no ADJ CLASSIF longer exists or it is no longer functioning. EG *...long defunct local authorities.*

defuse /diːˈfjuːz/, **defuses, defusing, defused**. 1 If V+O you **defuse** a dangerous or tense situation, you make it less dangerous or tense. EG *Lester's casual attitude defused the situation.*

2 If someone **defuses** a bomb, they remove the V+O fuse from it so that it cannot explode.

defy /dɪˈfaɪ/, **defies, defying, defied**. 1 If you V+O **defy** people or laws, you refuse to obey them. EG *...people who are intending to defy the law.*

2 If you **defy** someone to do something, you V+O+to-INF challenge them to do it when you think that they will be unable to do it or will be too frightened to do it. EG *I defy anyone to disprove it.*

3 If something **defies** description or understand- V+O ing, it is so strange or surprising that it is almost impossible to describe or understand. EG *...forces within the human character which defy rational analysis.*

degenerate, degenerates, degenerating, de-generated; pronounced /dɪˈdʒɛnəreɪt/ when it is a verb and /dɪˈdʒɛnərət/ when it is an adjective or a noun.

1 If someone or something **degenerates**, they V: OFT become worse. EG *The discussion degenerated into* +into/to *a row.* ◊ **degeneration** /dɪdʒɛnəreɪʃən/. EG *This* ◊ N UNCOUNT *disease causes physical and mental degeneration.*

2 If someone is **degenerate**, they show low stand- ADJ QUALIT ards of morality. EG *...the less degenerate men of earlier times.* ◊ **degeneracy** /dɪdʒɛnərəsi[1]/. EG ◊ N UNCOUNT *...the degeneracy of the age.*

3 A **degenerate** is someone who behaves in a way N COUNT that many people find shocking or disgusting.

degradation /dɛgrədeɪʃən/ is a state of poverty N UNCOUNT and dirt. EG *They forgot the squalor and degradation around them.*

degrade /dɪˈgreɪd/, **degrades, degrading, de-** V+O **graded**. If something **degrades** someone, it causes people to have less respect for them. EG *...films that degrade women.* ◊ **degrading.** EG *He denounced* ◊ ADJ QUALIT *the 'vicious and degrading cult of violence'.*

degree /dɪˈgriː/, **degrees**. 1 A **degree** is the N COUNT+SUPP amount of a feeling or quality that someone or something has or the extent to which something happens. EG *She admits to a degree of prejudice... This has been tried with varying degrees of success... The number of police carrying guns has increased to an alarming degree.* ● If something ● PHRASE

How many words on these pages could you use when talking about food?

happens **by degrees**, it happens slowly and gradually.

2 A **degree** is also **2.1** a unit of measurement that N COUNT is used when expressing temperatures; often written as '°', for example 23°. EG *The temperature was 23 degrees centigrade*. **2.2** a unit of measurement that is used when expressing angles and also latitude and longitude; often written as '°', for example 50°.

3 If you take a **degree**, you take a course of study N COUNT at a university or polytechnic. If you have a **degree**, you have gained a qualification by passing a course like this. EG *He had taken a degree in music at Cambridge*.

dehydrate /di:haɪdreɪt/, **dehydrates, dehydrating, dehydrated**. **1** When something such as food V+O : USU PASS **is dehydrated**, all the water is removed from it, often in order to preserve it. ◊ **dehydrated**. EG ◊ ADJ CLASSIF *...packets of dehydrated soup*.

2 If you **are dehydrated**, you have lost too much V+O : USU PASS water from your body so that you feel weak or ill.

deign /deɪn/, **deigns, deigning, deigned**. If you V+to-INF **deign** to do something, you do it even though you Formal think you are really too important to do such a thing. EG *...plays that no regular reviewer would deign to go to*.

deity /di:ɪtɪ, deɪ-/, **deities**. A **deity** is a god or N COUNT goddess. EG *...Roman deities... ...Blake's visions of* Formal *the Deity*.

dejected /dɪˈdʒɛktɪd/. If you are **dejected**, you ADJ QUALIT feel unhappy or disappointed about something. EG Formal *He has a dejected, saddened look... He walked off, dejected in defeat*. ◊ **dejectedly**. EG *'I can't do it,'* ◊ ADV *said the girl dejectedly*.

dejection /dɪˈdʒɛkʃəʰn/ is unhappiness and disap- N UNCOUNT pointment about something. EG *There was general* Formal *dejection over the siege of Jerusalem*.

delay /dɪˈleɪ/, **delays, delaying, delayed**. **1** If you V+-ING, V+O, **delay** doing something, you do not do it until a OR V later time. EG *Try and persuade them to delay some of the changes... She will delay starting for six months... Don't delay*.

2 To **delay** someone means to make them late or V+O to make them slow down. EG *I'm afraid I was slightly delayed*.

3 To **delay** something means to make it happen V+O later than was planned or expected. EG *The shock of the operation delayed his recovery*.

4 If there is a **delay**, something does not happen N COUNT OR until later than was planned or expected. EG *The* N UNCOUNT *delays were caused by events beyond our control... We shall inform you without delay*.

delectable /dɪˈlɛktəbəʰl/. **1** If you say that some- ADJ QUALIT one is **delectable**, you mean that they are very Literary attractive. EG *...the delectable Miss Haynes*.

2 Food that is **delectable** is very pleasant and ADJ QUALIT tasty. Literary

delegate, delegates, delegating, delegated; pronounced /dɛləgəʰt/ when it is a noun and /dɛləgeɪt/ when it is a verb.

1 A **delegate** is a person who is chosen to make N COUNT decisions on behalf of a group of other people, especially at a meeting. EG *...delegates to the annual party conference*.

2 If you **delegate** someone to do something, you V+O : formally ask them to do it on your behalf. EG *The* USU+to-INF *Bishop delegated me to approach the local press*.

3 If you **delegate** duties or responsibilities, you tell V+O OR V someone to do them on your behalf. EG *I employ staff and delegate all household tasks*.

delegation /dɛlɪˈgeɪʃəʰn/, **delegations**. A **delega-** N COUNT **tion** is a group of people who have been sent somewhere to speak or act on behalf of a larger group of people. EG *There was also a delegation from the British Isles*.

delete /dɪˈliːt/, **deletes, deleting, deleted**. If you V+O **delete** something that has been written down, you cross it out or remove it. EG *...a narrative from which some words have been deleted*.

deliberate, deliberates, deliberating, deliberated; pronounced /dɪˈlɪbərəʰt/ when it is an adjective and /dɪˈlɪbəreɪt/ when it is a verb.

1 If something that you do is **deliberate**, you ADJ CLASSIF planned or intended to do it, rather than doing it by accident. EG *It was a deliberate lie*. ◊ **deliberately**. EG *I've never deliberately hurt* ◊ ADV *anyone*.

2 An action or movement that is **deliberate** is ADJ QUALIT done slowly and carefully. EG *His manner was quiet, his speech deliberate*. ◊ **deliberately**. EG *He* ◊ ADV *climbed the stairs slowly and deliberately*.

3 If you **deliberate**, you think about something V carefully before making a decision. EG *We had been waiting for two days while the jury deliberated*.

deliberation /dɪˌlɪbəˈreɪʃəʰn/, **deliberations**. **1** N UNCOUNT **Deliberation** is careful consideration of a subject. EG *After considerable deliberation, I decided to accept the job*.

2 If you do something **with deliberation**, you do it PHRASE slowly and carefully. EG *John, with great deliberation, put his books into his briefcase*.

3 **Deliberations** are formal discussions. EG *I left* N PLURAL *the committee to its deliberations*.

delicacy /dɛlɪkəsɪ/, **delicacies**. **1** If something N UNCOUNT has **delicacy**, it is graceful and attractive. EG *...the ravishing beauty and delicacy of their features*.

2 If you do or say something with **delicacy**, you do N UNCOUNT it or say it carefully and tactfully because you do not want to offend someone. EG *With great delicacy, they refrained from asking the sex of his friend*.

3 A **delicacy** is a rare or expensive food that is N COUNT considered especially nice to eat. EG *...artichokes, smoked fish, and other delicacies*.

delicate /dɛlɪkəʰt/. **1** Something that is **delicate** is ADJ QUALIT narrow and graceful or attractive. EG *She had long delicate fingers*. ◊ **delicately**. EG *...delicately* ◊ ADV *veined pale skin*.

2 A colour, taste, or smell that is **delicate** is ADJ QUALIT pleasant and not strong or intense. EG *...a delicate pale cream colour*.

3 A **delicate** object is fragile and needs to be ADJ QUALIT handled carefully. EG *...delicate china*.

4 A **delicate** movement is gentle, controlled, and ADJ QUALIT not at all clumsy. EG *...delicate ballet steps*. ◊ **delicately**. EG *The princess took the pot delicate-* ◊ ADV *ly from him*.

5 Someone who is **delicate** is often ill. EG *She was a* ADJ QUALIT *very delicate child*.

6 If someone is **delicate** in their speech, they ADJ QUALIT choose their words carefully in order to avoid offending people. ◊ **delicately**. EG *She had deli-* ◊ ADV *cately hinted at his inadequacy*.

7 A **delicate** situation or problem needs very ADJ QUALIT careful and tactful treatment. EG *...the delicate sphere of race relations*. ◊ **delicately**. EG *...highly* ◊ ADV *sensitive and delicately balanced economic systems*.

8 A **delicate** sense or scientific instrument is ADJ QUALIT capable of noticing very small changes or differences. EG *Bees have a delicate sense of smell*.

delicatessen /dɛlɪkəˈtɛsəʰn/, **delicatessens**. A N COUNT **delicatessen** is a shop that sells unusual foods such as foreign cheeses and cold meats.

delicious /dɪˈlɪʃəs/. **1** Food that is **delicious** has a ADJ QUALIT very pleasant taste. EG *...a delicious cake*.

2 Something or someone that is **delicious** is very ADJ QUALIT nice or pleasant. EG *It is a delicious feeling*. Informal ◊ **deliciously**. EG *The sun felt deliciously warm*. ◊ ADV+ADJ

delight /dɪˈlaɪt/, **delights, delighting, delighted**.

1 **Delight** is a feeling of very great pleasure. EG N UNCOUNT *Frank discovered to his delight that the gun was real*.

2 If someone **takes a delight** or **takes delight** in PHRASE doing something, they get a lot of pleasure from doing it. EG *...sadistic friends who take delight in breaking bad news*.

3 You can refer to someone or something that N COUNT : gives you great joy or pleasure as a **delight**. EG OFT+SUPP

That was when I first discovered the delights of the city... Mrs Travers was a delight to interview.

4 If something **delights** you, it gives you a lot of v+o pleasure. EG *The thought of divorce neither distressed nor delighted her.*

5 If you **delight** in something, you get a lot of v+in/at pleasure from it. EG *Morris delighted in hard manual work.*

delighted /dɪˈlaɪtɪ²d/. If you are **delighted**, you ADJ QUALIT are extremely pleased and excited about something. EG *He was delighted with his achievement... He was delighted to meet them again.*
◇ **delightedly.** EG *She laughed delightedly.* ◇ ADV

delightful /dɪˈlaɪtful/. Someone or something that ADJ QUALIT is **delightful** is very pleasant. EG *Her children really are delightful... ...a delightful room.*
◇ **delightfully.** EG *...a delightfully smooth soup.* ◇ ADV+ADJ

delinquent /dɪˈlɪŋkwənt/, **delinquents.** You use ADJ CLASSIF **delinquent** to describe young people who are always committing minor crimes. EG *...families with delinquent children... ...delinquent behaviour.*
▸ used as a noun. EG *A few months of this may deter* ▸ N COUNT *some potential delinquents.* ◇ **delinquency** ◇ N UNCOUNT /dɪˈlɪŋkwənsɪ/. EG *...children taken into care be-* Formal *cause of their delinquency.* ● See also **juvenile delinquent**.

delirious /dɪˈlɪrɪəs/. **1** Someone who is **delirious** is ADJ CLASSIF unable to think or speak in a rational way, usually because they have a fever. ◇ **delirium** /dɪˈlɪrɪəm/. ◇ N UNCOUNT EG *We heard him babble in delirium.*

2 You can also describe someone who is extremely ADJ QUALIT excited and happy as **delirious**. EG *He sang before delirious crowds in a theatre.*

deliver /dɪˈlɪvə/, **delivers, delivering, delivered. 1** If you **deliver** something, **1.1** you take it to v+o someone's house or office. EG *He delivered newspapers as a boy.* **1.2** you give it to someone. EG v+o+A *Chance delivered his enemy into his hands.* Formal

2 If you **deliver** a lecture or speech, you give it. v+o

3 When someone **delivers** a baby, they help the v+o woman who is giving birth to the baby.

4 If you say that someone has **delivered the** PHRASE **goods**, you mean that they have done something that they promised to do. EG *The Department failed to deliver the goods.*

delivery /dɪˈlɪvə⁰rɪ¹/, **deliveries. 1** Delivery is N UNCOUNT the bringing of letters, parcels, or goods to someone's house or office. EG *All goods must be paid for before delivery.*

2 A **delivery** is something that is delivered to N COUNT someone. EG *We ordered an extra delivery of coal.*

3 Someone's **delivery** is the way in which they N UNCOUNT : give a speech. EG *His delivery was slow and ponder-* USU+SUPP *ous.*

4 Delivery is also the process of giving birth to a N COUNT OR baby. EG *It was a simple, routine delivery.* N COUNT

delta /ˈdɛltə/, **deltas.** A **delta** is an area of flat land N COUNT where a river spreads out into several smaller rivers before entering the sea.

delude /dɪˈljuːd/, **deludes, deluding, deluded.** If v+o OR v-REFL you **delude** someone, you make them believe something that is not true. EG *They are not deluded by our talk of freedom... It was no good deluding myself that he loved me.*

deluge /ˈdɛljuːdʒ/, **deluges, deluging, deluged. 1** N COUNT A **deluge** is a sudden, very heavy fall of rain. EG *The rain turned to a deluge.*

2 A **deluge** of things is a very large number of N PART them which arrive at the same time. EG *...a deluge of petitions to the King.*

3 If you **are deluged** with things, a very large v+o : USU number of them arrive at the same time. EG *They* PASS+with *were deluged with requests to play the song.*

delusion /dɪˈluːʒən/, **delusions.** A **delusion** is a N COUNT false belief. EG *...the delusion that slaughter in Britain is humane.*

de luxe /dɪˈ lʌks/. You use **de luxe** to describe ADJ CLASSIF things that are better and more expensive than

other things of the same kind. EG *...a de luxe version of the Ford Escort.*

delve /dɛlv/, **delves, delving, delved. 1** If you v+A **delve** into something, you try to discover more information about it. EG *One must delve more deeply to find the reasons.*

2 If you **delve** inside something such as a cupboard v+A or a bag, you search inside it.

demagogue /ˈdɛməgɒg/, **demagogues.** A **dema-** N COUNT **gogue** is a political leader who tries to win support by appealing to people's emotions rather than by using rational arguments; used showing disapproval.

demand /dɪˈmɑːnd/, **demands, demanding, de-** **manded. 1** If you **demand** something, **1.1** you ask v+o, for it very forcefully. EG *They are demanding* v+to-INF, *higher wages... I demand to see a doctor... She had* OR v+REPORT *been demanding that he visit her.* **1.2** you ask a v+QUOTE question in a forceful way. EG *'What have I done?' he demanded.*

2 If a job or situation **demands** something, that v+o thing is necessary for it. EG *He has most of the qualities demanded of a leader.*

3 A **demand** is a firm request for something. EG N COUNT *They feared what might happen if they refused his* +SUPP OR *demands... ...his demand for stronger armed forces.* REPORT

4 If there is **demand** for something, a lot of people N UNCOUNT : want to buy it or have it. EG *The demand for health* OFT+for *care is unlimited.* ● If something is **in demand**, a ● PHRASE lot of people want to buy it or have it.

5 The **demands** of something are the things that N COUNT : have to be done or provided for it. EG *The system* USU PLURAL *has always made heavy demands on those working in it.*

6 If something is available **on demand**, you can PHRASE have it whenever you ask for it. EG *Your money is available on demand.*

demanding /dɪˈmɑːndɪŋ/. **1** A **demanding** job or ADJ QUALIT task requires a lot of time, energy, or attention. EG *...women who are involved in demanding careers.*

2 People who are **demanding** are not easily ADJ QUALIT satisfied. EG *...an impatient and demanding public.*

demarcation /ˌdiːmɑːˈkeɪʃən/ is the action of N UNCOUNT showing or stating exactly where two things are separated or are different. EG *...the demarcation lines between ethnic groups.*

demean /dɪˈmiːn/, **demeans, demeaning, de-** V-REFL OR v+o **meaned.** If you **demean** yourself or **demean** Formal something, you do something which makes people have less respect for you or for that thing. EG *They all agreed that the President had demeaned himself as a man... He had demeaned his office by lying.* ◇ **demeaning** /dɪˈmiːnɪŋ/. EG *They regard* ◇ ADJ QUALIT *these jobs as demeaning and degrading.*

demeanour /dɪˈmiːnə/; spelled **demeanor** in N UNCOUNT : American English. Your **demeanour** is the way USU+POSS you behave, which gives people an impression of Formal your character and feelings. EG *...his usual calm demeanour... ...the vulgarity of his demeanour.*

demented /dɪˈmɛntɪ²d/. Someone who is **dement-** ADJ CLASSIF **ed** behaves in a wild or violent way, often because they are mad.

demise /dɪˈmaɪz/. The **demise** of something or N SING+SUPP someone is their end or death. EG *...the demise of* Formal *the British Empire.*

democracy /dɪˈmɒkrəsɪ¹/, **democracies. 1** De- N UNCOUNT **mocracy** is a system of government or organization in which people choose leaders or make important decisions by voting.

2 A **democracy** is a country in which the people N COUNT choose their government by voting for it.

democrat /ˈdɛməˌkræt/, **democrats.** A **democrat** N COUNT is a person who believes in the ideals of democracy, personal freedom, and equality.

What different style labels are used in the Extra Column on these pages?

democratic /dɛmə⁶krætɪk/. A **democratic** coun- ADJ CLASSIF
try, organization, or system is one in which leaders
are chosen or decisions are made by voting. EG
...democratic government. ◊ **democratically.** EG ◊ ADV
...a democratically elected government.

demolish /dɪ¹mɒlɪʃ/, **demolishes, demolishing,
demolished. 1** When a building **is demolished**, it v+o
is knocked down, often because it is old or dangerous. EG The old prison was demolished in 1890.
◊ **demolition** /dɛmə̃lɪʃə⁰n, di:-/. EG ...the demolition ◊ N UNCOUNT
of the old YMCA building.
2 If you **demolish** someone's idea, argument, or v+o
belief, you prove that it is completely wrong. EG A
week in Moscow demolished the myth that their
stage productions are not exciting. ◊ **demolition.** ◊ N UNCOUNT
EG ...the demolition of a beloved theory.

demon /di:mə⁰n/, **demons.** A **demon** is an evil N COUNT
spirit. EG ...a demon of wrath.

demonic /dɪ¹mɒnɪk/. Something that is **demonic** ADJ CLASSIF
is evil. EG ...demonic forces.

demonstrable /dɪ¹mɒnstrəbə⁰l/. Something that ADJ CLASSIF
is **demonstrable** can be shown to exist or to be
true. EG The economic advantages are clearly
demonstrable. ◊ **demonstrably.** EG Their vehicles ◊ ADV :
are demonstrably more reliable than ours. OFT+ADJ

demonstrate /dɛmənstreɪt/, **demonstrates,
demonstrating, demonstrated. 1** To **demon-** v+o OR
strate a fact or theory means to make it clear to V+REPORT
people. EG Her latest book demonstrates how important freedom is.
2 If you **demonstrate** something to someone, you v+o : OFT+to
show them how to do it or how it works. EG She is OR V+REPORT
demonstrating a new kind of cooker... She has been
demonstrating how you make bread.
3 If you **demonstrate** a particular skill, quality, or v+o
feeling, you show that you have it. EG She has not
demonstrated much generosity.
4 When people **demonstrate**, they take part in a v
march or a meeting to show their opposition to
something or their support for it.
◊ **demonstrator, demonstrators.** EG ...crowds of ◊ N COUNT
demonstrators.

demonstration /dɛmənstreɪʃə⁰n/, **demonstrations. 1** A **demonstration** is a public meeting or N COUNT
march which is held by people to show their
opposition to something or their support for it. EG
There was a series of demonstrations against the
visit.
2 A **demonstration** of something is a talk by N COUNT
someone who shows you how to do it or how it
works. EG ...a demonstration of the new machinery.
3 A **demonstration** of something such as a fact is N COUNT OR
a proof by someone that it exists or is true. EG It N UNCOUNT
was an unforgettable demonstration of the power
of reason.
4 Demonstration of a quality or feeling is an N COUNT OR
expression of it. EG ...spontaneous demonstrations of N UNCOUNT
affection.

demonstrative /dɪ¹mɒnstrətɪv/. Someone who is ADJ QUALIT
demonstrative shows affection freely and openly.
EG ...a demonstrative and sympathetic mother.

demoralize /dɪ¹mɒrəlaɪz/, **demoralizes, demor-** v+o
alizing, demoralized; also spelled **demoralise.** If
something **demoralizes** you, it makes you lose
confidence in what you are doing and makes you
feel depressed. EG People are demoralized by the
present climate of public opinion. ◊ **demoralized.** ◊ ADJ QUALIT
EG ...the stream of desperate and demoralized peo-
ple seeking work. ◊ **demoralization** ◊ N UNCOUNT
/dɪ¹mɒrəlaɪzeɪʃə⁰n/. EG ...the growing national mood
of doubt and demoralisation.

demote /dɪ¹məʊt/, **demotes, demoting, de-** v+o
moted. If someone in authority **demotes** you, they
reduce your rank, often as a punishment. EG He was
demoted to the rank of ordinary soldier.

demur /dɪmɜ:/, **demurs, demurring, demurred.** v
If you **demur**, you say that you do not agree with Formal
something or will not do something. EG Morris
invited her out for a meal. She demurred.

demure /dɪ¹mjʊə/. Someone, especially a young ADJ QUALIT
woman, who is **demure** is quiet and rather shy,
and behaves very correctly. EG ...a demure, sweet-
faced girl. ◊ **demurely.** EG She sat demurely by ◊ ADV
her mother.

den /dɛn/, **dens.** The **den** of a fox or wolf is its N COUNT
home.

denial /dɪ¹naɪəl/, **denials. 1** If you make a **denial** N COUNT OR
of something such as an accusation, you say that it N UNCOUNT
is not true. EG He made a personal denial of all the
charges against him.
2 If there is a **denial** of something that people N UNCOUNT :
think they have a right to, someone in authority OFT+of
refuses to let them have it. EG They protested
against the continued denial of civil liberties.

denigrate /dɛnɪ¹greɪt/, **denigrates, denigrating,** v+o
denigrated. If you **denigrate** someone or some- Formal
thing, you criticize them unfairly. EG To assert this
is to denigrate the effectiveness of the police.

denim /dɛnɪm/, **denims. 1 Denim** is a thick N UNCOUNT :
cotton cloth which is used to make clothes. EG USU N MOD
...denim jeans... ...a skirt made of black denim.
2 Denims are trousers made of denim. N PLURAL

denomination /dɪ¹nɒmɪneɪʃə⁰n/, **denomina-** N COUNT
tions. A **denomination** is a religious group within
a particular religion. EG ...young people of all de-
nominations.

denote /dɪ¹nəʊt/, **denotes, denoting, denoted. 1** v+o OR
If one thing **denotes** another, it is a sign or V+REPORT
indication of it. EG My identity was denoted by a Formal
plastic label on my wrist.
2 What a word or name **denotes** is what it means v+o
or refers to. EG 'Basic', as its name denotes, is a Formal
very straightforward set of computer instructions.

denounce /dɪ¹naʊns/, **denounces, denouncing,** v+o : OFT+as
denounced. If you **denounce** someone or something, you criticize them severely and publicly. EG A
mass meeting at Carnegie Hall denounced him as a
traitor.

dense /dɛns/, **denser, densest. 1** Something that ADJ QUALIT
is **dense** contains a lot of things or people in a
small area. EG ...a dense crowd... ...dense forest.
◊ **densely.** EG ...the most densely populated region ◊ ADV
in the country.
2 Dense fog or smoke is thick and difficult to see ADJ QUALIT
through.
3 If you say that someone is **dense**, you think that ADJ PRED
they are stupid and take a long time to understand Informal
simple things.

density /dɛnsɪ¹ti¹/, **densities. 1** The **density** of N UNCOUNT
something in a place is the extent to which it fills OR N COUNT
the place. EG Australia has a very low population
density... Traffic density was increasing.
2 The **density** of a substance or object is the N UNCOUNT
relation of its mass to its volume. EG ...the density of OR N COUNT
water. Technical

dent /dɛnt/, **dents, denting, dented. 1** If you **dent** v+o
something, you damage its surface by hitting it and
causing a bit of it to curve inwards. EG He pulled
back the covers and dented the pillow a little.
◊ **dented.** EG ...some dented oil drums. ◊ ADJ CLASSIF
2 A **dent** is a hollow made in the surface of N COUNT
something, which has been caused by hitting it. EG
...car owners searching for dents and scratches.

dental /dɛntə⁰l/ is used to describe things that ADJ CLASSIF :
relate to teeth. EG ...free dental treatment... Maggie ATTRIB
has a dental appointment.

dentist /dɛntɪst/, **dentists. 1** A **dentist** is a person N COUNT
who is qualified to treat people's teeth.
2 You refer to the place where a dentist works as N SING : the+N
the **dentist's** or the **dentist.** EG He's at the dentist's.

dentures /dɛntʃəz/ are artificial teeth used by N PLURAL
people who no longer have all their own teeth.

denude /dɪ¹nju:d/, **denudes, denuding, denuded.** v+o : USU
If something **is denuded**, everything is taken off it PASS, OFT+ of
or from it. EG The Christmas tree was soon denuded Formal
of its parcels.

denunciation /dɪˈnʌnsɪeɪʃən/, **denunciations.** N UNCOUNT OR N COUNT: USU+SUPP
Denunciation of someone or something is severe public criticism of them. EG ...*his denunciations of the errors of the previous government.*

deny /dɪˈnaɪ/, **denies, denying, denied. 1** If you V+O, **deny** something, you say that it is not true. EG *He denied that he was involved... Green denied doing anything illegal.* V+-ING, OR V+REPORT: ONLY that

2 If you **deny** someone something that they want, V+O+O you do not let them have it. EG *He has denied you access to information... Freedom is denied to the young for the same reason.* OR V+O+to

deodorant /diːˈəʊdərənt/, **deodorants. Deodor-** N MASS **ant** is a pleasant-smelling liquid that you put on your body, in order to reduce the smell of perspiration.

depart /dɪˈpɑːt/, **departs, departing, departed. 1** V: USU+A When someone or something **departs** from a place, they leave it. EG *She prepared to depart for Italy... The Express was scheduled to depart at six.*

2 If you **depart** from the normal way of doing V+from something, you do something slightly different. EG ...*their unwillingness to depart from traditional practice... We departed from the script to produce a startling finish.*

departed /dɪˈpɑːtɪd/. If you talk about **departed** ADJ CLASSIF friends or relatives, you mean the ones who have Formal died.

department /dɪˈpɑːtmənt/, **departments.** A de- N COUNT+SUPP **partment** is one of the sections in a large shop or an organization such as a university. EG ...*a Professor in the English department... the cosmetics department of Harrods... the local office of the Department of Health.* ◊ **departmental** ◊ ADJ CLASSIF /diːpɑːˈtmentəl/. EG ...*a departmental meeting.* ATTRIB

department store, department stores. A de- N COUNT **partment store** is a large shop which sells many different kinds of goods.

departure /dɪˈpɑːtʃə/, **departures. 1 Departure** N COUNT OR is the act of leaving a place. EG ...*the signal for* N UNCOUNT *departure... the week before their departure.*

2 If an action is a **departure** from what was N COUNT: previously planned or what is usually done, it is OFT+from different from it. EG *Does the budget represent a departure from stated Government policy?*

depend /dɪˈpend/, **depends, depending, depend-** **ed. 1** If you **depend** on someone or something, you V+on/upon need them in order to be able to survive. EG ...*the two persons on whom the child depended for survival... These factories depend upon natural resources.*

2 If you can **depend** on someone or something, you V+on/upon know that they will help you when you need them. EG *I knew I could depend on you.*

3 If you say that something **depends** on something V: OFT+on else, you mean that it will only happen if the OR V+REPORT: circumstances are right. EG *The success of the* ONLY WH *meeting depends largely on whether the chairman is efficient.*

4 You use an expression such as 'It depends' to PHRASE indicate that you are not sure what will happen or what is the best answer to give. EG *'What will you do?' - 'I don't know. It depends.'*

5 You use **depending on** to say that what happens PREP varies according to the circumstances. EG *This training takes a variable time, depending on the chosen speciality.*

dependable /dɪˈpendəbəl/. If someone or some- ADJ QUALIT thing is **dependable**, you know that they will always do what you need or expect them to do. EG *She was remarkably self-confident and dependable for her age... a dependable sort of car.*

dependant /dɪˈpendənt/, **dependants;** also N COUNT spelled **dependent.** Your **dependants** are the people who you support financially, such as your children. EG *Were you to be killed, your dependants could get compensation.*

dependence /dɪˈpendəns/; also spelled **depend-** N UNCOUNT **ance. Dependence** is a constant and regular need +on/upon that someone has for something in order to be able to live or work properly. EG ...*the increasing dependence of police forces on computers... ...depend-ence on pain-killing drugs.*

dependent /dɪˈpendənt/. **1** If you are **dependent** ADJ QUALIT: on someone or something, you need them in order OFT+on/upon to be able to survive. EG *West Europe was still heavily dependent on Middle Eastern oil.*

2 See also **dependant.**

depict /dɪˈpɪkt/, **depicts, depicting, depicted.** If you **depict** someone or something, **1** you draw V+O them in a painting or cartoon. EG *Haselden's cartoon depicted the British lion roaring triumphantly.*

2 you describe them. EG *Women are constantly* V+O: OFT+as *depicted as inferior to men.*

depiction /dɪˈpɪkʃən/, **depictions.** A **depiction** N COUNT OR of something is a picture of it or a written descrip- N UNCOUNT tion of it. EG ...*the depiction of Christ.*

deplete /dɪˈpliːt/, **depletes, depleting, depleted.** V+O If you **deplete** something, you reduce the amount of it that is available to be used. EG *We must be careful as we deplete our stocks of resources.* ◊ **depletion** /dɪˈpliːʃən/. EG ...*the depletion of raw* ◊ N UNCOUNT: *material reserves.* USU+SUPP

deplorable /dɪˈplɔːrəbəl/. If you say that some- ADJ QUALIT thing is **deplorable**, you mean that it is extremely Formal bad or unpleasant. EG *How did these deplorable conditions come about?*

deplore /dɪˈplɔː/, **deplores, deploring, deplored.** V+O If you **deplore** something, you think that it is Formal wrong or immoral. EG *We deplore waste.*

deploy /dɪˈplɔɪ/, **deploys, deploying, deployed.** V+O When a country **deploys** troops, resources, or equipment, it organizes them so that they are ready for immediate action. ◊ **deployment** ◊ N UNCOUNT /dɪˈplɔɪmənt/. EG ...*the deployment of nuclear weapons.*

deport /dɪˈpɔːt/, **deports, deporting, deported.** V+O When a government **deports** foreigners, it sends them out of the country because they have committed a crime or because they do not have official permission to be there. ◊ **deportation** ◊ N UNCOUNT /diːpɔːˈteɪʃən/, **deportations.** EG *They were pre-* OR N COUNT *pared to risk prison or deportation.*

deportment /dɪˈpɔːtmənt/. Your **deportment** is N UNCOUNT the way you behave, especially the way you walk Formal and move.

depose /dɪˈpəʊz/, **deposes, deposing, deposed.** If V+O: USU PASS a ruler or leader is **deposed**, they are removed from their position by force.

deposit /dɪˈpɒzɪt/, **deposits, depositing, deposit-** **ed. 1** If a substance is **deposited** somewhere, it is V+O: left there as a result of a chemical or geological USU PASS+A process. EG *Layers of sand were deposited on top of the peat.*

2 If you **deposit** something somewhere, you put it V+O: USU+A there, often so that it will be safe until it is needed again. EG *He deposited the case in the left luggage office.*

3 A **deposit** is an amount of a substance that has N COUNT been left somewhere as a result of a chemical or geological process. EG ...*rich mineral deposits.*

4 When talking about money, a **deposit** is **4.1** a N COUNT sum of money which you put in a bank account or other savings account. **4.2** part of the price of something which you pay when you agree to buy it. EG *We've saved enough for the deposit on a house.* **4.3** a sum of money which you give a person you rent or hire something from. The money is returned to you if you do not damage what you have rented.

depot /ˈdepəʊ/, **depots.** A **depot** is **1** a place where N COUNT goods and vehicles are kept when they are not being used. EG ...*airfields and supply depots.* **2** a bus American station or a railway station.

On these pages, which noun is often used in front of another noun?

depraved /dɪ'preɪvd/. If you describe someone as ADJ QUALIT
depraved, you think that they are morally bad. EG
*Few mothers are depraved enough to kill their
children.* ◇ **depravity** /dɪ'prævɪti¹/. EG *...a world* ◇ N UNCOUNT
of depravity and torture. Formal

deprecating /'deprəkeɪtɪŋ/. A **deprecating** ges- ADJ QUALIT
ture or remark shows that you think something is Formal
not very good. EG *Tom waved a deprecating hand.*

depreciate /dɪ'priːʃieɪt/, **depreciates, depreci-** v
ating, depreciated. When something **depreci-**
ates, it loses some of its value. EG *Property rarely
depreciates.* ◇ **depreciation** /dɪ'priːsi'eɪʃə⁰n/. EG ◇ N UNCOUNT
...the depreciation of currency. +SUPP

depress /dɪ'pres/, **depresses, depressing, de-**
pressed. 1 If something **depresses** you, it makes v+o
you feel sad and disappointed. EG *She lost the case,
which depressed her enormously.*

2 If something **depresses** prices or wages, it v+o
causes them to drop in value. EG *The current oil
glut has depressed prices still more.*

depressed /dɪ'prest/. **1** If you are **depressed**, you ADJ QUALIT
feel sad and disappointed.

2 A place that is **depressed** does not have as much ADJ QUALIT
business or employment as it used to. EG *...the
effects of living in depressed city areas.*

depressing /dɪ'presɪŋ/. Something that is **de-** ADJ QUALIT
pressing makes you feel sad and disappointed. EG
This was depressing news. ◇ **depressingly.** EG *It* ◇ ADV+ADJ
was all depressingly clear.

depression /dɪ'preʃə⁰n/, **depressions. 1 Depres-** N UNCOUNT
sion is great sadness and disappointment. OR N COUNT

2 A **depression** is a time when there is very little N COUNT
economic activity, which results in a lot of unemployment. EG *...during the depression of the 1930's.*

3 On a surface, a **depression** is an area which is N COUNT
lower than the rest of the surface. EG *...shallow
depressions in the ground.*

deprive /dɪ'praɪv/, **deprives, depriving, de-** v+o+of
prived. If you **deprive** someone of something, you
take it away from them or prevent them from
having it. EG *...to deprive a peasant of his land.*
◇ **deprivation** /deprɪ'veɪʃə⁰n/, **deprivations.** EG ◇ N UNCOUNT
...suffering years of deprivation and poverty. OR N COUNT

deprived /dɪ'praɪvd/. If you describe someone as ADJ QUALIT
deprived, you think that they do not have the
things that are essential in life. EG *...deprived children.*

dept is a written abbreviation for 'department';
mainly used as part of a name. EG *...Dept of English.*

depth /depθ/, **depths. 1** The **depth** of something is N UNCOUNT
1.1 the distance between its top and bottom OR N COUNT
surfaces. EG *None of the lakes was more than a few
yards in depth.* **1.2** the distance between the front
and the back of it. EG *...things buried in the depths
of your store cupboard.*

2 The **depth** of a situation or emotion is its great N UNCOUNT
degree or intensity. EG *The depth of his concern* +SUPP
was evident enough.

3 The **depths** of the ocean are the parts of it which N PLURAL
are a long way below the surface. the+N

4 If you are in the **depths** of despair, you are N PLURAL
extremely unhappy.

5 In the **depths** of winter means in the middle of N PLURAL
winter, when it is coldest. +SUPP

6 If you deal with a subject **in depth**, you deal with PHRASE
it very thoroughly and consider all the aspects of it.

7 If you are **out of** your **depth**, you are trying to PHRASE
deal with something that is too difficult for you to
cope with or understand.

deputation /depjə'teɪʃə⁰n/, **deputations.** A **depu-** N COUNT
tation is a small group of people who have been
asked to speak to someone on behalf of a larger
group of people, usually in order to make a complaint.

deputize /'depjʊ'taɪz/, **deputizes, deputizing,** v:OFT+for
deputized; also spelled **deputise.** If you **deputize**
for someone, you do something on their behalf, for
example attend a meeting.

deputy /'depjə'ti¹/, **deputies.** A **deputy** is the N COUNT
second most important person in an organization OR N MOD
or department. A deputy often acts on behalf of the
boss when the boss cannot be present. EG *He and
his deputy co-operated well... ...the Deputy Chairman of the Commission.*

deranged /dɪ'reɪndʒd/. Someone who is **de-** ADJ QUALIT
ranged behaves in a wild or strange way, often as
a result of mental illness.

derelict /'derə'lɪkt/. A **derelict** building or area of ADJ CLASSIF
land has not been used for some time and is in a
bad condition.

deride /dɪ'raɪd/, **derides, deriding, derided.** If v+o
you **deride** someone or something, you unkindly
laugh at them, saying that they are stupid or of no
value. EG *His sense of superiority makes him deride
her opinions.*

derision /dɪ'rɪʒə⁰n/. If you speak of someone or N UNCOUNT
something with **derision**, you show that you have
contempt for them, believing that they are stupid
or have no value. EG *They speak with derision of
amateurs.*

derisive /dɪ'raɪsɪv/. A **derisive** noise, expression, ADJ QUALIT
or remark shows the contempt that you have for
someone or something. EG *Maureen rocked with
derisive laughter.* ◇ **derisively.** EG *Desiree snorted* ◇ ADV
derisively.

derisory /dɪ'raɪzəri¹/. Something that is **derisory** ADJ QUALIT
is so small or inadequate that it seems silly or not
worth considering. EG *Fines for cruelty to animals
are derisory.*

derivation /derə'veɪʃə⁰n/, **derivations.** The N COUNT
derivation of a word is the original word or
expression that it comes from.

derivative /dɪrɪvətɪv/, **derivatives. 1** A **deriva-** N COUNT
tive is something which has developed from something else. EG *...the modern derivative of the fairy
story.*

2 A work or idea that is **derivative** is not new or ADJ QUALIT
original, but copies ideas that have been used
before; used showing disapproval.

derive /dɪ'raɪv/, **derives, deriving, derived. 1** If v+o:
you **derive** a particular feeling from someone or OFT+from
something, you get it from them. EG *They derive* Formal
enormous pleasure from their grandchildren.

2 If you say that something **derives** or **is derived** v-ERG+from
from another thing, you mean that it comes from
that thing. EG *The word 'detergent' is derived from
the Latin word for 'cleaner'... Wealth derives from
political power.*

derogatory /dɪrɒgətə⁰ri¹/. A **derogatory** remark ADJ CLASSIF
expresses your low opinion of someone or some-
thing.

descend /dɪ'send/, **descends, descending, de-**
scended. 1 If you **descend** or if you **descend** v OR v+o
something, you move downwards from a higher to Formal
a lower level. EG *The valley becomes more exquisite as we descend... They descended the stairs.*

2 If silence or unhappiness **descends** on people or v:OFT
places, it occurs or starts to affect them. EG *A* +on/upon
sinister silence descended upon the office. Literary

3 If you **descend** on a place, you arrive suddenly v:OFT
and often unexpectedly. EG *...the prospect of mil-* +on/upon
lions of pilgrims descending on Turin.

4 If you **descend** to something, you behave in a v+to
way that is considered unacceptable or unworthy
of you. EG *Gareth was vexed that he should descend
to such a stupid remark.*

5 See also **descended, descending.**

descendant /dɪ'sendə²nt/, **descendants.** Some- N COUNT
one's **descendants** are the people in later generations who are related to them.

descended /dɪ'sendɪ²d/. A person who is **de-** ADJ PRED
scended from someone who lived a long time ago +from
is related to them. EG *His family were descended
from kings.*

descending /dɪ'sendɪŋ/. When a group of things ADJ CLASSIF:
is arranged in **descending** order, each thing is ATTRIB
smaller in size or less in importance than the thing

before it. eg *Arrange the numbers in descending order.*

descent /dɪˈsɛnt/, **descents. 1** A **descent** is a movement from a higher to a lower level. eg *He saw an aircraft making a very steep descent.* `N COUNT: USU SING`

2 Your **descent** is the nationality or social status of the people that you are descended from. eg *...Americans of Irish descent.* `N UNCOUNT +SUPP`

describe /dɪˈskraɪb/, **describes, describing, described.** When you **describe** a person, thing, or event, you say what they are like or you say what happened. eg *Can you describe your son?... His ideas could hardly be described as original... He described how he was kidnapped.* `V+O: OFT+as; ALSO V+REPORT: ONLY WH`

description /dɪˈskrɪpʃəⁿn/, **descriptions. 1** A **description** is an account of what someone or something is like. eg *...a detailed description of the house... His description was remarkably accurate.* `N COUNT: OFT+of`

2 Description is the act of saying what someone or something is like. eg *The relationships in his family are so complex that description is almost impossible.* `N UNCOUNT`

3 Something of a particular **description** is something of that kind. eg *Her dress was too tight to have concealed a weapon of any description.* `N SING`

descriptive /dɪˈskrɪptɪv/. Writing that is **descriptive** describes what something is like. eg *...a descriptive article about Venice.* `ADJ QUALIT`

desecrate /ˈdɛsɪkreɪt/, **desecrates, desecrating, desecrated.** If someone **desecrates** something that is considered to be sacred or special, they deliberately damage it. eg *The men in Rodez had desecrated the church.* ◊ **desecration** /ˌdɛsəˈkreɪʃəⁿn/. eg *...the desecration of religious sites in Nigeria.* `V+O` ◊ `N UNCOUNT`

desert, deserts, deserting, deserted; pronounced /ˈdɛzət/ when it is a noun and /dɪˈzɜːt/ when it is a verb.

1 A **desert** is a large area of land where there is very little water or rain and very few plants. eg *...the Sahara Desert.* `N COUNT`

2 You can refer to any place where there is nothing good or interesting as a **desert**. eg *Our modern towns are concrete deserts created by modern planning.* `N COUNT+SUPP`

3 If people **desert** a place, they all leave it and it becomes empty. ◊ **deserted.** eg *...a deserted village.* `V+O` ◊ `ADJ CLASSIF`

4 If someone **deserts** you, they leave you and no longer help or support you. eg *She deserted her family and ran away with him.* ◊ **desertion** /dɪˈzɜːʃəⁿn/. eg *She could get a divorce on the grounds of desertion.* `V+O` ◊ `N UNCOUNT`

5 If you **desert** a political party or idea, you stop supporting it. eg *Owen deserted the Labour Party.* `V+O`

6 If someone **deserts** their job in the armed forces or if they **desert**, they leave their job without permission. ◊ **desertion.** eg *...the desertion of young conscripts.* ◊ **deserter** /dɪˈzɜːtə/, **deserters.** eg *...a deserter from the British army.* `V+O OR V` ◊ `N UNCOUNT` ◊ `N COUNT`

deserve /dɪˈzɜːv/, **deserves, deserving, deserved.** If you say that someone **deserves** a particular reward or punishment, you mean that they should be given this reward or punishment because of their qualities or actions. eg *These people deserve recognition for their talents... He deserves to get the sack.* `V+O OR V+to-INF`

deserved /dɪˈzɜːvd/. If you say that something is **deserved**, you mean that the person getting it is worthy of it. eg *It was a richly deserved honour.* ◊ **deservedly.** eg *The first prize was won, most deservedly, by Mrs Jones.* `ADJ QUALIT` ◊ `ADV`

deserving /dɪˈzɜːvɪŋ/. **1** If you describe someone or something as **deserving**, you mean that you think they should be helped. eg *Let us not forget the deserving poor... The proceeds will be given to a deserving charity.* `ADJ QUALIT Formal`

2 If someone is **deserving of** particular treatment, they have qualities or have done something which `PREP Formal`

makes it right for them to be treated in that way. eg *...those who see their behaviour as deserving of punishment.*

design /dɪˈzaɪn/, **designs, designing, designed.**
1 When you **design** something, **1.1** you plan it in your mind and make a detailed drawing of it from which it can be built or made. eg *The house was designed by local builders... Who designed the costumes?* **1.2** you plan, prepare, and decide on all the details of it. eg *Tests have been designed to assess mathematical ability.* `V+O` `V+O: USU PASS +to-INF`

2 Design is the process and art of planning and making detailed drawings of something. eg *...graphic and industrial design.* `N UNCOUNT`

3 The **design** of something is the way in which it has been planned and made. eg *The awkward design of the handles made it difficult to use.* `N UNCOUNT`

4 A **design** is **4.1** a drawing which someone produces to show how they would like something to be built or made. eg *He is submitting a design for the new building.* **4.2** a pattern of lines, flowers, or shapes which is used to decorate something. eg *They painted floral designs on the walls.* **4.3** the intention that someone has in their mind when they are doing something. eg *He failed in his design to become Prime Minister.* ● If something happens or is done **by design**, someone does it deliberately, rather than by accident. `N COUNT` `N COUNT: USU+SUPP` `N COUNT Formal` ● `PHRASE`

5 If something **is designed** for a purpose, it is intended for that purpose. eg *The laws were designed to protect women.* `V-PASS+for OR+to-INF`

designate, designates, designating, designated; pronounced /ˈdɛzɪɡneɪt/ when it is a verb, and /ˈdɛzɪɡnət/ when it is an adjective.
1 When you **designate** someone or something, **1.1** you formally give them a particular description or name. eg *The area was designated a national monument.* **1.2** you formally choose them to do a particular job. eg *I had been designated to read the lesson.* `V+O OR V+O+C` `V+O+O OR to-INF; ALSO V+O+C`

2 Designate is used to describe someone who has been formally chosen to do a particular job, but has not yet started doing it. eg *Mr Bell had been Attorney General designate.* `ADJ AFTER N`

designation /ˌdɛzɪɡˈneɪʃəⁿn/, **designations.** A **designation** is a description or name that is given to a person or thing. eg *No one would dare to apply the designation 'OAP' to a retired judge.* `N COUNT OR N UNCOUNT Formal`

designer /dɪˈzaɪnə/, **designers.** A **designer** is a person whose job is to design things by making drawings of them. eg *She wants to be a dress designer.* `N COUNT`

desirable /dɪˈzaɪərəbᵊl/. **1** Something that is **desirable** is worth having or doing because it is useful, necessary, or popular. eg *After an injury an X-ray is often desirable... one of the most desirable residences in London.* ◊ **desirability** /dɪˌzaɪərəˈbɪlɪti/. eg *...decisions about the desirability of an official policy.* `ADJ QUALIT` ◊ `N UNCOUNT: USU+SUPP`

2 Someone who is **desirable** is sexually attractive. `ADJ QUALIT`

desire /dɪˈzaɪə/, **desires, desiring, desired. 1** If you **desire** something, you want it. eg *He passionately desired to continue his career in politics.* ▶ used as a noun. eg *He had not the slightest desire to go on holiday.* ◊ **desired.** eg *This did not produce the desired effect... ...their desired goals.* `V+O OR V+to-INF: NO CONT` ▶ `N COUNT` ◊ `ADJ CLASSIF`

2 Desire for someone is a strong feeling of wanting to have sex with them. eg *Their desire for each other was as eager as ever.* ▶ used as a verb. eg *He still desired her, after all these years.* `N UNCOUNT OR N COUNT` ▶ `V+O: NO CONT`

3 If you say that something **leaves a lot to be desired** or **leaves a great deal to be desired**, you mean that it is not as good as it should be. eg *His work left much to be desired.* `PHRASE`

What are you desperate for if you are destitute?

desist /dɪzɪst, -sɪst/, **desists, desisting, desisted.** v:OFT+from
If you **desist** from doing something, you stop doing Formal
it. EG *They ought to desist from such foolish activities.*

desk /desk/, **desks.** A **desk** is a table, often with N COUNT
drawers, which you sit in order to write or work.
EG *...a beautiful mahogany desk.*

desolate /desəˈlət/. 1 A place that is **desolate** is ADJ QUALIT
empty of people and looks depressing. EG *The house
looked desolate, ready to be torn down.*
2 If someone is **desolate**, they feel very lonely and ADJ QUALIT
depressed.

desolation /desəˈleɪʃəⁿn/ is 1 a quality of a place N UNCOUNT
which makes it seem empty and frightening. EG
...the horror and desolation of the camp. 2 a feeling
of great unhappiness and despair.

despair /dɪˈspeə/, **despairs, despairing, des-**
paired. 1 **Despair** is the feeling that everything is N UNCOUNT
wrong and nothing can improve. EG *I was in
despair, all hope gone.*
2 If you **despair**, you feel that everything is wrong v:OFT+at
and that nothing will improve. EG *She despaired at
the thought of it.*
3 If you **despair** of something, you feel that there v+of
is no hope that it will happen or improve. EG *She
had despaired of completing her thesis.*

despatch /dɪspætʃ/. See **dispatch.**

desperate /despəⁿrəˈt/. 1 If you are **desperate**, ADJ QUALIT
you are in such a bad or frightening situation that
you will try anything to change it. EG *She was
desperate with fright.* ◊ **desperation** ◊ N UNCOUNT
/despəreɪʃəⁿn/. EG *Sam's desperation grew worse as
the day approached.*
2 A **desperate** action is one that you take when ADJ QUALIT
you are in such a bad or frightening situation that
you feel it is the only thing that you can try. EG *She
killed him in a desperate attempt to free herself.*
◊ **desperately.** EG *He will fight even more desper-* ◊ ADV
ately if trapped.
3 If you are **desperate** for something or **desper-** ADJ PRED:
ate to do something, you want to have it or do it OFT+for
very much indeed. EG *She was desperate to find a* OR to-INF
job... I was desperate for the money.
◊ **desperately.** EG *I desperately wanted to be on* ◊ ADV
my own.
4 A **desperate** situation is very difficult or danger- ADJ QUALIT
ous. EG *The situation had become desperate; we
were rapidly running out of money.*

despicable /despɪkəbəⁿl, dɪspɪk-/. A person or ADJ QUALIT
action that is **despicable** is extremely nasty or
evil. EG *He is too nice a man to do anything as
despicable as murder.*

despise /dɪˈspaɪz/, **despises, despising, des-** v+o
pised. If you **despise** someone or something, you
have a very low opinion of them and so dislike
them. EG *They despise them for their cowardice
and ignorance.*

despite /dɪˈspaɪt/. 1 You use **despite** to introduce PREP
a fact which makes the other part of the sentence
surprising. EG *Despite the difference in their ages
they were close friends.*
2 If you do something **despite** yourself, you do it PREP
although you did not really intend or expect to. EG
*Rose, despite herself, had to admit that she was
impressed.*

despondent /dɪˈspɒndəⁿnt/. If you are **despond-** ADJ QUALIT
ent, you are unhappy because you have difficulties
that you think you will not be able to overcome. EG
*They grew increasingly despondent about securing
any improvement.* ◊ **despondently.** EG *Fanny* ◊ ADV
sighed despondently. ◊ **despondency** ◊ N UNCOUNT
/dɪˈspɒndəⁿnsɪ/. EG *He was unable to hide his
despondency.*

despot /despɒt/, **despots.** A **despot** is a ruler or N COUNT
other person who has a lot of power and uses it Formal
unfairly or cruelly.

despotic /dəˈspɒtɪk/ is used to describe people or ADJ QUALIT
their behaviour when they use their power in an Formal
unfair or cruel way. EG *...oppression by despotic
governments.*

dessert /dɪzɜːt/, **desserts. Dessert** is something N UNCOUNT
sweet, such as fruit or a pudding, that you eat at the OR N COUNT
end of a meal. EG *For dessert there was ice cream.*

dessert spoon, dessert spoons. 1 A **dessert** N COUNT
spoon is a spoon which is about twice as big as a
teaspoon. You use it to eat puddings with.
2 A **dessert spoon** of food or liquid is the amount N PART
that a dessert spoon will hold. EG *Add two dessert
spoons of salt.*

destination /destɪneɪʃəⁿn/, **destinations.** The N COUNT
destination of someone or something is the place
to which they are going. EG *I reached my destination around half-past two.*

destined /destɪnd/. 1 If something is **destined** to ADJ CLASSIF:
happen, it is planned and will definitely happen. EG USU PRED
The station was destined for demolition... She felt +to-INF
she was destined to be unhappy for the rest of her OR+for
life.
2 If you are **destined** for a particular place, you ADJ CLASSIF:
are travelling towards it. EG *...passengers destined* USU PRED+for
for New York.

destiny /destɪⁿnɪ/, **destinies.** 1 Someone's **desti-** N COUNT+SUPP
ny is everything that will happen to them during
their life, especially when it is considered to be
controlled by someone or something else. EG *We
know we are in control of our own destiny.*
2 **Destiny** is the force which some people believe N UNCOUNT
controls the things that happen to you in your life.

destitute /destɪtjuːt/. Someone who is **destitute** ADJ QUALIT
has no money or possessions. EG *...destitute immigrants.* ◊ **destitution** /destɪtjuːʃəⁿn/. EG *The pea-* ◊ N UNCOUNT
santry hovered on the brink of destitution. Formal

destroy /dɪˈstrɔɪ/, **destroys, destroying, de-** v+o
stroyed. 1 To **destroy** something means 1.1 to
cause so much damage to it that it is completely
ruined. EG *Several buildings were destroyed by the
bomb.* 1.2 to cause it not to exist any more. EG *They
want to destroy the State... I don't wish to destroy a
life-long friendship.*
2 If you **destroy** an animal, you kill it because it is v+o
dangerous or very ill. EG *During the epidemic
farmers had to destroy entire herds of cattle.*
3 If someone or something **destroys** you, they ruin v+o
your life by making you so depressed that there
seems to be no hope for you in the future. EG *The
loss of his business and of his wife finally destroyed
him.*

destroyer /dɪˈstrɔɪə/, **destroyers.** 1 A **destroyer** N COUNT
is a small warship with a lot of guns.
2 You can refer to anything that destroys things or N COUNT
people as a **destroyer.** EG *Sunshine is a potent
destroyer of many bacteria.*

destruction /dɪˈstrʌkʃəⁿn/ is the act of destroying N UNCOUNT
something. EG *It will cause pollution and the destruction of our seas and rivers.*

destructive /dɪˈstrʌktɪv/. Something that is **de-** ADJ QUALIT
structive causes great damage or distress. EG *This
rocket has sufficient destructive power to blow a
battleship to pieces... Jealousy is destructive and
undesirable.* ◊ **destructiveness.** EG *...a monster of* ◊ N UNCOUNT
great potential destructiveness.

desultory /desəltⁿrɪ/. Something that is **desul-** ADJ QUALIT
tory is done without enthusiasm and in an un- Formal
planned and disorganized way. EG *There were some
desultory attempts to defend him.*

DET stands for determiner
A small group of words, such as 'a', 'the', 'this', and
'every', have the label DET in the Extra Column.
See the entry headed DETERMINERS for information about this group of words.

---

detach /dɪˈtætʃ/, **detaches, detaching, de-**
tached. 1 If you **detach** one thing from another v+o:
OFT+from

DETERMINERS

When you use a noun in English, you have to say how the noun relates to objects, events, or concepts in the real world. This is usually done by putting a determiner (DET) in front of the noun. The most typical, most common determiners are **the** (often called the 'definite article') and **a** or **an** (the 'indefinite article').

The definite article tells you that you should already know what the noun refers to. So that when someone says *I bought the table yesterday,* you know which table they are talking about. See the entry for **the** for more details about this.

The indefinite article tells you that you probably do not know what the noun refers to. So that when someone says *I bought a table yesterday,* you do not know which table they are talking about. See the entry for **a** for more details about this.

The determiners **all**, **some**, **any**, **another**, **each**, **every**, **either**, **neither**, and **no** are like **a** – they do not refer to specific items that you can identify individually.

The determiners **this**, **that**, **these**, and **those**, and the possessive determiners (DET POSS) **my**, **your**, **his**, **her**, **its**, **our**, and **their** are like **the**. In various ways these words tell you that you should be able to identify exactly what the noun refers to. You use **this** and **these** to refer to things that you consider to be relatively close to you. You use **that** and **those** to refer to things that you consider to be relatively far from you. The possessive determiners tell you who something belongs to. So that 'your book' belongs to you and 'my book' belongs to me.

When you want to refer very generally to something, you can use some nouns without a determiner. Uncountable nouns (N UNCOUNT), such as **rice**, **chemistry**, and **disappointment** are usually used without a determiner, unless you want to specify something very precisely. So you normally say *I like rice,* when you are thinking about rice in general, although you can also say *I cooked **this** rice for longer than usual,* when you are referring to the rice that you are eating. Plural countable nouns (N COUNT) such as **boys**, **parties**, and **lessons** are also often used without a determiner, unless you want to be more specific. So you can say *I like parties,* when you are thinking of parties in general, or you can say *I like **the** parties that my boss gives,* when you are thinking of particular kinds of parties.

Most determiners can be used with any noun, whether it is singular or plural or uncountable. There are, however, some which cannot. The determiners **a**, **another**, **each**, **every**, **either**, and **neither** are normally used with singular countable nouns, as in *She poured herself **another** cup of tea* and *I kept records on **each** child. **These** and **those** are normally used with nouns in the plural, as in *Who are **those** men over there?* **This** and **that** are used with uncountable nouns or singular countable nouns, as in *I've used **that** information many times since then* and ***That** night Kunta slept well.* The determiner **some** can be used with uncountable nouns or plural countable nouns, as in *I bought **some** meat for dinner* and *We've got **some** friends coming.*

There can only be one determiner in a noun group, and it is usually the first word in the group. But occasionally a predeterminer (PREDET) can come in front of the determiner. The words that are labelled as predeterminers in this dictionary are: **all**, **both**, **half**, **double**, **treble**, **quadruple**, **twice**, **such**, and **what**. As with the determiners, these words have other uses. The words **such** and **what** come in front of the determiner **a**, as in *There was **such** a noise in the room* and ***What** a mess!* The other predeterminers are usually used in front of words with a more specific meaning, such as **the**, **those**, and the possessive determiners. So you can say *He looked at **all** my paintings, They charged us **double** the price they should have done,* and ***Both** her parents are dead.*

thing that it is fixed to, you remove it. EG *The handle of the saucepan can be detached.*
2 If you **detach** yourself from something, you feel V-REFL: less involved in it. *...learning to detach ourselves* OFT+*from from the world.*

detachable /dɪˈtætʃəbəl/. Something that is **de-** ADJ CLASSIF **tachable** is made so that it can be removed from a larger object. EG *...detachable collars.*

detached /dɪˈtætʃt/. **1** A **detached** house is one ADJ CLASSIF that is not joined to any other house.
2 Someone who is **detached** is not personally ADJ QUALIT involved in something. EG *...the detached view that writers must take.*

detachment /dɪˈtætʃmənt/ is the feeling that you N UNCOUNT have of not being personally involved in something. EG *...his strange detachment from the world about him.*

detail /ˈdiːteɪl/, **details, detailing, detailed. 1** A **detail** is **1.1** an individual fact or feature which you N COUNT: notice when you look at something carefully, or OFT+*of* which you remember when you think about it. EG *I can still remember every single detail of that night... He described it down to the smallest detail.*
1.2 a fact or comment that is not of major impor- N COUNT tance to what is being discussed. EG *But those were details; what was important was that the rate of work failed to increase.*
2 Detail consists of all the small features which N UNCOUNT are often not noticed when people first look at something or think about it. EG *Attention to detail is vital in this job.*
3 If you **go into detail** or **go into details** about PHRASE something, you explain it thoroughly, including all the small pieces of information. EG *I don't want to go into detail about the actual methods used.*
4 If you examine or discuss something **in detail**, PHRASE you do it thoroughly. EG *His theory is examined in detail in chapter 12.*
5 Details about someone or something are facts or N PLURAL: pieces of information about them. EG *You can get* OFT+*about/of details of nursery schools from the local authority... He was interested in every detail about you.*
6 If you **detail** things, you list them and give V+O information about them. EG *I carefully detailed the* Formal *areas of the Avenue that I could see.*

detailed /ˈdiːteɪld/. Something that is **detailed** ADJ QUALIT contains a lot of details. EG *...a detailed map of the area... They gave a detailed account of what they had seen.*

detain /dɪˈteɪn/, **detains, detaining, detained.** If V+O you **detain** someone, **1** you force them to stay in a place. EG *We shall be obliged to detain you here while we continue the investigation.* **2** you delay them, for example by talking to them. EG *Well, I needn't detain you any longer.*

detect /dɪˈtekt/, **detects, detecting, detected.** If V+O you **detect** something, **1** you notice it, often when it is not very obvious. EG *These animals seem able to detect a shower of rain falling five miles away.* **2** you find it. EG *The submarines had to be detected and destroyed.*

detection /dɪˈtekʃən/ is **1** the act of noticing N UNCOUNT something. EG *The main detection device is sonar.* **2** the discovery of something in a place, especially when it is supposed to be hidden. EG *The submarines were able to withdraw without detection.*

detective /dɪˈtektɪv/, **detectives.** A **detective** is N COUNT someone whose job is to discover what has happened in a crime or other situation and to find the people involved. Some police officers are detectives. EG *He was being followed by a private detective.*

detector /dɪˈtektə/, **detectors.** A **detector** is an N COUNT: instrument which is used to find or measure some- USU+SUPP thing. EG *...a metal detector.*

detente /deɪˈtɒnt/; also spelled **détente. Detente** N UNCOUNT is a state of friendly relations between two coun- Formal tries when previously there had been problems between them.

detention /dɪˈtenʃən/ is the arrest or imprison- N UNCOUNT ment of someone, especially for political reasons. EG *It was obvious to his colleagues that his detention was politically motivated.*

deter /dɪˈtɜː/, **deters, deterring, deterred.** To V+O: **deter** someone means to persuade them not to do OFT+*from* something or to prevent them from doing it. EG *Such discrimination may deter more women from seeking work.*

detergent /dɪˈtɜːdʒənt/, **detergents. Detergent** N MASS is a chemical substance, usually a powder or liquid, which is used for washing things such as clothes or dishes. EG *Wash it with hot water and detergent.*

deteriorate /dɪˈtɪəriəreɪt/, **deteriorates, deteriorating, deteriorated.** If something **deterio-rates, 1** it becomes worse in condition. EG *His sight* V had begun to deteriorate.* ◊ **deterioration.** ◊ N UNCOUNT /dɪˌtɪəriəˈreɪʃən/. EG *She had suffered progressive deterioration of health.* **2** it becomes more difficult V or unpleasant. EG *The weather had deteriorated.*
◊ **deterioration.** EG *This speeded the deterioration* ◊ N UNCOUNT *of our relationship.*

determination /dɪˌtɜːmɪˈneɪʃən/. **1 Determina-** N UNCOUNT **tion** is the quality that you show when you have decided to do something and you will not let anything stop you. EG *Seeing my determination to leave, she demanded her money.*
2 The **determination** of something is the deciding N UNCOUNT or settling of it. EG *She is responsible for the* +SUPP *determination of wage levels within this company.*

determine /dɪˈtɜːmɪn/, **determines, determining, determined. 1** If something **determines** a V+O situation or result, it controls it or causes it. EG *Economic factors determine the progress which a society can make.*
2 If you **determine** something, **2.1** you find out the V+O facts about it. EG *It was in the public interest to determine exactly what happened... An X ray determined that no bones were broken.* **2.2** you decide it or settle it. EG *The date of the match is yet to be determined.*
3 If you **determine** to do something, you make a V+*to*-INF firm decision to do it. EG *He determined to become* Formal *commander-in-chief of the forces.*

determined /dɪˈtɜːmɪnd/. If you are **determined** ADJ QUALIT: to do something, you have made a firm decision to USU+*to*-INF do it and will not let anything stop you. EG *He is determined to win in the end.* ◊ **determinedly.** ◊ ADV *She determinedly kept the conversation going.*

deterrence /dɪˈterəns/ is the prevention of war N UNCOUNT by having weapons that are so powerful that people will not dare to attack you. EG *They believe that NATO's policy of deterrence is justified.*

deterrent /dɪˈterənt/, **deterrents. 1** A **deterrent** N COUNT is **1.1** a thing that prevents you from doing something by making you afraid of what will happen if you do it. EG *Severe punishment is the only true deterrent.* **1.2** a weapon or set of weapons that are intended to prevent enemies from attacking by making them afraid to do so. EG *...the nuclear deterrent.*
2 If something has a **deterrent** effect, it discour- ADJ CLASSIF: ages people from doing something they might want ATTRIB to do. EG *...the deterrent effect of nuclear weapons.*

detest /dɪˈtest/, **detests, detesting, detested.** If V+O you **detest** someone or something, you dislike them very much. EG *They detest the thought of living elsewhere.*

detestable /dɪˈtestəbəl/. If you say that someone ADJ QUALIT or something is **detestable**, you mean that you dislike them very strongly. EG *...a step-son he thought altogether detestable.*

detonate /ˈdetəneɪt/, **detonates, detonating,** V-ERG **detonated.** If you **detonate** a bomb or if it **deto-nates**, it explodes. EG *...land mines which could be detonated from inside the camp.* ◊ **detonation.** ◊ N UNCOUNT /ˌdetəˈneɪʃən/. EG *...the possible detonation of a nuclear weapon.*

detour /diːtʊə/, **detours.** A **detour** is a route N COUNT
which is not the shortest way from one place to
another. You often make a detour because you
want to avoid a traffic jam or because you want to
see the countryside. EG *He made a detour to pass
the house where Miss Lenaut lived.*

DET POSS stands for **possessive determiner**
The words 'my', 'your', 'his', 'her', 'its', 'our', and
'their' have the label DET POSS in the Extra Column.
See the entry headed DETERMINERS for more information.

---

detract /diˈtrækt/, **detracts, detracting, de-** V+from
tracted. If one thing **detracts** from another, it
makes the other thing seem less good than people
thought or than it really is. EG *This fact did not
detract from her sense of achievement.*

detriment /dɛtrəˈmənt/. If something happens to PHRASE
the **detriment** of someone or something, it causes Formal
harm or damage to them. EG *This discovery has
been exploited to the detriment of the poor peasants.*

detrimental /dɛtrɪmɛntəˈl/. Something that is ADJ QUALIT :
detrimental has harmful or damaging effects. EG OFT+to
*...actions which may be detrimental to the compa- Formal
ny.*

deuce /djuːs/ is the score in a game of tennis when N UNCOUNT
both players have forty points.

devalue /diːvæljuː/, **devalues, devaluing, de-**
valued. 1 If you **devalue** someone or something, V+O
you think that they are unimportant and so you do
not give them the respect that they deserve. EG
Scientific expertise has been devalued.

2 To **devalue** the currency of a country means to V+O
reduce its value in relation to other currencies. EG Technical
The President has devalued the dollar.
◊ **devaluation** /diːvæljuːˈeɪʃən/. EG *...the devalua-* ◊ N UNCOUNT
tion of sterling in November 1967.

devastate /dɛvəsteɪt/, **devastates, devastating,** V+O : OFT PASS
devastated. If something **devastates** a place, it
destroys it or damages it very badly. EG *A hurricane
had devastated the plantation.* ◊ **devastation** ◊ N UNCOUNT
/dɛvəsteɪʃən/. EG *...the threat of nuclear devastation.*

devastated /dɛvəsteɪtɪd/. If you are **devastated** ADJ PRED
by something, you are very shocked and upset by
it. EG *We were devastated by her decision.*

devastating /dɛvəsteɪtɪŋ/. 1 Something that is ADJ QUALIT
devastating destroys or severely damages something. EG *...devastating bombing raids.*

2 **Devastating** remarks indicate strongly that a ADJ QUALIT
point of view that has been expressed is wrong. EG
*He thought of the devastating witticisms with
which he would destroy his opponents.*

3 If you find something **devastating**, it makes you ADJ QUALIT
feel very shocked and upset. EG *It was a devastating
announcement.*

4 You can also use **devastating** to describe things ADJ QUALIT
that are very good or beautiful. EG *That's her most
devastating insight.* ◊ **devastatingly.** EG *She was* ◊ ADV+ADJ
devastatingly beautiful.

develop /dɪvɛləp/, **develops, developing, devel-**
oped. 1 When something **develops**, it grows or V-ERG : USU+A
changes over a period of time into a better or more
complete form. EG *The bud develops into a flower...
Her friendship with Harold developed slowly... We
had hopes of developing tourism on a big scale.*

2 If a problem **develops**, it starts to exists and V
gradually becomes more severe. EG *A new crisis
began to develop.*

3 If a country **develops**, it changes from being a V
poor or agricultural country to being an advanced
industrial country. ◊ **developing.** EG *Several indus-* ◊ ADJ CLASSIF :
trialized nations are supplying developing coun- ATTRIB
tries with new technology.

4 To **develop** an area of land means to build V+O
houses or factories on it.

5 To **develop** a characteristic, illness, or fault V+O
means to begin to have it. EG *She developed an
enormous appetite... Write to the manufacturer if
the machine develops the same fault again.*

6 If someone **develops** a new machine, they V+O
produce it by improving the original design. EG
*Their new engine was developed from a petrol
motor.*

7 If you **develop** an argument or idea, you begin to V+O
understand it better by saying more about it. EG
The rationale he developed was very interesting.

8 When a photographic film **is developed**, prints V+O
or negatives are made from it.

developer /dɪvɛləˈpə/, **developers.** 1 A **develop-** N COUNT
er is a person or a company that buys land in order
to build new houses or factories on it. EG *Villagers
are protesting about the destruction of their beautiful landscape by the developers.*

2 If a child is an early **developer**, he or she N COUNT+SUPP
develops physically or mentally earlier than others
of the same age. A late **developer** develops later
than others of the same age.

development /dɪvɛləˈpmənt/, **developments.** 1
Development is 1.1 the gradual growth or forma- N UNCOUNT
tion of something. EG *This can harm a child's* +SUPP
*psychological development... Some people expect
rapid economic development in Pakistan.* 1.2 the N UNCOUNT
process or result of improving a basic design. EG OR N COUNT
*...research and development... What have been the
major developments in aircraft engines in the last
decade?* 1.3 the process of making an area of land N UNCOUNT
or water more useful or profitable. EG *...Japanese* +SUPP
ventures for the development of Siberia.

2 A **development** is an event which is likely to N COUNT
have an effect on the situation in a particular place
or field of activity. EG *Recent developments in
Latin America suggest that the situation may be
improving.*

3 A **development** is also an area of houses or N COUNT
buildings which have been built by property developers. EG *Many people live in new housing developments.*

deviant /diːvɪənt/, **deviants.** A **deviant** is some- N COUNT
one whose behaviour or beliefs are not considered
by most people to be acceptable. ▶ used as an ▶ ADJ QUALIT
adjective. EG *To light a cigarette in company is
becoming a deviant act.*

deviate /diːvɪeɪt/, **deviates, deviating, deviated.** V : OFT+from
If you **deviate**, you change your ideas or behaviour
so that they are different from what they used to
be or from what people usually consider to be
acceptable. EG *He has not deviated from his view
that war can never be justified.*

deviation /diːvɪeɪʃən/, **deviations. Deviation** is N UNCOUNT
a difference in behaviour or belief from what OR N COUNT
people consider to be normal or acceptable. EG
*There was to be no deviation from the ruling
ideology.*

device /dɪvaɪs/, **devices.** 1 A **device** is an object N COUNT :
that has been made or built for a particular pur- USU+SUPP
pose, for example for recording or measuring
something. EG *A computer is a device for handling
or processing information... Firemen carry a little
alarm device in their pocket... ...pumps and other
devices.*

2 A **device** is also a method of getting what you N COUNT :
want or of getting something done. EG *They used* USU+SUPP
*television advertising as a device for stimulating
demand.*

3 If you **leave** someone **to their own devices**, PHRASE
they have to find something to occupy them because you do not give them anything to do. EG *The
children were left to their own devices.*

If you devour a book, do you eat it?

devil /dɛvə⁰l/, **devils. 1** In Christianity, the **Devil** is the most powerful evil spirit. N PROPER: the+N

2 You can use **devil** to refer to any evil spirit. N COUNT

3 You can also use **devil** to talk about people. For example, if you call someone a silly **devil**, you are saying that you think that they are silly. EG *You lucky devil!... The poor devil died of a heart attack.* N COUNT+SUPP Informal

4 When you want to emphasize how annoyed or surprised you are, you can start your sentence with a phrase such as **who the devil, where the devil,** or **why the devil.** EG *Where the devil did you get that cat?* PHRASE

devilish /dɛvə⁰lɪʃ/. A **devilish** idea or action is cruel or unpleasant. EG *What devilish impulse moved you to this?* ADJ QUALIT

devious /diːvɪəs/. **1** Someone who is **devious** is dishonest and does things in a secretive, often complicated way. EG *...consultants who are prepared to use devious means to justify their actions.* ADJ QUALIT

2 A **devious** route or path to a place involves many changes in direction rather than going in the straightest possible line. EG *She led him by devious ways to the meeting place.* ADJ QUALIT

devise /dɪˈvaɪz/, **devises, devising, devised.** If you **devise** a plan, system, or machine, you have the idea for it and you work out how you could create it. EG *It has been necessary to devise a system of universal schooling.* V+O

devoid /dɪˈvɔɪd/. If someone or something is **devoid** of a quality, they have none of it at all. EG *He was devoid of any talent whatsoever.* ADJ PRED+of Formal

devolution /diːvə⁷luːʃə⁰n/ is the transfer of authority or power from a central organization or government to smaller organizations or government departments. N UNCOUNT

devolve /dɪˈvɒlv/, **devolves, devolving, devolved.** If a responsibility or privilege **devolves** or **is devolved** upon a person or group, it is transferred to them from a more important or powerful person or group. EG *The necessity for making decisions devolves upon him.* V-ERG +upon/on/to Formal

devote /dɪˈvəʊt/, **devotes, devoting, devoted.** If you **devote** yourself, your time, or your energy to something, you spend a lot of your time or energy on it. EG *They have devoted all their time to helping the sick... He devoted himself to his studies.* V+O OR V-REFL+to

devoted /dɪˈvəʊtɪ²d/. **1** If you are **devoted** to someone, you love them very much. EG *He's devoted to his mother.* ADJ QUALIT OFT+to

2 You use **devoted** to describe activities which have involved a lot of someone's time and energy. EG *...years of devoted research.* ADJ QUALIT ATTRIB

devotee /dɛvə⁰tiː/, **devotees.** A **devotee** of a subject or activity is someone who is very enthusiastic about it. EG *The building has an enormous appeal for devotees of history.* N COUNT: OFT+SUPP

devotion /dɪˈvəʊʃə⁰n/ is **1** great love and affection for someone. EG *Their devotion to their children is plain to see.* **2** The giving of a lot of your time or energy to a particular activity. EG *It demands total devotion to the cause.* **3** strong religious feeling. EG *We watched them kneel in devotion.* N UNCOUNT OFT+to | N UNCOUNT OFT+to | N UNCOUNT

devour /dɪˈvaʊə/, **devours, devouring, devoured. 1** When one animal **devours** another, it eats it. EG *We came upon a black snake devouring a large frog.* V+O Formal

2 If you **devour** something, you eat it quickly and eagerly. EG *He sat by the fire, devouring beef and onions.* V+O Formal

3 If you **devour** a book or magazine, you read it quickly and eagerly. EG *As a boy I devoured Scott's novels.* V+O Formal

devout /dɪˈvaʊt/. Someone who is **devout** believes in God or a religion very deeply. EG *She was a devout Catholic.* ADJ QUALIT

dew /djuː/ is small drops of water that form on the ground and other surfaces outdoors during the night. N UNCOUNT

dexterous /dɛkstrəs/; also spelled **dextrous.** Someone who is **dexterous** is very skilful with their hands. ◊ **dexterity** /dɛksterɪtiː/. EG *...weaving in and out with great dexterity.* ADJ QUALIT Formal ◊ N UNCOUNT

diabetes /daɪəˈbiːtɪs, -tiːz/ is an illness in which someone's body is unable to control the level of sugar in their blood. N UNCOUNT

diabetic /daɪəˈbɛtɪk/, **diabetics. 1** A **diabetic** is a person who suffers from diabetes. N COUNT

2 Diabetic medicines or conditions are intended for or affect people who have diabetes. EG *...in a diabetic coma... ...diabetic chocolate.* ADJ CLASSIF: ATTRIB

diabolical /daɪəˈbɒlɪkə⁰l/. You use **diabolical** to emphasize how bad or unpleasant you think something is. EG *It gave men the pretext for all sorts of diabolical behaviour.* ADJ CLASSIF Informal

diagnose /daɪəˈgnəʊz/, **diagnoses, diagnosing, diagnosed.** When a doctor **diagnoses** an illness that someone has, he or she identifies exactly what is wrong. EG *The doctor has diagnosed it as rheumatism.* V+O:OFT+as

diagnosis /daɪəˈgnəʊsɪs/, **diagnoses** /daɪəˈgnəʊsiːz/. **Diagnosis** is identifying what is wrong with someone who is ill. EG *Joan's fever led to a diagnosis of pneumonia.* N UNCOUNT OR N COUNT

diagnostic /daɪəˈgnɒstɪk/. **Diagnostic** equipment or methods are used for discovering what is wrong with people who are ill. EG *...medical diagnostic devices.* ADJ CLASSIF

diagonal /daɪˈægənə⁰l/, **diagonals. 1** A **diagonal** line goes in a slanting direction. EG *There was a diagonal red line on the label.* ◊ **diagonally.** EG *We drove diagonally across the airfield.* ADJ CLASSIF ◊ ADV

2 A **diagonal** is a straight line that joins two opposite corners in a flat four-sided shape such as a square. N COUNT Technical

diagram /daɪəˈgræm/, **diagrams.** A **diagram** is a simple drawing consisting mainly of lines, often one which is used to explain how something works. EG *...a simple diagram showing compass directions.* ◊ **diagrammatic** /daɪəgrəˈmætɪk/. EG *The factors can be shown in diagrammatic form.* N COUNT: USU+SUPP ◊ ADJ CLASSIF

dial /daɪl/, **dials, dialling, dialled;** spelled **dialing** and **dialed** in American English. **1** On an instrument such as a clock or a meter, the **dial** is an indicator which shows you the time or a measurement. EG *...the luminous dial of his watch... The figures on the dial can be seen.* N COUNT

2 On a piece of equipment such as a radio or a time switch, the **dial** is the controlling part which you move in order to change the radio frequency or the timing. N COUNT

3 On some telephones, the **dial** is the circle that has holes in it and numbers behind the holes. You move the dial to ring the telephone number that you want to call. N COUNT

4 If you **dial** a number, you move the circle or press the buttons on the front of a telephone in order to phone someone. EG *Jim dialled his home number.* V+O OR V

dialect /daɪəlɛkt/, **dialects.** A **dialect** is a form of a language that is spoken by people living in a particular area. It has different pronunciations and words from other forms of the language. EG *...old ballads written in northern dialect.* N COUNT OR N UNCOUNT

dialogue /daɪəlɒg/, **dialogues;** spelled **dialog** in American English. **1 Dialogue** is communication or discussion between people or groups. EG *The union continued to seek dialogue with the authorities.* N UNCOUNT OR N COUNT

2 A **dialogue** is a conversation between two people, especially one in a book, film, or play. EG *...500 words of movie dialogue... Their dialogue was interrupted by Philip's voice.* N COUNT OR N UNCOUNT

diameter /daɪˈæmə³tə/, **diameters.** The **diameter** of a round object is the length of a straight line that can be drawn through the middle of it. EG *...a giant planet over 30,000 miles in diameter.* N COUNT

diametrically /daɪəˈmɛtrɪkliˈ/. If you say that PHRASE two things are **diametrically opposed** or **diametrically opposite**, you are emphasizing that they are completely different from each other. EG *The two systems are diametrically opposed.*

diamond /ˈdaɪəmənd/, **diamonds. 1** A **diamond** is N COUNT a hard, bright, precious stone that consists of pure carbon. Diamonds are used especially in jewellery. EG *...diamond brooches.*

2 If something has the shape of a **diamond**, it has N COUNT four straight sides of equal length, but the sides are not at right angles to each other as they are in a square. See picture at SHAPES.

3 Diamonds is one of the four suits of cards in a N UNCOUNT pack of playing cards. Each card in the suit is marked with one or more red symbols in the shape of a diamond.

4 A **diamond** is also one of the thirteen playing N COUNT cards in the suit of diamonds.

diaper /ˈdaɪəpə/, **diapers.** A **diaper** is a piece of N COUNT soft towel or absorbent paper, which you put round American a baby's bottom until it is old enough to use a toilet.

diaphragm /ˈdaɪəfræm/, **diaphragms. 1** Your N COUNT **diaphragm** is a muscle between your lungs and your stomach. It is used especially when you breathe deeply.

2 A **diaphragm** is a small, round contraceptive N COUNT device that a woman places inside her vagina.

diarrhoea /daɪəˈrɪə/; also spelled **diarrhea. Diar-** N UNCOUNT **rhoea** is an illness in which people get rid of a lot of faeces which are much more liquid than usual.

diary /ˈdaɪərɪˈ/, **diaries.** A **diary** is a book which N COUNT : has a separate space for each day of the year. You USU+POSS use a diary to write down your appointments and things you have to do in the future, or to record what happens in your life day by day. EG *Her diary gives an account of what happened.*

dice

dice /daɪs/, **dices, dicing, diced. Dice** is both the singular and the plural form of the noun.

1 A **dice** is a small cube made of wood or plastic, N COUNT which has from one to six spots on each of its six sides. You throw dice in games to decide, for example, who will start the game first or how many moves you can make. EG *They roll dice to see who will go first.*

2 When you **dice** food, you cut it into small cubes. V+O ◊ **diced.** EG *...diced potatoes.* ◊ ADJ CLASSIF

dicey /ˈdaɪsɪˈ/. Something that is **dicey** is slightly ADJ QUALIT dangerous or uncertain. EG *Hitch-hiking's a bit* Informal *dicey in this area.*

dichotomy /daɪˈkɒtəˈmiˈ/, **dichotomies.** If there N COUNT is a very great difference between two things, you Formal can say that there is a **dichotomy** between them. EG *The clearest dichotomy is between the winners and the losers.*

dictate, dictates, dictating, dictated; pronounced /dɪkˈteɪt/ when it is a verb and /ˈdɪkteɪt/ when it is a noun.

1 If you **dictate** something, you say it aloud for V+O OR V someone else to write down. EG *It took him a long time to dictate this letter.*

2 If you **dictate** to someone, you tell them what V+to, V+O, OR they must do. EG *The unions are hardly in a position* V+REPORT *to dictate to the Labour party... The printers tried*

to dictate how he should run his business... The law dictated that his right hand be cut off.

3 A **dictate** is an order which you have to obey. EG N COUNT *They obeyed the union's dictates and went on strike.*

dictation /dɪkˈteɪʃəˈn/, **dictations. 1 Dictation** is N UNCOUNT **1.1** the speaking aloud of words for someone else to write down. EG *Jill took down a story from Frank's dictation.* **1.2** the giving of orders in a forceful and commanding way. EG *The group resented dictation from above.*

2 A **dictation** is a test of your knowledge of a N COUNT OR foreign language, in which you have to write down N UNCOUNT a text that is read aloud to you.

dictator /dɪkˈteɪtə/, **dictators.** A **dictator** is a N COUNT ruler who has complete power in a country; used showing disapproval.

dictatorial /dɪktəˈtɔːrɪəl/. **1 Dictatorial** means ADJ QUALIT caused, controlled, or used by a dictator. EG *...dictatorial regimes.*

2 Dictatorial power or behaviour involves giving ADJ QUALIT orders to people in a forceful and often unfair way. EG *...the dictatorial power of central committees.*

dictatorship /dɪkˈteɪtəˈʃɪp/, **dictatorships. 1 Dic-** N UNCOUNT **tatorship** is government by a dictator. EG *Democracy soon gave way to dictatorship.*

2 A country that is a **dictatorship** is ruled by a N COUNT dictator.

diction /ˈdɪkʃəˈn/. You refer to how clearly some- N UNCOUNT one speaks or sings as their **diction.** EG *What was so striking was her magnificent diction.*

dictionary /ˈdɪkʃənəˈrɪ/, **dictionaries.** A **diction-ary** is **1** a book in which the words of a language N COUNT are listed alphabetically and their meanings are explained. **2** a book in which words in one lan- N COUNT guage are listed alphabetically and are followed by words which have the same meaning in another language. EG *...an English-French dictionary.* **3** an N COUNT+SUPP alphabetically ordered reference book on a particular subject. EG *...the Dictionary of National Biography.*

did /dɪd/ is the past tense of **do.**

didactic /dɪˈdæktɪk/. Something that is **didactic** ADJ QUALIT is intended to teach people a moral lesson. EG Formal *...authoritarian, didactic teaching.*

didn't /ˈdɪdəˈnt/ is the usual spoken form of 'did not'.

die /daɪ/, **dies, dying, died. 1** When people, ani- V mals, and plants **die**, they stop living. EG *He died of a heart attack.* ● If someone **dies** a violent or ● PHRASE unnatural **death**, they die in a violent or unnatural way. EG *I don't believe Davis died a natural death.*

2 If someone **is dying**, they are so ill or so badly V : ONLY CONT injured that they will not live much longer. EG *...an old woman dying of cancer.*

3 When emotions **die**, they become less intense V and disappear. EG *True love never dies.* Literary

4 If you say that you are **dying for** something or PHRASE **dying to do** something, you mean that you want Informal very much to have it or to do it. EG *I'm dying for a drink... They were all dying to go to Paris.*

5 If an idea or custom **dies hard**, it changes or PHRASE disappears very slowly. EG *Colonial traditions die hard.*

6 See also **dying.**

die away. If a sound **dies away**, it gradually PHRASAL VB : becomes fainter and finally disappears. EG *Now* V+ADV *that the cheers had died away, it seemed oddly quiet.*

die down. If something **dies down**, it becomes PHRASAL VB : quieter or less intense. EG *She waited until the* V+ADV *laughter had died down... The wind has died down.*

die out. If something **dies out**, it becomes less PHRASAL VB : and less common and eventually disappears. EG *He* V+ADV

If you are diffident, do you behave in a dictatorial way?

*thought the custom had died out a long time ago...
Many species died out.*

diesel /diːzəl/, **diesels.** 1 A **diesel** is a vehicle N COUNT
which has an engine in which a mixture of air and
heavy oil is made to burn by pressure rather than
by an electric spark.

2 **Diesel** or **diesel oil** is the heavy oil used in a N UNCOUNT
diesel engine.

diet /daɪət/, **diets, dieting, dieted.** 1 A **diet** is the N COUNT OR
food that a person or animal eats regularly. EG *Her* N UNCOUNT
*diet consisted of bread and lentils... Correct diet is
important.*   ◇ **dietary.** EG *We are working on* ◇ ADJ CLASSIF:
changing dietary habits. ATTRIB

2 If you are on a **diet**, you are eating special kinds N COUNT
of food because you want to lose weight. EG *'Have a
biscuit.' - 'No thanks, I'm on a diet.'* ▶ used as an ▶ ADJ CLASSIF:
adjective. EG *Saccharin is the main sweetener for* ATTRIB
diet drinks.

3 If you **are dieting**, you are eating special kinds V
of food because you want to lose weight.

differ /dɪfə/, **differs, differing, differed.** 1 If V OR V+from:
things **differ**, they are unlike each other in some RECIP
way. EG *Modern cars differ from the early ones in
many ways... Although our looks differ, we are both
attractive.*

2 If people **differ** about something, they disagree V
with each other about it. EG *We differ about moral
standards.*

difference /dɪfərəns/, **differences.** 1 The **dif-** N COUNT OR
ference between things is the way in which they N UNCOUNT:
are different from each other. EG *There is an* USU+SUPP
*essential difference between computers and hu-
mans... Look at their difference in size.*

2 If you say that something **doesn't make any** PHRASE
difference, you mean that it does not change the
situation in any way. EG *It makes no difference
whether he is a citizen or not.*

3 If you say that something **makes all the differ-** PHRASE
ence, you mean that it is very important in helping
you to achieve what you are trying to do. EG *That
extra money would have made all the difference.*

4 The **difference** between two amounts is the N SING:OFT
amount by which they differ. *between*

5 If people have their **differences**, they disagree N COUNT:
about things. USU PLURAL

different /dɪfərənt/. 1 If one thing is **different** ADJ QUALIT:
from another, it is unlike the other thing in some OFT+from/
way. EG *The meeting was different from any that* to/than
*had gone before... His message is very different to
theirs.*   ◇ **differently.** EG *...people who feel very* ◇ ADV
differently about things.

2 When you refer to two or more **different** things ADJ CLASSIF:
of a particular kind, you mean two or more sepa- ATTRIB
rate things of that kind. EG *I visited 21 different
schools.*

differentiate /dɪfərenʃieɪt/, **differentiates, dif-**
ferentiating, differentiated. 1 If you **differenti-** V+between;
ate between things or **differentiate** one thing ALSO V+O:
from another, you recognize or show the difference OFT+from
between them. EG *How can you differentiate between moral and religious questions?*

2 If a quality or aspect **differentiates** one thing V+O:
from another, it makes the two things different. EG OFT+from
What differentiates a sculpture from an object?
◇ **differentiation** /dɪfərenʃieɪʃən/. EG *...the differ-* ◇ N UNCOUNT
entiation of classes.

difficult /dɪfɪkəlt/. 1 Something that is **difficult** ADJ QUALIT:
is not easy to do, understand, or solve. EG *Many* OFT+to-INF
youngsters find it difficult to get jobs... That's a OR for
*very difficult question... This is bad for a child,
making it difficult for him to adjust.*

2 Someone who is **difficult** behaves in an unrea- ADJ QUALIT
sonable and unhelpful way. EG *...a difficult baby.*

difficulty /dɪfɪkəlti[1]/, **difficulties.** 1 A **difficulty** N COUNT
is something that is a problem for you. EG *There are
lots of difficulties that have to be overcome.*

2 If you have **difficulty** doing something, you are N UNCOUNT
not able to do it easily. EG *I was having difficulty
breathing... She spoke with difficulty.*

3 If you are **in difficulty** or **in difficulties**, you PHRASE
are in a situation in which you are having a lot of
problems. EG *He went to the aid of a swimmer in
difficulty.*

diffident /dɪfɪdənt/. Someone who is **diffident** is ADJ QUALIT
nervous and lacks confidence. EG *...a rather diffident, uncommunicative man.*   ◇ **diffidently.** EG *He* ◇ ADV
approached the desk diffidently.   ◇ **diffidence** ◇ N UNCOUNT
/dɪfɪdəns/. EG *She walked up with some diffidence.*

diffuse, diffuses, diffusing, diffused; pronounced /dɪfjuːz/ when it is a verb and /dɪfjuːs/
when it is an adjective.

1 When light **diffuses** or when something **diffuses** V-ERG
it, the light spreads in a lot of directions and shines Formal
faintly over a wide area. EG *The light was diffused
by leaves.*

2 If you **diffuse** knowledge or information or if it V-ERG
diffuses, it spreads to a lot of people over a wide Formal
area. EG *Fashion trends diffuse themselves rapidly
around the globe.*   ◇ **diffusion** /dɪfjuːʒən/. EG *...the* ◇ N UNCOUNT
diffusion of scientific knowledge.

3 Something that is **diffuse** is **3.1** vague and not ADJ QUALIT
easy to understand. EG *Modern anarchism has* Formal
become increasingly diffuse. **3.2** spread out over a Formal
large area rather than concentrated in one place.
EG *...a broad, diffuse organization... ...a faint and
diffuse glow of light.*

dig /dɪg/, **digs, digging, dug** /dʌg/. 1 If you **dig**, V OR V+O
you make a hole in the ground, using your hands or
a spade. EG *I was digging my garden... He dug a
little hole in the ground.*

2 If you **dig** into something, you search in it for V+A
something with your hand. EG *Thomas dug into the
bag and pulled out a sandwich.*

3 If you **dig** one thing into another, you press the V-ERG+A
first thing hard into the second. EG *She dug her
needle into her sewing... My corset was digging
into my stomach.*

4 A **dig** is an unpleasant remark which is intended N COUNT:
to hurt or embarrass someone. EG *Whenever she* OFT+at
can, she takes a dig at me.*

5 Your **digs** are a room in someone else's house N PLURAL:
which you pay to live in. EG *When I was working in* OFT in+N
Sheffield, I lived in digs. British

dig out. 1 If you **dig** someone or something **out** of PHRASAL VB:
somewhere, you get them out with some effort or V+O+ADV,
difficulty. EG *They worked all night, digging people* OFT+of
out of the rubble. 2 If you **dig** something **out**, you V+O+ADV
find it after it has been hidden or stored for a long
time. EG *We dug out our tour books and maps for
the holiday.*

dig up. 1 If you **dig** something **up**, you remove it PHRASAL VB:
from the ground where it has been buried. EG V+O+ADV
...digging up potatoes in the vegetable garden. 2 If V+O+ADV
you **dig up** information that is not widely known,
you discover it. EG *Journalists have dug up some
hair-raising facts about the company.*

digest, digests, digesting, digested; pronounced
/dɪdʒest/ when it is a verb and /daɪdʒest/ when it
is a noun.

1 When you **digest** food, you stomach removes the V+O
substances that your body needs and gets rid of the
rest.

2 If you **digest** information, you think about it and V+O
understand it. EG *I had heard it without having
actually digested what was said.*

3 A **digest** is a collection of pieces of writing, N COUNT:
which are published together in a shorter form USU+SUPP
than they originally appeared in.

digestion /dɪdʒestʃən/, **digestions.** 1 **Digestion** N UNCOUNT
is the process of digesting food. EG *A good walk aids
digestion.*

2 Your **digestion** is the system in your body which N COUNT
digests your food. EG *His digestion had always been
poor.*

digestive /dɪdʒestɪv/ means relating to the diges- ADJ CLASSIF:
tion of food. EG *...the digestive system.* ATTRIB

digit /dɪdʒɪt/, **digits.** A **digit** is 1 a written symbol N COUNT
for any of the ten numbers from 0 to 9. EG *11 is a*

two digit number. **2** a finger, thumb, or toe.

digital /dɪdʒɪtəºl/. **Digital** watches or clocks ADJ CLASSIF: show the time by displaying numbers rather than ATTRIB by using hands on a traditional clock face.

dignified /dɪgnɪfaɪd/. Someone who is **dignified** ADJ QUALIT is calmly impressive and worthy of respect. EG *She was tall, handsome, very dignified... ...a cool, dignified attitude... He composed a dignified letter to accompany his cheque.*

dignify /dɪgnɪfaɪ/, **dignifies, dignifying, digni-** V+O: **fied.** Something that **dignifies** a place makes it NO IMPER impressive. EG *They stood admiring the broad steps that dignified the front of the mansion.*

dignitary /dɪgnɪtəºriº/, **dignitaries.** A **dignitary** N COUNT: is someone who has a high rank in government or USU PLURAL in the Church.

dignity /dɪgnɪtiº/. **1** If someone has **dignity** or if N UNCOUNT: they show **dignity**, their behaviour or appearance USU+SUPP is serious, calm, and controlled. EG *There was something impressive about Julia's quiet dignity.* **2 Dignity** is also the quality of being worthy of N UNCOUNT: respect. EG *Don't discount the importance of human* USU+SUPP *dignity.*

digress /daɪgres/, **digresses, digressing, di-** V **gressed.** If you **digress**, you move away from the subject you are talking or writing about and talk or write about something different for a while. EG *I will digress slightly at this stage.* ◊ **digression** ◊ N COUNT OR /daɪgreʃəºn/, **digressions.** EG *This long digression* N UNCOUNT *has led me away from my main story.*

dike /daɪk/. See **dyke.**

dilapidated /dɪˈlæpɪdeɪtɪ²d/. A building that is ADJ QUALIT **dilapidated** is old and in bad condition.

dilate /dɪˈsleɪt/, **dilates, dilating, dilated.** When V-ERG your eyes **dilate**, the pupils of your eyes become wider or bigger. ◊ **dilated.** EG *She smiled, her eyes* ◊ ADJ QUALIT *bright and dilated.*

dilemma /dɪˈslemə/, **dilemmas.** A **dilemma** is a N COUNT difficult situation in which you have to choose between two or more alternatives. EG *It put me in a difficult moral dilemma.*

diligent /dɪlɪ²dʒəºnt/. Someone who is **diligent** ADJ QUALIT works hard and carefully, and tries to do everything that they are expected to do. EG *I have no doubt that diligent research will produce results.* ◊ **diligently.** EG *He read the Bible diligently.* ◊ ADV ◊ **diligence** /dɪlɪ²dʒəºns/. EG *I had been hoping to* ◊ N UNCOUNT *impress my new boss with my diligence.*

dilute /daɪljuːt/, **dilutes, diluting, diluted.** When V+O you **dilute** a liquid, you add water or another liquid to it in order to make it weaker.

dim /dɪm/, **dimmer, dimmest; dims, dimming, dimmed. 1** Something that is **dim** is **1.1** rather ADJ QUALIT dark because there is not much light in it. EG *The room was dim.* ◊ **dimly.** EG *...the dimly lit depart-* ◊ ADV *ment store.* ◊ **dimness.** EG *...in the dimness of the* ◊ N UNCOUNT *church.* **1.2** not very easy to see. EG *Bernard peered* ADJ QUALIT *at the dim figure by the bus-stop.* **2** If your memory of something is **dim**, you can ADJ QUALIT hardly remember it at all. EG *I only have a dim recollection of the production.* **3** If you describe someone as **dim**, you mean that ADJ QUALIT they are stupid. Informal **4** If a light **dims** or if you **dim** it, it becomes less V-ERG bright.

dime /daɪm/, **dimes.** A **dime** is an American coin N COUNT worth ten cents.

dimension /dɪˈslmenʃəºn/, **dimensions. 1** A par- N COUNT: ticular **dimension** of a situation is a fact or event USU+SUPP that affects the way you understand the situation. EG *Most of us were Catholic, and this added an extra dimension to the tension.* **2** The **dimensions** of a situation or problem are N COUNT: the extent or importance of it. EG *...a growing* USU PLURAL *awareness of the true dimensions of the threat.* **3** A **dimension** is a measurement in space such as N COUNT length, width, or height. EG *...a dimension of six metres.* **4** You can refer to the size of something as its N COUNT: USU PLURAL

dimensions. EG *These plants grew to magnificent dimensions.*

diminish /dɪmɪnɪʃ/, **diminishes, diminishing,** V-ERG **diminished.** When something **diminishes** or **is diminished,** it becomes reduced in size, importance, or intensity. EG *As she turned the knob, the sound diminished.* ◊ **diminished.** EG *...clear evi-* ◊ ADJ QUALIT *dence of diminished social tension.* ◊ **diminishing.** EG *...the diminishing importance of* ◊ ADJ QUALIT *universities.*

diminutive /dɪmɪnjuːtɪv/ means very small in- ADJ CLASSIF deed. EG *...Mrs Bradley, a diminutive figure in* Literary *black.*

dimple /dɪmpəºl/, **dimples.** A **dimple** is a small N COUNT hollow in someone's cheek or chin, often one that you can see when they smile.

dimpled /dɪmpəºld/. Something that is **dimpled** ADJ CLASSIF has small hollows in it. EG *...the child's dimpled cheeks.*

din /dɪn/. A **din** is a very loud and unpleasant noise N SING that lasts for a long time. EG *They were unable to* Informal *sleep because of the din coming from the bar.*

dine /daɪn/, **dines, dining, dined.** When you **dine,** V you have dinner. EG *They arrived at seven, in time* Formal *to dine at a splendid Hungarian restaurant.*

dine out. If you **dine out,** you have dinner away PHRASAL VB: from your home, usually at a restaurant. V+ADV

diner /daɪnə/, **diners.** A **diner** is **1** someone who N COUNT is having dinner in a restaurant. **2** a small, cheap American restaurant.

dinghy /dɪŋiº/, **dinghies.** A **dinghy** is a small boat N COUNT that you sail or row.

dingy /dɪndʒiº/, **dingier, dingiest. 1** A building or ADJ QUALIT place that is **dingy** is rather dark and depressing. EG *We drove through some of the dingiest streets of the town.* **2** Clothes or curtains that are **dingy** are dirty or ADJ QUALIT faded.

dining room, dining rooms. A **dining room** is N COUNT the room in a house where people have their meals, or a room in a hotel where meals are served.

dinner /dɪnə/, **dinners. 1 Dinner** is the main N UNCOUNT meal of the day. EG *I haven't had dinner yet.* OR N COUNT **2** A **dinner** is a formal social event in the evening N COUNT at which a meal is served. EG *Mrs Thatcher attended a dinner at the Mansion House last night.*

dinner jacket, dinner jackets. A **dinner jacket** N COUNT is a black jacket that a man wears with a bow tie at formal social events.

dinner party, dinner parties. A **dinner party** is N COUNT a social event where a small group of people are invited to have dinner and spend the evening at someone's house. EG *How about giving a dinner-party next week?*

dinosaur /daɪnəsɔː/, **dinosaurs. Dinosaurs** were N COUNT large reptiles which lived in prehistoric times and which are now extinct.

diocese /daɪəˈsɪs/, **dioceses.** A **diocese** is the N COUNT area over which a bishop has control.

dip /dɪp/, **dips, dipping, dipped. 1** If you **dip** V+O: OFT something into a liquid or powder, you put it into +in/into the liquid or powder and then quickly take it out again. EG *He dipped his pen in the ink.* **2** If something **dips,** it makes a downward move- V ment. EG *The plane's nose dipped.* **3** If a road **dips,** it goes down quite suddenly to a V lower level. EG *The railway dips between thick forests.* **4** A **dip** in a surface is a place in it that is lower N COUNT than the rest of the surface. EG *...a small dip in the ground.* **5** A **dip** is a thick creamy mixture which you eat by N COUNT OR scooping it up with raw vegetables or biscuits. EG N UNCOUNT *...tasty cheese dips.*

When your eyes dilate, does the size of your pupils diminish?

6 If you have a **dip**, you go for a quick swim. N COUNT

diphtheria /dɪpθɪərɪə, dɪf-/ is a dangerous infec- N UNCOUNT
tious disease.

diploma /dɪpləʊmə/, **diplomas**. A **diploma** is a N COUNT
qualification which is awarded to students by a
university or college. A diploma is not as high as a
degree. EG *She studied for a diploma in theology.*

diplomacy /dɪpləʊməsi¹/ is **1** the management of N UNCOUNT
relations between countries. EG *The crisis developed into a matter of high-level diplomacy between the two embassies.* **2** the skill of saying or
doing things without offending people. EG *You will
need to employ a great deal of tact and diplomacy
to put him politely in his place.*

diplomat /dɪpləˢmæt/, **diplomats**. A **diplomat** is
1 a senior government official who negotiates with N COUNT
another country on behalf of his or her own
country. Diplomats usually work as members of an
embassy.
2 You can also refer to someone who is skilful at N COUNT
saying and doing things that do not offend people
as a **diplomat**.

diplomatic /dɪpləˢmætɪk/. **1 Diplomatic** means ADJ CLASSIF :
relating to diplomacy and diplomats. EG *The gov-* ATTRIB
*ernment was reluctant to endanger its diplomatic
links with Britain.*
2 Someone who is **diplomatic** is able to be tactful ADJ QUALIT
and say or do things without offending people. EG
The secretary was diplomatic on the telephone.

dire /daɪə/ is used to emphasize how serious or ADJ CLASSIF :
terrible a situation is. EG *...countries in dire mis-* USU ATTRIB
ery... ...the dire consequences of his actions.

direct /dɪˢrɛkt/, **directs, directing, directed**. **1** ADJ CLASSIF,
Direct means going or aimed straight towards a ALSO ADV :
place or object. EG *Are there any direct flights to* USU+PREP
Athens?... Why hadn't he gone direct to the lounge?
◊ **directly**. EG *She turned her head and looked* ◊ ADV
directly at them.
2 You use **direct** to emphasize that no other ADJ CLASSIF :
person or situation is involved. EG *...the direct* ATTRIB OR ADV
*intervention of the managing director... ...as a
direct result of this information... Money
comes direct from industry.* ◊ **directly**. EG ◊ ADV
They negotiated directly with the leaders.
3 A **direct** attack or challenge is one made openly ADJ CLASSIF :
so that there is no doubt about what is being done. ATTRIB
EG *This move is a direct challenge to the government.*
4 Someone who is **direct** makes their opinions and ADJ QUALIT
wishes known in a very clear, open way.
◊ **directly**. EG *She never directly asked for money.* ◊ ADV
◊ **directness**. EG *Such directness embarrassed Ian.* ◊ N UNCOUNT
5 Something that **is directed** at a particular per- V+O+A
son or thing is aimed at them or is intended to
affect them. EG *...a question that John had evidently
directed at me... This is a fundamental question to
which we should all be directing our attention.*
6 If you **direct** someone somewhere, you tell them V+O : OFT+to
how to get there. EG *Can you direct me to the* Formal
cemetery?
7 If someone **directs** a project or a group of V+O
people, they organize it and are in charge of it. EG
No one seemed to be directing the operation.
8 If someone **directs** a film, play, or television V+O OR V
programme, they decide how it should be made
and performed.
9 If you **direct** someone to do something, you tell V+O+to-INF
them to do it. EG *She directed me to sit in the* Formal
waiting room.
10 Someone who is a **direct** descendant of a ADJ CLASSIF :
particular person is descended from that person ATTRIB
through their parents, grandparents and so on,
rather than through uncles, aunts, or cousins.
11 See also **directly**.

direction /dɪˢrɛkʃəˢn/, **directions**. **1** A **direction** N COUNT :
is **1.1** the general line that someone or something USU+SUPP
is moving or pointing in. EG *We ended up going in
the opposite direction from them... Pieces of jagged metal are sent flying in all directions.* **1.2** the

general way in which something develops or progresses. EG *The government has to guide the general direction of the economy.*
2 Directions are instructions that tell you what to N PLURAL
do or how to get to a place. EG *Follow the directions
that your doctor gives you... I asked a policeman
for directions to the hospital.*
3 The **direction** of a film, play, or television N UNCOUNT
programme is the work that the director does
while it is being made.
4 If you do something **under** someone else's **direc-** PHRASE
tion, they tell you what to do.

directive /dɪˢrɛktɪv/, **directives**. A **directive** is N COUNT
an official instruction that is given by someone in Formal
authority. EG *The government is obliged to take
action because of EEC directives.*

directly /dɪˢrɛktli¹/. **1** If something is **directly** ADV
above, below, or in front of something, it is in
exactly that position. EG *The sun was almost directly overhead... I saw him pass directly in front of the
window.*
2 If you say something will happen **directly**, you ADV
mean that it will happen very soon. EG *She's in a
meeting at the moment but she will be here
directly.*
3 You use **directly** to say that one thing happens ADV OR CONJ
immediately after another thing. EG *Newly married
girls go directly to live in the village of their new
husband... Directly he heard the door close he
picked up the telephone.*
4 See also **direct**.

director /dɪˢrɛktə/, **directors**. A **director** is **1** N COUNT
someone who is responsible for organizing and
leading a group of people who are working together. EG *He became artistic director of the Sadlers
Wells ballet in 1978.* **2** someone who is on the board
of a company or in charge of a government
organization. **3** someone who decides how a film,
play, or television programme is made or performed.

directory /dɪˢrɛktəˢri¹/, **directories**. A **directory** N COUNT
is a book which gives lists of information such as
people's names, addresses, and telephone numbers,
usually arranged in alphabetical order. EG *...the
Birmingham telephone directory.*

dirge /dɜːdʒ/, **dirges**. A **dirge** is a slow, sad song N COUNT
or piece of music, often performed at funerals.

dirt /dɜːt/ is **1** dust or mud on something which is N UNCOUNT
usually kept clean. EG *...sweeping up the dirt.* **2** the
earth on the ground. EG *...rough dirt roads.*

dirty /dɜːti¹/, **dirtier, dirtiest; dirties, dirtying,
dirtied**. **1** Something that is **dirty** has dust, mud, or ADJ QUALIT
stains on it and needs to be cleaned. EG *The
children were hot, dirty, and exhausted... ...dirty
marks on the walls.*
2 To **dirty** something means to make it dirty. EG V+O
She didn't like dogs; they dirtied her clothes.
3 A **dirty** action is unfair or dishonest. EG *They will* ADJ QUALIT :
use any dirty trick. ATTRIB
4 Dirty jokes, books, or language refer to sex in a ADJ QUALIT
way that many people find offensive.

disability /dɪsəbɪlə¹ti¹/, **disabilities**. A **disability** N COUNT OR
is a physical injury or mental illness that severely N UNCOUNT
affects your life. EG *...the disabilities suffered by the* Formal
elderly.

disable /dɪseɪbəˢl/, **disables, disabling, dis-** V+O
abled. If something **disables** you, it injures you
physically or mentally and severely affects your
life. EG *...if you are disabled by an accident at work.*

disabled /dɪseɪbəˢld/. **1** Someone who is **disabled** ADJ QUALIT
has a physical injury or mental illness that severe-
ly affects their life. EG *She has to look after a
disabled relative.*
2 The **disabled** are people who have a physical N PLURAL :
injury or mental illness that severely affects their the+N
lives. EG *...the variety of help available to the
disabled.*

disablement /dɪseɪbəˢlmə¹nt/ is the state of being N UNCOUNT
disabled or the act of becoming disabled. EG *...un-* Formal

able to work because of disablement caused by an accident.

disadvantage /dɪsə³dvɑːntɪdʒ/, **disadvantages.** N COUNT
1 A **disadvantage** is a part of a situation which causes problems. EG ...*the disadvantages of living in cities.*

2 If you are **at a disadvantage** in a situation, you PHRASE cannot succeed easily because you have a problem that other people do not have. EG *These restrictions put banks at a disadvantage.*

3 If something is **to** your **disadvantage**, it causes PHRASE problems for you or puts you in a worse position than other people. EG *The treaty was to our disadvantage.*

disadvantaged /dɪsə³dvɑːntɪdʒd/. People who ADJ QUALIT are **disadvantaged** live in bad conditions and cannot easily improve their situation. EG ...*disadvantaged children.*

disadvantageous /dɪsædvɑːnteɪdʒəs/. Some- ADJ QUALIT : thing that is **disadvantageous** causes problems or OFT+to puts someone in a worse position than other people. EG *This made the 1976 agreement disadvantageous to the British.*

disaffected /dɪsəfektɪ³d/. People who are **disaf-** ADJ QUALIT **fected** are dissatisfied with an organization or idea and no longer support it. EG *Our party gained four disaffected UP members.*

disaffection /dɪsəfekʃə⁰n/ is a feeling of dissatis- N UNCOUNT faction that people have with an organization or Formal idea, so that they no longer support it. EG *They were worried about the possibility of disaffection in the army.*

disagree /dɪsəgriː/, **disagrees, disagreeing, dis-**
agreed. 1 If you **disagree** with a person or idea, V : OFT+with/ you have a different opinion of what is true or about correct. EG *I disagree completely with John Taylor... He and I disagree about it.*

2 If you **disagree** with an action or decision, you v+with disapprove of it. EG *Benn disagreed with the abandonment of the project.*

3 If food or drink **disagrees** with you, it makes you v+with feel ill after you have eaten or drunk it. Informal

disagreeable /dɪsəgriːəbə⁰l/. **1** Something that is ADJ QUALIT **disagreeable** is unpleasant or annoying. EG ...*a very disagreeable smell.*

2 Someone who is **disagreeable** is unfriendly or ADJ QUALIT bad-tempered. ◊ **disagreeably.** EG *'I hate it,' she* ◊ ADV *said disagreeably.*

disagreement /dɪsəgriːmə³nt/, **disagreements.**
1 **Disagreement** is a situation in which people N UNCOUNT have different opinions and cannot reach a decision. EG *There was little disagreement over what needed to be done... The experts find themselves in total disagreement.*

2 A **disagreement** is an argument between peo- N COUNT : ple. EG *We had a serious disagreement about busi-* USU+SUPP *ness.*

disallow /dɪsəlaʊ/, **disallows, disallowing, dis-** v+o **allowed.** If an action or claim **is disallowed**, it is Formal not accepted or not approved by people in authority. EG *The appeals were disallowed by the court.*

disappear /dɪsəpɪə/, **disappears, disappearing,**
disappeared. 1 If someone or something **disap-**
pears, 1.1 they go where you can no longer see v : OFT+A them. EG *I saw him disappear round the corner.* **1.2** v they go where nobody can find them. EG *I shall disappear. You will not hear from me again.*
◊ **disappearance** /dɪsəpɪərəns/, **disappear-** ◊ N UNCOUNT **ances.** EG ...*the mysterious disappearance of* OR N COUNT *Halliday.*

2 If something **disappears**, it stops existing or v happening. EG *Some newspapers are going to disappear as a result of this strike.* ◊ **disappearance.** ◊ N UNCOUNT EG ...*the disappearance of the dinosaurs.*

disappoint /dɪsəpɔɪnt/, **disappoints, disap-** v+o **pointing, disappointed.** If things or people **disappoint** you, they do not satisfy you, because they are not as good as you had hoped, or do not do what

you want. EG *The results disappointed him... We must not disappoint the hopes of the people.*

disappointed /dɪsəpɔɪntɪ²d/. If you are **disap-** ADJ QUALIT **pointed**, you are sad because something that you wanted has not happened or because it is not as good as you hoped it would be. EG *She was disappointed that Ted had not come... My father was bitterly disappointed in me.*

disappointing /dɪsəpɔɪntɪŋ/. Something that is ADJ QUALIT **disappointing** is not as good or not as much as you expected it to be. EG ...*a disappointing book.*
◊ **disappointingly.** EG ...*the disappointingly small* ◊ ADV *crowd.*

disappointment /dɪsəpɔɪntmə³nt/, **disappoint-**
ments. 1 **Disappointment** is the state of feeling N UNCOUNT : disappointed. EG *To my disappointment, she came* USU+SUPP *with her mother.*

2 A **disappointment** is something which makes N COUNT you feel disappointed. EG *That defeat was a surprise and a disappointment.*

disapproval /dɪsəpruːvə⁰l/. If you express **disap-** N UNCOUNT **proval** of someone or something, you indicate that you do not like them or that you think they are wrong. EG ...*his disapproval of the President's policy.*

disapprove /dɪsəpruːv/, **disapproves, disap-** V : OFT+of **proving, disapproved.** If you **disapprove** of someone or something, you feel or show that you do not like them or that you think they are wrong. EG *The other teachers disapproved of his methods.*

disapproving /dɪsəpruːvɪŋ/. A **disapproving** ac- ADJ QUALIT tion or expression indicates that you do not like someone or something or that you think they are wrong. EG ...*a disapproving glance... My parents were slightly disapproving of Ellen.*
◊ **disapprovingly.** EG *He shook his head disap-* ◊ ADV *provingly.*

disarm /dɪsɑːm/, **disarms, disarming, dis-**
armed. 1 If you **disarm** people, you take away v+o their weapons. EG *The officer captured and disarmed the two men.*

2 If a country **disarms**, it gives up the use of v weapons, especially nuclear weapons.

3 If you **disarm** someone or **disarm** their anger or v+o hostility, you cause them to feel less angry or hostile. EG *They were so kind that it surprised and disarmed her.*

disarmament /dɪsɑːməmə³nt/ is a process in N UNCOUNT which countries agree to reduce the number of weapons that they have, especially nuclear weapons.

disarming /dɪsɑːmɪŋ/. If someone is **disarming**, ADJ QUALIT they cause you to feel less angry or hostile. EG ...*Harriet's disarming friendliness... ...a disarming smile.*

disarrange /dɪsəreɪndʒ/, **disarranges, disar-** v+o **ranging, disarranged.** To **disarrange** something Formal means to make it untidy. EG *The wind was disarranging her hair.*

disarray /dɪsəreɪ/. **1** If a group of people is **in** PHRASE **disarray** or has been thrown **into disarray**, they Formal have become confused and disorganized. EG *The Democratic Party was in disarray.*

2 If things or places are **in disarray**, they are very PHRASE untidy. EG ...*books in disarray.* Formal

disassociate /dɪsəsəʊʃɪeɪt/, **disassociates, dis-** V.REFL+from **associating, disassociated.** If you **disassociate** Formal yourself from a person or situation, you state or show that you are not involved with them, in order to avoid trouble or blame. EG *Democratic politicians wanted to disassociate themselves from the President.*

disaster /dɪzɑːstə/, **disasters. 1** A **disaster** is an N COUNT unexpected event which causes a lot of damage or

On these pages which adjective is always used in front of a noun?

suffering. EG ...*a natural disaster, an earthquake or a typhoon.*
2 If you say that something was a **disaster**, you mean that you think it was very unsuccessful or unpleasant. EG *The last day at the hotel was a disaster.* N COUNT
3 Disaster is something which affects you very badly. EG *They had led the country into economic disaster.* N UNCOUNT

disastrous /dɪzɑːstrəs/. **1** A **disastrous** event causes a lot of damage or suffering. EG ...*disastrous floods.* ◇ **disastrously.** EG *These diseases have increased disastrously.* ADJ QUALIT / ◇ ADV
2 If you say that something is **disastrous**, you mean that it is very unsuccessful or unpleasant. EG ...*a disastrous holiday.* ◇ **disastrously.** EG *The team performed disastrously.* ADJ QUALIT / ◇ ADV

disband /dɪsbænd/, **disbands, disbanding, disbanded.** If someone **disbands** an organization or group of people, the organization or group officially ceases to exist. EG *The regiment had been disbanded... They began to disband.* V-ERG

disbelief /dɪsbəˈliːf/ is not believing that something is true or real. EG *He shook his head in disbelief... I looked at it with disbelief.* N UNCOUNT

disbelieve /dɪsbəˈliːv/, **disbelieves, disbelieving, disbelieved.** If you **disbelieve** someone, you think that they are telling lies. EG *There is no reason to disbelieve him.* V+O / Formal

disc /dɪsk/, **discs;** spelled **disk** in American English. A **disc** is **1** a flat, circular shape or object. EG ...*a metal disc with a number stamped on it.* **2** a thin, circular piece of cartilage between the bones in your spine. **3** a gramophone record. N COUNT

discard /dɪskɑːd/, **discards, discarding, discarded.** If you **discard** something, you get rid of it or leave it because it is old, useless, or unwanted. EG *Pull off and discard the outer leaves.* ◇ **discarded.** EG ...*discarded newspapers.* V+O / ◇ ADJ CLASSIF

discern /dɪsɜːn/, **discerns, discerning, discerned.** If you **discern** something, **1** you can see it by looking carefully. EG *I could dimly discern his figure.* **2** you can notice it or understand it by careful thought or study. EG *Posy had not discerned the real reason... He is unable to discern what is actually happening.* V+O / Formal / V+O OR V+REPORT / Formal

discernible /dɪsɜːnəbəl/. If something is **discernible**, **1** you can see it by looking carefully. EG *Each pebble was clearly discernible.* **2** you can notice it or understand it by careful thought or study. EG *An element of envy is discernible in his attitude.* ADJ QUALIT / ADJ QUALIT : OFT+*in*

discerning /dɪsɜːnɪŋ/. Someone who is **discerning** is good at judging the quality of something. EG ...*discerning readers.* ADJ QUALIT

discharge, discharges, discharging, discharged; pronounced /dɪstʃɑːdʒ/ when it is a verb and /dɪstʃɑːdʒ/ when it is a noun.
1 When someone **is discharged** from hospital, prison, or the armed forces, they are officially allowed to leave. ▶ used as a noun. EG ...*from the time of his discharge until his re-arrest.* V+O : USU PASS / ▶ N UNCOUNT : USU+POSS
2 If someone **discharges** their duties or responsibilities, they carry them out satisfactorily. EG *He is unable to discharge the duties of his office.* V+O / Formal
3 To **discharge** an object or substance means to send it out from a place or container. EG *The city's sewage is discharged into huge lakes.* ▶ used as a noun. EG ...*the discharge of mercury from industrial premises.* V+O / Formal / ▶ N COUNT OR N UNCOUNT : USU+SUPP
4 A **discharge** is also a substance that comes out from a place. EG ...*a discharge from the nose.* N COUNT / Formal

disciple /dɪsaɪpəl/, **disciples.** A **disciple** is someone who believes, supports, and uses the ideas of their leader or superior. EG ...*Jesus and his disciples.* N COUNT

disciplinarian /dɪsɪplɪnɛərɪən/, **disciplinarians.** If someone in authority is a **disciplinarian**, they are strict and insist that people obey the rules. N COUNT

disciplinary /dɪsɪplɪnəri/ matters are concerned with rules, making sure that people obey them, and punishing people who do not. EG ...*forcing them to take disciplinary action against their own members.* ADJ CLASSIF : ATTRIB

discipline /dɪsɪplɪn/, **disciplines, disciplining, disciplined. 1 Discipline** is **1.1** the practice of making people obey rules and punishing them when they do not. EG *She was a harsh mother and imposed severe discipline.* **1.2** the quality of always behaving or working in a controlled way. EG *They admired our patience and discipline.* N UNCOUNT
2 The **discipline** of a particular activity is the system of rules or methods that is used in it. EG ...*the discipline of dancing...* ...*military discipline.* N UNCOUNT OR N COUNT
3 If you **discipline** someone, **3.1** you train them to behave or work in a controlled way. EG *They will have to discipline themselves.* **3.2** you punish them for behaving badly or breaking a rule. EG *They could be disciplined by the union if they refused to strike.* V+O OR V-REFL / V+O
4 A **discipline** is a subject that is studied in colleges and universities. EG ...*graduates of all disciplines.* N COUNT / Formal

disciplined /dɪsɪplɪnd/. Someone who is **disciplined** behaves or works in a controlled way. EG *Baker lives a disciplined life.* ADJ QUALIT

disc jockey, disc jockeys. A **disc jockey** is someone whose job is to play and introduce pop records on the radio or at a disco. N COUNT

disclaim /dɪskleɪm/, **disclaims, disclaiming, disclaimed.** If you **disclaim** knowledge of something or **disclaim** responsibility for it, you say that you did not know about it or are not responsible for it. EG *Tess disclaimed any knowledge of it... She disclaimed any wish to impose censorship on television.* V+O / Formal

disclose /dɪskləʊz/, **discloses, disclosing, disclosed.** If you **disclose** new or secret information, you tell it to someone. EG *I had no intention of disclosing their names... The English newspaper disclosed that the treaty had been signed.* ◇ **disclosure** /dɪskləʊʒə/, **disclosures.** EG *He feared it might lead to the disclosure of his visit to Rome... There were more disclosures about Casey in the press.* V+O OR V+REPORT / ◇ N UNCOUNT OR N COUNT / Formal

disco /dɪskəʊ/, **discos.** A **disco** is a place or event at which young people dance to pop records. EG ...*going out to a disco or a pub.* N COUNT

discolour /dɪskʌlə/, **discolours, discolouring, discoloured;** spelled **discolor** in American English.
If something **discolours** or if it **is discoloured** by something else, it changes its original colour and looks unattractive. EG *The pans may discolour inside.* ◇ **discoloured.** EG ...*discoloured teeth.* V-ERG / ◇ ADJ QUALIT

discomfort /dɪskʌmfət/, **discomforts. 1 Discomfort** is **1.1** an unpleasant or painful feeling in a part of your body. EG *He was conscious only of physical discomfort.* **1.2** a feeling of worry or embarrassment. EG *I no longer experienced discomfort in their presence.* N UNCOUNT
2 Discomforts are conditions which make you feel pain or unease. EG ...*the discomforts of life in India.* N PLURAL : +SUPP

disconcert /dɪskənsɜːt/, **disconcerts, disconcerting, disconcerted.** If something **disconcerts** you, it makes you feel worried or embarrassed. EG *Her cold stare disconcerted me.* V+O : USU PASS / Formal

disconcerting /dɪskənsɜːtɪŋ/. Something that is **disconcerting** makes you feel worried or embarrassed. EG ...*his disconcerting habit of pausing before he spoke.* ◇ **disconcertingly.** EG *Harold laughed disconcertingly loudly.* ADJ QUALIT / ◇ SUBMOD OR ADV

disconnect /dɪskənekt/, **disconnects, disconnecting, disconnected. 1** If you **disconnect** things that are joined, you pull them apart. EG *Can you disconnect all these tubes?* V+O
2 If you **disconnect** a piece of equipment, you V+O

detach it from its source of power, such as a gas or electricity supply. EG *I bent down to disconnect the plug.*

3 If a gas, electricity, water, or telephone company **disconnects** you, it turns off the connection to your house. EG *His telephone had been disconnected.* V+O : USU PASS

4 If a telephone operator **disconnects** you, he or she suddenly ends a call you are making. V+O

disconnected /dɪskəˈnektɪ³d/. **Disconnected** things are not linked in any way. EG *...a series of disconnected events... She gave disconnected answers.* ADJ CLASSIF

disconsolate /dɪskɒnsələ³t/. Someone who is **disconsolate** is very unhappy or disappointed. EG *...disconsolate passengers standing around.* ◇ **disconsolately.** EG *He walked disconsolately down the path.* ADJ QUALIT Formal ◇ ADV

discontent /dɪskəˈntent/ is the feeling of not being satisfied with your situation. EG *...their discontent with pay and conditions.* N UNCOUNT : USU+SUPP

discontented /dɪskəˈntentɪ³d/. If you are **discontented**, you are not satisfied with your situation. EG *Most of the people he saw looked discontented.* ADJ QUALIT

discontinue /dɪskəˈntɪnjuː/, **discontinues**, **discontinuing**, **discontinued**. If you **discontinue** an activity, you stop doing it. EG *Fanny wanted to discontinue her visits.* V+O Formal

discord /dɪskɔːd/, **discords**. **1** Discord is disagreement and unpleasantness between people. EG *He's been a source of discord and worry.* N UNCOUNT Literary

2 A **discord** is an unpleasant combination of musical notes. N COUNT Technical

discordant /dɪskɔːdəⁿnt/. **1** Things that are **discordant** are different from each other in an unexpected or unpleasant way. EG *...the discordant state of industrial relations.* ADJ QUALIT Formal

2 A sound that is **discordant** is unpleasant to listen to. ADJ QUALIT Formal

discotheque /dɪskəˈtek/, **discotheques**. A **discotheque** is a disco. N COUNT Formal

discount, discounts, discounting, discounted; pronounced /dɪskaunt/ when it is a noun and /dɪskaunt/ when it is a verb.

1 A **discount** is a reduction in the usual price of something. EG *Our clients receive a 50% discount.* N COUNT

2 If you **discount** someone or something, you reject or ignore them because you think they are not important. EG *I decided to discount the risks.* V+O

discourage /dɪskʌrɪdʒ/, **discourages**, **discouraging**, **discouraged**. **1** If someone or something **discourages** you, they cause you to lose your enthusiasm or become unwilling to do something. EG *Don't let friends discourage you.* ◇ **discouraging.** EG *...a difficult and discouraging task.* ◇ **discouraged.** EG *Whenever I feel discouraged, I read that letter.* ◇ **discouragement** /dɪskʌrɪdʒmə³nt/, **discouragements.** EG *The submarines were a constant discouragement to naval movements.* V+O ◇ ADJ QUALIT ◇ ADJ QUALIT ◇ N COUNT

2 To **discourage** an action or to **discourage** someone from doing it means to try and persuade them not to do it. EG *She wanted to discourage him from marrying the girl.* ◇ **discouragement.** EG *When I first started, I encountered opposition and discouragement.* V+O : OFT+*from* ◇ N UNCOUNT

discourse, discourses, discoursing, discoursed; pronounced /dɪskɔːs/ when it is a noun and /dɪskɔːs/ when it is a verb.

1 A **discourse** is a talk or piece of writing that teaches or explains something. EG *They listened to his discourse on human relations.* ▸ used as a verb. EG *Jeff discoursed impressively on Newton's theory of gravity.* N COUNT ▸ V+*on/upon* Formal

2 Discourse is spoken or written communication between people. EG *Let us switch the area of discourse to politics.* N UNCOUNT Formal

discover /dɪskʌvə/, **discovers**, **discovering**, **discovered**. **1** When you **discover** a fact that you did V+O OR V+REPORT

not know, you find out about it. EG *We discovered a way to get rid of it... I discovered that Zapp is Melanie's father.*

2 If you **discover** someone or something, you find them accidentally or by searching for them. EG *He was dead before anyone discovered him.* V+O

3 If someone **discovers** something that nobody knew about before, they are the first person to find it or find out about it. EG *Herschel discovered a new planet.* ◇ **discoverer** /dɪskʌvərə/, **discoverers.** EG *...the discoverer of penicillin, Sir Alexander Fleming.* V+O ◇ N COUNT

4 If you **discover** a feeling, you experience it for the first time. EG *She discovered the joy of writing.* V+O

5 If an artist or athlete **is discovered**, someone realizes how talented they are and helps them to become famous. V+O : USU PASS

discovery /dɪskʌvə³riː/, **discoveries**. A **discovery** is **1** the finding of an object or fact that nobody knew about. EG *New scientific discoveries are being made every day... ...the Chinese discovery of paper-making.* **2** the finding of an object or fact that you did not know about. EG *...the discovery that he wanted to hurt her.* N COUNT OR N UNCOUNT : USU+SUPP / N COUNT : USU+SUPP

discredit /dɪskredɪt/, **discredits**, **discrediting**, **discredited**. **1** To **discredit** someone means to cause them to lose the trust or respect of other people. EG *...efforts to discredit the government.* ◇ **discredited.** EG *...the discredited ambassador.* V+O Formal ◇ ADJ QUALIT

2 To **discredit** an idea or belief means to make it appear false or doubtful. EG *Scientific discoveries have discredited religious belief.* ◇ **discredited.** EG *...discredited theories.* V+O Formal ◇ ADJ QUALIT

3 Discredit is shame or disapproval. EG *It may bring discredit to our city.* N UNCOUNT Formal

4 If something is **to** your **discredit**, it causes people to lose respect for you. EG *To Monty's discredit, he refused.* PHRASE

discreet /dɪskriːt/. **1** Discreet behaviour involves being careful not to cause embarrassment or difficulties for someone. EG *Make discreet enquiries at his place of employment.* ◇ **discreetly.** EG *The king came discreetly up the back stairs.* ADJ QUALIT ◇ ADV

2 If you are **discreet**, you do not talk about secret or private matters. EG *I'll certainly be most discreet in my conversation.* ADJ QUALIT

3 Something that is **discreet** is intended not to attract a lot of attention. EG *...discreet advertisements in the newspapers.* ◇ **discreetly.** EG *...the discreetly shaded light.* ADJ QUALIT ◇ ADV

discrepancy /dɪskrepənsiː/, **discrepancies**. A **discrepancy** is a surprising difference between things that ought to be similar or the same. EG *...discrepancies between school records and examination results... ...discrepancies in Mr Casey's accounts.* N COUNT : OFT +*between/in*

discrete /dɪskriːt/. A **discrete** thing is separate and different from similar things. EG *...the two discrete hemispheres of the brain... ...mobility between discrete social classes.* ADJ CLASSIF : ATTRIB Formal

discretion /dɪskreʃəⁿn/. **1** Discretion is **1.1** the quality of not causing embarrassment or difficulties or of not revealing secrets. EG *The plan was carried out with maximum speed and discretion.* **1.2** the ability to judge a situation and to take suitable decisions or actions. EG *Use your discretion!* N UNCOUNT

2 If a decision is **at the discretion of** someone in authority, it depends on them and not on a fixed rule. EG *The issue of these cards is at the discretion of your bank manager.* PHRASE

discretionary /dɪskreʃənə³riː/ matters are not fixed by rules but are decided by the people in authority. EG *The University has funds for discretionary awards in special cases.* ADJ CLASSIF

Which word on these pages is spelled differently in British English and American English?

discriminate /dɪskrɪmɪneɪt/, **discriminates,** v : OFT +
discriminating, discriminated. 1 If you can **dis-** between
criminate between two things, you can recognize
and understand the difference between them. EG
...to discriminate between right and wrong.

2 To **discriminate** against someone or in favour of v : OFT
them means to unfairly treat them worse or better +against/
than other people. EG *The law discriminated* favour of
against women.

discriminating /dɪskrɪmɪneɪtɪŋ/. Someone who ADJ QUALIT
is **discriminating** recognizes and likes things that
are of good quality. EG *We offer choices to discrimi-*
nating readers.

discrimination /dɪskrɪmɪneɪʃə⁰n/ is **1** the prac- N UNCOUNT :
tice of unfairly treating someone worse or better USU + SUPP
than other people. EG *...discrimination against wom-*
en. **2** the ability to recognize and understand the N UNCOUNT :
difference between two things. EG *...discrimination* USU + SUPP
between the important and the trivial problems. **3** N UNCOUNT
the ability to recognize and like things that are of
good quality. EG *There was in Julie a coarseness*
and a lack of discrimination.

discursive /dɪskɜːsɪv/. If speech or writing is ADJ QUALIT
discursive, the ideas in it are not carefully ar- Formal
ranged and include unnecessary details. EG *They*
complained that my writing was becoming too
discursive.

discus /dɪskəs/, **discuses.** A **discus** is a heavy, N COUNT
circular object that is thrown as a sport.

discuss /dɪskʌs/, **discusses, discussing, dis-** v+o
cussed. If you **discuss** something, you talk about it
seriously with other people. EG *They said they had*
an important matter to discuss with you.

discussion /dɪskʌʃə⁰n/, **discussions. 1 Discus-** N UNCOUNT
sion is the act of talking seriously about something
with other people. EG *Ten hours were spent in*
discussion of Boon's papers... There was much
discussion between those inside and outside the
party.

2 A **discussion** is a serious conversation between N COUNT
people. EG *I had been involved in discussions about*
this with Ken and Frank... We're having a discus-
sion on leisure activities.

3 If something is **under discussion,** it is being PHRASE
talked about and no decision about it has been
reached yet. EG *...the weapons system under discus-*
sion.

disdain /dɪsdeɪn/, **disdains, disdaining, dis-**
dained. 1 If you feel **disdain** for someone or N UNCOUNT :
something, you think that they have little value or OFT + for
importance. EG *He spoke of the rebels with disdain.* Formal

◊ **disdainful** /dɪsdeɪnful/. EG *They tend to be* ◊ ADJ QUALIT
disdainful of their colleagues. ◊ **disdainfully.** EG ◊ ADV
She looked away disdainfully.

2 If you **disdain** something or **disdain** to do v+o OR
something, you reject it or refuse to do it because V + to-INF
you think that it is not important or is not good Formal
enough for you. EG *...disdaining the help of his son...*
Claire disdained to reply.

disease /dɪziːz/, **diseases. 1** A **disease** is an N COUNT OR
illness in living things that is caused by infection or N UNCOUNT
by a fault inside them. EG *I have a rare eye*
disease... ...conditions that cause disease and star-
vation.

2 You can refer to an attitude or habit that you N COUNT + SUPP
consider to be unnatural or harmful as a **disease.**
EG *You've caught the disease of the profession,*
suspicion.

diseased /dɪziːzd/. **1** Someone or something that is ADJ CLASSIF
diseased is affected by a disease. EG *...an old*
diseased tree.

2 If you say that someone has a **diseased** mind, ADJ QUALIT
you mean that they have strange or shocking ideas.

disembark /dɪsɪmbɑːk/, **disembarks, disem-** v : OFT + from
barking, disembarked. When you **disembark** Formal
from a ship or aeroplane, you get off it at the end of
your journey.

disenchanted /dɪsɪntʃɑːntɪd/. If you are **disen-** ADJ QUALIT
chanted with something, you no longer think that Formal

it is good or worthwhile. EG *Some young people are*
disenchanted with school.

disenchantment /dɪsɪntʃɑːntmə⁰nt/ is the feeling N UNCOUNT
of being disappointed with something and no long- Formal
er thinking that it is good or worthwhile. EG *...public*
disenchantment with the war.

disengage /dɪsɪ⁰ngeɪdʒ/, **disengages,** v+o OR
disengaging, disengaged. If you **disengage** V-REFL :
things that are connected, you separate them. EG OFT + from
Don't break or disengage the rope... Melanie at- Formal
tempted to disengage her arms from his grip... He
disengaged himself and jumped up.

disentangle /dɪsɪ⁰ntæŋgə⁰l/, **disentangles, dis-** v+o OR
entangling, disentangled. If you **disentangle** V-REFL :
something, you separate it from other things that it OFT + from
has become mixed with or attached to. EG *She*
disentangled her jacket from the coat-hanger...
Tom disentangled himself himself from his wife's
arms.

disfavour /dɪsfeɪvə/; spelled **disfavor** in American English.

Disfavour is **1** dislike or disapproval of someone N UNCOUNT :
or something. EG *...looking with disfavour at the* USU + POSS
glass in his hand. **2** the state of being disliked or N UNCOUNT
disapproved of by someone in authority. EG *He was*
in disfavour with his employer.

disfigure /dɪsfɪgə/, **disfigures, disfiguring, dis-** v+o : USU PASS
figured. To **disfigure** someone or something Formal
means to spoil their appearance. EG *His nose was*
disfigured in an accident.

disgrace /dɪsgreɪs/, **disgraces, disgracing, dis-**
graced. 1 Disgrace is a state in which people N UNCOUNT
disapprove of someone or stop respecting them. EG
My uncle brought disgrace on the family. ● If ● PHRASE
someone is **in disgrace,** other people disapprove
of them or stop respecting them. EG *He was sent*
back to his village in disgrace.

2 You say that something is a **disgrace** when you N SING : a + N
find it totally unacceptable. EG *They are destroying*
the country - it's a disgrace!

3 You say that someone is a **disgrace** to someone N SING :
else when their behaviour makes the other person a + N + to
feel ashamed. EG *You're a disgrace to the Italians.*

4 If you **disgrace** someone, you behave in a way v+o OR V-REFL
that causes them to be disapproved of by other
people. EG *Fanny disgraced herself in London.*

disgraceful /dɪsgreɪsful/. If you say that some- ADJ CLASSIF
thing is **disgraceful,** you think it is totally unacceptable. EG *...the disgraceful state of the prisons.*

◊ **disgracefully.** EG *She behaved disgracefully.* ◊ ADV

disgruntled /dɪsgrʌntə⁰ld/. If you are **disgrun-** ADJ QUALIT
tled, you are cross and dissatisfied about something. EG *The disgruntled passengers were guided*
to another plane.

disguise /dɪsgaɪz/, **disguises, disguising, dis-**
guised. 1 A **disguise** is clothing or a change in N COUNT
your appearance that is intended to prevent people
from recognizing you. EG *...the disguise he wore*
when he escaped.

2 If you are **in disguise,** you have changed your PHRASE
clothes or appearance to prevent people recognizing you. EG *The Emperor came aboard the ship in*
disguise.

3 If you **disguise** yourself or if you **are disguised** V-REFL :
as someone else, you dress like them and behave OFT + as
like them in order to deceive other people. EG *I*
disguised myself as a French priest.

4 If you **disguise** something, **4.1** you change it so v+o
that people do not recognize it. EG *He tried to*
disguise his voice. **4.2** you prevent other people
knowing about it. EG *It proved difficult to disguise*
her anxiety.

disgust /dɪsgʌst/, **disgusts, disgusting, disgust-**
ed. 1 Disgust is a feeling of strong dislike or N UNCOUNT
disapproval. EG *Many expressed disgust at the use*
of such weapons. ● If you do something **in disgust,** ● PHRASE
you do it because of a strong feeling of dislike or
disapproval. EG *He returned downstairs in disgust.*

2 Something that **disgusts** you causes you to have v+o a strong feeling of dislike or disapproval. EG *The attitudes of the tourists disgusted him even more.*

disgusted /dɪsgʌstɪ²d/. If you are **disgusted**, you have a strong feeling of dislike or disapproval. EG *She was disgusted with herself.* ADJ QUALIT

disgusting /dɪsgʌstɪŋ/. If you say that something is **disgusting**, you mean that it is extremely unpleasant. EG *The food was disgusting... ...his disgusting behaviour.* ◊ **disgustingly.** EG *She was disgustingly fat.* ADJ QUALIT ◊ SUBMOD

dish /dɪʃ/, **dishes, dishing, dished. 1** A **dish** is **1.1** a shallow container used for cooking or serving food. **1.2** food that is prepared in a particular style or combination. EG *...the traditional British dish of eggs and bacon.* N COUNT N COUNT : USU+SUPP

2 The **dishes** are all the objects that have been used to cook, serve, and eat a meal. EG *Rudolph stayed to dry the dishes after his mother had washed them.* ● If you **do the dishes**, you wash the objects that have been used to cook, serve, and eat a meal. N PLURAL : USU the+N ● PHRASE

dish out. If you **dish out** something, you give it to people. EG *...dishing out presents at Christmas.* PHRASAL VB : V+O+ADV

dish up. If you **dish up** food, you serve it to people. PHRASAL VB : V+O+ADV

dishcloth /dɪʃklɒθ/, **dishcloths.** A **dishcloth** is a cloth that you use for washing objects that have been used to cook, serve, and eat a meal. N COUNT

disheartened /dɪshɑːtə⁰nd/. If you are **disheartened**, you feel disappointed and have less hope or confidence. EG *He became disheartened after losing the money.* ADJ QUALIT Formal

disheartening /dɪshɑːtə⁰nɪŋ/. If something is **disheartening**, it makes you feel disappointed and have less hope or confidence. EG *Such a defeat is inevitably disheartening.* ADJ QUALIT Formal

dishevelled /dɪʃɛvə⁰ld/; spelled **disheveled** in American English. If someone is **dishevelled**, their appearance is very untidy. EG *...dirty and dishevelled travellers.* ADJ QUALIT

dishonest /dɪsɒnɪ³st/. **1** Someone who is **dishonest** lies, cheats, or does illegal things, and cannot be trusted. ◊ **dishonesty** /dɪsɒnə³stiˈ/. EG *The moneylender dare not admit his dishonesty.* ADJ QUALIT ◊ N UNCOUNT

2 A **dishonest** action involves lying, cheating, or doing illegal things. EG *It would be dishonest to claim that.* ADJ QUALIT

dishonour /dɪsɒnə/, **dishonours, dishonouring, dishonoured;** spelled **dishonor** in American English.

1 Dishonour is a state in which people disapprove of you and have no respect for you. EG *There are men who prefer death to dishonour.* N UNCOUNT Formal

2 If you **dishonour** someone, you do something that causes people to disapprove of them and to have no respect for them. EG *He taught her never to dishonour her family.* V+O Formal

dishwasher /dɪʃwɒʃə/, **dishwashers.** A **dishwasher** is a machine that washes objects that have been used to cook, serve, and eat a meal. N COUNT

disillusion /dɪsə¹luːʒə⁰n/, **disillusions, disillusioning, disillusioned. 1** If something **disillusions** you, it makes you feel disappointed because it is not as good as you expected. EG *They were bitterly disillusioned by the performance.* ◊ **disillusioning.** EG *...the disillusioning failure of the unit.* V+O ◊ ADJ QUALIT

2 Disillusion is the same as disillusionment. EG *...her growing disillusion with her husband.* N UNCOUNT

disillusioned /dɪsə¹luːʒə⁰nd/. If you are **disillusioned**, you feel disappointed because someone or something is not as good as you expected. EG *My father was thoroughly disillusioned with me.* ADJ QUALIT

disillusionment /dɪsə¹luːʒə⁰nmə²nt/ is a feeling of disappointment that you have when you discover that something is not as good as you expected it to be. EG *...public disillusionment with politics.* N UNCOUNT

disinclination /dɪsɪnklɪneɪʃə⁰n/ is a feeling that you do not want to do something. EG *...a disinclination to go out on winter evenings.* N UNCOUNT USU+to-INF

disinclined /dɪsɪnklaɪnd/. If you are **disinclined** to do something, you do not want to do it. EG *He was disinclined to talk about that.* ADJ PRED : USU+to-INF

disinfect /dɪsɪnfɛkt/, **disinfects, disinfecting, disinfected.** If you **disinfect** something, you clean it using a liquid that kills germs. EG *Wash the cuts and disinfect them.* V+O

disinfectant /dɪsɪnfɛktənt/ is a liquid which contains chemicals that kill germs. N MASS

disinherit /dɪsɪnhɛrɪt/, **disinherits, disinheriting, disinherited.** If someone **disinherits** their son or daughter, they legally arrange that, when they die, the son or daughter will not receive any of their money or property. V+O Formal

disintegrate /dɪsɪntɪ²greɪt/, **disintegrates, disintegrating, disintegrated. 1** If an object **disintegrates**, it breaks into many small pieces. EG *There was an explosion and the boat disintegrated.* V

2 If a relationship or organization **disintegrates**, it becomes very weak and unsuccessful. EG *They had seen marriages disintegrate under such pressure.* V :OFT+A

◊ **disintegration** /dɪsɪntɪ²greɪʃə⁰n/. EG *...the disintegration of the army.* ◊ N UNCOUNT

disinterest /dɪsɪntə⁰rɪ³st/ is a lack of interest or enthusiasm. EG *...the Government's disinterest in conservation.* N UNCOUNT

disinterested /dɪsɪntə⁰rɪ³stɪ²d/. Someone who is **disinterested** is **1** not involved in a situation and can make fair decisions or judgments about it. EG *I'm a disinterested observer.* **2** not interested in something. Some people think that it is not correct to use **disinterested** with this meaning. EG *Her mother had always been a little disinterested in her, preferring her brother's company.* ADJ QUALIT ADJ QUALIT

disjointed /dɪsdʒɔɪntɪ²d/ words or ideas are not connected in a sensible way and are difficult to understand. EG *...a number of disjointed statements.* ADJ QUALIT

disk /dɪsk/. See **disc.**

dislike /dɪslaɪk/, **dislikes, disliking, disliked. 1** If you **dislike** someone or something, you think that they are unpleasant and do not like them. EG *I dislike him intensely.* V+O

2 Dislike is the feeling of not liking someone or something. EG *...their dislike of authority.* N UNCOUNT : OFT+of/for

3 If you **take a dislike to** someone or something, you begin to dislike them. EG *This caused Brody to take an instant dislike to the man.* PHRASE

4 Your **dislikes** are the things that you do not like. EG *She has her likes and dislikes, as we all have.* N PLURAL

dislocate /dɪslə²keɪt/, **dislocates, dislocating, dislocated. 1** If you **dislocate** a part of your body, it is forced out of its normal position and causes you pain. EG *I had a nasty fall and dislocated my arm.* V+O

2 If a process **is dislocated**, something stops it from continuing normally. EG *The accident had dislocated the flow of vehicles.* ◊ **dislocation** /dɪslə²keɪʃə⁰n/. EG *...the serious dislocation to business.* V+O Formal ◊ N UNCOUNT

dislodge /dɪslɒdʒ/, **dislodges, dislodging, dislodged.** To **dislodge** someone or something from a place means to cause them to move from it. EG *Burr put his feet on the table, dislodging papers and books.* V+O

disloyal /dɪslɔɪə⁰l/. If you are **disloyal** to your friends, family, or country, you do not support them. EG *You wanted me to be disloyal to Gareth.* ◊ **disloyalty** /dɪslɔɪə⁰lti¹/. EG *...Haldane's disloyalty to the nation.* ADJ QUALIT OFT+to ◊ N UNCOUNT : OFT+to

dismal /dɪzmə⁰l/. Something that is **dismal 1** is rather unattractive and depressing. EG *...one dark, dismal day.* ◊ **dismally.** EG *It's a dismally dull* ADJ QUALIT ◊ ADV+ADJ

What is the difference between 'dishevelled' and 'disordered'?

place. **2** is unsuccessful and makes people lose ADJ QUALIT
hope or confidence. EG *Their record over the last
decade has been dismal.*

dismantle /dɪsmæntə⁰l/, **dismantles,** v+o
dismantling, dismantled. If you **dismantle** a
machine or structure, you separate it into its parts.
EG *The gun had to be dismantled and carried.*

dismay /dɪsmeɪ/, **dismays, dismaying, dis-**
mayed. 1 Dismay is a strong feeling of fear, N UNCOUNT
worry, or disappointment. EG *I realised with dismay
that he had gone... To their dismay, few companies
were keen... They looked at each other in dismay.*

2 If something **dismays** you, it makes you feel v+o
afraid, worried, or disappointed. ◇ **dismayed.** EG ◇ ADJ QUALIT
Barbara seemed dismayed at my views.

◇ **dismaying.** EG *...the dismaying complexity of the* ◇ ADJ QUALIT
problems.

dismember /dɪsmembə/, **dismembers, dis-** v+o
membering, dismembered. To **dismember** a Formal
person or animal means to tear their body to
pieces. EG *...a wild animal dismembering its prey.*

dismiss /dɪsmɪs/, **dismisses, dismissing, dis-** v+o
missed. 1 If you **dismiss** someone or something,
1.1 you decide or say that they are not important
or not good enough. EG *This plan was dismissed as
foolish.* **1.2** you stop thinking about them. EG *She
dismissed him from her mind.*

2 If you **are dismissed** from your job, your v+o : USU PASS
employers get rid of you. EG *They were dismissed
for refusing to join a union.*

3 If someone in authority **dismisses** you, they give v+o
you permission to go away. EG *Dismissing the other
children, she told me to wait.*

dismissal /dɪsmɪsə⁰l/, **dismissals. Dismissal** is
1 the act of getting rid of an employee. EG *They* N UNCOUNT
discussed the dismissal of a teacher... ...a tribunal OR N COUNT
dealing with unfair dismissals. **2** the act of stating N UNCOUNT
that someone or something is not important or not
good enough. EG *...this dismissal of the computer's
potential.*

dismissive /dɪsmɪsɪv/. If you are **dismissive** of ADJ QUALIT :
someone or something, your attitude indicates that OFT+*of*
you think they are not important or not good Formal
enough. EG *She is dismissive of the school.*

dismount /dɪsmaʊnt/, **dismounts, dismounting,** v : OFT+*from*
dismounted. If you **dismount** from a horse or a Formal
vehicle, you get down from it. EG *The police officer
dismounted from his bicycle.*

disobedience /dɪsə⁶biːdɪəns/ is deliberately not N UNCOUNT
doing what a person in authority or a rule says that
you should do. EG *She would tolerate no argument
or disobedience.*

disobedient /dɪsə⁶biːdɪənt/. If you are **disobedi-** ADJ QUALIT
ent, you deliberately do not do what a person in
authority or a rule says that you should do. EG *...a
disobedient child.*

disobey /dɪsə⁶beɪ/, **disobeys, disobeying, dis-** v+o OR V
obeyed. If you **disobey** a person in authority or an
order, you deliberately do not do what you have
been told to do. EG *It never occurred to them that
they could disobey their parents... If he disobeys,
he will be killed.*

disorder /dɪsɔːdə/, **disorders. 1** Something that is N UNCOUNT
in **disorder 1.1** is very untidy. EG *The room was in
dreadful disorder.* **1.2** is badly prepared or badly
organized. EG *They rushed after them in disorder.*

2 Disorder is a situation in which many people N UNCOUNT
behave violently. EG *...a serious risk of public disorder.*

3 A **disorder** is a problem or illness which affects N COUNT OR
a person's mind or body. EG *...painful stomach* N UNCOUNT :
disorders. USU+SUPP

disordered /dɪsɔːdəd/. **1** Something that is **disor-** ADJ QUALIT
dered is untidy and not neatly arranged. EG *...the
small disordered room.*

2 Someone who is mentally **disordered** has an ADJ CLASSIF
illness which affects their mind. EG *...the care of
mentally disordered patients.*

disorderly /dɪsɔːdəli¹/. **1** Something that is **disor-** ADJ QUALIT
derly is very untidy. EG *...their disorderly bedroom.*

2 People who are **disorderly** behave in an uncon- ADJ QUALIT
trolled or violent way. EG *...disorderly assemblies of
soldiers.*

disorganized /dɪsɔːgənaɪzd/; also spelled **disor-**
ganised. 1 Something that is **disorganized** is in a ADJ QUALIT
confused and badly prepared state. EG *Everything
was disorganised because he had got back late.*

2 If you are **disorganized,** you do not plan or ADJ QUALIT
arrange things well. EG *She is inclined to be disorganised and indecisive.*

disorientated /dɪsɔːrɪə⁰nteɪtɪ²d/ means the same ADJ QUALIT
as disoriented. EG *I stood there, feeling disorientated.*

disorientation /dɪsɔːrɪə⁰nteɪʃə⁰n/ is a feeling of N UNCOUNT
extreme confusion.

disoriented /dɪsɔːrɪə⁰ntɪ²d/. If you are **disorient-** ADJ QUALIT
ed, you are confused or lost and are not sure where
you are. EG *I woke up that afternoon, totally disoriented.*

disown /dɪsəʊn/, **disowns, disowning, dis-** v+o
owned. If you **disown** someone or something, you
formally end your connection with them. EG *If it
happened again her family would disown her.*

disparage /dɪspærɪdʒ/, **disparages, disparag-** v+o
ing, disparaged. If you **disparage** someone or Formal
something, you talk about them with disapproval
or lack of respect. ◇ **disparagement** ◇ N UNCOUNT
/dɪspærɪdʒmə⁰nt/. EG *...Bernstein's disparagement
of the myth.*

disparaging /dɪspærɪdʒɪŋ/. A **disparaging** re- ADJ QUALIT
mark or comment is critical and scornful of someone or something. EG *The newspaper had made
disparaging remarks about his wife.*

◇ **disparagingly.** EG *She spoke disparagingly of* ◇ ADV
the new house.

disparate /dɪspərə¹t/ is used to describe things ADJ QUALIT
that are very different from each other. EG *...dispar-* Formal
*ate social groups... ...a range of entirely disparate
reasons.*

disparity /dɪspærɪ²ti¹/, **disparities.** A **disparity** N COUNT OR
between things is a surprising or unfair difference N UNCOUNT :
between them. EG *...the disparity between rich and* OFT+
poor... ...the regional disparities in unemployment. *between/in*
Formal

dispassionate /dɪspæʃə⁰nə¹t/. Someone who is ADJ QUALIT
dispassionate is calm, reasonable, and not influenced by their emotions. EG *...a dispassionate observer.* ◇ **dispassionately.** EG *I shall judge your* ◇ ADV
problems dispassionately.

dispatch /dɪspætʃ/, **dispatches, dispatching,**
dispatched; also spelled **despatch** in British English.

1 If you **dispatch** someone or something to a v+o : USU+A
place, you send them there. EG *Troops were dis-* Formal
patched to the north coast.

2 A **dispatch** is an official report that is sent to a N COUNT
person or organization by their representative in Formal
another place. EG *...a dispatch from their office in
Rome.*

dispel /dɪspel/, **dispels, dispelling, dispelled.** To v+o
dispel an idea or feeling that someone has means
to stop them believing in it or feeling it. EG *Jenny
tried to dispel her illusions... All such doubts were
now dispelled.*

dispensable /dɪspensəbə⁰l/. Someone or some- ADJ QUALIT
thing that is **dispensable** is not really needed. EG
These were dispensable luxuries.

dispensation /dɪspenseɪʃə⁰n/, **dispensations.** A N COUNT OR
dispensation is special permission to do some- N UNCOUNT
thing that is normally not allowed. EG *For centuries* Formal
royal dispensation was required to hunt here.

dispense /dɪspens/, **dispenses, dispensing, dis-**
pensed. 1 To **dispense** something means to give it v+o
to people. EG *...a clinic at which advice was dis-* Formal
pensed.

2 Someone who **dispenses** medicine prepares it v+o
and gives it to people. EG *...a dispensing chemist.*

dispense with. If you **dispense with** some- PHRASAL VB :
V+PREP

thing, you stop using it or get rid of it because you no longer need it. EG *We decided to dispense with the services of Mrs Baggot.*

dispenser /dɪspensə/, **dispensers.** A **dispenser** N COUNT+SUPP is a machine or container from which you can get things. EG *...cash dispensers... ...paper napkins from the dispenser.*

disperse /dɪspɜːs/, **disperses, dispersing, dispersed.** 1 When a group of people **disperse** or V-ERG when someone **disperses** them, they go away in different directions. EG *Police used tear gas to disperse the mob.*

2 When something **disperses** or when you **dis-** V-ERG **perse** it, it spreads over a wide area. EG *Most of the pieces had dispersed.*

dispirited /dɪspɪrɪtɪd/. If you are **dispirited**, you ADJ QUALIT have lost your confidence or enthusiasm.

displace /dɪspleɪs/, **displaces, displacing, displaced.** 1 If one thing **displaces** another, it forces V+O : the other thing out of its position and occupies that NO IMPER position itself. EG *London displaced Antwerp as the commercial capital of Europe.*

2 If someone is **displaced**, they are forced to V+O : move away from the area or country where they NO IMPER live. ◊ **displacement** /dɪspleɪsmənt/. EG *...the* ◊ N UNCOUNT *displacement of large masses of people.*

display /dɪspleɪ/, **displays, displaying, displayed.** 1 If you **display** something, you put it in a V+O place where people can easily see it. EG *...a small museum where they could display the collection.* ▶ used as a noun. EG *He has all his tools on display.* ▶ N UNCOUNT

2 If you **display** a quality or emotion, you behave V+O in a way which shows that you have it. EG *...the hostility displayed by trade unions.* ▶ used as a ▶ N COUNT : noun. EG *...a spontaneous display of affection.* USU+SUPP

3 A **display** is 3.1 an arrangement of things that is N COUNT : intended to attract people's attention. EG *...displays* USU+SUPP *of sausages and cheese.* 3.2 a public event that is intended to entertain people. EG *...a firework display.*

displease /dɪspliːz/, **displeases, displeasing,** V+O **displeased.** If someone or something **displeases** you, you make them dissatisfied, annoyed, or upset. EG *What he saw did not displease him.*

◊ **displeased.** EG *'Why are you displeased with* ◊ ADJ PRED *me?' I pleaded.* +with

displeasure /dɪspleʒə/ is a feeling of dissatisfac- N UNCOUNT tion or annoyance. EG *Professor Aitken looked at me with displeasure.*

disposable /dɪspəʊzəbəl/. Something that is **dis-** ADJ CLASSIF **posable** is designed to be thrown away after it has been used. EG *...disposable nappies... ...disposable paper tissues.*

disposal /dɪspəʊzəl/. 1 If you have something **at** PHRASE your **disposal**, you can use it at any time and for any purpose. EG *...a cottage put at her disposal by a friend.*

2 **Disposal** is the act of getting rid of something. EG N UNCOUNT : *...the safe disposal of radioactive waste.* USU+SUPP

dispose /dɪspəʊz/, **disposes, disposing, dis-** PHRASAL VB : **posed.** If you **dispose of** something that you no V+PREP, longer want or need, you get rid of it, for example HAS PASS by throwing it away or by selling it. EG *He could dispose of the house and car.*

disposed /dɪspəʊzd/. 1 If you are **disposed** to do ADJ PRED something, you are willing to do it. EG *He seemed* +to-INF *disposed to chat.* Formal

2 If you are **well disposed** to someone, you feel PHRASE friendly towards them. Formal

disposition /dɪspəzɪʃən/, **dispositions.** 1 Some- N COUNT one's **disposition** is their character or mood. EG *Waddell was of a cheerful disposition.*

2 If you show a **disposition** to do something, you N UNCOUNT show a willingness to do it or a tendency to do it. EG +to-INF *Adam showed no disposition to move... Dixon had* Formal *been showing a disposition to tremble and stagger.*

dispossess /dɪspəzes/, **dispossesses, dispos-** V+O : USU PASS **sessing, dispossessed.** If you are **dispossessed**

of land or property, it is taken away from you. EG *Landowners could not be legally dispossessed.*

disproportionate /dɪsprəpɔːʃənət/. Something ADJ QUALIT that is **disproportionate** is surprising or unreasonable in amount or size. EG *A disproportionate number of people die shortly after retiring.*

◊ **disproportionately.** EG *There were dispropor-* ◊ ADV *tionately high costs.*

disprove /dɪspruːv/, **disproves, disproving, dis-** V+O OR **proved.** If you **disprove** an idea or belief, you V+REPORT show that it is not true. EG *They can neither prove* ONLY that *nor disprove that it is genuine.*

dispute, disputes, disputing, disputed; pro- nounced /dɪspjuːt/ when it is a noun and /dɪspjuːt/ when it is a verb.

1 A **dispute** is a disagreement or quarrel between N COUNT OR people or groups. EG *...disputes between unions and* N UNCOUNT *employers... There is some dispute about this.*

2 If people are **in dispute**, they disagree with each PHRASE other. EG *We're not really in dispute over this, actually.*

3 If something is **in dispute**, people disagree about PHRASE it.

4 If you **dispute** an opinion or action, you say that V+O OR you think it is untrue or incorrect. EG *I don't dispute* V+REPORT *that children need love.* ◊ **disputed.** EG *...a disput-* ◊ ADJ CLASSIF *ed decision.*

5 When people or animals **dispute** something, they V+O fight for control of it. EG *They continued to dispute the ownership of the territory.* ◊ **disputed.** EG ◊ ADJ CLASSIF *...the disputed provinces.*

disqualify /dɪskwɒlɪfaɪ/, **disqualifies, disquali-** V+O : **fying, disqualified.** If someone **is disqualified,** USU PASS+ they are officially stopped from doing something from because they have broken a law or rule. EG *Seven of them were disqualified from driving.*

◊ **disqualification** /dɪskwɒlɪfɪkeɪʃən/, **disquali-** ◊ N UNCOUNT **fications.** EG *He is liable to disqualification from all* OR N COUNT *official events.*

disquiet /dɪskwaɪət/ is a feeling of worry or N UNCOUNT anxiety. EG *Many physicists expressed extreme* Formal *disquiet about the idea.*

disregard /dɪsrɪgɑːd/, **disregards, disregard-** V+O **ing, disregarded.** If you **disregard** something, you ignore it or do not consider it seriously. EG *Men who disregarded the warning were beaten severely.* ▶ used as a noun. EG *The centre was built with* ▶ N UNCOUNT : *an obvious disregard for cost.* OFT+for/of

disrepair /dɪsrɪpeə/. If something is in **disre-** PHRASE **pair**, it is broken or has not been looked after Formal properly. EG *His cycle is in disrepair.*

disreputable /dɪsrepjʊtəbəl/. If someone or ADJ QUALIT something is **disreputable**, they are considered to be not respectable or not to be trusted. EG *...Ash and his disreputable friends.*

disrepute /dɪsrɪpjuːt/. If something is brought PHRASE **into disrepute** or falls **into disrepute**, it loses its Formal good reputation and is disapproved of. EG *He brought his profession into disrepute.*

disrespect /dɪsrɪspekt/. If someone shows **disre-** N UNCOUNT : **spect** for a person, law, or custom, they do not OFT+for behave in a correct or acceptable way.

◊ **disrespectful** /dɪsrɪspektfʊl/. EG *They are* ◊ ADJ QUALIT *arrogant and disrespectful to me.*

disrupt /dɪsrʌpt/, **disrupts, disrupting, dis-** V+O **rupted.** To **disrupt** an activity or system means to prevent it from continuing normally. EG *...attempts to disrupt meetings organized by their opponents.*

◊ **disruption** /dɪsrʌpʃən/, **disruptions.** EG *...the* ◊ N COUNT OR *disruption of rail communications... ...disruptions in* N UNCOUNT *routine.* ◊ **disruptive** /dɪsrʌptɪv/. EG *...children* ◊ ADJ QUALIT *who are disruptive in school.*

dissatisfaction /dɪsætɪsfækʃən/. If you feel **dis-** N UNCOUNT : **satisfaction** with something, you are not content- OFT+with ed or are not pleased with it. EG *There is wide-*

Find five words on these pages which mean the opposite if you take off the prefix 'dis-'.

spread *dissatisfaction with the existing political parties.*

dissatisfied /dɪssætɪsfaɪd/. If you are **dissatis-** ADJ QUALIT:
fied, you are not contented, or are not pleased with USU PRED
something. EG *All of them had been dissatisfied with* +with
their lives.

dissect /dɪˈsɛkt/, **dissects**, **dissecting**, **dissect-** v+o
ed. If someone **dissects** the body of a dead person
or animal, they cut it up carefully in order to
examine it. ◊ **dissection** /dɪˈsɛkʃəⁿn/. EG *...the* ◊ N UNCOUNT
dissection of the earthworm.

disseminate /dɪsɛmɪneɪt/, **disseminates**, **dis-** v+o
seminating, **disseminated**. To **disseminate** in- Formal
formation means to distribute it to many people. EG
...disseminating information among the villages.
◊ **dissemination** /dɪsɛmɪneɪʃəⁿn/. EG *...the printing* ◊ N UNCOUNT:
and dissemination of news. USU+SUPP

dissension /dɪsɛnʃəⁿn/ is disagreement and argu- N UNCOUNT
ment. EG *It would create dissension in the home.* Formal

dissent /dɪsɛnt/, **dissents**, **dissenting**, **dis-**
sented. 1 **Dissent** is strong disagreement with N UNCOUNT
established ideas. EG *Healthy societies can tolerate* Formal
dissent.
2 If someone **dissents**, they express strong dis- v
agreement with established ideas. EG *...anyone dis-* Formal
senting from the prevailing view. ◊ **dissenting**. EG ◊ ADJ CLASSIF:
There have been dissenting voices. ATTRIB

dissenter /dɪsɛntə/, **dissenters**. A **dissenter** is N COUNT
someone who expresses disagreement with estab- Formal
lished ideas. EG *...political and religious dissenters.*

dissertation /dɪsəteɪʃəⁿn/, **dissertations**. A **dis-** N COUNT
sertation is a long, formal piece of writing on a Formal
particular subject, especially for a university degree. EG *She wrote a dissertation on industrial
development.*

disservice /dɪsˈsɜːvɪs/. If you do someone a **dis-** N COUNT:
service, you do something that harms them. EG USU SING+to
They are guilty of a disservice to their community. Formal

dissident /dɪsɪdəⁿnt/, **dissidents**. A **dissident** is N COUNT
someone who criticizes their government or or- Formal
ganization. EG *...political dissidents.*

dissimilar /dɪsɪmɪlə/. If two things are **dissimi-** ADJ QUALIT:
lar, they are different from each other. EG *...a* OFT+to
proposal not dissimilar to that now adopted by the Formal
Government.

dissipate /dɪsɪpeɪt/, **dissipates**, **dissipating**, **dis-**
sipated. 1 If something **dissipates** or is **dissipat-** V-ERG
ed by something else, it gradually becomes less or Formal
disappears. EG *The heat was dissipated by cooling
systems.*
2 If someone **dissipates** money, time, or effort, v+o
they waste it in a foolish way. EG *He rapidly* Formal
dissipated his fortune.

dissociate /dɪsˈəʊʃɪeɪt, -sɪ-/, **dissociates**, **dissoci-**
ating, **dissociated**. 1 If you **dissociate** yourself V-REFL+from
from someone or something, you try to deny or end
any connection with them. EG *He did all he could to
dissociate himself from the Government.*
2 If you **dissociate** one thing from another, you v+o+from
consider the two things separately. EG *It is often
difficult to dissociate cause from effect.*

dissolution /dɪsəluːʃəⁿn/. The **dissolution** of an N UNCOUNT:
organization or legal relationship is the act of OFT+SUPP
officially ending it. EG *...the dissolution of the village* Formal
council.

dissolve /dɪzɒlv/, **dissolves**, **dissolving**, **dis-**
solved. 1 If you **dissolve** a solid substance or if it V-ERG
dissolves, you mix it with a liquid until it disappears. EG *Dissolve the sugar in the water.*
2 To **dissolve** an organization or legal relationship v+o
means to officially end it. EG *They wish to dissolve* Formal
their union with the United States.

dissolve in or **dissolve into**. If you **dissolve** PHRASAL VB:
into tears or laughter, you begin to cry or laugh, V+PREP
because you cannot control yourself. EG *Kiri dis-* Literary
solved in tears.

dissuade /dɪsweɪd/, **dissuades**, **dissuading**, **dis-** v+o:
suaded. If you **dissuade** someone from doing OFT+from
Formal

something, you persuade them not to do it. EG *I
tried to dissuade David from going.*

distance /dɪstəⁿns/, **distances**, **distancing**, **dis-**
tanced. 1 The **distance** between two places is the N COUNT OR
amount of space between them. EG *The town is* N UNCOUNT
some distance from the sea... Farmers were travel- +SUPP
ling long distances to get supplies.
2 **Distance** is the fact of being far away from N UNCOUNT
something in space or time. EG *...cut off from the
next community by distance.*
3 If you are **at a distance** from something, or if PHRASE
you see it or remember it **from a distance**, you
are a long way away from it in space or time. EG
From a distance, he heard Jack's whisper.
4 If you can hear or see something **in the dis-** PHRASE
tance, you can hear or see something that is far
away from you. EG *In the distance, she sees a cloud
of smoke.*
5 If something **distances** you from someone or v+o:
something, it causes you to feel less friendly to- OFT+from
wards them or less involved with them. EG *...dis-* Formal
tancing young people from their families.

distant /dɪstəⁿnt/. 1 Something that is **distant** is ADJ QUALIT
far away. EG *...a distant country... The planes were
distant from each other.*
2 An event or time that is **distant** is far away in ADJ QUALIT
the past or future. EG *He may return in the not too
distant future.*
3 A **distant** relative is one that you are not closely ADJ QUALIT
related to. ◊ **distantly**. EG *...an Italian family to* ◊ ADV
whom he was distantly related.
4 Someone who is **distant** is **4.1** unfriendly. EG ADJ QUALIT
Boylan was polite but distant. **4.2** not paying attention because they are thinking about something
else. EG *His eyes took on a distant look.*
◊ **distantly**. EG *Jennifer looked at herself, smiling* ◊ ADV AFTER
distantly. VB

distaste /dɪsteɪst/ is a feeling of dislike or disap- N SING+SUPP
proval. EG *She looked at him with distaste... ...his
distaste for money.*

distasteful /dɪsteɪstfʊl/. If you say that something ADJ QUALIT:
is **distasteful**, you dislike it or disapprove of it. EG OFT+to
...work that is distasteful to him.

distended /dɪstɛndɪ²d/. If a part of someone's ADJ QUALIT
body is **distended**, it is swollen and unnaturally Formal
large. EG *He had a grossly distended stomach.*

distil /dɪstɪl/, **distils**, **distilling**, **distilled**; spelled
distill in American English.
1 When a liquid **is distilled**, it is purified or v+o
concentrated by being heated until it becomes
steam and then being cooled until it becomes liquid
again. ◊ **distilled**. EG *Top up the car battery with* ◊ ADJ CLASSIF
distilled water. ◊ **distillation** /dɪstɪleɪʃəⁿn/. EG ◊ N UNCOUNT
Separate the alcohol from the water by distillation.
2 If you **distil** information from something, you v+o:
obtain it by careful study. EG *The record had been* OFT+from
distilled from conversations and correspondence. Formal

distinct /dɪstɪŋkt/. 1 If something is **distinct** from ADJ QUALIT:
another thing, there is an important difference OFT+from
between them. EG *Our interests were quite distinct
from those of the workers... The word is used in
three distinct senses.* ● If you refer to one thing **as** ● PREP
distinct from another, you are indicating exactly
which thing you mean by contrasting it with the
other. EG *...parliamentary (as distinct from presidential) systems.*
2 If something is **distinct**, you hear or see it ADJ QUALIT
clearly. EG *...a small but distinct voice.*
◊ **distinctly**. EG *Jones was distinctly seen at the* ◊ ADV
back door.
3 You can use **distinct** to emphasize that some- ADJ QUALIT:
thing is great enough in amount or degree to be ATTRIB
noticeable or important. EG *...a distinct possibility of
war.* ◊ **distinctly**. EG *...a distinctly different pic-* ◊ SUBMOD
ture.

distinction /dɪstɪŋkʃəⁿn/, **distinctions**. 1 A **dis-** N COUNT:OFT
tinction is a difference between similar things. EG +between
Remember the distinction between those words.
2 If you **draw** or **make a distinction** between two PHRASE

things, you say that the two things are different. EG
*I must make a distinction here between travellers
and tourists.*

3 Distinction is the quality of being excellent. EG N UNCOUNT
He is a man of distinction.

4 A **distinction** is also something that causes N UNCOUNT
someone to be respected or admired. EG *...the* OR N COUNT
distinction of being Gerran's son-in-law.

distinctive /dɪstɪŋktɪv/. Something that is **dis-** ADJ QUALIT
tinctive has special qualities that make it easily
recognizable. EG *Irene had a very distinctive voice.*
◊ **distinctively.** EG *...a distinctively African cul-* ◊ ADV
ture.

distinguish /dɪstɪŋgwɪʃ/, **distinguishes, distin-** V+O OR
guishing, distinguished. 1 If you can **distinguish** V+between
one thing from another, you can see or understand
the difference between them. EG *He had never been
capable of distinguishing between his friends and
his enemies... ...animals that cannot distinguish
colours.*

2 If a feature or quality **distinguishes** one thing V+O+from
from another, it causes the things to be recognized
as different. EG *...the characteristics that distinguish
birds from other animals.* ◊ **distinguishing.** EG *He* ◊ ADJ CLASSIF :
had no scars or distinguishing marks. ATTRIB

3 If you can **distinguish** something, you are just V+O
able to see it, hear it, or taste it. EG *The photograph
was poor and few details could be distinguished.*

4 If you **distinguish** yourself, you do something V-REFL
that causes other people to admire you. EG *...prison-
ers who had distinguished themselves in battle.*

distinguishable /dɪstɪŋgwɪʃəbəl/. If one thing is ADJ PRED :
distinguishable from another, you can see or OFT+from
understand the difference between them.

distinguished /dɪstɪŋgwɪʃt/. A **distinguished** ADJ QUALIT
person is very successful, famous or important. EG
...rushing to meet the distinguished visitors.

distort /dɪstɔːt/, **distorts, distorting, distorted. 1** V+O
To **distort** a fact or idea means to change it so
much that it becomes incorrect or untrue. EG
You're distorting his argument. ◊ **distorted.** EG ◊ ADJ QUALIT
They get a distorted picture of what's going on.
◊ **distortion** /dɪstɔːʃən/, **distortions.** EG *...this* ◊ N UNCOUNT
distortion of history... The report contained a num- OR N COUNT
ber of distortions.*

2 If something **distorts** or **is distorted**, it becomes V-ERG : USU
twisted into a different shape. EG *The objects were* PASS
scorched and distorted. ◊ **distorted.** EG *...her* ◊ ADJ QUALIT
distorted limbs. ◊ **distortion.** EG *...the distortion of* ◊ N UNCOUNT
his face. OR N COUNT

distract /dɪstrækt/, **distracts, distracting, dis-**
tracted. 1 If something **distracts** you or your V+O :
attention, it makes you stop concentrating on what OFT+from
you are doing. EG *It distracted them from their
work.* ◊ **distracting.** EG *...irrelevant or distracting* ◊ ADJ QUALIT
details.

2 If you try to **distract** someone, you try to stop V+O OR V-REFL
them feeling upset or worried. EG *Distract her with
a toy if you can.*

distracted /dɪstræktɪd/. If you are **distracted,** ADJ QUALIT
you are very worried or are thinking about some-
thing else. EG *During classes he was distracted and
strangely troubled.* ◊ **distractedly.** *She began* ◊ ADV
looking distractedly about her.*

distraction /dɪstrækʃən/, **distractions. 1** A **dis-**
traction is **1.1** something that takes your attention N COUNT OR
away from what you are doing. EG *It would be a* N UNCOUNT :
distraction from his political labours... She needed OFT+from
to work without interruption or distraction.* **1.2** an N COUNT OR
object or activity that is intended to entertain N UNCOUNT
people. EG *...the various distractions provided for
them.*

2 If someone or something **drives** you **to distrac-** PHRASE
tion, they annoy you continually. EG *They were
driven to distraction by the flies.*

distraught /dɪstrɔːt/. If someone is **distraught,** ADJ QUALIT
they are extremely upset or worried and cannot
think clearly. EG *'What can we do?' she asked,
turning a distraught face to me.*

distress /dɪstres/, **distresses, distressing, dis-** N UNCOUNT
tressed. 1 Distress is **1.1** extreme anxiety, sorrow, or pain. EG *Delays may cause distress to your
family... He was breathing fast and in obvious
distress.* **1.2** the state of being in extreme danger
and needing urgent help. EG *...an aircraft in distress... ...a distress signal.*

2 If someone or something **distresses** you, they V+O
cause you to be upset or worried. EG *I hate to
distress you like this, but it is important.*
◊ **distressing** /dɪstresɪŋ/. EG *It was a distressing* ◊ ADJ QUALIT
experience for me. ◊ **distressed** /dɪstrest/. EG *She* ◊ ADJ QUALIT
was distressed about having to leave home.

distribute /dɪstrɪbjuːt/, **distributes,**
distributing, distributed. 1 If you **distribute** V+O
things, you hand them to people. EG *The leaflets
were distributed by students.*

2 When goods **are distributed**, they are supplied V+O : USU+A
to the shops or businesses that use or sell them. EG
*They needed trucks to distribute their produce
over New York City.* ◊ **distribution** ◊ N SING : USU
/dɪstrɪbjuːʃən/. EG *...the manufacture and distribu-* the+N+OF
tion of products.

3 To **distribute** something also means to share it V+O
among the members of a group. EG *Profits should
be distributed between employers and workers.*
◊ **distribution.** EG *...a fairer distribution of wealth.* ◊ N UNCOUNT

distributor /dɪstrɪbjətə/, **distributors.** A **dis-** N COUNT
tributor is a person or company that supplies
goods to shops or other businesses.

district /dɪstrɪkt/, **districts.** A **district** is **1** an N COUNT+SUPP
area of a town or country. EG *...doctors in country
districts... ...a working class district of Paris.* **2** an
administrative area of a town or country. EG *...dis-
trict councils... ...the Southall district of London.*

distrust /dɪstrʌst/, **distrusts, distrusting, dis-** V+O
trusted. If you **distrust** someone or something,
you think that they are not honest, reliable, or safe.
EG *He keeps his savings under his mattress because
he distrusts the banks.* ► used as a noun. EG *...their* ► N UNCOUNT
distrust of politicians.

distrustful /dɪstrʌstfʊl/. If you are **distrustful** of ADJ QUALIT :
someone or something, you think that they are not OFT+of
honest, reliable, or safe. EG *Both parties were
distrustful of his policies.*

disturb /dɪstɜːb/, **disturbs, disturbing, dis-**
turbed. 1 If you **disturb** someone, you interrupt V+O
what they are doing and cause them inconvenience. EG *Sorry to disturb you... If she's asleep, don't
disturb her.*

2 If something **disturbs** you, it makes you feel V+O
upset or worried. EG *I was disturbed by some of the
speeches.*

3 To **disturb** something means to change its V+O
position or appearance. EG *The sand had not been
disturbed.*

4 To **disturb** a situation means to cause it to V+O
become less peaceful or organized. EG *...people who
disturb public order.*

disturbance /dɪstɜːbəns/, **disturbances. 1** A **dis-** N COUNT
turbance is an event in which people behave
violently in public. EG *...violent disturbances in
Liverpool.*

2 Disturbance is the act of making a situation less N UNCOUNT
peaceful, organized, or stable. EG *This would cause* OR N COUNT
*disturbance to the public... ...a disturbance of the
social order.*

3 You can use **disturbance** when you are talking N UNCOUNT
about extreme unhappiness or mental illness in a OR N COUNT
person. EG *This often causes serious emotional
disturbance.*

disturbed /dɪstɜːbd/. **1** Someone who is **dis-** ADJ QUALIT
turbed is **1.1** extremely unhappy or mentally ill.
EG *...emotionally disturbed youngsters.* **1.2** very

On these pages, which verb has a different past
tense in British English and American English?

worried about something. EG *They appeared disturbed by their powerlessness.*

2 If you say that a period of time is **disturbed**, you mean that the people involved are unhappy. EG *...his disturbed childhood.* ADJ QUALIT

disturbing /dɪstɜ:bɪŋ/. Something that is **disturbing** makes you feel worried or upset. EG *She has written two disturbing books.* ◊ **disturbingly**. EG *The radiation levels are disturbingly high.* ADJ QUALIT ◊ SUBMOD

disuse /dɪsju:s/ is the state of being no longer used. EG *These methods have fallen into disuse.* N UNCOUNT

disused /dɪsju:zd/. A **disused** place or building is empty and no longer used. EG *...a disused airfield near Lincoln.* ADJ CLASSIF

ditch /dɪtʃ/, **ditches**, **ditching**, **ditched**. **1** A **ditch** is a long narrow channel cut into the ground at the side of a road or field. EG *...a muddy ditch.* N COUNT

2 If you **ditch** someone, you end a relationship with them. EG *She ditched him for an older man.* V+O Informal

3 If you **ditch** something that is no longer of any use to you, you get rid of it. EG *He had decided to ditch the car.* V+O Informal

dither /dɪðə/, **dithers**, **dithering**, **dithered**. If you **are dithering**, you are hesitating because you are unable to make a quick decision. EG *After dithering about helplessly for a bit, he picked up the phone... You mustn't dither.* V:OFT+about

ditto /dɪtəʊ/. You use **ditto** to represent the word or phrase that you have just used in order to avoid repeating it. In written lists, **ditto** can be represented by a symbol (") underneath the word or phrase that you want to repeat. EG *...a cupboard door with mirror, a bathroom door ditto.*

divan /dɪvæn/, **divans**. A **divan** or a **divan bed** is a bed that has a thick base under the mattress. N COUNT

dive /daɪv/, **dives**, **diving**, **dived**. In American English, the form **dove** /dəʊv/ is sometimes used as the past tense.

1 If you **dive**, **1.1** you jump head-first into water with your arms held straight above your head. EG *She dived into the water and swam away.* ▸ used as a noun. EG *Ralph did a dive into the pool.* **1.2** you go under the surface of the sea or a lake, using special breathing equipment. EG *No one had ever dived there before.* ◊ **diving**. EG *...deep-sea diving.* V:OFT+into ▸ N COUNT V:USU+A ◊ N UNCOUNT

2 When birds and animals **dive**, they go quickly downwards, head-first, through the air or through water. EG *The fish dived down toward the reef.* V:USU+A

3 If you **dive** forwards or to one side, you jump or rush in that direction, for example in order to catch something. EG *He dived after the ball.* ▸ used as a noun. EG *He made a dive for the bag.* V+A ▸ N COUNT +SUPP

4 If you **dive** into something such as a bag, you put your hands into it quickly in order to get something out. EG *He suddenly dived into the chest and produced a shirt.* V+A

diver /daɪvə/, **divers**. A **diver** is a person who works under water, usually in the sea, using special breathing equipment. N COUNT

diverge /daɪvɜ:dʒ/, **diverges**, **diverging**, **diverged**. **1** If two things **diverge**, they are different or become different from one another. EG *...countries whose history and circumstances widely diverge... Their interests diverge from those of pensioners.* V OR V+from

2 Where two roads or paths **diverge**, they start leading in different directions. V:OFT+from

divergent /daɪvɜ:dʒənt/. Things that are **divergent** are different from each other. EG *...widely divergent religious groups.* ◊ **divergence** /daɪvɜ:dʒəns/, **divergences**. EG *...a sharp divergence of opinion.* ADJ QUALIT ◊ N UNCOUNT OR N COUNT

diverse /daɪvɜ:s, daɪvɜ:s/. People or things that are **diverse** are very different from each other. EG *...celebrities as diverse as Bob Dylan, Bob Hope, and Ronald Reagan... ...a man of diverse talents.* ADJ QUALIT

diversify /daɪvɜ:sɪfaɪ/, **diversifies**, **diversifying**, **diversified**. When a company or organization **diversifies**, it increases the variety of the things V OR V+O

that it makes or does. EG *Many car manufacturers are diversifying as rapidly as they can.* ◊ **diversification** /daɪvɜ:sɪfɪkeɪʃə⁰n/. EG *...the diversification of the range of studies.* ◊ N UNCOUNT

diversion /daɪvɜ:ʃə⁰n/, **diversions**. **1** A **diversion** is an action that attracts your attention away from what you are doing. EG *Billy created a welcome diversion by bringing in a shrew.* N COUNT

2 A **diversion** is also a special route arranged for traffic when the normal route cannot be used. EG *You can't go on, there's a diversion.* N COUNT

3 The **diversion** of something involves **3.1** changing its course or destination. EG *Possible diversions of the troop convoys were considered.* **3.2** changing the thing that it is used for. EG *Inflation and diversion of investment were having a bad effect.* N UNCOUNT OR N COUNT

diversity /daɪvɜ:sɪti/ is a range of different conditions, qualities, or types. EG *...the rich diversity of cultures and societies in the world.* N UNCOUNT

divert /daɪvɜ:t/, **diverts**, **diverting**, **diverted**. **1** If you **divert** something, **1.1** you change its course or destination. EG *The police were diverting the traffic.* **1.2** you cause it to be used for a different purpose. EG *We felt it desirable to divert funds from armaments to health and education.* V+O:USU+A V+O+A

2 If you **divert** someone's attention, you attract their attention away from a particular thing. EG *...diverting attention from the making of lethal weapons.* V+O:OFT+A

divest /daɪvest/, **divests**, **divesting**, **divested**. **1** If you **divest** yourself of something, you get rid of it. EG *She divested herself of her bag.* V-REFL+of Formal

2 If you **divest** someone or something of a position or quality, you cause them to lose it. EG *...divesting public housing of its welfare role.* V+O+of Formal

divide /dɪˈvaɪd/, **divides**, **dividing**, **divided**. **1** When something **divides** or **is divided**, it becomes separated into smaller parts. EG *...an attempt to divide the country into two social classes... The cells begin to divide rapidly.* V-ERG

2 If something **is divided** into several distinct parts, it consists of these parts. EG *The houses in Florence St are all divided into flats... The children are divided into three age groups.* V-PASS+into

3 If you **divide** something among a number of people, you give each of them part of it. EG *He divided his property among his brothers and sisters... The land was divided between the two brothers.* V+O:OFT +among/ between

4 If something **divides** two areas or **divides** an area into two, it forms a barrier or boundary which keeps the two areas separate from each other. EG *A line of rocks seemed to divide the cave into two.* V+O:USU+A

5 If people **divide** over something or if something **divides** people, it causes strong disagreement between them. EG *This question is dividing the people of Wales.* ◊ **divided**. EG *The conference was divided on many issues.* V-ERG ◊ ADJ CLASSIF

6 If you **divide** a larger number by a smaller number, you calculate how many times the smaller number can go exactly into the larger number. EG *Divide 35 by 7... Divide 7 into 35... 35 divided by 7 is 5.* V+O+by/into

7 A **divide** is a significant difference between two groups, especially one that causes conflict. EG *The divide between rich and poor was great... ...the religious divide.* N COUNT

divide up. If you **divide** something **up**, **1** you separate it into different parts. EG *We're dividing our group up.* **2** you share it out among a number of people. EG *The proceeds had to be divided up among about four hundred people.* PHRASAL VB: V+O+ADV V+O+ADV

dividend /dɪvɪdə⁰nd/, **dividends**. **1** A **dividend** is part of a company's profits which is paid to people who have shares in the company. N COUNT

2 If something **pays dividends**, it brings advantages at a later date. EG *The time she had spent learning German now paid dividends.* PHRASE

divine /di'vain/, **divines, divining, divined.** 1 ADJ CLASSIF
Something that is **divine** belongs or relates to a
god or goddess. EG *These men had been operating
under divine inspiration.* ◊ **divinely.** EG ...*a divine-* ◊ ADV
ly appointed prophet.
2 If you **divine** something, you guess it correctly. V+O OR
EG *She had divined something about me... She* V+REPORT
seemed to divine that it would be unpopular. Literary
diving board, diving boards. A **diving board** is N COUNT
a board high above a swimming pool from which
people can dive into the water.
divinity /di'vini'ti'/, **divinities.** 1 **Divinity** is the N UNCOUNT
study of the Christian religion. EG ...*a degree in
divinity.*
2 **Divinity** is also the quality of being divine. EG N UNCOUNT
The divinity of the Pharoah was not doubted.
3 A **divinity** is a god or goddess. N COUNT
divisible /di'vizə'bə'l/. A number that is **divisible** ADJ PRED :
by another number can be divided by that number. OFT+*by*
EG *24 is divisible by 3.*
division /di'viʒə'n/, **divisions.** 1 The **division** of
something is 1.1 the act of separating it into two or N UNCOUNT :
more different parts. EG ...*the division of physical* OFT+*into*
science into chemistry and physics. 1.2 the sharing N UNCOUNT
of it among a number of people. EG ...*the division of
responsibility.*
2 **Division** is the mathematical process of dividing N UNCOUNT
one number by another.
3 A **division** is a difference or conflict that exists N COUNT
between two groups. EG ...*class divisions... ...political
divisions between North and South... ...a division of
opinion.*
4 A **division** is also 4.1 a department in a large N COUNT
organization. EG ...*the BBC's engineering division.*
4.2 one of the groups of teams which make up a
football league or other sports league. The teams
in each division are considered to be about the
same standard. EG *United are top of the First
Division.*
division sign, division signs. A **division sign** is N COUNT
the symbol (÷) which is used between two num-
bers to show that the first number has to be divided
by the second.
divisive /di'vaisiv/. Something that is **divisive** ADJ QUALIT
causes hostility between people. EG ...*the Govern-* Formal
ment's divisive policy of confrontation.
divorce /di'vɔːs/, **divorces, divorcing, divorced.**
1 A **divorce** is the formal ending of a marriage by N COUNT OR
law. EG *I want a divorce... Divorce is on the* N UNCOUNT
increase.
2 When someone **divorces** their husband or wife V+O OR V :
or when a married couple **divorce**, their marriage RECIP
is legally ended. EG *I divorced him for cruelty.*
◊ **divorced.** EG ...*a divorced lady with two chil-* ◊ ADJ CLASSIF
dren... ...when my parents got divorced.
3 If you **divorce** one thing from another, you V+O :
consider or treat the two things as different and OFT+*from*
separate from each other. EG *I don't think it is* Formal
possible to divorce sport from politics.
divorcee /di'vɔːsiː/, **divorcees.** A **divorcee** is a N COUNT
person, especially a woman, who is divorced.
divulge /daivʌldʒ/, **divulges, divulging, di-** V+O OR
vulged. If you **divulge** a piece of information, you V+REPORT
tell someone about it. EG *I shall divulge the details* Formal
to no one.
D.I.Y. /diː ai wai/ is the activity of making or N UNCOUNT
repairing things yourself, especially in your home.
D.I.Y. is an abbreviation for 'do-it-yourself'. EG
...*D.I.Y. experts.*
dizzy /dizi'/. 1 If you feel **dizzy**, you feel that you ADJ QUALIT
are losing your balance and are about to fall. EG *I
felt dizzy and weak... I can't climb trees – I get
dizzy.* ◊ **dizziness.** EG *She was overcome by* ◊ N UNCOUNT
nausea and dizziness.
2 If you say that something has reached **dizzy** ADJ QUALIT :
heights, you mean that it is at a very high level ATTRIB
indeed. EG ...*the dizzy heights of success.* Literary

do /duː/, **does** /dʌz/, **doing, did** /dɪd/, **done** /dʌn/.
Do is both a main verb and an auxiliary verb. The

meanings of **do** as an auxiliary are given in paragraph 1.
1 **Do** is used as an auxiliary in the following ways: AUX
1.1 to form the negative of main verbs, by putting
'not' or '-n't' after the auxiliary and before the main
verb in its infinitive form. EG *You don't have to go.*
1.2 to form questions, by putting the subject after
the auxiliary and before the main verb in its
infinitive form. EG *What did he say?... Do you think
that's possible?* 1.3 to stand for, and refer back to, a
previous verbal group. EG *She meets lots more
people than I do... I like cooking and so does John.*
1.4 in question tags. EG *She made a lot of mistakes,
didn't she?... You don't know her, do you?* 1.5 to
give emphasis to the main verb when there is no
other auxiliary. EG *I did buy a map but I must have
lost it... Do sit down.* 1.6 with a negative to tell
someone not to behave in a certain way. EG *Don't
speak to me like that.*
2 When you **do** something, you perform an action, V+O
activity, or task. EG *What are you doing?... I do the
cooking and Brian does the cleaning... I've got to do
some work this morning.*
3 You can use **do** with a noun referring to a thing V+O
when you are talking about performing an action
or task involving that thing. EG *if some-
one **does** their teeth, they brush their teeth.* EG *She
had done her hair for the party... We have a man to
do the garden.*
4 If you **do** something about a problem, you take V+O :
action to try to solve it. EG *They promised that they* OFT+*about*
*were going to do something about immigration...
There's nothing I can do about it.*
5 You can use **do** to say that an action or event has V+O
a particular result or effect. EG *Their policies have
done more harm for the working class than ours...
They are afraid of what it might do to the children.*
6 If you ask someone what they **do**, you are asking V+O
what their job is. EG *What do you want to do when
you leave school?*
7 If someone **does** well or badly, they are success- V+A
ful or unsuccessful. EG *I didn't do very well in my
exams... It all depends how the Labour Party do at
this next election.*
8 If a person or organization **does** a particular V+O
service, they provide that service. EG *They do ferry
bookings to Ireland.*
9 If you **do** a subject, you study it at school or V+O
college. EG *I'm doing biology.*
10 You can use **do** when referring to the speed or V+NUMBER
rate that something or someone achieves or can
achieve. EG *The car's already doing 70 miles per
hour.*
11 If you say that something will **do** or will **do** you, V OR V+O
you mean that it is good enough for you. If you say
that something will not **do**, you mean that it is not
suitable or satisfactory. EG *No other school will do...
Two thousand will do me very well.*
12 **How do you do** is used as a formal way of CONVENTION
greeting someone when you meet them. When one
person says 'How do you do', the other person says
'How do you do' in reply.
13 **Do** is used in these phrases. 13.1 If you **do** your PHRASES
best to achieve something, you try as hard as you
can to achieve it. EG *We do our best to make sure
it's up to date information.* 13.2 If you ask someone
what they **did with** something, you are asking
them where they put it. EG *What did you do with the
keys?* 13.3 If you say that something is **the thing
to do** or **the best thing to do**, you mean that it
would be a very good idea to do it. EG *The best thing
to do is come in tomorrow morning.* 13.4 If you ask
what someone **is doing** in a particular place, you
are showing that you are surpised that they are
there. EG *What are you doing here, Francis? I*

Do you say 'How do you do?' to someone you
know very well?

thought you were still in London. **13.5** If you say PHRASE that someone **would do well** to do something, you mean that they ought to do it. EG *She would do well to steer clear of men.* **13.6** If you say that one thing **has to do with** or **is to do with** another thing, you mean that the first thing is connected or concerned with the second thing. EG *The basic argument has nothing to do with agriculture... It's got something to do with an economic crisis.* **13.7** If you say that you **could do with** something, you mean that you need it. EG *I think we could all do with a good night's sleep... The staff could probably do with some more money.*

14 A **do** is a party, dinner party, or other social N COUNT event. The plural is 'dos'. EG *We're going to a* Informal *formal do tonight.*

15 Do's and don'ts are things which you must and PHRASE must not do in a particular situation. EG *...lists of do's and don'ts for fitness.*

16 See also **doings, done.**

do away with. If someone or something **does** PHRASAL VB : **away with** a thing, they get rid of it. EG *Modern* V+ADV+PREP *medicines have not done away with disease.*

do down. If someone **does** you **down**, they PHRASAL VB : criticize you in order to make other people think V+O+ADV that you are unpleasant or unsuccessful. Informal

do for. If something **does for** you or if you **are** PHRASAL VB : **done for**, your life is ruined or ended. EG *She* V+PREP, *couldn't open the door. She was done for.* HAS PASS Informal

do in. To do someone **in** means to kill them. PHRASAL VB : *They might do you in one night while you're* V+O+ADV *sleeping.* Informal

do out of. If you **do** someone **out of** something, PHRASAL VB : you unfairly cause them not to have it. EG *He did* V+O+ADV *me out of £500.* +PREP Informal

do up. 1 If you **do** something **up**, you fasten it. EG PHRASAL VB : *He did his shoelaces up... Make sure you do your tie* V+O+ADV *up.* **2** If you **do up** an old building, you repair and V+O+ADV decorate it. EG *The theatre was horrible, done up as* Informal *cheaply as possible.* **3** If something **is done up** in a V+O+ADV, parcel or bundle, it is wrapped in something or tied USU PASS with something. EG *I gave her a box, nicely done up in flowered paper.*

do without. If you **do without** something, you PHRASAL VB : manage or survive in spite of not having it. EG V+PREP, *Many Victorian households did without a bathroom* HAS PASS *altogether.*

docile /dəʊsaɪl/. A person or animal that is **docile** ADJ QUALIT is quiet and easily controlled.

dock /dɒk/, **docks, docking, docked. 1** A **dock** is N COUNT an area in a harbour where ships go to be loaded, unloaded, or repaired. EG *...London Docks.*

2 When a ship **docks** or when it **is docked**, it V OR V-ERG : comes into a dock at the end of a voyage. EG *They* USU+A *docked at Southampton.*

3 In a law court, the **dock** is the place where the N SING : the+N person accused of a crime stands or sits. EG *...the people who should have been in the dock.*

4 If you **dock** someone's wages or money, you take V+O some of the money away. EG *He docked her pocket money until the debt was paid off.*

docker /dɒkə/, **dockers.** A **docker** is a person N COUNT who works in the docks.

doctor /dɒktə/, **doctors, doctoring, doctored. 1** N COUNT A **doctor** is someone who is qualified in medicine and treats people who are ill. EG *She felt so ill we had to call the doctor... ...Doctor Barker.*

2 When you go to the **doctor's**, you go to the N SING : the+N surgery or clinic where a doctor works.

3 The title **Doctor** is also given to someone who N COUNT has been awarded the highest academic degree by a university. EG *...Doctor Brian Smith, Physics Building... He is a doctor of philosophy.*

4 If someone **doctors** something, they deliberately V+O change it, usually in order to deceive people. EG *The despatch from Davis had been doctored.*

5 If someone **doctors** food or drink, they add a V+O poison or drug to it.

doctorate /dɒktərəʔt/, **doctorates.** A **doctorate** N COUNT is the highest degree awarded by a university. EG *...a doctorate in art.*

doctrinaire /dɒktrɪnɛə/. Someone who is **doctri-** ADJ QUALIT **naire** insists on principles or theories without Formal allowing arguments against them. EG *Their atti- tudes were condemned as doctrinaire.*

doctrine /dɒktrɪn/, **doctrines.** A **doctrine** is a N COUNT OR principle or belief, or a set of principles or beliefs. N UNCOUNT EG *...the doctrine of permanent revolution... ...Chris- tian doctrine.* ◇ **doctrinal** /dɒktraɪnᵊl/. EG *...doc-* ◇ ADJ CLASSIF : *trinal arguments between rival factions.* ATTRIB

document /dɒkjəmə²nt/, **documents, docu- menting, documented. 1** A **document** is an offi- N COUNT cial piece of paper with writing on it. EG *...docu- ments relating to the nineteenth century... ...travel documents.*

2 If you **document** something, you write down V+O facts and details about it, or record them on film or tape. EG *The films document the development of the railways.*

documentary /dɒkjə⁴mentə⁰ri¹/, **documen- taries. 1** A **documentary** is a radio or television N COUNT programme, or a film, which provides information about a particular subject. EG *...a television docu- mentary on the lives of the Royal Family.*

2 Documentary evidence consists of documents ADJ CLASSIF : rather than things that people say. EG *There is* ATTRIB *plenty of documentary evidence on the Roman Empire.*

documentation /dɒkjə⁴mentəɪʃə⁰n/ is documents N UNCOUNT that provide proof or evidence of something. EG *His story was backed by massive documentation.*

doddle /dɒdᵊl/. Something that is a **doddle** is N SING : a+N very easy to do. EG *Don't worry about it. It'll be a* Informal *doddle.* British

dodge /dɒdʒ/, **dodges, dodging, dodged. 1** If you V : USU+A **dodge**, you move suddenly in order to avoid being hit, caught, or seen. EG *He dodged into the post office.*

2 If you **dodge** something, **2.1** you avoid it by V+O quickly moving aside. EG *The Minister had to dodge flying tomatoes.* **2.2** you avoid thinking about it or dealing with it. EG *We cannot dodge this accusa- tion... This issue should not be dodged.*

dodgy /dɒdʒi¹/. Something that is **dodgy** seems ADJ QUALIT rather risky, dangerous, or unreliable. EG *It's a* Informal *rather dodgy plan, but it might just work... Relying* British *on the conscience of your rulers is a dodgy thing.*

doe /dəʊ/, **does.** A **doe** is an adult female deer, N COUNT rabbit, or hare.

does /dʌz/ is the third person singular of the present tense of **do.**

doesn't /dʌzə⁰nt/ is the usual spoken form of 'does not'.

dog /dɒg/, **dogs, dogging, dogged. 1** A **dog** is **1.1** N COUNT an animal that is often kept as a pet or used to guard or hunt things. EG *Their dog started barking at me.* **1.2** a male dog or fox.

2 If you **dog** someone, you follow them very closely V+O : OFT+A and never leave them. EG *He's been dogging me all day.*

3 If problems or injuries **dog** you, they keep V+O affecting you. EG *The project has been dogged by a number of technical problems... Bad luck has dog- ged me all year... Last winter's cricket tour was dogged by injuries to our best players.*

4 If you say that a particular way of life is **a dog's** PHRASE **life**, you mean that it is very unpleasant. EG *It's a dog's life being a football manager.*

5 See also **dogged.**

dog-collar, dog-collars. A **dog-collar** is a white N COUNT collar that is worn by priests and ministers of the Informal Christian Church.

dog-eared. A book or piece of paper that is **dog-** ADJ QUALIT **eared** has been used so much that the corners of the pages are turned down or crumpled.

dogged /dɒgɪd/ means showing determination to ADJ CLASSIF : continue with something, even if it is very difficult. ATTRIB

EG ...*his dogged refusal to admit defeat.*
◊ **doggedly.** EG *Karen doggedly continued to* ◊ ADV
search... They persisted doggedly in their campaign against the law.

doggerel /dɒgəᵇrəl/, is poetry which is silly or funny, often written quickly and not intended to be serious. EG *She wrote some doggerel about it.*

dogma /dɒgmə/, **dogmas.** A **dogma** is a belief or   N COUNT OR
a system of beliefs which a particular religious or   N UNCOUNT :
political group has. EG *He had no time for political*   USU+SUPP
or other dogmas... ...Christianity in the early days when there was less dogma.

dogmatic /dɒgmætɪk/. Someone who is **dogmat-**   ADJ QUALIT
ic about something is convinced that they are right about it and does not consider other points of view. EG *He was so dogmatic about it that I almost believed him... She was not impressed by his dogmatic assertions.* ◊ **dogmatically.** EG *He argued so* ◊ ADV
dogmatically... 'This stone,' he said dogmatically, 'is far older than the rest.'

dogsbody /dɒgzbɒdiᵇ/, **dogsbodies.** A **dogsbody**   N COUNT
is someone who has to do all the boring jobs that   Informal
nobody else wants to do. EG *I was employed as a*   British
general dogsbody on the project.

doings /duːɪŋz/. Someone's **doings** are their activi-   N PLURAL
ties. EG *...a magazine about the doings of royalty... He gave an admiring account of Larry's doings.*

do-it-yourself is the activity of making or repair-   N UNCOUNT
ing things yourself, especially in your home. EG *You can get them from good do-it-yourself shops.*

doldrums /dɒldrəmz/. If an area of activity is **in**   PHRASE
the doldrums, it is very quiet and nothing new or   Informal
exciting is happening. EG *The American market is in the doldrums... By and large, athletics were in the doldrums in the 1960s.*

dole /dəʊl/, **doles, doling, doled.** The **dole** is   N SING : the+N
money that is given regularly by the government   British
to people who are unemployed. EG *...dole money...
...lengthening dole queues.* ● Someone who is **on**   ● PHRASE
the dole is unemployed and receives money regu-
larly from the government. EG *He's spent the last year on the dole... They made him redundant but he wouldn't go on the dole.*

dole out. If you **dole** something **out**, you give a   PHRASAL VB :
certain amount of it to each person in a group. EG   V+O+ADV
The food was doled out.

doleful /dəʊlful/. A **doleful** expression or manner   ADJ QUALIT
is depressed and miserable. EG *...a doleful sigh.*
◊ **dolefully.** EG *'You're hopeless,' she said doleful-* ◊ ADV
ly.

doll /dɒl/, **dolls.** A **doll** is a child's toy which looks   N COUNT
like a small person or baby.

dollar /dɒlə/, **dollars.** A **dollar** is a unit of money   N COUNT
used in the USA, Canada, and some other countries.
EG *They spent half a million dollars on the campaign... Ethel gave him a dollar bill... The pound fell more than 25 per cent against the dollar.*

dolled up /dɒld ʌp/. When a woman gets **dolled**   ADJ PRED
up, she puts on smart clothes in order to look   Informal
attractive. EG *She was all dolled up in the latest fashion.*

dollop /dɒləp/, **dollops.** A **dollop** of soft or sticky   N PART
food is a small amount of it served in a lump. EG *...a*   Informal
dollop of ice-cream... ...stew with beans, topped up with a dollop of mashed potato.

dolphin /dɒlfɪn/, **dolphins.** A **dolphin** is a mam-   N COUNT
mal which lives in the sea and looks like a large fish.

dolt /dəʊlt/, **dolts.** If you call someone a **dolt,** you
mean that you think that they have done some-
thing stupid. EG *You would have to be a complete dolt to miss the turn-off.*

domain /dəʊ⁷meɪn/, **domains.** A **domain** is **1** a   N COUNT+SUPP
particular area of activity or interest. EG *This question comes into the domain of philosophy... The ultimate responsibility in this domain, as in all others, lay with the chairman.* **2** an area over   N COUNT+POSS
which someone has control or influence. EG *His domain extended to New York.*

domes   Ibn Tulun Mosque, Cairo

St Peter's dome, Rome

dome /dəʊm/, **domes.** A **dome** is a round roof. EG   N COUNT
...the dome of St Peter's.

domestic /dəᵇmestɪk/. **1 Domestic** activities,   ADJ CLASSIF :
events, and situations happen or exist within one   ATTRIB
particular country. EG *...foreign and domestic policy.*

2 Domestic duties and activities are concerned   ADJ CLASSIF :
with your home and family. EG *...domestic chores...*   ATTRIB
....domestic responsibilities.

3 Someone who is **domestic** enjoys doing things in   ADJ QUALIT
their home, for example cooking and cleaning. EG *She was never a very domestic sort of person.*

4 Domestic items and services are used in peo-   ADJ CLASSIF :
ple's homes rather than in factories or offices. EG   ATTRIB
...domestic appliances... ...a domestic water supply... ...coal for industrial and domestic use.

5 Domestic animals are not wild, and are kept as   ADJ CLASSIF
pets or are kept on farms to produce food.

domesticate /dəᵇmestɪkeɪt/, **domesticates,**   V+O
domesticating, domesticated. When people **domesticate** wild animals or plants, they bring them
under control and use them for work or for food.
◊ **domesticated.** EG *There were no domesticated* ◊ ADJ CLASSIF
animals for ploughing.

domesticity /dəʊmestɪsɪᵗtiᵇ, dɒm-/ is the habit of   N UNCOUNT
spending a lot of time at home with your family. EG   Formal
I had put off settling down to such domesticity.

dominance /dɒmɪnəns/. **1** If someone has **domi-**   N UNCOUNT :
nance over a person, place, or group, they have   OFT+over
power or control over them. EG *Their dominance over the party was eroded... The treaty gave them dominance of the sea routes.*

2 The **dominance** of something is the fact that it is   N UNCOUNT :
more important than other similar things. EG *...the*   USU+SUPP
dominance of economics in social sciences.

dominant /dɒmɪnənt/. Someone or something   ADJ QUALIT
that is **dominant** is more powerful, important, or
noticeable than other similar things. EG *The dominant personality in our firm was John Brown.*

dominate /dɒmɪneɪt/, **dominates, dominating,
dominated. 1** If someone or something **domi-**   V+O
nates a situation or event, they are the most
powerful or important thing in it. EG *These issues
dominated the election.* ◊ **domination** ◊ N UNCOUNT
/dɒmɪneɪʃəᵇn/. EG *...the company's increasing domination of the UK market.*

2 If one country **dominates** another, it has power   V+O

over it. ◇ **domination.** EG ...*the domination of* ◇ N UNCOUNT
Europe over the rest of the world.

3 If something **dominates** an area, it is so large v+o
that it can be seen from all over that area. EG *The
valley was dominated by the huge Benedictine
abbey.*

dominating /dɒmɪneɪtɪŋ/. Someone who is **domi-** ADJ QUALIT
nating has a very strong personality and influences other people a great deal.

domineering /dɒmɪnɪərɪŋ/. Someone who is ADJ QUALIT
domineering tries to control other people. EG
...*domineering husbands.*

dominion /dəˈmɪnjən/, **dominions. 1 Dominion** N UNCOUNT :
is control or authority that someone has over other OFT+*over*
people. EG *They now had dominion over a large* Formal
part of southern India.

2 A **dominion** is an area of land that is controlled N COUNT
by a ruler. EG ...*Britain's imperial dominions.* Formal

domino /dɒmɪnəʊ/, **dominoes. 1 Dominoes** are N COUNT
small rectangular blocks marked with two groups
of spots on one side. Dominoes are used for playing
games.

2 Dominoes is a game played using dominoes. N UNCOUNT

don /dɒn/, **dons, donning, donned. 1** A **don** is a N COUNT
lecturer at a university, especially Oxford or Cambridge.

2 If you **don** a piece of clothing, you put it on. EG V+O
The two men donned white cotton gloves. Literary

donate /dəʊneɪt/, **donates, donating, donated.** If V+O : OFT+*to*
you **donate** something to a charity or other organization, you give it to them. EG *The van was donated
to us by a local firm.*

donation /dəʊneɪʃəⁿn/, **donations.** A **donation** is N COUNT
an amount of money that is given to a charity or
other organization. EG *They received a large donation from one of the unions.*

done /dʌn/. **1 Done** is the past participle of **do**.

2 A task that is **done** has been completed. EG *When* ADJ PRED
her errand was done she ran home.

3 If you say that a situation or task is **over and** PHRASE
done with, you mean that it is finished and you
can forget about it.

4 You say **'Done'** when you are accepting a deal or CONVENTION
a bet. EG *'Shall we say two hundred pounds?' –
'Done.'*

donkey /dɒŋkiˈ/, **donkeys. 1** A **donkey** is an N COUNT
animal which is like a horse, but smaller and with
longer ears.

2 If you say that something has been happening for PHRASE
donkey's years, you mean that it has been hap- Informal
pening for a very long time. EG *She's been there
donkey's years.*

donor /dəʊnə/, **donors.** A **donor** is **1** someone N COUNT :
who lets a doctor take an organ or some blood USU+SUPP
from their body so that it can be given to a patient
who needs it. EG ...*kidney donors.* **2** someone who N COUNT
gives something such as money to a charity or
other organization. EG *About half this amount
comes from individual donors.*

don't /dəʊnt/ is the usual spoken form of 'do not'.

doodle /duːdəⁿl/, **doodles, doodling, doodled. 1** A N COUNT
doodle is a pattern or picture that you draw when
you are thinking about something else or when you
are bored.

2 When someone **doodles**, they draw doodles. EG *I* V
used to doodle on my papers.

doom /duːm/ a terrible state or event in the future N UNCOUNT
which you cannot prevent. EG *I felt as if I were
going to my doom.*

doomed /duːmd/. **1** If someone or something is ADJ PRED+*to*
doomed to an unpleasant or undesirable experi- OR *to*-INF
ence, they are certain to suffer it. EG *They are
doomed to failure... He was doomed to be killed in
a car crash.*

2 Something that is **doomed** is certain to fail or be ADJ CLASSIF
destroyed. EG *They informed the Prime Minister
that his government was doomed.*

doomsday /duːmzdeɪ/. **1 Doomsday** is the end of N UNCOUNT
the world.

2 If you say that something will or could happen PHRASE
until Doomsday, you mean that it will or could go
on for ever. EG *I could have knocked until Doomsday and Antonio would not have heard me.*

door /dɔː/, **doors. 1** A **door** is **1.1** a swinging or N COUNT
sliding piece of wood, glass, or metal, which is used
to open and close the entrance to a building, room,
cupboard, or vehicle. EG *My friend knocked on the
door... There was a knock at the door... He opened
the car door and got out.* **1.2** the space in a wall
which a door can close and through which you
enter a building or room. EG *As they passed through
the door, they saw Tom at the end of the room.*

2 Door is used in these phrases. **2.1** The person PHRASES
who lives **next door** to you lives in the house that
is next to yours. EG *She put a notice in the shop next
door... ...our next-door neighbour, Joan.* **2.2** When
you are **out of doors**, you are not inside a building,
but are in the open air. **2.3** If you **lay** the blame for
something **at** someone's **door**, you blame that
person for it. EG *Responsibility for the strike was
laid at the door of the employers.* **2.4** An event
which **opens the door to** something makes that
thing possible. EG *This new discovery will open the
doors to prosperity.* **2.5 at death's door**: see
death.

doorbell /dɔːbɛl/, **doorbells.** A **doorbell** is a bell N COUNT
on the outside of a house, which you ring when you
want the people inside to open the door.

doorknob /dɔːnɒb/, **doorknobs.** A **doorknob** is a N COUNT
round handle on a door.

doormat /dɔːmæt/, **doormats.** A **doormat** is a N COUNT
mat by a door which people can wipe their shoes
on before coming into the house.

doorstep /dɔːstɛp/, **doorsteps. 1** A **doorstep** is a N COUNT
step in front of a door on the outside of a building.

2 If a place is **on your doorstep**, it is very near to PHRASE
where you live.

door-to-door. Door-to-door activities involve go- ADJ CLASSIF :
ing from one house to another along a street, often ATTRIB
in order to try and sell something.

doorway /dɔːweɪ/, **doorways.** A **doorway** is a N COUNT
space in a wall which a door can close. EG *A child
stood in the doorway.*

dope /dəʊp/, **dopes, doping, doped. 1 Dope** is a N UNCOUNT
drug, often an illegal drug such as cannabis. EG Informal
Others sat around smoking dope.

2 If someone **dopes** you, they put a drug into your V+O
food or drink in order to make you unconscious. EG
She'd been heavily doped.

3 If you call someone a **dope**, you mean that you N COUNT
think they are stupid. Informal

dopey /dəʊpiˈ/. **1** Someone who is **dopey** is sleepy, ADJ QUALIT
especially because they have taken drugs or alco-
hol. EG *The pill had already made her dopey.*

2 If you describe someone as **dopey**, you mean that ADJ QUALIT
they are stupid. Informal

dormant /dɔːmənt/. Something that is **dormant** ADJ CLASSIF
has not been active or been used for a long time. EG
*The idea had lain dormant in Britain during the
fifties.*

dormitory /dɔːmɪˈtəⁿriˈ/, **dormitories.** A **dormi-** N COUNT
tory is **1** a large bedroom where several people
sleep, for example in a boarding school. **2** a building where students live, in an American college.

dormouse /dɔːmaʊs/, **dormice** /dɔːmaɪs/. A **dor-** N COUNT
mouse is a small furry animal. People think of it
as being a very sleepy animal.

dosage /dəʊsɪdʒ/, **dosages.** The **dosage** of a N COUNT
medicine or drug is the total amount of it that
should be taken over a period of time. EG ...*a daily
dosage of 150 mg.*

dose /dəʊs/, **doses, dosing, dosed. 1** A **dose** of a N PART
medicine or drug is a measured amount of it. EG
This is lethal to rats in small doses.

2 A **dose** of something is an amount of it which you N PART
get or need. EG *What we needed was a large dose of
courage.*

3 If you **dose** someone, you give them a medicine V+O,OR or drug. EG *He dosed himself with pills.* V-REFL : OFT+with

doss /dɒs/, **dosses, dossing, dossed.** If you **doss** PHRASAL VB : **down** somewhere, you sleep there because you V+ADV have nowhere else to sleep. Informal

dossier /ˈdɒsɪeɪ, -sɪə/, **dossiers.** A **dossier** is a N COUNT collection of papers containing information on a particular subject. EG *We have a hefty dossier on his exploits in the war.*

dot /dɒt/, **dots, dotting, dotted. 1** A **dot** is a very N COUNT small round mark. EG *She painted black dots for the clown's eyes.*

2 If things **dot** an area, they are scattered or V+O spread all over it. EG *Countless fishing villages dot the coast... The hills are dotted with trees.*

3 If you arrive somewhere **on the dot**, you arrive PHRASE there at exactly the right time.

dote /dəʊt/, **dotes, doting, doted.** If you **dote on** V+on/upon someone, you love them very much and cannot see their faults. ◇ **doting.** EG *...doting relatives who* ◇ ADJ CLASSIF : *keep spoiling them with presents.* ATTRIB

dotted /ˈdɒtɪ²d/. **Dotted** lines are lines which are ADJ CLASSIF : made of a row of dots. EG *The boundaries are* ATTRIB *shown on the map by dotted lines.*

dotty /ˈdɒtɪ¹/, **dottier, dottiest.** Someone who is ADJ QUALIT **dotty** is slightly mad. Informal

double /ˈdʌbə⁰l/, **doubles, doubling, doubled. 1** If PREDET OR one thing is **double** the amount or size of another QUANTIF thing, it is twice as large. EG *He needs to eat double that amount... We paid her double what she was getting before.*

2 You use **double** to describe **2.1** something that is ADJ CLASSIF : twice the normal size. EG *I asked for a double gin.* ATTRIB **2.2** something that consists of two things of the same kind. EG *The double doors were open.* **2.3** something that is intended to be used by two people. EG *...a double bed.*

3 You say **double** before a number or letter to ADJ CLASSIF : indicate that it occurs twice. EG *My phone number* ATTRIB *is nine, double three, two, four.*

4 If something **doubles** or if you **double** it, it V-ERG becomes twice as large as it was. EG *The world population is doubling every thirty-five years.*

5 If someone or something **doubles** as something V+as else, they have a second job or use as well as their main one. EG *This bedroom doubles as a study.*

6 Doubles is a game of tennis or badminton in N UNCOUNT which two people play against two other people. EG *Don't use this shot in mixed doubles.*

7 If you **bend double**, you bend right over. If you PHRASE **are bent double**, you are bent right over.

double up. If you **double up**, you bend your body PHRASAL VB : quickly. EG *He doubled up with laughter, holding his* V+ADV *stomach.* ◇ **doubled up.** EG *I was doubled up in* ◇ ADJ PRED *pain.*

double bass, double basses. A **double bass** is a N COUNT large stringed instrument shaped like a violin, which you play standing up. See picture at MUSICAL INSTRUMENTS.

double-breasted. A **double-breasted** jacket or ADJ CLASSIF coat has two very wide sections at the front which overlap when you button them up.

double-check, double-checks, double- V+O OR V **checking, double-checked.** If you **double-check** something, you examine or test it a second time to make sure that it is completely correct or safe. EG *The facts will be double-checked by more senior persons.*

double chin, double chins. Someone who has a N COUNT **double chin** has a fold of fat under their chin.

double cream is very thick cream. N UNCOUNT

double-cross, double-crosses, double- V+O **crossing, double-crossed.** If someone **double-** Informal **crosses** you, they pretend that they are doing what you had planned together, when in fact they are doing the opposite. EG *You want me to double-cross the man I work for?*

double-dealing is behaviour which is deliberate- N UNCOUNT ly deceitful. EG *They dismissed him for suspected double-dealing.*

double-decker, double-deckers. A **double-** N COUNT **decker** is a bus that has two floors.

double-glazing is an extra layer of glass which N UNCOUNT can be fitted to the windows in a house in order to keep the house warmer or quieter. EG *...a house with double-glazing.*

doubly /ˈdʌblɪ¹/. You use **doubly 1** to say that ADV+ADJ there are two aspects or features that have an effect or make something true. EG *...doubly handicapped children.* **2** to emphasize that something happens or is true to a greater degree than usual. EG *It was doubly difficult for Dora at her age.*

doubt /daʊt/, **doubts, doubting, doubted. 1** A N COUNT : **doubt** about something is a feeling of uncertainty USU PLURAL about it, for example about whether it is true or +about, OR possible. EG *Frank had no doubts about the outcome* N UNCOUNT *of the trial... I had moments of doubt.*

2 Doubt is used in these phrases. **2.1** If you say PHRASE **there is no doubt** about something or you **have no doubt** about it, you mean that you feel certain it is true. EG *There's no doubt that it's going to be difficult... Rose was mad, there was no doubt about it.* **2.2 No doubt** means probably or almost certain- ADV SEN ly. EG *As Jennifer has no doubt told you, we are leaving tomorrow.* **2.3** You say **without doubt** or ADV SEN **without a doubt** to emphasize that you think that what you are saying is definitely true. EG *Hugh Scanlon became without doubt one of the most powerful men in Britain.* **2.4** If something is shown ADV SEN to be true **beyond a doubt**, it is shown to be definitely true. EG *We have established the ownership beyond all doubt.* **2.5** If something is **in doubt** PHRASE or is **open to doubt**, it is considered to be uncertain or unreliable. EG *Devaluation had put Concorde's future in doubt.* **2.6** To **cast doubt** on PHRASE something means to cause people to suspect that it might not be true. EG *The new evidence cast doubt on Christine's story.* **2.7** If you are **in doubt** about PHRASE something, you feel unsure about it. EG *If in doubt, call the doctor... He left us in no doubt that he wanted results.* **2.8** to **give** someone **the benefit of the doubt**: see **benefit**.

3 If you **doubt** whether something is true or V+REPORT possible, you think that it is probably not true or possible. EG *I doubt if they will ever want vanilla pudding again... Maybe he changed his mind, but I doubt it.*

4 If you **doubt** something, you think that it might V+O not be true or might not exist. EG *...men who never doubt their own superiority.*

5 If you **doubt** someone or **doubt** their word, you V+O think that they may not be telling the truth. EG *I apologized for having doubted his word.*

doubtful /ˈdaʊtfʊl/. **1** Something that is **doubtful** ADJ QUALIT seems unlikely or uncertain. EG *The organisation has a doubtful future... It is doubtful whether the Chairman would approve.*

2 If you are **doubtful** about something, you are ADJ QUALIT : unsure about it. EG *I was a little doubtful about* USU PRED *accepting the job... He was doubtful of his talents.* +about/of ◇ **doubtfully.** EG *Ralph looked at him doubtfully.* ◇ ADV

doubtless /ˈdaʊtlɪ²s/ means probably or almost ADV SEN certainly. EG *Over 2,500 species are known and doubtless more are still to be discovered.*

dough /dəʊ/. **1 Dough** is a mixture of flour and N UNCOUNT water, and sometimes also sugar and fat, which can be cooked to make bread, pastry, or biscuits. EG *Shape the dough into rolls.*

2 You can refer to money as **dough**. EG *Twenty* N UNCOUNT *million bucks is a lot of dough.* Informal

doughnut /ˈdəʊnʌt/, **doughnuts.** A **doughnut** is a N COUNT lump or ring of sweet dough cooked in hot fat.

If you have doubts about something, would you double-check?

dour /dʊə/. Someone who is **dour** has a severe and   ADJ QUALIT
unfriendly manner. EG *She faced me with her usual*
dour expression. ◊ **dourly.** EG *'Yes,' said Christo-*   ◊ ADV
pher, smiling dourly.

douse /daʊs/, **douses, dousing, doused;** also
spelled **dowse. 1** If you **douse** a fire or a light, you   V+O
stop it burning or shining.
2 If you **douse** someone or something with liquid,   V+O
you throw the liquid over them. EG *She had doused*
herself with perfume.

dove, doves; pronounced /dʌv/ for paragraph 1
and /dəʊv/ for paragraph 2.
1 A **dove** is a type of pigeon. Doves are often used   N COUNT
as a symbol of peace.
2 In American English, **dove** is a past tense of
dive.

dowager /daʊədʒə/, **dowagers.** A **dowager** is an   N COUNT
old lady, especially a grand-looking one.   Literary

dowdy /daʊdɪ¹/, **dowdier, dowdiest.** Someone   ADJ QUALIT
who is **dowdy** is wearing dull and unfashionable
clothes.

down /daʊn/, **downs, downing, downed. 1 Down**   PREP, OR
means towards the ground or a lower level, or in a   ADV AFTER VB
lower place. EG *They walked down the steps... Shall*
I lift your suitcase down?... The rain came down in
sheets... the house down below.
2 You use **down** with verbs such as 'fall' or 'pull' to   ADV AFTER VB
say that something is destroyed or falls to the
ground. EG *The house fell down a week later... He*
burnt down his school.
3 If you put something **down**, you put it onto a   ADV AFTER VB
surface. EG *Put that book down.*
4 If you go **down** a road or river, you go along it. EG   PREP OR ADV
He walked down the road reading a newspaper...
I'm just going down to the shops... The library is
halfway down the street.
5 Down also means in the south or towards the   ADV
south. EG *There's a man down in Baltimore who*
does that... Did you have a good trip down?
6 If one thing has another thing **down** it, it has the   PREP
other thing on its surface from the top towards the
bottom. EG *...a girl with a pigtail down her back.*
7 If an amount of something goes **down**, it decreas-   ADV AFTER VB
es. EG *Sheila was trying to get her weight down...*
Tourism is down 40 percent.
8 If something is **down** on paper, it has been   ADJ PRED
written on the paper. EG *That date wasn't down on*
our news sheet.
9 Down to a particular detail means including   ADV+*to*
everything, even that detail. EG *Successful suicides*
seem to have been planned down to the last detail.
10 If you are **down** with an illness, you have that   ADV+*with*
illness. EG *She's down with the flu.*   Informal
11 If you are feeling **down**, you are feeling unhap-   ADJ PRED
py or depressed.   Informal
12 If you **down** a drink, you drink it quickly. EG *I*   V+O
poured him a whisky and he downed it at a gulp.
13 Down is the small, soft feathers on young birds.   N UNCOUNT
Down is used to make pillows or quilts.
14 Down is also used in phrasal verbs such as
'bring down' and 'calm down.'
15 up and down, ups and downs: see **up.**

downcast /daʊnkɑːst/. **1** If you are **downcast**,   ADJ QUALIT
you are feeling sad and pessimistic.   Formal
2 If your eyes are **downcast**, you are looking   ADJ CLASSIF
towards the ground, usually because you are feel-   Formal
ing sad or embarrassed. EG *The girl could only nod,*
her eyes downcast.

downfall /daʊnfɔːl/. **1** The **downfall** of a success-   N UNCOUNT
ful or powerful person or institution is their loss of   USU+POSS
success or power. EG *...the downfall of a dictator.*
2 The thing that was a person's **downfall** caused   N UNCOUNT
them to fail or lose power. EG *Bad publicity was our*   USU+POSS
downfall.

downgrade /daʊngreɪd/, **downgrades, down-**   V+O
grading, downgraded. If you **downgrade** something, you give it less importance than it used to
have or should have. EG *They were reluctant to*
downgrade the nuclear element of their defence.

downhearted /daʊnhɑːtɪ²d/. If you are **down-**   ADJ QUALIT
hearted, you are feeling sad and discouraged.   Outdated

downhill /daʊnhɪl/. **1** If something is moving   ADV AFTER VB
downhill, it is moving down a slope. EG *The chil-*   OR ADJ
dren were racing downhill on their sledges... ...a   CLASSIF :
downhill slope.   ATTRIB
2 If something is going **downhill**, it is becoming   ADV AFTER VB
worse or less successful. EG *Journalism is going*
downhill nowadays.
3 If you say that a task or situation is **downhill**   ADJ PRED
after a particular stage or time, you mean that it is
easy to deal with after that stage or time. EG *It was*
downhill all the way after that.

downpour /daʊnpɔː/, **downpours.** When there is   N COUNT
a **downpour**, a lot of rain falls fast and heavily.

downright /daʊnraɪt/. You use **downright** to   SUBMOD OR
emphasize that something is unpleasant or bad in   ADJ CLASSIF :
some way. EG *Some of the jobs were downright*   ATTRIB
disgusting... That's a downright lie.

Down's syndrome. If a baby is born with   N UNCOUNT
Down's syndrome, it has less than normal intelligence and develops a flat face and sloping eyes.

downstairs /daʊnsteəz/. **1** If you go **downstairs**   ADV AFTER VB
in a building, you go down a staircase towards the
ground floor. EG *He went downstairs and into the*
kitchen.
2 If someone or something is **downstairs** in a   ADV AFTER VB
building, they are on the ground floor. EG *Arthur*   OR
isn't downstairs; he is asleep in bed... ...the photo-   ADV AFTER N
graph on the piano downstairs.
3 A **downstairs** room or object is situated on the   ADJ CLASSIF
ground floor of a building. EG *...the downstairs*   ATTRIB
phone.

downstream /daʊnstriːm/. Something that is   ADV
moving **downstream** is moving towards the
mouth of a river, from a point further up the river.
EG *The soil is washed downstream.*

down-to-earth. Someone who is **down-to-earth**   ADJ QUALIT
is concerned with practical things and actions,
rather than with abstract theories. EG *...his warm,*
down-to-earth manner.

downtown /daʊntaʊn/ means in or towards the   ADV OR
centre of a large town or city. EG *We went down-*   ADJ CLASSIF :
town to buy a pair of shoes... ...downtown Belfast.   ATTRIB

downtrodden /daʊntrɒdə⁰n/. People who are   ADJ QUALIT
downtrodden are treated very badly by people
with power, and do not have the ability or the
energy to rebel.

downturn /daʊntɜːn/, **downturns.** If there is a   N COUNT :
downturn in something such as a country's econo-   USU SING
my, it becomes worse or less successful. EG *...a*
downturn in manufacturing and industry.

downward /daʊnwəd/, **downwards.** When it is
an adverb, the form **downwards** is normally used
in British English and **downward** in American
English.
1 If you move or look **downwards**, you move or   ADV AFTER VB
look towards the ground or a lower level. EG *It*   OR
glides gently downwards... My dad was lying face   ADV AFTER N
downward. ▸ used as an adjective. EG *...a downward*   ▸ ADJ CLASSIF :
glance.   ATTRIB
2 If an amount or rate moves **downwards**, it   ADV AFTER VB
decreases. EG *The long term trend in the suicide*
rate is downwards. ▸ used as an adjective. EG   ▸ ADJ CLASSIF :
Prices started a downward plunge.   ATTRIB
3 When you want to emphasize that a statement   PHRASE
applies to everyone in an organization, you can say
that it applies **from** its leader **downwards.** EG *The*
entire crew from Captain Imrie downwards be-
lieved that we were sinking.

downwind /daʊnwɪnd/. If something moves   ADV AFTER VB
downwind, it moves in the same direction as the
wind. EG *The sparks drifted downwind.*

downy /daʊni¹/. Something that is **downy** is   **1** ADJ CLASSIF
filled or covered with small soft feathers. EG *...thick*
downy feather beds. **2** covered with very fine hairs.
EG *...the downy head of the sleeping baby.*

dowry /dauəri¹/, **dowries.** A woman's **dowry** is N COUNT money or goods which her father gives to the man that she marries, in some countries.

dowse /daus/. See **douse**.

doze /dəuz/, **dozes, dozing, dozed.** When you V **doze**, you sleep lightly or for a short period. EG *Thomas dozed in the armchair.* ▸ used as a noun. ▸ N COUNT EG *I had a short doze at ten o'clock.*

doze off. If you **doze off**, you fall into a light PHRASAL VB : sleep. EG *He dozed off in front of the fire.* V+ADV

dozen /dʌzə⁰n/, **dozens. 1** If you have a **dozen** NUMBER things, you have twelve of them. See the entry headed NUMBER. EG *...a dozen eggs... ...a few dozen mats.*

2 You can use **dozens** to refer vaguely to a large N PART : number. EG *There had been dozens of attempts at* USU PLURAL *reform.*

dozy /dəuzi¹/. If you are **dozy**, you are feeling ADJ QUALIT sleepy and not very alert.

Dr, Drs. Dr is a written abbreviation for 'Doctor'. EG *Dr Franz was an economist of some standing.*

drab /dræb/. Something that is **drab** is dull and not ADJ QUALIT attractive or exciting. EG *...the drab old building... ...a drab brown dress.* ◊ **drabness.** EG *...the ugli-* ◊ N UNCOUNT *ness and drabness of most people's surroundings.*

draconian /drəˈkəuniən/. **Draconian** laws or ADJ CLASSIF : measures are extremely harsh or drastic. EG *There* ATTRIB *has been an overall growth in population, despite some draconian efforts to contain it.*

draft /drɑːft/, **drafts, drafting, drafted. 1** A N COUNT : **draft** of a letter, book, or speech is an early USU+SUPP version of it. EG *...the change from the first draft to the final printed version.*

2 When you **draft** a letter, book, or speech, you V+O write the first version of it. EG *They sat down and drafted a letter to the local newspaper.*

3 If you **are drafted**, you are ordered to serve in V+O : USU PASS one of the armed forces of your country. EG *I was* American *drafted into the navy.*

4 If you **draft** people somewhere, you move them V+O : OFT+A to another place so that they can do a specific job. EG *Extra staff were drafted from Paris to Rome.*

5 See also **draught**.

draftsman /drɑːftsmən/. See **draughtsman**.

drafty /drɑːfti¹/. See **draughty**.

drag /dræg/, **drags, dragging, dragged. 1** If you V+O : USU+A **drag** a heavy object somewhere, you pull it along the ground with difficulty. EG *He listened as the body was dragged up the stairs.*

2 If you **drag** someone somewhere, **2.1** you pull V+O+A them there roughly. EG *She grabbed her husband by the wrist and dragged him away.* **2.2** you make them go there. EG *I'm sorry to drag you to the telephone, but something awful has happened.*

3 If you **drag** yourself somewhere, you move there V-REFL+A slowly because you feel ill or weak or because you do not want to go there. EG *I was able to drag myself shakily to my feet.*

4 If an event or a period of time **drags**, it is very V boring and seems to last a long time. EG *The part of the play which drags is the last half-hour.*

5 If a man, especially an entertainer, is **in drag**, he PHRASE is wearing women's clothes.

6 If you take a **drag** on a cigarette or pipe, you N COUNT suck air through it. Informal

drag down. If something **drags** you **down**, it PHRASAL VB : makes you feel less able to succeed or progress. V+O+ADV

drag into. If you **drag** something **into** a discus- PHRASAL VB : sion or situation, you mention it or involve it when V+O++PREP it is not necessary or not desirable. EG *It was the politicians who were dragging politics into sport, not the sportsmen.*

drag on. If an event or process **drags on**, it PHRASAL VB : progresses very slowly and lasts a long time. EG V+ADV *Some legal cases have dragged on for years.*

drag out. 1 If you **drag** something **out**, you make PHRASAL VB : it last for longer than is necessary. EG *How could* V+O+ADV *we prevent them from dragging out the talks?* **2** If V+O+ADV you **drag** something **out** of someone, you persuade

them with great difficulty to tell it to you. EG *The truth had to be dragged out of him.*

dragon /drægən/, **dragons.** In stories and leg- N COUNT ends, a **dragon** is an animal like a big lizard. It has wings and claws, and breathes out fire.

dragonfly /drægənflaɪ/, **dragonflies.** A dragon- N COUNT **fly** is a brightly-coloured insect which is often found near water.

drain /dreɪn/, **drains, draining, drained. 1** If you V-ERG **drain** something or if it **drains**, liquid gradually flows out of it or off it. EG *...the complex problem of draining the marshes... Put those plates on the rack to drain.*

2 If a liquid **drains** somewhere, it flows there V-ERG+A gradually. EG *The sewage drains off into the river.*

3 If you **drain** a glass, you drink the whole of its V+O contents. EG *I picked up the glass and drained it.*

4 If a feeling **drains** out of you, it gradually V+A becomes less strong until you no longer feel it. EG *He felt the tension drain out of him.*

5 If something **drains** your strength or resources, V+O it gradually uses up your strength or resources and leaves you weaker. EG *The project is already drain-ing the charity's funds.* ◊ **drained.** EG *She looked* ◊ ADJ QUALIT *tired and drained.*

6 If something is a **drain** on your resources, it N SING : a+N gradually uses them up. EG *The banks are facing a very large drain on their funds.*

7 A **drain** is **7.1** a pipe that carries water or N COUNT sewage away from a place. **7.2** a metal grid in a road, through which rainwater can flow away into pipes.

8 If you say that something goes **down the drain**, PHRASE you mean that it is wasted or ruined. EG *That's just* Informal *money down the drain.*

drainage /dreɪnɪdʒ/ is **1** a system of pipes or N UNCOUNT ditches that are used for draining water or other liquids away from a place. EG *There is no drainage of any sort... Massive big drainage ditches take the water away.* **2** the process of draining water away, or the way in which a place drains. EG *Good drainage doesn't mean dry soil.*

draining board, draining boards. A draining N COUNT **board** is the place next to the sink where you put cups, plates, and cutlery to drain after washing them up.

drainpipe /dreɪnpaɪp/, **drainpipes.** A drainpipe N COUNT is a pipe attached to the side of a building, through which water flows from the roof into a drain.

drake /dreɪk/, **drakes.** A **drake** is a male duck. N COUNT

drama /drɑːmə/, **dramas. 1** A **drama** is a serious N COUNT play for the theatre, television, or radio. EG *I remember her acting in a drama called The Gar-den Party.*

2 You refer to plays in general and to all work in N UNCOUNT the theatre as **drama**. EG *...an expert on modern drama.*

3 You can refer to an exciting real-life situation as N COUNT a **drama**. EG *...the dramas of this village life.*

4 You can refer to the exciting aspects of a N UNCOUNT situation or activity as its **drama**. EG *...the drama of* +SUPP *politics.*

dramatic /drəmætɪk/, **dramatics. 1** A **dramatic** ADJ QUALIT change happens suddenly and is very noticeable. EG *I expect to see dramatic improvements.* ◊ **dramatically.** EG *The way in which information* ◊ ADV *is transmitted has changed dramatically.*

2 You can describe something as **dramatic** when ADJ QUALIT it is very exciting or impressive. EG *Landing on the moon was one of the most dramatic scientific adventures of this century.*

3 If you say or do something **dramatic**, you are ADJ QUALIT trying to surprise and impress people. EG *...a dra-matic gesture.* ◊ **dramatically.** EG *He paused* ◊ ADV

On these pages, which words can be spelled differently in British and American English?

dramatically... She stared into the distance, sighing dramatically.

4 Dramatic art or writing is connected with plays and the theatre. EG *...Browning's dramatic works.* ADJ CLASSIF: ATTRIB

5 Dramatics is the performing of plays. EG *...amateur dramatics.* N UNCOUNT

6 You can refer to emotional behaviour which is intended to impress people as **dramatics**; used showing disapproval. EG *George's dramatics were beginning to irritate me.* N PLURAL

dramatist /drǽmətɪst/, **dramatists.** A **dramatist** is someone who writes plays. N COUNT

dramatize /drǽmətaɪz/, **dramatizes, dramatizing, dramatized;** also spelled **dramatise.**
1 If you **dramatize** a book or story, you rewrite it as a play. EG *His ambition is to dramatise the great works of literature.* ◊ **dramatization** /drǽmətaɪzéɪʃᵊn/, **dramatizations.** EG *...a dramatization of the story of Ali Baba.* V+O ◊ N COUNT

2 If you **dramatize** an event or situation, you try to make it seem more serious or exciting than it really is. EG *The conflict has been dramatized in the newspapers.* V+O

drank /drǽŋk/ is the past tense of **drink.**

drape /dreɪp/, **drapes, draping, draped. 1** If you **drape** a piece of cloth somewhere, you place it there so that it hangs down. EG *He began to drape the shawl carefully over Gertrude's shoulders.* V+O+A

2 If something **is draped** with a piece of cloth, it is covered by it. EG *The walls were draped with banners... ...coffins draped with American flags.* V+O:OFT PASS+with/in

3 Drapes are curtains. EG *The drapes were drawn... Kitty pulled back the drapes.* N PLURAL American

drapery /dreɪpᵊriⁱ/, **draperies. 1** You can refer to cloth or clothing hanging in folds as **drapery** or **draperies.** EG *...fold upon fold of thick drapery... They wore layers of enfolding draperies.* N UNCOUNT OR N PLURAL

2 Drapery is also cloth that you buy in a shop. EG *She works in the drapery department.* N UNCOUNT British

drastic /drǽstɪk/. **1** A **drastic** course of action is extreme and is usually taken urgently. EG *This may force the Government to take drastic measures.* ADJ QUALIT

2 A **drastic** change is very significant and noticeable. EG *...the drastic decline in flat-building.* ◊ **drastically.** EG *Because of the snow, visibility was drastically reduced.* ADJ QUALIT ◊ ADV

draught /drɑːft/, **draughts;** spelled **draft** in American English. **1** A **draught** is a current of air coming into a room or a vehicle. EG *The draught from the window stirred the papers on her desk.* N COUNT

2 A **draught** of liquid or air is a large amount that you swallow or breathe in. EG *He gulped the brandy down in one draught.* N COUNT: USU+SUPP

3 Draught beer is served from barrels rather than bottles. ADJ CLASSIF: ATTRIB

4 Draughts is a game for two people, played with round pieces on a board. In America, draughts is called 'checkers'. N UNCOUNT British

draughtsman /drɑːftsmən/, **draughtsmen;** spelled **draftsman** in American English. A **draughtsman** is someone whose job is to prepare technical drawings. EG *My father worked as a draughtsman in a shipyard.* N COUNT

draughty /drɑːftiⁱ/, **draughtier, draughtiest;** spelled **drafty** in American English. If a room or building is **draughty**, it has currents of cold air blowing through it. ADJ QUALIT

draw /drɔː/, **draws, drawing, drew** /druː/, **drawn. 1** If you **draw** a picture, pattern, or diagram, you make it using a pencil, pen, or crayon. EG *She used to draw funny pictures of everybody... He drew a rough sketch on his pad.* V+O OR V

2 When vehicles or people **draw** away or **draw** near, they move away or move near. EG *The cab drew away from the kerb... Jack and Roger drew near... The slave drew back in fear.* V+A

3 When an event or period of time **draws to an end** or **draws to a close**, it finishes. PHRASE

4 If you **draw** someone or something in a particu- V+O+A

---

lar direction, you pull them there smoothly or gently. EG *He draws the document from its folder... She drew the comb lightly through her hair.*

5 When an animal **draws** a cart or other vehicle, it moves along pulling the vehicle behind it. V+O

6 If you **draw** a curtain or blind, you pull it across a window to cover it or uncover it. V+O

7 If someone **draws** a gun, sword, or knife, they pull it out of its holder so that it is ready to use. V+O OR V

8 If you **draw** a deep breath, you breathe in deeply. V+O

9 If you **draw** money out of a bank or building society, you take it out so that you can use it. V+O+A

10 If something **is drawn** from a particular thing or place, it is obtained from that thing or place. EG *The committee members are drawn from all sections of the local community.* V+O: USU PASS +from

11 If you **draw** a conclusion from facts that you know, you decide that it is the correct conclusion. EG *Unfortunately, they drew the wrong conclusions.* V+O

12 If you **draw** a distinction, comparison, or parallel between two things, you point out that it exists. V+O

13 If something that you do **draws** a particular reaction, that is the way that people react to it. EG *The mayor drew criticism for these excesses... The police drew praise for their handling of the riots.* V+O

14 If you **draw** people's **attention** to something, you make them aware of it. EG *He drew attention to the rising unemployment rates.* PHRASE

15 If something or someone **draws** you, they attract or interest you. EG *She was shy, and perhaps he was drawn to her for that reason.* V+O

16 In a game or competition, if one person or team **draws** with another one, they get the same number of points and nobody wins. V OR V+with: RECIP

17 A **draw** is the result of a game or competition in which two people or teams draw. N COUNT

18 See also **drawing, drawn.**

draw into. If you **draw** someone **into** something, you cause them to become involved in it. EG *She refused to be drawn into the conversation.* PHRASAL VB: V+O+PREP

draw on. 1 If you **draw on** something, you make use of it in order to do something. EG *...the kind of information an expert draws on... He was able to draw on vast reserves of talent.* **2** When someone **draws on** a cigarette, they breathe in through it and inhale the smoke. PHRASAL VB: V+PREP, HAS PASS / V+PREP

draw up. 1 When you **draw up** a document, list, or plan, you prepare it and write it out. EG *I was busy drawing up plans for the new course.* **2** When a vehicle **draws up**, it comes to a particular place and stops. EG *Just before eleven a bus drew up.* PHRASAL VB: V+O+ADV / V+ADV

draw upon. If you **draw upon** something, you make use of it in order to do something. EG *One had to draw upon some knowledge of human psychology.* PHRASAL VB: V+PREP, HAS PASS

drawback /drɔːbæk/, **drawbacks.** A **drawback** is a difficult or unpleasant aspect of something that makes it less acceptable or less desirable. EG *The major drawback of the system is that the funds are administered centrally.* N COUNT: USU+SUPP

drawer /drɔːᵊ/, **drawers.** A **drawer** is a box-shaped part of a desk or other piece of furniture. You pull it towards you to open it, so that you can take things out of it or put things in. EG *The letter had always been kept in a drawer in his study.* N COUNT

drawing /drɔːɪŋ/, **drawings. 1** A **drawing** is a picture made with a pencil, pen, or crayon. EG *On the cover was a drawing of five students.* N COUNT

2 Drawing is the skill or work of drawing pictures. EG *She had a passion for drawing and painting.* N UNCOUNT

drawing pin, drawing pins. A **drawing pin** is a short nail with a broad, flat top which you use for attaching papers to a vertical surface. See picture at PINS. N COUNT British

drawl /drɔːl/, **drawls, drawling, drawled.** If someone **drawls**, they speak slowly, with long vowel sounds. ▸ used as a noun. EG *McCord spoke in a soft drawl.* V OR V+QUOTE ▸ N SING+SUPP

drawn /drɔːn/. 1 **Drawn** is the past participle of draw.

2 A **drawn** curtain or blind has been pulled over a window to cover it. ADJ CLASSIF

3 If someone looks **drawn** or if their face looks **drawn**, they look very tired or ill. EG *There was a drawn and haggard look about his eyes.* ADJ QUALIT

drawn-out. You describe something as **drawn-out** when it lasts longer than you think it should. EG *He was tired of the long drawn-out arguments.* ADJ QUALIT

dread /dred/, **dreads, dreading, dreaded.** 1 If you **dread** something which is going to happen or which may happen, you feel very worried about it because you think that it will be very unpleasant. EG *She had begun to dread these excursions... Fanny dreaded seeing Thomas again, but felt that she had to... What woman does not dread that a lump will turn out to be cancer?* ▸ used as a noun. EG *Her dread of returning to school gets stronger... ...his dread that the child would be infected with the disease.* V+O, V+-ING, OR V+REPORT: ONLY that ▸ N UNCOUNT: OFT+of OR REPORT

2 If you say that you **dread to think** what is happening, you mean that you think that it is probably unpleasant or undesirable. EG *I dread to think what goes on in these schools.* PHRASE

dreaded /ˈdredɪd/ means terrible and greatly feared. EG *Consumption was the most dreaded disease of the time... ...the dreaded General van den Bergh.* ADJ CLASSIF: ATTRIB

dreadful /ˈdredful/. 1 If you say that something is **dreadful**, you mean that it is 1.1 very bad or unpleasant. EG *The weather was dreadful... ...that dreadful man!* ◊ **dreadfully.** *Ian was behaving dreadfully.* 1.2 of very poor quality. EG *She spoke dreadful English.* ADJ QUALIT ◊ ADV ADJ QUALIT

2 You can use **dreadful** to emphasize the degree or extent of something bad. EG *I was a dreadful coward... It'll be a dreadful waste.* ◊ **dreadfully.** EG *The girls were dreadfully dull companions.* ADJ QUALIT: ATTRIB ◊ SUBMOD

dream /driːm/, **dreams, dreaming, dreamed** or **dreamt. Dreamed** and **dreamt** are both used as the past tense and past participle of the verb.

1 A **dream** is 1.1 an imaginary series of events that you experience in your mind while you are asleep. EG *In his dream he was sitting in a theatre watching a play... I had a strange dream about you last night.* N COUNT

1.2 a situation or event which you often think about because you would very much like it to happen. EG *His dream of being champion had come true... ...a dream world.* N COUNT: OFT+SUPP

2 When you **dream**, 2.1 you see imaginary pictures and events in your mind while you are asleep. EG *That night I dreamt that I was beaten up by Ernest Hemingway.* 2.2 you think about a particular situation or event that you would very much like to happen. EG *He dreamed of having a car.* V: OFT+of/ about OR REPORT: ONLY that

3 If you say that you **would not dream of** doing something, you are emphasizing that you would not do it. EG *A lot of the boys would never dream of going away for residential courses.* PHRASE

4 If you say that you **never dreamed** that something would happen, you are emphasizing that you did not think it would happen. EG *It all seemed so permanent; we never dreamed that it was about to end.* PHRASE

5 If you describe your house or job as a **dream** house or a **dream** job, you mean that you are very pleased with it. ADJ CLASSIF: ATTRIB

dream up. If someone **dreams up** a plan, they invent it. EG *He would never dream up a desperate scheme like that on his own.* PHRASAL VB: V+ADV+O

dreamer /ˈdriːmə/, **dreamers.** Someone who is a **dreamer** looks forward to pleasant things that may never happen, rather than being realistic and practical. N COUNT

dreamily /ˈdriːmɪlɪ¹/. If you do something **dreamily**, you do it without concentrating, because you are thinking about something else. EG *He stared dreamily around him.* ADV

dreamt /dremt/ is a past tense and past participle of **dream**.

dreamy /ˈdriːmɪ¹/, **dreamier, dreamiest.** 1 If someone has a **dreamy** expression, they look as if they are thinking about something very pleasant. EG *...a dreamy smile of content... A dreamy look came into her eyes.* ADJ QUALIT

2 See also **dreamily.**

dreary /ˈdrɪərɪ¹/, **drearier, dreariest.** If something is **dreary**, it is so dull that it makes you feel bored or depressed. EG *They don't realise how dull and dreary their world is... I spent a dreary hour with him... They do only the dreariest jobs.* ◊ **drearily.** EG *He was dressed drearily in grey.* ADJ QUALIT ◊ ADV

dredge /dredʒ/, **dredges, dredging, dredged.** To **dredge** a harbour or a river means to clear a channel by removing mud from the bottom using a special machine. V+O

dregs /dregz/. 1 The **dregs** of a liquid are the last drops left at the bottom of a container, together with any solid bits that have sunk to the bottom. EG *She had drunk her coffee down to the dregs.* N PLURAL

2 If you talk about the **dregs** of a society or community, you are referring to the worst or most useless people in it. EG *...the dregs of humanity.* N PLURAL +SUPP

drenched /drentʃt/. If people or things are **drenched**, they have become very wet. EG *Joseph was drenched with sweat... ...scores of drenched people waiting for the bus.* ADJ QUALIT

dress /dres/, **dresses, dressing, dressed.** 1 A **dress** is a piece of clothing worn by a woman or girl. It covers her body and extends down over her legs. See picture at CLOTHES. EG *She was wearing a short black dress.* N COUNT

2 You can refer to clothes worn by men or women as **dress**. EG *He was in evening dress.* N UNCOUNT

3 When you **dress** or **dress** yourself, you put on your clothes. EG *When he had shaved and dressed, he went down to the kitchen.* V OR V-REFL

4 If you are **dressed**, you are wearing clothes rather than being naked, or wearing ordinary clothes rather than pyjamas or a nightdress. EG *Both men were fully dressed... Get dressed.* ADJ PRED

5 If you are **dressed** in a particular way, you are wearing clothes of a particular kind or colour. EG *He was dressed in a black suit.* ADJ PRED: USU+in

6 You say that someone **dresses** in a particular way when they usually wear that style of clothes. EG *He still dressed like a bank manager.* V+A

7 If you **dress** someone, for example a child, you put clothes on them. V+O

8 See also **dressing.**

dress up. If you **dress up** or **dress** yourself **up**, you put on different clothes, in order to make yourself look smarter than usual or to disguise yourself. EG *That evening they dressed themselves up in fancy clothes.* ◊ **dressed up.** EG *She was glad that she was all dressed up.* PHRASAL VB: V+ADV OR V-REFL+ADV ◊ ADJ CLASSIF

dresser /ˈdresə/, **dressers.** 1 A **dresser** is 1.1 a piece of furniture with cupboards or drawers in the lower part and shelves in the top part. 1.2 a chest of drawers, usually with a mirror on the top. N COUNT British American

2 You also use **dresser** to refer to the kind of clothes that a person wears. For example, if you say that someone is a neat dresser, you mean that they dress neatly. EG *Fisher was a smart dresser.* N COUNT+SUPP

dressing /ˈdresɪŋ/, **dressings.** 1 A **dressing** is a covering that is put on a wound to protect it while it heals. N COUNT

2 A **salad** dressing is a mixture of oil, vinegar, and herbs, which you pour over a salad. N MASS

dressing-down. If someone gives you a **dressing-down**, they speak angrily to you because you have done something bad or foolish. N SING

What kind of thing do *you* dream about?

dressing gown, dressing gowns. A **dressing** N COUNT **gown** is a loose-fitting coat which you wear over pyjamas or a nightdress when you are not in bed.

dressing room, dressing rooms. A **dressing** N COUNT **room** is a room in a theatre where performers can get dressed and put on their make-up.

dressing table, dressing tables. A **dressing** N COUNT **table** is a small table in a bedroom. It has drawers underneath and a mirror on top.

dressmaker /drɛsmeɪkə/, **dressmakers.** A N COUNT **dressmaker** is a woman who is paid to make women's or children's clothes.

drew /druː/ is the past tense of **draw.**

dribble /drɪbəᵘl/, **dribbles, dribbling, dribbled.** **1** When a liquid **dribbles** down a surface, it moves V-ERG : USU+A down it in a thin stream. EG *Condensation dribbled down the glass.* **2** A **dribble** of liquid is a small amount of it N PART dribbling somewhere. EG *...dribbles of blood.* **3** When a person or animal **dribbles**, saliva trick- V les from their mouth.

dried /draɪd/. **1 Dried** is the past tense and past participle of **dry.** **2 Dried** food is food that has been preserved by ADJ CLASSIF : having liquid removed from it. EG *...dried milk...* ATTRIB *...pieces of dried fruit.*

drier /draɪə/. See **dryer.**

drift /drɪft/, **drifts, drifting, drifted.** **1** When V+A something **drifts** somewhere, it is carried there by the wind or by water. EG *The clouds drifted away... A tiny fishing boat was drifting slowly along.* **2** A **drift** is the same as a snowdrift. EG *There were* N COUNT *two-foot drifts in some places.* **3** When people **drift** somewhere, they move there V+A slowly or gradually. EG *The crowd started to drift away.* **4** To **drift** towards a bad situation means to slowly V+A reach the stage where you are in this situation. EG *We are drifting towards disaster.* ▸ used as a noun. ▸ N SING+SUPP EG *...the drift to violence.* **5** When someone **drifts** or **drifts** around, they V : USU+A travel from place to place without a settled way of life. EG *They had drifted around in search of their great chance.* ◊ **drifter** /drɪftə/, **drifters.** EG *She* ◊ N COUNT *was a drifter with no family and no close friends.* **6** Someone's **drift** is the general line of argument N COUNT in what they are saying. EG *I was able to follow his drift pretty well.*

drift off. If you **drift off** to sleep, you gradually PHRASAL VB : fall asleep. V+ADV

driftwood /drɪftwʊd/ is wood which is floating on N UNCOUNT the sea or a river, or which has been carried by the water onto the shore.

drill /drɪl/, **drills, drilling, drilled.** **1** A **drill** is a N COUNT tool or machine that you use for making holes. EG *...an electric drill.* **2** When you **drill** into something or **drill** a hole in V OR V+O : something, you make a hole in it using a drill. OFT+A **3** When people **drill** for oil or water, they search V : OFT+for for it by drilling deep holes in the ground or in the bottom of the sea. **4** A **drill** is also **4.1** a way of teaching people to do N COUNT something by making them repeat it many times. EG *...spelling drills.* **4.2** a routine exercise that is N COUNT+SUPP intended to save people's lives by showing them what to do in a dangerous situation. EG *...a fire drill.* **5** If you **drill** people, you teach them to do some- V+O : OFT+in thing by making them repeat it many times. EG *He was not pleased at having to drill a squad of new recruits.*

drily /draɪliⁱ/. See **dry.**

drink /drɪŋk/, **drinks, drinking, drank** /dræŋk/, **drunk** /drʌŋk/. **1** When you **drink** a liquid, you V+O OR V take it into your mouth and swallow it. EG *We sat drinking coffee... He drank eagerly.* **2** To **drink** also means to drink alcohol. EG *She said* V *she didn't drink... You shouldn't drink and drive.* **3** A **drink** is **3.1** an amount of a liquid which you N COUNT

drink. EG *I asked for a drink of water.* **3.2** an alcoholic drink. EG *He poured himself a drink.* **4 Drink** is alcohol, for example beer, wine, or N UNCOUNT whisky. EG *We are trying to keep him away from drink... He eventually died of drink.*

drink to. If you **drink to** someone or something, PHRASAL VB : you raise your glass and say their name before V+PREP drinking, as a way of showing that you hope they will be happy or successful. EG *They agreed on their plan and drank to it.*

drinker /drɪŋkə/, **drinkers.** **1** A **drinker** is some- N COUNT one who drinks a lot of alcohol. EG *She had become a secret drinker.* **2** You can use **drinker** to say what kind of drink N COUNT+SUPP someone regularly drinks. For example, a coffee drinker is someone who regularly drinks coffee. EG *...a tea drinker... ...a beer drinker.*

drinking /drɪŋkɪŋ/ is the activity of drinking N UNCOUNT alcohol. EG *There had been some heavy drinking at the party.*

drip /drɪp/, **drips, dripping, dripped.** **1** When V-ERG liquid **drips**, it falls in small drops. EG *The rain was dripping down our necks.* **2** When something **drips**, drops of liquid fall from V it. EG *...the dripping of the cold water tap.* **3 Drips** are drops of liquid falling from a place. EG N COUNT *She placed a cup under the leak to catch the drips.*

drive /draɪv/, **drives, driving, drove** /drəʊv/, **driven** /drɪvəⁿn/. **1** When you **drive** a vehicle, you V+O OR V : operate it and control it so that it goes where you OFT+A want it to go. EG *It is her turn to drive the car... They drove to the temple... I have never learned to drive.* **2** If you **drive** someone somewhere, you take them V+O+A there in a car. EG *Can I drive you to the airport?* **3** A **drive** is a journey in a vehicle such as a car. EG N COUNT *It'll be a thirty mile drive.* **4** The **drive** to someone's house is a private road N COUNT that leads from a public road to the house. EG *There were several cars parked in the drive.* **5** If something **drives** a machine, it supplies the V+O power that makes it work. EG *Steam can be used to drive generators.* **6** If you **drive** a post or a nail into something, you V+O+A force it in by hitting it with a hammer. EG *...a stake driven into the gravel.* **7** If people or animals **are driven** somewhere, V+O+A they are forced to go there. EG *Half a million people had been driven out... We smoked constantly to drive away the mosquitoes.* **8** To **drive** someone into a particular state or V+O+A situation means to force them into it. EG *The* OR V+O+C *farming venture drove the company into debt... The tourists were beginning to drive me crazy.* **9** If someone **is driven** by a feeling or need, this is V+O : USU PASS what makes them behave as they do. EG *...a man driven by greed or envy.* **10** If someone has **drive**, they have energy and N UNCOUNT determination. EG *Northcliffe had great ability and drive.* **11** A **drive** is also a special effort made by a group N SING+SUPP of people in order to achieve something. EG *The Poles launched a tremendous investment drive.* **12** If you understand what someone **is driving at**, PHRASE you understand what they are trying to say. EG *She knew at once what I was driving at.* **13** See also **driving, drove.**

drivel /drɪvəᵘl/. You can describe something that N UNCOUNT someone has said or written as **drivel** when you think that it is very silly. EG *I've never heard such drivel.*

driven /drɪvəⁿn/ is the past participle of **drive.**

driver /draɪvə/, **drivers.** **1** A **driver** is someone N COUNT who drives a motor vehicle. EG *I hate being behind middle-aged drivers.* **2** A bus **driver** or a taxi **driver** is someone whose N COUNT+SUPP job is to drive a bus or a taxi.

driveway /draɪvweɪ/, **driveways.** A **driveway** is N COUNT a private road that leads from a public road to a house or garage. EG *The car turned into a dark driveway.*

driving /draɪvɪŋ/. **1** Driving is the activity of driving a car, or the way that you drive it. EG *I love driving... She was found guilty of dangerous driving.* N UNCOUNT

2 You describe something as the **driving** force behind something else when it is the main cause of it. EG *The union is the driving force behind the revolution.* ADJ CLASSIF: ATTRIB

driving licence, driving licences. A driving licence is a card showing that you are qualified to drive because you have passed a driving test. N COUNT: British

drizzle /drɪzə⁰l/, **drizzles, drizzling, drizzled. 1** Drizzle is light rain falling in very small drops. EG *He walked back through the fine drizzle.* N UNCOUNT

2 If it **is drizzling**, it is raining lightly. V

drone /drəun/, **drones, droning, droned. 1** If something **drones**, it makes a low, continuous humming noise. EG *The engine droned on and on.* V

▸ used as a noun. EG *...the drone of a bee... ...the steady drone of the traffic.* ▸ N SING+SUPP

2 A **drone** is a male bee. N COUNT

drone on. If someone **drones on**, they keep talking about something or reading something aloud in a boring way. EG *He droned on through several more pages of information.* PHRASAL VB: V+ADV

drool /druːl/, **drools, drooling, drooled. 1** If someone **drools**, they let saliva fall from their mouth, without being able to stop it. V

2 If you **drool** over someone or something, you look at them with uncontrolled pleasure; used showing disapproval. EG *Gaskell's drooling over you all the time.* V: OFT+over/at Informal

droop /druːp/, **droops, drooping, drooped.** If something **droops**, it hangs or leans downwards with no strength or firmness. EG *His shoulders drooped... His eyelids drooped as though he was on the verge of sleep.* ◊ **drooping.** EG *...drooping purple flowers... ...a drooping moustache.* V ◊ ADJ CLASSIF

drop /drɒp/, **drops, dropping, dropped. 1** If you **drop** something, you let it fall deliberately or by mistake. EG *Planes dropped huge quantities of incendiary bombs... He collided with a chair and dropped his cigar.* V+O

2 If something **drops**, it falls straight down. EG *Ash dropped from his cigarette.* V: USU+A

3 If a level or amount **drops**, it quickly becomes less. EG *The temperature of their bodies dropped ten degrees.* ▸ used as a noun. EG *...a drop in income... ...a voltage drop.* V: OFT+A ▸ N COUNT +SUPP

4 If your voice **drops** or if you **drop** your voice, you speak more quietly. V-ERG

5 If someone **drops dead**, they die suddenly. EG *The minister dropped dead at a public meeting.* PHRASE Informal

6 If you **drop** something that you are doing or dealing with, you stop doing it or dealing with it. EG *Most of the charges against him were dropped... I was certain he would drop everything to help.* V+O

7 If you **drop** a hint, you give someone a hint in a casual way. EG *Don't drop hints about promotion.* V+O

8 If the driver of a vehicle **drops** you somewhere, he or she stops the vehicle and you get out. EG *He ordered his taxi to drop him at the corner of the street.* V+O+A

9 If you **drop** someone **a line**, you write them a short letter. PHRASE Informal

10 A **drop** of a liquid is a very small amount of it shaped like a little ball. EG *A drop of blood slid down his leg.* N COUNT OR N PART

11 A **drop** of an alcoholic drink is a small amount of it in a glass. EG *A little drop of scotch would be very welcome.* N PART Informal

12 Drops are a kind of medicine which you put drop by drop into your ears, eyes, or nose. N COUNT: USU PLURAL

13 You use **drop** to talk about vertical distances. For example, a thirty-foot **drop** is a distance of thirty feet between the top of a cliff or wall and the bottom of it. N COUNT+SUPP

drop by. If you **drop by**, you visit someone PHRASAL VB: V+ADV

informally. EG *If there's anything you want to see, just drop by.*

drop in. If you **drop in** on someone, you visit them informally, usually without having arranged it before. EG *I thought I'd just drop in and see how you were.* PHRASAL VB: V+ADV, OFT+on Informal

drop off. 1 If you **drop off** to sleep, you go to sleep. EG *I was feeling tired enough to drop off to sleep at any moment.* **2** If the driver of a vehicle **drops** you **off** somewhere, he or she stops the vehicle and you get out. EG *I can drop Daisy off on my way home.* PHRASAL VB: V+ADV V+O+ADV

drop out. If you **drop out** of college or university, you leave it without finishing your course. EG *Some students drop out after a relatively short time.* PHRASAL VB: V+ADV, OFT+of

drop-out, drop-outs. 1 Drop-outs are people who reject the accepted ways of a society, for example by not having a regular job and by dressing in an untidy way; used showing disapproval. N COUNT Informal

2 Drop-outs are also young people who have left school or college before they have finished their studies. EG *...a high-school dropout.* N COUNT Informal

droppings /drɒpɪŋz/ are the faeces of birds and small animals. EG *...mouse droppings.* N PLURAL

drought /draut/, **droughts.** A **drought** is a long period of time during which no rain falls. EG *...the effects of famine and drought... Local problems include diseases and periodic droughts.* N UNCOUNT OR N COUNT

drove /drəuv/, **droves. 1 Drove** is the past tense of **drive**.

2 Droves of people are very large numbers of them. EG *They came in droves to see Australia's natural wonder.* N PLURAL

drown /draun/, **drowns, drowning, drowned. 1** When someone **drowns** or **is drowned**, they die because they have gone under water and cannot breathe. EG *A man fell from a bridge and drowned... I couldn't make myself drown the poor creature.* V-ERG

2 If something **drowns** a sound, it is louder than the sound and makes it impossible to hear it. EG *...the heckling which drowned his speech.* V+O: USU PASS

3 If you say that someone **is drowning** their **sorrows**, you mean that they are drinking a lot of alcohol in order to forget an unhappy experience. PHRASE Informal

drowse /drauz/, **drowses, drowsing, drowsed.** If you **drowse**, you are almost asleep or just asleep. EG *She drowsed in the sun.* V

drowsy /drauzi¹/, **drowsier, drowsiest.** If you are **drowsy**, you feel sleepy and cannot think clearly. EG *I became pleasantly drowsy.* ◊ **drowsiness.** EG *The sound of the waves lulled me into drowsiness... I must shake off this drowsiness...* ◊ **drowsily.** EG *I shook my head drowsily.* ADJ QUALIT ◊ N UNCOUNT ◊ ADV

drudge /drʌdʒ/, **drudges.** You can refer to someone as a **drudge** when they have to do a lot of very uninteresting work. N COUNT

drudgery /drʌdʒəri¹/ is uninteresting work that must be done. EG *...the drudgery of housework.* N UNCOUNT

drug /drʌg/, **drugs, drugging, drugged. 1** A **drug** is a chemical which is given to people in order to treat or prevent an illness or disease. EG *This drug is prescribed to treat hay fever.* N COUNT

2 Drugs are also substances that some people smoke or inject into their blood because of their stimulating effects. In most countries, these uses of drugs are illegal. EG *He was on drugs... She takes drugs... ...drug addiction.* N COUNT: USU PLURAL

3 If you **drug** a person or animal, you give them a chemical substance in order to make them sleepy or unconscious. ◊ **drugged.** EG *She spoke as if she was half asleep or drugged.* V+O ◊ ADJ CLASSIF

4 If food or drink **is drugged**, a chemical substance is added to it in order to make someone unconscious when they eat or drink it. EG *The sweets she had given them were drugged.* V+O: USU PASS

If an English film is dubbed into your language, what language would you hear?

drugstore /drʌgstɔː/, **drugstores**. In America, a N COUNT
drugstore is a shop where you can buy medicines
and other goods and also get drinks and snacks.

drum /drʌm/, **drums, drumming, drummed**. 1 N COUNT
A **drum** is a musical instrument consisting of a
skin stretched tightly over a round frame. You play
a drum by beating it rhythmically with sticks or
with your hands. See picture at MUSICAL INSTRU-
MENTS.

2 A **drum** is also a large cylindrical container in N COUNT
which fuel is kept. EG ...oil drums.

3 If you **drum** your fingers, you hit a surface with V+O OR V
them, making a continuous beating sound. EG He
drummed his fingers on the desk.

4 If something **is drumming** on a surface, it is V
hitting it regularly, making a continuous beating
sound. EG We sat listening to the rain drumming on
the roof.

drum into. If you **drum** something **into** some- PHRASAL VB :
one, you keep saying it to them until they under- V+O+PREP
stand it or remember it. EG These facts had been
drummed into him.

drum up. If you **drum up** support, you succeed PHRASAL VB :
in getting it. EG ...the patriotic fervour Hamilton had V+ADV+O
drummed up.

drummer /drʌmə/, **drummers**. A **drummer** is a N COUNT
person who plays a drum or drums in a band or
group.

drunk /drʌŋk/, **drunks**. 1 **Drunk** is the past
participle of **drink**.

2 If someone is **drunk**, they have drunk so much ADJ QUALIT
alcohol that they cannot speak clearly or behave
sensibly. EG He was never going to get drunk
again... He was so drunk he couldn't write a word.

3 A **drunk** is someone who is drunk or who often N COUNT
gets drunk. EG San Francisco has a lot of drunks.

drunkard /drʌŋkəd/, **drunkards**. A **drunkard** is N COUNT
someone who often gets drunk.

drunken /drʌŋkəⁿn/. 1 **Drunken** behaviour is ADJ CLASSIF :
clumsy, noisy, or foolish behaviour by someone ATTRIB
who is drunk. EG A long drunken party that had just
broken up... ...drunken whoops of laughter.

◇ **drunkenly**. EG Their parents fought drunkenly ◇ ADV
with each other. ◇ **drunkenness** /drʌŋkənnəs/. ◇ N UNCOUNT
EG They acquired a reputation for drunkenness and
crime.

2 A **drunken** person is drunk. EG ...stiffer penalties ADJ QUALIT :
for drunken drivers. ATTRIB

dry /draɪ/, **drier** or **dryer, driest; dries, drying,
dried**. 1 Something that is **dry** has no water or ADJ QUALIT
other liquid on it or in it. EG They threw onto the
fire some dry branches... He was rubbing himself
dry with a towel. ◇ **dryness**. EG ...the dryness of ◇ N UNCOUNT
the air.

2 When you **dry** something or when it **dries**, it V-ERG
becomes dry. EG He dried his feet with the towel...
The washing hung drying in the sun.

3 When the weather is **dry**, there is no rain. EG The ADJ QUALIT
night was dry and clear.

4 If you are on **dry land**, you are on the shore, PHRASE
rather than in a ship or boat.

5 Dry humour is subtle and sarcastic. EG I enjoyed ADJ QUALIT
her dry accounts of her work experiences. ◇ **drily** ◇ ADV
or **dryly**. EG 'Thank you,' I said drily. 'It must be
nice to be so culturally enlightened.'

6 Dry sherry or wine does not taste sweet. ADJ CLASSIF

7 See also **dried, dryer**.

dry out. If something **dries out**, it becomes PHRASAL VB :
completely dry. EG The material gets as hard as a V-ERG+ADV
brick when it dries out.

dry up. 1 If something **dries up**, it loses all its PHRASAL VB :
water or moisture. EG The pool dried up in the late V+ADV
summer... My mouth always dries up when I'm
nervous. ◇ **dried-up**. EG ...a dried-up piece of cake. ◇ ADJ CLASSIF

2 When you **dry up** after a meal or **dry** the dishes V+ADV OR
up, you wipe the water off the cutlery, plates, and V+O+ADV
cups when they have been washed. EG Would you
like me to dry up?... I started to dry up the cups. **3** V+ADV

If a supply or series of things **dries up**, it stops. EG
Orders dried up and costs continued to rise.

dry-clean, dry-cleans, dry-cleaning, dry- V+O : USU PASS
cleaned. When clothes **are dry-cleaned**, they are
cleaned with a liquid chemical rather than with
water. ◇ **dry-cleaning**. ...dry-cleaning fluid... I'm ◇ N UNCOUNT
taking a load of things to the dry-cleaning shop.

dryer /draɪə/, **dryers**; also spelled **drier**. 1 A N COUNT
dryer is a machine for drying clothes.

2 Dryer and **drier** are also the comparative forms
of **dry**.

dual /djuːəl/ means having two parts, functions, or ADJ CLASSIF :
aspects. EG The committee has a dual function... ATTRIB
...dual nationality... ...dual purpose furniture.

dual carriageway, dual carriageways. A **dual** N COUNT OR
carriageway is a road which has a strip of grass N UNCOUNT
or concrete down the middle to separate traffic British
going in opposite directions.

dub /dʌb/, **dubs, dubbing, dubbed**. 1 If something V+O+C :
is dubbed a particular name, it is given that name. USU PASS
EG London was dubbed 'the insurance capital of the
world'.

2 If a film **is dubbed**, the voices on the soundtrack V+O : USU PASS
are not those of the actors, but those of other
actors speaking in a different language. EG The
series is dubbed into six languages.

dubious /djuːbɪəs/. 1 You describe something as ADJ QUALIT
dubious when you think that it is not completely
honest, safe, or reliable. EG ...goods of dubious
origin... Here Halliday carried on his dubious trade.

2 If you are **dubious** about something, you are not ADJ PRED
sure about it. EG He was dubious about Baker's
choice of pilot. ◇ **dubiously**. EG They looked at ◇ ADV
him dubiously, not knowing how much to believe.

duchess /dʌtʃɪs/, **duchesses**. A **duchess** is a N COUNT
woman who has the same rank as a duke, or who is
a duke's wife or widow. EG ...the Duchess of Marl-
borough.

duck /dʌk/, **ducks, ducking, ducked**. 1 A **duck** is N COUNT
a very common water bird with short legs, webbed
feet, a short neck, and a large flat beak. The plural
form of 'duck' is either 'ducks' or 'duck'.

2 Duck also refers to the meat of a duck when it is N UNCOUNT
cooked and eaten. EG Gerald had ordered duck.

3 If you **take to** something **like a duck to water**, PHRASE
you discover that you are naturally good at it or Informal
that you like doing it.

4 If you **duck** your head or **duck**, you move your V+O OR V
head quickly downwards in order to avoid being
seen or hit by something. EG A gull flew so close
that she ducked.

5 If you **duck** into a place, you move there quickly, V+A
especially in order to escape danger. EG I ducked
into the shrubbery.

6 If you **duck** a duty or responsibility, you avoid it. V+O

duck out. If you **duck out** of something that you PHRASAL VB :
are supposed to do, you avoid doing it. EG I once V+ADV,
ducked out of an appointment I couldn't face. OFT+of

duckling /dʌklɪŋ/, **ducklings**. A **duckling** is a N COUNT
young duck.

duct /dʌkt/, **ducts**. A **duct** is 1 a pipe, tube, or N COUNT :
channel through which a liquid or gas is sent. 2 a OFT+SUPP
tube in your body that a liquid such as tears or bile
can pass through. EG ...an obstructed tear duct.

dud /dʌd/, **duds**. You say that something is **dud** or ADJ CLASSIF
a **dud** when it does not work properly. EG ...dud OR N COUNT
light bulbs... The new system is a dud. Informal

due /djuː/, **dues**. 1 If a situation, event, or state of PREP
affairs is **due to** something else, it happens or
exists as a result of it. EG Over 40 per cent of deaths
were due to this disease... There's still a good deal
of disruption due to the strike.

2 If something is **due** at a particular time, it is ADJ PRED
expected to happen or to arrive at that time. EG We USU+A
were due in at 2 a.m... What time is the bus due?... OR to-INF
The committee was due to meet on 22 August.

3 If you say that something will happen **in due** PHRASE
course, you mean that it will happen eventually, Formal

when the time is right. EG *All will be attended to in due course.*

4 Dues are sums of money that you pay regularly to an organization that you belong to. N PLURAL

5 If some money is **due** to you, you have a right to it. EG *You may get slightly less pension than the full amount due to you.* ADJ PRED : OFT+*to*

6 If you give something **due** consideration or **due** attention, you give it the amount of consideration or attention that it deserves. EG *After due consideration of the evidence, the meeting decided that no one had been to blame.* ADJ CLASSIF : ATTRIB

7 You say **'to give** them their **due'** when you are saying something good about people who have been criticized. EG *To give him his due, he had no idea that he was breaking the rules.* ADV SEN

8 You use **due** to talk about exact compass directions. For example, if a place is **due** north, it is exactly to the north of where you are. EG *They were travelling due east.* ADV

duel /djuːəl/, **duels. 1** A **duel** is a fight between two people in which they use guns or swords in order to settle a quarrel. EG *Feelings were so intense that they fought a duel.* N COUNT

2 You can refer to any conflict between two people as a **duel**. EG *The enemy pilot had fired too soon in the high-speed duel.* N COUNT

duet /djuːɛt/, **duets.** A **duet** is a piece of music sung or played by two people. N COUNT

duffel coat /dʌfəl kəʊt/, **duffel coats;** also spelled **duffle coat.** A **duffel coat** is a heavy coat with rod-shaped buttons and a hood. N COUNT

dug /dʌg/ is the past tense and past participle of **dig.**

duke /djuːk/, **dukes.** A **duke** is a nobleman with a rank just below that of a prince. EG *...the Duke of York... I was in the Duke's service.* N COUNT

dulcet /dʌlsɪt/. **Dulcet** sounds are gentle and pleasant to listen to; often used humorously. EG *I wake up to the dulcet tones of the Radio Four news.* ADJ CLASSIF : ATTRIB Literary

dull /dʌl/, **duller, dullest; dulls, dulling, dulled. 1** Something or someone that is **dull** is not interesting in any way. EG *I thought the book dull and unoriginal... It will be so dull here without you.* ADJ QUALIT
◊ **dullness.** EG *...the dullness of his life.* ◊ N UNCOUNT

2 You can say that someone is **dull** when they show no interest in anything. ◊ **dully.** EG *They stared dully down at the ground.* ADJ QUALIT ◊ ADV

3 A **dull** colour or light is not bright. EG *The sea had been a dull grey... On the opposite wall was a dull electric sign.* ◊ **dully.** EG *The lights of the houses gleamed dully.* ADJ QUALIT : ATTRIB ◊ ADV

4 You say that the weather is **dull** when it is rather cloudy. EG *It was a dull morning.* ADJ QUALIT

5 A **dull** sound is not clear or loud. EG *...a dull thud.* ADJ CLASSIF

6 Dull feelings are weak and not intense. EG *The dull ache in her side began again... I stared at her in dull discomfort.* ◊ **dully.** EG *His ankle throbbed dully.* ADJ CLASSIF : ATTRIB ◊ ADV

7 If something **dulls** a pain or feeling, it causes it to seem less intense. EG *In her experience, the taking of food dulled pain.* V+O

8 If something **dulls** or is **dulled**, it becomes less bright. EG *His eyes dulled.* V-ERG Literary

duly /djuːlɪ/. **1** If something is **duly** done, it is done in the correct way. EG *She was declared duly elected to Parliament.* ADV Formal

2 If something happens that was expected to happen, you can say that it **duly** happened. EG *De Gaulle duly attended the ceremony at the appointed time.* ADV

dumb /dʌm/, **dumber, dumbest. 1** Someone who is **dumb** is completely unable to speak. EG *She was deaf and dumb from birth.* ADJ CLASSIF

2 If someone is **dumb** on a particular occasion, they cannot speak because they are angry, shocked, or surprised. EG *We were struck dumb with horror.* ADJ PRED

3 Dumb also means stupid; an offensive use. EG *Get out of the way, you dumb idiot.* ADJ QUALIT

4 You can describe attitudes or feelings as **dumb** when they are expressed without words. EG *Silence can upset some people who interpret it as dumb insolence.* ADJ CLASSIF : ATTRIB

dumbfounded /dʌmfaʊndɪd/. If you are **dumbfounded**, you are so surprised that you cannot speak. EG *He was watching, dumbfounded.* ADJ CLASSIF

dumbly /dʌmlɪ/. If you do something **dumbly**, you do it without saying anything. EG *He stared dumbly at the wall.* ADV

dummy /dʌmɪ/, **dummies. 1** A baby's **dummy** is a rubber or plastic object that you give to it to suck so that it feels comforted and stays quiet. N COUNT British

2 A tailor's **dummy** is a large model that looks like a human being and that is used to display clothes in a shop. EG *...dummies dressed in military uniforms.* N COUNT

3 You use **dummy** to describe things that are not real. For example, a **dummy** car is not a real car, but one that has been made to look or behave like a real car. EG *...dummy doors... ...experiments with dummy animals.* ADJ CLASSIF : ATTRIB

dump /dʌmp/, **dumps, dumping, dumped.**
1 When unwanted waste matter is **dumped**, it is put somewhere and is intended to remain there for ever. EG *...chemicals dumped in unsuitable places.* ◊ **dumping.** EG *...the dumping of acid wastes in the North Sea.* V+O : USU+A ◊ N UNCOUNT

2 If you **dump** something somewhere, you put it there quickly and in a careless way. EG *She dumped her bag on Judy's table.* V+O : USU+A

3 A **dump** or a **rubbish dump** is a place where rubbish is left, for example on open ground outside a town. EG *...a large municipal dump.* N COUNT

4 You refer to a place as a **dump** when it is unattractive and unpleasant to live in. EG *She'll never want to endure that squalid little dump again... What a dump!* N COUNT Informal

5 If you are **in the dumps**, you feel depressed and miserable. PHRASE Informal

dumping ground, dumping grounds. If you refer to a place as a **dumping ground**, you mean that things are left there, usually in large quantities. EG *The house has become a dumping ground for stolen goods.* N COUNT+*for*

dumpling /dʌmplɪŋ/, **dumplings.** A **dumpling** is a small lump of dough that is cooked with meat and vegetables. N COUNT

dumpy /dʌmpɪ/, **dumpier, dumpiest.** Someone who is **dumpy** is short and fat. ADJ QUALIT

dun /dʌn/. Something that is **dun** is a dull greybrown colour. ADJ COLOUR

dunce /dʌns/, **dunces.** You call someone a **dunce** when they cannot learn what someone is trying to teach them. EG *I was such a dunce at school.* N COUNT

dune /djuːn/, **dunes.** A **dune** or a sand **dune** is a hill of sand near the sea or in a desert. N COUNT

dung /dʌŋ/ is faeces from large animals. N UNCOUNT

dungarees /dʌŋgəriːz/ are trousers attached to a piece of cloth which covers your chest and has straps going over your shoulders. See picture at CLOTHES. N PLURAL

dungeon /dʌndʒən/, **dungeons.** A **dungeon** is a dark underground prison in a castle. N COUNT

dunk /dʌŋk/, **dunks, dunking, dunked.** If you **dunk** something in a liquid, you put it in it for a short time. EG *I dunked my bread in the cocoa.* V+O+*in* Informal

dupe /djuːp/, **dupes, duping, duped. 1** If someone **dupes** you, they trick you. EG *I was duped into expressing my thoughts.* V+O : USU PASS+*into*

2 A **dupe** is someone who has been tricked. N COUNT

duplicate, duplicates, duplicating, duplicated;
pronounced /djuːplɪkeɪt/ when it is a verb and /djuːplɪkət/ when it is a noun or an adjective.

> Are a dustman's clothes likely to be dusty?

1 If you **duplicate** a piece of writing or a drawing, v+o you make exact copies of it using a machine. EG *The story was typed and duplicated.*

2 A **duplicate** is something that is identical to N COUNT something else. EG *In the room was a duplicate of the display panel.* ▶ used as an adjective. EG *...a* ▶ ADJ CLASSIF: *duplicate key... My bag contained the duplicate* ATTRIB *typescript of the book.*

3 If you have something **in duplicate**, you have PHRASE two identical copies of it. EG *Usually we ask for a draft in duplicate.*

4 When an activity **is duplicated**, two people or v+o two groups do the same thing. ◇ **duplication** ◇ N UNCOUNT /dju:plɪkeɪʃəⁿn/. EG *We try to avoid duplication of work.*

durable /djuəⁿrəbəⁿl/. Something that is **durable** ADJ QUALIT is strong and lasts a long time. EG *...well-finished and durable products.* ◇ **durability** ◇ N UNCOUNT /djuəⁿrəbɪlⁱti¹/. EG *...the durability of their love.*

duration /djuⁿreɪʃəⁿn/. The **duration** of something N SING: is the length of time during which it happens or the+N+of exists. EG *He was prepared to do this for the duration of the campaign.*

duress /djuəⁿres/. If you do something under N UNCOUNT **duress**, you are forced to do it, and do it very unwillingly. EG *...a decision made early in life under duress.*

during /djuəⁿrɪŋ/. Something that happens **during** PREP a period of time **1** happens continuously or several times in that period. EG *She heated the place during the winter with a huge wood furnace... Fred had worked a great deal with her at Oxford during the war.* **2** happens at some point in that period. EG *He had died during the night.*

dusk /dʌsk/ is the time just before night when it is N UNCOUNT not completely dark.

dusky /dʌski¹/. Something that is **dusky** is rather ADJ QUALIT dark. EG *...her dusky cheeks... ...the dusky room.*

dust /dʌst/, **dusts, dusting, dusted**. **1** Dust on a N UNCOUNT road or in the air consists of many tiny particles of earth or sand. EG *Each car threw up a cloud of white dust.*

2 Dust in a building consists of many tiny particles N UNCOUNT of dirt. EG *...the dust on the coffee table.*

3 Gold **dust** or chalk **dust** is fine powder consisting N UNCOUNT of tiny particles of gold or chalk.

4 When you **dust** furniture or other objects, you v+o OR v remove dust from them using a duster. EG *She lifted the jugs one by one as she dusted the shelf.*

5 If you **dust** a surface with a powder, you cover it v+o: lightly with the powder. EG *She put on lipstick and* OFT+with *dusted her face with powder.*

dustbin /dʌstbɪn/, **dustbins**. A **dustbin** is a large N COUNT container that you put rubbish in. You keep it British outside your house.

duster /dʌstə/, **dusters**. A **duster** is a cloth that N COUNT you use for removing dust from furniture and other objects.

dustman /dʌstməⁿn/, **dustmen**. A **dustman** is a N COUNT person whose job it is to take away the rubbish that British people keep in their dustbins.

dustpan /dʌstpæn/, **dustpans**. A **dustpan** is a N COUNT small flat container for sweeping dust and dirt into.

dust-up, dust-ups. A **dust-up** is a quarrel or fight. N COUNT EG *Another dust-up took place on the public beach.* Informal

dusty /dʌsti¹/, **dustier, dustiest**. Something that ADJ QUALIT is **dusty** is covered with dust. EG *We rode along a dusty mountain track... ...a room full of dusty, broken furniture.*

dutiful /dju:tɪful/. If you are **dutiful**, you do every- ADJ QUALIT thing that you are expected to do. EG *He was a dutiful son.* ◇ **dutifully**. EG *The audience dutifully* ◇ ADV *applauded.*

duty /dju:ti¹/, **duties. 1** Duty is the work that you N UNCOUNT have to do as your job. EG *He reported for duty at the manager's office.*

2 When policemen, doctors, or nurses are **on duty**, PHRASE they are working. When they are **off duty**, they

are not working. EG *A police constable on duty became suspicious... You can go off duty now.*

3 Your **duties** are the tasks which you do as part of N PLURAL your job. EG *Nursing auxiliaries help qualified nurses with their basic duties.*

4 If you say that something is your **duty**, you mean N SING+POSS that you ought to do it because it is your respon- sibility. EG *As a doctor, it was my duty to preserve life... I've always tried to do my duty.*

5 Duties are taxes which you pay to the govern- N COUNT ment on goods that you buy. EG *The government increased the duty on petrol.*

duty-bound. If you are **duty-bound** to do some- ADJ PRED thing, you must do it because it is your duty. EG *You* +to-INF *are duty-bound to stay by her sick bed.* Formal

duty-free. Duty-free goods are goods that you ADJ CLASSIF buy at airports or on planes or ships at a cheaper price than usual because you do not have to pay taxes on them. EG *...duty-free whisky.*

duvet /du:veɪ/, **duvets**. A **duvet** is a large bag N COUNT filled with feathers or similar material, which you British use to cover yourself in bed.

dwarf /dwɔ:f/, **dwarfs, dwarfing, dwarfed. 1** If v+o: USU PASS one thing **dwarfs** another thing, it is much bigger than the other thing and makes it look small. EG *David was dwarfed by a huge desk... Commercial buildings are beginning to dwarf the city churches.*

2 Dwarf plants or animals are much smaller than ADJ CLASSIF: other plants or animals of the same kind. EG *...dwarf* ATTRIB *wheat.*

3 A **dwarf** is a person who is much smaller than N COUNT most people.

dwell /dwel/, **dwells, dwelling, dwelled, dwelt** v+A /dwelt/. **Dwelled** and **dwelt** are both used as the Outdated past tense and past participle of the verb. If you **dwell** somewhere, you live there. EG *They still dwelt in their old abode.*

dwell on. If you **dwell on** something or **dwell** PHRASAL VB: **upon** it, you think, speak, or write about it a great V+PREP, deal. EG *She began to dwell on memories of her* HAS PASS *mother... So far we have dwelt upon the negative elements in the situation.*

dweller /dwelə/, **dwellers**. You use **dweller** to N COUNT+SUPP say where someone lives. For example, a city **dweller** is someone who lives in a city. EG *...slum dwellers... ...cave dwellers.*

dwelling /dwelɪŋ/, **dwellings**. A **dwelling** is a N COUNT house or other place where someone lives. EG *They* Formal *were five miles from the nearest dwelling.*

dwelt /dwelt/ is the past tense and past participle of **dwell**.

dwindle /dwɪndəⁿl/, **dwindles, dwindling, dwin-** v: OFT+A **dled**. If something **dwindles**, it becomes smaller or less strong. EG *Their small hoard of money dwindled... The stream had dwindled to a trickle.* ◇ **dwindling**. EG *...an area of rapidly dwindling* ◇ ADJ QUALIT *forest.*

dye /daɪ/, **dyes, dyeing, dyed. 1** If you **dye** v+o something such as hair or cloth, you change its colour by soaking it in a coloured liquid. ◇ **dyed**. ◇ ADJ CLASSIF EG *...a woman with dyed red hair.*

2 A **dye** is a substance which is mixed into a liquid N MASS and is used to change the colour of something such as cloth or hair.

dying /daɪɪŋ/. **1** Dying is the present participle of **die**.

2 The **dying** are people who are so ill or so badly N PLURAL: injured that they are likely to die soon. EG *She* the+N *cared for the poor, the diseased and the dying.*

3 A **dying** tradition or industry is becoming less ADJ CLASSIF: important and is likely to finish altogether. EG *Coal* ATTRIB *is by no means a dying industry.*

dyke /daɪk/, **dykes**; also spelled **dike**. A **dyke** is a N COUNT thick wall that prevents water flooding onto land from a river or from the sea.

dynamic /daɪnæmɪk/, **dynamics. 1** Someone who ADJ QUALIT is **dynamic** is full of energy. EG *The new President is a dynamic and able man.* ◇ **dynamically**. EG *We* ◇ ADV *would like to see them participate more dynami-cally.*

2 The **dynamics** of a society or a situation are the N PLURAL forces that cause it to change. EG *...the dynamics of industrial development.*

dynamism /daɪnəmɪzəᵊm/. Someone's **dyna-** N UNCOUNT **mism** is their energy or ability to produce new ideas.

dynamite /daɪnəmaɪt/, **dynamites, dynamiting, dynamited. 1 Dynamite** is an explosive. EG *...re-* N UNCOUNT *bels wielding sticks of dynamite.*

2 If you **dynamite** something, you blow it up using V+O dynamite. EG *They dynamited the houses.*

dynamo /daɪnəməu/, **dynamos.** A **dynamo** is a N COUNT device that uses the movement of a machine or vehicle to produce electricity.

dynasty /dɪnəsti¹/, **dynasties.** A **dynasty** is a N COUNT series of rulers of a country who all belong to the same family.

d'you is a short form of 'do you' used in questions in spoken English. EG *D'you know what I found?*

dysentery /dɪsəⁿntri¹/ is an infection that causes N UNCOUNT severe diarrhoea.

dyslexia /dɪsleksɪə/ is difficulty with reading, N UNCOUNT caused by a slight disorder of the brain.
◊ **dyslexic** /dɪsleksɪk/. EG *Her younger daughter* ◊ ADJ CLASSIF *was dyslexic... ...dyslexic pupils.*

E e

E, e /iː/, **E's, e's. 1 E** is the fifth letter of the N COUNT English alphabet.

2 E is a written abbreviation for 'east'.

each /iːtʃ/. **1** If you refer to **each** thing or **each** DET; person in a group, you are referring to every ALSO PRON : member of the group and considering them as OFT+*of* individuals. EG *Each county is subdivided into sever-al districts... Each day Kunta felt a little worse... There were peaches and pears. I opened two tins of each... They were all just sitting there, each of them thinking private thoughts.*

2 You use **each** to emphasize that you are refer- PRON ring to every individual thing or person in a group. EG *He offered me the tin of biscuits and my sister and I had one each... They cost eight pounds each.*

3 You use **each other** when you are saying that PRON each member of a group does something to the others or has a particular connection with the others. EG *She and John looked at each other... We know each other's minds very well.*

eager /iːgə/. If you are **eager** to do something, you ADJ QUALIT : want to do it very much. EG *The majority were* OFT+*to*-INF *eager to express their opinions... ...people eager for* OR *for* *a quick cure.* ◊ **eagerly.** EG *They began to talk* ◊ ADV *eagerly.* ◊ **eagerness.** EG *...my eagerness to* ◊ N UNCOUNT *learn... ...an eagerness for total freedom.*

eagle /iːgəᵊl/, **eagles.** An **eagle** is a large bird that N COUNT lives by eating small animals.

ear /ɪə/, **ears. 1** Your **ears** are the two parts of N COUNT your body, one on each side of your head, with which you hear sounds. See picture at THE HUMAN BODY.

2 You can use **ear** to refer to a person's willingness N SING+SUPP to listen to what someone is saying. EG *He tried to give a sympathetic ear at all times.*

3 The **ears** of a cereal plant such as wheat or N COUNT barley are the parts at the top of the stem, which contain the seeds or grains.

4 Ear is used in these phrases. **4.1** If you **keep** or PHRASES **have** your **ear to the ground**, you make sure that Informal you are well informed about what is happening. **4.2** If can you **play** a piece of music **by ear**, you can play it when you hear it or have heard it in the past, rather than by reading printed music. **4.3** If Informal you **turn a deaf ear** to something that is being said, you take no notice of it. EG *Young people sometimes seem to turn a deaf ear to the words of their anxious parents.* **4.4** When someone forgets Informal what you tell them, you can say that it **goes in one ear and out the other.**

eardrum /ɪədrʌm/, **eardrums.** Your **eardrums** N COUNT are thin pieces of tightly stretched skin inside your ears, which vibrate so that you can hear sounds.

earl /ɜːl/, **earls.** An **earl** is a British nobleman. N COUNT

earlier /ɜːli¹ə/ is the comparative of **early**. It is ADV AFTER VB, also used to refer to a point or period in time OR ADJ QUALIT : before the present or before the one that you are COMPAR talking about. EG *Her parents had died of cholera four years earlier... ...as I said earlier... ...in earlier times, when this fashion was popular.* ● **Earlier on** ● PHRASE means the same as 'earlier'. *I mentioned that problem earlier on.*

earlobe /ɪələub/, **earlobes.** Your **earlobes** are N COUNT the soft parts at the bottom of your ears.

early /ɜːli¹/, **earlier, earliest. 1 Early** means ADV OR near the beginning of a period of time, a process, ADJ QUALIT : or a piece of work. EG *I got up early... ...very early* ATTRIB *in the morning... ...early last week... ...in the early 1980s... The men realized this quite early on in their lives... ...in those early chapters, when he's writing about his family.*

2 If someone or something arrives or happens ADV AFTER VB **early**, they arrive or happen before the time that OR AFTER N was arranged or expected. EG *The day's practice ended early because of bad light... He knew he was three minutes early.*

3 You also use **early** to describe things that ADJ QUALIT : happen before the normal time. EG *...her husband's* ATTRIB OR *early death... Everyone went to sleep early.* ADV AFTER VB

4 As early as means at a particular time or period PHRASE that is surprisingly early. EG *As early as 1978 the United States had taken steps to counteract this.*

5 At the earliest means not before the date or PHRASE time mentioned. EG *No developments were expect-ed before August at the earliest.*

6 If you say that it is **early days**, you mean that it PHRASE is too soon for you to be completely sure about something. EG *Well, it's early days yet to say whether it works.*

7 bright and early: see **bright.** ● **early night**: see **night.** ● See also **earlier.**

earmark /ɪəmɑːk/, **earmarks, earmarking,** V+O : **earmarked.** If something **is earmarked** for a USU PASS+*for* particular purpose, it has been reserved for that purpose. EG *The fund contained more than $300,000 earmarked for sensitive political projects.*

earn /ɜːn/, **earns, earning, earned. 1** If you **earn** V+O money, you receive it in return for work that you do. EG *...the average worker, earning $15,058... They have to earn a living somehow.* ◊ **earner** /ɜːnə/, ◊ N COUNT **earners.** EG *Most wage earners can afford it.* +SUPP

2 If something **earns** money, it produces money as V+O profit. EG *Something is uneconomic when it fails to earn an adequate profit.*

3 If you **earn** something such as praise, you get it V+O because you deserve it. EG *He has earned his place in history... They earn acclaim wherever they go.*

earnest /ˈɜːnɪst/. 1 People who are **earnest** are ADJ QUALIT very serious in what they say and do. EG *She was approached by an earnest young man from the University... It is my earnest wish that you use this money to further your research.* ◊ **earnestly.** EG ◊ ADV *He was in a corner of the room talking earnestly to Julie.* ◊ **earnestness.** EG *...speaking with great* ◊ N UNCOUNT *earnestness.*

2 If you are **in earnest**, you are sincere in your PHRASE intentions. EG *Is the President in earnest about the desire to negotiate?*

3 If something happens **in earnest**, it happens to a PHRASE much greater extent and more seriously than before. EG *Work on the tunnel began in earnest soon after.*

earnings /ˈɜːnɪŋz/. Your **earnings** are the money N PLURAL that you earn by working. EG *...a tax form which shows your earnings in the previous year.*

earphone /ˈɪəfəʊn/, **earphones**. **Earphones** are N COUNT : equipment which you wear over your ears, so that USU PLURAL you can listen to a radio or a cassette recorder in private.

earplug /ˈɪəplʌg/, **earplugs**. **Earplugs** are small N COUNT : pieces of soft material which you put into your ears USU PLURAL to keep out noise, water, or cold air.

earring /ˈɪərɪŋ/, **earrings**. **Earrings** are pieces of N COUNT jewellery which you attach to your earlobes. See picture at JEWELLERY.

earshot /ˈɪəʃɒt/. If you are **within earshot** of PHRASE something, you are close enough to be able to hear it. If you are **out of earshot**, you are too far away to hear it. EG *There was no one within earshot... Keep him out of earshot if possible.*

ear-splitting. An **ear-splitting** noise is very ADJ CLASSIF loud. EG *...an ear-splitting shriek.*

earth /ɜːθ/, **earths**. 1 The **earth** is 1.1 the planet N PROPER on which we live. EG *The earth moves around the sun... ...man's life on Earth.* 1.2 the land surface on N SING : the+N which we live and move about. EG *For twenty minutes the earth shook.*

2 Earth is the substance on the land surface of the N UNCOUNT earth in which plants grow. EG *Beyond the pines were clumps of sand and earth... He was pulling dead roots from the earth.*

3 An **earth** is a wire which passes from a piece of N COUNT : electrical equipment into the ground and makes USU SING the equipment safe.

4 You use **on earth** for emphasis **4.1** with words PHRASE such as 'how', 'why', 'what', or 'where', or with negatives, usually in order to suggest that there is no obvious answer to a question or problem. EG *How on earth do we raise half a million dollars?... He was wondering what on earth he should do.* **4.2** after a noun group that contains a superlative adjective in order to emphasize the adjective. EG *He regarded film-making as the most glamorous job on earth.*

5 If you say that something costs **the earth**, you PHRASE mean that it costs a very large amount of money. Informal EG *If you go to a commercial photographer he'll charge the earth for it.*

6 the salt of the earth: see salt. ● See also **down-to-earth.**

earthen /ˈɜːθən/. 1 **Earthen** pots or bowls are ADJ CLASSIF : made of baked clay. ATTRIB

2 An **earthen** floor is made of hard earth. EG *The* ADJ CLASSIF : *earthen floor was covered with rugs and cushions.* ATTRIB

earthenware /ˈɜːθənwɛə/. **Earthenware** pots or ADJ CLASSIF : bowls are made of baked clay. EG *...a big earthen-* ATTRIB *ware jar.* ▶ used as a noun. EG *...bowls of glazed* ▶ N UNCOUNT *earthenware.*

earthly /ˈɜːθliˈ/. 1 **Earthly** means happening in ADJ CLASSIF : the material world of our life on earth and not in ATTRIB any spiritual life or life after death. EG *She believed that our earthly life is all that matters.*

2 If you say that there is no **earthly** reason for ADJ CLASSIF : ATTRIB

something, you are emphasizing that there is no reason at all for it.

earthquake /ˈɜːθkweɪk/, **earthquakes**. An **earth-** N COUNT **quake** is a shaking of the ground caused by movement of the earth's crust.

earthworm /ˈɜːθwɜːm/, **earthworms**. An **earth-** N COUNT **worm** is a kind of worm that lives under the ground.

earthy /ˈɜːθiˈ/. 1 Someone who is **earthy** does not ADJ QUALIT mind talking openly about things such as sex that other people feel embarrassed about. EG *...a buxom, earthy, attractive girl.*

2 Something that is **earthy** looks, smells, or feels ADJ QUALIT like earth. EG *...the subtle, earthy fragrance of wild thyme.*

ease /iːz/, **eases, easing, eased.** 1 Ease is lack of N UNCOUNT difficulty. EG *She performed this trick with ease... The boxes are designed to fit one inside the other for ease of transportation.*

2 If you have a life of **ease**, you have plenty of N UNCOUNT money and live comfortably. EG *I remember being* Formal *astounded by the quietness and ease of the place.*

3 If you are **at ease**, you feel confident and PHRASE comfortable. If you are **ill at ease**, you are anxious or worried. EG *He was at ease with strangers... Brody felt ill at ease and patronized... My smiling face set her at ease.*

4 If something **eases** a problem or an unpleasant V+O situation, it makes it less difficult or less unpleas- ant. EG *The bungalows were built in 1946 to ease the housing shortage... ...a powder which eased the pain.*

5 You say that something **eases** when it becomes V-ERG less in degree, quantity, or intensity. EG *The snow had eased... He had taken the drugs to ease the pain.*

6 If you **ease** something somewhere, you move it V+O+A there slowly and carefully. EG *I eased the back door open.*

ease off. If something **eases off**, it becomes less PHRASAL VB : in degree, quantity, or intensity. EG *The rain had* V+ADV *eased off.*

easel /ˈiːzəl/, **easels**. An **easel** is a wooden frame N COUNT that supports a picture which an artist is painting.

easily /ˈiːzɪliˈ/. 1 You use **easily** 1.1 to emphasize ADV that something is very likely to happen. EG *She might easily decide to cancel the whole thing.* **1.2** to emphasize that there can be no doubt that something is the case. EG *This car is easily the most popular model.* **1.3** to say that something happens more quickly than is usual or normal. EG *He tired very easily.*

2 See also **easy.**

east /iːst/; often spelled with a capital letter. 1 The N SING : the+N **east** is **1.1** the direction which you look towards in order to see the sun rise. EG *Ben noticed the first faint streaks of dawn in the east.* **1.2** the part of a place or country which is towards the east. EG *...the east of the country.*

2 East means towards the east or to the east of a ADV AFTER VB place or thing. EG *They were heading almost due east... There were areas of open country east of the river.*

3 The **east** part of a place or country is the part ADJ CLASSIF which is towards the east. EG *...East Africa... ...the east coast of South America.*

4 An **east** wind blows from the east. EG *There was a* ADJ CLASSIF : *cold blue sky and a biting east wind.* ATTRIB

5 The **East** is also used to refer to **5.1** the N SING : the+N countries in the southern and eastern part of Asia, including India, China, and Japan. EG *He was deeply interested in meditation, the East, and yoga.* **5.2** the USSR and other communist countries in the east- ern part of Europe. EG *...a breakthrough in East-West relations.*

6 See also **Far East, Middle East.**

Easter /ˈiːstə/ is a religious festival in March or N UNCOUNT April when Christians celebrate the death and resurrection of Christ.

Easter egg, Easter eggs. An **Easter egg** is a N COUNT chocolate egg that is given as a present at Easter.

easterly /iːstəliˈ/. **1** The most **easterly** of a group ADJ QUALIT of things or places is the one that is farthest to the east. EG *Greenwich is the most easterly of the Thames-side places.*

2 An **easterly** wind blows from the east. ADJ CLASSIF

eastern /iːstəⁿn/. **Eastern** means **1** in or from the ADJ CLASSIF : east of a region or country. EG *...a small town in* ATTRIB *Eastern Portugal.* **2** coming from or associated with the people or countries of the East, such as India, China, and Japan. EG *...Eastern philosophy.* **3** coming from or associated with the countries in the east of Europe and the USSR. EG *...the Eastern bloc.*

eastward /iːstwəd/, **eastwards. Eastward** or ADV AFTER VB **eastwards** means towards the east. EG *They trav- elled eastwards.* ▶ **Eastward** is also used as an ▶ ADJ CLASSIF : adjective. EG *...a grassy eastward slope.* ATTRIB

easy /iːziˈ/, **easier, easiest. 1** Something that is ADJ QUALIT **easy** can be done without difficulty or effort. EG *The house is easy to keep clean... How easy is it for novelists to get their work published?... This new dancing looked easy.* ◇ **easily.** EG *A baby buggy* ◇ ADV *can be easily carried on a bus or in a car.*

2 You can say **easier said than done** to indicate CONVENTION that it is difficult to do what someone has just suggested. EG *'Just relax.' - 'Easier said than done.'*

3 Easy also means relaxed. EG *They have a natu-* ADJ QUALIT *ral, easy confidence.* ◇ **easily.** EG *...a friendly man* ◇ ADV *who talked freely and easily.*

4 An **easy** life or time is comfortable and without ADJ QUALIT any problems. EG *I wanted to make life easier for you.*

5 If you **take it easy** or **take things easy,** you PHRASE relax and do not do very much. Informal

6 If you **go easy on** something, you avoid using too PHRASE much of it. EG *I suggested to him that he should go* Informal *easy on publicity for a while.*

7 See also **easily.**

easy chair, easy chairs. An **easy chair** is a N COUNT large, comfortable chair in which you can relax.

easy-going. Someone who is **easy-going** is not ADJ QUALIT easily annoyed, worried, or upset. EG *My father was a gentle, easy-going person.*

eat /iːt/, **eats, eating, ate** /eɪt, ɛt/, **eaten.** When V+O OR V you **eat** something, you put it into your mouth, chew it, and swallow it. EG *He began to eat his sandwich... He said he would eat at his hotel.*

eat into. If a substance such as acid or rust **eats** PHRASAL VB : **into** something, it destroys the surface of the thing. V+PREP

eat out. When you **eat out,** you have a meal at a PHRASAL VB : restaurant. V+ADV

eat up. If you **eat up** your food, you eat it all. EG PHRASAL VB : *He gave her a spoon to eat up the cream with...* V+O+ADV *'Eat up, girl, that's it,' he said.* OR V+ADV

eater /iːtə/, **eaters.** You use **eater** to refer to N COUNT+SUPP someone who eats in a particular way or eats a particular thing. EG *Tim was a slow eater... ...a meat eater.*

eau-de-cologne /əʊdəˈkəˌləʊn/ is a fairly weak, N MASS sweet-smelling perfume.

eaves /iːvz/. The **eaves** of a house are the lower N PLURAL : edges of its roof. the+N

eavesdrop /iːvzdrɒp/, **eavesdrops, eavesdrop-** V : OFT+on **ping, eavesdropped.** If you **eavesdrop,** you listen secretly to what other people are saying. EG *I don't like eavesdropping on people talking on the phone.* ◇ **eavesdropper** /iːvzdrɒpə/, **eavesdroppers.** EG ◇ N COUNT *There was an eavesdropper on the landing.*

ebb /ɛb/, **ebbs, ebbing, ebbed. 1** If a feeling or a V person's strength **ebbs,** it becomes weaker. EG *Only* Literary *then did the strength ebb from his fingers.*

2 If something is **at a low ebb,** it is not being very PHRASE successful or profitable. EG *George's fortunes at this time were at a low ebb.*

3 When the tide or the sea **ebbs,** its level falls. V ▶ used as a noun. EG *...the stormy ebb and flow of* ▶ N SING : *the sea.* the+N

4 You can talk about **the ebb and flow of** some- PHRASE thing when you want to describe a situation in which periods of progress and success are followed by periods of trouble or difficulty. EG *...the ebb and flow of political struggle.*

ebony /ɛbəniˈ/. **1 Ebony** is a very hard, dark- N UNCOUNT coloured wood.

2 Something that is **ebony** is a very deep black ADJ COLOUR colour. EG *...ebony eyes.*

ebullient /iˈbʌliˈənt/. Someone who is **ebullient** ADJ QUALIT is lively and full of enthusiasm. Formal

eccentric /iˈksɛntrɪk/ , **eccentrics. 1** Someone ADJ QUALIT who is **eccentric** has habits or opinions that other people think strange. EG *...a slightly eccentric Frenchman... ...eccentric right-wing views.* ◇ **eccentricity** /ɛksɛntrɪsɪtiˈ/, **eccentricities.** EG ◇ N UNCOUNT *...the eccentricity of Rose's behaviour... ...her hus-* OR N COUNT *band's eccentricities.*

2 An **eccentric** is a person who has habits or N COUNT opinions which other people think strange. EG *...a bunch of harmless eccentrics.*

ecclesiastical /iˈkliːziˈæstɪkəˈl/ means belonging ADJ CLASSIF to or connected with the Christian Church.

echelon /ɛʃəˈlɒn/, **echelons.** An **echelon** is a N COUNT+SUPP level of power or responsibility in an organization. Formal EG *...the higher echelons of the party.*

echo /ɛkəʊ/, **echoes, echoing, echoed. 1** An **echo** is **1.1** a sound which is caused when a loud, sharp N COUNT noise is reflected off a surface such as a wall. EG *Judy listened to the echo of her shoes clicking on the marble floors.* **1.2** an expression of an attitude N COUNT : or opinion which has already been expressed by USU+of someone else. EG *The echo of public sentiment in Congress was inevitable.* **1.3** a small detail or N COUNT+SUPP feature which reminds you of something else. EG *...echoes of the past.*

2 A sound that **echoes** is reflected off a surface V : USU+A such as a wall so that it can be heard again after the original sound has stopped. EG *The cry echoed back from the mountain.*

3 A place that **echoes** is one in which a sound V : USU+A continues or is repeated after the original sound has stopped. EG *The bamboo grove echoed with the screams of monkeys.* ◇ **echoing.** EG *...echoing* ◇ ADJ CLASSIF *halls.*

4 If you **echo** something that someone has said, V+O OR you repeat it. EG *'They lived in the open air, simply* V+QUOTE *under a tree.' - 'Under a tree,' echoed Etta.*

éclair /iˈkleə/, **éclairs.** An **éclair** is a long thin N COUNT cake made of very light pastry, which is filled with cream and usually has chocolate on top.

eclectic /iˈklɛktɪk/ means using what seems to be ADJ QUALIT best or most useful from several different sets of Formal ideas or beliefs. EG *...a doctrine that drew upon an eclectic mixture of both Western and Asian thought.*

eclipse /iˈklɪps/, **eclipses, eclipsing, eclipsed. 1** N COUNT When there is an **eclipse** of the sun, the moon comes between the earth and the sun, so that for a short time you cannot see part or all of the sun. When there is an **eclipse** of the moon, the earth comes between the sun and the moon, so that for a short time the earth's shadow covers the moon.

2 If someone or something suffers an **eclipse,** they N SING : lose some or all of their importance or influence. USU+POSS EG *...the eclipse of the national radical press.*

3 If something **eclipses** something else, the first V+O thing is more important or influential than the second thing, so that the second thing is no longer noticed. EG *Less talented artists were totally eclipsed.*

ecologist /iˈkɒləˌdʒɪst/, **ecologists.** An **ecologist** N COUNT is **1** a person who studies the pattern and balance of relationships between plants, animals, people, and their environment. EG *Ecologists estimate that* *half of the ancient woodlands in Britain are in danger of extinction.* **2** a person who believes that the environment and natural resources should be used properly and be preserved.

ecology /iˈkɒlədʒiˡ/. **1** When you talk about the N UNCOUNT **ecology** of a place, you are referring to the pattern and balance of relationships between all the plants, animals, and people there. EG *...the delicate ecology of the rainforest.* ◊ **ecological** /ˌiːkəˈlɒdʒɪkəˡl/. EG ◊ ADJ CLASSIF: *Use of nitrogen fertilizers has damaged the eco-* ATTRIB *logical balance in the lake.* ◊ **ecologically.** EG *...an* ◊ SUBMOD *ecologically sound system of farm management.*
2 Ecology is the study of the relationships between plants, animals, people, and their environment, and the balances between these relationships. EG *...the most recent research in ecology.*

economic /ˌiːkəˈnɒmɪk, ˌek-/, **economics. 1 Eco-** ADJ CLASSIF: **nomic** means concerned with the organization of ATTRIB the money, industry, and trade of a country, region, or social group. EG *What has gone wrong with the economic system during the last ten years?... ...a period of economic and industrial crisis.*
◊ **economically.** EG *Katanga was extremely un-* ◊ ADV *evenly developed economically.*
2 A business that is **economic** produces a profit. EG ADJ QUALIT *We have to keep fares high enough to make it economic for the service to continue.*
3 Economics is the study of the way in which N UNCOUNT money, industry, and trade are organized in a society. EG *...a degree in economics.*
4 The **economics** of a society or industry is the N UNCOUNT system of organizing money and trade in it. EG *...the* +SUPP *economics of the timber trade.*

economical /ˌiːkəˈnɒmɪkəˡl, ˌek-/. **1** Something that ADJ QUALIT is **economical** does not require a lot of money to operate. EG *This system was extremely economical because it ran on half-price electricity.*
◊ **economically.** EG *This courier service could be* ◊ ADV *most economically operated.*
2 If someone is **economical**, they spend money ADJ QUALIT carefully and sensibly. ◊ **economically.** EG *We* ◊ ADV *live very economically.*
3 Economical also means using the minimum ADJ QUALIT amount of something that is necessary. EG *She spoke in short, economical sentences.*
◊ **economically.** EG *The book is very economically* ◊ ADV *written.*

economist /iˈkɒnəmɪst/, **economists.** An econo- N COUNT mist is a person who studies, teaches, or writes about economics.

economize /iˈkɒnəmaɪz/, **economizes, econo-** V **mizing, economized;** also spelled **economise.** If you **economize**, you save money by spending it very carefully and not buying expensive things. EG *The loss of business was so great that they had to economize on staff.*

economy /iˈkɒnəmiˡ/, **economies. 1** The econo- N COUNT: my of a country or region is **1.1** the system USU SING according to which money, industry, and trade are organized there. EG *New England's economy is still largely based on manufacturing.* **1.2** the wealth that it gets from business and industry. EG *Unofficial strikes were damaging the British economy.*
2 Economy is careful spending or the careful use N UNCOUNT of things in order to save money. EG *His seaside shack was small, for reasons of economy.*
3 If you make **economies**, you save money, by not N PLURAL spending it on unnecessary things.

ecstasy /ˈekstəsiˡ/, **ecstasies. 1 Ecstasy** is a N UNCOUNT feeling of very great happiness. EG *On both faces were expressions of ecstasy.*
2 If you go **into ecstasies** about something, you PHRASE show how delighted you are about it. EG *Her mere proximity would send him into ecstasies.*

ecstatic /ɪkˈstætɪk/. If you are **ecstatic**, you feel ADJ QUALIT very enthusiastic and happy. EG *Eddie was ecstatic over his new rifle... ...a wild ecstatic happiness.*
◊ **ecstatically.** EG *...children jumping ecstatically* ◊ ADV *up and down.*

ecumenical /ˌiːkjuːˈmenɪkəˡl, ˌek-/ is used to de- ADJ CLASSIF scribe activities, ideas, and movements which try Formal to unite different Christian Churches. EG *...an ecumenical institute.*

-ed. 1 -ed is used to form the past tense and past SUFFIX participle of many verbs. EG *He blinked in the bright light... Tim dodged round the car... They had arrived two hours earlier.*
2 -ed is also added to nouns to form adjectives. SUFFIX These adjectives describe someone or something as having a particular feature or features. For example, a bearded man is a man with a beard and a fenced area is an area with a fence round it. Adjectives like these are often not defined in this dictionary, but are treated with the related nouns. EG *She put on a feathered hat.*

eddy /ˈediˡ/, **eddies, eddying, eddied.** If water or V : USU+A wind **eddies**, it moves round and round in no particular direction. EG *The wind whipped and eddied around the buildings.* ► used as a noun. EG ► N COUNT *...every trick and eddy of the tide.*

edge /edʒ/, **edges, edging, edged. 1** The **edge** of N COUNT: something is the place or line where it stops and USU+SUPP another thing begins. EG *Little children played in the sand at the water's edge... They lived in a cottage on the edge of the moors.*
2 The **edge** of a flat, solid object is its narrow side. N COUNT: EG *...the edge of a ruler.* USU+SUPP
3 If something **is edged** with a particular thing, it V+O: USU has that thing along its edge. EG *...a beautiful garden* PASS+with *edged with flowering trees.*
4 If you **edge** somewhere, you move there very V+A OR V+O+ slowly. EG *He edged away from the thug... I edged* A *my way to the window.*
5 If people are on the **edge** of an event or situation, N SING : the+N it is likely to happen to them soon. EG *The world had been brought to the edge of war.*
6 If you say that there is an **edge** to someone's N SING : an+N voice, you mean that they sound angry or bitter.
7 If you are **on edge**, you are tense, nervous, and PHRASE unable to relax. EG *She was worried that the prospect was setting his nerves on edge.*
8 If you have an **edge** over someone, you have an N SING : advantage that makes you more likely to be suc- OFT+over cessful than them.

edgeways /ˈedʒweɪz/. If you say that you **cannot** PHRASE **get a word in edgeways**, you mean that you are Informal unable to say anything because someone else is talking too much.

edging /ˈedʒɪŋ/, **edgings.** An **edging** is something N COUNT that is put along the sides of something else in order to make it look attractive. EG *...a blouse trimmed with bows and lace edgings.*

edgy /ˈedʒiˡ/. When you are **edgy**, you are nervous ADJ QUALIT and anxious. EG *Rick seemed very edgy.*

edible /ˈedɪbəˡl/. Something that is **edible** is safe ADJ CLASSIF to eat and not poisonous. EG *...edible mushrooms.*

edict /ˈiːdɪkt/, **edicts.** An **edict** is a command N COUNT given by someone in authority. EG *I told the factory* Formal *inspector we would defy his edict... ...banned by government edict.*

edifice /ˈedɪfɪs/, **edifices.** An **edifice** is **1** a large N COUNT and impressive building. EG *...a huge Victorian* Formal *edifice.* **2** a system of beliefs or a traditional N COUNT : institution. EG *The whole edifice of modern civiliza-* USU+SUPP *tion is beginning to sway.* Formal

edify /ˈedɪfaɪ/, **edifies, edifying, edified.** If some- V+O: thing **edifies** you, it teaches you something useful NO IMPER or interesting. EG *...a series of popular talks intend-* Formal *ed to edify and entertain.* ◊ **edifying.** EG *He may* ◊ ADJ QUALIT *come out with all sorts of edifying sentiments.*
◊ **edification** /ˌedɪfɪˈkeɪʃəˡn/. EG *...books bought for* ◊ N UNCOUNT *instruction or edification.*

edit /ˈedɪt/, **edits, editing, edited. 1** If you **edit** a V+O OR V text, you examine it and make corrections to it so that it is suitable for publication. ◊ **edited.** EG *This* ◊ ADJ CLASSIF *is the edited text.*
2 If you **edit** a book, you collect several pieces of V+O writing by different authors and prepare them for

publication. EG ...'The Save and Prosper Book of Money,' edited by Margaret Allen.

3 If you **edit** a film or a television or radio v+o programme, you choose some of the material that has been filmed or recorded and arrange it in a particular order.

4 Someone who **edits** a newspaper or magazine is v+o in charge of it.

edition /ɪˈdɪʃəⁿn/, **editions**. An **edition** is **1** a N COUNT+SUPP particular version of a book, magazine, or newspaper that is printed at one time. EG *the city edition of the New York Times.* **2** a single television or radio programme that is one of a series. EG *...tonight's edition of Kaleidoscope.*

editor /ˈɛdɪtə/, **editors**. An **editor** is **1** a person N COUNT who is in charge of a newspaper or magazine. EG *....the editor of a local newspaper.* **2** a journalist N COUNT: who is responsible for a particular section of a OFT+SUPP newspaper or magazine. EG *...the foreign editor.* **3** a N COUNT person whose job is to check texts and make changes and corrections before they are published.

4 a person who prepares a film or a radio or N COUNT television programme by selecting some of what has been filmed or recorded and putting it in a particular order.

editorial /ɛdɪˈtɔːrɪəl/, **editorials**. **1** Editorial ADJ CLASSIF: means **1.1** involved in preparing a newspaper, ATTRIB magazine, or book for publication. EG *Hearst expanded his editorial staff.* **1.2** involving the attitudes, opinions, and contents of a newspaper, magazine, or television programme. EG *...the paper's editorial policy.*

2 An **editorial** is an article in a newspaper which N COUNT gives the opinion of the editor or publisher on a topic or item of news.

editorship /ˈɛdɪtəʃɪp/. The **editorship** of a news- N SING: paper or magazine is the position and authority of USU+POSS its editor. EG *The paper was considerably improved under McPherson's editorship.*

educate /ˈɛdjʊkeɪt/, **educates, educating, edu-** **cated. 1** When someone, especially a child, **is** v+o **educated**, he or she is taught at a school or college. EG *He was educated at Eton.*

2 Educated people have reached a high standard ADJ QUALIT of learning. EG *...an educated man.*

3 To **educate** people also means to teach them v+o better ways of doing something or a better way of living. EG *Not enough is being done to educate smokers about the benefits of stopping the habit.*

education /ɛdjʊˈkeɪʃəⁿn/ consists of teaching peo- N UNCOUNT ple various subjects at a school or college. EG *...the government's policy on higher education.*

educational /ɛdjʊˈkeɪʃəⁿnəl, -ʃənəⁿl/ means con- ADJ CLASSIF cerned with and related to education. EG *...an educational institution.* ◊ **educationally.** EG *...a* ◊ ADV *school for the educationally subnormal.*

educationalist /ɛdjʊˈkeɪʃəⁿnəlɪst/, **educational-** N COUNT **ists.** An **educationalist** is a specialist in the theories and methods of education.

educator /ˈɛdjʊkeɪtə/, **educators**. An **educator** is N COUNT a person who educates people. EG *He was a distin-* Formal *guished educator.*

EEC /iː iː siː/. The **EEC** is an organization of N PROPER: Western European countries, including the UK, the+N that have joint policies on matters such as trade and agriculture. 'EEC' is an abbreviation for 'European Economic Community'.

eel /iːl/, **eels**. An **eel** is a long, thin, snake-like fish. N COUNT

eerie /ˈɪərɪ/. Something that is **eerie** is strange ADJ QUALIT and frightening. EG *...the eerie feeling that someone was watching me.* ◊ **eerily.** EG *The lights gleamed* ◊ ADV *eerily.*

efface /ɪˈfeɪs/, **effaces, effacing, effaced.** To v+o **efface** something means to rub it out or remove it. Formal EG *In the sand, all the footprints had effaced one another... He hoped to efface the memory of an embarrassing speech.*

effect /ɪˈfɛkt/, **effects, effecting, effected. 1** An N COUNT OR **effect** is **1.1** a change or event that is caused by N UNCOUNT: OFT+on

something or is the result of something. EG *This has the effect of separating students from teachers... ...the effect of noise on people in the factories... These measures did have some effect on rural poverty.* **1.2** an impression that a speaker or artist N COUNT deliberately creates. EG *Don't move, or you'll destroy the whole effect.* ● If you do something **for** ● PHRASE **effect**, you do it in order to impress people. EG *...a pause for effect.*

2 You add **in effect** to a statement to indicate that ADV SEN it is not precisely accurate but it is a reasonable description or summary of a situation. EG *In effect he has no choice.*

3 You use **to this effect, to that effect,** or **to the** PHRASE **effect that** when you are summarizing what someone has said, rather than repeating their actual words. EG *...a rumour to the effect that he had been drunk... He said, 'No, you fool, the other way!' or words to that effect.*

4 When something **takes effect** or **is put into** PHRASE **effect**, it starts to happen or to have some result. EG *The tax cuts take effect on July 1st... Signing the agreement was one thing, putting it into effect was another.*

5 If you **effect** something, you succeed in causing v+o it to happen. EG *Production was halted until repairs* Formal *could be effected.*

6 See also **sound effect.**

effective /ɪˈfɛktɪv/. **1** Something that is **effective** ADJ QUALIT works well and produces the results that were intended. EG *...the most effective ways of reducing pollution... In order to be effective we need your support.* ◊ **effectiveness.** EG *Methods vary in* ◊ N UNCOUNT *effectiveness.*

2 Effective also means having a particular role or ADJ CLASSIF: result in practice, though not officially. EG *He* ATTRIB *assumed effective command of the armed forces.*

3 When a law or an agreement becomes **effective**, ADJ PRED it begins officially to apply or be valid. EG *...a ceasefire, to become effective as soon as possible.*

effectively /ɪˈfɛktɪvliˈ/. **1** If something works ADV **effectively**, it works well. EG *...an attempt to make the system work more effectively.*

2 You can also use **effectively** to indicate that ADV what you are saying is a reasonable summary of a situation, although it is not precisely accurate. EG *The television was on, effectively ruling out conversation.*

effeminate /ɪˈfɛmɪnəˈt/. When people describe a ADJ QUALIT man or a boy as **effeminate**, they mean that he behaves, looks, or sounds like a woman or girl; an offensive word.

effete /ɪˈfiːt/. Someone who is **effete** is weak and ADJ QUALIT powerless. EG *...an effete middle-class aesthete.* Formal

efficient /ɪˈfɪʃəⁿnt/. A person, machine, or organi- ADJ QUALIT zation that is **efficient** does a job well and successfully, without wasting time or energy. EG *Engines and cars can be made more efficient... You need a very efficient production manager.* ◊ **efficiently.** ◊ ADV EG *You must work more efficiently.* ◊ **efficiency** ◊ N UNCOUNT /ɪˈfɪʃəⁿnsiˈ/. EG *...an increase in business efficiency.*

effigy /ˈɛfɪdʒiˈ/, **effigies**. An **effigy** is **1** a roughly N COUNT made figure that represents someone you strongly dislike. EG *The students burned effigies of the president.* **2** a statue or carving of a famous person. Formal EG *...unusually good fifteenth-century alabaster effigies.*

effluent /ˈɛflʊənt/, **effluents. Effluent** is liquid N UNCOUNT waste material that comes out of factories or OR N COUNT sewage works. EG *Our rivers are being poisoned by* Formal *industrial waste and untreated effluent.*

effort /ˈɛfət/, **efforts. 1** If you make an **effort** to N UNCOUNT do something, you try very hard to do it. EG *Little* OR N COUNT *effort has been made to investigate this claim...*

What kind of place would you describe as eerie?

...the efforts of governments to restrain inflation...
...a waste of effort.

2 If you do something with **effort**, it is difficult for N UNCOUNT
you to do. EG *Robert spoke with effort.*

3 If you describe an object or an action as a poor N COUNT :
effort or a feeble **effort**, you mean that it has not ADJ + N
been well made or well done. EG *It was a rather*
amateurish effort.

4 If you say that an action is an **effort**, you mean N SING : an + N
that an unusual amount of physical or mental
energy is needed to do it. EG *Getting up was an*
effort.

5 If you **make the effort** to do something, you use PHRASE
the extra energy that is needed to do it, even
though you may not really want to. EG *Having made*
the effort to find them, I was unwilling to let them
go.

6 If you say that something is **worth the effort**, PHRASE
you mean that it will justify the energy that you
have spent or will spend on it. EG *It's not worth the*
effort to get them to do the washing up.

effortless /ˈɛfətlɪʔs/. You describe an action as ADJ QUALIT
effortless when it is achieved very easily. EG *His*
rise in politics appears to have been effortless.
◇ **effortlessly**. EG *He finished his MA thesis almost* ◇ ADV
effortlessly.

effrontery /ɪˈfrʌntəᵊriˈ/ is bold, rude, or cheeky N UNCOUNT
behaviour. EG *He has the effrontery to use my* Formal
office without asking.

effusive /ɪˈfjuːsɪv/. A person who is **effusive** ADJ QUALIT
expresses pleasure, gratitude, or approval enthusi- Formal
astically. EG *Mrs Schiff was effusive in her con-*
gratulations... ...an effusive welcome.
◇ **effusively**. EG *The doctor thanked him effusive-* ◇ ADV
ly.

EFL /ˌiː ɛf ˈɛl/ is used to describe things that are
connected with the teaching of English to people
whose first language is not English. **EFL** is an
abbreviation for 'English as a Foreign Language'.
EG *...EFL dictionaries... ...an EFL teacher.*

e.g. /ˌiː ˈdʒiː/ is an abbreviation that means 'for
example'. It is used before a noun, or to introduce
another sentence. EG *...woollens and other delicate*
fabrics (e.g. lace)... He specialised in trivial knowl-
edge, e.g. that three MPs had glass eyes.

egalitarian /ɪˌgælɪˈteərɪən/. In an **egalitarian** ADJ QUALIT
system or society, all people are equal and have Formal
the same rights. EG *...a more egalitarian education-*
al system... ...egalitarian principles.

egg /ɛg/, **eggs, egging, egged.** An **egg** is **1** the N COUNT
rounded object produced by a female bird from
which a baby bird later emerges. Some other
creatures also lay eggs. EG *...birds' eggs... The*
alligator then lays her eggs... These eggs hatch into
larvae. **2** a hen's egg considered as food. EG *...a* N COUNT OR
dozen eggs... ...bacon and egg.   N UNCOUNT

egg on. If you **egg** someone **on**, you encourage PHRASAL VB :
them to do something daring or foolish. EG *Egged* V + O + ADV
on by Iago, Othello makes up his mind to kill
Desdemona.

eggcup /ˈɛgkʌp/, **eggcups.** An **eggcup** is a small N COUNT
container in which you put a boiled egg while you
eat it.

eggplant /ˈɛgplɑːnt/, **eggplants.** An **eggplant** is N COUNT OR
an aubergine. EG *I've made you that eggplant dip* N UNCOUNT
you like.   American

eggshell /ˈɛgʃɛl/, **eggshells.** An **eggshell** is the N COUNT OR
hard covering round an egg.   N UNCOUNT

egg-timer, egg-timers. An **egg-timer** is a device N COUNT
that helps you measure the time needed to boil an
egg.

ego /ˈiːgəʊ, ˈɛgəʊ/, **egos.** Your **ego** is your opinion of N COUNT
your own worth. EG *It was a blow to my ego, and*
meant I would have to look for a new job.

egoism /ˈiːgəʊɪzᵊm, ˈɛg-/ is the same as egotism. N UNCOUNT

egoist /ˈiːgəʊɪst, ˈɛg-/, **egoists.** An **egoist** is the N COUNT
same as an egotist.

egoistic /ˌiːgəʊˈɪstɪk, ˈɛg-/ means the same as egotis- ADJ QUALIT
tic.

egotism /ˈiːgətɪzᵊm, ˈɛg-/ is behaviour which N UNCOUNT
shows that you only care about yourself, or that
you believe that you are more important than
other people. EG *It was a piece of blatant egotism.*

egotist /ˈiːgətɪst, ˈɛg-/, **egotists.** An **egotist** is a N COUNT
person who acts selfishly and believes that he or
she is more important than other people.

egotistic /ˌiːgəˈtɪstɪk, ˈɛg-/. If you are **egotistic** or ADJ QUALIT
egotistical, you believe that you are more impor-
tant than other people. EG *Success makes a man*
egotistic.

eh /eɪ/. You say **eh 1** when you are asking someone to reply to you or to agree with you. EG *Looks*
good, eh?... Who knows we're here? Eh? **2** when
you are asking someone to repeat what they have
just said because you did not hear it the first time.
EG *'Well, I still have a chequebook.' – 'Eh?' – 'I said I*
still have a chequebook.'

eiderdown /ˈaɪdədaʊn/, **eiderdowns.** An **eider-** N COUNT
down is a bed covering that is filled with small soft
feathers or warm material.

eight /eɪt/ **eights. Eight** is the number 8: see the NUMBER
entry headed NUMBER. EG *...eight months of exile.*

eighteen /ˌeɪˈtiːn/ **eighteens. Eighteen** is the NUMBER
number 18: see the entry headed NUMBER.

eighteenth /ˌeɪˈtiːnθ/ **eighteenths.** The **eight-** ORDINAL
eenth item in a series is the one that you count as
number eighteen: see the entry headed NUMBER. EG
...the early eighteenth century.

eighth /eɪtθ/, **eighths. 1** The **eighth** item in a ORDINAL
series is the one that you count as number eight:
see the entry headed NUMBER. EG *...his room on the*
eighth floor.
2 An **eighth** is one of eight equal parts of some- N COUNT :
thing. EG *It was about an eighth of an inch thick.* USU + of

eightieth /ˈeɪtiˈɪθ/. The **eightieth** item in a series ORDINAL
is the one that you count as number eighty: see the
entry headed NUMBER. EG *I saw him at his eightieth*
birthday party.

eighty /ˈeɪtiˈ/ **eighties. Eighty** is the number 80: NUMBER
see the entry headed NUMBER.

either /ˈaɪðə, ˈiːðə/. **1** You use **either 1.1** in front of CONJ
the first of two or more alternatives, when you are
stating the only possibilities or choices that there
are. The other alternative is introduced by 'or'. EG *I*
was expecting you either today or tomorrow... You
either love him or you hate him... Either you eat
your spinach or you go without ice cream. **1.2** in a
negative statement in front of the first of two
alternatives, when you are emphasizing that the
negative statement refers to both the alternatives.
EG *Dr Kirk, you're not being either frank or fair... I*
wouldn't dream of asking either Mary or my
mother to take on the responsibility.

2 You can also use **either 2.1** to refer to one of two PRON OR DET
possible things, people, or situations, when you
want to say that it does not matter which one is
chosen or considered. EG *One speech by either of*
them stating the facts would have ended his uncer-
tainty... Either is acceptable... Either way, I can't
lose. **2.2** in a negative statement to refer to each of PRON OR DET
two things, people, or situations, when you are WITH BROAD
emphasizing that the negative statement includes NEG
both of them. EG *'Which one do you want?' – 'I don't*
want either.'... There was no sound from either of
the flats... She could not see either man.

3 You can use **either** by itself at the end of a ADV : WITH
negative statement **3.1** to indicate that there is a BROAD NEG
similarity between a person or thing that you have
just mentioned and one that was mentioned earlier, for example that the same fact is true about
both of them. EG *'I haven't got that address.' – 'No, I*
haven't got it either'... I can't play golf either. **3.2** to
indicate that you are adding an extra piece of
information. EG *Not only was he ugly, he was not*
very interesting to talk to either.

4 You can use **either** before a noun that refers to DET
each of two things when you are talking about both
of them. EG *The two ladies sat in large armchairs*

on either side of the stage... In either case the answer is the same.

eject /i'dʒɛkt/, **ejects, ejecting, ejected. 1** To v+o eject something means to push or send it out, usually with force. EG _The machine ejected a handful of cigarettes._

2 If you **eject** someone from a place, you force v+o them to leave. _We reserve the right to eject any objectionable person._

eke /iːk/, **ekes, eking, eked. 1** If you **eke** some- PHRASAL VB: thing **out**, you make your supply of it last as long as V+O+ADV possible. EG _Migrants send home cash that helps eke out low village incomes._

2 If you **eke out** a living, you manage to survive PHRASAL VB: with very little money. EG _In his early days he eked_ V+O+ADV _out a precarious living from designing book jackets._

elaborate, elaborates, elaborating, elaborated; pronounced /i'læbərət/ when it is an adjective and /i'læbəreɪt/ when it is a verb.

1 Something that is **elaborate** is very complex ADJ QUALIT because it has a lot of different parts. _...the elaborate network of canals... ...an elaborate ceremony._

◊ **elaborately.** EG _Every inch of its surface was_ ◊ ADV _elaborately decorated._

2 If you **elaborate** on an idea, or if you **elaborate** v+on OR V+O it, you give more details about it. EG _It isn't a statement I want to elaborate on... Some of these points will have to be further elaborated as we go along._ ◊ **elaboration** /i'læbəreɪʃəⁿ/, **elabora-** ◊ N COUNT OR **tions.** EG _An elaboration of this idea will follow in_ N UNCOUNT _Chapter 12._

3 To **elaborate** something also means to make it v+o more complex. EG _This type of plan could be elaborated._

elapse /i'læps/, **elapses, elapsing, elapsed.** v When a period of time **elapses**, it passes. EG _Too_ Formal _much time had elapsed since I had attempted any serious study._

elastic /i'læstɪk/. **1 Elastic** is a rubber material N UNCOUNT that stretches when you pull it and returns to its original size and shape when you let it go. EG _It snapped back like a piece of elastic._

2 Something that is **elastic** is able to stretch easily ADJ QUALIT and then return to its original size and shape. EG _...a softer, more elastic and lighter material._ ◊ **elasticity** /iːlæstɪsⁱtiⁱ, ɪlæstɪsⁱtiⁱ/. EG _The skin_ ◊ N UNCOUNT: _eventually loses its elasticity._ USU+SUPP

3 Elastic ideas and policies can change in order to ADJ QUALIT suit new circumstances. EG _Liberal policy was sufficiently elastic to accommodate both views._

elastic band, elastic bands. An **elastic band** is N COUNT the same as a rubber band.

elated /i'leɪtⁱd/. If you are **elated**, you are ex- ADJ QUALIT tremely happy and excited. EG _The members left the meeting elated._

elation /i'leɪʃəⁿ/ is a feeling of great happiness N UNCOUNT and excitement. EG _This little incident filled me with elation._

elbow /ɛlbəʊ/, **elbows, elbowing, elbowed. 1** N COUNT Your **elbow** is the part in the middle of your arm where your arm bends. See picture at THE HUMAN BODY. EG _She sat with her elbows on the table._

2 The **elbow** on a sleeve is the part that covers N COUNT your elbow. EG _...an old suit whose jacket had worn through at the elbows._

3 If you **elbow** someone away, you use one of your v+o+A elbows to push them out of the way. EG _Ralph elbowed him to one side._

elder /ɛldə/, **elders. 1** The **elder** of two people is ADJ QUALIT: the one who was born first. EG _...his elder brother..._ COMPAR _Posy was the elder of the two._

2 Your **elders** are people who are older than you. N COUNT: EG _Their father had taught them to show respect_ USU+POSS _towards their elders._ Formal

3 The **elders** of a tribe are the older members who N COUNT have influence and authority.

4 The **elders** of some Christian churches are N COUNT

people who hold positions of responsibility in these churches.

5 An **elder** is also a bush or small tree with small N COUNT white flowers and red or black berries.

elderly /ɛldəliⁱ/. **1 Elderly** people are old. EG _The_ ADJ QUALIT _coach was full of elderly ladies._

2 You can refer to old people in general as the N PLURAL: **elderly.** EG _...unless the elderly are adequately_ the+N _cared for._

3 Something that is **elderly** is rather old or old- ADJ QUALIT fashioned. EG _...elderly oil-fired steam engines._

eldest /ɛldⁱst/. The **eldest** person in a group is ADJ QUALIT: the one who was born before all the others. EG _Her_ SUPERL _eldest son was killed in the First War... Gladys was the eldest of four children._

elect /i'lɛkt/, **elects, electing, elected. 1** When v+o: people **elect** someone, they choose that person to OFT+as/to; represent them, by voting. EG _They met to elect a_ ALSO V+O+C _president... Why should we elect him Mayor?... You could be elected as an MP._ ◊ **elected.** EG _...a_ ◊ ADJ CLASSIF: _democratically elected government._ ATTRIB

2 If you **elect** to do something, you choose to do it. v+to-INF EG _...the questions he had elected to answer._ Formal

election /i'lɛkʃəⁿ/, **elections. 1** An **election** is N COUNT OR an organized process in which people vote to N UNCOUNT choose a person or group of people to hold an official position or to represent them in government. EG _Labour did badly in the election... I may vote for her at the next election._ ● See also **by-election, general election.**

2 When you talk about the **election** of a person or N SING: a political party, you are referring to their success USU+POSS in winning an election. EG _...within two months of her election as Tory leader... ...after the election of Mr Heath's government in 1970._

elector /i'lɛktə/, **electors.** The **electors** are the N COUNT people who have the right to vote in an election.

electoral /i'lɛktərəl/ means intended for an elec- ADJ CLASSIF: tion, happening in an election, or resulting from an ATTRIB election. EG _...a contribution to their electoral funds... ...electoral success._

electorate /i'lɛktⁿrəⁱt/, **electorates.** The **elec-** N COUNT: **torate** of a country or area is all the people in it USU the+N who have the right to vote in an election. EG _The Government was responsible to the electorate as a whole._

electric /i'lɛktrɪk/. **1** An **electric** device or ma- ADJ CLASSIF chine works by means of electricity. EG _...an electric fan._

2 Electric is used to describe other things that ADJ CLASSIF: relate to electricity. EG _...electric current._ ATTRIB

3 If you describe a situation as **electric**, you mean ADJ CLASSIF that people are very excited. EG _When Drew arrived, the atmosphere was already electric._

electrical /i'lɛktrɪkəⁿl/. **1 Electrical** devices or ADJ CLASSIF machines work by means of electricity. EG _...electrical equipment._ ◊ **electrically.** EG _...electrically_ ◊ ADV _operated windows._

2 Electrical engineers and industries are involved ADJ CLASSIF: in the production or maintenance of electricity or ATTRIB electrical goods.

electric chair. The **electric chair** is a method N SING: the+N of execution, used in some parts of the United States, in which a person is strapped to a special chair and killed by a powerful electric current.

electrician /ɪlɛktrɪʃəⁿn, iːlɛk-/, **electricians.** An N COUNT **electrician** is a person whose job is to install and repair electrical equipment.

electricity /ɪlɛktrɪsⁱtiⁱ, iːlɛk-/ is a form of energy N UNCOUNT that is used for heating and lighting, and to provide power for machines in houses and factories. EG _They generate the electricity in power stations... There were no telephones and no electricity._

electric shock, electric shocks. An **electric** N COUNT **shock** is a sudden painful feeling that you get when

If you have to eke out your money, are you likely to feel elated?

you touch something which is connected to a supply of electricity.

electrify /i'lektrıfaı/, **electrifies, electrifying, electrified.** 1 If something **electrifies** you, it v+o excites you a lot. EG ...the news that had electrified the world. ◇ **electrifying.** EG ...an electrifying ◇ ADJ QUALIT speech.

2 When something **is electrified**, it is altered so v+o: USU PASS that it operates by electricity or is connected to a supply of electricity. EG British Rail plans to electrify over 50 per cent of its network. ◇ **electrified.** ◇ ADJ CLASSIF: EG ...electrified wire netting. ATTRIB

electrocute /i'lektrə⁶kju:t/, **electrocutes, elec-** v+o OR V-REFL **trocuting, electrocuted.** If you **electrocute** yourself or if you **are electrocuted**, you are killed or badly injured by touching something that is connected to a source of electricity. EG Don't touch that wire, you'll electrocute yourself!... He fell and was electrocuted on the rails.

electrode /i'lektrəud/, **electrodes.** An **electrode** N COUNT is a small piece of metal or other substance that is used to take an electric current to or from a source of power or to or from a piece of equipment.

electron /i'lektron/, **electrons.** An **electron** is a N COUNT tiny particle of matter that is smaller than an Technical atom.

electronic /ilektronık, iːlek-/, **electronics.** 1 An ADJ CLASSIF **electronic** device has transistors, silicon chips, or valves which control and change the electric current passing through it. EG ...electronic equipment.

2 An **electronic** process or activity involves the ADJ CLASSIF: use of electronic devices. EG ...electronic surveil- ATTRIB lance. ◇ **electronically.** EG Each vehicle might be ◇ ADV electronically tracked.

3 **Electronics** is 3.1 the technology of using tran- N UNCOUNT sistors, silicon chips, or valves, especially in the manufacture of devices such as radios, televisions, and computers. EG ...the British electronics indus- try. 3.2 equipment that consists of electronic N PLURAL devices. EG The boat carries a mass of sophisticated electronics.

elegant /eligənt/. 1 Someone or something that is ADJ QUALIT **elegant** is pleasing and graceful in appearance. EG ...a tall, elegant woman... ...the little church with its elegant square tower. ◇ **elegantly.** EG ...an el- ◇ ADV egantly dressed woman. ◇ **elegance** /eligəns/. ◇ N UNCOUNT The street had retained some of its old elegance.

2 You can say that an idea or plan is **elegant** when ADJ QUALIT it is simple, clear, and clever. EG His proposal has an elegant simplicity.

elegiac /elıdʒaıək/. Something that is **elegiac** ADJ CLASSIF expresses or shows sadness. EG ...an elegiac mood. Literary

elegy /elıdʒi¹/, **elegies.** An **elegy** is a sad poem, N COUNT often about someone who has died.

element /elə¹mə²nt/, **elements.** 1 An **element** of N COUNT+SUPP something is a single part which combines with others to make up a whole. EG ...the different elements in the play... ...the basic elements of a job... Surprise would be an essential element in any such action.

2 The **elements** of a subject are the first and most N PLURAL important things that you need to know about it. EG +SUPP ...the elements of reading.

3 When you talk about **elements** within a society N COUNT+SUPP or organization, you are referring to groups of people who have similar aims, beliefs, or habits. EG ...sympathetic elements outside the party.

4 If something has an **element** of a particular N PART quality or emotion, it has a certain amount of this quality or emotion. EG It contains an element of truth... ...to add an element of suspense and mystery to my novels.

5 An **element** is a substance that consists of only N COUNT one type of atom. For example, gold, oxygen, and carbon are elements.

6 The **element** in an electric fire or water heater N COUNT is the metal part which changes the electric current into heat.

7 You can refer to the weather, especially when it N PLURAL: the+N

is stormy, as the **elements.** EG Her raincoat was buttoned tight against the elements.

8 If you say that someone is **in** their **element**, you PHRASE mean that they are doing something that they enjoy and do well.

elemental /elə¹mentə⁰l/. **Elemental** feelings and ADJ QUALIT behaviour are simple, basic, and forceful. EG ...out- Literary bursts of elemental rage.

elementary /elə¹mentə⁰ri¹/. Something that is ADJ QUALIT **elementary** 1 is very simple and straightforward. EG Most towns had taken some elementary precautions. 2 is of a simple or basic standard. EG ...elementary maths.

elephant /elı¹fənt/, **elephants.** An **elephant** is a N COUNT very large animal with a long trunk. Elephants are found in Africa and India.

elephantine /elıfæntaın/. Something that is **el-** ADJ CLASSIF **ephantine** is large and clumsy. EG ...Amelia's el- Literary ephantine foot... ...an elephantine attempt at gallantry.

elevate /elıveıt/, **elevates, elevating, elevated.** 1 When people or things **are elevated**, they are v+o+to/into: given greater status or importance. EG Someone NO IMPER described cricket as 'male idleness elevated into religion'.

2 To **elevate** something means to raise it to a v+o higher level. EG Earth movements elevated great areas of the seabed.

elevated /elıveıtı²d/. 1 A person or a job or role ADJ QUALIT: that is **elevated** is very important or of very high ATTRIB rank. EG ...some elevated person like the Home Secretary.

2 If thoughts or ideas are **elevated**, they are on a ADJ QUALIT high level morally or intellectually. EG Let's discuss it on a slightly more elevated plane.

3 You say that land or a building is **elevated** when ADJ CLASSIF it is higher than the surrounding area.

elevation /elı'veıʃə⁰n/, **elevations.** 1 The eleva- N UNCOUNT **tion** of someone or something is the act of raising +POSS them to a position of greater importance or higher Formal rank. EG ...the elevation of the standards of the average man... ...his elevation to the peerage.

2 The **elevation** of a place is its height above sea N COUNT level. EG ...a fairly flat plateau at an elevation of Formal about a hundred feet.

elevator /elə¹veıtə/, **elevators.** An **elevator** is a N COUNT device that moves up and down inside a tall American building and carries people from one floor to another.

eleven /ılevə⁰n/ **elevens.** Eleven is the number NUMBER 11: see the entry headed NUMBER. EG The flight had been postponed until eleven o'clock.

eleventh /ı'levə⁰nθ/, **elevenths.** 1 The **eleventh** ORDINAL item in a series is the one that you count as number eleven: see the entry headed NUMBER. EG ...the eleventh floor of the building.

2 An **eleventh** is one of eleven equal parts of N COUNT: something. USU+of

eleventh hour. The **eleventh hour** is the last N SING: the+N possible moment before something happens. EG I was asked, at the eleventh hour, to step in and direct the play.

elicit /ı'lısıt/, **elicits, eliciting, elicited.** 1 If you v+o: **elicit** a response or a reaction, you cause it to OFT+from happen by saying or doing something. EG Threats to Formal reinstate the tax elicited jeers from the opposition.

2 If you **elicit** a piece of information, you find it out v+o by asking careful questions. EG In five minutes she Formal had elicited all the Herriard family history.

eligible /elıdʒə³bə⁰l/. 1 Someone who is **eligible** ADJ CLASSIF: for something is qualified or suitable for it. EG You OFT+for OR may be eligible for a grant to help you study. to-INF ◇ **eligibility** /elıdʒəbılıti¹/. EG ...the eligibility of ◇ N UNCOUNT applicants.

2 An **eligible** man or woman is not yet married but ADJ QUALIT is considered to be a suitable marriage partner. EG ...an eligible bachelor.

eliminate /ı'lımı¹neıt/, **eliminates, eliminating, eliminated.** 1 To **eliminate** something means to v+o remove it completely, especially when it is something that you do not want or need. EG *Poverty must be eliminated.* ◇ **elimination** /ɪˈlɪmɪneɪʃəⁿn/. EG ...*the elimination of spelling errors.*

2 When a person or team **is eliminated** from a competition, they are defeated and so take no further part in the competition. EG *Four minor candidates were eliminated in the first round.*

elite /ɪˈliːt/, **elites. 1** An **elite** is a group of the most powerful, rich, or talented people in a place or community. EG ...*a small intellectual elite.*

2 Elite people or organizations are considered to be the best of their kind. EG ...*a small group of elite investment bankers... ...elite training establishments.*

elitism /ɪˈliːtɪzəⁿm/ is the belief that a society or country should be ruled by a small group of people who are considered to be superior to everyone else. EG *This kind of elitism is even more marked in public schools.* ◇ **elitist** /ɪˈliːtɪst/, **elitists.** EG *Conservationists are often branded as elitists... It had been a very elitist society.*

elixir /ɪˈlɪksɪə/, **elixirs.** An **elixir** is a liquid that is considered to have magical powers.

ellipse /ɪˈlɪps/, **ellipses.** An **ellipse** is an oval shape like a flattened circle.

elm /ɛlm/, **elms.** An **elm** is a kind of tree with broad leaves which it loses in winter. EG ...*a house surrounded by tall elms.*

elocution /ˌɛləkjuːʃəⁿn/ is the art of speaking clearly in public with a standard accent. EG *He taught elocution at a junior college.*

elongated /iːlɒŋɡeɪtɪd/. Something that is **elongated** is very long and thin.

elope /ɪˈləʊp/, **elopes, eloping, eloped.** When two people **elope**, they go away secretly together in order to get married, usually without their parents' permission. EG *Is it true you eloped with her to Florida?*

eloquent /ˈɛləkwəⁿnt/. People who are **eloquent** express themselves well when they are speaking and can persuade other people to do things. EG *He was tall, eloquent, and had fine manners... ...detailed and eloquent descriptions.* ◇ **eloquently.** EG *They spoke eloquently of their concern.* ◇ **eloquence** /ˈɛləkwəns/. EG *He may have inherited his eloquence from his father.*

else /ɛls/. **1** You use **else** after words such as 'anywhere', 'someone', and 'what' to refer in a vague way to another place, person, or thing. EG *Let's go somewhere else... I had nothing else to do... ...someone else's house... Who else was there?*

2 You use **or else 2.1** to introduce a statement that indicates the unpleasant results that will occur if someone does something. EG *You've got to be very careful in case you'll miss the turn-off into our drive.* **2.2** to introduce the second of two possibilities, when you are sure that there are only two but you do not know which one is true. EG *I think I was at school, or else I was staying with a school friend during the vacation.*

elsewhere /ɛlsweə/ means in other places or to another place. EG ...*in Europe and elsewhere... He can go elsewhere.*

ELT /iː ɛl tiː/ is an abbreviation for 'English Language Teaching'.

elucidate /ɪˈljuːsɪdeɪt/, **elucidates, elucidating, elucidated.** If you **elucidate** something, you make it easier to understand by explaining it fully. EG ...*a lesson elucidating the points that have been made in the previous lecture.* ◇ **elucidation** /ɪˈljuːsɪdeɪʃəⁿn/. EG *These are issues which deserve more thorough elucidation.*

elude /ɪˈluːd/, **eludes, eluding, eluded. 1** If a fact or idea **eludes** you, you cannot understand it or remember it. EG *She tried to remember the shape of his face, but it eluded her.*

2 If you **elude** someone or something, you avoid

them or escape from them. EG ...*the problems of eluding the police.*

elusive /ɪˈluːsɪv/. Something or someone that is **elusive** is difficult to find, achieve, describe, or remember. EG *Happiness is an elusive quality... Rommel remained as elusive as ever.*

emaciated /ɪˈmeɪsɪeɪtɪd/. Someone who is **emaciated** is extremely thin and weak because of illness or lack of food.

emanate /ˈɛmɒneɪt/, **emanates, emanating, emanated.** If a quality, idea, or feeling **emanates** from you, or if you **emanate** a feeling, it comes from you or was originally started by you. EG *These ideas are said to emanate from Henry Kissinger... He emanates concern.*

emancipate /ɪˈmænsɪpeɪt/, **emancipates, emancipating, emancipated.** To **emancipate** someone means to free them from unpleasant social, political, or legal restrictions. EG ...*a government determined to emancipate the poor.* ◇ **emancipation** /ɪˈmænsɪpeɪʃəⁿn/. EG *Marx spoke of the emancipation of mankind.*

embalm /ɪˈmbɑːm/, **embalms, embalming, embalmed.** When a dead person **is embalmed**, their body is preserved using spices, oils, or chemicals.

embankment /ɛmˈbæŋkməⁿnt/, **embankments.** An **embankment** is a thick wall built of earth, often supporting a railway line. EG *The car ran up an embankment covered with grass... ...a railway embankment.*

embargo /ɛmˈbɑːɡəʊ/, **embargoes.** An **embargo** is an order that is made by a government to stop trade with another country. EG *The states imposed an embargo on oil shipments... ...a trade embargo.*

embark /ɪˈmbɑːk/, **embarks, embarking, embarked. 1** If you **embark** on something new, difficult, or exciting, you start doing it. EG *Peru embarked on a massive programme of reform.*

2 When you **embark** on a ship, you go on board before the start of a voyage. EG *She had embarked on the S.S. Gordon Castle at Tilbury.* ◇ **embarkation** /ˌɛmbɑːˈkeɪʃəⁿn/. EG *They returned to their port of embarkation, Toulon.*

embarrass /ɪˈmbærəs/, **embarrasses, embarrassing, embarrassed. 1** If something **embarrasses** you, it makes you feel shy or ashamed. EG *It embarrasses me even to think about it... He had been highly embarrassed by this confession.*

2 If something **embarrasses** a politician or political party, it causes political problems for them. EG *The march could embarrass the government.*

embarrassed /ɪˈmbærəst/. If you are **embarrassed**, you feel shy or ashamed. EG *I felt really embarrassed about it... She had been too embarrassed to ask her friends... They were met with embarrassed silence.*

embarrassing /ɪˈmbærəsɪŋ/. Something that is **embarrassing** makes you feel embarrassed. EG *He said something that would be embarrassing for me to repeat.* ◇ **embarrassingly.** EG *Their possessions were embarrassingly few.*

embarrassment /ɪˈmbærəsməⁿnt/, **embarrassments. 1 Embarrassment** is a feeling of shyness or shame. EG *His cheeks were hot with embarrassment... ...her embarrassment at having to visit me.*

2 Someone or something that embarrasses people can be referred to as an **embarrassment.** EG *For Labour, it was a political embarrassment... He was an embarrassment to so many people.*

embassy /ˈɛmbəsɪ/, **embassies.** An **embassy** is **1** a group of government officials, headed by an ambassador, who represent their government in a foreign country. EG *She was attached to the Canadian embassy.* **2** the building in which an ambassador and his or her officials work.

Do eloquent people elucidate things well?

embattled /ɪ'bætəˀld/. An **embattled** person or ADJ CLASSIF
group is having a lot of problems or difficulties. EG
...supporting an embattled Labour Government.

embedded /ɪ'mbedɪd/. 1 If an object is **embed-** ADJ PRED + in
ded in something, it is fixed there firmly and
deeply. EG The boat lay with its rudder embedded in
mud.
2 If something such as an attitude or feeling is ADJ CLASSIF
embedded in a society or in someone's personality, it has become a permanent feature of it. EG ...a
deeply embedded feeling of guilt.

embellish /ɪ'mbelɪʃ/, **embellishes, embellish-**
ing, embellished. 1 If something **is embellished** V+O : USU
with other things such as decorations, they are PASS + with
added to it to make it more attractive. EG ...a dress Formal
embellished with tiny circular mirrors.
◊ **embellishment** /ɪ'mbelɪʃmə²nt/, **embellish-** ◊ N COUNT OR
ments. EG ...the embellishment of the church at N UNCOUNT
Chambery.
2 If you **embellish** a story or account, you make it V+O
more interesting by adding details which are pos- Formal
sibly untrue. EG ...embellished accounts of the day's
events. ◊ **embellishment.** EG ...copying articles ◊ N COUNT
from other papers and repeating them with embel-
lishments.

ember /ɛmbə/, **embers.** The **embers** of a fire are N COUNT :
the small hot pieces of wood or coal that remain USU PLURAL
and glow after the fire has finished burning.

embezzle /ɪ'mbezə³l/, **embezzles, embezzling,** V+O
embezzled. If someone **embezzles** money, they
steal it from an organization that they work for. EG
For years he'd been embezzling large sums of
money from the company. ◊ **embezzlement.** EG ◊ N UNCOUNT
He was prosecuted for embezzlement.

embitter /ɪ'mbɪtə/, **embitters, embittering,** V+O : USU PASS
embittered. If someone **is embittered** by what
happens to them, they feel angry and resentful
because of it. ◊ **embittered.** EG ...a disappointed ◊ ADJ QUALIT
and embittered man. ◊ **embittering.** EG ...an ◊ ADJ QUALIT
embittering experience.

emblazoned /ɪ'mbleɪzə²nd/ If designs or letters ADJ PRED : OFT
are **emblazoned** on something, they are clearly +on/with
drawn, printed, or sewn on it. EG ...a flag on which
the imperial eagle was emblazoned... ...sweatshirts
emblazoned with the name of their college.

emblem /ɛmblə²m/, **emblems.** An **emblem** is 1 a N COUNT :
design that represents a country or organization. EG USU + SUPP
The bald eagle remains the proud emblem of the
USA. **2** something that represents a quality or idea. N COUNT + SUPP
EG ...a ruler's staff, an emblem of kingship.

embodiment /ɪ'mbɒdɪ²mə²nt/. If you describe N SING :
someone or something as the **embodiment** of a OFT + SUPP
quality, principle, or idea, you mean that they have Formal
that quality, principle, or idea as their main feature
or as the basis for all they do. EG She was the
embodiment of loyalty.

embody /ɪ'mbɒdɪ²/, **embodies, embodying, em-**
bodied. 1 To **embody** a quality, principle, or idea V+O
means to have it as your main feature or basis. EG
...the institutions which embody traditional values.
2 If something **embodies** a particular thing, it V+O
contains or consists of that thing. EG These proposals were embodied in the Industrial Relations Act.

emboldened /ɪ'mbəʊldə²nd/ If you are **embold-** ADJ PRED : OFT
ened by something that happens, it makes you feel +by
confident enough to do something. EG Emboldened
by this success, he had begged a further favour.

embossed /ɛmbɒst/. An **embossed** design or ADJ CLASSIF
word sticks up slightly from the surface it has been
added to. EG ...embossed writing paper.

embrace /ɪ'mbreɪs/, **embraces, embracing,**
embraced. 1 When you **embrace** someone, you V OR V+O :
put your arms around them in order to show your RECIP
affection for them. EG We embraced each other.
▸ used as a noun. EG They greeted us with warm ▸ N COUNT
embraces.
2 If something **embraces** a group of people, things, V+O
or ideas, it includes them. EG The course embraces Formal
elements of chemistry, physics, and engineering.

3 If you **embrace** a religion, political system, or V+O
idea, you start believing wholeheartedly in it. EG Formal
She embraced the Catholic faith.

embroider /ɪ'mbrɔɪdə/, **embroiders, embroi-** V+O OR V
dering, embroidered. If you **embroider** something made of cloth, you sew a decorative design
onto it. ◊ **embroidered.** EG ...an embroidered ◊ ADJ CLASSIF
shirt... ...a veil embroidered with red flowers.

embroidery /ɪ'mbrɔɪdə²rɪ¹/ is 1 designs sewn on N UNCOUNT
cloth. EG ...fine linen, decorated with embroidery. **2**
cloth on which designs have been sewn. **3** the
activity of sewing designs on cloth. EG ...Jane's first
attempts at embroidery.

embroil /ɪ'mbrɔɪl/, **embroils, embroiling, em-** V+O :
broiled. When someone **is embroiled** in an argu- USU PASS + in
ment or fight, they become deeply involved in it. EG
It would be foolish to become embroiled in this
struggle.

embryo /ɛmbrɪəʊ/, **embryos.** 1 An **embryo** is an N COUNT
animal or human being which has not yet been
born and which is in the very early stages of
development.
2 Something that is **in embryo** is at a very early PHRASE
stage of its development. EG The electron microscope has been around, in embryo at any rate, for a
long time.

embryonic /ɛmbrɪɒnɪk/ means in a véry early ADJ CLASSIF :
stage of development. EG Embryonic peasant move- ATTRIB
ments began to emerge. Formal

emerald /ɛmə²rə²ld/, **emeralds.** 1 An **emerald** is N COUNT
a precious stone which is clear and bright green.
2 Something that is **emerald** is bright green in ADJ COLOUR
colour. EG ...over the emerald turf.

emerge /ɪ'mɜːdʒ/, **emerges, emerging,**
emerged. 1 When you **emerge,** you come out V : OFT + from/
from a place where you could not be seen. EG I saw out of
the woman emerge from a shop.
2 When you **emerge** from a situation or state, you V + from
stop being in it or experiencing it. EG Few emerge
from the experience unscathed.
3 If a fact **emerges** from a discussion or investiga- V + from
tion, it becomes known as a result of it. EG It OR REPORT :
emerged that she had been drinking. ONLY that
4 When something such as an industry or a politi- V
cal movement **emerges,** it comes into existence.
EG Large-scale industry emerged only gradually.
◊ **emergence** /ɪ'mɜːdʒəns/. EG ...the emergence of ◊ N SING
new ideas.

emergency /ɪ'mɜːdʒənsɪ¹/, **emergencies.** 1 An N COUNT OR
emergency is an unexpected and dangerous situa- N UNCOUNT
tion, which must be dealt with quickly. EG The bells
were only used in emergencies... ...what to do in
case of emergency.
2 Emergency action is taken immediately, be- ADJ CLASSIF :
cause an emergency has occurred. EG The plane ATTRIB
made an emergency landing.
3 Emergency equipment or supplies are intended ADJ CLASSIF :
for use in an emergency. EG ...emergency supplies ATTRIB
of food.

emergent /ɪ'mɜːdʒənt/. An **emergent** country, ADJ CLASSIF :
political group, or way of life is becoming powerful ATTRIB
or is coming into existence. Formal

emigrate /ɛmɪgreɪt/, **emigrates, emigrating,** V : OFT + to/
emigrated. If you **emigrate,** you leave your na- from
tive country to live in another country. EG He
received permission to emigrate to Canada.
◊ **emigration** /ɛmɪgreɪʃə⁰n/. EG ...the encourage- ◊ N UNCOUNT
ment given to peasant emigration.

émigré /ɛmɪgreɪ/, **émigrés.** An **émigré** is some- N COUNT
one who has left their country for political reasons. Formal
EG ...revolutionary émigrés from Russia.

eminent /ɛmɪnə²nt/. An **eminent** person is impor- ADJ QUALIT
tant and highly respected, especially because they
are very good at their profession. EG ...one of the
most eminent scientists in Britain. ◊ **eminence** ◊ N UNCOUNT
/ɛmɪnə²ns/. EG ...a statesman of great eminence.

eminently /ɛmɪnə²ntlɪ¹/ means very, or to a great SUBMOD
degree. EG Children are eminently practical. Formal

emissary /ˈɛmɪsəˈriˈ/, **emissaries.** An **emissary** N COUNT
is a messenger or representative who is sent by Formal
one government or leader to another.

emission /iˈmɪʃᵊn/, **emissions.** When there is an N COUNT OR
emission of gas or radiation, it is released into the N UNCOUNT
atmosphere. EG ...*emissions of sulphur.* Formal

emit /iˈmɪt/, **emits, emitting, emitted.** To **emit** a v+o
sound, a smell, a substance, heat, or light means to Formal
produce it or send it out. EG *He was heard to emit
heartbroken sighs... ...the rays of heat that are
emitted by the warm earth.*

emotion /iˈməʊʃᵊn/, **emotions.** An **emotion** is a N COUNT OR
feeling such as fear, love, anger, or jealousy. EG *It* N UNCOUNT
*wasn't proper for a man to show his emotions... She
looked around her without emotion.*

emotional /iˈməʊʃᵊnəl, -ʃᵊnᵊl/. **1 Emotional** ADJ CLASSIF
means relating to your emotions. EG ...*the emotional needs of children.* ◊ **emotionally.** EG *He felt* ◊ ADV
physically and emotionally exhausted.
2 When someone is **emotional**, they experience a ADJ QUALIT
strong emotion and show it openly, especially by
crying. EG *Nell was far more emotional about it
than he was.*

emotive /iˈməʊtɪv/. Something that is **emotive** is ADJ QUALIT
likely to make people feel strong emotions. EG *Sir
John used extremely emotive language.*

empathy /ˈɛmpəθiˈ/ is the ability to share another N UNCOUNT
person's feelings as if they were your own. Formal

emperor /ˈɛmpᵊrə/, **emperors.** An **emperor** is a N COUNT
man who rules an empire. EG ...*the Emperor of
Austria.*

emphasis /ˈɛmfəsɪs/, **emphases** /ˈɛmfəsiːz/. **Em-**
phasis is 1 special importance that is given to an N UNCOUNT
activity or to a part or aspect of something. EG *Too* OR N COUNT
*much emphasis is being placed on basic research...
The army has always laid great emphasis on the
use of helicopters.* **2** extra force that you put on a N UNCOUNT
word when you are speaking in order to make it OR N COUNT
seem more important. EG *'They had four cars,' he
repeated with emphasis.*

emphasize /ˈɛmfəsaɪz/, **emphasizes, emphasiz-** v+o OR
ing, emphasized; also spelled **emphasise.** To v+REPORT
emphasize something means to indicate that it is
particularly important or true. EG *John went on to
emphasise a point I'd already made... Mr
Thompson was at pains to emphasize that he was
threatening nobody.*

emphatic /iˈmfætɪk/. **1** An **emphatic** statement ADJ QUALIT
is one that is made forcefully and clearly. EG ...*an
emphatic refutation.*
2 If you are **emphatic**, you use forceful language, ADJ PRED
showing that you believe that what you are saying
is important. EG *But Wendy was emphatic. 'You
must do it,' she said.*
3 An **emphatic** way of speaking is one in which ADJ CLASSIF :
you speak slowly, adding extra stress to many ATTRIB
words in order to make them sound more important.

emphatically /iˈmfætɪkᵊliˈ/. **1** If you say some- ADV
thing **emphatically**, you say it in a way that shows
that you feel strongly about what you are saying. EG
'I hope it does,' she said emphatically.
2 You also use **emphatically** to indicate that ADV
something is definitely true. EG *She is emphatically
not a recluse.*

empire /ˈɛmpaɪə/, **empires.** An **empire** is **1** a N COUNT
number of nations that are all controlled by one
country. EG ...*the British Empire.* **2** a large group of
companies which is controlled by one person. EG
His publishing empire was flourishing.

empirical /iˈmpɪrɪkᵊl/. **Empirical** knowledge or ADJ CLASSIF
study comes from or involves practical experience Formal
rather than theories. EG ...*the empirical study of
anatomy.* ◊ **empirically.** EG *The theory could be* ◊ ADV OR
tested empirically. ADV SEN

empiricism /ɛmˈpɪrɪsɪzᵊm/ is the belief that peo- N UNCOUNT
ple should rely on practical experience rather than Technical
theories as a basis for knowledge and action.

employ /iˈmplɔɪ/, **employs, employing, em-**
ployed. 1 If you **employ** someone, you pay them to v+o:
work for you. EG *He was employed as a research* USU PASS+*as*
assistant.
2 To **employ** something means to use it. EG *If* v+o
nuclear weapons are employed the world will be Formal
*destroyed... You will need to employ a great deal of
tact.*

employee /ɛmplɔɪˈiː, iˈmplɔɪiː/, **employees.** An N COUNT
employee is a person who is paid to work for an
organization or for another person. EG ...*a BBC
employee.*

employer /iˈmplɔɪə/, **employers.** Your **employ-** N COUNT
er is the person or organization that you work for.
EG *The university is a major employer in the area.*

employment /iˈmplɔɪmᵊnt/ is the position of N UNCOUNT
having a paid job. EG *He had retired from regular
employment.*

empower /iˈmpaʊə/, **empowers, empowering,** v+o+to-INF :
empowered. When someone is **empowered** to do USU PASS
something, they are given the authority or power Formal
to do it. EG *The police are empowered to stop
anyone to search for illegal drugs.*

empress /ˈɛmprɪs/, **empresses.** An **empress** is a N COUNT
woman who rules an empire, or the wife of an
emperor.

emptiness /ˈɛmptiˈnɪs/. **1** A feeling of empti- N UNCOUNT
ness is an unhappy or frightening feeling that
nothing is worthwhile. EG *She showed no sign of the
inner sense of emptiness she felt.*
2 The **emptiness** of a place is the fact that it has N UNCOUNT
nothing in it. EG ...*the largely unexplored emptiness
of the Indian Ocean.*

empty /ˈɛmptiˈ/, **emptier, emptiest; empties,**
emptying, emptied. 1 A place, vehicle, or contain- ADJ QUALIT
er that is **empty** has no people or things in it. EG
The room was empty... ...two empty bottles.
2 A gesture, threat, or relationship that is **empty** ADJ QUALIT
has no real value, meaning, or effectiveness. EG
They ignored his threats as empty rhetoric.
3 If you describe a person's life or a period of time ADJ QUALIT
as **empty**, you mean that it has nothing interesting
or important in it. EG *How shall I exist during the
empty days ahead?*
4 If you **empty** a container, you remove its con- v+o : USU+A
tents. EG *She picked up an ashtray and emptied it
into a wastepaper basket.*
5 If you **empty** a substance or object out of a v+o+A
container, you pour or tip it out of the container. EG
You ought to empty the water out of those boots.
6 If a room or container **empties**, everyone or v
everything that is in it goes out of it. EG *The play
was over and the auditorium began to empty.*

empty-handed. If you come back from some- ADJ PRED
where **empty-handed**, you have failed to get what
you intended to get. EG *They were punished severely if they came back empty-handed.*

emulate /ˈɛmjəˈleɪt/, **emulates, emulating,** v+o
emulated. If you **emulate** someone or something, Formal
you imitate them because you admire them. EG ...*a
system that has been envied and emulated.*

enable /iˈneɪbᵊl/, **enables, enabling, enabled.** If v+o+to-INF
someone or something **enables** you to do some- Formal
thing, they make it possible for you to do it. EG ...*the
feathers that enable a bird to fly.*

enact /iˈnækt/, **enacts, enacting, enacted. 1** v+o
When a government **enacts** a proposal, they make Technical
it into a law.
2 If people **enact** a story or play, they act it. EG v+o
They enacted tales of feudal princes. Formal

enamel /iˈnæmᵊl/ is **1** a substance like glass N UNCOUNT
which can be heated and put onto metal, glass, or
pottery in order to decorate it. ◊ **enamelled** ◊ ADJ CLASSIF
/iˈnæmᵊld/. EG ...*scissors with enamelled handles.*

What do you call the wife of an emperor?

2 the hard white substance that forms the outer N UNCOUNT
part of a tooth.

enamoured /ɪˈnæməd/; spelled **enamored** in ADJ PRED : USU
American English. If you are **enamoured** of some- +of
one or something, you like them very much. EG *I
was, of course, always enamoured of the theatre.*

en bloc /ɒn blɒk/. If several people or things do ADV
something **en bloc**, they do it as a group. EG *...a* Formal
*system which teaches the young, en bloc, a number
of beliefs.*

encapsulate /ɪˈkæpsjəˌleɪt/, **encapsulates, en-** V+O
capsulating, encapsulated. If something **encap-** Formal
sulates facts or ideas, it contains or represents
them in a very small space or in a single object or
event. EG *A play was written, encapsulating the
main arguments.*

encase /ɪˈkeɪs/, **encases, encasing, encased.** V+O :
If something **is encased** in a container or ma- USU PASS+*in*
terial, it is completely enclosed within it or covered by it. EG *Her feet were encased in a pair of old
baseball boots.*

-ence, -ence and **-ency** are added to adjectives, SUFFIX
usually in place of -ent, to form nouns. These nouns
refer to states, qualities, attitudes, or behaviour.
For example, 'affluence' is the state of being
affluent, and 'complacency' is the attitude of someone who is complacent. Nouns like these are often
not defined in this dictionary, but are treated with
the related adjective. EG *...his abhorrence of war...
...the prevention of delinquency.*

enchanted /ɪˈntʃɑːntɪd/. 1 If you are **enchanted** ADJ QUALIT
by something, you think that it is lovely or delightful. EG *Sheila was enchanted by the prospect of a
journey.*

2 If you describe a place or event as **enchanted**, ADJ CLASSIF
you mean that it seems as lovely or strange as
something in a fairy story. EG *...an enchanted
island.*

enchanting /ɪˈntʃɑːntɪŋ/. Something that is **en-** ADJ QUALIT
chanting is lovely or delightful. EG *...the most
enchanting smile.*

encircle /ɪˈnsɜːkəl/, **encircles, encircling, en-** V+O
circled. If something **encircles** something else, it
completely surrounds it or encloses it. EG *The M5
and M6 motorways encircle Birmingham.*

enclave /ˈɛnkleɪv/, **enclaves.** You can refer to a N COUNT :
place as an **enclave** when it is surrounded by other USU+SUPP
places that are different, for example because Formal
they are inhabited by people of a different culture.
EG *...the cloistered enclaves of academic life.*

enclose /ɪˈkləʊz/, **encloses, enclosing, en-**
closed. 1 If an object **is enclosed** by something V+O :OFT+*in*/
solid, it is completely surrounded by it. EG *The* with
statue is enclosed in a heavy glass cabinet.
◊ **enclosed.** EG *The reaction takes place extremely* ◊ ADJ CLASSIF
rapidly within an enclosed space.

2 If you **enclose** something with a letter, you put it V+O
in the same envelope. EG *I enclose a small cheque.*
◊ **enclosed.** EG *The enclosed list gives details of* ◊ ADJ CLASSIF
the courses available.

enclosure /ɪˈkləʊʒə/, **enclosures.** An enclo- N COUNT
sure is an area of land that is surrounded by a wall
or fence and that is used for a special purpose. EG
...the public enclosure of a racecourse.

encode /ɪˈkəʊd/, **encodes, encoding, encoded.** V+O
If you **encode** a message or some information, you
put it into code.

encompass /ɪˈkʌmpəs/, **encompasses, en-** V+O
compassing, encompass. If something or some- Formal
one **encompasses** certain things, they have a wide
range that includes all those things. EG *...a policy
which encompasses all aspects of conservation.*

encore /ˈɒŋkɔː/, **encores.** An audience shouts 'En- CONVENTION
core!' at the end of a concert when they want the
performer to perform an extra item. ▶ An **encore** ▶ N COUNT
is this extra item. EG *...and lastly, for the encore, a
Brahms waltz.*

encounter /ɪˈkaʊntə/, **encounters, encounter-**
ing, encountered. 1 If you **encounter** someone, V+O : NO CONT
Formal

you meet them. EG *On their journey they encountered an English couple.* ▶ used as a noun. EG *That* ▶ N COUNT :
was my first encounter with the great man. OFT+with

2 If you **encounter** something, you experience it. V+O
EG *They've never encountered any discrimination.*
▶ used as a noun. EG *In their earliest encounters* ▶ N COUNT :
with stories, children want action. OFT+with

encourage /ɪˈkʌrɪdʒ/, **encourages, encourag-**
ing, encouraged. 1 If you **encourage** someone to V+O :
do something, you tell them that you think that OFT+*to*-INF
they should do it, or that they should continue
doing it. EG *Her husband encouraged her to get a
car.* ◊ **encouragement** /ɪˈkʌrɪdʒmənt/. EG ◊ N UNCOUNT
Many people sent messages of encouragement.

2 If you **encourage** a particular activity, you V+O : USU PASS
support it actively. EG *Group meetings in the factory were always encouraged.*

3 If something **encourages** an attitude or a kind of V+O
behaviour, it makes it more likely to happen. EG
Could the Scarman Report encourage racism?

4 Something that is **encouraging** gives you hope ADJ QUALIT
or confidence. EG *Her husband had some encouraging news.*
◊ **encouragingly.** EG *Rachel smiled encouraging-* ◊ ADV
ly.

encroach /ɪˈkrəʊtʃ/, **encroaches, en-**
croaching, encroached. 1 To **encroach** on some- V :OFT
thing means to take away part of it or to take more +*on/upon*
and more of it. EG *The new law doesn't encroach on
the rights of the citizen.* ◊ **encroachment** ◊ N COUNT OR
/ɪˈkrəʊtʃmənt/, **encroachments.** EG *...the Estab-* N UNCOUNT
*lishment's encroachments on traditional rights and
liberties.*

2 If someone or something **encroaches** on an area V :OFT
of land, they gradually occupy more and more of it. +*on/upon*
EG *They would not try to encroach in any way on
the estate.* ◊ **encroachment.** EG *...justifiable con-* ◊ N COUNT OR
cern about the encroachment on farming land that N UNCOUNT
might occur.

encrusted /ɪˈkrʌstɪd/. If a surface is **encrust-** ADJ QUALIT :
ed with something, it is covered with it. EG *The* OFT+with
statues are encrusted with jewels.

encumber /ɪˈkʌmbə/, **encumbers, encum-** V+O : USU
bering, encumbered. If something **encumbers** PASS+with
you, it makes it difficult for you to move or to take Formal
some action. EG *...passengers who were encumbered with suitcases.*

encumbrance /ɪˈkʌmbrəns/, **encumbrances.** N COUNT
An **encumbrance** is something or someone that Formal
encumbers you. EG *They are both encumbrances
and I don't want them around.*

-ency. See **-ence.**

encyclopedia /ɪnˌsaɪkləˈpiːdɪə/, **encyclopedias;** N COUNT
also spelled **encyclopaedia.** An **encyclopedia** is a
book or set of books in which many facts are
arranged for reference, usually in alphabetical
order.

end /ɛnd/, **ends, ending, ended.** 1 The **end** of a N SING : the+N
period of time, an event, or a piece of writing is the
last part of it. EG *...at the end of August... ...one
afternoon near the end of my stay... She read the
first draft from beginning to end.*

2 If something puts an **end** to an activity or N SING :
situation, the activity or situation stops. EG *He urged* OFT+*to/of*
an immediate end to all armed attacks.

3 The **end** of something long and narrow is one of N COUNT+SUPP
its two extreme points, or the place that is furthest
away from the point where it is attached to something else. EG *Sharpen a stick at both ends... The
end of its tail quivered.*

4 You can refer to one of the two extreme points of N COUNT+SUPP
a scale as one **end** of the scale. EG *...at the other
end of the social scale.*

5 The other **end** is one of two places that are N COUNT+SUPP
connected because people are communicating with
each other by telephone or in writing. EG *The
phone at the other end rang.*

6 An **end** is also the purpose for which something N COUNT :
is done. EG *...their use of industrial power for* USU+SUPP
political ends. ● If you consider something to be an ● PHRASE

end in itself, you consider it to be desirable, even though you do not achieve anything by it.

7 Someone's **end** is their death. EG *He did not deserve such a cruel end.* N COUNT Literary

8 When a situation or activity **ends** or when you **end** it, it stops. EG *The current agreement ends on November 24... ...a desperate initiative which ended in failure... He refused to end his nine-week-old hunger strike.* ◇ **ending.** EG *...the ending of all* ◇ N UNCOUNT *manufacture of nuclear weapons.* V-ERG

9 If a piece of writing or a performance **ends** in a particular way or if the writer or performer **ends** it in that way, its final part consists of the thing mentioned. EG *The play ends with all the children playing and reciting.* V OR V-ERG+ with/on

10 An object that **ends** with or in something has that thing on its tip, or as its last part. EG *Each finger ends with a sharp claw.* V+with/in

11 A journey, road, or area that **ends** at a particular place stops there and goes no further. EG *The trail ends one mile from Bakewell.* V : USU+A

12 End is also used in these phrases. **12.1** If something is **at an end**, it is finished and will not continue. EG *The service was nearly at an end.* **12.2** If something **comes to an end**, it stops and does not continue. EG *And here the story comes to an end.* **12.3** You say **at the end of the day** when you are talking about what appears to be the case after you have considered the relevant facts. EG *The question at the end of the day is whether the house is actually worth that amount.* **12.4 In the end** means finally, after a considerable time. EG *She went back to England in the end.* **12.5** If you manage to **make ends meet**, you have just enough money to buy necessary things. EG *Many were finding it difficult to make ends meet, especially those with young children.* **12.6 No end** means a lot. EG *It upset me no end... She had no end of trouble at school.* **12.7** When something happens for days or weeks **on end**, it happens continuously for that amount of time. EG *I don't see anybody for weeks on end.* PHRASES

13 to **get the wrong end of the stick**: see **stick**. ● **at a loose end**: see **loose**. ● See also **dead end**, **ending**, and **odds and ends**.

end up. If you **end up** in a particular place or situation, you are in that place or situation after a series of events, even though you did not intend to be. EG *Many of their friends have ended up in prison... We ended up taking a taxi there.* PHRASAL VB : V+ADV+A OR V+ADV+-ING

endanger /ɪˈndeɪndʒə/, **endangers**, **endangering**, **endangered**. If you **endanger** someone or something, you cause them to be in a dangerous situation in which they might be seriously harmed. EG *They claimed the herbicides did not endanger human life.* ◇ **endangered.** EG *...endangered species of animals.* ◇ ADJ QUALIT V+O

endear /ɪˈndɪə/, **endears**, **endearing**, **endeared**. If someone's behaviour **endears** them to you, it makes you fond of them. EG *This sort of talk did not endear him to Mr Lincoln.* V+O+to OR V-REFL+to Formal

endearing /ɪˈndɪərɪŋ/. If someone's behaviour is **endearing**, it makes you fond of them. EG *...an endearing smile.* ◇ **endearingly.** EG *...endearingly* ◇ ADV *childish behaviour.* ADJ QUALIT Formal

endearment /ɪˈndɪəməⁿnt/, **endearments**. **Endearments** are words or phrases that you use to show affection. EG *He held me close to him, murmuring endearments.* N COUNT OR N UNCOUNT Formal

endeavour /ɪˈndevə/, **endeavours**, **endeavouring**, **endeavoured**; spelled **endeavor** in American English.

If you **endeavour** to do something, you try to do it. EG *He endeavoured to adopt a positive but realistic attitude.* ► used as a noun. EG *...this exciting new field of endeavour... We must wish him good fortune in his endeavours.* V+to-INF ► N UNCOUNT OR N COUNT Formal

endemic /enˈdemɪk/. A condition or illness that is **endemic** in a particular place is found naturally or ADJ CLASSIF : OFT+in Formal

commonly among the people there. EG *Until the 1940's, malaria was endemic in Ceylon.*

ending /ˈendɪŋ/, **endings**. The **ending** of something such as a story or a play is the last part of it. EG *The best kind of story is the one with a happy ending.* N COUNT

endless /ˈendlɪˢs/. If you describe something as **endless**, **1** you mean that it lasts so long that it seems as if it will never end. EG *They spend their time in an endless search for food.* ◇ **endlessly.** EG ◇ ADV *She used to nag me endlessly about the family's money.* **2** you mean that it is very large or long, with no variation. EG *...an endless sandy waste.* ADJ CLASSIF ADJ CLASSIF

endorse /ɪˈndɔːs/, **endorses**, **endorsing**, **endorsed**. If you **endorse** someone or something, you say publicly that you support or approve of them. EG *The Germans and Italians endorsed the plan.* ◇ **endorsement** /ɪˈndɔːsməⁿnt/, **endorsements**. EG *...their public endorsement of Liberal candidates.* V+O ◇ N COUNT OR N UNCOUNT

endow /ɪˈndaʊ/, **endows**, **endowing**, **endowed**. **1** If someone or something **is endowed** with a quality, they have it or are given it. EG *O'Neill had been endowed with film star looks.* V+O : USU PASS+with Formal

2 If someone **endows** an institution, they give it a large amount of money to invest or use. V+O

endowment /ɪˈndaʊməⁿnt/, **endowments**. **1** An **endowment** is a gift of money that is made to an institution such as a school or hospital. N COUNT

2 Someone's **endowments** are their natural qualities and abilities. N COUNT Formal

end product. The **end product** of an activity or process is the thing that it produces. N SING

end result. You can describe the result of a lengthy process or activity as the **end result** of it. EG *This sense of one's own worth is the end result of years of loving care.* N SING

endure /ɪˈndjʊə/, **endures**, **enduring**, **endured**. **1** If you **endure** a painful or difficult situation, you bear it calmly and patiently. EG *It was more than I could endure.* ◇ **endurance** /ɪˈndjʊərəns/. EG ◇ N UNCOUNT *They admired the troops for their courage and endurance.* V+O

2 If something **endures**, it continues to exist. EG *...a city which will endure for ever.* ◇ **enduring.** EG ◇ ADJ QUALIT *...hopes for an enduring peace.* V

enemy /ˈenəmiᵃ/, **enemies**. **1** You can describe someone who intends to harm you as your **enemy**. EG *I have many enemies... ...an enemy of society.* N COUNT

2 In a war, the **enemy** is the army or country that your country is fighting. EG *After a fierce battle the enemy had been forced back... ...enemy aircraft.* N COLL : SING, the+N

energetic /ˌenəˈdʒetɪk/. **1** Someone who is **energetic 1.1** shows a lot of enthusiasm and determination. EG *He is an energetic campaigner in the cause of road safety.* ◇ **energetically.** EG *This right is* ◇ ADV *not merely questioned but energetically denied.* ADJ QUALIT **1.2** is lively and physically active. EG *...energetic young children.* ◇ **energetically.** EG *...acrobats* ◇ ADV *energetically tumbling across the stage.* ADJ QUALIT

2 An **energetic** activity involves a lot of physical movement. EG *Do something energetic, play golf, swim, or ski.* ADJ QUALIT

energy /ˈenədʒiᵃ/, **energies**. **1 Energy** is the ability and willingness to do lots of active things, because you do not feel at all tired. EG *He has neither the time nor the energy to play with the children... ...a woman of energy and ambition.* N UNCOUNT

2 Your **energies** are your effort and attention, which you direct towards a particular aim. EG *Men like Muhammed Abdu poured their energies into religious reform.* N COUNT+POSS

3 Energy is also power that is obtained from sources such as electricity, coal, or water, and that N UNCOUNT

If a meeting seems endless, do you find it enjoyable?

makes machines work or provides heat. EG ...*nuclear energy.*

enfold /ɪ'nfəʊld/, **enfolds, enfolding, enfolded. 1** V+O:OFT+*in* Formal
If you **enfold** something in your hand or in your arms, you put your hand or your arms around it. EG *Their arms reached out to enfold him.*
2 You can say that something **enfolds** you when it V+O is all around you. EG ...*this darkness that continually* Literary *enfolds me.*

enforce /ɪ'nfɔːs/, **enforces, enforcing, enforced.**
1 If people in a position of authority **enforce** a law V+O or rule, they make sure that it is obeyed. EG· ...*officials who refused to enforce the immigration laws.* ◊ **enforcement** /ɪ'nfɔːsmə²nt/. EG ...*the en-* ◊ N UNCOUNT: *forcement of public laws and regulations.* OFT+SUPP
2 If you **enforce** a particular condition, you force it V+O to be done or to happen. EG *He enforced high standards.* ◊ **enforced.** EG ...*a life of enforced* ◊ ADJ CLASSIF *inactivity*... ...*the enforced discipline of working* ATTRIB *life.* ◊ **enforcement** /ɪ'nfɔːsmə²nt/. EG ...*the en-* ◊ N UNCOUNT: *forcement of discipline.* OFT+SUPP

enforceable /ɪ'nfɔːsəbə²l/. A rule or agreement ADJ CLASSIF: that is **enforceable** can be enforced. EG ...*a civil* OFT+*by* *contract enforceable by law.*

engage /ɪ'ngeɪdʒ/, **engages, engaging, engaged. 1** If you **engage** in an activity, you do it. If V+*in/on* OR V- you **are engaged** in it, you are doing it. EG *It was* PASS+*in/on* *considered inappropriate for a former President to* Formal *engage in commerce... The work we're engaged on is a study of heat transfer.*
2 If something **engages** you or **engages** your V+O attention or interest, it keeps you interested in it Formal and thinking about it. EG *Boredom has a chance to develop if the child's interest is not engaged.*
3 If you **engage** someone **in conversation,** you PHRASE have a conversation with them. EG *This allowed* Formal *him to engage the woman in further conversation.*
4 If you **engage** someone to do a particular job, V+O you appoint them to do it. EG *No continental opera would engage an English singer.*

engaged /ɪ'ngeɪdʒd/. **1** When two people are ADJ CLASSIF: **engaged,** they have agreed to marry each other. OFT+*to* EG *A week later, Tony became engaged to Caroline.*
2 If a telephone or telephone line is **engaged,** it is ADJ CLASSIF: already being used, so you cannot speak to the USU PRED person you are trying to phone.
3 If a public toilet is **engaged,** it is already being ADJ PRED used by someone else.

engagement /ɪ'ngeɪdʒmə²nt/, **engagements.** N COUNT An **engagement** is **1** an arrangement that you Formal have made to do something at a particular time. EG *I phoned my wife to cancel our lunch engagement.*
2 an arrangement that has been made for a performer to perform somewhere on a particular occasion. EG *He is much in demand in America for television engagements.* **3** an agreement that two people have made with each other to get married. EG *Their engagement was officially announced on 5th August.* **4** the period of time during which two people are engaged. EG ...*a letter which she wrote to Harold during their engagement.*

engaging /ɪ'ngeɪdʒɪŋ/. Someone who is **engag-** ADJ QUALIT **ing** is pleasant and charming. EG *Peter was an engaging personality.*

engender /ɪ'ndʒendə/, **engenders, engender-** V+O **ing, engendered.** If someone or something **en-** Formal **genders** a particular feeling, atmosphere, or situation, they cause it to occur. EG *This engenders a sense of responsibility.*

engine /'endʒɪn/, **engines. 1** The **engine** of a car N COUNT or other vehicle is the part that produces the power which makes the vehicle move. EG *He couldn't get his engine started.*
2 An **engine** is also the large vehicle that pulls a railway train. EG ...*a steam engine.*

engineer /ˌendʒɪ'nɪə/, **engineers, engineering,** N COUNT **engineered. 1** An **engineer** is **1.1** a skilled person who uses scientific knowledge to design and construct machinery, electrical devices, or roads and bridges. **1.2** a person who repairs mechanical or electrical devices. EG ...*a telephone engineer.* **1.3** a person who is responsible for the engine of a ship while it is at sea.
2 If you **engineer** an event or situation, you cause V+O it to happen, in a clever or indirect way. EG *It was Dr Martin who had engineered Miss Jackson's dismissal.*

engineering /ˌendʒɪ'nɪərɪŋ/ is the work involved N UNCOUNT in designing and constructing machinery, electrical devices, or roads and bridges.

English /'ɪŋglɪʃ/. **1 English** means belonging or ADJ CLASSIF relating to England, or to its people or language. EG ...*the English language.*
2 English is the language that is spoken by people N UNCOUNT who live in Great Britain and Ireland, the United States, Canada, Australia, and many other countries. EG *Half the letter was in Swedish and the rest in English.*
3 The **English** are the people who live in England. N PLURAL

Englishman /'ɪŋglɪʃmə²n/, **Englishmen.** An N COUNT **Englishman** is a man who comes from England or Great Britain.

Englishwoman /'ɪŋglɪʃwʊmən/, **Englishwomen.** N COUNT An **Englishwoman** is a woman who comes from England or Great Britain.

engrave /ɪ'ngreɪv/, **engraves, engraving, en-** V+O : USU PASS **graved. 1** If you **engrave** something with a design + *with*; ALSO or inscription or if you **engrave** a design on it, you V+O+*on* cut the design into its surface. EG *They engraved on it, 'Dedicated to the Lord'.* ◊ **engraved.** EG ...*en-* ◊ ADJ CLASSIF *graved copper trays.*
2 If you say that something **is engraved** on your V+O+*on* : USU mind, memory, or heart, you mean that you will PASS never forget it. EG *This episode remains sharply* Literary *engraved on my mind.*

engraving /ɪ'ngreɪvɪŋ/, **engravings.** An **en-** N COUNT **graving** is a picture or design that has been either cut into a surface or printed from an engraved plate.

engrossed /ɪ'ngrəʊst/. If you are **engrossed** in ADJ PRED : OFT something, it holds your attention completely. EG + *in* *She was engrossed in her book.*

engulf /ɪ'ngʌlf/, **engulfs, engulfing, engulfed. 1** V+O To **engulf** something means to completely cover Literary and hide it. EG *The town was quickly engulfed in volcanic ash.*
2 If something such as a feeling **engulfs** you, you V+O are affected by it to a very great degree. EG *Panic* Literary *engulfed him*... ...*a world engulfed in hatred and intolerance.*

enhance /ɪ'nhɑːns/, **enhances, enhancing, en-** V+O **hanced.** To **enhance** something means to improve it. EG *It would enhance his standing in the community.*

enigma /ɪ'nɪgmə/, **enigmas.** Someone or some- N COUNT thing that is an **enigma** is mysterious and difficult to understand. EG *Mrs Yule remains an enigma, revealing nothing of herself.*

enigmatic /ˌenɪg'mætɪk/. Someone or something ADJ QUALIT that is **enigmatic** is mysterious and difficult to understand. EG ...*an enigmatic smile.* ◊ **enigmatically.** EG *'You can try,' he said enig-* ◊ ADV *matically.*

enjoy /ɪ'ndʒɔɪ/, **enjoys, enjoying, enjoyed. 1** If you **enjoy** something, **1.1** you find pleasure and V+O OR V+-ING satisfaction in doing it or experiencing it. EG *I enjoyed the holiday enormously... Painting is something that I really enjoy doing.* **1.2** you are lucky V+O enough to have it. EG *They enjoyed exceptional living standards.*
2 If you **enjoy** yourself, you do something you like V-REFL doing or you take pleasure in what you are doing. EG *He is thoroughly enjoying himself.*

enjoyable /ɪ'ndʒɔɪəbə²l/. Something that is **enjoy-** ADJ QUALIT **able** gives you pleasure. EG *We had an enjoyable day at Poole.*

enjoyment /ɪ'ndʒɔɪmə²nt/, **enjoyments. 1 En-** N UNCOUNT **joyment** is the feeling of pleasure that you have

when you do or experience something you like. EG
...*the enjoyment that reading brings.*

2 An **enjoyment** is an activity that gives you N COUNT
pleasure. EG *His enjoyments in life are limited to
fighting and drinking.*

enlarge /ɪˈnlɑːdʒ/, **enlarges, enlarging, en-** V-ERG
larged. 1 If you **enlarge** something, you make it
bigger. When something becomes bigger, you can
say that it **enlarges.** EG *The original windows were
enlarged by Christopher Wren... The pores enlarge
and secrete more oil.* ◊ **enlarged.** EG ...*abnormally* ◊ ADJ QUALIT
enlarged tonsils.

2 When a photograph **is enlarged**, a bigger print V+O
of it is made.

enlarge on or **enlarge upon.** If you **enlarge on** PHRASAL VB :
or **enlarge upon** a subject, you give more details V+PREP,
about it. EG *He enlarged on the glorious future he* HAS PASS
had in mind. Formal

enlargement /ɪˈnlɑːdʒmənt/, **enlargements. 1** N UNCOUNT
Enlargement is the process or result of making
something larger. EG ...*the enlargement of crowded
hospitals... The X-ray showed moderate enlargement of the heart.*

2 An **enlargement** is a photograph that has been N COUNT
made bigger. EG *Patrick is still looking at the
enlargements.*

enlighten /ɪˈnlaɪtən/, **enlightens, enlightening,** V+O
enlightened. To **enlighten** someone means to Formal
give them more knowledge about something. EG
The object is to amuse and enlighten the reader.
◊ **enlightening.** EG *It was a most enlightening* ◊ ADJ QUALIT
book. ◊ **enlightenment** /ɪˈnlaɪtənmənt/. EG *The* ◊ N UNCOUNT
*talks were intended to bring culture and enlighten-
ment to the hearers.*

enlightened /ɪˈnlaɪtənd/. If you describe some- ADJ QUALIT
one as **enlightened**, you mean that they have
sensible, modern attitudes and ways of dealing with
things. EG *Our enlightened social policies are much
admired.*

enlist /ɪˈnlɪst/, **enlists, enlisting, enlisted. 1** If V-ERG :
someone **enlists**, they join the army, navy, or air OFT+*in/into*
force. EG *He had enlisted in the Marines.*

2 If you **enlist** someone or **enlist** their help, you V+O
persuade them to help you. EG *He should try to
enlist the help of a doctor with an interest in sport.*

enliven /ɪˈnlaɪvən/, **enlivens, enlivening, enliv-** V+O
ened. If something **enlivens** an event or situation,
it makes it more lively or cheerful. EG *The journey
was enlivened by noisy goings-on in the next
carriage.*

en masse /ɒn mæs/. If a group of people do ADV
something **en masse**, they all do it together. EG
They threatened to resign en masse.

enmeshed /ɪˈnmeʃt/. If you are **enmeshed** in a ADJ PRED : USU
situation, you are involved in it and find it difficult +*in*
to escape from it. EG *At the time I was enmeshed in* Formal
a controversy over abortion.

enmity /ˈenmɪtiˈ/, **enmities. Enmity** is a long- N UNCOUNT
lasting feeling of hatred towards someone. EG *It had* OR N COUNT
earned him the enduring enmity of the farmers. Formal

ennoble /ɪˈnəʊbəˈl/, **ennobles, ennobling, enno-** V+O
bled. To **ennoble** someone or something means to Formal
make them more noble and dignified. EG *Suffering
does not ennoble people.*

ennui /ɒnwiː/ is a feeling of tiredness, boredom, N UNCOUNT
and dissatisfaction. Literary

enormity /ɪˈnɔːmɪtiˈ/. The **enormity** of some- N SING :
thing such as a problem or difficulty is its very *the*+N+*of*
large size or extent and its seriousness. EG *Smith did
not grasp the enormity of the danger involved.*

enormous /ɪˈnɔːməs/. **1** Something that is **enor-** ADJ QUALIT
mous is extremely large in size or amount. EG ...*an
enormous cat... We do an enormous amount of
research.*

2 Enormous is also used to emphasize the great ADJ QUALIT :
degree or extent of something. EG *To his enormous* ATTRIB
delight he was elected... ...an enormous success.
◊ **enormously.** EG *I admired her enormously...* ◊ ADV
...*an enormously long room.*

enough /ɪˈnʌf/. **1 Enough** means as much as you DET, OR PRON :
need. EG *I haven't enough room... I don't think I've* OFT+*of*
*really got enough information... I've got five thou-
sand dollars – I hope it's enough... I had not seen
enough of his work.* ▸ used after a noun. EG *The fact* ▸ ADJ AFTER N
that he did so much is proof enough. Formal

2 If you say that something is **enough**, you mean PRON : OFT+*of*,
that you do not want it to continue any longer or OR DET
get any worse. EG *I didn't want to stay any longer.
Two years was enough... I've had enough of the
both of you. Get out... Don't tell me. I've got enough
problems.* ▸ used as an adverb. EG *No. This thing is* ▸ ADV AFTER
complicated enough already. VB

3 You use **enough** to say that someone or some- ADV AFTER
thing has the necessary amount of a quality, or that ADJ/ADV/VB
something is happening to the necessary extent. EG
*He was old enough to understand... The student
isn't trying hard enough.*

4 You can also use **enough** to say that something is ADV AFTER
the case to a moderate or fairly large degree. EG *He* ADJ/ADV
was a nice enough boy.

5 You use expressions such as **strangely enough** ADV SEN
and **interestingly enough** to indicate that you
think a fact is strange or interesting. EG *Oddly
enough, I do believe you.*

6 If you say **'Enough is enough'**, you mean that CONVENTION
you want something that is happening to stop.

7 fair enough: see **fair.** • **sure enough**: see **sure.**

enquire /ɪˈnkwaɪə/. See **inquire.**

enquiry /ɪˈnkwaɪəriˈ/. See **inquiry.**

enrage /ɪˈnreɪdʒ/, **enrages, enraging, enraged.** V+O
If something **enrages** you, it makes you very
angry. EG *She was enraged by these remarks.*
◊ **enraged.** EG *Letters flooded in to MPs from* ◊ ADJ QUALIT
enraged constituents.

enrich /ɪˈnrɪtʃ/, **enriches, enriching, enriched.**
1 To **enrich** something means to improve its V+O
quality by adding something else to it. EG *He
enriched drab lives.* ◊ **enriched.** EG ...*enriched* ◊ ADJ QUALIT
breakfast cereals. ◊ **enrichment** /ɪˈnrɪtʃmənt/. ◊ N UNCOUNT
EG ...*the enrichment of human experience.*

2 To **enrich** someone means to make them richer. V+O
EG *The purpose of the colonies was to enrich the* Formal
colonists. ◊ **enrichment.** EG ...*the pursuit of per-* ◊ N UNCOUNT
sonal enrichment.

enrol /ɪˈnrəʊl/, **enrols, enrolling, enrolled;**
spelled **enroll** in American English.
If you **enrol** or **are enrolled** on a course, you V-ERG
officially join it and pay a fee. EG *I was enrolled at
the University of Vienna.* ◊ **enrolment** ◊ N UNCOUNT
/ɪˈnrəʊlmənt/. EG ...*the enrolment of pupils.*

en route /ɒn ruːt/. If you are **en route** to a place, ADV
you are travelling there. EG *You'll see plenty to
interest you en route.*

enshrined /ɪˈnʃraɪnd/. If something such as an ADJ CLASSIF
idea or a right is **enshrined** in a society or a law, it Formal
is permanent and protected. EG *The universities'
autonomy is enshrined in their charters.*

enslave /ɪˈnsleɪv/, **enslaves, enslaving, en-**
slaved. 1 To **enslave** someone means to make V+O : USU PASS
them into a slave. EG *He was enslaved and ill-
treated.* ◊ **enslaved.** EG ...*slave-owning govern-* ◊ ADJ CLASSIF
ments and enslaved peoples. ◊ **enslavement** ◊ N UNCOUNT
/ɪˈnsleɪvmənt/. EG ...*the enslavement of the whole
population.*

2 To **enslave** people also means to keep them in a V+O : USU PASS
situation from which they cannot escape. EG *Men
were enslaved by developing industrialism.*
◊ **enslavement.** EG ...*enslavement to the state.* ◊ N UNCOUNT

ensue /ɪˈnsjuː/, **ensues, ensuing, ensued.** If V
something **ensues**, it happens immediately after Formal
something else. EG *A shouting match ensued be-
tween us and the bus driver.* ◊ **ensuing.** EG *He* ◊ ADJ CLASSIF :
killed a policeman in the ensuing fight... ...the ATTRIB
ensuing months.

If you entertain people at your house, are you an
entertainer?

ensure /ɪnˈʃʊə, -ˈʃɔː/, **ensures, ensuring, en-** V+REPORT
sured; also spelled **insure** /ɪnˈʃʊə, -ˈʃɔː/ in American OR V+O
English. To **ensure** that something happens means
to make certain that it happens. EG *The first duty of
the state is to ensure that people are protected
from crime... The door did not lock, but at least it
ensured a reasonable amount of privacy... I shall
try to insure that your stay is a pleasant one.*

entail /ɪnˈteɪl/, **entails, entailing, entailed.** If V+O
something **entails** something else, it necessarily
involves it or causes it. EG *The move entailed
radical changes in lifestyle... ...my romantic notions
of what parenthood entailed.*

entangled /ɪnˈtæŋɡəld/. **1** If something becomes ADJ PRED : OFT
entangled in something such as a rope or a net, it +in
is caught and held by it. EG *The oar got entangled in
the weeds.*
2 If you are **entangled** in a difficult situation, you ADJ PRED : OFT
are involved in it and you find it hard to escape +in
from. EG *The country became entangled in a grave
economic crisis.*
3 If you are **entangled** with someone, you are ADJ PRED : OFT
involved in a relationship with them that causes +with
you problems. EG *She got entangled with a pretty
awful crook.*

entanglement /ɪnˈtæŋɡəlmənt/, **entangle-** N COUNT OR
ments. An **entanglement** is a relationship with N UNCOUNT
someone, often a sexual one, which you wish to
escape from. EG *For years Uncle Tom had avoided
entanglements. Then he met Effie Mansell.*

enter /ˈentə/, **enters, entering, entered. 1** When V OR V+O
you **enter** a place, you come into it or go into it. EG
*They stopped talking as soon as they saw Brody
enter... Tom timidly entered the bedroom.*
2 When you **enter** an organization, institution, or V+O
profession, you become a member of it or become
involved in it. EG *He decided to enter college... She
entered politics.*
3 When a new quality or feature **enters** something, V+O
it appears in it. EG *A note of resolution entered the
bishop's voice... A new factor has unfortunately
entered trade union negotiations.*
4 When something **enters** a new period in its V+O
development or history, it begins this period. EG
The industry entered a period of lower growth.
5 If you **enter** a competition or race or if you V+O OR V+for
enter for it, you take part in it. EG *I entered one or
two competitions and won prizes.*
6 When you **enter** something in a written set of V+O : OFT+in
records or a computer, you write it down or type it
in. EG *Enter it in the cash book.*

enter into. 1 When you **enter into** something PHRASAL VB :
important or complicated, you start doing it or V+PREP,
being involved in it. EG *The Labour Government* HAS PASS
refused to enter into negotiations. **2** Something V+PREP,
that **enters into** something else is a factor in it or HAS PASS
is involved in it. EG *Obviously personal relationships
enter into it.*

enterprise /ˈentəpraɪz/, **enterprises. 1** An **enter-** N COUNT :
prise is **1.1** a company or business. EG *...large* USU+SUPP
industrial enterprises. **1.2** something new, difficult,
or important that you do or try to do. EG *He had
doubts about the whole enterprise.*
2 Enterprise is **2.1** a system of business, especial- N UNCOUNT :
ly one in a particular country. EG *...private enter-* USU+SUPP
prise. **2.2** willingness to try out new ways of doing
and achieving things. EG *...men of enterprise, energy, and ambition.*

enterprising /ˈentəpraɪzɪŋ/. Someone who is **en-** ADJ QUALIT
terprising is willing to try out new ways of doing
and achieving things. EG *You are no longer the
enterprising cook that once you were.*

entertain /ˌentəˈteɪn/, **entertains, entertaining,** V+O OR V
entertained. 1 To **entertain** people means **1.1** to
do something that amuses or interests them and
gives them pleasure. EG *We entertained the guests
with a detailed description of the party.* **1.2** to give
them food and hospitality, for example at your
house. EG *She never entertained.*

2 If you **entertain** an idea or suggestion, you V+O :
consider it. EG *I wondered what could have led me* NO IMPER
to entertain so ludicrous a suspicion. Formal

entertainer /ˌentəˈteɪnə/, **entertainers.** An **en-** N COUNT
tertainer is a person whose job is to entertain
audiences, for example by telling jokes, singing, or
dancing.

entertaining /ˌentəˈteɪnɪŋ/. **1** People or things ADJ QUALIT
that are **entertaining** are amusing or interesting
and give people pleasure. EG *Films should be entertaining.*
2 Entertaining involves giving guests food and N UNCOUNT
talking to them. EG *...business entertaining.*

entertainment /ˌentəˈteɪnmənt/, **entertain-**
ments. 1 Entertainment consist of performances N UNCOUNT
or activities that give an audience pleasure. EG
*...the entertainment business... This was not Mor-
ris's idea of an evening's entertainment.*
2 An **entertainment** is a performance which N COUNT
people watch for pleasure. EG *...extravagant musical entertainments.*

enthral /ɪnˈθrɔːl/, **enthrals, enthralling, en-**
thralled; spelled **enthraling** and **enthraled** in
American English.
To **enthral** someone means to hold their attention V+O : USU PASS
and interest completely. ◊ **enthralled.** EG *400* ◊ ADJ QUALIT
*people listened enthralled to an account of their
journey.* ◊ **enthralling.** EG *...an enthralling story.* ◊ ADJ QUALIT

enthuse /ɪnˈθjuːz/, **enthuses, enthusing, en-** V+O
thused. If you **enthuse** over something, you say OR V+QUOTE
excitedly how wonderful or pleasing it is. EG
*...enthusing over a weekend spent in the Lake
District... 'Brilliant,' he enthused.*

enthusiasm /ɪnˈθjuːziæzəm/, **enthusiasms. 1** N UNCOUNT
Enthusiasm is great eagerness to do something or
to be involved in something. EG *He had embarked
with great enthusiasm on an ambitious project...
...her enthusiasm for the theatre.*
2 An **enthusiasm** is an activity or subject that N COUNT :
interests you a great deal. EG *Pop music and* USU+SUPP
football are her chief enthusiasms. Literary

enthusiast /ɪnˈθjuːziæst/, **enthusiasts.** An **en-** N COUNT :
thusiast is a person who is very interested in a USU+SUPP
particular activity or subject. EG *...a great soccer
enthusiast.*

enthusiastic /ɪnˌθjuːziˈæstɪk/. If you are **enthu-** ADJ QUALIT :
siastic about something, you want to do it very OFT+about
much or like it very much, and show this in an
excited way. EG *Sarah is very enthusiastic about
learning to read.* ◊ **enthusiastically.** EG *I re-* ◊ ADV
sponded very enthusiastically.

entice /ɪnˈtaɪs/, **entices, enticing, enticed.** If V+O
you **entice** someone away from a place or activity
or **entice** them into it, you tempt them away from
it or into it. EG *An attempt is being made to entice
otters back to the river.*

enticing /ɪnˈtaɪsɪŋ/. Something that is **enticing** is ADJ QUALIT
extremely attractive. EG *Tanya's invitation seemed* Literary
too enticing to refuse.

entire /ɪnˈtaɪə/ is used to refer to the whole of ADJ CLASSIF :
something. EG *We've covered the entire wall with* ATTRIB
*postcards... He had spent his entire career on Wall
Street.*

entirely /ɪnˈtaɪəli/ means completely, and not ADV
just partly. EG *It was entirely my own fault... I must
say I agree entirely... McGovern had told them
something entirely different.*

entirety /ɪnˈtaɪərɪti/. If something happens to PHRASE
something **in** its **entirety**, it happens to all of it. EG Formal
If published, it must be published in its entirety.

entitle /ɪnˈtaɪtəl/, **entitles, entitling, entitled. 1** V+O+to OR
If something **entitles** you to have or do something, to-INF
it gives you the right to have it or do it. EG *Their
qualifications entitle them to a higher salary...
Women aged 60 and over are entitled to free
prescriptions.*
2 If something such as a book, film, or painting is ADJ PRED+N
entitled 'Sunrise', its title is 'Sunrise'. EG *...a report* PROPER
entitled 'Attitudes Towards Geriatrics'.

entitlement /ɪˈntaɪtəᵊlməᵊnt/, **entitlements. En-** N UNCOUNT
titlement to something is the right to have it or do OR N COUNT
it. EG *...entitlements to welfare and tax benefits.* Formal

entity /ˈentɪˈtiˈ/, **entities.** An **entity** is something N COUNT :
that exists separately from other things and has a USU+SUPP
clear identity. EG *Increasingly, inner cities and* Formal
suburbs are separate entities.

entomology /ˌentəˈmɒlədʒiˈ/ is the study of in- N UNCOUNT
sects.

entourage /ˈɒntʊrɑːʒ/, **entourages.** The **entou-** N COUNT :
rage of someone famous or important is the group USU+POSS
of assistants, servants, or other people who travel
with them. EG *Among his entourage was a retired*
general.

entrails /ˈentreɪlz/. The **entrails** of people or N PLURAL
animals are their intestines. Literary

entrance, entrances, entrancing, entranced;
pronounced /ˈentrəns/ when it is a noun, and
/ɪˈntrɑːns/ when it is a verb.

1 An **entrance** is a way into a place, for example a N COUNT
door or gate. EG *...the entrance to the National*
Gallery.

2 Someone's **entrance** is their arrival in a room. EG N COUNT :
She had only broken off to acknowledge our en- USU+POSS
trance... Her father would make a sudden en-
trance.

3 If you gain **entrance** to a particular place, you N UNCOUNT
are able to go into it. EG *I denied him entrance.*

4 If you gain **entrance** to a profession, society, or N UNCOUNT
institution, you are accepted as a member of it. EG
Entrance to the professions is open to many more
people.

5 If something **entrances** you, it causes you to feel V+O : USU PASS
delight and wonder. EG *The man was so entranced*
and amused by the whole idea that he said he
would return. ◊ **entranced.** EG *Everyone sat* ◊ ADJ QUALIT
entranced. ◊ **entrancing.** EG *...the most entranc-* ◊ ADJ QUALIT
ing singers.

entrant /ˈentrənt/, **entrants.** An **entrant** is **1** a N COUNT
person who has recently become a member of an
institution such as a university. **2** a person who is
taking part in a competition. EG *Each entrant plays*
the music of their choice.

entrenched /ɪˈntrentʃt/. If something such as ADJ QUALIT
power, a custom, or an idea is **entrenched**, it is Formal
firmly established, so that it would be difficult to
change it. EG *...strongly entrenched ideas.*

entrepreneur /ˌɒntrəprəˈnɜː/, **entrepreneurs.** N COUNT
An **entrepreneur** is a person who sets up businesses.

entrust /ɪˈntrʌst/, **entrusts, entrusting, en-** V+O+to/with
trusted. If you **entrust** something important to
someone or if you **entrust** them with it, you make
them responsible for looking after it or dealing
with it. EG *Children are too young to be entrusted*
with family money... It was a task the Foreign
Secretary had entrusted to him.

entry /ˈentriˈ/, **entries. 1** An **entry** is **1.1** some- N COUNT
thing that you do in order to take part in a
competition, for example a piece of work or the
answers to a set of questions. EG *Here are some*
extracts from the five winning entries. **1.2** something written in a diary, account book, dictionary,
or encyclopedia. EG *Let me look up the entries for*
mid-June. **1.3** a way into a place, for example a
door or gate. EG *...the pretty screen at the entry to*
Hyde Park.

2 A person's **entry** is their arrival in a room. EG *At* N COUNT+POSS
Derek's entry a few heads turned.

3 If you are allowed **entry** into a country, building, N UNCOUNT
or enclosure, you are allowed to go in it. EG *Many of*
his associates were refused entry to Britain.

4 The words **no entry** are used on signs to indicate
that you are not allowed to go through a particular
door or gate.

5 Someone's **entry** into a society or group is the N UNCOUNT :
act of joining it. EG *...her entry into national politics.* OFT+into/to

6 Entry, in a competition, is the act of taking part N UNCOUNT

in it. EG *Entry is free to all readers... ...the entry*
form.

entwine /ɪˈntwaɪn/, **entwines, entwining, en-** V-ERG : OFT
twined. If you **entwine** something with something PASS+in/with
else, you twist it in and around it. EG *One second* Formal
later her fingers were entwined in my own.

enumerate /ɪˈnjuːməreɪt/, **enumerates, enu-** V+O
merating, enumerated. When you **enumerate** a Formal
list of things, you name each one in turn.

enunciate /ɪˈnʌnsɪeɪt/, **enunciates, enunciat-**
ing, enunciated. 1 When you **enunciate** a word V+O OR V
or part of a word, you pronounce it clearly. Formal

2 When you **enunciate** a thought, idea, or plan, V+O OR
you express it clearly and formally. EG *I enunciated* V+QUOTE
a general principle. Formal

envelop /ɪˈnveləp/, **envelops, enveloping, en-** V+O
veloped. If something soft **envelops** something
else, it covers or surrounds it completely. EG *Mist*
was rising, enveloping the grey tree trunks.

envelope /ˈenvələʊp, ˈɒn-/, **envelopes.** An **en-** N COUNT
velope is the rectangular paper cover in which
you send a letter or card to someone through the
post. EG *...a sealed envelope.*

enviable /ˈenvɪəbᵊl/. You describe something ADJ QUALIT
such as a quality as **enviable** when someone else
has it and you wish that you had it yourself. EG *She*
learned to speak foreign languages with enviable
fluency.

envious /ˈenvɪəs/. Someone who is **envious** of ADJ QUALIT
someone else envies them. EG *Ralph watched them,*
envious and resentful. ◊ **enviously.** EG *They were* ◊ ADV
watched enviously by the rest of the crowd.

environment /ɪˈnvaɪrənᵊməᵊnt/, **environments.**

1 Someone's **environment** is everything that af- N COUNT OR
fects their daily life, for example the place where N UNCOUNT :
they live, the people around them, and the things USU+SUPP
that they experience. EG *Could the college provide*
a stimulating environment?... Are we more influ-
enced by environment or heredity?

2 The **environment** is the natural world of land, N SING : the+N
sea, air, plants, and animals that exists around
towns and cities. EG *We are fighting pollution to*
protect the environment.

environmental /ɪˈnvaɪrənᵊmentᵊl/ means **1** ADJ CLASSIF :
concerned with or relating to the natural world. EG ATTRIB
...environmental pollution. **2** relating to the surroundings in which a person or animal lives. EG
Corals are very demanding in their environmental
requirements.

environmentalist /ɪˈnvaɪrənᵊmentəlɪst/, **envi-** N COUNT
ronmentalists. An **environmentalist** is a person
who wants to protect and preserve the natural
environment, for example by preventing pollution.

environs /ɪˈnvaɪrənz/. If you talk about a place N PLURAL
and its **environs**, you are referring to the place +POSS
and the area immediately surrounding it. EG *...Fleet* Formal
Street and its environs.

envisage /ɪˈnvɪzɪdʒ/, **envisages, envisaging, en-** V+O OR
visaged. If you **envisage** a situation or event, you V+REPORT
imagine it, or think that it is likely to happen. EG Formal
The last forecast envisaged inflation falling to
about 10 per cent... The party envisages that social-
ism can come without civil war.

envoy /ˈenvɔɪ/, **envoys.** An **envoy** is a diplomat N COUNT
sent to a foreign country.

envy /ˈenviˈ/, **envies, envying, envied.** If you V+O OR
envy someone, you wish that you had things or V+O+O
qualities that they have. EG *It would be unfair to*
envy him his good fortune. ▶ used as a noun. EG *Her* ▶ N UNCOUNT
undisputed good looks caused envy and admiration.

● If you have something that other people wish ● PHRASE
they had, you can say that it is **the envy of** these
people. EG *It has a robust economy that is the envy*
of its neighbours.

Where might you see the words 'no entry'?

ephemeral /ɪ'femərəl/. Something that is ADJ QUALIT
ephemeral lasts only for a short time. EG ...*the* Literary
ephemeral nature of fads and fashions.

epic /ɛpɪk/, **epics. 1** An **epic** is a long book, poem, N COUNT
or film which usually tells a story of heroic deeds.
EG ...*the latest James Bond epic.*

2 Something that is described as **epic** is considered ADJ CLASSIF
to be very impressive or ambitious. EG ...*his trium-*
phant return after his epic voyage.

epidemic /ɛpɪdemɪk/, **epidemics.** An **epidemic** N COUNT :
is an occurrence of a disease which affects a large OFT+SUPP
number of people and which spreads quickly. EG
...*an influenza epidemic.*

epilepsy /ɛpɪlepsɪ/ is a brain condition which N UNCOUNT
causes a person to suddenly lose consciousness and
sometimes to have fits.

epileptic /ɛpɪleptɪk/, **epileptics. 1** Someone who ADJ CLASSIF
is **epileptic** suffers from epilepsy. ▸ used as a ▸ N COUNT
noun. EG *He is an epileptic.*

2 Epileptic also means caused by epilepsy. EG ...*an* ADJ CLASSIF :
epileptic fit. ATTRIB

epilogue /ɛpɪlɒg/, **epilogues.** An **epilogue** is a N COUNT
passage or speech which is added to the end of a
book or play as a conclusion.

episcopal /ɪ'pɪskəpəl/ means belonging or relat- ADJ CLASSIF :
ing to a bishop. EG ...*dressed in his episcopal vest-* ATTRIB
ments. Formal

episode /ɛpɪsəʊd/, **episodes. 1** An **episode** is an N COUNT :
important or memorable event or series of events. OFT+SUPP
EG *A wartime episode had demonstrated his judge-*
ment of men.

2 An **episode** of a drama series on television or N COUNT
radio is one of the programmes or parts that it
consists of. EG ...*the end of the first episode.*

epitaph /ɛpɪtɑːf, -tæf/, **epitaphs.** An **epitaph** is N COUNT
something written on a person's gravestone, or a
sentence or short poem that sums up a dead
person's character.

epithet /ɛpɪθɛt/, **epithets.** An **epithet** is an adjec- N COUNT :
tive or a short descriptive phrase. EG *No one could* OFT+SUPP
have denied to him the epithet of handsome. Formal

epitome /ɪ'pɪtəmɪ/. If you say that someone or N SING :
something is the **epitome** of a particular thing, you the+N+of
mean that they are a perfect example of it. EG *He* Formal
was considered the epitome of a gentleman.

epitomize /ɪ'pɪtəmaɪz/, **epitomizes, epitomiz-** V+O
ing, epitomized; also spelled **epitomise.** If you
say that someone or something **epitomizes** a
particular thing, you mean that they are a perfect
example of it. EG *His failure epitomizes that of the*
whole movement.

epoch /iːpɒk/, **epochs.** An **epoch** is a long period N COUNT+SUPP
of time in history. EG *We are at the end of one* Formal
historical epoch, and at the dawn of another.

equable /ɛkwəbəl/. Someone who is **equable** is ADJ QUALIT
calm and reasonable, and does not get angry
quickly. EG *'Oh yes, sir.' Bond's voice was patient,*
equable. ◊ **equably.** EG *'It suits me,' I said equably.* ◊ ADV

equal /iːkwəl/, **equals, equalling, equalled;**
spelled **equaling** and **equaled** in American English.

1 If two things are **equal** or if one thing is **equal** to ADJ CLASSIF :
another, they are the same, usually in size, amount, OFT+to
or degree. EG *The cake was divided into twelve*
equal parts... This creed is held with equal fervour
by all political parties... They paid fines of 250
rupees each (equal to about three months' wages).

2 If people have **equal** rights, they have the same ADJ CLASSIF :
rights as each other. EG *There is a trend towards* ATTRIB
equal opportunities for men and women.

3 If you say that people are **equal,** you mean that ADJ PRED
everyone has or should have the same rights and
opportunities as each other.

4 Someone who is your **equal** has the same ability, N COUNT+POSS
status, or rights that you have. EG *We treat our*
enemies as equals.

5 If two people do something **on equal terms,** PHRASE
neither person has any advantage over the other.

EG *This law enables British shipbuilders to compete*
on equal terms with foreign yards.

6 If something **equals** a particular amount, it is the V+C
exact equivalent of it. EG *79 minus 14 equals 65.*

7 To **equal** something or someone means to be as V+O
good or as great as them. EG *There are few film*
artists who can equal this man for sheer daring...
Your folly is only equalled by your ignorance.

8 If someone is **equal** to a job or situation, they ADJ PRED+to
have the necessary abilities, strength, or courage Formal
to deal successfully with it. EG *The staff are not*
equal to all these demands.

equality /iː'kwɒlɪtɪ/ is the same status, rights, N UNCOUNT
and opportunities for all the members of a society
or group. EG ...*equality between men and women.*

equally /iːkwəlɪ/. **1 Equally** means **1.1** in sec- ADV
tions, amounts, or spaces that are the same size as
each other. EG *On his death the land was divided*
equally between them. **1.2** to the same degree or SUBMOD OR ADV
extent. EG ...*two equally qualified men... Are par-*
ents meant to love all their children equally? **1.3** to SUBMOD OR ADV
the same degree or extent as someone or some-
thing else that has just been mentioned. EG *He was*
a superb pianist. Irene was equally brilliant... This
applies equally to partnerships of a less emotional
nature.

2 Equally is also used to introduce a comment ADV SEN
which balances or contrasts with another comment that has just been made. EG *Each country*
must find its own solution to unemployment. Equal-
ly, each must find its own way of coping with
inflation.

equals sign, equals signs. An **equals sign** is the N COUNT
sign (=), which is used in arithmetic to indicate
that two numbers or sets of numbers are equal.

equanimity /ɛkwɒnɪmɪtɪ/ is a calm state of N UNCOUNT
mind. EG *They were content to accept their defeat* Formal
with equanimity.

equate /ɪ'kweɪt/, **equates, equating, equated.** If V+O+with/to
you **equate** one thing with another, you say or Formal
believe that it is the same thing. EG *It is imperative*
that war should on no account be equated with
glory.

equation /ɪ'kweɪʒən/, **equations.** An **equation** N COUNT
is a mathematical statement saying that two
amounts or values are the same, for example 6 x 4
= 12 x 2.

equator /ɪ'kweɪtə/. The **equator** is an imaginary N PROPER
line round the middle of the earth at an equal
distance from the North Pole and the South Pole.

equatorial /ɛkwətɔːrɪəl/ is used to describe ADJ CLASSIF :
places and conditions near or at the equator. EG ATTRIB
...*the equatorial lands in the Amazon and Congo*
basins.

equestrian /ɪ'kwɛstrɪən/ means connected with ADJ CLASSIF
the activity of riding horses. EG ...*an equestrian* ATTRIB
statue of the Duke of Wellington. Formal

equidistant /ɛkwɪdɪstənt/. A place that is equi- ADJ PRED
distant from two other places is the same distance
away from each of them.

equilibrium /iːkwɪlɪbrɪəm/ is a balance between N UNCOUNT
several different forces, groups, or aspects of a Formal
situation. EG *I believe this state of equilibrium will*
be maintained.

equine /ɛkwaɪn/ means connected with or relat- ADJ CLASSIF
ing to horses. EG ...*research into equine health.* Formal

equip /ɪ'kwɪp/, **equips, equipping, equipped. 1** V-REFL
If you **equip** yourself with something, or if some- OR V+O :
one **equips** you with it, you obtain it for a particu- OFT+with
lar purpose. EG *They equip themselves with a great*
variety of gadgets... The enemy troops were
equipped with tanks, aircraft and missiles.
◊ **equipped.** EG ...*a large and well equipped army...* ◊ ADJ QUALIT :
By contrast, their competitors were superbly USU ADV+ADJ
equipped.

2 If something **is equipped** with a particular thing V+O :
or device, it has it. EG *The card will be equipped* USU PASS+with
with a built-in computer chip.

3 If something **equips** you for a task or experi- V+O :

ence, it prepares you mentally for it. EG *Kindness* OFT+*for* *will not equip your children to stand on their own* OR *to*-INF *feet... Little in their history has equipped them for coping with this problem.* ◊ **equipped.** EG *They* ◊ ADJ QUALIT : *were ill equipped to deal with the situation... They* USU ADV+ADJ *are not equipped to face reality in any shape or form.*

equipment /ɪˈkwɪpmə²nt/ consists of the things N UNCOUNT which are needed for a particular activity. EG *...kitchen equipment... ...fire-fighting equipment.*

equitable /ˈɛkwɪtəbə⁰l/. In an **equitable** system ADJ QUALIT or arrangement, everyone is treated equally. EG Formal *...economic growth of a more balanced and equitable kind.* ◊ **equitably.** EG *...spreading work and* ◊ ADV *its benefits equitably through society.*

equivalence /ɪˈkwɪvələns/. If there is **equiva-** N UNCOUNT **lence** between two things, they have the same use, function, size, or value.

equivalent /ɪˈkwɪvələ²nt/, **equivalents**. If things ADJ CLASSIF are **equivalent**, they have the same use, function, size, or value. EG *Women were paid less than men doing equivalent work... His job was roughly equivalent to that of the State Department's chief.* ▸ used as a noun. EG *A good quilt is the equivalent of* ▸ N COUNT : *at least three blankets.* OFT+*of*

equivocal /ɪˈkwɪvəkə⁰l/. **1** If something that you ADJ QUALIT say is **equivocal**, it is deliberately vague or am- Formal biguous because you want to avoid speaking the truth. EG *He limited himself to an equivocal grunt.* **2 Equivocal** behaviour, attitudes, and events are ADJ QUALIT difficult to understand or explain. EG *...equivocal* Formal *and complex situations.*

equivocate /ɪˈkwɪvəkeɪt/, **equivocates, equivo-** V **cating, equivocated.** When someone **equivo-cates**, they deliberately use vague and ambiguous language in order to deceive people or to avoid speaking the truth. EG *The temptation to equivocate was especially strong.*

er /ə, ɜː/ is used in writing to represent the sound that people make **1** when they hesitate while they are deciding what to say next. EG *...and it was not until 1845 that, er, Texas became part of the USA.* **2** when they want to attract someone's attention before speaking. EG *Er, ladies and gentlemen, dinner is served.*

-er, -ers. 1 You add **-er** to adjectives that have one SUFFIX or two syllables in order to form comparative adjectives. You also add it to some adverbs that do not end in -ly in order to form comparative adverbs. EG *They are faced with a much harder problem... Alf kept putting bigger and bigger locks on the door... He apologized for not returning sooner.* **2 -er** is used in the following ways to form nouns. SUFFIX These nouns are often not defined in this dictionary, but are treated at the related words. **2.1 -er** is added to verbs to form nouns that refer to people or things that do a particular action. For example, a reader is someone who reads, and a money-saver is something that saves money. EG *I think I know what the questioner is getting at.* **2.2 -er** is used to form nouns that refer to a person who does a particular job. EG *My grandfather was a miner... She joined the theatre as a choreographer.* **2.3 -er** is used to form nouns that refer to a particular kind of person. For example, a pensioner is someone who is entitled to a pension.

era /ˈɪərə/, **eras**. An **era** is a period of time that is N COUNT : considered as a single unit because it has a particu- USU+SUPP lar feature that makes it remarkable in some way. EG *...the post-war era... Her candidacy marked the beginning of a new era for the party.*

eradicate /ɪˈrædɪkeɪt/, **eradicates, eradicating,** V+O **eradicated.** To **eradicate** something means to Formal destroy it or remove it completely. EG *...the failure of the welfare state to eradicate poverty... ...efforts to eradicate every trace of discrimination.* ◊ **eradication** /ɪˈrædɪkeɪʃə⁰n/. EG *...pest eradica-* ◊ N UNCOUNT *tion... ...the eradication of apartheid.*

erase /ɪˈreɪz/, **erases, erasing, erased. 1** If you V+O **erase** a thought or feeling, you destroy it so that you can no longer remember it or feel it. EG *He cannot erase the memories of childhood... Your fears must be erased.* **2** If you **erase** writing, you remove it by rubbing it V+O with a rubber or cloth. **3** To **erase** something also means to destroy or V+O remove it completely so that it no longer exists. EG Formal *...a campaign to erase hunger from the world.*

eraser /ɪˈreɪzə/, **erasers**. An **eraser** is a piece of N COUNT rubber which is used for rubbing out writing. American

erect /ɪˈrɛkt/, **erects, erecting, erected. 1** If you V+O **erect** something, **1.1** you build it. EG *It would be* V+O *splendid to erect a memorial to the regiment.* Formal ◊ **erection** /ɪˈrɛkʃə⁰n/. EG *...the erection of a grave-* ◊ N UNCOUNT *stone... The building was badly damaged shortly after its erection.* **1.2** you fit the pieces of it V+O together so that it is ready to be used. EG *Thirty beds had to be erected... This kind of tent is easily erected or folded away.* **2** People or things that are **erect** are straight and ADJ QUALIT upright. EG *In the door, small but erect, stood an old man... She held herself erect.* ◊ **erectly.** EG *Each* ◊ ADV *plant begins by growing erectly.*

erode /ɪˈrəʊd/, **erodes, eroding, eroded. 1** If V-ERG something **erodes** or **is eroded**, it is gradually USU PASS destroyed or removed. EG *Confidence in the dollar has eroded... Our freedom is being eroded.* **2** If rock or soil **erodes** or **is eroded** by the V-ERG : weather, sea, or wind, it is gradually destroyed or USU PASS removed. EG *The river has eroded the rocks... The cliffs have become eroded by wind and water.*

erosion /ɪˈrəʊʒə⁰n/. **1 Erosion** is the gradual N UNCOUNT : destruction or removal of something. EG *...the ero-* USU+SUPP *sion of individual freedom.* **2** When the **erosion** of rock or soil takes place, it is N UNCOUNT : gradually destroyed or removed by the weather, USU+SUPP sea, or wind. EG *...the loss of farmland by erosion.*

erotic /ɪˈrɒtɪk/. **1 Erotic** feelings and activities ADJ QUALIT involve sexual pleasure or desire. EG *...erotic dreams... ...an erotic experience.* ◊ **erotically.** EG ◊ ADV *He found her loose dress erotically appealing.* **2 Erotic** paintings, books, and films are intended ADJ QUALIT to produce feelings of sexual pleasure. EG *...an anthology of erotic verse... ...erotic photographs.*

eroticism /ɪˈrɒtɪsɪzə⁰m/ is **1** the erotic quality of N UNCOUNT something such as a book, picture, or sculpture. EG *The powerful eroticism of his painting was a revelation.* **2** sexual interest and excitement. EG *...the helpless rapture of adolescent eroticism.*

err /ɜː/, **errs, erring, erred. 1** If you **err**, you V make a mistake. EG *Undoubtedly we have erred in* Formal *giving such low status to our nurses.* ● If someone ● PHRASE says **to err is human**, they mean that it is natural for human beings to make mistakes. **2** If you **err on the side of** a particular way of PHRASE behaving, you tend to behave that way rather than the opposite way. EG *Often one finds that advisers err on the side of caution.*

errand /ˈɛrənd/, **errands**. If you go on an **errand** N COUNT or run an **errand** for someone, you go a short distance in order to do something for them, for example to buy something from a shop. EG *It was the children's job to run errands.*

erratic /ɪˈrætɪk/. Something that is **erratic** does ADJ QUALIT not follow a regular pattern, but happens at unexpected times or moves in an irregular way. EG *...the country's erratic attempts to move into the future... I made my erratic way through the dining room.* ◊ **erratically.** EG *Gaskell steered the boat errati-* ◊ ADV *cally towards the harbour.*

erroneous /ɪˈrəʊnɪəs/. **Erroneous** beliefs or ADJ QUALIT opinions are incorrect. EG *...the erroneous belief* Formal *that every man is a responsible human being.*

Does an escalator escalate?

◊ **erroneously.** EG *Some drinkers erroneously imagined that they had become wiser.*

error /ɛrə/, **errors.** 1 An **error** is a mistake. EG *The doctor committed an appalling error of judgement... ...errors in grammar.* N COUNT OR N UNCOUNT

2 If you do something **in error** or if something happens **in error**, it happens because of a mistake. EG *Another village had been wiped out in error.* PHRASE

3 **trial and error**: see **trial.**

erudite /ɛrjuːdaɪt/. People who are **erudite** show great academic knowledge. EG *...the erudite scholar Herbert Thurston.* ADJ QUALIT

erupt /iˈrʌpt/, **erupts, erupting, erupted.** 1 When something **erupts**, it happens suddenly and in an unexpected way. EG *The Cuban Missile Crisis had erupted... Spontaneous discussion erupted about colour prejudice.* V

2 When the people in a place suddenly become angry or violent, you can say that they **erupt** or that the place **erupts**. EG *The inhabitants had erupted in massive protests... The room erupted.* V+A

3 When war or fighting **erupts**, it suddenly begins. EG *...the urban riots that erupted this summer in Britain.* ◊ **eruption** /iˈrʌpʃəⁿn/, **eruptions.** EG *This may have stopped the eruption of a major war between the superpowers.* V / ◊ N UNCOUNT OR N COUNT

4 When a volcano **erupts**, it throws out lava, ash, and steam. EG *Six other volcanoes were still erupting.* ◊ **eruption.** EG *...the most violent eruption of Mount Etna... ...a volcano on the point of eruption.* V : NO IMPER / ◊ N UNCOUNT OR N COUNT

escalate /ɛskəleɪt/, **escalates, escalating, escalated.** If an unpleasant situation **escalates**, it becomes worse. EG *There is a danger that the conflict might escalate to a nuclear confrontation.* ◊ **escalation** /ɛskəleɪʃəⁿn/. EG *...the risk of escalation... ...a steady escalation of violence.* V-ERG / ◊ N UNCOUNT

escalator /ɛskəleɪtə/, **escalators.** An **escalator** is a moving staircase on which people can go up or down. EG *They got on the wrong escalator.* N COUNT

escapade /ɛskəpeɪd/, **escapades.** An **escapade** is an exciting and rather dangerous adventure. EG *She enjoyed the escapade... The whole school knew every detail of this mad escapade.* N COUNT

escape /iˈskeɪp/, **escapes, escaping, escaped.** 1 If you **escape** from something or someone that you do not like, you succeed in avoiding them or in getting away from them. EG *How does one escape from the influence of such ideas?... Ralph was thankful to have escaped responsibility... They cannot escape their enemies.* V : OFT+*from*; ALSO V+O : NO PASS

2 If you **escape** from a place such as a prison, you succeed in getting away from it. EG *On 7 October Eva escaped from prison... He escaped to Britain.* ► used as a noun. EG *They were now able to make their escape... The chances of escape were not high... ...escape stories.* ◊ **escaped.** EG *He had shot and killed two escaped convicts... He pretended to be the escaped officer.* V : OFT +*from/to* / ► N UNCOUNT OR N COUNT / ◊ ADJ CLASSIF : ATTRIB

3 You can also say that you **escape** when you survive something such as an attack or an accident. EG *Fortunately we all escaped unhurt... The minister escaped without a scratch.* V+C OR V+A

4 If something **escapes** you or **escapes** your notice, you do not know about it, do not remember it, or do not notice it. EG *I doubt that such tactics escaped their notice... Their names escaped him.* V+O

5 You can describe a way of avoiding difficulties or responsibilities as an **escape.** EG *Reading is an escape from reality.* N COUNT OR N UNCOUNT : OFT+*from*

6 When a gas or liquid **escapes**, it leaks from a pipe or container. EG *...air escaping from a tyre.* V

7 See also **fire escape.**

escapism /iˈskeɪpɪzəⁿm/ consists of thoughts or activities that involve pleasant or fantastic ideas instead of the uninteresting or unpleasant aspects of your life. EG *Thinking about the future is a form of escapism.* ◊ **escapist** /iˈskeɪpɪst/. EG *...an escapist fantasy... His pleasures are mostly escapist.* N UNCOUNT / ◊ ADJ QUALIT

escort, escorts, escorting, escorted; pronounced /ɛskɔːt/ when it is a noun, and /iˈskɔːt/ when it is a verb. ◊ ADV

1 An **escort** is a person who goes somewhere with you in order to protect you or guard you. EG *...a police escort.* ● If someone is taken somewhere **under escort**, they are accompanied by guards, either because they have been arrested or because they are very important. N COUNT / ● PHRASE

2 If you **escort** someone, you go somewhere with them, usually in order to make sure that they leave a place or get to their destination. EG *He escorted me to the door.* V+O+A

ESL /iː ɛs ɛl/ is used to describe things that are connected with the teaching of English to people whose first language is not English, and who need to speak and write English because they are living in a country where English is an important language or the official language. **ESL** is an abbreviation for 'English as a second language'.

esoteric /ɛsəʊtɛrɪk/. Something that is **esoteric** is understood by only a small number of people who have special knowledge of it. EG *It is written in an esoteric script that few people can read.* ADJ QUALIT Formal

ESP /iː ɛs piː/ is the teaching of English to students who need it for a particular purpose. **ESP** is an abbreviation for 'English for specific purposes' or 'English for special purposes'.

especial /iˈspeʃəⁿl/ means the same as special. EG *He took especial care to vary his routine.* ADJ QUALIT : ATTRIB

especially /iˈspeʃəliⁱ/. 1 You use **especially** to indicate that what you are saying applies more to one thing or situation than to any other. EG *He was kind to his staff, especially those who were sick or in trouble... Children's bones, especially, are very sensitive to radiation... Double ovens are a good idea, especially if you are cooking several meals at once.* ADV SEN

2 You use **especially** to emphasize a quality. For example, if you say that something is **especially** good, you mean that it is very good indeed. EG *He found his host especially irritating... They didn't find it especially hard to do these exams.* SUBMOD

espionage /ɛspɪɒnɑːʒ/ is the activity of finding out the political, military, or industrial secrets of your enemies or rivals by using spies. EG *The Swiss threatened to throw them in jail for espionage.* N UNCOUNT

espouse /iˈspaʊz/, **espouses, espousing, espoused.** If you **espouse** a policy, cause, or plan, you become interested in it and support it. EG *The ideas she espoused were incomprehensible to me.* V+O Formal

Esq. is sometimes written after a man's name if he has no other title. It is an abbreviation for 'esquire'. EG *...a postcard addressed to James Dickson, Esq.*

essay /ɛseɪ/, **essays.** An **essay** is a short piece of writing on a particular subject. Students write essays for their tutors to mark, and authors write them for publication. EG *I had to produce an essay on Herrick for my tutor... ...a volume of essays.* N COUNT

essayist /ɛseɪɪst/, **essayists.** An **essayist** is someone who writes essays for publication. EG *...the best political essayist in the country.* N COUNT

essence /ɛsəⁿns/. 1 The **essence** of something is its basic, central, and most important characteristic which gives it an individual identity. EG *Competition is the essence of all games.* N SING : USU+POSS

2 You use **in essence** to indicate that you are talking about the most important or central aspect of an idea, situation, or event. EG *But this is not in essence a book about religion.* ADV SEN Formal

essential /iˈsenʃəⁿl/, **essentials.** 1 Something that is **essential** is absolutely necessary. EG *Land is essential for food and for work... A degree is by no means an essential qualification for a journalist...It is essential to set your targets realistically...* ► used as a noun. EG *...other essentials such as fuel and clothing... I had only the bare essentials.* ADJ QUALIT : OFT+*for/to* OR to-INF / ► N COUNT : USU PLURAL

2 The **essential** aspects of something are its most basic or important aspects. EG *...the essential fea-* ADJ QUALIT : ATTRIB

ture of the situation... The people around me translated the essential points of the lectures into English.

3 Essentials are the most important principles, ideas, or facts involved in a particular subject. EG *Their laws deal with essentials, not appearances.* N PLURAL

essentially /ɪˈsɛnʃəˀliˀ/. You use **essentially 1** to emphasize a particular feature or quality that something or someone has, and to say that this feature or quality is their most important one. EG *Phyllis was essentially a soft, caring person... ...a country not essentially different from our own... Essentially, what you're saying is that a teacher shouldn't be afraid to admit ignorance.* **2** to indicate that what you are saying is true in general terms, and that other, more detailed factors are not necessary for you to be able to make your point. EG *Such theories are essentially correct.* ADV OR ADV SEN ADV

-est. You add **-est** to adjectives that have one or two syllables to form superlatives. You also add it to some adverbs that do not end in -ly. EG *...the hardest rock in the world... ...the prettiest girl she had ever seen... Children love simple toys best and play with them longest.* SUFFIX

establish /ɪˈstæblɪʃ/, **establishes, establishing, established.** **1** If you **establish** something such as an organization or a system, you create it and make it begin to operate. EG *He had set out to establish his own business.* ◊ **established.** EG *...the established institutions of society... This was a well-established custom among the prisoners.* V+O ◊ ADJ CLASSIF : ATTRIB

2 If you **establish** contact with a group of people, you start to have discussions with them. EG *We tried to establish contact with pressure groups.* V+O : OFT+with

3 If you **establish** that something is the case, you discover facts which show that it is definitely the case. EG *A court of enquiry established that there were faults on both sides... So far they have been unable to establish the cause of death.* V+REPORT OR V+O

4 If you **establish** yourself as something, or **establish** your reputation as something, you get a reputation for being that thing. EG *The Liberals established themselves as the major alternative... He quickly established his reputation as a radical.* V-REFL OR V+O : OFT+as

establishment /ɪˈstæblɪʃməˀnt/, **establishments.** **1** The **establishment** of an organization or system is the process by which it is created and begins to operate. EG *...the establishment of free trade unions.* N SING : the+N+of

2 An **establishment** is a shop or business. EG *At least one establishment in Savile Row now sells clothes off-the-peg.* N COUNT+SUPP

3 You refer to a group of people as the **establishment** when they have special power and influence in the running of a country or an organization. EG *It taught me more about the British Establishment... ...the university establishment.* N SING : the+N

estate /ɪˈsteɪt/, **estates.** **1** An **estate** is a large area of land in the country which is owned by one person or organization. EG *The colonel returned to his estate in Somerset.* N COUNT

2 A housing **estate** or factory **estate** is a large area of land, usually in or near a city, which has houses or factories on it. EG *...Singapore's industrial estates.* ● See also **real estate.** N COUNT+SUPP

3 Someone's **estate** is all the money and property that they leave when they die. EG *She left her estate to her grandchildren.* N COUNT

estate agent, estate agents. An **estate agent** is someone who works for a company that sells houses and land. N COUNT British

estate car, estate cars. An **estate car** is a car with a long body, a door at the rear, and space behind the back seats. N COUNT British

esteem /ɪˈstiːm/ is admiration and respect. EG *I know the high esteem you feel for our colleague here... Zapp had no great esteem for his fellow lecturers.* ● If you **hold** someone or something **in high esteem,** you admire and respect them very N UNCOUNT Formal ● PHRASE

much. EG *The organization was one which he held in high esteem.*

esteemed /ɪˈstiːmd/ is used to describe someone who you greatly admire and respect. EG *...our esteemed employer, Otto Gerran.* ADJ QUALIT Outdated

esthetic /ɛsˈθɛtɪk/. See **aesthetic.**

estimate, estimates, estimating, estimated; pronounced /ˈɛstɪmeɪt/ when it is a verb, and /ˈɛstɪməˀt/ when it is a noun.

1 If you **estimate** something such as an amount or a quantity, you calculate it approximately. EG *They were not able to estimate the cost... He estimated he would do the hundred miles by noon.* ◊ **estimated.** EG *In 1975 there were an estimated 6,000 children in community homes.* V+O OR V+REPORT ◊ ADJ CLASSIF

2 An **estimate** is **2.1** an approximate calculation, or the result obtained by such a calculation. EG *According to some estimates the number of farms has increased by 50 per cent.* **2.2** a judgement which you make about a person or a situation. EG *Thomas wasn't living up to my estimate of him.* N COUNT

3 If you get an **estimate** from someone such as a builder or plumber, they give you a written statement of how much a job is likely to cost. N COUNT

estimation /ˌɛstɪˈmeɪʃəˀn/, **estimations.** **1** Your **estimation** of a person or situation is the opinion that you have formed about them. EG *His comments were, in my estimation, correct and most useful.* N SING : USU+POSS

2 An **estimation** is an approximate calculation, or the result obtained by such a calculation. EG *...an estimation of the speed of the air leaving the lungs.* N COUNT : USU+SUPP

estranged /ɪˈstreɪndʒd/. **1** If you are **estranged** from your husband or wife, you are no longer living with him or her. EG *He was estranged from his second wife... ...her estranged husband.* ADJ CLASSIF

2 If you are **estranged** from your family or friends, you have quarrelled with them and do not meet them or speak to them. EG *He knows I am estranged from my father.* ADJ PRED : OFT+from

estuary /ˈɛstjʊəˀriˀ/, **estuaries.** An **estuary** is the wide part of a river where it joins the sea. N COUNT

etc /ɪtˈsɛtəˀrə/ is used at the end of a list to indicate that there are other items which you could mention if you had enough time or space. EG *...window frames, floorboards, beams, etc... She had to cook, do the cleaning, make beds etc, etc.*

etch /ɛtʃ/, **etchs, etching, etched.** **1** If you **etch** a design or pattern on a surface, you cut it into the surface by using acid or something sharp such as a knife. EG *The artists must have spent many hours etching the images on the walls.* V+O OR V

2 If something **is etched** on your memory, it has made such a strong impression on you that you cannot forget it. EG *His face will remain permanently etched on my memory.* V+O : USU PASS +on

etching /ˈɛtʃɪŋ/, **etchings.** An **etching** is a picture printed from a metal plate that has had a design cut into it. EG *His etchings and drawings never went out of fashion.* N COUNT

eternal /ɪˈtɜːnəˀl/. **1** If something is **eternal**, it lasts for ever. EG *...the promise of eternal bliss.* ◊ **eternally.** EG *Something remained eternally unspoiled in him.* ADJ CLASSIF ◊ ADV

2 You can also describe something as **eternal** when it seems to last for ever, because it is boring or annoying. EG *He was annoying me with his eternal whining.* ADJ CLASSIF

3 Eternal truths and values never change and are believed to be true and relevant in all situations. EG *...a society which lives by eternal principles.* ADJ CLASSIF

eternity /ɪˈtɜːnɪˀtiˀ/, **eternities.** **1 Eternity** is time without an end, or a state of existence that is outside time, especially the state which some people believe they will pass into after they have died. EG *The preacher promised us eternity.* N UNCOUNT

If you say that something is essentially correct, is it completely correct?

2 You can refer to a period of time as an **eternity** when it seems very long indeed because you are having a boring or unpleasant experience. EG *I lay there for an eternity, coughing and gasping.* `N COUNT : USU SING Informal`

ethic /ɛθɪk/, **ethics. 1** A particular **ethic** is an idea or moral belief that influences the behaviour, attitudes, and philosophy of life of a group of people. EG *...the American ethic of expansion and opportunity... ...the Protestant work ethic.* `N SING+SUPP`

2 Ethics are moral beliefs and rules about right and wrong. EG *...a rational, scientific code of ethics.* `N PLURAL`

ethical /ɛθɪkəl/ means influenced by or based on a system of moral beliefs about right and wrong. EG *...an ethical problem... He had no ethical objection to drinking.* ◊ **ethically.** EG *I found Captain Imrie's proposal ethically objectionable.* `ADJ CLASSIF : ATTRIB` `◊ SUBMOD`

ethnic /ɛθnɪk/ means connected with or relating to different racial groups of people. EG *...the ethnic composition of the voters of New York... ...ethnic minorities.* `ADJ CLASSIF : ATTRIB`

ethos /iːθɒs/. The **ethos** of a group of people or of a type of activity is the set of ideas and attitudes that is associated with it. EG *...the working-class ethos of 'togetherness'... ...the prevailing social ethos.* `N SING : USU+SUPP`

etiquette /ɛtɪkɛt/ is a set of customs and rules for polite behaviour. EG *...problems of etiquette... ...a book on etiquette.* `N UNCOUNT`

eulogy /juːlədʒɪ/, **eulogies.** A **eulogy** is a speech or piece of writing that praises someone or something. EG *Countless eulogies have been written about her... ...a eulogy to the Queen Mother.* `N COUNT Formal`

euphemism /juːfɪˈmɪzəm/, **euphemisms.** A **euphemism** is a polite word or expression that people use when they are talking about something which they or other people find unpleasant or embarrassing, such as death or sex. `N COUNT OR N UNCOUNT`

euphemistic /juːfɪˈmɪstɪk/. **Euphemistic** language consists of polite words or expressions for things that people find unpleasant or embarrassing. ◊ **euphemistically.** EG *Then came what the French euphemistically call 'the events of May' – the student revolution.* `ADJ QUALIT` `◊ ADV`

euphoria /juːfɔːrɪə/ is a feeling of great happiness. EG *She shared Dan's euphoria over the play.* `N UNCOUNT`

euphoric /juːfɒrɪk/. If you are **euphoric**, you are extremely happy. EG *...a euphoric moment... ...a feeling of euphoric triumph.* `ADJ QUALIT`

European /jʊərəpɪən/, **Europeans. 1 European** means coming from or relating to Europe. `ADJ CLASSIF`

2 A **European** is a person who comes from Europe. EG *She was the only European living in the neighbourhood.* `N COUNT`

euthanasia /juːθəneɪzɪə/ is the practice of painlessly killing someone who is ill in order to relieve their suffering when there is nothing more that can be done to help them. `N UNCOUNT`

evacuate /ɪˈvækjuˈeɪt/, **evacuates, evacuating, evacuated.** If people **evacuate** a place or if they **are evacuated** from it, they move out of it for a period of time, because it has become dangerous. EG *The entire complex was being evacuated... I was evacuated to Swindon in 1941.* ◊ **evacuation** /ɪˈvækjuˈeɪʃən/, **evacuations.** EG *Orders went out to prepare for the evacuation of the city.* `V+O : USU PASS` `◊ N UNCOUNT OR N COUNT`

evade /ɪˈveɪd/, **evades, evading, evaded. 1** If you **evade** something that you do not want to be involved with, you succeed in not becoming involved with it. EG *I evaded the issue... He had found a way of evading responsibility.* `V+O`

2 If you **evade** someone or something that is moving towards you, you succeed in not being touched or hit by them. EG *Tim tried to catch her arm but she evaded him.* `V+O`

3 If something such as success or love **evades** you, you never manage to achieve it. EG *Military glory had evaded him throughout his long career.* `V+O`

evaluate /ɪˈvæljuˈeɪt/, **evaluates, evaluating, evaluated.** If you **evaluate** something, you decide `V+O`

how significant or valuable it is after carefully studying its good and bad features. EG *He was asked to evaluate the situation... Football performance can never be truly evaluated.*

evaluation /ɪˈvæljuˈeɪʃən/, **evaluations.** An **evaluation** is a decision about how significant or valuable something is, based on a careful study of its good and bad features. EG *...a realistic evaluation of the working of Britain's economy... They can help develop our powers of critical evaluation.* `N COUNT OR N UNCOUNT`

evaporate /ɪˈvæpəreɪt/, **evaporates, evaporating, evaporated. 1** When a liquid **evaporates**, it changes into a gas, usually because it has been heated. EG *All the water has evaporated.* `V`
◊ **evaporation** /ɪˈvæpəreɪʃən/. EG *Be careful not to lose too much liquid by evaporation.* `◊ N UNCOUNT`

2 If a feeling or attitude **evaporates**, it gradually becomes less and eventually disappears altogether. EG *My nervousness evaporated.* `V`

evasion /ɪˈveɪʒən/, **evasions. Evasion** consists of deliberately not doing something that you ought to do or of deliberately avoiding talking about something. EG *He is guilty of gross tax evasion... ...an evasion of our responsibilities... He continued with his evasions and lies.* `N UNCOUNT OR N COUNT`

evasive /ɪˈveɪsɪv/. **1** If you are being **evasive**, you are deliberately not talking about something. EG *Victor became evasive... ...an evasive answer.* `ADJ QUALIT`
◊ **evasively.** EG *The Count had answered evasively.* ◊ **evasiveness.** EG *There was a certain evasiveness in Mary's replies.* `◊ ADV` `◊ N UNCOUNT`

2 If a ship or plane **takes evasive action**, it changes its position or course to avoid being hit by something that is coming towards it. `PHRASE`

eve /iːv/, **eves.** The **eve** of an event or occasion is the day before it. EG *...a devastating attack on the eve of the election.* ● See also **Christmas Eve, New Year's Eve.** `N COUNT : USU+SUPP`

even /iːvən/, **evens, evening, evened. 1** You use **even 1.1** to emphasize that what comes just after or just before it in the sentence is surprising. EG *Even Anthony enjoyed it... She liked him even when she was quarrelling with him... I often lend her money even now... No one dared even to whisper.* **1.2** to emphasize the fact that something is, for example, bigger, better, or worse than something else. EG *Barber had something even worse to tell me... ...an even brighter light... I must be even more tired than I thought.* `ADV SEN` `ADV+COMPAR`

2 You use **even if** or **even though** to indicate that a fact would not make what you are saying untrue or does not make it untrue. EG *Even if you disagree with her, she's worth listening to... I was always rather afraid of men, even though I had lots of boyfriends.* `CONJ`

3 You use **even so** to introduce a fact which seems surprising after what you have just said. EG *Their feathers are regularly shed and renewed. Even so they need constant care.* `ADV SEN`

4 When a measurement or rate is **even**, it stays at about the same level. EG *...an even body temperature.* ◊ **evenly.** EG *Mary was breathing quietly and evenly.* `ADJ QUALIT` `◊ ADV`

5 Surfaces that are **even** are smooth and flat. EG *The road wasn't very even.* `ADJ QUALIT`

6 If there is an **even** distribution of something, each person, group, or area involved has an equal amount or share. EG *The distribution of land was much more even than in Latin America.* ◊ **evenly.** EG *Opinion seems to be fairly evenly divided.* `ADJ QUALIT` `◊ ADV`

7 If a contest or competition is **even**, the people taking part are all as strong, skilful, or successful as each other. EG *Government and rebel soldiers are evenly matched.* ◊ **evenly.** `ADJ QUALIT` `◊ ADV`

8 If you say that you are going to **get even** with someone, you mean that you are going to harm them because they have harmed you. EG *I always knew that one day I would get even with her.* `PHRASE Informal`

9 If you say that there is an **even** chance of `ADJ CLASSIF` something happening, you mean that it is equally likely to happen or not to happen. EG *She would have had only an even chance of being saved.*

10 An **even** number can be divided exactly by the number two. EG *Houses with even numbers are on the right, those with odd numbers on the left.* ADJ CLASSIF

even out. When an amount of something **evens out** or when you **even** it **out**, each person, group, or area begins to receive an equal share of it. EG *Irrigation systems help to even out the supply of water over the growing season.* PHRASAL VB : V-ERG+ADV

evening /i:vnɪŋ/, **evenings.** The **evening** is the part of each day between the end of the afternoon and the time when you go to bed. EG *He arrived about six in the evening... Each evening he runs 5 miles... He was silently finishing his evening meal.* N COUNT OR N UNCOUNT

evening class, evening classes. An **evening class** is a course for adults that is taught in the evening rather than during the day. N COUNT

event /i'vent/, **events. 1** An **event** is something that happens, especially something unusual or important. EG *Next day the newspapers reported the event... ...the most important event in family life.* N COUNT

2 You can refer to all the things that are happening in a particular situation as **events.** EG *Events now moved swiftly... The authorities were quite unable to control events.* N PLURAL

3 In sport, an **event** is one of a series of races or other activities that are part of an organized occasion. EG *Lord Exeter presented the medals for this event.* N COUNT

4 You use an expression such as **in the event that** when you are talking about something that might happen in the future. EG *In the unlikely event that they give you any real trouble, give me a ring... In that event, we would take the matter to court.* PHRASE Formal

5 You say **at all events** or **in any event** when you are pointing out that something is definitely true, although there may be uncertainty about other things that you have mentioned. EG *In any event, it was something that had to be done.* ADV SEN

6 You say **in the event** when you are stating what actually happened, after you have been discussing what might have happened. EG *In the event, it turned out to be fun.* PHRASE Formal

eventful /i'ventful/. An **eventful** period of time is full of interesting, exciting, or important events. EG *...the most exhausting and eventful day of his life.* ADJ QUALIT

eventual /i'ventʃuʊəl/. The **eventual** result of a process or series of events is what happens or what has been achieved at the end of it. EG *...the company's eventual collapse in 1971... ...anxiety about the eventual outcome.* ADJ CLASSIF : ATTRIB

eventuality /i'ventʃuæli'ti'/, **eventualities.** An **eventuality** is a possible future event. EG *He was ready for any eventuality... We are insured against all eventualities.* N COUNT Formal

eventually /i'ventʃuʊəli'/. If something happens **eventually, 1** it happens after a lot of delays, caused for example by problems or arguments. EG *Rodin eventually agreed that Casson was right... Eventually they got through to the hospital.* **2** it happens at the end of a process or series of events, or as the final result of it. EG *The three firms eventually became Imperial Airways.* ADV OR ADV SEN ADV

ever /evə/. **1 Ever** means at any time. EG *I don't think I'll ever be homesick here... ...one of the best novels ever written... I am happier than I have ever been... The news is as awful as ever.* ADV

2 Ever also means all the time. You use it **2.1** in expressions like 'ever-increasing' and 'ever-present' to indicate that something exists all the time or continues doing something or being something all the time. EG *...an ever-increasing prison population... ...an ever-present sense of danger.* **2.2** to indicate someone's usual behaviour or character. EG *Ever unpredictable, James could be angry one moment and calm the next.* ADV

3 You also use **ever** in questions when you want to ADV AFTER WH

emphasize how surprised or shocked you are. EG *'I'm sorry. I'd rather not say.' - 'Why ever not?'... Who ever would have thought that?*

4 You use **ever since** to emphasize that something has been true all the time since the time mentioned, and is still true now. EG *'How long have you lived here?' - 'Ever since I was married.'... They were formed in the seventeenth century and have continued ever since.* CONJ, ADV, OR PREP

5 You use **ever so** and **ever such** to emphasize the degree of something. EG *They are ever so kind... I had ever such a nice letter from her.* PHRASE Informal

evergreen /evəgri:n/, **evergreens.** An **evergreen** is a tree or bush which has green leaves all the year round. EG *...forests of evergreens.* N COUNT

everlasting /evəla:stɪŋ/. Something that is **everlasting** continues to exist or to happen, and never ends. EG *...the everlasting snows of the mighty Himalayas.* ◇ **everlastingly.** EG *He was everlastingly optimistic.* ADJ CLASSIF Literary ◇ ADV

every /evri/. **1** You use **every** to indicate that you are referring to all the members of a group or all the parts of something and not only some of them. EG *She spoke to every person at the party... I have answered every single question... I loved every minute of it.* DET

2 You also use **every 2.1** in order to indicate that something happens at regular intervals. EG *They met every day... I visit her once every six months.* **2.2** in expressions such as 'every now and then' in order to indicate that something happens occasionally. EG *Every now and then she would cry out... Every so often, she spends a weekend in London.* DET

3 You use **every** to say how often something happens. For example, if something happens **every second** day or **every other** day, it happens on one day in each period of two days. If something happens **every third** day or **every fourth** year, it happens on one day in each period of three days or in one year in each period of four years. EG *We only save enough money to take a real vacation every other year... He shaved only every second day.* PHRASE

4 You use **every** in front of a number when you are saying what proportion of people or things something happens to or applies to. EG *One woman in every two hundred is a sufferer... Since 1976, nine women have lost jobs for every five men.* DET

5 If you say that something shows **every** sign of happening, or if you say that there is **every** chance that something will happen, you mean that it is very likely that it will happen. EG *They show every sign of continuing to succeed.* DET

6 If you say that someone has **every** reason to do something, you mean that they would be justified in doing it. EG *She had every reason to be pleased.* DET

everybody /evrɪbɒdi'/. See **everyone.**

everyday /evrɪdeɪ/. You use **everyday** to describe something which **1** is part of normal life, and is not especially interesting or unusual. EG *People could resume a normal everyday life... ...their role in everyday affairs.* **2** happens or is used each day. EG *Exercise is part of my everyday routine.* ADJ CLASSIF ATTRIB

everyone /evrɪwⁿn/. The form **everybody** is also used.
You use **everyone** or **everybody 1** to refer to all the people in a particular group. EG *Everybody in the office laughed... She was genuinely interested in everyone she met.* **2** to refer to all the people in the world. EG *Everyone has their own ideas about it... Everyone knows that.* PRON INDEF

everything /evrɪθɪŋ/. You use **everything 1** to refer to all the objects, actions, activities, or facts in a particular situation. EG *I don't agree with everything he says... I will arrange everything.* **2** to PRON INDEF

Is an ex-President still a President?

refer to all possible or likely actions, activities, or situations. EG *That's your answer to everything... You think of everything.* **3** to refer to a whole situation or to life in general. EG *Is everything all right?... Everything went on just as before.*

everywhere /ˈɛvrɪwɛə/. You use **everywhere** **1** ADV to refer to a whole area or to all the places in a particular area. EG *Everywhere in Asia it is the same... People everywhere are becoming aware of the problem.* **2** to refer to all the places that someone goes to. EG *Everywhere I went, people were angry or suspicious... She always carried a gun with her.*

evict /iˈvɪkt/, **evicts, evicting, evicted.** When V+O : USU PASS people **are evicted**, they are officially forced to leave the house where they are living. EG *If evicted, they would have nowhere else to go.* ◊ **eviction** ◊ N UNCOUNT /iˈvɪkʃəⁿ/, **evictions.** EG *The family faces eviction* OR N COUNT *for non-payment of rent... She described the evictions as 'an outrage'.*

evidence /ˈɛvɪdəns/. **1** Evidence is anything that N UNCOUNT you see, experience, read, or are told which causes USU+SUPP you to believe that something is true or has really happened. EG *We saw evidence everywhere that a real effort was being made to promote tourism... There was no evidence of quarrels between them.* **2** If you **give evidence** in a court of law, you PHRASE officially say what you know about something. EG *The doctor gave evidence at the inquest.* **3** If you say that someone or something is **in** PHRASE **evidence**, you mean that they are present and can be clearly seen. EG *Violence was particularly in evidence in the towns.*

evident /ˈɛvɪdənt/. If it is **evident** that something ADJ QUALIT exists or that something is true, people can easily see that it exists or is true. EG *It was evident that his faith in the Government was severely shaken... She took a sip with evident enjoyment.*

evidently /ˈɛvɪdəntliⁱ/. You use **evidently** **1** to ADV SEN say that something appears to be true. EG *They said it would come, but evidently they failed to send it.* **2** to say that something is obviously true. EG *I found her in bed, evidently in great pain.*

evil /ˈiːvəⁿl/, **evils.** **1** Evil is all the wicked and bad N UNCOUNT things that happen in the world. EG *...the conflict between good and evil.* **2** The **evils** of a situation or activity are all the N COUNT : things that are bad or harmful about it. EG *...a* USU+SUPP *sermon on the evils of drink.* **3** Someone who is **evil** is wicked and enjoys doing ADJ QUALIT things that harm other people. **4** Something that is **evil** causes a great deal of ADJ QUALIT harm to people. EG *Slavery was the most evil system of labour ever devised.*

evocation /ˌiːvəˈkeɪʃəⁿn/, **evocations.** An **evoca-** N COUNT OR **tion** of a place or a past event is an experience in N UNCOUNT : which you remember or think about this place or USU+SUPP event. EG *...evocations of rural America... It was* Formal *disturbing, this evocation of her youth.*

evocative /iˈvɒkətɪv/. Something that is **evoca-** ADJ QUALIT **tive** makes you remember or think about a place or a past event. EG *...an evocative description.* ◊ **evocatively.** EG *Old photographs are evocatively* ◊ ADV *displayed round the building.*

evoke /iˈvəʊk/, **evokes, evoking, evoked.** If V+O something **evokes** an emotion, memory, or re- Formal sponse, it causes it to be felt, remembered, or expressed. EG *The quarrel seemed to evoke the bitterest passions.*

evolution /ˌiːvəˈluːʃəⁿn/. **1** Evolution is a process of N UNCOUNT gradual change that takes place over many generations, during which animals and plants change some of their characteristics and sometimes develop into new species. EG *The processes of evolution are still going on.* ◊ **evolutionary** /ˌiːvəˈluːʃənəⁿriⁱ/. ◊ ADJ CLASSIF : EG *...evolutionary theory... These variations can* ATTRIB *produce evolutionary change.* **2** You can use **evolution** to refer to any gradual N UNCOUNT process of change and development. EG *Social* +SUPP

evolution has now become extremely rapid... ...the evolution of parliamentary democracy.

evolve /iˈvɒlv/, **evolves, evolving, evolved.** **1** V : OFT When animals and plants **evolve**, they gradually +into/from change and develop into different forms. EG *The earliest fish have evolved into some 30,000 different species.* **2** When something **evolves**, it gradually develops V-ERG from something simpler. EG *It was fascinating to see how the film evolved... How did Giotto evolve his very personal and original style?*

ewe /juː/, **ewes.** A **ewe** is an adult female sheep. N COUNT

ex- is added to nouns to indicate that someone or PREFIX something is no longer the thing referred to by the noun. For example, an ex-farmer is someone who is no longer a farmer. EG *...an ex-serviceman... ...his ex-wife.*

exacerbate /ɪⁱgˈzæsəbeɪt, ɪⁱkˈsæs-/, **exacerbates,** V+O **exacerbating, exacerbated.** If something **exac-** Formal **erbates** a bad situation, it makes it worse. EG *Withholding aid only exacerbates the problem... ...inadequacy exacerbated by muddle.*

exact /ɪⁱgˈzækt/, **exacts, exacting, exacted.** **1** Something that is **exact** is **1.1** correct or accurate, ADJ CLASSIF rather than approximate. EG *He noted the exact time... He searched for the exact word to define his feelings.* ◊ **exactness.** EG *He expressed himself* ◊ N UNCOUNT *with great exactness.* **1.2** correct and complete in ADJ CLASSIF every detail. EG *...an exact replica of Hamburg airport.* **2** You say **to be exact** when you want to indicate ADV SEN that you are giving more detailed information or are slightly correcting what you have said. EG *I thought that this would be possible, or to be more exact, I could see no reason why it should not be so.* **3** If someone **exacts** something from you, they V+O : demand and obtain it from you, because they are OFT+from more powerful than you are. EG *They exacted* Formal *absolute obedience from their followers.*

exacting /ɪⁱgˈzæktɪŋ/. **1** If something is **exacting,** ADJ QUALIT you have to work very hard to do it well. EG *...an exacting job... The task proved to be exacting.* **2** If someone is **exacting**, they insist that you work ADJ QUALIT very hard or with very great care. EG *Both were exacting bosses... The state of repair failed to measure up to their exacting standards.*

exactly /ɪⁱgˈzæktliⁱ/. **1** Exactly means precisely, ADV and not just approximately. EG *You've exactly one hour to do this... That's exactly what they told me... I don't know exactly where it is, but it's in the south of France.* **2** If you do something **exactly**, you do it very ADV accurately or precisely. EG *Sam answered the owl's cry, imitating it exactly... He did exactly as he was told.* **3** You can use **exactly** to emphasize how similar ADV something is to something else. EG *He's exactly like a little baby.* **4** You can say **'Exactly'** to express agreement CONVENTION with what has just been said or to confirm that it is true. EG *'Do you mean that we are stuck here?' – 'Exactly, my dear.'* **5** You can use **not exactly** to indicate that some- ADV OR thing is not true, but is almost true. EG *He didn't* CONVENTION *exactly block me, but he didn't move either... 'She's taken the day off.' – 'Is she sick?' – 'Not exactly.'*

exaggerate /ɪⁱgˈzædʒəreɪt/, **exaggerates, exag-gerating, exaggerated.** **1** If you **exaggerate**, you V OR V+O make the thing that you are talking about seem bigger, better, or worse than it actually is. EG *I am exaggerating a little... She did not exaggerate about the height of the tower... It is impossible to exag-gerate the horrors of the system.* ◊ **exaggeration** ◊ N COUNT OR /ɪⁱgˈzædʒəreɪʃəⁿn/, **exaggerations.** EG *Isn't that a* N UNCOUNT *bit of an exaggeration?... One can speak, without exaggeration, of a peaceful revolution.* **2** If something **exaggerates** a quality or feature, it V+O makes it seem more obvious or more important than it really is. EG *Ballet exaggerates ordinary body movements.*

3 An **exaggerated** expression or gesture is more ADJ QUALIT noticeable than it needs to be. EG *Brody heaved an exaggerated sigh.* ◊ **exaggeratedly.** EG *...an exag-* ◊ ADV *geratedly intense smile.*

exalted /ɪˈgzɔːltɪd/. Someone who is **exalted** is ADJ QUALIT very important. EG *I had never met so exalted a person... ...someone in his exalted position.*

exam /ɪˈgzæm/, **exams.** An **exam** is the same as N COUNT an examination in paragraph 1. Informal

examination /ɪgzæmɪˈneɪʃəⁿn/, **examinations. 1** N COUNT An **examination** is a formal test that you take to show your knowledge or ability in a particular subject. EG *...a three-hour written examination.*

2 If you make an **examination** of something, you N UNCOUNT look at it carefully. EG *Mrs Oliver devoted herself to* OR N COUNT *an examination of the address book... The weapon was taken away for examination.*

3 When you have a medical **examination**, a doctor N UNCOUNT looks at your body in order to check how healthy OR N COUNT you are. EG *A full examination of the chest failed to reveal anything wrong.*

4 When there is **examination** of an idea, proposal, N UNCOUNT or plan, it is considered very carefully. EG *...an* OR N COUNT *important case which deserves closer examination.*

examine /ɪˈgzæmɪn/, **examines, examining, ex-amined. 1** If you **examine** something, you look at V+O it carefully. EG *I examined the lighter, then handed it back... Government experts were still examining the wreckage of the plane.*

2 If a doctor **examines** you, he or she looks at your V+O body in order to check how healthy you are. EG *Each child is medically examined.*

3 If you **examine** an idea, proposal, or plan, you V+O consider it very carefully. EG *They agreed immedi-* N UNCOUNT *ately without having examined the proposition.* OR N COUNT

4 If a teacher **examines** you, he or she finds out V+O how much you know by asking you questions or by making you take an examination.

examiner /ɪˈgzæmɪnəʳ/, **examiners.** An **examin-** N COUNT **er** is a person who sets or marks an examination.

example /ɪˈgzɑːmpəⁿl/, **examples. 1** An **example** N COUNT of a particular kind of thing is a thing of that kind, which can be mentioned or pointed out in order to show the characteristics of that kind of thing. EG *It's a very fine example of traditional architecture... Could you give me an example of an application of this principle?*

2 You use **for example** to show that you are giving ADV SEN an example of a particular kind of thing. EG *Japan, for example, has two languages... In our library we have quite a lot of newspapers – The Times, for example, and the New York Times.*

3 If you say that someone is an **example** to other N COUNT people or sets an **example**, you mean that they behave in a way that other people copy or should copy. EG *They are a shining example to progressive people everywhere... She set such a good example to us all.* ● If you **follow** someone's **example**, you ● PHRASE behave in the same way that they do. EG *A number of people followed Shuttleworth's example and were subsequently arrested.*

4 If you **make an example of** someone, you PHRASE punish them severely so that other people will not behave in the same way. EG *It was decided to make an example of some of the top conspirators.*

exasperate /ɪˈgzɑːspəreɪt/, **exasperates, exas-** V+O **perating, exasperated.** If someone or something **exasperates** you, they annoy you and make you feel frustrated or upset. EG *She frequently exasper-ates her friends.* ◊ **exasperated.** EG *He had an* ◊ ADJ QUALIT *exasperated look on his face... ...overworked and exasperated teachers.* ◊ **exasperating.** EG *I have* ◊ ADJ QUALIT *seldom had a more exasperating day... She could be a most exasperating child.* ◊ **exasperation** ◊ N UNCOUNT /ɪˈgzɑːspəreɪʃəⁿn/. EG *He looked at the little boy in exasperation.*

excavate /ˈekskəveɪt/, **excavates, excavating,** V+O OR V **excavated.** When people **excavate** a piece of land, they remove earth carefully from it and look for the remains of pots, bones, or buildings, in order to discover information about the past. ◊ **excavation** /ekskəˈveɪʃəⁿn/, **excavations.** EG ◊ N COUNT OR *...the excavation of a Neolithic village... Post-war* N UNCOUNT *excavations revealed the foundations of an earlier church.*

exceed /ɪkˈsiːd/, **exceeds, exceeding, exceeded. 1** If something **exceeds** a particular amount or V+O number, it is greater than that amount or number. EG *Average annual temperatures exceed 20° centi-grade.*

2 If you **exceed** a limit or rule, you go beyond it. EG V+O *A motorist was caught exceeding the speed limit... The company is not allowed to exceed its budget.*

exceedingly /ɪkˈsiːdɪŋliʳ/ means very much in- SUBMOD deed. For example, someone who is exceedingly Outdated rich is very rich indeed. EG *The Colonel was ex-ceedingly wealthy... Doug is an exceedingly ami-able fellow.*

excel /ɪkˈsel/, **excels, excelling, excelled.** If V : OFT+at/in someone **excels** at something or **excels** in it, they are very good at it. *He excels at sports... It is in this area of running that women excel.*

excellence /ˈeksələns/. **1 Excellence** is the qual- N UNCOUNT ity of being extremely good at something. EG *Sport is an area in which excellence is still treasured.*

2 See also **par excellence.**

Excellency /ˈeksələnsiʳ/, **Excellencies.** People say **Your Excellency, His Excellency,** or **Excel-lency** when they are referring to or addressing important officials such as ambassadors. EG *His Excellency desires to see you... I shall do my best, Your Excellency.*

excellent /ˈeksələnt/. Something that is **excellent** ADJ QUALIT is very good indeed. EG *I think the teaching here is excellent... That's an excellent idea.* ◊ **excellently.** EG *The system works excellently...* ◊ ADV *There are some excellently preserved fossils here.*

except /ɪkˈsept/. You use **except** or **except for** to PREP OR CONJ introduce the only thing or person that a statement does not apply to. EG *All the boys except Piggy started to giggle... The classroom was silent, except for the busy scratching of pens on paper... There was little I could do except wait.*

excepted /ɪkˈseptɪd/. You use **excepted** after you PREP AFTER N have mentioned a person or thing to show that you do not include them in the statement you are making. EG *...a gentleman for whom other people - Rhoda excepted - put on their biggest smiles... It is more worth seeing than any city I ever saw, London excepted.*

excepting /ɪkˈseptɪŋ/. You use **excepting** to PREP introduce the only thing or person that prevents a statement from being completely true. EG *He was the only human male for miles around (excepting an old handyman).*

exception /ɪkˈsepʃəⁿn/, **exceptions. 1** An **excep-** N COUNT : **tion** is a thing, person, or situation that is not OFT+of/to included in a general statement. EG *Women, with a few exceptions, are not involved in politics... They are all, with the exception of one Swedish coin, of Portuguese origin... There is no exception to this rule.*

2 You use **without exception** to indicate that the ADV SEN statement you are making is true in all cases. EG *Almost without exception, the fastest-growing cities are in Africa.*

3 If you **take exception to** something, you feel PHRASE offended or annoyed by it, and usually complain about it. EG *There are three things you've just said that I take exception to.*

Do you make an example of someone who sets a good example?

exceptional /ɪ²ksɛpʃə⁰nəl, -ʃənə⁰l/. 1 Someone who is **exceptional** is unusually talented, clever, or gifted. EG *She was an exceptional teacher... My brother isn't exceptional; there are plenty of youngsters like him.* ADJ QUALIT

2 **Exceptional** situations, incidents, or events are unusual and only likely to happen very rarely. EG *Permission will be granted only in very exceptional circumstances.* ADJ QUALIT

exceptionally /ɪ²ksɛpʃə⁰nəli¹/. You use **exceptionally** 1 to emphasize how very good, important, or bad something is. EG *...an exceptionally fine meal... February had been exceptionally wet.* SUBMOD 2 to indicate that what you are talking about is unusual and is only likely to happen very rarely. EG *Exceptionally, with the approval of the University, a degree will be awarded to a candidate who did not take all the exams.* ADV SEN

excerpt /ɛksɜːpt/, **excerpts.** An **excerpt** is a short piece of writing or music which is taken from a larger piece. EG *Here are a few excerpts from her diary... You'll hear the oboe in this final excerpt.* N COUNT: OFT+*from*

excess, excesses; pronounced /ɛksɛs/ when it is an adjective, and either /ɪ²ksɛs/ or /ɛksɛs/ when it is a noun.

1 An **excess** of something is a larger amount than is needed, allowed, or usual. EG *Inflation results from an excess of demand over supply... This report should discourage us all from eating an excess of fat.* N SING: *an*+N ▸ used as an adjective. EG *The body gets rid of excess water through the urine.* ▸ ADJ CLASSIF: ATTRIB

2 If something is **in excess of** an amount, it is more than that amount. EG *...interest rates in excess of 20 per cent.* PREP Formal

3 If you do something **to excess**, you do it too much. EG *He spent all his time in the flat, cleaning and tidying it to excess.* PHRASE

4 **Excesses** are acts which are very extreme, irresponsible, cruel, or immoral. EG *...the worst excesses of the French Revolution.* N PLURAL

excessive /ɪ²ksɛsɪv/. If you describe something as **excessive**, you mean that it is too large or too extreme. EG *Their profits were excessive... ...excessive pessimism.* ADJ QUALIT ◇ **excessively.** EG *He walked excessively fast.* ◇ ADV

exchange /ɪ²kstʃeɪnd⁰ʒ/, **exchanges, exchanging, exchanged.** 1 If two or more people **exchange** things, they give them to each other at the same time. EG *The three of us exchanged addresses... Gertie and Dolly exchanged glances.* V+O ▸ used as a noun. EG *...an exchange of information.* ▸ N COUNT

2 If you **exchange** one thing for another, you replace it with it, because the other thing is more satisfactory or more useful. EG *The sales girl refused to exchange the sweater... She exchanged the jewels for money.* V+O: OFT+*for*

3 If you **exchange** your house or job with someone, you live or work in the place where they normally live or work, while they live or work in the place where you normally live or work. EG *The Ingrams exchanged houses with some friends who live in London.* V+O: OFT+*with* ▸ used as a noun. EG *...the exchange of visiting teachers.* ▸ N COUNT

4 An **exchange** is also a brief conversation. EG *Throughout these exchanges I had a curious feeling of detachment.* N COUNT Formal

5 If you give something to someone **in exchange for** something else, you give it to them because they are giving the other thing to you. EG *They sold textiles in exchange for agricultural products.* PHRASE

6 See also **stock exchange, telephone exchange**.

exchange rate, exchange rates. The **exchange rate** is the rate at which a sum of money of your country's currency is exchanged for an equivalent sum of money of another country's currency. N COUNT

excise /ɛksaɪz/ is a tax that the government of a country puts on goods which are produced for sale in that country. EG *...excise duties.* N UNCOUNT

excitable /ɪ²ksaɪtəbə⁰l/. If someone is **excitable**, they become excited very easily. EG *They were both very excitable... ...a highly excitable man.* ADJ QUALIT

excite /ɪ²ksaɪt/, **excites, exciting, excited.** 1 If something **excites** you, it makes you very interested and enthusiastic. EG *The idea of journalism excited me.* V+O

2 If something excites a feeling, emotion, or reaction, it causes it to happen. EG *These rumours excited suspicion.* V+O

excited /ɪ²ksaɪtɪ²d/. If you are **excited**, you are so happy that you are full of energy and cannot relax, usually because you are looking forward to something and cannot stop thinking about it. EG *He was so excited he could hardly sleep... There were hundreds of excited children to meet us.* ADJ QUALIT ◇ **excitedly.** EG *They were excitedly discussing plans for the weekend... They turned to each other, laughing excitedly.* ◇ ADV

excitement /ɪ²ksaɪtmə²nt/, **excitements.** 1 **Excitement** is the state of being excited. EG *Struggling to conceal his excitement, he accepted her invitation.* N UNCOUNT

2 **Excitements** are things that cause you to feel excited. EG *...all the excitements of London.* N COUNT Literary

exciting /ɪ²ksaɪtɪŋ/. Something that is **exciting** causes you to feel excited. EG *Growing up in the heart of London was exciting... It did not seem a very exciting idea.* ADJ QUALIT ◇ **excitingly.** EG *Life was excitingly unpredictable.* ◇ ADV

exclaim /ɪ²kskleɪm/, **exclaims, exclaiming, exclaimed.** When you **exclaim**, you say something suddenly and emphatically because you are excited, shocked, or angry. EG *'Oh, you poor child!' exclaimed Mrs Socket... All of the women exclaimed at how well formed the baby was.* V: OFT +*at/over*, ALSO V+QUOTE

> **EXCLAM** stands for **exclamation**
> Words and phrases which have the label EXCLAM in the Extra Column are exclamations such as **Oh dear!** and **Help!** which you use to show that you are angry, worried, and so on.

exclamation /ɛkskləmeɪʃə⁰n/, **exclamations.** An **exclamation** is a sound, word, or sentence that is spoken suddenly and emphatically in order to express excitement, admiration, shock, or anger. EG *He drew back with a sharp exclamation... They embraced him with exclamations of joy.* N COUNT

exclamation mark, exclamation marks. An **exclamation mark** is the sign (!). It is used in writing to show that a word, phrase, or sentence is an exclamation. N COUNT

exclude /ɪ²ksklu:d/, **excludes, excluding, excluded.** 1 If you **exclude** something from an activity or a piece of work, you deliberately do not include that thing in it. EG *For the moment we will exclude the special case of the religious wars.* V+O: OFT+*from*

2 If you **exclude** a possibility, you reject it after considering it carefully. EG *A fake call from some local phone box was not excluded.* V+O

3 If you **exclude** someone from a place or activity, you prevent them from entering the place or taking part in the activity. EG *...jobs from which the majority of workers are excluded.* V+O: OFT+*from*

excluding /ɪ²ksklu:dɪŋ/. You use **excluding** before you mention a person or thing to show that you are not including them in a statement that you are making. EG *We are open seven days a week, excluding Christmas Day.* PREP

exclusion /ɪ²ksklu:ʒə⁰n/. 1 When someone is prevented from entering a place or from taking part in an activity, you can refer to this as their **exclusion** from this place or activity. EG *...the laws relating to the admission and exclusion of aliens.* N UNCOUNT: USU+POSS

2 The **exclusion** of something from a speech, piece of writing, or activity is the act of deliberate- N UNCOUNT

ly not including it. EG ...*the exclusion of any mention of her good qualities.*

3 You say that something happens **to the exclusion of** other things when it happens to such a great extent that there is no chance for anything else to be considered or to be present. EG ...*the ability to concentrate on a problem to the exclusion of all other matters.*   PREP

exclusive /ɪ²kskluːsɪv/. **1** Something that is **exclusive** is **1.1** available only to people who are rich or who belong to a high social class. EG ...*an exclusive residential district.* **1.2** used or owned by only one person or group, and not shared with anyone else. EG *They have exclusive use of the machine.*   ADJ QUALIT / ADJ CLASSIF : ATTRIB

2 If two things are mutually **exclusive**, they cannot exist together. EG *There is no reason why these two functions should be mutually exclusive.*   ADJ CLASSIF

exclusively /ɪ²ˈkskluːsɪvliˀ/. You use **exclusively** to refer to situations or activities that involve only the things mentioned, and nothing else. EG ...*young people who devote their lives exclusively to sport.*   ADV

excrement /ɛkskrɪˈməˀnt/ is the solid waste matter that is passed out of your body through your bowels.   N UNCOUNT / Formal

excrete /ɪ²kskriːt/, **excretes, excreting, excreted.** When you **excrete** waste matter from your body, you get rid of it, usually by going to the lavatory or by sweating.   V+O OR V

excruciating /ɪ²kskruːʃieɪtɪŋ/. **1** Excruciating pain is very painful indeed. EG *I had the most excruciating cramp in my leg.* ◊ **excruciatingly.** EG *Walking was excruciatingly painful.*   ADJ QUALIT / ◊ SUBMOD

2 An **excruciating** situation or experience is extremely difficult to bear. EG ...*excruciating unhappiness.* ◊ **excruciatingly.** EG *It was an excruciatingly humiliating experience.*   ADJ QUALIT / ◊ SUBMOD

excursion /ɪ²kskɜːʃəˀn/, **excursions. 1** An **excursion** is a short journey, especially one that you make for a particular purpose. EG ...*a shopping excursion... ...excursions to deserted beaches.*   N COUNT

2 An **excursion** into something such as a new topic or a new experience is an attempt to develop it or understand it. EG ...*a rare excursion into contemporary music.*   N COUNT : OFT+*into*

excusable /ɪ²kskjuːzəbəˀl/. If a mistake or wrong action is **excusable**, you can forgive it, because of the circumstances in which it was made. EG *He made an excusable mistake.*   ADJ QUALIT

excuse, excuses, excusing, excused; pronounced /ɪ²kskjuːs/ when it is a noun and /ɪ²kskjuːz/ when it is a verb.

1 An **excuse** is a reason which you give in order to explain why something has been done, has not been done, or will not be done. EG *You don't have to make any excuses to me... There is no excuse for this happening in a new building.*   N COUNT

2 If you **excuse** yourself or **excuse** something wrong that you have done, you say why you did it, in an attempt to make yourself seem less bad. EG *I'm not going to try and excuse myself... The Vice-President admitted taking bribes, excusing it as a momentary weakness.*   V-REFL OR V+O

3 If you **excuse** someone for something wrong that they have done, you forgive them for it. EG *Such delays cannot be excused... I excused him much of his prejudice because I liked him.*   V+O : OFT+*for*, ALSO V+O+O

4 If you **excuse** someone from a duty or responsibility, you free them from it. EG ...*a certificate excusing him from games at school.*   V+O : OFT+*from*

5 If you ask someone to **excuse** you, you are asking them to allow you to leave. EG *Will you excuse me just a second?*   V+O

6 You say **excuse me** to show politeness in these ways: **6.1** to get someone's attention, especially when you want to ask them a question. EG *Excuse me, but is there a fairly cheap restaurant near here?* **6.2** before correcting someone. EG *Excuse me, but I think you have misunderstood.* **6.3** to apologize for disturbing or interrupting someone,   PHRASE

or for doing something slightly impolite such as burping or hiccupping. EG *Excuse me butting in.* **6.4** to indicate that you are about to leave the room. **6.5** to ask someone to repeat what they have just said.   CONVENTION / CONVENTION American

execrable /ɛksɪkrəbəˀl/. If you say that something is **execrable**, you mean that it is very bad or very unpleasant. EG *The food is execrable.*   ADJ QUALIT / Formal

execute /ɛksɪkjuːt/, **executes, executing, executed. 1** To **execute** someone means to kill them as a punishment. EG ...*the last woman to be executed in Britain.* ◊ **execution** /ɛksɪkjuːʃəˀn/, **executions.** EG ...*the execution of Charles I.*   V+O : USU PASS / ◊ N COUNT OR N UNCOUNT

2 If you **execute** a plan, you carry it out. EG ...*a carefully executed crime.* ◊ **execution.** EG ...*obstructing an officer in the execution of his duty.*   V+O / ◊ N UNCOUNT Formal

3 If you **execute** a difficult action or movement, you perform it. EG *The pilot began to execute a series of aerobatics.*   V+O

executioner /ɛksɪkjuːʃəˀnə/, **executioners.** An **executioner** is a person who has the job of executing criminals.   N COUNT

executive /ɪ²gzɛkjəˀtɪv/, **executives. 1** An **executive** is someone who is employed by a company at a senior level. EG ...*a senior executive.*   N COUNT

2 The **executive** sections and tasks of an organization are concerned with making important decisions. EG ...*our executive board.*   ADJ CLASSIF : ATTRIB

3 Executive goods are expensive and fashionable. EG ...*an executive chair.*   ADJ CLASSIF : ATTRIB

4 The **executive** of an organization such as a political party is a committee within that organization which has the authority to make important decisions. EG ...*the executive of the National Union of Teachers.*   N COLL

executor /ɪ²gzɛkjəˀtə/, **executors.** Your **executor** is the person who you appoint to deal with your affairs after your death.   N COUNT Legal

exemplary /ɪ²gzɛmpləriˀ/. If you describe someone or something as **exemplary**, you mean that they are excellent. EG *He had been an exemplary father.*   ADJ QUALIT Formal

exemplify /ɪ²gzɛmplɪfaɪ/, **exemplifies, exemplifying, exemplified. 1** If you say that someone or something **exemplifies** a situation or quality, you mean that they are a typical example of it. EG *He exemplified the new liberalism.*   V+O

2 If you **exemplify** something, you give an example of it. EG *I'm going to exemplify one or two of these points.*   V+O

exempt /ɪ²gzɛmpᵗt/, **exempts, exempting, exempted. 1** If you are **exempt** from a rule or duty, you do not have to obey it or perform it. EG *Harold was exempt from military service.*   ADJ PRED : USU+*from*

2 To **exempt** a person from a rule or duty means to state officially that they do not have to obey it or perform it. EG *Farmers were exempted from rates.* ◊ **exemption** /ɪ²gzɛmpʃəˀn/, **exemptions.** EG ...*exemption from jury service.*   V+O : OFT+*from* / ◊ N UNCOUNT OR N COUNT

exercise /ɛksəsaɪz/, **exercises, exercising, exercised. 1** Exercises are **1.1** energetic movements which you do in order to become fit or remain healthy. EG ...*gymnastic exercises.* **1.2** repeated actions which you do in order to practise for something such as playing a musical instrument. **1.3** operations or manoeuvres that are performed by a section of the army, navy, or air force. EG ...*peacetime exercises and training.*   N COUNT : USU PLURAL

2 Exercise is energetic movement that you do to keep healthy or to train for a sport. EG *I have had all the exercise I need for one day.*   N UNCOUNT

3 An **exercise** is a short piece of work that you do, for example in school, which is designed to help you learn something. EG ...*grammatical exercises.*   N COUNT

4 An **exercise** in something is an activity which is   N COUNT

Does exertion exhaust you?

planned to achieve a particular purpose. EG *The rally was organized by the state as an exercise in patriotism.*

5 When you **exercise**, you move your body ener- v getically in order to become fit and to remain healthy. EG *I could not fall asleep unless I exercised first.*

6 If you **exercise** authority, rights, or responsibil- v+o ities, you use them. EG *They exercise considerable* Formal *influence in all western countries... They had no intention of exercising restraint.* ▶ used as a noun. ▶ N SING : EG *..the exercise of personal responsibility.* the+N+of

7 If something **exercises** your mind, you think or v+o talk about it a great deal. EG *This problem has* Formal *exercised the minds of academics and politicians.*

exercise book, exercise books. An **exercise** N COUNT **book** is a small book with blank pages that pupils and students use for doing their schoolwork.

exert /ɪɡ'zɜːt/, **exerts, exerting, exerted. 1** If you v+o : USU+A **exert** influence or pressure, you use it in order to achieve something. EG *These departments exert pressure on the schools to get them to agree.*

2 If you **exert** yourself, you make a physical or v-REFL mental effort to do something. EG *He had to exert himself to make conversation with the visitor.*

exertion /ɪɡ'zɜːʃən/, **exertions. Exertion** is N UNCOUNT physical effort or exercise. EG *He was panting with* OR N COUNT *exertion... I was weakened by my exertions.*

exhale /ɪks'heɪl/, **exhales, exhaling, exhaled.** v OR v+o When you **exhale**, you breathe out. EG *He exhaled* Formal *slowly and smiled.* ◇ **exhalation** /ɛksəˈleɪʃən/, ◇ N UNCOUNT **exhalations.** EG *...a soft exhalation of breath.* OR N COUNT

exhaust /ɪɡ'zɔːst/, **exhausts, exhausting, ex- hausted. 1** If something **exhausts** you, it makes v+o you very tired. EG *She exhausted Nell both nervous- ly and physically.* ◇ **exhausted.** EG *All three men* ◇ ADJ QUALIT *were hot, dirty, and exhausted.* ◇ **exhausting.** EG ◇ ADJ QUALIT *...a difficult and exhausting job.*

2 If you **exhaust** money or food, you use or finish it v+o all. EG *They soon exhausted the food resources of the surrounding area.*

3 If you **exhaust** a subject, you talk about it so v+o much that there is nothing else to say about it. EG *...when the subject had been thoroughly exhausted.*

4 An **exhaust** or an **exhaust pipe** is a pipe which N COUNT carries the gas out of the engine of a motor vehicle. See picture at CAR.

5 Exhaust is the gas that is produced when the N UNCOUNT engine of a motor vehicle is running.

exhaustion /ɪɡ'zɔːstʃən/ is the state of being so N UNCOUNT tired that you have no energy left. EG *She was almost fainting with exhaustion.*

exhaustive /ɪɡ'zɔːstɪv/. An **exhaustive** study or ADJ QUALIT search is very thorough. EG *This list is by no means exhaustive.* ◇ **exhaustively.** EG *...exhaustively* ◇ ADV *researched evidence.*

exhibit /ɪɡ'zɪbɪt/, **exhibits, exhibiting, exhibit- ed. 1** If you **exhibit** an ability or feeling, it can be v+o easily seen by other people. EG *He still exhibited* Formal *signs of stress.*

2 When something **is exhibited**, it is put in a public v+o : USU PASS place so that people can come to look at it. EG *The paintings are exhibited in chronological sequence.*

3 An **exhibit** is **3.1** something that is put on show N COUNT to the public in a museum or art gallery. EG *Our local museum has over a thousand exhibits.* **3.2** something that a lawyer shows in court as evi- dence. EG *Exhibit number two is a diary belonging to the accused.*

exhibition /ɛksɪ'bɪʃən/, **exhibitions. 1** An **exhi-** N COUNT **bition** is a collection of pictures, sculptures, or other things displayed in a public place. EG *Did you see the Shakespeare exhibition?*

2 Exhibition is the showing of pictures, sculptures, N UNCOUNT or other things in a public place. EG *The film was refused a licence for public exhibition.*

3 If you **make an exhibition of** yourself, you PHRASE behave very stupidly or rudely in public.

exhibitionism /ɛksɪ'bɪʃənɪzəm/ is a type of be- N UNCOUNT haviour in which someone tries to get people's Formal attention all the time; used showing disapproval. ◇ **exhibitionist, exhibitionists.** EG *As a child I* ◇ N COUNT *was inclined to be an exhibitionist.*

exhibitor /ɪɡ'zɪbɪtə/, **exhibitors.** An **exhibitor** is N COUNT a person whose work is being shown in a public exhibition.

exhilarate /ɪɡ'zɪləreɪt/, **exhilarates, exhilarat-** v+o : USU PASS **ing, exhilarated.** If you **are exhilarated** by something, it gives you a strong feeling of happi- ness and excitement. EG *The refugees were exhila- rated by the news.* ◇ **exhilarated.** EG *He felt* ◇ ADJ QUALIT *exhilarated.* ◇ **exhilarating.** EG *...an exhilarating* ◇ ADJ QUALIT *experience.* ◇ **exhilaration** /ɪɡzɪlə'reɪʃən/. EG ◇ N UNCOUNT *There was a sense of exhilaration about being alone on the beach.*

exhort /ɪɡ'zɔːt/, **exhorts, exhorting, exhorted.** If v+o : you **exhort** someone to do something, you try hard OFT+to-INF to persuade them to do it. EG *I exhorted the men* Formal *not to drink too much.* ◇ **exhortation** ◇ N COUNT OR /ɛgzɔː'teɪʃən/, **exhortations.** EG *...fervent exhorta-* N UNCOUNT *tions to revolutionary action.*

exhume /ɛks'hjuːm/, **exhumes, exhuming, ex-** v+o **humed.** When a body **is exhumed**, it is taken out Formal of the ground where it is buried.

exile /ɛgzaɪl, ɛksaɪl/, **exiles, exiling, exiled. 1** If N UNCOUNT someone lives in **exile**, they live in a foreign country because they cannot live in their own country, usually for political reasons. EG *...eight whole months of exile.*

2 If someone **is exiled**, they are sent away from v+o their own country and are not allowed to return there. EG *I was exiled from Ceylon for a year.* ◇ **exiled.** EG *...the exiled King.* ◇ ADJ CLASSIF

3 An **exile** is someone who lives in exile. EG N COUNT *...political exiles.*

exist /ɪɡ'zɪst/, **exists, existing, existed.** If some- v : NO CONT thing **exists**, it is present in the world as a real, living, or actual thing. EG *That word doesn't exist in English... Nobody can actually know if God exists.*

existence /ɪɡ'zɪstəns/, **existences. 1 Existence** N UNCOUNT is the state of existing. EG *Do you believe in the existence of God?*

2 You refer to someone's way of life as an **exist-** N COUNT+SUPP **ence** when they live under difficult conditions. EG *The family lived a more or less vagabond exist- ence.*

existential /ɛgzɪ'stenʃəl/ means relating to hu- ADJ CLASSIF man existence and experience. Formal

existentialism /ɛgzɪ'stenʃəlɪzəm/ is a philo- N UNCOUNT sophical belief which stresses the importance of human experience and says that everyone is re- sponsible for the results of their own actions. ◇ **existentialist** /ɛgzɪ'stenʃəlɪst/, **existentialists.** ◇ N COUNT EG *...the writings of the existentialists.*

existing /ɪɡ'zɪstɪŋ/. You use **existing** to describe ADJ CLASSIF : something which is now in use or in operation. EG ATTRIB *We have to find ways of making the existing system work better.*

exit /ɛgzɪt, ɛksɪt/, **exits, exiting, exited. 1** An **exit** N COUNT is **1.1** a door in a public building through which you can leave. EG *He hurried towards the exit.* **1.2** a place on a motorway where traffic can leave the motorway.

2 When someone leaves a room, you can say that N SING they make an **exit**. EG *He made a hasty exit from the Men's Room.*

3 If you **exit** from a room, you leave it. EG *I exited* v : IF+PREP *from the surgery.* THEN from

exodus /ɛksədəs/. When there is an **exodus**, a lot N SING of people leave a place together. EG *...the massive exodus of refugees from the North.*

exonerate /ɪɡ'zɒnəreɪt/, **exonerates, exonerat-** v+o : **ing, exonerated.** To **exonerate** someone means OFT+from to show that they are not responsible for some- Formal thing wrong that has happened. EG *...to exonerate me from the crimes they had charged me with.*

exorbitant /ɪˈgzɔːbɪtənt/. If you describe some- ADJ QUALIT
thing as **exorbitant**, you mean that it is much
more expensive than it should be. EG *...an exorbitant rent.*

exorcism /ˈɛksɔːsɪzəm/ is the removing of evil N UNCOUNT
spirits from a place or person by using prayer. OR N COUNT
◇ **exorcist** /ˈɛksɔːsɪst/, **exorcists.** EG *They felt they* ◇ N COUNT
had to call in an exorcist.

exorcize /ˈɛksɔːsaɪz/, **exorcizes, exorcizing, ex-** V+O
orcized; also spelled **exorcise.** To **exorcize** an
evil spirit or to **exorcise** a place or person means
to force the spirit to leave the place or person by
means of prayers and religious ceremonies.

exotic /ɪˈgzɒtɪk/. Something that is **exotic** is un- ADJ QUALIT
usual and interesting because it comes from a
distant country. EG *...rich exotic foods.*

expand /ɪˈkspænd/, **expands, expanding, ex-** V-ERG
panded. If something **expands** or if you **expand**
it, 1 it becomes greater in number or amount. EG
*The city's population expanded by 12 per cent...
...major measures to expand the Royal Air Force.* 2
it becomes larger in size. EG *Natural materials
expand with heat... His business expanded rapidly.*

expand on or **expand upon.** If you **expand on** PHRASAL VB :
or **expand upon** something, you give more infor- V+PREP,
mation or details about it. EG *Perhaps you could* HAS PASS
expand on this a little bit.

expanse /ɪˈkspæns/, **expanses.** An **expanse** of N COUNT+of
sea, sky, or land is a very large amount of it. EG Written
...the wide expanse of snowy fields.

expansion /ɪˈkspænʃən/ is the process of becom- N UNCOUNT
ing greater in size or amount. EG *...the rapid expansion of British agriculture.*

expansionism /ɪˈkspænʃənɪzəm/ is the policy of N UNCOUNT
expanding the economy of a country or increasing
the amount of land that it rules. ◇ **expansionist.** ◇ ADJ CLASSIF
EG *...expansionist policies.*

expansive /ɪˈkspænsɪv/. If you are **expansive**, ADJ QUALIT
you talk a lot, because you are happy and relaxed.
EG *That week had made him jovial and expansive.*

expatriate /ɛksˈpætriˌət/, **expatriates.** An **expat-** N COUNT
riate is someone who is living in a country which
is not their own. EG *...British expatriates.*

expect /ɪˈkspɛkt/, **expects, expecting, expected.**
1 If you **expect** something to happen, you believe V+O+to-INF,
that it will happen. EG *Nobody expected the strike* V+to-INF,
to succeed... He didn't expect to be so busy... When OR V+REPORT
do you expect that this material will be available? ONLY that

2 If you **expect** something, 2.1 you believe that it is V+O
going to happen or arrive. EG *We are expecting
rain... Dr Willoughby was expecting him.*
◇ **expected.** EG *We would resist this expected* ◇ ADJ CLASSIF
attack. 2.2 you believe that it is your right to get it V+O, OR V :
or have it. EG *We expect sincerity from our politi-* OFT+to-INF
cians... I expect to be treated with respect.

3 If you **expect** someone to do something, you V+O+to-INF
require them to do it as a duty or obligation. EG *He
is expected to put his work before his family.*

4 If a woman **is expecting**, she is pregnant. EG V OR V+O :
She's expecting her third baby. ONLY CONT

5 If you say **'I expect'**, you mean that you think PHRASE
that what you are saying is likely to be correct. EG *I
expect he was trying to make me feel sorry for
him.*

6 If you say **'What do you expect?'** you mean that PHRASE
there is nothing surprising about a person's behaviour or a situation. EG *What could you expect from a
family like that?*

expectancy /ɪˈkspɛktənsɪ/ is the feeling that N UNCOUNT
something exciting or interesting is about to happen. ● See also **life expectancy.**

expectant /ɪˈkspɛktənt/. 1 If you are **expectant**, ADJ QUALIT
you are excited because you think something interesting is going to happen. EG *The assembly, sensing
a crisis, was tensely expectant.* ◇ **expectantly.** EG ◇ ADV
She looked at him expectantly.

2 An **expectant** mother or father is someone ADJ CLASSIF :
whose baby is going to be born soon. EG *Good* ATTRIB
nutrition is important to an expectant mother.

expectation /ˌɛkspɛkˈteɪʃən/, **expectations.** An N COUNT
expectation is 1 a strong hope that something will
happen. EG *The plan has succeeded beyond our
expectations... Living standards and expectations
are increasing.* 2 a belief that something is likely to
happen or should happen. EG *I was watched in the
expectation that I would go too far... ...women with
expectations of old-fashioned gallantry.*

expediency /ɪˈkspiːdɪənsɪ/ is behaviour in which N UNCOUNT
you do what is convenient, rather than what is Formal
morally right. EG *The government is torn between
principle and expediency.*

expedient /ɪˈkspiːdɪənt/, **expedients.** 1 An **ex-** N COUNT
pedient is an action or plan that achieves a Formal
particular purpose, but that may not be morally
acceptable. EG *Incomes controls were used only as
a short-term expedient.*

2 If it is **expedient** to do something, it is useful or ADJ QUALIT
convenient to do it. EG *The President did not find it* Formal
expedient to attend the meeting.

expedition /ˌɛkspɪˈdɪʃən/, **expeditions.** An N COUNT
expedition is 1 an organized journey that is made
for a particular purpose such as exploration. EG
*...the British expedition to Mount Everest... ...a
hunting expedition.* 2 a short journey or outing that
you make for pleasure. EG *...a shopping expedition.*

expel /ɪˈkspɛl/, **expels, expelling, expelled.** 1 If V+O : USU PASS
someone **is expelled** from a school or organiza-
tion, they are officially told that they no longer
belong to it, because they have behaved badly. EG
*He had been expelled from his previous school for
stealing.*

2 When people **are expelled** from a place, they V+O :
are made to leave it, usually by force. EG *Peasants* USU PASS+A
were expelled from their villages.

3 If a gas or liquid **is expelled** from a place, it is V+O
forced out of it. EG *Water is sucked in at one end* Formal
and expelled at the other.

expend /ɪˈkspɛnd/, **expends, expending, ex-** V+O
pended. To **expend** energy, time, or money Formal
means to spend it or use it. EG *They expend large
sums of money to maintain this beach.*

expendable /ɪˈkspɛndəbəl/, **expendables.** Some- ADJ CLASSIF
thing or someone that is **expendable** is no longer Formal
needed and can be got rid of. EG *My part would be
played and I would become expendable.*

expenditure /ɪˈkspɛndɪtʃə/, **expenditures.** Ex-
penditure is 1 the total amount of money that is N UNCOUNT
spent on something. EG *We restricted our expendi-* OR N COUNT
ture on food... ...public expenditure. 2 the using of N UNCOUNT
energy or time for a particular purpose. EG *This* +SUPP
was done with a minimum expenditure of energy.

expense /ɪˈkspɛns/, **expenses.** 1 Expense is the N UNCOUNT
money that something costs. EG *...the roads they're* OR N COUNT
building at vast expense... ...household expenses.
● If you **go to great expense** to do something, you ● PHRASE
spend a lot of money on it. EG *The Government has
gone to great expense to set up procedures.*

2 Your **expenses** are the money that you spend N PLURAL
while doing something connected with your work,
and which is paid back to you afterwards. EG
...travelling expenses.

3 The phrase **'at someone's expense'** is used in PHRASE
these ways: **3.1** If you do something **at someone's
expense**, they provide the money for you to do it.
EG *He circulated the document at his own expense.*
3.2 If you make a joke **at someone's expense**, you
do it to make fun of them or to make them seem
foolish. **3.3** If you achieve something **at someone's** PREP
expense, you do it in a way that harms them. EG
*They increase their own income at the expense of
the rural masses.*

expensive /ɪˈkspɛnsɪv/. Something that is **expen-** ADJ QUALIT
sive costs a lot of money. EG *...expensive clothes.*

If you say 'I expect it's true', do you feel sure that
it is true?

◊ **expensively.** EG *We can do that fairly easily and* ◊ ADV *not too expensively.*

experience /ɪˈkspɪərɪəns/, **experiences, experi-** N UNCOUNT : **encing, experienced.** 1 **Experience** is 1.1 the USU+SUPP fact of having worked at a particular kind of job for a period of time. EG *I had no military experience... She's had nine months experience.* 1.2 the act of seeing, doing, or feeling something or the fact of being affected by it. EG *...his experience of nature and natural forms... The new countries have no experience of democracy.* 1.3 the things that have happened to you or that you have done. EG *Everyone learns best from his own experience... ...speaking from personal experience.*

2 An **experience** is something that happens to you N COUNT+SUPP or something that you do, especially something unusual. EG *Moving house can be a traumatic experience... I was enjoying the experience of working with Tony.*

3 If you **experience** a situation or feeling, it V+O happens to you or you are affected by it. EG *Similar problems have been experienced by other students... Few of the soldiers had experienced combat... They experienced a mild burning sensation.*

experienced /ɪˈkspɪərɪənst/. You describe some- ADJ QUALIT one as **experienced** when they are skilled at a particular job because they have done it for a long time. EG *...an experienced lecturer.*

experiment /ɪˈkspɛrɪmənt/, **experiments, ex-** N COUNT OR **perimenting, experimented.** 1 An **experiment** N UNCOUNT is 1.1 a scientific test which is done in order to prove or discover something. EG *...experiments in physics.* 1.2 the trying out of a new idea or method to see what effect it has. EG *...the failure of this great experiment in industrial democracy.*

2 If you **experiment** with something or experi- V : USU+A **ment** on it, you do a scientific test on it in order to prove or discover something. EG *He experimented with young white rats.* ◊ **experimentation** ◊ N UNCOUNT /ɪˌkspɛrɪmɛnˈteɪʃən/. EG *...a place for medical experimentation.* ◊ **experimenter** /ɪˈkspɛrɪˈ ◊ N COUNT mɛntə/, **experimenters.** EG *Experimenters have licences granted by the Home Office.*

3 To **experiment** also means to try out a new idea V : USU+A or method to see what effects it has. EG *...small businesses anxious to experiment with computers.* ◊ **experimentation.** EG *...experimentation with* ◊ N UNCOUNT *cut-out shapes.*

experimental /ɪˈkspɛrɪˈmɛntəl/. 1 **Experimen-** tal means 1.1 involving the use of new ideas or ADJ QUALIT methods. EG *...experimental forms of teaching.* ◊ **experimentally.** EG *...the first parking meters,* ◊ ADV *introduced experimentally in 1958.* 1.2 relating to ADJ CLASSIF scientific experiments. ◊ **experimentally.** EG ◊ ADV *These are then measured experimentally and the results compared.*

2 An **experimental** action is done in order to see ADJ CLASSIF what effects it has. EG *He gave an experimental tug at Clarissa's bag.* ◊ **experimentally.** EG *He took* ◊ ADV *the rifle and held it experimentally to his shoulder.*

expert /ˈɛkspɜːt/, **experts.** 1 An **expert** is 1.1 a N COUNT person who is very skilled at doing something. EG *Experts were called in to dismantle the bomb.* 1.2 a person who has studied a particular subject and knows a lot about it. EG *...an expert on Eastern philosophy.*

2 Someone who is **expert** at doing something is ADJ QUALIT very skilled at it. EG *...expert acrobats... Get expert treatment from a specialist.* ◊ **expertly.** EG *Burke* ◊ ADV *drove expertly.*

expertise /ˌɛkspɜːˈtiːz/ is special skill or knowl- N UNCOUNT : edge. EG *...jobs which require a great deal of* USU+SUPP *managerial expertise.*

expiate /ˈɛkspɪeɪt/, **expiates, expiating, expi-** V+O **ated.** If you **expiate** guilty feelings or bad behav- Formal iour, you do something to indicate that you are sorry for what you have done. EG *He hoped to expiate his guilt over leaving her.* ◊ **expiation** ◊ N UNCOUNT

/ˌɛkspɪˈeɪʃən/. EG *He sought expiation by demanding punishment.*

expire /ɪˈkspaɪə/, **expires, expiring, expired.** 1 V When something **expires**, it reaches the end of the Formal period of time for which it is valid. EG *My passport is due to expire in three months.* ◊ **expiration** ◊ N UNCOUNT /ˌɛkspɪˈreɪʃən/. EG *...expiration of the legal waiting period.* ◊ **expiry** /ɪˈkspaɪəri/. EG *The French* ◊ N UNCOUNT *licences have no expiry date.*

2 When someone **expires**, they die. EG *The old lady* V *expired within the hour.* Literary

explain /ɪˈkspleɪn/, **explains, explaining, ex-** **plained.** If you **explain** something, 1 you give V+O : OFT+to; details about it so that it can be understood. EG *John* ALSO *went on to explain the legal situation... I explained* V+REPORT *that I was trying to write a book... Let me explain* OR QUOTE *to you about Jackie.* 2 you give people reasons for V+O, V-REFL, it. EG *He never wrote to me to explain his decision...* OR V *Just a minute. Let me explain.*

explain away. If you **explain away** a mistake, PHRASAL VB : you try to indicate that it is not very important or V+O+ADV that it is not really your fault. EG *...explaining away his department's latest blunder.*

explanation /ˌɛkspləˈneɪʃən/, **explanations.** If you give an **explanation**, 1 you say why something N COUNT OR happened. EG *There was no reasonable explanation* N UNCOUNT *for her decision... Enclose a note of explanation with the parcel... The time for lengthy explanations was over.* 2 you describe something in detail. EG *...a* N COUNT *scientific explanation of the universe.*

explanatory /ɪˈksplænətəri/. **Explanatory** ADJ CLASSIF statements are intended to make people under- Formal stand something by describing it or giving the reasons for it. EG *They produce free explanatory leaflets on heating.*

explicable /ˌɛksplɪkəbᵊl, ɪˈksplɪk-/. Something ADJ QUALIT that is **explicable** can be explained and under- Formal stood. EG *For no explicable reason your mind goes blank.*

explicit /ɪˈksplɪsɪt/. 1 Something that is **explicit** is ADJ QUALIT shown or expressed clearly and openly, without any attempt to hide anything. EG *...the explicit support of the Prime Minister.* ◊ **explicitly.** EG ◊ ADV *...explicitly violent scenes.*

2 If you are **explicit** about something, you express ADJ QUALIT yourself clearly and openly about it. EG *She was not explicit about what she really felt.* ◊ **explicitly.** EG ◊ ADV *This was explicitly admitted by the Premier.*

explode /ɪˈksploʊd/, **explodes, exploding, ex-** **ploded.** 1 When a bomb **explodes**, it bursts loudly V-ERG and with great force, often causing a lot of damage. EG *A bomb had exploded in the next street... They exploded a nuclear device.*

2 When something increases suddenly and rapidly, V you can say that it **explodes**. EG *The population was still exploding.*

3 You can say that a person **explodes** when they V+A express strong feelings suddenly and violently. EG *She exploded with rage.*

4 If you **explode** a theory, you prove that it is V+O wrong or impossible. EG *I could explode some of the myths about him.*

exploit, exploits, exploiting, exploited; pro- nounced /ɪkˈsplɔɪt/ when it is a verb and /ˈɛksplɔɪt/ when it is a noun. 1 If someone **exploits** you, they V+O treat you unfairly by using your work or your ideas and giving you very little in return. EG *Adults exploit children far too often.* ◊ **exploitation** ◊ N UNCOUNT /ˌɛksplɔɪˈteɪʃən/. EG *...to protect the public from commercial exploitation.*

2 If you **exploit** something such as a raw material V+O or an idea, you develop it in order to make money out of it. EG *Everyone is seeking to exploit opportunities for improving efficiency.* ◊ **exploitation.** EG ◊ N UNCOUNT *...the exploitation of the Earth's resources.*

3 Someone's **exploits** are the brave or interesting N COUNT : things that they have done. EG *...his exploits in the* USU PLURAL *War.*

exploitative /ɪˈksplɔɪtətɪv/. If you describe a person or organization as **exploitative**, you mean that they treat people unfairly because they are interested only in making money. EG ...*exploitative employment agencies.*   ADJ QUALIT Formal

exploiter /ɪˈksplɔɪtə/, **exploiters.** You refer to people as **exploiters** when they use other people or things in order to make money in an uncaring way. EG ...*the misuse of power by property-hungry exploiters.*   N COUNT

exploratory /ɪˈksplɒrətəˈriˈ/. **Exploratory** actions are done in order to discover something or to learn something. EG *An early exploratory expedition had failed.*   ADJ CLASSIF Formal

explore /ɪˈksplɔː/, **explores, exploring, explored.** 1 If you **explore** a place, you travel in it in order to find out what it is like. EG *He explored three continents by canoe.* ◇ **exploration** /ˌekspləˈreɪʃəⁿn/, **explorations.** EG ...*voyages of exploration... He had become fascinated by the great explorations of the past.* ◇ **explorer** /ɪˈksplɔːrə/, **explorers.** EG ...*an Arctic explorer.*   V+O ◇ N UNCOUNT OR N COUNT ◇ N COUNT

2 If you **explore** something with your hands, you touch it so that you can feel what it is like. EG *With widespread hands he explored the wet grass.*   V+O

3 If you **explore** an idea, you think about it carefully in order to decide whether it is a good one. EG *The conference explored the possibility of closer trade links.* ◇ **exploration.** EG ...*a fundamental exploration of the main alternatives.*   V+O ◇ N UNCOUNT OR N COUNT

explosion /ɪˈkspləʊʒəⁿn/, **explosions.** An **explosion** is 1 a sudden, violent burst of energy, for example one caused by a bomb. EG *Twenty men were killed in the explosion.* 2 a large and rapid increase in something. EG ...*the population explosion.* 3 a sudden and violent expression of anger. EG ...*an explosion of rage.* 4 an outbreak of protest or violence. EG ...*the explosion of mass protest.*   N COUNT   N COUNT+SUPP   N COUNT   N COUNT

explosive /ɪˈkspləʊsɪv/, **explosives.** 1 An **explosive** is a substance or device that can explode. 2 Something that is **explosive** 2.1 is capable of exploding or is likely to explode. EG ...*a powerful explosive device.* 2.2 involves an explosion or results from an explosion. EG *Modern bullets produce an explosive effect upon impact.* 2.3 happens suddenly and makes a loud noise. EG *The final applause was explosive.*   N COUNT OR N UNCOUNT   ADJ CLASSIF   ADJ CLASSIF   ADJ QUALIT

3 An **explosive** situation is likely to have serious or dangerous effects. EG *Unemployment has become the most explosive political issue.*   ADJ QUALIT

exponent /ɪˈkspəʊnənt/, **exponents.** 1 An **exponent** of an idea, theory, or plan is someone who supports it. EG ...*the leading exponents of apartheid.* 2 An **exponent** of a particular skill or activity is someone who is good at it. EG ...*the supreme exponent of the English humorous essay.*   N COUNT+SUPP   N COUNT+SUPP Formal

exponential /ˌekspəˈnenʃəˈl/ means growing or increasing very rapidly. EG *Computer technology is embarking on a period of exponential growth.* ◇ **exponentially.** EG *Money spent by Education Authorities has risen exponentially.*   ADJ CLASSIF Formal ◇ ADV

export, exports, exporting, exported; pronounced /ˈekspɔt/ when it is a noun and /ɪˈkspɔt/ when it is a verb.
1 To **export** products or raw materials means to sell them to another country and send them there. EG *Africa is exporting beef to Europe.* ▸ used as a noun. EG *They grow coffee and bananas for export.*   V+O OR V   ▸ N UNCOUNT

2 **Exports** are products or raw materials which are sold and sent to another country.   N COUNT

3 To **export** ideas or values means to introduce them into other countries. EG *The values of today's Europeans are now exported by them to all parts of the world.*   V+O

exporter /ˈekspɔtə/, **exporters.** An **exporter** is a country, firm, or person that sells and sends goods to another country.   N COUNT

expose /ɪˈkspəʊz/, **exposes, exposing, exposed.**
1 To **expose** something means to uncover it and   V+O

make it visible. EG *The rocks are exposed at low tide.*

2 If you **are exposed** to something dangerous or unpleasant, you are put in a situation in which it might harm you. EG *They had been exposed to radiation.*   V+O+to

3 If you **are exposed** to an idea or feeling, you experience it. EG *We are all exposed to grief.*   V+O+to: USU PASS

4 To **expose** a person or situation means to reveal the truth about them, especially when it involves dishonest or shocking behaviour. EG *He was eventually exposed in the perjury case.*   V+O

5 An **exposed** place has no natural protection against bad weather or enemies. EG *The house is in a very exposed position.*   ADJ QUALIT

exposé /ɛksˈpuːzeɪ/, **exposés.** An **exposé** is a piece of writing which reveals the truth about a situation or person, especially when it involves dishonest or shocking behaviour. EG ...*a lucid exposé of the hypocrisy surrounding the payment.*   N COUNT

exposition /ˌekspəˈzɪʃəⁿn/, **expositions.** An **exposition** is a detailed explanation of an idea or a discussion of a problem. EG ...*a clear exposition of the theory of evolution.*   N COUNT Formal

expostulate /ɪˈkspɒstjəˈleɪt/, **expostulates, expostulating, expostulated.** If you **expostulate**, you express strong disagreement with someone. EG *Sir William expostulated against this policy of suppression.*   V OR V+QUOTE Formal

exposure /ɪˈkspəʊʒə/, **exposures.** 1 **Exposure** to something is 1.1 a situation in which you are affected or influenced by something. EG *He was suffering from exposure to nuclear radiation... ...receiving maximum exposure to new ideas.* 1.2 the publicity given to something. EG ...*the widest possible exposure to scenes of casualties and damage.*   N UNCOUNT

2 The **exposure** of someone or something is the revealing of the truth about them, especially when it involves dishonest or shocking behaviour. EG ...*the public exposure of a president.*   N UNCOUNT

3 **Exposure** is the harmful effect on your body caused by very cold weather. EG *The group's leader died of exposure.*   N UNCOUNT

4 In photography, an **exposure** is a single photograph. EG ...*a camera capable of taking a hundred exposures before the film needs changing.*   N COUNT Technical

expound /ɪˈkspaʊnd/, **expounds, expounding, expounded.** If you **expound** an idea or opinion, you give a clear and detailed explanation of it. EG *He expounded his latest theory.*   V+O Formal

express /ɪˈkspres/, **expresses, expressing, expressed.** 1 When you **express** an idea or feeling or when you **express** yourself, you show people what you think or feel by saying or doing something. EG *They hooted their car horns to express their disapproval... I expressed myself better in French.*   V+O OR V-REFL

2 If an idea or feeling **expresses** itself in some way, it can be clearly seen in someone's actions or in its effects on a situation. EG *That increased confidence expressed itself in other ways.*   V-REFL: USU+A Formal

3 If you **express** a quantity in a particular form, you write it down in that form. EG *Here it is expressed as a percentage.*   V+O: USU+A Technical

4 An **express** command or order is one that is clearly stated. EG *This may not be published save by the express direction of the School.* ◇ **expressly.** EG *Jefferson had expressly asked her to invite Freeman.*   ADJ CLASSIF: ATTRIB Formal ◇ ADV

5 An **express** intention or purpose is a deliberate and specific one. EG *She came with the express purpose of causing trouble.* ◇ **expressly.** EG *They bought the house expressly for her.*   ADJ CLASSIF: ATTRIB ◇ ADV

6 An **express** service is one in which things are   ADJ CLASSIF:

If your face is expressionless, do people know what you are thinking?

sent or done faster than usual. EG ...*an express* ATTRIB
letter.

7 An **express** is a fast train or coach which stops N COUNT
at very few places.

expression /ɪ²kspreʃ³n/, **expressions. 1** An ex- N COUNT
pression is a word or phrase that is usually used in
a particular situation or by particular people, and
that you are quoting, explaining, or commenting
on. EG ...*slang expressions... The expression is 'fly in
the ointment'*.

2 The **expression** of ideas or feelings is **2.1** the act N UNCOUNT
of putting them into words by speaking or writing. OR N COUNT :
EG *We parted with many expressions of goodwill*. OFT+*of*

2.2 the act of showing them through your actions N COUNT :
or through artistic activities. EG *His carvings have* OFT+*of*
*become one of the finest expressions of African
art*.

3 Your **expression** is the way that your face shows N COUNT
what you are thinking or feeling. EG *He couldn't see* +SUPP OR
the expression on her face... Anthony's face N UNCOUNT
showed no expression.

4 Expression is the showing of feeling when you N UNCOUNT
are acting, singing, or playing a musical instrument. EG *The playing was flat, without expression*.

expressionless /ɪ²kspreʃ³nlɪ²s/. If someone's ADJ QUALIT
face or voice is **expressionless**, it shows no feelings. EG *His face was completely expressionless*.

expressive /ɪ²kspresɪv/. **1** Something that is ex- ADJ QUALIT
pressive indicates clearly a person's feelings or
intentions. EG *She had given Lynn an expressive
glance*. ◊ **expressively.** EG *He drew a finger* ◊ ADV
expressively across his throat.

2 Someone's **expressive** ability is their ability to ADJ CLASSIF
speak or write clearly and interestingly. EG ...*evaluating the child's expressive powers*.

expressway /ɪ²kspreswei/, **expressways.** An N COUNT
expressway is a wide road that is specially de- American
signed so that a lot of traffic can move along it
very quickly. EG ...*a four-lane expressway*.

expropriate /ɛksprəʊprɪeɪt/, **expropriates, ex-** V+O
propriating, expropriated. If someone **expro-** Formal
priates something, they take it away from the
person who it belongs to. EG *The surplus will be
expropriated by the government*.

expulsion /ɪ²kspʌlʃ³n/, **expulsions. Expulsion** N UNCOUNT
is **1** the expelling of someone from a school or OR N COUNT
organization. EG ...*his expulsion from the university*. Formal
2 the act of forcing people to leave a place. EG ...*the* Formal
expulsion of military advisers. **3** the act of forcing Formal
something out of a container or out of your body. EG
...*with each expulsion of breath*.

exquisite /ɪ²kskwɪzɪt, ɛkskwɪzɪt/. You describe
something as **exquisite 1** when it is extremely ADJ QUALIT
beautiful in appearance. EG *She has the most exquisite face... ...exquisite jewellery*. ◊ **exquisitely.** ◊ ADV
EG *Their children were exquisitely dressed*. **2** when ADJ QUALIT
it is very pleasant or satisfying. EG ...*sipping the
water slowly with exquisite relief*. ◊ **exquisitely.** ◊ ADV
EG ...*his exquisitely polite voice*.

extant /ɛkstænt, ɛkstənt/. Something that is ex- ADJ CLASSIF
tant still exists although it is very old. EG ...*one* Formal
Spanish law that is still extant in California.

extend /ɪ²kstend/, **extends, extending, extended. 1** If something **extends** for a particular dis- V+A
tance, it continues for that distance from a point or
central area. EG *The road now extends two kilometres beyond the River*.

2 If something **extends** from a surface or object, it V+A
sticks out from it. EG ...*metal slabs extending from
the wall*.

3 If something **extends** for a period of time, it V+A
continues for that time. EG *His working day often
extends well into the evening*.

4 If something **extends** to other people or things, it V+A
includes or affects them. EG *The consequences of
unemployment extend well beyond the labour market*.

5 If you **extend** something, **5.1** you make it bigger V+O
or longer. EG *Have you ever thought of extending*

your house? **5.2** you cause it to exist or be valid for V+O
a longer period of time. EG *The authorities extended her visa*. ◊ **extended.** EG ...*extended news* ◊ ADJ CLASSIF
bulletins. **5.3** you cause it to include or affect more V+O
people or things. EG *Congress wants the law extended to cover all states*.

6 If you **extend** a part of your body, you straighten V+O
it or stretch it out. EG *He extended his hand, and
Brody shook it*.

7 If you **extend** something to someone, you offer it V+O : OFT+*to*
to them in a polite or friendly way. EG *The invita-* Formal
tion she had extended was promptly accepted.

extension /ɪ²kstenʃ³n/, **extensions. 1** An exten- N COUNT
sion is a new room or building which is added to
an existing building. EG ...*a new extension to the
library*.

2 An **extension** is also **2.1** an extra period of time N COUNT OR
for which something continues to exist or be valid. N UNCOUNT
EG *He asked for extension of his residence permit*.
2.2 a development that includes or affects more
people, ideas, or activities. EG *Nationalist leaders
demanded the extension of democratic rights*.

3 A telephone **extension** is a telephone that is N COUNT
connected to the switchboard of an organization,
and that has a special number.

extensive /ɪ²kstensɪv/. Something that is **extensive 1** covers a large area. EG ...*an extensive* ADJ QUALIT
Roman settlement in north-west England. **2** is very ADJ QUALIT
great in effect. EG *Many buildings suffered extensive damage in the blast*. ◊ **extensively.** EG *The* ◊ ADV
aircraft were extensively modified. **3** contains ADJ QUALIT
many details, ideas, or items on a particular subject. EG *We had fairly extensive discussions*.
◊ **extensively.** EG *I have quoted extensively from* ◊ ADV
it in the following pages.

extent /ɪ²kstent/. **1** The **extent** of something is its N SING+POSS
length, area, or size. EG ...*to expand the empire to
its largest extent*.

2 The **extent** of a situation or difficulty is its size or N SING+POSS
scale. EG *The full extent of the problem is not yet
known*.

3 You use phrases such as **to a large extent**, **to** ADV SEN
some extent, or **to a certain extent** in order to
indicate that something is partly true, but not
entirely true. EG *Well I think to a certain extent it's
true*.

4 You use phrases such as **to what extent**, **to that** PHRASE
extent, or **to the extent that** when you are
discussing how true a statement is. EG *To what
extent are diseases linked with genes?... A computer is intelligent only to the extent that it can store
information*.

5 You use phrases such as **to the extent of**, **to the** PHRASE
extent that, or **to such an extent that** in order to
indicate that a situation has reached a particular
stage. EG *Sanitary conditions had deteriorated to
such an extent that there was widespread danger
of disease*.

exterior /ɪ²kstɪərɪə/, **exteriors. 1** The **exterior** of N COUNT
something is its outside surface. EG *Keep your car
exterior in good condition*.

2 Your **exterior** is your usual appearance or N COUNT+SUPP
behaviour, especially when it is very different from
your character. EG *Beneath his professional doctor's exterior, he was wildly fun-loving and reckless*.

3 You use **exterior** to describe something that is ADJ CLASSIF :
situated or happening outside something or some- ATTRIB
one. EG *Exterior drains must be kept clear*.

exterminate /ɪ²kstɜːmɪneɪt/, **exterminates, ex-** V+O : USU PASS
terminating, exterminated. When a group of
animals or people **is exterminated**, they are all
killed. EG *Fishing must stop before the species is
completely exterminated*. ◊ **extermination** ◊ N UNCOUNT
/ɪ²kstɜːmɪneɪʃ³n/. EG ...*a way to prevent the extermination of these animals*.

external /ɪ²kstɜːn³l/, **externals. 1 External** ADJ CLASSIF :
means happening, coming from, or existing outside USU ATTRIB
a place, person, or area of activity. EG ...*the exter-*

nal walls of the chimneys... They did it in response to external pressures. ◊ **externally.** EG *It should be applied externally.* ◊ ADV

2 External is used to describe people who come into an organization from outside in order to do a job there. EG *Their accounts are audited by a firm of external auditors.* ADJ CLASSIF: ATTRIB

3 When you talk about the **externals** of a situation, you are referring to features that are obvious but not very important. EG *The popular historian is concerned only with externals.* N PLURAL Formal

extinct /ɪ²kstɪŋkt/. **1** A species of animals that is **extinct** no longer has any living members. EG *The wolf is now nearly extinct... The dodo became extinct about 300 years ago.* ADJ CLASSIF

2 An **extinct** volcano does not erupt or is very unlikely to erupt. ADJ CLASSIF

extinction /ɪ²kstɪŋkᵏʃəⁿn/ is The **extinction** of a species of animal is the death of all its remaining members. EG *Apes are in danger of extinction.* N UNCOUNT

extinguish /ɪ²kstɪŋgwɪʃ/, **extinguishes, extinguishing, extinguished. 1** If you **extinguish** a fire or a light, you stop it burning or shining. EG *...a new method of extinguishing forest fires.* V+O Formal

2 If someone or something **extinguishes** an idea or feeling, they destroy it. EG *We have to extinguish the memory of the defeat.* V+O Formal

extinguisher /ɪ²kstɪŋgwɪʃə/. See **fire extinguisher**.

extol /ɪ²kstəʊl/, **extols, extolling, extolled.** If you **extol** something, you praise it enthusiastically, often in order to persuade other people to like it or approve of it. EG *Only a week or two later he was extolling the virtues of female independence.* V+O Formal

extort /ɪ²kstɔːt/, **extorts, extorting, extorted.** If someone **extorts** money from you, they get it from you by using force or threats. EG *They extorted every penny from us.* ◊ **extortion** /ɪ²kstɔːʃəⁿn/. EG *He faces trial on extortion charges.* V+O: OFT+from ◊ N UNCOUNT

extortionate /ɪ²kstɔːʃəⁿnət/. You describe something as **extortionate** when it is bigger or more costly than you consider to be fair. EG *...a worker making extortionate demands upon the employer.* ADJ QUALIT

extra /ekstrə/, **extras. 1** An **extra** thing, person, or amount is a thing, person, or amount that is added to others of the same kind. EG *Take an extra pair of shoes... You have to pay extra for breakfast.* QUANTIF, OR ADV AFTER VB

2 Extras are **2.1** things that are not necessary but that make something more comfortable, useful, or enjoyable. EG *With the extras, the car cost £4,000.* **2.2** additional amounts of money which are added to the price that you have to pay for something. EG *There are no hidden extras.* N COUNT: USU PLURAL

3 An **extra** is a person who plays an unimportant part in a film. N COUNT

4 If you are **extra** polite or **extra** careful, you are more polite or careful than usual. EG *He was extra polite to his superiors.* SUBMOD

extra- is used to form adjectives that describe something as being outside something else. For example, extra-parliamentary activities are political activities that take place outside parliament. EG *He was preoccupied with extra-theatrical problems.* PREFIX Formal

extract, extracts, extracting, extracted; pronounced /ɪ²kstrækt/ when it is a verb and /ekstrækt/ when it is a noun.

1 If you **extract** something from a place, you take it out or pull it out. EG *Mrs Oliver extracted a small notebook from her bag... He tried to extract his pole from the mud.* V+O: OFT+from Formal

2 To **extract** a raw material means to get it from the ground or from another substance. EG *The Japanese extract ten million tons of coal each year.* V+O

3 If you **extract** information from someone, you get it from them with difficulty. EG *Sir James had extracted from Francis a fairly detailed account.* V+O: OFT+from

4 If someone **extracts** an advantage from a situa- V+O+from Formal

tion, they use the situation in order to gain the advantage. EG *They will extract the maximum propaganda value from this affair.*

5 An **extract** from a piece of writing or music is a small part of it that is printed or played separately. EG *I would like to quote two extracts from the book.* N COUNT

extraction /ɪ²kstrækʃəⁿn/. **1** Your **extraction** is the country or people that your family originally comes from. EG *Alistair was of Scottish extraction.* N UNCOUNT Formal

2 The **extraction** of something from a place is the act or process of removing it. EG *...industries involved in mineral extraction.* N UNCOUNT

extractor /ɪ²kstræktə/, **extractors.** An **extractor** or **extractor fan** is a device that is fixed to a window or wall in order to draw steam or hot air out of a room or building. N COUNT

extra-curricular /ekstrə kərɪkjəˀlə/. **Extra-curricular** activities are activities for students that are not part of the course that they are doing. EG *We offer a wide range of extracurricular activities... ...informal, extra-curricular discussions about politics.* ADJ CLASSIF Formal

extradite /ekstrədaɪt/, **extradites, extraditing, extradited.** To **extradite** someone means to officially send them back to their own country so that they can be tried there for a crime that they have been accused of. ◊ **extradition** /ekstrədɪʃəⁿn/, **extraditions.** EG *France requested their extradition from the United States.* V+O Formal ◊ N UNCOUNT OR N COUNT

extramarital /ekstrəmærɪtəˀl/. You use **extramarital** to describe a sexual relationship between a married person and another person who is not their husband or wife. EG *...an extramarital affair.* ADJ CLASSIF Formal

extra-mural. You use **extra-mural** to refer to courses in a college or university which are involved mainly with part-time students. EG *...the Department of Extra-mural Studies.* ADJ CLASSIF: ATTRIB

extraneous /ɪ²kstreɪnɪəs/. Something that is **extraneous** happens or concerns things outside the situation or subject that you are talking about. EG *We must avoid all extraneous issues.* ADJ CLASSIF Formal

extraordinary /ɪ²kstrɔːdəⁿnəˀriⁱ/. **1** If you describe someone or something as **extraordinary**, you mean that they have some very special or extreme qualities. EG *My grandfather was a most extraordinary man.* ◊ **extraordinarily.** EG *...an extraordinarily beautiful girl.* ADJ QUALIT ◊ SUBMOD

2 You can also say that something is **extraordinary** when it is unusual or surprising in a particular situation. EG *What an extraordinary thing to say.* ◊ **extraordinarily.** EG *...extraordinarily high levels of radiation.* ADJ QUALIT ◊ SUBMOD

3 An **extraordinary** meeting is arranged specially to deal with a particular situation or problem. ADJ CLASSIF: ATTRIB

extravagance /ɪ²kstrævəˀgəns/, **extravagances. 1 Extravagance** is the spending of more money than is reasonable or than you can afford. EG *It is easy to criticize governments for extravagance and waste.* N UNCOUNT

2 An **extravagance** is something that you spend money on which you cannot really afford. EG *It was a little extravagance of my father to buy new plants every year.* N COUNT

extravagant /ɪ²kstrævəˀgənt/. **1** Someone who is **extravagant 1.1** spends more money than is reasonable or than they can afford. EG *He was extravagant and liked to live well.* ◊ **extravagantly.** EG *I lived extravagantly, taking cabs everywhere.* **1.2** uses more of something than is reasonable. EG *She considered him extravagant with electricity.* ADJ QUALIT ◊ ADV ADJ QUALIT

2 Something that is **extravagant 2.1** costs more money than is reasonable or than you can afford. EG *...extravagant gifts.* ◊ **extravagantly.** EG *...merchandise known to be extravagantly priced.* **2.2** uses more of something than is reasonable. EG ADJ QUALIT ◊ SUBMOD ADJ QUALIT

Does an extravaganza cost an extortionate amount of money?

...*machines that are extravagant in their requirements of energy.*

3 Extravagant behaviour is extreme and is done to create a particular effect. EG *He raised his eyebrows in extravagant surprise.* ◊ **extravagantly.** EG *Harold was extravagantly affectionate with his daughters.* ADJ QUALIT Formal ◊ SUBMOD

4 Extravagant ideas are unrealistic and impractical. EG ...*extravagant expectations.* ADJ QUALIT Formal

5 Extravagant entertainments or designs are elaborate and impressive. ◊ **extravagantly.** EG ...*extravagantly elaborate funerals.* ADJ QUALIT ◊ SUBMOD

extravaganza /ɪˈkstrævəgænzə/, **extravaganzas.** An **extravaganza** is a very elaborate and expensive public activity or performance. N COUNT

extreme /ɪˈkstriːm/, **extremes. 1 Extreme** means very great in degree or intensity. EG *He died in extreme poverty... You must proceed with extreme caution.* ◊ **extremely.** EG ...*an extremely difficult task... Ralph and I always got on extremely well.* ADJ QUALIT : ATTRIB ◊ SUBMOD

2 Things that are **extreme**, for example opinions, beliefs, or behaviour, are very severe, unusual, or unreasonable. EG *People are capable of surviving in extreme conditions... Their methods may seem extreme to many parents... ...the extreme Right Wing of the Party.* ADJ QUALIT

3 The **extreme** point, edge, or end of something is its furthest point, edge, or end. EG ...*the extreme south of the country.* ADJ CLASSIF : ATTRIB

4 An **extreme** of behaviour is one in which you show a quality or attitude to an unacceptable degree. EG *There's now a danger that we're going to the other extreme and being too lenient.* N COUNT

5 If you say that someone **is going to extremes**, or **is taking** something **to extremes**, you mean that their behaviour is extreme and unacceptable. PHRASE

6 You use **in the extreme** to emphasize how bad or undesirable something is. EG *I thought the suggestion dangerous in the extreme.* PHRASE Formal

extremism /ɪˈkstriːmɪzəm/ is the behaviour or beliefs of extremists. EG ...*political extremism.* N UNCOUNT

extremist /ɪˈkstriːmɪst/, **extremists.** An **extremist** is a person who wishes to bring about political or social change by using methods that other people consider too severe or unreasonable. EG ...*a bomb planted by Nationalist extremists.* ► used as an adjective. EG ...*political parties with extremist views.* N COUNT ► ADJ CLASSIF

extremity /ɪˈkstremɪti/, **extremities. 1** The **extremities** of something are its furthest ends or edges. EG ...*the northern extremity of the cathedral.* N COUNT : USU + POSS Formal

2 Your **extremities** are the outermost parts of your body, especially your hands and feet. EG *The warmth spread outwards till it reached his extremities.* N PLURAL

3 An **extremity** is a very serious situation. EG *She tried to remember how things had ever reached such an extremity.* N COUNT Formal

4 If you think that someone talks or behaves in an extreme way, you can talk about the **extremity** of their views or behaviour. N UNCOUNT Formal

extricate /ˈekstrɪkeɪt/, **extricates, extricating, extricated. 1** If you **extricate** someone from a difficult or serious situation, you free them from it. EG *She found it impossible to extricate herself from the relationship.* V + O OR V-REFL : OFT + from

2 If you **extricate** someone from a place where they are trapped or caught, you succeed in freeing them. EG *It was exceedingly difficult to extricate her from the hole.* V + O OR V-REFL : OFT + from

extrovert /ˈekstrəvɜːt/, **extroverts.** An **extrovert** is a person who is very active, lively, and sociable. ► used as an adjective. EG ...*a rather extrovert student.* N COUNT ► ADJ QUALIT

extrude /ɪˈkstruːd/, **extrudes, extruding, extruded.** When something **extrudes** or **is extruded**, it is forced or squeezed out through a small V-ERG Formal

opening. EG *As the eggs are extruded, the male fertilizes them.*

exuberant /ɪˈɡzjuːbəʳrənt/. Someone who is **exuberant** is full of energy, excitement, and cheerfulness. EG ...*the exuberant director of the Theatre Royal.* ◊ **exuberantly.** EG *Children danced exuberantly around the tree.* ◊ **exuberance** /ɪˈɡzjuːbəʳrəns/. EG *She always greeted him with the same exuberance.* ADJ QUALIT ◊ ADV ◊ N UNCOUNT

exude /ɪˈɡzjuːd/, **exudes, exuding, exuded. 1** If you say that someone **exudes** a quality or feeling, you mean that they seem to have it to a great extent. EG *She exuded vitality, enthusiasm, and generosity.* V + O Formal

2 If something **exudes** a liquid or a smell, the liquid or smell comes out of it. EG *Some frogs exude a poisonous chemical from their skins.* V-ERG Formal

exult /ɪˈɡzʌlt/, **exults, exulting, exulted.** If you **exult**, you feel and show great happiness and pleasure because of some triumph or success that you have had. EG *I exulted at my fortune... 'I've never played golf like I did last week,' he exulted.* ◊ **exultation** /ɪˈɡzʌlteɪʃəʳn/. EG *He spoke with an air of exultation.* V : USU + A OR V + QUOTE ◊ N UNCOUNT

exultant /ɪˈɡzʌltənt/. If you are **exultant**, you feel very happy and triumphant. EG *Her voice was loud and exultant.* ◊ **exultantly.** EG *She laughed again,* exultantly. ADJ QUALIT Formal ◊ ADV

eye /aɪ/, **eyes, eyeing** or **eying, eyed. 1** Your **eyes** are the two things in your face that you see with. See picture at THE HUMAN BODY. EG *She opened her eyes.* N COUNT

2 If you say that someone has an **eye** for something, you mean that they can recognize it and make good judgements about it. EG ...*a marvellous eye for detail.* N SING + for

3 If you **eye** something, you look at it carefully or suspiciously. EG *Posy was eyeing the man thoughtfully.* V + O : NO IMPER

4 Eye is also used in these phrases. **4.1** If you say that something happened **before** your **eyes**, you mean that you actually saw it happen. EG *Her father was murdered before her very eyes.* **4.2** If you **cast** or **run** your **eye over** something, you look quickly at every part of it. EG *He ran his eye over the article.* **4.3** If something **catches** your **eye**, you suddenly notice it. EG *The flowers in your window caught my eye.* **4.4** If you try to **catch** someone's **eye**, you try to attract their attention. **4.5** If you **clap, lay**, or **set eyes on** someone, you see them. EG *She was the most extraordinary person I had ever laid eyes on.* **4.6** If you **cry** your **eyes out**, you cry a lot. **4.7** If someone **has** their **eye on** you, they are watching you and making judgements about you. **4.8** If you say that something is true **in** a particular person's **eyes**, you mean that this is that person's opinion. EG *Her children could do no wrong in her eyes.* **4.9** If you **keep** your **eyes open** or if you **keep an eye out for** something, you are looking or watching for it carefully. EG *You'll have to keep your eyes open for trouble tonight.* **4.10** If you **keep an eye on** someone or something, you watch them and make sure that they are safe. EG *Can you keep an eye on the baby while I go shopping?* **4.11** If you say that there is **more** to a situation **than meets the eye**, you mean that it is more complicated than you originally thought. **4.12** If an event **opens** your **eyes**, it makes you aware that something is different from the way you thought it was. **4.13** If you don't **see eye to eye** with someone, you don't agree with them. **4.14** If you **shut** or **close** your **eyes to** something, you ignore it. EG *It is foolish to shut our eyes to the effects of unemployment.* **4.15** If you are **up to** your **eyes in** something, you are extremely busy dealing with it. EG *Sal is still up to her eyes in kids and housework.* **4.16** to **turn a blind eye**: see **blind**. PHRASES Outdated Informal

eyeball /ˈaɪbɔːl/, **eyeballs.** Your **eyeballs** are the N COUNT
parts of your eyes that are like white balls.

eyebrow /ˈaɪbraʊ/, **eyebrows.** Your **eyebrows** N COUNT
are the lines of hair which grow in an arch above
each of your eyes. See picture at THE HUMAN BODY.
● If something causes you to **raise an eyebrow** or ● PHRASE
to **raise** your **eyebrows**, it causes you to feel
surprised, shocked, or disapproving. EG *Eyebrows
were raised at their behaviour.*

eye-catching. Something that is **eye-catching** is ADJ QUALIT
very noticeable. EG *...an eye-catching poster.*

eyelash /ˈaɪlæʃ/, **eyelashes.** Your **eyelashes** are N COUNT
the hairs which grow on the edges of your upper
and lower eyelids.

eyelid /ˈaɪlɪd/, **eyelids. 1** Your **eyelids** are the two N COUNT
flaps of skin which cover your eyes when they are
closed.

2 If you **don't bat an eyelid** when something PHRASE
happens, you remain completely calm and are not Informal
at all shocked or surprised. EG *She didn't bat an
eyelid when she was given the bill.*

eye-opener. If you say that something is an **eye-** N SING : an+N
opener, you mean that you find it very surprising Informal
and that you have learned something from it which
you did not know before. EG *The book is quite an
eye-opener.*

eye-shadow is a substance which women put on N UNCOUNT
their eyelids in order to make them a different
colour.

eyesight /ˈaɪsaɪt/. Your **eyesight** is your ability to N UNCOUNT
see. EG *His eyesight was excellent.*

eyesore /ˈaɪsɔː/, **eyesores.** If you say that some- N COUNT
thing is an **eyesore**, you mean that it is extremely
ugly. EG *It's an architectural eyesore.*

eye-witness /ˈaɪwɪtnɪs/, **eye-witnesses.** An **eye-** N COUNT
witness is a person who has seen an event and can
therefore describe it, for example in a law court. EG
*'Planes plunged down from the skies,' recalled one
eyewitness.*

F f

F, f /ɛf/, **Fs, f's. 1 F** is the sixth letter of the N COUNT
English alphabet.
2 F is an abbreviation for 'Fahrenheit'.

fable /ˈfeɪbəl/, **fables.** A **fable** is a traditional N COUNT
story that is intended to teach a moral lesson and
often has animals as its main characters. EG *...a
children's fable.*

fabric /ˈfæbrɪk/, **fabrics. 1** A **fabric** is a type of N MASS
cloth or material. EG *...silks and other soft fabrics...
...a bit of fabric.*
2 The **fabric** of a society or system is its structure N SING :
and the customs that make it work successfully. EG the+N+of
...the priests who upheld the fabric of Roman Formal
society.
3 The **fabric** of a building is its walls, roof, and N SING :
other parts. EG *This amount was enough to main-* the+N+of
tain the fabric of the house. Formal

fabricate /ˈfæbrɪkeɪt/, **fabricates, fabricating,
fabricated. 1** If you **fabricate** information, you V+O
invent it in order to deceive people. EG *They* Formal
fabricated evidence and threatened witnesses.
◊ **fabrication** /fæbrɪˈkeɪʃən/, **fabrications.** EG ◊ N COUNT OR
The story was a fabrication... ...how truth differs N UNCOUNT
from falsehood and fabrication.
2 When objects **are fabricated**, they are made. EG V+O
New parts had to be fabricated out of scrap iron. Formal
◊ **fabrication.** EG *...the fabrication of metals and* ◊ N UNCOUNT
alloys.

fabulous /ˈfæbjʊləs/. **1** If you say that something ADJ QUALIT
is **fabulous**, you are expressing your admiration or Informal
approval of it. EG *What a fabulous place this is!*
2 If you talk about someone's **fabulous** wealth or ADJ CLASSIF :
fabulous beauty, you mean that they are extreme- ATTRIB
ly wealthy or beautiful. EG *...a woman of fabulous
beauty.* ◊ **fabulously.** EG *...a fabulously rich fami-* ◊ SUBMOD
ly.
3 Fabulous is also used to describe things that ADJ CLASSIF :
occur in traditional stories but are not real or true. ATTRIB
EG *...fabulous beasts.* Formal

facade /fəˈsɑːd/, **facades;** also spelled **façade.**
1 The **facade** of a large building is the outside N COUNT
surface of its front wall. EG *...the ornate facade of
the Palace.*
2 You say that something is a **facade** when it gives N SING
a wrong impression of the true nature of a situation. EG *...the grim facts behind the facade of
gaiety... The unity of the Party was a facade.*

face /feɪs/, **faces, facing, faced. 1** Your **face** is N COUNT
the front of your head from your chin to your
forehead. EG *Her face was sad... ...the expression on
her face... The wind blew snow in her face.*
2 The **face** of a cliff or a mountain is a side of it. EG N COUNT :
...the north face of the Eiger. USU+SUPP
3 The **face** of a clock or watch is the surface with N COUNT
numbers on it, which shows the time.
4 The **face** of a place or organization is its appear- N SING :
ance or nature. EG *The face of a city can change* the+N+of
completely in a year. Literary
5 If someone or something **faces** a particular V+O OR V+A
thing, person, or direction, their front is towards
that thing, person, or direction. EG *The two boys
faced each other... The seats face forward.*
6 If you **face** something difficult or unpleasant, or V+O
if you **are faced** with it, it is going to affect you or
you have to deal with it. EG *It is the biggest problem
he has ever faced... They face a sentence of ten
years in prison... You are faced with a choice.*
7 If you cannot **face** something, you do not feel V+O OR
able to do it or cope with it because it seems so V+-ING : WITH
unpleasant. EG *She could not face speaking to them.* BROAD NEG
8 If you **face** the truth, you accept it, although it is V+O
unpleasant. EG *We simply must face facts... Let's
face it, we all cheat.*
9 Face is also used in these phrases. **9.1** If PHRASES
someone or something is **face down**, their face or
front points downwards. If they are **face up**, their
face or front points upwards. EG *Philip lay face
down on the floor.* **9.2** If two people are **face to
face**, they are looking directly at each other. EG *I
suddenly came face to face with Karen.* **9.3** If you
are brought **face to face** with an unpleasant fact,
you cannot avoid it and have to deal with it. EG *It
brings patients face to face with their problems.* **9.4**
If you cannot **look** someone **in the face**, you are
too ashamed or embarrassed to look at them
directly. **9.5** If you say something **to** someone's
face, you say it directly to them, rather than when
they are not there. **9.6** To **show** your **face** some-

where means to go there. EG *She never showed her face in the town again.* **9.7** If you **make** or **pull a face**, you put on an ugly expression to show that you dislike something or to annoy someone. EG *She made monstrous faces at me.* **9.8** If you **lose face**, people lose respect for you. EG *He is afraid that he will lose face with the boss.* **9.9** If you do something to **save face**, you do it in order to avoid losing people's respect. EG **9.10** If you do something **in the face of** a particular problem or difficulty, you do it even though this problem or difficulty exists. EG *They carry on smiling in the face of adversity.* **9.11** If an action or belief **flies in the face of** accepted ideas, it seems to oppose or contradict them. EG *This proposal flies in the face of so many British political traditions.* **9.12** If you talk about **the face of the earth** or **the face of the world**, you mean the whole world. EG *...if men were to disappear from the face of the earth.* **9.13** You say **on the face of it** to indicate that you are describing what something seems to be like and that its real nature may be different. EG *On the face of it, it sounds like a good idea.* **9.14 at face value:** see **value.**

face up to. If you **face up to** a difficult situation, you accept it and deal with it. EG *They had to face up to many setbacks.* PHRASAL VB : V+ADV+PREP

faceless /ˈfeɪslɪs/. If you describe people as **faceless**, you mean that they are dull and boring and have no character or individuality. EG *...faceless bureaucrats in the Civil Service.* ADJ CLASSIF : ATTRIB

face-saving. A **face-saving** action is done in order to avoid losing people's respect. EG *As a face-saving gesture the British let the prisoner go.* ADJ CLASSIF : ATTRIB

facet /ˈfæsɪt/, **facets. 1** A **facet** of something is a part or aspect of it. EG *...every facet of their lives... ...an interesting facet of his character.* N COUNT

2 The **facets** of an object, especially a precious stone, are the flat surfaces on its outside. N COUNT

facetious /fəˈsiːʃəs/. You say that someone is being **facetious** when they make humorous remarks in a serious situation. EG *Mrs Pringle ignored this facetious interruption.* ◊ **facetiously.** EG *Frank suggested facetiously that we all go home.* ADJ QUALIT ◊ ADV

facial /ˈfeɪʃəl/ is used to describe things that relate to your face. EG *...facial muscles... ...changes in facial expression.* ADJ CLASSIF : ATTRIB

facile /ˈfæsaɪl/. A **facile** remark or argument is a simple and obvious one, rather than one that has been carefully thought about. EG *It would be facile to call it a conspiracy.* ADJ QUALIT

facilitate /fəˈsɪlɪteɪt/, **facilitates, facilitating, facilitated.** To **facilitate** an action or process means to make it easier for it to happen or be done. EG *...legislation to facilitate the sale of homes.* V+O Formal

facility /fəˈsɪlɪtɪ/, **facilities. 1 Facilities** are buildings or pieces of equipment which are provided for a particular purpose. EG *...the lack of play facilities for young children.* N COUNT : USU PLURAL +SUPP

2 A **facility** is an additional feature or service which is useful but not essential. EG *This tape recorder has a tape-slide facility.* N COUNT+SUPP

3 If you have a **facility** for something, you find it easy to do it well. EG *Meehan began to learn German and, having a facility for languages, was soon fluent in it.* N COUNT OR N UNCOUNT Formal

facsimile /fækˈsɪmɪlɪ/, **facsimiles.** A **facsimile** of something is an exact model or copy of it. EG *The Morning Star produced a facsimile of the letter.* N COUNT

fact /fækt/, **facts. 1** A **fact** is **1.1** a statement or piece of information that is true. EG *The report is full of facts and figures... He told me a few facts about her.* **1.2** a situation that exists or something that happened. EG *There was little warmth, owing to the fact that Smithy had left the door open... ...the fact of belonging to a certain race... ...to investigate the facts of the killing.* N COUNT

2 If you say that a story or statement is **fact**, you mean that it is true. EG *How much of the novel is fiction and how much is fact?* N UNCOUNT

3 You say **in fact, in point of fact, in actual fact,** or **as a matter of fact 3.1** to emphasize that something really happened or is true. EG *This is, in fact, what happened... In actual fact, we don't have all that much more leisure time than we used to.* **3.2** to introduce some information, especially more precise information. EG *It was terribly cold weather – a blizzard in fact... I don't think she mentioned it. In fact I don't think she knew... As a matter of fact, I just got it this afternoon.* ADV SEN

4 You say **the fact is** before reluctantly telling someone something true. EG *The fact is, we are rivals... The fact is that child rearing is a long, hard job.* PHRASE

5 You say **the fact remains** to emphasize what you think is important in a situation or argument. EG *We may have forgotten their true meaning but the fact remains that they exist.* PHRASE

6 If you say that you know something **for a fact,** you are emphasizing that you know that it is true. EG *I know for a fact that there's a place free.* PHRASE

faction /ˈfækʃən/, **factions.** A **faction** is an organized group of people within a larger group, who oppose some of the ideas of the larger group. EG *...arguments between rival factions.* N COLL

factor /ˈfæktə/, **factors.** A **factor** is one of the things that affects an event, decision, or situation. EG *Confidence is the key factor in any successful career... ...social and economic factors.* N COUNT+SUPP

factory /ˈfæktərɪ/, **factories.** A **factory** is a large building or group of buildings where machines are used to make goods in large quantities. EG *...a furniture factory... ...factory workers.* N COUNT

factual /ˈfæktʃʊəl/. Something that is **factual** contains or refers to facts and not theories or opinions. EG *...a factual account... ...an enormous amount of factual information.* ◊ **factually.** EG *...a factually accurate pamphlet.* ADJ CLASSIF ◊ ADV

faculty /ˈfækəltɪ/, **faculties. 1** Your **faculties** are your physical and mental abilities. EG *She was in full command of all her faculties... ...the faculty of imagination.* N COUNT

2 A **faculty** in a university or college is a group of related departments. EG *...the Arts Faculty... ...the Faculty of Engineering.* N COUNT

fad /fæd/, **fads.** A **fad** is something which is very popular for a short period of time. EG *The interest in things Japanese is not just a passing fad.* N COUNT

fade /feɪd/, **fades, fading, faded. 1** When a coloured object **fades,** it gradually becomes paler in colour. EG *The wallpaper may have faded.* ◊ **faded.** EG *...an old man in a faded blue shirt.* V-ERG ◊ ADJ QUALIT

2 When something that you are looking at **fades,** it slowly becomes less bright or clear until you cannot see it any longer. EG *Already the mountains are fading in the evening light.* V

3 When the light **fades,** it becomes darker, because the sun is going down. EG *The afternoon light was fading.* V

4 When a sound **fades,** it slowly becomes less loud until you cannot hear it. EG *The applause faded.* V

5 When a feeling, memory, or quality **fades,** it slowly becomes less intense. EG *My anger faded... Interest in the story will fade.* V

6 When someone's smile **fades,** they slowly stop smiling. V

fade away or **fade out.** When something **fades away** or **fades out,** it slowly becomes less intense or strong until it ends completely. EG *Your enthusiasm for running will soon fade away... The sound of the chopper had faded out... This sort of protest tends to fade out quickly.* PHRASAL VB : V+ADV

faeces /ˈfiːsiːz/; spelled **feces** in American English. **Faeces** is the solid waste that people get rid of from their body when they go to the toilet. N UNCOUNT Formal

fag /fæg/, **fags. 1** In British English, a **fag** is a cigarette. EG *...a packet of fags.* N COUNT Informal

2 In American English, a **fag** is a homosexual man; an offensive use. N COUNT Informal

faggot /fǽgət/, **faggots.** In American English, a ⬦ N COUNT
faggot is a homosexual man; an offensive use. Informal

Fahrenheit /fǽrənhəait/ is a scale for measuring N UNCOUNT
temperature, in which water freezes at 32 degrees
and boils at 212 degrees. EG ...*a temperature of 50°*
Fahrenheit.

fail /feɪl/, **fails, failing, failed.** 1 If someone **fails** V : USU + *to*-INF
to do something that they were trying to do, they
do not succeed in doing it. EG *Their party failed to*
win a single seat... The attempt to bribe the clerk
had failed. ⬦ **failed.** EG *He was a failed novelist* ⬦ ADJ CLASSIF :
and poet. ATTRIB

2 If someone **fails** to do something that they should V + *to*-INF
have done, they do not do it. EG *He was fined for*
failing to complete the census form.

3 If someone **fails** a test or examination, they do V + O OR V
not reach the standard that is required. EG *I passed*
the written part but failed the oral section.

4 If something **fails**, it stops working or functioning V
properly. EG *Her lighter failed... ...people whose*
sight is failing.

5 If someone **fails** you, they do not do what you V + O
expected or trusted them to do. EG *Our leaders have*
failed us.

6 If a quality or ability that you have **fails** you, you V + O OR V
lose it just when you need it. EG *At the last minute*
his courage failed him... His usually inventive im-
agination had failed for once.

failing /feɪlɪŋ/, **failings.** 1 A **failing** is a fault or N COUNT
unsatisfactory feature. EG *The present system has*
many failings... Being rude was one of Cindy's
failings.

2 If someone has **failing** health or **failing** eye- ADJ CLASSIF :
sight, their health or eyesight is getting worse. EG ATTRIB
He had given up his job because of failing health.

3 You say **'failing that'** to introduce an alterna- ADV SEN
tive, in case what you previously said is not possible. EG *Wear your national dress or, failing that, a*
suit.

failure /feɪljə/, **failures.** 1 **Failure** is a lack of N UNCOUNT
success in doing or achieving something. EG ...*a*
desperate initiative which ended in failure.

2 Someone who is a **failure** has not succeeded at N COUNT
something or at anything. EG *I felt such a failure.*

3 If something is a **failure**, it is unsuccessful. EG N COUNT
The meeting was a failure.

4 Someone's **failure** to do something is the fact N UNCOUNT
that they do not do it although they were expected + *to*-INF
to. EG *His friends remarked on his failure to appear*
at the party.

5 When there is a **failure**, something stops work- N UNCOUNT
ing or does not do what it is supposed to do. EG OR N COUNT
...*engine failure... ...the failure of the bank where he* + SUPP
kept his money.

6 If you have a **failure** of an ability or quality that N UNCOUNT
you normally have, you lose it. EG ...*a failure of* OR N COUNT
imagination... ...a sudden failure of nerve. + SUPP

faint /feɪnt/, **fainter, faintest; faints, fainting,**
fainted. 1 Something that is **faint** is not at all ADJ QUALIT
strong or intense. EG *There was a faint smell of*
gas... Her cries grew fainter... ...a faint hope.

2 A **faint** action is one that is done without much ADJ QUALIT
effort or enthusiasm. EG ...*a few faint protests... Her*
lips parted in a faint smile.

3 If you **faint**, you lose consciousness for a short V
time. EG *He nearly fainted from the pain.*

4 Someone who feels **faint** feels dizzy and un- ADJ QUALIT
steady.

5 You can use **faintest** in negative sentences to ADJ QUALIT :
emphasize the total absence of something. EG *He* SUPERL,
didn't have the faintest idea what to do... I never ONLY ATTRIB
felt the faintest desire to cry.

faintly /feɪntli¹/. 1 You can use **faintly** to indicate ADV + ADJ
that something is true only to a very slight degree.
EG *It was faintly possible.*

2 If something happens **faintly**, it happens with ADV
very little strength or intensity. EG *She turned and*
smiled faintly.

fair /feə/, **fairer, fairest; fairs.** 1 Something or ADJ QUALIT
someone that is **fair** is reasonable, right, and just.
EG *It wouldn't be fair to disturb the children... This*
isn't fair on anyone... ...a fairer share of profits...
She won't get a fair trial. ● You can say **to be fair** ● PHRASE
before making a statement which corrects a previ-
ous unfavourable and exaggerated one. EG *Well, to*
be fair, it only happened once.

2 You say **fair enough 2.1** to indicate that you PHRASE
accept what has been said or done so far, but that
you think more needs to be said or done. EG *All this*
is fair enough, but it touches only the surface of the
problem. **2.2** to indicate that you agree to what CONVENTION
someone has just said. EG ...*Thursday, yes, fair*
enough.

3 **Fair** also means **3.1** quite large. EG *We've got a* ADJ CLASSIF :
fair number of postgraduate students... ...a fair- ATTRIB
sized bedroom. **3.2** quite good. EG *I've think I've got* ADJ QUALIT :
a fair chance of evading them altogether. USU ATTRIB

4 A **fair** guess or idea is one that is likely to be ADJ QUALIT :
correct. EG *I had a pretty fair idea of the answer to* ATTRIB
this question.

5 Someone who is **fair** or who has **fair** hair has ADJ QUALIT
light, gold-coloured hair. EG *She was fair and blue-*
eyed.

6 **Fair** skin is pale in colour. EG *Unprotected fair* ADJ QUALIT
skin gets sunburned quickly.

7 When the weather is **fair**, it is not cloudy or ADJ CLASSIF
rainy. EG *It will be fair and warm.* Formal

8 A **fair** is **8.1** an event held in a park or field at N COUNT
which people pay to ride on various machines for British
amusement or try to win prizes in games. EG ...*the*
doll I won at the fair. **8.2** an event at which people British
display or sell goods. EG ...*the Leipzig Trade Fair.*

9 See also **fair play.**

fairground /feəgraund/, **fairgrounds.** A **fair-** N COUNT
ground is an area of land where a fair is being
held.

fairly /feəli¹/. 1 **Fairly** means to quite a large SUBMOD
degree. EG *The information was fairly accurate... I*
wrote the first part fairly quickly.

2 If something is said or done **fairly**, the statement ADV
or action is reasonable and just. EG *The car could*
fairly be described as sluggish and noisy... We want
it to be fairly distributed.

fairness /feənəs/. 1 **Fairness** is the quality of N UNCOUNT
being reasonable and just. EG *Even a child sees the*
fairness of reasonable penalties.

2 You say **in all fairness**, or **in fairness to** ADV SEN
someone, before a statement that corrects or balances a previous unfavourable one. EG *In all fair-*
ness, I must say that I was not the only one... Yet in
fairness to him, one must add that he was often
correct.

fair play. If you want **fair play**, you want every- N UNCOUNT
one to be treated in a reasonable and just way. EG
They appealed to his sense of fair play.

fairy /feəri¹/, **fairies. Fairies** are small, imagi- N COUNT
nary creatures with magical powers. They are
usually said to look like tiny girls with wings.

fairy tale, fairy tales. A **fairy tale** or a **fairy** N COUNT
story is a story for children involving magical
events and imaginary creatures such as fairies.

fait accompli /feɪt ɔ³kɒmpliː/. If something is a N SING
fait accompli, it has already been done and Formal
cannot be changed. EG *You've presented us with a*
fait accompli.

faith /feɪθ/, **faiths.** 1 If you have **faith** in someone N UNCOUNT :
or something, you feel confident and hopeful about USU + *in*
their ability or goodness. EG *I had faith in Alan – I*
knew he could take care of me.

2 A **faith** is a particular religion, such as Christian- N COUNT
ity or Buddhism. EG ...*its tolerant attitude to other*
faiths.

If you fall into a particular group, do you hurt
yourself?

3 Faith is also strong religious belief. EG *...the* N UNCOUNT *power of faith... ...her deep religious faith.*

4 If you break **faith** with someone, you fail to N UNCOUNT behave in the way that you promised or were expected to. If you keep **faith** with them, you continue to behave as you promised or were expected to. EG *They were forced to break faith with millions of decent, hard working citizens.*

5 If you do something **in good faith**, you sincerely PHRASE believe that it is the right thing to do in the circumstances. EG *The two doctors were acting in good faith.*

faithful /feɪθful/. **1** If you are **faithful** to a person, ADJ QUALIT organization, or idea, you remain firm in your support for them. EG *Bond remained faithful to his old teacher.* ◊ **faithfully.** EG *The party rallied* ◊ ADV *round him faithfully.*

2 People who firmly support a particular religion N PLURAL : or political party are sometimes referred to as the the+N **faithful.** EG *The bishop was condemned because he had led the faithful astray.*

3 Someone who is **faithful** to their husband, wife, ADJ CLASSIF or lover does not have a sexual relationship with anyone else. EG *She has been a faithful wife to him.*

4 A **faithful** account, translation, or adaptation of a ADJ QUALIT book represents the facts or the original book accurately. EG *Do you think the film was faithful to the book?* ◊ **faithfully.** EG *Their activities were* ◊ ADV *faithfully described in the newspapers.*

faithfully /feɪθfəˈliː/. You write **Yours faithfully** CONVENTION before your signature at the end of a formal letter, when you have started the letter with 'Dear Sir' or 'Dear Madam'.

fake /feɪk/, **fakes, faking, faked. 1** A **fake** is N COUNT something that is made to look like something valuable or real in order to deceive people. EG *They swore that the pictures were fakes.* ▸ used as an ▸ ADJ CLASSIF adjective. EG *...a fake passport.*

2 If someone **fakes** something, they make it look v+o like something valuable or real in order to deceive people. EG *...faking the fine furniture of the century before.* ◊ **faked.** EG *...faked pictures.* ◊ ADJ CLASSIF

3 Someone who is a **fake** is not the type of person N COUNT that they pretend to be. EG *I admit I'm a fake.*

4 If you **fake** a feeling or reaction, you pretend v+o that you are experiencing it when you are not. EG *Thomas faked a yawn.*

falcon /fɔːlkən/, **falcons.** A **falcon** is a bird of N COUNT prey that can be trained to hunt other birds and animals.

fall /fɔːl/, **falls, falling, fell** /fel/, **fallen** /fɔːlən/.

1 If someone or something **falls**, they move quick- v : USU+A ly downwards or towards the ground. EG *The cup fell from her hand and shattered on the floor... Tears fell from Mother's eyes... Part of the ceiling fell down... A bomb had fallen on the school.* ▸ used ▸ N SING as a noun. EG *He was rushed to hospital after a 40-foot fall.*

2 If someone or something that is standing **falls**, v they accidentally move or are pushed from their upright position so that they end up lying on the ground. EG *She lost her balance and fell... He tripped and fell down... ...a falling tree.* ▸ used as a ▸ N COUNT noun. EG *He asked her if she had had a fall.*

◊ **fallen.** EG *...to rescue people trapped inside* ◊ ADJ CLASSIF : *fallen buildings.* ATTRIB

3 When rain or snow **falls**, it comes down from the v sky. EG *The snow was still falling.*

4 If people in a position of power **fall**, they v suddenly lose that position. EG *The regime had fallen.* ▸ used as a noun. EG *This led to the* ▸ N SING+POSS *Government's fall.*

5 If a place **falls** in a war or election, an enemy v army or a different political party takes control of it. EG *Greater London will fall to Labour.* ▸ used as ▸ N SING+POSS a noun. EG *...the fall of France.*

6 If someone **falls** in battle, they are killed. EG *...the* v : USU+A *brave young men who have fallen in the struggle.* Literary

7 If something **falls** in amount, value, or strength, v

it decreases. EG *The value of the dollar has fallen... Their voices could be heard rising and falling.* ▸ used as a noun. EG *...a fall in moral standards.* ▸ N SING

◊ **falling.** EG *Some nations were uneasy about their* ◊ ADJ CLASSIF *falling birth rates.*

8 If silence or a feeling of sadness or tiredness v : USU+A **falls** on a group of people, they become silent, sad, Written or tired. EG *An expectant hush fell on the gathering.*

9 When light or shadow **falls** on something, it v+A covers it. EG *A shadow fell over her book and she looked up.*

10 When night or darkness **falls**, night begins and v it becomes dark.

11 You can use **fall** to show that someone or v+C OR V+A something passes into another state. For example, if someone **falls** ill, they become ill. EG *After a while I fell asleep... The crowd fell silent... Their ideas had fallen into disuse... He fell in love with her.*

12 If you say that something **falls** into a particular v+A group or category, you mean that it belongs in that group or category. EG *Human beings fall into two types.*

13 You can refer to a waterfall as the **falls**. EG N PLURAL *...Niagara Falls.*

14 Fall is the season between summer and winter. N UNCOUNT In the fall the weather becomes cooler. EG *In the* OR N COUNT *fall of 1941 he appointed a committee.* American

15 Fall is also used in these phrases. **15.1** If PHRASES something **falls to bits** or **falls to pieces**, it breaks into pieces because it is old or badly made. EG *The boots had all fallen to bits.* **15.2** If something **falls open**, it opens accidentally. EG *Ellen's mouth fell open and she began to snore.* **15.3** If someone's **face falls**, they suddenly look upset or disappointed. **15.4** to **fall flat**: see **flat.** ● to **fall into place**: see **place.**

fall about. If you say that people **are falling** PHRASAL VB : **about**, you mean that they are very amused by V+ADV something. EG *When he complained, they fell about* Informal *laughing.*

fall apart. 1 If something **falls apart**, it breaks PHRASAL VB : into pieces because it is old or badly made. EG V+ADV *...cheap beds that fell apart.* **2** If an organization or system **falls apart**, it becomes disorganized and unable to work effectively. EG *The nation is falling apart.*

fall away. If something **falls away** from the PHRASAL VB : surface that it is attached to, it breaks off. EG V+ADV *Patches of plaster had fallen away between the windows.*

fall back. If you **fall back**, you move quickly PHRASAL VB : away from someone or something. EG *I saw my* V+ADV *husband fall back in horror.*

fall back on. If you **fall back on** something, you PHRASAL VB : do it or use it after other things have failed. EG V+ADV+PREP *Often you give up and fall back on easier solutions.*

fall behind. If you **fall behind**, you do not make PHRASAL VB : progress or move forward as fast as other people. V+ADV EG *...children who fall behind with their reading.*

fall for. 1 If you **fall for** someone, you are PHRASAL VB : strongly attracted to them and start loving them. V+PREP EG *Richard fell for her the moment he set eyes on her.* **2** If you **fall for** a lie or trick, you believe it v+PREP even though it is not true. EG *The working class* Informal *were not going to fall for this one.*

fall in. If a roof or ceiling **falls in**, it collapses PHRASAL VB : and falls to the ground. V+ADV

fall in with. If you **fall in with** an idea, plan, or PHRASAL VB : system, you accept it and do not try to change it. EG V+ADV+PREP *Instead of challenging the lie, she falls in with it.*

fall off. If the degree, amount, or rate of some- PHRASAL VB : thing **falls off**, it decreases. EG *We knew that the* V+ADV *numbers of overseas students would fall off drastically.* ● See also **falling-off.**

fall on or **fall upon.** If your eyes **fall on** some- PHRASAL VB : thing or **fall upon** it, you suddenly see or notice it. V+PREP EG *His gaze fell on a small white bundle.*

fall out. 1 If something such as a person's hair or PHRASAL VB : V+ADV a tooth **falls out**, it becomes loose and separates from their body. EG *After about two weeks, the victim's hair starts to fall out.* **2** If you **fall out** with someone, you have an argument and stop being friendly with them. EG *I've fallen out with certain members of the band.* **3** See also **fallout**. `V+ADV OR V+ADV+with : RECIP`

fall over. 1 If someone or something that is standing **falls over**, they accidentally move or are pushed from their upright position so that they end up lying on the ground. EG *He pushed back his chair so hard that it fell over.* **2** If you **are falling over yourself** to do something, you are very keen to do it. EG *Producers were falling over themselves to hire girls who had acting experience.* `PHRASAL VB : V+ADV` `PHRASE Informal`

fall through. If an arrangement **falls through**, it fails to happen. EG *We wanted to book a villa but it fell through.* `PHRASAL VB : V+ADV`

fall to. If a responsibility or duty **falls to** someone, it becomes their responsibility or duty. EG *It fell to Philip Crow to act the part of host.* `PHRASAL VB : V+PREP Formal`

fall upon. See **fall on**.

fallacious /fəleɪʃəs/. A **fallacious** idea or argument is wrong because it is based on incorrect information or a fault in logic. EG *This point of view is exposed as fallacious by Emerson.* `ADJ CLASSIF Formal`

fallacy /fæləsɪ/, **fallacies.** A **fallacy** is an idea or argument which is incorrect or illogical. EG *It is a fallacy that women are more pure-minded than men... I spotted the fallacy in the argument.* `N COUNT Formal`

fallen /fɔːlən/ is the past participle of **fall.**

fallible /fælɪˈbəᵊl/. **1** If you say that someone is **fallible**, you mean that their judgement or knowledge is not perfect and they may make mistakes. **2** If you say that something is **fallible**, you mean that it is not perfect and may be wrong or unreliable. EG *Mary was conscious how fallible this method was.* `ADJ QUALIT Formal` `ADJ QUALIT Formal`

falling-off. If there is a **falling-off** in something, it decreases. EG *A falling-off in business was expected.* `N SING`

fallout /fɔːlaʊt/ is the radiation that affects an area after a nuclear explosion. `N UNCOUNT`

fallow /fæləʊ/. If land is lying **fallow**, it has been dug or ploughed but no crops have been planted in it, so that the soil has a chance to rest and improve. EG *...plots of fallow land.* `ADJ CLASSIF`

false /fɔls, fɔːls/. **1** If a statement is **false**, it is not true. EG *What you're saying is false.* ◊ **falsely.** EG *...falsely accusing him of a crime.* **2** If an idea or action is **false**, it is based on wrong information or beliefs. EG *I had a false impression of him... ...to save her from false imprisonment.* **3** **False** things are **3.1** made so that they appear real although they are not. EG *...false teeth... ...false eyelashes.* **3.2** intended to deceive people. EG *She travelled under a false name.* ● **under false pretences**: see **pretence**. **4** Behaviour that is **false** is not sincere and is often intended to deceive people. EG *...a false smile... ...false modesty.* ◊ **falsely.** EG *She laughed, falsely, to cheer him up.* `ADJ CLASSIF` `◊ ADV` `ADJ CLASSIF` `ADJ CLASSIF : USU ATTRIB` `ADJ QUALIT` `◊ ADV`

false alarm, false alarms. When you are warned of something dangerous and it does not happen, you say that the warning was a **false alarm.** `N COUNT`

falsehood /fɔlshʊd, fɔːl-/, **falsehoods. 1** The **falsehood** of something is the fact that it is untrue. EG *We must establish the truth or falsehood of the various rumours.* **2** A **falsehood** is a lie. EG *...exaggerations and falsehoods about the Indians.* `N UNCOUNT Formal` `N COUNT Formal`

false start, false starts. A **false start** is **1** an attempt to start something which fails because you were not properly ready to begin. EG *...natural speech with all its hesitations and false starts.* **2** a beginning of a race when one competitor moves before the starter has given the signal. `N COUNT`

falsetto /fɒlsɛtəʊ/, **falsettos.** If a man speaks or sings in a **falsetto**, he uses a high-pitched voice. EG `N COUNT`

I heard him singing in a clear, high falsetto... ...a falsetto whine.

falsify /fɔlsɪfaɪ, fɔːl-/, **falsifies, falsifying, falsified.** If someone **falsifies** information, they change it so that it is no longer true or correct, in order to deceive people. EG *The facts concerning my birth have been falsified.* ◊ **falsification** /fɔlsɪfɪkeɪʃᵊn, fɔːl-/, **falsifications.** EG *...falsification of accounts.* `V+O` `◊ N UNCOUNT OR N COUNT`

falsity /fɒlsɪˈtɪ, fɔːl-/. The **falsity** of something is the fact that it is untrue. EG *...the falsity of this evidence.* `N UNCOUNT`

falter /fɒltə, fɔːltə/, **falters, faltering, faltered. 1** If something **falters**, it becomes weaker or slower in an uneven way and may stop completely. EG *The engines faltered and the plane lost height... The organization's progress faltered.* **2** If you **falter**, **2.1** you lose confidence in what you are doing. EG *From that moment onwards he never faltered in his resolve.* **2.2** you stop saying something, because you are nervous or unhappy. EG *'Would you –' Rey faltered.* **2.3** you stop moving easily and start moving slowly and with difficulty. EG *Looking to his left, he saw Percy faltering.* `V` `V : OFT+in` `V OR V+QUOTE` `V`

fame /feɪm/. If you achieve **fame**, you become well known and admired by many people. EG *She was jealous of Ellen's fame... He rose rapidly to fame.* `N UNCOUNT`

famed /feɪmd/. If you are **famed** for something, you are well known and admired because of it. EG *The women there were famed for the pots they made... ...a great church, famed for its flower festivals.* `ADJ QUALIT : OFT+for Literary`

familial /fəmɪlɪəl/ means concerning families in general or one particular family. EG *...social and familial influences.* `ADJ CLASSIF : ATTRIB Formal`

familiar /fəmɪljə/. **1** If someone or something is **familiar** to you, you recognize them or know them well because you have seen, heard, or experienced them before. EG *His name was familiar to me... ...my pleasure at seeing all the familiar faces again.* ◊ **familiarity** /fəmɪlæˈrɪˈtɪ/. EG *...the familiarity of the surroundings.* **2** If you are **familiar** with something, you know it well. EG *I am of course familiar with your work.* ◊ **familiarity.** EG *...his familiarity with the system gave him a considerable advantage.* **3** If you behave in a **familiar** way towards someone, you treat them very informally like a close friend, so that you may offend them if they are not a close friend. EG *...disliking intensely the burly man's familiar tone.* ◊ **familiarly.** EG *He spoke of them casually and familiarly by their first names.* ◊ **familiarity.** EG *They greeted him with familiarity.* `ADJ QUALIT : OFT+to` `◊ N UNCOUNT` `ADJ PRED +with` `◊ N UNCOUNT +with` `ADJ QUALIT` `◊ ADV` `◊ N UNCOUNT`

familiarize /fəmɪljəraɪz/, **familiarizes, familiarizing, familiarized;** also spelled **familiarise.** If you **familiarize** yourself with something, or if someone **familiarizes** you with it, you learn all about it and get to know it. EG *He had to familiarize himself with the ship.* `V-REFL+with OR V+O+with`

family /fæmɪˈlɪ/, **families. 1** A **family** is a group of people who are related to each other, especially parents and their children. EG *...an English family on holiday... ...the Barrett family... He showed me photographs of his family... ...help offered by family and friends.* **2** When people talk about their **family**, they can also mean **2.1** their children. EG *...raising a family... ...mothers with large families... She has no family of her own.* **2.2** one line of their ancestors. EG *Her mother's family had lived there for generations.* **3** You can use **family** to describe **3.1** things that belong to a particular family. EG *Ben worked in the family business.* **3.2** things that are designed to be `N COLL N UNCOUNT` `N COLL N UNCOUNT` `N COLL` `N MOD`

Do you plant a family tree?

used or enjoyed by both parents and children. EG ...a *family car... ...family entertainment.*

4 A **family** of animals or plants is a group of N COUNT+SUPP related species. EG *It is a member of the sparrow family.*

family planning is the practice of using contra- N UNCOUNT ception to control the number of children in a family. EG ...*family planning clinics.*

family tree, family trees. A **family tree** is a N COUNT chart that shows all the people in your family over many generations and their relationships with one another.

famine /fæmɪn/, **famines**. **Famine** is a serious N UNCOUNT shortage of food in a country, which may cause OR N COUNT many deaths. EG ...*the effects of famine and drought... ...a severe famine.*

famished /fæmɪʃt/. If you say that you are **fam-** ADJ CLASSIF **ished**, you mean that you are very hungry. Informal

famous /feɪməs/. Someone or something that is ADJ QUALIT: **famous** is very well known. EG ...*a famous writer...* OFT+for *California is famous for raisins.*

fan /fæn/, **fans, fanning, fanned**. **1** If you are a N COUNT: **fan** of someone or something, you admire them USU+SUPP and support them. EG *I was a Beatles fan... ...football fans.*

2 A **fan** is also **2.1** a flat object that you hold in N COUNT your hand and wave in order to move the air and make yourself cooler. **2.2** a piece of electrical equipment with revolving blades which keeps a room or machine cool or gets rid of unpleasant smells.

3 If you **fan** yourself when you are hot, you wave a V-REFL OR V+O fan or other flat object in order to move the air and make yourself cooler. EG *She took up some sheets of paper and fanned herself with them.*

4 To **fan** a fire means to create a current of air so V+O that the fire burns more strongly. EG *The rush of air fed and fanned the fires.*

5 To **fan** fear, hatred, or passion means to cause V+O people to feel it more strongly. EG *Public hysteria fanned fears of an invasion.*

fan out. When people or things **fan out**, they PHRASAL VB: move forwards together from the same point, V+ADV while moving further apart from each other. EG *The five of us fanned out at intervals of not more than fifteen feet.*

fanatic /fənætɪk/, **fanatics**. **1** A **fanatic** is **1.1** a N COUNT person with strong religious or political beliefs who behaves in an extreme or violent way. **1.2** a person who is very enthusiastic about a subject or activity. EG ...*a sports fanatic.*

2 Fanatic means the same as fanatical. EG ...*a* ADJ QUALIT *fanatic hunter.*

fanatical /fənætɪkᵊl/. Someone who is **fanatical** ADJ QUALIT feels very strongly about something and behaves in an extreme way because of this. EG ...*fanatical rebels... Bill inspired fanatical devotion in his pu-pils.* ◊ **fanatically.** EG *He was fanatically against* ◊ ADV *intervention in the war.*

fanaticism /fənætɪsɪzᵊm/ is fanatical behaviour. N UNCOUNT EG *He took to abstract painting with an obsessive fanaticism.*

fanciful /fænsɪfʊl/. **1 Fanciful** ideas or stories ADJ QUALIT are based on someone's imagination and not on facts or reality. EG *He had heard fanciful tales about their work... It would not be fanciful to say that he hissed.*

2 Something that is **fanciful** is unusual and elabo- ADJ QUALIT rate rather than plain and simple; used showing disapproval. EG ...*fanciful architecture... He consid-ered this name far too fanciful.*

fancy /fænsɪ¹/, **fancies, fancying, fancied; fan-cier, fanciest**. **1** If you **fancy** something, you want V+O OR V+-ING to have it or do it. EG *She fancied a flat of her own...* Informal *I don't fancy going back alone.*

2 If you **fancy** someone, you feel attracted to them V+O in a sexual way. Informal

3 If you **fancy** yourself, you think that you are very V-REFL clever, attractive, or good at something, or think Informal

that you would be good at something if you tried it; used showing disapproval. EG *I've heard that this man Bond fancies himself with a pistol... We all fancied ourselves as leaders.*

4 If you **take a fancy to** someone or something, PHRASE you start liking them, usually for no understand- Informal able reason.

5 If something **takes** your **fancy**, you like it quite a PHRASE lot when you see it or think of it. EG *He paid £50 for* Informal *a painting that had taken his fancy.*

6 You say **'fancy'** when you want to express EXCLAM surprise. EG *Fancy seeing you here!... 'You're in* Informal *hospital.' – 'Well, fancy that.'*

7 If you **fancy** that something is the case, you think V+REPORT: or suppose that it is. EG *I fancied I could hear a* ONLY that *baby screaming.* Formal

8 A **fancy** is an idea that is unlikely or untrue. EG N COUNT OR *His mind was filled with weird fancies... It is* N UNCOUNT *difficult to separate fact from fancy... ...indulging in* Formal *a flight of fancy.*

9 Something that is **fancy** is special, unusual, and ADJ QUALIT elaborate. EG ...*fancy hats... ...good plain food: noth-* Informal *ing fancy.*

fancy dress is clothing that you wear for a party N UNCOUNT at which everyone tries to look like a person from a story, from history, or from a particular profes-sion. EG ...*ladies in fancy dress... ...a fancy dress ball.*

fanfare /fænfeə/, **fanfares**. A **fanfare** is a short, N COUNT loud tune played on trumpets to announce a special event. EG *The Queen's arrival was greeted with a fanfare.*

fang /fæŋ/, **fangs**. An animal's **fangs** are its long, N COUNT sharp teeth. EG *Most snakes withdraw their fangs after striking.*

fanlight /fænlaɪt/, **fanlights**. A **fanlight** is a N COUNT small window above a door.

fantasize /fæntəsaɪz/, **fantasizes, fantasizing**; V: OFT **fantasized**; also spelled **fantasise**. If you **fanta-** +about OR **size**, you think imaginatively about something that V+REPORT: you would like to happen but that is unlikely to ONLY that happen. EG ...*fantasizing about ripping down the iron bars of the jail... She had fantasized that she and Wendy would live in this house.*

fantastic /fæntæstɪk/. **1** People say that some- ADJ QUALIT thing is **fantastic** when they like it or admire it Informal very much. EG *He chewed it and said, 'Fantastic!'... He scored the most fantastic goal I have ever seen.*

2 You use **fantastic** when you want to emphasize ADJ QUALIT: the size, amount, or degree of something. EG ...*a* ATTRIB *fantastic amount of time... ...her fantastic power.* ◊ **fantastically.** EG *They were fantastically strict.* ◊ SUBMOD

3 You can describe something as **fantastic** when it ADJ QUALIT looks strange and wonderful. EG ...*fantastic images of gods.* ◊ **fantastically.** EG ...*fantastically shaped* ◊ SUBMOD *islands.*

4 If you say that a statement or story is **fantastic**, ADJ QUALIT you mean that it is very strange and difficult to believe. EG *He was in love with her – fantastic though that may seem.*

fantasy /fæntəsɪ¹/, **fantasies**. **1** A **fantasy** is a N COUNT situation or event that you think about or imagine, although it is unlikely to happen or be true. EG *That's supposed to be every schoolgirl's fantasy... ...fantasies about suicide.*

2 Fantasy refers to **2.1** stories or situations that N UNCOUNT people create from their imagination and that are OR N COUNT not based on reality. EG *To a child, fantasy and reality are very close to each other... His novels were fantasies.* **2.2** the activity of imagining things. N UNCOUNT EG *Everyone should indulge in fantasy on occasions.*

far /fɑː/, **farther** /fɑːðə/ or **further** /fɜːðə/, **far-thest** /fɑːᵊrᵊst/ or **furthest** /fɜːᵊrᵊst/. See separate entries for **further** and **furthest**. **Farther** and **farthest** are used mainly when talking about dis-tance.

1 If one place, thing, or person is **far** away from ADV another, there is a great distance between them. EG *He sat far away from the others... ...a villa not far*

*from Hotel Miranda... ...clouds drifting far above...
...a little farther south.*

2 If you ask how **far** away a place is, you are ADV
asking how great a distance away it is. If you ask
how **far** someone went, you are asking what
distance they travelled or what place they
reached. EG *How far is Amity from here?... Vita
went as far as Bologna.*

3 When there are two similar things somewhere, ADJ CLASSIF:
the **far** one is the one that is a greater distance ATTRIB
away from you. EG *...the far end of the room.*

4 You can use **far** to refer to the part of an area ADJ CLASSIF:
that is the greatest distance from the centre in a ATTRIB
particular direction. For example, the **far** north of
a country is the part that is the greatest distance to
the north. EG *...on the far right of the page.*

5 If something happens **far and wide**, it happens PHRASE
in a lot of places or over a large area. EG *People
would come from far and wide to hear him.*

6 A time or event that is **far** in the future or the ADV+ADV OR
past is a long time from the present. EG *The Fourth* ADV+PREP
*of July isn't far off... ...as far back as the twelfth
century.*

7 You can use **far** to indicate the extent or degree ADV
to which something happens. EG *Prices will not
come down very far... None of us would trust them
very far... ...using her methods as far as possible.*

8 If you ask or say how **far** someone or something ADV
gets or goes, you are talking about their level of
achievement or progress. EG *How far have you got
in developing this?... Selling programmes, that's
about as far as it goes.*

9 If you say that someone is going **too far**, you PHRASE
mean that they are behaving in an unacceptable or
extreme way. EG *The press went too far and
suffered accordingly.*

10 If you say that someone **goes so far as** to do PHRASE
something, you mean that what they do is surprising or extreme. EG *He went so far as to spit over the
wall.*

11 You can use **far** to emphasize that something is ADV
much greater or better than something else, or has
much more of a particular quality. EG *...a far
greater problem... It was far more than I expected... The firm had far outstripped its rivals.*

12 You can use **by far** or **far and away** to PHRASE
emphasize that something is the best, or has more
of a particular quality than anything else. EG *She
was by far the camp's best swimmer... This is far
and away the most important point.*

13 Someone or something that is **not far wrong**, PHRASE
not far out, or **not far off** is almost correct. EG
*...an answer that's not far wrong... He hadn't been
so far out, for Antonio had died.*

14 You can use **far from** to emphasize that PHRASE
something is the opposite of what it should be,
could be, or was expected to be. EG *His hands were
far from clean... Far from speeding up, the tank
slithered to a halt... It is not that you are ungener-
ous. Far from it.*

15 You use **far** in expressions such as 'as far as I ADV SEN
know' and 'so far as I remember' to indicate that
you are not absolutely sure and may be wrong. EG
*We only had one paper as far as I remember... As
far as they could see, the room was empty.*

16 So far means up until the present point in time PHRASE
or the present stage in a situation. EG *What do you
think of the town so far?... So far only two bodies
have been discovered.*

17 You say **'So far so good'** when what you are CONVENTION
doing has been successful or satisfactory up until
the time when you are speaking. EG *I tied him
quickly to a tree. So far so good.*

18 You can use **in so far as** or **insofar as** to CONJ
introduce a statement that limits the extent of Formal
another statement or gives a reason for it. EG
*Liberty is cherished only in so far as it costs
nothing.*

19 as far as something **is concerned**: see **concern**. ● **few and far between**: see **few**.

faraway /ˈfɑːrəweɪ/. **1** A **faraway** place or sound ADJ CLASSIF:
is a long distance away from you. EG *...news from* ATTRIB
*far-away villages... ...the faraway sound of a water-
fall.*

2 If someone has a **faraway** expression, they look ADJ CLASSIF:
as if they are thinking deeply about something and ATTRIB
are not paying attention to what is happening. EG
She had a faraway look in her eyes.

farce /fɑːs/, **farces**. **1** A **farce** is a humorous play N COUNT
in which the characters become involved in unlike-
ly and complicated situations.

2 If you say that something is a **farce**, you mean N COUNT
that it is very disorganized or unsatisfactory. EG *His
education had been a farce.*

farcical /ˈfɑːsɪkəl/. If you say that something is ADJ QUALIT
farcical, you mean that it is ridiculous, disorganized, or unsatisfactory. EG *The next ten minutes
were farcical... ...this farcical voyage to somewhere she did not want to go.*

fare /feə/, **fares, faring, fared**. **1** The **fare** is the N COUNT
money that you pay for a journey in a vehicle such
as a taxi, train, or aeroplane. EG *Coach fares are
cheaper than rail fares... What is the fare to
Weymouth?*

2 The **fare** served at a place such as a restaurant is N UNCOUNT
the food that is served there. EG *Army kitchens* Outdated
serve better fare than some hotels.

3 If you **fare** badly in a particular situation, you are V+A:
unsuccessful or are treated badly. If you **fare** well, OFT WITH
you are successful or are treated well. EG *How did* BROAD NEG
you fare with Sir Hugo?... They fared badly in the Outdated
1978 elections.

Far East. The **Far East** consists of all the N PROPER:
countries of Eastern Asia, including China and the+N
Japan.

farewell /feəˈwel/, **farewells**. **Farewell** means CONVENTION
goodbye. EG *Farewell, my dear child... He bade* Outdated
farewell to his family. ▸ used as a noun. EG *...tearful* ▸ N COUNT
farewells... ...the farewell party.

far-fetched. If you say that a statement, idea, or ADJ QUALIT
plan is **far-fetched**, you mean that it is exaggerated, unlikely, or impossible. EG *The theory is too far-
fetched to be considered.*

far-flung. 1 Far-flung places are a very long ADJ CLASSIF:
distance away. EG *...some far-flung corner of the* ATTRIB
world.

2 A **far-flung** empire or organization extends to ADJ CLASSIF:
distant places. EG *...the produce of a far-flung em-* ATTRIB
pire.

farm /fɑːm/, **farms, farming, farmed**. **1** A **farm** N COUNT
is an area of land consisting of fields and some
buildings, which is used for growing crops or
raising animals. EG *My father worked on a farm...
...farm buildings.*

2 If you **farm** an area of land, you grow crops or V+O OR V
raise animals on it. EG *The hill land is farmed by
Mike Keeble... ...those who have farmed for generations.*

farmer /ˈfɑːmə/, **farmers**. A **farmer** is a person N COUNT
who owns or manages a farm.

farmhand /ˈfɑːmhænd/, **farmhands**. A **farm-** N COUNT
hand is a person who is employed by a farmer to
work on a farm.

farmhouse /ˈfɑːmhaʊs/, **farmhouses**. A **farm-** N COUNT
house is a house on a farm, especially one where a
farmer lives.

farming /ˈfɑːmɪŋ/ is the activity of growing crops N UNCOUNT
or raising animals on a farm. EG *...an economy
based on farming and tourism... ...sheep farming.*

farmland /ˈfɑːmlænd/ is land which is farmed or N UNCOUNT
is suitable for farming. EG *...1500 acres of forest and
farmland.*

On these pages, what coin is no longer used in
Britain?

farmyard /fɑːmjɑːd/, **farmyards**. A **farmyard** is N COUNT
an area on a farm surrounded by buildings or walls.

far-off. 1 A **far-off** place is a long distance away. ADJ QUALIT
EG ...*a far-off country.*

2 A **far-off** time is a long time away in the future ADJ QUALIT
or the past. EG ...*looking back at that far-off day.*

far-reaching means affecting something greatly, ADJ QUALIT
in many ways, and for a long time. EG *It could have
far-reaching implications for the economy.*

far-sighted. If you say that someone is **far-** ADJ QUALIT
sighted, you mean that they are good at foreseeing what will happen in the future and making
suitable plans or decisions.

farther /fɑːðə/ is a comparative of **far**.

farthest /fɑːðɪ²st/ is a superlative of **far**.

farthing /fɑːðɪŋ/, **farthings**. In old British curren- N COUNT
cy, a **farthing** was a coin that was worth a quarter
of a penny.

fascinate /fæsɪneɪt/, **fascinates**, **fascinating**, V+O
fascinated. If something or someone **fascinates**
you, you find them very interesting. EG *I love
history, it fascinates me... I was fascinated by the
people dressed in white.* ◊ **fascinated**. EG *He* ◊ ADJ QUALIT
became fascinated with their whole way of life.
◊ **fascinating**. EG *It's a fascinating book.*
◊ **fascination** /fæsɪneɪ̩ʃə²n/. EG ...*Taylor's fascina-* ◊ N UNCOUNT
*tion with bees... Mildred was staring with fascina-
tion at the scene.*

fascist /fæʃɪst/, **fascists**. If you call someone a N COUNT
fascist, you mean that their opinions are very
right-wing, and that they believe in strong government and do not care about people's rights. EG *I
fought a war to get rid of Fascists like you.* ▸ used ▸ ADJ CLASSIF
as an adjective. EG ...*those fascist parents of yours.*

fashion /fæʃə²n/, **fashions**, **fashioning**, **fash-** N SING+SUPP
ioned. 1 If you do something in a particular
fashion, you do it in that way. EG *We talked in an
animated fashion... He greeted us in his usual
friendly fashion.*

2 **Fashion** is the area of activity that involves N UNCOUNT
styles of clothing and appearance. EG ...*hints on
fashion and cookery... ...the fashion industry.*

3 A **fashion** is a style of clothing or a way of N COUNT
behaving that is popular at a particular time. EG
...*the latest Parisian fashions... The Beatles set the
fashion for a generation.*

4 If something is **in fashion**, it is popular and PHRASE
approved of at a particular time. If it is **out of
fashion**, it is not popular or approved of. EG *Exotic
fruits are coming into fashion... She never wears a
hat. They're out of fashion.*

5 If you **fashion** something, you make it. EG *The* V+O
crew fashioned a raft from the wreckage. Outdated

6 See also **old-fashioned**.

fashionable /fæʃə²nəbə²l/. Something that is ADJ QUALIT
fashionable is popular or approved of at a particular time. EG ...*the striped shirts that were fashionable in 1963... ...the less fashionable parts of the
city.* ◊ **fashionably**. EG ...*fashionably dressed* ◊ ADV
ladies.

fast /fɑːst/, **faster**, **fastest**; **fasts**, **fasting**, **fasted**.

1 If something or someone is **fast**, they move, do ADJ QUALIT
something, or happen with great speed. EG ...*a fast
car... ...producing goods at a faster rate.* ▸ used as ▸ ADV
an adverb. EG *I ran as fast as I could... We are fast
becoming a nation fed on canned food.*

2 If you ask how **fast** something is moving, you ADV
want to know the speed at which it is moving.

3 If something happens **fast**, it happens very soon ADV
and without any delay. EG *She needed medical help
fast... Treat stains as fast as possible.*

4 If a watch or clock is **fast**, it is showing a time ADJ PRED
that is later than the real time.

5 If you **hold fast** to an idea or course of action, PHRASE
you firmly continue believing it or doing it. EG *He
was determined to hold fast to his beliefs.*

6 Someone who is **fast asleep** is completely PHRASE
asleep.

7 If you **fast**, you eat no food for a period of time, V

usually for religious reasons. EG *He fasts for a whole
day every week.* ▸ used as a noun. EG *During my* ▸ N COUNT
fast I lost fifteen pounds.

8 to **make a fast buck**: see **buck**. ● **thick and
fast**: see **thick**. ● See also **hard and fast**.

fasten /fɑːsə²n/, **fastens**, **fastening**, **fastened**. 1 V-ERG
If you **fasten** something, you fix it in a closed
position with a button, strap, or other device. EG *He
fastened his seat-belt... The case fastened at the
top.*

2 If you **fasten** one thing to another, you attach the V+O+A
first thing to the second thing. EG *The bench had
been fastened to the pavement.*

3 If you **fasten** your hands or teeth around or onto V-ERG+A
something, you grasp it firmly with your hands or
teeth. EG *He fastened his hands round the spear...
The snake's fangs fastened on the Count's arm.*

fasten on. If you **fasten on** to someone or PHRASAL VB:
something, you concentrate your attention on V+ADV:
them. EG *Once she had fastened on to a scheme she* OFT+*to*
did not let go.

fastening /fɑːsə²nɪŋ/, **fastenings**. A **fastening** is N COUNT
a device that keeps something in a fixed or closed
position. EG ...*the fastenings of her gown.*

fast food is hot food that is prepared and served N UNCOUNT
quickly after you order it. EG ...*fast-food restaurants.*

fastidious /fæstɪdɪəs/. Someone who is **fastidious** ADJ QUALIT
is fussy and likes things to be clean, tidy, and
properly done. EG ...*with noses wrinkled in fastidious distaste.* ◊ **fastidiously**. EG *The process was* ◊ ADV
fastidiously checked. ◊ **fastidiousness**. EG *I want* ◊ N UNCOUNT
you to overcome your fastidiousness.

fat /fæt/, **fatter**, **fattest**; **fats**. 1 A **fat** person has a ADJ QUALIT
lot of flesh on their body. EG ...*a small fat man...
Henry has grown fat.* ◊ **fatness**. EG *He was* ◊ N UNCOUNT
embarrassed to hear her discussing his fatness.

2 **Fat** is 2.1 the layer of flesh in the bodies of N UNCOUNT
animals and people which is used to store energy
and to keep them warm. 2.2 a substance used in N MASS
cooking which is obtained from vegetables or the
flesh of animals. EG ...*a smell of fried fat.* 2.3 a N MASS
substance contained in many foods and used by
your body to produce energy. EG ...*a diet containing
protein, fats, carbohydrates, and vitamins.*

3 A **fat** object is very thick or wide. EG ...*one fat* ADJ QUALIT
volume of a report... ...a fat briefcase.

4 A **fat** profit or fee is a large one. EG *The shoes* ADJ QUALIT:
made a fat profit for the manufacturer. ATTRIB

5 You use **a fat lot** to mean 'not any' or 'nothing'. PHRASE
For example, if you say that something is **a fat lot** Informal
of good or **a fat lot** of use, you mean that it is
completely useless. EG *A fat lot of good that would
be!... A fat lot that'll prove!*

fatal /feɪtə²l/. 1 A **fatal** action has very undesir- ADJ CLASSIF
able results. EG *I made the fatal mistake of letting
her talk... It would be fatal to bring in an outsider.*
◊ **fatally**. EG *Their leaders are fatally mistaken.* ◊ ADV

2 A **fatal** accident or illness causes someone's ADJ CLASSIF
death. EG ...*Pollock's fatal car crash.* ◊ **fatally**. EG ◊ ADV
Four men were fatally stabbed.

fatalism /feɪtəlɪzə²m/ is the belief that people N UNCOUNT
cannot prevent or control events. EG ...*the fatalism
of the masses.* ◊ **fatalist, fatalists**. EG *I've always* ◊ N COUNT
been a fatalist.

fatalistic /feɪtəlɪstɪk/. Someone who is **fatalistic** ADJ QUALIT
believes that people cannot prevent or control
events. EG *They're so fatalistic, they don't even
bother to vote.*

fatality /fətælɪ¹tɪ/, **fatalities**. 1 A **fatality** is a N COUNT
person's death that is caused by an accident or by
violence. EG *Fatalities from the use of pesticide are
rare.*

2 **Fatality** is the feeling or belief that people N UNCOUNT
cannot prevent or control events. EG *The modern* Formal
world is dominated by a sense of fatality.

fate /feɪt/, **fates**. 1 **Fate** is a power that is believed N UNCOUNT
by some people to control everything that happens.
EG *Fate was against me.*

2 Someone's **fate** is what happens to them. EG N COUNT+SUPP
Several other companies suffered a similar fate.

fated /feɪtɪ²d/. If you say that someone is **fated** to ADJ CLASSIF:
do something, or that an event is **fated**, you mean USU+*to*-INF
that nothing can be done to avoid or change what
will happen. EG *We were fated to dislike one
another.*

fateful /feɪtful/. If you describe an action or event ADJ QUALIT:
as **fateful**, you mean that it had important, and ATTRIB
often bad, effects on later events. EG *...when the
President made his fateful announcement.*

father /fɑːðə/, **fathers, fathering, fathered. 1** N COUNT OR
Your **father** is the man who is one of your parents. VOCATIVE

2 When a man **fathers** a child, he makes a woman V+O
pregnant and their child is born. EG *He fathered two* Literary
children.

3 The man who invented or started something is N SING:
sometimes referred to as its **father**. EG *Chaucer is* the+N+*of*
often said to be the father of English poetry.

4 In some Christian churches, priests are addressed or referred to as **Father**. EG *Good afternoon, Father... ...Father Drew.*

5 Christians often refer to God as our **Father** or N PROPER OR
address him as **Father**. EG *Heavenly Father, hear* VOCATIVE
our prayers.

Father Christmas is an imaginary old man with N PROPER
a long white beard and a red coat. Young children
believe that he brings them their presents at
Christmas.

fatherhood /fɑːðəhʊd/ is the state of being a N UNCOUNT
father. EG *Attitudes to fatherhood are changing.*

father-in-law, **fathers-in-law.** Someone's N COUNT
father-in-law is the father of their husband or
wife.

fatherless /fɑːðəlɪ²s/. You describe children as ADJ CLASSIF
fatherless when their father has died or does not
live with them.

fatherly /fɑːðəlɪ/. You say that someone behaves ADJ QUALIT:
in a **fatherly** way when they behave like a kind ATTRIB
father. EG *Let me give you some fatherly advice.*

fathom /fæðə⁰m/, **fathoms, fathoming, fath-
omed. 1** A **fathom** is a measurement of 1.8 metres N COUNT
or 6 feet, used when describing the depth of the Technical
sea.

2 If you **fathom** something or **fathom** it out, you V+O:
understand it as a result of thinking about it OFT+*out*;
carefully. EG *I couldn't fathom the meaning of her* ALSO V+WH
*remarks... She couldn't fathom why McCurry was
causing such a scene.*

fatigue /fətiːg/, **fatigues, fatiguing, fatigued. 1** N UNCOUNT
Fatigue is a feeling of extreme physical or mental
tiredness. EG *He was dizzy with hunger and fatigue.*

2 If something **fatigues** you, it makes you ex- V+O
tremely tired. EG *Some people say eating fatigues* Formal
them. ◊ **fatigued.** EG *She was utterly fatigued.* ◊ ADJ QUALIT

3 **Fatigue** in metal is a weakness caused by N UNCOUNT
repeated stress. It can sometimes cause the metal
to break.

fatten /fætə⁰n/, **fattens, fattening, fattened.** If V-ERG
you **fatten** an animal or if it **fattens**, it becomes
fatter as a result of eating more. EG *Soya is excellent for fattening pigs.*

fatten up. If you **fatten up** an animal, you feed it PHRASAL VB:
more food so that it reaches the weight that you V+O+ADV
want it to be. EG *Their cattle take twice as long to
fatten up as European cattle.*

fattening /fætə⁰nɪŋ/. Food that is **fattening** tends ADJ QUALIT
to make people fat.

fatty /fætɪ/, **fatties. 1** A fat person is sometimes N COUNT OR
called a **fatty**; an offensive use. EG *Shut up, Fatty.* VOCATIVE

2 **Fatty** food contains a lot of fat. ADJ QUALIT

fatuous /fætjʊəs/. If you say that a remark, action, ADJ QUALIT
or plan is **fatuous**, you mean that it is very silly
indeed.

faucet /fɔːsɪt/, **faucets.** A **faucet** is a device that N COUNT
you turn in order to control the flow of a liquid or American
gas from a pipe or container. Sinks and baths have
faucets attached to them.

fault /fɔːlt/, **faults, faulting, faulted. 1** If a bad or N SING+POSS
undesirable situation is your **fault**, you are the
cause of it or are responsible for it. EG *It was
entirely my own fault... It's all the fault of a girl
called Sarah.*

2 If you are **at fault**, you have done something PHRASE
wrong or have made a mistake. EG *It was 1976, I
believe, if my memory is not at fault.*

3 A **fault** in a person's character or in a system is a N COUNT
weakness or imperfection in it. EG *She is forever
telling me what my faults are.*

4 A **fault** in a machine or structure is a broken N COUNT
part or a mistake in the way it was made. EG
Computer faults are commonplace.

5 If you say that you cannot **fault** someone, you V+O:OFT+*on*
mean that they are doing something so well that
you cannot criticize them for it. EG *You can't fault
their psychology... I couldn't fault him on that one.*

6 If you **find fault** with something, you complain PHRASE
about it.

7 A **fault** is also a large crack in the surface of the N COUNT
earth. Technical

8 In tennis, a **fault** is a service that is wrong N COUNT
according to the rules.

faultless /fɔːltlɪ²s/. Something that is **faultless** ADJ CLASSIF
has no mistakes in it. EG *...two men who spoke to
him in faultless German.*

faulty /fɔːltɪ/. A machine or piece of equipment ADJ CLASSIF
that is **faulty** is not working properly. EG *We traced
the trouble to a faulty transformer.*

fauna /fɔːnə/. The **fauna** in a place are all the N PLURAL
animals, birds, fish, and insects there. EG *...the flora* Formal
and fauna of Africa.

faux pas /fəʊ pɑː/. A **faux pas** is a socially N COUNT
embarrassing action or mistake. The plural form is Formal
also **faux pas**. EG *They behaved as if they were
fearful of committing a faux pas.*

favour /feɪvə/, **favours, favouring, favoured;**
spelled **favor** in American English.

1 If you regard something or someone with **favour**, N UNCOUNT
you like or support them. EG *I think the company
will look with favour on your plan... Is this just an
attempt to win his favour?*

2 **In favour** is used in these ways. **2.1** If you are **in** PHRASES
favour of something, you support it and think that
it is a good thing. EG *They are in favour of reforming the tax laws.* **2.2** If you make a judgement **in**
someone's **favour**, you say that they are right. EG
The umpire ruled in her favour. **2.3** Something that
is **in** someone's **favour** gives them an advantage.
EG *The system is biased in favour of young people.*
2.4 If something is rejected **in favour of** something else, the second thing is done or chosen
instead of the first one. EG *The plans for a new
airport have been scrapped in favour of an extension to the old one.*

3 If something is **out of favour**, people no longer PHRASE
like or support it. If something is **in favour**,
people like it or support it. EG *Their views are very
much out of favour now.*

4 If you do someone a **favour**, you do something N COUNT
for them even though you do not have to. EG *I've
come to ask a favour.*

5 If you **favour** something, you like that thing V+O
more than the other choices available. EG *...those
who favour disarmament.*

6 Something that **favours** a person or event make V+O
it easier for that person to do something or for that
event to happen. EG *The weather favoured the
attacking army.*

7 If you **favour** someone, you treat them better or V+O
more kindly than you treat other people. EG *Parents may favour the youngest child in the family.*

8 If you **favour** someone with something such as V+O+*with*
your attention or your presence, you give them Formal

If you are fed up, have you had enough to eat?

that thing. EG *I cannot say why he believes this, for he does not favour us with his reasoning.*

favourable /feɪv°rəb°l/; spelled **favorable** in American English. **1** If you are **favourable** to ADJ QUALIT: something, you agree with it or approve of it. EG OFT+to *Most people were favourable to the idea... Her request met with a favourable response.* ◊ **favourably.** EG *Many reacted favourably to the* ◊ ADV *plan.*

2 If something makes a **favourable** impression on ADJ QUALIT you, you like it or approve of it. ◊ **favourably.** EG ◊ ADV *Her application had impressed him very favourably.*

3 If you present something in a **favourable** light, ADJ QUALIT you try to make people like it or approve of it. EG *We must try to present our profession in a more favourable light.*

4 Favourable conditions make something more ADJ QUALIT likely to succeed. EG *This creates an atmosphere favourable to expansion.*

5 If you make a **favourable** comparison between ADJ QUALIT one thing and another, you say that the first thing is at least as good as the second. ◊ **favourably.** EG ◊ ADV *...an education service which compares favourably with that of other countries.*

favourite /feɪv°rɪt/, **favourites;** spelled **favor-ite** in American English. **1** Your **favourite** thing of ADJ CLASSIF a particular type is the one that you like most. EG *What is your favourite television programme?... She's one of my favourite writers.*

2 The **favourite** in a race or contest is the person N COUNT or animal that is expected to win.

favouritism /feɪv°rɪtɪzm/; spelled **favoritism** in N UNCOUNT American English. **Favouritism** is the practice of unfairly helping or supporting one person or group more than another. EG *There must be no favourit-ism in the allocation of contracts.*

fawn /fɔːn/, **fawns, fawning, fawned. 1** Some- ADJ COLOUR thing that is **fawn** is a pale yellowish brown colour.

2 A **fawn** is a very young deer. N COUNT

3 If people **fawn** on a powerful or rich person, they v:OFT+on flatter him or her, usually in order to get some advantage for themselves.

fear /fɪə/, **fears, fearing, feared. 1 Fear** is the N UNCOUNT unpleasant feeling that you have when you think that you are in danger. EG *They huddled together, quaking with fear... She was brought up with no fear of animals.*

2 If you **fear** someone or something, you are v+o frightened because you think that they will harm you. EG *He fears nothing.*

3 If you **fear** something unpleasant, you think that v+o OR it might happen, or might have happened, and feel V+REPORT: worried about this. EG *An epidemic of plague was* ONLY that *feared... The new countries fear that their new-found independence might be lost.*

4 A **fear** is a thought that something unpleasant N COUNT might happen or might have happened. EG *My worst fears were quickly realized.*

5 If you **fear** for something, you think that it might v+for be in danger and are very worried. EG *Morris began to fear for the life of Mrs Reilly.* ▸ used as a noun. ▸N COUNT OR EG *They had fears for their health.* N UNCOUNT

6 If you do not take a particular course of action PHRASE **for fear** of something happening, you do not take it because you do not wish that thing to happen. EG *They did not mention it for fear of offending him.*

7 If you say that you **fear** that something is the v: case, you mean that you are sorry or sad that it is OFT+REPORT, the case. EG *It is usually, I fear, the parents who are* ONLY that responsible. Formal

fearful /fɪəful/. **1** Someone who is **fearful** is ADJ QUALIT afraid. EG *They are fearful of letting their feelings take over.* ◊ **fearfully.** EG *The boys looked at each* ◊ ADV *other fearfully.*

2 Something that is **fearful** is very unpleasant or ADJ QUALIT bad. EG *...the fearful risks of the operation.*

fearless /fɪəlɪˀs/. Someone who is **fearless** is not ADJ QUALIT afraid at all. EG *...fearless reporters.* ◊ **fearlessly.** ◊ ADV EG *If provoked, it defended itself fearlessly.*

fearsome /fɪəsəm/. Something that is **fearsome** ADJ QUALIT is terrible or frightening. EG *The dog had a fear-* Formal *some set of teeth.*

feasible /fiːzəb°l/. Something that is **feasible** can ADJ QUALIT be done, made, or achieved. EG *The electric car is technically feasible.* ◊ **feasibility** /fiːzəbɪlɪti/. EG ◊ N UNCOUNT *...the technical feasibility of a supersonic aircraft.*

feast /fiːst/, **feasts, feasting, feasted. 1** A **feast** N COUNT is a large and special meal. EG *...a wedding feast.*

2 If you **feast,** you take part in a feast. EG *The poor* v:OFT+off/on *starve while the rich feast... He sprawled there, feasting off cold roast duck.* ◊ **feasting.** EG *The* ◊ N UNCOUNT *feasting went on for hours.*

3 If you **feast** your **eyes** on something, you look at PHRASE it for a long time because you like it very much. EG *I feasted my eyes upon her lovely face.*

feat /fiːt/, **feats.** A **feat** is an impressive and N COUNT+SUPP difficult act or achievement. EG *...a brilliant feat of engineering.*

feather /feðə/, **feathers.** A bird's **feathers** are N COUNT the light, soft things that cover its body. EG *...ostrich feathers.* ◊ **feathered** /feðəd/. EG *...girls in feath-* ◊ ADJ CLASSIF: *ered head-dresses.* ATTRIB

feathery /feð°ri/. Something that is **feathery** ADJ QUALIT has an edge divided into lots of thin parts so that it looks soft. EG *...feathery palm trees.*

feature /fiːtʃə/, **features, featuring, featured. 1** N COUNT+SUPP A **feature** of something is some part or character-istic that it has. EG *The most important feature of our work must be parental involvement... Every car will have built-in safety features.*

2 Your **features** are your eyes, nose, mouth, and N PLURAL other parts of your face.

3 When a film or exhibition **features** someone or v+o something, they are an important part of it. EG *This film features two of my favourite actors.*

4 If you **feature** in something, you are an impor- v+in tant and noticeable part of it. EG *This is not the first time he has featured in allegations of violence.*

5 A geographical **feature** is something noticeable N COUNT+SUPP in a particular area of country, for example a hill or a river. EG *...the natural features of the land-scape.*

6 A **feature** is also **6.1** a special article in a N COUNT newspaper or magazine. EG *The local newspaper ran a feature on drug abuse.* **6.2** a special pro-gramme on radio or television.

7 You can also refer to a full-length film in a N COUNT cinema as a **feature** or a **feature** film.

February /februəri/ is the second month of the N UNCOUNT year in the Western calendar.

feces /fiːsiːz/. See **faeces.**

feckless /feklɪˀs/. Someone who is **feckless** lacks ADJ QUALIT strength of character, and cannot run their life Formal properly. EG *...children with drunken or feckless parents.*

fed /fed/ is the past tense and past participle of **feed.** ● See also **fed up.**

federal /fed°rəl/. In a **federal** country or system ADJ CLASSIF: of government, a group of states is controlled by a ATTRIB central government. EG *...the Federal Republic of Germany... ...a federal court.*

federation /fedəreɪʃ°n/, **federations.** A federa- N COUNT **tion** is **1** a group of organizations with a common interest. EG *...the National Federation of Women's Institutes.* **2** a federal country. EG *...the proposal to form a federation out of Northern and Southern Rhodesia.*

fed up. Someone who is **fed up** is bored or ADJ PRED annoyed. EG *You sound a bit fed up... They're* Informal *getting pretty fed up with him.*

fee /fiː/, **fees.** A **fee** is **1** a sum of money that you N COUNT pay to be allowed to do something. EG *...an entrance fee.* **2** the amount of money that a person or organization is paid for a particular job or service. EG *Agencies charge a fee to find an au pair.*

feeble /fíːbəºl/, **feebler**, **feeblest**. 1 Someone or ADJ QUALIT something that is **feeble** has very little power, strength, or energy. EG *The creature is physically feeble, with poor vision and dull senses... ...the feeble light of the bulb in the hallway.* ◊ **feebly.** EG ◊ ADV *It feebly beat its wings.*

2 You can describe something that someone says ADJ QUALIT as **feeble** when it is not effective, good, or convincing. EG *...feeble excuses... ...a feeble joke.* ◊ **feebly.** ◊ ADV EG *'They seemed all right to me,' I explained feebly.*

feed /fíːd/, **feeds**, **feeding**, **fed** /fed/. 1 If you **feed** V+O:OFT+A a baby or an animal, you give it food. EG *He had just* ALSO V+O+O *come back from feeding the ponies... She fed the baby some milk.* ▸ used as a noun. EG *What time is* ▸ N COUNT *his next feed?*

2 When an animal or baby **feeds**, it eats some- V:OFT+on/off thing. EG *Not all bats feed on insects.*

3 **Feed** is food that is given to an animal. N MASS

4 If you **feed** your family or a community, you V+O OR V-REFL supply or prepare food for them. EG *The farmers grew too little to feed even their own families.*

5 If something **feeds** on something else or **is fed** V+on by it, it grows stronger as a result of it. EG *Once the* OR V+O: *process has been started, it feeds on itself... The* USU PASS *fires were being fed by escaping gas.*

6 If you **feed** something into an object, you put it V+O: gradually into the object. EG *Extra gas was fed into* USU PASS+A *the pipeline... This data is fed into the computer.*

feedback /fíːdbæk/. When you get **feedback**, you N UNCOUNT get comments about something that you have done or made. EG *The more feedback we get from viewers, the better.*

feel /fíːl/, **feels**, **feeling**, **felt** /felt/. 1 If you **feel** a V+O, V+C, particular emotion or sensation, you experience it. OR V+A EG *Mrs Oliver felt a sudden desire to burst out crying... I felt angry... I was feeling hungry and sleepy... She felt a fool... I felt like a murderer.*

2 If you **feel** that something is the case, it is your V+REPORT: opinion that it is the case. EG *He felt I was making a* ONLY *that*; *terrible mistake... I felt obliged to invite him in...* ALSO V+C, OR *He felt it necessary to explain why he had come.* NO CONT V+O+C:

3 If you **feel** a particular way about something, you V+A:OFT+ have that attitude or reaction to it. EG *She knew* *about*; NO CONT *how I felt about totalitarianism.*

4 If you **feel like** doing something or having PHRASE something, you want to do it or have it. EG *Whenever I felt like talking these were ready to listen... I feel like a stroll.*

5 You use **feel** when describing something that you V+C OR V+ are touching or holding. For example, if something *like*: NO CONT **feels** heavy, it seems heavy when you pick it up. EG *It looks and feels like a normal fabric.* ▸ used as a ▸ N SING+SUPP noun. EG *...the cool feel of armchair leather.*

6 If you talk about how an experience **feels**, you V+C OR V+*like* are talking about the emotions and sensations that you have when you have the experience. EG *It felt good to be back... What does it feel like to watch yourself on TV?*

7 If you **feel** something, **7.1** you are aware that it is V+O, OR V-REFL touching you or happening to your body. EG *They* +-ING OR INF *felt the wind on their damp faces... She felt his hand pat hers... Rudolph could feel himself blushing.* **7.2** you are aware of it, even though you V+O cannot see or hear it. EG *He had felt Binta's presence in the hut.*

8 If you **feel** the effect or result of something, you V+O experience it. EG *We shan't feel the effect of the change for some years.*

9 If you **feel** a physical object, you touch it V+O deliberately, in order to find out what it is like. EG *Eric felt his face. 'I'm all rough. Am I bleeding?'*

10 If you **feel** for an object, you try to find it using V+*for* your hands rather than your eyes. EG *She felt in her bag for her key.*

11 The **feel** of something, for example a place, is N SING+SUPP the general impression that it gives you. EG *The Brazilian Amazon has the feel of a tropical wild west.*

12 If you **do not feel yourself**, you feel slightly ill. PHRASE

13 See also **feeling**, **felt**.

feeling /fíːlɪŋ/, **feelings**. 1 A **feeling** is an emo- N COUNT tion or attitude. EG *A feeling of panic was rising in* N UNCOUNT: *him... She tried to hide her feelings... She cried out* USU+SUPP *in a voice rich in real feeling, 'It means so much to me!'*

2 A **feeling** of, for example, hunger or tiredness is N COUNT+SUPP a physical sensation that you experience. EG *...an itchy feeling... ...feelings of nausea.*

3 If you have no **feeling** in a part of your body, you N UNCOUNT cannot tell when that part is being touched.

4 If you have a **feeling** that something is the case, N COUNT: OFT you think that it is probably the case. EG *My feeling* +REPORT *is that it would work very well... I have a nasty feeling you're right.*

5 **Feeling** for someone or something is affection N UNCOUNT for them. EG *He may be moved by feeling for his fellow-citizens.*

6 If you **hurt** someone's **feelings**, you upset them. PHRASE

7 **Bad feeling** is resentment or hostility which PHRASE exists between people.

8 If you have no **hard feelings** towards someone PHRASE who has quarrelled with you or upset you, you do not feel angry with them.

feet /fíːt/ is the plural of **foot**.

feign /feɪn/, **feigns**, **feigning**, **feigned.** If you V+O **feign** a feeling, you pretend that you are experien- Literary cing it. EG *She knew that her efforts to feign cheerfulness weren't convincing.* ◊ **feigned.** *'I* ◊ ADJ CLASSIF *thought you must know,' Dixon said with feigned surprise.*

feint /feɪnt/, **feints**, **feinting**, **feinted.** A **feint** is a N COUNT misleading action or movement, especially in boxing, which is intended to deceive your opponent. ▸ used as a verb. EG *Green feinted with his right.* ▸ V

feline /fíːlaɪn/. 1 **Feline** means belonging or relat- ADJ CLASSIF ing to the cat family.

2 If you describe someone as **feline**, you mean that ADJ QUALIT they look or move like a cat. EG *...her feline charm.*

fell /fel/, **fells**, **felling**, **felled.** 1 **Fell** is the past tense of **fall**.

2 If you **fell** a tree, you cut it down. V+O

3 If you **fell** someone, you knock them down. EG V+O *This blow would have felled most men.* Literary

fellow /feláʊ/, **fellows.** 1 A **fellow** is a man. EG N COUNT *Doug is an exceedingly amiable fellow... My dear* Informal *fellow, I really am sorry.*

2 You use **fellow** to describe people who have ADJ CLASSIF: something in common with you. EG *I've always* ATTRIB *trusted my fellow men... I had a conversation with a fellow passenger.* ▸ used as a plural noun. EG *He* ▸ N PLURAL *sought the approval of his fellows.* +POSS

3 A **fellow** of a society or academic institution is a N COUNT member of it. EG *...Sir George Porter, Fellow of the Royal Society.*

fellowship /feláʊºʃɪp/, **fellowships.** 1 **Fellowship** N UNCOUNT is a feeling of friendship that people have when they are doing something together. EG *...the atmosphere of cheerful good fellowship.*

2 A **fellowship** is a group of people that join N COUNT+SUPP together for a common purpose or interest. EG *...the Socialist Fellowship.*

felony /feləniˡ/, **felonies.** A **felony** is a very N COUNT serious crime such as murder or armed robbery. Legal

felt /felt/. 1 **Felt** is the past tense and past participle of **feel**.

2 **Felt** is a type of thick cloth made by pressing N UNCOUNT short threads together.

felt-tip. A **felt-tip** pen has a rod of fibres for a nib. ADJ CLASSIF

female /fíːmeɪl/, **females.** 1 You can refer to any N COUNT creature that can produce babies from its body or lay eggs as a **female**. EG *The male fertilizes the female's eggs.* ▸ used as an adjective. EG *...a female* ▸ ADJ CLASSIF *toad.*

2 Women and girls are sometimes referred to as N COUNT

Do you ever have to fend for yourself?

females. Some people find this use offensive. EG ...a *lone female staying at a hotel.* ▸ used as an adjective. EG *There are only nineteen female members of parliament.* ▸ ADJ CLASSIF

3 Something that is **female** concerns, relates to, or affects women rather than men. EG ...*female inventions... ...traditionally female areas of work.* ADJ CLASSIF: ATTRIB

feminine /fɛmɪnɪn/. Something that is **feminine** relates to or is considered typical of women, in contrast to men. EG *Society hasn't regarded science or engineering as feminine occupations... ...feminine clothes.* ADJ QUALIT

femininity /fɛmɪnɪnɪ¹tɪ¹/. 1 A woman's **femininity** is the fact that she is a woman. N UNCOUNT

2 **Femininity** is also the qualities that are considered to be typical of women. EG *The fashion industry responded to the new mood of femininity.* N UNCOUNT

feminism /fɛmɪnɪzə⁰m/ is the belief that women should have the same rights, power, and opportunities as men. N UNCOUNT

feminist /fɛmɪnɪst/, **feminists**. A **feminist** is a person who believes in and supports feminism. EG *Claudia thought of herself as a feminist.* ▸ used as an adjective. EG ...*the feminist response to the new law.* N COUNT; ▸ ADJ CLASSIF

fence /fɛns/, **fences, fencing, fenced**. 1 A **fence** is a barrier made of wood or wire supported by posts. N COUNT

2 If you **fence** an area of land, you surround it with a fence. ◇ **fenced**. EG ...*a fenced enclosure.* V+O; ◇ ADJ CLASSIF

3 If you **sit on the fence**, you avoid supporting any side in a discussion or argument. PHRASE

fence in. If you **fence** something **in**, you surround it completely with a fence. PHRASAL VB: V+O+ADV

fence off. If you **fence off** an area of land, you build a fence round it. PHRASAL VB: V+O+ADV

fencing /fɛnsɪŋ/. 1 **Fencing** is a sport in which two competitors fight each other using very thin swords. N UNCOUNT

2 You can also refer to materials that are used to make fences as **fencing**. EG ...*cedar wood fencing.* N UNCOUNT: USU+SUPP

fend /fɛnd/, **fends, fending, fended**. If you **fend for yourself**, you look after yourself without relying on help from anyone else. EG *Grown up children should leave home and fend for themselves.* PHRASE

fend off. 1 If you **fend off** someone who is attacking you, you use your arms or a stick to defend yourself. 2 If you **fend off** questions or requests, you avoid answering them. EG *She fended off all these claims.* PHRASAL VB: V+O+ADV

ferment, ferments, fermenting, fermented; pronounced /fɜːmɛnt/ when it is a noun and /fə⁵mɛnt/ when it is a verb.

1 **Ferment** is excitement and unrest caused by change or uncertainty. EG *Portugal was in ferment... ...the present ferment in education.* N UNCOUNT

2 When wine, beer, or fruit **ferments** or is **fermented**, a chemical change takes place in it. ◇ **fermented**. EG *He smelt the whiff of fermented apples.* ◇ **fermentation** /fɜːmɛnteɪʃə⁰n/. EG ...*the fermentation of wines.* V-ERG; ◇ ADJ CLASSIF; ◇ N UNCOUNT

fern /fɜːn/, **ferns**. A **fern** is a plant that has long stems with feathery leaves and no flowers. N COUNT

ferocious /fərəʊʃəs/. A **ferocious** animal, person, or action is fierce and violent. EG ...*two years of ferocious fighting.* ◇ **ferociously.** EG *The buck shook his antlers ferociously.* ADJ QUALIT; ◇ ADV

ferocity /fərɒsɪ¹tɪ¹/. When something is done with **ferocity**, it is done in a fierce and violent way. EG *The attack was resumed with a new ferocity.* N UNCOUNT

ferret /fɛrɪt/, **ferrets, ferreting, ferreted**. A **ferret** is a small, white, fierce animal. Ferrets are used for hunting rabbits and rats. N COUNT

ferret out. If you **ferret out** information, you discover it by searching thoroughly. EG ...*ferreting out the details of their private lives.* PHRASAL VB: V+O+ADV Informal

ferry /fɛrɪ¹/, **ferries, ferrying, ferried**. 1 A **ferry** is a boat that carries passengers or vehicles N COUNT OR by+N

across a river or a narrow bit of sea. EG ...*car ferries... We got back to London by train and ferry.*

2 To **ferry** people or goods somewhere means to transport them there. EG *They were ferried from one building to another.* V+O: USU+A

fertile /fɜːtaɪl/. 1 You describe land or soil as **fertile** when plants grow easily in it. ◇ **fertility** /fɜːtɪlɪtɪ¹/. EG ...*soil fertility.* ADJ QUALIT; ◇ N UNCOUNT

2 If someone has a **fertile** mind or imagination, they produce a lot of good or original ideas. ADJ QUALIT: ATTRIB

3 You describe a place or situation as **fertile** ground when you think that something is likely to succeed or develop there. EG *Britain is not fertile ground for news magazines.* ADJ QUALIT

4 A woman who is **fertile** can have babies. ◇ **fertility.** EG *Fertility rates have declined.* ADJ QUALIT; ◇ N UNCOUNT

fertilize /fɜːtɪlaɪz/, **fertilizes, fertilizing, fertilized;** also spelled **fertilise**. 1 When an egg or a plant is **fertilized**, sperm reaches the egg, or pollen reaches the reproductive part of the plant, so that young animals or plants can start to be produced. ◇ **fertilized.** EG *The fertilised egg remains where it is for one more week.* ◇ **fertilization** /fɜːtɪlaɪzeɪʃə⁰n/. EG ...*the small amount of pollen necessary for fertilization.* V+O: USU PASS; ◇ ADJ CLASSIF; ◇ N UNCOUNT

2 To **fertilize** land means to spread manure or chemicals on it in order to make plants grow well. V+O

fertilizer /fɜːtɪlaɪzə/, **fertilizers;** also spelled **fertiliser**. **Fertilizer** is a substance that you spread on the ground in order to make plants grow more successfully. N MASS

fervent /fɜːvənt/. Someone who is **fervent** about something has strong and enthusiastic feelings about it. EG ...*a fervent belief in God... He had been one of Lily's most fervent admirers.* ◇ **fervently.** EG *'Oh, I am glad!' Scylla said fervently.* ADJ QUALIT; ◇ ADV

fervour /fɜːvə/; spelled **fervor** in American English. **Fervour** is a very strong feeling in favour of something. EG *She was swept to power on a tide of patriotic fervour... 'She's marvellous,' said Mrs Moffatt with fervour.* N UNCOUNT Formal

fester /fɛstə/, **festers, festering, festered**. 1 When a wound **festers**, it becomes infected. EG ...*a painful, festering sore.* V

2 If an unpleasant situation, feeling, or thought **festers**, it grows worse. EG ...*the bitter row still festering between them.* V

festival /fɛstɪvə⁰l/, **festivals**. A **festival** is 1 an organized series of events such as musical concerts or drama productions. EG ...*the Edinburgh Festival... ...the London Film Festival.* 2 a day or time of the year when people have a holiday from work and celebrate some special event, especially a religious event. N COUNT

festive /fɛstɪv/. Something that is **festive** is full of colour and happiness, especially because of a holiday or celebration. EG ...*a festive occasion... They were in a festive mood.* ADJ QUALIT

festivity /fɛstɪvɪ¹tɪ¹/, **festivities**. 1 **Festivity** is the celebrating of something in a happy way. EG ...*four days of festivity.* N UNCOUNT

2 **Festivities** are things that people do in order to celebrate something. EG *The week is crammed with festivities.* N PLURAL

festooned /fɛstuːnd/. If something is **festooned** with objects, the objects are hanging over it in large numbers. EG *The counters were festooned with rainbow-coloured scarves.* V-PASS+with

fetch /fɛtʃ/, **fetches, fetching, fetched**. 1 If you **fetch** something or someone, you bring them from a place by going there in order to get them. EG *He fetched a bucket of water from the pond.* V+O: OFT+A; ALSO V+O+O

2 If something **fetches** a particular amount of money, it is sold for that amount. EG *His pictures fetch very high prices.* V+O

3 See also **far-fetched**.

fetch up. If you **fetch up** somewhere, you arrive there, usually without intending to. EG *She fell* PHRASAL VB: V+ADV American *through the rotten floorboards, finally fetching up on the ground floor.*

fetching /fetʃɪŋ/. If you say that a woman looks **fetching**, you mean that she looks attractive. EG *Melanie looked remarkably fetching in a white dress.* ADJ QUALIT

fête /feɪt/, **fêtes, fêting, fêted;** also spelled **fete. 1** A **fête** is an event that is held out of doors and includes competitions, entertainments, and the selling of homemade goods. EG *...the church fête.* N COUNT

2 If someone important is **fêted**, a public welcome is provided for them. EG *In New York, Karen Blixen was being fêted by everyone who knew her work.* V+O : USU PASS

fetid /fetɪd, fiː-/. **Fetid** water or air has a strong, unpleasant smell. ADJ CLASSIF

fetter /fetə/, **fetters, fettering, fettered. 1** If something **fetters** you, it prevents you from behaving in a free and natural way. EG *...the forces that fetter our souls.* V+O Literary

2 Fetters are things that prevent you from behaving in a free and natural way. EG *...freed from the fetters of control.* N COUNT : USU PLURAL Literary

fetus /fiːtəs/. See **foetus.**

feud /fjuːd/, **feuds, feuding, feuded.** A **feud** is a long-lasting and bitter dispute. EG *His feud with the Premier proceeded remorselessly.* ▸ used as a verb. EG *They are constantly feuding amongst themselves... He feuded with the formidable Ernest Bevin.* N COUNT ▸ V OR V+ with : RECIP

feudal /fjuːdəˀl/ means relating to the system of feudalism. EG *...a feudal society.* ADJ CLASSIF : ATTRIB

feudalism /fjuːdəˀlɪzəˀm/ was a system in which people were given land or protection by people of higher rank, and worked and fought for them in return. N UNCOUNT

fever /fiːvə/, **fevers. 1** If you have a **fever**, your temperature is higher than usual because you are ill. ● See also **hay fever, scarlet fever, yellow fever.** N COUNT OR N UNCOUNT

2 You can also refer to extreme excitement or agitation as a **fever**. EG *He stayed calm through the fever of the campaign.* N COUNT : USU+SUPP

feverish /fiːvərɪʃ/. **1 Feverish** emotion or activity shows great excitement or agitation. EG *...the feverish excitement in his voice... a feverish race against time.* ◆ **feverishly.** EG *They worked feverishly.* ADJ QUALIT ◇ ADV

2 If you are **feverish**, you are suffering from a fever. ADJ QUALIT

few /fjuː/, **fewer, fewest. 1 Few** is used **1.1** to refer to a small number of things or people. EG *The window opened a few inches... During the first few weeks, I didn't understand a word... A few were smoking.* **1.2** to indicate that the number of things or people that you are referring to is smaller than is desirable or than was expected. EG *Very few people survived... There are fewer trains at night... Few of them ever reach their potential.* QUANTIF OR PRON

2 You use **no fewer than** to suggest that a number is surprisingly large. EG *No fewer than five cameramen lost their lives.* PHRASE

3 You use **quite a few** and **a good few** when you are referring to quite a lot of things or people. EG *We had quite a few friendly arguments... I spent a good few years of my life there.* QUANTIF

4 Things that are **few and far between** are very rare or uncommon. PHRASE

fiancé /fiˈɒnseɪ/, **fiancés.** A woman's **fiancé** is the man to whom she is engaged to be married. N COUNT

fiancée /fiˈɒnseɪ/, **fiancées.** A man's **fiancée** is the woman to whom he is engaged to be married. N COUNT

fiasco /fiˈæskəʊ/, **fiascos** or **fiascoes.** When something fails completely, you can describe it as a **fiasco**. EG *The meeting was a fiasco.* N COUNT

fib /fɪb/, **fibs, fibbing, fibbed. 1** A **fib** is a small lie which is not very important. N COUNT Informal

2 If you **are fibbing**, you are telling lies. EG *It isn't true! You're fibbing!* V Informal

fibre /faɪbə/, **fibres;** spelled **fiber** in American English. **1** A **fibre** is a thin thread of a natural or artificial substance, especially one that is used to make cloth or rope. N COUNT

2 Fibre consists of the parts of plants or seeds that your body cannot digest. EG *Scientists are recommending people to eat more fibre.* N UNCOUNT

3 A **fibre** is also a thin piece of flesh like a thread which connects nerve cells in your body or which muscles are made of. EG *...nerve fibres.* N COUNT

fibreglass /faɪbəglɑːs/; spelled **fiberglass** in American English. **Fibreglass** is plastic strengthened with short threads of glass. N UNCOUNT

fibrous /faɪbrəs/. Something that is **fibrous** contains a lot of fibres. EG *They eat a great deal of fibrous twigs and woody material.* ADJ CLASSIF

fickle /fɪkəˀl/. Someone who is **fickle** keeps changing their mind about what they like or want. ◇ **fickleness.** EG *This serves to demonstrate the fickleness of public taste.* ADJ QUALIT ◇ N UNCOUNT

fiction /fɪkʃəˀn/, **fictions. 1 Fiction** consists of books and stories about imaginary people and events. EG *I enjoy reading fiction... ...a fiction writer.* N UNCOUNT

2 A **fiction** is something that you pretend is true, although you know that it is not true. EG *We had to keep up the fiction of being a normal couple... ...the replacement of facts by comforting fictions.* N UNCOUNT OR N COUNT

fictional /fɪkʃəˀnəl, -ʃənəˀl/. **1 Fictional** people and events occur in stories, plays, and films, and never actually existed or happened. EG *...a fictional composer called Moony Shapiro.* ADJ CLASSIF

2 Fictional means relating to fiction. EG *...the fictional treatment of adultery.* ADJ CLASSIF : ATTRIB

fictitious /fɪktɪʃəs/. Something that is **fictitious** is false or does not exist. EG *They bought the materials under fictitious names.* ADJ CLASSIF

fiddle /fɪdəˀl/, **fiddles, fiddling, fiddled. 1** If you **fiddle** with something, you keep moving it or touching it with your fingers. EG *He sat nervously fiddling with his spectacles.* V : OFT+ with

2 When people **fiddle** an account or bill, they alter it dishonestly or arrange it so that they get money for themselves. EG *He had fiddled the figures in the transaction.* ◇ **fiddling.** EG *A lot of fiddling goes on in these companies.* V+O Informal ◇ N UNCOUNT

3 A **fiddle** is a dishonest action or scheme in which a person gets money for himself or herself. EG *Laing had worked some fiddle.* N COUNT Informal

4 A **fiddle** is also a violin. N COUNT

5 If you **play second fiddle** to someone, your position is less important than theirs in something that you are doing together. PHRASE

fiddle about or **fiddle around.** If you **fiddle about** or **fiddle around** with something, you keep moving it or touching it with your fingers. PHRASAL VB : V+ADV, OFT+ with

fiddly /fɪdli/. You say that something is **fiddly** when it is difficult to use or do, because it involves small or complicated objects. EG *It is a very fiddly job.* ADJ QUALIT Informal

fidelity /fɪdelɪˀtiˀ/. **1** When you talk about the **fidelity** of a person or an animal, you are referring to the fact that they continue to be faithful or loyal to someone. EG *There's nothing like a dog's fidelity.* N UNCOUNT : OFT+ to Formal

2 When you talk about the **fidelity** of a report, translation, or adaptation, you are referring to its degree of accuracy. EG *...fidelity to the author's intentions.* N UNCOUNT : OFT+ to Formal

fidget /fɪdʒɪt/, **fidgets, fidgeting, fidgeted.** When people **fidget**, they keep moving their hands or feet or changing their position slightly, because they are nervous or bored. EG *The children are starting to fidget.* V

fidgety /fɪdʒɪtiˀ/. Someone who is **fidgety** keeps fidgeting. ADJ QUALIT

Which words on these pages can be spelled in two ways?

field /fiːld/, **fields, fielding, fielded. 1** A **field** is an area of land on which a crop is grown, or an area of grass where animals are kept. EG ...*fields of wheat... We pitched our tent in a field.* N COUNT

2 A sports **field** is an area of grass where a sport is played. EG ...*a football field.* N COUNT

3 A magnetic or gravitational **field** is an area in which magnetism or gravity is strong enough to have an effect. N COUNT+SUPP

4 Your **field** of vision or **field** of view is the whole area that you can see from a particular position or without turning your head. EG *A brown figure dressed in red crept into her field of vision.* N COUNT+SUPP

5 In a war, fighting takes place in the **field** or on the **field** of battle. EG *They needed a more effective way of using military forces in the field.* N SING : the+N

6 A particular **field** is a particular subject or area of activity or interest. EG *He doesn't seem to have done much in the political field... She is an expert in this field.* N COUNT+SUPP

7 A **field** trip or a **field** study involves research that is done in a real, natural environment rather than in a theoretical way. ADJ CLASSIF : ATTRIB

8 Something that is studied or tested **in the field** is studied or tested in a real, natural environment. PHRASE

9 The team that **is fielding** in a game of cricket, baseball, or rounders is the team that is trying to catch the ball, rather than batting. V : USU CONT

10 If you **have a field day**, you have a very pleasant time doing something that you have been given an opportunity to do. EG *The local papers had a field day.* PHRASE

field-glasses are binoculars. N PLURAL

field marshal, field marshals. A **field marshal** is an officer in the army who has the highest possible rank. EG ...*Field Marshal Montgomery.* N COUNT

fiend /fiːnd/, **fiends. 1** If you call someone a **fiend**, you mean that they are very wicked or cruel. EG *I have no idea who this murderous fiend may be.* N COUNT Literary

2 You can use **fiend** to describe someone who is very interested in a particular thing or likes it very much. For example, if you say that someone is a health **fiend**, you mean that they are very interested in good health. N COUNT+SUPP Informal

fiendish /fiːndɪʃ/. **1** Someone who is **fiendish** is very cruel. EG ...*a fiendish despot.* ADJ QUALIT

2 A **fiendish** problem or task is very difficult. EG ...*a task of fiendish complexity.* ◊ **fiendishly.** EG *This effect is fiendishly hard to achieve.* ADJ QUALIT ◊ SUBMOD Informal

fierce /fɪəs/, **fiercer, fiercest. 1** A **fierce** person or animal is very aggressive or angry. EG ...*fierce dogs.* ◊ **fiercely.** EG *'Don't assume anything!' said Martha fiercely.* ADJ QUALIT ◊ ADV

2 Something that is **fierce 2.1** involves strong feelings or great activity. EG ...*a fierce battle... ...the fierce loyalty of these people.* ◊ **fiercely.** EG ...*a fiercely dedicated group of people.* **2.2** is very strong or intense. EG ...*fierce heat... ...a fierce storm.* ◊ **fiercely.** EG *The fire was blazing fiercely.* ADJ QUALIT ◊ ADV ADJ QUALIT ◊ ADV

fiery /faɪəriː/, **fierier, fieriest. 1** Something that is **fiery 1.1** is burning strongly or contains fire. EG ...*clouds of fiery gas.* **1.2** is bright red in colour. EG *The tonsils become fiery red and swollen.* ADJ CLASSIF ADJ QUALIT

2 A **fiery** person behaves or speaks in an angry way. EG ...*this fiery young man... ...a fiery speech.* ADJ QUALIT

fifteen /fɪftiːn/, **fifteens.** Fifteen is the number 15: see the entry headed NUMBER. EG *We were married for fifteen years.* NUMBER

fifteenth /fɪftiːnθ/ **fifteenths.** The **fifteenth** item in a series is the one that you count as number fifteen: see the entry headed NUMBER. EG *The palace is supposed to have been built in the late fifteenth century.* ORDINAL

fifth /fɪfθ/, **fifths. 1** The **fifth** item in a series is the one that you count as number five: see the entry headed NUMBER. EG *We were sent to another office on the fifth floor.* ORDINAL

2 A **fifth** is one of five equal parts of something. EG N COUNT : USU+of

Only one fifth of the surface area of Africa is farmland.

fiftieth /fɪftiːəθ/ **fiftieths.** The **fiftieth** item in a series is the one that you count as number fifty: see the entry headed NUMBER. EG ...*the fiftieth anniversary of the Russian Revolution.* ORDINAL

fifty /fɪftiː/, **fifties.** Fifty is the number 50: see the entry headed NUMBER. EG *He pointed to some low buildings about fifty yards away.* NUMBER

fifty-fifty. 1 When something is divided **fifty-fifty** between two people, each person gets half of it. EG *Profits were to be split fifty-fifty between us.* ADV AFTER VB, OR ADJ CLASSIF

2 If the chances of something happening are **fifty-fifty**, it is equally likely to happen as not to happen. EG *We have little better than a fifty-fifty chance of survival.* ADJ CLASSIF

fig /fɪg/, **figs.** A **fig** is a soft, sweet fruit full of tiny seeds. Figs grow on trees in hot countries. N COUNT

fig., figs. Fig. is used to refer to a particular diagram. It is an abbreviation for 'figure'. EG *The piston moves into a horizontal position (see fig. 3).*

fight /faɪt/, **fights, fighting, fought** /fɔːt/. **1** If you **fight** something, you try in a determined way to prevent it or stop it. EG *We must fight discrimination... You can't fight against progress.* ▸ used as a noun. EG ...*the fight against illegal drugs.* V+O; ALSO V : OFT+against ▸ N COUNT

2 If you **fight** for something, you try in a determined way to get it or achieve it. EG *They will fight for their rights... Workers will have to fight to participate in the country's economic growth.* ▸ used as a noun. EG ...*the fight for equality.* V : OFT+for OR to-INF ▸ N COUNT

3 When people **fight**, they try to hurt each other physically. EG *I learned how to fight other boys... He had fought in the First World War... The men were going off to fight a battle.* ▸ used as a noun. EG *There would be fights sometimes between the workers.* ◊ **fighting.** EG *We were only metres away from the fighting.* V OR V+O ▸ N COUNT ◊ N UNCOUNT

4 When people **fight** about something, they quarrel. EG *They fought about money... It's nice not having to fight you about housework.* V OR V+O : OFT +about/over

5 If you **put up a fight**, you fight strongly against someone who is stronger than you are. PHRASE

6 When politicians **fight** an election, they try to win it. V+O

7 If you **fight** your **way** somewhere, you get there with great difficulty, for example because there are a lot of people in your way. PHRASE

8 When you **fight** an emotion or desire, you try very hard not to feel it, show it, or act on it. EG *He fought the urge to cry.* V+O

9 to **fight a losing battle**: see **battle**.

fight back. 1 If you **fight back** against someone who has attacked you or made difficulties for you, you try to protect yourself and stop them or beat them. EG *The importing countries could fight back with laws of their own.* **2** When you **fight back** an emotion or a desire, you try very hard not to feel it, show it, or act on it. EG *She fought back the tears.* PHRASAL VB : V+ADV V+ADV+O

fight off. 1 If you **fight off** something, for example an illness or an unpleasant feeling, you succeed in getting rid of it. EG *We can fight off most minor ailments.* **2** If you **fight off** someone who has attacked you, you succeed in driving them away by fighting them. PHRASAL VB : V+O+ADV V+O+ADV

fight out. When two people or groups **fight** something **out**, they fight or argue until one of them wins. EG ...*while the European nations were fighting it out on the battlefield.* PHRASAL VB : V+O+ADV

fighter /faɪtə/, **fighters. 1** A **fighter** or a **fighter plane** is a fast military aircraft that is used for destroying other aircraft. N COUNT

2 A **fighter** is also someone who fights. N COUNT

figment /fɪgmənt/, **figments.** If you say that something is a **figment** of someone's imagination, you mean that it does not really exist and they are imagining it. EG *I thought this man Broum was another figment of your imagination.* N COUNT : USU+of

figuratively /fɪɡəˈrətɪvli¹/. When someone is ADV speaking **figuratively**, they are using a word or expression with a more abstract or imaginative meaning than its usual one. EG *'She said I killed him.' – 'She was speaking figuratively.'*

figure /ˈfɪɡə/, **figures, figuring, figured. 1** A N COUNT **figure** is **1.1** a particular amount expressed as a number, especially a statistic. EG *...unemployment figures... The figure for 1983 was as low as 23 per cent.* **1.2** any of the ten written symbols from 0 to 9 that are used to represent a number. EG *...a three-figure number.*

2 An amount or number that is in **double figures** PHRASE is between ten and ninety-nine. An amount or number that is in **single figures** is between nought and nine. EG *The rate of inflation remains in double figures.*

3 When you **put a figure on** an amount, you say PHRASE exactly how much it is. EG *They said defence spending should be raised but put no figure on the increase they wanted.*

4 You refer to someone that you can see as a N COUNT **figure** when you cannot see them clearly, for example because they are a long way away. EG *I could see a small female figure advancing towards us.*

5 Someone who is referred to as a particular type N COUNT+SUPP of **figure** is well-known and important in some way. EG *He was a key figure in the independence struggle... ...one of the great theatrical figures of our time.*

6 Someone who is regarded as, for example, a N COUNT+SUPP mother **figure** or a hero **figure** is regarded as the type of person stated or suggested. EG *...authority figures.*

7 Your **figure** is the shape of your body. EG *She's* N COUNT *got a fabulous figure.*

8 A **figure** is also a drawing or diagram in a book. N COUNT EG *The original design was modified (see Figure 4.)*

9 If you **figure** that something is the case, you V+REPORT: think or guess that it is the case. EG *They figured it* ONLY *that* *was better to stay where they were.* Informal

10 A thing or person that **figures** in something V:USU+*in* appears in it or is included in it. EG *Loneliness figures quite a lot in his conversation.*

figure out. If you **figure out** a solution to a PHRASAL VB: problem or the reason for something, you work it V+ADV+O OR out. EG *She had not yet figured out what she was* V+ADV+ *going to do... We thought you'd figured it out by* Informal *now.*

figurehead /ˈfɪɡəhɛd/, **figureheads.** If you refer N COUNT to the leader of a movement or organization as a **figurehead**, you mean that he or she has little real power. EG *The president had become merely a figurehead.*

figure of speech, figures of speech. A **figure** N COUNT **of speech** is an expression or word that is used with a more abstract or imaginative meaning than its original one.

filament /ˈfɪləmə³nt/, **filaments.** A **filament** is a N COUNT very thin piece or thread of something.

filch /fɪltʃ/, **filchs, filching, filched.** If someone V+O **filches** something, they steal it. EG *The letters had* Informal *been filched from the private files of John D. Archbold.*

file /faɪl/, **files, filing, filed. 1** A **file** is **1.1** a box N COUNT or a folded piece of card in which someone keeps documents that belong together. EG *He closed the file and looked up at Rodin.* **1.2** a collection of information about a particular person or thing. EG *Get me the personal file on Viktor Kowalski.*

2 Something that is **on file** or **on the files** is PHRASE recorded in a collection of information. EG *The police had both men on their files.*

3 If you **file** a document, you put it in the correct V+O:OFT+ file. EG *Bills are not filed under B; but under U for* under *unpleasant.*

4 In computing, a **file** is a set of related data that N COUNT has its own name.

5 When you **file** a formal accusation, complaint, or V+O OR V+*for* request, you make it officially. EG *Adoption papers were duly filed by Mr and Mrs White in May 1974... I'm filing for divorce.*

6 When a group of people **files** somewhere, they V+A walk one behind the other in a line. EG *They filed out in silence.*

7 A group of people who are moving along **in** PHRASE **single file** are in a line, one behind the other.

8 A **file** is also a hand tool with rough surfaces N COUNT which is used for rubbing hard objects to make them smooth, shape them, or cut through them.

9 If you **file** an object, you smooth it, shape it, or V+O cut it with a file. EG *Kitty sat at the kitchen table filing her fingernails.*

filial /ˈfɪljəl/ means relating to the status or duties ADJ CLASSIF of a son or daughter. EG *...a sense of filial obligation.* Formal

filing cabinet, filing cabinets. A **filing cabinet** N COUNT is a piece of office furniture with deep drawers in which files are kept.

fill /fɪl/, **fills, filling, filled. 1** If you **fill** a contain- V+O: er or area, you put a large amount of something OFT+*with* into it, with the result that it is full. EG *Fill the teapot with boiling water.*

2 If an amount of things or an object **fills** a space V+O or area, it is so large that there is very little room left. EG *Enthusiastic crowds filled the streets.*

◊ **filled.** EG *They entered a large hall filled with* ◊ ADJ PRED *rows of desks.* +*with*

3 If a thing or a place **fills**, it becomes full of V:OFT+*with* things, people, or a substance. EG *Madeleine's eyes filled with tears... The place of assembly filled quickly.*

4 If something **fills** you with an emotion or if an V+O: emotion **fills** you, you experience this emotion OFT+*with* strongly. EG *His son's lies filled him with anger and contempt... A wave of panic filled her.*

5 If something **fills** a need or a gap, it puts an end V+O to this need or gap by existing or being active. EG *The Alliance filled the political vacuum.*

6 Something that **fills** a role or position performs a V+O particular function or has a particular place within a system. EG *It has filled this role in a most satisfactory way for many years.*

7 If you **have had your fill of** something, you do PHRASE not want to experience it or do it any more. EG *I'd had my fill of storms.*

8 See also **filling.**

fill in. 1 When you **fill in** a form, you write PHRASAL VB: information in the spaces on it. EG *Fill in your name* V+O+ADV *and address.* **2** If you **fill** someone **in**, you give V+O+ADV them detailed information about something. EG *I'll fill you in on the details now.* **3** If you **fill in** for V+ADV, someone else, you do the work that they normally OFT+*for* do because they are unable to do it on that day. **4** If PHRASE you **are filling in time**, you are doing something to use up some spare time while waiting for something else to happen.

fill out. 1 When you **fill out** a form, you write PHRASAL VB: information in the spaces on it. EG *I've filled out the* V+O+ADV *death certificate.* **2** If a fairly thin person **fills out,** V+ADV he or she becomes fatter.

fill up. 1 If you **fill up** a container, you put a large PHRASAL VB: amount of something into it, with the result that it V+O+ADV is full. EG *Fill up his seed bowl twice a day.* **2** If a V+ADV, place **fills up**, it becomes full of things or people. OFT+*with* EG *His office began to fill up with people.*

fillet /ˈfɪlɪt/, **fillets.** A **fillet** of fish or meat is a N COUNT OR piece that has no bones in it. N UNCOUNT

filling /ˈfɪlɪŋ/, **fillings. 1** A **filling** is a small N COUNT amount of metal or plastic that a dentist puts in a hole in a tooth.

2 The **filling** in a cake, pie, chocolate, or sandwich N MASS is the mixture inside it. EG *...delicious chocolates with cream fillings.*

Which word on these pages is an informal word meaning 'to steal'?

3 Food that is **filling** makes you feel full when you have eaten it. ADJ QUALIT

filling station, filling stations. A **filling station** is a place where you can buy petrol and oil for your car. N COUNT

film /fɪlm/, **films, filming, filmed. 1** A **film** consists of moving pictures that have been recorded so that they can be shown in a cinema or on television. EG *Shall we go and see a film?... The film was shot largely on location... The broadcast began with close-up film of babies crying.* N COUNT OR N UNCOUNT

2 If you **film** someone or something, you use a camera to take moving pictures which can be shown in a cinema or on television. EG *Joan ran ahead to film us... The TV crews couldn't film at night.* V+O OR V

3 A **film** is also the roll of thin plastic that you use in a camera to take photographs. EG *...a roll of film.* N COUNT OR N UNCOUNT

4 A **film** of powder, liquid, or grease is a very thin layer of it. N COUNT : USU+SUPP

filming /fɪlmɪŋ/ is the activity of making a film, including the acting, directing, and operating of the cameras. EG *I found filming terribly exhausting.* N UNCOUNT

filter /fɪltə/, **filters, filtering, filtered. 1** To **filter** a substance means to pass it through a device which is designed to remove particles from it. EG *Water would have to be filtered many times to remove any radioactive matter.* V+O

2 A **filter** is a device through which something is filtered. N COUNT

3 When light or sound **filters** into a place, it comes in faintly. EG *...with the morning light already filtering through the curtains.* V+A

4 When news or information **filters** through to people, it gradually reaches them. EG *Disturbing rumours filtered back from the East.* V+A

filter out. To **filter out** something from a substance means to remove it by passing the substance through a filter. EG *First we would have to filter out some of the tar particles.* PHRASAL VB : V+O+ADV

filth /fɪlθ/. **1 Filth** is a disgusting amount of dirt. EG *...the filth and decay of the villages.* N UNCOUNT

2 People refer to words or pictures as **filth** when they think that they describe or represent sex or nudity in a disgusting way. EG *...the filth the press printed about him.* N UNCOUNT

filthy /fɪlθɪ/, **filthier, filthiest. 1** Something that is **filthy** is very dirty indeed. EG *...a really filthy oven... Her sandals were filthy.* ADJ QUALIT

2 People describe words or pictures as **filthy** when they think that they describe or represent sex or nudity in a disgusting way. EG *I caught her reading a filthy book.* ADJ QUALIT

fin /fɪn/, **fins.** A fish's **fins** are flat objects like small wings sticking out of its body. Fins help the fish to swim and to keep its balance. N COUNT

final /faɪnᵊl/, **finals. 1** In a series of events, things, or people, the **final** one is the last one. EG *...on the final morning of the festival... We made our final attempt to beat the record.* ADJ CLASSIF : ATTRIB

2 Final also means **2.1** happening at the end of an event or series of events. EG *The final applause was explosive.* **2.2** the greatest or most severe that is possible. EG *He paid the final penalty for his crime.* ADJ CLASSIF : ATTRIB

3 If a decision is **final**, it cannot be changed or questioned. EG *The judges' decision is final... You'd be insane to let him have the final say.* ADJ CLASSIF

4 The **final** of a competition or sporting event is the last game or contest. The winner of the final wins the whole competition or event. EG *I'm trying to get tickets for the Cup Final.* N COUNT+SUPP

5 When university students take their **finals**, they take the last and most important examinations in their course. N PLURAL

finale /fɪnɑːlɪ/, **finales.** The **finale** of a show or piece of music is the last section of it. EG *...the Finale of Beethoven's Violin Concerto.* N COUNT

finalise /faɪnəlaɪz/. See **finalize.**

finalist /faɪnᵊlɪst/, **finalists.** A **finalist** is someone who takes part in the final of a competition or sporting event. EG *...an Olympic finalist.* N COUNT

finality /faɪnælᵊti/. If you say or do something with **finality**, you say or do it in a way that makes it clear that you will not say or do anything else relating to that matter. EG *Margaret said quietly but with finality: 'Well, we'll just have to disagree over this.'* N UNCOUNT

finalize /faɪnəlaɪz/, **finalizes, finalizing, finalized;** also spelled **finalise.** If you **finalize** something that you are arranging or organizing, you complete the arrangements for it. EG *I'm hoping to finalize things with the builders next week.* V+O

finally /faɪnəlɪ/. **1** If you say that something **finally** happened, you mean that it happened after a long delay. EG *One of them stared at me for a long time and finally asked whether I was Angela Davis... They finally realized that the whole thing was a joke.* ADV

2 You use **finally** to indicate that something is the last in a series. EG *Trotsky lived in Turkey, France, Norway and finally Mexico.* ADV

3 You also use **finally** to introduce a final point, question, or topic. EG *Finally, Carol, are you encouraged by the direction education is taking?... Let's come finally to the question of pensions.* ADV SEN

finance /faɪnæns, faɪnæns/, **finances, financing, financed. 1** When someone **finances** a project or purchase, they provide the money that is needed to pay for it. EG *A private company will finance and build the pipeline.* V+O

2 Finance for a project or purchase is the money that is needed to pay for it. EG *The Group raises finance for oil drilling... Obtaining finance may be difficult.* N UNCOUNT

3 Finance is also the management of money, loans, credit, and investment, especially on a national level. EG *...public-sector finance... ...a successful job in high finance.* N UNCOUNT

4 You can refer to the amount of money that you have as your **finances.** EG *Whether it can be done depends, of course, on your finances.* N PLURAL

financial /fɪnænʃᵊl/ means relating to or involving money. EG *The company was in deep financial difficulties... Let's talk in purely financial terms.* ADJ CLASSIF

◊ **financially.** EG *The venture was not financially successful.* ◊ ADV+ADJ

financier /fɪnænsɪə/, **financiers.** A **financier** is a person who provides money for projects or enterprises. N COUNT

finch /fɪntʃ/, **finches.** A **finch** is a small bird with a short strong beak. N COUNT

find /faɪnd/, **finds, finding, found** /faʊnd/. **1** If you **find** something, often something that you are looking for, you discover it, see it, or learn where it is. EG *Put things in a place where you can find them quickly... She found a crack in one of the tea-cups... She looked up to find Tony standing there.* V+O

2 If you **find** something that you need or want, you succeed in getting it. EG *He cannot find work... I had not yet found the answer... They don't guarantee to find me a job.* V+O, V+O+O OR V+O+for

3 If you **find** that something is the case, you become aware that it is the case. EG *When I got back, I found that the reading lamp would not work... They found it impossible to get a bank loan.* V+REPORT : ONLY that; ALSO V+O+C OFT+to-INF

4 You can use **find** when describing your reaction to something. For example, if you say that you **find** something frustrating, you mean that you think it is frustrating. EG *I don't find that funny at all... I found him a disappointment... Others may find them of value.* V+O+C OR V+O+A

5 If you **find** yourself doing something, you do it without intending to. EG *He found himself giggling uncontrollably.* V-REFL+-ING OR A

6 If you say that something **is found** in a particular place, you mean that it exists in that place. EG *Four different species of lungfish are found in Africa.* V+O : USU PASS+A

7 If you **find** your **way** somewhere, you get there PHRASE by choosing the right way to go.

8 If something **finds** its **way** somewhere, it eventually gets there. EG *I doubt whether much of the money found its way to Bernadette.* PHRASE

9 If you **find** the time to do something, you manage V+O : OFT+ to do it even though you are busy. EG *How do you* to-INF OR for *find time to write these books?*

10 If someone who is on trial **is found** guilty or **is** V+O+C : USU **found** not guilty, the court or the jury decides that PASS they are guilty or innocent. EG *He was found guilty of murder.*

11 If you describe something that has been discov- N COUNT ered as a **find**, you mean that it is interesting, good, or useful. EG *Among the finds so far are pottery and jewellery... Liz Pym, who plays the heroine, is a real find.*

12 to **find fault**: see **fault**.

find out. 1 If you **find out** a fact that you did not PHRASAL VB : already know, you learn it, often by making a V+ADV+O OR deliberate effort. EG *I found out the train times... We* V+ADV+ *found out that she was wrong.* **2** If you **find** V+O+ADV someone **out**, you discover that they have been doing something dishonest.

finding /faɪndɪŋ/, **findings.** Someone's **findings** N COUNT : are the information they get or the conclusions USU PLURAL they come to as the result of an investigation or some research. EG *...the findings of the committee... His findings were both surprising and significant.*

fine /faɪn/, **finer, finest; fines, fining, fined. 1** ADJ QUALIT : You use **fine** to describe something that is very USU ATTRIB good. EG *From the top there is a fine view... It is, I believe, the finest English painting of its time.*

2 If you say that something is **fine**, you mean that ADJ PRED it is satisfactory or acceptable. EG *'Do you want it stronger than that?' – 'No, that's fine.'... If you want to come, that's fine.* ▸ used as an adverb. EG *We get* ▸ ADV *on fine.*

3 If you say that you are **fine**, you mean that you CONVENTION are in good health and quite happy. EG *'How are you?' – 'Fine, thanks.'*

4 Something that is **fine** is very narrow or consists ADJ QUALIT of very narrow threads or pieces. EG *...fine string... ...fine hair.*

5 A **fine** substance consists of very small bits or ADJ QUALIT particles. EG *...handfuls of fine sand.* ◊ **finely.** EG ◊ ADV *...finely chopped meat.*

6 A **fine** adjustment, detail, or distinction is very ADJ QUALIT delicate, small, or exact. EG *Their eyes are trained to see the fine detail.* ◊ **finely.** EG *...finely balanced* ◊ ADV *systems.*

7 You describe the weather as **fine** when it is not ADJ CLASSIF raining, especially when it is also sunny. EG *...a fine summer's day.*

8 A **fine** is a punishment in which a person is N COUNT ordered to pay a sum of money. EG *He paid a £10,000 fine for income tax evasion.*

9 If you **are fined**, you are punished by being V+O : USU PASS ordered to pay a fine. EG *The demonstrators were fined £5 each for breach of the peace.*

fine art, fine arts. 1 You can refer to the N UNCOUNT producing of objects which are beautiful rather OR N PLURAL than useful as **fine art** or the **fine arts**. EG *...a fine art course.*

2 to **get** something **down to a fine art**: see **art**.

finery /faɪnəriˈ/ is clothing and jewellery that is N UNCOUNT beautiful and impressive. EG *The ladies were dressed up in all their finery.*

finesse /fɪnes/. If you do something with **finesse**, N UNCOUNT you do it with great skill and elegance or subtlety.

finger /fɪŋgə/, **fingers, fingering, fingered. 1** N COUNT Your **fingers** are the four long jointed parts at the end of your hand. You can also use **fingers** to refer to your fingers and your thumb, although **finger** in the singular never refers to your thumb. See picture at THE HUMAN BODY. EG *She ran her fingers through the cool grass... He held the handkerchief between his finger and thumb.*

2 If you **finger** something, you touch it or feel it V+O with your finger. EG *Eric fingered his split lip.*

3 Finger is also used in these phrases. **3.1** If you PHRASES put your **finger on** something such as a problem, you succeed in identifying it. EG *He immediately put his finger on what was wrong.* **3.2** If you say that someone did not **lay a finger on** someone else, you mean that they did not touch or harm them. EG *Stop yelling! He didn't lay a finger on you.* **3.3** If you say that someone did not **lift a finger** or **raise a finger** to help someone else, you mean that they did nothing at all to help them. EG *He's never raised a finger to help you with the baby.* **3.4** If you **point the finger** or **point a finger** at someone, you blame them or accuse them of something. **3.5** to **cross** your **fingers**: see **cross**. ● to have **green fingers**: see **green**.

fingernail /fɪŋgəneɪl/, **fingernails.** Your finger- N COUNT nails are the thin hard areas on the ends of your fingers.

fingerprint /fɪŋgəprɪnt/, **fingerprints, fingerprinting, fingerprinted. 1** A **fingerprint** is a N COUNT mark made by your finger which shows the lines on the skin. EG *He was careful, leaving no fingerprints.* ● When the police **take** your **fingerprints,** ● PHRASE they make you press your fingers onto an inky pad and then onto paper, so that they can see what your fingerprints look like.

2 If the police **fingerprint** you, they take your V+O fingerprints.

fingertip /fɪŋgətɪp/, **fingertips. 1** Your finger- N COUNT : tips are the ends of your fingers. EG *I probed* USU PLURAL *through his hair with my fingertips.*

2 If you say that someone is professional or an PHRASE artist **to** their **fingertips**, you mean that they are professional or an artist in every way possible.

3 If you have something **at your fingertips**, you PHRASE can reach it or make use of it quickly and easily. EG *The task is easier now, with calculators and computers at your fingertips.*

4 If you have some information **at your finger-** PHRASE tips, you know it very well and can easily pass it on. EG *Mrs Leach had the facts at her fingertips.*

finicky /fɪnɪkiˈ/. Someone who is **finicky** is fussy. ADJ QUALIT EG *He was a very finicky eater.*

finish /fɪnɪʃ/, **finishes, finishing, finished. 1** V+O ; ALSO V When you **finish** something that you are making OFT+-ING or doing, you make or do the last part of it, so that there is no more for you to do. EG *The building was finished in 1962... I've finished reading your book.* ● When you put the **finishing touches** to some- ● PHRASE thing, you do the last things that are needed in order to make it complete. EG *She had been putting the finishing touches to her make-up.*

2 When something **finishes**, it does not continue V : USU+A any longer. EG *The course starts in October and finishes in June.*

3 The **finish** of something is the end or the last N SING part of it.

4 If you **finish** work or school at a particular time, V+O : USU+A you stop working or studying at that time. EG *I finish work at 3.*

5 When you **finish** something that you have been V+O eating, drinking, or smoking, you eat, drink, or smoke the last part of it. EG *Brody finished his sandwich.*

6 The position that someone taking part in a race V+A OR V+C or competition **finishes** in is the position they are in at the end of the race or competition. EG *He finished fifth in the 1967 US Open.*

7 An object's **finish** is the appearance or texture of N UNCOUNT its surface. EG *Metallic finish is standard on this car.* OR N COUNT

8 See also **finished**.

finish off. 1 When you **finish off** something that PHRASAL VB : you are doing, you do the last part of it. EG *He* V+O+ADV

If you make a fine distinction, are you being finicky?

finished off his thesis. **2** When you **finish off** v+o+ADV
something that you have been eating or drinking.
you eat or drink the last part of it. EG *He finished off
the wine with a couple of swallows.*

finish up. 1 If you **finish up** in a particular place PHRASAL VB :
or situation, you are in that place or situation at the V+ADV+A OR
end of doing something. EG *She'll be going on tour,* V+ADV+-ING
*starting in Southampton and finishing up in Lon-
don... They finished up serving in a shop.* **2** If you v+o+ADV
finish up some food or drink that is left, you eat or
drink it all.

finish with. When you **finish with** someone or PHRASAL VB :
something, you stop dealing with them or being V+PREP,
involved with them. EG *I haven't finished with you* HAS PASS
yet.

finished /fɪnɪʃt/. **1** If you are **finished** with some- ADJ PRED : OFT
thing, you are no longer doing it or dealing with it, +with
or are no longer interested in it. EG *He won't be
finished for at least half an hour... He was finished
with marriage.*
2 Something that is **finished** no longer exists or is ADJ PRED
no longer happening. EG *All that is finished now.*
3 You also say that people or things are **finished** ADJ PRED
when they are no longer important or effective. EG
If that happens, Richard is finished.

finishing school, finishing schools. A **finish-** N COUNT OR
ing school is a private school where rich or upper- N UNCOUNT
class young women are taught behaviour and skills
that are considered to be suitable for them.

finite /faɪnaɪt/. Something that is **finite** has a ADJ CLASSIF
definite boundary beyond which it does not exist or Formal
a limit beyond which it cannot increase or develop.
EG *...a finite but unbounded universe... We have a
finite number of places.*

fir /fɜ:/, **firs.** A **fir** or a **fir tree** is a tall, pointed N COUNT
tree that grows mainly in cool countries.
fire /faɪə/, **fires, firing, fired. 1 Fire** is the hot, N UNCOUNT
bright flames produced by things that are burning.
2 A **fire** is **2.1** an occurrence of uncontrolled N COUNT OR
burning which destroys things. EG *A fire had severe-* N UNCOUNT
*ly damaged part of the school... His neighbour's
house is not insured against fire.* **2.2** a burning pile N COUNT
of wood or coal that you have set light to, often in
order to keep yourself warm. EG *He lit a fire and
cooked a meal.* **2.3** a device that uses electricity or N COUNT
gas to give out heat and warm a room. EG *She
switched on the electric fire.*
3 Fire is used in these phrases relating to burning. PHRASES
3.1 Something that is **on fire** is burning and is
being destroyed. EG *Two vehicles were on fire.* **3.2**
If something **catches fire,** it starts burning. EG *Will
the house catch fire?* **3.3** If you **set fire to** something, you start it burning in order to destroy it. EG
He set fire to the church.
4 If someone **fires** a gun or **fires** a bullet, they V OR V-ERG
cause a bullet to be sent from the gun that they are
using. People can also **fire** missiles and arrows. EG
I fired three or four times in quick succession.
◊ **firing.** EG *The firing stopped.* ◊ N SING
5 Shots fired from a gun or guns are referred to as N UNCOUNT
fire. EG *There was a burst of automatic rifle fire...
We climbed up the hill under fire.* ● If you **open** ● PHRASE
fire on someone, you start shooting at them.
6 If you **fire** questions or suggestions at someone, v+o : OFT+at
you say a lot of them quickly, one after another.
7 If your employer **fires** you, he or she dismisses v+o
you from your job. EG *Graffman fired him for* Informal
incompetence.
firearm /faɪərɑ:m/, **firearms. Firearms** are N COUNT :
guns, especially the sort that you can carry. EG *He* USU PLURAL
*got a fourteen-year sentence for illegal possession
of firearms.*
firebrand /faɪəbrænd/, **firebrands.** You describe N COUNT
someone as a **firebrand** when they are very active
in politics and try to make other people take strong
action. EG *He is represented by the media as a
dangerous firebrand.*
fire brigade, fire brigades. The **fire brigade** is N COUNT
an organization which puts out fires. EG *Smother*

the flames with a coat or blanket and call the fire
brigade.
firecracker /faɪəkrækə/, **firecrackers.** A **fire-** N COUNT
cracker is a firework that makes several loud
bangs when you light it. EG *People set off strings of
firecrackers.*
fire engine, fire engines. A **fire engine** is a N COUNT
large vehicle that carries firemen and equipment
for putting out fires.
fire escape, fire escapes. A **fire escape** is a N COUNT
metal staircase or ladder on the outside of a
building down which people can escape if there is a
fire.
fire extinguisher, fire extinguishers. A **fire** N COUNT
extinguisher is a metal cylinder which contains
water or chemicals at high pressure for putting out
fires.
fire-fighting is the work of putting out fires. EG N UNCOUNT
...fire-fighting equipment.
fireguard /faɪəgɑ:d/, **fireguards.** A **fireguard** is N COUNT
a screen made of strong wire mesh that you put in
front of a fire so that people cannot accidentally
burn themselves.
fire hydrant /faɪə haɪdrənt/, **fire hydrants.** A N COUNT
fire hydrant is a pipe in the street from which
firemen can obtain water that they can use to put
out a fire.
firelight /faɪəlaɪt/ is the light that comes from a N UNCOUNT
fire. EG *His face looked ruddy in the firelight.*
fireman /faɪəmə³n/, **firemen.** A **fireman** is a N COUNT
person whose job is to put out fires. Firemen also
rescue people or animals when they are trapped,
for example in burning buildings or cars. EG *Firemen turned their hoses on the flames.*
fireplace /faɪəpleɪs/, **fireplaces.** A **fireplace** is N COUNT
an opening in the wall of a room where you can
light a fire. EG *There was a portrait of his wife over
the fireplace.*
firepower /faɪəpauə/. The **firepower** of an army, N UNCOUNT
ship, tank, or aircraft is the amount of ammunition
it can fire. EG *They have greatly increased the
firepower of their fleet.*
fireproof /faɪəpru:f/. Something that is **fireproof** ADJ CLASSIF
cannot be damaged by fire. EG *...fireproof clothing.*
fireside /faɪəsaɪd/, **firesides.** If you sit by the N COUNT :
fireside in a room, you sit near the fire. EG *...sitting* USU SING
comfortably by his fireside... ...a fireside chat.
fire station, fire stations. A **fire station** is a N COUNT
building where fire engines are kept, and where
firemen wait until they are called to put out a fire.
firewood /faɪəwʊd/ is wood that has been cut into N UNCOUNT
pieces so that it can be burned on a fire. EG *...a
bundle of firewood.*
firework /faɪəwɜ:k/, **fireworks. Fireworks** are N COUNT
small objects with chemicals inside them that burn
with coloured sparks or smoke when you light
them. Some fireworks make loud noises. Fireworks
are lit to entertain people. EG *A few fireworks went
off... I had gone to watch the fireworks... ...a
firework display.*
firing squad, firing squads. A **firing squad** is a N COUNT
group of soldiers who are ordered to shoot dead a
person who has been found guilty of committing a
crime. ● If someone is executed **by firing squad,** ● PHRASE
they are shot by a firing squad. EG *He faces death
by firing squad.*
firm /fɜ:m/, **firms; firmer, firmest. 1** A **firm** is N COUNT
an organization which sells or produces something
or which provides a service which you pay for. EG
He was a partner in a firm of solicitors.
2 Something that is **firm 2.1** does not change its ADJ QUALIT
shape much when you press it, although it is not
completely hard. EG *...a firm mattress.* **2.2** does not ADJ QUALIT
shake or move when you put pressure on it. EG *...a
firm ladder.* ◊ **firmly.** EG *Each block rested firmly* ◊ ADV
on the block below it.
3 If you have a **firm** grasp of something, you are ADJ QUALIT
holding it tightly. EG *I took a firm hold on the rope.*
◊ **firmly.** EG *She grasped the cork firmly.* ◊ ADV

4 A **firm** push or pull is done with quite a lot of ADJ QUALIT
force but is controlled. EG ...*firm pressure.*
◊ **firmly.** EG *She closed the door firmly.*   ◊ ADV
5 A **firm** decision or opinion is definite and unlike- ADJ QUALIT
ly to change. EG ...*a person with firm views.*
◊ **firmly.** EG *His sister was firmly of the belief that* ◊ ADV
he was crazy.
6 Firm evidence or information is definitely true. ADJ QUALIT
EG *No firm evidence had come to light... By the*
weekend came firm news.
7 Someone who is **firm** behaves in a way that ADJ QUALIT
shows that they will not change their mind or that
they are in control. EG *Our present state of affairs*
demands firm leadership... 'No,' said Mother in a
firm voice. ◊ **firmly.** EG *I shall tell her quite firmly* ◊ ADV
that it is not any business of hers. ◊ **firmness.** EG ◊ N UNCOUNT
She treated the children with kindliness and firm-
ness.
8 If you **stand firm**, you refuse to change your PHRASE
mind. EG *The Government should stand firm*
against such threats.
9 If something relating to finance and trade is ADJ CLASSIF
firm, it is not decreasing in value or amount. EG
Investment remained firm despite the average
1.8% growth rate.
first /fɜːst/ **firsts. 1** The **first** thing, person, event, ORDINAL
or period of time is the one that happens or comes
before all the others of the same kind: see the
entry headed NUMBER. EG ...*the first man in space...*
...*the first two years of life.*
2 If you do something **first, 2.1** you do it before ADV
anyone else does it. EG *Ralph spoke first.* **2.2** you do ADV OR
it before you do other things. EG *We sent her a* ADV SEN
letter first... First I went to see the editor of the
Dispatch.
3 When something happens to you for the **first** ORDINAL
time, it has never happened to you before. When OR ADV
you do something for the **first** time, you have
never done it before. EG *For the first time in our*
lives something really exciting has happened...
Vita and Harold first met in the summer of 1910.
4 An event that is described as a **first** has never N SING : a+N
happened before and is important or exciting.
5 The **first** you hear of something or the **first** you PRON
know about it is the time when you first become
aware of it. EG *The first Mr Walker knew about it*
was when he saw it in the local paper.
6 You use **at first** when you are talking about what PHRASE
happens in the early part of an event or experi-
ence, in contrast to what happens later. EG *At first I*
was reluctant.
7 You say **first** when you are about to mention the ADV SEN
first in a series of items. EG *There were several*
reasons for this. First, four submarines had been
sighted.
8 The **first** thing, person, or place in a line is the ORDINAL
one that is nearest to you or nearest to something
else. EG *They took their seats in the first three rows.*
9 You use **first** to refer to the best or most ORDINAL
important thing or person of a particular kind. EG
She won first prize... The first duty of the state is to
ensure that law and order prevail.
10 If you put someone or something **first**, you treat ADV
them as more important than anything else. EG *Put*
your career first... Your family must always come
first.
11 First is also used in these phrases. **11.1** If you PHRASES
experience something **at first hand**, you experience it yourself rather than being told about it by
other people. **11.2** If you do something **first thing**,
you do it at the beginning of the day, before you do
anything else. EG *I'll tell her first thing tomorrow.*
11.3 If you say **'first things first'**, you mean that a
particular thing should be dealt with before anything else because it is the most important thing.
11.4 If you say that you **do not know the first**
thing about something, you mean that you know
absolutely nothing about it.

first aid is simple medical treatment which is N UNCOUNT
given as soon as possible to a person who is injured
or who has suddenly become ill. EG *The wounded*
were given first aid... ...my first-aid kit.
first-born. You can refer to someone's first child N SING OR
as their **first-born** or their **first-born** child. EG ADJ CLASSIF :
We'll stand by you. You are our first-born... ...his ATTRIB
first-born son. Literary
first-class. 1 If you describe something or some- ADJ QUALIT
one as **first-class**, you mean that they are excellent and of the highest quality. EG ...*a first-class*
administrator.
2 A **first-class** degree is a degree of the highest ADJ CLASSIF
class. EG ...*a first class honours degree in applied* ATTRIB
chemistry.
3 A **first-class** ticket allows you to travel in the ADJ CLASSIF
best type of accommodation on a train, aircraft, or
ship. EG ...*a first-class rail ticket.* ▸ used as an ▸ ADV AFTER
adverb. EG ...*the privilege of flying first class.* VB
4 First-class postage is the quicker and more ADJ CLASSIF, OR
expensive type of postage. ADV AFTER VB
first floor. The **first floor** of a building is **1** the N SING : the+N
floor immediately above the ground floor. EG ...*on* British
the first floor of the Museum... ...a first-floor suite. **2** American
the ground floor.
first-hand. First-hand information or experi- ADJ CLASSIF :
ence is gained directly, rather than from other ATTRIB
people or from books. EG *They have first-hand*
experience of charitable organizations. ▸ used as ▸ ADV
an adverb. EG *This sort of experience can only be*
gained first-hand.
firstly /fɜːstlɪ/. You use **firstly** when you are ADV SEN
about to mention the first in a series of items or
reasons. EG *There are two reasons. Firstly I have*
no evidence that the original document has been
destroyed.
first name, first names. Your **first name** is the N COUNT
first of the names that you were given when you
were born. You can also refer to all of your names
except your surname as your **first names**. EG
Nobody called Daintry by his first name because
nobody knew it.
first night, first nights. The **first night** of a N COUNT
show or play is the first public performance of it.
first-rate. If you describe someone or something ADJ CLASSIF
as **first-rate**, you mean that they are excellent and
of the highest quality. EG ...*a first-rate golfer...*
...*first-rate performances.*
first school, first schools. A **first school** is a N COUNT
school for children aged between five and eight or British
nine.
fiscal /fɪskəl/ is used to describe something that ADJ CLASSIF :
relates to government money, especially taxes. EG ATTRIB
...*fiscal controls.* Technical
fish /fɪʃ/, **fishes, fishing, fished. Fish** is the most
common form for the plural of the noun, but **fishes**
is also sometimes used.
1 A **fish** is a creature that lives in water and that N COUNT
has a tail and fins. EG *We didn't catch any fish.*
2 Fish is the flesh of a fish eaten as food. EG ...*fish* N UNCOUNT
and chips.
3 If you **fish**, you try to catch fish, either for food or V
as a sport or hobby. EG *They went fishing and*
caught half a dozen trout.
4 If you **fish** a particular area of water, you try to V+O
catch fish in it. EG *It was the first trawler ever to*
fish those waters.
5 If you **fish** for information or praise, you try to V+for
get it in an indirect way. EG *I think he was just*
fishing for compliments.
6 If you **fish** something out of a liquid or a V+O+A
container, you take it out or pull it out. EG *More* Informal
bodies have been fished out of the canal... She
fished out her cigarettes.

Name some of the fittings you might find in an
office.

fisherman /fɪʃəmə³n/, **fishermen**. A **fisherman** N COUNT is a man who catches fish as a job or for sport.

fishery /fɪʃə³rɪ¹/, **fisheries**. A **fishery** is an area N COUNT of the sea where fish are caught in large quantities.

fishing /fɪʃɪŋ/ is the sport, hobby, or business of N UNCOUNT catching fish. EG *Fishing has been a profitable industry lately... ...a small fishing boat.*

fishing rod, **fishing rods**. A **fishing rod** is a long N COUNT thin pole with a line and hook attached to it which is used for catching fish.

fishmonger /fɪʃmʌŋgə/, **fishmongers**. A **fish-** N COUNT **monger** is a shopkeeper who sells fish. British

fishy /fɪʃɪ¹/. **1** If something smells or tastes **fishy**, ADJ QUALIT it smells or tastes like fish. EG *It had a fishy flavour.*
2 If something seems **fishy** to you, you feel that ADJ QUALIT someone is not telling the truth or not behaving Informal honestly. EG *It all sounded very fishy to her.*

fission /fɪʃə³n/. Nuclear **fission** is the splitting of N UNCOUNT the nucleus of an atom to produce a large amount of energy or to cause a large explosion.

fissure /fɪʃə/, **fissures**. A **fissure** is a deep crack N COUNT in something, especially in rock or in the ground. Formal

fist /fɪst/, **fists**. You refer to someone's hand as N COUNT their **fist** when they have bent their fingers to- wards their palm. EG *She hit me with her fist... I shook my fist... The Marine held it tightly in his fist.*

fistful /fɪstful/, **fistfuls**. A **fistful** of things is the N PART number of them that you can hold in your fist. EG *He handed me a fistful of letters.*

fit /fɪt/, **fits**, **fitting**, **fitted**; **fitter**, **fittest**. In American English the form **fit** can also be used for the past tense and past participle of the verb.
1 If something **fits**, it is the right size and shape to V OR V+O : go onto a particular person's body or onto a OFT+A particular object. EG *The boots fitted Rudolph per- fectly... Does the lid fit?... The metal cover fits over the tap.*
2 If something is a good **fit**, it fits. N SING
3 If something **fits** into something else, it is small V+A enough to be able to go in it. EG *All my clothes fit into one suitcase.*
4 If you **fit** something into the right space or place, V+O+A you put it there. EG *Philip fitted his key into the lock.*
5 If you **fit** a piece of equipment or an extra part to V+O : OFT+to/ something, you fix it to it. EG *Castors can be fitted to* with *a bed to make it easier to pull... The kitchen has been fitted with a stainless steel sink.*
6 You can also say that something **fits** a person or V+O thing when it is suitable for them. EG *The descrip- tion fits women better than it fits men... ...the attempt to make the punishment fit the crime.*
7 If someone or something is **fit** for a particular ADJ PRED+for purpose, they are good enough for that purpose. EG OR to-INF *The houses are now fit for human habitation... She regarded herself as fit to be a governess.*
8 If someone **sees fit** or **thinks fit** to do some- PHRASE thing, they decide that it is the right thing to do. EG Formal *The present government has seen fit to cut back on spending.*
9 Someone who is **fit** is healthy and able to do ADJ QUALIT physical activities without getting tired. EG *She works hard at keeping fit.* ◊ **fitness**. EG *They were* ◊ N UNCOUNT *trained to a peak of physical fitness.*
10 If you say that someone is **as fit as a fiddle**, you PHRASE mean that they are very fit. Informal
11 If someone has a **fit**, they suddenly lose con- N COUNT sciousness and their body makes uncontrollable movements. EG *...an epileptic fit.* ● If you say that ● PHRASE someone will **have a fit** when they hear about Informal something, you mean that they will be very angry or shocked.
12 If you have a **fit** of coughing or laughter, you N COUNT+SUPP suddenly start coughing or laughing in an uncon- trollable way. EG *She had a coughing fit.*
13 If you do something in a **fit** of anger or panic, N COUNT+of you are very angry or afraid when you do it. EG *In a fit of rage, he had flung Paul's violin out of the window.*

14 Something that happens **in fits and starts** PHRASE keeps happening and then stopping again.
15 not in a fit state: see **state**. ● See also **fitted**, **fitter**, **fitting**.

fit in or **fit into**. **1** If you **fit** something **in** or **fit** it PHRASAL VB : **into** your schedule, you find time to do it or deal V+O+ADV OR with it. EG *You seem to fit in an enormous amount* V+O+PREP *every day.* **2** If you **fit in** or **fit into** a group, you V+ADV OR V+ are similar to the other people in the group. EG PREP *These children are unable to fit into ordinary society when they leave school.*

fitful /fɪtful/. Something that is **fitful** happens for ADJ CLASSIF irregular periods of time, rather than being con- tinuous. EG *He dozed off into a fitful sleep.*
◊ **fitfully**. EG *A pallid moon shone fitfully between* ◊ ADV *the clouds.*

fitted /fɪtɪ²d/ **1** If you are **fitted** to something or ADJ PRED+to **fitted** to do something, you have the right qualities OR to-INF for it. EG *Those best fitted to their surroundings will* Formal survive.
2 A **fitted** piece of clothing is designed so that it is ADJ CLASSIF : the same size and shape as your body. EG *Dolly* ATTRIB *wore a grey dress with a fitted bodice.*
3 A **fitted** carpet is cut to the same shape as a ADJ CLASSIF : room so that it covers the floor completely. ATTRIB
4 A **fitted** piece of furniture, for example a cup- ADJ CLASSIF : board, is designed to fill a particular space and is ATTRIB fixed in place. EG *...fitted wardrobes.*

fitter /fɪtə/, **fitters**. A **fitter** is a person whose job N COUNT is to put together, adjust, or install machinery or equipment. EG *He got a job as an electrical fitter.*

fitting /fɪtɪŋ/, **fittings**. **1** If you say that something ADJ QUALIT is **fitting**, you mean that it is right or suitable. EG *She said that I was the eldest and that it was fitting that I should go first.* ◊ **fittingly**. EG *The speech* ◊ ADV *was fittingly solemn.* Formal
2 A **fitting** is one of the smaller parts on the N COUNT outside of a piece of equipment or furniture, for example a handle or a tap. EG *They make fittings for car dashboards... ...light fittings.*
3 Fittings are things such as cookers or electric N PLURAL fires that are fixed inside a building but can be removed to another building. EG *Make sure you know what fixtures and fittings will be left at your new home.*
4 If someone has a **fitting**, they try on a piece of N COUNT clothing that is being made for them, to see if it fits. EG *Rhoda had been for several fittings for the fur coat.*

five /faɪv/, **fives**. **Five** is the number 5: see the NUMBER entry headed NUMBER. EG *Five inches of snow had fallen.*

fiver /faɪvə/, **fivers**. A **fiver** is five pounds, or a N COUNT note worth five pounds. EG *You owe me a fiver...* Informal *She took a fiver from her purse.*

fix /fɪks/, **fixes**, **fixing**, **fixed**. **1** If you **fix** some- V+O+A thing to something else, you attach it firmly to the other thing. EG *He had the sign fixed to the gate... She fixed a jewelled brooch on her dress.*
2 If you **fix** your eyes or attention on something, V+O+on/upon you look at it or think about it with complete attention. EG *She fixed her brown eyes upon him.*
3 If you **fix** the date or amount of something, you V+O decide exactly what it will be. EG *All that remained was to fix the date of the wedding.*
4 If you **fix** something which is damaged or which V+O will not work properly, you repair it. EG *I learned how to fix radios in the Army... He spent the afternoon getting his car fixed.*
5 To **fix** something also means to arrange for it to V+O happen. EG *Leave it to me. I'll fix it.*
6 If you say that a race or a competition **was** V+O : USU PASS **fixed**, you mean that someone unfairly arranged Informal for a particular competitor to win or lose.
7 If you **fix** a drink or food for someone, you V+O, V+O+O, prepare it for them. EG *Would you like me to fix you* OR V-REFL+O *a drink?... She fixed herself a plate of food.* Informal
8 A **fix** is an injection of a drug such as heroin. EG N COUNT *He inquired if I was in need of a fix.* Informal

9 See also **fixed**.

fix up. 1 If you **fix** someone **up** with something PHRASAL VB : they need, you provide it for them. EG *They told me* V+O+ADV *that they could fix me up with tickets.* 2 If you **fix** V+O+ADV something **up**, you arrange it. EG *The holiday is all fixed up.*

fixation /fɪkseɪʃəⁿn/, **fixations.** If you have a N COUNT : **fixation** on someone or something, you think USU+SUPP about them to an excessive degree. EG ...*fixations on brothers or sisters... ...the sport fixation of the British.*

fixed /fɪkst/. 1 A **fixed** amount, position, pattern, ADJ CLASSIF or method always stays the same. EG *The signal goes on sounding at fixed intervals... ...a fixed pattern of behaviour.*

2 If you say that someone has **fixed** ideas or ADJ QUALIT opinions, you mean that their ideas or opinions never change. EG *Children can be raised without fixed ideas and prejudices.*

3 You can say that something is **fixed** in your mind ADJ PRED or brain when you remember it very well. EG *The scene was firmly fixed in all our minds.*

fixedly /fɪksəˈdli¹/. If you stare **fixedly** at some- ADV one or something, you look at them steadily and continuously for a period of time.

fixture /fɪkstʃə/, **fixtures.** 1 A **fixture** is a piece N COUNT of furniture or equipment, for example a bath or sink, which is fixed inside a house or other building and which is left in place when you move. EG *Make sure you know what fixtures and fittings will be left at your new home... ...the light fixture on the ceiling.*

2 If you say that something or someone is a **fixture** N COUNT in a particular place or group, you mean that they are always there and it seems likely that they will always remain there. EG *Pool seems likely to become a fixture in working-class pubs.*

3 In sport, a **fixture** is a match or competition N COUNT which has been arranged to take place on a British particular date. EG *We had to cancel a lot of fixtures... Most athletic clubs produce their own fixture lists.*

fizz /fɪz/, **fizzes, fizzing, fizzed.** If a liquid, espe- v cially a drink, **fizzes**, it produces lots of little bubbles of gas and makes a hissing sound.

fizzle /fɪzəⁿl/, **fizzles, fizzling, fizzled.** If some- PHRASAL VB : thing **fizzles out**, it ends in a weak or disappoint- V+ADV ing way. EG *The strike fizzled out after three days.*

fizzy /fɪzi¹/. A **fizzy** drink or other liquid is full of ADJ QUALIT little bubbles of gas and makes a hissing sound. EG ...*fizzy lemonade.*

flabbergasted /flæbəgɑːstɪ²d/. If you are **flab-** ADJ CLASSIF **bergasted**, you are extremely surprised. EG *I stared at him, flabbergasted.*

flabby /flæbi¹/. **Flabby** people are fat and have ADJ QUALIT loose flesh on their bodies. EG *He was a flabby, pale-faced bachelor... ...her flabby arms.*

flaccid /flæsɪd/. Something that is **flaccid** is soft ADJ QUALIT and loose or limp, rather than firm. EG *Her lips* Formal *went flaccid, her eyes glazed over.*

flag /flæg/, **flags, flagging, flagged.** 1 A **flag** is a N COUNT piece of coloured cloth which can be attached to a pole and which is used as a sign, signal, or symbol of something, especially of a country. EG ...*a ship flying a foreign flag... The guard blew his whistle and waved his flag.*

2 If you **flag** or if your spirits **flag**, you begin to v lose enthusiasm or energy. EG *They showed signs of flagging... Your spirits may flag when faced with this new task.* ◊ **flagging.** EG *She tried to revive* ◊ ADJ CLASSIF *their flagging energies.*

flag down. If you **flag down** a vehicle, especially PHRASAL VB : a taxi, you wave at it as a signal for the driver to V+O+ADV stop.

flagon /flægəⁿn/, **flagons.** A **flagon** is 1 a wide N COUNT bottle in which cider or wine is sold. 2 a jug with a narrow neck in which wine is served.

flagpole /flægpəʊl/, **flagpoles.** A **flagpole** is a N COUNT tall pole on which a flag can be displayed.

flagrant /fleɪgrənt/ is used to describe bad ac- ADJ QUALIT : tions or situations which are not concealed in any ATTRIB way. EG ...*a flagrant violation of human rights... ...flagrant injustices.* ◊ **flagrantly.** EG *This legisla-* ◊ ADV *tion remains flagrantly unenforced.*

flagship /flægʃɪp/, **flagships.** A **flagship** is the N COUNT most important ship in a fleet, especially the one on which the commander of the fleet sails. EG ...*a replica of Christopher Columbus's flagship.*

flagstaff /flægstɑːf/, **flagstaffs.** A **flagstaff** is the N COUNT same as a flagpole.

flagstone /flægstəʊn/, **flagstones.** Flagstones N COUNT are big, flat, square pieces of stone which are used for paving.

flail /fleɪl/, **flails, flailing, flailed.** If you **flail** V-ERG your arms or legs about or if they **flail**, they wave about in a wild, uncontrolled way. EG *The baby flailed her little arms... ...his flailing arms.*

flair /fleə/. 1 If you have a **flair** for doing some- N SING + thing, you have a natural ability to do it. EG *He had* OFT+ *for,* *a flair for this branch of law... Wilson was im-* OR N UNCOUNT *pressed by his political flair.*

2 **Flair** is also the ability to do things in an original, N UNCOUNT interesting, and stylish way. EG *She showed her usual flair and cunning.*

flak /flæk/. 1 **Flak** is a large number of explosive N UNCOUNT shells being fired at planes from the ground. EG *I saw one of the Dakotas hit by flak.*

2 You can also refer to severe criticism as **flak**. EG N UNCOUNT *The President has already run into murderous* Informal *political flak over his decision.*

flake /fleɪk/, **flakes, flaking, flaked.** 1 A **flake** is N COUNT 1.1 a small thin piece of something that has broken off a larger piece. EG ...*flakes of burnt paper from a bonfire.* 1.2 a snowflake. EG *The first flakes began to flutter down.*

2 If something such as paint **flakes**, small thin V :OFT+A pieces of it come off. EG *The paint was flaking off the walls.*

flake out. If you **flake out**, you collapse, go to PHRASAL VB : sleep, or lose consciousness, usually because you V+ADV are very tired. Informal

flamboyant /flæmbɔɪənt/. 1 Someone who is ADJ QUALIT **flamboyant** behaves in a very noticeable, confi- dent, and exaggerated way. EG *He has been accused of being too flamboyant on stage... My father was capable of flamboyant generosity.*

2 Something that is **flamboyant** is very brightly ADJ QUALIT coloured or of a very noticeable shape or design. EG ...*a flamboyant quilted bathrobe.*

flame /fleɪm/, **flames.** 1 A **flame** is a quantity of N COUNT OR hot, bright, burning gas that comes in a pointed N UNCOUNT stream from something that is burning. EG *The flames and smoke rose hundreds of feet into the air... The aircraft disappeared in a ball of flame.*

2 If something is **in flames**, it is on fire. EG *My* PHRASE *parents' home was in flames.*

3 If something **bursts into flames**, it suddenly PHRASE starts burning fiercely. EG *The satellite burst into flames and disintegrated.*

4 An **old flame** is someone who you once had a PHRASE romantic relationship with. Outdated

flamenco /fləˈmɛŋkəʊ/, **flamencos.** A **flamenco** N COUNT OR is a Spanish dance that is danced to a special type N UNCOUNT of guitar music.

flaming /fleɪmɪŋ/. 1 **Flaming** is used to describe ADJ CLASSIF things that are burning and producing a lot of ATTRIB flames. EG ...*planes diving down with flaming wings.*

2 You describe something as **flaming**, **flaming** ADJ CLASSIF **red**, or **flaming orange** when it is bright red or USU ATTRIB bright orange in colour. EG ...*gorgeous flaming sunsets... She had flaming red hair.*

3 Some people use **flaming** as a mild swear word ADJ CLASSIF : when they are annoyed. EG *The flaming car's* ATTRIB *locked.* Informal

---

What is the difference between a flask and a flagon?

flamingo /fləˈmɪŋɡəʊ/, **flamingos** or **flamin-** N COUNT
goes. A **flamingo** is a bird with pink feathers, long
thin legs, and a curved beak.

flammable /ˈflæməbəl/. Something that is **flam-** ADJ QUALIT
mable can catch fire and burn easily.

flan /flæn/, **flans.** A **flan** is a kind of tart which N COUNT OR
has a base and sides of pastry or sponge cake, and N UNCOUNT
which is filled with fruit or something savoury. EG
...onion flan.

flank /flæŋk/, **flanks, flanking, flanked. 1** If V+O : USU PASS
something **is flanked** by things, it has them on +by/with
both sides of it, or sometimes on one side of it. EG
Billy was seated at the table, flanked by the two
women.
2 An animal's **flanks** are its sides. EG Their legs N COUNT
gripped the flanks of the ponies.
3 The **flank** of an army or fleet is one side of it N COUNT
when it is organized ready for battle. EG ...the
weaknesses of NATO's south-east flank.

flannel /ˈflænəl/, **flannels. 1 Flannel** is a light- N UNCOUNT
weight cloth used for making clothes. EG ...a grey
flannel suit.
2 Flannels are men's trousers made of flannel. EG N PLURAL
...a pair of pressed grey flannels.
3 A **flannel** is a small cloth that you use for N COUNT
washing yourself. British

flap /flæp/, **flaps, flapping, flapped. 1** If a piece V-ERG
of cloth or paper **flaps** or if you **flap** it, it moves
quickly up and down or from side to side, often
making a snapping sound. EG His long robes flapped
in the breeze.
2 When a bird **flaps** its wings, it moves them V-ERG OR V+A
quickly up and down. EG Its wings flapped weakly...
The pheasant flapped around for a few seconds.
3 If you **flap** your arms or hands, you move them V+O
quickly up and down as if they were wings.
4 A **flap** is a flat piece of something that can move N COUNT
freely up and down or from side to side because it
is attached by only one edge. EG ...looking out
through a tent flap... The men wore black shiny
caps, with broad flaps at the back.
5 Someone who is **in a flap** is in a state of great PHRASE
excitement or panic. Informal

flare /fleə/, **flares, flaring, flared. 1** A **flare** is a N COUNT
small device that produces a bright flame. Flares
are used as signals. EG He stood ready to fire a
warning flare.
2 If a flame or fire **flares**, the flame or flames V : OFT+up
suddenly become larger. EG The candle flared to a
bright light.
3 If something such as violence, conflict, or anger V : OFT+up
flares, it starts or becomes more violent. EG From
time to time violence flared... Fury flared up in his
mind.
4 If something such as a dress **flares**, it spreads V : OFT+out
outwards at one end to form a wide shape. EG She
pirouetted, making the skirt flare out.

flared /fleəd/. **Flared** skirts or trousers become ADJ CLASSIF :
wider towards the hem or towards the bottom of ATTRIB
the legs.

flash /flæʃ/, **flashes, flashing, flashed. 1** A **flash** N COUNT :
of light is a very bright light which appears sudden- USU+SUPP
ly and then disappears immediately. EG Suddenly
there was a flash of lightning.
2 If a light **flashes** or if you **flash** it, it shines V-ERG
brightly once or several times. EG I'll flash my
headlights to make sure he sees us.
3 If you say that something **flashes** past you, you V+A
mean that it moves very fast. EG Something white
flashed past the van.
4 In a flash means very quickly. EG I was out of the PHRASE
room in a flash. Written
5 Quick as a flash means immediately and quick- PHRASE
ly. EG Quick as a flash, Claud pulled the paper bag Written
out of his pocket.
6 If something **flashes** through your mind, you V+through
think of it suddenly and briefly. EG It flashed
through his mind that he might never get back.

7 If you have a **flash** of intuition or insight, you N COUNT+SUPP
suddenly guess or realise something.
8 If you **flash** a look or a smile at someone, you V+O+at
look or smile at them quickly and briefly. EG He Literary
flashed a conspiratorial grin at them.
9 If you say that someone's eyes **flash**, you mean V
that their eyes seem bright because they are Literary
experiencing a strong emotion. EG Her eyes flashed
as she demanded to know what I was laughing at.

flashback /ˈflæʃbæk/, **flashbacks.** A **flashback** is N COUNT
a scene in a film or a part of a novel or play in
which the plot suddenly changes to events in the
past.

flashbulb /ˈflæʃbʌlb/, **flashbulbs.** A **flashbulb** is N COUNT
a small lightbulb that can be fixed to a camera. It
makes a bright flash of light so that you can take
photographs indoors.

flashlight /ˈflæʃlaɪt/, **flashlights.** A **flashlight** is N COUNT
a torch, especially a large one.

flashy /ˈflæʃɪ/, **flashier, flashiest.** You describe ADJ QUALIT
something as **flashy** when it looks smart, bright, Informal
and expensive in a rather vulgar way. EG ...a flashy
sports car. ◊ **flashily.** EG He was dressed rather ◊ ADV
more flashily than usual.

flask /flɑːsk/, **flasks.** A **flask** is **1** a small, flat N COUNT
bottle that you use for carrying alcoholic drink
around with you. **2** a Thermos flask. EG ...a flask of
coffee.

flat /flæt/, **flats; flatter, flattest. 1** A **flat** is a set N COUNT
of rooms for living in, usually on one floor of a British
large building. EG ...a block of flats.
2 Something that is **flat 2.1** is not sloping or ADJ QUALIT
curved, or has no raised parts. EG Every flat surface
in our house is covered with junk... He took the
handkerchief and smoothed it flat. **2.2** is not as
round, pointed, or tall as things of its kind usually
are. EG ...a huge man with a broad flat nose... ...a flat
box.
3 If something is **flat** against a surface, all of it is ADV+PREP
touching the surface. EG She let the blade of her oar
rest flat upon the water.
4 A **flat** tyre does not have enough air inside it. ADJ CLASSIF
5 A **flat** refusal, denial, or rejection is definite and ADJ CLASSIF :
firm. EG Their earnest request met with a flat ATTRIB
refusal. ◊ **flatly.** EG She has flatly refused to go. ◊ ADV
6 If someone says something in a **flat** voice, they ADJ QUALIT
do not show any emotion in their voice. ◊ **flatly.** ◊ ADV
EG 'She is dead,' said Ash flatly.
7 If something is done in a particular amount of ADV AFTER N
time **flat**, it is done in exactly that amount of time.
EG They will be able to hit the targets in four
minutes flat.
8 If an event or an attempt to do something **falls** PHRASE
flat, it is unsuccessful.
9 In music, a **flat** is a note that is a semitone lower N COUNT, OR
than the note which is described by the same ADJ AFTER N
letter. It can be represented by the symbol 'b' after
the letter. EG ...the Sonata in B flat minor.
10 If a musical note is played or sung **flat**, it is ADV OR ADJ
slightly lower in pitch than it should be. QUALIT
11 A **flat** charge or fee is the same for everyone ADJ CLASSIF :
whatever the circumstances are. ATTRIB
12 A **flat** battery has lost some or all of its ADJ CLASSIF
electrical power.
13 If you do something **flat out**, you do it as fast or PHRASE
as hard as you can. EG Our staff are working flat Informal
out.

flatmate /ˈflætmeɪt/, **flatmates.** Someone's **flat-** N COUNT
mate is the person who shares a flat with them.

flatten /ˈflætən/, **flattens, flattening, flattened.**
1 If you **flatten** something or if it **flattens**, it V-ERG
becomes flat or flatter. EG The steel rod had been
slightly flattened.
2 If you **flatten** buildings or crops, you destroy V+O
them by knocking or pushing them down. EG Huge
areas of Queen Victoria Street were flattened by
bombs.
3 If you **flatten** yourself against something, you V-REFL+A
press yourself flat against it, for example in order

not to be seen. EG *She flattened herself against the door.*

4 If you **flatten** someone, you make them fall by hitting them violently. EG *I watched Carpentier flatten Wells in 73 seconds.* v+o Informal

flatten out. If you **flatten** something **out** or if it **flattens out**, it becomes flat or flatter. EG *The lump had flattened out, almost.* PHRASAL VB : V-ERG+ADV

flattened /flætəⁿnd/. A **flattened** object **1** has been squashed flat. EG *...flattened paper cups.* **2** has a flatter shape than usual. EG *...a grotesque creature with a flattened body.* ADJ CLASSIF : USU ATTRIB

flatter /flætə/, **flatters, flattering, flattered. 1** If you **flatter** someone, you say or imply that they are more attractive, important, or clever than they really are in order to please them or to persuade them to do something. EG *Ginny knew that he was saying all this just to flatter her.* v+o

2 If you **are flattered** by something that someone says or does, you are pleased because it makes you feel more important. EG *I was flattered that he remembered my name... I'm all the more flattered to be invited to your home.* V-PASS : OFT+REPORT : ONLY *that*

3 If you **flatter** yourself that something is the case, you believe, perhaps wrongly, something good about yourself or your abilities. EG *I rather flatter myself I've been reserved for a better fate.* V-REFL +REPORT : ONLY *that*

flattering /flætərɪŋ/. If you say that something is **flattering**, you mean that it makes someone appear more attractive or important than they really are. EG *...clothing which is stylish, well made and flattering... It is not a flattering picture.* ADJ QUALIT

flattery /flætəri¹/ is flattering words or behaviour. EG *He was immune to the flattery of political leaders.* N UNCOUNT

flaunt /flɔːnt/, **flaunts, flaunting, flaunted.** If you **flaunt** something desirable that you possess, you display it in a very obvious way. EG *They flaunt their engagement rings... The leader of the group wanted to flaunt his authority.* v+o

flavour /fleɪvə/, **flavours, flavouring, flavoured;** spelled **flavor** in American English.
1 The **flavour** of a food or drink is its taste. EG *...the flavour of the honey... Do you think that improves the flavour?* N COUNT OR N UNCOUNT

2 If you **flavour** food or drink, you add something to it to give it a particular taste. EG *Milk can be flavoured with vanilla.* v+o : OFT+with

3 You can refer to a special quality that something has as its **flavour**. EG *Pimlico has its own peculiar flavour and atmosphere... ...drama with an African flavour.* N UNCOUNT

flavouring /fleɪvəⁿrɪŋ/, **flavourings;** spelled **flavoring** in American English.
Flavouring is a substance that you add to food or drink to give it a particular taste. N MASS

flaw /flɔː/, **flaws. 1** If there is a **flaw** in something, there is something wrong with it which makes it ineffective, invalid, or unsatisfactory. EG *There is a flaw in this policy. We have no money to lend them... The law contained a flaw which made it unworkable.* N COUNT

2 A **flaw** in someone's character is an undesirable quality which they have, especially the only one they have. N COUNT

3 A **flaw** in a material such as cloth or glass or in a pattern is a small mark or damaged area that should not be there. N COUNT

flawed /flɔːd/. Something that is **flawed** has a flaw of some kind. EG *We are all flawed in some way... ...flawed arguments.* ADJ CLASSIF

flawless /flɔːlˀs/. Something that is **flawless** is perfect and has no flaws. EG *...a flawless performance... ...her flawless complexion.* ADJ CLASSIF

flax /flæks/ is a plant whose stem is used for making thread, rope, and cloth. N UNCOUNT

flaxen /flæksəⁿn/. **Flaxen** hair is pale yellow in colour. ADJ COLOUR Literary

flay /fleɪ/, **flays, flaying, flayed.** When someone **flays** a dead animal, they cut off its skin. v+o

flea /fliː/, **fleas. 1** A **flea** is a very small jumping insect that feeds on the blood of humans and animals. N COUNT

2 If you send someone away **with a flea in** their **ear**, you speak to them angrily and reject their suggestion or attempt to do something. EG *Don't blame me if you come back with a flea in your ear!* PHRASE

fleck /flɛk/, **flecks. Flecks** are small marks on a surface, or objects that look like small marks. EG *...the grey flecks in his eyes... Little flecks of white powder floated on top.* N COUNT

flecked /flɛkd/. If a surface is **flecked** with small marks, it is covered with them. EG *Her eyes were dull grey, and flecked with dots of milky white.* ADJ PRED+ with

fled /flɛd/ is the past tense and past participle of **flee**.

fledgling /flɛdʒlɪŋ/, **fledglings. 1** A **fledgling** is a young bird. N COUNT

2 You use **fledgling** to describe an inexperienced person or a new organization. EG *...fledgling industries.* ADJ CLASSIF : ATTRIB Literary

flee /fliː/, **flees, fleeing, fled** /flɛd/. **1** If you **flee**, you run away from someone or something. EG *Local tribesmen fled in fear... He had to flee to Tanzania... The gazelle fled from him.* v : OFT+A

2 If you **flee** a place, you leave it quickly because you are in danger. EG *He fled the country.* v+o : NO PASS

fleece /fliːs/, **fleeces, fleecing, fleeced. 1** A sheep's **fleece** is its wool. N COUNT

2 A **fleece** is a sheep's wool when it is cut off in one piece. N COUNT

3 If you **are fleeced**, someone gets a lot of money from you by tricking you or overcharging you. EG *The pensioners feel they are being fleeced.* v+o : USU PASS Informal

fleet /fliːt/, **fleets. 1** A **fleet** is a group of ships organized to do something together. EG *Britain had to increase her battle fleet... ...a trawling fleet.* N COUNT

2 You can also refer to a group of vehicles as a **fleet**. EG *Fleets of buses take them the rest of the way.* N COUNT

fleeting /fliːtɪŋ/ is used to describe things which last for only a very short time. EG *I got only fleeting glimpses of them.* ◊ **fleetingly.** EG *...a way to assert power, however fleetingly.* ADJ QUALIT : ATTRIB ◊ ADV

flesh /flɛʃ/, **fleshes, fleshing, fleshed. 1** Your **flesh** is the substance your body is made of, which comes between your bones and your skin. EG *The fangs are driven into the victim's flesh.* N UNCOUNT

2 You can also refer to a person's skin as their **flesh**. EG *...the whiteness of her flesh.* N UNCOUNT

3 Someone who is your **own flesh and blood** is a member of your own family. ● See also **flesh-and-blood.** PHRASE

4 If you see someone **in the flesh**, you actually see them rather than, for example, seeing them in a film or on television. PHRASE

5 The **flesh** of a fruit or vegetable is the soft inner part. N UNCOUNT

flesh out. If you **flesh** something **out**, you add more details to it. EG *We're now seeing the proposal fleshed out for the first time.* PHRASAL VB : V+O+ADV

flesh-and-blood means real and alive, rather than imaginary or artificial. EG *...a game between a computer and a flesh-and-blood chess master.* ADJ CLASSIF : ATTRIB

fleshy /flɛʃi¹/, **fleshier, fleshiest. 1 Fleshy** people have a lot of flesh on their bodies. EG *...a fleshy middle-aged official... ...her fleshy arms.* ADJ QUALIT

2 Fleshy leaves or stalks are thick. ADJ QUALIT

flew /fluː/ is the past tense of **fly.**

flex /flɛks/, **flexes, flexing, flexed. 1** A **flex** is a long, flexible plastic tube with two or three wires inside. It is used to carry electricity from a plug to an electrical appliance. EG *...a length of flex.* N COUNT OR N UNCOUNT

If you are fleshy, are you fat?

2 If you **flex** a muscle or a part of your body, you v+o
bend, move, or stretch it for a short time in order
to exercise it.

flexible /ˈfleksɪbəˀl/. **1** A **flexible** object or ma- ADJ QUALIT
terial can be bent easily without breaking. EG *The
tube is flexible but tough.*

2 A **flexible** system or arrangement can be ADJ QUALIT
changed and adapted to different conditions or
circumstances. EG *We need a more flexible
decision-making system... ...flexible working hours.*
◊ **flexibility** /ˌfleksəˈbɪlɪˀtiˀ/. EG *This called for* ◊ N UNCOUNT
some flexibility of approach.

flick /flɪk/, **flicks, flicking, flicked. 1** If some- V-ERG+A
thing **flicks** in a particular direction or if you **flick**
it, it moves with a short, sudden movement. EG *Its
tongue flicks in and out of its tiny mouth... ...flicking
its tail backwards and forwards.* ▸ used as a noun. ▸ N COUNT
EG *...a quick upward flick of the arm.*

2 If you **flick** something away or **flick** it off V+O+A
something else, you remove it with a quick movement of your finger or hand. EG *He flicked the dust
from his suit... She sat there, flicking ash into the
ashtray.*

3 If you **flick** something such as a whip or a towel, V+O :
you hold one end and move your hand quickly up OFT+with
and then forward, so that the other end moves or
hits something. EG *He flicked their bare arms with
a tea towel.* ▸ used as a noun. EG *He gave a flick of* ▸ N COUNT :
the whip. OFT+of

4 If you **flick** pages over or **flick** through a book or V+O : OFT+A;
magazine, you turn the pages quickly. EG *He flicked* ALSO V+A
through the passport, not understanding a word.
▸ used as a noun. EG *...a quick flick through the* ▸ N COUNT
pages. +SUPP

5 You also **flick** something when you hit it sharply V+O
with your fingernail by pressing the fingernail
against your thumb and suddenly releasing it. EG *I
flicked the hollow door with my finger.*

6 If you **flick** a switch or catch, you press it sharply V+O : OFT
so that it moves into a different position. EG *He* +on/off
*flicked a couple of light switches... She flicked on
the lamp.*

7 Some people refer to the cinema as the **flicks**. EG N PLURAL :
Sometimes she just went to the flicks... What's on at the+N
the flicks? Informal

flicker /ˈflɪkə/, **flickers, flickering, flickered. 1** v
If a light or flame **flickers**, it shines unsteadily,
with sudden changes in strength and brightness. EG
The candle flickered by the bed. ▸ used as a noun. ▸ N COUNT
EG *...a faint flicker of lightning.*

2 A **flicker** of a feeling happens or is noticeable N COUNT
only briefly. EG *There was a flicker of fear in the
man's eyes.* ▸ used as a verb. EG *A rather sad smile* ▸ V+A
flickered across her face.

3 You can also say that something **flickers** when it v
moves lightly and quickly, especially up and down
or backwards and forwards. EG *Her eyelids flickered and closed again.*

flier /ˈflaɪə/. See **flyer.**

flight /flaɪt/, **flights. 1** A **flight** is **1.1** a journey N COUNT
made by flying, especially in an aeroplane. EG *It
had been his first flight.* **1.2** an aeroplane that takes
you on a particular journey. EG *Can you tell me
what time Flight No. 172 arrives?*

2 Flight is the action of flying. EG *...a bird in flight...* N UNCOUNT
Supersonic flight is very expensive.

3 A **flight** of birds is a group of them flying N PART
together. EG *...a flight of duck.*

4 Flight is also the act of running away from a N UNCOUNT :
place or situation which you feel is dangerous or USU+SUPP
unpleasant. EG *He was born at sea during his
parents' flight from the revolution.*

5 A **flight** of steps or stairs is a row of them N COUNT :
leading from one level to another without changing USU+of
direction. EG *She led the way down a short flight of
steps.*

6 You can refer to an idea that is imaginative but N COUNT+of
not practical as a **flight** of fancy or a **flight** of the

imagination. EG *Despite his occasional flights of
fancy, he is an astute politician.*

flighty /ˈflaɪtiˀ/. People, especially women, are ADJ QUALIT
described as **flighty** when they are not serious, Outdated
steady, or reliable. EG *...the disrespectful way in
which these flighty females carry out their duties.*

flimsy /ˈflɪmziˀ/, **flimsier, flimsiest. 1** Something ADJ QUALIT
that is **flimsy** is easily damaged because it is badly
made or made of a weak material. EG *Poor people
can afford only flimsy houses of mud and straw.*

2 Flimsy cloth or clothing is thin and does not give ADJ QUALIT
much protection. EG *They stood shivering in flimsy
white muslin gowns.*

3 A **flimsy** excuse or **flimsy** evidence is not very ADJ QUALIT
good or convincing.

flinch /flɪntˀʃ/, **flinches, flinching, flinched. 1** If v
you **flinch** when you are startled or hurt, you
make a small, sudden movement without meaning
to. EG *The children flinched as the cold rain
splashed them.*

2 If you **flinch** from something unpleasant, you are V : OFT+from
unwilling to do it or think about it. EG *They flinched
from the prospect of starting again.*

fling /flɪŋ/, **flings, flinging, flung** /flʌŋ/. **1** If you V+O+A
fling something somewhere, you throw or move it
there suddenly and not at all carefully. EG *She took
off her hat, flinging it on the grass... She was
flinging a few things into her handbag... The woman flung her arms around him.*

2 If you **fling** yourself somewhere, you move or V-REFL+A
jump there with a lot of force. EG *He flung himself
down at Jack's feet.*

3 If you have a **fling, 3.1** you enjoy yourself briefly N COUNT
in an energetic way. EG *...a last fling at the disco.* **3.2** Informal
you have a brief romantic or sexual relationship. EG
She had a brief fling while her husband was away.

flint /flɪnt/, **flints. 1 Flint** is a very hard, greyish- N UNCOUNT
black stone. EG *...the grey flint parish church. ...a* OR N COUNT
wall made of flints.

2 A **flint** is also a small piece of flint which can be N COUNT
struck to produce sparks and used to light a fire.

flip /flɪp/, **flips, flipping, flipped. 1** If you **flip** V+through
through a book or file, you turn the pages or
documents quickly.

2 If you **flip** a switch or **flip** a light or machine on V+O : OFT
or off, you turn it on or off quickly. EG *He flipped off* +on/off
the outside light.

3 If you **flip** something into a different position, V+O+A
you turn it or move it into that position with a
quick push. EG *He flipped open his notebook.*

4 If you **flip** something somewhere, you hit it V+O+A
sharply so that it moves there through the air. EG
*He tore off the metal tab and flipped it into the
garbage can.*

flippant /ˈflɪpənt/. You say that someone is being ADJ QUALIT
flippant when they make remarks which show
that they are not taking something seriously, although they ought to. EG *John was offended by the
doctor's flippant attitude.* ◊ **flippancy** /ˈflɪpənsiˀ/. ◊ N UNCOUNT
EG *'This is no time for flippancy,' he said angrily.*

flipper /ˈflɪpə/, **flippers. 1** The **flippers** of an N COUNT :
animal such as a seal are the two or four flat limbs USU PLURAL
that it uses for swimming.

2 Flippers are also flat pieces of rubber that you N COUNT :
can wear on your feet to help you swim more USU PLURAL
quickly, especially underwater.

flirt /flɜːt/, **flirts, flirting, flirted. 1** If you **flirt** V OR V+with :
with someone, you behave as if you are sexually RECIP
attracted to them, in a not very serious way. EG *She
never even flirted with other men.* ◊ **flirtation** ◊ N COUNT OR
/flɜːˈteɪʃəˀn/, **flirtations.** EG *He had a mild flirtation* N UNCOUNT
with two Danish blondes.

2 If you describe someone as a **flirt**, you mean that N COUNT
they flirt a lot.

3 If you **flirt** with the idea of doing or having V+with
something, you consider doing or having it, without
making any definite plans. EG *Burlington has flirted
for years with the idea of a wood-burning electrical
generator.*

flirtatious /flɜːˈteɪʃəs/. Someone who is **flirta-** ADJ QUALIT
tious behaves towards someone as if they are
sexually attracted to them, in a not very serious
way. EG *She kept giving him flirtatious looks.*

flit /flɪt/, **flits, flitting, flitted. 1** To **flit** about V+A
means to fly or move quickly from one place to
another with small, light movements. EG *Bats flitted
about in the darkening sky.*
2 If an expression **flits** across your face or an idea V+A
flits through your mind, it is there for a short time
and then goes again. EG *An expression of pain
flitted across her face.*

float /fləʊt/, **floats, floating, floated. 1** If some- V : OFT+A
thing **is floating** in a liquid, it is lying or moving
slowly along on the surface. EG *There was seaweed
floating on the surface of the water.*
2 Something that **floats** through the air moves V : USU+A
slowly through it, because it is very light. EG *Six
dollar bills floated down on to the table.*
3 If a sound **floats** somewhere, it can be heard V+A
faintly there. EG *Their voices floated across the* Literary
graveyard.
4 A **float** is a light object that is used to help N COUNT
someone or something float in water.
5 A **float** is also a lorry on which people and N COUNT
displays are carried in a festival procession.

floating /ˈfləʊtɪŋ/. A **floating** voter is a person ADJ CLASSIF :
who is not a firm supporter of any political party. ATTRIB

flock /flɒk/, **flocks, flocking, flocked. 1** A **flock** N PART
of birds, sheep, or goats is a group of them. EG *...a
flock of seagulls... Shepherds moved with their
flocks to lowland pastures.*
2 Someone's **flock**, especially a clergyman's, is the N COLL+POSS
group of people that they are responsible for. EG *He* Outdated
looked severely at his flock.
3 If people **flock** to a place or event, a lot of them V+A OR *to*-INF
go there, because it is pleasant or interesting. EG
*Many thousands had flocked to Rome for the
festival... Crowds flocked to see the treasures.*

flog /flɒg/, **flogs, flogging, flogged. 1** If you **flog** V+O OR
something, you sell it. V+O+O
2 To **flog** someone means to hit them hard with a V+O
whip or stick as a punishment. EG *Frequently slaves
were flogged.* ◇ **flogging, floggings.** EG *He was* ◇ N UNCOUNT
sentenced to receive a public flogging. OR N COUNT

flood /flʌd/, **floods, flooding, flooded. 1** If there N COUNT
is a **flood**, a large amount of water covers an area
which is usually dry, for example when a river
overflows. EG *In 1975, floods in north-eastern India
made 233,000 people homeless.*
2 If something **floods** a place that is usually dry or V-ERG
if the place **floods**, it becomes covered with water.
EG *When we took the plug out the kitchen flooded.*
◇ **flooding.** EG *There has been heavy rain in many* ◇ N UNCOUNT
areas, resulting in widespread flooding.
3 If a river **floods**, it overflows, usually after very V
heavy rain.
4 A **flood** of things is a large number of them that N PART
come or occur. EG *She received a flood of grateful
letters.*
5 If people or things **flood** into a place, large V+A
numbers of them come there. EG *This brought more
and more migrants flooding into the cities.*
6 If you **flood** a place with things, you fill it with so V+O :
many of them that it cannot hold or deal with any OFT+*with*
more. EG *Manufacturers have been flooding India
with imports from Britain.*
7 If memories or anxieties come **flooding** back, V+O OR V+A
you suddenly remember them or feel them again
very strongly. EG *The memories flooded back as we
passed the old school.*
8 If light **floods** a place or **floods** into it, it V+O OR
suddenly fills it. EG *Daylight flooded the room.* V+*into*

floodgates /ˈflʌdgeɪts/. If someone or something PHRASE
opens the floodgates, they make it possible for a
large number of people to do something for the
first time. EG *They were afraid of opening the
floodgates to mass democracy.*

floodlight /ˈflʌdlaɪt/, **floodlights, floodlighting,**
floodlit. 1 Floodlights are powerful lamps which N COUNT :
are used to light sports grounds and the outsides of USU PLURAL
public buildings when it is dark.
2 If a building or place **is floodlit**, it is lit by V+O : USU PASS
floodlights. EG *The cathedral is floodlit at night.*

floor /flɔː/, **floors, flooring, floored. 1** The **floor** N COUNT
of a room is the flat part of it that you walk on. EG
The book fell to the floor.
2 The **floor** of a valley or forest, or of the sea, is N COUNT+SUPP
the ground at the bottom of it. EG *Fifty yards
farther out, the ocean floor dropped steeply.*
3 A **floor** of a building is all the rooms that are on a N COUNT
particular level. EG *My office is on the second floor.*
4 If a remark or question **floors** you, you are so V+O
surprised or confused by it that you are completely
unable to answer it.
5 See also **shop floor.**

floorboard /ˈflɔːbɔːd/, **floorboards. Floorboards** N COUNT :
are the long pieces of wood that a floor is made of. USU PLURAL
EG *The floorboards creaked.*

flop /flɒp/, **flops, flopping, flopped. 1** If you **flop** V+A
onto something, you sit or lie down suddenly and
heavily because you are tired. EG *She flopped into
an armchair.*
2 If something **flops** somewhere, it falls there V+A
untidily. EG *She tipped the pan over and a fish
flopped out.*
3 Something that is a **flop** is a total failure. EG *His* N COUNT
first play was a disastrous flop... So the brilliant Informal
invention was a flop economically.* ▸ used as a ▸ V
verb. EG *One of their space projects flopped.*

floppy /ˈflɒpiː/. Something that is **floppy** is loose ADJ QUALIT
rather than stiff, and tends to hang downwards. EG
...ladies in floppy hats.

flora /ˈflɔːrə/. The **flora** in a place are all the N PLURAL
plants there. EG *...the unnecessary destruction of* Formal
the flora and fauna of our countryside.

floral /ˈflɔːrəl/. **1 Floral** cloth, paper, or china has ADJ CLASSIF :
a pattern of flowers on it. EG *...floral dresses.* ATTRIB
2 You also use **floral** to describe something that is ADJ CLASSIF :
made of flowers. EG *...floral decorations.* ATTRIB

florid /ˈflɒrɪd/. **1** Something that is **florid** is com- ADJ QUALIT
plicated and extravagant rather than plain and Literary
simple. EG *...florid verse.*
2 Someone who is **florid** has a red face. EG *...a large* ADJ QUALIT
man with a florid complexion.

florist /ˈflɒrɪst/, **florists.** A **florist** is a shopkeeper N COUNT
who sells indoor plants and bunches of flowers.

flounce /flaʊns/, **flounces, flouncing, flounced.** V+A
When people, especially women, **flounce** somewhere, they walk there quickly in a way which
suggests that they are angry. EG *She flounced into
the bedroom, slamming the door behind her.*

flounder /ˈflaʊndə/, **flounders, floundering,**
floundered. 1 If you **flounder** when you are in V : USU+A
water, you move in an energetic, uncontrolled way,
trying not to sink. EG *Ahead, men were floundering
in the dark swamps.*
2 You can also say that someone **is floundering** V
when they cannot think what to say or do. EG
*Suddenly she asked me: 'What do you think?' I
floundered for a moment.*

flour /ˈflaʊə/ is a white or brown powder that is N UNCOUNT
made by grinding grain. It is used to make bread,
cakes, and pastry.

flourish /ˈflʌrɪʃ/, **flourishes, flourishing, flour-**
ished. 1 When you say that something **is flourish-** V
ing, you mean that it is active or successful, or is
developing quickly and strongly. EG *Democracy
cannot possibly flourish in such circumstances.*
◇ **flourishing.** EG *...flourishing industries.* ◇ ADJ QUALIT
2 If a plant or animal **flourishes**, it grows well or V
is healthy because the conditions are right for it. EG
In these waters, bacteria flourish.

Find two words on these pages with the same
pronunciation.

3 If you **flourish** an object, you wave it about so v+o
that people notice it. EG *She rushed in flourishing a
document.*

4 If you do something with a **flourish**, you do it N COUNT
with a bold waving or sweeping movement. EG *Jack
drew his knife with a flourish.*

flout /flaʊt/, **flouts, flouting, flouted.** If you **flout** v+o
a law, order, or rule of behaviour, you deliberately
disobey it. EG *We're prepared to flout their laws if
necessary.*

flow /fləʊ/, **flows, flowing, flowed. 1** If a liquid, v+A
gas, or electrical current **flows** somewhere, it
moves there steadily and continuously. You can
also say that a number of people or things **flow**
somewhere. EG *The river flows south-west to the
Atlantic Ocean... European scientists are flowing
into the United States.* ▸ used as a noun. EG *The* ▸ N COUNT
blood flow is cut off... There's a good flow of +SUPP
information.

2 If someone's hair or clothing **flows** about them, it v+A
hangs freely and loosely. EG *She let her hair down
so that it flowed over her shoulders.* ◊ **flowing.** EG ◊ ADJ CLASSIF
...women in long flowing robes.

3 If a quality or situation **flows** from something, it v+*from*
comes from it or results naturally from it. EG *The* Literary
love for one another flows from that unity.

4 If there is a **flow** of conversation, people are N SING+SUPP
talking without stopping. EG *She can keep up a non-
stop flow of baby talk.*

5 the ebb and flow of something: see **ebb.**

flower /flaʊə/, **flowers, flowering, flowered. 1** N COUNT
The **flowers** on a plant are the coloured or white
parts that grow on its stems. EG *The hawthorn has
white flowers in June.*

2 Flowers are small plants that are grown for N COUNT:
their **flowers**, as opposed to trees, shrubs, and USU PLURAL
vegetables. EG *He planted flowers on the banks... a
bunch of flowers.*

3 When a plant or tree **flowers**, its flowers appear v
and open.

4 When an idea, artistic style, or political move- v
ment **flowers**, it develops fully and becomes successful. EG *Liberties need to grow and flower in
times of peace.* ◊ **flowering.** EG *...the flowering of* ◊ N UNCOUNT:
socialist thought. OFT+SUPP

flowerbed /flaʊəbɛd/, **flowerbeds.** A **flowerbed** N COUNT
is an area of earth in which you grow plants.

flowered /flaʊəd/. **Flowered** cloth, paper, or ADJ CLASSIF
china has a pattern of flowers on it. EG *...a flowered
skirt.*

flowering /flaʊəᵊrɪŋ/. **Flowering** shrubs, trees, ADJ CLASSIF:
or plants produce flowers. ATTRIB

flowerpot /flaʊəpɒt/, **flowerpots.** A **flowerpot** is N COUNT
a small container which a plant is grown in.

flowery /flaʊəᵊriʲ/. **1** Something that is **flowery** ADJ QUALIT
1.1 has a sweet smell. EG *...a flowery perfume.* **1.2** ADJ CLASSIF
has a pattern of flowers on it. EG *...a flowery apron.*

2 Flowery speech or writing contains long, com- ADJ QUALIT
plicated words and literary expressions.

flown /fləʊn/ is the past participle of **fly.**

flu /fluː/ is an illness which is like a bad cold. When N UNCOUNT
you have flu, you feel weak and your muscles ache.

fluctuate /flʌktjʊeɪt/, **fluctuates, fluctuating,** v
fluctuated. If something **fluctuates**, its amount,
level, or nature keeps changing. EG *Prices fluctuated between 1970 and 1972... Friendships blos-
somed, fluctuated, and died.* ◊ **fluctuating.** EG ◊ ADJ CLASSIF
...fluctuating opinions. ◊ **fluctuation** /flʌkt ◊ N COUNT OR
jʊeɪʃᵊn/, **fluctuations.** EG *...fluctuations in tem-* N UNCOUNT
perature... ...sharp fluctuations in policy.

flue /fluː/, **flues.** A **flue** is a chimney or a pipe that N COUNT
acts as a chimney.

fluent /fluːənt/. **1** Someone who is **fluent** in a ADJ QUALIT:
language can speak or write it easily and correctly. OFT+*in*
EG *She was fluent in Spanish... people who spoke
fluent Portuguese.* ◊ **fluently.** EG *He spoke both* ◊ ADV
languages fluently. ◊ **fluency** /fluːənsiʲ/. EG *She* ◊ N UNCOUNT
could speak German with great fluency.

2 Someone whose speech, reading, or writing is ADJ QUALIT

fluent speaks, reads, or writes easily and clearly
with no hesitation or mistakes. ◊ **fluently.** EG *By* ◊ ADV
the time she was six she could read fluently.

fluff /flʌf/, **fluffs, fluffing, fluffed. 1 Fluff** is **1.1** N UNCOUNT
the small masses of soft, light thread that you find
on clothes or in dusty corners of a room. EG *He
brushed some fluff from his jacket.* **1.2** soft, newly
grown hair or fur. EG *...a tiny creature covered with
black fluff.*

2 If you **fluff** something or **fluff** it out, you shake it v+o:
or brush it in order to make it seem larger and OFT+*up/out*
lighter. EG *...birds fluffing their feathers... She
fluffed her hair out in big waves.*

3 If you **fluff** something that you are trying to do, v+o
you do it badly. EG *My co-star used to get very cross* Informal
if I fluffed my lines.

fluffy /flʌfiʲ/. Something that is **fluffy** is very soft ADJ QUALIT
and furry. EG *...a fluffy kitten... ...fluffy white robes.*

fluid /fluːɪd/, **fluids. 1** A **fluid** is a substance that N COUNT OR
can flow, especially a liquid. EG *...petrol and clean-* N UNCOUNT
ing fluids. ▸ used as an adjective. EG *After a month* ▸ ADJ PRED
it was still completely fluid at the centre.

2 Fluid movements are relaxed, smooth, and ADJ QUALIT
graceful.

3 A situation, idea, or arrangement that is **fluid** is ADJ QUALIT
not fixed and is likely to change often. EG *Opinion in
the trade unions is very fluid as regards this
question.* ◊ **fluidity** /fluːɪdɪtiʲ/. EG *...the fluidity of* ◊ N UNCOUNT
the situation.

fluid ounce, fluid ounces. A **fluid ounce** is a N COUNT
measurement of liquid. There are twenty fluid
ounces in a British pint, and sixteen in an American pint.

fluke /fluːk/, **flukes.** If something good that hap- N COUNT:
pens is a **fluke**, it happens accidentally rather than USU SING
because of someone's skill or plan. EG *The police* Informal
have stumbled on this man by a fluke.

flung /flʌŋ/ is the past tense of **fling.**

fluorescent /flʊəresᵊnt/. **1** Something that is ADJ CLASSIF
fluorescent looks very bright when light is shone
on it, as if it is shining itself. EG *...a fluorescent
orange circle fixed to a belt.*

2 A **fluorescent** light shines with a very hard, ADJ CLASSIF:
bright light. ATTRIB

fluoride /flʊəraɪd/ is a mixture of chemicals that N UNCOUNT
is sometimes added to a water supply or to toothpaste because it is thought to be good for people's
teeth.

flurry /flʌriʲ/, **flurries. 1** A **flurry** of activity or N COUNT:
speech is a short, vigorous amount of it. EG *There* USU+*of*
*was the usual flurry of activity in the hall... The
decision raised a flurry of objections.*

2 A **flurry** of snow or wind is a small amount of it N COUNT:
that moves suddenly and quickly along. EG *The* OFT+*of*
wind came at them in a flurry... ...snow flurries.

flush /flʌʃ/, **flushes, flushing, flushed. 1** If you v
flush, your face goes red because you are embarrassed or because you feel hot. ▸ used as a noun. EG ▸ N SING
There was a flush in his cheeks. ◊ **flushed.** EG *Her* ◊ ADJ QUALIT
face was hot and flushed... ...her flushed cheeks.

2 When you **flush** a toilet or when it **flushes**, the V-ERG
handle is pressed or pulled and water flows into the
toilet bowl.

3 If you **flush** something down the toilet, you put it v+o+A
into the toilet bowl and operate the handle so that
it is washed away.

4 If you **flush** people or animals out of a place, you v+o+A
force them to come out. EG *They went into the area
to flush out guerrillas who were sheltering there.*

5 If you are **in the first flush** of something, you PHRASE
are in the first stages of experiencing it. EG *...in the* Literary
first fine flush of liberation.

6 If something is **flush** with a surface, it is level ADJ PRED:
with it and does not stick up. OFT+*with*

flushed /flʌʃt/. Someone who is **flushed** with ADJ PRED:
success or pride is very pleased and excited as a OFT+*with*
result of achieving something. EG *He hurried
flushed with victory into the office.*

fluster /flʌstə/, flusters, flustering, flustered. V+O : USU PASS
If something or someone **flusters** you, they make
you feel nervous and confused. ▸ used as a noun. EG ▸ N SING : a+N
*...doing several things at once and not getting in a
fluster.* ◊ **flustered.** EG *He was so flustered he* ◊ ADJ QUALIT
forgot to close the door.

flute /fluːt/, flutes. A **flute** is a musical instrument N COUNT
in the shape of a long tube with holes in it. You
play it by blowing over a hole near one end while
holding it sideways to your mouth. See picture at
MUSICAL INSTRUMENTS.

fluted /fluːtɪd/. Something that is **fluted** has long ADJ CLASSIF
grooves cut or shaped into it. EG *...fluted columns.*

flutter /flʌtə/, flutters, fluttering, fluttered. 1 If V-ERG
something **flutters** or if you **flutter** it, it waves up
and down or from side to side with small quick
movements. EG *His long robe fluttered in the wind...
Courting male birds flutter their wings like chicks.*
▸ used as a noun. EG *He let her pass after one flutter* ▸ N SING
of her long dark eyelashes.
2 If something light such as a bird or a piece of V : USU+A
paper **flutters** somewhere, it moves through the
air with small quick movements. EG *The pieces of
paper flutter down like butterflies.*
3 A **flutter** of panic or excitement is a slight N SING :
feeling of panic or excitement. EG *He felt a flutter* OFT+SUPP
of panic.
4 If your heart or stomach **flutters**, you feel V : USU+A
excited, worried, or afraid. EG *His heart fluttered
with fear.*

flux /flʌks/. If something is in a state of **flux**, it is N UNCOUNT
changing constantly. EG *...years of political flux and
turmoil.*

fly /flaɪ/, flies, flying, flew /fluː/, flown /fləʊn/. 1 N COUNT
A **fly** is a small insect with two wings. EG *...the flies
that buzzed around their bodies.*
2 When a bird, insect, or aircraft **flies**, it moves V : USU+A
through the air. EG *My canary flew away.*
3 If you **fly** somewhere, you travel there in an V : USU+A
aircraft. EG *You can fly from Cardiff to Ostend.*
4 When someone **flies** an aircraft, they control its V+O OR V
movement in the air. ◊ **flying.** EG *Why don't you* ◊ N UNCOUNT
take up flying?
5 If you **fly** someone or something somewhere, you V+O+A
send them there by plane. EG *Exotic fruits were
specially flown in for the occasion.*
6 If something **flies** about, it moves about freely V : USU+A
and loosely. EG *He jumped onto the platform with
his cloak flying.*
7 When a flag **is flying** or when people **fly** a flag, V-ERG
it is displayed at the top of a pole.
8 If something **flies** in a particular direction, it V+A
moves there with a lot of speed or force. EG *His
glasses flew off and smashed on the rocks... Pieces
of jagged metal are sent flying in all directions.*
9 If you say that **time flies**, you mean that it seems PHRASE
to pass very quickly.
10 If you **fly** at someone or **let fly** at them, you V+at,
attack them, either by hitting them or by insulting OR PHRASE
them. EG *One day the man flew at me in a temper.*
11 The front opening on a pair of trousers is N COUNT
referred to as the **fly** or the **flies.**
12 See also **flying.** ● **as the crow flies**: see **crow.**
● **to fly in the face of** something: see **face.** ● **to fly
off the handle**: see **handle.** ● **a fly in the
ointment**: see **ointment.**

fly into. If you **fly into** a rage or a panic, you PHRASAL VB :
suddenly become very angry or anxious, and show V+PREP
this in your behaviour. EG *She flies into a temper if I
make a mistake.*

flyer /flaɪə/, flyers; also spelled **flier.** 1 If a bird N COUNT :
or insect is a skilled **flyer**, it can fly well or USU+SUPP
quickly. EG *Hawkmoths are among the swiftest
insect flyers.*
2 People who fly aircraft are sometimes referred N COUNT
to as **flyers.** EG *...dashing young flyers.*

flying /flaɪɪŋ/. 1 If you take a **flying** leap or jump, ADJ CLASSIF :
you run forward and jump. EG *She took a flying leap* ATTRIB
at the fence.

2 A **flying** animal is able to fly. EG *...flies and other* ADJ CLASSIF :
flying insects. ATTRIB
3 If you **get off to a flying start**, you start PHRASE
something very well, for example a race or a new
job.
4 A **flying** visit is a visit that lasts for a very short ADJ CLASSIF :
time. ATTRIB
5 See also **fly.** ● **with flying colours**: see **colour.**

flying saucer, flying saucers. Flying saucers N COUNT
are round flat spacecraft from other planets, which
some people say they have seen.

flyover /flaɪəʊvə/, flyovers. A **flyover** is a struc- N COUNT
ture which carries one road over the top of another
one.

foal /fəʊl/, foals. A **foal** is a very young horse. N COUNT

foam /fəʊm/, foams, foaming, foamed. 1 Foam N UNCOUNT
consists of a mass of small bubbles. It is formed
when air and a liquid are mixed together violently.
EG *She could see the line of white foam where the
waves broke on the beach.*
2 **Foam** or **foam rubber** is soft rubber full of small N UNCOUNT
holes which is used, for example, to make mat-
tresses and cushions. EG *...foam mattresses.*
3 If a liquid **is foaming**, it has lots of small bubbles V : USU+A
in it or on its surface. ◊ **foaming.** EG *He poured* ◊ ADJ CLASSIF
foaming champagne into her glass.

fob /fɒb/, fobs, fobbing, fobbed. If you ask for PHRASAL VB :
something and you **are fobbed off** with something V+O+ADV,
else, the thing that you are given is not very good USU+with
or is not really what you want. EG *He may try to fob
you off with a prescription for pills.*

focal point /fəʊkəˀl pɔɪnt/. The **focal point** of N SING
people's interest or activity is the thing they concentrate on or the place they are active in most. EG
*Dinner was the focal point of my day... The focal
point of these celebrations was the local church.*

focus /fəʊkəs/, focuses, focusing, focused. The
spellings **focusses, focussing,** and **focussed** are
also used.
1 When you **focus** a camera or telescope or **focus** V-ERG OR V :
your eyes on something, you adjust it or them so OFT+on
that you can clearly see the thing you want to look
at. EG *...when he saw me focusing the camera on
him... His eyes would not focus.*
2 If a photograph or a camera or telescope is **in** PHRASE
focus, the photograph or the thing you are looking
at is clear and sharp. If it is **out of focus**, the
photograph or the thing you are looking at is
blurred. EG *The only part of the picture which was
in clear focus was a small child.*
3 If you **focus** a ray of light, you make it narrower V+O : OFT+on
or direct it towards a particular point. EG *I focused
the beam of the spotlight on them.*
4 If you **focus** your attention on something, you V-ERG : USU+
look at it or concentrate on it. EG *As we cannot* on
*study all resources, I propose to focus attention on
one... Attention focused on the election.*
5 If special attention is being paid to someone or N UNCOUNT
something, you can say that they are the **focus** of
interest or attention. EG *Changes in the urban
environment are the focus of public interest and
discussion.*
6 The **focus** on a particular person or thing is the N UNCOUNT
fact that special attention is being paid to them. EG
*The focus on money and position tends to foster
rivalry.*

fodder /fɒdə/ is food that is given to animals such N UNCOUNT
as cows or horses.

foe /fəʊ/, foes. Your **foe** is your enemy. EG *Friends* N COUNT
became foes. Outdated

foetus /fiːtəs/, foetuses; also spelled **fetus.** A N COUNT
foetus is an unborn animal or human being in its
later stages of development.

fog /fɒg/, fogs. When there is **fog**, there are tiny N UNCOUNT
drops of water in the air which form a thick cloud OR N COUNT

Do you believe in flying saucers?

and make it difficult to see things. EG *The only accident I've ever had was in fog... Around midday, the fog lifted.*

foggy /fɒgiˈ/, **foggier, foggiest. 1** When it is foggy, there is fog. EG *...a foggy day.* ADJ QUALIT

2 When people say they **haven't the foggiest idea**, they are emphasizing that they do not know something. EG *I haven't the foggiest idea what it is.* PHRASE Informal

foghorn /fɒghɔːn/, **foghorns.** A **foghorn** is a loud N COUNT horn that is used when it is foggy to warn ships about the position of land and other ships.

foible /fɔɪbəl/, **foibles.** A **foible** is a habit or N COUNT tendency which is rather strange or foolish, but not serious. EG *She knows his moods and foibles.*

foil /fɔɪl/, **foils, foiling, foiled. 1** Foil is metal in N UNCOUNT the form of a sheet as thin as paper. It is used especially to wrap food in and keep it fresh. EG *...the foil wrapper of a bar of chocolate.*

2 If you **foil** someone's plan or attempt at some- v+o thing, you prevent them from being successful. EG *Their attempt to recapture Calais was foiled by a traitor.*

3 Something that is a good **foil** for something else N SING : contrasts with it and makes its good qualities more USU+for/to noticeable. EG *She had bronzed skin, for which her yellow swimsuit was a perfect foil.*

foist /fɔɪst/, **foists, foisting, foisted.** If you **foist** v+o+on something on someone, you force them to have it or experience it. EG *They were out to foist their views on the people.*

fold /fəʊld/, **folds, folding, folded. 1** If you **fold** a v+o : OFT+A piece of paper or cloth, you bend it so that one part of it covers another part. EG *Fold the sheet and blankets back at the top.*

2 If you **fold** something, you make it into a smaller v+o shape by folding it several times. EG *They folded the tent neatly.*

3 A **fold** is **3.1** one of the curved shapes that are N COUNT formed in a piece of cloth when it is not lying flat. EG *Snow had collected in the folds of my clothes.* **3.2** a bend that you make in a piece of paper or cloth when you fold it.

4 If you **fold** a piece of furniture or equipment, you v-ERG : USU+A change its shape by bending or closing parts of it. EG *The bed can be easily erected or folded away... The rear seat folds down.*

5 If you **fold** your arms or hands, you bring them v+o together and cross them or link them. EG *He sat with his arms folded across his chest.*

6 If a business or organization **folds**, it is unsuc- v cessful and has to close. EG *The project folded.*

7 You can refer to an organization or group as the N SING : the+N **fold** when you are talking about its members Literary leaving it or returning to it. EG *They wanted to entice the conservatives back to the fold.*

8 See also **folding.**

fold up. 1 If you **fold** something **up**, you make it PHRASAL VB : into a smaller shape by folding it several times. EG V+O+ADV *She folded up some shirts.* **2** If a business or v+ADV organization **folds up**, it is unsuccessful and has to close.

-fold combines with a number **1** to indicate that something has a particular number of kinds or parts. EG *The problems were two-fold: it was diffi- cult to get finance, and there weren't enough trained people available.* **2** to indicate that some- thing is multiplied a particular number of times. EG *Even if we multiplied it ten-fold, that would still only be thirty per cent.*

folder /fəʊldə/, **folders.** A **folder** is a thin piece of N COUNT cardboard folded into the shape of a container or cover, in which you can keep documents. EG *He took a sealed envelope from the folder on his desk.*

folding /fəʊldɪŋ/. A **folding** table, bicycle, or ADJ CLASSIF : other object is designed so that you can fold it into ATTRIB a smaller shape to make it easier to carry or store. EG *...folding chairs... ...folding steps.*

foliage /fəʊliˈɪdʒ/. The leaves of plants and trees N UNCOUNT are referred to as **foliage**. EG *...the dense foliage of the forest.*

folk /fəʊk/, **folks. 1** You can refer to people as N PLURAL : **folk**. EG *...old folk... ...country folk.* OFT+SUPP

2 Your **folks** are your close relatives, especially N PLURAL your parents. EG *I don't even have time to write Informal letters to my folks.* American

3 You can use **folks** to address a group of people. VOCATIVE EG *That's all for tonight, folks.*

4 Folk music, art, and customs are considered to ADJ CLASSIF : be traditional or typical of a particular community ATTRIB or nation. EG *...Russian folk songs.*

folklore /fəʊklɔː/. The traditional stories and cus- N UNCOUNT toms of a community or nation are referred to as its **folklore**. EG *...a flourishing oral tradition of folklore and song.*

follow /fɒləʊ/, **follows, following, followed. 1** If v+o OR v you **follow** someone, **1.1** you move along behind them. EG *He followed Sally into the yard... Lynn got up and made for the stairs. Marsha followed.* **1.2** you go to the place that they have recently gone to. EG *He followed them to Venice.*

2 An event or period of time that **follows** a v+o OR v particular event happens or comes after it. EG *In the days that followed, Keith and his mates could talk of nothing else... ...outings to the cinema followed by tea at Lyons Corner House... Famine and disease follow close behind.*

3 If you say that something **follows**, you mean that **3.1** it is true as a logical result of something else v : OFT being true. EG *Just because they are old, it doesn't* +REPORT follow that they have to be patronized. **3.2** it comes V OR V+O next in a piece of writing or speech. EG *I learned most of what follows from a parlourmaid called Louise.*

4 You use **as follows** to introduce **4.1** a list of PHRASE things. EG *The contents are as follows: one black desk, one grey wastepaper bin, two red chairs.* **4.2** a description of the way that something is done. EG *File your correspondence roughly as follows.*

5 If you **follow** something with your eyes, you v+o : USU+A watch it as it moves. EG *Its eyes followed her everywhere she moved.*

6 If you **follow** a path, river, or route, you go along v+o : USU+A it. EG *We followed a path up along the creek.*

7 If you **follow** someone's instructions, advice, or v+o example, you do what they say or do what they have done. EG *She promised to follow his advice.*

8 If you **follow** a particular course of action, you do v+o a particular thing, in a planned way. EG *This forced them to follow a tight money policy.*

9 If you manage to **follow** an explanation or the v+o OR v : plot of a story, you manage to understand it. EG USU WITH *They were having some difficulty in following the* BROAD NEG *plot... He didn't quite follow.*

10 If you **follow** a series of events or a television v+o serial, you take an interest in it and keep informed about what happens. EG *...the thousands of Ameri- can couples who followed the case with great interest.*

11 to follow suit: see **suit.** ● See also **following.**

follow up. 1 If you **follow** something **up**, you try PHRASAL VB : to find out more about it. EG *It's an idea which has* V+O+ADV *been followed up by a group of researchers at Birmingham.* **2** If you **follow** one thing **up** with v+o+ADV, another, you do the second thing after you have OFT+with done the first. EG *He followed up this criticism with a personal attack on the Prime Minister.* **3** See also **follow-up.**

follower /fɒləʊə/, **followers.** The **followers** of a N COUNT : person or belief are the people who support the USU+POSS person or belief. EG *...Freud and his followers... ...the followers of Chinese communism.*

following /fɒləʊɪŋ/. **1** The **following** day, week, ADJ CLASSIF : or year is the day, week, or year that comes after ATTRIB the one that you have just mentioned. EG *He died* the+ADJ *the following day... She intended to come on the following Friday.*

2 Following a particular event means after that PREP event. EG ...*the election of Harold Wilson to the leadership following Gaitskell's death.*

3 You can refer to the things that you are about to ADJ CLASSIF: mention as the **following** things. EG *This could be* ATTRIB; *achieved in the following way.* the+ADJ

4 A person or organization that has a **following** N SING has a group of people who support their beliefs or actions. EG *This religion is too stark to attract a large following.*

follow-up, follow-ups. Follow-up work or action ADJ CLASSIF: is done as a continuation or second part of some- ATTRIB thing that has been done previously. EG *He needed follow-up treatment from a specialist doctor...* ...*a follow-up survey.* ▸ used as a noun. EG *This confer-* ▸ N COUNT *ence is a follow-up to an earlier one in Gabon.*

folly /fɒli¹/, **follies.** If you say that an action N UNCOUNT or a **folly**, you mean that OR N COUNT way of behaving is **folly** it is foolish. EG *It would be folly to continue...* ...*to protect others against their follies or vices.*

fond /fɒnd/, **fonder, fondest. 1** If you are **fond** of ADJ PRED+of someone, you like them and have a feeling of affection for them. EG *I'm very fond of you.*

2 If you are **fond** of something, you like it. If you ADJ PRED+of are **fond** of doing something, you like doing it. EG *I am not fond of salad... Etta was fond of shopping.* ◊ **fondness.** EG ...*my fondness for red wine and* ◊ N UNCOUNT *black olives.*

3 You use **fond** to describe people or their actions ADJ QUALIT: or expressions when they show affection for some- ATTRIB one or something. EG *His fond parents looked on with a smile...* ...*looking at me with fond eyes.* ◊ **fondly.** EG *He used to gaze at the old car fondly.* ◊ ADV

4 Fond hopes, wishes, or expectations are unlikely ADJ CLASSIF: to be fulfilled. EG *One fond dream has been to* ATTRIB *harness the sun's rays.* ◊ **fondly.** EG *He had fondly* ◊ ADV *imagined that it would be a simple matter.*

fondle /fɒndə⁰l/, **fondles, fondling, fondled.** If V+O you **fondle** someone, you touch them or stroke them gently, usually to show your affection for them. EG *I began fondling her neck.*

font /fɒnt/, **fonts.** The **font** in a church is a bowl N COUNT which holds the water used for baptisms.

food /fuːd/, **foods. Food** is what people and ani- N MASS mals eat. EG ...*money for food or clothing...* ...*food supplies...* ...*health foods.*

foodstuff /fuːdstʌf/, **foodstuffs. Foodstuffs** are N COUNT: substances which people eat. EG *They produce* USU PLURAL *sugar and other basic foodstuffs.*

fool /fuːl/, **fools, fooling, fooled. 1** If you call N COUNT OR someone a **fool**, you mean that they are silly or VOCATIVE have done something silly. EG *Just look what you've done! You stupid fool!... She was sharp-witted and no fool.*

2 If you **make a fool of** someone, you make them PHRASE appear silly by telling people about something silly that they have done, or by tricking them in some way. EG *They threatened to publish his letters to her and make a fool of him before the world.*

3 If you **make a fool of** yourself, you behave in a PHRASE way that makes you appear silly. EG *He had never learned to dance and was not prepared to make a fool of himself.*

4 If you **play the fool**, you behave in a playful, PHRASE childish, and silly way.

5 If you **fool** someone, you deceive or trick them. V+O EG *He fooled them with false promises... Do not be fooled into thinking that the system is perfect.*

fool about or **fool around.** If you **fool about** or PHRASAL VB: **fool around**, you behave in a playful, childish, and V+ADV silly way. EG *He was always fooling about.*

foolhardy /fuːlhɑːdi¹/. **Foolhardy** behaviour is ADJ QUALIT foolish because it involves taking risks. EG *It was* Outdated *considered foolhardy for him to quit his job.*

foolish /fuːlɪʃ/. **1** If you say that someone's behav- ADJ QUALIT iour is **foolish**, you mean that it is not sensible and shows a lack of good judgement. EG *It would be foolish to tell such things to a total stranger... How foolish I was not to have bought it.* ◊ **foolishly.** EG ◊ ADV OR ADV SEN

They have acted a little foolishly... Foolishly, we said we would do the decorating. ◊ **foolishness.** ◊ N UNCOUNT EG *Have I killed him by my foolishness?*

2 You can also say that people or things are ADJ QUALIT **foolish** when they are so silly that they make you want to laugh. EG *They looked foolish...* ...*the foolish stick that he carried.* ◊ **foolishly.** EG *Would the* ◊ ADV *whole thing appear foolishly melodramatic?*

foolproof /fuːlpruːf/. A plan, system, or machine ADJ QUALIT that is **foolproof** is so good or easy to use that it cannot go wrong or be used wrongly. EG ...*foolproof safety devices.*

foot /fʊt/, **feet; foots, footing, footed.** The plural of the noun is **feet. Foots** is the third person singular of the verb in the phrase in paragraph 8.

1 Your **feet** are the parts of your body that are at N COUNT the ends of your legs and that you stand on. See picture at THE HUMAN BODY. EG *It fell to the floor at her feet.*

2 If you go somewhere **on foot**, you walk, rather PHRASE than using any form of transport. EG *The city should be explored on foot.*

3 When you are **on** your **feet**, you are standing up. PHRASE

4 If you get **to** your **feet**, you stand up. EG *He rose* PHRASE *hurriedly to his feet and ran from the room.*

5 The **foot** of something is the bottom or lower end N SING of it. EG ...*at the foot of the stairs... We camped at the foot of some hills... He sat at the foot of her bed.*

6 A **foot** is a unit for measuring length, equal to 12 N COUNT inches or 30.48 centimetres. The plural can be **foot** or **feet.** EG *We were a few feet away from the edge...* ...*a 40-foot fall.*

7 Foot or **feet** is also used in these phrases. **7.1** To PHRASES **set foot** in a place means to go there. EG *It was a* Formal *long time before I set foot in a theatre again.* **7.2** When someone or something is **on** their **feet** again after an illness or a difficult period of time, they have recovered. EG ...*an economic programme to put the country back on its feet.* **7.3** If you **put** your **feet up**, you relax by sitting or lying with your feet supported by something. **7.4** If someone in author- ity **puts** their **foot down**, they say that something must not happen or continue. **7.5** If you **put** your Informal **foot in it**, you cause embarrassment by doing or saying something tactless. **7.6** If someone has to **stand on** their **own two feet**, they have to be independent and manage their lives without help from other people.

8 If you **foot the bill** for something, you pay for it. PHRASE EG *They may no longer be willing to foot the bills.*

9 to **have** or **get cold feet**: see **cold**.

football /fʊtbɔːl/, **footballs. 1 Football** is a game N UNCOUNT played between two teams of eleven players who kick a ball around a field in an attempt to score goals. EG *The children are playing football...* ...*a football match.*

2 A **football** is the large ball which is used in the N COUNT game of football.

footballer /fʊtbɔːlə/, **footballers.** A **footballer** is N COUNT a person who plays football, especially as a profes- sion.

foothills /fʊthɪlz/ are hills at the base of a moun- N PLURAL tain or range of mountains. EG ...*exploring the foothills of the Himalayas.*

foothold /fʊthəʊld/, **footholds. 1 Footholds** are N COUNT ledges or hollows where you can put your feet when you are climbing. EG *He cut footholds in the side of the ravine.*

2 If a person or animal gets a **foothold** on a N SING vertical surface, they hold on to it with their feet or claws without slipping or falling. EG *They keep their foothold on the bark with their claws.*

3 You can also say that you get a **foothold** when N SING you establish yourself in a strong position from

Are you forbearing with people you are fond of?

which you can make progress. EG *I tried to find a way to gain a foothold in the organization.*

footing /fʊtɪŋ/. **1** If you lose your **footing**, your feet slip, and you fall. EG *He lost his footing, and stumbled to the floor... She regained her footing.* N UNCOUNT: USU+POSS

2 When an activity goes on in a particular way, you can say that it is on that kind of **footing**. EG *We've had to get this on a more official footing.* N SING+SUPP

3 If you are on a particular kind of **footing** with someone, you have that kind of relationship with them. EG *The school's constitution puts parents on an equal footing with staff.* N SING: OFT+*with*

footman /fʊtmən/, **footmen**. A **footman** is a male servant who does jobs such as opening doors or serving food. N COUNT

footnote /fʊtnəʊt/, **footnotes**. A **footnote** is a note at the bottom of a page in a book which provides more information about something that is mentioned on the page. N COUNT

footpath /fʊtpɑːθ/, **footpaths**. A **footpath** is a path for people to walk on, especially in the countryside. N COUNT

footprint /fʊtprɪnt/, **footprints**. **Footprints** are the marks that your feet leave in soft ground or when they are wet. EG *...footprints in the snow.* N COUNT: USU PLURAL

footstep /fʊtstɛp/, **footsteps**. **1** Your **footsteps** are the sounds that your feet make when you walk. EG *They heard footsteps and turned.* N COUNT: USU PLURAL

2 If you **follow in** someone's **footsteps**, you do the same things as they did earlier. EG *I'd have liked to have followed in my father's footsteps and been a gamekeeper.* PHRASE

footwear /fʊtwɛə/ refers to things that people wear on their feet, for example shoes, boots, and sandals. EG *...the footwear industry.* N UNCOUNT

for /fɔː/. **1** If something is intended or done **for** someone, they are intended to have it, use it, or benefit from it. EG *He left a note for her on the table... I am doing everything I can for you... He often cooked for himself.* PREP

2 If you work **for** someone, you are employed by them. EG *He works for British Rail.* PREP

3 You use **for** when you state **3.1** the purpose of something. EG *...a Stanley knife for cutting linoleum, etc... I walked two miles for a couple of pails of water... We met for lunch.* **3.2** the reason for something or the cause of it. EG *Money is the primary reason for a young man's leaving the village... This area is famous for its spring flowers.* ▸ used as a conjunction. EG *This was where he spent his free time, for he had nowhere else to go.* PREP ▸ CONJ

4 For is the preposition that you use after many nouns, adjectives, and verbs in order to introduce more information. EG *...their reputation for being fierce and warlike... ...his designs for the engine... You had to be ready for any emergency... They were aiming for a double share by 1985.* PREP

5 You use **for** when you say how something affects or relates to someone or what their attitude to it is. EG *I knew it was difficult for him to talk like this... It was a frightening experience for a boy.* PREP

6 You use **for** when you say that an aspect of someone or something is surprising in relation to other aspects of them. EG *She wore rather too much make-up for her age.* PREP

7 If you feel a particular emotion **for** someone, **7.1** you feel it about them. EG *I felt sorry for my wife... ...Kurt's contempt for people.* **7.2** you feel it on their behalf. EG *I'm delighted for you.* PREP

8 You use **for** after words such as 'time', 'space', or 'money' when you say how much of it there is and what use could be made of it. EG *There was room for a table... He didn't have the concentration required for doing the job.* PREP

9 If something lasts or continues **for** a period of time, that is how long it lasts or continues. EG *I have known you for a long time... ...for three days.* PREP

10 If something extends **for** a particular distance, PREP

that is how far it extends. EG *Black cliffs rose sheer out of the water for a hundred feet or more.*

11 If you give someone something **for** their birthday or **for** some other occasion, you give it on that occasion. EG *She had given him a dog for his birthday... What did you get for Christmas?* PREP

12 If something is planned **for** a particular time, it is planned to happen then. EG *The meeting has been scheduled for August 30.* PREP

13 You use expressions such as **for the first time** and **for the second time** when you are talking about how often something has happened. EG *The guide returned for the third time.* PHRASE

14 If you leave **for** a place or if you take a train, plane, or boat **for** a place, you are going there. EG *...one morning, before he left for the fields.* PREP

15 If something is bought, sold, or done **for** a particular amount of money, that is the cost of buying, selling, or doing it. EG *You can buy the paperback for about two pounds.* PREP

16 If you are **for** something, you are in favour of it. **For** is usually stressed when it is used with this meaning. EG *There was a majority of 294 for war, with only 6 voting against.* ● If you are **all for** something, you are very much in favour of it. PREP ● PHRASE

17 You use **for** after words such as 'argue' and 'vote' in order to introduce the thing that is being supported. EG *I had to vote for him on principle... This looked like a good case for the existence of telepathy.* PREP

18 You use **for** when you state the second part of a ratio. EG *About nine women have lost jobs for every five men.* PREP

19 If one word or expression has the same meaning as another one, you can say that the first one is another word or expression **for** the second one. EG *'Carte' is the French word for card.* PREP

20 for all: see **all**. ● **as for**: see **as**. ● **but for**: see **but**.

forage /fɒrɪdʒ/, **forages**, **foraging**, **foraged**. **1** When animals **forage**, they search for food. V

2 If you **forage** for something, you search busily for it. EG *She couldn't resist foraging around for paintings.* V+A

foray /fɒreɪ/, **forays**. **1** If a group of soldiers make a **foray** into an area, they make a quick attack, usually in order to steal supplies. N COUNT

2 If you make a **foray** somewhere, you go there briefly, usually in order to obtain something. EG *From time to time he made forays to the pavement booksellers.* N COUNT

3 If you make a **foray** into a particular area of activity, you try it for a short while. EG *It was his first foray into politics.* N COUNT+*into*

forbade /fəbæd, -beɪd/ is the past tense of **forbid**.

forbearance /fɔːbeərəns/ is patience and kindness. N UNCOUNT Formal

forbearing /fɔːbeərɪŋ/. Someone who is **forbearing** is patient and kind. ADJ QUALIT Formal

forbid /fəbɪd/, **forbids**, **forbidding**, **forbade** /fəbæd, -beɪd/, **forbidden**. **1** If you **forbid** someone to do something, you order them not to do it. EG *I forbid you to tell her... They had obtained a court order forbidding the sale.* V+O: OFT+*to*-INF

2 If something **forbids** an event or course of action, it makes it impossible for it to happen. EG *Mexico City's altitude forbids such exertions.* V+O Formal

3 If you say **God forbid** or **Heaven forbid** that a particular thing should happen, you mean that you hope that it will not happen. EG *God forbid that anything should happen to my father.* PHRASE

forbidden /fəbɪdən/. **1** If something is **forbidden**, you are not allowed to do it or have it. EG *It is forbidden to bathe in the sea here... Indoor football is forbidden.* ADJ PRED

2 A **forbidden** place is one that you are not allowed to visit or enter. EG *...forbidden ground.* ADJ CLASSIF

3 A **forbidden** subject is one that you are not allowed to mention. ADJ CLASSIF

forbidding /fə^bbɪdɪŋ/. Someone or something that ADJ QUALIT
is **forbidding** has a severe and unfriendly appearance. EG ...*a bleak, forbidding stretch of grey water.*

force /fɔːs/, **forces, forcing, forced. 1** If you V+O
force someone to do or to have something, you OR V-REFL :
make them do it or have it, although they are very OFT+*to*-INF
OR A
unwilling to. EG *They forced him to resign... She
forced herself to kiss her mother's cheek... ...the
campaign to force the closure of the factory... ...the
missiles which they are forcing upon Britain.*

2 If a situation or event **forces** you to do some- V+O+*to*-INF
thing, it makes it necessary for you to do it. EG OR A
*Weekend gales forced him to change his plans...
This forces us into specialization.*

3 If you **force** something into a particular position, V+O+A
you use a lot of strength to make it move there. EG *I
forced his head back.*

4 If you **force** a lock, a door, or a safe, you break V+O
the lock in order to open it.

5 If you **force** your **way** through or into a place, PHRASE
you have to push or break things that are in your
way in order to get there.

6 If something is done by **force**, strong and violent N UNCOUNT
physical action is used in order to do it. EG *We have
renounced the use of force to settle our disputes.*

7 Force is power or strength. EG *I hit him with all* N UNCOUNT
the force I could muster.

8 Someone or something that is referred to as a N COUNT :
force has a great effect or influence on a situation. USU+SUPP
EG *Britain is re-establishing itself as a powerful
force in world affairs.*

9 A **force** in physics is the pulling or pushing effect N COUNT OR
that something has on something else. EG ...*magnet-* N UNCOUNT
ic forces.

10 If something happens **by force of** a particular PHRASE
quality or action, it happens because of the nature
or intensity of that quality or action. EG *By sheer
force of will, he fought the urge to go after them.*

11 If you do something from **force of habit**, you do PHRASE
it because you have always done it in the past.

12 A law or system that is **in force** exists or is PHRASE
being used. EG ...*when the system comes into force.*

13 A **force** is an organized group of soldiers or N COUNT :
other armed people. EG ...*the United States armed* USU PLURAL
forces... ...a guerrilla force.

14 If you **join forces** with someone, you work PHRASE
together in order to achieve a common aim or
purpose.

forced /fɔːst/. **1** A **forced** action is one that you ADJ CLASSIF :
only do because you have to do it. EG *They prom-* ATTRIB
ised to abolish forced labour... ...a forced landing.

2 Something that is **forced** is done with an effort ADJ QUALIT
rather than being genuine and spontaneous. EG ...*a
forced smile... The conversations had been stiff,
forced, and uncomfortable.*

forceful /fɔːsful/. **1** Someone who is **forceful** ADJ QUALIT
expresses their opinions in a strong and confident
way. EG ...*a forceful and assertive man.*
◊ **forcefully.** EG *Her views were forcefully ex-* ◊ ADV
pressed.

2 Something that is **forceful** causes you to think or ADJ QUALIT
feel something very strongly. EG ...*a forceful reminder of the risks involved.* ◊ **forcefully.** EG *It* ◊ ADV
*forcefully struck the bishop that this was very
unusual.*

3 A **forceful** point or argument in a discussion is ADJ QUALIT
good and convincing.

forceps /fɔːsɪ²ps/ are an instrument consisting of N PLURAL
two long narrow arms. They are used by a doctor
for holding things. EG ...*a pair of forceps.*

forcible /fɔːsəbᵊl/. **1 Forcible** actions involve ADJ CLASSIF :
physical force or violence. EG ...*the forcible imposi-* ATTRIB
tion of military control. ◊ **forcibly.** EG *Children* ◊ ADV
were taken forcibly from their mothers.

2 A **forcible** reminder, example, or lesson is very ADJ QUALIT :
powerful. EG ...*a forcible reminder of the continuing* ATTRIB
strife there. ◊ **forcibly.** EG *This was brought home* ◊ ADV
to me forcibly by a personal experience.

3 A **forcible** expression of an opinion or wish is ADJ QUALIT :
ATTRIB

strong and emphatic. EG *The survey made certain
very forcible recommendations.* ◊ **forcibly.** EG ◊ ADV
This point has been forcibly expressed by Tories.

ford /fɔːd/, **fords.** A **ford** is a shallow place in a N COUNT
river or stream where you can cross safely on foot.

fore /fɔː/. When something or someone comes to PHRASE
the fore, they suddenly become important or
popular. EG *Andrew Young came to the fore during
the 1960s.*

forearm /fɔːrɑːm/, **forearms.** Your **forearms** N COUNT
are the parts of your arms between your elbows
and your wrists.

forebear /fɔːbeə/, **forebears.** Your **forebears** N COUNT :
are your ancestors. EG ...*the lands from which their* USU PLURAL
forebears had been driven. Formal

foreboding /fɔːbəʊdɪŋ/, **forebodings. Forebod-** N UNCOUNT
ing is a strong feeling that something terrible is OR N COUNT
going to happen. EG *Tim's absence filled her with
foreboding... ...beset by dismal forebodings.*

forecast /fɔːkɑːst/, **forecasts, forecasting, fore-**
casted. The forms **forecast** and **forecasted** are
both used as the past tense and past participle of
the verb.

1 A **forecast** is a prediction or statement of what is N COUNT :
expected to happen in the future. EG ...*forecasts of* USU+SUPP
*military involvement in British politics... ...the
weather forecast.*

2 If you **forecast** future events, you say what you V+O
think is going to happen. EG *It is almost impossible
to forecast the future development of a very young
child... Some warm weather had been forecast.*

forecourt /fɔːkɔːt/, **forecourts.** The **forecourt** of N COUNT
a large building is an open area at the front of it.

forefather /fɔːfɑːðə/, **forefathers.** Your **fore-** N COUNT :
fathers are your ancestors, especially your male USU PLURAL
ancestors. Formal

forefinger /fɔːfɪŋgə/, **forefingers.** Your **fore-** N COUNT
finger is the finger next to your thumb.

forefront /fɔːfrʌnt/. Someone or something that is N SING : *the*+N
in the **forefront** of an activity is advanced, active,
or important. EG *This was to place the company in
the forefront of computer manufacture.*

forego /fɔːgəʊ/, **foregoes, foregoing** /fɔːgəʊɪŋ/, V+O
forewent /fɔːwent/, **foregone** /fɔːgɒn/; also Formal
spelled **forgo.** If you **forego** something, you give it
up or do not insist on having it. EG *Lilian agreed to
forego her holiday.*

foregoing /fɔːgəʊɪŋ/. You can refer to something N SING : *the*+N
that has just been said as the **foregoing.** EG *In the* Formal
*foregoing we have seen how people differ in their
approach to problems.* ▸ used as an adjective. EG ▸ ADJ CLASSIF :
...*the foregoing analysis.* ATTRIB

foregone /fɔːgɒn/. If you say that the result of PHRASE
something is **a foregone conclusion**, you mean
that it is certain what the result will be. EG *The
outcome was assumed to be a foregone conclusion.*

foreground /fɔːgraʊnd/. The **foreground** of a N SING : *the*+N
picture is the part that seems nearest to you.

forehand /fɔːhænd/, **forehands.** A **forehand** is a N COUNT
shot in a game such as tennis in which the palm of
your hand faces the direction in which you are
hitting the ball.

forehead /fɒrɪd, fɔːhed/, **foreheads.** Your **fore-** N COUNT
head is the flat area at the front of your head
above your eyebrows and below where your hair
grows. See picture at THE HUMAN BODY. EG *He wiped
his forehead with the back of his hand... He kissed
her forehead.*

foreign /fɒrɪ¹n/. **1** Something that is **foreign** ADJ CLASSIF
belongs to or relates to a country that is not your
own. EG ...*a policy of restricting foreign imports...
...children from foreign countries.*

2 A **foreign** minister is a government minister ADJ CLASSIF :
who deals with matters that involve other coun- ATTRIB
tries besides his own. EG ...*the Belgian Foreign*

What does the prefix 'fore-' mean in words like
'forerunner', 'foresight', and 'forewarn'?

Minister... ...*the Foreign Secretary*... ...*the Foreign Office.*

3 A **foreign** object or substance is one that has got into something else, usually by accident, and should not be in it. EG *food containing foreign matter.* ADJ CLASSIF: ATTRIB Formal

4 You can say that something is **foreign** to a person or thing when it is not typical of them. EG *...that strange gloomy mood that was so foreign to him.* ADJ QUALIT: OFT+*to* Formal

foreigner /fɒrɪ¹nə/, **foreigners.** You refer to someone as a **foreigner** when they belong to a country that is not your own. EG *More than a million foreigners visit the USA every year.* N COUNT

foreman /fɔːmə¹n/, **foremen.** A **foreman** is a person, especially a man, who is in charge of a group of workers. N COUNT

foremost /fɔːməʊst/. **1** The **foremost** of a group of things is the most important or the best. EG *...India's foremost centre for hand-made shoes.* ADJ CLASSIF

2 First and foremost means more than anything else. EG *Rugby is first and foremost a team game.* ADV SEN

forename /fɔːneɪm/, **forenames.** Your **forename** is your first name. N COUNT Formal

forensic /fərɛnsɪk/. When a **forensic** analysis is done, objects are examined scientifically in order to discover information about a crime. EG *...the forensic department*... ...*the standard forensic tests for detecting the presence of blood.* ADJ CLASSIF: ATTRIB

forerunner /fɔːrʌnə/, **forerunners.** The **forerunner** of someone or something is a similar thing or person that existed before them. EG *...the forerunners of the International Socialists.* N COUNT: OFT+SUPP

foresee /fɔːsiː/, **foresees, foreseeing, foresaw** /fɔːsɔː/, **foreseen** /fɔːsiːn/. If you **foresee** something, you believe that it is going to happen. EG *Do you foresee any problems with the new system?*... *It was possible to foresee that the coming winter would be a hard one.* V+O OR V+REPORT

foreseeable /fɔːsiːəbəl/. **1** When you talk about the foreseeable future, you are referring to the period of time in the future during which it is possible to predict what will happen. EG *Nobody is likely to find a cure in the foreseeable future.* PHRASE

2 Something that is **foreseeable** can be expected to happen, and should not be a surprise. EG *...a perfectly foreseeable catastrophe.* ADJ QUALIT

foreshadow /fɔːʃædəʊ/, **foreshadows, foreshadowing, foreshadowed.** If one thing **foreshadows** another, it suggests that the other thing will happen. EG *These later movements had been foreshadowed in much of the work of the late 1950s.* V+O

foresight /fɔːsaɪt/ is the ability to see what is likely to happen in the future, which is shown in the action that someone takes. EG *He showed remarkable foresight*... ...*a lack of foresight.* N UNCOUNT

forest /fɒrɪ²st/, **forests.** A **forest** is a large area where trees grow close together. A **forest** is usually larger than a wood. EG *...a clearing in the forest.* N COUNT OR N UNCOUNT

forestall /fɔːstɔːl/, **forestalls, forestalling, forestalled.** If you **forestall** someone, you realize what they were intending to do and prevent them from doing it. V+O

forestry /fɒrɪstri¹/ is the science or skill of growing and taking care of trees in forests. N UNCOUNT

foretaste /fɔːteɪst/. You say that something is a **foretaste** of something that is going to happen when it is similar to it and shows you what it will be like. EG *The episode was a foretaste of the bitter struggle that was to come.* N SING+*of*

foretell /fɔːtel/, **foretells, foretelling, foretold** /fɔːtəʊld/. If you **foretell** something, you say correctly that it will happen in the future. EG *Who could ever foretell that Paul would turn traitor?* V+O OR V+REPORT Literary

forethought /fɔːθɔːt/ is the practice of thinking carefully about what will be needed, or about what the consequences of something will be. EG *With a bit of forethought, life can be made a lot easier.* N UNCOUNT

forever /fəˀrɛvə/. The form **for ever** is also used, except in paragraph 4.

1 Something that will happen or continue **forever** will always happen or continue. EG *They thought that their empire would last forever.* ADV

2 Something that has gone **forever** has disappeared completely and permanently. EG *This innocence is lost forever.* ADV

3 People say that something takes **for ever** or lasts **for ever** when they want to emphasize that it takes or lasts a very long time. EG *The next minutes lasted for ever.* ADV Informal

4 If you say that someone or something is **forever** doing a particular thing, you mean that they do it very often. EG *Babbage was forever spotting errors in their calculations.* ADV+-ING Informal

forewarn /fɔːwɔːn/, **forewarns, forewarning, forewarned.** If you **forewarn** someone, you warn them that something is going to happen. EG *We were forewarned that the food would be unusual.* V+O: OFT+REPORT, ONLY *that*

foreword /fɔːwɜːd/, **forewords.** The **foreword** to a book is an introduction either by the author or by someone else. N COUNT

forfeit /fɔːfɪt/, **forfeits, forfeiting, forfeited.** If you **forfeit** something, you have to give it up because you have broken a rule or done something wrong. EG *He has forfeited the right to be the leader of this nation.* V+O

forgave /fɔːgeɪv/ is the past tense of **forgive.**

forge /fɔːdʒ/, **forges, forging, forged.** **1** If someone **forges** banknotes, documents, or paintings, they copy them or make false ones in order to deceive people. EG *I learnt how to forge someone else's signature.* V+O

2 If you **forge** an alliance or relationship, you succeed in creating it. EG *They forged links with the French Communist Party.* V+O

3 A **forge** is a place where metal things such as horseshoes are made. N COUNT

forge ahead. If you **forge ahead** with something, you make a lot of progress. EG *They forged ahead, leaving countries like Britain behind.* PHRASAL VB: V+ADV

forger /fɔːdʒə/, **forgers.** A **forger** is someone who forges things such as banknotes, documents, or paintings. N COUNT

forgery /fɔːdʒəˀri¹/, **forgeries.** **1** **Forgery** is the crime of forging things such as banknotes, documents, or paintings. EG *...passport forgery.* N UNCOUNT

2 You can refer to a forged banknote, document, or painting as a **forgery.** N COUNT

forget /fəget/, **forgets, forgetting, forgot** /fəgɒt/, **forgotten** /fəgɒtə⁰n/. **1** If you **forget** something or **forget** how to do something, you cannot think of it or think how to do it, although you knew it or knew how to do it in the past. EG *I never forget a face... She had forgotten how to ride a bicycle.* ◊ **forgotten.** EG *...a forgotten event in her past.* V+O OR V+REPORT: NO CONT ◊ ADJ CLASSIF

2 If you **forget** something or **forget** to do something, you do not remember to consider it or do it. EG *I meant to see her on Friday, but I forgot all about it... I forgot to mention that John is a musician.* V+O; ALSO V: OFT+REPORT OR *to*-INF

3 If you **forget** something that you had intended to bring, you do not bring it because you did not think about it at the right time. EG *Sorry to disturb you – I forgot my key.* V+O

4 You can also say that someone **forgets** something or someone when they deliberately do not think about them any more. EG *If you want my advice I think you ought to forget her.* V+O

5 If you **forget** yourself, you behave in an uncontrolled or unacceptable way, which is not the way in which you usually behave. EG *'Oh darling!' cried Judy, forgetting herself.* V-REFL Formal

forgetful /fəgetfʊl/. **1** Someone who is **forgetful** often forgets things. EG *Be sure to remind your uncle – you know how forgetful he is.* ADJ QUALIT

◊ **forgetfulness.** EG *...his growing forgetfulness.* ◊ N UNCOUNT

2 Someone who is **forgetful** of a particular thing ADJ PRED+of
does not think about it or notice it. EG *Fiona,*
forgetful of the time, was still working away in the
library.

forgettable /fəgɛtəbəˀl/. Something that is **for-** ADJ QUALIT
gettable is not unusual or special in any way. EG
...forgettable men working at obscure jobs.

forgivable /fəgɪvəbəˀl/. If you say that something ADJ CLASSIF
is **forgivable**, you mean that you can understand it
and can forgive it. EG *Her lack of sympathy was*
perhaps forgivable.

forgive /fəgɪv/, **forgives, forgiving, forgave**
/fəːgeɪv/, **forgiven. 1** If you **forgive** someone who V+O:OFT+for;
has done something wrong, you stop being angry ALSO V+O+O
with them. EG *I'll never forgive you for what you*
did... I forgave him everything.

2 You use **forgive** in polite expressions like 'for- PHRASE
give me' and 'forgive the language' to apologize for
saying something that might seem rude, silly, or
too complicated. EG *Forgive my ignorance, but who*
is Jane Fonda?

3 If you say that someone could **be forgiven** for V-PASS:
doing something, you mean that such behaviour MODAL+V+for
would be reasonable in the circumstances. EG *We*
could be forgiven for thinking that we were still in
London.

forgiveness /fəgɪvnɪˀs/. If you ask someone for N UNCOUNT
their **forgiveness**, you are asking them to forgive
you for something wrong that you have done.

forgiving /fəgɪvɪŋ/. Someone who is **forgiving** is ADJ QUALIT
willing to forgive people. EG *...a forgiving father.*

forgo /fɔːgəʊ/. See **forego**.

forgot /fəgɒt/ is the past tense of **forget**.

forgotten /fəgɒtəˀn/ is the past participle of **for-**
get.

fork

fork /fɔːk/, **forks, forking, forked. 1** A **fork** is **1.1** N COUNT
a tool that you eat food with. It consists of three or
four prongs on the end of a handle. **1.2** a large tool
that you dig your garden with. It consists of three
or four long prongs attached to a long handle. See
picture at TOOLS.

2 A **fork** in a road, path, or river is the point at N COUNT
which it divides into two parts in the shape of a 'Y'.
▶ used as a verb. EG *...where the road forks.* ▶ V

fork out. If you **fork out** for something, you pay PHRASAL VB:
for it. EG *...the fortune I had already had to fork out* V+ADV OR
on her education. V+O+ADV
Informal

forked /fɔːkt/. Something that is **forked** divides ADJ CLASSIF
into two parts in the shape of a 'Y'. EG *...an adder's*
forked tongue.

forlorn /fəlɔːn/. **1** If you are **forlorn**, you are ADJ QUALIT
lonely and unhappy. EG *The child looked very*
forlorn... ...a forlorn cry. ◊ **forlornly.** EG *He was* ◊ ADV
standing forlornly by the ticket office.

2 A **forlorn** place looks deserted and not cared for. ADJ QUALIT
EG *...this grimy, forlorn industrial town.*

3 A **forlorn** attempt or hope has no chance of ADJ CLASSIF:
success. EG *...the forlorn hope of achieving full* ATTRIB
employment.

form /fɔːm/, **forms, forming, formed. 1** A par- N COUNT+SUPP
ticular **form** of something is a type or kind of it. EG
He begged for any form of transport that would

take him to the ferry... I never touch alcohol in any
form... ...money, in the form of coins, notes, or
cheques... The broadcast took the form of an
interview.

2 When people or things **form** a particular shape, V-ERG OR
they move or are arranged so that this shape is V-REFL:OFT+A
made. EG *They formed a ring... Long queues had*
formed... The men formed themselves into a line.

3 The **form** of something is its shape. EG *The* N COUNT
middle finger was touching the end of the thumb in
the form of a letter O.

4 You can refer to someone or something that you N COUNT
see as a **form**. EG *She gazed with deep affection at* Literary
his slumbering form.

5 If you say that a particular thing **forms** some- V+C
thing with a particular structure or function, you
mean that it has this structure or function. EG *The*
black leather chair folds back to form a couch...
...red rocks forming a kind of cave.

6 The things or people that **form** a particular thing V+C
are the things or people that it consists of. EG *The*
contents of the house will form the basis of a major
exhibition.

7 If you **form** an organization, group, or company, V+O
you start it. EG *The League was formed in 1959.*

8 When something natural **forms** or **is formed**, it V-ERG
begins to exist. EG *The islands are volcanic and*
were formed comparatively recently.

9 If you **form** an idea, relationship, or habit, you V+O
begin to have it. EG *He formed the habit of taking*
long solitary walks.

10 A **form** is a piece of paper with questions on it. N COUNT
You write the answers on the same piece of paper.
EG *Fill in this form... ...application forms.*

11 In a school, a **form** is a class, or all the classes N COUNT
containing children of a similar age. EG *...the fifth*
form.

12 Someone who is **on form** is performing their PHRASE
usual activity very well. Someone who is **off form**
is not performing as well as they usually do.

13 If someone's behaviour is **true to form**, it is PHRASE
typical of them. EG *Watson, true to form, made an*
instant decision.

formal /fɔːməˀl/. **1 Formal** speech or behaviour is ADJ QUALIT
very correct and serious rather than relaxed and
friendly, and is used especially in official situations.
In this dictionary, language of this kind is indicated
by the use of the word 'Formal' in the Extra
Column. EG *The letter was stiff and formal.*
◊ **formally.** EG *Everyone was formally lined up to* ◊ ADV
meet the king. ◊ **formality** /fəˀmælɪˀtiˀ/. EG *The* ◊ N UNCOUNT
elders conversed with strict formality.

2 A **formal** statement or action is an official one. ADJ CLASSIF:
EG *No formal declaration of war had been made.* ATTRIB
◊ **formally.** EG *He had already formally an-* ◊ ADV
nounced his candidacy.

3 Formal occasions are ones at which people wear ADJ QUALIT
smart clothes and behave correctly rather than in
a casual way. EG *...a formal dinner at Buckingham*
Palace... ...a formal dance.

4 Formal clothes are very smart clothes that are ADJ QUALIT
suitable for formal occasions. ◊ **formally.** EG *He* ◊ ADV
dressed rather formally.

5 A **formal** garden or room is arranged in a very ADJ CLASSIF
neat, regular way. EG *...formal flowerbeds.*

6 Formal education or training is given officially, ADJ CLASSIF:
usually in a school or college. EG *Faraday had no* ATTRIB
formal education... ...formal qualifications.

formality /fəˀmælɪtiˀ/, **formalities. 1 Formal-** N COUNT
ities are formal actions that are carried out on
particular occasions. EG *The pre-funeral formalities*
had to be attended to.

2 If you say that an action or procedure is just a N COUNT
formality, you mean that it must be done, although it will not have any effect on what is being

Has a forlorn place been forsaken?

decided or arranged. EG *He knew the interview was just a formality.*

3 See also **formal**.

formalize /fɔ:məlaɪz/, **formalizes, formalizing, formalized;** also spelled **formalise**. If you **formalize** a plan, idea, or arrangement, you make it clear and official. EG *Their marriage vows will be formalized.* v+o

format /fɔ:mæt/, **formats.** The **format** of something is the way in which it is arranged and presented. EG *They're producing material in all kinds of different formats.* N COUNT

formation /fəˈmeɪʃəˈn/, **formations. 1** The **formation** of something is its start or creation. EG *He had played a major role in the formation of the United Nations... ...the physical process of rock formation... ...the formation of new ideas.* N UNCOUNT +SUPP

2 If things are in a particular **formation**, they are arranged in a particular pattern. EG *...aircraft flying in formation.* N COUNT OR N UNCOUNT

3 A rock **formation** or a cloud **formation** is rock or clouds of a particular shape. N COUNT

formative /fɔ:mətɪv/. A **formative** period in your life has an important and lasting influence on your character and attitudes. EG *...where I spent my formative years.* ADJ CLASSIF: ATTRIB

former /fɔ:mə/. **1 Former** is used to describe **1.1** someone who used to have a particular job or position, but no longer has it. EG *...former President Theodore Roosevelt.* **1.2** something which someone used to have or which used to be a particular thing. EG *...their former home... The college was in fact a former mansion.* **1.3** a situation or period of time which came before the present one. EG *...a selection of items published in former years.* ADJ CLASSIF: ATTRIB

2 When two people or things have just been mentioned, you can refer to the one that was mentioned first as the **former**. EG *The former believe in a strong centralized government.* ▶ used as an adjective. EG *Lack of space forbids the former alternative.* N SING OR N PLURAL: the+N ▶ ADJ CLASSIF: the+ADJ+N

formerly /fɔ:məli¹/. If something happened or was true **formerly**, it happened or was true in the past. EG *Some of my salesmen formerly worked for this company.* ADV

formidable /fɔ:mɪdəbəˈl, fəˈmɪdəbəˈl/. Something that is **formidable** is **1** rather frightening because it is difficult to deal with or overcome. EG *He had earned the reputation of being a formidable opponent.* **2** very impressive because it is so good or great. EG *...the formidable army of brains that are at the Prime Minister's disposal.* ◇ **formidably.** EG *The jeeps came with army drivers, each formidably armed.* ADJ QUALIT ◇ ADV

formless /fɔ:mlɪ²s/. Something that is **formless** does not have a clear shape or structure. EG *...a group of formless shapes... ...formless chaos.* ADJ CLASSIF Formal

formula /fɔ:mjəˈlə/, **formulae** /fɔ:mjəˈli:/ or **formulas.** A **formula** is **1** a group of letters, numbers, or other symbols which represents a scientific or mathematical rule. EG *He knew the formula for converting kilometres into miles.* **2** a list of substances which tells you what amounts to mix together in order to make another substance. **3** a plan that is devised as a way of dealing with a problem. EG *...a peace formula.* N COUNT

formulate /fɔ:mjəˈleɪt/, **formulates, formulating, formulated. 1** If you **formulate** a plan or proposal, you invent it, thinking about the details carefully. EG *We had formulated our own strategy.* ◇ **formulation** /fɔ:mjəˈleɪʃəˈn/, **formulations.** EG *...the formulation of policy.* v+o ◇ N UNCOUNT OR N COUNT

2 If you **formulate** a thought or opinion, you express it in words. v+o

forsake /fəˈseɪk/, **forsakes, forsaking, forsook** /fəˈsʊk/, **forsaken. 1** If you **forsake** someone, you stop helping them or stop looking after them. EG *Their leaders have forsaken them.* v+o Literary

2 If you **forsake** something, you stop doing it or having it. EG *...if you forsake religion.* v+o Literary

forsaken /fəˈseɪkəˈn/. A **forsaken** place is no longer lived in or no longer looked after. EG *...a dusty, forsaken prairie village... ...a forsaken garden.* ADJ CLASSIF Literary

fort /fɔ:t/, **forts. 1** A **fort** is a strong building that is used as a military base. N COUNT

2 If you **hold the fort** for someone, you look after things for them while they are somewhere else. PHRASE Informal

forte /fɔ:teɪ/, **fortes.** You can say that an activity is your **forte** if you are very good at it. EG *Cooking is hardly my forte.* N COUNT+SUPP

forth /fɔ:θ/. **1** When someone goes **forth** from a place, they leave it. EG *The goats came bounding forth from their pens.* ADV AFTER VB Formal

2 When something is brought **forth**, it is brought out into a place where you can see it. EG *He reached into his briefcase and brought forth a file.* ADV AFTER VB Formal

3 back and forth: see **back**. ● **and so forth**: see **so**.

forthcoming /fɔ:θkʌmɪŋ/. **1** A **forthcoming** event is planned to happen soon. EG *...the forthcoming presidential election.* ADJ CLASSIF: ATTRIB Formal

2 When something such as help or information is **forthcoming**, it is provided or is made available. EG *No evidence was forthcoming.* ADJ PRED Formal

3 You say that a person is **forthcoming** when they willingly give you information. EG *He was not forthcoming on the way in which he had risen to power.* ADJ PRED Formal

forthright /fɔ:θraɪt/. Someone who is **forthright** shows clearly and strongly what they think and feel. EG *...his forthright opposition to the war.* ADJ QUALIT

forthwith /fɔ:θwɪθ, -wɪð/ means immediately. EG *He would take up his new duties forthwith.* ADV Formal

fortieth /fɔ:tɪ²θ/, **fortieths.** The **fortieth** item in a series is the one that you count as number forty: see the entry headed NUMBER. EG *...the fortieth president of the United States.* ORDINAL

fortification /fɔ:tɪfɪkeɪʃəˈn/, **fortifications. 1** **Fortifications** are buildings, walls, or ditches that are built to protect a place against attack. N COUNT: USU PLURAL

2 The **fortification** of a place is the act of fortifying it. EG *...the fortification of Florence.* N UNCOUNT Formal

fortify /fɔ:tɪfaɪ/, **fortifies, fortifying, fortified. 1** If people **fortify** a place, they make it better able to resist an attack, often by building a wall or ditch round it. EG *...the tiny fortified town.* v+o

2 Things, such as food or drinks, that **fortify** you make you feel stronger and more full of energy. v+o

fortitude /fɔ:tɪtju:d/. If someone shows **fortitude** when in pain or in danger, they do not complain and remain brave and calm. EG *Cal bore his pain with commendable fortitude.* N UNCOUNT Formal

fortnight /fɔ:tnaɪt/, **fortnights.** A **fortnight** is a period of two weeks. EG *I went to Rothesay for a fortnight.* N COUNT: USU SING

fortnightly /fɔ:tnaɪtli¹/. A **fortnightly** event or magazine happens or appears once a fortnight. EG *...a fortnightly newspaper... The therapy group meets fortnightly.* ADJ CLASSIF: ATTRIB OR ADV AFTER VB

fortress /fɔ:trɪ²s/, **fortresses.** A **fortress** is a castle or other large strong building which is difficult for enemies to enter. N COUNT

fortuitous /fəˈtju:ɪtəs/. You describe an event as **fortuitous** when it happens by chance and helps someone. EG *...a fortuitous discovery.* ADJ QUALIT Formal

fortunate /fɔ:tʃəˈnəˈt/. **1** Someone who is **fortunate** is lucky. EG *...those who are fortunate enough to get jobs.* ADJ QUALIT

2 You say that an event is **fortunate** when it is lucky for someone. EG *It was fortunate for Mr Fox that he decided to wait.* ◇ **fortunately** /fɔ:tʃəˈnətli¹/. EG *Fortunately she didn't mind.* ADJ QUALIT ◇ ADV SEN

fortune /fɔ:tʃəˈn/, **fortunes. 1 Fortune** or good **fortune** is good luck. Ill **fortune** is bad luck. EG *He has since had the good fortune to be promoted.* N UNCOUNT

2 If you talk about someone's **fortunes**, you are N PLURAL +POSS referring to the extent to which they are doing well or being successful. EG *In the following years, Victor's fortunes improved considerably.*

3 When someone **tells** your **fortune**, they look at PHRASE something such as playing cards and tell you what will happen to you in the future.

4 Someone who has a **fortune** has a very large N COUNT amount of money. EG *His father left him an immense fortune.*

5 You can refer to any large sum of money as a N SING : a+N **fortune**. EG *She earns a fortune.* Informal

fortune-teller, fortune-tellers. A **fortune-** N COUNT **teller** is someone who tells people's fortunes, often in exchange for money.

forty /fɔːtiʲ/, **forties. Forty** is the number 40: see NUMBER the entry headed NUMBER. EG *We have a nursery school for forty children.*

forum /fɔːrəm/, **forums.** A **forum** is a place or N COUNT event in which people exchange ideas and discuss things. EG *...Parliament's role as a forum for debate.*

forward /fɔːwəd/, **forwards, forwarding, for-** **warded. 1** If someone moves or faces **forward** or ADV AFTER VB **forwards**, they move or face in a direction that is OR in front of them. EG *Suddenly she leaned forward...* ADJ CLASSIF : *...his forward movement.* ● **backwards and for-** ATTRIB **wards**: see **backwards**.

2 Forward or **forwards** is also used to indicate ADJ AFTER N, that something progresses or becomes more mod- OR ADV ern. EG *Obviously it's a great step forward for you... ...moving society forward into a better world.*

3 If you look **forward** in time, you look into the ADV AFTER VB future. EG *When I was your age I could only look* OR *forward... ...forward planning.* ● to **look forward to** ADJ CLASSIF : something: see **look**. ATTRIB

4 If you put a clock or watch **forward**, you alter it ADV AFTER VB so that it shows a later time.

5 If you **forward** a letter that has been sent to V+O someone who has moved, you send it to them at the place where they are now living.

forwarding address, forwarding addresses. N COUNT A **forwarding address** is an address that you give to someone when you go and live somewhere else so that they can send your mail on to you. EG *She had gone to Spain, leaving no forwarding address.*

fossil /fɒsəl/, **fossils.** A **fossil** is the hardened N COUNT remains of a prehistoric animal or plant, or a print that it leaves in rock.

fossil fuel, fossil fuels. Fossil fuels are fuels N MASS such as coal, oil, and peat that are formed from the decayed remains of plants and animals.

fossilize /fɒsɪlaɪz/, **fossilizes, fossilizing, fossil-** V-ERG : **ized;** also spelled **fossilise.** When the remains of USU PASS an animal or plant **fossilize** or **are fossilized**, they become hard, or leave a print, and form a fossil. EG *...fossilised bones.*

foster /fɒstə/, **fosters, fostering, fostered. 1** ADJ CLASSIF : **Foster** parents are people who officially take ATTRIB someone else's child into their family for a period of time, without becoming the child's legal parents. The child is referred to as their **foster** child.
▶ used as a verb. EG *When they are fostered, boys* ▶ V+O OR V *have more behaviour problems than girls.*

2 If you **foster** a feeling, an activity, or an idea, you V+O help it to develop. EG *The local council has a policy of fostering music, drama, and crafts.*

fought /fɔːt/ is the past tense of **fight**.

foul /faʊl/, **fouler, foulest; fouls, fouling, fouled.**
1 You say that something is **foul** when it is dirty or ADJ QUALIT smells unpleasant. EG *The water in the pools be-* *came tepid and foul.*

2 Foul language contains swear words or rude ADJ QUALIT words.

3 If someone has a **foul** temper, they become ADJ QUALIT angry or violent suddenly and easily.

4 If you **fall foul of** someone or something, you PHRASE accidentally do something which gets you into trouble with them. EG *He was found drowned in a river after falling foul of local poachers.*

5 If you **foul** something, you make it dirty. EG *The* V+O *deck would soon be fouled with blood.*

6 In a game or sport, a **foul** is an action that is N COUNT against the rules. EG *The team's record of fouls was among the worst.*

foul up. If you **foul up** something such as a plan, PHRASAL VB : you spoil it by doing something wrong or stupid. EG V+O+ADV *So many good projects have been fouled up by* Informal *elementary mistakes.*

foul play is criminal violence or activity that N UNCOUNT results in a person's death. EG *There was no evi-* *dence of foul play.*

found /faʊnd/, **founds, founding, founded. 1** **Found** is the past tense and past participle of **find**.

2 If someone **founds** an institution or organization, V+O they create it, often by providing the necessary money. EG *The Constituency Labour Party was founded in 1918 by Walter Ayles and others.*
◊ **founding.** EG *He opposed the founding of the* ◊ N SING : *National Gallery.* the+N+of

3 If someone **founds** a town, important building, or V+O other place, they cause it to be built. EG *The theatre was founded in 1720.*

4 If something **is founded** on a particular thing, it V+O+on/ is based on it. EG *...a political system founded on* upon : USU PASS *force.* ● See also **well-founded.**

foundation /faʊndeɪʃəⁿn/, **foundations. 1** The N COUNT+SUPP **foundation** of something such as a belief or way of life is the basic idea, attitude, or experience on which it is built. EG *Respect for the law is the foundation of civilised living.*

2 The **foundations** of a building or other structure N PLURAL are the layers of bricks or concrete below the ground that it is built on.

3 When a new institution or organization is creat- N SING : ed, you can refer to this event as the **foundation** of the+N+of the institution or organization. EG *...since the foun-* *dation of the university.*

4 A **foundation** is an organization which provides N COUNT money for a special purpose such as research or a charity. EG *...the National Foundation for Educa-* *tional Research.*

5 If you say that a story, idea, or argument has no N UNCOUNT : **foundation**, you mean that there are no facts to USU WITH support it and prove that it is true. EG *The sugges-* BROAD NEG *tion is absurd and without foundation.*

founder /faʊndə/, **founders, foundering, found-** **ered. 1** The **founder** of an institution, organization, N COUNT : or building is the person who created it or caused it USU+POSS to be built. EG *...Thomas Kemp, the founder of Kemp Town.*

2 If something **founders**, it fails. EG *Without their* V *assistance the arrangement would have foundered pretty quickly.*

3 If a ship **founders**, it fills with water and sinks. V : USU+A

founder member, founder members. A **found-** N COUNT **er member** of a club, group, or organization is one of the original members.

foundry /faʊndriʲ/, **foundries.** A **foundry** is a N COUNT place where metal or glass is melted and formed into particular shapes.

fount /faʊnt/. If you describe a person or thing as N SING+of the **fount** of something, you mean that they are the Literary best source or supply of it. EG *...the Encyclopaedia Britannica, the fount of all knowledge.*

fountain /faʊntɪn/, **fountains.** A **fountain** is an N COUNT ornamental feature in a pool which consists of a spray or jet of water that is forced up into the air by a pump.

fountain pen, fountain pens. A **fountain pen** is N COUNT a pen that has a container inside which you fill with ink.

four /fɔː/, **fours. 1 Four** is the number 4: see the NUMBER entry headed NUMBER. EG *His mother died when he was four... ...a four-mile walk.*

Might you get a fracture in a fracas?

2 If you are **on all fours**, you are crawling or PHRASE leaning on your hands and knees. EG *Claud slipped through the hedge on all fours.*

four-letter word, four-letter words. Four- N COUNT **letter words** are short words that people consider to be rude or offensive, usually because they refer to sex or other bodily functions.

foursome /fɔːsəm/, **foursomes. A foursome** is a N COUNT group of four people. EG *We functioned well as a foursome.*

fourteen /fɔːtiːn/, **fourteens. Fourteen** is the NUMBER number 14: see the entry headed NUMBER. EG *He was the eldest of a family of fourteen children.*

fourteenth /fɔːtiːnθ/, **fourteenths.** The **four-** ORDINAL **teenth** item in a series is the one that you count as number fourteen: see the entry headed NUMBER. EG *...their son's fourteenth birthday.*

fourth /fɔːθ/, **fourths. 1** The **fourth** item in a ORDINAL series is the one that you count as number four: see the entry headed NUMBER. EG *My mother died just before my fourth birthday.*

2 A **fourth** is one of four equal parts of something. N COUNT : EG *They conceded him three-fourths or more of the* USU + of *spending cuts he sought.*

fowl /faʊl/, **fowls. Fowl** can also be used as the N COUNT OR plural form. N UNCOUNT
A **fowl** is a bird, especially one that can be eaten as food.

fox /fɒks/, **foxes, foxing, foxed. 1** A **fox** is a wild N COUNT animal which looks like a dog and has reddish-brown fur.

2 If something **foxes** you, you cannot understand it V+O or solve it. EG *We were foxed by the calculations...* Informal *Ah, now you've foxed me.*

fox-hunting is a sport in which people riding N UNCOUNT horses chase foxes across the countryside.

foyer /fɔɪeɪ, fɔɪə/, **foyers.** The **foyer** of a theatre, N COUNT cinema, or hotel is the large area just inside the main doors where people meet or wait.

fracas /frækɑː/. A **fracas** is a rough, noisy quarrel N SING or fight. EG *They got involved in another fracas.* Formal

fraction /frækʃəʰn/, **fractions. 1** You can refer to N PART a small amount or proportion of something as a **fraction** of it. EG *For a fraction of a second, I hesitated... The door opened a fraction.*

2 In arithmetic, a **fraction** is an exact division of a N COUNT number. For example, ½ and ⅓ are fractions of 1.

fractionally /frækʃəʰnəlɪ¹, -ʃənəʰlɪ¹/. **Fractional-** ADV **ly** means very slightly. EG *They're only fractionally different.*

fracture /fræktʃə/, **fractures, fracturing, frac-tured. 1** A **fracture** is a crack or break in N COUNT something, especially a bone. EG *...a fracture of the left shoulder blade.*

2 If something such as a bone **fractures** or **is** V-ERG **fractured**, it breaks. EG *...a fractured ankle.*

fragile /frædʒaɪl/. **Fragile** things are easily ADJ QUALIT spoilt, harmed, or broken. EG *...constructions built of fragile materials... ...extremely fragile econo-mies.* ◊ **fragility** /frəˈdʒɪlɪ¹tɪ¹/. EG *...the fragility of* ◊ N UNCOUNT *their communication links.*

fragment, fragments, fragmenting, fragment-ed; pronounced /frægməʰnt/ when it is a noun and /frægmɛnt/ when it is a verb.

1 A **fragment** of something is a small piece or part N COUNT of it. EG *...a small fragment of bone... This was only a fragment out of a long conversation with John.*

2 If something **fragments** or **is fragmented**, it V-ERG breaks or separates into small pieces. EG *Farms are constantly being fragmented into smaller holdings.*
◊ **fragmentation** /frægmɛnteɪʃəʰn/. EG *This led to* ◊ N UNCOUNT *its fragmentation into eight independent parties.* Formal

fragmentary /frægməʰntəʰrɪ¹/. Something that is ADJ QUALIT **fragmentary** is made up of small or unconnected pieces. EG *...the fragmentary evidence for this sto-ry.*

fragmented /frægmɛntɪd/. Something that is ADJ QUALIT **fragmented** consists of a lot of different parts

which seem unconnected with each other. EG *It's a book that is very fragmented in its structure.*

fragrance /freɪgrəns/, **fragrances.** You can re- N COUNT OR fer to a sweet or pleasant smell as a **fragrance**. EG N UNCOUNT *...a deep, musky fragrance.*

fragrant /freɪgrənt/. Something that is **fragrant** ADJ QUALIT has a sweet or pleasant smell. EG *...fragrant flowers.*

frail /freɪl/, **frailer, frailest. 1** Someone who is ADJ QUALIT **frail** is not strong or healthy. EG *...a frail old man.*

2 Something that is **frail** is easily broken or ADJ QUALIT damaged. EG *...a frail structure.*

frailty /freɪltɪ¹/, **frailties. 1** If you talk about the N PLURAL OR **frailties** or **frailty** of people, you are referring to N UNCOUNT their weaknesses. EG *...our vanities and frailties.*

2 Frailty is also the condition of being weak in N UNCOUNT health. EG *...the advanced age and frailty of some of the inhabitants.*

frame /freɪm/, **frames, framing, framed. 1** A N COUNT **frame** is **1.1** a hollow structure inside which you can fit something such as a window, door, or picture. EG *...gold-painted picture frames.* **1.2** an arrangement of bars that give an object its shape and strength. EG *...a bunk made of canvas laced to a steel frame.*

2 The **frames** of a pair of glasses are the wire or N PLURAL plastic part which holds the lenses in place. EG *...sunglasses with black frames.*

3 Your **frame** is your body. EG *His big frame was* N COUNT *gaunt and weak.* Literary

4 If you **frame** a picture or photograph, you put it V+O : USU PASS in a frame. EG *Are you having your picture profes-sionally framed?* ◊ **framed.** EG *...a framed photo-* ◊ ADJ CLASSIF *graph of her mother.*

5 If something **is framed** by a particular thing, it is V+O : USU PASS surrounded by that thing, and is noticeable or Written attractive as a result. EG *She stood framed in the doorway of the dining-room.*

6 If you **frame** something in a particular kind of V+O+A language, you express it in that way. EG *Laws are invariably framed in tortuous jargon.*

7 If you **are framed** by someone, they make it V+O seem that you have committed a crime, although Informal you haven't. EG *I was framed by the authorities.*

frame of mind. Your **frame of mind** is the N SING mood that you are in at a particular time. EG *I'm not in the right frame of mind for riddles, Tana.*

framework /freɪmwɜːk/, **frameworks. 1** A N COUNT **framework** is a structure that forms a support or frame for something. EG *There are nine large panels set in a richly carved framework.*

2 A **framework** is also a set of rules, ideas, or N COUNT+SUPP beliefs which you use in order to decide what to do. EG *They were able to absorb these changes within the framework of traditional institutions and ideas.*

franchise /fræntʃaɪz/, **franchises. 1** The **fran-** N SING **chise** is the right to vote in an election, especially one in which people elect a parliament. EG *...a policy of universal franchise.*

2 A **franchise** is an authority that is given by a N COUNT company to someone, allowing them to sell its goods or services. EG *...a farm equipment franchise.*

frank /fræŋk/, **franker, frankest.** If someone is ADJ QUALIT **frank**, they state things in an open and honest way. EG *John was perfectly frank with him... ...a frank discussion.* ◊ **frankness.** EG *He seemed to be* ◊ N UNCOUNT *speaking with complete frankness.*

frankly /fræŋklɪ¹/. **1** You use **frankly** when bold- ADV SEN ly stating a feeling or opinion. EG *Frankly, this has all come as a bit of a shock.*

2 If you say or do something **frankly**, you say or do ADV it in an open and honest way. EG *He asked me to tell him frankly what I wished to do.*

frantic /fræntɪk/. **1** If you are **frantic**, you are ADJ QUALIT behaving in a wild and desperate way because you are frightened or worried. EG *We were frantic with worry.* ◊ **frantically.** EG *...frantically searching for* ◊ ADV *David.*

2 When there is **frantic** activity, things are being ADJ QUALIT done hurriedly and in a rather disorganized way. EG

...a frantic week of high-level discussions.

◊ **frantically.** EG *They worked frantically through-* ◊ ADV
out the day.

fraternal /frəˈtɜːnəᵊl/ means having strong links ADJ CLASSIF
of friendship with another group of people. EG Formal
Fraternal greetings were received from the Com-
munist Party of the Soviet Union.

fraternity /frəˈtɜːnɪtiᵊ/, **fraternities. 1 Frater-** N UNCOUNT
nity refers to feelings of friendship between Formal
groups of people.

2 You can refer to a group of people who have the N COUNT :
same profession or interests as a particular **frater-** OFT+SUPP
nity. EG ...the banking fraternity. Formal

fraternize /ˈfrætənaɪz/, **fraternizes, fraterniz-** V OR V+with :
ing, fraternized; also spelled **fraternise.** If you RECIP
fraternize with someone, you associate with them
in a friendly way. EG *We fraternized with their sons*
and grandsons.

fraud /frɔːd/, **frauds. 1 Fraud** is the crime of N UNCOUNT
gaining money by deceit or trickery. EG *His closest*
adviser is under indictment for fraud.

2 A **fraud** is something that deceives people in a N COUNT
way that is illegal or immoral.

3 Someone who is a **fraud** is not the person they N COUNT
pretend to be or does not have the abilities or
status they pretend to have.

fraudulent /ˈfrɔːdjəᵊlənt/. Something that is ADJ CLASSIF
fraudulent is deliberately deceitful, dishonest, or
untrue. EG *The promise Mrs Haze had made was a*
fraudulent one.

fraught /frɔːt/. **1** If you say that something is ADJ PRED
fraught with problems or difficulties, you mean +with
that it is full of them. EG *Any further moves would*
be fraught with danger.

2 Someone who is **fraught** is very worried or ADJ QUALIT
anxious. EG *Everyone's rather tense and fraught*
tonight.

fray /freɪ/, **frays, fraying, frayed. 1** If something V-ERG
such as cloth or rope **frays**, its threads or strands
become worn and it is likely to tear or break. EG *His*
shirts were frayed.

2 If your nerves **fray** or your temper **frays**, you V-ERG
feel irritable and nervous because of mental strain
and anxiety.

3 You can refer to an exciting activity or argument N SING : the+N
that you are involved in as the **fray.** EG *I returned*
to the fray with renewed vigour.

freak /friːk/, **freaks. 1** People call someone a N UNCOUNT
freak 1.1 when their behaviour or attitudes are
regarded as very unusual. EG *A woman is consid-*
ered a freak if she decides to put her career first.
1.2 when they are physically abnormal in some
way. EG ...hair-raising freaks, including a two-
headed Indian.

2 You can also describe someone as a **freak** when N COUNT+SUPP
they are very enthusiastic about something. EG *He* Informal
was a real cleanliness freak.

3 A **freak** event or action is very unusual and very N MOD
unlikely to happen. EG *My mother died in a freak*
accident, struck by lightning at a picnic.

freakish /ˈfriːkɪʃ/. You describe something as ADJ QUALIT
freakish when it is very unusual. EG ...an isolated,
freakish event... ...freakish-looking people.

freckled /ˈfrekəᵊld/. Someone who is **freckled** has ADJ CLASSIF
freckles. EG ...her freckled face.

freckles /ˈfrekəᵊlz/ are small, light brown spots on N PLURAL
someone's skin, especially on their face. EG *She had*
red hair and freckles.

free /friː/, **freer** /ˈfriːə/, **freest** /ˈfriːɪst/; **frees,**
freeing, freed. 1 Someone or something that is ADJ QUALIT
free is not restricted, controlled, or limited. EG
Within the EEC there is free movement of labour...
We are free to regard such a view as mistaken...
...a free press.

2 Someone who is **free** is no longer a prisoner or a ADJ CLASSIF OR
slave. EG *I wish to return to London, this time as a* ADV AFTER VB
free man... One prisoner in seven had been set
free.

3 If you **free** a prisoner or a slave, you let them go V+O

or release them from prison. EG *Her sister was also*
arrested but was freed after three weeks.

4 If you **free** someone of something that is unpleas- V+O OR
ant or restricting, you remove it from them. EG V-REFL : OFT+A
...the attempt to free France of the Dictator.

5 A person or thing that is **free** of something ADJ PRED
unpleasant does not have it or is not affected by it. +of/from
EG *The area will be free of pollution by the year*
2000.

6 If you **free** someone or something, you cause V+O
them to become available for a task or purpose. EG
We could cut defence expenditure, freeing vital
resources for more useful purposes.

7 If you have a **free** period of time or are **free** at a ADJ CLASSIF
particular time, you are not busy then. EG *They*
don't have much free time... Are you free for
lunch?

8 A place, seat, or machine that is **free** is not ADJ CLASSIF
occupied or not being used by anyone.

9 If something is **free**, you can have it or use it ADJ CLASSIF
without paying for it. EG ...free school meals.

10 If you do something or get something **for free**, PHRASE
you do it without being paid or you get it without
having to pay for it. EG *I said I'd work for free.*

11 Something that is moved **free** is moved so that ADV AFTER VB
it is no longer attached to or trapped by something.
EG *I shook my jacket free and hurried off.*

12 If you **free** something, you remove or loosen it V+O
from the place in which it has been fixed or
trapped. EG *He freed his arms.*

13 When someone is using one of their hands to ADJ CLASSIF :
hold or do something, you can refer to their other ATTRIB
hand as their **free** hand. EG ...buttoning his overcoat
with his free hand.

14 You say **'Feel free'** to someone as an informal PHRASE
way of giving your permission. EG *'Is it OK if I take* Informal
this one?' – 'Yeah, feel free.'

15 free of charge: see **charge.** ● to give someone
a free hand: see **hand.**

-free combines with nouns to form adjectives that
indicate that something does not have the thing
mentioned. EG *Each submarine reported a trouble-*
free launch... ...error-free computer programs.

free agent, free agents. You say that someone is N COUNT
a **free agent** when they can do whatever they
want because they are not responsible to anyone.

free-and-easy. Free-and-easy people and ADJ QUALIT
things are casual and informal. EG ...a free-and-easy
relationship.

freebie /ˈfriːbiᵊ/, **freebies.** A **freebie** is something N COUNT
that you are given without having to pay for it, Informal
usually by a company.

freedom /ˈfriːdəm/, **freedoms. 1 Freedom** is the N UNCOUNT
state of being allowed to do or say what you want OR N COUNT
to. EG *Political freedom is still rare... ...freedom of*
speech... ...the erosion of basic freedoms.

2 When slaves or prisoners escape or are released, N UNCOUNT
they gain their **freedom.** EG *Many slaves buy their*
freedom with what they save from farming.

3 When someone or something has **freedom** of N UNCOUNT
movement, they can move about.

4 When there is **freedom** from something unpleas- N UNCOUNT
ant, people are not affected by it. EG ...freedom +from
from hunger and starvation.

freedom fighter, freedom fighters. Freedom N COUNT
fighters are people who are trying to overthrow
the government of their country using violent
methods; used showing approval.

free enterprise is an economic system in which N UNCOUNT
businesses compete for profit without much government control.

free-for-all, free-for-alls. A **free-for-all** is a N COUNT
disorganized fight, argument, or attempt to get
something, in which everybody joins in. EG *The*

fight turned into a free-for-all... This would result in a free-for-all on wage bargaining.

free kick, free kicks. When there is a **free kick** N COUNT in a game of football or rugby, the ball is given to a member of one side to kick without opposition because a member of the other side has broken a rule.

freelance /ˈfriːlɑːns/, **freelances.** A **freelance** ADJ CLASSIF journalist or photographer is not employed by one OR ADV organization, but is paid for each piece of work that they do by the organization that they do it for. EG *...freelance writing... I work freelance.* ▶ used as a ▶ N COUNT noun. EG *'Are you employed by Collins?' – 'No, I'm a freelance.'*

freely /ˈfriːliⁱ/. **1** You say that something is done ADV **freely** when it is done often or in large quantities. EG *He spends fairly freely... ...perspiring freely.*
2 Someone or something that can move or act ADV **freely** is not restricted, controlled, or limited by anything or anyone. EG *British goods were allowed to move freely from one state to another.*
3 If you can talk **freely**, you do not need to be ADV careful about what you say. EG *We are all comrades here and I may talk freely.*
4 Something that is **freely** available can be ob- ADV+ADJ tained easily. EG *These drugs are freely available in most cities.*
5 Something that is given or done **freely** is given ADV or done willingly. EG *...freely given affection.*

freer /ˈfriːə/ is the comparative of **free.**

free-range. Free-range eggs are produced by ADJ CLASSIF hens that can move and feed freely on an area of open ground.

freest /ˈfriːⁱst/ is the superlative of **free.**

freestyle /ˈfriːstaɪl/. **Freestyle** is used to describe N SING sports competitions, especially in swimming, wrestling, and skiing, in which competitors can use any style or method they like. EG *She won the 100 metres freestyle.*

freeway /ˈfriːweɪ/, **freeways.** A **freeway** is a road N COUNT which has several lanes and controlled places American where vehicles join it, so that people can travel quickly. EG *He turned off the freeway.*

free will. 1 If you believe in **free will**, you believe N UNCOUNT that people have a choice in what they do and that their actions have not been decided in advance by God or Fate.
2 If you do something **of your own free will**, you PHRASE do it by choice and not because you are forced to do it. EG *He has come back of his own free will.*

freeze /friːz/, **freezes, freezing, froze** /frəʊz/, **frozen** /ˈfrəʊzᵊn/. **1** When a liquid **freezes** or V-ERG when something **freezes** it, it becomes solid because it is very cold. EG *The water froze in the wells.*
2 If you **freeze** food, you preserve it by storing it at V-ERG a temperature below freezing point.
3 If you say that it will **freeze**, you mean that the V temperature outside will fall below freezing point. ▶ used as a noun. EG *...the forecasting of storms,* ▶ N COUNT *freezes, and droughts.*
4 If you **freeze**, you become very cold. EG *You'll* V *freeze to death out there.*
5 You can also say that someone **freezes** when V they suddenly stop moving and become completely still and quiet, for example because they have seen something dangerous. EG *Then she sensed something moving about. She froze.*
6 To **freeze** something such as wages or prices V+O means to state officially that they will not be allowed to increase for a fixed period of time. EG *Various attempts to control or freeze wages have failed.* ▶ used as a noun. EG *...a freeze in the nuclear* ▶ N COUNT *arms race.* +SUPP
7 See also **deep freeze, freezing, frozen.**

freezer /ˈfriːzə/, **freezers.** A **freezer** is a large N COUNT container in which you can store food for long periods of time, because the temperature inside is kept below freezing point.

freezing /ˈfriːzɪŋ/. **1** If you say that something is ADJ CLASSIF **freezing**, you mean that it is very cold indeed. EG *It's freezing outside... The water was black and freezing.*
2 If you say that you are **freezing**, you mean that ADJ PRED you feel unpleasantly cold.
3 Freezing is the same as freezing point. EG *The* N UNCOUNT *air temperature was now well below freezing.*

freezing point, freezing points. 1 Freezing N UNCOUNT **point** is 0° Celsius, the temperature at which water freezes. EG *The temperature was well above freezing point.*
2 The **freezing point** of a particular substance is N COUNT the temperature at which it freezes.

freight /freɪt/ refers to **1** the transportation of N UNCOUNT goods by lorries, trains, ships, or aeroplanes. EG *...one section going by air freight... ...freight charges.* **2** the goods transported by lorries, trains, ships, or aeroplanes. EG *...eight thousand tons of freight.*

freighter /ˈfreɪtə/, **freighters.** A **freighter** is a N COUNT ship or aeroplane that is designed to carry goods rather than people.

freight train, freight trains. A **freight train** is N COUNT a train that carries goods rather than people. American

French fries /frentʃ ˈfraɪz/ are long, thin pieces N PLURAL of potato fried in oil or fat. EG *...hamburgers and French fries.*

French window /frentʃ ˈwɪndəʊ/, **French win-** N COUNT : **dows. French windows** are glass doors which USU PLURAL you go through into a garden or onto a balcony.

frenetic /frɪˈnetɪk/. **Frenetic** activity or behav- ADJ QUALIT iour is fast, energetic, and often confused or uncontrolled.

frenzied /ˈfrenzɪd/. **Frenzied** actions are wild, ADJ QUALIT excited, and uncontrolled. EG *...frenzied cheers... ...a frenzied mob of students.* ◊ **frenziedly.** EG *I* ◊ ADV *scrambled frenziedly to the cave.*

frenzy /ˈfrenziⁱ/, **frenzies.** You say that someone N COUNT OR is in a **frenzy** when they are very excited and their N UNCOUNT behaviour is violent or uncontrolled. EG *It would drive Thomas into a frenzy... There was an element of frenzy and desperation in the singing.*

frequency /ˈfriːkwənsiⁱ/, **frequencies. 1** The fre- N UNCOUNT **quency** of an event is the number of times that it happens during a particular period. EG *Serious disasters appear to be increasing in frequency... ...the frequency of their appearance.*
2 The **frequency** of a sound or radio wave is the N COUNT OR rate at which it vibrates. A high frequency sound N UNCOUNT wave produces a high-pitched sound. Technical

frequent, frequents, frequenting, frequented; pronounced /ˈfriːkwənt/ when it is an adjective, and /frɪˈkwent/ when it is a verb.
1 You say that something is **frequent** when it ADJ QUALIT often happens. EG *George's absences were frequent... They move at frequent intervals... Etta was a frequent visitor there.* ◊ **frequently.** EG *This* ◊ ADV *question is frequently asked.*
2 If you **frequent** a place, you go there often and V+O spend a lot of time there. EG *Jo liked to frequent the bars... The restaurant was frequented by workmen.*

fresco /ˈfreskəʊ/, **frescoes.** A **fresco** is a picture N COUNT that is painted on a plastered wall while the plaster Technical is still wet.

fresh /freʃ/, **fresher, freshest. 1** A **fresh** thing or ADJ CLASSIF amount replaces or is added to a previous one. EG ATTRIB *He poured himself a fresh drink... Rose had given him fresh instructions.*
2 Something that is **fresh** has been done or experi- ADJ QUALIT enced recently. EG *...fresh footprints in the snow... Memories of the war are fresh in both countries.*
3 If food is **fresh**, it has been made or got recently, ADJ QUALIT and has not been tinned or frozen. EG *...fresh vegetables.*
4 If you describe something as **fresh**, you mean that it is **4.1** different in a new and exciting way. EG ADJ QUALIT *He has a fresh approach.* ◊ **freshness.** EG *This* ◊ N UNCOUNT *gives the novel freshness and charm.* **4.2** pleasant ADJ QUALIT

and clean in appearance. EG ...*the fresh dawn light.*
◊ **freshness.** EG ...*the freshness of the curtains.* ◊ N UNCOUNT
5 If something smells, tastes, or feels **fresh**, it is ADJ QUALIT
pleasant and refreshing. EG *The air is cool and
fresh... A piece of lemon gives it a fresh flavour.*
6 **Fresh** water is water that is not salty, for ADJ CLASSIF
example the water in streams and lakes.
7 If the weather is **fresh**, it is fairly cold and windy. ADJ QUALIT
8 If you are **fresh** from a place or experience, you ADJ PRED+
have been to the place or had the experience very PREP
recently. EG ...*coming fresh from the junior school.*

freshen /frɛʃəⁿn/, **freshens, freshening, freshened.** 1 If you **freshen** something, you make it v+o
cleaner and more pleasant. EG *Keith freshened
himself with a wash... The air freshened his lungs.*
2 If the wind **freshens**, it increases and becomes v
fairly strong.

freshen up. If you **freshen up**, you have a quick PHRASAL VB:
wash and make yourself look neat and tidy. EG V+ADV
*Sarah and Barry returned to their hotel to freshen
up.*

fresher /frɛʃə/, **freshers.** A **fresher** is a student N COUNT
who has just started university or college. British

freshly /frɛʃli¹/. You say that something is **fresh-** ADV
ly made or done when it has been recently made
or done. EG ...*freshly cooked food... ...a freshly
painted room.*

freshwater /frɛʃwɔːtə/. 1 A **freshwater** lake or ADJ CLASSIF:
pool contains water that is not salty. ATTRIB
2 A **freshwater** fish lives in a river, lake, or pool ADJ CLASSIF:
that is not salty. ATTRIB

fret /frɛt/, **frets, fretting, fretted.** If you **fret** v: OFT+
about something, you worry about it. EG *Daniel was* about/over
*fretting about money... 'Don't fret,' she said. 'He'll
be all right.*

fretful /frɛtful/. You say that someone is **fretful** ADJ QUALIT
when they behave in a way that shows that they
are worried or unhappy about something. EG ...*fretful babies.*

friar /fraɪə/, **friars.** A **friar** is a member of a N COUNT
Catholic religious order. Friars travel around
preaching Christianity.

friction /frɪkʃəⁿn/, **frictions.** 1 Friction is 1.1 the N UNCOUNT
force that prevents things from moving freely
when they are touching each other. 1.2 the rubbing
of one thing against another. EG *She rubbed her
hands as if trying to warm them by friction.*
2 Friction between people is disagreement and N UNCOUNT
quarrels. EG ...*friction between Healy and his col-* OR N PLURAL
leagues... ...family frictions.

Friday /fraɪdi¹/, **Fridays. Friday** is the day after N UNCOUNT
Thursday and before Saturday. EG *I came here on* OR N COUNT
Friday... Try and finish that by next Friday.

fridge /frɪdʒ/, **fridges.** A **fridge** is a large metal N COUNT
container in which you store food to keep it fresh. British
Fridges are kept cool by electricity. EG *He put the
milk back in the fridge.*

friend /frɛnd/, **friends.** 1 Your **friends** are the N COUNT
people who you know well and like to spend time
with. EG *He was my best friend at Oxford... ...an old
friend of the family.*
2 If you are **friends** with someone, you like each N PLURAL
other and enjoy spending time together. EG *You* OFT+with
used to be friends with him, didn't you?
3 If you **make friends** with someone, you begin a PHRASE
friendship with them. EG *Karen made friends with
some young Chinese girls.*
4 The people who help and support a cause or a N PLURAL
country are often referred to as its **friends.** EG *All* OFT+of
friends of Ireland should support us.
5 You can refer to an object that you know well or N COUNT
use a lot as your **friend.** EG *Use your old friend the
microscope.*

friendless /frɛndlɪ²s/. Someone who is **friend-** ADJ CLASSIF
less has no friends. EG *She remained friendless and
miserable.*

friendly /frɛndli¹/, **friendlier, friendliest;
friendlies.** 1 If you are being **friendly** to some- ADJ QUALIT
one, you are behaving in a kind and pleasant way

to them. EG *The women had been friendly to Lyn...
...a friendly smile.* ◊ **friendliness.** EG *The friendli-* ◊ N UNCOUNT
ness was gone from his voice.
2 If you are **friendly** with someone, you like each ADJ QUALIT
other and enjoy spending time together. EG *I became friendly with a young engineer.*
3 A **friendly** place or object makes you feel ADJ QUALIT
comfortable and relaxed. EG ...*a small room lit by
friendly lamps.*
4 A **friendly** fight or argument is one in which ADJ QUALIT
people are only amusing themselves and do not
intend to harm or offend each other.
5 A **friendly** is a sports match that is played for N COUNT
practice and not as part of a competition.

friendship /frɛndʃip/, **friendships.** 1 A **friend-** N COUNT
ship is a relationship between two people who like
each other and enjoy spending time together. EG
*My friendship with her had taught me a great
deal... ...the ability to form friendships.*
2 **Friendship** is the state of being friends with N UNCOUNT
someone. EG *Friendship is based on shared interests... He lost Britten's friendship.*
3 **Friendship** between countries is a relationship N UNCOUNT
in which they help and support each other. EG ...*his
efforts to promote Anglo-German friendship... ...our
friendship with America.*

frieze /friːz/, **friezes.** A **frieze** is a long, narrow N COUNT
strip of decoration, carving, or pictures along the
top of the walls of a room or on the outside walls of
a building.

frigate /frɪgəⁱt/, **frigates.** A **frigate** is a small, N COUNT
fast ship used by the navy to protect other ships.

fright /fraɪt/, **frights.** 1 **Fright** is a sudden feeling N UNCOUNT
of fear. EG *I heard Amy cry out in fright... He was
paralysed with fright.*
2 If someone **takes fright**, they experience a PHRASE
sudden feeling of fear. EG *The animals took fright
and ran away.*
3 A **fright** is an experience which gives you a N COUNT
sudden feeling of fear. EG *She gave me a nasty
fright with those rabbits.*

frighten /fraɪtəⁿn/, **frightens, frightening,** v+o
frightened. If something **frightens** you, it makes
you feel afraid or nervous. EG *Rats and mice don't
frighten me... The threat of prison did not frighten
them.*

frighten away. If you **frighten** someone **away,** PHRASAL VB:
you make them feel afraid so that they go away V+O+ADV
and do not harm you. EG *He waved his torch to
frighten away some animal.*

frighten into. If you **frighten** someone **into** PHRASAL VB:
doing something that they do not want to do, you V+O+PREP
make them do it by making them afraid not to do
it. EG *They tried to frighten me into talking.*

frighten off. To **frighten** a person **off** means to PHRASAL VB:
make them unwilling to become involved with V+O+ADV
someone or something. EG *Cliff was less encouraging, seeking to frighten him off.*

frightened /fraɪtəⁿnd/. If you are **frightened,** 1 ADJ QUALIT
you are afraid because of something that has
happened or that may happen. EG *The men led
their frightened families to safety... When you were
a child, were you frightened of the dark?* 2 you are ADJ PRED
worried or nervous about something. EG *I was
frightened of making a fool of myself... I am
frightened to look... They were frightened that you
might talk to the police.*

frightening /fraɪtəⁿnɪŋ/. Something that is ADJ QUALIT
frightening makes you feel afraid or worried. EG
...*the most frightening sight he had ever seen... It is
frightening to think what a complete search would
reveal.* ◊ **frighteningly.** EG *It was happening* ◊ ADV
frighteningly fast.

frightful /fraɪtful/. 1 If you say that something is ADJ QUALIT
frightful, you mean that it is very bad or unpleas- Informal

If you fritter your time away, are you frivolous?

ant. EG *The smell was frightful.* ◇ **frightfully.** EG ◇ ADV
She had behaved frightfully.

2 You can also use **frightful** to emphasize what ADJ CLASSIF : ATTRIB
you are saying. EG *It seems a frightful nuisance.*
◇ **frightfully.** EG *I'm frightfully sorry.* ◇ SUBMOD

frigid /frɪdʒɪd/. If a woman is **frigid**, she does not ADJ QUALIT
easily become sexually aroused.

frill /frɪl/, **frills.** **1** A **frill** is a long, narrow strip of N COUNT
cloth or paper with many folds, which is attached
to something as a decoration. EG *...a white pillow
with a blue frill round it.* ◇ **frilled** /frɪld/. EG *...a* ◇ ADJ CLASSIF
white frilled blouse.

2 If you say that something has no **frills**, you mean N PLURAL
that it is simple and has no unnecessary additions.
EG *...a house with no frills...* *...the necessities of life
but none of the frills.*

frilly /frɪlɪ¹/. **Frilly** clothes or objects are decorat- ADJ QUALIT
ed with many frills. EG *...a frilly nightdress.*

fringe /frɪndʒ/, **fringes.** **1** A **fringe** is **1.1** hair N COUNT
which is cut so that it hangs over your forehead. EG
Her hair was rather short and had a fringe in front.
1.2 a decoration attached to clothes and other
objects, consisting of a row of hanging strips or
threads. EG *...silk shawls with fringes.*

2 The **fringes** of a place are the parts that are N COUNT
farthest from its centre. EG *...on the western fringe
of London...* *...from the desert fringes of Mali right
across to Sudan.*

3 The **fringes** of an activity or organization are N COUNT :
the parts that are least typical, or most unusual or USU+SUPP
extreme. EG *...the radical fringe of the Labour
Party...* *...Julie's work in fringe theatre... Benn
remained on the fringes of the debate.*

fringed /frɪndʒd/. **1** If clothes or other objects ADJ CLASSIF
are **fringed**, they are decorated with a fringe. EG
...a fringed leather jacket.

2 If a place or object is **fringed** with things, they ADJ PRED+
form a border around it or are situated along its with/by
edges. EG *Her eyes were large, fringed with long
eyelashes...* *...a bay of blue water fringed by palm
trees.*

frisk /frɪsk/, **frisks, frisking, frisked.** **1** If some- V+O
one **frisks** you, they search you with their hands in Informal
order to see if you are hiding a weapon or something else in your clothes. EG *Two policemen
grabbed his arms while another one frisked him.*

2 When animals **frisk**, they run around in a happy, V
energetic way. EG *...his nine dogs frisking round
him.*

frisky /frɪskɪ¹/, **friskier, friskiest.** A **frisky** ani- ADJ QUALIT
mal or person is energetic and wants to have fun.
EG *...frisky young ponies...* *...the frisky schoolboy
lurking underneath.*

fritter /frɪtə/, **fritters, frittering, frittered.** N COUNT
Fritters consist of fruit, vegetables, or other food
dipped in batter and fried. EG *...corn fritters...
...banana fritters.*

fritter away. If you **fritter away** time or mon- PHRASAL VB :
ey, you waste it gradually on unimportant or V+O+ADV
unnecessary things. EG *She would not fritter away
her vacation on reading.*

frivolity /frɪvɒlɪ¹tɪ¹/ is rather silly, light-hearted N UNCOUNT
behaviour. EG *Harry tolerated the younger man's
frivolity.*

frivolous /frɪvələs/. **1** Someone who is **frivolous** ADJ QUALIT
behaves in a silly or light-hearted way, especially
when they should be serious or sensible. EG *Forgive
me. I didn't mean to sound frivolous... She is seen as
rather a frivolous writer.*

2 **Frivolous** objects and activities are amusing or ADJ QUALIT
silly, rather than useful or important. EG *I spend a
lot of my salary on frivolous things.*

frizzy /frɪzɪ¹/, **frizzier, frizziest.** **Frizzy** hair has ADJ QUALIT
a lot of stiff, wiry curls. EG *...a youth with a mop of
frizzy hair.*

fro /frəʊ/. **to and fro:** see **to**.

frock /frɒk/, **frocks.** A **frock** is a woman's or N COUNT
girl's dress. Outdated

frog

frog /frɒg/, **frogs.** **1** A **frog** is a small creature N COUNT
with smooth skin, big eyes, and long back legs
which it uses for jumping. Many frogs live near
water.

2 If you **have a frog in** your **throat**, you cannot PHRASE
speak properly because your throat is partly Informal
blocked by phlegm, for example when you have a
cold.

frogman /frɒgmə³n/, **frogmen.** A **frogman** is a N COUNT
person whose job is to work underwater, wearing
special rubber clothing and breathing equipment.

frog-march, frog-marches, frog-marching, V+O : USU+A
frog-marched. If you **are frog-marched** somewhere, you are forced to walk there by two people,
each holding one of your arms. EG *I was frog-
marched down to the police station.*

frolic /frɒlɪk/, **frolics, frolicking, frolicked.** V : USU+A
When animals or children **frolic**, they run around
and play in a lively way. EG *The children frolicked
on the sand.* ▸ used as a noun. EG *What started as a* ▸ N COUNT
frolic might turn into something different.

from /frɒm/. **1** You use **from** to say what the PREP
source of something is, or where it began. EG
*...wisps of smoke from a small fire... She came
from Ilford... Get the leaflet from a post office... She
got a postcard from them yesterday... ...a song
from his latest film... He was always sure of
sympathy from his mother.*

2 A person who is **from** a particular organization PREP
works for that organization. EG *This is Mr Castle
from the bank.*

3 If someone or something moves or is moved PREP
from a place, they leave it or are removed, so that
they are no longer there. EG *They drove down from
Leeds... We scrambled from our trucks and ran
after them... We went around clearing rubbish
from the fields.*

4 If something is taken **from** you, it is removed or PREP
stolen, and you no longer have it.

5 If you take something **from** an amount, you PREP
reduce the amount by that much. EG *This will be
deducted from your pension.*

6 If you are away **from** a place, you are not there. PREP
EG *They were away from home.*

7 If you return **from** doing something, you return PREP
after doing it. EG *The men had not yet come back
from fishing.*

8 If you see or hear something **from** a particular PREP
position, you are in that position when you see it or
hear it. EG *From the top of the bus you could look
down on people below.*

9 If something hangs or sticks out **from** an object, PREP
it is attached to it or held by it. EG *...buckets
hanging from a bamboo pole.*

10 You can use **from** when giving distances. For PREP
example, if a place is fifty miles **from** another
place, the distance between the two places is fifty
miles.

11 If a road goes **from** one place to another, you PREP
can travel along it between the two places. EG *...on
the main road from Paris to Marseilles.*

12 If something is made **from** a particular sub- PREP
stance, that substance is used to make it. EG *The
shafts were cut from heavy planks of wood.*

13 If something happens **from** a particular time, it PREP begins to happen then. EG *She was deaf from birth... We had no rain from March to October.*

14 If something changes **from** one thing to another, it stops being the first thing and becomes the second thing. EG *They enlarged the committee from 17 members to 30... ...translating from one language to another.* PREP

15 If one thing happens **from** another, it happens as a result of it. EG *From nervousness she said a few more stupid things... My eyes hurt from the wind.* PREP

16 You use **from** when you are giving the reason for an opinion. EG *I could see from her face that she felt disappointed... I am speaking from personal experience.* PREP

17 You say **from** one thing to another when you are stating the range of things that are possible. EG *The process takes from two to five weeks... The flowers may be anything from pink to crimson.* PREP

frond /frɒnd/, **fronds.** Fronds are long leaves with lots of spiky edges. EG *...palm fronds... ...huge fronds of seaweed.* N COUNT

front /frʌnt/, **fronts, fronting, fronted.** 1 The **front** of something is the part of it that faces you or faces forward, or that you normally see or use. EG *...jackets with six buttons down the front... The policeman searched the front of the car.* ▸ used as an adjective. EG *...the front gate... One of his front teeth was gone.* N COUNT : USU SING+SUPP ▸ ADJ CLASSIF: ATTRIB

2 If a person or thing is **in front**, they are ahead of other ones in a moving group, or further forward than other ones. EG *Jay walked in front and Simon and Val behind him. ...a lady in the row in front.* PHRASE

3 If you are **in front** in a competition or contest, you are winning. PHRASE

4 If someone or something is **in front of** a particular thing, they are facing it, ahead of it, or close to the front part of it. EG *A car was drawing up in front of the house... There was a man standing in front of me.* PREP

5 If you do something **in front of** someone else, you do it when they are present. EG *I couldn't tell you in front of Sam.* PREP

6 In a war, the **front** is the place where two armies are fighting. N COUNT : the+N

7 If you say that something happens on a particular **front**, you mean that it happens with regard to a particular situation or activity. EG *On the intellectual front, little advance has been made.* N COUNT : USU SING+SUPP

8 If someone puts on a **front**, they pretend to have a feeling or quality which they do not have. EG *...presenting a united front to the world.* N SING : a+N

9 In meteorology, a **front** is the line where a mass of cold air meets a mass of warm air. N COUNT Technical

10 A building that **fronts** a place is next to it and faces it. EG *This beach has two restaurants fronting it.* v+o

frontage /frʌntɪdʒ/, **frontages.** The **frontage** of a building is the wall which faces the street. EG *...the Victorian frontage of the Treasury.* N COUNT

frontal /frʌntəl/. 1 A **frontal** attack is direct and obvious. EG *...a frontal attack on the unions.* ADJ CLASSIF: ATTRIB

2 **Frontal** also means concerning the front of something. EG *...a frontal view.* ADJ CLASSIF: ATTRIB

frontier /frʌntɪə/, **frontiers.** 1 A **frontier** is a border between two countries. EG *...the frontier between the United States and Canada.* N COUNT

2 The **frontiers** of a subject or activity are the limits to which it can be known or done, or the boundary between it and something else. EG *They are doing work on the frontiers of discovery... ...crossing social frontiers.* N COUNT+SUPP

frontispiece /frʌntɪspiːs/, **frontispieces.** The **frontispiece** of a book is a picture at the beginning, opposite the page with the title on. N COUNT

front line, front lines. The **front line** is the place where two armies are fighting each other. EG *We came to within a mile of the front line... ...front-line troops.* N COUNT

front-page. **Front-page** articles or pictures are printed on the front page of a newspaper because they are very important or interesting. EG *Several papers carried front-page stories about the murdered girl.* ADJ CLASSIF: ATTRIB

frost /frɒst/, **frosts.** 1 When there is a **frost**, the temperature outside falls below freezing point and the ground is covered with ice crystals. EG *There was a touch of frost this morning... Even into April the frosts continued.* N COUNT OR N UNCOUNT

2 **Frost** is the thin layer of ice crystals that forms on the ground when there is a frost. EG *The lawn was sparkling with frost.* N UNCOUNT

frostbite /frɒstbaɪt/ is a condition caused by extreme cold which can damage your fingers, toes, and ears. EG *He was crippled with frostbite.* N UNCOUNT

frosted /frɒstɪd/. **Frosted** glass has a rough surface that you cannot see through. EG *...the frosted glass pane in the door.* ADJ CLASSIF: ATTRIB

frosty /frɒstiː/, **frostier, frostiest.** 1 If the weather is **frosty**, the temperature is below freezing. EG *...a still and frosty night.* ADJ QUALIT

2 If you say that someone is **frosty**, you mean that they are unfriendly or disapproving. EG *...a frosty glance.* ◇ **frostily.** EG *He smiled frostily.* ADJ QUALIT ◇ ADV

froth /frɒθ/, **froths, frothing, frothed.** 1 **Froth** is a mass of small bubbles on the surface of a liquid. N UNCOUNT

2 If a liquid **froths**, it has lots of small bubbles in it or on its surface. EG *...the water frothing at his feet.* v : USU+A

frothy /frɒθiː/. A **frothy** liquid has lots of bubbles on its surface. EG *...frothy beer.* ADJ QUALIT

frown /fraʊn/, **frowns, frowning, frowned.** When someone **frowns**, they move their eyebrows towards each other because they are annoyed, worried, or concentrating on something. EG *He frowned as though deep in thought... She frowned at him. 'What others?'* ▸ used as a noun. EG *...a frown of disappointment.* v : OFT+at ▸ N COUNT

frown on or **frown upon.** If something is **frowned on** or is **frowned upon**, people disapprove of it. EG *Non-membership of a union is frowned upon.* PHRASAL VB : V+PREP, OFT PASS

froze /frəʊz/ is the past tense of **freeze.**

frozen /frəʊzən/ 1 **Frozen** is the past participle of **freeze.**

2 If a lake or river is **frozen** or **frozen over**, its surface has turned into ice because the weather is very cold. EG *...the frozen canal... The Missouri was frozen over.* ADJ CLASSIF

3 **Frozen** food has been preserved by freezing. EG *...a packet of frozen peas... ...a frozen chicken.* ADJ CLASSIF : USU ATTRIB

4 If you are **frozen**, you are very cold. EG *'Poor Oliver,' she said. 'You're frozen.'* ADJ QUALIT

5 If you stand or sit **frozen**, you keep still or cannot move because of danger or fear. EG *The men sat frozen with terror.* ADJ PRED : USU +with

frugal /fruːgəl/. 1 People who are **frugal** eat very little and spend very little money on themselves. EG *She lived a careful, frugal life.* ◇ **frugally.** EG *He ate frugally.* ◇ **frugality** /fruːgælɪtiː/. EG *...the tendency towards frugality and simplicity.* ADJ QUALIT ◇ ADV ◇ N UNCOUNT

2 A **frugal** meal is small and inexpensive. EG *...his frugal breakfast.* ADJ QUALIT

fruit /fruːt/, **fruits.** The plural can be either **fruit** or **fruits**, but it is usually **fruit.**

1 A **fruit** is something which grows on a tree or a bush and which contains seeds or a stone covered by a substance that you can eat. Apples, oranges, grapes, and bananas are all fruit. N COUNT OR N UNCOUNT

2 The **fruit** or the **fruits** of an action or activity are its results or products, especially good or pleasant ones. EG *...the fruit of his visits to China... The fruits of our labours were tremendous.* ● If an action **bears fruit**, it produces good results. EG *The good work of this year will continue to bear fruit.* N UNCOUNT OR N PLURAL : USU+of ● PHRASE Formal

Do you get fruit from a fruit machine?

fruitcake /fruːtkeɪk/, **fruitcakes.** A **fruitcake** is N COUNT OR a cake that contains dried fruit. N UNCOUNT

fruitful /fruːtfʊl/. Something that is **fruitful** pro- ADJ QUALIT duces good and useful results. EG ...*hours of fruitful discussion*... ...*the fruitful use of funds.*

fruition /fruːɪʃəⁿn/. If something comes to **frui-** N UNCOUNT **tion**, it starts to succeed and produce the results Formal that were intended or hoped for. EG *At last his efforts were coming to fruition.*

fruitless /fruːtlɪⁱs/. Something that is **fruitless** ADJ QUALIT does not produce any results or achieve anything. EG ...*making fruitless inquiries*... ...*their fruitless search for the plane.*

fruit machine, fruit machines. A **fruit ma-** N COUNT **chine** is a machine used for gambling. You put in a British coin and then press buttons to try and get particu- lar patterns of symbols on a screen in order to win money.

fruity /fruːtiⁱ/, **fruitier, fruitiest.** 1 Something ADJ QUALIT that is **fruity** smells or tastes of fruit. EG ...*cheap, fruity wines.*

2 A **fruity** laugh or voice is rich and deep; used ADJ QUALIT showing approval.

frustrate /frʌstreɪt/, **frustrates, frustrating, frustrated.** 1 If a situation **frustrates** you, it V+O makes you feel upset and angry because you are unable to do what you would like to do. EG *The lack of money and facilities depressed and frustrated him.* ◊ **frustrated.** EG ...*the sobbing wife and the* ◊ ADJ QUALIT *angry, frustrated husband*... ...*a job in which you feel frustrated.* ◊ **frustrating.** EG *It was frustrating* ◊ ADJ QUALIT *to live at the sea's edge and be unable to swim.* ◊ **frustration** /frʌstreɪʃəⁿn/, **frustrations.** EG ◊ N UNCOUNT ...*screaming with frustration*... ...*the frustrations of* OR N COUNT *poverty.*

2 If someone or something **frustrates** a plan or V+O hope, they prevent the event that was planned or hoped for from taking place. EG *The government have frustrated further advance towards European union.* ◊ **frustrated.** EG ...*frustrated desires... Many* ◊ ADJ CLASSIF *frustrated poets end up as teachers.* ◊ **frustration.** EG ...*the frustration of hopes.* ◊ N UNCOUNT

fry /fraɪ/, **fries, frying, fried.** 1 When you **fry** V-ERG food, you cook it in a pan that contains hot fat or oil. EG *Ellen was frying an egg*... ...*the smell of frying onions.* ◊ **fried.** EG ...*fried potatoes.* ◊ ADJ CLASSIF

2 See also **small fry.**

frying pan, frying pans. 1 A **frying pan** is a flat, N COUNT metal pan with a long handle, in which you fry food.

2 If you say that doing something is jumping **out of** PHRASE **the frying pan into the fire,** you mean that doing it puts you in just as bad a position as you were in before.

ft is a written abbreviation for 'foot' or 'feet' in measurements. EG ...*cages less than 4 ft high and 2 ft wide*... ...*age 35, height 6 ft 3 in.*

fudge /fʌdʒ/, **fudges, fudging, fudged.** 1 **Fudge** N UNCOUNT is a soft, brown sweet made from butter, milk, and sugar.

2 If you **fudge** something, you avoid making clear V+O or definite decisions or statements about it. EG ...*an attempt to fudge this issue by concealing the facts.*

fuel /fjʊəl/, **fuels, fuelling, fuelled;** also spelled **fueling, fueled** in American English.

1 **Fuel** is a substance such as wood, coal, or petrol N MASS that is burned to supply heat or power. EG *The cost of fuel is a worry for old people*... ...*the increase in world fuel consumption.* ● See also **fossil fuel.**

2 A machine or vehicle that **is fuelled** by a V+O : USU PASS particular substance works by burning that sub- stance. EG ...*boilers fuelled by coal.*

3 If something **fuels** a situation or feeling, it causes V+O it to increase in intensity or scale. EG *Hugh's anger was fuelled by resentment.*

4 If something **adds fuel to** a conflict or an PHRASE unpleasant situation, it makes the situation worse. EG *The trouble will add fuel to the class war.*

fugitive /fjuːdʒɪtɪv/, **fugitives.** 1 A **fugitive** is N COUNT someone who is running away from or hiding from OR N MOD their enemies, from the police, or from an unpleas- ant situation. EG ...*political fugitives from Algeria*... ...*the hunt for a fugitive American.*

2 **Fugitive** also means lasting for only a very short ADJ CLASSIF time. EG ...*a fugitive smile*... ...*fugitive visits.* Literary

-ful, -fuls. -ful is used to form nouns that refer to SUFFIX the quantity of a substance that an object contains or can contain. For example, a handful of sand is the amount of sand that you can hold in your hand. EG ...*two cupfuls of sugar*... ...*every mouthful of food.*

fulcrum /fʌlkrəm, fʊlkrəm/. The **fulcrum** of N SING something that is balancing or being used as a Technical lever is the point at which it is supported or fixed.

fulfil /fʊlfɪl/, **fulfils, fulfilling, fulfilled;** also spelled **fulfill, fulfills** in American English.

1 If you **fulfil** a promise, request, or hope, you do V+O what was promised, asked, or hoped. EG *They failed to fulfil their promises to revive the economy*... *I had fulfilled many of my ambitions.*

2 If what you are doing **fulfils** you or if you **fulfil** V+O OR V-REFL yourself, you feel happy and satisfied with what you are doing. EG *This way of life no longer fulfils the individuals concerned.* ◊ **fulfilling.** EG *Jobs* ◊ ADJ QUALIT *should be made as creative and fulfilling as pos- sible.* ◊ **fulfilled.** EG *The children gain if both* ◊ ADJ QUALIT *parents are living fulfilled lives.*

3 If someone or something **fulfils** a role or func- V+O tion, they do whatever is required by it. EG *He could no longer fulfil his function as breadwinner for the family... Helicopters fulfilled a variety of roles.*

fulfilment /fʊlfɪlməⁿnt/; also spelled **fulfillment** in American English.

1 **Fulfilment** is a feeling of satisfaction that you N UNCOUNT get from doing or achieving something. EG *People find fulfilment in working for a common goal.*

2 When something happens that has been prom- N UNCOUNT : ised or hoped for, you can refer to this event as the USU+*of* **fulfilment** of the promise or hope. EG ...*the fulfil- ment of their dreams.*

full /fʊl/, **fuller, fullest.** 1 Something that is **full** ADJ QUALIT contains as much of a substance or as many objects as it can. EG *The bucket's almost full... All the car parks are absolutely full.*

2 If you say that something is **full** of things or ADJ PRED+*of* people, you mean that it contains a large number of them. EG ...*a garden full of pear and apple trees.*

3 If you say that someone or something is **full** of ADJ PRED+*of* feeling or quality, you mean that they have a lot of it. EG *I was full of confidence.*

4 You can use **full** to indicate the greatest extent ADJ CLASSIF : or amount of something that is possible. EG ...*a* ATTRIB *return to full employment... Make full use of your brains... The radio was playing at full volume.*

5 You say that something has been done **in full** PHRASE when everything that is necessary has been done. EG *The bill has been paid in full.*

6 Something that is done **to the full** is done to as PHRASE great an extent as is possible. EG *She wanted to exploit that opportunity to the full.*

7 You can use **full** to emphasize 7.1 that you are ADJ CLASSIF : referring to the whole of something, or to a com- ATTRIB plete thing. EG *I haven't got his full name*... ...*my last full day in Warsaw.* 7.2 the degree of a quality that ADJ CLASSIF : something has. EG ...*the full squalor of the buildings.* ATTRIB 7.3 the directness and force with which a person or ADV+PREP thing hits or looks at something. EG *My skis struck a woman full in the face.*

8 When machinery or equipment is **full** on, it is ADV AFTER VB working at its greatest power or intensity. EG *The gas fire was full on.*

9 If someone has a **full** life, they are always busy. ADJ QUALIT

10 If you describe a part of someone's body as **full**, ADJ QUALIT you mean that it is rounded and rather large. EG ...*her full red lips.*

11 When there is a **full** moon, the moon appears as ADJ CLASSIF a bright circle.

12 If you say that you know something **full well,** PHRASE

you are emphasizing that you are totally sure about it. EG *We know full well that Congress will spend every penny.*

13 to be **full of beans**: see **bean**. ● to **come full circle**: see **circle**.

full-blooded. Full-blooded is used to describe things that are intense or complete. EG *...without the full-blooded support of the Opposition parties.* ADJ CLASSIF ATTRIB

full-blown. Full-blown things are as intense as possible or have all the features they could have. EG *...a full-blown military operation.* ADJ CLASSIF: ATTRIB

full board. If you stay at a hotel that provides **full board**, you can get all your meals there. N UNCOUNT

full-length. 1 A **full-length** novel, film, or play is the normal length, rather than being shorter than normal. ADJ CLASSIF: ATTRIB

2 A **full-length** skirt or coat is quite long, rather than being short. ADJ CLASSIF: ATTRIB

3 A **full-length** mirror or portrait shows the whole of a person. ADJ CLASSIF: ATTRIB

4 Someone who is lying **full-length** is lying down flat and stretched out. ADV AFTER VB

full marks. 1 If you get **full marks** in a test or exam, you answer every question correctly. N PLURAL

2 If you say that someone gets **full marks** for something, you are praising them. EG *Mr Jenkins gets full marks for courage.* N PLURAL

fullness /fʊlnɪ²s/. **1** If you talk about the **fullness** of something, you mean that it is very strong or rich, or full of many things. EG *...the fullness of her love... ...life in all its fullness.* N UNCOUNT Literary

2 If you say that something will happen **in the fullness of time**, you mean that it will eventually happen, but probably after a long time. EG *The inspector's report, in the fullness of time, would reach headquarters.* PHRASE

full-page. A **full-page** advertisement, picture, or article covers a whole page of a newspaper or magazine. ADJ CLASSIF: ATTRIB

full-scale is used to describe things that have all the features they could have and that are done to the greatest extent possible. EG *It could turn into a full-scale war.* ADJ CLASSIF: ATTRIB

full-size. Full-size or **full-sized** things **1** have finished growing and will not become any larger. EG *...full-size trees.* **2** are the same size as the thing they represent. EG *...a full-size model of a vehicle.* ADJ CLASSIF ADJ CLASSIF: ATTRIB

full stop, full stops. A **full stop** is the dot (.) which you put as a punctuation mark at the end of a sentence when it is not a question or an exclamation. N COUNT British

full-time. 1 Full-time work or study takes up the whole of each normal working week rather than just part of it. EG *...a full-time job... ...full-time students... Bob and I worked full time.* ADJ CLASSIF, OR ADV AFTER VB

2 If you say that an activity or task is **a full-time job**, you mean that it takes up a lot of your time. EG *Answering letters was a full-time job.* PHRASE

3 In some sports such as football, hockey, and rugby, **full time** is the end of a match. N UNCOUNT

full up. If you say that something is **full up**, you are emphasizing that it contains as much of a substance or as many objects as it can. EG *The town's full up.* ADJ PRED

fully /fʊlɪ¹/. **1 Fully** means to the greatest degree or extent possible. EG *The secrets of its success ₣re still not fully understood... ...fully automatic washing machines.* ADV

2 You use **fully** to indicate that a process is completely finished. EG *It was weeks before he fully recovered... Barber isn't fully trained yet.* ADV

3 If you do something **fully**, you do not leave out or forget any details or aspects of it. EG *She answered his questions fully.* ADV

4 You can use **fully** to emphasize how great an amount is. EG *Fully one-quarter of the workers are Turks.* ADV+N

fully-fledged /fʌlɪ¹flɛdʒd/ means having completely developed into the type of thing or person ADJ CLASSIF: ATTRIB

mentioned. EG *...fully-fledged members of the association.*

fulsome /fʊlsəm/. **Fulsome** apologies or expressions of gratitude or admiration are very exaggerated or excessive. EG *...with fulsome compliments and extravagant gifts.* ADJ QUALIT Formal

fumble /fʌmbə²l/, **fumbles, fumbling, fumbled.** **1** If you **fumble** with an object or **fumble** in a container, you handle the object or search for something clumsily. EG *His awkwardness made him fumble with the key... He fumbled in his pocket for his whistle.* V: USU+A

2 If you **fumble** when you are trying to say something, you talk in a confused and unclear way. EG *Brody fumbled for words.* V OR V+O

fume /fju:m/, **fumes, fuming, fumed. 1 Fumes** are strong and unpleasant or harmful gases, smells, or smoke. EG *...the exhaust fumes of a car... ...tobacco fumes.* N PLURAL

2 If you **fume**, you show or express impatience and anger. EG *I was fuming with rage... He fumed: 'I have answered every question.'* V OR V+QUOTE

fun /fʌn/. **1** If you say that an activity is **fun**, you mean that it is enjoyable or amusing. EG *It's fun working for him... Tests are no fun.* N UNCOUNT

2 If you have **fun**, you enjoy yourself. EG *We had great fun on the beach... She wanted a bit more fun out of life.* N UNCOUNT

3 If you say that someone is **fun**, you mean that you enjoy being with them because they say and do interesting or amusing things. EG *She was great fun... He was fun to be with.* N UNCOUNT

4 If you say that something is a **fun** thing, you mean that you enjoy it. EG *Those were fun times.* ADJ CLASSIF Informal

5 If you do something **for fun** or **for the fun of it**, you do it in order to enjoy yourself and not because it is important or necessary. EG *...things that you do for fun in your spare time... You don't come to work just for the fun of it.* PHRASE

6 If you **make fun of** someone or something or **poke fun at** them, you tease them or make jokes about them. EG *Don't make fun of my father.* PHRASE

function /fʌŋkⁿʃəⁿn/, **functions, functioning, functioned. 1** The **function** of something or someone is the useful thing that they do or are intended to do. EG *The essential function of trade unions is to bargain with employers... The brain performs three functions: recording, recalling, and analysing... What is your main function in life?* N COUNT

2 If a machine or system **is functioning**, it is working or operating. EG *The phone didn't function at all... Only one hospital is functioning... ...an idea of how the civil service functions.* V

3 If someone or something **functions** as a particular thing, they do the work or fulfil the purpose of that thing. EG *The room had previously functioned as a playroom... I found myself functioning as an ambassador.* V+as

4 If you say that one thing is a **function** of another, you mean that its amount or nature depends on the other thing. EG *The supply of money was a function of the amount of gold discovered.* N COUNT: OFT SING+of Formal

5 A **function** is also a large formal dinner or party. EG *He had been invited to a function at the college.* N COUNT

functional /fʌŋkⁿʃəⁿnəl, -ʃənə²l/. **1** Something that is **functional 1.1** is intended to be useful rather than attractive. EG *...functional modern furniture.* ADJ QUALIT

1.2 is working or operating. EG *How long has the machine been functional?* ADJ CLASSIF

2 Functional also means relating to the way something works. EG *...a functional description of the motorcycle... ...functional efficiency.* ADJ CLASSIF

functionary /fʌŋkⁿʃənəⁿri¹/, **functionaries.** A **functionary** is a person who has an official admin- N COUNT Formal

If you poke fun at someone, are you being funny?

istrative job in an organization, especially in a government or a political party.

fund /fʌnd/, funds, funding, funded. **1** Funds N PLURAL are amounts of money that are available for spending. EG ...*how to raise funds for a commercial project.*

2 A **fund** is an amount of money that is collected N COUNT for a particular purpose. EG *He made a generous donation to our campaign fund.*

3 If you have a **fund** of something, you have a lot of N PART it. EG ...*a large fund of scientific knowledge.*

4 When a person or organization **funds** something, V+O they provide money for it. EG *The work is being funded both by governments and private industry.*
◊ **funding.** EG *They provide funding in the form of* ◊ N UNCOUNT *loans.*

fundamental /fʌndəmentəºl/, fundamentals. **1** ADJ CLASSIF If you describe something as **fundamental**, you mean that it is very important or basic. EG ...*the fundamental principles on which it is based... The differences are in some respects fundamental.*

2 The **fundamentals** of a subject or activity are its N PLURAL most important and basic parts. EG ...*the fundamentals of police work... Their test really gets down to fundamentals.*

fundamentalism /fʌndəmentəlɪzºm/ is belief in N UNCOUNT the original form of a religion, without accepting any later ideas. ◊ **fundamentalist** ◊ N COUNT /fʌndəmentəlɪst/, fundamentalists. EG ...*a funda-* OR N MOD *mentalist Christian.*

fundamentally /fʌndəmentəli/. You use **funda-mentally 1** to indicate that you are talking about ADV OR the real or basic nature of something. EG *Our* ADV SEN *criminal code is based fundamentally on fear... Fundamentally, we are not a part of the community.* **2** to indicate the extreme degree or extent of ADV something. EG *I disagreed fundamentally with the Party.*

fund-raising is the activity of collecting money N UNCOUNT for a particular purpose or organization.

funeral /fjuːnºrəl/, funerals. A **funeral** is the N COUNT ceremony that is held when the body of someone who has died is buried or cremated. EG *Both actresses attended the funeral... ...a funeral service.*

funereal /fjuːnɪərɪəl/. If you describe something ADJ QUALIT as **funereal**, you mean that it is very sad, serious, Literary and depressing. EG *The atmosphere in the cabin was almost funereal.*

fungus /fʌngəs/, fungi /fʌngaɪ/. **Fungi** are plants N COUNT OR such as mushrooms, toadstools, and mould which N UNCOUNT have no leaves or green colouring.

funk /fʌŋk/ is a style of music based on jazz and N UNCOUNT blues, with a strong, repeated bass part.

funky /fʌŋki/. **Funky** jazz, blues, or pop music ADJ QUALIT has a very strong, repeated bass part.

funnel

funnel /fʌnºl/, funnels, funnelling, funnelled; also spelled **funneling, funneled** in American English.

1 A **funnel** is an object with a wide, circular top N COUNT and a short tube at the bottom, which is used when pouring liquids, powders, or very small things into a container. EG *Fill a bottle through a funnel.*

2 A **funnel** is also a chimney on a ship or railway N COUNT engine powered by steam. EG ...*a ship with a yellow funnel.*

3 If something **funnels** or **is funnelled** some- V-ERG : USU+A where, it is directed through a narrow space. EG ...*gales funnelling between the islands.*

4 If you **funnel** money, information, or goods V+O+A somewhere, you cause them to be sent there from several sources. EG ...*funneling aid to the resistance groups.*

funnily /fʌnɪli/. You say **funnily enough** to ADV SEN indicate that, although something is surprising, it is true or it really did happen. EG *Funnily enough, old people seem to love bingo... Well, funnily enough, all seven of us went there, but separately.*

funny /fʌni/, funnier, funniest. **1** You say that ADJ QUALIT something is **funny 1.1** when it is strange, surprising, or puzzling. EG ...*a funny little white hat... It's a funny thing to write... It was funny that you met the same people... The funny thing is, we went to Arthur's house just yesterday.* **1.2** when it is amusing and makes you smile or laugh. EG *She laughed. 'What's funny?' he asked... It did look funny upside down... He told funny stories and made everyone laugh.*

2 If you feel **funny**, you feel slightly ill. EG *I just feel* ADJ PRED *a bit funny, it's difficult to describe.*

fur /fɜː/, furs. **1** Fur is **1.1** the thick hair that N UNCOUNT grows on the bodies of many animals. EG *Moles have short silky fur.* **1.2** the fur-covered skin of an N MASS animal that is used to make clothing or rugs. EG ...*a jacket edged with white fur... ...a fur coat.* **1.3** a N UNCOUNT soft, artificial material that looks like fur and is used to make clothing, rugs, toys, and seat covers.

2 A **fur** is a coat made from real or artificial fur, or N COUNT a piece of fur worn round a woman's neck. EG *Many women refused to buy furs... You can get a genuine fur in Jenners.*

furious /fjuərɪəs/. **1** Someone who is **furious** is ADJ QUALIT extremely angry. EG *I was furious and told them to get out of my house... She was furious with him.*
◊ **furiously.** EG *'Who is this man?' the Prince* ◊ ADV *exclaimed furiously.*

2 You can use **furious** to indicate that something ADJ CLASSIF : happens with great energy, speed, or violence. EG ATTRIB ...*a furious battle... ...the furious efforts they were making.* ◊ **furiously.** EG *She ran furiously up the* ◊ ADV *hill.*

furled /fɜːld/. If something such as an umbrella or ADJ CLASSIF a sail is **furled**, it is rolled or folded up because it is not being used. EG ...*a ship with its sails furled.*

furnace /fɜːnɪs/, furnaces. **1** A **furnace** is a N COUNT container in which a very hot fire is used to melt metal, burn rubbish, or produce steam. EG *He kicked the furnace door open and began shovelling coal... Gradually, coal furnaces were replaced by gas and electric ones.*

2 You can describe a room or vehicle as a **furnace** N COUNT when it is very hot inside it. EG *The car was a furnace when we got in again.*

furnish /fɜːnɪʃ/, furnishes, furnishing, fur-nished. **1** When you **furnish** a room or building, V+O you put furniture, carpets, curtains, and other things into it. EG *Do you enjoy decorating and furnishing a house?*

2 To **furnish** something means to provide it or V+O : supply it. EG *They were not prepared to furnish the* OFT + with *necessary troops... Luckily, they have furnished us* Formal *with a translation.*

furnished /fɜːnɪʃt/. **1** A **furnished** room or house ADJ CLASSIF is rented with furniture already in it. EG *They were living in a furnished flat near Finchley Station.*

2 When you say how a room or house is **furnished**, ADJ CLASSIF you are describing the kind or amount of furniture that it has in it. EG *The bedroom was scantily furnished... ...a large room furnished with low tables and cushions.*

furnishings /fɜːnɪʃɪŋz/. The **furnishings** of a N PLURAL room or house are the furniture, carpets, curtains, and decorations. EG *The tables and stools were the sole furnishings of the room.*

furniture /fɜːnɪtʃə/ consists of the large, movable N UNCOUNT objects such as tables, chairs, or beds that are used in a room. EG *She arranged the furniture... The only piece of furniture was an old wardrobe.*

furore /fjuəˈrɔːrɪ/, also spelled **furor** N SING /fjuərɔː/ in American English. A **furore** is a very angry or excited reaction by people to something. EG *The lecture caused an enormous furore... ...the present furore over drugs.*

furrow /fʌrəʊ/, **furrows, furrowing, furrowed.** N COUNT
1 A **furrow** is **1.1** a long line in the earth which a farmer makes in order to plant seeds in or to allow water to flow along. EG *...a field with parallel furrows running down it.* **1.2** a deep fold or line in the skin of someone's face. EG *...the deep furrows in his cheeks.*
2 When you **furrow** your brow or forehead or V-ERG when it **furrows**, it has deep folds because you are frowning. EG *The pain caused him to furrow his brow.*

furry /fɜːrɪ/, **furrier, furriest. 1** A **furry** animal ADJ QUALIT is covered with thick, soft hair. EG *It had a long furry tail.*
2 Something that is **furry** has a soft texture like ADJ QUALIT fur. EG *...a furry coat.*

further /fɜːðə/, **furthers, furthering, furthered.** **Further** is a comparative form of **far**, and is also a verb.
1 Further means to a greater degree or extent. EG ADV *The situation was further complicated by uncertainty about the future... He sank further into debt.*
2 If someone or something goes **further** or takes ADV something **further**, they progress to a more advanced stage. EG *They never got any further... He hoped the new offer would develop matters a stage further.*
3 If you say you will go **further** in a discussion, you ADV mean you will make a more extreme or more detailed statement. EG *I shall go further and say that Len was lying.*
4 A **further** thing or amount is an additional one. ADJ CLASSIF, OR EG *We need a further five hundred pounds... Do you* ADJ AFTER N *have nothing further to say?*
5 Further to is used in business letters to indicate PREP that you are referring to a previous letter or Formal conversation. EG *Further to your enquiry of the 16th, I am happy to enclose the new contract.*
6 Further means a greater distance than before ADV or than something else. EG *I walked further than I intended.* ● If something is **further on**, it is further ● PHRASE in the direction that you are going. EG *I found a tree a little further on.*
7 If you tell someone that a piece of information PHRASE must **not go any further**, you mean that they must not tell it to anyone else. EG *'This mustn't go any further.' - 'No, of course.'*
8 You can use expressions such as **'further** back' ADV+ADV and **'further** on' to refer to a time that is before or after the time you are talking about. EG *It has its origins much further back... Three years further on, Linda has no regrets.*
9 If you **further** something, you help it to progress, V+O to be successful, or to be achieved. EG *...a plot by Morris to further his career... ...furthering the cause of liberation.*

furtherance /fɜːðərəns/. If you do something in N UNCOUNT **furtherance** of something else, you do it in order +SUPP to help bring this other thing to be achieved. EG *He did it* Formal *solely in the furtherance of his own interests... ...acting in furtherance of a lawful trade dispute.*

further education is the education of people N UNCOUNT who have left school and want more qualifications, British at a lower level than a degree. EG *The state is pouring money into further education... We can give advice on further education courses throughout Britain.*

furthermore /fɜːðəmɔː/ is used to introduce a ADV SEN piece of information or an opinion that adds to or supports the previous one. EG *He carried out orders without questioning them. Furthermore, he was not bothered by hard work... It is nearly dark, and furthermore it's going to rain.*

furthest /fɜːðɪst/. **Furthest** is a superlative form of **far**.
1 Furthest means to a greater extent or degree ADV OR than ever before or than anything or anyone else. ADJ QUALIT : EG *...countries where commercialized farming has* SUPERL *advanced furthest... ...the furthest limits of democracy.*
2 The **furthest** one of a number of things is the ADJ CLASSIF OR one that is the greatest distance away from a ADV particular place. EG *She sat near the furthest window... ...the fields which lay furthest from his farm.*

furtive /fɜːtɪv/. You say that someone's behaviour ADJ QUALIT is **furtive** when they seem to be trying to do something secretly. EG *They suddenly looked furtive... ...a furtive glance.* ◊ **furtively.** EG *He* ◊ ADV *furtively handed over the letter... He looked round, furtively.*

fury /fjuərɪ/. **1 Fury** is violent or very strong N UNCOUNT anger. EG *He clenched his fists in fury... There was fury in Miss Lenaut's dark eyes... He looked up at us with fury.*
2 If you are **in a fury**, you are very angry. EG *The* PHRASE *women jumped on Willie in a fury... He flew into a fury.*

fuse /fjuːz/, **fuses, fusing, fused. 1** A **fuse** is a N COUNT safety device in an electric plug or circuit. It contains a piece of wire which melts when there is a fault so that the flow of electricity stops. EG *...to switch off the lamp and mend the fuse... Have you checked the fuse?*
2 When an electric device **fuses**, it stops working V-ERG because of a fault. EG *Several of the street lamps had fused.*
3 A **fuse** is also a device on a bomb or firework N COUNT which delays the explosion and gives people time to move away to a safe distance.
4 When objects **fuse** or **are fused**, they join V-ERG together physically because of heat or a biological process. EG *During fertilization the sperm and egg fuse.*
5 If you **fuse** two ideas, methods, or systems, you V-ERG combine them. EG *...the attempt to fuse new and old.*

fuselage /fjuːzɪlɑːʒ/, **fuselages.** The **fuselage** of N COUNT an aeroplane, missile, or rocket is its main part. EG *The big jet was still stuck, its fuselage and tail blocking runway three.*

fusion /fjuːʒən/, **fusions. 1** When two ideas, N UNCOUNT methods, or systems are combined, you can say OR N COUNT that there is a **fusion** of these ideas, methods, or systems. EG *...the fusion of radical and socialist ideals... The painting is a rich fusion of several elements.*
2 The process in which atomic particles combine N UNCOUNT and produce nuclear energy is called nuclear **fu-** Technical **sion.**

fuss /fʌs/, **fusses, fussing, fussed. 1** If you say N SING OR that someone is making a **fuss** about something, N UNCOUNT : you mean that they are behaving in an unneces- OFT+*about*/ sarily anxious, excited, or angry way. EG *They're* over *making a fuss about the wedding... He accepted the statement without fuss.*
2 If you **make a fuss of** someone, you pay a lot of PHRASE

What is the difference between 'furniture' and 'furnishings'?

attention to them. EG *They like to be flattered and made a fuss of.*

3 When people **fuss**, they behave in an unnecessarily anxious or excited way. EG *Stop fussing, mother... Ted fussed with his camera.*   v

fuss over. If you **fuss over** someone or something, you pay too much attention to them or worry about them too much. EG *She was inclined to fuss over her health.*   PHRASAL VB : V+PREP, HAS PASS

fussy /fʌsiˈ/, **fussier, fussiest. 1** Someone who is **fussy** is excessively nervous, concerned with details, or careful in choosing things. EG *I am very fussy about my food... ...a fat and fussy lady... He's not fussy who he rents his room to.* ◊ **fussily.** EG ◊ ADV *...fumbling fussily with his papers.*   ADJ QUALIT : OFT+*about*

2 If you describe clothes or furniture as **fussy**, you mean that they are too elaborate or have too much decoration. EG *...fussy lace curtains.* ◊ **fussily.** EG ◊ ADV *She was fussily dressed.*   ADJ QUALIT

futile /fjuːtaɪl/. If you describe an action or attempt as **futile**, you mean that it will not be successful or was not successful. EG *...a series of costly and futile wars... Lucy knew how futile it was to argue with her father.* ◊ **futility** /fjuːtɪlˈtiˈ/. EG ◊ N UNCOUNT *...the futility of their attempts.*   ADJ QUALIT

future /fjuːtʃə/, **futures. 1** The **future** is the period of time that will come after the present, or the things that will happen then. EG *It might be possible in the future... What plans do you have for the future?*   N SING : the+N

2 You use **in future** when you are telling someone what you want or expect to happen from now on.   ADV SEN

EG *Be more careful in future... More hospital officers will in future be temporarily attached to hospitals.*

3 Future things will happen or exist after the present time. EG *Let's meet again at some future date... ...future generations.*   ADJ CLASSIF : ATTRIB

4 Your **future** is your life or career after the present time. EG *I decided that my future lay in medicine.*   N COUNT : OFT+POSS

5 If something has a **future**, it is likely to be successful and to continue to exist. EG *Does the engine have a future?*   N SING : a+N

future tense. In grammar, the **future tense** is used to refer mainly to things that will come after the present, or the things that will happen then.   N SING : the+N

futuristic /fjuːtʃərˈɪstɪk/. You describe something as **futuristic** when it looks or seems unusual, like something from the future. EG *...the futuristic shape of the buildings.*   ADJ QUALIT

fuzz /fʌz/. **1 Fuzz** is a mass of short curly hairs or threads. EG *...the light, blond fuzz on his cheeks.*   N UNCOUNT

2 Some people refer to the police as the **fuzz**. EG *We thought you were the fuzz.*   N SING : the+N Informal

fuzzy /fʌziˈ/, **fuzzier, fuzziest. 1 Fuzzy** hair sticks up in a soft, curly mass.   ADJ QUALIT

2 If something looks **fuzzy**, its shape is blurred rather than being sharp and clear. EG *These photographs were less fuzzy.*   ADJ QUALIT

3 If you or your thoughts are **fuzzy**, you are confused and cannot think clearly. EG *My mind was tired and a bit fuzzy.*   ADJ QUALIT

G g

G, g /dʒiː/, **Gs, g's. 1 G** is the seventh letter of the English alphabet.   N COUNT

2 g is used after a number as an abbreviation for 'gram'. EG *...257g.*

gab /gæb/. If you say that someone has **the gift of the gab**, you mean that they have the ability to speak easily, confidently, and in a persuasive way.   PHRASE Informal

gabble /gæbəˈl/, **gabbles, gabbling, gabbled.** If you **gabble**, you say things so quickly that it is difficult for people to understand you. EG *'Look here,' he gabbled, 'It's about the Harvest Festival.'* ▸ used as a noun. EG *There was a gabble of conversation in the pub.*   V, V+QUOTE, OR V+O   ▸ N UNCOUNT

gable /geɪbəˈl/, **gables.** A **gable** is the triangular part at the top of the end wall of a building, between the two sloping sides of the roof. ◊ **gabled** /geɪbəˈld/. EG *...small gabled houses.*   N COUNT   ◊ ADJ CLASSIF

gadget /gædʒɪˈt/, **gadgets.** A **gadget** is a small machine or device. EG *...household gadgets.*   N COUNT

gaffe /gæf/, **gaffes.** A **gaffe** is something that you say or do which is considered to be socially incorrect. EG *I had no idea of the gaffe which I was committing.*   N COUNT

gag /gæg/, **gags, gagging, gagged. 1** A **gag** is a piece of cloth that is tied round or put inside someone's mouth in order to stop them from speaking.   N COUNT

2 If someone **gags** you, they tie a piece of cloth round your mouth. EG *She was gagged and blindfolded.*   V+O

3 If you **gag**, you choke and nearly vomit. EG *Dr. Hutchinson suddenly gagged. 'Too much wine. Forgive me.'*   V

4 A **gag** is also a joke, especially one told by a professional comedian. EG *Where do you get all these gags?*   N COUNT Informal

gaga /gɑːgɑː/. Someone who is **gaga** is senile. EG *She's seventy-seven and rather gaga.*   ADJ QUALIT Informal

gaggle /gægəˈl/, **gaggles.** You can use **gaggle** to refer to a group of people. EG *...a gaggle of little girls.*   N PART

gaiety /geɪəˈtiˈ/ is a feeling or attitude of liveliness and fun. EG *...fresh youthful gaiety.*   N UNCOUNT

gaily /geɪliˈ/. **1** If you do something **gaily**, you do it in a lively, happy way. EG *Off we set, with Pam chattering gaily all the way.*   ADV

2 Something that is **gaily** coloured or decorated is coloured or decorated in a bright, pretty way. EG *...donkeys pulling gaily painted carts.*   ADV

gain /geɪn/, **gains, gaining, gained. 1** If you **gain** a quality, you gradually get more of it. EG *The speaker began to gain confidence... ...if the baby fails to gain weight... The Opposition party is gaining in popularity.*   V+O OR V+*in*

2 If you **gain** from something, you get some advantage or benefit from it. EG *It is not only banks who will gain from the coming of electronic money... What has Britain gained by being a member of the EEC?*   V OR V+O : USU+A

3 A **gain** is an improvement, or something that is achieved. EG *The company has made notable gains in productivity.*   N COUNT

4 If you do something for **gain**, you do it in order to get some profit for yourself. EG *He did it for financial gain.*   N UNCOUNT Formal

5 If a clock or watch **gains**, it shows a time that is later than the real time.   V OR V+O

gain on. If you **are gaining on** someone or something that you are chasing, you are gradually catching them up.   PHRASAL VB : V+PREP

gait /geɪt/, **gaits.** Someone's **gait** is the way that they walk. EG *He moves with the slow confident gait of a successful man.*   N COUNT : USU SING+SUPP Formal

gala /gɑːlə/, **galas.** A **gala** is a special public celebration, entertainment, or performance. EG *...the special guest on a gala occasion.*   N COUNT

galactic /gəlæktɪk/ means relating to galaxies in space. ADJ CLASSIF: ATTRIB

galaxy /gæləksi[1]/, **galaxies.** A **galaxy** is a huge group of stars and planets that extends over many millions of miles. N COUNT

gale /geɪl/, **gales.** A **gale** is a very strong wind. N COUNT

gall /gɔːl/, **galls, galling, galled. 1** If you say that someone has the **gall** to do something dangerous or dishonest, you mean that they have the courage to do it. EG *They haven't the gall to steal.* N SING: the+N Formal

2 If something **galls** you, it makes you angry or annoyed. EG *It galled him to have to ask permission.* V+O Formal

gallant /gælənt/; also pronounced /gəlænt/ in rather old-fashioned English for paragraph 2.

1 Someone who is **gallant** is very brave and honourable when they are in danger or difficulty. EG *They have put up a gallant fight over the years.* ADJ QUALIT

◊ **gallantly.** EG *Gallantly they battled on.* ◊ ADV

2 A man who is **gallant** is kind, polite, and considerate towards women. ◊ **gallantly.** EG *He gallantly offered to carry her cases to the car.* ADJ QUALIT ◊ ADV

gallantry /gæləntri[1]/ is **1** bravery that is shown by someone who is in danger, especially in a war. EG *He was awarded the Military Cross for gallantry in combat.* **2** polite and considerate behaviour by men towards women. N UNCOUNT

gall bladder, gall bladders. Your **gall bladder** is the organ in your body which contains bile and is next to your liver. N COUNT

gallery /gælə[1]ri[1]/, **galleries. 1** A **gallery** is **1.1** a building or room that has exhibitions of works of art in it. EG *...pictures in the National Gallery.* **1.2** a place where works of art are displayed and sold. **1.3** a raised area at the back or the sides of a large room or hall. EG *...the public gallery at Parliament.* N COUNT

2 The **gallery** in a theatre is a raised area like a large balcony that usually contains the cheapest seats. EG *She always sat in the gallery.* N COUNT

galley /gæli[1]/, **galleys.** A **galley** is a small kitchen, especially in a ship or an aircraft. N COUNT

gallon /gælən/, **gallons.** A **gallon** is a unit of volume that is equal to eight pints. EG *...three gallons of water.* N PART

gallop /gæləp/, **gallops, galloping, galloped. 1** When a horse **gallops**, it runs very fast so that all four legs are off the ground at the same time in each stride. EG *The horse galloped down the road.* V: USU+A

▸ used as a noun. EG *All the animals broke into a gallop.* ▸ N SING

2 If you **gallop**, you ride a horse that is galloping. EG *He swung onto his horse, saluted, and galloped off.* V OR V+O: USU+A

3 A **gallop** is also a ride on a horse that is galloping. EG *...a brisk morning's gallop.* N COUNT

galloping /gæləpɪŋ/ is used to describe something that is increasing or developing very fast and is difficult to control. EG *The oil crisis brought galloping inflation on an international scale.* ADJ CLASSIF: ATTRIB

gallows /gæləʊz/. **Gallows** is both the singular and the plural form.

A **gallows** is a wooden frame used to execute criminals by hanging. N COUNT

galore /gəlɔː/ means existing in very large numbers. EG *...restaurants and night clubs galore.* ADJ AFTER N Outdated

galoshes /gəlɒʃɪz/ are waterproof shoes which people wear over their ordinary shoes to prevent them getting wet. EG *...a pair of galoshes.* N PLURAL

galvanize /gælvənaɪz/, **galvanizes, galvanizing, galvanized;** also spelled **galvanise.** To **galvanize** someone means to cause them to do something suddenly by making them feel excited, afraid, or angry. EG *The lecture galvanized several others into action.* V+O: OFT+into

galvanized /gælvənaɪzd/; also spelled **galvanised.** Galvanized metal has been covered with zinc in order to protect it from rust. EG *...a barn made out of galvanized iron.* ADJ CLASSIF: ATTRIB

gambit /gæmbɪt/, **gambits.** A **gambit** is something that you do or say for a particular purpose. EG N COUNT *...a good gambit for attracting attention... ...a conversational gambit.*

gamble /gæmbə[0]l/, **gambles, gambling, gambled. 1** A **gamble** is a risky action or decision that you take in the hope of gaining money or success. EG *We took a gamble, and lost... ...a gamble that paid off for us.* ▸ used as a verb. EG *I was gambling on the assumption that the file had been lost.* N COUNT: USU SING ▸ V OR V+O: OFT+on

2 If you **gamble**, you bet money in a game such as cards or on the result of a race or competition. EG *He gambled heavily on the horses.* ◊ **gambling.** EG *He used the firm's money to pay off gambling debts.* ◊ **gambler, gamblers.** EG *...a compulsive gambler.* V OR V+O: OFT +on ◊ N UNCOUNT ◊ N COUNT

gambol /gæmbə[0]l/, **gambols, gambolling, gambolled;** spelled **gamboling** and **gamboled** in American English.

If animals or people **gambol**, they run or jump about in a playful way. EG *...with his dogs gambolling round him.* V: USU+A

game /geɪm/, **games. 1** A **game** is **1.1** an activity or sport involving skill, knowledge, or chance, in which you follow rules and try to win against an opponent or try to solve a puzzle. EG *You need two people to play this game... ...a game like tennis... ...word games.* **1.2** a particular occasion on which a game is played. EG *Did you go to the baseball game?... This was our last game, which we lost 6 – 3.* **1.3** a part of a match, consisting of a fixed number of points. EG *Becker leads by four games to one.* **1.4** the equipment that you need to play a particular indoor game, for example a specially marked board, dice, or special cards. EG *...a box of toys and games.* **1.5** a way of behaving in which a person uses a particular plan, especially in order to gain an advantage. EG *...these games that politicians play... ...the power game.* N COUNT

2 Game is used in these phrases. **2.1** If you beat someone **at** their **own game**, you use the same methods that they have used, but more successfully, so that you gain an advantage over them. EG *The Japanese were beating the West at its own game.* **2.2** If you say **the game is up**, you mean that someone's secret plans or activities have been discovered. EG *The British realized that the game was up.* **2.3** If someone or something **gives the game away**, they reveal something such as information which is secret. EG *I always give the game away – you've only got to look at my face.* PHRASES

3 Game is wild animals or birds that are hunted for sport and sometimes cooked and eaten. EG *The men had gone to hunt wild game.* N UNCOUNT

4 If you describe someone as **game**, you mean that they are willing to do something new, unusual, or risky. ◊ **gamely.** EG *The vicar rose gamely to the challenge.* ADJ CLASSIF ◊ ADV

5 Games are **5.1** an organized event in which competitions in several sports take place. EG *...the Olympic Games.* **5.2** organized sports activities that children do at school. EG *I was hopeless at games at school.* N PLURAL

gamekeeper /geɪmkiːpə/, **gamekeepers.** A **gamekeeper** is a person who takes care of the wild animals or birds that are kept on someone's land for hunting. N COUNT

gammon /gæmən/ is meat from a pig which has been smoked or salted like ham. N UNCOUNT

gamut /gæmə[0]t/. The **gamut** of something is the wide variety of things that can be included in it. EG *...the entire gamut of London politics... Fathers can participate in the whole gamut of domestic work.* N SING: USU+of Literary

● If you **run the gamut** of something, you experience or express the wide variety of things that can be included in it. EG *She ran the gamut of all the illnesses that babies can have.* ● PHRASE

What kinds of food are mentioned on these pages?

gang /gæŋ/, **gangs, ganging, ganged.** A **gang** is 1 a group of criminals who work together to commit crimes. EG ...*a gang of terrorists.* 2 a group of people who go around together. EG *They stood around in gangs... ...fights with rival gangs.* N COLL

gang up. If people **gang up**, they unite against someone else, for example in a fight or argument. EG *National groups are ganging up to claim their rights.* PHRASAL VB : V+ADV Informal

gangling /gæŋglɪŋ/. You use **gangling** to describe a young person who is tall, thin, and clumsy. EG ...*a gangling twenty-year-old by the name of Pyle.* ADJ CLASSIF Written

gangrene /gæŋgriːn/ is bad decay that can occur in a part of a person's body if the blood stops flowing to it, for example as a result of illness or injury. N UNCOUNT

gangster /gæŋstə/, **gangsters.** A **gangster** is a member of an organized group of violent criminals. EG ...*a gangster film.* N COUNT

gangway /gæŋweɪ/, **gangways.** A **gangway** is 1 a passage left between rows of seats, for example in a theatre or aircraft, for people to walk along. 2 a short bridge or platform leading onto a ship. EG ...*walking down the gangway to the wharf.* N COUNT British

gaol /dʒeɪl/. See **jail.**

gaoler /dʒeɪlə/. See **jailer.**

gap /gæp/, **gaps.** A **gap** is 1 an empty space or hole in the middle of something solid or between two things. EG ...*a narrow gap in the mountains... She had gaps in her teeth... ...a gap in the hedge.* 2 a period of time when you are not busy or not doing something that you normally do. EG *After a gap of two years, she went back to college.* 3 the absence of something in a situation that prevents it from being satisfactory or complete. EG *This book fills a major gap... You may not get a pension if there are gaps in your record.* 4 a great difference between two things, people, or ideas. EG *The gap between rich and poor regions widened.* ● See also **generation gap.** N COUNT : USU+SUPP / N COUNT : USU+SUPP / N COUNT : USU+SUPP / N COUNT : USU+between

gape /geɪp/, **gapes, gaping, gaped.** 1 If you **gape**, you look at someone or something in surprise, with your mouth open. EG *Jackson gaped in astonishment at the result.* ◊ **gaping.** EG ...*gaping tourists.* 2 If something **gapes**, it opens wide or comes apart. EG *The front door gaped open... The shirt gaped to reveal his chest.* ◊ **gaping.** EG *The dressing gown had a gaping hole in it.* V : OFT+at / ◊ ADJ CLASSIF / V OR V+C / ◊ ADJ CLASSIF : ATTRIB

garage /gæraːʒ, -rɪdʒ/, **garages.** A **garage** is 1 a building in which you keep a car. See picture at HOUSE. 2 a place where you can get your car repaired, buy a car, or buy petrol. EG *It was Sunday and the garage was closed.* N COUNT

garb /gaːb/. Someone's **garb** is the clothes that they are wearing, especially clothes that are in a particular style or are part of a uniform. EG ...*a convict in striped prison garb... ...his habitual winter garb of cloak and gloves.* N UNCOUNT +SUPP Formal

garbage /gaːbɪdʒ/. 1 **Garbage** is rubbish, especially waste from a kitchen. EG ...*the garbage in the streets.* N UNCOUNT American

2 You can refer to ideas and opinions that are stupid or of no value as **garbage**. EG *He talked a lot of garbage on the subject.* N UNCOUNT Informal

garbled /gaːbəld/. If a message or explanation is **garbled**, the details are confused or wrong. EG *I got a garbled telephone message.* ADJ QUALIT

garden /gaːdən/, **gardens, gardening.** 1 A **garden** is a piece of land next to someone's house where they grow flowers, vegetables, or other plants, and which often includes a lawn. EG ...*sitting in the back garden... ...the vegetable garden.* N COUNT

2 If you **are gardening**, you are doing work in your garden such as weeding or planting. ◊ **gardening.** EG *It is too hot to do any gardening... ...gardening gloves.* V : USU CONT / ◊ N UNCOUNT

3 **Gardens** are a place like a park that has areas of N COUNT : USU PLURAL

plants, trees, and grass. EG ...*Kensington Gardens... ...the botanical gardens.*

gardener /gaːdənə/, **gardeners.** A **gardener** is 1 a person who is paid to work in someone else's garden. 2 someone who enjoys working in their garden as a hobby. EG *He was not a keen gardener.* N COUNT

garden party, garden parties. A **garden party** is a formal party that is held in a large private garden, usually in the afternoon. N COUNT

gargantuan /gaːgæntjuˈən/. Something that is **gargantuan** is very large. EG ...*a gargantuan meal.* ADJ QUALIT Literary

gargle /gaːgəl/, **gargles, gargling, gargled.** When you **gargle**, you wash your mouth by filling it with liquid, tilting your head back, and breathing out through your mouth, making a bubbling noise. V OR V+O

garish /geərɪʃ/. Something that is **garish** is very bright in colour and harsh to look at. EG ...*a garish yellow tie.* ADJ QUALIT

garland /gaːlənd/, **garlands.** A **garland** is a decoration in the shape of a circle made of flowers and leaves, which is worn round someone's neck or head. EG *He hung a garland of flowers round my neck.* N COUNT

garlic /gaːlɪk/ is the small round white bulb of an onion-like plant. Garlic has a very strong smell and taste and is used in cooking. EG *Add a crushed clove of garlic.* N UNCOUNT

garment /gaːmənt/, **garments.** A **garment** is a piece of clothing, for example a shirt, dress, skirt, or pair of trousers. EG *She wore a long smock-like garment in scarlet linen.* N COUNT Formal

garner /gaːnə/, **garners, garnering, garnered.** If you **garner** information, you collect it, often with some difficulty. EG *A certain amount can be garnered from the British press.* V+O Formal

garnish /gaːnɪʃ/, **garnishes, garnishing, garnished.** 1 A **garnish** is a small amount of food that you use to decorate food. EG ...*a garnish of parsley.* 2 If you **garnish** food, you decorate it with small amounts of a different food. EG *Garnish the fish with cucumber slices.* N COUNT OR N UNCOUNT / V+O : OFT+with

garret /gærɪt/, **garrets.** A **garret** is a very small room at the top of a house. N COUNT

garrison /gærɪsən/, **garrisons.** A **garrison** is a group of soldiers whose job is to guard a town or building. N COUNT

garrulous /gærələs/. Someone who is **garrulous** talks a lot. EG *She's only a foolish, garrulous woman.* ADJ QUALIT

garter /gaːtə/, **garters.** A **garter** is a piece of elastic worn round the top of a stocking or sock in order to prevent it slipping down. N COUNT

gas /gæs/, **gases; gasses, gassing, gassed.** The form **gases** is the plural of the noun; **gasses** is the 3rd person singular, present tense of the verb.

1 **Gas** is 1.1 a substance like air that is neither liquid nor solid and burns easily. It is used as a fuel for fires, cookers, and central heating in people's homes. EG *He remembered to turn the gas off before leaving home.* 1.2 any substance that is neither liquid nor solid, for example oxygen or hydrogen. EG *Helium is a gas at room temperature... ...deadly nerve gases.* ● See also **tear gas.** N UNCOUNT / N COUNT OR N UNCOUNT

2 **Gas** fires and **gas** cookers use gas as a fuel. N MOD

3 **Gas** is also the same as petrol. EG *Sorry I'm late. I had to stop for gas.* N UNCOUNT American

4 To **gas** a person or animal means to kill them by making them breathe poisonous gas. EG *She tried to gas herself.* V+O OR V-REFL

gas chamber, gas chambers. A **gas chamber** is a room that can be filled with poisonous gas in order to kill people or animals. N COUNT

gaseous /gæsɪəs, geɪʃəs/ is used to describe substances which are neither solid nor liquid. EG ...*liquid or gaseous fuels.* ADJ CLASSIF : ATTRIB Formal

gash /gæʃ/, **gashes, gashing, gashed.** 1 A **gash** is a long, deep cut in something. EG *Zeleika had a large gash in her head.* N COUNT : USU+SUPP

2 If you **gash** something, you make a long, deep cut in it. EG *He gashed his arm on a window last night.* V+O

gas mask, gas masks. A **gas mask** is a device N COUNT
that you wear over your face to protect you from
breathing poisonous gases.

gasoline /ˈɡæsəliˈn/ is the same as petrol. EG N UNCOUNT
...*soaring gasoline prices.* American

gasp /ɡɑːsp/, **gasps, gasping, gasped.** A **gasp** is N COUNT
a short quick breath of air that you take in through
your mouth, especially when you are surprised or
in pain. EG *I listened to him breathing in short
gasps...* ...*a gasp of horrified surprise.* ▸ used as a ▸ V OR
verb. EG *He was gasping for air... 'Call the doctor!'* V+QUOTE
she gasped.

gas station, gas stations. A **gas station** is a N COUNT
place where petrol is sold. American

gastric /ˈɡæstrɪk/ is used to describe processes, ADJ CLASSIF :
pains, or illnesses that occur in your stomach. EG ATTRIB
...*a gastric ulcer.*

gastronomic /ˌɡæstrəˈnɒmɪk/ means concerned ADJ CLASSIF :
with good food. EG ...*the gastronomic reputation of* ATTRIB
France. Formal

gate /ɡeɪt/, **gates.** A **gate** is **1** a structure like a N COUNT
door that is used at the entrance to a field, a
garden, or the grounds of a building. EG *The prison
gates closed behind him...* *The taxi swung in
through the gates of the vicarage.* **2** an official exit
in a large airport which passengers go through on
their way to the aeroplane. EG *Passengers on flight
BA504 should proceed to gate four.*

gateau /ˈɡætəʊ/, **gateaux;** also spelled **gâteau.** A N COUNT OR
gateau is a rich cake, usually with cream in it. EG N UNCOUNT
...*chocolate gateau.*

gatecrash /ˈɡeɪtkræʃ/, **gatecrashes, gate-** V+O OR V
crashing, gatecrashed. If someone **gatecrashes** Informal
a party, they go to it, even though they have not
been invited.

gatepost /ˈɡeɪtpəʊst/, **gateposts.** A **gatepost** is a N COUNT
post in the ground which a gate is fastened to.

gateway /ˈɡeɪtweɪ/, **gateways.** **1** A **gateway** is an N COUNT
entrance where there is a gate. EG *They passed
through an arched gateway.*
2 A **gateway** to somewhere is a place which you N COUNT+to
go through because it leads you to a much larger
place. EG ...*Sheremetyevo, the gateway to Moscow.*
3 If something is a **gateway** to a job, career, or N COUNT+to
other activity, it gives you the opportunity to
progress into that job or activity. EG ...*a world in
which examinations are the gateways to some
professions.*

gather /ˈɡæðə/, **gathers, gathering, gathered.** **1** V-ERG : USU+A
When people **gather** somewhere, they come to-
gether in a group. EG *The villagers gathered around
him...* *He whistled to gather the whole squad in a
group.* ◇ **gathered.** EG *All the family were gath-* ◇ ADJ PRED
ered to hear the solicitor read the will.
2 If you **gather** together a number of things that V+O : USU+A
you have spread out, you bring them together
again. EG *I gathered my maps together and tucked
them into the folder.*
3 If you **gather** things, you collect them from a V+O
number of different places. EG *They gathered berries and nuts...* *The team worked for about a year
and a half to gather data.*
4 If you say that something **is gathering dust**, you PHRASE
mean that it is not being used regularly. EG *My
briefcase was already beginning to gather dust.*
5 If something **gathers** speed, momentum, or V+O
force, it gradually becomes faster or more powerful. EG *The train gathered speed as it left the town.*
6 If you **gather** that something is true, you learn V+REPORT
from what someone says that it is true. EG *I* ONLY that
*gathered that they were not expected to eat with
us... His wife had been ill, I gather, for some time.*
7 If you **gather** a piece of cloth, you make a row of V+O
very small pleats in it by sewing a thread through
it and then pulling the thread tight. EG ...*a long
white dress gathered under the bosom.*

gather up. If you **gather up** a number of things, PHRASAL VB :
you bring them together into a group. EG *She* V+O+ADV
watched Willie gather up the papers.

gathering /ˈɡæðəˈrɪŋ/, **gatherings. 1** A **gather-** N COUNT
ing is a group of people who are meeting for a
particular purpose. EG ...*political and social gatherings.*
2 If you talk about the **gathering** dusk, you mean ADJ CLASSIF :
that it is gradually getting darker, usually because ATTRIB
it is nearly night. EG *We walked up the long Main
Street in the gathering dusk.*

gauche /ɡəʊʃ/. Someone who is **gauche** is awk- ADJ QUALIT
ward and uncomfortable in the company of other
people. EG *She seemed rather gauche and fat and to
have grown much shyer.*

gaudy /ˈɡɔːdiˈ/. Something that is **gaudy** is very ADJ QUALIT
brightly coloured; used showing disapproval. EG
...*young men in gaudy shirts.*

gauge /ɡeɪdʒ/, **gauges, gauging, gauged. 1** If V+O OR
you **gauge** an amount or quantity, you measure or V+REPORT
calculate it. EG *With a modern machine, you can
gauge the number of stitches... I could usually
gauge how many members were present.*
2 If you **gauge** people's feelings or actions, you V+O OR
carefully consider and judge them. EG ...*gauging* V+REPORT
*what the people wanted... I couldn't gauge how it
would affect me.*
3 A **gauge** is **3.1** a device that measures the N COUNT :
amount of something and shows the amount meas- OFT+SUPP
ured. EG *The fuel gauge dropped swiftly towards
zero.* See picture at CAR. **3.2** a fact that can be used
to judge a situation or a person's feelings. EG *The
increase in attendance was used as a gauge of the
course's success.*

gaunt /ɡɔːnt/. **1** Someone who is **gaunt** looks very ADJ QUALIT
thin and unhealthy. EG *She looked very weak, her
face gaunt and drawn.*
2 Something that is **gaunt** looks bare and unattrac- ADJ QUALIT
tive. EG ...*the gaunt outlines of the houses opposite.*

gauntlet /ˈɡɔːntlɪˈt/, **gauntlets. 1 Gauntlets** are N COUNT :
long, thick gloves that are worn for protection, for USU PLURAL
example by motorcyclists.
2 If you **throw down the gauntlet** to someone, PHRASE
you say or do something that challenges them to
argue, compete, or fight with you. If you **pick up
the gauntlet**, you accept their challenge. EG *Wendy now had to pick up the gauntlet thrown down by
her mother.*
3 If you **run the gauntlet**, you go through an PHRASE
unpleasant experience in which a lot of people
criticize or attack you. EG *In research, academics
run the gauntlet of their professional peers.*

gauze /ɡɔːz/ is a light, soft cloth with tiny holes in N UNCOUNT
it.

gave /ɡeɪv/ is the past tense of **give.**

gawky /ˈɡɔːkiˈ/. Someone who is **gawky** stands ADJ QUALIT
and moves awkwardly and clumsily. EG ...*a gawky
young woman.*

gawp /ɡɔːp/, **gawps, gawping, gawped.** If you V : OFT+at
are **gawping** at someone or something, you are
staring at them in a rude or stupid way. EG *Don't
stand there gawping, come away.*

gay /ɡeɪ/, **gays; gayer, gayest. 1** A person who is ADJ CLASSIF
gay is homosexual. EG *I've told them I'm gay.*
▸ used as a noun. EG ...*a holiday spot for gays.* ▸ N COUNT
2 Gay organizations and magazines are for homo- ADJ CLASSIF :
sexual people. EG *They have an active Gay Group.* ATTRIB
3 In slightly more old-fashioned English, a person ADJ QUALIT
who is **gay** is lively and enjoyable to be with. EG Outdated
Well, he's not the gayest of companions... ...*a gay,
carefree young woman.*
4 A place or a piece of music that is **gay** is lively ADJ QUALIT
and pleasant. EG *What gay and exciting place are
you taking me to?*
5 Something that is **gay** is brightly coloured and ADJ QUALIT
pretty. EG *Her dress was gay and flowered.*
6 See also **gaiety** and **gaily.**

Would you be pleased if someone referred to you
as gauche?

gaze /geɪz/, **gazes, gazing, gazed.** If you **gaze**, V+A you look steadily at someone or something for a long time. EG *She turned to gaze admiringly at her husband... He gazed down into the water.* ▸ used as ▸ N COUNT: a noun. EG *He sat without shifting his gaze from the* USU SING *television.*

gazelle /gə³zɛl/, **gazelles.** A **gazelle** is a kind of N COUNT small antelope.

GCE /dʒi: si: i:/, **GCEs.** 1 GCE is an abbreviation for 'General Certificate of Education'. The GCE is an examination in Britain which is usually taken at Ordinary level when leaving school and at Advanced level before going to University: see also **A level** and **O level.** EG *...good grades in GCE subjects.*

2 A GCE is a pass in an Ordinary level GCE N COUNT examination for a particular subject.

GCSE /dʒi: si: ɛs i:/ is an abbreviation for 'General Certificate of Secondary Education'. The GCSE is an examination in Britain introduced to replace the GCE Ordinary level examination in 1988.

gear /gɪə/, **gears, gearing, geared.** 1 A **gear** in a machine or vehicle is 1.1 a device or system which N COUNT controls the rate at which energy is converted into motion. Gears usually consist of moving wheels and levers which fit together. See picture at CAR. EG *...interlocking cogs and gears... John checked the gear on the bicycle.* 1.2 one of the different ranges N COUNT OR of speed or power which a machine or vehicle has. N UNCOUNT EG *We slow down to first gear and ten miles an hour.*

2 The **gear** for a particular activity is the equip- N UNCOUNT: ment and special clothes that you use. EG *...camping* USU+SUPP *gear.*

3 If someone or something **is geared** to a particu- V+O+A: USU lar purpose, they are organized or designed to be PASS suitable for that purpose. EG *They were not geared to armed combat... a policy geared towards rehabilitation.*

gear up. If someone **is geared up** to do some- PHRASAL VB: thing, they are prepared and able to do it. EG *Hotels* V+ADV OR *like this are not geared up to cater for parties like* V-REFL+ADV *ours.*

gearbox /gɪəbɒks/, **gearboxes.** A **gearbox** is the N COUNT system of gears in an engine or vehicle.

gee /dʒi:/. Some people say **gee** when they are EXCLAM surprised or excited. EG *Gee, what fun!* American

geese /gi:s/ is the plural of **goose.**

gel /dʒɛl/, **gels, gelling, gelled;** also spelled **jell.** 1 V If a liquid **gels**, it changes into a thicker, firmer substance rather like jelly.

2 If an unclear shape, thought, or idea **gels**, you V can see or understand it more clearly and definitely. EG *After talking to you things really began to gel.*

3 Gel is a thick oily substance, especially one that N MASS you use to keep your hair in a particular style.

gelatine /dʒɛləti:n/ is a clear, tasteless powder N MASS that is used to make liquids become firm. Gelatine is often used in cooking.

gelignite /dʒɛlɪgnaɪt/ is an explosive substance N UNCOUNT that is similar to dynamite.

gem /dʒɛm/, **gems.** 1 A **gem** is a jewel that is used N COUNT in jewellery. EG *...a bracelet of solid gold, studded with gems.*

2 If you refer to someone or something as a **gem**, N COUNT you think they are especially good or pleasing. EG *...this gem of wisdom... This house is a gem.*

gender /dʒɛndə/, **genders.** A person's **gender** is N UNCOUNT the sex that they belong to. Men belong to the male OR N COUNT gender and women belong to the female gender. EG *...differences of race or gender.*

gene /dʒi:n/, **genes.** Genes are parts of cells N COUNT: which control the physical characteristics, growth, USU PLURAL and development of living things. Genes are passed on from one generation to another.

genealogy /dʒi:ni¹ælədʒi¹/, **genealogies.** 1 Ge- N UNCOUNT **nealogy** is the study of the history of families. Formal ◊ **genealogist, genealogists.** EG *...an amateur* ◊ N COUNT

genealogist attempting to trace the family of his wife.

2 A **genealogy** is the history of a particular family, N COUNT describing who each person married and who their Formal children were.

genera /dʒɛnərə/ is the plural of **genus.**

general /dʒɛnə⁰rəl/, **generals.** 1 You use gener- al 1.1 when describing something that belongs or ADJ CLASSIF: relates to the whole of something rather than to its ATTRIB details or parts. EG *Their cost rose despite a general decline in their quality... The general standard of education there is very high... His general attitude suggested that he regarded me as a fool.* ◊ **generally.** EG *His account was generally accu-* ◊ ADV OR *rate... Wool and cotton blankets are generally* ADV SEN *cheapest.* 1.2 when describing several items or ADJ CLASSIF: activities, when there are too many of them or ATTRIB when they are not important enough to mention separately. EG *Put down telephone calls as part of your general business expenses.* ◊ **generally.** EG ◊ ADV SEN *It's wonderful for information on things generally.*

2 You also use **general** 2.1 to describe something ADJ QUALIT that involves or affects most people in a group. EG *There was a general movement to leave the table at this point... a topic of general interest.* ◊ **generally.** EG *When will this material become* ◊ ADV *generally available?* 2.2 to describe a statement ADJ QUALIT that involves only the main features of something and not its details. EG *Principles have to be stated in very general terms.* ◊ **generally.** EG *I'll say a few* ◊ ADV OR *words generally on grants... Generally speaking,* ADV SEN *your pronunciation of English is very good.* 2.3 to ADJ CLASSIF: describe a statement or opinion that is true or ATTRIB suitable in most situations. EG *As a general rule, consult the doctor if the baby has a temperature.* **2.4** to describe an organization or business that ADJ CLASSIF: offers a variety of services or goods. EG *...a general* ATTRIB *hospital... a general grocery store.* 2.5 to describe ADJ CLASSIF: a person's job, to indicate that they have complete ATTRIB responsibility for the administration of an organization. EG *...the general manager of the hotel... the General Secretary.* 2.6 to describe a person who ADJ CLASSIF does a variety of jobs which require no special skill ATTRIB or training. EG *...unskilled general labourers.*

3 You say in **general** 3.1 when you are talking PHRASE about the whole of a situation without going into details. EG *They want shorter shifts, and shorter working hours in general.* 3.2 when you are PHRASE referring to most people or things in a group. EG *...his contemptuous attitude to society in general.* **3.3** to indicate that a statement is true in most ADV SEN cases. EG *The industrial processes, in general, are based on man-made processes.*

4 A **general** is an officer who holds a high rank in N COUNT the armed forces, usually in the army. EG *...General Ravenscroft.*

general election, general elections. A gener- N COUNT **al election** is an election at which all the citizens of a country vote for people to represent them in the national parliament. EG *A general election was called.*

generality /dʒɛnəræli¹ti¹/, **generalities.** A gen- N COUNT OR **erality** is something that you say that is general N UNCOUNT and not very detailed. EG *She spoke in short simple* Formal *generalities.*

generalize /dʒɛnə⁰rəlaɪz/, **generalizes, gener-** V **alizing, generalized;** also spelled **generalise.** If you **generalize**, you say that something is true in most situations or for most people, especially when you have very little evidence for it. EG *I don't think you can generalize about that.* ◊ **generalization,** ◊ N COUNT OR **generalizations.** EG *It is easy to make sweeping* N UNCOUNT *generalizations about someone else's problems.*

generalized /dʒɛnə⁰rəlaɪzd/; also spelled **gener-** ADJ QUALIT **alised. Generalized** means 1 involving a large number of people or things. EG *The problem is one of generalized human needs.* 2 applying to a variety of situations or subjects. EG *...generalised remarks about the futility of love.*

general knowledge is knowledge about many different things, rather than about one particular subject. EG *Her general knowledge is amazing.*   N UNCOUNT

general practice, general practices. 1 General practice is the work of a doctor who treats people at a surgery or in their homes, not in a hospital, and who does not specialize in particular illnesses or methods of treatment.   N UNCOUNT British

2 A **general practice** is a place where such a doctor works. EG *Some hospital doctors are also attached to general practices.*   N COUNT

general practitioner. See GP.

general public. The **general public** is all the people in a society. EG *The lecture will interest both musicians and members of the general public.*   N COLL : the+N

generate /dʒenəreɪt/, **generates, generating, generated. 1** To **generate** something means to cause it to begin and develop. EG *This book will continue to generate excitement for a long time... Tourism will generate new jobs.*   V+O Formal

2 To **generate** energy means to produce it from fuel or from another source of power such as water. EG *...improved methods of generating electricity.*   V+O

generation /dʒenəreɪʃən/, **generations. 1** A **generation** is **1.1** all the people in a group or country who are of a similar age. EG *...an older generation of intellectuals... Few actresses of her generation could play the part well... Property is handed on from generation to generation.* **1.2** the period of time, usually considered to be about thirty years, that it takes for children to grow up and become adults and have children of their own. EG *We have had a generation of peace in Europe.* **1.3** a stage of development in the design and manufacture of machines or equipment. EG *...the new generation of missiles.*   N COUNT+SUPP / N COUNT / N COUNT+SUPP

2 The **generation** of energy is its production from fuel or from another source of power such as water. EG *Electric power generation had ceased.*   N UNCOUNT

generation gap. A **generation gap** is a difference in attitude and behaviour between older people and younger people.   N SING

generator /dʒenəreɪtə/, **generators.** A **generator** is a machine which produces electricity.   N COUNT

generic /dʒɪˈnerɪk/ means referring to or shared by a whole group of similar things. EG *Software is a generic term for the sets of programs which control a computer.*   ADJ CLASSIF : ATTRIB Formal

generosity /dʒenəˈrɒsɪtiˈ/ is the quality of being generous, especially in doing or giving more than is usual or expected. EG *You shouldn't take advantage of his generosity... ...the generosity with which she had shared her ideas.*   N UNCOUNT

generous /dʒenərəs/. **1** Someone who is **generous 1.1** gives more of something, especially money, than is usual or expected. EG *That's very generous of you... They aren't very generous with pensions.* ◊ **generously.** EG *She was paid generously to look after the children.* **1.2** is friendly, helpful, and willing to see the good qualities in people or things. EG *She was a kind and generous soul... The most generous interpretation is that he didn't know.*   ADJ QUALIT / ◊ ADV / ADJ QUALIT

2 Something that is **generous** is much larger in quantity than is usual or necessary. EG *...a generous donation to our campaign fund... ...a generous measure of cognac.* ◊ **generously.** EG *He was providing for them generously in his will.*   ADJ QUALIT / ◊ ADV

genetic /dʒɪˈnetɪk/, **genetics. 1 Genetics** is the study of how characteristics are passed from one generation to another by means of genes.   N UNCOUNT

2 Something that is **genetic** is concerned with genetics or with genes. EG *...genetic defects.*   ADJ CLASSIF

◊ **genetically.** EG *...genetically programmed behaviour.*   ◊ ADV

genial /dʒiːnɪəl/. Someone who is **genial** is kind and friendly. EG *...a genial smile.* ◊ **genially.** EG *He waved genially to people as they passed.*   ADJ QUALIT / ◊ ADV

geniality /dʒiːnɪˈælɪtiˈ/. EG *...his general air of geniality.*   ◊ N UNCOUNT

genital /dʒenɪtəl/, **genitals. 1** Someone's **genitals** are their external sexual organs.   N PLURAL

2 Genital means relating to a person's external sexual organs.   ADJ CLASSIF : ATTRIB

genius /dʒiːnɪəs/, **geniuses. 1 Genius** is **1.1** very great ability or skill in something. EG *...his genius for improvisation.* **1.2** an excellent quality which makes something distinct from everything else. EG *That is the genius of the system.*   N UNCOUNT

2 Someone who is a **genius** has very great natural ability and talent, especially for a particular subject or activity. EG *Beethoven was a genius.*   N COUNT

genocide /dʒenəˈsaɪd/ is the murder of a whole community or race.   N UNCOUNT Formal

genre /ʒɒnrə/, **genres.** A **genre** is a particular style of literature, art, or music. EG *...a whole new genre of sentimental fiction.*   N COUNT Formal

gent /dʒent/, **gents. 1** A **gent** is the same as a gentleman. EG *They are very tough gents.*   N COUNT Informal

2 A **gents** or the **gents** is a public toilet for men. EG *The gents was situated in a small yard outside.*   N SING British

genteel /dʒenˈtiːl/. Someone who is **genteel** is polite, respectable, and refined. EG *He came from a genteel family.*   ADJ QUALIT

gentle /dʒentəl/, **gentler, gentlest. 1** Someone who is **gentle** is kind, mild, and pleasantly calm. EG *...a gentle, sweet man... She had very gentle blue eyes.* ◊ **gently.** EG *'You have nothing to worry about,' he said gently.* ◊ **gentleness.** EG *...the virtues of gentleness and compassion.*   ADJ QUALIT / ◊ ADV / ◊ N UNCOUNT

2 Movements that are **gentle** are even and calm. EG *...the gentle rocking of his mother's chair... There was a gentle breeze.* ◊ **gently.** EG *I shook her gently and she opened her eyes.*   ADJ QUALIT / ◊ ADV

3 Scenery that is **gentle** has soft shapes and colours that people find pleasant and relaxing. EG *...a gentle little landscape... The beach stretched away in a gentle curve.* ◊ **gently.** EG *...gently sloping hills.*   ADJ QUALIT / ◊ ADV

4 Gentle jokes or hints are quite kind and not intended to hurt people. EG *...a very gentle parody of American life... I gave a gentle hint.*   ADJ QUALIT : ATTRIB

gentleman /dʒentəlmən/, **gentlemen. 1** A **gentleman** is **1.1** a man who comes from a family of high social standing. EG *...a country gentleman.* **1.2** a man who is well behaved, educated, and refined. EG *He was a terribly nice man – a real gentleman.*   N COUNT

2 You can refer politely to men as **gentlemen**. EG *...the gentlemen of the Press... Good afternoon, ladies and gentlemen.*   N COUNT

gentlemanly /dʒentəlmənliˈ/. A man who is **gentlemanly** has perfect manners and is very well-behaved. EG *...a courteous, gentlemanly gesture.*   ADJ QUALIT

gentry /dʒentriˈ/. The **gentry** are people of high social status.   N PLURAL Formal

genuine /dʒenjuɪn/. **1** Something that is **genuine** is real and exactly what it appears to be. EG *...genuine Ugandan food... She looked at me in genuine astonishment.* ◊ **genuinely.** EG *...genuinely democratic countries.*   ADJ CLASSIF / ◊ ADV : OFT+ADJ

2 If you describe a person as **genuine**, you mean that they are honest and sincere. EG *They seemed nice, genuine fellows.*   ADJ QUALIT

genus /dʒiːnəs/, **genera** /dʒenərə/. A **genus** is a class or group of similar animals or plants.   N COUNT Technical

geographic /dʒiːəˈgræfɪk/ or **geographical** /dʒiːəˈgræfɪkəl/. Something that is **geographic** or **geographical** involves geography. EG *...geographic and political boundaries... ...the characteristics of any geographical region.* ◊ **geographically.** EG *...geographically separated species.*   ADJ CLASSIF / ◊ ADV OR ADV SEN

Do you think that a geologist should know something about geography?

geography /dʒɪˈɒgrəfi¹/. **1 Geography** is the study of the countries of the world and of such things as land formations, seas, climate, towns, and population. ◊ **geographer, geographers.** EG ...*professional geographers.* N UNCOUNT / N COUNT

2 The **geography** of a place is the way that its physical features are arranged within it. EG ...*the geography of the United States.* N UNCOUNT OFT+SUPP

geology /dʒɪˈɒlədʒi¹/. **1 Geology** is the scientific study of substances such as rock and soil in order to find out about the origin, structure, and history of the earth. ◊ **geological** /dʒiːəˈlɒdʒɪkə⁰l/. EG ...*an interesting geological site.* ◊ **geologist, geologists.** EG *For many years these questions puzzled geologists.* N UNCOUNT ADJ CLASSIF N COUNT

2 The **geology** of an area is the structure of its land. N UNCOUNT : OFT+SUPP

geometric /dʒiːəˈmetrɪk/ or **geometrical** /dʒiːəˈmetrɪkə⁰l/. Something that is **geometric** or **geometrical** involves geometry or consists of regular shapes and lines. EG ...*geometric blocks of concrete... ...a geometrical problem... ...abstract geometrical designs.* ADJ CLASSIF : ATTRIB

geometry /dʒɪˈɒmɪ²tri¹/ is a mathematical science concerned with the measurement of lines, angles, curves, and shapes. N UNCOUNT

geranium /dʒɪˈreɪniəm/, **geraniums.** A **geranium** is a plant with small red, pink, or white flowers. N COUNT

geriatric /dʒɛriˈætrɪk/ is used to describe very old people, their illnesses, and their treatment. EG ...*a geriatric ward.* ADJ CLASSIF Technical

germ /dʒɜːm/, **germs. 1** A **germ** is a very small organism that causes disease. EG ...*a flu germ.* N COUNT

2 The **germ** of something is the beginning of it which may develop or become more important. EG *It contains the germ of an idea which might save us.* N COUNT : USU SING+of

German measles is a disease which gives you red spots and a sore throat. N UNCOUNT

germinate /dʒɜːmɪneɪt/, **germinates, germinating, germinated. 1** If a seed **germinates** or is **germinated**, it starts to grow. EG *You need cool, moist weather for the seed to germinate.* ◊ **germination** /dʒɜːmɪˈneɪʃə⁰n/. EG *Temperature is most important for seed germination.* V-ERG ◊ N UNCOUNT

2 If an idea, plan, or feeling **germinates**, or if someone or something **germinates** it, it comes into existence and begins to develop. EG *New concepts germinate before your eyes.* V-ERG Formal

gestation /dʒeˈsteɪʃə⁰n/ is **1** the process in which babies grow inside their mother's body before they are born. EG ...*the shortest gestation period in any mammal.* **2** the process in which an idea or plan develops. EG *The road had been sixty years in gestation.* N UNCOUNT Technical / Literary

gesticulate /dʒeˈstɪkjəleɪt/, **gesticulates, gesticulating, gesticulated.** If you **gesticulate**, you make movements with your arms or hands, often while you are talking. EG *We sometimes gesticulate even when talking on the telephone... Stuart gesticulated angrily.* ◊ **gesticulation** /dʒeˈstɪkjəˈleɪʃə⁰n/, **gesticulations.** EG ...*the gesticulations that accompany conversation.* V Formal ◊ N UNCOUNT OR N COUNT

gesture /dʒeˈstʃə/, **gestures, gesturing, gestured.** A **gesture** is **1** a movement that you make with your hands or your head to express emotion or to give information. EG *She made an angry gesture with her fist.* ▸ used as a verb. EG *She gestured that I ought to wait... He gestured to me to lie down... She gestured towards the bookshelves.* **2** something that you say or do in order to express your attitude or intentions. EG *The demonstration is a gesture of defiance... She thanked him for his thoughtful gesture.* N COUNT ▸ V+REPORT OR V+A N COUNT : USU+SUPP

get /get/, **gets, getting, got** /gɒt/. The form **gotten** /gɒtə⁰n/ is often used in American English for the past participle. In most of its uses **get** is a fairly informal word.

1 Get often has the same meaning as 'become'. For example, if someone **gets** bored, they become bored. If something **gets** cold, it becomes cold. EG *She began to get suspicious... If things get worse, you'll have to come home.* V+C

2 If you **get** into a particular state or situation, you allow or cause yourself to be in that state or situation. EG *He got into trouble with the police... I began to get in a panic.* V+A

3 If you **get** someone or something into a particular state or situation, you cause them to be in that state or situation. EG *The girl finally got the door open... He got her pregnant.* V+A OR C

4 If you **get** someone to do something, you cause them to do it by asking them or telling them to do it. EG *She gets Stuart to help her.* V+O+to+-INF

5 If you **get** something done, you cause it to be done. EG *I got safety belts fitted.* V+O +PAST PART

6 If you **get** somewhere, **6.1** you move there. EG *When the train stopped, he got off... Brody got out of bed... Nobody can get past.* **6.2** you arrive there. EG *When we got to Firle Beacon we had a rest... What time do they get back?* V+A

7 If you **get** someone or something into or out of a place, you succeed in moving them there. EG *I got Allen into his bunk.* V+O+A

8 If you **get** someone something, you bring it to them. EG *Get me a glass of water.* V+O+O OR V+O+for

9 Get is often used instead of 'be' to form passives. EG *Suppose someone gets killed... He failed to get re-elected.* AUX+PAST PART : FORMS PASS

10 If you **get** something, **10.1** you obtain it. EG *He's trying to get a flat... Get advice from your local health department... I am going to get a divorce... He got her a job with the telephone company.* **10.2** you receive it. EG *I got the anorak for Christmas... He was with us when we got the news... She ought to get at least eight pounds for it.* V+O, V+O+O, OR V+O+for V+O: NO IMPER, NO PASS

11 If you **get** the time or the opportunity to do something, you have the time or the opportunity to do it. EG *We get little time for sewing.* V+O : OFT+to-INF OR for

12 If you **get** an idea or feeling, you come to have it as the result of an experience. EG *She got a lot of fun out of sweeping the front porch... I got the impression he'd had a sleepless night.* V+O : OFT+A

13 If you **get** an illness or disease, you become ill with it. EG *She got chicken pox.* V+O : NO PASS

14 If you **get** to do something, **14.1** you eventually do it. EG *The Prime Minister got to hear of the rumours... I got to like the whole idea.* **14.2** you eventually succeed in doing it. EG *We never got to see the play.* V+to-INF

15 If you **get** moving or **get** going, you begin to move or to do something. EG *We can't seem to get moving.* V+-ING

16 If you **get** to a particular stage in something, you reach that stage. EG *You have got to an important stage in your career... I got as far as dismantling the plug.* V+A

17 When it **gets** to a particular time, it is that time. EG *It's getting late.* V+A

18 If you **get** a joke or **get** the point of something, you understand it. EG *I don't really get the point of the story.* V+O : NO IMPER, NO PASS

19 When you **get** a train or bus, you leave a place on it. EG *We got the train to Colchester.* V+O : NO PASS

20 If you **get** a person or an animal, you catch them or shoot them. EG *The police got him in the end.* V+O

21 If you say that something **is getting** to you, you mean that it is making you suffer physically or mentally. EG *The fatigue and backache are getting to me now.* V+to

22 If you say that someone's behaviour **gets** you, you mean that it annoys you. EG *What gets me is the way Janet implies that I'm lazy.* V+O : NO CONT Informal

23 You can use **you get** instead of 'there is' or 'there are' to say that something exists, happens, or can be experienced. EG *You get some rather curious effects.*

24 If you say that you are **getting somewhere**, PHRASE you mean that you are making progress. If you say that you are **getting nowhere**, you mean that you are making no progress.

25 See also **got**. ● to **get used to** something: see **used**. ● to **get your way**: see **way**.

get about or **get around**. 1 If you **get about** or PHRASAL VB: **get around**, you go to a lot of different places as V+ADV part of your way of life. 2 If news **gets about** or V+ADV: **gets around**, it is told to lots of people and OFT+REPORT becomes well known. 3 See also **get around**.

get across. If you **get** an idea or argument PHRASAL VB: **across**, you succeed in making people understand V-ERG+ADV it. EG *We managed to get our message across.*

get ahead. If you **get ahead**, you are successful PHRASAL VB: in your career. V+ADV

get along. If you **get along** with someone, you PHRASAL VB: have a friendly relationship with them. EG *They just* V+ADV OR *can't get along together.* V+ADV+*with*: RECIP

get around or **get round**. 1 If you **get around** a PHRASAL VB: difficulty or restriction or **get round** it, you over- V+PREP, come it. EG *To help get around this problem, some* HAS PASS *tanks are now equipped with radar.* 2 If news **gets** V+ADV: **around** or **gets round**, it is told to lots of people OFT+REPORT and becomes well known. EG *The word got round* *that Morris was going to England.* 3 When you V+ADV+*to* eventually **get around** to doing something or **get round** to it, you do it, when you were previously too busy to do it or were reluctant to do it. EG *I only got around to doing this a few days ago.* 4 See also **get about**.

get at. 1 If you manage to **get at** something, you PHRASAL VB: manage to reach it. EG *The goats bent down to get* V+PREP *at the short grass.* 2 If you ask someone what they V+PREP **are getting at**, you are asking them to explain what they mean. EG *I don't know what you are getting at.* 3 If you say that someone **is getting at** V+PREP, you, you mean that they are criticizing you or HAS PASS teasing you in an unkind way. Informal

get away. 1 If you **get away**, 1.1 you succeed in PHRASAL VB: leaving a place or person. EG *Last year, he was* V+ADV, *always trying to get away by five in the evening.* OFT+*from* 1.2 you go away to have a holiday. EG *Is there any* V+ADV *chance of you getting away this summer?* ● If you ● PHRASE **get away from it all**, you have a holiday in a place that is very different from the place where you live and work. 2 If you **get** someone **away** PHRASAL VB: if they **get away**, they escape. EG *They got away* V-ERG+ADV *through Mrs Barnett's garden.* ● See also **getaway**.

get away with. If you **get away with** some- PHRASAL VB: thing that you should not have done, you are not V+ADV+PREP punished for doing it. EG *He bribed her – and got away with it.*

get back. 1 If you **get back** to your previous PHRASAL VB: state or situation, you return to it. EG *Eddie wanted* V+ADV+*to* *to get back to sleep... Things would soon get back to normal.* 2 If you **get back** to what you were V+ADV+*to/* doing or talking about before, you start doing it or *into* talking about it again. EG *He got back to work again.* 3 If you **get back** something that you used V+O+ADV to have, you then have it again. EG *He would get back his old job.* 4 If you tell someone to **get back**, V+ADV you are telling them to move away from something or someone.

get by. If you **get by**, you succeed in surviving PHRASAL VB: and having a fairly satisfactory life. EG *He had* V+ADV, OFT+A *managed to get by without much reading or writing.*

get down. If a situation **gets** you **down**, it makes PHRASAL VB: you unhappy. EG *It isn't just the work that gets her* V+O+ADV *down.* Informal

get down to. When you **get down to** something, PHRASAL VB: you start doing it. EG *I got down to work.* V+ADV+PREP

get in. 1 When a political party or a politician PHRASAL VB: **gets in**, they are elected. EG *What would Labour do* V+ADV *if they got in, then?* 2 When a train, bus, or plane V+ADV **gets in**, it arrives somewhere. EG *What time does*

the coach get in? **3** If you **get** a remark **in**, you V+O+ADV; eventually succeed in making it when other people ALSO V+ADV are talking continuously. EG *'What I wanted to say,'* +QUOTE *I finally got in, 'is that I've a set of instructions at home.'*

get in on. If you **get in on** an activity, you start PHRASAL VB: taking part in it. EG *'He even gets in on the* V+ADV+PREP *photography shows,' she said indignantly.* Informal

get into. 1 If you **get into** an activity, you start PHRASAL VB: being involved in it. EG *I always get into arguments* V+PREP *with people... He was determined to get into poli- tics.* 2 If you **get into** a particular habit, you start V+PREP having it. EG *She'd got into the habit of sulking.* 3 If V+PREP you **get into** a school, college, or university, you are accepted there as a pupil or student. 4 If you V+PREP ask what has **got into** someone, you mean that Informal they are behaving in an unexpected way.

get off. 1 If someone is given a very small PHRASAL VB: punishment for breaking a law or rule, you can say V-ERG+ADV that they **got off** with this punishment. EG *He expressed relief that he had got off so lightly.* 2 If V+O+ADV/ you **get** something **off**, you remove it. EG *...stains* PREP *you can't get off your skin... Get your shirt off.* 3 If PHRASE you say **'Get off'** or **'Get your hands off'**, you are telling someone not to touch you, or not to touch something.

get off with. If you **get off with** someone, you PHRASAL VB: begin a romantic or sexual relationship with them. V+ADV+PREP EG *Mike thinks I'm trying to get off with his* Informal *girlfriend.*

get on. 1 If you **get on** with someone, you have a PHRASAL VB: friendly relationship with them. EG *Mother and I* V+ADV OR *get on very well... It is very important to get on* V+ADV+*with*: *with your employer.* 2 If you **get on** with some- RECIP thing, you continue doing it or start doing it. EG V+ADV, *Perhaps we can get on with the meeting now.* 3 If OFT+*with* someone who is doing a task **is getting on** well, V+ADV+A they are making good progress. EG *I always get on far better if I can draw a diagram.* 4 If you **get on**, V+ADV you are successful in your career. EG *She's got to study to get on.* 5 If you say that someone **is** V+ADV **getting on**, you mean that they are old. EG *She* Informal *must be getting on now, I suppose.* 6 If you **get** a V+O+ADV piece of clothing **on**, you put it on. EG *Get your coat on.* 7 **Getting on for** means the same as 'nearly' EG PHRASE *They have getting on for a hundred stores.* Informal

get on to. 1 If you **get on to** a particular topic, PHRASAL VB: you start talking about it in a lecture or conversa- V+ADV+PREP tion. EG *Somehow we got on to grandparents.* 2 If V+ADV+PREP you **get on to** someone, you contact them. EG *I'll get on to her right away.*

get out. 1 If you **get out** of an organization, you PHRASAL VB: withdraw from it. EG *The Common Market? The* V+ADV *sooner we get out the better.* 2 If you **get out** of V+ADV+*of* doing something, you avoid doing it. EG *She always got out of washing up.* 3 If news or information V+ADV **gets out**, it becomes known. EG *The word got out that he would go ahead with the merger.* 4 If you V+O+ADV **get** something **out**, you take it out of the thing in which it is kept or in which it is being carried. EG *He got out a book and read.* 5 If you **get** a stain V+O+ADV **out**, you remove it.

get over. 1 If you **get over** an unpleasant PHRASAL VB: experience or an illness, you recover from it. EG V+PREP *Have you got over the shock?* 2 If you **get over** a V+PREP problem, you overcome it. EG *One mother got over this problem by leaving her baby with someone else.*

get over with. If you decide to **get** something PHRASAL VB: unpleasant **over with**, you decide to do it or V+O+ADV+ undergo it. EG *Can we just get this questioning over* PREP *with?*

get round. See **get around**.

get through. 1 If you **get through** a task, you PHRASAL VB: succeed in completing it. EG *It is extremely difficult* V+PREP

Do people get together when they have a get-together?

to get through this amount of work in such a short time. **2** If you **get through** an unpleasant experi- V+PREP, ence or period of time, you succeed in living HAS PASS through it. EG *They helped me to get through that time.* **3** If you **get through** a large amount of V+PREP, something, you completely use it up. EG *I got* HAS PASS *through about six pounds worth of drink.* **4** If you **get through** to someone, **4.1** you succeed in mak- V+ADV+to ing them understand what you are trying to tell them. EG *Howard, how do I get through to you?* **4.2** V+ADV you succeed in contacting them on the telephone. EG *I finally got through at twenty past ten.*

get together. **1** When people **get together**, they PHRASAL VB: meet in order to discuss something or to spend V-ERG+ADV, time together. EG *I want a team of experts to be got* OFT+with *together.* ● See also **get-together.** **2** If you **get** V+O+ADV something **together**, you make it or organize it. EG *He's spent a whole afternoon trying to get the thing together.*

get up. **1** When you **get up**, **1.1** you rise to a PHRASAL VB: standing position after you have been sitting or V+ADV, OFT+A lying down. EG *The woman got up from her chair with the baby in her arms.* **1.2** you get out of bed. V+ADV OR EG *You've got to get up at eight o'clock.* **2** See also V+O+ADV **get-up.**

get up to. When you talk about what someone PHRASAL VB: **gets up to**, you are referring to what they do, V+ADV+PREP especially when it is something that you do not approve of. EG *When I found out what they used to get up to I was horrified.*

getaway /ɡetəweɪ/, **getaways.** When someone N COUNT makes a **getaway**, they leave a place in a hurry, often after committing a crime. EG *Duffield was already making his getaway down the stairs.*

get-together, get-togethers. A **get-together** is N COUNT an informal meeting or party. EG *We must have a get-together some evening.*

get-up, get-ups. A **get-up** is a strange or unusual N COUNT set of clothes. EG *...Albert Finney in a Mexican get-up.*

geyser /ɡiːzə/, **geysers.** A **geyser** is **1** a hole in N COUNT the Earth's surface from which hot water and steam are forced out. **2** a device for providing hot British water in a bathroom or kitchen.

ghastly /ɡɑːstliɪ/. **1** You describe things or people ADJ QUALIT as **ghastly** when you dislike them very much because of their appearance or behaviour. EG *...ghastly office blocks... ...those ghastly Hewson-Smarts.* **2** A **ghastly** experience or situation is very un- ADJ QUALIT pleasant. EG *We wouldn't be in this ghastly mess if you had kept quiet... ...the ghastly news of the murder.* **3** You also describe something as **ghastly** when it ADJ QUALIT looks strange or evil and makes you feel afraid. EG *The great fangs gleamed a ghastly white.* **4** You can say that someone looks **ghastly** when ADJ PRED they look very ill. Informal

ghetto /ɡetəʊ/, **ghettos** or **ghettoes.** A **ghetto** is N COUNT a part of a city in which many people of a particular race, religion, or nationality live. EG *...a black kid growing up in the ghetto.*

ghost /ɡəʊst/, **ghosts.** **1** When people think that N COUNT they see a **ghost**, they think that they can see a dead person behaving as if they were still alive. EG *...the ghost of Mrs Dowell... I don't believe in ghosts.* **2** A **ghost** of something is a faint trace of it. EG *We* N COUNT+of *haven't the ghost of a chance... ...a ghost of a smile.* Literary

ghostly /ɡəʊstliɪ/. Something that is **ghostly** is ADJ QUALIT frightening because it does not seem real or natural. EG *...ghostly rumbling noises.*

ghost town, ghost towns. A **ghost town** is a N COUNT town which used to be busy and prosperous but which people no longer live in.

ghoulish /ɡuːlɪʃ/. Something that is **ghoulish** is ADJ QUALIT concerned with torture or death. EG *Tim took a ghoulish interest in the murders.*

GI /dʒiː aɪ/, **GIs.** A **GI** is a soldier in the United N COUNT States army.

giant /dʒaɪənt/, **giants.** **1** A **giant** is an imaginary N COUNT person who is very big and strong, especially one mentioned in myths and children's stories. EG *...stories of cruel giants and wicked witches.* **2** Large business organizations are sometimes re- N COUNT+SUPP ferred to as **giants**. EG *...the electronics giant, Hitachi.* **3** Something that is much larger than usual can be N COUNT referred to as a **giant**. EG *...a giant of a man.* ▶ used ▶ ADJ CLASSIF: as an adjective. EG *...giant Christmas trees.* ATTRIB

gibber /dʒɪbə/, **gibbers, gibbering, gibbered.** V OR V+QUOTE When people **gibber**, they talk very fast in a confused manner. EG *...men gibbering in their terror.*

gibberish /dʒɪbəʳrɪʃ/. You describe what some- N UNCOUNT one says as **gibberish** when it does not make any sense. EG *He was talking gibberish.*

gibbon /ɡɪbən/, **gibbons.** A **gibbon** is an ape with N COUNT very long arms.

gibe /dʒaɪb/. See **jibe.**

giblets /dʒɪblɪʳts/ are the parts such as the heart N PLURAL and liver that you remove from inside a chicken or other bird before you cook it.

giddy /ɡɪdiɪ/, **giddier, giddiest.** **1** If you feel gid- ADJ QUALIT dy, you feel that you are about to fall over, usually because you are not well. ◇ **giddiness.** EG *...a* ◇ N UNCOUNT *sensation of extreme giddiness.* **2** If something makes you **giddy**, **2.1** you find it ADJ QUALIT very confusing. EG *It made me giddy to hear so much analysis.* **2.2** it makes you happy and excited. EG *The news made me giddy with excitement.*

gift /ɡɪft/, **gifts.** **1** A **gift** is something that you N COUNT give someone as a present. EG *...a gift from the Russian ambassador to Charles II... ...the gift of a handful of primroses.* **2** If you say that someone has a **gift** for doing N COUNT: something, you mean that they have a natural USU SING ability for doing it. EG *John has a real gift for* +for/of *conversation... ...his gifts as a story-teller.*

gifted /ɡɪftɪ²d/. **1** Someone who is **gifted** has a ADJ QUALIT natural ability to do something well. EG *She was a gifted actress.* **2** A **gifted** child is extremely intelligent. ADJ QUALIT

gig /ɡɪɡ/, **gigs.** A **gig** is a performance by pop N COUNT musicians. EG *They started out doing free gigs in* Informal *bars.*

gigantic /dʒaɪɡæntɪk/. Something that is **gigantic** ADJ QUALIT is extremely large. EG *...a gigantic rubbish heap... ...a gigantic effort.* ◇ **gigantically.** EG *The compa-* ◇ ADV *ny got away with gigantically inflated profits.*

giggle /ɡɪɡəⁿl/, **giggles, giggling, giggled.** **1** If V OR V+QUOTE you **giggle**, you make quiet laughing noises, be- cause you are amused or because you are nervous or embarrassed. EG *The absurd sound made her giggle... 'Oh dear,' she giggled, 'I forgot.'* ▶ used as a ▶ N COUNT noun. EG *...a nervous giggle.* **2** If someone has got the **giggles**, they cannot stop N PLURAL giggling. Informal

gilded /ɡɪldɪd/. If something is **gilded**, it has been ADJ CLASSIF covered with a thin layer of gold or gold paint. EG *...the ornate gilded mirror.*

gill /ɡɪl/, **gills.** Gills are the organs on the sides of N COUNT: a fish through which it breathes. USU PLURAL

gilt /ɡɪlt/. Something that is **gilt** is covered with a ADJ CLASSIF thin layer of gold or gold paint. EG *...paintings in dark gilt frames.* ▶ used as a noun. EG *The gilt had* ▶ N UNCOUNT *been chipped.*

gimmick /ɡɪmɪk/, **gimmicks.** A **gimmick** is an N COUNT unusual action, object, or device which is intended to attract attention or publicity. EG *The manufactur-er needed a new sales gimmick.*

gin /dʒɪn/, **gins.** Gin is a colourless alcoholic N MASS drink. EG *A gin and tonic, please.*

ginger /dʒɪndʒə/. **1** Ginger is the root of a plant, N UNCOUNT sometimes sold in the form of a powder, which has a spicy hot flavour and is used in cooking. **2** Something that is **ginger** is a bright orange- ADJ COLOUR brown colour. EG ...*a man with ginger hair... ...a ginger cat.*

ginger ale, ginger ales. Ginger ale is a fizzy N MASS non-alcoholic drink flavoured with ginger, which you usually add to an alcoholic drink such as whisky.

ginger beer, ginger beers. Ginger beer is a N MASS fizzy drink flavoured with ginger and sometimes slightly alcoholic, which you drink by itself.

gingerly /dʒɪndʒəli¹/. If you do something **gin-** ADV **gerly**, you do it in a careful, hesitant, and often nervous manner. EG *They walked gingerly over the rotten floorboards.*

gingham /gɪŋəm/ is cloth made of cotton which N UNCOUNT has a pattern of small squares or stripes. EG ...*a pink gingham shirt.*

gipsy /dʒɪpsi¹/. See gypsy. N COUNT

giraffe /dʒɪˈrɑːf, -ˈræf/, **giraffes. A giraffe** is a N COUNT large African animal with a very long neck, long legs, and dark patches on its yellowish body.

gird /gɜːd/, **girds, girding, girded.** If you say that PHRASE someone is **girding** their **loins** or **girding up** their Outdated **loins**, you mean that they are preparing to do something difficult or dangerous.

girder /gɜːdə/, **girders. A girder** is a long, thick N COUNT piece of steel or iron that is used in the framework of buildings and bridges.

girdle /gɜːdəⁱl/, **girdles. A girdle** is a piece of N COUNT woman's underclothing that fits tightly around her stomach and hips.

girl /gɜːl/, **girls. 1 A girl** is a female child. EG ...*a* N COUNT *girl of eleven... ...when you were a little girl... ...a girls' school.*

2 You can also refer to a young woman as a **girl.** EG N COUNT ...*a girl of nineteen... There were a lot of pretty girls there.*

3 Someone's daughter can be referred to as their N COUNT **girl.** EG *She has two girls and a boy.*

4 You can refer to a group of women as **girls.** EG N PLURAL *Come on, girls... ...the other girls at work.*

5 Older people sometimes address a woman or VOCATIVE female child as **my girl.** EG *My dear girl, what does* Outdated *it matter?*

girlfriend /gɜːlfrɛnd/, **girlfriends. 1 A** man's or N COUNT : boy's **girlfriend** is a girl or woman with whom he USU+POSS is having a romantic or sexual relationship. EG *His girlfriend walked out on him.*

2 A woman's **girlfriend** is a female friend. EG *She* N COUNT *went to the movies with some girlfriends.*

girlhood /gɜːlhʊd/ is the time during which a N UNCOUNT female person is a girl. EG *She had a healthy and happy girlhood.*

girlish /gɜːlɪʃ/. If you say that a woman's behav- ADJ QUALIT iour is **girlish**, you mean that she behaves like a young girl. EG *She felt a surge of girlish nervous-ness... ...a girlish laugh.*

giro /dʒaɪrəʊ/, **giros. 1 Giro** is a system by which N UNCOUNT a bank or post office can transfer money from one British account to another.

2 A giro or a **giro cheque** is a cheque that is given N COUNT by the government to a person who is unemployed British or ill.

girth /gɜːθ/, **girths. The girth** of something is the N COUNT measurement around it. EG ...*a 52-inch girth.* Formal

gist /dʒɪst/. **The gist** of a speech, conversation, or N SING : USU piece of writing is its general meaning. EG *We* the+N+of *began to get the gist of her remarks.*

give /gɪv/, **gives, giving, gave, given.** **Give** is one of the most common English verbs. It is often used with nouns to form expressions refer-ring to an action. For example, 'She gave a smile' means almost the same as 'She smiled'. Para-graphs 1 to 3 show how **give** is used in this way.

1 You use **give** to refer to an action, especially a V+O OR V+O+ physical action. EG *Jill gave an immense sigh... She* O *gave Etta a quick, shrewd glance... She gave the door a push... Any aircraft carrying the Prime Minister is given a thorough check.*

2 If you **give** a speech or a performance, you speak V+O, V+O+to, OR V+O+O

or perform in public. EG *He was due to give a lecture that evening.*

3 If something **is given** attention or thought, V+O+O, OR V+ people concentrate on it, deal with it, or think O+O about it. EG *She hadn't bothered to give it particular thought.*

4 You use **give** to say that a person does something V+O+O OR for someone else. For example, if you **give** some- V+O+to one help, you help them. EG *He gave her a lift back to London... ...a tutor who came to give lessons to my son.*

5 You use **give** to say that a person tells someone V+O, V+O+O, something or tells them to do something. For OR V+O+to example, if you **give** someone some news, you tell them some news. EG *That's the best advice I can give... Castle gave the porter the message... Marsha gave her name... 13% gave bad housing as their main source of worry.*

6 If you **give** someone something, **6.1** you offer it to V+O+O OR them as a present. EG *They gave me a handsome* V+O+to *little wooden box.* **6.2** you hand it over to them. V+O+O OR EG *Give me your key... Joe, give the Colonel another* V+O+to *coffee.* **6.3** you provide them with it or let them V+O+O have it. EG ...*without having been given the oppor-tunity to defend himself.*

7 If something **gives** a person or thing a particular V+O+O, V+O, feeling, quality, idea, or right, it causes that person OR V+O+to or thing to have it or experience it. EG *Working on the car has given me an appetite... What gave you that idea?... His leadership gives him the right to command.*

8 If you **give** a party, you organize it. EG *Every year* V+O, V+O+O, *he gives a lunch for his family and friends.* OR V+O+for

9 If you **give** something a value, you estimate that V+O, V+O+O, it has that value. EG *The polls had given the* OR V+to *President a 10 to 15 point lead.*

10 If something **gives**, it collapses or breaks under V pressure. EG *His legs gave beneath him.*

11 If you say that you **are given** to believe or PHRASE understand something, you mean that someone has Formal told it to you. EG *We are given to believe that patience is a virtue.*

12 If you say that you would **give** your **right arm** PHRASE or **give anything** to have or do something, you are emphasizing how very keen you are to have it or do it. EG *She said she would give anything to stay in China.*

13 People use **give** in expressions such as 'I don't V+O give a damn' to emphasize that they do not care Informal about something. EG *He didn't give a damn about his passengers.*

14 If someone **gives as good as** they **get**, they PHRASE fight or argue as well as the person they are fighting or arguing with.

15 Give or take is used to indicate that an amount PHRASE is approximate. For example, if you say that some-thing is fifty years old **give or take** a few years, you mean that it is approximately fifty years old.

16 Give way is used in these ways. **16.1** If PHRASE something **gives way** to something else, it is replaced by it. EG *Her look of joy gave way to one of misery.* **16.2** If a structure **gives way**, it collapses. EG *The floor gave way.* **16.3** If you **give way** to someone, you agree to allow them to do something, although you do not really want them to do it. EG *In the long run it proved easier to give way to his demands.* **16.4** If you **give way** when you are driving a car, you slow down or stop in order to allow other traffic to go in front of you.

17 See also **given.**

give away. 1 If you **give** something **away**, you PHRASAL VB : give it to someone, often because you no longer V+O+ADV want it. EG *She has given away jewellery worth millions of pounds.* **2** If you **give away** information V+O+ADV

> If you glare at someone, will they be pleased?

that should be kept secret, you reveal it to other people.

give back. If you **give** something **back**, you return it to the person who gave it to you. EG *If I didn't need the money, I would give it back again.* PHRASAL VB : V+O+ADV

give in. If you **give in**, 1 you admit that you are defeated or that you cannot do something. EG *We mustn't give in to threats.* **2** you allow something to happen that you do not want to happen, or agree to do something that you do not want to do. EG *We mustn't give in to threats.* PHRASAL VB : V+ADV / V+ADV, OFT+*to*

give off. If something **gives off** heat, smoke, or a smell, it produces it and sends it out into the air. EG *...the tremendous heat given off by the fire.* PHRASAL VB : V+O+ADV

give out. If you **give out** a number of things, you distribute them among a group of people. EG *Howard gave out drinks to his guests.* PHRASAL VB : V+O+ADV

give over. If something **is given over** to a particular use, it is used for that purpose. EG *...land given over to agriculture.* PHRASAL VB : V+O+ADV, USU PASS+*to*

give up. 1 If you **give up** something, you stop doing it or having it. EG *He gave up smoking to save money... She never completely gave up hope.* **2** If you **give up**, you admit that you cannot do something and stop trying to do it. EG *I don't know. I give up. What is it?* **3** If you **give up** your job, you resign from it. V+ADV+O / V+ADV / V+O+ADV

give up on. If you **give up on** something, you decide that you will never succeed in doing it, understanding it, or changing it, and you stop trying to. PHRASAL VB : V+ADV+PREP

give-and-take is a willingness to listen to other people's opinions and to make compromises. EG *...a give-and-take relationship.* N UNCOUNT

give-away. A **give-away** is something that reveals a truth that someone is trying to hide. EG *The give-away is the slight droop of the head... ...a give-away remark.* N SING

given /gɪvᵊn/. **1 Given** is the past participle of **give**.
2 A **given** date or time is one that has been fixed or decided on previously. EG *At a given moment we all cheered.* ADJ CLASSIF : ATTRIB
3 If you talk about **any given** society or **any given** time, you mean any society or time that can be mentioned. EG *One cannot look at the problems of any given society in isolation from the rest of the world.* PHRASE
4 If you say that something is the case **given** a particular thing, you mean that it is the case if you take that thing into account. EG *This was the best place to study, given my interest in Kant, Hegel, and Marx... It seemed churlish to send him away, given that he only wanted to take photographs.* PREP OR CONJ
5 If you say that someone is **given** to doing something, you mean that they often do it. EG *He was given to claiming that he was related to the Queen.* ADJ PRED+*to* Formal

glacial /gleɪsjᵊl/ means relating to glaciers or ice. EG *...a glacial landscape.* ADJ CLASSIF : ATTRIB

glacier /glæsjə/, **glaciers.** A **glacier** is a huge mass of ice which moves very slowly, often down a mountain valley. N COUNT

glad /glæd/, **gladder, gladdest. 1** If you are **glad** about something, you are happy and pleased about it. EG *I'm so glad that your niece was able to use the tickets... Ralph was glad of a chance to change the subject.* ◇ **gladly.** EG *He gladly accepted their invitation.* ADJ PRED+ *to*-INF, REPORT, OR PREP ◇ ADV
2 If you say that you are **glad** to do something, you mean that you are willing to do it. EG *Many people would be glad to work half time.* ◇ **gladly.** EG *We will gladly do it if it is within our power.* ADJ PRED +*to*-INF ◇ ADV

gladden /glædᵊn/, **gladdens, gladdening, gladdened.** If something **gladdens** you, it makes you happy and pleased. EG *It gladdened him to be home.* V+O

glade /gleɪd/, **glades.** A **glade** is a grassy space without trees in a wood or forest. EG *...a forest glade.* N COUNT Literary

glamorous /glæmərəs/. People, places, or jobs that are **glamorous** are attractive and exciting. EG *...the most glamorous star in motion pictures.* ADJ QUALIT

glamour /glæmə/; spelled **glamor** in American English. People, places, or jobs that have **glamour** are attractive and exciting. EG *Acapulco has lost much of its glamour... ...the superficial glamour of television.* N UNCOUNT

glance /glɑːns/, **glances, glancing, glanced. 1** If you **glance** at something, you look at it very quickly and then look away immediately. EG *Jacqueline glanced at her watch... Rudolph glanced around to make sure nobody was watching.* ▶ used as a noun. EG *He cast a quick glance at his friend.* V+A ▶ N COUNT : OFT+SUPP
2 If you **glance** through or **glance** at a newspaper or book, you spend a short time looking at it without reading it carefully. EG *During breakfast he glances through the morning paper.* V+*through/at*
3 If you can see or recognize something **at a glance**, you can see or recognize it immediately. EG *She can tell at a glance whether they are married to each other.* PHRASE
4 If you say that something seemed to be true **at first glance**, you mean that it seemed to be true when you first saw it or thought about it, but that your first impression was probably wrong. EG *At first glance the bullets looked the same as the others.* PHRASE

glance off. If an object **glances off** something, it hits it at an angle and bounces away in another direction. EG *The ball glanced off my fingertips.* PHRASAL VB : V+ADV/PREP

glancing /glɑːnsɪŋ/. A **glancing** blow hits something at an angle rather than from directly in front. EG *The glass hit him a glancing blow on the forehead.* ADJ CLASSIF : ATTRIB

gland /glænd/, **glands. Glands** are organs in your body that make substances for your body to use or allow substances to pass out of it. EG *...the thyroid gland.* ◇ **glandular** /glændjʊˈlə/. EG *...glandular changes.* N COUNT ◇ ADJ CLASSIF : ATTRIB

glare /gleə/, **glares, glaring, glared. 1** If you **glare** at someone, you look at them with an angry expression on your face. EG *The two brothers glared at each other.* ▶ used as a noun. EG *He shot a suspicious glare at me.* V : OFT+*at* ▶ N COUNT : USU+SUPP
2 If a light **glares**, it shines very brightly and makes it difficult for you to look in a particular direction. ▶ used as a noun. EG *The windows were tinted to reduce the glare.* ◇ **glaring.** EG *...the glaring lights of the fairground.* V : USU+A ▶ N UNCOUNT ◇ ADJ CLASSIF
3 If you are in the **glare** of publicity or public attention, you are constantly being watched and talked about by a lot of people. EG *At home he can relax once he's away from the glare of publicity.* N SING : *the*+N

glaring /gleərɪŋ/. If you refer to something bad as **glaring**, you mean that it is very obvious. EG *...glaring inequalities of wealth.* ◇ **glaringly.** EG *It was glaringly obvious that he had no idea what he was doing.* ADJ QUALIT ◇ ADV : USU+ADJ

glass /glɑːs/, **glasses. 1 Glass** is the hard transparent substance that windows and bottles are made from. EG *He sweeps away the broken glass... They crept up to the glass doors and peeped inside.* N UNCOUNT
2 A **glass** is a container made from glass which you can drink from. Glasses do not have handles. EG *I put down my glass and stood up.* N COUNT
3 You can use **glass** to refer to the contents of a glass, as in a **glass** of water or a **glass** of milk. EG *He poured Ellen a glass of wine.* N PART
4 Glass objects that you have in your house can be referred to as **glass.** EG *...a house crammed with beautiful furniture, glass and china.* N UNCOUNT
5 Glasses are two lenses in a frame that some people wear in front of their eyes in order to help them to see better. EG *...a girl with glasses... ...a pair of glasses.* N PLURAL
6 See also **dark glasses, magnifying glass.**

glasshouse /glɑːshaʊs/, **glasshouses.** A **glasshouse** is a large greenhouse. N COUNT

glassy /glɑːsiʼ/. 1 Something that is **glassy** is very smooth and shiny, like glass. EG *The boat lay motionless on the glassy sea.*   ADJ CLASSIF Literary

2 If you describe someone's eyes as **glassy**, you mean that they show no feeling or understanding in their expression. EG *He gazed at the street with dull, glassy eyes.*   ADJ QUALIT

glaze /ɡleɪz/, **glazes, glazing, glazed.** A **glaze** is a thin layer of a hard shiny substance on a piece of pottery.   N COUNT

glaze over. If someone's eyes **glaze over**, they become dull in appearance, usually because the person is no longer interested in what they are looking at or being told. EG *I can see people's eyes start to glaze over at the mention of Chomsky.*   PHRASAL VB : V+ADV

glazed /ɡleɪzd/. 1 If you describe someone's eyes as **glazed**, you mean that their expression is dull or dreamy, because they are tired or are having difficulty concentrating on something. EG *His eyes took on a slightly glazed, distant look.*   ADJ QUALIT

2 If a piece of pottery is **glazed**, it is covered with a thin layer of a hard shiny substance. EG *...glazed clay pots.*   ADJ CLASSIF

3 A **glazed** window or door has glass in it.   ADJ CLASSIF

gleam /ɡliːm/, **gleams, gleaming, gleamed.** 1 If an object or a surface **gleams**, it shines brightly because it is reflecting light. EG *He polished the gold until it gleamed.* ▶ used as a noun. EG *...a gleam of water.* ◊ **gleaming.** EG *...the gleaming brass on the altar.*   V   ▶ N COUNT   ◊ ADJ CLASSIF

2 When a small light shines brightly, you can say that it **gleams**. EG *The lighthouses of the islands gleam and wink above the surf.*   V

3 If your eyes or eyes **gleam** with a particular feeling, they show it. EG *His eyes gleamed with pleasure.* ▶ used as a noun. EG *A gleam of triumph crossed the woman's face.*   V : OFT+with   ▶ N COUNT : USU SING+of

glean /ɡliːn/, **gleans, gleaning, gleaned.** If you **glean** information about something, you obtain it slowly and with difficulty. EG *Much of the information he gleaned was of no practical use.*   V+O OFT+from

glee /ɡliː/ is a feeling of joy and excitement. EG *...the glee with which the media report scientific calamities.*   N UNCOUNT

gleeful /ɡliːfʊl/. Someone who is **gleeful** is full of joy and excitement, often because of someone else's foolishness or failure. ◊ **gleefully.** EG *He gleefully rubbed his hands.*   ADJ QUALIT   ◊ ADV

glen /ɡlen/, **glens.** A **glen** is a deep, narrow valley, especially in Scotland or Ireland.   N COUNT

glib /ɡlɪb/. You describe someone's behaviour as **glib** when they talk too quickly and confidently, often making difficult situations sound easy, so that you feel that you cannot trust them. ◊ **glibly.** EG *MacIver was always ready with glib promises.* ◊ **glibly.** EG *They still talk glibly of a return to full employment.*   ADJ QUALIT   ◊ ADV

glide /ɡlaɪd/, **glides, gliding, glided.** 1 If you **glide** somewhere, you move there smoothly and silently. EG *Tim glided to the door and down the stairs... The canoes glided by.*   V : USU+A

2 When birds or aeroplanes **glide**, they float on air currents. EG *...an owl gliding silently over the fields.*   V : USU+A

glider /ɡlaɪdə/, **gliders.** A **glider** is an aircraft without an engine. Gliders fly by floating on air currents.   N COUNT

glimmer /ɡlɪmə/, **glimmers, glimmering, glimmered.** 1 If something **glimmers**, it produces a faint, often unsteady light. EG *The pearl glimmered faintly as she moved.* ▶ used as a noun. EG *The sky was pink with the first, far-off glimmer of the dawn.* ◊ **glimmering.** EG *...the glimmering night sky.*   V   ▶ N COUNT : OFT+of   ◊ ADJ CLASSIF

2 A **glimmer** or a **glimmering** of something is a faint sign of it. EG *He showed no glimmer of interest in them... ...the first glimmering of hope.*   N COUNT+SUPP

glimpse /ɡlɪmpˢs/, **glimpses, glimpsing, glimpsed.** 1 If you **glimpse** something, you see it very briefly and not very well. EG *...a village they*   V+O

had glimpsed through the trees. ▶ used as a noun. EG *...the first glimpse I caught of Fanny.*   ▶ N COUNT : OFT+of

2 You can also say that you **glimpse** something when you experience or think about it briefly, especially when this makes you understand it better. EG *She glimpses something of what life ought to be about.* ▶ used as a noun. EG *...glimpses of his kindness.*   V+O   ▶ N COUNT : OFT+of

glint /ɡlɪnt/, **glints, glinting, glinted.** 1 If something **glints**, it produces or reflects a quick flash of light. EG *His spectacles glinted in the sunlight... The sun glinted on the walls.* ▶ used as a noun. EG *...a glint of metal.* ◊ **glinting.** EG *...a city of glinting glass and high towers.*   V : OFT+A   ▶ N COUNT   ◊ ADJ CLASSIF

2 If someone's eyes **glint**, they shine and express a particular emotion. EG *Her green eyes glinted with mockery.* ▶ used as a noun. EG *There was an ironic glint in his eyes.*   V   ▶ N COUNT

glisten /ɡlɪsəⁿn/, **glistens, glistening, glistened.** If something **glistens**, it shines or sparkles, because it is smooth, wet, or oily. EG *His face glistened with sweat.* ◊ **glistening.** EG *...glistening lips.*   V : OFT+A   ◊ ADJ CLASSIF

glitter /ɡlɪtə/, **glitters, glittering, glittered.** 1 If something **glitters**, it shines in a sparkling way. EG *Her jewellery glittered under the spotlight... Stars glittered in a clear sky.* ▶ used as a noun. EG *...the glitter of the sea.* ◊ **glittering.** EG *...glittering Christmas trees... ...a charming dress glittering with diamonds.*   V : OFT+A   ▶ N UNCOUNT   ◊ ADJ CLASSIF

2 If someone's eyes **glitter**, they are very bright and shiny because they are feeling a particular emotion. EG *Her eyes glittered as she described these wonders.* ▶ used as a noun. EG *He noticed a slight glitter in the whites of her eyes.* ◊ **glittering.** EG *Tony gazed with glittering eyes around him.*   V : OFT+A   ▶ N SING   ◊ ADJ QUALIT

3 You can describe something as **glittering** when it is very impressive. EG *...a glittering career.*   ADJ QUALIT : ATTRIB

gloat /ɡləʊt/, **gloats, gloating, gloated.** When someone **gloats**, they show great pleasure at their own success or at other people's failure. EG *They were gloating over my bankruptcy.* ◊ **gloating.** EG *...gloating self-satisfaction.*   V : OFT+over   ◊ ADJ CLASSIF : ATTRIB

global /ɡləʊbəⁿl/ means concerning or including the whole world. EG *...protests on a global scale.* ◊ **globally.** EG *This accounts for about half the wheat sold globally.*   ADJ CLASSIF   ◊ ADV

globe /ɡləʊb/, **globes.** 1 You can refer to the Earth as the **globe**. EG *...television pictures seen all over the globe... ...countries on the far side of the globe.*   N SING : the+N

2 A **globe** is a spherical object, usually fixed on a stand, with a map of the world on it.   N COUNT

3 Any object shaped like a ball can be referred to as a **globe**. EG *...the orange globe of the sun.*   N COUNT : USU+SUPP

globule /ɡlɒbjuːl/, **globules.** A **globule** is a tiny round particle of a substance, especially of a liquid. EG *...a globule of blood.*   N PART Formal

gloom /ɡluːm/. 1 **Gloom** is partial darkness in which there is still a little light. EG *He peered through the gloom at the dim figure... ...the gloom of their cell.*   N SING : the+N

2 **Gloom** is also 2.1 a feeling of unhappiness or despair. EG *He viewed the future with gloom.* 2.2 the quality that something has of making people feel depressed. EG *...the pervading gloom of the place.*   N UNCOUNT

gloomy /ɡluːmiʼ/, **gloomier, gloomiest.** 1 If a place is **gloomy**, it is almost dark so that you cannot see very well. EG *...the gloomy prison.*   ADJ QUALIT

2 You say that the weather is **gloomy** when it is cloudy and rather dark.   ADJ QUALIT

3 If someone is **gloomy**, they are unhappy and have no hope. EG *He looked gloomy... There was a*   ADJ QUALIT

Which words on these pages refer to lights shining?

gloomy silence. ◊ **gloomily.** EG 'Trouble,' Rudolph ◊ ADV
said gloomily.

4 If a situation is **gloomy**, it does not give you ADJ QUALIT
much hope of success or happiness. EG He could
only see the gloomy possibilities of modern science.

glorified /glɔːrɪfaɪd/ is used to say that something ADJ CLASSIF:
is not as important or impressive as its name ATTRIB
suggests. For example, if you say that a lake is a
glorified pond, you mean that it is not much bigger
than a pond.

glorify /glɔːrɪfaɪ/, **glorifies, glorifying, glori-** V+O
fied. If you **glorify** someone or something, you
praise them or make them seem important. EG His
newspapers glorified his charitable donations.
◊ **glorification** /glɔːrɪfɪkeɪʃəⁿn/. EG ...the glorifica- ◊ N UNCOUNT
tion of war. the+N+of

glorious /glɔːrɪəs/. **1** Something that is **glorious** is ADJ QUALIT
very beautiful and impressive. EG ...the most glori-
ous flowers I have ever seen. ◊ **gloriously.** EG ◊ ADV
...gloriously embroidered pictures.

2 Glorious events and experiences **2.1** make you ADJ QUALIT
very happy. EG ...a glorious carefree feeling of joy.
◊ **gloriously.** EG We got gloriously drunk. **2.2** ADJ QUALIT
involve great fame or success. EG ...the glorious
future opening before them.

3 If you describe the weather as **glorious**, you ADJ QUALIT
mean that it is hot and sunny. EG We had glorious
sunshine. ◊ **gloriously.** EG The first few days were ◊ ADV
gloriously hot.

glory /glɔːrɪ¹/, **glories, glorying, gloried. 1 Glo-** N UNCOUNT
ry is the fame and admiration that you get by
achieving something. EG The warriors valued glory
and honour above life itself... I did it for the
theatre, not for my own personal glory.

2 The **glory** of something is its great beauty or N UNCOUNT
impressiveness. EG ...the glory of the classical thea- +SUPP
tre.

3 The **glories** of a person or group of people are N PLURAL
the occasions on which they have done something +SUPP
famous or admirable. EG ...a shrine to the glories of
the French Army.

4 The **glories** of a culture or place are the things N PLURAL
that people find most attractive about it. EG ...the +POSS
glories of Venice.

glory in. If you **glory in** a situation or activity, PHRASAL VB:
you enjoy it very much. EG The women were V+PREP,
glorying in this new-found freedom. HAS PASS

gloss /glɒs/, **glosses, glossing, glossed.** A **gloss** N SING
is a bright shine on the surface of something. EG
The wood has a high gloss.

gloss over. If you **gloss over** a problem, a PHRASAL VB:
mistake, or an embarrassing moment, you try and V+ADV+O
make it seem unimportant by ignoring it or by
dealing with it very quickly. EG Truffaut glosses
over such contradictions.

glossary /glɒsəⁿrɪ¹/, **glossaries.** The **glossary** of N COUNT
a book or a subject is an alphabetical list of the
special or technical words used in it, with explanations of their meanings.

glossy /glɒsɪ¹/. **1** Something that is **glossy** is ADJ QUALIT
smooth and shiny. EG She had glossy brown hair.

2 Glossy magazines and photographs are pro- ADJ QUALIT:
duced on expensive, shiny paper. EG ...the fashion ATTRIB
models you see in glossy magazines.

glove /glʌv/, **gloves.** A **glove** is a piece of clothing N COUNT:
which covers your hand and wrist and has individ- USU PLURAL
ual sections for each finger. See picture at CLOTHES.
EG He pulled his gloves on... Wear rubber gloves or
you may scald yourself.

glove compartment, glove compartments. N COUNT
The **glove compartment** in a car is a small
cupboard or shelf below the front windscreen. See
picture at CAR.

glow /gləʊ/, **glows, glowing, glowed. 1** A **glow** is N COUNT:
a dull, steady light, for example the light produced USU SING
by a fire when there are no flames. EG ...the blue
glow of a police station light.

2 A **glow** on someone's face is the pink colour that N SING

it has when they are excited or when they have
done some exercise. EG The conversation brought a
glow to her cheeks.

3 A **glow** is also a strong feeling of pleasure or N SING:
satisfaction. EG I felt a glow of pleasure. USU+SUPP

4 If something **glows, 4.1** it produces a dull, steady V OR V+C
light. EG A cluster of stars glowed above us... They
blew into the charcoal until it glowed red. **4.2** it V OR V+C
looks bright by reflecting light. EG ...children's faces
glowing in the light of the fire. **4.3** it is bright, V
attractive, and colourful. EG The Church glowed
with colourful African patterns and fabrics.

5 If someone **glows** or their face **glows**, their face V:OFT+with
is pink as a result of excitement or physical
exercise. EG Aunt Agnes glowed with joy... Her face
glowed with a healthy red sheen.

6 See also **glowing.**

glower /glaʊə/, **glowers, glowering, glowered.** V:USU+A
If you **glower** at someone or something, you look
at them angrily. EG He glowered resentfully at Ash.

glowing /gləʊɪŋ/. A **glowing** description of some- ADJ QUALIT
one or something praises them very highly. EG ...the
book, of which I had read such glowing reports.

glow-worm, glow-worms. A **glow-worm** is a N COUNT
beetle which produces a greenish light from its
body.

glucose /gluːkəʊz, -əʊs/ is a type of sugar that N UNCOUNT
gives you energy. It is produced in your body from
the food that you eat and you can also buy it in the
form of a powder or tablets.

glue /gluː/, **glues, glueing** or **gluing, glued. 1** N MASS
Glue is a sticky substance used for joining things
together. EG The hat seems to be stuck on with glue.

2 If you **glue** one object to another, you stick them V+O+A
together using glue. EG A new piece was glued into
place.

3 If you say that something is **glued** to something ADJ PRED+to
else by a substance that is not glue, you mean that
it is firmly fixed to it. EG ...a chop glued to the plate
by a thick sauce.

4 If you say that someone is **glued** to the television ADJ PRED+to
or radio, you mean that they are giving it all their
attention. EG They were glued to their TV sets
watching the latest news.

5 If you say that someone's eyes are **glued** to ADJ PRED+to/
something, you mean that they are watching it on
with all their attention. EG Their eyes were glued to
the scene below.

glum /glʌm/, **glummer, glummest.** Someone ADJ QUALIT
who is **glum** is sad and quiet, because they are
disappointed or unhappy. EG Don't look so glum...
...his glum face. ◊ **glumly.** EG 'It's no use,' Eddie ◊ ADV
said glumly.

glut /glʌt/, **gluts.** A **glut** is a situation in which N COUNT
there is too much of something, especially goods or
raw materials, so that not all of it can be sold or
used. EG The oil glut has forced price cuts.

glutinous /gluːtɪnəs/. Something that is **glutinous** ADJ QUALIT
is very sticky. EG ...glutinous rice.

glutton /glʌtəⁿn/, **gluttons. 1** Someone who is a N COUNT
glutton eats too much in a greedy way.

2 If you say that someone is a **glutton** for some- N COUNT+for
thing, you mean that they enjoy or need it very
much. EG The British must be gluttons for satire.

gluttony /glʌtəⁿnɪ¹/ is the act or habit of eating N UNCOUNT
too much.

glycerine /glɪsəⁿriːⁿn/; spelled **glycerin** in Ameri- N UNCOUNT
can English. **Glycerine** is a thick, colourless liquid
that is used in making medicine, explosives, and
antifreeze.

gnarled /nɑːld/. **1** A **gnarled** tree is twisted and ADJ QUALIT
rough because it is old.

2 A **gnarled** person has rough swollen skin, as a ADJ QUALIT
result of old age or hard physical work. EG ...gnarled
peasant's hands.

gnash /næʃ/, **gnashes, gnashing, gnashed.** If V+O
you **gnash** your teeth, you bite and rub them
together hard because you are angry or in pain. EG
I lay gnashing my teeth in despair.

gnat /næt/, gnats. A **gnat** is a small flying insect N COUNT that bites people.

gnaw /nɔː/, gnaws, gnawing, gnawed. 1 If ani- V+O OR V+A mals or people **gnaw** something or **gnaw** at it, they bite it repeatedly. EG ...*watching her puppy gnaw a bone... The ant tried to gnaw through the thread.*

2 If a feeling **gnaws** at you or **gnaws** away at you, V+at/away it causes you to worry or suffer and is hard to get Literary rid of. EG *These desires gnaw away at us constantly.*

◊ **gnawing.** EG ...*gnawing doubts about the future* ◊ ADJ CLASSIF: *of civilisation.* ATTRIB

gnome /nəʊm/, gnomes. A **gnome** is an imagi- N COUNT nary creature in children's stories that is like a tiny old man with a beard and pointed hat. People sometimes have small statues of gnomes in their gardens.

go /gəʊ/, goes, going, went /wɛnt/, gone /gɒn/. In most cases the past participle of **go** is 'gone', but occasionally you use 'been': see **been.**

1 When you **go** somewhere, you move or travel V : USU+A there. EG *I went to Stockholm... She went into the sitting-room... He went to get some fresh milk... A car went by.*

2 When you **go**, you leave the place where you are. V EG *'I must go,' she said... Our train went at 2.25.*

3 You use **go** to say that someone leaves the place V+-ING OR for where they are and takes part in an activity. EG *Let's go fishing... They went for a walk.* ● If you ● V+-ING : advise someone not to **go** doing something, you WITH BROAD mean that they should not do it. EG *Don't go hiding* NEG *in the attic.* Informal

4 If you **go** and do a particular thing, you move V+and+INF : from one place to another in order to do the thing, NO CONT and you do it. EG *I'll go and see him in the morning.*
● If you say that someone **has gone and** done ● PHRASE something, you are expressing annoyance at what Informal they have done. EG *That idiot Antonio has gone and locked our door.*

5 If you **go** to school, church, or work, you attend it V+to regularly. EG *She went to London University.*

6 You can use **go** to say that someone is in a V+C particular state. For example, if someone **goes** naked, they are not wearing any clothes, and if they **go** unarmed, they are not carrying any weapons.

7 You can also use **go** to say that something does V+C not have something done to it. For example, if someone's words **go** unheard, they are not heard. EG *Halliday's absence had gone unnoticed... Her decision went unchallenged.*

8 You can also use **go** to mean become. For V+C example, if someone's hair **is going** grey, it is becoming grey. EG *The village thought we had gone crazy.*

9 If you say that a period of time **goes** quickly or V+A **goes** slowly, you mean that it seems to pass quickly or slowly.

10 If an event or activity **goes** well, it is successful. V+A If it **goes** badly, it is unsuccessful. EG *Everything went pretty smoothly... How did school go?... The way things are going, it'll be dark before we've finished.*

11 If a machine or device **is going**, it is working. EG V : OFT+A *The tape recorder was still going.*

12 You talk about how a story, song, saying, or V : OFT+QUOTE piece of writing **goes** just before quoting it or singing it. EG *As the song goes: I fell in love with eyes of blue.*

13 You use **go** before the word that represents a ◊ QUOTE noise that something makes. EG ...*American sirens which instead of going 'Ow-wow' go 'Whoop-whoop'.*

14 When a bell or alarm **goes**, it makes a noise. V

15 If you say that money **goes** in, into, or on V+in/into/on something, you mean that it is used for that purpose. EG *Most of the aid has gone into urban projects... 40% of his income goes on rent.*

16 If something **goes** to someone, it is given to V+to them. EG *The job is to go to a private contractor.*

17 If you say that someone or something **has got** PHRASE **to go**, you mean that they must be got rid of. EG *The last to be hired had to be the first to go.*

18 If you say that there is a particular thing **to go**, PHRASE you mean that it remains to be dealt with. If there is a particular period of time **to go**, that period of time remains to pass. EG *Eight down and two to go... There are still two years to go.*

19 If someone's sight or hearing **is going**, it is V getting worse.

20 If two things **go** together, 20.1 they look nice V OR V+with : when they are placed together. EG *I got the shoes to* RECIP, NO CONT *go with my coat.* 20.2 they are appropriate or suitable together. EG *White wine goes with fish.*

21 If something **goes** in a particular place, 21.1 it V+A fits in that place. EG *The silencer went on easily.* 21.2 it belongs there, because that is where you normally keep it. EG *Where do the pans go?*

22 When you talk about where a road or path **goes**, V+A you are referring to the place it leads to or passes through. EG *There's a little road that goes off to the right.*

23 You say **'here goes'** just before you do some- CONVENTION thing difficult, exciting, or dangerous. Informal

24 You say **there goes** a particular thing to PHRASE express disappointment when something happens Informal to prevent you getting it. EG *There goes my chance of a job.*

25 If someone asks **'Where do we go from here?'** PHRASE when a problem has not been solved satisfactorily, they mean 'What shall we do next?'

26 If you do something **as** you **go along**, you do it PHRASE without preparing it beforehand. EG *I was making it* Informal *up as I went along.*

27 If you say that something **goes to show** or **goes** PHRASE **to prove** something interesting, you mean that it shows or proves it. EG *All of which goes to show that people haven't changed.*

28 A **go** is an attempt at doing something. EG *He* N COUNT *passed the test first go... I'll have a go at mending it.* ● If you **have a go at** someone, you criticize ● PHRASE them. Informal

29 If you say that something happened **from the** PHRASE **word go**, you mean that it happened from the very beginning of a situation. EG *She complained from the word go.*

30 If you say that someone **is making a go** of a PHRASE business or relationship, you mean that they are Informal being successful.

31 If you say that someone is always **on the go**, PHRASE you mean that they are busy and active. Informal

32 See also **going, gone.** ● **to go easy on**something: see **easy.** ● **to go so far as** to do something: see **far.** ● **to go hungry:** see **hungry.** ● **to go without saying:** see **say.** ● **there you go:** see **there.**

go about. 1 If you **go about** a task in a particular PHRASAL VB : way, you deal with it in that way. EG *She told me* V+PREP *how to go about it.* 2 If you **go about** your usual V+PREP activities, you continue doing them. EG *He wanted to be left alone to go about his business.* 3 See also **go around.**

go after. If you **go after** something, you try to PHRASAL VB : get it. EG *My husband had gone after a job.* V+PREP

go against. 1 If something **goes against** an idea, PHRASAL VB : it conflicts with it. EG *When things go against my* V+PREP, wishes, I threaten to resign... The teaching of the* HAS PASS *Bible clearly goes against it.* 2 If you **go against** V+PREP someone's advice or wishes, you do something different from what they want you to do. EG *She went against the advice of her Cabinet and called a general election.* 3 If a decision **goes against** V+PREP someone, for example in a court of law, they lose.

If you go along with a decision, do you agree with it?

go ahead. 1 If someone **goes ahead** with something they have planned or suggested, they begin to do it or make it. EG *They are going ahead with the missile... 'Would you like to hear it?' – 'Go ahead.'* **2** If an organized event **goes ahead**, it takes place. EG *The May day marches could go ahead.* **3** See also **go-ahead**. PHRASAL VB: V+ADV, OFT+with / V+ADV

go along with. If you **go along with** a decision, policy, or idea, you accept it and obey it. EG *How could you go along with such a plan?* PHRASAL VB: V+ADV+PREP

go around, go round, or **go about. 1** If you **go around, go round,** or **go about** doing something, often something that other people disapprove of, you have the habit of doing it. EG *I don't go around deliberately hurting people's feelings.* **2** If you **go around, go round,** or **go about** with a person or group of people, you regularly meet them and go to different places with them. EG *He had no intention of letting her go around with those scruffy students.* **3** If a piece of news or a joke **is going around, is going round,** or **is going about,** it is being told by many people. PHRASAL VB: V+ADV+-ING / V+ADV OR V+ADV+with : RECIP / V+ADV/PREP

go back on. If you **go back on** a promise or agreement, you do not do what you promised or agreed to do. PHRASAL VB: V+ADV+PREP

go back to. 1 If you **go back to** a task or activity, you start doing it again. EG *She had gone back to staring out of the window.* **2** If you **go back to** something that was mentioned earlier in a discussion or talk, you discuss it again. EG *Going back to your point about standards, I agree that they have fallen.* **3** If something **goes back to** a particular time in the past, it was made, built, or started at that time. EG *The shop goes back to 1707.* PHRASAL VB: V+ADV+PREP / V+ADV+PREP / V+ADV+PREP

go before. Something that **has gone before** has happened or been discussed at an earlier time. EG *The meeting was unlike any that had gone before.* PHRASAL VB: V+ADV

go by. 1 If a period of time **has gone by,** it has passed. EG *Eight years went by and the children grew up.* **2** If you **go by** something, you use it as a basis for a judgement or action. EG *I try to go by reason as far as possible.* PHRASAL VB: V+ADV / V+PREP

go down. 1 If a price, amount, or level **goes down,** it becomes lower. EG *The average age of farmers has gone down.* **2** If a speech or performance **goes down** well, people like it and are impressed by it. **3** When the sun **goes down,** it sets. PHRASAL VB: V+ADV / V+ADV+A / V+ADV

go down with. If you **go down with** an illness, you catch it. PHRASAL VB: V+ADV+PREP

go for. 1 If you **go for** a particular type of product or way of doing something, you choose it. EG *...a tendency to go for grand projects.* **2** If you **go for** someone, you attack them. EG *He went for me with the bread-knife.* **3** If you say that a statement you have made about one person or thing **goes for** another person or thing, you mean that it is also true of this other person or thing. EG *The same goes for Bardolph.* PHRASAL VB: V+PREP / V+PREP / V+PREP

go in for. If you **go in for** something, **1** you decide to do it as your job. EG *I thought of going in for teaching.* **2** you often do it or have it. EG *They go in for vintage port.* PHRASAL VB: V+ADV+PREP / V+ADV+PREP

go into. 1 If you **go into** something, **1.1** you describe it in detail. EG *I won't go into what I've suffered.* **1.2** you examine or investigate it thoroughly. EG *My solicitors are going into the question of my jewellery.* **1.3** you decide to do it as your career. EG *Have you ever thought of going into journalism?* **2** The amount of time, effort, or money that **goes into** something is the amount that is used to produce it. EG *Three years of research went into the making of those films.* **3** If a vehicle **goes into** a particular kind of movement, it starts moving in that way. EG *The plane went into a nose dive.* PHRASAL VB: V+PREP / V+PREP, HAS PASS / V+PREP / V+PREP / V+PREP

go off. 1 If you **go off** someone or something, you stop liking them. EG *He's suddenly gone off the idea.* **2** If something **goes off, 2.1** it explodes. EG *I could* PHRASAL VB: V+ADV+O / V+ADV

hear the bombs going off. **2.2** it makes a sudden loud noise. EG *The alarm went off.* **2.3** it stops operating. EG *The light only goes off at night.* **3** If an organized event **goes off** well, it is successful. EG *The meeting went off well.* V+ADV / V+ADV / V+ADV+A

go off with. If someone **goes off with** something that belongs to someone else, they take it away with them. EG *She had let him go off with her papers.* PHRASAL VB: V+ADV+PREP

go on. 1 If you **go on** doing something, you continue to do it. EG *I went on writing... They can't go on with their examinations... There's no need to go on arguing about it.* **2** If you **go on** to do something, you do it after you have done something else. EG *He went on to get his degree.* **3** If you **go on** to a place, you go to it from the place that you have reached. EG *We had gone on to Clare's house.* **4** If you **go on,** you continue talking. EG *'You know,' he went on, 'it's extraordinary.'... 'Sounds serious,' I said. 'Go on.'* **5** If you **go on** about something or **go on** at someone, you talk about the same thing for a long time in an annoying way. EG *Don't go on about it... I went on at my father to have safety belts fitted.* **6** If you say that a particular activity **is going on,** you mean that it is taking place. EG *There's a big argument going on... A lot of cheating goes on.* ● See also **goings-on. 7** As time **goes on** means as time passes. EG *I get more depressed, as time goes on.* **8** You say **'Go on'** to someone to persuade or encourage them to do something. EG *Go on, have a biscuit.* **9** If you **go on** a piece of information, you base an opinion or judgement on it. EG *It's not much to go on.* **10** If a device or machine **goes on,** it begins operating. EG *The light goes on automatically.* PHRASAL VB: V+ADV+-ING OR with / V+ADV+to-INF / V+ADV+A / V+ADV, USU+QUOTE / V+ADV: OFT+about/at Informal / V+ADV / V+ADV / V+ADV, ONLY IMPER / V+PREP, HAS PASS / V+ADV

go out. 1 If you **go out** with someone, you spend time with them socially and often have a romantic or sexual relationship with them. EG *My parents wouldn't let me go out with boys... I went out with him a long time ago.* **2** If a light **goes out,** it stops shining. EG *The lights went out in the big tent.* **3** If a fire or a flame **goes out,** it stops burning. EG *The fire went out... My cigar's gone out.* **4** If something **goes out,** it stops being popular or stops being used. EG *Steam went out and diesel was introduced.* PHRASAL VB: V+ADV OR V+ADV+with : RECIP / V+ADV / V+ADV / V+ADV

go over. If you **go over** something, you examine, discuss, or think about it very carefully. EG *He went over this in his mind.* PHRASAL VB: V+PREP

go over to. 1 If someone **goes over to** a different way of doing things, they change to it. EG *We went over to the American system.* **2** If you **go over to** a group of people, you join them after previously belonging to a group with very different aims or ideas. EG *Anyone joining the police is going over to the other side.* PHRASAL VB: V+ADV+PREP / V+ADV+PREP

go round. If there is enough of something to **go round,** there is enough of it for everyone in a group to have some. ● See also **go around.** PHRASAL VB: V+ADV/PREP, NO CONT

go through. 1 If you **go through** an event or a period of time, especially an unpleasant one, you experience it. EG *I'm too old to go through that again.* **2** If you **go through** a number of things, you look at them in turn, especially in order to find a particular item. EG *Go through the files again.* **3** If you **go through** a list, story, or plan, you say it or describe it from beginning to end. EG *You'd better go through the names.* **4** If a law, agreement, or official decision **goes through,** it is approved and becomes official. EG *The adoption went through.* PHRASAL VB: V+PREP / V+PREP, HAS PASS / V+PREP, HAS PASS / V+ADV/PREP

go through with. If you **go through with** something, you do it even though it is difficult or unpleasant for you or other people. EG *Would he go through with the assassination?* PHRASAL VB: V+ADV+PREP

go towards. If an amount of money **goes towards** something, it is used as part of the cost of that thing. EG *It will go towards a deposit on the flat.* PHRASAL VB: V+PREP

go under. If a business or project **goes under,** it fails. PHRASAL VB: V+ADV

go up. 1 If a price, amount, or level **goes up,** it PHRASAL VB: V+ADV becomes higher than it was. EG *The price of food will go up.* **2** When a building or other structure **goes up**, it is built. **3** If something **goes up**, it explodes or starts to burn fiercely. EG *In seconds it had gone up in flames.* **4** If a shout or a cheer **goes up**, it is made by a lot of people together. V+ADV

go with. If one thing **goes with** another, you always get the second thing if you get the first one. EG *The house went with the job.* PHRASAL VB: V+PREP, NO CONT

go without. If you **go without** something, you do not get it. EG *If they couldn't get coal, they had to go without... The family went without food all day.* PHRASAL VB: V+ADV/PREP

goad /gəʊd/, **goads, goading, goaded.** If you **goad** someone, you make them feel a strong emotion such as anger, often causing them to react by doing something. EG *She was being goaded into denouncing her own friend.* V+O:USU+A

goad on. If you **goad** someone **on**, you encourage them. EG *...the spontaneous uprising of masses goaded on by student activists.* PHRASAL VB: V+O+ADV, USU PASS

go-ahead. 1 If you give someone the **go-ahead**, you give them permission or approval to start doing something. EG *He gave the go-ahead for the Manhattan Project.* N SING: the+N

2 A **go-ahead** person or organization is ambitious and tries hard to succeed, often by using new methods. ADJ QUALIT

goal /gəʊl/, **goals. 1** A **goal** in some games such as football or hockey is **1.1** the space into which the players try to get the ball in order to score a point for their team. **1.2** an instance in which a player succeeds in getting the ball into the goal, and the point they score by doing this. N COUNT

2 Something that is your **goal** is something that you hope to achieve. EG *They had at last achieved their goal of landing a man on the Moon.* N COUNT+SUPP

goalkeeper /gəʊlkiːpə/, **goalkeepers.** A **goalkeeper** is the player in a sports team whose job is to guard the goal. N COUNT

goalpost /gəʊlpəʊst/, **goalposts.** A **goalpost** is one of the two upright wooden posts that are connected by a crossbar and form the goal in games like football and hockey. N COUNT

goat /gəʊt/, **goats.** A **goat** is an animal with horns and a short tail. Goats are found in mountain areas or are kept on farms. N COUNT

gob /gɒb/, **gobs.** Someone's **gob** is their mouth; often used in a rude way. EG *You shut your gob!* N COUNT Informal

gobble /gɒbəl/, **gobbles, gobbling, gobbled.** If you **gobble** food, you eat it quickly and greedily. EG *Still hungry, I gobbled a second sandwich.* V+O

gobble down or **gobble up.** If you **gobble** food **down** or **gobble** it **up**, you eat all of it very quickly. EG *He gobbled down the eggs with satisfaction.* PHRASAL VB: V+ADV+O

gobbledygook /gɒbəldiˈguːk/; also spelled **gobbledegook.** Gobbledygook is language, often in official statements, which you cannot understand at all. EG *He talked complicated gobbledygook.* N UNCOUNT Informal

go-between, go-betweens. A **go-between** is a person who takes messages between people who are unable or unwilling to meet each other. EG *Fortunately I was there to act as a go-between.* N COUNT

goblet /gɒblɪt/, **goblets.** A **goblet** is a type of cup without handles and usually with a long stem, which is used for drinking wine out of. N COUNT

goblin /gɒblɪn/, **goblins.** A **goblin** is a small ugly creature in fairy stories. N COUNT

god /gɒd/, **gods. 1** The name **God** is given to the spirit or being who is worshipped as the creator and ruler of the world, especially by Christians, Jews, and Muslims. N PROPER

2 People sometimes use **God** in exclamations to emphasize something that they are saying, or to express surprise, fear, or excitement. Some people find this offensive. EG *My God, John, what are you doing here?* EXCLAM

3 The word **God** is also used in these phrases. **3.1** If you say **God help** someone, you mean that you hope they will not have to experience something PHRASES

unpleasant or dangerous, often when you are warning them. EG *He spoke sharply: 'God help them if that's whom they follow.'* **3.2** If you say **God forbid**, you are expressing your hope that something will not happen. EG *God forbid that anything should happen to my father.* **3.3** If you say **God knows**, you are emphasizing that you don't know something or that you find a fact very surprising. EG *He was interested in shooting and God knows what else... God knows how they knew I was coming.* **3.4** You use **to God** in expressions like **I pray to God** and **I hope to God** to emphasize what you are saying. EG *I hope to God she'll be happy.* **3.5** for **God's sake:** see sake. ● **thank God:** see thank. Formal

Informal

4 A **god** is **4.1** one of the spirits or beings that are believed in many religions to have power over a particular part of the world or nature. EG *...the Saxon god of war.* **4.2** someone who you admire very much and think is more important than anyone else. EG *When I was eight years old, my uncles were my gods.* N COUNT

godchild /gɒdtʃaɪld/, **godchildren** /gɒdtʃɪldrən/. If someone is your **godchild**, you are their godparent, which means that you agreed to take responsibility for their religious upbringing when they were baptized in a Christian church. N COUNT

goddaughter /gɒddɔːtə/, **goddaughters.** A **goddaughter** is a female godchild. N COUNT

goddess /gɒdɪs/, **goddesses.** A **goddess** is a female spirit or being that is believed in many religions to have power over a particular part of the world or nature. N COUNT

godfather /gɒdfɑːðə/, **godfathers.** A **godfather** is a male godparent. N COUNT

god-fearing. Someone who is **god-fearing** is religious and behaves according to the moral rules of their religion. ADJ QUALIT

god-forsaken. A **god-forsaken** place is not at all interesting and is very depressing. EG *The ranch was a lonely run-down god-forsaken place.* ADJ CLASSIF: ATTRIB

godless /gɒdlɪs/. A **godless** person does not believe in God and has no religion; often used showing disapproval. EG *These men were dirty, drunken, and both godless and lawless.* ADJ CLASSIF

godly /gɒdli/. Someone who is **godly** is deeply religious and shows obedience to the rules of their religion. ADJ QUALIT

godmother /gɒdmʌðə/, **godmothers.** A **godmother** is a female godparent. N COUNT

godparent /gɒdpɛərənt/, **godparents.** Someone's **godparent** is a man or woman who agrees to take responsibility for their religious upbringing when they are baptized in a Christian church. N COUNT

godsend /gɒdsɛnd/. If you describe something as a **godsend**, you mean that it helps you very much. EG *The extra twenty dollars a week was a godsend.* N SING: a+N

godson /gɒdsʌn/, **godsons.** A **godson** is a male godchild. N COUNT

-goer /gəʊə/, **-goers. -goer** is added to words such as 'theatre' and 'church' to form nouns that refer to people who regularly go to a particular place or event. EG *They were both enthusiastic playgoers.*

goggle /gɒgəl/, **goggles, goggling, goggled. 1** If you **goggle** at something, you stare at it with your eyes wide open. EG *She goggled at the dreadful suit.* V:OFT+at Informal

2 Goggles are large glasses that fit closely to your face around your eyes to protect them from such things as water, wind, or sparks. EG *She was wearing big green-tinted snow goggles.* N PLURAL

going /gəʊɪŋ/. **1** If you say that something **is going to** happen, **1.1** you mean that it will happen in the future, especially soon. EG *She told him she was going to leave her job.* **1.2** you mean that you are determined that it will happen. EG *I'm not going to be made a scapegoat.* PHRASE

Do polite people gobble their food?

2 If you **get going**, you start doing something, PHRASE especially after a delay.

3 If you **keep going**, you continue doing some- PHRASE thing, especially something difficult or tiring.

4 The **going** is the conditions that affect your N UNCOUNT ability to do something. EG *...when the going gets tough... It was hard going at first.*

5 You say **'That's good going'** or **'That's not bad** PHRASE **going'** when something has been done more quick- Informal ly or more successfully than expected.

6 The **going** rate for something is the usual ADJ CLASSIF : amount of money that you expect to pay or receive ATTRIB for it. EG *The going rate is about £1,000 a head.*

7 If you **have** something **going for** you, you have a PHRASE particular advantage or useful quality. EG *She had so much going for her in the way of wealth and success.*

8 See also **go**. ● **comings and goings**: see **coming**.

goings-on. You refer to activities that you think N PLURAL are strange or amusing, or that you do not approve of, as **goings-on**. EG *...an amusing story about goings-on at Harry's Bar.*

gold /gəʊld/, **golds. 1 Gold** is **1.1** a valuable N UNCOUNT yellow-coloured metal that is used for making jewellery, and as an international currency. EG *...gold bracelets.* **1.2** jewellery and other things that are made of gold. EG *They stole an estimated 12 million pounds worth of gold and jewels.*

2 Something that is **gold** is bright yellow in colour. ADJ COLOUR EG *...a cap with gold braid all over it.*

3 If you say that someone has **a heart of gold**, you PHRASE mean that they are very good, kind, and considerate.

4 If you say that a child or an animal is **as good as** PHRASE **gold**, you mean that it behaves very well.

5 A **gold** is a gold medal. EG *He won the gold at* N COUNT *Amsterdam in 1928.*

golden /ˈgəʊldəⁿn/. **1** Something that is **golden** is **1.1** bright yellow in colour and looks rather like ADJ COLOUR gold. EG *...a girl with bright golden hair.* **1.2** made of ADJ CLASSIF gold. EG *She wore a golden cross.*

2 You use **golden** to describe something that you ADJ QUALIT think will be successful or the best of its kind. EG *It's a golden opportunity.*

goldfish /ˈgəʊldfɪʃ/. **Goldfish** is both the singular and the plural form.

A **goldfish** is a small orange-coloured fish. People N COUNT keep goldfish in garden ponds or in a bowls.

gold medal, gold medals. If you win a **gold** N COUNT **medal**, you come first in a competition, especially a sports contest, and are given a medal made of gold as a prize.

goldmine /ˈgəʊldmaɪn/, **goldmines.** If you call a N COUNT business or activity a **goldmine**, you mean that it is very successful and produces large profits. EG *The company has bought Cosmopolitan, a future goldmine.*

gold-plated. Something that is **gold-plated** is ADJ CLASSIF covered with a very thin layer of gold. EG *...a bath with gold-plated taps.*

golf /gɒlf/ is a game in which you use long sticks N UNCOUNT called clubs to hit a small, hard ball into holes that are spread out over a large area of grassy land.

golf club, golf clubs. A **golf club** is **1** a long, thin, N COUNT metal stick with a piece of wood or metal at one end that you use to hit the ball in golf. **2** an organization whose members play golf. **3** a place where people play golf.

golf course, golf courses. A **golf course** is a N COUNT large area of grassy land that is specially prepared for playing golf on.

golfer /ˈgɒlfə/, **golfers.** A **golfer** is a person who N COUNT plays golf for pleasure or as a profession.

golfing /ˈgɒlfɪŋ/ is the activity of playing golf. EG N UNCOUNT *...a golfing holiday.*

gone /gɒn/. **1 Gone** is the past participle of **go**.

2 Someone or something that is **gone** is no longer ADJ PRED present or no longer exists. EG *He turned the corner*

and was gone... The days are gone when women worked for half pay.

3 If it is **gone** a particular time, it is later than that PREP time. EG *It's gone tea-time.*

gong /gɒŋ/, **gongs.** A **gong** is a flat, circular piece N COUNT of metal that you hit with a hammer to make a sound like a loud bell.

gonna /ˈgɒnə/ is used in written English to represent the words 'going to' pronounced informally or in a particular accent. EG *What are we gonna do?*

goo /guː/. You can use **goo** to refer to any thick, N UNCOUNT sticky substance, for example mud or paste. EG Informal *...animals sinking in the goo offshore.*

good /gʊd/, **better** /ˈbetə/, **best** /best/; **goods.** See also separate entries at **better** and **best**.

1 Something that is **good** is **1.1** pleasant and ADJ QUALIT enjoyable. EG *They had a good time... That's good news... Hello! It's good to see you.* **1.2** of a high quality or standard. EG *...a very good school... ...good agricultural land... She speaks good English.* **1.3** satisfactory or successful. EG *Develop a good relationship with the staff... Both policies make good sense.*

2 If you say that a situation or idea is **good**, you ADJ QUALIT mean it is desirable, acceptable, or right. EG *It's good that there are places like this... She takes on more work than is good for her... 'How is he?' - 'He's fine.' - 'Good.'* ● If you say **it's a good thing** ● PHRASE or **it's a good job** that something is the case, you mean it is fortunate that it is the case. EG *It's a good thing I wasn't there.*

3 Someone who is in a **good** mood is cheerful and ADJ QUALIT : pleasant to be with. ATTRIB

4 If you are **good** at something, you are skilful and ADJ QUALIT successful at doing it. EG *Alex is a good swimmer... Marcus was good with his hands... You were never any good at Latin.*

5 Someone who is **good** is **5.1** kind and thoughtful. ADJ QUALIT EG *He's always been good to me... It's good of you to come.* **5.2** morally correct in their attitudes and behaviour. EG *There was no trace of evil in her - she was good.*

6 A child or animal that is **good** is well-behaved ADJ QUALIT and obedient. EG *Were the kids good?*

7 Good is what is considered to be right according N UNCOUNT to moral standards or religious beliefs. EG *...the conflict between good and evil.*

8 If something is done for the **good** of a person or N SING+POSS organization, it is done in order to benefit them. EG *Casey should quit for the good of the agency... It was for her own good.*

9 If you say that something will **do** someone **good**, PHRASE you mean that it will benefit them or improve them. EG *It'll do you good to get a bit of fresh air!*

10 You use **good** with a negative to say that N UNCOUNT : something will not succeed or be of any use. EG *It's* WITH BROAD *no good worrying any more tonight... Even if I* NEG *came, what good would it do?*

11 People say **'Good for you'** to express approval CONVENTION of your actions.

12 You use **good** to emphasize the great extent or ADJ QUALIT : degree of something. EG *He took a good long look at* ATTRIB *it... ...a good while ago... Take good care of it, won't you?*

13 If something happens **for good**, the situation PHRASE never changes back to what it was before. EG *They had gone for good.*

14 You use **as good as** before an adjective or a PHRASE verb to indicate that something is almost true or almost the case. EG *Without her glasses she was as good as blind... He had as good as abdicated.*

15 If you **make good** some damage or a loss, you PHRASE try to repair the damage or replace what has been lost.

16 Goods are things that are made to be sold. EG *...a* N PLURAL *wide range of electrical goods.*

17 If you **deliver the goods** or **come up with the** PHRASE **goods**, you do what is expected or required of you. Informal

EG *Such an unwieldy banking system is unable to deliver the goods.*

18 so far so good: see **far**. ● **in good time**: see **time**.

good afternoon. You say **'Good afternoon'** in the afternoon when you are greeting someone. EG *Good afternoon. Could I speak to Mr Duff, please.*   CONVENTION Formal

goodbye /gʊdbaɪ/, **goodbyes. 1** You say **'Good-bye'** to someone when you or they are leaving, or at the end of a telephone conversation. EG *We said good-bye to Charlie and walked back.*   CONVENTION

2 A **goodbye** is the act of saying goodbye. EG *They said their good-byes at the front door.*   N COUNT

good evening. You say **'Good evening'** in the evening when you are greeting someone, or sometimes instead of 'Goodbye'. EG *Good evening, Mr Castle. I'm sorry I'm late.*   CONVENTION Formal

good-humoured. Someone who is **good-humoured** is pleasant and cheerful in their attitude and behaviour. EG *The crowds were patient and good-humoured.*   ADJ QUALIT

goodie /gʊdiˈ/. See **goody**.

good-looking. Someone who is **good-looking** has an attractive face.   ADJ QUALIT

good morning. You say **'Good morning'** in the morning when you are greeting someone. EG *Good morning, darling. Another beautiful day.*   CONVENTION

good-natured. A person or animal that is **good-natured** is friendly and pleasant and does not easily get angry.   ADJ QUALIT

goodness /gʊdnɪ²s/. **1** People say **'My goodness'** or **'Goodness'** to express surprise. EG *My goodness, this is a difficult one.* ● **thank goodness**: see **thank**.   EXCLAM

2 Goodness is the quality of being kind and considerate. EG *...a belief in the goodness of human nature.*   N UNCOUNT

goodnight /gʊdnaɪt/, **goodnights. 1** You say **'Goodnight'** to someone late in the evening, before going home or going to sleep. EG *We all said good night and went to our rooms.*   CONVENTION

2 A **goodnight** is the act of saying goodnight. EG *They just left. Not even a goodnight or a thank you.*   N COUNT

goods train, goods trains. A **goods train** is a train that transports goods and not people.   N COUNT

good-tempered. Someone who is **good-tempered** is cheerful and does not easily get angry.   ADJ QUALIT

goodwill /gʊdwɪl/ is kind feelings and helpful behaviour towards other people. EG *...the goodwill and cooperation of all who are involved.*   N UNCOUNT

goody /gʊdiˈ/, **goodies;** also spelled **goodie. 1** People, especially children, say **'goody'** to express their pleasure about something. EG *Oh goody, there's some cake!*   EXCLAM Informal

2 A **goody** is **2.1** a person, especially in a film or book, who works or fights for people or ideas that you approve of. **2.2** something pleasant, exciting, or attractive. EG *She opened the bag of goodies.*   N COUNT : USU PLURAL Informal

gooey /guːiˈ/. A **gooey** substance is very soft and sticky. EG *...gooey fudge.*   ADJ QUALIT Informal

goof /guːf/, **goofs, goofing, goofed.** If you **goof,** you make a foolish mistake. EG *They had their chance, and they goofed.*   V Informal

goose /guːs/, **geese** /giːs/. A **goose** is a large bird that has a long neck and webbed feet and makes a loud noise.   N COUNT

gooseberry /gʊzbə⁰riˈ/, **gooseberries. 1** A **gooseberry** is a small, round, green fruit that grows on a bush, has a sharp taste, and is covered with tiny hairs.   N COUNT

2 If you say that someone is **playing gooseberry**, you mean that they are an unwelcome third person in the company of two people who are in love with each other and who want to be alone together. EG *I'd hate to play gooseberry to you and your boyfriend.*   PHRASE

gooseflesh /guːsflɛʃ/ or **goose pimples** refers to a condition of your skin when you are cold or   N UNCOUNT

scared. The hairs on the skin stand up so that it is covered with tiny bumps. EG *The sudden chill raised gooseflesh on the girl's arms.*

gore /gɔː/, **gores, goring, gored. 1** If an animal **gores** someone, it wounds them badly with its horns or tusks. EG *...if a bull gores someone to death.*   V+O

2 Gore is unpleasant-looking blood from a person or animal, for example after they have been in an accident. EG *...lie dying in a pool of black gore.*   N UNCOUNT

gorge /gɔːdʒ/, **gorges, gorging, gorged. 1** A **gorge** is a deep, narrow valley with very steep sides, usually where a river passes through mountains. EG *The road winds through rocky gorges and hills.*   N COUNT

2 If you **gorge** or **gorge** yourself, you eat very greedily until you are so full that you cannot eat any more. EG *They gorged themselves on rich food.*   V OR V-REFL

gorgeous /gɔːdʒəs/. **1** If you say that something is **gorgeous,** you mean that you find it extremely pleasant or enjoyable. EG *'Look what David gave me.' – 'Oh it's absolutely gorgeous.'... Isn't it a gorgeous day?*   ADJ QUALIT Informal

2 If you say that someone is **gorgeous,** you mean that you find them extremely attractive.   ADJ QUALIT Informal

gorilla /gərɪlə/, **gorillas.** A **gorilla** is an animal which looks like a very large monkey with a black face and black fur. Gorillas live in African forests.   N COUNT

gorse /gɔːs/ is a dark green bush that grows wild and has sharp prickles and small yellow flowers.   N UNCOUNT

gory /gɔːriˈ/. **Gory** situations involve people being injured or dying in a horrible way. EG *The film contains no gory violence.*   ADJ QUALIT

gosh /gɒʃ/. You say **'Gosh'** to indicate how surprised or shocked you are about something. EG *Thirteen pounds! Gosh that's a lot.*   EXCLAM Informal

gosling /gɒzlɪŋ/, **goslings.** A **gosling** is a baby goose.   N COUNT

go-slow, go-slows. A **go-slow** is a protest by workers in which they deliberately work slowly in order to cause problems for their employers.   N COUNT

gospel /gɒspə⁰l/, **gospels. 1** The **Gospels** are the four books of the Bible which describe the life and teachings of Jesus Christ. EG *...the Gospel according to St Mark.*   N COUNT

2 A **gospel** is also a set of ideas that someone believes in very strongly and that they urge others to accept. EG *They continue to preach their gospel of self-reliance.*   N COUNT+SUPP

3 If you regard something as **gospel** or as **gospel** truth, you believe that it is completely true. EG *You can take it as gospel truth that he is busy.*   ADJ CLASSIF

4 Gospel music is a style of religious music that uses strong rhythms and people singing in harmony. It is especially popular among black Christians in the southern United States.   ADJ CLASSIF : ATTRIB

gossamer /gɒsəmə/. **1 Gossamer** is the very light, fine thread that spiders use to make cobwebs.   N UNCOUNT

2 You use **gossamer** to describe cloth that is very thin and delicate. EG *...a gossamer handkerchief.*   N MOD Literary

gossip /gɒsɪp/, **gossips, gossiping, gossiped. 1** **Gossip** is informal conversation or information about other people, often including comments about their private affairs. EG *...spreading scandal and gossip about their colleagues.*   N UNCOUNT

2 A **gossip** is **2.1** a person who enjoys talking about the private affairs of other people. EG *According to the gossips, Mrs Ede is absolutely furious.* **2.2** an informal conversation, especially about other people or local events. EG *...friendly gossips over our garden gates.*   N COUNT

3 If you **gossip,** you talk informally with someone, especially about other people or local events. EG *I mustn't stay gossiping with you any longer.*   V : USU+A

> Find three words beginning with 'good' which have nearly the same meaning.

gossip column, gossip columns. A **gossip column** is a part of a newspaper or magazine where the activities and private affairs of famous people are discussed. N COUNT

gossipy /ˈgɒsɪpiˈ/. 1 A **gossipy** person enjoys gossiping; used showing disapproval. EG *...a lot of gossipy old women.* ADJ QUALIT
2 Speech or writing that is **gossipy** is informal and full of news about your own affairs or about other people. ADJ QUALIT

got /gɒt/. 1 **Got** is the past tense and past participle of **get**.
2 **Got** is often used in spoken English after the verb 'have' in the expression **have got**, when 'have' alone would be correct but more formal. The form **have got** is used with the same meanings as the main verb 'have', in the senses of owning or possessing things: see **have**. EG *We haven't got a car... Have you got any brochures on Holland?... I've got nothing to hide... That door's got a lock on it.* V+O
3 **Got** is also used in the expression **have got to**, which is an informal way of saying 'have to' or 'must'. It is used mainly to indicate that it is necessary that something should be done. EG *We've got to get up early tomorrow... There's got to be some motive.* V+to-INF

gotta /ˈgɒtə/ is used in written English to represent the words 'got to' pronounced informally or in a particular accent. It is an informal way of saying 'have to' or 'must'. EG *I've gotta get back.*

gotten /ˈgɒtəᵉn/ is often used for the past participle of **get** in American English.

gouge /gaʊdʒ/, **gouges, gouging, gouged.** If you **gouge** something, you make a hole in it with a pointed object. EG *...gouging a trough in the lawn.* V+O : USU+A

gouge out. If you **gouge** something **out**, you force it out of a hole using your fingers or a sharp instrument. EG *...gouging out the dirt with a knife.* PHRASAL VB : V+O+ADV

gourd /gʊəd/, **gourds.** A **gourd** is a large fruit that is similar to a marrow. N COUNT

gourmet /ˈgʊəmeɪ/, **gourmets.** A **gourmet** is a person who knows a lot about good cooking and wine, and who enjoys eating good food. N COUNT

gout /gaʊt/ is a disease which causes someone's joints to swell painfully, especially in their toes. N UNCOUNT

govern /ˈgʌvᵊn/, **governs, governing, governed.** 1 Someone who **governs** a country rules the country, for example by making and revising the laws, managing the economy, and controlling public services. EG *Many civil servants are sure that they can govern better than the politicians.* V OR V+O
2 Something that **governs** an event or situation has control and influence over it. EG *Poverty governed our lives... ...rules governing the conduct of students.* V+O

governess /ˈgʌvᵊnɪˈs/, **governesses.** A **governess** is a woman who is employed by a family to live with them and educate their children. N COUNT

government /ˈgʌvᵊnᵊmᵊᶰt/, **governments.** 1 A **government** is the group of people who are responsible for governing a country or state. EG *The Wilson Government came to power in 1964... The government has had to cut back on public expenditure.* N COLL
2 **Government** is **2.1** the departments, ministries, and committees that carry out the decisions of the political leaders of a country. EG *...a cut in government spending.* **2.2** the activities and methods involved in governing a country or state. EG *Most of his ministers had no previous experience of government... ...the principle of government by the majority.* N UNCOUNT : USU N MOD ; N UNCOUNT

governor /ˈgʌvᵊnə/, **governors.** A **governor** is 1 a person who is responsible for the political administration of a region, especially of a state in the United States of America. EG *...former Governor John Connally of Texas.* 2 a person who is on a committee which controls an institution such as a N COUNT

school or a hospital. EG *...the Board of Governors.* 3 the person who is in charge of the administration of a prison.

gown /gaʊn/, **gowns.** A **gown** is 1 a long dress which women wear on formal occasions. EG *...a wedding gown.* 2 a loose piece of clothing like a long cloak, which is usually black and is worn on formal occasions by people such as judges and lawyers. N COUNT

GP, GPs. A **GP** is a doctor who does not specialize in any particular area of medicine, but who has a medical practice in which he or she treats all types of illness. **GP** is an abbreviation for 'general practitioner'. EG *...the GP's surgery.* N COUNT

grab /græb/, **grabs, grabbing, grabbed.** 1 If you **grab** something, you take it or pick it up suddenly and roughly. EG *She grabbed my arm.* V+O
2 If you **grab** at something, you try to take it or pick it up. EG *She fell on her knees to grab at the money.* ▸ used as a noun. EG *He made a grab for the knife.* V+at ; ▸ N COUNT
3 If you **grab** some food or sleep, you get it quickly, usually because you do not have much time. EG *I'll grab a sandwich before I go.* V+O
4 If you **grab** a chance or opportunity, you take advantage of it eagerly. EG *Why didn't you grab the chance to go to New York?* V+O OR V+at

grace /greɪs/, **graces, gracing, graced.** 1 If you refer to someone's **grace**, you are referring to the smooth, controlled, and attractive way they move. EG *She moved with an extraordinary grace.* N UNCOUNT
2 If you do something unpleasant **with good grace**, you do it without complaining. EG *They accept unhappiness with stoic good grace.* PHRASE
3 If you say that someone **had the grace** to do something, you mean that what they did showed that they were ashamed of something bad that they had done earlier; used showing approval. EG *At least he had the grace to drop his smile and look away from me.* PHRASE
4 If you say that something **graces** a place, you mean that it makes the place more pleasant or attractive. EG *...the plants that grace our conservatories.* V+O Formal
5 If you say that someone important will **grace** an event, you mean that they have kindly agreed to be present at it. EG *He had been invited to grace a function at the college.* V+O Formal
6 You use expressions such as **Your Grace** and **Her Grace** when you are addressing or referring to a duke, duchess, or archbishop. EG *His Grace will receive you now.*

graceful /ˈgreɪsfʊl/. 1 Someone or something that is **graceful** moves in a smooth and controlled way which is attractive to watch. EG *They're very graceful animals.* ◊ **gracefully.** EG *Learn how to move gracefully on a stage.* ADJ QUALIT ◊ ADV
2 Something that is **graceful** is attractive because it has a pleasing shape or style. EG *...graceful curves... ...graceful writing.* ADJ QUALIT
3 If a person's behaviour is **graceful**, it is polite, kind, and pleasant, especially in a difficult situation. EG *She turned with graceful solicitude to Anthea.* ◊ **gracefully.** EG *He accepted gracefully and gratefully.* ADJ QUALIT ◊ ADV

graceless /ˈgreɪslɪˈs/. 1 Something that is **graceless** is unattractive and not very interesting. EG *...a large, graceless industrial city.* ADJ QUALIT
2 If you describe someone as **graceless**, you mean that they behave impolitely. EG *He was so graceless, so eager to shock.* ADJ QUALIT Formal

gracious /ˈgreɪʃəs/. 1 If you say that someone is **gracious**, you mean that they are polite and pleasant, especially in the way that they treat people who have a lower social position than them. ◊ **graciously.** EG *She accepted the tribute graciously.* ADJ QUALIT ◊ ADV Formal
2 You use **gracious** to describe the comfortable ADJ QUALIT : ATTRIB

way of life of wealthy people, especially in former times. EG ...places of recreation and gracious living.

3 People use phrases such as '**Good gracious!**' and '**Goodness gracious!**' to express surprise or annoyance. EG Good gracious! I never knew that... 'You're short of money?' - 'Good gracious no!' EXCLAM Informal Outdated

gradation /grədeɪʃəⁿn/, **gradations.** A **gradation** is a small change, or one of the stages in the process of change. EG ...white bread and wholemeal bread, and many gradations between the two. N COUNT+SUPP

grade /greɪd/, **grades, grading, graded. 1** If you **grade** a number of things, you judge or measure their quality and give each of them a number or name that indicates how good or bad it is. EG The reports are graded 1 to 6. V+O : USU PASS

2 The **grade** of a product is its quality, usually when this has been officially judged or measured. EG ...ordinary grade petrol. N COUNT : OFT+SUPP

3 Your **grade** in an examination or piece of written work is the mark that you get. EG She passed the exams with good grades. N COUNT

4 Your **grade** in a company or organization is your level of importance or your rank. EG ...separate dining rooms for different grades of staff. N COUNT+SUPP

5 A **grade** in an American school is a class or a group of classes in which all the children are of a similar age. EG She had entered the sixth grade at eleven. N COUNT

6 If you **make the grade**, you succeed in something by reaching the standard that is required. EG She couldn't make the grade. PHRASE Informal

graded /greɪdɪⁿd/ is used to describe something that is gradually sloping or changing. EG ...a nicely graded curve. ADJ CLASSIF : ATTRIB

gradient /greɪdɪənt/, **gradients.** A **gradient** is a slope or the degree of steepness of a slope. EG The floor has a minimum gradient of one in five... ...roads with sharp bends and varying gradients. N COUNT

gradual /grædjuⁿəl/. Something that is **gradual** happens over a long period of time rather than suddenly. EG It's a process of gradual development. ADJ QUALIT

◊ **gradually.** EG Things change gradually in engineering. ◊ ADV

graduate, graduates, graduating, graduated; pronounced /grædjuət/ when it is a noun and /grædjueɪt/ when it is a verb.
1 A **graduate** is **1.1** a student who has successfully completed a first degree at a university or college. EG ...a psychology graduate of Stanford University. **1.2** in the United States, a student who has successfully completed high school. N COUNT / N COUNT+SUPP

2 Graduate means the same as postgraduate. EG ...graduate students in the philosophy department. N MOD

3 When a student **graduates**, he or she has successfully completed a degree course at a university or college and receives a certificate that shows this. EG She recently graduated from law school. V : USU+A

4 In the United States, when someone **graduates**, they have successfully completed high school and receive a certificate or diploma that shows this. V : USU+A

5 If you **graduate** from one thing to another, you go from a less important job or position to a more important one. EG Start on a local paper, and then graduate to a provincial paper. V : OFT+from/ to

graduated /grædjueɪtɪⁿd/ is used to describe something that increases by regular amounts or grades. EG ...graduated pensions. ADJ CLASSIF

graduation /grædjueɪʃəⁿn/ is **1** the successful completion of a course of study at a university or college, for which you receive a degree or diploma. EG He should get a good job after graduation. **2** a ceremony at university or college, at which degrees and diplomas are given to students who have successfully completed their studies. EG He had just attended his daughter's graduation. N UNCOUNT

graffiti /grəˈfiːtiⁱ/. **Graffiti** is words or pictures that are written or drawn on walls, signs, and posters in public places. Graffiti is usually rude, N UNCOUNT OR N PLURAL

funny, or contains a political message. EG ...walls covered with graffiti.

graft /grɑːft/, **grafts, grafting, grafted. 1** If you **graft** a part of one plant on to another plant, you join them together so that they will grow together and become one plant. V+O : OFT+onto

2 If you **graft** one idea or system on to another, you try to join one to the other. EG ...modern federal structures grafted on to ancient cultural divisions. V+O : OFT +on/upon

3 If doctors **graft** a piece of healthy skin or bone or a healthy organ to a damaged part of your body, they attach it by a medical operation in order to replace the damaged part. EG ...new veins grafted to his heart. V+O : OFT +to/onto

4 A **graft** is a piece of healthy skin or bone, or a healthy organ, which is attached to a damaged part of your body by a medical operation in order to replace it. EG Laverne had skin grafts on her thighs. N COUNT : OFT+SUPP

5 Graft means hard work. EG ...the hard graft of the working men. N UNCOUNT British

6 Graft is also the act of obtaining money dishonestly by using your position of political power. EG ...graft and corruption. N UNCOUNT

grain /greɪn/, **grains. 1** A **grain** of wheat, rice, or other cereal crop is a seed from it. EG ...no bigger than grains of rice. N PART OR N COUNT

2 Grain is a cereal crop, especially wheat or corn, that has been harvested to be used for food. EG We had surplus grain. N MASS

3 A **grain** of sand or salt is a tiny hard piece of it. N PART

4 A **grain** of a quality is a very small amount of it. EG He did not have a grain of humour... ...a grain of truth. N PART Literary

5 The **grain** of a piece of wood is the natural pattern and direction of lines in its surface. N COUNT

6 If you say that an idea or action **goes against the grain**, you mean that it is very difficult for you to accept it or do it, because it conflicts with your ideas or beliefs. EG However much it goes against the grain, we are compelled to concede that their methods may succeed. PHRASE

grained /greɪnd/ is used after adjectives and adverbs to describe substances that consist of particles of a particular size. EG ...a coarse grained clay. ADJ CLASSIF

grainy /greɪniⁱ/. Something that is **grainy** has a rough surface or texture. EG ...the grainy wood of the table. ADJ CLASSIF : ATTRIB

gram /græm/, **grams;** also spelled **gramme.** A **gram** is a very small unit of weight. One thousand grams are equal to one kilogram. EG ...500 grams of flour. N COUNT OR N PART

grammar /græmə/, **grammars. 1 Grammar** is **1.1** the rules of a language, relating to the way in which you can put words together in order to make sentences. **1.2** the way in which someone either obeys or does not obey the rules of grammar when they write or speak. EG I'm constantly having to correct their grammar. N UNCOUNT

2 A **grammar** is **2.1** a book that describes the rules of a language. EG ...an old French grammar. **2.2** a theory that is intended to explain the rules of a language. EG ...the theory of Case Grammar. N COUNT / N COUNT OR N UNCOUNT

grammar school, grammar schools. A **grammar school** is a school in Britain for children aged between eleven and eighteen who have a high academic ability. N COUNT

grammatical /grəmætɪkəⁿl/. **1 Grammatical** is used to describe something that relates to grammar. EG This sentence is very complex in its grammatical structure. ◊ **grammatically.** EG His English was usually grammatically correct. ADJ CLASSIF : ATTRIB ◊ ADV

2 If someone's language is **grammatical**, it is correct because it obeys the rules of grammar. EG He speaks perfectly grammatical English. ADJ QUALIT

Do grapefruit grow on grapevines?

gramme /græm/. See gram.

gramophone /ˈgræməfəʊn/, **gramophones**. A N COUNT
gramophone is an old-fashioned type of record
player.

gran /græn/, **grans**. Your **gran** is your grand- N COUNT OR
mother. VOCATIVE

granary /ˈgrænəri/, **granaries**. A **granary** is a N COUNT
building in which grain is stored.

grand /grænd/, **grander, grandest. 1** Buildings ADJ QUALIT
that are **grand** are splendid or impressive in size
and appearance. EG ...a grand palace... ...grand
architecture. ◊ **grandly**. EG Its interior is grandly ◊ ADV
elegant.
2 Plans and actions that are **grand** are intended to ADJ QUALIT :
achieve important results. EG ...the grand plot that ATTRIB
you two are hatching.
3 People, jobs, or appearances that are **grand** ADJ QUALIT
seem important or socially superior. EG ...all sorts of
grand people... The job isn't as grand as it sounds.
◊ **grandly**. EG He announced grandly that he 'had ◊ ADV
no time for women.'
4 Grand moments or activities are exciting and ADJ QUALIT :
important. EG Finally, the grand moment comes ATTRIB
when you make your first solo flight.
5 If you describe an experience as **grand**, you ADJ QUALIT
mean that it is very pleasant and enjoyable. EG Informal
We've had some grand times together, haven't we? Outdated
6 A **grand** total is the final amount of something. ADJ CLASSIF :
EG In 1886 Levers, the soap firm, spent a grand total ATTRIB
of 50 pounds on advertising.
7 A **grand** is a thousand dollars or pounds. EG That NUMBER
still leaves you with fifty grand. Informal

grandad /ˈgrændæd/, **grandads**; also spelled N COUNT OR
granddad. Your **grandad** is your grandfather. VOCATIVE

grandchild /ˈgrændtʃaɪld/, **grandchildren** N COUNT
/ˈgrændtʃɪldrən/. Someone's **grandchild** is the
child of their son or daughter.

granddaughter /ˈgrændɔːtə/, **granddaughters**. N COUNT
Someone's **granddaughter** is the daughter of their
son or daughter.

grandeur /ˈgrændʒə/ is **1** the quality in some- N UNCOUNT
thing, for example in a building or in scenery,
which makes it seem impressive and often elegant.
EG ...the grandeur of Lansdowne House. **2** great
importance and social status that a person has. EG
His wealth gave him grandeur.

grandfather /ˈgrændfɑːðə/, **grandfathers**. Your N COUNT
grandfather is the father of your father or mother.

grandfather clock, **grandfather clocks**. A N COUNT
grandfather clock is a clock in a tall wooden case
which stands upright on the floor.

grandiose /ˈgrændɪəʊs/ is used to describe some- ADJ QUALIT
thing which is bigger or more elaborate than
necessary and therefore seems ridiculous. EG
...grandiose architecture... ...grandiose schemes to
recycle everything.

grandma /ˈgrændmɑː/, **grandmas**. Your **grand- N COUNT OR
ma** is your grandmother. VOCATIVE

grandmother /ˈgrændmʌðə/, **grandmothers**. N COUNT
Your **grandmother** is the mother of your father or
mother.

grandpa /ˈgrændpɑː, ˈgræmpɑː/, **grandpas**. Your N COUNT OR
grandpa is your grandfather. VOCATIVE

grandparent /ˈgrændpeərənt/, **grandparents**. N COUNT :
Your **grandparents** are the parents of your father USU PLURAL
or mother.

grand piano, **grand pianos**. A **grand piano** is a N COUNT
large flat piano. See picture at MUSICAL INSTRU-
MENTS.

grandson /ˈgrændsʌn/, **grandsons**. Someone's N COUNT
grandson is the son of their son or daughter.

grandstand /ˈgrændstænd/, **grandstands**. A N COUNT
grandstand is a covered stand with several rows
of seats which provide a good view, for example at
racecourses or football grounds.

granite /ˈgrænɪt/ is a very hard rock which is N UNCOUNT
often used in building.

granny /ˈgræni/, **grannies**; also spelled **grannie**. N COUNT OR
Your **granny** is your grandmother. VOCATIVE

grant /grɑːnt/, **grants, granting, granted. 1** A N COUNT
grant is an amount of money that the government
gives to a person or to an organization for a
particular purpose such as education, welfare, or
home improvements. EG You may be eligible for a
grant to help you study.
2 If someone in authority **grants** you something V+O+O OR
such as a sum of money, they give it to you. EG V+O+to
Proposals have been made to grant each displaced
family £25,000... He was finally granted a visa.
3 If you **take it for granted** that something is true, PHRASE
you believe that it is true without thinking about it
or looking for proof. EG It is taken for granted that
every child should learn mathematics.
4 If you **take** someone **for granted**, you benefit PHRASE
from them without showing that you are grateful.
EG He just takes me absolutely for granted.
5 If you **grant** that something is true, you admit V+REPORT
that it is true. EG That joy ride, I grant you, was a ONLY that
silly stunt. ● You use **granted** or **granting** to say OR V+O
that something is true, before you make a com- ● CONJ
ment about it. EG Granted that he's in hospital, he Formal
can't do us much harm.

granulated /ˈgrænjʊleɪtɪd/. **Granulated** sugar is ADJ CLASSIF :
sugar which is in the form of coarse grains. ATTRIB

granule /ˈgrænjuːl/, **granules**. A **granule** is a N COUNT
small round piece of something. EG ...sea salt sold in
the form of granules.

grape /greɪp/, **grapes**. A **grape** is a small, round N COUNT :
fruit, green or purple in colour, which is eaten raw, USU PLURAL
used for making wine, or dried to make raisins,
sultanas, or currants. EG ...a bunch of grapes.

grapefruit /ˈgreɪpfruːt/, **grapefruits**. **Grapefruit**
can also be used as the plural form.
A **grapefruit** is a large, round, yellow fruit, similar N COUNT OR
to an orange, that has a sharp, sour taste. N UNCOUNT

grapevine /ˈgreɪpvaɪn/, **grapevines. 1** A **grape- N COUNT
vine** is a climbing plant on which grapes grow.
2 If people hear news on the **grapevine**, the news N SING : the+N
is passed from one person to another in casual
conversation. EG She heard something intriguing on
the grapevine.

graph /grɑːf, græf/, **graphs**. A **graph** is a math- N COUNT
ematical diagram, usually a line or curve, which
shows how two or more sets of numbers or measurements are related. EG ...a temperature graph.

graphic /ˈgræfɪk/, **graphics. 1** Descriptions or ADJ QUALIT
accounts that are **graphic** are very clear and
detailed. EG ...his graphic stories of persecution.
◊ **graphically**. EG The cruelty of this is graphically ◊ ADV
described by the old farmer.
2 Something that is **graphic** is concerned with ADJ CLASSIF :
drawing, especially the use of strong lines and ATTRIB
colours. EG ...graphic and industrial design.
3 Graphics are drawings and pictures that are N PLURAL
made using simple lines and sometimes strong
colours. EG ...computer generated graphics.

graphite /ˈgræfaɪt/ is a hard black substance that N UNCOUNT
is a form of carbon. It is used to make the centre
part of pencils.

grapple /ˈgræpəl/, **grapples, grappling, grappled. 1** If you **grapple** with someone, you take V : OFT+with
hold of them and struggle or fight with them. EG We
grappled with him and took the guns from them.
2 If you **grapple** with a problem, you try hard to V+with
solve it. EG I grappled with this moral dilemma.

grasp /grɑːsp/, **grasps, grasping, grasped. 1** If V+O OR V+
you **grasp** something, you take it with your hand for/at
and hold it firmly. EG Edward grasped Castle's arm.
● See also **grasping**.
2 A **grasp** is a firm hold or grip. EG The animal had N SING+SUPP
a powerful grasp.
3 If you **grasp** something complicated, you under- V+O OR
stand it. EG The concepts were difficult to grasp... I V+REPORT
grasped quite soon what was going on.
4 If you have a **grasp** of something, you have an N SING+SUPP

understanding of it. EG *He had a sound grasp of tactics.*

5 If something is **within** your **grasp**, it is likely PHRASE that you will achieve it. EG *A peaceful solution was within his grasp.*

6 If something is **in** your **grasp**, you hold it or PHRASE control it. If something escapes or slips **from** your **grasp**, you no longer hold it or control it. EG *They regretted letting her slip from their grasp.*

grasping /grɑːspɪŋ/. Someone who is **grasping** ADJ QUALIT wants to get as much money as possible; used showing disapproval.

grass /grɑːs/ is a very common plant with narrow N UNCOUNT leaves that forms a layer covering an area of ground. EG *They lay on the grass.*

grasshopper /grɑːshᵒɒpə/, **grasshoppers.** A N COUNT **grasshopper** is an insect which has long back legs and can jump high into the air. Grasshoppers make a high, vibrating sound.

grassland /grɑːsləᵊnd/, **grasslands. Grassland** N UNCOUNT is land which is covered with wild grass.   OR N COUNT

grass roots. The **grass roots** of an organization N PLURAL are the ordinary people in it, rather than its leaders. EG *...to strengthen democracy at the grass roots... ...grass-roots support for the new party.*

grassy /grɑːsiⁱ/. A **grassy** area of land is covered ADJ QUALIT in grass.

grate /greɪt/, **grates, grating, grated. 1** A **grate** N COUNT is a framework of metal bars in a fireplace, which holds the coal or wood. EG *A fire was burning in the grate.*

2 When you **grate** food such as cheese or carrot, V+O you rub it over a metal tool so that it is shredded into very small pieces. EG *...grated lemon peel.*

3 When something **grates** or when you **grate** it, it V-ERG makes a harsh, unpleasant sound because two surfaces are rubbing hard against each other. EG *He could hear her shoes grating on the steps.*

4 If a noise or someone's behaviour **grates** on you, V : OFT+*on* it irritates you. EG *That shrill laugh grated on her mother.*

5 See also **grating.**

grateful /greɪtful/. If you are **grateful** for some- ADJ QUALIT thing that someone has given you or done for you, you have friendly feelings towards them and wish to thank them. EG *I am ever so grateful to you for talking to me... I'd be so grateful if you could do it.*
◊ **gratefully.** EG *He accepted the money grateful-* ◊ ADV *ly.*

grater /greɪtə/, **graters.** A **grater** is a metal tool N COUNT with sharp, raised parts on its surface which is used for grating food.

gratify /grætɪfaɪ/, **gratifies, gratifying, grati- fied. 1** If you **are gratified** by something, it gives V+O you pleasure or satisfaction. EG *He was gratified* Formal *that his guess had been proved right.*
◊ **gratifying.** EG *It was gratifying to see so many* ◊ ADJ QUALIT *people present... It makes a gratifying change.*
◊ **gratification** /grætɪfɪkeɪʃᵊn/. EG *To my im-* ◊ N UNCOUNT *mense gratification, he fell into the trap.*

2 If you **gratify** a desire, you do what is necessary V+O to please the person who has that desire. EG *His* Formal *smallest wish must be gratified... Do gratify our curiosity.* ◊ **gratification.** EG *...action directed* ◊ N UNCOUNT *towards the gratification of desire.*

grating /greɪtɪŋ/, **gratings. 1** A **grating** is a flat N COUNT metal frame with rows of bars across it which is fastened over a window or over a hole in a wall or in the ground.

2 A **grating** sound is harsh and unpleasant. EG *...a* ADJ QUALIT *repulsive woman with a grating voice.*

gratitude /grætɪtjuːd/ is the state of feeling grate- N UNCOUNT ful. EG *People wish to show their gratitude for the help he has given them... I must express my gratitude to the BBC.*

gratuitous /grətjuːɪtəs/. An action that is **gratui-** ADJ QUALIT **tous** is unnecessary, and usually harmful or upset- Formal ting. EG *...gratuitous acts of vandalism.*

◊ **gratuitously.** EG *She had no wish to wound his* ◊ ADV *feelings gratuitously.*

grave /greɪv/, **graves; graver, gravest. 1** A N COUNT **grave** is a place where a dead person is buried. EG *Flowers had been put on the grave.*

2 You can refer to death as the **grave.** EG *He drank* N COUNT *himself into an early grave.*

3 If you say that someone who is dead would **turn** PHRASE **in** their **grave** if something happened, you mean that they would be very shocked or upset if they were alive. EG *Crewe would turn in his grave if that building came down.*

4 A situation or event that is **grave** is very serious ADJ QUALIT and worrying. EG *...grave mistakes... I had the gravest suspicions about the whole enterprise.*
◊ **gravely.** EG *His father was gravely ill.* ◊ ADV

5 A person who is **grave** is quiet and serious. ADJ QUALIT
◊ **gravely.** EG *Roger nodded gravely.* ◊ ADV

gravel /grævᵊl/ consists of very small stones. It is N UNCOUNT often used to make paths. EG *...the sound of his feet on the gravel.*

gravelled /grævᵊld/; spelled **graveled** in Ameri- ADJ CLASSIF can English. A **gravelled** path or road has a surface made of gravel.

gravelly /grævᵊliⁱ/. An area of land that is ADJ QUALIT **gravelly** is covered in small stones.

gravestone /greɪvstəun/, **gravestones.** A **grave-** N COUNT **stone** is a large piece of stone with words carved into it, which is placed by or on a grave.

graveyard /greɪvjɑːd/, **graveyards.** A **grave-** N COUNT **yard** is an area of land, often near a church, where dead people are buried.

gravitate /grævɪteɪt/, **gravitates, gravitating,** V+*towards/to* **gravitated.** If you **gravitate** towards a particular Formal place or activity, you are attracted by it and go to it or get involved in it. EG *The best reporters gravitate towards the centres of power.*

gravitation /grævɪteɪʃᵊn/ is the force which N UNCOUNT causes objects to be attracted towards each other Technical because they have mass. ◊ **gravitational** ◊ ADJ CLASSIF : /grævɪteɪʃᵊnᵊl, -ʃᵊnᵊl/. EG *...the earth's gravitation-* ATTRIB *al force.*

gravity /grævɪtiⁱ/. **1 Gravity** is the force which N UNCOUNT causes things to fall to the ground when you drop them, and to remain on the ground instead of floating in the air.

2 The **gravity** of a situation or event is its extreme N UNCOUNT importance and seriousness. EG *...the gravity of the* +SUPP *threat to shipping.*

gravy /greɪviⁱ/ is a thin savoury sauce that is N UNCOUNT served with meat.

gray /greɪ/. See **grey.**

graze /greɪz/, **grazes, grazing, grazed. 1** When V-ERG OR V+O an animal **grazes** or when someone **grazes** it somewhere, it eats the grass that is growing there. EG *The horses graze peacefully... The people of the town fought for the right to graze cattle on the Common... ...land grazed by sheep and cattle.*

2 If you **graze** a part of your body, you injure the V+O skin by scraping against something. EG *I grazed my legs as he pulled me up.*

3 A **graze** is a small wound caused by scraping N COUNT against something. EG *...cuts and grazes.*

4 If something **grazes** you, it touches you lightly as V+O it passes you. EG *Jones's shot only grazed him.*

grease /griːs/, **greases, greasing, greased. 1** N UNCOUNT **Grease** is **1.1** a thick, oily substance which is put on the moving parts of machines in order to make them work smoothly. **1.2** an oily substance that is produced by your skin. **1.3** animal fat that is produced by cooking meat.

2 If you **grease** something, you put grease or fat on V+O it. EG *Clean and grease the valve thoroughly.*

If you grieve, do you have a grievance?

greaseproof paper /ˈgriːspruːf ˈpeɪpə/ is a kind of N UNCOUNT
paper which does not allow grease to pass through
it and is used especially in cooking.

greasy /ˈgriːsiˈ, -ziˈ/. Something that is **greasy** is ADJ QUALIT
covered with grease or contains a lot of grease. EG
...greasy tools... ...greasy hamburgers.

great /greɪt/, **greater, greatest. 1** You use **great**
to describe something that is **1.1** very large in size. ADJ QUALIT
EG ...a great black cloud of smoke. **1.2** large in ADJ QUALIT
amount or degree. EG There is a great amount of
conflict... He had great difficulty in selling his
house... The heat was so great I took off my
sweater. **1.3** important, famous, or exciting. EG ADJ CLASSIF :
...the great cities of the Rhineland... ...the great USU ATTRIB
issues of the day. ◊ **greatness**. EG ...the greatness ◊ N UNCOUNT
of Germany.
2 A person who is described as **great** is successful, ADJ QUALIT
famous, and respected. EG ...a great actor.
◊ **greatness**. EG ...Boltzmann's greatness as a ◊ N UNCOUNT
physicist.
3 If you say that something is **great**, you mean that ADJ QUALIT
you think it is very good or nice. EG It's a great idea. Informal
▸ used as an exclamation. EG Great! Thanks very ▸ EXCLAM
much.
4 If you feel **great**, you feel very healthy and ADJ PRED
energetic. Informal
5 You also use **great** to emphasize the size or ADV+ADJ, OR
degree of a quality that something has. EG ...a great ADJ QUALIT :
big gaping hole... He was a great friend of Huxley. ATTRIB

great- is used before nouns that refer to relatives, PREFIX
such as 'aunt' or 'grandson', to indicate that a
relative is one generation further away than the
one that the noun refers to. For example, someone's great-aunt is the aunt of their mother or
father, and someone's great-grandson is the grandson of their son or daughter. EG ...our great-great-
grandparents.

greatly /ˈgreɪtliˈ/. You use **greatly** to emphasize ADV
the degree or extent of something. EG I was greatly Formal
influenced by Sullivan... He was not greatly surprised.

greed /griːd/ is an eager desire for more of N UNCOUNT
something such as food, money, or power than it is
necessary or fair for you to have.

greedy /ˈgriːdiˈ/, **greedier, greediest.** Someone ADJ QUALIT
who is **greedy** wants more of something such as
food, money, or power than it is necessary or fair
for them to have. EG People got richer and also
greedier. ◊ **greedily**. EG He slurped the soup ◊ ADV
greedily.

green /griːn/, **greener, greenest; greens. 1** ADJ COLOUR
Something that is **green** is the colour of grass or
leaves. EG She had blonde hair and green eyes.
2 A place that is **green** is covered with grass and ADJ COLOUR
trees and not with buildings; used showing approv-
al.
3 A **green** is **3.1** an area of grass in a town or N COUNT
village. EG ...the village green. **3.2** a smooth, flat
area of grass around a hole on a golf course.
4 You can refer to cooked cabbage as **greens**. N PLURAL
5 If someone is **green** with envy, they are very ADJ PRED
envious indeed. +with
6 If you describe someone as **green**, you mean that ADJ QUALIT
they have had very little experience. EG ...green
recruits, new to the traditions.
7 **Green** is also used of political movements whose ADJ CLASSIF
members are particularly concerned about pro-
tecting the environment.
8 **Greens** are members of green political move- N COUNT :
ments. EG ...the success of the Greens in Germany. USU PLURAL
9 If you say that someone has **green fingers** or, in PHRASE
American English, **a green thumb**, you mean that
they are very good at gardening.
10 If someone in authority gives you a **green light**, PHRASE
they give you permission to do something.

greenery /ˈgriːnəˈriˈ/. Plants or leaves that make N UNCOUNT
a place look attractive are referred to as **greenery**. EG ...the lush greenery of the region.

greengrocer /ˈgriːnɡrəʊsəˈ/, **greengrocers. 1** A N COUNT
greengrocer is a shopkeeper who sells fruit and British
vegetables.
2 You refer to a shop that sells fruit and vegetables N SING : the+N
as the **greengrocer's** or the **greengrocer**.

greenhouse /ˈgriːnhaʊs/, **greenhouses.** A **green-** N COUNT
house is a glass building in which you grow plants
that need to be protected from cold weather, wind,
or frost.

greenish /ˈgriːnɪʃ/ means slightly green in colour. ADJ COLOUR
EG ...a greenish blue.

greet /griːt/, **greets, greeting, greeted. 1** When V+O
you meet someone, you **greet** them by saying
something such as 'Hello' or 'How are you?', as a
way of being friendly.
2 If you **greet** something in a particular way, you V+O : USU+A
express your reaction to it. EG The news will be
greeted with shock and surprise.
3 If something **greets** you, it is the first thing you V+O
notice in a place. EG The smell of coffee greeted us Literary
as we entered.

greeting /ˈgriːtɪŋ/, **greetings.** A **greeting** is N COUNT OR
something that you say or do as a way of express- N UNCOUNT
ing friendliness when you meet someone. EG ...a
friendly greeting... She smiled in greeting.

gregarious /ɡrɪˈɡeəriəs/. Someone who is **gre-** ADJ QUALIT
garious enjoys being with other people. Formal

grenade /ɡrɪˈneɪd/, **grenades.** A **grenade** is a N COUNT
small bomb containing explosive that can be
thrown by hand or fired from a gun.

grew /gruː/ is the past tense of **grow.**

grey /greɪ/, **greyer, greyest; greys, greying;**
spelled **gray** in American English.
1 Something that is **grey** is the colour of ashes or ADJ COLOUR
of clouds on a rainy day. EG ...a grey suit... ...the
grey-haired driver.
2 If someone **is greying** or **is going grey**, their V : ONLY CONT
hair is becoming grey. EG She went grey in about a OR PHRASE
year. ◊ **greying**. EG ...a small, greying man... A ◊ ADJ CLASSIF :
strand of greying hair fell over her eyes. ATTRIB
3 If someone looks **grey**, their face is pale because ADJ QUALIT
they are tired, ill, or worried. ◊ **greyness**. EG ◊ N UNCOUNT
There was an awful greyness about his face.
4 If the weather is **grey**, the sky is very cloudy and ADJ QUALIT
the light is dull. EG ...a grey April afternoon.

grey area, grey areas. A **grey area** is a situa- N COUNT
tion or aspect of something that does not seem to
belong to any particular category, and so people
are not sure how to deal with it.

greyhound /ˈgreɪhaʊnd/, **greyhounds.** A **grey-** N COUNT
hound is a thin dog that can run very fast. Greyhounds sometimes run in races.

greyish /ˈgreɪɪʃ/; spelled **grayish** in American ADJ COLOUR
English. **Greyish** means slightly grey in colour.

grid /grɪd/, **grids.** A **grid** is a pattern or object N COUNT
which consists of straight lines that cross over
each other and form a series of squares. EG ...a grid
of small streets.

grief /griːf/. **1** **Grief** is extreme sadness. EG That N UNCOUNT
helped to ease his grief. Formal
2 If someone or something **comes to grief**, they PHRASE
fail or are harmed. EG I ran away once but came to Formal
grief.
3 Some people say **'Good grief'** to express surprise EXCLAM
or exasperation.

grievance /ˈgriːvəns/, **grievances.** A **grievance** N COUNT OR
is **1** a complaint that you make about something N UNCOUNT
which you feel is unfair. EG They may well have a
genuine grievance. **2** a feeling that something that
has been done is unfair. EG ...my family's grievance
against Mr Geard.

grieve /griːv/, **grieves, grieving, grieved. 1** If V : OFT+for/
you **grieve**, you feel very sad about something that over
has happened. EG She was grieving for the dead Formal
baby.
2 If something **grieves** you, it makes you feel very V+O :
sad. EG It grieves me to say this, but you must leave OFT+to-INF
now. Formal

grievous /griːvəs/. Something that is **grievous** is ADJ QUALIT extremely serious or worrying in its effects. EG ...a grievous mistake. ◊ **grievously.** EG He had been ◊ ADV grievously wounded. Formal

grill /grɪl/, **grills, grilling, grilled. 1** When you V-ERG **grill** food, you cook it using strong heat directly above or below it. ◊ **grilled.** EG ...a grilled chop. ◊ ADJ CLASSIF **2** A **grill** is **2.1** a part of a cooker that consists of a N COUNT metal shelf where food is cooked by strong heat from above. **2.2** a flat frame of metal bars on N COUNT which you cook food over a fire. **2.3** a dish which N COUNT OR consists of food that has been grilled. N UNCOUNT **3** If you **grill** someone about something, you ask V+O them many questions for a long period of time. EG Informal At the police station, she was grilled for twenty-four hours.

grille /grɪl/, **grilles.** A **grille** is a framework of N COUNT metal bars or wire which is placed in front of something such as a window or a piece of machinery, in order to protect it or to protect people. EG ...the protective grille at the back of the set.

grim /grɪm/, **grimmer, grimmest. 1** A situation ADJ QUALIT or piece of information that is **grim** is unpleasant, difficult to accept, and worrying. EG ...the grim facts... ...the grim aftermath of World War I. **2** A place that is **grim** is unattractive and depress- ADJ QUALIT ing in appearance. **3** If someone is **grim**, they are very serious or ADJ QUALIT stern, especially because they are worried or angry about something. EG ...his grim determination not to cry... ...grim-faced guards. ◊ **grimly.** EG ◊ ADV 'Smoke,' Eddie announced grimly.

grimace /ˈɡrɪmeɪs, ɡrɪˈmɑːs/, **grimaces, grimac-** N COUNT **ing, grimaced.** A **grimace** is an expression that you make by twisting your face in an ugly way because you are displeased, disgusted, or in pain. EG Thomas made a little grimace. Perhaps he thought the wine was sour. ▸ used as a verb. EG She made a ▸ V bad gear-change and grimaced.

grime /ɡraɪm/ is dirt which gathers on the surface N UNCOUNT of something. EG The windows were thick with grime.

grimy /ˈɡraɪmiˈ/. Something that is **grimy** is very ADJ QUALIT dirty. EG ...a grimy office.

grin /ɡrɪn/, **grins, grinning, grinned. 1** If you V:OFT+at **grin**, you smile broadly. EG He grinned at her. ▸ used as a noun. EG The pilot was unhurt and ▸ N COUNT climbed out with a cheerful grin. **2** If you **grin and bear it**, you mean PHRASE that you will accept a difficult or unpleasant situa- Informal tion without complaining because there is nothing you can do to make things better. EG I'd just have to grin and bear it for the next two hours.

grind /ɡraɪnd/, **grinds, grinding, ground** /ɡraʊnd/. **1** If you **grind** something such as corn or V+O pepper, you crush it between two hard surfaces or in a machine until it becomes a fine powder. EG ...freshly ground black pepper. **2** If you **grind** something into a surface, you press V+O+A it hard into the surface with small circular or sideways movements. EG He ground his cigarette in the ashtray. **3** If a machine **grinds**, it makes a harsh scraping V noise. EG The lift grinds in the shaft. **4** If something large **grinds to a halt** or **comes to** PHRASE **a grinding halt**, it stops. EG The huge coal cart would grind to a halt at our front door... Why doesn't the whole economy grind to a halt? **5** You can refer to routine work which you have to N SING do and which is tiring or boring as the **grind**. EG They then begin the long and tiresome grind of preparing themselves for college entrance. **6** See also **grinding**.

grind down. If you **grind** someone **down**, you PHRASAL VB: treat them very harshly, with the result that they V+O+ADV do not have the will to resist you. EG See how the working people of Britain are ground down.

grind up. If you **grind** something **up**, you crush it PHRASAL VB: V+O+ADV

until it becomes a fine powder, especially in a machine.

grinder /ˈɡraɪndə/, **grinders.** A **grinder** is a N COUNT machine or device which crushes something into small pieces. EG ...a coffee grinder.

grinding /ˈɡraɪndɪŋ/. You use **grinding** to de- ADJ CLASSIF: scribe a situation that never seems to change or ATTRIB end, and that makes you feel unhappy, tired, or bored. EG ...grinding poverty.

grip /ɡrɪp/, **grips, gripping, gripped. 1** If you V+O **grip** something, you take hold of it with your hand and continue to hold it firmly. EG Lomax gripped the boy's arm. **2** A **grip** is a firm, strong hold on something. EG I N COUNT: tightened my grip on the handrail. USU SING **3** A **grip** on someone or something is power and N SING+SUPP control over them. EG He now took a firm grip on the management side of the newspaper... She felt herself in the grip of a sadness she could not understand. **4** If something **grips** you, **4.1** it suddenly affects V+O:USU PASS you strongly. EG He seemed to be gripped by a powerful desire to laugh. **4.2** it keeps your atten- V+O:USU PASS tion concentrated on it. EG I was really gripped by the first few pages. ◊ **gripping.** EG ...a gripping ◊ ADJ QUALIT film. **5** If tyres or shoes have **grip**, they do not slip. N UNCOUNT **6** A **grip** is also a bag that you use when you are N COUNT travelling. **7 Grip** is also used in these phrases. **7.1** If you **get** PHRASES or **come to grips with** a problem or situation, you consider it seriously, and start taking action to deal with it. EG It's taken us eighteen years to get to grips with our inadequacies. **7.2** If you **get** or **take a grip on** yourself, you make an effort to control yourself. **7.3** If you **are losing** your **grip**, you are becoming less efficient and less confident, and less able to deal with things. EG I could see they thought I was losing my grip.

gripe /ɡraɪp/, **gripes, griping, griped.** If you V:OFT+about **gripe** about something, you keep complaining Informal about it. EG I guess you think I'm just griping because I wasn't elected captain.

grisly /ˈɡrɪzli/. Something that is **grisly** is ex- ADJ QUALIT tremely nasty and horrible. EG ...a grisly experiment.

grist /ɡrɪst/. If you say that something is **grist to** PHRASE **the mill**, you mean that it is something that can be used. EG All this conflict was grist to the mill for the various Left groups.

gristle /ˈɡrɪsəl/ is a tough, rubbery substance N UNCOUNT found in meat. Gristle is unpleasant to eat.

grit /ɡrɪt/, **grits, gritting, gritted. 1 Grit** consists N UNCOUNT of very small pieces of stone. **2** If people **grit** a road, they put grit on it in order V+O to make it less slippery in icy or snowy weather. **3 Grit** is also determination and courage. EG He has N UNCOUNT grit. **4** If you **grit** your **teeth**, **4.1** you press your upper PHRASE and lower teeth tightly together. EG She nodded at me sternly. I gritted my teeth, but she didn't notice my anger. **4.2** you decide to carry on in a difficult situation. EG We must just grit our teeth and carry on.

gritty /ˈɡrɪtiˈ/. **1** Something that is **gritty** is cov- ADJ QUALIT ered with grit or has a texture like grit. EG ...the gritty carpet. **2** Someone who is **gritty** is strong, determined, and ADJ QUALIT courageous. EG ...a gritty upholder of the law.

groan /ɡrəʊn/, **groans, groaning, groaned. 1** If V, V+QUOTE, you **groan**, you make a long, low sound because OR V+O you are in pain or unhappy, or because you disapprove of something. EG 'I'm sick,' he groaned. ▸ used as a noun. EG ...the groans of the wounded... ▸ N COUNT A chorus of groans greeted his joke.

Is a grotto grotty?

2 If something made of wood **groans**, it makes a loud creaking sound. EG *The wind roared, and the trees groaned.* `v`

grocer /grəʊsə/, **grocers**. **1** A **grocer** is a shopkeeper who sells foods such as flour, sugar, and tinned foods. `N COUNT`

2 You refer to a shop where groceries are sold as the **grocer's** or the **grocer**. `N SING : the+N`

grocery /grəʊsə⁰ri¹/, **groceries**. **1** A **grocery** is a grocer's shop. `N COUNT` `American`

2 Groceries are foods such as flour, sugar, and tinned foods. EG *...a shopping-basket containing groceries.* `N PLURAL`

groggy /grɒgi¹/. If you feel **groggy**, you feel weak and ill. EG *I expect you're feeling a bit groggy with the injections.* `ADJ QUALIT` `Informal`

groin /grɔɪn/, **groins**. Your **groin** is the part of your body where your legs meet. `N COUNT`

groom /gru⁴m/, **grooms**, **grooming**, **groomed**. **1** A **groom** is **1.1** a person whose job is to look after the horses in a stable. **1.2** the same as a bridegroom. EG *The wedding feast went on until midnight but the bride and groom left before that.* `N COUNT`

2 If you **groom** an animal, you clean its fur, usually by brushing it. `v+o`

3 If you **groom** a person for a special job, you prepare them for it by teaching them the skills they will need. EG *I had been chosen to be groomed as editor.* `v+o : OFT+ for/as`

groomed /gru:md/. Someone who is well **groomed** is clean and smart in appearance. `ADJ QUALIT : USU WITH ADV`

groove /gru:v/, **grooves**. A **groove** is a deep line cut into a surface. EG *...a steel plate with grooves cut in it.* ◊ **grooved** /gru:vd/. EG *...the grooved rock.* `N COUNT` ◊ `ADJ QUALIT`

grope /grəʊp/, **gropes**, **groping**, **groped**. **1** If you **grope** for something that you cannot see, you try to find it by moving your hands around in order to feel it. EG *I groped for the timetable I had in my pocket.* `v : OFT+ for`

2 If you **grope** your way to a place, you move there holding your hands in front of you and feeling the way because you cannot see anything. EG *I groped my way out of bed and downstairs.* `v+o+A OR V+A`

3 If you **grope** for something such as the solution to a problem, you try to think of it, when you have no real idea what it could be. EG *We are groping for ways to get the communities together... 'I mean...' She groped for words.* `v : OFT+ for`

gross /grəʊs/, **grosser**, **grossest**; **grosses**, **grossing**, **grossed**. **1** You use **gross** to describe something unacceptable or unpleasant that is very great in amount or degree. EG *...children whose parents are guilty of gross neglect... ...gross inequalities in wealth, power and privilege.* `ADJ CLASSIF : ATTRIB`

◊ **grossly**. EG *...grossly unfair social conditions... They were both grossly overweight.* ◊ `ADV : OFT+ ADJ`

2 Speech or behaviour that is **gross** shows lack of taste, or is very rude. EG *He felt he had said something gross, indecent.* `ADJ QUALIT`

3 Something that is **gross** is very large and ugly. EG *...the gross architecture of the Piccadilly frontages.* `ADJ QUALIT`

4 Gross is also used to describe **4.1** someone's total earnings, before any necessary deductions are made. EG *His gross income will very likely exceed $900,000 this year.* **4.2** the total amount of something, after all the relevant amounts have been added together. EG *...the gross national product.* **4.3** the total weight of something, including its container or wrapping. EG *...8,000 merchant ships with a gross tonnage of 20 million.* `ADJ CLASSIF : ATTRIB OR ADV` `ADJ CLASSIF : ATTRIB` `ADJ CLASSIF : ATTRIB OR ADV`

5 If you **gross** an amount of money, you earn that amount money in total. EG *The film grossed a quarter of a billion dollars in America.* `v+o` `Formal`

6 A **gross** is a group of 144 things. The plural is also **gross**. EG *He bought them by the gross.* `N COUNT`

grotesque /grəʊtesk/. Something that is **grotesque** is **1** very exaggerated so that it is ridiculous or frightening. EG *...grotesque comedy.* `ADJ QUALIT`

◊ **grotesquely**. EG *I knew I had been perfectly ridiculous, over-acting grotesquely.* **2** very ugly in appearance. EG *...grotesque figures carved into the stonework.* ◊ `ADV` `ADJ QUALIT`

grotto /grɒtəʊ/, **grottoes** or **grottos**. A **grotto** is a small attractive cave. `N COUNT`

grotty /grɒti¹/. Something that is **grotty** is unpleasant or of poor quality. EG *...a grotty little building.* `ADJ QUALIT` `Informal`

grouchy /graʊtʃi¹/. Someone who is **grouchy** is bad-tempered and complains a lot. `ADJ QUALIT` `Informal`

ground /graʊnd/, **grounds**, **grounding**, **grounded**. **1** The **ground** is the surface of the earth. EG *He set down his bundle carefully on the ground... He keeled over unconscious and fell to the ground.* `N SING : the+N`

2 Ground is land. EG *...a rocky piece of ground... They spend their lives below ground.* `N UNCOUNT`

3 A **ground** is **3.1** an area of land or sea which is used for a particular purpose. EG *...a burial ground... ...fishing grounds.* **3.2** an area of land where sport is played. EG *...football grounds.* `N COUNT+SUPP`

4 The **grounds** of a building are the land which surrounds it and which is owned by the same people. EG *...the school grounds.* `N PLURAL : USU+SUPP`

5 A particular type of **ground** is **5.1** a place or situation in which ideas, attitudes, or organizations can develop. EG *Britain is not fertile ground for news magazines.* **5.2** a subject or range of subjects. EG *This course covers the same ground as the undergraduate degree in Social Administration.* `N COUNT OR N UNCOUNT +SUPP` `N UNCOUNT +SUPP`

6 Something that is **grounds** or a **ground** for something else is a reason or justification for it. EG *You have no real grounds for complaint... Adultery was a ground for divorce.* ● You can use on **grounds of**, **on the grounds of**, and on the **grounds that** to introduce the reason for a particular action. EG *He was always declining their invitations on grounds of ill health... She was prohibited from speaking on the grounds that it would stir up trouble.* `N COUNT OR N UNCOUNT +SUPP` `Formal` ● `PHRASE`

7 If you gain **ground**, you make progress or get an advantage. EG *Godley's views are gaining political ground... He tried to regain lost ground.* `N UNCOUNT`

8 If aircraft or pilots **are grounded**, they have to remain on the ground. `v+o`

9 If an argument or opinion **is grounded** in or on something, it is based on that thing or results from it. EG *...a delusion grounded in fear.* `v+o : OFT+ in/ on`

10 Ground is also the past tense and past participle of **grind**.

11 Ground is also used in these phrases. **11.1** If you **go to ground**, you hide somewhere for a period of time. EG *All the people involved have gone to ground in cheap hotels.* **11.2** If you **run** someone or something **to ground**, you find them after a long and difficult search. EG *It was run to ground in the nearby woods.* **11.3** If you **break fresh ground** or **break new ground**, you make a new discovery or start a new activity. **11.4** If you **get** something **off the ground**, you get it started. EG *There was a hurry to get the new film off the ground.* **11.5** If you **stand** your **ground** or **hold** your **ground**, you do not retreat or give in when people are opposing you; used showing approval. EG *Laing held his ground. 'We seek only to reverse the discrimination which already exists.'* **11.6** If you **cut** or **dig the ground from under** someone's **feet**, you do something that destroys their chance of success. `PHRASES`

12 to **have** your **ear to the ground**: see **ear**. ● **thin on the ground**: see **thin**. ● See also **home ground**.

ground floor. The **ground floor** of a building is the floor that is level with the ground outside. EG *There's a bathroom on the ground floor.* `N SING` `British`

grounding /graʊndɪŋ/. A **grounding** in a subject is a course of instruction in the basic facts or principles of the subject. EG *Schools must provide a* `N SING : OFT+ in` *firm grounding in the basics, reading, writing, arithmetic.*

groundless /graʊndlɪ²s/. A fear, suspicion, or ADJ QUALIT claim that is **groundless** is not based on reason or Formal evidence. EG *Your fears are groundless... His allegations, when investigated, prove groundless.*

ground level is used to refer to the ground or to N UNCOUNT the floor of a building which is at the same level as the ground. EG *...an explosion at ground level.*

ground rules. The **ground rules** for something N PLURAL are the basic principles on which future action will be based. EG *They sat down to work out the ground rules for the project.*

groundsheet /graʊndʃiːt/, **groundsheets.** A N COUNT **groundsheet** is a piece of waterproof material which you put on the ground to sleep on when you are camping.

groundsman /graʊndzmən/, **groundsmen.** A N COUNT **groundsman** is a person whose job is to look after a park or sports ground.

groundswell /graʊndswɛl/. A **groundswell** is N SING+SUPP the rapid growth of a feeling or opinion about something in a society or group of people. EG *There was a groundswell of outrage against him.*

groundwork /graʊndwɜːk/ is early work on N SING something which forms the basis for further work or study. EG *The previous president had already provided the groundwork for economic progress.*

group /gruːp/, **groups, grouping, grouped.** 1 A **group** is 1.1 a number of people or things which N COLL are together in one place at one time. EG *...a small* OR N PART *group of boys... ...a group of buildings... They were all standing in a group in the centre of the room.* 1.2 a set of people or things which have something N COLL+SUPP in common. EG *children of his age group... We feel it's wrong for one group of people to take land from another... A parents' action group has accused the local authority of breaking the law.* 1.3 a N COUNT number of musicians who perform pop music together. EG *...a pop group.* 1.4 See also **pressure group.**

2 When you **group** a number of things or people V-ERG : USU+A together or when they **group** together, they all come together in one place or within one organization. EG *They encouraged workers and consumers to group together... Occupations are grouped into separate categories.*

grouping /gruːpɪŋ/, **groupings.** A **grouping** is a N COUNT+SUPP set of people or things which have something in common. EG *Lawyers and government officials were the largest groupings.*

grouse /graʊs/, **grouses, grousing, groused. Grouse** is both the singular and the plural form of the noun.

1 A **grouse** is a small fat bird. Grouse are often N COUNT shot for sport and can be eaten.

2 If you **grouse**, you complain. EG *It was a sad end* V OR V+QUOTE *to her career but she never grumbled or groused.*

grove /grəʊv/, **groves.** A **grove** is a group of trees N COUNT that are close together. EG *...an olive grove.*

grovel /grɒvə²l/, **grovels, grovelling, grovelled;** spelled **groveling** and **groveled** in American English.

If you **grovel**, 1 you behave very humbly towards V someone, for example because they are important or because you are frightened of them; used showing disapproval. ◊ **grovelling.** EG *He sent a letter* ◊ ADJ QUALIT *of grovelling apology to the publisher.* 2 you crawl V+A on the floor, for example in order to find something. EG *He was grovelling under his desk for a dropped pencil.*

grow /grəʊ/, **grows, growing, grew** /gruː/, **grown.** 1 When people, animals, or plants **grow**, V : USU+A they increase in size. EG *Babies who are small at birth grow faster... ...fast-growing weeds.*

2 If a plant or tree **grows** in a particular place, it is V : USU+A alive there. EG *An oak tree grew at the edge of the lane... ...an old brick wall with things growing up it.*

3 When you **grow** plants, you put seeds or young V+O

plants in the ground and look after them as they develop. EG *The district grew peas on a large scale.* ◊ **grower, growers.** EG *My father was a great rose* ◊ N COUNT *grower.* +SUPP

4 If a man **grows** a beard or a moustache, he V+O allows the beard or moustache to develop by not shaving.

5 If someone or something **grows** into a particular V+C, V+to-INF, state or condition, they change gradually until they OR V+A are in that state or condition. EG *The sun grew so hot that they were forced to stop working... I grew to dislike working for the cinema.*

6 If an idea, feeling, amount, or problem **grows**, it V gradually becomes stronger or greater. EG *There is a growing awareness of the difficulties... Jobs in industry will grow by 11 per cent... Refugees were posing a growing problem.*

7 If one idea, plan, or policy **grows** out of another, V : OFT+out it develops from it. EG *Out of this would grow a* of/from *broad socialist programme.*

8 If a place or organization **grows**, it increases in V size, wealth, or importance. EG *...the fast-growing New York investment bank.*

9 See also **grown.**

grow apart. If people **grow apart**, they gradual- PHRASAL VB : ly start to have different interests and opinions V+ADV from each other.

grow into. When children **grow into** a piece of PHRASAL VB : clothing that is too big for them, they become V+PREP bigger so that it fits them properly.

grow on. If someone or something **grows on** PHRASAL VB : you, you start to like them more and more. EG *She* V+PREP *was someone whose charm grew very slowly on* Informal *you.*

grow out of. 1 If you **grow out of** a type of PHRASAL VB : behaviour or an interest, you stop behaving in that V+ADV+PREP way or having that interest. EG *I've rather grown out of my taste for the bizarre.* 2 If a child **grows** V+ADV+PREP **out of** a piece of clothing, they become so big that it no longer fits them properly.

grow up. 1 When someone **grows up**, they PHRASAL VB : gradually change from being a child into being an V+ADV adult. EG *They grew up in the early days of television.* 2 If something **grows up**, it starts to exist and V+ADV becomes stronger. EG *The idea has grown up that science cannot be wrong.* 3 If you tell someone to V+ADV **grow up**, you are telling them to stop being silly or childish. 4 See also **grown-up.**

growl /graʊl/, **growls, growling, growled.** 1 V When a dog or other animal **growls**, it makes a low rumbling noise, usually because it is angry. EG *The dog growled at me.* ▶ used as a noun. EG *He did* ▶ N COUNT *not hear the growl of the leopard.*

2 If someone **growls** something, they say it in a V+O, V+ low, rough, and rather angry voice. EG *'There's a* QUOTE, OR V *visitor here,' he growled.* ▶ used as a noun. EG ▶ N COUNT *'Yeah,' said John in a low growl.*

3 If something **growls**, it makes a deep rumbling V noise. EG *The thunder still growled in the distance.* Literary ▶ used as a noun. EG *The engine's pitch changed* ▶ N COUNT *from a low murmur to an urgent growl.*

grown /grəʊn/. A **grown** man or woman is a ADJ CLASSIF : physically and mentally mature adult. EG *It re-* ATTRIB *quires a child's spontaneity and a grown man's decisiveness.* ● See also **grow.**

grown-up, grown-ups. 1 A **grown-up** is the same N COUNT as an adult; used especially by children. EG *Until the* Informal *grown-ups come to fetch us we'll have fun.*

2 If you say that someone is **grown-up**, you mean 2.1 that they are physically and mentally mature. ADJ CLASSIF EG *...older couples with grown-up children.* 2.2 that ADJ QUALIT they behave in an adult way, especially when they are in fact still a child. EG *Your brother's awfully grown-up for his age.*

Which words on these pages can you use to talk about people complaining or being angry?

growth /grəʊθ/, **growths.** 1 The **growth** of something such as an industry or organization is its development in size, wealth, or importance. EG *Its economic growth rate is second only to Japan's... ...the growth of political opposition... Computing remains a growth area.* N UNCOUNT: USU+SUPP

2 A **growth** in an amount of something is an increase in it. EG *...India's population growth... ...a growth in research expenditure.* N UNCOUNT +SUPP

3 **Growth** in a person, animal, or plant is the process of increasing in size and development. EG *He noticed that this drug seemed to inhibit bacterial growth.* N UNCOUNT: USU+SUPP

4 A **growth** is an abnormal lump that grows inside or on a person, animal, or plant. EG *...an ache where a growth was removed.* N COUNT

grub /grʌb/, **grubs, grubbing, grubbed.** 1 A **grub** is a young insect which has just come out of an egg and looks like a short fat worm. N COUNT

2 **Grub** is food. EG *It sounds fun. Can I come? I'll bring my own grub.* N UNCOUNT Informal

3 If you **grub** about for something, you search for it by moving things or digging. EG *The fish grubs around on the river bed.* V :OFT+ about/around

grubby /grʌbi¹/, **grubbier, grubbiest.** A person or object that is **grubby** is rather dirty. EG *...grubby clothes... ...their grubby hands.* ADJ QUALIT

grudge /grʌdʒ/, **grudges, grudging, grudged.** 1 If you have a **grudge** against someone, you have unfriendly feelings towards them because they have upset you or harmed you in the past. EG *They had to do it, and I bear them no grudge... It isn't in her nature to hold grudges.* N COUNT: OFT+against

2 If you **grudge** someone something, you give it to them very unwillingly or you are displeased that they have it. EG *We need not grudge them their mindless pleasures... Not that I grudge the use of my kitchen to you.* V+O+O OR V+O+to

grudging /grʌdʒɪŋ/. A **grudging** feeling or action is one that you feel or do very unwillingly. EG *Others stood watching with grudging respect.* ADJ QUALIT

◊ **grudgingly.** EG *'Okay,' he said grudgingly, 'I suppose I was to blame.'* ◊ ADV

gruel /gruəl/ is a cheap food made by boiling oats with water or milk. N UNCOUNT

gruelling /gruəlɪŋ/; spelled **grueling** in American English. Something that is **gruelling** is extremely difficult and tiring. EG *I was exhausted after a gruelling week.* ADJ QUALIT

gruesome /gruːsəm/. Something that is **gruesome** involves death or injury and is very unpleasant and shocking. EG *...gruesome tales of child murder.* ADJ QUALIT

gruff /grʌf/. If someone's voice is **gruff**, they speak in a low, rough, unfriendly voice. EG *He hid his feelings behind a kind of gruff abruptness.* ADJ QUALIT

◊ **gruffly.** EG *She said gruffly, 'Put on your clothes.'* ◊ ADV

grumble /grʌmbə¹l/, **grumbles, grumbling, grumbled.** If you **grumble**, you complain about something, usually in a low voice and not forcefully. EG *They will grumble about having to do the work... 'It's awful,' Posy grumbled.* ▸ used as a noun. EG *There were angry grumbles from the British ranks.* ◊ **grumbling.** EG *There was more grumbling at the Cabinet's decision.* V, V+about, OR V+QUOTE ▸ N COUNT ◊ N UNCOUNT

grumpy /grʌmpi¹/. Someone who is **grumpy** is bad-tempered and rather miserable. EG *Don't be so grumpy and cynical about it.* ADJ QUALIT

grunt /grʌnt/, **grunts, grunting, grunted.** 1 If you **grunt**, you make a low rough noise, usually because you are uninterested or disapproving. EG *His father looked up and grunted, then went back to his work.* ▸ used as a noun. EG *He gave a sceptical grunt.* V, V+QUOTE, OR V+O ▸ N COUNT

2 When a pig **grunts**, it makes a low rough noise. ▸ used as a noun. EG *It sounded like a pig's grunt.* V ▸ N COUNT

guarantee /gærənti¹/, **guarantees, guaranteeing, guaranteed.** 1 If something **guarantees** something else, it is certain to cause that thing to V+O

happen. EG *Equality does not guarantee happiness in love... This method guarantees success.*

2 If you **guarantee** something, you promise that it will definitely happen, or that you will do or provide it. EG *I'm not guaranteeing that this will work... They guarantee to hold interest rates down until next year... Advertisers were guaranteed a weekly circulation of 250,000.* V+O :OFT+ REPORT OR to-INF; ALSO V+ O+O

3 If you say that you **guarantee** that something will happen, or that it **is guaranteed** to happen, you mean that you are certain that it will happen. EG *You should have one evening off a week, but you can't guarantee it... This state of affairs is guaranteed to continue indefinitely.* V+REPORT: ONLY that, V+O, OR V-PASS+to-INF

4 Something that is a **guarantee** of something else makes it certain that it will happen or that it is true. EG *There is no guarantee that they are telling the truth... The jury system is one of the guarantees of democracy.* N COUNT: USU+REPORT OR of

5 A **guarantee** is also 5.1 a promise that something will definitely happen. EG *We want some guarantee that an enquiry will be held... They gave guarantees of full employment.* 5.2 a written promise by a company that if their product or work has any faults within a particular time, it will be repaired or replaced free of charge. EG *How long does the guarantee last?* N COUNT: USU+REPORT OR of N COUNT

6 If a company **guarantees** their product or work, they give a written promise that if it has any faults within a particular time it will be repaired or replaced free of charge. V+O

guard /gɑːd/, **guards, guarding, guarded.** 1 If you **guard** a place, person, or object, you watch and protect them. EG *Scotland Yard sent an officer to guard his house.* V+O

2 If you **guard** someone, you watch them to stop them from escaping. EG *She had been locked in her room and was guarded night and day.* V+O

3 A **guard** is 3.1 a person who is guarding a person, place, or object. 3.2 an organized group of soldiers or policemen that protect or watch someone or something. EG *They will give him an armed guard.* 3.3 a railway official on a train. N COUNT N COLL N COUNT

4 If you **guard** something important or secret, you protect or hide it. EG *The contents of the lists were a closely guarded secret.* V+O

5 A **guard** is also a device which covers a dangerous part of something. EG *When the guard is taken off the motor the machine can't start.* N COUNT

6 **Guard** is also used in these phrases. 6.1 If you **stand guard**, you stand near a person or place and watch or protect them. EG *You will be expected to stand guard over the village.* 6.2 Someone who is **on guard** is on duty and responsible for guarding a particular place or person. 6.3 If you are **on your guard**, you are being very careful because you think a situation might become difficult or dangerous. EG *Busy parents have to be on their guard against being bad-tempered with their children.* 6.4 If you **catch** someone **off guard**, you surprise them by doing something when they are not expecting it. EG *I didn't want to be caught off guard in the middle of the night.* PHRASES

guard against. If you **guard against** something, you are careful to avoid it happening, or to avoid being affected by it. EG *...ideas which the trained mind of a judge knows to guard against.* PHRASAL VB: V+PREP, HAS PASS

guarded /gɑːdɪ¹d/. Someone who is **guarded** is careful not to show their feelings or give away information about something. EG *The play got very guarded reviews.* ◊ **guardedly.** EG *'Do you ever hear from your sister?' - 'Sometimes,' Rudolph said guardedly.* ADJ QUALIT ◊ ADV

guardian /gɑːdɪən/, **guardians.** A **guardian** is 1 someone who has been legally appointed to look after a child, usually when the child's parents have died. EG *He became the legal guardian of his brother's daughter.* 2 someone who is considered to N COUNT: OFT+POSS protect or defend a person or thing. EG *...guardians of morality.*

guerrilla /gərɪlə/, **guerrillas**; also spelled **gue-** N COUNT **rilla**. A **guerrilla** is a person who fights as part of an unofficial army. EG *...guerilla attacks.*

guess /gɛs/, **guesses**, **guessing**, **guessed**. 1 If V·SPEECH, you **guess** something, 1.1 you give an answer or an V+at, OR V opinion about something when you do not know whether it is correct. EG *She guessed that she was fifty yards from shore... We can only guess at the number of deaths it has caused.* 1.2 you give the V OR V+O correct answer to a problem or question when you did not know it for certain. EG *How did you guess?... I had guessed the identity of her lover.*

2 A **guess** is an attempt to give the right answer to N COUNT something when you do not know it. EG *I don't know the name but I'll take a guess at it... I'll give you two guesses.*

3 You say **I guess** 3.1 to indicate that you think PHRASE that something is true or likely. EG *I guess I got the* Informal *news a day late... 'What's that?' – 'Some sort of* American *blackbird, I guess.'... 'Sure?' – 'I guess so.'* 3.2 to Informal indicate what you are thinking, especially when American you have made a decision. EG *I guess I won't wake him up yet.*

4 If you **keep** someone **guessing**, you do not tell PHRASE them what they want to know. EG *'Have you told them where you are living?' – 'Not yet. Let's keep them guessing a while longer.'*

5 You say **'guess what'** to draw attention to CONVENTION something exciting, surprising, or interesting that Informal you are about to tell someone. EG *Guess what, you're going to be a granny!*

6 If you say that something is **anyone's guess** or PHRASE **anybody's guess**, you mean that nobody can be Informal certain about what is really the case. EG *What would have happened is anyone's guess.*

guesswork /gɛswɜːk/ is the process or result of N UNCOUNT trying to guess something without knowing all the facts. EG *This is pure guesswork at this stage.*

guest /gɛst/, **guests**. A **guest** is 1 someone who is N COUNT staying in your home or is at an occasion because you have invited them. EG *...wedding guests.* 2 someone who is staying in a hotel. 3 someone who visits a place or appears on a radio or television show because they have been invited. EG *We're here as guests of the National Theatre.*

guest house, **guest houses**. A **guest house** is a N COUNT small hotel.

guest of honour, **guests of honour**; spelled **guest of honor** in American English. The **guest of honour** is the most important guest N COUNT at a dinner or other social occasion.

guest-room, **guest-rooms**. A **guest-room** is a N COUNT bedroom in someone's house for visitors to sleep in.

guffaw /gəfɔː/, **guffaws**, **guffawing**, **guffawed**. N COUNT A **guffaw** is a very loud laugh. EG *Martin let out a delighted guffaw.* ► used as a verb. EG *He guffawed* ► V *and thumped his friend on the shoulder.*

guidance /gaɪdəns/ is help and advice. EG *We* N UNCOUNT *would appreciate guidance from an expert in this field.*

guide /gaɪd/, **guides**, **guiding**, **guided**. 1 A **guide** is 1.1 someone who shows places such as cities or N COUNT museums to tourists. 1.2 someone who shows N COUNT people the way to a place in a difficult or danger-ous region. 1.3 the same as a guidebook. EG *...a* N COUNT *guide to New York City.* 1.4 a book which gives N COUNT you information or instructions to help you do or understand something. EG *This book is meant to be a practical guide to healthy living.* 1.5 something N SING : a + N that can be used to help you plan your actions. EG *As a rough guide, 1 cubic foot stores 25lb frozen food.*

2 A **guide** or a **girl guide** is a girl who belongs to N COUNT the Girl Guides Association, an organization which British encourages girls to become disciplined and to learn practical skills.

3 If you **guide** someone round a city, museum, or V+O:USU+A building, you show it to them and explain points of interest. ◊ **guided**. EG *We went on a guided tour of* ◊ ADJ CLASSIF : *Paris.* ATTRIB

4 To **guide** someone or something means to cause V+O them to move in the right direction. EG *He took Julie's arm and guided her through the doorway... Men crossing the ocean would use the stars to guide them.*

5 If you **guide** someone, you influence their actions V+O or decisions. EG *Politicians will in the end always be guided by changes in public opinion.* ◊ **guiding**. EG ◊ ADJ CLASSIF : *The guiding principle of the family was Catholi-* ATTRIB *cism.*

guidebook /gaɪdbʊk/, **guidebooks**. A **guidebook** N COUNT is a book which gives information for tourists about a town, area, or country.

guideline /gaɪdlaɪn/, **guidelines**. A **guideline** is N COUNT : a piece of advice about how to do something. EG USU PLURAL *...government pay guidelines... ...guidelines for the control of dogs in public places.*

guild /gɪld/, **guilds**. A **guild** is an organization of N COUNT people who do the same job or share an interest. Formal

guile /gaɪl/ is the quality of being very cunning N UNCOUNT and good at deceiving people. Literary

guillotine /gɪlətiːn/, **guillotines**. A **guillotine** is N COUNT 1 a device consisting of a blade in a large frame which was used to execute people, especially in France in the past. 2 a device used for cutting and trimming paper.

guilt /gɪlt/ is 1 an unhappy feeling that you have N UNCOUNT because you believe that you have done something wrong. EG *I had agonizing feelings of shame and guilt.* 2 the fact that you have done something wrong or have broken a law. EG *He at last made a public admission of his guilt.*

guiltless /gɪltlɪs/. If someone is **guiltless**, they ADJ CLASSIF have not done anything wrong. EG *Nor were gov-* Formal *ernments guiltless in this matter.*

guilty /gɪltiˈ/. 1 If you feel **guilty**, you feel unhap- ADJ QUALIT py because you believe that you have done some-thing wrong. EG *They feel guilty about seeing her so little.* ◊ **guiltily**. EG *I blushed and looked away* ◊ ADV *guiltily.*

2 You use **guilty** to describe an action or fact that ADJ CLASSIF you feel guilty about. EG *...a guilty secret.* ATTRIB

3 If you have a **guilty conscience**, you feel guilty PHRASE about something that you have done. EG *Some children get a guilty conscience about not learning enough.*

4 If someone is **guilty**, 4.1 it is officially stated that ADJ CLASSIF they have committed a crime or offence. EG *He was* OFT+of *found guilty of passing on secret papers to a foreign power.* 4.2 they have done something wrong. EG *He was guilty of an important misjudg-ment.*

guinea /gɪniˈ/, **guineas**. A **guinea** is an old Brit- N COUNT ish unit of money that was worth 21 shillings.

guinea pig, **guinea pigs**. A **guinea pig** is 1 a N COUNT small furry animal without a tail. Guinea pigs are often kept as pets. 2 a person that is used in an experiment. EG *...experimentation on human guinea pigs.*

guise /gaɪz/, **guises**. You use **guise** to refer to the N COUNT+SUPP outward appearance or form of something. EG *They will form new political groupings, or old ones in new guises... A lot of nonsense was talked, under the guise of philosophy.*

guitar /gɪtɑː/, **guitars**. A **guitar** is a wooden N COUNT musical instrument with six strings. You play the guitar by plucking or strumming the strings. See picture at MUSICAL INSTRUMENTS.

guitarist /gɪtɑːrɪst/, **guitarists**. A **guitarist** is N COUNT someone who plays the guitar.

Would you see a gymnast at a gymkhana?

gulf /gʌlf/, **gulfs.** A gulf is 1 an important or significant difference between two people, things, or groups. EG *The gulf between the cultures was too great to be easily bridged.* 2 a large area of sea which extends a long way into the surrounding land. EG *...the Gulf of Mexico.*   N COUNT : OFT+*between*   N COUNT

gull /gʌl/, **gulls.** A gull is a common sea bird.   N COUNT

gullet /gʌlɪʔt/, **gullets.** Your gullet is the tube which goes from your mouth to your stomach.   N COUNT

gullible /gʌləbəˀl/. Someone who is gullible is easily tricked because they are too trusting.   ADJ QUALIT

gully /gʌliˀ/, **gullies.** A gully is a long narrow valley with steep sides.   N COUNT

gulp /gʌlp/, **gulps, gulping, gulped.** 1 If you gulp something, you drink or eat it very fast by swallowing large quantities of it at once. EG *She gulped her coffee.* ▸ used as a noun. EG *She took a gulp of whisky... He finished his drink in one gulp.* 2 If you gulp, you swallow air, because you are nervous. ▸ used as a noun. EG *I gave a little gulp.*   V+O   ▸ N COUNT   V   ▸ N COUNT

gulp down. If you gulp something down, you quickly drink or eat it all by swallowing large quantities of it at a time. EG *The old man gulped down his coffee.*   PHRASAL VB : V+O+ADV

gum /gʌm/, **gums, gumming, gummed.** 1 Gum is 1.1 a kind of sweet which you chew for a long time but do not swallow. 1.2 a type of glue that you use to stick paper together. 2 If you gum something to something else, you stick it to something else. EG *...false eyelashes gummed together by lumps of mascara.* 3 Your gums are the areas of firm, pink flesh inside your mouth, above your top teeth and below your bottom teeth.   N UNCOUNT   V+O+A   N COUNT : USU PLURAL

gumboot /gʌmbuːt/, **gumboots.** Gumboots are long rubber boots which you wear to keep your feet dry.   N COUNT : USU PLURAL

gun /gʌn/, **guns, gunning, gunned.** 1 A gun is a weapon consisting mainly of a metal tube from which bullets are fired. 2 If you jump the gun, you do something before the proper time. EG *Newspapers began to jump the gun and talk about resignations.* 3 If you stick to your guns, you continue to have your own opinion about something even though other people tell you that you are wrong. EG *People who lean towards strictness should stick to their guns and raise their children that way.*   N COUNT   PHRASE Informal   PHRASE Informal

gun down. If you gun someone down, you shoot them and injure them severely or kill them.   PHRASAL VB : V+O+ADV

gunboat /gʌnbəʊt/, **gunboats.** A gunboat is a small ship which has several large guns fixed on it.   N COUNT

gunfire /gʌnfaɪə/ is the repeated shooting of guns, especially in a battle. EG *...listening for the bursts of gunfire.*   N UNCOUNT

gunge /gʌndʒ/ is a soft or sticky mass of something. EG *It's solidifying into a sort of brown gunge.*   N UNCOUNT Informal

gunman /gʌnmᵊn/, **gunmen.** A gunman is someone who uses a gun to commit a crime.   N COUNT

gunner /gʌnə/, **gunners.** A gunner is a member of the armed forces who is trained to use guns.   N COUNT

gunpoint /gʌnpɔɪnt/. If someone does something to you at gunpoint, they are threatening to shoot you if you do not obey them. EG *He held the three men at gunpoint.*   PHRASE

gunpowder /gʌnpaʊdə/ is an explosive substance.   N UNCOUNT

gunshot /gʌnʃɒt/, **gunshots.** A gunshot is the firing of a gun. EG *...the sound of gunshots.*   N COUNT

gurgle /gɜːɡəˀl/, **gurgles, gurgling, gurgled.** 1 When water gurgles, it makes a rippling, bubbling sound. EG *The waves swept back with a gurgling, sucking sound.* 2 When a baby gurgles, it makes a bubbling sound in its throat. EG *Kicking and gurgling, his little brother looked up at him.* ▸ used as a noun. EG *...gurgles of pleasure.*   V   V OR V+QUOTE   ▸ N COUNT

guru /gʊˀruː/, **gurus.** A guru is 1 a spiritual leader and teacher, especially in Hinduism. 2 an adviser whom a group of people respect greatly. EG *She has become the guru of many a modern mother-to-be.*   N COUNT   EG

gush /gʌʃ/, **gushes, gushing, gushed.** 1 When liquid or gas gushes out of something, it flows out very quickly and in large quantities. EG *Blood gushed from the wounds.* ▸ used as a noun. EG *...a gush of smoke.* 2 If someone gushes, they express their admiration or pleasure in a very exaggerated way. EG *'Amy!' he gushed. 'How good to see you again.'* ◊ **gushing.** EG *He arrived in the company of a large gushing female.*   V+A   ▸ N SING : OFT+*of*   V OR V+QUOTE   ◊ ADJ QUALIT

gust /gʌst/, **gusts.** 1 A gust is a short, strong, sudden rush of wind. EG *...a sudden gust of wind.* 2 If you feel a gust of emotion such as anger, you feel the emotion suddenly and intensely. EG *A gust of pure happiness swept through her.*   N COUNT : OFT+*of*   N SING+*of*

gusto /gʌstəʊ/. If you do something with gusto, you do it very energetically and enthusiastically. EG *We ate with gusto.*   N UNCOUNT

gusty /gʌstiˀ/ is used to describe weather in which there are very strong, irregular winds. EG *...gusty winds.*   ADJ QUALIT

gut /gʌt/, **guts, gutting, gutted.** 1 Your guts are your internal organs, especially your intestines. 2 When someone guts a dead fish, they remove all the organs from inside it. 3 The gut is the tube inside your body through which food passes while it is being digested. 4 Guts is courage. EG *Sam hasn't got the guts to leave his dad.* 5 A gut feeling or reaction is based on instinct or emotion rather than on reason. EG *My immediate gut reaction was to refuse.* 6 If a building is gutted, the inside of it is destroyed. EG *The whole house was gutted by fire.* 7 If you hate someone's guts, you dislike them very intensely.   N PLURAL   V+O   N SING Formal   N UNCOUNT Informal   N MOD   V+O : USU PASS   PHRASE Informal

gutter /gʌtə/, **gutters.** A gutter is 1 the edge of a road next to the pavement, where rain water collects and flows away. EG *The motorbike lay on its side in the gutter.* 2 a plastic or metal channel fixed to the edge of the roof of a building, which rain water drains into.   N COUNT

guttering /gʌtᵊrɪŋ/ consists of the plastic or metal channels fixed to the edge of the roof of a building, which rain water drains into.   N UNCOUNT

guttural /gʌtᵊrəl/. Guttural sounds are harsh sounds that are produced at the back of a person's throat. EG *...a strange, loud, guttural cry.*   ADJ QUALIT

guy /gaɪ/, **guys.** 1 A guy is a man. EG *...the guy who drove the bus... He's a nice guy.* 2 Americans sometimes address a group of people as guys or you guys.   N COUNT Informal   VOCATIVE Informal

guzzle /gʌzᵊl/, **guzzles, guzzling, guzzled.** If you guzzle something, you drink or eat it quickly and greedily. EG *The wine was being guzzled like lemonade.*   V+O OR V Informal

gym /dʒɪm/, **gyms.** 1 A gym is a gymnasium. EG *He was always at the gym.* 2 Gym means gymnastics. EG *We did an hour of gym... She wore white gym shoes.*   N COUNT   N UNCOUNT

gymkhana /dʒɪmkɑːnɑː/, **gymkhanas.** A gymkhana is an event in which people ride horses in competitions.   N COUNT

gymnasium /dʒɪmneɪzɪəm/, **gymnasiums.** A gymnasium is a building or large room which is used for physical exercise and usually has equipment such as bars and ropes in it.   N COUNT

gymnast /dʒɪmnæst/, **gymnasts.** A gymnast is someone who is trained in gymnastics.   N COUNT

gymnastic /dʒɪmnæstɪk/, **gymnastics.** 1 Gymnastics are physical exercises, often using equipment such as bars and ropes, which develop your strength and agility. 2 Gymnastic is used to describe things relating to gymnastics. EG *He shows great gymnastic ability.*   N PLURAL   ADJ CLASSIF : ATTRIB

gynaecology /gaɪnəkɒlədʒi¹/; also spelled **gyne-** N UNCOUNT
cology. Gynaecology is the branch of medical Technical
science which deals with diseases and medical
conditions that only women have.
◊ **gynaecologist, gynaecologists.** EG ...*an emi-* ◊ N COUNT
nent gynaecologist. ◊ **gynaecological.** EG ...*the* ◊ ADJ CLASSIF
gynaecological ward.
gypsy /dʒɪpsi¹/, **gypsies;** also spelled **gipsy.** A N COUNT
gypsy is a member of a race of people who travel

from place to place in caravans rather than living
in one place.
gyrate /dʒaɪreɪt/, **gyrates, gyrating, gyrated.** If V
something **gyrates,** it turns round and round in a Formal
circle, usually very fast. EG ...*a small gyrating*
plastic advertisement for a brand of lager.
◊ **gyration** /dʒaɪreɪʃə⁰n/, **gyrations.** EG ...*their* ◊ N COUNT OR
bodily gyrations and contortions. N UNCOUNT

H h

H, h /eɪtʃ/, **Hs, h's** /eɪtʃɪz/. **H** is the eighth letter of N COUNT
the English alphabet.
ha /hɑ:/; also spelled **hah.** You say **ha** to show that EXCLAM
you are very surprised, pleased, or annoyed about Informal
something. EG '*Ha!*' *she said,* '*Isn't that wonderful?*'...
Hah! Scared you, didn't I? ● See also **ha ha.**
haberdashery /hæbədæʃə⁰ri¹/ is **1** buttons, zips, N UNCOUNT
thread, and other small things that you need for British
sewing. **2** men's clothing sold in a shop. American
habit /hæbɪt/, **habits. 1** A **habit** is **1.1** something N COUNT OR
that you do often or regularly. EG *I got into the habit* N UNCOUNT :
of studying at the library... More out of habit than OFT+SUPP
anything else, I stopped and went in. **1.2** an action N COUNT :
that someone has done many times before and OFT+SUPP
finds difficult to stop, especially when this action is
considered to be bad. EG *He had a nervous habit of*
biting his nails.
2 If you are **in the habit of** doing something, or if PHRASE
you **make a habit** of doing it, you do it regularly
and often. EG *Once a month Castle was in the habit*
of taking Sarah for an excursion... They made a
habit of lunching together twice a week.
3 A **habit of mind** is the kind of thought, feeling, or PHRASE
attitude that someone generally has. EG *Resistance*
is a natural habit of mind in people who have been
oppressed.
4 A drug **habit** is an addiction to a drug. EG *Groups* N COUNT+SUPP
exist to help those who want to kick the marijuana
habit.
5 A **habit** is also a piece of clothing shaped like a N COUNT
long loose dress, which a nun or monk wears.
habitable /hæbɪtəbə⁰l/. If a place is **habitable,** it ADJ CLASSIF
is good enough for people to live in. EG *A few flats*
were made habitable.
habitat /hæbɪtæt/, **habitats.** The **habitat** of an N COUNT+SUPP
animal or plant is the natural environment in
which it normally lives. EG ...*the open woodland*
that is their natural habitat.
habitation /hæbɪteɪʃə⁰n/, **habitations. 1** Habita- N UNCOUNT
tion is the human activity of living somewhere. EG
...*to see whether the houses are fit for human*
habitation.
2 A **habitation** is a place where people live. EG N COUNT
...*squalid human habitations.* Formal
habitual /həbɪtjʊ⁰əl/. **1** A **habitual** action is one ADJ CLASSIF
that someone usually or often does. EG '*Sorry I'm*
late,' *David said with his habitual guilty grin.*
◊ **habitually.** EG *Anybody who habitually keeps his* ◊ ADV
office door shut is suspect.
2 A **habitual** criminal or liar commits crimes or ADJ CLASSIF :
tells lies very often. ATTRIB
hack /hæk/, **hacks, hacking, hacked. 1** If you V+O OR V+A
hack something, you cut it using a sharp tool, such
as an axe or knife, with strong, rough strokes. EG
They were ambushed and hacked to death...
...*hacking away at the branches.*
2 A **hack** is a professional writer who produces N COUNT
work fast, without worrying very much about the Informal
quality of it. EG ...*a hack writer, scribbling madly to*
keep to the deadline.

3 When someone **hacks** a computer system, **3.1** V+A OR V+O
they write programs for the system. **3.2** they try to V+O
break into the system, especially in order to get
secret or confidential information that is stored
there.
hack through. If you **hack through** something PHRASAL VB :
such as jungle, you move through it by cutting V+PREP
down branches and bushes.
hacker /hækə/, **hackers.** A computer **hacker** is **1** N COUNT
someone who uses a computer a lot, especially so
much that they have no time to do anything else. **2**
someone who tries to break into computer systems, especially in order to get secret or confidential information that is stored there.
hackneyed /hæknɪd/. An expression that is ADJ QUALIT
hackneyed is boring because it has been used
many times before. EG '*Of course I love you. With*
all my heart.' *The hackneyed phrase came unin-*
tended to his lips.
hacksaw /hæksɔ:/, **hacksaws.** A **hacksaw** is a N COUNT
small saw used for cutting metal.
had /hæd/ is the past tense and past participle of
have.
haddock /hædək/. **Haddock** is both the singular N COUNT OR
and the plural form. N UNCOUNT
A **haddock** is a kind of sea fish. EG *Would you like*
smoked haddock this evening?
hadn't /hædə⁰nt/ is the usual spoken form of 'had
not'.
haemoglobin /hi:mə⁰glอʊbɪn, hem-/; also spelled N UNCOUNT
hemoglobin. Haemoglobin is a substance that Technical
carries oxygen in red blood cells.
haemophilia /hi:mə⁰fɪliə, hem-/; also spelled N UNCOUNT
hemophilia. Haemophilia is an inherited disease,
usually affecting men, in which a person's blood
does not clot properly, so that they continue to
bleed for a long time if they are injured.
haemophiliac /hi:mə⁰fɪliæk, hem-/, **haemophili-** N COUNT
acs; also spelled **hemophiliac.** A **haemophiliac** is
a person who suffers from haemophilia.
haemorrhage /hemə⁰rɪdʒ/, **haemorrhages,** N COUNT OR
haemorrhaging, haemorrhaged; also spelled N UNCOUNT
hemorrhage. A **haemorrhage** is serious bleeding
inside a person's body. EG *He had died of a brain*
haemorrhage. ▸ used as a verb. EG *She began to* ▸ V
haemorrhage badly.
haemorrhoids /hemə⁰rɔɪdz/; also spelled **hem-** N PLURAL
orrhoids. Haemorrhoids are painful swellings Medical
that appear in the veins inside a person's anus.
hag /hæg/, **hags.** If you call a woman a **hag,** you N COUNT
mean that you think she is ugly and unpleasant; an
offensive word.
haggard /hægəd/. Someone who is **haggard** looks ADJ QUALIT
very tired and worried. EG *There was a haggard*
look about his eyes.
haggis /hægɪs/ is a Scottish dish made with oat- N UNCOUNT
meal and the internal organs of a sheep or calf.
haggle /hægə⁰l/, **haggles, haggling, haggled.** If V OR V+with :
you **haggle,** you argue about the cost of something RECIP

that you are buying. EG *They haggled with shop-keepers in the bazaar.*

hah /hɑ:/. See **ha**.

ha ha /hɑ: hɑ:/. 1 **Ha ha** is used in writing to CONVENTION represent the sound that people make when they laugh.

2 You sometimes say **ha ha** sarcastically, when CONVENTION you are not amused and are only pretending to laugh. EG *I watched as the man made mistakes. 'Ha ha,' I sneered to myself.*

hail /heɪl/, **hails, hailing, hailed. 1 Hail** consists N SING of tiny balls of ice that fall like rain from the sky. EG *The hail battered on the windows.*

2 When it **hails**, hail falls from the sky. EG *It hailed* V *all afternoon.*

3 A **hail** of small objects is a large number of them N PART that fall down on you at the same time with great force. EG *He was dead, killed in a hail of bullets.*

4 If you **hail** someone, you call to them. EG *A voice* V+O *hailed him from the steps.* Literary

5 If you **hail** a taxi, you wave at it in order to stop it V+O and ask the driver to take you somewhere.

6 If you **hail** a person, event, or achievement as V+O+as important or successful, you praise them publicly. EG *They were hailed as heroes... The discovery was hailed as the scientific sensation of the century.*

hailstone /heɪlstəʊn/, **hailstones. Hailstones** N COUNT are tiny balls of ice that fall from the sky when it hails.

hailstorm /heɪlstɔ:m/, **hailstorms.** A **hailstorm** N COUNT is a storm during which it hails.

hair /heə/, **hairs. 1 Hairs** are the long, fine, N COUNT thread-like things that grow in large numbers on your head and on other parts of your body. EG *...black hairs on the back of his hands.*

2 Your **hair** is the large number of hairs that grow N UNCOUNT in a mass on your head. See picture at THE HUMAN BODY. EG *...a young woman with long blonde hair.*

3 **Hairs** are also very fine thread-like pieces of N COUNT material that grows on some insects and plants. EG *The adult beetle has silken hairs on its body.*

4 **Hair** is used in these phrases. 4.1 Something that PHRASES makes your **hair stand on end** shocks or horrifies you. EG *She did it with an ease that made his hair stand on end.* 4.2 If you **let** your **hair down**, you relax completely and enjoy yourself. 4.3 If you say that someone is **splitting hairs**, you mean that they are making very fine distinctions that are not necessary. EG *Am I splitting hairs here? I think not, because this is an important distinction.*

hairbrush /heəbrʌʃ/, **hairbrushes.** A **hairbrush** N COUNT is a brush that you use to brush your hair. See picture at BRUSHES.

haircut /heəkʌt/, **haircuts. 1** If you have a **haircut**, someone cuts your hair for you. EG *He needed a haircut.*

2 A **haircut** is also the style in which your hair has N COUNT been cut. EG *The girls had short, neat haircuts.*

hairdo /heədu:/, **hairdos.** A **hairdo** is the style in N COUNT which your hair has been cut and arranged. EG *I* Informal *went to a salon and had a new hairdo.*

hairdresser /heədresə/, **hairdressers. 1** A **hair-** N COUNT **dresser** is a person who cuts, washes, and styles people's hair.

2 A **hairdresser** or a **hairdresser's** is a shop N COUNT where a hairdresser works. EG *...going to the hairdresser.*

hairdryer /heədraɪə/, **hairdryers;** also spelled N COUNT **hairdrier.** A **hairdryer** is a machine that you use to dry your hair.

hairless /heəlɪs/. A part of your body that is ADJ CLASSIF **hairless** has no hair on it. EG *...his hairless chest.*

hairline /heəlaɪn/, **hairlines. 1** Your **hairline** is N COUNT the edge of the area where your hair grows on the front part of your head. EG *His hairline was receding.*

2 A **hairline** crack or gap is very narrow or fine. ADJ CLASSIF: EG *...a tiny hairline fracture.* ATTRIB

hairnet /heənet/, **hairnets.** A **hairnet** is a small N COUNT net that some women wear over their hair in order to keep it tidy.

hairpin /heəpɪn/, **hairpins. 1** A **hairpin** is a thin N COUNT piece of bent metal that women use to hold their hair in position.

2 A **hairpin** bend is a very sharp bend in a road, N COUNT where the road turns back in the opposite direction.

hair-raising. Something that is **hair-raising** is ADJ QUALIT very frightening or disturbing. EG *The ride was bumpy and at times hair-raising.*

hair's breadth. A **hair's breadth** is a very small N SING : a+N degree or amount. EG *A national strike has been averted by no more than a hair's breadth.*

hair slide, hair slides. A **hair slide** is a decora- N COUNT tive clip that girls and women put in their hair to hold it in position.

hairstyle /heəstaɪl/, **hairstyles.** Your **hairstyle** N COUNT is the style in which your hair has been cut or arranged. EG *...a new hairstyle.*

hairy /heəri¹/, **hairier, hairiest. 1** Someone or ADJ QUALIT something that is **hairy** is covered with hair. EG *...a big, hairy man.*

2 If you describe a situation as **hairy**, you mean ADJ QUALIT that it is exciting, worrying, and rather frightening. Informal EG *It got a little hairy when we drove him to the station with less than two minutes to spare.*

halcyon /hælsɪən/. A **halcyon** time is a peaceful ADJ CLASSIF : or happy one. EG *...the halcyon days of his late* ATTRIB *teens.* Formal

hale /heɪl/. If you describe someone as **hale**, you ADJ QUALIT mean that they are healthy. EG *They had hale old* Literary *parents who lived on farms in the country.*

half /hɑ:f/, **halves** /hɑ:vz/. **1 Half** of an amount or PRON, PREDET, object is one of the two equal parts that together OR N COUNT make up the amount or object. EG *Roughly half are French... The house was half a mile away... ...half a million men... Half his front teeth were missing... ...the two halves of the brain... I went to Poland four and a half years ago.*

2 You can also use **half** to describe a half of ADJ CLASSIF: something. EG *...a half chicken... The picture* ATTRIB *wouldn't end for another half hour.*

3 **Half** is also used in these phrases. **3.1** If PHRASES something is divided **in half**, it is divided into two equal parts. EG *He tore it in half.* **3.2** If you increase something **by half**, half of the original amount is added to it. If you decrease it **by half**, half of the original amount is taken away from it. EG *She reckoned she cut her costs by half.* **3.3** If you say Informal that someone is **too** clever **by half** or **too** arrogant **by half**, you mean that you dislike their cleverness or arrogance. **3.4** If two people **go halves**, they divide the cost of something equally between them.

4 A **half** is **4.1** half a pint of beer, lager, or cider. EG N PART *...a half of lager.* **4.2** a half-price ticket on a bus or N COUNT train, especially one for a child.

5 You also use **half** to say that something is only ADV partly the case or happens to only a limited extent. EG *He half expected to see Davis there... His eyes were half-closed... ...his half empty glass.*

6 You can use **half** to say that someone has ADV parents of different nationalities. For example, if +ADJ CLASSIF you are **half** German, one of your parents is German.

7 You use **half** to refer to a time that is thirty ADV minutes after a particular hour. For example, if it is **half** past two, thirty minutes have passed since two o'clock. See the entry headed TIME.

8 **half the battle:** see **battle**.

half-baked. Ideas, opinions, or plans that are ADJ QUALIT **half-baked** have not been properly thought out, and so are usually stupid or impractical. EG *...your half-baked political opinions.*

half board. If you stay at a hotel and have **half** N UNCOUNT **board**, you have your breakfast and evening meal at the hotel, but not your lunch.

half-brother, half-brothers. Your **half-brother** N COUNT is a boy or man who has the same mother or the same father as you have.

half-caste. Someone who is **half-caste** has par- ADJ CLASSIF ents who come from different races. EG *Half-caste children were taken forcibly from their parents and sold as slaves.*

half-day, half-days. A **half-day** is a day when N COUNT you work only in the morning or in the afternoon, but not all day. EG *Saturday is his half-day.*

half-hearted. Someone or something that is **half-** ADJ QUALIT **hearted** shows no real effort, interest, or enthusi-asm. EG *She made a half-hearted attempt to break away.* ◊ **half-heartedly.** EG *I stayed home, study-* ◊ ADV *ing half-heartedly.*

half-life, half-lives. The **half-life** of a radioactive N COUNT substance is the amount of time that it takes to lose Technical half its radioactivity. EG *...a half-life of 30 years.*

half-mast. If a flag is flying **at half-mast**, it is PHRASE flying from the middle of the mast as a sign that someone important has died.

halfpenny /heɪpniˈ/, **halfpennies** or **halfpence.** N COUNT A **halfpenny** is a small British coin which used to be worth one half of a penny.

half-price. If something is **half-price**, it costs ADJ CLASSIF only half what it usually costs. EG *...half-price elec-tricity.*

half-sister, half-sisters. Your **half-sister** is a N COUNT girl or woman who has the same mother or the same father as you have.

half-term is a short holiday in the middle of a N UNCOUNT school term. EG *It's half-term next week.*

half-timbered. Buildings that are **half-timbered** ADJ CLASSIF have wooden beams showing in the brick and plaster walls.

half-time is the short period of time between the N UNCOUNT two parts of a sports match, when the players have a short rest.

halfway /hɑːfweɪ/. 1 **Halfway** means 1.1 at the ADV : middle of a place or of a distance between two OFT+PREP points. EG *She was half-way up the stairs.* 1.2 at the OR+ADV middle of a period of time or of an event. EG *Dr O'Shea usually fell asleep halfway through the programme.*
2 If you **meet** someone **halfway**, you accept some PHRASE of the points they are making so that you can come to an agreement.

half-yearly. A **half-yearly** event happens twice ADJ CLASSIF : a year, with six months between each event. ATTRIB

hall /hɔːl/, **halls.** 1 A **hall** is 1.1 the area just inside N COUNT the front door of a house. EG *We began bringing down our suitcases and putting them in the hall.* 1.2 a large building or a room in a building which is N COUNT used for public events such as concerts, exhibi-tions, and meetings. EG *We organized a concert in the village hall.* 1.3 a building where a local N COUNT+SUPP government authority has its main offices. EG *...the town hall.*
2 Students who live **in hall** live in university or PHRASE college accommodation.
3 A **hall** is also a large house on a country estate. N COUNT EG *'I don't own Barrett Hall,' I said.*

hallelujah /hælɪˈluːjə/; also spelled **halleluiah** CONVENTION and **alleluia.** Some Christians say **hallelujah** in church as an exclamation of praise and thanks to God.

hallmark /hɔːlmɑːk/, **hallmarks.** A **hallmark** is
1 the most typical quality or feature of something N COUNT+SUPP or someone. EG *...the kind of subtlety that was the hallmark of Elgar.* 2 an official mark put on things N COUNT made of gold, silver, or platinum that indicates the quality of the metal and where the object was made.

hallo /həˈləʊ/. See **hello.**

hall of residence, halls of residence. Halls of N COUNT **residence** are blocks of rooms or flats, usually built by universities or colleges, in which students live.

hallowed /hæləʊd/. If something is **hallowed**, it is ADJ QUALIT respected and revered, usually because it is old or important. EG *...those hallowed offices on State Street.*

Halloween /hæləʊiːn/; also spelled **Hallowe'en.** N UNCOUNT **Halloween** is October 31st. It is traditionally said to be the night on which ghosts and witches can be seen, and so children often dress up as ghosts and witches.

hallucinate /həˈluːsɪneɪt/, **hallucinates, halluci-** V **nating, hallucinated.** If you **hallucinate**, you see things that are not really there, either because you are ill or because you have taken a drug. EG *She barked at me and I knew she must be hallucinat-ing.*

hallucination /həˌluːsɪˈneɪʃəˀn/, **hallucinations.** N COUNT OR A **hallucination** is what you see when you are N UNCOUNT hallucinating. EG *...a bizarre hallucination.*

hallway /hɔːlweɪ/, **hallways.** A **hallway** is the N COUNT entrance hall of a house or other building.

halo /heɪləʊ/, **haloes** or **halos.** A **halo** is a circle N COUNT of light that is drawn in pictures round the heads of saints or angels to show that they are holy.

halt /hɒlt/, **halts, halting, halted.** 1 When you V-ERG **halt** or when something **halts** you, you stop mov-ing and stand still. EG *He took a step and halted... He tried to push past, but the girl halted him.*
2 When growth, development, or activity **halts** or V-ERG when you **halt** it, it stops completely. EG *...if popula-tion growth were to halt overnight... The firm ran into foreign exchange problems which halted its imports of nylon.*
3 If someone or something comes **to a halt**, they PHRASE stop moving. EG *The car slowed, and came to a halt opposite her.*
4 If growth, development, or activity comes **to a** PHRASE **halt**, it stops completely. EG *The comment brought conversation to a halt.*
5 If you **call a halt** to something, you decide not to PHRASE continue with it. EG *Surely it is time to call a halt to these practices?*

halting /hɒltɪŋ, hɔːl-/. If you speak in a **halting** ADJ QUALIT way, you speak uncertainly with a lot of pauses. EG *...his halting admission of guilt.* ◊ **haltingly.** EG *He* ◊ ADV *answered haltingly.*

halve /hɑːv/, **halves, halving, halved.** 1 When V-ERG you **halve** something or when it **halves**, it is reduced to half its previous size or amount. EG *This could halve rail fares... If that happened, sales would halve overnight.*
2 If you **halve** something, you divide it into two V+O equal parts. EG *Halve the avocado pears and re-move the stones.*
3 **Halves** is the plural of **half.**

ham /hæm/, **hams, hamming, hammed.** 1 **Ham** N UNCOUNT is salted meat from a pig's leg. EG *...legs of ham hanging behind the counter... ...a ham sandwich.*
2 If actors or actresses **ham it up**, they exaggerate PHRASE every emotion and gesture when they are acting. EG *She was obviously hamming it up for the benefit of the watching tourists.*

hamburger /hæmbɜːgə/, **hamburgers.** A **ham-** N COUNT **burger** is minced meat which has been shaped into a flat disc. Hamburgers are fried or grilled and often eaten in a bread roll.

hamlet /hæmlɪˀt/, **hamlets.** A **hamlet** is a very N COUNT small village.

hammer /hæmə/, **hammers, hammering, ham-** N COUNT **mered.** 1 A **hammer** is 1.1 a tool that you use for hitting things. It consists of a heavy piece of metal at the end of a handle. See picture at TOOLS. 1.2 a heavy weight attached to a piece of wire, that is thrown as a sport.
2 If you **hammer** something such as a nail, you hit V+O it with a hammer.

Will you find a hallmark in a hall?

3 If you **hammer** a surface or **hammer** on it, you make a noise by hitting it several times with your fist. EG *Men used to hammer on our door late at night.* v+o OR v+A

4 If you **hammer** an idea into people, you keep repeating it forcefully so that it will have an effect on them. EG *...ideas hammered into their heads by a stream of movies.* v+o+A

hammer away. If you **hammer** away at some work or activity, you work at it constantly and with great energy. EG *They all hammer away at their thesis.* PHRASAL VB : V+ADV, OFT+*at*

hammer out. If you **hammer** something **out**, you reach an agreement about it after a long or difficult discussion. EG *...procedures hammered out over recent years.* PHRASAL VB : V+o+ADV

hammock /hǽmək/, **hammocks.** A **hammock** is a piece of strong cloth which is hung between two supports and is used as a bed. N COUNT

hamper /hǽmpə/, **hampers, hampering, hampered.** **1** If you **hamper** a person or their actions, you restrict them by making their development, progress, or movement more difficult. EG *They were hampered by a constant stream of visitors.* v+o

2 A **hamper** is a large basket with a lid, used especially for carrying food in. EG *We packed a big wicker hamper and went for a picnic.* N COUNT

hamstring /hǽmstrɪŋ/, **hamstrings, hamstringing, hamstrung.** **1** A **hamstring** is a tendon behind your knee which joins the muscles of your thigh to the bones of your lower leg. EG *...a hamstring injury.* N COUNT

2 If you **hamstring** someone, you make it very difficult for them to take any action. EG *If you made the law too precise, you would so hamstring the medical profession that patients would go untreated.* v+o Formal

hand /hænd/, **hands, handing, handed.** **1** Your **hands** are the parts of your body at the end of your arms. Each hand has four fingers and a thumb. See picture at THE HUMAN BODY. EG *He took her hand and squeezed it.* N COUNT

2 If someone has a **hand** in an action or situation, they are actively involved in it. EG *I had a hand in drafting the appeal... The hand of the military in shaping government policy was obvious.* N SING

3 If you ask someone for a **hand** with something, you are asking them to help you. EG *Give me a hand with this desk, will you?* ● to **lend a hand**: see **lend.** N SING : a+N

4 A **hand** is someone who is employed to do hard physical work. N COUNT

5 The **hands** of a clock or watch are the thin pieces of metal or plastic that point to the numbers in order to show what time it is. N COUNT

6 If you **hand** something to someone, you give it to them. EG *Could you hand me that piece of wood?... I examined the lighter, then handed it back.* v+o+*to* OR v+o+o

7 **Hand** is used in the following ways after different prepositions. **7.1** Something that is **at hand** or that is **close at hand** is very near in time or place. EG *I picked up a book that happened to lie at hand.* **7.2** If you do something **by hand**, you do it using your hands rather than using a machine. **7.3** If you have some time **in hand**, you have some time free. EG *He arrived with half an hour in hand and went for a walk.* **7.4** The job or problem **in hand** is the one that you are dealing with at the moment. EG *Let's get on with the job in hand.* **7.5** If someone is **on hand**, they are near and ready to help. **7.6** If you reject an idea **out of hand**, you reject it immediately and completely. **7.7** If you have something **to hand**, you have it ready to use when needed. EG *...using the material most readily to hand.* PHRASES

8 **Hand** is also used in these phrases. **8.1** If someone gives you **a free hand**, they allow you to do a particular task exactly as you want. **8.2** You use **on the one hand** when mentioning one aspect of a situation. Then you use **on the other hand** PHRASES

when mentioning another, contrasting aspect. EG *John had great difficulties playing cricket. But on the other hand, he was an awfully good rugby player.* **8.3** Two people who are **hand in hand** are holding each other's hand. **8.4** Two things that **go hand in hand** are closely connected. EG *Military superiority went hand in hand with organizational superiority.* **8.5** If you **force** someone's **hand**, you force them to act sooner than they want to. **8.6** If a person or a situation **gets out of hand**, you are no longer able to control them or it. **8.7** If you **know** a place **like the back of** your **hand**, you know it extremely well. **8.8** If you **take** someone **in hand**, you take control over them, especially in order to improve them. **8.9** If you **try** your **hand** at a new activity, you attempt to do it. EG *I had tried my hand at milking years ago.*

9 **Hands** is used in these phrases. **9.1** You say **'Hands off'** to tell someone not to touch something. **9.2** If you receive bad treatment **at** someone's **hands**, they treat you badly. EG *...brutality at the hands of angry parents.* **9.3** If something is **in the hands** of a particular person, the person has it, or has power or responsibility over it. EG *This law leaves too much power in the hands of the judges.* **9.4** If you have a responsibility or problem **on** your **hands**, you have to deal with it. When it is **off** your **hands**, it is no longer your responsibility. EG *They've still got an economic crisis on their hands.* **9.5** If a possession **changes hands**, it is sold or given from one person to another. **9.6** If you **get** or **lay** your **hands on** something, you manage to find it or obtain it. EG *I wondered how I could lay my hands on the money to buy equipment.* **9.7** If you **have** your **hands full**, you are very busy. **9.8** Two people who **are holding hands** are holding each other's hand. **9.9** If you **wash** your **hands** of someone or something, you refuse to take any more responsibility for them. PHRASES

hand down. If you **hand** something **down**, you give it or leave it to people who belong to a younger generation. EG *Such knowledge was handed down from father to son.* PHRASAL VB : V+o+ADV, USU PASS

hand in. If you **hand in** something you have written, you give it to someone in authority. EG *I haven't yet marked the work you handed in... I was tempted to hand in my resignation at once.* PHRASAL VB : V+o+ADV

hand on. If you **hand** something **on** to someone, you give it or leave it to them. EG *Property is something handed on from generation to generation.* PHRASAL VB : V+o+ADV, OFT+*to*

hand out. **1** If you **hand out** a set of things, you give one to each person in a group. EG *Hand out the books.* **2** When people in authority **hand out** advice or punishment, they give it to people. EG *Family doctors handed out information on treatment.* **3** See also **handout.** PHRASAL VB : V+o+ADV v+o+ADV

hand over. **1** If you **hand** something **over** to someone, you give it to them. EG *Samuel was clearly about to hand over large sums of money to this man.* **2** If you **hand over** to someone, you give them the responsibility for dealing with something which you were previously responsible for. EG *Sir John handed over to his deputy and left.* PHRASAL VB : V+o+ADV, OFT+*to* v+ADV OR v+o+ADV, OFT+*to*

handbag /hǽndbæg/, **handbags.** A **handbag** is a small bag in which a woman carries things such as her money and keys. See picture at BAGS. N COUNT

handbook /hǽndbʊk/, **handbooks.** A **handbook** is a book that gives you advice and instructions about something. EG *...the official handbook for the airport.* N COUNT : OFT+SUPP

handbrake /hǽndbreɪk/, **handbrakes.** A **handbrake** is a brake which is operated by the hand of the person driving a vehicle. See picture at CAR. EG *Mr Boggis released the handbrake.* N COUNT

handclap /hǽndklæp/. A **slow handclap** is slow rhythmic clapping by an audience to show that they do not like what they are seeing or hearing. PHRASE British

handcuff /ˈhændkʌf/, **handcuffs, handcuffing, handcuffed. 1 Handcuffs** are two metal rings N PLURAL which are joined by a short chain and which can be locked round someone's wrists, usually by the police.

2 If you **handcuff** someone, you put handcuffs V+O : USU PASS around their wrists. EG *They were searched and handcuffed.*

handful /ˈhændful/, **handfuls. 1** A **handful** of N PART something is the amount of it that you can hold in your hand. EG *Roger gathered a handful of stones.*

2 If there is only a **handful** of people or things, N PART : SING there are not very many of them. EG *The firm employs only a handful of workers.*

3 If you describe a child as a **handful**, you mean N COUNT that he or she is difficult to control. Informal

handicap /ˈhændikæp/, **handicaps, handicap-** N COUNT **ping, handicapped. 1** A **handicap** is **1.1** a physical or mental disability which prevents you from living a totally normal life. EG *These changes have made the campus an easier place for people with handicaps.* **1.2** an event or situation that makes it difficult for you to do something. EG *His chief handicap is that he comes from a broken home.*

2 If an event or a situation **handicaps** someone, it V+O makes it difficult for them to do something. EG *We were handicapped by the darkness.*

3 A **handicap** is also a disadvantage that is given N COUNT to someone who is good at a particular sport, in order to make the competition between them and the other competitors more equal.

handicapped /ˈhændikæpt/. **1** Someone who is ADJ QUALIT **handicapped** has a physical or mental disability that prevents them living a totally normal life. EG *A friend of his had a handicapped daughter.*

2 You can refer to people who are handicapped as N PLURAL : **the handicapped.** EG *...establishments for the men-* the+N *tally or physically handicapped.*

handicraft /ˈhændikrɑːft/, **handicrafts. Handi-** N COUNT : **crafts** are **1** activities such as embroidery and USU PLURAL pottery which involve making things with your hands in a skilful way. EG *She teaches handicrafts.* **2** the objects that are produced by people doing handicrafts. EG *Handicrafts were produced by families to be sold in local shops.*

handiwork /ˈhændiwɜːk/. If you refer to some- N UNCOUNT thing as your **handiwork**, you mean that you made +POSS it yourself. EG *He stood back and surveyed his handiwork.*

handkerchief /ˈhæŋkətʃiːf/, **handkerchiefs.** A N COUNT **handkerchief** is a small square piece of fabric which you use for blowing your nose.

handle /ˈhændəl/, **handles, handling, handled. 1** N COUNT A **handle** is **1.1** a lever or other small object that is attached to a door or window and is used for opening and closing it. EG *He tugged at the metal handle.* **1.2** the part of an object that you hold in order to carry it or use it. EG *...a broom handle.*

2 If you **fly off the handle**, you suddenly and PHRASE completely lose your temper. Informal

3 When you **handle** something, you hold it and V+O move it about in your hands. EG *Glass. Handle with Care.*

4 When you **handle** something such as a weapon, V-ERG car, or horse, you use or control it effectively. EG IF V THEN+A *She had handled a machine gun herself... This car handles very nicely.*

5 If you **handle** a problem or difficult situation, you V+O deal with it successfully. EG *You don't have to come. Hendricks and I can handle it.* ◊ **handling.** ◊ N UNCOUNT EG *His handling of these important issues was* USU+of *condemned by the opposition.*

6 If you **handle** a particular area of work, you have V+O responsibility for it. EG *He handles all the major accounts.*

7 If you can **handle** people, you establish a good V+O relationship with them so that they respect you and do what you want them to. EG *The principal was a genius in the way he handled us.*

handlebar /ˈhændəlbɑː/, **handlebars.** The N COUNT : **handlebars** of a bicycle consist of a curved metal USU PLURAL bar with handles at each end. The handlebars are attached to the front of the bicycle and are turned in order to steer it. See picture at BICYCLE.

handler /ˈhændlə/, **handlers.** A **handler** is **1** N COUNT+SUPP someone who is in charge of an animal as part of their work. **2** someone who deals with a particular type of object as part of their work. EG *...baggage handlers.*

handmade /ˌhændˈmeɪd/. If something is **hand-** ADJ CLASSIF **made**, it is made by someone without using machines. EG *...beautiful handmade clothes.*

handout /ˈhændaʊt/, **handouts. 1** A **handout** is N COUNT money, clothing, or food which is given free to poor people. EG *We said that we wouldn't be relying on handouts from anyone for our future.*

2 A **handout** is also **2.1** a document which gives N COUNT information about a particular company or event, and is used to publicize the company or event. EG *...a pile of unread public relations handouts and shiny magazines.* **2.2** a summary of the information in a lecture or talk, which is given to the audience.

hand-picked. If someone is **hand-picked**, they ADJ CLASSIF have been very carefully chosen for a particular purpose or for a particular job. EG *Each of the officers had been hand-picked by the general.*

handrail /ˈhændreɪl/, **handrails.** A **handrail** is a N COUNT long piece of metal or wood which is fixed near stairs or high places, which people can hold for support as they walk. EG *I had to cling with both hands to the handrails.*

handshake /ˈhændʃeɪk/, **handshakes.** If you give N COUNT someone a **handshake**, you take their right hand with your right hand and hold it firmly or move it up and down. You do this as a sign of greeting or to show that you have agreed about something. EG *He came to the door to welcome me with a handshake.*

handsome /ˈhænsəm/. **1** A man who is **handsome** ADJ QUALIT has an attractive face with regular features. EG *He was a tall, dark, and undeniably handsome man.*

2 A woman who is **handsome** has an attractive, ADJ QUALIT smart appearance, usually with features that are large and regular rather than small and delicate. EG *...a strikingly handsome woman.*

3 A building or garden that is **handsome** is large ADJ QUALIT and well made with an attractive appearance. EG *...handsome big apartment buildings.* ◊ **handsomely.** EG *...handsomely sized rooms.* ◊ ADV

4 A **handsome** sum of money is a large or ADJ CLASSIF : generous amount. EG *The rate of return on these* ATTRIB *farmers' outlay was a handsome 57 per cent.*

handstand /ˈhændstænd/, **handstands.** If you do N COUNT a **handstand**, you balance upside down on your hands with your body and legs straight up in the air.

hand-to-hand. A **hand-to-hand** fight is one in ADJ CLASSIF : which people are fighting very close together, with ATTRIB OR ADV their hands or sometimes with knives.

hand-to-mouth. A **hand-to-mouth** existence is a ADJ CLASSIF : way of life in which you have hardly enough food ATTRIB OR ADV or money to live on.

handwriting /ˈhændraɪtɪŋ/. Someone's **hand-** N UNCOUNT **writing** is their style of writing with a pen or pencil rather than with a typewriter. EG *He looked at his son's laborious handwriting.*

handwritten /ˌhændˈrɪtən/. A piece of writing ADJ CLASSIF that is **handwritten** is one that has been written using a pen or pencil.

handy /ˈhændi/, **handier, handiest. 1** Something ADJ QUALIT that is **handy** is useful and easy to use. EG *An electric kettle is very handy.* ● If you say that ● PHRASE something will **come in handy**, you mean that it Informal

Is this book handwritten?

will be useful. EG *Rick's raft came in handy for shipping camera gear up the river.*

2 Someone who is **handy** with a particular tool is skilful at using it. EG *He was handy with an axe.* ADJ QUALIT Informal

3 A thing or place that is **handy** is nearby and convenient. EG *I looked to see whether there was a glass handy.* ● If you **keep** something **handy**, you keep it easily available so that you can use it when you need it. ADJ QUALIT Informal ● PHRASE

handyman /hændi¹mæn/, **handymen**. A **handy-man** is a man who is good at making things or repairing things. N COUNT

hang /hæŋ/, **hangs**, **hanging**, **hung** /hʌŋ/, **hanged**. **Hung** is the past tense and past participle of the verb, except in paragraph 3, where the form **hanged** is used.

1 If you **hang** something on a hook or rail, you place it so that its highest part is supported and the rest of it is not. EG *He was hanging his coat in the hall.* V+O+A

2 If something **is hanging** somewhere, the top of it is attached to something and the rest of it is free and unsupported. EG *...some washing hanging on a line.* V+A

3 To **hang** someone means to kill them by tying a rope around their neck and taking away the support from under their feet so that they hang in the air. EG *Rebecca Smith was hanged in 1849... He tried to hang himself.* V+O OR V-REFL

4 If a future event or a possibility **hangs** over you, it worries you. EG *...the threat of universal extinction hanging over all the world today.* V+over

5 If you **get the hang of** something, you begin to understand how to do it. EG *Once you have got the hang of it, you'll be alright.* PHRASE Informal

6 See also **hanging**.

hang about or **hang around**. If you **hang about** or **hang around** somewhere, you stay in a particular place doing nothing, often because you are waiting for someone. EG *We would have to hang around for a while... I enjoyed hanging around Parliament listening to debates.* PHRASAL VB : V+ADV/PREP Informal

hang on. 1 If you ask someone to **hang on**, you mean you want them to wait for a moment or stop what they are doing or saying. EG *Hang on a minute.* **2** If you **hang on**, you manage to survive until the situation you are in improves. EG *I can't keep hanging on here much longer.* **3** If something **hangs on** something else, it depends on it. EG *Everything hangs on money at the moment.* CONVENTION Informal PHRASAL VB : V+ADV V+PREP

hang onto. If you **hang onto** something, **1** you hold it very tightly. EG *Claude hung on to Tom's shoulder.* **2** you keep it or try to keep it. EG *Fear is a powerful motive for hanging on to power.* PHRASAL VB : V+PREP V+PREP

hang out. When you **hang out** washing, you hang it on a clothes line to dry. PHRASAL VB : V+O+ADV

hang round. See **hang around**.

hang up. 1 If you **hang** something **up**, you place it so that its highest part is supported and the rest of it is not. EG *Howard hangs up his scarf on the hook behind the door.* **2** Something that is **hanging up** somewhere has been put there so that it does not touch the ground. EG *There are some old tools hanging up in the shed.* **3** When you **hang up** at the end of a phone call, you put back the receiver. PHRASAL VB : V+ADV V+ADV V+ADV OR V+O+ADV

hang up on. If you **hang up on** someone, you end a phone call to them suddenly and unexpectedly by putting back the receiver. PHRASAL VB : V+ADV+PREP

hangar /hæŋə/, **hangars**. A **hangar** is a large building in which aircraft are kept. N COUNT

hanger /hæŋə/, **hangers**. A **hanger** is the same as a coat hanger. EG *He took off his shirt, put it on a hanger, and hung it in the wardrobe.* N COUNT

hanger-on, hangers-on. A **hanger-on** is a person who tries to be friendly with a richer or more important person or group, especially for his or her own advantage. EG *...a small group of writers, artists and assorted hangers-on.* N COUNT

hang-glider, hang-gliders. A **hang-glider** is a type of large kite, which someone can hang from and use to help them fly through the air. N COUNT

hang-gliding is the activity of flying in a hang-glider. N ING

hanging /hæŋɪŋ/, **hangings. 1 Hanging** is the practice of executing people by hanging them. EG *Every one of them was in favour of hanging.* N UNCOUNT

2 A **hanging** is the act or occasion of killing a person by hanging them. EG *The crowds at Tyburn used to find a hanging entertaining.* N COUNT OR N UNCOUNT

3 A **hanging** is also a large piece of cloth that you put as a decoration on a wall or as a curtain over a window. EG *...silk and damask hangings.* N COUNT : OFT+SUPP

hangman /hæŋmə³n/, **hangmen**. A **hangman** is a man whose job is to execute people by hanging them. N COUNT

hangover /hæŋəʊvə/, **hangovers. 1** A **hangover** is a headache and feeling of sickness that you have in the morning if you have drunk a lot of alcohol the night before. N COUNT

2 A **hangover** from the past is something that results from ideas or attitudes which people had in the past but which are no longer generally held. EG *This feeling should be attributed to habit, a hangover from earlier, more primitive times.* N COUNT+SUPP

hang-up, hang-ups. If you have a **hang-up** about something, you have a feeling of fear, embarrassment, or worry about it. EG *He's got a hang-up about flying.* N COUNT Informal

hank /hæŋk/, **hanks.** A **hank** is an amount of wool, rope, or string that has been loosely wound. N COUNT Technical

hanker /hæŋkə/, **hankers, hankering, hankered.** If you **hanker** after something or for something, you have a great desire for it. EG *We always hankered after a bungalow of our own.* V+after/for

hankering /hæŋkə³rɪŋ/, **hankerings.** A **hankering** for something is a great desire for it. EG *If you give way to this hankering for food you will become fat.* N COUNT+for

hanky /hæŋki¹/, **hankies;** also spelled **hankie.** A **hanky** is the same as a handkerchief. N COUNT Informal

haphazard /hæphæzəd/. Something that is **haphazard** is not organized or not arranged according to a plan. EG *It was done on a haphazard basis.* ADJ QUALIT

◊ **haphazardly.** EG *...all the papers haphazardly strewn on desks.* ◊ ADV

hapless /hæpli³s/. A **hapless** person is very unlucky. EG *...the hapless victim of a misplaced murder attempt.* ADJ CLASSIF : ATTRIB Literary

happen /hæpə³n/, **happens, happening, happened. 1** When something **happens**, it occurs or is done without being planned. EG *The explosion had happened at one in the morning... ...a court of inquiry into what happened.* V : OFT+A

2 When something **happens** to someone or something, it takes place and affects them, often in an unpleasant way. EG *...all the ghastly things that had happened to him.* V+to

3 If you **happen** to do something, you do it as a result of chance. EG *He happened to be at their base when the alert began.* V+to-INF

4 You say **as it happens** before a statement in order to introduce a new fact. EG *As it happens, I brought the note with me.* ADV SEN

happening /hæpə³nɪŋ/, **happenings.** A **happening** is something that happens, often in a way that is unexpected or hard to explain. EG *...some very bizarre happenings in Europe.* N COUNT

happy /hæpi¹/, **happier, happiest. 1** Someone who is **happy** has feelings of pleasure, often because something nice has happened. EG *...a happy smile... The old man's not very happy.* ◊ **happily.** EG *We laughed and chatted happily together.* ADJ QUALIT ◊ ADV

◊ **happiness.** EG *Money did not bring happiness.* ◊ N UNCOUNT

2 A time or place that is **happy** is an atmosphere in which people feel happy. EG *...a happy childhood... ...the happiest time of their lives.* ADJ QUALIT

3 If you are **happy** about a situation or arrange- ADJ PRED +about/with ment, you are satisfied with it. EG *We are not too happy about this turn of events... Are you happy with that, Diana?*

4 If you say you are **happy** to do something, you mean that you are very willing to do it. EG *I was happy to work with George.* ADJ PRED +*to*-INF

5 You use **happy** in greetings to say that you hope someone will enjoy a special occasion. EG *Happy birthday!... Happy New Year!* ● **many happy returns:** see **return.** ADJ QUALIT: ATTRIB

6 You use **happy** to describe something that is very suitable, appropriate, or fortunate. EG *I appreciate that this is not a happy comparison.* ◊ **happily.** EG *That trend reversed itself, happily.* ADJ QUALIT: ATTRIB Formal ◊ ADV SEN

happy-go-lucky. Someone who is **happy-go-lucky** enjoys life and does not worry about the future. ADJ QUALIT

harangue /həˈræŋ/, **harangues, haranguing, harangued.** A **harangue** is a long, forceful speech that someone makes in order to persuade other people to accept their opinions. EG *...blazing harangues about the wickedness of the Government.* ▸ used as a verb. EG *Smith harangued his fellow students and persuaded them to walk out.* N COUNT ▸ V+O

harass /ˈhærəs/, **harasses, harassing, harassed.** If you **harass** someone, you trouble them or annoy them. EG *Some governments have chosen to harass and persecute the rural poor.* V+O

harassed /ˈhærəst/. Someone who is **harassed** feels worried and under pressure because they have too much to do. EG *As the pressure gets worse, people get more harassed and work is rushed.* ADJ QUALIT

harassing /ˈhærəsɪŋ/. Something that is **harassing** makes you feel worried and under pressure because you have too many jobs to do or too many problems to cope with. EG *I have had a particularly busy and harassing day.* ADJ QUALIT

harassment /ˈhærəsməᵊnt/ is behaviour which is intended to trouble or annoy someone. EG *...alleged police brutality and harassment.* N UNCOUNT

harbinger /ˈhɑːbɪndʒə/, **harbingers.** A person or thing that is a **harbinger** of something is a sign that is going to happen in the future. EG *The sudden oil price rise was a harbinger of future problems.* N COUNT: USU+*of* Formal

harbour /ˈhɑːbə/, **harbours, harbouring, harboured;** spelled **harbor** in American English. **1** A **harbour** is an area of water at the coast which is protected from the sea by land or strong walls, so that boats can be left there safely. N COUNT

2 If you **harbour** a strong emotion, you have it in your mind over a long period of time. EG *I was unable to dismiss the fears I harboured for my safety.* V+O Literary

3 If you **harbour** someone who is wanted by the police, you hide them secretly in your house. EG *You could get into trouble for harbouring her.* V+O

hard /hɑːd/, **harder, hardest. 1** If something feels **hard** when you touch it, it is very firm and is not easily bent, cut, or broken. EG *The green fruits were as hard as rocks... The ground was baked hard.* ◊ **hardness.** EG *We gave them cushions to ease the hardness of the benches.* ADJ QUALIT ◊ N UNCOUNT

2 If something is **hard** to do or to understand, it is difficult. EG *He found it hard to make friends... That is a very hard question to answer.* ADJ QUALIT

3 If you try **hard** to do something or if you concentrate **hard,** you make a great effort or pay great attention. EG *I cannot stand upright, no matter how hard I try... He had worked hard all his life... Think hard about what I'm offering.* ADV

4 Hard work involves a lot of effort. EG *This has been a long hard day.* ADJ QUALIT

5 Hard also means **5.1** with a lot of force. EG *She slammed the door hard.* **5.2** with great severity. EG *The government's first reaction to the riots was to clamp down hard.* ADV

6 Someone who is **hard** shows no kindness or ADJ QUALIT

sympathy. EG *His hard grey eyes began to soften a little.*

7 If you are **hard** on someone, you treat them severely or unkindly. EG *Don't be hard on her.* ADJ PRED+*on*

8 If something is **hard** on a person or thing, it causes them suffering or damage. EG *This arrangement seemed rather hard on the women... This work's hard on the feet.* ADJ PRED+*on*

9 If your life is **hard,** it is difficult and unpleasant. ADJ QUALIT

10 A **hard** winter or **hard** frost is very cold or severe. ADJ QUALIT

11 Hard facts are definitely true. EG *We have no hard evidence to indicate that he is the culprit.* ADJ CLASSIF: ATTRIB

12 Hard drugs are very strong illegal drugs such as heroin or cocaine. ADJ CLASSIF: ATTRIB

13 You can refer to very extreme members of political parties as the **hard** left or the **hard** right. ADJ CLASSIF: ATTRIB

14 If you are **hard pushed, hard put,** or **hard pressed** to do something, you have great difficulty doing it. EG *One would be hard put to think of a better plan.* ● See also **hard-pressed.** PHRASE

15 If you feel **hard done by,** you feel that you have not been treated fairly. PHRASE

16 to **follow hard on the heels of** something: see **heel.**

hard and fast. Hard and fast rules cannot be changed and should be obeyed. EG *There isn't any hard and fast rule about this.* ADJ CLASSIF: ATTRIB

hardback /ˈhɑːdbæk/, **hardbacks.** A **hardback** is a book which has a stiff hard cover. EG *...a hardback edition... The book was published in hardback.* N COUNT OR in+N

hardboard /ˈhɑːdbɔːd/ is a material made by pressing small pieces of wood very closely together. You buy it in thin, flexible sheets. N UNCOUNT

hard-boiled. A **hard-boiled** egg has been boiled in its shell until the yolk and the white are hard. ADJ CLASSIF

hard cash is money in the form of notes and coins as opposed to a cheque or a credit card. N UNCOUNT

hard core. The **hard-core** members of a group are the ones who are most involved with the activities of the group. N MOD OR N SING

harden /ˈhɑːdᵊn/, **hardens, hardening, hardened. 1** When something **hardens** or when you **harden** it, it becomes stiff or firm. EG *The glue dries very fast and hardens in an hour.* V-ERG

2 When you **harden** your ideas or attitudes or when they **harden,** they become fixed and you become determined not to change them. EG *The organization has hardened its attitude to the crisis.* ◊ **hardening.** EG *It would almost certainly result in a hardening of Allied opposition and determination.* V-ERG ◊ N UNCOUNT

3 When events **harden** people or when people **harden,** they become less sympathetic and gentle than they were before. EG *Life in the camp had hardened her considerably.* V-ERG

hard-headed. Someone who is **hard-headed** does not allow emotion to affect their actions. EG *...this hard-headed brother of mine.* ADJ QUALIT

hard-hearted /hɑːd ˈhɑːtɪd/. Someone who is **hard-hearted** has no sympathy for people and does not care if they are hurt or unhappy. EG *I'm not a hard-hearted man.* ADJ QUALIT

hard labour; spelled **hard labor** in American English. **Hard labour** is hard physical work which people have to do as punishment for a crime. EG *He was condemned to six months hard labour.* N UNCOUNT

hard line. If someone takes a **hard line** on something, they have a firm policy which they refuse to change. EG *He applauded the president's hard line on the issue.* N SING

hard luck. You can say '**Hard luck**' to someone to say that you are sorry they have not got something that they wanted. CONVENTION Informal

---

What phrase might you use to show sympathy with someone?

hardly /hɑːdli¹/. 1 You use **hardly** to say that [ADV BRD NEG] something is only just true. EG *I was beginning to like Sam, though I hardly knew him... The boy was hardly more than seventeen... She had hardly any money... Her bedroom was so small that she could hardly move in it.*

2 If you say **hardly** had one thing happened when [ADV BRD NEG] something else happened, you mean that the first event was followed immediately by the second. EG *Hardly had he uttered the words when he began laughing.*

3 You can use **hardly** in an ironic way to empha- [ADV BRD NEG] size that something is certainly not true. EG *In the circumstances, it is hardly surprising that he re- signed.*

hard of hearing. If someone is **hard of hearing**, [ADJ QUALIT] they are deaf.

hard-pressed. If someone is **hard-pressed**, they [ADJ QUALIT] are under a great deal of strain and worry. EG *...hard-pressed clergymen.*

hardship /hɑːdʃɪp/, **hardships. Hardship** is the [N UNCOUNT] situation someone is in when they are suffering [OR N COUNT] from great difficulties and problems in life, often because they do not have enough money. EG *...a period of considerable hardship and unhappiness... You know the hardships we have suffered.*

hard shoulder. The hard shoulder is the area at [N SING : the+N] the side of a motorway where you are allowed to stop if your car has broken down.

hard-up. If you are **hard-up**, you have very little [ADJ QUALIT] money. EG *I know we're all hard up, but everybody can afford a drink now and then.*

hardware /hɑːdwɛə/. 1 **Hardware** is tools and [N UNCOUNT] equipment for use in the home and garden.

2 Computer **hardware** is the machinery of a [N UNCOUNT] computer as opposed to the programs that are written for it. EG *Computer technology in all its phases from hardware to software has become less expensive.*

hard-wearing. Something that is **hard-wearing** [ADJ QUALIT] is strong and well made so that it lasts for a long time. EG *These blankets are hard-wearing, but not so warm as wool.*

hardy /hɑːdi¹/, **hardier, hardiest. 1** People and [ADJ QUALIT] animals that are **hardy** are strong and able to endure difficult conditions. EG *Their children are remarkably hardy.*

2 Plants that are **hardy** are able to survive frost [ADJ QUALIT] and cold weather. EG *Strawberries are hardy and easy to grow in all soils.*

hare /hɛə/, **hares, haring, hared. 1** A **hare** is an [N COUNT] animal like a large rabbit with long ears, long legs, and a small tail.

2 If you **hare** off or **hare** away somewhere, you [V+A] run off very fast. EG *They took one look at him and hared off.*

harebrained /hɛəbreɪnd/. Plans or ideas that are [ADJ QUALIT] **harebrained** are foolish and not likely to succeed. EG *...harebrained schemes.*

harem /hɛərəm, hɑːriːm/, **harems.** A **harem** is a [N COUNT] group of wives or mistresses belonging to one man, especially in Muslim societies. EG *...a harem of more than a hundred wives.*

haricot /hærɪkəʊ/, **haricots. Haricots** or **haricot** [N COUNT : beans** are small, pale beans. They are usually sold [USU PLURAL] dried.

hark /hɑːk/, **harks, harking, harked.** If someone [PHRASAL VB : or something **harks back** to an event or situation [V+ADV+to] in the past, they remember or remind you of it. EG *Increasingly she harked back to our 'dear little cottage'.*

harlequin /hɑːlɪkwɪn/ means having a lot of [ADJ CLASSIF : different colours. EG *...a harlequin jacket.* [ATTRIB]

harm /hɑːm/, **harms, harming, harmed. 1** To [V+O] **harm** someone means to cause them physical injury. EG *I stood very still, hoping they wouldn't harm my sister and me.* ▸ used as a noun. EG *He* ▸ [N UNCOUNT] *went in danger of physical harm.*

2 To **harm** something means to damage it or make [V+O]

it less effective or successful. EG *Washing cannot harm the fabric... This can harm a child's psycho- logical development.* ▸ used as a noun. EG *Much* ▸ [N UNCOUNT] *harm has been done to the earth's environment... Do prisons do more harm than good?*

3 If you say that someone or something will **come** [PHRASE] **to no harm** or that **no harm will come** to them, you mean that they will not be hurt or damaged.

4 If you say that someone or something is **out of** [PHRASE] **harm's way,** you mean that they are in a safe place. EG *The presents were now hidden under the sink, out of harm's way.*

5 If you say **there is no harm in** doing something, [PHRASE] you mean that you want to do it and you do not think that you will be blamed for doing it. EG *There's no harm in asking.*

harmful /hɑːmfʊl/. Something that is **harmful** [ADJ QUALIT] has a bad effect on someone or something else. EG *...the harmful effects of eating too many eggs... Too much salt can be harmful to a young baby.*

harmless /hɑːmlɪ³s/. 1 Something that is **harm-** [ADJ QUALIT] **less** is safe to use, touch, or be near. EG *...harmless butterflies.* ◊ **harmlessly.** EG *The rocket thudded* ◊ [ADV] *harmlessly to the ground.*

2 An action or activity that is **harmless** is unlikely [ADJ QUALIT] to annoy other people or make them worried or upset. EG *Singing in the bath gives him a little harmless pleasure.* ◊ **harmlessly.** EG *His column* ◊ [ADV] *deals harmlessly with the antics of film stars.*

harmonica /hɑːmɒnɪkə/, **harmonicas.** A **har-** [N COUNT] **monica** is a small musical instrument. You play it by moving it across your lips and blowing and sucking air through it.

harmonious /hɑːməʊnɪəs/. 1 A relationship, [ADJ QUALIT] agreement, or discussion that is **harmonious** is friendly and peaceful. EG *...a generally harmonious debate.* ◊ **harmoniously.** EG *Harold and I worked* ◊ [ADV] *harmoniously together.*

2 Something that is **harmonious** has parts which [ADJ QUALIT] go well together and which are in proportion to each other. EG *The different parts of the garden fit together in a harmonious way.*

3 Musical notes that are **harmonious** produce a [ADJ QUALIT] pleasant sound when played together. EG *...a harmo- nious musical chord.*

harmonize /hɑːmənaɪz/, **harmonizes, harmo-** [V OR V+with : **nizing, harmonized;** also spelled **harmonise.** If [RECIP] two or more things **harmonize** with each other, they fit in well with each other. EG *Such events harmonized with one's view of society.*

harmony /hɑːməni¹/, **harmonies. 1** If people are [N UNCOUNT] living in **harmony** with each other, they are in a state of peaceful agreement and co-operation. EG *Industry and the universities have worked together in harmony... ...people living in harmony with their environment.*

2 **Harmony** is the pleasant combination of differ- [N UNCOUNT] ent notes of music played at the same time. EG [OR N COUNT] *They sing in harmony... ...the harmonies of Ravel and Debussy.*

3 The **harmony** of something is the way in which [N UNCOUNT] its parts are combined into a pleasant arrange- [+SUPP] ment. EG *...the harmony of nature.*

harness /hɑːnɪ³s/, **harnesses, harnessing, har- nessed. 1** If you **harness** something such as a [V+O] natural source of energy, you bring it under your control and use it. EG *Techniques harnessing the energy of the sun are being developed.*

2 A **harness** is **2.1** a set of straps which fit under a [N COUNT] person's arms and round their body in order to hold equipment in place or to prevent them from moving too much. EG *A seat and harness for a child are essential in a family car.* **2.2** a set of leather straps and metal links fastened round a horse's head or body so that the horse can pull a carriage, cart, or plough.

3 If you **harness** a horse or other animal, you put a [V+O:OFT+to] harness on it. EG *...a dog harnessed to a sledge.*

harp /hɑːp/, **harps, harping, harped.** A **harp** is a N COUNT large musical instrument consisting of a row of strings stretched from the top to the bottom of a frame, which you play by picking at the strings with your fingers. See picture at MUSICAL INSTRU- MENTS.

harp on. If you **harp on** about something, you PHRASAL VB : keep on talking about it; used showing disapproval. V+ADV/PREP EG *She continued to harp on the theme of her wasted life.*

harpoon /hɑːpuːn/, **harpoons.** A **harpoon** is a N COUNT spear with a long rope attached to it, which is fired by people hunting whales.

harpsichord /hɑːpsɪkɔːd/, **harpsichords.** A N COUNT **harpsichord** is a musical instrument which looks like a small piano. When you press the keys, strings are plucked mechanically rather than hit by ham- mers as in a piano.

harrowing /hærəʊɪŋ/. A situation or event that is ADJ QUALIT **harrowing** is very upsetting or disturbing. EG *...a harrowing experience... The film is deeply harrow- ing.*

harry /hæri¹/, **harries, harrying, harried.** If you V+O **harry** someone, you constantly tell them what to Formal do, so that they feel anxious or annoyed. EG *He set to work harrying people for donations.* ◊ **harried.** ◊ ADJ QUALIT EG *...a waiter with a full tray and a harried expres- sion.*

harsh /hɑːʃ/, **harsher, harshest.** 1 A condition or ADJ QUALIT way of life that is **harsh** is severe and difficult. EG *His family wouldn't survive the harsh winter.* ◊ **harshness.** EG *...the harshness of their nomadic* ◊ N UNCOUNT *life.*

2 Behaviour and actions that are **harsh** are cruel ADJ QUALIT and unkind. EG *...her harsh, cold, contemptuous attitude.* ◊ **harshly.** EG *He thinks you've marked* ◊ ADV *his essay rather harshly.* ◊ **harshness.** EG *Dis-* ◊ N UNCOUNT *obedience is treated with special harshness.*

3 Something such as a light or a sound that is ADJ QUALIT **harsh** is very bright or loud, so as to be unpleasant. EG *Harsh daylight fell into the room... She spoke in a harsh whisper.* ◊ **harshly.** EG *'What is it?' he said* ◊ ADV *harshly.*

harvest /hɑːvɪst/, **harvests, harvesting, har- vested.** 1 The **harvest** is the cutting or picking of N SING : the+N crops at the time of year when they are ripe. EG *Their stock of rice wouldn't last until the harvest.* ▸ used as a verb. EG *We harvested what we could* ▸ V+O *before the rains came.*

2 A **harvest** is a year's crops that have ripened so N COUNT that they can be cut or picked. EG *Their sons always came home to help bring in the harvest.*

has /hæz/ is the third person singular of the present tense of **have.**

has-been, has-beens. A **has-been** is a person N COUNT who was once important or successful, but who is Informal now thought to be unimportant. EG *She was no longer dismissed as a political has-been.*

hash /hæʃ/. 1 If you **make a hash of** a job, you do PHRASE the job very badly. EG *At first I thought I would* Informal *make a terrible hash of it.*

2 **Hash** is a dish made from small lumps of meat N UNCOUNT fried with onions, potatoes, or other ingredients. EG *...corned beef hash.*

hasn't /hæzəⁿt/ is the usual spoken form of 'has not'.

hassle /hæsəⁿl/, **hassles, hassling, hassled.** 1 If N COUNT OR N you say that something is a **hassle**, you mean that N UNCOUNT it is difficult and annoying to do. EG *Washing is a* Informal *real hassle in a house with one cold tap.*

2 A **hassle** is also an argument. EG *I didn't want any* N COUNT OR *hassle from the other women.* N UNCOUNT

3 If someone **hassles** you, they keep annoying you, V+O for example by telling you to do things that you do Informal not want to do. EG *Oh God, she's back again to hassle me.*

haste /heɪst/. 1 **Haste** is the quality of doing N UNCOUNT things quickly. EG *I immediately regretted my*

haste... The old men began interrupting each other in their haste to explain what had happened.

2 If you do something **in haste**, you do it in a hurry. PHRASE EG *It was written quickly and published in haste.*

3 To **make haste** means to act quickly in doing PHRASE something. EG *Make haste, all of you, and get ready.* Outdated

hasten /heɪsəⁿn/, **hastens, hastening, hastened.** 1 If you **hasten** something, you make it happen V+O faster or sooner. EG *Two factors hastened the* Formal *formation of the new party.*

2 If you **hasten** to do something, you are quick to V+to-INF do it. EG *He hastened to remark that he was not against television.*

3 If you **hasten** somewhere, you hurry there. EG *He* V+A *hastened back into the forest.* Literary

hasty /heɪsti¹/, **hastier, hastiest.** 1 If you are ADJ QUALIT **hasty**, you do things suddenly and quickly, often without thinking properly about them. EG *Don't be hasty. It's not so easy to find another job... He made a hasty, unsuitable marriage.* ◊ **hastily.** EG *Philip* ◊ ADV *hastily changed the subject.*

2 A **hasty** action is done quickly because you do ADJ QUALIT not have much time. EG *...a hasty meal.* ◊ **hastily.** ◊ ADV EG *He dressed himself hastily.*

hat /hæt/, **hats.** 1 A **hat** is a covering that you N COUNT wear on your head, especially when you are out of doors. See picture at CLOTHES.

2 **Hat** is used in these phrases. **2.1** If you ask PHRASES someone to **keep** something **under** their **hat**, you are asking them to keep it secret. **2.2** If you describe something as **old hat**, you mean that it is so well-known and familiar that it has become uninteresting and boring. **2.3** If you say that some- one **is talking through** their **hat**, you mean that they are talking nonsense.

hatch /hætʃ/, **hatches, hatching, hatched.** 1 V-ERG : When a baby bird, insect, or other animal **hatches** IF V OFT+out or when it **is hatched**, it comes out of its egg by breaking the shell. EG *The larva hatches out and lives in the soil... ...newly hatched chicks.*

2 When an egg **hatches**, it breaks open and a baby V bird, insect, or other animal comes out. EG *After ten days, the eggs hatch.*

3 If you **hatch** a plot or a scheme, you think of it V+O and work it out. EG *I've heard about the grand plot that you two gentlemen are hatching.*

4 A **hatch** is **4.1** an opening in the deck of a ship, N COUNT which is used for people to come on deck or go below, or during loading and unloading cargo. EG *Hendricks poked his head through the forward hatch.* **4.2** an opening in a wall, especially one between a kitchen and a dining room, which you use to pass food through.

hatchback /hætʃbæk/, **hatchbacks.** A **hatch-** N COUNT **back** is a car with an extra door at the back which opens upwards.

hatchet /hætʃɪ²t/, **hatchets.** 1 A **hatchet** is a N COUNT small axe.

2 If two people **bury the hatchet**, they become PHRASE friendly again after a quarrel or disagreement. EG *Now that our fight was over we were glad to bury the hatchet.*

hate /heɪt/, **hates, hating, hated.** 1 If you **hate** V+O someone, you have an extremely strong feeling of dislike for them. EG *You really hate her, don't you?... She was aware of what she was doing and she hated herself for it.* ◊ **hated.** EG *...the most* ◊ ADJ QUALIT *hated man in America.*

2 If you say that you **hate** something, you mean V+O, V+-ING, that you find it very unpleasant. EG *I used to hate* OR V+to-INF *going to lectures... I hate milk... I would hate to move to another house.*

3 **Hate** is a strong feeling of dislike for someone or N UNCOUNT something. EG *He was a violent bully, destructive*

Do you use a musical instrument to harp on about something?

and full of hate... ...highly charged scenes of love and hate.

4 You can use an expression such as **'I hate to disturb you'**, or **'I hate to trouble you'** when you are apologizing to someone for what you are going to say next. EG *I hate to wake you up, but there's something urgent I've got to tell you.* PHRASE

5 You say **'I hate to say it'** to introduce something that you regret having to say because you feel that it is unpleasant or unfair. EG *There is unfortunately – I hate to say it – a substantial amount of racism in our cities.* PHRASE

hateful /ˈheɪtfʊl/. Someone or something that is **hateful** is extremely unpleasant. EG *It was going to be a hateful week.* ADJ QUALIT Outdated

hatred /ˈheɪtrɪ²d/ is an extremely strong feeling of dislike for someone or something. EG *...their hatred of technology... She felt hatred towards his sister.* N UNCOUNT : USU+SUPP

haughty /ˈhɔːtiˈ/, **haughtier, haughtiest.** Someone who is **haughty** is very proud and thinks that they are better than other people; used showing disapproval. EG *He had an air of haughty aloofness.* ADJ QUALIT

◊ **haughtily.** EG *'Very well,' he replied haughtily.* ◊ ADV

haul /hɔːl/, **hauls, hauling, hauled. 1** If you **haul** a heavy object somewhere, you pull it there using a lot of effort. EG *They hauled the pilot clear of the wreckage... Ralph hauled himself onto the platform.* V+O+A OR V-REFL+A

2 If you say that a journey or a struggle is a **long haul**, you mean that it takes a long time and a big effort. EG *We began the long haul up the cobbled street... ...as women begin the long haul to equality.* PHRASE

haul up. If someone **is hauled up** before a court of law, they are made to appear before the court. EG *He got hauled up in court for assaulting a student.* PHRASAL VB : V+O+ADV : OFT PASS

haunch /hɔːntʃ/, **haunches.** Your **haunches** are your buttocks and the tops of your legs. EG *He squatted down on his haunches.* N COUNT : USU PLURAL

haunt /hɔːnt/, **haunts, haunting, haunted. 1** If a place **is haunted**, people believe that a ghost appears there regularly. EG *The building was supposed to be haunted by the ghost of a leper.* V+O : USU PASS

2 If something unpleasant **haunts** you, you keep thinking about or worrying about it over a long period of time. EG *...a mystery that had haunted me for most of my life.* V+O

3 A problem that **haunts** a person or organization regularly causes difficulties for them over a period of time. EG *Lack of money haunted successive projects.* V+O Literary

4 Someone's **haunt** is a place which they often visit. EG *The pottery seems to be a favourite haunt among the children... Their old haunts have been ruined by becoming too popular.* N COUNT+SUPP

haunted /ˈhɔːntɪ²d/. **1** A **haunted** building or other place is one where people believe that a ghost regularly appears. EG *...a haunted house.* ADJ CLASSIF

2 Someone who has a **haunted** expression looks very worried or troubled. EG *Her face took on a haunted quality.* ADJ QUALIT

haunting /ˈhɔːntɪŋ/. Something that is **haunting** has a quality such as great beauty or sadness that makes a strong impression on you and remains in your thoughts. EG *He repeated the haunting melody.* ADJ QUALIT

have. See the entry on the next two pages.

haven /ˈheɪvə²n/, **havens.** You can refer to a place where people feel safe and secure as a **haven**. EG *They have made the park a haven for weary Londoners.* N COUNT

haven't /ˈhævə²nt/ is the usual spoken form of 'have not'.

haversack /ˈhævəsæk/, **haversacks.** A **haversack** is a canvas bag that you wear on your back and use to carry things in when you are out walking. N COUNT

havoc /ˈhævək/. **1** **Havoc** is a state of great disorder. EG *After the havoc of the war, England had to be rebuilt.* N UNCOUNT

2 If one thing **plays havoc with** another, it causes a lot of disorder and confusion. EG *The anxieties of the last few days had played havoc with his working hours.* PHRASE

hawk /hɔːk/, **hawks, hawking, hawked. 1** A **hawk** is a large bird with a short hooked bill and sharp claws. Hawks eat small birds and animals. EG *A hawk hovered, motionless, in the blue sky.* N COUNT

2 If you **watch** someone **like a hawk**, you watch them very carefully so that you will know if they do something wrong. PHRASE

3 If you **hawk** something around, you try to sell it by taking it around to various people who might be interested in buying it; often used showing disapproval. EG *His writings were being hawked round German publishers.* V+O : USU+A

hawthorn /ˈhɔːθɔːn/, **hawthorns.** A **hawthorn** is a small tree which has sharp thorns and white flowers. N COUNT OR N UNCOUNT

hay /heɪ/ is grass which has been cut and dried so that it can be used to feed animals. EG *About 30 or 40 bales of hay were scattered about the barn.* N UNCOUNT

hay fever is an illness similar to a cold, in which people sneeze a lot. People get hay fever in the summer because they are allergic to some types of pollen. N UNCOUNT

haystack /ˈheɪstæk/, **haystacks. 1** A **haystack** is a large pile of hay in a field, which has been built into a stack. N COUNT

2 If you say that trying to find something is like looking for **a needle in a haystack**, you mean that it is extremely difficult to find so you are very unlikely to find it. PHRASE

haywire /ˈheɪwaɪə/. If something goes **haywire**, it becomes completely disordered or out of control. ADJ PRED Informal

hazard /ˈhæzəd/, **hazards, hazarding, hazarded. 1** A **hazard** is something which could be dangerous to you. EG *...a natural hazard, like an earth tremor... Drinking alcohol is a real health hazard if carried to excess.* N COUNT

2 If you **hazard** a guess, you make a suggestion which is only a guess and which might be wrong. EG *'How much do you think he makes a year?' – 'Fifteen thousand,' Rudolph hazarded... As to the author of the letter, I will hazard a guess that it is Howard.* V+QUOTE OR V+O

hazardous /ˈhæzədəs/. Something that is **hazardous** is dangerous to people's health or safety. EG *...hazardous chemicals... Breathing smoky air may be hazardous to health.* ADJ QUALIT

haze /heɪz/ is a kind of mist caused by heat or dust in the air. EG *...in the golden morning haze... The room became cloudy with a blue haze of smoke.* N UNCOUNT +SUPP

hazel /ˈheɪzə²l/, **hazels. 1** A **hazel** is a kind of small tree which produces nuts. N COUNT OR N UNCOUNT

2 **Hazel** eyes are greenish-brown in colour. ADJ COLOUR

hazelnut /ˈheɪzə²lnʌt/, **hazelnuts. Hazelnuts** are nuts from a hazel tree. N COUNT

hazy /ˈheɪziˈ/, **hazier, haziest. 1** When the sky or a view is **hazy**, you cannot see it clearly because there is haze in the air. EG *...a hazy blue view beyond railings on a mountain pass.* ADJ QUALIT

2 If you are **hazy** about things or if your thoughts are **hazy**, you are unclear or confused about them. EG *She was hazy about her mother's origins... The details are getting a bit hazy in my mind now.* ADJ PRED

he /hiː/ is used as the subject of a verb. You use **he** **1** to refer to a man, boy, or male animal who has already been mentioned, or whose identity is known. EG *Bill had flown back from New York and he and his wife took me out to dinner.* **2** to refer to a person whose sex is not known or is not stated. EG *A teacher should do whatever he thinks best.* PRON : SING Outdated

head /hed/, **heads, heading, headed. 1** Your **head** is the part of your body which has your eyes, mouth, and brain in it. See picture at THE HUMAN BODY. EG *She shook her head.* N COUNT

2 The **head** of something is the top or most N SING+SUPP

HAVE

have /hæv/, **has, having, had**.

Have is one of the most important verbs in English. It is very common and has a large number of different uses, the most important of which are explained here.

In speech, and very informal writing, **have** is reduced to the sound /v/ spelled **'ve**.

'Have' as an auxiliary

1 When you want to show that an event that happened in the past is still important at the time you are speaking or writing, you use **have** followed by the past participle form of a verb. For example: *It hasn't rained for a month . . . She has never been to Rome . . . They have just bought a new car.*

2 The use of **had** as an auxiliary shows that an action happened earlier than another action which was also in the past. For example: *I had just finished when you arrived . . . Officials said that the two men had at last signed an agreement.*

3 The use of **having** as an auxiliary shows that one action had already happened before another action began. For example: *We were home by 8, having come straight from the station . . . Having been warned beforehand, I knew how he would react.*

'Have' meaning 'must'

4 When you want to say that something must be done or must happen, you can use **have** followed by the to-infinitive of another verb. For example: *We had to learn it in school . . . He had to sit down because he felt dizzy . . . I have to speak to your father . . . You have to be careful of your facts.*

'Have' with nouns

5 When you want to talk about something that happens as if it were an event, instead of using a verb you can use **have** followed by a noun. So that, instead of saying: *I strolled round the garden this morning,* you can say *I had a stroll round the garden this morning.*

Other examples of this are:
She was invited to the party / She had an invitation to the party . . .
A lot of people commented on my work / I had a lot of comments on my work.

You also find this use of **have** with nouns which do not have a corresponding verb, as in: *The children are having a party . . . What effect will this have on transport?*

'Have' replacing 'be'

6 You can make some statements more personal by using **have** instead of **be**. So that instead of saying: *There is no alternative,* you can say *You have no alternative*; and instead of: *There were students living with us,* you can say *We had students living with us.*

'Have' replacing other verbs

7 In normal speech or writing you can often use **have** where in more restricted or more formal language you would use a more specific verb. So you are more likely to say: *I have a sandwich every lunchtime;* than *I eat a sandwich every lunchtime.*

Other examples are:
I had a boring afternoon, rather than *I spent a boring afternoon.*
I had an operation last year, rather than *I underwent an operation last year.*

This feature of the use of **have** is particularly common where it is very obvious from the context what the meaning of the whole phrase is. Where doubt or confusion could be caused, speakers will probably choose the more specific verb, if it is important to be understood!

'Have' meaning 'own'

8 You can use **have** to make statements about things that you possess or about people and things that are closely associated with you. For example: *What is the point of having a mink coat? . . . He had a small hotel . . . She had a successful career.*

The following sentences with **have** would be equally correct with **have got**, especially in spoken English: *They don't have any money . . . We had no regrets at all . . . They have one daughter . . . I have lots of friends.*

'Have' in phrases

9 Have is often followed by an object and a verb which can be either a past participle or a to-infinitive.

When it is followed by a past participle, it can mean that you arrange for something to happen. For example: *You should have your car cleaned . . . Make sure you have that shirt washed for next Monday . . . Isn't it time you had your hair cut?*

Or it can mean that something happens to you without you doing anything about it: *She had her purse stolen . . . Children love to have stories read to them.*

When **have** is followed by a to-infinitive, it means that you are responsible for something. For example: *She had a huge department to administer . . . They have a lot of shopping to do . . . I've never had so much work to finish.*

10 Here are a number of expressions which use **have**:

If you **have it in for someone**, you want to make life difficult for them because you dislike them or they have upset you.

If you **have been had**, you have been deliberately tricked by someone, who has, for example, sold you something at too high a price.

If you are **had up for something**, you appear in court for a crime that you have committed.

If you say that you **have had it**, you mean that you are too exhausted to continue doing something.

If you **have on** something such as a dress or a shirt, you are wearing it.

If you **are having** someone **on**, you are teasing them.

important end of it. EG *Howard stood at the head of the stairs... ...standing at the head of the queue.*

3 When you toss a coin and it comes down **heads**, ADV AFTER VB you can see the side of the coin which has a person's head on it.

4 The **head** of a company or organization is the N COUNT+SUPP person in charge of it. EG *...the head of the English department.* ▶ used as an adjective. EG *...the head* ▶ ADJ CLASSIF: *gardener.* ATTRIB

5 In a school, the **head** is the head teacher. EG *I had* N COUNT *coffee with the head after school.*

6 If you **head** an organization, you are in charge of V+O it. EG *The firm is headed by John Murray.*

7 If something **heads** a list, it is at the top of it. V+O

8 You can mention the title of a piece of writing by V+O+C: saying how it **is headed**. EG *...an article headed 'An* USU PASS *Open Letter to the Prime Minister.'*

9 If you **head** in a particular direction, you go in V+A that direction. EG *Julie headed for the cupboard.*

10 If you **are heading** for an unpleasant situation, V+*for*: you are behaving in a way that makes the situation ONLY CONT more likely. EG *You may be heading for disaster.*

11 When you **head** a ball, you hit it with your head. V+O

12 Head is also used in these phrases. **12.1** The PHRASES cost or amount **a head** or **per head** is the cost or amount for each person. EG *The meal will cost £9 a head.* **12.2** If you say something **off the top of your head**, you say it without thinking about it before you speak. **12.3** If someone says to you **'On your own head be it'**, they mean that any unpleasant or bad results of your action will be your responsibility. **12.4** If you are laughing, crying, or Informal shouting your **head off**, you are doing it very noisily. EG *It woke up and started screaming its head off.* **12.5** If you **bite** or **snap** someone's **head** Informal **off**, you speak to them very angrily. **12.6** If something **comes** or **is brought to a head**, it reaches a state where you have to do something urgently about it. EG *Anti-British feeling came to a head in the 1890's.* **12.7** If you **get** a fact or idea **into** your **head**, you start thinking that it is true. If you **get** a fact or idea **into** someone else's **head**, you make them think that it is true. **12.8** If alcohol **goes to** your **head**, it makes you drunk. **12.9** If praise or success **goes to** your **head**, it makes you conceited. **12.10** If you **keep** your **head**, you stay calm. If you **lose** your **head**, you panic. **12.11** If you Informal say you could not **make head nor tail of** something, you mean you could not understand it at all. **12.12** When people **put** their **heads together**, they try to solve a problem together. **12.13** If you say Informal that someone is **off** their **head**, you mean that they are behaving in a very stupid way.

13 See also **heading**.

headache /hɛdeɪk/, **headaches. 1** A **headache** is N COUNT a pain that you feel in your head. EG *She took an aspirin to relieve her headache.*

2 If you say that something is a **headache**, you N COUNT mean that it causes you difficulty or worry. EG *Rivalry between the two industries presents a big headache for government.*

headdress /hɛddrɛs/, **headdresses.** A **head-** N COUNT **dress** is something that people sometimes wear on their heads for decoration. EG *The dancers wore face masks and tall head-dresses.*

head-first. If you fall somewhere **head-first**, ADV AFTER VB your head is the part of your body that is furthest forward as you fall. EG *He had fallen head-first into the ditch.*

headgear /hɛdgɪə/. You can refer to hats or other N UNCOUNT things worn on people's heads as **headgear.**

heading /hɛdɪŋ/, **headings.** A **heading** is the title N COUNT of a piece of writing, written or printed at the top of it. EG *The figures were put forward under the heading 'World Fuel Requirements in the 1990's'.*

headlamp /hɛdlæmp/, **headlamps.** A **headlamp** N COUNT is a headlight.

headland /hɛdlɔ³nd/, **headlands.** A **headland** is N COUNT a narrow piece of land which sticks out into the sea. EG *A road was built across the headland.*

headless /hɛdlɪ²s/. A **headless** body has no head. ADJ CLASSIF

headlight /hɛdlaɪt/, **headlights.** A car's **head-** N COUNT: **lights** are the large bright lights at the front of it. USU+POSS See picture at CAR. EG *All the cars had their headlights on.*

headline /hɛdlaɪn/, **headlines. 1** A **headline** is N COUNT the title of a newspaper story, printed in large letters at the top of the story. EG *The headlines that day were full of news of the kidnapping.*

2 The **headlines** are also the main points of the N PLURAL news which are read on radio or television. EG *And now for the main headlines again.*

headlong /hɛdlɒŋ/. **1** If you move **headlong** in a ADV AFTER VB particular direction, you move there very quickly. EG *The frightened elephants ran headlong through the forest.*

2 If you rush **headlong** into something, you do it ADV AFTER VB quickly without thinking carefully about it. EG *Don't* OR ADJ CLASSIF *rush headlong into buying new furniture... ...a headlong rush to sell.*

headmaster /hɛdmɑːstə/, **headmasters.** A N COUNT **headmaster** is a man who is the head teacher of a school.

headmistress /hɛdmɪstrɪ²s/, **headmistresses.** A N COUNT **headmistress** is a woman who is the head teacher of a school.

head of state, heads of state. A **head of state** is N COUNT the leader of a country, for example a president, king, or queen.

head-on. 1 If two vehicles hit each other **head-on**, ADV AFTER VB they hit each other with their front parts pointing OR ADJ towards each other. EG *The motor cycle ran head-* CLASSIF: *on into the lorry... ...a head-on collision.* ATTRIB

2 A **head-on** disagreement is firm and direct and ADJ CLASSIF: has no compromises. EG *...a head-on confrontation* ATTRIB, OR *with the unions... It had to meet the threat head-on.* ADV AFTER VB

headphones /hɛdfəʊnz/ are small speakers N PLURAL which you wear over your ears in order to listen to music or speech without other people hearing it.

headquarters /hɛdkwɔːtəz/. The **headquarters** N PLURAL of an organization are the main offices where the leaders of the organization work. EG *The bank had its headquarters in Paris... Captain Meadows was ordered to report to headquarters the following day.*

headroom /hɛdruː⁴m/ is the amount of space N UNCOUNT below a roof or a bridge. EG *Maximum headroom 2.6 metres.*

headscarf /hɛdskɑːf/, **headscarves.** A **head-** N COUNT **scarf** is a scarf which is worn on the head by women.

headstand /hɛdstænd/, **headstands.** If you do a N COUNT **headstand**, you balance upside down with your head and your hands on the ground and your legs up in the air.

head start, head starts. If you have a **head start** N COUNT on other people, you have an advantage over them in a competition or race. EG *A university degree would give you a head start in getting a job.*

headstone /hɛdstəʊn/, **headstones.** A **head-** N COUNT **stone** is a large stone at one end of a grave, usually with the name of the dead person carved on it.

headstrong /hɛdstrɒŋ/. Someone who is **head-** ADJ QUALIT **strong** is determined to do what they want and will not let anyone stop them. EG *Luce was stubborn and headstrong.*

head teacher, head teachers. A **head teacher** N COUNT is a teacher who is in charge of a school.

headway /hɛdweɪ/. If you **make headway**, you PHRASE make progress towards achieving something. EG *The emergency services began to make some headway in restoring order to the devastated area.*

Is it safe to believe in hearsay?

headwind /hɛdwɪnd/, **headwinds**. A **headwind** N COUNT
is a wind which blows in the opposite direction to
the one in which you are moving.

heady /hɛdi/. 1 A **heady** experience makes you ADJ QUALIT :
feel very excited and full of energy. EG ...the heady ATTRIB
days of the sixties.

2 A **heady** drink or atmosphere strongly affects ADJ QUALIT
your physical senses, for example by making you
feel drunk or excited. EG ...heady perfumes.

heal /hiːl/, **heals, healing, healed**. 1 When an V-ERG
injury **heals** or when something **heals** it, it becomes healthy and normal again. EG His leg needs
support while the bone is healing.

2 If someone **heals** you when you are ill, they v+o
make you well again. ◊ **healer, healers**. EG Some ◊ N COUNT
were treated by traditional healers.

3 When a process or the passage of time **heals** v+o
something that has been damaged, it restores it. EG
...damage to the ecology that would take a hundred
years to heal.

heal up. When an injury **heals up**, it becomes PHRASAL VB :
completely healthy again. EG His hoof had healed V+ADV
up.

health /hɛlθ/. 1 Your **health** is the condition of N UNCOUNT
your body. EG Cigarette smoking is dangerous to
your health... My mother was in poor health.

2 **Health** is a state in which you are fit and well N UNCOUNT
and not ill. EG They were glowing with health... ...a
soldier who was nursed back to health.

3 When you **drink to** someone's **health** or **drink** PHRASE
their **health**, you have a drink as a sign of wishing
that they will be healthy and happy.

4 The **health** of an organization or system is the N UNCOUNT :
success that it has and the fact that it is working USU+SUPP
well. EG ...the health of the British film industry.

health food is food which has been made or N MASS
grown without any chemicals, and which some
people eat because they believe it is better for
their health than ordinary food.

healthy /hɛlθi/, **healthier, healthiest**. 1 Some- ADJ QUALIT
one who is **healthy** is well and is not suffering
from any illness. EG ...a healthy baby... As a result of
the diet, he feels fitter and healthier. ◊ **healthily**. ◊ ADV
EG It is perfectly possible to live healthily on a
meat-free diet.

2 If a feature or quality that you have is **healthy**, it ADJ QUALIT
shows that you are well. EG The children have
healthy appetites... ...healthy skin. ◊ **healthily**. EG ◊ ADV+ADJ
...the dreamless slumber of the healthily tired man.

3 Something that is **healthy** is good for you and ADJ QUALIT
likely to make you healthy. EG ...healthy seaside air.

4 An organization or system that is **healthy** is ADJ QUALIT
successful. EG ...a healthy economy.

5 A **healthy** amount of something is a large ADJ QUALIT
amount that is a sign of success. EG ...healthy
profits.

heap /hiːp/, **heaps, heaping, heaped**. 1 A **heap** of N COUNT
things is an untidy pile of them. EG Brody picked up OR N PART
the heap of papers and piled them on top of a
radiator... ...a compost heap. ● If someone col- ● PHRASE
lapses **in a heap**, they fall heavily and do not
move.

2 If you **heap** things in a pile, you arrange a lot of v+o+A
them in a large pile. EG ...food heaped on platters...
We sat on cushions heaped on the floor.

3 If you **heap** praise or criticism on someone or v+o+on/upon
something, you give them a lot of praise or criticism. EG Burgin heaped scorn on such styles of
painting and sculpture.

4 **Heaps** of something or a **heap** of something is a N PART
large quantity of it. EG We've got heaps of time. Informal

heap up. If you **heap** things **up**, you make them PHRASAL VB :
into a pile. Heap up the flour round the sides of the V+O+ADV
bowl.

heaped /hiːpt/. 1 A **heaped** spoonful is so full that ADJ CLASSIF
its contents rise higher than the top of its sides. EG
Add one heaped tablespoon of salt.

2 If a surface is **heaped** with things, it has a lot of ADJ CLASSIF
OFT+with

them on it in a pile. EG The desk was heaped with
magazines.

hear /hɪə/, **hears, hearing, heard** /hɜːd/. 1 When v+o or v :
you **hear** sounds, you are aware of them because NO IMPER
they reach your ears. EG He heard a distant voice
shouting... Etta hated to hear Mrs Hochstadt talk
like that... She could hear clearly.

2 When a judge or a court **hears** a case or **hears** v+o
evidence, they listen to it officially in order to
make a decision about it.

3 If you **hear** from someone, you receive a letter v+from :
or a telephone call from them. EG They'll be NO CONT,
delighted to hear from you again. NO IMPER

4 If you **hear** some news or information, you learn v+o,
it because someone tells it to you or it is mentioned V+REPORT,
on the radio or television. EG I was glad to hear that OR V+about/of
things are quietening down... My first meeting with
the woman confirmed everything I had heard
about her... When he came to hear of their difficulties, he volunteered help.

5 If you **have heard of** someone or something, you PHRASE
know that they exist, but you do not know any
details about them. EG The vast majority of these
students had never heard of the Marshall plan.

6 If you **won't hear of** someone doing something, PHRASE
you refuse to let them do it. EG Her father had
refused to hear of such a thing.

hearer /hɪərə/, **hearers**. Your **hearers** are the N COUNT
people who are listening to you speak. EG He was Formal
shocked by the violent reactions of some of his
hearers.

hearing /hɪərɪŋ/, **hearings**. 1 **Hearing** is the N UNCOUNT
sense which people and animals have that makes it
possible for them to be aware of sounds. EG Her
limbs were weak, her hearing almost gone. ● See
also **hard of hearing**.

2 If you are **in** or **within** someone's **hearing**, you PHRASE
are so close to them that they can hear what you
are saying. EG She began to grumble about it within
his hearing.

3 A **hearing** is an official meeting held to collect N COUNT
facts about an incident or problem. EG I wish these
hearings had been televised.

4 If you get **a hearing** or **a fair hearing**, you have PHRASE
the opportunity to give your opinion about something. EG She believed in giving a fair hearing to all
sides of the question.

hearing aid, hearing aids. A **hearing aid** is an N COUNT
instrument that helps deaf people to hear better.

hearsay /hɪəseɪ/ is information which you have N UNCOUNT
been told indirectly, but which you do not personally know to be true. EG 'Everything else I know is
hearsay,' she said.

hearse /hɜːs/, **hearses**. A **hearse** is a large car N COUNT
that carries the coffin at a funeral.

heart /hɑːt/, **hearts**. 1 Your **heart** is the organ in N COUNT
your chest that pumps the blood around your body.
EG She could hear her heart beating... ...the first
successful human heart transplant.

2 You can also talk about someone's **heart** 2.1 N COUNT :
when you are referring to their emotions. EG ...the USU+POSS
troubled heart of the younger man... She knew all Literary
the secrets of my heart. 2.2 when you are describ- N COUNT OR
ing their character and attitudes. EG He's got a very N UNCOUNT
soft heart.

3 **Heart** is also used in various expressions to refer N UNCOUNT
to courage and determination. EG It was a bad time
and people were losing heart... No one had the
heart to tell her.

4 The **heart** of something is the most central and N SING+of
important part of it. EG ...the heart of the problem...
...lyrics that get right to the heart of the matter.

5 The **heart** of a place is its centre. EG Thousands N SING+of
of protesters marched into the heart of San Francisco.

6 The **heart** of a vegetable such as a cabbage or N COUNT+SUPP
lettuce is the group of leaves in its centre.

7 A **heart** is also a shape with an outline made up N COUNT
of two curves going upwards and then meeting at a

point at the bottom. It is often coloured red or pink and is used to represent love. See picture at SHAPES.

8 Hearts is one of the four suits in a pack of N UNCOUNT playing cards. Each card in the suit is marked with one or more red symbols in the shape of a heart.

9 A **heart** is also one of the thirteen playing cards N COUNT in the suit of hearts.

10 Heart is also used in these phrases. **10.1** If you PHRASES say that someone is a particular kind of person **at heart**, you mean that this is what they are really like. EG *He was at heart a kindly man.* **10.2** If you know something such as a poem **by heart**, you have learnt it so well that you can remember it perfectly. EG ...*learning by heart the dates of battles.* **10.3** If you have a **change of heart**, your feelings about something change and you act in a different way. EG *He has declared his change of heart on this matter.* **10.4** If you say something **from the heart** or **from the bottom of** your **heart**, you are being sincere. **10.5** If your **heart isn't in** what you are doing, you have very little enthusiasm for it. EG *The children soon sensed that his heart was not in it.* **10.6** What you think or feel **in your heart of hearts** is what you secretly really think or feel. EG *In his heart of hearts, he didn't trust the authorities.* **10.7** If someone can do something **to** their **heart's content**, they can do it as much as they want. EG *Jack could talk and plan to his heart's content.* **10.8** If someone **breaks** your **heart**, they make you very unhappy, for example because you love them and they do not love you. EG *She said that I had broken her heart.* **10.9** If something **breaks** your **heart**, it makes you very sad. EG *Though it breaks my heart to say it, the American ship is prettier.* **10.10** If something is **close to** or **dear to** your **heart**, you care deeply about it. **10.11** If your **heart leaps**, you suddenly feel very excited and happy. If your **heart sinks**, you suddenly feel very disappointed or unhappy. EG *I found there were six of us auditioning and my heart sank.* **10.12** If you have **set** your **heart on** something, you want it very much. EG *She had set her heart on going.* **10.13** If you **take** an experience **to heart**, you are deeply affected and upset by it.

heart attack, heart attacks. If someone has a N COUNT **heart attack**, their heart begins to beat irregularly or fails to pump blood properly, so that it causes them a lot of pain. People often die of heart attacks.

heartbeat /hɑːtbiːt/, **heartbeats. 1** Your **heart-** N SING **beat** is the regular movement of your heart as it pumps blood around your body. EG *He could hear the pounding rhythm of her heartbeat.*

2 A **heartbeat** is one of the movements of your N COUNT heart.

heartbreak /hɑːtbreɪk/ is very great sadness or N UNCOUNT unhappiness. EG *All of Allen's work is about heartbreak.*

heartbreaking /hɑːtbreɪkɪŋ/. Something that is ADJ QUALIT **heartbreaking** makes you feel extremely sad and upset. EG ...*a heartbreaking letter from an American friend whose wife had died.*

heartbroken /hɑːtbrəʊkⁿn/. Someone who is ADJ QUALIT **heartbroken** is extremely sad and upset. EG *Sylvia would be heartbroken if one of her cats died.*

hearten /hɑːtⁿn/, **heartens, heartening, heart-** V+O : USU PASS **ened.** When something such as good news **heartens** you, it encourages you and makes you cheerful. EG *I am very heartened by her success in the last election.* ◊ **heartening.** EG ...*some heartening* ◊ ADJ QUALIT *news.*

heartfelt /hɑːtfelt/. You use **heartfelt** to describe ADJ CLASSIF : something that someone feels or believes deeply ATTRIB and sincerely. EG ...*a heartfelt wish that it will never happen.*

hearth /hɑːθ/, **hearths.** A **hearth** is the floor of a N COUNT fireplace. EG *A bright fire was burning in the hearth.*

heartland /hɑːtlænd/, **heartlands.** The **heart-** N COUNT OR **land** or **heartlands** of a country, region, or conti- N PLURAL nent are the most central parts of it. EG ...*the* +SUPP *industrial heartlands of western Europe.*

heartless /hɑːtlɪˀs/. Someone who is **heartless** is ADJ QUALIT cruel and unkind. EG ...*a heartless cynic... She sat there, mocking me with her heartless eyes.* ◊ **heartlessly.** EG ...*defenceless creatures being* ◊ ADV *heartlessly destroyed.*

heartrending /hɑːtrendɪŋ/. Something that is ADJ QUALIT **heartrending** makes you feel great sadness and pity. EG *Isabel's sigh was heartrending.*

hearty /hɑːtiˈ/, **heartier, heartiest. 1** Someone ADJ QUALIT or something that is **hearty** is loud, cheerful, and energetic. EG *He had a big hearty laugh... ...hearty soccer fans.* ◊ **heartily** /hɑːtɪliˈ/. EG *Etta laughed* ◊ ADV *heartily... 'Now then,' she cried heartily, 'who's for a lovely drink?'*

2 Hearty feelings or opinions are strongly felt or ADJ CLASSIF : held. EG *I have a hearty hatred of all examinations.* ATTRIB ◊ **heartily.** EG *Why should one pretend to like* ◊ ADV *people one actually heartily dislikes?*

heat /hiːt/, **heats, heating, heated. 1** When you V+O **heat** something, you raise its temperature by using a flame, a cooker, or other special piece of equipment. EG *Don't heat more water than you need... ...accommodation that is difficult to heat.*

2 Heat is **2.1** warmth or the quality of being hot. EG N UNCOUNT *Water retains heat much longer than air... ...loss of body heat.* **2.2** the temperature of something that N UNCOUNT is warm. EG *It should be equivalent to blood heat.* +SUPP **2.3** a source of heat, for example a cooking ring on N SING a stove. EG *Don't put pans straight on to a high heat.*

3 The **heat** is very hot weather. EG *You shouldn't go* N SING *out in this heat.*

4 You also use **heat** to refer to a state of strong N UNCOUNT emotional feeling, especially anger or excitement. +SUPP EG *'You're a fool,' Boylan said, without heat.*

5 The **heat** of a particular activity or time is the N SING : point at which there is the greatest activity and *the*+N+*of* excitement. EG *Last week, in the heat of the election campaign, the Prime Minister left for Venice.*

6 A **heat** is a race or competition whose winners N COUNT take part in the next one with winners of similar races or competitions. This continues until there is the right number of competitors for a final race or competition. ● See also **dead heat**.

7 See also **heated, heating**.

heat up. 1 When something **heats up**, it gradual- PHRASAL VB : ly becomes hotter. EG *The air over the great land* V+ADV *mass heats up in the summer.* **2** When you **heat up** V+O+ADV food that has already been cooked, you make it hot again. EG *He debated heating up the pot roast.*

heated /hiːtⁿd/. If someone is **heated** about some- ADJ QUALIT thing, they are angry and excited about it. EG *He became quite heated... ...a heated argument.* ◊ **heatedly.** EG *Naturalists argued heatedly about* ◊ ADV *the issue for nearly a century.*

heater /hiːtə/, **heaters.** A **heater** is a piece of N COUNT equipment which is used to warm the air in a room or to heat water. EG ...*a water heater... Mel had left the car heater on.* ● See also **immersion heater**.

heath /hiːθ/, **heaths.** A **heath** is an area of open N COUNT land covered with rough grass or heather.

heathen /hiːðⁿn/, **heathens.** Christians used to N COUNT refer to people from other countries who were not Outdated Christian as **heathens**. EG *He was sent out to convert the heathens.* ▶ used as an adjective. EG ▶ ADJ CLASSIF ...*the ancient heathen inhabitants of this place.*

heather /heðə/ is a plant with small flowers that N UNCOUNT grows wild on hills and moorland.

heating /hiːtɪŋ/ is the process, system, or equip- N UNCOUNT ment involved in keeping a room or building warm. EG *The rent was £7 a week including heating.* ● See also **central heating**.

heatwave /hi:tweɪv/, **heatwaves.** A **heatwave** is N COUNT a period of time when the weather is much hotter than usual.

heave /hi:v/, **heaves, heaving, heaved. 1** If you V OR V+O **heave** something that is heavy or difficult to move, you push, pull, or lift it using a lot of effort. EG *I threw the rope around the tree and heaved with all my might... Lee heaved himself with a groan from his chair.* ▶ used as a noun. EG *With one single* ▶ N COUNT *determined heave I pulled everything down.*

2 If something **heaves,** it moves up and down or in V and out with large regular movements. EG *I staggered across the heaving deck... His shoulders heaved silently.*

3 To **heave** also means to vomit or feel sick. EG *The* V *sight of the soapy scum made her stomach heave.*

4 If you **heave a sigh,** you give a big sigh. EG *They* PHRASE *all heaved a sigh of relief when he finally departed.*

heaven /hevə⁰n/, **heavens. 1 Heaven** is where N PROPER God is believed to live, and where good people are believed to go when they die.

2 If you say that a place or a situation is **heaven,** N UNCOUNT you mean that it gives you a lot of pleasure. EG *Mrs* Informal *Duncan's cottage is just heaven... Kelmscott is a heaven on earth.*

3 The **heavens** are the sky. EG *The moon was high* N PLURAL : *in the heavens... The man continued to gesticulate* the+N *sadly towards the heavens.* Literary

4 You say **'heaven knows'** to emphasize that you PHRASE do not know something or that you find something very surprising. EG *Heaven knows what I would do without it... He ended up, heaven knows why, in the Geological Museum.*

5 You say **'good heavens'** or **'heavens'** to express EXCLAM surprise or to emphasize that you agree or disagree with someone. EG *Heavens, is that the time?... 'Oh, good heavens, no,' said Etta with a light laugh.*

● **thank heavens:** see **thank.** ● **for heaven's sake:** see **sake.**

heavenly /hevə⁰nli¹/. **1** You use **heavenly** to ADJ CLASSIF : describe things relating to heaven. EG *The heavenly* ATTRIB *spirits were displeased with the people.*

2 If you describe something as **heavenly,** you ADJ QUALIT mean that it is very pleasant and enjoyable. EG *...a* Informal *big steaming pot of the most heavenly stew.*

heaven-sent. Something that is **heaven-sent** is ADJ CLASSIF unexpected but very welcome because it happens at just the right time. EG *...the latest heaven-sent triumph of advanced technology.*

heavenward /hevə⁰nwəd/; also **heavenwards.** ADV **Heavenward** means up towards the sky or to Literary heaven. EG *Mr Menzies turned his eyes heavenward... The old lady's husband had departed heavenwards during the night.*

heavily /hevɪli¹/. If someone says something ADV **heavily,** they say it in a slow way which shows a feeling such as sadness, tiredness, or annoyance. EG *'I don't understand you,' he said heavily.*

heavy /hevi¹/, **heavier, heaviest. 1** Something that is **heavy 1.1** weighs a lot. EG *He dumped the* ADJ QUALIT *heavy suitcases by the door.* **1.2** is great in amount, ADJ QUALIT degree, or intensity. EG *There would be heavy casualties... ...a heavy responsibility.* ◊ **heavily.** EG ◊ ADV *It began to rain more heavily... He smoked heavily all his life.* **1.3** has a solid, thick appearance rather ADJ QUALIT than being light and delicate. EG *...spectacles with heavy black frames... He had a heavy, sullen face.* ◊ **heavily.** EG *I've never seen anyone so heavily* ◊ ADV *built move quite so fast.*

2 If you ask how **heavy** something is, you are ADJ PRED asking how much it weighs.

3 Something that is **heavy** with things is full of ADJ PRED them or loaded with them. EG *The trees were heavy* +with *with fruit and blossoms.* Literary

4 If a person's breathing is **heavy,** it is very loud ADJ QUALIT and deep. EG *She lay sleeping, her breathing heavy.* ◊ **heavily.** EG *She sighed heavily.* ◊ ADV

5 A **heavy** substance or material is thick and solid ADJ QUALIT

in texture. EG *...heavy clay soil... ...a heavy tweed coat.*

6 A **heavy** movement or action is done with a lot of ADJ QUALIT : force or pressure. EG *A heavy blow with a club* ATTRIB *knocked him senseless.* ◊ **heavily.** EG *He sat down* ◊ ADV *heavily.*

7 You say that a period of time or a schedule is ADJ QUALIT **heavy** when it involves a lot of work. EG *I've had a heavy week.*

8 Heavy work requires a lot of strength or energy. ADJ QUALIT

9 If you are **heavy** on something, you use too much ADJ PRED+on of it. EG *You've been a bit heavy on the mascara,* Informal *haven't you?*

10 Air or weather that is **heavy** is unpleasantly ADJ QUALIT still, hot, and damp.

11 If your heart is **heavy,** you are sad about ADJ QUALIT something.

12 to **make heavy weather** of something: see **weather.**

heavy-duty. A **heavy-duty** machine is strong ADJ CLASSIF : and can be used a lot or used to do very hard work. ATTRIB

heavy-handed. Someone who is **heavy-handed** ADJ QUALIT acts or speaks forcefully and without any care or thought. EG *We are incensed at the government's heavy-handed economic policies.*

heavy industry, heavy industries. Heavy in- N UNCOUNT **dustry** is industry in which large machines are OR N COUNT used to produce a raw material such as steel, or to make large objects.

heavy metal is a style of rock music with a N UNCOUNT strong, fast beat, which is played very loudly on electric guitars and drums.

heavyweight /hevi¹weɪt/, **heavyweights.** A N COUNT **heavyweight** is a boxer or wrestler in the heaviest class. EG *...a heavyweight boxing champion.*

heck /hek/. **1** Some people use **the heck** in EXCLAM questions after words such as 'how', 'why', or Informal 'what', to emphasize that they are angry or surprised. EG *Why the heck is she so polite?*

2 People use **a heck of** to emphasize the amount PHRASE or size of something. EG *Jean has done a heck of a* Informal *lot for us.*

heckle /hekə⁰l/, **heckles, heckling, heckled.** If V OR V+O people **heckle** public speakers or performers, they interrupt them by making loud, unfriendly remarks. EG *He went to heckle at their meetings.* ◊ **heckling.** EG *Despite the heckling, the meeting* ◊ N UNCOUNT *was a success.* ◊ **heckler, hecklers.** EG *There was* ◊ N COUNT *already a crowd of hecklers there when I arrived.*

hectic /hektɪk/. A situation that is **hectic** is very ADJ QUALIT busy and involves a lot of rushed activity. EG *It's been pretty hectic at the office.*

he'd /hi:d/ is **1** the usual spoken form of 'he had', especially when 'had' is an auxiliary verb. EG *He said he'd told them.* **2** a spoken form of 'he would'. EG *He said that he'd give me a lift.*

hedge /hedʒ/, **hedges, hedging, hedged. 1** A N COUNT **hedge** is a row of bushes along the edge of a garden, field, or road.

2 If you **hedge,** you avoid answering a question or V : OFT+on committing yourself to something. EG *Politicians are known for hedging on promises.*

3 If something **is hedged** about, **hedged** around, V-PASS+A : or **hedged** in with things, it is affected by things OFT+with which prevent or restrict its freedom or development. EG *The concessions were hedged around with many restrictions... We feel hedged in by fear.*

4 If you **hedge** your **bets,** you avoid the risk of PHRASE losing a lot by supporting more than one person or Informal thing in a situation.

hedgehog /hedʒhɒg/, **hedgehogs.** A **hedgehog** is N COUNT a small brown animal with sharp spikes covering its back.

hedgerow /hedʒrəʊ/, **hedgerows.** A **hedgerow** N COUNT is a row of bushes, trees, and plants, usually growing along a country lane or between fields.

hedonism /hi:də⁰nɪzə⁰m, hed-/ is the belief that N UNCOUNT gaining pleasure is the most important thing in life. Formal

◊ **hedonistic** /hiːdɔ°nɪstɪk, hɛd-/. EG ...*lives of* ◊ ADJ CLASSIF
unending hedonistic delight.

heed /hiːd/, **heeds, heeding, heeded. 1** If you V+O
heed someone's advice or warning, you pay atten- Formal
tion to it and do what they suggest. EG *David wished*
that he had heeded his father's warnings.

2 If you **take heed** of what someone says or if you PHRASE
pay heed to them, you consider carefully what
they say. EG *Take heed of these warnings.*

heedless /hiːdlɪ²s/. If you are **heedless** of some- ADJ CLASSIF :
one or something, you do not take any notice of OFT+*of*
them. EG *She stood glued to the radio, heedless of* Formal
the bustle about her... ...heedless passers-by hurry-
ing through the market place.

heel /hiːl/, **heels. 1** Your **heel** is **1.1** the back part N COUNT
of your foot, just below your ankle. See picture at
THE HUMAN BODY. EG *One of his heels had got*
blistered on the walk. **1.2** the raised part on the
bottom of your shoe at the back. EG *All I could hear*
was the click of my own heels on the linoleum.

2 Heel is used in these phrases. **2.1** If you **dig** your PHRASES
heels in, you refuse to do something such as
change your opinions or plans. EG *Organizations*
employing volunteers are beginning to dig their
heels in about the new regulations. **2.2** If one event
or situation **follows hard on the heels of** another,
it happens very quickly after it. EG *Cultural isola-*
tion has followed quickly on the heels of economic
recession. **2.3** If you **turn** or **swing on** your **heel**,
you suddenly turn round, often because you are
angry or surprised. EG *He swung round upon his*
heel and surveyed the young man. **2.4** If you **take** Literary
to your **heels**, you run away.

hefty /hɛftɪ¹/, **heftier, heftiest.** Someone or some- ADJ QUALIT
thing that is **hefty** is very large in size, weight, or Informal
amount. EG *...a broad, hefty Irish nurse... We sell*
them at a hefty profit.

heifer /hɛfə/, **heifers.** A **heifer** is a young cow. N COUNT

height /haɪt/, **heights. 1** The **height** of a person N UNCOUNT
or thing is its measurement from the bottom to the OR N COUNT
top. EG *The redwood grows to 100 metres in height...* +SUPP
He was of medium height... This enables them to
grow to considerable heights.

2 Height is the quality of being tall. EG *You'll* N UNCOUNT
recognize her because of her height.

3 A particular **height** is the distance that some- N UNCOUNT
thing is above the ground. EG *The aircraft reaches* OR N COUNT
its maximum height of 80,000 feet in about ten +SUPP
minutes... The bag had been dropped from about
shoulder height. ● If something **gains height**, it ● PHRASE
moves to a higher position above the ground. If it
loses height, it moves to a lower position. EG *The*
plane began to lose height on its approach to
Heathrow.

4 You use **heights** to refer to the top of a hill or N PLURAL
cliff. EG *...fierce fighting on the heights above the*
bay.

5 Something that is at its **height** is at its most N SING+POSS
successful, powerful, or intense. EG *The group had*
at its height 500 members... It is the height of the
tourist season.

6 You can use **height** to emphasize how extreme a N SING :
quality is. For example, if you say that something is the+N+*of*
the **height** of absurdity, you mean that it is ex- Formal
tremely absurd. EG *It seemed to me the height of*
luxury.

7 If something reaches great **heights**, it becomes N PLURAL
very extreme or intense. EG *Love must soar to the* +SUPP
greatest heights of sacrifice.

heighten /haɪtə°n/, **heightens, heightening,** V-ERG
heightened. When something **heightens** a feeling
or state or when it **heightens**, it increases in
degree or intensity. EG *We should try to calm*
people's fears rather than heighten them through
uncertainty... As their hardship heightened, so did
their desperation and anger. ◊ **heightened.** EG *She* ◊ ADJ CLASSIF :
is in a state of heightened emotion. ATTRIB

heinous /heɪnəs, hiː-/ means extremely evil. EG ADJ QUALIT
...heinous crimes. Formal

heir /ɛə/, **heirs.** Someone's **heir** is the person who N COUNT
will inherit their money, property, or title when
they die. EG *...Thompson's son and heir... The*
Prince of Wales is heir to the throne.

heiress /ɛərɪ²s/, **heiresses.** An **heiress** is a wom- N COUNT
an who will inherit property, money, or a title.

heirloom /ɛəluːm/, **heirlooms.** An **heirloom** is N COUNT
an ornament or other object that has belonged to a
family for a very long time. EG *...jewels and other*
family heirlooms.

held /hɛld/ is the past tense and past participle of
hold.

helicopter /hɛlɪkɒptə/, **helicopters.** A **helicop-** N COUNT
ter is an aircraft with large blades which rotate
above it rather than wings.

hell /hɛl/. **1 Hell** is the place where wicked people N PROPER
are believed to go when they die.

2 If you say that a situation is **hell**, you mean that it N UNCOUNT
is extremely unpleasant. EG *War is hell... I don't* Informal
know how I've stuck it. It's been hell. ● If you say ● PHRASE
that **all hell broke loose**, you mean that there was
suddenly a lot of arguing or fighting. EG *When*
Darwin asserted that men were descended from
apes, all hell broke loose.

3 Hell is a swear word used by some people to EXCLAM
express annoyance or to emphasize what they are
saying.

4 Hell is also used in these phrases. **4.1** If someone PHRASES
gives you **hell**, they are very severe and cruel to Informal
you. EG *I bet these ladies gave their secretaries hell.*
4.2 Something that **plays hell** with something else Informal
has a bad effect on it. EG *The new extension will*
play hell with the plumbing. **4.3** Some people say Informal
'go to hell' when they are angrily telling someone
to go away; a rude expression. **4.4** If you **get the** Informal
hell out of a place, you leave it very quickly. EG
Get the hell out of here! **4.5** If someone says **'to** Informal
hell with' something, they are saying that they do
not care about it and do not want any more to do
with it. EG *To hell with university.* **4.6** Some people Informal
use **the hell** in questions after words such as 'how',
'why', or 'what', to emphasize how angry or surprised they are. EG *How the hell should I know?* **4.7** Informal
If someone does something **for the hell of it**, they
do it for fun or for no particular reason. EG *I don't*
want to offend people for the hell of it. **4.8** People Informal
use **a hell of** or **one hell of** to emphasize the
amount or size of something. EG *There was a hell of*
a lot of traffic... The government was in one hell of
a mess. **4.9** Some people use **like hell** to empha- Informal
size how strong an action or quality is. EG *It was*
beginning to hurt like hell... It's cold as hell out
here.

he'll /hiːl/ is the usual spoken form of 'he will'. EG
He'll have to go to hospital, won't he?

hellish /hɛlɪʃ/. If you describe something as **hell-** ADJ QUALIT
ish, you mean that it is extremely unpleasant. EG Informal
It's hellish being a student without a grant.

hello /hə²ləʊ/, **hellos;** also spelled **hallo** and **hullo.**

1 You say **'Hello'** when you are greeting someone CONVENTION
or starting a telephone conversation, for example.
EG *'Hello,' Lynn said. 'Hello,' said the girl... He lifted*
the receiver and said 'Hello,' but no one replied.
▶ used as a noun. EG *Do come over and say hello to* ▶ N COUNT
the group.

2 You can call **'hello'** to attract someone's atten- CONVENTION
tion. EG *'Hello, can I come in?' I called. 'Is anyone*
here?'

helmet /hɛlmɪt/, **helmets.** A **helmet** is a type of N COUNT
hard hat which you wear to protect your head.

help /hɛlp/, **helps, helping, helped. 1** If you **help** V+O OR V :
someone, you make it easier for them to do some- OFT+INF
thing, for example by doing part of the work or by OR *to*-INF
giving them advice or money. EG *Something went*
wrong with his machine so I helped him fix it... The

Which words on these pages refer only to
women?

courier helped everyone out of the coach... This organization may be able to help you with such information.

2 If something **helps**, it makes it easier for you to get something, do something, or bear something. EG *I've got 40 pence, will that help?* V OR V+O: OFT+INF OR to-INF

3 If something **helps** to achieve a particular result, it is one of the things that together achieve it. EG *One of the things that can help to keep prices down is high productivity... Having a job helps keep them off the streets.* V+to-INF OR -INF; ALSO V+O+to-INF OR -INF

4 If you **help** yourself, you serve yourself some food or drink. EG *Mr Stokes helped himself to some more rum.* V-REFL: OFT+to

5 If you can't **help** the way you feel or the way you behave, you cannot change it or stop it happening. EG *You can't help who you fall in love with... I can't help feeling that it was a mistake to let him go.* V+O OR V+-ING

6 If you give **help** to someone, you help them. EG *The organization gives help to single women.* N UNCOUNT

7 If you say that someone or something is a **help**, you mean that they help you to do something. EG *He was a great help with some of the problems.* N SING: a+N

8 If something **is of help**, it makes things easier or better. EG *Having a sober mind around might prove to be of some help.* PHRASE

9 **Help** is also the assistance that someone gives when they go to rescue a person who is in danger. EG *I thought I'd better yell for help.* N UNCOUNT

10 You shout **'Help!'** when you are in danger, in order to attract someone's attention. EXCLAM

help out. If you **help out** or **help** someone **out**, you help them by doing some work for them or lending them money. PHRASAL VB: V+ADV OR V+O+ADV

helper /hɛlpə/, **helpers**. A **helper** is a person who helps another person or group with a job. EG *All the helpers for this organization are voluntary.* N COUNT

helpful /hɛlpful/. **1** If someone is **helpful**, they help you by doing work for you or by giving you advice or information. EG *They were all very pleasant and extremely kind and helpful.* ADJ QUALIT

◊ **helpfully.** EG *Doctor Percival said helpfully, 'I'd advise you not to go'.* ◊ **helpfulness.** EG *I was greatly impressed by the efficiency and helpfulness of the stage crew.* ◊ ADV ◊ N UNCOUNT

2 Something that is **helpful** makes a situation more pleasant or more easy to tolerate. EG *It is often helpful during an illness to talk to other sufferers... None of these suggestions is very helpful.* ADJ QUALIT

helping /hɛlpɪŋ/, **helpings**. A **helping** of food is the amount of it that you get in a single serving. EG *I gave him a second helping of pudding.* N PART

helpless /hɛlpləs/. If you are **helpless**, you are unable to do anything useful or unable to protect yourself, for example because you are very weak. EG *He was helpless to resist... ...a helpless baby... Sam raised his arms in a helpless gesture.* ADJ QUALIT

◊ **helplessly.** EG *She stood there helplessly crying... His wrist hung helplessly at his side.* ◊ ADV

◊ **helplessness.** EG *She took advantage of my utter helplessness.* ◊ N UNCOUNT

hem /hɛm/, **hems, hemming, hemmed. 1** The **hem** of a skirt or dress is the bottom edge of it, which is folded over and sewn. N COUNT

2 If you **hem** a piece of cloth, you sew the edge of it to make it neat and prevent it from fraying. V OR V+O

hem in. If you **are hemmed in** by something, you are completely surrounded by it so that you cannot move. EG *The Princess's car was hemmed in by the crowd.* PHRASAL VB: V+O+ADV

hemisphere /hɛmɪsfɪə/, **hemispheres**. A **hemisphere** is one half of the earth. EG *...the greatest empires in the western hemisphere.* N COUNT Formal

hemoglobin /hiːməˈɡləʊbɪn, hɛm-/. See **haemoglobin**.

hemophilia /hiːməˈfɪlɪə, hɛm-/. See **haemophilia**.

hemorrhage /hɛmərɪdʒ/. See **haemorrhage**.

hemorrhoids /hɛməˈrɔɪdz/. See **haemorrhoids**.

hen /hɛn/, **hens**. A **hen** is **1** a female chicken. People often keep hens for their eggs. **2** the female of any bird. EG *...a hen pheasant.* N COUNT

hence /hɛns/. **1 Hence** means for the reason just mentioned or as a result of the fact just mentioned. EG *The computer has become smaller and cheaper and hence more available to a greater number of people.* ADV SEN Formal

2 If you say that something will happen a number of hours, days, or years **hence**, you mean that it will happen that number of hours, days, or years after the time when you are speaking. EG *The tunnel will open in 1993, seven years hence.* ADV AFTER N Formal

henceforth /hɛnsˈfɔːθ/ means from this time on. EG *Henceforth his life would never be the same again.* ADV SEN Formal

henchman /hɛntʃmə³n/, **henchmen**. The **henchmen** of a powerful person are people employed by that person to do violent or dishonest work; used showing disapproval. EG *He signed the papers and left it to his henchmen to do the work.* N COUNT

hepatitis /hɛpəˈtaɪtɪs/ is a serious disease which causes a person's liver to become inflamed. N UNCOUNT

her /hɜː/. **1 Her** is used as the object of a verb or preposition. You use **her** to refer to a woman, girl, or female animal who has already been mentioned, or whose identity is known. **Her** is also sometimes used to refer to a nation, ship, or car. EG *I knew your mother. I was at school with her... They gave her the job.* PRON: SING

2 You also use **her** to indicate that something belongs or relates to a woman, girl, or female animal who has already been mentioned, or whose identity is known. **Her** is also sometimes used to indicate that something belongs or relates to a nation, ship, or car. EG *Her face was very red... Britain must, of course, expand her air power.* DET POSS

3 You also use **her** in some titles when you are referring to a woman with that title. EG *...Her Majesty the Queen.*

herald /hɛrəld/, **heralds, heralding, heralded. 1** Something that **heralds** a future event or situation is a sign that it is going to happen or appear. EG *His rise to power heralded the end of the liberal era.* V+O

▸ used as a noun. EG *The festival was the herald of a new age.* ▸ N COUNT+of

2 If an important event or action **is heralded**, announcements have been made about it so that everyone knows about it. EG *Every reduction in taxation is heralded as a new achievement... ...the royal couple's much heralded world tour.* V+O: USU PASS+as

herb /hɜːb/, **herbs**. A **herb** is a plant which is used to add flavour to food, or as a medicine. EG *...dried herbs and spices... ...herb tea.* ◊ **herbal** /hɜːbə³l/. EG *...herbal medicine.* N COUNT ◊ ADJ CLASSIF: ATTRIB

herculean /hɜːkjəˈliːən/. A **herculean** task or effort requires great strength or effort. EG *You must make a herculean effort not to talk to them about it.* ADJ CLASSIF ATTRIB Literary

herd /hɜːd/, **herds, herding, herded. 1** A **herd** is a large group of animals of one kind that live together. EG *...a herd of goats.* N PART

2 If you **herd** people or animals, you make them move together to form a group. EG *...men herding cattle... The chained people were herded back into the dark cellar.* V+O: OFT+A

here /hɪə/. **1** You use **here 1.1** when you are referring to the place where you are or to a place which has been mentioned. EG *She left here at eight o'clock... Elizabeth, come over here... You've been here for a number of years. **1.2** when you are pointing to a place that is near you, in order to draw someone's attention to it. EG *You have to sign here and acknowledge the receipt. **1.3** to indicate that the person or thing that you are talking about is near you or being held by you. EG *What can you do with this thing here?... I have here a very important message that has just arrived.* ADV

2 You can also use **here** to refer to the time, ADV situation, or subject that you have come to or that you are dealing with. EG *I think that what we're talking about here is role-playing... The autumn's really here at last.*

3 You use **here is** or **here are** to draw attention to PHRASE something or to introduce something. EG *Now here is the News... Here she is... Here's how it's done.*

4 You say **'Here'** or **'Here you are'** when you are CONVENTION offering or giving something to someone. EG *He pushed a piece of paper across the table. 'Here you are. My address.'... Here, hold this while I go and get a newspaper.*

5 You say **'Here we are'** when you have just found CONVENTION something that you have been looking for.

6 Something that is happening **here and there** is PHRASE happening in several different places. EG *Panic here and there was only to be expected.*

7 You say **'Here's to us'** or **'Here's to your new** CONVENTION **job'**, for example, as a toast in order to wish success or happiness to someone.

hereby /hɪəbaɪ/. You use **hereby** in formal state- ADV ments and documents to emphasize that a state- Formal ment or declaration is official. EG *I hereby resign.*

hereditary /hɪ²redɪtə⁰ri¹/. **1** A characteristic or ADJ CLASSIF illness that is **hereditary** is passed on to a child from its parents before it is born. EG *...a progressive, hereditary disease of certain glands.*

2 A title or position in society that is **hereditary** is ADJ CLASSIF passed on as a right from parent to child. EG *...the hereditary right to belong to the House of Lords.*

heredity /hɪ²redɪ¹ti¹/ is the process by which N UNCOUNT characteristics are passed on from parents to their children before the children are born. EG *Do you think we are influenced more by environment or heredity?*

heresy /herə¹si¹/, **heresies**. Heresy is **1** a belief, N UNCOUNT opinion, or way of behaving that disagrees with OR N COUNT beliefs that are generally accepted. EG *...bitter complaints about the heresies of the group.* **2** a belief, opinion, or way of behaving that seriously disagrees with the principles of a particular religion. EG *He was tried for heresy in the ecclesiastical courts.*

heretic /herə¹tɪk/, **heretics**. A **heretic** is **1** a N COUNT person who has beliefs or opinions that most people think are wrong. EG *His views are portrayed as those of an unrealistic leftist heretic.* **2** a person who belongs to a particular religion, but whose beliefs seriously disagree with the principles of that religion. EG *They were denounced as heretics and burned at the stake.*

heretical /hɪ²retɪkə⁰l/. A belief or action that is ADJ CLASSIF **heretical 1** disagrees with beliefs that are generally accepted. EG *...heretical opinions.* **2** seriously disagrees with the principles of a particular religion. EG *The bishops jailed him for heretical and blasphemous words.*

heritage /herɪtɪdʒ/. A country's **heritage** is all N SING+POSS the qualities and traditions that have continued over many years, especially when they are considered to be of historical importance. EG *...a building that may one day be part of Britain's national heritage.*

hermit /hɜ:mɪt/, **hermits**. A **hermit** is a person N COUNT who lives alone, away from people and society.

hero /hɪərəʊ/, **heroes**. **1** A **hero** is **1.1** the main N COUNT male character in a book, play or film, who is admired or respected for his good qualities. EG *Robert Powell plays Alec, the hero of the play.* **1.2** someone who has done something brave or good and is admired by a lot of people. EG *...one of the heroes of the Battle of Britain.*

2 If you describe someone as your **hero**, you mean N COUNT+POSS that you admire them greatly. EG *Bill Hook was my first rugby hero.*

heroic /hɪ²rəʊɪk/, **heroics**. **1** Actions that are **heroic 1.1** are brave and courageous. EG *...truly* ADJ QUALIT *heroic work by army engineers.* ◊ **heroically**. EG ◊ ADV

They fought heroically. **1.2** involve great effort and ADJ QUALIT determination to succeed. EG *...a heroic stand against undemocratic provocation.* ◊ **heroically**. ◊ ADV EG *The boys heroically kept the secret even from their parents.*

2 Heroic people are very brave and courageous. EG ADJ CLASSIF : *They are heroic figures in the fight against cancer.* ATTRIB

heroin /herəʊɪn/ is a powerful drug which some N UNCOUNT people take for pleasure, but which they can become addicted to. EG *...an overdose of heroin.*

heroine /herəʊɪn/, **heroines**. A **heroine** is **1** the N COUNT main female character in a book, play or film, who is admired or respected for her good qualities. EG *...Adah, the heroine of the book.* **2** a woman who has done something brave or good and is admired by a lot of people. EG *...the heroine of their great 1967 election triumph.*

heroism /herəʊɪzə⁰m/ is great courage and brav- N UNCOUNT ery. EG *...an act of heroism.*

heron /herən/, **herons**. A **heron** is a kind of large N COUNT bird which eats fish.

herring /herɪŋ/, **herrings**. **Herring** can also be N COUNT used as the plural form.
A **herring** is a kind of long silver-coloured fish that lives in the sea. ● See also **red herring**.

hers /hɜ:z/. You use **hers** to indicate that some- PRON POSS : thing belongs or relates to a woman, girl, or female SING animal who has already been mentioned, or whose identity is known. **Hers** is also sometimes used to indicate that something belongs or relates to a nation, ship, or car. EG *He laid his hand on hers... You were an old friend of hers.*

herself /hɜ²self/. **1** You use **herself** as the object PRON REFL of a verb or preposition to refer to the same SING woman, girl, or female animal who is mentioned as the subject of the clause, or as a previous object in the clause. **Herself** is also sometimes used in relation to a nation, ship, or car. EG *She groaned and stretched herself out flat on the sofa... Barbara stared at herself in the mirror... On the way home Rose bought herself a piece of cheese for lunch.*

2 You also use **herself** to emphasize the female PRON REFL : subject or object of a clause, and to make it clear SING who you are referring to. EG *Sally herself came back... How strange that he should collide with Melanie Byrd herself... Their audience was of middle-aged women like herself.*

3 If a girl or woman does something **herself**, she PRON REFL : does it without any help or interference from SING anyone else. EG *She had printed the little card herself.*

he's /hi:z/ is the usual spoken form of 'he is' or 'he has', especially when 'has' is an auxiliary verb. EG *He's a reporter... I hope he's got some money left.*

hesitancy /hezɪtənsi¹/ is unwillingness to do N UNCOUNT something. EG *...an air of childlike hesitancy.*

hesitant /hezɪtə⁰nt/. If you are **hesitant** about ADJ QUALIT doing something, you do not do it quickly or immediately, for example because you are uncertain, embarrassed, or worried about it. EG *He seemed hesitant to confirm the bad news... ...a hesitant, almost boyish smile.* ◊ **hesitantly**. EG ◊ ADV *'Maybe you could teach me,' said Marsha hesitantly.*

hesitate /hezɪteɪt/, **hesitates, hesitating, hesitated. 1** If you **hesitate**, you pause slightly while V you are doing something or just before you do it, usually because you are uncertain, embarrassed, or worried about it. EG *She put her hand on the phone, hesitated for a moment, then picked up the receiver... I said: 'What was all that about?' He hesitated. 'I'm sorry. I'd rather not say.'*

2 If you **hesitate** to do something, you are unwill- V+to-INF ing to do it because you are not certain whether it is correct or right. EG *I would hesitate to say*

What is the name for a female hero?

precisely what a fantasy is... Don't hesitate to go to a doctor if you have any unusual symptoms.

hesitation /hɛzɪteɪʃəⁿn/, **hesitations. 1 Hesitation** is **1.1** a pause or slight delay in something that you are doing. EG *'Well, no,' Karen said, with some hesitation... ...a slight hesitation.* **1.2** an unwillingness to do something. EG *After some hesitation he agreed to allow me to write the article... The calm voice of authority overrode the teacher's hesitations.* N UNCOUNT OR N COUNT

2 If you **have no hesitation in** saying something, you are certain that you are right to say it. EG *They had no hesitation in describing the situation as ridiculous.* PHRASE

heterogeneous /hetəˈrəʊdʒiːnɪəs/. Something that is **heterogeneous** consists of many different types of things. EG *Arts and sciences are contained in one heterogeneous collection, the South Kensington Museum.* ADJ QUALIT Formal

heterosexual /hetəˈrəˈsɛksjuᵊl/. **1** A **heterosexual** relationship is a sexual relationship between a man and a woman. ADJ CLASSIF

2 Someone who is **heterosexual** is sexually attracted to people of the opposite sex. ADJ CLASSIF

het up /het ʌp/. If you get **het up**, you get very excited or anxious about something. EG *...when he gets all het up about some business problem.* ADJ PRED Informal

hew /hjuː/, **hews, hewing, hewed, hewn** /hjuːn/. If someone **hews** stone, they cut large pieces out of it roughly. EG *...hewn stone.* V+O Formal

hey /heɪ/. You say or shout **'hey'** to attract someone's attention or show how surprised, interested, or annoyed you are. EG *'Hey, Ben!' he called. There was no reply... Hey, Dad, what's for dinner?* CONVENTION Informal

heyday /heɪdeɪ/. The **heyday** of a person, nation, or organization is the time when they are most powerful, successful, or popular. EG *...the heyday of Christianity.* N SING+POSS

hi /haɪ/. You say **'hi'** **1** when you are greeting someone. EG *'Hi, Uncle Harold,' Thomas said... Hi, there, Mr Swallow, good to see you.* **2** when you are trying to attract someone's attention. EG *Ralph jumped to his feet. 'Hi! You two!'* CONVENTION Informal Outdated

hiatus /haɪeɪtəs/. A **hiatus** is a pause in which nothing happens. EG *There came a pause, a hiatus. He stared out of the window.* N SING Formal

hibernate /haɪbəneɪt/, **hibernates, hibernating, hibernated.** Animals that **hibernate** spend the winter in a state like a deep sleep. EG *Squirrels don't hibernate.* ◊ **hibernation** /haɪbəneɪʃəⁿn/. EG *...a brown bear emerging from hibernation.* V ◊ N UNCOUNT

hiccup /hɪkʌp/, **hiccups, hiccupping, hiccupped;** also spelled **hiccough. Hiccups** are repeated little choking sounds in your throat. You sometimes get hiccups if you have been eating or drinking too quickly. ▸ used as a verb. EG *She turned over on her side, hiccupped once or twice and went to sleep.* N COUNT: USU PLURAL ▸ V

hid /hɪd/ is the past tense of **hide.**

hidden /hɪdᵊn/. **1 Hidden** is the past participle of **hide.**

2 Something that is **hidden** is not easily noticed. EG *...the hidden disadvantages of a cheque book.* ADJ CLASSIF

3 A place that is **hidden** is difficult to find. EG *...hidden valleys.* ADJ CLASSIF

hide /haɪd/, **hides, hiding, hid** /hɪd/, **hidden** /hɪdᵊn/. **1** If you **hide** something, you put it in a place where it cannot easily be seen or found. EG *The women managed to steal and hide a few knives.* V+O

2 If you **hide** or if you **hide** yourself, you go somewhere where you cannot easily be seen or found. EG *There was nowhere to hide.* V OR V-REFL

3 If you **hide** your feelings or information, you keep it a secret, so that no one knows about it. EG *I couldn't hide this fact from you.* V+O

4 If something **hides** an object, it covers it and prevents it from being seen. EG *Much of his face was hidden by a beard.* V+O

5 A **hide** is the skin of a large animal, which is used for making leather. N MASS

6 See also **hidden, hiding.**

hideous /hɪdɪəs/. Something that is **hideous** is extremely unpleasant or ugly. EG *They're not like dogs, they're ugly, hideous brutes... ...the hideous conditions of trench warfare.* ◊ **hideously.** EG *...hideously mutilated bodies... ...a hideously difficult task.* ADJ QUALIT ◊ SUBMOD

hiding /haɪdɪŋ/, **hidings. 1** If someone is in **hiding,** they have secretly gone somewhere where they cannot be seen or found. EG *He has not been heard from since going into hiding in June.* N UNCOUNT

2 If you give someone a **hiding,** you hit them many times as a punishment. EG *He told us to stop, or else we'd get a good hiding.* N COUNT Informal

hierarchy /haɪərɑːkiˈ/, **hierarchies. 1** A **hierarchy** is a system in which people have different ranks or positions depending on how important they are. EG *...the hierarchy of the Episcopal Church.* ◊ **hierarchical** /haɪərɑːkɪkᵊl/. EG *...ancient hierarchical societies.* N COUNT Formal ◊ ADJ QUALIT

2 The **hierarchy** is the group of people who have the power in an organization. EG *The university hierarchy decided that it was best to ignore the situation.* N COUNT Formal

hieroglyphics /haɪərəglɪfɪks/ are written symbols or words which you cannot understand. EG *On the blackboards were hieroglyphics which I was told were called logarithms.* N COUNT

hi-fi /haɪfaɪ/, **hi-fis.** A **hi-fi** is a set of equipment which you use to play records and tapes, and which produces stereo sound of good quality. EG *...listening to classical music on the hi-fi.* N COUNT

high /haɪ/, **higher, highest; highs. 1** A **high** structure or mountain measures a great amount from the bottom to the top. EG *...the high walls of the prison.* ADJ QUALIT

2 You use **high** to say how much something measures from the bottom to the top. EG *...a low mud wall about 10 centimetres high... ...a 200 foot high crag.* ADJ AFTER N

3 If something is **high,** it is a long way above the ground, above sea level, or above a person. EG *The bookshelf was too high for him to reach... I threw the shell high up into the air.* ADJ QUALIT

4 High also means great in amount, degree, or intensity. EG *Ceramic materials will withstand high temperatures... Her works fetch high prices... ...areas of high unemployment.* ADJ QUALIT

5 You can use **high** with numbers. For example, if a number or level is **in the high** eighties, it is more than eighty-five, but not as much as ninety. PHRASE

6 If someone has a **high** position in a profession or society, they have an important position in it. EG *She is high enough up in the company to be able to help you... ...high social status.* ADJ QUALIT

7 If people have a **high** opinion of you, they respect you very much. ADJ QUALIT

8 If the quality or standard of something is **high,** it is very good indeed. EG *...high-quality colour photographs.* ADJ QUALIT

9 If someone has **high** principles or standards, they are morally good. ADJ QUALIT

10 A **high** sound is close to the top of a particular range of notes. EG *...a high squeaky voice.* ADJ QUALIT

11 If your spirits are **high,** you are happy and confident about the future. EG *They were not at all depressed, but in high spirits.* ADJ QUALIT

12 If you are **high** on drugs, you are under the influence of drugs. ADJ QUALIT Informal

13 A **high** is the greatest level or amount that something reaches or has reached. EG *Prices on the stock exchange reached another record high last week.* N COUNT+SUPP

14 High also means advanced or complex. EG *...a successful job in high finance... The questions he'd asked were at a higher level than other people's.* ADJ CLASSIF ATTRIB

15 If you say that **it is high time** something was PHRASE done, you mean that it should be done now, and that it should have been done before now. EG *It's high time that we did something about improving the situation.*

highbrow /haɪbraʊ/. If you describe something as **highbrow**, you mean that it is intellectual, academic, and difficult to understand. EG *...highbrow radio programmes.* ADJ QUALIT

high-class. Something that is **high-class** is of very good quality and of high social status. EG *...big hotels and high-class restaurants.* ADJ QUALIT

higher /haɪə/. **1 Higher** is the comparative form of **high**.
2 A **higher** exam or qualification is of an advanced standard or level. EG *They have their first degrees and are studying for higher degrees.* ADJ CLASSIF : ATTRIB

higher education is education at universities, colleges, and polytechnics. EG *...the government's policy on higher education.* N UNCOUNT

high-heeled /haɪ hi:ld/. **High-heeled** shoes have a narrow high heel at the back. They are usually worn by women. ADJ CLASSIF

high heels are high-heeled shoes. N PLURAL

highlands /haɪləndz/ are mountainous areas of land. EG *...the highlands of New Guinea.* N PLURAL

highlight /haɪlaɪt/, **highlights, highlighting, highlighted. 1** If you **highlight** a point or problem, you draw attention to it. EG *The survey highlighted the needs of working women.* V+O
2 A **highlight** is the most interesting or exciting part of something. EG *This visit provided the real highlight of the morning.* N COUNT+SUPP
3 Highlights in a person's hair are thin streaks of lighter colour that have been made by dyeing the hair. EG *...blonde highlights.* N PLURAL

highly /haɪlɪ/. **1** You use **highly 1.1** to emphasize that a particular quality exists to a great degree. EG *The report is highly critical of these policies... It is highly improbable that they will accept... ...highly-educated people.* **1.2** to indicate that something is very important. EG *...a highly placed negotiator... ...a very highly classified document.* ADV+ADJ
2 If you praise someone **highly** or speak **highly** of them, you praise them a lot. EG *They spoke highly of Harold... Ross Thompson obviously thought very highly of him.* ADV

highly-strung. Someone who is **highly-strung** is very nervous and easily upset. ADJ QUALIT

high-minded. Someone who is **high-minded** has strong moral principles. EG *...high-minded idealists from overseas.* ADJ QUALIT

Highness /haɪnɪs/, **Highnesses.** You use expressions such as **Your Highness** and **His Highness** when you are addressing or referring to a prince or princess. EG *...Her Royal Highness, Princess Alexandra.*

high-pitched. A sound that is **high-pitched** is very high and shrill. EG *...a high-pitched whine.* ADJ QUALIT

high point, high points. The **high point** of an event or period of time is the most exciting or enjoyable part of it. EG *His speech was the high point of the evening.* N COUNT+SUPP

high-powered. 1 A machine or piece of equipment that is **high-powered** is very powerful and efficient. EG *...high-powered microscopes.* ADJ QUALIT
2 An activity that is **high-powered** is very advanced and successful. EG *...high-powered advertising... The course is high-powered.* ADJ QUALIT

high-rise. High-rise buildings are very tall modern buildings. EG *...high-rise flats.* ADJ CLASSIF : ATTRIB

high school, high schools. A **high school** is **1** a school in Britain for people aged between eleven and eighteen. **2** a school in the United States for people aged between fifteen and eighteen. N COUNT OR N UNCOUNT

high-spirited. Someone who is **high-spirited** is very lively. ADJ QUALIT

high street, high streets. The **high street** of a town is the main street where most of the shops N COUNT

and banks are. EG *They had a little flat off Kensington High Street.*

high tea is a large meal that some people eat in the late afternoon, often with tea to drink. N UNCOUNT British

high technology is the practical use of advanced scientific research and knowledge, especially in relation to electronics and computers. EG *...a new leap forward into an age of high technology... ...high-technology equipment.* N UNCOUNT

high tide is the time at which the sea is at its highest level at the coast each day before it starts to fall again. EG *...a pool which the sea only reached at high tide.* N UNCOUNT

highway /haɪweɪ/, **highways.** A **highway** is **1** a large road that connects towns or cities. EG *...interstate highways.* **2** a main road. EG *She was charged with obstructing the highway.* N COUNT American Formal

hijack /haɪdʒæk/, **hijacks, hijacking, hijacked.** If someone **hijacks** a plane, they illegally take control of it by force while it is on a journey. EG *A Pan Am aircraft was hijacked on its way to Singapore.* V+O

hike /haɪk/, **hikes, hiking, hiked. 1** A **hike** is a long walk in the country. EG *We're going on a four mile hike tomorrow.* N COUNT
2 If you **hike**, you go on long country walks for pleasure. EG *She was in Switzerland, hiking.* ◊ **hiker, hikers.** EG *I watched the hikers scrambling up the gully.* ◊ **hiking.** EG *We have maps of the area where we hope to do some hiking.* V ◊ N COUNT ◊ N UNCOUNT

hilarious /hɪleərɪəs/. Something that is **hilarious** is extremely funny and makes you laugh a lot. EG *...the hilarious tale of how Uncle Harold got stuck in a lift.* ◊ **hilariously.** EG *These words are now hilariously old-fashioned.* ADJ QUALIT ◊ SUBMOD

hilarity /hɪlærɪtɪ/ is great amusement and laughter. EG *The noise of hilarity in the restaurant below kept him awake until the small hours.* N UNCOUNT

hill /hɪl/, **hills.** A **hill** is an area of land that is higher than the land that surrounds it, but not as high as a mountain. EG *I started to walk up the hill... ...the Malvern Hills of Worcestershire.* N COUNT

hillock /hɪlək/, **hillocks.** A **hillock** is a small hill. EG *The view was broken up into many little valleys and small hillocks.* N COUNT Literary

hillside /hɪlsaɪd/, **hillsides.** A **hillside** is the side of a hill. EG *...the steep hillsides of North Wales... ...a hillside town.* N COUNT

hilltop /hɪltɒp/, **hilltops.** A **hilltop** is the top of a hill. EG *...the hilltop village of Combe.* N COUNT

hilly /hɪlɪ/, **hillier, hilliest.** Land that is **hilly** has many hills. EG *They drove around the hilly area behind the town.* ADJ QUALIT

hilt /hɪlt/, **hilts. 1** The **hilt** of a sword, dagger, or knife is its handle. N COUNT
2 If you support or defend someone **to the hilt**, you give them all the support that you can. EG *She had backed me to the hilt in all my projects.* PHRASE Informal

him /hɪm/ is used as the object of a verb or preposition. You use **him** to refer to a man, boy, or male animal who has already been mentioned or whose identity is known, or to someone whose sex is not known or stated. EG *He asked if you'd ring him back when you got in... There's no need for him to worry.* PRON : SING

himself /hɪmself/. **1** You use **himself** as the object of a verb or preposition to refer to the same man, boy, male animal, or person who is mentioned as the subject of the clause, or as a previous object in the clause. EG *Mr Boggis introduced himself... ...his lack of confidence in himself.* PRON REFL SING
2 You also use **himself** to emphasize the male subject or object of a clause, and to make it clear who you are referring to. EG *Forman himself became Minister of International Affairs... It was* PRON REFL SING

If you hire something, does it belong to you?

easy for a clever young man like himself to make a good living.

3 If a man or boy does something **himself**, he does it without any help or interference from anyone else.   PRON REFL: SING

hind /haɪnd/. The **hind** legs of an animal are at the back of its body. EG *Kangaroos' hind legs are enormously powerful.*   ADJ CLASSIF: ATTRIB

hinder /ˈhɪndə/, **hinders, hindering, hindered.** If something **hinders** you, it makes it more difficult for you to do something. EG *Her career was not hindered by the fact that she had three children.*   V+O

hindrance /ˈhɪndrəns/, **hindrances. 1** A **hindrance** is a person or thing that makes it more difficult for you to do something. EG *New ideas may be more of a hindrance than an asset.*   N COUNT

2 Hindrance is the act of hindering someone or something. EG *Now they can construct tunnel systems without hindrance.*   N UNCOUNT

hindsight /ˈhaɪndsaɪt/. If you can understand something with **hindsight**, you can understand it after it has happened. EG *With the benefit of hindsight, what lessons could we learn from their mistakes?*   N UNCOUNT

Hindu /ˈhɪnduː, hɪnˈduː/, **Hindus. 1** A **Hindu** is a person who believes in Hinduism.   N COUNT

2 Something that is **Hindu** belongs or relates to Hinduism. EG *...Hindu civilization.*   ADJ CLASSIF

Hinduism /ˈhɪnduːɪzəm/ is an Indian religion. Hinduism has many gods and teaches that people live again after they die.   N UNCOUNT

hinge /hɪndʒ/, **hinges, hinging, hinged.** A **hinge** is a piece of metal, wood or plastic that is used to join two things together so that one of them can swing freely. EG *The door was ripped from its hinges.*   N COUNT

hinge on or **hinge upon.** If something **hinges on** or **hinges upon** a fact or event, it depends on it. EG *Everything hinged on what happened to the United States economy.*   PHRASAL VB: V+PREP

hinged /ˈhɪndʒd/. Something that is **hinged** is joined to something by means of a hinge. EG *...the hinged flap of the counter.*   ADJ CLASSIF

hink /hɪŋk/, **hinks, hinking, hinked.** If you **hink**, you think hopefully and unrealistically about something.   V OR V+REPORT

hint /hɪnt/, **hints, hinting, hinted. 1** A **hint** is a suggestion about something that is made in an indirect way. EG *As yet no hint had appeared as to who was going to be the next Foreign Secretary.*   N COUNT

● If you **drop a hint**, you suggest something in an indirect way. EG *He had dropped several hints that he knew where Mary was.* ● If you **take a hint**, you understand something that someone is suggesting indirectly to you. EG *She may take the hint and become more organized.*   ● PHRASE   ● PHRASE

2 If you **hint** at something, you suggest something in a very indirect way. EG *Harold hinted at what she had already guessed... I tried to hint that I deserved an increase in salary.*   V+at, OR V+REPORT: ONLY that

3 A **hint** is also a helpful piece of advice. EG *The magazine had the usual hints on fashion and cookery.*   N COUNT: USU PLURAL

4 A **hint** of something is a very small amount of it. EG *There was a hint of disapproval in her face.*   N PART

hip /hɪp/, **hips.** Your **hips** are the two areas at the sides of your body between the tops of your legs and your waist. EG *Her waist was slender, her hips curved... She put her hand on her hip.*   N COUNT

hippie /ˈhɪpiː/, **hippies;** also spelled **hippy.** A **hippie** is someone who has rejected conventional ideas about dress and social values and wants to live a different kind of life based on love. EG *...hippies in a commune... ...the hippy generation.*   N COUNT

hippo /ˈhɪpəʊ/, **hippos.** A **hippo** is a hippopotamus.   N COUNT

hippopotamus /ˌhɪpəˈpɒtəməs/, **hippopotamuses** or **hippopotami.** A **hippopotamus** is a large animal with short legs and thick, wrinkled skin. Hippopotamuses live near rivers in Africa.   N COUNT

hippy /ˈhɪpiː/. See **hippie.**

hire /haɪə/, **hires, hiring, hired. 1** If you **hire** something, you pay money to use it for a period of time. EG *We hired a car and drove across the island.*   V+O

▶ used as a noun. EG *Hire of a van costs about £30 a day.*   ▶ N UNCOUNT +SUPP

2 If something is **for hire**, you can hire it. EG *...boats for hire.*   PHRASE

3 If you **hire** someone, you pay them to do a job for you. EG *You've got to hire a private detective to make enquiries.*   V+O

hire out. If you **hire out** something, you allow it to be used in return for payment. EG *Holborn library hires out pictures.*   PHRASAL VB: V+O+ADV

hire purchase is a way of buying goods gradually. You make regular payments to the seller until you have paid the full price and the goods belong to you. EG *Have you bought anything on hire purchase?*   N UNCOUNT

his /hɪz/. **1** You use **his** to indicate that something belongs or relates to a man, boy, or male animal who has already been mentioned or whose identity is known, or to someone whose sex is not known or stated. EG *His name was Simon.* ▶ used as a pronoun. EG *Willie had a job on a new magazine that a friend of his had just started.*   DET POSS   ▶ PRON POSS: SING

2 You also use **his** in some titles when you are referring to a man with that title. EG *...his Lordship.*   DET POSS

hiss /hɪs/, **hisses, hissing, hissed. 1** To **hiss** means to make a sound like a long 's'. EG *If you shove a hot frying pan into water it will hiss and buckle.* ▶ used as a noun. EG *...the soft hiss of roasting meat.*   V   ▶ N COUNT

2 If you **hiss**, you say something in a strong, angry whisper. EG *He pointed a shaking finger at my friend and hissed through clenched teeth: 'You, you get out!'*   V+QUOTE

3 When an audience **hisses** a performance, they express their dislike of it by making long loud 's' sounds. EG *His public appearances were frequently hissed.*   V+O OR V

historian /hɪˈstɔːrɪən/, **historians.** A **historian** is a person who studies history. EG *...art historians.*   N COUNT

historic /hɪˈstɒrɪk/. Something that is **historic** is important in history. EG *What we are talking about was a historic change.*   ADJ QUALIT

historical /hɪˈstɒrɪkəl/. **1 Historical** people or situations existed in the past and are considered to be a part of history. EG *...actual historical events... ...autographs and manuscripts of historical interest.*   ADJ CLASSIF: ATTRIB

◊ **historically.** EG *Historically, Labour was strongly opposed to the powers of the Lords.*   ◊ ADV SEN OR ADV

2 Historical books and pictures describe or represent real people or things that existed in the past. EG *...historical novels.*   ADJ CLASSIF: ATTRIB

history /ˈhɪstərɪ/, **histories. 1** You can refer to the events of the past as **history**. EG *...one of the most dramatic moments in Polish history... Each city has its own history and character.* ● Someone who **makes history** does something very important and significant. ● If you **go down in history**, people in the future remember you because of things that you have done.   N UNCOUNT   ● PHRASE   ● PHRASE

2 History is also a subject studied in schools, colleges, and universities that deals with the past. EG *I adored history and hated geography... ...a history book, not a novel.* ● See also **natural history**.   N UNCOUNT

3 A **history** is a description of the important events that have happened in a particular subject. EG *...a television history of the United States.*   N COUNT+SUPP

4 If someone has a **history** of something, that thing has happened frequently in their life. EG *There is a family history of coronary heart disease... Both he and Nick have similar histories of success.*   N COUNT+of

5 The **history** of a person or thing is a set of facts that are known about their past. EG *I'd like to look at his medical history.*   N COUNT: USU+POSS

histrionic /hɪstrɪˈɒnɪk/. **Histrionic** behaviour is ADJ QUALIT: very dramatic and seems full of emotion, but is not ATTRIB sincere. EG *...a flamboyant, histrionic gesture.* Formal
◊ **histrionically.** EG *She sighed histrionically.* ◊ ADV

hit /hɪt/, **hits, hitting.** The form **hit** is used in the present tense and is the past tense and past participle of the verb.
1 If you **hit** someone or something, you deliberate- V+O ly touch them with a lot of force using your hand or an object. EG *He hit the burglar on the head with a candlestick... He never hit the ball very far.*
2 When something **hits** something else, it touches V+O it with a lot of force. EG *The truck had hit a wall... Enormous hailstones hit the roof of the car.*
3 If a bomb or other missile **hits** its target, it V+O reaches it. EG *Three ships were hit.* ▸ used as a ▸ N COUNT noun. EG *The tanks were designed to withstand anything except a direct hit.*
4 If something **hits** a person, place, or thing, it V+O affects them very badly. EG *Spectator sport has been badly hit by the increase in ticket prices.*
5 When a feeling or an idea **hits** you, it suddenly V+O affects you or comes into your mind. EG *The shock of her death kept hitting me afresh... Suddenly it hit me: my diary had probably been read by everyone in the office.*
6 A **hit** is a record, play, or film that is very N COUNT popular and successful. EG *The play became a tremendous hit... ...a hit single.*
7 If you **hit the roof**, you react to something very PHRASE angrily. Informal
8 If two people **hit it off**, they like each other and PHRASE become friendly as soon as they meet. Informal

hit back. If you **hit back** at someone who has PHRASAL VB: criticized or harmed you, you criticize or harm V+ADV, them in return. OFT+*at*

hit on or **hit upon.** If you **hit on** an idea or hit PHRASAL VB: **upon** it, you think of it. EG *He hit on the idea of* V+PREP, *cutting a hole in the door to allow the cat to get in* HAS PASS *and out.*

hit and miss. Something that is **hit and miss** ADJ QUALIT happens in an unplanned way, so that you never know what the result will be. EG *The service here is very hit and miss, isn't it?*

hit-and-run. A **hit-and-run** car accident is one in ADJ CLASSIF: which the driver does not stop. EG *...killed in a hit-* ATTRIB *and-run accident.*

hitch /hɪtʃ/, **hitches, hitching, hitched.** 1 A N COUNT **hitch** is a slight problem or difficulty. EG *There had also been one or two technical hitches.*
2 If you **hitch** or **hitch** a lift, you hitch-hike. EG *He* V OR V+O: *hitched south towards Italy.* OFT+*A*
3 If you **hitch** something onto something else, you V+O+A hook it or fasten it there. EG *...ponies hitched to rails.*

hitch up. If you **hitch up** a piece of clothing, you PHRASAL VB: pull it up into a higher position. EG *He hitched up* V+O+ADV *his trousers.*

hitch-hike, hitch-hikes, hitch-hiking, hitch- V : USU+A **hiked.** If you **hitch-hike**, you travel by getting lifts in other people's cars, which you ask for by standing at the side of the road with your thumb held out. EG *She went off with a friend intending to hitch-hike to Turkey.* ◊ **hitch-hiker, hitch-hikers.** EG ◊ N COUNT *...foreign hitch-hikers in Sardinia.*

hi tech /haɪ tek/. Something that is **hi tech** uses ADJ QUALIT very modern methods and equipment.

hither /ˈhɪðə/ is used to describe movement to- ADV wards the place where you are at present. EG *...my* Literary *journey hither.* ● Something that moves **hither** ● PHRASE **and thither** moves in all directions. EG *She ran* Literary *hither and thither in the orchard.*

hitherto /ˌhɪðəˈtuː/. If something has been happen- ADV ing **hitherto**, it has been happening until now. EG Formal *She had hitherto been relatively nice to me.*

hit list, hit lists. A **hit list** is a list that terrorists N COUNT have of the people they intend to kill.

hit or miss. Something that is **hit or miss** ADJ QUALIT happens in an unplanned way, so that you never

know what the result will be. EG *We are working on a rather hit-or-miss basis at the moment.*

hive /haɪv/, **hives.** 1 A **hive** is a beehive. EG *There* N COUNT *must be sixty thousand bees in that hive.*
2 You describe a place as a **hive** of activity when N COUNT+*of* there is a lot of activity there. EG *Calcutta is a hive of industry and trade.*

h'm; also spelled **hm.** You say **'h'm'** when you are hesitating, for example because you are thinking about something.

HMS is used before the names of ships in the British Royal Navy. **HMS** is an abbreviation for 'Her Majesty's Ship' or 'His Majesty's Ship'. EG *...HMS Churchill.*

hoard /hɔːd/, **hoards, hoarding, hoarded.** 1 If V+O you **hoard** things, you save or store them, often in secret. EG *Is it better to spend your money today or hoard every penny in the bank for tomorrow?*
2 A **hoard** is a store of things you have saved. EG *...a* N PART *small hoard of coins.*

hoarding /ˈhɔːdɪŋ/, **hoardings.** A **hoarding** is a N COUNT: very large notice board that stands at the sides of USU PLURAL roads and is used for displaying advertisements and posters. EG *I scanned the hoardings for election posters.*

hoarse /hɔːs/, **hoarser, hoarsest.** If your voice is ADJ QUALIT **hoarse**, it sounds rough and unclear. EG *When he spoke his voice was hoarse with rage.* ◊ **hoarsely.** ◊ ADV EG *'Go in there,' he whispered hoarsely.*
◊ **hoarseness.** EG *I noticed a peculiar hoarseness* ◊ N UNCOUNT *in Johnny's voice.*

hoary /ˈhɔːrɪ/. 1 Something that is **hoary** is grey- ADJ QUALIT ish white. EG *...a clump of hoary juniper bushes.* Literary
2 A **hoary** problem or subject is old and familiar. ADJ QUALIT EG *They discussed the hoary old problem.*

hoax /həʊks/, **hoaxes.** A **hoax** is a trick in which N COUNT someone tells people something that is not true. EG *It wasn't a hoax, there really was a fire.*

hob /hɒb/, **hobs.** A **hob** is a surface on top of a N COUNT cooker which can be heated. EG *The stew sim- mered on the hob.*

hobble /ˈhɒbəl/, **hobbles, hobbling, hobbled.** 1 If V : USU+A you **hobble**, you walk in an awkward way with small steps, for example because your feet are injured. EG *He hobbled along as best he could.*
2 If you **hobble** an animal, you tie its legs together V+O so that it cannot run away. EG *They were hobbled by straps around their legs.*

hobby /ˈhɒbɪ/, **hobbies.** A **hobby** is something N COUNT that you enjoy doing in your spare time, such as collecting stamps or painting. EG *Music is his chief hobby.*

hock /hɒk/ is a type of dry white wine from N MASS Germany. EG *...a glass of hock.*

hockey /ˈhɒkɪ/ is an outdoor game, played be- N UNCOUNT tween two teams of 11 players who use long curved sticks to hit a small ball and try to score goals.
● See also **ice hockey.**

hoe /həʊ/, **hoes, hoeing, hoed.** 1 A **hoe** is a N COUNT gardening tool with a long handle and a small square blade, which is used to remove small weeds.
2 If you **hoe** a field, you use a hoe on the weeds or V OR V+O soil there.

hog /hɒg/, **hogs, hogging, hogged.** 1 A **hog** is a N COUNT male pig that has been castrated.
2 If you **hog** something, you take all of it in a V+O selfish or impolite way. EG *...a huge lorry hogging* Informal *the centre of the road.*
3 If you **go the whole hog**, you do something bold PHRASE or extravagant in the most complete way possible. Informal

ho ho /həʊ həʊ/ is used, especially in writing, to CONVENTION represent laughter.

hoist /hɔɪst/, **hoists, hoisting, hoisted.** 1 If you V+O+A **hoist** something heavy somewhere, you lift it or

If you hit the roof, do you touch it?

pull it up there. EG *She hoisted the child onto her shoulder.*

2 If you **hoist** a flag or a sail, you pull it up to its correct position by means of ropes. EG *The American flag was hoisted.* v+o

3 A **hoist** is a machine for lifting heavy things. EG *...an electric hoist.* N COUNT

hold /həʊld/, **holds, holding, held** /held/. **1** When you **hold** something, you have your fingers or arms firmly round it. You can also **hold** things with other parts of your body, for example your mouth. EG *He was holding a bottle of milk... I held the picture up to the light... He held her in his arms.* ▸ used as a noun. EG *She resumed her hold on the rope.* ● If you **hold tight**, you hold something very firmly, especially so that you do not fall. v+o: USU+A

2 If you **hold** someone or **hold** them prisoner, you keep them as a prisoner. EG *I was held overnight in a cell.* v+o: USU+A; ALSO V+O+C

3 If you **hold** your body or part of your body in a particular position, you keep it in that position. EG *Etta held her head back... Mrs Patel held herself erect.* v+o+A; OR V-REFL+A

4 If you **hold** power or office, you have it. EG *...one of the greatest Prime Ministers who ever held office.* v+o

5 If you **hold** a qualification, licence, or other official document, you have it. v+o

6 If you **hold** an event such as a meeting or a party, you organize it and it takes place. EG *He had promised he would hold elections in June.* v+o

7 If you **hold** a conversation with someone, you talk with them. v+o

8 If something **holds** a particular quality or characteristic, it has it. EG *These legends hold a romantic fascination for many Japanese... We will have to see what the future holds.* v+o

9 If you **hold** a particular opinion or belief, you have it. EG *People who hold this view are sometimes dismissed as cranks... Marxists hold that people are all naturally creative.* v+o OR V+REPORT: ONLY *that*

10 You can also use **hold** to say that you consider someone or something to have a particular quality. For example, if you **hold** someone responsible for something, you consider them responsible for it. EG *The government is destroying every institution and value they hold dear.* v+o+A OR V+O+C

11 If someone asks you to **hold** the line when you have made a telephone call, they are asking you to wait until they can connect you. v+o OR V

12 If you **hold** someone's interest or attention, you do or say something which keeps them interested. v+o

13 If a group of fighters **hold** a place, they prevent it from being captured. v+o

14 Something that **holds** something else keeps it fixed or supported in position. EG *There was just a rail holding it... There were tremendous pillars holding up high ceilings.* v OR V+O

15 If something **holds** a particular amount of something, it can contain that amount. EG *The theatre itself can hold only a limited number of people.* v+o

16 If an offer or invitation still **holds**, it is still available for you to accept. v

17 If your luck **holds** or if the weather **holds**, it remains good. EG *If my luck continues to hold, I think I've got a fair chance.* v

18 The **hold** of a ship or aeroplane is the place where cargo or luggage is stored. N COUNT

19 If you have a **hold** over someone, **19.1** you know something about them that you can use in order to make them do something for you. **19.2** you have power or control over them. EG *The party tightened its hold on the union.* N SING+*over*; N SING: OFT+*on/over*

20 If you take **hold** of something, you put your hand tightly round it. EG *She took hold of my wrist... He still had hold of my jacket.* N UNCOUNT: OFT+*of*

21 When something takes **hold**, it starts to have a great effect. EG *Then the fire took hold.* N UNCOUNT

22 If you **get hold of** something or someone, you manage to get them or find them. EG *Can you get hold of a car this weekend?* PHRASE

23 **Hold** is also used in these phrases. **23.1** If you say to people **'Hold it'** or **'Hold everything'**, you are telling them to stop what they are doing. **23.2** If you **hold still** or **hold steady**, you do not move. EG *'Oh! do hold still!' she cried.* **23.3** If you **hold** your **own**, you are not defeated by someone or do not do worse than them. EG *She was still able to hold her own with the Prime Minister.* PHRASES

hold against. If someone has done something wrong and you **hold** it **against** them, you treat them more severely because they did it. EG *His refusal to cooperate will be held against him.* PHRASAL VB: V+O+PREP

hold back. 1 If you **hold back** or if something **holds** you **back**, you hesitate before you do something because you are not sure whether it is the right thing to do. EG *Police have held back from going into such a holy place.* **2** If you **hold** someone or something **back**, you prevent them from advancing or increasing. EG *If she is ambitious, don't try to hold her back... The rise in living standards has been held back for so long.* **3** If you **hold** something **back**, you do not tell someone the full details about something. PHRASAL VB: V-ERG+ADV; V+O+ADV; V+O+ADV

hold down. If you **hold down** a job, you manage to keep it. EG *He was surprised to find her holding down a successful job in high finance.* PHRASAL VB: V+O+ADV

hold off. 1 If you **hold off** something such as an army, you prevent it from coming too close to you. **2** If the rain **holds off**, it does not rain although you had expected it to. PHRASAL VB: V+O+ADV; V+ADV

hold on. 1 If you **hold on**, you put or keep your hand firmly round something. EG *He tried to pull free but she held on tight.* **2** If you ask someone to **hold on**, you are asking them to wait for a short time. EG *Hold on a moment, please.* PHRASAL VB: V+ADV; V+ADV, OFT+*to*

hold onto. If you **hold onto** something, **1** you put or keep your hand firmly round it. EG *He has to hold onto something to steady himself.* **2** you keep it. EG *Politicians want to hold on to power at all costs.* PHRASAL VB: V+PREP; V+PREP

hold out. 1 If you **hold out** your hand or something that you have in your hand, you move it away from your body, usually towards someone. EG *'John?' Esther held out the phone.* **2** If you **hold out** for something, you want it and refuse to accept anything else. EG *Women all over the country are holding out for more freedom.* **3** If you **hold out**, you manage to resist an enemy or opponent. EG *I can't hold out forever.* PHRASAL VB: V+O+ADV; V+ADV, OFT+*for*; V+ADV

hold up. 1 If someone or something **holds** you **up**, they delay you. EG *The whole thing was held up about half an hour.* **2** If you **hold up** something as being good or bad, you mention it to other people in order to influence their opinions. EG *Their ways are held up to scorn... What do you hold up to the children as being desirable goals?* **3** See also **hold-up**. PHRASAL VB: V+O+ADV; V+O+ADV+A

hold with. If you do not **hold with** something, you do not approve of it. EG *...a man who did not hold with these notions.* PHRASAL VB: V+PREP, WITH BROAD NEG

holdall /ˈhəʊldɔːl/, **holdalls**. A **holdall** is a large bag in which you carry things. N COUNT

holder /ˈhəʊldə/, **holders**. A **holder** is **1** a container in which you put an object, usually in order to protect it or to keep it in place. EG *The cup was held in a brown plastic holder.* **2** someone who owns something or has control of it. EG *I require the licence number and the full name of the holder... ...ticket-holders.* **3** someone who has a particular opinion. EG *...holders of anti-government opinions.* N COUNT: OFT+SUPP

holding /ˈhəʊldɪŋ/, **holdings**. **1** If you have a **holding** in a company, you own shares in it. EG *We should sell the government holding in British Gas.* N COUNT+SUPP

2 A **holding** is also an area of farm land which is rented or owned by the person who cultivates it. EG *78 per cent of holdings are below 5 hectares.* N COUNT

3 You use **holding** to describe a temporary action. ADJ CLASSIF: ATTRIB which is intended to prevent a situation from becoming worse. EG *The rest of the campaign was a holding operation.*

hold-up, hold-ups. A **hold-up** is **1** a situation in N COUNT which someone is threatened with a weapon in order to make them hand over money. EG *...the victim of a masked hold-up.* **2** something which causes a delay. EG *He may be delayed by some hold-up in the department... ...traffic hold-ups.*

hole /həʊl/, **holes, holing, holed. 1** a **hole** is **1.1** a N COUNT hollow space in something solid, with an opening on one side. EG *What do you recommend for filling holes and cracks?... ...a deep hole in the ground.* **1.2** an opening in something that goes right through it. EG *He was wearing grey socks with holes in them.*

2 If you **pick holes in** an argument or theory, you PHRASE find weak points in it. EG *...when someone really* Informal *picks holes in their argument.*

3 You can describe an unpleasant place as a **hole.** N COUNT EG *Why don't you leave this awful hole and come to* Informal *live with me.*

4 If a building or a ship **is holed**, holes are made in V+O : USU PASS it by guns or other weapons. EG *The buildings were holed by shells.*

hole up. If you **hole up** somewhere, you hide PHRASAL VB : yourself there. EG *San Francisco was where she* V+ADV+A *holed up.* Informal

holiday /hɒlɪdɪ/, **holidays, holidaying, holi-** dayed. A **holiday** is **1** a period of time during N COUNT OR which you are relaxing and enjoying yourself away N UNCOUNT from home. EG *I went to Marrakesh for a holiday... Remember to turn off the gas when you go on holiday.* **2** a period of time during which you are N COUNT OR not working or attending school, college, or univer- N UNCOUNT sity. EG *New Year's Day is a national holiday.* ● See also **bank holiday.**

holiday camp, holiday camps. A **holiday camp** N COUNT is a place which provides holiday accommodation and entertainment for large numbers of people.

holidaymaker /hɒlɪdɪmeɪkə/, **holidaymakers.** N COUNT A **holidaymaker** is a person who is away from home on holiday. EG *The sundeck was crowded with holidaymakers.*

holiness /həʊlɪnɪs/. **1 Holiness** is the state or N UNCOUNT quality of being holy and dedicated to God. EG *She could feel the holiness of the place.*

2 You use expressions such as **Your Holiness** and **His Holiness** when you are addressing or refer- ring to the Pope or to leaders of some other religions.

holler /hɒlə/, **hollers, hollering, hollered.** If you V : OFT+QUOTE **holler,** you shout or weep loudly. EG *You should* Informal *have heard him holler!... 'Fishing?' she hollered.* American *'On Sunday?'*

hollow /hɒləʊ/, **hollows, hollowing, hollowed. 1** ADJ CLASSIF Something that is **hollow** has a hole or space inside it. EG *...a hollow tube... ...a large hollow container.*

2 A surface that is **hollow** or **hollowed** curves ADJ QUALIT inwards or downwards. EG *...a lean, hollow-cheeked man... ...a cadaverous face, hollowed by illness.*

3 A **hollow** is an area that is lower than the N COUNT surrounding surface. EG *Davis hid in a hollow surrounded by bracken.*

4 A situation or opinion that is described as **hollow** ADJ QUALIT has no real value, worth, or effectiveness. EG *Their* Formal *independence is hollow... His outward optimism rang hollow.* ◊ **hollowness.** EG *...the hollowness of* ◊ N UNCOUNT *his victory.* +SUPP

5 If someone gives a **hollow** laugh, they laugh in a ADJ CLASSIF : way that shows that they do not really find some- ATTRIB thing funny. ◊ **hollowly.** EG *He laughed hollowly.* ◊ ADV *'And what a mess we made of that!'*

6 A **hollow** sound goes on for some time after it ADJ QUALIT has been made, like an echo. ◊ **hollowly.** EG *His* ◊ ADV *footsteps sounded hollowly on the uncarpeted stairs.*

hollow out. If you **hollow** something **out**, you PHRASAL VB : remove the inside part of it. EG *The kids had* V+ADV *hollowed out tunnels through the maize.*

holly /hɒlɪ/ is a kind of small evergreen tree with N UNCOUNT hard, prickly leaves and red berries.

holocaust /hɒləkɔːst/, **holocausts.** A **holocaust** N COUNT OR is very great destruction and loss of life, especially N UNCOUNT in war or by fire. EG *He claimed that the world was about to be consumed in a nuclear holocaust.*

hologram /hɒləgræm/, **holograms.** A **hologram** N COUNT is a three-dimensional photographic image created by laser beams.

holster /həʊlstə/, **holsters.** A **holster** is a holder N COUNT for a gun, which is worn on a belt round someone's waist or on a strap below their arm.

holy /həʊlɪ/, **holier, holiest. 1** Something that is ADJ QUALIT **holy** relates to God or to a particular religion. EG *...holy pictures and statues.*

2 Someone who is **holy** leads a pure and good life ADJ QUALIT which is dedicated to God or to a religion.

homage /hɒmɪdʒ/ is a way of behaving towards N UNCOUNT : someone which shows that you respect or honour USU+*to* them very much. EG *The young soldiers gathered to pay homage to their heroes.*

home /həʊm/, **homes, homing, homed. 1** Your **home** is **1.1** the place where you live and feel that N UNCOUNT you belong. EG *The old man wants to die in his own* OR N COUNT *home... ...a normal home life... He stayed at home to care for the children.* **1.2** the area or country N UNCOUNT where you were born or where your home is. EG *For most English children, home is a town or city... My own home town is thousands of miles away.*

2 Home means to or at the place where you live. ADV AFTER VB EG *I want to go home... Here we are, home at last.*

3 You can use **at home** to refer to things that PHRASE happen in your own country, rather than in a foreign country. EG *Newspapers both at home and abroad ignored the incident.*

4 If you are **at home** in a particular situation, you PHRASE feel comfortable and relaxed in it. EG *I felt at home at once, because I recognized familiar faces.* ● If ● CONVENTION you say to a guest **'Make yourself at home'**, you are inviting them to feel relaxed in your home. EG *Make yourself at home. I'll be back in half an hour.*

5 Home also means relating to your own country ADJ CLASSIF : rather than to foreign countries. EG *The govern-* ATTRIB *ment had promised to maintain an expanding home market.*

6 If you **make** your **home** somewhere, you start PHRASE living there. EG *Tramps have made their homes in warehouses on the river bank.*

7 When someone **leaves home**, they leave their PHRASE parents' home and go to live somewhere else.

8 A **home** is also a building where people who N COUNT : cannot look after themselves live and are looked USU+SUPP after by other people. EG *...a children's home... ...a home for the elderly.*

9 The **home** of something is the place where it N SING+SUPP began or where it is found. EG *...that home of free enterprise, the United States.*

10 If you **bring** or **drive** something **home to** PHRASE someone, you make them understand how impor- tant or serious it is. EG *We must bring home to everyone the dangers of any other course of ac- tion... He raised his voice to drive home the point.*

11 A **home** game is played on your team's own ADJ CLASSIF : ground. EG *They watched every single game, home* ATTRIB *or away.*

12 See also **homing.**

home in. If a missile **homes in** on something, it PHRASAL VB : finds it. EG *It can thus home in on the target with* V+ADV+PREP *pinpoint accuracy.*

home-brew is beer made in someone's home N UNCOUNT rather than in a brewery.

homecoming /həʊmkʌmɪŋ/, **homecomings.** N COUNT OR Your **homecoming** is your return to your home or N UNCOUNT your country after you have been away for a long

If you are homesick, do you need a holiday?

time. EG *There were 120,000 people at his home-coming.*

home economics is a subject studied at school N UNCOUNT and college in which students are taught how to run a house well and efficiently.

home ground, home grounds. 1 If you are **on** PHRASE **home ground, 1.1** you are near where you live and so know where you are. **1.2** you are discussing a subject that you know about.

2 A sports team's **home ground** is their own N COUNT playing field.

home-grown fruit and vegetables have been ADJ CLASSIF grown in your own garden, area, or country.

home help, home helps. A **home help** is a N COUNT person employed by a local government authority to help people who are old or ill with their house-work.

homeland /ˈhəʊmlənd/, **homelands.** Your N COUNT **homeland** is your native country.

homeless /ˈhəʊmlɪs/. **1** If people are **homeless,** ADJ CLASSIF they have nowhere to live. EG *Floods in north-eastern India made 233,000 people homeless.*

◇ **homelessness.** EG *For a growing number of* ◇ N UNCOUNT *young people, homelessness is becoming a way of life.*

2 You can refer to people who are homeless as **the** N PLURAL: **homeless.** EG *We were running homes for the* the+N *homeless.*

homely /ˈhəʊmli/. **1** If something is **homely,** it is ADJ QUALIT simple and ordinary. EG *We stayed in the Hotel Claravallis, a homely and comfortable establish-ment.*

2 If someone is **homely,** they are not very attrac- ADJ QUALIT tive to look at. EG *Paul is a homely, shy, stammer-* American *ing boy.*

home-made. Something that is **home-made** has ADJ CLASSIF been made in somebody's home, rather than in a shop or factory. EG *...homemade bread.*

homeopath /ˈhəʊmiˈəˌpæθ/, **homeopaths;** also N COUNT spelled **homoeopath.** A **homeopath** is someone who treats illness by homeopathy.

homeopathy /ˌhəʊmiˈɒpəθi/; also spelled N UNCOUNT **homoeopathy. Homeopathy** is a way of treating illness in which the patient is given very small amounts of drugs. ◇ **homeopathic** ◇ ADJ CLASSIF /ˌhəʊmiˈəˌpæθɪk/. EG *...homeopathic remedies.*

homeowner /ˈhəʊməʊnə/, **homeowners.** A N COUNT **homeowner** is someone who owns their own home.

homesick /ˈhəʊmsɪk/. If you are **homesick,** you ADJ QUALIT are feeling unhappy because you are away from home. EG *The smell of the grass made her home-sick for her parents' farm.* ◇ **homesickness.** EG *...a* ◇ N UNCOUNT *sudden spasm of homesickness.*

homespun /ˈhəʊmspʌn/. Beliefs, opinions, or com- ADJ CLASSIF ments that are **homespun** are simple and uncom-plicated. EG *They believed in simple living and homespun virtues.*

homestead /ˈhəʊmstɛd/, **homesteads.** A **home-** N COUNT **stead** is a farmhouse and the land around it. American

home truth, home truths. Home truths are N COUNT: unpleasant facts that you learn about yourself, USU PLURAL usually from someone else.

homeward /ˈhəʊmwəd/ means going towards ADJ CLASSIF: home. EG *The tank blew up on its homeward* ATTRIB *journey.* ▸ **Homeward** or **homewards** is also used ▸ ADV AFTER as an adverb. EG *The time had come to drive the* VB *goats homewards.*

homework /ˈhəʊmwɜːk/ is **1** work that teachers N UNCOUNT give to pupils to do at home. EG *He never did any homework and he got terrible results in school.* **2** research that someone does, usually in preparation for a written article or speech. EG *Aiken did his homework and worked out a convincing commer-cial case.*

homicidal /ˌhɒmɪˈsaɪdəl/. Someone who is **homi-** ADJ CLASSIF **cidal** is likely to kill someone. EG *...homicidal maniacs.*

homicide /ˈhɒmɪsaɪd/, **homicides. Homicide** is N UNCOUNT the crime of murder. EG *...countries where theft and* OR N COUNT *homicide are unknown today.* American

homily /ˈhɒmɪli/, **homilies.** A **homily** is a speech N COUNT in which someone complains about something or Formal tells people how they ought to behave. EG *We listened to her homily about the rising cost of living.*

homing /ˈhəʊmɪŋ/. **1** A weapon that has a **homing** ADJ CLASSIF: system is able to guide itself to a particular posi- ATTRIB tion. EG *Even small missiles have built-in homing devices.*

2 An animal that has a **homing** instinct has the ADJ CLASSIF: ability to remember and return to a place where it ATTRIB has been in the past.

homoeopath /ˈhəʊmiˈəˌpæθ/. See **homeopath.**

homogeneity /ˌhɒmədʒɪˈniːɪti, ˌhəʊ-/ is the qual- N UNCOUNT: ity of being homogeneous. EG *...emphasis on the* USU+SUPP *unity of the nation and the homogeneity of society.*

homogeneous /ˌhɒməˈdʒiːnɪəs, ˌhəʊ-/. A thing or ADJ QUALIT group that is **homogeneous** has parts or members which are all the same. EG *The working class is not very homogeneous.*

homogenous /hɒˈmɒdʒənəs/ means the same as ADJ QUALIT homogeneous.

homosexual /ˌhəʊməˈsɛksjuəl, ˌhɒm-/, **homosex-** ADJ CLASSIF **uals.** Someone who is **homosexual** is sexually attracted to someone of the same sex. ▸ used as a ▸ N COUNT noun. EG *...clubs and bars for homosexuals.* ◇ **homosexuality** /ˌhəʊməˌsɛksjuˈælɪti, ˌhɒm-/. EG ◇ N UNCOUNT *...the reform of the laws on homosexuality.*

honest /ˈɒnɪst/. **1** Someone who is **honest** about ADJ QUALIT something is completely truthful about it and does not hide anything. EG *At least you're honest about why you want the money... To be perfectly honest, up until three weeks ago I had never set foot in a nightclub... Not all scientists are as honest as Pasteur was.* ◇ **honestly.** EG *Philip had answered* ◇ ADV *them honestly.*

2 You say **'honest'** to emphasize that you are ADV SEN telling the truth. EG *It's true as I'm sitting here,* Informal *Mabel, honest it is.*

3 Someone who is **honest** does not cheat or break ADJ QUALIT the law and can be trusted with money and other valuable things. EG *He's very honest in money matters.* ◇ **honestly.** EG *If he couldn't get rare* ◇ ADV *shrubs honestly, he would steal them.*

4 Some people say **'honest to God'** or **'honest to** ADV SEN **goodness'** to express annoyance or impatience. EG Outdated *Honest to God, how can you believe such rubbish?*

honestly /ˈɒnɪstli/. You use **honestly 1** to em- ADV OR phasize that you are telling the truth. EG *He didn't* ADV SEN *honestly think he would miss them... I'll go if you like. I don't mind, honestly.* **2** to indicate that you CONVENTION are annoyed or impatient. EG *Honestly, Flora, this is* OR ADV SEN *getting ridiculous.*

honesty /ˈɒnɪsti/ is the quality of being honest. EG N UNCOUNT *I sat quietly admiring Claudia's honesty.* ● If you ● ADV SEN say something **in all honesty,** you are being completely truthful. EG *In all honesty he had to admit that he was glad.*

honey /ˈhʌni/. **1 Honey** is a sweet sticky yellowish N UNCOUNT substance that is made by bees. EG *...tea sweetened with honey.*

2 You can call someone **honey** as a sign of VOCATIVE affection. EG *Hi there, honey.* American

honeybee /ˈhʌnibiː/, **honeybees.** A **honeybee** is N COUNT a bee that makes honey.

honeycomb /ˈhʌnikəʊm/, **honeycombs.** A N COUNT OR honeycomb is a wax structure made by bees. It N UNCOUNT contains lots of six-sided holes where the bees store honey.

honeyed /ˈhʌnɪd/. If someone speaks **honeyed** ADJ CLASSIF words or speaks with a **honeyed** voice, what they say is soft and pleasant to listen to. EG *She was soothed by his honeyed words.*

honeymoon /ˈhʌnimuːn/, **honeymoons.** A **honey-** N COUNT **moon** is **1** a holiday taken by a man and a woman who have just got married. EG *They spent their* *honeymoon at Petersburg, Florida.* **2** a period of time after the start of a new job or new government when everyone is pleased with the person or people concerned. EG *The honeymoon period is over.*

honeysuckle /hʌnɪsʌkəʰl/ is a climbing plant N UNCOUNT with sweet-smelling flowers.

honk /hɒŋk/, **honks, honking, honked.** If you V-ERG **honk** the horn of a vehicle or if it **honks**, it produces a short loud sound.

honor /ɒnə/. See **honour**.

honorable /ɒnəʰrəbəʰl/. See **honourable**.

honorary /ɒnəʰrəri¹/. **1** An **honorary** title or ADJ CLASSIF: **honorary** membership of a group is given to ATTRIB someone for a special reason without them needing to have the qualifications that are usually necessary. EG *...an honorary degree.*

2 An **honorary** job is an official job that is done ADJ CLASSIF: without payment. EG *...the honorary Treasurer.* ATTRIB

honour /ɒnə/, **honours, honouring, honoured;** spelled **honor** in American English. **1** Honour is a N UNCOUNT feeling of pride that you have when you behave in the best way so that people admire or respect you. EG *A debt is a thing of family honour... He was able to withdraw from the battle with honour.*

2 An **honour** is a special award or job that is given N COUNT to someone. EG *It was a richly deserved honour.*

3 If you describe something that has happened to N SING you as an **honour**, you mean that you are very Formal pleased and proud about it. EG *He is one of the most interesting people I have had the honour of meeting... She did me the honour of attending my exhibition.*

4 If something is arranged **in** your **honour**, it is PHRASE arranged specially for you. EG *I arranged to give a party in her honour.*

5 If something is arranged **in honour of** an event, PREP it is arranged to celebrate the event. EG *The ceremony was held in honour of the Queen's birthday.*

6 You address a judge in court as **your honour**. EG VOCATIVE *Is there any evidence of this, your honour?* American

7 Honours is a type of university degree which is N UNCOUNT of a higher standard than an ordinary degree. EG *...a* British *first class honours degree in French.*

8 If you **do the honours** at a social occasion, you PHRASE pour drinks for people or serve food. Informal

9 If you **honour** someone, **9.1** you give them public V+O praise or a medal because they have done something good or brave. EG *The people came to honour their leader... In 1949, he was honoured by the Grand Cross.* **9.2** you treat them with special attention and respect. ◊ **honoured.** EG *Rose was* ◊ ADJ CLASSIF: *the honoured guest.* ATTRIB

10 If you **honour** an arrangement or promise, you V+O keep to it and do not change your mind. EG *The* Formal *government has solemn commitments and must honour them.*

honourable /ɒnəʰrəbəʰl/; spelled **honorable** in American English. **1** Someone or something that is ADJ QUALIT **honourable** is honest and worthy of respect. EG *...an honourable man... Major Vane had always tried to do the honourable thing.* ◊ **honourably.** EG ◊ ADV *He served his master honourably until his death.*

2 Honourable is used as part of a title. EG *...the* ADJ CLASSIF: *Honourable Miss Sparrow.* ATTRIB

hood /hʊd/, **hoods.** A **hood** is **1** a part of a coat or N COUNT cloak which you pull up to cover your head. EG *He held both sides of the parka hood closed against the snow.* **2** a covering on a vehicle or a piece of equipment, which is usually curved and can be moved. EG *...a pram which had its hood folded down.* **3** the bonnet of a car. American

hooded /hʊdɪ²d/. **1** A **hooded** piece of clothing has ADJ CLASSIF: a hood. EG *...a hooded duffel coat.* ATTRIB

2 Someone with **hooded** eyes has large eyelids that ADJ CLASSIF: are partly closed. ATTRIB

hoodwink /hʊdwɪŋk/, **hoodwinks, hoodwinking,** V+O **hoodwinked.** If you **hoodwink** someone, you trick

or deceive them. EG *He is too often hoodwinked by flashy external appearances.*

hoof /huːf/, **hoofs** or **hooves** /huːvz/. The **hooves** N COUNT: of an animal such as a horse are the hard parts of USU PLURAL its feet.

hook /hʊk/, **hooks, hooking, hooked. 1** A **hook** is N COUNT a bent piece of metal or plastic that is used for holding things. EG *Howard hangs up his coat on the hook behind the door... ...curtain hooks.*

2 If you **hook** one thing onto another, you attach it V+O+A there using a hook. EG *One after the other they were hooked to the moving cable.* ● See also **hooked.**

3 If you **hook** your arm, leg, or foot round an V+O+A object, you place it like a hook round the object in order to move it or hold it. EG *She hooked her foot under a cane stool, drawing it nearer.*

4 Hook is used in these phrases. **4.1** If you take the PHRASES phone **off the hook**, you take the receiver off the part that it normally rests on, so that the phone will not ring. **4.2** If someone **gets off the hook**, they manage to get out of a difficult or dangerous situation. EG *He felt he had got off the hook perhaps too easily.*

hook up. If you **hook up** a computer or other PHRASAL VB: electronic machine, you connect it to other similar V+O+ADV, machines or to a central power supply. ● See also USU PASS **hook-up.**

hook and eye, hooks and eyes. A **hook and eye** N COUNT is a small metal hook and bar that together form a fastening for clothes such as dresses or skirts.

hooked /hʊkt/. **1** Something that is **hooked** is ADJ CLASSIF shaped like a hook. EG *...huge hooked claws.*

2 A **hooked** nose is large and curved. ADJ CLASSIF

3 If you are **hooked** on something, **3.1** you like it or ADJ PRED: enjoy it so much that it takes up a lot of your OFT+*on* interest and attention. EG *They're the sweetest kids ever. I'm really hooked on those kids.* **3.2** you are addicted to it. EG *...hooked on heroin.*

hooker /hʊkə/, **hookers.** In American English, a N COUNT **hooker** is a prostitute; an offensive use. Informal

hook-up, hook-ups. A **hook-up** is an electronic or N COUNT radio connection between computers, satellites, or radios.

hooligan /huːlɪgən/, **hooligans.** A **hooligan** is a N COUNT young person who behaves in a noisy and violent way in public places. ● **hooliganism** ◊ N UNCOUNT /huːlɪgənɪzəʰm/. EG *...football hooliganism.*

hoop /huːp/, **hoops.** A **hoop** is a large ring made of N COUNT wood, metal, or plastic. EG *...boys holding hoops, kites, and marbles.* ● **hooped** /huːpt/. EG *...hooped* ◊ ADJ CLASSIF *earrings.*

hooray /həˈreɪ/. People sometimes shout '**Hoo-** EXCLAM **ray!**' when they are very happy and excited.

hoot /huːt/, **hoots, hooting, hooted. 1** If you **hoot** V OR V-ERG the horn on a vehicle or if it **hoots**, it makes a loud noise. EG *Tug boats hooted at it... He hoots the horn.* ▸ used as a noun. EG *I heard a hoot and saw Martin* ▸ N COUNT *driving by.*

2 If you **hoot**, you make a loud high-pitched noise, V: USU+A for example when you are laughing. EG *They point-* Literary *ed and hooted with enjoyment.* ▸ used as a noun. EG ▸ N COUNT *At this Etta gave a hoot of laughter.*

3 When an owl **hoots**, it makes a sound like a long V 'oo'. EG *Outside, an owl hooted among the pines.* ▸ used as a noun. EG *He heard the hoot of an owl.* ▸ N COUNT

hooter /huːtə/, **hooters. 1** A **hooter** on a car or N COUNT other vehicle is a device such as a horn or a siren.

2 In British English, you can refer to someone's N COUNT nose as their **hooter**, especially if it is very large. Informal

hoover /huːvə/, **hoovers, hoovering, hoovered. 1** N COUNT A **Hoover** is a vacuum cleaner. EG *There was no* Trademark *Hoover for the carpets.*

2 If you **hoover** a carpet, you clean it using a V OR V+O

Find two things that make the same sort of noise, and two noises that they make.

vacuum cleaner. EG *She began the daily round of washing and hoovering.*

hooves /huːvz/ is a plural of **hoof.**

hop /hɒp/, **hops, hopping, hopped. 1** If you **hop**, you move along jumping on one foot. ▸ used as a noun. EG *They began jumping up and down together in short hops.* V:USU+A ▸ N COUNT

2 When birds and some small animals **hop**, they move in small jumps using both feet together. EG *A hare hopped straight into the doorway.* ▸ used as a noun. EG *...a bird so heavy that it could make only short, low hops through the brush.* V:USU+A ▸ N COUNT

3 If you **hop** somewhere, you move there quickly or suddenly. EG *He hopped out of bed... Let's hop in my car and drive out there.* V+A Informal

4 Hops are flowers that are dried and used for making beer. EG *...the hop gardens of Sussex.* N COUNT: USU PLURAL

5 Someone who is **hopping mad** is very angry or annoyed. PHRASE Informal

hope /həʊp/, **hopes, hoping, hoped. 1** If you **hope** that something is true or will happen, you want it to be true or to happen and usually believe that it is possible. EG *She hoped she wasn't going to cry... I sat down, hoping to remain unnoticed... He paused, hoping for evidence of interest... I hope I didn't wake you... 'You haven't lost the ticket, have you?' – 'I hope not.'* V+REPORT: ONLY that; ALSO V+to-INF OR for

2 Hope is a feeling of confidence that what you want to happen might happen. EG *She never completely gave up hope... Do you see any cause for hope for a settlement?... ...his hopes of a reconciliation.* N UNCOUNT OR N COUNT

3 If there is a **hope** of something desirable happening, there is a chance that it will happen. EG *Technical co-operation is the only hope for progress... There is no hope of regular employment as an agricultural labourer.* N SING+SUPP

4 Hope is also used in these phrases. **4.1** If you **hope for the best**, you hope that everything will happen in the way that you want it to. **4.2** If you do something **in the hope** of achieving a particular thing, you do it because you hope to achieve that thing. EG *Tourists were waiting outside the palace in the hope of getting a look at the king.* **4.3** If you **hold out hope**, you tell someone that what they want to happen might happen. **4.4** If something **raises** your **hopes**, it gives you a stronger feeling that what you want to happen will happen. EG *The new agreement raised hopes for conditions of prosperity.* PHRASES

hopeful /həʊpfʊl/, **hopefuls. 1** If you are **hopeful**, you are fairly confident that something that you want to happen will happen. EG *He sounded hopeful that she would come.* ADJ QUALIT

2 Something that is **hopeful** gives you the feeling that what you want to happen will happen. EG *...the most astonishing and hopeful results.* ADJ QUALIT

3 If you refer to someone as a **hopeful**, you mean that they have an ambition that they want to achieve and that there is a possibility that they will achieve it. EG *Almost a hundred hopefuls stood in a queue outside the theatre.* N COUNT

hopefully /həʊpfəliː/. **1** If you do something **hopefully**, you do it in a way which shows that you are fairly confident that what you want to happen will happen. EG *He smiled hopefully in their direction.* ADV

2 You say **hopefully** when mentioning something that you hope and are fairly confident will happen. Some careful speakers of English think that this use of **hopefully** is not correct, but it is very frequently used. EG *The new legislation, hopefully, will lead to some improvements.* ADV SEN

hopeless /həʊplɪˀs/. **1** If you feel **hopeless**, you feel desperate because there seems to be no possibility of comfort or success. EG *I walked away in an agony of hopeless grief and pity.* ◊ **hopelessly.** EG *She shook her head hopelessly.* ◊ **hopelessness.** EG *...the hopelessness of the poor.* ADJ QUALIT ◊ ADV ◊ N UNCOUNT

2 Something that is **hopeless** is certain to fail or to be unsuccessful. EG *I knew my love was as hopeless as ever... The situation was hopeless.* ADJ CLASSIF

3 If someone is **hopeless** at something, they do it very badly. EG *He was hopeless at games.* ADJ QUALIT Informal

4 You use **hopeless** to emphasize how bad an event or situation is. EG *Her room is in a hopeless muddle.* ◊ **hopelessly.** EG *She was hopelessly impulsive.* ADJ CLASSIF: ATTRIB ◊ SUBMOD

horde /hɔːd/, **hordes.** A **horde** is a large crowd of people. EG *...hordes of screaming children... ...rioting hordes.* N COUNT OR N PART

horizon /həraɪzəˀn/, **horizons. 1** The **horizon** is the line in the far distance where the sky seems to touch the land or the sea. EG *...the smoke on the horizon.* N COUNT

2 If you say that something is **on the horizon**, you mean that it is almost certainly going to happen or appear soon. EG *A new type of drug is on the horizon.* PHRASE

3 Your **horizons** are the limits of what you want to do or of what you are interested or involved in. EG *...the spontaneous expansion of human horizons.* N COUNT: USU PLURAL

horizontal /hɒrɪzɒntəˀl/. Something that is **horizontal** is flat and level with the ground, rather than at an angle to it. EG *...horizontal stripes.* ◊ **horizontally.** EG *The lower branches spread out almost horizontally.* ADJ CLASSIF ◊ ADV

hormone /hɔːməʊn/, **hormones.** A **hormone** is a chemical that is produced in your body. EG *...the male hormone testosterone.* ◊ **hormonal** /hɔːməʊnəˀl/. EG *...hormonal changes.* N COUNT ◊ ADJ CLASSIF

horn /hɔːn/, **horns. 1** The **horn** on a car or other vehicle is the thing that makes a loud noise as a signal or warning; also used of the button that you press in order to operate it. See picture at CAR. EG *A car passed him at top speed, sounding its horn.* N COUNT

2 Horns are the hard pointed things that stick out of the heads of cows, deer, and some other animals. EG *...the horns of a bull.* N COUNT: USU PLURAL

3 Horn is the hard substance that the horns of animals are made of. People use horn to make objects such as spoons or ornaments. N UNCOUNT

4 A **horn** or a **French horn** is a brass musical instrument that you play by blowing into it. It consists of a long metal tube wound round in a circle with a funnel at one end. N COUNT

horn-rimmed /hɔːn rɪmd/ spectacles have plastic frames that look as though they are made of horn. EG *She wore enormous horn-rimmed glasses.* ADJ CLASSIF

horoscope /hɒrəskəʊp/, **horoscopes.** Your **horoscope** is a forecast of events that will happen to you in the future. Horoscopes are based on the position of the stars when you were born. N COUNT

horrendous /həˀrendəs/. Something that is **horrendous** is very unpleasant and shocking. EG *...the horrendous murder of a prostitute.* ADJ QUALIT

horrible /hɒrəˀbəˀl/. **1** Something that is **horrible 1.1** is very unpleasant. EG *The hotel was horrible... I've never had such a horrible meal.* **1.2** causes you to feel great shock, fear, and disgust. EG *...an imaginary torture, perhaps, but all the more horrible.* ◊ **horribly.** EG *The man had begun to scream horribly.* ADJ QUALIT Informal ◊ ADV

2 You use **horrible** to emphasize how bad something is. EG *Everything's in a horrible muddle... I've got a horrible suspicion this thing won't work.* ◊ **horribly.** EG *I am horribly timid... Everything has gone horribly wrong.* ADJ QUALIT: ATTRIB ◊ SUBMOD Informal

horrid /hɒrɪd/. **1** Something that is **horrid** is very unpleasant. EG *Tea always tastes horrid out of Thermos flasks... ...a horrid little flat.* ADJ QUALIT Informal

2 If you describe a person as **horrid**, you mean that they behave in a very unpleasant way. EG *...her horrid parents... I don't mean to be horrid to you.* ADJ QUALIT Informal

horrific /hɒˀrɪfɪk/. Something that is **horrific** is so unpleasant that people are horrified and shocked by it. EG *It was one of the most horrific experiences of my life.* ADJ QUALIT

horrify /ˈhɒrɪfaɪ/, **horrifies, horrifying, horri-** v+o : USU PASS
fied. If you **are horrified** by something, it makes
you feel very alarmed and upset. EG *He was horri-*
fied by their poverty... Both Mr Faulds and his
daughter were horrified at the proposal.
◊ **horrifying.** EG *...horrifying stories... ...brutal* ◊ ADJ QUALIT
beatings and horrifying torture sessions.

horror /ˈhɒrə/, **horrors. 1 Horror** is a strong N UNCOUNT
feeling of alarm caused by something extremely
unpleasant. EG *The boys shrank away in horror...*
These policies arouse in many people a horror and
an anger that cannot be suppressed.
2 If you have a **horror** of something, you are afraid N SING :
of it or dislike it strongly. EG *Despite a horror of* a+N+of
violence, John allowed himself to be drafted into
the army.
3 You can refer to extremely unpleasant experi- N COUNT :
ences as **horrors.** EG *Sometimes his mind would* USU PLURAL
dwell on the horrors he had been through.
4 If you talk about the **horror** of something un- N SING :
pleasant, you are emphasizing that it is very un- the+N+of
pleasant. EG *They will never forget the blood and*
horror of the battle.
5 A **horror** film or story is intended to be very N MOD
frightening and is often about ghosts, witches, or
imaginary monsters.

hors d'oeuvre /ˌɔːˈdɜːv/, **hors d'oeuvres. Hors** N COUNT :
d'oeuvres are dishes of cold food that you eat USU PLURAL
before the main course of a meal.

horse /hɔːs/, **horses. A horse** is a large animal N COUNT
which you can ride. Some horses are used for
pulling ploughs and carts. EG *He was seen riding a*
horse through the streets of London.

horseback /ˈhɔːsbæk/. If you are **on horseback,** PHRASE
you are riding a horse. EG *The crowds were dis-*
persed by policemen on horseback.

horseman /ˈhɔːsmən/, **horsemen. 1 A horseman** N COUNT
is a man who is riding a horse.
2 If you say that a man is a good **horseman,** you N COUNT :
mean that he can ride a horse well. ADJ+N

horseshoe /ˈhɔːsʃuː/, **horseshoes. A horseshoe** is N COUNT
a piece of metal shaped like a U which is fixed to a
horse's hoof.

horticulture /ˈhɔːtɪkʌltʃə/ is the study and prac- N UNCOUNT
tice of growing flowers, fruit, and vegetables.
◊ **horticultural** /ˌhɔːtiˈkʌltʃərəl/. EG *...the Royal* ◊ ADJ CLASSIF
Horticultural Society.

hose /həʊz/, **hoses, hosing, hosed. 1 A hose** is a N COUNT
long, flexible pipe made of rubber or plastic, along
which water is carried.
2 If you **hose** something, you wash it or spread v+o
water on it using a hose. EG *Hose the soil well*
immediately after planting rose bushes.

hose down. If you **hose** something **down,** you PHRASAL VB :
clean it using a hose. EG *Could you not get the* v+o+ADV
sanitation department to hose the place down?

hosiery /ˈhəʊzɪˈɔriˈ/ is garments such as tights and N UNCOUNT
stockings that are for sale in a shop. Formal

hospice /ˈhɒspɪs/, **hospices. A hospice** is a hospi- N COUNT
tal where dying people receive special care.

hospitable /ˈhɒspɪtəbəˡl, hɒspɪtˈ/. If you are **hos-** ADJ QUALIT
pitable, you are friendly and welcoming to guests
or strangers. EG *Mr Steinberg was a good-natured*
and hospitable man... She behaved in a generous
and hospitable fashion. ◊ **hospitably.** EG *'You* ◊ ADV
must have a drink!' cried Bill hospitably.

hospital /ˈhɒspɪtəˡl/, **hospitals. A hospital** is a N COUNT OR
place where sick people are looked after by doc- N UNCOUNT
tors and nurses. EG *I was working at the hospital...*
...a psychiatric hospital... I used to visit him in
hospital.

hospitality /ˌhɒspɪtælɪˈtiˈ/ is friendly, welcoming N UNCOUNT
behaviour towards guests or strangers. EG *I thanked*
him for his hospitality.

hospitalize /ˈhɒspɪtəlaɪz/, **hospitalizes, hospital-** v+o : USU PASS
izing, hospitalized. If someone **is hospitalized,** American
they are sent to hospital. EG *She contracted pneu-*
monia and had to be hospitalized.

◊ **hospitalization** /ˌhɒspɪtəlaɪzeɪʃˈəˈn/. EG *...the first* N UNCOUNT
60 days of hospitalization.

host /həʊst/, **hosts. 1** The **host** at a party is the N COUNT
person who has invited the guests. EG *Drinks were*
being prepared by the host... We ended up having a
tremendous row with our host.
2 A **host** country or organization provides the N COUNT :
facilities for an event, or gives people from another USU N MOD
country a place to live. EG *...the attitude of the host*
community to the refugees... Within a week his
host country had supplied him with accommoda-
tion.
3 The **host** of a radio or television show is the N COUNT
person who introduces it and talks to the people
who appear in it.
4 A **host** of things is a lot of them. EG *I'm sure the* N PART
audience has a host of questions for our team of Formal
experts.

hostage /ˈhɒstɪdʒ/, **hostages. A hostage** is some- N COUNT
one who has been captured by a person or organization and who may be killed or injured if people
do not do what the person or organization wants. EG
An agreement was reached that freed the 52
hostages. ● If someone **is taken hostage** or **is** ● PHRASE
held hostage, they are captured and kept as a
hostage. EG *He had been taken hostage by terror-*
ists... They are being held hostage until our de-
mands are met.

hostel /ˈhɒstəˡl/, **hostels. A hostel** is a house N COUNT
where people can stay cheaply for a short time.
Hostels are usually owned by local government
authorities or charities.

hostess /ˈhəʊstɪˈs/, **hostesses. 1** The **hostess** at a N COUNT
party is the woman who has invited the guests. EG
My hostess greeted me with unexpected warmth.
2 A **hostess** at a night club or dance hall is a N COUNT
woman who is paid by a man to be his companion
for the evening.

hostile /ˈhɒstaɪl/. **1** Someone who is **hostile** is ADJ QUALIT
unfriendly and aggressive. EG *Frank was a re-*
served, almost hostile person... I was in a depressed
and hostile mood.
2 If you are **hostile** to someone or something, you ADJ QUALIT
disagree with them or disapprove of them. EG *...a*
new government that is hostile to us.
3 **Hostile** situations and conditions make it difficult ADJ QUALIT
for you to achieve something. EG *...hostile weather...*
...the problem of running machinery in hostile
environments.

hostility /hɒstɪlɪˈtiˈ/, **hostilities. 1 Hostility** is N UNCOUNT
1.1 unfriendly and aggressive behaviour. EG *Their*
friendship is regarded with suspicion and hostility.
1.2 opposition to something that you do not approve of. EG *American spokesmen made clear their*
hostility to the new proposals.
2 You can refer to fighting between two countries N PLURAL
or groups as **hostilities.** EG *Both sides wanted a* Formal
cessation of hostilities.

hot /hɒt/, **hotter, hottest; hots, hotting, hotted. 1** ADJ QUALIT
Something that is **hot** has a high temperature. EG
The metal is so hot I can't touch it... ...hot water.
2 If it is **hot,** the temperature of the air is high. EG ADJ QUALIT
...a fine, hot August day.
3 If you are **hot,** your body is at an unpleasantly ADJ PRED
high temperature. EG *Hot and perspiring, John*
toiled up the hill.
4 Food that is **hot** has a strong, burning taste ADJ QUALIT
caused by spices. EG *...hot curries.*
5 If you say that someone is **hot** on something, you ADJ PRED :
mean that they know a lot about it. EG *I'm not so hot* OFT+on
on linguistic theory. Informal
6 Someone who has a **hot** temper gets angry very ADJ QUALIT
easily.

hot up. When an event **hots up,** there begins to PHRASAL VB :

> Would you expect a hostile person to give you
> hospitality?

house

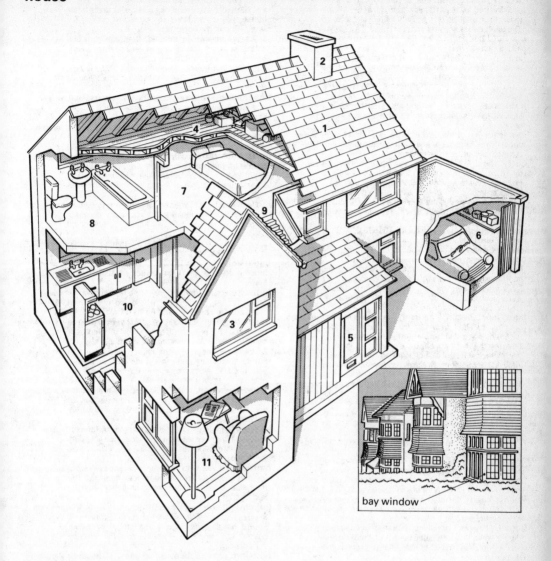

bay window

1	roof		
2	chimney	7	bedroom
3	window	8	bathroom
4	loft	9	staircase
5	front door	10	kitchen
6	garage	11	sitting room/living room

be a lot of activity and excitement. EG *Now the pace really began to hot up.* V-ERG+ADV Informal

hotbed /hɒtbɛd/, **hotbeds.** If you say that a place is a **hotbed** of a particular kind of activity, you mean that a lot of this activity happens there. EG *The universities are hotbeds of intrigue.* N COUNT+*of*

hot dog, hot dogs. A **hot dog** is a long bread roll with a sausage in it. N COUNT

hotel /hⁿəʊtɛl/, **hotels.** A **hotel** is a building where people stay, for example on holiday, paying for their rooms and meals. N COUNT

hotelier /hⁿəʊtɛliə/, **hoteliers.** A **hotelier** is a person who owns or manages a hotel. N COUNT

hothouse /hɒthaʊs/, **hothouses.** A **hothouse** is a heated glass building in which plants and flowers grow. N COUNT

hot line, hot lines. A **hot line** is a direct telephone line by which heads of government can contact each other in an emergency. N COUNT: USU *the*+N

hotly /hɒtli¹/. 1 If you say something **hotly**, you say it angrily. EG *'I don't mind going,' said Jack hotly... ...a claim which the USA has hotly denied.* ADV

2 If something is **hotly** discussed or disputed, people discuss or dispute it in a lively way, because they feel strongly about it. EG *...the hotly debated question of abortion.* ADV

hot-water bottle, hot-water bottles. A **hot-water bottle** is a rubber container which you fill with hot water and put in a bed to make it warm. N COUNT

hound /haʊnd/, **hounds, hounding, hounded.** 1 A **hound** is a type of dog that is often used for hunting or racing. EG *...large packs of hounds.* N COUNT

2 If someone **hounds** you, they constantly disturb you or criticize you; used showing disapproval. EG *He was hounded by the press.* V+O

hour /aʊə/, **hours.** 1 An **hour** is a period of sixty minutes. EG *They slept for two hours... We talked for hours.* ● See also **lunch hour, rush-hour.** N COUNT

2 Something that happens **on the hour** happens at one o'clock, at two o'clock, and so on at regular intervals of one hour. EG *Buses for London leave on the hour.* PHRASE

3 You can refer to a particular time in the day as a particular **hour.** EG *There was little traffic at this hour.* ● See also **eleventh hour.** N COUNT+SUPP Literary

4 If something happens in **the small hours**, it happens in the early morning after midnight. EG *The noise kept him awake until the small hours.* PHRASE

5 You can refer to the period of time that something happens each day as the **hours** that it happens. EG *...our demands for shorter working hours.* ● See also **opening hours.** N PLURAL

hourly /aʊəli¹/. 1 An **hourly** event happens once every hour. EG *There is an hourly bus service.* ADJ CLASSIF: ATTRIB

2 Your **hourly** earnings are the amount of money that you earn each hour. EG *Their average hourly earnings were £5.00.* ADJ CLASSIF: ATTRIB

house, houses, housing, housed; pronounced /haʊs/ when it is a singular noun and /haʊz/ when it is a verb. The plural of the noun is pronounced /haʊzɪz/.

1 A **house** is **1.1** a building in which people live. EG *He has a house in Pimlico... It only takes 35 minutes from my house.* ● See also **boarding house, public house. 1.2** a company, especially one which publishes books, lends money, or designs clothes. EG *...a University Publishing House.* N COUNT+SUPP

2 If someone tells you to **set** or **put** your **own house in order**, they mean that you should arrange your own affairs properly before you tell others how to arrange theirs. ● to **set up house**: see **set up.** PHRASE

3 The group of people who make a country's laws are often referred to as a **House.** EG *...the House of Assembly... ...twenty-two members drawn from both Houses.* N COUNT Formal

4 In a theatre or cinema, the **house** is the part where the audience sits. EG *We stood at the back of the packed house.* ● If a performance **brings the** N COUNT ● PHRASE Informal

house down, the audience claps and cheers loudly for a long time. EG *There was one scene which never failed to bring the house down.*

5 If you are given something at a restaurant **on the house**, you do not have to pay for it. EG *You try some – it's on the house.* PHRASE Informal

6 When someone **is housed**, they are provided with a house or flat to live in. EG *They are better housed than ever before.* V+O: USU PASS

7 If a building **houses** something, that thing is kept in the building. EG *This is the building which houses the library.* V+O Formal

houseboat /haʊsbəʊt/, **houseboats.** A **houseboat** is a small boat on a river or canal which people live in. N COUNT

housebound /haʊsbaʊnd/. Someone who is **housebound** is unable to go out of their house because they are ill or old. ADJ CLASSIF

household /haʊshəʊld/, **households. 1** A **household** is all the people in a family or group who live together in a house. EG *He loved being part of a huge household... Only 8 per cent of households owned a fridge.* N COUNT

2 The **household** is your home and everything that is connected with looking after it. EG *My daughter managed the entire household... ...household chores.* N SING

3 Someone or something that is a **household** name is very well known and often talked about. N MOD

householder /haʊshəʊldə/, **householders.** A **householder** is the legal owner or tenant of a house. N COUNT

housekeeper /haʊskiːpə/, **housekeepers.** A **housekeeper** is a person whose job is to cook, clean and look after a house for its owner. N COUNT

housekeeping /haʊskiːpɪŋ/. 1 **Housekeeping** is the work and organization involved in running a home, including the cooking and cleaning. N UNCOUNT

2 The **housekeeping** is the money that you use to buy food, cleaning materials, and other things that you need in your home. EG *She spent all the housekeeping on a new coat.* N SING: *the*+N

house-to-house. If the police carry out a **house-to-house** search, they search all the houses in an area. EG *We've not got the manpower to do a house-to-house check.* ADJ CLASSIF: ATTRIB

housewife /haʊswaɪf/, **housewives.** A **housewife** is a married woman who does not normally have a job outside her home. EG *I was a housewife and mother of two small children.* N COUNT

housework /haʊswɜːk/ is the work such as cleaning and cooking that you do in your home. EG *The men shared all the housework, including washing and ironing.* N UNCOUNT

housing /haʊzɪŋ/ is 1 the buildings that people live in. EG *...bad housing and poverty... There is a severe housing shortage.* 2 the job of providing houses for people to live in. EG *...the housing department.* N UNCOUNT

housing estate, housing estates. A **housing estate** is a large number of houses or flats built close together at the same time. N COUNT

hovel /hʌvəˀl, hɒv-/, **hovels.** A **hovel** is a small hut that people live in and that is in bad condition. EG *They lived in overcrowded hovels.* N COUNT

hover /hɒvə/, **hovers, hovering, hovered.** 1 When a bird or insect **hovers**, it stays in the same position in the air by moving its wings very quickly. V

2 If someone **is hovering**, **2.1** they are waiting in one place, for example because they cannot decide what to do. EG *A figure hovered uncertainly in the doorway... His hand was hovering over the telephone.* **2.2** they are unable to make a decision V: OFT+A

Would you like to live in a hovel?

about something. EG *We hovered between the two possibilities.*

hovercraft /h<u>o</u>vəkrɑːft/, **hovercrafts. Hover-** N COUNT **craft** can also be the plural form.
A **hovercraft** is a vehicle that can travel across land and water by floating on a cushion of air.

how /hau/. 1 You use **how** in questions when you WH : ADV are asking someone about the way or manner in which something is done. EG *How did you know about this?... How did they behave towards me?*
2 If you talk about **how** something is done, 2.1 you WH : CONJ are talking about the way or manner in which it is done. EG *Tell me how to get there... A lot depends on how the Americans handle the situation.* 2.2 you are talking about the fact that it is done. EG *Do you remember how you and I planned to live in Venice?*
3 You use **how** 3.1 when you are asking someone WH : ADV whether something is or was successful or enjoyable. EG *'How did school go?' - 'It was all right.'... How was Paris?* 3.2 when you are asking about someone's health, or referring to it. EG *'How are you?' - 'Fine, thanks.'... I'm going to see how Davis is.* ● **'How do you do?'** is a polite way of greeting ● CONVENTION someone when you meet them for the first time.
4 You can use **how** to emphasize an adjective, WH : ADV adverb, or statement. EG *How pretty you look!... How I dislike that man!*
5 You use **how** when you are asking someone to WH : ADV tell you something such as a measurement or a person's age. EG *How old are you?... How far is Amity from here?* ● If you ask **how much** some- ● PHRASE thing is, you are asking what its price is, because you want to buy it. EG *How much is it?*
6 You can say **'How can** you' or **'How could** you' PHRASE to indicate that you are surprised at what someone has done or said. EG *'I'm bored.' - 'How can you be bored?'*
7 You can say **how about** something or **how** PHRASE **would you** like something when you are making a suggestion or an offer. EG *If there isn't a playgroup locally, how about starting one?... How would you fancy a few months on the continent?*
8 You can say **'How about you?'** when you are CONVENTION asking someone what they think or want. EG *How about you, Dorothy, what do you want?*

however /hauɛvə/. 1 You use **however** when you ADV SEN are adding a comment which is surprising or which contrasts with what has just been said. EG *I felt that I would not be sufficiently experienced. However Jenkins seemed to have confidence in me... Losing at games doesn't seem to matter to some women. Most men, however, can't stand it.*
2 You can use **however** to emphasize that the WH : ADV degree of something, for example size or effort, cannot change a situation. EG *She could not remember, however hard she tried.*
3 You can use **or however many** or **or however** PHRASE **much** at the beginning of a clause to indicate that Informal you do not know the exact quantity or size of something, and that it is not important. EG *...the twelve or eleven people on the jury or however many there are.*

howl /haul/, **howls, howling, howled.** 1 If an V animal such as a wolf or a dog **howls**, it utters a long, loud, crying sound. EG *Jackals howled among the ruins.* ◊ **howling.** EG *He could hear the* ◊ N UNCOUNT *howling of hyenas.*
2 If someone **howls**, they weep loudly because V they are very unhappy or in pain. EG *I put back my head and howled.* ▸ used as a noun. EG *He gave a* ▸ N COUNT *howl of pain.* ◊ **howling.** EG *...the endless howling* ◊ N UNCOUNT *of their children.*
3 When the wind **howls**, it blows hard and makes a V loud noise. ◊ **howling.** EG *...torrential rain and* ◊ ADJ CLASSIF *howling winds.*

howl down. If people **howl** you **down**, they shout PHRASAL VB : loudly in order to prevent you from speaking. EG *He* V+O+ADV *was howled down by monarchists.*

HP is an abbreviation for 'hire purchase'.

HQ, HQs. HQ is an abbreviation for 'headquarters'.

hr, hrs. hr is a written abbreviation for 'hour'. EG *He won the Cardiff run in 2hrs 26mins 4secs... ...a 6hr sea crossing.*

HRH is an abbreviation for 'His Royal Highness' or 'Her Royal Highness'. It is used as part of the title of a prince or princess. EG *...HRH Prince Charles.*

hub /hʌb/, **hubs.** 1 The **hub** of a wheel is the part N COUNT which is at the centre. EG *...the hub of a bicycle wheel.*
2 If you describe a place as the **hub** of a district, N COUNT+of you mean that it is the most important area of the district. EG *Amity would one day be the hub of commerce on Long Island.*

huddle /hʌdəⁿl/, **huddles, huddling, huddled.** 1 If V+A you **huddle** somewhere, you sit, stand, or lie there holding your arms and legs close to your body, because you are cold or frightened. EG *She huddled among the untidy bedclothes.* ◊ **huddled.** EG *In the* ◊ ADJ CLASSIF *evening he would sit huddled near the stove.*
2 If people **huddle** together or **huddle** round V+A something, they stand, sit, or lie close to each other, because they are cold or frightened. EG *The people huddled around their fires.* ◊ **huddled.** EG ◊ ADJ CLASSIF *We sat huddled together.*
3 A **huddle** of people or things is a small group N COUNT standing or sitting close together. EG *They flopped down in a huddle... ...a huddle of huts.*

hue /hjuː/, **hues.** A **hue** is a colour. EG *Mrs Par-* N COUNT *tridge's face took on a deeper hue.* Literary

huff /hʌf/, **huffs, huffing, huffed.** 1 If someone is PHRASE **in a huff**, they are behaving in a bad-tempered way because they are annoyed or offended. EG *The people all left in a huff.*
2 If someone **is huffing and puffing**, they are PHRASE expressing their annoyance or dissatisfaction in a silly and unnecessary way. EG *The politicians still huffed and puffed, but were ignored.*

hug /hʌg/, **hugs, hugging, hugged.** 1 When you V OR V+O : **hug** someone, you put your arms around them and RECIP hold them tightly because you like them or are pleased to see them. EG *During our infancy, our parents cuddle and hug us... In an instant we were hugging and kissing.* ▸ used as a noun. EG *He* ▸ N COUNT *greeted his mother with a hug.*
2 If you **hug** something, you hold it close to your V+O body with your arms tightly round it. EG *...a basket of provisions which she hugged tight on her lap.*

huge /hjuːdʒ/. Something that is **huge** is extremely ADJ QUALIT large in size, amount, or degree. EG *Huge wooden earrings dangled from her ears... A huge industry has been built up... Huge numbers of children are leaving school.* ◊ **hugely.** EG *...a hugely expensive* ◊ ADV *machine... He was having a hugely enjoyable time.*

huh /hʌ, hə/. Some people say **'huh?'** at the end of American a question. EG *'You been away, huh?' - 'Yes,' I said.* Informal

hulk /hʌlk/, **hulks.** You can refer to something or N COUNT someone that is large, clumsy, and heavy as a **hulk.** EG *Her pupils were raw-boned hulks with red hair and freckles... The Abbey is a great cross-shaped, blackish hulk.*

hulking /hʌlkɪŋ/. A **hulking** person is extremely ADJ CLASSIF : large and heavy. ATTRIB

hull /hʌl/, **hulls.** The **hull** of a boat or ship is the N COUNT main part of its body. See picture at YACHT.

hullabaloo /hʌləbəluː/, **hullabaloos.** If you make N COUNT a **hullabaloo**, you make a lot of noise or fuss about Outdated something. EG *You can't imagine what a hullabaloo they've been making about it at College.*

hullo /həⁿləu/. See **hello.**

hum /hʌm/, **hums, humming, hummed.** 1 If V something **hums**, it makes a low continuous noise. EG *The air-conditioning hummed.* ▸ used as a noun. ▸ N COUNT EG *The only sound she heard was the hum of a machine in the basement.*
2 When you **hum**, you sing a tune with your lips V OR V+O closed. EG *I began to hum... She continued to hum the song.*

human body

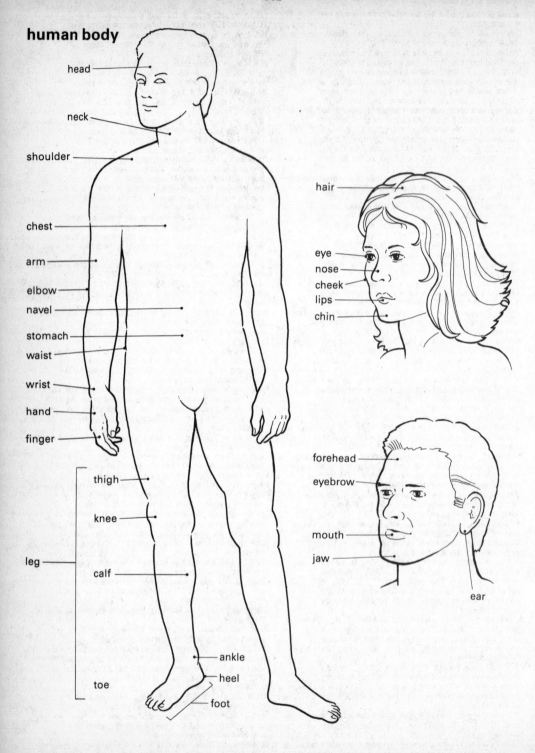

head

neck

shoulder

chest

arm

elbow

navel

stomach

waist

wrist

hand

finger

thigh

knee

leg

calf

toe

ankle

heel

foot

hair

eye

nose

cheek

lips

chin

forehead

eyebrow

mouth

jaw

ear

3 If you say that a place is **humming** with some- ADJ PRED: thing, you mean that it is full of activity. EG *The* OFT+*with* *area is usually humming with shoppers.*

human /hju:mən/, **humans. 1 Human** means ADJ CLASSIF relating to or concerning people. EG *He had no regard for human life... ...the human body... ...one of the most exciting periods in human history.*

2 You can refer to people as **humans** when you N COUNT are comparing them with animals or machines. EG *Could a computer ever beat a human at chess?*

human being, human beings. A **human being** N COUNT is a man, woman, or child. EG *A dog eats far more meat than a human being.*

humane /hju:meɪn/. Someone who is **humane** is ADJ QUALIT kind, thoughtful, and sympathetic. EG *He's one of the most humane people I have ever worked with... ...the humane treatment of psychiatric patients.*
◊ **humanely.** EG *Animals must be killed humanely.* ◊ ADV
◊ **humaneness.** EG *...the moral necessity for* ◊ N UNCOUNT *humaneness towards all people.*

humanism /hju:mənɪzəm/ is the belief that peo- N UNCOUNT ple can achieve happiness and fulfilment without having a religion. ◊ **humanist, humanists.** EG ◊ N COUNT *...the humanist's belief in man.*

humanitarian /hju:mænɪteəriən/, **humanitar-** N COUNT **ians.** A **humanitarian** is someone who works to improve the welfare of mankind and to end suffer- ing and pain. ▸ used as an adjective. EG *...liberal* ▸ ADJ CLASSIF *and humanitarian opinions.*

humanity /hju:mænɪtiɪ/, **humanities. 1 Human-** N UNCOUNT **ity** is the same as mankind. EG *...a crime against humanity... ...a triumph for humanity.*

2 A person's **humanity** is their state of being a N UNCOUNT human being, rather than an animal or an object. Formal EG *They denied him his humanity.*

3 Humanity is also the quality of being kind, N UNCOUNT thoughtful, and sympathetic. EG *...a man of remark- able humanity.*

4 The **humanities** are subjects such as literature, N PLURAL philosophy, and history which are concerned with human ideas and behaviour. EG *She has a back- ground in humanities and modern languages.*

humanly /hju:mənlɪ/. If something is **humanly** PHRASE **possible**, it is possible for people to do it. EG *People were asked to reply within twenty-four hours whenever this was humanly possible.*

human nature is the natural qualities and ways N UNCOUNT of behaviour that most people have. EG *You can't change human nature.*

human race. You can refer to the whole of N SING:*the+N* mankind as the **human race.** EG *The future of the human race might now be at stake.*

human rights are the basic rights which most N PLURAL nations agree that all people should have. EG *...a violation of human rights.*

humble /hʌmbəl/, **humbler, humblest. 1** Some- ADJ QUALIT one who is **humble** is not proud and does not believe that they are better or more important than other people. EG *We were taught to be humble, truthful, and generous... Jim bore this with humble patience.* ◊ **humbly.** EG *'You know much more* ◊ ADV *about it, Sir, than I do,' said John humbly.*

2 People with low social status are sometimes ADJ QUALIT described as **humble.** EG *...men and women from very humble backgrounds.*

3 People use **humble** in expressions such as **my** ADJ QUALIT **humble opinion** when they are expressing an opinion politely but firmly. EG *My humble opinion is that an analysis would be very useful.*

humbug /hʌmbʌg/, **humbugs. 1** A **humbug** is a N COUNT hard striped sweet that tastes of peppermint.

2 If you describe speech or writing as **humbug,** N UNCOUNT you mean that you think it is dishonest and intend- Outdated ed to deceive people. EG *...parliamentary humbug.*

humdrum /hʌmdrʌm/. Something that is **hum-** ADJ QUALIT **drum** is ordinary and dull. EG *...their humdrum lives.*

humid /hju:mɪd/. In **humid** places, the weather is ADJ QUALIT hot and damp. EG *...humid jungles... Singapore was dank and humid.*

humidity /hju:mɪdɪtiɪ/ is dampness in the air. EG N UNCOUNT *...diseases and weeds, encouraged by heat and humidity.*

humiliate /hju:mɪlɪeɪt/, **humiliates, humiliat-** V+O **ing, humiliated.** If you **humiliate** someone, you do or say something that makes them feel ashamed or stupid. EG *She had humiliated him in front of his friends.* ◊ **humiliated.** EG *I could die. I* ◊ ADJ QUALIT *feel so humiliated.*

humiliating /hju:mɪlɪeɪtɪŋ/. Something that is **hu-** ADJ QUALIT **miliating** embarrasses you and makes you feel ashamed and stupid. EG *He said it was humiliating for him that his wife should go out to work.*

humiliation /hju:mɪlɪeɪʃən/, **humiliations. 1** N UNCOUNT **Humiliation** is the embarrassment that you feel when you are made to appear helpless or stupid. EG *The prisoners suffered constant public humiliation.*

2 A **humiliation** is an experience in which you are N COUNT humiliated. EG *Taylor's humiliations had taken place in public.*

humility /hju:mɪlɪtiɪ/. Someone who has **humil-** N UNCOUNT **ity** is not proud and does not believe that they are better or more important than other people. EG *He has sufficient humility to acknowledge his own imperfections.*

humor /hju:mə/. See **humour.**

humorist /hju:mərɪst/, **humorists.** A **humorist** is N COUNT an entertainer or writer who makes jokes or writes in a humorous way.

humorous /hju:mərəs/. **1** Something that is **hu-** ADJ QUALIT **morous** is amusing. EG *...humorous books.*

2 Someone who is **humorous** is amusing and witty. ADJ QUALIT EG *They were imaginative, quick, and humorous.*
◊ **humorously.** EG *They often humorously referred* ◊ ADV *to themselves as caretakers.*

humour /hju:mə/, **humours, humouring, hu-** **moured;** spelled **humor** in American English.

1 Humour is the ability to see when something is N UNCOUNT funny and to say amusing things. EG *My grand- mother had a kind of heavy humour... ...a great sense of humour.*

2 If something has **humour**, it is funny and makes N UNCOUNT you want to laugh. EG *She could appreciate the humour of the remark.*

3 Humour is also things that people say or write N UNCOUNT which make you laugh. EG *...the difference between English and American humour.*

4 If you are in a good **humour**, you are cheerful N UNCOUNT and behave pleasantly to people. If you are in a bad +SUPP **humour**, you are unhappy and behave unpleasant- ly. EG *This put Etta into a good humour... The work was proceeding with efficiency and good humour... I am in a bad humour today.*

5 If you **humour** someone who is behaving V+O strangely or unreasonably, you try to please them, so that they will not become upset or behave unpleasantly. EG *He had bought it to humour Julie... Maybe if I humor him he'll go away.*

humourless /hju:məlɪs/; spelled **humorless** in ADJ CLASSIF American English. Someone who is **humourless** is very serious about everything and does not find things amusing.

hump /hʌmp/, **humps, humping, humped. 1** A N COUNT **hump** is a small hill or raised piece of ground. EG *...the humps and hollows of the old golf course.*

2 A camel's **hump** is the large lump on its back. N COUNT

3 If you **hump** something heavy somewhere, you V+O carry it there with difficulty. EG *You will probably* Informal *have to hump your own luggage.*

humpbacked /hʌmpbækt/. A **humpbacked** ani- ADJ CLASSIF: mal has a lump on its back. ATTRIB

hunch /hʌntʃ/, **hunches, hunching, hunched. 1** N COUNT If you have a **hunch** that something is true, you Informal feel strongly that it is true, although you have no proof. EG *Morris had a hunch that she was a good cook... Watson frequently acted on a hunch.*

2 If you **hunch** somewhere, you draw your shoulders towards each other and lower your chin towards your chest. EG *She hunched down in her seat... I was cold as I hunched over my meagre fire.*   V:USU+A

◊ **hunched.** EG *His eyes fell on Laing, hunched in a corner.*   ◊ ADJ CLASSIF

hundred /hʌndrəˈd/, **hundreds. 1** A **hundred** or one **hundred** is the number 100. See the entry headed NUMBER. EG *There are more than two hundred languages spoken in Nigeria.*   NUMBER

2 You can use **hundreds** to mean an extremely large number. EG *He handed me hundreds of forms.*   N PART: PLURAL

3 If you say that something is **a hundred per cent** true or **a hundred per cent** accurate, you mean that it is completely true or accurate. EG *Your assessment of Otto is a hundred per cent wrong... I agree one hundred per cent with Carol.*   PHRASE Informal

hundredth /hʌndrədθ/, **hundredths. 1** The **hundredth** item in a series is the one that you count as number one hundred. See the entry headed NUMBER. EG *...the hundredth anniversary of tennis championships at Wimbledon.*   ORDINAL

2 A **hundredth** is one of a hundred equal parts of something. EG *...one hundredth of a second... These simple organisms are no more than one or two hundredths of a millimetre across.*   N COUNT: USU+of

hundredweight /hʌndrədweɪt/, **hundredweights.** The plural can be either **hundredweight** or **hundredweights.**
A **hundredweight** is a unit of weight that is equal to 112 pounds in Britain and to 100 pounds in the United States. EG *The tenor bell in St Paul's Cathedral weighs sixty-two hundredweight.*   N COUNT OR N PART

hung /hʌŋ/ is the past tense and past participle for most of the senses of **hang.**

hunger /hʌŋgə/, **hungers, hungering, hungered. 1** Hunger is **1.1** the feeling of weakness or discomfort that you get when you need something to eat. EG *Babies show their hunger by waking up to be fed.* **1.2** a serious lack of food which causes suffering or death. EG *There were families dying of hunger and disease.*   N UNCOUNT

2 If you **hunger** for or **hunger** after something, you want it very much. EG *...Spaniards who hunger for Flamenco music.* ▸ used as a noun. EG *What gives people the hunger for power?*   V+for/after Formal ▸ N UNCOUNT: OFT+for

hungry /hʌŋgri¹/, **hungrier, hungriest. 1** When you are **hungry**, you want food. EG *I'm tired and hungry and I want some supper... ...a hungry baby.*   ADJ QUALIT

◊ **hungrily.** EG *I ate hungrily.*   ◊ ADV

2 If people **go hungry**, they suffer from hunger. EG *...sad reports of children going hungry.*   PHRASE

3 If you are **hungry** for something, you want it very much. EG *They were hungry for news.*   ADJ QUALIT: OFT+for

hung up. If you are **hung up** on something or **hung up** about it, you are anxious about it. EG *You're hung up about your father.*   ADJ QUALIT Informal

hunk /hʌŋk/, **hunks.** A **hunk** of something is a large piece of it. EG *...a hunk of brown bread.*   N PART

hunt /hʌnt/, **hunts, hunting, hunted. 1** When people **hunt**, they chase wild animals in order to kill them, either for food or as a sport. Some wild animals also **hunt** other animals for food. EG *The men had gone to the forest to hunt wild game... Hyenas usually hunt at night.* ▸ used as a noun. EG *They sighted a zebra and the hunt began.*   V OR V+O ▸ N COUNT

◊ **hunting.** EG *...communities who live by hunting... ...a hunting expedition.*   ◊ N UNCOUNT

2 In Britain, when people **hunt**, they chase and kill foxes as a sport. ◊ **hunting.** EG *The squire was killed in a hunting accident.*   V ◊ N UNCOUNT

3 If you **hunt** a criminal or an enemy, you search for them in order to catch or defeat them. EG *Two helicopters were hunting a submarine.*   V+O

4 If you **hunt** for something, you try to find it. EG *The kids hunted for treasure... She began hunting frantically in the back of the car... I'm still job hunting.* ▸ used as a noun. EG *...the hunt for the missing child.*   V:USU+for ▸ N COUNT: USU SING

hunt down. If you **hunt** someone or something **down**, you succeed in finding them after you have been searching for them. EG *It was obvious that they had hunted down their victims.*   PHRASAL VB: V+O+ADV

hunter /hʌntə/, **hunters. 1** A **hunter** is a person who hunts wild animals for food or as a sport.   N COUNT

2 People who search for things of a particular kind are often referred to as **hunters**. EG *...bargain hunters... ...fossil hunters.*   N COUNT+SUPP

huntsman /hʌntsmən/, **huntsmen.** A **huntsman** is a person who hunts wild animals, especially one who hunts foxes using dogs.   N COUNT

hurdle /hɜːdəˈl/, **hurdles. 1** A **hurdle** is a difficulty that you must overcome in order to achieve something. EG *The Government had got over their first important hurdle.*   N COUNT

2 Hurdles are fences that runners jump over in some races.   N COUNT

hurl /hɜːl/, **hurls, hurling, hurled. 1** If you **hurl** something, you throw it with a lot of force. EG *I took all his books and hurled them out of the window.*   V+O:USU+A

2 If you **hurl** abuse or insults at someone, you shout abuse or insults at them. EG *Abuse was hurled at the police.*   V+O:USU+A

hurray /həreɪ/ and **hurrah** /hərɑː/ mean the same as hooray.   CONVENTION

hurricane /hʌrɪkəˈn, -keɪn/, **hurricanes.** A **hurricane** is an extremely violent wind or storm. EG *The island is in the path of the hurricane.*   N COUNT

hurried /hʌrɪd/. Something that is **hurried** is done very quickly or suddenly. EG *...a hurried lunch... ...a hurried glance.* ◊ **hurriedly.** EG *He had dressed hurriedly.*   ADJ QUALIT ◊ ADV

hurry /hʌri¹/, **hurries, hurrying, hurried. 1** If you **hurry** somewhere, you go there quickly. EG *He hurried off down the street... The people hurried home.*   V:USU+A

2 If you **hurry** to do something, you start doing it as soon as you can. *They hurried to help him.*   V:USU+to-INF

3 If you **hurry** someone or something, you try to make them do something more quickly. EG *Efforts to hurry them only make them angry.*   V+O OR V+O+A

4 If you are in a **hurry**, you need to do something quickly. If you do something in a **hurry**, you do it quickly. EG *She was always in a hurry... Otto had to leave in a great hurry... In the middle of all this hurry, he dropped the bag.*   N SING

5 Hurry is used in these phrases. **5.1** If you say to someone **'There's no hurry'** or **'I'm in no hurry'**, you are telling them that there is no need to do something immediately. EG *There's no hurry. You've got until nine o'clock.* **5.2** If you say **'What's the hurry?'**, you want to know why something must be done quickly. EG *'Drink up, Sarah!' - 'What's the hurry?'* **5.3** You can also say that you are **in no hurry** to do something when you are very unwilling to do it. EG *He was in no hurry to confront Abraham Chase.*   CONVENTION Informal / CONVENTION Informal / PHRASE Informal

hurry up. If you tell someone to **hurry up**, you are telling them to do something more quickly. EG *Hurry up, it's getting late... You can hurry the process up by leaving the door open.*   PHRASAL VB: V+ADV OR V+O+ADV

hurt /hɜːt/, **hurts, hurting.** The form **hurt** is used in the present tense and is also the past tense and past participle of the verb.

1 If you **hurt** yourself or **hurt** a part of your body, you injure yourself. EG *How did you hurt your finger?*   V-REFL OR V+O

2 If a part of your body **hurts**, you feel pain there. EG *My leg was beginning to hurt.*   V

3 If you **hurt** someone else, you cause them to feel pain. EG *Did I hurt you?... Stop it! You're hurting!*   V+O

4 If you **hurt** someone or **hurt** their feelings, you make them unhappy by being unkind to them. EG

If someone called you a hypocrite, would you feel hurt?

She was easily hurt by an unkindness... He didn't want to hurt her feelings.
5 If you are **hurt, 5.1** you have been injured. EG *The soldier was obviously badly hurt.* **5.2** you are upset because of something that someone has said or done. EG *His mother was deeply hurt... ...a tone of hurt surprise.* ADJ QUALIT
6 Hurt is the damage to someone's feelings when they think that they have been treated badly. EG *...feelings of anger and hurt.* N UNCOUNT
7 You can say that something **hurts** someone or something when it has a bad effect on them. EG *These policies could destroy small businesses and hurt consumers.* V+O

hurtful /hɜːtful/. Something that is **hurtful** is unkind and makes you feel unhappy and upset. EG *Some of the things they say are hurtful.* ADJ QUALIT

hurtle /hɜːtəⁱl/, **hurtles, hurtling, hurtled.** If something **hurtles**, it moves very quickly, often in a dangerous way. EG *He didn't like hurtling along rough dirt roads at fifty miles an hour... He watched the plane as it hurtled down the runway.* V : USU+A

husband /hʌzbənd/, **husbands.** A woman's **husband** is the man she is married to. N COUNT : OFT+POSS

hush /hʌʃ/, **hushes, hushing, hushed.** 1 If you say **'Hush!'** to someone, you are telling them to be quiet. CONVENTION
2 You say that there is **hush** or a **hush** when it is quiet and peaceful. EG *An expectant hush fell on the gathering.* N SING

hush up. If people in authority **hush** something **up**, they prevent the public from knowing about it. EG *The police had hushed the matter up.* PHRASAL VB : V+O+ADV

hushed /hʌʃt/. 1 A **hushed** place is quiet and peaceful. EG *We walked in silence through the hushed valley.* ADJ QUALIT Literary
2 If you say something in a **hushed** voice, you say it very quietly. EG *In the hotel lobby, people were talking in hushed tones.* ADJ QUALIT Literary

husk /hʌsk/, **husks. Husks** are the outer coverings of grains or seeds. N COUNT

husky /hʌskiⁱ/, **huskier, huskiest.** If someone's voice is **husky**, it sounds rough or hoarse. ADJ QUALIT

hustle /hʌsəⁱl/, **hustles, hustling, hustled.** If you **hustle** someone somewhere, you make them move there quickly, usually by pulling or pushing them. EG *He hustled Fanny through the door.* V+O : USU+A

hut /hʌt/, **huts.** A **hut** is 1 a small house with only one or two rooms which is usually made of wood, mud, or grass. 2 a small shed or shelter. N COUNT

hyacinth /haɪəsɪnθ/, **hyacinths.** A **hyacinth** is a plant with a lot of small, sweet-smelling flowers growing closely around a single stem. N COUNT

hybrid /haɪbrɪd/, **hybrids.** 1 A **hybrid** is an animal or plant that has been bred from two different types of animal or plant. ▸ used as an adjective. EG *...hybrid roses.* N COUNT Technical ▸ ADJ CLASSIF
2 Anything that is a mixture of two different things can be called a **hybrid.** EG *...a hybrid of business and art.* ▸ used as an adjective. EG *...hybrid systems of heat storage.* N COUNT ▸ ADJ CLASSIF

hydro-electric /haɪdrəʊ ɪˈlektrɪk/. **Hydro-electric** power is electrical power obtained from the energy of running water. *...a hydro-electric project.* ADJ CLASSIF : ATTRIB

hydrogen /haɪdrədʒəⁿn/ is the lightest gas and the simplest chemical element in nature. Hydrogen and oxygen make water. N UNCOUNT

hygiene /haɪdʒiːn/ is the practice of keeping yourself and your surroundings clean, especially in order to prevent illness or the spread of diseases. EG *...personal hygiene.* N UNCOUNT

hygienic /haɪdʒiːnɪk/. Something that is **hygienic** is clean and unlikely to cause illness. EG *It's more hygienic to use disposable paper tissues.* ADJ QUALIT

hymn /hɪm/, **hymns.** A **hymn** is a song that Christians sing in order to praise God. N COUNT

hyper- is used to form adjectives that describe someone as having too much of a particular qual- PREFIX

ity. For example, someone who is hyper-cautious is too cautious. EG *I find that a bit hypercritical... Emily is fastidious and hypersensitive.*

hypermarket /haɪpəmɑːkɪt/, **hypermarkets.** A **hypermarket** is a very large supermarket. N COUNT

hyphen /haɪfəⁿn/, **hyphens.** A **hyphen** is a sign used to join words together to make compounds. The word 'left-handed' has a hyphen in the middle of it. Hyphens can also be used to indicate that the first part of a word is at the end of one line and the second part is at the beginning of the next line. N COUNT

hypnosis /hɪpnəʊsɪs/. 1 **Hypnosis** is the practice or skill of hypnotizing people. N UNCOUNT
2 If you are **under hypnosis**, you have been hypnotized. EG *Is it true that a person could be made to commit a crime under hypnosis?* PHRASE

hypnotic /hɪpnɒtɪk/. Something that is **hypnotic** makes you feel as if you are hypnotized. EG *The rhythmic clapping was having a hypnotic effect on Ginny.* ADJ QUALIT

hypnotism /hɪpnətɪzəⁿm/ is the same as hypnosis. ◊ **hypnotist, hypnotists.** EG *Some hypnotists can hypnotize people who are not prepared for it.* N UNCOUNT ◊ N COUNT

hypnotize /hɪpnətaɪz/, **hypnotizes, hypnotizing, hypnotized;** also spelled **hypnotise.**
1 If someone **hypnotizes** you, they put you into a state in which you seem to be asleep but in which you can see or hear certain things and respond to some things that are said to you. EG *I was able to hypnotize him into doing things against his own will.* V+O
2 If you **are hypnotized** by something, you are so fascinated by it that you cannot think of anything else. EG *The child was hypnotized by the machine.* V+O : USU PASS

hypochondriac /haɪpəkɒndrɪæk/, **hypochondriacs.** A **hypochondriac** is someone who continually worries about their health, often when there is nothing wrong with them. EG *He was a bit of a hypochondriac.* N COUNT

hypocrisy /hɪpɒkrəsiⁱ/ is behaviour in which someone pretends to have beliefs, principles, or feelings that they do not really have; used showing disapproval. EG *...social injustice and official hypocrisy... Many people have dismissed his criticism as hypocrisy.* N UNCOUNT

hypocrite /hɪpəkrɪt/, **hypocrites.** If you call someone a **hypocrite**, you mean that they are pretending to have beliefs, principles, or feelings that they do not really have; used showing disapproval. EG *They were nothing but a lot of hypocrites.* N COUNT

hypocritical /hɪpəkrɪtɪkəⁿl/. If someone is being **hypocritical**, they are pretending to have beliefs, principles, or feelings that they do not really have; used showing disapproval. EG *They send you their love. It would be hypocritical of me to do the same.* ADJ QUALIT

hypodermic /haɪpədɜːmɪk/. A **hypodermic** needle or syringe is a medical instrument with a hollow needle, which is used to inject drugs into a person's body. See picture at NEEDLES. ADJ CLASSIF

hypothesis /haɪpɒθɪsɪs/, **hypotheses** /haɪpɒθɪsiːz/. A **hypothesis** is an idea which is suggested as a possible explanation for something, but which has not yet been proved to be correct. EG *People have proposed all kinds of hypotheses about what these things are.* N COUNT Formal

hypothetical /haɪpəθetɪkəⁿl/. Something that is **hypothetical** is based on possible situations rather than actual ones. EG *Let me put a hypothetical question to you.* ADJ CLASSIF Formal

hysteria /hɪstɪəriːə/. 1 **Hysteria** among a group of people is a state of uncontrolled excitement, anger, or panic. EG *...a growing climate of hysteria and racialism... ...this current hysteria about shortage of petrol.* N UNCOUNT
2 A person who is suffering from **hysteria** is in a state of violent and disturbed emotion as a result of shock. EG *...her thin shoulders shaking convulsively in hysteria.* N UNCOUNT Medical

hysterical /hɪstɛrɪkə⁰l/. 1 Someone who is **hys-** ADJ QUALIT
terical is 1.1 in a state of uncontrolled excitement,
anger, or panic. EG ...*a mob of hysterical vigilan-*
tes... ...*Farlow's hysterical letter.* 1.2 in a state of ADJ CLASSIF
violent and disturbed emotion as a result of shock.
EG ...*stress leading to irrational and hysterical be-*
haviour. ◊ **hysterically.** EG *A man was screaming* ◊ ADV
hysterically.
2 **Hysterical** laughter is loud and uncontrolled. ADJ CLASSIF
◊ **hysterically.** EG *We laughed hysterically at* ◊ ADV
their startled expressions.

3 If you describe something as **hysterical**, you ADJ QUALIT
mean that it is extremely funny. ◊ **hysterically.** ◊ ADV+ADJ
EG ...*jokes which people find hysterically funny.* Informal
hysterics /hɪstɛrɪks/. If someone is in **hysterics** N PLURAL
or having **hysterics**, 1 they are in a state of
uncontrolled excitement, anger, or panic. EG *If she*
didn't get home early, there would probably be
hysterics from her mother. 2 they are laughing Informal
loudly in an uncontrolled way. EG *The audience was*
in hysterics.

I i

I, i /aɪ/, **I's, i's.** I is the ninth letter of the English N COUNT
alphabet.
I /aɪ/ is used as the subject of a verb. A speaker or PRON : SING
writer uses **I** to refer to himself or herself. EG *I like*
your dress... He and I were at school together.
-ibility, -ibilities. -ibility is added in place of SUFFIX
'-ible' at the end of adjectives to form nouns. These
nouns are often not defined in this dictionary, but
are treated with the related adjectives. EG ...*the*
need to provide flexibility... ...*the impossibility of*
any change.
ice /aɪs/, **ices, icing, iced.** 1 Ice is 1.1 water that N UNCOUNT
has frozen and become solid. 1.2 pieces of ice that
you use to keep food or drink cool. EG ...*two tall*
glasses of pineapple juice, soda and ice.
2 If you **ice** cakes, you cover them with icing. V+O
3 An **ice** is an ice cream. EG *He bought ices and* N COUNT
lollipops for the children.
4 If you do something to **break the ice**, you make PHRASE
people feel relaxed and comfortable, for example
at the beginning of a party. EG *A cigarette was often*
the means of breaking the ice.
5 See also **iced, icing.**
ice over or **ice up.** If something **ices over** or PHRASAL VB :
ices up, it becomes covered with a layer of ice. EG V+ADV
The road becomes treacherous when it is iced
over.
iceberg /aɪsbɜːg/, **icebergs.** An **iceberg** is a N COUNT
large, tall mass of ice floating in the sea. ● **tip of**
the iceberg: see **tip.**
ice-box, ice-boxes. An **ice-box** is a large metal N COUNT
container in which you store food to keep it fresh. American
Ice-boxes are kept cool by electricity.
ice-cold. Something that is **ice-cold** is very cold ADJ CLASSIF
indeed. EG ...*ice-cold beer.*
ice cream, ice creams. 1 Ice cream is a very N UNCOUNT
cold, sweet-tasting food. EG *For dessert there was*
vanilla ice cream.
2 An **ice cream** is a portion of ice cream, usually N COUNT
wrapped in paper or in a container. EG *They spent*
all their pocket money on sweets and ice-creams.
ice cube, ice cubes. An **ice cube** is a small N COUNT
square block of ice that you put into a drink to
make it cold.
iced /aɪst/. 1 An **iced** drink has been made very ADJ CLASSIF :
cold. EG ...*an iced beer.* ATTRIB
2 An **iced** cake is covered with icing. ADJ CLASSIF
ice hockey is a game played on ice by two teams. N UNCOUNT
Each team tries to score goals by using long sticks
to hit a small, flat object called the puck into a
goal.
ice lolly, ice lollies. An **ice lolly** is a piece of N COUNT
flavoured ice or ice cream on a stick.
ice-skate, ice-skates, ice-skating, ice-skated. 1 N COUNT
Ice-skates are shoes with a metal bar attached to
them that you wear when you skate on ice.
2 If you **ice-skate**, you move about on ice wearing V

ice-skates. ◊ **ice-skating.** EG *I like to watch soccer* ◊ N UNCOUNT
and ice-skating.
icicle /aɪsɪkə⁰l/, **icicles.** An **icicle** is a long point- N COUNT
ed piece of ice that hangs down from a surface in
cold weather. EG *Huge gleaming icicles hung half-*
way down her windows.
icing /aɪsɪŋ/. 1 Icing is a sweet substance made N UNCOUNT
from powdered sugar that is used to cover cakes as
a decoration. EG ...*cake covered in chocolate icing.*
2 If you describe something as **the icing on the** PHRASE
cake, you mean that it is an extra unnecessary
detail that has been added to something. EG *All*
further changes are icing on the cake.
icon /aɪkɒn/, **icons**; also spelled **ikon.** An **icon** is a N COUNT
picture of Christ or of a saint painted on a wooden
panel. Icons are regarded as holy by many Orthodox Christians. EG ...*an icon of the face of Christ.*
icy /aɪsiˈ/. 1 Icy air or water is extremely cold. EG ADJ QUALIT
As I opened the door a gust of icy air struck me...
...*an icy shower.*
2 An **icy** road has ice on it. EG *We made our way* ADJ QUALIT
along the icy, muddy lanes.
3 If someone's manner or way of speaking is **icy**, ADJ QUALIT
they indicate their dislike or anger in a quiet,
controlled way. EG *Bowman spoke with an icy calm.*
◊ **icily.** EG *'That is quite out of the question,' said* ◊ ADV
Thomas icily.
I'd /aɪd/ is 1 the usual spoken form of 'I had',
especially when 'had' is an auxiliary verb. EG *I'd*
just had a letter from her. 2 the usual spoken form
of 'I would'. EG *I'd like to make my views clear.*
idea /aɪdɪə/, **ideas.** 1 An **idea** is 1.1 a plan, N COUNT
suggestion, or possible course of action. EG *That's a*
good idea... I suddenly had the idea of cutting a
hole in the door... It's a good idea to get some
instruction... I don't like the idea of going to ask for
money. 1.2 an opinion or belief about what something is like or should be like. EG *They had many*
ideas on how films should be made... People had
some odd ideas about village children... ...*the idea*
of happiness... What's your idea of a good party?
2 If you have an **idea** of something or an **idea** that N SING OR
something is true, you know about it to some N UNCOUNT
extent. EG *He has a good idea of how the Civil* +SUPP
Service functions... Have you any idea how much it
would cost?... My friends had an idea that some-
thing was wrong.
3 If you **have no idea** about something, you do not PHRASE
know about it at all. EG *'How much does he earn?' –*
'I've no idea.'... They'd no idea it was there.
4 If someone **gets the idea**, they understand how PHRASE
to do something or they understand what you are Informal
telling them.
5 The **idea** of a particular course of action is its N SING : the+N
aim or purpose. EG *The idea is to try and avoid*
further expense.
ideal /aɪdɪəl/, **ideals.** 1 An **ideal** is a principle, N COUNT
idea, or standard that seems perfect to you so that

you try to achieve it. EG *He believed in parliamentary democracy as an ideal... ...the ideal of marriage as a permanent bond.*

2 Your **ideal** of something is the person or thing N SING that seems to you to be the best possible example of it. EG *He idolizes her as his feminine ideal.*

3 The **ideal** person or thing for a particular ADJ CLASSIF: purpose is the best one for it. EG *He is the ideal* OFT+*for person for the job.*

4 An **ideal** society or world is the best possible ADJ CLASSIF: kind of society or world that you can imagine. EG ATTRIB *That would be the simplest solution in an ideal world.*

idealise /aɪdɪəlaɪz/. See **idealize**.

idealism /aɪdɪəlɪzəm/ is the behaviour and be- N UNCOUNT liefs of someone who has ideals. EG *...the idealism and action of the young people of Britain.*

◊ **idealist** /aɪdɪəlɪst/ **idealists.** EG *He was a ro-* ◊ N COUNT *mantic idealist, almost a dreamer.*

idealistic /aɪdɪəlɪstɪk/. An **idealistic** person has ADJ QUALIT ideals, and bases their behaviour on these ideals. EG *We need to attract idealistic young people into politics... Teachers are often very idealistic.*

idealize /aɪdɪəlaɪz/, **idealizes, idealizing, ideal-** V+O OR V **ized;** also spelled **idealise.** If you **idealize** some-one or something, you think of them or represent them as being perfect or much better than they really are. EG *Romantic love and motherhood are sentimentally idealized.* ◊ **idealized.** EG *The boy* ◊ ADJ CLASSIF *yearned to be like his idealized father.*

ideally /aɪdɪəliⁱ/. **1** If you say that **ideally** some- ADV SEN thing should happen, you mean that you would like it to happen in this way, although it may not be possible. EG *The government should ideally be run by the people... Ideally, we would like to start at the beginning.*

2 If you say that someone or something is **ideally** ADV+PAST suited or **ideally** located, you mean that they are PART in the best possible situation or position. EG *He considered himself ideally suited for the job of Prime Minister.*

identical /aɪdentɪkəl/. Things that are **identical** are **1** exactly the same in every detail. EG *...two* ADJ CLASSIF *women in identical pinafores... Chemically, it is almost identical to limestone... India's internal structure can never be identical with Europe's.* ◊ **identically.** EG *All of them were identically* ◊ ADV *dressed for the occasion.* **2** very similar indeed. EG ADJ CLASSIF *The houses in this colony were all identical.*

identical twin, identical twins. Identical N COUNT: **twins** are twins who are the same sex and look USU PLURAL exactly like each other.

identifiable /aɪdentɪfaɪəbəl/. Something that is **identifiable 1** can be easily recognized because it ADJ CLASSIF has a particular quality. EG *...a much more easily identifiable hand signal.* **2** can be named. EG *They* ADJ QUALIT *were convinced that certain identifiable groups were threatening them.*

identification /aɪdentɪfɪkeɪʃən/. **1** The **identifi-** N UNCOUNT **cation** of people and things is the process of recognizing or choosing them because they have a particular quality. EG *...the identification of require-ments and resources.*

2 Your **identification** of a particular person or N UNCOUNT thing is your ability to name them because you know them. EG *...the identification, examination, and disposal of a dead body.*

3 If someone asks you for **identification**, they are N UNCOUNT asking you for something such as a driving licence, passport, or identity card, which proves who you are. EG *Could I ask you to show me some identifica-tion?*

4 Identification with someone or something is a N UNCOUNT feeling of sympathy and support for them. EG *These* +*with conditions gave us a strong identification with our people and our history.*

identify /aɪdentɪfaɪ/, **identifies, identifying, identified. 1** If you can **identify** someone or V+O something, you can recognize them or name them.

EG *An individual bird can identify the call of its own species... The guard had been identified as Victor Kowalski.*

2 Something that **identifies** you makes you easy to V+O recognize, because it makes you different in some way. EG *Wear on your third finger an iron ring, which will identify you.*

3 If you **identify** facts, you notice them and realize V+O that they are important. EG *The report does clearly identify the fact that there is racial inequality.*

4 If you **identify** with someone or something, you V+O: feel that you understand them. EG *He couldn't* OFT+*with identify with other people's troubles.*

5 If you **are identified** with someone or some- V+O: USU thing, you are very closely involved with them. EG PASS+*with During the 1950's he was identified with certain radical causes.*

6 If you **identify** one thing with another, you V+O+*with consider them to be the same thing. EG *If I pro-* Formal *tested he would at once identify me with his stern father.*

identity /aɪdentɪtiⁱ/, **identities.** Your **identity** is **1** who you are. EG *I had guessed the identity of her* N COUNT+POSS *lover... Glenn whipped off the mask to reveal his identity.* **2** all the qualities, beliefs, and ideas which N COUNT OR make you feel that you belong to a particular N UNCOUNT group. EG *...our identity as black people.... ...a region with its own cultural identity.*

identity card, identity cards. Your **identity** N COUNT **card** is a card that has your name, photograph, age, address, and other information on it. In some countries you have to carry an identity card in order to prove who you are.

ideological /aɪdɪəlɒdʒɪkəl/. Something that is ADJ CLASSIF **ideological** relates to principles or beliefs. EG *...the ideological aspects of the dispute... ...ideological assertions of national solidarity.* ◊ **ideologically.** ◊ ADV EG *I was ideologically attracted to Liberalism.*

ideology /aɪdɪˈɒlədʒiⁱ/, **ideologies.** An **ideology** N COUNT is a set of beliefs, especially the political beliefs on +SUPP OR which people, parties, or countries base their ac- N UNCOUNT tions. EG *...the capitalist ideology of the West.*

idiocy /ɪdɪəsiⁱ/, **idiocies.** The **idiocy** of something N UNCOUNT is the total stupidity of it. EG *...the idiocy of the* OR N COUNT *plan... ...her contempt for parliamentary idiocy.* Formal

idiom /ɪdɪəm/, **idioms. 1** The **idiom** of something N COUNT+SUPP such as speech, writing, or music is its particular Formal style. EG *The Beatles changed for ever the idiom of popular music... ...a church in the idiom of the thirteenth century.*

2 An **idiom** is a group of words which have a N COUNT different meaning when used together from the one they would have if you took the meaning of each word individually. EG *The idiom 'ladies' man' is untranslatable into Japanese.*

idiomatic /ɪdɪəˈmætɪk/. Language that is **idio-** ADJ QUALIT **matic** uses words in a way that sounds natural to native speakers of the language. EG *Her English was fluent and idiomatic.*

idiosyncrasy /ɪdɪəˈsɪŋkrəsiⁱ/, **idiosyncrasies.** N COUNT Someone's **idiosyncrasies** are their own rather unusual habits or likes and dislikes. EG *She adjusted magnificently to her husband's many idiosyncra-sies.*

idiosyncratic /ɪdɪəˈsɪŋkrætɪk/. If someone's be- ADJ QUALIT haviour or likes and dislikes are **idiosyncratic,** they are personal to them, and are often rather unusual. EG *...Michelangelo's highly idiosyncratic style of painting.*

idiot /ɪdɪət/, **idiots.** If you call someone an **idiot,** N COUNT you mean that you think they have done something very stupid. EG *That idiot Antonio has gone and locked our door.*

idiotic /ɪdɪˈɒtɪk/. If you describe someone or ADJ QUALIT something as **idiotic,** you mean that they are extremely stupid. EG *It was an idiotic question to ask... It was just one of his idiotic jokes.*

idle /aɪdəl/. **1** Someone who is **idle 1.1** is not doing ADJ QUALIT anything, especially when they should be doing something. EG *A healthy child cannot be idle; he has to be doing something all day long.* ◊ **idly.** EG ◊ ADV *...those who sit idly by while you slave over a hot stove.* ◊ **idleness.** EG *No one can afford to pay* ◊ N UNCOUNT *troops to sit about in idleness.* **1.2** does not have a ADJ PRED job. EG *There are 13,000 idle in a workforce of 170,000.*

2 Machines or factories that are **idle** are not ADJ PRED working or being used. EG *The machinery could not be converted, and so stood idle.*

3 If you say that it is **idle** to do something, you ADJ CLASSIF mean that it is not worth doing it, because no useful Formal result would be achieved. EG *It would be idle to look for a solution at this stage.*

4 You use **idle** to describe **4.1** something that you ADJ CLASSIF: do for no particular reason, often simply because ATTRIB you have nothing better to do. EG *Sudhir and Judy carried on long, idle conversations.* ◊ **idly.** EG *She* ◊ ADV *glanced idly down the list of contents.* **4.2** some- ADJ CLASSIF: thing that someone has said or done that you do not ATTRIB treat seriously. EG *This is no idle bluff.*

idle away. If you **idle away** a period of time, you PHRASAL VB: spend it doing very little. EG *...three old men, idling* V+O+ADV *away the summer afternoon under the trees.*

idler /ˈaɪdlə/, **idlers.** If you call someone an **idler**, N COUNT you mean that they are lazy and should be work- ing. EG *...a state full of idlers.*

idol /ˈaɪdəʊl/, **idols. 1** An **idol** is someone such as a N COUNT film star or pop star, who is greatly admired or loved by the public. EG *...young pop idols... Django Reinhardt is evidently Chris Goddard's idol.*

2 An **idol** is also a statue that is worshipped by N COUNT people who believe that it is a god. EG *They set up stone pillars for idol worship.*

idolatry /aɪˈdɒlətri/. Someone who practises N UNCOUNT **idolatry** worships idols. Formal

idolize /ˈaɪdəlaɪz/, **idolizes, idolizing, idolized;** V+O also spelled **idolise.** If you **idolize** someone such as a film star or pop star, you admire them or love them very much. EG *They idolize Bob Dylan.*

idyll /ˈɪdɪl/, **idylls.** An **idyll** is a situation which is N COUNT idyllic. EG *...the myth of an unchanging idyll of rural England.*

idyllic /ɪˈdɪlɪk/. Something that is **idyllic** is ex- ADJ QUALIT tremely pleasant and peaceful without any difficul- ties. EG *...an idyllic place to raise a young child... ...an idyllic country holiday.*

i.e. /ˌaɪ ˈiː/ is used to introduce a word or sentence which gives more information about the meaning of what you have just said. EG *To keep a dog costs twice as much, i.e. £110 a year.*

if /ɪf/. **1** You use **if** to mention an event or situation CONJ that might happen, might be happening, or might have happened. EG *If all goes well, Voyager 2 will head on to Uranus... If unemployment remains at present levels for a few more years, democracy could become unworkable... If any questions occur to you, then don't hesitate to write... If I could afford it I would buy a boat.*

2 You use **if** in indirect questions. EG *I asked her if I* CONJ *could help her... I wonder if you'd give the children a bath?*

3 You can use **if** in sentences in which you mention CONJ a possible exception to a general statement you have already made. EG *It was an excellent concert. If I had any disappointment at all it was the end.*

4 You can use **if** to introduce a comment or make CONJ a request. EG *If you don't mind my saying so, I think you are partly responsible... If you can sign that for me. Thank you.*

5 You use **if not 5.1** to suggest that an amount, CONJ degree, or time might be even bigger, better, or sooner than the one you have mentioned. EG *They have hundreds of thousands if not millions of pounds of investment... I'd like to see you tonight, if not sooner.* **5.2** to mention a state of affairs that does not exist, when saying that a less extreme one does. EG *Her voice was, if not perfect, at least nearly so.*

6 You say **'if I were you'** to someone when you ADV SEN are giving them advice. EG *If I were you I'd take the money.*

7 You use **'if anything'** after a negative statement ADV SEN to say that something different is true. EG *It certain- ly wasn't an improvement. We were, if anything, worse off than before.*

8 You use **if ever** to emphasize the description of a CONJ person or thing that you are giving. EG *She was a hopeless figure if ever I saw one.*

9 You use **if only 9.1** to introduce one reason for CONJ doing something, when you realize it may not be a very good one. EG *I'll have a glass myself, if only to stop you from drinking it all.* **9.2** to express a wish or desire, especially one that cannot be fulfilled. EG *If only she could have lived a little longer.*

10 You use **as if 10.1** when describing the way CONJ that something is done. EG *She folded her arms as if she were cold.* **10.2** to emphasize that something is not the case, for example that something is not important. EG *He keeps worrying about what wine to buy. As if it mattered!*

igloo /ˈɪgluː/, **igloos.** An **igloo** is a dome-shaped N COUNT house made out of blocks of snow.

ignite /ɪgˈnaɪt/, **ignites, igniting, ignited.** When V-ERG you **ignite** something or when it **ignites**, it starts burning or it explodes. EG *The device was supposed to ignite the fireworks.*

ignition /ɪgˈnɪʃən/ **ignitions. 1** The **ignition** in a N COUNT: car is the part of the engine where the fuel is USU SING ignited, and which starts the engine when you start the car; also used of the keyhole in the dashboard in which you put the key to start it. See picture at CAR. EG *Have you switched the ignition on?*

2 Ignition is the process by which a car engine is N UNCOUNT started. EG *...electronic ignition.*

ignoble /ɪgˈnəʊbəl/. An **ignoble** person behaves ADJ QUALIT in a way that is considered dishonourable. EG Formal *There's something cowardly and ignoble about such an attitude.*

ignominious /ˌɪgnəˈmɪnɪəs/. **Ignominious** behav- ADJ QUALIT iour is considered shameful or morally unaccep- Formal table. EG *The marriage was considered especially ignominious since she was of royal descent.* ◊ **ignominiously.** EG *They were ignominiously* ◊ ADV *defeated in the general election.*

ignorant /ˈɪgnərənt/. Someone who is **ignorant** of ADJ QUALIT: something does not know about it. EG *The masses* OFT+*of* *were largely ignorant of the options open to them... ...his idea that ordinary people are ignorant.* ◊ **ignorance** /ˈɪgnərəns/. EG *Individuals suffer* ◊ N UNCOUNT: *through ignorance of their rights.* OFT+*of*

ignore /ɪgˈnɔː/, **ignores, ignoring, ignored. 1** If V+O you **ignore** someone or something that you have seen, heard, or experienced, you act as if they are not there, or as if the event has not happened. EG *Ralph ignored Jack's question... The President can- not rudely ignore any head of state who chooses to come here... I ignored him and looked at Judith.*

2 If you **ignore** something that you have been V+O advised or told to do, you deliberately do not do it. EG *The Government ignored his advice.*

3 Something that **ignores** an important aspect of a V+O situation fails to take it into account. EG *These proposals ignore the court's existing power.*

ikon /ˈaɪkɒn/. See **icon.**

ill /ɪl/, **ills. Worse** /wɜːs/ and **worst** /wɜːst/ are often used as the comparative and superlative of **ill** when it is an adjective or adverb.

1 Someone who is **ill** is suffering from a disease or ADJ QUALIT: health problem which makes them unable to work USU PRED or to live normally. EG *I feel ill... Don't refreeze food. It could make you ill... She is ill with cancer.*

● If you **fall ill** or **are taken ill**, you become ill ● PHRASE

Can you read something that is illegible?

suddenly. EG *She was taken ill on holiday and they had to find a doctor.*

2 Difficulties or problems can be referred to as **ills.** EG *...the necessary ills of old age... No ill had yet come to Sarah's child.*   N UNCOUNT OR N PLURAL Literary

3 If something **bodes ill** or **augurs ill** for you, it gives you a reason to fear that something harmful might happen. EG *She had a sullen expression which might bode ill.*   PHRASE Literary

4 You can use **ill** to describe something that is done badly. EG *The programme was ill researched.*   ADV Literary

5 If you **speak ill of** someone, you criticize them. EG *Don't expect me to speak ill of my employer.*   PHRASE

6 You can use **ill** to describe harmful or unpleasant things. EG *Did you get any ill effects when you had your blood transfusion?... ...protection against ill fortune and disaster.*   ADJ CLASSIF : ATTRIB

I'll /aɪl/ is the usual spoken form of 'I will' or 'I shall'. EG *I'll ring you tomorrow morning.*

ill- is added to words, especially adjectives and past participles, to add the meaning 'badly' or 'inadequately'. For example, 'ill-written' means badly written, and 'ill-judged' means judged with insufficient care or judgement.

ill-advised. An action that is **ill-advised** is not sensible or wise. EG *It is ill-advised to attempt competition.*   ADJ QUALIT

ill at ease. Someone who is **ill at ease** feels uncomfortable or embarrassed. EG *He was ill at ease with people whom he didn't understand.*   ADJ PRED

illegal /ɪˈliːgəl/. **1** If an activity or possession is **illegal**, the law says that you are not allowed to do it or have it. EG *It is illegal in many countries for women to work on night shifts... Marijuana is illegal in the United States.* ◊ **illegally.** EG *...illegally parked cars.*   ADJ CLASSIF ◊ ADV

2 An **illegal** organization is one which a government says must not exist. EG *...the Haganah, the illegal Jewish defence force.*   ADJ CLASSIF

3 An **illegal** action or system is one which breaks an international law or agreement. EG *...the illegal colonial regime.* ◊ **illegally.** EG *Their country had been illegally occupied for many years.*   ADJ CLASSIF ◊ ADV

4 An **illegal** immigrant is a person who has entered a country without an official permit.   ADJ CLASSIF : ATTRIB

illegible /ɪˈledʒɪbəl/. Writing that is **illegible** is so unclear that you cannot read it. EG *...a suitcase with illegible labels.*   ADJ QUALIT

illegitimate /ˌɪlɪˈdʒɪtɪmət/. **1** A person who is **illegitimate** was born of parents who were not legally married to each other. EG *...an illegitimate child.* ◊ **illegitimacy** /ˌɪlɪˈdʒɪtɪməsɪ/. EG *Victoria was not told of her illegitimacy until she was 25.*   ADJ CLASSIF ◊ N UNCOUNT

2 An **illegitimate** activity is not allowed or approved of by law or social customs. EG *All parties regarded the treaty as illegitimate and not binding.*   ADJ CLASSIF

ill-equipped. Someone who is **ill-equipped** to do something does not have the ability, the qualities, or the equipment necessary to do it. EG *The police were plainly ill-equipped to deal with the riot.*   ADJ QUALIT

ill-fated. If you describe something as **ill-fated**, you mean that it has a tragic or unlucky outcome. EG *Alice recounted the story of her ill-fated boating expedition.*   ADJ CLASSIF

ill-health. If you are in a state of **ill-health**, you have an illness. EG *Throughout his career he had suffered from ill-health.*   N UNCOUNT

illicit /ɪˈlɪsɪt/. An **illicit** activity or substance is not allowed or not approved of by the laws and social customs of a country. EG *They were prosecuted for illicit liquor selling.*   ADJ CLASSIF : ATTRIB

illiterate /ɪˈlɪtərət/, **illiterates.** Someone who is **illiterate** does not know how to read or write. EG *40 per cent of the country is reckoned to be illiterate.*   ADJ CLASSIF
▸ used as a noun. EG *...the teaching of adult illiterates.* ◊ **illiteracy** /ɪˈlɪtərəsɪ/. EG *...adult illiteracy.*   ▸ N COUNT ◊ N UNCOUNT

illness /ˈɪlnɪs/, **illnesses.** **1 Illness** is the experience of being ill for a period of time. EG *During his last illness we only saw him twice.*   N UNCOUNT OR N COUNT

2 An **illness** is a particular disease that people can suffer from, such as a cold, measles, or pneumonia. EG *She died of a mysterious illness.*   N COUNT

illogical /ɪˈlɒdʒɪkəl/. If a feeling or action is **illogical**, it is not reasonable or sensible, because you are not considering properly all the aspects of a situation. EG *...the illogical reactions of the male sex... It is clearly illogical to maintain such a proposition.* ◊ **illogically.** EG *I felt illogically that my own years there counted for nothing.*   ADJ QUALIT ◊ ADV

ill-treat, ill-treats, ill-treating, ill-treated. If someone **ill-treats** you, they treat you cruelly. EG *The man had been ill-treated in prison.*   V+O

illuminate /ɪˈluːmɪneɪt/, **illuminates, illuminating, illuminated.** **1** If you **illuminate** something, you shine light on it. EG *Lamps were arranged to illuminate his work.* ◊ **illuminated.** EG *...illuminated advertising.*   V+O ◊ ADJ CLASSIF

2 If you **illuminate** something that is difficult to understand, you make it easier to understand by explaining it or giving examples. EG *Their doctrine illuminates much that might seem obscure in the Muslim teaching.* ◊ **illuminating.** EG *...Basil Spence, in his illuminating book on the subject.*   V+O ◊ ADJ QUALIT

illumination /ɪˌluːmɪˈneɪʃən/, **illuminations.** **1 Illumination** is the lighting that a place has. EG *The dusty bulb gave barely adequate illumination.*   N UNCOUNT

2 Illuminations are coloured lights which are put up in towns, especially at Christmas, as a decoration.   N PLURAL

illusion /ɪˈluːʒən/, **illusions.** An **illusion** is **1** an idea or belief which you think is true but which is in fact false. EG *We have an illusion of freedom.* **2** something that looks like one thing but is really another thing or is not there at all. EG *The garden through the windows was merely a clever optical illusion.* **3** a magic trick in which the audience is fooled by the skill of the magician's actions.   N COUNT OR N UNCOUNT / N COUNT / N COUNT

illusory /ɪˈluːzərɪ/. Something that is **illusory** seems to be true or possible, but is false or impossible in reality. EG *...illusory hopes that he would soon find a new job.*   ADJ CLASSIF Formal

illustrate /ˈɪləstreɪt/, **illustrates, illustrating, illustrated.** **1** If you **illustrate** a point that you are making, you make it clear by using examples, stories, or diagrams. EG *The Muslims tell a story to illustrate the fact that power changes people... Nothing illustrates his selfishness more clearly than his behaviour to his wife.*   V+O

2 If you **illustrate** a book, you put pictures or diagrams into it. ◊ **illustrated.** EG *...illustrated books of fairy tales.*   V+O ◊ ADJ CLASSIF

illustration /ˌɪləˈstreɪʃən/, **illustrations.** **1** An **illustration** of a point is an example or a story which is used to make the point clear. EG *I've included a few specific examples as illustrations of the difficulty of our work.*   N COUNT : OFT+of

2 An **illustration** in a book is a picture or diagram. EG *...a cookery book with marvellous colour illustrations.*   N COUNT

3 Illustration is the activity or process of illustrating. EG *...evening classes in drawing and illustration.*   N UNCOUNT

illustrative /ˈɪləstrətɪv/. An **illustrative** picture or action is an example or explanation of something. EG *These incidents are illustrative of the range of political actions being undertaken.*   ADJ CLASSIF Formal

illustrator /ˈɪləstreɪtə/, **illustrators.** An **illustrator** is an artist who draws pictures and diagrams for books and magazines. EG *...an illustrator of children's books.*   N COUNT

illustrious /ɪˈlʌstrɪəs/. An **illustrious** person is extremely well known and famous. EG *He was determined not to be outdone by his more illustrious partner... ...a long and illustrious career as a radio producer.*   ADJ QUALIT : ATTRIB

ill-will is a feeling of hostility towards someone. EG *He assured me he felt no ill-will toward me.*   N UNCOUNT

I'm /aɪm/ is the usual spoken form of 'I am'. EG *I'm not blaming you... I'm afraid I can't come.*

image /ˈɪmɪdʒ/, **images.** 1 If you have an **image** N COUNT of someone or something, you have a picture or USU+SUPP idea of them in your mind. EG *To most people, the term 'industrial revolution' conjures up images of smoky steel mills or clanking machines... They feel under pressure to conform to our image of them.*

2 The **image** of a person or organization is the way N COUNT: that they appear to other people. EG *His attempts to* USU+POSS *improve the Post Office's image were criticised as 'gimmicks'.*

3 An **image** is also **3.1** a picture or theme in a N COUNT work of art such as a painting or a book. EG *He was one of the few painters who produced convincing images of life in contemporary America.* **3.2** a picture that you see of someone or something. EG *...a musical sound track accompanying the visual image... He began to dress, never taking his eyes off his image in the mirror.*

imagery /ˈɪmɪdʒrɪ/ is 1 the mental pictures that N UNCOUNT are created in your mind by poetic language. EG *He argued that Shakespeare's plays were patterns of imagery.* 2 ideas or themes that are represented in visual art such as pictures and statues.

imaginable /ɪˈmædʒɪnəbəl/. You use **imagi-** ADJ CLASSIF: **nable** when referring to the most extreme exam- ATTRIB, OR ple of a particular thing that you can think of. EG ADJ AFTER N *...the narrowest imaginable range of interests... ...every bit of information imaginable.*

imaginary /ɪˈmædʒɪnəⁿrɪ/. Something that is **im-** ADJ CLASSIF **aginary** exists only in your mind and not in real life. EG *Many children develop fears of imaginary dangers... He was playing an imaginary trumpet.*

imagination /ɪˌmædʒɪˈneɪʃəⁿn/, **imaginations.** Your **imagination** is 1 the ability that you have to N COUNT OR form ideas of new or exciting things. EG *He has a* N UNCOUNT *marvellous imagination... These plans reveal a complete failure of imagination.* 2 the part of your N COUNT: mind which you use to form pictures or ideas of USU+POSS things that do not necessarily exist in real life. EG *They are creations of our imagination.* 3 some- N UNCOUNT thing that you think of that does not exist in real +POSS life or that never happened. EG *There's nothing there – it's just your imagination.*

imaginative /ɪˈmædʒɪnətɪv/. Someone who is **im-** ADJ QUALIT **aginative** is easily able to form ideas of new or exciting things in their mind. EG *...an imaginative writer... ...imaginative and original theories.*
◊ **imaginatively.** EG *...an imaginatively designed* ◊ ADV *bathroom.*

imagine /ɪˈmædʒɪn/, **imagines, imagining, im-** **agined.** 1 If you **imagine** something, **1.1** you think V+O, about it and your mind forms a picture or idea of it. V+REPORT, EG *Not one of us could imagine what he'd meant...* OR V+-ING *Try to imagine you're sitting on a cloud... Can you imagine standing up there and giving a speech?* **1.2** V+O OR you think that you have seen or heard something, V+REPORT although actually you haven't. EG *'I saw a thing on the mountain.' – 'You only imagined it.'... He imag- ined he saw things.*

2 If you **imagine** that something is true, you think V+REPORT: that it is true. EG *I should imagine he wants you to* ONLY that, *hold his hand... He was much more generous than* NO CONT *people imagined.*

imbalance /ɪmˈbæləns/, **imbalances.** If there is N COUNT OR an **imbalance** in a situation, things are not evenly N UNCOUNT or fairly arranged. EG *...the imbalance between the rich and poor countries.*

imbecile /ˈɪmbɪsiːl, -saɪl/, **imbeciles.** If you call N COUNT someone an **imbecile**, you are saying that you think that they are stupid; an offensive word. EG *For two years that imbecile spent his money like water.*

imbibe /ɪmˈbaɪb/, **imbibes, imbibing, imbibed.** 1 V+O OR V If you **imbibe** alcohol, you drink it. EG *He had* Formal *imbibed some much stronger beers in his young days in Manchester.*

2 If you **imbibe** ideas or arguments, you listen to V+O them and believe that they are right or true. EG *You* Formal *have been imbibing too many of their doctrines.*

imbue /ɪmˈbjuː/, **imbues, imbuing, imbued.** If V+O you **imbue** something or someone with a particu- lar quality, you give them that quality so that they become filled with it. EG *...Mondrian's desire to imbue his art with mystical properties.* ◊ **imbued.** ◊ ADJ PRED EG *...a unified society deeply imbued with Marxist* +with *convictions.*

imitate /ˈɪmɪteɪt/, **imitates, imitating, imitated.**
1 If you **imitate** a person, group, or society, you V+O behave in the same way as they do. EG *Other societies have begun to imitate the wastefulness of the West... The University of London imitated the German tradition of scholarship.*

2 If you **imitate** a person or animal, you copy the V+O way they speak or behave, often in order to be amusing. EG *'Sidney, you'll kill him,' he said, trying to imitate the girl's voice.*

imitation /ɪmɪˈteɪʃəⁿn/, **imitations.** 1 An imita- N COUNT tion is **1.1** something which is a copy of something else. EG *Computers so far are just bad imitations of our brains.* **1.2** something that you do in order to copy the way someone else speaks or behaves. EG *'Come here, my dear,' she said, giving a reasonable imitation of Isabel Travers.*

2 **Imitation** is behaviour which is modelled on N UNCOUNT someone else's behaviour. EG *Boys can be seen to pat one another on the head in imitation of what their fathers do.*

3 Imitation things are not genuine but are made ADJ CLASSIF: to look as if they are genuine. EG *...a pocket diary* ATTRIB *bound in black imitation leather.*

imitative /ˈɪmɪtətɪv/. Behaviour that is **imitative** ADJ QUALIT copies someone else's behaviour. Formal

imitator /ˈɪmɪteɪtə/, **imitators.** An **imitator** of N COUNT someone is a person who copies them or behaves in the same way as them. EG *...successful designers and their imitators.*

immaculate /ɪˈmækjʊⁿlɪt/. Something that is **im-** **maculate** is 1 absolutely clean or tidy. EG *Her* ADJ CLASSIF *apartment was immaculate.* ◊ **immaculately.** EG ◊ ADV *Sir Oswald was immaculately dressed.* 2 perfect, ADJ CLASSIF with no mistakes at all. EG *Your timing and tech- nique will have to be immaculate.*

immaterial /ɪməˈtɪərɪəl/. Something that is **im-** ADJ CLASSIF **material** is not important or not relevant. EG *The price was immaterial.*

immature /ɪməˈtjʊə, -tʃʊə/. 1 Something that is ADJ CLASSIF **immature** is not yet fully developed. EG *...an imma- ture organism... ...the baby's immature digestive system.*

2 If you describe someone as **immature**, you mean ADJ QUALIT that they are not sensible enough to behave prop- erly. EG *I was too immature to understand.*
◊ **immaturity** /ɪmətjʊərɪˈtiː/. EG *There were com-* ◊ N UNCOUNT *plaints about my immaturity and lack of judge- ment.*

immeasurable /ɪˈmeʒəⁿrəbəl/. An amount or dis- ADJ CLASSIF tance that is **immeasurable** is too large to be measured or counted. EG *The gap between them now seems immeasurable.*

immeasurably /ɪˈmeʒəⁿrəbliː/. You use **immeas-** ADV+ADJ **urably** to emphasize that something has a particu- lar quality to a very great extent. EG *Paul Getty had always been immeasurably rich.*

immediacy /ɪˈmiːdɪəsɪ/. When you talk about the N UNCOUNT **immediacy** of something, you mean that it seems Formal to be happening now or that it makes you feel directly involved with it. EG *It is the immediacy of events which makes television so popular.*

immediate /ɪˈmiːdɪət/. 1 Immediate means **1.1** ADJ CLASSIF: happening without any delay. EG *They called for an* USU ATTRIB *immediate meeting of the Security Council... My immediate reaction was one of relief.* **1.2** actually ADJ CLASSIF: existing now, and needing to be dealt with quickly. ATTRIB EG *...the immediate needs of people in western*

What is the difference between an imaginary diamond and an imitation one?

society... He was occupied with more immediate matters.

2 You use **immediate** to describe someone or something that is very near in time or position to another person or thing. EG Charlie was more honest than his immediate predecessor... To the immediate south we can see the mountains. ADJ CLASSIF: ATTRIB

3 Your **immediate** family are the people who are very closely related to you, such as your parents, children, brothers, and sisters. ADJ CLASSIF: ATTRIB

immediately /ɪˈmiːdɪətlɪ/. **1** If something happens **immediately**, it happens without any delay. EG I have to go to Brighton immediately. It's very urgent... She finished her cigarette, then lit another one immediately. ADV

2 You use **immediately 2.1** when talking about something that can be understood or used without any delay. EG The connection was not immediately apparent. **2.2** when talking about something that is closely and directly involved in a situation. EG The countries most immediately threatened are those to the south. **2.3** when talking about someone or something that is very near in time or position to another person or thing. EG The church is immediately on your right... The sequence of events immediately preceding the tragedy is uncertain. ADV / ADV / ADV+PREP

3 You also use **immediately** when you are saying what happens or is done as soon as something else has happened. EG Immediately I finish the show I get changed and go home. CONJ

immemorial /ɪmɪˈmɔːrɪəl/. **1** If something has been happening **from time immemorial**, it has been happening for longer than anyone can remember. EG Indian villages have governed themselves from time immemorial. PHRASE

2 You use **immemorial** to describe something that is so old that nobody can remember a time when it did not exist. EG ...the immemorial custom of all Western societies. ADJ CLASSIF: ATTRIB

immense /ɪˈmens/. Something that is **immense** is extremely large. EG Squids grow to an immense size... This development has been of immense importance. ADJ QUALIT

immensely /ɪˈmenslɪ/ means to a very great extent or degree. EG The issue is immensely complex... I enjoyed the course immensely. ADV

immensity /ɪˈmensɪtɪ/. The **immensity** of something is the very large size or extent of it. EG ...the immensity of the building. N UNCOUNT +SUPP

immerse /ɪˈmɜːs/, **immerses, immersing, immersed. 1** If you **immerse** yourself in something, you become completely involved in it. EG That year I immersed myself totally in my work. ◊ **immersed.** EG He became immersed in the activities of the union. ◊ **immersion** /ɪˈmɜːʃən/. EG ...their total immersion in European history. V-REFL+in / ◊ ADJ PRED / ◊ N UNCOUNT

2 If you **immerse** something in a liquid, you put it into the liquid so that it is completely covered. EG Ebony hairbrushes shouldn't be immersed in water. ◊ **immersion.** EG Treat sprained ankles by immersion in cold water. V+O: USU+in / ◊ N UNCOUNT

immersion heater, immersion heaters. An **immersion heater** is an electric heater which is used to provide hot water. N COUNT

immigrant /ˈɪmɪgrənt/, **immigrants.** An **immigrant** is a person who has come to live in a country from another country. EG ...a Russian immigrant... ...immigrant communities in London. N COUNT

immigration /ɪmɪˈgreɪʃən/ is **1** the coming of people into a country in order to live and work there. EG ...government controls on immigration. **2** the control section at a port, airport or international border, where officials check the passports of people who wish to come into the country. N UNCOUNT / N UNCOUNT

imminent /ˈɪmɪnənt/. Something that is **imminent** is certain to happen very soon. EG I believed that war was imminent... ...his imminent departure. ◊ **imminence** /ˈɪmɪnəns/. EG They seemed unaware of the imminence of the invasion. ADJ CLASSIF / ◊ N UNCOUNT +of

immobile /ɪˈməʊbaɪl/. Someone or something that is **immobile** is **1** completely still. EG Boylan sat immobile, staring straight ahead. ◊ **immobility** /ɪməʊˈbɪlɪtɪ/. EG She had drugged herself into immobility with sleeping pills. **2** unable to move. EG Sea-snakes have fangs that are short and immobile. ADJ PRED / ◊ N UNCOUNT / ADJ CLASSIF

immobilize /ɪˈməʊbɪlaɪz/, **immobilizes, immobilizing, immobilized;** also spelled **immobilise. 1** If you **immobilize** something, you completely stop it from moving. EG When you ring the alarm it immobilizes the lift. V+O

2 Something that **immobilizes** someone stops them from working efficiently. EG They must cast off those bureaucratic practices that immobilize them. V+O

immodest /ɪˈmɒdɪst/. **1** Behaviour that is **immodest** shocks or embarrasses some people because they think that it is rude. EG Breast feeding in public may seem immodest to some people. ADJ QUALIT

2 Someone who is **immodest** often says that they are very clever or important. EG He said it might be immodest for him to quote the next two lines of the review. ADJ QUALIT

immoral /ɪˈmɒrəl/. If you describe someone or their behaviour as **immoral**, you mean that they are morally wrong. EG ...the cruel and immoral use of animals in medical research... ...an immoral seducer of youth. ◊ **immorality** /ɪmɒˈrælɪtɪ/. EG ...the immorality of apartheid. ADJ QUALIT / ◊ N UNCOUNT

immortal /ɪˈmɔːtəl/. Someone or something that is **immortal 1** is famous and will be remembered for a long time. EG The play contained one immortal line. ◊ **immortality** /ɪmɔːˈtælɪtɪ/. EG You're not going to achieve immortality by writing a book like that. **2** lives for ever and never dies. EG ...old legends of immortal creatures. ADJ CLASSIF / ◊ N UNCOUNT / ADJ CLASSIF

immortalize /ɪˈmɔːtəlaɪz/, **immortalizes, immortalizing, immortalized;** also spelled **immortalise.** If someone or something is **immortalized**, for example in a book or film, they are remembered for a very long time. EG We talked about her gangster parts immortalised on film. V+O: USU PASS+A

immovable /ɪˈmuːvəbəl/. **1** Something that is **immovable** is fixed and cannot be moved. EG ...an immovable pillar. ADJ CLASSIF

2 Feelings or opinions that are **immovable** are firm and will not change. EG ...fossilised ways and immovable conservatism. ADJ CLASSIF

immune /ɪˈmjuːn/. **1** If you are **immune** to a particular disease, you cannot be made ill by it. EG She thought that women might be immune to lung cancer. ◊ **immunity** /ɪˈmjuːnɪtɪ/. EG Babies receive immunity to a variety of infections... ...the immunity of some crops against pests and diseases. ADJ PRED+to / ◊ N UNCOUNT: OFT+to/against

2 If you are **immune** to a situation or to people's behaviour, you are not affected by it. EG He was immune to the flattery of political leaders. ◊ **immunity.** EG This immunity to criticism is built into them. ADJ PRED: OFT+to / ◊ N UNCOUNT: OFT+to

3 Someone or something that is **immune** from a process or situation is able to escape it. EG ...targets that the West had considered immune from air attack. ◊ **immunity, immunities.** EG He had been granted immunity from prosecution. ADJ PRED: OFT+from / ◊ N UNCOUNT OR N COUNT

immunize /ˈɪmjənaɪz/, **immunizes, immunizing, immunized;** also spelled **immunise.** If you **are immunized** against a disease, you are made immune to it, usually by being given an injection. EG They should have their children immunised against diphtheria. ◊ **immunization** /ɪmjənaɪˈzeɪʃən/, **immunizations.** EG Measles can be prevented by immunization. V+O: OFT+against / ◊ N UNCOUNT OR N COUNT

immutable /ɪˈmjuːtəbəl/. Something that is **immutable** will never change. EG ...behaving according to a set of immutable rules. ADJ CLASSIF Formal

impact /ˈɪmpækt/, **impacts. 1** If something has an **impact** on a situation or person, it has a great effect on them. EG ...the impact of computing on N COUNT+SUPP routine office work... British authors make relatively little impact abroad.

2 Impact is **2.1** the action of one object hitting another. EG Many modern bullets produce an explosive effect upon impact. **2.2** the force with which one object hits another. EG Hill 402 seemed to crumble with the impact of enemy artillery fire. N UNCOUNT

impacted /ɪmpæktɪ²d/. An **impacted** tooth is unable to grow through your gum properly. EG ...an impacted wisdom tooth that had to be taken out. ADJ CLASSIF : USU ATTRIB

impair /ɪmpeə/, **impairs, impairing, impaired.** If you **impair** something, you damage or weaken it so that it stops working properly. EG His digestion had been impaired by his recent illness. ◊ **impaired.** EG ...children with impaired hearing. V+O · ◊ ADJ CLASSIF

impale /ɪmpeɪl/, **impales, impaling, impaled.** If you **impale** something, you pierce through it with a sharp pointed object. EG He cut off a piece of the meat and impaled it on his fork. V+O OR V-REFL : OFT+A Formal

impart /ɪmpɑːt/, **imparts, imparting, imparted.**
1 If you **impart** information to people, you tell it to them. EG He had a terrible piece of news to impart. V+O : OFT+to Formal
2 If something **imparts** a particular quality, it gives that quality to another thing. EG Peas and carrots impart a delicious flavour to stews. V+O Formal

impartial /ɪmpɑːʃə⁰l/. Someone who is **impartial** is able to act fairly because they are not involved in a particular situation. EG He gave an impartial view of the state of affairs in Northern Ireland. ◊ **impartially.** EG These men will judge the people impartially. ◊ **impartiality** /ɪmpɑːʃiælɪ¹ti¹/. EG ...the impartiality of the law. ADJ CLASSIF · ◊ ADV · ◊ N UNCOUNT

impassable /ɪmpɑːsəbə⁰l/. A road or path that is **impassable** is impossible to travel over because it is blocked or in bad condition. ADJ CLASSIF

impasse /ɒmpæs/. An **impasse** is a difficult situation in which it is impossible to make any progress. EG The government had reached an impasse... I see no way out of this impasse. N SING Formal

impassioned /ɪmpæʃənd/. When you speak in an **impassioned** way, you express powerful emotion. EG After three hours of impassioned debate the motion was defeated. ADJ QUALIT Formal

impassive /ɪmpæsɪv/. If your face is **impassive**, it does not show any emotion. EG Ruth smiled her usual impassive smile and said nothing. ◊ **impassively.** EG He looked at me impassively. ADJ CLASSIF · ◊ ADV

impatient /ɪmpeɪʃənt/. **1** Someone who is **impatient 1.1** is annoyed because they have had to wait too long for something, or because they are not getting what they want. EG He became impatient. 'Well, can you do it?' ◊ **impatiently.** EG Oliver stood waiting impatiently. ◊ **impatience** /ɪmpeɪʃəns/. EG Chris watched me with some impatience. **1.2** is easily irritated by people or situations. EG He was very impatient with students who could not follow him. ◊ **impatiently.** EG 'I know, I know,' Vaughan said impatiently. ◊ **impatience.** EG There was increasing impatience with the reluctance of the party to grant these reforms. ADJ QUALIT · ◊ ADV · ◊ N UNCOUNT · ADJ QUALIT : OFT+with · ◊ ADV · ◊ N UNCOUNT
2 If you are **impatient** to do something or **impatient** for something to happen, you are eager to do it or for it to happen and do not want to wait. EG Philip was impatient to inspect his place of work. ◊ **impatiently.** EG He looked forward impatiently to Kumar's next visit. ◊ **impatience.** EG There is always a certain impatience to try out an idea to see if it works... He was awaiting the outcome with impatience. ADJ QUALIT : OFT+to-INF OR for · ◊ ADV · ◊ N UNCOUNT +SUPP

impeccable /ɪmpekəbə⁰l/. Something that is **impeccable** is perfect. EG He had impeccable manners... He stood before them, impeccable as ever in his elegant suit. ◊ **impeccably.** EG As usual, he was impeccably dressed. ADJ CLASSIF · ◊ ADV

impede /ɪmpiːd/, **impedes, impeding, impeded.** To **impede** someone or something means to make their movement or development difficult. EG Their advance was seriously impeded by the bad weath- V+O Formal

er... ...procedures that would impede an effective investigation.

impediment /ɪmpedɪmə²nt/, **impediments. 1** Something that is an **impediment** to a person or thing makes their movement or development difficult. EG The new taxes were a major impediment to economic growth. N COUNT : OFT+to Formal
2 A speech **impediment** is a disability such as a stammer which makes speaking difficult. N COUNT : USU+SUPP

impel /ɪmpel/, **impels, impelling, impelled.** When an emotion **impels** you to do something, it affects you so strongly that you feel forced to do it. EG I feel impelled to express grave doubts about the project... What were the motives that impelled Geoffrey to act? V+O : USU+to-INF Formal

impending /ɪmpendɪŋ/. You use **impending** to describe something that is going to happen very soon. EG We were well aware of impending disaster. ADJ CLASSIF : ATTRIB Formal

impenetrable /ɪmpenɪtrəbə⁰l/. Something that is **impenetrable** is **1** solid and impossible to get through. EG ...an impenetrable wall... ...immense tracts of impenetrable jungle. **2** impossible or very difficult to understand. EG The law seems mysterious and impenetrable. ADJ QUALIT

IMPER stands for **imperative**

The imperative form of the verb is used when you are giving a command or making a suggestion to someone, such as Keep off the grass or Come at about 6 o'clock.

The verb is used without inflections, and there is no need for a subject, because you are talking or writing directly to someone.

In a verb entry some meanings have the label ONLY IMPER in the Extra Column. This means that for these meanings the imperative is normally the only form used. An example of a verb meaning labelled ONLY IMPER is **see 20**. You say See p. 19 when you are telling readers that they should look at p. 19 for further details of something.

Some meanings of verbs have the label NO IMPER in the Extra Column. This means that they are not normally used in the imperative. An example of a verb meaning labelled NO IMPER is **see 1**. You do not usually say to someone 'See me' although you can, of course, say 'Look at me' and 'Watch me'.

---

imperative /ɪmperətɪv/, **imperatives. 1** Something that is **imperative** is extremely important and needs to be dealt with before anything else. EG It's imperative that we take care of Liebermann immediately. ▶ used as a noun. EG Any species' first imperative is to survive. ADJ QUALIT : USU PRED · ▶ N COUNT Formal
2 In grammar, an **imperative** is a verb in the form that is typically used for giving orders. N COUNT

imperceptible /ɪmpəseptɪbə⁰l/. Something that is **imperceptible** happens or exists without being felt or noticed. EG ...an almost imperceptible sensation. ◊ **imperceptibly.** EG Gradually, almost imperceptibly, the sun warmed us up. ADJ CLASSIF · ◊ ADV

imperfect /ɪmpɜːfɪ²kt/. **1** Something that is **imperfect** has faults or problems. EG We live in an imperfect society... The examination system is imperfect. ADJ QUALIT
2 In grammar, the **imperfect** or the **imperfect** tense is used in describing continuous or repeated actions in the past. N SING : the+N

imperfection /ɪmpəfekʃə⁰n/, **imperfections. 1** An **imperfection** in someone or something is a fault or weakness that they have. EG ...his human N UNCOUNT OR N COUNT

If something is impending, when will it happen?

imperfection... Americans do not tolerate such imperfections in themselves.
2 An **imperfection** in something is a small mark N COUNT or damaged area which may spoil its appearance. EG *...an imperfection on the surface.*

imperfectly /ɪmpɜːˈfɛktlɪ¹/. If you do something ADV **imperfectly**, you do not do it completely or perfectly. EG *...a world which we only imperfectly understand.*

imperial /ɪmpɪərɪəl/. **1 Imperial** is used **1.1** to ADJ CLASSIF : describe an empire. EG *...the decline of Britain as* ATTRIB *an imperial power.* **1.2** to describe something that relates to an emperor or empress. EG *...the Imperial Palace.*
2 The **imperial** system of measurement is the ADJ CLASSIF : system where length is measured in inches, feet, ATTRIB and yards, weight is measured in ounces and pounds, and the volume of liquids is measured in pints and gallons.

imperialism /ɪmpɪərɪəlɪzə⁰m/ is a system of rule N UNCOUNT in which a rich and powerful country controls other countries in order to become richer and more powerful. EG *...British imperialism in India.*
◊ **imperialist** /ɪmpɪərɪəlɪst/. EG *...the imperialist* ◊ ADJ CLASSIF *ruling classes.*

imperil /ɪmpɛrɪ¹l/, **imperils**, **imperilling**, v+o **imperilled**; spelled **imperiling** and **imperiled** in Formal American English.
Something that **imperils** you puts you in danger. EG *...a political crisis which had imperilled the future of the party.*

imperious /ɪmpɪərɪəs/. An **imperious** person is ADJ QUALIT proud and expects to be obeyed. EG *All his imperi-* Formal *ous orders were obeyed.*

imperishable /ɪmpɛrɪʃəbə⁰l/. Something that is ADJ CLASSIF **imperishable** cannot disappear or be destroyed. Formal EG *There was a certain quality which was imperishable.*

impersonal /ɪmpɜːˈsɒnə⁰l/. **1** A place or an activ- ADJ QUALIT ity that is **impersonal** makes you feel that you are not important and do not matter. EG *...the rules and regulations of a vast, impersonal organization... ...dull, repetitive, impersonal work.*
2 An **impersonal** feeling or action does not relate ADJ CLASSIF to any particular person. ◊ **impersonally.** EG ◊ ADV *...written examinations marked impersonally and with no knowledge of the candidate.*

impersonate /ɪmpɜːˈsəneɪt/, **impersonates**, **im-personating**, **impersonated**. If you **impersonate** someone, **1** you pretend that you are that person, v+o usually by disguising yourself. EG *I ought to be arrested for impersonating an officer.* **2** you imi- v+o tate them in order to be amusing or as an entertainment. EG *...Senator Johnson was brilliantly im-personated by an actor.* ◊ **impersonation** ◊ N COUNT OR /ɪmpɜːˈsəneɪʃə⁰n/, **impersonations.** EG *...Harry's* N UNCOUNT *impersonation of a Russian prince.*

impertinent /ɪmpɜːˈtɪnənt/. Someone who is **im-** ADJ QUALIT **pertinent** speaks or behaves rudely. EG *...imperti-nent questions.* ◊ **impertinence** /ɪmpɜːˈtɪnəns/. EG ◊ N UNCOUNT *They might be offended by such impertinence.*

impervious /ɪmpɜːˈvɪəs/. **1** If you are **impervious** ADJ QUALIT : to someone's actions, you are not affected or USU PRED+*to* influenced by them. EG *I became impervious to influence of any kind... They were impervious to any outside pressures.*
2 Something that is **impervious** to water does not ADJ CLASSIF : allow water to pass through it. EG *The upper walls* USU PRED+*to* *are impervious to water.*

impetuous /ɪmpɛtjʊəs/. Someone who is **impetu-** ADJ QUALIT **ous** acts quickly and suddenly without thinking. EG *I thought scientists were never impetuous.*

impetus /ɪmpɪ¹təs/ is an important effect which N UNCOUNT strongly influences a situation and causes some- +SUPP thing to happen. EG *The present conflict might* Formal *provide fresh impetus for peace talks.*

impinge /ɪmpɪnd⁰ʒ/, **impinges**, **impinging**, **im-** v+on/upon **pinged**. Something that **impinges** on you has an Formal effect on you, often by restricting the way that you

can behave. EG *Your political opinions will neces-sarily impinge on your public life.*

implacable /ɪmplækəbə⁰l/. Someone who is **im-** ADJ QUALIT **placable** has a strong feeling of anger, disapproval, or resentment that you are unable to change. EG *...our most implacable opponent... ...the implacable hatred that workers feel for their employers.*
◊ **implacably.** EG *They are implacably hostile.* ◊ ADV

implant, **implants**, **implanting**, **implanted**; pro-nounced /ɪmplɑːnt/ when it is a verb, and /ɪmplɑːnt/ when it is a noun.
1 If someone **implants** something into a person's v+o : body, they put it there by means of an operation. EG OFT+*in/into* *They implanted electrodes in the skull of a bull.*
2 An **implant** is something that is implanted into a N COUNT person's body. EG *...hormone implants.*
3 If you **implant** an idea or attitude in people, you v+o : make it become accepted or believed. EG *...parents* OFT+*in/into* *requiring teachers to implant religious attitudes in their children.*

implausible /ɪmplɔːzə⁰bə⁰l/. Something that is ADJ QUALIT **implausible** is not easy to believe, and therefore unlikely to be true or genuine. EG *It's an extremely likeable but very implausible romantic thriller.*

implement, **implements**, **implementing**, **im-plemented**; pronounced /ɪmplɪ¹mə⁰nt/ when it is a verb, and /ɪmplɪ¹mənt/ when it is a noun.
1 If you **implement** a plan, system, or law, you v+o carry it out. EG *...policies that they would like to see implemented in the next parliament.*
◊ **implementation** /ɪmplɪ¹mə⁰nteɪʃə⁰n/. EG *...the* ◊ N UNCOUNT *implementation of the desired reforms.*
2 An **implement** is a tool or other piece of N COUNT equipment. EG *...producing basic agricultural imple-ments for underdeveloped areas.*

implicate /ɪmplɪkeɪt/, **implicates**, **implicating**, v+o : **implicated**. If you **implicate** someone in an un- OFT PASS+*in* pleasant event or situation, you show that they have been involved in it. EG *He was implicated in the horrendous murder of a teacher.*

implication /ɪmplɪkeɪʃə⁰n/, **implications. 1** An N COUNT **implication** is something that is suggested or implied by a particular situation, event, or statement. EG *Spencer began to query the political implications of Macaulay's statement.*
2 If something appears to be the case **by implica-** PHRASE **tion**, you think that it is probably true because of another fact that you have just mentioned. *Many are saying her policies have failed and, by implica-tion, so has she.*

implicit /ɪmplɪsɪt/. **1** Something that is **implicit** is ADJ CLASSIF expressed in an indirect way. EG *...advertisements containing implicit racial prejudice... Although it wasn't spoken, it was implicit in her attitude that she thought I had failed.* ◊ **implicitly.** EG *Nobody* ◊ ADV *questioned the implicitly accepted dogma.*
2 If you have an **implicit** belief or faith in some- ADJ QUALIT thing, you believe it completely and have no doubts about it. ◊ **implicitly.** EG *I believe implicitly in the* ◊ ADV *concept of Europe.*

implore /ɪmplɔː/, **implores**, **imploring**, **im-** v+o+*to*-INF **plored**. If you **implore** someone to do something, OR V+QUOTE you desperately beg them to do it. EG *She tele-* Formal *phoned me to implore me to come.*

imply /ɪmplaɪ/, **implies**, **implying**, **implied. 1** If v+REPORT you **imply** that something is true, you suggest that OR V+O it is true without actually saying so. EG *At one point she implied she would marry me... In Malta this gesture implies heavy sarcasm.* ◊ **implied.** EG ◊ ADJ CLASSIF *...implied criticism.*
2 When one situation **implies** another, it suggests v+o OR that the second situation is true as a consequence V+REPORT of the first one being true. EG *All these require-* ONLY *that* *ments imply a reduction in government spending... These discoveries imply that the sea-bed is rich in fossil fuels.*

impolite /ɪmpəlaɪt/. Someone who is **impolite** is ADJ QUALIT rather rude and offends people. EG *It was very impolite of him to ask.*

import, imports, importing, imported; pronounced /ɪmˈpɔːt/ when it is a verb, and /ˈɪmpɔːt/ when it is a noun.

1 If you **import** goods or services, you buy them from another country and have them sent to your own country. EG *The government had an interest in importing scientific equipment... ...imported sugar.* ► used as a noun. EG *The import of cotton goods went up sharply in 1859.* ◊ **importation** /ˌɪmpɔːˈteɪʃⁿn/. EG *...the illegal importation of drugs into Britain.* V+O

► N UNCOUNT

◊ N UNCOUNT

2 An **import** is a product or raw material which you buy from another country for use in your own country. EG *They blamed the closure on cheap imports and the recession.* N COUNT

important /ɪmˈpɔːtənt/. **1** Something that is **important** is very significant, valuable, or necessary. EG *This is the most important part of the job... It is important to get on with your employer and his wife... Your child's health is more important than the doctor's feelings.* ◊ **importantly.** EG *The problems the Chinese face differ importantly from those facing Africa.* ◊ **importance.** EG *Here I would stress the importance of mathematics to the whole of science... ...an attempt to assess Stonehenge's historic importance.* ADJ QUALIT

◊ ADV

◊ N UNCOUNT +SUPP

2 Things that are **important** to you have great significance for you and you consider them very seriously. EG *I realize how important it is for me to have a job... It was important to me to know.* ADJ QUALIT

3 Someone who is **important** has influence or power. EG *He wasn't anyone important in the firm... ...the list of important people who are coming on state visits.* ◊ **importance.** EG *Was he related to anyone of importance?* ADJ QUALIT

◊ N UNCOUNT

importer /ɪmˈpɔːtə/, **importers.** An **importer** is a person, country, or firm which buys goods or services from another country for use in its own country. EG *Many western countries have ceased to be major food importers.* N COUNT

impose /ɪmˈpəʊz/, **imposes, imposing, imposed.**
1 If you **impose** something on people, you use your authority to force people to accept it. EG *She was a harsh mother and imposed severe discipline on her children... ...the proposal to impose a 20p admission charge for museums... ...parents who impose religion on their children.* ◊ **imposition** /ˌɪmpəˈzɪʃⁿn/. EG *...the imposition of a wages freeze.* V+O: OFT+on/upon

◊ N UNCOUNT: USU+of

2 If something **imposes** an unpleasant effect, it causes this effect. EG *...the restraint imposed on them by the government... Overcrowding imposes mental strains.* V+O: OFT+on/upon

3 If someone **imposes** on you, they unreasonably expect you to do something for them when you do not really want to. EG *She would hate to feel that she was imposing on anyone.* ◊ **imposition, impositions.** EG *I'd be so grateful, though really it's an imposition.* V OR V-REFL: OFT+on

◊ N COUNT

4 If something **imposes** itself on a situation or activity, it becomes noticeable as a strong factor in the situation. EG *The logic of party organization imposes itself even on anarchic movements.* V-REFL: OFT+on

imposing /ɪmˈpəʊzɪŋ/. Someone or something that is **imposing** has an impressive appearance or manner. EG *Mrs Sabawala's house was large and imposing.* ADJ QUALIT

impossible /ɪmˈpɒsəbⁿl/. **1** Something that is **impossible** cannot be done, cannot happen, or cannot be believed. EG *It was an impossible task... Staying awake all night was virtually impossible.* ◊ **impossibly.** EG *He had impossibly thin legs.* ◊ **impossibility** /ɪmˌpɒsəˈbɪlɪtiⁱ/, **impossibilities.** EG *...the impossibility of change.* ADJ QUALIT

◊ ADV+ADJ

◊ N UNCOUNT OR N COUNT

2 A situation that is **impossible** is one that you find very difficult and are unable to decide on or improve. EG *They are in an impossible position on this matter.* ◊ **impossibly.** EG *Flats make life impossibly restrictive for energetic young children.* ADJ QUALIT

◊ ADV+ADJ

3 If you describe someone as **impossible**, you ADJ QUALIT

mean that they are very difficult to deal with, usually because of their bad behaviour or strong views. EG *...my impossible daughter... You're an impossible man to please.* ◊ **impossibly.** EG *She was impossibly rude to Miss Cormorant.* ◊ ADV+ADJ

impostor /ɪmˈpɒstə/, **impostors;** also spelled **imposter.** If someone is an **impostor**, they are dishonestly pretending to be someone else in order to get something that they want. EG *This is not Doctor Malcolm, he is an impostor.* N COUNT

impotent /ˈɪmpətənt/. **1** Someone who is **impotent** has no power to influence people or events. EG *Those who do not conform must be rendered impotent.* ◊ **impotence** /ˈɪmpətəns/. EG *...the impotence and inactivity of the left-wing parties in Europe.* ADJ QUALIT Formal

◊ N UNCOUNT

2 If a man is **impotent**, he is unable to reach an orgasm when having sex. ◊ **impotence.** EG *...impotence and frigidity in adults.* ADJ CLASSIF

◊ N UNCOUNT

impound /ɪmˈpaʊnd/, **impounds, impounding, impounded.** If policemen or other officials **impound** something that you own, they take legal possession of it. EG *Security Police had come to our house and impounded all our belongings.* V+O Formal

impoverish /ɪmˈpɒvərɪʃ/, **impoverishes, impoverishing, impoverished.** To **impoverish** someone or something means to make them poor. EG *They were impoverished by a prolonged spell of unemployment.* ◊ **impoverished.** EG *...an impoverished Third World country... ...a spiritually impoverished way of life.* ◊ **impoverishment** /ɪmˈpɒvərɪʃmənt/. EG *...a period of very severe impoverishment.* V+O

◊ ADJ QUALIT

◊ N UNCOUNT

impracticable /ɪmˈpræktɪkəbⁿl/. A course of action that is **impracticable** is impossible to do. EG *It would be impracticable to ban all food additives.* ADJ CLASSIF

impractical /ɪmˈpræktɪkⁿl/. An idea or course of action that is **impractical** is not sensible, realistic, or practical. EG *...a totally impractical view... To expect automatic protection is impractical.* ADJ QUALIT

imprecise /ˌɪmprɪˈsaɪs/. Something that is **imprecise** is not clear or accurate. EG *My ideas about it were imprecise... ...imprecise data.* ADJ QUALIT

impregnable /ɪmˈpregnəbⁿl/. **1** Something that is **impregnable** is so strong or solid that it cannot be broken into. EG *They will establish impregnable fortresses to defend themselves.* ADJ CLASSIF

2 A person or group that is **impregnable** cannot be affected or overcome by anyone. EG *They are virtually impregnable to attack from any other party.* ADJ CLASSIF

impregnate /ˈɪmpregneɪt/, **impregnates, impregnating, impregnated.** If you **impregnate** something with a substance, you make the substance pass into it and spread through it. EG *...paper that has been impregnated with chemicals.* V+O: OFT+with

impresario /ˌɪmprɪˈsɑːriⁱəʊ/, **impresarios.** An **impresario** is a person whose job is to manage a theatre or music company. EG *...a successful West End impresario.* N COUNT

impress /ɪmˈpres/, **impresses, impressing, impressed.** **1** If you do something that **impresses** someone, you make them admire you and respect you. EG *I was hoping to impress my new boss with my diligence... I was greatly impressed by the pianist.* V+O: OFT+A

2 If you **impress** something on someone, you make them understand the importance of it. EG *She impressed on the Government the danger of making too many cuts.* V+O+on/upon Formal

impression /ɪmˈpreʃⁿn/, **impressions.** **1** An **impression** that you have of someone or something is the way that they look or seem to you. EG *The immediate impression of the bedroom is one of sheer 1950s Hollywood.* N COUNT: USU+SUPP

If you are impudent, what kind of impression do you make?

2 Your **impression** of a situation, place, or person N COUNT : is the opinion that you have about it. EG *My* USU+SUPP *impression is that contemporary British authors have a lot to learn from American writing... Reporters wanted my personal impressions of China.*

3 When something gives a particular **impression**, N SING : it causes people to believe that something is true, USU+SUPP often when it is not actually true. EG *They give the impression of not working... I had the impression that he didn't trust me.* ● If you are **under the** ● PHRASE **impression** that something is true, you believe that it is true. EG *They were under the impression I had come to stay.*

4 The **impression** that something makes on peo- N COUNT : ple is the effect that it has on their ideas or USU+SUPP attitudes. EG *I left thinking that I had created quite a good impression.* ● If you **make an impression**, ● PHRASE you have a strong effect on people when you meet them, causing them to notice you and remember you. EG *She did not fail to make an impression.*

5 An **impression** by someone is an amusing N COUNT imitation of a well-known person. EG *Have you seen her impressions of the TV newscasters?*

impressionable /ɪmpreʃənəbəʰl/. Someone who ADJ QUALIT is **impressionable** is easy to influence. EG *...an impressionable young girl.*

impressive /ɪmpresɪv/. Someone or something ADJ QUALIT that is **impressive** impresses you, usually because they are very important. EG *She was a very impressive woman... ...an impressive international reputation... The list of speakers was impressive.* ◊ **impressively.** EG *The Mysore Palace was im-* ◊ ADV *pressively elegant and massive.*

imprint, imprints, imprinting, imprinted; pronounced /ɪmprɪnt/ when it is a noun, and /ɪmprɪnt/ when it is a verb.

1 If something leaves an **imprint** on your mind or N COUNT : on a place, it has a strong effect on it. EG *These* USU+SUPP *things have left a deep imprint on our thinking... The town still bears the imprint of its industrial origins.*

2 If something **is imprinted** on your memory, it is V+O+A : so firmly fixed in your memory that you will not USU PASS forget it. EG *This is a sunset that will be forever imprinted in the mind.*

3 An **imprint** is a mark or outline made by N COUNT pressure of an object on a surface. EG *In its centre was the imprint of his hand.*

4 If an object **is imprinted** onto a surface, it is V+O+A : pressed hard onto the surface so that it leaves a USU PASS mark or an outline. EG *...the hand imprinted in the sand.*

imprison /ɪmprɪzəʰn/, **imprisons, imprisoning, imprisoned. 1** If someone **imprisons** you, they V+O lock you up in prison.

2 A condition or situation that **imprisons** you V+O restricts your freedom. EG *...the conditions that imprison the industrial worker today.*

imprisonment /ɪmprɪzəʰnməʰnt/ is the state of N UNCOUNT being imprisoned. EG *They were sentenced to life imprisonment.*

improbable /ɪmprɒbəbəʰl/. **1** Something that is ADJ QUALIT **improbable** is unlikely to be true or to happen. EG *His explanation seems highly improbable.*

2 If you describe something as **improbable**, you ADJ QUALIT mean that you find it strange, unusual, or ridiculous. EG *...the gaudiest and most improbable water wheel the world has ever seen.*

impromptu /ɪmprɒmptjuː/. An **impromptu** ac- ADJ CLASSIF tion is done without planning or organizing it in USU ATTRIB advance. EG *I got drawn into a kind of impromptu* Formal *party downstairs.*

improper /ɪmprɒpə/. **1** If you describe someone's ADJ QUALIT behaviour as **improper**, you mean that it is rude or shocking because it is not the correct way to behave. EG *Charlotte thought my mirth improper.*

2 Improper activities are illegal or dishonest. EG ADJ CLASSIF *...allegations of improper business dealings.*

◊ **improperly.** EG *There were charges that Hugel* ◊ ADV *had improperly provided them with cash.*

3 Improper conditions or methods of treatment ADJ CLASSIF are not suitable or adequate for a particular purpose. EG *...the cruel and improper treatment of cattle.* ◊ **improperly.** EG *Bottled milk, improperly* ◊ ADV *handled, is a lethal carrier of disease.*

improve /ɪmpruːv/, **improves, improving, improved. 1** If something **improves** or if you im- V-ERG **prove** it, it gets better. EG *The weather improved later in the day... These houses have been improved by the addition of bathrooms.* ◊ **improved.** ◊ ADJ CLASSIF EG *In underdeveloped countries, improved health and education are urgently needed.*

2 If you **improve** at a skill or in an area of V-ERG knowledge, you get better at it by practising or studying. EG *She went to the club to improve her tennis... His French was improving.*

3 If you **improve** after an illness or an injury, your V health gets better. EG *She may improve with medical treatment.*

4 If something **improves** someone, it changes V+O OR V-REFL them so that they have a better character or a better social status. EG *He is enjoying his job, getting on and improving himself.*

5 If you **improve** on an achievement, you achieve V+on/upon : a better standard or result than the previous one. HAS PASS EG *He thinks he's improving on my work... Our techniques are already far advanced and being improved on daily.*

improvement /ɪmpruːvməʰnt/, **improvements.** N UNCOUNT **Improvement** in someone or something is a OR N COUNT change which improves their quality or condition. EG *The Company made a significant improvement in the wages of its employees... ...the gradual improvement of relations between East and West... Life there would be such an improvement on Paris.*

improvise /ɪmprəvaɪz/, **improvises, improvising, improvised. 1** If you **improvise** something, V OR V+O you make it or do it using whatever you have or without planning it in advance. EG *We had to improvise as we went along... The sisters helped me improvise a curtain in front of the toilet.* ◊ **improvised.** EG *Tanks were crossing the river* ◊ ADJ CLASSIF *on improvised bridges.*

2 When musicians **improvise**, they play music V OR V+O without set music, using their imagination. When actors **improvise**, they act without set words, using their imagination. EG *He could improvise quite ambitiously on classical themes.* ◊ **improvisation** /ɪmprəvaɪzeɪʃəʰn/, **improvisa-** ◊ N UNCOUNT **tions.** EG *...actors playing out improvisations.* OR N COUNT

imprudent /ɪmpruːdəʰnt/. **Imprudent** behaviour ADJ QUALIT is not sensible or carefully thought out. EG *It would be imprudent of you to make enemies of those who can help you.*

impudent /ɪmpjʊdəʰnt/. Someone who is **impu-** ADJ QUALIT **dent** behaves or speaks rudely or disrespectfully. EG *The impudent child extended her legs across my lap.* ◊ **impudently.** EG *...somebody who impudent-* ◊ ADV *ly defies my orders.*

impulse /ɪmpʌls/, **impulses. 1** If you have an N COUNT **impulse** to do something, you have a sudden desire to do it. EG *I had a sudden impulse to turn around and walk out.* ● If you do something **on** ● PHRASE **impulse**, you do it suddenly without planning. EG *On a sudden impulse, he went into the library.*

2 An **impulse** is a short electrical signal that is N COUNT sent along a wire or nerve or through the air.

impulsive /ɪmpʌlsɪv/. Someone who is **impulsive** ADJ QUALIT does things suddenly without thinking about them carefully first. EG *Alice's overdose was an impulsive act.* ◊ **impulsively.** EG *She kissed him impulsively* ◊ ADV *on the mouth.*

impunity /ɪmpjuːnɪʰtiʰ/. If you do something PHRASE wrong **with impunity**, you are not punished for Formal doing it. EG *Landlords were simply ignoring the law with impunity.*

impure /ɪmpjʊə/. 1 A substance that is **impure** is ADJ CLASSIF not of good quality because it has other substances mixed with it.

2 Impure thoughts and actions are concerned with ADJ CLASSIF sex and are regarded as sinful.

impurity /ɪmpjʊərɪ'ti¹/, **impurities**. An **impu- N COUNT rity** is a substance that is present in another substance making it of a low quality. EG *There are traces of impurities in the gold.*

in /ɪn/. 1 Something that is **in** something else is PREP, OR enclosed by it or surrounded by it. EG *We put them* ADV AFTER VB *away in a big box... We've just found a body in the water... She opened her bag and put her diary in.*

2 If something is **in** a place, it is there. EG *I wanted* PREP *to play in the garden... She locked herself in the bathroom... In Hamburg the girls split up... I could not sleep because of the pain in my feet.*

3 If you are **in**, you are present at your home or ADV AFTER VB place of work. EG *He's never in when I phone.*

4 When someone comes **in**, they enter a room or ADV AFTER VB building. EG *There was a knock at Howard's door. 'Come in,' he shouted... He had his meals brought in... The children run in and out all the time.*

5 If a train, boat, or plane is **in** or has come **in**, it ADV AFTER VB has arrived somewhere. EG *The train's not in yet.*

6 Something that is **in** a window, especially a shop PREP window, is just behind the window so that you can see it from outside. EG *How much is the hat in the window?*

7 When you see something **in** a mirror, you see its PREP reflection.

8 If you are **in** a piece of clothing, you are wearing PREP it. EG *Martin was in his pyjamas.*

9 If something is **in** a book, film, play, or picture, PREP, OR you can read it or see it there. EG *She dies in the* ADV AFTER VB *last act... In Chapter 7 this point is discussed in detail.*

10 If something is **in** a group or collection, it is part PREP of it. EG *She waited in the queue.*

11 If you are **in** something such as a play or a race, PREP you are one of the people taking part. EG *She took part in a marathon.*

12 You also use **in** when you are talking about PREP time. **12.1** If something happens **in** a particular year, month, or season, it happens during that time. EG *In 1872, Chicago was burned to the ground... It'll be warmer in the spring.* **12.2** If you do something **in** a particular period of time, that is how long it takes you to do it. EG *I told him the money would be paid back in six months.* **12.3** If something will happen **in** a particular length of time, it will happen after that length of time. EG *In another five minutes it'll be pitch dark.*

13 If something happens **in** a particular situation, it PREP happens during it or when it is going on. EG *He escaped in the confusion... In these circumstances prices and profits would remain stable.*

14 If you are **in** a particular state or situation, that PREP is your present state or situation. EG *We are in a position to advise our Indian friends... We might be in a state of near chaos again... You can't go home in all this rain.*

15 You use **in** to say that an emotion, desire, or PREP reaction causes someone to do something. For example, if you do something **in** surprise, you do it because you are surprised. EG *He shook his head in admiration... In his excitement, Billy had forgotten the letter... In an effort to conceal my thinness, I had worn two layers of clothing.*

16 You use **in** to specify a general subject or field PREP of activity. EG *...recent advances in mathematics... He plans to make his career in music.*

17 You use **in** to indicate how many people or PREP things do something. EG *Students flocked to the SDP in considerable numbers.*

18 You use **in** to give someone's approximate age. PREP For example, if someone is **in** their fifties, they are between 50 and 59 years old. EG *In her twenties and thirties she had had no difficulty in finding jobs.*

19 You use **in** to indicate how someone is express- PREP ing something. EG *I need your complaints in writing... She spoke in a calm, friendly voice... They were speaking in French.*

20 You use **in** to describe the arrangement or PREP shape of something. For example, if things are **in** a row, they are arranged to form a row. If something is **in** a ball, its shape is that of a ball. EG *The students sit in a circle on the floor.*

21 If something is **in** a particular colour, it has that PREP colour. EG *We put up curtains in yellow and orange.*

22 You use **in** to specify what something relates to. PREP EG *It grew to eight metres in length... We need a change in direction... She was dismissed for slackness in her duties.*

23 You use **in** to express a ratio, proportion, or PREP probability. EG *Only one acre in five was previously uncultivated... He has only a one in ten chance of being reunited with his family.*

24 Something that is **in** or that is the **in** thing is ADJ CLASSIF fashionable. EG *Bright colours are in this year.* Informal

25 When the sea or tide comes **in**, the sea moves ADV AFTER VB towards the shore rather than away from it.

26 You use **in** with a present participle to indicate PREP + -ING that when you do something, something else happens as a consequence. EG *Babbage rejected the obvious, and in doing so achieved his magnificent insight.*

27 If you say that someone **is in for** a shock or a PHRASE surprise, you mean that they are going to experience it.

28 If you **have it in for** someone, you dislike them PHRASE and try to cause problems for them. Informal

29 If you are **in on** something, you are involved in PHRASE it or know about it. EG *I'd like to be in on the scheme.*

30 You use **in that** to explain a statement you have CONJ just made. EG *He's a good listener in that he never interrupts you with thoughts of his own.*

in. is a written abbreviation for 'inch'. The plural can be **in.** or **ins.** EG *...6 x 4 ins.*

in- is added to some adjectives, adverbs, and nouns PREFIX to form other adjectives, adverbs, and nouns that have the opposite meaning. For example, something that is incorrect is not correct. EG *He was obviously insincere... 'No, Father,' she said, almost inaudibly... ...a source of political instability.*

inability /ɪnəbɪlɪ'ti¹/. If you refer to someone's N UNCOUNT **inability** to do something, you are referring to the + to-INF fact that they are unable to do it. EG *She despises her husband for his inability to work.*

inaccessible /ɪnə³ksesə¹bəˀl/. If something is **in- accessible**, 1 it is impossible to reach or very ADJ QUALIT difficult to reach. EG *...the most inaccessible reaches of the jungle.* ◊ **inaccessibility** ◊ N UNCOUNT /ɪnə³ksesə¹bɪlɪ¹ti¹/. EG *The hilltop church attracted good congregations, in spite of its inaccessibility.* **2** ADJ QUALIT you are unable to understand or appreciate it. EG Formal *The music of Bartok is considered inaccessible by many people.*

inaccuracy /ɪnækjə⁴rəsi¹/, **inaccuracies**. 1 The N UNCOUNT **inaccuracy** of something is the fact that it is inaccurate. EG *...the inaccuracy of my estimates.*

2 An **inaccuracy** is a statement that is inaccurate. N COUNT EG *The report contained a number of inaccuracies.*

inaccurate /ɪnækjə⁴rə¹t/. Something that is **inac- ADJ QUALIT curate** is not correct or precise. EG *...a wildly inaccurate editorial.*

inaction /ɪnækʃəⁿn/. If you refer to someone's N UNCOUNT **inaction**, you are referring to the fact that they are doing nothing. EG *We do not accept this as an excuse for government inaction.*

inactive /ɪnæktɪv/. A person, animal, or thing that ADJ CLASSIF is **inactive** is not doing anything. EG *Crocodiles are inactive for long periods.* ◊ **inactivity** ◊ N UNCOUNT

What is the difference between an inborn quality and an inbred one?

/ɪnæktɪvɪ¹ti¹/. EG *The dry season was traditionally a time of inactivity.*

inadequacy /ɪnædɪ¹kwəsi¹/, **inadequacies. 1** The N UNCOUNT inadequacy of something is the fact that there is OR N COUNT not enough of it or that it is not good enough. EG *Parents are complaining at the inadequacy of education facilities in Britain.*

2 If someone has feelings of **inadequacy**, they feel N UNCOUNT that they do not have the qualities and abilities necessary to do something or to cope with life.

3 An **inadequacy** is a weakness or fault in a N COUNT person or thing. EG *...the inadequacies of a superficial education.*

inadequate /ɪnædɪ¹kwə¹t/. **1** If something is **inadequate**, ADJ QUALIT there is not enough of it or it is not good enough. EG *His income is inadequate to meet his basic needs... ...an inadequate and hurried lunch.*

◊ **inadequately.** EG *Many elderly people live in* ◊ ADV *inadequately heated accommodation.*

2 If someone feels **inadequate**, they feel that they ADJ QUALIT do not have the qualities or abilities necessary to do something or to cope with life. EG *He makes me feel totally inadequate.*

inadvertently /ɪnəd¹vɜ:təntli¹/. If you do something ADV inadvertently, you do it without intending to do it. EG *...a dog that has been kicked inadvertently by a friend.*

inadvisable /ɪnəd¹vaɪzəbə⁰l/. A course of action ADJ QUALIT : that is **inadvisable** is not sensible and should not USU PRED be done. EG *It is inadvisable to plant lettuces too early.*

inalienable /ɪneɪljənəbə⁰l/. An **inalienable** right ADJ CLASSIF : is one that cannot be taken away. EG *...the inalienable* USU ATTRIB *right to do anything you want.* Formal

inane /ɪneɪn/. **Inane** remarks or actions are silly. ADJ QUALIT EG *She sat through the lesson making inane remarks.* ◊ **inanely.** EG *He smiled rather inanely.* ◊ ADV

inanimate /ɪnænɪmə¹t/. An **inanimate** object has ADJ CLASSIF no life.

inappropriate /ɪnəprəʊprɪə¹t/. Something that is ADJ CLASSIF inappropriate is not suitable. EG *...a small suitcase full of inappropriate clothes.*

inarticulate /ɪnɑ:tɪkjə⁰lə¹t/. If you are **inarticulate**, ADJ QUALIT you are unable to express yourself easily or well in speech. EG *He became inarticulate in his anger... ...inarticulate sounds.*

inasmuch /ɪnə¹zmʌtʃ/; also spelled **in as much.** CONJ You use **inasmuch as** when you are giving the Formal reason for something. EG *The outcome of this was important inasmuch as it showed just what human beings were capable of.*

inattention /ɪnətenʃə⁰n/ is lack of attention to N UNCOUNT what is being said or done. EG *...scolding the maid for inattention.*

inattentive /ɪnətentɪv/. Someone who is **inattentive** ADJ QUALIT is not paying attention to what is being said or done. EG *...children who are inattentive and doing poorly in school.*

inaudible /ɪnɔ:də¹bəl/. A sound that is **inaudible** ADJ CLASSIF is not loud enough to be heard. EG *Her voice became inaudible.*

inaugural /ɪnɔ:gjⁱ⁰ərəl/. An **inaugural** meeting or ADJ CLASSIF : speech is the first one of a new organization or ATTRIB leader. EG *...his inaugural address as President.*

inaugurate /ɪnɔ:gjⁱ⁰əreɪt/, **inaugurates, inaugurating, inaugurated. 1** When new leaders are V+O inaugurated, they are officially established in their new position at a special ceremony.

◊ **inauguration** /ɪnɔ:gjⁱ⁰əreɪʃə⁰n/. EG *...the inauguration* ◊ N UNCOUNT : *of a new President.* USU+SUPP

2 If you **inaugurate** a system or organization, you V+O start it. EG *They undertook to inaugurate measures* Formal *to control and protect shipping.*

inborn /ɪm¹bɔ:n/. **Inborn** qualities are believed to ADJ CLASSIF be natural ones with which you are born. EG *...our inborn hatred for freaks and outcasts.*

inbred /ɪm¹bred/. **1** An **inbred** quality is an ADJ CLASSIF inborn one. EG *...the inbred suspicion of strangers.* Formal

2 People who are **inbred** have ancestors who are ADJ CLASSIF

all closely related to each other. EG *...the inbred royal family.*

inbuilt /ɪm¹bɪlt/. An **inbuilt** quality is one that ADJ CLASSIF someone or something has from the time they were born or produced. EG *The child has got an inbuilt feeling of inferiority.*

incalculable /ɪŋ¹kælkjələbə⁰l/. Something that is ADJ CLASSIF **incalculable** is so great that it cannot be estimated. EG *The loss to the race as a whole is incalculable.*

incantation /ɪŋ¹kænteɪʃə⁰n/, **incantations.** An N COUNT **incantation** is a series of words that a person says or sings as a magic spell.

incapable /ɪŋ¹keɪpəbə⁰l/. **1** Someone who is **incapable** ADJ PRED+of of doing something is unable to do it. EG *She is incapable of grasping what self-discipline means.*

2 An **incapable** person is weak and helpless or ADJ CLASSIF stupid. EG *He's both incapable and dishonest.*

incapacitate /ɪŋ¹kə³pæsɪteɪt/, **incapacitates, incapacitating, incapacitated.** If you **are** **inca-** V+O : USU PASS **pacitated** by something, it weakens or harms you Formal so much that you become unable to do things. EG *...those not yet incapacitated by seasickness.*

incapacity /ɪŋ¹kə³pæsɪ¹ti¹/. The **incapacity** of a N UNCOUNT person, society, or system is their inability to do Formal something. EG *Growing incapacity is expected with increasing age... ...her incapacity to forgive herself.*

incarcerate /ɪŋ¹kɑ:səreɪt/, **incarcerates, incar-** V+O **cerating, incarcerated.** If someone is **incarcer-** Formal **ated**, they are put in prison. ◊ **incarceration** ◊ N UNCOUNT /ɪŋ¹kɑ:səreɪʃə⁰n/. EG *...the incarceration of political dissenters.*

incarnation /ɪŋ¹kɑ:neɪʃə⁰n/, **incarnations. 1** You N COUNT+of can describe someone as the **incarnation** of a particular quality to emphasize that they have that quality very strongly. EG *...Miss Lenaut, that incarnation of feminine beauty.*

2 An **incarnation** is an instance of being alive on N COUNT earth in a particular form. Some religions believe that people have several incarnations. EG *Perhaps they were lovers in a previous incarnation.*

incautious /ɪŋ¹kɔ:ʃəs/. Someone who is **incautious** ADJ QUALIT does not take enough care over what they say or do. EG *...an incautious remark.*

incendiary /ɪnsendjəri¹/. **Incendiary** attacks or ADJ CLASSIF : weapons involve setting fire to something. EG *...a* ATTRIB *huge incendiary bomb that exploded in the street.*

incense, **incenses, incensing, incensed;** pronounced /ɪnsens/ when it is a noun and /ɪnsens/ when it is a verb.

1 **Incense** is a substance that is burned for its N UNCOUNT sweet smell, often during a religious ceremony.

2 Something that **incenses** you makes you ex- V+O tremely angry. EG *The proposed pay freeze has incensed the men.* ◊ **incensed.** EG *Korean* ◊ ADJ QUALIT : *businessmen are particularly incensed at the gov-* USU PRED *ernment's new policy.*

incentive /ɪnsentɪv/, **incentives.** An **incentive** is N COUNT OR something that encourages you to do something. EG N UNCOUNT *Money is being used as an incentive... He has no incentive to make permanent improvements.*

inception /ɪnsepʃə⁰n/. The **inception** of an insti- N UNCOUNT tution or activity is the start of it. EG *He has been* +POSS *associated with Everyman Opera since its incep-* Formal *tion in 1952.*

incessant /ɪnsesənt/. An **incessant** activity con- ADJ QUALIT tinues without stopping. EG *...long centuries of almost incessant warfare.* ◊ **incessantly.** EG *She* ◊ ADV *drank tea incessantly.*

incest /ɪnsest/ is a crime in which someone has N UNCOUNT sex with a person they are closely related to, for example their brother or sister.

incestuous /ɪnsestjuəs/. **1** An **incestuous** rela- ADJ CLASSIF tionship is one involving incest.

2 An **incestuous** group of people is a small group ADJ QUALIT of people who all know each other well and do not associate with anyone outside the group.

inch /ɪntʃ/, **inches, inching, inched. 1** An **inch** is N COUNT an unit for measuring length, approximately equal to 2.54 centimetres. There are twelve inches in a foot. EG *A standard bed is 6 feet 3 inches long... Five inches of snow had fallen... ...searching every inch of the car.*

2 If you **inch** somewhere, you move there very slowly and carefully. EG *You can only enter the caves by inching through a narrow tunnel on your stomach... Howard inched the van forward.*   V-ERG+A

incidence /ˈɪnsɪdəns/. The **incidence** of something is how often it occurs. EG *There is a high incidence of heart disease among middle-aged men.*   N SING+*of*

incident /ˈɪnsɪdənt/, **incidents**. An **incident** is an event, especially one involving violence or something unpleasant. EG *...a succession of bizarre incidents... ...a shooting incident... ...the recent small-pox incident.*   N COUNT / Formal

incidental /ɪnsɪˈdentᵊl/. Something that is **incidental** happens or exists in connection with something else that is more important. EG *...incidental expenses... ...incidental music for a film.*   ADJ CLASSIF: ATTRIB

incidentally /ɪnsɪˈdentᵊliˈ/. You use **incidentally** when you add something to what you are saying or when you change the subject. EG *Incidentally, I suggest that you have the telephone moved to the sitting-room.*   ADV SEN

incinerate /ɪnˈsɪnəreɪt/, **incinerates**, **incinerating**, **incinerated**. If you **incinerate** something, you burn it completely. EG *Tons of paper are incinerated every year.*   V+O / Formal

incinerator /ɪnˈsɪnəreɪtə/, **incinerators**. An **incinerator** is a furnace for burning rubbish.   N COUNT

incipient /ɪnˈsɪpɪənt/. An **incipient** condition or quality is one that is starting to happen or appear. EG *...a good way of curing incipient baldness.*   ADJ CLASSIF: ATTRIB / Formal

incision /ɪnˈsɪʒᵊn/, **incisions**. An **incision** is a careful cut made in something, for example by a surgeon. EG *...an incision between the fifth and sixth ribs.*   N COUNT / Formal

incisive /ɪnˈsaɪsɪv/. Speech or writing that is **incisive** is clear and forceful. EG *...an incisive critique of our society.*   ADJ QUALIT

incite /ɪnˈsaɪt/, **incites**, **inciting**, **incited**. If you **incite** someone to behave in a particular way or **incite** particular behaviour, you encourage someone to behave in that way. EG *...inciting people to acts of violence... He was accused of inciting violence.* ◊ **incitement** /ɪnˈsaɪtmᵊnt/. EG *I have been convicted of incitement to murder.*   V+O: OFT+*to-INF* OR A / ◊ N UNCOUNT: USU+*to*

inclination /ɪŋklɪˈneɪʃᵊn/, **inclinations**. An **inclination** is a feeling that makes you act or want to act in a particular way. EG *People decide on their aims in life according to their inclinations... Some parents have no time or inclination to play with their children.*   N COUNT OR N UNCOUNT

incline, **inclines**, **inclining**, **inclined**; pronounced /ˈɪŋklaɪn/ when it is a noun and /ɪŋˈklaɪn/ when it is a verb.
1 An **incline** is land that slopes at an angle. EG *They walked down a steep incline.*   N COUNT
2 If you **incline** your head, you bend your neck so that your head is leaning forward.   V+O / Formal

inclined /ɪŋˈklaɪnd/. **1** If you are **inclined** to behave in a particular way, **1.1** you often behave in that way. EG *My father was inclined to be very moody.* **1.2** you want to behave in that way. EG *Only do the dusting when you feel inclined.*   ADJ PRED / +*to-INF* / ADJ PRED
2 If you say that you are **inclined** to have a particular opinion, you are saying that you have this opinion. EG *I'm inclined to agree with you.*   ADJ PRED / +*to-INF* / Formal
3 Someone who is mathematically **inclined** or artistically **inclined**, for example, has a natural ability to do mathematics or art.   ADJ PRED
4 Something that is **inclined** in a particular direction is sloping in this direction. EG *The southern hemisphere is inclined towards the sun.*   ADJ CLASSIF+A

include /ɪnˈkluːd/, **includes**, **including**, **included**. **1** If one thing **includes** another, it has the other thing as one of its parts. EG *The four-man*   V+O crew included one Briton... The proposals included the nationalization of major industries.*
2 If you **include** one thing in another, you make it part of the other thing. EG *Carpets and curtains are to be included in the purchase price.*   V+O+A

included /ɪnˈkluːdɪd/. You use **included** to emphasize that someone or something is part of the group of people or things that you are referring to. EG *All of us, myself included, had been totally committed to the project.*   ADJ AFTER N

including /ɪnˈkluːdɪŋ/. You use **including** to say that someone or something is part of the group of people or things that you are referring to. EG *Nine persons were injured, including two wounded by gunfire... ...a home with 5 rooms (not including the bathroom).*   PREP

inclusion /ɪnˈkluːʒᵊn/. The **inclusion** of one thing in another is the act of making it a part of the other thing. EG *...the inclusion of the Old Testament in the Christian Bible.*   N UNCOUNT

inclusive /ɪnˈkluːsɪv/. **1** A price that is **inclusive** includes all the goods and services that are being offered. EG *It's a fully inclusive price... ...£168 (inclusive of tax).*   ADJ CLASSIF
2 You use **inclusive** to say that you are including the things mentioned when you refer to a series of things. EG *...ages 17 to 27 inclusive.*   ADJ AFTER N

incognito /ɪŋˈkɒɡniːtəʊ/. Someone famous who is travelling **incognito** is travelling in disguise or using another name so that they will not be recognized.   ADV AFTER VB

incoherent /ɪŋkəʊˈhɪərənt/. If someone is **incoherent**, they are talking in an unclear way. EG *He moved among his guests, stammering incoherent apologies... He was quite incoherent with joy.* ◊ **incoherently.** EG *Marcus stood up, muttering incoherently.*   ADJ QUALIT / ◊ ADV

income /ˈɪŋkəm/, **incomes**. A person's **income** is the money that they earn or that they get from other sources such as investments.   N COUNT

incoming /ˈɪŋkʌmɪŋ/. **1** An **incoming** tide or wave is going towards the shore.   ADJ CLASSIF: ATTRIB
2 An **incoming** plane, vehicle, or passenger is arriving at a place.   ADJ CLASSIF: ATTRIB
3 An **incoming** message, report, or phone call is one that you receive.   ADJ CLASSIF: ATTRIB
4 An **incoming** official or government has just been appointed or elected.   ADJ CLASSIF: ATTRIB

incomparable /ɪnˈkɒmpᵊrəbᵊl/. Something that is **incomparable** is very good or great in degree. EG *...a movement of incomparable grace... ...a writer of incomparable prose.* ◊ **incomparably.** EG *The private schoolboy enjoys an incomparably superior education.*   ADJ CLASSIF / Formal / ◊ SUBMOD

incompatible /ɪŋkəmˈpætᵊbᵊl/. Two things that are **incompatible** are unable to exist together because they are completely different. EG *Their styles of life were incompatible... ...his actions are totally incompatible with the group's safety.* ◊ **incompatibility** /ɪŋkəmpætəˈbɪlɪtiˈ/. EG *There is a fundamental incompatibility between the management and the unions.*   ADJ CLASSIF: OFT+*with* / ◊ N UNCOUNT

incompetent /ɪŋˈkɒmpɪtənt/. Someone who is **incompetent** does their job badly or does a particular thing badly. EG *Our secret services and our navy are completely incompetent.* ◊ **incompetence** /ɪŋˈkɒmpɪtəns/. EG *Graffman fired him for incompetence.*   ADJ QUALIT / ◊ N UNCOUNT

incomplete /ɪŋkəmˈpliːt/. Something that is **incomplete 1** does not have all the parts that it should have. EG *...a short and incomplete account of my life.* **2** is not as great in extent, degree, or amount as it could be. EG *...the consequences of incomplete military success.* ◊ **incompletely.** EG *...incompletely cooked meat.*   ADJ QUALIT / ADJ CLASSIF / ◊ ADV

If you were travelling incognito, would you try to be inconspicuous?

incomprehensible /ɪŋˈkɒmprɪhensəˈbəºl/. ADJ CLASSIF Something that is **incomprehensible** is impossible to understand. EG *A great deal of Caine's language was incomprehensible to me.*

incomprehension /ɪŋˈkɒmprɪhenʃəºn/ is the N UNCOUNT state of being unable to understand something. EG *He went on staring in incomprehension.*

inconceivable /ɪŋˈkənsiːvəbəºl/. If you describe ADJ QUALIT something as **inconceivable**, you mean that you cannot believe that it could possibly be true. EG *He found it inconceivable that Belov was insane.*

inconclusive /ɪŋˈkənkluːsɪv/. 1 If a discussion is ADJ QUALIT **inconclusive**, it does not lead to any decision. 2 If evidence, an experiment, or a result is **incon-** ADJ CLASSIF **clusive**, it has not proved anything.

incongruous /ɪŋˈkɒŋgruːəs/. Something that is ADJ QUALIT **incongruous** seems strange because it does not fit in with the rest of the situation. EG *He was an incongruous figure among the tourists.* ◊ **incongruously.** EG *...a fat lady, dressed incon-* ◊ ADV *gruously in black satin.* ◊ **incongruity** ◊ N UNCOUNT /ɪŋˈkɒŋgruːːɪtiˈ/, **incongruities.** EG *We were both* OR N COUNT *conscious of the incongruity of the situation... ...looking for contradictions and incongruities.*

inconsequential /ɪŋˈkɒnsiˈkwenʃəºl/. Something ADJ QUALIT that is **inconsequential** is not very important. EG *...some inconsequential conversation.*

inconsiderable /ɪŋˈkənsɪdəˈrəbəºl/. If you de- ADJ CLASSIF scribe something as not **inconsiderable**, you mean that it is large. EG *The country's not inconsiderable army was mobilized.*

inconsiderate /ɪŋˈkənsɪdəˈrəºt/. People who are ADJ QUALIT **inconsiderate** do not care how their behaviour affects other people.

inconsistent /ɪŋˈkənsɪstənt/. 1 Someone who is ADJ QUALIT **inconsistent** behaves differently in a particular situation each time it happens; used showing disapproval. EG *The blame was laid on an inconsistent government... There's such an inconsistent lot, young people.* ◊ **inconsistency** /ɪŋˈkəˈnsɪstənsiˈ/, ◊ N UNCOUNT **inconsistencies.** EG *His life was full of inconsisten-* OR N COUNT *cies.* 2 If you say things that are **inconsistent**, they ADJ QUALIT contradict each other. EG *Some of your answers are rather inconsistent.* ◊ **inconsistency, inconsist-** ◊ N UNCOUNT **encies.** EG *...the complete inconsistency between* OR N COUNT *the two views expressed by John.* 3 Something that is **inconsistent** with a particular ADJ PRED set of ideas, beliefs, or values is not in accordance + with with them. EG *...a monarch whose behaviour they judged to be inconsistent with Hindu religious values.*

inconspicuous /ɪŋˈkənspɪkjuːəs/. Something that ADJ QUALIT is **inconspicuous** is not at all noticeable. EG *I have asked the children to make themselves as inconspicuous as possible.* ◊ **inconspicuously.** EG *He* ◊ ADV *slipped into the nearest bar as inconspicuously as he could.*

incontinent /ɪŋˈkɒntɪnənt/. Someone who is **in-** ADJ CLASSIF **continent** is unable to control their bladder or bowels. ◊ **incontinence** /ɪŋˈkɒntɪnəns/. EG *Incon-* ◊ N UNCOUNT *tinence can become a real problem in old age.*

incontrovertible /ɪŋˈkɒntrəvɜːtəˈbəºl/. **Incon-** ADJ CLASSIF **trovertible** evidence or proof shows that some- Formal thing is definitely true. EG *His picture collection was incontrovertible evidence of his wealth.*

inconvenience /ɪŋˈkənviːnjəns, -viːnjəns/, **incon-** N UNCOUNT **veniences, inconveniencing, inconvenienced.** 1 OR N COUNT If someone or something causes **inconvenience**, they cause problems or difficulties. EG *I'm very sorry to have caused so much inconvenience... You have to put up with these inconveniences as best you can.* 2 If you **inconvenience** someone, you cause prob- V+O lems or difficulties for them. EG *All the residents have been inconvenienced by the road works.*

inconvenient /ɪŋˈkənviːnjənt, -viːnjənt/. Some- ADJ QUALIT thing that is **inconvenient** causes problems or difficulties for you. EG *You live quite a long way out.*

Don't you find it a bit inconvenient?... I seem to have come at an inconvenient time.

incorporate /ɪŋˈkɔːpəreɪt/, **incorporates, incor-** **porating, incorporated.** 1 If something is **incor-** V+O+into/in **porated** into another thing, it becomes a part of that thing. EG *They were incorporated into the Zulu Empire... ...legislation compelling manufacturers to incorporate safety features in all new cars.* ◊ **incorporation** /ɪŋˈkɔːpəreɪʃəºn/. EG *...the incor-* ◊ N UNCOUNT *poration of Austria into the German Empire.* 2 If something **incorporates** another thing, it V+O includes that thing as one of its parts. EG *These houses usually incorporated a long gallery.*

incorrect /ɪŋˈkərekt/. Something that is **incor-** ADJ CLASSIF **rect** is wrong or untrue. EG *Sonny dismissed the information as incorrect... ...spelling mistakes and incorrect English.* ◊ **incorrectly.** EG *The problem* ◊ ADV *has been incorrectly defined.*

incorrigible /ɪŋˈkɒrɪdʒəˈbəºl/. Someone who is ADJ CLASSIF **incorrigible** has faults or bad habits that will never change. EG *...incorrigible criminals... 'Oh, James, you are incorrigible!' she said.*

incorruptible /ɪŋˈkərʌptəˈbəºl/. Someone who is ADJ CLASSIF **incorruptible** cannot be bribed or persuaded to do things that they should not do. EG *They were both wise and incorruptible men.*

increase, increases, increasing, increased; pronounced /ɪŋˈkriːs/ when it is a noun and /ɪŋˈkriːs/ when it is a verb. 1 If something **increases** or if you **increase** it, it V-ERG becomes larger in amount. EG *Crime has increased by three per cent in the past year... ...men seeking to increase their knowledge.* ◊ **increased.** EG ◊ ADJ CLASSIF *...increased productivity.* ◊ **increasing.** EG *Japa-* ◊ ADJ CLASSIF *nese industry is making increasing use of robots.* 2 An **increase** is a rise in the number, level, or N COUNT amount of something. EG *At the meeting they demanded a sharp increase in wages.* 3 If something is **on the increase**, it is becoming PHRASE more frequent. EG *Crime is on the increase.*

increasingly /ɪŋˈkriːsɪŋliˈ/. You use **increasing-** SUBMOD OR ADV **ly** to indicate that a situation or quality is becoming greater in intensity or more common. EG *It was becoming increasingly difficult to find jobs... The cases he dealt with increasingly repelled him... Men increasingly find that they need more training.*

incredible /ɪŋˈkredəˈbəºl/. 1 Something that is **incredible** is 1.1 amazing or very unusual. EG *They* ADJ CLASSIF *were wearing incredible uniforms... It was an incredible experience.* ◊ **incredibly.** EG *Upstairs,* ◊ ADV SEN *incredibly, the beds were already made.* 1.2 very ADJ CLASSIF great in amount or degree. EG *They get an incredible amount of money.* ◊ **incredibly.** EG *The water* ◊ SUBMOD *was incredibly hot... I'm in an incredibly privileged position.* 2 You can use **incredible** to say that you think that ADJ CLASSIF something cannot possibly be true. EG *You've no basis for this incredible suggestion.*

incredulous /ɪŋˈkredjəˈləs/. If someone is **in-** ADJ QUALIT **credulous**, they are unable to believe what they have just heard because it is very surprising or shocking. EG *'You left her all alone?' He sounded incredulous.* ◊ **incredulously.** EG *I stared at him* ◊ ADV *incredulously.* ◊ **incredulity** /ɪŋˈkrɪˈdjuːlɪtiˈ/. EG *I* ◊ N UNCOUNT *read the document with incredulity.*

increment /ɪŋˈkrəməºnt/, **increments.** An **in-** N COUNT **crement** is an addition to something, especially a regular addition to someone's salary.

incriminate /ɪŋˈkrɪmɪneɪt/, **incriminates, in-** V+O **criminating, incriminated.** If something **in-** **criminates** you, it provides evidence that you are the person responsible for a crime. EG *They raided his laboratory to seize any papers that might incriminate them.* ◊ **incriminating.** EG *They* ◊ ADJ QUALIT *began a search for incriminating evidence.*

incubate /ɪŋˈkjəˈbeɪt/, **incubates, incubating,** **incubated.** 1 When a bird **incubates** its eggs or V-ERG Technical when they **incubate**, it keeps them warm until they hatch.

2 The time that an infection or virus takes to **incubate** is the time that it takes to affect people and make them ill. *v Technical*

incubator /ɪŋˈkjəˈbeɪtə/, **incubators**. An **incubator** is a piece of hospital equipment in which an ill or very weak baby is kept for a time after it is born. *N COUNT*

inculcate /ɪŋˈkʌlkeɪt, ɪŋˈkʌlkeɪt/, **inculcates**, **inculcating**, **inculcated**. If you **inculcate** an idea or an opinion in someone, you teach it to them so that it becomes fixed in their mind. *EG We want to inculcate the values of marriage and family life into our children.* *v+o: USU+in/into Formal*

incumbent /ɪŋˈkʌmbənt/, **incumbents**. **1** If it is **incumbent** on you to do something, it is your duty or responsibility to do it. *EG It was incumbent on editors to exercise discretion.* *ADJ PRED Formal*

2 An **incumbent** is the person who is holding a particular post. *EG ...the new incumbent.* *N COUNT Formal*

incur /ɪŋˈkɜː/, **incurs**, **incurring**, **incurred**. If you **incur** something unpleasant, it happens because of something you do. *EG ...the risk of incurring her displeasure... ...business expenses incurred outside the office.* *v+o Formal*

incurable /ɪŋˈkjʊərəbəˌl/. **1** If someone has an **incurable** disease, they cannot be cured of it. *EG ...incurable cancer.* *ADJ CLASSIF*

2 You can use **incurable** to describe people who will never change their attitudes or habits. *EG ...incurable optimists.* ◊ **incurably**. *EG ...the incurably servile housekeeper.* *ADJ CLASSIF: ATTRIB ◊ ADV+ADJ*

incursion /ɪŋˈkɜːʃˈn/, **incursion**. An **incursion** is a small military invasion into another country. *EG ...their incursion into Yugoslavia.* *N COUNT+SUPP*

indebted /ɪndetˈd/. If you are **indebted** to someone, **1** you are grateful to them for something. *EG I am indebted to Bob Waller for many of the ideas expressed here.* ◊ **indebtedness**. *EG I readily acknowledge my indebtedness to my friends.* **2** you owe them money. *EG His company became indebted to the bank.* ◊ **indebtedness**. *EG Home ownership involves higher indebtedness than renting.* *ADJ PRED+to ◊ N UNCOUNT ADJ PRED American ◊ N UNCOUNT*

indecency /ɪndiːsˈnsiˈ/. The **indecency** of something or someone is the fact that they are morally or sexually offensive. *N UNCOUNT*

indecent /ɪndiːsənt/. Something that is **indecent 1** is shocking because it relates to naked people or sexual acts. *EG ...indecent jokes.* **2** breaks rules of good behaviour or morality. *EG The rush to become a White House correspondent was indecent.* *ADJ QUALIT ADJ QUALIT*

indecipherable /ɪndɪsaɪfəˈrəbəˌl/. **1** If writing is **indecipherable**, you cannot read it. *ADJ QUALIT Formal*

2 If the expression on a person's face or a gesture is **indecipherable**, you cannot understand it. *EG An indecipherable glance passed between them.* *ADJ QUALIT Formal*

indecision /ɪndɪsɪʒˈn/ is uncertainty about what you should do. *EG She felt ill with anxiety and indecision.* *N UNCOUNT*

indecisive /ɪndɪsaɪsɪv/. If you are **indecisive**, you do not find it easy to make decisions. *EG There was nothing dithering or indecisive about them.* *ADJ QUALIT*

indeed /ɪndiːd/. **1** You use **indeed 1.1** to confirm or agree with something that has just been said. *EG 'I think you knew him.' – 'I did indeed.' 1.2* to add a comment or statement which strengthens the point you have already made. *EG This act has failed to bring women's earnings up to the same level. Indeed the gulf is widening.* *ADV SEN*

2 You also use **indeed** at the end of a clause to give extra force to the word 'very', or to emphasize a particular word. *EG We have very little information indeed... Thank you very much indeed... The possibility of rescue now seemed remote indeed.*

3 You can also use **indeed** to express anger, indignation, or scorn about something. *EG 'She wants to go too.' – 'Does she indeed!'* *EXCLAM Spoken*

indefatigable /ɪndiˈfætɪgəbəˌl/. You use **indefatigable** to describe people who do something a lot and never get tired of doing it. *EG All through her life she was an indefatigable traveller.* *ADJ CLASSIF Formal*

indefensible /ɪndiˈfensəbəˌl/. Statements, actions, or ideas that are **indefensible** cannot be justified because they are completely wrong or unacceptable. *EG He denounced the judge's savage attack as totally indefensible.* *ADJ QUALIT Formal*

indefinable /ɪndiˈfaɪnəbəˌl/. A quality or feeling that is **indefinable** cannot easily be described. *EG ...the indefinable quality of leadership.* ◊ **indefinably**. *EG Terry had somehow indefinably altered.* *ADJ CLASSIF ◊ ADV*

indefinite /ɪndefɪnɪt/. **1** If something is **indefinite**, people have not decided when it will end. *EG I was going to have to leave for an indefinite period... Members of the union began an indefinite strike this morning.* *ADJ CLASSIF*

2 Actions, events, or situations that are **indefinite** are not exact or clear. *EG Milner advised him not to answer so indefinite a proposal.* *ADJ QUALIT*

indefinite article, **indefinite articles**. The **indefinite article** is a term used in grammar for the words 'a' and 'an'. In this dictionary 'a' and 'an' are described as DET. See the entry headed DETERMINERS for more information. *N COUNT: USU the+N*

indefinitely /ɪndefɪnɪtliˈ/. If something will continue **indefinitely**, it will continue until there is a reason for it to change or end. *EG The Regency Hotel was closed indefinitely.* *ADV*

indelible /ɪndelɪbəˌl/. **1** If a mark or stain is **indelible**, it cannot be removed or washed out. *EG His fingertips had turned an indelible black.* *ADJ CLASSIF*

2 **Indelible** pens and pencils make marks that cannot be removed or washed out. *ADJ CLASSIF*

3 Memories, impressions, or details that are **indelible** will never be forgotten. *EG ...all the indelible memories of childhood.* ◊ **indelibly**. *EG The number was indelibly printed on her brain.* *ADJ CLASSIF ◊ ADV*

indelicate /ɪndelɪkɪt/. Behaviour that is **indelicate** is rude or offensive. *EG Simon was hungry, but felt it would be indelicate to make too much fuss about it.* *ADJ QUALIT Formal*

indentation /ɪndenteɪʃˈn/, **indentations**. An **indentation** is a dent or groove in the surface or edge of something. *EG The high heels of her boots made little indentations in the carpet.* *N COUNT*

independence /ɪndɪpendəns/. **1** If a country has **independence**, it is not ruled by any other country. *EG The country has had 24 years of independence.* *N UNCOUNT*

2 If you refer to someone's **independence**, you are referring to the fact that they are independent. *EG She shows great independence of mind.* *N UNCOUNT*

independent /ɪndɪpendənt/. **1** Something that is **independent** exists, happens, or acts separately from other people, groups, or things. *EG Two independent studies came to the same conclusions... ...20 clinics which are independent of the National Health Service.* ◊ **independently**. *EG Agriculture developed independently in many different parts of the globe... This decision was taken quite independently of any other organization.* *ADJ CLASSIF: OFT+of ◊ ADV*

2 If you are **independent**, **2.1** you form your own opinions and arrange your own life, rather than relying on other people or copying them. *EG They wanted to encourage independent thought. 2.2* you can support yourself financially. *EG I became financially independent.* *ADJ QUALIT*

3 An **independent** school, broadcasting company, or other organization does not receive money from the government. *ADJ CLASSIF*

4 **Independent** countries and states are not ruled *ADJ CLASSIF* by other countries and have their own government.

5 An **independent** inquiry or opinion is held by people who are not involved in a situation and so are able to make a fair judgement. EG *He backs the need for an independent inquiry into charity law.* ADJ CLASSIF: ATTRIB

indescribable /ɪndɪˈskraɪbəbəˀl/. Something that is **indescribable** is too intense or extreme to be described properly. EG *...the indescribable sadness of those final pages... The smell was indescribable.* ADJ CLASSIF
◊ **indescribably**. EG *The air was getting indescribably foul... ...an indescribably sad cry.* ◊ SUBMOD

indestructible /ɪndɪˈstrʌktəbəˀl/. Something that is **indestructible** cannot be destroyed. EG *Our friendship is indestructible.* ADJ CLASSIF

indeterminate /ɪndɪˈtɜːmɪnət/. If something is **indeterminate**, you are not able to say exactly what it is. EG *...a figure of indeterminate sex, encased in a quilted body suit.* ADJ QUALIT

index /ˈɪndɛks/, **indexes, indexing, indexed; indices** /ˈɪndɪsiːz/. The plural form of the noun is usually **indexes** for paragraph 1 and **indices** for paragraph 2.
1 An **index** is **1.1** an alphabetical list that is sometimes printed at the back of a book to tell you where to find information about particular things or people in the book. **1.2** a collection of cards with information on them, arranged in alphabetical order. N COUNT
2 An **index** is also a system by which changes in the value of something can be compared or measured. EG *...a 0.3 per cent rise in the wholesale prices index.* N COUNT
3 If you **index** a book or collection of information, you provide an index for it. V+O

index finger, index fingers. Your **index finger** is the finger that is next to your thumb. N COUNT

indicate /ˈɪndɪkeɪt/, **indicates, indicating, indicated.** **1** If something **indicates** that something is true, it gives you information which makes you decide that it is true. EG *These studies indicate that it's best to change your car every two years... This absurd action indicated the level of their intelligence.* V+REPORT OR V+O
2 If you **indicate** something to someone, you show them where it is, especially by pointing to it. EG *She sat down in the armchair that Mrs Jones indicated.* V+O
3 If you **indicate** a particular fact, you mention it in a brief, often general, way. EG *As I have already indicated, there is now more competition for jobs than there used to be... I indicated that I had not seen enough of his work to be able to judge it.* V+O OR V+REPORT
4 If something **indicates** something else, it is a sign of that thing. EG *An erect tail on a cat indicates aggression... The lights above the lift doors indicated that the lift was ascending.* V+O OR V+REPORT
5 When someone who is driving a car **indicates**, they show which way they are going to turn by making lights on the car flash or by signalling with their hand. V+O OR V+REPORT

indication /ɪndɪˈkeɪʃəˀn/, **indications.** An **indication** is a sign which gives you an idea of what someone feels, what is happening, or what is likely to happen. EG *The President gave a clear indication yesterday of his willingness to meet the visitors... All the indications are that both sides will soon reach an agreement... There was no indication that he ever noticed my absence.* N COUNT OR N UNCOUNT

indicative /ɪnˈdɪkətɪv/. **1** If something is **indicative** of something else, it is a sign of that thing. EG *He regarded their action as indicative of their lack of courage.* ADJ PRED+of
2 If a verb is in the **indicative**, it is in the form used for making statements. N SING: the+N

indicator /ˈɪndɪkeɪtə/, **indicators.** **1** An **indicator** is something which tells you what something is like, what is happening, or what is likely to happen. EG *Price is not always an indicator of quality.* N COUNT Formal
2 A car's **indicators** are the lights at the front and N COUNT

back which are used to show when it is turning left or right. See picture at CAR.

indices /ˈɪndɪsiːz/ is a plural of **index**.

indict /ɪnˈdaɪt/, **indicts, indicting, indicted.** When someone **is indicted** for a crime, they are officially charged with it. EG *The General was indicted for treason.* V+O: USU PASS Formal

indictment /ɪnˈdaɪtmənt/, **indictments.** **1** If you say that something is an **indictment** of something else, you mean that it shows how bad that thing is. EG *It is a striking indictment of our educational system that so many children cannot read or write.* N COUNT+SUPP
2 An **indictment** is an official charge of a crime made against a person. EG *Robbins is under indictment for fraud.* N COUNT OR N UNCOUNT Formal

indifferent /ɪnˈdɪfərənt/. **1** If you are **indifferent** to something, you have no interest in it. EG *Children fail to progress if their parents seem indifferent to their success.* ADJ QUALIT: OFT+to
◊ **indifferently**. EG *Mark smiled at me briefly, indifferently, and hurried away.* ◊ ADV
◊ **indifference** /ɪnˈdɪfərəns/. EG *...Aitken's indifference to criticism.* ◊ N UNCOUNT
2 If you describe things or people as **indifferent**, you mean that they are not of a very good standard. EG *He was a gifted painter but an indifferent actor.* ADJ QUALIT

indigenous /ɪnˈdɪdʒɪnəs/. Something that is **indigenous** is originally from the country in which it is found, rather than having come there from another country. EG *...the indigenous population... The elephant is indigenous to India.* ADJ CLASSIF Formal

indigestible /ɪndɪˈdʒɛstəbəˀl/. Food that is **indigestible** cannot be digested easily. ADJ QUALIT

indigestion /ɪndɪˈdʒɛstʃəˀn/ is pain that you get in your abdomen when you find it difficult to digest food. EG *Food that is too fatty may cause indigestion.* N UNCOUNT

indignant /ɪnˈdɪgnənt/. If you are **indignant**, you are shocked and angry. EG *Many taxpayers are indignant at what they regard as an illegal use of public funds.* ◊ **indignantly**. EG *'Why not?' cried Judy indignantly.* ADJ QUALIT ◊ ADV

indignation /ɪndɪgˈneɪʃəˀn/ is the feeling of shock and anger which you have when you think that what someone has done is unjust or unfair. EG *She seethed with indignation.* N UNCOUNT

indignity /ɪnˈdɪgnɪtiˀ/, **indignities.** An **indignity** is something that makes you feel embarrassed or humiliated. EG *He hated the rules and the petty indignities of prison life... ...the indignity of slavery.* N COUNT OR N UNCOUNT

indigo /ˈɪndɪgəʊ/. Something that is **indigo** is a dark purplish-blue in colour. EG *...an indigo sky.* ADJ COLOUR

indirect /ɪndaɪˈrɛkt/. **1** Something that is **indirect** is not done or caused directly, but by means of something or someone else. EG *A sudden increase in oil prices would have serious indirect effects.* ◊ **indirectly**. EG *I suppose I was indirectly responsible for the whole thing.* ADJ CLASSIF ◊ ADV
2 An **indirect** route or journey does not use the shortest way between two places. ADJ CLASSIF
3 An **indirect** answer or reference does not directly mention the thing that is actually being talked about. ADJ QUALIT

indirect object. See object.

indiscreet /ɪndɪˈskriːt/. If you are **indiscreet**, you talk about or do things openly when you should have kept them secret. EG *...an indiscreet comment.* ADJ QUALIT

indiscretion /ɪndɪˈskrɛʃəˀn/, **indiscretions.** **Indiscretion** is behaviour that is unacceptable by being incautious, tactless, or by revealing secrets. EG *How could she commit such an indiscretion?* N UNCOUNT OR N COUNT

indiscriminate /ɪndɪˈskrɪmɪnɪˀt/. An **indiscriminate** action does not involve any careful thought or choice. EG *...indiscriminate slaughter... Television watchers tend to be indiscriminate in their viewing habits.* ◊ **indiscriminately**. EG *He reads widely and indiscriminately.* ADJ QUALIT ◊ ADV

indispensable /ɪndɪˈspɛnsəbəˀl/. If something is **indispensable**, it is absolutely essential. EG *In my* ADJ CLASSIF: OFT+to *job, a telephone is indispensable... Energy is indispensable to modern industrial societies.*

indisputable /ˌɪndɪspjuːtəbəl/. If a fact is **indisputable**, it is obviously and definitely true. EG *We're going to have a very hard time. That's indisputable... This is a work of indisputable genius.* ◊ **indisputably.** EG *The book is indisputably a masterpiece.* ◊ ADV — ADJ CLASSIF

indissoluble /ˌɪndɪsɒljəbəl/. A relationship or link that is **indissoluble** can never be ended. EG *...the indissoluble ties of mother to child.* — ADJ CLASSIF / Formal

indistinct /ˌɪndɪstɪŋkt/. Something that is **indistinct** is unclear and difficult to see or hear. EG *His words were faint and often indistinct... ...an indistinct footpath.* ◊ **indistinctly.** EG *I mumbled indistinctly through a mouthful of food.* ◊ ADV — ADJ QUALIT

indistinguishable /ˌɪndɪstɪŋwɪʃəbəl/. If two things are **indistinguishable**, they are so similar that it is impossible to tell them apart. EG *Some synthetic meat is indistinguishable from the natural product in taste.* — ADJ CLASSIF: OPT+*from*

individual /ˌɪndɪvɪdjuəl/, **individuals**. 1 **Individual** means relating to one particular person or to each person separately, rather than to a large group. EG *...the preservation of individual liberty... ...individual tuition... We can identify each individual whale by its song.* ◊ **individually.** EG *The children can work individually or in small groups... Each fruit should be wrapped individually in paper.* 2 An **individual** is a person. EG *...the freedom of the individual... Fourier seems to be a somewhat eccentric individual.* — ADJ CLASSIF: ATTRIB / ◊ ADV / N COUNT

individualist /ˌɪndɪvɪdjəlɪst/, **individualists**. If you are an **individualist**, you like to do things in your own way. EG *Academics are such individualists.* — N COUNT

individualistic /ˌɪndɪvɪdjəlɪstɪk/. If you are **individualistic**, you like to do things in your own way. EG *Lions are highly individualistic animals.* — ADJ CLASSIF

individuality /ˌɪndɪvɪdjuælɪtɪ/. If something has **individuality**, it is different from all other things and is therefore more noticeable and interesting. EG *The advertisement lacks any individuality.* — N UNCOUNT

indivisible /ˌɪndɪvɪzɪbəl/. If something is **indivisible**, it cannot be divided into different parts. EG *...the ancient Greek belief that the atom is indivisible.* — ADJ CLASSIF

indoctrinate /ˌɪndɒktrɪneɪt/, **indoctrinates**, **indoctrinating**, **indoctrinated**. If you **indoctrinate** someone, you teach them a particular belief with the aim that they will only accept that belief and will not accept any other; used showing disapproval. ◊ **indoctrination** /ˌɪndɒktrɪneɪʃən/. EG *It is difficult to overcome the early indoctrination of children.* — v+o / ◊ N UNCOUNT

indolent /ˈɪndələnt/. Someone who is **indolent** is lazy. EG *...an indolent girl with a moody mouth... ...an indolent smile.* ◊ **indolence** /ˈɪndələns/. EG *...the indolence of his movements.* — ADJ QUALIT / Formal / ◊ N UNCOUNT

indomitable /ɪndɒmɪtəbəl/. Someone who is **indomitable** never admits that they have been defeated. EG *The boy had been kept alive by his indomitable spirit.* — ADJ QUALIT / Formal

indoor /ˈɪndɔː/. You use **indoor** to describe things which are situated or happen inside a building rather than outside. EG *...indoor games such as table tennis. ...indoor swimming pools.* — ADJ CLASSIF: ATTRIB

indoors /ˌɪndɔːz/. If something happens **indoors**, it happens inside a building. EG *The concert is held indoors when it rains... We'd better go indoors.* — ADV AFTER VB

indubitable /ɪndjuːbɪtəbəl/. Something that is **indubitable** is definite and cannot be doubted. ◊ **indubitably.** EG *There was Thomas, dirty and muddy but indubitably alive.* — ADJ CLASSIF / Formal / ◊ ADV

induce /ɪndjuːs/, **induces**, **inducing**, **induced**. 1 To **induce** a particular state or condition means to cause it. EG *...pills guaranteed to induce sleep... Failure induces a total sense of inferiority.* 2 To **induce** someone to do something means to — v+o / v+o+*to*-INF

persuade or influence them to do it. EG *What on earth had induced her to marry a man like that?*

inducement /ɪndjuːsmənt/, **inducements**. An **inducement** is something that is offered to someone in order to persuade them to do something. EG *These tax advantages provide the main inducement to become a home-owner.* — N COUNT

indulge /ɪndʌldʒ/, **indulges**, **indulging**, **indulged**. 1 If you **indulge** in something or **indulge** a hobby or interest, for example, you allow yourself to have or do something that you enjoy. EG *Let us indulge in a little daydreaming... Jack had spent the previous three weeks indulging his passion for climbing... He indulged himself by smoking another cigarette.* 2 If you **indulge** someone or their wishes, you let them have or do whatever they want. EG *He was usually prepared to indulge his sister if it did not mean a great deal of trouble.* — v+*in*, v+o, OR v-REFL / v+o

indulgence /ɪndʌldʒəns/, **indulgences**. 1 An **indulgence** is something that you allow yourself to do or have because it gives you pleasure. EG *Smoking was his one indulgence.* 2 **Indulgence** is the act of indulging yourself or another person. EG *Simon listened to her with indulgence.* — N COUNT / N UNCOUNT

indulgent /ɪndʌldʒənt/. If you are **indulgent**, you treat a person with special kindness. EG *He was an indulgent father, ever ready to provide new clothes.* ◊ **indulgently.** EG *He smiled indulgently at her.* — ADJ QUALIT / ◊ ADV

industrial /ɪndʌstrɪəl/. 1 You use **industrial** to describe things which relate to industry or are used in it. EG *...industrial robots... ...industrial and technical change.* 2 An **industrial** city or country is one in which industry is important or highly developed. — ADJ CLASSIF: ATTRIB / ADJ CLASSIF: USU ATTRIB

industrial action. When a group of workers take **industrial action**, they go on strike or take other action as a way of protesting about their pay or working conditions. — N UNCOUNT

industrial estate, **industrial estates**. An **industrial estate** is an area which has been specially planned for a lot of factories. — N COUNT

industrialise /ɪndʌstrɪəlaɪz/. See **industrialize**.

industrialism /ɪndʌstrɪəlɪzəm/ is the state of having an economy based on industry. EG *...as men were enslaved by developing industrialism.* — N UNCOUNT

industrialist /ɪndʌstrɪəlɪst/, **industrialists**. An **industrialist** is a person who owns or controls large amounts of money or property in industry. — N COUNT

industrialize /ɪndʌstrɪəlaɪz/, **industrializes**, **industrializing**, **industrialized**; also spelled **industrialise**. When a country **industrializes** or when it **is industrialized**, it develops a lot of industries. ◊ **industrialized.** EG *...the industrialized world... ...those societies which became industrialized during the last century.* ◊ **industrialization** /ɪndʌstrɪəlaɪzeɪʃən/. EG *...the rising cost of industrialization.* — v-ERG / ◊ ADJ CLASSIF: ATTRIB / ◊ N UNCOUNT

industrial relations. When you refer to **industrial relations**, you are referring to the relationship between employers, workers, and trade unions in industry. EG *...the future of industrial relations in Britain.* — N PLURAL

industrious /ɪndʌstrɪəs/. Someone who is **industrious** works very hard. EG *...an industrious student.* — ADJ QUALIT

industry /ˈɪndəstrɪ/, **industries**. 1 **Industry** is the work and processes involved in manufacturing things in factories. EG *Japanese industry is making increasing use of robots.* 2 An **industry** consists of all the people and the processes that are involved in manufacturing or producing a particular thing. EG *...the oil industry.* — N UNCOUNT / N COUNT

Is everyone in an industry industrious?

3 Industry is also the quality of working very N UNCOUNT hard. EG ...*the old virtues of self-reliance, industry,* Formal *and frugality.*

inedible /ɪnˈɛdɪbəl/. Something that is **inedible** is ADJ CLASSIF too nasty or poisonous to eat.

ineffective /ɪnɪˈfɛktɪv/. Something that is **inef-** ADJ QUALIT **fective** has no effect. EG *The therapy was obviously ineffective.* ◇ **ineffectiveness.** EG *He was disgust-* ◇ N UNCOUNT *ed by the ineffectiveness of the government.*

ineffectual /ɪnɪˈfɛktʃuəl/. Something that is **inef-** ADJ QUALIT **fectual** fails to do what it is supposed to do. EG *...ineffectual policies.* ◇ **ineffectually.** EG *...trying* ◇ ADV *ineffectually to brush the mud off his jacket.*

inefficient /ɪnɪˈfɪʃənt/. **1** A person, organization, ADJ QUALIT or system that is **inefficient** achieves results slowly and not in the most economical way. EG *...inefficient farming.* ◇ **inefficiently.** EG *She* ◇ ADV *works slowly and inefficiently.* ◇ **inefficiency** ◇ N UNCOUNT /ɪnɪˈfɪʃənsi/. EG *He criticised the inefficiency of public authorities.*
2 An **inefficient** machine or piece of equipment ADJ QUALIT does not work effectively and wastes energy.

inelegant /ɪnˈɛlɪgənt/. Something that is **inel-** ADJ QUALIT **egant** is not attractive or graceful. EG *Glass chandeliers have been replaced by inelegant plastic ones... ...his inelegant dressing gown.*

ineligible /ɪnˈɛlɪdʒəbəl/. If you are **ineligible** for ADJ CLASSIF : something, you are not qualified for it or entitled to OFT+*for* it. EG *I am ineligible for unemployment benefit.* Formal

inept /ɪˈnɛpt/. Someone who is **inept** does some- ADJ QUALIT thing with a complete lack of skill. EG *...the government's inept handling of the crisis.*

ineptitude /ɪˈnɛptɪtjuːd/ is a complete lack of skill. N UNCOUNT EG *...his record of political ineptitude.* Formal

inequality /ɪnɪˈkwɒlɪti/, **inequalities. 1 In-** N UNCOUNT **equality** is a difference in social status, wealth, or OR N COUNT opportunity between groups in a society. EG *...but inequality is the great problem here... We found great inequalities of opportunity.*
2 An **inequality** is also a difference in the size or N COUNT OR amount of two or more things. N UNCOUNT

ineradicable /ɪnɪˈrædɪkəbəl/. Something that is ADJ CLASSIF **ineradicable** cannot be removed. EG *...an ineradi-* Formal *cable tendency to be frivolous.*

inert /ɪˈnɜːt/. Someone or something that is **inert** ADJ CLASSIF does not move at all and appears to be lifeless. EG *I carried her, still inert, up the stairs to her room.*

inertia /ɪˈnɜːʃə/. If you have a feeling of **inertia** N UNCOUNT you feel very lazy and unwilling to do anything. EG *Though I wanted to go, I stayed from sheer inertia.*

inescapable /ɪnɪˈskeɪpəbəl/. If something, espe- ADJ CLASSIF cially a fact, is **inescapable**, it cannot be avoided. EG *...an inescapable conclusion.*

inestimable /ɪnˈɛstɪməbəl/. Something that is ADJ CLASSIF **inestimable** is extremely great or good. EG *Maria's* Formal *advice proved of inestimable value.*

inevitable /ɪnˈɛvɪtəbəl/. **1** If something is **inevi-** ADJ CLASSIF **table**, it is certain to happen and cannot be prevented or avoided. EG *If this policy continues, then violence is inevitable... It's inevitable that you should feel indignant.* ◇ **inevitability** ◇ N UNCOUNT /ɪnˌɛvɪtəˈbɪlɪti/. EG *You must recognize the inevitability of change.*
2 The **inevitable** is something that is certain to N SING : *the*+N happen and cannot be prevented or avoided. EG *I suddenly became fatalistic, resigning myself to the inevitable.*
3 You can also use **inevitable** humorously to ADJ CLASSIF : describe something that happens so regularly that ATTRIB you are able to predict it. EG *We went inside for the inevitable cup of tea.*

inevitably /ɪnˈɛvɪtəbli/. If something **inevitably** ADV OR happens or will happen, it is the only possible ADV SEN result. EG *Inevitably, a shouting match ensued between us... A household of this size inevitably has problems.*

inexcusable /ɪnɪkˈskjuːzəbəl/. Something that is ADJ QUALIT **inexcusable** is too bad to be justified or tolerated.

EG *The local paper declared such waste inexcusable.*

inexhaustible /ɪnɪgˈzɔːstəbəl/. If something is ADJ CLASSIF **inexhaustible**, there is so much of it that it cannot be used up. EG *The sun is an inexhaustible source of energy... His patience must be inexhaustible.*

inexorable /ɪnˈɛksərəbəl/. Something that is **in-** ADJ CLASSIF **exorable** cannot be prevented from continuing. EG Formal *...the inexorable rise in the cost of living.*
◇ **inexorably.** EG *These facts led inexorably to one* ◇ ADV *conclusion.*

inexpensive /ɪnɪkˈspɛnsɪv/. Something that is ADJ QUALIT **inexpensive** does not cost much. EG *...an inexpensive wine.*

inexperience /ɪnɪkˈspɪəriəns/. If you refer to N UNCOUNT someone's **inexperience**, you are referring to the fact that they are inexperienced. EG *You're bound to make a few mistakes through inexperience.*

inexperienced /ɪnɪkˈspɪəriənst/. If you are **inex-** ADJ QUALIT **perienced**, you have little or no experience of a particular situation or activity. EG *...an inexperienced swimmer.*

inexplicable /ɪnɪkˈsplɪkəbəl/. If something is **in-** ADJ QUALIT **explicable**, you cannot explain why it happened or why it is true. EG *I still find this incident inexplicable.* ◇ **inexplicably.** EG *Anita had inexplicably* ◇ ADV *disappeared.*

inextricably /ɪnɪkˈstrɪkəbli/. If two or more ADV things are **inextricably** linked, they cannot be separated. EG *Social and economic factors are inextricably linked.*

INF stands for **infinitive**
Verbs in English have two infinitive forms. One is the simple form of the verb, for example 'understand'. And the other is the simple form with 'to', for example 'to understand'.
When **+INF** is used in the Extra Column, it means that the word is followed by a verb in the infinitive without 'to'. So the label for **make 8** says V+O+INF. This means that this meaning of 'make' is followed by the infinitive, as in *They made me **feel** guilty* and *I couldn't make her **change** her mind.*
When **+***to*-INF is used in the Extra Column, it means that the word is followed by a verb in the infinitive with 'to'. So the label for **got 3** says V+*to*-INF. This means that this meaning of 'got' is usually followed by the infinitive with 'to', as in *We've got **to go** now* and *They'd got **to catch** a bus at 6.*
And the label for **glad 3** says ADJ PRED+*to*-INF. This means that this meaning of 'glad' is usually followed by the infinitive with 'to', as in *I'd be glad **to help*** and *She was glad **to see** us.*

---

infallible /ɪnˈfælɪbəl/. Someone or something that ADJ CLASSIF is **infallible** is never wrong. EG *Doctors aren't infallible... ...an infallible cure for rheumatism.*

infamous /ˈɪnfəməs/. **Infamous** people or things ADJ CLASSIF are well-known because they are evil or connected with something evil. EG *How well I remember that infamous night.*

infancy /ˈɪnfənsi/. **1** Your **infancy** is the period in N UNCOUNT your life when you are a very young child. EG *The child died in infancy... He came to England in his infancy.*
2 If something is **in** its **infancy**, it has only just PHRASE started. EG *This research is only in its infancy.*

infant /ˈɪnfənt/, **infants.** An **infant** is a very young N COUNT child or baby. EG *...a newborn infant.* Formal

infantile /ˈɪnfəntaɪl/. **1** You use **infantile** to de- ADJ QUALIT scribe behaviour or disease which very young Formal children have. EG *...infantile paralysis.*
2 Someone who is **infantile** behaves in a foolish ADJ QUALIT and childish way. EG *You're so horribly infantile!*

infantry /ˈɪnfəntri¹/. The **infantry** are the soldiers N COLL
in an army who fight on foot rather than in tanks
or on horses.

infant school, infant schools. An **infant school** N COUNT
is a school for children between the ages of five British
and seven.

infatuated /ɪnˈfætjʊeɪti³d/. If you are **infatuated** ADJ PRED :
with someone, you have a strong feeling of love or USU + with
passion for them that other people think is ridiculous. EG He was for several years infatuated with
her.

infatuation /ɪnfætjʊˈeɪʃə⁰n/. An **infatuation** for N SING
someone is a strong feeling of love or passion for
them that other people think is ridiculous. EG This is
not love but a foolish infatuation.

infect /ɪnˈfɛkt/, **infects, infecting, infected.** 1 To V+O :
infect people, animals, plants, or food means to OFT+with
cause them to suffer from germs or to carry
germs. EG Imported birds can infect their owners
with an unpleasant illness. ◇ **infected.** EG ...infect- ◇ ADJ CLASSIF
ed milk... ...a man limping on a badly infected leg.
2 When a feeling or influence **infects** people, V+O
places, or things, it spreads to them. EG Pessimism
had a way of infecting everyone.

infection /ɪnˈfɛkʃə⁰n/, **infections.** 1 An **infection** N COUNT OR
is a disease caused by germs. EG I had an ear N UNCOUNT
infection... ...chest infections... Radiation lessened
bodily resistance to infection.
2 **Infection** is the state of becoming infected. EG N UNCOUNT
There is little risk of infection.

infectious /ɪnˈfɛkʃəs/. 1 If you have an **infectious** ADJ QUALIT
disease, other people can catch it from you, even if
they do not touch you.
2 If a feeling is **infectious**, it spreads to other ADJ QUALIT
people. EG Don't you find her enthusiasm infec-
tious?... What an infectious laugh she has!

infer /ɪnˈfɜː/, **infers, inferring, inferred.** If you
infer that something is the case, 1 you decide that V+REPORT OR
it is true, on the basis of information you have. EG V+O+from
He can infer that if the battery is dead then the
horn will not sound... As a result of this simple
statement, I could infer a lot about his former
wives. 2 you say something to suggest that it is the V+REPORT
case without actually saying so directly. Many
people consider that this use is wrong, and that the
right word to use is 'imply'. EG I do not want to infer
by this criticism that there is something fundamentally wrong with the system.

inference /ˈɪnfə⁰rəns/, **inferences.** 1 An **infer-** N COUNT
ence is a conclusion that you draw about something. EG The inferences drawn from data have led
to some major changes in our policy.
2 **Inference** is the act of drawing conclusions N UNCOUNT
about something. EG We should understand the
importance of the industrial revolution and, by
inference, the coming computer revolution.

inferior /ɪnˈfɪərɪə/, **inferiors.** 1 Someone who is ADJ QUALIT :
inferior is less important than other people or has OFT+to
a lower position in society. EG Charlie, aged sixteen,
felt inferior to lads of his own age... Mary does not
rebel against her inferior status. ◇ **inferiority** ◇ N UNCOUNT
/ɪnfɪɔrɪˈɒrɪti¹/. EG ...feelings of inferiority... ...an inferiority complex.
2 Your **inferiors** are people who have a lower N COUNT :
position or status than you. EG He complained of the USU+POSS
slackness and stupidity of his inferiors.
3 Something that is **inferior** is of worse quality ADJ QUALIT :
than something else of a similar type. EG It was a OFT+to
cheap and inferior product.

infernal /ɪnˈfɜːnə⁰l/. You use **infernal** to describe ADJ CLASSIF :
something that is very unpleasant, especially when ATTRIB
you are angry about it. EG Will you stop that Outdated
infernal noise?

inferno /ɪnˈfɜːnəʊ/, **infernos.** You can refer to a N COUNT
very large dangerous fire as an **inferno**. Literary

infertile /ɪnˈfɜːtaɪl/. 1 Someone who is **infertile** is ADJ CLASSIF
unable to have or produce babies. EG She learned
she was infertile. ◇ **infertility** /ɪnfɜːtɪlˈɪti¹/. EG ◇ N UNCOUNT
...an infertility clinic.

2 **Infertile** soil is of poor quality, and so plants ADJ QUALIT
cannot grow in it. EG ...infertile tropical soils.
◇ **infertility.** EG There were few farms there ◇ N UNCOUNT
because of the infertility of the soil.

infested /ɪnˈfɛsti³d/. If a plant or area is **infested** ADJ PRED
with insects, rats, or other pests, many of them are
on it or in it, usually causing damage. EG ...broad
beans infested with blackfly.

infidelity /ɪnfɪˈdɛlɪti¹/, **infidelities.** When **infi-** N UNCOUNT
delity occurs, a person who is married or who has OR N COUNT
a steady relationship with someone has sex with
another person. EG ...a widow who discovers her
late husband's infidelity.

in-fighting is rivalry or quarrelling between N UNCOUNT
members of the same organization.

infiltrate /ˈɪnfɪltreɪt/, **infiltrates, infiltrating,** V+O OR
infiltrated. If people **infiltrate** an organization, V+into
they join it secretly in order to spy on its activities
or to influence its decisions. EG The organization
was infiltrated by the police... Some of them infiltrated into its highest councils. ◇ **infiltration** ◇ N UNCOUNT
/ɪnfɪlˈtreɪʃə⁰n/. EG ...the infiltration of the party by
extreme left-wing groups.

infinite /ˈɪnfɪnə¹t/. Something that is **infinite** 1 is ADJ CLASSIF
extremely large in amount or degree. EG Qualified
doctors are found in an infinite variety of careers.
◇ **infinitely.** EG The process of unloading had been ◇ SUBMOD
infinitely easier than putting the stuff on. 2 has no ADJ CLASSIF
limit, end, or edge. EG ...that desert land of infinite
blue air.

infinitesimal /ɪnfɪnɪˈtɛsɪmə⁰l/. Something that is ADJ CLASSIF
infinitesimal is extremely small. EG The chances Formal
that the company will have any problems are
infinitesimal.

infinitive /ɪnˈfɪnɪtɪv/, **infinitives.** The **infinitive** N COUNT
or the **infinitive** form of a verb is the form which
does not have inflections, such as do, take, and eat.
The infinitive can either be used on its own or with
to in front of it. The infinitive is abbreviated to INF
in the Extra Column in this dictionary. See the
entry headed INF for more information.

infinity /ɪnˈfɪnɪti¹/ is 1 a number that is larger N UNCOUNT
than any other number and can never be given an
exact value. EG ...an infinity of possible combinations. 2 a point that is further away than any other
point and can never be reached. EG There was
nothing but darkness stretching away to infinity.

infirm /ɪnˈfɜːm/. 1 A person who is **infirm** is weak ADJ QUALIT
or ill. EG His grandfather was over eighty years of Formal
age, infirm and totally blind. ◇ **infirmity** ◇ N COUNT OR
/ɪnˈfɜːmɪti¹/, **infirmities.** EG ...physical infirmity or N UNCOUNT
weakness... ...the infirmities of old age.
2 The **infirm** are people who are infirm. EG ...the N PLURAL :
needs of the old and infirm. the+N

infirmary /ɪnˈfɜːmə⁰ri¹/, **infirmaries.** Some hos- N COUNT
pitals are called **infirmaries**. EG ...Manchester Outdated
Royal Infirmary.

inflame /ɪnˈfleɪm/, **inflames, inflaming, in-** V+O
flamed. Something that **inflames** someone makes
them very angry or excited. EG Her question
seemed to inflame him all the more.

inflamed /ɪnˈfleɪmd/. If part of your body is **in-** ADJ QUALIT
flamed, it is red and often hot and swollen, be- Formal
cause of an infection or an injury.

inflammable /ɪnˈflæməbə⁰l/. An **inflammable** ADJ QUALIT
material or chemical burns easily.

inflammation /ɪnfləˈmeɪʃə⁰n/. An **inflammation** N UNCOUNT
is a painful redness or swelling of part of the body. OR N SING
EG Some children have inflammation of the ears
when they have colds.

inflammatory /ɪnˈflæmətə⁰ri¹/. An **inflamma-** ADJ QUALIT
tory speech or action is likely to make people very
angry or hostile. EG ...an inflammatory speech
about terrorists.

If you are informative, are you an informer?

inflatable /ɪnˈfleɪtəbəl/. An **inflatable** object can ADJ CLASSIF be filled with air. EG ...*inflatable lifejackets.*

inflate /ɪnˈfleɪt/, **inflates, inflating, inflated.** V-ERG When you **inflate** something or when it **inflates**, it becomes bigger as it is filled with air or another gas. EG ...*a rubber dinghy that took half a hour to inflate.*

inflated /ɪnˈfleɪtɪd/ 1 An **inflated** object has been ADJ CLASSIF filled with air until it is firm. EG ...*the large inflated tyre they used as a raft.*
2 If you have an **inflated** opinion of yourself, you ADJ QUALIT think you are much more important than you really are. EG ...*his inflated self-image.*
3 An **inflated** price or salary is higher than is ADJ QUALIT considered reasonable. EG ...*food and clothing which had to be bought at inflated prices.*

inflation /ɪnˈfleɪʃən/ is a general increase in the N UNCOUNT prices of goods and services in a country. EG *Chile has reduced its inflation in the past year from a hundred per cent to fifty.*

inflationary /ɪnˈfleɪʃənəri/. An **inflationary** ac- ADJ QUALIT tion or event causes inflation. EG ...*inflationary* Formal *wage demands... ...inflationary economic policies.*

inflect /ɪnˈflekt/, **inflects, inflecting, inflected.** V If a word **inflects**, its ending or form changes in order to show its grammatical function. If a language **inflects**, it has words in it that change their endings or forms in order to show their grammatical functions. ◊ **inflected.** EG *German is an* ◊ ADJ CLASSIF *inflected language.*

inflection /ɪnˈflekʃən/, **inflections;** also spelled N COUNT OR **inflexion.** An **inflection** is 1 the way that you N UNCOUNT change the sound of your voice when you speak. EG *She spoke in a low voice, always without inflection.*
2 a change in the form of a word that shows its grammatical function, for example a change that makes a noun plural or makes a verb into the past tense.

inflexible /ɪnˈfleksɪbəl/. Something that is **inflex-** ADJ QUALIT **ible** cannot be altered. EG *Nursery schools have inflexible hours.* ◊ **inflexibility** /ɪnfleksɪˈbɪlɪti/. ◊ N UNCOUNT EG ...*dogmatic inflexibility in the face of change.*

inflexion /ɪnˈflekʃən/. See **inflection.**

inflict /ɪnˈflɪkt/, **inflicts, inflicting, inflicted.** If V+O: you **inflict** something unpleasant on someone, you OFT+*on/upon* make them suffer it. EG ...*the suffering that would be inflicted upon innocent people. ...the dreadful way she had inflicted her problems on him.*

influence /ˈɪnfluəns/, **influences, influencing, influenced.** 1 **Influence** is power that you have N UNCOUNT which makes it likely that other people will agree with you or do what you want. EG *The government would use its influence to try to make the negotiations successful... Moscow retains some influence over their affairs.* ● If you are **under the influ-** ● PHRASE **ence** of someone or something, you are being affected or controlled by them. EG *He was under the influence of friends who were highly conservative... They were deeply under the influence of alcohol.*
2 The **influence** that someone or something has N COUNT on people or situations is the effect that they have on them. EG *His teachings still exert a strong influence... ...the influence of religion on society.*
3 Someone or something that is an **influence** on N COUNT+SUPP people or things has an effect on them. EG *He was a bad influence on the children... ...influences in drama and literature.*
4 If you **influence** a person, thing, or situation, you V+O have an effect on the way that person acts or on what happens. EG *I didn't want him to influence me in my choice... Is British art influenced at all by American painting?*

influential /ɪnfluˈenʃəl/. Someone who is **influ-** ADJ QUALIT **ential** has a lot of influence over people. EG ...*a powerful and influential politician.*

influenza /ɪnfluˈenzə/ is the same as flu. EG *She* N UNCOUNT *died in the great influenza epidemic.* Formal

influx /ˈɪnflʌks/. An **influx** of people or things into N SING+SUPP a place is their steady arrival there in large numbers. EG ...*a massive influx of refugees from neighbouring countries.*

info /ˈɪnfəʊ/ is the same as information. EG ...*the* N UNCOUNT *info on where the meeting was.* Informal

inform /ɪnˈfɔːm/, **informs, informing, informed.** V+O: USU+*of,* If you **inform** someone of something, you tell them REPORT, about it. EG *He intended to see Barbara to inform* OR QUOTE *her of his objections... I informed her that I was unwell... 'They are late,' he informed her.* ● See also **informed.**

informal /ɪnˈfɔːməl/. 1 You use **informal** to de- ADJ QUALIT scribe behaviour or speech that is relaxed and casual rather than correct and serious. In this dictionary, language of this kind is indicated by the word 'Informal' in the Extra Column. EG ...*a relaxed and quite informal discussion.* ◊ **informally.** EG ◊ ADV ...*people talking informally together.*
◊ **informality** /ɪnfɔːˈmælɪti/. EG ...*an atmosphere* ◊ N UNCOUNT *of informality.*
2 You also use **informal** to describe 2.1 relaxed ADJ QUALIT social occasions, where you do not have to wear smart clothes or behave correctly. EG ...*an informal party.* 2.2 clothes that are suitable for wearing ADJ QUALIT when you are relaxing, but not for formal occasions. ◊ **informally.** EG *The producer was infor-* ◊ ADV *mally dressed in a blue silk shirt open at the neck.*
2.3 something that is done unofficially. EG *We have* ADJ CLASSIF *informal contacts with over 500 firms.*
◊ **informally.** EG *Germany and Russia agreed* ◊ ADV *informally to abide by the agreement.*

informant /ɪnˈfɔːmənt/, **informants.** An **inform-** N COUNT **ant** is 1 someone who gives another person a piece of information. 2 the same as an informer.

information /ɪnfəˈmeɪʃən/. If you have **informa-** N UNCOUNT **tion** about something, you know something about it. EG *I'm afraid I have no information on that... She provided me with a very interesting piece of information about his past.*

informative /ɪnˈfɔːmətɪv/. Something that is **in-** ADJ QUALIT **formative** gives you useful information. EG ...*an informative guidebook... Nothing that she said was very informative.*

informed /ɪnˈfɔːmd/. If you make an **informed** ADJ CLASSIF: guess about something, you use your knowledge to ATTRIB decide what you think the answer should be.

informer /ɪnˈfɔːmə/, **informers.** An **informer** is N COUNT someone who tells the police that another person has done something illegal.

infra-red /ɪnfrə ˈred/. **Infra-red** light is below the ADJ CLASSIF colour red in the spectrum and cannot be seen. EG ...*infra-red photography.*

infrequent /ɪnˈfriːkwənt/. If something is **infre-** ADJ QUALIT **quent**, it does not happen often. EG ...*her sister's infrequent letters.* ◊ **infrequently.** EG *My parents* ◊ ADV *were only able to visit us infrequently.*

infringe /ɪnˈfrɪndʒ/, **infringes, infringing, in-** **fringed.** 1 If you **infringe** a law or an agreement, V+O you break it. EG *They occasionally infringe the law* Formal *by parking near a junction.*
2 If you **infringe** people's rights or **infringe** on V+O OR them, you do not allow the people the rights or V+*on/upon* freedom that they are entitled to. EG *They were citizens with legal rights, which were being infringed... We must fight them when they infringe on our children's right to freedom.*

infringement /ɪnˈfrɪndʒmənt/, **infringements.** 1 If an action is an **infringement** of your rights, it N COUNT OR restricts you unfairly. EG *The new law is an in-* N UNCOUNT: *fringement on free speech.* USU+*of/on*
2 An **infringement** of a law, rule, or agreement is N COUNT OR the breaking of it. EG ...*small infringements of* N UNCOUNT: *prison discipline.* USU+*of*

infuriate /ɪnˈfjʊərieɪt/, **infuriates, infuriating,** V+O **infuriated.** If something or someone **infuriates** you, they make you extremely angry. EG *Is he trying to infuriate me? He's succeeding... Old jeans*

and T-shirts infuriated him. ◊ **infuriated.** EG ...a ◊ ADJ QUALIT
small group of infuriated little boys.

infuriating /ɪnfjʊəriˈeɪtɪŋ/. Something that is **in-** ADJ QUALIT
furiating annoys you very much. EG ...her infuriating habit of criticizing people all the time.

-ing is added to verbs **1** to form present partici- SUFFIX
ples. EG I was walking along the road... She sat by
the window, drinking coffee. **2** to form uncountable
nouns that refer to activities. Nouns like these are
often not defined in this dictionary, but are treated
with the related verbs. EG Farming was something I
really enjoyed... We need to spend more money on
advertising.

-ING stands for **present participle**

When a verb is followed by another verb, sometimes the second verb must be in the form that
ends in '-ing'. In these cases the label in the Extra
Column will include + -ING. An example is **enjoy 1**,
where the Extra Column says V+O OR V+ -ING,
showing that the verb can be followed either by an
object or by a form ending in '-ing', as in You're
interesting and I enjoy talking to you and They
enjoyed reading novels when they were young.
ING is also used as part of the label for some nouns.
See the entry headed NOUNS for information about
this.

---

ingenious /ɪndʒiːnjəs, -nɪəs/. An **ingenious** idea, ADJ QUALIT
plan, or device is very clever. EG ...an ingenious
method of forecasting economic trends.
◊ **ingeniously.** EG The hangers were ingeniously ◊ ADV
fixed to the wardrobe by pieces of wire.

ingenuity /ɪndʒɪˈnjuːɪtiˈ/ is cleverness and skill at N UNCOUNT
inventing things or working out plans. EG With a bit
of ingenuity you can do almost anything.

ingenuous /ɪndʒenjuːəs/. Someone who is **in-** ADJ QUALIT
genuous is innocent, trusting, and not capable of
deceiving people. EG His expression was frank,
ingenuous, and engaging.

ingrained /ɪŋˈɡreɪnd/. If habits and beliefs are ADJ QUALIT :
ingrained, they are difficult to change or destroy. OFT+in
EG The belief that one should work hard is ingrained in our culture.

ingratiate /ɪŋˈɡreɪʃiˈeɪt/, **ingratiates, ingratiat-** V.REFL :
ing, ingratiated. If you try to **ingratiate** yourself USU+with
with other people, you try to make them like you;
used showing disapproval. EG They resented his
knack for ingratiating himself with officers.
◊ **ingratiating** /ɪŋˈɡreɪʃiˈeɪtɪŋ/. EG ...an ingratiat- ◊ ADJ QUALIT
ing smile.

ingratitude /ɪŋˈɡrætɪtjuːd/ is the lack of gratitude N UNCOUNT
for something that has been done for you. EG I was
shocked and enraged at such ingratitude.

ingredient /ɪŋˈɡriːdɪənt/, **ingredients. 1** The **in-** N COUNT
gredients of something that you cook or prepare
are the different foods that you use. EG Mix the
ingredients to a soft dough.
2 An **ingredient** of a situation is one of the N COUNT+SUPP
essential parts of it. EG The most essential ingredient in economic progress is investment.

inhabit /ɪnˈhæbɪt/, **inhabits, inhabiting, inhabit-** V+O : USU PASS
ed. If a place or region is **inhabited**, people live
there. EG The town was a seaside resort, inhabited
by fishermen and hoteliers.

inhabitant /ɪnˈhæbɪtənt/, **inhabitants.** The **in-** N COUNT
habitants of a place are the people who live there.

inhale /ɪnˈheɪl/, **inhales, inhaling, inhaled.** When V OR V+O
you **inhale** or when you **inhale** smoke, fumes, or a
smell, you breathe in. EG She put the cigarette
between her lips and inhaled deeply.

inherent /ɪnˈhɪərənt, -ˈher-/. Qualities or character- ADJ CLASSIF :
istics that are **inherent** in something are a neces- OFT+in
sary and natural part of it. EG ...the dangers inherent in this kind of political system... ...my inherent

laziness. ◊ **inherently.** EG Power stations are ◊ ADV
themselves inherently inefficient.

inherit /ɪnˈherɪt/, **inherits, inheriting, inherit-**
ed. 1 If you **inherit** something such as a position, V+O :
situation, or attitude, you take it over from people OFT+from
who came before you. EG They inherited a weak
economy... ...traditions inherited from the past.
2 If you **inherit** money or property, you receive it V+O
from someone who has died.
3 If you **inherit** a characteristic or quality, you are V+O
born with it, because your parents or ancestors had
it. EG This kind of brain damage may be inherited.

inheritance /ɪnˈherɪtəⁿns/, **inheritances. 1** An
inheritance is **1.1** money or property which you N COUNT OR
receive from someone who is dead. EG He had no N UNCOUNT
motive for depriving his son of the inheritance...
...the customs of inheritance in Asia. **1.2** a situation N SING+SUPP
or thing which you have taken over from people Formal
who came before you. EG ...our alphabet, an inheritance from the Greeks.
2 Inheritance is also the fact of being born with N UNCOUNT
characteristics or qualities which your parents or +SUPP
ancestors had. EG To what extent does human
nature depend on genetic inheritance?

inheritor /ɪnˈherɪtə/, **inheritors.** Someone who is N COUNT+SUPP
an **inheritor** of something inherited it from people
who came before them. EG ...the inheritors of a
literary tradition.

inhibit /ɪnˈhɪbɪt/, **inhibits, inhibiting, inhibited.** V+O
If something **inhibits** an action or the development of something, it prevents it or slows it down.
EG The drugs with which the animals are fed inhibit
their development.

inhibited /ɪnˈhɪbɪtɪ'd/. If you are **inhibited**, you ADJ QUALIT
find it difficult to behave naturally and to show
your real feelings. EG Her severe upbringing had
left her inhibited.

inhibition /ɪnhⁱˈbɪʃəⁿn/, **inhibitions. Inhibitions** N COUNT OR
are feelings of fear or embarrassment that make it N UNCOUNT
difficult for you to behave naturally. EG ...a child
who is free from inhibitions... She's prepared to
argue without inhibition.

inhospitable /ɪnhɒspɪtəbəⁿl/. **1** If a place is **in-** ADJ QUALIT
hospitable, it is unpleasant for people to live in. EG
...inhospitable deserts.
2 If you are **inhospitable**, you do not like having ADJ QUALIT
guests and do not make people feel welcome when
they visit you. EG I don't like to be inhospitable, but
I've got an awful lot to do.

inhuman /ɪnhjuːmən/. **1** Behaviour that is **inhu-** ADJ QUALIT
man is extremely cruel or brutal. EG ...barbarous
and inhuman atrocities.
2 Something that is **inhuman** is not human, and is ADJ CLASSIF
therefore strange or frightening. EG Their faces
looked inhuman, covered with scarlet and black
paint.

inhumane /ɪnhjuːmeɪn/. A way of treating people ADJ QUALIT
or animals that is **inhumane** is extremely cruel.

inhumanity /ɪnhjuːmænɪ'tiˈ/ is extreme cruelty N UNCOUNT
or the lack of kind feelings towards people. EG
...man's inhumanity to man.

inimical /ɪnɪmɪkəⁿl/. Conditions that are **inimical** ADJ CLASSIF :
to something make it hard for it to survive. EG The USU PRED+to
very nature of society is inimical to freedom. Formal

inimitable /ɪnɪmɪtəbəⁿl/. If someone has an **in-** ADJ CLASSIF
imitable quality or characteristic, that quality is Formal
very good or is very typical of that person. EG The
Welsh Rugby team have their own inimitable style.

iniquitous /ɪnɪkwɪtəs/. If you describe something ADJ QUALIT
as **iniquitous**, you mean that it is very bad and Formal
unfair. EG ...this iniquitous policy.

iniquity /ɪnɪkwɪ'tiˈ/, **iniquities.** An **iniquity** is N COUNT OR
something that is very wicked or unjust. EG We N UNCOUNT
fought a revolution to put an end to such in- Formal
iquities... ...Rose's iniquity and selfishness.

How is someone related to their in-laws?

initial /ɪnɪʃᵊl/, **initials, initialling, initialled;** spelled **initialed** and **initialing** in American English.

1 You use **initial** to describe something that happens at the beginning of a process, in contrast to what happens later. EG ...*the initial stages of learning English... My initial reaction was one of great relief.* ADJ CLASSIF: ATTRIB

2 Your **initials** are the set of capital letters which begin each of your names, or begin your first names. For example, if your full name is Karen Anne Fox, your initials are K.A.F. N PLURAL

3 When you **initial** a document, you write your initials on it in order to show that you have seen it or have officially approved it. *He picked up his pen and initialed the papers.* V+O

initially /ɪnɪʃᵊlɪ/ means in the early or original stages of a process. EG *I don't remember who initially conceived the idea.* ADV

initiate, initiates, initiating, initiated; pronounced /ɪnɪʃɪeɪt/ when it is a verb, and /ɪnɪʃɪᵊt/ when it is a noun.

1 If you **initiate** something, you cause it to start. *We should initiate direct talks with the trades unions.* ◊ **initiation** /ɪnɪʃɪeɪʃᵊn/. EG ...*the initiation of a new revolutionary practice.* V+O ◊ N UNCOUNT +of

2 If you **initiate** someone into a type of knowledge or into a group, you conduct a ceremony or teach them special things so that they become a member of a group. EG *To understand, one must be initiated into great mysteries.* ◊ **initiation.** EG ...*an initiation ceremony.* V+O+into ◊ N UNCOUNT

3 An **initiate** is a person who has recently been allowed to join a particular group and who has been taught special things. EG ...*an initiate into the world of politics.* N COUNT

initiative /ɪnɪʃɪᵊtɪv/, **initiatives. 1** An **initiative** is an important act, which is an attempt to solve a problem. EG ...*launching various initiatives to tackle real or imagined problems.* N COUNT: USU PLURAL

2 If you have the **initiative**, you are in a stronger position than the people you are competing with or fighting against. EG *They had lost the initiative.* N SING: the+N

3 If you **take the initiative** in a situation, you are the first person to do something. EG *In Sweden employers have taken the initiative in promoting health insurance schemes.* PHRASE

4 If you have **initiative**, you are able to decide what to do, and to take action, without needing other people to tell you what to do. N UNCOUNT

5 If you **use** your **initiative**, or if you do something **on** your **own initiative**, you make decisions or take action using your own judgement rather than being told what to do. EG *In special circumstances we have to use our initiative... In 1912 he had gone to Berlin on his own initiative.* PHRASE

inject /ɪndʒekt/, **injects, injecting, injected. 1** If you **inject** someone with a liquid, you use a syringe to get it into their blood. EG *She injected a sleeping drug into my arm... Animals were injected with various doses.* V+O: OFT +into/with

2 If you **inject** something such as excitement or interest into a situation, you add it. EG *She was trying to inject some fun into the grim proceedings.* V+O: OFT+into

3 If you **inject** money into a business or organization, you provide more money for it. EG *Enormous sums of money are injected each year into teaching.* V+O: OFT+into

injection /ɪndʒekʃᵊn/, **injections. 1** If you have an **injection**, someone puts a liquid into your blood using a syringe, especially in order to prevent you getting an illness. EG *You had a smallpox injection when you were five.* N COUNT

2 An **injection** of money into a business or organization is the putting of extra money into it. EG *They only survived because of massive injections of commercial funds.* N COUNT+of

injunction /ɪndʒʌŋkʃᵊn/, **injunctions.** An **injunction** is a formal order, especially one issued N COUNT

by a court of law in order to stop someone doing something. EG *We will apply to the courts for an injunction against the march.*

injure /ɪndʒə/, **injures, injuring, injured.** If you **injure** someone, you damage a part of their body. EG *I feared they might injure themselves... Peter injured his right hand in an accident... She was not badly injured.* V+O OR V-REFL

injury /ɪndʒərɪ/, **injuries.** An **injury** is damage done to a person's body. EG *The earthquake caused many deaths and severe injuries... Louis received an injury to his head... He was weakened by illness and injury.* N COUNT OR N UNCOUNT

injustice /ɪndʒʌstɪs/, **injustices. 1 Injustice** is unfairness and lack of justice in a situation. EG *There's social injustice everywhere... He contemplated the injustices of life.* N UNCOUNT OR N COUNT

2 If you say that you have **done** someone an **injustice**, you mean that your opinion about them was too severe or harsh. EG *I feel I've done him rather an injustice.* PHRASE

ink /ɪŋk/, **inks. Ink** is the coloured liquid used for writing or printing. EG *Please write in ink.* N MASS

inkling /ɪŋklɪŋ/. If you **have an inkling** of something, you suspect what it is or suspect that it is the case. EG *He had an inkling of what was going on... I had no inkling that she was interested in me.* PHRASE

inky /ɪŋkɪ/ means **1** very black, like ink. EG ...*inky forests of evergreens on the mountains... an inky sky.* **2** covered in ink. EG ...*an inky handkerchief.* ADJ COLOUR Literary / ADJ QUALIT

inland /ɪnlᵊnd/ means away from the coast, towards the middle of a country. EG *The Sahara was once an inland sea... Donkeys bear goods inland to the towns and villages.* ADJ CLASSIF: ATTRIB OR ADV

in-laws. Your **in-laws** are the parents of your husband or wife, and possibly his or her other close relatives too. N PLURAL

inlet /ɪnlᵊt/, **inlets.** An **inlet** is a narrow strip of water which goes from a sea or lake into the land. N COUNT

inmate /ɪnmeɪt/, **inmates.** The **inmates** of an institution such as a prison or a psychiatric hospital are the people living there. EG *In prison you learned about other inmates and their crimes.* N COUNT

inmost /ɪnməʊst/ means the same as innermost. EG *You read my inmost thoughts.* ADJ CLASSIF: ATTRIB

inn /ɪn/, **inns.** An **inn** is a small hotel or a pub, usually an old one. EG ...*the Pilgrim's Inn.* N COUNT Outdated

innate /ɪneɪt/. An **innate** quality or ability is one which a person is born with. EG *They believed intelligence was innate, and unlikely to change... ...an innate talent for music.* ◊ **innately.** EG *I don't think that anybody is innately good.* ADJ CLASSIF ◊ ADV

inner /ɪnə/. **1** You use **inner** to describe a part of something which is contained or enclosed inside the outer part. EG *There were several flats overlooking the inner courtyard.* ADJ CLASSIF: ATTRIB

2 Inner feelings are feelings which you have but do not show to other people. EG ...*his inner feelings of failure... ...inner doubts.* ADJ CLASSIF ATTRIB

inner city, inner cities. You use **inner city** to refer to the centre of a large city where people live and where there are often social and economic problems. EG *This is one of the most serious problems in the inner cities... ...the problems for inner-city children.* N SING: the+N, OR N PLURAL

innermost /ɪnəməʊst/. Your **innermost** thoughts and feelings are your most personal and secret ones. EG ...*her innermost wishes.* ADJ CLASSIF ATTRIB Literary

innings /ɪnɪŋz/. **Innings** is both the singular and the plural form. N COUNT
An **innings** is a period in a game of cricket during which a particular player or team is batting.

innocent /ɪnəsᵊnt/, **innocents. 1** If someone is **innocent**, they are not guilty of a crime. EG *He was accused of a crime of violence of which he was innocent... ...the suffering that would be inflicted upon innocent people.* ◊ **innocence** /ɪnəsᵊns/. EG *He desperately protested his innocence.* **1.2** they have no experience or knowledge of the more ADJ CLASSIF ◊ N UNCOUNT / ADJ QUALIT complex or unpleasant aspects of life. EG *I was very young, and very innocent.* ◊ **innocence.** EG *He had*   N UNCOUNT *a peculiar air of childlike innocence.*

2 An **innocent** is a person who has no experience   N COUNT or knowledge of the more complex or unpleasant   Literary aspects of life. EG *He was a financial genius but a political innocent.*

3 An **innocent** remark or action is not intended to   ADJ QUALIT offend or upset people, although it may do so. EG *It was an innocent question.* ◊ **innocently.** EG *'What*   ◊ ADV *did I do wrong?' asked Howard, innocently.*

innocuous /ɪnɒkjuːəs/. Something that is **innocu-**   ADJ QUALIT **ous** is not at all harmful. EG *Most of these substances are relatively innocuous.*

innovate /ɪnəˈveɪt/, **innovates, innovating, in-**   V **novated.** To **innovate** means to introduce changes and new ideas. EG *...the industry's capacity to respond swiftly to market changes and to innovate.* ◊ **innovator** /ɪnəˈveɪtə/, **innovators.** EG *The Pope*   ◊ N COUNT *thought of himself as an innovator.*

innovation /ɪnəˈveɪʃəⁿn/, **innovations. 1** An **in-**   N COUNT **novation** is a new thing or a new way of doing something. EG *...a series of remarkable innovations in textile manufacturing.*

2 Innovation is the introduction of new things or   N UNCOUNT new ways of doing things. EG *...a period of technological innovation.*

innovative /ɪnəvətɪv/. **1** Something that is **inno-**   ADJ QUALIT **vative** is new and original. EG *...their innovative campaign style... ...innovative ideas.*

2 Someone who is **innovative** introduces changes   ADJ QUALIT and new ideas. EG *...a pioneering and innovative banker.*

innovatory /ɪnəvətɔːri¹, ɪnəveɪtɔːri¹/ means the   ADJ QUALIT same as innovative. EG *His music was innovatory in its time.*

innuendo /ɪnjuːˈɛndəʊ/, **innuendoes** or **innuen-**   N UNCOUNT **dos.** Innuendo is indirect reference to something   OR N COUNT rude or unpleasant. EG *...a campaign of innuendo and gossip... He became a target for sexual innuendoes.*

innumerable /ɪnjuːmərəbəⁿl/ means too many to   ADJ CLASSIF be counted. EG *The industrial age has brought innumerable benefits.*

inoculate /ɪnɒkjuˈleɪt/, **inoculates, inoculating,**   V+O : OFT **inoculated.** If you **are inoculated** against a dis-   +against/with ease, you are injected with a weak form of the disease as a way of protecting you against it. ◊ **inoculation** /ɪnɒkjuˈleɪʃəⁿn/, **inoculations.** EG   ◊ N COUNT OR *...prevention of disease by inoculation... ...inocula-*   N UNCOUNT *tions against tetanus.*

inoffensive /ɪnəfɛnsɪv/. Someone or something   ADJ QUALIT that is **inoffensive** is harmless or not unpleasant. EG *...a nice, quiet, inoffensive little fellow.*

inordinate /ɪnɔːdɪnɪt/ means much greater than   ADJ CLASSIF : you would expect. EG *The idea of this gave me*   USU ATTRIB *inordinate pleasure... Colin always spent an inordi-*   Formal *nate length of time in the bathroom.* ◊ **inordinately.** EG *...an achievement of which I*   ◊ ADV+ADJ *was inordinately proud.*

inorganic /ɪnɔːˈgænɪk/. **Inorganic** substances are   ADJ CLASSIF substances such as stone and metal that do not come from living things. EG *...inorganic materials... ...inorganic fertilizers.*

input /ɪnpʊt/, **inputs. Input** consists of **1** informa-   N UNCOUNT tion or resources that a group or project receives.   OR N COUNT EG *The project requires the input of more labour.* **2**   N UNCOUNT information that is put into a computer.

inquest /ɪnkwɛst/, **inquests.** An **inquest** is an   N COUNT official inquiry to find out what caused someone's death. EG *There have been demands from his family for an inquest.*

inquire /ɪnˈkwaɪə/, **inquires, inquiring, in-**   V+A, OR **quired;** also spelled **enquire** /ɪ²nˈkwaɪə/. If you   V.SPEECH : **inquire** about something, you ask for information   ONLY WH about it. EG *'What will it cost?' inquired Miss*   Formal *Musson... He inquired whether it was possible to leave his case at the station... He went to enquire about the times of trains to Edinburgh.*

inquire after. If you **inquire after** someone,   PHRASAL VB : you ask for information about them, for example   V+PREP, about their health. EG *She enquired after Mrs*   HAS PASS *Carstair's daughter, who had just had a baby.*

inquire into. If you **inquire into** something, you   PHRASAL VB : investigate it carefully. EG *The police inquired into*   V+PREP, *the deaths of two young girls.*   HAS PASS

inquiring /ɪnˈkwaɪərɪŋ/. **1** If you have an **inquir-**   ADJ QUALIT **ing** mind, you have a great interest in learning   ATTRIB new things.

2 An **inquiring** expression shows that you want to   ADJ QUALIT know something. EG *...the people's inquiring faces.* ◊ **inquiringly.** EG *I looked at her inquiringly.*   ◊ ADV

inquiry /ɪ¹nˈkwaɪəri¹/, **inquiries;** also spelled **en-** **quiry** /ɪ¹n¹kwaɪəri¹/, especially for paragraph 1.1. **1** An **inquiry** is **1.1** a question which you ask   N COUNT someone in order to get some information. EG *This is what I have been able to learn in my enquiries... I shall make some enquiries.* **1.2** an official investi- gation into something. EG *Opposition MPs have called for an inquiry... ...a public enquiry.*

2 Inquiry is the process of asking about something   N UNCOUNT in order to find out information about it. EG *On further enquiry, however, I discovered that there had been nobody at home that evening.*

inquisitive /ɪnˈkwɪzɪtɪv/. If you are **inquisitive**   ADJ QUALIT you like finding out about things. EG *He tried not to sound inquisitive.* ◊ **inquisitively.** EG *I glanced*   ◊ ADV *inquisitively through the open doorway.*

inroads /ɪnrəʊdz/. If something **makes inroads**   PHRASE into something else, it starts affecting it or destroy- ing it. EG *Our party hasn't made great inroads in Scotland... They are highly sensitive to any inroads upon their independence.*

insane /ɪnseɪn/. **1** Someone who is **insane** is mad.   ADJ CLASSIF EG *Some went insane.* ◊ **insanity** /ɪnsæni¹ti¹/. EG   ◊ N UNCOUNT *He saw the beginnings of insanity in her.*

2 If you describe something or someone as **insane,**   ADJ QUALIT you mean that they are very foolish. EG *This idea is*   Informal *totally insane... You'd be insane to do that.* ◊ **insanely.** EG *I must admit that I was insanely*   ◊ ADV *jealous.* ◊ **insanity.** EG *I laughed at the insanity of*   ◊ N UNCOUNT *it all.*

insatiable /ɪnseɪʃi¹əbəⁿl/. A desire or greed that is   ADJ CLASSIF **insatiable** is very great. EG *...an insatiable curios- ity... ...an insatiable appetite for power.* ◊ **insatiably.** EG *She was insatiably curious.*   ◊ ADV

inscribe /ɪnskraɪb/, **inscribes, inscribing, in-**   V+O+A **scribed.** If some words **are inscribed** on an   OR V+O+O : object or if an object **is inscribed** with some   USU PASS words, the words are written or carved on the   Formal object. EG *The names of the dead were inscribed on the wall... ...a ring inscribed 'To My Darling'.*

inscription /ɪnskrɪpʃəⁿn/, **inscriptions.** An **in-**   N COUNT **scription** is words that are written or carved on something. EG *The inscription above the door was in English.*

inscrutable /ɪnskruːtəbəⁿl/. Someone who is **in-**   ADJ QUALIT **scrutable** does not show by their words or behav- iour what they are really thinking. EG *The candi- dates are pretty inscrutable.*

insect /ɪnsɛkt/, **insects.** An **insect** is a small   N COUNT animal that has six legs. Most insects have wings. Ants, flies, butterflies, and beetles are all insects.

insecticide /ɪnsɛktɪsaɪd/, **insecticides. Insecti-**   N MASS **cide** is a chemical that is used to kill insects.

insecure /ɪnsɪkjʊə/. **1** If you feel **insecure,** you   ADJ QUALIT feel that you are not good enough in some way, or are not loved. EG *What had I done to make you so insecure and frightened?* ◊ **insecurity**   ◊ N UNCOUNT /ɪnsɪ²kjʊəri¹ti¹/. EG *...feelings of insecurity.*

2 Something that is **insecure** is not safe or well-   ADJ QUALIT protected. EG *Their place in society is insecure.* ◊ **insecurity.** EG *...financial insecurity.*   ◊ N UNCOUNT

What will kill an insect?

insensitive /ɪnsɛnsɪtɪv/. Someone who is **insensitive** is not aware of other people's feelings, and does not realize when they have upset or annoyed people. EG ...*bad-mannered, loud, insensitive oafs...* ...*the insensitive attitude of the government.* ◊ **insensitivity** /ɪnsɛnsɪtɪvɪ¹ti¹/. EG *There were times when he showed a curious insensitivity.* ADJ QUALIT ◊ N UNCOUNT

inseparable /ɪnsɛpə⁰rəbə⁰l/. 1 If two things are **inseparable**, they are so closely connected that they cannot be considered separately. EG *Culture is inseparable from class... The social and ecological costs are inseparable.* ADJ CLASSIF : OFT+*from* Formal

2 Friends who are **inseparable** are always together. EG *Soon they were inseparable.* ADJ QUALIT Formal

insert /ɪnsɜːt/, **inserts, inserting, inserted. 1** If you **insert** an object into something, you put the object inside it. EG *He inserted the wooden peg into the hole.* V+O : USU+A

2 If you **insert** a comment in a piece of writing or a speech, you include it. EG *The President inserted one unscripted item in his speech.* V+O

inshore /ɪnʃɔː/ means in the sea but quite close to the land. EG ...*inshore fishermen... These fish are not found inshore.* ADJ CLASSIF : ATTRIB OR ADV

inside /ɪnsaɪd/, **insides. 1** Something or someone that is **inside** a place, container, or object is surrounded by its sides. EG *Two minutes later we were inside the taxi... You left your lighter inside... It is a fruit with a seed inside.* ► used as an adjective. EG *The door had no inside bolt.* PREP OR ADV ► ADJ CLASSIF : ATTRIB

2 The **inside** of something is the part or area that its sides surround or contain. EG *The inside of my mouth was dry... ...the inside of the castle.* N COUNT

3 You can also say that someone is **inside** when they are in prison. ADV Informal

4 On a wide road, the **inside** lanes are the ones which are closest to the edge of the road. ADJ CLASSIF : ATTRIB

5 **Inside** information is obtained from someone who is involved in a situation and therefore knows a lot about it. ADJ CLASSIF : ATTRIB

6 If you are **inside** an organization, you belong to it. EG *Nobody inside the company will be surprised.* PREP

7 If you say that someone has a feeling **inside** them, you mean that they have not expressed this feeling. EG *His true feelings keep surging up inside him... I always felt inside that I wanted to write.* PREP OR ADV

8 If something such as a piece of clothing is **inside out**, the inside part has been turned so that it faces outwards. PHRASE

9 Your **insides** are your internal organs, especially your stomach. EG *What we all need is a bit of food in our insides.* N PLURAL : USU+POSS Informal

insider /ɪnsaɪdə/, **insiders**. An **insider** is someone who is involved in a situation and who knows more about it than other people. EG *According to one insider, the government is getting worried.* N COUNT

insidious /ɪnsɪdi¹əs/. Something that is **insidious** is unpleasant and develops gradually without being noticed. EG *The leaflets were a more insidious form of propaganda.* ADJ QUALIT

insight /ɪnsaɪt/, **insights**. If you gain **insight** into a complex situation or problem, you gain an understanding of it. EG ...*a number of interesting psychological insights.* N UNCOUNT OR N COUNT

insignia /ɪnsɪgniə/. **Insignia** is both the singular and the plural form. An **insignia** is a badge or sign which shows that a person or object belongs to a particular organization. EG ...*military insignia... ...a plane bearing the insignia of the Condor Legion.* N COUNT

insignificant /ɪnsɪgnɪfɪkənt/. Something that is **insignificant** is not at all important. EG *Whatever I write seems so insignificant... ...an insignificant minority.* ◊ **insignificance** /ɪnsɪgnɪfɪkəns/. EG *This emergency plunges all her other problems into insignificance.* ADJ QUALIT ◊ N UNCOUNT

insincere /ɪnsɪnsɪə/. Someone who is **insincere** is not sincere. EG ...*people whose admiration is extravagant and often insincere.* ◊ **insincerity** ADJ QUALIT ◊ N UNCOUNT

/ɪnsɪnsɛrɪ¹ti¹/. EG *The young are quick to recognize insincerity.*

insinuate /ɪnsɪnjueɪt/, **insinuates, insinuating, insinuated. 1** If you **insinuate** that something is true, you hint in an unpleasant way that it is true. EG *He insinuated that my wife had betrayed my trust in her.* V+REPORT : ONLY *that*

2 If you **insinuate** yourself into a particular position, you manage slowly and cleverly to get yourself into that position; used showing disapproval. EG *He eventually insinuated himself into a key position in the Party.* V-REFL+*into*

insipid /ɪnsɪpɪd/. 1 If you describe someone or something as **insipid**, you mean that they are dull and boring. EG *I used to find him insipid.* ADJ QUALIT

2 Food or drink that is **insipid** has very little taste. EG ...*gigantic insipid tomatoes, huge flavourless lettuces.* ADJ QUALIT

insist /ɪnsɪst/, **insists, insisting, insisted. 1** If you **insist** that something is true, you say it very firmly and refuse to change your mind. EG *She insisted that Jim must leave... 'But you know that she's innocent,' the girl insisted.* V+REPORT : ONLY *that*, OR V+QUOTE

2 If you **insist** on something, you say that you must do it or have it, and refuse to give in. EG *He insisted on paying for the meal... We were right to insist on reform.* V+*on*

insistence /ɪnsɪstəns/ Someone's **insistence** on something is the fact that they keep saying firmly that it must be done. EG ...*my insistence on secrecy.* N UNCOUNT : OFT+*on*

insistent /ɪnsɪstənt/. 1 Someone who is **insistent** keeps saying firmly that something must be done. EG *There have been insistent demands that more should be done to provide for poor families.* ◊ **insistently.** EG *No-one has spoken more insistently on the subject of education than her.* ADJ QUALIT ◊ ADV

2 If you describe a noise or action as **insistent**, you mean that it continues for a long time and gets your attention. EG ...*the insistent ringing of the telephone.* ◊ **insistently.** EG *I tugged insistently at his jacket.* ADJ QUALIT ◊ ADV

in situ /ɪn sɪtjuː/. If something remains **in situ**, especially while something is done to it, it remains where it is. EG *They will carry out further analysis in situ.* ADV Formal

insofar as /ɪnsə⁰fɑːr ə³z/. You use **insofar as** when giving the reason for something or when showing the extent of something. EG ...*contemptuous of the traditional culture, except insofar as it provided precious metals.* CONJ Formal

insolent /ɪnsələnt/. Someone who is **insolent** is very rude or impolite. EG ...*an insolent remark.* ◊ **insolence** /ɪnsələns/. EG *I was taken to the headmistress for my insolence.* ADJ QUALIT ◊ N UNCOUNT

insoluble /ɪnsɒljʊbə⁰l/. An **insoluble** problem is so difficult that it is impossible to solve. EG *The problems confronting this country are insoluble.* ADJ CLASSIF

insolvent /ɪnsɒlvənt/. Someone who is **insolvent** does not have enough money to pay their debts. EG *He revealed that he was insolvent by 1.2m pounds.* ADJ CLASSIF Formal

insomnia /ɪnsɒmniə/. Someone who suffers from **insomnia** finds it difficult to sleep. N UNCOUNT

insomniac /ɪnsɒmniæk/, **insomniacs**. An **insomniac** is a person who finds it difficult to sleep. N COUNT

inspect /ɪnspɛkt/, **inspects, inspecting, inspected. 1** If you **inspect** something, you look at every part of it carefully. EG *She inspected his scalp for lice.* ◊ **inspection** /ɪnspɛkʃə⁰n/, **inspections**. EG *Closer inspection revealed crabs among the rocks.* V+O ◊ N UNCOUNT OR N COUNT

2 When officials **inspect** a place, they visit it in order to find out whether regulations are being obeyed. EG *The fire prevention branch inspects factories and all sorts of public buildings.* ◊ **inspection.** EG ...*carrying out an inspection of the kitchen.* V+O ◊ N COUNT OR N UNCOUNT

inspector /ɪnspɛktə/, **inspectors**. An **inspector** is **1** an official whose job is to find out whether organizations are obeying official regulations. EG N COUNT

...*the factory inspector... The inspector's report was released to the public.* **2** an officer in the police force. EG ...*Inspector Flint.*

inspiration /ˌɪnspɪˈreɪʃən/, **inspirations.** **1** If you N UNCOUNT get **inspiration** from someone or something, you get new ideas from them which make you enthusiastic and encourage you to do something. EG *I have derived inspiration from Freud.*

2 The **inspiration** for something such as a piece of N SING+SUPP work or a theory is the thing that provides the basic idea or example for it. EG *He was later to become the inspiration for the comic strip character, Superman... The British Civil Service provided the inspiration for the system in India.*

3 If you get **inspiration**, you suddenly think of a N UNCOUNT good idea. EG *I had an inspiration... He paused,* OR N COUNT *searching for inspiration.*

inspire /ɪnˈspaɪə/, **inspires, inspiring, inspired.**
1 If someone or something **inspires** you to do V+O: something, they make you want to do it by giving OFT+*to*-INF you new ideas and enthusiasm. EG *Not even Churchill could inspire the Party to reform... They were too gloomy to be inspired by his enthusiasm... The strikes appear to be politically inspired.*

2 Someone or something that **inspires** a particular V+O:OFT+*in* emotion in people makes them feel this emotion. EG ...*a man who inspired confidence in women.*

inspired /ɪnˈspaɪəd/. **1** Someone who is **inspired** ADJ QUALIT is brilliant and very creative in their work. EG *As an architect, he was an inspired amateur... ...works of inspired beauty.*

2 An **inspired** guess is very clever and accurate. ADJ QUALIT EG *It was just an inspired guess.*

inspiring /ɪnˈspaɪərɪŋ/. Something or someone ADJ QUALIT that is **inspiring** is exciting and makes you enthusiastic and interested. EG *It was an inspiring occasion... I'm afraid it may not be inspiring to watch.*

instability /ˌɪnstəˈbɪlɪtiˈ/, **instabilities. Instabil-** N UNCOUNT **ity** is a lack of stability in a place, situation, or OR N COUNT person. EG *Various signs of political instability began to appear.*

install /ɪnˈstɔːl/, **installs, installing, installed. 1** V+O OR If you **install** a piece of equipment in a place, you V+O+A put it there so that it is ready to be used. EG *We have just installed central heating.*

2 If you **install** someone in an important job or V+O OR position, you officially give them the job or posi- V+O+A tion. EG *He installed a man named Briceland as head of the advertisement department.*

3 If you **install** yourself in a place, you settle there V-REFL+A and make yourself comfortable. EG *By now he was installed at number 7 New King Street.*

installation /ˌɪnstəˈleɪʃən/, **installations. 1** An N COUNT **installation** is a place that contains equipment and machinery which are being used for a particular purpose. EG ...*North Sea oil and gas installations... ...missile installations.*

2 The **installation** of a piece of equipment in- N UNCOUNT volves putting it into place and making it ready for use. EG ...*the installation of the colour TV.*

instalment /ɪnˈstɔːlməˈnt/, **instalments;** spelled **installment** in American English. **1** If you pay for N COUNT something in **instalments**, you pay small sums of money at regular intervals over a period of time. EG *I paid one hundred dollars in four monthly instalments.*

2 If a story is published in **instalments**, part of it is N COUNT published each day, week, or month. EG ...*the first instalment of the story.*

instance /ˈɪnstəns/, **instances. 1** You use **for** ADV SEN **instance** when mentioning a particular event, situation, or person that is an example of what you are talking about. EG *I mean, for instance, a man like Tom... For instance, an electric fire is a relatively expensive method of heating a room.*

2 An **instance** is a particular example of an event, N COUNT situation, or person. EG *I do not think that in this instance the doctor was right... ...instances of government injustice.*

3 You say **in the first instance** when mentioning PHRASE something that should be done first before any- Formal thing else. EG *The library will supply a list of addresses to which you should apply in the first instance.*

instant /ˈɪnstənt/, **instants. 1** An **instant** is an N COUNT: extremely short period of time. EG *Bal hesitated for* USU SING *an instant... It was all gone in a single instant.*

2 If you say that something happened at a particu- N SING+SUPP lar **instant**, you are referring to the actual moment at which it happened. EG *At that instant, an angry buzzing began.*

3 If you do something **the instant** something else CONJ happens, you do it as soon as it happens. EG *She must have dashed out the instant I grabbed the phone.*

4 If you say that something must be done **this** PHRASE **instant**, you mean that it must be done immediately.

5 You use **instant** to describe something that ADJ CLASSIF happens immediately without any delay. EG *Herschel did not have instant success.* ◊ **instantly.** EG *He was killed instantly.* ◊ ADV

6 Instant food is food that has been specially made ADJ CLASSIF so that you can prepare it with very little time and effort. EG ...*instant coffee.*

instantaneous /ˌɪnstənˈteɪnɪəs/. Something that is ADJ CLASSIF **instantaneous** happens immediately and very quickly. EG ...*an instantaneous look of happiness... Death was instantaneous.* ◊ **instantaneously.** EG ◊ ADV *The pain passed instantaneously.*

instead /ɪnˈsted/. If you do one thing **instead of** PREP OR another or if you do it **instead**, you do the first ADV SEN thing rather than the second thing. EG *If you want to have your meal at seven o'clock instead of five o'clock, you can... Instead of going straight to work, he took a bus into town... Robert had a great desire to turn away from her but instead he took her and led her towards the house.*

instep /ˈɪnstep/, **insteps.** Your **instep** is the mid- N COUNT dle part of your foot, where it curves upwards.

instigate /ˈɪnstɪɡeɪt/, **instigates, instigating, in-** V+O **stigated.** If you **instigate** an event or situation, Formal you cause it to happen by your own effort or work. EG *Sir Ernest Cassel instigated the Anglo-German talks of 1912.* ◊ **instigation** /ˌɪnstɪˈɡeɪʃən/. EG *One* ◊ N UNCOUNT *husband, at the instigation of his wife, called the police.* ◊ **instigator** /ˈɪnstɪɡeɪtə/, **instigators.** EG ◊ N COUNT *The instigator of the plot was Colonel Fletcher.*

instil /ɪnˈstɪl/, **instils, instilling, instilled;** spelled V+O: **instill, instills** in American English. If you **instil** OFT+*in/into* an idea or feeling into someone, you make them think it or feel it. EG *The presence of the guard was supposed to instil awe and fear in us.*

instinct /ˈɪnstɪŋkt/, **instincts. 1** An **instinct** is the N COUNT OR natural tendency that a person has to behave or N UNCOUNT react in a particular way without thinking about it or planning it. EG ...*a fundamental instinct for survival... She knew, by instinct, that he wouldn't come back... ...the maternal instinct.*

2 If it is your **instinct** to do something in a N COUNT: particular situation, you want to do it or feel that it USU+*to*-INF is right. EG *My first instinct was to resign... She really ought to trust Nick's instincts in these matters.*

instinctive /ɪnˈstɪŋktɪv/. An **instinctive** feeling, ADJ CLASSIF idea, or action is one that you have or do without thinking logically about it. EG *Brody took an instinctive dislike to the man... My instinctive reaction was to take a couple of rapid steps backwards.* ◊ **instinctively.** EG *Charles instinctively under-* ◊ ADV *stood I wanted to be alone.*

institute /ˈɪnstɪtjuːt/, **institutes, instituting, in-** **stituted. 1** An **institute** is an organization set up N COUNT to do a particular type of work, especially research

If something is installed, is it an instalment?

or teaching. EG *I visited a number of research institutes in Asia... ...the Massachusetts Institute of Technology.*

2 If you **institute** a system, rule, or course of action, you start it. EG *Mr Wilson was in Opposition when the scheme was instituted.* v+o Formal

institution /ɪnstɪtjuːʃəⁿn/, **institutions. 1** An **institution** is a custom or a system that is considered an important or typical feature of a society, usually because it has existed for a long time. EG *...the institution of marriage.* N COUNT

2 An **institution** is also **2.1** a large organization, for example a university, bank, or church. EG *These universities accept lower grades than the more prestigious institutions... ...financial institutions.* **2.2** a building where certain people are kept or looked after, for example people who are mentally ill or children who have no parents. EG *He may end up in a mental institution.* N COUNT

institutional /ɪnstɪtjuːʃəⁿnəl, -ʃənəⁿl/ means **1** relating to a large organization, for example a university, bank, or church. EG *...institutional reform.* **2** relating to a building where people are kept or looked after. EG *The child has been in institutional care for many years.* ADJ CLASSIF: ATTRIB

institutionalized /ɪnstɪtjuːʃəⁿnəlaɪzd/; also spelled **institutionalised. 1** If someone is **institutionalized**, they have been living in an institution for a long time and so they find it hard to look after themselves. EG *...institutionalized children.* ADJ CLASSIF

2 If a custom or a system is **institutionalized**, it is part of the social system of a society. EG *...institutionalized religion.* ADJ CLASSIF

instruct /ɪnstrʌkt/, **instructs, instructing, instructed. 1** If you **instruct** someone to do something, you tell them to do it. EG *'Breathe in,' he instructed her... I've been instructed to take you to London.* v+o+to-INF, QUOTE, OR REPORT Formal

2 Someone who **instructs** people in a subject or skill teaches it to them. v+o

instruction /ɪnstrʌkʃəⁿn/, **instructions. 1** An **instruction** is something that someone tells you to do. EG *She was only following the instructions of her supervisor.* N COUNT

2 Instructions are clear and detailed information on how to do something, especially written information. EG *Read the instructions before you switch on the engine.* N PLURAL

3 Instruction in a subject or skill is teaching that someone gives you about it. N UNCOUNT

instructive /ɪnstrʌktɪv/. Something that is **instructive** gives you useful information. EG *His seminars were instructive and illuminating occasions.* ADJ QUALIT

instructor /ɪnstrʌktə/, **instructors.** An **instructor** is a person who teaches you something, especially a skill such as driving or skiing. EG *...a Swiss ski instructor.* N COUNT

instrument /ɪnstrəməⁿnt/, **instruments. 1** An **instrument** is **1.1** a tool or device that is used to do a particular task. EG *...surgical instruments... ...instruments of torture.* **1.2** a device that is used for making measurements of something such as speed, height, or sound. EG *The co-pilot was watching a panel of instruments.* N COUNT

2 A musical **instrument** is an object such as a piano, guitar, or violin, which you play in order to produce music. EG *...stringed instruments.* N COUNT

3 Something that is an **instrument** for achieving a particular aim is used by people to achieve that aim. EG *Incomes policy is a weak instrument for reducing inflation... The Labour Party is the only instrument of change open to them.* N COUNT+SUPP Formal

instrumental /ɪnstrəˈmentəⁿl/. **1** Someone or something that is **instrumental** in a process or event helps to make it happen. EG *The organization was instrumental in getting a ban on certain furs.* ADJ QUALIT

2 Instrumental music is performed by instruments and not by voices. ADJ CLASSIF

insubordination /ɪnsəbɔːdɪneɪʃəⁿn/ is disobedient behaviour. EG *...charges of insubordination.* N UNCOUNT Formal

insubstantial /ɪnsəbstænʃəⁿl/. Something that is **insubstantial** is not very large, solid, or strong. EG *...a feathery, insubstantial plant... ...slender and insubstantial structures.* ADJ QUALIT

insufferable /ɪnsʌfəⁿrəbəⁿl/. If you find someone or something **insufferable**, you find them very unpleasant or annoying. EG *He was becoming an insufferable pest with his stealing.* ADJ CLASSIF

insufficient /ɪnsəfɪʃəⁿnt/. Something that is **insufficient** is not enough for a particular purpose. EG *Insufficient research has been done... These steps will be insufficient to change our economic decline.* ADJ CLASSIF OFT+for OR to-INF

◊ **insufficiently.** EG *My hand had proved insufficiently strong to open the door.* ◊ ADV

insular /ɪnsjʊlə/. People who are **insular** are unwilling to meet new people or to consider new ideas. EG *He lived a rather insular life.* ADJ QUALIT

insulate /ɪnsjʊˈleɪt/, **insulates, insulating, insulated. 1** If you **insulate** a person from harmful things, you protect them from those things. EG *The leaders were able to insulate the local population from these dangerous influences... ...in a sheltered, womb-like world, insulated against the events of life outside.* v+o: OFT+from/ against Formal

2 If a material or substance **insulates** something, it keeps the thing warm by covering it in a thick layer. EG *The function of a mammal's hair is to insulate the body.* v+o

3 If you **insulate** a tool or electrical device, you cover it with rubber or plastic in order to prevent electricity passing through it and giving the person using it an electric shock. EG *...two small electrical screwdrivers with insulated handles.* v+o

insulation /ɪnsjʊˈleɪʃəⁿn/ is a thick layer of a material or substance, which keeps something warm. EG *...a long roll of roof insulation.* N UNCOUNT

insult, insults, insulting, insulted; pronounced /ɪnsʌlt/ when it is a verb and /ɪnsʌlt/ when it is a noun.

1 If you **insult** someone, you say something rude about them, or offend them by doing something that shows you have a low opinion of them. EG *You don't have to apologize to me. You didn't insult me... He feels deeply insulted.* ◊ **insulting.** EG *He did use insulting language.* v+o ◊ ADJ QUALIT

2 An **insult** is a rude remark about someone or an action that offends them. EG *The older boys yelled out insults... I would take it as an insult if you left.* N COUNT

● You say **'to add insult to injury'** when mentioning an action or fact that makes a situation you are involved in even more unfair or unpleasant. EG *To add insult to injury, the penalty was awarded to the other side.* ● PHRASE

insuperable /ɪnsjuːpəⁿrəbəⁿl/. A problem that is **insuperable** cannot be solved. EG *It would be an insuperable barrier to unity.* ADJ CLASSIF Formal

insupportable /ɪnsəpɔːtəbəⁿl/. If you find something **insupportable**, you find it so unpleasant that you cannot accept it. EG *Accusations of that kind are quite insupportable... The strain would be insupportable.* ADJ CLASSIF Formal

insurance /ɪnʃʊərəns, -ʃɔː-/. **1 Insurance** is an agreement in which you pay a fixed sum of money to a special company, usually each year. Then, if you become ill or if your property is damaged or stolen, the company pays you a sum of money. EG *...private health insurance... ...insurance companies.* ● See also **national insurance.** N UNCOUNT

2 If you do something as an **insurance** against something unpleasant, you do it in order to protect yourself in case the unpleasant thing happens, or in order to prevent it from happening. EG *They build up supplies as an insurance against drought.* N SING: USU+against

insure /ɪnʃʊə, -ʃɔː-/, **insures, insuring, insured. 1** If you **insure** yourself or your property, you pay money to an insurance company so that, if you become ill or if your property is damaged or stolen, v+o OR V-REFL the company will pay you a sum of money. EG *Insure your baggage before you leave home.* ◊ **insured.** EG *The house is not insured against fire.* ◊ ADJ PRED

2 If you do something to **insure** against something V+*against* unpleasant happening, you do it in order to protect yourself in case it happens, or in order to prevent it from happening. EG *In years of good rainfall they expand their stocks to insure against drought.*

3 See also **ensure.**

insurgent /ɪnˈsɜːdʒənt/, **insurgents. Insurgents** N COUNT : are people who are fighting against the govern- USU PLURAL ment or army of their own country. EG *Insurgents partially damaged the embassy.*

insurmountable /ɪnsəˈmaʊntəbəˀl/. A problem ADJ CLASSIF that is **insurmountable** cannot be solved. EG *The* Formal *bureaucratic obstacles to this proved insurmountable.*

insurrection /ɪnsəˈrekʃəˀn/, **insurrections.** An N COUNT OR **insurrection** is violent action that is taken by a N UNCOUNT large group of people against the rulers of their country. EG *We are not prepared for an armed insurrection... Such policies were intended to prevent insurrection.*

intact /ɪnˈtækt/. Something that is **intact** is com- ADJ QUALIT : plete and has not been damaged or changed in any USU PRED way. EG *...the only window that remained intact... They are fighting to keep village life intact.*

intake /ˈɪnteɪk/, **intakes. 1** Your **intake** of food, N UNCOUNT drink, or air is the amount that you eat, drink, or +SUPP breathe in, or the process of taking it into your body. EG *Nurses kept measuring her fluid intake.*

2 The people who are accepted into an institution N COUNT : or organization at a particular time are referred to USU+SUPP as a particular **intake.** EG *...the army's huge emergency intake of soldiers.*

intangible /ɪnˈtændʒɪbəˀl/. A quality or idea that is ADJ QUALIT **intangible** is hard to define or explain. EG *...a vast and intangible subject.*

integral /ˈɪntɪˀgrəl/. Something that is an **integral** ADJ CLASSIF : part of something else is an essential part of it. EG OFT+*to* *The Young Socialists were an integral feature of the Labour movement... The concept of loyalty is integral to the story.*

integrate /ˈɪntɪˀgreɪt/, **integrates, integrating, integrated. 1** If people **integrate** into a social V-ERG+*into*; group, they mix with people in that group. EG ALSO *...helping the individual integrate quickly into the* V OR V+*with* : *community... ...ways of integrating handicapped* RECIP *children into ordinary schools.* ◊ **integration** ◊ N UNCOUNT /ˌɪntɪˀˈgreɪʃəˀn/. EG *He campaigned for the integration of immigrants into British society.*

2 If you **integrate** things, you combine them so V+O that they are closely linked or so that they form one thing. EG *The two regional railway systems were integrated.*

integrated /ˈɪntɪˀgreɪtɪˀd/. An **integrated** institu- ADJ CLASSIF : tion is intended for use by people of all races or ATTRIB groups. EG *...an integrated school for Protestants and Catholics.*

integrity /ɪnˈtegrɪtiˀ/. **1 Integrity** is the quality of N UNCOUNT being honest and firm in your moral principles. EG *He was particularly respected for his integrity... My husband was a man of the highest integrity.*

2 The **integrity** of something such as a group of N UNCOUNT people is its quality of being one united or connect- +POSS ed thing. EG *They were totally committed to the* Formal *survival and integrity of the nation.*

intellect /ˈɪntɪˀlekt/, **intellects. Intellect** is **1** the N UNCOUNT ability to think and to understand ideas and infor- OR N COUNT mation. EG *...the intellect of modern man... ...the idea of computers with intellects.* **2** the quality of N UNCOUNT being very intelligent or clever. EG *He was born into a family noted for its intellect.*

intellectual /ɪntɪˀˈlektʃʊˀəl/, **intellectuals. 1 In-** ADJ CLASSIF : **tellectual** means involving a person's ability to ATTRIB think and to understand ideas and information. EG *...children in need of extra emotional or intellectual stimulation... ...his tremendous intellectual*

powers. ◊ **intellectually.** EG *...an intellectually* ◊ ADV *challenging occupation.*

2 An **intellectual** is someone who spends a lot of N COUNT time studying and thinking about complicated ideas. EG *...scholars and intellectuals.* ▸ used as an ▸ ADJ QUALIT adjective. EG *...all the intellectual Oxford people... ...an intellectual conversation.*

intelligence /ɪnˈtelɪdʒəˀns/. **1** Someone's **intelli-** N UNCOUNT **gence** is their ability to understand and learn things. EG *...a person of average intelligence... She prided herself on her intelligence.*

2 Intelligence is the ability to think and under- N UNCOUNT stand instead of doing things by instinct or auto- matically. EG *Do hedgehogs have intelligence?... ...computer intelligence.*

3 Intelligence is also information that is gathered N UNCOUNT by the government or the army about their coun- try's enemies. EG *...American intelligence services.*

intelligent /ɪnˈtelɪdʒəˀnt/. **1** Someone who is **intel-** ADJ QUALIT **ligent** has the ability to understand and learn things well. EG *Jo is an intelligent student... ...a very intelligent question.* ◊ **intelligently.** EG *They dealt* ◊ ADV *with that problem intelligently.*

2 An animal or computer that is **intelligent** has ADJ CLASSIF the ability to think and understand instead of doing things by instinct or automatically. EG *We have shown that computers can be intelligent.*

intelligentsia /ɪnˌtelɪˀˈdʒentsɪə/. The **intelligent-** N COLL : *the*+N **sia** in a community are the most educated people Formal in it.

intelligible /ɪnˈtelɪdʒəbəˀl/. Something that is **in-** ADJ QUALIT **telligible** can be understood. EG *Make sure that your letters are intelligible... Describe it in a way that would be intelligible to an outsider.*

intend /ɪnˈtend/, **intends, intending, intended. 1** V+*to*-INF If you **intend** to do something, you have decided to OR -ING do it or have planned to do it. EG *This is my job and I intend to do it... He had intended staying longer... He woke later than he had intended.*

2 If you **intend** something or to have a V+O+*to*-INF, particular effect or function, you have planned that *as,* OR it should happen or should have this effect or REPORT : function. EG *We never intended the scheme to be* ONLY *that* *permanent... It is intended as a handbook, for frequent reference... It had been intended that a second group should be assembled.*

3 Something that **is intended** for a particular V+O : USU person or purpose has been planned or made for PASS+*for* that person or purpose. EG *The man had drunk what had been intended for me... They are not yet intended for use.*

intended /ɪnˈtendɪˀd/. You use **intended** to de- ADJ CLASSIF : scribe the thing that you are trying or planning to ATTRIB achieve, do, or affect. EG *What is the intended result?... ...your intended trip abroad... ...his intended ruin.*

intense /ɪnˈtens/. **1** Something that is **intense** is ADJ QUALIT very great in strength or degree. EG *The effects of the drug are intense and brief... ...the intense heat... The row caused her intense unhappiness.* ◊ **intensely.** EG *She had suffered intensely.* ◊ ADV ◊ **intensity** /ɪnˈtensɪˀtiˀ/. EG *The debates are re-* ◊ N UNCOUNT *newed with great intensity.*

2 If you describe a person as **intense**, you mean ADJ QUALIT that they seem very serious all the time. EG *It was like Jane to be so intense and dramatic about the future.*

intensify /ɪnˈtensɪfaɪ/, **intensifies, intensifying,** V-ERG **intensified.** If you **intensify** something or if it **intensifies**, it becomes greater in strength or degree. EG *In the late 1960s the pressures suddenly intensified.* ◊ **intensified.** EG *...intensified interna-* ◊ ADJ CLASSIF : *tional competition.* ATTRIB

intensive /ɪnˈtensɪv/. An **intensive** activity in- ADJ QUALIT volves the concentration of energy or people on one particular task in order to try to achieve a great deal in a short time. EG *...the last intensive preparation for my exams... ...an intensive struggle against racism.* ◊ **intensively.** EG *The land was developed very intensively in the mid 1930s.* ◊ ADV

intensive care is extremely thorough care pro- N UNCOUNT vided by hospitals for people who are so ill that they would die if they were not being looked after.

intent /ɪntent/, **intents.** 1 A person's **intent** is N UNCOUNT their intention to do something. EG *The conference* Formal *declared its intent to organize a national movement... They signed a declaration of intent.*

2 When you look **intent**, you show that you are ADJ QUALIT paying great attention to someone or something. EG *He gazed at their intent faces... She was brushing her hair, intent on her face in the mirror.* ◊ **intently.** EG *I stood behind a parked van, watch-* ◊ ADV *ing intently.*

3 If you are **intent** on doing something, you are ADJ PRED determined to do it. EG *They were intent on keeping* +on/upon *what they had.*

4 You use the phrase **to all intents and purposes** ADV SEN to suggest that a situation is not exactly as you describe it but the effect is the same as if it were. EG *She was to all intents and purposes the infant's mother.*

intention /ɪntenʃəᵒn/, **intentions.** An **intention** N COUNT OR that you have is an idea or plan of what you are N UNCOUNT going to do. EG *He confirmed his intention to leave next April... He was suspicious of the government's intentions... She had no intention of spending the rest of her life working as a waitress.*

intentional /ɪntenʃəᵒnəl, -ʃənᵒl/. Something that ADJ CLASSIF is **intentional** is deliberate. EG *...intentional misrepresentation.* ◊ **intentionally.** EG *I banged the door.* ◊ ADV *Not intentionally.*

inter- is used to form adjectives that describe PREFIX something as moving, existing, or happening between similar things or groups of people. For example, inter-governmental relations are relations between governments. EG *...intercontinental missiles... ...inter-state roads... ...inter-racial marriages.*

interact /ɪntərækt/, **interacts, interacting, interacted.** 1 When people **interact** with each V OR V + with: other, they communicate or work together. EG RECIP *Mothers and babies interact in a very complex way.* ◊ **interaction** /ɪntərækʃəᵒn/, **interactions.** ◊ N UNCOUNT EG *There is a need for more interaction between* OR N COUNT *staff and children.*

2 When one thing **interacts** with another, the two V OR V + with: things react together and affect each other's devel- RECIP opment or nature. EG *The bacteria's genes interact with those of many plants.* ◊ **interaction.** EG *...a* ◊ N UNCOUNT *method of encouraging the interaction of ideas.* OR N COUNT

interactive /ɪntəræktɪv/. **Interactive** use of a ADJ CLASSIF computer is use in which the user and the comput- Technical er communicate directly with each other via a keyboard and a screen. EG *...interactive graphic systems... ...interactive computer games.*

intercede /ɪntəsiːd/, **intercedes, interceding,** V : OFT + with **interceded.** If you **intercede** with a person, you Formal talk to them in order to try to end a disagreement that they have with another person. EG *Ten years before, I had interceded for him with his employer.*

intercept /ɪntəsept/, **intercepts, intercepting,** V+O **intercepted.** If you **intercept** someone or something that is travelling from one place to another, you stop them. EG *The car was intercepted and stopped by a policeman.*

intercession /ɪntəseʃəᵒn/, **intercessions. Inter-** N UNCOUNT **cession** is an act of trying to end a disagreement OR N COUNT between two people, usually by talking to one of Formal them. EG *Through the intercession of a friend, my request was granted.*

interchange /ɪntətʃeɪndᵒʒ/, **interchanges.** 1 The N UNCOUNT **interchange** of things, people, or ideas is the OR N COUNT exchange of things, people, or ideas. EG *...a regular* +SUPP

forum for the interchange of information and ideas... ...interchange between the classes.

2 An **interchange** on a motorway is a junction N COUNT where it meets a main road or another motorway.

interchangeable /ɪntətʃeɪndᵒʒəbᵒl/. Things that ADJ CLASSIF are **interchangeable** can be exchanged with each other without making any difference to a situation. EG *We tend to use these terms as if they were freely interchangeable... ...interchangeable forms of energy.* ◊ **interchangeably.** EG *In many of the* ◊ ADV speeches, the word 'fascist' was used interchangeably with the word 'racist'.*

intercom /ɪntəkɒm/, **intercoms.** An **intercom** is N COUNT a device which people use to communicate with each other when they are in different rooms. It is usually like a box with a microphone for talking into and a loudspeaker to hear the reply. EG *A voice on the intercom said, 'It's Mr Vaughan.'*

interconnect /ɪntəkənekt/, **interconnects,** V OR V + with : **interconnecting, interconnected.** Things that RECIP; ALSO **interconnect** or that **are interconnected** are V-PASS connected to each other or with each other. EG *The nervous system is a complicated network of interconnecting parts... Monarch, court and government were all interconnected.*

intercontinental /ɪntəkɒntɪnentᵒl/ is used to ADJ CLASSIF describe something that exists or happens between continents. EG *...an intercontinental flight.*

intercourse /ɪntəkɔːs/ is the act of having sex. EG N UNCOUNT *He had had sexual intercourse with her.*

interdependent /ɪntədɪˈpendənt/. People or ADJ CLASSIF things that are **interdependent** all depend on each other. EG *Plants and animals are strongly interdependent.* ◊ **interdependence** ◊ N UNCOUNT /ɪntədɪˈpendəns/. EG *...the interdependence of* Formal *economies.*

interest /ɪntrᵊᵉst/, **interests, interesting, interested.** 1 If you have an **interest** in something, N SING OR you want to learn or hear more about it. EG *None of* N UNCOUNT them had the slightest interest in music... Brody was beginning to lose interest.*

2 Your **interests** are the things that you spend N COUNT time on because you enjoy them. EG *He had two consuming interests: rowing and polo.*

3 Something that is of **interest** attracts your N UNCOUNT attention because it is exciting or unusual. EG *There was nothing of any great interest in the paper today.*

4 If something **interests** you, you want to learn V+O more about it or to continue doing it. EG *Young men should always look for work which interests them.*

5 If you **interest** someone in something, you V+O : OFT+in persuade them to do it or to buy it. EG *Can I interest you in yet another horror movie?*

6 If you have an **interest** in something being done, N COUNT : you want it to be done because you will benefit OFT+in from it. EG *They had no interest in the overthrow of the established order... They would protect the interests of their members.* ● Something that is **in** ● PHRASE **the interests** of a person or group will benefit them in some way. EG *It is not in the interests of any of us to have a weak government.* ● See also **vested interest.**

7 If you do something **in the interests** of a PHRASE particular thing, you do it in order to achieve or preserve this thing. EG *She was prepared to sacrifice this principle in the interests of domestic harmony.*

8 Someone who has **interests** in a particular type N PLURAL of business owns companies or shares of this type. EG *...an industrialist with business interests in Germany.*

9 **Interest** is money that you receive if you have N UNCOUNT invested a sum of money, or money that you pay if you have borrowed money. EG *...the interest you pay on your mortgage... ...high interest rates.*

interested /ɪntrᵊᵉstɪ²d/. 1 Someone who is **interested** in something 1.1 wants to know more ADJ QUALIT : about it. EG *I'm very interested in birds... She was* USU PRED + in genuinely *interested in everyone she met... He looked interested.* **1.2** thinks that it is important and worth giving attention to. EG *We are interested only in the efficiency of the company as a whole.* ADJ PRED+in

2 Someone who is **interested** in doing something wants to do it. EG *My sister is interested in becoming a nurse... No. I'm not interested.* ADJ PRED : USU+in

3 An **interested** party or group of people is affected by or involved in a particular event or situation. EG *We talked to a group of scientists who know about this work, and other interested parties.* ADJ CLASSIF : ATTRIB

interesting /ɪntəˈrəˈstɪŋ/. If you find something **interesting**, it attracts or holds your attention, for example because you think it is exciting or unusual. EG *That's a very interesting question... He was not very interesting to talk to... It must be quite interesting for you.* ADJ QUALIT

interestingly /ɪntəˈrəˈstɪŋliˈ/. You use **interestingly** to introduce a piece of information that you think is interesting and unexpected. EG *Interestingly enough, America is now dependent on Africa for 40% of its oil imports.* ADV SEN

interfere /ɪntəˈfɪə/, **interferes, interfering, interfered.** **1** If you **interfere** in a situation, you try to influence it or become involved in it although it does not really concern you; used showing disapproval. EG *My mother interferes in things... They didn't interfere with us and we didn't interfere with them... Don't interfere.* V : USU+A

2 Something that **interferes** with a situation, process, or activity has a damaging effect on it. EG *Child-bearing will not interfere with a career.* V : OFT+with

interference /ɪntəˈfɪərəns/. **1 Interference** is the act of interfering in something. EG *I wanted to do the thing on my own without outside interference or help... They didn't want any interference from their national government.* N UNCOUNT

2 When there is **interference**, a radio signal is affected by other radio waves so that it cannot be received properly. N UNCOUNT

interfering /ɪntəˈfɪərɪŋ/. An **interfering** person tries to get involved in other people's affairs, especially when their advice is not wanted. EG *...an interfering old woman.* ADJ QUALIT

interim /ɪntərɪm/ is used to describe things that are intended to be used only until something more permanent is arranged or produced. EG *...a temporary or interim arrangement... ...an interim loan... ...an interim report.* ADJ CLASSIF : ATTRIB

interior /ɪntɪərɪə/, **interiors.** **1** The **interior** of something is the inside part of it. EG *Very little is known about the deep interior of the earth... The castle has its interior well preserved.* N COUNT

2 You use **interior** to describe something that is inside a building or vehicle. EG *...an interior room without windows.* ADJ CLASSIF : ATTRIB

3 The **interior** of a country or continent is the central area of it. EG *The interior of the island consists largely of swamps.* N SING : the+N

4 An **interior** minister or political department deals with affairs in their own country. EG *The Interior Department framed a criminal code forbidding church services.* ADJ CLASSIF : ATTRIB

interject /ɪntədˈʒɛkt/, **interjects, interjecting, interjected.** If you **interject**, you say something and interrupt someone else who is speaking. EG *'No, no,' interjected Schmidt... If I may interject a word here.* V, V+QUOTE, OR V+O Formal

interjection /ɪntədˈʒɛkʃəˈn/. **1** An **interjection** is something you say which interrupts someone else who is speaking. EG *The bishop was prepared for this interjection.* N COUNT Formal

2 In grammar, an **interjection** is a word or expression which you use to express a strong feeling such as surprise, pain, or horror, and which you often say loudly and emphatically. In this dictionary words like this are described as EXCLAM in the Extra Column. N COUNT

interlock /ɪntəlɒk/, **interlocks, interlocking, interlocked.** Things that **interlock** with each other fit into each other so that they are firmly joined together. EG *All the units interlock with one another rigidly... He interlocked his fingers.* V-ERG : ALSO V OR V+with : RECIP

interloper /ɪntələʊpə/, **interlopers.** An **interloper** is a person who interferes in something or who is in a place where they are not supposed to be. EG *Any interloper who heckled would be removed from the meeting.* N COUNT

interlude /ɪntəluːd/, **interludes.** An **interlude** is a short period of time when an activity or event stops for a break. EG *After this interlude, the band started up again.* N COUNT

intermarry /ɪntəmæriˈ/, **intermarries, intermarrying, intermarried.** When people from different social, racial, or religious groups **intermarry**, they marry each other. V OR V+with : RECIP

intermediary /ɪntəmiːdjəriˈ/, **intermediaries.** An **intermediary** is a person who passes messages or proposals between two people or groups. EG *He dealt through an intermediary with Beaverbrook himself... This spirit serves as an intermediary between men and the gods.* N COUNT

intermediate /ɪntəmiːdɪət/, **intermediates.** **1** An **intermediate** stage or position is one that occurs between two other stages or positions. EG *One group of animals developed into another by way of intermediate forms.* ADJ CLASSIF : ATTRIB

2 Intermediate students are no longer beginners, but are not yet advanced. EG *...an English course, intermediate level, for adult students.* ADJ CLASSIF

interminable /ɪntɜːmɪnəbəˈl/. Something that seems **interminable** seems to continue for a very long time. EG *I was glad of company for this interminable flight.* ◊ **interminably.** EG *MPs argued each point interminably.* ADJ CLASSIF ◊ ADV

intermingle /ɪntəmɪŋgəˈl/, **intermingles, intermingling, intermingled.** When people or things **intermingle**, they mix with each other. EG *The police intermingled with the crowds.* V OR V+with : RECIP Formal

intermission /ɪntəmɪʃəˈn/, **intermissions.** An **intermission** is an interval between two parts of a play. N COUNT American

intermittent /ɪntəmɪtənt/. Something that is **intermittent** happens occasionally rather than continuously. EG *I became aware of a faint, intermittent noise, somewhere outside.* ◊ **intermittently.** EG *The magazine had been published intermittently since the war.* ADJ QUALIT ◊ ADV

intern /ɪntɜːn/, **interns, interning, interned.** To **intern** someone means to put them in prison, for political reasons. EG *They were interned for subversive activities.* V+O Formal

internal /ɪntɜːnəˈl/. **1** You use **internal 1.1** to describe things that exist or happen inside a place, person, or object. EG *You should lag internal pipes to prevent them from freezing.* ◊ **internally.** EG *The house has been rebuilt internally.* **1.2** to describe the political and commercial activities inside a country. EG *...the internal politics of France.* **1.3** to describe something that exists or happens within a particular organization. EG *...an internal bank memorandum.* ADJ CLASSIF : ATTRIB ◊ ADV ADJ CLASSIF : ATTRIB ADJ CLASSIF : ATTRIB

2 Internal ideas or images exist in your thoughts or in your mind. EG *We have both external and internal values.* ADJ CLASSIF Formal

international /ɪntənæʃənəˈl/, **internationals.** **1 International** means involving different countries. EG *...international affairs... They signed an international agreement on nuclear waste.* ◊ **internationally.** EG *She's an internationally famous historian.* ADJ CLASSIF ◊ ADV

2 An **international** is a sports match between teams from two countries. N COUNT

If something happens at intervals, does it happen in an interval?

internment /ɪntɜːnmənt/ is imprisonment for N UNCOUNT
political reasons. EG ...the internment of human- Formal
rights activists... ...two years of internment.

interpersonal /ɪntəpɜːsəʰnəl/ means relating to ADJ CLASSIF :
relationships between people. EG ...interpersonal ATTRIB
relationships... ...interpersonal skills.

interplay /ɪntəpleɪ/. The **interplay** between two N UNCOUNT :
or more things is the way that they react with each USU+of/
other and have an effect on each other. EG ...the between
interplay between practical and theoretical con- Formal
straints... ...the interplay of market forces.

interpose /ɪntəpəʊz/, **interposes, interposing,** V OR V+QUOTE
interposed. If you **interpose**, you interrupt with a Formal
comment or question. EG 'Enough of this!' interposed Miss Musson.

interpret /ɪntɜːprɪt/, **interprets, interpreting,**
interpreted. 1 If you **interpret** something in a V+O : OFT+as
particular way, you decide that this is its meaning
or significance. EG I'm not quite sure how to interpret that question... The election result is being
interpreted as a serious setback for the government.
2 If you **interpret** what someone is saying, you V+O OR V
translate it immediately into another language. EG
Paul had to interpret for us.

interpretation /ɪntɜːprɪteɪʃəʰn/, **interpreta-**
tions. 1 An **interpretation** of something is an N COUNT OR
explanation of what it means. EG This passage is N UNCOUNT
open to a variety of interpretations.
2 A performer's **interpretation** of a piece of N COUNT OR
music or a dance is the particular way in which N UNCOUNT
they choose to perform it. EG Do you find his
interpretation of Chopin satisfactory?

interpreter /ɪntɜːprɪtə/, **interpreters.** An **inter-** N COUNT
preter is a person whose job is to listen to what
someone is saying and translate it immediately
into another language. EG I talked to him through
an interpreter.

interrelate /ɪntəriˈleɪt/, **interrelates, interre-** V-ERG :
lating, interrelated. If two or more things **inter-** USU PASS
relate or **are interrelated**, there is some kind of Formal
connection between them, so that they have an
effect on one another. EG These courses interrelate
in a variety of ways... All three factors are interrelated.

interrogate /ɪntərəgeɪt/, **interrogates, interro-** V+O
gating, interrogated. If someone, especially a
police officer or an army officer, **interrogates**
you, they question you thoroughly for a long time,
in order to get information from you. EG They had
been interrogated for 20 hours about political demonstrations. ◊ **interrogation** /ɪntərəgeɪʃəʰn/, **in-** ◊ N COUNT OR
terrogations. EG Waddell had undergone a lengthy N UNCOUNT
interrogation... We've had him under interrogation
for 36 hours.

interrogative /ɪntərɒgətɪv/, **interrogatives.** 1 ADJ CLASSIF
An **interrogative** sentence is one that has the
form of a question.
2 An **interrogative** is a word such as 'who', 'how', N COUNT
or 'why', which can be used to ask a question.

interrogator /ɪntərəgeɪtə/, **interrogators.** An N COUNT
interrogator is a person who questions someone
thoroughly for a long time.

interrupt /ɪntərʌpt/, **interrupts, interrupting,**
interrupted. 1 If you **interrupt** someone who is V+O,
speaking, you say or do something that causes V+QUOTE,
them to pause or stop. EG Sorry to interrupt you... OR V
'Mother!' interrupted Delia.
2 If you **interrupt** an activity, you temporarily V+O
prevent it from continuing. EG Bain had interrupted
his holiday to go to Hamburg.

interruption /ɪntərʌpʃəʰn/, **interruptions.** 1 An N COUNT
interruption is something which temporarily prevents an activity from continuing. EG She hates
interruptions when she's working.
2 **Interruption** is the act of interrupting someone N UNCOUNT
or something. EG We should be safe from interruption.

intersect /ɪntəsekt/, **intersects, intersecting,**
intersected. 1 When roads **intersect**, they cross V OR V+O :
each other. EG The highway intersected Main Street RECIP
in a busy crossing.
2 If an area **is intersected** by roads or railways, V+O : USU PASS
they cross it and divide it into smaller areas. EG The
marshes were intersected by a maze of ditches.

intersection /ɪntəsekʃəʰn/, **intersections.** An N COUNT :
intersection is a place where roads cross each OFT+of/with
other. EG ...a city at the intersection of three
motorways.

interspersed /ɪntəspɜːst/. If something is **inter-** ADJ PRED
spersed with other things, these things occur at +with/by
various points in it. EG ...shabby shops and houses
interspersed with modern offices and banks... ...a
story interspersed with long silences.

intertwine /ɪntətwaɪn/, **intertwines, intertwin-** V-ERG; ALSO
ing, intertwined. If two things **intertwine** or **are** V OR V+with :
intertwined, they are joined together in a very RECIP
close or complicated way. EG Their tails intertwine... Reality and art are intertwined.

interval /ɪntəvəl/, **intervals.** 1 An **interval** is the N COUNT : OFT
period of time between two events or dates. EG +between/of
...the interval between supper and bedtime... ...after
an interval of ten years.
2 At a play or concert, an **interval** is a break N COUNT
between two of the parts. EG The audience were
going out for the interval... ...the tea interval.
3 If something happens at **intervals**, it happens PHRASE
several times, with gaps or pauses in between. EG
At intervals, the carriage was halted... They kept
coming back at six-month intervals.
4 If things are placed at particular **intervals**, PHRASE
there are spaces between them. EG They were
scattered through the forest, at varying intervals.
5 In music, an **interval** is the difference in pitch N COUNT
between two notes. Technical

intervene /ɪntəviːn/, **intervenes, intervening,**
intervened. 1 If you **intervene**, you take action in V : OFT+in
a situation that you were not originally involved in.
EG Two officers intervened to stop their recording...
The State may intervene in disputes between employers and workers. ◊ **intervention** ◊ N UNCOUNT
/ɪntəvenʃəʰn/, **interventions.** EG He was against OR N COUNT
American intervention in the war.
2 If you **intervene** when someone is talking, you V OR V+QUOTE
interrupt them by saying something. EG 'Yes,' intervened Grant, 'but you had it.' ◊ **intervention,** ◊ N UNCOUNT
interventions. ...the angry interventions of Lord OR N COUNT
Grant.
3 You can say that an event **intervenes** when it V
delays something or prevents it from happening. EG
This will produce a result unless the weather
intervenes.
4 If an event happens a particular number of days V
or years after another event, you can say that that
number of days or years **intervenes** between the
two events. EG Ten years had intervened since she
had last seen Joe.

intervening /ɪntəviːnɪŋ/. 1 An **intervening** peri- ADJ CLASSIF
od of time is one which separates two events or ATTRIB
points in time. EG What happened in the intervening years?
2 An **intervening** object or area exists between ADJ CLASSIF :
two others. EG The intervening space consists of ATTRIB
empty windows.

interview /ɪntəvjuː/, **interviews, interviewing,**
interviewed. 1 An **interview** is 1.1 a formal N COUNT OR
meeting at which someone is asked questions in N UNCOUNT
order to find out if they are suitable for a job or for
a course of study. EG I had an interview for a job on
a newspaper... He was invited for interview at
three universities. 1.2 a conversation in which a N COUNT
journalist asks a famous person questions. EG ...my
interview with the Duke... ...a television interview.
2 If an employer **interviews** you, he or she asks V+O
you questions in order to find out whether you are
suitable for a job. EG I was once interviewed for a
part in a film.

3 When a famous person **is interviewed**, a jour-   v+o : usu pass
nalist asks this person a series of questions. eg
*Hopkins was interviewed by Wyndham for Queen
magazine.* ◇ **interviewer** /ɪntəvjuːə/, **interview-** ◇ n count
ers. eg *Television interviewers were being too
aggressive.*

interwoven /ɪntəwəʊvⁿn/. If things are **inter-** adj classif
woven, they are joined together in a very close
and complicated way. eg *Social and international
unity have become interwoven.*

intestine /ɪntestɪn/, **intestines.** Your **intestines** n count :
are the tubes in your body through which food   usu plural
from your stomach passes. eg *...pains in the intes-
tine.* ◇ **intestinal** /ɪntestɪnəl/. eg *...the cause of* ◇ adj classif :
serious intestinal infections... ...an enzyme which   attrib
exists in the intestinal lining.

intimacy /ɪntɪˈməsi/, **intimacies. 1** When there n uncount :
is **intimacy** between people, they have a close   oft+
relationship. eg *...the intimacy between mother and*   between/with
*child... Never before had he known such intimacy
with another person.*
2 Intimacies are things that are said or done by n count :
people in a close relationship. eg *I like sharing*   usu plural
these little intimacies.

intimate, intimates, intimating, intimated;
pronounced /ɪntɪˈmət/ when it is an adjective or
noun, and /ɪntɪmeɪt/ when it is a verb. **1** If two adj qualit
people have an **intimate** relationship, they are
very good friends. eg *...her best and most intimate
friend.* ◇ **intimately.** eg *I don't know any girls* ◇ adv
intimately.
2 Your **intimates** are your close friends. eg *He let* n count
one or two intimates know his good news.   Literary
3 If you are **intimate** with someone, you have a adj classif
sexual relationship with them. eg *He had been*   Formal
intimate with a number of women.
4 Intimate things are very personal and private. adj qualit
eg *...the most intimate details of their personal
lives.* ◇ **intimately.** eg *...women talking intimately* ◇ adv
to other women.
5 An **intimate** place or occasion has a pleasant adj qualit
and friendly atmosphere. eg *...small and intimate
night clubs... ...an intimate meal with the family.*
6 An **intimate** connection between ideas or or- adj qualit :
ganizations is very strong or close. eg *...its intimate*   usu attrib
bonds with government. ◇ **intimately.** eg *These* ◇ adv
two questions are intimately linked.
7 If you have an **intimate** knowledge of something, adj qualit :
you know it in great detail. eg *...someone with an*   attrib
intimate knowledge of the station. ◇ **intimately.** ◇ adv
eg *He knew the contents of the files intimately.*
8 If you **intimate** something, you tell it to some- v+o or
one, often in an indirect way. eg *Forbes intimated* v+report :
that he would prefer to do this later.   only that
  Formal

intimation /ɪntɪmeɪʃⁿn/, **intimations.** An **inti-** n count+supp
mation of something is an indication or feeling   Formal
that it is likely to exist, happen, or be true. eg *For
the first time I felt some intimation of danger...
...the first intimations of a new idea.*

intimidate /ɪntɪmɪdeɪt/, **intimidates, intimidat-** v+o
ing, intimidated. If you **intimidate** someone, you
frighten them, sometimes as a deliberate way of
making them do something. eg *In 1972 his neighbours intimidated his family into leaving.*
◇ **intimidation** /ɪntɪmɪdeɪʃⁿn/. eg *Young suffered* ◇ n uncount
imprisonment and intimidation.

intimidated /ɪntɪmɪdeɪtᵻd/. If people are **intimi-** adj qualit
dated, they feel afraid and have no confidence in
themselves. eg *Theo was intimidated by so many
strangers.*

intimidating /ɪntɪmɪdeɪtɪŋ/. If something is **in-** adj qualit
timidating, it causes you to feel afraid and to lose
confidence in yourself. eg *The rooms were huge
and intimidating.*

into /ɪntuː/. **1** If you put one thing **into** another prep
thing, you put it inside the other thing, so that it is
enclosed or surrounded. eg *Pour some water into a
glass... He slipped the note into his pocket.*
2 If you go **into** a place or vehicle, you move from prep

being outside it to being inside it. eg *He walked into
a police station... They got into the car.*
3 If one thing gets **into** another thing, it enters it prep
and becomes part of it. eg *Drugs may get into the
milk... ...Britain's entry into the Common Market.*
4 If you are walking or driving a vehicle and you prep
bump **into** something or crash **into** something, you
hit it accidentally. eg *I bumped into a chair.*
5 When you get **into** a piece of clothing, you put it prep
on. eg *She changed into her best dress.*
6 If someone or something gets **into** a particular prep
state, they start being in that state. eg *The Labour
Government came into power in 1974... The assembly was shocked into silence.*
7 If something changes **into** a new form or shape, prep
it then has this new form or shape. eg *The bud
develops into a flower... The play was made into a
movie... He folded his newspaper into a neat rectangle... I tore her letter into eight pieces.*
8 An investigation **into** a subject or event is prep
concerned with that subject or event. eg *...research
into emotional problems... Some MPs demanded a
full enquiry into the incident.*
9 If you are very interested in something and like it prep
very much, you can say that you are **into** it. eg   Informal
Teenagers are into those romantic novels.

intolerable /ɪntɒlərəbⁿl/. If something is **intol-** adj qualit
erable, it is so bad or so severe that people can no
longer accept it. eg *All my employees found it
intolerable... ...the things that made his life intolerable... ...an intolerable dullness.* ◇ **intolerably.** eg ◇ adv
The days were still intolerably hot.

intolerant /ɪntɒlərənt/. If you are **intolerant**, you adj qualit
disapprove of behaviour and opinions which are
different from your own. eg *He was intolerant of
other people's weakness... We are giving support to
intolerant regimes.* ◇ **intolerance** /ɪntɒlərəns/. eg ◇ n uncount
*She accused the men of ignorance and intoler-
ance... ...religious intolerance.*

intonation /ɪntəⁿneɪʃⁿn/, **intonations.** Intona- n uncount
tion is the way that your voice rises and falls when or n count
you speak. eg *...their accents and intonations... ...a
Northern intonation.*

intone /ɪntəʊn/, **intones, intoning, intoned.** If v+o or
you **intone** something, you say it in a slow and v+quote
serious way, not allowing your voice to rise and fall   Literary
very much. eg *He was intoning, '...and so it is my
privilege and pleasure'... They intoned the afternoon prayers.*

intoxicated /ɪntɒksɪkeɪtᵻd/. **1** If someone is **in-** adj qualit
toxicated, they are drunk. eg *Thompson went into*   Formal
town and got very intoxicated.
2 If you are **intoxicated** by an event, idea, or adj pred
feeling, it makes you very excited so that you +by/with
behave in an extreme way. eg *Intoxicated by
victory, he was dancing... They became intoxicated
with pride.*

intoxicating /ɪntɒksɪkeɪtɪŋ/. **1** An **intoxicating** adj qualit
drink contains alcohol and can make you drunk. eg   Formal
...the intoxicating wine.
2 Something that is **intoxicating** causes you to be adj qualit
very excited and to behave in an uncontrolled or
foolish way. eg *...her intoxicating beauty.*

intoxication /ɪntɒksɪkeɪʃⁿn/ is **1** the state of n uncount
being drunk. eg *They were in an advanced state of*   Formal
intoxication. **2** the state of being so excited that you Formal
behave in an uncontrolled or foolish way. eg *...the
intoxication of success.*

intractable /ɪntræktəbⁿl/. **1 Intractable** people adj qualit
are stubborn and difficult to influence or control. eg   Formal
On one issue Luce was intractable.
2 Intractable problems seem impossible to deal adj qualit
with. eg *Labour problems can be more intractable.*

intransigent /ɪntrænsɪdʒənt/. If someone is **in-** adj qualit
transigent, they refuse to change their behaviour   Formal

Are there any intransitive verbs on these pages?

or opinions; used showing disapproval. EG ...*their intransigent attitude over our debts.*
◊ **intransigence** /ɪntrænsɪdʒəns/. EG *The party is forced into violence by the intransigence of its opponents.* ◊ N UNCOUNT +POSS

intransitive /ɪntrænsɪtɪv/. An **intransitive** verb ADJ CLASSIF does not have an object. In this dictionary v is used in the Extra Column to show that a verb is intransitive. See the entry headed VERBS for more information.

intrepid /ɪntrepɪd/. An **intrepid** person acts ADJ QUALIT bravely, ignoring difficulties and danger. EG *This* Literary *intrepid woman was unlikely to hand over her money... ...the route of those intrepid explorers.*

intricacy /ɪntrɪkəsɪ/, **intricacies. 1** The **intrica-** N PLURAL : **cies** of a situation are its complicated or subtle USU +*of* details. EG ...*the intricacies of American politics.*
2 When you talk about the **intricacy** of something, N UNCOUNT you are referring to the fact that it has many parts or details. EG ...*the technical intricacy of modern industry.*

intricate /ɪntrɪkə¹t/. Something that is **intricate** ADJ QUALIT has many small parts or details. EG *They were painted in intricate patterns... ...long, intricate discussions.* ◊ **intricately.** EG ...*intricately patterned* ◊ ADV *necklaces... ...an intricately carved door.*

intrigue, intrigues, intriguing, intrigued; pronounced /ɪntriːg/ when it is a noun and /ɪntriːg/ when it is a verb.
1 Intrigue is the making of secret plans that are N UNCOUNT intended to harm other people. EG ...*a great deal of* OR N COUNT *political intrigue... ...financial intrigues.*
2 If someone or something **intrigues** you, you are v+o fascinated by them and curious about them. EG *The idea seemed to intrigue him... I was intrigued by the small brown paper packet.* ◊ **intrigued.** EG ◊ ADJ PRED *Intrigued, I followed the instructions.*
◊ **intriguing.** EG *This intriguing woman was an* ◊ ADJ QUALIT *exceptional mathematician... That sounds most intriguing.*

intrinsic /ɪntrɪnsɪk/. The **intrinsic** qualities of ADJ CLASSIF : something are the important and basic qualities of ATTRIB it. EG ...*the intrinsic idiocy of the plan... ...objects* Formal *which have no intrinsic value.* ◊ **intrinsically.** EG ◊ ADV *His material was intrinsically interesting.*

introduce /ɪntrədjuːs/, **introduces, introducing, introduced. 1** If you **introduce** someone to a v+o : OFT+*to* person they do not know, you tell them each other's name, so that they can get to know each other. EG *Hogan introduced him to Karl... At a party in Hollywood, I was introduced to Charlie Chaplin.*
2 If you **introduce** yourself to someone you do not V-REFL know, you tell them your name, so that you can get to know them. EG *I had better introduce myself. I am Mark Rodin... A man came up and introduced himself as the Bishop.*
3 If you **introduce** a speaker to an audience, you v+o tell the audience who the speaker is and what they are going to talk about.
4 When someone **introduces** a television or radio v+o programme, they say a few words at the beginning of it to tell you what it will be about.
5 If you **introduce** something to a place, situation, v+o or system, you take it there or use it there for the first time. EG *Rabbits had been introduced into Australia by Europeans... Banks will soon introduce new savings plans.*
6 If you **introduce** someone to something, you v+o+*to* cause them to learn about it or experience it for the first time. EG *We introduced them to the new methods... He was first introduced to politics as a child.*

introduction /ɪntrədʌkʃə⁰n/, **introductions. 1** N UNCOUNT The **introduction** of something into a place or +SUPP system is the act of taking it there or using it there for the first time. EG *The Government saw the introduction of new technology as vital.*
2 Your **introduction** to something is the occasion N SING : USU+*to*

when you experience it for the first time. EG *This was my first real introduction to agriculture.*
3 The **introduction** to a book or talk is the first N COUNT part, which tells you what the rest of the book or talk is about. EG *Johnston contributes a delightful introduction to Smith's book.*
4 Books which explain the basic facts about a subject often have **Introduction** as part of their title. EG *An Introduction to English Literature.*
5 An **introduction** is also the act of telling two N COUNT people each other's names so that they can get to know each other. EG *Sam got to his feet and I made the introductions.*

introductory /ɪntrəˈdʌktəriː/. **Introductory** re- ADJ CLASSIF : marks, books, or courses are intended to give you a ATTRIB general idea of a particular subject, often before more detailed information is given. EG *After the introductory speeches Hughes began his talk... ...a good introductory chapter on forests.*

introspection /ɪntrəˈspekʃə⁰n/ is the act of exam- N UNCOUNT ining your own thoughts, ideas, and feelings. EG *I* Formal *simply hadn't time for introspection.*

introspective /ɪntrəˈspektɪv/. **Introspective** ADJ QUALIT people spend a lot of time examining their own Formal thoughts, ideas, and feelings. EG *The boy was downcast and introspective.*

introvert /ɪntrəˈvɜːt/, **introverts.** An **introvert** is N COUNT a quiet, shy person who spends a lot of time alone. Formal EG ...*a bashful introvert.*

introverted /ɪntrəˈvɜːtɪ²d/. **Introverted** people ADJ QUALIT are quiet, shy, and spend a lot of time alone. EG *He* Formal *was without doubt the most introverted boy in my school... During pregnancy, a woman often becomes introverted.*

intrude /ɪntruːd/, **intrudes, intruding, intruded.**
1 If you **intrude** on someone, you disturb them V : OFT when they are in a private place or having a +*on/upon* private conversation. EG *He felt that he couldn't intrude... I don't want to intrude on your family.*
2 If something **intrudes** on your mood or your life, v+*on* it disturbs it or has an unpleasant effect on it. EG *I shall not intrude on your grief.*
3 You can say that someone **is intruding** when v : OFT they enter a place without permission. EG *I heard* +*on/upon* *peals of laughter from the intruding children.*

intruder /ɪntruːdə/, **intruders.** An **intruder** is a N COUNT person who enters a place without permission. EG *An intruder had come into his home.*

intrusion /ɪntruːʒə⁰n/, **intrusions. 1** If someone N COUNT OR disturbs you when you are in a private place or N UNCOUNT having a private conversation, you can describe their behaviour as an **intrusion**. EG *I must ask your pardon for this intrusion.*
2 An **intrusion** is also something that affects your N COUNT OR mood or your life in an unwelcome way. EG *I resent* N UNCOUNT *the intrusion of the outside world.*

intrusive /ɪntruːsɪv/. If someone or something is ADJ QUALIT **intrusive**, they disturb your mood or life in an unwelcome way. EG ...*this intrusive insect... ...Gordon's intrusive interest in our religious activities.*

intuit /ɪntjuːɪt/, **intuits, intuiting, intuited.** If you v+o OR **intuit** something, you guess it by using your feel- V+REPORT ings, rather than your knowledge. EG *She intuited* Formal *that Peter would be glad to see her.*

intuition /ɪntjuːɪʃə⁰n/, **intuitions.** Your **intuition** N UNCOUNT is a feeling that something is true or exists al- OR N COUNT though you have no evidence or proof of it. EG *My intuition told me to stay away... ...arguments based on intuition... I've got an intuition that something is wrong.*

intuitive /ɪntjuːɪtɪv/. **Intuitive** ideas or feelings ADJ QUALIT tell you that something is true or exists although Formal you have no evidence or proof of it. EG *I got a strong intuitive feeling that he was lying... ...his intuitive understanding of nature.* ◊ **intuitively.** ◊ ADV EG *I felt intuitively that they would not return.*

inundate /ɪnʌndeɪt/, **inundates, inundating, inundated. 1** If you are **inundated** with things, you v+o : USU PASS receive so many of them that you cannot deal with +*with*

them all. EG *She was inundated with telephone calls... They had been inundated with applications.*
2 If an area of land **is inundated**, it becomes v+o : USU PASS covered with water. EG *...inundated areas... ...the* Formal *floods that inundate northern India every year.*

inure /ɪnjʊə/, **inures, inuring, inured.** If you v-REFL+*to* **inure** yourself to something unpleasant, you ex- Formal perience it so often that you learn to accept it. EG *...people who inure themselves to tragedy... ...a man who was inured to disappointment.*

invade /ɪnveɪd/, **invades, invading, invaded. 1** v+o To **invade** a country means to enter it by force with an army. EG *...Kennedy's secret plan to invade Cuba... ...the invading forces.* ◊ **invader** /ɪnveɪdə/, ◊ N COUNT : **invaders.** EG *The invaders had been defeated.* USU PLURAL
2 If people or animals **invade** a place, they enter it v+o in large numbers. EG *The town was invaded by reporters... ...pests that invade the home.*
3 If someone or something **invades** your privacy, v+o they disturb you when you want to be alone.

invalid, invalids; pronounced /ɪnvəlɪd/ in paragraph 1 and /ɪnvælɪd/ in paragraphs 2 and 3.
1 An **invalid** is someone who is very ill or disabled N COUNT and who needs to be cared for by someone else. EG *The family treated her like an invalid... ...her invalid mother.* ◊ **invalidity** /ɪnvəlɪdɪ¹tɪ¹/. EG *...an* ◊ N MOD *invalidity pension.*
2 If an argument, conclusion or result is **invalid**, it ADJ CLASSIF is not correct or not reasonable. EG *The comparison is invalid.* ◊ **invalidity.** EG *My experiments show* ◊ N UNCOUNT *the invalidity of his argument.*
3 If an official process, contract, or document is ADJ CLASSIF **invalid**, it has not followed the laws or regulations and is not legally acceptable. EG *The marriage was invalid... The court ruled his election invalid.*

invalidate /ɪnvælɪdeɪt/, **invalidates, invalidating, invalidated. 1** If something **invalidates** an v+o argument, conclusion, or result, it proves that it is Formal wrong. EG *Such exceptions do not invalidate the rule.*
2 If something **invalidates** an official process, v+o contract, or document, it causes it to be legally Formal unacceptable. EG *The marriage would invalidate any earlier will.*

invaluable /ɪnvæljuᵊəbᵊl/. If someone or some- ADJ CLASSIF thing is **invaluable**, they are extremely useful. EG *This experience proved invaluable later on... He was an invaluable source of information.*

invariable /ɪnveərɪəbᵊl/. Something that is **in-** ADJ CLASSIF **variable** always happens or never changes. EG *They followed an invariable routine.* ◊ **invariably** ◊ ADV /ɪnveərɪəblɪ¹/. EG *The conversation invariably returns to politics... Our receptionists are almost invariably female.*

invasion /ɪnveɪʒᵊn/, **invasions. 1** When there is N COUNT OR an **invasion** of a country, an army enters it by N UNCOUNT force. EG *...the invasion of Europe by the Allies in 1944... It enabled us to remain free from invasion.*
2 You can describe the arrival of large numbers of N UNCOUNT things or people in a place as an **invasion**. EG *...the* +SUPP *invasion of Italian movies in the fifties.*

invective /ɪnvektɪv/. **Invective** consists of rude N UNCOUNT and unpleasant things that people say when they Formal are very angry or annoyed with someone. EG *...women hurling invective at us... A torrent of invective awaited them.*

invent /ɪnvent/, **invents, inventing, invented. 1** v+o If you **invent** something, you are the first person to think of it or make it. EG *...the men who invented the sewing machine... ...a game he had invented... He invented this phrase himself.*
2 If you **invent** a story or excuse, you try to v+o persuade people that it is true when it is not, often for dishonest reasons. EG *...lies invented for a political purpose.*

invention /ɪnvenʃᵊn/, **inventions. 1** An **inven-** N COUNT **tion** is a machine or system that has been invented by someone. EG *He was working on his invention...*

Writing was the most revolutionary of all human inventions.
2 If you refer to someone's account of something as N COUNT an **invention**, you mean that it is not true and that they have made it up. EG *The account was a deliberate and malicious invention.*
3 When someone creates something that has never N UNCOUNT existed before, you can refer to this event as the +SUPP **invention** of the thing. EG *...the invention of printing.*
4 Invention is also the ability to invent things or to N UNCOUNT have clever and original ideas. EG *...his powers of invention.*

inventive /ɪnventɪv/. An **inventive** person is ADJ QUALIT good at inventing things or has clever and original ideas. EG *He is inventive in dealing with physical problems.* ◊ **inventiveness.** EG *The musicians can* ◊ N UNCOUNT *play, even if they do lack inventiveness.*

inventor /ɪnventə/, **inventors.** An **inventor** is a N COUNT person who has invented something, or whose job is to invent things. EG *...Cockerell, the inventor of the hovercraft... ...inventors and engineers.*

inventory /ɪnvə²ntrɪ¹/, **inventories.** An **inven-** N COUNT **tory** is a written list of all the objects in a Formal particular place. EG *...compiling an inventory of the treasures that lay hidden in the ship.*

inverse /ɪnvɜːs/. **1** If there is an **inverse** relation- ADJ CLASSIF ship between two things, one of them decreases as Formal the other increases. EG *The time spent varies in inverse proportion to the amount of work done.*
2 The **inverse** of something is its exact opposite. EG N SING *It represents the inverse of everything I find worth* Formal *preserving.* ▸ used as an adjective. EG *The inverse* ▸ ADJ CLASSIF : *case is also worth considering.* ATTRIB

inversion /ɪnvɜːʃᵊn/, **inversions.** When there is N UNCOUNT an **inversion** of something, it is changed into its OR N COUNT : opposite. EG *...this curious inversion of facts... ...an* USU+SUPP *inversion of the expected order.* Formal

invert /ɪnvɜːt/, **inverts, inverting, inverted.** If v+o you **invert** something, you turn it upside down or Formal back to front. EG *The chairs are inverted on the tables.* ◊ **inverted.** EG *It was shaped like an* ◊ ADJ CLASSIF *inverted cone.* ● See also **inverted commas.**

invertebrate /ɪnvɜːtɪbreɪt, -brə¹t/, **inver-** N COUNT **tebrates.** An **invertebrate** is a creature that does Technical not have a spine, for example an insect, a worm, or an octopus. EG *...other floating invertebrates.*

inverted commas are the punctuation marks N PLURAL (' and ' or " and ") that are used in writing to indicate where speech or a quotation begins and ends.

invest /ɪnvest/, **invests, investing, invested. 1** If v+o OR v : you **invest** an amount of money, you pay it into a OFT+*in* bank or buy shares with it, so that you will receive a profit. EG *...investing in stocks and shares... £20 million of public money had been invested.* ◊ **investor** /ɪnvestə/, **investors.** EG *The investor is* ◊ N COUNT *entitled to a reasonable return on his money.*
2 If you **invest** money, time, or energy in some- v+o OR v : thing, you use it to try and make the thing success- OFT+*in* ful. EG *They are willing to invest energy in a* Formal *European disarmament campaign... They have failed to invest in job creation in the cities.*
3 If you **invest** in something useful, you buy it v+*in* OR because it will be more efficient or cheaper over a v+o+*in* period of time. EG *Good shoes are worth investing in even though they are expensive.*
4 To **invest** someone with rights or responsibilities v+o+*with* means to give them to them legally or officially. EG Formal *The law invests the shareholders alone with legal rights.*

investigate /ɪnvestɪgeɪt/, **investigates, investi-** v+o OR v **gating, investigated.** If you **investigate** an event, situation, or person, you try to find out all the facts about them. EG *He had come to investigate*

If something is invaluable, is it also valuable?

a murder... I sent my men to investigate.
◊ **investigation** /ɪnvestɪgeɪʃən/, **investigations.** ◊ N COUNT OR
EG *Sherman ordered an investigation into her* N UNCOUNT
death... ...the results of their investigations.

investigative /ɪnvestɪgətɪv/. **Investigative** ac- ADJ CLASSIF:
tivities involve trying to find out all the facts about ATTRIB
events, situations, or people. EG *He was doing* Formal
investigative work on Kennedy... ...investigative
reporters.

investigator /ɪnvestɪgeɪtə/, **investigators.** An N COUNT
investigator is someone whose job is to investigate events, situations, or people. EG *Aircraft acci-*
dent investigators got to the scene quickly.

investment /ɪnvestmənt/, **investments. 1** In- N UNCOUNT
vestment is the activity of buying shares or of
putting money into a bank account in order to
obtain a profit. EG *We aim to encourage invest-*
ment.
2 An **investment** is **2.1** the amount of money you N COUNT
put into a bank account or buy shares with. EG *...a*
better return on the investment. **2.2** something that Informal
you buy. EG *The tractors proved a superb invest-*
ment.
3 If you make an **investment** of time or effort in N UNCOUNT
something, you spend time or effort in order to +SUPP
achieve something. EG *It might be a better invest-*
ment of time to teach the children to cook.

inveterate /ɪnvetərət/. You use **inveterate** to ADJ CLASSIF:
say that someone has been doing something for a ATTRIB
long time and that they are not likely to stop doing Formal
it. For example, an inveterate liar is someone who
has always told lies and who will probably continue
to tell lies. EG *Hubert had been an inveterate*
hunter... ...their inveterate distrust of others.

invidious /ɪnvɪdɪəs/. **1** An **invidious** task or job is ADJ QUALIT
unpleasant to do, because it is likely to make you
unpopular. EG *The role of a critic can be an*
invidious one.
2 An **invidious** comparison or decision is an unfair ADJ CLASSIF
one because the things involved are not similar or
are almost equal in value or quality. EG *He defend-*
ed American police against invidious comparisons
with Scotland Yard... This involves an invidious
choice.

invigilator /ɪnvɪdʒɪleɪtə/, **invigilators.** An in- N COUNT
vigilator is someone who supervises the people
taking an examination. The invigilator makes sure
that the examination starts and finishes at the
correct time and that nobody cheats.

invigorating /ɪnvɪgəreɪtɪŋ/. Something that is ADJ QUALIT
invigorating makes you feel more energetic. EG
The air here is invigorating... ...an invigorating
bath... You will find it an invigorating experience.

invincible /ɪnvɪnsəˈbəl/. **1** An **invincible** army ADJ CLASSIF
or sports team is very powerful and difficult to
defeat. EG *They are invincible in battle... ...an army*
of invincible strength.
2 If someone has an **invincible** belief or attitude, it ADJ CLASSIF:
cannot be changed. EG *...their invincible contempt* ATTRIB
for foreigners.

inviolable /ɪnvaɪələbəl/. If a law or principle is ADJ CLASSIF
inviolable, you cannot or must not break it. EG Formal
Tradition was considered inviolable.

inviolate /ɪnvaɪələt/. If something is **inviolate**, it ADJ CLASSIF
cannot be harmed or affected. EG *...leaving the* Formal
truth inviolate... ...its walls inviolate as a fortress.

invisible /ɪnvɪzəˈbəl/. **1** If something is **invisible**, ADJ CLASSIF
you cannot see it, because it is hidden or because it
is very small or faint. EG *Her legs were invisible*
beneath the table... ...hairs invisible to the naked
eye. ◊ **invisibly.** EG *...draw the lines almost* ◊ ADV
invisibly pale. ◊ **invisibility** /ɪnvɪzəˈbɪlɪtiˈ/. EG ◊ N UNCOUNT
The main advantage is the submarine's invisibility.
2 In stories, **invisible** people or things cannot be ADJ CLASSIF
seen by anybody. EG *He waves his magic wand and*
turns himself invisible.

invitation /ɪnvɪteɪʃən/, **invitations. 1** An invita- N COUNT
tion is a written or spoken request to come to an
event such as a party, a meal, or a meeting. EG

Cindy accepted invitations to cocktail parties and
private dinners... I had an invitation to go and talk
to the cadets.
2 The card or paper on which an invitation is N COUNT
written is also called an **invitation**. EG *...engraved*
invitations... Jenny was waving the invitation.
3 Behaviour that encourages you to do something N SING+to-INF
is sometimes referred to as an **invitation**. EG *She* OR to
declined the invitation to address him as 'Charles'...
Houses left unlocked are an open invitation to
burglary.

invite /ɪnvaɪt/, **invites, inviting, invited. 1** If you V+O:OFT+to
invite someone to something such as a party or
meal, you ask them to come to it. EG *Invite her to*
the party... Leggett invited me for lunch at the
hotel.
2 If someone **invites** you to do something, they V+O:
formally ask you to do it. EG *I was invited to attend* OFT+to-INF
future meetings... He was invited for interview. OR for
3 If someone **invites** discussion or criticism, they V+O
encourage you to discuss or criticize what they Formal
have said or done. EG *He stopped speaking and*
invited discussion.
4 If someone or something **invites** confidence or V+O
disbelief, they cause you to feel confident in them, Formal
or to disbelieve them. EG *This kind of statement*
invites disbelief.
5 If something **invites** danger or trouble, it makes V+O
danger or trouble more likely. EG *To speak of it to* Formal
others would invite danger.

inviting /ɪnvaɪtɪŋ/. If you say that something is ADJ QUALIT
inviting, you mean that it is attractive and desirable. EG *The place was green and inviting... ...large*
dark eyes, shy but inviting. ◊ **invitingly.** EG *The* ◊ ADV
packet of cigarettes lay invitingly open.

invocation /ɪnvəkeɪʃən/, **invocations.** An invo- N COUNT OR
cation is a spoken request to a god for help or N UNCOUNT
forgiveness. EG *They murmured invocations to the*
gods.

invoice /ɪnvɔɪs/, **invoices.** An **invoice** is an offi- N COUNT
cial document that lists the goods or services that
you have received from a person or company and
says how much money you owe for them. EG *His*
firm sent you an invoice for it six months ago.

invoke /ɪnvəuk/, **invokes, invoking, invoked. 1** V+O
If you **invoke** a law, you use it to justify what you Formal
are doing. EG *The Government invoked the Emer-*
gency Powers Act.
2 If you **invoke** a principle, proverb, famous per- V+O
son, or book, you quote them or use them as Formal
examples to support your argument. EG *They in-*
voke Lenin and Trotsky... The phrase invoked was
'the country is going to the dogs'.
3 If you **invoke** feelings of a particular kind, you V+O
cause someone to feel them. EG *They tried to* Formal
invoke popular enthusiasm for the war.

involuntary /ɪnvɒləntəˈriˈ/. **Involuntary** actions ADJ CLASSIF
are done suddenly and without intention because
people are unable to control themselves. EG *There*
were one or two involuntary exclamations.
◊ **involuntarily.** EG *I shivered involuntarily.* ◊ ADV

involve /ɪnvɒlv/, **involves, involving, involved.**
1 If a situation or activity **involves** someone or
something, **1.1** it includes or uses them as a neces- V+O OR V+-ING
sary part. EG *Caring for a one-year-old involves*
changing nappies... Some of the experiments in-
volve the equipment you've seen. **1.2** it concerns V+O
or affects them. EG *Workers are never told about*
things which involve them.
2 If you **involve** yourself in something, you take V-REFL:
part in it. EG *They involve themselves deeply in* OFT+in/with
community affairs.
3 If you **involve** someone else in something, you V+O:OFT+in
get them to take part in it. EG *Did you have to*
involve me in this?
4 If a book, play, or film **involves** you, it makes V+O
you feel that you are taking part in the events it
describes or shows. EG *...the ability of the film to*
involve you imaginatively.

involved /ɪnvɒlvd/. **1** If someone or something is ADJ PRED: **involved** in or with a situation or activity, they are OFT+in/with taking part in it. EG *Should religious leaders get involved in politics?... ...companies involved in producing the aircraft... He is involved with editing... ...the large number of people involved.*

2 If you are deeply or intensely **involved** in ADJ PRED: something, you feel very strongly or enthusiastical- OFT+with/in ly about it. EG *I was deeply involved in my work... She became terribly involved with writing.*

3 The things **involved** in a task, situation, or ADJ PRED: system are the things that are required in order to OFT+in achieve it or understand it, or the problems that it causes. EG *There is quite a lot of work involved... What is involved in making a television programme?... Explain the principles involved.*

4 If you describe a situation or activity as **in-** ADJ QUALIT **volved**, you mean that it is very complicated;. EG *We had long, involved discussions.*

5 If you are **involved** with another person, you are ADJ PRED: having a close relationship with them. EG *He had* OFT+with *become involved with her in Brussels.*

involvement /ɪnvɒlvmənt/. **1** Your **involvement** N UNCOUNT: in something is the fact that you are taking part in OFT+in/ it. EG *...parental involvement in schools... ...the* of/with *active involvement of workers.*

2 Involvement is also the concern and enthusiasm N UNCOUNT: that you feel about something. EG *...his deep in-* OFT+with/in *volvement with socialism.*

invulnerable /ɪnvʌlnə⁰rəbə⁰l/. If someone or ADJ CLASSIF something is **invulnerable**, they cannot be harmed or damaged. EG *The nuclear submarine is almost invulnerable to attack.* ◇ **invulnerability** ◇ N UNCOUNT /ɪnvʌlnə⁰rəbɪlɪ'tɪ¹/. EG *Parents have a feeling of invulnerability.*

inward /ɪnwəd/, **inwards**. **1** Your **inward** ADJ CLASSIF: thoughts or feelings are the ones that you do not ATTRIB express or show to other people. EG *...my inward happiness... She hid an inward amusement.* ◇ **inwardly**. EG *I remained inwardly unconvinced.* ◇ ADV

2 If something moves or faces **inward** or **inwards**, ADV AFTER VB it moves or faces towards the inside or centre of something. EG *The door swung inward... His cell faced inwards.*

3 An **inward** movement is one towards the inside ADJ CLASSIF: or centre of something. EG *...the inward flow of air.* ATTRIB

iodine /aɪədiːn/ is a dark-coloured substance used N UNCOUNT in medicine and photography.

ion /aɪən/, **ions**. Ions are electrically charged N COUNT atoms. EG *...calcium ions... ...ions of nitrogen.* Technical

-ion, -ions. See **-ation**.

iota /aɪəʊtə/. You can refer to an extremely small N PART amount of something as an **iota**. EG *I don't feel one iota of guilt... I don't think you've changed an iota.*

IOU /aɪ əʊ juː/, **IOUs**. An **IOU** is a written promise N COUNT to pay back money that you have borrowed. **IOU** is an abbreviation for 'I owe you'. EG *He wrote out an IOU for five thousand dollars.*

IQ /aɪ kjuː/, **IQs**. Your **IQ** is your level of intelli- N UNCOUNT gence, which is measured by a special test. **IQ** is an +SUPP abbreviation for 'intelligence quotient'. EG *He had an IQ of 50... The IQ of our students is quite low.*

irascible /ɪræsɪ¹bə⁰l/. An **irascible** person be- ADJ QUALIT comes angry very easily. EG *He is irascible and* Formal *violent....Jeff's irascible outbursts.*

irate /aɪreɪt/. If you are **irate**, you are very angry ADJ QUALIT about something. EG *The Bishop looked irate...* Formal *...calming down irate customers... ...an irate letter.*

ire /aɪə/ is anger. EG *He incurred the ire of the* N UNCOUNT authorities. Literary

iridescent /ɪrɪdesənt/. Something that is **irides-** ADJ CLASSIF **cent** has bright colours that seem to keep chang- Literary ing. EG *...the iridescent blue and orange glow... ...iridescent feathers.*

iris /aɪrɪs/, **irises**. **1** The **iris** in your eye is the N COUNT round coloured part. EG *...eyelids dropping over blue irises.*

2 An **iris** is also a tall plant with long leaves and N COUNT large purple, yellow, or white flowers.

Irish /aɪrɪʃ/. **1** Something that is **Irish** **1.1** belongs ADJ CLASSIF or relates to the whole of Ireland, to its people, or to its language. EG *She spoke with an Irish accent.* **1.2** belongs or relates to the Republic of Ireland. EG *...the Irish Prime Minister.*

2 The **Irish** are the people who come from Ireland. N PLURAL: EG *The majority of the Irish accept these proposals.* the+N

Irishman /aɪrɪʃmə³n/, **Irishmen**. An **Irishman** is N COUNT a man who comes from Ireland.

Irishwoman /aɪrɪʃwʊmən/, **Irishwomen**. An N COUNT **Irishwoman** is a woman who comes from Ireland.

irk /ɜːk/, **irks**, **irking**, **irked**. If something **irks** V+O: you, it irritates or annoys you. EG *...twisting his* NO IMPER *shoulders as if his jacket irked him... Such tactics clearly irked Gordon.*

irksome /ɜːksəm/. If something is **irksome**, it ADJ QUALIT irritates or annoys you. EG *I found Clare's methods rather irksome... ...an irksome responsibility.*

iron /aɪən/, **irons**, **ironing**, **ironed**. **1 Iron** is a N UNCOUNT hard, dark metal found in rocks. It is used to make objects such as gates and fences, and also to make other metals such as steel. Small amounts of iron occur in your blood and in food. EG *...a lump of iron... ...an iron bar... ...the iron and steel industries... Seaweed has a high iron content.*

2 An **iron** is an electrical device with a handle and N COUNT a heated flat metal base. You rub an iron over clothes to remove creases. EG *If it's cotton or linen, use a hot iron.*

3 If you **iron** clothes, you remove the creases from V+O them using an iron. EG *I can't iron shirts.* ● See also **ironing, ironing board**.

4 You can use **iron** to describe the character or ADJ CLASSIF: behaviour of someone who is very firm in their ATTRIB decisions and actions, and who can control their feelings. EG *He was able to enforce his iron will... ...her iron composure... ...iron discipline.*

iron out. If you **iron out** difficulties, you get rid PHRASAL VB: of them successfully. EG *I thought most of our* V+O+ADV *problems were ironed out.*

Iron Curtain. **1** The **Iron Curtain** refers to the N PROPER: border between the Soviet Union and its East the+N European allies and the Western European countries. EG *...the Soviet side of the Iron Curtain.* ● If ● PHRASE something happens **behind the Iron Curtain**, it happens in the Soviet Union or in one of the East European countries that are allied to it. EG *Sales of his novels were most brisk behind the Iron Curtain.*

2 The **Iron Curtain** countries are the Soviet Union N MOD and its East European allies.

ironic /aɪrɒnɪk/. **1** If someone makes **ironic** re- ADJ QUALIT marks or gestures, they are joking or really mean the opposite of what they say. EG *It was possible that his thanks were ironic... ...an ironic smile.*

2 An **ironic** situation is strange or amusing be- ADJ QUALIT cause it is very unusual or is the opposite of what was expected. EG *It is ironic that the people who complain most loudly are the ones who do least to help.*

ironical /aɪrɒnɪkə⁰l/ means the same as ironic. ADJ QUALIT

ironically /aɪrɒnɪkə⁰lɪ¹/. **1** You say **ironically** to ADV SEN draw attention to an unusual or amusing aspect of a situation. EG *Ironically, the intelligence chief was the last person to hear the news.*

2 If you say something **ironically**, you are joking ADV or you really mean the opposite of what you say. EG *'Do you want to search the apartment?' she enquired ironically.*

ironing /aɪənɪŋ/ is the activity of using a hot iron N UNCOUNT to remove creases from clothes. EG *She's doing the ironing.*

ironing board, ironing boards. An **ironing** N COUNT **board** is a long, narrow board covered with cloth, on which you iron clothes.

If you are irascible, are you easily irked?

ironwork /aɪənwɜːk/ refers to objects or parts of N UNCOUNT buildings that are made of iron. EG ...*brick houses with painted ironwork*... ...*ironwork gates.*

irony /aɪrəni¹/, **ironies. 1** Irony is a way of N UNCOUNT speaking which indicates that you are joking or that you really mean the opposite of what you say. EG *She said with slight irony, 'Bravo'... She spoke simply, without irony.*

2 The **irony** of a situation is an unusual or unexpec- N COUNT OR ted aspect of it. EG *The irony is that many politi-* N UNCOUNT cians agree with him... History has many ironies.

irrational /ɪræʃəⁿəl, -ʃənəⁿl/. **Irrational** feelings ADJ QUALIT or behaviour are not based on logical reasons or clear thinking. EG *His anxiety was irrational...* ...*an irrational child.* ◇ **irrationally.** EG *They were* ◇ ADV *accused of acting irrationally.* ◇ **irrationality** ◇ N UNCOUNT /ɪræʃəⁿnælˈiti¹/. EG ...*the irrationality of contempo- rary economics.*

irreconcilable /ɪrekənsaɪləbəⁿl/. **1** If two ideas ADJ CLASSIF or actions are **irreconcilable**, they are so differ- Formal ent from each other that it is not possible or reasonable to believe, accept, or do both of them. EG *Their views had been irreconcilable from the beginning.*

2 An **irreconcilable** disagreement is so serious ADJ CLASSIF that it cannot be settled. EG ...*an irreconcilable clash of loyalties.*

irreducible /ɪrɪdjuːsɪˈbəⁿl/. Something that is **ir-** ADJ CLASSIF **reducible** cannot be reduced in amount or cannot Formal be made simpler. EG ...*the irreducible essence of art.*

irrefutable /ɪrɪfjuːtəbəⁿl/. A statement that is ADJ CLASSIF **irrefutable** cannot be denied or cannot be shown Formal to be incorrect. EG *That is an opinion, not an irrefutable fact... His argument is virtually irrefu- table.*

irregular /ɪregjəˈləˈ/, **irregulars. 1** Something ADJ QUALIT that is **irregular** is not smooth or straight, or does not form a regular pattern. EG ...*its rough, irregular surface...* ...*dark, irregular markings on the photos.* ◇ **irregularly.** EG ...*irregularly shaped fields.* ◇ ADV ◇ **irregularity** /ɪregjəˈlærɪti¹/, **irregularities.** EG ◇ N COUNT OR *The whole building was full of holes and* N UNCOUNT *irregularities.*

2 Irregular actions happen with different periods ADJ QUALIT of time between them. EG ...*feeding them at irregu- lar intervals... The newspaper's appearance be- came increasingly irregular.* ◇ **irregularly.** EG *He* ◇ ADV *went home, irregularly, at weekends.* ◇ **irregularity.** EG *These illnesses can be caused* ◇ N COUNT OR *by irregularity in feeding. This is more likely to* N UNCOUNT *produce irregularities of heart rate.*

3 Irregular behaviour is considered to be unusual ADJ QUALIT or not acceptable. EG *It isn't signed. This is irregu- lar...* ...*his irregular working hours.* ◇ **irregularity.** EG *The report revealed a large* ◇ N COUNT OR *number of irregularities.* N UNCOUNT

4 An **irregular** verb, noun, or adjective does not ADJ CLASSIF inflect in the same way as most other verbs, nouns, or adjectives in the language.

irrelevance /ɪreləvəns/. The **irrelevance** of N UNCOUNT something is the fact that it is not connected with +SUPP what you are talking about or dealing with. EG *'By the way,' he added with apparent irrelevance, 'will you be locking it?'*

irrelevancy /ɪreləvənsi¹/, **irrelevancies.** You N COUNT can refer to something that you think has no useful Formal purpose as an **irrelevancy**. EG *School is an irrel- evancy... He should not waste his time with irrel- evancies.*

irrelevant /ɪreləvənt/. If you say that something ADJ QUALIT is **irrelevant**, you mean that it is not connected with what you are talking about or dealing with, and is therefore not important. EG *The book was full of irrelevant information... He felt that right and wrong were irrelevant to the situation.*

irreligious /ɪrɪlɪdʒəs/. An **irreligious** person ADJ QUALIT does not have a religion. EG *My family were com-*

pletely irreligious... ...*an irreligious society...* ...*irre- ligious attitudes.*

irremediable /ɪrəˈmiːdjəbəⁿl/. If a situation or ADJ CLASSIF state is **irremediable**, it is very bad and cannot be Formal made better. EG *Irremediable damage has been done.*

irreparable /ɪrepəˈrəbəⁿl/. **Irreparable** damage ADJ CLASSIF is so severe that it cannot be repaired or put right Formal again. EG *She has done irreparable harm to her reputation... I had made an irreparable mistake.*

irreplaceable /ɪrɪpleɪsəbəⁿl/. If things are **irre-** ADJ CLASSIF **placeable**, they are so special that they cannot be replaced if they are lost or destroyed. EG *My jewellery is totally irreplaceable.*

irrepressible /ɪrɪpresɪˈbəⁿl/. **Irrepressible** peo- ADJ QUALIT ple are lively, energetic, and cheerful. EG *Basil is irrepressible, funny, and affectionate.*

irreproachable /ɪrɪprəʊtʃəbəⁿl/. If someone's be- ADJ CLASSIF haviour or character is **irreproachable**, it is so good or correct that it cannot be criticized. EG ...*McKinley's irreproachable character... He had done an irreproachable job of presiding over the tribunal.*

irresistible /ɪrɪzɪstəbəⁿl/. **1** If your wish to do ADJ QUALIT something is **irresistible**, it is so strong that you cannot prevent yourself doing it. EG *The urge to laugh was irresistible...* ...*an irresistible desire to sing.*

2 If you describe someone or something as **irre-** ADJ QUALIT **sistible**, you mean that you find them very attrac- tive or interesting. EG *He found her irresistible... His charm was irresistible to them.* ◇ **irresistibly.** EG ◇ SUBMOD *The songs are irresistibly catchy.*

3 An **irresistible** force cannot be stopped or ADJ CLASSIF controlled. EG ...*an irresistible attack... They put irresistible pressure upon the government.* ◇ **irresistibly.** EG *The waves take you irresistibly* ◇ ADV *onwards.*

irresolute /ɪrezəluːt/. If you are **irresolute**, you ADJ QUALIT cannot decide what to do. EG *He stood irresolute at* Formal *the top of the stairs.*

irrespective /ɪrɪspektɪv/. If something is true or PREP if it happens **irrespective** of other things, those Formal things do not affect it or are not considered to be important. EG *They demanded equal pay irrespec- tive of age or sex...* ...*available to all students, irrespective of where they live.*

irresponsible /ɪrɪspɒnsɪˈbəⁿl/. People who are ADJ QUALIT **irresponsible** do things without properly consider- ing their possible consequences; used showing dis- approval. EG *You've behaved like an irresponsible idiot... It would be irresponsible of me to encourage you...* ...*the irresponsible application of technology.* ◇ **irresponsibly.** EG ...*acting unfairly and irrespon-* ◇ ADV *sibly.* ◇ **irresponsibility** /ɪrɪspɒnsɪbɪlˈiti¹/. EG ◇ N UNCOUNT ...*youthful irresponsibility.*

irretrievable /ɪrɪtriːvəbəⁿl/. **Irretrievable** harm ADJ CLASSIF is so severe that it cannot be put right again. EG Formal ...*the irretrievable damage done to the Earth.* ◇ **irretrievably.** EG *The war was irretrievably lost.* ◇ ADV

irreverent /ɪrevəˈrənt/. If you are **irreverent**, ADJ QUALIT you do not show the respect for someone or something that other people expect you to show. EG ...*rude and irreverent comments.* ◇ **irreverence** ◇ N UNCOUNT /ɪrevəˈrəns/. EG *His irreverence has frequently landed him in trouble.*

irreversible /ɪrɪvɜːsɪˈbəⁿl/. Situations that are ADJ CLASSIF **irreversible** cannot be changed, stopped, or im- proved. EG *We've done something irreversible... The damage may be irreversible...* ...*irreversible changes to the climate...* ...*an irreversible decision.*

irrevocable /ɪrevəkəbəⁿl/. Actions or decisions ADJ CLASSIF that are **irrevocable** cannot be stopped or Formal changed. EG *The US has given its irrevocable commitment to the Russians.* ◇ **irrevocably.** EG ◇ ADV *The world had changed irrevocably.*

irrigate /ɪrɪgeɪt/, **irrigates, irrigating, irri-** V+O **gated.** To **irrigate** land means to supply it with water in order to help crops to grow. EG *A small*

pump will irrigate about an acre of land... You had to work hard to irrigate the fields. ◇ **irrigated**. EG ◇ ADJ CLASSIF ...the irrigated areas of the Ganges plain.
◇ **irrigation** /ɪrɪgeɪʃəⁿn/. EG ...a complex irrigation ◇ N UNCOUNT system... ...the area under irrigation.

irritable /ɪrɪtəbəⁿl/. If you are **irritable**, you ADJ QUALIT easily become annoyed. EG Judy was feeling hot, tired, and irritable. EG 'What do you ◇ ADV want me to do?' she said irritably. ◇ **irritability** ◇ N UNCOUNT /ɪrɪtəbɪliˈtiˈ/. EG ...periods of irritability.

irritant /ɪrɪtənt/, **irritants. 1** If something con- N COUNT tinually annoys you, you can refer to it as an Formal **irritant**. EG Lack of national independence was a strong irritant.
2 An **irritant** is also a substance which causes a N COUNT part of your body to become itchy or sore. EG Its Formal juice is a serious irritant... ...irritant gases.

irritate /ɪrɪteɪt/, **irritates, irritating, irritated.**
1 If something **irritates** you, it gradually makes v+o you slightly angry, because you do not like it but cannot stop it continuing. EG His style irritated some officials. ◇ **irritated**. EG Dixon, irritated by ◇ ADJ QUALIT this question, said nothing... ...an irritated gesture.
◇ **irritating**. EG I found it irritating to be with the ◇ ADJ QUALIT men... ...an irritating noise. ◇ **irritatingly**. EG She ◇ SUBMOD was irritatingly slow. OR ADV
2 If something **irritates** a part of your body, it v+o causes it to be itchy or sore. EG The detergent can irritate sensitive feet. ◇ **irritating**. EG Their ◇ ADJ QUALIT irritating bites leave large red patches.

irritation /ɪrɪteɪʃəⁿn/, **irritations. 1 Irritation** is N UNCOUNT a feeling of slight anger because something that you do not like continues to happen. EG I began to feel the same irritation with all of them... ...showing no irritation at her behaviour.
2 If you have **irritation** in a part of your body, you N UNCOUNT have an itchy, sore, or painful feeling there. EG ...eye irritation.
3 An **irritation** is something that causes you to be N COUNT slightly angry because you do not like it but cannot stop it continuing. EG The weather was a slight irritation... ...the irritations of everyday existence.

is /ɪz/ is the third person singular of the present tense of **be**.

-ise, -ises, -ising, -ised. See **-ize**.

-ish is used to form adjectives. You use it **1** to SUFFIX indicate that something has a quality to a limited extent. For example, 'reddish' means slightly red. EG He had a yellowish complexion... He was a biggish fellow. **2** to indicate that someone or something has the qualities of a particular kind of thing or person. For example, someone who is childish behaves like a child. EG She was a beautiful kittenish creature.

Islam /ɪzlɑːm/ is the religion of the Muslims, N UNCOUNT which teaches that there is only one God and that Mohammed is His prophet.

Islamic /ɪzlæmɪk/ means belonging or relating to ADJ CLASSIF: Islam. EG ...Islamic laws... ...Islamic countries. ATTRIB

island /aɪlənd/, **islands. An island** is a piece of N COUNT land that is completely surrounded by water. EG There are pigs on the island... ...the island of Cyprus... ...the Channel Islands.

islander /aɪləndə/, **islanders. Islanders** are peo- N COUNT ple who live on an island. EG The islanders had never seen a car... ...the Falkland Islanders.

isle /aɪl/, **isles. An isle** is an island. EG ...a desert N COUNT isle... ...the Isle of Wight... ...the British Isles. Literary

-ism, -isms. -ism is used to form nouns that refer SUFFIX to **1** political or religious movements and beliefs. EG ...the emergence of nationalism... ...the importance of Hinduism as a unifying force. **2** attitudes and behaviour. EG Clem's eyes gleamed with fanaticism... ...an opportunity for heroism... He had begun to regret his criticisms.

isn't /ɪzəⁿnt/ is the usual spoken form of 'is not'. EG It isn't dark... That's right, isn't it?

isolate /aɪsəleɪt/, **isolates, isolating, isolated. 1** V+O OR V-REFL If something **isolates** you or if you **isolate** your-

self, you are physically or socially set apart from other people. EG His wealth isolated him... They isolated themselves in order to build a new society.
2 If you **isolate** an idea or word, you consider it v+o: separately from the other ideas or words that are OFT+from connected with it or close to it. EG I isolated that sentence from the rest of the text.
3 If you **isolate** a substance, you separate it from v+o: other substances so that you can examine it in OFT+from detail. EG You can isolate genes and study how they work.
4 If you **isolate** a sick person or animal, you keep v+o them apart from other people or animals, so that their illness does not spread. EG David had to be isolated for whooping cough.
5 If you **isolate** people, **5.1** you cause them to lose v+o their friends or supporters because you are opposed to them and want to weaken them. EG Could we isolate the administration, and thus force it to accept our demands? **5.2** you cause them to stop liking you or supporting you because you do things that they do not approve of. EG One by one, the chairman isolated all the good people in the firm.

isolated /aɪsəleɪtɪⁿd/. **1** An **isolated** place is a long ADJ QUALIT way away from any town or village. EG ...an isolated farmhouse.
2 If you feel **isolated**, you feel lonely and without ADJ PRED friends or help. EG I had become isolated, defensive, and humourless.
3 An **isolated** example or incident is one that is ADJ CLASSIF: rare and that is not part of a general pattern. EG ...a ATTRIB few isolated acts of violence.

isolation /aɪsəleɪʃəⁿn/. **1 Isolation** is a state in N UNCOUNT which you feel separate from other people, because you live far away from them or because you do not have any friends. EG ...the isolation of city life... ...mothers living in isolation and poverty.
2 If something exists or happens **in isolation**, it PHRASE exists or happens separately from other things of the same kind. EG A single country acting in isolation is vulnerable to competition... These questions can't be answered in isolation from each other.

issue /ɪʃuː/, **issues, issuing, issued. 1** An **issue** is N COUNT: an important problem or subject that people are USU+SUPP discussing or arguing about. EG I raised the issue with him... ...the issue of immigration.
2 If something is the **issue**, it is the thing you N SING: the+N consider to be the most important part of a situation or discussion. EG That's just not the issue... You cannot go on evading the issue.
3 The thing **at issue** is the thing that is being PHRASE argued about. EG The point at issue is this.
4 If you **make an issue of** something, you make a PHRASE fuss about it. EG She didn't want to make an issue of it... Some people make such an issue of everything.
5 An **issue** of a magazine or newspaper is a N COUNT particular edition of it. EG The article had appeared in the previous day's issue.
6 If someone **issues** a statement, they make it v+o formally or publicly. EG They issued a serious warning... The rebels issued a proclamation.
7 If someone **issues** something to you or **issues** v+o: you with it, they officially give it to you. EG Radios OFT+to/with were issued to the troops... She was issued with travel documents.
8 When something **issues** from a place, it comes v+from out of it. EG ...the smells issuing from the kitchen. Literary

-ist, -ists. -ist is added to nouns, often in place of SUFFIX '-ism', to form nouns and adjectives. The nouns refer to people who have particular beliefs, jobs, or interests. For example, a pacifist believes in pacifism and a journalist works in journalism. These count nouns and adjectives are often not defined in this dictionary, but are treated with the nouns from

What do you find in italics in this dictionary?

which they are derived. EG *She was a committed fatalist... ...imperialist sentiments... ...a nuclear physicist... ...a professional pianist.*

isthmus /ɪsθ⁰məs/, **isthmuses.** An **isthmus** is a narrow area of land connecting two larger areas. EG *...the Isthmus of Panama.* N COUNT Formal

it /ɪt/ is used as the subject of a verb or as the object of a verb or preposition.
1 You use **it** **1.1** to refer to an object, animal, or other thing that has already been mentioned or whose identity is known. **It** can also be used to refer to a child. EG *...a tray with glasses on it... The man went up to the cat and started stroking it... The strike went on for a year before it was settled.* PRON : SING
1.2 to refer to a situation or fact, or to say something about a situation or fact. EG *She was frightened, but tried not to show it... It was very pleasant at the Hochstadts... It took Simon some time to work out what she meant... He found it hard to make friends... It was a pity that her spelling was so bad... It doesn't matter.*
2 You also use **it**, mainly as the subject of the verb 'be', **2.1** when you are making statements about the weather, the time, the date, or the day of the week. EG *It's hot... It's raining here... It is nearly one o'clock... It's the 6th of April today.* **2.2** when you are stating or asking who is speaking on the telephone or who is present. EG *It's me – Mary... Who is it?* **2.3** when you are emphasizing or drawing attention to something. EG *It's my mother I'm worried about.* PRON : SING

italics /ɪtælɪks/ are letters which have been printed so that they slope to the right. Italics are often used to emphasize a word or sentence. The examples in this dictionary are printed in italics. N PLURAL

itch /ɪtʃ/, **itches, itching, itched.** **1** When you **itch** or when a part of your body **itches**, you have an unpleasant feeling on your skin that makes you want to scratch. EG *At first, you will itch... My toes are itching like mad.* ▸ used as a noun. EG *...an itch that must be scratched.* V ▸ N COUNT
2 If you **itch** to do something, you are very eager or impatient to do it. EG *I was itching to get away.* ▸ used as a noun. EG *....the itch to travel... I've had an itch to go there.* V+*to*-INF Informal ▸ N SING : OFT+*to*-INF

itchy /ɪtʃɪ¹/. If you are **itchy** or if a part of your body is **itchy**, you have an unpleasant feeling on your skin that makes you want to scratch. EG *Don't you feel all itchy?... My skin became dry and itchy.* ADJ QUALIT

it'd /ɪtə⁰d/ is **1** a spoken form of 'it would'. EG *If I went on the train, it'd be cheaper.* **2** a spoken form of 'it had', especially when 'had' is an auxiliary verb. EG *It'd just been killed.*

item /aɪtəm/, **items. 1** An **item** is **1.1** one of a collection or list of objects. EG *The first item he bought was a clock... ...a list of household items.* **1.2** one of a number of matters that you are dealing with. EG *I had two items of business to attend to before lunch.* N COUNT
2 An **item** in a newspaper or magazine is a report or article. EG *...an item in the Sacramento Times.* N COUNT

itemize /aɪtəmaɪz/, **itemizes, itemizing, itemized;** also spelled **itemise.** If you **itemize** a number of things, you make a list of them. EG *The contents of his pockets were itemized and confiscated.* V+O

itinerant /ɪˈtɪnərənt/. **Itinerant** workers travel around a region, working for short periods in different places. EG *...itinerant vegetable sellers... ...itinerant preachers.* ADJ CLASSIF : ATTRIB Formal

itinerary /ɪˈtɪnərəri¹/, **itineraries.** An **itinerary** is a plan of a journey, including the route and the places that will be visited. EG *A detailed itinerary is supplied.* N COUNT

it'll /ɪtə⁰l/ is a spoken form of 'it will'. EG *It'll be quite interesting.*

its /ɪts/. You use **its** to indicate that something belongs or relates to a thing, place, animal, or child that has just been mentioned or whose identity is known. See **it**. EG *The creature lifted its head... The group held its first meeting last week.* DET POSS

it's /ɪts/ is **1** the usual spoken form of 'it is'. EG *It's very important... It's snowing.* **2** a spoken form of 'it has', especially when 'has' is an auxiliary verb. EG *It's been nice talking to you.*

itself /ɪtsɛlf/. **1** You use **itself** as the object of a verb or preposition when the same thing, animal, or child is also the subject of the clause. See **it**. EG *Britain must bring itself up to date... It wraps its furry tail around itself.* PRON REFL : SING
2 You can use **itself** to emphasize the subject or object of a clause and to make it clear what you are referring to. EG *The town itself was very small... Growing up in London was itself exciting.* PRON REFL : SING
3 If you say that something has a particular quality **in itself**, you are emphasizing that it has this quality because of its own nature, regardless of any other factors. EG *The process is, in itself, an act of worship.* PHRASE

-ity, -ities. -ity is added to adjectives, sometimes in place of '-ous', to form nouns. These nouns usually refer to a state or quality. For example, 'tranquillity' refers to the state of being tranquil. Nouns of this kind are not usually defined in this dictionary, but are treated with the related adjectives. EG *The function of their bones is to give rigidity... ...a tradition of political neutrality... About this there is unanimity among sociologists.* SUFFIX

I've /aɪv/ is the usual spoken form of 'I have', especially when 'have' is an auxiliary verb. EG *I've never met her... I've only been there once.*

ivory /aɪvə⁰ri¹/. **1 Ivory** is the hard white bone which forms the tusks of elephants. It is valuable, and is often used to make ornaments. EG *Gold, slaves and ivory were sent north... ...an ivory dealer... ...ivory chess sets.* N UNCOUNT
2 Ivory is also a creamy-white colour. EG *...ivory teeth... ...her ivory legs.* ADJ COLOUR

ivy /aɪvɪ¹/ is a plant that grows up walls and trees and has small, shiny leaves with several pointed edges. EG *...a broken ivy branch.* N UNCOUNT

-ize, -izes, -izing, -ized; also spelled **-ise, -ises, -ising, -ised.** Verbs that can end in either '-ize' or '-ise' are dealt with in this dictionary as ending in '-ise'. SUFFIX

Some verbs ending in **-ize** are derived from adjectives. These verbs describe the processes by which things or people are changed to a particular state or condition. For example, when something is popularized, it becomes popular. EG *Parliament finally legalized trade unions... Most of the country had been industrialized.*

J j

J, j /dʒeɪ/, **Js, j's. J** is the tenth letter of the English N COUNT alphabet.

jab /dʒæb/, **jabs, jabbing, jabbed. 1** If you **jab** V+O+A something somewhere, you push it there with a quick, sudden movement. EG *She jabbed her knitting needles into a ball of wool... He jabbed his finger at me... ...jabbing the knife into the fruit.*

2 A **jab** is an injection of a substance into your N COUNT blood to prevent illness. EG *Everyone was queueing* Informal *up to have their jabs.* British

jabber /dʒæbɪt/, **jabbers, jabbering, jabbered.** V : OFT+A Someone who **is jabbering** is talking very quickly OR V+O and excitedly. EG *She was jabbering in Italian to her* Informal *husband.*

jack /dʒæk/, **jacks.** A **jack** is **1** a mechanical N COUNT device that is used to lift a heavy object off the ground. **2** a playing card with a picture of a young man on it. Jacks are higher than the ten and lower than the queen. EG *...the jack of clubs.*

jacket /dʒækɪt/, **jackets. 1** A **jacket** is a short N COUNT coat with long sleeves and an opening at the front. See picture at CLOTHES. EG *He wore a tweed sports jacket... From his jacket pocket he took out a small screwdriver.* ● See also **dinner jacket, lifejacket.**

2 The **jacket** of a baked potato is its skin. EG N COUNT *...potatoes in their jackets.*

3 The **jacket** of a book is the paper cover that N COUNT protects the book. EG *...colourful book jackets.*

jack-knife /dʒæknaɪf/, **jack-knifes, jack-knifing, jack-knifed; jack-knives. Jack-knives** is the plural of the noun.

1 If an articulated lorry **jack-knifes,** the trailer V swings round at a sharp angle to the cab in an uncontrolled way. EG *Traffic was stopped after an articulated truck jack-knifed in heavy rain.*

2 A **jack-knife** is a large knife with a blade that N COUNT can be folded into the handle.

jackpot /dʒækpɒt/, **jackpots.** A **jackpot** is the N COUNT most valuable prize in a game or lottery.

jade /dʒeɪd/ is a hard green stone that is used for N UNCOUNT making jewellery and ornaments.

jaded /dʒeɪdɪᵈd/. If you are **jaded,** you have no ADJ QUALIT enthusiasm because you are tired and bored. EG *...jaded housewives who'd like to try something different... They are getting a little jaded.*

jagged /dʒægɪᵈd/. Something that is **jagged** has a ADJ QUALIT rough, uneven shape with lots of sharp points. EG *...the jagged outline of the crags... ...small pieces of jagged metal.*

jaguar /dʒægjuᵊə/, **jaguars.** A **jaguar** is a large N COUNT animal which is a member of the cat family and has dark spots on its back.

jail /dʒeɪl/, **jails, jailing, jailed;** also spelled **gaol** in British English. **1** A **jail** is a place where people N COUNT OR are kept locked up, usually because they have been N UNCOUNT found guilty of a crime. EG *...women who spent years in jail... He went to jail for attempted robbery... ...a heavy jail sentence.*

2 If someone **is jailed,** they are put into jail. EG *He* V+O : USU PASS *was jailed for five years.*

jailer /dʒeɪlə/, **jailers;** also spelled **gaoler** in N COUNT British English. A **jailer** is a person who is in Outdated charge of a jail.

jam /dʒæm/, **jams, jamming, jammed. 1** Jam is N MASS a food that is made by cooking fruit with sugar. Usually you spread jam on bread. EG *...pots of raspberry and blackcurrant jam.*

2 If you **jam** something somewhere, you push it V+O+A there roughly. EG *Then he jammed his hat back on... Reporters jammed microphones in our faces.*

3 If something **jams** or if you **jam** it, it becomes V-ERG : OFT+A fixed in position and cannot move freely or work

properly. EG *The machines jammed and broke down... I jammed the window shut.*

4 If a road **is jammed** with vehicles, it is filled V+O : USU PASS completely with them, so that the traffic cannot move. EG *The town was jammed with traffic.*

5 If you **jam** a lot of things into a place, they are V+O pressed tightly together so that they can hardly move. EG *The fridge won't work properly if you jam in too much food.*

6 A **jam** is a situation where there are so many N COUNT vehicles on a road that none of them can move. EG *There were traffic jams, and police clearing people away.*

7 If you are in a **jam,** you are in a very difficult N COUNT situation. EG *He finds himself in exactly the same* Informal *jam as his brother was in ten years before.*

8 To **jam** a radio, radar, or electronic signal means V+O to prevent it from being received or heard clearly. This happens because other signals are being transmitted on the same wavelength.

jamboree /dʒæmbɒriː/, **jamborees.** A **jamboree** N COUNT is a party or celebration which a large number of people go to. EG *...an open-air jamboree that attracted 250,000 people.*

jam-packed. A place that is **jam-packed** is so full ADJ CLASSIF of people or things that there is no room for any Informal more. EG *The streets were jam-packed that day.*

jangle /dʒæŋgᵊl/, **jangles, jangling, jangled.** If V-ERG metal objects **jangle,** they make a ringing noise by hitting against each other. EG *I ran upstairs, the keys jangling in my pockets.* ▶ used as a noun. EG ▶ N SING *...the jangle of armour.*

janitor /dʒænɪtə/, **janitors.** A **janitor** is a person N COUNT whose job is to look after a building.

January /dʒænjuᵊəriː/ is the first month of the N UNCOUNT year in the Western calendar. EG *On 24 January Harold left for Constantinople.*

jar /dʒɑː/, **jars, jarring, jarred. 1** A **jar** is a glass N COUNT container with a lid that is used for storing food such as jam. EG *I was having trouble unscrewing the tops of fruit jars, jam jars and so on.*

2 If something **jars** on you, you find it unpleasant V : OFT+on or annoying. EG *The harsh, metallic sound jarred on her.... He had a way of speaking that jarred.*

◊ **jarring.** EG *...a jarring office block.* ◊ ADJ QUALIT

3 If something **jars** you, it gives you an unpleasant V+O shock. EG *This thought jarred me... He was evidently jarred by my appearance.* ◊ **jarring.** EG *...a* ◊ ADJ QUALIT *jarring experience.*

4 If things **jar** or if something **jars** them, they V-ERG strike against each other with quite a lot of force. EG *The house shook and his bones were jarred.*

▶ used as a noun. EG *Knocks and jars can cause* ▶ N COUNT *weakness in the spine.*

jargon /dʒɑːgᵊn/ is language containing words N UNCOUNT : that are used in special or technical ways. Jargon USU+SUPP is used to talk about particular subjects. EG *...complex legal jargon... They use so much professional jargon.*

jaundice /dʒɔːndɪs/ is an illness that makes your N UNCOUNT skin and eyes yellow.

jaundiced /dʒɔːndɪst/. A **jaundiced** attitude or ADJ QUALIT view is unenthusiastic or pessimistic. EG *He takes a* Literary *rather jaundiced view of societies and clubs.*

jaunt /dʒɔːnt/, **jaunts.** A **jaunt** is a short journey N COUNT which you go on for pleasure. EG *We went on a motor jaunt to Marrakesh.*

jaunty /dʒɔːntiː/ means cheerful, full of confi- ADJ QUALIT dence, and energetic. EG *She adjusted her hat to a jaunty angle... He spoke suddenly in a jaunty tone.*

javelin /dʒævᵊlɪn/, **javelins.** A **javelin** is a long N COUNT spear that is used in sports competitions.

jaw /dʒɔː/, **jaws. 1** Your **jaw** is **1.1** the lower part N COUNT
of your face below your mouth. Your jaw moves up
and down when you eat. See picture at THE HUMAN
BODY. EG *His jaw dropped in surprise.* **1.2** one of the
two bones in your head which your teeth are
attached to. EG *...the upper jaw... The panther held a
snake in its jaws.*

2 If you talk about the **jaws** of something unpleas- N PLURAL
ant such as death or hell, you are referring to a +SUPP
dangerous or unpleasant situation. EG *The nation* Literary
has been snatched out of the jaws of war.

jazz /dʒæz/, **jazzes, jazzing, jazzed. Jazz** is a N UNCOUNT
style of music that has an exciting rhythm and is
usually played with drums, saxophones, and trumpets. EG *...a jazz concert.*

jazz up. If you **jazz** something **up**, you make it PHRASAL VB :
look more interesting, colourful, or exciting. EG V+O+ADV
They've certainly jazzed this place up since the last Informal
time I was here.

jazzy /dʒæziʹ/, **jazzier, jazziest. 1** If you describe ADJ QUALIT
something as **jazzy**, you mean that it is colourful
and modern. EG *He was dressed in a jazzy suit and a
large yellow cravat.*

2 Music that is **jazzy** is in the style of jazz. EG *...a* ADJ CLASSIF
large orchestra playing jazzy rhythms.

jealous /dʒeləs/. If you are **jealous, 1** you feel ADJ QUALIT
anger or bitterness towards someone who has
something that you would like to have. EG *I often
felt jealous because David could go out when he
wished... They may feel jealous of your success.* **2** ADJ QUALIT
you feel that you must try to keep something that
you have, because you think someone else might
take it away from you. EG *She was a very jealous
woman... He was jealous of his wife and suspected
her of adultery.* ◊ **jealously.** EG *They were jealous-* ◊ ADV
ly guarding their independence.

jealousy /dʒeləsiʹ/, **jealousies. Jealousy** is **1** the N UNCOUNT
feeling of resentment and bitterness that you have OR N COUNT
when you think someone is trying to take away
something that you feel belongs to you. EG *Hate,
jealousy, the desire to kill all rose to the surface...
He was good at talking me out of my suspicions
and jealousies.* **2** the feeling you have when you
wish that you could have the qualities or possessions that someone else has. EG *We often feel
jealousy of our brothers and sisters.*

jeans /dʒiːnz/ are casual trousers that are made of N PLURAL
strong blue denim. EG *Three young men came out,
all in jeans... ...a pair of jeans.*

jeep /dʒiːp/, **jeeps.** A **jeep** is a small four-wheeled N COUNT
vehicle that can travel over rough ground. EG *A
jeep pulled up and a marine jumped out.*

jeer /dʒɪə/, **jeers, jeering, jeered.** If you **jeer** at V : OFT+at
someone, you say rude and insulting things to OR V+O
them. EG *Boys had jeered at him at school... He was
jeered and booed as a traitor.* ▸ used as a plural ▸ N PLURAL
noun. EG *...the taunts and jeers of passers-by.*
◊ **jeering.** EG *...the jeering crowd.* ◊ ADJ CLASSIF

jell /dʒel/. See **gel**.

jelly /dʒeliʹ/, **jellies. 1 Jelly** is **1.1** a clear food N MASS
made from gelatine, which is usually sweetened,
flavoured with fruit juices, and eaten as a dessert.
1.2 a kind of jam made by boiling fruit juice and
sugar. EG *...slices of bread, smeared with butter and
jelly.*

2 If your legs or arms feel like **jelly**, they feel very N UNCOUNT
weak, often because you are ill or afraid.

jellyfish /dʒeliʹfɪʃ/. **Jellyfish** is both the singular N COUNT
and the plural form.
A **jellyfish** is a creature that lives in the sea and
has a body that looks like clear jelly. Some jellyfish
can sting you.

jeopardize /dʒepədaɪz/, **jeopardizes, jeopardiz-** V+O
ing, jeopardized; also spelled **jeopardise.** If you
jeopardize something, you do something that may
destroy or damage it. EG *This judgment may jeopardize his job... I didn't want to jeopardize my
relationship with my new friend.*

jeopardy /dʒepədiʹ/. If someone or something is PHRASE
in jeopardy, they are in a dangerous situation. EG
*She had placed herself in jeopardy in order to save
my life... Their future is in jeopardy.*

jerk /dʒɜːk/, **jerks, jerking, jerked. 1** If you **jerk** V-ERG : USU+A
something, you pull it or move it suddenly and
forcefully. EG *He jerked the boy savagely to his
feet... The door of the van was jerked open... He
jerked his head around to stare at me.* ▸ used as a ▸ N COUNT
noun. EG *The man pulled the girl back with a jerk.*

2 If you **jerk** in a particular direction or in a V+A
particular way, you move with a very sudden and
quick movement. EG *She jerked away from him...
Jerking suddenly awake, he lay very still and
listened.*

3 If you call someone a **jerk**, you mean that they N COUNT
are very stupid; an offensive use.

jerky /dʒɜːkiʹ/, **jerkier, jerkiest.** Movements that ADJ QUALIT
are **jerky** are very sudden and abrupt. EG *She lit a
cigarette with quick, jerky movements.*

jersey /dʒɜːziʹ/, **jerseys. 1** A **jersey** is a piece of N COUNT
clothing made of knitted wool, that covers the
upper part of your body and your arms and does
not open at the front. EG *She pulled on her striped
jersey and her jeans.*

2 Jersey is a knitted woollen fabric used especially N UNCOUNT
to make women's clothing.

jest /dʒest/, **jests.** A **jest** is an amusing comment N COUNT
or a joke. EG *His Lordship hoped that a jest would* Outdated
be excused. ● If you say something **in jest**, you do ● PHRASE
not mean it seriously, but want to be amusing. EG *It
was said half in jest.*

jet /dʒet/, **jets, jetting, jetted. 1** A **jet** is a very N COUNT
fast modern aeroplane. EG *She woke just as the big* OR by+N
jet from Hong Kong touched down.

2 If you **jet** somewhere, you travel there in a fast V+A
aeroplane. EG *A Pennsylvania teenager jets regularly to a doctor in Frankfurt, Germany.*

3 A **jet** of water or gas is a strong, fast, thin stream N COUNT
of it. EG *He blew a jet of water into the air.*

4 Jet is a hard black stone that is used in jewellery. N UNCOUNT

jet-black. Something that is **jet-black** is very ADJ COLOUR
dark black in colour. EG *His hair was jet black.*

jet engine, jet engines. A **jet engine** is an N COUNT
engine in which hot air and gases are pushed out at
the back. Jet engines are used for most modern
aeroplanes.

jetlag /dʒetlæg/ is a feeling of confusion and N UNCOUNT
tiredness that people experience after a long journey in an aeroplane. EG *With jet-lag still a problem,
I almost fell asleep during the meeting.*

jet set. The **jet set** are rich and successful people, N SING : the+N
especially young people, who live in a luxurious
way. EG *...the whole French and Italian jet set.*

jettison /dʒetɪsᵊn, -zᵊn/, **jettisons, jettisoning,** V+O
jettisoned. If you **jettison** something, you deliber- Formal
ately reject it or throw it away. EG *...ideas too
valuable, too sacred, to jettison... I also thought it
was time to jettison the blue overcoat.*

jetty /dʒetiʹ/, **jetties.** A **jetty** is a wide stone wall N COUNT
or wooden platform at the edge of the sea or a
river, where boats can wait while people get on
and off. EG *The boat was tied up alongside a
crumbling limestone jetty.*

Jew /dʒuː/, **Jews.** A **Jew** is a person who believes N COUNT
in and practises the religion of Judaism.

jewel /dʒuːəl/, **jewels.** A **jewel** is a precious stone N COUNT
such as a diamond or ruby that is used to decorate
valuable things that you wear, such as rings or
necklaces. EG *She was wearing even more jewels
than the Queen Mother!... ...a jewel box.*

jewelled /dʒuːəld/; spelled **jeweled** in American ADJ CLASSIF :
English. **Jewelled** items and ornaments are deco- ATTRIB
rated with precious stones. EG *...a jewelled brooch.*

jeweller /dʒuːələ/, **jewellers;** spelled **jeweler** in N COUNT
American English. A **jeweller** is a person who
buys, sells, and repairs jewellery and watches.

jewellery

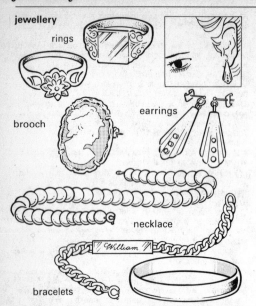

rings

earrings

brooch

necklace

bracelets

William

---

jewellery /dʒuːəˡlri¹/; spelled **jewelry** in Ameri- N UNCOUNT can English. **Jewellery** consists of ornaments such as rings, bracelets, and necklaces which are often made of valuable metal such as gold, and which are sometimes decorated with precious stones. EG *She thought some of her jewellery was missing... ...a jewellery box.*

Jewess /dʒuːˡs/, **Jewesses**. A **Jewess** is a wom- N COUNT an or girl who is Jewish. Formal

Jewish /dʒuːɪʃ/. A person or thing that is **Jewish** ADJ CLASSIF belongs or relates to the religion of Judaism or to people who follow this religion. EG *Jewish schol- ars... ...a beautiful Jewish woman... ...a Jewish wed- ding... ...Jewish teaching.*

jibe /dʒaɪb/, **jibes**; also spelled **gibe**. A **jibe** is a N COUNT rude or insulting remark about someone. EG *He swallowed and tried to smile at the jibe.*

jiffy /dʒɪfi¹/. If you say that you will do something PHRASE **in a jiffy**, you mean that you will do it quickly and Informal very soon. EG *I'll be back in a jiffy.*

jig /dʒɪg/, **jigs**, **jigging**, **jigged**. 1 A **jig** is a lively N COUNT folk dance, popular in the past among country people.

2 To **jig** means to dance or move in an uneven V : OFT+A way, especially bouncing up and down. EG *Others began to jig and stamp and shuffle.*

jiggle /dʒɪgəˡl/, **jiggles**, **jiggling**, **jiggled**. If you V+O **jiggle** something, you move it quickly from side to Informal side. EG *She jiggled the front door handle.*

jigsaw /dʒɪgsɔː/, **jigsaws**. A **jigsaw** or **jigsaw** N COUNT **puzzle** is a game using a picture on cardboard or wood that has been cut up into odd shapes. You have to make the picture again by putting the pieces together correctly.

jilt /dʒɪlt/, **jilts**, **jilting**, **jilted**. If you **jilt** someone V+O who you have promised to marry, you end your Outdated relationship with them suddenly; used showing disapproval. EG *He had jilted her to marry a maidservant.*

jingle /dʒɪŋgəˡl/, **jingles**, **jingling**, **jingled**. 1 V-ERG When something **jingles** or when you **jingle** it, it makes a gentle ringing noise, like small bells. EG *...waving her arms in the air so that her charm bracelet jingled.* ▸ used as a noun. EG *I can hear the* ▸ N SING *jingle of bracelets coming up behind me in the dark.*

2 A **jingle** is a short and simple tune, often with N COUNT

words, used to advertise a product on radio or television.

jinx /dʒɪŋks/, **jinxes**. A **jinx** is bad luck, or a thing N COUNT : or person that is thought to bring bad luck. EG USU SING *...Muck Hall: the farm with the jinx on it.*

jittery /dʒɪtəˡri¹/. Someone who is **jittery** feels ADJ QUALIT extremely nervous. EG *The postponement had* Informal *made them jittery.*

job /dʒɒb/, **jobs**. 1 A **job** is 1.1 the work that a N COUNT person does regularly in order to earn money. EG *Gladys finally got a good job as a secretary.* 1.2 a N COUNT particular task. EG *There are always plenty of jobs to be done round here... ...a repair job.*

2 The **job** of a particular person or thing is their N COUNT+POSS duty or function. EG *It's not their job to decide what ought to be the law.*

3 If you say that you had a **job** doing something, N SING you are emphasizing how difficult it was to do. EG *I* Informal *had a job sneaking into the house unnoticed.*

4 If you say that someone **is doing** a good job or is PHRASE **making a good job of** something, you mean that they are doing something well. EG *Daddy thought we'd made a very good job of the bathroom.* ● **it's a good job**: see good.

5 If you say that something is **just the job**, you PHRASE mean that it is exactly what you wanted or needed. Informal

jobless /dʒɒblɪˢs/. 1 Someone who is **jobless** does ADJ CLASSIF not have a job, even though they would like one. EG *During the depression millions were jobless and homeless.*

2 The **jobless** are people who are jobless. EG *We* N PLURAL : the *have to do more for the poor and the jobless.* +N

job lot, **job lots**. A **job lot** is a number of cheap N COUNT things of poor quality which are sold together, for example in an auction. EG *He bought a job lot of 50 books for £3.*

job sharing is the arrangement by which two N UNCOUNT people work part-time at the same job, for example one person working in the morning and the other in the afternoon.

jockey /dʒɒki¹/, **jockeys**, **jockeying**, **jockeyed**. 1 N COUNT A **jockey** is someone who rides a horse in a horse race.

2 If people **jockey for position**, they try to get into PHRASE a better position than their rivals. EG *Rival trade union organizations continuously jockey for posi- tion.*

jocular /dʒɒkjəˡlə/. 1 Someone who is **jocular** is ADJ QUALIT cheerful and often makes jokes. EG *The resem- blance was noted by a jocular English visitor.*

2 Something that is **jocular** is intended to make ADJ QUALIT people laugh. EG *...a jocular remark.*

jodhpurs /dʒɒdpəz/ are special trousers that you N PLURAL wear when you are riding a horse.

jog /dʒɒg/, **jogs**, **jogging**, **jogged**. 1 If you **jog**, you V : OFT+A run slowly, often as a form of exercise. EG *...people who jog or play squash... He jogged off down the lane.* ▸ used as a noun. EG *I speeded up to a jog and* ▸ N SING *moved up the road briskly.* ◇ **jogger** /dʒɒgə/, ◇ N COUNT **joggers**. EG *...a couple of track-suited joggers.* ◇ **jogging** /dʒɒgɪŋ/. EG *...the current enthusiasm* ◇ N UNCOUNT *for jogging.*

2 If you **jog** something, you push or bump it slightly V+O so that it shakes or moves. EG *She jogged her cup of chocolate... Be careful not to jog the table.*

3 If something or something **jogs** your **memory**, PHRASE they remind you of something. EG *He had demon- strated the sound to jog my memory.*

join /dʒɔɪn/, **joins**, **joining**, **joined**. 1 If one person V OR V+O : or thing **joins** another, the two people or things RECIP come together. EG *He went for a walk before joining his brother for tea... The helicopter was quickly joined by a second... The Missouri joins the Mississippi at St Louis.*

2 If you **join** a queue, you go and stand at the end of V+O

If you think that something is beyond a joke, do you think that it is funny?

it. EG *They went off to join the queue for coffee...*
The van joined the row of cars.

3 If you **join** a club, society, or organization, you v+o
become a member of it. EG *We both joined the*
Labour Party... He's joined the army.

4 If you **join** an activity, you become involved with v+o
it. EG *They were invited to join the feasting.* ● to
join forces: see **force**.

5 If you **join** two things, you fasten or fix them v+o:usu+a
together. EG *Cut them down the middle and join the*
two outside edges together.

6 If a line, a path, or a bridge **joins** two things, it v+o:usu+a
connects them. EG *Draw a straight line joining*
these two points... The cities are joined by telecom-
munication links.

7 A **join** is a place where two things are fastened N count
or fixed together. EG *The repair was done so well,*
you could hardly see the join.

join in. If you **join in** an activity, you become phrasal vb :
involved in it. EG *He took his coat off and joined in* v+adv/prep
the work... Parents should join in these discussions.

join up. **1** If someone **joins up**, they become a phrasal vb :
member of the army, the navy, or the air force. EG v+adv
At eighteen, just before joining up and going British
abroad, I met Elizabeth. **2** If you **join up** two v+o+adv
things, you fasten or fix them together. EG *I used to*
join up all his paper clips in a long chain.

joiner /dʒɔɪnə/, **joiners.** A **joiner** is a person who N count
makes wooden window frames, door frames, and British
doors.

joint /dʒɔɪnt/, **joints. 1** Joint means shared by or adj classif :
belonging to two or more people. EG *We have* attrib
opened a joint account at the bank... The presenta-
tion was a joint effort. ◊ **jointly.** EG *It was built* ◊ adv
jointly by France and Germany.

2 A **joint** is **2.1** a part of your body such as your N count
elbow or knee where two bones meet and are able
to move together. EG *He can feel the rheumatism in*
his joints... the joints of the fingers. **2.2** the place
where two things are fastened or fixed together. EG
Cracks appeared at the joints between the new
plaster and the old.

3 A **joint** of meat is a fairly large piece of meat N count
which is suitable for roasting. EG *...a joint of roast*
beef.

4 You can refer to a night club or other place N count
where people go for entertainment as a **joint.** EG Informal
He was employed in a poky little jazz joint in San
Francisco.

5 Some people refer to a cigarette which contains N count
cannabis as a **joint.** Informal

jointed /dʒɔɪntɪ²d/. Something that is **jointed** has adj classif
joints that move. EG *The doll had jointed legs and*
arms.

joke /dʒəʊk/, **jokes, joking, joked. 1** A **joke** is N count
something that is said or done to make you laugh,
for example a funny story. EG *Dave was telling me*
this joke about a penguin.

2 If you **joke**, you tell funny stories or say things v : oft
that are amusing and not serious. EG *They never* +about/with
joked about sex... Don't worry, I was only joking.

3 If you say that someone or something is a **joke**, N sing : a+N
you mean that they are ridiculous and not worthy Informal
of respect. EG *His colleagues regard him as a joke.*

4 If you say that a situation has gone **beyond a** phrase
joke, you mean that it has become annoying or
worrying. EG *The whole thing is getting beyond a*
joke.

5 If you say that something is **no joke**, you mean phrase
that it is very difficult and unpleasant. EG *It's no* Informal
joke running up mountains at the age of forty six!

6 You say '**You're joking**' or '**You must be** convention
joking' when someone has just said something
very surprising.

joker /dʒəʊkə/, **jokers. 1** Someone who is a **joker** N count
likes making jokes or doing amusing things. EG *I*
enjoyed working with Hitchcock. He was a great
joker.

2 The **joker** in a pack of cards is a card which does N count

not belong to any of the four suits. In many card
games it can be used instead of any card.

jokey /dʒəʊkiˈ/. Something that is **jokey** is amus- adj qualit
ing and does not have any serious meaning. EG Informal
They all had jokey nicknames.

jokingly /dʒəʊkɪŋliˈ/. If you say or do something adv
jokingly, you do it to amuse someone or without
seriously meaning it. EG *My friend said jokingly that*
George had lost around two hundred pounds.

jollity /dʒɒlɪtiˈ/ is cheerful behaviour. EG *He ad-* N uncount
mired her high spirits and her jollity. Outdated

jolly /dʒɒliˈ/, **jollier, jolliest. 1** Someone who is adj qualit
jolly is happy and cheerful. EG *Buddy's mother was*
a jolly, easy-going woman.

2 An event that is **jolly** is lively and enjoyable. EG adj qualit
At Christmas we have an awfully jolly time: tree, Outdated
carols and all that stuff.

3 You can use **jolly** to emphasize something. EG *We* submod
provide a jolly good service, I think... It was jolly Informal
decent of him to think of me, I must say. British

4 You can use **jolly well** to emphasize what you adv
are saying, especially when you are annoyed or Informal
upset. EG *I'm jolly well not going to ring her up!* British

jolt /dʒəʊlt/, **jolts, jolting, jolted. 1** If something v-erg
jolts or if you **jolt** it, it moves suddenly and
violently. EG *She jolted his arm... ...enormous loads*
that jolted and swayed. ▸ used as a noun. EG *I came* ▸ N count
down slowly at first, but then with a jolt.

2 If you **are jolted** by something, it gives you an v+o : usu pass
unpleasant surprise or shock. EG *I was jolted awake*
by a bright light. ▸ used as a noun. EG *The aim of* ▸ N sing
Detention Centres is to give kids a jolt.

jostle /dʒɒsəˈl/, **jostles, jostling, jostled.** If peo- v+o or v
ple **jostle** or **jostle** each other, **1** they bump
against each other or push each other in a crowd.
EG *Pedestrians jostled them on the pavement.* **2**
they compete with each other for attention or for a
reward. EG *Photographers, models, and singers, all*
jostled for money and fame.

jot /dʒɒt/, **jots, jotting, jotted.** If you **jot** some- v+o+a
thing down, you write it down in the form of a short
informal note. EG *I asked you to jot down a few*
ideas... I jot odd notes in the back of the diary.

journal /dʒɜːnəˈl/, **journals.** A **journal** is **1** a N count
magazine for people with a particular interest. EG
...a trade journal. **2** an account which you write of
your daily activities. EG *For nearly three months he*
had been keeping a journal.

journalism /dʒɜːnəˈlɪzə²m/ is the job of collect- N uncount
ing, writing, and publishing news in newspapers
and magazines and on television and radio. EG *Have*
you ever thought of going into journalism?

journalist /dʒɜːnəˈlɪst/, **journalists.** A **journalist** N count
is a person who works on a newspaper or maga-
zine and writes articles for it. EG *She worked as a*
journalist on The Times.

journalistic /dʒɜːnəˈlɪstɪk/ means relating to the adj classif
work of a journalist. EG *I had no journalistic experi-* attrib
ence in Britain... ...journalistic investigations.

journey /dʒɜːniˈ/, **journeys, journeying, jour-** N count
neyed. 1 When you make a **journey**, you travel
from one place to another. EG *He went on a journey*
to London... She'll want her supper straightaway
after that long journey. ● If you **break** your ● phrase
journey somewhere, you stop there for a short
time so that you can have a rest. EG *He is staying in*
Singapore, where he is breaking his journey home
to Australia.

2 If you **journey** somewhere, you travel there. EG v+a
The nights became colder as they journeyed north. Literary

jovial /dʒəʊviəl/. Someone who is **jovial** behaves adj qualit
in a cheerful and happy way. EG *He was a big,*
heavy, jovial man... ...a jovial smile.

jowl /dʒaʊl/, **jowls.** Your **jowls** are the lower N count :
parts of your cheeks, covering your jawbones. EG usu plural
...an old woman with heavy jowls and a double
chin.

joy /dʒɔɪ/, **joys. 1** Joy is a feeling of great happi- N uncount
ness. EG *She shouted with joy when I told her she*

was free... His face showed his joy the moment he saw me... Her look of joy gave way to one of misery.

2 Something that is a **joy** makes you feel happy or gives you great pleasure. EG *She discovered the joy of writing... His one joy is playing squash.*   N COUNT+SUPP

joyful /dʒɔɪful/. **1** Something that is **joyful** causes happiness and pleasure. EG *I still felt sad even after you'd announced the joyful tidings.*   ADJ QUALIT

2 Someone who is **joyful** is extremely happy. EG *The joyful parents named him Lexington.*   ADJ QUALIT

◊ **joyfully.** EG *We welcomed him joyfully to the club.*   ◊ ADV

joyless /dʒɔɪlɪˀs/. Something or someone that is **joyless** produces or experiences no pleasure. EG *...years and years of joyless married life... I hope I never become as joyless as they have become.*   ADJ QUALIT

joyous /dʒɔɪəs/ means extremely happy and enthusiastic. EG *I spread my arms wide and felt joyous and exalted and free.* ◊ **joyously.** EG *He flung back the curtains joyously and let the sunlight pour in.*   ADJ QUALIT Literary   ◊ ADV

joyride /dʒɔɪraɪd/, **joyrides.** If someone goes for a **joyride**, they drive around for pleasure in a car that they have just stolen. EG *That joyride was a silly stunt.*   N COUNT

JP, JPs. A **JP** is a local magistrate in Britain. **JP** is an abbreviation for 'Justice of the Peace'.   N COUNT

jubilant /dʒuːbɪlənt/. If you are **jubilant**, you feel extremely happy and successful. EG *...a jubilant Labour Party Conference.*   ADJ QUALIT

jubilation /dʒuːbɪleɪʃəˀn/ is a feeling of great happiness and success. EG *There was a general air of jubilation.*   N UNCOUNT Formal

jubilee /dʒuːbɪliː, dʒuːbɪliː/, **jubilees.** A **jubilee** is a special anniversary of an event, especially the 25th or 50th anniversary. EG *...the college's silver jubilee year.*   N COUNT

Judaism /dʒuːdeɪɪzəˀm/ is the religion of the Jewish people, which is based on the Old Testament of the Bible and on the Jewish book of laws and traditions.   N UNCOUNT

judge /dʒʌdʒ/, **judges, judging, judged. 1** A **judge** is **1.1** the person in a court of law who decides how the law should be applied to people, for example how criminals should be punished. EG *Last week she appeared before a judge... Judge Arnason set Miss Davis free on bail.* **1.2** a person who decides who will be the winner of a competition. EG *The panel of judges consisted of a variety of famous people.*   N COUNT

2 If someone is a good **judge** of something, they can understand it and make decisions about it. If they are a bad **judge** of something, they cannot understand it or make decisions about it. EG *He was a good judge of character... Nick, a perfect judge of such matters, had ordered a light French wine.*   N COUNT+SUPP

3 If you **judge** a competition, you decide who the winner is. EG *The competition was judged by the local mayor.*   V+O

4 If you **judge** something, you form an opinion about it by thinking carefully about it. EG *It's impossible to judge her age... The operation must be judged a failure... He judged it wiser to put a stop to this quarrel... I'm not in a position to judge.*   V+O, V+O+C, OR V

5 If you **judge** someone, you decide whether they are good or bad after you have thought about their character, behaviour, and life style. EG *She seemed to be watching him, judging him... Social workers declare that they are not out to judge people, but simply want to help.*   V+O

6 You use **judging from** or **judging by** to mention the reasons that cause you to believe something. EG *There was some great national celebration in town, judging by the firework displays everywhere... He was extremely attractive, to judge from the newspaper photographs.*   PREP

judgement /dʒʌdʒməˀnt/, **judgements;** also spelled **judgment. 1** A **judgement** is **1.1** an opinion that you have or give after thinking carefully   N COUNT: OFT+SUPP

about something. EG *I shall make my own judgement on this matter when I see the results... In our judgment, her plan has definitely succeeded.* **1.2** a decision made by a judge or by a court of law. EG *The final judgment will probably be made in court... Mr Justice Dillon gave his judgement the week before.*   N COUNT OR N UNCOUNT

2 Judgement is **2.1** the ability to make sensible guesses about a situation or sensible decisions about what to do. EG *This is a case that calls for judgement rather than expert knowledge... My father did not permit me to question his judgement... ...an error of judgement.* **2.2** the process of deciding how good something or someone is. EG *I have a great fear of judgment... During her career a scientist must survive many judgments.*   N UNCOUNT   N UNCOUNT OR N COUNT

3 If you **pass judgement** on something, you give your opinion about it, especially if you are making a criticism. EG *I can't pass judgement until I know all the facts.*   PHRASE

4 If you **reserve judgement** about something, you do not give an opinion about it until you know more about it. EG *Jenny was still reserving judgment until she could check out the details.*   PHRASE

5 If something is **against** your **better judgement**, you believe that it would be more sensible not to do it.   PHRASE

6 A **judgement** is also something unpleasant that happens to you and that is considered to be a punishment from God. EG *War is a judgement on us all for our sins.*   N COUNT

judicial /dʒuːdɪʃəˀl/ means **1** relating to judgement in a court of law. EG *The two territories had differing political, judicial, and educational systems.* **2** showing or using judgement in thinking about something. EG *...the young man's calm judicial gaze... ...examined with judicial care.*   ADJ CLASSIF: ATTRIB Formal   Literary

judiciary /dʒuːdɪʃəriˀ/. The **judiciary** is the branch of authority in a country which is concerned with justice and the legal system.   N SING: the+N Formal

judicious /dʒuːdɪʃəs/. An action or decision that is **judicious** shows good judgement and sense. EG *They made judicious use of government incentives... ...surveying them with a judicious eye.* ◊ **judiciously.** EG *You put your case most judiciously.*   ADJ QUALIT Formal   ◊ ADV

judo /dʒuːdəʊ/ is a sport in which two people fight each other and each tries to throw the other one to the ground.   N UNCOUNT

jug /dʒʌg/, **jugs. 1** A **jug** is a container which is used for holding and pouring liquids. EG *...a big white jug full of beer... ...the milk jug.*   N COUNT

jug

2 You can use **jug** to refer to the contents of a jug, as in a **jug** of water or a **jug** of milk.   N PART

juggernaut /dʒʌgənɔːt/, **juggernauts.** A **juggernaut** is a very large lorry.   N COUNT British

juggle /dʒʌgəˀl/, **juggles, juggling, juggled. 1** If you **juggle**, you throw things into the air, catching each one and throwing it up again so that there are several of them in the air at the same time.   V OR V+O

2 If you **juggle** numbers or ideas, or **juggle** with them, you rearrange them repeatedly in order to   V+O OR V+with

What months of the year are on these pages?

make them fit the pattern that you want them to fit. EG *Both of them juggle their working hours to be with the children... He was still juggling with figures and possibilities.*

juggler /dʒʌglə/, **jugglers.** A **juggler** is someone who juggles in order to entertain people. N COUNT

jugular /dʒʌgjoᵘlə/, **jugulars.** Your **jugular** or **jugular vein** is a large vein in your neck that carries blood from your head back to your heart. N COUNT

juice /dʒuːs/, **juices.** 1 **Juice** is the liquid that can be obtained from a fruit or a plant. EG *Try squeezing a little lemon juice and garlic into it... two glasses of pineapple juice.* N MASS

2 The **juices** of a joint of meat are the liquid that comes out of it when you cook it. EG *...spooning the juices over the top of a leg of lamb.* N COUNT OR N UNCOUNT

3 The **juices** in your stomach are the fluids that help you to digest food. EG *...digestive juices.* N PLURAL

juicy /dʒuːsiᶦ/, **juicier, juiciest.** 1 A fruit or other food that is **juicy** has a lot of juice in it. EG *...juicy, ripe tomatoes.* ADJ QUALIT

2 Something that is described as **juicy** 2.1 is very interesting and enjoyable. EG *The title part of the play is the juiciest for an actor.* 2.2 describes or represents sexual behaviour in a way that people consider to be pleasing or exciting. EG *He describes some juicy scenes in the 'Priest of Love'.* ADJ QUALIT Informal / Informal

jukebox /dʒuːkbɒks/, **jukeboxes.** A **jukebox** is a large record player in pubs and bars. You put a coin in and choose the record that you want to hear. EG *...the noise of reggae music from the jukebox.* N COUNT

July /dʒɔᵘlaɪ/ is the seventh month of the year in the Western calendar. EG *On leaving school in July 1942, Tony very much wanted to join the RAF.* N UNCOUNT

jumble /dʒʌmbᵊl/, **jumbles, jumbling, jumbled.**
1 A **jumble** is a lot of different things that are all mixed together in a confused or untidy way. EG *...a chaotic jumble of motor vehicles of every description... ...a jumble of colours and patterns and noises and smells.* N PART OR N SING

2 If you **jumble** things, or **jumble** them **up,** you mix them together so that they are not in the correct order. EG *The bits and pieces were jumbled up with a lot of stuff that would never be needed again.* V+O : OFT+up, USU PASS

jumble sale, jumble sales. A **jumble sale** is an event that is held to raise money, usually for a charity. People bring old things that they do not want any more, and other people buy them for small amounts of money. N COUNT

jumbo /dʒʌmbəʊ/, **jumbos.** 1 **Jumbo** means very large; used especially in advertising. EG *...jumbo steaks... ...a jumbo vacuum cleaner.* ADJ CLASSIF : ATTRIB

2 A **jumbo** or a **jumbo jet** is a very large jet aeroplane. N COUNT

jump /dʒʌmp/, **jumps, jumping, jumped.** 1 If you **jump** somewhere, 1.1 you push your feet against the ground and go into the air. EG *He jumped down from the terrace... The horse jumps over a small stream.* ▶ used as a noun. EG *It was a spectacular jump.* 1.2 you move there quickly and suddenly. EG *Ralph jumped to his feet... He jumped up and went across to the large bookcase.* V : USU+A / ▶ N COUNT / V+A

2 If you **jump** something such as a fence, you jump over it or across it. V+O

3 If you **jump,** your body makes a sudden movement because you have just been badly frightened or surprised by something. EG *A sudden noise made me jump... I spoke so loudly that they jumped.* V

4 If an amount or level **jumps,** it increases by a large amount in a short time. EG *The population jumped to nearly 10,000.* ▶ used as a noun. EG *...a massive jump in expenditure.* V : USU+A / ▶ N COUNT : USU+SUPP

5 If someone **jumps** a queue, they move to the front of it before it is their turn to do so; used showing disapproval. V+O

6 If you **keep one jump ahead** of an opponent or PHRASE

rival, you manage always to be in a better position than they are.

7 to **jump to a conclusion:** see **conclusion.** ● to **jump the gun:** see **gun.** ● to **jump out of** your **skin:** see **skin.**

jump at. If you **jump at** an offer or opportunity, you accept it eagerly as soon as it is offered to you. EG *I suggested it to him, and he jumped at the idea.* PHRASAL VB : V+PREP, HAS PASS

jumper /dʒʌmpə/, **jumpers.** A **jumper** is 1 a piece of clothing made of knitted wool, that covers the upper part of your body and your arms and does not open at the front. 2 a pinafore dress. N COUNT British / American

jumpy /dʒʌmpiᶦ/, **jumpier, jumpiest.** If you are **jumpy,** you are nervous or worried about something. EG *The very thought of it makes me feel slightly jumpy.* ADJ QUALIT Informal

junction /dʒʌŋkʃᵊn/, **junctions.** A **junction** is a place where roads or railway lines join. EG *She began walking towards the junction of Cortez Avenue and Main Street.* N COUNT

juncture /dʒʌŋktʃə/, **junctures.** At a particular **juncture** means at a particular point in time, especially when it is a very important time in a series of events. EG *She knew that any move on her part at this juncture would be interpreted as a sign of weakness.* PHRASE Formal

June /dʒuːn/ is the sixth month of the year in the Western calendar. EG *Labour was defeated in the General Election of 19 June 1970.* N UNCOUNT

jungle /dʒʌŋgᵊl/, **jungles.** 1 A **jungle** is a forest in a hot country where tall trees and other plants grow very closely together. EG *...the Amazon jungle... ...immense tracts of impenetrable jungle.* N COUNT OR N UNCOUNT

2 You can refer to a situation where everything is very complicated as a **jungle.** EG *He'd never have got anywhere in the jungle of real politics.* N SING+SUPP

junior /dʒuːnjə/, **juniors.** 1 Someone who is **junior** holds an unimportant position in an organization or profession. EG *She's a junior minister at the Home Office... We could give the job to somebody more junior.* ▶ used as a noun. EG *Police officers later blamed their juniors for not spotting these clues.* ADJ QUALIT / ▶ N COUNT

2 If you are someone's **junior,** you are younger than they are. EG *She was married at the age of seventy-seven to a man seventeen years her junior.* N SING+POSS

junior school, junior schools. A **junior school** in England or Wales is a school for children between the ages of about seven and eleven. N COUNT OR N UNCOUNT

junk /dʒʌŋk/ is 1 an amount of old or useless things. EG *Look, get that junk off the table, will you!* 2 second-hand goods that are being sold cheaply. EG *We got most of our furniture from junk shops and jumble sales.* N UNCOUNT Informal / N MOD Informal

junk food is food that is not very good for your health but is easy and quick to prepare. N MASS

junkie /dʒʌŋkiᶦ/, **junkies.** A **junkie** is someone who is addicted to a drug that they inject into their body. EG *Of course I'm worried. You're turning into a junkie.* N COUNT Informal

jurisdiction /dʒʊəᵊrɪsdɪkʃᵊn/ is the power that a court of law or someone in authority has to carry out legal judgements or enforce laws. EG *The Governor had no jurisdiction over prices.* N UNCOUNT

juror /dʒʊərə/, **jurors.** A **juror** is a member of a jury. EG *The jurors gave their verdict.* N COUNT

jury /dʒʊəriᶦ/, **juries.** A **jury** is 1 a group of people in a court of law who listen to the facts about a crime and decide whether the person accused is guilty or not. EG *A jury would never convict on that evidence... ...trial by jury.* 2 a group of people who decide who the winner of a competition is. EG *We'd like to test the opinion of our jury in Broadcasting House.* N COLL

just /dʒʌst/. 1 If you say that something has **just** happened, you mean that it happened a very short time ago. EG *I've just sold my car... She had only just moved in.* ADV

2 If you say that you are **just** doing something, you mean that you will finish doing it very soon. If you ADV

say that you are **just** going to do something, you mean that you will do it very soon. EG *I'm just making us some coffee, Chris... They were just about to leave when there was a knock on the door.*

3 You can also use **just** to emphasize that something happens or happened at exactly the moment you are talking about. EG *The telephone rang just as I was about to serve up the dinner... Judy didn't like to tell him just then.* ADV

4 Just now means **4.1** a very short time ago. EG *She was here just now.* **4.2** at the present time. EG *Nasty weather we're having just now.* PHRASE

5 You say **just a minute**, **just a moment**, or **just a second** when you are asking someone to wait for a short time. EG *'Have you got John's address?' – 'Just a minute. I'll have a look.'* CONVENTION

6 You also use **just 6.1** to indicate that something is no more important, interesting, difficult, or great than you say it is. EG *It's just a story... It is not just a children's film... Just add boiling water.* **6.2** to indicate that you are talking about a small part or sample, not the whole of an amount. EG *These are just a few of the enquiries.* **6.3** to indicate that what you are saying is the case, but only by a very small degree or amount. EG *The heat was just bearable... He could only just hear them... It might just help.* **6.4** to give emphasis to what you are saying. EG *I just know there's something wrong... Just listen to that noise.* ADV

7 Just also means exactly or precisely. EG *That's just what I wanted to hear... Rattlesnake is just like chicken, only tougher... She was as fat as he was and just as unattractive... The real debate is about just how much money you should spend.* ADV

8 If you say that someone is **just** the person, you mean that they are the right person. If something is **just** the thing, it is the right thing. EG *He knew just the place... Sam would be just the person!* ADV

9 If you say that you can **just** imagine something, you mean that it is easy for you to imagine it. EG *Ah yes, I can just see him as a dentist.* ADV

10 You also use **just** when you are politely making a request, interrupting someone, or changing the subject. EG *Can I just use your lighter please?* ADV

11 You use **just about** to say that something is so close to a particular level or state that it can be regarded as having reached it. EG *She was just about his age... Everything is just about ready.* PHRASE

12 Someone or something that is **just** is reasonable and fair. EG *...a just punishment... ...a just and civilised society.* ◊ **justly**. EG *I believe that I have acted justly.* ADJ QUALIT ◊ ADV

justice /dʒʌstɪs/, **justices**. **1 Justice** is **1.1** fairness in the way that people are treated. EG *The concept of justice is very basic in human thought... ...economic justice.* **1.2** the system that a country uses in order to make sure that people obey the law. EG *The courts are a very important part of our British system of justice.* N UNCOUNT

2 The **justice** of a claim, argument, or cause is its quality of being reasonable and right. EG *They believe in the justice of their cause.* N UNCOUNT +SUPP

3 If a criminal **is brought to justice**, he or she is tried in a court of law and punished. EG *The murderer will in time be brought to justice.* PHRASE

4 If you **do justice to** something, you deal with it properly and completely. EG *I am the only man in Europe capable of doing it justice, of making a perfect job of it.* PHRASE

5 A **justice** is a judge. EG *...justices of the Supreme Court.* N COUNT American

Justice of the Peace, Justices of the Peace. A **Justice of the Peace** is a local magistrate in Britain. N COUNT

justifiable /dʒʌstɪfaɪəbəˀl/. An opinion, action, or fact that is **justifiable** is acceptable or correct because there is a good reason for it. EG *I hope this is a justifiable interpretation.* ◊ **justifiably**. EG *The Government is justifiably unpopular.* ADJ QUALIT ◊ ADV

justification /dʒʌstɪfɪkeɪʃəˀn/, **justifications**. A **justification** for something is a good reason or explanation for it. EG *We all have justifications for what we do... There was no justification for higher interest rates.* N COUNT OR N UNCOUNT

justified /dʒʌstɪfaɪd/. **1** If you think that someone is **justified** in doing something, you think that they have good reasons for doing it. EG *I think he was quite justified in refusing to help her.* ADJ PRED

2 An action that is **justified** is reasonable and acceptable. EG *In these circumstances, massive industrial action is justified and necessary.* ADJ QUALIT

justify /dʒʌstɪfaɪ/, **justifies, justifying, justified.** If someone **justifies** a particular action or idea, they give a good reason why it is sensible or necessary. EG *The decision has been fully justified... I'm not going to try and justify myself... How did they justify putting that thing on a gallery wall?* V+O, V-REFL, OR V+-ING

jut /dʒʌt/, **juts, jutting, jutted.** If something **juts** out, it sticks out above or beyond a surface. EG *The living room window juts out... A line of rocks jutted into the sea.* V+A

juvenile /dʒuːvəˀnaɪl/, **juveniles. 1 Juvenile** activity or behaviour involves young people who are not adults. EG *...the increase in juvenile crime... ...juvenile offenders.* ADJ CLASSIF : ATTRIB

2 You can say that someone is **juvenile** when they are behaving in a silly way. EG *Mike has a somewhat juvenile sense of humour.* ADJ QUALIT

3 A **juvenile** is a child or young person who is not yet old enough to be regarded as an adult. EG *17% of all crime in 1983 was committed by juveniles.* N COUNT Legal

juvenile delinquent, juvenile delinquents. A **juvenile delinquent** is a young person who is guilty of committing crimes, especially vandalism or violence. N COUNT

juxtapose /dʒʌkstəpəʊz/, **juxtaposes, juxtaposing, juxtaposed.** If you **juxtapose** two things or ideas, you put them next to each other, often in order to emphasize the difference between them. EG *She juxtaposes her photographs with illustrations of flowers.* ◊ **juxtaposition** /dʒʌkstəpəzɪʃəˀn/, **juxtapositions.** EG *...the juxtaposition of extreme wealth and poverty.* V+O OR V+O+with : RECIP Formal ◊ N COUNT OR N UNCOUNT

K k

K, k /keɪ/, **Ks, k's. K** is the eleventh letter of the English alphabet. N COUNT

kaleidoscope /kəlaɪdəˀskəʊp/, **kaleidoscopes. 1** A **kaleidoscope** is a tube that you hold in your hand. When you look through one end and turn the tube, you see a pattern of colours which keeps changing. N COUNT

2 You can refer to any pattern of colours that keeps changing as a **kaleidoscope**. EG *Alongside the railway line, in a kaleidoscope of colours, cars and lorries swept by.* N SING+SUPP Literary

kangaroo /kæŋgəruː/, **kangaroos.** A **kangaroo** is a large Australian animal which moves by jumping N COUNT on its back legs. Female kangaroos carry their babies in a pouch on their stomachs.

karate /kərɑːtiː/ is a sport in which people fight using their hands, elbows, feet, and legs. `N UNCOUNT`

kebab /kəˈbæb/, **kebabs**. A **kebab** consists of small pieces of meat and sometimes vegetables that have been put on a thin metal rod and grilled. `N COUNT`

keel /kiːl/, **keels**, **keeling**, **keeled**. If you say that something is **on an even keel**, you mean that it is working or proceeding smoothly and satisfactorily. EG *Most governments are able to keep their economies on an even keel.* `PHRASE`

keel over. If something **keels over**, it falls over sideways. EG *The pillar was liable to keel over at any moment... One of the athletes suddenly keeled over.* `PHRASAL VB : V+ADV`

keen /kiːn/, **keener**, **keenest**. 1 If you are **keen** to do something, you want to do it very much. EG *Her solicitor was keener to talk than she was... He didn't seem all that keen on having it... He's not keen for Charlotte to know.* `ADJ PRED : OR to-INF OR on`

2 You use **keen** to show that someone enjoys a particular sport or activity and does it a lot. For example, if someone is a **keen** golfer, they enjoy playing golf very much. EG *He was not a keen gardener... Boys are as keen on cooking as girls are.* `ADJ QUALIT : ATTRIB OR ADJ PRED+on`

3 **Keen** people are enthusiastic and are interested in everything they do. EG *They were highly-motivated students, very keen.* `ADJ QUALIT`

4 If you have a **keen** interest or a **keen** desire, your interest or desire is very strong. EG *He took a keen interest in domestic affairs... She had a keen desire to see the union brought under the rule of law.* ◊ **keenly.** EG *I was keenly interested in outdoor activities.* `ADJ QUALIT : USU ATTRIB` ◊ `ADV`

5 If you are **keen** on someone, you find them very attractive. EG *Molly was very keen on the music master.* `ADJ PRED+on Informal`

6 If you have **keen** sight or hearing, for example, you can see or hear very well. EG *It takes a keen eye to spot them... ...people with keen powers of observation.* `ADJ QUALIT`

7 You say that a contest is **keen** when the competitors are trying very hard and it is not clear who will win. EG *The competition for the first prize was keen.* ◊ **keenly.** EG *...a keenly contested football match.* `ADJ QUALIT` ◊ `ADV`

keenly /kiːnliː/. If you watch or listen **keenly**, you watch or listen with great concentration. EG *He was watching Tortyev keenly.* ● See also **keen**. `ADV`

keep /kiːp/, **keeps**, **keeping**, **kept** /kɛpt/. 1 To **keep** someone or something in a particular state or place means to cause them to remain in that state or place. EG *They had been kept awake by nightingales... She kept her arm around her husband as she spoke... He bought a guard dog to keep out intruders... Sorry to keep you waiting.* `V+O+A, V+O+C, OR V+O+-ING`

2 If you **keep** in a particular state or place, you remain in that state or place. EG *They've got to hunt for food to keep alive... Keep in touch... They kept away from the forest.* `V+C OR V+A`

3 If you **keep** doing something, **3.1** you do it repeatedly. EG *I keep making the same mistake.* **3.2** you continue doing it without stopping. EG *The men just kept walking... Keep searching.* `V+-ING`

4 If you **keep** something, you continue to have it. EG *Why didn't Daddy let me keep the ten dollars?... She would not be able to keep her job.* `V+O`

5 If you **keep** something in a particular place, you have it there so that you can use it whenever you need it. EG *...the shelf where the butter and cheese were kept... Keep a spare key in your bag.* `V+O : USU+A`

6 **Keep** is used with some nouns to indicate that someone does something or continues to do it. For example, if you **keep** a grip on something, you continue to hold or control it. EG *They would keep a look-out for him.* `V+O : NO PASS`

7 To **keep** someone or something from doing a particular thing means to prevent them from doing it. EG *She had to hold the boy tight, to keep him from falling.* `V+O :`

8 If something **keeps** you, it makes you arrive somewhere later than expected. EG *Am I keeping you from your party?... What kept you?* `V+O : OFT+from`

9 When you **keep** something such as a promise or an appointment, you do what you said you would do. EG *Hearst kept his word.* `V+O`

10 If you **keep** something from someone, you do not tell them about it. EG *Why did you keep it from me?* ● If you **keep** something **to yourself**, you do not tell anyone about it. EG *They keep their discoveries to themselves.* `V+O+from` ● `PHRASE`

11 If you **keep yourself to yourself**, you do not talk much to other people. `PHRASE`

12 If you **keep** a record of a series of events, you make a written record of it. EG *We keep a record of the noise levels... I did not keep any notes.* `V+O`

13 People who **keep** animals own them and take care of them. EG *My dad kept chickens.* `V+O`

14 Your **keep** is the cost of food and other things that you need in your daily life. EG *The grant includes £19 for your keep during the vacation.* `N SING+POSS`

15 If food **keeps**, it stays in good condition. `V : NO CONT`

16 If you ask someone how they **are keeping**, you are asking if they are well. `V+A : ONLY CONT`

17 If you **keep at it**, you continue doing something that you have started. EG *You've just got to keep at it.* `PHRASE`

18 If a sign on a piece of land says **'Keep Out'**, it is warning you not to go onto the land.

19 If you say that something is **in keeping** with something else, you mean that it seems right or suitable with it. If it is **out of keeping**, it does not seem right or suitable. EG *Her white socks and brown shoes were not quite in keeping with her beautiful satin evening dress... In keeping with the government policy of non-interference, they refused to take any action.* `PHRASE`

keep back. If you **keep** some information **back**, you do not tell everything that you know about something. EG *You can't write an autobiography without keeping something back.* `PHRASAL VB : V+O+ADV`

keep down. If you **keep** the number or size of something **down**, you do not allow it to get bigger. EG *The French are very concerned to keep costs down.* `PHRASAL VB : V+O+ADV`

keep off. If you **keep** something **off**, you prevent it from reaching you and harming you. EG *They built a bamboo shelter to keep the rain off.* `PHRASAL VB : V+O+ADV/ PREP`

keep on. 1 If you **keep on** doing something, **1.1** you continue doing it without stopping. EG *They kept on walking for a while in silence.* **1.2** you do it repeatedly. EG *I kept on getting up and staring out of the window.* 2 If someone **keeps on** about something, they talk about it often or for a long time, in an irritating way. EG *She kept on about the car.* `PHRASAL VB : V+ADV+-ING` `V+ADV, OFT+about`

keep on at. If someone **keeps on at** you, they repeatedly ask or tell you to do something, in an irritating way. `PHRASAL VB : V+ADV+PREP`

keep to. 1 If you **keep to** a rule, plan, or agreement, you do exactly what you are expected or supposed to do. EG *We must keep to the deadlines.* 2 If you **keep** something to a particular number or quantity, you limit it to that number or quantity. EG *Keep it to a minimum.* `PHRASAL VB : V+PREP, HAS PASS` `V+O+PREP`

keep up. 1 If one person or thing **keeps up** with another, the first one moves, progresses, or increases as fast as the second. EG *I started to run, so that she had to hurry to keep up with me... Pensions were increased to keep up with the rise in prices.* 2 If you **keep up** with what is happening, you make sure that you know about it. EG *Even friends have trouble keeping up with each other's whereabouts.* 3 If you **keep** something **up**, **3.1** you continue to do it or provide it. EG *She kept up a steady moaning... He was unable to keep up the* `PHRASAL VB : V+ADV, OFT+with` `V+ADV, OFT+with` `V+O+ADV` *payments.* **3.2** you prevent it from becoming less. EG *It's important to keep up the standard.*

keeper /kiːpə/, **keepers. 1** A **keeper** is a person N COUNT who takes care of the animals in a zoo.

2 If you say that you **are not** someone's **keeper**, PHRASE you mean that you are not responsible for what they do or for what happens to them. EG *She was not her sister's keeper.*

keep-fit is the activity of keeping your body in N UNCOUNT good condition by doing special exercises.

ken /kɛn/. If something is **beyond** your **ken**, you PHRASE do not have enough knowledge to be able to Formal understand it.

kennel /kɛnəºl/, **kennels. 1** A **kennel** is a small N COUNT hut made for a dog to sleep in.

2 A **kennels** is a place where people can leave N SING their pet dogs when they go on holiday, or where dogs are bred. EG *He had arranged to leave Towser at a kennels.*

kept /kɛpt/ is the past tense and past participle of **keep.**

kerb /kɜːb/, **kerbs;** spelled **curb** in American N COUNT English. The **kerb** is the raised edge between a pavement and a road. EG *The taxi pulled into the kerb... She was standing on the kerb.*

kernel /kɜːnəºl/, **kernels. 1** The **kernel** of a nut is N COUNT the part that is inside the shell.

2 You can refer to the most basic part of some- N COUNT+of thing as its **kernel.** EG *...the men who form the* Formal *kernel of this army... There is a kernel of truth in what you say.*

kerosene /kɛrəsiːn/ is a liquid that is used as a N UNCOUNT fuel in some heaters and lamps. American

kestrel /kɛstrəl/, **kestrels.** A **kestrel** is a small N COUNT falcon.

ketchup /kɛtʃəp/ is a thick, cold sauce made from N UNCOUNT tomatoes.

kettle /kɛtəºl/, **kettles.** A **kettle** is a covered N COUNT round container that you use for boiling water. It has a handle on top and a spout. EG *They put the kettle on to make a cup of tea.*

key /kiː/, **keys. 1** A **key** is **1.1** a specially shaped N COUNT piece of metal which you place in a lock and turn in order to open or lock a door, a drawer, or a suitcase. EG *He locked the bag and put the key in his pocket... I've lost the key to the filing cabinet.* **1.2** a specially shaped piece of metal or plastic which you turn, for example in order to wind up a clock.

2 The **keys** of a typewriter, computer keyboard, or N COUNT cash register are the buttons that you press in order to operate it. See picture at TYPEWRITER.

3 The **keys** of a piano or organ are the black and N COUNT white bars that you press in order to play it.

4 In music, a **key** is a scale of musical notes that N UNCOUNT starts at one particular note. EG *...the key of D.* OR N COUNT

5 The **key** to a map, diagram, or technical book is N COUNT a list of the symbols and abbreviations used in it, with explanations of what they mean.

6 The **key** things or people in a group are the most ADJ CLASSIF : important ones. EG *The country's key industries are* ATTRIB *coal, engineering, and transport... Unemployment was a key issue during the election campaign.*

7 The **key** to a desirable situation or result is the N COUNT : way in which it can be achieved. EG *Education* USU the+N *became the key to progress.*

keyboard /kiːbɔːd/, **keyboards. 1** The **keyboard** N COUNT of a typewriter or a computer terminal is the set of keys that you press in order to operate it.

2 The **keyboard** of a piano or organ is the set of N COUNT black and white keys that you press in order to play it. EG *She reached out her hands to the keyboard and began to play.*

keyhole /kiːhəʊl/, **keyholes.** A **keyhole** is the N COUNT hole in a lock that you put a key in.

keynote /kiːnəʊt/, **keynotes.** The **keynote** of an N COUNT : activity or policy is the most important part of it. USU SING EG *The keynote for Labour policy, he saw, was planning.*

key-ring, key-rings. A **key-ring** is a ring which N COUNT you use to keep your keys together.

kg is an abbreviation for 'kilogram'. EG *It weighs only 20 kg.*

khaki /kɑːkiː[1]/. Something that is **khaki** is ADJ COLOUR yellowish-brown in colour. EG *...khaki shorts... The boys looked smart in khaki and polished brass.*

kibbutz /kɪbʊts/, **kibbutzes** or **kibbutzim** N COUNT /kɪbʊtsiːm/. A **kibbutz** is a place of work in Israel, for example a farm or factory, where the workers live together and share all the duties and income. EG *He wrote to the Jewish agency asking to visit a kibbutz.*

kick /kɪk/, **kicks, kicking, kicked. 1** If you **kick** V+O someone or something, you hit them with your foot. EG *He protested violently, and threatened to kick me... We caught sight of Christopher, kicking a tin can down the High Street.* ▶ used as a noun. EG ▶ N COUNT *He gave him a good kick.*

2 If you **kick,** you move your feet violently or V : OFT+A suddenly, for example when you are dancing or swimming. EG *Simon was floating in the water and kicking with his feet.*

3 If someone **gets a kick** from something, they get PHRASE a feeling of intense pleasure or excitement from it. Informal EG *They loved debate, and got a kick out of court proceedings.*

4 If someone does something **for kicks,** they do it PHRASE because they find it exciting. Informal

5 If you say that you **kicked** yourself or **could** V-REFL **have kicked** yourself, you mean that you were Informal very annoyed with yourself because you did something wrong. EG *I kicked myself for not having thought of it earlier.*

6 If you **kick** a habit, such as smoking, you give it V+O up. Informal

7 See also **free kick.**

kick about or **kick around.** If something is PHRASAL VB : **kicking about** or **is kicking around,** it is lying V+ADV, ONLY somewhere and has been forgotten. EG *His old bike* CONT *has been kicking about among the bushes for days.* Informal

kick off. 1 When you **kick off** an event or a PHRASAL VB : discussion, you start it. EG *They kicked off a two-* V+ADV OR *month tour of the U.S. with a party in Washington.* V+O+ADV **2** See also **kick-off.** Informal

kick out. If you **kick** someone **out** of a place, you PHRASAL VB : force them to leave. EG *He kicked me out... She* V+O+ADV *kicked me out of the room.* Informal

kick up. If you **kick up** a fuss or a row, you get PHRASAL VB : very annoyed or upset about something. EG *When I* V+ADV+O *told him, he kicked up a fuss.* Informal

kick-off, kick-offs. Kick-off or the **kick-off** is N COUNT OR the time at which a game of football officially N UNCOUNT starts. EG *Kick-off is at 2.30.*

kid /kɪd/, **kids, kidding, kidded. 1** You can refer N COUNT to a child as a **kid.** EG *...five-year-old kids... I can* Informal *remember the feelings I had when I was a kid... ...his wife and kids.*

2 Young people who are no longer children are N COUNT sometimes referred to as **kids.** EG *GM's college kids* Informal *pay only $1,200 tuition.* American

3 You can refer to your younger brother or sister ADJ CLASSIF : as your **kid** brother or **kid** sister. EG *Are you going* ATTRIB *to bring your kid brother along?* Informal

4 If you **are kidding,** you are saying something V : ONLY CONT that is not really true, as a joke. EG *They're not sure* Informal *whether I'm kidding or not... I'm not kidding, Jill. He could have taken it if he'd wanted.* ● You can ● PHRASE say **'No kidding'** to emphasize that what you are saying is true, or that you mean it. EG *No kidding, Ginny, you look good.*

5 If you **kid** someone, you tease them. EG *Tim's* V+O *friends kidded him about his odd clothes.*

6 If people **kid** themselves, they allow themselves V-REFL to believe something that is not true because they OFT+REPORT

> What do you think 'kilo-' means in 'kilogram' and 'kilometre'?

wish that it was true. EG *They like to kid themselves they're keeping fit.*

7 A **kid** is also a young goat. N COUNT

kidnap /kɪdnæp/, **kidnaps, kidnapping, kidnapped.** **1** If someone **kidnaps** you, they take you V+O away by force, usually in order to demand money from your family, employers, or government. EG *He was kidnapped by terrorists just over a month ago.*
◊ **kidnapping, kidnappings.** EG *...the kidnapping* ◊ N UNCOUNT *of a royal child... They charged me with murder* OR N COUNT *and kidnapping.* ◊ **kidnapper** /kɪdnæpə/, **kidnappers.** EG *I had given up all hope of tracing her kidnapper.*

2 Kidnap is the crime of kidnapping someone. EG N UNCOUNT *...the threat of kidnap or assassination... ...a kidnap victim.*

kidney /kɪdniˈ/, **kidneys.** Your **kidneys** are the N COUNT two organs in your body that produce urine. EG *He had kidney trouble.*

kill /kɪl/, **kills, killing, killed.** **1** When someone or V+O, V-REFL, something **kills** a person, animal or plant, they OR V cause the person, animal, or plant to die. EG *She killed him with a hammer... He had tried to kill himself five times... Her mother was killed in a car crash... The sun had killed most of the plants... ...a desire to kill.*

2 The act of killing an animal after hunting it is N COUNT referred to as the **kill.** EG *The hunters move in for the kill... The female lions make the majority of kills.*

3 If you say that something **is killing** you, you V+O : USU CONT mean that it is causing you great pain. EG *These* Informal *shoes are killing me.*

4 If something **kills** an activity, process, or feeling, V+O it prevents it from continuing. EG *His behaviour outraged me and killed our friendship... These latest measures killed all hope of any relaxation of the system.*

5 When you **kill time**, you occupy yourself by PHRASE doing something unimportant or uninteresting while you are waiting for something. EG *He spent long hours keeping out of the way, killing time.*

6 to **kill two birds with one stone**: see **bird.** ● See also **killing.**

kill off. If you **kill** something **off**, you completely PHRASAL VB : destroy it. EG *This discovery killed off one of the* V+O+ADV *last surviving romances about the place... The bacteria had been killed off.*

killer /kɪlə/, **killers.** **1** A **killer** is a person who N COUNT has killed someone. EG *He became a ruthless killer.*

2 You can refer to anything that causes death as a N COUNT **killer.** EG *The lion is one of the most efficient killers in the animal world... Heart disease is the major killer of our time.*

killing /kɪlɪŋ/, **killings.** **1** A **killing** is an act in N COUNT which one person deliberately kills another. EG *...a brutal killing which had occurred in the neighbourhood... The killings were random, gruesome, and baffling.*

2 If you **make a killing**, you make a large profit PHRASE very quickly and easily. Informal

kiln /kɪln/, **kilns.** A **kiln** is an oven in which you N COUNT bake things such as pottery and bricks.

kilo /kiːloʊ/, **kilos.** A **kilo** is the same as a kilo- N COUNT gram. EG *...a kilo of fresh strawberries.* OR N PART

kilogram /kɪləˈgræm/, **kilograms;** also spelled N COUNT **kilogramme.** A **kilogram** is a metric unit of OR N PART weight that is a thousand grams and is equal to 2.2 pounds. Its abbreviation is 'kg'.

kilometre /kɪləˈmiːtə, kɪlɒmɪtə/, **kilometres;** N COUNT spelled **kilometer** in American English. A **kilometre** is a metric unit of distance that is a thousand metres. Its abbreviation is 'km'. EG *We could see rain falling about a kilometre away.*

kilt /kɪlt/, **kilts.** A **kilt** is a short pleated skirt that N COUNT is sometimes worn by Scotsmen. Kilts can also be worn by women and girls.

kin /kɪn/. Your **kin** are your relatives. See also N UNCOUNT **next of kin.** Outdated

kind /kaɪnd/, **kinds; kinder, kindest. 1** If you talk N COUNT OR about a particular **kind** of thing, you are talking N UNCOUNT about one of the classes or sorts of that thing. EG +SUPP *Was he carrying a weapon and, if so, what kind of weapon?... ...processes of an entirely new kind... He had a seizure of some kind... These thoughts weren't the kind he could share with anyone.*

2 You use **kind of** when you want to say that PHRASE something can be roughly described in a particular Informal way. EG *He spoke in a kind of sad whisper.*

3 In American English, **kind of** is used to say that PHRASE something is partly true or partly the case. EG *I felt* Informal *kind of sorry for him.*

4 You use **of a kind** to say that something belongs PHRASE to a particular class of things but that it is not really satisfactory. EG *A solution of a kind has been found to this problem.*

5 Payment **in kind** is payment in the form of goods PHRASE or services, rather than money.

6 Someone who is **kind** is gentle, caring, and ADJ QUALIT helpful. EG *We were much kinder to one another after that night... It was kind of you to come.*
◊ **kindly.** EG *'You're not to blame yourself, Smithy,'* ◊ ADV *Rick said kindly.* ◊ **kindness.** EG *He treated his* ◊ N UNCOUNT *labourers with kindness and understanding.*

7 If someone asks you if you would **be kind** PHRASE **enough** to do something or **be so kind as** to do it, they are asking you politely but rather firmly to do it. EG *Before you go to bed, would you be kind enough to close the window.*

8 See also **kindly, kindness.**

kindergarten /kɪndəgɑːtᵊn/, **kindergartens.** A N COUNT OR **kindergarten** is a school for young children who N UNCOUNT are not old enough to go to a primary school.

kind-hearted. Someone who is **kind-hearted** is ADJ QUALIT kind, loving, and gentle.

kindle /kɪndᵊl/, **kindles, kindling, kindled. 1** If V+O something **kindles** an idea or feeling in you, it Literary makes you begin to have that idea or feeling. EG *...the aspirations kindled in us in early childhood.*

2 If you **kindle** a fire, you light wood, coal, or V+O paper in order to start it.

kindling /kɪndlɪŋ/ is small pieces of dry wood that N UNCOUNT you use to start a fire. EG *They would pull up the blackened stalks for kindling.*

kindly /kaɪndliˈ/. **1** Someone who is **kindly** is ADJ QUALIT : kind, caring, and sympathetic. EG *Being a kindly* ATTRIB *and reasonable man, he at once apologized... The students were watching her with kindly interest.*
◊ **kindliness.** EG *...the great virtues of humility and* ◊ N UNCOUNT *kindliness.*

2 If you ask someone to **kindly** do something, you ADV+INF are asking them to do it in a way that shows that you are angry or annoyed with them. EG *Kindly take your hand off my knee.*

3 If someone **looks kindly** on something, they PHRASE approve of it. EG *The White House will look more kindly on a robust economy.*

4 If someone **does not take kindly to** something, PHRASE they do not like it. EG *They are unlikely to take kindly to this suggestion.*

5 See also **kind.**

kindness /kaɪndnɪˈs/, **kindnesses.** A **kindness** is N COUNT a helpful or considerate act. EG *She thanked them both many times for all their kindnesses.* ● See also **kind.**

kindred /kɪndrɪˈd/. Someone that you describe as ADJ CLASSIF : a **kindred** spirit has the same view of life or the ATTRIB same interests that you have. EG *When I saw his work I recognized him as a kindred spirit... They must have recognised each other as kindred souls.*

king /kɪŋ/, **kings. 1** A **king** is a man who is the N COUNT head of his country. He is a member of the royal family. EG *...King Arthur... Three Saxon kings are buried here... ...the King of Spain.*

2 In chess, the **king** is the most important piece. N COUNT When you are in a position to capture your opponent's king, you win the game.

3 A **king** is also a playing card with a picture of a king on it. N COUNT

kingdom /kɪŋdəm/, **kingdoms. 1** A **kingdom** is a country or region that is ruled by a king or queen. EG ...*the United Kingdom.* N COUNT

2 All the animals in the world, including the birds, fish, and insects, can be referred to together as the animal **kingdom**. All the plants can be referred to as the plant **kingdom**. EG *This creature has the largest eyes in the whole animal kingdom.* N SING+SUPP

kingfisher /kɪŋfɪʃə/, **kingfishers.** A **kingfisher** is a brightly-coloured bird which lives near rivers and lakes and catches fish. N COUNT

king-size. King-size things or **king-sized** things are of the largest size that you can get. EG ...*his king-size bed...* ...*king-size cigarettes.* ADJ CLASSIF: ATTRIB

kinky /kɪŋkiˈ/. If you describe someone's behaviour as **kinky**, you mean that it is strange, and probably connected with unusual sexual practices. EG *There must be something very kinky going on.* ADJ QUALIT Informal

kinship /kɪnʃɪp/. **1 Kinship** is the relationship between members of the same family. EG *Their ties of kinship mean a lot to them.* N UNCOUNT Formal

2 If you feel **kinship** with someone, you feel close to them, because you have a similar background or similar feelings or ideas. EG *He felt a deep kinship with the other students.* N UNCOUNT +SUPP Literary

kiosk /kiːɒsk/, **kiosks.** A **kiosk** is a small shop where you can buy things such as sandwiches or newspapers through an open window. EG *We were eating hamburgers at an all-night kiosk.* N COUNT

kipper /kɪpə/, **kippers.** A **kipper** is a herring which has been preserved by being hung in smoke. N COUNT

kiss /kɪs/, **kisses, kissing, kissed. 1** If you **kiss** someone, you touch them with your lips to show affection or to greet them. EG *He bent down and kissed his wife on the cheek... I kissed her goodbye and drove away... They stopped and kissed.* ▸ used as a noun. EG *Give me a kiss... They long for a mother's goodnight kiss.* V+O OR V: RECIP ▸ N COUNT

2 If you **kiss** an object, you touch it lightly with your lips, usually as a sign of reverence. EG *She had always wanted to kiss the Pope's ring.* V+O

kit /kɪt/, **kits. 1** A **kit** is a group of items that are kept together because they are used for similar purposes. EG ...*my first-aid kit...* ...*a tool kit.* N COUNT+SUPP

2 Your **kit** is the special clothing that you use when you take part in a sport. EG *Have you brought your squash kit?* N UNCOUNT USU+SUPP

3 A **kit** is also a set of parts that can be put together in order to make something. EG ...*a do-it-yourself radio kit...* ...*people who build their cars from kits.* N COUNT

kitchen /kɪtʃɪn/, **kitchens.** A **kitchen** is a room that you use for cooking and for household jobs such as washing dishes. See picture at HOUSE. EG *Brody went into the kitchen and opened the refrigerator... She left the cheese on the kitchen table.* N COUNT

kite /kaɪt/, **kites.** A **kite** is an object consisting of a light frame covered with paper or cloth. It has a long string attached to it. You hold the string and the kite flies in the air. N COUNT

kitten /kɪtˠən/, **kittens.** A **kitten** is a very young cat. N COUNT

kitty /kɪtiˈ/, **kitties.** A **kitty** is an amount of money consisting of contributions from several people, which is spent on things that they will share or use together. EG *After we paid the phone bill there was nothing left in the kitty.* N COUNT: USU SING

kiwi /kiːwiˈ/, **kiwis.** A **kiwi** is a type of bird that lives in New Zealand. Kiwis cannot fly. N COUNT

kiwi fruit, kiwi fruits. Kiwi fruit is often also used as the plural form.
A **kiwi fruit** is a fruit with a brown hairy skin and green flesh. N COUNT

Kleenex /kliːnɛks/, **Kleenexes. Kleenex** can also be used as the plural form.
Kleenex is soft tissue paper that is used as a N UNCOUNT OR N COUNT Trademark

handkerchief. EG ...*a packet of Kleenex... Have you got a Kleenex?*

km is a written abbreviation for 'kilometres' or 'kilometre'. EG *My older sister lives about 10km from our village.*

knack /næk/. If you have the **knack** of doing something, you are able to do it, although other people find it difficult. EG *He had the knack of balancing his pile of objects perfectly... Others seem to have a knack for combining colours and patterns.* N SING: USU+of//for

knackered /nækəd/. If you are **knackered**, you are exhausted. ADJ PRED Informal

knead /niːd/, **kneads, kneading, kneaded.** When you **knead** dough, you press and squeeze it with your hands so that it becomes smooth and ready to cook. V+O

knee /niː/, **knees. 1** Your **knee** is the place where your leg bends. See picture at THE HUMAN BODY. EG *Your knee's bleeding... Kindly take your hand off my knee.* N COUNT

2 The **knee** of a piece of clothing is the part that covers your knee. EG *There was a triangular tear at the knee of his trousers.* N COUNT

3 If you have something on your **knee**, it is resting on the upper part of your legs when you are sitting down. EG *She sat with Marcus by her side and Maria on her knee.* N COUNT

4 If you are on your **knees**, you are kneeling. EG *Kurt threw himself on his knees... The woman got up off her knees.* N PLURAL

5 If something **brings** a country **to** its **knees**, it weakens and almost destroys it. EG *The cost of the war would have brought the kingdom to its knees.* PHRASE

kneecap /niːkæp/, **kneecaps.** Your **kneecaps** are the bones at the front of your knees. N COUNT

knee-deep. If you are **knee-deep** in something, it is as high as your knees. EG *He stood there knee-deep in the grass.* ADJ PRED+in

knee-high. If something is **knee-high**, it is as high as your knees. EG *I crept through a mass of knee-high nettles.* ADJ CLASSIF

kneel /niːl/, **kneels, kneeling, knelt** /nɛlt/, **kneeled. Knelt** and **kneeled** can both be used as the past tense and past participle.

1 If you **are kneeling**, your legs are bent under you and your knees are touching the ground and supporting the rest of your body. EG *Ralph was kneeling by the fire.* ◊ **kneeling.** EG *The kneeling figure was Mary Darling.* V ◊ ADJ CLASSIF: ATTRIB

2 If you **kneel** or **kneel** down, you bend your legs and lower your body until your knees are touching the ground. EG *I knelt down beside her... Together they kneeled in prayer.* V: OFT+down

knew /njuː/ is the past tense of **know.**

knickers /nɪkəz/ are a piece of underwear worn by women and girls. Knickers have holes for your legs and elastic around the top. EG ...*a pair of knickers.* N PLURAL

knick-knacks /nɪk næks/ are small ornaments. EG *Their house was full of plants and attractive knick-knacks.* N PLURAL

knife /naɪf/, **knives** /naɪvz/; **knifes, knifing, knifed. Knives** is the plural form of the noun and **knifes** is the third person singular of the present tense of the verb.

1 A **knife** is an object that you hold in your hand and use to cut things. A knife consists of a sharp, flat piece of metal attached to a handle. EG ...*knives and forks...* ...*men armed with knives...* ...*a knife blade.* See picture at WEAPONS. N COUNT

2 To **knife** someone means to attack and injure them with a knife. EG *Rausenberger had been knifed and robbed near his home.* ◊ **knifing,** ◊ **knifings.** EG *There were often knifings or brawls.* V+O ◊ N COUNT

What title is a knight given?

3 See also **carving knife**, **jack-knife**, **penknife**, **pocket knife**.

knight /naɪt/, **knights, knighting, knighted. 1** In medieval times, a **knight** was a man of noble birth, who served his king or lord in battle, riding a horse. EG ...*knights in armour*.   N COUNT

2 In modern times, a **knight** is a man who has been given a knighthood.   N COUNT

3 In chess, a **knight** is a piece that is shaped like a horse's head.   N COUNT

4 If a man **is knighted**, he is given a knighthood. EG *He was knighted by Queen Anne in 1705*.   V+O : USU PASS

knighthood /naɪthʊd/, **knighthoods**. A **knight-hood** is a title that is given to a man by a British king or queen for his outstanding achievements or for service to his country. A man who has been given a knighthood puts 'Sir' in front of his name.   N COUNT

knit /nɪt/, **knits, knitting, knitted. 1** When someone **knits** something, they make it from wool or a similar thread using knitting needles or a machine. EG *She wore a scarf that she had knitted... I had just finished knitting her a cardigan... The old lady sat in her doorway and knitted.*   ◊ **knitted**. EG ...*a knitted shawl*.   V+O, V+O+O, V+O+*for*, OR V ◊ ADJ CLASSIF

2 If you **knit** your **brows**, you frown because you are angry or worried. EG *He sat there knitting his brows and twisting his napkin.*   PHRASE Literary

3 A group of people who are close-**knit**, closely **knit**, or tightly **knit** feel closely linked to each other. EG *It's a very close-knit community... They live in tightly knit families.*   ADJ QUALIT

knitting /nɪtɪŋ/ is **1** something that is being knitted. EG *She picked up her knitting.* **2** the action or process of knitting.   N UNCOUNT

knitting needle, **knitting needles**. A **knitting needle** is a long thin stick made of plastic or metal, with a point at one end. You use two knitting needles when you are knitting. See picture at NEEDLES.   N COUNT

knitwear /nɪtwɛə/ is clothing that has been knitted. EG ...*the family knitwear business.*   N UNCOUNT

knives /naɪvz/ is the plural of **knife**.

knob /nɒb/, **knobs**. A **knob** is **1** a round handle on a door or drawer. EG *He turned the knob and the door burst open... ...mahogany cabinets with polished brass knobs.* **2** a rounded lump on a flat surface or on top of a stick or post. EG *Her umbrella is elegantly capped with a glass knob... The bed had one gilt knob missing.* **3** a round switch, for example on a television or radio. EG ...*the knobs on his tape recorder.*   N COUNT

knobbly /nɒbliː/. Something that is **knobbly** has large lumps on it, making it uneven rather than smooth. EG ...*her knobbly old hand.*   ADJ QUALIT

knock /nɒk/, **knocks, knocking, knocked. 1** If you **knock** at a door or window, you hit it, usually several times, in order to attract someone's attention. EG *He knocked softly on the door.* ▸ used as a noun. EG *There was a knock at the door.*   V : OFT+*at/on* ▸ N COUNT

2 If you **knock** something, you hit it roughly, so that it moves or falls over. EG *In the excitement he knocked over his chair... The glass had been knocked out from windows.* ▸ used as a noun. EG *Knocks can cause weaknesses in the spine.*   V+O : USU+A ▸ N COUNT

3 If you **knock** someone down or **knock** them unconscious, you hit them very hard, so that they fall or become unconscious. EG *Dad knocked him to the floor... Rudolph had seen him knock Thomas unconscious with one blow of his fist.*   V+O+A OR V+O+C

4 If you **knock** an attitude or kind of behaviour out of someone, you cause them to lose it or stop it, by treating them roughly. EG *All this training might knock the enthusiasm out of him a bit... He was to knock the foolishness out of me eventually.*   V+O+*out of* Informal

5 If you **knock** someone or something, you criticize them. EG *He was always knocking the performance of fellow-actors.*   V+O Informal

6 If someone receives a **knock**, they have an unpleasant experience which seriously affects   N COUNT

their plans or their way of life. EG *She has suffered some hard knocks.*

knock about or **knock around. 1** If someone **is knocked about** or **is knocked around**, they are hit several times. EG *He did not like the thought of a woman being knocked about.* **2** Someone who **has knocked about** or **has knocked around** has had experience in a lot of different places or situations. EG *I'm a bachelor, I've knocked about the world a bit, known a few women.* **3** If you **knock about** or **knock around** with someone, you spend your spare time with them. EG *Who's she knocking around with now?*   PHRASAL VB : V+O+ADV, USU PASS Informal / V+ADV/PREP Informal / V+ADV, OFT+*with* Informal

knock back. If you **knock back** a drink, you drink it quickly. EG *He won't be too happy if he finds me knocking back his whisky.*   PHRASAL VB : V+O+ADV Informal

knock down. 1 If a vehicle **knocks** someone **down**, it hits them so that they fall and are injured or killed. EG *He was knocked down by a bus.* **2** If you **knock down** a building or part of a building, you deliberately destroy it or remove it. EG *I'd knock the wall down between the two rooms.*   PHRASAL VB : V+O+ADV

knock off. 1 If someone **knocks** an amount **off** the price of something, they reduce the price by that amount. EG *He knocked £50 off the price, because it was slightly scratched.* **2** If someone **knocks** something **off**, they steal it. EG *He was planning to knock off a few videos that weekend.* **3** When people **knock off**, they finish work at the end of the day or before a break. EG *We knock off at 5.*   PHRASAL VB : V+O+ADV/ PREP / V+O+ADV Informal / V+ADV Informal

knock out. 1 If someone **knocks** you **out**, they make you unconscious by hitting you. EG *He hit me so hard he knocked me out.* **2** If a drug **knocks** you **out**, you become unconscious after taking it. EG *The tablet had knocked her out for four hours.* **3** If a person or team **is knocked out** of a competition, they are defeated in a game, so that they do not play any more games. **4** See also **knockout**.   PHRASAL VB : V+O+ADV / V+O+ADV / V+O+ADV : OFT+*of*

knocker /nɒkə/, **knockers**. A **knocker** is a piece of metal attached to the door of a building, which you use to hit the door in order to attract the attention of the people inside.   N COUNT

knock-on. If something has a **knock-on** effect, it causes a series of events to happen, one after another. EG *We need to find a solution that doesn't have so many knock-on effects.*   ADJ CLASSIF : ATTRIB

knockout /nɒkaʊt/, **knockouts. 1** In boxing, a **knockout** is a blow that makes one of the boxers fall to the floor and not be able to stand up before the referee has counted to ten. EG *Davies won by a knockout.*   N COUNT

2 A **knockout** competition is one in which the winner of each match goes on to the next round, until one competitor or team is the winner.   ADJ CLASSIF : ATTRIB

knoll /nəʊl/, **knolls**. A **knoll** is a small hill. EG ...*a grassy knoll on the outskirts of Waltham.*   N COUNT Literary

knot /nɒt/, **knots, knotting, knotted. 1** A **knot** is a place in a piece of string, rope, or cloth where one end has been passed through a loop and pulled tight. You tie a knot in order to join two things together or to keep something firmly in place. EG *He had tied a crude knot... The knot of her head-scarf hung beneath her chin.*   N COUNT

2 If you **knot** a piece of string, rope, or cloth, you pass one end of it through a loop and pull it tight.   ◊ **knotted**. EG ...*a knotted handkerchief.*   V+O ◊ ADJ CLASSIF

3 If you **knot** something around something else, you fasten it to it by tying a knot. EG *He knotted a towel about his neck... I set off with the rope knotted round my waist.*   V+O+A

4 A **knot** of people is a group of them standing very close together. EG ...*watched by a knot of sightseers.*   N PART

5 If you say that you have a **knot** in your stomach, you mean that your stomach feels uncomfortable because you are anxious or afraid. EG *Gant felt the knot of tension harden in his stomach.*   N COUNT+SUPP

6 A **knot** in a piece of wood is a small hard area where a branch used to grow.   N COUNT

7 A **knot** is also a unit of speed. The speed of ships N COUNT and aircraft is measured in knots. EG ...*an underwater object moving at over 150 knots.*

knotty /nɒti¹/. A **knotty** problem is difficult to ADJ QUALIT : solve. EG *He and Don had solved many a knotty* ATTRIB *problem in this room... ...a knotty question.* Informal

know /nəʊ/, **knows**, **knowing**, **knew** /njuː/, **known**. **1** If you **know** something, you have it V+O; ALSO V : correctly in your mind. EG *I don't know her ad-* USU+REPORT; *dress... I knew that she had recently graduated* NO CONT, *from law school... We knew what to expect... No* NO IMPER *one knew how to repair it... 'Will they come back?' – 'I don't know.'*

2 If you **know** of something or **know** about it, you V+of/about : have heard about it. EG *Many people did not even* NO CONT, *know of their existence... Claud knew about the* NO IMPER *killing.*

3 If you **let** someone **know** about something, you PHRASE tell them about it. EG *I'll find out about the car and let you know what happened.*

4 If you **know** a language, you can understand it V+O : NO CONT, and speak it. EG *Shanti knew a few words of* NO IMPER *English.*

5 If you **know** about a subject, you have studied it V OR and have some knowledge of it. EG *He knew about* V+O+about : *pictures... They knew a lot about films... I don't* NO CONT, *know much about physics, I'm afraid.* NO IMPER

6 If you **know** someone, you have met them and V+O : NO CONT talked to them. EG *Do you know David?*

7 If you **know** a place or a thing, you are familiar V+O : NO CONT with it. EG *He knew London well.*

8 If you **get to know** a person or place, you find PHRASE out what they are like. EG *I'd like the chance to get to know him.*

9 You use **know** in the passive to say what people V-PASS+as call someone or something. For example, if a forest **is known** as the Big Thicket, people call it the Big Thicket.

10 If you **know better** than someone else, your PHRASE ideas are more sensible or more correct than theirs. EG *The experts, who knew better, laughed at the idea.*

11 If you say that someone ought to **know better**, PHRASE you mean that they ought to behave in a more sensible and acceptable way. EG *Brian is old enough to know better.*

12 If you say that a particular person **knows best**, PHRASE you mean that they are always right about what should be done. EG *Parents always know best.*

13 You say **'you know' 13.1** to emphasize or draw attention to what you are saying. EG *You were very naughty, you know... You know, most of the time he seems like a fool.* **13.2** to fill a gap in a conversation, for example when you are uncertain about what you are going to say next. EG *She thought a lot about her appearance, you know, and spent a lot of her money on clothes.* **13.3** to try to explain more clearly what you mean. EG *...the old desk. You know, the one that's broken.*

14 You say **'I know' 14.1** to indicate that you CONVENTION agree with what has just been said. EG *'It's quite extraordinary.' – 'I know.'* **14.2** to indicate that you realize or accept that something is true. EG *I get frightened in the night sometimes – it's silly, I know.*

15 You say **'You never know'** to indicate that, CONVENTION although it is uncertain what will happen, there is some hope that things might turn out well. EG *Well, I can't promise anything, but you never know.*

16 Some people say **'God knows'** or **'Heaven** CONVENTION **knows'** to emphasize that they do not know some- OR PHRASE thing. EG *God knows why they did it... What would* Informal he do with them? *Heaven only knows.*

17 Someone who is **in the know** has information PHRASE about something that only a few people have.

18 See also **knowing, known.**

know-how. Someone who has **know-how** knows N UNCOUNT methods of doing something, especially something Informal scientific or technical. EG *They now had the facilities and knowhow to produce advanced weapons.*

knowing /nəʊɪŋ/. A **knowing** gesture or remark ADJ CLASSIF : shows that you understand something, for example ATTRIB why someone has done something, even though it has not actually been mentioned directly. EG *This is usually greeted with deep sighs and knowing looks... ...a knowing smile.*

knowingly /nəʊɪŋli¹/. **1** If you do something ADV wrong **knowingly**, you do it knowing that it is wrong. EG *They knowingly broke laws that ban trade in rare reptiles.*

2 If you look, smile, or wink **knowingly**, you do it ADV in a way that shows that you understand something, even though it has not actually been mentioned directly. EG *The girls looked knowingly at each other.*

knowledge /nɒlɪdʒ/. **1 Knowledge** is information N UNCOUNT : and understanding about a subject, which someone USU+SUPP has in their mind. EG *...advances in scientific knowledge... All knowledge comes to us through our senses... He is the only person I know with a real knowledge of income-tax legislation.*

2 If you say that something is true **to** your **knowl-** ADV SEN **edge**, you mean that you know that it is true. EG *Of these thirty-seven couples, thirty-five, to my knowledge, are still married.*

3 If you say that something is true **to the best of** ADV SEN your **knowledge**, you mean that you think that it is true, but you do not know definitely that it is true. EG *This is a play which to the best of my knowledge has never been performed in Britain.*

knowledgeable /nɒlɪdʒəbəl/. You describe ADJ QUALIT someone as **knowledgeable** when they know a lot about many different things or a lot about a particular subject. EG *He was surprisingly knowledgeable about what was going on in the theatre.*

known /nəʊn/. **1 Known** is the past participle of **know.**

2 If something is **known** to people, they are aware ADJ CLASSIF of it and have information about it. EG *There's no known cure for a cold... ...the most dangerous substance known to man.*

3 If you **let it be known** that something is the PHRASE case, you make sure that people know it, without Formal telling them directly. EG *She let it be known that she wanted to leave China.*

4 See also **well-known.**

knuckle /nʌkəl/, **knuckles.** Your **knuckles** are N COUNT : the rounded pieces of bone where your fingers join USU PLURAL your hands, and where your fingers bend. EG *As he fell, he scraped the skin off his knuckles... Her hands were clasped so violently that the knuckles showed white.*

Koran /kɔːrɑːn/. The **Koran** is the sacred book on N PROPER : which the religion of Islam is based. the+N

kosher /kəʊʃə/. **Kosher** food is approved of by the ADJ CLASSIF laws of Judaism. EG *They all buy kosher meat.*

kow-tow /kaʊ taʊ/, **kow-tows**, **kow-towing**, V : OFT+to **kow-towed.** If you **kow-tow** to someone, you Informal behave very humbly and respectfully towards them, especially because you hope to get something from them. EG *He rather resents having to kow-tow to anyone.*

L l

L, l /ɛl/, **Ls, l's.** **1** L is the twelfth letter of the N COUNT
English alphabet.
2 L is the symbol for 'learner driver'. In Britain, a
large red 'L' on a white background is attached to
cars in which people are learning to drive.
3 L or l is also an abbreviation for 'litre'.

lab /læb/, **labs.** A **lab** is the same as a laboratory. N COUNT
EG *Your X-rays have just come back from the lab.* Informal

label /leɪbəˀl/, **labels, labelling, labelled;** spelled
labeling and **labeled in American English.**
1 A **label** is a piece of paper or plastic that is N COUNT
attached to an object to give information about it,
for example to say what it is, who owns it, or how
you should use it. EG *The bottles got wet and all the
labels came off.*
2 If you **label** something, you attach a label to it. EG V+O OR
...the brown pot labelled 'Salt'. V+O+C
3 If people **label** you as something, they describe V+O : OFT+as
you or think of you in that way, even though you do OR V+O+C
not agree with their opinion; used showing disapproval. EG *I wasn't going to be labelled mad... Once
you are labelled as a secretary you will never
become anything else... His behaviour is labelled
deviant.* ▸ used as a noun. EG *He was not willing to* ▸ N COUNT
accept the label of anarchist. +SUPP

labor /leɪbə/. See **labour.**

laboratory /ləˀbɒrətəˀriˀ/, **laboratories.** A **labora-** N COUNT
tory is **1** a building or a room that contains special
scientific equipment. Scientists use laboratories to
do experiments or for research. EG *The geologists
took the samples back to the laboratory.* **2** a room
in a school or university which contains scientific
equipment, and where students are taught about
science subjects such as chemistry. ● See also
language laboratory.

laborious /ləˀbɔːrɪəs/. Something that is **labo-** ADJ QUALIT
rious takes a lot of effort. EG *Clearing the forest is a
laborious business.* ◊ **laboriously.** EG *...laboriously* ◊ ADV
hand-written books.

labour /leɪbə/, **labours, labouring, laboured;**
spelled **labor in American English.**
1 Labour is very hard work, especially work that N UNCOUNT
does not need a lot of skill. EG *I really enjoy manual* OR N COUNT
*labour... a pleasant distraction from his political
labours.* ● If you do something as a **labour of love,** ● PHRASE
you do it because you really want to, even though it
involves hard work and you will get no reward for
it.
2 People who **labour** work hard using their hands. V : USU+A
EG *He was sent to labour as a peasant in a com-* Formal
mune.
3 If you **labour** at something, you do it with V+A
difficulty. EG *Tim had laboured over a letter to
Gertrude.* ◊ **laboured.** EG *McKellen's breathing* ◊ ADJ QUALIT
was laboured.
4 Labour is used to refer to **4.1** the workers of a N UNCOUNT
country or industry, considered as a group. EG *...a
shortage of skilled labour.* **4.2** the work done by a
group of workers. EG *They are threatening a withdrawal of labour in support of their claims.*
5 If you **labour** under a delusion or misapprehen- V+under
sion, you continue to believe something which is
not true. EG *He laboured under the misapprehension that nobody liked him.*
6 If you **labour** a point or an argument, you talk V+O
about it in great and unnecessary detail. EG *There is
no need to labour the point.*
7 Labour is also the last stage of pregnancy, in N UNCOUNT
which the baby is gradually pushed out of the
womb by the mother. EG *She was in labour for
seven hours.*

labourer /leɪbəˀrə/, **labourers.** A **labourer** is a N COUNT
person who does a job which involves a lot of hard
physical work. EG *...a farm labourer.*

labyrinth /læbəˀrɪnθ/, **labyrinths.** A **labyrinth** is N COUNT
a complicated series of narrow corridors or
streets, through which it is difficult to find your
way. EG *He wandered through the labyrinths of the
Old Town.*

lace /leɪs/, **laces, lacing, laced.** **1 Lace** is very N UNCOUNT
delicate cloth which is made with a lot of holes in
it. EG *...a white lace handkerchief.*
2 Laces are pieces of cord or string that are put N COUNT :
through holes along the two edges of something USU PLURAL
and tied in order to fasten the two edges together.
EG *He spent ten minutes tying the laces of his shoes.*
3 If you **lace** food or drink with alcohol or a drug, V+O :
you put a small amount of it into the food or drink. OFT+with
EG *...coffee laced with brandy.*

lace up. If you **lace** something **up,** you fasten it PHRASAL VB :
by pulling two ends of a lace tight and tying them V+O+ADV
together. EG *He bent and laced up his shoes.*

lacerate /læsəreɪt/, **lacerates, lacerating, lac-** V+O
erated. If something **lacerates** your skin, it cuts it
deeply. ◊ **lacerated.** EG *I could not shave my* ◊ ADJ CLASSIF
lacerated face. ◊ **laceration** /læsəˀreɪʃəˀn/, **lac-** ◊ N COUNT
erations. EG *The pain of my lacerations had be-
come less.*

lace-up, lace-ups. Lace-ups or lace-up shoes N COUNT :
are shoes which are fastened with laces. USU PLURAL

lack /læk/, **lacks, lacking, lacked.** **1** If there is a N SING OR
lack of something, there is not enough of it, or N UNCOUNT :
there is none at all. EG *I hated the lack of privacy in* USU+of
the dormitory... Lack of proper funding is making
our job more difficult.*
2 If something happens **for** or **through lack of** PHRASE
something, it happens because there is not enough
of it. EG *His department was shut down for lack of
funds.*
3 If you say that there is **no lack of** something, you PHRASE
mean that there is a great deal of it, and perhaps
more than you need. EG *There was no lack of
schools to choose from.*
4 If you **lack** something, you do not have it. EG *They* V+O
*lack the confidence to make friends... The adver-
tisement lacks any individuality.*
5 If you say that something **is lacking,** you mean V : ONLY CONT
that it does not exist, or there is not enough of it. EG
*'What is lacking in this case,' he concluded, 'is a
corpse.'*
6 If someone or something is **lacking** in a particu- ADJ PRED+in
lar quality, they do not have it or do not have
enough of it. EG *Philip was not lacking in intelligence or ability.*

lackey /lækiˀ/, **lackeys.** If you call someone a N COUNT
lackey, you mean that they follow someone's
orders completely, without ever questioning them;
used showing disapproval. EG *They said that the
police were lackeys of the Establishment.*

laconic /ləˀkɒnɪk/. Someone who is **laconic** uses ADJ QUALIT
very few words to say something, so that they
seem very casual. EG *...the laconic entries in his
diary.* ◊ **laconically.** EG *Sam was laconically* ◊ ADV
directed to an office in a nearby street.*

lacquer /lækə/, **lacquers, lacquering, lac-** N MASS
quered. **1 Lacquer** is **1.1** a special type of paint
which is put on wood or metal in order to protect it
and make it shiny. EG *The red lacquer work on the
upper walls was badly chipped.* **1.2** a liquid which
some women put on their hair to hold their hairstyle neatly in place.
2 If you **lacquer** wood or metal, you cover it with V+O

lacquer in order to protect it and make it shiny. ◊ **lacquered.** EG *...a lacquered box.* [◊ ADJ CLASSIF]

lacy /leɪsi^1/. Something that is **lacy** is made from lace or has pieces of lace attached to it. EG *...a lacy dress... She was propped up against lacy pillows.* [ADJ CLASSIF]

lad /læd/, **lads.** A **lad** is a boy or young man. EG *He used to collect stamps when he was a lad.* [N COUNT]

ladder /lædə/, **ladders. 1** A **ladder** is a piece of equipment used for climbing up something such as a wall or a tree. It consists of two long pieces of wood, metal, or rope with steps fixed between them. [N COUNT]

2 When someone keeps moving to higher levels in a society or an organization, you can refer to their progress as a **ladder**. EG *Joining the golf club takes you up the social ladder a little bit more.* [N SING : *the*+N]

3 A **ladder** in a pair of tights or stockings is a torn part where some of the vertical threads have broken, leaving only the horizontal threads. [N COUNT]

laden /leɪdə^{0}n/. If someone is holding or carrying a lot of heavy things, you can say that they are **laden** with them. EG *Ken arrived laden with presents... The trees were laden with fruit.* [ADJ CLASSIF : USU PRED+*with*; Literary]

ladle /leɪdə^{0}l/, **ladles, ladling, ladled. 1** A **ladle** is a large, round, deep spoon with a long handle, used for putting food such as soup or stew into bowls. [N COUNT]

2 If you **ladle** food such as soup or stew, you serve it using a large spoon such as a ladle. EG *'Plenty here,' said the man, ladling the soup into bowls.* [V+O : USU+A]

lady /leɪdi^1/, **ladies. 1** You can use **lady** as a polite way of referring to a woman. EG *...a rich American lady... ...a little old lady... ...a lady novelist... ...elderly ladies living on their own.* [N COUNT]

2 You can say **'ladies'** when you are addressing a group of women. EG *'Ladies,' George appealed, 'Could I have your attention, please?'... Good evening, ladies and gentlemen.* [VOCATIVE]

3 If you say that a woman is a **lady**, you mean that she behaves in a polite, dignified, and graceful way. EG *Many of the farmers' wives were trying to be ladies.* [N COUNT; Outdated]

4 A **lady** is a woman from the upper classes. EG *I rode in her carriage like a lady... The lords and ladies are all gathered at the palace.* [N COUNT]

5 Lady is a title used in front of the names of some women from the upper classes. EG *...Lady Diana Cooper.*

6 A **ladies** is a public toilet for women. EG *Where's the ladies, please?* [N SING : USU *the*+N]

7 Ladies' or **lady's** is used to describe something that belongs to girls or women, or something that is done or used by them. EG *She sang in a ladies' choir... ...Mellifont Ladies' College.* [ADJ CLASSIF : ATTRIB]

ladylike /leɪdi^{1}laɪk/. If you say that a woman or girl is **ladylike**, you mean that she behaves in a polite, dignified, and graceful way. EG *She took little ladylike sips of the cold drink.* [ADJ QUALIT]

lag /læg/, **lags, lagging, lagged. 1** If you **lag** behind someone or something, you move or progress more slowly than they do. EG *He set off at a brisk walk, Kate lagging behind... Britain's economic development must lag behind that of almost every other industrial nation.* [V : OFT *behind*]

2 When something such as trade or investment **lags**, there is less of it than there was before. EG *Production lagged and unemployment rose.* [V : OFT *behind*]

3 A time **lag** is a period of time between two related events. EG *There will be a one-year lag between the time I write this book and its publication... ...a small time lag.* [N COUNT+SUPP]

4 If you **lag** a pipe, a hot water tank, or the inside of a roof, you cover it with a special material to prevent heat escaping from it. [V+O]

lager /lɑːgə/, **lagers. Lager** is a kind of light beer. EG *...a bottle of ice-cold lager.* [N MASS]

lagoon /lə^{3}guːn/, **lagoons.** A **lagoon** is an area of calm sea water that is separated from the ocean by reefs or sand. [N COUNT]

laid /leɪd/ is the past tense and past participle of **lay.**

laid up. If you are **laid up**, you have to stay in bed because you are ill. EG *He had been laid up for five days with a bad cold.* [ADJ CLASSIF]

lain /leɪn/ is the past participle of **lie** in some of its meanings.

lair /lɛə/, **lairs.** A **lair** is a place where a wild animal lives, usually a place which is underground or well-hidden. EG *...animals that refuse to come out of their lairs.* [N COUNT]

lake /leɪk/, **lakes.** A **lake** is a large area of fresh water, surrounded by land. [N COUNT]

lamb /læm/, **lambs. 1** A **lamb** is a young sheep. [N COUNT]

2 Lamb is the flesh of a sheep or lamb eaten as food. EG *...roast lamb.* [N UNCOUNT]

lame /leɪm/. **1** If you are **lame**, you are unable to walk properly because an injury or illness has damaged one or both of your legs. EG *The illness left her permanently lame... ...a lame horse.* [ADJ QUALIT]

2 If you describe an excuse, argument, or remark as **lame**, you mean that it is poor or weak. EG *My lame excuse was that I had too much else to do.* [ADJ QUALIT]

◊ **lamely.** EG *'I didn't recognize you,' Claude said lamely.* [◊ ADV]

lament /ləment/, **laments, lamenting, lamented.** If you **lament** something, you express your sadness or regret about it. EG *He laments the changing pattern of life in the countryside.* ▸ used as a noun. EG *'It's a dying industry,' is his lament.* [V-SPEECH OR V; Literary; ▸ N COUNT]

lamentable /ləmentəbə^{0}l, læməntəbə^{0}l/. If you describe something as **lamentable**, you mean that it is very unfortunate or disappointing. EG *...the lamentable state of the industry in the Sixties.* [ADJ CLASSIF : USU ATTRIB; Formal]

◊ **lamentably.** EG *...the lamentably inadequate plans for retraining officers.* [◊ SUBMOD OR ADV SEN]

lamp /læmp/, **lamps.** A **lamp** is a device which produces light by using electricity or by burning oil or gas. EG *She turned on the bedside lamp... ...the street lamp outside Mrs Flanagan's house.* [N COUNT]

lamp-post, lamp-posts. A **lamp-post** is a tall metal or concrete pole beside a road with a light at the top. [N COUNT]

lampshade /læmpʃeɪd/, **lampshades.** A **lampshade** is a covering that is fitted round an electric light bulb in order to decorate it and make the light less harsh. [N COUNT]

land /lænd/, **lands, landing, landed. 1 Land** is an area of ground with few or no buildings on it. EG *It's good agricultural land... ...a piece of land.* [N UNCOUNT]

2 If you refer to someone's **land** or **lands**, you mean an area of land which they own. [N COUNT+POSS]

3 Land or the **land** refers to the part of the world that is solid ground rather than sea or air. EG *We turned away from land and headed out to sea.* [N UNCOUNT, OR N SING : *the*+N]

4 A particular **land** is a particular country. EG *...a land where there is never any rain... Australia is the land of opportunities.* [N COUNT : USU+SUPP; Literary]

5 If someone or something **lands** somewhere, **5.1** they come down to the ground or in water after moving through the air. EG *The last man slipped and landed in the water.* **5.2** they arrive there after a journey by air. EG *His plane lands at six-thirty.* [V : USU+A]

6 To **land** people or goods somewhere means to unload them there at the end of a journey, especially a journey by ship. [V+O : USU+A]

7 If you **land** in an unpleasant situation or if something **lands** you in it, you come to be in it. EG *That would have landed him in jail.* [V-ERG+A; Informal]

8 If you **land** someone with something that causes difficulties, you cause them to have to deal with it. EG *...when a clergyman is landed with a huge rectory... You landed us with that awful man.* [V+O+*with*; Informal]

land up. If you **land up** in a particular place or situation, you arrive in it after a long journey or at [PHRASAL VB : V+ADV, OFT+A]

Is your country landlocked?

the end of a long series of events. EG *She landed up in Rome.*

landed /lændɪ²d/. **Landed** people own a lot of land. EG *...landed gentry.* ADJ CLASSIF: ATTRIB

landing /lændɪŋ/, **landings**. 1 In a house or other building, a **landing** is an area at the top of a staircase, with rooms leading off it. N COUNT

2 A **landing** is also a place with a wooden platform where boats stop to let people get on or off. N COUNT

3 When the pilot of an aircraft makes a **landing**, he brings the aircraft down to the ground. EG *We had to make an emergency landing.* N COUNT OR N UNCOUNT

landlady /lændleɪdɪ¹/, **landladies**. A **landlady** is N COUNT
1 a woman who owns a house, flat, or room that other people live in, in return for payment of rent.
2 a woman who owns or runs a pub.

landlocked /lændlɒkt/. A country that is **land-locked** is surrounded by other countries and does not have its own sea coast. ADJ CLASSIF

landlord /lændlɔːd/, **landlords**. A **landlord** is 1 a man who owns a house, flat, or room that other people live in, in return for payment of rent. 2 a man who owns or runs a pub. N COUNT

landmark /lændmɑːk/, **landmarks**. 1 A **land-mark** is a building or feature of the land which is easily noticed and which you can use to judge your position. EG *The Chamberlain tower is a landmark visible for miles.* N COUNT

2 You can also refer to an important stage in the development of something as a **landmark**. EG *The discovery of penicillin was a landmark in medicine.* N COUNT: USU+SUPP

landscape /lændskeɪp/, **landscapes**, **landscaping**, **landscaped**. 1 The **landscape** is everything that you can see when you look across an area of land, including hills, rivers, buildings, and trees. EG *...the beauty of the Welsh landscape.* N COUNT

2 A **landscape** is a painting which shows a scene in the countryside. EG *She painted landscapes and portraits.* N COUNT

3 If you **landscape** an area of land, you alter it by planting trees and bushes there to produce a pleasing effect. EG *...landscaped grounds.* V+O

landslide /lændslaɪd/, **landslides**. 1 In an election, a **landslide** is a victory in which a person or political party gets far more votes or seats than their opponents. EG *Taylor should win by a land-slide... ...a landslide victory.* N COUNT

2 A **landslide** is also a large amount of earth and rocks falling down a cliff or down the side of a mountain. EG *The slightest noise might set off a landslide.* N COUNT

lane /leɪn/, **lanes**. 1 A **lane** is a narrow road in the country. EG *She turned and went back down the lane... ...Park Lane.* N COUNT

2 Roads, race courses, and swimming pools are sometimes divided into **lanes**. These are parallel strips separated from each other by lines or ropes. EG *He changed lanes to make a left turn.* N COUNT

language /læŋgwɪdʒ/, **languages**. 1 A **language** is a system of communication which consists of a set of sounds and written symbols which are used by the people of a particular country for talking or writing. EG *...the English language... ...a foreign language... I can speak six languages.* N COUNT

2 **Language** is the ability to use words in order to communicate. Human beings have this ability but animals do not. EG *This research helps teachers to understand how children acquire language.* N UNCOUNT

3 You can refer to the words used in connection with a particular subject as the **language** of that subject. EG *...the language of sociology.* N UNCOUNT +SUPP

4 When you talk about the **language** of a piece of writing or a speech, you are referring to the style in which it is written or spoken. EG *I admire the directness of the language.* N UNCOUNT

5 **Language** is also used to refer to other means of communication such as sign language, computer languages, and animal language. N UNCOUNT OR N COUNT

language laboratory, **language laboratories**. A **language laboratory** is a room in a college or school in which people can learn to improve their knowledge of languages by listening to tape record-ings, recording their own voices, and having their mistakes corrected. N COUNT

languid /læŋgwɪd/. Someone who is **languid** shows little energy or interest and is slow and casual in their movements. EG *...a languid wave of the hand.* ◊ **languidly**. EG *He looked up languidly.* ADJ QUALIT Literary ◊ ADV

languish /læŋgwɪʃ/, **languishes**, **languishing**, **languished**. You say that people **languish** when they are forced to remain and suffer in an unpleas-ant situation. EG *A few people enjoyed rich lifestyles while the majority languished in poverty.* V: USU+A Literary

languor /læŋgə/ is a feeling of not having any energy or interest in anything. EG *...the languor of the summer afternoon.* N UNCOUNT Literary⁴·⁴

lanky /læŋkɪ¹/. Someone who is **lanky** is tall and thin and moves rather awkwardly. EG *Quentin was a lanky boy with long skinny legs.* ADJ QUALIT

lantern /læntən/, **lanterns**. A **lantern** is a lamp consisting of a metal frame with glass sides and an oil lamp or candle inside. Lanterns were used in former times. N COUNT

lap /læp/, **laps**, **lapping**, **lapped**. 1 Your **lap** is the flat area formed by your thighs when you are sitting down. EG *Her youngest child was asleep in her lap... He placed the baby on the woman's lap.* N COUNT+POSS

2 In a race, you say that a competitor has complet-ed a **lap** when he or she has gone round the course once. N COUNT

3 If you **lap** another competitor in a race, you pass them while they are still on the previous lap. V+O

4 When water **laps** against something, it touches it gently and makes a soft sound. EG *Waves lapped against the side of the boat.* V+A OR V+O

5 When an animal **laps**, it drinks. EG *The cat was lapping at a saucer of milk.* V+O OR V+A

lap up. 1 When an animal **laps up** a drink, it drinks it up very eagerly. EG *The cat was lapping up the milk as if it had not fed for days.* **2** If someone **laps up** information or attention, they accept it eagerly, often when it is not really true or sincere. EG *It was a lie, but millions of newspaper readers lapped it up.* PHRASAL VB: V+O+ADV V+O+ADV

lapel /lə³pel/, **lapels**. The **lapels** of a jacket or coat are the two parts at the front that are folded back on each side and join on to the collar. N COUNT

lapse /læps/, **lapses**, **lapsing**, **lapsed**. 1 A **lapse** is an unexpected piece of bad behaviour by some-one who usually behaves well. EG *I intended to make up for this lapse in manners at the next party.* N COUNT

2 If you have a **lapse** of memory or a **lapse** of concentration, you forget to do something or fail to concentrate on something. N COUNT+SUPP

3 If you **lapse** into a particular kind of behaviour, you start behaving that way. EG *He lapsed into an unhappy silence... She keeps lapsing into jargon.* V+into

4 A **lapse** of time is a period of time that is long enough for a situation to change. EG *After a certain lapse of time it would be safe for Daisy to return... He was not conscious of the time lapse.* ▸ used as a verb. EG *Hours lapsed between each phone call.* N SING+SUPP ▸ V

5 If a situation, relationship, or legal contract **lapses**, it is allowed to end or to become invalid rather than being continued. EG *...traditions which had never lapsed... He allowed his membership of the union to lapse.* V

larch /lɑːtʃ/, **larches**. A **larch** is a tree with needle-shaped leaves. N COUNT

lard /lɑːd/ is soft white fat obtained from pigs. It is used in cooking. N UNCOUNT

larder /lɑːdə/, **larders**. A **larder** is a room or cupboard in which food is kept. EG *...a well-stocked larder... Some cheese had vanished from the lar-der.* N COUNT

large /lɑːdʒ/, **larger, largest. 1** Something that is ADJ QUALIT **large** is greater in size or amount than is usual or average. EG ...*a large house... ...a large and well equipped army... She made a very large amount of money.*

2 You use **by and large** to indicate that a state- ADV SEN ment is mostly true but is not completely true. EG *By and large, they were free to do as they wished.*

3 You use **at large** to indicate that you are talking PHRASE about most of the people mentioned. EG *There has been unrest in the country at large.*

4 If you say that a dangerous person or animal is **at** PHRASE **large**, you mean that they have escaped and have not yet been captured.

largely /lɑːdʒliʲ/. **1** You use **largely** to say that a ADV statement is mostly true but is not completely true. EG *The evidence shows them to be largely correct... Her work is largely confined to the cinema.*

2 You also use **largely** to introduce the main ADV OR reason for an event or situation. EG *We were there* ADV SEN *largely because of the girls... He was acquitted, largely on the evidence of a tape recording.*

large-scale. 1 A **large-scale** action or event ADJ QUALIT : happens over a wide area or involves a lot of ATTRIB people or things. EG ...*large-scale forest fires... ...a large-scale farming operation.*

2 A **large-scale** map or diagram represents a ADJ QUALIT : small area of land or a building or a machine on a ATTRIB scale that is large enough for small details to be shown.

lark /lɑːk/, **larks, larking, larked. 1** A **lark** is a N COUNT small brown bird that has a pleasant song.

2 If you do something for a **lark**, you do it because N COUNT you think it is amusing, rather than for any serious Informal purpose. EG *For a lark, she walked in and asked his* British *name... To me the whole thing was just a lark.*

lark about. If you **lark about**, you enjoy yourself PHRASAL VB : doing silly things. V+ADV

larva /lɑːvə/, **larvae** /lɑːviː/. A **larva** is an insect N COUNT at the stage of its life when it looks like a short, fat worm. This is the stage after it has developed from an egg and before it changes into an adult.

lascivious /ləsɪvɪəs/. **Lascivious** people have a ADJ QUALIT strong desire for sex. EG *He wanted to protect Frances from unscrupulous or lascivious men.*

laser /leɪzə/, **lasers.** A **laser** is a narrow beam of N COUNT concentrated light that is used especially for cutting very hard materials and in surgery. Lasers are produced by special machines which are also called **lasers.** EG *A laser beam would cut into it... ...experiments with laser weapons.*

lash /læʃ/, **lashes, lashing, lashed. 1** Your N PLURAL **lashes** are the hairs that grow on the edge of your eyelids.

2 A **lash** is **2.1** the thin strip of leather at the end of N COUNT a whip. EG *He gasped as the lash hit him.* **2.2** a blow with a whip on someone's back as a punishment. EG ...*a public flogging of thirty-nine lashes.*

3 If someone **lashes** you, they hit you with a whip. V+O

4 If the wind or rain **lashes** something, it hits it V+O OR V+A violently. EG *High winds lashed the branches of the* Literary *elm.*

5 If you **lash** one thing to another, you tie them V+O+*to/* firmly together. EG *We lashed our boats together.* *together*

lash out. 1 If you **lash out**, you try to hit PHRASAL VB : someone with your hands or feet or with a weapon. V+ADV EG *When cornered, they lash out with savage kicks.*

2 You can also say that someone **lashes out** when V+ADV, they criticize or scold people in an angry way. EG USU+*at/* *Harris lashed out against the Committee.* *against*

lass /læs/, **lasses.** In some parts of Britain, a N COUNT young woman or girl is referred to as a **lass.** EG *She'd worked on the farm as a lass.*

last /lɑːst/, **lasts, lasting, lasted. 1** You use **last** ORDINAL to describe the most recent period of time, event, or thing. EG *I went to a party last night... ...the last four years... Thanks for your last letter.*

2 The **last** thing or part is **2.1** the one that comes ORDINAL at the end. EG *He missed the last bus... I saw the last*

five minutes of it... *Hooper was the last to leave.* **2.2** the one at the end of a row of things. EG ...*the last classroom along that passage... ...the last of a string of islands.* **2.3** the only one that remains. EG *She removed the last traces of make-up... Otto drank the last of the brandy.*

3 You can use **last** to emphasize that you do not ORDINAL want to do something or that something is unlikely to happen or be true. EG *The last thing I want to do is offend you... I would be the last to suggest that.*

4 If something **last** happened on a particular ADV occasion, it has not happened since then. EG *They last saw their homeland nine years ago.*

5 If something happens **last**, it happens after ADV everything else. EG *He added the milk last.*

6 If something **lasts**, **6.1** it continues to exist or V : USU+A happen. EG *His speech lasted for exactly fourteen minutes... Profits are as high as ever. It won't last.* **6.2** it continues to be in good condition. EG *A fresh pepper lasts about three weeks.*

7 If a quantity of something **lasts** for a period of V+A OR time, there is enough of it for someone to use V+O+A during that period. EG *A cheap box of toothpowder lasts two years... He had only £8 left to last him till he reached Bury.*

8 Last is also used in these phrases. **8.1** You use PHRASES **before last** to refer to the thing, event, or person immediately before the most recent one. For example, the year **before last** was the one before the most recent one. **8.2** You use **last but** with a number when referring to a thing that comes before the final one in a series. For example, there are two things after the **last** thing **but** two. EG ...*during the last day but one of the trial.* **8.3** You use **the last** to indicate that something did not happen or exist again after a particular time, or that it will never happen or exist again. EG *That was the last I ever saw of Northcliffe.* **8.4** If something happens **last thing**, it happens at the end of a period of time. EG ...*the sink where we all had to wash last thing at night.* **8.5** If you **leave** something **till last**, you deal with it after everything else. **8.6** You use expressions such as **to the last detail** or **to the last man** to emphasize that you are including every single thing or person. EG *The robbery was planned down to the last detail... State the actual amount down to the last 10p.*

9 At last is used in these ways. **9.1** If you say that PHRASE something has happened **at last** or **at long last**, you mean it has happened after you have been waiting for it for a long time. EG *I'm free at last... At long last I've found a girl that really loves me.* **9.2** Literary **At last** also means at the end of a long period of time. EG *At last Ralph stopped work and stood up.*

last-ditch. You can refer to your final attempt to ADJ CLASSIF : do something that you have previously failed to do ATTRIB as a **last-ditch** attempt. EG *The Treasury made a last-ditch attempt to intervene.*

lasting /lɑːstɪŋ/. Something that is **lasting** con- ADJ CLASSIF : tinues to exist or to have an effect for a very long ATTRIB time. EG *This may provide a lasting solution to our problems... ...lasting friendships.*

lastly /lɑːstliʲ/. You use **lastly 1** when you want to ADV SEN make a final point that is connected with the other ones you have already mentioned. EG *Lastly, I would like to ask you about your future plans.* **2** ADV when you are saying what happens after everything else in a series of actions or events. EG *Lastly he jabbed the knife into the trunk of the tree.*

last-minute. A **last-minute** action is done just ADJ CLASSIF : before something else happens, usually before ATTRIB something important which is planned to happen at a fixed time. EG ...*a last-minute attempt to stop the school being closed... We have some last-minute details to talk over.*

latch /lætʃ/, **latches, latching, latched.** 1 A latch is a fastening on a door or gate. It consists of a metal bar which is held in place to lock the door and which you lift in order to open the door. N COUNT

2 If you **latch** a door or gate, you fasten it by means of a latch. ◇ **latched.** EG *Both doors were open and latched in position.* V+O ◇ ADJ CLASSIF

3 If a door with a lock that locks automatically is **on the latch**, the lock has been set so that it does not lock automatically when you shut the door. EG *He closed the door and left it on the latch in case Tom had forgotten his key.* PHRASE

latch onto. If you **latch onto** someone or something, you become very involved with them, because you are interested in them or find them useful. EG *She latched onto someone with a family business.* · PHRASAL VB : V+PREP, HAS PASS Informal

late /leɪt/, **later, latest.** 1 **Late** means near the end of a period of time, a process, or a piece of work. EG *Very late at night, I got a phone call... Decker arrived in late September... ...Picasso's late work... ...in the late afternoon... ...late in 1952.* ADV OR ADJ QUALIT : ATTRIB

2 If you are **late** for something or if you arrive **late**, you arrive after the time that was arranged. EG *I was ten minutes late for my appointment... I apologise for my late arrival.* ADJ QUALIT : OFT ATTRIB, OR ADV

3 If it is **too late** for something, that thing is no longer possible or useful. If something happens **too late**, the right time for it has passed. EG *It's too late to change that now... I realized my mistake too late.* PHRASE

4 You use **late** to describe things that happen after the normal time. EG *We had a late lunch at the hotel... ...if you get up late.* ADJ QUALIT OR ADV

5 **As late as** means at a particular time or period that is surprisingly late. EG *Even as late as 1950 coal provided over 90% of our energy.* PREP

6 You use **late** when you are talking about someone who is dead, especially someone who has died recently. EG *...the late Harry Truman.* ADJ CLASSIF : ATTRIB

7 Something that has been happening **of late** has been happening recently. EG *My wife has been rather tired of late.* PHRASE Formal

8 See also **later, latest.**

latecomer /leɪtkʌmə/, **latecomers.** A latecomer is someone who arrives after the time that they should have arrived. N COUNT

lately /leɪtliʲ/. If something has happened **lately**, it has happened recently. EG *John has seemed worried lately.* ADV

latent /leɪtənt/ is used to describe something which is hidden and not obvious at the moment, but which may develop further in the future. EG *I believe that everyone has a latent mathematical ability.* ADJ CLASSIF

later /leɪtə/. 1 **Later** is the comparative of **late.**

2 You use **later** or **later on** to refer to a time or situation that is after the one that you have been talking about or after the present one. EG *Four weeks later... Later on this evening, we shall have some music... See you later... We will discuss this in more detail in a later chapter.* ADV OR ADJ CLASSIF : ATTRIB

3 You also use **later** to refer to the last part of someone's life or to the last part of a period of time. EG *This may cause illness in later life... ...the later eighteenth century.* ADJ CLASSIF : ATTRIB

lateral /lætəʳrəl/ is used to describe something which relates to the sides of something, or to describe a sideways movement. EG *All of these primitive sea creatures had well developed lateral fins.* ADJ CLASSIF : ATTRIB

latest /leɪtiʲst/. 1 **Latest** is the superlative of **late.**

2 You use **latest** to describe something that is the most recent thing of its kind. EG *...the latest news... ...her latest book... ...the latest fashions from Paris.* ADJ QUALIT : SUPERL

3 You use **at the latest** to emphasize that something must happen at or before a particular time and not after that time. EG *Changes will become necessary by the autumn at the latest.* PHRASE

lathe /leɪð/, **lathes.** A **lathe** is a machine which is used for shaping wood or metal. It works by turning the wood or metal continually against a tool which cuts it. N COUNT

lather /lɑːðə/, **lathers, lathering, lathered.** 1 **Lather** is a white mass of bubbles which is produced by mixing soap or washing powder with water. EG *It is important when washing clothes to maintain a good lather throughout the wash.* N SING OR N UNCOUNT

2 If you **lather** something, you rub soap or washing powder into it or on it until a lather is produced, in order to clean it. EG *Lather the carpet with a sponge and rub gently until the stain has gone.* V+O

Latin /lætɪn/. 1 **Latin** is the language which the ancient Romans used to speak. N UNCOUNT

2 **Latin** is used to refer to people who come from the countries where French, Italian, Spanish, and Portuguese are spoken. EG *He had Latin blood... ...the Latin nations.* ADJ CLASSIF

Latin American, Latin Americans. 1 **Latin American** means relating or belonging to the countries of South and Central America. EG *...Latin American countries.* ADJ CLASSIF

2 A **Latin American** is someone who lives in or comes from South or Central America. N COUNT

latitude /lætɪtjuːd/, **latitudes.** 1 The **latitude** of a place is its distance to the north or south of the Equator: compare **longitude.** EG *We are at the precise latitude of Corfu.* N COUNT OR N UNCOUNT

2 **Latitude** is freedom to choose the way in which you do something. EG *She was given considerable latitude in how she spent the money.* N UNCOUNT Formal

latrine /lətriːn/, **latrines.** A **latrine** is a hole in the ground which is used as a toilet, for example when you are camping. N COUNT

latter /lætə/. 1 When two people, things, or groups have just been mentioned, you refer to the one that was mentioned second as the **latter.** EG *They were eating sandwiches and little iced cakes, (the latter obtained from Mrs Kaul's bakery).* ▸ used as an adjective. EG *The novel was made into a film in 1943 and again in 1967: I prefer the latter version to the former.* N SING OR N PLURAL : the+N ▸ ADJ CLASSIF

2 You use **latter** to describe the second part of a period of time. EG *By the latter half of July the total was well over two million.* ADJ CLASSIF

3 **Latter** also means recent. EG *He was the sort of admirer she had been having in these latter years.* ◇ **latterly.** EG *I have found that latterly this rapport is getting less and less.* ADJ CLASSIF : ATTRIB ◇ ADV Formal

latter-day is used to describe something or someone that is a modern equivalent of something or someone in the past. EG *...the latter-day martyr, Edith Cavell.* ADJ CLASSIF : ATTRIB

lattice /lætɪs/, **lattices.** A **lattice** is a pattern or structure made of strips which cross over each other diagonally leaving holes in between. A lattice can be used as a framework or as a decoration. EG *Their houses are in traditional style of clay over a lattice of bamboo.* N COUNT

laudable /lɔːdəbəl/. If you describe something as **laudable**, you mean that it deserves to be praised or admired. EG *The programme was inspired by laudable motives of improving housing conditions.* ADJ QUALIT Formal

laugh /lɑːf/, **laughs, laughing, laughed.** 1 When you **laugh**, you make the sound by which people show that they are happy or amused. EG *He grinned, then started to laugh... The young men laughed at his jokes.* ▸ used as a noun. EG *'Hurry up,' said Tony with a laugh... It was a terrible laugh, very quiet and intense.* V ▸ N COUNT

2 **Laugh** is used in these expressions. 2.1 If you **laugh your head off**, you laugh very loudly for a long time. 2.2 If you **laugh out loud** or **laugh aloud**, you laugh loudly at something, especially when this is an unusual thing to do, for example when you are on your own. EG *It's rare to come across any book which makes you laugh out loud.* 2.3 When comedians **get** or **raise a laugh**, they PHRASES Informal

succeed in making their audience laugh. EG *His act would always get a huge laugh.* **2.4** If you do something **for a laugh** or **for laughs**, you do it as a joke or for fun. EG *I gave him the wrong address just for a laugh.* **2.5** If someone **has the last laugh**, they succeed after appearing to have been defeated. EG *Henry had outlived all the others to have the last laugh.*   Informal

laugh at. If you **laugh at** someone or something, you mock them or make jokes about them. EG *I don't think it's nice to laugh at people's disabilities.*   PHRASAL VB : V+PREP, HAS PASS

laugh off. If you **laugh off** a serious situation, you try to suggest that it is amusing and unimportant, for example by making a joke about it. EG *Despite being in trouble with the Government, Northcliffe attempted to laugh the matter off.*   PHRASAL VB : V+O+ADV

laughable /ˈlɑːfəbəl/. You say that something is **laughable** when it seems amusing because it is so obviously unsuccessful, foolish, or poor in quality. EG *It's almost laughable to talk about a 'policy'.* ◇ **laughably.** EG *They appear almost laughably pompous.*   ADJ QUALIT   ◇ ADV

laughing stock. If someone is a **laughing stock**, they have been made to seem ridiculous. EG *Arthur was the laughing stock of the neighbourhood.*   N SING

laughter /ˈlɑːftə/ is the act of laughing, or the sound of people laughing. EG *Mr Evans heard laughter and applause as the speaker ceased... We roared with laughter.*   N UNCOUNT

launch /lɔːntʃ/, **launches, launching, launched.** **1** When a **ship is launched**, it is put into water for the first time.   V+O : OFT PASS

2 To **launch** a rocket, missile, or satellite means to send it into the air or into space. EG *Soviet rockets launched more satellites into orbit.* ▶ used as a noun. EG *They gave only a few minutes' warning of the missile launch.*   V+O   ▶ N COUNT

3 To **launch** a large and important activity, for example a political movement or a military attack, means to start it. EG *The government has launched a massive literacy campaign... Guerrilla attacks were launched against the police.*   V+O

4 If a company **launches** a new product, it starts to make it available to the public. EG *A magazine called 'The Week' was launched in January 1964.* ▶ used as a noun. EG *We are already selling millions of copies just one year after the launch.*   V+O   ▶ N COUNT

5 A **launch** is a large motor-boat.   N COUNT

launch into. If you **launch into** a speech, fight, or other activity, you start it enthusiastically. EG *He launched into a long speech about the dangers of taking drugs.*   PHRASAL VB : V+PREP, HAS PASS

launder /ˈlɔːndə/, **launders, laundering, laundered.** When you **launder** clothes, sheets, and towels, you wash and iron them.   V+O   Outdated

launderette /lɔːndəˈrɛt/, **launderettes.** A **launderette** is a shop in which there are washing machines and dryers which people can pay to use to wash and dry their clothes.   N COUNT

laundry /ˈlɔːndri/, **laundries.** **1 Laundry** is **1.1** dirty clothes, sheets, and towels that are being washed or are about to be washed. EG *The washing machine takes about two hours to do my laundry.* **1.2** clean clothes, sheets, and towels that have been washed. EG *...laundry hung out to dry in the sun.*   N UNCOUNT, OR N SING : the+N

2 A **laundry** is **2.1** a firm that washes and irons clothes, sheets, and towels for people. **2.2** a room in a house or hotel where clothes, sheets, and towels are washed.   N COUNT

laurel /ˈlɒrəl/, **laurels.** **1** A **laurel** is a small evergreen tree with shiny leaves.   N COUNT

2 If you say that someone **is resting on** their **laurels**, you mean that they feel so satisfied with what they have already achieved that they are not bothering to make any more effort. EG *We have no cause to rest on our laurels.*   PHRASE

lava /ˈlɑːvə/ is a kind of rock which comes out of a volcano in the form of a very hot liquid, and gradually cools and becomes solid.   N UNCOUNT

lavatory /ˈlævətəri/, **lavatories.** A **lavatory** is a toilet.   N COUNT

lavender /ˈlævɪndə/ is a garden plant that has sweet-smelling, bluish-purple flowers on long stalks.   N UNCOUNT

lavish /ˈlævɪʃ/, **lavishes, lavishing, lavished.** **1** If you are **lavish** with your money or time, you are very generous in the way that you spend it for other people's benefit. EG *...the lavish hospitality of Indian princes.* ◇ **lavishly.** EG *Rich merchants lavishly entertained travelling tradesmen.*   ADJ QUALIT   ◇ ADV

2 If you **lavish** money, affection, or time on someone or something, you spend a lot of money on them or give them a lot of affection or attention. EG *Everything was lavished on her one and only child... He lavished presents on her.*   V+O+on/upon

3 Something that is **lavish 3.1** is very large in amount. EG *The meal, he said, would be nothing fancy, but the portions would be lavish.* ◇ **lavishly.** EG *They were lavishly paid.* **3.2** has an appearance of great wealth and extravagance. EG *...lavish funeral parlours.* ◇ **lavishly.** EG *The building has been lavishly restored to a fresh brilliance.*   ADJ QUALIT   ◇ ADV   ADJ QUALIT   ◇ ADV

law /lɔː/, **laws.** **1** The **law** is a system of rules that a society or government develops in order to deal with business agreements, social relationships, and crime. EG *It's against the law to demonstrate here... She was caught breaking the law... Every company must by law submit accounts annually.*   N SING : the+N, OR N UNCOUNT

2 A particular type of **law**, for example company **law** or criminal **law**, is the group of rules in a system of law which deals with a particular set of agreements, relationships, or crimes. EG *She's the Senate's expert on constitutional law... The soldiers faced charges under military law.*   N UNCOUNT +SUPP

3 A **law** is **3.1** one of the rules in a system of law which deals with a particular type of agreement, relationship, or crime. EG *Many of the laws passed by Parliament are never enforced... ...immigration laws.* **3.2** a rule or set of rules for good behaviour which seems right and important for moral, religious, or emotional reasons. EG *Children soon accept social laws.*   N COUNT

4 Law or **the law** is all the professions which deal with advising people about the law, representing people in court, or giving decisions and punishments. EG *I was planning a career in law... There are curious parallels between medicine and the law... ...a New York law firm.*   N UNCOUNT, OR N SING : the+N

5 Law is the study of systems of law and how laws work. EG *A degree in law would be an advantage in the job market.*   N UNCOUNT

6 Some people refer to government authorities, especially the police, as the **law**. EG *He found himself in trouble with the law again.*   N SING : the+N Informal

7 When someone **lays down the law**, they give other people orders because they think that they are right and the other people are wrong; used showing disapproval.   PHRASE

8 A **law** is also **8.1** a natural process or pattern in which a particular cause always leads to a particular effect and nothing can stop it happening. EG *...the laws of nature... The laws that govern the behaviour of light are universal.* **8.2** a scientific rule that people have invented to describe and explain the way that nature works. EG *...the second law of heat distribution.*   N COUNT+SUPP

law-abiding. Someone who is **law-abiding** always obeys the law. EG *...respectable, law-abiding citizens.*   ADJ QUALIT USU ATTRIB

law and order. When people talk about **law and order**, they are referring to **1** the acceptance and obeying of the laws of a country by the people who live there. EG *There were periods of unrest and a*   N UNCOUNT

Do lawyers lay down the law?

breakdown of law and order. **2** the use of strict laws as a way of controlling a society, especially when the police or the army are used. EG *Are they not prepared to enforce law and order among their own people?*

law court, law courts. A **law court** is a place N COUNT where legal matters are decided by a judge and jury or by a magistrate.

lawful /lɔːfʊl/. **Lawful** activities, organizations, ADJ CLASSIF and products are allowed by law. EG *...lawful publi-* Formal *cations... Use all lawful means to persuade employ-* *ers.* ◇ **lawfully.** EG *The tenant cannot be lawfully* ◇ ADV *evicted.*

lawless /lɔːlɪ²s/. **Lawless** actions break the laws ADJ CLASSIF of a country or state. EG *...the lawless activities of* Formal *these gangs.* ◇ **lawlessness.** EG *...our disapproval* ◇ N UNCOUNT *of lawlessness and violence.*

lawn /lɔːn/, **lawns.** A **lawn** is an area of grass that N COUNT OR is kept cut short. A **lawn** is usually part of a garden N UNCOUNT or park. EG *I'm going to mow the lawn.*

lawnmower /lɔːnməʊə/, **lawnmowers.** A N COUNT **lawnmower** is a machine for cutting grass on lawns.

lawsuit /lɔːsuːt/, **lawsuits.** A **lawsuit** is a case in N COUNT a court of law which concerns a dispute between Formal two people, rather than the prosecution of a crimi-nal by the police. EG *He had sought to bring a lawsuit against the airline.*

lawyer /lɔːjə, lɔɪə/, **lawyers.** A **lawyer** is a per- N COUNT son who is qualified to advise people about the law and represent them in court. EG *I sought the advice of a lawyer.*

lax /læks/. If you say that someone's behaviour or ADJ QUALIT a system is **lax**, you mean that rules are not being obeyed or standards are not being maintained. EG *Standards are regarded by some experts as being far too lax... Procedures are lax, discipline is weak.*

laxative /læksətɪv/, **laxatives.** A **laxative** is N COUNT something that you eat or drink which stops you being constipated.

lay /leɪ/, **lays, laying, laid** /leɪd/. **Lay** is also the past tense of the verb **lie** in some meanings.
1 If you **lay** something somewhere, you place it V+O+A there so that it rests there. EG *She laid the baby gently down on its bed... She laid a hand on his shoulder.*
2 When you **lay** the table, you arrange the knives, V+O forks, plates, and other things on a table before a meal. EG *I'm not laying a place at table for him.*
3 If you **lay** something such as a carpet or a cable, V+O you put it on or in the ground in its proper position. EG *They're laying water pipes and electricity ca-bles.*
4 When a female bird or animal **lays** an egg, the V+O OR V egg comes out of its body.
5 If you **lay** a trap, **5.1** you hide a trap and set it in V+O order to catch an animal. **5.2** you deceive someone in order to catch them or get them to do what you want. EG *He walked right into the trap I had laid for him.*
6 If you **lay hold of** someone or something, you PHRASE grab them and hold them tight.
7 If you **lay** the basis for something, you make V+O preparations for it in order to make sure that it will happen in the way you want it to. EG *Her new policy helped to lay the foundations of electoral success.*
8 If you **lay** something on someone, you cause V+O+*on/upon* them to be affected by it. EG *Women lay most of the blame on men... A curse has been laid on those who violated the tomb of the King.*
9 If you **lay emphasis on** something, you empha- PHRASE size it. EG *His lawyer will lay great emphasis on his state of mind at the time.*
10 If you **lay** someone **open to** criticism or attack, PHRASE you do something which is likely to make people criticize or attack them. EG *That kind of behaviour can lay you open to the charge of wasting the company's time.*
11 You use **lay** to describe people who are **11.1** ADJ CLASSIF : ATTRIB

involved with a Christian church but are not mem-bers of the clergy, monks, or nuns. EG *...a lay preacher.* **11.2** not trained or qualified in a particu-lar subject or activity. EG *The computer has be-come much more accessible to the lay person.*
12 to **lay claim to**: see **claim**.

lay before. If you **lay** an idea or problem **before** PHRASAL VB : someone, you present it to them, for example in V+O+PREP order to obtain their approval or advice. EG *What* Formal *exactly was the scheme he intended to lay before them?*

lay down. 1 If rules or people in authority **lay** PHRASAL VB : **down** what people must do, they tell people what V+O+ADV they must do. EG *...the conditions laid down by the Department of Health.* ● to **lay down the law:** see **law. 2** If someone **lays down** their life in a war or PHRASE struggle, they are killed while fighting for some- Literary thing.

lay into. If you **lay into** someone, you start PHRASAL VB : attacking them physically or criticizing them se- V+PREP, verely. HAS PASS

lay off. 1 If workers **are laid off** by their PHRASAL VB : employers, they are told to leave their jobs, usually V+O+ADV because there is no more work for them to do. **2** If V+ADV/PREP, you tell someone to **lay off**, you are telling them to USU IMPER leave you alone. **3** See also **layoff.**

lay on. If you **lay on** food, entertainment, or a PHRASAL VB : service, you provide it, especially in a generous V+O+ADV way. EG *We laid on a great show for them.*

lay out. 1 If you **lay out** a group of things, you PHRASAL VB : spread them out and arrange them. EG *Clothes,* V+O+ADV *jewels, and ornaments were laid out on the ground.*
2 You can describe the design of a garden, V-PASS+ADV building, or town by saying how it **is laid out.** EG *Their settlement is laid out traditionally as a small village.* **3** See also **layout.**

layabout /leɪəbaʊt/, **layabouts.** If you say that N COUNT someone is a **layabout**, you mean that they are Informal idle and lazy. EG *He's just a drunken layabout.*

lay-by, lay-bys. A **lay-by** is a short strip of road N COUNT by the side of a main road, where cars can stop for a while. EG *Pull into the next lay-by.*

layer /leɪə/, **layers.** A **layer** is a flat piece of N COUNT : something or a quantity of something that covers a USU+SUPP surface or that is between two other things. EG *A fine layer of dust covered everything... He wrapped each component in several layers of foam rubber.*

layman /leɪmə³n/, **laymen.** A **layman** is a person N COUNT who is not qualified or experienced in a particular subject or activity. EG *...a task for industrial experts rather than for laymen.*

layoff /leɪⁱɒf/, **layoffs.** When there are **layoffs** in N COUNT a company, people are told to leave their jobs, usually because there is no more work for them to do. EG *Textile companies announced 2,000 fresh layoffs last week.*

layout /leɪⁱaʊt/, **layouts.** The **layout** of a garden, N COUNT+SUPP building, or piece of writing is the way in which the parts of it are arranged. EG *He knew the airport layout intimately.*

laze /leɪz/, **lazes, lazing, lazed.** If you **laze** some- V : OFT+A where or **laze** about, you relax and do nothing. EG *...lazing by the hotel pool.*

lazy /leɪzi¹/, **lazier, laziest. 1** Someone who is ADJ QUALIT **lazy** tries to avoid doing any work or making any effort to do something. EG *His maths teacher thought he was bright but lazy.* ◇ **laziness.** EG *Only* ◇ N UNCOUNT *laziness prevented him from doing it.*
2 Lazy actions are done slowly without making ADJ QUALIT : very much effort. EG *She gave a lazy smile.* ATTRIB ◇ **lazily.** EG *Philip was lazily combing his hair.* ◇ ADV

lb, lbs. You use **lb** as a written abbreviation for 'pound' when you are describing the weight of something. The plural can be either 'lb' or 'lbs'. EG *...a 2lb bag of sugar... ...a fish weighing about 10 lbs.*

lead, leads, leading, led /led/; pronounced /liːd/ except in paragraphs 19 and 20, where it is pro-nounced /led/.
1 If you **lead** a group of moving people, you walk V+O : USU+A; ALSO V

or ride in front of them. EG *He led a demonstration through the City.*

2 If you **lead** someone somewhere, you take them there. EG *My mother takes me by the hand and leads me downstairs.* ● If you **lead the way**, you go in front of someone in order to show them where to go. EG *I led the way to Andrew's cabin.* `V+O+A` ● `PHRASE`

3 If something such as a road, pipe, or wire **leads** somewhere, it goes there. EG *The steps lead down to his basement. ...the main street leading to the centre of the city.* `V+A`

4 If a door or gate **leads** to a place, you can get to the place by going through it. EG *There was a gate on our left leading into a field.* `V+to/into`

5 If you **are leading** in a race or competition, you are winning. EG *Becker leads by five games to four.* `V`

6 In a race or competition, if you have the **lead** or are in the **lead**, you are winning. EG *This win gave him the overall lead... The USSR was well in the lead.* `N SING`

7 If you **lead** a group of people or an organization, you are officially in charge of it. EG *The Labour Party was led by Wilson.* `V+O OR V`

8 If you **lead** an activity, you start it or guide it. EG *The rioting was led by students.* `V+O`

9 If you **take the lead**, you start doing something before other people do. EG *It was France who took the lead in the development of the airbus.* `PHRASE`

10 If you give a **lead**, you do something which is considered to be a good example to follow. EG *The European Community should give a lead... Other firms are now following the company's lead.* `N COUNT`

11 You can use **lead** when saying what sort of life someone has. For example, if you **lead** an exciting life, your life is exciting. `V+O`

12 If something **leads** to an unpleasant situation, it causes that situation to happen. EG *...a drinking spree which had led to his court appearance.* `V+to`

13 If something **leads** you to do something, it influences or affects you so that you do that thing. EG *Recent evidence is leading historians to reassess that event... This led him to an obsession with art.* `V+O+to-INF OR V+O+A`

14 A dog's **lead** is a long, thin chain or piece of leather which you attach to the dog's collar so that you can keep the dog under control. `N COUNT`

15 A **lead** in a piece of electrical equipment is a piece of wire which supplies electricity to the equipment. `N COUNT`

16 The **lead** in a play or film is the most important role in it. EG *Richard was signed up to play the lead.* `N SING : the+N`

17 The **lead** singer in a pop group is the one who sings the main tunes. `ADJ CLASSIF : ATTRIB`

18 A **lead** is also a piece of information which may help the police to find out who committed a crime. `N COUNT`

19 **Lead** is a soft, grey, heavy metal. `N UNCOUNT`

20 The **lead** in a pencil is the centre part of it which makes a mark on paper. `N COUNT`

21 See also **leading**.

lead off. 1 If a road or corridor **leads off** from a place, it starts at that place and goes away from it. EG *...a side street leading off from a road of shops.* **2** If a room **leads off** a place, there is an entrance to it in that place. EG *...rooms leading off the courtyard.* `PHRASAL VB : V+ADV+A` `V+PREP`

lead up to. 1 Events that **lead up to** a situation happen one after the other until that situation is reached. EG *...the chain of events that led up to her death.* **2** If you **lead up to** a particular subject in a conversation, you gradually guide the conversation to a point where you can introduce that subject. EG *Ever since you came in you've been leading up to this one question.* `PHRASAL VB : V+ADV+PREP`

leaden /lɛdᵊn/. **1** A **leaden** sky or sea is dark grey and has no movement of clouds or waves. `ADJ CLASSIF Literary`
2 If your movements are **leaden**, you are moving slowly and heavily, because you are tired. EG *He took two leaden steps forward.* `ADJ QUALIT Literary`
3 You can describe a conversation as **leaden** when it is very dull. `ADJ QUALIT Literary`

leader /liːdə/, **leaders. 1** The **leader** of an organization or a group of people is the person who is in charge of it. EG *...the leader of the Labour Party... He didn't know how to be a decisive leader.* `N COUNT`
2 The **leader** in a race or competition is the person who is winning at a particular time. `N COUNT`

leadership /liːdəʃɪp/. **1** You can refer to the people who are in charge of a group or organization as the **leadership**. EG *...the gap between the leadership and the men they represent.* `N SING : the+N`
2 If a group of people is under your **leadership**, you are their leader. EG *...an independent group under the leadership of Jones... ...the election of Wilson to the leadership of the Labour Party.* `N SING`
3 Someone who shows **leadership** shows that they have the qualities of a good leader. EG *...a task calling for energy and firm leadership.* `N UNCOUNT`

leading /liːdɪŋ/. **1** The **leading** people or things in a group are the most important ones. EG *A demand for change came from leading politicians.* `ADJ CLASSIF : ATTRIB`
2 The **leading** role in a play or film is the main one. EG *She played the leading role in The Winter's Tale... ...their leading lady, Yvonne Printemps.* `ADJ CLASSIF : ATTRIB`
3 The **leading** person or thing in a line of moving people or things is the one that is at the front of the line. EG *The leading car was full of security men.* `ADJ CLASSIF : ATTRIB`

leaf /liːf/, **leaves** /liːvz/; **leafs, leafing, leafed.** **Leaves** is the plural of the noun. **Leafs** is the third person singular, present tense, of the phrasal verb.
1 The **leaves** of a tree or plant are the parts that are flat, thin, and usually green. Many trees and plants lose their leaves in the autumn and grow new leaves in the spring. `N COUNT`
2 When trees are **in leaf**, they have leaves on their branches. `PHRASE`

leaf through. If you **leaf through** a book or newspaper, you turn the pages quickly without looking at them carefully. EG *While he is waiting he leafs through a magazine.* `PHRASAL VB : V+PREP`

leaflet /liːflɪt/, **leaflets, leafleting, leafleted. 1** A **leaflet** is a little book or a piece of paper containing information about a particular subject. EG *The company produces a little leaflet called 'Protect your Pipes from Frost'.* `N COUNT`
2 If you **leaflet** a place, you distribute leaflets there, especially as part of a campaign. EG *All the local houses and shops had been leafleted.* `V+O`

leafy /liːfiː/, **leafier, leafiest. 1** **Leafy** trees and plants have a lot of leaves. EG *...leafy green vegetables.* `ADJ QUALIT`
2 You say that a place is **leafy** when there are a lot of trees and plants there. EG *...a leafy suburb.* `ADJ QUALIT`

league /liːg/, **leagues. 1** A **league** is a group of people, clubs, or countries that have joined together for a particular purpose or because they share a common interest. EG *...the National Book League... ...the football league.* `N COLL`
2 If you are **in league with** someone, you are working with them for a particular purpose, often secretly. EG *They are in league with the police.* `PHRASE`

leak /liːk/, **leaks, leaking, leaked. 1** If a container or other object **leaks**, there is a hole or crack in it which liquid or gas can pass through. EG *The roof leaks... ...leaking drain pipes.* ▸ used as a noun. EG *I fixed a small leak in the roof of her shed.* `V` ▸ `N COUNT`
2 When liquid or gas **leaks** through an object or **leaks** out of it, it passes through a hole or crack in it. EG *The water was still slowly leaking out.* ▸ used as a noun. EG *There's been a gas leak.* `V : USU+A` ▸ `N COUNT`
3 If someone **leaks** a piece of secret information, they let the public know about it. EG *He made sure the story was leaked to the media.* ▸ used as a noun. EG *...the possibility of a security leak.* `V+O : OFT+to` ▸ `N COUNT`

leak out. If information that you want to keep secret **leaks out**, it becomes known to other `PHRASAL VB : V+ADV`

When is the next leap year?

people. EG *News of their engagement leaked out just before Christmas.*

leakage /liːkɪdʒ/, **leakages**. If there is a **leakage** N COUNT of liquid or gas, an amount of it comes out of an object through a crack or hole. EG *A leakage in the hydraulic system was diagnosed.*

leaky /liːki¹/, **leakier**, **leakiest**. Something that is ADJ QUALIT **leaky** has holes or cracks in it which liquids or gases can pass through. EG *...a leaky roof.*

lean /liːn/, **leans**, **leaning**, **leaned**, **leant** /lɛnt/. **Leaned** and **leant** are both used as the past tense and past participle of the verb.

1 When you **lean** in a particular direction, you V+A bend your body in that direction. EG *He was sitting on the edge of his chair and leaning eagerly forwards... I leaned out of the window.*

2 If you **lean** on something, you rest against it so V+A OR that it partly supports your weight. If you **lean** an V+O+A object on something, you place the object so that its weight is partly supported by the thing it is resting against. EG *He leaned against a tree... He leaned the bike against a railing.*

3 If you **lean** towards a particular idea or action, V+towards you approve of it and behave in accordance with it. EG *...parents who naturally lean towards strictness.*

4 If you **lean** on someone, **4.1** you try to influence V+on/upon them by threatening them. EG *They can lean on the administration by threatening to withhold their subscriptions.* **4.2** you depend on them for support and encouragement. EG *They lean heavily upon each other for support.*

5 Someone who is **lean** is thin but looks strong and ADJ QUALIT fit. EG *...a lean, handsome man.*

6 **Lean** meat does not have very much fat. ADJ QUALIT

7 A **lean** period of time is one in which people do ADJ QUALIT not have very much food, money, or success. EG *In the lean years, crop failures are common.*

leaning /liːnɪŋ/, **leanings**. If you have a **leaning** N COUNT+SUPP towards a particular belief or type of behaviour, you tend to have that belief or to behave in that way. EG *...their different political leanings.*

leant /lɛnt/ is one of the forms of the past tense and past participle of **lean.**

leap /liːp/, **leaps**, **leaping**, **leaped** /liːpt/ or /lɛpt/, **leapt** /lɛpt/. **Leaped** and **leapt** are both used as the past tense and past participle of the verb.

1 If you **leap** somewhere, **1.1** you jump high in the V+O OR V: air or jump a long distance. EG *Some monkeys can* USU+A *leap five metres from one tree to another... They leaped into the water.* ▸ used as a noun. EG *She took* ▸ N COUNT *a flying leap at the fence.* **1.2** you move there V+A suddenly and quickly. EG *She leapt into a taxi and headed for the Bronx.*

2 You can say that things **leap** when they suddenly V+A advance or increase by a large amount. EG *The number of computers in the world is leaping upwards daily.* ▸ used as a noun. EG *...an economic* ▸ N COUNT: *leap forward... ...a leap in oil prices.* USU+SUPP

3 You can say that your **heart leaps** when you PHRASE experience a sudden strong feeling of surprise, Literary fear, or happiness. EG *My heart leapt at the thought of seeing her again.*

leap at. If you **leap at** a chance or opportunity, PHRASAL VB : you accept it quickly and eagerly. EG *David would* V+PREP *have leaped at the chance to go.*

leapt /lɛpt/ is one of the forms of the past tense and past participle of **leap.**

leap year, **leap years**. A **leap year** is a year in N COUNT which there are 366 days instead of 365. There is a leap year every four years.

learn /lɜːn/, **learns**, **learning**, **learned**, **learnt**. **Learned** and **learnt** are both used as the past tense and past participle of the verb.

1 If you **learn** facts or **learn** a skill, you obtain V+O, knowledge of the facts or gain the skill as a result V+to-INF, OR V of studying or training. EG *Children learn foreign languages very easily... He had never learnt to read and write... The best way to learn is by*

practical experience. ◊ **learner, learners.** EG *She* ◊ N COUNT *is a very slow learner.*

2 If you **learn** something such as a poem or the V+O script of a play, you study or repeat the words so much that you can remember them without looking at them. EG *We have to learn the whole poem.*

3 You say that people **learn** to behave in a V+to-INF particular way when they gradually start behaving that way as a result of a change in their attitudes. EG *Women must learn to value themselves as individuals... If only these people could learn to live together.*

4 If you **learn** of something, you find out about it, V+of, usually by being told about it. EG *They offered help* V+REPORT, *as soon as they learnt of the accident... She was* OR V+O extremely upset to learn that he had died... ...the night when he learned the truth about Sam.*

5 See also **learning**.

learned /lɜːnɪ¹d/. 1 Someone who is **learned** has ADJ QUALIT gained a lot of knowledge by studying, and is respected for this. EG *...the learned professions.*

2 **Learned** books or papers have been written by ADJ QUALIT: someone with a lot of academic knowledge. EG ATTRIB *...new ideas announced in learned journals.*

learning /lɜːnɪŋ/ is knowledge that has been N UNCOUNT gained through studying. EG *...a man of learning.*

learnt /lɜːnt/ is one of the forms of the past tense and past participle of **learn.**

lease /liːs/, **leases**, **leasing**, **leased**. 1 A **lease** is a N COUNT legal agreement by which the owner of a building or piece of land allows someone else to use it for a period of time in return for money. EG *The house was let on a 99-year lease.*

2 If you **lease** property from someone or if they V+O, V+O+O, **lease** it to you, they allow you to use it in return for OR V+O+to money. EG *They leased a house at Cospoli... He had persuaded the local council to lease him a house.*

3 If you say that someone who seemed to be failing PHRASE or becoming weaker has been given **a new lease of life,** you mean that they are now more lively or successful. EG *After her marriage it was as though she'd got a new lease of life.*

least /liːst/. 1 You use **at least** **1.1** to say that the ADV SEN number or amount mentioned is the smallest that is likely, and that the actual number or amount may be greater. EG *He drank at least half a bottle of whisky a day... I must have slept twelve hours at least.* **1.2** to say that something is the minimum which should be done, although in fact you think that more than this ought to be done. EG *Go to see the administrator or at least write a letter.* **1.3** to indicate an advantage that exists in spite of the disadvantage or bad situation that has just been mentioned. EG *The process looks rather laborious but at least it is not dangerous.*

2 You can also use **at least** when you want to ADV SEN correct something that you have just said. EG *A couple of days ago I spotted my ex-wife; at least I thought I did, I wasn't sure.*

3 You use **least** **3.1** to say that an amount of QUANTIF something is as small as it can be. EG *...the thinner animals, who had the least muscle over their bones.* **3.2** to say that something is true to as small ADV SUPERL a degree or extent as is possible. EG *He came out when I least expected it... They're the ones who need it the least.* **3.3** to say that something has less SUBMOD of a particular quality than most other things of its kind. EG *...one of the smallest and least powerful of the African states.* **3.4** to emphasize that a particu- ADJ QUALIT lar situation or thing is much less important or SUPERL serious than other ones. EG *That was the least of her worries.*

4 **Least** is also used in these phrases. **4.1** You can PHRASES use **in the least** and **the least bit** to emphasize a negative. EG *I don't mind in the least, I really don't... She wasn't the least bit jealous.* **4.2** If you say that something is **the least that** someone **can do,** you mean that they should do that even if they cannot do anything more. EG *And if I can't protect them*

from something, the least I can do is warn them that there is a danger. **4.3** You can use **to say the least** to suggest that a situation is actually much more extreme or serious than you say it is. EG *...a development which will have, to say the least, intriguing effects.* **4.4** You can use **not least** when giving an important example or reason. EG *...all western countries, not least the USA.* **4.5** You can use **least of all** after a negative statement to emphasize that it applies especially to a particular person or thing. EG *Nobody seemed amused, least of all Jenny.*

leather /lɛðə/ is the specially treated skin of N UNCOUNT animals. It is used for making shoes, clothes, bags, and furniture. EG *...leather jackets.*

leathery /lɛðəriˡ/. If the texture of something is ADJ QUALIT **leathery**, it is tough, like leather. EG *The wrinkled, leathery face broke into a smile.*

leave /liːv/, **leaves, leaving, left** /lɛft/. **1** When v+o OR v you **leave** a place, you go away from it. EG *They left the house to go for a walk after tea... My train leaves at 11.30.*

2 If you **leave** a person or thing somewhere, they v+o : USU+A remain there when you go away. EG *Leaving Rita in a bar, I made for the town library... Leave your phone number with the secretary... I had left my raincoat in the restaurant.*

3 If you **leave** a place or institution, you go away v+o OR v permanently from it. EG *What do you want to do when you leave school?... She told him she was going to leave her job... She wanted to leave China altogether.*

4 If someone **leaves** their husband or wife, they v+o OR v stop living with him or her and finish the relation-ship. EG *My husband had left me for another woman.*

5 If you **leave** a particular amount of something, v+o : OFT+A you do not use it, and so it remains available to be used later. EG *Leave some of the stew for the boys... I meant to leave myself with fifteen pounds a week.* ● See also **left 2**.

6 If something **leaves** a mark, effect, or impres- v+o sion, it causes that mark, effect, or impression to remain as a result. EG *I didn't want him to leave a trail of wet footprints... Does it leave a stain?*

7 To **leave** someone or something in a particular v+o+A, state or position means to cause them to remain or v+o+C, ORV+o+o be in that state or position. EG *Who left the gates open?... The result has left everybody dissatisfied... You are left with two alternatives.*

8 If you **leave** a space or gap in something, you v+o deliberately make that space or gap. EG *Remember to leave a space between the fridge and the wall.*

9 If you **leave** something to someone, you give v+o+to/with them the responsibility for dealing with it. EG *He said the whole business should be left to the courts... Leave it with me, I'll fix it... He left it to us to try and sort it out.*

10 If you **leave** something until a particular time, v+o : OFT+A you delay dealing with it. EG *Why do you always leave things to the last minute?*

11 If you **leave** a particular subject, you stop v+o talking about it and start discussing something else. EG *Let's leave the budget and go on to another question. I want to leave that for the moment.*

12 If you **leave** property or money to someone, you v+o, v+o+o, arrange for it to be given to them after you have ORV+o+to died. EG *She did not leave a very large legacy.*

13 Leave is **13.1** a period of time when you do not N UNCOUNT have to do your usual job, but which is not a +SUPP holiday. EG *She was granted a year's maternity leave... ...sick leave.* **13.2** a period of time when you are on holiday from your job. EG *He'd come over on leave from Northern Ireland... He asked for forty-eight hours' leave.*

14 Leaves is also the plural form of **leaf**.

leave behind. 1 If you **leave** someone or some- PHRASAL VB : thing **behind**, you go away permanently from V+O+ADV them. EG *I hated having to leave behind all my*

friends. **2** If you **leave** an object or a situation v+o+ADV **behind**, it remains after you have left a place. EG *Millie had left her watch behind... ...leaving behind an unsolved mystery.*

leave off. 1 If you **leave** someone or something PHRASAL VB : **off** a list, you do not include them in that list. EG V+O+PREP *Hopper was too important to be left off the guest list.* **2** If you continue doing something **from** PHRASE **where** you **left off**, you start doing it again at the point where you had previously stopped doing it. EG *He sat down at the piano again and started playing from where he left off.*

leave out. 1 If you **leave** someone or something PHRASAL VB : **out**, you do not include them in something. EG *One* V+O+ADV *or two scenes in the play were left out.* **2** If you PHRASE **feel left out**, you feel unhappy because you have not been included in a group or activity.

lecherous /lɛtʃərəs/. A man who is **lecherous** ADJ QUALIT behaves towards women in a way which shows that he is thinking of them in a sexual way; used showing disapproval.

lectern /lɛktəˢn/, **lecterns**. A **lectern** is a high N COUNT sloping desk on which someone puts their notes or a book when they are standing up and talking or reading to an audience.

lecture /lɛktʃə/, **lectures, lecturing, lectured. 1** N COUNT A **lecture** is a talk that someone gives in order to teach people about a particular subject. EG *...a series of lectures on literature... I went to a lecture he gave at the African Institute.* ▸ used as a verb. ▸ V EG *He lectured on Economic History at the Univer-sity.*

2 If someone **lectures** you about something, they v+o+A criticize you or tell you how you should behave. EG *I had always been lectured about not talking with my mouth full.* ▸ used as a noun. EG *He'll give her a* ▸ N COUNT *lecture on accepting her responsibilities.*

lecturer /lɛktʃərə/, **lecturers**. A **lecturer** is a N COUNT person who teaches at a university or college. EG *...a lecturer in sociology.*

lectureship /lɛktʃəʃɪp/, **lectureships**. A **lecture-** N COUNT **ship** is the position of lecturer at a university or college. EG *She was offered a lectureship at Bir-mingham University.*

led /lɛd/ is the past tense and past participle of **lead**.

ledge /lɛdʒ/, **ledges**. A **ledge** is **1** a narrow, flat N COUNT place in the side of a cliff or mountain. EG *Only a bird could get to that ledge.* **2** a narrow shelf along the bottom edge of a window. EG *...students sitting on the window ledges.*

ledger /lɛdʒə/, **ledgers**. A **ledger** is a book in N COUNT which a company or organization writes down the amounts of money it spends and receives.

leek /liːk/, **leeks**. A **leek** is a long thin vegetable N COUNT which is white at one end and has long green leaves.

leer /lɪə/, **leers, leering, leered.** If someone v : OFT+at **leers** at you, they smile in an unpleasant way, usually because they are sexually interested in you. EG *He leaned over and leered at them, saying, 'Good morning, little girls.'* ▸ used as a noun. EG *He* ▸ N COUNT *was staring down with a leer on his face.*

left /lɛft/. **1 Left** is the past tense and past participle of **leave**.

2 If there is a certain amount of something **left** or ADJ PRED **left over**, it remains after the rest has gone or been used. EG *I only had two pounds left... He drained what was left of his drink... We had a bit of time left over.*

3 Left is one of two opposite directions, sides, or N UNCOUNT OR positions. If you are facing north and you turn to N SING the left, you will be facing west. In the word 'to', the 't' is to the left of the 'o'. EG *There was a gate on our left leading into a field... His was the third door to*

Which word on these pages is used in Britain but not in America?

the left. ▶ used as an adverb or an adjective. EG *He* ▶ ADV OR *turned left and began strolling down the street...* ADJ CLASSIF: *She came forward looking neither right nor left...* ATTRIB *In his left hand he clutched a book.*

4 The **Left** is used to refer to the people or groups N COLL: who support socialism rather than capitalism. EG SING, *the*+N *This fear is by no means confined to the extreme left.*

left-hand is used to describe something which is ADJ CLASSIF: on the left side. EG *She noted it down on the left-* ATTRIB *hand side of the page.*

left-handed. Someone who is **left-handed** uses ADJ CLASSIF their left hand rather than their right hand for OR ADV activities such as writing or throwing a ball. EG *...left-handed batsmen... They both play golf left-handed.*

leftist /ˈleftɪst/, **leftists.** **1** Socialists and commun- N COUNT ists are sometimes referred to as **leftists**.

2 People and organizations connected with social- ADJ CLASSIF: ism and communism are sometimes described as ATTRIB **leftist**.

left-luggage office, left-luggage offices. A N COUNT **left-luggage office** is a place in a railway station British or airport where you can pay to leave your luggage for a short period of time.

leftover /ˈleftəʊvə/, **leftovers.** **1** You can refer to N PLURAL food that remains uneaten after a meal as the **leftovers**. EG *The dogs eat the leftovers.*

2 You use **leftover** to describe an amount of ADJ CLASSIF: something that remains after the rest of it has been ATTRIB used. EG *...a bottle of left-over perfume.*

left-wing. 1 Left-wing people have political ideas ADJ QUALIT that are close to socialism or communism. EG *...left-wing journalists.*

2 The **left wing** of a political party consists of the N SING: *the*+N members of it whose beliefs are closer to socialism or communism than those of its other members. EG *...the left wing of the Labour Party.*

left-winger, left-wingers. A **left-winger** is a N COUNT person whose political beliefs are close to social- ism or communism, or closer to them than most of the other people in the same group or party.

leg /leg/, **legs. 1** Your **legs** are the two long parts N COUNT of your body that are connected to your hips and have your feet at the end of them. See picture at THE HUMAN BODY.

2 The **legs** of an animal, bird, or insect are the thin N COUNT parts of its body that it uses to stand on or to move across the ground. EG *...creatures with short legs and long tails.*

3 The **legs** of a pair of trousers are the parts that N COUNT cover your legs.

4 A **leg** of lamb or pork is a piece of meat that N COUNT+SUPP consists of the thigh of a sheep, lamb, or pig.

5 The **legs** of a piece of furniture such as a table or N COUNT+SUPP chair are the thin vertical parts that touch the floor and support the furniture's weight.

6 A **leg** of a long journey is one part of it. EG *They* N COUNT *set off on the first leg of their 12,000 mile journey.*

7 Leg is also used in these phrases. **7.1** If you **pull** PHRASES someone's **leg**, you tell them something untrue as a Informal joke. EG *'You're pulling my leg.' – 'No, it's true.'* **7.2** If you say that someone **does not have a leg to stand on**, you mean that what they have done or said cannot be justified or proved. **7.3** If you say that something is **on** its **last legs**, you mean that it is in a very bad condition and will soon fall to pieces or stop working. EG *Most of the houses were on their last legs.*

legacy /ˈlegəsɪ/, **legacies. 1** A **legacy** is money or N COUNT property which you receive after someone has died because they said in their will that you should have it. EG *All I've got is that little legacy my aunt left me. ...a legacy of five thousand pounds.*

2 A **legacy** of an event or period of history is N COUNT+SUPP something that exists after it and as a result of it. EG *These characteristics of British industry are a legacy of pre-war unemployment.*

legal /ˈliːgəl/. **1 Legal** is used to describe things ADJ CLASSIF: that relate to the law. EG *...the British legal system...* ATTRIB *...legal obligations... ...a legal dispute.*

2 An action or situation that is **legal** is allowed by a ADJ CLASSIF law. EG *Capital punishment is legal in many coun-tries.* ◊ **legally.** EG *We are not legally married.* ◊ ADV

legality /lɪˈgælɪtɪ/. If you talk about the **legality** N UNCOUNT of an action or situation, you are talking about +SUPP whether it is legal or not. EG *He disputed the legality of the invasion.*

legalize /ˈliːgəlaɪz/, **legalizes, legalizing, legal-ized;** also spelled **legalise.** If an action or situation **is legalized**, a law is V+O passed that makes it legal. EG *The government had finally legalized trade unions.*

legend /ˈledʒənd/, **legends. 1** A **legend** is a very N COUNT OR old story that may be based on real events. EG *The* N UNCOUNT *original inhabitants, according to legend, were blacksmiths.*

2 If you refer to someone as a **legend**, you mean N COUNT that they are very famous and admired. EG *Brook has become something of a legend.*

legendary /ˈledʒəndərɪ/. A **legendary** person or ADJ CLASSIF thing is **1** very famous. EG *...one of his many legendary acts of courage.* **2** described in an old legend. EG *...the legendary king.*

legible /ˈledʒəbəl/. If a piece of writing is **legible**, ADJ QUALIT it is written or printed clearly enough to be read. EG *...a crumpled but still legible document.*

legion /ˈliːdʒən/, **legions. 1** A **legion** of people is a N COUNT large number of them. EG *...legions of foreign* OR N PART visitors.

2 If you say that things of a particular kind are ADJ PRED **legion**, you mean that there are a great number of Formal them. EG *Stories about him are legion.*

legislate /ˈledʒɪsleɪt/, **legislates, legislating,** V **legislated.** When a government or state **legis-** Formal **lates**, it passes a new law. EG *Parliament must eventually legislate against fox-hunting.*

legislation /ˌledʒɪsˈleɪʃən/ consists of a law or N UNCOUNT laws passed by a government or state. EG *...tax* +SUPP *legislation... ...the introduction of legislation to gov-ern industrial relations.*

legislative /ˈledʒɪslətɪv/ means involving or relat- ADJ CLASSIF ing to the process of making and passing laws. EG ATTRIB *The Government should consider further legisla-* Formal *tive reforms... ...a legislative assembly.*

legislator /ˈledʒɪsleɪtə/, **legislators.** A **legislator** N COUNT is a person who is involved in making or passing Formal laws. EG *Many of the legislators who drafted the bill are landowners.*

legislature /ˈledʒɪslətʃə/, **legislatures.** The **leg-** N COUNT: **islature** of a state or country is the group of USU *the*+N people there who have the power to make and pass Formal laws.

legitimate /lɪˈdʒɪtɪmət/. Something that is **legiti-mate** is **1** reasonable and acceptable. EG *Religious* ADJ CLASSIF *leaders have a legitimate reason to be concerned.* ◊ **legitimacy** /lɪˈdʒɪtɪməsɪ/. EG *...the legitimacy of* ◊ N UNCOUNT *our complaint.* **2** allowed or justified by law. EG *...a* ADJ CLASSIF *legitimate business transaction.* ◊ **legitimacy.** ◊ N UNCOUNT *They challenge the very legitimacy of the govern-ment.*

leisure /ˈleʒə/. **1 Leisure** is time when you are not N UNCOUNT working and can do things that you enjoy doing. EG *Not everybody wants more leisure.*

2 If someone does something **at leisure** or **at** their PHRASE **leisure**, they do it slowly, taking as much time as they want. EG *Now I can read at leisure.*

leisurely /ˈleʒəlɪ/. A **leisurely** action is done in a ADJ QUALIT relaxed way without hurrying. EG *My wife went off for a leisurely walk round the gardens.* ▶ used as ▶ ADV an adverb. EG *He strolled leisurely away from the bar.*

lemon /ˈlemən/, **lemons. 1** A **lemon** is a bright N COUNT OR yellow fruit with sour juice. EG *...slices of lemon.* N UNCOUNT

2 Lemon is a drink that tastes of lemons. EG *...a* N UNCOUNT *glass of lemon.*

lemonade /lɛmɔneɪd/ is a colourless, sweet, fizzy N UNCOUNT drink.

lend /lɛnd/, **lends, lending, lent** /lɛnt/. **1** If you V+O+O **lend** someone money or **lend** them something that OR V+O+*to* you own, you allow them to have it or use it for a period of time. EG *I had to lend him a pound... She was reading a book I had lent her... ...lending money to Poland.*

2 If you **lend** your support to a person or group, V+O+*to,* you support them. EG *He was there lending advice* V+O+O, *and support.* OR V+O

3 If something **lends** a particular quality to some- V+O+O thing else, it gives it that quality. EG *Tradition lends* OR V+O+O *order to the world... It would lend credibility to her arguments.*

4 If something **lends** itself to being dealt with or V-REFL+*to* considered in a particular way, it is easy to deal with it or consider it in that way. EG *...problems which do not lend themselves to simple solutions... This model lends itself to the process of duplication.*

5 If you **lend** someone **a hand**, you help them. EG PHRASE *You may have to lend a hand with the training.*

length /lɛŋkθ/, **lengths. 1** The **length** of some- N UNCOUNT thing is the amount that it measures from one end OR N COUNT to the other. EG *It grows to a length of three or four* +SUPP *metres... The snake was a metre and a half in length.*

2 If something happens or exists along the **length** N SING : of something, it happens or exists for the whole *the*+N+*of* way along it. EG *They travelled the length of the island... ...looking down the length of the boulevard.*

3 If you say that something happens throughout PHRASE **the length and breadth** of a country, you are Literary emphasizing that it happens everywhere in it.

4 If you swim a **length** in a swimming pool, you N COUNT swim from one end to the other.

5 A **length** of wood, string, cloth, or other material N COUNT+SUPP is a long piece of it. EG *...a length of rope... ...a short length of steel chain.*

6 The **length** of an event, activity, or situation is N UNCOUNT the amount of time for which it lasts. EG *The length* OR N COUNT *of the visit depends on you... It is foolish to expect* +SUPP *to be happy for any length of time.*

7 The **length** of something is also its quality of N UNCOUNT being long. EG *I hope the length of this letter will make up for my not having written earlier.*

8 If someone does something **at length, 8.1** they PHRASE do it after a long interval or period of time. EG Written *There was another silence. At length Claire said, 'You mean you're not going?' 8.2* they do it for a long time. EG *He spoke at some length about the press... He studied the pictures at length.*

9 If someone **goes to great lengths** to achieve PHRASE something, they try very hard and perhaps do extreme things in order to achieve it. EG *He was willing to go to great lengths to avoid admitting his error... They will go to considerable lengths to buy petrol.*

lengthen /lɛŋkθən/, **lengthens, lengthening,** V-ERG **lengthened.** When something **lengthens** or is **lengthened**, it becomes longer. EG *The waiting lists are lengthening... The money has been spent on lengthening the runway.*

lengthy /lɛŋkθiː/, **lengthier, lengthiest.** Some- ADJ QUALIT thing that is **lengthy** lasts for a long time. EG *This is a lengthy process for the patient... ...lengthy explanations... ...a lengthy wait at the airport.*

lenient /liːnɪənt/. When someone in authority is ADJ QUALIT **lenient**, they are not as strict or as severe as expected. EG *Fines were low and magistrates often too lenient.* ◊ **leniently.** EG *Offenders had been* ◊ ADV *treated leniently by the judge.*

lens /lɛnz/, **lenses.** A **lens** is a thin, curved piece N COUNT of glass or plastic which is part of something such as a camera, telescope, or pair of glasses. When you look through a lens, things appear clearer, larger, or smaller. See picture at CAMERAS. ● See also **contact lens**.

lent /lɛnt/. **1 Lent** is the past tense and past participle of **lend**.

2 In the Christian calendar, **Lent** is the period of N UNCOUNT forty days before Easter, during which some Christians give up something that they enjoy.

lentil /lɛntɪl/, **lentils. Lentils** are dried seeds N COUNT : taken from a lentil plant which are cooked and USU PLURAL eaten.

leopard /lɛpəd/, **leopards.** A **leopard** is an ani- N COUNT mal that looks like a large cat with yellow fur and black spots. Leopards live in Africa and Asia.

leotard /liːɔtɑːd/, **leotards.** A **leotard** is a tight- N COUNT fitting piece of clothing that some people wear when they practise dancing or do exercises.

leper /lɛpə/, **lepers.** A **leper** is a person who has N COUNT leprosy. EG *...a leper hospital.*

leprosy /lɛprɔsiː/ is a serious infectious disease N UNCOUNT that damages people's skin and flesh.

lesbian /lɛzbɪən/, **lesbians.** A **lesbian** is a homo- N COUNT sexual woman. ▸ used as an adjective. EG *...lesbian* ▸ ADJ CLASSIF *activities.*

less /lɛs/. **1 Less** means **1.1** not as much in QUANTIF amount or degree as before or as something else. EG *A shower uses less water than a bath... We had less than three miles to go... Sixty per cent of them are aged 20 or less... With practice it becomes less of an effort.* **1.2** not having as much of a quality as SUBMOD before or as something else. EG *From this time on, I felt less guilty... Fires occurred less frequently outside this area... ...the less developed countries.*

2 If you do something **less** than before or **less** than ADV : COMPAR someone else, you do it to a smaller extent or not as often. EG *You probably use them less than I do... The more I hear about him, the less I like him.*

3 You use **less and less** to say that something is PHRASE becoming smaller all the time in degree or amount. EG *He found them less and less interesting... There is less and less freedom for children... They had less and less to talk about.*

4 You use **less than** to say that something does not PHRASE have a particular quality. For example, if you say that something is **less than** perfect, you are emphasizing that it is not perfect. EG *It would have been less than fair.*

5 You can use **no less** as an emphatic way of ADV SEN expressing surprise or admiration at the importance of someone or something. EG *...the President of the United States, no less.*

6 You can use **no less than** before an amount to PHRASE indicate that you think the amount is surprisingly large. Some people consider that it is incorrect to use 'no less than' when referring to a number of things rather than to an amount of something. EG *By 1880, there were no less than fifty-six coal mines... ...no less than 40 per cent of the material.*

7 Less also means the same as minus. EG *He earns £200 a week, less tax.*

8 more or less: see **more**. ● See also **lesser**.

-less is added to nouns in order to form adjectives SUFFIX that describe something or someone as not having the thing that the noun refers to. EG *...meaningless sounds... ...landless peasants.*

lessen /lɛsən/, **lessens, lessening, lessened.** If V-ERG something **lessens** or is **lessened**, it becomes smaller in amount or degree. EG *Separating the sick from the healthy lessens the risk of infection... Their financial hardship has lessened.* ◊ **lessening.** EG *...a lessening of his power... ...less-* ◊ N UNCOUNT *ening of taxation.* +SUPP

lesser /lɛsə/ is used to indicate that something is ADJ CLASSIF : smaller in degree, importance, or amount than COMPAR something else that is mentioned. EG *These customs are common in Czechoslovakia and to a lesser extent in Hungary and Romania... ...charges of attempted murder and lesser crimes.*

If the rain lets up, does it lessen?

lesson /lɛsən/, **lessons.** 1 A **lesson** is a short period of time during which people are taught about a particular subject or taught how to do something. EG ...*tennis lessons*... ...*a history lesson.* N COUNT

2 If an experience teaches you a **lesson**, it makes you realize the truth or realize what should be done. EG *The lesson of that bizarre episode is that Mr Smith is not to be trusted... This is a lesson that every generation has to learn.* N COUNT

3 If you **teach** someone a **lesson**, you punish them for something that they have done in order to make sure that they do not do it again. PHRASE

lest /lɛst/. If you do something **lest** something unpleasant should happen, you do it to try to prevent the unpleasant thing from happening. EG *I had to grab the iron rail at my side lest I slipped off.* CONJ Formal

let /lɛt/, **lets, letting.** The form **let** is used in the present tense and is the past tense and past participle of the verb.

1 If you **let** something happen, you allow it to happen without doing anything to stop it. EG *People here sit back and let everyone else do the work... She kept lifting handfuls of sand and letting it pour through her fingers.* V+O: USU+INF, NO PASS

2 If you **let** someone do something, you give them your permission to do it. EG *My parents wouldn't let me go out with boys.* V+O: USU+INF, NO PASS

3 If you **let** someone in, out, or through, you allow them to go there, for example by opening a door or moving out of the way. EG *'I rang the bell,' Rudolph said, 'and your friend let me in.'... I asked him to stop the car and let me out.* V+O+A

4 You can use **let me** in discussions before saying something. EG *Richard, let me start by asking you, what is the Institute's main aim?* PHRASE

5 You use **let's** or **let us** when you are making a suggestion about what you and the people you are talking to should do. EG *Let's go... Let's wait for Guy... Let us give her one more chance.* PHRASE

6 If you say **let** someone do something, **6.1** you are saying that you think they should do it. EG *If she insists on going so early, let her take a taxi.* **6.2** you mean that you do not care if they do it. EG *Let them think what they want.* V+O+INF: ONLY IMPER

7 If you **let go** of someone or something, you stop holding them. EG *Let go of me... They let go of the chains and stumbled to their feet.* PHRASE

8 If you **let** a person or animal **go**, you allow them to leave or to escape. PHRASE

9 If you say that something is not the case, **let alone** something else, you mean that since the first thing is not the case, the second thing cannot be, because it is more difficult or unusual. EG *I had never seen him, let alone spoken to him... The story was not worth reading, let alone filming.* PHRASE

10 If you **let** your house or land to someone, you allow them to use it in exchange for regular payments. EG *The cottage was let to an actress.* V+O

let down. 1 If you **let** someone **down**, you disappoint them, usually by not doing something that you said you would do. EG *They felt strongly that the school system had let them down.* ● See also **letdown.** 2 If you **let down** something filled with air, such as a tyre, you allow air to escape from it. PHRASAL VB: V+O+ADV

let in. If something **lets in** water or air, it has a hole or crack which allows the water or air to get into it. EG *My old boots had been letting in water.* PHRASAL VB: V+O+ADV

let in for. If you wonder what you have **let** yourself **in for**, you think that you may be getting involved in something difficult or unpleasant. EG *What have we let ourselves in for?* PHRASAL VB: V+O+ADV+ PREP Informal

let in on or **let into.** If you **let** someone **in on** a secret or **let** someone **into** a secret, you tell it to them. EG *He didn't want to let Uncle Harold in on the news just yet.* PHRASAL VB: V+O+ADV+ PREP, OR V+O+PREP

let off. 1 If you **let** someone **off** a duty or task, you say that they do not have to do it. EG *We have* PHRASAL VB: V +O+ADV/PREP

been let off our homework because of the concert.

2 If you **let** someone **off**, you give them no punishment, or a less severe punishment than they expect. EG *He let me off with a reprimand.* 3 If you **let off** a gun or a bomb, you fire the gun or cause the bomb to explode. V+O+ADV

let on. If you do not **let on** about something secret, you do not tell anyone about it. EG *Don't let on we went to that dance.* PHRASAL VB: V+ADV, WITH BROAD NEG

let out. 1 If you **let** water, air, or breath out, you allow it to come out freely. EG *He let the water out and refilled the bath... Piggy let out his breath with a gasp.* 2 If you **let out** a sound, you make that sound. EG *She let out a terrible shriek.* PHRASAL VB: V+O+ADV

let up. If something **lets up**, it stops or becomes less. EG *Day followed day and still the heat did not let up.* ● See also **let-up.** PHRASAL VB: V+ADV

letdown /lɛtdaʊn/, **letdowns.** If you say that something is a **letdown**, you mean that it is disappointing. EG *For the visitor expecting something special, this is rather a let-down.* N COUNT: USU a+N Informal

lethal /liːθəl/. Something that is **lethal** can kill people or animals. EG *The chemical is lethal to rats but safe for cattle... ...a lethal weapon.* ADJ QUALIT

lethargic /lɪˈθɑːdʒɪk/. Someone who is **lethargic** has no energy or enthusiasm. EG *I often feel tired and lethargic.* ◊ **lethargy** /lɛθədʒɪ/. EG *He was determined to shake them out of their lethargy.* ADJ QUALIT Formal ◊ N UNCOUNT

let's /lɛts/ is the usual spoken form of 'let us'.

letter /lɛtə/, **letters.** 1 When you write a **letter**, you write a message on paper and then send it to someone. EG *She wrote a letter to Harold... Peter received a letter from his wife... They informed Victor by letter.* N COUNT OR by+N

2 **Letters** are written symbols which represent the sounds of a language. N COUNT

letterbox /lɛtəbɒks/, **letterboxes.** A **letterbox** is 1 a rectangular hole in a door through which letters are delivered. 2 a large metal container in the street into which you post letters. N COUNT

lettering /lɛtərɪŋ/ is writing in which the letters are not joined to each other. EG *Underneath it, in smaller lettering, was a name.* N UNCOUNT +SUPP

lettuce /lɛtɪs/, **lettuces.** A **lettuce** is a plant with large green leaves that you eat in salads. N COUNT OR N UNCOUNT

let-up, let-ups. If there is a **let-up** of something, there is less of it. EG *There was a noticeable let-up of violence.* N UNCOUNT OR N COUNT

leukaemia /luːˈkiːmɪə/; also spelled **leukemia.** **Leukaemia** is a disease of the blood, which can kill people. N UNCOUNT

level /lɛvəl/, **levels, levelling, levelled;** spelled **leveling** and **leveled** in American English.

1 A **level** is a point on a scale, for example a scale of amount, importance, or difficulty. EG *Mammals maintain their body temperature at a constant level... ...a high level of unemployment... ...an intermediate level English course.* N COUNT+SUPP

2 The **level** of a lake or river, or the **level** of a liquid in a container, is the height of its surface. EG *The level of the lake continues to rise... Check the oil level and tyre pressure of your car regularly.* ● See also **sea level.** N SING: the+N

3 If one thing is at the **level** of another thing, it is at the same height as the other thing. EG *He had a pile of books which reached to the level of his chin.* N SING+SUPP

4 If one thing is **level** with another thing, it is at the same height as the other thing. EG *He had his hands in front of him, level with his chest.* ADJ PRED: OFT+with

5 If something such as trade stays **level** with something else, it gets larger or smaller at the same rate as the other thing. EG *Food production is going to keep level with population growth.* ADJ PRED: OFT+with

6 If you are going somewhere and you draw **level** with someone, you get closer to them until you are at their side. EG *Coming towards me was a man and when we drew level, I smiled.* ADV AFTER VB

7 Something that is **level** is completely flat, with no ADJ QUALIT

part higher than any other. EG *The floor is quite level.*

8 If you **level** an area of land, you make it flat. EG V+O *...gardeners digging and levelling the ground.*

9 If people **level** something such as a building or a wood, they knock it down completely so that there is nothing left. EG *Specially built tractors levelled more than 1,000 acres of forest.*   V+O

10 If you **level** a criticism or accusation at or against someone, you criticize or accuse them. EG *...criticisms he has levelled against gangsters... Serious charges were levelled at television during the sixties.*   V+O+at/ against

level off or **level out.** **1** If something **levels off** or **levels out**, it stops increasing or decreasing. EG *Economic growth was starting to level off.* **2** When an aircraft **levels off** or **levels out**, it travels horizontally after it has been travelling upwards or downwards. EG *The plane levelled off at 35,000 feet.*   PHRASAL VB : V+ADV

level crossing, level crossings. A **level crossing** is a place where a railway line crosses a road at the same level.   N COUNT British

level-headed. Someone who is **level-headed** can act calmly in difficult situations.   ADJ QUALIT

lever /liːvəˈ/, **levers.** **1** A **lever** is **1.1** a handle or bar that you pull or push in order to operate a piece of machinery. EG *Howard pushes the gear lever in.* **1.2** a bar, one end of which is placed under a heavy object so that when you press down on the other end you can move the object. EG *There was nothing rigid to serve as a lever.*   N COUNT

2 A **lever** is also something that you can use as a means of getting someone to do something. EG *Industrial action may be threatened as a political lever.*   N COUNT : USU+SUPP

leverage /liːvəˈrɪdʒ/ is **1** the ability to influence people. EG *Relatively small groups can exert immense political leverage.* **2** the force that is applied to an object when a lever is used.   N UNCOUNT : USU+SUPP

levity /levɪˈtiː/ is behaviour in which someone treats serious matters in a light-hearted way. EG *I've been appalled by the levity with which some politicians discuss this issue.*   N UNCOUNT Formal

levy /leviː/, **levies, levying, levied.** **1** A **levy** is a sum of money that you have to pay, for example as a tax to the government.   N COUNT

2 When a government or organization **levies** a tax or other sum of money, it demands it from people.   V+O

liability /laɪəbɪlˈɪtiː/, **liabilities.** **1** If you say that someone or something is a **liability**, you mean that they cause a lot of problems or embarrassment. EG *Colley was an asset in the drawing room but a liability on any battlefield.*   N COUNT

2 A company's **liabilities** are the sums of money which it owes. EG *The company has had to undertake heavy liabilities.*   N COUNT : USU PLURAL Technical

3 If you have **liability** for something such as a debt or an accident, you are legally responsible for it.   N UNCOUNT Legal

liable /laɪəbˈl/. **1** Something that is **liable** to happen is very likely to happen. EG *I feel that the play is liable to give offence to many people.*   ADJ PRED +to-INF

2 If people or things are **liable** to something, they are likely to experience it or do it. EG *I was liable to sea-sickness... ...an improved design which is less liable to error.*   ADJ PRED+to Formal

3 If you are **liable** for something such as a debt, you are legally responsible for it.   ADJ PRED : OFT+for

liaise /liːˈeɪz/, **liaises, liaising, liaised.** When organizations or people **liaise** with each other, they work together and keep each other fully informed. EG *Members can help by liaising with the press.*   V+with/ between

liaison /liːˈeɪzɒn/, **liaisons.** **1** Liaison is cooperation and the exchange of information between different organizations or between different sections of an organization. EG *...liaison between the army and the government... ...a need to maintain liaison with local organizations with similar objectives.*   N UNCOUNT

2 A **liaison** is a sexual relationship which is regarded as immoral. EG *The security services had discovered his liaison with Miss Keeler.*   N COUNT Formal

liar /laɪəˈ/, **liars.** A **liar** is someone who tells lies. EG *You're a liar... He called me a liar.*   N COUNT

libel /laɪbˈl/, **libels.** Libel or a **libel** is something written which wrongly accuses someone of something, and which is therefore against the law. EG *Hinds brought an action for libel against him... This was a gigantic libel.*   N UNCOUNT OR N COUNT

libellous /laɪbˈləs/; spelled **libelous** in American English. If something written is **libellous**, it wrongly accuses someone of something, and is therefore against the law. EG *...libellous comments... We must be careful not to say anything libellous.*   ADJ QUALIT

liberal /lɪbˈrəl/, **liberals.** **1** Someone who is **liberal** is tolerant of different kinds of behaviour or opinions. EG *My school was traditional, but more liberal than other public schools... ...a liberal democracy.* ▶ used as a noun. EG *...a pair of enlightened liberals.*   ADJ QUALIT ▶ N COUNT

2 Liberal also means giving, using, or taking a lot of something. EG *Could any man make a more liberal offer?... ...a liberal provision of guns.*   ADJ QUALIT

◊ **liberally.** EG *Tim helped himself liberally to some more wine.*   ◊ ADV

liberalism /lɪbˈrəlɪzəm/ is the belief that people should have a lot of political freedom.   N UNCOUNT

liberalize /lɪbˈrəlaɪz/, **liberalizes, liberalizing,** also spelled **liberalise.** When a country or government **liberalizes** its laws or its attitudes, it makes them less strict and allows people more freedom. EG *There was a move to liberalize the state abortion laws.* ◊ **liberalization** /lɪbˈrəlaɪzeɪʃˈn/. EG *He called for the liberalization of the laws relating to immigration.*   V+O OR V   ◊ N UNCOUNT

liberate /lɪbˈreɪt/, **liberates, liberating, liberated.** **1** To **liberate** someone means to help them to achieve a freer and happier way of life. EG *He claimed that socialism alone could liberate black people... ...liberating people from poverty.* ◊ **liberation** /lɪbˈreɪʃˈn/. EG *...the women's liberation movement.*   V+O : OFT+from Formal   ◊ N UNCOUNT

2 If prisoners **are liberated**, they are released from prison.   V+O Formal

3 To **liberate** a place means to free it from the political or military control of another country. EG *...the hero who liberated Cuba.* ◊ **liberation.** EG *...wars of national liberation.*   V+O Formal   ◊ N UNCOUNT

liberated /lɪbˈreɪtɪd/. You say that people are **liberated** when they do not accept all the ideas and ways of behaviour which are traditional in their society. EG *...a liberated couple.*   ADJ QUALIT

libertarian /lɪbˈteəˈrɪən/, **libertarians.** Someone who is **libertarian** believes in the idea of people being free to think and behave in the way that they want. ▶ used as a noun. EG *Education is a topic in which libertarians have taken a close interest.*   ADJ CLASSIF Formal   ▶ N COUNT

liberty /lɪbˈtiː/, **liberties.** **1 Liberty** is **1.1** the freedom to live your life in the way that you want, especially without a lot of interference from the government. EG *...respect for individual liberty... ...increasing attacks on their liberties.* **1.2** the freedom to go wherever you want, which you lose when you are a prisoner. EG *...that fundamental aspect of imprisonment, the loss of liberty.*   N UNCOUNT OR N PLURAL Formal   N UNCOUNT Formal

2 A criminal who is **at liberty** has not yet been caught, or has escaped from prison. EG *Only one important figure remains at liberty.*   PHRASE Formal

3 If you are not **at liberty** to do something, you have not been given permission to do it.   PHRASE Formal

4 You say that someone **is taking a liberty** when they do or say something that involves another person without asking the person's permission first. EG *I took the liberty of looking you up in the*

> Which word on these pages has two different plurals?

phone book... He was not the sort of man with whom one took liberties.

librarian /laɪbreəriən/, **librarians.** A **librarian** N COUNT is a person who is in charge of a library or who has been trained to do responsible work in a library.

library /laɪbrərɪ¹/, **libraries. 1** A **library** is an N COUNT institution or a part of an institution that keeps books and newspapers for people to read. Most libraries allow their members to borrow books for certain periods of time. EG *... public libraries... ...a library book... ...a new extension to the library.*

2 A **library** is also a private collection of books or N COUNT : gramophone records. USU+SUPP

libretto /lɪbretəʊ/, **librettos** or **libretti.** The **li-** N COUNT **bretto** of an opera or musical play is the words that are sung and spoken in it.

lice /laɪs/ is the plural of **louse.**

licence /laɪsəns/, **licences;** spelled **license** in American English. **1** A **licence** is an official docu- N COUNT ment which gives you permission to do, use, or own something. EG *...a driving licence... The first page carried the licence number and the full name of the holder.*

2 If someone does something **under licence,** they PHRASE do it by special permission from a government or other authority. EG *Badgers can be killed under licence in those areas.*

3 See also **off-licence.**

license /laɪsəns/, **licenses, licensing, licensed.** V+O If a government or other authority **licenses** a person, organization, or activity, they officially give permission for the person or organization to do something, or for the activity to take place. EG *The Royal College examines and licenses surgeons.*

◊ **licensing.** EG *...a licensing authority... ...licensing* ◊ ADJ CLASSIF : *controls.* ATTRIB

licensed /laɪsənst/. **1** If you are **licensed** to do ADJ CLASSIF something, you have official permission from a government or other authority to do it. EG *These men are licensed to carry firearms... You must be licensed to drive... ...a licensed pilot.*

2 If something that you own or use is **licensed,** you ADJ CLASSIF have official permission to own it or use it. EG *The car is licensed and insured.*

3 If a restaurant or hotel is **licensed,** it has a ADJ CLASSIF licence to sell alcoholic drinks.

licensing hours are the times of the day when a N PLURAL pub is allowed to sell alcoholic drinks. British

licensing laws are the laws which control the N PLURAL selling of alcoholic drinks. British

licentious /laɪsentʊəs/. If you describe a person ADJ QUALIT as **licentious,** you mean that they are very immor- Formal al, especially in their sexual behaviour.

lick /lɪk/, **licks, licking, licked. 1** When you **lick** V+O something, you move your tongue across its sur- face. EG *He licked the last of the egg off his knife... The cat was licking its paw... All I do is lick stamps and address envelopes.* ▸ used as a noun. EG *...a few* ▸ N COUNT *licks and nibbles.*

2 If you **lick** your **lips,** you move your tongue PHRASE across your lips, often when you see food that attracts you. EG *She looked at the plate and licked her lips.*

3 If you **lick** someone, you easily defeat them in a V+O fight or competition. EG *I'm sure you could lick both* Informal *of them.*

4 If you say that someone is **licking** their **wounds,** PHRASE you mean that they are recovering after being defeated or humiliated. EG *She'd rather be left alone to lick her wounds in solitude.*

5 If you **lick** something **into shape,** you improve it PHRASE so that it is ready to be used.

licorice /lɪkərɪs, -ɪʃ/. See **liquorice.**

lid /lɪd/, **lids. 1** A **lid** is the top of a box or other N COUNT container which can be removed or raised when you want to open the container. EG *I lifted the lid... She was opening and closing the lid of her tin.*

2 Your **lids** are the same as your eyelids. EG *She* N COUNT : *looked round from under half-closed lids.* USU PLURAL

lie /laɪ/. The forms **lie, lies, lying, lay** /leɪ/, **lain** /leɪn/ are used for the verb in paragraphs 1 to 6 and for the phrasal verbs. The forms **lie, lies, lying, lied** are used for the verb in paragraph 8. **Lies** is also the plural form of the noun in para- graph 7.

1 If you **are lying** somewhere, you are in a V+A OR V+C horizontal position and are not standing or sitting. EG *Judy was lying flat on the bed... I lay there trying to remember what he looked like... She lay ill for days... Lie on your side.*

2 If an object **lies** in a particular place, it is in a flat V+A OR V+C position in that place. EG *The weapon was found lying in a ditch... ...the folder lying open before him... The coffin lay undisturbed for centuries.*

3 If you say that a place **lies** in a particular V+A position, you mean that it is situated there. EG *The bridge lies beyond the docks... This town lies at the southernmost tip of the island.*

4 If you say that the cause of something or the V+A solution to a problem **lies** somewhere, you are Formal indicating what you think the cause or solution is. EG *The causes of this lie deep in the history of society... Its attraction lay in its simplicity.*

5 If something **lies** ahead or **lies** before you, it is V+A going to happen in the future. EG *Endless hours of pleasure lie before you... ...an unwelcome foretaste of what lay in store.*

6 You can use **lie** to say what position someone is V+C in during a competition. For example, if they **are lying** third, they are third.

7 A **lie** is something that someone says which they N COUNT know is untrue. EG *You're telling lies now.* ● See also **white lie.**

8 If someone **is lying,** they are saying something V OR V+QUOTE which they know is untrue. EG *You lied to me... 'Certainly not,' I lied.*

9 See also **lying.**

lie about or **lie around. 1** If you **lie about** or **lie** PHRASAL VB : **around,** you spend your time relaxing and being V+ADV lazy. EG *We lay around smoking... ...lying about in* Informal *their rooms.* **2** If things are left **lying about** or V+ADV **lying around,** they are left somewhere in an untidy way. EG *The bottles were left lying around overnight.*

lie down. 1 When you **lie down,** you move into a PHRASAL VB : horizontal position, usually in order to rest or sleep. V+ADV EG *He lay down on the couch.* ● See also **lie-down.**

2 If you **take** unfair treatment **lying down,** you PHRASE accept it without complaining or resisting. EG *She* Informal *was never one to take bullying lying down.*

lie with. If the responsibility for something **lies** PHRASAL VB : **with** you, it is your responsibility. EG *Are you* V+PREP *saying that the fault generally lies with the man-* Formal *agement?*

lie-down. If you have a **lie-down,** you lie down on N SING : a+N a bed and rest. Informal

lie-in. If you have a **lie-in,** you stay in bed later N SING : a+N than usual in the morning. EG *The meeting's not* Informal *until ten o'clock, so I can have a lie-in.*

lieutenant, lieutenants; pronounced /leftenənt/ in British English and /luːtenənt/ in American English.

A **lieutenant** is a junior officer in the army or N COUNT navy. EG *...Lieutenant Lawton.*

life /laɪf/, **lives** /laɪvz/. The form **lives** is also the third person singular of the present tense of the verb 'live' and is then pronounced /lɪvz/.

1 Life is **1.1** the quality which people, animals, and N UNCOUNT plants have when they are not dead and which objects and substances do not have. EG *...her last hours of life... How far do we allow a doctor to have power over life and death?* **1.2** things which are N UNCOUNT : alive. EG *Is there life on Jupiter?... ...plant life.* OFT+SUPP

2 Someone's **life** is **2.1** their state of being alive. EG N COUNT : *She had risked her life to save mine... He nearly* USU+POSS *lost his life.* **2.2** the period of time during which they are alive. EG *People spend their lives worrying*

about money... I've never boiled a potato in my life... I've had such a fascinating life.

3 Life is also the events and experiences that happen to people, either generally or in a particular place. EG *Life is probably harder for women... I don't know what you want out of life... Sport has always been a part of university life.* N UNCOUNT

4 If you say that an activity or interest is someone's **life**, you mean that they spend most of their time on it. EG *Fishing was their entire life.* N UNCOUNT +POSS

5 A person or place that is full of **life** is full of activity and excitement. N UNCOUNT

6 The **life** of a machine, object, or substance is the period of time that it lasts for. EG *Underlays double the life of a carpet.* N SING

7 Life is also used in these phrases. **7.1** If someone or something that has become inactive **comes to life**, they become active. EG *Their political movement came to life again.* **7.2** If you **hold on** to something **for dear life**, you hold on very tightly because it is important that you do not let go. EG *I held on to the ledge for dear life.* **7.3 For life** means for the rest of a person's life. EG *If you help me, I'll be your friend for life.* **7.4** If you say that you cannot **understand** or remember something **for the life of you**, you mean that you cannot understand or remember it, however hard you try. EG *I can't for the life of me see why you want them.* **7.5** If you **live** your **own life**, you live in the way that you want to, without other people's advice or interference. EG *She was 18 after all, entitled to live her own life.* **7.6** If you describe a situation as **a matter of life and death**, you mean that someone may die if people do not act immediately. EG *Phone an ambulance. It's a matter of life and death.* **7.7** If someone **takes** a person's **life**, they kill that person. EG *On the eve of his conviction, he took his own life.* **7.8** to **risk life and limb**: see limb. ● See also **way of life**. PHRASES / Informal / Informal / Formal

lifebelt /laɪfbɛlt/, **lifebelts**. A **lifebelt** is a large ring used to keep a person afloat and prevent them from drowning when they fall into the sea or other deep water. N COUNT

lifeboat /laɪfbəʊt/, **lifeboats**. A **lifeboat** is **1** a large boat which is sent out from a port or harbour in order to rescue people who are in danger at sea. **2** a small boat which is carried on a ship and which people on the ship use to escape when the ship is in danger of sinking. N COUNT

lifebuoy /laɪfbɔɪ/, **lifebuoys**. A **lifebuoy** is the same as a lifebelt. N COUNT

life-cycle, **life-cycles**. The **life-cycle** of an animal or plant is the series of changes and developments that it passes through from the beginning of its life until its death. EG *...the life-cycle of the salmon... They complete their life-cycle in a single growing season.* N COUNT : USU + POSS

life expectancy, **life expectancies**. The **life expectancy** of a person, animal, or plant is the length of time that they are normally likely to live. EG *Women have a longer life expectancy than men.* N COUNT OR N UNCOUNT

life form, **life forms**. A **life form** is any living thing such as an animal or plant. EG *Many of the deep-sea life forms feed directly on bacteria.* N COUNT + SUPP

lifeguard /laɪfgɑːd/, **lifeguards**. A **lifeguard** is a person at a beach or swimming pool whose job is to rescue people when they are in danger of drowning. N COUNT

life imprisonment. When criminals are sentenced to **life imprisonment**, they are sentenced to stay in prison for the rest of their lives, although they are usually released after several years. N UNCOUNT

lifejacket /laɪfdʒækət/, **lifejackets**. A **lifejacket** is a sleeveless jacket which you wear in order to stay afloat in the water when you are in danger of drowning. N COUNT

lifeless /laɪflɪs/. **1** A person or animal that is **lifeless** is dead. EG *...the lifeless body of Lieutenant Dowling.* ADJ CLASSIF / Literary

2 You can use **lifeless** to describe machines and objects when you want to emphasize that they are not living things. EG *...a lifeless chunk of rock.* ADJ CLASSIF

3 A **lifeless** place or area does not have anything living or growing there. EG *...a time when the earth was completely lifeless.* ADJ CLASSIF

4 You can also say that people or things are **lifeless** when you find them dull and not lively or exciting. EG *The characters in the novel are lifeless... ...a lifeless voice.* ADJ QUALIT

lifelike /laɪflaɪk/. **1** Something that is **lifelike** has the appearance of being alive. EG *...extremely lifelike computer-controlled robots.* ADJ QUALIT

2 A **lifelike** painting or acting performance is very realistic. ADJ QUALIT

lifeline /laɪflaɪn/, **lifelines**. **1** You refer to something as a **lifeline** when it is very important in helping people to survive, or in helping an activity to continue. EG *The household became my lifeline, my only link with the outside world... ...the oil lifeline of Western Europe.* N COUNT : USU + SUPP

2 A **lifeline** is also a rope which you throw to someone when they are in danger of drowning. N COUNT

lifelong /laɪflɒŋ/ means existing or happening for the whole of a person's life. EG *...her friend and lifelong companion.* ADJ CLASSIF ATTRIB

life science, **life sciences**. The **life sciences** are sciences such as zoology, botany, and anthropology, which are concerned with human beings, animals, and plants. N COUNT : USU PLURAL

life sentence, **life sentences**. When criminals receive a **life sentence**, they are sentenced to stay in prison for the rest of their lives, although they are usually released after several years. N COUNT

life-size. **Life-size** or **life-sized** paintings, sculptures, or models are the same size as the person or thing that they represent. EG *...a life-size inflatable whale... ...a life-size statue.* ADJ CLASSIF

lifespan /laɪfspæn/, **lifespans**. **1** The **lifespan** of a person, animal, or plant is the period of time during which they are alive. EG *...the human lifespan... In our brief life-span we normally experience only a few of these problems.* N COUNT + SUPP

2 The **lifespan** of a product, organization, or idea is the period of time during which it exists or is used. EG *This job had a planned life-span of five years.* N COUNT + SUPP

life style, **life styles**. Your **life style** is the way you live, for example the conditions you live in and the things you normally do. EG *...this highly urban lifestyle... This will affect the life-styles of many people.* N COUNT + SUPP

lifetime /laɪftaɪm/, **lifetimes**. **1** A **lifetime** is the length of time that someone is alive. EG *I have spent a lifetime in politics... I've seen a lot of changes in my lifetime.* N COUNT

2 The **lifetime** of something is the period of time that it lasts. EG *...during the lifetime of this parliament.* N SING + POSS

lift /lɪft/, **lifts**, **lifting**, **lifted**. **1** If you lift something, you move it to another position, usually upwards. EG *He lifted the glass to his mouth... She lifted down the wooden boxes.* V+O : USU+A

2 If you lift a part of your body, you move it to a higher position. EG *He lifted his hand to ring the doorbell... She lifted her feet on to the settee.* V+O

3 If you **lift** your eyes or your head, you look up. EG *She lifted her eyes from the ground and fixed them on me.* V+O / Literary

4 A **lift** is a device like a large box that moves up and down inside a tall building and carries people from one floor to another. EG *I took the lift to the eighth floor.* N COUNT / British

5 If you give someone a **lift**, you take them in your car from one place to another in order to help N COUNT : USU a+N

Find two words on these pages which refer to the same thing.

them. EG *He gave her a lift back to London that night... She offered me a lift home.*

6 When fog or mist **lifts**, it disappears or moves v upwards. EG *Around midday, the fog lifted.*

7 If people in authority **lift** a law or rule that v+o prevents people from doing something, they end it. EG *He lifted the ban on the People's Party.*

8 If you **lift** a piece of writing or music that has v+o: been written by someone else, you copy it and use OFT+*from* it in your own work. EG *Most of the article was lifted from a woman's magazine.*

lift-off, lift-offs. Lift-off or a **lift-off** is the N UNCOUNT launching of a rocket into space. OR N COUNT

ligament /lɪgəmə³nt/, **ligaments.** A **ligament** is N COUNT a band of strong tissue in your body, which connects bones. EG *He had torn a ligament in his knee playing squash.*

light /laɪt/, **lights, lighting, lighted, lit** /lɪt/; **lighter, lightest.** The forms **lighted** and **lit** are both used as the past tense and past participle of the verb, although **lit** is more usual.

1 Light is the brightness that lets you see things, N UNCOUNT and that comes from the sun, the moon, lamps, or fire. EG *We are dependent on the sun for heat and light... By the light of a torch, she began to read.*

2 A **light** is anything that produces light, especially N COUNT an electric bulb. EG *She went into her daughter's room and turned on the light.*

3 A place or object that **is lit** by something has v+o light shining in it or on it. EG *...a room lit by candles.*
◇ **lighted.** EG *He looked up thoughtfully at the* ◇ ADJ CLASSIF: *lighted windows.* ATTRIB

4 If a building or room is **light**, it has a lot of ADJ QUALIT natural light in it, for example because it has large windows.

5 If it is **light**, it is daytime. ADJ PRED

6 If there is a particular **light** in someone's eyes, N SING+SUPP their eyes show a particular emotion. EG *I could see* Literary *a questioning and reproachful light in Jane's eyes.*

7 If you **light** something, you make it start burning. v+o EG *She stopped and lit a match... Light the gas fire if you feel chilly.* ◇ **lighted.** EG *...a lighted candle.* ◇ ADJ CLASSIF

8 If someone asks you for a **light**, they want some N SING:a+N matches or a cigarette lighter in order to start their cigarette burning.

9 If you **set light to** something, you make it start PHRASE burning.

10 Light is also used in these phrases. **10.1** If PHRASES someone **sees the light**, they finally realise or understand something they ought to. **10.2** If a new event or piece of information **throws** or **casts light on** something, it makes it easier to understand. EG *His diaries throw a new light upon certain incidents.* **10.3** If something **comes to light** or **is brought to light**, it becomes known. EG *It has come to light that he was lying.* **10.4** When you talk about **the light at the end of the tunnel**, you are referring to the end of an unpleasant situation, which you are looking forward to. EG *There was no victory in sight, no light at the end of the tunnel.* **10.5 First light** is the time in the early morning Formal when the sun begins to rise. EG *They attacked at first light.* **10.6** If someone **goes out like a light**, Informal they fall asleep or become unconscious very quickly. **10.7 green light:** see **green**.

11 If you see something in a particular **light**, you N SING+SUPP think about it in that way. EG *We were now seeing things in a different light... He appeared that day in the worst possible light.*

12 In the light of something means considering it PHRASE or taking it into account. EG *This development is significant in the light of what happened later.*

13 Something that is **light 13.1** does not weigh very ADJ QUALIT much. EG *The bag was very light, as though there were nothing in it.* ◇ **lightness.** EG *...the extreme* ◇ N UNCOUNT *lightness of this particular shoe.* **13.2** is not very ADJ QUALIT great in amount, degree, or intensity. EG *A light rain was falling... The traffic on the highway was light that day.*

14 Light colours are very pale. EG *...light blue eyes.* ADJ QUALIT

15 Light work does not involve much physical ADJ QUALIT effort. EG *He has grown much weaker and is now capable of only light work.*

16 Movements and actions that are **light** are ADJ QUALIT graceful or gentle and are done with very little force or effort. EG *She runs up the stairs two at a time with her light graceful step.* ◇ **lightly.** EG *He* ◇ ADV *kissed his wife lightly on the cheek.* ◇ **lightness.** ◇ N UNCOUNT EG *For a heavy man he moves with surprising lightness and speed.*

17 Light books, plays, or pieces of music entertain ADJ QUALIT you without making you think very deeply. EG *...light entertainment and comedy.*

18 If you speak in a **light** way, you sound as if you ADJ QUALIT do not think that what you are saying is important or serious. EG *...a cool, light, insolent voice.* ◇ **lightly.** EG *He said sorry as lightly as possible.* ◇ ADV

19 See also **lighting, lightly.**

light up. 1 If something **lights up** something PHRASAL VB: else, it shines light on all of it. EG *The fire was still* V+O+ADV *blazing, lighting up the sky.* **2** If your face or eyes V+ADV **light up**, you suddenly look very happy. EG *His face lit up at the sight of Cynthia.* **3** If you **light up** a V+O+ADV cigarette or pipe, you start smoking. EG *George lit* OR V+ADV *up and puffed away for a while.*

light bulb, light bulbs. A **light bulb** is the round N COUNT glass part of an electric light or lamp which light shines from.

lighten /laɪtə³n/, **lightens, lightening, light- ened. 1** When something **lightens** or when you V-ERG **lighten** it, it becomes less dark in colour. EG *After the rain stops, the sky lightens a little... Constant exposure to the sun had lightened my hair.*

2 You also say that you **lighten** something when v+o you make it less heavy. EG *They began to lighten their products in an effort to increase sales.*

3 If someone's face or expression **lightens**, it V-ERG becomes more cheerful, happy, and relaxed. EG *Her whole expression lightened.*

lighter /laɪtə/, **lighters. 1** A **lighter** or a **ciga-** N COUNT **rette lighter** is a small device which produces a flame that you can light a cigarette or pipe with. EG *Can I use your lighter?*

2 Lighter is the comparative of **light.**

light-fingered. If you say that someone is **light-** ADJ CLASSIF **fingered**, you mean that they steal things. Informal

light-headed. If you are **light-headed**, you feel ADJ QUALIT rather dizzy and faint.

light-hearted. 1 Someone who is **light-hearted** ADJ QUALIT is cheerful and happy. EG *He was in a light-hearted mood.* ◇ **light-heartedly.** EG *She flirted with them* ◇ ADV *light-heartedly and enjoyed herself enormously.*

2 Something that is **light-hearted** is entertaining ADJ QUALIT or amusing, and not serious. EG *Let me finish with a slightly more light-hearted question.*

lighthouse /laɪthaʊs/, **lighthouses.** A **light-** N COUNT **house** is a tower in or near to the sea which contains a powerful flashing lamp. Lighthouses are used to guide ships or to warn them of danger.

light industry, light industries. Light **indus-** N COUNT OR **try** is industry in which only small items are made, N UNCOUNT for example household goods and clothes.

lighting /laɪtɪŋ/. The **lighting** in a place is the N UNCOUNT way that it is lit, for example by electric lights or candles, or the quality of the light in it. EG *...artificial lighting... ...poorly designed street lighting.*

lightly /laɪtli¹/. If you say that something is not ADV done **lightly**, you mean that it is not done without serious thought. EG *This is not a charge to make lightly against the government... He knew it was not being said lightly.* ● See also **light.**

lightning /laɪtnɪŋ/. **1 Lightning** is the very bright N UNCOUNT flashes of light in the sky that you see during a thunderstorm. EG *...a flash of lightning... He was struck by lightning, and nearly died.*

2 Lightning describes things that happen very ADJ CLASSIF: quickly or last for only a short time. EG *He drew his* ATTRIB *gun with lightning speed.*

lightning conductor, lightning conductors. A   N COUNT
lightning conductor is a long, thin piece of metal   British
that is placed on top of a building and that goes as
far as the ground. It allows lightning to reach the
ground safely without damaging the building.

lightning rod, lightning rods. A **lightning rod**   N COUNT
is the same as a lightning conductor.   American

lightweight /ˈlaɪtweɪt/. Something that is **light-**   ADJ QUALIT
weight weighs less than most other things of the
same type. EG ...a grey lightweight suit... ...light-
weight cameras.

light-year, light-years. 1 A **light-year** is the   N COUNT
distance that light travels in a year.   Technical

2 You can use **light-years** to mean a very long   N COUNT :
time. EG Last Tuesday seemed light-years away   USU PLURAL
already.   Informal

likable /ˈlaɪkəbəl/. See likeable.

like /laɪk/, **likes, liking, liked.** 1 If you say that   PREP
one person or thing is **like** another, you mean that
they have similar characteristics. EG He looked like
Clark Gable... She's very like her younger sister...
She's nothing like I imagined... 'I'm glad you came.'
– 'Yes. It was like old times.'... The lake was like a
bright blue mirror.

2 If you ask someone what something is **like**, you   PREP
are asking them to describe it or to give their
opinion of it. EG What was Essex like?... What did
they taste like?... I don't remember what she was
like.

3 You can use **like** to introduce an example of the   PREP
thing that you have just mentioned. EG You only get
them in big countries, like Africa or India... They
knew very little about home activities like cooking.

4 You can use **like** to say that something is true of   PREP
a particular thing because it is true of all things of
that kind. EG There's no point in stirring up a lot of
publicity about a foolish thing like this.

5 You can use **like** to say that someone or some-   PREP
thing is in the same situation as another person or
thing. EG He, like everybody else, had worried about
it... She died in childbirth, like Sir Thomas More's
wife Jane.

6 If you say that someone is behaving **like** a   PREP
particular person or thing, you mean that what
they are doing is what that person or thing typically does. EG You're behaving like a perfect idiot...
She began to shake like a jelly.

7 If you say **and the like** after mentioning some   PHRASE
things or people, you are indicating that there are
other similar things or people that can be included
in what you are saying. EG ...the activities of ruthless mine owners and the like.

8 You say **'like this', 'like that'**, or **'like so'** when   PHRASE
you are showing someone how something is done.
EG Twist it round and put it on here, like that.

9 You also use **'like this'** or **'like that'** when you   PHRASE
are drawing attention to something that you are
doing or that someone else is doing. EG Stop laughing like that!... Does he often talk like this?

10 If you say that something is **like** you remem-   CONJ
bered it or **like** you imagined it, you mean that it is   Informal
the way you remembered or imagined it. EG Is it
like you remembered it?... It didn't work out quite
like I intended it to.

11 You can sometimes use **nothing like** instead of   PHRASE
'not' when you want to emphasize a negative
statement. EG The cast is nothing like as numerous
as one might suppose... There is nothing like
enough practice given in solving problems.

12 You use **something like** to indicate that a   PHRASE
number or quantity is an estimate, not an exact
figure. EG Something like ninety per cent of the
crop was destroyed.

13 If you **like** something, you find it pleasant or   V+O :
attractive, or you approve of it. EG I like reading...   OFT+-ING
She's a nice girl, I like her... They didn't like what   OR to-INF;
they saw... What is it you like about them?... A   ALSO V+-ING OR
strike is going to take place whether we like it or   to-INF
not... Her folks like her to get in early.

14 If you say that you would **like** something or   V+O,
would **like** to do something, you are expressing a   V+to-INF, OR
wish or desire. EG I'd like to marry him... Would you   V+O+to-INF
like some coffee?... He would have liked a pint of
beer before he started... Do what you like... He can
stay here if he likes... I'd like you to come.

15 You say **if you like** when you are offering to do   ADV SEN
something for someone. EG I'll drive, if you like.

16 See also **liking.**

-like. You can add **-like** to a noun when you want
to describe something as similar to the thing
referred to by the noun. EG The landscape has a
dream-like air... ...a rock-like hump.

likeable /ˈlaɪkəbəl/; also spelled **likable.** If you   ADJ QUALIT
describe someone or something as **likeable**, you
mean that they are pleasant and therefore easy to
like. EG ...a very attractive and likeable young man.

likelihood /ˈlaɪklihʊd/. The **likelihood** of some-   N SING :
thing happening is the fact that it is likely to   USU+of
happen. EG There is every likelihood that she will   OR REPORT
succeed... This increases the likelihood of an attack.

likely /ˈlaɪkli/, **likelier, likeliest.** 1 If something   ADJ QUALIT
is **likely**, it is probably true or will probably
happen. EG What kind of change is likely?... It
seemed hardly likely that they would agree.

2 If you are **likely** to do something, you will   ADJ PRED
probably do it. EG They were not likely to forget it.   + to-INF

3 **Very likely** or **most likely** means probably. EG   ADV SEN
Very likely none of them would know the name.

4 You use **likely** to describe people or things who   ADJ CLASSIF :
will probably be suitable for a particular purpose.   ATTRIB
EG The local committee is always looking out for
likely recruits... ...likely candidates for appeal.

5 If you say to someone that what they have just   PHRASE
told you is **a likely story**, you are saying in a
humorous way that you don't believe it.

like-minded. People who are **like-minded** have   ADJ CLASSIF
similar opinions, ideas, or interests to each other.
EG ...Hubbard and his like-minded colleagues.

liken /ˈlaɪkən/, **likens, likening, likened.** If you   PHRASAL VB :
liken something to something else, you say that it   V+O+PREP
is similar to it in some way. EG It has a mildly nutty
taste which has been likened to new potatoes.

likeness /ˈlaɪknɪs/, **likenesses.** 1 If one thing has   N SING :
a **likeness** to another, it is similar to it in appear-   OFT+to
ance. EG ...a china dog that bore a likeness to his
aunt... The boy's likeness to her son was startling.

2 If you say that a picture of someone is a good   N COUNT :
likeness of them, you mean that it looks very   OFT+of
much like them. EG The portrait shows a lot of
talent. A very good likeness.

likewise /ˈlaɪkwaɪz/. 1 You use **likewise** when   ADV SEN
you are comparing two things and saying that they
are similar. EG In Yugoslavia there was a special
local way of doing it, likewise in Italy.

2 If you do one thing, and someone else **does**   PHRASE
likewise, they do the same thing. EG He is relaxing
and invites them to do likewise.

liking /ˈlaɪkɪŋ/. 1 If you have a **liking** for someone   N SING+SUPP
or something, you like them. EG I took an enormous
liking to Davies the moment I met him... She was
developing a liking for Scotch.

2 If something is **to** your **liking**, you like it. EG   PHRASE
Organising Christmas relief funds was more to his
liking than the routine work on Capitol Hill... Did
they find the temperature to their liking?

3 If something is too big or too fast **for** your **liking**,   PHRASE
you would prefer it to be smaller or slower. EG You
are progressing too fast for his liking.

lilac /ˈlaɪlək/, **lilacs.** 1 A **lilac** is a small tree. It has   N COUNT OR
pleasant-smelling flowers, which are also called   N UNCOUNT
lilac. EG ...lilac bushes in the garden.

2 Something that is **lilac** is pale pinkish-purple in   ADJ COLOUR
colour. EG ...her plain lilac dress.

If something is likely to happen, do you think it will
happen?

Lilo /ˈlaɪləʊ/, **Lilos.** A **Lilo** is a long, flat plastic mattress that you fill with air and use for lying on, for example when you are camping or at the seaside. N COUNT Trademark

lilt /lɪlt/, **lilts.** If you say that someone speaks with a **lilt**, you mean that the pitch of their voice rises and falls in a pleasant way, as if they were singing. EG There was something familiar in the lilt of her voice... ...his Irish lilt. N COUNT

lilting /ˈlɪltɪŋ/. A **lilting** voice or song rises and falls in pitch in a pleasant way. EG The lark sings its lilting song... She spoke to him in her lilting Arabic. ADJ CLASSIF

lily /ˈlɪlɪ/, **lilies.** A **lily** is a plant with large flowers that are often white. The flowers are also called **lilies.** EG She added a wild lily to her bouquet. N COUNT

limb /lɪm/, **limbs. 1** Your **limbs** are your arms and legs. EG He was very tall with long limbs... We cough, yawn, and stretch our limbs. N COUNT

2 The **limbs** of a tree are its branches. EG Thick smoke rose into the tree's upper limbs. N COUNT Literary

3 If you say that someone has gone **out on a limb**, you mean that they have done or said something that is risky or extreme. EG I never heard him go out on a limb like that before. PHRASE

4 If someone **risks life and limb**, they do something very dangerous that may cause them to die or be seriously injured. PHRASE

-limbed is used after an adjective to indicate that a person or animal has limbs of a particular type or appearance. EG The female athlete tends to be longer limbed... ...loose-limbed, well-built kids.

limber /ˈlɪmbə/, **limbers, limbering, limbered.** If you **limber up**, you prepare for a sport by practising or doing exercises. EG We had no time to limber up on the practice range. PHRASAL VB : V+ADV

limbo /ˈlɪmbəʊ/. **1** If you are in **limbo**, you are in a situation where you do not know what will happen next and you have no control over things. EG Refugees may remain in limbo for years. N UNCOUNT

2 The **limbo** is a West Indian dance in which you have to pass under a low bar while leaning backwards. The bar is moved nearer to the floor each time you go under it. N SING : the+N

lime /laɪm/, **limes. 1** A **lime** is **1.1** a small round fruit that has a dark green skin and tastes like a lemon. **1.2** a large tree with pale green leaves which is often planted in parks in towns and cities. EG ...the long avenue of limes. N COUNT

2 Lime or **lime juice** is a non-alcoholic drink that is made from the juice of limes. N UNCOUNT

3 Lime is also **3.1** a chemical substance which you spread onto soil in order to improve its quality. **3.2** a white-coloured rock used for building or for making cement. EG ...a lime quarry. **3.3** a white substance used for painting walls. N UNCOUNT

limelight /ˈlaɪmlaɪt/. If someone is in the **limelight**, a lot of attention is being paid to them, because they are famous or because they have done something very unusual or exciting. EG He was only happy when he was in the limelight. N SING : the+N

limerick /ˈlɪmərɪk/, **limericks.** A **limerick** is a humorous poem which has five lines and a special rhythm and way of rhyming. N COUNT

limestone /ˈlaɪmstəʊn/ is a white-coloured rock which is used for building and making cement. N UNCOUNT

limit /ˈlɪmɪt/, **limits, limiting, limited. 1** A **limit** is the greatest amount, extent, or degree of something that is possible or allowed. EG There is no limit to the risks they are prepared to take... The powers of the human brain are stretched to the limit... ...a motorist exceeding the speed limit. N COUNT : USU+SUPP

2 The **limits** of a situation are the facts involved in it which make only some actions or results possible. EG ...the problems of applying that system within the limits of a weekly, two-hour meeting. N PLURAL

3 If you **limit** something, you do something to ensure that it will not become greater than a particular amount or degree. EG The government V+O

plans to limit military expenditure... Japanese exports would be limited to 1.68m vehicles.

4 If someone or something **limits** you, they reduce the number of things that you can have or do. EG Why should the people of this country limit me that way? ◇ **limiting.** EG Many of these customs were narrow and limiting. V+O / ◇ ADJ QUALIT

5 If you **limit** yourself or **limit** your actions, you deal only with particular things or people. EG Will he limit himself to seeing that the enterprise is approved?... I am limiting my observations to the Christian faith. V+O OR V-REFL : USU+to

6 If something **is limited** to a particular place or group of people, it exists only in that place, or is had or done only by that group. EG This problem is not limited to Sweden. V+O : USU PASS+to

7 If you add **within limits** to a statement, you mean that it applies only to reasonable or normal situations. EG Within limits, the higher the temperature, the quicker the chemical reaction. ADV SEN

8 If a place is **off limits**, you are not allowed to go there. PHRASE

9 You say that someone **is the limit** when you are very annoyed with them. PHRASE Informal

limitation /ˌlɪmɪˈteɪʃən/, **limitations. 1 Limitation** is the control or reduction of something. EG ...the limitation of trade union power... ...arms limitation talks. N UNCOUNT

2 If you talk about the **limitations** of someone or something, you mean that they can only do some things and not others, or that they can only achieve a fairly low degree of success or excellence. EG It's important to know your own limitations... The technique has its limitations. N PLURAL : USU+POSS

3 When there are **limitations** on something, it is not allowed to grow or extend beyond certain limits. EG All limitations on earnings must cease... I am willing to accept certain limitations on my freedom. N COUNT : USU PLURAL

limited /ˈlɪmɪtɪd/. **1** Something that is **limited** is not very large in amount or degree, or not large enough. EG The choice was very limited... ...a painter of limited abilities. ADJ QUALIT

2 A **limited** company is one in which the shareholders are legally responsible for only a part of any money that it may owe to other people or companies, for example if it goes bankrupt. EG The Foundation had become a limited company... ...Hourmont Travel Limited. ADJ CLASSIF British

limitless /ˈlɪmɪtlɪs/. You say that something is **limitless** when it is extremely large in amount or number. EG ...the computer's limitless memory... ...our limitless fascination with toys and games. ADJ CLASSIF Literary

limp /lɪmp/, **limps, limping, limped; limper, limpest. 1** If you **limp**, you walk with difficulty or in an uneven way because one of your legs or feet is hurt. EG He picked up his bag and limped back to the road... Two of the dogs were limping badly. V : OFT+A

▶ used as a noun. EG He walks with a limp... She had a slight limp. ▶ N COUNT : USU SING

2 If someone is **limp**, they have no strength or energy in their body, so that they can be moved easily. EG Her hand felt limp and damp. ◇ **limply.** EG The tiny baby lay limply on her arm. ADJ QUALIT / ◇ ADV

3 Something that is **limp** is soft and not stiff or firm. EG ...a dressing-gown of limp, shiny fabric. ◇ **limply.** EG The rope fell limply to the ground. ADJ QUALIT / ◇ ADV

line /laɪn/, **lines, lining, lined. 1** A **line** is a long, thin mark on a surface, or something that looks long and thin. EG ...a diagonal red line on the label... ...a straight line joining those two points... ...the hard thin line of Lynn's mouth. N COUNT

2 If there are **lines** on someone's face, their face has wrinkles or creases in it. N COUNT : USU PLURAL

3 A **line** of people or things is a number of them positioned one behind another or side by side in a row. EG ...long lines of poplar trees... The men formed themselves into a line. ● See also **picket line.** N COUNT OR N PART

4 A **line** is also **4.1** one of the rows of words or N COUNT symbols in a piece of writing. EG *I have read every line... They sang the next line of the song.* **4.2** a sentence or remark that is said by an actor in a play or film. EG *She found it impossible to remember her lines.*

5 You can refer to a long piece of string or wire as N COUNT: a **line** when it is being used for a particular USU+SUPP purpose. EG *...washing hanging on a line... The fish was heavy at the end of my line... ...a fallen power line... ...a telephone line.*

6 Line is also used to refer to a route, for example: **6.1** a particular route along which something N COUNT moves. EG *Wireless waves travel in straight lines.* **6.2** a route along which people move or send N COUNT: messages or supplies. EG *All lines of communication* USU PLURAL *had been cut... ...the supply lines to enemy forma-* +SUPP *tions.* **6.3** a railway track. EG *...repairs to the line* N COUNT *beyond Tring.* **6.4** a particular route along which a N COUNT train, coach, or bus service regularly operates. EG *They took the wrong line on the London Tube.*

7 You can use **line** to refer to **7.1** the edge, outline, N COUNT+SUPP or shape of something. EG *...the firm, delicate lines of Paxton's buildings... ...a superb line from nose to brow, a real conqueror's face.* **7.2** the boundary between areas occupied by enemy armies during a war. EG *They were dropped by parachute behind enemy lines.* ● See also **front line**.

8 The **line** between two classes or types of people N COUNT+SUPP or things is the point at which they are divided or considered different. EG *The traditional social dividing lines are becoming blurred... She will be living below the poverty line.*

9 A particular **line** of research or argument, for N COUNT+SUPP example, is a particular series or type of thing that is done or said. EG *...his particular line of research... ...future lines of development.*

10 The **line** that someone takes on a problem or N COUNT+SUPP topic is their attitude or policy towards it. EG *...the official line of the Labour Party... The President takes a much harder line.*

11 Your **line** of business or work is the kind of N SING+POSS work that you do. EG *A man in my line of business has to take precautions... Well, it's not my line, really, is it?*

12 A particular **line** is also a particular type of N COUNT product that a company makes or sells. EG *Unprofitable lines will be discontinued.*

13 A particular **line** of people or things is a series N SING+SUPP of similar people or things that existed one after another. EG *...the long line of American Presidents.*

14 If people or things **line** a road or room, they are V+O present in large numbers along its edges or sides. EG *The streets were lined with cars... Trophies lined the walls of her bedroom.*

15 If you **line** a container or a piece of clothing, V+O: you put a layer of something such as paper or cloth OFT+*with* on the inside surface of it. EG *Line the cupboards and drawers with paper... ...a coffin lined with velvet... ...a pair of thick fur-lined boots.*

16 If something **lines** a container or an area inside V+O a person, animal, or plant, it forms a layer on the inside surface. EG *...tiny hairs lining the nose.*

17 Line is used after 'in' in these phrases. **17.1** PHRASES When people or cars are **in line**, they are in a row one behind another, waiting for something. EG *We had to wait in line at the counter.* **17.2** If you are in **line for** something, you are likely to get it. EG *You are next in line for promotion.* **17.3** If one thing is **in line** with another, the two things are next to each other or form part of a straight row. EG *She shifted her chair to bring it in line with her neighbours.* **17.4** If one person or group is **in line** with others, it is doing the same thing as the others. EG *Africa may bring itself in line with the rest of the world on this matter.* **17.5** If something is done **in line** with a policy, guideline, or standard, it is done following that policy, guideline, or standard. **17.6** If you keep someone **in line**, you make them behave

in the way that they are supposed to. **17.7** You can use **line** to say what sort of thing you are referring to. For example, something **in the** sports **line** means something connected with sports. EG *Call me if anything in the electrical line has to be done.*

18 Line is used after 'on' in these phrases. **18.1** If PHRASES you are **on line** when using a large computer, you type on a keyboard with a screen directly into the computer. **18.2** If your job, career, or reputation is **on the line**, you may lose it or harm it as a result of doing something brave or foolish. EG *I didn't dare fight and put my job on the line, so I went along with them.*

19 Line is also used in these phrases. **19.1** If you PHRASES **draw the line** at a particular activity, you refuse to do it, because it is more than you are prepared to do. EG *There is a point at which they will have to draw the line.* **19.2** If something happens somewhere **along the line**, it happens during a process or activity. EG *We slipped up somewhere along the line... He had fought us all along the line.* **19.3** If something happens **on** or **along** particular **lines**, it happens in that way. EG *The population is split along religious lines... He thinks along the same lines as you.* **19.4** You use the phrases **on the lines of** and **along the lines of** when you are giving a general description of what someone has said or of what you want. EG *Driberg opened with a question on the lines of: 'What do you think about the present political situation?'* **19.5** If someone is **on the right lines**, they are thinking or acting in a way that is sensible or likely to produce useful results. EG *Do his policies strike you as being on the right lines?* **19.6** If someone is **out of line** or **steps out of line**, they do not behave in the way that they are supposed to. **19.7** to **drop** someone a **line**: see **drop**. ● to **read between the lines**: see **read**. ● See also **lined, lining, hard line, hot line, party line**.

line up. 1 If people **line up** or if you **line** them PHRASAL VB: **up**, they stand in a row or form a queue. EG *They* V-ERG+ADV *lined us up and marched us off.* **2** If something **is** V+ADV+O: **lined up** for someone, it is arranged for them. EG *A* OFT PASS *formal farewell party was lined up.* **3** See also **line-up**.

linear /lɪniˈə/. **1** A **linear** process is one in which ADJ CLASSIF something progresses straight from one stage to Formal another. EG *...linear thinking... ...events occurring simultaneously rather than in a linear sequence.* **2** A **linear** shape or form consists of lines, especial- ADJ CLASSIF ly straight lines. Formal **3 Linear** movement is movement in a straight ADJ CLASSIF line. EG *...turning linear motion into rotary motion.* Formal

lined /laɪnd/. **1** If someone's face or skin is **lined**, ADJ QUALIT it has wrinkles or lines on it. EG *Their faces are lined, immeasurably sad.* **2 Lined** paper has lines printed across it. EG *He* ADJ CLASSIF *was writing on a lined pad.*

linen /lɪnɪn/. **1 Linen** is a kind of cloth that is used N UNCOUNT for making tea-towels, tablecloths, sheets, and clothes. EG *...a white linen suit.* **2** You can refer to tablecloths, sheets, and similar N UNCOUNT things that are used in a house as **linen**. EG *...bed linen... ...the linen cupboard.*

liner /laɪnə/, **liners**. **1** A **liner** is a large ship in N COUNT which people travel long distances. **2** A bin **liner** or a dustbin **liner** is a plastic bag that N COUNT+SUPP you put inside a waste-bin or dustbin so that the rubbish can be easily taken out. EG *...black polythene bin liners.*

linesman /laɪnzməᶻn/, **linesmen**. A **linesman** is N COUNT an official who assists the referee or umpire in games such as football and tennis by watching the boundary line of the field or court and indicating when the ball goes outside it.

Can you be a linguist if you speak only one language?

line-up, line-ups. The **line-up** for a sports event or other public activity is the people who are going to take part in it. EG ...*the line-up for the next game.* N COUNT Informal

linger /lɪŋgə/, **lingers, lingering, lingered.** 1 When ideas, practices, or feelings **linger**, they continue to exist for a long time. EG *The resentment and the longings lingered... This tradition apparently manages to linger on.* ◊ **lingering.** EG *There was no lingering sense of guilt.* V:OFT+on ◊ ADJ CLASSIF: ATTRIB

2 If you **linger** somewhere, you stay there for a longer time than is necessary, for example because you are enjoying yourself. EG *Davis lingered for a moment in the bar... ...lingering over their meals.* V+A

lingerie /lɒnʒəri/ is women's underwear and night-clothes. N UNCOUNT Formal

linguist /lɪŋgwɪst/, **linguists.** A **linguist** is 1 someone who can speak several languages. 2 someone who studies or teaches linguistics. N COUNT

linguistic /lɪŋgwɪstɪk/, **linguistics.** 1 **Linguistics** is the study of the way in which language works. EG ...*a broad introduction to linguistics.* N UNCOUNT

2 **Linguistic** studies, developments, or ideas relate to language or linguistics. EG ...*linguistic development between the ages of nought and four.* ◊ **linguistically.** EG ...*conversations which are linguistically perfect.* ADJ CLASSIF ◊ ADV

lining /laɪnɪŋ/, **linings.** 1 A **lining** is a layer of cloth attached to the inside of something in order to make it thicker or more slippery, or to protect it. EG ...*a white cloak with a scarlet lining... ...the lining of the case.* N COUNT OR N UNCOUNT

2 The **lining** of your stomach or nose, for example, is the layer of flesh on the inside. N COUNT

link /lɪŋk/, **links, linking, linked.** 1 You say that two things **are linked** when there is a relationship between them, for example because one causes the other. EG *Evidence has been offered linking the group to a series of bomb attacks.* ▶ used as a noun. EG *There seems to be a link between the rising rate of unemployment and the rise in crime... We have very close links with industry.* V+O:OFT+ with/to ▶ N COUNT: OFT+ between/with

2 You say that two places or objects **are linked** when there is a physical connection between them so that you can travel or communicate between them. EG ...*a canal linking the Pacific and Atlantic oceans... The television camera had been linked to a computer.* ▶ used as a noun. EG *They opened a rail link between the two towns... A telephone link between Washington and Moscow was established.* V+O:OFT+to ▶ N COUNT: USU+between

3 If you **link** two things, you join them by putting part of one through the other one, or by knotting them together. EG *She linked her hand through the crook of his elbow.* ◊ **linked.** EG *They walked along, arms linked.* V+O:OFT+A ◊ ADJ CLASSIF

4 A **link** is also one of the rings in a chain. N COUNT

link up. If you **link up** two items or places, you connect them to each other in some way. EG *This computer can be linked up to other computers.* PHRASAL VB: V+O+ADV

linkage /lɪŋkɪdʒ/, **linkages.** The **linkage** between two things is the connection between them. EG ...*the linkage between causes and effects.* N UNCOUNT OR N COUNT

lino /laɪnəʊ/ is the same as linoleum. EG ...*a landing with cracked lino on the floor.* N UNCOUNT

linoleum /lɪnəʊliəm/ is a floor covering which is made of cloth covered with a hard shiny substance. EG ...*shiny linoleum floors.* N UNCOUNT Formal

lion /laɪən/, **lions.** 1 A **lion** is a large, wild member of the cat family which is found in Africa. Lions have yellowish fur, and male lions have long hair on their head and neck. N COUNT

2 If someone gets the **lion's share** of something, they get the largest part of it, leaving very little for other people. EG *The lion's share of investment has gone to a few favoured companies.* N PART

lioness /laɪənɪˀs/, **lionesses.** A **lioness** is a female lion. N COUNT

lip /lɪp/, **lips.** 1 Your **lips** are the top and bottom edges of your mouth. See picture at THE HUMAN N COUNT: USU PLURAL

BODY. EG *He had a freshly lit cigarette between his lips.*

2 **Lip** is used in these phrases. 2.1 If you say that something is **on everyone's lips**, you mean that many people are talking about it. 2.2 If you say to someone **'my lips are sealed'**, you mean that you will keep a secret that they have just told you. 2.3 If you **keep a stiff upper lip**, you do not show any emotion, even though it is difficult not to. PHRASE CONVENTION PHRASE

lip-read, lip-reads, lip-reading. If someone can **lip-read**, they can understand what are you saying by watching the way your lips move. Deaf people sometimes do this. V

lip-service. If you say that someone pays **lip-service** to an idea, you mean that they pretend to be in favour of it, but they do not do anything to support it; used showing disapproval. EG *Our major political parties pay lip-service to the ideal of community participation.* N UNCOUNT

lipstick /lɪpstɪk/, **lipsticks. Lipstick** is a coloured substance which women put on their lips. EG *She was wearing lipstick and mascara.* N MASS

liqueur /lɪkjʊə/, **liqueurs.** A **liqueur** is a strong alcoholic drink with a sweet taste, which is often drunk after a meal. N MASS

liquid /lɪkwɪd/, **liquids.** 1 A **liquid** is a substance such as water which is not solid and which flows and can be poured. N MASS

2 Something that is **liquid** is in the form of a liquid rather than being solid or a gas. EG ...*liquid polish.* ADJ CLASSIF

liquidate /lɪkwɪdeɪt/, **liquidates, liquidating, liquidated.** 1 When someone **liquidates** people who are causing problems, they get rid of them by killing them. EG *All his supporters were expelled, exiled, or liquidated.* V+O

2 When a company **is liquidated**, it is closed down, usually because it has large debts and cannot repay them. ◊ **liquidation** /lɪkwɪdeɪʃəⁿn/. EG *By April 1969, the group faced liquidation.* V+O Technical ◊ N UNCOUNT

liquidizer /lɪkwɪdaɪzə/, **liquidizers.** A **liquidizer** is an electrical machine that you use to crush food and make it liquid. N COUNT

liquor /lɪkə/, **liquors. Liquor** is strong alcoholic drink. EG *Drinking cheap liquor made their heads ache... I never touch hard liquor.* N MASS American

liquorice /lɪkərɪs, -ɪʃ/; also spelled **licorice. Liquorice** is a firm black substance with a strong taste, which is used for making sweets. N UNCOUNT

lisp /lɪsp/, **lisps, lisping, lisped.** 1 If someone has a **lisp**, they pronounce the sounds 's' and 'z' as if they were 'th'. For example, they say 'thing' instead of 'sing'. N COUNT: USU SING

2 When someone **lisps**, they speak with a lisp. EG *'Thay yeth,' she lisped.* V OR V+QUOTE

list /lɪst/, **lists, listing, listed.** 1 A **list** is a set of things which are written down one below the other. EG *Look at your list of things to be mended... Find out all their names and make a list.* ● See also **short-list.** N COUNT: OFT+of

2 To **list** a set of things means to mention them all one after the other. EG *There was a label on each case listing its contents.* V+O

3 If something **is listed**, it is included as an item on a list. EG *He is still listed in the files by his code name, the Jackal.* V+O: USU PASS

listed /lɪstɪ³d/. **Listed** buildings are protected by law from being demolished or altered, because they are old or important. ADJ CLASSIF British

listen /lɪsəⁿn/, **listens, listening, listened.** 1 If you **listen** to someone who is talking or **listen** to a sound, you give your attention to the person or the sound. EG *Paul, are you listening?... Listen carefully to what he says... They listen to some music or read until I put them to bed... 'Listen,' Claude whispered, 'I've got something to tell you.'* V:OFT+to

2 If you **listen** for a sound, you keep alert and are ready to hear it if it occurs. EG *She sat quite still, listening for her baby's cry.* V+for

3 To **listen** to someone also means to believe them V:OFT+to

or accept their advice. EG *No one here will listen to you, not without proof... He refused to listen to reason.*

listen in. If you **listen in** to a private conversation, you secretly listen to it. PHRASAL VB : V+ADV

listener /lɪsəᵒnə/, **listeners. 1** Your **listeners** are the people who are listening to you when you are explaining or describing something. EG *She told the tale so well that both her listeners were enchanted.* N COUNT

2 People who listen to the radio are often referred to as **listeners**. EG *We've had a number of letters from listeners about the future of British industry.* N COUNT

listless /lɪstlɪ²s/. If you are **listless**, you have no energy or enthusiasm. EG *She became listless and bored.* ◊ **listlessly.** EG *Rose watched him listlessly.* ADJ QUALIT ◊ ADV

lit /lɪt/ is a past tense and past participle of **light.**

liter /liːtə/. See **litre**.

literacy /lɪtəᵒrəsi¹/ is the ability to read and write. EG *Mass literacy was only possible after the invention of printing.* N UNCOUNT

literal /lɪtəᵒrəl/. **1** If you use a word or expression in its **literal** sense, you use it with its most basic meaning or with its main meaning. EG *She was older than I was, and not only in the literal sense.* ADJ CLASSIF : USU ATTRIB

2 If you make a **literal** translation of something written or spoken in a foreign language, you translate each word, rather than trying to give the general meaning using words that sound natural. EG *...a literal translation from the German.* ADJ CLASSIF : ATTRIB

3 If you say that something is a **literal** fact or the **literal** truth, you are emphasizing that it is true. ADJ CLASSIF : USU ATTRIB

literally /lɪtəᵒrəli¹/. **1** You use **literally** **1.1** to emphasize that what you are saying is actually true, even though it seems surprising or exaggerated. EG *I have literally begged my son for help... They were literally starving to death.* **1.2** to indicate that a word or expression which has more than one meaning is being used in its most basic sense, rather than in a more abstract, metaphorical sense. EG *They are people who have literally and spiritually left home.* ADV

2 People sometimes add **literally** to an exaggerated statement to make it even more exaggerated. EG *They are literally willing to sell you the shirt off their backs.* ADV Informal

3 If you translate a word or expression **literally**, you translate it giving its most simple or basic meaning. EG *...a wati-pulka (literally 'big man').* ADV

4 If you **take** something **literally**, you think that a word or expression is being used with its most simple or basic meaning. EG *Don't misunderstand or take that too literally.* PHRASE

literary /lɪtəᵒrəri¹/. **1 Literary** means concerned with or connected with the writing, study, or appreciation of literature. EG *...his genuine pleasure at her literary success... The text has some literary merit... ...literary critics.* ADJ CLASSIF : ATTRIB

2 Literary words and expressions are rather unusual ones which are used to create a special effect in a poem, speech, or novel. In this dictionary, words and expressions of this kind are indicated by the use of the word 'Literary' in the Extra Column. ADJ QUALIT

literate /lɪtəᵒrə¹t/. **1** Someone who is **literate** is able to read and write. EG *Only half the children in this class are literate.* ADJ CLASSIF

2 If you say that someone is highly **literate**, you mean that they are well educated and intelligent. EG *...the children of highly literate parents.* ADJ QUALIT

literature /lɪtəᵒrətʃə/. **1** Novels, plays, and poetry are referred to as **literature**. EG *I envy you having a friend with whom you can discuss art and literature... ...a degree in English Literature.* N UNCOUNT

2 Books and articles about a particular subject are referred to as the **literature** on this subject. EG *The recent literature on animal behaviour is extensive.* N UNCOUNT +SUPP

3 Literature is also printed information that is produced by people who are trying to sell you something or to give you advice. EG *All major political parties print literature for hopeful candidates.* N UNCOUNT : USU+SUPP

litigation /lɪtɪgeɪʃəᵒn/ is the process of fighting or defending a case in a civil court of law. EG *It was not unusual for the bank to be involved in litigation over failed companies.* N UNCOUNT Formal

litre /liːtə/, **litres;** spelled **liter** in American English. **1** A **litre** is a metric unit of volume that is equal to a thousand cubic centimetres or 1.76 pints. EG *...a litre of wine.* N PART

2 You use **litre** when talking about the capacity of a car engine. For example, if a car has a 2 **litre** engine, its engine's cylinders have a capacity of 2 litres. EG *...a 1.3 litre Vauxhall Astra.* N COUNT+SUPP

litter /lɪtə/, **litters, littering, littered. 1 Litter** is rubbish, such as bits of paper and old bottles, which is left lying around outside. EG *There were piles of litter in the streets.* N UNCOUNT

2 If a number of things **litter** a place or if the place **is littered** with them, they are scattered around in it, in an untidy way. EG *Papers littered every surface... The floor was littered with ashtrays.* V+O

3 A **litter** is a group of animals born to the same mother at the same time. EG *It was the finest puppy in a litter of six.* N COUNT

litter bin, litter bins. A **litter bin** is a container, usually outside or in a public building, into which people can put rubbish. N COUNT British

little /lɪtəᵒl/. For paragraphs 6 and 8, the comparative is **less** and the superlative is **least**. See separate entries for **less** and **least**.

1 Little things are small in size. EG *...a little table with a glass top... ...those little dark villages... ...little groups of people.* ADJ QUALIT : USU ATTRIB

2 A **little** child is very young. EG *...two little girls... I often heard him do that when I was little.* ADJ QUALIT

3 Your **little** sister or brother is younger than you are. EG *My little brother loves school.* ADJ QUALIT : ATTRIB

4 A **little** distance, period of time, or event is short in length. EG *...after he had walked for a little way... She lay awake a little while longer... ...a little chat.* ADJ QUALIT : ATTRIB

5 You use **little** to indicate that something is not serious or important. EG *Don't bother me with little things like that... ...annoying little mishaps.* ADJ CLASSIF : ATTRIB

6 You also use **little** to emphasize that there is only a very small amount of something. EG *John and I had very little money left... Little of the equipment was standardized... There is little to worry about... She ate little.* QUANTIF

7 If something happens **little by little**, it happens very gradually. EG *Then I learnt, little by little, the early history of her family.* PHRASE

8 Little means not very often or to only a small extent. EG *Richardson interrupted very little... She seemed little changed.* ADV BRD NEG

9 A little of something is a small amount of it. EG *He spoke a little French... The waiter poured a little of the wine into a glass.* QUANTIF

10 A little or **a little bit** means to a small extent or degree. EG *He frowned a little and then closed his eyes... I felt a little uncomfortable... I thought he was a little bit afraid.* PHRASE

11 If you do something **a little**, you do it for a short time. EG *He walked about a little.* PHRASE

little finger, little fingers. Your **little finger** is the smallest finger on your hand. N COUNT

live, lives, living, lived. The word **live** is pronounced /lɪv/ when it is a verb and /laɪv/ when it is an adjective or adverb. The word **lives** is pronounced /lɪvz/ when it is a verb and /laɪvz/ when it is the plural of **life**.

1 If someone **lives** in a particular place, their home is there. EG *Where do you live?... I used to live in Grange Road... My grandmother lived with us for 15 years.* V+A

How many little fingers do you have?

2 If you **live** in particular circumstances or **live** a v+a or v+o particular kind of life, you are in those circumstances or your life is of that kind. EG *We lived very simply... They are forced to live entirely artificial lives... We live in a technological society... Many people do not live by these standards.*

3 To **live** means to be alive. EG *Women seem to live* v: no cont *longer than men... She lost her will to live... I hope I shall live to see peace.*

4 Live animals or plants are alive, rather than adj classif: being dead or artificial. EG *They grasp live snakes* attrib *while dancing to bring rain.*

5 A **live** television or radio programme is one in adj classif which an event is broadcast at the time that it or adv happens, rather than being recorded first. EG *...live pictures of a man walking on the moon... The concert will be broadcast live on Radio Three.*

6 A **live** performance is one that is done in front of adj classif an audience, rather than being a recorded one. EG or adv *...live theatre... I would like to perform live as much as possible.*

7 A **live** wire or piece of electrical equipment is adj classif directly connected to a source of electricity.

8 Live bullets, bombs, or missiles have not yet adj classif exploded or been fired.

9 If you **live it up**, you have a very enjoyable and phrase exciting time, for example by going to lots of Informal parties. EG *They were living it up in Amsterdam.*

10 Lives is the plural of **life**.

11 See also **living**.

live down. If you are unable to **live down** a phrasal vb: mistake or failure, you are unable to make people v+o+adv forget that you did it. EG *If you were beaten by Jack, you'd never live it down.*

live for. If you **live for** a particular thing, it is the phrasal vb: most important thing in your life. EG *...a man who* v+prep *lived for pleasure.*

live in. If someone **lives in**, they live in the place phrasal vb: where they work or study. EG *The rest of the* v+adv *students tend to live in.* ● See also **live-in.**

live off. If you **live off** a particular source of phrasal vb: money, you get from it the money that you need. EG v+prep *They were living off welfare.*

live on. 1 If you **live on** a particular amount of phrasal vb: money, you have that amount of money to buy v+prep things. EG *I don't have enough to live on.* **2** If you v+prep **live on** a particular kind of food, it is the only kind of food you eat. EG *She lived on berries and wild herbs.* **3** If something **lives on**, it is remembered v+adv, oft+a for a long time or it continues to exist in some form. EG *The Marilyn Monroe legend lives on in Hollywood.*

live out. 1 If you **live out** your life in a particular phrasal vb: place or in particular circumstances, you stay in v+o+adv, that place or remain in those circumstances until usu+a the end of your life. EG *He lived out the remaining years of his life in London.* **2** If someone **lives out,** v+adv they do not live in the place where they work or study.

live together. If two people **live together**, they phrasal vb: live in the same house and have a sexual relation- v+adv ship but are not married to one another.

live up to. If someone or something **lives up to** phrasal vb: people's expectations, they are as good as they v+adv+prep were expected to be. EG *She succeeded in living up to her extraordinary reputation.*

live with. 1 If you **live with** someone, you live in phrasal vb: the same house as them and have a sexual relation- v+prep ship with them but are not married to them. **2** If v+prep, you have to **live with** an unpleasant situation, you has pass have to accept it and carry on with your life or work. EG *They have to live with the consequences of their decision.*

live-in. Live-in boyfriends or girlfriends live in adj classif: the same house as the person they are having a attrib sexual relationship with. Informal

livelihood /laɪvlɪhʊd/, **livelihoods.** Your liveli- n count or **hood** is the job or other source of income which n uncount gives you the money to buy the things that you

need. EG *...their fear of losing their livelihood... Their principal livelihood was in the sea.*

lively /laɪvli¹/, **livelier, liveliest. 1** You describe adj qualit people as **lively** when they behave in an enthusias- tic and cheerful way. EG *Her parents were lively, eccentric, and attractive individuals... Four lively youngsters suddenly burst into the room.*

2 You say that a place, event, or book is **lively** adj qualit when there are lots of interesting and exciting things happening in it. EG *...a lively debate... It should be a lively evening.*

3 Someone who has a **lively** mind is intelligent and adj qualit interested in a lot of different things.

4 You use **lively** to describe a feeling when it is a adj qualit: strong and enthusiastic one. EG *She took a lively* attrib *interest in everything... ...an institution for which I have a lively admiration.*

liven /laɪv³n/, **livens, livening, livened. 1** If a phrasal vb: place or event **livens up** or if you **liven** it **up**, it v-erg+adv becomes more interesting and exciting. EG *There are lots of new shops and things. The place is really livening up.*

2 If people **liven up** or if something **livens** them v-erg+adv **up**, they become more cheerful and energetic. EG *At least the incident livened her up.*

liver /lɪvə/, **livers. 1** Your **liver** is a large organ n count in your body which processes your blood and helps to clean unwanted substances out of it.

2 Liver is the liver of some animals, especially n uncount lambs, pigs, and cows, which is cooked and eaten.

livestock /laɪvstɒk/. Animals such as cattle and n uncount sheep which are kept on a farm are referred to as or n plural **livestock.** EG *They encourage farmers to keep more livestock.*

livid /lɪvɪd/. **1** Someone who is **livid** is extremely adj qualit angry. EG *He said, 'No, you won't.' I was absolutely* Informal *livid.*

2 Something that is **livid** is an unpleasant dark adj qualit purple or greyish blue colour. EG *...livid bruises.* Literary

living /lɪvɪŋ/. **1** A **living** person or animal is alive. adj classif EG *I have no living relatives... She had been in Amity for as long as anyone living could remem- ber.*

2 The work that you do for a **living** or to earn your n sing **living** is the work that you do to earn the money that you need in your daily life. EG *I never expected to earn my living as an artist... He made a modest living by painting... What do you do for a living?*

3 You use **living 3.1** when you are talking about n uncount the quality of people's daily lives. EG *The quality of* +supp *urban living has been damaged by excessive noise levels... ...the demand for better living standards.* **3.2** when you are talking about places where adj classif: people sleep, eat, and relax when they are not attrib working. EG *...the living quarters of the hotel staff... We are trying to improve living conditions at sea.*

4 within living memory: see **memory.** ● See also **cost of living, standard of living.**

living-room, living-rooms. The **living-room** in n count a house is the room where people sit and relax.

lizard /lɪzəd/, **lizards.** A **lizard** is a small animal n count with short legs, a long tail, and a rough, dry skin.

-'ll is a short form of 'will' or 'shall' used in spoken English and informal written English. EG *He'll come back... They'll spoil our picnic... That'll be all right.*

load /ləʊd/, **loads, loading, loaded. 1** If you **load** v+o or a vehicle or container or **load** things into it, you v+o+a put things into it. EG *...when they came to load the van with their things... They were ordered to begin loading the lorries... We started loading the pheas- ants into the sacks.*

2 A **load** is something which is being carried n count somewhere. EG *We took up our heavy load and trudged back... Its load of minerals was dumped at sea.*

3 When someone **loads** a gun, they put a bullet in it v+o so that it is ready to use.

4 When someone **loads** a camera, computer, or v+o

tape recorder or **loads** film or tape into it, they put film or tape into it so that it is ready to use.

5 If people talk about **loads** of something or a **load** of something, they mean a lot of it. EG *We talked about loads of things.* N PART Informal

6 People say that something is **a load of rubbish** or **a load of junk** as a way of expressing their disapproval of it. EG *You paid twenty pounds for a load of junk like this?* PHRASE Informal

7 See also **workload**.

loaded /ˈləʊdɪd/. **1** If something is **loaded** with things, it has a large number of them in it or on it. EG ...*a truck loaded with bricks*... ...*waitresses with loaded trays.* ADJ QUALIT: OFT+ *with*

2 If you are **loaded** with things or **loaded down** with them, you are carrying a lot of them. EG *A man precedes him up the stairs, loaded with bundles*... *She was loaded down with parcels.* ADJ PRED: OFT+ *with*

3 If you say that someone is **loaded**, you mean that they have a lot of money. ADJ PRED Informal

4 A **loaded** remark or question has more significance, meaning, or purpose than it appears to have. ADJ QUALIT

loaf /ləʊf/, **loaves** /ləʊvz/. A **loaf** of bread is bread in a shape that can be cut into slices. N COUNT OR N PART

loan /ləʊn/, **loans, loaning, loaned**. **1** A **loan** is a sum of money that you borrow. EG *They found it impossible to get a bank loan*... *The government had to make a further loan of 3.3m pounds to save the industry.* N COUNT

2 If someone gives you a **loan** of something or if you have the **loan** of it, you borrow it from them. EG *He asked for the loan of twelve dozen glasses.* N SING+ *of*

3 If something is **on loan**, it has been borrowed. EG *Most of his books are on loan from the library.* PHRASE

4 If you **loan** something to someone, you lend it to them. EG *He never loaned his car to anybody*... *I'll loan you fifty dollars.* V+O+ *to* OR V+O+O

loath /ləʊθ/; also spelled **loth**. If you are **loath** to do something, you are unwilling to do it. EG *Governments have been loath to impose any sanctions.* ADJ PRED + *to*-INF

loathe /ləʊð/, **loathes, loathing, loathed**. If you **loathe** something or someone, you dislike them very much. EG *I particularly loathed team games at school.* V+O

loathing /ˈləʊðɪŋ/ is a feeling of great dislike and disgust. EG *He remembered his school days with loathing*... *She had a loathing for the smell of cooking.* N UNCOUNT

loathsome /ˈləʊðsəm/. If you say that someone or something is **loathsome**, you mean that they are horrible and you dislike them very much. EG *I hate the loathsome way you use other people.* ADJ QUALIT

loaves /ləʊvz/ is the plural of **loaf**.

lob /lɒb/, **lobs, lobbing, lobbed**. **1** If you **lob** something, you throw it so that it goes quite high in the air. EG *She wrapped a piece of paper round a stone and lobbed it into the next garden.* V+O: USU+A

2 If you **lob** the ball in a game of tennis, you hit it high into the air so that it lands behind your opponent. EG *Miss Evert reached to lob a return of Miss Wade's.* ▶ used as a noun. EG ...*high lobs to the backhand corner.* V+O OR V ▶ N COUNT

lobby /ˈlɒbɪ/, **lobbies, lobbying, lobbied**. **1** The **lobby** of a hotel or other large building is the area behind the main door which has corridors and staircases leading off it. EG *I rushed into the hotel lobby.* N COUNT

2 A **lobby** is also a group of people who try to persuade a government or council that a particular thing should be done. EG ...*an increasingly strong and well organized lobby for the abolition of film censorship*... ...*the anti-nuclear lobby.* N COLL+SUPP

3 If you **lobby** a member of a government or council, you try to persuade them that a particular thing should be done. EG *He lobbied the Home Secretary, ministers, and other members of parliament*... *We should all be lobbying for stricter controls on guns.* V+O OR V+A

lobe /ləʊb/, **lobes**. The **lobe** of your ear is the soft part at the bottom. N COUNT

lobster /ˈlɒbstə/, **lobsters**. A **lobster** is a sea creature that has a hard shell, two large claws, and eight legs. N COUNT

local /ˈləʊkəl/, **locals**. **1** A **local** council is responsible for the government of a small part of a country, for example a town or a county. EG *Some local councils give grants to parents with low incomes*... ...*local government.* ◊ **locally**. EG *Should housing policy be decided nationally or locally?* ADJ CLASSIF: ATTRIB ◊ ADV

2 Local means existing in or belonging to the area where you live or work. EG *Members are drawn from all sections of the local community*... ...*a picture in the local paper*... *Telephone your local police station.* ◊ **locally**. EG *Everything we used was bought locally.* ADJ CLASSIF: USU ATTRIB ◊ ADV

3 You can refer to the people who live in a particular district as the **locals**. EG *The locals view these road improvements with alarm.* N COUNT: USU PLURAL Informal

4 A **local** anaesthetic affects only one part of your body. ADJ CLASSIF Medical

locality /ləʊˈkælɪtɪ/, **localities**. A particular locality is a small area of a country or city. EG ...*the anxiety of people living in the same locality.* N COUNT

localized /ˈləʊkəlaɪzd/; also spelled **localised**. Something that is **localized** exists or occurs only in one place or in one part of your body. EG ...*localized problems of erosion*... ...*a localized pain in the back of her head.* ADJ CLASSIF

locate /ləʊˈkeɪt/, **locates, locating, located**. **1** If you **locate** something or someone, you find them. EG *He located a better restaurant in the next street*... *If you do locate him, call me.* V+O Formal

2 If something **is located** in a particular place, it is in that place. EG *The house was located in the heart of the city.* V-PASS+A Formal

location /ləʊˈkeɪʃən/, **locations**. **1** A particular **location** is a particular place, especially the place where something happens or where something is situated. EG *Election officials ran out of ballot papers at six locations*... *The new job involves a new employer, a new location, and a new set of colleagues*... ...*the size and location of your office.* N COUNT+SUPP

2 If a film is made **on location**, it is made away from a studio. PHRASE

loch /lɒx/, **lochs**. A **loch** is a large area of water in Scotland that is completely or almost completely surrounded by land. EG ...*Loch Lomond.* N COUNT

lock /lɒk/, **locks, locking, locked**. **1** When you **lock** a door, a drawer, or a suitcase, you fasten it by means of a key. EG *Lock the door after you leave.* ◊ **locked**. EG *I tried the front door, and found that it was locked*... ...*the locked cupboard.* V+O ◊ ADJ CLASSIF

2 If you **lock** something in a cupboard, a room, or a drawer, you put it inside and lock the door of the cupboard or room, or lock the drawer. EG *He had locked all his papers in the safe*... *He locked them away in a drawer.* V+O: USU+A

3 You say that something **locks** or **is locked** in a position or place when it moves into that position or place and is held firmly there. EG *Smoothly the rod locked into place.* V-ERG: USU+A

4 You say that people **are locked** in a fight or argument when they are fighting or arguing and cannot stop. EG *Rebel groups and government forces are locked in a fierce battle for control of the country.* V-PASS+A

5 The **lock** on a door, a drawer, or a suitcase is the part which you use to keep it shut and to prevent other people from opening it. To open it, you must first turn a key in the lock. EG *The key rattling in the lock startled me.* ● If something is **under lock and key**, it is in a room or container which has N COUNT ● PHRASE

Where does a lodger lodge?

been locked. EG *She would keep any sensitive documents under lock and key.*

6 A **lock** is also a place on a canal or river where walls have been built with gates at each end so that boats can move to a higher or lower section of the canal or river, by gradually changing the water level inside the gates. N COUNT

7 A **lock** of hair is a small bunch of hairs on someone's head. EG *A lock of hair had fallen down over her eyes... He shook his black locks.* N COUNT

8 If you gain or lose something **lock, stock, and barrel**, you gain or lose every single part of it. EG *I got it for £5000, lock, stock and barrel, a sixty-five-acre Suffolk farm.* PHRASE

lock in. If you **lock** someone **in**, you put them in a place and lock the door so that they cannot get out. PHRASAL VB : V+O+ADV

lock out. If you **lock** someone **out**, you prevent them from getting into a place by locking the doors. EG *She had been locked out of the house.* PHRASAL VB : V+O+ADV : OFT+*of*

lock up. 1 You can say that someone **is locked up** when they are put in prison or in a special psychiatric hospital. EG *The idea of being locked up in jail filled her with horror... They locked him up as a madman.* **2** When you **lock up**, you make sure that all the doors and windows of a building are properly closed or locked so that burglars cannot get in. PHRASAL VB : V+O+ADV ; V+ADV OR V+O+ADV

3 See also **lockup**.

locker /lɒkə/, **lockers.** A **locker** is a small cupboard in which you can keep your personal belongings and which you lock with a key. Lockers are often provided in schools and railway stations. N COUNT

locket /lɒkɪ²t/, **lockets.** A **locket** is a piece of jewellery containing something such as a picture which a woman wears on a chain round her neck. N COUNT

lockup /lɒkʌp/, **lockups.** A **lockup** is a jail or cell. EG *They hustled him off and put him in the lockup.* N COUNT American

locomotive /ləʊkəməʊtɪv/, **locomotives.** A **locomotive** is a railway engine. N COUNT Formal

locust /ləʊkəst/, **locusts. Locusts** are insects that live in hot countries and fly in large groups. They eat crops and can cause a lot of damage. N COUNT

lodge /lɒdʒ/, **lodges, lodging, lodged. 1** A **lodge** is **1.1** a small house at the entrance to the grounds of a large house. **1.2** a hut in the country or in the mountains where people stay when they go to shoot animals for sport. EG *They went to a shooting lodge in Scotland for the weekend.* N COUNT ; N COUNT : USU+SUPP

2 If you **lodge** in someone else's house, you live there, often for only a short period of time. EG *He had arranged for me to lodge with his daughter.* V+A

3 If something **lodges** somewhere or **is lodged** there, it becomes stuck there. EG *The bullet had lodged a quarter of an inch from his spine... I had somehow got the bone lodged in my throat.* V-ERG+A

4 If something **lodges** in your mind or heart or **is lodged** there, you remember it for a long time afterwards. EG *Facts don't lodge easily in my mind.* V-ERG+A

5 If you **lodge** a complaint, protest, or accusation, you formally make it. EG *I was going to ring you to lodge a formal complaint... ...the charges that had been lodged against them.* V+O Formal

lodger /lɒdʒə/, **lodgers.** A **lodger** is a person who you allow to live in a part of your house in return for money. EG *She allowed her student lodgers a lot of freedom.* N COUNT

lodging /lɒdʒɪŋ/, **lodgings. 1** If you are provided with **lodging**, you are provided with a place to stay for a period of time. EG *They were offered free lodging in first-class hotels.* N UNCOUNT

2 If you live in **lodgings**, you live in a room or rooms in someone's house and you pay them money to live there. EG *They have to find lodgings in the village.* N COUNT : USU PLURAL

loft /lɒft/, **lofts.** A **loft** is the space inside the sloping roof of a house or other building. People sometimes keep things in lofts. N COUNT

lofty /lɒfti¹/, **loftier, loftiest. 1** Something that is **lofty** is very high. EG *We explored lofty corridors... ...a lofty platform.* ADJ QUALIT Literary

2 A **lofty** idea or aim is noble, important, and admirable. EG *...trying to maintain a lofty principle... Such lofty goals justify any means.* ADJ QUALIT Literary

3 Someone who behaves in a **lofty** way behaves in a proud and rather unpleasant way, as if they are very important. EG *She hated his lofty manner.* ◊ **loftily.** EG *'I can't permit that,' Otto said loftily.* ADJ QUALIT Formal ◊ ADV

log /lɒg/, **logs, logging, logged. 1** A **log** is a piece of a thick branch or the trunk of a tree which has fallen or been cut down. EG *He threw another log on the fire.* N COUNT

2 A **log** is also an official written account which describes the important events that happen each day, for example on board a ship. EG *The Controller entered this in his log.* N COUNT

3 If you **log** an event or fact, you record it officially in writing. EG *The death must be logged.* V+O

log in or **log into**; also **log on.** When someone **logs into** a computer system or **logs in**, they gain access to the system, usually by giving a special word or name that it will accept. PHRASAL VB : V+PREP OR V+ADV Technical

log out. When someone who is using a computer system **logs out**, they finish using the system, by giving a special word. PHRASAL VB : V+ADV Technical

loggerheads /lɒgəhɛdz/. If people are **at loggerheads**, they disagree strongly with each other. EG *He and Thomas were continually at loggerheads.* PHRASE

logic /lɒdʒɪk/. **1 Logic** is a method of reasoning that involves a series of statements, each of which must be true if the statement before it is true. N UNCOUNT

2 If you refer to the **logic** of a conclusion, you are referring to the fact that it has been correctly worked out according to the laws of logic. EG *It is difficult to believe, and yet the logic of the deduction is undeniable.* N UNCOUNT

3 Different kinds of **logic** are different ways of thinking about things that are characteristic of particular people, groups, or activities. EG *Economic logic dictated the policy of centralization.* N UNCOUNT +SUPP

logical /lɒdʒɪkə⁰l/. **1** In a **logical** argument or analysis, each statement is true if the statement before it is true. EG *I made little attempt at logical argument... This is a masterly, logical analysis of the procedure.* ◊ **logically.** EG *Everything has to be logically analysed.* ADJ CLASSIF ◊ ADV

2 A **logical** conclusion or result is the only one that can reasonably result from a particular set of facts or from a particular event. EG *There is only one logical conclusion... To him violence was a logical inevitability.* ◊ **logically.** EG *It follows logically that one of them is lying.* ADJ CLASSIF ◊ ADV

3 You can say that a course of action is **logical** when it seems reasonable or sensible in the circumstances. EG *Wouldn't it have been more logical for them to make the arrest downstairs?... It seemed a logical idea to everyone but my mother.* ◊ **logically.** EG *Therefore, logically, he had to go.* ADJ QUALIT ◊ ADV SEN

logistic /ləˈdʒɪstɪk/, **logistics. 1** You can refer to the skilful organization of something that involves a lot of people or equipment as the **logistics** of it. EG *...the tiresome logistics of modern broadcasting... Logistics and transport remained a problem.* N PLURAL Formal

2 Logistic or **logistical** means relating to the organization of something complicated. EG *...faced with daunting logistic and administrative problems.* ADJ CLASSIF ATTRIB Formal

logo /ləʊgəʊ/, **logos.** The **logo** of a company or organization is the special design or way of writing its name that it puts on all its products and possessions. EG *You will be welcome at all hotels displaying our logo.* N COUNT

loincloth /lɔɪnklɒθ/, **loincloths.** A **loincloth** is a piece of cloth that covers a man's sexual parts. It is sometimes worn by men in very hot countries. N COUNT

loins /lɔɪnz/. Someone's **loins** are the front part of N PLURAL their body between their waist and thighs, especial-Literary ly their sexual parts.

loiter /lɔɪtə/, **loiters, loitering, loitered.** If you V:OFT+A **loiter** somewhere, you remain there or walk up and down without any real purpose. EG *Remember not to loiter on the way.*

loll /lɒl/, **lolls, lolling, lolled. 1** If you **loll** some-V+A where, you sit or lie in a very relaxed position. EG *The students lolled in the grass... ...lolling about in the summer sun.*
2 If your head or tongue **lolls,** it hangs down V:OFT+A loosely. EG *...feeling so sleepy, head lolling, eyes closing... Her tongue lolled out, her eyes were rolled back.*

lollipop /lɒlɪpɒp/, **lollipops.** A **lollipop** is a sweet N COUNT consisting of a hard disc or ball of a sugary substance on the end of a stick. EG *She was sitting on the front step sucking a lollipop.*

lolly /lɒli¹/, **lollies. 1** A **lolly** is. **1.1** a piece of N COUNT flavoured ice or ice cream on a stick. **1.2** a lollipop. Informal
2 You can also refer to money as **lolly.** EG *They* N UNCOUNT *took all his lolly and his clothes.* Informal

lone /ləʊn/. A **lone** person or thing is alone or is ADJ CLASSIF: the only one in a particular place or group. EG *They* ATTRIB *saw ahead a lone figure walking towards them... They made an attack on the area's lone hospital.*

lonely /ləʊnli¹/, **lonelier, loneliest. 1** Someone ADJ QUALIT who is **lonely** is unhappy because they are alone or do not have any friends. EG *I didn't feel lonely at all... ...lonely widows.* ◊ **loneliness.** EG *They suffer* ◊ N UNCOUNT *from isolation, poverty and loneliness.*
2 A **lonely** situation or period of time is one in ADJ QUALIT which you feel alone and unhappy. EG *...that lonely night in Dakota.*
3 A **lonely** place is one where very few people ADJ QUALIT come and which is a long way from places where people live. EG *...lonely country roads.*

loner /ləʊnə/, **loners.** A **loner** is a person who N COUNT prefers to be alone rather than be with other people.

lonesome /ləʊnsə⁰m/. **1** Someone who is **lone-** ADJ QUALIT **some** is unhappy because they are alone or do not American have any friends. EG *I get lonesome sometimes.* Informal
2 A **lonesome** place is one where very few people ADJ QUALIT come and which is a long way from places where American people live. EG *...a lonesome valley.* Informal

long /lɒŋ/, **longer** /lɒŋgə/, **longest** /lɒŋgɪ¹st/; **longs, longing, longed. 1** You use **long** to say that ADV a great amount of time passes while something is happening or is in existence. EG *I haven't known her long... Sorry it took so long... Our oil won't last much longer... I had guessed long ago... Not long after our arrival a curious thing happened.*
2 A **long** event or period of time lasts or takes a ADJ QUALIT: great amount of time. EG *There was a long pause...* USU ATTRIB *They are demanding longer holidays.*
3 You use **for long** when you are saying that PHRASE something happens or is the case for a great amount of time. EG *Men have been indoctrinated for too long... It didn't stay there for long.*
4 You use **long** when asking questions or giving ADV, OR information about amounts of time. EG *'How long* ADJ AFTER N *have you been married?' – 'Five years.'... His speeches are never less than two hours long.*
5 Something that **no longer** happens used to PHRASE happen in the past but does not happen now. EG *We can no longer afford to live there... I couldn't stand it any longer.*
6 If you say that something will happen **before** PHRASE **long,** you mean that it will happen soon. EG *They're bound to catch him before long.*
7 You use **long** to emphasize that something happens for the whole of a particular time. For example, if something happens all day **long,** it happens throughout the day. EG *We row all day long.*
8 Something that is **long** measures a great distance ADJ QUALIT from one end to the other. EG *She had long dark*

hair... ...a long line of cars... ...long tables... It may look a long way on the map but it isn't.
9 You use **long** when giving information or asking ADJ AFTER N questions about how much something measures from one end to the other. EG *...an area 3,000 feet long and 900 feet wide... How long is that side?*
10 A **long** book or other piece of writing contains a ADJ QUALIT: lot of words. EG *...an enormously long novel.* USU ATTRIB
11 If you say that one thing is true **as long as** or **so** CONJ **long as** another thing is true, you mean that it is true if or when the other thing is true. EG *We were all right as long as we kept our heads down.*
12 You can say **'So long'** as a way of saying CONVENTION goodbye. Informal
13 If you **long** for something, you want it very V+*for* much. EG *They longed for green trees and open* OR *to*-INF *spaces... They're longing to see you.*
14 See also **longing.**

long-distance. **Long-distance** travel or commu- ADJ CLASSIF: nication is travel or communication between ATTRIB places that are far apart. EG *...long-distance motor coaches... ...long-distance phone calls.*

long-drawn-out. A **long-drawn-out** process or ADJ CLASSIF: conflict lasts an unnecessarily long time. EG *...a* ATTRIB *long-drawn-out struggle.*

longevity /lɒndʒevɪ¹ti¹/ is long life. EG *...improved* N UNCOUNT *health resulting in increased longevity.* Formal

longing /lɒŋɪŋ/, **longings.** A **longing** is a rather N COUNT OR sad feeling of wanting something very much, espe- N UNCOUNT cially something that you are unlikely to get. EG *People have a longing for normality... He gazed with longing and apprehension into the future.*

longingly /lɒŋɪŋli¹/. If you think **longingly** about ADV something you want, you think about it with a feeling of desire. EG *I began to think longingly of bed... I eyed the cold drinks longingly.*

longitude /lɒŋɪtjuːd/, **longitudes.** The **longitude** N COUNT OR of a place is its distance to the west or east of a line N UNCOUNT passing through Greenwich in England: compare **latitude.**

long-lasting, longer-lasting. Something that is ADJ QUALIT **long-lasting** lasts for a long time. EG *The failure of the dam is unlikely to have long-lasting environmental consequences... Solid rubber is longer-lasting.*

long-life. **Long-life** milk, fruit juice, and batteries ADJ CLASSIF: last longer than ordinary kinds. ATTRIB

long-lived. Something that is **long-lived** lives or ADJ QUALIT lasts for a long time. EG *Bats are surprisingly long-lived creatures... ...a long-lived rebellion.*

long-lost is used to describe someone or some- ADJ CLASSIF: thing that has not been seen for a long time. EG *She* ATTRIB *greeted me like a long-lost daughter... These pictures were based on a long-lost mosaic.*

long-range. 1 A **long-range** piece of military ADJ CLASSIF: equipment is able to hit a target a long way away, ATTRIB or to travel a long way. EG *...a modern long-range strategic missile... ...long-range bombers.*
2 A **long-range** plan or prediction relates to a ADJ CLASSIF: period extending a long time into the future. EG ATTRIB *...the necessity for long-range planning.*

long-sighted. If you are **long-sighted,** you can- ADJ QUALIT not see things near you clearly, but you can see things a long way away.

long-standing. Something that is **long-standing** ADJ QUALIT has existed for a long time. EG *...his long-standing reputation as a scholar... ...a long-standing feud.*

long-suffering. Someone who is **long-suffering** ADJ QUALIT patiently bears continual trouble or bad treatment. EG *...his noble, long-suffering wife.*

long-term. 1 **Long-term** things are intended to ADJ QUALIT: continue or to be effective for a long time in the USU ATTRIB future. EG *...hopes for a long-term solution to the problem... I hesitated before making a long-term commitment of this importance.*

If you are a loner, are you lonesome?

2 When you talk about what happens in the **long** N SING : the+N **term**, you are talking about what happens over a long period of time. EG *The results, in the long term, were successful.*

long wave is a range of radio waves which are N UNCOUNT used for broadcasting.

long-winded. If you describe something that has ADJ QUALIT been written or said as **long-winded**, you mean that it contains many more words than are necessary and is therefore boring. EG *...long-winded prayers.*

loo /luː/, **loos.** People sometimes refer to a toilet as N COUNT the **loo**. EG *I think she's in the loo... He wanted to go* Informal *to the loo.*

look /luk/, **looks, looking, looked. 1** If you **look** in V : USU+A a particular direction, you turn your eyes in that direction so that you can see what is there. EG *She turned to look out of the window... They looked at each other... He blushed and looked away.* ▶ used ▶ N SING as a noun. EG *Take a good look... Did you have a look at the shop?*

2 To **look** at something also means to read or V+at examine it, usually not thoroughly. EG *'I'd like to look at his medical history,' Percival said.* ▶ used ▶ N SING as a noun. EG *Tony, I've had a look at that book you wrote... You should let a doctor have a look at her.*

3 If you give someone a **look**, you look at them N COUNT : with an expression on your face that shows what USU+SUPP you are thinking. EG *Don't give me such severe looks. What have I done?*

4 If you **look** for someone or something, you try to V : OFT+for find them. EG *I've been looking for you... She looked around for some paper... ...people looking for work.*

5 If you **look** at a subject, problem, or situation, you V+at think about it or study it. EG *Let's look at the implications of these changes.* ▶ used as a noun. EG ▶ N SING *We have to take a hard look at the whole situation.*

6 If you **look** at a situation from a particular point V+at of view, you judge it or consider it from that point of view. EG *If you're a Democrat, you look at things one way, and if you're a Republican you look at them very differently.*

7 You say **'look'** or **'look here'** when you want CONVENTION someone to pay attention to what you are saying, often when you are angry or upset. EG *Look, Mrs Kintner, you've got it wrong.*

8 You also use **look** to draw attention to something, V+at OR WH : when you are surprised or angry, or when you are ONLY IMPER giving an example of something. EG *Goodness, look at the time. I promised I'd be home at six... Now look what you've done... I mean, look at fortune tellers.*

9 If a window, room, or building **looks** out onto a V+A particular thing, it has a view of that thing. EG *The kitchen window looks out onto a yard.*

10 You use **look** when describing something's V+C OR appearance or someone's appearance or expres- V+as if/like sion. For example, if something **looks** nice, its appearance is nice. EG *You look very pale... He looked as if he hadn't slept very much... 'What does he look like?' – 'Pale, thin, dark-haired.'*

11 If someone or something has a particular **look**, N SING+SUPP they have that appearance or expression. EG *He didn't have the look of a man who was thinking... There is a nervous look in their eyes.* ● You say **by** ● PHRASE **the look of** or **by the looks of** something or someone when you are giving an opinion about them which is based on their appearance. EG *It's been there all summer by the look of it.*

12 When you refer to someone's **looks**, you are N PLURAL referring to how beautiful or handsome they are. EG *She had lost her looks... I didn't marry him for his looks... ...his good looks and charm.*

13 You use **look** to say how something seems to V+C OR you. For example, if a situation **looks** bad, it seems V+as if/like bad. If it **looks** as if something is the case, it seems as if it is the case. EG *The plan looks impressive enough on paper... Looks like we're going to be late... It looks like a good book.*

look after. 1 If you **look after** someone or PHRASAL VB : something, you do what is necessary in order to V+PREP, keep them safe, well, or in good condition. EG *Your* HAS PASS *husband ought to be looking after the baby.* **2** If V+PREP, you **look after** something, you are responsible for HAS PASS it and deal with it. EG *The duty of the local authority is to look after the interests of local people.*

look back. 1 If you **look back**, you think about PHRASAL VB : things that happened in the past. EG *People can* V+ADV *often look back and reflect on happy childhood memories.* **2** If you say that someone did some- PHRASE thing and **never looked back**, you mean that they then became very successful. EG *He borrowed $10,000 to start his Hollywood restaurant and never looked back.*

look down on. If you **look down on** someone or PHRASAL VB : something, you think that they are inferior or V+ADV+PREP unimportant. EG *Farm labourers used to be looked down on.*

look forward to. If you **are looking forward to** PHRASAL VB : something, you want it to happen because you V+ADV+PREP think you will enjoy it. EG *I'm quite looking forward to it... I look forward to seeing you in Washington.*

look into. If you **look into** something, you find PHRASAL VB : out about it and examine the facts. EG *A working* V+PREP, party was set up to look into the problem.* HAS PASS

look on. 1 If you **look on** while something hap- PHRASAL VB : pens, you watch it. EG *His parents looked on with a* V+ADV triumphant smile.* **2** If you **look on** something as a V+PREP+A, particular thing, you think of it as that thing. EG *She* HAS PASS looked on us as idiots.*

look out. You say **'look out'** to warn someone CONVENTION that they are in danger. EG *'Look out,' I said. 'There's something coming.'* ● See also **lookout.**

look out for. If you **look out for** a particular PHRASAL VB : thing, you make sure that you notice it when it is V+ADV+PREP there. EG *It's a film we shall look out for in the next couple of months.*

look round. If you **look round** a building or PHRASAL VB : place, you walk round it and look at the different V+PREP parts of it.

look through. If you **look through** something, PHRASAL VB : you examine all of it in order to find what you are V+PREP looking for. EG *He looked through the clothing on the bed.*

look to. 1 If you **look to** someone for something PHRASAL VB : such as help or advice, you expect or hope that V+PREP, they will provide it. EG *Many people in the commu-* OFT+to-INF *nity will be looking to us for leadership.* **2** If you OR for **look to** the future, you think about it, often with a V+PREP particular emotion. EG *Some New Englanders look to the future with a certain anxiety.*

look up. 1 If you **look up** a piece of information, PHRASAL VB : you find it out by looking in a book. EG *He consulted* V+O+ADV *his dictionary to look up the meaning of 'apotheo-sis'.* **2** If you **look** someone **up**, you visit them after V+O+ADV you have not seen them for a long time. EG *It was* Informal such a fine day he thought he'd look me up.* **3** If a V+ADV, situation **is looking up**, it is improving. EG *Things* USU CONT are looking up.* Informal

look upon. If you **look upon** something as a PHRASAL VB : particular thing, you think of it as that thing. EG V+PREP+A, *Houses are looked upon as investments.* HAS PASS

look up to. If you **look up to** someone, you PHRASAL VB : respect and admire them. EG *His younger brothers* V+ADV+PREP look up to him.*

look-alike, look-alikes. A person's **look-alike** is N COUNT someone who looks very like them. EG *It was only the Minister's look-alike.*

look-in. If you fail to do something because too N SING : a+N, many other people are doing it, you can say that WITH you did not get a **look-in**. EG *James talks so much* BROAD NEG that all the others barely get a look-in.* Informal

lookout /lukaut/, **lookouts. 1** A **lookout** is **1.1** a N COUNT place from which you can see clearly in all direc-tions. EG *...a lookout platform.* **1.2** someone who is watching for danger. EG *Two of the burglars were tipped off by a lookout and escaped.*

2 If you are **on the lookout** or are **keeping a** PHRASE

lookout for something, you are paying attention so that you will notice it when it appears or happens. EG *I'm on the lookout for a second-hand car... She sat a little distance away keeping a lookout for danger.*

loom /lu:m/, **looms, looming, loomed. 1** You say v: USU+A that something **looms** when it appears as a tall, unclear shape, often in a frightening way. EG *As you get closer they loom above you like icebergs.*

2 You can say that an event or situation **looms** v when it will soon happen and it will bring you problems. EG *The next general election loomed.*

● You say that a problem or situation **looms large** ● PHRASE when you are worrying about it a lot. EG *The meeting loomed large.*

3 A **loom** is a machine that is used for weaving N COUNT thread into cloth.

loom up. You say that something **looms up** when PHRASAL VB: it appears as a tall, unclear shape, often in a v+ADV frightening way. EG *...a huge Victorian edifice that loomed up in front of us.*

loony /lu:niᵃ/, **loonies. 1** You describe behaviour ADJ QUALIT or ideas as **loony** when they seem mad or eccen- Informal tric. EG *There seems to be this loony idea that you have to be passionately in love to get married.*

2 You call someone a **loony** when they behave in a N COUNT way that seems mad or eccentric. EG *He's probably* Informal *a loony, poor old soul... They sent me to this loony doctor.*

loop /lu:p/, **loops, looping, looped. 1** A **loop** is a N COUNT curved or circular shape in something long, for example in a piece of string. EG *...loops of blue and pink ribbon.*

2 If you **loop** something such as rope around an v+o: USU+A object, you tie a length of it in a loop around the object. EG *The king had pearls looped round his neck.*

3 If something **loops**, it goes in a circular direction v: OFT+A that makes the shape of a loop. EG *Birds loop and weave through the tall trees.*

loophole /lu:phəʊl/, **loopholes.** A **loophole** in the N COUNT law is a small mistake or omission which allows you to avoid doing something that the law intends you to do. EG *A number of obvious loopholes exist for tax avoidance.*

loose /lu:s/, **looser, loosest. 1** Something that is **loose** is **1.1** not firmly held in place. EG *The* ADJ QUALIT *doorknob is loose and rattles... ...loose strands of copper wire.* ◊ **loosely.** EG *Willie held the phone* ◊ ADV *loosely.* **1.2** not attached to anything else. EG *...a* ADJ CLASSIF *few loose sheets of paper.*

2 Loose clothes are rather large and do not fit ADJ QUALIT closely to your body. EG *...a loose cotton shirt.* ◊ **loosely.** EG *His black garments hung loosely* ◊ ADV *from his powerful shoulders.*

3 When a woman's hair is **loose**, it is hanging ADJ CLASSIF freely round her shoulders rather than being tied back. EG *She shook her hair loose.*

4 If you set animals **loose**, you release them when ADJ CLASSIF they have been tied up or kept in a box or cage. EG *He had taken some white rats into church and let them loose on the floor.*

5 You say that people cut **loose** or are set **loose** ADJ PRED when they become free from the influence or authority of other people. EG *The younger genera- tion have tended to cut loose from the influence of class background.*

6 If a dangerous person is **on the loose**, they are PHRASE free and there is a possibility that you might meet them and be harmed by them. EG *A bandit leader was on the loose in the hills.*

7 People refer to a woman as a **loose** woman when ADJ QUALIT: they consider that she is sexually promiscuous; ATTRIB used showing disapproval. Outdated

8 A **loose** organization or administration is not ADJ QUALIT strictly controlled. EG *A loose grouping of 'radicals' was formed which met once a week... The country has a loose federal structure.*

9 If you are **at a loose end**, you have nothing to do PHRASE and are bored.

loosen /lu:sən/, **loosens, loosening, loosened. 1** V-ERG If you **loosen** something or if it **loosens**, it be- comes less firm or less tightly held in place. EG *The tyre on one of his wheels had loosened... The wind had loosened some leaves.*

2 If you **loosen** your clothing or **loosen** something v+o that is tied or fastened, you undo it slightly. EG *He loosened his seat-belt... He took off his jacket and loosened his tie.*

loosen up. If you **loosen up** or if something PHRASAL VB: **loosens** you **up**, you become calmer and less V-ERG+ADV worried than you were. EG *Her second drink loos-* Informal *ened her up... As the day wore on he loosened up and became more chatty.*

loot /lu:t/, **loots, looting, looted. 1** When people v+o OR v **loot** shops or houses, they steal things from them during a battle or a riot. EG *Shops were looted and wrecked in London.* ◊ **looting.** EG *There was* ◊ N UNCOUNT *widespread looting of stores and shops.*

2 Stolen money or goods can be referred to as **loot.** N UNCOUNT EG *He told his wife where the loot was hidden.* Informal

lop /lɒp/, **lops, lopping, lopped.** If you **lop** a tree, v+o you cut off some of its branches.

lop off. If you **lop** something **off**, you cut it away PHRASAL VB: from what it was attached to, usually with a quick, v+o+ADV strong stroke.

lope /ləʊp/, **lopes, loping, loped.** When people or v+A animals **lope**, they run in an easy and relaxed way, taking long steps. EG *The dog started to lope alongside my car.*

lopsided /lɒpsaɪdⁱd/. Something that is **lopsided** ADJ QUALIT is uneven because its two sides are different from each other. EG *...a lopsided smile.*

loquacious /ləˈkweɪʃəs/. People who are **loqua-** ADJ QUALIT **cious** talk a lot. EG *He is an easy, loquacious man.* Formal

lord /lɔːd/, **lords. 1 Lord** is the title used in front of the name of some British peers. EG *...Lord Harewood... ...Lord Alfred Douglas.*

2 In Britain, judges, bishops, and some members of the nobility are addressed as 'my **Lord'.**

3 Lord is also used in the title of officials of very high rank in Britain. EG *...The Lord Mayor of London... ...the Lord Chief Justice.*

4 A **lord** is a man who has a high rank in the N COUNT British nobility. EG *...lords and ladies.*

5 The word **lord** is often used in expressions such N COUNT as 'lord and master' and 'lord of the manor' to refer to men who are in positions of authority.

6 In the Christian church, people refer to God and N PROPER to Jesus Christ as **Lord.**

7 You can say **'good Lord!'** or **'oh Lord!'** when you EXCLAM are surprised, amused, shocked, or worried about something. EG *'Good Lord!' I said. 'You still here?'*

Lordship /lɔːdʃɪp/, **Lordships.** Your **Lordship** or his **Lordship** is a respectful way of addressing or talking about a judge, bishop, or lord. EG *I'm sorry, sir, his Lordship is in his bath... Their Lordships were late for dinner.*

Lord's Prayer. The **Lord's Prayer** is a very N SING: the+N important Christian prayer that was originally taught by Jesus Christ to his disciples.

lore /lɔː/. The **lore** of a particular country or N UNCOUNT culture is the traditional stories and history of it. EG +SUPP *...Jewish mystical lore.* ● See also **folklore.**

lorry /lɒriⁱ/, **lorries.** A **lorry** is a large vehicle N COUNT that is used to transport goods by road. British

lose /lu:z/, **loses, losing, lost** /lɒst/. **1** If you **lose** v+o something, **1.1** you do not know where it is, for example because you have forgotten where you put it. EG *You haven't lost the ticket, have you?* **1.2** you no longer have it, although you would like to have it, often because it has been taken away from you or destroyed. EG *I might lose my job... ...a*

If you lopped a leg off a chair, would it be lopsided?

complete list of all the goods lost in the fire... He lost the use of his legs. **1.3** you have less of it than you used to have. EG *He has lost a lot of weight... Brody was beginning to lose interest.*

2 If you **lose** a close relative or friend, he or she v+o : NO CONT dies. EG *I lost my father when I was nine.*

3 If you **lose** an opportunity or **lose** time, you v+o waste it. EG *Bill lost no time in telling everyone about his idea... He will lose his chances of promotion.*

4 If a business **loses** money, it earns less money v+o than it spends.

5 If you **have** something **to lose**, you are in a PHRASE position where you may suffer if you do something unsuccessfully. EG *The price was too high and he had too much to lose... They had absolutely nothing to lose.*

6 If you **lose sight of** something, you can no longer PHRASE see it.

7 If you **lose sight of** an aim, argument, or idea, PHRASE you gradually forget about it. EG *We've lost sight of moral values.*

8 If a clock or watch **loses** time, it shows a time v+o that is earlier than the real time.

9 If you **lose** a competition or argument, someone v+o OR V does better than you and defeats you. EG *They expected to lose the election.* ◊ **losing.** EG *He'd* ◊ ADJ CLASSIF : *never played on a losing side.* ATTRIB

10 If you **lose** your way, you get lost when you are v+o trying to go somewhere.

11 See also **lost.** ● to **lose face:** see **face.** ● to **lose** your **head:** see **head.** ● to **lose** your **nerve:** see **nerve.** ● to **lose** your **temper:** see **temper.** ● to **lose touch:** see **touch.**

lose out. If you **lose out**, you suffer a loss or PHRASAL VB : disadvantage. EG *They did not lose out in the* V+ADV *struggle to keep up with inflation.*

loser /ˈluːzə/, **losers. 1** The **loser** of a game, N COUNT contest, or struggle is the person who is defeated. ● Someone who is a **good loser** accepts the fact ● PHRASE that they have lost a game or contest and does not complain. Someone who is a **bad loser** hates losing and complains a lot when they do.

2 You say that someone or something is a **loser** N COUNT when they are always unsuccessful or when they Informal seem likely to be unsuccessful. EG *You're a loser, Bill... He avoided losers.*

3 If someone is the **loser** as the result of an action N COUNT : or event, they are in a worse situation because of the+N it. EG *She will be the loser if she fails to respond to your friendly overtures.*

loss /lɒs/, **losses. 1 Loss** is the fact of no longer N UNCOUNT : having something or of having less of it than you OFT+of had before. EG *...temporary loss of vision... ...the loss of liberty... ...heat loss.*

2 Loss of life occurs when many people die, for N UNCOUNT example in a battle or a disaster. EG *The loss of life* OR N COUNT *was appalling... Artillery fire caused heavy losses.*

3 The **loss** of a close relative or friend is his or her N UNCOUNT death. EG *...the loss of my daughter and husband.* +SUPP

4 If a business makes a **loss**, it earns less money N COUNT OR than it spends. EG *The company announced a huge* N UNCOUNT *loss for the first half of the year.*

5 If you are **at a loss**, you do not know what to do. PHRASE EG *I was at a complete loss as to how I could lay my hands on the money.*

6 If you **cut** your **losses**, you stop trying to do PHRASE something, in order to prevent the bad situation you are in from becoming worse. EG *You ought to cut your losses and start again.*

7 If you say that someone or something is a **dead** PHRASE **loss**, you mean that they are completely useless or Informal unsuccessful.

lost /lɒst/. **1 Lost** is the past tense and past participle of **lose.**

2 If you are **lost**, you do not know where you are or ADJ CLASSIF : you are unable to find your way. EG *There was that* USU PRED *time when we got lost out in Dennington.*

3 If you say that you would be **lost** without ADJ PRED +without

someone or something, you mean that you would be unhappy or unable to work properly without them. EG *I am lost without him.*

4 If something is **lost**, you cannot find it. EG ADJ CLASSIF *Shopping lists on old envelopes tend to get lost.*

5 If advice or a comment is **lost** on someone, they ADJ PRED+on do not understand it, or they pay no attention to it. EG *The lesson was not lost on the committee.*

6 If you tell someone to **get lost**, you are rudely PHRASE telling them to go away. Informal

lost property consists of things that people have N UNCOUNT lost or accidentally left in a public place, for example at a railway station. Lost property is kept safe in a special office so that people can collect it. EG *...a lost property office.*

lot /lɒt/, **lots. 1** A **lot** of something or **lots** of N PART something is a large amount of it. EG *We owed a lot of money... This is a subject that worries a lot of people... I feel that we have a lot to offer... ...a big house with lots of windows.*

2 A **lot** means to a great extent or degree. EG *The* PHRASE *man in the photograph looked a lot like Mr Williams... The weather's a lot warmer there... Thanks a lot.*

3 If you do something **a lot**, you do it often or for a PHRASE long time. EG *He laughs a lot.*

4 When you refer to the **lot**, you are referring to N SING : the+N the whole of a particular amount of something. EG Informal *Wilks bet his last ten pounds and lost the lot.*

5 You can refer to a particular group of people as a N SING+SUPP particular **lot.** EG *They were a rather arrogant* Informal *boring lot.*

6 You can refer to a set or group of things as a N COUNT particular **lot.** EG *...two sets of cards, one lot written* OR N PART *in blue, the other in red... I get two lots of everything.*

7 Your **lot** is the kind of life you have. EG *She was* N COUNT+POSS *quite content with her lot.*

8 A **lot** in an auction is one of the objects or groups N COUNT of objects that are being sold. EG *Lot No 359 was a folder of 11 original sketches.*

9 If people **draw lots** or **cast lots** to decide who PHRASE will do something, each of them takes a stick or piece of paper from a container. The person who takes the stick or piece of paper that is different from the others is chosen.

10 See also **parking lot.**

loth /ləʊθ/. See **loath.**

lotion /ˈləʊʃən/, **lotions.** A **lotion** is a liquid that N MASS you use on your skin or hair. EG *...a bottle of suntan lotion... ...a tube of hand lotion.*

lottery /ˈlɒtəri/, **lotteries. 1** When a **lottery** is N COUNT held, people buy tickets with different numbers on them. Several numbers are chosen and the people whose tickets have these numbers on them win prizes. EG *...a lottery ticket.*

2 If you describe a contest as a **lottery**, you mean N SING : a+N that the result depends entirely on luck or chance, rather than being decided in a fairer way; used showing disapproval. EG *The British election system will become a lottery.*

loud /laʊd/, **louder, loudest. 1** You say that a ADJ QUALIT noise is **loud** when the level of sound is very high. OR ADV For example, thunder is loud and your voice is loud when you shout. EG *His voice was loud and savage... There was a loud explosion... He spoke louder.* ◊ **loudly.** EG *The audience laughed loudly.* ◊ ADV

2 If someone is **loud** in their support or condemna- ADJ QUALIT : tion of something, they express their opinion often OFT+in and in a strong way. EG *Northcliffe's newspapers were loud in their condemnation of British sentimentality.* ◊ **loudly.** EG *Most people loudly allege* ◊ ADV *that all this is just another excuse.*

3 If you say something **loud and clear**, what you PHRASE say can be easily understood. EG *The message goes out loud and clear.*

4 If you say something **out loud**, you say it, rather PHRASE than just thinking it. EG *She was praying out loud... I laughed out loud at the thought.*

5 You say that a piece of clothing is **loud** when it ADJ QUALIT
has very bright colours or a large, bold pattern;
used showing disapproval. EG *...young men in loud
shirts and jackets.*

loud-mouthed /laʊdmaʊðd/. Someone who is ADJ QUALIT
loud-mouthed talks a lot, especially in an unpleasant, offensive, or stupid way. EG *...a loud-mouthed,
hard-drinking actor.*

loudspeaker /laʊdspiːkə/, **loudspeakers.** A N COUNT
loudspeaker is a piece of equipment that makes
your voice sound louder. EG *He made an announcement over the loudspeaker.*

lounge /laʊndʒ/, **lounges, lounging, lounged. 1** N COUNT
A **lounge** is a room in a house, hotel, or club where
people sit and relax.

2 A **lounge** at an airport is a very large room for N COUNT
passengers to wait in. EG *...the arrivals lounge.*

3 The **lounge** or **lounge bar** in a pub or hotel is a N COUNT
comfortably furnished bar where the drinks are British
more expensive than in the other bars.

4 If you **lounge** somewhere, you lean against V : USU+A
something or lie on something in a comfortable
and lazy way. EG *She lounged on the rug.*

lounge about or **lounge around.** If you **lounge** PHRASAL VB :
about or **lounge around,** you spend your time in a V+ADV/PREP
relaxed and lazy way; usually used showing disapproval. EG *...people who were lounging about, apparently with nothing to do.*

louse /laʊs/, **lice** /laɪs/. **Lice** are small insects N COUNT
that live on the bodies of people or animals.

lousy /laʊziˈ/. **1** If you describe something as ADJ QUALIT
lousy, you mean that it is of very bad quality or Informal
that you do not like it at all. EG *The hotels are
lousy... ...a lousy hockey game.*

2 If you feel **lousy,** you feel ill. EG *I feel really lousy* ADJ PRED
tonight. Informal

lout /laʊt/, **louts.** If you call a young man a **lout,** N COUNT
you mean that he behaves in an impolite or
aggressive way. EG *...gangs of drunken louts.*

lovable /lʌvəbˀl/. Someone who is **lovable** has ADJ QUALIT
attractive qualities, and it is easy to like them very
much. EG *...a mischievous but lovable child.*

love /lʌv/, **loves, loving, loved. 1** If you **love** V+O
someone, **1.1** you feel romantically or sexually
attracted to them, and they are very important to
you. EG *I do not think I love him enough to marry
him... 'I love you, Albert.' – 'I love you too, Mabel.'*
1.2 you feel that their happiness is very important
to you, and so you behave in a kind and caring way
towards them. EG *He gave us a little baby. A little
baby to love... They make us feel safe and secure,
loved and wanted.*

2 If you **love** something, **2.1** you feel that it is V+O
important and want to protect it. EG *They don't love
their village in the way that their parents did.* **2.2**
you like it very much. EG *We both love dancing... I
love Haydn and Schubert.*

3 Love is **3.1** a very strong feeling of affection N UNCOUNT :
towards someone who you are romantically or OFT+*for*
sexually attracted to. EG *Her love for him never
wavered... You are not marrying for love... ...a
Russian love song.* **3.2** the feeling that a person's N UNCOUNT
happiness is very important to you, and the way
you show this feeling in your behaviour towards
them. EG *...maternal love... Children need love and
understanding.* **3.3** a strong liking for something or N UNCOUNT :
enjoyment of it. EG *...a man with a genuine love of* OFT+*of*
literature... It was designed and built with love.

4 If you would **love** to have or to do something, you V+O OR
very much want to have it or to do it. EG *I would* V+*to*-INF
*love a photograph of Edith Evans... Posy said she'd
love to stay.*

5 Some people use **love** as an affectionate way of VOCATIVE
addressing someone. Men usually address only Informal
women and children as **love.** EG *Thanks a lot, love.*

6 In tennis, **love** is a score of zero. NUMBER

7 You can write **love** or **love from,** followed by CONVENTION
your name, as an informal way of ending a letter to

a friend or relation. EG *Hope you are all well at
home. Love, Dan.*

8 If you **send** someone your **love** or say **'give** PHRASE
them my love', you ask another person to tell
them that you are thinking about them with affection. EG *They send you their love.*

9 If you are **in love** with someone, you feel PHRASE
romantically or sexually attracted to them, and
they are very important to you. EG *They are in love
with each other and wish to marry.*

10 If you **fall in love** with someone, you start to be PHRASE
in love with them. EG *I fell madly in love with Ellen
the first time I saw her.*

11 When two people **make love,** they have sex. PHRASE

12 If you have **a love-hate relationship** with PHRASE
someone or something, you have strong feelings of
both love and hate towards them.

13 a **labour of love:** see **labour.** ● See also **loving.**

love affair, love affairs. A **love affair** is a N COUNT
romantic and often sexual relationship between
two people who love each other but who are not
married to each other.

loveless /lʌvlɪˀs/. In a **loveless** relationship or ADJ CLASSIF :
situation, there is no love. EG *...a loveless marriage.* ATTRIB

love letter, love letters. A **love letter** is a letter N COUNT
that you write to someone in order to tell them that
you love them.

love life, love lives. Someone's **love life** is the N COUNT
part of their life that consists of their romantic and
sexual relationships. EG *He had a very emotional
lovelife and was always changing partners.*

lovely /lʌvliˀ/, **lovelier, loveliest. 1** Someone or ADJ QUALIT
something that is **lovely** is very beautiful and
therefore pleasing to look at or listen to. EG *'Doesn't
she look lovely, Albert?' she whispered... To me
Hong Kong was one of the loveliest places in the
world.* ◊ **loveliness.** EG *Coffee was being handed* ◊ N UNCOUNT
out by a girl of film-star loveliness.

2 If you describe something as **lovely,** you are ADJ QUALIT
saying how much you like it. EG *'What a lovely
surprise!' she said... Lovely day, isn't it?... It was
lovely to hear from you again.*

3 You can describe someone as **lovely** when you ADJ QUALIT
like them very much because they are friendly,
kind, and generous. EG *We've got lovely neighbours... She's the sweetest, loveliest person.*

love-making refers to romantic activities, espe- N UNCOUNT
cially sexual activities, that take place between
two people. EG *...ardent love-making.*

lover /lʌvə/, **lovers. 1** Your **lover** is someone who N COUNT
you are having a sexual relationship with but are
not married to. EG *Jenny and I were lovers.*

2 You can refer to people as **lovers** when they are N COUNT
in love with each other. EG *...young lovers.* Outdated

3 You can also use **lover** to refer to someone who N COUNT+SUPP
enjoys something very much. For example, an art
lover is someone who enjoys art. EG *...a music
lover.*

loving /lʌvɪŋ/. **1** Someone who is **loving** feels or ADJ QUALIT
shows love to other people. EG *...a loving, beautiful
wife.* ◊ **lovingly.** EG *For a moment she looked at* ◊ ADV
her grandson lovingly.

2 Loving actions are done with great enjoyment ADJ CLASSIF :
and care, especially by someone with special ATTRIB
knowledge or understanding. EG *...tending the gardens with loving care.* ◊ **lovingly.** EG *The Society* ◊ ADV
of Antiquaries have lovingly restored the building.

low /ləʊ/, **lower, lowest; lows. 1** Something that
is **low 1.1** measures a short distance from the ADJ QUALIT
bottom to the top, or from the ground to the top. EG
...a low brick wall... ...a low table... ...low hills. **1.2** is ADJ QUALIT
close to the ground. EG *She made a low curtsey... I* OR ADV
*asked him to fly low over the beach... He bent
lower and lower.* **1.3** is close to the bottom of ADJ QUALIT
something. EG *She saw the scar low on his spine.* OR ADV

Should you always try to write lucidly?

2 A dress or blouse that is described as **low** leaves a woman's neck and the top part of her chest bare. EG ...*a low neckline... Her dress was cut low in front.*   ADJ QUALIT OR ADV

3 Low means small in amount, value, or degree. EG ...*workers on low incomes... Temperatures are lower on the continent in winter than in Britain... ...low expectations... ...a low tar cigarette.*   ADJ QUALIT

4 You can use **low** with numbers. For example, if a number or level is **in the low** twenties, it is more than twenty, but not as much as twenty-five. EG *The temperature is in the low eighties.*   PHRASE

5 If a supply of something is **low** or if you are **low** on a particular type of thing, you do not have much of it left. EG *We're a bit low on claret.*   ADJ PRED

6 If the quality or standard of something is **low**, it is bad. EG ...*a low standard of living... ...low-grade material.*   ADJ QUALIT

7 Low is used to describe people who are near the bottom of a particular scale or system. EG ...*a junior executive of a fairly low grade... ...the lowest 85 per cent of the working population.*   ADJ QUALIT

8 If you have a **low** opinion of someone, you disapprove of them or dislike them.   ADJ QUALIT

9 You also use **low** to describe people and actions which are not respectable and which you disapprove of. EG ...*mixing with low company... Well I'm not doing that. I haven't sunk that low.*   ADJ QUALIT OR ADV

10 If a sound is **low**, **10.1** it is deep. EG ...*a long low note on the horn.* **10.2** it is quiet or soft. EG *Smithy spoke to him in a low and urgent voice... He turned the radio on low.*   ADJ QUALIT / ADJ QUALIT OR ADV

11 A light that is **low** is dim rather than bright.   ADJ QUALIT

12 Someone who is feeling **low** is depressed.   ADJ QUALIT

13 A **low** is the worst or smallest level that something has ever reached. EG *Output was at a record low.*   N COUNT+SUPP

14 If you **are lying low**, you are avoiding being seen in public. EG *She'll have to lie low for a couple of years.*   PHRASE Informal

low-cut dresses and blouses leave a woman's neck, shoulders, and the top part of her chest bare.   ADJ QUALIT

lower /ˈləʊə/, **lowers, lowering, lowered. 1 Lower** is the comparative of **low**.

2 Lower is used to describe **2.1** the bottom one of a pair of things. EG *Thomas was lying in the lower bunk... Jane sucked at her lower lip.* **2.2** the less important one of two organizations or systems that work together. EG *He could argue his case in the lower court.* **2.3** the bottom part of something. EG *The bullet had penetrated the lower left corner of his back.*   ADJ CLASSIF: ATTRIB

3 Lower also describes people or things that are less important than other people or things. EG ...*the lower levels of the organization.*   ADJ CLASSIF: ATTRIB

4 If you **lower** something, **4.1** you move it slowly downwards. EG *He lowered his glass... Lynn lowered herself into the water.* **4.2** you make it less in amount, value, or quality. EG *The voting age was lowered to eighteen... Mexican hotels are lowering their rates sharply.* ◊ **lowering.** EG ...*the lowering of examination standards.*   V+O / V+O / ◊ N SING +SUPP

5 If you **lower** your eyes, you look downwards. EG *She lowered her eyes and remained silent.*   V+O

6 If you **lower** your voice, you speak more quietly.   V+O

lower class, lower classes. The **lower class** or **lower classes** are the social class that is below the middle class. EG *I'm one of the lower classes and I'm proud of it... ...lower-class families.*   N COUNT: USU PLURAL

low-key. Something that is **low-key** or **low-keyed** is not obvious or intense. EG *The organization lent us support in its own low-key way.*   ADJ QUALIT

lowlands /ˈləʊləⁿdz/. A flat area of land that is approximately at sea level is sometimes referred to as the **lowlands**. EG ...*the Scottish Lowlands... The cattle are brought down to the lowlands.*   N PLURAL

lowly /ˈləʊlɪ¹/, **lowlier, lowliest.** Something that is **lowly** is low in rank, status, or importance. EG ...*a lowly employee... ...his lowly social origins.*   ADJ QUALIT

low-paid. When workers earn only a small amount of money, you can say that they are **low-paid** or that their jobs are **low-paid**. EG ...*low-paid workers... ...women in low paid jobs.*   ADJ QUALIT

low tide is the time at which the sea is at its lowest level at the coast each day before it starts to rise again. EG *The rocks are exposed at low tide.*   N UNCOUNT

loyal /ˈlɔɪəl/. Someone who is **loyal** remains firm in their friendship or support for someone or something. EG *Most Tories remained loyal to the Government... ...a loyal friend.* ◊ **loyally.** EG *For thirty years she had served him loyally.*   ADJ QUALIT: OFT+to / ◊ ADV

loyalty /ˈlɔɪəltɪ¹/, **loyalties. 1 Loyalty** is behaviour in which you stay firm in your friendship or support for someone or something. EG *I am convinced of your loyalty to the cause.*   N UNCOUNT

2 Loyalties are feelings of friendship, support, or duty towards someone or something. EG ...*an issue that transcended party loyalties... ...their loyalties to the church.*   N COUNT: USU PLURAL

lozenge /ˈlɒzɪ²ndʒ/, **lozenges. 1** A **lozenge** is a tablet which you can suck when you have a cough or sore throat. EG ...*throat lozenges.*   N COUNT

2 A **lozenge** is also a shape like a square which usually has two corners pointing up and down that are further apart than the corners that point sideways.   N COUNT

LP /ˌel ˈpiː/, **LPs.** An **LP** is a record which has about 25 minutes of music or speech on each side.   N COUNT

L-plate /ˈel pleɪt/, **L-plates. L-plates** are square white pieces of plastic or metal with a red 'L' on them which you attach to the front and back of a car when you are learning to drive.   N COUNT

LSD /ˌel es ˈdiː/ is a very powerful drug which causes strong hallucinations.   N UNCOUNT

Ltd is written after the name of a company. **Ltd** is an abbreviation for 'limited'. EG ...*Cobuild Ltd.*

lubricate /ˈluːbrɪkeɪt/, **lubricates, lubricating, lubricated.** If you **lubricate** part of a machine, you put a substance such as oil onto it so that it moves smoothly. EG *The chain might need lubricating.* ◊ **lubrication** /ˌluːbrɪˈkeɪʃəⁿn/. EG ...*the lubrication system of the engine.*   V+O / ◊ N UNCOUNT

lucid /ˈluːsɪd/. **1** Writing or speech that is **lucid** is clear and easy to understand. EG ...*a brief and lucid account.* ◊ **lucidly.** EG *Her ideas are very lucidly set out in his book.* ◊ **lucidity** /luːˈsɪdɪ¹tɪ¹/. EG *He expresses himself with quiet lucidity.*   ADJ QUALIT Formal / ◊ ADV / ◊ N UNCOUNT

2 When someone who has been ill or confused is **lucid**, they are able to think clearly again. EG *There was a ringing in my head, yet I was lucid.* ◊ **lucidity.** EG *In one of his moments of lucidity, he came upstairs to talk.*   ADJ QUALIT Formal / ◊ N UNCOUNT

3 Things that are **lucid** are very bright and clear. EG ...*a lucid light.*   ADJ QUALIT Literary

luck /lʌk/. **1 Luck** or good **luck** is success that does not come from your own abilities or efforts. EG *I had some wonderful luck... He wished me luck.*   N UNCOUNT

2 Bad luck is lack of success or bad things that happen to you, that have not been caused by yourself or other people. EG *One spring we had a lot of bad luck.*   PHRASE

3 Luck is used in these phrases. **3.1** If you say **'Bad luck'** or **'Hard luck'** to someone, you are expressing sympathy when they have failed to do something or failed to get something. EG *Tough luck, Barrett. You played a great game.* **3.2** If you say **'Good luck'** or **'Best of luck'** to someone, you are saying that you hope that they will be successful. EG *Good luck to you, my boy... Best of luck with the exams.* **3.3** If you say that someone is **in luck**, you mean that they are lucky on a particular occasion. **3.4** If you say that someone **is pushing** their **luck**, you mean that they are taking a risk and may get into trouble. **3.5** When someone **tries** their **luck** at something, they try to succeed at it. EG *He came to England to try his luck at a musical career.* **3.6** You can add **with luck** or **with any luck** to a statement to indicate that you hope that a particu-   CONVENTION / CONVENTION / PHRASE / PHRASE / PHRASE / ADV SEN Informal

lar thing will happen. EG *This one should work with a bit of luck... With any luck they might forget all about it.*

luckily /lʌkılıˈ/. You can add **luckily** to what you ADV SEN are saying to indicate that you are glad that something happened. EG *Luckily, Saturday was a fine day... Luckily, Joe came to my rescue... Luckily for you, I happen to have the key.*

luckless /lʌklıˈs/. If someone is **luckless** or if ADJ QUALIT something that they do is **luckless**, they are unsuc- Literary cessful or unfortunate. EG *This trip of ours has been singularly luckless.*

lucky /lʌkiˈ/, **luckier, luckiest. 1** You say that ADJ QUALIT someone is **lucky 1.1** when they have something that is very desirable, or when they are in a very desirable situation. EG *I'm lucky in having an excellent teacher... He was the luckiest man in the world. **1.2** when they always seem to have good luck. EG Are you lucky at cards?*

2 If you describe an event or situation as **lucky**, ADJ QUALIT you mean that it had good effects or consequences, although it happened by chance and not as a result of planning or preparation. EG *It's lucky I'm here... It was lucky that I had cooked a big joint... ...a lucky guess.*

3 People describe something that they wear or ADJ CLASSIF have with them as **lucky** when they believe that it helps them to be successful. EG *...his lucky sweater.*

4 If you say that someone **will be lucky** to do PHRASE something, you mean it is very unlikely that they Informal will be able to do it. EG *We will be lucky to get five pounds for it.*

lucrative /luːkrətıv/. Something that is **lucrative** ADJ QUALIT earns you a lot of money. EG *It had been an exciting* Formal *and lucrative business... ...the lucrative trade in tea and porcelain.*

ludicrous /luːdıkrəs/. If you describe something ADJ QUALIT as **ludicrous**, you mean that it is extremely foolish, unreasonable, or unsuitable. EG *I had a ludicrous feeling of pride in him... ...one teacher for every 100 pupils, it was ludicrous.* ◇ **ludicrously.** EG *...a* ◇ ADV *ludicrously low price.*

lug /lʌg/, **lugs, lugging, lugged.** If you **lug** a V+O:USU+A heavy object from one place to another, you carry Informal it there with difficulty. EG *She lugged the suitcase out into the hallway.*

luggage /lʌgıdʒ/ consists of the suitcases and N UNCOUNT bags that you have with you when you are travelling. EG *They did not have much luggage.* ● See also **left-luggage office.**

lugubrious /ləˈguːbrıəs/. You describe someone ADJ QUALIT or something as **lugubrious** when they are sad Formal and dull, and not lively or cheerful. EG *...a lugubrious face... ...lugubrious hymns.*

lukewarm /luːkwɔːm/. **1** Something that is **luke- ADJ QUALIT warm** is only slightly warm. EG *...lukewarm water.*

2 If you describe someone as **lukewarm**, you ADJ QUALIT mean that they do not show much enthusiasm or interest. EG *...her parents' lukewarm response... He was lukewarm about the committee.*

lull /lʌl/, **lulls, lulling, lulled. 1** A **lull** is a period N COUNT: of quiet or of little activity. EG *...a lull in the* USU+SUPP *conversation... After a lull of several weeks, there has been a resumption of bombing.*

2 If you describe a situation as the **lull before the** PHRASE **storm**, you mean that you think something very unpleasant is going to happen soon.

3 If something **lulls** you, **3.1** it causes you to feel V+O: calm or sleepy. EG *...lulling us into slumber.* **3.2** it USU+into causes you to feel safe and secure. EG *He had lulled me into thinking that I had won.*

lullaby /lʌləbaı/, **lullabies.** A **lullaby** is a quiet N COUNT song which you sing to help a child go to sleep.

lumber /lʌmbə/, **lumbers, lumbering, lum- N UNCOUNT bered. 1 Lumber** consists of **1.1** tree trunks, logs, American or planks of wood that have been roughly cut up. EG *...piles of lumber... ...a lumber company.* **1.2** old British and unwanted things, especially old pieces of furniture. EG *...the lumber room.*

2 If someone **lumbers** from one place to another, V+A they move there very slowly and clumsily. EG *He lumbered upstairs looking for the bathroom... Donkeys lumbered by.*

lumber with. If you **are lumbered with** some- PHRASAL VB: thing such as a duty, you have to deal with it even V+O+PREP, though you do not want to. EG *Women are still* OFT PASS lumbered with the cooking and cleaning.

luminous /luːmınəs/. Something that is **luminous** ADJ QUALIT shines or glows, especially in the dark. EG *...the luminous hands of my watch.*

lump /lʌmp/, **lumps, lumping, lumped. 1** A N COUNT **lump** is a piece of a solid substance, of any shape OR N PART or size. EG *...lumps of clay... ...a lump of butter.*

2 A **lump** on or in someone's body is a small, hard N COUNT piece of flesh that is formed as a result of an injury or an illness. EG *...a small lump, a little growth just above the right eye.*

3 A **lump** of sugar is a small amount of sugar N PART shaped like a cube. EG *Black coffee, two lumps, please.*

4 If you **lump** different people or things together, V+O+with/ you consider them in the same way or combine together them into one large group. EG *'Don't lump me and Dave together,' he interrupted... The old rural counties were lumped together into new units.*

5 If you say that someone will **have to lump it,** PHRASE you mean that they must accept a situation or Informal decision whether they like it or not. EG *'He won't like that.' – 'Then he'll lump it.'*

lump sum, lump sums. A **lump sum** is an N COUNT amount of money that is paid as a large amount on a single occasion rather than as smaller amounts on several separate occasions. EG *He has been offered a tax-free lump sum of $4,000.*

lumpy /lʌmpiˈ/. Something that is **lumpy** contains ADJ QUALIT lumps or is covered with lumps. EG *...sitting on his lumpy mattress... ...a big bowl of lumpy porridge.*

lunacy /luːnəsiˈ/ is **1** very strange or foolish N UNCOUNT behaviour. EG *This comment would have seemed sheer lunacy to his ancestors... It would be lunacy to marry.* **2** severe mental illness. Outdated

lunar /luːnə/ means concerning the moon or trav- ADJ CLASSIF: el to the moon. EG *...the lunar surface... ...the lunar* ATTRIB spacecraft. Formal

lunatic /luːnətık/, **lunatics. 1** If you describe N COUNT someone as a **lunatic**, you mean that they behave Informal in a stupid and annoying way. EG *The man's a bloody lunatic.*

2 A **lunatic** is also someone who is mad. EG *Out of a* N COUNT dozen patients, three or four were lunatics. Outdated

3 If you say that a proposal or an action is **lunatic**, ADJ QUALIT you mean that it is foolish and likely to be dangerous. EG *This Government's policies are lunatic.*

lunatic asylum, lunatic asylums. A **lunatic** N COUNT **asylum** is a place where people were locked up in former times when they were considered to be mad.

lunatic fringe. If you refer to a group of people N SING: the+N as the **lunatic fringe**, you mean that they are very extreme in their opinions or behaviour. EG *...the lunatic fringe of the movement.*

lunch /lʌntʃ/, **lunches, lunching, lunched. 1** N UNCOUNT **Lunch** is a meal that you have in the middle of the OR N COUNT day. EG *What did you have for lunch?... We had a late lunch... After lunch I went to see our doctor.*

2 When you **lunch**, you eat lunch, especially at a V:USU+A restaurant. EG *Why don't you two lunch with me* Formal *tomorrow?... She was lunching off beer and cheese rolls in a pub.*

luncheon /lʌntʃəˈn/, **luncheons. 1** A **luncheon** is N COUNT a formal meal in the middle of the day. EG *I had met him at a civic luncheon... ...a luncheon party.*

2 Luncheon is the meal that you eat in the middle N UNCOUNT of the day. EG *I was planning something hot for luncheon.*

lunch hour, lunch hours. Your **lunch hour** is the period in the middle of the day when you stop work in order to have a meal. EG *The secretaries were just back from their lunch hour.*   N COUNT

lunchtime /lʌntˈʃtaɪm/, **lunchtimes. Lunchtime** is the time in the middle of the day when people have lunch. EG *She's going to see him at lunchtime.*   N COUNT OR N UNCOUNT

lung /lʌŋ/, **lungs.** Your **lungs** are the two parts of your body inside your chest which fill with air when you breathe. EG *She filled her lungs with smoke... ...lung cancer.*   N COUNT : USU PLURAL

lunge /lʌndʒ/, **lunges, lunging, lunged.** If you **lunge** in a particular direction, you move there suddenly and clumsily. EG *He lunged toward me.* ▸ used as a noun. EG *When he makes a lunge at you, run.*   V : USU+A   ▸ N COUNT : USU SING

lurch /lɜːtʃ/, **lurches, lurching, lurched. 1** To **lurch** means to make a sudden, jerky movement. EG *He lurched and fell... The boat lurched ahead.* ▸ used as a noun. EG *With a tremendous lurch he fell over me.*   V : USU+A   ▸ N COUNT
2 If you **lurch** from one thing to another, you suddenly change your opinions, attitude, or behaviour. EG *After lurching away from Socialism in 1976, they now seem to be lurching back.*   V+A
3 If someone **leaves** you **in the lurch**, they go away or stop helping you at a very difficult or dangerous time. EG *It's the whole theatre group he's leaving in the lurch.*   PHRASE Informal

lure /lʊə/, **lures, luring, lured. 1** To **lure** someone means to attract them and cause them to do something or go somewhere. EG *The price also lures students... Why else had Halliday come up, if not to lure me away?*   V+O : USU+A
2 A **lure** is an attractive quality that something has. EG *Many economists have succumbed to the fatal lure of mathematics.*   N COUNT+SUPP

lurid /lʊərɪd/. Something that is **lurid 1** involves a lot of violence or sex; used showing disapproval. EG *...lurid stories about the war... ...lurid novels.* **2** is very brightly coloured. EG *...lurid polyester skirts.* ◊ **luridly.** EG *...a luridly coloured advertisement.*   ADJ QUALIT   ADJ QUALIT   ◊ ADV

lurk /lɜːk/, **lurks, lurking, lurked. 1** To **lurk** somewhere means to wait there secretly so that you cannot be seen. EG *Wild boars and wolves lurked near the isolated camp.*   V : USU+A
2 If something such as a memory, suspicion, or danger **lurks**, it exists, but you are only slightly aware of it. EG *...outdated prejudices lurking in the minds of individuals.*   V : USU+A

luscious /lʌʃəs/. **1** If you describe something as **luscious**, you mean that you find it extremely attractive. EG *...a luscious car... She was looking luscious in faded overalls and a flannel shirt.*   ADJ QUALIT
2 Luscious food is juicy and delicious. EG *...a basket of luscious figs.*   ADJ QUALIT

lush /lʌʃ/, **lusher, lushest. 1** You describe fields or gardens as **lush** when the grass or plants there are very healthy and are growing well and thickly. EG *...a landscape of lush green meadows.*   ADJ QUALIT
2 You can describe places or ways of life as **lush** when they are very rich and full of luxury. EG *...lush restaurants in London and Paris.*   ADJ QUALIT

lust /lʌst/, **lusts, lusting, lusted. 1 Lust** is a feeling of strong sexual desire for someone; used showing disapproval.   N UNCOUNT
2 A **lust** for something is a very strong and eager desire to possess or gain it; used showing disapproval. EG *...the lust for power.*   N COUNT : OFT+*for*

lust after or **lust for. 1** If you **lust after** something or **lust for** it, you have a very strong desire to possess it. EG *They lusted after the gold of El Dorado.*   PHRASAL VB : V+PREP, HAS PASS
2 If you **lust after** someone or **lust for** them, you feel a very strong sexual desire for them. EG *How I lusted for that girl!*   V+PREP, HAS PASS

lustful /lʌstfʊl/ means feeling or expressing strong sexual desire. EG *...lustful thoughts.*   ADJ CLASSIF

lustre /lʌstə/; spelled **luster** in American English.
1 Lustre is gentle shining light that is reflected from a surface, for example from polished metal. EG *...the lustre of encrusted gold.*   N UNCOUNT Literary
2 You can refer to the qualities of something that make it interesting and exciting as its **lustre**. EG *...the tarnished lustre of his name.*   N UNCOUNT Literary

lusty /lʌsti¹/, **lustier, lustiest. Lusty** means healthy and full of strength and energy. EG *...a strong and lusty boy of whom any father could be proud.* ◊ **lustily.** EG *They stood waving their Union Jacks and singing lustily.*   ADJ QUALIT   ◊ ADV

luxuriant /lʌgzjʊərɪənt, lʌgʒ-/. **1** You can describe plants, trees, and gardens which are large, healthy, and growing well as **luxuriant**. EG *...luxuriant forests.*   ADJ QUALIT
2 You can also use **luxuriant** to describe someone's hair when it is very thick and healthy. EG *...his pale lined face and luxuriant, flowing hair.*   ADJ QUALIT

luxuriate /lʌgzjʊərɪeɪt, lʌgʒ-/, **luxuriates, luxuriating, luxuriated.** If you **luxuriate** in something, you relax in it and enjoy it very much. EG *...bath tubs in which you could lie back and luxuriate... I luxuriated in my retirement.*   V : USU+*in*

luxurious /lʌgzjʊərɪəs, lʌgʒ-/. **1** Something that is **luxurious** is very comfortable and expensive. EG *...big, luxurious cars.* ◊ **luxuriously.** EG *We lived luxuriously.*   ADJ QUALIT   ◊ ADV
2 Luxurious actions express great pleasure and comfort. EG *She took a deep luxurious breath.* ◊ **luxuriously.** EG *She stretched luxuriously.*   ADJ QUALIT   ◊ ADV

luxury /lʌkʃə⁰ri¹/, **luxuries. 1 Luxury** is very great comfort, especially among beautiful and expensive surroundings and possessions. EG *We lived in great luxury... ...a life of ease and luxury.*   N UNCOUNT
2 A **luxury** is **2.1** something expensive which is not necessary but which gives you pleasure. EG *Her mother provided her with clothes and little luxuries.* **2.2** a pleasure which you do not often have the opportunity to enjoy. EG *Privacy was an unknown luxury.*   N COUNT   N SING+SUPP
3 Luxury is used, especially in advertising, to describe expensive things which are very comfortable or of a special design. EG *...luxury hotels... ...a luxury car.*   ADJ CLASSIF ATTRIB

-ly is added to adjectives to form adverbs. For example 'loudly' means in a loud way, and 'rudely' means in a rude way. Adverbs like these are often not defined in this dictionary but are treated with the related adjectives. EG *He walked slowly down the street... 'I was hoping you would,' Morris said mischievously.*   SUFFIX

lying /laɪɪŋ/. **1 Lying** is the present participle of **lie**.
2 A **lying** person is dishonest or deceitful. EG *...those lying journalists.*   ADJ CLASSIF ATTRIB
3 Lying is the act of telling lies. EG *She's incapable of lying.*   N UNCOUNT

lynch /lɪntˈʃ/, **lynchs, lynching, lynched.** If an angry crowd of people **lynch** someone, they kill them because they believe that they have committed a crime. EG *At one point he was in danger of being lynched.*   V+O

lyric /lɪrɪk/, **lyrics. 1 Lyric** poetry is written in a simple and direct style, and is usually about love.   ADJ CLASSIF ATTRIB
2 The **lyrics** of a modern song are its words. EG *The lyrics are maddeningly memorable.*   N PLURAL

lyrical /lɪrɪkə⁰l/. **1** Something that is **lyrical** is **1.1** poetic and musical. EG *He tries to bring into his plays a special lyrical quality.* **1.2** very romantic. EG *...a dreamy, lyrical study of the Covent Garden flower market.*   ADJ CLASSIF   ADJ QUALIT
2 If you are **lyrical** about something, you are very enthusiastic and eager about it. EG *Ned was growing lyrical.* ◊ **lyrically.** EG *It was Johnson, I remembered, who had written so lyrically about Woolley.*   ADJ PRED   ◊ ADV

M m

M, m /ɛm/, **Ms, m's.** **1 M** is the thirteenth letter of N COUNT the English alphabet.

2 m is a written abbreviation for 'metres' or 'metre'.

M.A. /ɛm eɪ/, **M.A.s.** An **M.A.** is a higher degree in N COUNT the arts or social sciences. **M.A.** is an abbreviation for 'Master of Arts'. EG ...an M.A. in Applied Linguistics.

ma'am /mɑːm/ is a spoken abbreviation for 'mad- VOCATIVE am'. EG A gentleman has called, ma'am. Outdated

mac /mæk/, **macs.** A **mac** is the same as a N COUNT mackintosh. EG They wore their plastic macs... She Informal was pulling on her old mac. British

macabre /məkɑːbrəʰ/ events or stories are very ADJ QUALIT strange and horrible, and usually involve death or injury. EG ...macabre sacrifices... ...a macabre story.

macaroni /mækərəʊniʰ/ is a kind of pasta made N UNCOUNT in the shape of short hollow tubes.

machete /məʃetiʰ/, **machetes.** A **machete** is a N COUNT large knife with a broad blade.

machine /məʃiːn/, **machines, machining, machined.** **1** A **machine** is a piece of equipment N COUNT which uses electricity or power from an engine. EG She took the paper out of the roller and shut the machine... The machine is beyond repair.

2 If you **machine** something, you make it, cut it, or V+O change its shape using a machine. ◇ **machining.** ◇ N UNCOUNT EG The work of machining a part is very slow.

3 You also use **machine** to refer to a well- N COUNT+SUPP controlled system or organization. EG ...the might of the enemy war machine... They had perfected their own propaganda machine.

machine gun, machine guns. A **machine gun** N COUNT is a gun which works automatically and which fires a lot of bullets very quickly one after the other. EG ...bursts of machine-gun fire.

machinery /məʃiːnəʰriʰ/. **1** If you talk about **ma- N UNCOUNT chinery**, you are referring to machines in general, or to machines that are used in a factory. EG Machinery is being introduced to save labour... ...the export of textile machinery to India.

2 The **machinery** of a government or organization N UNCOUNT is the system that it uses in order to deal with +SUPP things. EG The party controls the state machinery... We need to discuss ways of improving the machinery of government.

machismo /mætʃɪzməʊ, -kɪz-/ is aggressively N UNCOUNT masculine behaviour or attitudes; used showing disapproval. EG ...the powerful machismo of the hero.

macho /mætʃəʊ/. You describe a man as **macho** ADJ QUALIT when you think that he behaves or dresses in an Informal aggressively masculine way; used showing disapproval. EG He emerged with a macho swagger... They were dressed in macho leather.

macintosh /mækɪntɒʃ/. See **mackintosh**.

mackerel /mækəʰrəl/, **mackerels.** A **mackerel** N COUNT OR is a kind of fish. The plural form of 'mackerel' is N UNCOUNT either 'mackerel' or 'mackerels'. EG ...shoals of mackerel.

mackintosh /mækɪntɒʃ/, **mackintoshes;** also N COUNT spelled **macintosh**. A **mackintosh** is a raincoat, especially one made from a particular kind of waterproof cloth. EG He took off his black mackintosh.

mad /mæd/, **madder, maddest. 1** Someone who is ADJ CLASSIF **mad** has a mind that does not work in a normal way, so that their behaviour is very strange and sometimes frightening. EG Rose was mad, there was no doubt about it... She was married to a man who'd gone mad. ◇ **madness.** EG ...the terrible ◇ N UNCOUNT madness that overtook the king.

2 You can also say that someone is **mad 2.1** when ADJ QUALIT they do or say things that you think are very foolish. EG You must be mad!... They think I am mad to live in such a place. ◇ **madness.** EG It is ◇ N UNCOUNT madness for them to remain unarmed. **2.2** when ADJ PRED they are very angry. EG He got pretty mad... They're mad at me for getting them up so early.

3 You use **mad** to describe behaviour that is wild ADJ CLASSIF: and uncontrolled. EG I was dashing around in the ATTRIB usual mad panic... ...the mad whirl of pleasure.

4 If you say that someone is **driving** you **mad** or PHRASE that they **will drive** you **mad**, you mean that they are annoying you very much by their behaviour. EG These blinking kids will drive me mad.

5 If you are **mad** about something or someone, you ADJ PRED like them very much indeed. EG For years he's been +about mad about opera... I'm mad about you. Informal

6 If you do something **like mad**, you do it very PHRASE energetically or enthusiastically. EG They were still Informal arguing like mad at six in the evening.

7 When an audience **goes mad**, they cheer and PHRASE clap very enthusiastically. EG Thousands of people Informal are ready to go mad at the mere sight of him.

madam /mædəʰm/. People sometimes address a VOCATIVE woman as **Madam** when they are being very formal and polite. 'Dear Madam' is often used at the beginning of letters. EG Dear Madam, Thank you for your letter replying to our advertisement... 'Yes, madam,' Harry Standish said.

madden /mædəʰn/, **maddens, maddening, mad- V+O dened.** If something **maddens** you, it makes you feel very angry or annoyed. EG The colonel's calmness maddened Pluskat. ◇ **maddening.** EG It ◇ ADJ QUALIT makes a maddening clicking noise... Lady Sackville Outdated was a maddening person to live with.

made /meɪd/ is the past tense and past participle of **make**.

-made combines with words such as 'factory' to indicate that something has been made or produced in a particular way or at a particular place. EG It's factory-made... Locally-made goods had to pay internal customs duties. ● See also **handmade**, **home-made**, **man-made**, **self-made**.

made-to-measure. A **made-to-measure** suit or ADJ CLASSIF shirt is one that is made by a tailor to fit you exactly, rather than one that you buy in a shop.

madhouse /mædhaʊs/, **madhouses.** If you say N COUNT: that a place is a **madhouse**, you mean that it is full USU SING of noise and confusion. EG This place will be a madhouse when all the kids arrive.

madly /mædliʰ/. **1** If you do something **madly**, you ADV do it very quickly, because you are eager, excited, or afraid. EG We began rushing around madly in the dark.

2 If you are **madly in love** with someone, you are PHRASE very much in love with them. EG I fell madly in love with Ellen the first time I ever saw her.

madman /mædmaʰn/, **madmen. 1** A **madman** is N COUNT a man who is mad. EG They locked him up as a madman.

2 You can refer to someone who behaves in a very N COUNT foolish or irresponsible way as a **madman**. EG I have had enough trouble with that madman Smith.

magazine /mægəziːn/, **magazines. 1** A **maga- N COUNT zine** is a publication with a paper cover which is issued regularly, usually weekly or monthly, and which contains articles, stories, photographs and advertisements. EG I got the recipe from a woman's magazine... ...a magazine article.

2 On radio or television, a **magazine** is a pro- N COUNT gramme with interesting stories about people and events. EG *Newsbeat is the popular news magazine on Radio 1.*

maggot /ˈmægət/, **maggots.** A **maggot** is a tiny N COUNT creature that looks like a very small worm. Maggots turn into flies.

magic /ˈmædʒɪk/. 1 In fairy stories, **magic** is a N UNCOUNT special power that can make apparently impossible things happen. For example, it can control events in nature or make people disappear. EG *He could see the magic beginning to do its work... She was accused of inflicting bad fortune on them through evil magic.* ▸ used as an adjective. EG *...the* ▸ ADJ CLASSIF : *magic forest... How fast the magic potion worked!* ATTRIB
2 **Magic** is also the art and skill of performing N UNCOUNT tricks to entertain people, for example by seeming to make things appear and disappear. EG *He was in his bedroom practising magic tricks.*
3 The **magic** of something is a special quality that N UNCOUNT makes it seem wonderful and exciting. EG *...the magic of theatre... They need a bit of magic in their lives.* ▸ used as an adjective. EG *That was a* ▸ ADJ QUALIT *truly magic moment.*

magical /ˈmædʒɪkəl/. 1 Something that is **magi-** ADJ CLASSIF **cal** uses magic or is able to produce magic. EG *I used to believe my mother had magical powers... ...a stream of magical water.*
2 You can also say that something is **magical** ADJ QUALIT when it has a special mysterious quality that makes it seem wonderful and exciting. EG *The journey had lost all its magical quality.*
◊ **magically.** EG *The horizon was magically filling* ◊ ADV *with ships.*

magician /məˈdʒɪʃən/, **magicians.** A **magician** N COUNT is 1 a person who performs tricks as a form of entertainment. EG *This process is very effectively used by stage magicians.* 2 a man in a fairy story who has magic powers.

magistrate /ˈmædʒɪstreɪt/, **magistrates.** A **mag-** N COUNT **istrate** is an official who acts as a judge in a law court which deals with less serious crimes or disputes. EG *You'll have to appear before the magistrate... ...the magistrates' court.*

magnanimous /mægˈnænɪməs/. If you are **mag-** ADJ QUALIT **nanimous**, you are generous towards someone, especially after you have beaten them in a fight or contest. EG *We must encourage new regimes to be magnanimous towards their former oppressors.*

magnate /ˈmægneɪt/, **magnates.** A **magnate** is N COUNT+SUPP someone who has become very powerful in a business or industry because they have earned a lot of money from it. EG *...a rich shipping magnate... ...a press magnate.*

magnet /ˈmægnɪt/, **magnets.** A **magnet** is a N COUNT piece of iron or other material which attracts iron or steel towards it. EG *The pin was extracted with a magnet.*

magnetic /mægˈnetɪk/. 1 Something that is **mag-** ADJ CLASSIF **netic** has the power of a magnet to attract iron or steel towards it. EG *He took a carving knife from a magnetic board on the wall.*
2 If you say that someone is **magnetic** or has ADJ QUALIT : **magnetic** qualities, you mean that they have ATTRIB unusual and exciting qualities that people find attractive. EG *Without magnetic appeal, the politician is unlikely to succeed.*

magnetic tape, magnetic tapes. Magnetic N UNCOUNT **tape** is narrow plastic tape covered with a magnet- OR N COUNT ic substance. It is used for recording sounds, film, or computer information.

magnetism /ˈmægnɪtɪzəm/. 1 **Magnetism** is a N UNCOUNT power that attracts some substances towards others. EG *...the forces of electricity and magnetism.*
2 If someone has **magnetism**, they have unusual N UNCOUNT and exciting qualities which people find very attractive. EG *He had immense personal magnetism.*

magnification /ˌmægnɪfɪˈkeɪʃən/, **magnifica-** tions. 1 **Magnification** is the process by which N UNCOUNT something is made to appear bigger than it actually is, as, for example, when you use a microscope.

2 The **magnification** of a microscope, telescope, N UNCOUNT or pair of binoculars is the degree to which it can OR N COUNT magnify things. EG *All the images, even under the highest magnification, were simply points of light.*

magnificent /mægˈnɪfɪsənt/. Something that is ADJ QUALIT **magnificent** is extremely good, beautiful, or impressive. EG *It's a magnificent book... Her dress is magnificent.* ◊ **magnificently.** EG *They per-* ◊ ADV *formed magnificently... He was magnificently dressed.*

magnify /ˈmægnɪfaɪ/, **magnifies, magnifying, magnified.** 1 When a microscope or magnifying V+O glass **magnifies** an object, it makes it appear bigger than it actually is. EG *The lenses magnified his eyes to the size of dinner plates.*
2 To **magnify** something also means to make it V+O seem more important than it actually is. EG *His fears have greatly magnified the true dangers... Minor advances were magnified into victories.*

magnifying glass, magnifying glasses. A N COUNT **magnifying glass** is a piece of glass which makes objects appear bigger than they actually are.

magnitude /ˈmægnɪtjuːd/ is the great size or great N UNCOUNT importance of something. EG *They do not recognize the magnitude of the problem.*

magpie /ˈmægpaɪ/, **magpies.** A **magpie** is a bird N COUNT with black and white markings and a long tail.

mahogany /məˈhɒgənɪ/ is a dark reddish-brown N UNCOUNT wood that is used to make furniture. EG *...a tall mahogany bookcase.*

maid /meɪd/, **maids.** A **maid** is a woman who N COUNT works as a servant in a hotel or private house. EG *The maid will bring you your wine in a moment.*

maiden /ˈmeɪdən/, **maidens.** 1 A **maiden** is a N COUNT young girl or woman, especially a beautiful one. EG Literary *Maidens performed graceful dances.*
2 The **maiden** voyage or flight of a ship or ADJ CLASSIF : aeroplane is the first official journey that it makes ATTRIB with passengers.

maiden aunt, maiden aunts. A **maiden aunt** is N COUNT an aunt who is quite old but is not married. Outdated

maiden name, maiden names. A woman's N COUNT **maiden name** is the surname she had before she got married and took her husband's surname. EG *My maiden name was Byers.*

mail /meɪl/, **mails, mailing, mailed. 1 Mail** is N UNCOUNT the letters and parcels that the post office delivers to you. EG *If there's anything urgent in the mail, I'll deal with it... Minnie was alone in the post office, sorting mail.*
2 The **mail** is the system used by the post office for N SING : *the+N* collecting and delivering letters and parcels. EG OR *by+N* *Send it to me by mail.*
3 If you **mail** something, you post it. EG *The books* V+O *had to be mailed directly from the publisher.*

mailbag /ˈmeɪlbæg/, **mailbags.** A **mailbag** is a N COUNT large bag that is used by the post office for carrying letters and parcels.

mailbox /ˈmeɪlbɒks/, **mailboxes.** A **mailbox** is 1 N COUNT a box outside your house where the postman American delivers letters. 2 a large container in the street American where people can post letters.

mailing list, mailing lists. A **mailing list** is a N COUNT list of names and addresses that an organization has so that it can send people information. EG *Does anyone wish to be put on the mailing list?*

mailman /ˈmeɪlmən/, **mailmen.** A **mailman** is a N COUNT man whose job is to deliver letters and parcels that American are sent by post.

mail order is a system of buying goods in which N UNCOUNT you choose what you want from a firm's catalogue and the firm sends you what you have ordered by post. EG *The record is available by mail order... ...a mail-order firm.*

maim /meɪm/, **maims, maiming, maimed.** If V+O someone **maims** another person, they injure them so badly that they cannot use part of their body properly for the rest of their life. EG *These people kill and maim innocent civilians.*

main /meɪn/, **mains.** 1 The **main** thing is the most important thing in a particular situation. EG *What are the main reasons for going to university?... Mrs Foster hurried through the main entrance.* ADJ CLASSIF : ATTRIB

2 If you say that something is true **in the main**, you mean that it is generally true, although there may be exceptions. EG *The Worthingtons are in the main decent, friendly folk... In the main, overseas students want to be on campus.* ADV SEN Formal

3 The **mains** are the pipes or wires which supply gas, water, or electricity to buildings, or which take sewage from them. EG *The radio we have at home plugs into the mains... You needn't turn off the mains water.* N PLURAL : the+N

4 A **main** is a large pipe which carries gas, water, or sewage, and is connected to smaller pipes which link it to buildings. EG *A bulldozer had cut a gas main.* N COUNT

main clause, main clauses. In grammar, a **main clause** is a clause that can stand alone as a complete sentence. N COUNT

mainframe /meɪnfreɪm/, **mainframes.** A **mainframe** is a large computer which can be used by many people at the same time, and which can do very large or complicated tasks. N COUNT

mainland /meɪnlə³nd/. The **mainland** is the large main part of a country or continent, in contrast to the islands that form smaller parts of the country or continent. EG *The motorboat was waiting to ferry him back to the mainland.* ▶ used as an adjective. EG *...the coast of mainland Greece.* N SING : the+N ▶ ADJ CLASSIF : ATTRIB

mainly /meɪnliː/. You use **mainly** to say that a statement is true in most cases or to a large extent. EG *The political groups have more power, mainly because of their larger numbers... I'll be concentrating mainly on French and German... ...a queue of people, mainly children and old men.* ADV

main road, main roads. A **main road** is a large important road that leads from one town or city to another. EG *We turned off the main road shortly after Alcester.* N COUNT

mainspring /meɪnsprɪŋ/. The **mainspring** of something is the most important reason for it or the thing that is essential to it. EG *Technology was the mainspring of economic growth.* N SING+SUPP Formal

mainstay /meɪnsteɪ/, **mainstays.** The **mainstay** of something is the part of it which is the most important source of its strength or effectiveness. EG *Homemade chocolate cookies were the mainstay of my diet.* N COUNT+SUPP Formal

mainstream /meɪnstriːm/. The **mainstream** is the group of people or ideas that most people agree with, and which is therefore regarded as being normal and conventional. EG *We feel isolated from the mainstream of social life in the community.* ▶ used as an adjective. EG *...mainstream political parties... ...mainstream education.* N SING : USU+SUPP ▶ ADJ CLASSIF : ATTRIB

maintain /meɪnteɪn/, **maintains, maintaining, maintained.** 1 If you **maintain** something, you continue to have it, and do not let it stop or grow weaker. EG *I wanted to maintain my friendship with her... For twenty-five years they had failed to maintain law and order.* V+O

2 If you **maintain** something at a particular rate or level, you keep it at that rate or level, and do not let it become less. EG *One has to maintain the temperature at a very high level.* V+O+A

3 If you **maintain** someone, you provide them with money and the things that they need. EG *I need the money to maintain me until I start a job.* V+O

4 If you **maintain** something such as a building, vehicle, road, or machine, you keep it in good condition by regularly checking it and doing necessary repairs. EG *...the rising cost of maintaining the equipment.* V+O

5 If you **maintain** that something is true, you state your opinion or belief very strongly. EG *Mrs Camish* V+REPORT : ONLY that

always maintained that he had been a brilliant thinker.

maintenance /meɪntɪ⁶nəns/. 1 The **maintenance** of something such as a building, road, vehicle, or machine is the process of keeping it in good condition by regularly checking it and doing necessary repairs. EG *He learnt tractor maintenance... Who's responsible for the maintenance and care of the buildings?* N UNCOUNT

2 **Maintenance** is also money that someone gives to a person who they are legally responsible for but are not living with, in order to pay for necessary things such as food and clothes. For example, a man may have to pay maintenance to his ex-wife after a divorce. N UNCOUNT British

3 The **maintenance** of a state or process consists of making sure that it continues and does not stop or become weaker. EG *...the maintenance of law and order... ...the maintenance of an effective incomes policy.* N SING : the+N+of

maisonette /meɪzənet/, **maisonettes.** A **maisonette** is a small flat on two floors of a larger building. EG *She shared an upper maisonette with two other girls.* N COUNT British

maize /meɪz/ is a tall plant which produces sweet corn. EG *...a field planted with maize.* N UNCOUNT

majestic /mədʒestɪk/. Something or someone that is **majestic** is very beautiful, dignified, and impressive. EG *...the majestic proportions of the great Pyramid... She looked majestic in her large, soft hat.* ◊ **majestically.** EG *Wet clouds, heavy with rain, moved majestically overhead.* ADJ QUALIT ◊ ADV

Majesty /mædʒɪ²stiː¹/, **Majesties.** You use expressions such as **Your Majesty, Her Majesty**, or **Their Majesties** when you are addressing or referring to Kings or Queens; compare **Royal Highness.** EG *...Her Majesty the Queen... Thank you, Your Majesty.*

major /meɪdʒə/, **majors, majoring, majored.** 1 You use **major** to describe something which is more important, serious, or significant than other things. EG *Jones was to play a major part in the improvement of the paper... One major factor was the revolution in communications... Finding a solicitor had been a major problem.* ADJ QUALIT : ATTRIB

2 A **major** is an army officer of medium rank. EG *...Major Burton-Cox.* N COUNT

3 A **major** key is one of the two types of key in which most European music is written. It is based on a scale of notes in which the third note is two tones higher than the first note. EG *They're both in D major.* ADJ CLASSIF

4 If you **major** in a particular subject, you study it as your main subject at university. EG *I decided to major in French.* V+in American

majority /mədʒɒrɪ¹tiː¹/, **majorities.** 1 The **majority** of people or things in a group is a number of them that form more than half of the group. EG *...mass movements involving the overwhelming majority of the people... ...the principle of government by the majority.* ● If a group is **in a majority** or **in the majority**, they form more than half of a larger group. N SING : USU+of ● PHRASE

2 A **majority** is the difference between the number of votes that the winner gets in an election and the number of votes that the next person or party gets. EG *I was beaten by a large majority... Benn was returned by a majority of 15,479.* N COUNT : USU SING+SUPP

make /meɪk/, **makes, making, made** /meɪd/. 1 You can use **make** to say that someone performs an action. For example, if you say that someone **makes** a suggestion, you mean that they suggest something. EG *You've got to make a start somewhere... He made the shortest speech I've ever heard... He had two phone calls to make... We have* V+O

If someone is maintained by you, do they give you money?

got to make a really serious effort... I made the wrong decision... He felt I was making a terrible mistake.

2 If something **makes** you do something, it causes you to do it. EG *What makes you ask that?... A sudden noise made Brody jump.*   V+O+INF : IF PASS THEN +to-INF

3 If someone **makes** you do something, they force you to do it. EG *Make him listen!... They were made to sit and wait.*   V+O+INF : IF PASS THEN +to-INF

4 You use **make** to say that someone or something is caused to be a particular thing or to have a particular quality. For example, if something **makes** someone a star, it causes them to become a star. If something **makes** someone happy, it causes them to be happy. EG *I'd like to do something to make the world a better place... The cold was making Posy irritable... He feared the story had made things worse... Jack was the first to make himself heard... The army made a man of me... They're making the old kitchen into a little bedroom.*   V+O+C, V+O+of, OR V+O+into

5 You use **make** to say how well or how badly someone does something. For example, if you **make** a success of something, you do it well. EG *Let's not make a mess of this.*   V+O+of

6 If you **make** something, you produce it or construct it. EG *I like making cakes... ...the greatest film ever made... You can make petroleum out of coal... Martin, can you make us a drink?*   V+O : OFT+A, OR V+O+O

7 If something **is made** of a particular substance, that substance was used to form or construct it. EG *The houses were made of brick... ...a rug made of scraps of old clothes... What is it made of?*   V-PASS+of

8 If someone or something **makes** a sound, they produce it or cause it to happen. EG *Try not to make so much noise.*   V+O

9 You use **make** to say what two numbers add up to. For example, if two numbers **make** 12, they add up to 12.   V+C

10 You can use **make** to say what the result of a calculation is. For example, if you **make** the answer to a calculation 144, you calculate it to be 144. EG *I make it thirty-five.*   V+O+C

11 You can use **make** to say what time your watch says it is. For example, if you **make** it 4 o'clock, your watch says it is 4 o'clock.   V+O+C

12 If you **make** money, you get it by working for it or by investing money. EG *He was making ninety dollars a week... She made a £200 profit.*   V+O

13 You can use **make** to say that someone or something has the right qualities for a particular task or role. For example, if you say that someone would **make** a good secretary, you mean that they have the right qualities to be a good secretary. EG *Do garden tools make good gifts?*   V+C OR V+O+C

14 If one part or aspect of something **makes** that thing, it is responsible for the success of that thing. EG *Nicholson's acting really makes the film.*   V+O

15 If you **make** a place, you manage to get there. EG *I made Ramsdale by dawn.*   V+O : USU+A

16 To **make it** means to succeed in getting somewhere in time to do something. EG *We only just made it.*   PHRASE Informal

17 You can also say that someone **makes it** when they are successful in doing something. EG *Blake failed to make it as a commercial airline pilot.*   PHRASE Informal

18 If you are invited to an event and you can **make it**, you are able to attend. EG *The Baxters couldn't make it, I'm afraid.*   PHRASE Informal

19 If you **have got it made**, you are certain to be successful.   PHRASE Informal

20 If you **make** friends or enemies, you cause people to become your friends or enemies. EG *Roger made a number of enemies... Karen made friends with several children.*   V+O

21 The **make** of a product is the name of the company that manufactured it. EG *She couldn't tell what make of car it was.*   N COUNT+SUPP

22 If you **make do** with something, you use it only   PHRASE

because you do not have anything better. EG *We had to make do with cheap lodgings.*

23 to **make good**: see **good**. ● to **make way**: see **way**. ● See also **making**.

make for. **1** If you **make for** a place, you move towards it. EG *We joined the crowd making for the exit.* **2** If something **makes for** a particular situation, that situation is likely to result from it. EG *What are the values that make for happy family life?*   PHRASAL VB : V+PREP   Informal

make of. If you ask someone what they **make of** something, you want to know **1** what their impression or opinion of it is. EG *He didn't know what to make of his new boss.* **2** if they understand what it means. EG *Can you make anything of it?*   PHRASAL VB : V+O+PREP

make off. If you **make off**, you leave somewhere as quickly as possible, often in order to escape. EG *The vehicle made off at once.*   PHRASAL VB : V+ADV

make off with. If you **make off with** something, you steal it. EG *Otto made off with the last of the brandy.*   PHRASAL VB : V+ADV+PREP

make out. **1** If you can **make** something **out**, you can see it, hear it, or understand it. EG *He could just make out the number plate of the car... She tried to make out what was being said... I can't make it out if Nell likes him or not.* **2** If you **make out** that something is the case, you try to cause people to believe that it is the case. EG *People tried to make out that the play was about Britain... He's not really as hard as people make out.* **3** When you **make out** a form or cheque, you write on it all the necessary information. EG *Did you make out a receipt?*   PHRASAL VB : V+O+ADV, OR V+ADV+REPORT : ONLY WH   V+ADV +REPORT, ONLY that   V+O+ADV

make up. **1** The people or things that **make up** something form that thing. EG *...the various groups which make up society... All substances are made up of molecules.* **2** If you **make up** something such as a story, you invent it, sometimes in order to deceive people. **3** If you **make** yourself **up**, you put cosmetics such as powder or lipstick on your face.   PHRASAL VB : V+ADV+O   V+O+ADV   V-REFL+ADV

◊ **made up.** EG *She had magnificent eyes, heavily made up.* ● See also **make-up**. **4** If you **make up** something, you prepare it by putting different things together. EG *...making up a package large enough for a month.* **5** If you **make up** an amount, you add something to it so that it is as large as it should be. EG *Government would have to make up the difference out of its welfare budget.* **6** If two people **make up** or **make** it **up**, they become friends again after they have had a quarrel. EG *He and Frank made it up.* **7** To **make up** for something that is lost or missing means to replace it or to compensate for it. EG *If babies put on very little weight at first, eventually they will gain rapidly to make up for it.* **8** If you **make it up to** someone for disappointing them, you do something for them to show how sorry you are.   ◊ ADJ CLASSIF   V+O+ADV   V+O+ADV   V+ADV OR V+O+ADV   V+ADV : USU+for   PHRASE

make-believe. You refer to someone's behaviour as **make-believe** when they pretend that things are better or more exciting than they really are. EG *His whole life these days was a game of make-believe.*   N UNCOUNT

maker /ˈmeɪkə/, **makers**. The **maker** of something is the person or company that makes it. EG *In the studio with me is film maker and critic, Iain Johnstone... The makers of the programme seemed to lose confidence in it... The maker's label was carefully removed.*   N COUNT+SUPP

makeshift /ˈmeɪkʃɪft/. Something that is **makeshift** is temporary and of poor quality, but you use it because nothing better is available. EG *Youths erected makeshift barricades... The accommodation was makeshift.*   ADJ QUALIT

make-up. **1 Make-up** is substances such as lipstick, eye-shadow, and mascara, which women use to make themselves look more attractive, or which actors use when they are acting. EG *...eye make-up... She had a lot of make-up on.*   N UNCOUNT

2 Someone's **make-up** is their character. EG *There*   N UNCOUNT +SUPP *are things in my make-up which do not bear close examination.*

3 The **make-up** of something is the different parts that it consists of, and the way these parts are arranged. EG *...the psychological make-up of primitive man.* N UNCOUNT +SUPP

making /meɪkɪŋ/, **makings. 1 Making** is the act or process of producing something. EG *At the end of his life he turned to the making of beautiful books... People should be involved in all decision-making which affects them.* N UNCOUNT +SUPP

2 If a problem is **of** your **own making**, it has been caused by you alone and not by anyone else. EG *The trouble here is of the President's own making.* PHRASE

3 When you describe someone as something **in the making**, you mean that they are gradually becoming that thing. EG *...an economist in the making.* PHRASE

4 If something **is the making of** a person or thing, it is the reason that they are successful. EG *The description of Belfast is the making of the book.* PHRASE

5 If you say that a person or thing has **the makings of** something, you mean that they seem likely to develop in that way. EG *She perceived that here might be the makings of the friendship that had so eluded her in the past.* PHRASE

maladjusted /mæləd-ʒʌstɪ²d/. **Maladjusted** children have psychological problems and behave in ways which are not acceptable to society. ADJ CLASSIF

malady /mælədi¹/, **maladies. A malady** is an illness. EG *Was she affected by the same malady?* N COUNT Outdated

malaise /mɔ³leɪz/ is a state in which people feel dissatisfied or unhappy but do not know exactly what is wrong. EG *Malaise had set in with the coming of the twentieth century.* N UNCOUNT Formal

malaria /mɔleɔrɪə/ is a disease which people get from mosquitoes and which causes periods of fever and shivering. N UNCOUNT

male /meɪl/, **males. 1 A male** is an animal that belongs to the sex that cannot have babies or lay eggs. EG *The males establish a breeding territory.* ▸ used as an adjective. EG *...male hamsters.* N COUNT ▸ ADJ CLASSIF

2 You can refer to a man or a boy as a **male**. EG *...the average American male.* ▸ used as an adjective. EG *Your boss is almost certainly there because he is male.* N COUNT ▸ ADJ CLASSIF

3 Something that is **male** concerns or affects men rather than women. EG *...the production of male hormones... ...male unemployment.* ADJ CLASSIF : ATTRIB

male chauvinism is the belief which some men have that men are naturally better and more important than women. N UNCOUNT

male chauvinist, male chauvinists. A male chauvinist is a man who believes that men are naturally better and more important than women. EG *The men in my office are all blatant male chauvinists.* ▸ used as an adjective. EG *I hope this won't be taken as a male chauvinist remark.* N COUNT ▸ ADJ CLASSIF : ATTRIB

malevolent /mɔ³levɔlɔnt/. If someone is **malevolent**, they want to cause harm. EG *These people seemed hard and malevolent... His face was malevolent.* ◊ **malevolence** /mɔ³levɔlɔns/. EG *...the victims of his malevolence.* ADJ QUALIT Formal ◊ N UNCOUNT

malformed /mælfɔːmd/. If something is **malformed**, it does not have the shape that it is supposed to have. EG *...his hideously malformed legs.* ADJ QUALIT Formal

malfunction /mælfʌŋkʃɔ⁰n/, **malfunctions, malfunctioning, malfunctioned.** If a machine or a computer **malfunctions**, it fails to work properly. ▸ used as a noun. EG *...a malfunction of the generator.* V ▸ N COUNT

malice /mælɪs/ is a desire to cause harm to people. EG *He chuckled with malice... 'So I notice,' he added with a touch of malice.* N UNCOUNT

malicious /mɔlɪʃɔs/. If talk or behaviour is **malicious**, it is intended to harm someone or their reputation. EG *Their talk was slightly malicious and gossipy... ...cold-blooded malicious cruelty.* ADJ QUALIT

malign /mɔlaɪn/, **maligns, maligning, maligned. 1** If you **malign** someone, you say unpleasant and untrue things about them. EG *He had maligned both women... ...the countries maligned by his newspapers.* V+O Formal

2 Malign behaviour is intended to harm someone. EG *His speeches are open to all sorts of malign interpretation.* ADJ QUALIT Formal

malignant /mɔlɪgnɔnt/. **1** If behaviour is **malignant**, it is harmful and cruel. EG *...the consequence of a malignant plot.* ADJ QUALIT

2 If a disease is **malignant**, it is uncontrollable and likely to cause death. EG *I was certain that you had a malignant growth in your larynx.* ADJ CLASSIF

malinger /mɔlɪŋgɔ/, **malingers, malingering, malingered.** If you **malinger**, you pretend to be ill in order to avoid working. EG *I'm not malingering, really I'm not.* V : USU CONT

mallet /mælɪ¹t/, **mallets. A mallet** is a wooden hammer with a square head. See picture at TOOLS. N COUNT

malnourished /mælnʌrɪʃt/. If someone is **malnourished**, they are physically weak because they have not eaten enough food. EG *The majority of the population is malnourished.* ADJ QUALIT Formal

malnutrition /mælnjuːtrɪʃɔ⁰n/ is physical weakness caused by not eating enough food. EG *He is showing the first signs of malnutrition.* N UNCOUNT Formal

malpractice /mælpræktɪs/, **malpractices. Malpractice** is behaviour in which someone breaks the law or the rules of their profession in order to gain some personal advantage. EG *A doctor who refused to give treatment is on trial for medical malpractice.* N UNCOUNT OR N COUNT Legal

malt /mɔlt/ is a substance made from grain that has been put in water and then dried in a hot oven. Malt is used in the making of whisky, beer, and other alcoholic drinks. EG *...a bottle of malt whisky.* N UNCOUNT

maltreat /mæltriːt/, **maltreats, maltreating, maltreated.** If people or animals are **maltreated**, they are treated unkindly or violently. EG *We do not intervene unless the children are being physically maltreated.* V+O : USU PASS

mammal /mæmɔ⁰l/, **mammals. Mammals** are particular types of animals. Female mammals give birth to babies rather than laying eggs, and feed their young with milk from their bodies. Human beings, dogs, lions, and whales are all mammals. N COUNT

mammoth /mæmɔθ/, **mammoths. 1 Mammoth** means very large indeed. EG *...the immense foyer with its mammoth mirrors... ...a mammoth task.* ADJ CLASSIF : ATTRIB

2 Mammoths were animals like elephants with very long tusks and long hair. Mammoths no longer exist. N COUNT

man /mæn/, **men** /men/; **mans, manning, manned. Men** is the plural of the noun. **Mans** is the 3rd person singular, present tense, of the verb. N COUNT

1 A man is **1.1** an adult male human being. EG *Larry was a handsome man in his early fifties... Every man, woman, and child will be taken care of.* **1.2** a human being of either sex. EG *All men are born equal... ...a deserted island where no man could live.*

2 You can refer to human beings in general as **man**. EG *Why does man seem to have more diseases than animals?... ...the most dangerous substance known to man.* N UNCOUNT

3 A woman's **man** is her husband, lover, or boyfriend. EG *Can I bring my man?* N COUNT+POSS Informal

4 The **men** in an army are the ordinary soldiers as opposed to the officers. EG *In all, some 70,000 officers and men died.* N PLURAL

5 People sometimes address a man as **'man'**, especially when they are angry or impatient with him. EG *For heaven's sake, man, can't you see she's had enough?* VOCATIVE

Name three mammals that are *not* mentioned on these pages.

6 If someone **mans** a machine, they operate it. EG v+o
They manned the phones all through the night.
7 If people talk to each other **man to man**, they PHRASE
talk honestly and openly, treating each other as
equals. EG *...a man-to-man discussion.*
8 If you **are man enough** to do something, you PHRASE
have the necessary courage to do it; used showing
approval. EG *He's not man enough for the job.*
9 **the man in the street**: see **street**. See also
manned, **right-hand man**.
-man combines with numbers to indicate that
something involves or is designed for the number
of people mentioned. EG *The delegates voted to
select a new, 20-man Central Committee first...
...one-man shows and exhibitions.*

manage /mænɪdʒ/, **manages**, **managing**, **man-**
aged. **1** If you **manage** to do something, you v+to-INF,
succeed in doing it. EG *How he managed to find us is* v+o, OR v
*beyond me... Did you manage to get anything to
eat?... We'll manage it somehow, I'm sure.*
2 If someone **manages** an organization, business, v+o
or system, they are responsible for controlling it.
EG *She manages a chain of pet shops.*
3 If you say that you can **manage** a period of time, v+o OR v+A
you mean that you can spend that time doing
something. EG *I wish you could manage the time to
come and talk to us... I could manage from about
half-past seven till nine.*
4 When people **manage**, they are able to continue v
with an acceptable way of life, although they do
not have much money. EG *I don't want charity. I
can manage... I've always managed on a teacher's
salary.*
manageable /mænɪdʒəbəl/. You say that some- ADJ QUALIT
thing is **manageable** when you can deal with it
because it is not too big or complicated. EG *It is a
perfectly manageable task.*
management /mænɪdʒmənt/, **managements**. **1** N UNCOUNT
The **management** of a business or other organization is the controlling and organizing of it. EG *She
began to take over the management of the estate...
It's a question of good management.*
2 The people who control an organization can also N UNCOUNT
be referred to as the **management**. EG *...a failure* OR N COUNT
*of communication between management and the
workforce... They are part of my management
team.*
3 Your **management** of something is the way that N UNCOUNT
you control or organize it. EG *The author's manage-* Formal
*ment of the plot is admirable... ...the management
of money.*
manager /mænɪdʒə/, **managers**. **1** The **manag-** N COUNT
er of an organization or of part of an organization
is the person who is responsible for running it. EG
*What you need is advice from your bank manag-
er... ...the general manager of Philips Ltd in Singapore.*
2 The **manager** of a pop star or other entertainer N COUNT
is the person who looks after the star's business
interests.
3 The **manager** of a sports team is the person who N COUNT
is responsible for organizing and training it. EG
...Don Revie, England's soccer team manager.
manageress /mænɪdʒəres/, **manageresses**. A N COUNT
manageress is a woman who is responsible for
running a shop or office. EG *The manageress was
tall and terrifying... ...the manageress of a bookshop.*
managerial /mænɪdʒɪərɪəl/ means relating to ADJ CLASSIF:
the work of a manager or manageress. EG *...techni-* ATTRIB
*cal and managerial skills... She was promoted into
some kind of managerial job.*
managing director, **managing directors**. The N COUNT
managing director of a company is a director
who is also responsible for the way that the company is managed. EG *He's now managing director of
English National Opera.*
mandarin /mændərɪn/, **mandarins**. A **manda-** N COUNT
rin is a small orange which is easy to peel.

mandate /mændeɪt/, **mandates**. **1** A govern- N COUNT
ment's **mandate** is the authority that it has to Formal
carry out particular policies as a result of winning
an election. EG *The President, strengthened by a
powerful conservative mandate, has called for
increases in defence spending.*
2 A **mandate** is also a task that you are instructed N COUNT
to carry out. EG *Peter's mandate was to find the* Formal
best available investment.
mandatory /mændətəʳriʰ/. If something is **man-** ADJ CLASSIF
datory, there is a law stating that it must be done.
EG *The testing of cosmetics is not mandatory here.*
mane /meɪn/, **manes**. A horse's or lion's **mane** is N COUNT
the long thick hair that grows from its neck.
man-eating. A **man-eating** animal is an animal ADJ CLASSIF:
which has eaten human beings and is very danger- ATTRIB
ous. EG *...man-eating lions.*
maneuver /mənuːvə/. See **manoeuvre**.
manfully /mænfʊliʰ/. If you do something **man-** ADV
fully, you do it in a very determined way; often
used humorously. EG *I could see Simon manfully
wielding a shovel.*
mangle /mæŋgəʳl/, **mangles**, **mangling**, **man-** v+o : USU PASS
gled. If something **is mangled**, it is so crushed or
twisted that you cannot see what its original shape
was. EG *...the mangled cabs of overturned lorries.*
mango /mæŋgəʊ/, **mangoes** or **mangos**. A **man-** N COUNT
go is a large, sweet yellowish fruit which grows in
hot countries.
mangy /meɪndʒiʰ/. A **mangy** animal has lost a lot ADJ QUALIT
of its hair through disease, or has not been properly looked after by its owner. EG *Rose was sitting in
her rocking chair with a mangy cat upon her knee.*
manhandle /mænhændəʳl/, **manhandles**, **man-** v+o
handling, **manhandled**. If you **manhandle** someone, you treat them very roughly, for example
when you are taking them somewhere. EG *He had
been manhandled on the street by police.*
manhole /mænhəʊl/, **manholes**. A **manhole** is a N COUNT
covered hole in the ground that leads to a drain or
sewer. EG *...an open manhole... ...manhole covers.*
manhood /mænhʊd/ is **1** the state of being a man N UNCOUNT
rather than a boy. EG *...the dubious rewards of
manhood.* **2** the period of a man's life during which
he is a man rather than a boy. EG *He had millions of
dollars to play with in his early manhood.*
man-hour, **man-hours**. You use **man-hour** to N COUNT :
refer to the amount of time that a piece of work USU PLURAL
will take. For example, if a job takes 15 man-hours,
it takes one person 15 hours to do it or three people
five hours to do it. EG *One firm spent a total of
370,000 man-hours on the job.*
manhunt /mænhʌnt/, **manhunts**. A **manhunt** is N COUNT
a search for someone who has escaped or disappeared. EG *...the biggest manhunt the country had
known.*
mania /meɪnɪə/, **manias**. **1** A **mania** for some- N COUNT OR
thing is a strong liking for it. EG *...the British mania* N UNCOUNT :
for television... She had a mania for cleanliness. OFT+for
2 A **mania** is also a mental illness. EG *...persecution* N UNCOUNT
mania... ...the symptoms of religious mania.
maniac /meɪnɪæk/, **maniacs**. A **maniac** is a mad N COUNT
person who is violent and dangerous. EG *She was
attacked by a maniac.*
manic /mænɪk/. You use **manic** to describe some- ADJ QUALIT
one's behaviour when they do something extreme-
ly quickly or energetically, often because they are
very excited or anxious. EG *Weston finished his
manic typing.*
manicure /mænɪkjʊə/, **manicures**, **manicuring**, v+o
manicured. If you **manicure** your hands or nails,
you care for them by softening the skin and cutting
and polishing the nails. EG *She was sitting manicuring her nails.* ▶ used as a noun. EG *His sister gave* ▶ N COUNT OR
him a manicure once a month. N UNCOUNT
manifest /mænɪfest/, **manifests**, **manifesting**,
manifested. **1** If something is **manifest**, people ADJ QUALIT
can easily see that it exists or that it is true. EG *...his* Formal
manifest disapproval... ...an intense patriotism

which is made manifest in the teaching in their schools. ◊ **manifestly.** EG *Hopper was manifestly too important to be left off the guest list.* ◊ ADV

2 If you **manifest** something or if it **manifests** itself, people are made aware of it. EG *It was a question of how we should manifest our resistance... His inventiveness most often manifested itself as a skill in lying.* V+O OR V-REFL Formal

manifestation /mænɪfesteɪʃⁿn/, **manifestations.** A **manifestation** is a sign that something is happening or that something exists. EG *...the first manifestations of the Computer Revolution.* N COUNT+SUPP Formal

manifesto /mænɪfestəʊ/, **manifestos** or **manifestoes.** A **manifesto** is a written statement published by a group of people, especially a political party, in which they say what their aims and policies are. EG *...Shirley Williams' election manifesto.* N COUNT

manifold /mænɪfəʊld/. Things that are **manifold** are of many different kinds. EG *Her good works were manifold... His manifold absurdities might have been forgotten.* ADJ CLASSIF Literary

manila /mənɪlə/; also spelled **manilla.** A **manila** envelope or folder is made from a strong brown paper. EG *...a stack of manila envelopes.* ADJ CLASSIF: ATTRIB

manipulate /mənɪpjʊleɪt/, **manipulates, manipulating, manipulated. 1** If you **manipulate** people, you skilfully cause them to behave in the way that you want them to; used showing disapproval. EG *Small children sometimes manipulate grown-ups.* ◊ **manipulation** /mənɪpjʊleɪʃⁿn/, **manipulations.** EG *...his unscrupulous manipulation of people.* V+O ◊ N UNCOUNT OR N COUNT

2 If you **manipulate** a situation or system, you cause it to develop or operate in the way that you want it to. EG *The job of a manager is to manipulate and control a complex system.* ◊ **manipulation.** EG *...the careful manipulation of circumstances.* V+O ◊ N UNCOUNT OR N COUNT

3 If you **manipulate** a piece of equipment, you control it in a skilful way. EG *Lawrence manipulated the knobs on his tape recorder.* ◊ **manipulation.** EG *I had bent to watch the mechanic's manipulations.* V+O ◊ N COUNT OR N UNCOUNT

manipulative /mənɪpjʊlətɪv/ is used to describe behaviour in which someone skilfully causes people to behave in the way that he or she wants them to; used showing disapproval. EG *...the manipulative powers of the ruler.* ADJ QUALIT Formal

manipulator /mənɪpjʊleɪtə/, **manipulators.** A **manipulator** is a person who skilfully controls events, systems, or people. EG *...the expert financial manipulator.* N COUNT

mankind /mænkaɪnd/. You can refer to all human beings as **mankind** when you are considering them as a group. EG *You have performed a valuable service to mankind.* N UNCOUNT

manly /mænlɪ/. People describe a man's behaviour or character as **manly** when they think that it is typical of a man rather than a woman or boy; used showing approval. EG *He laughed a deep, manly laugh.* ADJ QUALIT

man-made. Something that is **man-made** is made by people, rather than formed naturally. EG *We live in an entirely man-made environment... ...man-made fibres.* ADJ CLASSIF

manned /mænd/. A **manned** vehicle is controlled by people travelling in it. EG *They released special underwater manned vehicles.* ADJ CLASSIF

manner /mænə/, **manners. 1** The **manner** in which you do something is the way that you do it. EG *They filed the report in a routine manner... Their manner of rearing their young is extremely unusual.* N SING+SUPP

2 Your **manner** is the way in which you behave and talk. EG *The judge had been impressed by his manner... He was fat, with a lazy manner.* N SING

3 If you have good **manners**, you behave and speak very politely. EG *She had beautiful manners...* N PLURAL

His manners were charming. ● See also **table manners.**

4 The **manner** of person you are is the kind of person that you are. EG *What manner of man is he?* N SING+of Literary

5 All **manner of** objects or people means objects or people of many different kinds. EG *There were four canvas bags filled with all manner of tools.* PHRASE

6 You say **in a manner of speaking** to indicate that what you have just said is not absolutely or literally true, but is nevertheless true in a general way. EG *If he hadn't been her boss, in a manner of speaking, she would have reported him to the police.* ADV SEN

mannered /mænəd/. If someone's speech or behaviour is **mannered**, it is very artificial, as if they were trying to impress people; used showing disapproval. EG *His conversation is a trifle mannered.* ADJ QUALIT Formal

mannerism /mænərɪzⁿm/, **mannerisms.** A **mannerism** is a gesture or way of speaking which is very characteristic of a person and which they often use. EG *As she grew older, her mannerisms became more pronounced.* N COUNT

mannish /mænɪʃ/. People describe a woman as **mannish** when they think that she looks or behaves more like a man than a woman; often used showing disapproval. EG *Her voice was low and almost mannish... ...her mannish shirt and tie.* ADJ QUALIT

manoeuvre /mənuːvə/, **manoeuvres, manoeuvring, manoeuvred;** spelled **maneuver** in American English. **1** If you **manoeuvre** something into or out of a place, you skilfully move it into or out of the place. EG *Hooper started the car and manoeuvred it out of the parking space.* ▶ used as a noun. EG *Most people seem to manage this manoeuvre without causing havoc.* V OR V+O: USU+A ▶ N COUNT

2 A **manoeuvre** is also something clever which you do in order to change a situation and make things happen the way that you want them to. EG *These results have been achieved by a series of political manoeuvres.* N COUNT

3 If you have **room for manoeuvre**, you have the opportunity to change your plans if it becomes necessary or desirable. EG *That doesn't leave you much room for manoeuvre.* PHRASE

4 When military **manoeuvres** take place, soldiers and equipment are moved around in a large area of countryside in order to train the soldiers to fight battles. N PLURAL

manor /mænə/, **manors.** A **manor** is a large private house and land in the country, especially one which was built in the Middle Ages. EG *...the restoration of their ancient halls and manors.* N COUNT

manpower /mænpaʊə/. People refer to workers as **manpower** when considering them as a means of producing goods. EG *The country is in need of skilled manpower... We've not got the manpower to do a regular check.* N UNCOUNT

mansion /mænʃⁿn/, **mansions.** A **mansion** is a large house. EG *...a late eighteenth-century mansion... ...a few old wooden mansions.* N COUNT

manslaughter /mænslɔːtə/ is the killing of a person by someone who may intend to hurt or injure them but who does not intend to kill them: compare **murder.** EG *He was sentenced to two years for manslaughter.* N UNCOUNT Legal

mantelpiece /mæntⁿlpiːs/, **mantelpieces;** also spelled **mantlepiece.** A **mantelpiece** is a wood or stone shelf over a fireplace. EG *There was a Chinese clay horse on the mantelpiece.* N COUNT

manual /mænjuːⁿl/, **manuals. 1 Manual** work is work in which you use your hands or your physical strength rather than your mind. ADJ CLASSIF

2 Manual also means operated by hand, rather than by electricity or by a motor. EG *...a manual* ADJ CLASSIF: ATTRIB

Find two words on these pages which are pronounced the same.

system. ◇ **manually.** EG *Such pumps can be* ◇ ADV *operated manually.*

3 A **manual** is a book which tells you how to do N COUNT something or how a machine works. EG *The instruction manuals are printed in German.*

manufacture /mænjəˈfæktʃə/, **manufactures, manufacturing, manufactured. 1** When people V+O **manufacture** things, they make them in a factory. EG *Many companies were manufacturing desk calculators... ...manufactured goods.* ▶ used as a noun. ▶ N UNCOUNT EG *...the manufacture and maintenance of vehicles.* ◇ **manufacturing.** EG *India and China had built up* ◇ N UNCOUNT *important manufacturing industries.*

2 If you **manufacture** information, you invent it. V+O EG *She had manufactured the terrorist story to put everyone off.*

manufacturer /mænjəˈfæktʃərə/, **manufacturers.** A **manufacturer** is a person or organization N COUNT that owns a business that makes goods in large quantities. EG *I'm a manufacturer of farm machinery... ...a furniture manufacturer.*

manure /mənjʊə/ is animal faeces, sometimes N UNCOUNT mixed with chemicals, that is spread on the ground in order to make plants grow healthy and strong. EG *...the powerful odour of horse manure.*

manuscript /mænjəˈskrɪpt/, **manuscripts.** A N COUNT **manuscript** is I a handwritten or typed document, especially the typed version of a book before it is printed. EG *I suggest that you offer your manuscript to a publisher at a later date.* **2** an old document that was written by hand before printing was invented. EG *...a medieval manuscript.*

many /menɪ/. The comparative of **many** is **more**, and the superlative is **most**. These words are dealt with separately in this dictionary.

1 If there are **many** people or **many** things, there QUANTIF are a lot of them. EG *Many people have been killed... ...the many brilliant speeches that had been made... Many of the old people were blind.*

2 You use **a good many** or **a great many** to PHRASE emphasize that you are referring to a very large number of things or people. EG *The information has proved useful to a great many people.*

3 You also use **many** to ask how great a quantity QUANTIF is, or to give information about it. EG *How many children has she got?... I used to get a lot of sweets. As many as I liked.*

4 many happy returns: see **return**. ● **in so many words**: see **word**.

map

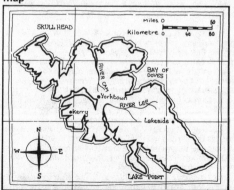

map /mæp/, **maps, mapping, mapped.** A **map** is N COUNT a drawing of an area as it would appear if you saw it from above. Maps show an area's main features, or give special information about it. EG *Maps can be obtained from the Tourist Office... On the map it is quite a brief strip of road... Look at the rainfall maps on page nineteen.*

map out. If you **map out** a plan or task, you work PHRASAL VB: V+O+ADV out in detail how you will do it. EG *They met and mapped out their task.*

maple /meɪpəl/, **maples.** A **maple** is a kind of N COUNT tree with five-pointed leaves.

mar /mɑː/, **mars, marring, marred.** To **mar** V+O something means to spoil its appearance. EG *Graffiti marred the sides of buildings.*

marathon /mærəθən/, **marathons. 1** A **mara-** N COUNT **thon** is a race in which people run about 26 miles (about 42 km) along roads. EG *...the London Marathon.*

2 A **marathon** job or task takes a long time to do ADJ CLASSIF : and is very tiring. EG *You need stamina to get* ATTRIB *through such a marathon production.*

marauder /məˈrɔːdə/, **marauders. Marauders** N COUNT are people who go around looking for something to steal or kill. EG *We were safe from marauders.*

marauding /məˈrɔːdɪŋ/. A **marauding** person or ADJ CLASSIF : animal is one that roams around looking for some- ATTRIB thing to steal or kill. EG *The countryside was being ravaged by marauding bands.*

marble /mɑːbəl/, **marbles. 1 Marble** is a very N UNCOUNT hard rock which is used to make statues and parts of houses. EG *...a monument in black marble.*

2 Marbles is a children's game played with small N UNCOUNT balls made of coloured glass. You roll a ball along the ground and try to hit an opponent's ball with it.

3 A **marble** is one of the small balls used by N COUNT children in the game of marbles.

march /mɑːtʃ/, **marches, marching, marched. 1** N UNCOUNT **March** is the third month of the year in the western calendar. EG *He was assassinated in March 1978.*

2 When soldiers **march**, they walk with quick V : USU+A regular steps, as a group. EG *They marched through Norway.* ▶ used as a noun. EG *We were woken in* ▶ N COUNT *the middle of the night for a long march.*

3 When a large group of people **march**, they walk V : USU+A somewhere together in order to protest about something. EG *The crowds of demonstrators marched down the main street.* ▶ used as a noun. ▶ N COUNT EG *A million people took part in last year's march.*

4 If you **march** somewhere, you walk there quick- V+A ly, for example because you are angry. EG *He marched out of the store.*

5 If you **march** someone somewhere, you force V+O+A them to walk there with you by grasping their arm tightly. EG *He took me by the arm and marched me out of the door.*

6 The **march** of something is its steady develop- N SING+SUPP ment or progress. EG *...the march of science... ...the slow march to socialism.*

mare /meə/, **mares.** A **mare** is an adult female N COUNT horse. EG *Pa was harnessing his mare.*

margarine /mɑːdʒəriːn/ is a yellow substance N UNCOUNT that looks like butter but is made from vegetable oil and animal fats. You can spread it on bread or use it for cooking.

margin /mɑːdʒɪn/, **margins. 1 Margin** is used to N COUNT : refer to the amount by which someone wins a USU+SUPP contest. For example, if there are two candidates in an election, and one receives 8765 votes and the other 6789 votes, the winner wins by a margin of 1976 votes. EG *They won by the small margin of five seats.*

2 If there is a **margin** of something, there is more N COUNT : than you need, and this extra amount allows you USU SING+SUPP more freedom. EG *What is the margin of safety?*

3 The **margins** on a written or printed page are N COUNT the blank spaces at each side. EG *They get a red tick in the margin to show that it's right.*

4 The **margin** of an area is the edge of it. EG *...the* N COUNT : *east margin of the river... We came to the margin* USU+*of* *of the wood.* Formal

5 The **margin** of a group, activity, or situation is N COUNT : the part that is least typical of it. EG *There were* OFT+*of* *multitudes of people living on the margin of soci-* Formal *ety.*

marginal /mɑːdʒɪnəˀl/. 1 Something that is **mar-**   ADJ QUALIT
ginal is small and not very important. EG *The*
effect will be marginal... ...making marginal adjust-
ments.

2 A **marginal** seat or constituency is a political   ADJ QUALIT
constituency where elections are usually won by a   British
very small majority, so that control often changes
from one party to another.

marginally /mɑːdʒɪnəˀliˀ/ means to only a small   SUBMOD
extent. EG *The prices of new houses are marginally*
higher than old houses.

marigold /mærɪˀgəʊld/, **marigolds**. A **marigold**   N COUNT
is a type of yellow flower.

marijuana /mærɪhˀuɑːnə/ is a type of drug which   N UNCOUNT
is is smoked in cigarettes. Marijuana is illegal in
Britain. EG *The room reeked of marijuana.*

marina /məriːnə/, **marinas**. A marina is a small   N COUNT
harbour where people keep boats.

marinate /mærɪneɪt/, **marinates, marinating,**   V-ERG
marinated. If you **marinate** meat or fish or if it
marinates, you keep it in a mixture of vinegar, oil,
and spices before cooking it, so that it develops a
special flavour.

marine /məriːn/, **marines. 1** A **marine** is **1.1** a   N COUNT
soldier in the American Marine Corps. **1.2** a British
soldier who serves with the navy.

2 **Marine** is used to describe things relating to the   ADJ CLASSIF :
sea. EG *...marine life... ...marine biology.*   ATTRIB

marital /mærɪtəˀl/ means relating to marriage. EG   ADJ CLASSIF :
...marital problems.   ATTRIB

marital status. If someone asks what your   N UNCOUNT
marital status is, they want to know whether you   Formal
are married, single, or divorced.

maritime /mærɪtaɪm/ is used to describe things   ADJ CLASSIF :
relating to the sea and to ships. EG *...the National*   ATTRIB
Maritime Museum.

marjoram /mɑːdʒəˀrəm/ is a kind of herb.   N UNCOUNT

mark /mɑːk/, **marks, marking, marked. 1** A   N COUNT
mark is a small part of a surface which has
changed its colour, for example because something
has been spilled on it. EG *...grease marks... Does it*
leave a mark?... I'm sorry, there seems to be a
dirty mark on it.

2 If a substance **marks** a surface, it damages it in   V-ERG
some way. EG *Vinegar, lemon juice, egg and salt*
can mark cutlery.

3 A **mark** is also a written or printed symbol, for   N COUNT
example a letter of the alphabet. EG *McNicoll made*
a few marks on the page with his pen.

4 When a teacher gives you a **mark, 4.1** he or she   N COUNT
gives you a point for a correct answer in a test or
examination. EG *You need 120 marks out of 200 to*
pass. **4.2** he or she gives you a number or letter to
indicate how good or bad your work is.

5 When something reaches a particular **mark,** it   N COUNT+SUPP
reaches that stage. EG *Unemployment is well over*
the three million mark... Once past the halfway
mark he found that he was running more easily.

6 If something has the **marks** of a particular kind   N PLURAL
of thing, it has that thing's most typical features. EG   +SUPP
The scene bore all the marks of a country wedding.

7 You can use **mark** to say what an action is   N COUNT+of
intended to express. For example, if you do something as a mark of friendship, you do it to show that
you feel friendly towards someone. EG *I took this*
smile as a mark of recognition.

8 If you **mark** something, you put a written symbol   V+O : USU PASS
on it. EG *...reports marked Top Secret... See that*
everything is marked with your initials.

9 When a teacher **marks** a student's work, he or   V+O
she decides how good it is and writes a number or
letter on it to indicate this opinion.

10 If something **marks** a place or position, it shows   V+O
where something else is or where it used to be. EG
The area of burned clay marks the position of
several Roman furnaces.

11 An event that **marks** a particular stage or time   V+O
is a sign that something different is about to
happen. EG *The film marks a turning point in*

Allen's career... Her resignation marks the end of
an era.

12 If you do something to **mark** an important   V+O
event, you do it to commemorate this event. EG *The*
concert is to mark the 75th Anniversary year of the
composer's death.

13 If a particular quality **marks** a person's life or   V+O
career, the person often shows this quality during
their life or career. EG *His cricket has always been*
marked by courage and determination.

14 Something that **marks** you as a particular type   V+O+as
of person indicates that you are that type of
person. EG *These signs marked him as a bachelor*
eager to wed.

15 **Mark** is used in these phrases. **15.1** If you are   PHRASES
slow off the mark, you respond to a situation
slowly. If you are **quick off the mark**, you respond
to a situation quickly. EG *Neighbours were always*
quick off the mark to ask him round when his wife
was away. **15.2** If you **make** or **leave** your **mark**
on something, you have an important influence on
it. EG *...a scholar who has made his mark in*
history... These policies have left indelible marks
on British society. **15.3** If something is **wide of the**
mark, it is a long way from being correct. EG *His*
assessment of the situation might be rather wide of
the mark. **15.4** If you **are marking time**, you are
doing something uninteresting or unimportant
while you wait for something else to happen. EG *I've*
been marking time reading books.

16 See also **marked, marking**.

mark off. If you **mark off** an item on a list, you   PHRASAL VB :
put a line through it or next to it, to show that it has   V+O+ADV
been dealt with. EG *Each day was marked off with a*
neat X.

marked /mɑːkt/. If you describe something as   ADJ QUALIT
marked, you mean that it is very obvious and
easily noticed. EG *He has shown marked improve-*
ments in spelling and writing. ◊ **markedly**   ◊ SUBMOD
/mɑːkɪˀdlɪˀ/. EG *Business in Nigeria is markedly*   OR ADV
different from that in Europe.

marker /mɑːkə/, **markers**. A **marker** is an ob-   N COUNT
ject which is used to show the position of something. EG *The post served as a boundary marker.*

market /mɑːkɪt/, **markets, marketing, mar-**
keted. 1 A **market** is a place, usually in the open   N COUNT
air, where lots of different goods are bought and
sold. EG *These women sell fish in the markets... ...a*
cattle market... ...a market stall.

2 The **market** for a product is the number of   N COUNT :
people who want to buy it. EG *...the declining*   USU SING+SUPP
commercial vehicle market... There is a vast over-
seas market.

3 To **market** a product means to sell it in an   V+O
organized way and on a large scale. EG *The felt-tip*
pen was first marketed by a Japanese firm.

4 If something is **on the market**, it is available for   PHRASE
people to buy. EG *It's one of the slowest cars on the*
market... It's been on the market for three years.

5 See also **black market, Common Market**.

marketable /mɑːkɪtəbəˀl/. If a product is **mar-**   ADJ QUALIT
ketable, it can be sold, because people want to buy
it. EG *It was their only marketable commodity.*

marketing /mɑːkɪtɪŋ/ is the part of business   N UNCOUNT
which is concerned with the way a product is sold,
for example its price and the way it is advertised.
EG *...the importance of effective marketing... ...mar-*
keting directors.

market place, market places. 1 The **market**   N SING : the+N
place is the activity of buying and selling, and the
places where this occurs. EG *Its products must*
compete in the international market place.

2 A **market place** is a small open area in a town   N COUNT
where lots of goods are bought and sold. EG *Beggars*
crowded in every market-place.

What is your marital status?

market research is the activity of collecting N UNCOUNT
and studying information about what people want,
need, and buy.

marking /mɑːkɪŋ/, **markings. 1 Markings** are N COUNT :
coloured shapes or designs on the surface of some- USU PLURAL
thing. EG *Look at the markings on the petals.*
2 Marking is the work a teacher does when he or N UNCOUNT
she reads a student's work and gives it a grade.

marksman /mɑːksmən/, **marksmen.** A **marks-** N COUNT
man is a person who can shoot very accurately
with a gun.

marmalade /mɑːməleɪd/ is a food like jam made N MASS
from oranges, lemons, or grapefruit and usually
eaten on bread or toast at breakfast.

maroon /mərʊːn/. Something that is **maroon** is ADJ COLOUR
dark reddish-purple in colour. EG *...a maroon jacket.*

marooned /mərʊːnd/. If you are **marooned** in a ADJ CLASSIF
place, you cannot leave it, for example because it
is surrounded by water. EG *...a story about a group
of young boys marooned on a desert island.*

marquee /mɑːkiː/, **marquees.** A **marquee** is a N COUNT
large tent which is used at a fair, garden party, or
other outdoor event, usually for eating and drinking in.

marquis /mɑːkwɪs/, **marquises;** also spelled N COUNT
marquess. A **marquis** is a male member of the
nobility. EG *...the Marquis of Stafford.*

marriage /mærɪdʒ/, **marriages. 1** A **marriage**
is **1.1** the relationship between a husband and wife. N COUNT
EG *It has been a happy marriage... Her fifth marriage lasted only a month.* **1.2** the act of marrying
someone. EG *Victoria's marriage to her cousin was* N UNCOUNT
not welcomed by her family.
2 Marriage is the state of being married. EG *I* N UNCOUNT
never wanted marriage.

married /mærɪd/. **1** If you are **married**, you have ADJ CLASSIF :
a husband or wife. EG *She's married to an English-* OFT+to
*man... He was thirty-five, married with two chil-
dren... ...a young married woman.*
2 If you **get married**, you marry someone. EG *I'm* PHRASE
getting married... We decided to get married.
3 You use **married** to describe things that involve ADJ CLASSIF :
marriage. EG *...their early married life.* ATTRIB

marrow /mærəʊ/, **marrows. 1** A **marrow** is a N COUNT OR
long, thick, green vegetable with soft white flesh, N UNCOUNT
which you can cook and eat. British
2 Marrow is the soft, fatty substance which fills N UNCOUNT
the space at the centre of the bones of humans and
animals. EG *...a bone marrow transplant.*

marry /mærɪ/, **marries, marrying, married. 1** V OR V+O :
When a man and a woman **marry**, they become RECIP
each other's husband and wife during a special
ceremony. EG *They are in love with each other and
wish to marry... I want to marry you.*
2 When a clergyman or registrar **marries** two V+O
people, he or she is in charge of the ceremony
during which the two people become husband and
wife.
3 If you **marry** two things together, you succeed in V+O:OFT+A
joining them together. EG *...the marrying together* Formal
of a number of different scientific disciplines.
4 See also **married.**

marsh /mɑːʃ/, **marshes.** A **marsh** is an area of N COUNT OR
land which is very wet and muddy. EG *I went off* N UNCOUNT
*into the marsh... ...a dense plantation bounded by
marsh.*

marshal /mɑːʃəl/, **marshals, marshalling,**
marshalled; spelled **marshaling** and **marshaled**
in American English. **1** If you **marshal** things or V+O
people, you gather them together and organize
them. EG *He hesitated, marshalling his thoughts...
Shipping was being marshalled into convoys... He
tried to marshal support.*
2 A **marshal** is an official who helps to organize a N COUNT
public event. EG *If you undergo difficulties, please
contact the nearest marshal.*
3 In the United States, a **marshal** is a police officer N COUNT
who controls and organizes a particular district.
4 See also **field marshal.**

marshmallow /mɑːʃmæləʊ/, **marshmallows. 1** N UNCOUNT
Marshmallow is a soft, spongy, sweet food.
2 Marshmallows are sweets made from marsh- N COUNT
mallow.

marshy /mɑːʃɪ/. **Marshy** land is covered in ADJ QUALIT
marshes. EG *...a stretch of marshy coastline.*

martial /mɑːʃəl/ is used to describe things that ADJ CLASSIF :
relate to soldiers, war, or military matters. EG ATTRIB
...martial music. ● See also **court-martial.** Formal

martial arts. The **martial arts** are the tech- N PLURAL
niques of self-defence that come from the Far East,
for example karate and judo.

martyr /mɑːtə/, **martyrs, martyring, mar-** N COUNT
tyred. A **martyr** is someone who was killed because of his or her religious beliefs. EG *St Sebastian
was a Christian martyr.* ● used as a verb. EG *This is* ▶ V+O :
where St Peter was supposed to have been mar- USU PASS
tyred.

martyrdom /mɑːtədəm/ is the murder of some- N UNCOUNT
one because of his or her religious beliefs. EG *...the
martyrdom of St Thomas.*

marvel /mɑːvəl/, **marvels, marvelling, mar-**
velled; spelled **marveling** and **marveled** in
American English. **1** If you **marvel** at something, it V :OFT+at
fills you with surprise or admiration. EG *Early* OR REPORT,
travellers marvelled at the riches of Mali... We ONLY that
*marvelled that so much could happen in such a
short time.*
2 A **marvel** is something that makes you feel great N COUNT
surprise or admiration. EG *Paestum is one of the
marvels of Greek architecture... It's a marvel that
I'm still alive.*

marvellous /mɑːvələs/; spelled **marvelous** in ADJ QUALIT
American English. If you say that people or things
are **marvellous**, you mean that they are wonderful and that you are very pleased indeed with them.
EG *Two ounces! Oh, Robin, that's marvellous!...
Flora, you're marvellous.* ◇ **marvellously.** EG *I* ◇ SUBMOD
slept marvellously well.

Marxism /mɑːksɪzəm/ is a political philosophy N UNCOUNT
based on the writings of Karl Marx. Marxism states
that the struggle between people of different social
classes is the most important part of history.

Marxist /mɑːksɪst/, **Marxists. 1** Something that ADJ CLASSIF
is **Marxist** is based on or relates to Marxism. EG
...Marxist theory... ...the Marxist Workers' League.
2 A **Marxist** is a person who believes in Marxism. N COUNT
EG *The Marxists were forced to revise their plans.*

marzipan /mɑːzɪpæn/ is a paste made of al- N UNCOUNT
monds, sugar, and egg. It is sometimes put on top
of cakes, or used to make small sweets.

mascara /mæskɑːrə/ is a substance which women N UNCOUNT
put on their eyelashes in order to make them look
thicker or a different colour.

mascot /mæskət/, **mascots.** A **mascot** is an N COUNT
animal, toy, or doll which is thought to bring good
luck. EG *Many of them have dolls as mascots... The
regimental mascot is a goat called Winston.*

masculine /mæskjəlɪn/. **1** Something that is ADJ QUALIT
masculine relates to or is considered typical of
men, in contrast to women. EG *I think it must have
something to do with masculine pride.*
2 If you describe a woman as **masculine**, you ADJ QUALIT
mean that she has a lot of qualities which make
her seem more like a man. EG *...a rather masculine-
looking lady.*

masculinity /mæskjəlɪnɪtɪ/. **1 Masculinity** is N UNCOUNT
the fact of being a man. EG *In society we assume
that masculinity has certain characteristics.*
2 A man's **masculinity** consists of the qualities, N UNCOUNT :
especially sexual qualities, which are considered to USU+POSS
be typical of men. EG *Some men measure their
masculinity by anything from their jobs to their
drinking habits.*

mash /mæʃ/, **mashes, mashing, mashed.** If you V+O
mash vegetables, you crush them after they have
been cooked. EG *Mash the lentils well.* ◇ **mashed.** ◇ ADJ CLASSIF
EG *...mashed potatoes.*

mask /mɑːsk/, **masks, masking, masked.** 1 A   N COUNT
mask is something which you wear over your face
in order to hide or protect it or to make yourself
look different. EG *The thieves were wearing
masks... ...a surgical mask.* ● See also **gas mask**.

2 If you **mask** something, you cover it so that it is   V+O
difficult to see. EG *Her eyes were masked by huge,
round sunglasses.*

3 If you **mask** your feelings, you behave in a way   V+O
which hides them. EG *Our opponents mask their
antagonism behind sweet words.* ▸ used as a noun.   ▸ N COUNT :
EG *He may learn to conceal his annoyance with a*   USU+SUPP
mask of politeness.

masked /mɑːskt/. Someone who is **masked** is   ADJ CLASSIF
wearing a mask. EG *Three armed and masked men
suddenly burst in.*

masochism /mæsəˈkɪzəᵘm/ is behaviour in which   N UNCOUNT
someone gets pleasure and satisfaction from suffering physically or mentally. ◇ **masochist,**   ◇ N COUNT
masochists. EG *Unless you are a complete masochist, you are unlikely to derive much pleasure
from the show.*

masochistic /mæsəˈkɪstɪk/. **Masochistic** behav-   ADJ QUALIT
iour is behaviour in which a person suffers physical
or mental pain in order to feel pleasure or satisfaction. EG *There are some actors with strong masochistic streaks who wish to hear only criticisms.*

mason /ˈmeɪsəᵘn/, **masons.** A **mason** is a person   N COUNT
who is skilled at making things out of stone. EG *He
carved marble faster than any mason.*

masonry /ˈmeɪsənriː/ is bricks or pieces of stone   N UNCOUNT
which form part of a wall or building. EG *Large
chunks of masonry were beginning to fall.*

masquerade /mæskəˈreɪd/, **masquerades, mas-**   V+AS/UNDER
querading, masqueraded. If you **masquerade** as
something, you pretend to be that thing. EG *He
might try to masquerade as a policeman... He
might be masquerading under an assumed name.*

mass /mæs/, **masses, massing, massed.** 1 A   N PART : SING
mass of something is a large amount of it. EG *Bruce
stuffed a mass of papers into his briefcase... ...a
mass of long grey hair.*

2 When people talk about **masses** of something,   N PART :
they mean a great deal of it. EG *They ate masses*   PLURAL
and masses of food... They've got simply masses of   Informal
money.

3 A **mass** is **3.1** an amount of a solid substance, a   N COUNT
liquid, or a gas. EG *The base of the rock cracked*   Formal
*and the whole mass toppled into the sea... ...a mass
of warm air laden with water vapour.* **3.2** a large
area of land. EG *...the great land mass of Asia.*

4 You use **mass** to describe something which   ADJ CLASSIF :
involves or affects a very large number of people.   ATTRIB
EG *...the power of mass communication... ...mass
unemployment.*

5 The **masses** are the ordinary people in society   N PLURAL :
considered as a group. EG *We want to produce*   the+N
opera for the masses.

6 When people or things **mass** or when you **mass**   V-ERG
them, they gather together into a large crowd or
group. EG *The students massed in Paris... The
general was massing his troops.*

7 The **mass** of an object is the amount of physical   N UNCOUNT
matter that it has. EG *The velocity depends on the*   OR N COUNT
mass of the object.   Technical

8 **Mass** is a ceremony in some Christian churches   N UNCOUNT
during which people eat bread and drink wine in   OR N COUNT
order to remember the last meal of Jesus Christ.

9 See also **massed.**

massacre /ˈmæsəkə/, **massacres, massacring,**   N COUNT OR
massacred. A **massacre** is the killing of a very   N UNCOUNT
large number of people in a violent and cruel way.
EG *...the massacre of a village.* ▸ used as a verb. EG   ▸ V+O
Their tanks massacred more than 32,000 people.

massage /ˈmæsɑːdᵌ/, **massages, massaging,**   V+O
massaged. If you **massage** someone, you rub a
part of their body in order to make them relax or
to stop their muscles from being painful. EG *Could*

you massage the back of my neck? ▸ used as a   ▸ N UNCOUNT
noun. EG *We can relax our muscles by massage.*   OR N COUNT

masse. See **en masse.**

massed /mæst/. You use **massed** to describe   ADJ CLASSIF :
large groups of people or things that have been   ATTRIB
collected or brought together. EG *...the massed
groups of rival supporters... ...massed brass bands.*

massive /ˈmæsɪv/. Something that is **massive** is   ADJ CLASSIF
extremely large in size, quantity, or extent. EG *He
opened the massive oak front doors... ...a massive
increase in oil prices.* ◇ **massively.** EG *We invest-*   ◇ ADV
ed massively in West German machinery.

mass media. The **mass media** are television,   N COLL : the+N
radio, and newspapers. EG *The mass media now
play an increasing role in shaping our opinions.*

mass noun, mass nouns. In grammar, a **mass**   N COUNT
noun is a noun which usually has no plural, but
which can have a plural in certain circumstances,
for example when you mean measures or brands of
the thing that the word stands for. Nouns of this
type are described as N MASS in this dictionary. See
the entry headed NOUNS for more information.

mass-produce,   **mass-produces,**   **mass-**   V OR V+O
producing, mass-produced. When people **mass-**
produce something, they make it in large quantities by repeating the same process many times.
EG *...a contract for mass-producing cheap computers... ...a vaccine which can be mass-produced
cheaply.* ◇ **mass-produced.** EG *...cheap mass-*   ◇ ADJ CLASSIF
produced exports. ◇ **mass-production.** EG *Soon*   ◇ N UNCOUNT
the car will go into mass-production.

mast /mɑːst/, **masts.** 1 The **masts** of a sailing   N COUNT
ship or yacht are the tall upright poles that are
used to support its sails. See picture at YACHT.

2 A radio or television **mast** is a very tall pole that   N COUNT
is used as an aerial to transmit sound or television
pictures.

master /ˈmɑːstə/, **masters, mastering, mas-**   N COUNT
tered. 1 A **master** is a man who has authority   Outdated
over a servant. EG *Sometimes there was no dispute
between a master and his slave.*

2 If you are **master** of a situation, you have   N UNCOUNT+of
complete control over it. EG *This was before man
was total master of his environment.*

3 If you **master** a difficult situation, you succeed in   V+O
controlling it. EG *Confrontations must be mastered
as they arise.*

4 If you **master** something, you learn how to do it   V+O
properly or manage to understand it completely. EG
*Slowly, one begins to master the complex skills
involved... I mastered the local dialect.*

5 You use **master** to describe someone who is   ADJ CLASSIF :
extremely skilled in a job or activity. EG *...master*   ATTRIB
bakers... ...a master plumber.

6 A **master** is also a male teacher at a school. EG   N COUNT :
...the science master... ...a master at the Agricultur-   OFT+SUPP
al Training Centre. ● See also **headmaster.**   British

masterful /ˈmɑːstəfʊl/. Someone who is **master-**   ADJ QUALIT
ful behaves in a way which shows that they can
control people or situations. EG *His voice had
become more masterful.*

masterly /ˈmɑːstəliː/. If you describe an action as   ADJ QUALIT
masterly, you mean that it is done extremely well.
EG *It was a masterly performance.*

mastermind /ˈmɑːstəmaɪnd/, **masterminds,**
masterminding, masterminded. 1 If you   V+O
mastermind a complicated activity, you plan it in
detail and make sure that it happens successfully.
EG *A young accountant masterminded the take-over
of the company.*

2 The **mastermind** of a complicated activity is the   N COUNT
person who is responsible for planning and organizing it. EG *The mastermind of the expedition was a
Frenchman.*

Do people mass-produce masterpieces?

Master of Arts, Masters of Arts. A **Master of** N COUNT
Arts is a person with an M.A. degree.
Master of Science, Masters of Science. A N COUNT
Master of Science is a person with an M.Sc.
degree. EG *He's a Master of Science now.*
masterpiece /mɑːstəpiːs/, **masterpieces. 1** A N COUNT
masterpiece is an extremely good painting, novel,
film, or other work of art. EG *It is one of the great
masterpieces of European art.*
2 An artist's, writer's, or composer's **masterpiece** N COUNT + POSS
is the best work that they have ever produced. EG
'Gulliver's Travels' is Swift's masterpiece.
3 If an action is especially clever, you can describe N COUNT :
it as a **masterpiece** of that kind of action. EG *...a* OFT + of
speech which was a masterpiece of ambiguity.
mastery /mɑːstə⁰riː/. **1 Mastery** of a skill or art N UNCOUNT :
is excellence in it. EG *...his mastery of the language.* OFT + of/over
2 Mastery is also complete power or control over N UNCOUNT :
something. EG *His sons were struggling to obtain* OFT + of/over
mastery of the country.
mat /mæt/, **mats. 1** A **mat** is a small piece of N COUNT
cloth, card, or plastic which you put on a table,
usually in order to protect it. EG *She set his food on
the mat before him... ...beer mats.*
2 A **mat** is also a small piece of carpet or other N COUNT
thick material which you put on the floor for
protection, decoration, or comfort.
3 See also **matt, matted, matting.**
match /mætʃ/, **matches, matching, matched. 1** N COUNT
A **match** is an organized game of football, cricket,
chess, or other sport. EG *...a football match.*

matches

2 A **match** is also one of the small, thin sticks of N COUNT
wood that produce a flame when you strike them
against the side of a matchbox. EG *Don't strike a
match if you smell gas... ...a box of matches.*
3 If one thing **matches** another, the two things are V OR V+O :
the same as one another, or have similar qualities. RECIP
EG *The captain's feelings clearly matched my own...
Sometimes his inner thoughts and his outer actions
do not match.*
4 If you **match** one thing with another, you decide V+O OR
that one is suitable for the other, or that there is a V+O+with :
connection between them. EG *All you have to do is* RECIP; ALSO
correctly match the famous personalities with the V+O+up
towns they come from.
5 If one thing **matches** another thing or if the two V OR V+O :
things **match,** they have the same colour or de- RECIP
sign. EG *All her towels match... She was dressed in a
yellow sari with yellow ribbons to match.*
6 If you **match** something, you are as good as it, or V+O
equal to it in speed, size, or quality. EG *They are
trying to upgrade their cars to match the foreign
competition... She walked at a pace that Morris's
short legs could hardly match.*
7 If you say that something **is no match for** PHRASE
another thing, you mean that it is inferior to it. EG *A
machine gun is no match for a tank.*

8 See also **matched, matching.**
matchbox /mætʃbɒks/, **matchboxes.** A **match-** N COUNT
box is a small box that you buy that contains
matches.
matched /mætʃt/. **1** If you say that two people are ADJ CLASSIF :
well **matched,** you mean that they are suited to ADV + ADJ
one another and are likely to have a happy and
successful relationship. EG *I thought we were perfectly matched.*
2 If two people or groups are well **matched,** they ADJ CLASSIF :
have the same strength or ability. EG *Government* ADV + ADJ
and rebel soldiers are evenly matched.
matching /mætʃɪŋ/. You use **matching** to de- ADJ CLASSIF :
scribe something which is the same colour or ATTRIB
design as something else. EG *...a blue jacket with
matching shirt.*
matchless /mætʃlɪ²s/. You use **matchless** to de- ADJ CLASSIF
scribe something that is so good that you think Formal
nothing else could be as good. EG *...men and women
of matchless honesty.*
mate /meɪt/, **mates, mating, mated. 1** Someone's N COUNT :
mate is their friend; used mainly by men. EG *He* OFT + POSS
supposed his old mate Kowalski would be with Informal
them... He went off with his mate.
2 An animal's **mate** is its sexual partner. EG *The* N COUNT :
females are about half the size of their mates. OFT + POSS
3 When a male animal and a female animal **mate,** V OR V + with :
they have sex. EG *The majority of amphibians mate* RECIP
in water. ◊ **mating.** EG *...the mating season...* ◊ ADJ CLASSIF :
Mosquitoes use sound as a mating call. ATTRIB
4 The **mate** or **first mate** on a ship is the officer N SING
who is next in importance to the captain.
material /mətɪəriəl/, **materials. 1** A **material** is N COUNT OR
a solid substance, especially one which can be used N UNCOUNT
in making things. EG *We need a cheap abundant
material to make the electrodes... ...synthetic substitutes for natural materials.*
2 Material is cloth. EG *The sleeping bags are made* N UNCOUNT
of quilted or acrylic material. OR N COUNT
3 Ideas or information that can be used as a basis N UNCOUNT
for a book, play, or film can be referred to as
material. EG *She hoped to find material for some
articles... They researched a lot of background
material.*
4 You use **material** to describe something which is ADJ CLASSIF :
concerned with possessions, money, and conditions ATTRIB
in which people live, rather than with their emotional or spiritual life. EG *...the material comforts of
life... ...material possessions.* ◊ **materially.** EG ◊ ADV
*...conditions which they found materially adequate
but spiritually impoverished.*
5 Materials are the equipment or things that you N PLURAL :
need for a particular activity. EG *I packed all my* USU + SUPP
books and writing materials... ...cleaning materials.
materialise /mətɪəriəlaɪz/. See **materialize.**
materialism /mətɪəriəlɪzə⁰m/ is the attitude that N UNCOUNT
someone has when they think that money and
possessions are the most important things in life. EG
*They were determined to renounce the material-
ism of the society they had been brought up in.*
◊ **materialist** /mətɪəriəlɪst/, **materialists.** EG *He* ◊ N COUNT
*was an atheist and a materialist... ...the materialist
way of life.*
materialistic /mətɪəriəlɪstɪk/. A **materialistic** ADJ QUALIT
person or society thinks that money and posses-
sions are the most important things in life. EG *This
society has made people greedy and materialistic.*
materialize /mətɪəriəlaɪz/, **materializes, ma-** V
terializing, materialized; also spelled **materialise.** If a possible event **materializes,** it actually
happens. EG *Fortunately, the attack did not materialize.*
maternal /mətɜːnə⁰l/ is used to describe things ADJ CLASSIF :
relating to a mother. EG *...maternal feelings... When* ATTRIB
*the baby arrived, she slipped into the maternal role
with ease... ...my maternal grandmother.*
maternity /mətɜːnɪ²tiː/ is used to describe things ADJ CLASSIF :
relating to the help and medical care given to a ATTRIB
woman when she is pregnant and when she gives

birth. EG ...*maternity hospitals*... ...*increases in maternity allowances*... *Until now women have been granted a year's maternity leave after giving birth.*

math /mæθ/ is the same as mathematics. EG ...*methods for teaching English or math.* N UNCOUNT American

mathematical /ˌmæθəˈmætɪkəl/. 1 Something that is **mathematical** involves numbers and calculations. EG ...*mathematical calculations*... ...*a mathematical formula.* ADJ CLASSIF: ATTRIB

2 If you have a **mathematical** mind, you are clever at doing calculations or understanding problems that involve numbers. ◊ **mathematically**. EG *Here's a problem for those of you who are mathematically inclined.* ADJ QUALIT: ATTRIB ◊ ADV

mathematician /ˌmæθəməˈtɪʃən/, **mathematicians**. A **mathematician** is a person who studies problems involving numbers and calculations. N COUNT

mathematics /ˌmæθəˈmætɪks/ is a subject which involves the study of numbers, quantities, or shapes. EG ...*professor of mathematics at Cambridge.* N UNCOUNT

maths /mæθs/ is the same as mathematics. EG ...*a maths teacher.* N UNCOUNT British

matinee /ˈmætɪneɪ/, **matinees**; also spelled **matinée**. A **matinee** is a play or film which is performed or shown in the afternoon. N COUNT

matrices /ˈmeɪtrɪsiːz/ is the plural of **matrix.**

matriculate /məˈtrɪkjəleɪt/, **matriculates**, **matriculating**, **matriculated**. If you **matriculate**, you register as a student at a university. ◊ **matriculation** /məˌtrɪkjəˈleɪʃən/. EG *Work for a degree counts only from the date of matriculation.* V Formal ◊ N UNCOUNT

matrimony /ˈmætrɪmənɪ/ means the same as marriage. EG ...*a proposal of matrimony.* ◊ **matrimonial** /ˌmætrɪˈməʊnɪəl/. EG ...*matrimonial difficulties*... ...*the matrimonial home*... ...*family and matrimonial law.* N UNCOUNT Formal ◊ ADJ CLASSIF: ATTRIB

matrix /ˈmeɪtrɪks/, **matrices** /ˈmeɪtrɪsiːz/. A **matrix** is the environment or context in which something such as a society develops and grows. EG *Attitudes are formed in a matrix of psychological and social complications.* N COUNT+SUPP Formal

matron /ˈmeɪtrən/, **matrons**. 1 In a hospital, the **matron** is a senior nurse who is usually in charge of all the nursing staff. N COUNT

2 At a boarding school, the **matron** is a woman who looks after the health and hygiene of the children. N COUNT

matt /mæt/; also spelled **mat**. A **matt** colour, paint, or surface is dull rather than shiny. EG ...*matt black*... *Raspberries have a matt, spongy surface.* ADJ CLASSIF

matted /ˈmætəd/. Something that is **matted** is twisted together untidily. EG *Their hair was matted and dirt caked their faces.* ADJ QUALIT

matter /ˈmætə/, **matters**, **mattering**, **mattered**. 1 A **matter** is an event or situation which you have to deal with, especially one that involves problems. EG *It was a purely personal matter... She's very honest in money matters... This is a matter for the police.* ● **a matter of life and death**: see **life**. N COUNT+SUPP

2 You use **matters** to refer to the situation that you are talking about or that you are involved in. EG *The absence of electricity made matters worse.* N PLURAL

3 You can use **matter** to refer in a general way to all substances or to any substance. EG *An atom is the smallest indivisible particle of matter... The termites feed on vegetable matter.* N UNCOUNT Formal

4 You can refer to books and other things that people read as reading **matter**. EG *He came into contact with a great variety of reading matter.* N UNCOUNT +SUPP Formal

5 You say 'What's **the matter**?' or 'Is anything **the matter**?' when you think that someone has a problem and you want to know what it is. EG *What's the matter, Cynthia? You sound odd... What's the matter with your hand?... We told them that there was nothing the matter.* PHRASE

6 If something **matters** to you, it is important to you. EG *My family were all that mattered to me... Your happiness, that's the only thing that matters.* V : NO CONT

7 If something does not **matter**, it is not important because it does not have an effect on the situation. EG *It does not matter which method you choose.* V WITH BROAD NEG : NO CONT

8 You use **no matter** in expressions such as 'no matter how' and 'no matter what' to indicate that something is true or happens in all circumstances. EG *I told him to report to me after the job was completed, no matter how late it was... They smiled continuously, no matter what was said.* PHRASE

9 You say **no matter what** to indicate that something is definitely going to happen. EG *They're going to win no matter what.* PHRASE

10 **Matter** is also used in these phrases. 10.1 If you do something **as a matter of** principle or policy, you do it for that reason or purpose. EG *Men were prepared to go to prison as a matter of principle, rather than pay this tax... Merchant banks recruit women as a matter of policy.* 10.2 You use **matter** in expressions such as 'a matter of days' when you are drawing attention to how short a period of time is. EG *Within a matter of weeks she was crossing the Atlantic.* 10.3 If you say that something is just **a matter of time**, you mean that it is certain to happen at some time in the future. EG *It appeared to be only a matter of time before they were caught.* 10.4 If you say that something is just **a matter of** doing something, you mean it is easy and can be done just by doing that thing. EG *Skating's just a matter of practice.* 10.5 If you say that a statement is **a matter of opinion**, you mean that people disagree about it or that you do not accept it. EG *'City are as good a team as United.' – 'That's a matter of opinion.'* 10.6 You say **for that matter** to emphasize that a statement you have made about one thing is also true about another. EG *He's shaking with the cold. So am I, for that matter.* 10.7 You say **the fact of the matter is** or **the truth of the matter is** to emphasize that you are telling the truth. EG *I exhausted myself too early, that's the truth of the matter.* 10.8 If you say that something is **another matter** or **a different matter**, you mean that it is very different from the situation that you have just discussed or is an exception to a rule. EG *But Asia was another matter altogether.* 10.9 **as a matter of course**: see **course**. ● **as a matter of fact**: see **fact**. PHRASES

matter-of-fact. Someone who is **matter-of-fact** shows no emotion in their speech or behaviour, especially in a situation where people expect them to be emotional. EG *'I see,' she said, trying to seem matter-of-fact... She said it calmly and firmly in a matter-of-fact voice.* ADJ QUALIT

matting /ˈmætɪŋ/ is strong thick material, usually made from a material like rope or straw, which is used as a floor covering. EG *There was rush matting on the floor... ...coconut matting.* N UNCOUNT

mattress /ˈmætrəs/, **mattresses**. A **mattress** is a large, flat cushion the same size as a bed, which is put on a bed to make it soft to lie on. N COUNT

mature /məˈtjʊə/, **matures**, **maturing**, **matured**; **maturer**, **maturest**. 1 When a child or young animal **matures**, it becomes an adult. EG *She had matured into a self-possessed and articulate young woman.* V

2 When something **matures**, it reaches a state of complete development. EG *The new seeds matured in 120 days.* V

3 If someone **matures**, they become more fully developed in their personality and emotional behaviour. EG *He had matured and quietened down considerably.* V

4 If you describe someone as **mature**, you mean that they are fully developed and balanced in their personality and emotional behaviour. EG *She's in* ADJ QUALIT

If something is matted, is it made of matting?

some ways mature and in some ways rather a child.

5 If something such as wine or cheese **matures** or **is matured**, it is left for a time to allow its full flavour or strength to develop. EG *This whisky achieves its taste and colour by being matured in old wood.*   V-ERG

6 Cheese or wine that is **mature** has been left to allow its full flavour or strength to develop.   ADJ QUALIT

mature student, mature students. In a British college or university, a **mature student** is a student who is over 25 years old.   N COUNT

maturity /mətjʊəri'ti¹, -tʃʊə-/. **1 Maturity** is the state of being fully developed or adult. EG *Only half of the young birds may live to reach maturity.*   N UNCOUNT

2 If someone has **maturity**, they are fully adult in their personality and emotional behaviour. EG *I have long felt that you lacked maturity.*   N UNCOUNT

maul /mɔːl/, **mauls, mauling, mauled.** If someone is **mauled** by an animal, they are savagely attacked and badly injured by it.   V+O : USU PASS

mausoleum /mɔːsəliəm/, **mausoleums.** A **mausoleum** is a building which contains the grave of a famous person or the graves of a rich family.   N COUNT

mauve /məʊv/, **mauves.** Something that is **mauve** is of a pale purple colour. EG *...mauve writing paper.*   ADJ COLOUR

maverick /mævə⁰rɪk/, **mavericks.** If you say that someone is a **maverick**, you mean that they think and act independently, and do not always do the same as the group that they belong to. ▸ used as an adjective. EG *He is a self-confessed maverick Marxist.*   N COUNT Literary ▸ ADJ CLASSIF : ATTRIB

max. is a written abbreviation for 'maximum'. EG *...max. 17°C... The cost will be £90 max.*   EG

maxim /mæksɪm/, **maxims.** A **maxim** is a rule for good or sensible behaviour, which is often in the form of a proverb or short saying. EG *Instant action: that's my maxim.*   N COUNT

maximize /mæksɪmaɪz/, **maximizes, maximizing, maximized;** also spelled **maximise.** If you **maximize** something, you make it as great in amount or importance as you can. EG *The company's main objective is to maximize profits.*   V+O

maximum /mæksɪməm/. The **maximum** amount of something is the largest amount that is possible or allowed. EG *The plan must be carried out with maximum speed... They held the prisoner under maximum security conditions... Never exceed the maximum daily dosage of 150 mg.* ▸ used as a noun. EG *Conscription should be limited to a maximum of six months' service.*   ADJ CLASSIF : ATTRIB ▸ N SING

may /meɪ/. **1** If you say that something **may** happen, you mean that it is possible that it will happen. EG *We may be here a long time... You may be right... We may never know the truth.*   MODAL

2 If you say that something **may** be true, you mean that there is a possibility that it is true, but you are not certain. If you say that something **may** have happened, you mean that it is possible that it happened. EG *This may or may not be true... You may think it's silly, Edward, but it's what I did... A gigantic meteorite may have wiped out the dinosaurs 65 million years ago.*   MODAL

3 If something **may** be done, it is possible to do it. EG *The fat in our diet may be reduced by buying low-fat milk.*   MODAL

4 If someone **may** do something, they are allowed to do it. EG *If the verdict is unacceptable, the defendant may appeal... May I have a word with you, please?... I'll take a seat, if I may.*   MODAL

5 You can use **may** when saying that, although something is true, something else which contrasts with it is also true. EG *They may be seven thousand miles away but they know what's going on over here... Ingenious though these techniques may be, they can hardly be regarded as practical.*   MODAL

6 If you do something so that a particular thing **may** happen, you do it so that it becomes possible   MODAL

for that thing to happen. EG *They struggle to cure diseases so that people may live longer.*

7 You use **may** to express a wish that something will happen. For example, if you say 'May you always be happy', you are expressing a wish that someone will always be happy. EG *Long may it continue.*   MODAL Formal

8 May is the fifth month of the year in the Western calendar. EG *The meeting is on the 5th of May.*   N UNCOUNT

maybe /meɪbiː/. You use **maybe 1** to indicate that something is possible or may be true, but you are not certain. EG *Maybe he'll be prime minister one day... Well, maybe you're right... Maybe I ought to grow a moustache.* **2** to indicate that you are making a rough guess at a number or quantity, rather than stating it exactly. EG *There were maybe half a dozen men there... He's in his fifties, I'd say. Fifty-five, maybe.*   ADV SEN

mayhem /meɪhem/ is a situation in which there is no order, and a lot of people behave in an uncontrolled way. EG *The kids began to create mayhem in the washrooms.*   N UNCOUNT

mayonnaise /meɪəneɪz/ is a pale, thick sauce which is often eaten with salads. It is made from egg yolks and oil.   N UNCOUNT

mayor /meə/, **mayors.** The **mayor** of a town or city is the person who has been elected to be its head for one year and to represent it at some official occasions.   N COUNT

mayoress /meəri's/, **mayoresses.** A **mayoress** is the wife of a mayor.   N COUNT

maze

maze /meɪz/, **mazes. 1** A **maze** is a system of complicated passages which it is difficult to find your way through. EG *Some mice were trained to find their way through a simple maze.*   N COUNT

2 A **maze** of ideas or subjects is a large number of them connected with each other in a complicated way. EG *He lost himself in a maze of thoughts.*   N COUNT+of

me /miː/ is used as the object of a verb or preposition. A speaker or writer uses **me** to refer to himself or herself. EG *He told me about it... He looked at me reproachfully.*   PRON : SING

meadow /medəʊ/, **meadows.** A **meadow** is a field which has grass and flowers growing in it.   N COUNT

meagre /miːgə/; spelled **meager** in American English. If you describe something as **meagre**, you mean that it is very small. EG *...a meagre crop of potatoes... ...his meagre wages.*   ADJ QUALIT

meal /miːl/, **meals. 1** A **meal** is an occasion when people eat or the quantity of food that they eat on that occasion. EG *We always had three good meals a day... ...a simple meal of bread and cheese... When the meal was over, Thomas went out... ...the evening meal.*   N COUNT

2 If you say that someone is **making a meal of** something, you mean that they are using more time and energy to do it than is necessary.   PHRASE Outdated

mealtime /miːltaɪm/, **mealtimes.** A **mealtime** is an occasion when you eat breakfast, lunch, or   N COUNT OR N UNCOUNT dinner. EG *I had a glass of juice three times a day at mealtimes... She looked forward to mealtimes.*

mean /miːn/, **means, meaning, meant** /ment/; **meaner, meanest. 1** If you ask what a word, v+o : NO CONT expression, or gesture **means**, you want it to be explained to you. EG *What does 'imperialism' mean?... What is meant by the term 'mental activity'?*

2 If you ask someone what they **mean**, you are v+o : OFT+*by*, asking them to explain exactly what they are OR V+REPORT: referring to or intending to say. EG *But what do we* ONLY *that* *mean by 'education'?... I know the guy you mean... I thought you meant you wanted to take your own car... You mean that she disliked Celia?*

3 You say **'I mean' 3.1** when you are explaining ADV SEN something more clearly or justifying something that you have said. EG *Does she drink? Heavily, I mean... If you haven't any climbing boots, you can borrow them. I mean dozens of people have got boots.* **3.2** when you are correcting something that you have just said. EG *This is Herbert, I mean Humbert.*

4 If something **means** a lot to you, it is important v+o : OFT+*to*, to you. EG *These were the friends who had meant* NO CONT *most to her since childhood.*

5 If one thing **means** another, it shows that the v+o OR second thing exists, is true, or will happen. EG *A cut* V+REPORT: *in taxes will mean a cut in government spending...* ONLY *that*, *Water running down the outside of a wall may* NO CONT *mean that the gutters are blocked.*

6 If you **mean** what you say, you are serious about v+o it and are not joking, exaggerating, or just being polite. EG *I'm going. I mean it... Anyone can programme a computer. And I do mean anyone.*

7 If you **mean** to do something, you intend to do it. v+*to*-INF: EG *I meant to ring you but I'm afraid I forgot... I'm* NO IMPER *sorry, I didn't mean to be rude.*

8 If something **is meant** to happen, **8.1** it is v+o+*to*-INF intended to happen. EG *Sorry, I'm not very good at* OR *for*: *drawing, but that's meant to be a cube... 'That* USU PASS, *hurts!' – 'It's meant to!'... His smile was meant for* NO IMPER *me.* **8.2** it is strongly expected to happen or exist. V-PASS+*to*-INF EG *Are parents meant to love all their children equally?... I found a road that wasn't meant to be there.*

9 You can use **mean** when you are talking about V-PASS+*to*-INF the reputation of a person or thing. For example, if something **is meant** to be good, it has a reputation for being good. If it **is meant** to be reliable, it has a reputation for being reliable. EG *They're meant to be excellent cars.*

10 A **means** of doing something is a method or N COUNT+SUPP object which makes it possible. **Means** is both the singular and the plural form. EG *Scientists are working to devise a means of storing this type of power... We have the means to kill people on a massive scale... An attempt was made to sabotage the ceremony by violent means.* ● If something is a ● PHRASE **means to an end**, you do it only because it will enable you to achieve what you want. EG *I never enjoyed college, it was just a means to an end.*

11 If you do something **by means of** a particular PREP method or object, you do it using that method or object. EG *The rig is anchored in place by means of steel cables.*

12 You say **'by all means'** as a way of telling CONVENTION someone that you are willing to allow them to do Formal something. EG *'May I go now?' – 'Yes, yes, by all means.'... By all means take a day's holiday.*

13 By no means is used to emphasize that some- PHRASE thing is not true. EG *It is by no means certain that this is what he did.*

14 You can refer to the money that someone has as N PLURAL their **means**. EG *Sutcliffe has a house in Mayfair so* Formal *he obviously has means.*

15 Someone who is **mean 15.1** is unwilling to spend ADJ QUALIT much money or to use very much of a particular thing. EG *I used to be very mean about hot water.* ◊ **meanness.** EG *These employers were famous for* ◊ N UNCOUNT

their meanness. **15.2** is unkind to someone. EG *She had apologized for being so mean to Rudolph.* ◊ **meanness.** EG *...his meanness to his sisters.* ◊ N UNCOUNT

16 No mean is used to indicate **16.1** that a person PHRASE is good at something. EG *Sir George Gilbert Scott,* Formal *himself no mean architect, approved the plans.* **16.2** that an achievement is a great one. EG *Per-* Formal *suading John to come was no mean feat.*

meander /miˈændə/, **meanders, meandering, meandered. 1** If a river or road **meanders** some- V : USU+A where, it has a lot of bends in it. EG *A stream meandered towards the sea.*

2 If you **meander** somewhere, you travel or move v+A there slowly. EG *We meandered along eating nuts and blackberries.*

meaning /miːnɪŋ/, **meanings. 1** The **meaning** of N COUNT OR a word, expression, or gesture is the thing that it N UNCOUNT refers to or expresses. EG *The word 'guide' is used with various meanings... Do you know the meaning of the phrase 'cock-and-bull story'?*

2 The **meaning** of what someone says or of N UNCOUNT something such as a book or film is the thought or OR N COUNT idea that it is intended to express. EG *The meaning of the remark was clear... I don't understand the meaning of Pollock's paintings.*

3 If something has **meaning**, it seems to be N UNCOUNT worthwhile and to have a real purpose. EG *We yearn for beauty, truth, and meaning in our lives... My prayers had real meaning for me at a very early age.*

meaningful /miːnɪŋful/. **1** A **meaningful** sen- ADJ QUALIT tence or event has a meaning that you can understand. EG *Nobody has ever explained electricity to me in a meaningful way... ...the difficulties of achieving meaningful results from scientific surveys.*

2 A **meaningful** look, expression, or remark is ADJ QUALIT intended to express an attitude or opinion. EG *They exchanged meaningful glances.* ◊ **meaningfully.** ◊ ADV EG *'Goodnight, and call again. Anytime,' Boon added meaningfully.*

3 A **meaningful** relationship, experience, or ac- ADJ QUALIT tion is serious and important in some way. EG *He felt the need to establish a more meaningful relationship with people... ...meaningful discussions.* ◊ **meaningfully.** EG *At least you'd be filling your* ◊ ADV *time meaningfully.*

meaningless /miːnɪŋlɪs/. **1** Something that is ADJ QUALIT **meaningless 1.1** has no meaning. EG *These songs are largely meaningless.* **1.2** has no importance or relevance. EG *Taxes made the bonus meaningless.*

2 If you feel that your work or life is **meaningless**, ADJ QUALIT you feel that it has no purpose and is not worthwhile. EG *People arrive at a factory and perform a totally meaningless task from eight to five.*

meant /ment/ is the past tense and past participle of **mean.**

meantime /miːntaɪm/. **In the meantime** means ADV SEN in the period of time between two events. EG *At long last we were released. In the meantime, our friends had informed the newspapers... I will call Doctor Ford. In the meantime you must sleep.*

meanwhile /miːnwaɪl/ means **1** while something ADV SEN else is happening. EG *She ate an olive. Nick, mean-while, was talking about Rose.* **2** in the period of time between two events. EG *But meanwhile a number of steps will have to be taken.*

measles /miːzəlz/ is an infectious illness that N UNCOUNT gives you red spots on your skin. ● See also **German measles.**

measly /miːzliː/. A **measly** amount of something ADJ QUALIT is very small or inadequate. EG *One measly tomato,* Informal *that's all we've had from this plant!*

measurable /meʒərəbl/. If something is ADJ CLASSIF **measurable**, it is large enough to be noticed or to Formal

If someone's friendship means a lot to you, is it meaningful?

be significant. EG *Some measurable progress had been made.*

measure /mɛʒə/, **measures, measuring, measured.** 1 When you **measure** something, you find v+o out how big or great it is by using an instrument or device. You can measure the length of something by using a ruler, for example. EG *He measured the diameter of the artery... The explosive force is measured in tons.*

2 If something **measures** a particular distance, its v+c length, width, or depth is that distance. EG *...small slivers of glass measuring a few millimetres across... ...a square area measuring 900 metres on each side.*

3 A **measure** of something is a certain amount of N PART : SING it. EG *Everyone is entitled to some measure of* Formal *protection.*

4 A **measure** of a strong alcoholic drink such as N PART brandy or whisky is an amount of it in a glass. EG *He poured himself a generous measure of cognac.*

5 Something that is a **measure** of something else N SING+*of* shows how great it is. EG *It is a measure of their achievement that the system has lasted so long.*

6 A **measure** is also an action carried out by a N COUNT : government or other authority in order to achieve USU PLURAL a particular result. EG *Measures had been taken to* Formal *limit the economic decline.*

7 If something is done **for good measure**, it is ADV SEN done in addition to a number of other actions, in order to make a situation more complete or satisfactory. EG *The waiter had taken away the plates, and, for good measure, had removed his glass.*

8 See also **measuring, tape measure.**

measure up. If someone or something **meas-** PHRASAL VB : **ures up** to a standard or to someone's expecta- V+ADV, tions, they are good as is required or expected. EG USU+*to* *The state of repair failed to measure up to their exacting standards.*

measured /mɛʒəd/. A **measured** way of speak- ADJ CLASSIF ing or moving is careful and deliberate. EG *...walk-* Literary *ing at the same measured pace.*

measurement /mɛʒəmə²nt/, **measurements.** 1 N COUNT A **measurement** is a result that you obtain by measuring something. EG *Check the measurements first... ...the exact measurements of the office.*

2 **Measurement** is the activity of measuring N UNCOUNT : something. EG *...the first actual measurement of the* OFT+*of* *speed of sound.*

3 Your **measurements** are the size of your chest, N PLURAL waist, hips, and other parts of your body.

MEASUREMENT

This entry shows some ways of expressing measurements such as sizes, distances, weights, and temperatures.

In speech, the actual words that refer to the unit of measurement, for example 'metres', 'miles', 'kilos', 'litres', or 'degrees', are often left out when it is obvious what you are measuring and what units of measurement you are using. When measurements are used like adjectives in front of a noun, you never use the plural form, so that you say 'a two-litre bottle' and 'a twenty-mile walk'.

Here are some ways of saying how big something is. EG *It was ten feet in height... The visitor was six feet tall... ...people who are over six foot... ...heavy planks of wood about three inches thick... ...a tiny cell four feet wide and seven long... ...a block of ice one cubic foot in size.*

Here are some ways of saying how heavy something is. EG *The largest brain possessed by any dinosaur weighed about a kilogram... ...14,000 tons of potatoes... ...a sixteen-ounce bar of soap.*

Here are some ways of saying how hot something

is. EG *...a temperature of four hundred degrees centigrade... The temperature touched 100° Fahrenheit in Los Angeles that day... It had been fourteen below zero when they woke up... The temperature was well above freezing point.*

In the following examples, the speaker is referring to clothing sizes or shoe sizes. EG *'What size do you take?' - 'Ten.'... ...a size 9 shoe.*

---

measuring /mɛʒə²rɪŋ/. A **measuring** jug or ADJ CLASSIF : spoon is one that is specially designed for measur- ATTRIB ing quantities, especially in cooking.

meat /miːt/, **meats. Meat** is the flesh of a dead N MASS animal that people cook and eat.

mecca /mɛkə/, **meccas.** If you say that a place is N COUNT a **mecca** for people of a particular kind, you mean +SUPP : that many of them go there because there is USU SING something there that interests or attracts them. EG *The United States is still a mecca for film-makers.*

mechanic /mɪ²kænɪk/, **mechanics.** 1 A **mechan-** N COUNT **ic** is someone whose job is to repair and maintain machines and engines.

2 The **mechanics** of something are the way in N PLURAL : which it works or the way in which it is done. EG *the*+N *...the mechanics of reading.*

mechanical /mɪ²kænɪkə⁰l/. 1 A **mechanical** de- ADJ CLASSIF vice has moving parts and uses power in order to do a particular task. EG *They were using a mechanical shovel to clear up the streets.*

◇ **mechanically.** EG *The glass doors slid open* ◇ ADV *mechanically as she approached them.*

2 Someone who has a **mechanical** mind under- ADJ CLASSIF : stands how machines work and knows how to ATTRIB repair them. EG *...a given level of mechanical ability.*

3 If someone's behaviour is **mechanical**, they are ADJ QUALIT doing something without thinking about it, because they have done it many times before. EG *When invention is left out, dancing becomes mechanical and dull.* ◇ **mechanically.** EG *'How are you?' - 'Oh,* ◇ ADV *fine, thanks,' said Philip mechanically.*

mechanism /mɛkənɪzə⁰m/, **mechanisms.** A **mechanism** is 1 a part of a device or machine that N COUNT : does a particular task. EG *...a locking mechanism...* USU+SUPP *...steering mechanisms in cars.* 2 a way of getting N COUNT+SUPP something done within a system. EG *There's no mechanism for changing the decision.* 3 a part of N COUNT+SUPP your behaviour that is automatic and that helps you to survive or to cope with a difficult situation. EG *During this regime, the defence mechanism of disbelief operated.*

mechanize /mɛkənaɪz/, **mechanizes, mecha-** V+O OR V **nizing, mechanized;** also spelled **mechanise.** If a type of work **is mechanized**, it is organized so that it is done by machines. ◇ **mechanized.** EG *House-* ◇ ADJ QUALIT *work has become highly mechanised.*

◇ **mechanization** /mɛkənaɪzeɪʃə⁰n/. EG *...the* ◇ N UNCOUNT *mechanisation of the postal service.*

medal /mɛdə⁰l/, **medals.** A **medal** is a small N COUNT piece of metal with a design on it. Medals are given as awards for bravery or as prizes in sporting events. EG *He won six gold medals.*

medallion /mɪ²dæljən/, **medallions.** A **medal-** N COUNT **lion** is a round piece of metal which is worn as an ornament on a chain round a person's neck.

medallist /mɛdə⁰lɪst/, **medallists.** A **medallist** is N COUNT a person who has won a medal in sport. EG *She's an Olympic medallist.*

meddle /mɛdə⁰l/, **meddles, meddling, meddled.** V : OFT+*in*/ If you **meddle** in something, you try to influence or *with* change it without being asked to; used showing disapproval. EG *I dared not meddle with my wife's plans.*

media /miːdɪə/. You can refer to television, radio, N COLL : *the*+N and newspapers as the **media.** EG *These problems have been exaggerated by the media.*

mediaeval /mɛdiːvəl/. See **medieval**.

mediate /miːdɪˈeɪt/, **mediates, mediating, mediated.** If you **mediate** between two groups who are involved in a dispute, you try to settle the dispute by finding things that they can both agree to. EG *I mediated for him in a quarrel with his brother... He called on the Red Cross to try to mediate the dispute.* ◊ **mediator, mediators.** EG *Tom Hagen was busy trying to find a mediator satisfactory to both parties.* V: OFT+*between*; ALSO V+O ◊ N COUNT

medic /mɛdɪk/, **medics.** A **medic** is a doctor or medical student. EG *Navy medics operated on the foot... We had more law students than medics.* N COUNT Informal

medical /mɛdɪkəl/, **medicals.** 1 **Medical** means relating to the treatment of illness and injuries and to the prevention of illness. EG *She had to undergo medical treatment... The medical profession was baffled... ...the medical care of babies.* ADJ CLASSIF : ATTRIB

2 A **medical** is a thorough examination of your body by a doctor. EG *They were all set to give him a medical.* N COUNT

medication /mɛdɪkeɪʃəˈn/, **medications.** Medication is medicine that is used to cure an illness. EG *The doctor can prescribe medication to relieve the symptoms... Don't forget your medication.* N UNCOUNT OR N COUNT

medicinal /mɛdɪsɪnəl/. A **medicinal** substance is used to treat and cure illness. EG *...a medicinal herb... ...the medicinal qualities of a plant.* ADJ CLASSIF

medicine /mɛdɪsɪn/, **medicines.** 1 **Medicine** is the treatment of illness and injuries by doctors and nurses. EG *...the professions of medicine and dentistry... ...the importance of preventative medicine.* N UNCOUNT

2 A **medicine** is a substance that you drink or swallow in order to cure an illness. EG *...a medicine for his cold... ...cough medicines... ...the cupboard where the medicines were kept.* N MASS

medieval /mɛdiːvəl/; also spelled **mediaeval. Medieval** means belonging or relating to the period between about 1100 AD and about 1500 AD, especially in Europe. EG *...a medieval church... ...medieval German literature.* ADJ CLASSIF

mediocre /miːdɪəʊkə/. Something that is **mediocre** is of poor quality. EG *He spent much of his time reading mediocre paperbacks.* ◊ **mediocrity** /miːdɪɒkrɪˈtiˈ, mɛd-/. EG *He was dismayed by the mediocrity of the people working with him.* ADJ QUALIT ◊ N UNCOUNT

meditate /mɛdɪteɪt/, **meditates, meditating, meditated.** 1 If you **meditate** on something, you think about it very carefully and deeply for a long time. EG *He was left alone to meditate on his sins.* ◊ **meditation** /mɛdɪteɪʃəˈn/, **meditations.** EG *I hope we will not disturb your meditations.* V : OFT+*on/upon* ◊ N UNCOUNT OR N COUNT

2 If you **meditate**, you remain in a calm, silent state for a period of time, often as part of a religious training or so that you are better able to deal with the problems and difficulties of everyday life. ◊ **meditation.** EG *He was deeply interested in meditation and yoga.* V ◊ N UNCOUNT

meditative /mɛdɪtətɪv/. A **meditative** action shows that you are thinking carefully about something. EG *Daniel took a meditative sip of tea... We were both quiet and meditative.* ◊ **meditatively.** EG *He was leaning meditatively on his elbow.* ADJ CLASSIF ◊ ADV

medium /miːdɪəm/, **mediums.** 1 Something that is of **medium** size, degree, or intensity is at the middle point on a scale; for example, it is neither large nor small, or neither light nor dark. EG *...a medium screwdriver... He was of medium height... ...medium brown.* ADJ CLASSIF : USU ATTRIB

2 A **medium** is something that you can use to communicate or express things. EG *...sending messages through the medium of paper and printed word... ...the major broadcasting medium.* N COUNT Formal

3 A **medium** is also a person who claims to be able to speak to people who are dead and to receive messages from them. N COUNT

medium wave is a range of radio waves which are used for broadcasting. N UNCOUNT

meek /miːk/. Someone who is **meek** is timid and does what other people say. EG *...a meek suggestion.* ADJ QUALIT ◊ **meekly.** EG *'I'm sorry dear,' Gretchen said meekly.* ◊ ADV

meet /miːt/, **meets, meeting, met** /mɛt/. 1 If you **meet** someone, 1.1 you happen to be in the same place as them and start talking to them. EG *I met a Swedish girl on the train... They met each other at a party in London.* 1.2 you both go separately to the same place at the same time, so that you can talk or do something together. EG *They met every day... Meet me under the clock.* 1.3 you are introduced to them and begin talking to them. EG *Come and meet Tony and Rick.* V OR V+O : RECIP, NO PASS / V OR V+O : RECIP, NO PASS / V+O : NO PASS

2 If you **meet** someone who is coming to see you or if you **meet** their train, plane, or bus, you go to the station, airport, or bus-stop in order to be with them when they arrive there. V+O

3 When a group of people **meet**, they gather together for a purpose. EG *Teachers in Tokyo met to discuss our methods.* V

4 If you **meet** with someone, you have a meeting with them. EG *We can meet with the professor Monday night.* V+*with* American

5 If something **meets** a need, requirement, or condition, it is large enough or good enough to fulfil it. EG *His income is inadequate to meet his basic needs.* V+O

6 If you **meet** a problem or challenge, you deal satisfactorily with it. V+O

7 If you **meet** the cost of something, you provide the money for it. V+O

8 If you **meet** a situation, attitude, or problem, you experience it. EG *Where had I met this kind of ignorance before?* V+O

9 If something **meets** with a particular reaction or is **met** with that reaction, it gets that reaction from people. EG *All appeals for aid meet with refusal... His approaches had been met with ill-concealed disdain.* V-ERG+*with*

10 If you **meet** with success, you are successful. If you **meet** with failure, you are unsuccessful. V+*with*

11 When a moving object **meets** another object, it hits it or touches it. EG *The heavy club met his head with a crack.* V OR V+O : RECIP

12 If your eyes **meet** someone else's, you both look at each other at the same time. EG *Their eyes meet, and they smile.* V OR V+O : RECIP

13 The place where two areas or lines **meet** is the place where they are next to one another or join together. EG *...where this road meets the one from Lairg.* V OR V+O : RECIP

14 to **make ends meet**: see **end**. ● to **meet** someone **halfway**: see **halfway**. ● See also **meeting.**

meet up. If you **meet up** with someone, you both go separately to the same place at the same time, so that you can talk or do something together. EG *We planned to meet up with them in Florence.* PHRASAL VB : V+ADV : OFT+*with*

meeting /miːtɪŋ/, **meetings.** 1 A **meeting** is an event in which a group of people discuss proposals and make decisions together. EG *The committee will consider the proposal at its next meeting... A meeting of physicists had been called.* N COUNT

2 You can refer to the people attending a meeting as the **meeting**. EG *The meeting agreed with him.* N SING : *the*+N

3 A **meeting** is also an event in which you meet someone. EG *Christopher Milne vividly remembers his first meeting with Alice.* N COUNT

megalomaniac /mɛgələˈmeɪniæk/, **megalomaniacs.** A **megalomaniac** is someone who enjoys being powerful, or who believes that they are more powerful or important than they really are. N COUNT

Find a word on these pages which has two different plurals.

megaphone

lots of people of different kinds get mixed together in it. EG *The city is a melting pot of races.*

member /mɛmbə/, **members.** 1 A **member** of a group is one of the people, animals, or things belonging to the group. EG *Babies usually have milder colds than older members of the family... ...junior members of staff... The weaver bird is a member of the sparrow family.* N COUNT+SUPP

2 A **member** of an organization is a person who has joined the organization. EG *...members of trade unions... He shared the disillusionment of many Party members.* N COUNT : USU+SUPP

3 A **member** country or **member** state is one of the countries that has joined an international organization. EG *All the member countries are under pressure to conform.* ADJ CLASSIF : ATTRIB

4 A **member** is also a Member of Parliament. EG *...John Parker, the Labour member for Dagenham.* N COUNT

Member of Parliament, Members of Parliament. A **Member of Parliament** is a person who has been elected to represent people in a country's parliament. N COUNT

membership /mɛmbəʃɪp/, **memberships.** 1 **Membership** of an organization is the state of being a member of it. EG *Deacon was questioned about his membership of the Nationalist Party... ...membership fees.* N UNCOUNT

2 The **membership** of an organization is the people who belong to it. EG *Membership declined to half a million.* N COUNT OR N UNCOUNT

membrane /mɛmbreɪn/, **membranes.** A **membrane** is a thin piece of skin which connects or covers parts of a person's or animal's body. EG *...the delicate membranes of the throat.* N COUNT Formal

memento /mɪmɛntəʊ/, **mementos** or **mementoes.** A **memento** is an object which you keep because it reminds you of a person or a special occasion. EG *...the Presley badge, a memento of the singer's farewell concert.* N COUNT : OFT+of

memo /mɛməʊ/, **memos.** A **memo** is an official note from one person to another within the same organization. EG *He wrote a memo to the War Department asking for more soldiers.* N COUNT

memoirs /mɛmwɑːz/. The book which someone writes about their experiences is called their **memoirs.** EG *He was writing his memoirs of his career abroad.* N PLURAL : USU+POSS

memorable /mɛmərəbəl/. Something that is **memorable** is likely to be remembered because it is special or unusual. EG *...a memorable train journey.* ADJ QUALIT

memorandum /mɛmərændəm/, **memoranda** or **memorandums.** A **memorandum** is an official note or report from one person to another within the same organization. EG *He received a disturbing memorandum from the chief agent of the Party... ...an office memorandum.* N COUNT Formal

memorial /mɪmɔːrɪəl/, **memorials.** 1 A **memorial** is a structure built in order to remind people of a famous person or event. EG *...a memorial to Queen Alexandra... ...a war memorial.* N COUNT

2 A **memorial** event, object, or prize is in honour of someone who has died, so that they will be remembered. EG *The book won the 1981 George Orwell Memorial Prize... ...funerals and memorial services.* ADJ CLASSIF : ATTRIB

memorize /mɛməraɪz/, **memorizes, memorizing, memorized;** also spelled **memorise.** If you **memorize** something, you learn it thoroughly so that you can remember it exactly. EG *I was able to read a whole page and memorise it in under three minutes.* V+O

memory /mɛmərɪ/, **memories.** 1 Your **memory** is 1.1 your ability to remember things. EG *...people who have good memories.* 1.2 the things that you can remember. EG *A few things stand out in my memory... 'Gregory Temple?' he said aloud, searching his memory.* N COUNT / N SING+POSS

2 A **memory** is something that you remember N COUNT+SUPP

---

megaphone /mɛgəfəʊn/, **megaphones.** A **megaphone** is a cone-shaped device for making your voice sound louder in the open air. You speak into the small end. N COUNT

melancholy /mɛlənkɒlɪ/. 1 If you feel **melancholy**, you feel sad. EG *...a deep, melancholy voice.* ADJ QUALIT Literary

▸ used as a noun. EG *When he left, she sank into melancholy.* ▸ N UNCOUNT

2 You describe something as **melancholy** when it makes you feel sad. EG *We acquainted him with the melancholy truth.* ADJ QUALIT Literary

mellow /mɛləʊ/, **mellows, mellowing, mellowed.** 1 **Mellow** light is soft and golden. EG *...the mellow sunlight.* ADJ QUALIT

2 **Mellow** stone or brick has a pleasant soft colour because it is old. EG *...a strange Tudor building in mellow brick.* ADJ QUALIT : ATTRIB

3 A **mellow** sound is smooth and pleasant to listen to. EG *...sophisticated rhythms and a mellow sound.* ADJ QUALIT

4 If someone **mellows** or **is mellowed** by something such as age or alcohol, they become more pleasant or relaxed. EG *He mellowed considerably as he got older... He says that age should have mellowed me.* V-ERG

melodious /mɪləʊdɪəs/. A **melodious** sound is pleasant to listen to. EG *...a low melodious laugh.* ADJ QUALIT Formal

melodrama /mɛlɔˈdrɑːmə/, **melodramas.** A **melodrama** is a story or play in which a lot of exciting or sad things happen and in which people's emotions are very exaggerated. EG *...a wildly old-fashioned melodrama about a female spy.* N COUNT OR N UNCOUNT

melodramatic /mɛlɔˈdrəmætɪk/. **Melodramatic** behaviour is behaviour in which someone treats a situation as much more serious than it really is. EG *'I've called the police.' – 'Must you be so melodramatic?'* ADJ QUALIT

melody /mɛlədɪ/, **melodies.** A **melody** is a tune. EG *...a simple melody composed by Ronnie Bond.* N COUNT Literary

melon /mɛlən/, **melons.** A **melon** is a large juicy fruit which has a thick green or yellow skin. N COUNT OR N UNCOUNT

melt /mɛlt/, **melts, melting, melted.** 1 When something **melts** or when you **melt** it, it changes from a solid to a liquid because it has been heated. EG *The snow and ice had melted... Melt the margarine in a saucepan.* V-ERG

2 When something **melts** or **melts** away, it gradually disappears. EG *Lynn's inhibitions melted... Their differences melted away.* V : OFT+away

3 If you **melt** into a crowd of people or into your surroundings, you become not at all noticeable. EG *They often wanted to melt into the teeming millions.* V+into

melt down. If you **melt down** an object made of metal or glass, you heat it until it melts. EG *Railings were melted down for cannon.* PHRASAL VB : V+O+ADV

melting pot, melting pots. If you describe a place or situation as a **melting pot**, you mean that N COUNT : USU SING

about the past. EG *My memories of a London childhood are happy ones.*

3 You can refer to the **memory** of a dead person as a way of referring to that person. EG *It is an insult to the memory of the brave men who died for their country.* N SING : USU+POSS

4 A computer's **memory** is the part of the computer where information is stored. N COUNT

5 Memory is also used in these phrases. **5.1** If you **lose** your **memory**, you can no longer remember things that you used to know. EG *...a story about somebody who's lost his memory.* **5.2** If you **commit** something **to memory**, you learn it thoroughly so that you can remember it exactly. **5.3** If you do something **from memory**, for example recite a poem or play a piece of music, you do it without looking at anything written or printed. EG *The next day he received the following letter (I quote from memory).* **5.4** If something has happened **within living memory**, there are people alive who can remember it happening. EG *The earthquake in San Francisco is well within living memory.* **5.5** If you do something **in memory** of someone who has died, you do it so that people will remember that person. EG *A fund was launched to set up a monument in memory of the dead men.* PHRASES

men /mɛn/ is the plural of **man**.

menace /ˈmɛnɪs/, **menaces, menacing, menaced. 1** Something or someone that is a **menace** is likely to cause serious harm to a person or thing. EG *These riots are a menace to democracy... ...the menace of totalitarianism.* N COUNT

2 Menace is the quality of being or appearing threatening. EG *There was anger and menace in his eyes.* N UNCOUNT

3 If something **menaces** something else, it is likely to harm it. EG *...the formidable threat that menaces Europe.* V+O

4 If someone **menaces** you, they threaten to harm you. EG *We were menaced by drunks.* V+O

menacing /ˈmɛnɪsɪŋ/. If someone's behaviour is **menacing**, they seem to be intending to harm you. EG *He advanced on me in a menacing fashion.*
◊ **menacingly**. EG *Joy scowled at him and waved her knife menacingly.* ADJ QUALIT ◊ ADV

mend /mɛnd/, **mends, mending, mended. 1** If you **mend** something that is damaged or not working, you do something to it so that it works again or is like it was before. EG *I mended some toys for her... He spent the evening mending socks.* V+O

2 If you are **on the mend**, you are recovering from an illness or an injury. EG *He had some colour in his cheeks and was plainly on the mend.* PHRASE Informal

3 If someone **mends** their **ways**, they begin to behave well after they have been behaving badly. EG *You've got to mend your ways or, next time, you will be sent to prison.* PHRASE

mending /ˈmɛndɪŋ/ is **1** the repairing of clothes that have got holes in them. **2** clothes that you have collected together to be mended. EG *...his mother's basket of mending.* N UNCOUNT

menfolk /ˈmɛnfəʊk/. When women refer to their **menfolk**, they mean the men in their family or community. EG *The wives and mothers would do anything to protect their menfolk.* N PLURAL +POSS

menial /ˈmiːnɪəl/. **Menial** work is boring and tiring, and the people who do it have a low status. EG *...menial tasks.* ADJ QUALIT

meningitis /ˌmɛnɪndʒˈaɪtɪs/ is a serious infectious illness which affects your brain and spinal cord. N UNCOUNT

menopause /ˈmɛnəʊpɔːz/. The **menopause** is the time during which a woman stops menstruating, usually when she is about fifty years old. N SING OR N UNCOUNT

men's room, men's rooms. The men's room is a toilet for men in a public building such as a restaurant. N COUNT American

menstrual /ˈmɛnstrʊəl/ means relating to menstruation. EG *...the menstrual cycle.* ADJ CLASSIF : ATTRIB

menstruate /ˈmɛnstrʊeɪt/, **menstruates, menstruating, menstruated.** When a woman **menstruates**, blood comes from her womb. Women who are fertile menstruate regularly once a month. ◊ **menstruation** /ˌmɛnstrʊˈeɪʃən/. EG *...the onset of menstruation.* V Technical ◊ N UNCOUNT

menswear /ˈmɛnzwɛə/ is clothing for men. N UNCOUNT

-ment, -ments. -ment is used to form nouns that refer to actions or states. For example, 'bombardment' refers to the bombarding of a place, and 'disenchantment' refers to the state of being disenchanted. When these nouns are formed from verbs, they are often not defined in this dictionary, but are treated with the related verb. EG *...the commencement of the flight... ...disillusionment with politics... Tree diseases are largely a result of mismanagement.* SUFFIX

mental /ˈmɛntəl/. **1 Mental** means **1.1** relating to the process of thinking or to intelligence. EG *...mental effort... ...one's mental ability.* ◊ **mentally.** *She looked at the bouquets, mentally pricing the blooms.* **1.2** relating to the health of a person's mind. EG *...mental illness... ...the mental health of children.* ◊ **mentally.** EG *He was a sick man, mentally and physically.* ADJ CLASSIF : ATTRIB ◊ ADV ADJ CLASSIF : ATTRIB ◊ ADV

2 A **mental** act is one that involves only thinking and not physical action. EG *...mental arithmetic.* ◊ **mentally.** EG *I have kicked myself mentally a hundred times for that stupidity.* ADJ CLASSIF : ATTRIB ◊ ADV

mental hospital, mental hospitals. A mental hospital is a hospital for people who are suffering from mental illness. N COUNT

mentality /mɛnˈtælɪtiː/, **mentalities.** Your **mentality** is your attitudes or ways of thinking; often used showing disapproval. EG *She says I have a slave mentality.* N COUNT+SUPP

mention /ˈmɛnʃən/, **mentions, mentioning, mentioned. 1** If you **mention** something, you say something about it, usually briefly. EG *Penny decided not to mention her cold... I mentioned to Tom that I was thinking of going back to work.* V+O OR V+REPORT : OFT+to

2 A **mention** is a reference to something or someone. EG *My brother used to go purple in the face at the very mention of my name... Mention was made earlier of the new university course in Japanese.* N COUNT OR N UNCOUNT : OFT+of

3 You say **'don't mention it'** as a polite reply to someone who has just thanked you for doing something. CONVENTION

4 You use **not to mention** when adding something to a list in an emphatic way. EG *He's always travelling to Buenos Aires and Delhi, not to mention London and Paris.* PHRASE

mentor /ˈmɛntɔː/, **mentors.** Someone's **mentor** is a person who teaches them and gives them advice. EG *...Harold, my mentor from my student days.* N COUNT Formal

menu /ˈmɛnjuː/, **menus.** A **menu** is a list of the kinds of food that you can eat in a particular restaurant. EG *He ordered the most expensive items on the menu.* N COUNT

MEP /ˌɛm iː ˈpiː/, **MEPs.** An **MEP** is a person who has been elected to the European Parliament. **MEP** is an abbreviation for 'Member of the European Parliament'. N COUNT

mercenary /ˈmɜːsɪnəriː/, **mercenaries. 1** A **mercenary** is someone who is paid to fight for countries or groups that they do not belong to. N COUNT

2 Someone who is **mercenary** is interested only in the money they can get; used showing disapproval. ADJ QUALIT

merchandise /ˈmɜːtʃəndaɪz/ is goods that are sold. EG *I'd like to examine the merchandise.* N UNCOUNT

merchant /ˈmɜːtʃənt/, **merchants. 1** A **merchant** is a person who buys or sells goods in large quantities, especially one who imports and exports them. EG *...a textile merchant.* N COUNT : USU+SUPP

Do men refer to other men as 'menfolk'?

2 Merchant seamen or ships are involved in carrying goods for trade. EG *He served for many years in the British Merchant Navy.* ADJ CLASSIF: ATTRIB

merchant bank, merchant banks. A **merchant bank** is a bank that deals mainly with businesses and investment. N COUNT

merciful /mɜːsiˈful/. 1 You describe an event or situation as **merciful** when you think it is fortunate or lucky, especially because it stops someone suffering. EG *Death came as a merciful release.* ADJ QUALIT
◇ **mercifully.** EG *He lay down and soon fell into a mercifully dreamless sleep... Mercifully, I hadn't yet had a puncture.* ◇ ADV OR ADV SEN
2 Someone who is **merciful** shows kindness and forgiveness to people who are in their power. EG *I begged him to be merciful.* ADJ QUALIT

merciless /mɜːsiˈlɪs/. Someone who is **merciless** is very strict or cruel and does not show any forgiveness towards people. EG *He had a reputation as a merciless foe of gambling.* ◇ **mercilessly.** EG *Unarmed peasants were beaten mercilessly.* ADJ QUALIT ◇ ADV

mercury /mɜːkjʊˈriˈ/ is a silver-coloured metal that exists as a liquid. It is used, for example, in thermometers. N UNCOUNT

mercy /mɜːsiˈ/, **mercies.** 1 If you show **mercy** to someone, you do not punish them or treat them as severely as you could. EG *He pleaded for mercy.* N UNCOUNT
2 If you describe an event or situation as a **mercy**, you mean that it is fortunate. EG *What a mercy it was that Maisie had given up drinking... Be thankful for small mercies.* N COUNT
3 If you are **at the mercy of** someone or something, they have complete power over you. EG *This action would leave them at the mercy of industrialised countries.* PHRASE

mere /mɪə/, **merest.** The superlative form **merest** is used to give emphasis, rather than in comparisons.
Mere is 1 used to emphasize how unimportant or minor something or someone is. EG *They were mere puppets manipulated by men in search of power... He had found out only by the merest accident.* **2** used when a quality or action that is usually unimportant has a very strong effect. EG *They feared the impact the mere presence of a political prisoner would have... The merest suggestion of marital infidelity enrages him.* **3** used to emphasize how small a particular amount or quantity is. EG *In Tanganyika, a mere 2 per cent of the population lived in towns.* ADJ CLASSIF: ATTRIB

merely /mɪəliˈ/. 1 You use **merely** 1.1 to emphasize that something is only the thing you say it is and not something better or more important. EG *This is not genuine. It's merely a reproduction... We accept ideas like this merely because they have never been challenged... 'I killed him,' said Stevens, as casually as if they were merely discussing the weather.* 1.2 to emphasize that a particular amount or quantity is very small. EG *January was merely a month away.* ADV
2 You use **not merely** before the less important of two statements, as a way of emphasizing the more important statement. EG *Much of this new industry was not merely in India; it was Indian-owned... The saints have known God – not merely believed in him.* ADV

merge /mɜːdʒ/, **merges, merging, merged.** 1 If one thing **merges** with another or if you **merge** them, they combine together to make one whole thing. EG *They advised their clients to merge with another company... The borough of Holborn was merged with St Pancras and Hampstead... The voices merged with one another.* V-ERG; ALSO V OR V+with: RECIP
2 If something **merges** into the darkness or the background, you can no longer see it clearly as a separate object. EG *They were painted so that they would merge into the landscape.* V+into

merger /mɜːdʒə/, **mergers.** When a **merger** takes place, two companies or organizations join N COUNT

together. EG *...a merger between the two organizations.*

meringue /məˈræŋ/, **meringues.** A **meringue** is a type of crisp, sweet, white cake made by baking a mixture of sugar and egg white. N COUNT

merit /merɪt/, **merits, meriting, merited.** 1 If something has **merit**, it is good or worthwhile. EG *...a work of high literary merit... There is undoubtedly some merit in this argument.* N UNCOUNT Formal
2 The **merits** of something are its advantages or good qualities. EG *...the relative merits of cinema and drama... The first version certainly has the merit of being clear.* N COUNT: USU+POSS
3 If you judge something **on** its **merits**, you base your decision about it on how good or worthwhile it is, rather than on your personal feelings. EG *We endeavour to assess any case on its merits.* PHRASE
4 If something **merits** a particular treatment, it is good enough or important enough to be treated in this way. EG *This experiment merits closer examination... It was not important enough to merit a special discussion.* V+O ◇ ADV

mermaid /mɜːmeɪd/, **mermaids.** In stories, a **mermaid** is a woman with a fish's tail instead of legs, who lives in the sea. N COUNT

merrily /merɪliˈ/. If you do something **merrily**, you do it without realizing that there are a lot of problems that you have not thought about. EG *Before you skip merrily on to the next page, pause.* ADV
● See also **merry**.

merriment /merɪmənt/ is laughter. EG *She put a hand to her mouth to stifle her merriment.* N UNCOUNT Formal

merry /meriˈ/. 1 If you are **merry**, you are 1.1 happy and cheerful. EG *My in-laws, a merry band from Bath, had joined us... ...his merry blue eyes.* ◇ **merrily.** EG *Dr Mason laughed merrily.* 1.2 slightly drunk. EG *Harvey was getting quite merry.* ADJ QUALIT ◇ ADJ PRED Informal
2 A **merry** sound or sight makes you feel cheerful. EG *...merry music.* ◇ **merrily.** EG *The fire was burning merrily.* ADJ QUALIT ◇ ADV
3 People say **Merry Christmas** to each other at Christmas time. CONVENTION
4 See also **merrily**.

merry-go-round, merry-go-rounds. A **merry-go-round** is a large circular platform with wooden or plastic animals and vehicles on it which children ride on as it turns round. N COUNT

mesh /meʃ/, **meshes, meshing, meshed.** 1 Mesh is material like a net made from wire, thread, or plastic. EG *...a fence made of stout wire mesh.* N UNCOUNT
2 If two things **mesh** or **mesh** together, they fit together closely. V OR V+with: RECIP

mesmerize /mezməraɪz/, **mesmerizes, mesmerizing, mesmerized;** also spelled **mesmerise.** If you **are mesmerized** by something, you are so interested in it or so attracted to it that you cannot think about anything else. EG *Blanche was mesmerized by his voice.* V+O: USU PASS

mess /mes/, **messes, messing, messed.** 1 If you say that something is a **mess**, you mean that it is in a very untidy state. EG *I know the place is a mess, but make yourself at home... They went back to see how much mess they'd left behind... We cleared up the mess.* N SING OR N UNCOUNT
2 If you describe a situation as a **mess**, you mean that it is full of problems and trouble. EG *My life is such a mess... It seemed a way out from the mess I'd got myself into.* N COUNT: USU SING
3 If something is **in a mess**, it is untidy or disorganized. EG *Her hair was in a terrible mess... The US economy is now in a mess.* PHRASE
4 A **mess** is also a room or building in which members of the armed forces eat. EG *...a bomb attack on an officers' mess.* N COUNT

mess about or **mess around.** 1 If you **mess about** or **mess around**, 1.1 you do things without any particular purpose and do not achieve anything. EG *Some of the lads had been messing around when they should have been working at the other* PHRASAL VB: V+ADV Informal *house.* **1.2** you interfere with things and make them worse or untidy. EG *She didn't want you coming and messing about with things.* **2** If you **mess** someone **about** or **mess** them **around,** you are not honest with them or continually change plans which affect them.   V+ADV, USU+*with* / V+O+ADV Informal

mess up. **1** If you **mess up** something that has been carefully made or done, you spoil it. EG *That will mess up the whole analysis.* **2** If you **mess up** a room, you make it untidy or dirty. EG *I was used to him messing up the kitchen.*   PHRASAL VB: V+O+ADV Informal

mess with. If you **mess with** someone or something dangerous, you become involved with them. EG *We don't mess with heroin or any of that stuff.*   PHRASAL VB: V+PREP, HAS PASS Informal

message /mɛsɪdʒ/, **messages.** **1** A **message** is **1.1** a piece of information or a request that you send to someone or leave for them when you cannot speak to them directly. EG *Oh, there was a message. Professor Marvin rang. He'd like to meet you on Tuesday... He sent a message to Sir Ian Hamilton saying he was returning.* **1.2** an idea that someone tries to communicate to people, for example in a play or a speech. EG *The play's message is that in the end good and right always triumph.*   N COUNT

2 If you say that someone **has got the message,** you mean that they have understood what you have been trying to tell them. EG *If we keep complaining, hospitals, doctors and nurses will eventually get the message.*   PHRASE Informal

messenger /mɛsɪndʒə/, **messengers.** A **messenger** is someone who takes a message to someone else or who takes messages regularly as their job. EG *By the time the messenger reached him, the damage had been done.* ● If you send something **by messenger**, a messenger delivers it for you. EG *...a note which had just arrived by messenger.*   N COUNT / ● PHRASE

Messrs /mɛsəz/ is the plural of 'Mr.' **Messrs** is used especially in the names of businesses. EG *Messrs Brant and Prout are dealers in hats.*

messy /mɛsiˈ/. **1 Messy** activities make people or places dirty or untidy. EG *I hate picnics; they're so messy.*   ADJ QUALIT

2 Someone who is **messy** leaves things in a dirty or untidy state. EG *Sometimes I'm neat, sometimes I'm messy.*   ADJ QUALIT

3 Something that is **messy** looks unpleasant because it is dirty, untidy, or sticky. EG *...messy bits of food... I disliked the messy farmyard.*   ADJ QUALIT

4 A **messy** situation is confused or complicated, and involves trouble for people. EG *Brown had been caught in a messy diplomatic dispute.*   ADJ QUALIT Informal

met /mɛt/ is the past tense and past participle of **meet.**

metabolism /mɪˈtæbəlɪzəˈm/, **metabolisms.** Your **metabolism** is the chemical process in your body that causes food to be used for growth and energy. EG *Some people's metabolism is more efficient than others.*   N UNCOUNT OR N COUNT Technical

metal /mɛtˈəl/, **metals. Metal** is a hard substance such as iron, steel, copper, or lead. EG *...a metal spoon... It was made of glass and metal.*   N MASS

metallic /mɪˈtælɪk/. **1** A **metallic** sound is like one piece of metal hitting another. EG *I heard the metallic click of a door handle.*   ADJ QUALIT

2 Metallic things or colours shine like metal. EG *Her hair was a metallic gold.*   ADJ CLASSIF

3 Metallic things consist of metal. EG *...metallic ores.*   ADJ CLASSIF Technical

metalwork /mɛtˈəlwɜːk/ is the activity of making objects out of metal. EG *She's good at woodwork and metalwork.*   N UNCOUNT

metamorphose /mɛtəmɔːfəʊz/, **metamorphoses, metamorphosing, metamorphosed.** When someone or something **metamorphoses** or is **metamorphosed,** they change into something completely different. EG *The headstrong girl metamorphoses into the loving wife and mother.*   V-ERG: OFT+*into* Formal

metamorphosis /mɛtəmɔːfəsɪs/, **metamorphoses** /mɛtəmɔːfəsiːz/. When a **metamorphosis** occurs, a person or thing changes into something completely different. EG *Science fiction may be undergoing a metamorphosis.*   N COUNT OR N UNCOUNT Formal

metaphor /mɛtəfəˈ/, **metaphors. 1** A **metaphor** is an imaginative way of describing something by saying that it is something else which has the qualities that you are trying to describe. For example, if you want to say that someone is very shy and timid, you might say that they are a mouse.   N COUNT OR N UNCOUNT

2 If you consider one thing to be a **metaphor** for another, you consider it to be a symbol of the other thing. EG *She sees the play as a metaphor for the prisons we create for ourselves.*   N COUNT OR N UNCOUNT Literary

metaphorical /mɛtəfɒrɪkəˈl/. You use the word **metaphorical** to indicate that you are not using words with their ordinary meaning, but are trying to describe something by using an image or symbol. EG *I had sprouted metaphorical wings.*   ADJ CLASSIF

◊ **metaphorically.** EG *I was literally as well as metaphorically wrapped in cotton wool... I was speaking metaphorically.*   ◊ ADV

mete /miːt/, **metes, meting, meted.** If you **mete out** a particular punishment, you officially order that someone shall be punished that way. EG *Magistrates meted out fines of as much as £1,000.*   PHRASAL VB: V+ADV, OFT+*to* Formal

meteor /miːtɪəˈ/, **meteors.** A **meteor** is a piece of rock or metal that burns very brightly when it enters the earth's atmosphere from space.   N COUNT

meteoric /miːtɪɒrɪk/. A **meteoric** rise to power or success happens very quickly. EG *He enjoyed a meteoric rise to power in Callaghan's government.*   ADJ CLASSIF

meteorite /miːtɪəraɪt/, **meteorites.** A **meteorite** is a large piece of rock or metal from space that has landed on the earth.   N COUNT

meteorological /miːtɪərəlɒdʒɪkəˈl/ means relating to the weather or to weather forecasting. EG *Meteorological conditions were reasonably good.*   ADJ CLASSIF: ATTRIB Technical

meter /miːtə/, **meters, metering, metered. 1** A **meter** is a device that measures and records something such as the amount of gas or electricity that you have used. EG *Someone comes to read the gas and electricity meters.*   N COUNT

2 If the gas, electricity, or water supplied to your house **is metered,** the amount you use is measured and recorded by a meter.   V+O

3 See also **metre, parking meter.**

method /mɛθəd/, **methods.** A **method** is a particular way of doing something. EG *...a change in the method of electing the party's leader... No one knows why they use this method.*   N COUNT: OFT+SUPP; ALSO N UNCOUNT

methodical /mɪˈθɒdɪkəˈl/. Someone who is **methodical** does things carefully and in a particular order. EG *With methodical thoroughness they demolished the prison.* ◊ **methodically.** EG *He worked quickly and methodically.*   ADJ QUALIT / ◊ ADV

meticulous /mɪˈtɪkjɔˈləs/. A **meticulous** person does things very carefully and with great attention to detail. EG *He had prepared himself with meticulous care.* ◊ **meticulously.** EG *...meticulously folded newspapers.*   ADJ QUALIT / ◊ ADV

metre /miːtə/, **metres;** spelled **meter** in American English. A **metre** is a unit of length equal to 100 centimetres. EG *The blue whale grows to over 30 metres long.*   N COUNT

metric /mɛtrɪk/ means relating to the system of measurement that uses metres, grammes, and litres. EG *...the new metric sizes for clothes.*   ADJ CLASSIF

metro /mɛtrəʊ/, **metros.** The **metro** is the underground railway system in some cities, for example in Paris.   N COUNT: USU *the*+N

metropolis /mɪˈtrɒpəlɪs/, **metropolises.** A **metropolis** is a very large city.   N COUNT

metropolitan /mɛtrəpɒlɪtəˈn/ means belonging to or typical of a large busy city. EG *...seven*   ADJ CLASSIF: ATTRIB

Can you eat microchips?

metropolitan districts in the Midlands... ...the metropolitan delights of cinemas and theatres.

mew /mju:/, **mews, mewing, mewed. 1** When a cat **mews**, it makes a soft high-pitched noise. EG *The cat was mewing for its supper.*

2 A **mews** is a quiet, old yard or street surrounded by houses. EG *...a rear exit into a quiet mews... ...a tiny mews flat.*

mg is a written abbreviation for 'milligram' or 'milligrams'. EG *It contained 65mg of Vitamin C.*

miaow /mi¹au/, **miaows, miaowing, miaowed.** When a cat goes **'miaow'**, it makes a short high-pitched sound. EG *That sounds like the miaow of a cat.* ▸ used as a verb. EG *There was a cat miaowing outside the front door.*

mice /mais/ is the plural of **mouse.**

mickey /mɪki¹/. If you **take the mickey** out of someone, you make fun of them. EG *You're always taking the mickey.*

micro /maikrəu/, **micros.** A **micro** is a small computer.

micro- is used to form nouns that refer to a very small example of a particular type of thing. For example, a microcomputer is a very small computer. EG *...the invention of the microcassette... ...diseases caused by micro-organisms.*

microbe /maikrəub/, **microbes.** A **microbe** is a very small living thing, which you can see only if you use a microscope. EG *...the microbes in the human gut.*

microchip /maikrə⁶tʃip/, **microchips.** A **microchip** is a small piece of silicon, for example inside a computer, on which electronic circuits are printed.

micro-computer, micro-computers. A **micro-computer** is a small computer.

microcosm /maikrə⁶kɒzə⁶m/, **microcosms.** A place or event that is a **microcosm** of a larger one has all the main features of the larger one and seems like a smaller version of it. EG *Bristol was a microcosm of urban England in the 1970s... Man was regarded as a microcosm of the universe.*

microfiche /maikrə⁶fi:ʃ/, **microfiches.** A **microfiche** is a small sheet of film on which information is stored in very small print. You read the information by putting the microfiche into a machine which magnifies it and projects it. EG *The Periodicals Catalogue is now on microfiche.*

microphone

microphone /maikrə⁶fəun/, **microphones.** A **microphone** is a device that is used to make sounds louder or to record them on a tape recorder.

microprocessor /maikrə⁶prəusɛsə/, **microprocessors.** A **microprocessor** is a microchip which can be programmed to do a large number of tasks or calculations.

---

microscope

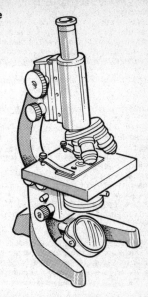

microscope /maikrə⁶skəup/, **microscopes.** A **microscope** is an instrument which magnifies very small objects so that you can study them. EG *The slides are carefully prepared and examined under the microscope.*

microscopic /maikrə⁶skɒpik/. **1** Something that is **microscopic** is very small. EG *...microscopic forms of life... No-one could decipher my microscopic script.*

2 A **microscopic** examination of something is very detailed. EG *...a microscopic study of medieval customs.*

microwave /maikrə⁶weiv/, **microwaves.** A **microwave** or a **microwave oven** is a cooker which cooks food very quickly by short-wave radiation rather than by heat.

mid-. 1 mid- is used to form nouns or expressions that refer to the middle part of a period of time. For example the mid-eighteenth century was the middle part of the eighteenth century. EG *It was mid-winter... ...studies published in the mid-1970s... ...the mid-morning sun.*

2 mid- is also used to form nouns or adjectives that refer to the middle part of a place. For example, the mid-Atlantic is the middle of the Atlantic. EG *...the Dyfi Valley in mid-Wales... ...mid-ocean ridges.*

mid-air. If something happens in **mid-air**, it happens in the air rather than on the ground. EG *The bird turned in mid-air and darted away... ...a mid-air collision.*

midday /mɪddei/ is twelve o'clock in the middle of the day. EG *Just before midday the telephone rang... ...a midday meal.*

middle /mɪdə⁶l/, **middles. 1** The **middle** of something is the part of it that is furthest from its edges, ends, or outside surface. EG *In the middle of the lawn was a great cedar tree... He sat down in the middle of the front row... ...the white lines painted along the middle of the highway.*

2 The **middle** thing or person in a row or series is the one that has an equal number of things or people on each side, or before it and after it. EG *...the middle button of her black leather coat... She was the middle child of the three.*

3 Your **middle** is the front part of your body at

Right margin grammar codes:
V
N COUNT
N COUNT
N COUNT
PHRASE Informal
N COUNT
PREFIX
N COUNT
N COUNT
N COUNT
N COUNT:
OFT+of
N COUNT OR
N UNCOUNT
N COUNT
N COUNT
N COUNT
ADJ CLASSIF
ADJ CLASSIF
N COUNT
PREFIX
PREFIX
N UNCOUNT
N UNCOUNT
N COUNT:
USU SING+SUPP
ADJ CLASSIF:
ATTRIB
N COUNT:
USU+POSS

your waist. EG *He had a large green towel wrapped round his middle.*

4 The **middle** of an event or period of time is the part that comes after the first part and before the last part. EG *We landed at Canton in the middle of a torrential storm... ...the middle of December.*   N SING : the+N+of

▸ used as an adjective. EG *...the middle fortnight of July... He was in his middle thirties.*   ▸ ADJ CLASSIF : ATTRIB

5 If you are **in the middle of** doing something, you are busy doing it. EG *I'm in the middle of washing up.*   PHRASE

6 The **middle** course or way is a moderate course of action that lies between two opposite and extreme courses. EG *Between Fascism or revolution there is a middle course.*   ADJ CLASSIF : ATTRIB

middle age is the period in your life when you are between about 40 and 60 years old. EG *...a grave, courteous man in late middle age.*   N UNCOUNT

middle-aged. Someone who is **middle-aged** is between the ages of about 40 and 60. EG *...a middle-aged businessman.*   ADJ CLASSIF

Middle Ages. In European history, the **Middle Ages** were the period between about 1100 AD and about 1500 AD.   N PLURAL : the+N

middle class, middle classes. The **middle class** or the **middle classes** are the people in a society who are not working class or upper class, for example managers, doctors, and lawyers. EG *...the new Indian middle classes... ...middle class families. Watson's upbringing was comfortably middle-class.*   N COUNT : OFT PLURAL

middle distance. The **middle distance** is the area or space between the foreground and the distance in a view or in a painting. EG *He stood at the gate, gazing into the middle distance.*   N SING : the+N

Middle East. The **Middle East** is a part of Asia. It includes Iran and all the countries in Asia that are to the west and south-west of Iran.   N PROPER : the+N

Middle Eastern means coming from or relating to the Middle East. EG *...Middle Eastern oil.*   ADJ CLASSIF : ATTRIB

middleman /mɪdəˀlmæn/, **middlemen.** A **middleman** is someone who buys things from the people who produce them and sells them to other people at a profit; often used showing disapproval.   N COUNT

middle name, middle names. A person's **middle name** is a name that they have which comes between their first name and their surname.   N COUNT

middle-of-the-road politicians or opinions are moderate, and usually between two political extremes. EG *...middle-of-the-road Labour MPs.*   ADJ QUALIT

middle school, middle schools. A **middle school** is a state school in Britain that children go to between the ages of 8 or 9 and 12 or 13.   N COUNT

middling /mɪdlɪŋ/ means of average quality. EG *...a woman of middling intellectual attainments.*   ADJ CLASSIF : ATTRIB

midge /mɪdʒ/, **midges. Midges** are very small flying insects which can bite people.   N COUNT

midget /mɪdʒɪt/, **midgets.** A **midget** is a very small person.   N COUNT

midnight /mɪdnaɪt/. **1 Midnight** is twelve o'clock in the middle of the night. EG *It was nearly midnight.*   N UNCOUNT

2 Midnight events happen at midnight or in the middle of the night. EG *We were always having midnight parties on beaches.*   N MOD

midriff /mɪdrɪf/, **midriffs.** Your **midriff** is the middle of your body, between your waist and your chest. EG *He was up to his midriff in hot water.*   N COUNT

midst /mɪdst/. **1** If you are **in the midst of** a group of people or things, you are in the middle of them. EG *I found him in the midst of a group of his friends... ...sitting in the midst of a pile of presents.*   PREP

2 If one event happens **in the midst of** another event, it happens while that event is taking place. If you are **in the midst of** doing something, you are doing it at the moment. EG *In the midst of this humiliating scandal, news arrived of Mr Hodge's resignation... Brody was in the midst of swallowing a bite of egg salad sandwich.*   PREP

3 You say that someone is **in** your **midst** in order to draw attention to the fact that they are in your group. EG *We have in our midst two Nobel prize-winners.*   PHRASE Formal

midsummer /mɪdsʌmə/ is the period in the middle of the summer. EG *...a hot midsummer day in July.*   N UNCOUNT

midway /mɪdweɪ/ means in the middle of a place, distance, or period of time. EG *St Germain is midway between Cherbourg and Granville... She arrived midway through the afternoon.*   ADV : USU+PREP

midweek /mɪdwiːk/. If you do something **midweek,** you do it in the middle of the week. EG *The Councils meet midweek... ...a midweek film.*   ADV OR ADJ CLASSIF : ATTRIB

midwife /mɪdwaɪf/, **midwives.** A **midwife** is a nurse who advises pregnant women and helps them to give birth.   N COUNT

might /maɪt/. **Might** is sometimes considered to be the past form of **may,** but in this dictionary the two words are dealt with separately.

1 If you say that something **might** happen, you mean that it is possible that it will happen. EG *I might even lose my job... I might go to a concert tonight... I thought I might find you here.*   MODAL

2 If you say that something **might** be true, you mean that there is a possibility that it is true, but you are not certain. If you say that something **might** have happened, you mean that it is possible that it happened. EG *Don't eat it. It might be a toadstool... He might well have said that. I just don't remember.*   MODAL

3 If you say that something **might** have happened, you mean that it was possible for it to have happened although it did not in fact happen. EG *A lot of men died who might have been saved.*   MODAL

4 If you ask if you **might** do something, you are asking very politely if someone will allow you to do it. EG *Might I suggest that you offer your manuscript to another publisher?... She asked the man's wife if she might borrow a pen.*   MODAL Formal

5 If you say to someone that they **might** do something, **5.1** you are suggesting that they do it. EG *The other thing you might find out is who owns the land.* **5.2** you are telling them in an angry way that they ought to do it. If you tell someone that they **might** have done something, you are telling them in an angry way that they ought to have done it. EG *You might do the washing up for a change!... You might have told me.*   MODAL

6 You can use **might** when saying that, although something is true, something else which contradicts it or contrasts with it is also true. EG *They might preach liberty, equality, and fraternity, but their record on human rights is pretty awful.*   MODAL

7 You use **might** in expressions such as 'I might have known' and 'I might have guessed' to indicate that you are not surprised at a disappointing event or fact. EG *I might have known he wouldn't come.*   MODAL

8 Might is the power or strength that someone has. EG *I tied the rope around the tree and heaved with all my might.*   N UNCOUNT +SUPP Literary

mightily /maɪtɪliˀ/ means to a great extent or degree. EG *Things have changed mightily since then... He's going to complain mightily.*   ADV Outdated

mightn't /maɪtəˀnt/ is a spoken form of 'might not'. EG *It mightn't be true at all.*

might've /maɪtəv/ is an informal form of 'might have', especially when 'have' is an auxiliary verb. EG *Someone might've written you a cheque.*

mighty /maɪtiˀ/, **mightier, mightiest. 1** Something that is **mighty** is **1.1** very powerful or strong. EG *...this mighty nation... We're dealing with forces that are mightier than ourselves.* **1.2** very large and impressive. EG *...a mighty ship... two of Asia's mightiest rivers, the Ganges and the Brahmaputra.*   ADJ QUALIT Literary

---

Is a middle-of-the-road politician likely to be militant?

2 Mighty also means the same as very. EG *It's* SUBMOD *going to be mighty embarrassing... It was mighty* American *generous of you.*

migraine /ˈmiːgreɪn, maɪ-/, **migraines. Migraine** N UNCOUNT is an extremely painful headache that makes you OR N COUNT feel very ill. EG *Do you suffer from migraine?... The experience had brought on one of her migraines.*

migrant /ˈmaɪgrənt/, **migrants. A migrant** is a N COUNT person who moves from one place to another, especially in order to find work. EG *...migrants looking for a place to live... ...migrant workers.*

migrate /maɪˈgreɪt/, **migrates, migrating, mi-** grated. **1** If people **migrate**, they move from one V : USU+A place to another, especially in order to find work. EG *Millions have migrated to the cities.*
◊ **migration** /maɪˈgreɪʃə⁰n/, **migrations.** EG *Migra-* ◊ N UNCOUNT *tion for work is accelerating in the Third World.* OR N COUNT
2 When animals **migrate**, they go and live in a V different area for part of the year, usually in order to breed or to find new feeding grounds. EG *Every spring they migrate towards the coast.*
◊ **migration.** EG *Swallows begin their migration* ◊ N UNCOUNT *south in early autumn.* OR N COUNT

mike /maɪk/, **mikes. A mike** is a microphone. EG N COUNT *Is the mike turned on?* Informal

mild /maɪld/, **milder, mildest. 1** Something that ADJ QUALIT is **mild** is not strong and does not have any powerful or harmful effects. EG *...a mild detergent... ...mild bleach... A slight fever often accompanies a mild infection.* ◊ **mildly.** EG *Judy mildly pro-* ◊ ADV *tested... The skin may become mildly infected.*
2 If someone is **mild**, they are gentle and kind. EG ADJ QUALIT *...my wife's mild nature... His eyes were no longer mild but glittered with fury.* ◊ **mildly.** EG *'No need* ◊ ADV *to shout,' he said mildly.* ◊ **mildness.** EG *The* ◊ N UNCOUNT *Colonel spoke with great mildness.*
3 Mild weather is warmer than usual, especially in ADJ QUALIT the winter or autumn. EG *The weather was comparatively mild through December.*
4 Mild qualities, attitudes, or emotions are not ADJ QUALIT very great or extreme. EG *It was of mild academic interest only... We looked at each other in mild astonishment.* ◊ **mildly.** EG *It was mildly amusing.* ◊ SUBMOD

mildew /ˈmɪldjuː/ is a soft white fungus that grows N UNCOUNT on things when they are warm and damp. EG *The hall smelt of mildew.*

mildly /ˈmaɪldliː/. **1** See **mild**.
2 You say **to put it mildly** when you are describ- PHRASE ing something less strongly or less critically than it deserves. EG *He and Connally are, to put it mildly, furious.*

mile /maɪl/, **miles. A mile** is a unit of distance N COUNT that is 1760 yards. A mile is equal to 1.6 kilometres. EG *The island is 16 miles wide... It'll be a thirty mile drive from here.*
2 You can refer to a long distance as **miles**. EG N PLURAL *'Frogstone Road? Where's that?' - 'Miles away.'... I had walked for miles and miles.*
3 If you say that you **are miles away**, you mean PHRASE that you are not concentrating on what is happen- Informal ing around you, but are thinking about something else.

mileage /ˈmaɪlɪdʒ/, **mileages. 1** Your **mileage** is N COUNT OR the distance that you have travelled, measured in N UNCOUNT miles. EG *The approximate mileage for the complete journey is 200 miles.*
2 The amount of **mileage** that you get out of a N UNCOUNT particular course of action is how useful it is to you. +SUPP EG *There is more mileage in this policy.*

milestone /ˈmaɪlstəʊn/, **milestones. 1** If you re- N COUNT+SUPP fer to an event as a **milestone**, you mean that is is an important event in the history or development of something. EG *The conference in 1913 was a milestone in the history of the party.*
2 A **milestone** is also a stone by the side of a road showing the distances to particular places.

milieu /ˈmiːljɜː/, **milieux** or **milieus. The milieu** N COUNT : in which you live or work is the group of people USU+SUPP Formal

that you live among or work among. EG *I was born in a social milieu where education was a luxury.*

militant /ˈmɪlɪtənt/, **militants.** Someone who is ADJ QUALIT **militant** is very active in trying to bring about extreme political or social change. EG *...militant trade unionists.* ▸ used as a noun. EG *...a number of* ▸ N COUNT *well-known militants.* ◊ **militantly.** EG *They be-* ◊ ADV *came militantly nationalistic.* ◊ **militancy** ◊ N UNCOUNT /ˈmɪlɪtənsɪ/. EG *The League is well known for its militancy.*

military /ˈmɪlɪtə⁰rɪ/. **1 Military** means relating to ADJ CLASSIF : the armed forces of a country. EG *...military lead-* ATTRIB *ers... ...direct military action.* ◊ **militarily.** EG ◊ ADV *Britain was no longer a militarily powerful nation.*
2 The **military** are the armed forces of a country, N COLL : the+N especially the officers of high rank. EG *The politicians and the military will do nothing.*

militate /ˈmɪlɪteɪt/, **militates, militating, mili-** V+against tated. If something **militates** against something Formal else, it makes it less likely to happen or succeed. EG *Family tensions can militate against learning for many youngsters.*

militia /mɪˈlɪʃə/, **militias. A militia** is an organi- N COUNT OR zation that operates like an army but whose mem- N UNCOUNT bers are not professional soldiers. EG *...a building guarded by the local police and militia.*

milk /mɪlk/, **milks, milking, milked. 1 Milk** is N UNCOUNT the white liquid produced by cows, goats, and some other animals. People drink milk, and use it to make butter, cheese, and yoghurt. EG *He only drinks milk in tea or coffee... ...a glass of milk.*
● See also **skimmed milk.**
2 When someone **milks** a cow or goat, they get V+O OR V milk from it by pulling its udders. ◊ **milking.** EG *I* ◊ N UNCOUNT *had to install milking equipment.*
3 Milk is also **3.1** the white liquid from a woman's N UNCOUNT breasts which babies drink. EG *A mother's milk takes care of the baby for many months.* **3.2** a white liquid produced inside coconuts.
4 If you **milk** a situation or place, you get as much V+O benefit or profit as you can from it, without caring about the effects on other people. EG *The island was milked by the invaders for five centuries.*

milkman /ˈmɪlkmə⁰n/, **milkmen. A milkman** is a N COUNT person who delivers milk to people's homes.

milk-shake, milk-shakes. A milk-shake is a N MASS cold drink made by mixing milk with ice cream and a flavouring. EG *We had a strawberry milkshake.*

milky /ˈmɪlkiː/. **1** Something that is **milky** is a pale ADJ COLOUR white colour. EG *...clouds of milky smoke.*
2 A drink or food that is **milky** contains a lot of ADJ QUALIT milk. EG *We always had milky coffee at lunchtime.*

mill /mɪl/, **mills, milling, milled. 1 A mill** is **1.1** a N COUNT building in which grain is crushed to make flour. EG *He sends his crop to a large mill instead of grinding it himself.* ● See also **windmill. 1.2** a factory used N COUNT+SUPP for making materials such as steel, wool, or cotton. EG *He had worked in a steel mill.*
2 A **mill** is also a small device used for grinding N COUNT+SUPP coffee beans or spices into powder. EG *...a pepper mill.*
3 If you **mill** something such as wheat, you crush V+O and grind it in a mill. EG *Flour is made by milling grain until a fine powder is formed.*
4 grist to the mill: see **grist.** ● See also **milling, run-of-the-mill.**

mill about or **mill around.** When a crowd of PHRASAL VB : people **mill about** or **mill around**, they move V+ADV/PREP around in a disorganized way. EG *Students and staff were milling about.*

millennium /mɪˈlenɪəm/, **millennia** or **millen-** N COUNT niums. A **millennium** is a period of a thousand Formal years. EG *...a landscape that had remained unchanged for millennia.*

milligram /ˈmɪlɪgræm/, **milligrams;** also spelled N COUNT **milligramme. A milligram** is a metric unit of OR N PART weight that is equal to one thousandth of a gramme. EG *...0.3 milligrams of mercury.*

millilitre /ˈmɪlili:tə/, **millilitres;** spelled **millili-** N COUNT
ter in American English. A **millilitre** is a metric OR N PART
unit of volume for liquids and gases that is equal to
one thousandth of a litre. EG ...45 millilitres of
alcohol.

millimetre /ˈmɪlimi:tə/, **millimetres;** spelled N COUNT
millimeter in American English. A **millimetre** is OR N PART
a metric unit of length that is equal to one tenth of
a centimetre. EG ...a silicon chip less than a millimetre thick.

milling /ˈmɪlɪŋ/. The people in a **milling** crowd ADJ CLASSIF:
move around in a disorganized way. EG She escaped ATTRIB
unnoticed into the milling crowds.

million /ˈmɪljən/, **millions.** 1 A **million** or one NUMBER
million is the number 1,000,000. See the entry
headed NUMBER. EG ...30 million dollars... ...£980
millions... 'How much?' - 'Half a million.'

2 A **million** or **millions** is often used to mean an N PART:
extremely large number. EG ...millions of mosqui- USU PLURAL
toes... Her books still give pleasure to millions.

millionaire /ˌmɪljəˈneə/, **millionaires.** A **million-** N COUNT
aire is a very rich person, especially one who has
property worth millions of pounds or dollars.

millionth /ˈmɪljənθ/, **millionths.** 1 The **millionth** ORDINAL
item in a series is the one you count as number one
million. See the entry headed NUMBER. EG Six years
later the one-millionth Ford rolled off an assembly
line.

2 A **millionth** is one of a million equal parts of N COUNT:
something. EG ...a millionth of a second... ...one ten USU +of
millionth of an inch.

millstone /ˈmɪlstəʊn/, **millstones.** If you describe PHRASE
something as **a millstone round** your **neck,** you
mean that it is a very unpleasant problem or
responsibility that you cannot escape from. EG The
debt becomes an even bigger millstone round the
poor man's neck.

mime /maɪm/, **mimes, miming, mimed.** 1 N UNCOUNT
Mime is the use of movements and gestures to OR N COUNT
express something or tell a story without using
speech. EG ...the re-telling of legends in mime and
song... In a brilliant mime, he showed how he
managed to support the tray.

2 If you **mime** something, you describe or express V+O; ALSO V
it using mime rather than speech. EG 'Dinner,' I OFT+-ING
said, and mimed cutting meat... They all vigorously OR REPORT
mimed that I should speak quietly.

mimic /ˈmɪmɪk/, **mimics, mimicking, mim-**
icked. 1 If you **mimic** someone's actions or voice, V+O
you imitate them in an amusing or entertaining
way. EG I can mimic Cockney speech reasonably
well... He mimicked the President cruelly.

2 A **mimic** is a person who is able to mimic people. N COUNT
EG One of my brothers is a wonderful mimic.

mimicry /ˈmɪmɪkriʲ/ is the action of mimicking N UNCOUNT
someone or something. EG ...his fine talent for
mimicry... ...adolescent mimicry of adult behaviour.

min. is 1 a written abbreviation for 'minimum'. 2 a
written abbreviation for 'minute' or 'minutes'.

minaret /ˌmɪnəˈret/, **minarets.** A **minaret** is a N COUNT
tall, thin tower which is part of a mosque.

mince /mɪns/, **minces, mincing, minced.** 1 N UNCOUNT
Mince is meat which has been cut into very small British
pieces.

2 If you **mince** meat, you cut it into very small V+O
pieces. EG Mince the lean meat finely. ◊ **minced.** ◊ ADJ CLASSIF:
EG ...minced beef. ATTRIB

3 If you **do not mince** your **words,** you tell PHRASE
someone something unpleasant in a very forceful
and direct way. EG They certainly don't mince their
words, do they?

4 If you **mince** your way somewhere, you walk V OR V+O
with quick small steps in a very affected or effeminate way. EG Off he goes, mincing his way across
the department store.

mincemeat /ˈmɪnsmiːt/. 1 **Mincemeat** is a sticky N UNCOUNT
mixture of small pieces of dried fruit. It is usually
cooked in pastry to make mince pies.

2 **Mincemeat** is also meat such as lamb or beef N UNCOUNT
which has been minced. American

mincer /ˈmɪnsə/, **mincers.** A **mincer** is a ma- N COUNT
chine which cuts meat into very small pieces.

mind /maɪnd/, **minds, minding, minded.** 1 Your N COUNT:
mind is your ability to think, including all the OFT+SUPP
thoughts that you have. EG All this confusion in the
minds of young people was bound to lead to
violence... Somewhere at the back of my mind, I
had the feeling I'd seen him before... Anne's got a
scientific mind.

2 **Mind** is used in these phrases about thoughts and PHRASES
memory. 2.1 If your **mind is on** something, you
are thinking about it. EG Her mind was not on the
announcements she was making. 2.2 If something
takes your **mind off** a problem, it helps you to
forget about it for a while. 2.3 If something **comes**
to mind or **crosses** or **enters** your **mind,** you
think of it suddenly and without making any effort.
EG I just pick up whatever groceries come to mind...
Scotland springs to mind as an example... The
thought never crossed my mind. 2.4 If you tell
someone to **bear** something **in mind** or to **keep** it
in mind, you are telling them that they should
remember it because it is important or relevant. EG
Bear in mind that these are sixty-five-year-old men.

3 **Mind** is used in these phrases about worrying. PHRASES
3.1 If something is **on** your **mind,** you are worried
or concerned about it and think about it a lot. EG
Let's hear what's on your mind. 3.2 If something
happens which causes you to stop worrying about
something, you can say it is **a load off your mind,**
or **a weight off your mind.**

4 **Mind** is used in these phrases about people's PHRASES
intentions. 4.1 If you **have** something **in mind,** you
intend or want to have it or to do it. EG It will be up
to her to tell you what she has in mind. 4.2 If you
say you **have a mind to** do something, you mean
that you would quite like to do it, although you will
probably not do it. EG If they had a mind to, they
could easily get it published... I've a good mind to
punish you for behaving so badly... I had half a
mind to walk out there and then. 4.3 If you **put**
your **mind to** something, you devote a lot of your
energy, effort, and attention to it. EG You could get
a job in London, if you put your mind to it.

5 **Mind** is used in these phrases about opinions and PHRASES
decisions. 5.1 You use **to my mind** to indicate that
you are giving your own opinion. EG The worst part
of air travel to my mind is the hanging around in
airport lounges. 5.2 If you have **an open mind,** you
do not form an opinion about something or make a
decision about it until you know all the facts. EG The
committee tried to keep an open mind. 5.3 If you
have **a closed mind,** you are unwilling to consider
or accept new ideas. 5.4 When you **make** your
mind up, you decide which of a number of possible
things you will have or will do. EG We have to make
up our minds quickly, or they'll go without us... My
mind's made up. 5.5 If you **change** your **mind,** you
change a decision you have made or an opinion
that you had. EG All of a sudden I changed my mind
and decided not to go anywhere. 5.6 If you are **in**
two minds about something, you are uncertain
whether or not to do it. EG I was very much in two
minds whether to apply for the Cambridge job.

6 **Mind** is also used in these phrases. 6.1 If you say PHRASES
that nobody **in** their **right mind** would do something, you mean that you would be very surprised if
anyone did it because you think it is foolish or
unreasonable. EG What woman in her right mind
would marry a man like that? 6.2 If you see
something in your **mind's eye,** you imagine it and
have a clear picture of it in your mind. EG In her
mind's eye, she had pictured herself in the new

If you wouldn't mind some mineral water, would
you be very thirsty?

house. **6.3** Your **state of mind** is your mental state at a particular time. EG *She was in a fairly disturbed state of mind.*

7 If you say that you do not **mind** something, you mean that you are not annoyed or bothered by it. EG *I don't mind personal questions at all... You probably do mind, but you're too polite to say so... I don't mind walking... I hope you don't mind, I came early... Do you mind if I stay here?* V+O; ALSO V: OFT+-ING OR REPORT: USU WITH BROAD NEG

8 If you are offered a choice and you say '**I don't mind**', you mean that you will be happy with any of the things offered. EG *'Tea or coffee?' – 'I don't mind.'* CONVENTION

9 If you say that you **wouldn't mind** something, you mean that you would quite like it. EG *I wouldn't mind a Renault myself.* PHRASE

10 You say **never mind** **10.1** to try and make someone feel better when they have failed to do something or when something unpleasant has happened to them. **10.2** to indicate that something is not important, especially when someone is apologizing to you. EG *Some of their towels are soaking wet, but never mind.* **10.3** to tell someone that they need not do something, because it is not important or because you will do it yourself. EG *What's it like? Oh, never mind, I'll go and see for myself... Never mind about those, Sam!* PHRASE Spoken

11 If you tell someone to **mind** something, you are warning them to be careful so that they do not get hurt or do not damage something. EG *Mind the ice on the step as you go... Mind my specs!* ● You say '**mind out**' as an urgent warning to someone that they are about to get hurt or to damage something. V+O: ONLY IMPER ● EXCLAM Informal British

12 You use **mind** when you are reminding someone of something they must do. EG *Mind you watch that programme tonight.* V+REPORT ONLY IMPER

13 If you **mind** a child or something such as a shop or luggage, you look after it for someone else for a while. EG *She can get a neighbour to come in and mind the child... My mother is minding the office.* V+O

14 You use **mind you** to emphasize the piece of information that you are adding or the point that you are making, especially when it contrasts with what you have just said. EG *Charles is fit and well. Not happy, mind you, just fit and well.* ADV SEN

15 to **mind** your **own business**: see **business**.

minded /mˈaɪndɪd/. If someone is **minded** to do something, they want or intend to do it. EG *...a country which seems minded to offer total resistance... He can stop here if he is so minded.* ADJ PRED: USU+to-INF Formal

minder /mˈaɪndə/, **minders**. A **minder** is **1** a person whose job is to look after someone, for example a child or an old person. EG *...a baby-minder.* **2** a person whose job is to protect someone such as a businessman. N COUNT+SUPP N COUNT Informal

mindful /mˈaɪndfʊl/. If you are **mindful** of something, you think about it and consider it when taking action. EG *Be mindful of the needs of others.* ADJ PRED+of OR REPORT

mindless /mˈaɪndlɪˀs/. **1 Mindless** actions are regarded as stupid and destructive. EG *...mindless violence... the mindless pollution of our cities.* ADJ CLASSIF: ATTRIB

2 A **mindless** job or activity is one that is so simple or is repeated so often that you do not need to think about it. EG *...mindless routine tasks.* ADJ CLASSIF

mine /mˈaɪn/, **mines, mining, mined.** **1** A speaker or writer uses **mine** to indicate that something belongs or relates to himself or herself. EG *Margaret was a very old friend of mine... I took her hands in mine... He gave it to me, it's mine.* PRON POSS

2 A **mine** is a place where people dig deep holes and tunnels under the ground in order to get out coal, diamonds, or gold. EG *...a coal mine.* N COUNT

3 If you **mine** coal, diamonds, or gold, you obtain that substance from the ground by digging deep holes and tunnels. EG *They mine their own coal and ore... ...mining for gold.* V+O; ALSO V: OFT+for

4 A **mine** is also a bomb which is hidden in the ground or in water and which explodes when people or things touch it. N COUNT

5 If you **mine** an area of land or water, you place mines there. EG *Eight miles of ground had been heavily mined.* V+O

6 If you say that someone is a **mine of information**, you mean that they know a great deal. PHRASE

7 See also **mining**.

minefield /mˈaɪnfiːld/, **minefields.** **1** A **minefield** is an area of land or water where explosive mines have been hidden. N COUNT

2 If you describe a situation as a **minefield**, you mean that it is full of hidden dangers or problems. EG *This could be a political minefield.* N COUNT: USU+SUPP

miner /mˈaɪnə/, **miners**. A **miner** is a person who works underground in mines in order to obtain coal, diamonds, or gold. EG *My grandfather was a coal miner.* N COUNT

mineral /mˈɪnəˀrəl/, **minerals**. A **mineral** is a substance such as tin, salt, uranium, or coal that is formed naturally in rocks and in the earth. EG *...a continent exceptionally wealthy in minerals... ...rich mineral deposits.* N COUNT

mineral water is water that comes out of the ground naturally and is often considered healthy to drink. N UNCOUNT

mingle /mˈɪŋgəˀl/, **mingles, mingling, mingled.** **1** If things such as sounds, feelings, or smells **mingle** or **are mingled**, they become mixed together. EG *His cries mingled with theirs... Sand and dust mingled with the blood.* ◊ **mingled.** EG *He loved the mingled smell of jasmine and food in the air... John watched her with mingled dismay and pleasure.* V OR V+with: RECIP ◊ ADJ CLASSIF

2 If you **mingle**, you move around within a group of people and chat to people you do not know. EG *Get out and mingle a bit... She invited me to drop in and mingle with the guests.* V: OFT+with

mini- is used to form nouns that refer to something which is a smaller or less important version of something else. For example, a mini-computer is a computer which is much smaller than a normal computer. EG *He was taken to school by minibus... ...the Chancellor's mini-budget.* PREFIX

miniature /mˈɪnɪtʃəˀ/, **miniatures.** **1** A **miniature** thing is a small copy of something that is usually much larger. EG *...tiny squares and miniature archways... They look like miniature sharks.* ADJ CLASSIF: ATTRIB

2 If you describe one thing as another thing **in miniature**, you mean that it is smaller than the other thing, but otherwise exactly the same. EG *It was an Austrian chalet in miniature.* PHRASE

3 A **miniature** is a very small, detailed painting, often of a person. EG *I collect early English miniatures.* N COUNT

miniaturize /mˈɪnɪtʃəraɪz/, **miniaturizes, miniaturizing, miniaturized;** also spelled **miniaturise.** If you **miniaturize** a machine, you produce a very small version of it. EG *We miniaturize spacecraft components.* ◊ **miniaturized.** EG *...a miniaturized video recorder... ...miniaturized telescoping systems.* ◊ **miniaturization** /mˈɪnɪtʃəraɪzeɪʃəˀn/. EG *...the miniaturization of electronic components.* V+O ◊ ADJ CLASSIF ATTRIB ◊ N UNCOUNT

minibus /mˈɪnɪˈbʌs/, **minibuses.** A **minibus** is a van with seats in the back, which is used as a small bus. EG *We went to school by minibus.* N COUNT, OR by+N

minimal /mˈɪnɪməˀl/. Something that is **minimal** is very small in quantity or degree. EG *My knowledge of German was minimal.* ◊ **minimally.** EG *At that stage the welfare state was only minimally developed.* ADJ CLASSIF ◊ ADV Formal

minimize /mˈɪnɪmaɪz/, **minimizes, minimizing, minimized;** also spelled **minimise.** If you **minimize** something, **1** you reduce it to the smallest amount or degree possible, or prevent it increasing beyond that amount or degree. EG *Our aim must be to minimize the risks... Crop rotations will help to minimise disease.* **2** you make it seem smaller or less important than it really is. EG *He was careful to minimise his role in these proceedings.* V+O

minimum /mɪnɪməᵍm/. **1** The **minimum** amount ADJ CLASSIF: of something is the smallest that is possible, al- ATTRIB lowed, or required. EG *...the minimum level of taxation... You need a minimum deposit of $20,000... He only aims to study for the minimum time.*

2 The **minimum** is the smallest amount of some- N SING: thing that is possible, allowed, or required. EG *Two* USU+SUPP *hundred pounds is the bare minimum... Practise each day for a minimum of twenty minutes.*

mining /maɪnɪŋ/ is the industry and activities N UNCOUNT connected with getting coal, diamonds, or other minerals from the ground. EG *...coal mining... ...mining areas... ...a mining engineer.*

minister /mɪnɪstə/, **ministers, ministering, ministered. 1** A **minister** is a person who is in N COUNT charge of a particular government department. EG *...the minister for Scottish affairs.* ● See also **Prime Minister.**

2 A **minister** in a church, especially a Protestant N COUNT church, is a member of the clergy.

minister to. If you **minister to** people or to PHRASAL VB: their needs, you make sure that they have every- V+PREP, thing they need or want. EG *Anne had spent her life* HAS PASS *ministering to the needs of her husband.* Formal

ministerial /mɪnɪstɪərɪəl/ means relating to a ADJ CLASSIF: government minister or government ministry. EG ATTRIB *We cannot afford a ministerial crisis.*

ministrations /mɪnɪstreɪʃə°nz/. A person's **mini-** N PLURAL: **strations** are the things that they do to help or USU+POSS care for someone in a particular situation. EG *I* Formal *thanked him for his spiritual ministrations.*

ministry /mɪnɪstriꞌ/, **ministries. 1** A **ministry** is N COUNT: a government department that deals with a par- USU+SUPP ticular area of administration within a country. EG *...the Ministry of Energy... The ministry will have no alternative but to cut its expenditure.*

2 The **ministry** of a member of the clergy or of a N COUNT religious person is the work that they do according to their religious beliefs. EG *The central message of Christ's ministry was the concept of grace.*

3 The **ministry** consists of members of the clergy, N SING: the+N usually Protestant ones. EG *Michael had intended to join the ministry.*

mink /mɪŋk/, **minks. 1** Mink is a very expensive N UNCOUNT fur that is used to make coats or hats.

2 A **mink** is a small furry animal. N COUNT

minor /maɪnə/, **minors. 1** You use **minor** to ADJ QUALIT: describe something that is not as important, seri- USU ATTRIB ous, or significant as other things of the same sort. EG *The police were called to quell a minor disturbance... ...minor injuries... ...a rather minor artist.*

2 A **minor** key is one of the two types of key in ADJ CLASSIF which most European music is written. It is based on a scale of notes in which the third note is one and a half tones higher than the first note. EG *...Chopin's Scherzo in B flat minor.*

3 A **minor** is a person who is still legally a child. In N COUNT Britain, people are minors until they reach the age of eighteen.

minority /maɪˀnɒrɪˀtiꞌ/, **minorities. 1** The **minor-** N SING: USU+*of* **ity** of people or things in a group is a number of them that form less than half of the whole group. EG *Only a small minority of children get a chance to benefit from this system... They are a minority group.* ● If a group is **in a minority** or **in the** ● PHRASE **minority,** they form less than half of a larger group. EG *Artistic people are in a tiny minority in this country.*

2 A **minority** is a group of people of a particular N COUNT race or religion who live in a place where most of the people around them are of a different race or religion. EG *Our aim is to improve relations between police and the ethnic minorities.*

mint /mɪnt/, **mints, minting, minted. 1** Mint is a N UNCOUNT type of herb that is used in cooking. EG *...a sprig of mint... ...mint tea.*

2 A **mint** is a sweet with a peppermint flavour. EG N COUNT *...a packet of mints.*

3 The place where the official coins of a country N SING: the+N

are made is called the **mint.** EG *The Mint has decided to issue the new coins next year.*

4 When coins or medals **are minted,** they are V+O: USU PASS made in a mint. EG *One of the coins, dated 1693, was minted in Portuguese Africa.*

5 If something is in **mint condition,** it is in very PHRASE good condition, as if it was new.

minus /maɪnəs/, **minusses** or **minuses. 1** You use **minus** to show that one number is being subtracted from another. For example, 'five minus three' means the same as 'three subtracted from five'. You represent this in figures as '5 – 3'. EG *Twenty-eight minus two is twenty-six.*

2 A **minus** is a minus sign. EG *There should be a* N COUNT *minus there.*

3 Minus is used when you talk about tempera- ADJ CLASSIF: tures. For example, **minus** four means four de- ATTRIB grees less than zero. EG *Temperatures there are colder than minus 20°C.*

4 Minus is also used in grading work in schools ADJ AFTER N and colleges. An A minus is a better grade than a B plus, but it is not as good as an A.

minuscule /mɪnəskjuːl/. Something that is **mi-** ADJ QUALIT **nuscule** is very small indeed. EG *He had to live in this minuscule room.*

minus sign, minus signs. A minus sign is the N COUNT sign (–) which is put between two numbers in order to show that the second number is being subtracted from the first one.

minute, minutes; pronounced /mɪnɪt/ when it is a noun and /maɪnjuːt/ when it is an adjective.

1 A **minute** is one of the sixty equal parts of an N COUNT hour. EG *Davis was ten minutes late... An accident had taken place only a few minutes before... This will take about twenty minutes to do.*

2 You can use **a minute** to mean a short time. EG N SING: *Will you excuse me if I sit down for a minute?...* USU a/one+N *Wait there a minute... Can I just finish doing this? I* Spoken *won't be a minute.*

3 Minute is also used in these phrases. **3.1** If you PHRASES do something the **minute** that something else happens, you do it as soon as the other thing happens. EG *Ask for help the minute you're stuck.* **3.2** If you do something **at the last minute,** you do it at the last possible time that it can be done. EG *They were only rescued at the last minute... Why do you always leave things to the last minute?* ● See also **last-minute. 3.3** If you say that something must be done **this minute,** you mean that it must be done immediately. EG *She doesn't have to make a decision this minute.* **3.4** If you say that something will happen at **any minute,** you mean that it is likely to happen very soon. EG *Mrs Curry was going to cry any minute.* **3.5** See also **up-to-the-minute.**

4 The **minutes** of a meeting are the written N PLURAL records of what is said or decided there. EG *You must learn how to take minutes.*

5 Something that is **minute** is extremely small. EG ADJ QUALIT *...minute amounts of fluoride... I had remembered in minute detail everything that had happened.*

minutely /maɪnjuːtliꞌ//. **1** If you examine some- ADV thing **minutely,** you examine it very carefully, paying attention to small details. EG *She began examining it minutely from all angles.*

2 Minutely also means very slightly. EG *His fingers* ADV *trembled minutely.*

minutiae /maɪnjuːʃiː-, -ʃɪaɪ/ are small, unimpor- N PLURAL tant details. EG *He has little time for the minutiae of* Formal *the game.*

miracle /mɪrəkə°l/, **miracles. 1** A **miracle** is a N COUNT wonderful and surprising event, often one which people believe was caused by God. EG *People said that it was a miracle of God... ...a miracle cure.*

2 You can refer to a very surprising and fortunate N COUNT

If someone is mischievous, are they misbehaving?

event as a **miracle**. EG *My father got a job. It was a miracle.*

miraculous /mɪrækjəˈləs/. 1 Something that is ADJ CLASSIF **miraculous** has been caused by a miracle. EG *...the miraculous powers of the saint.*

2 You can describe something that is very surpris- ADJ QUALIT ing and fortunate as **miraculous**. EG *I had been expecting some miraculous change to occur.*

◊ **miraculously**. EG *This time, the door miracu-* ◊ ADV OR *lously opened... It seemed, miraculously, that* ADV SEN *everyone was satisfied.*

3 You can also use **miraculous** to describe some- ADJ QUALIT thing that is extremely beautiful. EG *...fossils of a near miraculous perfection.*

mirage /mɪrɑːʒ/, **mirages**. A **mirage** is 1 an N COUNT image which you see in the distance or in the air in very hot weather, but which does not actually exist. 2 something in the future that you look forward to, but that never actually happens. EG *The promised land turns out to be a mirage.*

mirror /mɪrə/, **mirrors, mirroring, mirrored**. 1 N COUNT A **mirror** is a flat piece of glass which reflects light, so that when you look at it you can see yourself reflected in it. EG *She stared at herself in the mirror.*

2 If water **mirrors** something, it reflects it, like a V+O mirror. EG *The clear water mirrored the blue sky.* Literary

3 If one thing **mirrors** another thing, it has similar V+O : IF PASS features to it, and therefore seems like a copy of it. THEN + *in/by* EG *In the country political allegiances mirrored* Formal *existing divisions in society.*

mirth /mɜːθ/ is amusement which you express by N UNCOUNT laughing. EG *His anger gave place to mirth.* Literary

mis- is used at the beginning of words to indicate PREFIX that something is done badly or wrongly. For example, if you mismanage something, you man- age it badly. EG *He had misjudged the situation... ...the risks of miscalculation... ...the misuse of psy- chiatry.*

misadventure /mɪsədˈvɛntʃə/, **misadventures**. N COUNT OR A **misadventure** is an unfortunate incident. EG *...a* N UNCOUNT *funny story about a friend's misadventure... ...a* Formal *verdict of death by misadventure.*

misapprehension /mɪsæprɪˈhɛnʃəᵘn/, **misap-** N COUNT OR **prehensions**. A **misapprehension** is a wrong N UNCOUNT idea or impression that you have about something. EG *I was still under a misapprehension as to the threat contained in the letter.*

misappropriate /mɪsəˈprəʊprɪˈeɪt/, **misappro-** V+O **priates, misappropriating, misappropriated**. If Formal you **misappropriate** money, you take it and use it for your own purposes, although it does not belong to you. ◊ **misappropriation** /mɪsəprəʊprɪˈeɪʃəᵘn/. ◊ N UNCOUNT EG *He had been held responsible for the misappro- priation of certain funds.*

misbehave /mɪsbɪˈheɪv/, **misbehaves, misbe-** V **having, misbehaved**. If someone, especially a child, **misbehaves**, they behave in a way that is not acceptable to other people. EG *When children misbehave, their parents shouldn't become angry.*

misbehaviour /mɪsbɪˈheɪvjə/, spelled N UNCOUNT **misbehavior** in American English. **Misbehaviour** is behaviour that is not acceptable to other people.

miscalculate /mɪsˈkælkjəˈleɪt/, **miscalculates**, V OR V+O **miscalculating, miscalculated**. If you **miscal- culate**, you make a mistake in judging a situation or in making a calculation. EG *He badly miscalcu- lated the response to his proposal.* ◊ **miscalculation** /mɪsˈkælkjəˈleɪʃəᵘn/, **miscalcu-** ◊ N COUNT OR **lations**. EG *These miscalculations had serious con-* N UNCOUNT *sequences.*

miscarriage /mɪsˈkærɪdʒ/, **miscarriages**. If a N COUNT OR woman has a **miscarriage**, she gives birth to a N UNCOUNT foetus before it is properly formed, with the result that it cannot live.

miscarry /mɪsˈkærɪ/, **miscarries, miscarrying, miscarried**. 1 If a woman **miscarries**, she has a V miscarriage. EG *Emma miscarried and nearly died.*

2 If a plan **miscarries**, it goes wrong and fails. EG V *Our scheme had miscarried.*

miscellaneous /mɪsəˈleɪnɪəs/. **Miscellaneous** ADJ QUALIT groups of things or people are very different from each other. EG *...a miscellaneous collection of tools... ...miscellaneous enemies of authority.*

mischief /mɪstʃɪf/ is 1 eagerness to have fun, N UNCOUNT especially by embarrassing people or by playing tricks. EG *Her face was kind, her eyes full of mischief... There was about him an air of mischief.* 2 naughty behaviour by children. EG *He was old enough to get into mischief and get beaten.*

mischievous /mɪstʃɪvəs/. 1 A **mischievous** per- ADJ QUALIT son is eager to have fun, especially by embarrass- ing people or by playing tricks. EG *He was saucy and mischievous... ...a mischievous smile.* ◊ **mischievously**. EG *Kitty winked mischievously.* ◊ ADV 2 A **mischievous** child is often naughty but does ADJ QUALIT not do any real harm.

misconceived /mɪskənˈsiːvd/. A plan or method ADJ QUALIT : that is **misconceived** is not the right one for a USU PRED particular situation and is therefore not likely to succeed. EG *Their whole approach was miscon- ceived.*

misconception /mɪskənˈsɛpʃəᵘn/, **misconcep-** N COUNT **tions**. A **misconception** is a wrong idea that you have about something. EG *Another misconception is that cancer is infectious... People have the oddest misconceptions about doctors.*

misconduct /mɪsˈkɒndʌkt/ is bad or unacceptable N UNCOUNT behaviour, especially by a professional person. EG *They were victims of government misconduct.*

misdemeanour /mɪsdəˈmiːnə/, **misdemean-** N COUNT OR **ours**; spelled **misdemeanor** in American English. N UNCOUNT A **misdemeanour** is an act that people consider to Formal be shocking or unacceptable. EG *They listened to accounts of his misdemeanours.*

misdirect /mɪsdɪˈrɛkt/, **misdirects, misdi- recting, misdirected**. 1 If someone's energy or V+O : USU PASS qualities **are misdirected**, they are used wrongly Formal or inappropriately. EG *Those qualities of leadership could be misdirected.* ◊ **misdirected**. EG *...a* ◊ ADJ CLASSIF *misdirected economic system.*

2 If you **misdirect** someone, you send them to the V+O wrong place. EG *Passengers for half a dozen flights had been misdirected to the same gate.*

miser /maɪzə/, **misers**. A **miser** is a person who N COUNT enjoys saving money and hates spending it; used showing disapproval. EG *Soon she discovered she had married a miser.*

miserable /mɪzᵊrəbᵊl/. 1 If you are **miserable**, ADJ QUALIT you are very unhappy. EG *Rudolph felt depressed and miserable... They all had miserable faces.* ◊ **miserably**. EG *He looked up miserably.* ◊ ADV 2 If you describe a place or situation as **miserable**, ADJ QUALIT you mean that it makes you feel depressed. EG *Being without a grant is really miserable.*

3 You can describe the weather as **miserable** ADJ QUALIT when it is raining or cold. EG *...a miserable Monday morning.*

4 You can describe something as **miserable** when ADJ CLASSIF you think that it is too small. EG *He was given a miserable little room.* ◊ **miserably**. EG *There was* ◊ SUBMOD *one miserably small piece left.*

5 A **miserable** failure is very disappointing or ADJ CLASSIF : humiliating. EG *The play was a miserable failure.* ATTRIB ◊ **miserably**. EG *I failed miserably.* ◊ ADV

miserly /maɪzəlɪ/. Someone who is **miserly** is ADJ QUALIT very mean and hates spending money. EG *...a miserly old lady.*

misery /mɪzᵊrɪ/, **miseries**. 1 **Misery** is 1.1 N UNCOUNT great unhappiness. EG *I am ill with misery... ...the* OR N COUNT *miseries of unemployment.* 1.2 the unpleasant N UNCOUNT living conditions of people who are very poor. EG *They argued for a law to insure people against poverty and misery.*

2 If someone **makes** your **life a misery**, they PHRASE make you unhappy by behaving in an unpleasant way towards you.

misfire /mɪsfaɪə/, **misfires, misfiring, mis-** v
fired. If a plan **misfires**, it goes wrong. EG *The use
of force in support of their demands had misfired.*

misfit /mɪsfɪt/, **misfits.** A **misfit** is a person who N COUNT
is not easily accepted by other people, often be-
cause their behaviour is very different from everyone else's. EG *In such societies there have always
been misfits.*

misfortune /mɪsfɔːtʃən/, **misfortunes.** A **mis-** N COUNT OR
fortune is something very undesirable that hap- N UNCOUNT
pens to you. EG *The violinist had the misfortune to
turn over two pages at once... They had suffered
their share of misfortune.*

misgiving /mɪsgɪvɪŋ/, **misgivings.** If you have N PLURAL
misgivings about something, you are worried or OR N UNCOUNT
unhappy about it. EG *The firm's collapse seemed to
confirm their misgivings... I was filled with misgiving about the whole venture.*

misguided /mɪsgaɪdɪd/. **Misguided** opinions and ADJ QUALIT
attitudes are wrong, because they are based on
wrong information or beliefs. EG *...Sir Terence's
view was misguided... ...misguided idealism... ...a
misguided genius.*

mishap /mɪshæp/, **mishaps.** A **mishap** is an N COUNT OR
unfortunate but not very serious event that hap- N UNCOUNT
pens to you. EG *Tell your mother you have arrived
here without mishap... Loss of your property and
other mishaps can spoil your stay.*

misinform /mɪsɪnfɔːm/, **misinforms, misin-** v+o : USU PASS
forming, misinformed. If you **are misinformed**, +about
you are told something that is wrong or inaccurate.
EG *Unfortunately we were misinformed about the
purpose of the fund.*

misinformation /mɪsɪnfəmeɪʃən/ is deliberate- N UNCOUNT
ly incorrect information. EG *...a piece of blatant
misinformation.*

misinterpret /mɪsɪntɜːprɪt/, **misinterprets,** v+o
misinterpreting, misinterpreted. If you **misin-**
terpret something, you understand it wrongly. EG
*He saw the smile and misinterpreted it as friendli-
ness.* ◊ **misinterpretation** /mɪsɪntɜːprɪteɪʃən/, ◊ N UNCOUNT
misinterpretations. EG *The new version was less OR N COUNT
open to misinterpretation... ...their misinterpretation of Scripture.*

misjudge /mɪsdʒʌdʒ/, **misjudges, misjudging,** v+o
misjudged. If you **misjudge** someone or something, you form an incorrect idea or opinion about
them. EG *I had rather misjudged the timing of the
operation.*

misjudgement /mɪsdʒʌdʒmənt/, **misjudge-** N COUNT OR
ments; also spelled **misjudgment.** A **misjudge-** N UNCOUNT
ment is the forming of an incorrect idea or opinion
about someone or something. EG *They were guilty
of a serious misjudgement.*

mislay /mɪsleɪ/, **mislays, mislaying, mislaid.** If v+o
you **mislay** something, you lose it, because you put
it somewhere and then forget where it is. EG *I fear I
have mislaid my bus ticket.*

mislead /mɪsliːd/, **misleads, misleading, misled** v+o
/mɪsled/. If you **mislead** someone, you make them
believe something which is not true. EG *The public
has been misled by the optimism surrounding the
agreement... They were misled into buying a car.*

misleading /mɪsliːdɪŋ/. Something that is **mis-** ADJ QUALIT
leading gives you a wrong idea or impression. EG
...misleading information.

misled /mɪsled/ is the past tense and past participle of **mislead.**

mismanage /mɪsmænɪdʒ/, **mismanages, mis-** v+o
managing, mismanaged. If you **mismanage**
something, you organize or deal with it badly. EG
*The local people thought that education was being
mismanaged.* ◊ **mismanagement** ◊ N UNCOUNT
/mɪsmænɪdʒmənt/. EG *...economic mismanagement.*

misnomer /mɪsnəʊmə/, **misnomers.** A **misno-** N COUNT
mer is a word or expression that describes some- Formal
thing wrongly or inaccurately. EG *The very term
'positive discrimination' is a misnomer.*

misplaced /mɪspleɪst/. A **misplaced** feeling or ADJ QUALIT
action is inappropriate, or is directed towards the
wrong thing or person. EG *Her fears had been
ludicrously misplaced... ...misplaced loyalties.*

misprint /mɪsprɪnt/, **misprints.** A **misprint** is a N COUNT
mistake in the way something is printed, for exam-
ple a spelling mistake. EG *There was a misprint in
her name.*

misread, misreads, misreading. Misread is
used in the present tense, when it is pronounced
/mɪsriːd/, and is also the past tense and past
participle, when it is pronounced /mɪsred/.
1 If you **misread** a situation or someone's behav- v+o
iour, you do not understand it properly. EG *Their
behaviour was usually misread as indifference... He
was unconsciously misreading their actions.*
2 If you **misread** something that has been written v+o
or printed, you read it wrongly, so that you think it
says something that it does not say. EG *She had
misread a date in the Tour Book.*

misrepresent /mɪsreprɪzent/, **misrepresents,** v+o
misrepresenting, misrepresented. If you **mis-**
represent someone, you give a wrong account of
what they have said or written. EG *Witnesses claim
to have been seriously misrepresented... He says
that I have misrepresented his views.*
◊ **misrepresentation** /mɪsreprɪzenteɪʃən/, **mis-** ◊ N UNCOUNT
representations. EG *All political policies are open OR N COUNT
to misrepresentation.*

miss /mɪs/, **misses, missing, missed. 1** You use
Miss before the name of a girl or unmarried
woman when you are speaking to her or referring
to her. EG *Good morning, Miss Haynes... I do not
know very much about Miss Ravenscroft.*
2 If you **miss** something, **2.1** you do not notice it. EG v+o
*He doesn't miss much... You can't miss it, it's on the
first floor.* **2.2** you fail to hit it when you have v+o OR v
aimed something at it. EG *She had thrown her plate
at his head and missed.* ▸ used as a noun. EG *We had* ▸ N COUNT
a few near misses in the first raid.
3 If you **miss** someone, you feel sad that they are v+o OR v+-ING
no longer with you. If you **miss** something, you feel
sad that you no longer have it or experience it. EG
*The two boys miss their father a great deal... I
knew I should miss living in the Transkei.*
4 If you **miss** a chance or opportunity, you fail to v+o
take advantage of it. EG *It was a good opportunity
which it would be a pity to miss.*
5 If you **miss** something such as a bus, plane, or v+o
train, you arrive too late to catch it. EG *She was
going to miss her plane if her husband didn't hurry.*
6 If you **miss** something such as a meeting or an v+o
activity, you do not go to it or do not experience it.
EG *I couldn't miss a departmental meeting... I tried
to cheer her up, telling her she wasn't missing
much.*
7 If you **give** something **a miss**, you decide not to PHRASE
do it or not to go to it. EG *I know you want to go, but* Informal
I'd advise you to give it a miss.
8 See also **missing, hit and miss.**

miss out. 1 If you **miss out** something or some- PHRASAL VB :
one, you do not include them in something. EG *You* v+o+ADV
*can miss out a surprising number of words and still
be understood.* **2** If you **miss out** on something v+ADV,
interesting or useful, you do not become involved OFT+*on*
in it or get it, when other people do. EG *I miss out on
all these kind of opportunities.*

misshapen /mɪsʃeɪpən/. Something that is **mis-** ADJ QUALIT
shapen does not have a normal or natural shape.
EG *Her misshapen old fingers twitched at her beads.*

missile /mɪsaɪl/, **missiles.** A **missile** is **1** a N COUNT
weapon that moves long distances through the air
and explodes when it reaches its target. EG *...nu-
clear missiles.* ● See also **cruise missile. 2** any
object that you throw at someone as a weapon. EG

Name five words on these pages that are still
words if you take 'mis-' away.

Demonstrators attacked police using sticks and assorted missiles.

missing /mɪsɪŋ/. 1 If someone or something is **missing**, they are not in the place where you expect them to be, and you cannot find them. EG *She thought some of her jewellery was missing... I want to report a missing person... ...Larry Burrows, missing since 1971.* ADJ CLASSIF

2 If a part of something is **missing**, it has been removed and has not been replaced. EG *The car was a wreck, with all its wheels missing.* ADJ CLASSIF

mission /mɪʃəⁿn/, **missions.** 1 A **mission** is **1.1** an important task that you are given to do, especially one that involves travelling to another country. EG *He has been on confidential missions to Berlin.* **1.2** a group of people who have been sent to a foreign country to carry out an official task. EG *He became head of the Ugandan mission there.* **1.3** a special journey made by a military aeroplane or by a space rocket. EG *...a bombing mission.* N COUNT : USU+SUPP — N COUNT

2 If you have a **mission**, there is something that you believe it is your duty to try to achieve. EG *...one of those girls who had a mission in life.* N UNCOUNT : USU+SUPP

3 A **mission** is also **3.1** the activity of a group of Christians who have been sent to a place to teach people about Christianity. EG *They conducted five-day evangelistic missions around Britain.* **3.2** a building or group of buildings in which missionary work is carried out. N COUNT

missionary /mɪʃənⁿri¹/, **missionaries.** A **missionary** is a Christian who has been sent to a foreign country to teach people about Christianity. EG *One of the college girls became a missionary and went out to Africa.* N COUNT

misspend /mɪsspend/, **misspends, misspending, misspent.** If you say that someone has **misspent** time or **misspent** money, you mean that they have wasted it, and could have used it in better ways. EG *I'll tell him about my misspent life... They have misspent their scarce funds on facilities that nobody needs.* V+O

mist /mɪst/, **mists, misting, misted.** 1 Mist consists of a large number of tiny drops of water in the air. When there is a mist, you cannot see very far. EG *Everything was shrouded in mist... ...the mists of early morning.* N UNCOUNT OR N COUNT

2 If your eyes **mist**, you cannot see easily, because there are tears in your eyes. EG *Grandpa's eyes still misted over when he told the tale.* V : OFT+over

mist over or **mist up.** When a piece of glass **mists over** or **mists up**, it becomes covered with tiny drops of moisture, so that you cannot see through it easily. EG *His spectacles misted over.* PHRASAL VB : V+ADV

mistake /mɪsteɪk/, **mistakes, mistaking, mistook** /mɪstʊk/, **mistaken** /mɪsteɪkən/. 1 A **mistake** is an action or opinion that is wrong, or that is not what you intended to do. EG *He had made a terrible mistake... We made the mistake of leaving our bedroom window open... I said there must be some mistake because it wasn't my birthday... ...a spelling mistake.* ◆ If you accidentally do something that you did not intend to do, you can say that you did it **by mistake**. EG *I opened the door into the library by mistake.* N COUNT — ● PHRASE

2 If you **mistake** something, you are wrong about it. EG *At first he thought he had mistaken the address... I think you're mistaking how far the responsibility goes.* V+O OR V+REPORT : ONLY WH Formal

3 If you **mistake** someone or something for another person or thing, you wrongly think that they are the other person or thing. EG *You mustn't mistake lack of formal education for lack of wisdom.* V+O+for

4 If you say **there's no mistaking** someone or something, you mean that they can be easily recognized or understood. EG *There was no mistaking her... There can be no mistaking his meaning.* PHRASE

mistaken /mɪsteɪkən/. 1 If you are **mistaken** about something, you are wrong about it. EG *I told her she must be mistaken... How could she have* ADJ PRED : OFT+about/in

been mistaken about a thing like this?... I had been mistaken in believing Nick was mad.*

2 If you have a **mistaken** belief or opinion, you believe something which is not true. EG *The discovery of adrenalin came about through a mistaken impression.* ◇ **mistakenly.** EG *The parents may mistakenly believe that they are to blame for their child's illness.* ADJ QUALIT — ◇ ADV

mister /mɪstə/. See **Mr.**

mistletoe /mɪsəⁿltəʊ/ is a plant with white berries on it, which grows on trees. Mistletoe is used in Britain as a Christmas decoration. N UNCOUNT

mistook /mɪstʊk/ is the past tense of **mistake.**

mistress /mɪstrɪ²s/, **mistresses.** 1 A man's **mistress** is a woman he is having a sexual relationship with, but who is not married to him. EG *He keeps a mistress.* N COUNT

2 A **mistress** in a school is a female schoolteacher. EG *...the French mistress.* N COUNT : USU+SUPP

3 A servant's **mistress** is the woman who has authority over the servant. EG *She was only carrying out her mistress's orders.* N COUNT

4 If a woman is the **mistress** of a situation, she has complete control over it. EG *Etta was now the acknowledged mistress of the situation.* N COUNT+of

mistrust /mɪstrʌst/, **mistrusts, mistrusting, mistrusted. Mistrust** is the feeling that you have towards someone who you do not trust. EG *She gazed on me with a sudden fear and mistrust.* ▸ used as a verb. EG *The child soon learns to mistrust offers of affection.* N UNCOUNT — ▸ V+O

misty /mɪsti¹/. If it is **misty**, there is a lot of mist in the air. EG *...a misty autumn morning... The night was cold and misty... We drove through the misty streets.* ADJ QUALIT

misunderstand /mɪsʌndəstænd/, **misunderstands, misunderstanding, misunderstood** /mɪsʌndəstʊd/. If you **misunderstand** someone, you do not understand properly what they say or write. EG *Don't misunderstand me; we're not making any promises... She misunderstood my question.* V+O OR V

misunderstanding /mɪsʌndəstændɪŋ/, **misunderstandings.** 1 A **misunderstanding** is a failure to understand something such as a situation or a person's remarks. EG *This was a minor misunderstanding which could be instantly cleared up... ...a source of suspicion and misunderstanding.* N COUNT OR N UNCOUNT

2 If two people have a **misunderstanding**, they have a disagreement or a slight quarrel. EG *They usually sort out their misunderstandings.* N COUNT

misuse, misuses, misusing, misused; pronounced /mɪsjuːs/ when it is a noun and /mɪsjuːz/ when it is a verb. The **misuse** of something is the use of it in an incorrect, improper, or careless way or for a wrong or dishonest purpose. EG *...the misuse of company funds... She cared deeply about words, and hated their misuse.* ▸ used as a verb. EG *In some cases, pesticides are deliberately misused.* N UNCOUNT OR N COUNT — ▸ V+O

mitigate /mɪtɪgeɪt/, **mitigates, mitigating, mitigated.** To **mitigate** something means to make it less unpleasant, serious, or painful. EG *They should endeavour to mitigate distress... ...an attempt to mitigate the unfavourable reaction.* V+O Formal

mitigating /mɪtɪgeɪtɪŋ/. **Mitigating** circumstances make a crime easier to understand, and may result in the person responsible being punished less severely. EG *They may deny the offence or plead mitigating circumstances.* ADJ CLASSIF ATTRIB Formal Legal

mitten /mɪtəⁿn/, **mittens. Mittens** are gloves which have one section that covers your thumb and another section for your four fingers together. See picture at CLOTHES. N COUNT : OFT PLURAL

mix /mɪks/, **mixes, mixing, mixed.** 1 If you **mix** two substances, you stir or shake them together. EG *The mug had been used for mixing flour and water... They drink whisky mixed with beer.* V-ERG : ALSO V OR V+with : RECIP

2 If you **mix** something, you make it by stirring or V+O, V+O+O, OR V+O+for shaking other things together. EG *She mixed Clara a drink... He carefully mixed the cement.*

3 A **mix** is a powder containing the correct amounts of all the substances that you need in order to make something. You buy the mix in a packet and add water or another liquid to the powder. EG *...cake mixes... She bought a packet of cement mix.* N MASS+SUPP

4 A **mix** is also two or more things combined together. EG *We should try and keep a broad mix of subjects in our schools... I find the mix of politics and literature very interesting.* N COUNT: USU SING+SUPP

5 If you **mix** two activities or **mix** one activity with another, you do them both at the same time. EG *...the concern for mixing study with work.* V+O OR V+with : RECIP

6 If you **mix** with other people, you meet them and talk to them at a social event such as a party. EG *He was making no effort to mix.* V : OFT+with

7 See also **mixed**.

mix up. 1 If you **mix up** two things or people, you confuse them, so that you think that one of them is the other one. EG *People even mix us up and greet us by each other's names.* **2** If you **mix up** a number of things that are in a special order or arrangement, you change the order or arrangement. EG *The letters had got too mixed up to be sorted out easily.* **3** See also **mixed up, mix-up.** PHRASAL VB : V+O+ADV

mixed /mɪkst/. **1** You use **mixed** to describe something which **1.1** consists of different things of the same general kind. EG *...a mixed salad... ...mixed nuts.* **1.2** involves people from two or more different races. EG *...a mixed marriage... He is of mixed parentage: half English, half Dutch.* ADJ CLASSIF : ATTRIB / ADJ CLASSIF

2 Mixed education or accommodation is intended for both males and females. EG *...a mixed school.* ADJ CLASSIF

3 Feelings or reactions that are **mixed** consist of some good and some bad things. EG *He has mixed feelings towards his wife.* ADJ QUALIT

mixed bag. If you describe a situation or a group of things or people as a **mixed bag**, you mean that it contains some good things and some bad ones. EG *...a mixed bag of amateurs and old professionals... It's very much a mixed bag of activities and interests.* N SING

mixed doubles is a match in some sports, especially tennis and badminton, in which a man and a woman play as partners against another man and woman. N UNCOUNT

mixed up. 1 If you are **mixed up**, you are confused, often because of emotional or social problems. EG *I got mixed up and forgot which one I'd gone to first... Tim was in a strange mixed-up frame of mind.* ADJ QUALIT

2 If you are **mixed up** in a crime or a scandal, you are involved in it. EG *I wasn't mixed up in it myself.* ADJ PRED : OFT+in

mixer /mɪksə/, **mixers.** A **mixer** is a machine used for mixing things together. EG *...a food mixer... ...the big cement mixers.* N COUNT+SUPP

mixing bowl, mixing bowls. A **mixing bowl** is a large bowl used for mixing ingredients when cooking. N COUNT

mixture /mɪkstʃə/, **mixtures. 1** A **mixture** of things consists of several different things together. EG *I swallowed a mixture of pills... At the conference you could hear an amazing mixture of languages... She stared at the cold green soup in a mixture of disgust and hunger.* N SING+of

2 A **mixture** is a substance that consists of other substances which have been stirred or shaken together. EG *...a mixture of water and household bleach... Take care not to spill the mixture.* N COUNT

mix-up, mix-ups. A **mix-up** is a mistake in something that was planned. EG *Due to some administrative mix-up the letters had not been sent.* N COUNT Informal

ml is an abbreviation for **1** 'millilitre' or 'millilitres'. EG *...180ml of water.* **2** 'mile' or 'miles'.

mm is an abbreviation for 'millimetre' or 'millimetres'. EG *...35mm film... ...standard mirror sizes: 760 x 460mm.*

Mm is used to represent a sound that you make when someone is talking, to indicate that you are listening to them, that you agree with them, or that you are preparing to say something. EG *'That's what you said, isn't it?' - 'Mm, yes. I suppose so.'*

moan /məʊn/, **moans, moaning, moaned. 1** If you **moan, 1.1** you make a low and miserable cry because you are in pain or suffering. EG *Otto moaned from the pain.* ► used as a noun. EG *Each time she moved her leg she let out a moan.* **1.2** you speak in a way which indicates that you are very unhappy or anxious. EG *'What am I going to do?' she moaned.* V / ► N COUNT / V+QUOTE OR REPORT : ONLY that

2 If you **moan** about something, you complain about it. EG *My brother's moaning about money again.* ► used as a noun. EG *There are the usual moans if tea is late on the table.* V : OFT+about Informal / ► N COUNT

moat /məʊt/, **moats.** A **moat** is a deep, wide ditch which people used to dig round a hill or castle and fill with water, in order to protect the place. N COUNT

mob /mɒb/, **mobs, mobbing, mobbed. 1** A **mob** is a large, disorganized, and often violent crowd of people. EG *The police faced a mob throwing bricks and petrol bombs.* N COUNT

2 If people **mob** a person, they gather round the person in a large crowd, in order to express feelings of anger or admiration. EG *Pop stars are always moaning about being mobbed by their fans.* V+O

mobile /məʊbaɪl/, **mobiles. 1** Something that is **mobile** is able to move freely or to be moved easily. EG *Most antelopes are fully mobile as soon as they are born... The squadron was protected by a highly mobile air defence.* ◊ **mobility** /məʊbɪlɪtiʔ/. EG *With the aeroplane, people achieved a physical mobility never before dreamed of.* ADJ QUALIT / ◊ N UNCOUNT

2 If you are **mobile, 2.1** you can move or travel easily from place to place. EG *Many seventy-year-olds are mobile: my mother runs her own car.* **2.2** you are able to move to a different job or social class. EG *...socially mobile business leaders.* ◊ **mobility.** EG *...growing affluence, opportunity, and social mobility.* ADJ PRED / ADJ PRED / ◊ N UNCOUNT

3 A **mobile** is a light structure which hangs from a ceiling as a decoration. It usually consists of several small objects which move as the air around them moves. N COUNT

mobilize /məʊbɪlaɪz/, **mobilizes, mobilizing, mobilized;** also spelled **mobilise. 1** If you **mobilize** a group of people, you encourage them all to do something. EG *The Trade Union Congress is prepared to mobilize the whole movement to defeat the bill.* ◊ **mobilization** /məʊbɪlaɪzeɪʃəˀn/. EG *The building of the canal required the mobilization of large masses of labour.* V+O / ◊ N UNCOUNT

2 If a country **mobilizes** or **mobilizes** its armed forces, its armed forces are given orders to prepare to fight a war. ◊ **mobilization.** EG *Defence chiefs urged mobilization at once.* V OR V+O Formal / ◊ N UNCOUNT

moccasin /mɒkəsɪn/, **moccasins. Moccasins** are soft leather shoes which have a low heel and a raised seam at the front above the toe. See picture at SHOES. N COUNT

mock /mɒk/, **mocks, mocking, mocked. 1** If you **mock** someone, you make them appear foolish, for example by saying something funny about them, or by imitating their behaviour. EG *He felt that Mrs Mount was mocking him a little... ...an unsympathetic teacher who had mocked her domestic ambitions.* ◊ **mocking.** EG *She stared at him in her mocking way.* V+O OR V+QUOTE / ◊ ADJ QUALIT

2 You use **mock** to describe something which is deliberately not genuine. EG *He shook his head with mock disapproval... Robert squealed in mock terror... ...mock Tudor houses.* ADJ CLASSIF : ATTRIB

If you are mixed up, has there been a mix-up?

MODAL VERBS

A small group of words in English are often called modal verbs or modal auxiliaries (MODAL). They are: **can, could, may, might, must, ought, shall, should, will,** and **would**. **Be to** and **have to** are also often called modals, but we do not label them as modals in this dictionary. See the entries for **be** and **have**.

The verbs **dare, need,** and **used to**, which some grammars call modals, are called semi-modals in this dictionary. See the entry headed SEMI-MODALS for information about them.

Modals behave rather differently from ordinary verbs:

Followed by an infinitive

Apart from **ought**, modals are followed only by a verb in the infinitive form without **to**. For example: *I must go . . . He will come . . . They should arrive soon.*

Ought is followed by a verb in the infinitive form with **to**, as in: *She ought to get there by 6.*

No inflections

Modals do not inflect – that is, they do not change their form for the third person singular. So: *I can swim . . . He can swim.*
Compare: *I swim . . . He swims.*

In questions

Modals come before the subject in questions. So: *Will you meet me at 6 o'clock? . . . What time will you meet me?*

With ordinary verbs the auxiliary **do** is used. For example: *Do you swim?*

In negative clauses

Modals come before the word **not** in negative clauses. Often **not** is abbreviated to **n't** and is added to the modal: *She wouldn't tell me where she had been.*

The forms **can't, won't,** and **shan't** are often used instead of **cannot, will not,** and **shall not**. For example: *I can't remember her name . . . They won't be here on time . . . I shan't give you a present this year.*

Used on their own

Modals can be used as a verbal group on their own following a full verbal group in order to make a contrast. For example: *I haven't strangled him yet, but I might . . . I'd love to have lunch with you but I can't.*

Used in question tags

Modals are used in question tags. For example: *You will come, won't you? . . . You won't be late, will you?*

3 A **mock** examination or battle is not real but is ADJ CLASSIF: intended to be like the real event so that people ATTRIB can practise and prepare for the real event.

mockery /mɒkə⁰ri¹/. **1 Mockery** is the scornful N UNCOUNT attitude that you express in your speech or behaviour when you think someone is foolish, stupid, or inferior. EG *There was a tone of mockery in his voice... He had ignored Helen's mockery.*

2 If something **makes a mockery of** something, it PHRASE makes it appear foolish and worthless. EG *The strikers were making a mockery of our efforts to build up employment.*

3 If you describe an event or situation as a **mock-** N SING:a+N **ery**, you mean that it is very unsuccessful. EG *The examination was a mockery.*

mock-up, mock-ups. A **mock-up** of something N COUNT such as a machine or building is a model of it which is made to do tests on or to show people what it will look like. EG *Here's a mock-up of the central section of the submarine.*

modal /mɒʊdə⁰l/, **modals.** In grammar, a **modal** N COUNT or a **modal verb** is a word such as *can* or *would* which is used in a verbal group and which expresses ideas such as possibility, intention, and necessity. See the entry headed MODAL VERBS for grammatical information about them.

MODAL stands for **modal verb**
The verbs *can, could, may, might, must, ought to, shall, should, will,* and *would* are labelled MODAL in the Extra Column.
See the entry headed MODAL VERBS for information about them.

---

mod cons /mɒd kɒnz/. If a house has all **mod** N PLURAL **cons**, it has all the modern facilities such as hot Informal water and heating that make it pleasant to live in. British

mode /mɒʊd/, **modes.** A **mode** of life or behav- N COUNT iour is a particular way of living or behaving. +SUPP: ...*conventionally acceptable modes of life... the* OFT+*of* *mode of action which protesters adopt today... She always chose this mode of transport.*

model /mɒdə⁰l/, **models, modelling, modelled;** spelled **modeling, modeled** in American English.

1 A **model** is **1.1** a physical representation that N COUNT shows what an object looks like or how it works. EG ...*scale models of well known Navy ships... I had a model theatre, for which I used to design scenery.*

1.2 a system that is being used and that people N COUNT+SUPP might want to copy in order to achieve similar Formal results. EG *This system seemed a relevant model for the new Africa.*

2 Something that is a **model** of clarity or a **model** N COUNT+*of* of fairness is extremely clear or extremely fair. EG *She's a model of discretion.*

3 A **model** wife or a **model** teacher is an excellent ADJ CLASSIF: wife or an excellent teacher. EG *Jane has turned* ATTRIB *into a model mother... They are model students.*

4 If you **model** yourself on someone, you copy the V-REFL+*on* way that they do things, because you admire them and want to be like them. EG *The children have their parents on which to model themselves.*

5 A **model** is also a particular type of machine, for N COUNT example a car or washing machine. EG *The Granada is the most popular model.*

6 A person who is a **model 6.1** poses for a painter N COUNT or photographer as a job. EG *She was one of Rossetti's favourite models.* **6.2** displays clothes by wearing them, especially in a fashion show. EG *She's a fashion model.*

7 If you **model** clothes, you display them by V+O OR V wearing them. EG *He models cardigans in knitting books.* ◊ **modelling.** EG *Tom says she's not to do* ◊ N UNCOUNT *modelling while she's still at school.*

8 If you **model** shapes or figures, you make them V+O out of a substance such as clay or wood. EG *The*

children were asked to model an aeroplane out of balsa wood.

moderate, moderates, moderating, moder- **ated;** pronounced /mɒdərə⁰t/ when it is an adjective or noun, and /mɒdəreit/ when it is a verb. **1** ADJ QUALIT Political opinions or policies that are **moderate** are not extreme and are concerned with slow or small changes in the system. EG ...*a woman with moderate views... The movement drew its support from moderate conservatives.*

2 A **moderate** is a person whose political opinions N COUNT and activities are not extreme. EG *The moderates have plenty to be anxious about.*

3 A **moderate** amount of something is neither ADJ QUALIT large nor small. EG *The sun's rays, in moderate* USU ATTRIB *quantities, are important for health... There's a big dining room and a moderate sized kitchen.*

4 If you **moderate** something or if it **moderates,** it V-ERG becomes less extreme or violent and more acceptable. EG *She had been given instructions to moderate her tone... The bad weather had moderated.*

moderately /mɒdərətli¹/. Something that is **mod-** SUBMOD **erately** good or that happens **moderately** fast, for example, is fairly good or happens fairly fast. EG *Her handwriting was moderately good... ...a moderately long beard.*

moderation /mɒdəreiʃə⁰n/ is control of your be- N UNCOUNT haviour that stops you acting in an extreme way. EG *He has not displayed the same moderation in his political behaviour as in his private life.* ● If you ● PHRASE drink alcohol or smoke **in moderation,** you do not drink or smoke too much.

modern /mɒdə⁰n/. **1 Modern** means relating to ADJ CLASSIF: the present time. EG *Marx still has much to say to* ATTRIB *the modern world... The social problems in modern society are mounting.*

2 Something that is **modern** is new and involves ADJ QUALIT the latest ideas and latest equipment. EG *Japan successfully built up a modern capitalist economy... 'Did you like Stockholm?' – 'Yes, it's very modern, isn't it?'* ◊ **modernity** /mɒ⁷dɜːni¹ti¹/. EG ...*indus-* ◊ N UNCOUNT *tries half way between tradition and modernity.*

modern-day. You use **modern-day** to describe ADJ CLASSIF: something in the present that is very similar to ATTRIB something that happened in the past. EG *He was convinced that he was a modern-day Messiah.*

modernize /mɒdənaiz/, **modernizes, moderniz-** V+O **ing, modernized;** also spelled **modernise.** If you **modernize** something such as a system or a factory, you change it by replacing old methods or equipment with new ones. EG ...*a twenty year programme to modernise Britain's transport system.* ◊ **modernization** /mɒdənaizeiʃə⁰n/. EG ◊ N UNCOUNT ...*plans for modernisation of the Post Office.*

modern languages. If you study **modern lan-** N PLURAL **guages,** you study the modern European languages such as French, German, and Russian.

modest /mɒdi²st/. **1** A **modest** house or flat is not ADJ QUALIT large or expensive. EG *He moved from his hotel suite into a modest flat.*

2 Something that is **modest** is quite small in ADJ QUALIT amount. EG ...*a small theatre with a modest budget.* ◊ **modestly.** EG *He still gambled modestly.* ◊ ADV

3 Someone who is **modest 3.1** does not talk much ADJ QUALIT about their abilities, qualities, or possessions; used showing approval. EG *He's got a drawer full of medals but he's too modest to wear them.* ◊ **modestly.** EG *He talks quietly and modestly* ◊ ADV *about his farm.* ◊ **modesty** /mɒdi²sti¹/. EG *The* ◊ N UNCOUNT *real secret of his power was his modesty and his total lack of vanity.* **3.2** is shy and easily embar- ADJ QUALIT rassed, especially by nudity or things relating to sex. EG *That such a modest man should be unclothed seems highly improbable.* ◊ **modestly.** EG ◊ ADV *They slipped out of their garments modestly.*

Is Britain a monarchy?

◊ **modesty.** EG *She covered herself with a sheet, respecting my modesty.*

modicum /mɒdɪkəm/. A **modicum** of something N PART : SING is a small amount of it. EG *...a designer with a* Formal *modicum of good taste.*

modification /mɒdɪfɪkeɪʃəⁿn/, **modifications.** A N COUNT OR **modification** to something is a small change N UNCOUNT which you make to it in order to improve it. EG *The engine was pulled apart for modifications... I said I thought the idea might need modification.*

modify /mɒdɪfaɪ/, **modifies, modifying, modi-** V+O **fied.** If you **modify** something, you change it slightly, often in order to improve it. EG *The present Government has modified this approach... The aircraft were extensively modified and improved.*

module /mɒdjuːl/, **modules.** A **module** is a part N COUNT of a spacecraft which can do certain things inde- Technical pendently, often away from the main part of the spacecraft.

mohair /məʊheə/ is a kind of very soft wool. EG *...a* N UNCOUNT *mohair coat.*

moist /mɔɪst/, **moister, moistest.** Something that ADJ QUALIT is **moist** is slightly wet. EG *...moist black earth... His eyes grew moist.*

moisten /mɔɪsəⁿn/, **moistens, moistening,** V+O **moistened.** If you **moisten** something, you make it slightly wet. EG *The girl moistened her lips.*

moisture /mɔɪstʃə/ is tiny drops of water in the N UNCOUNT air, on a surface, or in the ground. EG *The kitchen's stone floor was shiny with moisture... Trees have enormous roots that can reach out for moisture far below the surface.*

molar /məʊlə/, **molars.** Your **molars** are the N COUNT large teeth at the side of your mouth.

mold /məʊld/. See **mould.**

moldy /məʊldɪ/. See **mouldy.**

mole /məʊl/, **moles.** 1 A **mole** is a dark spot or N COUNT small, dark lump on someone's skin which is permanent. EG *She had a tiny mole on her cheek.*
2 A **mole** is also a small animal with black fur that N COUNT lives in tunnels in the ground.
3 If you refer to someone as a **mole**, you mean that N COUNT they are secretly working against the government or some other organization of which they are a member. EG *There is some gossip in Westminster that there is a mole in the Thatcher cabinet.*

molecule /mɒlɪkjuːl/, **molecules.** A **molecule** is N COUNT the smallest amount of a chemical substance Technical which can exist by itself without changing or breaking apart. EG *The haemoglobin molecule con- tains only four atoms of iron.* ◊ **molecular** ◊ ADJ CLASSIF : /məⁿlekjəˡlə/. EG *...molecular biology.* ATTRIB

molehill /məʊlhɪl/, **molehills.** 1 A **molehill** is a N COUNT small pile of earth on the ground that has been left by a mole that has been digging there.
2 If you say that someone is **making a mountain** PHRASE **out of a molehill**, you mean that they are making an unimportant fact or difficulty seem very seri- ous.

molest /məˡlest/, **molests, molesting, molested.**
1 Someone who **molests** children touches them in V+O a sexual way against their will and can be arrested Formal by the police for this. ◊ **molestation** ◊ N UNCOUNT /mɒlesteɪʃəⁿn/. EG *...child molestation.* ◊ **molester** ◊ N COUNT /məˡlestə/, **molesters.** EG *...child molesters.*
2 If someone **molests** you, they annoy you and V+O prevent you from doing something, often by using Formal physical violence. EG *They feared they would be molested by the angry crowd.*

mollify /mɒlɪfaɪ/, **mollifies, mollifying, molli-** V+O **fied.** If you **mollify** someone, you do something to Formal make them less upset or angry. EG *Mrs Pringle allowed herself to be mollified.* ◊ **mollified.** EG *She* ◊ ADJ PRED *appeared slightly mollified.*

molt /məʊlt/. See **moult.**

molten /məʊltəⁿn/. **Molten** rock or metal has ADJ QUALIT been heated to a very high temperature and has become a hot, thick, sticky liquid. EG *...a great mass of molten rock.*

mom /mɒm/, **moms.** Some people refer to their VOCATIVE mother as **mom.** EG *When I was born, Mom was* OR N COUNT *forty and Dad forty-six... 'Hey, mom,' said Billy,* Informal *'what's that around your neck?'* American

moment /məʊməⁿnt/, **moments.** 1 A **moment** is 1.1 a very short period of time. EG *She hesitated for* N COUNT *only a moment... A few moments later he heard footsteps... I'll come back to that in a moment... It causes me moments of acute embarrassment.* 1.2 N SING+SUPP the point in time at which something happens. EG *At that precise moment, Miss Pulteney came into the office... ...the moment of death... ...at such a critical moment in his career.*
2 **Moment** is used in these phrases. 2.1 If you say PHRASES that something is true or is happening **at the moment**, you mean that it is true or is happening now. EG *The biggest problem at the moment is unemployment... I'm sorry, but she's not in at the moment.* 2.2 If you do something **at the last moment**, you do it at the last possible time that it can be done. EG *We escaped from Saigon at the last moment.* 2.3 If you say that you do not believe something **for one moment**, you are emphasizing that you do not believe it at all. EG *I didn't believe for a moment that he was an actor.* 2.4 If you say that you cannot do something **for the moment**, you mean that you cannot do it now, but you will probably be able to do it later. EG *I don't want to discuss this for the moment.* 2.5 If one thing happens **the moment** something else happens, the two things happen at exactly the same time. EG *The moment I saw this, it appealed to me.* 2.6 If you say that someone or something **has** their **moments**, you mean that they are occasionally successful or interesting, although not very often. EG *The film had its moments.*

momentary /məʊməntəⁿriː/. Something that is ADJ CLASSIF **momentary** lasts for only a few seconds. EG *There was a momentary pause.* ◊ **momentarily** ◊ ADV /məʊməntˡeəⁿˡliː/. EG *I had momentarily forgotten.*

momentous /məˡmentəs/. Something that is mo- ADJ CLASSIF **mentous** is very important, often because of the Formal effect that it will have in the future. EG *There was no doubt it would be a momentous occasion.*

momentum /məˡmentəm/ is 1 the ability that N UNCOUNT something has to keep developing. EG *It was neces- sary to crush the rebel movement before it had a chance to gather momentum.* 2 the ability that an object has to continue moving as a result of the speed it already has. EG *...the momentum of the rocket.*

monarch /mɒnək/, **monarchs.** A **monarch** is a N COUNT king, queen, or other royal person who reigns over a country.

monarchist /mɒnəkɪst/, **monarchists.** A mon- N COUNT **archist** is a person who believes that their country Formal should have a monarch.

monarchy /mɒnəkiː/, **monarchies.** A monar- N COUNT : **chy** is a system in which a monarch reigns over a USU the+N, country and in which the next monarch will be OR N UNCOUNT another member of the same family. EG *We want to abolish the monarchy... I have never been an opponent of monarchy... ...the English monarchy.*

monastery /mɒnəstriː/, **monasteries.** A monas- N COUNT **tery** is a building or collection of buildings in which a group of monks live.

Monday /mʌndiː/, **Mondays. Monday** is one of N UNCOUNT the seven days of the week. It is the day after OR N COUNT Sunday and before Tuesday. Most people start their week's work on a Monday. EG *It was cold last Monday... ...a plan for reducing ticket prices on Mondays.*

monetary /mʌnɪtəⁿriː/ means relating to money, ADJ CLASSIF : especially the total amount of money in a country. ATTRIB EG *Washington's tight monetary policy... ...mon-* Formal *etary value... ...the monetary system.*

money /mʌniː/. 1 **Money** consists of the coins or N UNCOUNT bank notes that you use when you buy something.

EG *I spent all my money on sweets... I had very little money left... They may not accept English money.*
2 If you **make money**, you obtain money by PHRASE earning it or by making a profit. EG *To make money you've got to take chances.*
3 If you **get** your **money's worth**, you get good PHRASE value for the money that you spend. EG *I always Informal insist on getting my money's worth.*

MONEY

This entry shows some of the ways in which you can refer to money.

When you express amounts of money in writing, the main unit of currency that you are using is usually shown by a symbol or letter in front of the figures. For example, £100 means one hundred pounds, $100 means one hundred dollars, and $2.50 means two dollars and fifty cents. If an amount of money consists of only a smaller unit, for example only pence or cents, then the symbol or letter usually follows the figures. For example, 50p means fifty pence.

When you express amounts of money in speech, you sometimes leave out the words that refer to the unit of currency, although you can say them after the numbers. For example, you write £10 but you say 'ten pounds'.

The following examples show a few ways of expressing amounts of money. EG *He was making ninety dollars a week... It costs 35 pounds a kilo... ...a million and a half dollars... ...the ten-cent packet of balloons... The machine wouldn't take 10p pieces... Total British losses were close to a quarter of a million pounds.*

---

mongrel /mʌŋgrəl/, **mongrels**. A **mongrel** is a N COUNT dog with parents of different breeds. EG *If you want a dog, you can get a mongrel from a pet store.*

monitor /mɒnɪtə/, **monitors, monitoring, monitored**. **1** If you **monitor** something, you check v+o regularly how it is changing or developing over a period of time. EG *The child's progress is being monitored.*
2 If you **monitor** sounds, especially radio broad- v+o casts, you record them or listen carefully to them in order to obtain information. EG *They were getting news by monitoring BBC broadcasts.*
3 A **monitor** is a machine that is used to check or N COUNT record things. EG *The patient was connected to the monitor.*

monk /mʌŋk/, **monks**. A **monk** is a member of a N COUNT male religious community.

monkey /mʌŋki/, **monkeys**. A **monkey** is an N COUNT animal which has a long tail and lives in hot countries. Monkeys climb trees.

mono /mɒnəʊ/ is used to describe a record or a ADJ CLASSIF system of playing music in which all the sound is OR N UNCOUNT directed through one speaker only.

monogamy /mə'nɒgəmi/ is the custom of being N UNCOUNT married to only one person at a particular time. EG Formal *Lifelong monogamy has other drawbacks.*
◊ **monogamous** /mə'nɒgəməs/. EG *...monogamous* ◊ ADJ CLASSIF *marriage.*

monogrammed /mɒnəgræmd/. Something that ADJ CLASSIF is **monogrammed** is marked with a design that includes a person's initials. EG *...his monogrammed hair brushes.*

monolithic /mɒnə'lɪθɪk/. **1** An organization or ADJ QUALIT system that is **monolithic** is very large and gives the impression that it will never change. EG *...the monolithic character of the main political parties.*
2 Something that is **monolithic** is very large and ADJ QUALIT impressive. EG *...the great monolithic rock.*

monologue /mɒnəlɒg/, **monologues**. A **mono-** N COUNT OR **logue** is a long speech by one person, for example N UNCOUNT in a play. EG *He went into a long monologue, only part of which I understood.*

monopolize /mə'nɒpəlaɪz/, **monopolizes, mo-** v+o **nopolizing, monopolized**; also spelled **monopolise**. If you **monopolize** something, you control it completely and prevent other people having a share in it. EG *The Dutch wanted to monopolize the profitable spice trade from the East.*

monopoly /mə'nɒpəli/, **monopolies**. **1** A **mo-** N COUNT : **nopoly** on a particular subject or activity is com- OFT+*on/of* plete control of it by one person or a group of people. EG *I don't believe the medical profession has a monopoly on morality.*
2 A **monopoly** of an industry is control of most of N COUNT OR the industry by only one or a few large firms. N UNCOUNT

monosyllable /mɒnə'sɪləbəl/, **monosyllables**. N COUNT : If someone speaks in **monosyllables**, they speak OFT PLURAL using only very short words, for example 'yes' or 'no'. EG *He was answering only in monosyllables.*

monotone /mɒnətəʊn/, **monotones**. A **monotone** N COUNT is a sound which does not vary at all in tone or loudness and is very boring to listen to. EG *He droned on in a steady monotone.*

monotonous /mə'nɒtənəs/. Something that is ADJ QUALIT **monotonous** has a dull and regular pattern which never changes and is very boring. EG *...people who have monotonous jobs... Barrack life is shown to be squalid and monotonous.* ◊ **monotony** ◊ N UNCOUNT : /mə'nɒtəni/. EG *...the monotony of work on the OFT+*of* assembly line.*

monsoon /mɒnsu:n/, **monsoons**. The **monsoon** is N COUNT the season in Southern Asia when there is a lot of very heavy rain. EG *Even during the monsoons the afternoons were warm and clear.*

monster /mɒnstə/, **monsters**. **1** A **monster** is a N COUNT large imaginary creature that looks very frightening. EG *...Dracula, Frankenstein, and every horrible monster you could think of.*
2 Monster means extremely large. EG *...the mon-* ADJ CLASSIF : ster Piccadilly Hotel. ATTRIB
3 If you describe someone as a **monster**, you mean N COUNT OR that they are cruel, frightening, or evil. EG *You're a* VOCATIVE *monster. A detestable, abominable monster.*

monstrosity /mɒnstrɒsɪti/, **monstrosities**. A N COUNT **monstrosity** is something that is large and extremely ugly. EG *...a monstrosity of a house he bought near Leatherhead.*

monstrous /mɒnstrəs/. **1** If you describe a situa- ADJ QUALIT tion or event as **monstrous**, you mean that it is extremely shocking or unfair. EG *The court's judgement was absolutely monstrous.*
2 Something that is **monstrous** is **2.1** extremely ADJ QUALIT ugly and frightening. EG *...this dense and monstrous urban wilderness.* **2.2** extremely large. EG *They went from one building to another in a fleet of monstrous vehicles.*

month /mʌnθ/, **months**. A **month** is **1** one of the N COUNT twelve periods of time that a year is divided into, for example January or February. EG *It's happened three times this month... I'm going away later in the month... The pay will be five hundred pounds a month... ...the month of March.* **2** a period of about four weeks. EG *He was kidnapped just over a month ago... Four months later she died.*

monthly /mʌnθli/. You use **monthly** to describe ADJ CLASSIF : something that happens, is done, or appears once a ATTRIB OR ADV month or every month. EG *...a monthly meeting... My monthly income was two hundred pounds... Most of our staff are paid monthly.*

monument /mɒnjə'mənt/, **monuments**. A N COUNT **monument** is **1** a large structure, usually made of stone, which is built to remind people of an event in history or of a famous person. EG *Across the*

Give four examples of monosyllables on these pages.

north side of the grass is the monument to F D
Roosevelt. **2** a very old building, castle or bridge
which is regarded as an important part of a
country's history. EG ...an ancient monument.

monumental /mɒnjə'mentə⁰l/. **1** A **monumental**   ADJ CLASSIF:
building or sculpture is very large and historically   ATTRIB
or artistically important. EG ...the monumental facade of the Royal School.

2 A **monumental** book or musical work is very   ADJ CLASSIF:
impressive and likely to be important for a long   USU ATTRIB
time. EG ...Wedderburn's monumental work, 'The
Worker and the Law'.

3 You can also use **monumental** to describe   ADJ CLASSIF:
something that you think is very extreme. EG That   USU ATTRIB
night there was a monumental hailstorm... It was a
case of monumental bad manners.

moo /muː/, **moos, mooing, mooed.** If a cow **moos,**   v
it makes the noise that cows typically make.
▶ used as a noun. EG The cow gave a low moo.   ▶ N COUNT

mooch /muːtʃ/, **mooches, mooching, mooched.**   v+A
If you **mooch** about, you walk about slowly with no   Informal
particular purpose. EG He mooched about the house
in his pyjamas... Jack and I, hands in pockets,
mooched silently up the lane.

mood /muːd/, **moods. 1** Your **mood** is the way you   N COUNT
are feeling about things at a particular time, especially how cheerful or how angry you are. EG He
was always in a good mood... She was in one of her
bad moods... I wasn't in the mood for helping.

2 If you are in a **mood,** you are angry and   N COUNT
impatient. EG When Chris was in one of his moods,
he was unpleasant to everyone.

3 The **mood** of a group of people is the way that   N SING:
they think and feel about something. EG The debate   USU+SUPP
took place amid a mood of growing political despair... The mood of this week's meeting has been
one of cautious optimism.

moody /muːdiː/, **moodier, moodiest.** Someone
who is **moody 1** is depressed or unhappy, so that   ADJ QUALIT
they do not talk very much or are impatient with
other people. EG He's only moody because things
aren't working out at home. ◊ **moodily.** EG She   ◊ ADV
drank her coffee moodily. **2** often changes in their   ADJ QUALIT
feelings, for example from being cheerful to being
angry, within a short period of time. EG He was
generally moody and unpredictable.

moon /muːn/, **moons. 1** The **moon** is **1.1** the round   N SING: the+N
object in the sky that you can often see at night. EG
...television pictures of a man walking on the moon.
1.2 the particular shape or appearance of the   N SING
moon. EG The sky was a brilliant silver from the full
moon... ...a crescent moon.

2 A **moon** is an object like a small planet that   N COUNT
travels round a planet. EG ...Jupiter's four moons.

3 If you are **over the moon,** you are very pleased   PHRASE
about something. EG I was over the moon to get   Informal
your letter.

4 If you say that something happens **once in a**   PHRASE
blue moon, you mean that it happens very rarely.

moonbeam /muːnbiːm/, **moonbeams.** A **moon-**   N COUNT
beam is a ray of light from the moon.

moonless /muːnlɪ³s/. A **moonless** sky or night is   ADJ CLASSIF
dark because there is no moon in the sky.

moonlight /muːnlaɪt/, **moonlights, moonlight-**
ing, moonlighted. 1 Moonlight is the light that   N UNCOUNT
comes from the moon at night. EG The field looked
like water in the moonlight... Our meeting took
place by moonlight.

2 If you **moonlight,** you have a second job in   v
addition to your main job, often without informing   Informal
your main employers or the tax office. EG She
moonlighted as a waitress.

moonlit /muːnlɪt/. Something that is **moonlit** is lit   ADJ CLASSIF
up or made bright by moonlight. EG I've spent many
a moonlit night here.

moor /muə, mɔː/, **moors, mooring, moored. 1** A   N COUNT
moor is a high area of open and uncultivated land
that is covered mainly with grass and heather. EG

The mists had vanished from the moor... He used to
go for long walks on the moors.

2 If a boat **is moored,** it is attached to the land   v+o: USU PASS
with a rope. EG Boats were moored on both sides of
the river.

mooring /muərɪŋ, mɔː-/, **moorings.** A **mooring** is   N COUNT
the place on land where a boat can be tied. EG
During the storm, boats were torn from their
moorings.

moorland /muələ³nd, mɔː-/, **moorlands. Moor-**   N UNCOUNT
land is land which consists of moors. EG ...the   OR N PLURAL
beauty of Britain's moorlands.

moose /muːs/. **Moose** is both the singular and the   N COUNT
plural form. A **moose** is a large North American
deer that has very flat antlers.

mop /mɒp/, **mops, mopping, mopped. 1** A **mop**   N COUNT
is a tool for washing floors. It consists of a sponge
or a cluster of pieces of string attached to a long
handle.

2 If you **mop** a floor, you clean it with a mop.   v+o

3 If you **mop** a liquid from a surface or if you **mop**   v+o: OFT+A
the surface, you wipe the surface with a dry cloth
in order to remove the liquid. EG He mopped the
sweat from his face... Mop it with a tissue... He
mopped his sweating brow.

4 A **mop** of hair is a large amount of loose or   N PART
untidy hair. EG ...a coarse mop of black hair.

mop up. If you **mop up** a liquid, you wipe it with   PHRASAL VB:
a cloth or sponge so that the liquid is absorbed. EG   V+O+ADV
Mother started mopping up the oil.   OR V+ADV

mope /məup/, **mopes, moping, moped.** If you   v
mope, you feel miserable and are not interested in
anything. EG He just sits about, moping in an
armchair.

moped /məuped/, **mopeds.** A **moped** is a type of   N COUNT
small motorcycle.

moral /mɒrə⁰l/, **morals. 1 Morals** are principles   N PLURAL
and values based on what a person or society
believes are the right or acceptable ways of behaving. EG Business morals nowadays are very low...
Films like this are a danger to public morals.

2 Moral means concerned with whether people's   ADJ CLASSIF:
behaviour is right or acceptable. EG I'm in a moral   ATTRIB
dilemma... I have noticed a fall in moral standards... He feels responsible for her moral welfare.

3 Moral courage or duty is based on what you   ADJ CLASSIF:
believe is right or acceptable, rather than on what   ATTRIB
the law says should be done. EG He had that moral
courage which enables a man to stand alone... It is
our moral duty to stay.

4 Someone who is **moral** behaves in a way that   ADJ QUALIT
they know is right or acceptable.

5 If you give **moral support** to someone, you   PHRASE
encourage them in what they are doing by expressing approval and enthusiasm. EG I looked across to
give moral support to my colleagues.

6 The **moral** of a particular situation, story, or   N SING
event is what you learn from it about how you
should or should not behave. EG The moral is clear:
you must never marry for money.

morale /mɒraːl/ is the amount of confidence and   N UNCOUNT
optimism that you have in a difficult, dangerous, or
important situation. EG The morale of the men was
good... The past 15 months have destroyed morale.

moralise /mɒrəlaɪz/. See **moralize.**

moralist /mɒrəlɪst/, **moralists.** A **moralist** is   N COUNT
someone who has strong ideas about right and
wrong behaviour. EG My grandfather was a stern
moralist.

moralistic /mɒrəlɪstɪk/. If you are **moralistic,**   ADJ QUALIT
you make strong or harsh judgements about people
on the basis of your own beliefs about what is right;
used showing disapproval. EG She had rebuked
David for his moralistic attitude to his clients.

morality /mə'rælɪ³tiː/, **moralities. 1 Morality** is   N UNCOUNT
the idea that some behaviour is right and accept-
able and that other behaviour is wrong. EG ...the
decline in traditional morality.

2 A **morality** is a system of principles and values   N COUNT concerning people's behaviour, which is generally accepted by a society or by a particular group of people. EG *Conflicts must arise between the two moralities.*

3 When you talk about the **morality** of something, N UNCOUNT you are talking about how right or acceptable it is. EG *...arguments concerning the morality of taking part in a war.*

moralize /mɒrəlaɪz/, **moralizes, moralizing,** V : USU+A **moralized**; also spelled **moralise.** If someone **moralizes**, they tell people what they think is right or wrong, especially in a particular situation; used showing disapproval. EG *...moralizing about the dangers of drink.*

morally /mɒrəliˈ/. **1** You use **morally** when you ADV+ADJ are talking about whether people's behaviour is right or acceptable. EG *It is morally wrong not to do more to help the poor.*
2 If you behave **morally**, you behave in a way that ADV you believe is right or acceptable. EG *I try to live morally.*

morass /mɒræs/, **morasses.** If you describe a N COUNT : situation as a **morass**, you mean that it is extreme- USU SING+SUPP ly complicated and confused. EG *These men are usually bogged down in a morass of paperwork.*

moratorium /mɒrətɔːrɪəm/, **moratoriums.** A N COUNT : **moratorium** on a particular activity is the stop- OFT+*on* ping of it for a fixed period of time as a result of an Formal official agreement. EG *The meeting did agree to extend the moratorium on the building of new warships.*

morbid /mɔːbɪd/. If you say that someone or ADJ QUALIT something is **morbid**, you mean that they have too great an interest in unpleasant things, especially in death. EG *It's morbid to dwell on cemeteries and suchlike... ...morbid imaginations.*

more /mɔː/. **1 More** means a greater number or QUANTIF amount than before or than something else. EG *Do you spend more time teaching, or doing research?... Better management may enable one man to milk more cows... Most men still earn much more than their wives... He saw more than 800 children dying of starvation.*
2 If something happens **more, 2.1** it happens to a ADV : COMPAR greater extent. EG *The books that are true to life will attract them more.* **2.2** it continues to happen. EG *They talked a bit more... I apologized and thought no more about it... The employers don't want quality work any more.* ● If you do something ● PHRASE **once more** or **twice more**, you do it again once or twice. EG *She wanted to perform it once more before she died.*
3 More is also used to refer to an additional thing QUANTIF or amount of something. EG *In the next hour he found two more diamonds... Have some more coffee, Vicar... I wanted to find out more about her.*
4 You can use **more** in front of adjectives or SUBMOD adverbs to form comparatives. EG *Your child's health is more important than the doctor's feelings... Next time, I will choose more carefully.*
5 You use **more and more** to indicate that some- PHRASE thing is becoming greater in amount, extent, or degree all the time. EG *More and more people grew ill... They began to dance, slowly at first, then more and more quickly.*
6 If you say that something is **more** one thing **than** PHRASE another, you mean that it is like the first thing rather than the second. EG *He always seemed old to me, more like a grandfather than a father... They were more amused than concerned.*
7 If something is true **more or less**, it is true in a ADV SEN general way, but is not completely true. EG *Brian more or less implied that we were lying.*
8 If something is **more than** a particular thing, it PHRASE has greater value or importance than this thing. EG *It wasn't much more than a formality... This is more than a hunter's job... At the moment our tree looks like nothing more than a branch.*
9 You can also use **more than** to emphasize that PHRASE

something is true to a greater degree than is necessary or than is said. EG *You'll have more than enough money for any equipment you need... This was a more than generous arrangement.*

10 You use **what is more** to introduce an addition- ADV SEN al piece of information which supports or empha- sizes the point you are making. EG *What's more, he adds, there are no signs of a change.*

moreover /mɔːrəʊvə/ is used to introduce a piece ADV SEN of information or an opinion that adds to or sup- Formal ports the previous statement. EG *They have accused the Government of corruption. Moreover, they have named names.*

morgue /mɔːg/, **morgues.** A **morgue** is a build- N COUNT ing where dead bodies are kept before being cremated or buried. EG *...the city morgue.*

morning /mɔːnɪŋ/, **mornings.** **1** The **morning** is **1.1** the part of each day between the time that N COUNT OR people usually wake up and noon or lunchtime. EG N UNCOUNT *She left after breakfast on Saturday morning... I was reading the morning paper.* **1.2** the part of a N COUNT day between midnight and noon. EG *She died in the very early hours of this morning... It was five o'clock in the morning.*
2 If you say that something will happen **in the** PHRASE **morning**, you mean that it will happen during the morning of the following day. EG *You'll feel awful in the morning if you drink so much.*

morning sickness is a feeling of sickness that N UNCOUNT some women have in the morning in the first few months of pregnancy.

moron /mɔːrɒn/, **morons.** If you describe some- N COUNT one as a **moron**, you mean that they are very Informal stupid. EG *Louise is in love with that moron.*

moronic /məˈrɒnɪk/. If you say that someone is ADJ QUALIT **moronic**, you mean that they are very stupid. Informal

morose /mərəʊs/. Someone who is **morose** is ADJ QUALIT miserable, bad-tempered, and not willing to talk much to other people. EG *He was morose and silent.*
◊ **morosely.** EG *The man followed me morosely* ◊ ADV *round the museum.*

morphine /mɔːfiːn/ is a drug which is used to N UNCOUNT relieve pain.

morsel /mɔːsəl/, **morsels.** A **morsel** of some- N PART thing, especially food, is a very small piece or amount of it. EG *He had a morsel of food caught between one tooth and another.*

mortal /mɔːtəl/, **mortals.** **1** When you describe ADJ CLASSIF people as **mortal**, you are referring to the fact that they have to die and cannot live forever. EG *Remember that you are mortal... There was no mortal man who could hurt them now.*
2 You can refer to a **mortal** to emphasize that you N COUNT are talking about an ordinary person, rather than someone who has power or has achieved something. EG *He passed first time, something which we mortals couldn't manage.*
3 If someone receives a **mortal** wound or blow, ADJ CLASSIF they die as a result of it. ◊ **mortally.** EG *Blake was* ◊ ADV *mortally wounded.*
4 If two people are in **mortal** combat, they are ADJ CLASSIF : trying to kill each other. EG *They were locked in* ATTRIB *mortal combat.*
5 A **mortal** enemy or threat is extremely serious ADJ CLASSIF : and causes you to feel strong fear or hatred. EG ATTRIB *They regard the police as their mortal enemies... We are all in mortal danger.*

mortality /mɔːtælɪtiˈ/ is **1** the fact that all people N UNCOUNT must die. EG *...man contemplating his own mortal- ity.* **2** the number of people who die within a particular period of time or on a particular occa- sion. EG *Infant mortality on the island has been reported at 200 per 1,000 births.*

mortar /mɔːtə/, **mortars.** **1** A **mortar** is a short N COUNT cannon which fires missiles high into the air for a

What is your mother-tongue?

short distance. EG *We returned fire with mortars and machine-guns.*

2 Mortar is a mixture of sand, water, and cement, N UNCOUNT which is put between bricks to make them stay firmly together. EG *The new buildings were solid brick and mortar.*

mortgage /mɔ:gɪdʒ/, **mortgages, mortgaging, mortgaged. 1** A **mortgage** is a loan of money N COUNT which you get from a bank or building society in order to buy a house. EG *We can't get a mortgage... ...mortgage repayments.*

2 If you **mortgage** your house or land, you use it as V+O a guarantee to a company in order to borrow Technical money from them. EG *He will have to mortgage his land for a loan.*

mortify /mɔ:tɪfaɪ/, **mortifies, mortifying, mor-** V+O : USU PASS **tified.** If you **are mortified**, you feel very offended, ashamed, or embarrassed. EG *She was deeply mortified at this rebuff.* ◊ **mortifying.** EG *There* ◊ ADJ QUALIT *were some mortifying setbacks.* ◊ **mortification** ◊ N UNCOUNT /mɔ:tɪfɪkeɪʃəⁿn/. EG *Davie was hiding his head in his hands with mortification.*

mortuary /mɔ:tʃuəriⁱ/, **mortuaries.** A **mortu-** N COUNT **ary** is a special room in a hospital where dead bodies are kept before being buried or cremated.

mosaic /məʊzeɪɪk/, **mosaics.** A **mosaic** is a de- N COUNT OR sign made of small coloured pebbles or pieces of N UNCOUNT coloured glass set in concrete or plaster. EG *...a Roman mosaic... ...walls covered with mosaics.*

Moslem /mɒzləⁿm/. See **Muslim.**

mosque /mɒsk/, **mosques.** A **mosque** is a build- N COUNT ing where Muslims go to worship.

mosquito /məˈski:təʊ/, **mosquitoes** or **mosqui-** N COUNT **tos. Mosquitoes** are small insects which live in damp places and bite people in order to suck their blood. EG *...hands covered with mosquito bites.*

moss /mɒs/, **mosses. Moss** is a very small soft N MASS green plant which grows on damp soil, or on wood or stone. EG *The bark was covered with moss.*

mossy /mɒsiⁱ/, **mossier, mossiest.** Something ADJ QUALIT that is **mossy** is covered with moss. EG *...a flight of mossy stone steps... ...a long mossy path.*

most /məʊst/. **1 Most** of a group of things or QUANTIF people means nearly all of them, or the majority of them. **Most** of something means nearly all of it. EG *Most Arabic speakers understand Egyptian... I saw most of the early Shirley Temple films... He used to spend most of his time in the library.*

2 The **most** means **2.1** a larger amount than QUANTIF anyone or anything else. EG *This is the area that attracts the most attention.* **2.2** the largest amount that is possible. EG *The most I could learn was that Lithgow had been sacked.*

3 You can use **most** in front of adjectives or SUBMOD adverbs to form superlatives. EG *It was one of the most important discoveries ever made... These are the works I respond to most strongly.*

4 Most means to a greater degree or extent than ADV SUPERL anything else. EG *What he most feared was being left alone... I liked him the most... Which do you value most - wealth or health?*

5 You can use **most** to emphasize an adjective or SUBMOD adverb. For example, if you say that something is Formal **most** interesting, you mean that it is very interesting. EG *The trading results show a most encouraging trend... I would most certainly love a drink... He always acted most graciously.*

6 You use **at most** when stating the maximum PHRASE number that is possible or likely. EG *I only have fifteen minutes or twenty minutes at the most... There would be at most a hundred people listening.*

7 If you **make the most of** something, you get the PHRASE maximum use, help, or advantage from it. EG *Governments should face up to the situation and make the most of it.*

-most is used to form adjectives that describe SUFFIX something as being further in a particular direction than other things of the same kind. For example, the northernmost part of a country is the part that is furthest to the north. EG *...the southern-most tip of the island... ...the innermost room of the castle... ...the topmost branches of a tree.*

mostly /məʊstliⁱ/ is used to indicate that a state- ADV OR ment is generally true, for example true about the ADV SEN majority of a group of things or people, or true most of the time. EG *The men at the party were mostly fairly young... A rattlesnake hunts mostly at night... They were mostly women.*

MOT /em əʊ ti:/, **MOTs.** An **MOT** is a British test N COUNT which is made each year on all road vehicles that are more than 3 years old, in order to check that they are safe to drive. EG *Our ageing minibus failed its MOT.*

motel /məʊtel/, **motels.** A **motel** is a hotel intend- N COUNT ed for people who are travelling by car, which has space to park cars near the rooms.

moth /mɒθ/, **moths.** A **moth** is an insect like a N COUNT butterfly, which usually flies about at night.

mothball /mɒθbɔ:l/, **mothballs. Mothballs** are N COUNT small white balls made of a special chemical, which you can put amongst clothes or blankets in order to keep moths away.

moth-eaten. Clothes that are **moth-eaten** look ADJ QUALIT very old and ragged with holes in. EG *...moth-eaten sweaters and worn-out shoes.*

mother /mʌðə/, **mothers, mothering, moth-** **ered. 1** Your **mother** is the woman who gave birth N COUNT OR to you. EG *I always did everything my mother told* VOCATIVE *me... You are looking wonderful, Mother.*

2 If you **mother** someone, **2.1** you look after them V+O : USU PASS and bring them up, usually when you are their mother. EG *Female monkeys who were badly moth-ered became bad mothers themselves.* **2.2** you V+O treat them with great care and affection, and often spoil them. EG *Both the other senior typists tended to mother me.*

motherhood /mʌðəhʊd/ is the state of being a N UNCOUNT mother. EG *...girls preparing for motherhood.*

mother-in-law, mothers-in-law. Someone's N COUNT **mother-in-law** is the mother of their husband or wife.

motherless /mʌðələs/. If someone is **mother-** ADJ CLASSIF **less**, their mother has died, or has left them and gone away. EG *What a bad thing it is to leave a child motherless.*

motherly /mʌðəliⁱ/. A **motherly** person shows ADJ QUALIT warm, kind, and protective feelings like those of a mother. EG *...a plump, motherly woman... Motherly hands touched him lightly, lovingly.*

mother-of-pearl is the hard, smooth substance N UNCOUNT which forms a layer on the inside of the shells of some shellfish. It is often used to make buttons or to decorate things.

mother-to-be, mothers-to-be. A **mother-to-be** N COUNT is a woman who is pregnant, especially for the first time.

mother-tongue, mother-tongues. Your N COUNT **mother-tongue** is the language that you learnt from your parents when you were a child.

motif /məʊti:f/, **motifs.** A **motif** is a design which N COUNT : is used as a decoration. EG *There were white* USU+SUPP *curtains with black and red motifs on them.*

motion /məʊʃəⁿn/, **motions, motioning, mo-** **tioned. 1 Motion** is the process of continually N UNCOUNT changing position or moving from one place to another. EG *The bed swayed with the motion of the ship... Just keep moving, stay in motion.* ● See also **slow motion.**

2 A **motion** is an action, gesture, or movement. EG N COUNT : *He made stabbing motions with his spear... With a* USU+SUPP *quick motion of her hands, she did her hair up in a knot... He made chewing motions with his jaws.*

3 A **motion** in a meeting or debate is a formal N COUNT proposal which the people present discuss and then vote on. EG *He proposed the motion that 'the Public Schools of England should be abolished.'*

4 If you **motion** to someone, you make a move- V+to OR ment with your hand in order to show them what V+O+to

they should do. EG *He motioned Tom to follow him...*
He shook hands and motioned him to a seat.

5 If you **go through the motions,** **5.1** you say or do PHRASE
something that is expected of you, without being
very sincere or serious about it. EG *Major Hawks*
went through the motions of advising me to quit.
5.2 you pretend to do something by making the
movements associated with a particular action. EG
He laughed and went through the motions of
aiming a slow punch at my jaw.
6 A process or event that is **in motion** is happen- PHRASE
ing already. EG *The changes are already in motion...*
...helping to set the programmes in motion.

motionless /ˈməʊʃ°nlɪ°s/. Someone or something ADJ CLASSIF
that is **motionless** is not moving at all. EG *Rudolph*
sat motionless... ...queues of motionless cars.

motivate /ˈməʊtɪveɪt/, **motivates, motivating,**
motivated. **1** If you **are motivated** by something, V+O: USU PASS
especially an emotion, it causes you to behave in a
particular way. EG *...people motivated by envy and*
the lust for power... My decision to make this trip
was motivated by a desire to leave the country.
◊ **motivation** /ˌməʊtɪˈveɪʃ°n/, **motivations.** EG ◊ N COUNT OR
There's a political motivation for these actions... N UNCOUNT
What was the motivation to stay at school?
2 If you **motivate** someone, you make them feel V+O
determined to do something. EG *You have first got*
to motivate the children and then to teach them.
◊ **motivated.** EG *...highly motivated and enthusias-* ◊ ADJ QUALIT
tic people. ◊ **motivation.** EG *She insists her* ◊ N UNCOUNT
success is due to motivation rather than brilliance.

motive /ˈməʊtɪv/, **motives.** Your **motive** for do- N COUNT
ing something is your aim or purpose in doing it. EG
Was there some sinister motive for their action?... I
urge you to question his motives.

motley /ˈmɒtlɪ°/. A **motley** collection of people or ADJ QUALIT:
things is one in which the people or things are all ATTRIB
very different from each other. EG *...a motley*
collection of hats and coats.

motor /ˈməʊtə/, **motors, motoring, motored.** **1** A N COUNT
motor is a part of a machine or vehicle that uses
electricity or fuel to produce movement, so that
the machine or vehicle can work. EG *He got into the*
car and started the motor... ...an electric motor.
2 Motor means relating to vehicles with a petrol ADJ CLASSIF:
engine or diesel engine. EG *...the decline of the* ATTRIB
motor industry... ...a motor mechanic.
3 If you **are motoring** somewhere, you are travel- V: USU+A
ling there in a car. EG *They spent a week motoring* Outdated
through Italy. ● See also **motoring.**

motorbike /ˈməʊtəbaɪk/, **motorbikes.** A **motor-** N COUNT
bike is the same as a motorcycle. EG *...youths riding* British
up and down on powerful motorbikes. Informal

motor car, motor cars. A **motor car** is the same N COUNT
as a car. Formal

motorcycle /ˈməʊtəsaɪk°l/, **motorcycles.** A N COUNT
motorcycle is a two-wheeled vehicle that has an
engine. EG *...cars and motorcycles for hire.*

motorcyclist /ˈməʊtəsaɪklɪst/, **motorcyclists.** A N COUNT
motorcyclist is a person who rides a motorcycle.
EG *...police motorcyclists.*

motoring /ˈməʊtə°rɪŋ/ means relating to cars and ADJ CLASSIF:
to driving. EG *...motoring offences.* ATTRIB

motorist /ˈməʊtə°rɪst/, **motorists.** A **motorist** is a N COUNT
person who drives a car.

motorized /ˈməʊtə°raɪzd/; also spelled **motor-** ADJ CLASSIF
ised. **Motorized** vehicles have engines. EG *...motor-*
ized transport.

motorway /ˈməʊtəweɪ/, **motorways.** A **motor-** N COUNT
way is a big road that has been specially built for British
fast travel over long distances.

mottled /ˈmɒt°ld/. Something that is **mottled** is ADJ QUALIT
covered with areas or spots of a different colour. EG
...a mottled camouflage jacket.

motto /ˈmɒtəʊ/, **mottoes** or **mottos.** A **motto** is a N COUNT
short sentence or phrase that expresses a rule for
good or sensible behaviour. EG *...the school motto,*
'To strive, to seek, to find.'

mould /məʊld/, **moulds, moulding, moulded;**
spelled **mold** in American English.
1 If you **mould** someone, you influence them over V+O
a long period of time so that their character
develops in a particular way. EG *...the desire to*
mould the child into a disciplined creature.
2 If you **mould** something, you create it or change V+O
it over a long period of time. EG *We have spent the* Formal
past year creating and moulding this industry...
Television plays a dominant role in moulding pub-
lic opinion.
3 If you **mould** a substance such as plastic or clay, V+O
you make it into a particular shape. EG *...clay*
moulded into pots.
4 A **mould** is a container that you use to make N COUNT
something into a particular shape. You pour a
liquid substance into the mould, and when the
substance becomes solid you take it out and it has
the same shape as the mould.
5 If a person fits into or is cast in a **mould** of a N COUNT:
particular kind, they are of a particular type, USU+SUPP
usually a common type. EG *He doesn't fit into the*
mould of the typical retired army officer... She
won't have the guts to break out of the mould and
move to another firm.
6 Mould is a soft grey, green, or blue substance N MASS
that sometimes forms on old food or on damp walls
or clothes. EG *...nasty green mould... Peanuts, when*
they go bad, produce a mould.

mouldy /ˈməʊldɪ°/; spelled **moldy** in American ADJ QUALIT
English. Something that is **mouldy** is covered with
mould. EG *...mouldy fruit.*

moult /məʊlt/, **moults, moulting, moulted;** V
spelled **molt** in American English. When an animal
or bird **moults,** it loses its fur, hair, or feathers so
that new fur, hair, or feathers can grow.

mound /maʊnd/, **mounds.** A **mound** is **1** a pile of N COUNT
earth which is like a very small hill. EG *...a large*
circular mound of earth... ...a few grass mounds. **2** N PART
a large and rather untidy pile of things. EG *He lay in*
his bunk under a mound of blankets... ...mounds of
tasteless rice.

mount /maʊnt/, **mounts, mounting, mounted.** **1** V+O
If you **mount** a campaign or a particular course of
action, you prepare it and carry it out. EG *We*
mounted a sustained attack on the government...
No rescue operations could be mounted.
2 If you **mount** an exhibition or display, you V+O
organize and present it. EG *We mounted an exhibi-*
tion of recent books.
3 If something **is mounting,** it is increasing. EG V
Social problems in modern society are mounting...
The temperature mounted rapidly. ◊ **mounting.** ◊ ADJ CLASSIF:
EG *Everywhere there is mounting unemployment.* ATTRIB
4 If you **mount** something such as a staircase or a V+O
platform, you go up to the top of it. EG *Walter* Formal
mounted the steps and pressed the bell.
5 When someone **mounts** a horse, they climb on to V+O OR V
its back so that they can ride it. EG *The brothers*
watched as she mounted the mare. ● See also
mounted.
6 If you **mount** an object in a particular place, you V+O: USU+A
fix it there firmly. EG *The sword was mounted in a*
mahogany case.
7 Mount is used as part of the name of a mountain.
EG *...Mount Erebus.*
8 If you **mount a guard** over something, you get PHRASE
someone to guard it. If you **mount guard** over
something, you guard it yourself. EG *Strong police*
guards were mounted at all hospitals... She had
been asked to mount guard over a number of dogs.

mount up. If something **mounts up,** it increases. PHRASAL VB:
EG *The soil becomes more and more acidic as* V+ADV
pollution mounts up.

Should you eat mousse if it is mouldy?

mountain /ˈmaʊntɪn/, **mountains**. 1 A **mountain** N COUNT
is a very high piece of land with steep sides which
are difficult to climb. EG ...*a pleasant hotel in the
mountains... ...a mountain road... ...the Rocky
Mountains.*

2 You can refer to a very large amount of some- N PART
thing as a **mountain** of it. EG ...*a mountain of
rubble... ...mountains of letters and memoranda.*

3 to **make a mountain out of a molehill**: see
molehill.

mountaineer /ˌmaʊntɪˈnɪə/, **mountaineers**. A N COUNT
mountaineer is a person who climbs mountains.

mountaineering /ˌmaʊntɪˈnɪərɪŋ/ is the activity N UNCOUNT
of climbing mountains as a hobby or sport.

mountainous /ˈmaʊntɪnəs/. 1 A **mountainous** ADJ QUALIT
area has a lot of mountains. EG *I was walking
through mountainous country.*

2 A **mountainous** thing or person is unusually ADJ CLASSIF :
large or high. EG ...*ranks of mountainous females.* ATTRIB

mountainside /ˈmaʊntɪnsaɪd/, **mountainsides**. A N COUNT
mountainside is one of the steep sides of a
mountain. EG ...*hurtling down the mountainside.*

mounted /ˈmaʊntɪ²d/. **Mounted** police or soldiers ADJ CLASSIF :
ride horses when they are on duty. ATTRIB

mourn /mɔːn/, **mourns**, **mourning**, **mourned**. 1 V+O OR V+for
If you **mourn** someone who has died or **mourn** for
them, you are very sad and think about them a lot.
EG *I remained to mourn him in Chicago... I shall
always love Guy and mourn for him.* ● See also
mourning.

2 If you **mourn** something or **mourn** for it, you are V+O OR V+for
very sad because you no longer have it. EG *I
mourned for the loss of my beauty.*

mourner /ˈmɔːnə/, **mourners**. A **mourner** is a N COUNT
person who attends a funeral. EG *I went out into the
garden to join the mourners.*

mournful /ˈmɔːnfʊl/. 1 If you are **mournful**, you ADJ QUALIT
are very sad. EG *Jefferson looked mournful... He* Literary
addressed Thomas in a mournful voice.

◊ **mournfully**. EG *He shook his head mournfully.* ◊ ADV

2 A **mournful** sound seems very sad. EG *The little* ADJ QUALIT
train kept up its mournful howl. Literary

mourning /ˈmɔːnɪŋ/. 1 **Mourning** is behaviour in N UNCOUNT
which you show sadness about a person's death. EG
Beards were shaved off as a sign of mourning.

2 If you are **in mourning**, you are wearing special PHRASE
clothes or behaving in a special way because a
member of your family has died. EG *He was in
mourning for his wife.*

mouse /maʊs/, **mice** /maɪs/. A **mouse** is a very N COUNT
small furry animal with a long tail. EG *The cat was
there to keep the mice out of the kitchen.*

moussaka /muːˈsɑːkə/, **moussakas**. **Moussaka** is N MASS
a cooked dish consisting of layers of meat and
aubergines.

mousse /muːs/, **mousses**. **Mousse** is a sweet, N MASS
light food made from eggs and cream. EG ...*chocolate mousse.*

moustache /məˈstɑːʃ/, **moustaches**; spelled **mus-** N COUNT
tache /ˈmʌstæʃ/ in American English. A man's
moustache is the hair that grows on his upper lip.
EG ...*a tall man with a moustache.*

mousy /ˈmaʊsi¹/. **Mousy** hair is a dull, light brown ADJ QUALIT
colour.

mouth, **mouths**, **mouthing**, **mouthed**. The noun
is pronounced /maʊθ/ in the singular and /maʊðz/
in the plural. The verb is pronounced /maʊð/.

1 Your **mouth** is your lips, or the space behind N COUNT
your lips where your teeth and tongue are. You use
your mouth for eating and speaking. See picture at
THE HUMAN BODY. EG *She opened her mouth to say
something, then closed it... Mr Geard had his
mouth full of sponge cake.*

2 The **mouth** of a cave or hole is the entrance to it. N COUNT :
EG *There was a vicious snarling in the mouth of the* USU+of
shelter.

3 The **mouth** of a river is the place where it flows N COUNT :
into the sea. EG *We lived near the mouth of the* USU+of
Bashee River.

4 If you **mouth** something, you form words with V+O OR
your lips without making any sound. EG *She* V+QUOTE
mouthed the word no... Jane mouthed 'Water?'

5 **shut** your **mouth**: see **shut**. ● **by word of
mouth**: see **word**. ● See also **hand-to-mouth**,
loud-mouthed, **open-mouthed**, **mouth-watering**.

mouthful /ˈmaʊθfʊl/, **mouthfuls**. 1 A **mouthful** of N COUNT
food or drink is an amount that you put or have in OR N PART
your mouth. EG *He took another mouthful of whisky... 'Don't you like me?' she asked between mouthfuls.*

2 If you say that a name or phrase is a bit of a N COUNT
mouthful, you mean that it is long or difficult to Informal
say.

mouth organ, **mouth organs**. A **mouth organ** is N COUNT
a small musical instrument. You play it by moving
it across your lips and blowing and sucking air
through it.

mouthpiece /ˈmaʊθpiːs/, **mouthpieces**. 1 The N COUNT
mouthpiece of a telephone is the part that you
speak into. EG *She had her hand over the mouthpiece.*

2 The **mouthpiece** of something such as a musical N COUNT
instrument is the part that you put into your mouth.

3 The **mouthpiece** of a person or organization is N COUNT :
the person who publicly states their opinions and USU+SUPP
policies. EG *He became the official mouthpiece of
the leadership.*

mouthwash /ˈmaʊθwɒʃ/, **mouthwashes**. **Mouth-** N MASS
wash is a liquid that you rinse your mouth with, in
order to clean and freshen it.

mouth-watering. **Mouth-watering** food looks ADJ QUALIT
or smells extremely delicious. EG ...*mouth-watering
ingredients like raisins.*

movable /ˈmuːvəbəˀl/; also spelled **moveable**. ADJ CLASSIF
Something that is **movable** can be moved from
one place to another. EG *The room is divided by
movable screens.*

move /muːv/, **moves**, **moving**, **moved**. 1 When V-ERG
you **move** something or when it **moves**, its position changes or keeps changing. EG *Workmen were
moving a heavy wardrobe in a bedroom... I'll have
to move the car... The curtains behind began to
move.*

2 When you **move**, 2.1 you change your position or V : USU+A
go to a different place. EG *I was so scared I couldn't
move... He moved eagerly towards the door to
welcome his visitors... He could hear Felicity moving about upstairs.* ▸ used as a noun. EG *They had* ▸ N SING
*been watching his every move... For a good half
hour neither she nor any of the others made a
move.* 2.2 you act or begin to do something. EG *If* V
we are going to go ahead, let's move fast.

3 If you **move** or if you **move** house, you go and V : USU+A :
live in a different house, taking your possessions ALSO V+O
with you. EG *My parents moved from Hyde to
Stepney... They had decided to retire from farming
and move away.* ▸ used as a noun. EG *I wrecked a* ▸ N COUNT
good stereo on my last move. ◊ **moving**. EG ◊ N UNCOUNT
Moving costs have risen considerably.

4 If you **move** or **are moved** from one place or job V-ERG : OFT+A
to another, you go from one place or job to
another. EG *Executives are being moved around
from one company to another... He'd moved to the
BBC from publishing.* ▸ used as a noun. EG *Regular* ▸ N COUNT
moves for junior executives are a company policy.

5 If you are **on the move**, you are going from one PHRASE
place to another. EG *Billie Jean is constantly on the
move.*

6 If you **move** towards a particular state, activity V+A
or opinion, you start to be in that state, do that
activity, or have that opinion. EG *We are moving
rapidly into the nuclear age... Public opinion was
moving strongly in favour of disarmament.* ▸ used ▸ N COUNT
as a noun. EG *This was the first step in his move
away from the Labour party.*

7 If a situation **is moving**, it is developing or V
progressing. EG *Events now moved swiftly... A
writer must keep the story moving.*

8 If something **moves** you to do something, it   v+o+to-INF
influences you and causes you to do it. EG *What has*   Formal
moved the President to take this step?

9 If something **moves** you, it causes you to feel a   v+o
deep emotion, usually sadness or sympathy. EG *The*
whole incident had moved her profoundly.
◊ **moved.** EG *He was too moved to speak.*   ◊ ADJ QUALIT

10 If you **move** a motion or amendment at a   v+o
meeting, you formally propose it so that everyone
present can vote for or against it.

11 A **move** is also **11.1** an action that you take in   N COUNT
order to achieve something. EG *Accepting this job*
was a very good move... For six days neither side
made a move. **11.2** an act of putting a counter or
chess piece in a different position on the board
when it is your turn to do so in a game. EG *Whose*
move is it?

12 If you tell someone to **get a move on**, you are   PHRASE
telling them to hurry.   Informal

13 See also **moving**.

move down. If you **move down**, you go to a   PHRASAL VB:
lower level, grade, or class. EG *When they fail their*   V+ADV, USU+A
mathematics exams they move down a year.

move in. **1** If you **move in** somewhere, you begin   PHRASAL VB:
to live in a different house or place. EG *He moved in*   V+ADV
with Mrs Camish. **2** If soldiers or police **move in**,
they go towards a place or person in order to
attack them or deal with them. EG *They were under*
orders to move in from France.

move off. When vehicles or people **move off**,   PHRASAL VB:
they start moving away from a place. EG *The*   V+ADV
gleaming fleet of cars prepared to move off.

move on. When you **move on**, **1** you leave a   PHRASAL VB:
place and go somewhere else. EG *After three weeks*   V+ADV
in Hong Kong, we moved on to Japan. **2** you finish
one thing and start doing something else. EG *Can we*
move on to the second question?

move out. If you **move out**, you leave the house   PHRASAL VB:
or place where you have been living, and go and   V+ADV
live somewhere else.

move up. If you **move up**, you go to a higher   PHRASAL VB:
level, grade, or class. EG *The Vice-President should*   V+ADV/PREP
move up into the Presidency... ...moving up the
scale.

moveable /muːvəbə⁰l/. See **movable**.

movement /muːvmə²nt/, **movements**. **1** Move-   N UNCOUNT
ment involves **1.1** changing position or going from   OR N COUNT
one place to another. EG *He heard movement in the*
hut... ...the soft movement of the flags... Tom lit a
cigarette with quick, jerky movements. **1.2** transporting goods from one place to another. EG *...the*
movement of oil cargoes. **1.3** a gradual development or change in an attitude, opinion, or policy. EG
...the party's general leftward movement... There
was a movement towards a revival of conscription.

2 Your **movements** are everything which you do   N PLURAL
or plan to do during a period of time. EG *I don't*
know why you have any interest in my movements.

3 A **movement** is also a group of people who share   N COUNT:
the same beliefs, ideas, or aims. EG *...the Trade*   USU+SUPP
Union Movement... ...the successful movement to
abolish child labour.

4 A **movement** of a piece of classical music is one   N COUNT
of its major sections. EG *There is an immensely*
long first movement.

movie /muːviˡ/, **movies**. **1** A **movie** is a cinema   N COUNT
film. EG *...a war movie... I went to a movie.*

2 The cinema is sometimes called the **movies**. EG   N PLURAL:
We decided to spend the afternoon at the movies...   the+N
...going to the movies.   American

moving /muːvɪŋ/. **1** Something that is **moving**   ADJ QUALIT
causes you to feel a deep emotion, usually sadness
or sympathy. EG *There is a moving account of his*
father's death. ◊ **movingly.** EG *Her childhood is*   ◊ ADV
movingly described.

2 A **moving** model or part of a machine is able to   ADJ CLASSIF:
move. EG *These devices have no moving parts.*   ATTRIB

3 See also **move**.

mow /məʊ/, **mows, mowing, mowed, mown**
/məʊn/. **Mowed** and **mown** are both used as the
past participle.

1 If you **mow** an area of grass, you cut it using a   v+o OR V
lawnmower. EG *Everyone was mowing their lawns.*

2 If you **mow** corn or wheat, you cut it.   v+o OR V

mow down. To **mow down** a large number of   PHRASAL VB:
people means to kill them all violently at one time.   V+O+ADV
EG *Several children had strayed onto an airport*
runway and been mown down by a jet.

mower /məʊə/, **mowers**. A **mower** is a machine   N COUNT
for cutting grass, corn, or wheat.

MP /ɛm piː/, **MPs**. An **MP** is a person who has   N COUNT
been elected to represent people in a country's
parliament. **MP** is an abbreviation for 'Member of
Parliament'. EG *...the MP for South East Bristol.*

mph is an abbreviation for 'miles per hour'. **mph** is
used after a number to indicate the speed of
something. EG *These cars are reasonably economi-*
cal at a steady 56 mph.

Mr /mɪstə/. **1 Mr** is used before a man's name
when you are speaking or referring to him. EG *...Mr*
Jenkins... ...Mr John Watson.

2 Mr is sometimes used before words like 'president' and 'chairman' when you are addressing the
person who holds that position. EG *Yes, Mr Presi-*
dent.

Mrs /mɪsɪz/ is used before the name of a married
woman when you are speaking or referring to her.
EG *...Mrs Carstairs.*

Ms /məz/ is used before a woman's name when
you are speaking or referring to her, especially in
written English. If you use **Ms**, you are not specifying whether the woman is married or not.

M.Sc. /ɛm ɛs siː/, **M.Scs.** An **M.Sc.** is a higher   N COUNT
degree in a scientific subject. **M.Sc.** is an abbreviation for 'Master of Science'.

much /mʌtʃ/. For paragraphs 1, 2, and 4, the
comparative is **more** and the superlative is **most**.
See separate entries for **more** and **most**.

1 You use **much** to emphasize that something is   ADV
true to a great extent. EG *Myra and I are looking*
forward very much to the party... He is very much
at ease in life... In Vienna, the travellers stopped
for a much-needed rest... Now I feel much more
confident.

2 If something does not happen **much**, it does not   ADV
happen very often. EG *She doesn't talk about them*
much.

3 If one thing is **much** the same as another thing, it   ADV
is very similar to it. EG *The landscape was then*
much as it is today... The two poems convey much
the same emotional tone.

4 You also use **much** to refer to a large amount or   QUANTIF
proportion of something. EG *We hadn't got much*
money... Much of the recent trouble has come from
outside... There wasn't much to do... She had en-
dured so much.

5 You also use **much** when you ask questions or   QUANTIF
give information about the size of an amount. EG
How much money have you got left?... How much
did he tell you?... He's done as much as I have.

6 Much is also used in these phrases. **6.1** If you say   PHRASE
that something is **not so much** one thing as
another, you mean that it is more like the second
thing than the first. EG *It was not so much an*
argument as a monologue. **6.2** If you say **so much**   PHRASE
for a particular thing, you mean that it has not
been successful or helpful. EG *So much for the*
experts and their learning. **6.3** If you say that   CONJ
much as one thing is true, another thing is not
true, you mean that although the first thing is true,
the second thing is not true. EG *Much as she likes*
him she would never consider marrying him. **6.4**   PHRASE
Nothing much means an amount that is so small

How many abbreviations are there on these
pages?

that it is not important. EG *There's nothing much left.* **6.5** If a situation or action is **too much** for PHRASE you, it is so difficult, tiring, or upsetting that you cannot cope with it. EG *The long journey each day might prove too much for him.* **6.6** If you describe PHRASE something as **not much of a** particular type of thing, you mean that it is small or of poor quality. EG *It wasn't much of a garden.* **6.7** If you do not so PHRASE **much as** do a particular thing, you do not even do that, when you were expected to do more. EG *John strolled by without so much as a glance of recognition.* **6.8** You say **'I thought as much'** after you CONVENTION have just been told something that you had expected or guessed. **6.9 a bit much**: see **bit**. ● **not up to much**: see **up**.

muchness /mˈʌtʃnɪ²s/. If two or more things are PHRASE **much of a muchness**, they are very similar. EG *In* Informal *general appearance the men were all much of a muchness.*

muck /mʌk/, **mucks, mucking, mucked. Muck** N UNCOUNT is **1** dirt or some other unpleasant substance. EG Informal *There was muck everywhere.* **2** manure. EG *...a* Informal *muck heap.*

muck about or **muck around.** If you **muck** PHRASAL VB: **about** or **muck around**, you behave in a stupid V+ADV way and waste time. EG *She was mucking about* Informal *with a jug of flowers on the table.*

muck out. If you **muck out** a stable, pigsty, or PHRASAL VB: cow shed, you clean it. V+O+ADV

muck up. If you **muck** something **up**, you do it PHRASAL VB: very badly or fail when you try to do it. EG *'How was* V+O+ADV *the exam?' - 'I mucked it up.'* Informal

mucky /mˈʌki¹/. **1** Something that is **mucky** is ADJ QUALIT very dirty. EG *...mucky fields.* Informal **2** A **mucky** book or film describes or shows a lot of ADJ QUALIT sex; used showing disapproval. Informal

mucus /mˈjuːkəs/ is a liquid that is produced in N UNCOUNT some parts of your body, for example your nose. Formal

mud /mʌd/ is a wet, sticky mixture of earth and N UNCOUNT water. EG *She was covered in mud.*

muddle /mˈʌdəl/, **muddles, muddling, muddled.** **1** A **muddle** is a state of disorder or untidiness. EG N COUNT OR *With the right government, the country wouldn't* N UNCOUNT *be in such a muddle... ...the worsening muddle of her finances.* **2** If you **muddle** things, you cause them to become V+O mixed up or in the wrong order. EG *I wish you wouldn't muddle my books and drawings.* **3** If you **muddle** ·someone, you cause them to V+O become confused. EG *Don't muddle her with too many suggestions.* ◊ **muddled.** EG *I'm sorry. I* ◊ ADJ QUALIT *thought I had. I'm getting muddled.* **4** A **muddle** is also a state of confusion in the mind. N COUNT OR EG *I have got into a muddle.* N UNCOUNT

muddle along. If you **muddle along**, you live or PHRASAL VB: exist without a proper plan or purpose in your life. V+ADV EG *The church has lost its way, muddling along from Sunday to Sunday.*

muddle through. If you **muddle through**, you PHRASAL VB: manage to do something even though you do not V+ADV really know how to do it properly. EG *The children are left to muddle through on their own.*

muddle up. If you **muddle** things **up**, you cause PHRASAL VB: them to become mixed up or in the wrong order. EG V+O+ADV *Later they may muddle up your names with those of your cousins.* ◊ **muddled up.** EG *You've got the* ◊ ADJ QUALIT *story muddled up.*

muddy /mˈʌdi¹/, **muddier, muddiest; muddies, muddying, muddied. 1** Something that is **muddy** ADJ QUALIT contains mud or is covered in mud. EG *...a muddy ditch... ...the muddy floor.* **2** A **muddy** colour is dull and brownish. EG *The* ADJ QUALIT *landscape turns a mottled, muddy brown.* **3** If you **muddy** a situation or issue, you make it V+O less clear and less easy to understand. EG *The issue has been muddied by allegations of bribery.*

mudguard /mˈʌdgɑːd/, **mudguards. The mud-** N COUNT **guards** on a bicycle or other vehicle are the metal or plastic parts above the tyres, which prevent mud from the road from being splashed up onto the rider or the vehicle. EG *...a racing model with no mudguards and special tyres.* See picture at BICYCLE.

muesli /mˈjuːzli¹/ is a mixture of chopped nuts, N UNCOUNT dried fruit, and grains that you eat for breakfast with milk or yoghurt.

muffin /mˈʌfɪn/, **muffins.** A **muffin** is a kind of N COUNT small, round bread roll which you eat hot.

muffle /mˈʌfəl/, **muffles, muffling, muffled.** If V+O something **muffles** a sound, it makes the sound quieter and more difficult to hear. EG *The snow muffled the sound of our footsteps.*

muffled /mˈʌfəld/. **1** A **muffled** sound is quiet, ADJ QUALIT dull, or difficult to hear, rather than being clear and sharp. EG *'I don't know,' he said in a muffled voice... ...a muffled explosion.* **2** If you are **muffled** or **muffled up**, you are ADJ PRED wearing thick, warm clothes, and very little of your body or face can be seen. EG *He was heavily muffled in a black overcoat... ...a boy muffled up in a blue scarf.*

muffler /mˈʌflə/, **mufflers.** A **muffler** is a scarf. N COUNT EG *...with a long, knitted muffler around her neck.* Outdated

mug /mʌg/, **mugs, mugging, mugged. 1** A **mug** N COUNT is a large, deep cup with straight sides. EG *...a chipped mug.* **2** You can also use **mug** to refer to a mug and its N PART contents, or to the contents only. EG *He sipped at his mug of coffee.* **3** If someone **mugs** you, they attack you in order to V+O steal your money. EG *They lurk in dark side streets* Informal *and mug passers-by.* ◊ **mugging, muggings.** EG ◊ N UNCOUNT *There has been a great increase in vandalism and* OR N COUNT *muggings.* ◊ **mugger, muggers.** EG *Gangs of* ◊ N COUNT *teenage muggers roam the streets.* **4** If you say that someone is a **mug**, you mean that N COUNT they are stupid and easily deceived by other peo- Informal ple. EG *'All right,' he said, like the mug he was, 'I won't say anything.'*

muggy /mˈʌgi¹/. If the weather is **muggy**, it is ADJ QUALIT unpleasantly warm and damp. EG *...the muggy, perfumed air of West Africa.*

mule /mjuːl/, **mules.** A **mule** is an animal pro- N COUNT duced by a horse and a donkey.

mull /mʌl/, **mulls, mulling, mulled.** If you **mull** PHRASAL VB: something **over**, you think about it for a long time, V+O+ADV often before deciding what to do. EG *I sat there and tried to mull things over in my mind.*

multi- means 'many'. It is added to the beginning PREFIX of nouns and adjectives. EG *...multilateral... ... multi-storey.*

multifarious /mˌʌltɪfˈɛəri¹əs/. **Multifarious** things ADJ CLASSIF are of many different kinds. EG *...pursuing their* Formal *multifarious hobbies and interests.*

multilateral /mˌʌltɪlˈætərəl/. Something that is ADJ CLASSIF **multilateral** involves at least three different countries or groups of people. EG *...multilateral nuclear disarmament.*

multinational /mˌʌltɪnˈæʃənəl/, **multinationals. 1** A **multinational** company has branches in many ADJ CLASSIF different countries. EG *Many of the West's large multinational companies have operations in Africa.* ▸ used as a noun. EG *Trade in bananas is dominated* ▸ N COUNT *by three huge food multinationals.* **2** You use **multinational** to describe something ADJ CLASSIF that involves several different countries. EG *...the multinational forces deployed under the treaty.*

multiple /mˈʌltɪpəl/. You use **multiple** to de- ADJ CLASSIF: scribe things that consist of many parts, involve ATTRIB many people, or have many uses. EG *There have been several multiple collisions in fog this winter... ...multiple locks on the doors.*

multiple-choice. When you do a **multiple-** ADJ CLASSIF **choice** test or question, you have to choose the correct answer from several possible answers that are listed on the question paper.

multiple sclerosis /mʌltɪpəl sklərəʊsɪs/ is a N UNCOUNT serious disease of the nervous system, which affects your ability to move.

multiplication /mʌltɪplɪkeɪʃən/. 1 **Multiplica-** N UNCOUNT **tion** is the process of calculating the total of one number multiplied by another number. EG ...*multiplication and division.*

2 The **multiplication** of things of a particular kind N UNCOUNT is a large increase in the number or amount of +SUPP them. EG ...*the multiplication of universities.*

multiplication sign, multiplication signs. A N COUNT **multiplication sign** is the sign (x) which is put between two numbers to show that they are being multiplied.

multiplicity /mʌltɪplɪsɪti/. A **multiplicity** of N SING+of things is a large number or a large variety of them. Formal EG ...*the multiplicity of languages spoken in Africa.*

multiply /mʌltɪplaɪ/, **multiplies, multiplying, multiplied. 1** When something **multiplies** or is V-ERG **multiplied**, it increases greatly in number or amount. EG *The shops began to multiply, eventually springing up in almost every town in the area.*

2 When animals **multiply**, they increase in num- v ber by giving birth to large numbers of young. EG *The creatures began to multiply very rapidly.*

3 If you **multiply** one number by another, you V+O:OFT+by calculate the total which you get when you add the number to itself a particular number of times. For example, 2 multiplied by 3 is equal to 2 plus 2 plus 2, which equals 6. EG *Multiply this figure by the number of years you have worked.*

multitude /mʌltɪtjuːd/, **multitudes.** A **multitude** N PART OR of things or people is a very large number of them. N COUNT EG *It didn't work out quite like I intended it to, for a* Formal *multitude of reasons... 'We are keeping our options open,' he had told the assembled multitude.*

mum /mʌm/, **mums. 1** Your **mum** is your moth- N COUNT OR er. EG *My mum used to live here... I've been put in* VOCATIVE *the special class, Mum.* Informal

2 If you **keep mum** about something, you don't tell PHRASE anyone about it. Informal

mumble /mʌmbəl/, **mumbles, mumbling,** V OR V-SPEECH : **mumbled.** If you **mumble**, you speak very quietly ONLY that and indistinctly so that the words are difficult to understand. EG *Stop mumbling, for goodness sake... He took my hand and mumbled, 'Don't worry.'... I mumbled something about having an appointment.*

mummified /mʌmɪfaɪd/. A **mummified** dead ADJ CLASSIF body has stayed preserved for a long time, especially because special oils were rubbed into it.

mummy /mʌmi/, **mummies. 1 Mummy** means N COUNT OR mother; used especially by children. EG *Mummy put* VOCATIVE *me on the train at Victoria.* Informal

2 A **mummy** is a dead body which was preserved N COUNT long ago by being rubbed with special oils and wrapped in cloth. EG ...*a gilded Egyptian mummy case.*

mumps /mʌmps/ is a disease that causes a painful N UNCOUNT swelling of the glands in the neck.

munch /mʌntʃ/, **munches, munching,** V+O OR V **munched.** If you **munch** something, you chew it steadily and thoroughly. EG *The father and son sat there, munching bread and butter.*

mundane /mʌndeɪn/. Something that is **mun-** ADJ QUALIT **dane** is very ordinary, and not interesting or unusual. EG ...*mundane tasks such as washing up.*

municipal /mjuːnɪsɪpəl/ means associated with ADJ CLASSIF : or belonging to a city or town which has its own ATTRIB local government. EG ...*a big municipal housing scheme... ...the municipal gardens.*

munificent /mjuːnɪfɪsənt/. Someone who is **mu-** ADJ QUALIT **nificent** is very generous. Formal

munitions /mjuːnɪʃənz/ are bombs, guns, and N PLURAL other military supplies. EG ...*munitions factories.*

mural /mjʊərəl/, **murals.** A **mural** is a picture N COUNT which is painted on the wall of a room or building.

murder /mɜːdə/, **murders, murdering, mur-** **dered. 1 Murder** is the deliberate and unlawful N UNCOUNT OR N COUNT

killing of a person. EG ...*attempted murder... ...the rising number of murders in San Francisco.*

2 To **murder** someone means to kill them deliber- V+O OR V ately and unlawfully. EG *His father, mother, and sister were all murdered by the terrorists.*

◊ **murderer, murderers.** EG *I want to track down* ◊ N COUNT *the murderers of my son.*

3 If you say that someone **gets away with mur-** PHRASE **der**, you mean that they do whatever they like and Informal nobody punishes them.

murderous /mɜːdərəs/. 1 Someone who is **mur-** ADJ CLASSIF **derous** is likely to murder someone or wants to murder someone. EG ...*murderous savages... The girl might have murderous tendencies.*

2 A **murderous** attack or other action results in ADJ CLASSIF the death of many people. EG ...*murderous guerrilla raids.*

murk /mɜːk/. You can refer to the darkness or the N SING : the+N thick mist somewhere as the **murk**. EG *Through the murk the dull red sun was visible.*

murky /mɜːki/. 1 Places that are **murky** are ADJ QUALIT dark and rather unpleasant. EG *We looked out into the murky streets.*

2 Water that is **murky** is dark in colour and has a ADJ QUALIT lot of mud or leaves in it. EG ...*murky ponds.*

3 You also use **murky** to describe something that ADJ QUALIT you suspect is dishonest or morally wrong. EG Literary ...*murky goings-on in a local picture gallery.*

murmur /mɜːmə/, **murmurs, murmuring, murmured. 1** If you **murmur** or if you **murmur** V, V+O, something, you say it very quietly. EG *'Darling,' she* OR V+QUOTE *murmured... 'I suggest we climb Ben Nevis tomorrow.' They murmured agreement.*

2 A **murmur** is 2.1 something that someone says N COUNT which can hardly be heard. EG *There were murmurs of sympathy.* 2.2 a continuous, quiet, indis- N SING+SUPP tinct sound. EG ...*the murmur of waves on a beach.*

muscle /mʌsəl/, **muscles, muscling, muscled. 1** A **muscle** is a piece of flesh inside your body N COUNT OR which is able to become smaller and to get bigger N UNCOUNT again. Your muscles enable you to make movements. EG *The boys couldn't help admiring their bulging muscles.*

2 If someone has **muscle**, they have power, which N UNCOUNT enables them to do something difficult. EG *The* Informal *campaign was valueless without the muscle of an organisation behind it.*

muscle in. If you **muscle in** on something or PHRASAL VB : **muscle** your way in, you force your way into a V+ADV+on situation when you have no right to and when you OR V+O+ADV are not welcome. EG *They are jealous of your success and resent the way you are muscling in on their territory.*

muscular /mʌskjələ/. 1 **Muscular** means involv- ADJ CLASSIF : ing or affecting your muscles. EG *Great muscular* ATTRIB *effort is needed... ...muscular pains.*

2 Someone who is **muscular** has strong, firm ADJ QUALIT muscles. EG ...*a short but muscular man of 35... ...his muscular arms.*

muscular dystrophy /mʌskjələ dɪstrɒfi/ is a N UNCOUNT serious disease in which your muscles become gradually weaker.

muse /mjuːz/, **muses, musing, mused. 1** If you V : USU+A, **muse**, you think about something slowly or without OR V+QUOTE a serious purpose. EG *She lay musing for a while... 'I* Literary *can't see him as a family man,' she mused.*

2 A **muse** is an imaginary force which is believed N COUNT to give people inspiration and creative ideas, espe- Formal cially for poetry or music. EG ...*the muse of music.*

museum /mjuːzɪəm/, **museums.** A **museum** is a N COUNT building where large numbers of interesting and valuable objects are kept and displayed to the public. EG ...*classical sculpture in the British Museum.*

Are all mummies mummified?

musical instruments

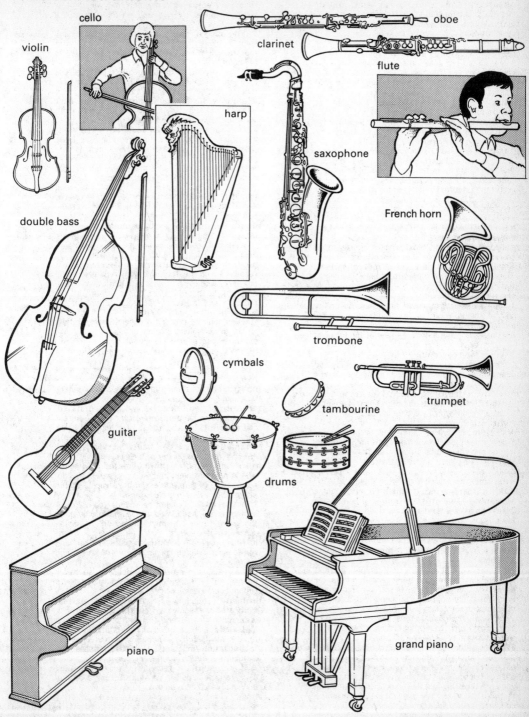

cello

oboe

violin

clarinet

flute

harp

saxophone

French horn

double bass

trombone

cymbals

trumpet

tambourine

guitar

drums

piano

grand piano

mush /mʌʃ/. If you refer to a substance as **mush**, N UNCOUNT
you mean that it is in the form of a thick soft paste. OR N SING
EG *He gulped down the tasteless mush.* Informal

mushroom /mʌʃruˈm/, **mushrooms, mush-**
rooming, mushroomed. 1 A **mushroom** is a N COUNT
fungus with a short stem and a round top. You can
eat mushrooms. EG *...a mushroom quiche.*

2 A **mushroom** cloud is a large cloud of dust which N MOD
rises into the sky after a nuclear explosion.

3 If something **mushrooms**, it grows or appears v
very quickly. EG *The organization quickly mush-*
roomed into a mass movement of the middle
classes... Factories mushroomed everywhere.

mushy /mʌʃiˈ/. **1** Vegetables and fruit that are ADJ QUALIT
mushy have become too soft.

2 Stories that are **mushy** are very sentimental; ADJ QUALIT
used showing disapproval. EG *The film is a mushy,*
but strangely moving story of young love.

music /mjuːzɪk/ is **1** sounds that are put together N UNCOUNT
in a pattern and performed by people who are
singing or playing instruments. EG *...dance music...*
...the music of Irving Berlin. **2** the art of creating or
performing music. EG *He plans to make his career*
in music... One of his granddaughters was having
her music lesson. **3** symbols written on paper
which represent musical sounds. EG *Not one of*
them could read a note of music... She placed the
music on the piano.

musical /mjuːzɪkəˈl/, **musicals. 1** You use **musi-** ADJ CLASSIF :
cal to describe things that are concerned with ATTRIB
playing or studying music. EG *...a musical career...*
...one of London's most important musical events.
◊ **musically.** EG *There is a lot going on musically* ◊ ADV
every night in London.

2 Someone who is **musical** has a natural ability ADJ QUALIT
and interest in music. EG *He came from a musical*
family.

3 Sounds that are **musical** are tuneful and pleasant ADJ QUALIT
to hear. EG *A musical bell softly sounded some-*
where in the passageway.

4 A **musical** is a play or film that uses singing and N COUNT
dancing in the story. EG *She appeared in the*
musical 'Oklahoma'.

musical instrument, musical instruments. A N COUNT
musical instrument is an object such as a piano,
guitar, or violin which you play in order to produce
music.

musician /mjuːzɪʃəˈn/, **musicians.** A **musician** is N COUNT
a person who plays a musical instrument as their
job, or plays it well as a hobby. EG *The musicians*
began packing their instruments away.

musk /mʌsk/ is a substance which has a strong, N UNCOUNT
sweet smell and is used to make perfume.

Muslim /muzlɪm, mʌz-/, **Muslims;** also spelled N COUNT
Moslem. A **Muslim** is a person who believes in
Islam and lives according to its rules. EG *...a pious*
Muslim on his way to Mecca. ▸ used as an ▸ ADJ CLASSIF
adjective. EG *...the medieval Muslim philosophers.*

muslin /mʌzlɪn/ is a very thin cotton material. N UNCOUNT

mussel /mʌsəˈl/, **mussels.** A **mussel** is a kind of N COUNT
shellfish.

must /mʌst/. **1** If you say that something **must** MODAL
happen, you mean that it is very important or
necessary that it happens. If you say that something **must** not happen, you mean that it is very
important or necessary that it does not happen. EG
Your family and children must always come first...
You must learn to remain calm... You mustn't
worry about me... Things must change.

2 If you say that you **must** do something, you mean MODAL
that you want to do it and intend to do it fairly soon. Informal
EG *I must come over and see you when he's away.*

3 If you tell someone that they **must** do something, MODAL
you are suggesting that they should do it or inviting Informal
them to do it. EG *You must play at the ship's*
concert... You must come and visit me.

4 You ask why someone **must** do something when MODAL
you are angry or upset about it and do not under-

stand why they are doing it. EG *Why must she be so*
nasty to me?

5 You say **'if you must'** when you cannot stop CONVENTION
someone from doing something that you think is
wrong or stupid. EG *Write and ask them yourself if*
you must.

6 You say **'if you must know'** when telling CONVENTION
someone something that you did not really want
them to know. EG *If you must know, I'm going to*
help him look for an apartment.

7 If you say that something **must** be true, you MODAL
mean that it is very likely that it is true. If you say
that something **must** have happened, you mean
that it is very likely that it happened. EG *You must*
be very fond of her... You must be Florrie Brown...
We must have taken the wrong road.

8 If you say that something **must** be true or **must** MODAL
have happened in order for something else to be
possible, you mean that the second thing is only
possible if the first thing is true or has happened. EG
In order to qualify for Unemployment Benefit, you
must have paid at least 26 contributions.

9 If you say that something is a **must**, you mean N SING : a+N
that it is absolutely necessary. EG *Rubber gloves* Informal
are a must if your skin is sensitive to washing
powders.

mustaché /mʌstæʃ/. See **moustache.**

mustard /mʌstəd/ is a yellow or brown paste N UNCOUNT
which tastes hot and spicy and is usually eaten with
meat. EG *...hot dogs dripping with mustard.*

muster /mʌstə/, **musters, mustering, mus-**
tered. 1 If you **muster** something such as strength v+o
or energy, you use or gather as much as you can in ◊ ADJ CLASSIF
order to do something. EG *I hit him with all the*
force I could muster... The group cannot muster
sufficient working class support.

2 When soldiers **muster** or **are mustered**, they V-ERG
gather in one place in order to take action. EG *An*
enormous convoy mustered in the city.

mustn't /mʌsəˈnt/ is the usual spoken form of
'must not'.

must've /mʌstəˈv/ is a spoken form of 'must
have', when 'have' is an auxiliary verb.

musty /mʌstiˈ/. Something that is **musty** smells ADJ QUALIT
stale and damp. EG *...musty old books.*

mutate /mjuːteɪt/, **mutates, mutating, mutated.** V : OFT+*into*
If an animal or plant **mutates**, it develops different Technical
characteristics as the result of a change in its
genes. ◊ **mutated.** EG *...a mutated flu virus.*
◊ **mutation** /mjuːteɪʃəˈn/, **mutations.** EG *The rate* ◊ N COUNT OR
at which mutations occur is fairly regular. N UNCOUNT

mute /mjuːt/, **mutes, muting, muted. 1** Someone ADJ CLASSIF
who is **mute** is silent and does not speak. EG *Sally* Formal
was staring at him, mute and awestruck... Fanny
clasped her hands in mute protest.

2 If you **mute** a noise or sound, you make it v+o
quieter. EG *She had closed all the windows to mute* Formal
the sounds from the town. ◊ **muted.** EG *People* ◊ ADJ CLASSIF
spoke in muted voices.

muted /mjuːtɪˈd/. **1 Muted** colours are soft and ADJ CLASSIF
gentle. EG *...a muted colour scheme of cream and*
white.

2 If a reaction is **muted**, it is not very strong or ADJ QUALIT
intense. EG *On the whole, criticism was muted...*
...muted enthusiasm. ● See also **mute.**

mutilate /mjuːtɪleɪt/, **mutilates, mutilating,**
mutilated. 1 If someone **is mutilated**, their body v+o : USU PASS
is damaged very severely. EG *Both bodies had been*
mutilated... They tortured and mutilated their vic-
tims. ◊ **mutilated.** EG *...photos of mutilated bodies.* ◊ ADJ CLASSIF
◊ **mutilation** /mjuːtɪleɪʃəˈn/, **mutilations.** EG *...the* ◊ N COUNT OR
death or mutilation of innocent men and women. N UNCOUNT

2 If you **mutilate** something, you deliberately v+o : USU PASS
damage it and spoil it. EG *Almost every book had*
been mutilated in some way.

If criticism is muted, is it mute?

mutinous /mjuːtɪnəs/. A person who is **mutinous** ADJ CLASSIF
is likely to disobey or rebel against the people in Formal
authority. EG *The crew were restive and mutinous.*

mutiny /mjuːtɪniʲ/, **mutinies, mutinying, muti-** N COUNT OR
nied. A **mutiny** is a rebellion by a group of people N UNCOUNT
against a person in authority. EG *It's like a slave
ship after a successful mutiny... Mutiny can lead to
riot.* ▸ used as a verb. EG *He shot himself when his* ▸ V
regiment mutinied.

mutter /mʌtə/, **mutters, muttering, muttered.** V : OFT + to;
If you **mutter**, you speak very quietly so that you ALSO
cannot easily be heard, often in a cross or unfriend- V-SPEECH :
ly way. EG *Denis could be heard muttering to* ONLY that
*himself about my stupidity... He refused her invita-
tion with a muttered excuse... 'Sorry,' he muttered.*
▸ used as a noun. EG *...a quick low mutter.* ▸ N COUNT

mutton /mʌtən/. **1 Mutton** is meat from an adult N UNCOUNT
sheep. EG *...a leg of mutton.*
2 If you describe a woman as **mutton dressed as** PHRASE
lamb, you mean that she is trying to look younger Informal
than she really is.

mutual /mjuːtʃuʲəl/. You use **mutual 1** to de- ADJ CLASSIF :
scribe something that two or more people do to USU ATTRIB
each other or for each other, or a feeling that they
have towards each other. EG *They are in danger of
mutual destruction... I didn't like him and I was
sure the feeling was mutual.* **2** to describe something which two or more people share. EG *They had
discovered a mutual interest in rugby football... He
sent a mutual friend to ask me to reconsider my
decision.*

mutually /mjuːtʃuʲəliʲ/. **1** You use **mutually** when ADV + ADJ
describing a situation in which two or more people
feel the same way about each other. EG *He enjoyed
a mutually respectful relationship with them.*
2 If two things are **mutually exclusive** or **mutu-** PHRASE
ally contradictory, they cannot both be true or
both exist somewhere at the same time. EG *The
principles on which it is based are mutually contradictory.*

muzzle /mʌzəl/, **muzzles, muzzling, muzzled. 1** N COUNT
The **muzzle** of an animal such as a dog or a wolf is
its nose and mouth.
2 A **muzzle** is a wire cover or a strap that is put N COUNT
over a dog's nose and mouth so that it cannot bite
people or bark.
3 If you **muzzle** a dog, you put a muzzle over its V + O
nose and mouth.
4 The **muzzle** of a gun is the open end where the N COUNT
bullets come out when it is fired.

muzzy /mʌziʲ/. Someone who feels **muzzy** is ADJ QUALIT
unable to think clearly, because they are ill or have
drunk a lot of alcohol.

my /maɪ/. **1** A speaker or writer uses **my** to DET POSS
indicate that something belongs or relates to himself or herself. EG *My name is Alan Jones... I closed
my eyes... My mother died in 1945.*
2 You use **my** in some titles when you are talking
to someone with that title. EG *I can, my Lord.*

myopic /maɪɒpɪk/. Someone who is **myopic** is ADJ CLASSIF
unable to see things which are far away from Formal
them. EG *She thinks Dolly is myopic and should see
a good optician.*

myriad /mɪriʲəd/, **myriads.** A **myriad** of people N PART
or things is a very large number of them. EG *...a* Literary
*myriad of political action groups... ...myriads of
tiny yellow flowers.* ▸ used as an adjective. EG ▸ ADJ CLASSIF
*...myriad pots of paint... ...embroidered with a myri-
ad pearls.*

myself /maɪself/. A speaker or writer uses **my-** PRON REFL :
self 1 as the object of a verb or preposition in a SING
clause where 'I' is the subject or 'me' is a previous
object. EG *If you do not help me, I will kill myself... I
was thoroughly ashamed of myself... I poured myself a small drink.* **2** to emphasize the subject or
object of a clause. EG *I myself feel that Muriel*

*Spark is very underrated... I find it a[...]
myself... My first pupil today is a Pole like [...]*
in expressions such as 'I did it myself' in o[...]
say that he or she did something without any[...]
or interference from anyone else. EG *I dealt with[...]
myself.*

mysterious /mɪstɪəriʲəs/. **1** Something that is ADJ QUALIT.
mysterious is strange and is not known about or
understood. EG *Their grandson died of a mysterious
illness... ...mysterious black boxes covered with
wires.* ◊ **mysteriously.** EG *The American had* ◊ ADV
mysteriously disappeared.
2 If you are **mysterious** about something, you ADJ QUALIT
deliberately do not talk about it, especially when
you want people to be curious about it. EG *Stop
being so mysterious.* ◊ **mysteriously.** EG *They* ◊ ADV
smiled mysteriously and said nothing.

mystery /mɪstəriʲ/, **mysteries. 1** A **mystery** is N COUNT
something that is not understood or known about.
EG *These two deaths have remained a mystery...
...to probe the mysteries of the universe.*
2 If you talk about the **mystery** of someone or N UNCOUNT
something, you are talking about how difficult they +SUPP
are to understand or to know about. EG *The place
continues to fascinate visitors, cloaked in its mystery... ...the mystery of God.*
3 A **mystery** person or thing is one whose identity ADJ CLASSIF :
or nature is not known. EG *...the mystery voice... ...a* ATTRIB
mystery tour... ...a mystery package.

mystic /mɪstɪk/, **mystics. 1** A **mystic** is a reli- N COUNT
gious person who spends a lot of time praying and
meditating.
2 Mystic means the same as mystical. EG *...a* ADJ QUALIT :
performer in a mystic rite. ATTRIB

mystical /mɪstɪkəl/. Something that is **mystical** ADJ QUALIT :
involves spiritual powers and influences that most ATTRIB
people do not understand. EG *...religious and mystical experiences.*

mysticism /mɪstɪsɪzəm/ is religious belief which N UNCOUNT
cannot be explained very easily and is very profound and personal.

mystify /mɪstɪfaɪ/, **mystifies, mystifying, mys-** V + O
tified. If something **mystifies** you, you find it
impossible to explain or understand. EG *They say
that they are mystified by the decision.*
◊ **mystified.** EG *I felt a bit mystified.* ◊ ADJ QUALIT

mystique /mɪstiːk/ is an atmosphere of mystery N UNCOUNT
and importance or difficulty which is associated Formal
with a particular person or thing. EG *...the mystique
surrounding doctors.*

myth /mɪθ/, **myths.** A **myth** is **1** an untrue belief N COUNT
or explanation. EG *...myths about the causes of
cancer... ...the myth of love at first sight.* **2** a story N COUNT OR
which has been made up to explain how the world N UNCOUNT
began or to justify religious beliefs. EG *...Greek
myths... ...queens in history, legend, and myth.*

mythic /mɪθɪk/. Something that is **mythic** exists ADJ CLASSIF :
in a myth or is like something in a myth. EG *My* ATTRIB
husband has none of the attributes of a mythic Formal
lover.

mythical /mɪθɪkəl/. Something that is **mythical** ADJ CLASSIF :
1 is imaginary and only exists in myths. EG *...mythi-* USU ATTRIB
cal monsters. **2** is untrue or does not exist. EG *They
trekked out to the west coast in search of the
mythical opportunities there.*

mythology /mɪθɒlədʒiʲ/. **1 Mythology** refers to N UNCOUNT
stories that have been made up in the past to
explain how the world began or to justify religious
beliefs. EG *Prometheus in Greek mythology brought
fire to man.* ◊ **mythological.** EG *Jupiter was the* ◊ ADJ CLASSIF :
Roman mythological king of the heavens. ATTRIB
2 You can also use **mythology** to refer to beliefs N UNCOUNT
that a lot of people have about something which
are not true. EG *...the whole mythology of national
greatness.*

N n

N, n /ɛn/, Ns, n's. 1 N is the fourteenth letter of N COUNT
the English alphabet.
2 N is also a written abbreviation for 'north'.

N stands for **noun**
Words which are labelled N in the Extra Column
are nouns.
See the entry headed NOUNS for information about
them.

---

nadir /ˈneɪdɪə, næ-/. The **nadir** of something is its N SING : USU+
worst time. EG *The fortunes of Trotskyism reached* POSS
their nadir... The government was at the nadir of Literary
its unpopularity.

nag /næg/, **nags, nagging, nagged. 1** If someone v+o OR v
nags you, they keep complaining to you in an
irritating way. EG *He used to nag me endlessly*
about money... Daddy, you don't have to nag at me.
2 If a doubt or suspicion **nags** at you, you keep v+at
thinking and worrying about it. EG *Something that*
she had said had been nagging at him. ◊ **nagging.** ◊ ADJ
EG *I have a nagging suspicion that one of the wheels* CLASSIF :
is loose... She had a nagging sense of inadequacy. ATTRIB

nail /neɪl/, **nails, nailing, nailed. 1** A **nail** is a N COUNT
small piece of metal with a sharp end. You hit the
nail with a hammer in order to push it into
something. See picture at TOOLS. EG *...the mirror*
that hung from a nail on the wall. ● If you say that ● PHRASE
someone has **hit the nail on the head,** you mean
that what they have said is exactly right. ● **a nail**
in another thing's **coffin**: see **coffin.**
2 If you **nail** something somewhere, you attach it v+o+A
there using a nail or nails. EG *They nail plastic*
sheets over their windows... There were signs
nailed to the trees.
3 Your **nails** are the thin hard areas that cover the N COUNT
ends of your fingers and toes. EG *He keeps biting his*
nails... ...her long red nails.

nail down. If you **nail** something **down,** you fix it PHRASAL VB :
firmly to the floor with nails. V+O+ADV

nail up. If you **nail** something **up,** you fix it to a PHRASAL VB :
vertical surface using nails. EG *...the warning notice* V+O+ADV
that he had nailed up on the pole.

nail brush, nail brushes. A **nail brush** is a small N COUNT
brush that you use for cleaning your nails.

nail file, nail files. A **nail file** is a small strip of N COUNT
metal that you rub on the end of your nails to make
them smooth and give them a rounded shape.

nail polish is the same as nail varnish. N UNCOUNT

nail varnish is a thick liquid that women paint on N UNCOUNT
their nails.

naive /naɪˈiːv/; also spelled **naïve.** Someone who is ADJ QUALIT
naive believes that things are much less complicated or difficult than they really are. EG *You're*
surely not so naive as to think that this will change
anything. ◊ **naively.** EG *They naively assume that* ◊ ADV
things can only get better. ◊ **naivety** /naɪˈiːvətiˈ/; ◊ N UNCOUNT
also spelled **naïvety** or **naïveté.** EG *In this he*
showed political naivety.

naked /ˈneɪkɪd/. **1** Someone who is **naked** is not ADJ CLASSIF
wearing any clothes. EG *He was naked except for a*
pair of underpants... ...the men's naked bodies.
◊ **nakedness.** EG *They seized towels to hide their* ◊ N UNCOUNT
nakedness.
2 You describe objects as **naked** when they are not ADJ CLASSIF :
covered, especially when you would expect them ATTRIB
to be covered. EG *...naked light bulbs... Never look*
for a gas leak with a naked flame.
3 Naked emotions are easily noticed, because they ADJ CLASSIF :
ATTRIB

are strongly felt. EG *His face broke into an expres-*
sion of naked anxiety.
4 If someone shows **naked** aggression, hostility, or ADJ CLASSIF :
greed, they do not try to hide their aggressive, ATTRIB
hostile, or greedy behaviour. EG *The home employ-*
ment offered to housewives is naked exploitation...
...naked dictatorship.
5 If you can see something with the **naked** eye, you ADJ CLASSIF :
can see it without using a microscope, binoculars, ATTRIB
or a telescope. EG *...microscopic hairs, invisible to*
the naked eye.

name /neɪm/, **names, naming, named. 1** The N COUNT :
name of a person, thing, or place is the word or USU+POSS
group of words that you use to identify them. EG *His*
name is Richard Arnason.
2 If you **name** someone or something, **2.1** you give v+o+c
them a name. EG *She wanted to name the baby*
Colleen. **2.2** you identify them by saying their v+o OR v+o+
name. EG *...a Minister, whom he did not name...* as
...various flowers: roses, tulips and snapdragons, to
name only a few. ● See also **named.**
3 If you **name** someone or something after a v+o+after/
person or thing, you give them the same name as for
that person or thing. EG *The College in Holborn is*
named after her.
4 If you **name** something, for example a date for a v+o
meeting or the price of some goods, you say what
you want it to be. EG *He named a price he thought*
would scare me off.
5 You can refer to someone's reputation as their N COUNT
name. EG *Grey spoke out in public to clear*
Haldane's name... They were giving the country a
bad name.
6 You can say that someone is a **name** or a big N COUNT :
name when they have become famous. USU+SUPP
7 Name is also used in these phrases. **7.1** If you PHRASES
mention someone **by name,** you say their name
rather than referring to them in a more indirect
way. **7.2** You can use **by name** or **by the name of** Formal
when you are saying what someone is called. EG
...the grocer, Jackson by name... ...a Swedish engi-
neer by the name of George Scheutz. **7.3** If you
call someone **names,** you insult or offend them by
using unpleasant words to describe them. **7.4** Something that exists **in name only** does not have the
status or position that it is officially supposed to
have. EG *Many of these branches are inactive,*
existing in name only. **7.5** If something is registered or recorded **in** your **name,** it officially belongs to you or has been reserved for you. **7.6** If you
do something **in the name of** an ideal or a group
of people, you do it because you believe in the ideal
or represent the people. EG *The group claims to*
speak in the name of 'the simple people of the
country'. **7.7** If you **make a name for yourself,**
you do something very well and become well-
known and admired for it. EG *George Eliot had*
already made a name for herself as a writer.
8 See also **brand name, Christian name, maiden**
name.

named /neɪmd/. When you say what a person, ADJ PRED
thing, or place is **named,** you give their name. EG
...a lecturer named Harold Levy.

name-dropping is the habit of referring to fa- N UNCOUNT
mous people as though they were your friends, in
order to impress people. EG *There was a good deal*
of academic name-dropping.

nameless /ˈneɪmlɪs/. **1** You describe people and ADJ CLASSIF :
things as **nameless** when you do not know their ATTRIB
name or when they have not been given a name. EG
...the nameless ones who built the village... ...a new
and nameless disease.

2 If you say that someone or something will remain **nameless**, you mean that you will not say their name, because you do not want to cause embarrassment. EG *We spend half our time cleaning up after others, who shall be nameless... I remember one movie, which shall remain nameless, that was described as 'two hours of boredom'.*   ADJ PRED

3 A **nameless** emotion is one that you cannot describe or explain. EG *He felt a nameless terror and sensed that death was near.*   ADJ CLASSIF : ATTRIB · Literary

namely /neɪmli¹/. You use **namely** to introduce detailed information about what you have just said. EG *...three famous physicists, namely Simon, Kurte and Mendelsohn... He could not do anything more than what he had promised – namely, to look after Charlotte's estate.*   ADV SEN

namesake /neɪmseɪk/, **namesakes.** Your **namesake** is someone who has the same name as you. EG *Remember what happened to your namesake.*   N COUNT + POSS

nanny /næni¹/, **nannies.** A **nanny** is a woman who is paid by parents to look after their children.   N COUNT

nanny goat, nanny goats. A **nanny goat** is a female goat.   N COUNT

nap /næp/, **naps, napping, napped. 1** A **nap** is a short sleep that you have during the day. EG *It was time for her to take a nap.* ► used as a verb. EG *That afternoon while Wendy was napping, I went to the cellar.*   N COUNT ►V

2 If you **are caught napping**, something happens to you when you are not prepared for it.   PHRASE Informal

nape /neɪp/, **napes.** The **nape** of your neck is the back of it.   N COUNT : USU SING + of

napkin /næpkɪn/, **napkins.** A **napkin** is a small piece of cloth or paper that you use when you are eating to protect your clothes, or to wipe your mouth or hands.   N COUNT

nappy /næpi¹/, **nappies.** A **nappy** is a piece of soft thick cloth or paper which is fastened round a baby's bottom in order to soak up its urine and faeces. EG *I seem to spend all day changing nappies.*   N COUNT British

narcissus /nɑːsɪsəs/, **narcissi** /nɑːsɪsɪ⁵/. A **narcissus** is a yellow, white, or orange flower that looks like a daffodil. The plural form is either 'narcissus' or 'narcissi'.   N COUNT

narcotic /nɑːkɒtɪk/, **narcotics. Narcotics** are drugs which make you sleepy and unable to feel pain. Some people become addicted to narcotics.   N COUNT

narrate /nəreɪt/, **narrates, narrating, narrated.** If you **narrate** a story, you tell it. EG *He narrated this tale with great effect.* ◊ **narration** /nəreɪʃəⁿn/. EG *The richness of the novel comes from his narration.*   V+O   ◊ N UNCOUNT Formal

narrative /nærətɪv/, **narratives.** A **narrative** is a story or an account of events or experiences. EG *...the narrative of her battle against depression.*   N COUNT

narrator /nəreɪtə/, **narrators.** The **narrator** of a story is the person who is telling it.   N COUNT

narrow /nærəʊ/, **narrower, narrowest; narrows, narrowing, narrowed. 1** Something that is **narrow** has a very small distance from one side to the other. EG *We turned into a narrow lane... The stream became narrower.* ◊ **narrowness.** EG *...the narrowness of the tunnels.*   ADJ QUALIT   ◊ N UNCOUNT

2 If something **narrows**, it becomes less wide. EG *The river narrowed and curved sharply to the left.*   V

3 If you **narrow** your eyes or if they **narrow**, you almost close them. EG *'I want you back here in five minutes,' he growled, narrowing his eyes.*   V-ERG

4 If you describe someone's ideas, attitudes, or beliefs as **narrow**, you mean that they are concerned with only a few aspects of something and ignore the more important aspects. EG *I think you are taking too narrow a view.* ◊ **narrowness.** EG *He criticized the narrowness of the range of opinion represented.*   ADJ QUALIT   ◊ N UNCOUNT

5 If the difference between two things **narrows** or if the range of something **narrows**, it becomes smaller. EG *The gap between the rich and the poor*   V-ERG

is narrowing. ◊ **narrowing.** EG *...the narrowing of the individual's field of choice.*   ◊ N UNCOUNT + SUPP

6 If you have a **narrow** victory, you just succeed in winning. If you have a **narrow** defeat, someone just beats you. EG *It was a narrow victory, by only five votes.* ◊ **narrowly.** *The motion was narrowly defeated.*   ADJ QUALIT : ATTRIB   ◊ ADV

7 If you have a **narrow** escape, something very unpleasant nearly happens to you. EG *...narrow misses.* ◊ **narrowly.** EG *He narrowly escaped being run over.*   ADJ QUALIT : ATTRIB   ◊ ADV

narrow down. If you **narrow** something **down**, you reduce it to a small number of things. EG *They had narrowed the choice down to a dozen sites.*   PHRASAL VB : V+O+ADV

narrow-minded. If you say that someone is **narrow-minded**, you mean that they are unwilling to consider new ideas or other people's opinions. EG *How narrow-minded he had become... ...a narrow-minded approach to broadcasting.*   ADJ QUALIT

nasal /neɪzəⁿl/. **1** You produce **nasal** sounds when air passes through your nose as well as your mouth when you are speaking. EG *He spoke in a nasal voice... ...singing in a nasal tone.*   ADJ QUALIT

2 Nasal also means relating to your nose. EG *...the nasal passages... ...nasal discharge.*   ADJ CLASSIF : ATTRIB

nasturtium /nəstɜːʃəⁿm/, **nasturtiums.** A **nasturtium** is a brightly-coloured garden flower.   N COUNT

nasty /nɑːsti¹/, **nastier, nastiest. 1** Something that is **nasty** is very unpleasant to see, experience, or feel. EG *This place has a nasty smell... I got a nasty feeling that I was being followed.*   ADJ QUALIT : USU ATTRIB

2 You can also describe things as **nasty** when you think that they are unattractive or in bad taste. EG *It's a tacky, nasty little movie.*   ADJ QUALIT : USU ATTRIB

3 A **nasty** problem or question is a difficult and worrying one. EG *This presented a nasty problem to Mayor Lindsay.*   ADJ QUALIT : USU ATTRIB

4 You describe a disease or injury as **nasty** when it is serious or looks very unpleasant. EG *Rats carry very nasty diseases... A nasty bruise rose where the handbag had landed.*   ADJ QUALIT : USU ATTRIB

5 You describe someone's behaviour as **nasty** when they behave in an unkind and unpleasant way. EG *Why must she be so nasty to me?* ◊ **nastily.** EG *He was staring at them nastily.*   ADJ QUALIT : USU ATTRIB   ◊ ADV

nation /neɪʃəⁿn/, **nations. 1** A **nation** is a country, together with its social and political structures. EG *...a powerful nation... ...the great accomplishments of their nation.*   N COUNT

2 The people who live in a country are sometimes referred to as the **nation.** EG *He appealed to the nation for self-restraint... ...the whole British nation.*   N SING : the+N

national /næʃəⁿnəl, -ʃənⁿl/, **nationals. 1** National means relating to the whole of a country, rather than to part of it or to several countries. EG *It made the headlines in the national newspapers... ...special stamps to mark national and international events.* ◊ **nationally.** EG *Should housing policy be decided nationally or locally?*   ADJ CLASSIF : USU ATTRIB   ◊ ADV

2 National is also used to describe things that are typical of the people of a particular country. EG *Common sense is certainly a national characteristic... ...national dress.*   ADJ CLASSIF : ATTRIB

3 You refer to someone as a **national** of a country when they are a citizen of that country and are staying in a different country. EG *Much of the workforce was made up of foreign nationals... ...a German national.*   N COUNT + SUPP

national anthem, national anthems. A country's **national anthem** is its official song. National anthems are often played on public occasions.   N COUNT

National Health Service. In Britain, the **National Health Service** is a system which provides free or cheap medical care for everybody. It is paid for by taxes.   N PROPER : the+N

national insurance is the system by which a government collects money regularly from em-   N UNCOUNT ployers and employees so that money can be paid to people who are ill, unemployed, or retired.

nationalise /nǽʃ°nəlaɪz/. See **nationalize**.

nationalism /nǽʃ°nəlɪz°m/ is 1 a desire for the political independence of a group of people who have the same religion, language, or culture. EG ...nineteenth-century Czech nationalism. 2 a great love for your country which may make you believe that it is better or more important than other countries.   N UNCOUNT

nationalist /nǽʃ°nəlɪst/, **nationalists**. 1 Nationalist ideas or movements are connected with attempts to obtain political independence for a particular group of people. EG ...the nationalist movements of French West Africa.   ADJ CLASSIF: ATTRIB

2 A **nationalist** is a person with nationalist beliefs. EG ...a great Indonesian nationalist.   N COUNT

nationalistic /nǽʃ°nəlɪstɪk/. Someone who is **nationalistic** is very proud of their country and believes that it is better or more important than other countries. EG ...an attempt to arouse nationalistic passions against the foreigner.   ADJ QUALIT

nationality /nǽʃ°nǽlɪ'tiɪ/, **nationalities**. You use **nationality** to refer to the country that people belong to. For example, someone who has British nationality is legally a British citizen. EG ...an identity card proving Belgian nationality... ...scientists of different nationalities.   N UNCOUNT OR N COUNT

nationalize /nǽʃ°nəlaɪz/, **nationalizes**, **nationalizing**, **nationalized**; also spelled **nationalise**. If a government **nationalizes** a private company or industry, that company or industry becomes owned by the state and controlled by the government. EG The revolutionary government has nationalized the mines. ◊ **nationalized**. EG Gas and coal are nationalized industries. ◊ **nationalization** /nǽʃ°nəlaɪzeɪʃ°n/. EG He argued for nationalisation on grounds of efficiency.   V+O   ◊ ADJ CLASSIF   ◊ N UNCOUNT

national park, national parks. A national park is a large area of land which is protected by the government of a country because of its natural beauty, its plants, or its animals.   N COUNT

national service is a period of service in a country's armed forces, which young people in many countries have to do by law.   N UNCOUNT

nationwide /neɪʃ°nwaɪd/. A nationwide activity happens in all parts of a country. EG ...a nationwide campaign to recruit women into trade unions. ▸ used as an adverb. EG She had lectured nationwide to various organizations.   ADJ CLASSIF: ATTRIB   ▸ ADV

native /neɪtɪv/, **natives**. 1 Your native country is the country where you were born. EG She made her way home to her native Russia.   ADJ CLASSIF: ATTRIB

2 A **native** of a country or region is someone who was born there. EG ...John Magee, a native of Northern Ireland. ▸ used as an adjective. EG They took on low paid work that native Britons would not touch.   N COUNT+SUPP   ▸ ADJ CLASSIF: ATTRIB

3 Your **native** language is the first language that you learned to speak when you were a child. EG She had spoken in her native language... He read a poem in his native Hungarian.   ADJ CLASSIF: ATTRIB

4 A **native** speaker of a language is someone who has spoken that language since childhood, rather than learning it later.   ADJ CLASSIF: ATTRIB

5 Animals or plants that are **native** to a region live or grow there naturally and have not been brought there by people. EG These are the only lilies native to Great Britain.   ADJ CLASSIF: OFT+to Formal

natter /nǽtə/, **natters**, **nattering**, **nattered**. When people **natter**, they talk casually for a long time about unimportant things. EG We just want to natter together about old times. ▸ used as a noun. EG They like to have a bit of a natter.   V Informal   ▸ N SING : a+N

natural /nǽtʃ°rə°l/, **naturals**. 1 If you say that someone's behaviour is **natural** in particular circumstances, you mean that it is the way people normally behave in those circumstances. EG She's upset. It's natural, isn't it? Today's the funeral... It is   ADJ QUALIT: USU PRED

natural for trade unions to adopt an aggressive posture.

2 You also say that someone's behaviour is **natural** when they are not trying to hide anything or pretend in any way. EG ...walking in a relaxed, natural manner... There was something not quite natural about her behaviour. ◊ **naturalness**. EG I was impressed by their ease and naturalness.   ADJ QUALIT   ◊ N UNCOUNT

3 A **natural** ability or way of behaving is one that you were born with and have not learned. You can also use **natural** to describe a person with a particular natural ability. EG He had a natural gift for making things work... Follow your own natural inclinations... She was a natural organizer.   ADJ CLASSIF: ATTRIB

4 If you say that someone is a **natural**, you mean that they seem to have been born with the ability to do something well. EG He is a great craftsman, a natural.   N COUNT : USU a +N Informal

5 **Natural** is used to describe things that exist in nature and that were not made or caused by people. EG ...protection from natural disasters such as earthquakes.   ADJ CLASSIF: ATTRIB

6 If someone died of **natural causes**, they died because they were ill and not because they committed suicide, were murdered, or were killed in an accident. EG The post-mortem showed that death was due to natural causes.   PHRASE

7 Someone's **natural** mother or father is their real mother or father, rather than someone who has adopted or fostered them. EG She claimed Prince Yousoupoff as her natural father.   ADJ CLASSIF: ATTRIB

8 A **natural** note in music is not a sharp or a flat. EG ...B natural.   ADJ AFTER N

natural gas is gas which is found underground or under the sea. It is collected and stored, and piped into people's houses to be used for cooking and heating.   N UNCOUNT

natural history is the study of animals, plants, and other living things.   N UNCOUNT

naturalised /nǽtʃrəlaɪzd/. See **naturalized**.

naturalist /nǽtʃrəlɪst/, **naturalists**. A naturalist is a person who studies plants, animals, and other living things.   N COUNT

naturalized /nǽtʃrəlaɪzd/; also spelled **naturalised**. If you are a **naturalized** citizen of a country, you have legally become a citizen of a country that you were not born in. EG ...a naturalized British subject.   ADJ CLASSIF: ATTRIB

naturally /nǽtʃrəli/. 1 You use **naturally** to indicate that you think that something is very obvious and not at all surprising. EG Dena was crying, so naturally Hannah was upset... 'Do you propose to take account of that?' – 'Naturally.'   ADV SEN

2 If one thing develops **naturally** from another, it develops as a normal result of it. EG This leads us fairly naturally into what career advisers call careers counselling.   ADV

3 If something happens or exists **naturally**, it happens or exists in nature and was not made or caused by people. EG He found some rock that does not occur naturally within 30 kilometres... They tried to reproduce artificially what they had observed to happen naturally.   ADV

4 You say that someone is behaving **naturally** when they are not trying to hide anything or to pretend in any way. EG The children were too frightened to behave naturally.   ADV

5 You can also use **naturally** to talk about qualities that people were born with, rather than qualities that they have learned or acquired later in their life. EG ...people who are naturally brilliant... She had a naturally cheerful and serene expression.   ADV+ADJ

6 If something **comes naturally** to you, you find   PHRASE

Find a word on these pages which means 'dark blue'.

that you can do it easily. EG *Politics came naturally to Tony.*

natural resources are all the land, forests, N PLURAL minerals, and sources of energy that occur naturally in a country or in the world, and that can be used by people. EG *They plan to open up the region with its wealth of natural resources.*

nature /ˈneɪtʃə/, **natures**. 1 **Nature** is all the N UNCOUNT animals, plants, and other things in the world that are not made by people, and all the events and processes that are not caused by people. EG *...the diversity of nature... A sunset is one of the most beautiful sights in nature... It's Nature's way of being sure that life will continue.*

2 The **nature** of something is its basic quality or N UNCOUNT character. EG *...the unique nature of Elizabethan* +SUPP *painting... Such a situation is by nature painful... These problems are political in nature.*

3 If you say that something is of a particular N SING+SUPP **nature**, you are saying what characteristic or quality it has. EG *They suffered injuries of a very serious nature... The music he played was of a romantic nature.*

4 Someone's **nature** is their character, which they N SING+SUPP show by their behaviour. EG *Rob had a very sweet nature... ...a woman with a wildly passionate nature... He eventually revealed his real nature.*

5 **Nature** is used in these phrases. 5.1 If you say PHRASES that something has a particular characteristic **by** its **nature** or **by** its **very nature**, you mean that things of that type always have that characteristic. EG *Trade unions are by their nature conservative bodies.* 5.2 If a way of behaving is **in** someone's **nature**, they behave like that because it is a part of their character. EG *It was not in her nature to tell lies.* 5.3 If someone has a particular characteristic **by nature**, it is a part of their character. EG *I am an optimist by nature... He was polite by nature.* 5.4 If you talk about someone's **better nature**, you are referring to their feelings of kindness and their desire to help other people. 5.5 If a way of behaving is **second nature** to you, you behave like that almost without thinking about it, because you have done it so many times before. ● See also **human nature**.

naughty /ˈnɔːti/. 1 You say that small children ADJ QUALIT are **naughty** when they behave badly or are disobedient. EG *Don't be a naughty boy.*

2 You describe books, pictures, or words as **naugh-** ADJ QUALIT ty when they are slightly rude or indecent. EG *...little boys who use naughty words... It's rather a naughty play.*

nausea /ˈnɔːzɪə, -sɪə/. If you have a feeling of N UNCOUNT **nausea**, you feel as if you are going to vomit.

nauseate /ˈnɔːzɪeɪt, -sɪ-/, **nauseates**, **nauseating**, **nauseated**. If something **nauseates** you, 1 it V+O makes you feel as if you are going to vomit. EG *The thought of food nauseated him.* ◊ **nauseating**. EG ◊ ADJ QUALIT *...an incredibly nauseating candy bar.* 2 it makes V+O you feel strong disgust or dislike. EG *This type of newspaper nauseated her.* ◊ **nauseating**. EG *...his* ◊ ADJ QUALIT *utterly nauseating hypocrisy.*

nautical /ˈnɔːtɪkəl/. **Nautical** people and things ADJ CLASSIF: are involved with ships. EG *...an elderly man in a* ATTRIB *nautical uniform.*

naval /ˈneɪvəl/. **Naval** people and things belong to ADJ CLASSIF: a country's navy. EG *...a French naval officer... ...US* ATTRIB *naval forces.*

navel /ˈneɪvəl/, **navels**. Your **navel** is the small N COUNT hollow in the middle of the front of your body. See picture at THE HUMAN BODY.

navigate /ˈnævɪgeɪt/, **navigates**, **navigating**, **navigated**. 1 When someone **navigates**, they V OR V+O work out which direction a ship, plane, or car should go, using maps and instruments. EG *Sailors used to navigate by the stars... Distances that cannot be navigated unless you have a good map.* ◊ **navigation** /ˌnævɪˈgeɪʃən/. EG *You can't teach* ◊ N UNCOUNT *navigation in the middle of a storm.*

2 If you **navigate** a difficult or dangerous place, V+O you travel through it carefully in order to be safe. EG *Until then no ship had been large enough to navigate the Atlantic.*

navigator /ˈnævɪgeɪtə/, **navigators**. A **navigator** N COUNT is someone who works out the direction in which a ship or plane should go. EG *He had many years experience as a navigator.*

navy /ˈneɪvɪ/, **navies**. 1 A country's **navy** is the N COLL : USU part of its armed forces that fights at sea. EG *My* the+N *father's in the Navy... ...Captain Jensen of the US Navy.*

2 Something that is **navy** or **navy-blue** is dark ADJ COLOUR blue in colour. EG *...a navy-blue jumper.*

NB. You write **NB** to draw someone's attention to what you are going to write next. EG *Total cost: £500. NB. The following items are not included.*

N COLL stands for **collective noun**
Nouns which have the label N COLL in the Extra Column are words like 'navy', 'audience', and 'committee' which refer to groups of people or things. Words such as 'herd' and 'flock' are called collective nouns in some grammars, but we call them partitive nouns (N PART) in this dictionary.
See the entry headed NOUNS for more information.

N COUNT stands for **countable noun**
Nouns which have the label N COUNT in the Extra Column are nouns which regularly use both a singular form and a plural form.
See the entry headed NOUNS for more information.

-nd. You add **-nd** to most numbers written in SUFFIX figures and ending in 2 in order to form ordinal numbers. 2nd is pronounced the same as 'second'. EG *...2nd October 1957... ...42nd Street... ...the 132nd Psalm.*

NE is an abbreviation for 'north-east'.

near /nɪə/, **nearer**, **nearest**; **nears**, **nearing**, **neared**. 1 If something is **near** a place or thing or PREP,ADV **near to** it, it is only a short distance from it. EG *He* AFTER VB, OR *stood near the door... I wish I lived nearer London...* ADJ QUALIT *He pulled her nearer to him.* ◊ **nearness**. EG *All* ◊ N UNCOUNT *the while I was acutely aware of her nearness...* +SUPP *Her heart leapt with terror at the nearness of her* Literary *enemy.*

2 If you are **near** a particular situation or state or PREP **near to** it, you have almost reached it. EG *Her father was angry, her mother near tears... I was very near to giving in to their demands.*

3 If something is similar to something else, you can PREP, OR say that it is **near** it or **near to** it. EG *Most views* ADV AFTER VB *were fairly near the truth... He is the nearest we have to an English Leonardo da Vinci.* ● If you say ● PHRASE that something is **the nearest thing** to a particular type of thing, you mean that it is almost that thing, and there is nothing else more similar. EG *He is the nearest thing we have to a genius.*

4 Your **near** relatives are the people who are most ADJ QUALIT closely related to you, for example your parents ATTRIB and grandparents.

5 If something happens **near** a particular time or PREP **near to** it, it happens just before or just after that time. EG *...near the beginning of the play.*

6 If a time or event is **near**, it will happen very ADV AFTER VB soon. EG *...as her wedding day drew near.* ● If you ● PHRASE say that something will happen **in the near future**, you mean that it will happen quite soon. EG *These things will be available to us all in the very near future.*

7 You can also use **near** to say that something ADJ CLASSIF : almost has a particular quality or almost happens. ATTRIB OR ADV +ADJ

EG *...a state of near chaos... ...our near catastrophic economic troubles.*

8 You use **near** in expressions such as **near enough** and **as near as makes no difference** in order to say that something is almost true. EG *He paid £100, or as near as makes no difference.* PHRASE Informal

9 If you say that something was **a near thing**, you mean that it was almost an accident or a disaster. PHRASE

10 You can use **nowhere near** to emphasize that something is not the case. For example, if you say that something is **nowhere near** ready, you mean that it will not be ready for a long time. EG *Lions are nowhere near as fast as the cheetah.* PHRASE Informal

11 If you **are nearing** a place, you are approaching it. EG *As they neared the harbour, it began to rain.* V+O

12 If someone or something **is nearing** a particular stage or point in time, they will soon reach it. EG *...anybody nearing the age of retirement.* V+O

nearby /nɪəbaɪ/. **Nearby** things and places are only a short distance away. EG *...Nottingham and nearby towns... There was a river nearby... Nearby a tractor was pulling a plough.* ADJ CLASSIF OR ADV

nearly /nɪəli¹/. **1 Nearly** means not completely or not exactly. EG *Brody had been there for nearly an hour... It was nearly dark... I can nearly swim a mile... They seem to be nearly always male... Nearly everybody went out of business... She was nearly as tall as he was.* ADV

2 You use **not nearly** to emphasize that something is not the case. For example, if you say that something is 'not nearly big enough', you are emphasizing that it is much too small. EG *I haven't spent nearly long enough here... They don't have nearly so many foods to choose from as we do.* PHRASE

nearside /nɪəsaɪd/. The **nearside** of a vehicle is the side that is nearest to the edge of the road when the vehicle is being driven normally. N SING

neat /niːt/, **neater, neatest. 1** Something that is **neat** is tidy and smart. EG *His clothes were neat... This is not a neat household... She had small, neat writing.* ◇ **neatly.** EG *Mother's clothes hung neatly in a row.* ◇ **neatness.** EG *Their desks are models of neatness... I was pleased at the neatness of the stitches.* ADJ QUALIT ◇ ADV ◇ N UNCOUNT

2 Someone who is **neat** is careful and tidy in their appearance and behaviour. EG *Ethel was clean and neat and politely spoken.* ADJ QUALIT

3 If you drink an alcoholic drink **neat**, you drink it without anything else added to it. EG *She takes her whisky neat... He gulped the neat brandy down in one draught.* ADJ CLASSIF

nebulous /nebjə⁴ləs/. **Nebulous** ideas are vague and not precise. EG *It's a very nebulous concept... I had a nebulous notion of a life after death.* ADJ QUALIT Formal

necessarily /nesi¹sə⁰rɪ¹li¹, nesi¹seri¹li¹/. **1** If you say that something is not **necessarily** the case, you mean that it is not always the case. If you say that something is **necessarily** the case, you are emphasizing that it is always the case. EG *Fleas are not necessarily associated with dirt... Documentaries don't necessarily need interviewers... The secular historian is necessarily concerned only with externals.* ADV : OFT WITH BROAD NEG

2 If something **necessarily** happens in particular circumstances, it must happen in those circumstances. EG *Growth has necessarily levelled off.* ADV Formal

necessary /nesə⁰sə⁰ri¹/. **1** Something that is **necessary** is needed in order to get the result or effect that you want. EG *Are we teaching undergraduates the necessary skills?... Make a soft dough, using a little more water if necessary... ...the colours and patterns necessary for perfect camouflage... I don't want to stay longer than necessary... It is necessary to examine this claim before we proceed any further.* ADJ CLASSIF

2 You can also say that something is **necessary** when it must happen or exist in particular circumstances and cannot be any different. EG *There is no* ADJ CLASSIF Formal

necessary connection between industrial democracy and productivity.

necessitate /nɪ²sesɪ¹teɪt/, **necessitates, necessitating, necessitated.** If something **necessitates** a particular course of action, it makes it necessary. EG *The Government's action had necessitated a by-election... This job would necessitate working with his hands.* V+O OR V+ING Formal

necessity /nɪ²sesɪ¹ti¹/, **necessities. 1 Necessity** is the need to do something. EG *...the necessity of keeping water uncontaminated... She went to work not out of choice but necessity.* N UNCOUNT

2 Necessities are things that you must have, such as food and clothing. EG *They were supplied with all the necessities of life.* N COUNT

3 You say **of necessity** to emphasize that something must happen or must be the case. EG *The account given here is of necessity extremely brief... Since my French was so poor our conversation was, of necessity, limited.* PHRASE Formal

neck /nek/, **necks, necking, necked. 1** Your **neck** is the part of your body which joins your head to the rest of your body. See picture at THE HUMAN BODY. EG *She threw her arms around his neck... The cat had a blue collar round its neck.* ● If something goes **down** your **neck**, it goes inside your collar and down your back. EG *The rain was dripping down our necks.* N COUNT : OFT + POSS ● PHRASE

2 The **neck** of a dress or shirt is the part which is round your neck or just below it. EG *...a dress with a lace neck... His shirt was open at the neck.* N COUNT

3 The **neck** of a bottle is the long narrow part at one end. N COUNT : USU + SUPP

4 Neck is used in these phrases. **4.1** If you say that you are **up to** your **neck** in problems, you mean that you are deeply involved in them and cannot get away from them. EG *You were up to your neck in trouble with the press.* **4.2** If you say that someone is **breathing down** your **neck**, you mean that they are watching you very closely and checking everything that you do. EG *They should not have their parents breathing down their necks all the time.* **4.3** If you **risk** your **neck**, you do something very dangerous in order to achieve something or to help someone. EG *I thanked him for risking his neck for me.* **4.4** If you **stick** your **neck out**, you do or say something that makes you likely to be criticized or harmed. EG *He was pleased to let someone else stick their neck out and take responsibility.* **4.5 by the scruff of** your **neck**: see **scruff.** ● **a millstone round** your **neck**: see **millstone.** PHRASES Informal / Informal / Informal / Informal

5 If two people **are necking**, they are kissing each other passionately. V : USU CONT Outdated

necklace /nekli¹s/, **necklaces.** A **necklace** is a piece of jewellery, such as a chain or string of beads, which a woman wears round her neck. See picture at JEWELLERY. N COUNT

neckline /neklaɪn/, **necklines.** The **neckline** of a dress or blouse is the top edge at the front. EG *...a mini-dress with a plunging neckline.* N COUNT

necktie /nektaɪ/, **neckties.** A **necktie** is the same as a tie. N COUNT American

née /neɪ/ is used before a name to indicate that it was a woman's surname before she got married. EG *...Jane Carmichael, née Byers.* Formal

need /niːd/, **needs, needing, needed. 1** If you **need** something, it is necessary for you to have it. EG *These animals need food throughout the winter... If you need any help, just give me a ring... Children need to feel they matter to someone... You don't need a degree in mathematics to run a computer.* V+O OR V+to-INF

2 If you **need** to do something, you must do it. EG *Before we answer this question, we need to look briefly at the world environment... You might need to visit a specialist.* V+to-INF

If someone needles you, do they stick a needle into you?

3 If you tell someone that they **need not** do something, you are saying that there is no good reason why they should do it. EG *You needn't worry.* SEMI-MODAL: WITH BROAD NEG

4 If you say that something **need not** be the case, you mean that it might happen or be the case, but it is not definite or unavoidable. EG *It needn't cost very much.* SEMI-MODAL: WITH BROAD NEG

5 If you say that something that has happened **need not** have happened, you mean that it could have been avoided or prevented. EG *People died of diseases that need not have proved fatal.* SEMI-MODAL: WITH BROAD NEG

6 If you say that something **needs** a particular action or that an action **needs** doing, you mean that this action is necessary. EG *The shed needs a good clean out... Keep a list of all the jobs that need doing... The top rim needs to be cut off.* V+O, V+-ING, OR V+to-INF

7 Your **needs** are the things that you need to have in order to have a satisfactory way of life. EG *She learned how to provide for her own needs.* N COUNT: USU PLURAL

8 A **need** is also a strong feeling that you must have something or must do something. EG *I began to feel the need of somewhere to retreat... Their need for money is rising fast... She felt no need to speak.* N SING: OFT+of/for OR to-INF

9 You use the expression **if need be** to say that an action will be carried out if it is considered to be necessary. EG *She said she would stay with me for months and years if need be.* PHRASE

10 If someone or something is **in need of** something, they need it. EG *I am badly in need of advice... The hospital was in need of decorating.* PREP

11 People **in need** do not have enough money, or need help of some kind. PHRASE

12 If you have **no need** of something, it is not necessary for you to have it. If there is **no need** for you to do something or if you have **no need** to do it, it is not necessary for you to do it. EG *The country had no need of Western weapons... There is no need to go into details.* PHRASE

13 If you tell someone that there is **no need** to do something, you are telling them to stop doing it because it annoys you. EG *There's no need to get so worked up about it.* PHRASE Informal

needle /ni:də⁰l/, **needles**, **needling**, **needled**. **1** A **needle** is a small, very thin piece of polished metal which is used for sewing. It has a sharp point at one end and a hole in the other end for a thread to go through. N COUNT

needles

sewing needle

knitting needles

hypodermic needle

2 You can refer to knitting needles as **needles**. N COUNT

3 The **needle** in a record player is the small pointed instrument that touches the record and picks up the sound signals. N COUNT

4 A **needle** is also the part of a syringe which a doctor or nurse sticks into your body. N COUNT

5 On an instrument that measures something such as speed, weight, or electricity, the **needle** is the thin piece of metal or plastic which moves back- N COUNT

wards and forwards on the dial and shows the measurement.

6 The **needles** of a pine tree are its very thin pointed leaves. EG *There was nothing on the ground except a thick layer of pine needles.* N COUNT

7 If someone **needles** you, they annoy you by criticizing you repeatedly. EG *She was needling me about Doris.* V+O Informal

8 a needle in a haystack: see **haystack**. ● See also **pins and needles**.

needless /ni:dli²s/. **1** Something that is **needless** is completely unnecessary. EG *The result was needless slaughter... It was a needless risk to run.* ADJ CLASSIF

◇ **needlessly.** EG *This may upset a mother needlessly.* ◇ ADV

2 You say **needless to say** to emphasize that what you are saying is obvious. EG *I left college in disgrace (needless to say without my Diploma)... This new social awareness will, needless to say, bring big changes.* ADV SEN

needlework /ni:də⁰lwɜ:k/ is **1** sewing or embroidery that is done by hand. EG *...the basket in which she kept her needlework.* **2** the activity of sewing or embroidering. EG *The girls spend much time doing needlework.* N UNCOUNT

needn't /ni:də⁰nt/ is the usual spoken form of 'need not'.

needy /ni:di¹/, **needier**, **neediest**. **1** Someone who is **needy** is very poor and does not have proper housing or enough food or clothing. EG *...helping needy old people throughout the world... They are among the neediest children in Britain.* ADJ QUALIT

2 Needy people are sometimes referred to as the **needy.** EG *It is important to serve everybody, not just the needy.* N PLURAL: the+N

NEG stands for **negative**

1. NEG is used in the Extra Column beside words such as 'nothing', 'nobody' and 'never' to tell you that the word makes the clause negative and that no other negative word is used in the same clause. So you say *There was **nobody** in the room.* You do not say 'There wasn't nobody in the room'.

2. See the entry at **not** for more information about how we make clauses and phrases negative.

3. NEG is also used in the labels ADV BRD NEG and BROAD NEG. See the entries for ADVERBS and for BROAD NEG for more information.

---

negate /nɪ²geɪt/, **negates**, **negating**, **negated**. If you **negate** something that someone has done, you cause it to have no value or effect. EG *The denial of the importance of minorities negates all our efforts on their behalf.* V+O Formal

negative /negətɪv/, **negatives**. **1** Negative is used to describe something that gives or suggests the answer 'no'. EG *We expected to receive a negative answer.* ◇ **negatively.** EG *The public responded negatively.* ADJ CLASSIF ◇ ADV

2 If an answer is **in the negative**, it is 'no'. EG *This question had been answered in the negative.* PHRASE

3 If you say that someone is **negative** or that they have a **negative** attitude, you mean that they consider only the disadvantages and bad aspects of a situation, rather than the advantages and good aspects. EG *No one else I met ever had such a negative view of Alice Springs... He was especially negative about my written work.* ADJ QUALIT

4 If a medical or other scientific test is **negative**, it shows that something has not happened or is not present. EG *...a negative pregnancy test.* ADJ CLASSIF

5 A **negative** is the image that is first produced when you take a photograph. The negative of a black-and-white photograph is dark in the places where the final photograph is light. N COUNT

6 A **negative** number is less than zero. ADJ CLASSIF

neglect /nɪˈglɛkt/, **neglects, neglecting, ne-** V+O
glected. 1 If you **neglect** someone or something,
you do not look after them or give them the
attention they deserve. EG ...*the farmer who ne-*
glects his crops. ◇ **neglected.** EG *The child looked* ◇ ADJ QUALIT
neglected, scruffy and unloved.
2 If you **neglect** to do something, you fail to do it. V+to-INF OR V
EG *I neglected to bring a gift... I feel I'm neglecting* +O
my duty.
3 Neglect is failure to look after someone or N UNCOUNT
something properly. EG *It was the mother's neglect*
of her infant that caused its death... ...estates suffer-
ing from vandalism and neglect.

neglectful /nɪˈglɛktfʊl/. **1** You describe someone ADJ QUALIT
as **neglectful** when they do not look after some-
one or something properly. EG ...*a neglectful father.*
2 If you are **neglectful** of something, you do not ADJ QUALIT :
give it the attention that it should be given. EG *He* OFT+*of*
had been neglectful of his duties.

negligee /ˈnɛglɪʒeɪ/, **negligees;** also spelled N COUNT
négligée. A woman's **negligee** is a dressing gown
made of very thin material.

negligent /ˈnɛglɪdʒənt/. When someone is **negli-** ADJ QUALIT :
gent, they do not do something that they ought to USU PRED
do, or do not show care for something that they are
responsible for. EG *He has to prove that he has not*
been negligent. ◇ **negligently.** EG *They may act* ◇ ADV
foolishly or negligently. ◇ **negligence** ◇ N UNCOUNT
/ˈnɛglɪdʒəns/. EG *The chairman of the Party had*
been dismissed for negligence.

negligible /ˈnɛglɪdʒəbəl/. Something that is **neg-** ADJ CLASSIF
ligible is so small or unimportant that it is not
worth considering or worrying about. EG *The cost in*
human life has been negligible.... This would have
a negligible effect on the temperature.

negotiable /nɪˈgəʊʃəbəl/. Something that is **ne-** ADJ CLASSIF
gotiable can be changed or agreed by means of
discussion. EG *The price is negotiable.*

negotiate /nɪˈgəʊʃɪeɪt/, **negotiates, negotiating,**
negotiated. 1 If you **negotiate** an agreement or a V+O :
deal, you obtain it by having discussions with other OFT+*with*
people. EG *He negotiated a trade agreement with*
Brazil.
2 If you **negotiate** for something, you try to obtain V : OFT+*for/*
it by having discussions with other people. EG *Paul* *with*
is negotiating for a job worth £18,000... The Nation-
al Council negotiates directly with the British Gas
Corporation.
3 If you **negotiate** an obstacle or difficult piece of V+O
ground, you succeed in moving around it or over it.
EG *Patrick is not sure whether he can negotiate the*
turn at the bottom.

negotiation /nɪˈgəʊʃɪeɪʃən/, **negotiations. Ne-** N COUNT :
gotiations are discussions that take place between USU PLURAL
people with different interests, in which they try to
reach an agreement. EG *The early stages of their*
negotiations with the Government were unsuccess-
ful. ▸ used as an uncount noun. EG *We need to allow* ▸ N UNCOUNT
more time for negotiation.

negotiator /nɪˈgəʊʃɪeɪtə/, **negotiators. Negotia-** N COUNT
tors are people who take part in negotiations in
business, politics, or international affairs. EG *They*
acted as negotiators in all dealings with other
villages... ...trade union negotiators.

Negro /ˈniːgrəʊ/, **Negroes.** A **Negro** is someone N COUNT
with black skin who comes from Africa or whose
ancestors came from Africa. Some people find this
word offensive.

neigh /neɪ/, **neighs, neighing, neighed.** When a V
horse **neighs,** it utters a loud sound.

neighbour /ˈneɪbə/, **neighbours;** also spelled
neighbor in American English. **1** Your **neigh-** N COUNT
bours are the people who live near you, especially
the people who live next door to you. EG *Don't be*
afraid of what the neighbours will think.
2 Your **neighbour** is also the person who is N COUNT+POSS
standing or sitting next to you. EG *Rudolph turned*
his head towards his neighbour.

3 You can refer to something which stands next to N COUNT+POSS
something else of the same kind as its **neighbour.**
The young plant risks being overshadowed by its
neighbours.
4 A country's **neighbours** are the countries that N COUNT+POSS
are next to it. EG ...*battles between Angola and her*
neighbours.

neighbourhood /ˈneɪbəhʊd/, **neighbourhoods;**
also spelled **neighborhood** in American English.
1 A **neighbourhood** is a part of a town where N COUNT
people live. EG *She'd just moved into the neighbour-*
hood... ...a wealthy neighbourhood... ...my neigh-
bourhood grocery.
2 If something is **in the neighbourhood** of a place, PHRASE
it is near to it. EG *We were heading for a destination*
in the neighbourhood of the Lofoten Islands.

neighbouring /ˈneɪbərɪŋ/; also spelled **neigh-** ADJ CLASSIF :
boring in American English. You use **neighbour-** ATTRIB
ing to describe places and things that are near to
the place or thing that you are talking about. EG
Families came from neighbouring villages to look
at her.

neighbourly /ˈneɪbəli/; also spelled **neighborly** ADJ QUALIT
in American English. If people who live near you
are **neighbourly,** they are kind, friendly, and
helpful to you. EG *That's a neighbourly thing to do.*

neither /ˈnaɪðə, ˈniːðə/. **1** You use **neither** in front CONJ : NEG
of the first of two or more words or expressions
when you are saying that two or more things are
not true or do not happen. The other things are
introduced by 'nor'. EG *He spoke neither English*
nor French... She neither drinks, smokes, nor eats
meat... The Englishman was neither gratified nor
displeased.
2 You also use **neither** to refer to both of two PRON SING :
things or people, when you are making a negative NEG, OFT+*of*;
statement about both of them. EG *Neither of us was* ALSO DET
having any luck... Neither was suffering pain.
3 If you say that one thing is not the case and CONJ : NEG
neither is another, you mean that the second thing
is also not the case. EG *'I don't normally drink at*
lunch.' – 'Neither do I.'
4 If you say that a fact is **neither here nor there,** PHRASE
you mean that it does not matter, because it is not
relevant.

neolithic /ˌniːəˈlɪθɪk/ means relating to the period ADJ CLASSIF
long ago when people first started farming but still
used stone weapons and tools. EG ...*in neolithic*
times... ...neolithic weapons... ...neolithic settle-
ments.

neon /ˈniːɒn/. **1 Neon** is a gas which exists in very N UNCOUNT
small amounts in the atmosphere. It is used in glass
tubes to make bright lights and signs.
2 Neon signs and places are lit by neon lights. EG N UNCOUNT :
...*a neon city.* OFT N MOD

neon light, neon lights. A **neon light** is a bright N COUNT OR
electric light that consists of a glass tube filled with N UNCOUNT
the gas neon. Neon lights are sometimes bent into
shapes or letters to form signs. EG *The front of the*
building glittered with bright neon lights.

nephew /ˈnɛvjuː, ˈnɛf-/, **nephews.** Someone's N COUNT
nephew is the son of their sister or brother.

nerve /nɜːv/, **nerves. 1** A **nerve** is a long, thin N COUNT
fibre in your body that transmits messages and
feelings between your brain and other parts of
your body. EG ...*the optic nerves... ...a network of*
nerve fibres.
2 If you talk about someone's **nerves,** you are N PLURAL
referring to how able they are to remain calm and
not become worried or tense in a dangerous or
stressful situation. EG *Hoping to calm our nerves,*
we decided to spend the afternoon at the lake... She
had strong nerves... All during lunch he had been in
a state of nerves.
3 Nerve is the courage and determination that you N UNCOUNT

Can you think of six nouns which end in '-ness'?

need in order to be able to do something, especially something difficult or dangerous. EG *Nobody had the nerve to remind him that he was several hours late... His nerve began to crack.*

4 Nerve is also used in these phrases. **4.1** If PHRASES someone or something **gets on** your **nerves,** they Informal annoy or irritate you very much. EG *He got on my nerves tonight with his fishing stories.* **4.2** If you **lose** your **nerve,** you suddenly panic and become afraid about something that you are doing. EG *The men inside the building lost their nerve and opened fire on the crowd.* **4.3** If you say that someone **had a nerve** or **had the nerve** to do something, you mean that they have made you angry or shocked by doing something rude or disrespectful. EG *He had the nerve to say Fleet Street was corrupting me... She has a nerve to ask.*

nerve-racking. Something that is **nerve-** ADJ QUALIT **racking** makes you feel very tense and worried. EG *It was a nerve-racking period for us all.*

nervous /nɜːvəs/. **1** If you are **nervous,** you are ADJ QUALIT worried and frightened, and show this in your behaviour. EG *Both actors were exceedingly nervous on the day of the performance.* ◇ **nervously.** ◇ ADV EG *He laughed nervously and asked me what I meant.* ◇ **nervousness.** EG *'Pa,' Rudolph began,* ◇ N UNCOUNT *trying to conquer his nervousness.*

2 A **nervous** person is very tense and easily upset. ADJ QUALIT: EG *She was a particularly nervous woman.* ATTRIB

3 If you are **nervous** about something, you feel ADJ PRED rather afraid or worried about it. EG *People are so* +about/of *nervous about believing anything to be right... He's nervous of thieves in that little shop of his.*

4 A **nervous** illness or condition affects your ADJ CLASSIF: emotions and your mental state. EG *She had suf-* ATTRIB *fered a lot of nervous strain.*

nervous breakdown, nervous breakdowns. A N COUNT **nervous breakdown** is an illness in which some-one suffers from deep depression, worry, and tired-ness, and so has psychiatric treatment. EG *You'll give yourself a nervous breakdown going on work-ing like this.*

nervous system, nervous systems. Your **nerv-** N COUNT **ous system** is all the nerves in your body together with your brain and spinal cord, which control your movement and reflexes as well as your feelings.

nervous wreck, nervous wrecks. If you say N COUNT that someone is a **nervous wreck,** you mean that Informal they are extremely nervous or worried. EG *I waited so long that by the time my turn came I was a nervous wreck.*

-ness, -nesses. -ness is added to adjectives to SUFFIX form nouns. These nouns usually refer to a state or quality. For example 'sadness' is the state of being sad and 'kindness' is the quality of being kind. Nouns formed in this way are often not defined in this dictionary but are treated with the related adjectives. EG *The aim of life is happiness... ...the smallness of the school... He was aware of his weaknesses.*

nest /nɛst/, **nests, nesting, nested. 1** A **nest** is N COUNT **1.1** a place that a bird makes to lay its eggs in, using things like twigs, leaves, moss, and mud. **1.2** the place that groups of insects or other animals make, in which they live and give birth to their young. EG *We had a wasp's nest in the roof.*

2 When a bird **nests** somewhere, it builds a nest V:USU+A and settles there to lay its eggs. EG *Hornbills nest in holes in trees.*

nestle /nɛsəl/, **nestles, nestling, nestled. 1** If V+A OR you **nestle** somewhere, you move into a comfort- V+O+A able position, often by pressing against someone or something soft. EG *They nestled together on the sofa... ...nestling against his body.*

2 If something **nestles** somewhere, it is in that V+A place or position and seems safe or sheltered. EG *...a house with other houses nestling against it on both sides... A village nestled in the hills to their right.*

net /nɛt/, **nets, netting, netted;** also spelled **nett** in British English for paragraphs 5 and 6.

1 Net is a kind of cloth made of very fine threads N UNCOUNT that are woven together so that there are small equal spaces between them and you can see through the cloth. EG *All the windows have net curtains.* ● See also **netting.**

2 A **net** is a piece of netting which is in a particular N COUNT shape and is used for a particular purpose, for example to keep something in place, or across the centre of a tennis court. EG *...a net to cover the plants... ...a butterfly trapped in a net.*

3 If you **net** something, you manage to get it, often V+O by using skill. EG *He was netting his largest fortune.*

4 If you **net** a particular amount of money, you V+O: gain it as profit when all expenses have been paid. OFT+*for,* EG *The plastics began netting £1 billion a year for* OR V+O+O *the company.*

5 A **net** result or amount is one that is final, when ADJ CLASSIF: everything necessary has been considered or in- ATTRIB OR cluded. EG *That gave him a net profit of just over* ADJ AFTER N *23%... The net result is a massive labour surplus.*

6 The **net** weight of something is its weight without ADJ CLASSIF: its container or wrapping. EG *If you look at the* ATTRIB OR label, *you'll see it says 450 g net.* ADJ AFTER N

netball /nɛtbɔːl/ is a game played by two teams of N UNCOUNT seven players, usually women. Each team tries to score goals by throwing a ball through a net which is at the top of a pole at each end of the court.

nett /nɛt/. See **net.**

netting /nɛtɪŋ/ is material made of pieces of N UNCOUNT thread or string, or metal wires, that are woven or knotted together so that there are equal spaces between them. EG *The dog scratched impatiently at the netting... ...wire netting on the windows.*

nettle /nɛtəl/, **nettles.** A **nettle** is a wild plant N COUNT with spiky leaves covered with little hairs, usually ones that sting. EG *...fields covered with stinging nettles.*

network /nɛtwɜːk/, **networks. 1** A **network** is N COUNT: **1.1** a large number of lines or things such as roads USU+SUPP or veins that look like lines, which cross each other or meet at many points. EG *...a network of tiny red veins running over her white skin... ...the network of back streets in the Latin Quarter.* **1.2** a large number of people or organizations that have a connection with each other and work together as a system. EG *...a network of clinics... ...the public telephone network.*

2 A radio or television **network** is a company or N COUNT: group of companies that usually broadcasts the OFT MOD+N same programmes at the same time in different parts of the country. EG *She gave an informal interview on a national television network.*

neurological /njʊərəˈlɒdʒɪkəl/ is used to de- ADJ CLASSIF scribe things relating to the nervous system. EG *...a* Medical *progressive neurological disease.*

neurosis /njʊərˈəʊsɪs/, **neuroses** /njʊərˈəʊsiːz/. N UNCOUNT **Neurosis** is a mental illness which causes people OR N COUNT to have continual and unreasonable fears and worries. EG *Such problems can distort personality and lead to neurosis.*

neurotic /njʊərˈɒtɪk/. If you say that someone is ADJ QUALIT **neurotic,** you mean that they continually show a lot of unreasonable anxiety about something. EG *They are becoming neurotic about their careers.*

neutral /njuːtrəl/, **neutrals. 1** A country or per- ADJ CLASSIF son that is **neutral** does not officially support anyone in a disagreement or war. EG *Throughout the hostilities this group remained neutral... Be-cause I was neutral in the conflict I was a welcome visitor.* ▸ used as a noun. EG *The neutrals can give* ▸ N COUNT *useful advice.* ◇ **neutrality** /njuːˈtrælɪtɪ/. EG *We* ◇ N UNCOUNT *have a tradition of political neutrality for our civil servants.*

2 If someone is **neutral** or if something that they ADJ CLASSIF do is **neutral,** they do not show any emotions or opinions. EG *I waited, but her eyes were neutral...*

*Their decision was neutral on this question...
'Look,' she said in a neutral voice.*

3 Neutral is the position between the gears of a car or other vehicle, in which the gears are not connected to the engine. EG *I pushed the handle into neutral.*   N UNCOUNT

4 The **neutral** wire in an electric plug is the wire that is not earth or live and that is needed to complete the circuit so that the electric current can flow.   ADJ CLASSIF

5 Neutral is used **5.1** to describe things that are pale grey or brown in colour. EG *The water was of a pale, neutral colour, a sort of ashen grey.* **5.2** to describe things that contain no colour at all or that are suitable to be used for any colour. EG *...a neutral shoe cream.*   ADJ QUALIT / ADJ CLASSIF

neutralize /njuːtrəlaɪz/, **neutralizes, neutralizing, neutralized**; also spelled **neutralise**. To neutralize something means to prevent it from having any effect or from working properly. EG *Their aim is to neutralize the Council's campaign... All aircraft were neutralized until repairs could be effected.*   V+O

neutron /njuːtrɒn/, **neutrons**. A **neutron** is an atomic particle that has no electrical charge.   N COUNT / Technical

neutron bomb, neutron bombs. A **neutron bomb** is a nuclear weapon that is designed to kill people and animals without a large explosion and without destroying buildings.   N COUNT

never /nevə/. **1 Never** means **1.1** at no time in the past or at no time in the future. EG *I've never been to Europe... I shall never forget this day... I never eat breakfast on Sundays.* **1.2** not in any circumstances at all. EG *What is morally wrong can never be politically right.*   ADV : NEG

2 Never ever is an emphatic expression for 'never'. EG *She never ever wears a hat.*   PHRASE / Informal

3 You use **never** with the simple past tense to mean 'did not'. EG *My bus never arrived... Good gracious! I never knew that.*   ADV : NEG / Informal

4 If you say **'Well I never'**, you are indicating that you are surprised. EG *Well, I never. It's Mrs Oliver.*   EXCLAM / Informal

5 never mind: see **mind**.

never-ending. If you describe something as **never-ending**, you are emphasizing that it lasts a very long time, often when you find it depressing or boring. EG *It was a drab, never-ending afternoon... ...the never-ending flow of refugees.*   ADJ CLASSIF

nevertheless /nevəðəles/ means in spite of what has just been said. EG *She saw Clarissa immediately, but nevertheless pretended to look around for her.*   ADV SEN

new /njuː/ **newer, newest; news**. The form **news** is used for the noun in paragraphs 7 to 10.

1 Something that is **new 1.1** has been recently made or created, or is in the process of being made or created. EG *...smart new houses... I haven't really had a new idea in years... ...a new type of bandage that stops minor bleeding almost immediately.* **1.2** has not been used or owned by anyone else. EG *There was another sign advertising new and used tractors... They cost over twenty dollars new.* **1.3** is different from what you had, used, or experienced before. EG *Not long after that, he got a new job... The villagers were suspicious of anything new.*   ADJ QUALIT / ADJ CLASSIF / ADJ CLASSIF : ATTRIB

◊ **newness**. EG *...the newness and strangeness of her surroundings.* **1.4** has only recently been discovered. EG *In 1781 an astronomer named William Herschel discovered a new planet.*   ◊ N UNCOUNT / ADJ CLASSIF : ATTRIB

2 When you refer to the beginning of a **new** day or period of time, you are referring to the beginning of the next day or period of time. EG *...on the eve of a new era... A new phase was about to start.*   ADJ CLASSIF : ATTRIB

3 New is also used to show that something has only just happened. For example, a **new** parent has only recently become a parent. EG *...from the new mother's point of view... Thousands were there to hear the new party leader.*   ADJ CLASSIF : ATTRIB

4 If you are **new** to a situation or place or if the situation or place is **new** to you, you have not   ADJ PRED : USU + to

experienced it or seen it before. EG *...a person who's new to the job of teaching... I'm new here... ...a part of England completely new to him.*

5 If you say that something is **as good as new**, you mean that it is now in very good condition, after it has been damaged and then repaired.   PHRASE

6 See also **newly**.

7 News is **7.1** information about a recent event or a recently changed situation. EG *I've got some good news for you... ...after receiving the news of my acceptance.* **7.2** information that is given in newspapers and on radio and television about recent events in the country or the world. EG *...a half hour of world and domestic news... It was on the news at 9.30... He's recently been in the news again.*   N UNCOUNT, OR N SING : the + N

8 If you say **'That's news to me'** when someone tells you something, you mean that you did not know it and you are rather surprised by it.   CONVENTION

newborn /njuːbɔːn/. A **newborn** baby is one that has been born recently.   ADJ CLASSIF

newcomer /njuːkʌmə/, **newcomers**. A **newcomer** is a person who has recently arrived to live in a place, joined an organization, or started a job. EG *...newcomers to the neighbourhood.*   N COUNT

new-fangled. You can describe an idea or piece of machinery that has been recently created or invented as **new-fangled**, often when you think it is unnecessary or too complicated. EG *...a new-fangled Japanese camera... No doubt they'll produce some new-fangled gadget to dispose of it.*   ADJ CLASSIF : ATTRIB / Informal

new-found. A **new-found** quality, ability, or person is one that you have discovered recently. EG *...this new-found confidence... ...new-found friends.*   ADJ CLASSIF : ATTRIB

newly /njuːliɪ/ is used before past participles to indicate that an action is very recent. EG *...the newly-married couple... ...newly discovered evidence... ...her newly acquired food mixer.*   ADV

new moon, new moons. The moon is a **new moon** when it is a thin crescent shape at the start of its four-week cycle of appearing to become larger and then smaller.   N COUNT : USU SING

news agency, news agencies. A **news agency** is an organization which collects news stories from all over the world and sells them to newspapers, magazines, and television and radio stations.   N COUNT

newsagent /njuːzeɪdʒənt/, **newsagents**. A **newsagent** or **newsagent's** is a shop which sells newspapers and magazines, and often cigarettes, sweets, and stationery.   N COUNT

newscaster /njuːzkɑːstə/, **newscasters**. A **newscaster** is a person who reads the news on a television or radio broadcast.   N COUNT

newsflash /njuːzflæʃ/, **newsflashes**. A **newsflash** is an interruption that is made to a radio or television programme to announce an important piece of news.   N COUNT

newsletter /njuːzletə/, **newsletters**. A **newsletter** is a printed sheet or several sheets of paper containing information about an organization that is sent regularly to its members. EG *Members receive a newsletter three times a year.*   N COUNT

newsmen /njuːzmen/ are reporters who work for newspapers, television, or radio. EG *Newsmen had been barred from the trial.*   N PLURAL

newspaper /njuːspeɪpə/, **newspapers**. **1** A **newspaper** is **1.1** a number of large sheets of folded paper on which news, advertisements, and other information is printed. Some newspapers are produced every day from Monday to Saturday, and others once a week. EG *...a weekly newspaper... ...a newspaper article... ...copies of France's leading daily newspaper Le Figaro.* **1.2** an organization that produces a newspaper. EG *I work for a newspaper.*   N COUNT

2 Newspaper consists of pieces of old newspapers,   N UNCOUNT especially when they are being used for another purpose such as wrapping things up. EG *Wedge it with a wad of newspaper.*

newsprint /njuːzprɪnt/ is the cheap, fairly rough N UNCOUNT paper on which newspapers are printed. EG *...reading through stacks of newsprint.*

newt /njuːt/, **newts**. A **newt** is a small animal with N COUNT a moist skin, short legs, and a long tail. Newts live partly on land and partly in water.

New Testament. The **New Testament** is the N PROPER: part of the Bible that deals with the life of Jesus the+N Christ and with Christianity in the early Church.

new wave, new waves. A **new wave** is a move- N COUNT ment in art, music, or film, which introduces new ideas instead of following traditional ideas. EG *...one of the young producers from the new wave of British music.*

New Year is the time when people celebrate the N UNCOUNT, OR start of a year. EG *We had a marvellous time over* N SING: the+N *New Year... Happy New Year!*

New Year's Day is the first day of a year. In N UNCOUNT Western countries this is January 1st.

New Year's Eve is the last day of the year, the N UNCOUNT day that comes before New Year's Day.

next /nɛkst/. **1** The **next** period of time, event, ORDINAL person, or thing is the one that happens or comes immediately after the present one or after the previous one. EG *The next five years are of vital importance... The next day, I left better prepared... I'm getting married next month... My pulse was 40 one minute and 100 the next... I may vote for her at the next election... My next question is, 'What is art?'... What's next on the agenda?*

2 The **next** place or person is the one that is ORDINAL: nearest to you or the first one that you come to. EG the+ORDINAL *The telephone was ringing in the next room... Pull into the next lay-by.*

3 The thing that happens **next** is the thing that ADV happens immediately after something else. EG *The audience does not know what is going to happen next... It's your turn next.*

4 When you **next** do something, you do it for the ADV first time since you last did it. EG *It was some years later when I next saw her.*

5 You use **next** to say that something has more of ADV+SUPERL a particular quality than all other things except one. For example, the thing that is **next** best is the one that is best except for one other thing. EG *The best kind of story is the one with a happy ending; the next best is the one with an unhappy ending.*

6 You use **after next** in expressions such as 'the PHRASE week after next' or 'the month after next' which refer to the period of time after the next one. For example, when it is May, the month after next is July. EG *He had to go there the week after next.*

7 If one thing is **next to** another thing, it is at the PREP side of it. EG *She went and sat next to him... There was a bowl of goldfish next to the bed.*

8 You can also use **next to** to mean almost. EG *I* PHRASE *knew next to nothing about him... The photographs were next to useless but they were all we had.*

next door. A house that is **next door** to your ADV OR house is on one side of it. EG *She lived next door to* ADJ CLASSIF: *the Wilsons... I'm going next door to tell them to be* ATTRIB *quiet... ...our next-door neighbour, Joan.*

next of kin. Your **next of kin** is the person who is N SING OR your closest relative. EG *The only next of kin seems* N UNCOUNT *to be a cousin in Droitwich.* Formal

NHS /ɛn eɪtʃ ɛs/ is an abbreviation for 'National Health Service'. EG *...free NHS dental treatment.*

nib /nɪb/, **nibs**. The **nib** on a fountain pen is the N COUNT small pointed piece of metal at the end, where the ink comes out as you write.

nibble /nɪbəl/, **nibbles, nibbling, nibbled. 1** If you **nibble** something, or **nibble** at it, **1.1** you eat it V+O; ALSO V: slowly by taking small bites out of it. EG *Just nibble* USU+at/on *a piece of bread... She nibbled at her food.* **1.2** you V+O OR V+at bite it very gently. EG *She nibbled my ear lobe playfully.*

2 When a mouse or other small animal **nibbles** V+O OR something, it takes small bites out of it quickly and V+at/on repeatedly. EG *It was nibbling the end of a leaf.*

3 A **nibble** is a gentle or quick bite of something. N COUNT EG *A few licks and nibbles quickly put him off.*

nice /naɪs/, **nicer, nicest. 1** If you say that ADJ QUALIT something is **nice**, you mean that you find it enjoyable, pleasant, or attractive. EG *It would be nice to see you... Did you have a nice time at the party?... How nice you look... It doesn't taste very nice... We had a nice long chat... It's so nice and peaceful here.* ◊ **nicely.** EG *I always think Bessie* ◊ ADV *dresses very nicely.*

2 If you say that someone does or says something ADJ QUALIT **nice**, you mean that they are being kind and thoughtful. EG *It's nice of you to say that... How nice of you to come.*

3 If you say that someone is **nice**, you mean that ADJ QUALIT they are friendly and pleasant and that you like them. EG *He was a terribly nice man.*

4 If you are **nice** to someone, you behave in a ADJ PRED: friendly and pleasant or polite way towards them. USU+to EG *Promise me you'll be nice to her when she comes back... I wish I'd been nicer to him.* ◊ **nicely.** EG *You may go if you ask nicely.* ◊ ADV

nicely /naɪsli/. Something that is happening or ADV AFTER VB working **nicely** is working in a satisfactory way or in the way that you want it to happen. EG *You need some form of identification. Your driver's licence will do nicely... He thought he could manage quite nicely without them.*

nicety /naɪsɪti/, **niceties**. A **nicety** is a small N COUNT: detail, especially concerning polite behaviour. EG USU PLURAL *Here the niceties of etiquette must be observed.* +SUPP

niche /niːʃ/, **niches. 1** A **niche** is a hollow area in N COUNT a wall which can be used to hold a statue, or a natural hollow part in a cliff. EG *...the little statue of the saint in his niche near the pulpit.*

2 If you say that you have found your **niche** in life, N COUNT you mean that you have a job or position which is exactly suitable for you. EG *You can then find your own niche in public life.*

nick /nɪk/, **nicks, nicking, nicked. 1** If you **nick** V+O OR V-REFL something, you make a small cut into the surface of it. EG *He shaved badly, nicking himself in a couple of places.*

2 A **nick** is a small cut made in the surface of N COUNT something. EG *I felt with my fingers for nicks in the metal.*

3 If someone **nicks** something, they steal it. EG *My* V+O typewriter had been nicked. Informal

4 If something happens **in the nick of time**, it PHRASE happens successfully, but at the last possible mo- Informal ment. EG *We got there in the nick of time.*

5 If you say that something is **in good nick**, you PHRASE mean that it is in good condition. If it is **in bad** Informal **nick**, it is in bad condition.

nickel /nɪkəl/, **nickels. 1** Nickel is a silver- N UNCOUNT coloured metal that can be mixed with other metals to form an alloy.

2 A **nickel** is an American or Canadian coin that is N COUNT worth five cents.

nickname /nɪkneɪm/, **nicknames, nicknaming, nicknamed. 1** A **nickname** is an informal name N COUNT for someone, especially one that is used by their friends or relations. EG *...Graham Rathbone, whose nickname was Raffy.*

2 If you **nickname** someone or something, you V+O+C give them an informal name. EG *For a brief while, Mrs Thatcher was nicknamed 'Tina'.*

nicotine /nɪkətiːn/ is an addictive substance that N UNCOUNT is contained in tobacco. EG *...teeth browned by nicotine.*

niece /niːs/, **nieces.** Someone's **niece** is the N COUNT daughter of their sister or brother.

niggle /nɪɡəl/, **niggles, niggling, niggled. 1** If V+O OR V something **niggles** you, it makes you worry slightly over a long time. EG *The question niggled at the* *back of his mind.* ◊ **niggling.** EG *...little niggling* ◊ ADJ CLASSIF : *doubts.* ATTRIB

2 If you **niggle** or if you **niggle** a person, you v, v+o, or criticize the person or fuss about small things. EG v+REPORT : *Critics niggled that the rapid production of planes* ONLY that *was dangerous.*

3 A **niggle** is a small worry or doubt that you keep N COUNT thinking about. EG *There is not the slightest niggle at the back of your mind that you should be spending your time more usefully?*

night /naɪt/, **nights. 1** The **night** is **1.1** the part of N COUNT OR each period of twenty-four hours when it is dark N UNCOUNT outside, especially the time when most people are sleeping. EG *He went out late at night when the streets were empty... We walked for six days and six nights... The storm lasted all night long... He woke in the night with a dreadful pain... I cannot sleep at nights.* **1.2** the period of time between the end of the afternoon and midnight, or between the end of the afternoon and the time when you go to bed. EG *I was out that night... I went on Saturday night.*

2 Night is used in these phrases. **2.1** If it is a PHRASES particular time **at night**, it is between the time when it gets dark and midnight. EG *...eleven o'clock at night.* **2.2** If something happens **day and night** or **night and day**, it happens all the time without stopping. EG *They were being guarded night and day.* **2.3** If you **have an early night**, you go to bed early. If you **have a late night**, you go to bed late.

nightcap /naɪtkæp/, **nightcaps.** A **nightcap** is a N COUNT drink that you have just before you go to bed.

nightclub /naɪtklʌb/, **nightclubs.** A **nightclub** is N COUNT a place where people go in the evening or late at night to drink and to dance or see a show.

nightdress /naɪtdrɛs/, **nightdresses.** A **night-** N COUNT **dress** is a sort of dress that women or girls wear in bed.

nightfall /naɪtfɔːl/ is the time of day when it N UNCOUNT starts to get dark. EG *By nightfall I was feeling sleepy... We wanted to get out before nightfall.*

nightgown /naɪtgaʊn/, **nightgowns.** A **night-** N COUNT **gown** is the same as a nightdress. American

nightie /naɪti¹/, **nighties.** A **nightie** is a night- N COUNT dress. Informal

nightingale /naɪtɪŋgeɪl/, **nightingales.** A **night-** N COUNT **ingale** is a small brown European bird. The male nightingale is considered to sing very beautifully.

nightlife /naɪtlaɪf/ is the entertainment and social N UNCOUNT activities that are available at night in towns and cities, such as nightclubs, theatres, and bars. EG *...the exotic nightlife of Montmartre.*

nightly /naɪtli¹/. A **nightly** event happens every ADJ CLASSIF : night. EG *I was watching the nightly television* ATTRIB OR ADV *news... My mother prayed nightly.*

nightmare /naɪtmɛə/, **nightmares.** A **night-** N COUNT **mare** is **1** a very frightening dream. EG *He rushed to her room when she had nightmares and com- forted her.* **2** a very frightening or unpleasant situation or time. EG *The first day was a nightmare.*

nightmarish /naɪtmɛərɪʃ/. If you describe a ADJ QUALIT : situation or event as **nightmarish**, you mean that USU ATTRIB it is extremely frightening. EG *I had nightmarish visions of what could go wrong.*

night school, night schools. Night school is a N UNCOUNT school where adults can go to educational courses OR N COUNT in the evenings.

night shift, night shifts. A **night shift** is a N COUNT OR period of work that is done regularly at night as N UNCOUNT part of a job, for example in a hospital or factory.

night-time is the part of the day between the N UNCOUNT time when it gets dark and the time when it gets light again. EG *Who would see smoke at night-time?*

night-watchman /naɪt wɒtʃmə²n/, **night-** N COUNT **watchmen.** A **night-watchman** is a person whose job is to guard buildings at night.

nil /nɪl/. **1** If you say that something is **nil**, you N UNCOUNT mean that it does not exist at all. EG *You can reduce the danger to almost nil.*

2 Nil also means the same as nought; often used in N UNCOUNT scores of sports games. EG *Wales beat England three nil... The number rose from nil to 120 in four years.*

nimble /nɪmbə¹l/, **nimbler, nimblest. 1** Someone ADJ QUALIT who is **nimble** is able to move their fingers, hands, or legs quickly and easily. EG *By now, he was quite nimble on his wooden leg.* ◊ **nimbly.** EG *Nimbly,* ◊ ADV *he swung himself out of the car.*

2 Someone who has a **nimble** mind is very quick ADJ QUALIT and clever in the way that they think.

nine /naɪn/, **nines. Nine** is the number 9: see the NUMBER entry headed NUMBER. EG *It had been nine years since she had seen her brother.*

nineteen /naɪntiːn/, **nineteens. Nineteen** is the NUMBER number 19. See the entry headed NUMBER. EG *The ceremony was performed at the same time in nineteen other countries.*

nineteenth /naɪntiːnθ/, **nineteenths.** The **nine-** ORDINAL **teenth** item in a series is the one that you count as number nineteen. See the entry headed NUMBER. EG *...the industrialism of the nineteenth century.*

ninetieth /naɪntɪ²θ/, **ninetieths.** The **ninetieth** ORDINAL item in a series is the one that you count as number ninety. See the entry headed NUMBER. EG *In his ninetieth year he had lost the ability to speak.*

ninety /naɪnti¹/, **nineties. Ninety** is the number NUMBER 90. See the entry headed NUMBER. EG *He was making ninety dollars a week... 'Eighty nine and I'll never live to be ninety,' he wheezed.*

N ING

Nouns which have the label N ING in the Extra Column are the names of activities such as 'cara- vanning' and 'windsurfing', where no verb 'to cara- van' or 'to windsurf' is given in the dictionary. See the entry headed NOUNS for more information.

---

ninth /naɪnθ/, **ninths. 1** The **ninth** item in a series ORDINAL is the one that you count as number nine. See the entry headed NUMBER. EG *...the ninth floor of the Hotel.*

2 A **ninth** is one of nine equal parts of something. N COUNT : EG *In exchange for this work they get one ninth of* USU+of *the crop.*

nip /nɪp/, **nips, nipping, nipped. 1** If you **nip** v+A somewhere, usually somewhere nearby, you go Informal there quickly or for a short time. EG *I'll just nip out and post these letters.*

2 If you **nip** someone or something, you pinch v+o : OFT+A them or bite them lightly. EG *The horse nipped me on the back of the head.* ▸ used as a noun. EG *He* ▸ N COUNT *gave her a nip on the lips.*

nipple /nɪpə²l/, **nipples. 1** The **nipples** on your N COUNT body are the two small pieces of slightly hard flesh on your chest. Babies suck milk through the nip- ples on their mothers' breasts. EG *Infection can enter the breast through the nipple.*

2 A **nipple** is also a piece of rubber or plastic in the N COUNT shape of a nipple which is fitted to the top of a baby's bottle.

nit /nɪt/, **nits. 1** If you call someone a **nit**, you N COUNT/ mean that they are stupid or silly. EG *You're* VOCATIVE *choking her, you nit!* Informal British

2 Nits are the eggs of a kind of louse that N COUNT : sometimes lives in people's hair. EG *The school* USU PLURAL *doctor looks to see if you have nits in your hair.*

nitrogen /naɪtrəʤə³n/ is a colourless element N UNCOUNT that has no smell and is usually found as a gas. It forms about 78% of the earth's atmosphere, and is found in all living things.

Do people go out at night in their nightdresses?

N MASS stands for **mass noun**
Nouns which have the label **N MASS** in the Extra Column are usually found in the singular form, and are not countable. But when you are talking about types of them or measures of them, you can use the plural. So you normally say *I drink coffee in the mornings and tea in the afternoons.* But you can also say *They stock teas and coffees from all over the world.*
See the entry headed NOUNS for more information.

N MOD stands for **noun modifier**
Some nouns have the label N MOD in the Extra Column. These are nouns which usually come just in front of other nouns, and are therefore used rather like adjectives.
See the entry headed NOUNS for more information.

no /nəʊ/. 1 You use **no** 1.1 to say that something is not true, to refuse an offer, or to refuse permission. EG *'Did you see that programme last night?' – 'No, I didn't.'... 'They go round kissing one another when they meet.' – 'No they don't.' – 'Yes they do. I've seen them doing it.'... 'Do you want a biscuit?' – 'No thanks.'... 'Can I come too?' – 'No.'* 1.2 to indicate that you do not want someone to do something. EG *'No!' I shrieked. 'Don't!'* CONVENTION: NEG

2 If you say that someone **will not take no for an answer**, you mean that they go on trying to make you agree to something even after you have refused. PHRASE

3 You also use **no** 3.1 to say that you agree with a negative statement that someone else has made. EG *'It's not difficult, you see.' – 'No, it must be quite easy when you know how.'* 3.2 as a way of introducing a correction to what you have just said. EG *...500 grams, no, a little less than that.* 3.3 to express shock or disappointment at something. EG *'Michael's fallen off his bike.' – 'Oh no, not again.'* CONVENTION: NEG

4 You use **no** to indicate that there is not even one thing of a particular kind or not even a small amount of a particular thing. For example, if someone has no job or no money, they do not have a job or do not have any money. EG *He has given no reason for his decision... I do it all on my own. I have no help at all.* DET: NEG

5 You use **no** to emphasize that someone or something is not a particular kind of person or thing. For example, if you say that someone is no fool, you mean that they are definitely not a fool. EG *She is no friend of mine.* DET: NEG

6 You use **no** when emphasizing that something does not exceed a particular amount or number, or does not have more of a particular quality than something else. For example, something that is no bigger than a fingernail is not bigger than a fingernail. EG *The whole gun was no longer than eighteen inches... Winners will be notified by post no later than 31st August... a job that was no better than a common labourer's.* SUBMOD +COMPAR: NEG

7 No is also used, especially on notices, to say that a particular thing is forbidden. EG *No smoking... No talking once we're inside.* DET: NEG Formal

8 If you say **there is no** doing a particular thing, you mean that it is impossible to do that thing. EG *There's no arguing with my father.* PHRASE

No., Nos. No. is a written abbreviation for 'number'. EG *He lives at No. 14 Sumatra Road.*

nobility /nəʊbɪlˈtiʲ/. 1 Nobility is 1.1 the quality of being noble and admirable in behaviour. EG *He had nobility in defeat... He followed his principles* N UNCOUNT with nobility. 1.2 the condition of belonging to the nobility of a society. EG *...the silken rope which was the privilege of nobility.*

2 The **nobility** of a society are all the people who have titles and high social rank. N COLL: the+N

noble /nəʊbəʳl/, **nobler, noblest; nobles.** 1 Someone who is **noble** 1.1 is honest, brave, and unselfish, and deserves admiration and respect. EG *Among them were some of the greatest and noblest men in our history... ...a man of noble character.* ◊ **nobly.** EG *She had nobly served the cause of Christianity.* 1.2 belongs to a high social class and has a title. EG *...young men of noble birth.* ▸ used as a noun. EG *Every noble in the land wanted to marry the king's daughter.* ADJ QUALIT ◊ ADV ADJ CLASSIF ▸ N COUNT

2 Something that is **noble** is very impressive in quality or appearance. EG *...an old man with a noble head and a bristling moustache... ...one of the noblest collections of art in England.* ADJ QUALIT

nobody /nəʊbəʳdiʲ/, **nobodies.** 1 Nobody means not a single person. See also **no-one.** EG *Nobody seems to notice... There was nobody on the bridge at all.* PRON INDEF: NEG

2 Someone who is a **nobody** is not at all important. EG *Miss Watkins was a nobody; no family, no close friends.* N COUNT: OFT a+N

nocturnal /nɒktɜːʳnəʳl/. 1 Nocturnal events happen during the night. EG *...your nocturnal sightseeing tour of our city.* ADJ CLASSIF: USU ATTRIB

2 An animal that is **nocturnal** is active mostly at night. EG *Their nocturnal habits make long-eared owls hard to see.* ADJ CLASSIF

nod /nɒd/, **nods, nodding, nodded.** 1 If you **nod,** 1.1 you move your head quickly down and up to show that you are answering 'yes' to a question, or to show agreement, understanding, or approval. EG *'Is it true?' She nodded... He nodded his head... I nod in agreement.* 1.2 you bend your head once in a particular direction in order to indicate something or to give someone a signal to do something. EG *'Ask him,' said Ringbaum, nodding towards Philip.* 1.3 you bend your head once to someone as a way of saying hello or goodbye. EG *They all nodded a final goodnight... I nodded to the ladies and sat down.* V OR V+O V+A V OR V+O

2 If something **nods,** it bends or moves gently up and down. EG *There was not even a little breeze to make the poppies nod.* V

3 A **nod** is a quick movement of your head down and up. EG *From time to time, he gave him an encouraging nod.* N COUNT: OFT a+N

nod off. If you **nod off,** you fall asleep while you are sitting down, especially when you had not intended to fall asleep. EG *His remarks left delegates nodding off.* PHRASAL VB: V+ADV Informal

nodule /nɒdjuːʳl/, **nodules.** A **nodule** is a small round lump on something, often on the root of a plant. EG *...bacteria in the root nodules of beans.* N COUNT

no-go area, no-go areas. A **no-go area** is a place which is controlled by a group of people who use force to prevent other people from entering it. EG *90 per cent of the country had become no-go areas.* N COUNT

noise /nɔɪz/, **noises.** 1 A **noise** is a sound that someone or something makes. EG *A sudden noise made Brody jump... The branches snapped with a dry cracking noise... Dolphins produce a great variety of noises.* N COUNT

2 Noise is a loud or unpleasant sound. EG *Try not to make so much noise... ...the noise of the radio next door... Our washing machine is making a terrible noise.* N UNCOUNT OR N COUNT

noiseless /nɔɪzlɪʳs/. Something that is **noiseless** does not make any sound. EG *...a totally noiseless fan.* ADJ QUALIT

noisy /nɔɪziʲ/, **noisier, noisiest.** 1 Someone or something that is **noisy** makes a lot of noise, especially loud or unpleasant noise. EG *The audience was large and noisy.* ◊ **noisily.** EG *My sister was crying noisily.* ADJ QUALIT ◊ ADV

2 A place that is **noisy** is full of a lot of noise, ADJ QUALIT
especially loud or unpleasant noise. EG *They complained that Canton was hot and noisy and they
wanted to leave.*

nomad /nəʊmæd/, **nomads**. A **nomad** is a person N COUNT
who belongs to a tribe which travels from place to
place rather than living in one place all the time.

nomadic /nəʊmædɪk/. People who are **nomadic** ADJ CLASSIF
travel from place to place rather than living in one
place all the time. EG *These tribes have a nomadic
way of life.*

no-man's land is land that is not owned or N UNCOUNT
controlled by anyone, for example the land between two boundaries.

nominal /nɒmɪnəl/. **1** You use **nominal** to de- ADJ CLASSIF
scribe a position or characteristic which something
is supposed to have but which it does not have in
reality. EG *We were directing the operation, though
under the nominal leadership of a guerrilla general.* ◊ **nominally**. EG *Dad, nominally a Methodist,* ◊ ADV
entered churches only for weddings and funerals.

2 A **nominal** price or sum of money is very small ADJ CLASSIF :
in comparison with the real cost or value of the ATTRIB
thing you are buying or selling. EG *At a nominal
price, the settlers got the rest of the land.*

nominate /nɒmɪneɪt/, **nominates**, **nominating**, V+O :
nominated. If you **nominate** someone for a job or USU+for/to
to a position, you formally choose them to hold that
job or position or suggest them as a candidate. EG
*Trade unions nominate representatives to public
bodies... I've been nominated for a Senior Lectureship.*

nomination /nɒmɪneɪʃən/, **nominations**. **1** A N COUNT
nomination is an official suggestion of someone as
a candidate in an election or for a job. EG *...a list of
nominations for senior lectureships.*

2 The **nomination** of someone to a job or position N UNCOUNT
is their appointment to the job or position. EG OR N COUNT
*...Judge O'Connor's nomination to the Supreme
Court.*

nominee /nɒmɪniː/, **nominees**. A **nominee** is N COUNT
someone who is nominated for something. EG *Dave
is this year's nominee for the Exchange scheme.*

non-. **1** non- is used to form adjectives that de- PREFIX
scribe something as not having a particular quality
or feature. For example, a non-nuclear war is a
war fought without nuclear weapons. EG *...non-
violent demonstrations... ...non-industrial societies.*

2 non- is also used to form nouns. These nouns PREFIX
refer **2.1** to situations in which a particular kind of
action is not taken. *...a non-aggression pact... ...non-
payment of fines.* **2.2** to people who do not belong
to a particular group. EG *...non-car-owners... ...non-
Christians... To the non-angler this can be very
puzzling.*

non-alcoholic. A **non-alcoholic** drink does not ADJ CLASSIF
contain alcohol.

nonchalant /nɒnʃələnt/. Someone who is **non-** ADJ QUALIT
chalant behaves calmly and in a way which
suggests that they do not care much about things.
EG *He tried to sound cheerful and nonchalant.*
◊ **nonchalantly.** EG *The officer waved a hand* ◊ ADV
nonchalantly. ◊ **nonchalance** /nɒnʃələns/. EG *The* ◊ N UNCOUNT
*answers are given with so much confidence and
such nonchalance.*

noncommittal /nɒnkəmɪtəl/. If someone is **non-** ADJ QUALIT
committal, they do not express their opinion or
decision firmly. EG *On planning the government is
studiously noncommittal... I received a noncommittal letter in return.*

nonconformist /nɒnkənfɔːmɪst/, **nonconform-** N COUNT
ists. A **nonconformist** is someone who behaves in
an unusual or rebellious way. EG *...the persecution
of non-conformists and minorities.* ▶ used as an ▶ ADJ QUALIT
adjective. EG *I've got rather nonconformist ideas on
this.*

nondescript /nɒndɪskrɪpt/. Something that is ADJ QUALIT
nondescript is fairly dull and uninteresting in
appearance or design. EG *...a complex of nonde-

script buildings... The women were dressed in
nondescript clothes.*

none /nʌn/. **1 None** means not a single thing or PRON : NEG,
person, or not even a small amount of a particular OFT+of
thing. EG *None of these suggestions is very helpful...
None of us were allowed to go... I have answered
every single question. My opponent has answered
none... 'You had no difficulty in finding it?' – 'None
at all.'*

2 If you say that you will **have none of** something, PHRASE
you mean that you refuse to tolerate it. EG *I'll have Informal
none of this nonsense.*

3 You use **none too** to mean 'not at all'. For PHRASE
example, **none too** sure means not at all sure. EG Formal
*We're none too sure what we're arguing about... He
hauled her none too gently to her feet.*

nonentity /nɒnentɪtɪ/, **nonentities**. If you refer N COUNT
to someone as a **nonentity**, you mean that they
are not special or important in any way. EG *Grant
came from a family of nonentities.*

nonetheless /nʌnðəles/ means in spite of what ADV SEN
has just been said. EG *She couldn't act at all.* Formal
*Nonetheless she was a big box office attraction... It
was not an impossible task, but they failed nonetheless.*

non-event, non-events. If you describe some- N COUNT
thing that happens as a **non-event**, you mean that
it is not at all interesting or exciting.

non-existent. Something that is **non-existent** ADJ CLASSIF
does not exist in a particular place or does not
exist at all. EG *Medical facilities are poor or non-
existent in most rural areas.*

non-fiction is writing that gives information or N UNCOUNT
describes real events, rather than telling an invented story. EG *...works of non-fiction... ...non-fiction
books.*

non-nuclear means not using or involving nu- ADJ CLASSIF
clear weapons or nuclear power. EG *...the deploy-* ATTRIB
ment of non-nuclear weapons.

no-nonsense. A **no-nonsense** person is firm and ADJ CLASSIF :
efficient. EG *I liked his no-nonsense approach to the* ATTRIB
whole matter.

nonplussed /nɒnplʌst/. If you are **nonplussed** ADJ QUALIT
when something happens, you feel confused and
unsure how to react. EG *'I've heard nothing about
this,' he said, nonplussed.*

nonsense /nɒnsəns/. **1** You use **nonsense** to
refer to **1.1** words that do not mean anything. EG N UNCOUNT
*You can confuse the computer program by typing
in nonsense.* **1.2** something spoken or written that N UNCOUNT
you think is untrue or stupid. EG *A lot of nonsense is* OR EXCLAM
*talked about the temperature of wine... 'I am her
father.' – 'Nonsense,' he said. 'You are not.'* **1.3** N UNCOUNT
something that you think is foolish or that you
disapprove of. EG *Stop this nonsense, Louisa, for
God's sake... We were warned not to get involved
in any sort of publicity nonsense.*

2 To **make nonsense of** something or to **make a** PHRASE
nonsense of it means to cause it to become
ridiculous or pointless. EG *The rest of his policies
made nonsense of his call for moderation.*

nonsensical /nɒnsensɪkəl/. Something that is ADJ QUALIT
nonsensical is stupid or ridiculous. EG *This attitude
seemed nonsensical to the general public.*

non-smoker, non-smokers. A **non-smoker** is N COUNT
someone who does not smoke.

non-starter, non-starters. If a plan or idea is a N COUNT
non-starter, it has no chance of success. EG *Such a
policy is really a complete non-starter.*

non-stick. A **non-stick** saucepan, frying-pan, or ADJ CLASSIF
baking tin has a layer of a special substance on its
inside which prevents food from sticking to it.

non-stop. A **non-stop** activity continues without ADJ CLASSIF
any pauses or breaks. EG *They keep up a non-stop* OR ADV

If something is a non-event, does it happen?

conversation... ...taking the non-stop flight to London... Carter laughed non-stop for several minutes.

non-violent. Non-violent actions, especially actions intended to bring about political change, do not involve hurting people or damaging things. EG It is to be a peaceful, non-violent protest. ◇ **non-violence.** EG ...my commitment to the principles of non-violence. _ADJ CLASSIF_ ◇ _N UNCOUNT_

non-white, non-whites. Someone who is **non-white** belongs to a race of people who are not of European origin. ▸ used as a noun. EG Such economic policies are hurting non-whites badly. _ADJ CLASSIF_ ▸ _N COUNT_

noodles /nu:dⁿlz/ are long thin pieces of pasta. _N PLURAL_

nook /nʊk/, **nooks.** If you talk about **every nook and cranny** of a place, you are emphasizing that you mean every part of it or every space in it. EG Toddlers are real explorers. They poke into every nook and cranny. _PHRASE_

noon /nu:n/ is twelve o'clock in the middle of the day. EG The visitor turned up at noon. _N UNCOUNT_

noonday /nu:ndeɪ/ means happening in the middle part of the day. EG ...a flash brighter than the noonday sun. _N MOD Literary_

no-one /nəʊ wʌn/ means not a single person. See also **nobody.** EG They had seen no-one else all afternoon... Sorry, there's no-one here called Nikki. _PRON INDEF : NEG_

noose /nu:s/, **nooses.** A **noose** is a loop at the end of a piece of rope, especially one used to hang someone. _N COUNT_

nor /nɔ:/. You use **nor** 1 after 'neither' in order to introduce the second thing that a negative statement applies to. EG Neither Margaret nor John was there... My father could neither read nor write. 2 after a negative statement in order to add something else that the negative statement applies to. EG Melanie was not to be found – not that day, nor the next day, nor the day after that... I could not afford to eat in restaurants and nor could anyone I knew. _CONJ : NEG_

norm /nɔ:m/, **norms.** 1 **Norms** are ways of behaving that are considered normal in a particular society or place. EG ...the conventional norms of polite European society. 2 If you say that a situation is the **norm**, you mean that it is usual and expected. EG In Russia, working wives have been the norm for many years. _N COUNT : USU PLURAL_ _N SING : the+N_

normal /nɔ:mⁿl/. Something that is **normal** is usual and ordinary, and what people expect. EG Can she lead a normal life?... This is a perfectly normal baby... I've got used to it, it seems normal now. _ADJ QUALIT_

normality /nɔ:mælɪˈtiˈ/ is a situation in which everything is normal and as people expect. EG People have a longing for normality. _N UNCOUNT_

normally /nɔ:məliˈ/. 1 If you say that a particular thing **normally** happens, you mean that it is what usually happens. EG I don't normally drink at lunch... Meetings are normally held three or four times a year... Normally, I keep these at home. 2 If something happens **normally**, it happens in a way that is usual and that people expect. EG The important thing is that she's eating normally. _ADV OR ADV SEN_ _ADV_

north /nɔ:θ/; often spelled with a capital letter. 1 The **north** is 1.1 the direction which is on your left when you are looking towards the direction where the sun rises. EG The land to the north and east was low-lying... ...Norwegian airfields in the far north. 1.2 the part of a place or country which is towards the north. EG ...a man from somewhere in the north of England. 2 **North** means towards the north or to the north of a place or thing. EG They were heading north... It's 150 miles north of Salisbury. 3 The **north** part of a place or country is the part which is towards the north. EG ...a flat in north London... ...the mountains of North Arizona. 4 A **north** wind blows from the north. _N SING : the+N_ _ADV_ _ADJ CLASSIF : ATTRIB_ _ADJ CLASSIF_

north-east; often spelled with a capital letter or capital letters. 1 The **north-east** is 1.1 the direction which is halfway between north and east. EG Our route lay somewhere to the north-east... We _N SING : the+N_

attack from the north-east. 1.2 the part of a place or country which is towards the north-east. EG ...the north-east of England... ...kids in the North-East. 2 **North-east** means towards the north-east or to the north-east of a place or thing. EG Turn left and go north-east towards the station... It's a small town about fifteen kilometers northeast of Uppsala. 3 The **north-east** part of a place or country is the part which is towards the north-east. EG The oldest part is close to the north-east entrance... ...in north-east Brazil. 4 A **north-east** wind blows from the north-east. _ADV_ _ADJ CLASSIF : ATTRIB_ _ADJ CLASSIF_

north-eastern means in or from the north-east of a region or country. EG ...floods in north-eastern India. _ADJ CLASSIF : ATTRIB_

northerly /nɔ:ðəliˈ/. 1 A **northerly** point, area, or direction is to the north or towards the north. EG ...the wet, northerly slopes... We proceeded along a more northerly route. 2 A **northerly** wind blows from the north. _ADJ QUALIT_ _ADJ CLASSIF_

northern /nɔ:ðⁿn/ means in or from the north of a region or country. EG ...the high mountains of northern Japan... ...the Northern Hemisphere. _ADJ CLASSIF : ATTRIB_

North Pole. The **North Pole** is the place on the surface of the earth which is farthest towards the north. _N PROPER : the+N_

northward /nɔ:θwəd/ or **northwards** means towards the north. EG They had fled northwards towards Kurnal. ▸ **Northward** is also used as an adjective. EG ...the northward drift of the massive Himalayan chain. _ADV AFTER VB_ ▸ _ADJ CLASSIF_

north-west; often spelled with a capital letter or capital letters. 1 The **north-west** is 1.1 the direction which is halfway between north and west. EG At the bridge the lake curves to the north-west. 1.2 the part of a place or country which is towards the north-west. EG ...a hilly area in the north-west. 2 **North-west** means towards the north-west or to the north-west of a place or thing. EG Some 300 miles north-west of Kampala, there is an abandoned village. 3 The **north-west** part of a place or country is the part which is towards the north-west. EG ...a Roman settlement in north-west England... ...the north-west frontier of India. 4 A **north-west** wind blows from the north-west. _N SING : the+N_ _ADV_ _ADJ CLASSIF : ATTRIB_ _ADJ CLASSIF_

north-western means in or from the north-west of a region or country. EG ...a cattle station in Northwestern Australia. _ADJ CLASSIF_

nose /nəʊz/, **noses, nosing, nosed.** 1 Your **nose** is the part of your face which sticks out above your mouth. You use it for smelling and breathing. See picture at THE HUMAN BODY. EG Johnny punched me in the nose. 2 The **nose** of a car or plane is the front part of it. EG He thrust the nose of his plane upward. 3 **Nose** is also used in these phrases. 3.1 If you say that someone **has a nose for** something, you mean that they have a natural ability to find it or recognize it. EG The young have a sensitive nose for insincerity. 3.2 If you **keep** your **nose out** of something, you do not interfere in it. 3.3 If someone **pokes** or **sticks** their **nose into** something, they try to interfere in it or to find out what is happening, when it does not concern them. EG He shouldn't poke his nose into their business. 3.4 If you say that something **gets up** your **nose**, you mean that it annoys you. 3.5 If you **pay through the nose** for something, you pay a very high price for it. EG Country people have to pay through the nose for their goods. 3.6 If something is happening **under** your **nose**, it is happening in front of you and it should be obvious to you. EG Cheating was going on under the teacher's nose. 3.7 If you **look down** your **nose at** someone or something, you think that they are inferior; used showing disapproval. 3.8 If someone **turns up** their **nose at** something, they reject it because they think that it _N COUNT_ _N COUNT+SUPP_ _PHRASES Informal_ is not good enough for them; used showing disapproval.

nose about or **nose around.** If you **nose about** PHRASAL VB: or **nose around**, you look around a place that V+ADV/PREP belongs to someone else to see if you can find Informal something interesting. EG *Stay outside the door and see that no one comes nosing around.*

nosebleed /nəʊzbliːd/, **nosebleeds.** If you have a N COUNT **nosebleed**, blood comes out from inside your nose, usually because it has been hit.

nosedive /nəʊzdaɪv/, **nosedives, nosediving,** N COUNT **nosedived.** If a plane does a **nosedive**, it flies very fast towards the ground, pointing downwards. EG *The plane went into a deliberate nose-dive.* ▸ used ▸ V as a verb. EG *Suddenly, it nosedived towards the roof of a school.*

nosey /nəʊzi¹/. See **nosy.**

nostalgia /nɒstældʒɪ²ə/ is an affectionate and N UNCOUNT: slightly sad feeling that you have for the past. EG OFT+*for* *...nostalgia for the good old days.*

nostalgic /nɒstældʒɪk/. If you feel **nostalgic**, you ADJ QUALIT are thinking affectionately and rather sadly about a happier time in the past. EG *He was full of memories, nostalgic for the past... She knew some of the tunes they were playing, nostalgic reminders of her youth.* ◇ **nostalgically.** EG *...talking nostalgi-* ◇ ADV *cally of the good old days.*

nostril /nɒstrɪl/, **nostrils.** Your **nostrils** are the N COUNT two openings at the end of your nose, which you breathe through. EG *...with the smell of smoke in my nostrils.*

nosy /nəʊzi¹/, **nosier, nosiest;** also spelled **nosey.** ADJ QUALIT Someone who is **nosy** tries to find out about things which do not concern them; used showing disapproval. EG *'Who was it?' – 'Don't be so nosy.'*

not /nɒt/. 1 You use **not** to make clauses or NEG sentences negative. **Not** is often shortened to **n't** in informal English. When the verb has an auxiliary or modal auxiliary, you add **not** between the auxiliary and the main verb. EG *I haven't tried to telephone him... She couldn't hear the orchestra properly.*
If the verb does not already have an auxiliary, you need to add 'do'. EG *I don't agree with everything he says... She did not answer.*
When the main verb is 'be', you use **not** without an auxiliary. EG *There wasn't enough room for everybody... It's not unusual.*
2 When **not** is used with verbs such as 'want', NEG 'think', and 'seem', the negative effect of **not** belongs to the clause or infinitive that follows the verb. For example, 'I don't think she's here' means 'I think she's not here'.
3 You use **not**, usually in the form **n't**, in question NEG: tags after a positive statement. EG *That's a new one,* AFTER MODAL *isn't it?... You've seen this, haven't you?* OR AFTER AUX
4 You can use **not** to make questions 4.1 express- NEG ing surprise or annoyance. EG *Don't they realize it's against the law?* 4.2 politely suggesting something. EG *Shouldn't you go and see him?*
5 You can use **not** to represent the negative of a NEG word, group, or clause that has just been used. EG *'Do you know how much it is?' – 'I'm afraid not.'... They'd know if it was all right or not.*
6 You can use **not** before 'all', 'every', or 'always' NEG when you are referring to only some members of a group or some occasions. EG *Not all scientists are honest... Not everyone agrees with me.*
7 You can use **not** or **not even** in front of 'a' or NEG 'one' as emphatic ways of saying that there is none at all of what is being mentioned. EG *The day was very still. There was not even a little breeze... Not one part was missing.*
8 You can use **not** when you are contrasting NEG something that is untrue with something that is true. EG *We wept, not because we were frightened but because we were ashamed.*
9 You use **not that** to introduce a negative clause CONJ: NEG that decreases the importance of the previous

statement. EG *Bob helped him. Not that it was difficult.*

10 **Not at all** is 10.1 an emphatic way of saying CONVENTION: 'No'. EG *'Does that seem nonsense to you?' – 'Not at* NEG *all.'... 'Would you mind?' – 'Not at all.'* 10.2 a polite Formal way of acknowledging a person's thanks. EG *'Thanks.' – 'Not at all.'*

11 **if not**: see **if.** ● **nothing if not**: see **nothing.**

notable /nəʊtəbə⁰l/. Something or someone that is ADJ QUALIT **notable** is important or interesting. EG *With a few notable exceptions this trend has continued... Watermouth is notable for experimental forms of teaching.*

notably /nəʊtəbli¹/. You use **notably** 1 before ADV giving an important or typical example of something that you are talking about. EG *Some people, notably his business associates, had begun to distrust him.* 2 to emphasize the degree of a quality or SUBMOD action. EG *So far, Wall Street has been notably unimpressed.*

notch /nɒtʃ/, **notches, notching, notched.** 1 A N COUNT **notch** is a small V-shaped cut in the surface or edge of something. EG *Carve notches at either end of a stick and wind the thread round them.*
2 You can refer to a particular level on a scale, for N COUNT example a scale of achievement, as a **notch**. EG *My regard for Smithy went up another notch.*

notch up. If you **notch up** a particular score or PHRASAL VB: total, you achieve it. EG *The Tory candidate had* V+O+ADV *notched up eleven hundred votes.*

note /nəʊt/, **notes, noting, noted.** 1 A **note** is 1.1 N COUNT a short letter, usually an informal one. EG *She left a note saying she would see us again... She wrote a note to the chief of police.* 1.2 something that you write down to remind you about something, for example what someone said or what you intend to do. EG *I'll make a note of that... I took notes at the lecture.* 1.3 a short piece of additional information that is given in a book or article. EG *Yugoslavia is a different matter (see note on the Yugoslav situation, below).* 1.4 a piece of printed paper that is used as money. EG *...a five pound note.*
2 If you **make** or **keep a mental note** of some- PHRASE thing, you make an effort to remember it. EG *He made a mental note to tell Lamin later how these men were.*
3 If you **compare notes** with someone, you talk to PHRASE them about something and find out whether they have the same opinion, information, or experiences of it as you. EG *There are a few things we might compare notes on.*
4 If you **note** a fact, 4.1 you become aware of it. EG V+O OR *It is important for us to note three basic facts...* V+REPORT *Note that the report does not carry any form of official recommendation... His audience, I noted with regret, were looking bored.* 4.2 you mention it in order to draw people's attention to it. EG *A government report released last week noted an alarming rise in racial harassment.*
5 If you **take note** of something, you pay attention PHRASE to it because you think that it is important. EG *I had to start taking some note of political developments.*
6 A **note** is also 6.1 a sound of a particular pitch, N COUNT especially one made by a musical instrument or a singer. EG *The slow music rang out, note by solemn note.* 6.2 a written symbol that represents a sound of a particular pitch and length. EG *Not one of them could read a note of music.*
7 A **note** of a particular kind is 7.1 a quality in N SING+SUPP someone's voice that shows how they are feeling. EG *There was a note of triumph in her voice.* 7.2 an atmosphere or mood. EG *Sensing this would be a good note on which to end the interview, I got up... On a more serious note, I must warn you of the risks involved in this project.*

Which meaning of 'notice' will you find on a noticeboard?

note down. If you **note** something **down,** you write it down so that you have a record of it. EG *I'll give you time to note down where to send them.*   PHRASAL VB : V+O+ADV

notebook /nǝutbuk/, **notebooks.** A **notebook** is a small book for writing notes in.   N COUNT

noted /nǝuti²d/. Someone or something that is **noted** is well-known and admired for something that they do or have. EG *...a Scottish family noted for its intellect... ...a noted American writer.*   ADJ CLASSIF : OFT+*for* Formal

notepad /nǝutpæd/, **notepads.** A **notepad** is a pad of paper that you write notes or letters on.   N COUNT

notepaper /nǝutpeɪpǝ/ is paper that you write letters on.   N UNCOUNT

noteworthy /nǝutwɜːðiˡ/. A **noteworthy** fact or event is interesting or significant. EG *It was noteworthy that the Count was the only person there.*   ADJ QUALIT

nothing /nʌθɪŋ/. **1** You use **nothing** when you are referring to no things, for example no objects, no events, or no ideas. EG *She shook the bottle over the glass; nothing came out... The man nodded but said nothing... There's nothing to worry about.*   PRON INDEF : NEG

2 If you say that someone or something is **nothing,** you mean that they are very unimportant. EG *In those days time was nothing. Now it is everything... 'What's the matter with you?' Claud asked. 'It's nothing,' he gasped. 'I'll be all right in a minute.'*   PRON INDEF : NEG Informal

3 Nothing is also used in these phrases. **3.1** If you say that an action was done **for nothing,** you mean that it was done either without a good reason or without achieving any worthwhile results. EG *Now they're killing our soldiers. For nothing.* **3.2** If you say about a story or rumour that there is **nothing in it,** you mean that it is untrue. **3.3** If you say about something that you have done that there was **nothing to it,** you mean that it was very easy. **3.4** You use **nothing of the sort** to emphasize a refusal or a negative statement. EG *You will do nothing of the sort... Although we think we are progressing, we may be doing nothing of the sort.* **3.5** You use **nothing if not** to emphasize that someone or something has a particular quality. For example, if you say that someone is **nothing if not** considerate, you mean that they are very considerate. **3.6 Nothing but** a particular thing means only that thing. EG *She could see nothing but his head... ...thirty years of nothing but war.* **3.7** If you say that **there is nothing for it** but to take a particular action, you mean that it is the only possible action that you can take, even though you would prefer not to. EG *There was nothing for it now except to go straight ahead with the plan.*   PHRASES   British

notice /nǝutɪs/, **notices, noticing, noticed. 1** If you **notice** something, you become aware of it. EG *I suddenly noticed a friend in the front row... She noticed him scratching his head... She noticed that he was staring at her.*   V+O : OFT+-ING OR INF; ALSO V OR V+REPORT

2 Notice is used in these phrases relating to awareness. **2.1** If you **take no notice** of someone or something, you do not allow them to affect what you think or do. EG *Take no notice of him. He's always rude to people.* **2.2** If you **take notice** of something, you behave in a way that shows you are aware of it. EG *I hope the heads of schools will take notice of my comments.* **2.3** If something **comes to** your **notice** or **is brought to** your **notice,** you become aware of it, for example because someone points it out to you. EG *Many cases have come to my notice... We bring to the notice of the committee things that ought to be done.* **2.4** If something **escapes** your **notice,** you do not recognize it or realize it. EG *It did not escape her notice that he kept glancing at her.*   PHRASES

3 If someone gets **notice** from other people, they receive attention and are admired or respected. EG *He achieved some public notice in later life.*   N UNCOUNT

4 A **notice** is a written announcement which is put in a place where it can be read by everyone. EG *At the main entrance, there was a large notice which said 'Visitors welcome at any time.'*   N COUNT

5 If you give **notice** about something that is going to happen, you give a warning in advance that it is going to happen. EG *The union was to give 28 days' notice of strikes... She could have done it if she'd had a bit more notice... They will eject without notice any undesirable person.*   N UNCOUNT : USU+SUPP

6 Notice is also used in these phrases relating to advance warnings or information. **6.1** If something can or must be done **at short notice** or **at a moment's notice,** it can or must be done with very little advance warning. EG *It's going to be difficult to fix things at such short notice... It is there ready to be switched on at a moment's notice.* **6.2** If a situation will exist **until further notice,** it will continue until someone changes it and informs people. EG *The beaches are closed until further notice.* **6.3** If an employer **gives** a worker **notice,** the employer tells the worker that he or she must leave within a fixed period of time. EG *She had been given two weeks' notice at the Works.* **6.4** If you **hand in** your **notice,** you tell your employer that you intend to leave your job soon, after a fixed period of time.   PHRASES

noticeable /nǝutɪsǝbǝˡl/. Something that is **noticeable** is very obvious, so that it is easy to see or recognize. EG *It did not have any noticeable effect upon the rate of economic growth.* ◊ **noticeably.** EG *As they climbed higher, the air became noticeably cooler.*   ADJ QUALIT   ◊ ADV

noticeboard /nǝutɪsbɔːd/, **noticeboards.** A **noticeboard** is a board on a wall, which people pin notices to.   N COUNT British

notification /nǝutɪfɪkeɪʃǝºn/. If you are given **notification** of something, you are officially informed of it. EG *You will be sent notification of the results of your interview by post.*   N UNCOUNT

notify /nǝutɪfaɪ/, **notifies, notifying, notified.** If you **notify** someone of something, you officially inform them of it. EG *The Housing Department is notified of all planning applications... He wrote to notify me that the cheque had arrived.*   V+O : OFT+*of* OR REPORT

notion /nǝuʃǝºn/, **notions.** A **notion** is a belief or idea. EG *...the notion that the earth was flat... He had only the vaguest notion of what it was about.*   N COUNT : USU+REPORT OR *of*

notoriety /nǝutǝraɪˡtiˡ/ is the fact of being well known for something that is bad or undesirable. EG *...terrorists who acquired international notoriety for the kidnapping of government figures.*   N UNCOUNT

notorious /nǝˡtɔːrɪǝs/. Someone or something that is **notorious** is well known for something that is bad or undesirable. EG *The area was notorious for murders... ...his notorious arrogance.*   ADJ QUALIT : OFT+*for*

◊ **notoriously.** EG *Here, rainfall is notoriously variable and unreliable.*   ◊ SUBMOD

notwithstanding /nɒtwɪθstændɪŋ, -wɪð-/. If something is true **notwithstanding** a particular thing, it is true in spite of that thing. EG *Computing remains a growth area in which, notwithstanding economic recessions, the outlook looks bright.*   PREP Formal

nought /nɔːt/, **noughts. Nought** is the number 0. See the entry headed NUMBER. EG *...nought point two.*   NUMBER

noun /naʊn/, **nouns.** In grammar, a **noun** is a word which is used to refer to a person, a thing, or an abstract idea such as a feeling or quality. In this dictionary, the abbreviation N is used in the grammar notes to mean 'noun'. See the entry headed NOUNS for information about nouns.   N COUNT

nourish /nʌrɪʃ/, **nourishes, nourishing, nourished. 1** To **nourish** people or animals means to provide them with food. EG *They had grown stronger now that they were better nourished... ...nourishing their young on small insects.*   V+O

2 If you **nourish** a feeling or belief, you encourage it to grow or survive. EG *She had nourished dreams of escape.*   V+O Literary

nourishing /nʌrɪʃɪŋ/. Food that is **nourishing** makes you strong and healthy. EG *Ham sandwiches are nourishing and filling... ...a nourishing diet.*   ADJ QUALIT

NOUNS

Nouns are the words that you use when you are referring to people, things, and abstract ideas such as feelings and qualities.

A lot of the grammar of nouns is in the way we measure and count them. There are three types of choice:

1 at word level: does the noun have singular and plural forms, or just one form?

2 at noun group level: does the noun go with 'a' or 'some'? Can it occur on its own?

3 at clause level: does the noun go with a singular or a plural verb? (Only the present tense of verbs shows this choice.)

Countable nouns

The most common nouns in English are countable nouns (N COUNT). These are nouns that have both a singular and a plural form. The plural is usually made by adding **-s** to the singular, but if you look at the first line of each entry, you will see exactly how to spell the plural.

When countable nouns are used in the singular, they must have a determiner, such as **a**, **the**, or **my** in front of them. So you say: *. . . the house . . .   . . . a friend . . .*
. . . his dog.

When you want to use an adjective to tell you more about the noun, you put the determiner before the adjective: *. . . a clean shirt . . .   . . . that little boy . . .*
. . . her pretty green dress.

When a countable noun is used in the plural, it can have a determiner, but only when you want to pick out some rather than all of the particular item. So you can say:
. . . tables . . .   . . . the tables . . .   . . . those tables . . .   . . . her tables.

Countable nouns go with the same number choice in verbs. For example: *The house is on fire . . .   The table is dirty . . .   Those flowers are lovely.*

Uncountable nouns

Many nouns are uncountable nouns (N UNCOUNT). These are nouns which have only one form. Examples are: *hatred, rice, information, news, furniture.*

You cannot put numbers in front of an uncountable noun, so you cannot say 'one furniture'. You have to say 'one piece of furniture' or 'two items of news', and so on. See the section which follows on partitive nouns.

Uncountable nouns are not usually used with the determiners **a** and **the**, unless extra information about the noun is being given. So you would normally say: *They sell furniture.* But you can also say: *. . . the furniture I want for my bedroom.*

In the same way you would normally say: *She felt hatred towards his sister.* But you can also say: *I have a hatred of all examinations.*

Uncountable nouns take a verb in the singular. For example: *The furniture is needed urgently.*

Mass nouns

There is a large group of nouns which are very similar to uncountable nouns, but which can also be used occasionally as countable nouns. These are called mass nouns (N MASS). 'Cheese' is a typical example of a mass noun. There are two forms, 'cheese' and 'cheeses'. You usually say: *I like cheese,* and in this case you are referring to cheese in general. Here the noun is like an uncountable noun because it is used without a determiner. However, when you want to refer to different types of cheese, you can say: *There's a shop in Harborne that sells more than a hundred cheeses.* Here it is used like a countable noun in the plural.

Again, you usually say: *I take sugar in tea.* However, when you want to say how much sugar you take, you can say: *I take three sugars in tea,* meaning that you take three spoonfuls or three lumps of sugar.

'Cheese' goes with a singular verb, and 'cheeses' goes with a plural.

Singular nouns

A few nouns are used in the singular form only (N SING). They must have a determiner An example is 'jumble', where you can say: *... the jumble which covers my desk ... ... a chaotic jumble of papers.*

For some nouns it is important which determiner you use, and in that case we say so in the Extra Column. For example, the Extra Column label for **harvest 1** says N SING: *the*+N, as in: *Our rice won't last until the harvest.*

And the Extra Column label for **bother 4** says N SING: *a*+N, as in: *It's a bit of a bother ... Sorry to be a bother, but could you help me?*

These nouns go with singular verbs.

Collective nouns

There is a small group of nouns, such as 'committee' and 'audience', which vary from the usual pattern of countable nouns. They have both singular and plural forms. They need a determiner in the singular.

Their singular form can occur with either a singular or a plural verb. This is because you can think of 'a committee' or 'an audience' as either a complete group or as a number of individual members. Nouns like this are often called 'collective nouns' in grammars; they are given the label N COLL in this dictionary. You can say: *The committee is meeting at the moment,* or: *The committee are meeting at the moment.*

In the same way you can say: *The audience was very enthusiastic, or: The audience were very enthusiastic.*

These nouns also have the normal pattern of countable nouns. So you say: *Their local committees are held every month.*

Turn over for more information about nouns.

MORE ABOUT NOUNS

Plural nouns

Some nouns are only used as plurals (N PLURAL).

They usually end in -s, as in: *clothes, scissors.*

They take determiners, just like countable plurals. However, when they modify other nouns they usually drop the -s, as in: *. . . trouser pocket . . .   . . . spectacle case.*

But a few do not, as in: *a clothes shop.*

Some plural nouns, such as **trousers**, **glasses**, and **scissors**, refer to a single object which has two main parts. With these, you often use the phrase **a pair of**, as in: *a pair of scissors . . .   . . . a pair of jeans . . .   . . . a pair of knickers.*

Similar to these nouns are a few words like **police** which do not end in -s but which behave like plural nouns.

Noun modifiers

A small group of nouns are not used very often on their own, but are more frequently used in front of another noun as if they were adjectives (N MOD). An example of a noun which is used in this way is **capacity**, as in: *a capacity audience . . .   . . . a capacity crowd.*

Another example is **steel 1**, where the Extra Column says N UNCOUNT: USU N MOD. This means that 'steel' is often used like an adjective in phrases such as: *steel rods . . .   . . . a steel bar . . .   . . . a steel works.*

It is also occasionally used as a straightforward noun, as in: *He works in a factory that makes steel.*

Proper nouns

A few nouns in this dictionary are proper nouns (N PROPER), which refer to a particular person, place, or institution. Proper nouns have a capital letter as their first letter. They each have a unique form.

Most proper nouns are used on their own, with no **a** or **the** in front of them: *Father Christmas, Heaven, Hell.*

A few proper nouns, however, always have **the** in front of them, because it is part of their name. So you say: *The Bible, The Continent, The Channel.*

Proper nouns usually take a singular verb, unless their form is clearly plural.

Partitive nouns

A number of nouns are partitive nouns (N PART). They are countable nouns.

They allow us to measure and count things that are normally expressed by uncountable nouns, and to group countable things together. The partitive construction uses the preposition **of** after the partitive noun.

Some partitive nouns allow you to measure things: *. . . two pints of beer . . .   . . . five tons of coal . . .   . . . three spoons of sugar.*

Other partitive nouns allow you to refer to individual items of something that is usually expressed by an uncountable noun: ... *a bit of paper* ... ... *a small piece of string* ... ... *an interesting bit of news*.

Some partitive nouns are followed by countable nouns in the plural, and refer to people, things, or animals which are together in a group: ... *a crowd of tourists* ... ... *a bunch of flowers* ... ... *a herd of cows* ... ... *a huge flock of sheep*.

When it is obvious what is being counted or measured, the 'of' phrase can be omitted. For example: *Two pints, please* ... *Those roses are lovely, I'll have a bunch*.

Nouns with supporting words

Many nouns, of different types, are typically used not by themselves but with supporting words or phrases in the language round about them. These nouns have +SUPP in the Extra Column.

The supporting language can come before or after the noun. If it comes before, it is usually in the form of an adjective or another noun. For example, **album 2** usually has a noun before it which tells you what type of album it is: *stamp album* ... ... *photograph album*.

If the supporting words come after the noun, they are usually in the form of a relative clause or a prepositional group, often one that starts with **of**. For example, **torrent 2** is usually followed by a phrase starting with **of**: *a torrent of oaths* ... ... *a torrent of bitter invective*.

Some nouns can have the supporting words either before or after them. For example, as in **way 2**: *He smiled in a superior way* ... ... *a strange way of grinning* ... *I don't like the way doctors talk to you*.

The examples which are given for each word give the most typical supporting structures, showing how the word is most frequently used.

'-ing' nouns

The **-ing** form of verbs is often used to describe activities. For example, if you ski, you can say that you 'like skiing' or that you 'go skiing every year'. This is a normal use of the **-ing** form of a verb: it behaves like an uncountable noun, but it can also be used with 'go'.

Some words are most frequently used in the **-ing** form. For example, the verb 'to caravan' is rare, yet the form 'caravanning' is quite common, as in: *I like caravanning* ... *They go caravanning every summer*.

Words of this type, where no verb is given but where the **-ing** form can be used with **be, like**, or **go**, are given in the dictionary with the label N ING in the Extra Column.

nourishment /nʌrɪʃmə²nt/ is the food that people and animals need to grow and remain healthy. EG *She had recovered sufficiently to take some nourishment... The seeds are full of nourishment.* — N UNCOUNT

novel /nɒvə⁰l/, **novels.** 1 A **novel** is a book that tells an invented story. EG *...reading a novel by Henry James.* — N COUNT
2 Something that is **novel** is unlike anything that has been done or created before. EG *...a novel experience... ...novel teaching methods.* — ADJ QUALIT

novelist /nɒvə⁰lɪst/, **novelists.** A **novelist** is a person who writes novels. — N COUNT

novelty /nɒvə⁰lti¹/, **novelties.** 1 **Novelty** is the quality of being different, new, and unusual. EG *He became interested because of the novelty of the problem... After twenty years, and hundreds of talks, the novelty had definitely worn off.* — N UNCOUNT
2 A **novelty** is **2.1** something that is unusual. EG *The car was still a novelty at that time.* — N COUNT **2.2** a cheap, unusual object that is sold as a gift or souvenir.

November /nəʊvembə/ is the eleventh month of the year in the Western calendar. EG *The agreement ends on November 24.* — N UNCOUNT

novice /nɒvɪs/, **novices.** 1 A **novice** is someone who is not experienced at the job or activity that they are doing. EG *He's still a novice as far as film acting is concerned... ...novice riders.* — N COUNT
2 A **novice** in a monastery or convent is a person who is preparing to become a monk or nun. — N COUNT

now /naʊ/. 1 You use **now** to refer to the present time, often in contrast to a time in the past or the future. EG *It is now just after one o'clock... I'm going home now... She has three children now... It's two weeks now since I wrote to you... Now is the time to find out... From now on, you are free to do what you like.* — ADV
2 You can also use **now** when telling a story or giving an account to refer to a particular time in the past. EG *They were walking more slowly now.* — ADV
3 If you say that something will happen **any day now** or **any time now**, you mean that it will happen very soon. EG *Any day now, the local authority is going to close it down.* — PHRASE
4 If you say that something happens **now and then**, **every now and then**, or **now and again**, you mean that it happens sometimes but not very often or not regularly. EG *Every now and then there is a confrontation.* — PHRASE
5 **Now** also means as a result of what has recently happened. EG *I was hoping to see you tomorrow. That won't be possible now.* — ADV
6 You can use **now that** or **now** when you are talking about the effect of an event or change. EG *Now that she's found him, she'll never let him go... I like him a lot now he's older.* — CONJ
7 You can also use **now 7.1** to add emphasis to a statement, remark, request, or command. EG *I ran downstairs. Now this was something the intruder had not expected... They call themselves men! Now, in my day, men were men!... 'I gave it back.' – 'Did you now?'... I must get back to work. Run along, now... Now, come on. Be sensible.* — Spoken **7.2** when you are searching for something or thinking what to say next. EG *I've got her address somewhere. Now let me see.* — Spoken Informal
8 You can say **now, now** when you are trying to calm someone or are warning them not to behave in a particular way. EG *'Now, now,' the doctor said, taking her gently by the hand. 'You mustn't get so upset.'* — CONVENTION Spoken Outdated
9 You say **now then** to attract people's attention. EG *Now then, who's for a cup of tea?* — Spoken

nowadays /naʊədeɪz/ means at the present time, in contrast with what happened in the past. EG *Nowadays most babies in this country are born in a hospital... Why don't we ever see Jim nowadays?* — ADV

nowhere /nəʊweə/. 1 You use **nowhere** to say that a suitable or relevant place does not exist. EG *There was nowhere to hide... She had nowhere else to go... Nowhere have I seen any mention of this.* — ADV : NEG
2 If you say that someone or something appears **from nowhere** or **out of nowhere**, you mean that they appear suddenly and unexpectedly. — PHRASE
3 If you say that a place is **in the middle of nowhere**, you mean that it is a long way from other places. EG *I spent hours waiting for a bus in the middle of nowhere.* — PHRASE Informal
4 If you say that you **are getting nowhere** or that something **is getting** you **nowhere**, you mean that you are not achieving anything or having any success. EG *Without them I would be nowhere... Calling me names will get you nowhere.* — PHRASE
5 If you say that something is **nowhere near** the case, you are emphasizing that it is not the case at all. EG *Lions are nowhere near as fast as the cheetah... One visit is nowhere near enough.* — PHRASE

noxious /nɒkʃəs/. A **noxious** gas or substance is harmful or poisonous. EG *...a cloud of noxious paraffin vapour.* — ADJ CLASSIF : USU ATTRIB Formal

nozzle /nɒzə⁰l/, **nozzles.** A **nozzle** is a narrow end piece fitted to a hose or pipe to control the flow of a liquid coming out of it. EG *The water shoots out of the nozzle in a powerful jet.* — N COUNT

> **N PART** stands for **partitive noun**
> 1 Nouns which have the label N PART in the Extra Column refer to a part or portion of something. For example, *...a **slice** of cake...* and *...a **piece** of advice.*
> 2 N PART is also used for words that group countable things together. For example, *...**masses** of people...* and *...**flocks** of sheep.*
> See the entry headed NOUNS for more information.

> **N PLURAL** stands for **plural noun**
> Nouns which have the label N PLURAL in the Extra Column always have a plural verb when they are the subject of a clause.
> See the entry headed NOUNS for more information.

> **N PROPER** stands for **proper noun**
> Nouns which have the label **N PROPER** in the Extra Column are the names of particular people, places, or organizations.
> See the entry headed NOUNS for more information.

> **N SING** stands for **singular noun**
> Nouns which have the label **N SING** in the Extra Column are normally only used in the singular. They always have a determiner such as 'a', 'the', and 'her' in front of them.
> See the entry headed NOUNS for more information.

nuance /nju:ɑ:ns/, **nuances.** A **nuance** is a slight difference in sound, appearance, feeling, or meaning. EG *He practised until he could imitate every nuance of Hall's speech.* — N COUNT OR N UNCOUNT

nuclear /nju:klɪə/ means relating to the energy that is produced when the nuclei of atoms are split — ADJ CLASSIF : ATTRIB

> Does a novelist write about novelties?

NUMBER

Numbers have the label NUMBER in the Extra Column. Most numbers behave in the following ways:

1 They occur in noun groups, coming before any adjectives in the group but after a determiner such as **the** or **these**. For example: *the two old chairs . . . . . . his five older sisters.*

2 Numbers can be the head of a noun group when the context makes it clear what the number refers to: *There were three in the room.*

3 Numbers can be used in front of prepositional phrases beginning with **of**: *There are eleven of us in the team . . . They are two of the nicest people I know.*

How to say numbers aloud:

For numbers greater than a hundred, it is usual to say 'and' before the part of the number which is less than a hundred. For example, 351 is said as 'three hundred and fifty-one' and 49,280 is said as 'forty-nine thousand two hundred and eighty'.

There are different ways of saying numbers greater than a hundred. For example, 250 can be said as 'two hundred and fifty', 'two fifty', or 'two five oh'. For longer numbers such as telephone numbers, it is usual to say the figures individually. For example, you would say the number 131274 as 'one three one two seven four'.

The number 0 is usually said as 'oh', although 'zero', 'nought', and 'nothing' are sometimes used instead.

NUMBERS		ORDINALS		FRACTIONS	
0	zero, nought, nothing				
1	one	1st	first		
2	two	2nd	second	$1/2$	a half
3	three	3rd	third	$1/3$	a third
4	four	4th	fourth	$1/4$	a quarter
5	five	5th	fifth	$1/5$	a fifth
6	six	6th	sixth	$1/6$	a sixth
7	seven	7th	seventh	$1/7$	a seventh
8	eight	8th	eighth	$1/8$	an eighth
9	nine	9th	ninth	$1/9$	a ninth
10	ten	10th	tenth	$1/10$	a tenth
11	eleven	11th	eleventh	etc	etc
12	twelve	12th	twelfth		
13	thirteen	13th	thirteenth		
14	fourteen	14th	fourteenth		
15	fifteen	15th	fifteenth		
16	sixteen	16th	sixteenth		
17	seventeen	17th	seventeenth		
18	eighteen	18th	eighteenth		
19	nineteen	19th	nineteenth		
20	twenty	20th	twentieth		
21	twenty-one	21st	twenty-first		
22	twenty-two	22nd	twenty-second		
30	thirty	30th	thirtieth		
40	forty	40th	fortieth		
50	fifty	50th	fiftieth		
60	sixty	60th	sixtieth		
70	seventy	70th	seventieth		
80	eighty	80th	eightieth		
90	ninety	90th	ninetieth		
100	a hundred	100th	hundredth		
101	a hundred and one	101st	hundred and first		
200	two hundred	200th	two hundredth		
1,000	a thousand	1,000th	thousandth		
1,001	a thousand and one	etc	etc		
10,000	ten thousand				
100,000	a hundred thousand				
1,000,000	a million				
1,000,000,000	a billion				

or combined. EG *...nuclear energy... ...nuclear weapons... ...nuclear war... ...nuclear physics.*

nuclear-free. A **nuclear-free** place is a place where nuclear weapons or nuclear energy are forbidden. EG *...if Europe becomes a nuclear-free zone.* ADJ CLASSIF: ATTRIB

nuclear reactor, nuclear reactors. A **nuclear reactor** is a machine which is used to produce nuclear energy. N COUNT

nucleus /njuːklɪəs/, **nuclei** /njuːklɪaɪ/. **1** The **nucleus** of an atom or cell is the central part of it. EG *...hydrogen nuclei.* N COUNT

2 The **nucleus** of a group of people or things is a small number of people or things which form the most important part of the group. EG *These people formed the nucleus of the American Vegetarian Movement.* N COUNT: OFT + of

nude /njuːd/, **nudes. 1** Someone who is **nude** or **in the nude** is not wearing any clothes. EG *They lay nude on the beach.* ADJ CLASSIF OR PHRASE

2 A **nude** is a picture or statue of a person who is not wearing any clothes. N COUNT

nudge /nʌdʒ/, **nudges, nudging, nudged. 1** If you **nudge** someone, you push them gently, usually with your elbow, in order to draw their attention to something or to make them move. EG *The girls grinned and nudged each other.* ▶ used as a noun. EG *Neil, give your companion a nudge.* V+O ▶ N COUNT

2 If you **nudge** someone into doing something, you gently persuade them to do it. EG *People began to nudge the couple into going away.* ▶ used as a noun. EG *I just gave Stroud a nudge in the right direction.* V+O+A ▶ N COUNT

nudity /njuːdɪˈtiː/ is the state of wearing no clothes. EG *The boys treated nudity as a natural thing.* N UNCOUNT

nugget /nʌgɪt/, **nuggets.** A **nugget** of information is an interesting or useful piece of information. EG *Where had he picked up that little nugget?* N COUNT

nuisance /njuːsəns/, **nuisances.** If you say that someone or something is a **nuisance**, you mean that they annoy you or cause you problems. EG *It was a nuisance for them to have all these visitors sitting around... I'm sorry to be such a nuisance.* N COUNT: USU SING

● If you **make a nuisance of** yourself, you behave in a way that annoys other people. EG *...teenagers who make nuisances of themselves.* ● PHRASE

numb /nʌm/, **numbs, numbing, numbed. 1** If a part of your body is **numb**, it cannot feel anything. EG *My shoulder no longer hurt – it was completely numb.* ADJ CLASSIF

2 If you are **numb** with shock or fear, you are so shocked or frightened that you cannot think clearly or feel any emotion. EG *Numb with shock, Kunta stood watching blankly.* ADJ QUALIT: OFT + with

3 If something such as a blow or cold weather **numbs** a part of your body, it makes it unable to feel anything. EG *Her fingers were numbed by the frost... A stone numbed his shoulder.* V+O

4 If an experience **numbs** you, you can no longer think clearly or feel any emotion. EG *We are numbed by repeated disappointments.* ◊ **numbed.** EG *He stood there in a numbed daze.* V+O ◊ ADJ QUALIT

number /nʌmbə/, **numbers, numbering, numbered. 1** A **number** is any of the words such as 'two', 'nine', or 'eleven', or the symbols such as 1, 3, or 47. You use numbers to say how many things you are referring to or where something comes in a series. EG *...a two-figure number... Your licence number is here... He lives at number 19 New King Street.* N COUNT

2 Someone's **number** is the series of digits that you dial when you telephone them. EG *Ring me tomorrow. Here's my number... He did not know the man's telephone number.* N COUNT: OFT + POSS

3 If you refer to the **number** of things or people in a situation, you are referring to how many things or people there are. EG *A surprising number of men never marry... ...cities with large numbers of chil-* N PART OR N COUNT + SUPP

dren in care... They were produced in vast numbers.* ● A **number** of things means several things. EG *A number of people disagreed.* ● Any **number** of things means a large quantity of them. EG *The work can be done in any number of ways.* ● PHRASE ● PHRASE

4 If a group of people or things **numbers** a particular amount, there are that many of them. EG *The force numbered almost a quarter of a million men.* V+C

5 If you **number** something, you give it a number in a series and write that number on it. EG *I haven't numbered the pages yet.* V+O

6 If someone or something **is numbered** among a particular group, they are considered to belong in that group. EG *She can be numbered among the great musicians of our time.* V+O+among: USU PASS

7 If you say that someone's **days are numbered**, you mean that they will not survive or be successful for much longer. PHRASE

8 A **number** is also a short piece of music or a song. N COUNT Informal

number one means better, more important, or more popular than anything else of its kind. EG *They regard unemployment as their number one priority.* ADJ CLASSIF Informal

number plate, number plates. The **number plates** of a vehicle are the signs on the front and back that show its registration number. See picture at CAR. N COUNT British

numeracy /njuːmərəsiː/ is the ability to do arithmetic. N UNCOUNT

numeral /njuːmərəl/, **numerals.** A **numeral** is a symbol used to represent a number. EG *My clock has Roman numerals.* N COUNT Formal

numerate /njuːmərəˈt/. Someone who is **numerate** is able to do arithmetic. ADJ CLASSIF

numerical /njuːmerɪkəˈl/ means expressed in numbers or relating to numbers. EG *...numerical data.* ◊ **numerically.** EG *...a numerically small group.* ADJ CLASSIF ◊ ADV

numerous /njuːmərəs/. **1** If you refer to **numerous** things or people, you mean a lot of things or people. EG *We had numerous discussions on the meaning of communism... George was the only survivor of her numerous children.* QUANTIF

2 If people or things are **numerous**, there are a lot of them. EG *Small enterprises have become more numerous.* ADJ QUALIT

nun /nʌn/, **nuns.** A **nun** is a member of a female religious community. N COUNT

N UNCOUNT stands for **uncountable noun**
Nouns which have the label N UNCOUNT in the Extra Column do not have plural forms. They are not usually used with determiners such as 'a' or 'this' unless they have a supporting word or phrase.
See the entry headed NOUNS for more information.

---

nurse /nɜːs/, **nurses, nursing, nursed. 1** A **nurse** is a person whose job is to care for people who are ill. EG *She's a trained nurse... Nurse Lore was on the telephone.* N COUNT

2 If you **nurse** someone, you care for them while they are ill. EG *She nursed him devotedly.* V+O

3 If you **nurse** an emotion or desire, you feel it strongly for a long time. EG *Wilson had long nursed a desire to build his own yacht.* V+O

4 See also **nursing.**

nursery /nɜːsəˈriː/, **nurseries. 1** A **nursery** is a place where very young children can be looked N COUNT

If you are training to be a nurse, do you go to a nursery school?

after while their parents are at work or doing something else.

2 Nursery education is the education of children who are between three and five years old. N MOD

3 A plant **nursery** is a place where plants are grown in order to be sold. N COUNT

nursery rhyme, nursery rhymes. A **nursery rhyme** is a poem or song for young children, especially one that is old or well-known. N COUNT

nursery school, nursery schools. A **nursery school** is a school for children who are between three and five years old. N COUNT OR N UNCOUNT

nursing /nɜːsɪŋ/. **1 Nursing** is the profession of looking after people who are ill. N UNCOUNT

2 A **nursing** mother feeds her baby with milk from her breasts. ADJ CLASSIF: ATTRIB

nursing home, nursing homes. A **nursing home** is a private hospital, especially one for old people. N COUNT

nurture /nɜːtʃə/, **nurtures, nurturing, nurtured. 1** If you **nurture** a young child or a young plant, you care for it while it is growing and developing. EG ...a mother's duty to nurture her children. V+O Formal

2 If you **nurture** plans, ideas, or people, you encourage their development and success. EG After spending two years nurturing this project, Bains came to England. V+O Formal

nut /nʌt/, **nuts. 1 Nuts** grow on trees. They have hard shells and firm insides that can be eaten. EG ...cashew nuts... ...gathering berries, nuts and fruit... The cake has chopped nuts in it. N COUNT: USU PLURAL

2 A **nut** is also a small piece of metal with a hole in it which a bolt screws into. Nuts and bolts are used to fasten things together. See picture at TOOLS. EG Take your spanner and tighten the nut. N COUNT

3 If you say that someone is a **nut**, or that they are **nuts** or **off** their **nut**, you mean that they are mad N COUNT, ADJ PRED,

or very foolish. EG You must have been nuts to leave this place... I think he's off his nut. OR PHRASE Informal

nutcase /nʌtkeɪs/, **nutcases.** If you say that someone is a **nutcase**, you mean that they behave in a mad or foolish way. N COUNT Informal Outdated

nutmeg /nʌtmɛg/ is a spice. N UNCOUNT

nutrient /njuːtrɪənt/, **nutrients. Nutrients** are substances that help plants and animals to grow. EG Excessive rainfall washes out valuable minerals and nutrients from the soil. N COUNT

nutrition /njuːtrɪʃən/ is the healthiness of the food that you eat. EG Children need education in good nutrition... ...improvements in nutrition. N UNCOUNT

nutritious /njuːtrɪʃəs/. Food that is **nutritious** contains substances which help your body to be healthy. EG The seeds are tasty and nutritious. ADJ QUALIT

nutshell /nʌtʃɛl/. You use **in a nutshell** to indicate that you are saying something in the briefest way possible. EG That, in a nutshell, is what we're trying to do here. ADV SEN

nutter /nʌtə/, **nutters.** If you call someone a **nutter**, you mean that they are mad or very foolish. N COUNT Informal

nutty /nʌti¹/, **nuttier, nuttiest. 1** If you describe someone or something as **nutty**, you mean that they are very foolish. EG ...this nutty idea he has. ADJ QUALIT Informal

2 Food that is **nutty** tastes of nuts. EG ...rice with a pleasantly nutty taste. ADJ QUALIT

nuzzle /nʌzəl/, **nuzzles, nuzzling, nuzzled.** If you **nuzzle** someone, you gently rub your nose and mouth against them, often to show affection. EG 'Ellen,' he said, nuzzling her neck... The dog began to nuzzle at his coat. V+O OR V+A

NW is an abbreviation for 'north-west'.

nylon /naɪlɒn/ is a strong type of artificial cloth. EG ...a dress made of nylon... ...nylon stockings. N UNCOUNT

O o

O, o /əʊ/, **O's, o's. 1 O** is the fifteenth letter of the English alphabet. N COUNT

2 O is used in exclamations, especially when you are expressing strong feelings. EG O God, I want to go home... O the joy of those Saturday afternoons... 'He's not the Chancellor now.' – 'O yes, he is.' EXCLAM

O stands for object

Objects are the words in a sentence which represent the people or things affected by the verb. Many verbs have an object, as in *I like Italy... All children like Italian ice cream.* Some verbs can have two objects, one of which refers to the person or thing that something is done to and the other refers to the person who is concerned with the result of the action. EG *She gave **me** some good advice... Can you give **me a few examples**?*

All prepositions are followed by objects, as in *They went into **the room**... I saw her car coming down the **High Street** towards **me**.*

See the entry headed VERBS for more information about verbs that have objects.

---

oaf /əʊf/, **oafs.** If you call someone an **oaf**, you mean that they are clumsy and stupid. EG Paul, you are a big oaf! N COUNT OR VOCATIVE

oak /əʊk/, **oaks. 1** An **oak** or an **oak tree** is a large tree that often grows in woods and forests. N COUNT

2 Oak is the wood from oak trees, which is strong and hard. EG ...a square oak table. N UNCOUNT

OAP /əʊ eɪ piː/, **OAPs.** An **OAP** is a man over the age of 65 or a woman over the age of 60. **OAP** is an abbreviation for 'old-age pensioner'. N COUNT British

oar /ɔː/, **oars.** An **oar** is a long pole that is used for rowing a boat. The oar is fixed across the side of the boat, and when you pull one end of it, the other end moves in the opposite direction through the water, causing the boat to move. N COUNT

oasis /əʊeɪsɪs/, **oases** /əʊeɪsiːz/. **1** In a desert, an **oasis** is a small area where water and plants are found. N COUNT

2 You can refer to any pleasant place or situation as an **oasis** when it is surrounded by unpleasant ones. EG The town was an oasis of prosperity in a desert of poverty. N COUNT

oat /əʊt/, **oats. Oats** are the grains of a cereal. You use oats for making porridge or for feeding animals. N COUNT: USU PLURAL

oath /əʊθ/, **oaths** /əʊðz/. **1** An **oath** is a formal promise. EG ...an oath of allegiance. ● If someone is **on oath** or **under oath**, they have made a promise, especially a promise to tell the truth in a court of law. EG ...witnesses under oath. N COUNT ● PHRASE

2 An **oath** is also an offensive expression or a swear-word. EG He was answered with a torrent of French oaths. N COUNT Outdated

oatmeal /ˈəʊtmiːl/. 1 **Oatmeal** is a coarse flour N UNCOUNT made by crushing oats. EG ...*oatmeal biscuits.*

2 Something that is **oatmeal** is a very pale, creamy ADJ COLOUR brown colour. EG ...*an oatmeal coat and brown trousers.*

obedient /əˈbiːdɪənt/. Someone who is **obedient** ADJ QUALIT does the things they are told to do. EG *She was an obedient little girl.* ◊ **obediently.** EG '*Try it,'* ◊ ADV *Clem ordered. Obediently I picked up the cup.*

◊ **obedience** /əˈbiːdɪəns/. EG *She failed to show* ◊ N UNCOUNT *proper obedience and respect to the elders.*

obese /əʊˈbiːs/. Someone who is **obese** is very fat. ADJ QUALIT EG *If they overeat, they are very likely to become* Formal *obese.* ◊ **obesity** /əʊˈbiːsɪˈtiˈ/. EG *Obesity is a health* ◊ N UNCOUNT *hazard.*

obey /əˈbeɪ/, **obeys, obeying, obeyed.** If you V+O OR V **obey** a person, a command, or an instruction, you do what you are told to do. EG *The troops were reluctant to obey orders... They obeyed me without question... Don't question anything, just obey!*

obituary /əˈbɪtjuˈəriˈ/, **obituaries.** An **obituary** is N COUNT a piece of writing about the character and achievements of someone who has just died. EG *I read Sewell's obituary in the Daily News.*

object, objects, objecting, objected; pronounced /ˈɒbdʒɪkt/ when it is a noun and /əˈbdʒɛkt/ when it is a verb. 1 An **object** is anything that has a fixed N COUNT shape or form, that you can touch or see, and that is not alive. EG ...*the shabby, black object he was carrying... ...mats, bowls, and other objects.*

2 Someone's **object** or the **object** of what they are N COUNT : doing is their aim or purpose. EG *The minder's* USU+POSS *object is to keep the child asleep... She would journey for months with the sole object of filming a rare creature.*

3 The **object** of a feeling, a wish, or a kind of N COUNT : behaviour is the thing or person that it is directed USU+*of* towards. EG *young Eileen, the object of his desires... This did not prevent him being the object of ridicule... She became an object of worship.*

4 In grammar, the object of a verb or a preposition N COUNT is the word or phrase which completes the structure begun by the verb or preposition. See the entry headed VERBS for more information.

5 If you **object** to something, **5.1** you do not like it V+*to* or do not approve of it. EG *This was exactly what he objected to in Christine... He would never object to sharing whatever he had.* **5.2** you say that you do V : OFT+*to* not like it or do not approve of it. EG *We object to* OR REPORT : *the selection of Haldane... You may object that the* ONLY *that* *system makes boys effeminate... The men objected and the women supported them.* ◊ **objector** ◊ N COUNT /əˈbdʒɛktə/, **objectors.** EG ...*her refusal to listen to objectors.*

objection /əˈbdʒɛkʃən/, **objections. 1** If you N COUNT make or raise an **objection** to something, you say that you do not like it or do not approve of it. EG *They raised objections to Seagram's bid... The objection that he had no experience was ignored.*

2 If you **have no objection** to something, you do PHRASE not dislike it or do not disapprove of it. EG *He had no real objection to drinking.*

objectionable /əˈbdʒɛkʃənəbəl/. If you describe ADJ QUALIT someone or something as **objectionable,** you Formal mean that you think they are offensive and unacceptable. EG ...*politicians whose views he found objectionable... ...a vulgar and objectionable person.*

objective /əˈbdʒɛktɪv/, **objectives. 1** Your **objec-** N COUNT **tive** is what you are trying to achieve. EG ...*Mobil's primary objective is to win... We shall never achieve our objectives.*

2 Information that is **objective** is based on facts. EG ADJ CLASSIF *There is no objective evidence... ...a search for objective data.*

3 If you describe a person as **objective,** you mean ADJ QUALIT that they are trying to be fair and to base their opinions on facts, rather than on personal feelings. EG ...*a book on communism written by an astonish-*

ingly objective author. ◊ **objectively.** EG *It was* ◊ ADV *desirable to view these things objectively.*

◊ **objectivity.** EG *Historians strive after objectiv-* ◊ N UNCOUNT *ity.*

obligation /ɒblɪˈɡeɪʃən/, **obligations.** An **obliga-** N COUNT OR **tion** is something that you must do because you N UNCOUNT have promised to do it or because it is your duty to do it. EG *He had to go home because of family obligations... We are under no obligation to give him what he wants.*

obligatory /əˈblɪɡətəˈriˈ/. If something is **obliga-** ADJ CLASSIF **tory,** you must do it, because there is a rule or a law about it. EG *It is not obligatory to answer.*

oblige /əˈblaɪdʒ/, **obliges, obliging, obliged. 1** If V+O+*to*-INF something **obliges** you to do something, it makes you feel that you must do it. EG *Politeness obliged me to go on with the conversation... ...if your business obliges you to stay until tomorrow.*

◊ **obliged.** EG *I felt obliged to invite him into the* ◊ ADJ PRED *parlour.* +*to*-INF

2 If you **oblige** someone, you are helpful to them V+O OR V by doing what they have asked you to do. EG '*Who did you ask?' – 'Jim. He's only too glad to oblige.'*

obliging /əˈblaɪdʒɪŋ/. Someone who is **obliging** is ADJ QUALIT willing and eager to be helpful. EG *Mr Carston is a very obliging gentleman.*

oblique /əˈbliːk/. 1 If you describe a statement or ADJ QUALIT comment as **oblique,** you mean that it is indirect and therefore difficult to understand. EG ...*an oblique compliment... Alexander took this as an oblique reference to his own affairs.*

2 An **oblique** line is one that slopes at an angle, ADJ CLASSIF rather than being vertical or horizontal. EG ...*a script which had oblique strokes after every phrase.*

obliterate /əˈblɪtəreɪt/, **obliterates, obliterat-** V+O **ing, obliterated.** If something **obliterates** an object or place, it destroys it completely. EG *I watched bombs obliterate the villages.*

oblivion /əˈblɪvɪən/ is 1 the state of not being N UNCOUNT aware or conscious of what is happening around you. EG *I sank back into oblivion.* 2 the state of having been forgotten or of no longer being considered important. EG *This art faded into oblivion years ago.*

oblivious /əˈblɪvɪəs/. If you are **oblivious** of ADJ PRED something, you are not aware of it. EG *She seemed* USU+*to/of* *oblivious of the attention she was drawing to herself... He was totally oblivious to the fact that he had almost been killed.*

oblong /ˈɒblɒŋ/, **oblongs.** An **oblong** is a shape N COUNT which has two long sides and two short sides and in which all the angles are right angles. See picture at SHAPES. ▸ used as an adjective. EG ...*an oblong table.* ▸ ADJ CLASSIF

obnoxious /əˈbnɒkʃəs/. If you describe someone ADJ QUALIT as **obnoxious,** you mean that you think they are very unpleasant. EG *He has some obnoxious qualities, but he is reliable.*

oboe /ˈəʊbəʊ/, **oboes.** An **oboe** is a wooden musical N COUNT instrument that is shaped like a tube. You play it by blowing through a reed inserted at its top. See picture at MUSICAL INSTRUMENTS.

obscene /əˈbsiːn/. Something that is **obscene** ADJ QUALIT shocks and offends people, because it involves sex in a way that people find unpleasant. EG *The Herald had been prosecuted for printing obscene advertising... ...huge paintings, many of them obscene.*

obscenity /əˈbsɛnɪˈtiˈ/, **obscenities. 1 Obscenity** N UNCOUNT is behaviour that shocks and offends people because it involves sex in a way that people find unpleasant. EG *Existing laws on obscenity are to be tightened.*

2 An **obscenity** is a word or expression that is rude N COUNT : and offensive because it relates to sex or bodily USU PLURAL functions. EG *They started yelling obscenities.*

If you have no objection to someone, do you think they are obnoxious?

obscure /ə'bskjʊə/, **obscurer, obscurest; ob-**
scures, obscuring, obscured. 1 Something that is
obscure 1.1 is known by only a few people. EG   ADJ QUALIT
...*obscure operas... ...experts in obscure subjects...*
...*some obscure country.*   ◇ **obscurity**   ◇ N UNCOUNT
/ə'bskjʊərɪ'tiː¹/. EG *He has risen from obscurity to*
international fame. **1.2** is complex and difficult to   ADJ QUALIT
understand. EG ...*obscure points of theology...*
France's relationship to the new organization is
extremely obscure.   ◇ **obscurity.** EG *Dixon didn't*   ◇ N UNCOUNT
mind the obscurity of the reference. **1.3** is difficult   ADJ QUALIT
to see. EG *He saw the hideous, obscure shape rise*
slowly to the surface.   ◇ **obscurity.** EG *He peered*   ◇ N UNCOUNT
into the obscurity beneath the trees.
2 To **obscure** something means **2.1** to make it   V+O
difficult to understand. EG *Words that obscure the*
truth must be discarded. **2.2** to prevent it from
being seen or heard properly. EG *Some areas were*
obscured by patches of fog.

obsequious /ə'bsiːkwɪəs/. People who are **obse-**   ADJ QUALIT
quious are too eager to help you, to listen to what
you say, or to agree with you; used showing disapproval. EG ...*obsequious shop assistants.*

observable /ə'bzɜː'vəbə¹l/. Something that is **ob-**   ADJ CLASSIF
servable can be seen. EG *It is an action that is*
observable in almost all countries in the world.

observance /ə'bzɜːvəns/. The **observance** of a   N UNCOUNT
law or custom is the practice of obeying or follow-   +SUPP
ing it. EG ...*observance of speed limits and traffic*
lights.

observant /ə'bzɜːvənt/. Someone who is **obser-**   ADJ QUALIT
vant has the ability to notice things that are not
usually noticed. EG *You're very observant, Cathy.*

observation /ɒbzəveɪʃə⁰n/, **observations. 1** Ob-   N UNCOUNT
servation is the action or process of carefully
watching someone or something, especially in order to learn something about them. EG ...*informa-*
tion gathered by observation or experiment... She
was put under observation in a nursing home.
2 An **observation** is **2.1** something that you have   N COUNT
learned by seeing or watching something and
thinking about it. EG ...*clinical observations.* **2.2** a
comment or remark. EG *We listened to Mama's*
tearful observations on the subject.
3 Observation is also the ability to notice things   N UNCOUNT
that are not usually noticed. EG ...*keen powers of*
observation... ...a talent for observation.

observatory /ə'bzɜːvətə⁰riː¹/, **observatories.** An   N COUNT
observatory is a special building with telescopes
that scientists use to study the sun, the moon, the
planets, and the stars.

observe /ə'bzɜːv/, **observes, observing, ob-**   V+O
served. 1 If you **observe** someone or something,
1.1 you watch them carefully. EG *By observing your*
boss's moods, you will soon discover when to talk
and when to keep quiet. **1.2** you see them or notice   Formal
them. EG *He looked out through the window and*
observed me walking along the boat deck.
2 You can use **observe** when you are quoting a   V+QUOTE
remark or comment that someone has made. EG   OR REPORT
'People aren't interested in spiritual things,' ob-   Formal
served the actress.
3 If you **observe** something such as a law or   V+O
custom, you obey it or follow it. EG *I didn't enjoy the*
party, but the conventions had been observed.

observer /ə'bzɜːvə/, **observers.** An **observer** is   N COUNT
1 someone who spends time studying the latest
news about a subject or an area of activity. EG
...*political observers.* **2** someone who sees or notices something. EG *A casual observer may get the*
wrong impression.

obsess /ə'bsɛs/, **obsesses, obsessing, obsessed.**   V+O : OFT PASS
If something **obsesses** you or if you **are obsessed**   +with
with it, you keep thinking about it and find it
difficult to think about anything else. EG *He became*
obsessed with a girl reporter... The image of Mad-
eleine obsessed him.

obsession /ə'bsɛʃə⁰n/, **obsessions.** When some-   N COUNT
one cannot stop thinking about something, you can

say that they have an **obsession** about it. EG
Taylor's fascination with bees developed into an
obsession.

obsessional /ə'bsɛʃə⁰nəl, -ʃənə⁰l/ means the same   ADJ QUALIT
as obsessive. EG ...*an obsessional need to win.*

obsessive /ə'bsɛsɪv/. You say that an attitude or   ADJ QUALIT
kind of behaviour is **obsessive** when someone
keeps thinking or behaving in a particular way and
seems unable to stop it. EG *Obsessive tidiness in the*
office is a bad sign.   ◇ **obsessively.** EG *He was*   ◇ ADV
obsessively interested in every single detail about
my early life.

obsolete /ɒbsəliːt/. Something that is **obsolete** is   ADJ CLASSIF
no longer needed because something newer or
more efficient has been invented. EG *The Falcon*
missile was now obsolete... ...*obsolete systems.*

obstacle /ɒbstəkə⁰l/, **obstacles. 1** An **obstacle** is   N COUNT
an object that makes it difficult for you to go where
you want to go, because it is in your way. EG *Bats*
can sense obstacles in their path.
2 You can refer to anything that makes it difficult   N COUNT :
for you to do something as an **obstacle.** EG ...*the*   USU+SUPP
bureaucratic obstacles to getting her son over from
Jamaica.

obstetrician /ɒbstetrɪʃə⁰n/, **obstetricians.** An   N COUNT
obstetrician is a doctor who is specially trained to
deal with pregnant women and childbirth.

obstinate /ɒbstɪnə¹t/. If you describe someone as   ADJ QUALIT
obstinate, you mean that they are very determined to do what they want, and will not change
their mind or be persuaded to do something else;
used showing disapproval. EG ...*an obstinate, rebel-*
lious child with a violent temper.   ◇ **obstinacy**   ◇ N UNCOUNT
/ɒbstɪnəsi¹/. EG ...*the obstinacy of the Transport*
Minister.

obstruct /ə'bstrʌkt/, **obstructs, obstructing, ob-**
structed. 1 If something **obstructs** a road or path,   V+O
it blocks it, so that people or vehicles cannot get
past. EG *The crash obstructed the road for several*
hours.
2 If someone **obstructs** something such as justice   V+O
or progress, they prevent it from happening or
developing. EG *It is a crime for the President to*
obstruct justice.

obstruction /ə'bstrʌkʃə⁰n/, **obstructions. 1** An   N COUNT
obstruction is something that blocks a road or
path. EG *The obstructions could take weeks to clear.*
2 Obstruction is the act of deliberately delaying   N UNCOUNT
something or preventing something from happen-
ing. EG *The unions faced legal obstruction.*

obstructive /ə'bstrʌktɪv/. Someone who is **ob-**   ADJ QUALIT
structive deliberately causes difficulties for other
people. EG *He behaved in a very obstructive fash-*
ion... ...*the obstructive tactics of the authorities.*

obtain /ə'bteɪn/, **obtains, obtaining, obtained.** If   V+O
you **obtain** something, you get it or achieve it. EG   Formal
She obtained her degree in 1951... These books can
be obtained from the Public Library.

obtainable /ə'bteɪnəbə⁰l/. Something that is **ob-**   ADJ CLASSIF :
tainable can be obtained. EG *Savings up to 65% are*   USU PRED
obtainable under this scheme.

obtrusive /ə'btruːsɪv/. Something that is **obtru-**   ADJ QUALIT
sive is noticeable in an unpleasant way. EG *Equally*
obtrusive was the graffiti that had started to ap-
pear.   ◇ **obtrusively.** EG *Hawke got up and walked*   ◇ ADV
obtrusively out of the building.

obvious /ɒbvɪəs/. **1** If something is **obvious,** you   ADJ QUALIT
can easily see it or understand it. EG *It was painfully*
obvious that I knew very little about it... There's no
obvious answer... ...*obvious similarities.*
2 If you describe something that someone says as   ADJ QUALIT
obvious, you mean that it is unnecessary and
shows lack of imagination. EG *Tove made such an*
obvious remark... You shouldn't tell such obvious
lies. ● If you say that someone **is stating the** ● PHRASE
obvious, you mean that they are saying something
that everyone knows already.

obviously /ɒbvɪəsli¹/. **1** You say **obviously** when   ADV SEN
you are stating something that you expect people

to know already. EG *Obviously I don't need to say how important this project is.*

2 You can also use **obviously** to indicate that something is easily seen, noticed, or recognized. EG *The soldier was obviously badly hurt.* ADV

occasion /əkeɪʒ⁰n/, **occasions, occasioning, occasioned. 1** The **occasion** when something happens is the time when it happens. EG *I met him only on one occasion.* N COUNT

2 An **occasion** is also an important event, ceremony, or celebration. EG *They have the date fixed for the big occasion... ...an important social occasion.* N COUNT

3 An **occasion** for doing something is an opportunity for doing it. EG *For the girls, nature study was an occasion for lazy walks and idle picnics... He had never had occasion to use his gun.* N SING+SUPP OR N UNCOUNT +to-INF Formal

4 If something happens **on occasion** or **on occasions**, it happens sometimes, but not very often. EG *You have on occasions surprised people.* PHRASE Formal

5 When someone does what is necessary to deal with a difficult situation, you say that they **rise to the occasion**. EG *Dekker had risen to the occasion with an insight that surprised us all.* PHRASE

6 To **occasion** something means to cause it. EG *...deaths occasioned by police activity... The discovery occasioned me no surprise... ...the frustration they occasioned in the lessons.* V+O, V+O+O, OR V+O+A Formal

occasional /əkeɪʒ⁰nəl, -ʒən⁰l/ means happening or being present sometimes, but not regularly or often. EG *...an occasional trip as far as Aberdeen... Apart from the occasional article, he hadn't published anything.* ADJ CLASSIF : ATTRIB ◇ **occasionally.** EG *Friends visit them occasionally... He was arrogant and occasionally callous.* ◇ ADV

occult /ɒkʌlt/. Someone who is interested in the **occult** is interested in supernatural or magical forces. EG *...enthusiasm for astrology and the occult.* N SING : the+N ▸ used as an adjective. EG *...the fantastic occult powers that he was said to possess.* ▸ ADJ CLASSIF : ATTRIB

occupant /ɒkjʊ⁴pənt/, **occupants. 1** The **occupants** of a building or room are the people who live or work there. EG *A tidy office means that the occupant doesn't want things disturbed.* N COUNT

2 You can also refer to someone who is in a room or chair at a particular time as its **occupant**. EG *The room's sole occupants were the boy and a dog.* N COUNT

occupation /ɒkjʊ⁴peɪʃ⁰n/, **occupations. 1** Your **occupation** is your job or profession. EG *...a poorly paid occupation.* N COUNT OR N UNCOUNT

2 An **occupation** is also something that you do for pleasure. EG *Riding was her favourite occupation.* N COUNT

3 When a foreign army moves into a country and takes control of it, you can refer to this as the **occupation** of that country. EG *...the French occupation of North Africa... Holland came under German occupation.* N UNCOUNT +SUPP

occupational /ɒkjʊ⁴peɪʃ⁰nəl, -ʃən⁰l/ means relating to a person's job or profession. EG *...occupational hazards... ...an occupational pension scheme.* ADJ CLASSIF : ATTRIB

occupier /ɒkjʊ⁴paɪə/, **occupiers.** The **occupier** of a house, flat, or piece of land is the person who lives or works there. EG *The occupier of the premises has applied for planning permission.* N COUNT Formal

occupy /ɒkjʊ⁴paɪ/, **occupies, occupying, occupied. 1** The people who **occupy** a building are the people who live there or work there. EG *Houses occupied by the aged must be centrally heated.* V+O

2 If something such as a seat **is occupied**, someone is using it, so that it is not available for anyone else to use. EG *At the pub, his usual corner seat was occupied.* V-PASS

3 When people **occupy** a place or a country, they move into it and gain control of it. EG *The students occupied the Administration Block.* V+O

4 If you say that something **occupies** a particular place in a system, process, or plan, you mean that it has that place. EG *The demonstration occupies a central place in their political campaign.* V+O

5 If you **occupy** yourself in doing something, you V-REFL OR V+O

are busy doing it. EG *They were occupying themselves in growing their own food... It was just a matter of keeping her occupied.*

6 If something **occupies** you, it requires your efforts, attention, or time. EG *That work was to occupy him for the rest of his life... His attention was occupied with other matters.* V+O : IF PASS THEN+ with/in

7 If something **occupies** a particular period of time, it happens while that amount of time passes. EG *The episode occupied many millions of years.* V+O

occur /ə⁷kɜː/, **occurs, occurring, occurred. 1** When an event **occurs**, it happens. EG *The attack occurred about six days ago... ...the changes which have occurred in the past fifty years.* V : USU+A

2 You can also say that something **occurs** when it exists or is present in a particular place. EG *...two other commonly occurring weeds... Racism and sexism occur in all institutions.* V : USU+A

3 If a thought or idea **occurs** to you, you suddenly think of it or realize it. EG *As soon as that thought occurred to him, he felt worse... It had never occurred to her that he might insist on paying.* V+to : NO CONT

occurrence /ə⁷kʌrəns/, **occurrences. 1** An **occurrence** is something that happens. EG *...weeks before the tragic occurrence.* N COUNT Formal

2 The **occurrence** of something is the fact that it happens, or the fact that it is present in a particular situation. EG *We may reduce the occurrence of cancer by fifty per cent.* N UNCOUNT +SUPP

ocean /əʊʃ⁰n/, **oceans. 1** The **ocean** is the sea. EG *...in the depths of the ocean.* N SING : the+N Literary

2 Ocean is part of the name of five very large areas of sea. EG *...the Atlantic Ocean.* N COUNT

o'clock /əklɒk/. You use **o'clock** after numbers from one to twelve to say what time it is. For example, if you say that it is three o'clock, you mean that it is three hours after midday or three hours after midnight; see the entry headed TIME. EG *At two o'clock in the morning Castle was still awake... It was 11 o'clock at night.* ADV AFTER NUMBER

octagon /ɒktəgən/, **octagons.** An **octagon** is a flat geometrical shape that has eight straight sides. N COUNT

octagonal /ɒktægən⁰l/. Something that is **octagonal** has eight sides. EG *...the octagonal tower.* ADJ CLASSIF

octave /ɒktɪv/, **octaves.** An **octave** is the musical interval between the first note and the eighth note of a scale. N COUNT

October /ɒktəʊbə/ is the tenth month of the year in the Western calendar. EG *They will be on show at the Museum until October.* N UNCOUNT

octopus /ɒktəpəs/, **octopuses.** An **octopus** is a sea creature with eight tentacles which it uses to catch food. N COUNT

oculist /ɒkjʊ⁴lɪst/, **oculists.** An **oculist** is an optician. N COUNT American

odd /ɒd/, **odder, oddest; odds. 1** If you say that someone or something is **odd**, you mean that they are strange or unusual. EG *We thought she was rather odd... There's something odd about its shape... It was odd that she still lived at home.* ADJ QUALIT ◇ **oddly.** EG *The drug made him behave quite oddly... Marsha found the play oddly disappointing.* ◇ ADV ◇ **oddness.** EG *...the slight oddness in her voice.* ◇ N UNCOUNT

2 You say **'oddly enough'** before adding a surprising piece of information to what you have been talking about. EG *Oddly enough, it was through him that I met Carson.* ADV SEN

3 You use **odd** before a noun to indicate that you are not mentioning the type, size, or quality of something, because it is not important. EG *You can add bones, the odd vegetable, and herbs... ...odd bits of glass... He did odd jobs about the place to earn a bit of money.* ● See also **odds and ends.** ADJ CLASSIF : ATTRIB Informal

4 You say that two things are **odd** when they do not belong to the same set or pair. EG *...odd socks.* ADJ CLASSIF : ATTRIB

What does 'oct-' mean in words like 'octagon', 'octave', and 'octopus'?

5 In a group of people or things, the **odd** one **out** is PHRASE the one that is different from all the others. EG *I was the odd one out; all my friends were in couples.*

6 Odd numbers, such as 3, 17, and 129, cannot be ADJ CLASSIF: divided exactly by the number two. ATTRIB

7 You use **odd** after a number to indicate that it is ADV AFTER only approximate. EG *We first met twenty odd* NUMBER *years ago... Thirty odd pounds, isn't it?* Informal

8 You refer to the probability of something happen- N PLURAL: ing as the **odds** that it will happen. In gambling, if the+N you bet one pound on a horse whose odds are '10 to 1', you will receive ten pounds if the horse wins. EG *Nobody will put money on a horse at those odds.*

9 If you say that the **odds are** that something will PHRASE happen, or that the **odds are in favour of** it happening, you mean that it is likely to happen. If you say that the **odds are against** it, you mean that it is unlikely to happen. EG *The odds are that they will succeed... The odds are against children learning in this environment.* ● See also **odds-on**.

10 When something happens **against** the **odds**, it PHRASE happens although it had seemed impossible or extremely unlikely. EG *She managed to do it against all the odds... ...working against appalling odds.*

11 If you are **at odds** with someone, you are PHRASE disagreeing or quarrelling with them. EG *She is at odds with her boss... The allies are at odds over how to respond to the threat.*

oddity /ˈɒdɪti/, **oddities. 1** An **oddity** is someone N COUNT or something that is very strange. EG *A career woman is still regarded as something of an oddity... ...the oddities and absurdities of the language.*

2 The **oddity** of something is the fact that it is very N UNCOUNT strange. EG *...the oddity of her behaviour.*

oddment /ˈɒdmənt/, **oddments. Oddments** are N COUNT: things that remain after other things have been USU PLURAL used. EG *...old postcards and scraps, all sorts of oddments... ...oddments of furniture.*

odds and ends. You refer to a group of things as N PLURAL **odds and ends** when you are not saying exactly Informal what they are, because it is not important or necessary to do so. EG *I had a trunk filled with various odds and ends that I would need for camping.*

odds-on. If there is an **odds-on** chance that some- ADJ CLASSIF thing will happen, it is very likely that it will Informal happen. EG *It was odds-on that there was no killer... Calderwood is the odds-on favourite to win.*

odious /ˈəʊdɪəs/. You describe people or things as ADJ QUALIT **odious** when you find them extremely unpleasant. EG *I shouldn't dream of telling the odious woman anything of the sort.*

odour /ˈəʊdə/, **odours;** spelled **odor** in American N COUNT: English. An **odour** is a smell, especially a strong USU+SUPP one. EG *...the warm odour of freshly-baked scones...* Formal *The noise was as appalling as the odour.*

of /əv/. **1** You use **of** after nouns referring to PREP quantities, groups, or amounts. EG *...a collection of essays... ...jewellery worth millions of pounds... ...25 gallons of hot water... ...a big piece of apple pie.*

2 You use **of** after a noun referring to a container PREP to form an expression referring to the container and its contents. EG *...a cup of tea.*

3 You use **of** to specify an amount, value, or age. EG PREP *...a price increase of 2%... ...a town of 13,000 people... ...at the age of five... ...a boy of nineteen.*

4 You use **of** to say that something consists of a PREP particular thing. EG *...strong feelings of jealousy... ...an atmosphere of co-operation... ...gifts of olive oil.*

5 You use **of** to say that someone or something has PREP a particular characteristic or quality. EG *...men of matchless honesty... She helped him to a gin and tonic of giant proportions.*

6 You use **of** to say that something is made from a PREP particular substance. EG *They are usually made of cotton... ...a disc of steel.*

7 You use **of** when you are talking about one or PREP more things among a number of similar ones. EG

This is the first of a series of programmes... Many of the students come from other countries.

8 You use **of** to say that something represents or PREP describes something. EG *...a map of Sweden... ...Mrs Jarrow's account of what happened.*

9 You use **of** when giving your opinion about PREP someone's action. For example, if you say 'That was nasty of him', you mean that what he did was nasty. EG *It was kind of her to take me in.*

10 You use **of 10.1** to say who has the belief, PREP attitude, or characteristic mentioned. EG *...the religious beliefs of the peasant communities... ...the disapproving stares of Rummidge students... ...the average age of commercial farmers... ...the size of the crowd.* **10.2** to say who something belongs to or is controlled by. EG *Imagine a child of yours doing that... ...the Conservative government of Mr Heath.* **10.3** to say what something is a part or a feature of. EG *She clutched the sleeve of his robe... ...the corners of a triangle... ...Act V of Macbeth.* **10.4** to say what group or organization someone belongs to. EG *...the General Secretary of the Tobacco Workers' Union... He was a member of a famous golf club.* **10.5** to say what place a person or organization is connected with. EG *...the Mayor of Moscow... ...the University of California.*

11 You can use **of** after words such as 'town' and PREP 'village' to introduce the name of a place. EG *...the village of Fairwater Green.*

12 You use **of** to say what something relates to or PREP is concerned with. EG *...the whole concept of economic growth... ...the Department of Employment... ...their hopes of a reconciliation... ...the cause of the infection... ...cancer of the stomach.*

13 You use **of** after nouns that have been formed PREP from verbs. The noun group following 'of' is either the object or the subject of the verb. For example, 'the kidnapping of a royal child' refers to a royal child being kidnapped; 'the arrival of the next train' refers to the next train arriving.

14 You use **of** when saying who did or made PREP something. For example, you can refer to the people who organize a meeting as 'the organizers of the meeting'.

15 You use **of** to say that something resembles the PREP thing that is mentioned after 'of'. For example, something that is the colour **of** blood is the same colour as blood. EG *...a boil the size of a golf ball.*

16 You can also use **of** to say that something is like PREP the thing that is mentioned before 'of'. For example, 'a giant of a man' means 'a man like a giant.'

17 You use **of 17.1** to say that something happened PREP at a particular time. EG *...the recession of 1974-75... ...the great conflicts of the past ten years.* **17.2** to say that something is the best or worst thing to happen during a particular time. EG *That was the highlight of the morning.* **17.3** after words like 'day' and 'time' to say when something happened. EG *...on the day of his inauguration... ...at the time of the earthquake.* **17.4** to say what date it is. EG *...the 17th of June.*

18 You also use **of** to say what illness someone died PREP from. EG *She died of pneumonia.*

off /ɒf/. **1** When something is taken **off** something PREP OR ADV else or when it moves or comes **off** it, it is taken away or it moves away so that it is no longer on the other thing or attached to it. EG *He took his hand off her arm... He was wiping sweat off his face... Miss Archer fell off her chair... The paint was peeling off... Get the car off the road.*

2 When you take **off** a piece of clothing, you ADV remove it from your body. EG *He took off his jacket... Let me help you off with your coat.*

3 When you go **off**, you leave a place. EG *He started* ADV AFTER VB *the motor and drove off abruptly... When are you off to America?... I had to send Matthew off to bed.*

4 You can say that someone is **off** somewhere or ADV+A OR -ING **off** doing something when they are in a different place from yourself. EG *She's off in Florida at some labour conference... A lot of men were off fighting.*

5 When you get **off** a bus, train, or plane, you get out of it. EG *The train stopped and people got off.* PREP, OR ADV AFTER VB

6 If you keep **off** a street or piece of land, you do not go onto it. EG *I kept off the main roads... You have no right to keep people off your land.* PREP

7 If an area of land is walled **off** or fenced **off**, it has a wall or fence around it or in front of it. ADV AFTER VB

8 If something is **off** a coast, it is in the sea and close to the coast. EG *...submarines off the Norwegian coast... ...two islands off the mainland of China.* PREP

9 If a building is **off** a road, it is near it but not next to it. EG *...a hotel just off the Via Condotti.* PREP

10 You can use **off** in these ways when you are talking about not working. **10.1** If you have some time **off**, you do not go to work for a period of time. EG *I would love to have a year off.* **10.2** If it is your day **off**, it is the day when you do not normally work. EG *Tonight is his night off.* **10.3** If you are **off** work, you are not working because you are ill. ADV ADV PREP

11 If you keep **off** a subject, you do not talk about it. EG *She kept off the subject of marriage.* PREP

12 If something such as a machine or an electric light is **off**, it is not functioning. EG *Boylan switched off the headlights. He turned the radio off.* ADJ PRED OR ADV AFTER VB

13 If an agreement or an arranged event is **off**, it has been cancelled. EG *I presume the deal is off.* ADJ PRED OR ADV AFTER VB

14 If food or drink is **off**, it tastes and smells unpleasant because it is going bad. EG *The wine was off.* ADJ PRED

15 If something is a long time **off**, it will not happen for a long time. EG *Control over the mind is not as far off as we think.* ADV OR PREP

16 If you are **off** something, you have stopped using it or liking it. EG *My father was off alcohol... He's gone off liberty.* PREP Informal

17 If you say that someone's behaviour is **a bit off**, you mean that you find it unacceptable and rude. PHRASE Informal

18 If an amount of money is taken **off** the price of something, it costs that amount less than it did before. EG *I knocked 100 pounds off the price.* PREP OR ADV

19 If you obtain something **off** someone, you obtain it from them. EG *I'd never buy anything off him.* PREP Informal

20 If you say that something happens **off and on**, you mean that it happens occasionally. PHRASE

offal /ɒfɔ°l/ refers to the heart, liver, and other internal organs of animals, which people cook and eat. EG *...offal mixed with onions and oatmeal.* N UNCOUNT

off-chance. If you do something **on the off-chance**, you do it because you hope that it will succeed or be useful, although you think that this is unlikely. EG *He collected an enormous amount of information on the off-chance that he might later have a use for it.* PHRASE

off-colour. If you are **off-colour**, you are slightly ill. EG *He's been a bit off-colour for two days.* ADJ PRED

off-day, off-days. If you have an **off-day**, you do not work or perform as well as usual. EG *We all have our off-days, of course.* N COUNT Informal

offence /ɔ°fens/, **offences;** spelled **offense** in American English. **1** An **offence** is a crime. EG *They were arrested for drug offences... Thirteen people were charged with offences including obstruction and resisting arrest.* N COUNT Formal

2 If you give **offence**, you upset or embarrass someone. EG *The play is liable to give offence to many people... His calmly rational voice robbed his words of all offence.* N UNCOUNT : USU+SUPP

3 If you **take offence**, you are upset by something that someone says or does. EG *He was always so quick to take offence.* PHRASE

offend /ɔ°fend/, **offends, offending, offended. 1** If you **offend** someone, you upset or embarrass them. EG *They took care never to offend their visitors.* ◊ **offended.** EG *Clarissa looked offended.* V+O ◊ ADJ PRED

2 If something **offends** a law, rule, or principle, it breaks it. EG *This process offends every known* V+O OR V+against Formal

natural law... It would offend against her conventions.

3 To **offend** also means to commit a crime. EG *Criminals who offend again when they're released.* V Formal

offender /ɔ°fendə/, **offenders. 1** An **offender** is someone who has committed a crime. EG *In 1965, 42% of convicted offenders ended up in prison... ...the treatment of young offenders.* N COUNT Formal

2 You can refer to something that causes a particular kind of harm as an **offender**. EG *Television is the worst offender of the lot.* N COUNT+SUPP

offending /ɔ°fendɪŋ/. You use **offending** to describe something that is causing a problem. EG *Smear the juice on the offending areas... He tapped the offending bulge with a pencil.* ADJ CLASSIF : ATTRIB

offense /ɔ°fens/. See **offence**.

offensive /ɔ°fensɪv/, **offensives. 1** Something that is **offensive** upsets or embarrasses people because it is rude or insulting. EG *That was an extremely offensive remark... Some of the advertisements were highly offensive.* ◊ **offensively.** EG *The examiners were often offensively rude to candidates.* ADJ QUALIT ◊ ADV

2 An **offensive** is a strong attack against someone. EG *...the enemy's air offensive... ...a propaganda offensive against the government.* ▶ used as an adjective. EG *We took immediate offensive action.* N COUNT ▶ ADJ CLASSIF : OFT ATTRIB

3 If you **go on the offensive** or **take the offensive**, you attack or criticize someone before they have the chance to do it to you. EG *He went on the offensive, giving details of blacks being victimized.* PHRASE

offer /ɒfə/, **offers, offering, offered. 1** If you **offer** something to someone, you ask them if they would like to have it or to use it. EG *...an apple which he offered to his friend... I was offered a place at Harvard University... Meadows stood up and offered her his chair.* V+O : USU+O; ALSO V+O+O

2 If you **offer** to do something, you say that you are willing to do it. EG *Gopal offered to take us to Mysore... 'We could take it for you,' offered Dolly.* V+to-INF OR QUOTE

3 An **offer** is something that someone says they will give you or do for you if you want them to. EG *She accepted the offer of a cigarette... ...Kirk's offer to take me to the clinic.* N COUNT : OFT+SUPP

4 If you **offer** someone information, advice, or praise, you give it to them. EG *...offering him advice about accommodation... They didn't ask Liebermann's name and Liebermann didn't offer it.* V+O+O; ALSO V+O : OFT+to

5 If you **offer** someone love or friendship, you show them that you love them or feel friendly towards them. EG *If you tell me the facts, I might be able to offer you more sympathy... Her blue eyes seemed to offer friendship.* V+O+O; ALSO V+O : OFT+to

6 If something **offers** a service, opportunity, or product, it provides it. EG *The new car plant offers the prospect of 5,000 jobs... ...the facilities and equipment offered by the playgroup.* V+O+O; ALSO V+O : OFT+to

7 An **offer** in a shop is a specially low price for a product, or something extra that you get by buying the product. EG *...cut price offers... ...special offers.* N COUNT+SUPP

8 If something is **on offer**, **8.1** it is available to be used or bought. EG *...the weird and wonderful range of gear on offer.* **8.2** its price is specially reduced for a period of time. EG *This item is on offer for a limited period.* PHRASE

9 If you **offer** an amount of money for something, you say that you will pay that much to buy it. EG *I'll offer you nine pounds for it.* V+O OR V+O+O : USU+for

10 An **offer** is also the amount of money that you say that you will pay to buy something. EG *Murgatroyd's offer was the most attractive.* N COUNT

offering /ɒfɔ°rɪŋ/, **offerings. 1** You can refer to something that has been specially produced as an **offering**. EG *...last week's offerings of caviar and* N COUNT

smoked salmon... ...the latest offering from Wilko Johnson.
2 An **offering** is also something that is offered to a N COUNT god as a sacrifice. EG ...sacred offerings on the altar.

off-hand. 1 If someone behaves in an **off-hand** ADJ QUALIT way, they are not friendly or polite, and show little interest in what other people are doing or saying. EG He became increasingly off-hand with Victoria... ...the off-hand contempt with which she treated most men.
2 If you say something **off-hand**, you say it without ADV OR needing to think very hard. EG Off-hand, I can think ADV SEN of three examples.

office /ɒfɪs/, **offices. 1** An **office** is a room or a N COUNT part of a building where people work sitting at desks. EG He called me into his office... You didn't go to the office today?
2 You can refer to the people who work in your N COLL office as the **office**. EG The whole office knows that.
3 An **office** is also **3.1** a department of an N COUNT + organization, especially the government, where USU + SUPP people deal with a particular kind of administrative work. EG ...your local education office... ...the tax office. **3.2** a small building or room where people can go for information, tickets, or a service of some kind. EG ...the ticket office... ...the enquiry office.
4 Someone who holds **office** has an important job N UNCOUNT or a position of authority in government or in an organization. EG The President of the BMA holds office for one year... ...Baldwin's second term of office as Premier. ● When someone is **in office**, ● PHRASE they are in a position of authority to which they were elected or appointed. If they are **out of office**, they are no longer in such a position of authority. EG ...during his first year in office.
● When someone **takes office**, they are elected or ● PHRASE appointed to a position of authority and begin to do their duties. EG The new Conservative Government took office.

officer /ɒfɪsə/, **officers. 1** In the armed forces, an N COUNT **officer** is a person in a position of authority. EG ...a retired army officer.
2 People with responsible positions in organiza- N COUNT : tions, especially government organizations, are USU + SUPP also referred to as **officers**. EG ...a Careers Officer... ...prison officers.
3 Members of the police force are sometimes N COUNT OR referred to as **officers**. EG Inspector Darroway was VOCATIVE the officer in charge of the investigation... Listen, Officer, why do you need all this information?

official /əfɪʃəl/, **officials. 1** Something that is ADJ CLASSIF **official** is approved by the government or by someone else in authority. EG The official figures for the year were published in January... Arabic is the official language of Morocco.
2 Official is used to describe **2.1** things which are ADJ CLASSIF : used by people in authority as part of their job or ATTRIB position. EG ...the Prime Minister's official residence. **2.2** activities which people in authority perform as part of their job or position. EG ...an official visit to Tanzania.
3 The **official** time when something happens is the ADJ CLASSIF : time when it is formally recognized as happening, ATTRIB for example at a public ceremony. EG ...the official opening of the new bridge. ◊ **officially**. EG The ◊ ADV war officially ended the following year.
4 The **official** reason or explanation for something ADJ CLASSIF : is something incorrect that people are told in the ATTRIB hope that they will believe it, because the truth is embarrassing. EG Visiting his aunt was only the official motive. ◊ **officially**. EG Officially she ◊ ADV SEN shares a flat with some girlfriend.
5 An **official** is a person who holds a position of N COUNT authority in an organization. EG ...government officials... ...trade union officials.

officialdom /əfɪʃəldəm/. You use **officialdom** to N UNCOUNT refer to officials in government and other organizations, especially when you disapprove of their rules

and regulations, their slowness, or their unhelpfulness. EG This leaves the individual at the mercy of officialdom.

officious /əfɪʃəs/. Someone who is **officious** is too ADJ QUALIT eager to tell people what to do; used showing disapproval. EG ...officious interference by managers.

offing /ɒfɪŋ/. If you say that something is **in the** PHRASE **offing**, you mean that it is likely to happen soon. EG War was already in the offing.

off-licence, **off-licences. An off-licence** is a N COUNT shop which sells beer, wine, and other alcoholic British drinks.

offload /ɒfləʊd/, **offloads, offloading, offloaded.** V+O : If you **offload** something that you do not want, you OFT + onto get rid of it, especially by giving it to someone else. Informal

off-peak. Off-peak things are available at a time ADJ CLASSIF : when there is little demand for them, so that they ATTRIB are cheaper than usual. EG ...off-peak electricity.

off-putting. You describe someone as **off-** ADJ QUALIT **putting** when you find them rather unpleasant and do not want to know them better. EG She has a rather off-putting manner.

offset /ɒfsɛt/, **offsets, offsetting.** The form **off-** V+O : OFT PASS **set** is used in the present tense and is also the past tense and past participle.
If one thing **is offset** by another, its effect is reduced by the other thing, so there is no great advantage or disadvantage as a result. EG They argued that their wage increases would be offset by higher prices.

offshoot /ɒfʃuːt/, **offshoots.** If one thing is an N COUNT + SUPP **offshoot** of another thing, it has developed from the other thing. EG Afrikaans is an offshoot of Dutch.

offshore /ɒfʃɔː/. Something that is **offshore** is ADJ CLASSIF situated in the sea near to the coast. EG ...offshore OR ADV oil terminals... The boats waited offshore.

offside /ɒfsaɪd/. **1** The **offside** of a vehicle is the N SING side of it that is furthest from the pavement when British you are driving. EG The mini had touched the offside of the truck with its nearside wing.
2 If a player in a game of football or hockey is ADJ CLASSIF **offside**, they have broken the rules by moving too OR ADV far forward.

offspring /ɒfsprɪŋ/. Your **offspring** are your N COUNT : children. 'Offspring' is both the singular and the USU + POSS plural form. EG How do parents pass genes on to Formal their offspring?

off-white. Something that is **off-white** is not pure ADJ COLOUR white, but slightly grey or yellow. EG ...a tatty off-white dress... ...bits of paper, some white, some off-white.

often /ɒfən/. **1** If something happens **often**, it ADV happens many times or much of the time. EG We often get very wet cold winters here... It's not often you meet someone who's really interested... She didn't write very often.
2 You use **often** when you are asking or talking ADV about how frequently something happens. EG How often do you need to weigh the baby?... John came as often as he could.
3 Often is also used in these phrases. **3.1** If you say PHRASE that something happens **more often than not**, you mean that it usually happens. EG More often than not the patient recovers. **3.2** If you say that something happens **as often as not**, you mean that it happens fairly often. EG These paintings, as often as not, ended up in America. **3.3** If you say that something happens **every so often**, you mean that it happens occasionally. EG Every so often, she spends a weekend in London.

ogle /əʊgəl/, **ogles, ogling, ogled.** If someone V+O **ogles** someone else, they stare at them, especially in a way that indicates a sexual interest; used showing disapproval. EG The men ogled her lasciviously... ...the ladies ogling their hero.

ogre /əʊgə/, **ogres. An ogre** is a character in fairy N COUNT stories who is large, cruel, and frightening.

oh /əʊ/. You use **oh** 1 to introduce a response or a EXCLAM comment on something that has just been said. EG *'I'll give it to you now.' – 'Oh thanks.'... 'I have a flat in London.' – 'Oh yes, whereabouts?'... 'How's your brother then?' – 'Oh he's fine.'* 2 when you are hesitating while speaking. EG *It was about, oh, half past five when I got home.* 3 to express a feeling such as surprise, pain, annoyance, or joy. EG *She covered her face with her hands and cried, 'Oh! Oh!'... 'He wants to see you immediately,' I said. 'Oh!' she said. Her smile vanished.*

oil /ɔɪl/, **oils, oiling, oiled. 1 Oil** is **1.1** a smooth, N UNCOUNT thick, sticky liquid that is used as a fuel and for lubricating machines. Oil is found underground, and it can also be manufactured. EG *...alternatives to coal and oil.* **1.2** a smooth, thick, sticky liquid N UNCOUNT: that is made from plants or animals. Some oils are USU+SUPP used for cooking. EG *...cooking oil... ...olive oil.* **1.3** a N UNCOUNT smooth, thick liquid that is often scented and that +SUPP you rub into your skin or add to your bath. EG *...some sort of delicious bath oil.*

2 If you **oil** a machine, you put oil into it in order to V+O make it work smoothly. EG *He has to oil and wind the clock... The gun was kept well oiled.*

3 If you **oil** your skin or your hair, you rub oil onto V+O it. EG *He had wavy, oiled hair.*

4 Oils are **4.1** oil paintings. EG *...an exhibition of* N COUNT: *watercolours and oils by Turner... ...small oils of an* USU PLURAL *early period.* **4.2** oil paints. EG *...trying to capture* N PLURAL *the scene in oils.*

oilfield /ɔɪlfiːld/, **oilfields. An oilfield** is an area N COUNT of land or part of the seabed where oil is found and from which it is removed.

oil paint, oil paints. Oil paint is a thick paint N MASS used by artists. It is made from a coloured powder and linseed oil.

oil painting, oil paintings. An oil painting is a N COUNT painting that has been painted using oil paint. EG *...really valuable oil paintings.*

oil slick, oil slicks. An oil slick is a layer of oil N COUNT that is floating on top of the sea or a lake as the result of an accident, usually one involving an oil tanker.

oil well, oil wells. An oil well is a hole which is N COUNT drilled into the ground or the seabed in order to remove the oil which lies underground.

oily /ɔɪliʰ/. **1** Something that is oily **1.1** is covered ADJ QUALIT with oil. EG *...oily rags... ...oily fried potatoes.* **1.2** ADJ CLASSIF looks or feels like oil. EG *...an oily substance.*

2 You describe someone as **oily** when you find ADJ QUALIT them unpleasant because they flatter people or behave in an excessively polite way.

ointment /ɔɪntməˀnt/, **ointments. 1** An **oint-** N MASS **ment** is a smooth thick substance that is put on sore skin or a wound to help it heal. EG *...zinc ointment... ...a tube of sunburn ointment.*

2 You describe something as a **fly in the oint-** PHRASE **ment** when it spoils a situation and prevents it from being as successful as you had hoped. EG *The only fly in the ointment was that his own son refused to co-operate.*

OK /əʊ keɪ/. See **okay**.

okay /əʊkeɪ/, **okays, okaying, okayed;** also spelled **OK. 1** If you say that something is **okay**, ADJ CLASSIF: you mean that it is acceptable. EG *I asked Jenny* USU PRED, *how she thought it all went. 'Okay,' she said... I'll* OR ADV *have another coffee and then I'll be going, if that's* Informal *okay... She wanted to know if the trip was OK with the government.*

2 If you say that someone is **okay**, you mean that ADJ CLASSIF: they are safe and well. EG *'Where's Jane?' – 'Just* USU PRED *back there. She's okay. Just shocked.'* Informal

3 You can say **okay 3.1** when you are agreeing to CONVENTION something. EG *'I'll be back at a quarter past one.' –* Informal *'OK. I'll see you then.'... 'I must go and make a phone call.' – 'Yeah OK.'* **3.2** to check whether the person you are talking to understands what you have just said and accepts it. EG *I'll be back in fifteen minutes. OK?* **3.3** as a way of stopping

people from arguing with you or criticizing you by showing that you accept their point, so that you can go on and say something more. EG *'You said you didn't look at it!' – 'Okay, so I did glance at it.'*

4 You can also use **okay** to indicate to someone CONVENTION that you want to start talking about something else Informal or doing something else. EG *Okay, do you mind if we speak a bit of German now?*

5 If someone in authority **okays** something, they V+O officially agree to it or allow it to happen. EG *I'm* Informal *blowed if I know why, but I'll okay this overdraft.*

▸ used as a noun. EG *I don't want to go on before* ▸ N SING: *he's given the OK.* the+N

old /əʊld/, **older, oldest. 1** Someone who is **old** has ADJ QUALIT lived for many years and is no longer young. EG *...his old mother... I'm too old, Mr Gerran.*

2 You can refer to people who are old as the **old**. EG N PLURAL: *...the particular needs of the old and infirm.* the+N

3 Something that is **old 3.1** has existed for a long ADJ QUALIT time and is no longer new. EG *...a massive old building of crumbling red brick... ...an old joke.* **3.2** ADJ QUALIT is no longer in a good condition because of its age or because it has been used a lot. EG *...wardrobes full of old clothes.* **3.3** is now no longer used or has ADJ CLASSIF been replaced by something else. EG *I was directed* ATTRIB *into the old dining room... ...his old job at the publishing company.*

4 If you say that someone or something is a ADJ QUALIT particular number of years **old**, you mean that they have lived or existed for that length of time. EG *She's about 50 years old... How old are you?... She was a couple of years older than me.*

5 If someone is an **old** friend of yours, they have ADJ QUALIT: been your friend for a long time. ATTRIB

6 In the old days means many years ago, before PHRASE things changed. EG *Hong Kong was a shopper's paradise in the old days.*

7 You can use **old** to express affection or familiar- ADJ CLASSIF: ity when you are talking to or about someone you ATTRIB know. EG *I got a letter from good old Lewis.* Informal

8 You use **any old** to emphasize that the quality or PHRASE type of something is not important. EG *Any old* Informal *board will do.*

old-age pensioner, old-age pensioners. An N COUNT **old-age pensioner** is the same as an OAP.

olden /əʊldəˀn/. **In the olden days** means long PHRASE ago in the past. Informal

old-fashioned. 1 Something that is **old-** ADJ QUALIT **fashioned** is no longer considered appropriate in style or design, because it has been replaced by something that is more modern. EG *He was wearing old-fashioned plastic-rimmed glasses.*

2 If you are **old-fashioned**, you believe in and ADJ QUALIT behave according to the values and standards of the past. EG *I am very old-fashioned... ...old-fashioned ideas.*

old hand, old hands. An old hand is a person N COUNT who is very skilled at something because they have a lot of experience. EG *...a few old hands in the press corps.*

old maid, old maids. People sometimes refer to N COUNT an old or middle-aged woman as an **old maid** when she has never been married and they think that she will never get married; an offensive expression.

old man. Someone's **old man** is their father or N SING their husband. EG *The first letter I got from my old* Informal *man told me how proud he was of me.*

old master, old masters. An old master is **1** a N COUNT famous painter of the past. **2** a painting by a famous painter of the past. EG *...reproductions of old masters.*

Old Testament. The Old Testament is the first N PROPER: part of the Bible. It contains Jewish writings, the+N mostly about the history of the Jewish people.

If someone is an old hand at something, are they omniscient?

old wives' tale, old wives' tales. An **old wives'** N COUNT
tale is a common belief that is based on traditional
ideas and that is often considered to be foolish or
superstitious.

old woman, old women. If you call someone, N COUNT
especially a man, an **old woman**, you mean that Informal
they are very fussy. EG *He's a bit of an old woman.* Outdated

O level, O levels. An **O level** is an educational N COUNT
qualification in a particular subject. O levels are
awarded in England, Wales, and Northern Ireland.
Schoolchildren usually take O level examinations
at the age of 15 or 16, after studying for them for 2
or 3 years. O level examinations are being replaced by GCSE examinations. EG *...minimum qualifications of five O levels... ...O-level Maths.*

olive /ɒlɪv/, **olives. 1** An **olive** is a small green or N COUNT
black fruit that has a bitter taste. Olives are often
eaten as a snack or with a meal.

2 Something that is **olive** or **olive green** is ADJ COLOUR
yellowish-green in colour. EG *...olive green towels.*

olive oil is oil that is obtained by pressing olives. It N UNCOUNT
is used for putting on salads or for cooking.

-ological is used to replace '-ology' at the end of SUFFIX
nouns in order to form adjectives. These adjectives
describe something as relating to a particular
science or subject. For example, 'geological'
means relating to geology. Adjectives formed in
this way are not usually defined in this dictionary,
but are treated with the related nouns. EG *...bacte-
riological research... ...the Zoological Society.*

-ologist, -ologists. -ologist is used to replace SUFFIX
'-ology' at the end of nouns in order to form other
nouns that refer to people who are concerned with
a particular science or subject. For example, a
'biologist' is concerned with biology. Nouns formed
in this way are not usually defined in this dictionary, but are treated with the nouns ending in
'-ology'. EG *...a well known anthropologist... ...ama-
teur geologists.*

Olympic /əlɪmpɪk/, **Olympics. 1 Olympic** means ADJ CLASSIF :
relating to the Olympic Games. EG *...fencing to* ATTRIB
Olympic standard... ...an Olympic finalist.

2 The **Olympics** are the Olympic Games. EG *Didn't* N PLURAL
she win a gold medal at the Olympics?

Olympic Games. The **Olympic Games** are a N PLURAL
set of international sports competitions which take the+N
place every four years, each time in a different
country.

omelette /ɒmlɪʔt/, **omelettes;** also spelled **ome-** N COUNT
let in American English. An **omelette** is a food
made by beating eggs and cooking them in a flat
pan.

omen /əʊməʔn/, **omens.** An **omen** is something N COUNT
that is thought to indicate what is going to happen
in the future. EG *An eclipse of the sun is the worst of
bad omens... It was a good omen for the trip.*

ominous /ɒmɪnəs/. Something that is **ominous** is ADJ QUALIT
worrying or frightening because it makes you think
that something unpleasant is going to happen. EG
There was an ominous silence. ◇ **ominously.** EG ◇ ADV
Black clouds were piling up ominously.

omission /əˈmɪʃəʔn/, **omissions. 1** An **omission** N COUNT
is something that has not been included or not been
done, either deliberately or accidentally. EG *The
reports were full of errors and omissions.*

2 Omission is the act of not including someone or N UNCOUNT
something or of not doing something. EG *...the
omission of women from these studies.*

omit /əˈmɪt/, **omits, omitting, omitted. 1** If you V+O
omit something, you do not include it, either
deliberately or accidentally. EG *Two groups were
omitted from the survey – the old and women.*

2 If you **omit** to do something, you do not do it. EG V+to-INF
He omitted to say whether the men were armed. Formal

omnibus /ɒmnɪbəʔs/, **omnibuses.** An **omnibus** is N COUNT
1 a book which contains a large collection of
stories or articles, often by the same person or
about the same subject. **2** a radio or television
broadcast which contains two or more similar

programmes that were originally broadcast separately.

omnipotent /ɒmnɪpətənt/. Someone or some- ADJ CLASSIF
thing that is **omnipotent** has complete power over Formal
things or people. EG *...an omnipotent central committee... ...an omnipotent and perfect deity.*

omniscient /ɒmnɪsɪənt/. Someone who is **omnis-** ADJ CLASSIF
cient knows or seems to know everything. EG *The* Formal
*woman goes as a patient to an omniscient profes-
sional... ...faith in an omniscient God.*

omnivorous /ɒmnɪvərəs/. An **omnivorous** per- ADJ CLASSIF
son or animal eats all kinds of food, including both Technical
meat and plants. EG *...the change from a vegetarian
to an omnivorous diet.*

on /ɒn/. **1** If you are standing or resting **on** PREP
something, it is underneath you and is supporting
your weight. EG *They were sitting on chairs...
Large, soft cushions lay on the floor... ...a cow
grazing on a hill.*

2 If something is **on** a surface or object, it is stuck PREP
to it or attached to it. EG *...the posters on the walls...
...the light on the ceiling... ...the buttons on a shirt.*

3 If there is something **on** a piece of paper, it has PREP
been written or printed there. EG *...the table on the
back page of the book... ...a card with his name on...
She wrote it down on a piece of paper.*

4 You use **on** to say what part of your body is PREP
supporting your weight. For example, you can lie
on your back or stand **on** one leg.

5 If someone has a particular expression **on** their PREP
face, they have that expression. EG *She had a
puzzled expression on her face.*

6 If a building is **on** a road, it is next to it. EG *The* PREP
house is on Pacific Avenue.

7 If you get **on** a bus, train, or plane, you get into it PREP
in order to travel somewhere. If you are **on** it, you
are travelling in it.

8 You can use **on** when mentioning the area of PREP
land where someone works or lives. For example,
someone can work **on** a farm or a building site, or
live **on** a housing estate.

9 If you put, drop, or throw something **on** a surface, PREP
you move it or drop it so that it is then supported
by the surface. EG *Put the tray on the bed, please...
He dropped it on the floor.*

10 When you put **on** a piece of clothing, you place ADV
it over a part of your body in order to wear it. If
you have it **on**, you are wearing it. EG *She put her
shoes on... She had her coat on.*

11 You can say that you have something **on** you if PREP
you are carrying it in your pocket or in a bag.

12 If you hurt yourself **on** something, you hurt PREP
yourself by accidentally hitting it with a part of
your body. EG *He cut himself on the gatepost.*

13 Books, discussions, or ideas **on** a particular PREP
subject are concerned with that subject. EG *...books
on philosophy, art, and religion.*

14 If information is **on** tape or **on** computer, that is PREP
the way that it is stored.

15 If something operates **on** a particular system or PREP
principle, that is how it operates. EG *They work on a
rota system.*

16 When you watch television or listen to the radio, PREP
you see things **on** television or hear things **on** the
radio. EG *His first film was shown on television
yesterday.*

17 When a musical instrument is played, you say PREP
that music is played **on** it. EG *...waltzes played on
the violin.*

18 When an activity involving a lot of people is ADV AFTER VB
taking place, you can say that it is **on**. EG *The war
was on then.*

19 When a play or film is being shown, you can say ADV AFTER VB
that it is **on**. EG *What's on at the Odeon?*

20 If something such as a machine or an electric ADV AFTER VB
light is **on**, it is functioning. EG *A tap had been left
on.*

21 If something happens **on** a particular day or PREP
date, that is when it happens. EG *...on the first day of*

term... ...on Thursday night... Caro was born on April 10th.

22 You use **on** when mentioning an event that was PREP followed by another one. For example, if something happened **on** someone's return, it happened just after they returned. EG 'It's so unfair,' Clarissa said on her return... On being called 'young lady', she laughed.

23 If you say, for example, that someone worked ADV AFTER VB **on** or chattered **on**, you mean that they continued working or chattering.

24 If you say that something goes **on and on**, you PHRASE mean that it continues for a very long time. EG The list goes on and on.

25 If you say that something happens **on and off**, PHRASE you mean that it happens occasionally.

26 If something happens **from** a particular time PHRASE **on**, it starts to happen at that time, and continues afterwards. EG From now on, you are free to do what you like.

27 If something affects you, you can say that it has PREP an effect **on** you. EG The effect on the environment could be considerable.

28 If you are **on** a council or committee, you are a PREP member of it.

29 Someone who is taking a medicine or drug PREP regularly is **on** that medicine or drug.

30 If you are **on** a particular kind of income, that is PREP the kind of income that you have. EG ...people on a low income.

31 Taxes or profits that are obtained from some- PREP thing are referred to as taxes or profits **on** it. EG ...a new sales tax on luxury goods... Profits on books will be down... You pay interest on your mortgage.

32 When you buy something, you spend money **on** PREP it. EG ...the amount of money he spent on clothes... Why waste money on them?

33 When you pay for something that someone else PREP receives, you can say that it is **on** you. EG The Informal drinks were always on him.

34 When you spend time **on** something, you spend PREP time doing it or making it. EG I spent a lot of time on this picture.

35 If you say that someone's eyes are **on** some- PREP thing, you mean that they are looking at it.

36 If you are very busy, you can say that you **have** PHRASE **a lot on**. If you are not busy, you can say that you Informal **do not have much on**.

37 If you say that someone goes **on** at you, you ADV AFTER VB mean that they keep criticizing you, complaining +at to you, or asking you to do something. EG I went on Informal at my father to have seat belts fitted... He's always on at me about the way I dress.

38 If you say that someone is **on** about something, ADV AFTER VB you mean that they are talking about it. EG He's +about always on about yoga... What are you on about? Informal

39 If you say that something **is not on**, you mean PHRASE that it is unacceptable or impossible. EG That sort of Informal writing just isn't on.

40 and so on: see **so**.

once /wʌns/. **1** If something happens **once**, it ADV happens one time only, or one time within a particular period of time. EG I've been out with him once, that's all... Some trees only bear fruit once every twenty-five years.

2 If something was **once** true, it was true at some ADV time in the past, but is no longer true. EG Texas was once ruled by Mexico.

3 If something happens **once** another thing has CONJ happened, it happens immediately afterwards. EG Once inside her flat, she glanced at the clock.

4 Once is also used in these phrases. **4.1** If you do PHRASES something **at once**, you do it immediately. EG They set to work at once... I knew at once that something was wrong. **4.2** If several things happen **at once** or **all at once**, they all happen at the same time. EG Everybody is talking at once. **4.3** If something happens **once again** or **once more**, it happens again. EG She wanted to see him once more

before she died. **4.4** If a situation exists **once again** or **once more**, it exists again, after not existing for a while. EG But now companies are once again queueing to join the scheme. **4.5** If you have done something **once or twice**, you have done it a few times, but not very often. EG She had been to London once or twice before. **4.6** If something happens **once in a while**, it happens occasionally but not very often. EG Once in a while she'd give me some lilacs to take home. **4.7** If you say that something happened **for once**, you are emphasizing that it does not usually happen. EG For once Castle went without his lunch. **4.8** If something happens **once and for all**, it happens completely or finally. EG They had to be defeated once and for all. **4.9 Once upon a time** is used at the beginning of a children's story to indicate that the events in it are supposed to have taken place a long time ago.

oncoming /ˈɒnkʌmɪŋ/ means moving towards ADJ CLASSIF: you. EG ...the oncoming waves... ...oncoming traffic. ATTRIB

one /wʌn/, **ones**. **1 One** is the number 1: see the NUMBER entry headed NUMBER. EG ...one hundred miles... Of these four suggestions, only one is correct... The two friends share one job... The road goes from one side of the town to the other.

2 If you refer to the **one** person or thing of a NUMBER particular kind, you mean the only person or thing of that kind. EG Their one aim in life is to go to University... She is the one person with enough medical knowledge to make it possible.

3 You can use **one**. **3.1** instead of 'a' to emphasize NUMBER the adjective or expression that follows it. EG There Informal was one hell of a row when they came on. **3.2** in Formal front of someone's name to indicate that you have not met them or heard of them before. EG The big man is one Bert Lance, a friend of the President.

4 You can also use **one** to refer to a thing or person PRON: of a particular kind, especially when you want to HAS PLURAL describe them or to give new information about them. EG These trousers aren't as tight as the other ones... ...buying old houses and building new ones... Oh, that's a difficult one to answer, isn't it.

5 You can use **one** when referring to a time in the NUMBER past or the future. For example, if you say that you did something **one** day, you mean that you did it on a day in the past. If you say that you will do something **one** day, you mean that you will do it on a day in the future. EG One day, she went for a swim in the ocean... One evening, I had a visit from Henry Cox... One day you and I must have a long talk together.

6 You can also use **one** after an adjective as a way PRON+SUPP: of addressing or referring to someone you are fond HAS PLURAL of or admire. EG Come along now, little ones, off to Outdated bed.

7 You can use **one** after a verb that means 'hit', to PRON: SING indicate that one blow is given. EG Go on, thump Informal him one.

8 One is also a personal pronoun and can be used PRON: SING as a subject or an object. A speaker or writer uses Formal **one** to refer to people in general, for example in statements about what usually happens in a particular situation. EG One can eat well here... The law should guard one against this sort of thing.

9 One is also used in these phrases. **9.1** If you say PHRASES that someone is **not one** to do something, you mean that they are not likely to do it, because of their character or habits. EG Uncle Harold was not one to underestimate the problem. **9.2 One or two** means a very few. EG One or two of the girls help in the kitchen. **9.3** If you are or have **one up on** Informal someone, you have an advantage over them. **9.4 A hundred and one** or **a thousand and one** means a great many. EG There must be a thousand and one books of this sort on the market. **9.5** When people Formal

What phrase can you use at the beginning of a children's story?

are **at one**, they are in agreement with each other.

9.6 You can use **for one** to emphasize that a particular person is definitely behaving or reacting in a particular way, whatever other people are doing. EG *But I for one feel very grateful and very satisfied.* **9.7** one thing **after another**: see another. ● **one another**: see another. ● **one after the other**: see other. ● See also **number one**.

one-man. A **one-man** performance is given by one man, rather than by several people. EG *...a one-man show.* ADJ CLASSIF: ATTRIB

one-off, one-offs. A **one-off** is something that happens or is made only once. EG *'A one-off,' he said delightedly. 'A tailor-made gun.'* ▶ used as an adjective. EG *...one-off projects.* N COUNT Informal ▶ ADJ CLASSIF: ATTRIB

one-parent family, one-parent families. A **one-parent family** consists of a child or children living with only one of their parents. N COUNT

onerous /ɒnərəs, əʊ-/. Work that is **onerous** is difficult and unpleasant. EG *...the onerous duties of postal delivery.* ADJ QUALIT Formal

one's /wʌnz/. **1** A speaker or writer uses **one's** to indicate that something belongs or relates to people in general. See paragraph 8 of the entry for **one**. EG *Naturally, one wanted only the best for one's children.* DET POSS Formal

2 One's is also a spoken form of 'one is' or 'one has', especially when 'has' is an auxiliary verb. EG *One's never quite sure exactly how things are going to turn out... One's got to pay for it.* Formal

oneself /wʌˈnself/. **1** A speaker or writer uses **oneself** as the object of a verb or preposition in a clause where 'one' is the subject or a previous object. See paragraph 8 of the entry for **one**. EG *One must keep such interests to oneself.* PRON REFL: SING

2 Oneself is also used to emphasize the subject or object of a clause. EG *Others might find odd what one finds perfectly normal oneself.* PRON REFL: SING

one-sided. 1 In a **one-sided** activity or relationship, one of the people involved does much more than the other. EG *...a one-sided correspondence... ...one-sided conversations.* ADJ QUALIT

2 A **one-sided** argument or report considers only some of the facts involved in a situation or problem, and is therefore not acceptable. EG *The report is one-sided in its interpretation of the evidence.* ADJ QUALIT

one-time. You use **one-time** to indicate that someone used to have a particular job, position, or role. EG *...Fred Dunn, a onetime farm worker.* ADJ CLASSIF: ATTRIB

one-to-one. In a **one-to-one** relationship, you deal with only one other person. EG *...one-to-one tuition.* ADJ CLASSIF: ATTRIB

one-way. 1 One-way streets are streets along which vehicles can drive in only one direction. ADJ CLASSIF: ATTRIB

2 If you buy a **one-way** ticket, you can use it to travel to a place, but not to travel back again. EG *...a one-way ticket to Jersey.* ADJ CLASSIF: ATTRIB

one-woman. A **one-woman** performance is given by one woman, rather than by several people. ADJ CLASSIF: ATTRIB

ongoing /ɒnɡəʊɪŋ/. An **ongoing** situation has been happening for quite a long time and is continuing to happen. EG *...an ongoing economic crisis... ...ongoing projects.* ADJ CLASSIF: ATTRIB

onion /ʌnjən/, **onions.** An **onion** is a small, round vegetable. It is white with a brown, papery skin, and has a strong smell and taste. N COUNT OR N UNCOUNT

onlooker /ɒnlʊkə/, **onlookers.** An **onlooker** is someone who watches an event without taking part in it. EG *She blew a kiss to the shivering onlookers.* N COUNT

only /əʊnliˈ/. In written English, 'only' is usually placed immediately before the word it qualifies. In spoken English, you can use stress to indicate what 'only' qualifies, so its position is not so important.

1 You use **only** to indicate the one thing that is involved or that happens in a particular situation. EG *He read only paperbacks... I'm only interested in facts... Only Mother knows... The video is to be used for teaching purposes only... She could only obey.* ADV

2 You say that one thing will happen **only if** CONJ

another thing happens when you want to indicate that it will not happen unless the other thing happens. EG *I will come only if nothing is said to the press... These snakes only attack if they feel cornered or threatened.*

3 If you talk about the **only** thing involved in a particular situation, you mean that there are no others. EG *I was the only one smoking... It was the only way out.* ADJ CLASSIF: ATTRIB

4 Someone who is an **only** child has no brothers or sisters. ADJ CLASSIF: ATTRIB

5 You can use **only** to emphasize that something is unimportant or small. EG *It was only a squirrel... I was only joking... We only paid £26... It only took half an hour.* ADV

6 You can use **only** to emphasize how recently something happened. EG *This beetle has only recently been discovered... I've only just arrived.* ADV

7 You say that something is **only just** the case to emphasize that it is very nearly not the case. EG *He could only just hear them... The heat was only just bearable.* PHRASE

8 You use **not only** to introduce the first of two linked statements when the second is even more surprising or extreme than the first. EG *Chimpanzees not only use tools but make them.* PHRASE

9 If you say that someone **has only** to do one thing in order to achieve or prove something, you are emphasizing how easily or quickly it can be done. EG *You've only got to read the newspapers to see what can happen to hitch-hikers.* PHRASE

10 You can use **only** to emphasize a wish or hope. EG *I only wish I had the money.* ● **if only**: see **if**. ADV

11 You can use **only** to add a comment which slightly changes or corrects what you have just said. EG *Snake is just like chicken, only tougher.* CONJ Informal

12 You can use **only** to introduce the reason why something is not done. EG *'That's what I'm trying to do,' said Mrs Oliver, 'only I can't get near enough.'* CONJ Informal

13 You can use **only** before an infinitive to introduce an event which happens immediately after the previous one, and which is rather surprising or unfortunate. EG *He broke off, only to resume almost at once... I had tried this years before, only to receive a polite refusal.* ADV + to-INF

14 You can use **only** to emphasize that you think a course of action or type of behaviour is reasonable in a particular situation. EG *It is only natural that she will have mixed feelings about your promotion.* ADV + ADJ

15 You use **only too** to emphasize that something happens to a greater extent than is expected or wanted. EG *He is normally only too pleased to help... She remembered that night only too clearly.* PHRASE

onrush /ɒnrʌʃ/. You say that there is an **onrush** of a feeling or emotion when it develops suddenly and quickly. EG *...the onrush of her tears... ...an onrush of pain.* N SING + *of* Formal

onset /ɒnset/. The **onset** of something unpleasant is the beginning of it. EG *...the onset of war... ...his brave response to the onset of blindness.* N SING: the + N + *of*

onslaught /ɒnslɔːt/, **onslaughts.** An **onslaught** is a violent attack. EG *...a co-ordinated onslaught on enemy airfields.* N COUNT + SUPP

onto /ɒntʊ/; also spelled **on to. 1** If someone or something moves **onto** an object or is put **onto** it, the object is then underneath them and supporting them. EG *I got onto the bed... She spooned a portion of potato onto his plate... I ran out onto the porch.* PREP

2 When you get **onto** a bus, train, or plane, you get into it in order to travel somewhere. PREP

3 If you fasten something **onto** something else, you fasten it to it. EG *I bent a pin and tied it onto a piece of string.* PREP

4 If you hold **onto** something, you hold it firmly. EG *I was still holding onto her shoulders... ...clinging onto his shirt.* PREP

5 If someone who is speaking gets **onto** or moves **onto** a different subject, they begin talking about it. EG *Let's move onto another question.* PREP

onus /ˈəʊnəs/. If you say that the **onus** is on N SING someone to do something, you mean that it is their Formal duty or responsibility to do it. EG *The onus was on me to earn enough to support the family.*

onward /ˈɒnwəd/, **onwards**. When it is an adverb, the form **onwards** is normally used in British English, and **onward** in American English or formal British English.

1 If something happens from a particular time ADV **onwards** or **onward**, it begins to happen at that time and continues happening afterwards. EG *From 1968 onwards the situation began to change... From that time onward he had never spoken to her again.*

2 If someone or something moves **onwards** or ADV OR **onward**, they continue travelling or moving for- ADJ CLASSIF : ward. EG *We travelled from China to India, and* ATTRIB *onwards to East Africa... ...as she ploughed inexorably onward... ...the onward motion of the boat.*

3 You can say that things move **onwards** or ADV OR **onward** when they continue to develop or pro- ADJ CLASSIF : gress. EG *...this onward march of the Labour move-* ATTRIB *ment.*

ooh /uː/. People say **ooh** when they are surprised EXCLAM or when something pleasant or unpleasant sudden- Informal ly happens. EG *Ooh, you are awful... Ooh, that feels nice.*

oops /ʊps, uːps/. You say **oops** to indicate that EXCLAM there has been a slight accident or mistake. EG Informal *Oops, sorry... Oops! He's fallen down.*

ooze /uːz/, **oozes, oozing, oozed. 1** When a thick, V-ERG sticky liquid **oozes** from an object or when the object **oozes** it, the liquid flows slowly from the object. EG *...blood oozing from his wounds... His sandals oozed black slime.*

2 You can refer to mud or any similar sticky N UNCOUNT substance as **ooze**.

3 If someone **oozes** a quality or feeling, they show V+O OR it very strongly, often when they do not really feel V+*with* it. EG *His letter, oozing remorse, appeared in all the newspapers... Her voice oozed with politeness.*

opal /ˈəʊpəl/, **opals**. An **opal** is a precious stone. N COUNT OR Opals are mainly whitish or colourless, but colours N UNCOUNT can be seen in them.

opaque /əʊˈpeɪk/. **1** If an object or substance is ADJ QUALIT **opaque**, you cannot see through it. EG *...the opaque windows of the jail... ...the opaque water.*

2 You can say that something is **opaque** when it is ADJ CLASSIF difficult to understand. EG *Their intentions re-* Formal *mained opaque... Jimmy was opaque to her.*

open /ˈəʊpən/, **opens, opening, opened. 1** When V-ERG you **open** something such as a door or the lid of a box, or when it **opens**, you move it so that it no longer covers a hole or gap. EG *Elizabeth opened the door and went in... The door opened almost before Brody had finished knocking.* ▸ used as an ▸ ADJ CLASSIF adjective. EG *...the open window.*

2 When you **open** a cupboard, container, or letter, V+O you move, remove, or cut part of it so that you can take out what is inside. EG *Open the tool-box... I opened a can of beans.* ▸ used as an adjective. EG ▸ ADJ CLASSIF *Boylan couldn't get the bottle open... He tore open the envelope.*

3 When you **open** a book, you move its covers V+O apart in order to read or write on the pages inside. EG *He opened the book at random.* ▸ used as an ▸ ADJ CLASSIF adjective. EG *...the open Bible.*

4 When you **open** your mouth, you move your lips V+O and teeth apart. EG *She opened her mouth to say something, then closed it.* ▸ used as an adjective. EG ▸ ADJ CLASSIF *Angelica looked at me with her mouth open.*

5 When you **open** your eyes, you move your eyelids V+O upwards so that you can see. EG *She opened her eyes and looked at me.* ▸ used as an adjective. EG ▸ ADJ CLASSIF *...lying with his eyes wide open.*

6 If you have an **open** mind or are **open** to ideas or ADJ QUALIT suggestions, you are prepared to consider any ideas or suggestions.

7 If you describe someone as **open**, you mean that ADJ QUALIT

they are honest and do not try to hide anything. EG *They looked at her with open curiosity.*

◊ **openness.** EG *...their relaxed openness.* ◊ N UNCOUNT

8 If you say that a person, idea, or system is **open** ADJ PRED+*to* to something such as criticism or blame, you mean they could be treated in the way indicated. EG *The proposals were certainly open to criticism... Such a description is open to misunderstanding.*

9 When a shop, office, or public building **opens** or **is opened, 9.1** its doors are unlocked, the people in V-ERG it start working, and customers can use it. EG *When does the library open?* ▸ used as an adjective. EG ▸ ADJ CLASSIF *The Tate Gallery is open 10 a.m. - 6 p.m.* **9.2** it V-ERG starts operating for the first time. EG *They're opening an office in Birmingham.*

10 When someone important **opens** a building or a V+O public area, they declare officially in a public ceremony that it is ready to be used or to start operating. ▸ used as an adjective. EG *Lord* ▸ ADJ PRED *Shawcross declared the hotel open.* ◊ **opening.** EG ◊ N UNCOUNT *...the opening of the new theatre.* +SUPP

11 When a public event such as a conference or a V play **opens**, it begins to take place or to be performed. EG *The UN General Assembly opens in New York later this month.* ◊ **opening.** EG *...the* ◊ N UNCOUNT *opening of 'Nicholas Nickleby' on Broadway.*

12 The person who **opens** an event is the first one V+O to speak or do something. EG *Senator Denton opened the hearing by reminding us of our duty.*

13 If you **open** an account with a bank, you begin V+O to use their services by giving them some of your money to look after or invest.

14 If you **open** something that is blocked, you V+O remove the thing that is blocking it. EG *It took three days to clear the snow and open the road to traffic.* ▸ used as an adjective. EG *Route Nine is now open.* ▸ ADJ CLASSIF

15 If a room or door **opens** into or onto a place, V+A you can go straight to that place from the room or through the door. EG *These rooms have doors opening directly onto the garden.*

16 When flowers **open**, they change from being V buds and their petals spread out.

17 If something that you are wearing is **open**, it is ADJ CLASSIF not fastened. EG *...an open black raincoat... ...an open-necked shirt.*

18 An **open** area of land or sea is a large area that ADJ CLASSIF : has few things such as buildings or islands in it. EG ATTRIB *The road stretched across open country.*

◊ **openness.** EG *...the openness of Vincent Square.* ◊ N UNCOUNT

19 You can use **open** to describe something that is ADJ CLASSIF : not covered or enclosed. EG *...an open car... Never* ATTRIB *dry clothes in front of an open fire.*

20 If you do something **in the open**, you do it out of PHRASE doors rather than in a building. EG *The children enjoyed sleeping out in the open.*

21 If an attitude or situation is brought out **into the** PHRASE **open**, people are told about it and it is no longer kept secret.

22 If a course of action is **open** to you, it is possible ADJ PRED+*to* for you to do it. EG *We should use the opportunities now open to us.*

23 If a meeting, competition, or invitation is an ADJ CLASSIF **open** one, anyone is allowed to take part in it or accept it. EG *Most Council meetings are open to the public... ...the Women's Open Golf Championship.*

24 If you describe a situation or topic as **open**, you ADJ CLASSIF mean that it is still being considered and no decision has been made about it yet. EG *I let joining the Party remain an open question... They had left their options open.*

25 See also **opening, openly**.

open out. If a road or passage **opens out**, it PHRASAL VB : gradually becomes larger or wider. V+ADV

open up. 1 When an opportunity **opens up** or PHRASAL VB : when a situation **opens up** an opportunity, that V-ERG+ADV

If someone is opinionated, are they open-minded?

opportunity is given to you. EG *All sorts of possibilities began to open up.* **2** If a place **opens up** or if v-ERG+ADV someone **opens** it **up**, people can then get to it or trade with it more easily. EG *Brunel opened up the West.* **3** When someone **opens up** a building or v+o+ADV **opens up**, they unlock the door and open it so that OR V+ADV people can get in.

open air. If you are in the **open air**, you are N SING: the+N outside rather than in a building. EG *Dry clothes in the open air, if possible... ...open-air swimming pools.*

open day, open days. An **open day** is a special N COUNT day when the public are allowed to visit a particular school or other institution. EG *You can meet the teacher on open days.*

open-ended. An **open-ended** discussion or activ- ADJ CLASSIF ity is started without the intention of achieving a particular decision or result.

opening /ˈəʊpᵊnɪŋ/, **openings. 1** The **opening** ADJ CLASSIF: item or part of something is the item or part that ATTRIB comes first. EG *...his opening remarks... ...the opening scene of the play.*

2 The **opening** of a book or film is the first part of N SING it. EG *The main characters are established in the opening of the book.*

3 An **opening** is a hole or empty space through N COUNT which things can pass. EG *We slid through the opening into the field.*

4 An **opening** is also **4.1** an opportunity to do N COUNT something. EG *Charlotte herself provided me with an opening.* **4.2** a job that you can apply for. EG *There were openings in the police force.*

5 See also **open.**

opening hours. The **opening hours** of a shop, N PLURAL bank, library, or pub are the times when it is open for business. EG *Banks often have very short opening hours.*

openly /ˈəʊpᵊnli¹/. If you do something **openly**, ADV you do it without trying to hide anything. EG *His mother wept openly... Margaret was openly angry at the other women.*

open-minded. Someone who is **open-minded** is ADJ QUALIT willing to listen to other people's ideas and consider them. EG *...an intelligent, open-minded man... ...an open-minded approach to new techniques.*

open-mouthed. If someone is looking **open-** ADJ CLASSIF **mouthed** at something, their mouth is open because they are very surprised. EG *She was staring open-mouthed at a picture of her father.*

open-plan. An **open-plan** building has just one ADJ CLASSIF large area on each storey, rather than several separate rooms. EG *...an open-plan office.*

opera /ˈɒpᵊrə/, **operas.** An **opera** is a musical N COUNT OR entertainment that is like a play except that most N UNCOUNT of the words are sung. EG *...choruses from Verdi's operas... ...a book on Italian opera.*

operate /ˈɒpəreɪt/, **operates, operating, operat-** ed. **1** If a business or organization **operates** in a v-ERG place, it carries out its work there. EG *...the multinational companies which operate in their country... He operates an Afghan news service here.* ◇ **operation.** EG *...our first year of operation.* ◇ N UNCOUNT

2 The way that something **operates** is the way that v it works or has an effect. EG *We discussed how language operates... ...the way calculators operated... Laws of the same kind operate in nature.*

3 When you **operate** a machine or device, you v-ERG make it work. EG *...how to operate the safety equipment.* ◇ **operation.** EG *...instructions for the* ◇ N UNCOUNT *operation of machinery.*

4 When surgeons **operate**, they cut open a pa- v tient's body in order to remove, replace, or repair a diseased or damaged part of it. EG *They operated but it was too late... His knees have been operated on three times.*

operatic /ɒpəˈrætɪk/ means relating to opera. EG ADJ CLASSIF: *...operatic roles... ...the local operatic society.* OFT ATTRIB

operating theatre, operating theatres. An **op-** N COUNT **erating theatre** is a room in a hospital where surgeons carry out operations.

operation /ɒpəˈreɪʃᵊn/, **operations. 1** An **opera-** N COUNT: **tion** is a planned activity that involves many USU+SUPP complicated actions. EG *...the biggest police operation in French history... ...military operations in Europe... ...a rescue operation.*

2 Businesses or companies are sometimes referred N COUNT: to as **operations**. EG *...Multiponics, a large-scale* USU+SUPP *farming operation.*

3 In a hospital, an **operation** is a form of treat- N COUNT ment in which a surgeon cuts open a patient's body in order to remove, replace, or repair a diseased or damaged part. EG *Her mother was about to undergo a major operation... ...heart operations.*

4 If something is **in operation**, it is working or PHRASE being used. EG *...gas drilling rigs in operation in the USA... The plans were put into operation at once.*

5 See also **operate.**

operational /ɒpəˈreɪʃᵊnəl, -ʃənᵊl/. **1** A machine ADJ CLASSIF or piece of equipment that is **operational** is working or able to be used. EG *...fifty operational warships... The system is not yet operational.*

2 Operational actions or difficulties occur while a ADJ CLASSIF: plan or system is being carried out. ATTRIB

operative /ˈɒpᵊrətɪv/, **operatives. 1** Something ADJ CLASSIF that is **operative** is working or having an effect. EG *The scheme was fully operative by 1975.*

2 An **operative** is a worker. EG *...each operative on* N COUNT *a production line.* Formal

operator /ˈɒpəreɪtə/, **operators. 1** An **operator** is N COUNT a person who works at a telephone exchange or at the switchboard of an office or hotel. EG *He dialled the operator... ...telephone operators.*

2 An **operator** is also **2.1** someone who is em- N COUNT+SUPP ployed to operate or control a machine. EG *...computer operators.* **2.2** someone who runs a business. EG *...tour operators... ...casino operators.*

operetta /ɒpəˈretə/, **operettas.** An **operetta** is a N COUNT OR type of opera which is light-hearted and often N UNCOUNT comic and has some of the words spoken rather than sung.

ophthalmic /ɒfˈθælmɪk/ means relating to or con- ADJ CLASSIF: cerned with the medical care of your eyes. EG *...an* ATTRIB *ophthalmic optician.* Formal

opinion /əˈpɪnjən/, **opinions. 1** Your **opinion** on N COUNT: something is what you think about it. EG *The* OFT+POSS *students were eager to express their opinions... Information of this nature was valuable, in his opinion... We have a high opinion of you.*

2 If someone **is of the opinion** that something is PHRASE the case, they think that it is the case. EG *He is of* Formal *the opinion that money is not important.*

3 You can refer to the beliefs or views that people N UNCOUNT have as **opinion.** EG *...changes in public opinion... Difficulties arise where there's a difference of opinion.*

opinionated /əˈpɪnjəneɪtɪ²d/. You say that some- ADJ QUALIT one is **opinionated** when they have firm opinions and refuse to accept that they may be wrong; used showing disapproval. EG *...this inexperienced but opinionated newcomer.*

opinion poll, opinion polls. An **opinion poll** N COUNT involves asking people for their opinion on a particular subject, especially one concerning politics.

opium /ˈəʊpɪəm/ is a drug made from the seeds of N UNCOUNT a type of poppy. It is used in medicines, and for pleasure. Opium is illegal in many countries.

opponent /əˈpəʊnᵊnt/, **opponents. 1** A politician's N COUNT: **opponents** are other politicians who belong to a USU+POSS different party or have different aims or policies. EG *...their political opponents.*

2 In a game, your **opponent** is the person who is N COUNT: playing against you. EG *He beat his opponent three* USU+POSS *sets to love.*

3 The **opponents** of an idea or policy do not agree N COUNT: OFT+of with it and do not want it to be carried out. EG ...a leading opponent of the budget cuts.

opportune /ɒpətjuːn/ means happening at a convenient time. EG It was most opportune that Mrs Davenport should arrive... The call came at an opportune moment.   ADJ QUALIT Formal

opportunism /ɒpətjuːnɪzəᵘm/. If you describe someone's behaviour as **opportunism**, you mean that they take advantage of any opportunity that occurs in order to gain money or power; used showing disapproval. EG ...a piece of cheap, cynical opportunism. ◊ **opportunist** /ɒpətjuːnɪst/, **opportunists.** EG ...the intrigues of a business opportunist.   N UNCOUNT Formal   ◊ N COUNT

opportunistic /ɒpətjuːnɪstɪk/. If you describe someone's behaviour as **opportunistic**, you mean that they take advantage of any opportunity that occurs in order to gain money or power; used showing disapproval. EG ...an opportunistic foreign policy.   ADJ QUALIT Formal

opportunity /ɒpətjuːnɪ¹ti¹/, **opportunities.** An **opportunity** is a situation in which it is possible for you to do something that you want to do. EG It will give you an opportunity to meet all kinds of people... They would return to power at the first opportunity... ...equality of opportunity.   N COUNT OR N UNCOUNT

oppose /əpəʊz/, **opposes, opposing, opposed.** If you **oppose** someone or **oppose** what they want to do, you disagree with what they want to do and try to prevent them from doing it. EG My father opposed my wish to become a sculptor... He opposed the founding of the Gallery.   V+O

opposed /əpəʊzd/. **1** If you are **opposed** to something, you disagree with it or disapprove of it. EG I am opposed to capital punishment... They were violently opposed to the idea.   ADJ PRED: USU+to

2 You say that two ideas or systems are **opposed** when they are opposite to each other or very different from each other. EG ...two bitterly opposed schools of socialist thought... ...a strategy which is diametrically opposed to that of the previous government.   ADJ CLASSIF: OFT+to

3 You use **as opposed to** when you want to make it clear that you are talking about a particular thing and not something else. EG There's a need for technical colleges as opposed to universities.   PREP

opposing /əpəʊzɪŋ/. **Opposing** ideas or tendencies are totally different from each other. EG We held opposing points of view... I feel there are two opposing tendencies in your work.   ADJ CLASSIF: ATTRIB

opposite /ɒpəzɪt, -sɪt/, **opposites.** **1** If one thing is **opposite** another, it is on the other side of a space from it. EG The hotel is opposite a railway station... Lynn was sitting opposite him... The man opposite lifted down her case.   PREP OR ADV

2 The **opposite** side or part of something is the side or part that is farthest away from you. EG ...on the opposite side of the street... She burst in through the opposite door.   ADJ CLASSIF: USU ATTRIB

3 **Opposite** is used to describe things of the same kind which are as different as possible in a particular way. For example, north and south are opposite directions, and winning and losing are opposite results in a game. EG I wanted to impress them but probably had the opposite effect... Paul turned and walked in the opposite direction... Holmes took the opposite point of view.   ADJ CLASSIF: ATTRIB

4 If two things of the same kind are completely different in a particular way, you can say that one is the **opposite** of the other. EG My interpretation was the absolute opposite of Olivier's... My brother is just the opposite. He loves sport.   N COUNT: USU the+N

5 The **opposite sex** refers to men if you are talking about women. It refers to women if you are talking about men. EG The teenage period is crucial in learning about the opposite sex.   PHRASE

opposite number, opposite numbers. Your **opposite number** is a person who does the same job as you, but works in a different department, firm,   N COUNT+POSS

or organization. EG My opposite numbers in industry don't have this problem.

opposition /ɒpəzɪʃəᵘn/. **1** When there is **opposition** to a plan or proposal, people disapprove of it and try to prevent it being carried out. EG It was only built after much opposition from the planners.   N UNCOUNT

2 The **opposition** refers to **2.1** the politicians or political parties that form part of a country's parliament but are not in the government. EG ...the leader of the Opposition... ...two new opposition parties. **2.2** all the people who disagree strongly with a person or an idea. EG The opposition consisted of chiefs and elders. **2.3** the person or team you are competing against in a sports event. EG One player broke through the opposition's defence.   N COLL : SING

oppress /əᵊpres/, **oppresses, oppressing, oppressed.** **1** To **oppress** someone means to treat them cruelly or unfairly. EG ...institutions that oppress women. ◊ **oppressed.** EG ...the sufferings of oppressed people everywhere. ◊ **oppressor, oppressors.** EG They didn't have the will to stand up against their foreign oppressors.   V+O   ◊ ADJ CLASSIF   ◊ N COUNT

2 If something **oppresses** you, it makes you feel depressed and uncomfortable. EG Somehow the room oppressed him.   V+O

oppression /əᵊpreʃəᵘn/. **1** **Oppression** is the cruel or unfair treatment of a group of people. EG ...the oppression of the weak and defenceless.   N UNCOUNT

2 **Oppression** is also a feeling of depression, especially one caused by a place or situation. EG Passing the place, my sense of oppression increased.   N UNCOUNT

oppressive /əᵊpresɪv/. **1** You say that the weather is **oppressive** when it is hot and humid. EG ...the oppressive heat of the plains. ◊ **oppressively.** EG The room was oppressively hot.   ADJ QUALIT   ◊ SUBMOD

2 An **oppressive** situation makes you feel depressed or uncomfortable. EG The silence became oppressive.   ADJ QUALIT

3 Laws, societies, and customs that are **oppressive** treat people cruelly and unfairly. EG ...an oppressive bureaucracy... ...the present oppressive system.   ADJ QUALIT

opt /ɒpt/, **opts, opting, opted.** If you **opt** for something, you choose it. If you **opt** to do something, you choose to do it. EG My father left the choice of career to me, and I opted for law... ...those who opt to cooperate with the regime.   V+for OR to-INF

opt out. If you **opt out** of something, you choose to be no longer involved in it. EG He tried to opt out of political decision-making.   PHRASAL VB : V+ADV, OFT+of

optical /ɒptɪkəᵊl/. **1** **Optical** instruments, devices, or processes involve or relate to vision or light. EG ...an optical microscope.   ADJ CLASSIF: ATTRIB

2 **Optical** means relating to the way that things appear to people. EG ...an optical illusion.   ADJ CLASSIF: ATTRIB

optician /ɒptɪʃəᵊn/, **opticians.** An **optician** is someone whose job involves testing people's eyesight or providing glasses and contact lenses.   N COUNT

optimism /ɒptɪmɪzəᵘm/ is the feeling of being hopeful about the future. EG I felt cheerful and full of optimism... There was a definite air of optimism at the headquarters. ◊ **optimist**, /ɒptɪmɪst/ **optimists.** EG I'm an optimist by nature.   N UNCOUNT   ◊ N COUNT

optimistic /ɒptɪmɪstɪk/. Someone who is **optimistic** is hopeful about the future. EG ...an optimistic estimate. ◊ **optimistically.** EG It might work, she thought optimistically.   ADJ QUALIT   ◊ ADV

optimum /ɒptɪməm/ means the best that is possible. EG The optimum feeding time is around dawn... ...in optimum conditions.   ADJ CLASSIF: ATTRIB Formal

option /ɒpʃəᵊn/, **options. 1** An **option** is something that you can choose to do in preference to one or more alternatives. EG He had, I would say, two options... ...the option of another referendum.   N COUNT

2 If you have the **option** to do something, you can   N SING

If you have the option to do something, do you do it?

choose whether to do it or not. EG *He was given the option: give them up or lose your job... ...mothers who have no option but to work.*

optional /ɒpʃəⁿnəl, -ʃənəⁿl/. If something is option- ADJ CLASSIF
al, you can choose whether or not you do it or have
it. EG *Games are optional at this school.*

opulent /ɒpjəⁿlənt/. 1 Someone who is opulent is ADJ QUALIT
very wealthy. EG *...all the advantages of an opulent* Formal
society. ◇ **opulence** /ɒpjəⁿlɒns/. EG *His eyes had* ◇ N UNCOUNT
never beheld such opulence.

2 If you describe an object as **opulent**, you mean ADJ QUALIT
that it looks grand and expensive. EG *...the magnifi-* Formal
cently opulent marble altar.

or /ɔː, ə/. 1 You use **or** 1.1 to link a number of CONJ
alternatives. EG *Do you want your drink up there or
do you want to come down for it?... Have you any
brothers or sisters?* **1.2** to give another alternative,
when the first alternative is introduced by 'either'
or 'whether'. EG *Most aircraft accidents occur at
either take-off or landing... He didn't know whether
to laugh or cry... We'd better wait and see whether
or not the operation was successful.* **1.3** between
two numbers to indicate that you are giving an
approximate amount. EG *You are supposed to polish your car three or four times a year.*

2 You also use **or** to introduce a comment which CONJ
corrects or modifies what you have just said. EG
*The company is paying the rent or at least contrib-
uting to it... ...Margaret. Or Molly as she was called.*

3 If you say that someone should do something **or** CONJ
something unpleasant will happen, you are warning them that if they do not do it, the unpleasant
thing will happen. EG *Don't put anything plastic in
the oven or it will probably start melting.*

4 You can also use **or** to introduce something CONJ
which is an explanation or justification for a statement you have just made. EG *He can't be that bad,
can he, or they wouldn't have allowed him home.*

5 or else: see **else. • or other:** see **other. • or so:**
see **so. • or something:** see **something.**

-or, -ors. -or is added to some verbs to form nouns. SUFFIX
These nouns refer to people who do a particular
kind of work or take a particular kind of action.
For example, a supervisor is someone whose job is
to supervise people, and a demonstrator is someone who takes part in a demonstration. Nouns like
these are sometimes not defined in this dictionary,
but are treated with the related verbs. EG *He
worked as a translator... ...the instigator of the
plot... ...the conquerors of Peru.*

oral /ɔːrəl/, **orals. 1 Oral** is used to describe things ADJ CLASSIF :
that involve speaking rather than writing. EG *...an* ATTRIB
oral test in German... ...oral reports. ◇ **orally.** EG ◇ ADV
The candidate will be examined orally.

2 An **oral** is an oral test or examination. EG *In some* N COUNT
examinations the oral follows a written paper.

3 Oral medicines are ones that you swallow. EG ADJ CLASSIF
...an oral vaccine. ◇ **orally.** EG *...a pill taken orally.* ◇ ADV

orange /ɒrɪndʒ/, **oranges. 1** Something that is EG ADJ COLOUR
orange is of a colour between red and yellow. EG
...an orange silk scarf.

2 An **orange** is a round fruit that is juicy and N COUNT OR
sweet. It has a thick orange skin and is divided into N UNCOUNT
sections inside.

3 Orange is a drink made from oranges or tasting N UNCOUNT
of oranges. EG *...gin and orange.*

oration /ɔːreɪʃən/, **orations.** An **oration** is a for- N COUNT
mal public speech. EG *...a funeral oration.* Formal

orator /ɒrətə/, **orators.** An **orator** is someone N COUNT
who is skilled at making speeches. EG *He is a
marvellous orator.*

oratory /ɒrətəⁿriⁱ/ is the art of making formal N UNCOUNT
speeches. EG *He roused the troops with his oratory.* Formal

orbit /ɔːbɪt/, **orbits, orbiting, orbited. 1** An **orbit** N COUNT OR
is the curved path in space that is followed by an N UNCOUNT
object that is going round a planet, a moon, or the
sun. EG *...the orbit of Mercury... How much does it
cost to put a satellite into orbit?*

2 If something such as a satellite **orbits** a planet, a V+O OR V
moon, or the sun, it goes round and round it.

orbital /ɔːbɪtəⁿl/. An **orbital** road goes all the way ADJ CLASSIF :
round a large city. ATTRIB

orchard /ɔːtʃəd/, **orchards.** An **orchard** is an N COUNT
area of land on which fruit trees are grown. EG *...an
apple orchard.*

orchestra /ɔːkɪⁿstrə/, **orchestras.** An **orchestra** N COUNT
is a large group of musicians who play a variety of
different instruments together. An orchestra usually plays classical music. EG *The orchestra played
the Russian national anthem.*

orchestral /ɔːkɛstrəⁿl/ means consisting of or ADJ CLASSIF :
relating to the music played by an orchestra. EG ATTRIB
...Mozart's orchestral pieces.

orchestrate /ɔːkɪⁿstreɪt/, **orchestrates, orches-
trating, orchestrated. 1** If you **orchestrate** V+O
something, you organize it very carefully in order
to produce a particular result or situation. EG *He
personally orchestrated that entire evening.*
◇ **orchestrated.** EG *...a brilliantly orchestrated* ◇ ADJ QUALIT
campaign of persuasion and protest.* ATTRIB

2 If you **orchestrate** a piece of music, you rewrite V+O
it so that it can be played by an orchestra.

orchid /ɔːkɪd/, **orchids.** An **orchid** is a plant with N COUNT
beautiful and unusual flowers.

ordain /ɔːdeɪn/, **ordains, ordaining, ordained. 1** V+O : USU PASS
When someone **is ordained**, they are made a
member of the clergy in a religious ceremony. EG
*When I was first ordained, I served as a hospital
chaplain.*

2 If someone in authority **ordains** something, they V+O OR
order that it shall happen. EG *Lady Sackville or-* V+REPORT :
dained complete discretion... The law ordained that ONLY that
she should be executed. Formal

ordeal /ɔːdiːl/, **ordeals.** An **ordeal** is a difficult N COUNT
and extremely unpleasant experience. EG *He de-
scribed the rest of his terrible ordeal.*

order /ɔːdə/, **orders, ordering, ordered. 1** If you CONJ
do something **in order** to achieve a particular
thing, you do it because you want to achieve that
thing. EG *He had to hurry in order to reach the next
place on his schedule... Rose trod with care, in
order not to spread the dirt... They are learning
English in order that they can study engineering.*

2 If someone in authority gives you an **order**, they N COUNT
tell you to do something. EG *George went away to
carry out this order... An official inquiry was set up
on the orders of the Minister of Health.* • If you are • PHRASE
under orders to do something, you have been told
to do it by someone in authority.

3 If someone in authority **orders** people to do V+O :
something or **orders** something to be done, they OFT+ *to*-INF
tell people to do it. EG *He ordered me to fetch the* OR A; ALSO
books... The Captain ordered the ship's masts to be V+QUOTE OR
cut down... Sherman ordered an investigation into REPORT :
her husband's death... He ordered me out of the ONLY *that*
*building... 'Sit down!' he ordered... The prime minis-
ter ordered that they be taken to women's prisons.*

4 When you **order** something that you are going to V+O OR V
pay for, you ask for it to be brought to you or sent
to you. EG *Davis had ordered a second whisky... I'll
order now... She ordered an extra delivery of coal.*

5 Something that is **on order** at a shop has been PHRASE
asked for but has not yet been supplied.

6 An **order** is something that you ask to be brought N COUNT
to you or sent to you, and that you are going to pay
for. EG *A waiter came to take their order... We will
continue to deal with overseas orders.*

7 If a set of things are arranged or done in a N UNCOUNT
particular **order**, one thing is put first or done first,
another thing second, another thing third, and so
on. EG *The names are not in alphabetical order.* • If • PHRASE
a set of things are done, arranged, or dealt with **in
order**, they are done, arranged, or dealt with
according to the correct sequence.

8 Order is **8.1** the situation that exists when N UNCOUNT
everything is in the correct place or is done at the
correct time. EG *I felt it would create some order in*

our lives... Gretchen combed her hair into some sort of order. **8.2** the situation that exists when people live together peacefully rather than fighting or causing trouble. EG *...the task of restoring order.*
● If you **keep order** or **keep** people **in order**, you ● PHRASE prevent people from behaving in an excited or violent way.

9 A machine or device that is **in working order** is PHRASE functioning properly and is not broken. EG *He was always finding cars in good working order.*

10 A machine or device that is **out of order** is PHRASE broken and does not work.

11 At a meeting, if you describe someone or their PHRASE behaviour as being **out of order**, you mean that Formal they are doing something incorrect according to the rules of the meeting. EG *The resolution was ruled out of order.*

12 When people talk about a particular **order**, they N SING+SUPP mean the way society is organized at a particular time. EG *They don't accept the existing order.*

13 An **order** is also a group of monks or nuns who N COUNT live according to rules laid down by the person who started the group.

14 If you refer to something of a particular **order**, N SING+SUPP you mean something of a particular quality, Formal amount, or degree. EG *...a thinker of the highest order.* ● You use **in the order of** or **of the order** ● PREP **of** when giving an approximate figure. EG *Britain's contribution is something in the order of 5 per cent.*

15 a tall order: see **tall.** ● See also **law and order, mail order, postal order, standing order.**

order about or **order around.** If you **order** PHRASAL VB : someone **about** or **order** them **around**, you al- V+O+ADV ways tell them what to do, in an unsympathetic way.

ordered /ɔːdəd/. An **ordered** society or system is ADJ QUALIT well organized or arranged. EG *In Mrs Kaul's house everything was well ordered.*

orderly /ɔːdəliˈ/, **orderlies.** **1** Something that is ADJ QUALIT **orderly** is well organized or arranged. EG *...a system of orderly government.* ◊ **orderliness.** EG ◊ N UNCOUNT *We pride ourselves on the orderliness of our way of life.*

2 An **orderly** is an untrained male hospital attend- N COUNT ant. EG *I sat at the end of the ward with the orderly.*

ORDINAL stands for **ordinal number**

Numbers such as 'first', 'third', 'fifth', and 'tenth' are called ordinal numbers. They usually come after a determiner such as 'the' and 'my' and before a noun, as in *...the fifth house on the right* and *...my second child.*
Ordinals can also behave like pronouns, and so can be used without a following noun, especially when it is obvious what you are talking about. For example, Beethoven's Ninth Symphony is often referred to simply as *Beethoven's Ninth.*
See the entry headed NUMBER for more information.

---

ordinarily /ɔːdɪˈnerɪliˈ/. If something **ordinarily** ADV OR happens or is **ordinarily** the case, it usually hap- ADV SEN pens or is usually the case. EG *This room was ordinarily used by the doctor... Ordinarily, of course, we would use the telephone.*

ordinary /ɔːdɪˈnriˈ/. **1** Something that is **ordinary** ADJ QUALIT is not special or different in any way. EG *...ordinary everyday objects... What do ordinary people really think about universities?... She is likeable enough, but very ordinary.*

2 Something that is **out of the ordinary** is unusual PHRASE or different. EG *I'd like to bring her something a little out of the ordinary.*

3 An **ordinary** degree is an undergraduate degree ADJ CLASSIF : that is lower than an honours degree. ATTRIB

ordination /ɔːdɪneɪʃəˈn/, **ordinations.** When N COUNT OR someone's **ordination** takes place, they are made N UNCOUNT a member of the Christian clergy in a special ceremony. EG *...the ordination of women.*

ore /ɔː/, **ores. Ore** is rock or earth from which N MASS metal can be obtained. EG *...iron ore.*

organ /ɔːgən/, **organs.** **1** An **organ** is a part of N COUNT your body that has a particular purpose or func- tion, for example your heart or your lungs. EG *Children's bones and organs are very sensitive to radiation.*

2 An **organ** is also a large musical instrument with N COUNT pipes of different lengths through which air is forced. You play the organ rather like a piano, using keys and pedals.

3 You refer to a newspaper as an **organ** of a N COUNT : particular organization when the organization uses USU+SUPP it as a means of giving information or influencing people. EG *They decided to close the newspaper and launch it again as a government organ.*

organic /ɔːgænɪk/. **1** Something that is **organic** is ADJ CLASSIF produced by or found in plants or animals. EG *The rocks were carefully searched for organic remains.*

2 Organic gardening or farming uses only natural ADJ CLASSIF : animal and plant products and does not use fertiliz- ATTRIB ers or pesticides containing artificial chemicals.
◊ **organically.** EG *Buy organically grown vegeta-* ◊ ADV *bles if possible.*

3 Change or development that is **organic** happens ADJ CLASSIF gradually and naturally rather than suddenly. EG Formal *Instead of organic growth, there have been abrupt changes.*

4 If you describe a structure or society as **organic**, ADJ CLASSIF you mean that it consists of many parts which all Formal contribute to the way the whole structure or soci- ety works.

organisation /ɔːgənaɪzeɪʃəˈn/. See **organization.**

organisational /ɔːgənaɪzeɪʃəˈnəl, -ʃənəˈl/. See **or- ganizational.**

organise /ɔːgənaɪz/. See **organize.**

organism /ɔːgənɪzəˈm/, **organisms.** An **organ-** N COUNT **ism** is an animal or plant, especially one that is so small that you cannot see it without a microscope. EG *These creatures are descended from simpler organisms like corals.*

organist /ɔːgənɪst/, **organists.** An **organist** is N COUNT someone who plays the organ.

organization /ɔːgənaɪzeɪʃəˈn/, **organizations;** also spelled **organisation.** **1** An **organization** is a N COUNT group of people who do something together regu- larly in an organized way. Businesses and clubs are organizations. EG *...student organizations... ...the World Health Organisation.*

2 The **organization** of a system is the way in N UNCOUNT : which its different parts are related and how they USU+SUPP work together. EG *There has been a total change in the organization of society.*

3 The **organization** of an activity or public event N UNCOUNT involves making all the arrangements for it. EG *I* USU+SUPP *don't want to get involved in the actual organisa- tion of things.*

organizational /ɔːgənaɪzeɪʃəˈnəl, -ʃənəˈl/; also ADJ CLASSIF spelled **organisational. Organizational** means **1** ATTRIB relating to the way that things are planned and arranged. EG *...an organizational genius named Alfred P. Sloan.* **2** relating to organizations. EG *The group has no political or organisational links with the terrorists.*

organize /ɔːgənaɪz/, **organizes, organizing, or-** **ganized;** also spelled **organise. 1** If you **organize** V+O an activity or public event, you make all the arrangements for it. EG *We organized a concert in the village hall... I thought that meeting was badly*

What is the difference between 'ornamental' and 'ornate'?

organized. ◊ **organizer, organizers.** EG *...the* N COUNT
organizers of the conference.

2 If you **organize** things, you arrange them so that V+O
they are in a sensible order or in sensible places. EG
He's better able now to organise his thoughts.

3 When workers or employees **organize**, they V
form themselves into a group such as a trade union
in order to have more power to get things they
want. EG *Their poverty prevents them from organizing effectively to improve their wages.*

organized /ɔːgənaɪzd/; also spelled **organised. 1** ADJ CLASSIF :
Organized activities are planned and controlled. ATTRIB
EG *...an organized holiday... ...organized crime...*
...organized games.

2 You say that people or things are **organized** ADJ QUALIT
when you admire them because they work in an
efficient and effective way. EG *How organised you
are!*

orgasm /ɔːgæzəm/, **orgasms.** An **orgasm** is the N COUNT
moment of greatest pleasure and excitement during sexual activity.

orgy /ɔːdʒiː/, **orgies. 1** An **orgy** is a party in which N COUNT
people behave in a very uncontrolled way. EG
...sexual orgies... ...a drunken orgy.

2 You can refer to a period of intense and extreme N COUNT+SUPP
activity as an **orgy** of that activity. EG *...an orgy of
destruction.*

orient /ɔːrɪənt/, **orients, orienting, oriented.** If V-REFL
you **orient** yourself to a new situation, you learn Formal
about it and prepare to deal with it. EG *The raw
newcomer has to orient himself.* ● See also **oriented.**

oriental /ɔːrɪentəl/. Something that is **oriental** ADJ CLASSIF
comes from or is associated with eastern and
south-eastern Asia, especially China and Japan. EG
...Oriental philosophy... ...her oriental features.

orientate /ɔːrɪenteɪt/, **orientates, orientating,** V-REFL
orientated. When you **orientate** yourself, you
discover where you are by looking at a map, or by
searching for familiar places or objects.

orientated /ɔːrɪenteɪtɪd/ means the same as ori- ADJ CLASSIF :
ented. EG *...a commercially orientated theory...* OFT+*towards/*
...career-orientated women... ...an industry orien- *to*
tated towards quick, easy profits.

orientation /ɔːrɪenteɪʃən/. The **orientation** of N UNCOUNT
an organization or system is the activities that it is +SUPP
concerned with and the aims that it has. EG *...the
party's revolutionary orientation.*

oriented /ɔːrɪentɪd/. You use **oriented** to indi- ADJ CLASSIF :
cate what someone or something is interested in or OFT+*towards/*
concerned with. For example, if someone is politi- *to*
cally **oriented**, they are interested in politics. EG
*...export-oriented industries... ...a society oriented
towards information.*

origin /ɒrɪdʒɪn/, **origins. 1** You can refer to the N COUNT OR
beginning or cause of something as its **origin** or its N UNCOUNT :
origins. EG *The unrest has its origins in economic* USU+POSS
*problems... ...the origin of the universe... ...a word
of recent origin.*

2 When you talk about a person's **origin** or ori- N COUNT OR
gins, you are referring to the country, race, or N UNCOUNT :
social class of their parents or ancestors. EG *...a* USU+SUPP
*woman of Pakistani origin... ...your working-class
origins... His origins were humble.*

original /ɒrɪdʒɪnəl/, **originals. 1** You use **origi-** ADJ CLASSIF :
nal to describe the form or use that something had ATTRIB
when it first existed, or something that existed at
the beginning of a process. EG *They will restore the
house to its original state... The original idea came
from Dr Ball.* ◊ **originally.** EG *It was originally a* ◊ ADV
toy factory.

2 You refer to a work of art or a document as an N COUNT
original when it is genuine and not a copy. EG *The
original is in the British Museum.* ▶ used as an ▶ ADJ CLASSIF
adjective. EG *...working on original documents.*

3 An **original** piece of writing or music was ADJ CLASSIF
written recently and has not been published or
performed before. EG *...her first collection of short
stories, some original, some reprinted.*

4 If you describe someone, their ideas, or their ADJ QUALIT
work as **original**, you mean that they are very
imaginative and clever. EG *...a daring and original
idea.* ◊ **originality** /ɒrɪdʒɪˈnælɪtiː/. EG *...a sculptor* ◊ N UNCOUNT
of genius and great originality.

originate /ɒrɪdʒɪneɪt/, **originates, originating,** V : USU+A
originated. If something **originated** at a particular time or in a particular place, it began to happen
or exist at that time or in that place. EG *These
beliefs originated in the 19th century.*

originator /ɒrɪdʒɪneɪtə/, **originators.** The origi- N COUNT
nator of something such as an idea or scheme is
the person who first thought of it or began it. EG
The originator of the idea was a young professor.

ornament /ɔːnəmənt/, **ornaments. 1** An **orna-** N COUNT
ment is **1.1** a small object that you display in your
home because it is attractive. EG *...painted china
ornaments.* **1.2** an object such as a piece of jewellery that someone wears in order to look attractive.

2 Ornament refers to decorations and designs on N UNCOUNT
a building or piece of furniture which make it more
elaborate. EG *...different styles of ornament.*

ornamental /ɔːnəmentəl/. Something that is or- ADJ CLASSIF
namental is intended to be attractive rather than
useful. EG *...an ornamental pond.*

ornamented /ɔːnəmentɪd/. If something is orna- ADJ CLASSIF :
mented with attractive objects or patterns, it is USU+*with*
decorated with them. EG *The sand was ornamented
with shells and seaweed.*

ornate /ɔːneɪt/. Something that is **ornate** has a lot ADJ QUALIT
of decoration on it. EG *...ornate necklaces.*

ornithology /ɔːnɪθɒlədʒiː/ is the study of birds. EG N UNCOUNT
I've taken up ornithology. Formal

orphan /ɔːfən/, **orphans, orphaned. 1** An **orphan** N COUNT
is a child whose parents are dead. EG *She became
an orphan at twelve.*

2 If a child **is orphaned.** its parents die. EG *We* V-PASS
adopted the twins when they were orphaned.

orphanage /ɔːfənɪdʒ/, **orphanages.** An **orphan-** N COUNT
age is a place where orphans are looked after.

orthodox /ɔːθədɒks/. **1 Orthodox** beliefs, meth- ADJ QUALIT :
ods, or systems are the ones that most people have ATTRIB
or use. EG *...orthodox medicine.*

2 People who are **orthodox** believe in the older ADJ QUALIT
and more traditional ideas of their religion or
political party. EG *...Orthodox Jews... ...a fairly
orthodox socialist.*

orthodoxy /ɔːθədɒksiː/, **orthodoxies. 1** An **ortho-** N COUNT
doxy is an accepted view about something. EG *...the
prevailing orthodoxy on this problem.*

2 Orthodoxy is **2.1** traditional and accepted be- N UNCOUNT
liefs. EG *...Islamic orthodoxy... ...Marxist orthodoxy.* +SUPP
2.2 the degree to which a person believes in and N UNCOUNT :
supports the ideas of their religion or political USU+POSS
party. EG *...the rigid orthodoxy of Mr Mzali.*

oscillate /ɒsɪleɪt/, **oscillates, oscillating, oscil-**
lated. 1 If something **oscillates**, it moves repeat- V : USU+A
edly from one position to another and back again. Formal
EG *Its wings oscillate up and down.*

2 If you **oscillate** between two moods, attitudes, or V+*between*
types of behaviour, you keep changing from one to Formal
the other and back again. EG *His mood oscillated
between co-operation and aggression.*

ostensible /ɒstensɪbəl/. If you refer to the **osten-** ADJ CLASSIF :
sible purpose, cause, or nature of something, you ATTRIB
are referring to the one that it seems or is said to Formal
have, which you think may not be the real one. EG
...the ostensible purpose of his excursion.
◊ **ostensibly.** EG *Rose left the room, ostensibly to* ◊ ADV OR
explain about dinner to the cook. ADV SEN

ostentation /ɒstenteɪʃən/. You say that some- N UNCOUNT
one's behaviour is **ostentation** when they do Formal
things in order to impress other people with their
wealth or importance. EG *More than two telephones
is pure ostentation.*

ostentatious /ɒstenteɪʃəs/. **1** You say that some- ADJ QUALIT
thing is **ostentatious** when it costs a lot of money Formal

and is intended to impress people. EG ...*a magnificent and ostentatious palace.*

2 People who are **ostentatious** try to impress other people with their wealth or importance. ADJ QUALIT: Formal ◊ **ostentatiously.** EG *They were never ostentatiously dressed.*

3 You can describe an action as **ostentatious** when it is done in an exaggerated way in order to attract people's attention. EG ...*an ostentatious gesture.* ◊ **ostentatiously.** EG *I started ostentatiously clearing the table.* ADJ QUALIT: Formal ◊ ADV

ostracize /ɒstrəsaɪz/, **ostracizes, ostracizing, ostracized;** also spelled **ostracise.** If you **are ostracized,** people deliberately behave in an unfriendly way towards you and do not allow you to take part in their social activities. EG *Their children were ostracized by teachers and pupils alike.* V+O : USU PASS Formal

ostrich /ɒstrɪtʃ/, **ostriches.** An **ostrich** is a large African bird that cannot fly. N COUNT

other /ʌðə/, **others. Other** cannot be used after the determiner 'an'. See **another.**

1 Other people or other things are not the people or things that you have just mentioned or have just been talking about. EG *There were some other people in the compartment... There was no other way to do it... ...toys, paints, books and other equipment... Results in other countries are impressive... Some projects are shorter than others.* ADJ CLASSIF : ATTRIB, OR PRON : HAS PLURAL

2 When you have mentioned the first of two things, you refer to the second one as the **other** one. EG *He had his papers in one hand, his hat in the other... They have two daughters, one a baby, the other a girl of twelve.* ADJ CLASSIF : ATTRIB, OR PRON : HAS PLURAL

3 The **other** people or things in a group are the rest of them. EG ...*the other members of the class... I shall wait until the others come back.* ADJ CLASSIF : ATTRIB OR N PLURAL

4 You refer to **other** people or **others** when you are talking about people in general, as opposed to yourself. EG *One ought not to inflict one's problems on other people... Working for others can be most fulfilling.* ADJ CLASSIF : ATTRIB OR N PLURAL

5 If you say that you did something the **other** day or the **other** week, you mean that you did it recently. EG *I saw Davis the other day.* ADJ CLASSIF : ATTRIB

6 Nothing **other than** a particular thing means only that thing. No one **other than** a particular person means only that person. EG *She never discussed it with anyone other than Derek... I don't have a thing with me other than this coat... There's no choice other than to reopen his case.* PHRASE : WITH BROAD NEG

7 You say **none other than** a particular person when you want to emphasize how surprising it is that this person is present or involved. EG *It was none other than the famous Mr Victor Hazel.* PHRASE

8 You use **every other** when talking about the intervals at which something occurs. For example, if something happens **every other** day, it could happen on the 1st, 3rd, 5th, etc of a particular month. EG *Their local committees are usually held every other month.* PHRASE

9 Other is also used in these phrases. **9.1** You use **one after the other** to emphasize that actions or events happen with very little time between them. EG *Stone, Prattley and Unwin came forward one after the other... We saw the three plays one after the other.* **9.2** You say **or other** after words such as 'some', 'something', or 'somehow' to emphasize that you cannot or do not want to be more precise about the information that you are giving. EG *For some reason or other your name was omitted... Somehow or other, he reached the Alps.* **9.3** You use **one or other** to refer to one or more things or people in a group, when it does not matter which one is thought of or chosen. EG *One or other current must be altered.* **9.4 each other:** see **each.** ● **in other words:** see **word.** PHRASES

otherwise /ʌðəwaɪz/. **1** You use **otherwise** after stating a situation or fact, in order to say what the result or consequence would be if this situation or ADV SEN

fact was not the case. EG *It's perfectly harmless, Mabel, otherwise I wouldn't have done it... Wash five times a day. You're not properly clean otherwise.*

2 You use **otherwise** when stating the general condition or quality of something after you have mentioned an exception to this general condition or quality. EG *The cement is slightly cracked but otherwise in good condition... That was a sudden outbreak in an otherwise blameless career.* ADV SEN OR SUBMOD

3 Otherwise also means in a different way. EG *Stiff and formal, the man was incapable of acting otherwise.* ADV Formal

4 You use **or otherwise** as a way of referring to things of a different sort in addition to the sort you have just mentioned. EG *It had no effect on its users, beneficial or otherwise... Both sides understand, consciously or otherwise, the limitations of the treaty.* PHRASE

otter /ɒtə/, **otters.** An **otter** is a small animal with a long tail. Otters swim well and catch and eat fish. N COUNT

ouch /aʊtʃ/. People say **'Ouch!'** when they suddenly feel pain. EXCLAM

ought /ɔːt/. **1** If you say that someone **ought** to do something, you mean that it would be a good idea or the right thing to do. EG *She ought to see the doctor... Oughtn't we to phone for the police?... 'I don't care,' he said. 'Well, you ought to,' she said... It's getting late; I think I ought to go.* MODAL

2 If you say that someone **ought** to have done something, you mean that it would have been a good idea or the right thing to do. EG *I ought to have said yes... I ought not to have come here.* MODAL

3 If you say that something **ought** to be true, you mean that you expect it to be true. EG *It ought to be quite easy... He ought to be out of jail by now.* MODAL

oughtn't /ɔːtəˀnt/ is a spoken form of 'ought not'.

ounce /aʊns/, **ounces. 1** An **ounce** is a unit of weight used in Britain and the USA. There are sixteen ounces in a pound, and one ounce is equal to 28.35 grams. See the entry headed MEASUREMENT. EG ...*an ounce of tobacco... The baby gains 6 to 8 ounces a week.* ● See also **fluid ounce.** N COUNT OR N PART

2 You can also refer to a very small amount of something as an **ounce.** EG ...*using every ounce of strength he possessed... ...anyone with an ounce of intelligence.* N PART : USU SING Informal

our /aʊə/. A speaker or writer uses **our** to describe something that belongs or relates both to himself or herself and to one or more other people. EG ...*our children... This could change our lives.* DET POSS

ours /aʊəz/. A speaker or writer uses **ours** to refer to something that belongs or relates both to himself or herself and to one or more other people. EG *It is a very different country from ours.* PRON POSS

ourselves /aʊəsɛlvz/. **1** A speaker or writer uses **ourselves** as the object of a verb or preposition in a clause where 'we' is the subject or 'us' is a previous object. See **we.** EG *We almost made ourselves ill... In 1968 we built ourselves a new surgery.* PRON REFL : PLURAL

2 Ourselves is also used to emphasize the subject or object of a clause. EG *In teaching, we ourselves have to do a lot of learning.* PRON REFL : PLURAL

3 A speaker or writer also uses **ourselves** in expressions such as 'we did it ourselves' in order to say that he or she, together with one or more other people, did something without any help or interference from anyone else. PRON REFL : PLURAL

-ous is added to some nouns to form adjectives that describe qualities. For example, someone who is courageous shows courage and someone who is envious feels envy. EG ...*scandalous stories... ...a mountainous region... ...a hazardous journey.* SUFFIX

In what country do you find the outback?

oust /aʊst/, **ousts, ousting, ousted.** If you **oust** v+o
someone from a job or a place, you force them to Formal
leave it. EG ...the coup which ousted the President...
...ousting peasants from their lands.

out /aʊt/. **1** When you go **out** of a place or get **out** ADV : OFT+of
of something such as a vehicle, you leave it, so that
you are no longer inside it. EG She rushed out of the
house... The lift doors opened and they stepped out
into the foyer... She's just got out of bed.
2 If you are **out**, you are not at home or not at your ADV AFTER VB
usual place of work. EG He came when I was out...
Joe is out looking for her.
3 If you are in a building and you look **out** of the ADV AFTER VB :
window, you look through the window at things OFT+PREP
that are outside the building. EG She stared out at
the rain... I was standing looking out over the view.
4 You can use **out** to indicate that something is ADV AFTER VB
happening outside a building rather than inside it.
EG Many people were sleeping out... It's hot out.
5 If you take something **out** of a container or place, ADV AFTER VB :
you remove it from the container or place. EG She OFT+of
opened a box and took out a cigarette... He got out
a book and read.
6 If someone or something is kept **out** of a place, ADV AFTER VB :
they are prevented from going into it. EG It's OFT+of
designed to keep out intruders.
7 If a light is **out**, it is no longer shining. EG The ADV AFTER VB
lights went out.
8 If a fire or cigarette is **out**, it is no longer ADV AFTER VB
burning. EG He helped to put the fire out.
9 If flowers are **out**, their petals have opened. EG ADJ PRED
The daffodils were out.
10 If workers are **out**, they are on strike. EG The ADJ PRED
men stayed out for nearly a month. Informal
11 If you say that a proposal or suggestion is **out**, ADJ PRED
you mean that it is unacceptable. EG That's right
out, I'm afraid.
12 If you say that something such as a type of ADJ PRED
clothing is **out**, you mean that it is unfashionable.
EG Romance is making a comeback. Reality is out.
13 When the sea or tide goes **out**, the sea moves ADV AFTER VB
away from the shore rather than towards it.
14 If you say that a calculation or measurement is ADJ PRED
out, you mean that it is incorrect. EG It's only a
couple of degrees out.
15 If someone is **out** to do something, they intend ADJ PRED+for
to do it. EG They're out to use your house as a free OR TO-INF
hotel. Informal
16 Out of is used in these ways. **16.1** You use **out** PREP
of to say what emotion or motive causes someone
to do something. For example, if you do something
out of pity, you do it because you pity someone. EG
He wrote that review out of pure spite. **16.2** If you
get something such as pleasure or an advantage
out of something, you get it as a result of being
involved in that thing. **16.3** If you are **out of**
something, you no longer have any of it. EG We're
out of paper. **16.4** If something is made **out of** a
particular material, it is made from it. EG You can
make petroleum out of coal. **16.5** If you pay for
something **out of** a particular sum of money, you
pay for it using some of that money. EG Is he paying
for your trip out of parish funds? **16.6** If you get
some information **out of** someone, you persuade or
force them to tell it to you. EG You're not going to
get anything out of her. **16.7** If you are **out of** the
rain, the sun, or the wind, you are sheltered from it.
16.8 You use **out of** to indicate what proportion of
a group of things something is true of. For example, if something is true of one **out of** five things, it
is true of one fifth of all things of that kind.

out-. You can use **out-** to form verbs that describe PREFIX
an action as being done better by one person than
by another. For example, if you can outswim
someone, you can swim further or faster than they
can. EG Surely you can outfight him... She managed
to outrun them.

out-and-out. You use **out-and-out** to emphasize ADJ CLASSIF :
that someone or something has all the characteris- ATTRIB
tics of a particular type of person or thing. EG He's
an out-and-out villain... ...an out-and-out triumph.

outback /aʊtbæk/. The parts of Australia where N SING : the+N
very few people live are referred to as the **out-**
back.

outboard motor, outboard motors. An out- N COUNT
board motor is a motor with a propeller that you
can fix to the back of a small boat.

outbreak /aʊtbreɪk/, **outbreaks.** An **outbreak** of N COUNT+SUPP
something unpleasant is a sudden occurrence of it.
EG ...the outbreak of war... ...outbreaks of disease.

outbuilding /aʊtbɪldɪŋ/, **outbuildings. Out-** N COUNT :
buildings are small buildings such as barns or USU PLURAL
stables that are part of a larger property.

outburst /aʊtbɜːst/, **outbursts. 1** An **outburst** is N COUNT
a sudden and strong expression of emotion, espe-
cially anger. EG I apologize for my outburst just
now.
2 An **outburst** of violent activity is a sudden period N COUNT+SUPP
of this activity. EG There followed an outburst of
shooting.

outcast /aʊtkɑːst/, **outcasts.** An **outcast** is some- N COUNT
one who is rejected by a group of people. EG They
are treated as outcasts.

outcome /aʊtkʌm/, **outcomes.** The **outcome** of N COUNT :
an action or process is the result of it. EG Nobody USU SING+of
dared predict the outcome of the election.

outcrop /aʊtkrɒp/, **outcrops.** An **outcrop** is a N COUNT :
large area of rock that sticks out of the ground. EG USU+SUPP
...a massive outcrop of granite.

outcry /aʊtkraɪ/, **outcries.** An **outcry** is a strong N COUNT
reaction of disapproval or anger by many people.
EG The experiments continued, despite the public
outcry against them.

outdated /aʊtdeɪtɪ²d/. If you say that a word, idea, ADJ QUALIT
or way of behaving is **outdated**, you mean that it is
old-fashioned and no longer useful. In this dictionary, language of this kind is indicated by the use of
the word 'Outdated' in the Extra Column. EG ...out-
dated methods of management.

outdo /aʊtduː/, **outdoes, outdoing, outdid, out-** v+o
done. If you **outdo** someone, you are more successful than they are at a particular activity. EG A
heavy person can outdo a lighter one in such jobs.

outdoor /aʊtdɔː/. **Outdoor** activities or clothes ADJ CLASSIF :
take place or are used in the open air, rather than ATTRIB
in a building. EG ...outdoor work... He was fully
dressed in his outdoor clothes.

outdoors /aʊtdɔːz/. If something exists or happens ADV AFTER VB
outdoors, it exists or happens in the open air,
rather than in a building. EG School classes were
held outdoors... Let them go outdoors and play.

outer /aʊtə/. The **outer** parts of something are the ADJ CLASSIF :
parts which contain or enclose the other parts, and ATTRIB
which are furthest from the centre. EG Peel off the
outer plastic cover of the flex... ...the building's
outer walls.

outermost /aʊtəməʊst/. The **outermost** thing in ADJ CLASSIF :
a group of things is the one that is furthest from the ATTRIB
centre. EG The outermost wall is 150 metres away.

outer space refers to the area outside the Earth's N UNCOUNT
atmosphere where the other planets and the stars
are situated. EG ...radiation in outer space.

outfit /aʊtfɪt/, **outfits. 1** An **outfit** is a set of N COUNT :
clothes. EG She wore a black ski outfit... I can't USU+SUPP
afford a new evening outfit.
2 You can refer to an organization as an **outfit**. EG I N COUNT
joined this outfit hoping to go abroad... ...a couple of Informal
guys from a security outfit.

outgoing /aʊtgəʊɪŋ/, **outgoings. 1** You use **out-** ADJ CLASSIF :
going to describe **1.1** someone who is leaving an ATTRIB
important job. EG ...the outgoing president in his last
days of office. **1.2** something that is leaving a place.
EG ...outgoing mail... ...incoming and outgoing passengers.
2 Someone who is **outgoing** is very friendly and ADJ QUALIT
eager to meet and talk to people. EG Adler was an
outgoing, sociable kind of man.
3 Your **outgoings** are the amounts of money N PLURAL

which you spend. EG *Try to reduce as many outgo-ings as possible.*

outgrow /ˈaʊtgrəʊ/, outgrows, outgrowing, out-grew, outgrown. 1 If you **outgrow** a piece of v+o clothing, you get bigger and can no longer wear it. EG *Small children outgrow their shoes at a fast rate.*
2 If you **outgrow** a way of behaving, you stop v+o behaving in that way because you are older and more mature. EG *She had now outgrown her ju-venile sense of humour.*

outhouse /ˈaʊthaʊs/, outhouses. An **outhouse** is N COUNT a small building or shed attached to a house or in its garden.

outing /ˈaʊtɪŋ/, outings. An **outing** is an occasion N COUNT on which you leave your house, school, or place of work, usually for an enjoyable activity. EG *...family outings on the River Thames... We went on a theatre outing.*

outlandish /aʊtˈlændɪʃ/. If you describe something ADJ QUALIT as **outlandish**, you mean that it very unusual or strange. EG *He was ashamed of his father's outland-ish looks... ...an outlandish idea.*

outlast /aʊtˈlɑːst/, outlasts, outlasting, out-v+o lasted. If one thing **outlasts** another, it lives or exists longer than the other thing. EG *Even those trees would outlast him... She had not yet outlasted her usefulness to the party.*

outlaw /ˈaʊtlɔː/, outlaws, outlawing, outlawed. 1 v+o When something **is outlawed**, it is made illegal. EG *...legislation which will outlaw this system... The use of poison gas was outlawed.*
2 An **outlaw** is a criminal who is hiding from the N COUNT authorities. EG *...a band of outlaws.* Outdated

outlay /ˈaʊtleɪ/, outlays. An **outlay** is an amount N COUNT : of money that is invested in a project or business. USU+SUPP EG *...an initial outlay for clothing and books... ...a* Formal *total outlay of £72,550.*

outlet /ˈaʊtlɪᵗt/, outlets. 1 An **outlet** is an activity N COUNT which allows you to express your feelings or ideas. EG *They can find no outlet for their grievances... Competitiveness can find an outlet in sport.*
2 An **outlet** is also a hole or pipe through which N COUNT water or air can flow away. EG *...the sewage outlet... ...an outlet pipe.*

outline /ˈaʊtlaɪn/, outlines, outlining, outlined. 1 v+o If you **outline** an idea or plan, you explain it in a very general way. EG *I outlined my reasons.* ► used ► N SING as a noun. EG *...a brief outline of European art.* ● If ● PHRASE you describe something **in outline**, you describe it in a very general way.
2 You say that an object **is outlined** when you can v+o : USU PASS see its general shape because there is a light behind it. EG *He was clearly outlined in the light of a lamp.* ► used as a noun. EG *He saw the outline of a* ► N SING *house against the sky.*

outlive /aʊtˈlɪv/, outlives, outliving, outlived. 1 v+o If you **outlive** someone, you are still alive after they have died. EG *Olivia outlived Pepita by eight-een years.*
2 If something **outlives** something else, it still v+o exists when the other thing no longer exists. EG *The organization had outlived its usefulness.*

outlook /ˈaʊtlʊk/. 1 Your **outlook** is your general N UNCOUNT attitude towards life. EG *My whole outlook on life* +SUPP *had changed... They are European in outlook.*
2 The **outlook** of a situation is the way it is likely to N SING+SUPP develop. EG *The economic outlook is bright.*

outlying /ˈaʊtlaɪɪŋ/. **Outlying** places are far away ADJ CLASSIF : from the main cities of a country. EG *...teachers* ATTRIB *from outlying villages.*

outmoded /aʊtˈməʊdɪ²d/. Something that is **out-** ADJ QUALIT **moded** is old-fashioned and no longer useful. EG *...outmoded techniques.*

outnumber /aʊtˈnʌmbə/, outnumbers, outnum-v+o bering, outnumbered. If one group of people or things **outnumbers** another, it has more people or things in it than the other group. EG *The men outnumbered the women by four to one... They are outnumbered by the Democrats.*

out of date. Something that is **out of date** is old-ADJ QUALIT fashioned and no longer useful. EG *It wasn't pub-lished until 1972, by which time it was out of date... This is rather an out-of-date concept.*

out of doors means outside a building rather than ADV inside it. EG *Hunting dogs should be kept out of doors... We sat out-of-doors beneath the trees.*

out-of-the-way. **Out-of-the-way** places are not ADJ QUALIT often visited. EG *Our expeditions have been to some out-of-the-way places.*

out of work. Someone who is **out of work** does ADJ CLASSIF not have a job. EG *...out-of-work actors.*

out-patient, out-patients. An **out-patient** is N COUNT someone who receives treatment at a hospital but does not stay there overnight. EG *The psychiatrists dealt with her as an out-patient... ...an out-patient clinic.*

outpost /ˈaʊtpəʊst/, outposts. An **outpost** is a N COUNT small settlement in a foreign country or a distant area. EG *...a trading outpost.*

outpouring /ˈaʊtpɔːrɪŋ/, outpourings. 1 An **out-** N COUNT+SUPP **pouring** of something is a large amount of it that is produced very rapidly. EG *...a prolific outpouring of ideas and energy... ...an outpouring of wild ru-mours.*
2 Someone's **outpourings** are strong feelings that N PLURAL they express in speech or writing in an uncon-+SUPP trolled way. EG *...the hysterical outpourings of fanat-ics... ...John's sentimental outpourings.*

output /ˈaʊtpʊt/, outputs. 1 You use **output** to N UNCOUNT refer to the amount of something that a person or OR N COUNT thing produces. EG *The party maintains a constant output of pamphlets... Their total industrial output grew at an annual rate of 7%.*
2 The **output** of a computer is the information that N UNCOUNT it displays on a screen or prints on paper as a OR N COUNT result of a particular program.

outrage /ˈaʊtreɪdʒ/, outrages, outraging, out-raged. 1 If something **outrages** you, it makes you v+o extremely shocked and angry. EG *The idea out-raged me... One woman was outraged by this response.* ◇ **outraged.** EG *...the expression of* ◇ ADJ QUALIT *outraged dignity on his face.*
2 **Outrage** is a strong feeling of anger and shock. N UNCOUNT EG *Benn shared this sense of outrage.*
3 An **outrage** is an act or event which people find N COUNT very shocking, especially one that involves vio-lence. EG *There have been more reports of bomb outrages in Falmouth... 'It's an outrage!' says Howard. 'Who invited him?'*

outrageous /aʊtˈreɪdʒəs/. If you describe some-ADJ QUALIT thing as **outrageous**, you mean that you find it very shocking. EG *She used to say some outrageous things... ...outrageous crimes.* ◇ **outrageously.** EG ◇ ADV OR *He was behaving outrageously.* SUBMOD

outright /ˈaʊtraɪt/. 1 You use **outright** to describe ADJ CLASSIF : actions and behaviour that are open and direct, ATTRIB OR ADV rather than indirect. EG *...an outright refusal... ...out-right hostility... If I ask outright I get nowhere.*
2 **Outright** also means complete and total. EG *...an* ADJ CLASSIF : *outright victory... The government has banned it* ATTRIB OR ADV *outright.* ● If someone **is killed outright,** they die ● PHRASE immediately rather than being injured and dying slowly.

outset /ˈaʊtsɛt/. If something happens **at the out-** PHRASE **set** of an event, process, or period of time, it happens at the very beginning of it. If something happens **from the outset,** it happens from the beginning onwards. EG *You should explain this to him at the outset... The police had participated from the outset.*

outside /aʊtˈsaɪd/. 1 The **outside** of a container or N COUNT OR building is the part which surrounds or encloses ADJ CLASSIF : the rest of it. EG *...the outside of the bottle...* ATTRIB

Is an outsider out of doors?

Examine the property closely from the outside...
...a wooden shed that stood against the outside wall.

2 If you are **outside**, you are not inside a building ADV, PREP, OR but are quite close to it. EG *Let's go outside... It was* ADJ CLASSIF: *dark outside... There was a demonstration outside* ATTRIB *the Social Security office... ...an outside lavatory.*

3 If you are **outside** a room, you are not in it but ADV OR PREP are in the hall or corridor next to it. EG *He's on the landing outside.*

4 When you talk about the **outside** world, you are ADJ CLASSIF referring to things that happen or exist in places other than your own home or community. EG *They don't want to go out into the outside world.*

5 People or things **outside** a country, town, or PREP, region are not in it. EG *Nobody outside California* OR ADV+of *knew about him... ...a small village just outside Birmingham... We live outside of London.*

6 On a wide road, the **outside** lanes are the ones ADJ CLASSIF: which are closest to its centre. ATTRIB

7 People who are **outside** a group or organization PREP OR are not members of it. EG *The bill was supported by* ADJ CLASSIF: *a mass movement outside Parliament... Since 1974,* ATTRIB *no outside body has questioned the advice.*

8 Something that is **outside** a particular range of PREP things is not included within it. EG *The pipeline was outside his range of responsibility.*

9 Something that happens **outside** a particular PREP period of time does not happen during that time. EG *You'll have to do it outside office hours.*

outsider /aʊtsaɪdə/, **outsiders**. An **outsider** is **1** N COUNT someone who is not involved with a particular group or organization. EG *...an independent committee of seven outsiders.* **2** someone who is not accepted by a group, or who feels that they do not belong in it. EG *...the sense of being out of place, of being an outsider.*

outsize /aʊtsaɪz/. **1** Outsize or outsized things ADJ CLASSIF: are much larger than usual. EG *...a blonde with* ATTRIB *outsize spectacles... ...an outsized envelope.*

2 Outsize clothes are specially made for very ADJ CLASSIF: large people. ATTRIB

outskirts /aʊtskɜːts/. The **outskirts** of a city or N PLURAL: town are the parts that are furthest from its centre. USU the+N+of EG *The garage was on the outskirts of town... They should reach the outskirts of London on May 27th.*

outsmart /aʊtsmɑːt/, **outsmarts**, **outsmarting**, v+o **outsmarted**. If you **outsmart** someone, you cleverly defeat them or gain an advantage over them. EG *The council outsmarted us by releasing their own press statement.*

outspoken /aʊtspəʊkən/. If you are **outspoken**, ADJ QUALIT you give your opinions about things openly, even if they shock people. EG *You are younger and more outspoken than they are... ...clear, outspoken statements.*

outstanding /aʊtstændɪŋ/. **1** If you describe a ADJ QUALIT person or their work as **outstanding**, you mean that they are very good, especially when compared to others. EG *She would never be an outstanding actress... His war record was outstanding.*
◊ **outstandingly.** EG *...an outstandingly successful* ◊ SUBMOD *director.*

2 Outstanding also means very obvious or impor- ADJ CLASSIF: tant. EG *There are significant exceptions, of which* ATTRIB *oil is the outstanding example.*

3 Money that is **outstanding** has not yet been paid ADJ CLASSIF and is still owed to someone. EG *There is fifty pounds outstanding... ...£280 in outstanding fines.*

outstretched /aʊtstretʃt/. If your arms or hands ADJ CLASSIF are **outstretched**, they are stretched out as far as possible. EG *...balancing himself with outstretched arms... He sat there, hand outstretched in greeting.*

outstrip /aʊtstrɪp/, **outstrips**, **outstripping**, out- v+o **stripped**. If one thing **outstrips** another thing, it becomes larger in amount or more successful than the other thing. EG *His wealth far outstripped Northcliffe's... His newspaper outstripped its rivals in circulation.*

outward /aʊtwəd/, **outwards. 1** If something ADV AFTER VB moves or faces **outwards** or **outward**, it moves or faces away from the place you are in or the place you are talking about. EG *He swam outwards into the bay... The door opened outwards.*

2 An **outward** journey is a journey that you make ADJ CLASSIF: away from a place that you are intending to return ATTRIB OR ADV to later. EG *It was time to begin the outward trek... Our journey outwards was delayed at the airport.*

3 The **outward** feelings or qualities of someone or ADJ CLASSIF: something are the ones they appear to have, rather ATTRIB than the ones they actually have. EG *I said it with what I hoped was outward calm.* ◊ **outwardly.** EG ◊ ADV *He is seething, but outwardly he remains composed... Outwardly they have much in common.*

4 The **outward** features of something are the ones ADJ CLASSIF: that you can see from the outside. EG *...the outward* ATTRIB *and visible signs of the disease.*

outweigh /aʊtweɪ/, **outweighs**, **outweighing**, v+o **outweighed**. If you say that the advantages of an Formal action **outweigh** the disadvantages, you mean that the advantages are more important than the disadvantages, and that the action is worth doing. EG *The benefits from the medicine outweigh the risks of treatment.*

outwit /aʊtwɪt/, **outwits**, **outwitting**, **outwitted**. v+o If you **outwit** someone, you cleverly defeat them or gain an advantage over them. EG *They managed to outwit Bill and get inside.*

outworn /aʊtwɔːn/. An **outworn** idea or method ADJ CLASSIF is old-fashioned and no longer useful. EG *...an out-* Formal *worn superstition.*

oval /əʊvəl/, **ovals**. An **oval** is a shape that is like N COUNT: a circle, but is wider in one direction than the OFT N MOD other. See picture at SHAPES. EG *...an oval mirror.*

ovary /əʊvəriɪ/, **ovaries**. A woman's **ovaries** are N COUNT the two organs in her body that produce eggs. Technical

ovation /əˈveɪʃən/, **ovations**. An **ovation** is a N COUNT long burst of applause. EG *The crowd broke into a* Formal *thunderous ovation.* ● If you receive a **standing** ● PHRASE **ovation**, the audience stand up and applaud you. EG *Joan got the loudest and longest standing ovation I have heard.*

oven /ʌvən/, **ovens**. An **oven** is a cooker or part N COUNT of a cooker that is like a box with a door. You put food inside the oven in order to cook it. EG *She took the pie out of the oven.*

over /əʊvə/. **1** If one thing is **over** another thing, PREP **1.1** it is directly above it, with a space between them. EG *I had reached the little bridge over the stream... ...the monument over the west door.* **1.2** it is supported by it and its ends are hanging down on each side of it. EG *Leave it to dry over the back of the sofa.* **1.3** it covers it. EG *Her hair hung down over her eyes... Place a piece of blotting paper over the stain... She was wearing a short robe over her bathing suit... Students were spraying paint over each other.*

2 If you look **over** or talk **over** an object, you look PREP or talk across the top of it. EG *The ponies would come and look over the wall... She was watching him over the rim of her cup.*

3 If you look **over** a piece of writing or a collection PREP of things, you quickly look at all the writing or all the things. EG *He ran his eye over one particular paragraph.*

4 If a window has a view **over** a piece of land, you PREP can see the land through the window. EG *The windows look out over a park.*

5 All **over** a place means in every part of it. EG *I've* PREP *been all over Austria... They come from all over the world.*

6 If you go **over** to a place, you go to it. EG *The* ADV AFTER VB *doctor walked over to the door... I've got some friends coming over tonight... Liz, come over here.*

7 If someone or something moves **over** an area or PREP surface, they move across it. EG *She ran back, skipping over the grass... His pen moved rapidly over the paper.*

8 If you go **over** something such as a river, bridge, PREP, or boundary, you cross it. EG ...*on the way back over* OR ADV+PREP *the Channel... We crossed over into Tennessee very late that night.*

9 If something is on the opposite side of a road or PREP river, you can say that it is **over** the road or river. EG *Eastwards over the Severn lie the hills.*

10 If something is **over** in a particular position, it is ADV+PREP a short distance away from you. EG *Mr Stryker was standing over by the window.*

11 Over there means in a place a short distance PHRASE away from you, or in another country. **Over here** means near you, or in the country you are in. EG *Who's the woman over there?... Are you over here on a trip?*

12 If someone or something gets **over** a barrier, PREP they get to the other side of it by going across the top of it. EG *Castle stepped over the dog... They throw their rubbish over the fence into the neighbour's garden.*

13 If you lean **over**, you bend your body in a ADV AFTER VB, particular direction. If you are leaning **over** an OR PREP object, you have bent your body and the top part of it is above the object. EG *Pat leaned over and picked it up... He crouched over a typewriter.*

14 If something rolls **over** or is turned **over**, its ADV AFTER VB position changes so that the part that was facing upwards is now facing downwards. EG *He flicked over the page... She tipped the pan over.*

15 If something is **over** a particular amount, PREP OR ADV measurement, or age, it is more than that amount, measurement, or age. EG *They paid out over 3 million pounds... ...people aged 80 or over... She did it for over a week.*

16 Over and above something means in addition PREP to it. EG *They have difficulties over and above the usual disadvantages suffered by poor children.*

17 If you say that an activity is **over** or **all over**, ADV you mean that it is completely finished. EG *Rodin's search was over... Why worry her when it's all over?*

18 If someone has control or influence **over** other PREP people, they are able to control them or influence them. EG ...*his authority over them.*

19 You also use **over** to indicate what a disagree- PREP ment or feeling relates to or is caused by. EG ...*disagreements over administrative policies... They were always quarrelling over women... ...the anxiety which the Commander suffered over it... I found him still chuckling over a telephone call he had received.*

20 If something happens **over** a period of time or PREP **over** a meal or a drink, it happens during that time or during that meal or drink. EG *He'd had flu over Christmas... ...a process developed over many decades... I was going to read it over lunch.*

21 If you say that something is happening **all over** PHRASE **again**, you mean that it is happening again, and you are implying that it is tiring, boring, or unpleasant. EG *The whole thing began all over again.*

22 If you say that something happened **over and** PHRASE **over** or **over and over again**, you mean that it happened many times. EG *I read it over and over again... Over and over, the same stories kept cropping up.*

over-. You can add **over-** to an adjective or verb to PREFIX indicate that a quality exists or an action is done to too great an extent. For example, if you say that someone is being over-cautious, you mean that they are being too cautious. EG ...*an over-confident young man... ...over-ripe fruit... My mother had always over-protected me.*

overall, overalls; pronounced /əʊvərˈɔːl/ when it is an adjective or an adverb and /ˈəʊvərˌɔːl/ when it is a noun.

1 You use **overall** to indicate that you are talking ADJ CLASSIF : about a situation in general or about the whole of ATTRIB something. EG ...*the overall pattern of his life... The overall impression was of a smoky industrial city.*

▸ used as an adverb. EG *Overall, imports account for* ▸ ADV SEN *half of our stock.*

2 Overalls consist of a single piece of clothing that N PLURAL combines trousers and a jacket. You wear overalls over your clothes in order to protect them from dirt while you are working.

3 An **overall** is a piece of clothing shaped like a N COUNT coat that you wear over your clothes in order to protect them from dirt while you are working.

overawe /əʊvərˈɔː/, **overawes, overawing, over-** V+O : USU PASS **awed.** If you **are overawed** by something, you are very impressed by it and a little afraid of it. EG *Don't be overawed by what the experts say.*

overbalance /əʊvəˈbæləns/, **overbalances,** V **overbalancing, overbalanced.** If you **overbalance**, you fall over or nearly fall over, because you are not in a steady position.

overbearing /əʊvəˈbeərɪŋ/. Someone who is ADJ QUALIT **overbearing** tries to make other people do what he or she wants in an unpleasant and forceful way. EG ...*her jealous, overbearing mother-in-law.*

overboard /əʊvəˈbɔːd/. **1** If you fall **overboard**, ADV AFTER VB you fall over the side of a ship into the water. EG *He had to hang on to avoid being washed overboard.*

2 If you **throw** a plan or idea **overboard**, you PHRASE abandon it because you think that it is no longer Informal useful. EG *They threw Baldwin's policy overboard.*

overcame /əʊvəˈkeɪm/ is the past tense of **overcome.**

overcast /əʊvəˈkɑːst/. If it is **overcast**, there are a ADJ QUALIT lot of clouds in the sky and the light is poor. EG *It was a warm day, but overcast... ...the grey, overcast sky.*

overcoat /əʊvəˈkəʊt/, **overcoats.** An **overcoat** is N COUNT a thick, warm coat that you wear in winter.

overcome /əʊvəˈkʌm/, **overcomes, overcoming, overcame** /əʊvəˈkeɪm/. The form **overcome** is used in the present tense and is also the past participle.

1 If you **overcome** a problem or a feeling, you V+O successfully deal with it or control it. EG *I was still trying to overcome my fear of the dark... We tried to overcome their objections to the plan.*

2 If you **are overcome** by a feeling, you feel it V+O : USU PASS very strongly. EG *I was overcome by a sense of failure... He was overcome with astonishment.*

overcrowded /əʊvəˈkraʊdᵻd/. If a place is **over-** ADJ QUALIT **crowded**, there are too many things or people in it. EG ...*overcrowded cities... ...the overcrowded sitting-room.*

overcrowding /əʊvəˈkraʊdɪŋ/. You say that N UNCOUNT there is **overcrowding** when more people are living in a place than it was designed for. EG *There is serious overcrowding in our prisons.*

overdo /əʊvəˈduː/, **overdoes** /əʊvəˈdʌz/, **overdo-** **ing, overdid** /əʊvəˈdɪd/, **overdone** /əʊvəˈdʌn/. **1** If V+O someone **overdoes** something, they behave in an exaggerated way. EG *Wish them luck, but don't overdo it or they may become suspicious.*

2 If you **overdo** an activity, you try to do more V+O than you can physically manage. EG *Don't overdo it. It's very hot in the sun.*

overdone /əʊvəˈdʌn/. If you say that food is **over-** ADJ PRED **done**, you mean that it has been cooked for too long.

overdose /əʊvəˈdəʊs/, **overdoses.** If someone N COUNT takes an **overdose** of a drug, they take more of it than is safe. EG *Alice took an overdose after a row with her mother... ...an overdose of sleeping pills.*

overdraft /əʊvəˈdrɑːft/, **overdrafts.** An **over-** N COUNT **draft** is an arrangement with a bank that allows you to spend more money than you have in your account. EG *She asked for a fifty-pound overdraft.*

overdue /əʊvəˈdjuː/. **1** If a person, bus, or train is ADJ QUALIT **overdue**, they have not arrived and it is after the

If it is overcast, do you wear an overcoat?

time when they were expected to arrive. EG
They're half an hour overdue. I wish they'd come.

2 If you say that a change or an event is **overdue**, ADJ QUALIT
you mean that it should have happened before
now. EG *Reform in all these areas is long overdue.*

3 If something borrowed or due to be paid is ADJ QUALIT
overdue, it is now later than the date when it
should have been returned or paid. EG *The rent on
his apartment was three weeks overdue... ...over-
due library books.*

overestimate /əʊvərˈɛstɪmeɪt/, **overestimates,**
overestimating, overestimated. 1 If you **over-** V+O
estimate something, you think that it is greater in
amount or importance than it really is. EG *We
greatly overestimated the time this would take... It
is possible to overestimate the problem.*

2 If you **overestimate** someone, you think that V+O
they have more of a skill or quality than they
really have. EG *Her confidence drained away and
he knew he had overestimated her.*

overflow, overflows, overflowing, overflowed;
pronounced /əʊvəˈfləʊ/ when it is a verb and
/ˈəʊvəfləʊ/ when it is a noun.

1 If a liquid or a river **overflows**, it flows over the V OR V-ERG
edges of the container it is in or the place where it
is. EG *He was careful to see that the jar did not
overflow... Rivers often overflow their banks.*

2 When people **overflow** a place, there are too V OR V-ERG
many of them in it and some of them have to go
outside. EG *The crowd overflowed the auditorium.*

3 If something **is overflowing** with things, it is too V+with :
full of them. EG *The table was overflowing with* USU CONT
clothes. ● If you say that something is filled **to** ● PHRASE
overflowing or full **to overflowing**, you mean
that it is extremely full. EG *The ashtrays were full to
overflowing.*

4 If someone **is overflowing** with a feeling, they V : OFT+with
are experiencing it very strongly and show this in
their behaviour. EG *...a nurse overflowing with love.*

5 An **overflow** is a hole or pipe through which N COUNT
liquid can flow out of a container when it gets too
full. EG *...the sink overflow... ...overflow pipes.*

overgrown /əʊvəˈɡrəʊn/. If a place is **over-** ADJ QUALIT
grown, it is thickly covered with plants because it
has not been looked after. EG *...a large house,
overgrown with brambles... ...the overgrown path.*

overhang /əʊvəˈhæŋ/, **overhangs, overhanging,** V+O OR V
overhung /əʊvəˈhʌŋ/. If one thing **overhangs**
another, **1** it sticks out sideways above it. EG *...a
tree which overhung the lake... ...the shadow of an
overhanging rock.* **2** it is supported by it and hangs
down its sides. EG *...wet clothes overhang the tub.*

overhaul /əʊvəˈhɔːl/, **overhauls, overhauling,**
overhauled. 1 If you **overhaul** a piece of equip- V+O
ment, you clean it, check it thoroughly, and repair
any faults. EG *The engines were overhauled before
our departure.*

2 If you **overhaul** a system or method, you exam- V+O
ine it carefully and change it in order to improve it.
EG *The company needs to overhaul its techniques
and methods.* ▶ used as a noun. EG *...a major* ▶ N COUNT
overhaul of the country's educational system.

overhead, overheads; pronounced /əʊvəˈhɛd/
when it is an adverb and /ˈəʊvəhɛd/ when it is an
adjective or a noun. **1** If something is **overhead**, it ADV OR
is above you or above the place that you are ADJ CLASSIF :
talking about. EG *Seagulls were circling overhead...* ATTRIB
The guard switched on an overhead light.

2 The **overheads** of a business are its regular and N PLURAL
essential expenses. EG *...reducing expenditure on
overheads.*

overhear /əʊvəˈhɪə/, **overhears, overhearing,** V+O
overheard /əʊvəˈhɜːd/. If you **overhear** someone,
you hear what they are saying when they are not
talking to you and they do not know that you are
listening. EG *Judy overheard him telling the children about it... I was too far away to overhear their
conversation.*

overheat /əʊvəˈhiːt/, **overheats, overheating,** V-ERG
overheated. If a piece of equipment **overheats**, it
becomes hotter than it should, usually because
there is a fault in it. EG *The appliances might
overheat and catch fire.*

overhung /əʊvəˈhʌŋ/ is the past tense and past
participle of **overhang.**

overjoyed /əʊvədˈʒɔɪd/. If you are **overjoyed**, you ADJ PRED
are extremely pleased about something. EG *Francis
was overjoyed to see him... They were overjoyed at
this treatment.*

overland /əʊvəˈlænd/. An **overland** journey is ADJ CLASSIF OR
made across land rather than by ship or aeroplane. ADV AFTER VB
EG *...an overland march across the desert... You
travelled overland to India?*

overlap; overlaps, overlapping, overlapped;
pronounced /əʊvəˈlæp/ when it is a verb and
/ˈəʊvəlæp/ when it is a noun.

1 If one thing **overlaps** another, one part of it V OR V+O :
covers a part of the other thing. EG *The circles* RECIP
overlap... A quilt must overlap the sides of the bed.

2 If two ideas or activities **overlap**, they involve V, V+O,
some of the same subjects, people, or periods of OR V+with :
time. EG *We worked overlapping shifts so there* RECIP
were always two of us on duty. ▶ used as a noun. ▶ N UNCOUNT
There is no overlap between our material and that OR N COUNT
of Lipset.

overload /əʊvəˈləʊd/, **overloads, overloading,**
overloaded. 1 If you **overload** a vehicle, you put V+O : USU PASS
more things or people into it than it was designed
to carry. EG *...little boats overloaded with desperate
people.*

2 If you **overload** an electrical system, you con- V+O
nect too many appliances to it and damage it. EG
*Your fuse has blown because you have overloaded
the circuit.*

3 If you **overload** someone with work or problems, V+O : USU PASS
you give them more work or problems than they +with
can cope with. EG *Medical services were overloaded with casualties.*

overlook /əʊvəˈlʊk/, **overlooks, overlooking,**
overlooked. 1 If a building or window **overlooks** a V+O
place, you can see the place clearly from the
building or window. EG *Elegant buildings overlooked the square... ...a room which overlooked the
garden.*

2 If you **overlook** a fact or problem, you ignore it, V+O
do not notice it, or do not realize its importance. EG
They overlook the enormous risks involved.

3 If you **overlook** someone's faults or bad behav- V+O
iour, you forgive them and do not criticize them. EG
I decided to overlook his unkindness.

overnight /əʊvəˈnaɪt/. **1 Overnight** means during ADV OR
all of the night. EG *If you leave your bike here* ADJ CLASSIF :
overnight, it's likely to disappear... Soak the raisins ATTRIB
overnight in water... ...an overnight stay.

2 Overnight cases or clothes are ones that you ADJ CLASSIF :
take when you go and stay somewhere for one or ATTRIB
two nights. EG *He packed a little overnight bag.*

3 You can say that something happened **overnight** ADV
when it happened very quickly and unexpectedly.
EG *The colonel became a hero overnight... You
can't expect these problems to be solved overnight.*

overpass /əʊvəˈpɑːs/, **overpasses.** An **overpass** N COUNT
is a structure which carries one road over the top American
of another one.

overpopulated /əʊvəˈpɒpjʊˈleɪtɪ²d/. A city or ADJ CLASSIF
country that is **overpopulated** has too many people living in it.

overpopulation /əʊvəˈpɒpjʊˈleɪʃə⁰n/. If there is N UNCOUNT
overpopulation in a place, there are too many
people living there. EG *Many problems are caused
by poverty and overpopulation.*

overpower /əʊvəˈpaʊə/, **overpowers, over-**
powering, overpowered. 1 If you **overpower** V+O
someone, you seize them despite their struggles
because you are stronger than they are. EG *They
easily overpowered her and dragged her inside.*

2 If an emotion or sensation **overpowers** you, it V+O

affects you very strongly. EG *Occasionally this desire overpowers me and leads me to be cruel.*
◊ **overpowering.** EG *...an overpowering feeling of failure... ...an overpowering anger.* ◊ ADJ QUALIT

overran /əʊvəræn/ is the past tense of **overrun.**

overrate /əʊvəreɪt/, **overrates, overrating,** V+O
overrated. If you **overrate** something, you think it is better or more important than it really is. EG *They overrate the extent of political freedom in England.* ◊ **overrated.** EG *They feel that maths is somewhat overrated as a school subject.* ◊ ADJ QUALIT

override /əʊvəraɪd/, **overrides, overriding, overrode** /əʊvərəʊd/, **overridden** /əʊvərɪdə⁰n/. 1 V+O
You say that something **overrides** other things when people decide that it is more important than these things. EG *The day-to-day struggle for survival overrode all other things... These common interests override the divisions between them.*
2 If you **override** a person or their decisions, you V+O cancel their decisions because you have more authority than they have. EG *Will they dare override what the people decide?*

overriding /əʊvəraɪdɪŋ/ means more important ADJ CLASSIF: than anything else in a particular situation. EG *The* ATTRIB *overriding need in the world is to promote peace.*

overrule /əʊvəru:l/, **overrules, overruling,** V+O
overruled. If someone in authority **overrules** a person or **overrules** their decisions, they officially decide that their decisions are incorrect or not valid. EG *The judgement was overruled by the Supreme Court... Frank was overruled by the planners in Berlin.*

overrun /əʊvərʌn/, **overruns, overrunning, overran** /əʊvəræn/, **overrun.** 1 If an army **over-** V+O **runs** a country, it succeeds in occupying it very quickly. EG *The north was overrun by the advancing troops.*
2 If animals or plants **overrun** a place, they spread V+O quickly all over it. EG *The city is overrun by rodents.*
3 If an event or meeting **overruns**, it continues for V OR V+O a longer time than it was intended to. EG *I think we've overrun our time, haven't we?*

overseas /əʊvəsi:z/. 1 You use **overseas** to de- ADJ CLASSIF: scribe things that happen or exist in foreign coun- ATTRIB OR ADV tries that you must cross the sea to get to. EG *There is a vast overseas market for our goods... Roughly 4 million Americans travel overseas each year.*
2 An **overseas** student or visitor comes from a ADJ CLASSIF: foreign country that you must cross the sea to get ATTRIB to.

oversee /əʊvəsi:/, **oversees, overseeing, over-** V+O **saw** /əʊvəsɔ:/, **overseen.** If someone in authority **oversees** a job or an activity, they make sure that it is done properly. EG *We need a guy to oversee our operations in Guyana.*

overseer /əʊvəsi:ə/, **overseers.** An **overseer** is N COUNT someone whose job is to make sure that employees are working properly.

overshadow /əʊvəʃædəʊ/, **overshadows, over-** **shadowing, overshadowed.** 1 You say that one V+O thing **overshadows** another when it is much taller than the other thing and is close to it. EG *...the elm trees overshadowing the school.*
2 If someone or something **is overshadowed** by V+O : USU PASS another person or thing, they are less successful, important, or impressive than the other person or thing. EG *She was sometimes overshadowed by the more talkative members... This incident was soon overshadowed by a greater drama.*
3 If an unpleasant event or feeling **overshadows** V+O : USU PASS something, it affects it and makes it less happy or enjoyable. EG *The closing entry of the diary is overshadowed by Pepys's fear of his failing eyesight.*

overshoot /əʊvəʃu:t/, **overshoots, overshooting,** V+O OR V **overshot** /əʊvəʃɒt/. If you **overshoot** a place that you want to get to, you go too far or too fast and

pass the place by mistake. EG *Natalie's glider overshot the landing zone and crashed into a field.*

oversight /əʊvəsaɪt/, **oversights.** An **oversight** N COUNT OR is something which you do not do and which you N UNCOUNT should have done. EG *My oversight was in not remembering to inform the authorities... Through some administrative oversight, he was released.*

oversimplify /əʊvəsɪmplɪfaɪ/, **oversimplifies,** V+O OR V **oversimplifying, oversimplified.** If you **over-** **simplify** something, you describe or explain it so simply that what you say is no longer true or reasonable. EG *We may have oversimplified the discussion by ignoring this.* ◊ **oversimplified.** EG ◊ ADJ QUALIT *...an oversimplified view of the world.*

oversize /əʊvəsaɪz/. You say that things are ADJ CLASSIF **oversize** or **oversized** when they are too big, or much bigger than usual. EG *...a girl in an oversize pair of slacks... ...an oversized tent.*

oversleep /əʊvəsli:p/, **oversleeps, oversleep-** V **ing, overslept** /əʊvəslɛpt/. If you **oversleep**, you sleep longer than you intended to. EG *Some mornings I oversleep and miss breakfast.*

overstate /əʊvəsteɪt/, **overstates, overstating,** V+O **overstated.** If you **overstate** something, you de- scribe or explain it in a way that exaggerates its importance or a quality that it has. EG *Its effect on history cannot be overstated... She may be overstating the case.*

overstep /əʊvəstɛp/, **oversteps, overstepping,** PHRASE **overstepped.** If you **overstep the mark**, you behave in an unacceptable way. EG *Last week he overstepped the mark and there will be trouble.*

overt /əʊvɜ:t/. An action or attitude that is **overt** ADJ QUALIT is done or shown in an open and obvious way. EG *...overt hostility... ...overt acts of violence.*
◊ **overtly.** EG *His jokes got more overtly malicious.* ◊ ADV

overtake /əʊvəteɪk/, **overtakes, overtaking,** **overtook** /əʊvətʊk/, **overtaken.** 1 If you **over-** V+O OR V **take** a moving vehicle or person, you pass them because you are moving faster than they are. EG *The truck had overtaken us... I was overtaken by a car.*
2 If an event **overtakes** you, it happens unexpect- V+O edly or suddenly. EG *...all the changes that have overtaken Shetland recently.*
3 If a feeling **overtakes** you, it affects you very V+O strongly. EG *Utter weariness overtook me.* Literary

overthrow, overthrows, overthrowing, over- **threw** /əʊvəθru:/, **overthrown. Overthrow** is pronounced /əʊvəθrəʊ/ when it is a verb and /əʊvəθrəʊ/ when it is a noun. 1 When a govern- V+O ment or a leader **is overthrown**, they are re- moved by force. EG *He was arrested for attempting to overthrow the regime.* ▸ used as a noun. EG *...the* ▸ N COUNT *overthrow of the dictator.*
2 If an idea, value or standard is **overthrown**, it is V+O : USU PASS replaced by another one. EG *Laws are openly violated, standards of behaviour are overthrown.*

overtime /əʊvətaɪm/ is time that you spend at N UNCOUNT your job in addition to your normal working hours. EG *He had been putting in overtime whenever he could.* ▸ used as an adverb. *They often worked* ▸ ADV *overtime.*

overtone /əʊvətəʊn/, **overtones.** If something N COUNT: has **overtones** of an idea or quality, it suggests USU PLURAL that idea or quality but does not openly express it. +SUPP EG *The play has heavy political overtones... ...a pleasure that carried no overtones of fear.*

overtook /əʊvətʊk/ is the past tense of **overtake.**

overture /əʊvətjʊə/, **overtures.** 1 An **overture** is N COUNT a piece of music, often one that is the introduction to an opera or play. EG *...Elgar's 'Cockaigne' Overture.*
2 If you make **overtures** to someone, you behave N PLURAL: in a friendly or romantic way towards them. EG *Mrs* USU+SUPP

If you make overtures to someone, do you play them a piece of music?

Thorne had made overtures of friendship... He feared they would reject his overtures.

overturn /ˌəʊvəˈtɜːn/, **overturns, overturning, overturned.** 1 If something **overturns** or if you V-ERG **overturn** it, it turns upside down or on its side. EG *She overturned the chairs and hurled the cushions about... His car crashed into a tree and overturned.*
2 If someone who has more authority or power V+O than you **overturns** your decision, they change it. EG *If they persist in their attitude he can't overturn their decision.*
3 To **overturn** a government or system means to V+O remove it or destroy it. EG *The unrest might have overturned the military rulers.*

overview /ˈəʊvəvjuː/, **overviews.** An **overview** of N COUNT : a situation is a a general understanding or descrip- USU SING +of tion of it as a whole. EG *...a short report giving a useful overview of recent developments.*

overweight /ˌəʊvəˈweɪt/. If someone is **over-** ADJ QUALIT **weight**, they are too fat, and therefore unhealthy. EG *Nearly half the people in this country are overweight... ...an overweight schoolgirl.*

overwhelm /ˌəʊvəˈwelm/, **overwhelms, over-** **whelming, overwhelmed.** 1 If you **are over-** V+O : USU PASS **whelmed** by a feeling or event, it affects you very strongly and suddenly. EG *He was overwhelmed by the intensity of her love... The horror of it all had overwhelmed me.*
2 If a group of people **overwhelm** a place or V+O another group, they gain complete control or victo- ry over them. EG *Their mission was to seize the bridges and overwhelm the garrison.*

overwhelming /ˌəʊvəˈwelmɪŋ/. 1 Something that ADJ QUALIT is **overwhelming** affects you very strongly. EG *...an overwhelming sense of powerlessness... The city is overwhelming and a little frightening.*
◊ **overwhelmingly.** EG *They had been overwhelm-* ◊ ADV *ingly appreciative.*
2 You can use **overwhelming** to say that one part ADJ CLASSIF of something is much greater than the rest of it. EG *An overwhelming majority of people are in favour of this plan.* ◊ **overwhelmingly.** EG *It is still an* ◊ ADV+ADJ *overwhelmingly rural country.*

overwork /ˌəʊvəˈwɜːk/, **overworks, over-** **working, overworked.** 1 If you **are overworking** V-ERG or **are overworked**, you are working too hard. EG *You look tired. Have you been overworking?... They were overworked and poorly paid.* ▸ used as ▸ N UNCOUNT a noun. EG *...a body made weak through undernour- ishment and overwork.*
2 If you **overwork** something, you use it too much. V+O EG *Farmers have overworked the soil.*
◊ **overworked.** EG *'Crisis' has become one of the* ◊ ADJ QUALIT *most overworked words of modern politics.*

overwrought /ˌəʊvəˈrɔːt/. Someone who is **over-** ADJ QUALIT **wrought** is very upset and uncontrolled in their behaviour. EG *Don't let people see you in this overwrought state.*

ow /aʊ/. People say **'Ow!'** when they suddenly feel EXCLAM pain. EG *Ow! You're hurting me!*

owe /əʊ/, **owes, owing, owed.** 1 If you **owe** V+O : OFT+ to; money to someone, they have lent it to you and you ALSO V+O+O have not yet paid it back. EG *I still owe you seven pounds... I paid Gower what I owed him.*
2 If you **owe** a quality or ability to someone or V+O+ to something, they are responsible for giving it to you.

EG *She owed her technique entirely to his teach- ing... The plains owe their fertility to the minerals deposited there by the river.*
3 If you say that you **owe** someone gratitude, V+O+O OR respect, or loyalty, you mean that they deserve it V+O+ to from you. EG *We owe you our thanks, Dr Marlowe...* Formal *Neither he nor Melanie owe me any explanation.*
4 You use **owing to** when you are introducing the PREP reason for something. EG *I missed my flight owing to a traffic hold-up... There was some difficulty, owing to Baldwin's precarious position.*

owl /aʊl/, **owls.** An **owl** is a bird with a flat face N COUNT and large eyes, which hunts small animals at night.

own /əʊn/, **owns, owning, owned.** 1 You use **own** ADJ CLASSIF : **1.1** to emphasize that something belongs to a ATTRIB, ONLY particular person. EG *She'd killed her own chil-* AFTER POSS *dren... His background was similar to my own.* **1.2** to emphasize that something is typical of a particu- lar person or thing. EG *Each city has its own peculiarities... His style is distinctive, very much his own.* **1.3** to emphasize that someone does something without any help from other people. EG *They are expected to make their own beds... I said 'What about lunch?' and he said, 'Oh, get your own.'*
2 When you are **on** your **own**, you are alone. EG *She* PHRASE *lived on her own... ...sitting on his own.*
3 If you do something **on** your **own**, you do it PHRASE without any help from other people. EG *We want to write a book on our own.*
4 If you say that you have a particular thing **of** PHRASE your **own**, you are emphasizing that you have it, rather than someone else. EG *She has troubles of her own... This type of glass has a colour and character all of its own.*
5 If you **get** your **own back** on someone who has PHRASE harmed you or tricked you, you harm them or trick Informal them in return.
6 If you **own** something, it is your property, V+O because you bought it or someone gave it to you. EG *...a huge old house owned by an Irish doctor... Who owns the land here?*
7 to **hold** your **own**: see **hold**.

own up. If you **own up** to something wrong that PHRASAL VB : you have done, you admit that you did it. EG *They* V+ADV, *don't want to own up to this... Was Bert owning up* OFT+ to *to Mrs Welch?*

owner /ˈəʊnə/, **owners.** The **owner** of something N COUNT : is the person to whom it belongs. EG *The owner of* USU+SUPP *the store was at his desk... The average car owner drives 10,000 miles per year.*

ownership /ˈəʊnəʃɪp/ is the state of owning some- N UNCOUNT thing. EG *...public ownership of land... ...the desire for home ownership.*

ox /ɒks/, **oxen.** An **ox** is a bull that has been N COUNT castrated. Oxen are used for pulling vehicles or carrying things. EG *...a plough pulled by two oxen.*

oxygen /ˈɒksɪdʒən/ is a colourless gas that exists N UNCOUNT in large quantities in the air. All plants and animals need oxygen in order to live. Without oxygen, nothing can burn.

oyster /ˈɔɪstə/, **oysters.** An **oyster** is a large, flat N COUNT shellfish. Some oysters can be eaten, others pro- duce pearls.

oz is a written abbreviation for 'ounce' or 'ounces'. EG *...3 oz of butter.*

P p

P, p /piː/, **Ps, p's. 1 P** is the sixteenth letter of the N COUNT
English alphabet.

2 p is an abbreviation for 'pence' or 'penny'. EG *It's
only 10p... ...a 50p piece.*

3 You write **p.** before a number as an abbreviation
for 'page'. The plural form is 'pp.'. EG *See p. 72...
...Tables I and II on pp. 40-43.*

pace /peɪs/, **paces, pacing, paced. 1** The **pace** of N UNCOUNT :
something is the speed at which it happens or is USU+SUPP
done. EG *...the pace of change... The sale resumed at
a brisk pace... He sets the pace.*

2 Your **pace** is the speed at which you walk. EG *He* N SING :
proceeds at a leisurely pace... He quickened his USU+SUPP
pace.

3 If something **keeps pace** with something else PHRASE
that is changing, it changes quickly in response to
it. EG *Earnings have not kept pace with inflation...
Any country which fails to keep pace with these
developments will soon be in trouble.*

4 If you **keep pace** with someone who is walking PHRASE
or running, you succeed in going as fast as them, so
that you remain close to them.

5 If you do something **at** your **own pace**, you do it PHRASE
at a speed that is comfortable for you. EG *It's best to
let him do the job at his own pace.*

6 If you take a number of **paces**, you walk that N COUNT
number of steps. EG *He took two quick paces
forward.*

7 A **pace** is also the distance that you move when N COUNT
you take one step. EG *He stopped when he was a
few paces away.*

8 If you **pace** a small area, you keep walking up V+O OR V+A
and down it, because you are anxious or impatient.
EG *She paced the room angrily... Harold paced
nervously up and down the platform.*

pacifism /pæsɪfɪzəm/ is the belief that war and N UNCOUNT
violence are always wrong. ◊ **pacifist** /pæsɪfɪst/, ◊ N COUNT
pacifists. EG *I was accused of being a pacifist.*

pacify /pæsɪfaɪ/, **pacifies, pacifying, pacified.** If V+O
you **pacify** someone who is angry or upset, you
succeed in making them become calm. EG *The
manager was trying hard to pacify our clients.*

pack /pæk/, **packs, packing, packed. 1** When V+O OR V
you **pack** a bag or when you **pack**, you put your
belongings in a bag, because you are leaving a
place or going on holiday. EG *He packed his bags
and left.* ◊ **packing.** EG *Have you started your* ◊ N UNCOUNT
packing?

2 When people **pack** things, for example in a V+O
factory, they put them into containers or parcels so
that they can be transported and sold.

3 If people or things **are packed** into a place or V-ERG+A OR V
pack a place, there are so many of them that the +O
place is full. EG *About 300 of us were packed into a
half-built mansion... Thirty thousand people packed
into the stadium to hear him.*

4 A **pack** is a bag containing your belongings that N COUNT
you carry on your back when you are travelling.

5 A **pack** of things is a packet of them. EG *...a pack* N COUNT
of cigarettes. American

6 A **pack** of playing cards is a complete set of N COUNT
playing cards.

7 A **pack** of wolves or dogs is a group of them that N COUNT
hunt together. EG *They hunt in packs.* OR N PART

8 You can refer to a group of people who go N COUNT
around together as a **pack**. EG *The boys always* OR N PART
went about as a pack... They're like a pack of kids.

9 See also **packed, packing.**

pack in. If you say that someone **has packed** PHRASAL VB :
something **in**, you mean that they have stopped V+O+ADV
doing it. EG *It's a good job. I don't think he'd pack it* Informal
in. British

pack off. If you **pack** someone **off** somewhere, PHRASAL VB :
you send them there to stay for a period of time. EG V+O+ADV
They pack their sons off to boarding school... I Informal
packed her off to bed.

pack up. If you **pack up** your belongings or if PHRASAL VB :
you **pack up**, you put all your belongings in a case V+O+ADV
or bag, because you are leaving. EG *Once term* OR V+ADV
finishes we all pack up and go home.

package /pækɪdʒ/, **packages, packaging, packaged. 1** A **package** is a small parcel. EG *...a small* N COUNT
package wrapped in tissue paper.

2 Some Americans refer to a packet as a **package**. N COUNT
EG *...a package of cigarettes.* American

3 When something **is packaged**, it is put into V+O : USU PASS
packets to be sold. EG *The cereal is packaged in
plain boxes.*

4 A **package** is also a set of suggestions that are N COUNT
presented together and must be accepted or reject-
ed as a group. EG *...the announcement of a fresh
package of spending cuts... They offered a package
worth sixty million dollars.*

package holiday, package holidays. A **pack-** N COUNT
age holiday or a **package tour** is a holiday
arranged by a travel company in which your travel
and your accommodation are booked for you.

packaging /pækɪdʒɪŋ/ is the container that some- N UNCOUNT
thing is sold in. EG *...disposable packaging.*

packed /pækt/. **1** A place that is **packed** is very ADJ QUALIT
crowded. EG *The theatre was packed... ...a vast
room packed with excited people... ...a packed
courtroom.*

2 Something that is **packed** with things contains a ADJ PRED :
very large number of them. EG *The book is packed* OFT+with
full of information.

packed lunch, packed lunches. A **packed** N COUNT
lunch is food, for example sandwiches, which you
take to work, to school, or on an outing and eat as
your lunch.

packet /pækɪt/, **packets. 1** A **packet** is a small N COUNT
container in which a quantity of something is sold.
Packets are either small boxes made of thin cardboard, or bags or envelopes made of paper or
plastic. EG *The room was littered with cups and
cigarette packets... Check the washing instructions
on the packet.*

2 When you refer to a **packet** of something, you N PART
are referring to a packet and its contents, or to the
contents only. EG *...a packet of cigarettes... ...a
packet of crisps... ...a packet of carrot seed.*

3 A **packet** is also a small flat parcel. N COUNT

packing /pækɪŋ/ is the paper, plastic, or other N UNCOUNT
material which is put round things that are being
sent somewhere. ● See also **pack.**

packing case, packing cases. A **packing case** N COUNT
is a large wooden box in which things are put so
that they can be stored or taken somewhere.

pact /pækt/, **pacts.** A **pact** is a formal agreement N COUNT
between two or more people or governments to do
a particular thing or to help each other. EG *A pact
was signed banning all military activity... ...a non-
aggression pact between the two countries.*

pad /pæd/, **pads, padding, padded. 1** A **pad** is a N COUNT
fairly thick, flat piece of a material such as cloth or
foam rubber. Pads are used, for example, to clean
things or protect things. EG *Dab the wound with a
cotton wool pad soaked in antiseptic... Elbow pads
and knee pads are essential on a skateboard.*

2 A **pad** of paper is a number of pieces of paper N COUNT
which are fixed together along the top or the side,
so that each piece can be torn off when it has been
used. EG *He took a pad and pencil from his pocket.*

3 A helicopter **pad** or a launch **pad** is an area of N COUNT flat, hard ground from which helicopters take off or rockets are launched. EG *The helicopter was in the air, hovering about a metre above the pad.*

4 You can refer to the place where you live as your **pad**, especially if it is a flat. EG *...his bachelor pad in Davies Street.* N COUNT Informal

5 When someone **pads** somewhere, they walk there with steps that are fairly quick and heavy but not very loud. EG *Harold padded out of the room.* V+A

6 A cat's or dog's **pads** are the soft, fleshy parts on the bottom of its paws. N COUNT : USU PLURAL

padded /ˈpædɪ'd/. Something that is **padded** has soft material on it or inside it which makes it less hard, protects it, or gives it a different shape. EG *The steering wheel is padded with real leather... ...a padded bra... ...a padded sofa.* ADJ CLASSIF

padding /ˈpædɪŋ/ is soft material which is put on something or inside it in order to make it less hard, to protect it, or to give it a different shape. EG *...a jacket with padding at the shoulders.* N UNCOUNT

paddle /ˈpædə'l/, **paddles, paddling, paddled.** **1** A **paddle** is a short pole with a wide, flat part at one end or at both ends, which you hold in your hands and use as an oar to move a small boat through water. N COUNT

2 If you **paddle** a boat, you move it through water using a paddle. EG *The people paddle from place to place in canoes.* V+O OR V+A

3 If you **paddle,** you walk or stand in shallow water at the edge of the sea, for pleasure. EG *It was too cold for paddling.* ▶ used as a noun. EG *We had a bit of a paddle.* V ▶ N SING

paddock /ˈpædək/, **paddocks.** **1** A **paddock** is a small field where horses are kept. N COUNT

2 At a race course, the **paddock** is the place where the horses are kept just before each race. N COUNT

paddy /ˈpædɪ'/, **paddies.** A **paddy** or a **paddy field** is a field that is kept flooded with water and is used for growing rice. N COUNT

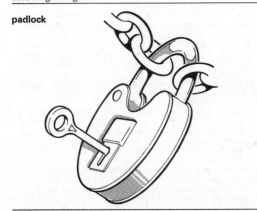
padlock

padlock /ˈpædlɒk/, **padlocks.** A **padlock** is a lock which is used for fastening two things or two parts of something together. It consists of a block of metal with a U-shaped bar attached to it. One end of the bar is released when the padlock is unlocked with a key. N COUNT

paediatrician /ˌpiːdɪəˈtrɪʃə'n/, **paediatricians;** also spelled **pediatrician.** A **paediatrician** is a doctor who specializes in treating sick children. N COUNT

pagan /ˈpeɪgə'n/, **pagans.** **1** Some people use **pagan** to describe religious beliefs and practices that do not belong to any of the main religions of the world. EG *...an ancient pagan festival... ...pagan gods.* ADJ CLASSIF

2 A **pagan** is a person who has pagan beliefs or takes part in pagan practices. EG *They burnt thousands of pagans and heretics.* N COUNT

page /peɪdʒ/, **pages.** **1** A **page** is one side of one of the pieces of paper in a book, magazine, or newspaper. Each page usually has a number printed at the top or bottom. EG *The story appeared on the front page of the Daily Mail... For details of pensions, see page 16.* N COUNT

2 The **pages** of a book, magazine, or newspaper are the pieces of paper it consists of. EG *Ellen aimlessly turned the pages of her magazine.* N COUNT

pageant /ˈpædʒə'nt/, **pageants.** **1** A **pageant** is a show, often performed out of doors, which is made up of historical or literary scenes. N COUNT

2 You can refer to any grand and colourful ceremony as a **pageant.** EG *...the pageant of the Duke's immense, sumptuous funeral.* N COUNT Literary

pageantry /ˈpædʒə'ntrɪ'/. You can refer to grand and colourful ceremonies as **pageantry.** EG *The week was crammed with festivities and pageantry.* N UNCOUNT

paid /peɪd/. **1** **Paid** is the past tense and past participle of **pay.**

2 If you do **paid** work or if you are a **paid** worker, you receive money for the work that you do. EG *You may be doing some paid work after retirement... Most of the work is done by paid staff.* ADJ CLASSIF : USU ATTRIB

3 If you are well **paid,** you receive a lot of money for the work that you do. If you are badly **paid,** you do not receive much money for it. EG *Secretaries are pretty well paid these days... ...women in low paid jobs.* ADJ CLASSIF

4 If you have **paid** holiday or **paid** leave, you are given your wages or salary even though you are not at work. ADJ CLASSIF : ATTRIB

paid-up. If you are a **paid-up** member of a group, you have paid the money required to be a member. EG *Over three million people in Britain are paid-up members of conservation groups.* ADJ CLASSIF : ATTRIB

pail /peɪl/, **pails.** A **pail** is a bucket, usually made of metal or wood. EG *...metal pails filled with milk.* N COUNT Outdated

pain /peɪn/, **pains, paining, pained.** **1** If you have **pain** or a **pain,** you have an unpleasant feeling in a part of your body because you are ill or have been hurt. EG *He was in pain... She complained of severe pains in her chest... ...acute abdominal pain.* N UNCOUNT OR N COUNT

2 **Pain** is also the feeling of unhappiness that you have when something unpleasant or upsetting happens. EG *How well I understood the confusion and pain of her parents... ...the pain of realizing that she had failed.* N UNCOUNT

3 If something **pains** you, it makes you feel upset or unhappy. EG *It pained him that his father talked like that... Such remarks always pained him.* V+O : NO CONT

4 **Pains** is used in these phrases. **4.1** If you **take pains** to do something, you try hard to do it successfully or well. EG *She took great pains to conceal this from her parents... She always took great pains with her make-up.* **4.2** Someone who is **at pains** to do something is very eager and anxious to do it. EG *She was at pains to show that she cared nothing for them.* **4.3** If you say that you got a particular thing **for** your **pains,** you mean that you got it as a reward for something you did, and you think that you deserved a much better reward. EG *A cup of tea was all I got for my pains.* PHRASES / Formal

5 If you say that someone is a **pain** or a **pain in the neck,** you mean that you find them very annoying or irritating. PHRASE Informal

pained /peɪnd/. Someone who looks or sounds **pained** seems rather upset or offended. EG *She raised her eyebrows and looked pained... ...a pained expression.* ADJ QUALIT

painful /ˈpeɪnful/. **1** If a part of your body is **painful,** it hurts. EG *My back is so painful that I cannot stand upright any more.* ADJ QUALIT

2 You say that things are **painful 2.1** when they cause you physical pain. EG *My boots are still painful... ...a long and painful illness.* ◇ **painfully.** EG *She struck him, quite painfully, with the ruler.* ADJ QUALIT / ◇ ADV

2.2 when they are upsetting, unpleasant, or difficult. EG *...the painful process of growing up... It was* ADJ QUALIT

painful to admit that I was wrong... Progress had
been slow and painful. ◊ **painfully.** EG *I was* ◊ ADV+ADJ
always painfully aware of my shortcomings.

painless /ˈpeɪnlɪs/. Something that is **painless 1** ADJ QUALIT
causes or involves no physical pain. EG *...painless
childbirth.* ◊ **painlessly.** EG *My tooth came out* ◊ ADV
quite painlessly. **2** does not involve much effort or ADJ QUALIT
unhappiness. EG *...the painless way to learn Ger-
man... There is no painless transition to socialism.*
◊ **painlessly.** EG *Industrialization in western coun-* ◊ ADV
tries was achieved painlessly.

painstaking /ˈpeɪnsteɪkɪŋ/. Someone who is ADJ QUALIT
painstaking carries out tasks extremely carefully
and thoroughly. EG *He had been an efficient and
painstaking worker... The picture had been cleaned
with painstaking care.* ◊ **painstakingly.** EG *He* ◊ ADV
painstakingly records details of every race.

paint /peɪnt/, **paints, painting, painted. 1 Paint** N MASS
is a coloured liquid that you put onto a surface
using a brush in order to protect the surface or to
make it look nice. EG *...a tin of pink paint... ...non-
drip paints.*

2 Paint is also a coloured liquid or thick paste, or a N MASS
coloured substance that can be mixed with a liquid,
which you use to make a picture or a design. EG
*...tubes of oil paint... In the art room, the brushes
and paints had been set out.*

3 A covering of dried paint on an object is often N SING : the+N
referred to as the **paint.** EG *The paint was flaking
off the walls.*

4 When you **paint** something or **paint** a picture of V+O OR V
it, you make a picture of it on paper or canvas
using paint. EG *Whistler painted his mother in a
rocking chair... I tried to paint a picture of a
pigeon... He painted a little.*

5 When you **paint** a wall or an object, you cover it V+O OR
with paint. EG *The rooms were painted green.* V+O+C
◊ **painted.** EG *...painted furniture... ...white-painted* ◊ ADJ CLASSIF :
passages. ATTRIB

6 When you **paint** a design or message on a V+O+A
surface, you put it on the surface using paint. EG
...white lines painted along the middle of the road.
◊ **painted.** EG *...the wastebasket with the painted* ◊ ADJ CLASSIF
roses.

7 If a woman **paints** her lips or nails, she puts V+O
lipstick or nail varnish on them. EG *Taking out her
lipstick, she began to paint her lips.*

8 See also **painting.**

paintbrush /ˈpeɪntbrʌʃ/, **paintbrushes. A paint-** N COUNT
brush is a brush which you use for putting paint
onto something. See picture at BRUSHES.

painter /ˈpeɪntə/, **painters. A painter** is **1** an N COUNT
artist who paints pictures. EG *...a landscape painter.*
2 someone whose job is painting the walls, doors,
and other parts of buildings.

painting /ˈpeɪntɪŋ/, **paintings. 1 A painting** is a N COUNT
picture which someone has produced using paint.
EG *...a large painting by Rossetti... ...a painting of a
horse... ...oil paintings.*
2 Painting is **2.1** the activity of painting pictures. N UNCOUNT
2.2 the activity of painting parts of buildings.

paintwork /ˈpeɪntwɜːk/. The **paintwork** of a N UNCOUNT
building or vehicle is the covering of paint on it or
the parts that are painted. EG *Use warm water and
detergent to wash paintwork... The paintwork was
chipped.*

pair /peə/, **pairs, pairing, paired. 1** You refer to N PART
two things as a **pair** when they are the same size
and shape and they are intended to be used together. EG *He bought a pair of boots... Dragonflies have
two pairs of wings.*

2 You also use **pair** when you are referring to N COUNT :
certain objects which have two main parts of the USU+of
same size and shape. EG *...a pair of trousers... ...a
pair of scissors... ...a pair of sunglasses.*

3 You can refer to two people as a **pair** when they N COLL
are standing or walking together or when they
have some kind of relationship with each other. EG

They were a sinister pair... They'd always been a
devoted pair.
4 See also **au pair.**

pair off. When people **pair off** or **are paired** PHRASAL VB :
off, they become grouped in pairs. EG *They'll* V-ERG+ADV
*probably pair off for company... People are paired
off according to their level of competence.*

pajamas /pəˈdʒɑːməz/. See **pyjamas.**

pal /pæl/, **pals.** Your **pal** is your friend. EG *Where's* N COUNT
your pal tonight?... I had a pal with me... Is he a pal Informal
of yours? Outdated

palace /ˈpælɪs/, **palaces. A palace** is a very large, N COUNT
grand house, especially one which is the home of a
king, queen, or president. EG *The palace ceased to
be a royal residence in 1960... The Queen appeared
on the balcony of Buckingham Palace.*

palatable /ˈpælətəbəl/. **1** If you describe food or ADJ QUALIT
drink as **palatable,** you mean that it tastes quite Formal
pleasant. EG *The food looked quite palatable.*
2 If you describe something such as an idea as ADJ QUALIT
palatable, you mean that you are willing to accept Formal
it. EG *The truth is not always palatable.*

palate /ˈpælət/, **palates. 1** Your **palate** is the top N COUNT
part of the inside of your mouth.
2 You can also refer to someone's ability to judge N COUNT
good food and wine as their **palate.** EG *All that junk
food must have ruined my palate.*

palatial /pəˈleɪʃəl/. If a house is **palatial,** it is ADJ QUALIT
large and splendid like a palace.

pale /peɪl/, **paler, palest. 1** Something that is **pale** ADJ QUALIT
is whitish, or not strong or bright in colour. EG *He
had on a pale blue shirt... The house is built of pale
stone.*
2 If someone looks **pale,** their face looks a lighter ADJ QUALIT
colour than usual, because they are ill, frightened,
or shocked. EG *You look awfully pale: are you all
right?... Joan collapsed, pale and trembling.*
◊ **paleness.** EG *Symptoms are unusual paleness* ◊ N UNCOUNT
and tiredness.
3 A **pale** light is very weak and dim. EG *I looked* ADJ CLASSIF
down at the beach in the pale light. Literary

pall /pɔːl/, **palls, palling, palled. 1** If something V
palls, it becomes less interesting or less enjoyable.
EG *It's one of the few delights that never palls...
George's jokes were beginning to pall.*
2 A **pall** of smoke is a thick cloud of smoke above a N COUNT :
place or in it. EG *A pall of smoke hung over the* USU SING+of
entire area.

pallid /ˈpælɪd/. Someone or something that is **pal-** ADJ QUALIT
lid is unattractively or unnaturally pale in appear- Literary
ance. EG *...his pallid face... ...a pallid moon.*

pallor /ˈpælə/ is an unhealthy paleness in some- N SING
one's face. EG *I was struck by her pallor.* Literary

palm /pɑːm/, **palms. 1** A **palm** or a **palm tree** is N COUNT
a tree that grows in hot countries. It has long
leaves growing at the top, and no branches. EG *He
sat in the shade beneath the palms.*
2 The **palm** of your hand is the flat surface which N COUNT+POSS
your fingers can bend towards. EG *She placed the
money in his palm... Claud spat on the palms of his
hands and rubbed them together.*

palpable /ˈpælpəbəl/. Something that is **palpable** ADJ QUALIT
is so obvious or intense that it is easily noticed. EG Formal
*The president's scepticism was palpable... ...a pal-
pable lie.* ◊ **palpably.** EG *It was palpably unjust.* ◊ ADV+ADJ

paltry /ˈpɔːltri/. A **paltry** sum of money is one ADJ QUALIT :
that you consider to be very small. EG *...a paltry* ATTRIB
wage... The deal cost him a paltry £100.

pamper /ˈpæmpə/, **pampers, pampering, pam-** V+O
pered. If you **pamper** someone, you treat them
too kindly and do too much for them in order to
make them comfortable.

pamphlet /ˈpæmflɪt/, **pamphlets. A pamphlet** is N COUNT
a very thin book, with a paper cover, which gives
information about something.

If a house is palatial, is it a palace?

pan /pæn/, **pans**. A **pan** is a round metal container N COUNT
with a long handle, which is used for cooking things
in, usually on top of a cooker. EG *He started tipping
beans into a pan... ...pots and pans.*

panacea /pænəsɪə/, **panaceas**. A **panacea** is N COUNT
something that is supposed to be a cure for any
problem or illness. EG *...an obsession with technology as a panacea for life's ills... There are no easy
solutions and certainly no political panaceas.*

panache /pənæʃ, -nɑːʃ/. If you do something with N UNCOUNT
panache, you do it in a confident, stylish, and
elegant way. EG *He made his final speech with
more panache than he had ever shown before...
The boy danced with equal energy but less panache.*

pancake /pænkeɪk/, **pancakes**. A **pancake** is a N COUNT
thin, flat, circular piece of cooked batter. Pancakes
are usually folded and eaten hot with a sweet or
savoury filling.

panda /pændə/, **pandas**. A **panda** or a **giant** N COUNT
panda is a large animal rather like a bear, which
has black and white fur and lives in China.

pandemonium /pændəˈməʊnɪəm/. If there is N UNCOUNT
pandemonium in a place, the people there are
behaving in a very confused and noisy way. EG
*When the spectators heard about this, pandemo-
nium broke loose... Pandemonium followed. The
cavalry were called out.*

pander /pændə/, **panders**, **pandering**, **pan-** V+to
dered. If you **pander** to someone or to their
wishes, you do everything that they want; used
showing disapproval. EG *Big business firms pander
to the teenagers of today... They pander to their
children's slightest whim.*

pane /peɪn/, **panes**. A **pane** of glass is a flat sheet N COUNT
of glass in a window or door. EG *Smash a pane in
the window and climb in... ...small square panes of
green glass.*

panel /pænəl/, **panels**. 1 A **panel** is a small group N COLL
of people who are chosen to do something, for
example to discuss something in public or to make
a decision about something. EG *...questions answered by a panel of experts... ...an interviewing
panel for a new teacher.*

2 A **panel** is also a flat, rectangular piece of wood N COUNT
or other material that forms part of a larger object
such as a door. EG *There were glass panels in the
front door... ...a ceiling with painted panels.*

3 A control **panel** or instrument **panel** is a board N COUNT :
or surface which contains switches and controls to USU+SUPP
operate a machine or piece of equipment. EG *The
instrument panel is just forward of the wheel.*

panelled /pænəld/; spelled **paneled** in American
English. 1 A **panelled** room has decorative wood- ADJ CLASSIF
en panels covering its walls. EG *His office was
panelled in dark wood.*

2 A **panelled** door does not have a flat surface but ADJ CLASSIF :
has square or rectangular areas set into its surface. USU ATTRIB

panelling /pænəlɪŋ/; spelled **paneling** in Ameri- N UNCOUNT
can English. **Panelling** consists of boards or strips
of wood covering a wall inside a building. EG *...the
hall, with its panelling and its splendid carved oak
screen.*

pang /pæŋ/, **pangs**. A **pang** is a sudden, strong N COUNT :
feeling, for example of sadness or pain. EG *She felt a* USU+of
*sudden pang of regret... He was conscious of a
sharp pang of guilt... ...hunger pangs.*

panic /pænɪk/, **panics**, **panicking**, **panicked**. 1 N UNCOUNT
Panic is a very strong feeling of anxiety or fear, OR N COUNT
especially one that makes you act without thinking
carefully. EG *Sandy was close to panic... These
rumours spread panic... Some of them got into their
cars and took off in a panic.*

2 If you **panic**, you suddenly become very anxious V
or afraid, and often act quickly and without thinking carefully. EG *She panicked as his hand closed on
her wrist... Don't panic. Sit still and keep calm.*

panic-stricken. Someone who is **panic-stricken** ADJ CLASSIF
is very anxious or afraid, and is often acting

without thinking carefully. EG *...a panic-stricken
crowd... She heard a rustle behind her and turned,
panic-stricken.*

panorama /pænərɑːmə/, **panoramas**. A **panora-** N COUNT :
ma is a view in which you can see a long way over OFT+of
a wide area of land. EG *...a vast panorama of
windswept mountain tops... ...every bend in the
road revealing fresh panoramas of empty beaches.*

panoramic /pænəræmɪk/. If you have a **panora-** ADJ CLASSIF
mic view, you can see a long way over a wide
area. EG *...a panoramic view of the valley.*

pansy /pænzi¹/, **pansies**. A **pansy** is a small N COUNT
garden flower with large, round petals.

pant /pænt/, **pants**, **panting**, **panted**. 1 **Pants** N PLURAL
are a piece of underwear which have two holes to
put your legs through and elastic around the top. EG
...a pair of pants.

2 In America, trousers are referred to as **pants**. EG N PLURAL
He fumbled in his pants pocket for his whistle. American

3 If you **pant**, you breathe quickly and loudly with V OR V+QUOTE
your mouth open, because you have been doing
something energetic. EG *We lugged the branch
along, panting and puffing... 'Let me go,' she panted.*

panther /pænθə/, **panthers**. A **panther** is a large N COUNT
wild animal that belongs to the cat family. Pan-
thers are usually black.

panties /pæntiz/ are pants worn by women or N PLURAL
girls. EG *Gretchen was pulling on her panties.*

pantomime /pæntəˈmaɪm/, **pantomimes**. A N COUNT
pantomime is a funny musical play for children.
Pantomimes are based on fairy stories and are
usually performed at Christmas.

pantry /pæntri¹/, **pantries**. A **pantry** is a small N COUNT
room where food is kept, in a house. EG *A pint of
milk had disappeared from the pantry.*

papal /peɪpə¹l/ is used to describe things relating ADJ CLASSIF :
to the Pope. EG *...a papal election.* ATTRIB

paper /peɪpə/, **papers**, **papering**, **papered**. 1 N UNCOUNT
Paper is a material that you write on or wrap
things with. The pages of this book are made of
paper. EG *Rudolph picked up the piece of paper and
gave it to her... ...a paper bag.*

2 A **paper** is a newspaper. EG *I read about the riots* N COUNT
in the papers... Where do you get your daily paper?

3 **Papers** are sheets of paper with information on N PLURAL
them. EG *He consulted the papers on his knee.*

4 Your **papers** are official documents, for example N PLURAL
your passport or identity card, which prove who
you are or give you official permission to do
something. EG *One of the men in the car had no
papers... ...false papers.*

5 A **paper** is also **5.1** a part of a written examina- N COUNT
tion in which you answer a number of questions in
a particular period of time. EG *He failed the history
paper... You have two hours for each paper.* **5.2** a
long essay written on an academic subject. EG *...a
paper on linguistics and literary criticism.*

6 **Paper** agreements, qualifications, or profits are N MOD
ones that are stated by official documents to exist,
although they have no real effectiveness or existence. EG *My paper qualifications declared me to be
a doctor.*

7 If you put your thoughts down **on paper**, you PHRASE
write them down. EG *He had put his suggestions
down on paper.*

8 If something seems to be the case **on paper**, it PHRASE
seems to be the case from what you read or hear
about it, but it may not really be the case. EG *The
project looks impressive enough on paper.*

9 If you **paper** a wall, you put wallpaper on it. EG V+O
The lounge was papered and painted first.

paper over. If you **paper over** a difficulty, you PHRASAL VB :
try to hide it by giving the impression that things V+ADV+O
are going well. EG *There is no papering over the
fact that basic disputes exist.*

paperback /peɪpəbæk/, **paperbacks**. A **paper-** N COUNT
back is a book with a paper cover. EG *'The Honor-* OR in+N
ary Consul' is now available in paperback.

paper boy, paper boys. A **paper boy** is a boy who delivers newspapers to people's homes.   N COUNT

paperclip

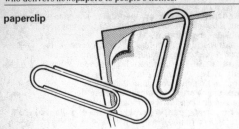

paper clip, paper clips. A **paper clip** is a small piece of bent wire that is used to fasten papers together.   N COUNT

paper shop, paper shops. A **paper shop** is the same as a newsagent's.   N COUNT

paperweight /ˈpeɪpəweɪt/, **paperweights.** A **paperweight** is a small, heavy object which you place on papers to prevent them from being disturbed or blown away.   N COUNT

paperwork /ˈpeɪpəwɜːk/ is the routine part of a job which involves writing or dealing with letters, reports, and records. EG *There was a single desk where all the paperwork seemed to be done.*   N UNCOUNT

papier-mâché /ˌpæpjeɪˈmæʃeɪ/ is a mixture of pieces of paper and glue, which is used to make objects such as bowls, ornaments, and models. EG *...papier-mâché boxes lacquered with flowers.*   N UNCOUNT

paprika /ˈpæprɪkə/ is a red powder that is used for flavouring food.   N UNCOUNT

par /pɑː/. If you say that something is **on a par** with something else, you mean that the two things are equally good or equally bad. EG *He put Warhol on a par with Titian... Forcing a child to learn is on a par with forcing a man to adopt a religion.*   PHRASE

parable /ˈpærəbl̩/, **parables.** A **parable** is a short story which is told in order to make a moral or religious point.   N COUNT

parachute /ˈpærəʃuːt/, **parachutes.** A **parachute** is a device which enables you to jump from an aircraft and float to the ground. It consists of a large circle of thin cloth attached to your body by strings.   N COUNT

parade /pəˈreɪd/, **parades, parading, paraded.** 1 A **parade** is 1.1 a line of people or vehicles moving somewhere together, for example through the streets of a town, to celebrate a special day or event. EG *When the war was over there was a parade in London.* 1.2 an occasion on which soldiers march together in front of important people or the public. ● When soldiers are **on parade**, they are standing or marching together on a formal occasion.   N COUNT   ● PHRASE

2 When people **parade** or **are paraded**, they walk together in a formal group, so that other people can see them. EG *The army paraded round the square... The captured criminals were paraded in chains through the streets.*   V-ERG+A

3 If you **parade** something, you show it to people in order to impress them. EG *She seldom or never paraded this knowledge.*   V+O

paradise /ˈpærədaɪs/, **paradises.** 1 According to some religions, **Paradise** is a wonderful place where people go after they die, if they have led good lives.   N PROPER

2 You can refer to a place or situation that seems perfect as **paradise** or a **paradise**. EG *...the palm-fringed paradise of Mauritius... 'That must have been interesting.' – 'For me it was paradise.'*   N UNCOUNT OR N SING

3 You can also use **paradise** to indicate that a place is very attractive to a particular kind of person. For example, you can say that a river where there is a lot of fish is an 'angler's paradise'. EG *Hong Kong was a shopper's paradise then.*   N COUNT+SUPP

paradox /ˈpærədɒks/, **paradoxes.** 1 You describe something as a **paradox** when it involves two facts which you would not expect to be both true or two qualities which you would not expect to exist together. EG *It was crowded and yet at the same time peaceful. This was a paradox she often remarked on.*   N COUNT

2 A **paradox** is also a statement which contradicts itself.   N COUNT OR N UNCOUNT

paradoxical /ˌpærədɒksɪkl̩/. You say that something is **paradoxical** when it involves two facts which you would not expect to be both true or two qualities which you would not expect to exist together. EG *It's paradoxical that the loneliest people live in the most crowded places.*   ADJ QUALIT

◊ **paradoxically** /ˌpærədɒksɪkl̩i/. EG *Paradoxically, he represented both escape and safety.*   ◊ ADV SEN

paraffin /ˈpærəfɪn/ is a strong-smelling liquid which is used as a fuel in heaters and lamps.   N UNCOUNT

paragon /ˈpærəgɒn/, **paragons.** If you describe someone as a **paragon**, you mean that they are perfect or that they have as much of a particular quality as anyone can have. EG *He was a paragon of honesty.*   N COUNT : USU+SUPP

paragraph /ˈpærəgrɑːf/, **paragraphs.** A **paragraph** is a section of a piece of writing. A paragraph always begins on a new line. In this dictionary, a **paragraph** is one of the sections of an entry numbered 1, 2, 3, and so on.   N COUNT

parallel /ˈpærəlel/, **parallels, paralleling, paralleled;** also spelled **parallelling** and **parallelled** in British English. 1 A **parallel** is something that is very similar to something else, but that exists or happens in a different place or at a different time. EG *It is not difficult to find a living parallel for these prehistoric creatures... We must search many past centuries for a parallel.* ● If you say that something has **no parallel**, you mean that there is nothing else like it or nothing else as good. EG *...a book which has no parallel in the English language.*   N COUNT   ● PHRASE

2 If you show that there are **parallels** between two things, you show that they are similar in some ways. EG *There are curious parallels between medicine and law... His career and attitudes have interesting parallels with Potter's... We can draw parallels here with the Antarctic.*   N COUNT : USU PLURAL +between +with

3 If something **parallels** something else, it is as good as that thing or similar to it. EG *...computers with intellects paralleling Man's... His career has almost exactly paralleled that of Hopper.*   V+O

4 If you refer to a **parallel** event or situation, you are referring to one that happens at the same time as another, or one that is similar to another. EG *...an endless process of destruction and a parallel process of re-creation.*   ADJ CLASSIF : OFT+with/to

5 If two lines or two long objects are **parallel**, they are the same distance apart all along their length. EG *The boys were marching in two parallel lines... Vanderhoff Street ran parallel to Broadway.*   ADJ CLASSIF : OFT+to/with

paralyse /ˈpærəlaɪz/, **paralyses, paralysing, paralysed;** spelled **paralyze** in American English. 1 If something **paralyses** you, it causes you to have no feeling in your body or in part of it, and to be unable to move. EG *A stroke paralysed half his face... Wasps catch spiders and paralyse them with a sting.* ◊ **paralysed.** EG *...a person paralysed from the neck down.*   V+O   ◊ ADJ CLASSIF

2 You can say that people, places, or organizations **are paralysed** by something when it makes them unable to act or function properly. EG *She was paralysed by uncertainty... Great cities are paralysed by strikes and power failures.* ◊ **paralysed.** EG *What he saw left him paralysed with fright.*   V+O : USU PASS   ◊ ADJ PRED +with

paralysis /pəˈræləsɪs/ is the loss of feeling in your body or in part of it, and the inability to move. EG   N UNCOUNT

One drop of this poison would be enough to induce
paralysis and blindness.

parameter /pərǽmətə/, **parameters. Param-** N COUNT:
eters are factors or limits which affect the way USU PLURAL
that something can be done or made. EG *It is* Formal
necessary to be aware of all the parameters that
have a bearing on the design process... ...a solution
that falls within certain parameters.

paramilitary /pærəmɪ́lɪtəˀrɪ́/. A **paramilitary** ADJ CLASSIF:
organization behaves like an army but is not the ATTRIB
official army of a country. EG *...a paramilitary*
terrorist group.

paramount /pǽrəmaʊnt/. Something that is ADJ CLASSIF
paramount or of **paramount** importance is more
important than anything else. EG *The interests of*
the child are paramount.

paranoia /pærənɔ́ɪə/. Someone who suffers from N UNCOUNT
paranoia wrongly believes that other people are
trying to harm them.

paranoid /pǽrənɔɪd/. If you say that someone is ADJ QUALIT
paranoid, you mean that they are extremely suspicious, distrustful, and afraid of other people. EG
You're getting paranoid... ...a paranoid terror of
young people.

parapet /pǽrəpɪ́t/, **parapets**. A **parapet** is a low N COUNT
wall along the edge of a bridge, roof, or balcony. EG
They leaned over the low stone parapet and stared
into the pool.

paraphernalia /pærəfənéɪlɪə/. You can refer to N UNCOUNT:
a large number of objects that someone has with USU+SUPP
them or that are connected with a particular
activity as **paraphernalia**. EG *The girls gathered*
together their hockey sticks, satchels, and other
paraphernalia.

paraphrase /pǽrəfreɪz/, **paraphrases, para-**
phrasing, paraphrased. 1 A **paraphrase** of N COUNT
something written or spoken is the same thing
expressed in a different way. EG *This article was a*
close paraphrase of Dixon's own original article.
2 If you **paraphrase** someone or **paraphrase** V+O OR V
something that they have said or written, you
express what they have said or written in a different way. EG *We must, to paraphrase Socrates, bring*
out the knowledge that people have inside them...
...paraphrasing a poem.

parasite /pǽrəsaɪt/, **parasites**. 1 A **parasite** is a N COUNT
small animal or plant that lives on or inside a
larger animal or plant and gets its food from it.
◊ **parasitic** /pærəsɪ́tɪk/. EG *...tiny parasitic insects.* ◊ ADJ CLASSIF
2 If you call someone a **parasite**, you mean that N COUNT
they get money or other things from other people
without doing anything in return; used showing
disapproval. ◊ **parasitic**. EG *...their parasitic ex-* ◊ ADJ QUALIT
ploitation of the masses.

parasol /pǽrəsɒl/, **parasols**. A **parasol** is an N COUNT
object like an umbrella that provides shade from
the sun. Large parasols are often placed over
tables out of doors.

paratroops /pǽrətruːps/. The form **paratroop** is N PLURAL
used before a noun.
Paratroops are soldiers who are trained to be
dropped by parachute into battle or into enemy
territory. EG *...paratroop attacks.*

parcel /páːsəˀl/, **parcels**. A **parcel** is something N COUNT:
wrapped in paper. EG *He started undoing a little* OFT+*of*
parcel tied with string... Charities sent parcels of
clothes. ● **part and parcel**: see **part**.

parched /páːtʃt/. 1 If the ground or plants are ADJ QUALIT
parched, they are very dry, because there has
been no rain. EG *...the parched plains of India.*
2 If your mouth, throat, or lips are **parched**, they ADJ QUALIT
are unpleasantly dry. EG *She touched her wet*
fingertips to her parched lips.
3 If you say that you are **parched**, you mean that ADJ PRED
you are very thirsty. Informal

parchment /páːtʃmənt/. 1 In former times, N UNCOUNT
parchment was the skin of a sheep or goat that
was used for writing on.
2 **Parchment** is a kind of thick yellowish paper. N UNCOUNT

pardon /páːdəˀn/, **pardons, pardoning, par-**
doned. 1 You say '**Pardon?**' or '**I beg your** CONVENTION
pardon?' when you have not heard or understood
what someone has just said and you want them to
repeat it. EG *'How old is she?' - 'Pardon?' - 'I said*
how old is she?'
2 People also say '**I beg your pardon?**' when they CONVENTION
are surprised or offended by something that someone has just said. EG *'Where the devil did you get*
her?' - 'I beg your pardon?'
3 You say '**I beg your pardon**' or '**I do beg your** CONVENTION
pardon' as a way of apologizing for accidentally
doing something wrong, for example disturbing
someone or making a mistake. EG *It is treated in*
the sentence as a noun - I beg your pardon - as an
adjective.
4 Some people say '**Pardon me**' instead of 'Excuse CONVENTION
me'. EG *Pardon me, Sergeant, I wonder if you'd do*
me a favour?
5 If you **pardon** someone, you forgive them or do V+O
not punish them for doing something bad or wrong.
EG *I hope that poor fellow may be pardoned for*
whatever crime he has committed. ▸ used as a ▸ N UNCOUNT
noun. EG *I had to beg her pardon.* OR N COUNT

pardonable /páːdəˀnəbəˀl/. You describe some- ADJ QUALIT
one's bad behaviour as **pardonable** when you can
understand why they behaved like that and think
that they should be forgiven in the circumstances.
EG *It was an exaggeration, but a pardonable one.*

pare /peə/, **pares, paring, pared**. When you **pare** V+O
something, you cut off its skin or its outer layer. EG
Mother was paring apples.

pare down. If you **pare** something **down**, 1 you PHRASAL VB:
make it smaller by cutting thin pieces off it. EG V+O+ADV
...pared-down fingernails. 2 you reduce it. EG *I had* V+O+ADV
pared my possessions down to almost nothing.

parent /peərənt/, **parents**. 1 Your **parents** are N COUNT
your father and mother. EG *Her parents are well-*
off... ...the bond between parents and children.
◊ **parental** /pərentəˀl/. EG *...lack of parental con-* ◊ ADJ CLASSIF:
trol... ...parental love. ATTRIB
2 The **parent** organization of a particular organiza- N MOD
tion created it and usually still controls it. EG
Subsidiaries are represented on the board of direc-
tors of the parent company.

parenthood /peərənthʊd/ is the state of being a N UNCOUNT
parent. EG *...the responsibility of parenthood.*

par excellence /páːr eksəlɑːns/. You say that ADJ AFTER N
something is a particular kind of thing **par excel-**
lence in order to emphasize that it is the best
possible example of that kind of thing. EG *She was*
strongly committed to her job, a policewoman par
excellence.

parish /pǽrɪʃ/, **parishes**. 1 A **parish** is a village N COUNT
or part of a town which has its own church and
clergyman. EG *...the parish of St Mark's, Sambourne*
Fishley... ...the parish church.
2 A **parish** is also a small country area which has N COUNT
its own elected council. EG *Stroud parish has a*
population of 20,000... ...a parish councillor.

parishioner /pərɪ́ʃənə/, **parishioners**. A clergy- N COUNT
man's **parishioners** are the people who live in his
parish, especially the ones who go to his church. EG
She had been one of his parishioners in Shropshire.

parity /pǽrɪ́tiˀ/. If there is **parity** between two N UNCOUNT:
things, they are equal. EG *...the theoretical parity in* OFT+
powers between the two Houses of Parliament... between/with
Women workers at the factory went on strike for Formal
parity with men.

park /páːk/, **parks, parking, parked**. 1 A **park** is N COUNT
a public area of land with grass and trees, usually
in a town, where people go in order to relax and
enjoy themselves. EG *She took her children for a*
walk in the park... ...Hyde Park.
2 A private area of grass and trees around a large N COUNT
country house can also be referred to as a **park**. British
3 When you **park** a vehicle or **park** somewhere, V+O; ALSO
you drive the vehicle into a position where it can V: USU+A
stay for a period of time, and leave it there. EG *She*

parked in front of the library. ◊ **parked.** EG *We* ◊ ADJ CLASSIF
could see the lights of a parked car. ◊ **parking.** EG ◊ N UNCOUNT
...a 'No parking' sign.

4 See also **car park**, **national park**.

parka /pɑːkə/, **parkas.** A **parka** is a jacket or coat N COUNT
which has a quilted lining and a hood with fur
round the edge.

parking lot, parking lots. A **parking lot** is an N COUNT
area of ground where people can leave their cars. American

parking meter, parking meters. A **parking** N COUNT
meter is a device next to a parking space which
you have to put money into when you park there.

parking ticket, parking tickets. A **parking** N COUNT
ticket is a piece of paper with instructions to pay a
fine, which a traffic warden puts on your car when
you have parked it somewhere illegally.

parkland /pɑːklɑ³nd/ is land with grass and trees N UNCOUNT
on it. EG *...twenty-five acres of parkland.*

parlance /pɑːləns/. You use **parlance** in phrases PHRASE
such as **'in common parlance'** or **'in medical** Formal
parlance' when you want to indicate what kind of
people normally use an expression that you are
using. EG *In common parlance that's known as
having your cake and eating it... ...the National
Economic Development Council ('Neddy' in popular parlance).*

parliament /pɑːləˡmənt/, **parliaments. 1** The N COUNT OR
parliament of a country is the group of people N UNCOUNT
who make or change its laws. EG *...the creation of
Welsh and Scottish parliaments... He was the second farm-worker to get into Parliament.* ● See also
Member of Parliament.
2 If something happens in a particular **parlia-** N COUNT+SUPP
ment, it happens during the time when a parliament is doing its work. EG *They discussed the
policies that they would like to see implemented in
the next parliament.*

parliamentary /pɑːləˡmentəˡriˡ/ is used to de- ADJ CLASSIF:
scribe things that are connected with a parliament ATTRIB
or with Members of Parliament. EG *...the start of
each parliamentary session... He was a Liberal
parliamentary candidate.*

parlour /pɑːlə/, **parlours**; spelled **parlor** in N COUNT
American English. A **parlour** is a sitting-room. Outdated

parochial /pəˡrəʊkɪəl/. If you describe someone ADJ QUALIT
as **parochial**, you mean that they are too concerned with their own local affairs and interests
when they should be thinking about more important things. EG *This is a narrow and parochial view.*

parody /pærədiˡ/, **parodies. 1** A **parody** is a N COUNT OR
humorous piece of writing, drama, or music which N UNCOUNT
copies the style of a well-known person or represents a familiar situation in an exaggerated way. EG
*...a parody of American life... ...real modern verse,
not parody.*
2 You can describe something as a **parody** of a N COUNT :
particular kind of thing when it is a very poor USU+of
example of it. EG *...a scruffy parody of a wig... Her
face was twisted into the parody of a smile.*

parole /pərəʊl/. When prisoners are given **parole**, N UNCOUNT
they are released before their prison sentence is
due to end, on condition that they behave well. EG
Prisoners are entitled to apply for parole.
● Prisoners who are **on parole** have been given ● PHRASE
parole.

paroxysm /pærəksɪzə⁰m/, **paroxysms. 1** A **par-** N COUNT+of
oxysm of rage or jealousy is a sudden, very strong
feeling of rage or jealousy. EG *In a sudden paroxysm of rage, Wilt hurled the vase across the room.*
2 A **paroxysm** is also a series of violent, uncontrol- N COUNT :
lable movements that your body makes because OFT+of
you are coughing, laughing, or in great pain. EG *...a
painful paroxysm of coughing... ...three men in
paroxysms of laughter.*

parquet /pɑːkeɪ/ is a floor covering made of small N UNCOUNT :
rectangular blocks of wood fitted together in a USU N MOD
pattern. EG *...the highly polished parquet floor.*

parrot /pærət/, **parrots, parroting, parroted. 1** N COUNT
A **parrot** is a tropical bird with a curved beak and

brightly-coloured or grey feathers. Parrots can be
kept as pets and sometimes copy what people say.
2 If you **parrot** what someone else has said, you V+O
repeat it, often without really understanding what
it means.
3 If you learn or repeat something **parrot fashion**, PHRASE
you learn or repeat it accurately but without really
understanding what it means.

parry /pæriˡ/, **parries, parrying, parried. 1** If V+O
you **parry** a question or argument, you cleverly OR V+with
avoid answering it or dealing with it. EG *Instead of
answering he parried with another question.*
2 If you **parry** a blow from someone who is V+O OR V
attacking you, you push aside their arm or weapon
so that you are not hurt.

parsimonious /pɑːsɪməʊnɪəs/. Someone who is ADJ QUALIT :
parsimonious is very unwilling to spend money. Formal

parsley /pɑːsliˡ/ is a small plant with curly leaves N UNCOUNT
that are used for flavouring or decorating savoury
food.

parsnip /pɑːsnɪp/, **parsnips.** A **parsnip** is a long, N COUNT OR
thick, pale cream vegetable that grows under the N UNCOUNT
ground.

parson /pɑːsə⁰n/, **parsons.** A **parson** is a vicar or N COUNT
other clergyman. Outdated

part /pɑːt/, **parts, parting, parted. 1** If something N PART OR
is **part** of something else or is a **part** of it, **1.1** it is N UNCOUNT
one of the pieces or areas that the other thing
consists of. EG *The bridge is part of the main road...
The head is the most sensitive part of the body... I
don't know this part of London very well... Unscrew the plug. It is now in two parts.* **1.2** it is one
of the aspects, things, or sections that the other
thing consists of. EG *Economic measures must form
part of any solution to this crisis... Finding the
money would be the hard part... The first part of
that statement is a lie.*
2 A particular **part** of a period of time is one of the N PART
shorter periods that it consists of. EG *...the latter
part of the twentieth century.*
3 A **part** for a machine or vehicle is one of the N COUNT
pieces that is used to make it or to replace a
broken piece. EG *...a group of workers who make
parts for generators.*
4 **Part** of something is some of it. EG *Part of the* N UNCOUNT
ceiling collapsed... My brothers went to school for OR N PART
*part of the day and to work for the rest of it... A
sizeable part of the labour force now live in the
cities.*
5 If you say that something is **part** one thing, **part** ADV
another, you mean that it is to some extent the first
thing and to some extent the second thing. EG *This
extraordinary document is part fiction and part
fact.*
6 You can use **part** when you are talking about the N PART
proportions of substances in a mixture. For exam- Technical
ple, if some instructions say that you should use
two **parts** disinfectant to three **parts** water, you
can mix two cups of disinfectant with three cups of
water, or two pints of disinfectant with three pints
of water. EG *Mix together equal parts of salt and
soda crystals.*
7 A **part** in a play or film is one of the roles in it N COUNT
which an actor or actress can perform. EG *She
plays the part of the witch.*
8 Your **part** in something that happens is your N SING :
involvement in it. EG *He was arrested for his part in* USU+POSS
the demonstrations.
9 If you **play** a large or important **part** in some- PHRASE
thing, you are very involved in it and have an
important effect on what happens. EG *Men should
play a bigger part in children's upbringing.*
10 If you **take part** in an activity, you do it PHRASE
together with other people. EG *I asked her if she'd
take part in a discussion about the uprising... They*

Do you get a parking ticket from a parking
meter?

want to take an active part in their country's affairs.

11 If you say that you **want no part of** something, you mean that you do not want to be involved in it at all. PHRASE

12 When you are describing people's thoughts or actions, you can say **for** her **part** or **for** my **part**, for example, to introduce what a particular person thinks or does. EG *Christopher's family despised my family, and my family, for their part, hated Christopher's.* PHRASE Formal

13 If you talk about a feeling or action **on** someone's **part**, you are referring to something that they feel or do. EG *I consider this a gross oversight on your part.* PHRASE Formal

14 **For the most part** means mostly or usually. EG *The forest is, for the most part, dark and wet.* PHRASE

15 **In part** means to some extent but not completely. EG *The improvement was brought about in part by the Trade Union Movement.* PHRASE

16 If you say that something is **part and parcel** of something else, you are emphasizing that it is involved or included in it. EG *These things are part and parcel of my everyday life.* PHRASE

17 If you say that something happened for **the best part** or **the better part** of a period of time, you mean that it happened for most of that time. EG *The men stayed for the best part of a year.* PHRASE

18 If things that are next to each other **part** or if you **part** them, they move in opposite directions, so that there is a space between them. EG *Ralph's lips parted in a delighted smile... Rudolph went to the window and parted the curtains.* V-ERG

19 If your hair **is parted** in the middle or at one side, it is combed in two different directions so that there is a straight line running from the front of your head to the back. V+O : USU PASS

20 When two people **part**, they leave each other. EG *A year ago they had parted for ever... I parted from them on excellent terms.* ● to **part company**: see **company**. V OR V+*from* : RECIP Formal

21 If you **are parted** from someone you love, you are prevented from being with them. V+O : USU PASS

22 See also **parting, partly**.

part with. If you **part with** something that is valuable or that you would prefer to keep, you give it or sell it to someone else. EG *She didn't want to part with the money.* PHRASAL VB : V+PREP

partial /pɑːʃəºl/. 1 A **partial** thing, state, or quality is not complete or whole. EG *I could give it only partial support... ...a partial solution... ...partial victory.* ADJ CLASSIF : USU ATTRIB

2 If you are **partial** to something, you like it very much. EG *The vicar is very partial to roast pheasant... George is not partial to the married state.* ADJ PRED+*to* Formal

3 Someone who is **partial** supports a particular person or thing, for example in a competition or dispute, when they should be completely fair and unbiased. EG *Children feel insecure with parents who are partial.* ADJ QUALIT

partially /pɑːʃəºli¹/ means to some extent, but not completely. EG *...a horse partially hidden by the trees... Dolly might have been partially responsible for it... He refused, partially because he was too tired.* ADV

participant /pɑːtɪsɪpənt/, **participants.** Someone who is a **participant** in an activity takes part in it. EG *She was a willing participant in these campaigns... The participants were mainly teenagers.* N COUNT : OFT+*in*

participate /pɑːtɪsɪpeɪt/, **participates, participating, participated.** If you **participate** in an activity, you take part in it. EG *We asked high school students to participate in an anti-drugs campaign.* ◇ **participation** /pɑːtɪsɪpeɪʃəºn/. EG *The success of the festival depended upon the participation of the whole community.* V : USU+*in* ◇ N UNCOUNT

participle /pɑːtɪsɪpəºl/, **participles.** In grammar, a **participle** is a form of a verb that can be used in compound tenses of the verb. There are two participles in English: the past participle, which usually ends in '-ed', and the present participle, which usually ends in '-ing'. N COUNT

particle /pɑːtɪkəºl/, **particles.** A **particle** of something is a very small piece or amount of it. EG *...particles of metal... ...food particles.* N PART OR N COUNT

particular /pətɪkjə⁴lə/, **particulars.** 1 If you refer to a **particular** thing, you are emphasizing that you are talking about only one thing in a group of similar things, and not about the others. EG *Let me ask you about one particular artist... She wasn't, at that particular moment, watching the cat at all.* ADJ CLASSIF : ATTRIB

2 If a person or thing has a **particular** quality or possession, it is distinct and belongs only to them. EG *It is important to discuss a child's particular problems and interests... Each species has its own particular place on the reef.* ADJ CLASSIF : ATTRIB

3 You use **in particular** to indicate that what you are saying applies especially to one thing or person. EG *Joan Greenwood in particular I thought was wonderful... This gesture is found in particular in Brazil... ...Africans, and in particular African women.* ADV SEN

4 You can use **particular** to emphasize that something is greater or more intense than usual. EG *The shortage of airfields gave particular concern.* ADJ QUALIT : ATTRIB

5 **Particulars** are facts or details about something or someone. EG *Renshaw jotted down a few particulars in his notebook.* N PLURAL Formal

6 If you say that someone is **particular**, you mean that they choose things and do things very carefully, and are not easily satisfied. EG *They're quite particular about their personnel.* ADJ PRED : OFT+*about*

particularly /pətɪkjə⁴ləli¹/. 1 You use **particularly** to indicate that what you are saying applies especially to one thing or situation. EG *It was hard for children, particularly when they were ill... He was challenged by the workers, particularly Gibson... He particularly dislikes quiz shows.* ADV

2 **Particularly** also means more than usually or normally. EG *She was looking particularly attractive today... This is not particularly difficult to do.* SUBMOD

parting /pɑːtɪŋ/, **partings.** 1 **Parting** is an occasion when one person leaves another. EG *She felt unable to bear the strain of parting... George said no more until their final parting.* N UNCOUNT OR N COUNT

2 The **parting** in someone's hair is the line running from the front to the back of their head where their hair has been combed in opposite directions. N COUNT

partisan /pɑːtɪzæn/, **partisans.** 1 Someone who is **partisan** strongly supports a particular person or cause. EG *There are real dangers in a partisan Civil Service... ...partisan political passions.* ▸ used as a noun. EG *He was a partisan of General Jackson.* ADJ QUALIT ▸ N COUNT

2 A **partisan** is also a member of an unofficial armed force that is formed in a country to fight enemy soldiers who are occupying it. EG *...those who fought in the hills as partisans.* N COUNT

partition /pɑːtɪʃəºn/, **partitions, partitioning, partitioned.** 1 A **partition** is a wall or screen that separates one part of a room or vehicle from another. EG *In one corner behind a partition was a lavatory... David tapped on the glass partition and the car stopped.* N COUNT

2 If you **partition** a room, you separate one part of it from another by means of a partition. EG *They had partitioned the inside into offices.* V+O

3 **Partition** is the dividing of a country into parts so that each part becomes an independent country. EG *...the partition of India in 1947.* ▸ used as a verb. EG *One plan involved partitioning the country.* N UNCOUNT ▸ V+O

partitive /pɑːtɪtɪv/, **partitives.** In grammar, a **partitive** is a word or expression that comes before a noun and indicates that part of a thing is being referred to rather than the whole of it. See the entry headed NOUNS for more information. N COUNT OR ADJ CLASSIF : ATTRIB

partly /pɑːtli¹/ means to some extent, but not completely. EG *The brass handles are partly obscured by white paint... The actors were not happy,* ADV *partly because of the scenery... This is partly a political and partly a legal question.*

partner /pɑːtnə/, **partners, partnering, partnered.** 1 Your **partner** is 1.1 the person you are married to or are having a romantic or sexual relationship with. EG *A marriage is likely to last if you and your partner are similar in personality.* 1.2 the person you are doing something with, for example dancing with or playing with in a game against two other people. EG *May I be your partner?... ...dance partners.* N COUNT

2 The **partners** in a business are the people who share the ownership of it. EG *She was a partner in a firm of solicitors... ...the senior partner.* N COUNT

3 The **partner** of a country or organization is another country or organization with which they have an alliance or agreement. EG *This move will not please Britain's EEC partners.* N COUNT

4 If you **partner** someone, you are their partner in a game or at a social occasion. EG *He found himself partnering Mrs Keppel at bridge.* V+O

partnership /pɑːtnəʃɪp/, **partnerships. Partnership** is a relationship in which two or more people, organizations, or countries work together as partners. EG *...new forms of partnership between management and workers... We are going into partnership... Our aim is to establish a working partnership with the teachers.* N UNCOUNT OR N COUNT

part of speech, parts of speech. A **part of speech** is a particular grammatical class of word, for example noun, adjective, or verb. N COUNT

partridge /pɑːtrɪdʒ/, **partridges.** A **partridge** is a wild bird with brown feathers, a round body, and a short tail. N COUNT

part-time. If someone is a **part-time** worker or has a **part-time** job, they work for only a part of each day or week. EG *We employ five part-time receptionists.* ▸ used as an adverb. EG *40 per cent of women work part-time.* ADJ CLASSIF : USU ATTRIB ▸ ADV

party /pɑːtiˈ/, **parties.** 1 A **party** is a political organization whose members have similar aims and beliefs, usually an organization that tries to get its members elected to the government of a country. EG *He's a member of the Labour Party... The PDG is not a political party... ...party leaders... The party does well in local elections.* N COUNT

2 A **party** is also a social event, often in someone's home, at which people enjoy themselves doing things such as eating, drinking, dancing, talking, or playing games. EG *...a birthday party... They gave a farewell party for her.* ● See also **garden party**. N COUNT

3 A **party** of people is a group of people who are doing something together, for example travelling together. EG *He took a party of Americans on a tour... ...rescue parties.* N PART OR N COUNT

4 One of the people involved in a legal agreement or dispute can be referred to as a particular **party**. EG *He is obviously within his rights in expecting the guilty party to pay up.* ● See also **third party**. N COUNT+SUPP Formal

5 Someone who **is a party** to an action or agreement is involved in it, and therefore partly responsible for it. EG *They simply wouldn't be a party to such a ridiculous enterprise.* PHRASE

party line, party lines. 1 The **party line** on a particular issue is the official view taken by a political party, which its members are expected to support. EG *They could be guaranteed to trot out the party line on all issues.* N SING : the+N

2 A **party line** is a telephone line shared by two or more houses or offices. N COUNT

pass /pɑːs/, **passes, passing, passed.** 1 To **pass** someone or something means to go past them without stopping. EG *We passed the New Hotel... ...a passing car... Please let us pass.* V+O OR V

2 When someone or something **passes** in a particular direction, they move in that direction. EG *They passed through an arched gateway... Slabs of toffee pass along a conveyor belt.* V+A

3 If something such as a road or pipe **passes** along V+A

a particular route, it goes along that route. EG *The stream and road pass through green fields... The pipe passed under the city sewer.*

4 If you **pass** something to someone, you take it in your hand and give it to them. EG *She passed me her glass... Pass the sugar, please.* V+O : OFT+*to*, OR V+O+O

5 If you **pass** something such as a rope through, over, or round something, you put one end of it through, over, or round that thing. EG *Pass the string under the hook.* V+O+A

6 If something **passes** from one person to another, the second person then has it instead of the first. EG *Her property passes to her next of kin.* V+*to*

7 If you **pass** the ball to someone in your team in a game such as football, hockey, or rugby, you kick, hit, or throw it to them. V+O : USU+A, OR V+A

8 When a period of time **passes**, it happens and finishes. EG *The time seems to have passed so quickly... The crisis passed.* ◊ **passing.** EG *The passing of time brought news of them.* V ◊ N UNCOUNT +SUPP

9 If you **pass** a period of time in a particular way, you spend it in that way. EG *Men pass their lives farming their small plots of land.* V+O+-ING OR V+O+A

10 If you **pass** through a stage of development or a period of time, you experience it. EG *Mrs Yule had to pass through a few years of bitterness... This area has not passed through the agricultural revolution.* V+*through*

11 If someone or something **passes** a test or **is passed** by someone, they are considered to be of an acceptable standard. EG *I passed my driving test in Holland... You have to get 120 marks out of 200 to pass... This drug has been passed by the US Food and Drug Administration.* V+O OR V-ERG

12 If an amount **passes** a particular total or level, it becomes greater than that total or level. EG *...when unemployment passed 2 million.* V+O

13 When people in authority **pass** a new law or a proposal, they formally agree to it or approve it. EG *Many of the laws passed by Parliament are never enforced.* V+O

14 When a judge **passes** sentence on someone, he or she says what their punishment will be. V+O

15 If someone or something **passes** for a particular thing or **passes** as it, they are accepted to be that thing, even though they do not have all the right qualities. EG *...that brief period that passes for summer in those regions... A strip of space 4 feet wide passed as a kitchen.* V+*for/as*

16 If something **passes** without comment or reaction or **passes** unnoticed, nobody comments on it, reacts to it, or notices it. EG *Social change was so slow that it passed unnoticed.* V+A OR V+C

17 A **pass** in a game such as football, hockey, or rugby is the act of kicking, hitting, or throwing the ball to someone in your team. N COUNT

18 A **pass** in an examination or test is a successful result in it. EG *She got a grade A pass in physics.* N COUNT

19 A **pass** is also a document that allows you to do something. EG *I have a pass to go from New York to East Hampton.* N COUNT

20 A **pass** in a mountainous area is a narrow way between two mountains. EG *...the Khyber Pass.* N COUNT

21 to **pass judgement**: see **judgement**. ● to **pass the time**: see **time**. ● to **pass water**: see **water**. ● See also **passing**.

pass around. See pass round.

pass away. If you say that someone **passed away**, you mean that they died. EG *Your husband sent it to us shortly before he passed away.* PHRASAL VB : V+ADV Outdated

pass by. If you **pass by** something, you go past it. EG *We pass by another marker... I was just passing by and I saw your car.* PHRASAL VB : V+ADV/PREP

pass off. If you **pass** something **off** as another thing, you convince people that it is that other PHRASAL VB : V+O+ADV+*as*

If you have a part-time job, do you work all the time?

thing. EG *The man who made the cabinet passed it off as an antique.*

pass on. If you **pass** something **on** to someone, you give it to them after you have used it or been given it. EG *He handed a sheet to Lee to pass on to me... Philip assured her that he had passed on the invitation.*   PHRASAL VB : V+O+ADV, OFT+*to*

pass out. If you **pass out**, you faint or collapse. EG *I thought I was going to pass out.*   PHRASAL VB : V+ADV

pass over. If you **pass over** a topic in a conversation, you do not discuss it. EG *He passed over the events of that week.*   PHRASAL VB : V+PREP

pass round or **pass around.** If a group of people **pass** something **round** or **pass** it **around**, they each take it and then give it to the next person. EG *Pass the matches round.*   PHRASAL VB : V+O+ADV/ PREP

pass up. If you **pass up** a chance or an opportunity, you do not take advantage of it. EG *I wouldn't have passed up the chance for a million dollars.*   PHRASAL VB : V+O+ADV

passable /ˈpɑːsəbəl/. **1** If you say that something is **passable**, you mean that its quality is satisfactory. EG *...some passable small restaurants... They make a passable imitation of the Spanish drink.*   ADJ QUALIT

2 If a road or path is **passable**, it is not completely blocked, and people can still use it. EG *Many of these roads are not passable in bad weather.*   ADJ PRED

passage /ˈpæsɪdʒ/, **passages. 1** A **passage** is **1.1** a long, narrow space with walls or fences on both sides, which connects one place or room with another. EG *At the end of the narrow passage was a bathroom... We went along a little passage to the garden.* **1.2** an empty space that allows you to move through a crowd of people or things. EG *Her aides had to go on ahead of her to clear a passage.* **1.3** a long, narrow hole or tube in your body, which air or liquid can pass along. EG *...the nasal passages... ...the passages into the lungs.*   N COUNT   N SING   N COUNT : USU+SUPP

2 A **passage** in a book, speech, or piece of music is a section of it that you are considering separately from the rest. EG *There's one brilliant passage in the book, where the Italian finds the money... The flute and oboe have long solo passages.*   N COUNT

3 The **passage** of someone or something is **3.1** their movement from one place to another. EG *The wind of the train's passage ruffled his hair.* **3.2** their progress from one stage in their development or situation to another. EG *...his rapid passage into senior philosophical circles.*   N UNCOUNT +POSS

4 A **passage** is also a journey by ship. EG *The passage across to Belfast was very rough.*   N COUNT

5 The **passage** of a period of time is its passing. EG *...despite the passage of two thousand years.*   N SING : the+N+of

passageway /ˈpæsɪdʒweɪ/, **passageways.** A **passageway** is a long, narrow space with walls or fences on both sides, which connects one place or room with another.   N COUNT

passenger /ˈpæsɪndʒə/, **passengers.** A **passenger** in a vehicle such as a bus, boat, or plane is a person who is travelling in it, but who is not the driver or a member of the crew. EG *The ferry service handles 400 passengers a week.*   N COUNT

passer-by /ˌpɑːsə ˈbaɪ/, **passers-by.** A **passer-by** is a person who is walking past someone or something. EG *One of the boys stopped a passer-by and asked him to phone an ambulance.*   N COUNT

passing /ˈpɑːsɪŋ/. **1 Passing** feelings, activities, or fashions last for only a short period of time. EG *...the passing whims of her mother.*   ADJ CLASSIF : ATTRIB

2 If you mention something **in passing**, you mention it briefly while you are talking or writing about something else. EG *We can note, in passing, the rapid expansion of private security organisations.*   PHRASE

3 See also **pass.**

passion /ˈpæʃən/, **passions. 1 Passion** is **1.1** a feeling of very strong sexual attraction for someone. EG *I felt such extraordinary passion for this girl.* **1.2** a very strong feeling about something or a strong belief in something. EG *Anna hated them*   N UNCOUNT OR N PLURAL

with passion... ...their attempt to arouse nationalistic passions against the foreigner.

2 If you have a **passion** for something, you have a very strong interest in it and like it very much. EG *She had developed a passion for gardens... Biology is their great passion at the moment.*   N COUNT+SUPP

passionate /ˈpæʃənət/. A **passionate** person **1** has very strong feelings about something or a strong belief in something. EG *...a passionate social reformer... ...a passionate speech.* ◊ **passionately.** EG *People care deeply and passionately about this issue.* **2** has strong romantic or sexual feelings and expresses them in their behaviour. EG *...a passionate and lonely woman... ...passionate love.* ◊ **passionately.** EG *They were kissing passionately.*   ADJ QUALIT   ◊ ADV   ADJ QUALIT   ◊ ADV

passive /ˈpæsɪv/. **1** Someone who is **passive** does not react or show their feelings when things are said to them or done to them. EG *She was so enraged that she could remain passive no longer.* ◊ **passively.** EG *They accept passively every law that is passed.*   ADJ QUALIT   ◊ ADV

2 In grammar, the **passive** is the form of the verb which is made up of the auxiliary verb 'be' and the past participle of a main verb. See the entry headed VERBS for more information.   N UNCOUNT

passport /ˈpɑːspɔːt/, **passports. 1** A **passport** is an official document containing your name, photograph, and personal details, which you need to show when you enter or leave a country. EG *My husband has a British passport.*   N COUNT

2 If you say that a thing is a **passport** to an achievement, you mean that this thing makes it possible. EG *The right contacts were the only passports to success.*   N COUNT+*to*

password /ˈpɑːswɜːd/, **passwords.** A **password** is a secret word or phrase that you must know in order to be allowed to enter a place such as a military base, or allowed to use a computer system.   N COUNT

past /pɑːst/. **1** The **past** is the period of time before the present, and the things that happened in that period. EG *He was highly praised in the past as head of the National Security Agency... ...the great Sanskrit dramas of the past.*   N SING : the+N

2 Your **past** consists of all the things that happened to you before the present time. EG *He never discussed his past... ...Britain's imperial past.*   N SING : USU+POSS

3 Past things are things that happened or existed before the present time. EG *He refused to answer questions about his past business dealings... They criticised past Governments for spending £3,500m on military aid... ...in past centuries.*   ADJ CLASSIF : ATTRIB

4 You use **past** to talk about an amount of time that has finished. If you talk about the **past** week or the **past** five years, for example, you mean the week or five years before the present week or year. EG *I've spent the past eight years at sea... He'd been through such a lot in the past hour.*   ADJ CLASSIF : ATTRIB

5 You use **past** when you are telling the time. For example, if it is twenty **past** six, it is twenty minutes after six o'clock. EG *It's ten past eleven... ...half past eight... It's quarter past.*   PREP OR ADV

6 If something such as a situation or feeling is **past**, it no longer exists. EG *All danger was now past... ...things one remembers, although they are past and gone.*   ADJ PRED

7 If you go **past** something, you go near it and then continue moving until you are on the other side of it. EG *He walked past Lock's hat shop... He drove straight past me... People ran past laughing.*   PREP OR ADV

8 If something is **past** a place, it is situated on the other side of it. EG *Past Doctor Ford's surgery was the grocer's.*   PREP

9 If you say that someone is **past it**, you mean that they no longer have the skill or energy to do something because they are too old.   PHRASE Informal

10 If you say that you **would not put it past** someone to do something, you mean that you   PHRASE would not be surprised if they did it, because of their character or previous actions. EG *I wouldn't put it past him to shoot the husband and the wife.*

pasta /pæstə/ is a type of food made from a N UNCOUNT mixture of flour, eggs, and water that is formed into different shapes. Spaghetti, macaroni, and noodles are types of pasta.

paste /peɪst/, **pastes, pasting, pasted. 1 Paste** is
1.1 a soft, wet, often sticky mixture of a substance N UNCOUNT and a liquid, which can be spread easily. EG *Mix* OR N COUNT *together the flour and the water to form a paste.*
1.2 a soft, smooth, sticky mixture of food that you N UNCOUNT spread onto bread or toast. EG *...sandwiches filled with duck paste.*
2 If you **paste** something on a surface or if you V+O+A **paste** a surface with it, you put glue or paste on it and stick it on the surface. EG *Labels were pasted to some of the clippings... The children were busy pasting gold stars on a chart.*
3 Paste is also a hard shiny glass that is used for N UNCOUNT making imitation jewellery. EG *...sparkling like a paste brooch.*

pastel /pæstəᵒl/, **pastels. 1 Pastel** colours are ADJ CLASSIF : pale rather than dark or bright. EG *...pastel shades* ATTRIB *of pink, blue, and brown.* ► used as a noun. EG *Our* ► N COUNT : *new range of paints includes some new subtle* USU PLURAL *pastels.*
2 Pastels are also small sticks of different col- N COUNT : oured chalks that are used for drawing pictures. USU PLURAL

pasteurized /pɑːstjəraɪzd/. **Pasteurized** milk or ADJ CLASSIF cream has had bacteria removed from it by means of a special heating process.

pastime /pɑːstaɪm/, **pastimes. A pastime** is N COUNT something that you do because you enjoy it or are interested in it, rather than as part of your job. EG *...leisurely pastimes, like gardening, woodwork, music and toy-making.*

pastoral /pɑːstəᵒrəl/. The **pastoral** duties and ADJ CLASSIF : activities of clergy in the Christian churches relate ATTRIB to the general needs of people, rather than just their religious needs. EG *...a pastoral visit.*

past participle, past participles. In grammar, N COUNT the **past participle** of a verb is a form which usually ends in '-ed' or '-en'. It is used to form some tenses and the passive voice, and can also be used like an adjective in front of nouns.

pastry /peɪstri¹/, **pastries. 1 Pastry** is a food N MASS made of flour, fat, and water that is mixed into a dough and then rolled flat. It is used for making pies and flans.
2 A **pastry** is a small cake made with sweet pastry. N COUNT EG *...pastries filled with custard or whipped cream.*

past tense. In grammar, the **past tense** is used to N SING : *the*+N refer mainly to things that happened or existed before the time when you are speaking or writing.

pasture /pɑːstʃə/, **pastures. Pasture** is land that N UNCOUNT has grass growing on it and that is used for farm OR N COUNT animals to graze on. EG *...five acres of pasture... ...the lush green pastures of Ireland.*

pasty, pasties; pronounced /peɪsti¹/ when it is an adjective and /pæsti¹/ when it is a noun.
1 If you are **pasty** or if you have a **pasty** face, you ADJ QUALIT look pale and unhealthy. EG *They looked pasty and red-eyed because they'd been up all night.*
2 A **pasty** is a small pie which consists of pastry N COUNT folded around meat, vegetables, or cheese.

pat /pæt/, **pats, patting, patted. 1** If you **pat** V+O something, you tap it or hit it lightly, usually with your fingers. EG *He patted the tree trunk softly.*
► used as a noun. EG *...a friendly pat on the shoulder.* ► N COUNT
2 A **pat** of butter or something else soft is a small N PART lump of it.
3 A **pat** answer or remark is something you say ADJ CLASSIF : that sounds prepared, for example an answer to a ATTRIB question that you are expecting to be asked. EG *I unfailingly gave my pat reply.*

patch /pætʃ/, **patches, patching, patched. 1** A N COUNT **patch** is **1.1** a piece of material which you use to cover a hole in something. EG *I mended holes in the*

sheets by sewing on square patches. **1.2** a small piece of material which you wear to cover an injured eye. EG *...an eye patch.*
2 If you **patch** something that has a hole in it, you V+O mend it by fastening a patch over the hole. EG *They patched the leaking roof... Anne sat by the fire, patching a pair of jeans.*
3 A **patch** on a surface is a part of it which is N COUNT+SUPP different in appearance from the area around it. EG *...the damp patch at the corner of the ceiling... ...patches of snow... He had a bald patch.*
4 You can refer to a part of something which you N COUNT+SUPP are considering separately from the rest as a **patch.** EG *There are some wonderful patches in this poem... ...the difficult patches in their relationship.*
5 If you say that someone or something **is not a** PHRASE **patch on** someone or something else, you mean Informal that they are not nearly as good as the other person or thing. EG *Joe's not a patch on his father.*

patch together. If you **patch** something **to-** PHRASAL VB : **gether,** you form it from a number of parts in a V+O+ADV quick or careless way. EG *A new government was patched together with the help of the military.*

patch up. 1 If you **patch up** something which is PHRASAL VB : damaged, you mend it or patch it so that it can be V+O+ADV used. EG *They have to patch up the mud walls that the rains have battered.* **2** If you **patch up** a V+O+ADV quarrel or relationship with someone, you try to be friends again and not to quarrel any more. EG *They tried to patch things up.*

patchwork /pætʃwɜːk/. **1** A **patchwork** quilt or ADJ CLASSIF : dress has been made by sewing together small ATTRIB pieces of material of different colours. EG *...a patch-work skirt... ...patchwork cushions.*
2 If you refer to something as a **patchwork,** you N SING+SUPP mean that it is made up of different parts or pieces. EG *...this marvellous patchwork of meadows and marsh.*

patchy /pætʃi¹/. **1** Something that is **patchy** is not ADJ QUALIT spread evenly, but is scattered around in small quantities. EG *If you dye clothes in too small a pan, the colour will be patchy.*
2 If you describe information or knowledge as ADJ QUALIT **patchy,** you mean that it is incomplete or unsatis-factory, for example because it is not correct in all parts. EG *The evidence is a bit patchy... He has a rather patchy grasp of history.*

pâté /pæteɪ/ is a mixture of meat, fish, or vegeta- N MASS bles with various flavourings, which is blended into a paste and eaten cold. EG *...chicken liver pâté.*

patent /peɪtəᵒnt/, **patents, patenting, patented;** also pronounced /pætəᵒnt/ in paragraphs 1 and 2.
1 A **patent** is an official right to be the only person N COUNT or company allowed to make or sell a new product for a certain period of time. EG *The first English patent for a typewriter was issued in 1714... To protect his new invention he took out a patent on it... ...drugs whose patents had expired.*
2 If you **patent** something, you obtain a patent for V+O it. EG *In the early 1870s he patented the sugar cube... I never attempted to patent the idea.*
3 You can use **patent** to say that something is ADJ CLASSIF : obvious. EG *...a patent impossibility in such a small* ATTRIB *room... This is patent nonsense... ...the patent hon-* Formal *esty of Butler.* ◊ **patently.** EG *Anne was patently* ◊ ADV annoyed.
4 **Patent** or **patent leather** is leather or plastic N UNCOUNT : which has a shiny surface and is used especially to USU N MOD make shoes and handbags. EG *...a pair of black patent leather shoes.*

paternal /pətɜːnəᵒl/ is used to describe things ADJ CLASSIF : relating to a father. EG *...lack of paternal love... ...a* ATTRIB *paternal duty... ...our paternal grandmother.*

path /pɑːθ/, **paths. 1** A **path** is **1.1** a long, thin line N COUNT of ground that has been marked by people walking,

What food is mentioned on these pages?

for example through a forest or up a mountain. EG
The path was easy to follow, then it just stopped.
1.2 a strip of ground for people to walk on. Paths
are often covered with concrete or gravel and
made in gardens, parks, or along the sides of roads.
EG *He went up the path to his front door.*

2 Your **path** is the space ahead of you which you N COUNT+POSS
are moving towards. EG *On arrival he found his
path barred... It moves forward killing anything in
its path.* ● If you **cross** someone's **path** or if your ● PHRASE
paths cross, you meet them by chance. EG *Our
paths had crossed many years before.*

3 The **path** of something is the line which it moves N COUNT+POSS
along in a particular direction. EG *The bullet had
scored its path across the skin of the fruit... The
flight path of the 747 carried it directly overhead.*

4 A **path** that you take is a particular course of N COUNT+SUPP
action or way of doing something. EG *I criticized the
path the government was taking... He saw public
ownership as one of many paths to achieving a
socialist society.*

pathetic /pəˈθɛtɪk/. If you describe someone or
something as **pathetic, 1** you mean that they are ADJ QUALIT
sad and weak or helpless, and that they make you
feel pity and sadness. EG *It was pathetic to see a
man to whom reading meant so much become
almost totally blind... The kitten was so tiny and
pathetic.* ◊ **pathetically.** EG *He looked pathetical-* ◊ ADV
ly defenceless. **2** you mean that they are so bad or ADJ QUALIT
weak that they make you feel impatient or angry.
EG *Our efforts so far have been rather pathetic... It
was a stupid pathetic joke.*

pathological /ˌpæθəˈlɒdʒɪkəl/. **1** You use **patho-** ADJ CLASSIF
logical to describe people who behave in an
extreme way and cannot control themselves easily.
EG *...a pathological liar... He has a pathological urge
to succeed... ...a pathological fear of being late.*

2 Pathological also means relating to pathology. ADJ CLASSIF :
EG *...pathological changes in the nervous system...* ATTRIB
...a pathological deviation from normal sexual dev- Medical
elopment.

pathology /pəˈθɒlədʒiˈ/ is the branch of medicine N UNCOUNT
that is concerned with the study of the way diseas- Medical
es and illnesses develop.

pathos /ˈpeɪθɒs/ is a quality in a situation, film, or N UNCOUNT
play that makes people feel sadness and pity. EG Formal
*...the pathos of his situation... They have eyes full of
sadness and pathos... ...a scene of real pathos.*

pathway /ˈpɑːθweɪ/, **pathways.** A **pathway** is a N COUNT
path which you can walk along or a route which
you can take. EG *Marsha could make out a possible
pathway through the wire.*

patience /ˈpeɪʃəns/. **1** If you have **patience,** you N UNCOUNT
are able to stay calm and not get annoyed, for
example when you are waiting for something. EG *It
took a vast amount of patience not to shout at
him... Paul was waiting his turn with patience... I've
lost all patience with him and his excuses.*

2 If you **try** someone's **patience,** you annoy them PHRASE
so much that it is very difficult for them to stay
calm. EG *I tried her patience to the limit.*

3 Patience is also a card game for only one N UNCOUNT
player.

patient /ˈpeɪʃənt/, **patients. 1** If you are **patient,** ADJ QUALIT
you are able to stay calm and not get annoyed, for
example when you are waiting for something. EG
He was very patient with me... Just be patient.
◊ **patiently.** EG *He answered my questions patient-* ◊ ADV
ly... James waited patiently for her to finish.

2 A **patient** is a person who is receiving medical N COUNT
treatment from a doctor or hospital, or who is
registered with a particular doctor. EG *...a consultant who treats kidney patients at the Manchester
Royal Infirmary.*

patio /ˈpætɪəʊ/, **patios.** A **patio** is an area of N COUNT
paving or concrete in a garden close to a house,
where people can sit in chairs. EG *She was sitting in
a deck chair on the patio.*

patriot /ˈpætrɪət, ˈpeɪt-/, **patriots.** Someone who is N COUNT
a **patriot** loves their country and feels very loyal
towards it. EG *...Swiss patriots.*

patriotic /ˌpætrɪˈɒtɪk, ˌpeɪt-/. Someone who is **pat-** ADJ QUALIT
riotic loves their country and feels very loyal
towards it. EG *...a patriotic song... ...patriotic fervour... Perhaps I'm old-fashioned and patriotic.*

patriotism /ˈpætrɪətɪzəm, ˈpeɪt-/ is love for your N UNCOUNT
country and loyalty towards it. EG *Her patriotism
would not permit her to buy a foreign car.*

patrol /pəˈtrəʊl/, **patrols, patrolling, patrolled. 1** V+O OR V+A
When soldiers, police, or guards **patrol** an area or
building, they move around it in order to make
sure that there is no trouble there. EG *I saw men
patrolling the streets with rifles on their backs...
...the policeman who is patrolling in a dangerous
area.* ► used as a noun. EG *An entire platoon was* ► N COUNT
*ambushed during a patrol... The police came in a
black patrol car.*

2 People who are **on patrol** are patrolling an area. PHRASE
EG *Two policemen on patrol saw the boy running
away.*

3 A **patrol** is also a group of soldiers or vehicles N COUNT
that are patrolling an area.

patron /ˈpeɪtrən/, **patrons.** A **patron** is **1** a person N COUNT :
who supports and gives money to artists, writers, USU+POSS
or musicians. EG *His portraits did not always please
his patrons... ...an entrepreneur and patron of the
arts.* **2** an important person who is interested in a
particular charity, group, or campaign and who
allows his or her name to be used for publicity. EG
*Our Chamber Music Society has the Lord Mayor as
its patron.* **3** a person who uses a particular shop or Formal
hotel, especially one who uses it frequently. EG
Patrons are requested to wear neat attire.

patronage /ˈpætrənɪdʒ/ is the support and money N UNCOUNT
given by someone to a person or a group such as a
charity. EG *...public patronage of the arts... Dalton
the physicist received lavish patronage.*

patronize /ˈpætrənaɪz/, **patronizes, patronizing,
patronized;** also spelled **patronise. 1** If someone V+O OR V
patronizes you, they speak or behave towards you
in a way which seems friendly, but which shows
that they think they are superior to you in some
way; used showing disapproval. EG *She seemed to
think that experience gave her the right to patronise... Don't patronize me!* ◊ **patronizing** ◊ ADJ QUALIT
/ˈpætrənaɪzɪŋ/. EG *Their smile was rather patronizing... ...a patronizing attitude.*

2 Someone who **patronizes** artists, writers, or V+O
musicians supports them and gives them money. EG Formal
Henry VII patronized a Flemish artist, Mabuse.

patron saint, patron saints. The **patron saint** N COUNT+SUPP
of a place, an activity, or a group of people is
someone, usually a saint, who is believed to give
them special help and protection. EG *...the patron
saint of the abbey... ...St Hubert, patron saint of
hunters.*

patter /ˈpætə/, **patters, pattering, pattered. 1** If V+A
something **patters** on a surface, it hits it quickly
several times, making quiet, tapping sounds. EG
*Spots of rain pattered on the window... Dead leaves
pattered against the walls... I heard her feet pattering about upstairs.*

2 A **patter** is a series of quick, quiet, tapping N SING
sounds. EG *They heard a patter of paws on matting
as the dog came to meet them... They fell with a
soft patter, like raindrops on dry leaves.*

3 An entertainer's **patter** or a salesperson's **patter** N COUNT :
is a speech or talk that he or she has learned and USU+SUPP
says quickly in order to entertain or influence
people. EG *He gave the usual patter about watertight boxes... Bill kept up a steady patter.*

pattern /ˈpætən/, **patterns, patterned. 1** A **pat-** N COUNT :
tern is a particular way in which something is OFT+SUPP
usually done or organized. EG *Over the next few
months their work pattern changed... ...behaviour
patterns... It fits in with the pattern of her family
life.*

2 A **pattern** is also **2.1** an arrangement of lines or N COUNT shapes, especially a design in which the same shape is repeated at regular intervals over a surface. EG *Jack was drawing a pattern in the sand with his forefinger... ...a frock with a pattern of little red apples.* **2.2** a diagram or shape that you can use as a guide when you are making something such as a model or a piece of clothing. EG *...sewing patterns.*

3 If something new **is patterned** on something V-PASS+*on* else that already exists, it is deliberately made so that it has similar features to it. EG *The 'Daily Dispatch' was patterned on the British press.*

patterned /pætəᵊnd/. Something that is **pat-** ADJ CLASSIF **terned** is covered with a pattern or design. EG *...patterned carpets... ...ties patterned with flowers.*

paunch /pɔːntʃ/, **paunches.** If a man has a N COUNT **paunch**, he has a fat stomach.

pauper /pɔːpə/, **paupers.** A **pauper** is a very poor N COUNT person. EG *Jefferson died a pauper.*   Outdated

pause /pɔːz/, **pauses, pausing, paused. 1** If you V **pause** while you are speaking, you stop speaking for a short time, often in order to think before you continue. EG *He paused and then went on in a low voice.*

2 If you **pause** while you are moving or doing V something, you stop for a moment. EG *He paused with a hand on the doorknob... He does not pause for breath until he reaches the top floor... He can do this without pausing in his work.*

3 A **pause** is **3.1** a moment of silence when a N COUNT sound, for example speech or music, stops before beginning again. EG *She continued after a pause... My signal will be three knocks, a pause, then two more.* **3.2** a short period when you stop doing what you are doing, for example to have a rest, before continuing again. EG *He went on for 35 minutes without a pause... The insect moves slowly, with frequent pauses to gather strength.*

pave /peɪv/, **paves, paving, paved. 1** When a V+O : OFT PASS road or an area of ground **is paved**, it is covered with blocks of stone or concrete, so that it is suitable for walking or driving on. ◊ **paved.** EG *...a* ◊ ADJ CLASSIF *steep causeway paved with slabs of granite.*

2 If one thing **paves the way** for another, it PHRASE creates a situation in which the other thing is more likely to happen or more able to happen. EG *His work paved the way for Burkitt's theories.*

pavement /peɪvmənt/, **pavements.** A **pave-** N COUNT **ment** is a path with a hard surface, usually by the side of a street. EG *He was standing on the pavement outside the bank.*

pavilion /pəvɪljən/, **pavilions.** A **pavilion** is a N COUNT building on the edge of a sports field where players British can change their clothes and wash.

paving stone, paving stones. Paving stones N COUNT : are flat pieces of stone, usually square in shape, USU PLURAL that are used for making pavements.

paw /pɔː/, **paws, pawing, pawed. 1** The **paws** of N COUNT an animal such as a cat, dog, or bear are its feet, which have claws for gripping things and soft pads for walking on. EG *...a black cat with white paws.*

2 If an animal **paws** something, it draws its paw or V+O OR V+*at* hoof over it or hits at it. EG *...bulls pawing the earth... The dog pawed at the door again.*

pawn /pɔːn/, **pawns, pawning, pawned. 1** If you V+O **pawn** something that you own, you leave it with a pawnbroker, who gives you money for it and who can sell it if you do not pay back the money before a certain time. EG *Brian didn't have a watch – he had pawned it some years ago.*

2 In chess, a **pawn** is the smallest and least N COUNT valuable playing piece. Each player has eight pawns at the start of the game.

3 If you refer to someone as a **pawn**, you mean N COUNT that another person is using them for his or her own advantage. EG *We are simply pawns in the hands of larger powers... Their players were being used as pawns to gain international support.*

pawnbroker /pɔːnbrəʊkə/, **pawnbrokers.** A N COUNT **pawnbroker** is a person who will lend you money if you give them something that you own. The pawnbroker can sell that thing if you do not pay back the money before a certain time.

pay /peɪ/, **pays, paying, paid** /peɪd/. **1** When you V+O OR **pay** an amount of money to someone, you give it to V+O+O; ALSO them because you are buying something from V : OFT+A them or because you owe it to them. When you **pay** a bill or a debt, you pay the amount that is required or owed. EG *He had paid £5,000 for the boat... ...money to pay the window cleaner... He paid his bill and left... Pay me five pounds... Willie paid for the drinks... I'll pay by cheque.* ● to **pay through the nose**: see **nose.**

2 When your employers **pay** you, they give you V+O, V+O+O, your wages or salary. EG *She was being paid sixty* OR V+A *dollars a week... The company pays well.*

3 Someone's **pay** is the money that they receive as N UNCOUNT their wages or salary. EG *The pay is dreadful... She lost three weeks' pay... ...a pay rise of £20 a week.*

4 If a job, deal, or investment **pays** a particular V+O OR V+A amount, it brings you that amount of money. EG *She complained about her job and how poorly it paid... A day's work pays £2,500.*

5 If a course of action **pays**, it results in some V : OFT+*to*-INF advantage or benefit for you. EG *It pays to keep on the right side of your boss.*

6 If you **pay** for something that you do or have, you V+*for/with* suffer as a result. EG *He paid dearly for his mis-* OR V+O *take... The men paid with their lives... You failed, and you must pay the penalty.*

7 You use **pay** with some nouns to indicate that V+O something is given or done. EG *It would be nice if* OR V+O+O *you paid me a visit... I paid little attention to what I heard... It was probably the greatest compliment I could have paid her.*

8 If you **pay** your **way**, you pay for things that you PHRASE need rather than letting other people pay for them.

9 See also **paid.**

pay back. 1 If you **pay back** some money that PHRASAL VB : you have borrowed from someone, you return it to V+O+ADV them. EG *I'll pay you back next week.* **2** If you **pay** V+O+ADV someone **back** for doing something unpleasant to you, you make them suffer for what they did.

pay off. 1 If you **pay off** a debt, you give someone PHRASAL VB : all the money that you owe them. EG *He had used* V+O+ADV *the firm's money to pay off gambling debts.* **2** If an V+ADV action **pays off**, it is successful. EG *It was a risk and it paid off.* **3** See also **payoff.**

pay out. If you **pay out** money, usually a large PHRASAL VB : amount, you spend it on a particular thing or V+O+ADV activity. EG *He had paid out good money to educate Julie at a boarding school.*

pay up. If you **pay up**, you give someone the PHRASAL VB : money that you owe them. EG *Pay up, son, and* V+ADV *come along quietly.*

payable /peɪəbəᵊl/. **1** If an amount of money is ADJ PRED **payable**, it has to be paid or it can be paid. EG *The interest payable on these loans was vast... This allowance is payable whether she lives with the man or not.*

2 If a cheque is made **payable** to you, it has your ADJ PRED+*to* name written on it to indicate that you are the person who will receive the money. EG *Cheques should be made payable to Trans Euro Travel Ltd.*

payment /peɪmənt/, **payments. 1 Payment** is N UNCOUNT the act of paying money to someone or of being paid. EG *Was the payment of rent optional?... When can I expect payment?*

2 A **payment** is an amount of money that is paid to N COUNT someone. EG *Some said that social security payments were too high.*

payoff /peɪɒf/, **payoffs. 1** A **payoff** is a result of a N COUNT particular action, usually a good one. EG *Some carry*

*out research and hope that there could be a
practical pay-off.*

2 A **payoff** is also a payment made to someone N COUNT
when they have been dismissed from their job. EG
*The casualties received generous redundancy pay-
offs.*

payroll /ˈpeɪrəʊl/, **payrolls.** If you are on an N COUNT
organization's **payroll**, you are employed and paid
by that organization.

PC /piː siː/, **PCs.** A **PC** is a male police officer of N COUNT
the lowest rank in Britain. **PC** is an abbreviation
for 'police constable'. EG ...*PC Cooper.*

pea /piː/, **peas. Peas** are small, round, green seeds N COUNT :
which are eaten as a vegetable. EG ...*a packet of* USU PLURAL
frozen peas.

peace /piːs/. 1 If you have **peace**, you are not N UNCOUNT
being disturbed, and you are in calm, quiet surroundings. EG *I shall need some peace and quiet in
which to practise... Go away and leave us in
peace... He returned to the peace of his village.*

2 If you have a feeling of **peace** or if you are at N UNCOUNT
peace, you feel contented and calm and not at all
worried. EG ...*the search for inner peace... For your
own peace of mind you should find out what
happened... ...a child at peace with her surroundings.*

3 When a country is at **peace**, it is not involved in a N UNCOUNT
war. EG *Their activities threaten world peace...
...peace negotiations... ...in times of peace.*

4 If there is **peace** among a group of people or if N UNCOUNT
they live at **peace** with each other, they live or
work together in a friendly way and do not quarrel.
EG *She had done it for the sake of peace in the
family... ...the peace and good order of society.*

5 If you **make peace** with someone or **make** your PHRASE
peace with them, you put an end to your quarrel
with them, often by apologizing. EG *He went to her
room to make peace.*

peaceable /ˈpiːsəbəl/. Someone who is **peaceable** ADJ QUALIT
tries to avoid quarrelling or fighting with other
people. EG ...*peaceable citizens.*

peaceful /ˈpiːsfʊl/. 1 A **peaceful** place or time is ADJ QUALIT
quiet, calm, and undisturbed. EG *It's so nice and
peaceful here... ...peaceful parks and gardens... It
was a peaceful Christmas.* ◊ **peacefully.** EG *They* ◊ ADV
lived there peacefully, happily.

2 Someone who feels or looks **peaceful** is calm ADJ QUALIT
and not at all worried. EG *He looked peaceful as he
lay there.* ◊ **peacefully.** EG *That night he slept* ◊ ADV
peacefully.

3 **Peaceful** people are not violent and try to avoid ADJ QUALIT
quarrelling or fighting with other people. EG ...*the
most peaceful nation on earth... ...peaceful demonstrations in Bonn.*

peach /piːtʃ/, **peaches.** 1 A **peach** is a soft, round, N COUNT
juicy fruit with sweet yellow flesh and pinky-
orange skin. Peaches grow in warm countries. EG
...*the best peaches I ever tasted.*

2 Something that is **peach** is pale pinky-orange in ADJ COLOUR
colour. EG ...*soft peach chiffon.*

peacock /ˈpiːkɒk/, **peacocks.** A **peacock** is a N COUNT
large bird. The male has a very long tail which it
can spread out like a fan and which is marked with
beautiful blue and green spots.

peak /piːk/, **peaks, peaking, peaked.** 1 The **peak** N COUNT :
of a process or an activity is the point at which it is USU SING
at its strongest, most successful, or most fully
developed. EG *They were trained to a peak of
physical fitness... Computer technology has not yet
reached its peak.*

2 When someone or something **peaks**, they reach V
the highest value or the highest level of success. EG
The annual workload peaks at harvest time.

3 The **peak** level or value of something is its ADJ CLASSIF :
highest level or value. EG ...*the peak voltage... ...a* ATTRIB
peak output of 165 cars per day.

4 The **peak** of a mountain is the pointed top of it; N COUNT
also sometimes used of the mountain itself. EG *It is
one of the highest peaks in the Alps.*

5 The **peak** of a cap is the part at the front that N COUNT
sticks out above your eyes. EG *He wore a brown
cloth cap with the peak pulled down over his eyes.*

peaked /piːkt/. A **peaked** cap has a pointed or ADJ CLASSIF :
rounded part that sticks out above your eyes. ATTRIB

peal /piːl/, **peals, pealing, pealed.** 1 When bells V
peal, they ring one after the other, making a
musical sound. EG *Nearby church bells pealed
across the quiet city.* ▶ used as a noun. EG ...*a peal* ▶ N COUNT
of bells.

2 A **peal** of laughter or thunder consists of a long, N COUNT+SUPP
loud series of sounds. EG ...*bursting into peals of
laughter... I was woken up by that peal of thunder.*

peanut /ˈpiːnʌt/, **peanuts. Peanuts** are small oval- N COUNT :
shaped nuts that grow under the ground. Peanuts USU PLURAL
are often eaten as a snack, especially roasted and
salted.

pear

pear /peə/, **pears.** A **pear** is a sweet, juicy fruit N COUNT
which is narrow near its stalk, and wider and
rounded at the bottom. Pears have white flesh and
thin green or yellow skin.

pearl /pɜːl/, **pearls.** A **pearl** is a hard, round N COUNT
object which is shiny and creamy white in colour.
Pearls grow inside the shell of an oyster and are
used for making expensive jewellery. EG *She was
wearing a string of pearls.* ● See also **mother-of-
pearl**.

pearly /ˈpɜːliˈ/. Something that is **pearly** has the ADJ CLASSIF
appearance of pearls. EG ...*pearly teeth... ...pearly
pink light... ...pearly water... ...pearly skies.*

peasant /ˈpezəˈnt/, **peasants.** A **peasant** is a N COUNT
person who works on the land, especially one who
owns a small piece of land in a poor country.

peasantry /ˈpezəˈntriˈ/. All the peasants in a N COLL
country are referred to as the **peasantry.** EG *The* Outdated
middle classes were no friends of the peasantry.

peat /piːt/ is black or brown decaying plant ma- N UNCOUNT
terial which is found under the ground in some
cool, wet regions. Peat can be added to soil to help
plants grow, or can be burnt on fires instead of
coal.

pebble /ˈpebəˈl/, **pebbles.** A **pebble** is a smooth, N COUNT
round stone which is found on seashores and river
beds. EG ...*the pebbles on the beach.*

peck /pek/, **pecks, pecking, pecked.** 1 If a bird V+O OR V :
pecks something, it moves its beak forward quick- USU+A
ly and bites at it. EG ...*a plump brown hen, pecking
around for grains of corn... Larger birds may peck
holes in their eggs.* ▶ used as a noun. EG *It hopped* ▶ N COUNT
over and made a quick peck at the ground.

2 If you **peck** someone on the cheek, you give V+O : USU+A
them a quick, light kiss. ▶ used as a noun. EG *She* ▶ N COUNT
gave him a peck on the cheek.

peckish /ˈpekɪʃ/. If you say that you are feeling ADJ PRED
peckish, you mean that you are fairly hungry. EG Informal
Well, children, I expect you're feeling rather peck- British
ish.

peculiar /prˈkjuːlɪə/. 1 If you describe someone or ADJ QUALIT
something as **peculiar**, you mean that they are
strange, often in an unpleasant way. EG *That lemon
is a very peculiar shape... He was wearing a*

peculiar suit... She gave him a peculiar look.

◊ **peculiarly.** EG Molly is behaving rather peculiar- ◊ ADV
ly these days.

2 If you say that you feel **peculiar**, you mean that ADJ PRED
you feel slightly ill or dizzy. EG Seeing blood makes
me feel a bit peculiar inside.

3 If something is **peculiar** to a particular thing, ADJ CLASSIF:
person, or situation, it belongs or relates only to OFT+to
that thing, person, or situation. EG ...the style of
decoration peculiar to the late 1920s.

◊ **peculiarly.** EG It's an idiom that people recog- ◊ ADV
nise as peculiarly English... ...that peculiarly feminine form of love.

peculiarity /pɪˌkjuːlɪˈærɪˈtiˈ/, **peculiarities. 1** A N COUNT:
peculiarity that someone or something has is a USU+POSS
strange or unusual habit or characteristic. EG It was
one of Boylan's peculiarities that he wanted to
humiliate her.

2 A **peculiarity** is also a thing or quality which N COUNT:
belongs or relates only to that person or thing. EG USU+POSS
Each city has its own peculiarities, its own history
and character... Is this form of politeness really a
British peculiarity?

3 Peculiarity is the quality of being strange, often N UNCOUNT
in an unpleasant way. EG ...the peculiarity of the
colonial situation.

pedal /ˈpedəˈl/, **pedals, pedalling, pedalled;**
spelled **pedaling** and **pedaled** in American English. **1** The **pedals** on a bicycle are the two parts N COUNT
that you push with your feet in order to make the
bicycle move. See picture at BICYCLE.

2 When you **pedal** a bicycle, you push the pedals V+O OR V
around with your feet to make it move. EG It was
time to pedal the three miles to the restaurant...
His legs were aching from pedalling too fast.

3 A **pedal** in a car or on a machine is a lever that N COUNT
you press with your foot in order to control the car
or machine.

pedant /ˈpedənt/, **pedants.** If you say that some- N COUNT
one is a **pedant**, you mean that they are too
concerned with unimportant details or traditional
rules, especially in connection with academic subjects. EG ...some pedant muttering something about
'only canvas would be used by real artists.'

pedantic /pɪˈdæntɪk/. If you describe someone as ADJ QUALIT
pedantic, you mean that they are too concerned
with unimportant details or traditional rules, especially in connection with academic subjects. EG ...a
fussy and pedantic middle-aged clerk.

peddle /ˈpedəˈl/, **peddles, peddling, peddled. 1** V+O
Someone who **peddles** drugs sells illegal drugs.

2 If someone **peddles** an idea or piece of informa- V+O
tion, they try hard to get people to accept it. EG
...the unreliable gossip that had been peddled for so
long... ...those who peddled this solution.

peddler /ˈpedlə/, **peddlers.** A drug **peddler** is a N COUNT:
person who sells illegal drugs. USU+SUPP

pedestal /ˈpedɪˈstəˈl/, **pedestals. 1** A **pedestal** is N COUNT
the base on which a statue or a column stands. EG
At the top of the steps was a bust of Shakespeare
on a pedestal.

2 If you **put** someone **on a pedestal**, you admire PHRASE
them too much and do not think that they have any
bad qualities at all. EG I put you on a pedestal: I
would have died for you.

pedestrian /pɪˈdestrɪən/, **pedestrians. 1** A pe- N COUNT
destrian is a person who is walking rather than
travelling in a vehicle, especially in a town. EG
Pedestrians jostled them on the pavement.

2 If you describe something as **pedestrian**, you ADJ QUALIT
mean that it is ordinary and not at all interesting.
EG He brings a touch of style to a government
whose members are pretty pedestrian.

pedestrian crossing, pedestrian crossings. A N COUNT
pedestrian crossing is a place where pedestrians
can cross a street and where motorists must stop
to let them cross.

pediatrician /ˌpiːdɪətrɪˈʃəˈn/. See paediatrician.

pedigree /ˈpedɪgriː/, **pedigrees. 1** If a dog, cat, or N COUNT
other animal has a **pedigree**, its ancestors are
known and recorded. An animal is considered to
have a good pedigree when all its known ancestors
are of the same type. EG ...fine dogs with pedigrees.

2 A **pedigree** animal is descended from animals ADJ CLASSIF:
which have all been of a particular type, and is ATTRIB
therefore considered to be of good quality.

3 Someone's **pedigree** is their background or N COUNT:
ancestry. EG He had a criminal pedigree... ...party USU+SUPP
activists with middle class pedigrees.

pee /piː/, **pees, peeing, peed.** Some speakers Informal
think that this word is rude.

When someone **pees**, they urinate. The little boys V
looked anxiously around for somewhere to pee.
▸ used as a noun. EG I need a pee. ▸ N SING: a+N

peek /piːk/, **peeks, peeking, peeked.** If you **peek** V: USU+A
at something or someone, you have a quick look at Informal
them, often secretly. EG He peeked through the
bedroom door. ▸ used as a noun. EG I took a peek at ▸ N COUNT:
the list. USU a+N

peel /piːl/, **peels, peeling, peeled. 1** The **peel** of a N UNCOUNT
fruit such as a lemon or an apple is its skin. EG USU+SUPP
...grated lemon peel.

2 When you **peel** fruit or vegetables, you remove V+O
their skins. EG I found Jane peeling potatoes.

3 If a painted surface **is peeling** or if the paint is V: OFT+off,
peeling off it, the paint is coming off it in patches. USU CONT
EG The paint was peeling off the woodwork... ...peel-
ing yellow walls.

4 If you **are peeling** or if your skin **is peeling**, V: USU CONT
small pieces of skin are coming off your body,
usually because you are sunburnt. EG Her nose was
peeling.

peel off. 1 If you **peel** something **off** a surface, PHRASAL VB:
you pull it off gently in one piece. EG I peeled some V+O+ADV/
moss off the wood... Peel off the outer plastic PREP
cover. **2** If you **peel off** a tight piece of clothing, PHRASAL VB:
you take it off, especially by turning it inside out. EG V+O+ADV
She peeled off her sweater.

peelings /ˈpiːlɪŋz/. Potato **peelings** are pieces of N PLURAL
skin peeled from potatoes. +SUPP

peep /piːp/, **peeps, peeping, peeped. 1** If you V: USU+A
peep at something, you have a quick look at it,
often secretly. EG They crept up to the glass doors
and peeped inside. ▸ used as a noun. EG I was ▸ N COUNT
allowed in to have a peep at the painting.

2 If something **peeps** out from behind or under V+A
something, a small part of it is visible or becomes Literary
visible. EG The sun was just peeping over the
horizon... ...a paper peeping out from under his
arm.

3 If you say that you haven't heard a **peep** out of N SING: a+N
someone, you mean that they have not said any- Informal
thing or made any noise.

peer /pɪə/, **peers, peering, peered. 1** If you **peer** V+A
at something, you look at it very hard, usually
because it is difficult to see very clearly. EG Howard
sat peering through the windscreen.

2 A **peer** is a member of the nobility. N COUNT

3 Your **peers** are the people who are the same age N COUNT:
as you or who have the same status as you. EG USU PLURAL
...comparing students with their peers outside uni- Formal
versity.

peerage /ˈpɪərɪdʒ/, **peerages. 1** A **peerage** is the N COUNT
rank of being a peer. EG ...an heir to a peerage.

2 The peers of a country are referred to as the N SING: the+N
peerage. EG ...his elevation to the peerage.

peer group, peer groups. Your **peer group** is N COUNT
the group of people you know who are the same Technical
age as you or who have the same social status as
you.

peeved /piːvd/. If you are **peeved** about some- ADJ QUALIT
thing, you are annoyed about it. EG He was rather Informal
peeved to discover that they had gone.

If you put someone on a pedestal, are they a
statue?

peevish /píːvɪʃ/. Someone who is **peevish** is bad- ADJ QUALIT
tempered. EG *Patty was peevish because the cous-*
ins took little notice of her. ◊ **peevishly.** EG ◊ ADV
'Where have you been?' she asked peevishly.

peg /pɛg/, **pegs, pegging, pegged. 1** A **peg** is **1.1** N COUNT
a small hook or knob that is attached to a wall or
door and is used for hanging things on. EG *He takes*
his coat from the peg. **1.2** a wooden or plastic
object used for attaching washing to a clothes line.

pegs

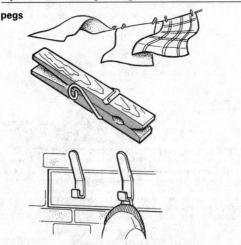

2 If you **peg** something somewhere, you fix it there V+O+A
with pegs. EG *Mamma came out and pegged wet*
clothes on the line.

3 If the price or amount of something **is pegged** at V+O : USU PASS
a particular level, it is fixed at that level. EG *Its cost* +at/to
was pegged at $750 million.

pejorative /pədʒɒrətɪv/. A **pejorative** word or ADJ QUALIT
expression is one that expresses criticism. EG *...the* Formal
pejorative term 'junk food'.

pelican /pɛlɪkən/, **pelicans.** A **pelican** is a large N COUNT
water bird. It catches fish and keeps them in the
bag-like bottom part of its beak.

pelican crossing, pelican crossings. A **peli-** N COUNT
can crossing is a place where pedestrians can
cross a road by pressing a button which operates
traffic lights to stop the traffic.

pellet /pɛlɪt/, **pellets.** A **pellet** is a small ball of N COUNT :
paper, mud, lead, or other material. EG *...a pellet of* USU+SUPP
mud... ...shotgun pellets.

pelt /pɛlt/, **pelts, pelting, pelted. 1** If you **pelt** V+O+with
someone with things, you throw things at them. EG
He was pelted with eggs.

2 If it **is pelting** with rain or if the rain **is pelting** V : OFT+down
down, it is raining very hard. Informal

3 If you **pelt** somewhere, you run there very fast. V+A
EG *I pelted up the stairs.* Informal

4 Something that is moving **at full pelt** is moving PHRASE
very fast indeed. EG *He drove away at full pelt.* Informal

pelvis /pɛlvɪs/, **pelvises.** Your **pelvis** is the wide, N COUNT
curved group of bones at the level of your hips.

pen /pɛn/, **pens, penning, penned. 1** A **pen** is a N COUNT
long thin object which you use to write in ink.

2 If someone **pens** a letter, article, or book, they V+O
write it. EG *Infuriated, he penned a blistering reply.* Literary

3 A **pen** is also a small area with a fence round it in N COUNT
which farm animals are kept for a short time.

4 If people or animals **are penned** somewhere or V+O:OFT+up,
are penned up, they are forced to remain in a USU PASS
very small area. EG *...the boredom of endless hours*
penned up in a hot and dusty railway carriage.

penal /píːnəl/. **1 Penal** means relating to the ADJ CLASSIF :
punishment of criminals. EG *...the British penal* ATTRIB
system... ...Howard's book on penal reform.

2 A **penal** institution or colony is one where ADJ CLASSIF :
criminals are imprisoned or kept. ATTRIB

penalize /píːnəlaɪz/, **penalizes, penalizing, pe-** V+O : USU PASS
nalized; also spelled **penalise.** If someone **is pe-**
nalized for something, they are made to suffer
some disadvantage because of it. EG *It would be*
unfair to penalise those without a job... You will be
penalized if you touch the ball with your hand.

penalty /pɛnəlti/, **penalties. 1** A **penalty** is a N COUNT
punishment that someone is given for doing some-
thing which is against a law or rule. EG *There are*
now stiffer penalties for drunken drivers.

2 In games such as football, rugby, and hockey, a N COUNT
penalty is a chance to score a goal without being
prevented by other players. A penalty is given
when a member of the other team commits a foul.

3 The **penalty** that you pay for something you N COUNT
have done is something unpleasant that you experience as a result. EG *I had to pay the penalty for the*
wrong decisions I made.

penance /pɛnəns/. If you do **penance** for some- N UNCOUNT
thing wrong that you have done, you do something
that you find unpleasant to show that you are sorry.
EG *As penance for his condescension, he forced*
himself to be pleasant to them.

pence /pɛns/ is a plural form of **penny.**

pencil /pɛnsəl/, **pencils, pencilling, pencilled.**
1 A **pencil** is an object that you write or draw with. N COUNT
It consists of a thin piece of wood with a rod of
graphite in the middle. ● If you write or draw ● PHRASE
something **in pencil**, you do it using a pencil.

2 If you **pencil** something, you write it using a V+O
pencil. EG *He pencilled his initials at the end.*
◊ **pencilled.** EG *...a pencilled note.* ◊ ADJ CLASSIF

pendant /pɛndənt/, **pendants.** A **pendant** is an N COUNT
ornament on a chain that you wear round your
neck. EG *...an amethyst pendant.*

pending /pɛndɪŋ/. **1** Something that is **pending** ADJ CLASSIF
1.1 is going to happen soon. EG *He knew my* Formal
examination was pending. **1.2** is waiting to be dealt Formal
with or settled. EG *...a pending lawsuit.*

2 If something is done **pending** a future event, it is PREP
done until that event happens. EG *An interim gov-* Formal
ernment is to be set up, pending elections.

pendulum /pɛndjʊləm/, **pendulums. 1** The **pen-** N COUNT
dulum of a clock is a rod with a weight at the end
which swings from side to side in order to make
the clock work.

2 You can use the idea of a **pendulum** and the way N SING : the+N
it swings regularly as a way of talking about +SUPP
regular changes in a situation or in people's opinions. EG *...the pendulum of fashion... Now the pendu-*
lum is swinging in the other direction.

penetrate /pɛnɪtreɪt/, **penetrates, penetrating,**
penetrated. 1 If someone or something **pen-** V+O OR V+A
etrates an area that is difficult to get into, they
succeed in getting into it or through it. EG *They*
penetrated into territory where no man had ever
gone before... The sun was not high enough yet to
penetrate the thick foliage overhead.
◊ **penetration** /pɛnɪtreɪʃən/. EG *...the penetration* ◊ N UNCOUNT
of hostile defences.

2 If someone **penetrates** an enemy group or a V+O
rival organization, they succeed in joining it in
order to get information or cause trouble.

penetrating /pɛnɪtreɪtɪŋ/. **1** A **penetrating** ADJ QUALIT
sound is loud and usually high-pitched. EG *...his*
penetrating voice.

2 If someone gives you a **penetrating** look, it ADJ QUALIT
makes you think that they know what you are
thinking. EG *...his penetrating gaze... ...those gentle*
but penetrating brown eyes.

3 Someone who has a **penetrating** mind under- ADJ QUALIT
stands and recognizes things quickly and thoroughly. EG *...a penetrating question.*

pen-friend, pen-friends. A **pen-friend** is some- N COUNT
one, especially a foreigner, who you write letters to
and receive letters from, although the two of you
may never have met.

penguin /ˈpɛŋgwɪn/, **penguins.** A **penguin** is a N COUNT black and white bird found mainly in the Antarctic. Penguins cannot fly.

penicillin /ˌpɛnɪˈsɪlɪn/ is an antibiotic. N UNCOUNT

peninsula /pɪˈnɪnsjələ/, **peninsulas.** A **peninsu-** N COUNT la is an area of land that is almost surrounded by water.

penis /ˈpiːnɪs/, **penises.** A man's **penis** is the part N COUNT of his body that he uses when urinating and when having sex.

penitent /ˈpɛnɪtənt/. Someone who is **penitent** is ADJ QUALIT very sorry for something wrong that they have Literary done. EG We sat silent, penitent for having missed his point.

penitentiary /ˌpɛnɪˈtɛnʃəri/, **penitentiaries.** A N COUNT **penitentiary** is a prison. American

penknife /ˈpɛnnaɪf/, **penknives.** A **penknife** is a N COUNT small knife with a blade that folds back into the handle.

pen name, pen names. A writer's **pen name** is N COUNT the name that he or she uses on books and articles instead of his or her real name.

penniless /ˈpɛnɪlɪs/. Someone who is **penniless** ADJ QUALIT has hardly any money at all.

penny /ˈpɛni/, **pennies** or **pence** /pɛns/. The plural form is **pennies** except for sense 1.2 where it is **pence.**
1 A **penny** is 1.1 a British coin which is worth one N COUNT hundredth of a pound. 1.2 the amount of money which a penny is worth. EG ...a ten pence coin... They only cost a few pence. 1.3 a British coin used before 1971 that was worth one twelfth of a shilling. 1.4 a coin that is worth one cent. American
2 **Penny** is also used in these phrases. 2.1 If you PHRASES say **the penny dropped**, you mean that someone suddenly understood or realized something. EG I detected a sweetish, acrid odour and the penny dropped. Chloroform. 2.2 If you say to someone who has been quiet and thoughtful **'a penny for your thoughts'**, you are asking them to tell you what they are thinking about. 2.3 If you say that Outdated you are going to **spend a penny**, you mean that British you are going to the toilet. 2.4 Things that are said to be **two a penny** or **ten a penny** are very common and easy to get. EG We have fifty men like that – drivers are two a penny.

penny-pinching is the practice of spending very N UNCOUNT little money. EG Good preventive health care means we cannot allow penny-pinching. ▸ used as ▸ ADJ QUALIT an adjective. EG ...penny-pinching miserly old men.

pension /ˈpɛnʃən/, **pensions, pensioning, pen-** N COUNT **sioned.** Someone who has a **pension** regularly receives a sum of money from the state or from a former employer because they have retired or because they are widowed or disabled. EG ...an old age pension... ...a retired judge living on a state pension.

pension off. If someone is **pensioned off**, they PHRASAL VB : are made to retire from work and are given a V+O+ADV, pension. EG We were pensioned off at the age of USU PASS fifty.

pensioner /ˈpɛnʃənə/, **pensioners.** A **pensioner** N COUNT is someone who receives a pension, especially a pension paid by the state to retired people.

pensive /ˈpɛnsɪv/. Someone who is **pensive** is ADJ QUALIT thinking deeply about something. EG Jefferson looked pensive. 'What's wrong?' asked Tyler.
◊ **pensively.** EG He gazed pensively at the water. ◊ ADV

pentathlon /pɛnˈtæθlən/, **pentathlons.** A **pen-** N COUNT **tathlon** is a sports competition in which each person must compete in five different athletic events.

penthouse /ˈpɛnthaʊs/, **penthouses.** A **pent-** N COUNT **house** or a **penthouse** apartment or suite is a OR N MOD luxurious flat or set of rooms at the top of a tall building.

pent-up /pɛnt ʌp/. **Pent-up** emotions or energies ADJ CLASSIF : have been held back and not expressed or re- USU ATTRIB leased. EG ...pent-up frustrations... ...sports in which they can get rid of some of their pent-up energy.

penultimate /pɪˈnʌltɪmət/. The **penultimate** ADJ CLASSIF thing in a series of things is the last but one. EG Formal ...the penultimate paragraph of the letter.

people /ˈpiːpəl/, **peoples, peopling, peopled.** 1 N PLURAL **People** are men, women, and children. EG There were 120 people at the lecture... Talk to the people concerned and see how they feel... The amount of potatoes people buy has dropped... ...young people.
2 When you refer to the **people**, you are referring N PLURAL to ordinary men and women in contrast to the the+N upper classes or the government. EG Power to the people!
3 You sometimes use **people** to refer to the N PLURAL members of a particular group of people. EG He Spoken spoke at length and I think people got rather bored.
4 A **people** is all the men, women, and children of N COUNT a particular country or race. EG ...the beliefs of various peoples across the world.
5 If a place or country is **peopled** by a particular V+O : USU PASS group of people, that group of people live there. EG +by/with ...Istanbul, now peopled by 4 million Turks.

pepper /ˈpɛpə/, **peppers, peppering, peppered.**
1 **Pepper** is a hot-tasting powder which is used to N UNCOUNT flavour food. EG ...pepper and salt.
2 A **pepper** is a hollow red or green vegetable. EG N COUNT OR ...a salad of green peppers. N UNCOUNT
3 If something is **peppered** with small objects, a V+O : USU PASS lot of those objects hit it or are scattered on it. EG I +with felt my fingers being peppered with small, hot fragments.
4 If one thing is **peppered** with other things, it has ADJ PRED a lot of those other things in it. EG His French is +with heavily peppered with Americanisms.

peppermint /ˈpɛpəmɪnt/, **peppermints.** 1 N UNCOUNT **Peppermint** is a strong flavouring that makes your mouth feel cold. EG ...peppermint candy.
2 A **peppermint** is a peppermint-flavoured sweet. N COUNT

pep talk /pɛp tɔːk/, **pep talks.** A **pep talk** is a N COUNT speech which is intended to encourage a group of Informal people to make more effort or to feel more confident.

per /pɜː/. You use **per** to express rates and ratios. PREP For example, if something costs £50 **per** year, you must pay £50 each year for it. If a vehicle is travelling at 40 miles **per** hour, it travels 40 miles each hour. EG The dwellings have more than six people per room... ...an income of less than £1000 per person.

per annum /pɜː ˈænəm/. A particular amount **per** ADV **annum** means that amount each year. EG It costs £125 per annum.

perceive /pəˈsiːv/, **perceives, perceiving, per-** **ceived.** 1 If you **perceive** something, you see, V+O OR notice, or realize it, especially when it is not V+REPORT obvious. EG Many insects can perceive colours that are invisible to us... They failed to perceive that this was what I objected to.
2 If you **perceive** someone or something as doing V+O : OFT+as a particular thing, it is your opinion that they do this thing. EG It is important that the president be perceived as moving the country forward... This theory expresses the truth as I perceive it.

per cent /pəˈsɛnt/. You use **per cent** to talk about PHRASE amounts. For example, if an amount is 10 **per cent** of a larger amount, it is equal to 10 hundredths of the larger amount. EG 45 per cent of Americans were against it... A good tumbler drier can reduce ironing by 80 per cent.

percentage /pəˈsɛntɪdʒ/, **percentages.** A **per-** N COUNT : **centage** is a fraction of an amount expressed as a OFT+of particular number of hundredths of that amount. EG ...areas with a high percentage of immigrants.

What is the penultimate headword on these pages?

perceptible /pəsɛptɪbəºl/. Something that is **per-** ADJ QUALIT
ceptible can only just be seen or noticed. EG *There
was a barely perceptible flicker of light.*

perception /pəsɛpʃəºn/, **perceptions. 1** Someone N UNCOUNT
who has **perception** realizes or notices things that
are not obvious. EG *...a person of extraordinary
perception... This requires a good deal of perception.*

2 A **perception** is an opinion that you have formed N COUNT
as a result of noticing something. EG *...representing
his perceptions through his painting... My perception of her had changed.*

3 Perception is the recognition of things using N UNCOUNT
your senses, especially the sense of sight. EG *...vis-
ual perception... ...the perception of movement.*

perceptive /pəsɛptɪv/. Someone who is **percep-** ADJ QUALIT
tive is good at noticing or realizing things, especially things that are not obvious. EG *...a perceptive
critic... She made a very perceptive comment.*

perch /pɜːtʃ/, **perches, perching, perched. 1** If V+A
you **perch** on a wall or table, you sit on the very
edge of it. EG *Dr Quilty perched on the corner of his
desk... They gathered round the tables or perched
at the bar.* ◊ **perched.** EG *Flora, perched on the* ◊ ADJ PRED
side of the bath, laughed.   +A

2 If you **perch** one thing on another, you put it on V-ERG+A
the top or edge of the other thing, so that it looks as
if it might fall off. EG *He would take out his
spectacles and perch them on the end of his nose...
The building perches precariously within a few
feet of a sudden drop.* ◊ **perched.** EG *...a little* ◊ ADJ PRED
village perched above the lake.   +A

3 When a bird **perches** on a branch or a wall, it V:USU+A
stands there.

4 A **perch** is **4.1** a short rod for a bird to stand on. N COUNT
EG *...a large cage with perches.* **4.2** a high place
where someone is sitting. EG *He climbed all the way
to his favourite perch near the top.*

percolator /pɜːkəleɪtə/, **percolators.** A **percola-** N COUNT
tor is a special piece of equipment for making and
serving coffee.

percussion /pəkʌʃəºn/. The **percussion** in an N SING : the+N,
orchestra or band consists of the instruments that OR N UNCOUNT
are hit, for example drums and cymbals. EG *We had
Dailey on percussion, and Flannery on the clarinet.*
See picture at MUSICAL INSTRUMENTS.

peremptory /pərɛmptəºriʲ/. Someone who does ADJ QUALIT
something in a **peremptory** way does it in a way Formal
that shows that they expect to be obeyed immediately; used showing disapproval. EG *Our conversation was interrupted by a peremptory thudding at
the door.* ◊ **peremptorily.** EG *'Come!' he said* ◊ ADV
peremptorily.

perennial /pɪˈrɛnɪəl/, **perennials. 1** A **perennial** ADJ CLASSIF
situation is one that keeps occurring or that never
ends. EG *...the perennial problems of isolation in old
age... ...a perennial feature of British politics.*

2 A **perennial** is a plant that lives for several N COUNT
years. EG *Garlic is a hardy perennial.*

perfect, perfects, perfecting, perfected; pronounced /pɜːfɪ²kt/ when it is an adjective or a
noun, and /pəfɛkt/ when it is a verb.

1 Something that is **perfect** is as good as it can ADJ CLASSIF
possibly be. EG *She speaks perfect English... This
was the perfect moment to move in... I've got the
perfect solution... ...a perfect example of fair play.*

2 You can use **perfect** to give emphasis to the ADJ CLASSIF :
noun following it. EG *They may be perfect stran-* ATTRIB
*gers... I have a perfect right to be here... It makes
perfect sense... 'Never,' I said with perfect calm.*

3 If you **perfect** something, you improve it so that V+O
it becomes as good as it can possibly be. EG *She
hoped to perfect her technique.*

4 In grammar, the **perfect** tense of a verb in ADJ CLASSIF :
English is the tense that is formed with the present ATTRIB
tense of the auxiliary 'have' and the past participle
of the main verb.

perfection /pəfɛkʃəºn/ is the quality of being N UNCOUNT
perfect. EG *...gardens of incredible perfection...*

...the perfection of its shimmering colours. ● If ● PHRASE
something is done **to perfection**, it is done so well
that it could not be done any better. EG *The dress
fitted her to perfection.*

perfectionist /pəfɛkʃənɪst/, **perfectionists.** N COUNT
Someone who is a **perfectionist** refuses to do or
accept anything that is not perfect.

perfectly /pɜːfɪ²ktºliʲ/. **1** You can use **perfectly** to SUBMOD
emphasize an adjective or adverb. EG *It's a perfect-
ly reasonable question... I'll be perfectly frank with
you... I knew perfectly well it was a trap.*

2 If something is done **perfectly**, it is done so well ADV
that it could not possibly be done better. EG *The
plan worked perfectly... The climate suited Len
perfectly... She understood him perfectly.*

perforated /pɜːfəreɪtɪd/. Something that is **perfo-** ADJ CLASSIF
rated has had a number of small holes made in it.
EG *...a perforated steel plate.*

perforation /pɜːfəreɪʃəºn/, **perforations. Perfo-** N COUNT :
rations are small holes that are made in some- USU PLURAL
thing, especially in paper.

perform /pəfɔːm/, **performs, performing, performed. 1** When you **perform** a task or action, V+O
especially a complicated one, you do it. EG *About
200 heart operations a year are performed at the
Brook Hospital... The ceremony was performed in
nineteen other countries.*

2 If something **performs** a particular service or V+O
function, it does it. EG *Their organization performs
a vital service.*

3 If you **perform** a play, a piece of music, or a V+O OR V
dance, you do it in front of an audience. EG *He
performed for them a dance of his native Samoa...
We had to perform on stage.*

4 If someone or something **performs** well, they V+A
work or function well. If they **perform** badly, they
work or function badly. EG *...the difficulty of finding
a rifle which will perform satisfactorily under
those conditions.*

performance /pəfɔːməns/, **performances. 1** A N COUNT
performance consists of entertaining an audience
by doing something such as singing, dancing, acting a play, or acting a role in a play. EG *I think
Roger Rees gives a remarkable performance...
...an amateur performance of 'Macbeth'... ...excel-
lent performances from both actresses... ...with two
performances on Wednesdays.*

2 Someone's or something's **performance** is how N UNCOUNT :
successful they are. EG *...Britain's poor economic* USU+SUPP
*performance in the 1970's... ...after a disappointing
performance in the 220-yards semi-final.*

3 A car's **performance** is its ability to go fast and N UNCOUNT
accelerate quickly. EG *...high performance cars.*

4 The **performance** of a task or action is the doing N SING : USU+of
of it. EG *...the performance of his Presidential
duties... ...another machine will then repeat the
performance.*

performer /pəfɔːmə/, **performers.** A **performer** N COUNT
is a person who acts, sings, or does other entertainment in front of audiences.

perfume /pɜːfjuːm/, **perfumes.** A **perfume** is **1** a N MASS
pleasant-smelling liquid which you put on your
body to make yourself smell nice. EG *...a bottle of
perfume... ...an expensive perfume.* ◊ **perfumed** ◊ ADJ QUALIT
/pɜːfjuːmd/. EG *...a perfumed towel.* **2** a pleasant N COUNT
smell. EG *The familiar perfumes of wild flowers
filled her nostrils.* ◊ **perfumed.** EG *...the perfumed* ◊ ADJ QUALIT
air.   Literary

perfunctory /pəfʌŋktəºriʲ/. A **perfunctory** ac- ADJ QUALIT
tion is done quickly and carelessly. EG *Max gave his* Formal
wife a perfunctory kiss.

perhaps /pəhæps/. **1** You use **perhaps** to indicate ADV SEN
that you are not sure whether something is true,
correct, possible, or likely to happen. EG *Perhaps
Andrew is right after all... Perhaps I'll come.
Perhaps not... Not many people used to go there,
perhaps because it was on the edge of town...
There are perhaps fifty women here.*

2 You also use **perhaps** to add politeness to a ADV SEN request, an offer, or an opinion. EG *Perhaps I might keep these, for a day or two?... Perhaps I had better explain what we try to do here... I think that's perhaps her finest picture.*

peril /ˈpɛrɪl/, **perils.** 1 A **peril** is a great danger. EG *...the perils of being a fugitive... The arms race is the greatest single peril now facing the world... They placed themselves in great peril by openly opposing him.* N COUNT OR N UNCOUNT Literary

2 If you say that someone does something **at their peril,** you are warning them that they will probably suffer as a result of doing it. EG *You become neglectful at your peril.* PHRASE Literary

perilous /ˈpɛrɪləs/. Something that is **perilous** is very dangerous. EG *The perilous journey was over.* ◊ **perilously** . EG *It came perilously close to destruction... ...stepping perilously near the crate.* ADJ QUALIT Literary ◊ ADV

perimeter /pəˈrɪmɪtə/, **perimeters.** The **perimeter** of an area of land is the whole of its outer edge or boundary. EG *...the perimeter of the clearing... ...dog patrols around the perimeter fence.* N COUNT

period /ˈpɪərɪəd/, **periods.** 1 A particular **period** is a particular length of time. EG *...over a period of several months... ...long periods of rain... ...a short period of time... ...in the Edwardian period.* N COUNT : USU+SUPP

2 At a school or college, a **period** is one of the parts that the day is divided into. EG *There were five periods of French a week.* N COUNT

3 Period costumes, objects, and houses were made at an earlier time in history, or look as if they were made then. EG *...period furniture.* ADJ CLASSIF : ATTRIB

4 A woman's **period** is the bleeding from her womb that happens each month. N COUNT

5 A **period** is also a full stop. N COUNT

periodic /ˌpɪərɪˈɒdɪk/. A **periodic** event or situation happens occasionally, at fairly regular intervals. EG *...periodic droughts.* ADJ CLASSIF : ATTRIB

periodical /ˌpɪərɪˈɒdɪkəl/, **periodicals.** 1 A **periodical** is a magazine, especially a serious or academic one. N COUNT

2 Periodical means the same as periodic. EG *These mood shifts are periodical and recurring.* ◊ **periodically** /ˌpɪərɪˈɒdɪkəliˈ/. EG *We met them periodically during the summer break.* ADJ CLASSIF : ATTRIB ◊ ADV

peripheral /pəˈrɪfərəl/. 1 A **peripheral** thing or part of something is of little importance compared with other things or parts. EG *...the peripheral features of religion.* ADJ QUALIT Formal

2 Peripheral also means on or relating to the edge of an area. EG *This gives greater peripheral vision... ...Russia's peripheral provinces.* ADJ CLASSIF Formal

periphery /pəˈrɪfəriˈ/, **peripheries.** 1 The **periphery** of an area is the edge of it. EG *The cost of land on the periphery of Calcutta went up.* N COUNT : USU the+N Formal

2 The **periphery** of a field of activity is the part of it that is not as important or basic as the main part. EG *...people working on the periphery of education.* N COUNT : USU the+N

periscope /ˈpɛrɪskəʊp/, **periscopes.** A **periscope** is a vertical tube through which people in a submarine can see above the surface of the water. N COUNT

perish /ˈpɛrɪʃ/, **perishes, perishing, perished.** 1 If people or animals **perish,** they die as a result of an accident or as a result of very hard conditions. EG *All the passengers and crew members perished.* v Literary

2 If something **perishes,** it comes to an end or is destroyed for ever. EG *The old religion is perishing.* v Literary

3 If rubber **perishes,** it starts to fall to pieces. v

perishable /ˈpɛrɪʃəbəl/. **Perishable** types of food go bad quite quickly. EG *In the Third World, all perishable food has to be eaten within twenty-four hours.* ADJ QUALIT

perjury /ˈpɜːdʒəriˈ/. If someone who is giving evidence in a court of law commits **perjury,** they lie. EG *She was charged with perjury.* N UNCOUNT Legal

perk /pɜːk/, **perks, perking, perked.** A **perk** is something extra, such as a car, that your employers give you in addition to your salary. EG *There are nice perks too, such as help with your mortgage.* N COUNT Informal

perk up. When someone **perks up,** they become PHRASAL VB : V-ERG+ADV

more cheerful. EG *John was being a misery. He perked up when we got there, though.*

perky /ˈpɜːkiˈ/, **perkier, perkiest.** If someone is **perky,** they are cheerful and lively. ADJ QUALIT

perm /pɜːm/, **perms, perming, permed.** If you have a **perm,** your hair is treated with chemicals and then curled so that the curls last for several months. ▶ used as a verb. EG *She had her hair permed.* N COUNT ▶ V+O : USU PASS

permanent /ˈpɜːmənənt/. 1 Something that is **permanent** lasts for ever or for a very long time. EG *Some drugs taken in large quantities cause permanent brain damage.* ◊ **permanently.** EG *My imprisonment was likely to scar me permanently.* ◊ **permanence** /ˈpɜːmənəns/. EG *People have a need for permanence.* ADJ QUALIT ◊ ADV ◊ N UNCOUNT

2 A **permanent** feature of a situation or place is present all the time. EG *...the only permanent water supply... I began to live in an almost permanent state of fear.* ◊ **permanently.** EG *The doors were kept permanently locked.* ADJ CLASSIF ◊ ADV

permeate /ˈpɜːmɪeɪt/, **permeates, permeating, permeated.** 1 If an idea, feeling, or attitude **permeates** something, it affects every part of it or is present throughout it. EG *...the extent to which secrecy permeates every part of our society.* V+O OR V+through Formal

2 If a liquid, smell, or flavour **permeates** something, it spreads through it. EG *Damp can easily permeate the wood... Dangerous chemicals may permeate through the soil into rivers.* V+O OR V+through Formal

permissible /pəˈmɪsəbəl/. If something is **permissible,** it is allowed by the rules. EG *...the maximum permissible levels of radiation... It was permissible to ask a question.* ADJ CLASSIF Formal

permission /pəˈmɪʃən/. If you are given **permission** to do something, someone says that they will allow you to do it. EG *I have permission to tell you... He refused permission for Biddle to enter Britain... You can't go without permission.* N UNCOUNT

permissive /pəˈmɪsɪv/. A **permissive** society allows things which other people disapprove of, especially freedom in sexual behaviour. EG *...the frequency of divorce within the permissive society.* ◊ **permissiveness.** EG *...sexual permissiveness.* ADJ QUALIT ◊ N UNCOUNT

permit, permits, permitting, permitted; pronounced /pəˈmɪt/ when it is a verb, and /ˈpɜːmɪt/ when it is a noun.

1 If you **permit** something, you allow it. EG *Her father would not permit her to eat sweets... He permitted himself a slight smile... The doctor has permitted him only two meals a day.* V+O OFT+to-INF; ALSO V+O+O Formal

2 If something **permits** a particular thing to happen, it makes it possible for it to happen. EG *Our regulations permit us to get rid of him... Had time permitted, we would have stayed longer... The timetable permits teams only a few weeks for preparation.* V+O OFT+to-INF; ALSO V OR V+O+O Formal

3 A **permit** is an official document which says that you may do something, for example work in a foreign country. EG *She could not get in without a permit... ...work permits.* N COUNT

permutation /ˌpɜːmjuːˈteɪʃən/, **permutations.** A **permutation** is one of the ways in which a number of things can be arranged. EG *You can form any number of permutations out of these symbols.* N COUNT Formal

pernicious /pəˈnɪʃəs/. If you describe something as **pernicious,** you mean that it is very harmful. EG *This had a pernicious influence on countless generations... ...pernicious institutions and teachings.* ADJ QUALIT Literary

pernickety /pəˈnɪkɪtiˈ/. Someone who is **pernickety** worries too much about small, unimportant details. EG *You can't be so pernickety about everything!* ADJ QUALIT Informal

perpendicular /ˌpɜːpənˈdɪkjələ/. Something that is **perpendicular** is tall and points straight up, ADJ CLASSIF Formal

If you commit perjury, do you perpetrate a crime?

rather than being sloping. EG ...*the perpendicular cliff-face*... ...*the supporting perpendicular stones.*

perpetrate /ˈpɜːpɪtreɪt/, **perpetrates**, **perpe-** V+O : USU PASS
trating, **perpetrated**. If someone **perpetrates** a   Formal
crime, they do it. EG ...*a fraud perpetrated by lawyers.* ◊ **perpetrator** /ˈpɜːpɪtreɪtə/, perpetra- ◊ N COUNT
tors. EG ...*the perpetrator of the crime.*

perpetual /pəˈpetjuəl/. A **perpetual** situation or ADJ CLASSIF :
quality never ends or changes. EG *These bats live in*   ATTRIB
deep caves in perpetual darkness... She had me in   Formal
perpetual fear. ◊ **perpetually.** EG *The younger* ◊ ADV
children seemed to be perpetually hungry... She was perpetually answering the doorbell.

perpetuate /pəˈpetjueɪt/,   **perpetuates,** V+O
perpetuating, perpetuated. If someone or some-   Formal
thing **perpetuates** a situation or belief, they cause
it to continue. EG ...*an education system that perpetuates inequality.*

perplexed /pəˈplekst/. If you are **perplexed**, you ADJ QUALIT
do not understand something or you do not know
what to do. EG *For a moment Mr Adams looked perplexed... He said in a perplexed voice: 'Sir?'.*

perplexing /pəˈpleksɪŋ/. If something is **perplex-** ADJ QUALIT
ing, you do not understand it or do not know how to
deal with it. EG ...*a perplexing and difficult problem.*

perplexity /pəˈpleksɪtiˈ/ is the feeling of being N UNCOUNT
perplexed. EG *She looked at us in some perplexity.*

persecute /ˈpɜːsɪkjuːt/, **persecutes, persecuting,** V+O
persecuted. If someone **persecutes** you, they
treat you cruelly and unfairly, usually because they
do not approve of your beliefs. EG *Members of these
sects are ruthlessly persecuted and suppressed.*

persecution /ˌpɜːsɪkjuːˈʃəˈn/, **persecutions.** Per- N UNCOUNT
secution is cruel and unfair treatment of a person   OR N COUNT
or group, usually because other people do not
approve of their beliefs. EG ...*the persecution of minorities.*

persevere /ˌpɜːsɪˈvɪə/, **perseveres, persevering,** V : OFT+*with*
persevered. If you **persevere** with something,
you keep trying to do it and do not give up. EG *Don't
give up - just persevere. You'll win in the end.*
◊ **perseverance** /ˌpɜːsɪˈvɪərəns/. EG *I underestimat-* ◊ N UNCOUNT
ed his perseverance.

persist /pəˈsɪst/, **persists, persisting, persisted.**
1 If something **persists**, especially something un- V
desirable, it continues to exist. EG *Political differences still persist... The pain persisted until the
morning.*
2 If you **persist** in doing something, you continue V : USU+A
to do it, even though it is difficult or other people   ALSO V+QUOTE
are against it. EG *People still persist in thinking that
standards are going down... He persisted with his
policy of conciliation... 'And what,' persisted
Casson, 'is to prevent us?'*

persistent /pəˈsɪstənt/. 1 Something that is **per-** ADJ QUALIT
sistent continues to exist or happen for a long
time. EG *How do you get rid of a persistent nasty
smell?* ◊ **persistently.** EG ...*persistently rattling* ◊ ADV
window frames. ◊ **persistence** /pəˈsɪstəns/. EG ◊ N UNCOUNT
*Because of the persistence of the depression, I saw
my doctor.*
2 Someone who is **persistent** continues trying to ADJ QUALIT
do something, even though it is difficult or other
people are against it. EG *I think you have to be
persistent if people say no to you.* ◊ **persistently.** ◊ ADV
EG ...*policemen who tried persistently to force their
way into his house.* ◊ **persistence.** EG *In the end* ◊ N UNCOUNT
our persistence was rewarded.

person /ˈpɜːsəˈn/, **persons.** The form **persons** is
only used in very formal or legal language, and the
word 'people' is normally used instead to refer to
more than one person: see **people.**
1 A **person** is a man or a woman. EG *There was far* N COUNT
*too much meat for one person... I want to see the
person responsible for accounts... She was a charming person.*
2 You can use **person** in expressions such as 'I'm N COUNT+SUPP
an outdoors person' or 'I'm not a coffee person' Informal

when you are saying whether or not you like a
particular activity or thing.
3 If you do something **in person**, you do it yourself PHRASE
rather than letting someone else do it for you. EG
He wished he had gone to the house in person.
4 If you hear or see someone **in person**, you are PHRASE
present to hear or see them, rather than hearing
them on the radio or seeing them on television. EG
Now I had the chance to hear her speak in person.
5 You use **in the person of** in front of someone's PREP
name when you want to say that they are the thing
you are referring to. EG *We had, in the person of
Susan Smith, an outstanding leader.*
6 In grammar, a **person** is a person in a conversation. The first **person** is the speaker, the second
person is the person being spoken to, and the third
person is another person mentioned in the conversation.

-person, -persons. -person is used instead of SUFFIX
'-man' or '-woman' in words such as 'spokesman' or
'chairwoman' when you want to refer to a person
who does a particular job or activity but you do not
want to indicate their sex. EG *He spoke to CND
chairperson Joan Ruddock.*

personage /ˈpɜːsənɪdʒ/, **personages.** A person- N COUNT
age is a famous or important person. EG ...*a distin-*   Formal
guished personage.

personal /ˈpɜːsəˈnəl/. 1 A **personal** opinion, qual- ADJ CLASSIF :
ity, or thing belongs or relates to a particular   ATTRIB
person rather than to other people. EG *My personal
view is that he should resign... It's a matter of
personal preference... ...his personal belongings.*
2 If you give something your **personal** care or ADJ CLASSIF :
attention, you deal with it yourself rather than   ATTRIB
letting someone else deal with it. EG *The book was
translated from the German under the personal
supervision of the author.*
3 **Personal** matters relate to your feelings, rela- ADJ QUALIT
tionships, and health, which you may find embarrassing. EG ...*the most intimate details of their
personal lives... ...personal problems.*
4 **Personal** comments refer to someone's appear- ADJ QUALIT
ance or character in an offensive way. EG *I think
we're getting too personal.*
5 **Personal** hygiene involves keeping your body ADJ CLASSIF :
clean.   ATTRIB

personal assistant, personal assistants. A N COUNT
personal assistant is a person who does secretarial and administrative work for someone.

personality /ˌpɜːsəˈnælɪˈtiˈ/, **personalities.** 1 N COUNT
Your **personality** is your whole character and +SUPP
nature. EG *He has a wonderful personality... He*   OR N UNCOUNT
*never began to understand her complicated per-
sonality.*
2 You can refer to a famous person, especially in N COUNT
entertainment, broadcasting, or sport, as a **personality.** EG ...*a television personality.*

personalized /ˈpɜːsəˈnəlaɪzd/; also spelled **per-** ADJ CLASSIF
sonalised. Something that is **personalized** 1 has
its owner's initials or name on it. EG ...*personalized
pens.* 2 has been designed specially for one person.
EG ...*a personalized service.*

personally /ˈpɜːsəˈnəliˈ/. 1 You use **personally** to ADV SEN
emphasize that you are giving your own opinion. EG
Well, personally, I feel that this is very difficult.
2 If you do something **personally**, you do it ADV
yourself rather than letting someone else do it. EG
*Since then I have undertaken all the enquiries
personally.*
3 Something that affects you or that applies to you ADV
personally affects you or applies to you rather
than to other people. EG *I wasn't referring to you
personally... It would be unjust for him to bear
personally the great expenses involved.*
4 If you **take** something that someone says **per-** ADV
sonally, you are upset because you think that they
are criticizing you in particular.

personal pronoun, personal pronouns. In N COUNT
grammar, **personal pronouns** refer to people and

things. Personal pronouns are labelled PRON in the Extra Column. See the entry headed PRONOUNS for more information.

personify /pə'sɒnɪfaɪ/, **personifies, personify-** v+o **ing, personified.** If you say that someone **personifies** a particular quality, you mean that they seem to have that quality to a very large degree. EG *He seemed to personify the evil that was in the world.*

personnel /pɜːsə'nel/. The **personnel** of an or- N PLURAL ganization are the people who work for it. EG *We've* Formal *advertised for extra security personnel... ...military personnel... I hadn't got the personnel to cope with it.*

perspective /pə'spektɪv/, **perspectives. 1** A **per-** N COUNT : **spective** is a particular way of thinking about USU+SUPP something, especially one that is influenced by your beliefs or experiences. EG *He wanted to leave the country in order to get a better perspective on things... It was impossible for me to identify with his religious perspective.*

2 If you get something **into perspective**, you judge PHRASE its real importance by considering it in relation to everything else. EG *It will help to put in perspective the vast gulf that separates existing groups.*

3 Perspective is a method by which things in the N UNCOUNT background of a picture are made to look further away than things in the foreground.

perspiration /pɜːspə'reɪʃə⁰n/ is the liquid which N UNCOUNT comes out in drops on the surface of your skin Formal when you are hot or frightened. EG *There were beads of perspiration on his upper lip.*

perspire /pə'spaɪə/, **perspires, perspiring, per-** v **spired.** When you **perspire**, a liquid comes out in Formal drops on the surface of your skin. EG *Hot and perspiring, John toiled up the dusty ascent.*

persuade /pə'sweɪd/, **persuades, persuading, persuaded. 1** If someone or something **persuades** v+o : you to do something, they cause you to do it by USU+to-INF; giving you a good reason for doing it. EG *Marsha* ALSO V+O+A *was trying to persuade Posy to change her mind... ...as the threat of unemployment persuades workers to moderate their pay demands... He is the sort of man that could be persuaded into anything.*

2 If someone **persuades** you that something is v+o OR true, they cause you to believe that it is true, V-REFL : usually by talking to you. EG *We worked hard to* OFT+REPORT *persuade them that we were genuinely interested...* OR of *I had persuaded myself that I could continue like this.* ◇ **persuaded.** EG *Few of them are persuaded* ◇ ADJ PRED *of the benefits of the shop.*

persuasion /pə'sweɪʒə⁰n/, **persuasions. 1 Per-** N UNCOUNT **suasion** is the act of persuading someone to do something or to believe that something is true. EG *They didn't need much persuasion... I had to adopt other methods of persuasion.*

2 If you are of a particular **persuasion**, you have a N COUNT+SUPP particular set of beliefs. EG *...people of different* Formal *political persuasions... ...those who were not of the Roman Catholic persuasion.*

persuasive /pə'sweɪsɪv/. Someone or something ADJ QUALIT that is **persuasive** is likely to persuade someone to believe or do a particular thing. EG *...a very persuasive argument... You were very useful, Jimmie, very persuasive.*

pertain /pə'teɪn/, **pertains, pertaining, per-** v+to **tained.** Something that **pertains** to something else Formal belongs or relates to it. EG *...documents pertaining to the suspects.*

pertinent /'pɜːtɪnənt/. Something that is **perti-** ADJ QUALIT **nent** is relevant to a particular subject. EG *I asked* Formal *him a lot of pertinent questions about the original production.*

perturbed /pə'tɜːbd/. Someone who is **perturbed** ADJ PRED is worried. EG *She was perturbed about a rash* Formal *which had come out on her face.*

peruse /pə'ruːz/, **peruses, perusing, perused.** If v+o you **peruse** a piece of writing, you read it to find Formal out what it says. EG *He took the letter and perused*

it... Having perused its contents, he flung down the paper.

pervade /pə'veɪd/, **pervades, pervading, per-** v+o **vaded.** Something that **pervades** a place or thing Formal is a noticeable feature throughout it. EG *An atmosphere of contentment pervades the school... A strong smell of fish pervaded the coach.*

pervasive /pə'veɪsɪv/. Something that is **perva-** ADJ QUALIT **sive** is present or felt throughout a place or thing. Formal EG *...a pervasive atmosphere of fear... ...the Church's all-pervasive influence.*

perverse /pə'vɜːs/. Someone who is **perverse** ADJ QUALIT deliberately does things that are unreasonable or that will result in harm. EG *It would be perverse to refuse... He takes a perverse delight in irritating people.* ◇ **perversely.** EG *They persisted, perverse-* ◇ ADV *ly, in trying to grow grain.*

perversion /pə'vɜːʃə⁰n/, **perversions. 1** A **per-** N COUNT OR **version** is a sexual desire or action that is consid- N UNCOUNT ered abnormal and unacceptable.

2 The **perversion** of something is the changing of N COUNT OR it so that it is no longer what it should be. EG *...the* N UNCOUNT *systematic perversion of the truth.*

perversity /pə'vɜːsɪ'tiʲ/. Someone who shows **per-** N UNCOUNT **versity** deliberately does things that are unreasonable or that other people do not want them to do. EG *...her perversity as a child... Some perversity in my nature caused me to refuse.*

pervert, perverts, perverting, perverted; pronounced /pə'vɜːt/ when it is a verb, and /'pɜːvɜːt/ when it is a noun.

1 If you **pervert** something, for example a process v+o or society, you interfere with it so that it is not Formal what it used to be or should be. EG *Traditional ceremonies were perverted into meaningless rituals.*

2 A **pervert** is a person whose behaviour, especial- N COUNT ly sexual behaviour, is harmful or disgusting.

perverted /pə'vɜːtɪ²d/. **1** Someone who is **pervert-** ADJ QUALIT **ed** has disgusting behaviour or ideas, especially sexual ones.

2 Something that is **perverted** is wrong, unnatural, ADJ QUALIT or harmful. EG *...the inventions of a perverted imagination... ...a perverted form of love.*

pessimism /'pesɪmɪzə⁰m/ is the belief that bad N UNCOUNT things are going to happen. EG *His pessimism was unjustified.* ◇ **pessimist** /'pesɪmɪst/, **pessimists.** ◇ N COUNT EG *Pessimists tell us that the family is doomed.*

pessimistic /pesɪ'mɪstɪk/. Someone who is **pessi-** ADJ QUALIT **mistic** thinks that bad things are going to happen. EG *Success now seemed very remote and Bernard felt pessimistic... This is too pessimistic a view.* ◇ **pessimistically.** EG *'Well, let's get it over with,'* ◇ ADV *he said pessimistically.*

pest /pest/, **pests. 1** A **pest** is an insect or small N COUNT animal which damages crops or food supplies. EG *Cold kills off lots of diseases and pests in the soil.*

2 You refer to someone, especially a child, as a N COUNT **pest** when they keep bothering you. Informal

pester /'pestə/, **pesters, pestering, pestered.** If v+o : OFT+A you **pester** someone, you keep asking them to do something, or you keep bothering them. EG *Everyone pestered me so much that I gave it up... For years Desiree had been pestering him to take her to Europe.*

pesticide /'pestɪsaɪd/, **pesticides. Pesticides** are N MASS chemicals which farmers put on their crops to kill harmful animals, especially insects.

pet /pet/, **pets, petting, petted. 1** A **pet** is a tame N COUNT animal that you keep in your home to give you company and pleasure. EG *It is against the rules to keep pets... ...his pet dog.*

2 Someone's **pet** theory, project, or subject is one ADJ CLASSIF : that they particularly support or like. EG *We were* ATTRIB *listening to a gardener with his pet theories.*

What is the connection between 'pharmaceuticals' and a 'pharmacist'?

3 If you **pet** a person or animal, you pat or stroke   v+o
them affectionately.

4 If two people, especially a teenage couple, **are**   v
petting, they are kissing and stroking each other.   Informal

petal /petə⁰l/, **petals**. The **petals** of a flower are   N COUNT
the thin coloured or white parts which together
form the flower. EG ...rose petals.

peter /pi:tə/, **peters, petering, petered**. If some-   PHRASAL VB :
thing **peters out**, it gradually comes to an end. EG   V+ADV
The tracks petered out a mile or two later... The
meeting petered out after two hours.

petite /pəti:t/. A woman who is **petite** is small and   ADJ QUALIT
slim. EG ...his petite bride.

petition /pɪ'tɪʃə⁰n/, **petitions, petitioning, peti-**   N COUNT
tioned. **1** A **petition** is **1.1** a document signed by a
lot of people which asks a government or other
official group to do something. EG He presented a
petition signed by 10,357 electors. **1.2** an applica-   Formal
tion to a court of law for some legal action to be
taken. EG She has filed a petition for divorce... The
court ordered him to pay the costs of the petition.

2 If you **petition** someone in authority, you make a   V+O OR V
formal request to them. EG It is my duty to petition   Formal
the court to declare this action illegal.

petrified /petrɪfaɪd/. If you are **petrified**, you are   ADJ QUALIT
extremely frightened. EG If I hadn't been alone I   Informal
wouldn't have been nearly so petrified.

petrol /petrəl/ is a liquid which is used as a fuel   N UNCOUNT
for motor vehicles. EG ...a petrol pump.   British

petroleum /pə'trəʊlɪəm/ is oil which is found   N UNCOUNT
under the surface of the earth or under the sea bed.
Petrol and paraffin are obtained from petroleum.

petrol station, petrol stations. A **petrol sta-**   N COUNT
tion is a garage by the side of the road where   British
petrol is sold and put into vehicles.

petticoat /petɪ'kəʊt/, **petticoats**. A **petticoat** is a   N COUNT
piece of clothing like a thin skirt, which is worn
under a skirt or dress.

petty /petɪ¹/, **pettier, pettiest**. **1 Petty** things are   ADJ QUALIT
small and unimportant. EG But these were petty
details... ...petty problems.

2 If you describe someone's behaviour as **petty**,   ADJ QUALIT
you mean that they care too much about unimpor-
tant things and perhaps that they are unnecessarily unkind. EG ...petty jealousies.

petty cash is money that is kept in the office of a   N UNCOUNT
company, ready to be used for making small
payments when necessary.

petulant /petjə⁰lənt/. Someone who is **petulant** is   ADJ QUALIT
unreasonably angry and upset in a childish way. EG
With a petulant snarl, I pushed the door.
◊ **petulantly**. EG 'Oh, why do you say that?' I cried   ◊ ADV
petulantly.

pew /pju:/, **pews**. A **pew** is a long wooden seat   N COUNT
with a back, which people sit on in church.

pewter /pju:tə/ is a grey metal made by mixing   N UNCOUNT
tin and lead. EG ...pewter plates.

phantom /fæntə⁰m/, **phantoms**. **1** A **phantom** is   N COUNT
a ghost. EG He was staring at her as if she were a   Literary
phantom.

2 You use **phantom** to describe something which   ADJ CLASSIF :
you think you see or hear but which is not real. EG   ATTRIB
...a phantom presence.   Literary

pharmaceutical /fɑːməsjuːtɪkə⁰l/, **pharmaceu-**   ADJ CLASSIF :
ticals. **1 Pharmaceutical** means connected with   ATTRIB
the industrial production of medicines. EG ...the   Formal
world's largest pharmaceutical company.

2 Pharmaceuticals are medicines. EG ...the sale of   N PLURAL
pharmaceuticals.   Formal

pharmacist /fɑːməsɪst/, **pharmacists**. A **phar-**   N COUNT
macist is a person who is qualified to prepare and
sell medicines.

pharmacy /fɑːməsɪ¹/, **pharmacies**. A **pharmacy**   N COUNT
is a shop where medicines are sold.

phase /feɪz/, **phases, phasing, phased**. **1** A   N COUNT :
phase is a particular stage in a process or in the   USU+SUPP
gradual development of something. EG When this
happens, society enters a dangerous phase... ...the
second phase of the Revolution.

2 If you **phase** an action or change over a period of   V+O
time, you cause it to happen in stages. EG The
reduction in nuclear weapons would be phased
over approximately ten years... ...the phased introduction of new technology.

phase in. If you **phase in** something, for exam-   PHRASAL VB :
ple a new way of doing something, you introduce it   V+O+ADV,
gradually. EG ...in the 1970's, when Britain phased in   HAS PASS
the EEC system.

phase out. If you **phase** something **out**, you   PHRASAL VB :
gradually stop using it. EG This type of weapon was   V+O+ADV,
now being finally phased out.   HAS PASS

Ph.D. /pi: eɪtʃ di:/, **Ph.D.s**. A **Ph.D.** is a degree   N COUNT
awarded to people who have done advanced re-
search into a particular subject. **Ph.D.** is an abbreviation for 'Doctor of Philosophy'. EG He's got a
Ph.D. in psychology... ...Jenny Remfrey, Ph.D.

pheasant /fezə⁰nt/, **pheasants**. **Pheasant** can   N COUNT
also be used as the plural form.
A **pheasant** is a long-tailed bird. Pheasants are
often shot as a sport or for eating.

phenomena /fɪ'nɒmɪnə/ is the plural of **phenom-**
enon.

phenomenal /fɪ'nɒmɪnə⁰l/. Something that is   ADJ QUALIT
phenomenal is so great or good that it is very
unusual indeed. EG It was a phenomenal success...
...the phenomenal growth of international trade.
◊ **phenomenally**. EG It's phenomenally expensive.   ◊ SUBMOD

phenomenon /fɪ'nɒmɪnən/, **phenomena**   N COUNT :
/fɪ'nɒmɪnə/. A **phenomenon** is something that is   USU+SUPP
observed to happen or exist. EG ...animals and
plants and other natural phenomena... Is this concern about energy a recent phenomenon?

phew /fju:/ is used to represent the soft whistling   EXCLAM
sound that you make when you breathe out quickly,
for example when you are very hot or when you
are relieved. EG 'Phew,' she said, 'it's hot out.'

philanthropist /fɪlænθrəpɪst/, **philanthropists**.   N COUNT
A **philanthropist** is someone who freely gives
money to people who need it. EG ...wealthy philanthropists... ...the great philanthropists of the past.

philanthropy /fɪlænθrəpɪ¹/ is the giving of money   N UNCOUNT
to people who need it, without wanting anything in
return. EG ...an organization noted for its philanthropy... ...acts of philanthropy or affection.

philistine /fɪlɪstaɪn/, **philistines**. If you call   N COUNT
someone a **philistine**, you mean that they do not
admire or recognize good art, music, or literature.
EG What does a lousy little philistine like you know
about it? ► used as an adjective. EG From Chelsea   ► ADJ QUALIT
he raged at a philistine public.

philosopher /fɪlɒsəfə/, **philosophers**. **1** A **phi-**   N COUNT
losopher is a person who creates or studies theo-
ries about basic things such as the nature of
existence or how people should live. EG ...the Greek
philosopher Thales.

2 If you refer to someone as a **philosopher**, you   N COUNT
mean that they think deeply and seriously about
life and other basic matters.

philosophic /fɪlɒsɒfɪk/ means the same as philo-   ADJ CLASSIF
sophical.

philosophical /fɪlɒsɒfɪkə⁰l/. **1 Philosophical**   ADJ CLASSIF :
means concerned with or relating to philosophy. EG   ATTRIB
They used to have long philosophical conversations... ...philosophical and religious ideas.

2 Someone who is **philosophical** does not get   ADJ QUALIT
upset when disappointing or disturbing things happen; used showing approval. EG He was a placid boy
with a philosophical approach to life.
◊ **philosophically**. EG He accepted their conclu-   ◊ ADV
sion philosophically.

philosophy /fɪlɒsəfɪ¹/, **philosophies**. **1 Philoso-**   N UNCOUNT
phy is the study or creation of theories about basic
things such as the nature of existence or how
people should live. EG ...an expert on Eastern philosophy... ...a series of philosophy lectures.

2 A **philosophy** is **2.1** a particular set of ideas that   N COUNT+SUPP
a philosopher has. EG ...the political philosophies of
the West. **2.2** a particular theory that someone has

PHRASAL VERBS

A phrasal verb (PHRASAL VB) is a combination of two words which has a single meaning. One word is a verb, and the other word is either a preposition or an adverb, such as **in**, **back**, and **down**. So you have phrasal verbs such as **take in**, **take back**, and **take down**. In some cases, you can have both an adverb and a preposition, as in **look forward to** and **get in on**. You will find phrasal verbs at the end of the entries which deal with the verb. So phrasal verbs starting with **take**, such as **take back**, **take down**, **take in**, and so on are explained at the end of the entry for **take**.

Types of phrasal verb

There are a number of common types of phrasal verb:

+ADV means that there is an adverb.

+PREP means that there is a preposition, which of course will always have an object.

+ADV/PREP means that the particle can be used either as an adverb or as a preposition.

v used on its own means that the verb is intransitive.

+o means that the verb is transitive.

These combine to give the following patterns:

V+ADV

The verb is intransitive and is followed by an adverb. For example: *The plane took off two hours late.*

V+PREP

The verb is intransitive and is followed by a prepositional group, as in: *They looked round the Cathedral.*

V+PREP, HAS PASS

The prepositional object can become the subject of a passive clause. For example: *She's looking after her sister's children ... The children were always well looked after.*

V+ADV+PREP

The verb is intransitive and is followed by both an adverb and a prepositional group. The preposition always comes after the adverb: *I began to look forward to their visits.*

V+ADV/PREP

The verb is intransitive and is followed by a word that can be either an adverb or a preposition. For example: *The road to Lutterworth branches off here.* ('off' is an adverb) ... *It branches off the main road.* ('off' is a preposition)

V+O+ADV

The verb is transitive and is followed by an adverb: *Some women choose to stay at home and bring up their children ... The children were brought up by their mother.*

The object can normally come before or after the adverb, unless it is a pronoun, in which case it must come before the adverb. So: *They took him on.*

V+ADV+O

In a small group of verbs, the object always comes after the adverb, except when it is a pronoun. For example: *I am trying to give up smoking.*

V+O+PREP

The verb is transitive and is followed by a prepositional group: *We talked Donald into agreement.*

V+O+ADV+PREP

The verb is transitive and is followed by both an adverb and a prepositional group. The preposition always comes after the adverb, but the object can come before or after the adverb. For example: *She took her unhappiness out on her husband. / She took out her unhappiness on her husband.*

V+O+ADV/PREP

The verb is transitive and is followed by a word that can be either an adverb or a preposition. For example: *I crossed my name off the list ... She crossed her name off.*

V−ERG+ADV

The verb is ergative and is followed by an adverb. So: *The rioters burned down five shops ... The house burned down in a few minutes.*

V−ERG+PREP

The verb is ergative and is followed by a preposition: *The workers' demands centred around pay and conditions ... Much of her teaching is centred around the family situation.*

about how to live or how to deal with a particular situation. EG ...*new philosophies of child rearing.*

phlegm /flɛm/ is the thick yellowish substance N UNCOUNT that develops in your throat and at the back of your nose when you have a cold.

phlegmatic /flɛgmætɪk/. Someone who is **phleg-** ADJ QUALIT **matic** stays calm even when upsetting or exciting Formal things happen. EG *He was a phlegmatic, rather unemotional man.*

phobia /fəʊbɪə/, **phobias.** A **phobia** is an irration- N COUNT al fear or hatred of something. EG *I've got a phobia about spiders.*

phone /fəʊn/, **phones, phoning, phoned. 1** The N SING : the+N **phone** is an electrical system that you use to talk OR by+N to someone else in another place, by dialling a number on a piece of equipment and speaking into it. EG *Most of the work is carried out over the phone... We have heard from her by phone a couple of times... I must go and make a phone call... Could you give me her Frau Doring's phone number?* **2** A **phone** is the piece of equipment that you use N COUNT : when you talk to someone by phone. EG *I'm scared* USU the+N *to answer the phone... The phone rang... She picked up the phone and dialled a number.* **3** When you **phone** someone, you dial their phone V+O OR V number and speak to them by phone. EG *I went back to the motel to phone Jenny... Harland phoned to tell me what time the bus was due.* **4** If you are **on the phone, 4.1** you are speaking to PHRASE someone by phone. EG *I spent an hour on the phone trying to sort things out.* **4.2** you have a phone in your home or place of work, so that you can be contacted by phone. EG *Are you on the phone?*

phone up. When you **phone** someone **up,** you PHRASAL VB : dial their phone number and speak to them by V+O+ADV phone. EG *I must phone her up tonight.* OR V+ADV

phone book, phone books. A **phone book** is a N COUNT book that contains an alphabetical list of the names, addresses, and telephone numbers of the people in a town or area.

phone booth, phone booths. A **phone booth** is 1 N COUNT a place in a station, hotel, or other public building where there is a public telephone. **2** A small shelter American in the street in which there is a public telephone.

phone box, phone boxes. A **phone box** is a small N COUNT shelter in the street in which there is a public British telephone. EG *Every phone box in Selly Oak had been vandalized.*

phone-in, phone-ins. A **phone-in** is a pro- N COUNT gramme on radio or television in which people telephone with questions or opinions and their calls are broadcast. EG ...*a late-night phone-in pro-gramme.*

phonetic /fəˈnɛtɪk/, **phonetics. 1 Phonetics** is N UNCOUNT the study of speech sounds. Technical **2 Phonetic** means relating to the sound of a word ADJ CLASSIF : or to the sounds that are used in languages. EG ATTRIB ...*phonetic spelling.* Technical

phoney /fəʊnɪ/, **phoneys; phonier, phoniest;** ADJ CLASSIF also spelled **phony. 1** Something that is **phoney** is Informal false rather than genuine. EG *He gave a phony name and address.* **2** Someone who is **phoney** is insincere or preten- ADJ QUALIT tious. EG *He thought all grown-ups were phony...* Informal ...*your phoney manners.* ▶ used as a noun. EG *I* ▶ N COUNT *suddenly realized what a phoney he is.*

phosphorescent /fɒsfərɛsənt/. Something that is ADJ CLASSIF **phosphorescent** glows with a soft light but gives Formal out little or no heat. EG ...*a phosphorescent gas.*

photo /fəʊtəʊ/, **photos.** A **photo** is the same as a N COUNT photograph. EG *I took a magnificent photo of him.* Informal

photocopier /fəʊtəˈkɒpɪə/, **photocopiers.** A N COUNT **photocopier** is a machine which quickly copies documents onto paper by photographing them.

photocopy /fəʊtəˈkɒpɪ/, **photocopies, photo-copying, photocopied. 1** A **photocopy** is a copy of N COUNT a document made using a photocopier. EG *We need to make a photocopy to send to staff members.*

2 If you **photocopy** a document, you make a copy V+O of it using a photocopier.

photogenic /fəʊtəˈdʒɛnɪk/. Someone who is ADJ QUALIT **photogenic** looks nice in photographs. EG *Photo-genic girls were sought for a series of adverts.*

photograph /fəʊtəgrɑːf, -græf/, **photographs, photographing, photographed. 1** A **photograph** N COUNT is a picture that is made using a camera. EG *I take photographs of things that interest me... They contacted the police after seeing his photograph in a newspaper.* **2** When you **photograph** someone or something, V+O you use a camera to obtain a picture of them. EG *She photographed the pigeons in Trafalgar Square.*

photographer /fəˈtɒgrəfə/, **photographers.** A N COUNT **photographer** is someone who takes photographs, especially as a job. EG ...*Robert L. Beck, photogra-pher for Life magazine.*

photographic /fəʊtəˈgræfɪk/. **1 Photographic** ADJ CLASSIF : means connected with photographs or photogra- ATTRIB phy. EG ...*expensive photographic equipment.* **2** If you have a **photographic** memory, you are ADJ CLASSIF : able to remember things in great detail after you ATTRIB have seen them.

photography /fəˈtɒgrəfɪ/ is the skill, job, or pro- N UNCOUNT cess of producing photographs. EG *Fox-Talbot was a pioneer of photography.*

Photostat /fəʊtəˈstæt/, **Photostats.** A **Photostat** N COUNT is a particular type of photocopy. EG ...*a photostat of* Trademark *the report.*

phrasal verb /freɪzəl vɜːb/, **phrasal verbs.** A N COUNT **phrasal verb** is a combination of a verb and an adverb or preposition, used together to have a particular meaning. In this dictionary, phrasal verbs have the label PHRASAL VB in the Extra Column. See the entry headed PHRASAL VERBS for more information.

phrase /freɪz/, **phrases, phrasing, phrased. 1** A N COUNT **phrase** is **1.1** a short group of words that people often use as a way of referring to something or saying something, especially a group of words that is memorable or whose meaning is not obvious from the words contained in it. Phrases are la-belled PHRASE in the Extra Column. See the entry headed PHRASES for more information. EG *People still use the phrase 'doctor's orders'... It was Asa Briggs who originally coined the phrase 'redrawing the map of learning'.* **1.2** a small group of words which forms a unit, either on its own or within a sentence. EG *My German was practically nil – a few phrases here and there.* **2** If you **phrase** something in a particular way, you V+O+A express it in words in that way. EG *The moment I'd said it, I could see that I'd phrased it wrong.* **3** A **turn of phrase** is a particular way of express- PHRASE ing something in words. EG *You have a nice turn of phrase.* ● **to coin a phrase:** see **coin.**

phrase book, phrase books. A **phrase book** is a N COUNT book used by people travelling abroad which has lists of useful words and expressions in a foreign language, together with the translation of each word or expression. EG ...*a French phrase book.*

phraseology /freɪzɪˈɒlədʒɪ/. If something is ex- N UNCOUNT pressed using a particular type of **phraseology,** it +SUPP is expressed in words and expressions of that style Formal and type. EG ...*the sort of phraseology used by some journalists.*

physical /fɪzɪkəl/. **1 Physical** qualities, actions, ADJ CLASSIF : or things are connected with a person's body, USU ATTRIB rather than with their mind. EG *All his physical and emotional needs would be attended to... He never used physical punishment on me.* ◊ **physically.** EG ◊ ADV *He looked physically fit... She didn't attract me physically.* **2 Physical** also means **2.1** relating to the struc- ADJ CLASSIF

PHRASES

A phrase is a group of words that you use together. The meaning of the whole phrase is often difficult to guess from the usual meanings of the words. Phrases in the dictionary have the label PHRASE in the Extra Column. The best way to find a phrase in the dictionary is to guess which is the least common word in it, and to look up that word. When all the words seem to be equally common, the phrase will usually be found at either a verb or a noun.

1 Some phrases normally occur at a particular place in the structure of a clause. For example, the phrase **for life** is usually an adjunct. So you say: *He'll be a friend for life.* Whenever possible, the explanation shows you where the phrase is typically used in a clause, and the examples always show this.

2 In many phrases, one or more of the words can inflect, so that the verb can change from present to past or the noun from singular to plural. So that in the phrase **to break your heart**, you can say: *She said that I had broken her heart* or *Their hearts were broken by the news.*

3 Phrases are often followed by a particular grammatical structure. So that you usually '**take delight in** doing something' rather than just 'take delight' or even 'take delight in something'. For example: *She takes a positive delight in being criticized.* The dictionary entry shows the phrase in its typical structure. For example, the dictionary entry for the phrase **turn a deaf ear** says 'If you **turn a deaf ear** to something that someone says, you refuse to pay attention to it'.

---

ture, size, or shape of something that can be touched and seen. EG ...*the physical characteristics of the earth...* ...*the physical size of a computer.* **2.2** connected with physics or the laws of physics. EG ...*basic physical laws.*
3 Physical things can be touched and seen. EG ...*a step towards the replacement of physical money by electronic money...* ...*an opportunity for children to look at the nature of the physical world around them.* ◊ **physically.** EG *Some religions suppose that there is a Heaven physically above the earth.* [ADJ CLASSIF : ATTRIB] [◊ ADV]

physician /fɪˈzɪʃəʰn/, **physicians.** A **physician** is a doctor. EG ...*consultant physicians in geriatric medicine.* [N COUNT American]

physicist /ˈfɪzɪsɪst/, **physicists.** A **physicist** is a person who studies physics. EG ...*a well-known nuclear physicist.* [N COUNT]

physics /ˈfɪzɪks/ is the scientific study of forces and qualities such as heat, light, sound, pressure, gravity, and electricity, and the way that they affect objects. EG *According to our present ideas of physics, nothing can travel faster than light...* ...*nuclear physics.* [N UNCOUNT]

physiology /ˌfɪzɪˈɒlədʒiʲ/. **1 Physiology** is the scientific study of how people's and animals' bodies function, and of how plants function. [N UNCOUNT]
2 The **physiology** of an animal or plant is the way that it functions. EG *He was interested in the physiology of bulls.* ◊ **physiological** /ˌfɪzɪəˈlɒdʒɪkəʰl/. EG ...*physiological changes.* [N SING+POSS] [◊ ADJ CLASSIF]

physiotherapist /ˌfɪzɪəʊˈθerəpɪst/, **physiotherapists.** A **physiotherapist** is a person whose job is doing physiotherapy. [N COUNT]

physiotherapy /ˌfɪzɪəʊˈθerəpiʲ/ is medical treatment which involves doing exercises or having part of your body massaged or warmed. [N UNCOUNT]

physique /fɪˈziːk/, **physiques.** Someone's **physique** is the shape and size of their body; used [N COUNT OR N UNCOUNT]

especially of a man's body. EG ...*a good-looking lad with a fine physique, powerful and attractive.*

pi /paɪ/ is a number, approximately 3.142, which is equal to the circumference of a circle divided by its diameter. It is usually represented by the Greek letter π.

pianist /ˈpɪənɪst/, **pianists.** A **pianist** is a person who plays the piano. [N COUNT]

piano /pɪˈænəʊ/, **pianos.** A **piano** is a large musical instrument with a row of black and white keys. When these keys are pressed down by the player's fingers, little hammers hit wire strings and different notes are played. See picture at MUSICAL INSTRUMENTS. EG *I play the piano.* ● See also **grand piano**. [N COUNT]

pick /pɪk/, **picks, picking, picked. 1** If you **pick** a particular person or thing, you choose that one. EG *Next time let's pick somebody else... I could not have picked a better way to travel.* ● If you **pick and choose**, you carefully choose only things that you really want and reject the others. EG *A good secretary can pick and choose her job.* [V+O] [● PHRASE]
2 If you are told to **take** your **pick**, you can choose any one that you like from a group of things. EG *Take your pick. Choose whichever one of the three methods you fancy.* [PHRASE]
3 When you **pick** flowers, fruit, or leaves, you break them off the plant or tree and collect them. EG ...*the woods where we picked blackberries... How nice of the children to pick her some flowers.* [V+O, V+O+O, OR V+O+for]
4 If you **pick** something from a place, you remove it from there with your fingers or your hand. EG *He picked his blazer off a chair... She picked a cigarette from her box and lit it.* [V+O+A]
5 If you **pick** your nose or teeth, you remove dirt from your nostrils or food from your teeth. EG *He had just had a meal and was picking his teeth.* [V+O]
6 If you **pick** a fight or quarrel with someone, you deliberately cause one. EG *He had ceased to pick quarrels with her.* [V+O: OFT+with]
7 If someone such as a thief **picks** a lock, they [V+O]

open it without a key, for example by using a piece of wire.

8 If you **pick** your **way** across an area, you walk PHRASE across it very carefully in order to avoid obstacles or dangerous things. EG *He began to pick his way over the rocks.*

9 A **pick** is the same as a pickaxe. N COUNT

10 to **pick** someone's **brains**: see **brain**. ● to **pick holes in** something: see **hole**. ● to **pick** someone's **pocket**: see **pocket**. ● See also **hand-picked**.

pick at. If you **pick at** the food that you are PHRASAL VB : eating, you eat only very small amounts of it. EG V+PREP *Laing was picking morosely at his salad.*

pick on. If you **pick on** someone, you criticize PHRASAL VB : them unfairly or treat them unkindly. EG *Why are* V+PREP, *you always picking on me?* HAS PASS Informal

pick out. If you **pick out** someone or something, **1** you recognize them when it is difficult to see PHRASAL VB : them, for example because they are among a large V+O+ADV group. EG *Ralph picked out Jack easily, even at that distance.* **2** you choose them from a group of V+O+ADV people or things. EG *This is the job they picked out for me.*

pick up. **1** When you **pick** something **up**, you lift PHRASAL VB : it up. EG *He stooped down to pick up the two* V+O+ADV *pebbles... The telephone rang and Judy picked it up.* **2** When you **pick up** something or someone V+O+ADV that is waiting to be collected, you go to the place where they are and take them away, often in a car. EG *I might get my brother to come and pick me up.* **3** If someone **is picked up** by the police, they are V+O+ADV, arrested and taken to a police station. EG *I don't* USU PASS *want you to be picked up for drunkenness.* **4** If you V+ADV+O **pick up** something such as a skill or an idea, you Informal acquire it without effort. EG *Did you pick up any Swedish?... I may pick up a couple of useful ideas for my book.* **5** If you **pick up** someone you do not V+O+ADV know, you talk to them and try to start a sexual Informal relationship with them. EG *I doubt whether Tony ever picked up a woman in his life.* **6** If a piece of V+ADV+O equipment, for example a radio or a microphone, **picks up** a signal or sound, it receives it or detects it. EG *It was easier to pick up Radio Luxembourg than the Light Programme.* **7** If trade or the V+ADV economy of a country **picks up**, it improves. EG *The economy is picking up.* **8** When you **pick up** PHRASE **the pieces** after a disaster, you do what you can to get the situation back to normal again. EG *When the confusion dies down, we can try to pick up the pieces.* **9** When a vehicle **picks up speed**, it begins PHRASE to move more quickly. **10** See also **pick-up.**

pickaxe /ˈpɪkæks/, **pickaxes**; spelled **pickax** in N COUNT American English. A **pickaxe** is a tool consisting of a curved, pointed piece of metal with a long handle joined to the middle. Pickaxes are used for breaking up rocks or the ground.

picker /ˈpɪkə/, **pickers**. A fruit **picker** or cotton N COUNT+SUPP **picker** is a person who picks fruit or cotton, usually for money. EG *...strawberry pickers.*

picket /ˈpɪkɪt/, **pickets, picketing, picketed**. **1** V+O OR V When a group of people, usually trade union members, **picket** a place of work, they stand outside it in order to protest about something, to prevent people from going in, or to persuade the workers to join a strike. EG *The plan was to picket docks and power stations.* ◊ **picketing**. EG *...before the mass* ◊ N UNCOUNT *picketing and its consequent mass arrests began.* ▸ used as a noun. EG *...the historic picket at Saltley* ▸ N COUNT *coke depot.* **2 Pickets** are people who are picketing a place of N COUNT work. EG *We could hear the chanting of the pickets.*

picket line, picket lines. A **picket line** is a N COUNT group of pickets outside a place of work. EG *The engineering union have joined them on the picket line.*

pickle /ˈpɪkəl/, **pickles, pickling, pickled**. **1** N COUNT OR **Pickles** are vegetables or fruit, sometimes cut into N UNCOUNT pieces, which have been kept in vinegar or salt

water for a long time so that they have a strong, sharp taste. EG *...a jar of pickles.*
2 When you **pickle** food, you keep it in vinegar or V+O salt water so that it does not go bad and it develops a strong, sharp taste. EG *...pickled herring.*
3 If you are in a **pickle**, you are in a difficult and N SING awkward situation. EG *So how did you get yourself* Informal *in this pickle?*

pickpocket /ˈpɪkpɒkɪt/, **pickpockets**. A **pick-** N COUNT **pocket** is a person who steals things from people's pockets or handbags in public places.

pick-up, pick-ups. A **pick-up** or a **pick-up truck** N COUNT is a small truck with low sides that can be easily loaded and unloaded.

picnic /ˈpɪknɪk/, **picnics, picnicking, picnicked**. N COUNT When people have a **picnic**, they eat a meal out of doors, usually in a field or wood or at the beach. EG *They often went on picnics... We used to take a* ▸ picnic lunch and eat it on the beach.* ▸ used as a ▸ V : USU+A verb. EG *The woods might be full of people picnicking.*

picnicker /ˈpɪknɪkə/, **picnickers**. A **picnicker** is N COUNT someone who is having a picnic.

picture /ˈpɪktʃə/, **pictures, picturing, pictured**. **1** N COUNT A **picture** consists of lines and shapes that are drawn, painted, or printed on a surface and that show a person, thing, or scene. EG *It is the single most important picture Picasso ever painted... Most of my pictures are engravings or screen prints... He picked up a book to look at the pictures.*
2 A **picture** is also **2.1** a photograph. EG *We all had* N COUNT *our pictures taken.* **2.2** an image which you see on a television screen. EG *We have all seen television news pictures of their forces in action.*
3 If someone or something **is pictured** in a V+O : newspaper or magazine, they appear in a photo- USU PASS+A graph in it. EG *Murray was pictured in The Times sharing a platform with Mostyn.*
4 You can also refer to a film as a **picture**. EG *We* N COUNT *worked together in the last picture I made.*
5 If you go to the **pictures**, you go to see a film at a N PLURAL : cinema. EG *She met him at the pictures... Will you* the+N *take me to the pictures?* British
6 If you have a **picture** of something in your mind, N COUNT **6.1** you have an idea or memory of it in your mind as if you were actually seeing it. EG *A picture flashed through Kunta's mind of the panther springing at him.* **6.2** you have an impression or belief about it. EG *They can get quite a distorted picture of what's going on.*
7 If you **picture** something in your mind, you think V+O of it so that you have a clear idea of what it is like. EG *He could picture all too easily the consequences of being caught.*
8 If you give a **picture** of what something is like, N COUNT : you describe it in words or represent it in a film. EG USU SING+SUPP *Mr Hamilton gives a most interesting picture of Monty's family background... You paint a rather bleak picture.*
9 When you refer to the **picture** in a particular N SING : place, you are referring to the situation there. EG *In* USU the+N *Nigeria, the picture appears to be different.*
10 Picture is also used in these phrases. **10.1** If PHRASES you **get the picture**, you understand the situation, Informal especially one which someone is describing to you. EG *I get the picture. You want to keep the whole thing quiet.* **10.2** If you **put** someone **in the picture**, you tell them about a situation which they need to know about. EG *Let me put you in the picture about the situation there.* **10.3** If you say that someone is **in the picture**, you mean that they are involved in the situation that you are talking about. If you say that they are **out of the picture**, you mean that they are not involved in the situation. EG *She hated being out of the picture.*

If you get the picture, do you buy it?

10.4 You use **picture** to describe what someone looks like. For example, if you say that someone is **a picture of** health or **the picture of** misery, you mean that they look extremely healthy or extremely miserable. EG *Vidal was a picture of sophisticated detachment.*

picture rail, picture rails. A **picture rail** is a N COUNT narrow piece of wood which is fixed to the walls of some rooms just below the ceiling. Pictures can be hung from it using string and hooks.

picturesque /pɪktʃəˈresk/. A place that is **pictur-** ADJ QUALIT **esque** is attractive and interesting to look at, usually because it is old and unspoiled. EG *...a small hotel overlooking the picturesque fishing harbour of Zeebrugge.*

piddling /ˈpɪdlɪŋ/ means small or unimportant. EG ADJ CLASSIF: *...piddling little jobs... They gave her a piddling sum* USU ATTRIB *by way of compensation.* Informal

pie /paɪ/, **pies. 1** A **pie** consists of meat, vegeta- N COUNT OR bles, or fruit, which is baked in pastry. EG *...chicken* N UNCOUNT *pie... ...a piece of apple pie.*

2 If you describe an idea, plan, or promise as **pie in** PHRASE **the sky**, you mean that you think that it is very unlikely to happen. EG *Can society really believe in the pie-in-the-sky promises of Professor Grant?*

piece /piːs/, **pieces, piecing, pieced. 1** A **piece** of N PART something is **1.1** a bit or part of it that has been broken off, torn off, or cut off. EG *He came back dragging a great big piece of a tree... ...folded pieces of cloth... She cut the cake and gave me a piece... He tore both letters into small pieces.* **1.2** one of the individual parts or sections which it is made of, especially a part that can be removed. EG *Piece by piece he assembled the rifle... ...like pieces fitting into a jigsaw puzzle.*

2 You use **piece** to refer to an individual object of N PART a particular type. EG *The only piece of clothing she bought was a jumper... ...each piece of furniture... ...the most important piece of apparatus.*

3 You use **piece** to refer to an individual group of N PART facts or an individual action or product. EG *...a valuable piece of information... ...a thoughtful piece of research... ...this piece of advice... ...a piece of music... Meeting Mrs Hooke was a piece of good fortune.*

4 A **piece** is also **4.1** something that is written or N COUNT created, for example an article, play, or short musical composition. EG *...a thoughtful piece about President Roosevelt... It was a classic piece called Forever Is For Us.* **4.2** an object, for example a vase or a table, that is considered valuable or interesting. EG *...a piece from Chippendale's Chinese period.*

5 You can refer to specific coins as **pieces**. For N COUNT+SUPP example, a 10p **piece** is a coin that is worth 10p. EG *The machine wouldn't take 10p pieces... ...a lighter that was no bigger than a 50p piece.*

6 The **pieces** which you use when you play a board N COUNT game such as chess or backgammon are the specially shaped objects which you move around on the board.

7 Piece is also used in these phrases. **7.1** If PHRASES someone or something is still **in one piece** after a dangerous journey or experience, they are safe and not damaged or hurt. **7.2** If something is smashed **to pieces**, is taken **to pieces**, or falls **to pieces**, it is broken or comes apart so that it is in separate pieces. EG *The poster had been ripped to pieces... He took to pieces and reassembled an entire engine.* **7.3** If you **go to pieces**, you are so Informal upset or nervous that you lose control of yourself and cannot do what you should do. EG *He did not go to pieces as I feared he might.* **7.4** If someone Informal **tears** you **to pieces** or **pulls** your work **to pieces**, they criticize you or your work very severely. **7.5** **bits and pieces**: see **bit.** ● **a piece of cake**: see **cake.** ● **to pick up the pieces**: see **pick up.**

piece together. 1 If you **piece together** the PHRASAL VB: truth about something, you gradually discover it. EG V+O+ADV

She had not yet been able to piece together exactly what had happened. **2** If you **piece** something V+O+ADV **together**, you gradually make it by joining several things or parts together. EG *She pieced together the torn-up drawing.*

piecemeal /ˈpiːsmiːl/. A **piecemeal** change or ADJ CLASSIF OR process happens gradually, usually at irregular ADV AFTER VB intervals. EG *...the piecemeal accumulation of land... Films are financed piecemeal; the distributor doles out money little by little.*

piecework /ˈpiːswɜːk/. If you do **piecework**, you N UNCOUNT are paid according to the amount of work that you do rather than the length of time that you work.

pier /pɪə/, **piers.** A **pier** is a large structure which N COUNT sticks out into the sea at a seaside town and which people can walk along.

pierce /pɪəs/, **pierces, piercing, pierced.** If a V+O OR V+A sharp object **pierces** something or if you **pierce** something with a sharp object, the object goes into it and makes a hole in it. EG *When the snake's fangs pierce its victim's flesh, the venom is injected... The pointed end of the stick pierced through its throat into its mouth.*

pierced /pɪəst/. A **pierced** object has had holes ADJ CLASSIF made in it deliberately. EG *...pierced wooden screens... ...pierced ears.*

piercing /ˈpɪəsɪŋ/. **1** A **piercing** sound or voice is ADJ QUALIT high-pitched and very sharp and clear in an unpleasant way. EG *I was jolted out of my exhaustion by piercing screams.*

2 If someone's eyes are **piercing**, they are bright ADJ QUALIT and seem to look at you very intensely. EG *He had piercing blue eyes.*

3 A **piercing** wind makes you feel very cold. ADJ QUALIT

piety /ˈpaɪəti/ is strong religious belief, or reli- N UNCOUNT gious behaviour. EG *...men of true piety.*

piffling /ˈpɪflɪŋ/. Something that is **piffling** is ADJ QUALIT small or unimportant, and ridiculous. EG *The steps* Informal *taken are so piffling in the face of the enormity of the problem.*

pig /pɪg/, **pigs. 1** A **pig** is a pink or black animal N COUNT with short legs and not much hair on its skin. Pigs are often kept on farms for their meat.

2 If you call someone a **pig**, you mean that you N COUNT think they are unpleasant in some way, especially Informal that they are greedy or unkind; an offensive use.

3 If you **make a pig of** yourself, you eat a great PHRASE deal; used showing disapproval. Informal

pigeon /ˈpɪdʒɪn/, **pigeons.** A **pigeon** is a bird, N COUNT usually grey in colour, which has a fat body. Pigeons often live in towns.

pigeon-hole, pigeon-holes. A **pigeon-hole** is one N COUNT of the sections in a frame on a wall where letters and messages can be left for someone. EG *Howard strolled over to the rows of pigeon-holes to collect his mail.*

piggyback /ˈpɪgibæk/, **piggybacks.** If you give N COUNT someone a **piggyback**, you carry them high on your back, supporting them under their knees.

piggybank /ˈpɪgibæŋk/, **piggybanks.** A N COUNT **piggybank** is a small container shaped like a pig, with a slot in it to put coins in. Children use piggybanks to save money in.

pig-headed. Someone who is **pig-headed** refuses ADJ QUALIT to change their mind about things; used showing disapproval. EG *...sheer pig-headed determination.*

piglet /ˈpɪglɪt/, **piglets.** A **piglet** is a young pig. N COUNT

pigment /ˈpɪgmənt/, **pigments.** A **pigment** is a N COUNT OR substance that gives something a particular colour. N UNCOUNT EG *It forms part of the red pigment of blood.* Formal

pigsty /ˈpɪgstaɪ/, **pigsties. 1** A **pigsty** is a hut with N COUNT a yard where pigs are kept on a farm.

2 If you describe a room or a house as a **pigsty**, N COUNT you mean that it is very dirty and untidy. Informal

pigtail /ˈpɪgteɪl/, **pigtails.** A **pigtail** is a length of N COUNT hair that has been divided into three and then plaited. EG *...a girl with a blonde pigtail down her back.*

pilchard /ˈpɪltʃəd/, **pilchards.** A **pilchard** is a N COUNT small fish that lives in the sea. EG ...*tins of pilchards.*

pile /paɪl/, **piles, piling, piled.** 1 A **pile** of things N PART is **1.1** a quantity of them which form a mass that is high in the middle and has sloping sides. EG *There in front of me was a great pile of old tin cans... ...a pile of sand.* **1.2** a quantity of them which have been put neatly somewhere so that each thing is on top of the one below. EG *He lifted a pile of books from the bedside table.*

2 If you **pile** a quantity of things somewhere, you V+O+A put them there so that they form a pile. EG *Brody picked up the heap of papers and piled them on top of a radiator... Her hair was piled high on her head.*

3 If a surface **is piled** with a quantity of things, it is V+O : USU PASS covered with piles of them. EG *His desk was piled* +with *with papers.*

4 If you talk about **piles** of something or a **pile** of N PART something, you mean a large amount of it. EG *He's* Informal *got an enormous pile of money stashed away.*

5 If a group of people **pile** into or out of a vehicle, V+A they all get into it or out of it in a rather disorganized way. EG *The troops piled into the coaches.*

6 Piles are painful swellings that appear in the N PLURAL veins inside a person's anus.

7 The **pile** of a carpet or of a fabric such as velvet N UNCOUNT is its soft surface, which consists of lots of little threads standing on end. EG *...a luxurious deep pile carpet.*

pile up. 1 If you **pile up** a quantity of things or if PHRASAL VB : they **pile up**, you put them somewhere or they V-ERG+ADV collect somewhere, forming a pile. EG *All her possessions were piled up there... The papers she was meant to be reading piled up untouched on her desk.* **2** If things **pile up** or if someone **piles** them V-ERG+ADV **up**, more and more of them happen or are acquired. EG *All these disasters piled up on the unfortunate villagers... Last year the company piled up losses totalling £4 billion.*

pile-up, pile-ups. A **pile-up** is a road accident in N COUNT which several vehicles crash into each other. EG *There had been a twenty-car pile-up on the M1.*

pilgrim /ˈpɪlgrɪm/, **pilgrims.** A **pilgrim** is a per- N COUNT son who makes a journey to a holy place for a religious reason.

pilgrimage /ˈpɪlgrɪmɪdʒ/, **pilgrimages.** A **pil-** N COUNT OR **grimage** is a journey that someone makes to a N UNCOUNT holy place for a religious reason. EG *She made the pilgrimage to Lourdes... ...a place of pilgrimage.*

pill /pɪl/, **pills.** 1 A **pill** is a small, round mass of N COUNT medicine that you swallow without chewing. EG *I took a sleeping pill.*

2 The **pill** is a type of pill that some women take N SING : the+N regularly so that they do not become pregnant. EG *I'm not on the pill.*

pillage /ˈpɪlɪdʒ/, **pillages, pillaging, pillaged.** N UNCOUNT **Pillage** is the stealing of property in a violent way, Outdated usually by a group of people. ▶ used as a verb. EG ▶ V+O *They pillaged and looted every house in the village.*

pillar /ˈpɪlə/, **pillars.** 1 A **pillar** is a tall, narrow, N COUNT solid structure, which is usually used to support part of a building. EG *I fell asleep leaning against a pillar on someone's porch.*

2 If you describe someone as a **pillar** of a group N COUNT : that they belong to, you mean that they are an USU+of active and important member of it. EG *I thought you had to be a pillar of the community to foster children... ...pillars of society.*

pillar box, pillar boxes. A **pillar box** is a tall red N COUNT cylinder with a narrow hole in it where you can put British letters to be collected by a postman. Pillar boxes are found in streets.

pillion /ˈpɪljən/. When you ride **pillion** on a motor- ADV AFTER VB cycle, you sit behind the person who is controlling it.

pilloried /ˈpɪlərid/. If someone **is pilloried**, they V-PASS are criticized severely, especially in newspapers or Formal on radio and television. EG *He was pilloried and his resignation demanded.*

pillow /ˈpɪləʊ/, **pillows.** A **pillow** is a rectangular N COUNT cushion which you rest your head on when you are in bed.

pillowcase /ˈpɪləʊkeɪs/, **pillowcases.** A **pillow-** N COUNT **case** is a cover for a pillow, which can be removed and washed.

pillowslip /ˈpɪləʊslɪp/, **pillowslips.** A **pillowslip** is N COUNT the same as a pillowcase.

pilot /ˈpaɪlət/, **pilots, piloting, piloted.** 1 A **pilot** is N COUNT a person who is trained to fly an aircraft. EG *...an experienced pilot.*

2 When someone **pilots** an aircraft, they act as its V+O pilot. EG *...a jolly man who piloted his own airplane.*

3 If you **pilot** a new law or scheme, you try to V+O introduce it. EG *He was keen to see through the Bill which John Silkin was piloting.*

4 A **pilot** scheme or study is used to test whether a ADJ CLASSIF : particular scheme or product will be successful, ATTRIB before it is introduced on a large scale. EG *This year we are trying a pilot scheme whereby the university leases one or two houses for students.*

pilot light, pilot lights. A **pilot light** is a small N COUNT gas flame in a cooker, boiler, or fire which burns all the time and which lights the main large flame when the gas is turned fully on.

pimp /pɪmp/, **pimps.** A **pimp** is a man who N COUNT controls prostitutes, gets clients for them, and Informal takes a large part of their earnings.

pimple /ˈpɪmpəl/, **pimples.** A **pimple** is a small N COUNT red spot, especially one on your face.

pimply /ˈpɪmpli/. Someone who is **pimply** has a ADJ QUALIT lot of pimples, especially on their face. EG *He was an ugly, pimply little boy.*

pin /pɪn/, **pins, pinning, pinned.** 1 A **pin** is a very N COUNT small, thin rod of metal with a point at one end. Pins can be stuck through things, for example through two pieces of cloth, in order to fasten them together. ● See also **drawing pin, safety pin**.

pins

pin

safety pin

drawing pin

2 If you **pin** something somewhere, you fasten it V+O+A there with a pin, a drawing pin, or a safety pin. EG *She wore a white rose pinned to her blouse.*

3 If someone **pins** you in a particular position, they V+O+A hold you or press down on you firmly so that you cannot move. EG *His strong arms were around me, pinning me down.*

4 If someone **pins** the blame for something on you, V+O+on/upon they say, often unfairly, that you did it or caused it. Informal EG *You can't pin that on me.*

5 If you **pin** your hopes on something, you hope V+O+on/upon very much that it will produce the result you want, because it is the only thing that is likely to. EG *He pinned his hopes on the prospect of a split in the opposition party.*

pin down. 1 If you try to **pin down** something PHRASAL VB :

If someone's face is pinched, has someone else pinched it?

which is hard to describe, you try to say exactly v+o+ADV
what it is or what it is like. EG *The courts have
found obscenity impossible to pin down as a punishable offence.* **2** If you **pin** someone **down**, you v+o+ADV
force them to make a definite statement, which
they have been trying to avoid doing. EG *He was
anxious to pin the Minister down to some definite
commitment.*

pin up. **1** If you **pin up** a poster or a notice, you PHRASAL VB:
pin it to a wall so that it can be seen easily. EG *The* v+o+ADV
*map was pinned up and became the centre of
attention.* **2** If you **pin up** part of a piece of v+o+ADV
clothing, you pin the bottom of it to a higher part of
it. EG *The hem was pinned up.* **3** See also **pin-up**.

pinafore /pɪnəfɔː/, **pinafores.** A **pinafore** or a N COUNT
pinafore dress is a dress with no sleeves, which a
woman or girl wears over a blouse or sweater.

pincer /pɪnsə/, **pincers.** **1 Pincers** are a tool N PLURAL
consisting of two pieces of metal that are hinged in
the middle. Pincers are used for gripping things or
for pulling things out. See picture at TOOLS. EG *...a
pair of pincers.*
2 The **pincers** of a crab or a lobster are its front N COUNT :
claws. USU PLURAL

pinch /pɪntʃ/, **pinches, pinching, pinched.** **1** If v+o
you **pinch** someone, you squeeze a part of their
body between your thumb and first finger. EG *Dr.
Hochstadt pinched Judy's cheek as she passed.*
▸ used as a noun. EG *She gave my wrist a little* ▸ N COUNT
pinch.
2 A **pinch** of something is the amount of it that you N PART
can hold between your thumb and your first finger.
EG *Season with salt and a pinch of cinnamon.* ● to
take something **with a pinch of salt**: see **salt**.
3 If someone **pinches** something, they steal it. EG *I* v+o
pinched fourpence from the box. Informal
4 At a pinch means if absolutely necessary and if PHRASE
there is no alternative. EG *At a pinch the new* Informal
doctor would do.
5 If you **are feeling the pinch**, you do not have as PHRASE
much money as you used to, and so you cannot buy
things you would like to buy. EG *The big fashion
establishments have been feeling the pinch lately.*

pinched /pɪntʃt/. If someone's face is **pinched**, it ADJ QUALIT
looks thin and pale, usually because they are ill or
cold. EG *He lay on his bed, looking pinched and
worn.*

pincushion /pɪnkʊʃən/, **pincushions.** A **pin-** N COUNT
cushion is a very small cushion that you stick pins
and needles into so that you can get them easily
when you need them.

pine /paɪn/, **pines, pining, pined.** **1** A **pine** or a N COUNT
pine tree is a tall evergreen tree which has long,
thin, sharp leaves and a fresh smell.
2 Pine is the pale-coloured wood of pine trees, N UNCOUNT
which is often used for making furniture. EG *...sit-
ting at the pine table.*
3 If you **are pining** for something, you want it very v+*for*
much and feel sad because you cannot have it. EG OR *to*-INF :
Most of them were pining to be recognized and USU CONT
admitted as citizens... Helen pines for you.

pine away. If someone **pines away**, they gradu- PHRASAL VB :
ally become weaker and die because they are very v+ADV
unhappy. EG *I believe she actually pined away – lost
her will to live.*

pineapple /paɪnæpəl/, **pineapples.** A **pineapple** N COUNT OR
is a large oval fruit that grows in hot countries. It is N UNCOUNT
sweet, juicy, and yellow inside and has a thick,
brownish skin. EG *...a slice of pineapple.*

ping /pɪŋ/, **pings, pinging, pinged.** If a bell or a v
piece of metal **pings**, it makes a short, high-
pitched noise. EG *The bell pings; the lift doors open.*
▸ used as a noun. EG *There is a loud ping from the* ▸ N COUNT
alarm clock.

ping-pong /pɪŋ pɒŋ/ is the game of table tennis. N UNCOUNT

pink /pɪŋk/, **pinker, pinkest; pinks.** **1** Something ADJ COLOUR
that is **pink** is of a colour between red and white.
EG *...the white and pink blossom of orchard apples...*

*...brilliant reds and pinks and oranges... The bath-
room was decorated in pink.*
2 If you go **pink**, your face turns a slightly redder ADJ COLOUR
colour than usual because you are embarrassed or
angry, or because you are doing something energetic. EG *He went very pink, and looked away.*
3 Pinks are small plants that people grow in their N COUNT
gardens. Pinks have sweet-smelling pink, white, or
red flowers.

pinkish /pɪŋkɪʃ/ means slightly pink in colour. EG ADJ COLOUR
...a faint pinkish glow.

pinnacle /pɪnəkəl/, **pinnacles.** **1** A **pinnacle** is a N COUNT
pointed cone-shaped piece of stone or rock. EG *...the
pinnacles of St John's Church... ...the white pinnacles of the distant mountains.*
2 The **pinnacle** of something is the best or highest N COUNT :
level of it. EG *These newspapers were regarded as* USU SING+*of*
*the pinnacle of journalism... The civil service was
the pinnacle of his employment hopes.*

pinpoint /pɪnpɔɪnt/, **pinpoints, pinpointing, pinpointed.** **1** If you **pinpoint** something, you discov- v+o
er or explain exactly what it is. EG *You can pinpoint
any danger and we can deal with it... In their book,
Jackson and Marsden pinpointed the difference.*
2 If you **pinpoint** the position of something, you v+o
discover or show its exact position. EG *'Just here,'
he said, pinpointing it on the map.*

pins and needles. If you get **pins and needles** N PLURAL
in part of your body, you feel sharp tingling pains
there for a while because it has been in an
awkward or uncomfortable position.

pin-stripe. Pin-stripe cloth or **pin-striped** cloth ADJ CLASSIF :
has very narrow vertical stripes. EG *He wore a pin-* ATTRIB
*stripe suit... ...a black jacket and pin-striped trou-
sers.*

pint /paɪnt/, **pints.** **1** A **pint** is **1.1** in Britain, a unit N PART
of measurement for liquids that is equal to one-
eighth of an imperial gallon or 568 cubic centimetres. EG *...one pint of milk.* **1.2** in America, a unit of
measurement for liquids that is equal to one-eighth
of an American gallon or 473 cubic centimetres.
2 If you have a **pint** in a pub, you have a pint of N COUNT
beer. EG *He likes having a couple of pints with his
lunch.*

pin-up, pin-ups. A **pin-up** is a picture of an N COUNT
attractive woman or man. EG *The bathroom wall
was plastered with pin-ups of film stars.* ▸ used as ▸ ADJ CLASSIF :
an adjective. EG *...pin-up girls.* ATTRIB

pioneer /paɪənɪə/, **pioneers, pioneering, pioneered.** **1** Someone who is referred to as a **pio-** N COUNT
neer in a particular area of activity is one of the
first people to be involved in it and develop it. EG
He was a pioneer of photography.
2 Someone who **pioneers** a new activity, invention, v+o
or process is one of the first people to do it. EG *...a
hospital which pioneered open heart surgery in
this country.* ◇ **pioneering.** EG *...a pioneering and* ◇ ADJ CLASSIF :
innovative banker. ATTRIB
3 A **pioneer** is also one of the first people to live or N COUNT
farm in a particular place. EG *They all went out as
pioneers, with little or nothing.*

pious /paɪəs/. Someone who is **pious** is very ADJ QUALIT
religious and moral. EG *Mrs Smith was a very pious
woman who attended Church services regularly.*

pip /pɪp/, **pips, pipping, pipped.** **1** A **pip** is one of N COUNT
the small hard seeds in a fruit such as an apple,
orange, or pear.
2 The **pips** on the radio are a series of short, high- N COUNT
pitched sounds that are used as a time signal.
3 If you **pip** someone **at the post**, you just beat PHRASE
them in a competition or in a race to achieve Informal
something.

pipe /paɪp/, **pipes, piping, piped.** **1** A **pipe** is a N COUNT
long, round, hollow object, usually made of metal
or plastic, through which a liquid or gas can flow.
EG *...hot water pipes.*
2 To **pipe** a liquid or gas somewhere means to v+o : USU+A
transfer it from one place to another through a
pipe. EG *Hot water is piped to all the rooms.*

pipe

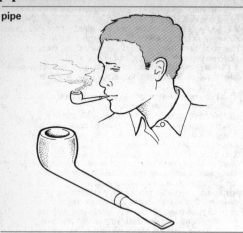

3 A **pipe** is also an object which is used for N COUNT smoking tobacco. You put the tobacco into the cup-shaped part at the end of the pipe, light it, and breathe in the smoke through a narrow tube. EG *He was sitting in his armchair, smoking a pipe and reading the paper.*

4 Pipes are the same as bagpipes. N PLURAL

5 If someone **pipes** something, they say it in a V+O OR high-pitched voice. EG *'It's for you,' he piped, wav-* V+QUOTE *ing a purple envelope.* Written

6 See also **piping, piping hot.**

piped music is music which is played through N UNCOUNT loudspeakers in some supermarkets, restaurants, and other public places.

pipe dream, pipe dreams. A **pipe dream** is a N COUNT hope or plan that you have which you know will never really happen. EG *He considered such hopes to be pipe dreams.*

pipeline /ˈpaɪplaɪn/, **pipelines. 1** A **pipeline** is a N COUNT large pipe which is used for carrying oil or gas over a long distance, often underground.

2 If you say that something is **in the pipeline**, you PHRASE mean that it is already planned or begun and will be completed soon. EG *More improvements were in the pipeline.*

piper /ˈpaɪpə/, **pipers.** A **piper** is a musician who N COUNT plays the bagpipes.

piping /ˈpaɪpɪŋ/. **1 Piping** is metal, plastic, or N UNCOUNT another substance made in the shape of a pipe or tube. EG *...a length of steel piping.*

2 If someone speaks in a **piping** voice, they speak ADJ CLASSIF: in a high-pitched voice. EG *In a piping voice she* ATTRIB *ordered me to sit down.* Written

piping hot. Food or water that is **piping hot** is ADJ CLASSIF very hot. EG *...mugs of piping hot coffee.*

piquant /ˈpiːkənt, -kɑːnt/. **1** Food that is **piquant** ADJ QUALIT has a pleasantly spicy taste. EG *...piquant crab soup* Formal *with chilli.* ◊ **piquancy** /ˈpiːkənsɪ/. EG *...using* ◊ N UNCOUNT *herbs or spices to give variety and piquancy.*

2 Something that is **piquant** is interesting and ADJ QUALIT exciting. EG *...a piquant face with large appealing* Formal *dark-blue eyes.* ◊ **piquancy.** EG *Argument adds* ◊ N UNCOUNT *piquancy to the contest.*

pique /piːk/ is the feeling of anger and resentment N UNCOUNT that you have when your pride is hurt. EG *He withdrew from the contest in a fit of pique.*

piqued /piːkt/. If someone is **piqued**, they are ADJ QUALIT angry and resentful because their pride has been hurt.

piracy /ˈpaɪrəsɪ/. **1 Piracy** was robbery carried N UNCOUNT out by pirates.

2 You can also refer to the illegal copying of things N UNCOUNT: such as video tapes and computer programs as USU+SUPP **piracy.** EG *...software piracy.*

piranha /pɪˈrɑːnə/, **piranhas.** A **piranha** is a N COUNT small, fierce fish from South America.

pirate /ˈpaɪrət/, **pirates, pirating, pirated. 1** N COUNT **Pirates** were sailors who attacked other ships and stole property from them.

2 Someone who **pirates** video tapes, cassettes, V+O books, or computer programs copies and sells them when they have no right to do so. ◊ **pirated.** ◊ ADJ CLASSIF EG *There were a lot of pirated editions.*

3 Pirate is used to describe illegal copies of things. ADJ CLASSIF: EG *...pirate videos.* ATTRIB

pirouette /ˌpɪruˈet/, **pirouettes.** In ballet, a **pirou-** N COUNT **ette** is a fast turn of the dancer's body which is done on the toes or on the ball of the foot.

piss /pɪs/, **pisses, pissing, pissed**; a very infor- Informal mal, rude word which many speakers avoid using.

1 To **piss** means to urinate. V

2 If someone has a **piss**, they urinate. N SING: *a*+N

3 Piss is urine. N UNCOUNT

piss down. If it **is pissing down**, it is raining PHRASAL VB: hard. V+ADV

piss off. If someone tells a person to **piss off**, PHRASAL VB: they are telling the person in a rude way to go V+ADV, away. USU IMPER

pissed /pɪst/; a very informal, rude word. Some- ADJ PRED one who is **pissed** is drunk. Informal

pissed off; a very informal, rude word. If someone ADJ PRED is **pissed off** with something, they feel bored and Informal irritated by it.

pistol /ˈpɪstəl/, **pistols.** A **pistol** is a small gun N COUNT that you hold in your hand.

piston /ˈpɪstən/, **pistons.** A **piston** is a cylinder or N COUNT metal disc that is part of an engine. Pistons slide up and down inside tubes and cause various parts of the engine to move.

pit /pɪt/, **pits, pitting, pitted. 1** A **pit** is **1.1** a large N COUNT hole that is dug in the ground. EG *The pit was stacked with ammunition.* **1.2** a small, shallow hole in the surface of something. EG *...scratches and pits on the enamel.*

2 A **pit** is also a coal mine. EG *...the men coming* N COUNT *home from the pit.*

3 A gravel **pit** or clay **pit** is a very large hole that N COUNT+SUPP is left where gravel or clay has been dug from the ground.

4 If you have a feeling in **the pit of your stomach**, PHRASE you have a physical feeling inside your body at the front, usually because you are afraid or anxious. EG *...the ache in the pit of her stomach.*

5 In motor racing, the **pits** are the areas at the side N PLURAL: of the track where drivers stop for refuelling and *the*+N repairs during races.

6 If you describe someone or something as **the** PHRASE **pits**, you mean that they are the worst of their Informal kind. EG *That first week is the pits, isn't it?*

7 If you **pit** your **wits against** someone, you PHRASE compete with them in a test of knowledge or intelligence.

8 See also **pitted.**

pitch /pɪtʃ/, **pitches, pitching, pitched. 1** A foot- N COUNT: ball **pitch**, hockey **pitch**, or cricket **pitch** is an USU+SUPP area of ground that is marked out and used for playing that particular game.

2 If you **pitch** something somewhere, you throw it V+O: USU+A with quite a lot of force, usually aiming it carefully. EG *He was pitching a penny at a crack in the sidewalk.*

3 If someone or something **pitches** somewhere, V+A they fall forwards suddenly and with a lot of force. EG *He suddenly pitched headlong to the ground.*

4 If someone **is pitched** into a new situation, they V+O: USU+A are suddenly forced into it. EG *This pitched him into the political arena.*

5 The **pitch** of a sound is its degree of highness or N UNCOUNT lowness. EG *Her voice dropped to a lower pitch.*

Is 'pitiless' the opposite of 'pitiful'?

6 If something reaches a high **pitch**, it reaches a high level or degree. EG *Excitement about the wedding is now at fever pitch... Her frustration mounted to such a pitch of anger that she could no longer keep silent.* N SING: USU+SUPP

7 If you **pitch** something at a particular level or degree of difficulty, you set it at that level. EG *Her lectures are pitched directly at the level of the students.* V+O+A

8 When you **pitch** a tent, you put it into an upright position using the poles and fix it securely to the ground. EG *They pitched their tents at the edge of the field.* V+O

pitch in. If you **pitch in**, you join in an activity. EG *They will be expected to pitch in and make their own beds.* PHRASAL VB: V+ADV Informal

pitch-black. If a place or the night is **pitch-black** or **pitch-dark**, it is completely dark. EG *We started off through the pitch-black woods.* ADJ CLASSIF

pitched battle, pitched battles. A **pitched battle** is a very fierce and violent fight. EG *Police fought a pitched battle with about 40 youths.* N COUNT

pitcher /pɪtʃə/, **pitchers.** **1** A **pitcher** is a jug. EG *...a pitcher of water.* N COUNT American

2 In baseball, the **pitcher** is the person who throws the ball to the person who is batting. N COUNT

pitchfork /pɪtʃfɔːk/, **pitchforks.** A **pitchfork** is a large fork with a long handle and two prongs that is used for lifting hay or grass. N COUNT

piteous /pɪtɪəs/. Something that is **piteous** is so sad that you feel great pity for the person involved. EG *There were piteous sounds of suffering and pain.* ADJ QUALIT Literary

pitfall /pɪtfɔːl/, **pitfalls.** The **pitfalls** involved in doing something are the ways in which you might fail or be harmed, or the things you might do wrong. EG *...the pitfalls of pursuing such a drastic policy... We must bear in mind the pitfalls and try to avoid them.* N COUNT: USU PLURAL

pith /pɪθ/. The **pith** of an orange, lemon, or other citrus fruit is the white substance between the peel and the inside of the fruit. N UNCOUNT

pithy /pɪθi/. A **pithy** comment or piece of writing is short, direct, sensible, and memorable. EG *...her brisk, pithy, ironic observations... ...pithy working-class humour.* ADJ QUALIT

pitiable /pɪtɪəbəl/. Someone who is **pitiable** is in such a sad or weak situation that you feel pity for them. EG *She was in a pitiable plight.* ADJ QUALIT

pitiful /pɪtɪful/. Someone or something that is **pitiful** is so sad, weak, or small that you feel pity for the person involved. EG *...his thin, bony legs and his pitiful arms... ...the pitiful sound of a human being in pain.* ◊ **pitifully.** EG *He looks pitifully thin.* ◊ ADV ADJ QUALIT

pitiless /pɪtɪlɪs/. Someone or something that is **pitiless** shows no feelings of pity or mercy. EG *His face was cool and pitiless... ...enduring the pitiless rain upon their bare backs.* ADJ CLASSIF

pittance /pɪtəns/. If you receive a **pittance**, you receive only a very small amount of money. EG *They are tired of working for a pittance.* N SING: a+N

pitted /pɪtɪd/. If the surface of something is **pitted**, it is covered with a lot of small, shallow holes. EG *The walls were pitted with bullet holes... His face was pitted and unshaven.* ADJ CLASSIF

pity /pɪti/, **pities, pitying, pitied.** **1** If you feel **pity** for someone, you feel very sorry for them. N UNCOUNT

2 If you **pity** someone, you feel very sorry for them. EG *She pitied him with her whole heart... I know how horrible it is to be pitied.* V+O

3 If you say that it is a **pity** that something is the case, you mean that you feel disappointed about it. EG *It will be a terrible pity if this should happen... Pity you missed that film last night.* N SING: a+N

4 If you add **more's the pity** to a comment, you are expressing your disappointment or regret about something. EG *'I didn't write that letter.' – 'More's the pity. If you had, you might have a job now.'* ADV SEN

5 If you **take pity on** someone, you feel sorry for PHRASE

them and help them. EG *A man who spoke English took pity on us and it was all sorted out.*

pivot /pɪvət/, **pivots, pivoting, pivoted.** **1** A **pivot** is the pin or the central point on which something balances or turns. EG *The compass needle swung round on its pivot.* N COUNT

2 If something **pivots**, it balances or turns on a central point. EG *Michael stopped, pivoted and walked back in.* V

3 The **pivot** in a situation is the most important thing which everything else is based on or arranged around. EG *We were important, essential, the pivot of their lives.* N COUNT

pizza /piːtsə/, **pizzas.** A **pizza** is a flat, round piece of dough covered with tomatoes, cheese, and other kinds of food, and then baked in an oven. N COUNT OR N UNCOUNT

placard /plækɑːd/, **placards.** A **placard** is a large notice that is carried in a march or demonstration or is displayed in a public place. EG *...placards which declared 'Troops off Campus Now!'* N COUNT

placate /pləkeɪt/, **placates, placating, placated.** If you **placate** someone, you try to stop them feeling angry or resentful by doing or saying things that will please them. EG *...the desire of politicians to placate the public.* V+O

place /pleɪs/, **places, placing, placed.** **1** A **place** is any point, building, area, town, or country. EG *The cellar was a very dark place... ...photographs of places taken during his travels abroad... Do you know a place called The Farmer's Inn?... ...a meeting place... Please give your name, address, age, place of birth, and religion... We were looking for a good place to camp... Of course it was no place to raise a child... The saloon, I decided, was the place for me.* N COUNT: OFT+SUPP

2 You can refer to the position where something was, or where it should be, as its **place**. EG *She put the book back in its place on the shelf... Don't park your car in the wrong place.* N COUNT+SUPP

3 If something is **in place**, it is in its correct or usual position. If it is **out of place**, it is not in its correct or usual position. EG *He held the handle in place while the glue set... Jane screwed the grille back into place... She was slightly out of breath but not one hair was out of place.* PHRASE

4 If things are **all over the place**, they are in many different places. EG *We have shops in Paris, New York and all over the place... There were clothes and old shoes all over the place.* PHRASE

5 Place can be used after 'any', 'no', 'some', or 'every' to mean 'anywhere', 'nowhere', 'somewhere', or 'everywhere'. EG *You are not going any place... He had no place else to go.* N SING American Informal

6 Your **place** is the house, flat, or room where you live. EG *Could I stay at your place for a bit, Rob?... What sort of place do they have?* N COUNT: USU+POSS Informal

7 Your **place** at a table, in a classroom, or in a hotel, for example, is a space, seat, or room that is intended for you to use or that you normally use. EG *I had a place reserved at the Youth Hostel in Stockholm... I took my place in class... Mrs Kaul had to leave her place and go to the back of the room.* N COUNT: USU+POSS

8 A **place** at a table is also a space with a knife, fork, and other things arranged on it, so that one person can sit down and eat. EG *Every day 12 places are laid for dinner.* N COUNT

9 If you have a **place** on a committee or at a college, for example, you are a member of the committee or are accepted by the college as a student. EG *I got a place at a teachers' training college... ...university places.* N COUNT

10 Someone's or something's **place** in a society, system, or situation, is their position or role in relation to other people or things. EG *Britain's place in the world... Frank felt it was not his place to raise any objection... The demonstration occupies a central place in their political campaign...* N COUNT+SUPP

One day we shall change places, and you will stay at home and I shall go to work.

11 Your **place** in a competition or on a scale is N COUNT your position at the end of the competition or on the scale. First place is the winning or top position. EG *She took first place in the Crafts Fair... The US leapt from sixth place to second.*

12 A good **place** to do something in a situation or N COUNT : activity is a good time or stage at which to do it. EG USU SING+SUPP *This could be a very good place to start... This is not the place for a detailed description of his problems.*

13 Your **place** in a book or speech is the point that N COUNT+POSS you have reached in reading or speaking it. EG *Her finger was pressed to the page as if marking her place... He lost his place in his notes.*

14 If you cannot understand something complicat- PHRASE ed and then everything **falls into place**, you suddenly understand how the different parts of it are connected and it becomes clearer. EG *...the incident on the bus, the police searches – it all fell into place.*

15 You say **in the first place** when you are PHRASE talking about the beginning of a situation or about the situation as it was before a series of events. EG *Nobody can remember what was agreed in the first place... How did she become interested in the French Revolution in the first place?*

16 You say **in the first place** and **in the second** ADV SEN **place** to introduce the first and second in a series of points or reasons. EG *...information that, in the first place, would have been very difficult for me to obtain and, in the second place, would have been useless anyhow.*

17 When something **takes place**, it happens. EG PHRASE *The next attack took place four hours later... The talks will take place in Vienna... Profound political changes have been taking place in the country.*

18 If you **place** something somewhere, you put it V+O+A there neatly or carefully. EG *She placed the music on the piano and sat down... Chairs had been placed in rows all down the room.*

19 If you **place** a person or thing in a particular V+O+A state, you cause them to be in it. EG *The agreement was not placed at risk... Chamberlain placed the Cabinet in a difficult situation.*

20 If you **place** responsibility, pressure, blame, or a V+O+on/upon restriction on someone, you make them have it or be affected by it. EG *The responsibility placed upon us is too heavy to bear... Renewed pressure will be placed on the Government this week... Vita is placing most of the blame on her mother.*

21 If you **place** emphasis on something, you em- V+O+on/upon phasize it. EG *The New Left placed much emphasis on the role of culture.*

22 If you **place** an order for goods or an advert in a V+O newspaper, for example, you ask a company to send you the goods or you ask the newspaper to publish the advert.

23 If you recognize someone but you cannot **place** V+O them, you cannot remember exactly who they are or where you have met them before. EG *She was looking at me as if she could not quite place me.*

24 If you say how many decimal **places** there are N COUNT in a number, you are saying how many numbers there are to the right of the decimal point.

25 Place is also used in these phrases. **25.1** If one PHRASES thing is used **in place of** another, or if it **takes the place of** the other thing, it replaces the other thing. EG *This task is carried out by robots in place of human workers... Armed soldiers were soon to take the place of diplomats.* **25.2** If you **put** some- one **in** their **place**, you show them that they are less important or clever than they think they are. EG *I decided to put this upstart politely in his place.* **25.3** If someone or something is **out of place** in a situation, they are unsuitable or do not fit easily into it. EG *I never overcame the sense of being out*

of place, of being an outsider... The degree of detail seems out of place in a book so limited on scope.

placed /pleɪst/. If someone is well **placed**, they ADJ PRED have more advantages or resources than other people. EG *How well are we placed with regard to America?... As for finance, we're better placed than people think.*

placement /pleɪsmənt/, **placements. 1** The N UNCOUNT **placement** of something is the act of putting it in a +SUPP particular place. EG *I spent a week directing the placement of the boulders.*

2 If someone gets a **placement**, they get a job for a N COUNT period of time which will give them experience in the work they are training for. EG *Amongst other placements, he spent some months at the Chil- dren's Hospital.*

placid /plæsɪd/. **1** Someone who is **placid** is calm ADJ QUALIT and does not easily become excited, angry, or upset. EG *He was a placid boy with a philosophical approach to life.*

2 A **placid** place is calm and peaceful. EG *...the ADJ QUALIT placid harbour waters.*

plagiarism /pleɪdʒərɪzəm/ is the practice of N UNCOUNT using or copying someone else's idea or work and pretending that you thought of it or created it. EG *It was a shameless piece of plagiarism.*

plague /pleɪg/, **plagues, plaguing, plagued. 1** A N COUNT OR **plague** is a very infectious disease that spreads N UNCOUNT quickly and kills large numbers of people.

2 A **plague** of unpleasant things is a large number N COUNT+of of them that arrive or happen at the same time. EG *...a plague of locusts.*

3 If unpleasant things **plague** you, they keep V+O happening and cause you a lot of trouble or suffer- ing. EG *The system is plagued by technical faults... He suffered severe back injuries, which plague him to this day.*

4 If you **plague** someone, you keep bothering them V+O : or asking them for something. EG *The readers were* OFT+with *urged to plague their MP with letters of protest.*

5 If you say that you **avoid** someone or something PHRASE **like the plague**, you are emphasizing that you deliberately avoid them completely.

plaice /pleɪs/. **Plaice** is both the singular and the N COUNT OR plural form. A **plaice** is a kind of flat fish. EG *Cod,* N UNCOUNT *haddock, and plaice are excellent all-purpose fish.*

plain /pleɪn/, **plains; plainer, plainest. 1** A **plain** N COUNT is a large, flat area of land with very few trees on it. EG *...vast plains covered in yellow grasses.*

2 A **plain** object or surface is entirely in one colour ADJ CLASSIF and has no pattern, design, or writing on it. EG *Put it* ATTRIB *in a plain envelope.*

3 Plain things are very simple in style. EG *She felt* ADJ QUALIT *ashamed of her plain dress... I enjoy good plain food; nothing fancy.*

4 If a fact or situation is **plain**, it is easy to ADJ QUALIT : recognize or understand. EG *It was plain that Eddie* USU PRED *wanted to get back to sleep... Their difficulty is plain.*

5 Plain statements are direct and easy to under- ADJ QUALIT stand. EG *...a plain statement of fact.*

6 You can use **plain** before a noun or an adjective ADJ CLASSIF : in order to emphasize it. EG *Petty is the wrong* ATTRIB *word. It's plain meanness... Logical judgment can* OR SUBMOD *also be just plain wrong.*

7 A woman or girl who is **plain** is not at all ADJ QUALIT beautiful. EG *...a plain plump girl with pigtails.*

8 plain sailing: see **sailing**.

plain-clothes. Plain-clothes police officers are ADJ CLASSIF : wearing ordinary clothes instead of a uniform. EG ATTRIB *Lebel ordered a plain-clothes detective to check into the hotel.*

plainly /pleɪnlɪ/. **1** If you say that something is ADV SEN **plainly** the case, you mean that it is obviously the case. EG *He was plainly angry.*

> Find two words on these pages which are pronounced in the same way.

2 If you can see, hear, or smell something **plainly**, ADV
you can see, hear, or smell it easily. EG *You could
see the oysters quite plainly, lying all over the seabed.*

3 If you say something **plainly**, you say it in a way ADV
that is easy to understand and cannot be mistaken.

plaintiff /ˈpleɪntɪf/, **plaintiffs.** A **plaintiff** is a N COUNT
person who brings a legal case against someone in Legal
a court of law.

plaintive /ˈpleɪntɪv/. A **plaintive** sound or voice is ADJ QUALIT
sad and high-pitched. EG *...a plaintive wail.*

plait /plæt/, **plaits, plaiting, plaited. 1** If you V+O : USU PASS
plait three or more lengths of hair or rope togeth-
er, you twist them over and under each other to
make one thick length. EG *Her thick brown hair
was plaited in a single braid down her back... ...long
ropes of plaited rushes.*

2 A **plait** is a length of hair or rope that has been N COUNT
plaited. EG *...her long gold plaits, each tied with a
red ribbon.*

plan /plæn/, **plans, planning, planned. 1** A **plan** N COUNT
is a method of achieving something that you have
worked out in detail beforehand. EG *I told them of
my plan... ...a plan to give women more power...
...her plan for union reform.*

2 If you **plan** what you are going to do, you decide V+O OR V+*for*
in detail what you are going to do. EG *At breakfast I
planned my day... We must plan for the future.*

3 If you **plan** to do something, you intend to do it. V+*to*-INF
EG *What do you plan to do after college?... I was* OR V+O
planning a career in law. ◊ **planned.** EG *...news of* ◊ ADJ CLASSIF
the planned sale of 50,000 acres of state forests.

4 If you have **plans**, you are intending to do a N PLURAL
particular thing. EG *The gales forced him to change
his plans... He was making plans to sell his house.*

5 When you **plan** something that you are going to V+O
make, build, or create, you decide what the main
parts of it will be and how they will be arranged. EG
*How do you plan a book?... ...the art of planning
gardens.*

6 A **plan** is also **6.1** a list or diagram of the main N COUNT
parts that are going to be included in something,
for example in a piece of writing. EG *...a plan of a
story.* **6.2** the shape and design of a garden, building, or group of buildings. EG *...the plan and overall
design of the building.* **6.3** a detailed drawing that
shows what each floor of a building looks like from
above. EG *Make a neat plan of your new home.*

7 A **plan of action** or a **plan of campaign** is a PHRASE
series of actions that you have decided to take in
order to achieve something. EG *His plan of campaign is to cycle into town and collect the money
personally.*

8 If something happens **according to plan**, it PHRASE
happens in the way that it was intended to happen.
EG *The whole thing was going according to plan.*

9 See also **planning**.

plan on. If you **plan on** doing something, you PHRASAL VB :
intend to do it. EG *I plan on staying in London for* V+PREP,
the foreseeable future. HAS PASS

plan out. If you **plan out** what you are going to PHRASAL VB :
do, you decide in detail what you are going to do. EG V+O+ADV
I hadn't even planned out the route yet.

plane /pleɪn/, **planes, planing, planed. 1** A N COUNT
plane is a vehicle with wings and one or more OR *by*+N
engines, which can fly through the air. EG *We went
by plane... We bought the cigarettes on the plane.*

2 A **plane** is also a flat surface. EG *...an elaborate* N COUNT
structure of coloured planes. Technical

3 You can refer to a particular level of something N COUNT+SUPP
as a particular **plane**. EG *She tried to lift the* Literary
*conversation onto a more elevated plane... Such
poetry belongs to another class, another plane of
sensitivity.*

4 A **plane** is also a tool that has a flat bottom with N COUNT
a sharp blade in it. You move the plane over a
piece of wood in order to remove thin pieces of its
surface.

5 If you **plane** a piece of wood, you make it smaller V+O
or smoother by using a plane.

planet /ˈplænɪt/, **planets.** A **planet** is a large, N COUNT
round object in space that moves around a star.
The Earth is a planet. EG *They have the capacity to
kill every human being on the planet... ...the orbit
of the planet Mars.*

planetarium /ˌplænɪˈteəriəm/, **planetariums.** A N COUNT
planetarium is a building where lights are shone
on the ceiling to represent the planets and the
stars and to show how they appear to move.

planetary /ˈplænɪtəri/ means relating to or be- ADJ CLASSIF :
longing to planets. EG *...the planetary exploration* ATTRIB
programme.

plank /plæŋk/, **planks.** A **plank** is a long rectan- N COUNT
gular piece of wood.

planner /ˈplænə/, **planners. 1** The **planners** in N COUNT :
local government are the people who decide how USU PLURAL
land should be used and what new buildings should
be built. EG *...architects and planners.*

2 A **planner** is a person who works out in detail N COUNT
what is going to be done in the future. EG *...TV
programme planners.*

planning /ˈplænɪŋ/. **1 Planning** is the process of N UNCOUNT
deciding in detail how to do something before you
actually start to do it. EG *The project is still in the
planning stage.* ● See also **family planning**.

2 Planning is also control by the local government N UNCOUNT
of the way that land is used in an area and of what
new buildings are built there. EG *...the concrete
deserts created by modern planning at its worst.*

plant /plɑːnt/, **plants, planting, planted. 1** A N COUNT
plant is a living thing that grows in the earth and
has a stem, leaves, and roots. EG *...alpine herbs and
plants... ...a tall banana plant... ...plant pots.*

2 When you **plant** a seed, plant, or young tree, you V+O
put it into the ground so that it will grow there. EG *I
spent weeks planting potatoes one spring... Each
autumn we planted primroses in the garden.*

3 When someone **plants** land with a particular V+O :
type of plant or crop, they put plants or seeds into USU+*with*
the land to grow them there. EG *...small front
gardens planted with rose trees.*

4 A **plant** is also a factory or a place where power N COUNT
is generated. EG *...the re-opening of a nuclear plant
after an accident.*

5 Plant is large machinery that is used in indus- N UNCOUNT
trial processes. EG *The company plans to spend* Technical
nearly £1 billion on new plant and equipment.

6 If you **plant** something somewhere, you put it V+O+A
there firmly. EG *I planted my deckchair beside
hers... 'Hello,' he said, planting a kiss on her cheek.*

7 If someone **plants** something such as a bomb V+O : USU+A
somewhere, they hide it in the place where they
want it to function. EG *They had planted the bomb
beneath the house... I haven't planted a microphone in your desk.*

8 If you **plant** something such as a weapon or V+O : USU+A
drugs on someone, you put it amongst their belongings or in their house or office so that they will be
wrongly accused of a crime. EG *I'm convinced the
evidence was planted in John's flat.*

9 If an organization **plants** an informer or a spy V+O : USU+A
somewhere, they send that person there so that
they can do something secretly. EG *The CIA had
planted its agents in all the strategic areas.*

plant out. When you **plant out** young plants, you PHRASAL VB :
plant them in the ground in the place where they V+O+ADV
are to be left to grow. EG *We had to rear it in a
nursery and plant it out.*

plantation /plɑːnˈteɪʃ⁰n/, **plantations.** A **planta-** N COUNT
tion is **1** a large piece of land, especially in a
tropical country, where crops such as cotton, tea,
or sugar are grown. EG *...rubber plantations.* **2** a
large number of trees that have been planted
together. EG *...conifer plantations.*

planter /ˈplɑːntə/, **planters.** A **planter** is a person N COUNT+SUPP
who owns or manages a plantation in a tropical
country. EG *...Indian tea planters.*

plaque /plæk, plɑːk/, plaques. 1 A **plaque** is a flat N COUNT piece of metal, wood, or stone, which is fixed to a wall or monument in memory of a famous person or event. EG ...*a memorial plaque at the crematorium... A plaque marks the site of Chippendale's workshops.*

2 Plaque is a substance that forms on the surface N UNCOUNT of your teeth. It consists of saliva, bacteria, and food.

plasma /plæzmə/ is the clear fluid part of blood N UNCOUNT which contains the corpuscles and cells.

plaster /plɑːstə/, plasters, plastering, plastered. 1 **Plaster** is a smooth paste made of sand, N UNCOUNT lime, and water which dries and forms a hard layer. Plaster is used to cover walls and ceilings inside buildings. EG *The walls were in a dreadful condition – the plaster was peeling off.*

2 If you **plaster** a wall or ceiling, you cover it with V+O a layer of plaster. EG ...*a wall that was poorly plastered.*

3 A **plaster** is a strip of sticky material used for N COUNT covering small cuts or sores on your body. EG *I dabbed the cut and applied a plaster.*

4 If you have a leg or arm **in plaster**, you have a PHRASE cast made of plaster of Paris around your leg or arm, in order to protect a broken bone and allow it to mend. EG ...*a fractured ankle encased in plaster.*

5 See also **plastered**.

plaster cast, plaster casts. A **plaster cast** is a N COUNT case made of plaster of Paris, which is used for protecting broken bones by keeping part of the body stiff and rigid.

plastered /plɑːstəd/. 1 If something is **plastered** ADJ PRED+to to a surface, it is sticking to the surface. EG *His wet hair was plastered to his forehead.*

2 If something is **plastered** with a sticky sub- ADJ PRED stance, it is covered with the substance. EG *Her* +with *back was thickly plastered with suntan oil.*

3 If a surface is **plastered** with posters or notices, ADJ PRED it is covered with them. EG *The walls of his tiny* +with *shop were plastered with pictures of actors and actresses.*

4 If someone is **plastered**, they are very drunk. EG ADJ PRED *You can't go and get plastered before church!* Informal

plaster of Paris /plɑːstər əv pærɪs/ is a type of N UNCOUNT plaster made from white powder and water which dries quickly and is used to make plaster casts.

plastic /plæstɪk/, plastics. **Plastic** is a material N UNCOUNT which is produced by a chemical process and OR N COUNT which is used to make many objects. It is light in weight and does not break easily. EG *The roofs are covered in winter by sheets of plastic... What's special about this new type of plastic?* ▸ used as an ▸ ADJ CLASSIF adjective. EG *Village potters become redundant as cheap plastic bowls and buckets flood the market... ...a plastic bag... The plastic seating was uncomfortable.*

Plasticine /plæstɪsiːn/ is a soft coloured sub- N UNCOUNT stance like clay which children use for making Trademark little models.

plastic surgery is the practice of performing N UNCOUNT operations to repair or replace skin which has been damaged, or to improve people's appearance by changing features of their body. EG *One of the survivors needed plastic surgery.*

plate /pleɪt/, plates, plating, plated. 1 A **plate** is N COUNT 1.1 a round or oval flat dish that is used to hold food. EG *The dirty plates have been stacked in a pile on the kitchen table... He looked at the food on his plate... ...plates of sandwiches.* 1.2 a flat sheet of metal, especially on machinery or a building. EG *We got into the cellar through a round hole covered by a metal plate.* 1.3 a small flat piece of metal with someone's name written on it, which you usually find beside the front door of an office or house. EG *I read her name on the polished brass plate.* ● See also **number plate**.

2 Plate is dishes, bowls, and cups that are made of N UNCOUNT precious metal, especially silver, gold, or pewter.

EG *We would prefer church plate and other treasures to be stored in bank vaults.*

3 Metal that **is plated** is covered with a thin layer V+O : USU PASS of a precious metal such as gold or silver. ▸ used as ▸ ADJ CLASSIF an adjective. EG ...*gold-plated brooches.*

4 A **plate** in a book is a picture or photograph N COUNT which takes up a whole page and is usually printed on better quality paper than the rest of the book.

5 A dental **plate** is a piece of plastic which is N COUNT shaped to fit inside a person's mouth and which a set of false teeth is attached to.

6 If you **have a lot on** your **plate**, you have a lot of PHRASE work to do or a lot of things to deal with. EG *I know* Informal *you've got a lot on your plate – so take it easy.*

7 If something **is handed** to you **on a plate**, you PHRASE get it very easily. EG *She got handed the job on a plate.*

plateau /plætəʊ/, plateaus or plateaux. 1 A N COUNT **plateau** is a large area of high and fairly flat land.

2 If you say that an activity or process has reached N COUNT a **plateau**, you mean that it has reached a stage where there is no further change or development. EG *In the seventies the US space programme seemed to have reached a plateau of development.*

plate glass is thick glass made in large, flat N UNCOUNT pieces, which is used especially to make large windows and doors. EG ...*a new plate-glass window.*

platform /plætfɔːm/, platforms. 1 A **platform** is N COUNT 1.1 a flat structure, usually made of wood, which people stand on when they make speeches or give a performance. EG *The speaker mounted the platform.* 1.2 a flat raised structure or area, usually one which something can stand on or land on. EG ...*helicopter landing platforms... ...loading platforms.*

2 A **platform** in a railway station is the area N COUNT beside the rails where you wait for or get off a train. EG *Jordache paced nervously up and down the platform.*

3 You can say that someone has a **platform** when N COUNT : they have an opportunity to tell people what they USU+SUPP think or want. EG *It provides a platform for the consumer's viewpoint.*

4 The **platform** of a political party is what they N COUNT+SUPP say they will do if they are elected. EG *He campaigned on a socialist platform.*

5 In a bus, the **platform** is the area of floor at the N SING : the+N front or back where you get on and off.

platinum /plætɪnəm/. 1 **Platinum** is a very valu- N UNCOUNT able, silvery-grey metal. It is often used for making jewellery.

2 Platinum hair is very fair, almost white. EG ...*a* ADJ COLOUR *platinum blonde.*

platitude /plætɪtjuːd/, platitudes. A **platitude** is N COUNT a statement which is considered boring and mean- Formal ingless because it has been made many times before in similar situations. EG ...*empty platitudes about democracy.*

platonic /plətɒnɪk/. **Platonic** relationships or ADJ CLASSIF feelings of affection do not involve sex. EG *Her interest in him was entirely platonic.*

platoon /plətuːn/, platoons. A **platoon** is a small N COLL group of soldiers which is commanded by a lieutenant. EG *In his platoon he had thirty-two men.*

platter /plætə/, platters. A **platter** is a large, flat N COUNT plate used for serving food. EG *There were five* Outdated *kinds of cheese on a wooden platter.*

plausible /plɔːzəbəl/. An explanation or state- ADJ QUALIT ment that is **plausible** seems likely to be true or valid. EG *Such a theory seems very plausible... ...a plausible answer.*

play /pleɪ/, plays, playing, played. 1 When chil- V : USU+A dren **play**, they spend time with their toys or taking part in games. EG *The kids went off to play* on the swings... I played with the children all day... Her grandchildren enjoy playing with her old toys.

2 When you **play** a sport, game, or match, you take part in it. EG *I played squash three times a week... Do you play chess?... I used to play for the village cricket team.* v+o or v

3 When one person or team **plays** another, they compete against them in a sport or game. EG *Did you see McEnroe playing Connors the other day?* v+o or V+against

4 If you **play** a joke or a trick on someone, you deceive them or give them a surprise in a way that you think is funny, but that often causes problems for them or annoys them. EG *I presumed someone was playing a rather silly joke.* v+o

5 You can use **play** to say how someone behaves, when they are deliberately behaving in a certain way. For example, if someone **plays** safe, they do not take any risks. If they **play** the innocent, they pretend to be innocent. EG *They would play it cool if they saw the boys again... Don't you play the wise old professor with me, Franz... This year we're playing host to the New Sussex Opera.* v+o+c or V+c Informal

6 A **play** is a piece of writing which is performed in a theatre, on the radio, or on television. EG *Wesker has written four major plays since then... I saw the play a couple of years ago.* N COUNT

7 If an actor **plays** a role or character in a play or film, he or she performs the part of that character. EG *Brutus was played by James Mason... I was asked to play in a revival of 'Ghosts'.* v+o or V+A

8 If you **play** a musical instrument or **play** a tune on it, you produce music from it. EG *Out on the balcony, a man stood playing a trombone... Doesn't he play beautifully?... The child played him a tune.* v+o, v+A, or V+o+o

9 If you **play** a record or tape, you listen to it on a record player, tape recorder, or cassette player. EG *I'll play you the tape in a minute.* v+o or V+o+o

10 When light **plays** somewhere, it moves about on a surface in an unsteady way. EG *The glossy patches of sunshine played over their bodies.* v+A Literary

11 When something **comes into play** or is **brought into play**, it begins to be used or to have an effect. EG *Computer systems were brought into play to draw up attack strategies.* PHRASE Formal

12 If something or someone **plays a part** or **plays a role** in a situation, they are involved in it and have an effect on it. EG *Examinations seem to play a large part in education... Television plays a dominant role in moulding public opinion.* PHRASE

13 If you **play for time**, you try to delay something happening, so that you can prepare for it or prevent it from happening. EG *She was playing for time, half hoping that he would forget all about it.* PHRASE

play along. If you **play along** with a person or with their plans, you agree with them and do what they want, even though you are not sure whether they are right. EG *I'll play along with them for the moment.* PHRASAL VB: V+ADV, USU+with

play at. **1** If you **play at** an activity, you do it without effort or seriousness. EG *They played at being huntsmen.* **2** If you ask **what** someone is **playing at**, you are angry because you think that they are doing something stupid or wrong. EG *What do you think you're playing at?... I don't know what the police are playing at.* PHRASAL VB: V+PREP CONVENTION Informal

play back. When you **play back** a tape or film, you listen to the sounds or watch the pictures after recording them. PHRASAL VB: V+o+ADV

play down. If you **play down** something, you try to make people think that it is less important than it really is. EG *He played down his recent promotion.* PHRASAL VB: V+o+ADV

play off against. If you **play** people **off against** each other, you make them compete or argue, so that you gain some advantage. EG *Annie played one parent off against the other.* PHRASAL VB: V+o+ADV +PREP

play on. If you **play on** people's weaknesses or faults, you deliberately use them in order to PHRASAL VB: V+PREP, HAS PASS

achieve what you want. EG *He used to play on their prejudices and their fears.*

play up. 1 If something such as a machine or a part of your body **is playing up** or **is playing** you **up**, it is not working properly. EG *Our phone is playing up again... Is your leg still playing you up?* PHRASAL VB: V+ADV OR V+o+ADV

2 When children **are playing up**, they are being naughty and are difficult to control. PHRASE Informal

play upon. To **play upon** something means the same as to play on it. EG *He found himself in a position to play upon the fears of his colleagues.* V+PREP, HAS PASS Formal

playboy /pleɪbɔɪ/, **playboys**. A **playboy** is a rich man who spends most of his time enjoying himself in expensive ways. N COUNT

player /pleɪə/, **players. 1** In sports, a **player** is a person who takes part in a sport or game. EG *...Gerald Davies, the former Welsh rugby player.* N COUNT

2 You can use **player** to refer to a musician. For example, a piano **player** is someone who plays the piano. EG *He's one of the most original guitar players in jazz.* N COUNT

3 A **player** is also an actor. EG *The players came on stage with their backs to the audience.* N COUNT Outdated

4 See also **record player**.

playful /pleɪful/. **1** Someone who is **playful** is friendly and jokes a lot. EG *He was just being playful... She gave Philip's hand a little playful squeeze.* ◇ **playfully.** EG *Elaine kissed Harold playfully on the cheek.* ADJ QUALIT ◇ ADV

2 An animal that is **playful** is lively and cheerful. EG *...a playful kitten.* ADJ QUALIT

playground /pleɪgraʊnd/, **playgrounds**. A **playground** is a piece of land where children can play. EG *He could hear the children in the playground nearby... ...a school playground.* N COUNT

playgroup /pleɪgruːp/, **playgroups**. A **playgroup** is an informal kind of school for very young children where they learn things by playing. N COUNT OR N UNCOUNT

playhouse /pleɪhaʊs/, **playhouses**. A **playhouse** is a theatre. EG *...London playhouses.* N COUNT Outdated

playing card, playing cards. Playing **cards** are thin pieces of cardboard with numbers or pictures printed on them, which are used to play various games. EG *...a pack of playing cards.* N COUNT

playing field, playing fields. A playing **field** is a large area of grass where people play sports. N COUNT

playmate /pleɪmeɪt/, **playmates**. A child's **playmate** is another child who often plays with him or her. EG *Over the summer my playmates were my cousins.* N COUNT

playoff /pleɪɒf/, **playoffs**. A **playoff** is an extra game which is played to decide the winner of a sports competition when two or more people have got the same score. N COUNT

play on words. A **play on words** is a clever and amusing use of a word with more than one meaning, or a word that sounds like another word, so that what you say has two different meanings. N SING

playpen /pleɪpen/, **playpens**. A **playpen** is a small structure which is designed for a baby or young child to play safely in. It has bars or a net round the sides and is open at the top. N COUNT

plaything /pleɪθɪŋ/, **playthings**. A **plaything** is a toy or other object that a child plays with. EG *I used to get them new playthings to keep them quiet.* N COUNT Formal

playtime /pleɪtaɪm/ is a period of time between lessons at school when children can play outside. N UNCOUNT

playwright /pleɪraɪt/, **playwrights**. A **playwright** is a person who writes plays. N COUNT

plc /piː el siː/. is an abbreviation for 'public limited company'. It is used after the name of a company whose shares can be bought by the public. EG *...National Westminster Bank plc.*

plea /pliː/, **pleas. 1** A **plea** is an intense, emotional request for something. EG *She at last responded to his pleas for help.* N COUNT

2 In a court of law, a **plea** is the answer which someone gives when they have been charged with a crime, in which they say whether they are guilty N COUNT Legal or not. EG *I agreed to enter a plea of guilty if the Crown would drop the charge against my friend.*

plead /pliːd/, **pleads, pleading, pleaded. 1** If you plead with someone to do something, you ask them in an intense, emotional way to do it. EG *He was pleading with her to control herself... She wrote to the Prime Minister pleading for restraint... 'Take me with you,' he pleaded.* V+A OR V+QUOTE

2 If someone, especially a lawyer, **pleads** someone else's case or cause, they speak in support or defence of that person. EG *Of course his mother does her best to plead his case... Who will plead for us?* V+O OR V+A Formal

3 If you **plead** a particular thing as the reason for doing or not doing something, you give it as your excuse. EG *The Government might find it convenient to plead ignorance... I pleaded that I felt ill.* V+O OR V+REPORT: ONLY *that*

4 When someone charged with a crime **pleads** guilty or not guilty in a court of law, they officially state that they are guilty or not guilty of the crime. EG *'How do you plead?' - 'Not guilty.'* V+C OR V

pleading /pliːdɪŋ/, **pleadings. 1** A **pleading** expression or gesture shows that you want something very much. EG *Then he saw his brother's pleading expression and his heart softened.* ADJ CLASSIF: ATTRIB

2 Pleading is asking someone in an intense, emotional way to do something. EG *After days of tearful pleading and sulking, she stayed... It was hard to resist his daughter's pleadings.* N UNCOUNT OR N PLURAL

pleasant /plɛzənt/, **pleasanter, pleasantest. 1** Something that is **pleasant** is nice and enjoyable or attractive. EG *...a pleasant chat... It was pleasant to sit under the apple tree.* ◇ **pleasantly.** EG *I was pleasantly surprised... ...a pleasantly nutty taste.* ADJ QUALIT ◇ ADV

2 Someone who is **pleasant** is friendly and likeable. EG *They were pleasant lads... Dr Lake wrote a very pleasant letter to my father.* ◇ **pleasantly.** EG *'Please come in,' she said pleasantly.* ADJ QUALIT ◇ ADV

pleasantry /plɛzəntri¹/, **pleasantries. Pleasantries** are casual, friendly remarks which you say in order to be polite. EG *We stood exchanging a few pleasantries.* N COUNT Formal

please /pliːz/, **pleases, pleasing, pleased. 1** You say **please 1.1** when you are politely asking someone to do something. EG *'Follow me, please,' the guide said... Please don't interfere, Boris.* **1.2** when you are politely asking for something. EG *Hello. Could I speak to Sue, please?* **1.3** when you are accepting something politely. EG *'Do you want some milk?' - 'Yes please.'* **1.4** to attract someone's attention; used especially by children to attract the attention of a teacher or other adult. EG *Please, miss, why is that wrong?* ADV SEN / ADV SEN / CONVENTION / CONVENTION

2 If someone or something **pleases** you, they make you feel happy and satisfied. EG *You're an impossible man to please, Emmanuel... Neither idea pleased me... Rose was anxious to please.* V+O OR V

3 You use **please** in expressions such as 'as she pleases' and 'whatever you please' to indicate that someone can do or have whatever they want. EG *Judy had a right to come and go as she pleased... He can get anyone he pleases to work with him.* V OR V+O

4 You say **if you please** as a very polite and formal way of attracting someone's attention. EG *Captain Imrie stopped me at the door. 'If you please, Dr Marlowe, a word with you.'* CONVENTION Formal

5 You say **'please yourself'** to indicate that you do not mind or care whether the person you are talking to does a particular thing or not. EG *'Do you mind if I wait?' I asked. Melanie shrugged: 'Please yourself.'* CONVENTION Informal

pleased /pliːzd/. **1** If you are **pleased**, you are happy about something or satisfied with something. EG *She seemed very pleased that he had come... He was pleased with my progress... She did not look at all pleased.* ADJ PRED

2 You say **'Pleased to meet you'** as a polite way of greeting someone who you are meeting for the first time. CONVENTION

pleasing /pliːzɪŋ/. Something that is **pleasing** gives you pleasure and satisfaction. EG *...a pleasing piece of news... It has a pleasing smell.* ADJ QUALIT Formal

pleasurable /plɛʒərəbəl/. Something that is **pleasurable** is pleasant and enjoyable. EG *...a pleasurable sensation... Not every child expects reading to be pleasurable.* ADJ QUALIT Formal

pleasure /plɛʒə/, **pleasures. 1 Pleasure** is **1.1** a feeling of happiness, satisfaction, or enjoyment. EG *McPherson could scarcely conceal his pleasure at my resignation... I can't understand how people can kill for pleasure.* **1.2** the activity of enjoying yourself rather than working. EG *She is a disciplined creature who will put duty before pleasure... He set off on another of his European pleasure tours.* N UNCOUNT

2 A **pleasure** is an activity or experience that you find very enjoyable and satisfying. EG *What a pleasure it would be to hunt in these forests!... Will you do me the pleasure of joining me in a drink?... ...the pleasures of choral singing.* N COUNT USU+SUPP

3 You can say **'It's a pleasure'** or **'My pleasure'** as a polite way of replying to someone who has just thanked you for doing something. EG *'Thank you for talking to us about your research.' - 'It's a pleasure.'* CONVENTION

4 You can say **'With pleasure'** as a polite way of saying that you are very willing to do something. EG *'Could you help?' - 'With pleasure.'* CONVENTION Formal

pleat /pliːt/, **pleats.** A **pleat** in a piece of clothing is a permanent fold that is made in the cloth. N COUNT

pleated /pliːtɪd/. A **pleated** piece of clothing has pleats in it. EG *...a brown pleated skirt.* ADJ CLASSIF

pledge /plɛdʒ/, **pledges, pledging, pledged. 1** A **pledge** is a solemn promise to do something. EG *The Government should fulfil its 1979 Manifesto pledge... He gave a pledge to handle the affair in a friendly manner.* N COUNT: OFT+REPORT

2 If you **pledge** something, you promise solemnly that you will do it or give it. EG *They will pledge $1 million to fund the project... The government pledged to reduce the level of imports... He has pledged that the ban will be lifted after two years.* V+O, V+to-INF, OR V+REPORT: ONLY *that*

3 If you **pledge** yourself to something, you commit yourself to following a particular course of action or to supporting a particular person, group, or idea. EG *The new organization pledged itself to the revolutionary overthrow of the dictator.* V-REFL+to OR to-INF

plentiful /plɛntɪfʊl/. Something that is **plentiful** exists in large amounts or numbers. EG *Food became more plentiful each day.* ADJ QUALIT

plenty /plɛnti¹/. If there is **plenty** of something, there is a large amount of it. If there are **plenty** of things, there is a large number of them. EG *We've got plenty of time... There are always plenty of jobs to be done... They would have plenty to eat.* QUANTIF

pleurisy /plʊəri¹si¹/ is a serious illness in which a person's lungs are inflamed and breathing is difficult. N UNCOUNT

pliable /plaɪəbəl/. **1** If something is **pliable**, you can bend it easily without breaking it. EG *...a soft and pliable material.* ADJ QUALIT

2 Someone who is **pliable** can be easily influenced and controlled by other people. EG *I am too passive and pliable.* ADJ QUALIT

pliant /plaɪənt/. **1** Someone who is **pliant** can be easily influenced and controlled by other people. EG *The Democrats may not be as pliant as they appear... She was pliant and docile.* ADJ QUALIT

2 If something is **pliant**, you can bend it easily without breaking it. ADJ QUALIT

pliers /plaɪəz/ are a tool used for holding or pulling out things such as nails, or for bending or cutting wire. See picture at TOOLS. EG *Use a pair of pliers.* N PLURAL

If a lawyer pleads a case, is he pleading?

plight /plaɪt/. If you refer to someone's **plight**, N SING+POSS you mean that they are in a difficult situation that Formal is full of problems. EG ...the plight of the mentally handicapped... He had heard of my plight through an acquaintance.

plimsoll /plɪmsəl/, **plimsolls**. **Plimsolls** are N COUNT shoes made of canvas with flat rubber soles, which people wear for sports and leisure.

plod /plɒd/, **plods**, **plodding**, **plodded. 1** If some- V : USU+A one **plods** along, they walk slowly and heavily. EG He plodded along the road.

2 If you say that someone **plods** on or **plods** along V+A with a job, you mean that they work slowly and without enthusiasm. EG He plodded on in the Board of Trade.

plonk /plɒŋk/, **plonks**, **plonking**, **plonked. 1** If V+O+A you **plonk** something somewhere, you put it or Informal drop it there heavily and carelessly. EG Bottles of beer were plonked on the wooden table... ...plonking himself down in the middle of the room.

2 Plonk is cheap or poor quality wine. EG Shall we N UNCOUNT get a bottle of plonk? Informal

plop /plɒp/, **plops**, **plopping**, **plopped. 1** A **plop** is N COUNT a soft gentle sound, like the sound made by something light dropping into water. EG My hat landed with a plop in the bucket.

2 If something **plops** into a liquid, it drops into it V+A with a soft gentle sound. EG Great big tears plopped into her soup.

plot /plɒt/, **plots**, **plotting**, **plotted. 1** A **plot** is a N COUNT secret plan by a group of people to do something that is illegal or wrong. EG Another plot to assassinate the General was uncovered.

2 If people **plot** something or **plot** to do something, V+O, they plan secretly to do it. EG They were accused of V+to-INF, plotting to assassinate the President... Anyone con- OR V+against victed of plotting against the king will be executed.

3 The **plot** of a film, novel, or play is the story and N COUNT the way in which it develops. EG They were having some difficulty in following the plot.

4 A **plot** of land is a small piece of land. EG His land N COUNT is split up into several widely scattered plots.

5 When someone **plots** the position or course of a V+O plane or ship, they mark it on a map or chart in order to see what course or direction it is taking. EG They plotted the new positions of each vessel.

6 When you are drawing a graph, you **plot** the V+O points on it by marking them at the correct places to form the graph. EG These figures can be plotted on a graph.

plough /plaʊ/, **ploughs**, **ploughing**, **ploughed**; also spelled **plow** in American English.

1 A **plough** is a large farming tool with sharp N COUNT blades which is attached to a tractor or an animal such as a horse. A plough is pulled across the soil to turn it over, usually before seeds are planted.

2 When someone **ploughs** an area of land, they V+O OR V turn over the soil using a plough. EG A small tractor can plough an acre in six to nine hours.

3 If you **plough** on, you continue moving or trying V+A to complete something, although it needs a lot of effort. EG The fighters ploughed on to their destination airfields... My mother ploughed her way through the list of recipes.

4 If one thing **ploughs** into another, it crashes into V+into it. EG The car wavered crazily before ploughing into the bank.

5 If someone **ploughs** money into a business or V+O : company, they invest large sums of money in it. EG USU+into ...the huge sums of money which were ploughed into computing.

plough up. If an area of land is **ploughed up**, PHRASAL VB : the soil is turned over using a plough. EG Nearly V+ADV, half of his grassland was ploughed up to grow corn. USU PASS

ploughman's lunch /plaʊmənz lʌntʃ/, **plough-** N COUNT **man's lunches**. A **ploughman's lunch** or a British **ploughman's** is a snack consisting of bread, cheese and pickles. It is usually bought and eaten in a pub.

plow /plaʊ/. See **plough**.

ploy /plɔɪ/, **ploys**. A **ploy** is a way of behaving that N COUNT you have planned carefully in order to get something you want. EG This was a tactful ploy to get Thomas to mention his present salary... This headache was clearly a delaying ploy.

pluck /plʌk/, **plucks**, **plucking**, **plucked. 1** If you V+O **pluck** a fruit, flower, or leaf, you take it in your Literary hand and pull it in order to remove it from its stalk where it is growing. EG He plucked a tomato and offered it to Hilda.

2 If you **pluck** something from somewhere, you V+O OR V : take hold of it and pull it with a sharp movement. USU+A EG He laughed and plucked the paper from my Written hand... Rough hands plucked at my jacket.

3 If you **pluck** a chicken or other dead bird, you V+O pull its feathers out to prepare it for cooking.

4 If someone **plucks** their eyebrows, they pull out V+O some of the hairs using tweezers, in order to look more attractive.

5 If you **pluck** a guitar or other stringed musical V+O OR V+A instrument, you use your fingers to pull the strings and let them go, so that they make a sound.

6 Pluck is courage. EG Why don't you ask her? N UNCOUNT You've got no pluck.

7 If you **pluck up the courage** to do something PHRASE frightening, you make an effort to be brave enough to do it. EG I eventually plucked up enough courage to go in.

plucky /plʌki[1]/. Someone who is **plucky** has cour- ADJ QUALIT age. EG This schoolgirl story featured a plucky Outdated heroine.

plug /plʌg/, **plugs**, **plugging**, **plugged. 1** A **plug** N COUNT is **1.1** a small plastic object with metal pieces which fit into the holes in a socket and connect the wire from a piece of electrical equipment to the electricity supply. EG This lamp doesn't have a plug... Do you know how to change a plug? **1.2** a Informal socket that is a source of electricity, usually in the wall of a room. EG ...electricity from a plug in the garage.

plugs

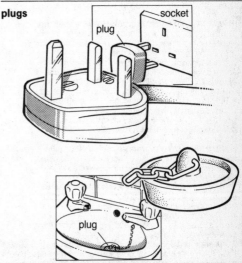

2 A **plug** is also a thick, circular piece of rubber or N COUNT plastic that you use to block the hole in a bath or sink when it is filled with water.

3 If you **plug** a hole, you block it with something. EG V+O He plugged the cracks with paper... Have you plugged all the leaks?

4 If someone **plugs** a book or film, they praise it in V+O order to encourage people to buy it or see it. EG The Informal radio stations are plugging the record like mad.

▸ used as a noun. EG *Can I quickly give our new show a plug?* ▸ N COUNT

plug in. If you **plug in** a piece of electrical equipment, you push its plug into an electric socket so that it can work. EG *I plugged in the kettle... She plugged the lamp into a wall-socket.* PHRASAL VB : V+O+ADV OR V+O+PREP

plughole /plʌghəʊl/, **plugholes.** A **plughole** is a small hole in a bath or sink which allows the water to flow away. N COUNT

plum /plʌm/, **plums. 1** A **plum** is a small, sweet fruit with a smooth red or yellow skin and a stone in the middle. EG ...*a basket of plums... ...plum jam.* N COUNT

2 A **plum** job is a very good job that a lot of people would like. EG *They held most of the plum jobs... She was given a plum part: the lead in a £3m film.* N MOD

plumage /pluːmɪdʒ/. A bird's **plumage** is all the feathers on its body. EG ...*a bird of brilliant plumage... Its plumage had turned grey.* N UNCOUNT

plumb /plʌm/, **plumbs, plumbing, plumbed.** If someone **plumbs the depths** of an unpleasant emotion, they experience it to an extreme degree. EG *The story shows how she plumbs the depths of humiliation.* PHRASE

plumber /plʌmə/, **plumbers.** A **plumber** is a person whose job is to connect and repair things such as water and drainage pipes, baths, and toilets. EG *The plumbers came to mend the pipes.* N COUNT

plumbing /plʌmɪŋ/. **1** The **plumbing** in a building consists of the water and drainage pipes, baths, and toilets in the building. EG *Will it need new wiring and plumbing?* N UNCOUNT

2 Plumbing is the work of connecting and repairing things such as water and drainage pipes, baths, and toilets. EG ...*minor plumbing repairs.* N UNCOUNT

plume /pluːm/, **plumes. 1** A **plume** is **1.1** a large, often brightly coloured bird's feather. EG ...*an ostrich plume.* **1.2** a bunch of long, thin strands of material, tied at one end and flowing loosely at the other. Plumes are usually attached to soldiers' helmets and horses' heads as decoration. EG ...*four horses with black plumes.* N COUNT Formal

2 A **plume** of smoke is a large quantity of it that rises into the air in a small column. EG *The last plume of blue smoke curled away.* N COUNT+of

plummet /plʌmɪt/, **plummets, plummeting, plummeted. 1** If something **plummets** downwards, it falls very quickly. EG *The explosion sent the aircraft plummeting towards the sea.* V+A

2 If an amount, rate, or price **plummets**, it decreases quickly and suddenly. EG *The price of paper plummeted... His popularity has plummeted.* V

plump /plʌmp/, **plumper, plumpest; plumps, plumping, plumped.** Someone who is **plump** is rather fat. EG ...*a plump, red-faced man.* ADJ QUALIT

plump for. If you **plump for** someone or something, you choose them, often after hesitating or thinking carefully. EG *She plumped for the eclair.* PHRASAL VB : V+PREP

plump up. If you **plump up** a cushion or pillow, you squeeze and shake it back into a rounded shape. EG *He plumped up the cushions and switched on the lamp.* PHRASAL VB : V+O+ADV

plunder /plʌndə/, **plunders, plundering, plundered. 1** If someone **plunders** a place or plunders things from a place, they steal things from it. EG *The conquerors plundered their wealth and burnt their cities... Imperialist governments plunder the weaker nations.* V+O OR V Literary

2 Plunder is **2.1** the activity of stealing property from people or places. EG ...*the savage burning and plunder of the commercial centre of town.* **2.2** the property that is stolen. EG *He escaped with his plunder.* N UNCOUNT / N SING

plunge /plʌndʒ/, **plunges, plunging, plunged. 1** If something **plunges** in a particular direction, it falls in that direction. EG *They plunged into the pool together... The car plunged into the river.* ▸ used as a noun. EG *They were relying on the plunge into icy waters to kill me.* V+A / ▸ N COUNT

2 If you **plunge** an object into something, you push V+O+A

it quickly or violently into it. EG *She plunged her hands into her coat pockets... He plunged the knife into her breast.*

3 To **plunge** someone or something into a state means to cause them suddenly to be in that state. EG *The hall was plunged into darkness... ...the danger of plunging society into chaos and anarchy.* V-ERG+A

4 If you **plunge** into an activity, you suddenly get very involved in it. EG *She plunged bravely into the debate.* V+into

5 If an amount or rate **plunges**, it decreases quickly and suddenly. EG *Sales have plunged by 24%.* ▸ used as a noun. EG *Prices started a downward plunge.* V / ▸ N COUNT

6 If you **take the plunge**, you decide to do something that you consider difficult or risky. EG *Take the plunge and start your own firm... We took the plunge and got married.* PHRASE

plunger /plʌndʒə/, **plungers.** A **plunger** is a device for unblocking pipes and sinks. It consists of a rubber cup on the end of a stick. You press it up and down over the pipe or the hole in the sink, and the suction moves the blockage. EG ...*a sink plunger.* N COUNT

pluperfect /pluːpɜːfi²kt/ is the term used in grammar for the tense of a verb describing actions that were completed before another event in the past happened. The pluperfect in English is formed using 'had' followed by the past participle of the verb, as in the sentences 'I had gone by then' and 'She'd eaten them before I arrived'. N SING : the+N

plural /plʊərəl/, **plurals. 1** In grammar, **plural** is the term used for a noun, pronoun, determiner, adjective, or verb when it refers to two or more people, things, or groups. EG *Use the first person plural... The singular is 'louse' and the plural is 'lice'.* ADJ CLASSIF OR N COUNT

2 Plural also means **2.1** consisting of more than one person or thing. EG *The only plural occupancy of the throne was during the reign of William and Mary.* **2.2** consisting of different kinds of people or things. EG *A democratic society is a plural society... We need a plural system of education, with different kinds of institutions.* ADJ CLASSIF : ATTRIB Formal / Formal

plus /plʌs/. **1** You say **plus** or write a **plus** sign (+) to show that one number or quantity is being added to another. EG *That's seventy-two plus ninety-six... ...5 + 3.*

2 You use **plus** after a number to show that the actual number or quantity is greater than the one mentioned. EG ...*my 25 years plus as a police officer... They take the exams at 13 plus.* ADJ AFTER N

3 Teachers use **plus** in grading work in schools and colleges. 'B plus' is a better grade than 'B', but it is not as good as 'A'.

4 You can also use **plus** to add an item to one or more that you have already mentioned. EG *Now five people, plus Val, are missing... He wore strange scarves and beads, plus he was English.* PREP OR CONJ

plush /plʌʃ/. Something that is **plush** is very smart, comfortable, and expensive. EG ...*his plush car with reclining seats.* ADJ QUALIT

plus sign, plus signs. A **plus sign** is the sign (+) which is put between two numbers in order to show that the second number is being added to the first one. N COUNT

plutonium /pluːtəʊnɪəm/ is a radioactive element used especially as a fuel in nuclear power stations. N UNCOUNT

ply /plaɪ/, **plies, plying, plied. 1** If you **ply** someone with food or drink, you keep giving them more of it. EG *Dolly plied me with sweets.* V+O+with

2 If you **ply** someone with questions, you keep asking them questions. EG *I plied him with questions about his novel.* V+O+with

3 If a ship or boat **plies** somewhere, it makes regular journeys there. EG ...*a new passenger liner* V+O OR V+A

If you take the plunge, do you fall?

to ply the North Atlantic route... ...the ferry that plies between Dover and Boulogne.
4 If you **ply** a trade, you do a particular kind of v+o work regularly as your job. EG *They received a warning not to ply their trade in the town.*
5 Ply is the thickness of wool, thread, or rope, which is measured by the number of strands it is made from. EG *...four-ply wool.*

plywood /plaɪwʊd/ is wood that consists of thin N UNCOUNT layers of wood stuck together. EG *...the flimsy plywood door.*

p.m. /piː ɛm/ after a number refers to a particular ADV time between noon and midnight. EG *Some of the shops stay open until 7 p.m.*

pneumatic /njuːmætɪk/. **1** A **pneumatic** drill is ADJ CLASSIF: operated by compressed air and is very powerful. ATTRIB
2 Pneumatic means filled with air. EG *...a pneu-* ADJ CLASSIF: *matic chair.* ATTRIB

pneumonia /njuːməʊnɪə/ is a serious disease N UNCOUNT which affects your lungs and makes it difficult for you to breathe. EG *She nearly died of pneumonia.*

PO /piː əʊ/ is an abbreviation for 'Post Office'.

poach /pəʊtʃ/, **poaches, poaching, poached. 1** If v+o OR v someone **poaches** fish, animals, or birds, they illegally catch them on someone else's property. EG *He had been poaching deer.*
2 If someone **poaches** an idea or a book, they v+o dishonestly or illegally use the idea or publish the book. EG *Meanwhile, their company implacably poach the masterpieces.*
3 When you **poach** an egg, you remove its shell v+o and cook the egg gently in boiling water. EG *...poached eggs and beans.*
4 If you **poach** food such as fish, you cook it gently v+o in boiling water or milk. EG *...poached salmon.*

poacher /pəʊtʃə/, **poachers.** A **poacher** is some- N COUNT one who illegally catches fish, birds, or animals on someone else's property.

PO Box is used before a number to refer to an address to which you can send letters or money, which the Post Office keeps until they are collect-ed by the person who has paid for the service. EG *...PO Box 48.*

pocket /pɒkɪt/, **pockets, pocketing, pocketed. 1** N COUNT A **pocket** is **1.1** a small bag that is sewn into a piece of clothing, and that is used for carrying small things such as money or a handkerchief. EG *She put her hand in her coat pocket.* **1.2** a pouch or bag which is attached to a suitcase or car door, for example, and which is used for putting things in.
2 If someone **pockets** something, they put it in v+o their pocket. EG *I locked the door and pocketed the key.*
3 You can say that someone who steals something v+o **pockets** it. EG *...servants who pocketed household funds for their own use.*
4 You use **pocket** to describe something that is N MOD small enough to fit into a pocket. EG *...a pocket calculator... ...a pocket torch.*
5 A **pocket** of something is a small area of it. EG *We* N PART *sat in the pocket of warmth by the fire.*
6 Pocket is also used in these phrases. **6.1** If you PHRASES say that people **live in each other's pockets,** you Informal mean that they are always together and depend on each other too much. **6.2** If someone **picks** your **pocket,** they steal something from your pocket. **6.3** If you are **out of pocket,** you have less money than you should have, usually because you have paid for something for someone else. EG *I don't want you to end up out of pocket.*

pocketbook /pɒkɪtbʊk/, **pocketbooks.** A **pocket-** N COUNT **book** is **1** a small book or notebook. **2** a wallet or American small case which is used for carrying money and papers.

pocket knife, pocket knives. A **pocket knife** is N COUNT the same as a penknife.

pocket money is money which a child is given by N UNCOUNT his or her parents every week. EG *When he was ten, his pocket money was 50p a week.*

pod /pɒd/, **pods.** A **pod** is a seed container that N COUNT grows on some plants such as peas or beans.

podgy /pɒdʒɪ/. Someone who is **podgy** is fairly ADJ QUALIT fat. EG *...a small, podgy girl.* Informal

poem /pəʊɪm/, **poems.** A **poem** is a piece of N COUNT writing in which the words are arranged in short lines which often rhyme. EG *...a selection of Robert Browning's poems.*

poet /pəʊɪt/, **poets.** A **poet** is a person who writes N COUNT poems. EG *...the Soviet poet, Yevtushenko.*

poetic /pəʊɛtɪk/. **1** Something that is **poetic** is ADJ QUALIT very beautiful, expressive, and sensitive. EG *...a poetic and beautiful picture of the landscape... ...great poetic speeches.* ◊ **poetically.** EG *...a* ◊ ADV *poetically true vision of Australia.*
2 Poetic also means relating to poetry. EG *...a* ADJ CLASSIF: *poetic tradition older than writing.* ATTRIB

poetical /pəʊɛtɪkəl/ means the same as poetic. ADJ

poetry /pəʊɪtrɪ/. **1 Poetry** is poems, considered N UNCOUNT as a form of literature. EG *...a book of poetry... ...poetry recitals.*
2 You can also refer to a quality of beauty or N UNCOUNT greatness that people see or experience in some- +SUPP thing as **poetry.** EG *...the poetry of human exist-ence.*

poignant /pɔɪnjənt/. Something that is **poignant** ADJ QUALIT makes you feel very sad. EG *His cry of protest is still poignant today.* ◊ **poignantly.** EG *He poignantly* ◊ ADV *describes poverty as it existed in his own child-hood.* ◊ **poignancy** /pɔɪnjənsɪ/. EG *It was a* ◊ N UNCOUNT *moment of extraordinary poignancy.* Formal

point /pɔɪnt/, **points, pointing, pointed. 1** A N COUNT: **point** is something that you say which expresses a USU+SUPP particular fact, idea, or opinion. EG *That's a very good point... We had a long argument on this point... I want to make several quick points... Let me tell you a little story to illustrate my point... I see your point... I take your point about needing new recordings... To prove his point, Mr Higgerson gave me the letter.*
2 If you say that someone has a **point,** you mean N COUNT: that you accept that what they have said is impor- USU a+N tant or should be considered. EG *You've got a point there.*
3 The **point** is the most important part of what you N SING : the+N are saying or discussing. EG *The point was that Dick could not walk... You've all missed the point... Philip, I may as well come straight to the point. I'm pregnant.*
4 If you say that something is **beside the point,** PHRASE you mean that it is not relevant to the subject that you are discussing. If it is **to the point,** it is relevant. EG *In art as a whole the notion of taste is beside the point... His letters are intelligible and to the point.*
5 A **point** is also a detail, aspect, or quality of N COUNT+SUPP something or someone. EG *The two books have some interesting points in common... This is just a minor point of criticism... The court dismissed the charges on a technical point... That's his best point, I think... Your strong points are your speed and accuracy... The main point on the agenda was left till the end of the meeting... Experts are still arguing over the finer points of how it operates.*
6 If you **make a point of** doing something, you do PHRASE it in a very deliberate or obvious way. EG *You make a point of forgetting everything I have said... I made a special point of being sociable.*
7 If you ask what the **point** of something is, or say N SING : that there is no **point** in it, you are talking about USU+SUPP what its purpose is or how useful it is. EG *I didn't see the point of boring you with all this... There was not much point in thinking about it.*
8 A **point** is also a particular place or position N COUNT+SUPP where something happens, often marked on a drawing or map by a dot or other symbol. EG *We were nearing the point where the lane curved round to the right... Her gaze shifted to a point over my left shoulder... The missile can strike at almost*

any point on the globe... The circle passes through those two points.

9 The **points** of a compass are the 32 marks on it that show the directions, especially North, South, East, and West. N COUNT+SUPP

10 The **point** of something such as a pin, needle, or knife is the thin, sharp end of it. EG *His moustache had been rolled into two tight points... It just has a short point.* N COUNT

11 On a railway track, the **points** are the levers and rails at a place where two tracks join or separate. N COUNT : USU PLURAL

12 The decimal **point** in a number is the dot that separates the whole numbers from the fractions. EG *...four point eight.*

13 You also use **point** to refer to a particular time or moment, or a particular stage in the development of something. EG *At one point, I was dreadfully rude... At the point of death, the woman suddenly clutched his hand... Do you ever reach a point where you just can't agree with her?... The strikers brought the economy to crisis point... His dinner had been the high point of his evening... I could not fall asleep unless I exercised to the point of exhaustion.* N SING+SUPP

14 If you are **on the point of** doing something, you are just going to do it. EG *As they were on the point of setting out, a light rain began to fall... Capitalism was on the point of collapse.* PHRASE

15 If you say that something is true **up to a point**, you mean that it is true to a certain extent but not completely. EG *He is right, but only up to a point.* PHRASE

16 In some sports, competitions, and games, a **point** is one of the single marks that are added together to give the total score. EG *The panel of judges gave him the highest points.* N COUNT

17 A **point** is also an electric socket. EG *The room has a wash-basin and an electric-shaver point.* N COUNT

18 If you **point** at something, you hold out your finger or an object such as a stick towards the thing, in order to show someone where it is or to make them notice it. EG *'Over there,' she said and pointed to the door... He pointed a finger at my friend and hissed with rage.* ● to **point the finger at** someone: see **finger**. V : USU+at/to; ALSO V+O : USU+at

19 If you **point** something at someone, you aim the tip or end of it towards them. EG *They were horrified when I told them I had actually pointed a gun at someone.* V+O+A

20 If something **points** to a place or **points** in a particular direction, it shows where that place is or faces in that direction. EG *There was a street sign that pointed down towards the cemetery... One of its toes pointed backwards.* V+A

21 If something **points** to a particular situation, it suggests that the situation exists or is likely to occur. EG *Her questions point to a desire to know some vital truth... This activity points to the likelihood that an armed revolution is imminent.* V+to

22 to **be a case in point**: see **case**. ● **in point of fact**: see **fact**. ● **a sore point**: see **sore**. ● See also **focal point, pointed, vantage point**.

point out. 1 If you **point out** an object or place, you make people look at it or show them where it is. EG *On car journeys we all used to shout and point out lovely places along the way... I can always recognize plants after they have been pointed out to me.* **2** If you **point out** a fact or mistake, you inform someone about it or draw their attention to it. EG *Mr Merritt pointed this problem out to you the other day... She pointed out that he was wrong.* PHRASAL VB : V+O+ADV OR V+ADV

point-blank. 1 If you say something **point-blank**, you say it very directly or rudely, without explaining or apologizing. EG *She asked him point-blank if I was with him on Saturday... ...a point-blank refusal to discuss the matter.* ADV OR ADJ CLASSIF : ATTRIB

2 If you shoot someone or something **point-blank**, you shoot them when the gun is touching them or ADV OR ADJ CLASSIF : ATTRIB

extremely close to them. EG *He shot him in the brain, point-blank... ...shooting at point-blank range.*

pointed /ˈpɔɪntɪd/. **1** Something that is **pointed** has a point at one end. EG *His daughter has a pointed nose... ...pointed trees.* ADJ CLASSIF

2 Pointed comments or behaviour express criticism, warning, or unpleasantness in a very obvious way. EG *Etta gave a pointed look in their direction... She made two pointed comments.* ◊ **pointedly.** EG *'How old is he?' Freya asked pointedly.* ADJ QUALIT ◊ ADV

pointer /ˈpɔɪntə/, **pointers. 1** A **pointer** is a piece of advice or information which helps you to understand a situation or to find a way of making progress. EG *She gave him a few more pointers... ...a list of things that seemed to be pointers to the truth of what happened.* N COUNT

2 A **pointer** is also a long, thin piece of wood or metal that is used to point at something such as a chart on a wall or a dial on a machine. EG *The pointer on the weighing machine is not accurate.* N COUNT

pointless /ˈpɔɪntlɪ²s/. Something that is **pointless** has no use, sense, or purpose. EG *...pointless violence... It was pointless to protest.* ◊ **pointlessly.** EG *He had pointlessly hurt her.* ADJ QUALIT ◊ ADV

point of view, points of view. 1 You can refer to the opinions or attitudes that someone has about something as their **point of view**. EG *We understand your point of view... An outsider who can offer a fresh point of view may stimulate new ideas.* N COUNT

2 If you consider something **from a** particular **point of view**, you are using one aspect of a situation in order to judge the situation. EG *From the commercial point of view, they have little to lose... We'll consider the problem from the point of view of the way it was handled.* PHRASE

poise /pɔɪz/ is a calm, dignified, self-controlled manner. EG *She received me with incredible poise for one so young.* N UNCOUNT

poised /pɔɪzd/. **1** If a part of your body is **poised**, it is completely still but ready to move at any moment. EG *He waited with fingers poised over the keys... I saw her hand poised to strike.* ADJ PRED

2 If you are **poised** to do something, you are ready to take action at any moment. EG *...powerful military forces, poised for invasion... His party seems poised to return to power.* ADJ PRED : USU+to-INF OR for

3 If you are **poised**, you are calm, dignified, and self-controlled. EG *She was poised and diplomatic on the telephone.* ADJ PRED

poison /ˈpɔɪzə⁰n/, **poisons, poisoning, poisoned.**

1 Poison is a substance that harms or kills people or animals if they swallow it or absorb it. EG *It was deadly poison and if he drank it he'd die.* N MASS

2 If someone **poisons** another person, they kill the person or make them ill by means of poison. EG *He had been poisoned with strychnine.* ◊ **poisoning.** EG *The poisoning had not been accidental.* V+O ◊ N UNCOUNT

3 If you **are poisoned** by a substance, it makes you very ill. EG *You can be poisoned by agricultural and industrial wastes.* ◊ **poisoning.** EG *These swans died of lead poisoning... ...food poisoning.* V+O : USU PASS ◊ N UNCOUNT

4 If food, drink, or a weapon **is poisoned**, it has poison added to it. EG *...a poisoned whisky bottle.* V+O : USU PASS

5 If water, air, or land **is poisoned**, it is damaged by harmful substances such as chemicals. EG *...our poisoned air and polluted streams and lakes.* V+O : USU PASS

6 Something that **poisons** a good situation or relationship spoils it or destroys it. EG *...the despair that poisoned the Romantic movement.* V+O Literary

poisonous /ˈpɔɪzə⁰nəs/. **1** Something that is **poisonous** will kill you or make you ill if you swallow or absorb it. EG *...a poisonous plant.* ADJ QUALIT

2 An animal that is **poisonous** produces a poison that will kill you or make you ill if you are bitten by ADJ QUALIT

If people are poles apart, are they a long way from each other?

the animal. EG ...one of the most poisonous snakes in the world... ...poisonous spiders.

3 If you describe something as **poisonous**, you mean that it is extremely unpleasant and likely to spoil or destroy a good relationship or situation. EG The article contained some poisonous allegations about his social behaviour. ADJ QUALIT Formal

poke /pəʊk/, **pokes, poking, poked. 1** If you **poke** someone or something, you quickly push them with your finger or with a sharp object. EG People poked the students with their umbrellas... You almost poked my eye out... Ralph began to poke little holes in the sand. ▸ used as a noun. EG Len gave him an affectionate poke. V+O:USU+A ▸ N COUNT

2 If you **poke** one thing into another, you push the first thing into the second thing. EG Never poke scissors into an electric socket. V+O+A

3 If something **pokes** out of or through another thing, you can see part of it appearing from behind or underneath the other thing. EG ...cotton wool poking out of his ear... ...a shoot poking through the earth... Blades of grass poked up between the paving stones. V+A

4 If you **poke** your head through an opening or if it **pokes** through an opening, you push it through, often so that you can see something more easily. EG The driver slowed down and poked his head out of the window... His secretary poked her head through the door. V-ERG+A

5 to **poke fun at** someone: see **fun**.

poke about or **poke around**. If you **poke about** or **poke around** for something, you search for it, usually by moving lots of objects around. EG He was lying flat on his stomach, poking around under the bed with his arm. PHRASAL VB: V+ADV, USU+A Informal

poke at. If you **poke at** something, you make lots of little pushing movements at it with a sharp object. EG The chef poked at his little pile of ashes. PHRASAL VB: V+PREP

poker /pəʊkə/, **pokers. 1 Poker** is a card game that people usually play in order to win money. N UNCOUNT

2 A **poker** is a metal bar which you use to move coal or wood in a fire. EG She prodded the fire gently with the poker. N COUNT

poky /pəʊki¹/, **pokier, pokiest.** A room or house that is **poky** is uncomfortably small. EG Her flat has three poky little rooms. ADJ QUALIT Informal

polar /pəʊlə/. **1 Polar** describes the area around the North and South Poles. EG ...the melting of the polar ice caps. ADJ CLASSIF: ATTRIB

2 Polar is also used to describe things which are completely opposite in character, quality, or type. EG ...the polar extremes of 'totalitarianism' and 'democracy.' ADJ CLASSIF: ATTRIB Formal

polar bear, polar bears. A **polar bear** is a large white bear which lives near the North Pole. N COUNT

polarize /pəʊləraɪz/, **polarizes, polarizing, polarized;** also spelled **polarise.** If people **polarize** or if something **polarizes** them, they form into two separate groups with opposite opinions or positions. EG In Britain the political debate is polarized between two major parties... Media coverage helps to polarize the public's views on the subject. V-ERG

◊ **polarization** /pəʊləraɪzeɪ¹ʃə⁰n/. EG ...a growing polarisation between rich and poor countries. ◊ N UNCOUNT

pole /pəʊl/, **poles. 1** A **pole** is a long, thin piece of wood or metal, used especially for supporting things. EG ...tent poles... ...telegraph poles. N COUNT

2 The earth's **poles** are the two opposite ends of its axis. N COUNT+SUPP

3 If you say that two people are **poles apart**, you mean that they have completely different beliefs and opinions. EG Politically they were poles apart. PHRASE

police /pəˈliːs/, **polices, policing, policed. 1** The **police** are **1.1** the official organization that is responsible for making sure that people obey the law. EG The police were called... Three police cars arrived. **1.2** the men and women who are members of this organization. EG 280 people were arrested and 117 police injured. N PLURAL: the+N N PLURAL

2 To **police** a place means to preserve law and order in it by means of the police or the army. EG It is impossible to police such a vast area. V+O

police force, police forces. A **police force** is the police organization in a particular country or area. EG We have the finest police force in the world. N COUNT

policeman /pəˈliːsmə³n/, **policemen** /pəˈliːsmə³n/. A **policeman** is a man who is a member of the police force. EG He had been a policeman for six years. N COUNT

police officer, police officers. A **police officer** is a policeman or policewoman. N COUNT

police station, police stations. A **police station** is the local office of a police force in a particular area. EG A youth was being questioned at Cannon Row police station. N COUNT

policewoman /pəˈliːswʊmən/, **policewomen** /pəˈliːswɪmɪn/. A **policewoman** is a woman who is a member of the police force. N COUNT

policy /pɒlɪsi¹/, **policies. 1** A **policy** is a set of ideas or plans that is used as a basis for making decisions, especially in politics, economics, or business. EG There is no change in our policy... ...a policy of reconciliation... ...economic and foreign policy... They oppose Conservative policies. N COUNT OR N UNCOUNT

2 An insurance **policy** is a document which shows the agreement that you have made with an insurance company. EG ...a life assurance policy... This service is free to policy holders. N COUNT Technical

polio /pəʊlɪəʊ/ is a serious infectious disease caused by a virus. It often causes paralysis. EG She had been crippled by polio. N UNCOUNT

polish /pɒlɪʃ/, **polishes, polishing, polished. 1 Polish** is a substance that you put on the surface of an object in order to clean it, protect it, and make it shine. EG Use wax polish on wooden furniture... ...shoe polish. N UNCOUNT

2 If you **polish** something, **2.1** you put polish on it. EG Leather needs polishing with good quality cream. ◊ **polished**. EG She slipped on the polished wooden floor. **2.2** you rub it with a cloth to make it shine. EG I polished my glasses with a handkerchief. V+O ◊ ADJ QUALIT V+O

3 If you say that something has **polish**, you mean that it is elegant and of good quality. EG It's an honest book but it hasn't got polish. N UNCOUNT

polish off. If you **polish** something **off**, you finish it completely and quickly. EG Last year's papers were polished off in half an hour... I had no trouble polishing off the pudding. PHRASAL VB: V+O+ADV Informal

polished /pɒlɪʃt/. **1** Someone who is **polished** shows confidence and sophistication. EG He had the most polished, sophisticated manner. ADJ QUALIT

2 If you describe an ability or skill as **polished**, you mean that it is of a very high standard. EG My German was not very polished... ...polished actors. ADJ QUALIT

polite /pəlaɪt/, **politer, politest. 1** Someone who is **polite** has good manners and is not rude to other people. EG He was very polite to his superiors... It's polite to ask before you help yourself... ...a polite refusal. ◊ **politely.** EG He thanked me politely. ◊ **politeness.** EG I do expect reasonable politeness and consideration. ADJ QUALIT ◊ ADV ◊ N UNCOUNT

2 You refer to people who consider themselves to be socially superior as **polite** society and **polite** company. EG ...the conventional norms of polite European society. ADJ CLASSIF: ATTRIB

politic /pɒlɪtɪk/, **politics. Politic** is an adjective and **politics** is a plural noun or an uncount noun.

1 Politics are the actions or activities which people use to achieve power in a country, society, or organization. EG Emily has never had the slightest interest in politics... He was active in Liberal politics... ...local politics... ...office politics. N PLURAL OR N UNCOUNT

2 Your **politics** are your beliefs about how a country ought to be governed. EG I have no politics... Her politics could be described as radical. N PLURAL

3 Politics is the study of the ways in which a country is governed. EG ...a lecturer in politics. N UNCOUNT

4 If you say that something is **politic**, you mean ADJ QUALIT that it seems to be the most sensible thing to do in Formal the circumstances. EG *It might be more politic to tell him yourself than let him find out from someone else.*

political /pɒlɪtɪkəᵘl/. **1 Political** means relating ADJ CLASSIF: to politics. EG *...the major political parties... ...politi-* USU ATTRIB *cal developments... He was sent to jail for his political views... ...demands for political and religious freedom.* ◇ **politically.** EG *...a country which* ◇ ADV *is politically stable and prosperous.*
2 Someone who is **political** is interested in politics ADJ QUALIT and holds strong beliefs about it. EG *He was always very political.*

political prisoner, political prisoners. A po- N COUNT litical prisoner is someone who has been imprisoned because they have expressed views that criticize or disagree with their own government.

politician /pɒlɪtɪʃəⁿn/, **politicians.** A **politician** N COUNT is a person whose job is in politics, especially a member of parliament. EG *...Labour and Tory politicians.*

politicize /pɒlɪtɪsaɪz/, **politicizes, politicizing,** v+o **politicized;** also spelled **politicise.** If you **politi- cize** someone or something, you make them more political. EG *The British people were politicized by their wartime experiences.* ◇ **politicization** ◇ N UNCOUNT /pɒlɪtɪsaɪzeɪʃəⁿn/. EG *...the increasing politicization* Formal *of the country.*

poll /pəʊl/, **polls, polling, polled. 1** A **poll** is a N COUNT survey in which people are asked their opinions about something, usually in order to find out how popular something is or to predict what will happen in the future. EG *Last year the polls gave the President a 10 to 15 point lead.* ● See also **opinion poll**.
2 If you **are polled** on something, you are asked v+o : USU PASS what you think about it as part of a survey. EG *A majority of those polled wanted 'stricter law enforcement'.*
3 The **polls** means a political election. EG *The party* N PLURAL : *won a convincing victory at the polls with an* the+N *overall majority of ninety-seven seats.*
4 If a political party or a candidate **polls** a v+o particular number of votes, they get that number of votes in an election. EG *In 1959 they only polled 43.7% of the votes.*

pollen /pɒlən/ is a fine powder produced by N UNCOUNT flowers. It fertilizes other flowers of the same species so that they produce seeds.

pollinate /pɒlɪneɪt/, **pollinates, pollinating, pol-** v+o **linated.** To **pollinate** a plant or tree means to fertilize it with pollen. EG *The plant may pollinate itself.* ◇ **pollination** /pɒlɪneɪʃəⁿn/. EG *Planting* ◇ N UNCOUNT *trees in groups helps pollination.*

polling day is the day on which people vote in an N UNCOUNT election.

pollutant /pəluːtənt/, **pollutants.** A **pollutant** is a N COUNT substance that pollutes the environment, especially a poisonous chemical. EG *The main pollutants in this country are sulphur dioxide and smoke.*

pollute /pəluːt/, **pollutes, polluting, polluted.** To v+o **pollute** the water, air, or atmosphere means to make it dirty and dangerous to live in or to use. EG *Our water supply is becoming polluted with nitrates.*

pollution /pəluːʃəⁿn/ is **1** the process of polluting N UNCOUNT the water, air, or atmosphere. EG *...changes in the climate due to pollution of the atmosphere by industrial waste.* **2** the unpleasant substances that pollute the water, air, or atmosphere. EG *They didn't seem to notice the pollution and the noise.*

polo /pəʊləʊ/ is a game played between two teams N UNCOUNT of players. The players ride horses and use wooden hammers with long handles to hit a ball.

polo-necked /pəʊləʊ nɛkt/. A **polo-necked** ADJ CLASSIF : sweater has a thick fold of material at the top ATTRIB which covers most of a person's neck.

poltergeist /pɒltəgaɪst/, **poltergeists.** A **polter-** N COUNT **geist** is an invisible force which is believed to move furniture or throw objects around, and which is often thought of as a type of ghost.

poly /pɒliᶦ/, **polys.** A **poly** is the same as a N COUNT polytechnic. EG *...a poly student.* Informal

polyester /pɒliˈɛstə/ is a type of cloth used espe- N UNCOUNT cially to make clothes. EG *...polyester skirts.*

polystyrene /pɒliˈstaɪriːn/ is a very light, plastic N UNCOUNT substance used especially to make containers or as an insulating material. EG *...white polystyrene ceiling tiles... ...foam polystyrene.*

polytechnic /pɒliˈtɛknɪk/, **polytechnics.** A N COUNT **polytechnic** is a college in Britain where you can go to study after leaving school. EG *...a course in drama at Manchester Polytechnic.*

polythene /pɒliˈθiːn/ is a type of plastic made into N UNCOUNT thin sheets or bags and used especially to keep food fresh. EG *...a polythene bag.*

polyunsaturated /pɒliˈʌnsætjəˈreɪtɪᵈd/. **Polyun-** ADJ CLASSIF **saturated** oils and margarines are made mainly from vegetable fats and are considered healthier than those made from animal fats.

pomegranate /pɒmiˈgrænɪt/, **pomegranates.** A N COUNT **pomegranate** is a round fruit with a thick, reddish skin. It contains lots of small seeds with juicy flesh around them.

pomp /pɒmp/ is the use of a lot of ceremony, fine N UNCOUNT clothes, and decorations, especially on a special occasion. EG *...coming ashore with pomp and ceremony... ...the pomp of Queen Elizabeth's court.*

pompous /pɒmpəs/. **1** Someone who is **pompous** ADJ QUALIT behaves in a very serious way because they think they are more important than they really are; used showing disapproval. EG *Anything I say about it is bound to sound pompous... ...a pompous document of over 500 pages.* ◇ **pompously.** EG *They puffed* ◇ ADV *pompously at fat German cigars.* ◇ **pomposity** ◇ N UNCOUNT /pɒmpɒsɪ'tiᶦ/. EG *They were annoyed by my pom-* Formal *posity, my insistence on taking the blame for the whole affair.*
2 A **pompous** building or ceremony is very grand ADJ QUALIT and elaborate. EG *...the pompous splendour of Hyde Park Hotel... ...a pompous celebration.*

pond /pɒnd/, **ponds.** A **pond** is a small area of N COUNT water that is smaller than a lake. EG *...an ornamental pond in the garden.*

ponder /pɒndə/, **ponders, pondering, pondered.** V : USU+A ; If you **ponder**, you think about something careful- ALSO V+O ly. EG *Hooper seemed to ponder for a moment, then* Literary *he nodded... Mary pondered upon the meaning of life... I pondered the ethics of the situation.*

ponderous /pɒndəᵘrəs/. **1** Speech or writing that ADJ QUALIT is **ponderous** is very dull and serious. EG *He spoke* Literary *in a slow, ponderous way.* ◇ **ponderously.** EG *She* ◇ ADV *nodded ponderously.*
2 An object that is **ponderous** is large and heavy. ADJ QUALIT EG *...ponderous royal tombs.* Literary
3 A **ponderous** action is very slow or clumsy. EG ADJ QUALIT *...taking a ponderous swing at the ball.* Literary ◇ **ponderously.** EG *Slowly, ponderously, the vehi-* ◇ ADV *cle shifted a few inches.*

pong /pɒŋ/, **pongs, ponging, ponged. 1** A **pong** is N COUNT an unpleasant smell. EG *There was a pong in the* British *room.* Informal
2 If you say that something **pongs**, you mean that v it has an unpleasant smell. EG *Take that thing away!* British *It pongs!* Informal

pontoon /pɒntuːn/, **pontoons.** A **pontoon** is a N COUNT floating platform, often one used to support a bridge. EG *...pontoon bridges.*

pony /pəʊniᶦ/, **ponies.** A **pony** is a type of small N COUNT horse. EG *Two girls rode up on small ponies.*

ponytail /pəʊniteɪl/, **ponytails.** A **ponytail** is a N COUNT hairstyle in which someone's hair is tied up at the

> What is an informal word for a polytechnic?

back of the head and hangs down like a tail. EG *She had her hair tied back in a ponytail.*

poodle /puːdᵊl/, **poodles.** A **poodle** is a type of N COUNT dog with thick curly hair.

pooh /puː/. You say **'Pooh'** to express your disgust EXCLAM at an unpleasant smell. EG *Pooh! It really stinks in* Informal *here!*

pool /puːl/, **pools, pooling, pooled.** 1 A **pool** is 1.1 N COUNT a small area of still or slow-moving water. EG *...long stretches of sand with rocks and pools.* 1.2 a swimming pool. EG *She went swimming in the hotel pool.*

2 A **pool** of liquid or light is a small area of it. EG *He* N COUNT+of *was lying dead in a pool of blood... A spotlight threw a pool of violet light onto the stage.*

3 A **pool** of people, money, or things is a number of N COUNT+SUPP them that are collected together to be used or shared by several people or organizations. EG *...car pools... ...a pool of agricultural workers.*

4 If people **pool** their money, knowledge, or equip- V+O ment, they allow it to be collected and used or shared by all of them. EG *We pooled our money, bought a van, and travelled... Families pooled their food resources in a common kitchen.*

5 **Pool** is a game. Players use long, thin sticks to N UNCOUNT hit coloured balls with numbers on them into six holes around the edges of a table. EG *...a pool table.*

6 If you do the **pools**, you take part in a gambling N PLURAL: competition in which people try to win money by the+N guessing correctly the results of football matches. British EG *...pools coupons... They won £300,000 on the Pools.*

poor /pʊə, pɔː/, **poorer, poorest.** 1 Someone who ADJ QUALIT is **poor** has very little money and few possessions. EG *I was a student then, and very poor... ...a poor family... He was now one thousand pounds poorer.*

2 The **poor** are people who are poor. EG *The* N PLURAL: *children of the poor are more likely to get diseases.* the+N

3 A **poor** country or place is inhabited by people ADJ QUALIT with very little money and few possessions. EG *...a shop in a poor part of Stratford... ...aid to the poorer countries.*

4 You can use **poor** to describe someone who you ADJ CLASSIF: are expressing sympathy for. EG *Poor old Dennis,* ATTRIB *he can't do a thing right.*

5 If you describe something as **poor**, you mean that ADJ QUALIT it is of a low quality or standard or that it is in bad condition. EG *...books in a very poor condition... In spite of poor health, I was able to continue work-ing... The pay was poor... ...poor weather condi-tions.* ◊ **poorly.** EG *...poorly designed equipment.* ◊ ADV

6 You also use **poor** to describe someone who is ADJ QUALIT: not very skilful in a particular activity. For exam- ATTRIB ple, a **poor** cook cooks badly. EG *She was a very poor swimmer... I am a poor businessman.* ◊ **poorly.** EG *I spoke Spanish so poorly.* ◊ ADV

7 If something is **poor** in a particular quality or ADJ PRED+in substance, it contains very little of the quality or substance. EG *The water was poor in oxygen... Their food was poor in nutritive value.*

poorly /pʊəliː, pɔː-/. If someone is **poorly**, they ADJ PRED are ill. EG *Your brother's had an operation and he's* Informal *quite poorly.* British

pop /pɒp/, **pops, popping, popped.** 1 **Pop** is N UNCOUNT modern music that usually has a strong rhythm and uses electronic equipment. EG *...pop music... ...pop concerts... ...a pop group.*

2 You can refer to fizzy drinks such as lemonade as N MASS **pop.** EG *...soda pop.* Informal

3 Some people call their father **Pop.** EG *Pop and I* N PROPER *went for walks.* OR VOCATIVE

4 **Pop** is used to represent a short sharp sound, for example the sound made by bursting a balloon or by pulling a cork out of a bottle. EG *The cork came out with a loud pop.* ▶ used as a verb. EG *The engine* ▶ V *began coughing and popping... The cork popped and flew out of the bottle.*

5 If your eyes **pop**, you look very surprised or V Informal

excited. EG *His mouth hung open and his eyes popped.*

6 If you **pop** something somewhere, you put it V+O+A there quickly. EG *He popped a piece of gum into his* Informal *mouth... I popped a note through her letter box.*

7 If you **pop** into or out of a place, you quickly go in V+A or out. EG *Suddenly she popped out from behind a bush... Why don't you pop in for a coffee... I'm just popping out for a haircut.*

pop up. If someone or something **pops up**, they PHRASAL VB: appear in a place or situation unexpectedly. EG *He's* V+ADV *one of those rare types who pops up every so often.*

popcorn /pɒpkɔːn/ is a snack which consists of N UNCOUNT grains of maize that are heated until they burst and become large and light. EG *...a bag of popcorn.*

Pope /pəʊp/, **Popes.** The **Pope** is the head of the N COUNT OR Roman Catholic Church. EG *...Pope John Paul II.* N PROPER

poplar /pɒplə/, **poplars.** A **poplar** is a type of tall, N COUNT thin tree.

popper

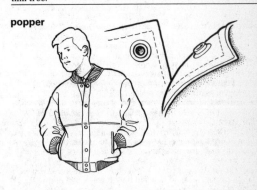

popper /pɒpə/, **poppers.** A **popper** is a device for N COUNT fastening clothes. It consists of two pieces of plastic British or metal, one with a small lump on it and the other with a small hole in it. You press the two bits together in order to fasten the popper.

poppy /pɒpiː/, **poppies.** A **poppy** is a plant with a N COUNT large, delicate, red flower.

populace /pɒpjʊləs/. The **populace** of a country N SING: the+N is its people. EG *They represented only a fraction of* Formal *the general populace... The populace went wild.*

popular /pɒpjʊlə/. 1 Something that is **popular** is ADJ QUALIT enjoyed or liked by a lot of people. EG *The Tower of London is the most popular tourist attraction in Britain... Swimming is very popular with all ages.* ◊ **popularity** /pɒpjʊlærɪtiː/. EG *...the popularity* ◊ N UNCOUNT *of science fiction films.*

2 **Popular** ideas or attitudes are approved of or ADJ CLASSIF: held by most people. EG *Contrary to popular belief,* ATTRIB *science does not offer us certainties... ...the popular image of feminism.*

3 **Popular** newspapers and television programmes ADJ CLASSIF are aimed at ordinary people and not at specialists ATTRIB in a particular subject. EG *The popular press is obsessed with the Royal Family... ...a series of popular talks on medicine.*

4 Someone who is **popular** is liked by most people. ADJ QUALIT EG *He became a popular Governor... He has always been popular among Conservatives.* ◊ **popularity.** ◊ N UNCOUNT EG *...his immense popularity with radio audiences.*

5 **Popular** is used to describe political activities ADJ CLASSIF: which involve all people, and not just members of ATTRIB political parties. EG *This is not a mere party issue,* Formal *but deserves wider popular debate... ...their advoca-cy of popular democracy.*

popularize /pɒpjʊləraɪz/, **popularizes, popular-izing, popularized;** also spelled **popularise.** 1 To V+O **popularize** something means to make a lot of people interested in it and able to enjoy it. EG *Television has done a great deal to popularize snooker.*

2 To **popularize** an academic subject or scientific idea means to make it more easily understandable to ordinary people. EG *Scientific notions soon become inaccurate when they are popularized.* v+o Formal

popularly /pɒpjəˈlɒli¹/. You use **popularly** to indicate **1** that a name or title is used by most people, although it is not the official name or title. EG *This theory was popularly called the Big Bang.* **2** that an idea is believed by most people, although it may not be true. EG *It is popularly believed that eating carrots makes you see better in the dark.* ADV

populate /pɒpjəˈleɪt/, **populates, populating, populated. 1** If an area **is populated** by people or animals, those people or animals live there, often in large numbers. EG *The town is heavily populated by immigrants... ...the rabbits that thickly populated the area.* ◊ **populated.** EG *...the densely populated countryside.* v+o : USU PASS ◊ ADJ QUALIT

2 To **populate** an area means to cause plants, animals, or people to live there. EG *Convicts from France were sent to populate the islands.* v+o

population /pɒpjəˈleɪʃ⁰n/, **populations.** The **population** of a country or area is **1** all the people who live in it. EG *The country is unable to feed its population... Kandahar has a population of 230,000... ...the increase in population.* **2** all the people or animals of a particular type in it. EG *...a prison population of 44,000... In these areas, populations of mosquitoes are greatly reduced.* N COUNT OR N UNCOUNT N COUNT : USU+SUPP

populous /pɒpjəˈləs/. A **populous** country or area has a lot of people living in it. EG *...the less populous areas of London.* ADJ QUALIT Formal

porcelain /pɔːsⁱliⁿn/ is a hard, shiny substance made by heating clay. It is used to make cups, plates, and ornaments. EG *...antique pottery and porcelain... ...a porcelain statue.* N UNCOUNT

porch /pɔːtʃ/, **porches.** A **porch** is **1** a sheltered area at the entrance to a building. It has a roof and sometimes has walls. EG *...a big house with a glass porch.* **2** a raised platform built along the outside wall of a house and often covered with a roof. EG *She sat beside me on the back porch.* N COUNT American

porcupine /pɔːkjəˈpaɪn/, **porcupines.** A **porcupine** is an animal with many long, thin, sharp spikes on its back. N COUNT

pore /pɔː/, **pores, poring, pored. 1** Your **pores** are the small holes in your skin. EG *...the pores round his nose.* N COUNT

2 The **pores** of a plant are the small holes on its surface. EG *...mushrooms with minute yellow pores.* N COUNT

3 Pores in rocks or soil are the tiny gaps or cracks in them. EG *...water trapped in pores in rocks.* N COUNT

pore over. If you **pore over** information, you look at it and study it very carefully. EG *Monks pored over ancient texts... We pored over our maps.* PHRASAL VB : V+PREP, HAS PASS

pork /pɔːk/ is meat from a pig, usually fresh and not smoked or salted. EG *...pork chops.* N UNCOUNT

porn /pɔːn/ means the same as pornography. EG *...porn shops... ...porn movies.* N UNCOUNT Informal

pornography /pɔːˈnɒgrəfi¹/ refers to books, magazines, and films that are designed to cause sexual excitement by showing naked people or referring to sexual acts. EG *...pornography in the cinema.* ◊ **pornographic** /pɔːnəˈgræfɪk/. EG *...pornographic films and magazines.* N UNCOUNT ◊ ADJ QUALIT

porous /pɔːrəs/. Something that is **porous** has many small holes in it, which water and air can pass through. EG *The volcanic rocks are porous.* ADJ QUALIT

porpoise /pɔːpəs/, **porpoises.** A **porpoise** is a sea animal that looks similar to a dolphin. N COUNT

porridge /pɒrɪdʒ/ is a thick, sticky food made from oats cooked in water or milk. N UNCOUNT

port /pɔːt/, **ports. 1** A **port** is **1.1** a town by the sea or on a river, which has a harbour. EG *...a fishing port... It is the major port on this coastline.* **1.2** a harbour area with docks and warehouses, where ships load or unload goods or passengers. N COUNT

2 The **port** side of a ship is the left side when you ADJ CLASSIF : ATTRIB

are facing towards the front of it. EG *A wave caught the trawler on her port bow.* ▸ used as a noun. EG *...a hundred yards to port.* ▸ N UNCOUNT

3 Port is a type of strong, sweet red wine. EG *...a glass of port.* N MASS

portable /pɔːtəbə⁰l/. A machine or device that is **portable** is designed to be easily carried or moved. EG *...a little portable TV... ...portable typewriters... ...a portable radio.* ADJ CLASSIF

portal /pɔːtə⁰l/, **portals.** A **portal** is a large, impressive doorway at the entrance to a building. EG *...villas with huge marble portals.* N COUNT Literary

portent /pɔːtɛnt/, **portents.** A **portent** is something that indicates what is likely to happen in the future. EG *Are dreams a portent of things to come?.. ...a hopeful portent.* N COUNT Formal

portentous /pɔːtɛntəs/. Something that is **portentous** is important in indicating or affecting future events. EG *Its consequences were historically portentous.* ADJ QUALIT Formal

porter /pɔːtə/, **porters.** A **porter** is **1** a person whose job is to be in charge of the entrance of a building such as a hotel. EG *...throwing open doors like a hotel porter.* **2** a person whose job is to carry things, for example to carry people's luggage at a railway station. EG *...railway porters.* N COUNT

portfolio /pɔːtˈfəʊliəʊ/, **portfolios.** A **portfolio** is **1** a thin, flat case for carrying papers or drawings in. **2** a set of drawings or paintings that represent an artist's work. EG *...a portfolio of photographs.* N COUNT

porthole /pɔːthəʊl/, **portholes.** A **porthole** is a small round window on the side of a ship or aircraft. EG *...the portholes of the cabin.* N COUNT

portico /pɔːtɪkəʊ/, **porticos** or **porticoes.** A **portico** is a large, covered area at the entrance to a building, with pillars supporting the roof. EG *...a palace with a huge marble portico.* N COUNT Formal

portion /pɔːʃⁿn/, **portions, portioning, portioned. 1** A **portion** of something is a part of it. EG *...the lower portion of the counter... Divide the cake into eight portions... A large portion of this money would come to her.* N PART

2 A **portion** is the amount of food that is given to one person at a meal. EG *He held out his plate for a second portion... ...a small portion.* N PART

portion out. If you **portion out** something, you share it out among a group of people. EG *...the food that Tim was carefully portioning out.* PHRASAL VB : V+O+ADV

portly /pɔːtli/, **portlier, portliest.** Someone who is **portly**, especially a man, is rather fat. EG *...portly middle-aged gentlemen.* ADJ QUALIT Outdated

portrait /pɔːtrɪ¹t/, **portraits.** A **portrait** is a painting, drawing, or photograph of someone. EG *...a famous portrait of the musician... She painted landscapes and portraits.* N COUNT

portray /pɔːtreɪ/, **portrays, portraying, portrayed. 1** When an actor or actress **portrays** someone, he or she plays that person in a play or film. EG *In her final sketch she portrayed a temperamental countess... The animals were portrayed by actors in masks.* v+o

2 When a writer or artist **portrays** something, he or she writes a description or produces a painting of it. EG *...writers who tried to portray London in words.* v+o

3 If you **portray** someone or something in a certain way, you give a particular impression of them by emphasizing some of their features. EG *Advertising tends to portray women in a very traditional role... Minor mishaps were portrayed as major tragedies.* v+o+A

portrayal /pɔːtreɪəl/, **portrayals. 1** An actor's **portrayal** of a character in a play or film is the way that he or she portrays the character. EG *He* N COUNT : USU+*of*

Find an outdated word on these pages to describe someone who is fat.

got the award for his portrayal of Willy Loman in
'Death of a Salesman'.

2 An artist's **portrayal** of something is a drawing,   N COUNT:
painting, or photograph of it. ...*an eye-catching*   USU+*of*
portrayal of the beautiful Madame Chiang.

3 The **portrayal** of something in a book or film is   N COUNT:
3.1 the act of describing it or showing it. EG   USU+*of*
...*portrayals of sexual behaviour.* **3.2** the way that it
is made to appear. EG ...*his portrayal by the media
as an enemy of democracy.*

pose /pəʊz/, poses, posing, posed. **1** If you **pose**   V : USU+A
for a photograph or painting, you stay in a particu-
lar position so that someone can photograph you or
paint you. EG *The bride and groom posed for the
photograph.*

2 You can say that people **are posing** when they   V
behave in an exaggerated way because they want
other people to admire them. ◊ **poser, posers.** EG   ◊ N COUNT
You're always posing. How I hate posers.

3 If you **pose** as someone, you pretend to be that   V+*as*
person in order to deceive people. EG ...*an agent
posing as a telephone engineer.*

4 If something **poses** a problem or a danger, it is   V+O
the cause of the problem or danger. EG *The ship's
length must pose considerable steering problems...
He posed a serious threat to their authority.*

5 If you **pose** a question, you ask it. EG *This brings*   V+O
me back to the question you posed earlier.   Formal

6 Your **pose** is the way that you stand, sit, or lie,   N COUNT+SUPP
especially when you are being photographed. EG
...*hundreds of photographs in various poses.*

7 A **pose** is also a way of behaving that is intended   N COUNT:
to impress or deceive people. EG ...*his pose as the*   USU+SUPP
champion of the proletariat.

posh /pɒʃ/. **1** If you describe something as **posh,**   ADJ QUALIT
you mean that it is smart, fashionable, and expen-   Informal
sive. EG *She had stayed in posh hotels.*

2 If you describe a person as **posh,** you mean that   ADJ QUALIT
they belong to the upper classes. EG ...*your posh*   Informal
friends... ...putting on her posh voice.

position /pəzɪʃəⁿn/, positions, positioning, positioned. **1** The **position** of someone or something is
1.1 the place where they are. EG *They tell the time*   N COUNT OR
by the position of the sun... The house is in a very   N UNCOUNT
*exposed position... He had shifted position from the
front to the back of the room.* **1.2** the way in which   N COUNT+SUPP
they are sitting or lying, or the direction in which
they are facing. EG *I helped her to a sitting position... Hold it in an upright position... He pushed the
catch down into the ready position.*

2 If someone or something is **in position**, they are   PHRASE
in their correct or usual place. EG *By 8.05 the
groups were in position... Keep it in position with a
rubber band.*

3 If you **position** something somewhere, you put it   V+O
there. EG *Mel positioned his car alongside the*   OR V-REFL:
foreman's... The boy positioned himself near the   USU+A
door.

4 Your **position** in society is the importance that   N COUNT+SUPP
you have in it. EG *Women hold a strong position in
Aboriginal society... ...people in positions of power
and influence.*

5 A **position** in a company or organization is a job   N COUNT
or post in it. EG ...*top management positions... Thorn*   Formal
lost his position as steward.

6 Your **position** in a race or competition is your   N COUNT+SUPP
place among the winners at the end, or your place
at some time during the event. EG *She sprinted hard
to hold third position.*

7 Your **position** at a particular time is the situa-   N COUNT+SUPP
tion that you are in. EG *It puts me in a rather
difficult position... You are in the fortunate position
of having no responsibilities.*

8 If you are **in a position** to do something, you are   PHRASE
able to do it. If you are **in no position** to do it, you
are unable to do it. EG *I would then be in a position
to do that for her... He's in a good position to
predict the election results... They were in no
position to help.*

9 If you say that you are **in no position** to criticize   PHRASE
someone, you mean that you do not want to,
because you are equally guilty or wrong. EG ...*nor
are we in any position to reproach them.*

10 Your **position** on a particular subject or situa-   N COUNT+SUPP
tion is your attitude towards it or your opinion of it.   Formal
EG ...*if you take a multilateralist position... What is
their position on the proposed sale of aircraft?*

positive /pɒzɪtɪv/. **1** If you are **positive** about   ADJ PRED :
something, you are completely sure about it. EG *He*   OFT+REPORT
was positive that he had seen it in the newspaper...   OR *about*
'Are you sure you don't want her address?' –
'Positive.'

2 If you have a **positive** attitude to things, you are   ADJ QUALIT
hopeful and confident. EG *I began to feel more
positive... ...positive feelings about life.*

3 If you make a **positive** decision or take **positive**   ADJ QUALIT
action, you do something definite in order to deal
with a task or problem. EG *They have a positive
policy of preventative dental care.*

4 Feelings or actions that are considered morally   ADJ QUALIT
good or socially useful are sometimes described as
positive. EG ...*positive feelings like tenderness and
joy... Being creative and productive are seen as
positive values.*

5 If the response to something is **positive,** it shows   ADJ QUALIT
agreement, approval, or encouragement. EG *Public
response was positive.* ◊ **positively.** EG *Thomson*   ◊ ADV
*replied positively: 'There will be no change in
policy.'*

6 Positive evidence gives definite proof of the   ADJ CLASSIF:
truth or identity of something. EG *I was looking for*   ATTRIB
*some positive evidence that Barney came to the
flat.* ◊ **positively.** EG *The body has been positively*   ◊ ADV
identified.

7 If a medical or scientific test is **positive,** it shows   ADJ CLASSIF
that something has happened or is present. EG ...*a
positive pregnancy test.*

8 A **positive** number is greater than zero.   ADJ CLASSIF

9 You can use **positive** to describe a surprising or   ADJ CLASSIF:
unexpected pleasant quality that something has. EG   ATTRIB
*I find cooking a positive pleasure... Life in a town
brings positive advantages to children.*

positively /pɒzɪtɪvli¹/. You use **positively 1** to   ADV SEN
emphasize that you really mean what you are
saying. EG *It's quite positively the last time that
you'll see me.* **2** to emphasize that something really   ADV
is the case, although it may sound surprising or
extreme. EG *Her friends had been positively abusive... I didn't object. I positively approved her
initiative.*

POSS stands for **possessive**

Some nouns have the label +POSS in the Extra
Column. This means that there is either a possessive form before it or a prepositional group immediately after it.

1 The possessive form can be a possessive determiner (DET POSS), such as *my, your, her, his, its,
our, their.* For example, ...*her relatives... ...our
house.*

2 The possessive form can be a noun or a name
with an apostrophe *"s"*, such as *the writer's, someone's, John's,* and *Professor Smith's.* If the noun is
plural, or if it already ends in 's', the possessive is
formed by adding only an apostrophe, as in *I've
read all Dickens' books... ...the teachers' strike.*

3 The prepositional group following the noun must
begin with 'of', as in *They said a prayer for the
souls of the men who had drowned.*

---

possess /pəzɛs/, possesses, possessing, pos-
sessed. **1** If you **possess** something, you have it or   V+O : NO CONT,
  NO IMPER

own it. EG *How I longed to possess a suit like that... They were found guilty of possessing petrol bombs.*

2 If something **possesses** a particular feature or quality, it has that feature or quality. EG *For hundreds of years London possessed only one bridge... Television possesses a superficial magic.*   v+o : NO CONT, NO IMPER Formal

3 If you **possess** a quality or ability, you have that quality or ability. EG *He possessed the qualities of a war leader... ...skills they do not possess.*   v+o : NO CONT, NO IMPER

4 If a feeling or belief **possesses** you, it strongly influences your behaviour or thinking. EG *A violent rage possessed him... I was possessed with the notion that I was not alone.*   v+o : NO CONT, NO IMPER Literary

possession /pəzeʃ°n/, **possessions. 1** Possession is the state of having or owning something. EG *Freedom depended on the possession of land... The possession of a degree does not guarantee you a job... They took possession of the island.*   N UNCOUNT USU+POSS

2 If something is in your **possession** or if you are **in possession** of it, you have it or have obtained it. EG *I had in my possession a portion of the money... The document came into the possession of the Daily Mail... MacDonald has been in possession of the letter for some weeks.*   PHRASE Formal

3 Your **possessions** are the things that you own or have with you at a particular time. EG *He had few possessions... Check your possessions on arrival.*   N COUNT : USU PLURAL

possessive /pəzesɪv/. **1** Someone who is **possessive** about another person wants all that person's love and attention. EG *She was very possessive about Rod.* ◊ **possessiveness.** EG *...a child's possessiveness towards its mother.*   ADJ QUALIT ◊ N UNCOUNT

2 When people are **possessive** about things that they own, they do not like other people to use them. EG *I am possessive about my car.*   ADJ QUALIT

3 **Possessive** is a grammatical term used to describe words that indicate the person or thing that an object, feature, or quality belongs to.   ADJ CLASSIF OR N COUNT

possessor /pəzesɔ/, **possessors.** The **possessor** of something is the person who has it or owns it. EG *I was the proud possessor of two tickets to the opera.*   N COUNT : USU+POSS Formal

possibility /pɒsɪbɪlɪˈtiˈ/, **possibilities. 1** If you say there is a **possibility** that something is true, you mean that it might be true. EG *We must accept the possibility that we might be wrong.*   N COUNT : OFT+REPORT OR SUPP

2 If there is a **possibility** of something happening, it might happen. EG *There was now no possibility of success.*   N COUNT : OFT+of OR REPORT

3 If there is a **possibility** of someone doing something, they could do it and might do it. EG *I considered the possibility of joining the Communist Party... That was one of the possibilities that was suggested.*   N COUNT+SUPP

possible /pɒsɪb°l/, **possibles. 1** If it is **possible** to do something, it can be done. EG *It is possible for us to measure my progress... They are doing everything possible to take care of you... They wished, where possible, to avoid new conflicts... Whenever possible, loads were flown in... 'When do you want to go?' - 'This weekend, if possible.'*   ADJ CLASSIF

2 A **possible** event is one that might happen. EG *His staff warned him of the possible consequences.*   ADJ CLASSIF

3 If you describe someone as, for example, a **possible** Prime Minister, you mean that he or she may become the Prime Minister. EG *America and Russia were both possible financiers of the dam.*   ADJ CLASSIF ATTRIB

4 If you say that it is **possible** that something is true or correct, you mean that although you do not know whether it is true or correct, you accept that it might be. EG *It is possible that he said these things... That's one possible answer.*   ADJ CLASSIF

5 If you do something **as soon as possible**, you do it as soon as you can. If you get **as much as possible** of something, you get as much of it as you can. EG *Go as soon as possible... I like to know as much as possible about my patients... He sat as far away from the others as possible.*   PHRASE

6 If you describe something as **the best possible**   PHRASE

or **the worst possible** thing, you mean that no other thing of that kind could be better or worse. EG *We provide the best possible accommodation for our students... ...the harshest possible conditions.*

7 If you describe someone or something as a **possible**, you mean that they are one of several people or things that could be chosen for a particular job or purpose. EG *He sounds like a possible... The first three houses were all possibles.*   N COUNT

possibly /pɒsɪbliˈ/. **1** You use **possibly** to indicate that you are not sure whether something is true or might happen. EG *Television is possibly to blame for this... The threat was possibly not very great... This must have been a little reading-room, possibly Leo's study.*   ADV SEN

2 You use **possibly** to emphasize that you are surprised, puzzled, or shocked by something that you have seen or heard. EG *How could it possibly accomplish anything?... I wondered what he could possibly be doing it for.*   ADV+INF

3 You use **possibly** to emphasize that someone has tried their hardest to do something, or has done it as well as they can. EG *He planned to come back as soon as he possibly could... I have made myself as comfortable as I possibly can... He will do everything he possibly can to aid you.*   ADV+MODAL

4 You use **possibly** with a negative modal, to emphasize that something definitely cannot happen or definitely cannot be done. EG *I can't possibly stay in all the weekend... Nobody could possibly tell the difference.*   ADV

post /pəʊst/, **posts, posting, posted. 1** The **post** is the public service or system by which letters and parcels are collected and delivered. EG *You'll get these through the post... There is a cheque for you in the post... Winners will be notified by post.*   N SING : the+N OR by+N British

2 You can refer to letters and parcels that are delivered to you as your **post**. EG *There is some post for you... Rose was reluctant to answer her post.*   N UNCOUNT

3 If you **post** a letter or parcel, you send it to someone by putting it in a post-box or by taking it to a post office. EG *I'm going to post a letter... I'll be glad to post you details... Post it to the social security office.*   v+o, v+o+o, OR V+o+to

4 If you **keep** someone **posted**, you keep giving them the latest information about a situation that they are interested in. EG *David promised to keep them posted.*   PHRASE

5 A **post** is a strong, upright pole made of wood or metal that is fixed into the ground. EG *A dog sat chained to a post outside.* ● See also **lamp-post.**   N COUNT

6 A **post** in a company or organization is a job or official position in it. EG *...a post at the High School... She is well qualified for the post.*   N COUNT Formal

7 In a battle, a soldier's or sailor's **post** is the place where he or she has been told to remain and to do his or her job. EG *Every man was at his post... He had to leave his post and flee.*   N COUNT+POSS

8 If you **are posted** somewhere, you are sent there by the organization that you work for. EG *I have been posted to Paris.*   v+o+A : USU PASS

post- is used to form words that describe something as taking place after a particular date, event, or period. For example, post-school education is education that you receive after you have left school. EG *...the post-1918 period... ...a post-election survey.*   PREFIX

postage /pəʊstɪdʒ/ is the money that you pay for sending letters and parcels by post. EG *Send 25p extra for postage and packing.*   N UNCOUNT

postage stamp, postage stamps. A **postage stamp** is a small piece of gummed paper that you buy from the post office and stick on an envelope or parcel before you post it.   N COUNT

Where would you put a postcode?

postal /pəʊstəºl/ is used to describe things con- ADJ CLASSIF:
nected with the public service of carrying letters ATTRIB
and parcels from one place to another. EG ...increas-
es in postal charges... ...the postal service.

postal order, postal orders. A **postal order** is a N COUNT
piece of paper representing a sum of money which British
you can buy at a post office and send to someone as
a way of sending them money by post.

post-box, post-boxes. A **post-box** is a metal box N COUNT
with a hole in it, which you put letters into to be
collected by a postman.

postcard /pəʊstkɑːd/, **postcards.** A **postcard** is a N COUNT
piece of thin card, often with a picture on one side,
which you can write on and send to people without
using an envelope. EG I sent her a postcard from
Eastbourne.

postcode /pəʊstkəʊd/, **postcodes.** Your **post-** N COUNT
code is a short sequence of numbers and letters at British
the end of your address, which helps the post office
to sort the mail.

poster /pəʊstə/, **posters.** A **poster** is a large N COUNT
notice or picture that you stick on a wall or
noticeboard, often in order to advertise something.
EG ...cinema posters... ...colourful posters of Paris
and Venice.

posterity /pɒsterɪ¹ti¹/. You can refer to everyone N UNCOUNT
who will be alive in the future as **posterity.** EG This Formal
fine building should be preserved for posterity.

postgraduate /pəʊstgrædjuːət/, **postgraduates.** N COUNT
A **postgraduate** is a student with a first degree
from a university who is studying or doing research at a more advanced level. ▶ used as an ▶ ADJ CLASSIF:
adjective. EG ...postgraduate students... Many stu- ATTRIB
dents go on and do postgraduate work.

posthumous /pɒstjʊ⁴məs/ is used to describe ADJ CLASSIF
something that happens after someone's death but
that relates to something that they did before they
died. EG ...a posthumous award for bravery... ...a
posthumous publication. ◊ **posthumously.** EG ...a ◊ ADV
posthumously published article.

posting /pəʊstɪŋ/, **postings.** A **posting** is a job N COUNT
that you are given by your employers, which
involves going to a different town or country. EG
I've been given an overseas posting to Japan.

postman /pəʊstməºn/, **postmen.** A **postman** is a N COUNT
man whose job is to collect and deliver letters and
parcels that are sent by post.

postmark /pəʊstmɑːk/, **postmarks.** A **postmark** N COUNT
is a mark which is printed on letters and parcels at
a post office. It shows the time and place at which
something is posted.

postmaster /pəʊstmɑːstə/, **postmasters.** A N COUNT
postmaster is a man who is in charge of a post Outdated
office.

postmistress /pəʊstmɪstrɪ²s/, **postmistresses.** N COUNT
A **postmistress** is a woman who is in charge of a Outdated
post office.

post-mortem /pəʊst mɔːtəm/, **post-mortems.** A N COUNT
post-mortem is a medical examination of a dead
person's body in order to find out how they died.

post office, post offices. 1 The **Post Office** is N SING: the+N
the national organization that is responsible for
postal services.
2 A **post office** is a building where you can buy N COUNT
stamps, post letters and parcels, and use other
services provided by the national postal service.

postpone /pəºstⁱpəʊn/, **postpones, postponing,** V+O: OFT+A
postponed. If you **postpone** an event, you arrange
for it to take place at a later time than was
originally planned. EG Could you postpone your
departure for five minutes?... The flight had been
postponed until eleven o'clock. ◊ **postponement** ◊ N COUNT OR
/pəºstⁱpəʊnməºnt/, **postponements.** EG ...the post- N UNCOUNT
ponement of the wedding.

postscript /pəʊstskrɪpt/, **postscripts.** A **post-** N COUNT
script is a message written at the end of a letter
after you have signed your name. You usually
write 'PS' in front of it.

posture /pɒstʃə/, **postures, posturing, postured.**
1 Your **posture** is the position or manner in which N UNCOUNT:
you stand or sit. EG ...his stiff, upright posture... USU+SUPP
...hands held out in the imploring posture of a
beggar.
2 A **posture** is also an attitude that you have N COUNT+SUPP
towards something. EG They are trying to adopt a
more co-operative posture.
3 You say that someone **is posturing** when they V: USU CONT
are trying to give a particular impression in order Formal
to deceive people. EG ...posturing to project an air of
knowledge.

post-war is used to describe things that happen, ADJ CLASSIF:
exist, or are made in the period immediately after ATTRIB
a war, especially the 1939-45 war. EG ...a postwar
building... ...a relic of the postwar era.

posy /pəʊzi¹/, **posies.** A **posy** is a small bunch of N COUNT
flowers. EG ...posies of wild flowers.

pot /pɒt/, **pots, potting, potted.** 1 A **pot** is a deep N COUNT
round container used for cooking, especially one OR N PART
used for cooking stews and soups. EG ...clay pots.
2 You can refer to a teapot or coffee pot as a **pot.** N COUNT
You can also refer to the tea or coffee inside it as a OR N PART
pot. EG I'll go and make a fresh pot of tea.
3 A **pot** is also a deep bowl or cylindrical container N COUNT
for paint or some other thick liquid. EG There were OR N PART
old paint pots stacked on the shelves.
4 You can refer to a flowerpot as a **pot.** EG Pots of N COUNT
geraniums stood on the window-sill.
5 If you **pot** a plant, you put it into a flowerpot V+O
filled with earth, so that it can grow there.
◊ **potted.** EG ...watering the potted plants. ◊ ADJ CLASSIF
6 Cannabis is sometimes referred to as **pot.** EG He N UNCOUNT
was said to have smoked pot occasionally. Informal
7 See also **chimney pot, melting pot, potted.**

potato /pəteɪtəʊ/, **potatoes.** A **potato** is a round N COUNT OR
white vegetable with a brown or red skin. Potatoes N UNCOUNT
grow underground. EG ...baked potatoes.

potent /pəʊtəºnt/. 1 Something that is **potent** is ADJ QUALIT
very effective and powerful. EG Potent new weap-
ons will shortly be available... ...a potent argument.
◊ **potency** /pəʊtəºnsi¹/. EG Princess Ida's spell lost ◊ N UNCOUNT:
its potency... ...the potency of history. USU+POSS
2 A man who is **potent** is capable of having sex. EG ADJ QUALIT
In early adulthood you are at your most potent.
◊ **potency.** EG ...sexual potency. ◊ N UNCOUNT

potentate /pəʊtəºnteɪt/, **potentates.** A **potentate** N COUNT
is a ruler who has direct power over his people. Formal

potential /pətenʃəºl/. 1 You use **potential** to ADJ CLASSIF:
describe something as capable of becoming a ATTRIB
particular kind of thing. EG All 92 countries are
customers or potential customers of the United
States... ...potential sources of food production.
◊ **potentially.** EG Electricity is potentially danger- ◊ SUBMOD
ous, so treat it with respect.
2 Your **potential** is the range of abilities and N UNCOUNT
talents that you have, although these abilities and +SUPP
talents may not be in full use yet. EG Many children
do not achieve their potential.
3 If you say that someone or something has **poten-** N UNCOUNT
tial, you mean that they have the necessary ability +SUPP
or quality to be successful or to develop in a
particular way. EG Has this woman got executive
potential?... The land has great strategic potential.

potentiality /pətenʃæli¹ti¹/, **potentialities.** If N COUNT OR
something has **potentiality** or **potentialities,** it is N UNCOUNT
capable of being used or developed in particular +SUPP
ways. EG ...the realization of human potentiality... Formal
He was swift to publicise the potentialities of
motoring and flight.

pothole /pɒthəʊl/, **potholes.** A **pothole** is a large N COUNT
hole in the surface of a road, caused by traffic and
bad weather. EG ...ground that is riddled with potholes.

potion /pəʊʃəºn/, **potions.** A **potion** is a drink that N COUNT
contains medicine, poison, or something that is
supposed to have magic powers. EG ...a medicine
chest stuffed with potions and ointments... ...love
potions.

potted /pɒtɪ²d/. **1 Potted** meat or fish has been cooked and put into a small sealed container. EG ...potted shrimps. _ADJ CLASSIF: ATTRIB_

2 A **potted** biography or history contains the main facts about someone or something in a short and simplified form. EG ...potted character studies of famous authors. _ADJ CLASSIF: ATTRIB_

potter /pɒtə/, **potters, pottering, pottered.** A **potter** is someone who makes pottery. _N COUNT_

potter about. If you **potter about** or **potter around**, you pass the time in a gentle, unhurried way, doing pleasant but unimportant things. EG He loved to potter around in the garden. _PHRASAL VB: V+ADV/PREP British_

pottery /pɒtə°ri¹/, **potteries. 1 Pottery** is **1.1** pots, dishes, and other objects which are made from clay and then baked in an oven until they are hard. EG ...a sale of antique pottery and porcelain. **1.2** the craft or activity of making pottery. EG My hobbies are pottery and basket-weaving. _N UNCOUNT_

2 A **pottery** is a factory or workshop where pottery is made. _N COUNT_

potty /pɒti¹/, **potties. 1** A **potty** is a deep bowl which a small child uses instead of a toilet. _N COUNT_

2 If you say that someone is **potty**, you mean that they are crazy or foolish. EG They thought she was potty... I think it's a potty idea. _ADJ QUALIT Informal_

pouch /paʊtʃ/, **pouches. 1** A **pouch** is a flexible container like a small bag. EG He took the cards and put them in the leather pouch on his belt... ...a tobacco pouch. _N COUNT_

2 A **pouch** is also a pocket of skin on some animals. Female kangaroos have pouches on their stomachs in which their babies grow. _N COUNT_

poultry /poʊltri¹/. **Poultry** is both the singular and the plural form.

1 You can refer to chickens, ducks, and other birds that are kept for their eggs and meat as **poultry**. EG They keep poultry. _N PLURAL_

2 You can also refer to the meat of these birds as **poultry**. EG They sell a wide range of cooked, frozen and fresh poultry. _N UNCOUNT_

pounce /paʊns/, **pounces, pouncing, pounced. 1** When an animal or bird **pounces** on something, it leaps on it and grabs it. EG He had seen leopards pouncing on young baboons. _V : OFT +on/upon_

2 If someone **pounces** on you, they come towards you suddenly and take hold of you. EG The police were about to pounce upon us. _V : OFT +on/upon_

3 If you **pounce** on something such as a mistake, you draw attention to it. EG Local politicians are quick to pounce on any trouble. _V : OFT +on/upon_

pound /paʊnd/, **pounds, pounding, pounded. 1** A **pound** is a unit of money which is used in Britain. One British pound is divided into a hundred pence. Many other countries have a unit of money called a **pound**. EG I was paid fifty pounds a week... ...his thirty-five thousand pound house. _N COUNT_

2 The British currency system is sometimes referred to as the **pound**. EG ...a 13% fall in the pound against the dollar. _N SING : the+N_

3 A **pound** is also a unit of weight used mainly in Britain, America, and other countries where English is spoken. One pound is equivalent to 0.454 kilograms. EG ...one pound of rice... He weighs about 140 pounds. _N COUNT OR N PART_

4 If you **pound** something or **pound** on it, you hit it loudly and repeatedly. EG In frustration she would pound the dining-room table... They began pounding on the walls. ◊ **pounding.** EG The pounding of the drums grew louder. _V+O OR V+A ◊ N UNCOUNT_

5 If you **pound** something, you crush it into a paste or a powder or into very small pieces. EG The women of the village pounded grain in their mortars. _V+O_

6 If your heart **is pounding**, it is beating with an unusually strong and fast rhythm. EG My heart pounded with joy. ◊ **pounding.** EG I felt only the pounding of my heart. _V ◊ N UNCOUNT_

pour /pɔ:/, **pours, pouring, poured. 1** If you **pour** a liquid or other substance, you make it flow steadily out of a container by holding the container at an angle. EG The waiter poured the wine into her glass... ...a machine that poured grain into sacks. _V+O : USU+A_

2 If you **pour** someone a drink, you fill a cup or glass with the drink so that they can drink it. EG He poured Ellen a glass of wine... Lally poured herself another cup of tea... She poured a drink for herself. _V+O+O, V+O, OR V+O+for_

3 When a liquid or other substance **pours** somewhere, for example through a hole, it flows there quickly and in large quantities. EG The rain poured through a hole in the roof... The sweat began to pour down his face. _V+A_

4 When it rains very heavily, you can say that it **is pouring**. EG In London it poured all the time... It was absolutely pouring with rain. ◊ **pouring.** EG Don't go out in the pouring rain. _V OR V+A ◊ ADJ CLASSIF: ATTRIB_

5 If people or animals **pour** into or out of a place, they go there quickly and in large numbers. EG Refugees are now pouring into this country. _V+A_

6 If information **pours** into or out of a place, a lot of it is obtained or given. EG Messages of encouragement poured in from people of all kinds... ...the lies that poured from headquarters. _V+A_

7 If you **pour** money or energy into an activity or organization, you use a lot of money or energy in order to do the activity or help the organization. EG The state is pouring money into further education... They poured their energies into religious reform. _V+O+into_

pour out. 1 If you **pour out** a drink, you fill a cup or glass with it. EG Castle poured out two glasses of whisky. **2** If you **pour out** your thoughts, feelings, or experiences, you tell someone all about them. EG I was on the verge of pouring out all my feelings. _PHRASAL VB : V+O+ADV_

pout /paʊt/, **pouts, pouting, pouted.** If you **pout**, you stick out your lips as a way of showing that you are annoyed. EG She tossed back her hair and pouted. ◊ **pouting.** EG ...girls with pouting mouths... ...a pouting blonde. _V ◊ ADJ CLASSIF_

poverty /pɒvəti¹/ is the state of being extremely poor. EG There are thousands living in poverty. _N UNCOUNT_

poverty-stricken. Poverty-stricken people or places are extremely poor. EG ...this small poverty-stricken town. _ADJ CLASSIF_

powder /paʊdə/, **powders, powdering, powdered. 1 Powder** consists of many tiny particles of a solid substance. EG Their bones turn to powder... ...washing powders. _N MASS_

2 A **powdered** substance is one which is in the form of a powder. EG ...powdered milk. _ADJ CLASSIF: ATTRIB_

3 If you **powder** yourself, you cover parts of your body with scented powder. EG She lightly powdered her face. ◊ **powdered.** EG You could see each wrinkle on her powdered face. _V+O OR V-REFL ◊ ADJ CLASSIF_

power /paʊə/, **powers, powering, powered. 1** If someone has **power**, they have a lot of control over people and activities. EG ...his yearning for power... It gave the President too much power. _N UNCOUNT_

2 If you have the ability or opportunity to do something, you can refer to this as a **power**. EG They did not have the power of speech... They lose the power to walk... They were equals except in earning power. ● If it is **in** or **within** your **power** to do something, you are able to do it. EG It may not be within their power to help... I did everything in my power to console her. _N UNCOUNT +SUPP ● PHRASE_

3 If someone in authority has the **power** to do something, they have the legal right to do it. EG ...the court's power to punish young offenders... The Government curbed the Lords' powers. _N COUNT OR N UNCOUNT +SUPP_

4 When people take **power** or come to **power**, they take charge of a country's affairs. EG The Wilson Government came to power in 1964... The Tories were restored to power for more than four _N UNCOUNT_

Are the 'powers that be' powerful?

years. ● If a group of people are **in power**, they ●PHRASE
are in charge of a country's affairs. EG *The Tories
were in power at the time.*

5 If you talk about **the powers that be**, you are PHRASE
referring to the people in authority. EG *He was
commissioned to write this report by the powers
that be.*

6 The **power** of something is the physical strength N UNCOUNT
that it has to move or damage things. EG *I underes-* +SUPP
timated the power of the explosion.

7 Power is the energy that is obtained, for exam- N UNCOUNT
ple, by burning a fuel or by using the wind or the
sun. EG *...steam power... ...a cheap source of power.*

8 Electricity is often referred to as **power**. EG N UNCOUNT
*Water and power have still not reached some rural
areas... ...a power failure.*

9 The device that **powers** a machine provides the v+o
energy that the machine needs in order to work. EG
*Its radar equipment was powered by a nuclear
reactor.*

powerful /pauəful/. **1** A **powerful** person or ADJ QUALIT
organization is able to control or influence people
and events. EG *They organize themselves into powerful and effective trade unions... ...the most powerful government in western Europe.* ● See also **all-
powerful.**

2 You say that someone's body is **powerful** when it ADJ QUALIT
is physically strong. EG *He had broad shoulders and
powerful arms.* ◊ **powerfully.** EG *They were* ◊ ADV
young, powerfully built men.

3 If a person or animal gives you a **powerful** blow ADJ QUALIT
or kick, they hit you or kick you with great force.
EG *The stallion will attack with powerful kicks and
bites.*

4 You can say that a machine or a substance is ADJ QUALIT
powerful when it is effective because it is very
strong. EG *...a powerful engine... ...a powerful and
quick-acting medicine.*

5 A **powerful** smell is strong and unpleasant. ADJ QUALIT
◊ **powerfully.** EG *...a room smelling powerfully of* ◊ ADV
cats.

6 A **powerful** voice is loud and can be heard from ADJ QUALIT
a long way away.

7 You describe a piece of writing, speech, or work ADJ QUALIT
of art as **powerful** when it has a strong effect on
people's feelings or beliefs. EG *I find his argument
very powerful... He produced a series of extraordinarily powerful paintings.*

powerless /pauələs/. **1** Someone who is **power-** ADJ CLASSIF
less is unable to control or influence events. EG
*Without the support of the party, the Cabinet is
powerless.* ◊ **powerlessness.** EG *She experienced* ◊ N UNCOUNT
an overwhelming sense of powerlessness.

2 If you are **powerless** to do something, you are ADJ PRED
completely unable to do it. EG *I stood there watch-* +to-INF
ing, feeling powerless to help.

power station, power stations. A power sta- N COUNT
tion is a place where electricity is generated.

pp. is the plural of **p.** and means 'pages'.

practicable /præktɪkəbəºl/. If a task, plan, or ADJ CLASSIF
idea is **practicable**, people are able to carry it out Formal
successfully. EG *The noise will be reduced as far as
is practicable.*

practical /præktɪkəºl/, **practicals.** **1** The **practi-** ADJ CLASSIF :
cal aspects of something involve real situations ATTRIB
and events, rather than just ideas and theories. EG
*The SDP faces practical difficulties of organization
and finance... Much of the information was of no
practical use... Practical experience of broadcasting would be valuable.*

2 You describe people as **practical** when they ADJ QUALIT
make sensible decisions and deal effectively with
problems. EG *Try to be as methodical and practical
about it as you can... What a practical mind you
have.*

3 You can also describe someone as **practical** ADJ QUALIT
when they are good at doing jobs with their hands.

4 Practical ideas and methods are likely to be ADJ QUALIT
effective or successful in a real situation. EG *Their*

*ideas are too opposed to our way of thinking to be
considered practical... How long will it be before
nuclear fusion becomes practical?*

5 You can describe clothes and things in your ADJ QUALIT
house as **practical** when they are suitable for a
particular purpose rather than fashionable or attractive. EG *Ceramic tiles are very hard on the feet,
though practical.*

6 A **practical** is an examination or a lesson in N COUNT
which you make things or do experiments rather
than simply write.

practicality /præktɪkælɪti¹/, **practicalities.** The N COUNT OR
practicalities of a situation are the practical N UNCOUNT
aspects of it, as opposed to its theoretical aspects.
EG *He turned out to know very little about the
practicalities of teaching... That idea is impractical, but practicality isn't everything.*

practical joke, practical jokes. A practical N COUNT
joke is a trick that is intended to embarrass
someone or make them look ridiculous.

practically /præktɪkəºli/ means almost, but not ADV
completely or exactly. EG *The town was practically
deserted... He knew practically no English... She
practically forced him into joining the army.*

practice /præktɪs/, **practices.** **1** You can refer to N COUNT
something that people do regularly as a **practice**.
EG *Benn began the practice of holding regular
meetings... ...the ancient Japanese practice of binding the feet from birth.*

2 The work done by doctors is referred to as the N UNCOUNT
practice of medicine. People's religious activities +SUPP
are referred to as the **practice** of a religion. EG
*...the practice of the Christian religion... They lived
on their earnings from private medical practice.*

3 Practice is regular training or exercise in N UNCOUNT
something, or a lot of experience in it. EG *I help
them with their music practice... Skating's just a
matter of practice... With practice it becomes less
of an effort.*

4 A doctor's or lawyer's **practice** is his or her N COUNT
business, often shared with other doctors or lawyers. EG *...a medical practice... ...a doctor with a
private practice.*

5 Practice is used in these phrases. **5.1** If you **put** PHRASE
a belief or method **into practice**, you behave or
act in accordance with it. EG *He had not yet
attempted to put his principles into practice... I'm
not sure how effective these methods will be when
put into practice.* **5.2** What happens **in practice** is ADV SEN
what actually happens, in contrast to what is
supposed to happen. EG *In practice, he exerted little
influence over the others... What it means in practice is that he does twice the work for half the
money.* **5.3** If you are **out of practice** at doing PHRASE
something, you have not had much experience of it
recently.

6 See also **practise.**

practise /præktɪs/, **practises, practising, practised;** also spelled **practice, practices, practic-
ing, practiced** in American English.

1 If you **practise** something, you keep doing it v+o OR v
regularly in order to be able to do it better. EG *I
played the piece I had been practising for months...
These are quite hard to do until you've practised a
bit.*

2 You say that an activity **is practised** when v+o : USU PASS
people do it regularly, for example as a custom. EG
*These crafts were practised by many early cul-
tures... ...a charming custom still practised in the
suburbs.*

3 Someone who is **practised** at doing something is ADJ CLASSIF
good at it because they have had a lot of experi-
ence of it. EG *A practised burglar rarely leaves any
trace of his presence... His was a practised performance.*

4 When people **practise** something such as a v+o
religion, they take part in the activities associated
with it. EG *They have managed to practise their
religion for years... We have never been allowed to*

practise democracy. ● to **practise what** you **preach**: see **preach**.

5 If something cruel is regularly done to people, you can say that it **is practised** on them. EG *I am horrified at the cruelty practised on these helpless victims... Torture was certainly practised in these countries.* v+o+A: USU PASS

6 Someone who **practises** medicine or law works as a doctor or a lawyer. EG *He went on to study law and practise it... He's in Hull practising medicine now.* ◊ **practising**. EG *He is now a practising doctor in Essex.* v+o ◊ ADJ CLASSIF: ATTRIB

practitioner /præktɪʃə⁰nə/, **practitioners**. Doctors are sometimes referred to as **practitioners** or medical **practitioners**. N COUNT: USU+SUPP Formal

pragmatic /prægmætɪk/. A **pragmatic** way of dealing with something is based on practical considerations, rather than theoretical ones. EG *He argued the case for increased state intervention on wholly pragmatic grounds... ...pragmatic reasons for their behaviour.* ◊ **pragmatically**. EG *We have to be ready to tackle situations pragmatically.* ADJ QUALIT ◊ ADV

pragmatism /prægmətɪzə⁰m/ is a way of thinking or of dealing with problems in a practical way, rather than by using theory or abstract principles. N UNCOUNT Formal

prairie /preəri¹/, **prairies**. A **prairie** is a very large area of flat, grassy land in North America. EG *...days of travel across the prairies.* N COUNT OR N UNCOUNT

praise /preɪz/, **praises, praising, praised. 1** If you **praise** someone or something, you express approval for their achievements or qualities. EG *Sylvia had a stern father who never praised her... They praised his speech for its clarity and humour.* v+o

2 Praise is what you say or write about someone when you are praising them. EG *Three entrants were singled out for special praise... She finds it hard to give praise.* N UNCOUNT

3 If you **sing** someone's **praises**, you praise them in an enthusiastic way. EG *Liz is forever singing your praises.* PHRASE

praiseworthy /preɪzwɜːði¹/. If you say that something is **praiseworthy**, you mean that it is very good and deserves to be praised. EG *...a praiseworthy action.* ADJ QUALIT Formal

pram /præm/, **prams**. A **pram** is a baby's cot on wheels. EG *...a young mother pushing a pram.* N COUNT

prance /prɑːns/, **prances, prancing, pranced. 1** If someone **prances**, they walk or move around with exaggerated movements because they want people to look at them and admire them. EG *...young girls who pranced around town.* v+A

2 When a horse **prances**, it moves with quick, high steps. v: USU+A

prank /præŋk/, **pranks**. A **prank** is a childish trick. EG *...a boyish prank.* N COUNT Outdated

prawn /prɔːn/, **prawns**. A **prawn** is a small shellfish, similar to a shrimp. N COUNT

pray /preɪ/, **prays, praying, prayed. 1** When people **pray**, they speak to God in order to give thanks or to ask for his help. EG *He kneeled down and prayed to Allah... The men prayed for forgiveness... She prayed that God would send her the necessary strength.* v: USU+A OR REPORT: ONLY that

2 When someone wants something very much, you can say that they **pray** for it. EG *He got what he had prayed for, the command of a division... Praying she would not see me, I hurried inside.* v+for OR REPORT: ONLY that

prayer /preə/, **prayers. 1 Prayer** is the activity of praying to God. EG *Her eyes were shut and her lips were moving in prayer.* N UNCOUNT

2 If you **say** your **prayers**, you pray. PHRASE

3 A **prayer** is **3.1** the words that you say when you pray on a particular occasion. EG *I made a brief prayer for her recovery.* **3.2** a set form of words which is used during a religious service. EG *He repeated his favourite passage of the Passover Prayer.* N COUNT

4 You can refer to a strong hope that you have as a N COUNT

prayer. EG *My one prayer is that I don't live to be really old.*

5 A short religious service can be referred to as **prayers**. EG *There were family prayers every morning.* N PLURAL

pre- is used to form words that describe something as taking place before a particular date, event, or period. For example, a pre-lunch meeting is a meeting that you have before your lunch. EG *...pre-1914 Europe... ...the pre-Christmas period... ...pre-trial interviews.* PREFIX

preach /priːtʃ/, **preaches, preaching, preached. 1** When a member of the clergy **preaches** a sermon or **preaches**, he or she gives a talk on a religious or moral subject during a church service. EG *The chaplain preached to a packed church.* v+o OR v

2 When people **preach** a belief or a course of action, they try to persuade other people to accept the belief or to take the course of action. EG *They preach peace while preparing for war... He used to go round the villages preaching Socialism.* v+o

3 If someone gives you advice in a boring, moralizing way, you can say that they **are preaching** at you. v: OFT+at

4 If you say that someone **practises what** they **preach**, you mean that they behave in the way that they encourage other people to behave in; used showing approval. PHRASE

preacher /priːtʃə/, **preachers**. A **preacher** is a person, usually a member of the clergy, who preaches sermons as part of a church service. N COUNT

preamble /priːæmbə⁰l/, **preambles**. A **preamble** is an introduction that comes before something you say or write. EG *...an intensely long preamble... Philip said quickly without preamble, 'Somebody shot your father.'* N COUNT OR N UNCOUNT

precarious /prɪkeərɪəs/. **1** Something that is **precarious** is in a dangerous position because it is not securely held in place and seems likely to fall. EG *The streams have to be crossed by precarious rows of bricks... The monkeys cling to their mother's fur in a most precarious fashion.* ◊ **precariously**. EG *For the rest of the journey I sat precariously on the roof of the cabin.* ADJ QUALIT ◊ ADV

2 If your situation is **precarious**, you are not in complete control of events and might fail in what you are doing. EG *The management was in a precarious position... Life will be more precarious in the year 2000 than it is now.* ◊ **precariously**. EG *I found myself living, somewhat precariously, from one assignment to another.* ADJ QUALIT ◊ ADV

precaution /prɪkɔːʃə⁰n/, **precautions**. A **precaution** is an action that is intended to prevent something dangerous or unpleasant from happening. EG *I had taken the precaution of swallowing two sea sickness tablets... ...fire precautions... As a precaution he had put his wallet in his briefcase... These precautions proved unnecessary.* N COUNT: USU+SUPP

precautionary /prɪkɔːʃənə⁰ri¹/. **Precautionary** actions are taken in order to prevent something dangerous or unpleasant from happening. EG *I would have to take precautionary steps to keep him out... Precautionary measures were unnecessary.* ADJ CLASSIF Formal

precede /prɪsiːd/, **precedes, preceding, preceded. 1** If one event or period of time **precedes** another, it happens before it. EG *...the drop in temperature that precedes a heavy thunderstorm... The children's dinner was preceded by games.* v+o Formal

2 If you **precede** someone somewhere, you go in front of them. EG *She preceded him across the hallway... We were preceded by a huge man called Teddy Brown.* v+o Formal

3 A sentence, paragraph, or chapter that **precedes** another one is written or printed just before it. v+o

Where would you put a preamble?

◊ **preceding.** EG ...*the activities we discussed in the preceding chapter.*

precedence /ˈprɛsɪdəns/. If one thing **takes precedence** over another, it is regarded as more important than the other thing. EG *The peaceful ordering of society takes precedence over every other consideration.* PHRASE Formal

precedent /ˈprɛsɪdənt/, **precedents.** 1 A **precedent** is an action or official decision that can be referred to in order to justify taking a similar action or decision. EG *The Supreme Court had already set a precedent... This case was something of a precedent.* N COUNT Formal

2 If there is a **precedent** for something, that thing has happened before, or something similar to it has happened before. EG *There was no precedent for the riots... She set a precedent for women runners... He broke with precedent by making his maiden speech on a controversial subject.* N COUNT OR N UNCOUNT Formal

precept /ˈpriːsɛpt/, **precepts.** A **precept** is a general rule that helps you to decide how you should behave in particular circumstances. EG *...precepts of tolerance and forgiveness.* N COUNT Formal

precinct /ˈpriːsɪŋkt/, **precincts.** 1 A shopping **precinct** is a specially built shopping area in the centre of a town, in which cars are not allowed. N COUNT British

2 In the United States, a **precinct** is a part of a city which has its own police force and fire service. EG *...police at work patrolling the 12th precinct.* N COUNT American

3 The **precincts** of an institution are its buildings and land. EG *Gambling is prohibited within the precincts of the University.* N PLURAL Formal

precious /ˈprɛʃəs/. 1 If you describe something as **precious**, you mean that it is valuable and useful and should not be wasted or used badly. EG *The one resource more precious than any other was land... They have lost precious working time.* ADJ QUALIT

2 **Precious** objects and materials are worth a lot of money because they are rare. EG *Salt is nearly as precious as gold in many places.* ADJ QUALIT

3 You say that things are **precious** when they are very important to you, often because you associate them with special events or people. EG *I imagine he treasures that letter as one of the precious mementoes of his Presidency.* ADJ QUALIT

4 People sometimes use **precious** to express their dislike for things which other people think are important. EG *I'm sick and tired of your precious brother-in-law... How sentimental you are about your precious ideas.* ADJ CLASSIF : ATTRIB Informal

5 If you describe someone as **precious**, you mean that they behave in a formal and unnatural way. EG *...that rather precious but oddly likeable young man... He has a slightly precious prose style.* ADJ QUALIT

6 If you say that there is **precious little** of something, you mean that there is very little of it. EG *There's precious little they can learn from us... He was a man with no charm and precious few virtues.* PHRASE

precious metal, precious metals. A **precious metal** is a valuable metal such as gold or silver. N COUNT OR N UNCOUNT

precious stone, precious stones. A **precious stone** is a valuable stone that is used for making jewellery. Diamonds, rubies, and sapphires are precious stones. N COUNT

precipice /ˈprɛsɪpɪs/, **precipices.** A **precipice** is a very steep cliff on a mountain. EG *I looked over the precipice.* N COUNT

precipitate /prɪˈsɪpɪteɪt/, **precipitates, precipitating, precipitated.** If something **precipitates** a new event or situation, it causes it to happen, usually suddenly and unexpectedly. EG *This would precipitate an economic crisis... The explosion was precipitated by the start of police enquiries.* V+O Formal

precipitous /prɪˈsɪpɪtəs/. A **precipitous** area of land is high and has very steep sides. EG *...precipitous hillsides... We bumped over the precipitous road to the ferry.* ADJ CLASSIF

précis /ˈpreɪsiː/. **Précis** is both the singular and the plural form. It is pronounced /ˈpreɪsiːz/ in the plural. ◊ ADJ CLASSIF ATTRIB

A **précis** is a short piece of writing which contains the main points of a book or report, but not the details. EG *...a comprehensive précis of the main points of the case.* N COUNT

precise /prɪˈsaɪs/. 1 You use **precise** to emphasize that you are describing something correctly and exactly. EG *At that precise moment we were interrupted by the telephone... The precise nature of the disease has not yet been established.* ADJ CLASSIF : ATTRIB

2 Something that is **precise** is exact and accurate in all its details. EG *Mr Jones gave him precise instructions... The timing had to be very precise... Try to be reasonably precise.* ADJ QUALIT

3 You say '**to be precise**' to indicate that you are giving more detailed or accurate information about what you have just said. EG *I have to be up early - 4 a.m. to be precise.* PHRASE

precisely /prɪˈsaɪsli/. 1 **Precisely** means accurately and exactly. EG *He made the knots precisely, losing no time... Let me explain to you precisely what I am going to do.* ADV

2 You can use **precisely** 2.1 to emphasize that you are giving a complete and correct explanation of something. EG *He was furious, precisely because he had not been consulted.* 2.2 to confirm that what someone has just said is true. EG *'So he's a professional assassin?' - 'Precisely.'* ADV

CONVENTION

precision /prɪˈsɪʒən/. If you do something with **precision**, you do it exactly as it should be done. EG *The attack was carried out with clockwork precision... He had established a reputation for unfailing precision in his job.* N UNCOUNT

preclude /prɪˈkluːd/, **precludes, precluding, precluded.** If something **precludes** an event or action, it prevents the event or action from happening. EG *This should not preclude a search for a better hypothesis... It sets limits on the powers of the Government, and precludes it from acting unconstitutionally.* V+O : OFT+*from* Formal

precocious /prɪˈkəʊʃəs/. **Precocious** children behave in a way that makes them seem older than they really are. EG *I have a brilliant, precocious pupil in my class.* ◊ **precociously.** EG *...his precociously articulate children.* ADJ QUALIT ◊ ADV

preconceived /ˌpriːkənˈsiːvd/. If you have **preconceived** ideas about something, you have already decided about it before you have had enough information or experience to form a fair opinion. EG *The development of the idea depended on getting away from preconceived notions.* ADJ CLASSIF : ATTRIB

preconception /ˌpriːkənˈsɛpʃən/, **preconceptions.** Your **preconceptions** about something are beliefs that you have about it before you have had enough information or experience to form a fair opinion. EG *He tries to deny information that challenges his preconceptions.* N COUNT

precondition /ˌpriːkənˈdɪʃən/, **preconditions.** If one thing is a **precondition** for another thing, it must happen or be done before the second thing can happen or exist. EG *Economic growth was regarded as the precondition for greater equality... Protection of the environment is a precondition of a healthy society.* N COUNT : USU+*for/of* Formal

precursor /prɪˈkɜːsə/, **precursors.** If something is a **precursor** of something more important, it is similar to it and happens or exists before it. EG *Railways were the precursors of modern transport.* N COUNT : OFT+*of/to* Formal

predator /ˈprɛdətə/, **predators.** A **predator** is an animal that kills and eats other animals. EG *The whiting is a major predator on smaller fish.* N COUNT

predatory /ˈprɛdətərɪ/. 1 **Predatory** animals live by killing other animals for food. ADJ CLASSIF : ATTRIB

2 **Predatory** people are eager to gain something out of someone else's weakness or suffering. EG *Her sharp dark eyes held a somewhat predatory expression.* ADJ CLASSIF : ATTRIB

predecessor /priːˈdiseso/, **predecessors. 1** Your   N COUNT+POSS
predecessor is the person who had your job
before you. EG *She wasn't being paid the same wage
as her predecessor.*

2 The **predecessor** of an object or machine is the   N COUNT+POSS
object or machine that it replaced.

predestination /priːˌdestɪneɪʃən/ is the belief that   N UNCOUNT
people have no control over events because they
have already been decided by God or by fate.

predestined /priːˈdestɪnd/. If you say that a situa-   ADJ CLASSIF
tion was **predestined**, you mean that it could not
have been prevented or altered because it had
already been decided by God or by fate. EG *I was
predestined to be a slave.*

PREDET stands for **predeterminer**
Words which have the label PREDET in the Extra
Column are words which come before a determiner in a noun group. In this dictionary the words 'all,
both, half, double, treble, twice, such,' and 'what'
are called predeterminers.
See the entry headed DETERMINERS for more information.

---

predetermined /priːdɪˈtɜːmɪnd/. If you say that   ADJ CLASSIF
something is **predetermined**, you mean that its   Formal
form or nature was decided by previous events or
by people rather than by chance. EG *He believes
that we're all genetically predetermined... The
energy industries expanded at their own predetermined rate.*

predicament /prɪˈdɪkəmənt/, **predicaments.** If   N COUNT+SUPP
you are in a **predicament**, you are in an unpleasant difficult situation. EG *He hasn't realized his
predicament... We are in a worse predicament
than ever.*

predicative /prɪˈdɪkətɪv/. In grammar, if an ad-   ADJ CLASSIF :
jective is in **predicative** position, it comes after a   ATTRIB
verb.

predict /prɪˈdɪkt/, **predicts, predicting, predict-**   V-SPEECH
ed. If you **predict** an event, you say that it will
happen. EG *He predicted a brilliant future for the
child... The government predicts that the region
will draw 500,000 tourists a year... You can't predict
what they are going to do.*

predictable /prɪˈdɪktəbəl/. Something that is   ADJ QUALIT
predictable happens in a way that you can know
about in advance. EG *The outcome is not always
predictable... Certain conditions have led to fairly
predictable kinds of behaviour.* ◊ **predictably.** EG   ◊ ADV SEN
Predictably, the affair went hopelessly wrong...   OR ADV
...situations where everyone behaves predictably.
◊ **predictability** /prɪˌdɪktəˈbɪlɪtiˈ/. EG *It happened*   ◊ N UNCOUNT
month by month, with boring predictability.

prediction /prɪˈdɪkʃən/, **predictions.** If you   N COUNT OR
make a **prediction** about something, you say what   N UNCOUNT
you think will happen. EG *...a prediction of the likely
outcome of the next election... That's a very confident prediction... ...methods of prediction.*

predilection /priːdɪˈlekʃən/, **predilections.** If   N COUNT
you have a **predilection** for something, you have a   Formal
strong liking for it. EG *...the American predilection
for salads with every meal.*

predispose /priːdɪˈspəʊz/, **predisposes, predis-**   V+O+to-INF
posing, predisposed. If something **predisposes**   OR to
you to think or behave in a particular way, it is one
of the reasons why you think or behave in that
way. ◊ **predisposed.** EG *She was predisposed to be*   ◊ ADJ PRED
critical.

predisposition /priːdɪspəˈzɪʃən/, **predisposi-**   N COUNT :
tions. If you have a **predisposition** to behave in a   USU+SUPP
particular way, you tend to behave like that be-   Formal
cause of the kind of person that you are. EG *She
may have inherited a predisposition to murder the
man she marries.*

predominance /prɪˈdɒmɪnəns/. **1** If there is a   N UNCOUNT :
predominance of one type of person or thing,   USU+of
there are many more of that type than of any other   Formal
type. EG *...the predominance of traders and
businessmen in the party's ranks.*

2 If someone or something has **predominance**,   N UNCOUNT
they have the most power or importance among a   Formal
group of people or things. EG *We now have total
predominance in the European market.*

predominant /prɪˈdɒmɪnənt/. If something is   ADJ CLASSIF
predominant, it is more important or noticeable   Formal
than other things of the same kind. EG *Italian opera
became predominant at the end of the 17th century... The predominant mood among policy-makers
is one of despair.*

predominantly /prɪˈdɒmɪnəntli/. You use **pre-**   ADV
dominantly to indicate which feature or quality is
most noticeable in a situation. EG *The debates were
predominantly about international affairs... Their
first reaction was predominantly one of dismay.*

predominate /prɪˈdɒmɪneɪt/, **predominates,**
predominating, predominated. 1 If one type of   V
person or thing **predominates** in a group, there   Formal
are more of that type in the group than any other
type. EG *In most churches, women predominate in
the congregations.*

2 When a feature or quality **predominates**, it is   V
the most noticeable one in a situation. EG *Feelings*   Formal
rather than facts predominate.

pre-eminent /priːˈemɪnənt/. If someone or some-   ADJ CLASSIF
thing is **pre-eminent** in a group, they are more
important, powerful, or capable than other people
or things in the group. EG *For the next thirty years
Bryce was the pre-eminent figure in Canadian
economic policy.* ◊ **pre-eminence** /priːˈemɪnəns/.   ◊ N UNCOUNT
EG *No one doubted his pre-eminence in financial*   Formal
matters.

preen /priːn/, **preens, preening, preened. 1**   V-REFL
When people **preen** themselves, they spend time
making themselves look neat and attractive. EG *He
preened himself in front of the mirror.*

2 When birds **preen** their feathers, they clean   V+O OR V
them and arrange them neatly using their beaks.
EG *A peacock pecked and preened on the lawn.*

prefab /ˈpriːfæb/, **prefabs.** A **prefab** is a house   N COUNT
built with parts which have been made in a factory   British
and then quickly put together.

prefabricated /priːˈfæbrɪkeɪtɪd/. **Prefabricated**   ADJ CLASSIF :
buildings are built with parts which have been   ATTRIB
made in a factory so that they can be easily carried
and put together.

preface /ˈprefɪs/, **prefaces, prefacing, pref-**   N COUNT :
aced. 1 A **preface** is an introduction at the begin-   OFT+to
ning of a book, which explains what the book is
about or why it was written. EG *Granville-Barker
had written a fine preface to the play.*

2 If you **preface** an action or speech with some-   V+O+with/by
thing else, you do or say this other thing first. EG   Formal
Each girl prefaced her remarks with 'sorry'.

prefect /ˈpriːfekt/, **prefects.** A **prefect** is an older   N COUNT
pupil at a British school who does special duties
and helps the teachers to control the younger
pupils.

prefer /prɪˈfɜː/, **prefers, preferring, preferred.**   V+O : USU+to
If you **prefer** one thing to another, you like the   OR to-INF; ALSO
first thing better, so you are more likely to choose   V+to-INF
it if there is a choice. EG *I prefer Barber to his*   OR REPORT :
deputy... A glass of sherry? Or would you prefer a   ONLY that
*cocktail?... The Head Master prefers them to act
plays they have written themselves... They prefer
to suffer deprivation rather than claim legal aid...
I'd prefer that he remain forgotten.*

preferable /ˈprefərəbəl/. If you say that one   ADJ CLASSIF
thing is **preferable** to another, you mean that it is   USU PRED+to
more desirable or suitable. EG *Gradual change is*

If one person in a group predominates, is he or
she pre-eminent?

preferable to sudden, large-scale change... Many people find this method immensely preferable.

◊ **preferably.** EG Clean the car from the top, preferably with a hose and warm water. ◊ ADV SEN

preference /ˈprefərəns/, **preferences.** 1 If you N COUNT OR have a **preference** for something, you would like N UNCOUNT to have it or do it rather than something else. EG Employers may show a preference for those with the same outlook... I continue to live in this country by preference... I took the non-stop flight to London, in preference to the two-stage journey via New York... Each of us has personal preferences for certain types of entertainment.

2 If you give **preference** to someone, you choose N UNCOUNT them rather than choosing someone else. EG Preference was given to those who had overseas experience.

preferential /ˌprefəˈrenʃəl/. If you get **preferen-** ADJ CLASSIF **tial** treatment, you are treated better than other ATTRIB people and therefore have an advantage over them. EG Disabled people at work should have preferential treatment.

prefix /ˈpriːfɪks/, **prefixes.** A **prefix** is a letter or N COUNT group of letters which is added to the beginning of a word in order to make a new word. See below.

> ## PREFIX
> Some letters or groups of letters are labelled PREFIX in the Extra Column. This means that they are not usually used by themselves as words, but they are put immediately in front of a word to form a new word. Sometimes the new word is written as one word, and sometimes the two parts are joined by a hyphen. An example of a group of letters which is labelled **PREFIX** is 'pre-', which forms words that describe something as happening or belonging before a certain time or event. So, for example, 'pre-war' means 'before the war' and 'pre-1960' means 'before 1960'.

pregnancy /ˈpregnənsiː/, **pregnancies. Preg-** N UNCOUNT **nancy** is the condition of being pregnant or the OR N COUNT period of time during which a female is pregnant. EG The breasts enlarge during pregnancy... She has had fifteen pregnancies.

pregnant /ˈpregnənt/. If a woman or female ani- ADJ CLASSIF mal is **pregnant**, she has a baby or babies developing in her body. EG She married and immediately got pregnant... She was three months pregnant... My mother was pregnant with me at the time.

prehistoric /ˌpriːhɪˈstɒrɪk/. **Prehistoric** people ADJ CLASSIF and things existed at a time before information ATTRIB was written down. EG ...prehistoric hunters... ...prehistoric cooking pots.

prejudice /ˈpredʒʊdɪs/, **prejudices.** 1 **Prejudice** N UNCOUNT is an unreasonable dislike of someone or some- OR N COUNT thing, for example of a particular group of people. EG Prejudice against women is becoming less severe... ...racial prejudice... Barber was a man of strong prejudices.

2 If people show **prejudice** in favour of someone N UNCOUNT or something, they prefer them, often unreasonably, to other people or other things of the same kind. EG There was some regrettable prejudice in favour of middle class children.

prejudiced /ˈpredʒʊdɪst/. A person who is **preju-** ADJ QUALIT **diced** against someone has an unreasonable dislike of them. A person who is **prejudiced** in favour of someone has an unreasonable preference for them. EG People were prejudiced against her... She had been prejudiced in his favour from the start... We all know how difficult it is to reason with a prejudiced person.

preliminary /prɪˈlɪmɪnəriː/, **preliminaries.** ADJ QUALIT : **Preliminary** activities or discussions take place in ATTRIB preparation for an event before it starts. EG ...preliminary arrangements... Preliminary discussions on Stage III had already begun. ▶ used as a noun. ▶ N COUNT : EG He spent a long time on polite preliminaries. USU PLURAL Secondary education is a necessary preliminary for university education.

prelude /ˈpreljuːd/, **preludes.** You can describe N COUNT : an event as a **prelude** to a more important event USU + to when it happens before it and acts as an introduction to it. EG This speech has been hailed by his friends as the prelude to his return to office.

premature /ˈpremətjʊə/. 1 Something that is ADJ CLASSIF **premature** happens earlier than usual or earlier than people expect. EG This disease produces premature aging... ...the premature departure of the visitors. ◊ **prematurely.** EG The warden ◊ ADV retired prematurely with a nervous disorder.

2 You can say that something is **premature** when ADJ QUALIT it happens too early and is therefore inappropriate. EG The final word 'goodbye' had been premature... It's a bit premature to be thinking about having one's biography written.

3 A **premature** baby is born before the date when ADJ CLASSIF it was due to be born.

premeditated /priːˈmedɪteɪtɪd/. An action that is ADJ CLASSIF **premeditated** is planned or thought about before it is done. EG ...a premeditated act of murder.

premier /ˈpremjə/, **premiers.** 1 The leader of the N COUNT government of a country is sometimes referred to as the country's **premier.** EG ...the French premier... ...Premier Francisco Pinto Balsemao.

2 **Premier** is used to describe something that is ADJ CLASSIF : considered to be the best or most important thing ATTRIB of a particular type. EG The article referred to Hull as Europe's premier port.

premiere /ˈpremiɛə, ˈpremiə/, **premieres.** The N COUNT **premiere** of a new play or film is the first public performance of it. EG The film had its world premiere at San Sebastian.

premiership /ˈpremjəʃɪp/. The **premiership** is N UNCOUNT the position of being the leader of a government. EG He should never have been considered for the premiership... ...in the later years of his premiership.

premise /ˈpremɪs/, **premises.** 1 The **premises** of N PLURAL a business or an institution are all the buildings and land that it occupies on one site. EG Some of the food was grown on the premises... In 1971 the firm moved to new premises in Bethnal Green.

2 A **premise** is something that you suppose is true N COUNT : and that you use as a basis for developing an idea. USU + SUPP EG ...if one accepts the premise that all knowledge Formal comes to us through our senses... I'm questioning whether the whole premise is correct.

premium /ˈpriːmɪəm/, **premiums.** 1 A **premium** N COUNT is **1.1** an extra sum of money that you have to pay for something in addition to the normal cost. EG Investors were willing to pay a premium for companies that offered such a potential for growth. **1.2** a sum of money that you pay regularly to an insurance company for an insurance policy. EG ...tax relief on life insurance premiums.

2 If something is **at a premium, 2.1** it is being sold PHRASE at a higher price than usual, for example because it is in short supply. EG Fertilizer is sold at a premium by government officials. **2.2** it is wanted or needed, but is difficult to get or achieve. EG Student flats are at a premium.

3 To **put** or **place a high premium** on a quality or PHRASE characteristic means to make it especially important or to regard it as especially important. EG This system places an enormous premium on learning efficiency.

premium bond, premium bonds. Premium N COUNT **bonds** are numbered tickets that are sold by the government in Britain. Each month, a computer randomly selects several numbers, and the people whose tickets have those numbers win money.

premonition /prɛmənɪʃəⁿn/, **premonitions.** If   N COUNT :
you have a **premonition**, you have a feeling that   USU+SUPP
something is going to happen, often something
unpleasant. EG ...a premonition of failure... He had a
sudden terrible premonition that she had run away.

prenatal /priːneɪtᵊl/ is used to describe things   ADJ CLASSIF :
relating to the medical care of women during   ATTRIB
pregnancy. EG ...prenatal classes for expectant
mothers.

preoccupation /priːɒkjəˈpeɪʃəⁿn/, **preoccupa-**   N COUNT OR
tions. If you have a **preoccupation** with some-   N UNCOUNT
thing, you keep thinking about it because it is
important to you. EG ...Alexander's preoccupation
with the past... Keeping warm was Morris's main
preoccupation in his first few days there.

preoccupied /priːˈɒkjəˈpaɪd/. Someone who is   ADJ QUALIT :
preoccupied is thinking a lot about something,   OFT+with
and so hardly notices other things. EG His wife
becomes more and more preoccupied with the
children... She seemed rather preoccupied and
distant.

preoccupy /priːɒkjəˈpaɪ/, **preoccupies, preoc-**   V+O
cupying, preoccupied. If something **preoccupies**
you, you think about it a lot. EG This is a question
which increasingly preoccupies me.

PREP stands for **preposition**
Words that are labelled PREP in the Extra Column
are prepositions such as 'for', 'with', and 'from'.
Prepositions always have an object.
1 The object can be a noun, noun group, or pronoun, as in ...the search **for** truth...helping learners
with real English ...I've never thought **about** it.
2 The object can be a clause with a verb in the
'-ing' form, as in **By** doing this, he achieved his
aim.

---

preparation /prɛpəreɪʃəⁿn/, **preparations.**   N UNCOUNT :
The **preparation** of something is the activity of   USU+SUPP
getting it ready. EG Benn was involved in the
preparation of Labour's manifesto... ...food preparation... Education should be a preparation for life.
2 Preparations are all the arrangements that are   N PLURAL
made for a future event. EG He'll have to make
preparations for the funeral... Elaborate preparations were being made to get me out.
3 A **preparation** is a mixture that has been   N COUNT
prepared for use as food, medicine, or a cosmetic.   Formal
EG ...beauty preparations.

preparatory /prəˈpærətᵊriˈ/. **Preparatory** ac-   ADJ CLASSIF :
tions are done before doing something else, as a   ATTRIB
preparation for it. EG ...a preparatory report... ...pre-   Formal
paratory language courses.

preparatory school, preparatory schools. A   N COUNT OR
preparatory school is the same as a prep school.   N UNCOUNT
Formal

prepare /prɪˈpeə/, **prepares, preparing, pre-**
pared. 1 If you **prepare** something, you make it   V+O
ready for something that is going to happen. EG A
room has been prepared for you... He had spent
days preparing the site of the statue... Schools have
to prepare children for life in the community.
2 If you **prepare** for an event or action that will   V : OFT+for
happen soon, you get yourself ready for it. EG The   OR to-INF; ALSO
guests prepared for their departure... I jumped up   V-REFL+for
and prepared to defend myself... Prepare yourself
for a shock.
3 When you **prepare** food, you get it ready to be   V+O
eaten, for example by cooking it. EG He had spent
all morning preparing the meal... She had prepared
a thermos of hot onion soup.

prepared /prɪˈpeəd/. **1** If you are **prepared** to do   ADJ PRED
something, you are willing to do it if necessary. EG   +to-INF
What sort of risks are you prepared to take?... I'm
prepared to say I was wrong... Many countries
seem prepared to consider nuclear energy.
2 If you are **prepared** for something, you are   ADJ PRED :
OFT+for

ready for it because you think that it might happen.
EG I was not really prepared for her fits of boredom... Be prepared for power cuts by buying lots of
candles.
3 Something that is **prepared** has been done or   ADJ CLASSIF
made beforehand, so that it is ready when it is
needed. EG He read out a prepared statement... ...a
specially prepared fluorescent screen.

preponderance /prɪˈpɒndᵊrəns/. If there is a   N UNCOUNT :
preponderance of one type of person or thing in a   USU+of
group, there are more of that type than of any   Formal
other. EG There is a definite preponderance of
women among those who study English Literature.

preposition /prɛpəzɪʃəⁿn/, **prepositions.** A   N COUNT
preposition is a word such as 'by', 'for', 'into', or
'with', which usually has a noun group as its object.
Words which are prepositions have PREP in the
Extra Column. See the entry headed PREP for more
information.

preposterous /prɪˈpɒstᵊrəs/. If you describe   ADJ QUALIT
something as **preposterous**, you mean that it is
extremely unreasonable and foolish. EG The situation was preposterous... ...a preposterous idea.

prep school, prep schools. A **prep school** is a   N COUNT OR
private school in Britain where children are edu-   N UNCOUNT
cated until the age of 11 or 13.

prerequisite /priːˈrɛkwɪzɪt/, **prerequisites.** If   N COUNT :
one thing is a **prerequisite** for another, it must   USU+SUPP
happen or exist before the other thing is possible.   Formal
EG Confidence is a prerequisite for mastering other
more formal skills... Ownership of great estates
was a prerequisite of power.

prerogative /prɪˈrɒgətɪv/, **prerogatives.** If   N COUNT :
something is the **prerogative** of a particular per-   USU+of
son or group, it is a privilege or a power that only   Formal
they have. EG ...luxuries which were considered the
prerogative of the rich.

prescribe /prɪˈskraɪb/, **prescribes, prescribing,**
prescribed. 1 If a doctor **prescribes** medicine or   V+O
treatment for you, he or she tells you what medicine or treatment to have. EG Her doctor prescribed
a sedative.
2 If someone **prescribes** an action or duty, they   V+O
state formally that it must be carried out. EG The   Formal
factory laws prescribed a heavy fine for contraven-
tion of this rule. ◇ **prescribed.** EG The list of   ◇ ADJ CLASSIF :
prescribed duties has been drawn up by the federa-   ATTRIB
tion.

prescription /prɪˈskrɪpʃəⁿn/, **prescriptions. 1** A   N COUNT
prescription is **1.1** a piece of paper on which a
doctor has written the name of a medicine you
need. You give it to a chemist in exchange for the
medicine. EG ...a prescription for sleeping tablets.
1.2 medicine which a doctor has told you to take. EG
I'm not sleeping even with the prescription
Ackerman gave me.
2 If a medicine is available **on prescription**, you   PHRASE
can get it from a chemist if a doctor gives you a
prescription for it. EG ...a drug which used to be
available only on prescription.

presence /prɛzᵊns/, **presences. 1** If you talk   N UNCOUNT
about someone's **presence** in a place, you are   +POSS
referring to the fact that they are there. EG He tried
to justify his presence in Belfast... He was aware of
her presence... He had to cope with the presence of
her family.
2 If you are **in** someone's **presence**, you are in the   PHRASE
same place as they are. EG I felt comfortable in her
presence... Haldane repeated his statement in the
presence of the chairman.
3 If you say that someone has **presence**, you mean   N UNCOUNT
that they impress people by their appearance and
manner. EG He had tremendous physical presence.
4 A **presence** is a person or creature that you   N COUNT

Who do you give a prescription to?

cannot see, but that you are aware of. EG ...*a mysterious winged presence, felt rather than seen.*

presence of mind is the ability to act quickly N UNCOUNT and sensibly in a difficult situation. EG *Richard had the presence of mind to step forward and pick it up.*

present, presents, presenting, presented; pronounced /ˈprezənt/ when it is an adjective or noun, and /prɪˈzent/ when it is a verb.

1 You use **present** to describe people and things ADJ CLASSIF: that exist now, rather than those that existed in the ATTRIB past or those that may exist in the future. EG *The present system has many failings... The present chairperson is a woman... Economic planning cannot succeed in present conditions.* ● **The present** ● PHRASE **day** is the period of history that is taking place now. EG *This tradition has continued till the present day.* ● See also **present-day**.

2 The **present** is the period of time that is taking N SING : the+N place now and the things that are happening now. EG *We have to come to terms with the present.*

3 If something is happening **at present**, it is PHRASE happening now. EG *He is at present serving a life sentence... I don't want to get married at present.*

4 If a situation exists **for the present**, it exists now PHRASE but is likely to change. EG *For the present she continues with the antibiotics... That's all for the present, Miss Livingstone.*

5 If someone is **present** at an event, they are ADJ PRED there. EG *He had been present at the dance... There was a photographer present.*

6 A **present** is something that you give to some- N COUNT one, for example at Christmas or when you visit them. EG *I gave him an atlas as a birthday present... He had brought home a present for her.*

7 If you **present** someone with something such as V+O+with, OR a prize, or if you **present** it to them, you formally V+O : OFT+to give it to them. EG *He presented her with a signed copy of his book... One of his constituents presented a petition to Parliament.*

8 If something **presents** a difficulty or a challenge, V+O+OFT+to, it causes it or provides it. EG *The tornado presented* OR V+O+with *the island with severe problems... Everest presented a challenge to Hillary.*

9 When you **present** information, you give it to V+O : OFT+to, people in a formal way. EG *...a way of presenting* OR V+O+with *new material... Our teachers were trying to present us with an accurate picture of history.*

10 If you **present** someone or something in a V+O+A particular way, you describe them in that way. EG *Her lawyer wanted to present her in the most favourable light... They present the British as the colonialist oppressor.*

11 If you **present** yourself somewhere, you official- V-REFL+A ly arrive there, for example for an appointment. EG *The next morning I presented myself at their offices.*

12 If an opportunity **presents** itself, it occurs, often V-REFL when you do not expect it. EG *Was he going to do it again if the opportunity presented itself?*

13 If someone **presents** a programme on televi- V+O sion or radio, they introduce each part of it or each person on it. EG *...'University Link', compiled and presented by Dr Brian Smith.*

14 If you **present** someone to an important person, V+O you officially introduce them. EG *May I present Mr* Formal *Rudolph Wallace.*

presentable /prɪˈzentəbəl/. If you say that some- ADJ QUALIT one or something is **presentable**, you mean that they are quite attractive or quite good, and are suitable for other people to see. EG *She looked quite presentable... ...some of his more presentable pictures.*

presentation /ˌprezənˈteɪʃən/, **presentations. 1** N UNCOUNT : The **presentation** of information is the process of OFT+of making it available to people, for example by broadcasting it or printing it. EG *...the collection and presentation of statistical data.*

2 Presentation is the appearance of something N UNCOUNT

and the impression that it gives to people. EG *Presentation is very important in cooking.*

3 A **presentation** is **3.1** a formal event in which N COUNT someone is given something such as a prize. EG *I said I would not be able to attend the presentation.*

3.2 a lecture or a talk about something. EG *Darwin* N COUNT *was urged to deliver a presentation on the subject* Formal *to the Linnean Society.* **3.3** something that is N COUNT+SUPP performed before an audience, for example a play Formal or a ballet. EG *He directed a theatrical presentation of 'Danton's Death'.*

present-day. You use **present-day** to describe ADJ CLASSIF : people and things that exist now. EG *...present-day* ATTRIB *Japanese children... ...social conditions in present-day India.*

presenter /prɪˈzentə/, **presenters.** A **presenter** N COUNT is a person who introduces a television or radio programme, especially a programme that gives news or information.

presently /ˈprezəntliˈ/. **1** You use **presently** to ADV SEN indicate that something happened quite a short OR ADV time after the time or event that you have just mentioned. EG *Presently I got the whole story.*

2 If you say that something will happen **presently**, ADV you mean that it will happen quite soon. EG *He will be here presently.*

3 If you say that something is **presently** happen- ADV ing, you mean that it is happening now. EG *...the oil rigs that are presently in operation.*

present participle, present participles. The N COUNT **present participle** of an English verb is the form that ends in '-ing'. It is used to form some tenses, and to form adjectives and nouns from a verb.

present tense. The **present tense** of a verb is N SING : the+N used mainly when you want to talk about things that happen or exist at the time of speaking or writing.

preservative /prɪˈzɜːvətɪv/, **preservatives.** A N MASS **preservative** is a chemical that prevents things from decaying. Some preservatives are added to food, and others are used to treat wood or metal.

preserve /prɪˈzɜːv/, **preserves, preserving, preserved. 1** If you **preserve** a situation or condi- V+O tion, you make sure that it remains as it is, and is not changed or ended. EG *We are interested in preserving world peace... I stood there, determined to preserve my dignity.* ◊ **preservation** ◊ N UNCOUNT /ˌprezəˈveɪʃən/. EG *...the preservation of democracy.*

2 If you **preserve** something, you take action to V+O save it or protect it from damage. EG *...a big house which had been preserved as a museum... ...a paint spray which would preserve it from corrosion.*

3 If you **preserve** food, you prevent it from V+O decaying so that you can store it for a long time. EG *Deep freezing is the simplest way of preserving food.*

4 Preserves are foods such as jam and marma- N MASS lade that are made by cooking fruit with a large amount of sugar and that can be stored for a long time.

preserved /prɪˈzɜːvd/. Something that is well ADJ QUALIT **preserved** is in good condition or is unchanged even though it is very old. EG *There are some excellently preserved fossilized tree stumps.*

preside /prɪˈzaɪd/, **presides, presiding, presid-** V : USU **ed.** If you **preside** over a formal meeting or event, +over/at you are in charge or act as the chairperson. EG *He* Formal *had presided over a seminar for theoretical physicists.*

presidency /ˈprezɪdənsiˈ/. The **presidency** is the N SING : the+N, position of being the president of a country. EG *He is* OR N UNCOUNT *to be nominated for the presidency.*

president /ˈprezɪdənt/, **presidents. 1** The **presi-** N COUNT **dent** of a country that has no king or queen is the person who has the highest political position and is the leader of the country. EG *The French president arrived in the United States this week... ...the assassination of President Kennedy.*

2 The **president** of an organization is the person N COUNT who has the highest position in it. EG ...*the former President of the Royal Academy.*

presidential /prɛzɪdɛnʃəˀl/. **Presidential** activi- ADJ CLASSIF : ties or things relate or belong to a president. EG ATTRIB ...*the next presidential election*... ...*John Kennedy's presidential airplane.*

press /prɛs/, **presses, pressing, pressed. 1** If V+O+A you **press** one thing against another, you hold it or push it firmly against the other thing. EG *Stroganov pressed his hand to his heart*... *She pressed her palms together*... *The animal presses itself against a tree trunk.*

2 If you **press** a button or switch, you push it with V+O your finger in order to make a machine or device work. EG *He could press the buzzer and wake her*... *Mrs Carstairs pressed an electric bell.* ▶ used as a ▶ N COUNT noun. EG *All this can be called up at the press of the right button.*

3 If you **press** on something or **press** it, you push V : USU+A hard against it with your hand or your foot. EG *The* OR V+O *driver may press harder on the accelerator*... *She pressed down upon the velvet cloth*... ...*pressing the mattress with his fingers.*

4 If you **press** clothes, you iron them in order to V+O get rid of the creases. EG *He always pressed his trousers before wearing them.*

5 If you **press** for something, you try hard to V+*for* persuade someone to give it to you or to agree to it. EG *He pressed for full public ownership*... *The labourers formed a union to press for higher wages.*

6 If you **press** someone, you try hard to persuade V+O : USU+A them to do something or to tell you something. EG *He pressed me to have a cup of coffee with him*... *Don't press me on this point.*

7 If you **press** something on someone, you give it V+O+*on/upon* to them and insist that they take it. EG *His aunt was pressing upon him cups of tea and cookies.*

8 If you **press** charges against someone, you make V+O an official accusation against them which has to be decided in a court of law. EG *They decided against pressing charges.*

9 The **Press** refers to **9.1** newspapers. EG ...*the* N COLL : SING, British press... ...*an amusing story in the press.* *the*+N *Press comments could be merciless.* **9.2** journalists. EG *I got to know a lot of the American press*... *Granville-Barker would never meet the press.*

10 If someone **gets a good press**, they are praised PHRASE in the newspapers, or on television or radio. If they **get a bad press**, they are criticized in the newspapers, or on television or radio. EG *Civil servants tend to get rather a poor press*... *I hope he'll get a fairer press in his own country.*

11 A printing **press** is a machine used for printing N COUNT books, newspapers, and leaflets. EG *Since then the presses have scarcely stopped turning.*

12 See also **pressing, pressing**.

press on. If you **press on**, you continue doing PHRASAL VB : something in spite of difficulties. EG *They coura-* V+ADV *geously pressed on with their vital repair work.*

press conference, press conferences. When a N COUNT famous person such as a politician or film star gives a **press conference**, he or she holds a meeting in order to answer questions put by newspaper and television reporters.

pressed /prɛst/. If you say that you are **pressed** ADJ PRED : for money or **pressed** for time, you mean that you OFT+*for* do not have enough money or time at the moment. EG *He was always pressed for money.*

pressing /prɛsɪŋ/. Something that is **pressing** ADJ QUALIT needs to be dealt with immediately. EG *I remembered a pressing appointment with the doctor.*

pressure /prɛʃə/, **pressures, pressuring, pressured. 1** Pressure is **1.1** force that you produce N UNCOUNT when you press hard on something. EG *It took a bit of pressure to make the lid close*... *He disliked the pressure of her hand*... *It bent when pressure was put upon it.* **1.2** the force that a quantity of gas or N UNCOUNT liquid has on a surface that it touches. EG *I'll just* +SUPP

check the tyre pressure... The water pressure may need adjusting.* ● See also **blood pressure**.

2 If someone puts **pressure** on you, they try to N UNCOUNT persuade you to do something. EG *For a long time* USU+SUPP *he's been trying to put pressure on us to go*... *The main pressure for change is coming from the unions*... ...*under pressure from feminists.*

3 If you feel **pressure**, you feel that you must do a N UNCOUNT lot of tasks or make a lot of decisions, especially OR N PLURAL when you have very little time. EG *Parents can suffer from too much pressure*... *We do our best work under pressure*... ...*the pressures of public life.*

4 If you **pressure** someone to do something, you V+O : try forcefully to persuade them to do it. EG *The* USU+*to*-INF *children are not pressured to eat*... *Some young* OR *into* *people are pressured into staying on at school.*

pressure cooker, pressure cookers. A pres- N COUNT **sure cooker** is a large saucepan with a lid that fits tightly, in which you can cook food quickly using steam at high pressure.

pressure group, pressure groups. A **pressure** N COUNT **group** is an organized group of people who are trying to persuade a government or other authority to do something, for example to change a law. EG *There followed six years of campaigning by pressure groups.*

pressurize /prɛʃəraɪz/, **pressurizes, pressuriz-** V+O : **ing, pressurized;** also spelled **pressurise.** If you USU+*to*-INF **pressurize** someone to do something, you try OR *into* forcefully to persuade them to do it. EG *It was a move designed to pressurise workers to return earlier.*

pressurized /prɛʃəraɪzd/; also spelled **pressur-** ADJ CLASSIF **ised.** The pressure inside a **pressurized** container or area is different from the pressure outside it. EG ...*the pressurized cabin of a Boeing 707.*

prestige /prɛstiːʒ/. If you have **prestige,** other N UNCOUNT people admire you because of your position in society or the high quality of your work. EG *He is looking for a job with some prestige attached to it.*

prestigious /prɛstɪdʒɪˀəs/. Something that is ADJ QUALIT **prestigious** is important, influential, and admired by people. EG ...*one of the most prestigious universities in the country.*

presumably /prɪˈzjuːməbliˀ/. If you say that ADV SEN something is **presumably** the case, you mean that you think it is the case, although you are not certain. EG *Presumably they're a bit more expensive*... *The bomb was presumably intended to go off while the meeting was in progress.*

presume /prɪˈzjuːm/, **presumes, presuming, presumed. 1** If you **presume** that something is V : the case, you think that it is the case, although you USU+REPORT : are not certain. EG *I presume you know why I am* ONLY *that* *here*... *If you do not come, I shall presume the deal is off*... *You are married, I presume?*

2 If something **is presumed** to be the case, people V+O+*to*-INF believe that it is the case, although they are not OR C : USU PASS certain. EG ...*Larry Burrows, missing and presumed dead since 1971*... *He got away and is presumed to be living in Spain.*

presumption /prɪˈzʌmpʃəˀn/, **presumptions.** A N COUNT : **presumption** is something that is presumed by USU+SUPP someone to be true. EG ...*based on the presumption that heaven has four walls.*

presumptuous /prɪˈzʌmptjʊəs/. If you describe ADJ QUALIT someone's behaviour as **presumptuous,** you mean that they are doing things that they have no right or authority to do. EG *It is dangerous and presumptuous to interfere between parents and children.*

presuppose /priːsəˈpəʊz/, **presupposes, presup-** V+O OR **posing, presupposed.** If one thing **presupposes** V+REPORT : another, the first thing cannot be true or exist ONLY *that* unless the second is true or exists. EG *The whole* Formal

---

If you presume that something is the case, are you presumptuous?

myth of the Ascension presupposes there is a Heaven physically above the Earth... All arguments must presuppose logic.

pretence /pri'tɛns/, **pretences;** spelled **pretense** in American English. **1** A **pretence** is an action or way of behaving that is intended to make people believe something that is not true. EG *She leapt up with a pretence of eagerness... Work is not available to them even though we make a pretence that it is.* N COUNT OR N UNCOUNT

2 If you do something **under false pretences**, you do it when people do not know the truth about you and your intentions. EG *I felt that I was taking money under false pretences.* PHRASE

pretend /pri'tɛnd/, **pretends, pretending, pretended.** If you **pretend** that something is the case, you act in a way that is intended to make people believe that it is the case, although in fact it is not. EG *Her father tried to pretend that nothing unusual had happened... Philip politely pretended not to have heard this remark... He pretended to fall over.* V+REPORT: ONLY *that*, OR V+*to*-INF

pretension /pri'tɛnʃən/, **pretensions.** Someone with **pretensions** claims or pretends that they are more important than they really are. EG *He has pretensions to greatness... He is evidently a person of some social pretension.* N UNCOUNT OR N COUNT

pretentious /pri'tɛnʃəs/. If you say that someone or something is **pretentious**, you mean that they try to seem important or significant, but you do not think that they are. EG *...one of the most pretentious films of all time.* ADJ QUALIT

pretext /'pri:tɛkst/, **pretexts.** A **pretext** is a reason which you pretend has caused you to do something. EG *The Government invented a 'plot' as a pretext for arresting opposition leaders... They withdrew their support on an ideological pretext.* N COUNT

pretty /'prɪtɪ/, **prettier, prettiest. 1** If you describe someone, especially a girl, as **pretty**, you mean that they are nice to look at and attractive in a delicate way. EG *Who's that pretty little girl?... She looked pretty in her long white dress.* ◊ **prettily.** EG *She smiled prettily.* ADJ QUALIT   ◊ ADV

2 A place or a thing that is **pretty** is nice to look at in a rather conventional way. EG *...a very pretty garden... The wallpaper was very pretty, covered in roses.* ◊ **prettiness.** EG *...the fairy-tale prettiness of the town.* ADJ QUALIT   ◊ N UNCOUNT

3 You can use **pretty** before an adjective or adverb to mean 'quite' or 'rather'. EG *I thought it was pretty good... I'm pretty certain she enjoys it.* SUBMOD Informal

4 Pretty much or **pretty well** means 'almost'. EG *I felt pretty much the same... She hated pretty well all of them.* PHRASE Informal

prevail /pri'veɪl/, **prevails, prevailing, prevailed. 1** If a custom or belief **prevails** in a particular place at a particular time, it is normal or most common in that place at that time. EG *...the traditions that have prevailed in Britain since the 17th century.* ◊ **prevailing.** EG *The prevailing view shifted still further.* V+A   ◊ ADJ CLASSIF: ATTRIB

2 If a proposal or a principle **prevails**, it gains influence or is accepted, often after an argument. EG *In the end, common sense prevailed... Political arguments had prevailed over economic sense.* V: OFT+*over*

prevalent /'prɛvələnt/. A condition or belief that is **prevalent** is very common. EG *...the liberal atmosphere prevalent in the late 1960s... ...one theory prevalent among scientists.* ◊ **prevalence** /'prɛvələns/. EG *...the prevalence of snobbery in Britain.* ADJ QUALIT   ◊ N SING: the+N+of Formal

prevaricate /pri'værɪkeɪt/, **prevaricates, prevaricating, prevaricated.** If you **prevaricate**, you do not give a direct, truthful answer or a firm decision when people want one. EG *The doctors prevaricated, arguing the need for additional tests.* V

prevent /pri'vɛnt/, **prevents, preventing, prevented. 1** If you **prevent** someone from doing something, you do not allow them to start doing it. EG *My only idea was to prevent him from speaking... Have you been instructed to prevent me entering?* V+O+*from* OR -ING

2 If people or things **prevent** something from happening, they ensure that it does not happen. EG *It was not enough to prevent war... ...a layer of fat beneath the skin that prevents their body heat from escaping.* V+O: OFT+*from* OR -ING

preventative /pri'vɛntətɪv/ means the same as **preventive.** EG *...preventative medicine.* ADJ CLASSIF: ATTRIB

prevention /pri'vɛnʃən/ is action that prevents something from happening. EG *...the prevention of cruelty to animals... ...fire prevention.* N UNCOUNT OFT+*of*

preventive /pri'vɛntɪv/. **Preventive** actions are intended to help prevent things such as disease or crime. EG *Preventive measures are essential... ...preventive medicine.* ADJ CLASSIF: ATTRIB

preview /'pri:vju:/, **previews.** A **preview** is an opportunity to see something such as a film or an art exhibition before it is officially shown to the public. EG *Welcome to the press preview of the Seyer Street exhibition.* N COUNT

previous /'pri:vɪəs/. **1** A **previous** event or thing is one that happened or came before the one that you are talking about. EG *He had children from a previous marriage... We were always told how valuable our previous career experience would be.* ADJ CLASSIF: ATTRIB

2 You refer to the period of time or the thing immediately before the one that you are talking about as the **previous** one. EG *They had arrived the previous night... The previous Government had decided to build it.* ADJ CLASSIF: ATTRIB

previously /'pri:vɪəslɪ/. **1 Previously** means at some time before the period that you are talking about. EG *I had previously lived the life of a miser... He was previously British consul in Atlanta.* ADV

2 You can use **previously** to say how much earlier one event was than another event. EG *This load had been dispatched three months previously... They had retired ten years previously.* ADV

pre-war /'pri: wɔː/. **Pre-war** things existed before a war, especially the 1939-45 war. EG *...the prewar telephone network.* ADJ CLASSIF: ATTRIB

prey /preɪ/, **preys, preying, preyed. 1** The creatures that an animal hunts and eats in order to live are its **prey.** EG *The mole seeks its prey entirely underground.* ● See also **bird of prey.** N UNCOUNT +POSS

2 If someone or something **falls prey to** a person or their action, they are taken control of by that person. EG *...to help prevent the company falling prey to a Stock Exchange raid.* PHRASE

prey on. 1 An animal that **preys on** another kind of animal lives by catching and eating this kind of animal. EG *The amphibians were hunters, preying on worms and insects.* **2** If something **preys on** your mind, you cannot stop thinking and worrying about it. EG *Barton reluctantly agreed, but the decision preyed on his mind.* PHRASAL VB: V+PREP, HAS PASS   V+PREP

price /praɪs/, **prices, pricing, priced. 1** The **price** of something is the amount of money that you must pay in order to buy it. EG *The price of firewood has risen steeply... The price is still only £1.05... Petrol will continue to drop in price.* ● See also **cut-price.** N COUNT: USU+SUPP, OR N UNCOUNT

2 The **price** that you pay for something that you want is an unpleasant thing that you have to do or suffer in order to get it. EG *This was the price that had to be paid for progress... This is a small price to pay for freedom... The price of such protection was an inevitable dependence.* N SING+SUPP

3 If you want something **at any price**, you are determined to get it, even if unpleasant things happen as a result. EG *...the desire to win at any price... His slogan is peace at any price.* PHRASE

4 If you get something that you want **at a price**, you get it but something unpleasant happens as a result. EG *Ford's grip on the market is one obtained at a price.* PHRASE

5 If something **is priced** at a particular amount, it costs that amount to buy. EG *The least expensive* V+O: USU PASS will be priced at £7,000... ...reasonably priced accommodation.

priceless /praɪslɪ's/. Something that is **priceless** ADJ CLASSIF
1 is worth a very large amount of money. EG ...a beautiful priceless sapphire. 2 is extremely useful. EG This priceless asset has enabled him to win innumerable tournaments.

pricey /praɪsɪ¹/. If you say that something is ADJ QUALIT **pricey**, you mean that it is expensive. EG The book Informal was a bit pricey.

prick /prɪk/, **pricks, pricking, pricked. 1** If you V+O : USU+A **prick** something or **prick** holes in it, you make small holes in it with a sharp object such as a pin. EG Prick the apples all over, using the prongs of a fork... I pricked little holes in the wrapping... He pricked himself with the needle.

2 If something sharp **pricks** you, it sticks into you V+O or presses your skin and causes you pain. EG Sharp thorns pricked his knees.

3 If tears **prick** your eyes, you feel small, sharp V+O pains in your eyes because you are about to cry. Literary

4 A **prick** is a small, sharp pain that you get when N COUNT something pricks you. EG ...the sharp pricks as the pellets struck his hands.

prick up. 1 If an animal **pricks up** its **ears**, its PHRASE ears suddenly point straight up. **2** If you **prick up** PHRASE your **ears**, you suddenly listen eagerly when you hear something interesting or important. EG He pricked up his ears at the sound of his father's voice.

prickle /prɪkə⁰l/, **prickles, prickling, prickled. 1 Prickles** are small, sharp points that stick out N COUNT : from leaves or from the stalks of plants. OFT PLURAL

2 If your skin **prickles**, it feels as if a lot of small, V : OFT+ with sharp points are being stuck into it, either because of something touching it or because you feel a strong emotion. EG The shirt I was wearing made my skin prickle... My skin prickled with fear.

▸ used as a noun. EG I felt a prickle of pleasure. ▸ N COUNT

prickly /prɪklɪ¹/. **1** Something such as a plant that ADJ QUALIT is **prickly** has a lot of sharp points sticking out from it. EG ...prickly thorn bushes.

2 Someone who is **prickly** loses their temper very ADJ QUALIT easily. EG ...a prickly and tiresome man.

pride /praɪd/, **prides, priding, prided. 1 Pride** is N UNCOUNT a feeling of satisfaction which you have because you or people close to you have done something good or possess something good. EG His mother looked at him with affection and pride... She pointed with pride to the fine horses she had trained.

2 If you **take pride** in something that you have or PHRASE do, you feel pleased and happy because of it. EG I take great pride in the success of my children.

3 If you **pride** yourself on a quality or skill that you V-REFL+ on have, you are very proud of it. EG Mrs Hochstadt prided herself on her intelligence... They prided themselves on being patient.

4 Someone or something that is your **pride and** PHRASE **joy** is very important to you and makes you feel very happy. EG Their baby daughter was their pride and joy.

5 Pride is also **5.1** a sense of dignity and self- N UNCOUNT respect. EG My pride did not allow me to complain too often... Pride alone prevented her from giving up. **5.2** a feeling of being superior to other people. EG There is a lot of pride in the phrase 'no one can fool me'.

6 If you **swallow** your **pride**, you decide that you PHRASE have to do something that you are rather ashamed to do. EG He swallowed his pride and accepted the money.

7 If something has **pride of place**, it is the most PHRASE important thing in a group of things. EG Musical compositions take pride of place in the festivities.

priest /priːst/, **priests.** A **priest** is **1** a member of N COUNT the Christian clergy in the Catholic, Anglican, or Orthodox church. **2** a man in many non-Christian religions who has particular duties and responsibil-

ities in the place where people worship. EG ...a Buddhist priest.

priestess /priːstes/, **priestesses.** A **priestess** is N COUNT a woman in a non-Christian religion who has particular duties and responsibilities in the place where people worship.

priesthood /priːsthʊd/. The **priesthood** is the N SING : the+N position of being a priest. EG ...the responsibilities of the priesthood.

priestly /priːstlɪ¹/ is used to describe things that ADJ CLASSIF belong or relate to a priest. EG ...priestly duties... ...a ATTRIB priestly blessing.

prig /prɪg/, **prigs.** If you call someone a **prig**, you N COUNT mean that they are irritating because they behave in a very moral way and disapprove of other people's behaviour. EG Jason was a self-righteous prig.

priggish /prɪgɪʃ/. If you describe someone as ADJ QUALIT **priggish**, you mean that they are irritating because they are very moral and disapproving.

prim /prɪm/. If you describe someone as **prim**, ADJ QUALIT you mean that they behave very correctly and are easily shocked by anything rude or improper; often used showing disapproval. EG ...a prim, severe woman. ◊ **primly.** EG His sister sat primly with her legs ◊ ADV together.

prima donna /priːmə dɒnə/, **prima donnas. 1** A N COUNT **prima donna** is the main female singer in an opera.

2 If you describe someone as a **prima donna**, you N COUNT mean that they are difficult to deal with because their moods change suddenly. EG Bob was a prima donna who played heartily at office politics.

primaeval /praɪmiːvə⁰l/. See primeval.

primarily /praɪmərəlɪ¹/. You use **primarily** to ADV indicate the most important feature of something or reason for something. EG These linguists were concerned primarily with the structure of languages... The issue was primarily a political one.

primary /praɪmərɪ¹/, **primaries. 1** You use **pri-** ADJ CLASSIF **mary** to describe something that is extremely USU ATTRIB important or most important for someone or something. EG One of Europe's primary requirements was minerals... She gets her primary satisfaction from her career.

2 Primary education is given to pupils between ADJ CLASSIF the ages of 5 and 11 in Britain. ATTRIB

3 A **primary** is an election in an American state in N COUNT which people vote for someone to become a candidate for a political office.

primary colour, primary colours. The **prima-** N COUNT **ry colours** are red, yellow, and blue. They can be mixed together in different ways to make all other colours.

primary school, primary schools. A **primary** N COUNT OR **school** is a school in Britain for children between N UNCOUNT the ages of 5 and 11.

primate /praɪmeɪt, -mə¹t/, **primates.** A **primate** N COUNT is a member of the group of mammals which includes humans, monkeys, and apes.

prime /praɪm/, **primes, priming, primed. 1** You ADJ CLASSIF use **prime** to describe **1.1** something that is most ATTRIB important in a situation. EG What was said was of prime importance... Maths is no longer a prime requirement for a career in accountancy. **1.2** something that is of the best possible quality. EG He wants his herd delivered in prime condition. **1.3** an example of a particular kind of thing that is absolutely typical. EG We had, a few years ago, a prime example of the power of the press to embarrass.

2 Someone's or something's **prime** is the stage in N SING+POSS their existence when they are at their strongest, most active, or most successful. EG I had been a

Should a Prime Minister be principled?

good player in my prime... ...machines past their prime.

3 If you **prime** someone about something, you give v+o:usu+a them information about it beforehand, so that they are prepared for it. EG *I had primed him for this meeting... He is well primed to enter the profession.*

4 If you **prime** wood, you cover it with special v+o paint to prepare it for the main layer of paint.

Prime Minister, Prime Ministers. . The lead- N PROPER er of the government in some countries is called OR N COUNT the **Prime Minister**. EG *The Prime Minister publicly deplored the affair... ...the Prime Minister of France.*

primeval /praɪmiːvəl/; also spelled **primaeval.** ADJ CLASSIF You use **primeval** to describe things that belong to ATTRIB a very early period in the history of the world. EG *...primeval forests... ...our primeval ancestors.*

primitive /prɪmɪtɪv/. **1 Primitive** means **1.1** ADJ CLASSIF: belonging to a society of people who live in a very USU ATTRIB simple way, usually without industries or a writing system. EG *...anthropologists who have studied primitive tribes... The most commonly cited example of a primitive device is the abacus.* **1.2** of an early type. EG *...primitive insect-eating mammals... ...primitive microprocessors.*

2 If you describe something as **primitive**, you ADJ QUALIT mean that it is very simple in style or very old-fashioned. EG *The sleeping accommodation is somewhat primitive.*

primrose /prɪmrəʊz/, **primroses.** A **primrose** is N COUNT a wild plant which has pale yellow flowers in spring.

prince /prɪns/, **princes.** A **prince** is **1** a male N COUNT member of a royal family, especially the son of the king or queen of a country. EG *...Prince Charles.* **2** the male royal ruler of a small country or state.

princely /prɪnsliː/. **1** Something that is **princely** ADJ CLASSIF belongs to a prince or is suitable for a prince. EG *...the princely courts of Asia.*

2 A **princely** sum of money is a large sum of ADJ QUALIT: money. EG *We're managing to sell them at a* ATTRIB *princely £25 a time.*

princess /prɪnses/, **princesses.** A **princess** is a N COUNT female member of a royal family, usually the daughter of a king or queen or the wife of a prince. EG *...Princess Mary, only daughter of King George V... ...the Prince and Princess of Wales.*

principal /prɪnsɪpəl/, **principals. 1 Principal** ADJ CLASSIF: means main or most important. EG *Political domi-* ATTRIB *nation was rarely their principal aim... ...the principal character in James Bernard Fagan's play.*

2 The **principal** of a school or college is the N COUNT person in charge of it.

principality /prɪnsɪpælɪtiː/, **principalities.** A N COUNT **principality** is a country that is ruled by a prince. EG *...the principality of Monaco.*

principally /prɪnsɪpəliː/ means more than any- ADV thing else. EG *He dealt principally with Ethiopia... ...a protein which occurs principally in wheat.*

principle /prɪnsɪpəl/, **principles. 1** A **principle** N COUNT OR is a general belief that you have about the way you N UNCOUNT should behave, which influences your behaviour. EG *...a man of high principles... She abandoned her principles... Our party remains a party of principle.*

● If you do something **on principle**, you do it ● PHRASE because of a particular belief that you have. EG *I had to vote for him, of course, on principle.*

2 A **principle** is also **2.1** a general rule about how N COUNT+SUPP something should be done. EG *...the principles of formal logic... ...a party organized on Leninist principles.* **2.2** a general scientific law which explains how something happens or works. EG *...the principle of acceleration.*

3 If you agree with something **in principle**, you PHRASE generally agree to the idea of it but may be unable or unwilling to support it in practice. EG *We are willing, in principle, to look afresh at the 1921 constitution.*

principled /prɪnsɪpəld/. **Principled** behaviour is ADJ QUALIT based on moral principles. EG *...the principled stand we have taken on matters of contemporary concern... I forgot you were so high principled.*

print /prɪnt/, **prints, printing, printed. 1** If v+o someone **prints** a book, newspaper, or leaflet, they produce it in large quantities by a mechanical process. EG *I asked him for an estimate to print a weekly paper for me.* ◊ **printing.** EG *Universal* ◊ N UNCOUNT *literacy was only possible after the invention of printing... ...a printing press.*

2 If someone **prints** a speech or a piece of writing, v+o they include it in a newspaper or magazine. EG *The paper printed a big exclusive story about Margaret Thatcher... This interview was not printed in the national press.*

3 The letters and numbers on a page of a book or N UNCOUNT newspaper are referred to as the **print**. EG *The print is rather poor... ...paragraphs in bold print.*

4 If something appears **in print**, it appears in a PHRASE book or newspaper. EG *He admitted it in print.*

5 If a book is **out of print**, it is no longer available PHRASE from a publisher.

6 A **print** is **6.1** a picture that is copied from a N COUNT painting by photography or made mechanically from specially prepared surfaces. **6.2** one of the photographs from a film that has been developed. EG *...simple black and white prints.*

7 If you **print** a pattern on cloth, you reproduce it v+o many times on the cloth, usually by using dye and special machinery. EG *...a pattern which is printed onto the fabric by hand.*

8 A **print** is also a footprint or a fingerprint. EG *His* N COUNT: *feet left prints in the soft soil.* OFT PLURAL

9 If you **print** when you write something, you write v OR v+o in letters that are not joined together. EG *There was an envelope on her desk with her name printed on it... As long as you print clearly, you don't have to type.*

print out. When information from a computer is PHRASAL VB: **printed out**, it is reproduced on paper. ● See also V+O+ADV **printout.**

printer /prɪntə/, **printers.** A **printer** is **1** a N COUNT person or machine that prints books, newspapers, or leaflets. **2** a machine that is connected to a computer and that prints out information from the computer on paper.

printout /prɪntaʊt/, **printouts.** A **printout** is a N COUNT OR piece of paper on which information from a com- N UNCOUNT puter has been printed. EG *...a printout of the result.*

prior /praɪə/. **1** If something happens **prior to** a PREP particular time or event, it happens before that Formal time or event. EG *It occurred in Dallas, just prior to President Kennedy's assassination.*

2 You use **prior** to describe something that has ADJ CLASSIF: happened or been planned earlier. EG *No prior* ATTRIB *knowledge should be required... I have a prior engagement... ...without prior warning.*

3 A **prior** claim or duty is more important than ADJ CLASSIF: other claims or duties. EG *There are many others* ATTRIB *who have a prior claim... He feels a prior obligation to his job as a journalist.*

priority /praɪɒrɪtiː/, **priorities. 1** Something that N COUNT+SUPP is a **priority** must be done or dealt with as soon as possible. EG *Getting food was the main priority... Factories seemed to be China's highest priority.*

▶ used as an adjective. EG *The waiting list contains* ▶ ADJ CLASSIF: *a thousand priority cases.* ATTRIB

2 When you talk about someone's **priorities**, you N PLURAL are talking about which tasks or things they consider most important and which they consider less important. EG *We must find out the priorities of the public... I have a different order of priorities... He had his priorities right.*

3 If someone or something has **priority** or is given N UNCOUNT **priority** over other things, they are considered more important than other things and are therefore dealt with first. EG *These children are given priority when day nursery places are allocated.*

prise /praɪz/, prises, prising, prised; also spelled   V+O+A
prize. If you **prise** something open or **prise** it away from a surface, you force it to open or force it to come away from the surface. EG *He prised the lids off both tins of paint... I prised her arms free.*

prism /prɪzəm/, **prisms**. A **prism** is an object   N COUNT
made of clear glass or plastic which has many straight sides. It separates the light which passes through it into the colours of the rainbow.

prison /prɪzən/, **prisons**. 1 A **prison** is a building   N COUNT OR
where criminals are kept in order to punish them   N UNCOUNT
and to protect other people from them. EG *I had never before been inside a prison... He died in prison... He was sent to prison for two years.*
2 You can describe your situation as a **prison**   N SING
when it makes you feel unhappy and you cannot   Literary
easily escape from it. EG *The Kirks' marriage had become a prison.*

prisoner /prɪzənə/, **prisoners**. 1 A **prisoner** is   N COUNT
1.1 a person who is kept in a prison as a punishment. EG *He was the only prisoner permitted to enter my cell.* 1.2 a person who has been captured by an enemy, for example in war.
2 If someone **is taken prisoner**, they are cap-   PHRASE
tured.

prisoner of war, prisoners of war. A **prisoner**   N COUNT
of war is a soldier who is captured by the enemy during a war and is kept as a prisoner until the end of the war.

pristine /prɪstiːn/. Something that is **pristine** is   ADJ CLASSIF
extremely clean or new. EG *He wiped his fingers on*   Formal
his pristine handkerchief.

privacy /praɪvəsiˈ, prɪvəsiˈ/. If you have **privacy**,   N UNCOUNT
you are alone or you can be alone, so that you can do things without other people seeing you or disturbing you. EG *I hated the lack of privacy in the dormitory... ...the privacy of your own home... Take it home and read it in privacy.*

private /praɪvəˈt/, **privates**. 1 Something that is   ADJ CLASSIF:
private is for the use of one person or group only,   USU ATTRIB
rather than for the general public. EG *All rooms have got private bath and WC... The fields were private property.*
2 **Private** is used to describe services that you pay   ADJ CLASSIF :
for or industries that are owned by an individual   ATTRIB
person or group, rather than services and industries that are controlled by the state. EG *...private education... ...private health insurance.*
◊ **privately**. EG *...privately owned firms.*   ◊ ADV
3 **Private** discussions take place between a small   ADJ CLASSIF :
group of people and are kept secret from other   ATTRIB
people. EG *I have asked the editors to apply to the Prime Minister for a private interview.*
◊ **privately**. EG *The notion was discussed privately*   ◊ ADV
between the two men at lunch.
4 If you do something **in private**, you do it without   PHRASE
other people being present, usually because it is something that you want to keep secret. EG *Could we talk to you in private?*
5 **Private** activities and belongings are connected   ADJ CLASSIF :
with your personal life rather than with your work   ATTRIB
or business. EG *She never spoke about her private life... I have an official diary and a private diary.*
6 Your **private** thoughts or plans are things that   ADJ CLASSIF :
are personal and that you do not talk about to other   ATTRIB
people. EG *He was deep in his own private thoughts... He was engaged in a private quest of his own.* ◊ **privately**. EG *Privately Ben felt close to*   ◊ ADV
despair.
7 If you describe a place as **private**, you mean that   ADJ QUALIT
it is quiet and you can be alone there without being disturbed. EG *...a private place of meditation.*
8 Someone who is a **private** person is very quiet   ADJ QUALIT
by nature and does not share their thoughts and feelings with other people. EG *Away from the glare of publicity he becomes an intensely private man.*
9 A **private** is a soldier who has the lowest rank in   N COUNT
an army.

private school, private schools. A **private**   N COUNT
school is a school which is not supported financially by the government and which parents have to pay for their children to go to.

privation /praɪveɪʃən/, **privations**. If you suffer   N UNCOUNT
privation or **privations**, you are deprived of   OR N COUNT
things that you need in life. EG *Life was riddled with*   Formal
privation... ...the privations of frontier life.

privatize /praɪvətaɪz/, **privatizes, privatizing**,   V+O
privatized; also spelled **privatise**. If a government **privatizes** a company, industry, or service that is owned and controlled by the state, it changes its ownership so that it is then owned by an individual or group. EG *Now the company is being privatised.* ◊ **privatization**   ◊ N UNCOUNT
/praɪvətaɪzeɪʃən/. EG *...the privatisation of the telephone service.*

privet /prɪvɪt/ is a type of bush with small leaves   N UNCOUNT
that stay green all year round. It is often grown in gardens to form hedges. EG *...houses separated by privet hedges.*

privilege /prɪvɪˈlɪdʒ/, **privileges**. 1 A **privilege**   N COUNT OR
is a special right or advantage that only one person   N UNCOUNT
or group has, so that they are in a better position than other people. EG *The privileges of these prisoners included being allowed daily visits... The children would resent any special privileges given to the staff... ...the power and privilege which they had once enjoyed.*
2 If you describe something that you have the   N SING :
opportunity to do as a **privilege**, you mean that   USU+SUPP
you are very pleased to have the opportunity to do it, because most people never have it. EG *Some years ago I had the privilege of meeting the world's oldest man... It was a privilege to work with such a great actress.*

privileged /prɪvɪˈlɪdʒd/. Someone who is **privi-**   ADJ QUALIT
leged has an advantage or opportunity that most other people do not have. EG *I am privileged to have worked with her so often... It was expensive and available only to the privileged few.*

privy /prɪviˈ/. If you are **privy** to something   ADJ PRED+to
secret, you have been allowed to know about it. EG   Formal
Very few of them were privy to the details of the conspiracy.

prize /praɪz/, **prizes, prizing, prized**. 1 A **prize** is   N COUNT
something of value, for example money or a trophy, that is given to someone who has the best results in a competition or game, or as a reward for doing good work. EG *I entered two competitions and won prizes... My pig won first prize at Skipton Fair... ...Nobel Prize winners.*
2 You use **prize** to describe things that are of such   ADJ CLASSIF :
good quality that they win prizes or deserve to win   ATTRIB
prizes. EG *...prize carnations.*
3 Something that **is prized** is wanted and admired   V+O : USU PASS
because it is considered to be very valuable or good in quality. EG *These fish are highly prized for their excellent flavour.*
4 See also **prise**.

pro /prəʊ/, **pros**. 1 A **pro** is a professional. EG *He's*   N COUNT
a pro and I'm only an amateur.   Informal
2 The **pros and cons** of something are its advan-   PHRASE
tages and disadvantages, which you consider so that you can make a sensible decision. EG *The pros and cons of strike action were discussed.*

pro- is used to form adjectives that describe people   PREFIX
as supporting something such as a country, person, or idea. For example, a pro-government newspaper is one that supports the government of its country. EG *...the Government's pro-American policy... ...the pro-nuclear lobby.*

probability /prɒbəbɪlɪˈtiˈ/, **probabilities**. 1 The   N COUNT OR
probability of something happening is how likely   N UNCOUNT
it is to happen, which is sometimes expressed as a

If you are in the process of doing something, have you finished it?

fraction or a percentage. EG *He must calculate the probability of failure... It had a high probability of succeeding.*

2 The **probability** that something will happen is N COUNT OR the fact that it is likely to happen. EG *The real* N UNCOUNT *source of his gloom was the probability that Kathy would not come... The probability is that they will find themselves in debt.*

3 If you say that something is true **in all probabil-** ADV SEN **ity**, you mean that you think it is very likely to be true. EG *They could, in all probability, perform any kind of calculation.*

probable /ˈprɒbəᵊl/. If you say that something is ADJ QUALIT **probable**, you mean that it is likely to be true or likely to happen. EG *It seems very probable that they are descended from a single ancestor... This is the most probable interpretation of the situation... The Belgians face a probable general election this autumn.*

probably /ˈprɒbəbliᵊ/. If you say that something is ADV SEN **probably** the case, you mean that you think it is likely to be the case, although you are not sure. EG *He probably kept your examination papers... Next year I shall probably be looking for a job... The owner is probably a salesman.*

probation /prəˈbeɪʃᵊn/ is **1** a period of time N UNCOUNT during which a person who has committed a crime has to obey the law and be supervised by a probation officer, rather than being sent to prison. EG *I wondered whether Daniel would be let off on probation.* **2** a period of time during which someone is judging your character and ability while you work, in order to see if you are suitable for that type of work. EG *He was a mechanic who was on probation.*

probation officer, probation officers. A **pro-** N COUNT **bation officer** is a person whose job is to supervise and help people who have committed crimes and been put on probation.

probe /prəʊb/, **probes, probing, probed. 1** If you V : OFT+A, **probe**, you ask questions or make enquiries in OR V+O order to discover facts about something. EG *She had learnt not to probe too far... We were probing for information relevant to our needs... ...to probe the mysteries of the universe.* ▸ used as a noun. EG *...a* ▸ N COUNT *probe into suspected drug dealing in Florida.*

2 A **probe** is a long thin metal instrument that N COUNT doctors and dentists use to examine very delicate parts of the body.

3 If you **probe** something, you poke it with some- V+O OR V+A thing long and thin in order to examine it. EG *The bird was probing the mound with its bill... I probed through his hair with my fingertips.*

problem /ˈprɒbləm/, **problems. 1** A **problem** is N COUNT **1.1** a situation that is unsatisfactory and causes difficulties for people. EG *They have financial problems... ...to help solve the problem of racism... The problem is that she can't cook.* **1.2** a puzzle that requires logical thought or mathematics to solve it. EG *...the development of problem-solving programs.*

2 Problem children are difficult for people to deal ADJ CLASSIF : with. EG *...the destructive behaviour of problem* ATTRIB *children.*

3 You can say **'No problem'** as a way of telling CONVENTION someone that you can easily do something for Informal them and will do it. Spoken

problematic /ˌprɒbləˈmætɪk/. Something that is ADJ QUALIT **problematic** involves problems and difficulties. EG Formal *...the problematic nature of the relationship.*

problematical /ˌprɒbləˈmætɪkᵊl/ means the ADJ QUALIT same as problematic. Formal

procedure /prəˈsiːdʒə/, **procedures.** A **pro-** N COUNT OR **cedure** is a way of doing something, especially the N UNCOUNT usual or correct way. EG *...the proper procedure to be followed in decision-making... ...a procedure for recording drugs administered... This was not standard procedure.*

proceed, proceeds, proceeding, proceeded. The verb is pronounced /prəˈsiːd/; the plural noun

in paragraph 5 is pronounced /ˈprəʊsiːdz/.

1 If you **proceed** to do something, you do it after V+to-INF doing something else. EG *He proceeded to explain... ...and then proceeds to throw stones through the windows.*

2 If you **proceed** with a course of action, you V : OFT+A continue with it. EG *It is necessary to examine this* Formal *claim before we proceed any further.*

3 If an activity, process, or event **proceeds**, it goes V on and does not stop. EG *Preparations were proceeding on schedule.*

4 If you **proceed** in a particular direction, you go V : USU+A in that direction. EG *...as we were proceeding along* Formal *Chiswick High Street.*

5 The **proceeds** of an event or activity are the N PLURAL money that has been obtained from it. EG *The proceeds will be given away to a deserving charity.*

proceeding /prəˈsiːdɪŋ/, **proceedings. 1** You can N COUNT : refer to an organized series of events that happen USU PLURAL in a place as the **proceedings**. EG *Millions of* Formal *people watched the proceedings on television.*

2 Legal **proceedings** are legal action taken N PLURAL against someone. EG *I shall institute proceedings* Formal *against you for unfair dismissal.*

process /ˈprəʊsɛs/, **processes, processing, pro-** N COUNT : **cessed. 1** A **process** is **1.1** a series of actions USU+SUPP which are carried out in order to achieve a particular result. EG *It has been a long process getting this information... ...industrial processes... The best solution can only be found by a process of trial and error.* **1.2** a series of things which happen naturally and result in a biological or chemical change. EG *...the digestive processes.*

2 If you **are in the process of** doing something, PHRASE you have started to do it and are still doing it. EG *She is still in the painful process of growing up.*

3 If you are doing something and you do something PHRASE else **in the process**, you do the second thing as a result of doing the first thing. EG *I got him out, but overbalanced in the process and fell.*

4 When raw materials or foods **are processed**, V+O they are treated chemically or industrially before they are used or sold. EG *...chemically processed food.* ◊ **processing.** EG *...the processing and stor-* ◊ N UNCOUNT *ing of radioactive materials.*

5 When people **process** information, they put it V+O through a system or into a computer in order to deal with it. EG *Your application will take a few weeks to process... Ten computers are processing the data.* ● See also **word processing**.

procession /prəˈsɛʃᵊn/, **processions.** A **proces-** N COUNT **sion** is a group of people who are walking, riding, or driving in a line as part of a public event. EG *Lady Branwell led the procession through the main street of the village.*

proclaim /prəˈkleɪm/, **proclaims, proclaiming,** V-SPEECH **proclaimed.** If people **proclaim** something, they Formal formally make it known to the public. EG *The Government proclaimed a state of emergency.*

proclamation /ˌprɒkləˈmeɪʃᵊn/, **proclamations.** N COUNT A **proclamation** is a public announcement about something important. EG *The king issued a proclamation outlawing the rebels.*

procreate /ˈprəʊkrɪeɪt/, **procreates, procreat-** V OR V+O **ing, procreated.** When animals or people **procre-** Formal **ate**, they produce young animals or babies.

◊ **procreation** /ˌprəʊkrɪˈeɪʃᵊn/. EG *...the natural* ◊ N UNCOUNT *process of procreation.*

procure /prəˈkjʊə/, **procures, procuring, pro-** V+O **cured.** If you **procure** something, you obtain it. EG Formal *It would be necessary to procure more grain.*

prod /prɒd/, **prods, prodding, prodded. 1** If you V+O : USU+A **prod** someone or something, you give them a quick push with your finger or with a pointed object. EG *She prodded a bean with her fork... He prodded Kunta roughly towards the raised platform.* ▸ used as a noun. EG *Mrs Travers gave her a* ▸ N COUNT *prod.*

2 If you **prod** someone who has not yet done V+O+A

something that they should do, you remind them to do it. EG ...*companies who prod the ministry into action every now and again.* ▸ used as a noun. EG ▸ N COUNT *The Home Office took their time replying, despite numerous prods from Mr Harper.*

prodigal /prɒdɪgəl/. If you describe someone as a ADJ CLASSIF **prodigal** son or daughter, you mean that they left Literary their family but have now returned.

prodigious /prədɪdʒəs/. Something that is **prodi-** ADJ QUALIT **gious** is amazingly great. EG ...*a prodigious store of* Formal *information... ...prodigious amounts of food.*

produce, produces, producing, produced; pronounced /prədjuːs/ when it is a verb, and /prɒdjuːs/ when it is a noun.

1 To **produce** something means to cause it to V+O happen. EG *All our efforts have not produced an agreement... This drug has produced terrible effects on children.*

2 If you **produce** something, you make or create it. V+O EG ...*factories producing electrical goods... These artists produce works of great beauty.*

3 When things or people **produce** something, it V+O comes from them or slowly forms from them, especially as the result of a biological or chemical process. EG *The sun produces light and heat... Parents are responsible for the offspring they produce.*

4 If you **produce** evidence or an argument, you V+O : OFT show it or explain it to people in order to make +*for/against* them agree with you. EG *He produces no evidence for his belief.*

5 If you **produce** an object from somewhere, you V+O : USU+A bring it out so that it can be seen. EG *Poirot produced the letter from his pocket.*

6 If someone **produces** a play, film, programme, V+O or record, they organize it and decide how it should be done. EG *The film was directed, written and produced by Mel Brooks.*

7 **Produce** is food or other things that are grown in N UNCOUNT large quantities to be sold. EG *They go to market to buy supplies and sell their produce.*

producer /prədjuːsə/, **producers**. **1** A **producer** N COUNT is a person whose job is organizing plays, films, programmes, or records. EG ...*a TV producer.*

2 A **producer** of a food or material is a company N COUNT : or country that provides or grows a large amount USU+SUPP of it. EG *The Soviet Union is the world's leading crude oil producer... ...producers of consumer goods.*

product /prɒdʌkt/, **products**. **1** A **product** is N COUNT : something that a company makes. EG *There are* USU PLURAL *masses of car-cleaning products available.*

2 Something or someone that is a **product** of a N COUNT+*of* particular situation or process exists or has particular qualities as a result of that situation or process. EG *The uniformity of the dancers was the product of hours of training... She is a product of the 1970s... ...a product of the party's weakness.*

production /prədʌkʃən/, **productions**. **1** **Pro-** N COUNT **duction** is **1.1** the process of manufacturing or growing something in large quantities. EG ...*more efficient methods of production.* **1.2** the amount of goods manufactured or grown by a company or country. EG *Industrial production has fallen by 20% over two years.* **1.3** the making of plays, films, programmes, or records. EG ...*members of the production crew and the cast.*

2 The **production** of something is its creation as N UNCOUNT the result of a natural process. EG ...*the production* +SUPP *of electricity.*

3 A **production** is a play, opera, or other show that N COUNT is performed. EG ...*Peter Hall's production of The Tempest at the Old Vic.*

production line, production lines. A **produc-** N COUNT **tion line** is an arrangement of machines in a factory where the products pass from machine to machine until they are finished. EG ...*cars coming off the production line at British Leyland.*

productive /prədʌktɪv/. **1** Something or someone ADJ QUALIT that is **productive** manufactures or grows a large amount of goods. EG *Agriculture and industry both grew more productive.*

2 If a meeting or a relationship is **productive**, ADJ QUALIT good or useful things happen as a result of it. EG ...*a productive friendship.*

productivity /prɒdʌktɪvɪtiː/ is the rate at which N UNCOUNT goods are produced. EG *There have been enormous increases in agricultural productivity.*

Prof. is an abbreviation for 'professor'. You write it in front of a professor's name. EG ...*Prof. Brewer.*

profess /prəfɛs/, **professes, professing, pro-** **fessed**. **1** If you **profess** to do or have something, V+*to*-INF you claim that you do it or have it. EG *Nell didn't* OR V+O like her, or professed not to... ...his professed com-* Formal *mitment to the school.*

2 If you **profess** a feeling or opinion, you openly V+O express it. EG *Many have professed disgust at this* Formal *use of weapons.*

profession /prəfɛʃən/, **professions**. **1** A **profes-** N COUNT **sion** is a type of job that requires special training and that has a fairly high status, for example the job of doctor or lawyer. EG *She decided on law or journalism as her profession.* ● If you are, for ● PHRASE example, a teacher or a lawyer, you can say that you are a teacher **by profession** or a lawyer **by profession**.

2 You can use **profession** to refer to all the people N COLL who have the same profession. EG *The medical profession are doing a very difficult job.*

professional /prəfɛʃənəl, -ʃənəl/, **profession-** **als**. **1** **Professional** means relating to a person's ADJ CLASSIF : work, especially work that requires special train- ATTRIB ing. EG *I sought professional advice.*

◊ **professionally**. EG *They are professionally* ◊ ADV *qualified.*

2 You use **professional** to describe things that ADJ CLASSIF : people do to earn money rather than as a hobby. ATTRIB For example, a **professional** actor does acting as a job. EG ...*a professional painter.*

◊ **professionally**. EG *He played the oboe profes-* ◊ ADV *sionally.*

3 **Professional** people have jobs that require ADJ CLASSIF : special training and that have a fairly high status. ATTRIB EG *The flat is ideal for the professional single person... ...two busy professional people.*

4 If something that someone does or produces is ADJ QUALIT **professional**, it is of a very high standard. EG *He had typed the whole scheme out in a very professional manner.*

5 A **professional** is **5.1** someone who has a job N COUNT that requires special training and has a fairly high status. EG ...*nurses, doctors, social workers, and other professionals.* **5.2** someone who plays a sport to earn money rather than as a hobby. EG *He has 17 championship victories as a professional plus two amateur titles.* **5.3** someone who does their work very skilfully.

professionalism /prəfɛʃənəlɪzəm/. Someone's N UNCOUNT **professionalism** is the skilful way in which they do a job. EG *The paper was produced with incredible speed and professionalism by the students.*

professor /prəfɛsə/, **professors**. **1** A **professor** N COUNT in a British university has the highest rank of the teachers in a department. EG ...*the Professor of English at Strathclyde University... ...Professor Cole.*

2 A **professor** in an American or Canadian univer- N COUNT sity or college is a teacher there.

proffer /prɒfə/, **proffers, proffering, proffered**. **1** If you **proffer** something to someone, you hold it V+O OR towards them so that they can take it or touch it. EG V+O+O *He put down his luggage and proffered his pass-* Formal *port... ...before he could proffer her one of them.*

Does a professor profess to do something?

2 If you **proffer** something to someone, you offer it v+o:oft+to, to them. EG *The solution he proffered to the banks* or v+o+o *was a novel one... She had already proffered her* Formal *resignation... Society proffers him no reward.*

proficient /prəfɪʃənt/. If you are **proficient** in ADJ QUALIT: something, you can do it quite well. EG *They were* oft+in/at *all proficient in needlework... ...a proficient swimmer.* ◊ **proficiency** /prəfɪʃənsi¹/. EG ...*your profi-* ◊ N UNCOUNT: *ciency in English... Technical proficiency is essen-* oft+in *tial.*

profile /prəʊfaɪl/, **profiles. 1** Your **profile** is the N COUNT outline of your face as it is seen when someone is looking at you from the side. EG *She glanced at his haughty profile.* ● If you see someone **in profile,** ● PHRASE you see them from the side. EG *She sat observing his face in profile.*

2 A **profile** of someone is a short article or N COUNT programme in which their life and character are described. EG *She wanted to write profiles of the founders of the Party.*

3 If you **keep a low profile,** you avoid doing things PHRASE that will make people notice you. EG *Keep a low profile until you have had time to settle in.*

profit /prɒfɪt/, **profits, profiting, profited. 1** A N COUNT OR **profit** is an amount of money that you gain when N UNCOUNT you are paid more for something than it cost you to make it, get it, or do it. EG *The company made a profit of 113 per cent... The profits are used to buy more equipment... ...to make as much profit as he can.*

2 If you **profit** from something, you benefit or gain v+from/by something from it. EG *I profited from his advice...* Formal *They had profited by their experience.*

profitable /prɒfɪtəbəºl/. Something that is **profitable 1** makes a profit. EG *The farm is a highly* ADJ QUALIT *profitable business... It was more profitable to export the crops.* ◊ **profitably.** EG *Can the motor* ◊ ADV *vehicle industry operate profitably?* **2** is useful and ADJ QUALIT results in some benefit for you. EG *He certainly made profitable use of the lessons he had learnt.* ◊ **profitably.** EG *There was little I could profitably* ◊ ADV *do sitting at my desk.*

profound /prəfaʊnd/. **1** You use **profound** to ADJ QUALIT emphasize the great degree or intensity of something. EG ...*in a state of profound shock... The war was to have a profound effect on all our lives.* ◊ **profoundly.** EG *I found the film profoundly* ◊ ADV *moving.* Formal

2 A **profound** idea or work is serious and shows ADJ QUALIT great intellectual understanding. EG *It's a profound book... ...a very profound question.*

profuse /prəfjuːs/ is used to indicate that a quan- ADJ QUALIT tity of something is very large. EG *There were* Formal *profuse apologies for its absence.* ◊ **profusely.** EG ◊ ADV *He was bleeding profusely.*

profusion /prəfjuːʒəºn/. If there is a **profusion** of N PART:SING something or if it occurs in **profusion,** there is a OR N UNCOUNT very large quantity of it. EG ...*a profusion of new* Formal *words... Daffodils grow in enormous profusion under the trees... ...the profusion of colour.*

prognosis /prɒgnəʊsɪs/, **prognoses** N COUNT /prɒgnəʊsiːz/. A **prognosis** is a prediction about Formal the future of someone or something, especially about whether a patient will recover from an illness. EG *It was a serious heart defect; the prognosis was poor, even with treatment.*

program /prəʊgræm/, **programs, programming, programmed. 1** A **program** is a set of N COUNT instructions that a computer follows in order to perform a particular task.

2 When you **program** a computer, you give it a set v+o of instructions to make it able to perform a particular task. EG *Can computers be programmed to hold intelligent conversations?* ◊ **programming.** EG ◊ N UNCOUNT ...*computer programming.*

3 See also **programme.**

programme /prəʊgræm/, **programmes, programming, programmed;** also spelled **program** in American English. **1** A **programme** of actions N COUNT: USU+SUPP

or events is a series of actions or events that are planned to be done. EG ...*a programme of modernization... They have embarked on an ambitious energy programme... ...their programme of meetings, talks and exhibitions.*

2 A television **programme** or radio **programme** N COUNT is something that is broadcast on television or radio. EG ...*the last programme in our series on education... ...gardening programmes.*

3 A theatre **programme** or concert **programme** N COUNT is a booklet or sheet of paper which gives information about the play or concert you are attending.

4 When you **programme** a machine or system, v+o: you set its controls so that it will work in a USU+to-INF particular way. EG *The radiators are programmed to come on at six every morning.*

programmer /prəʊgræmə/, **programmers.** A N COUNT computer **programmer** is a person whose job involves writing programs for computers.

progress, progresses, progressing, progressed; pronounced /prəʊgres/ when it is a noun, and /prəgres/ when it is a verb.

1 Progress is **1.1** the process of gradually getting N UNCOUNT nearer to achieving something or completing something. EG *She is making good progress with her German... They came in from time to time to check on my progress.* **1.2** changes and advances in a society that make life better or more civilized. EG ...*technological progress... ...the progress in transportation.*

2 The **progress** of a situation or action is the way N SING: in which it develops. EG *He followed the progress of* the+N+of *hostilities with impatience.*

3 If something is **in progress,** it is happening. EG PHRASE *The battle was still in progress.*

4 To **progress** means **4.1** to become more ad- v:USU+A vanced, skilful, or higher in rank over a period of time. EG *You're not progressing quickly enough... Technology did not progress any further for centuries.* **4.2** to continue. EG *My impressions changed as* v *the trip progressed.*

5 If you **progress** to something which naturally v+to comes after what you previously did or had, you start doing it or having it. EG *From there we progressed to a discussion on politics.*

progression /prəgreʃəºn/, **progressions. 1** A N COUNT+SUPP **progression** is a gradual development from one Formal state to another. EG *The progression from one extreme to the other is gradual.*

2 A **progression** of things is a number of things N COUNT+of which come one after the other. EG *It is part of a* Formal *connected progression of events.*

progressive /prəgresɪv/. **1** Someone who is **pro-** ADJ QUALIT **gressive** or has **progressive** ideas has modern ideas about how things should be done. EG *Some young parents are eager to be progressive.*

2 A **progressive** change happens gradually over a ADJ CLASSIF period of time. EG ...*the progressive industrialization of our society.* ◊ **progressively.** EG *It became* ◊ ADV *progressively easier to see.*

prohibit /prəhɪbɪt/, **prohibits, prohibiting, pro-** v+o: **hibited.** If someone **prohibits** something, they oft+from forbid it or make it illegal. EG *The country has a law prohibiting employees from striking... She believes that nuclear weapons should be totally prohibited... ...to prohibit the use of lead in petrol.*

prohibition /prəʊɪbɪʃəºn/, **prohibitions. 1** A **pro-** N COUNT **hibition** is a law or rule forbidding something. EG Formal *Of course, some of these prohibitions have social value... ...a prohibition on nuclear weapons.*

2 The **prohibition** of something is the forbidding of N UNCOUNT it. EG ...*the prohibition of strikes.*

prohibitive /prəhɪbɪtɪv/. If the cost of something ADJ QUALIT is **prohibitive,** it is so high that you cannot afford it. EG *The cost of making them by hand is prohibitive... ...the prohibitive price of domestic labour.*

project, projects, projecting, projected; pronounced /prɒdʒekt/ when it is a noun, and /prədʒekt/ when it is a verb.

1 A **project** is **1.1** a large-scale attempt to do or achieve something, which is carefully planned and will take some time. EG ...*the cancellation of the Blue Streak Missile project.* **1.2** a detailed study of a subject by a pupil or student. EG *He's doing a project on Scottish oil.* `N COUNT`

2 If something **is projected**, it is planned to happen in the future. EG *There were demonstrations against the projected visit.* `V+O : USU PASS`

3 If a future amount **is projected**, it is estimated. EG *The population of Calcutta is projected to rise to seventy million people.* `V+O : USU PASS`

4 If you **project** a light, film, or picture onto a screen or wall, you make it appear there. EG *The images were projected on a screen.* `V+O`

5 If someone **projects** you as a particular thing, they try to make people believe that you are that thing. EG *He had projected himself as a reformer.* `V+O OR V-REFL : USU+as`

6 If something **projects**, it sticks out above or beyond a surface or edge. EG *He could see the end of a spear projecting over the rock.* `V : USU+A Formal`

projection /prəʤɛkʃəⁿn/, **projections**. **1** A **projection** is an estimate of a future amount. EG *The company made projections of sales of 3000 aircraft.* `N COUNT`

2 A **projection** is also a part of something that sticks out. EG ...*the projection on the mantelpiece.* `N COUNT Formal`

3 The **projection** of a film or picture is the act of projecting it onto a screen or wall. EG ...*a projection room...* ...*arranges the hire and projection of films.* `N UNCOUNT`

projector /prəʤɛktə/, **projectors**. A **projector** is a machine that projects films or slides onto a screen or wall. `N COUNT`

proletarian /prəʊlɪtɛərɪən/ means relating to the proletariat. EG ...*establishing a new proletarian party...* ...*proletarian violence...* ...*the proletarian masses.* `ADJ CLASSIF : ATTRIB Technical`

proletariat /prəʊlɪtɛərɪət/. You can refer to working-class people, especially industrial workers, as the **proletariat**. EG *He identified himself with the proletariat and their struggles.* `N COLL : SING Technical`

proliferate /prəˈlɪfəreɪt/, **proliferates, proliferating, proliferated.** If things **proliferate**, they increase in number very quickly. EG *Polytechnics proliferated all over the country.* ◊ **proliferation** /prəˌlɪfəreɪʃəⁿn/. EG *We can prevent the proliferation of nuclear weaponry.* `V Formal` ◊ `N UNCOUNT : OFT+of`

prolific /prəˈlɪfɪk/. A **prolific** writer, artist, or composer produces a large number of works. `ADJ QUALIT`

prologue /prəʊlɒg/, **prologues**. A **prologue** is a speech or section that introduces a play or book. `N COUNT`

prolong /prəˈlɒŋ/, **prolongs, prolonging, prolonged.** To **prolong** something means to make it last longer. EG *All the time people are seeking to prolong life.* `V+O`

prolonged /prəˈlɒŋd/. A **prolonged** event or situation continues for a long time, or for longer than expected. EG ...*a prolonged and bitter struggle...* ...*a prolonged period of uncertainty.* `ADJ QUALIT`

promenade /prɒmənɑːd/, **promenades**. At a seaside town, the **promenade** is a raised road or path next to the beach. `N COUNT : USU the+N`

prominent /prɒmɪnənt/. **1** Someone who is **prominent** is important. EG ...*US Senators and other prominent American personalities.* ◊ **prominence** /prɒmɪnəns/. EG *Alan Travers had risen to prominence in his wife's organisation.* `ADJ QUALIT` ◊ `N UNCOUNT`

2 Something that is **prominent** is very noticeable or is an important part of something else. EG *There were two prominent landmarks.* ◊ **prominently.** EG ...*a large photograph prominently displayed in her front room... In the labour market before 1974, women figured prominently.* `ADJ QUALIT` ◊ `ADV`

promiscuous /prəmɪskjʊəs/. Someone who is **promiscuous** has sex with many different people; used showing disapproval. EG ...*when young people engage in promiscuous behaviour.* ◊ **promiscuity** /prɒmɪskjuːˈɪtiˈ/. EG *Parents often worry about sexual promiscuity when their children reach adolescence.* `ADJ QUALIT` ◊ `N UNCOUNT`

promise /prɒmɪs/, **promises, promising, promised. 1** If you **promise** that you will do something, you say to someone that you will definitely do it. EG *Promise me you'll go... I'll be back at one, I promise... 'I won't fail you', he promised... I promised to take the children to the fair.* `V : OFT +REPORT, QUOTE, OR to-INF; ALSO V+O+REPORT OR QUOTE`

2 If you **promise** someone something, you tell them that you will definitely give it to them or make sure that they have it. EG *I promised him a canary for his birthday... The government promise better homes for all who need them.* `V+O+O OR V+O+A`

3 If a situation or event **promises** to have a particular quality or to be a particular thing, it shows signs that it will have that quality or be that thing. EG *The debate promises to be lively... Early mist had promised a clear day.* `V+to-INF OR V+O`

4 A **promise** is a statement which you make to someone in which you say that you will definitely do something or give them something. EG *They tried to break the promises made in negotiations... They fulfilled their promise to revive trade.* `N COUNT`

5 If someone or something shows **promise**, they seem likely to be very good or successful. EG *She showed considerable promise as a tennis player... The relationship held little promise of happiness.* `N UNCOUNT`

promising /prɒmɪsɪŋ/. Someone or something that is **promising** seems likely to be very good or successful. EG *I consulted the menu. It looked promising...* ...*a most promising new actress.* `ADJ QUALIT`

promote /prəməʊt/, **promotes, promoting, promoted. 1** If people **promote** something, **1.1** they help it to happen, increase, or spread. EG *The government could do more to promote economic growth.* **1.2** they try to make it popular or successful. EG *The new town was vigorously promoted as an ideal place to settle.* `V+O`

2 If someone **is promoted**, they are given a more important job in the organization they work for. EG *He had recently been promoted to captain.* `V+O : OFT+to`

promoter /prəməʊtə/, **promoters. 1** A **promoter** is a person who helps organize and finance an event, especially a sports event. EG ...*a bullfight promoter...* ...*concert promoters.* `N COUNT`

2 The **promoter** of a cause or idea tries to make it become popular. EG *She was a tireless promoter of new causes.* `N COUNT`

promotion /prəməʊʃəⁿn/, **promotions. 1** If you are given **promotion**, you are given a more important job in the organization you work for. EG *What, if any, are your chances of promotion?* `N UNCOUNT OR N COUNT`

2 The **promotion** of a product, event, or idea is an attempt to make it popular or successful, especially by advertising. EG *There are government controls on the promotion of cigarettes.* `N UNCOUNT`

3 A **promotion** is a publicity campaign that is intended to increase the sales of a product. `N COUNT`

prompt /prɒmpt/, **prompts, prompting, prompted. 1** If something **prompts** someone to do something, it causes them to decide to do it and then to do it. EG *The Times article prompted him to call a meeting of the staff... My choice was prompted by a number of considerations.* `V+O : OFT+to-INF OR A`

2 If you **prompt** someone who has just stopped talking, you say something to indicate that you wish them to continue talking. EG *'Yes?' Morris prompted, after a pause.* `V+O OR V+QUOTE`

3 A **prompt** reaction or action comes or is done without any delay. EG *Professor Hamburg got a prompt reply... She requires prompt medical attention.* `ADJ QUALIT : USU ATTRIB`

4 You use **prompt** to talk about exact times. For example, if you say that something will happen at 8 o'clock **prompt**, you mean that it will happen at exactly 8 o'clock. `ADV`

Where would you find a promenade?

PRONOUNS

A pronoun is a word that is used to refer to people or things without naming or describing them. Pronouns are used in similar ways to noun groups, and so a pronoun can be the subject, object, or complement of a clause, or the object of a preposition. Most pronouns are used in place of complete noun groups, and so they are not normally used with determiners or adjectives. The pronouns **one** and **ones** are different, however, because they are used in place of a noun rather than a complete noun group. See the dictionary entry for **one** for an explanation of its uses.

1 Personal pronouns (PRON) refer to people and things. When the pronoun is the subject of a clause, the words **I**, **you**, **he**, **she**, **it**, **we**, and **they** are used. When the pronoun is the object of a clause, or when it comes after a preposition, the words **me**, **you**, **him**, **her**, **it**, **us**, and **them** are used. For example: *I gave him a record for Christmas and he gave me a book.*

2 The possessive form (PRON POSS) is used to show who something belongs to. The possessive pronouns are **mine**, **yours**, **his**, **hers**, **its**, **ours**, and **theirs**. Possessive pronouns stand as full noun groups: *Although yours is new, I still prefer mine.* See also the entry headed DETERMINERS for information about the words **my**, **your**, **his**, **her**, **its**, **our**, and **their**, which are labelled DET POSS in this dictionary.

3 Relative pronouns (PRON REL) introduce relative clauses. The pronouns **who**, **whose**, and **whom** refer back to people, **which** refers back to things, and **that** refers back to either people or things. At the same time these words introduce subordinate clauses in a sentence, giving extra information about the people or things they refer to. For example: *You are the only person who knows anything about me . . . There's one question which I'd like to ask you . . . . . . ice cream that Mum had made.*

4 Reflexive pronouns (PRON REFL) are formed by adding 'self' or 'selves' to other pronouns: **myself**, **yourself**, **himself**, **herself**, **itself**, **ourselves**, **yourselves**, and **themselves**. They are used as the objects of clauses or prepositions when they refer to the same person or thing as the subject of the clause. For example: *He bought himself a tie . . . She poured herself a drink . . . They treated themselves to a good meal.* Reflexive pronouns can also be used to add emphasis when you are saying that a particular person or thing did something: *He baked the bread himself . . . I myself saw the accident . . . You yourself said it's only a routine check.*

5 The words **this**, **that**, **these**, and **those** can be used as pronouns (also PRON) to refer to things that have already been mentioned in the conversation, or to things that are around you in the real world. They can be used as the subject or object of a clause. For example: *She gave me this for my birthday . . . These are for you.*

6 There is a group of words, also labelled PRON, which are usually used in front of nouns but which can, when it is obvious what they refer to, be used on their own. Examples are **all**, **both**, **few**, and **none**, as in: *All were waiting silently . . . He got angry with both of them . . . Many of us tried but few succeeded . . . None could afford to buy books.*

7 There is a small class of indefinite pronouns (PRON INDEF) which you use when you cannot or do not want to refer to any particular person or thing by name. These are: **anybody**, **anyone**, **anything**, **everybody**, **everyone**, **everything**, **nobody**, **no-one**, **nothing**, **somebody**, **someone**, and **something**. If you want to modify an indefinite pronoun with an adjective, you have to put the adjective after the pronoun, and not before it. So you say: *It's nothing serious, I hope?*

prompting /prɒmpᵊtɪŋ/, **promptings.** If you re-   N UNCOUNT
spond to **prompting**, you do what someone encour-   OR N COUNT
ages or reminds you to do. EG *She did it without any*
prompting.

promptly /prɒmpᵊtliʲ/. If you do something
promptly, 1 you do it immediately. EG *He slapped* ADV
her and she promptly burst into tears... When you
receive orders you must obey them promptly with-
out question. 2 you do it at exactly the time that   ADV
has been arranged. EG *I arrived at the gates*
promptly at six o'clock.

PRON stands for **pronoun**
Words which are labelled PRON in the Extra Column are pronouns.
See the entry headed PRONOUNS for more information.

---

prone /prəʊn/. 1 If someone or something is   ADJ PRED+ to
prone to something, they have a tendency to be   TO-INF
affected by it or to do it. EG *He was prone to*
indigestion... A computer was fairer and less prone
to error... They were prone to argue.
2 If you are lying **prone**, you are lying flat with the   ADJ CLASSIF
front of your body facing downwards. EG *She was*   Formal
lying prone on the floor.

prong /prɒŋ/, **prongs.** The **prongs** of a fork are   N COUNT
the long, thin pointed parts.

PRON INDEF stands for **indefinite pronoun**
There are 12 words labelled PRON INDEF in the
Extra Column - 'anybody, anyone, anything, everybody, everyone, everything, nobody, no-one, nothing, somebody, someone, something'.
See the entry headed PRONOUNS for more information.

---

pronoun /prəʊnaʊn/, **pronouns.** In grammar, a   N COUNT
pronoun is a word that is used to replace a noun or
a noun group that has already been mentioned or
that will be mentioned later. 'He', 'she', and 'them'
are all pronouns. Words that are pronouns have the
label PRON in the Extra Column. See the entry
headed PRONOUNS for more information.

pronounce /prənaʊns/, **pronounces, pronounc-**
ing, pronounced. 1 To **pronounce** a word means   V+O
to say it in the way it is usually said or in a
particular way. EG *I can't pronounce his name...*
...the town of Ixtlan, pronounced East-lon.
2 If you **pronounce** something to be true, you   V+O+C
formally state that it is true. EG *The victim was*   Formal
pronounced dead on arrival at the hospital.
3 If someone **pronounces** a verdict or opinion on   V+O,
something, they formally give their verdict or   V+QUOTE,
opinion. EG *'Are the people ready to pronounce*   OR V+on
their verdict?' - *'Guilty.'... She was asked to pro-*   Formal
nounce on the merits of an antique vase.

pronounced /prənaʊnst/. Something that is **pro-**   ADJ QUALIT
nounced is very noticeable. EG *He spoke with a*
pronounced English accent.

pronouncement /prənaʊnsməᵊnt/, **pronounce-**   N COUNT
ments. A **pronouncement** is a formal or official
statement. EG *...official pronouncements made by*
politicians.

PRON POSS stands for **possessive pronoun**
There are seven words labelled PRON POSS in the
Extra Column - 'mine, yours, hers, his, its, ours,
theirs'.
See the entry headed PRONOUNS for more informa-
tion.

PRON REFL stands for **reflexive pronoun**
There are nine words labelled PRON REFL in the
Extra Column - 'myself, yourself, herself, himself,
itself, oneself, ourselves, themselves, yourselves'.
See the entry headed PRONOUNS for more informa-
tion.

PRON REL stands for **relative pronoun**
There are ten words labelled PRON REL in the
Extra Column - 'that, when, where, whereby,
wherein, which, who, whom, whose, why'.
See the entry headed PRONOUNS for more informa-
tion.

---

pronunciation /prənʌnsɪeɪʃᵊn/, **pronuncia-**
tions. 1 The **pronunciation** of a word or language   N UNCOUNT
is the way in which it is usually pronounced. EG   OR N COUNT
...the recommended American pronunciation.
2 Someone's **pronunciation** of a word is the way   N COUNT :
in which they pronounce it. EG *He tried to correct*   USU SING+POSS
Francois's pronunciation.

proof /pruːf/, **proofs. 1 Proof** is a fact or a piece   N UNCOUNT
of evidence which shows that something is true or   OR N COUNT
exists. EG *Do you have any proof of that allega-*
tion?... He hadn't any proof that Davis had not died.
2 The **proofs** of a printed publication are a first   N COUNT
copy of it that is printed so that mistakes can be
corrected before more copies are printed.

-proof combines with nouns to form adjectives
which indicate that something cannot be damaged
by a particular thing or person. EG *This building's*
supposed to be earthquake-proof... Can these con-
tainers be made vandal-proof? ● See also **fire-**
proof, waterproof.

prop /prɒp/, **props, propping, propped.** 1 If you   V+O+A
prop an object on or against something, you support it by putting something underneath it or by
resting it against something. EG *She propped her*
chin on her hand and gazed at him... His gun lay
propped against the wall.
2 Someone or something that is a **prop** for a   N COUNT+SUPP
system, institution, or person is the main thing that
makes it able to survive. EG *They ceased to be the*
prop of the imperial administration... Discussing
everything was the prop of their marriage.
3 A **prop** is also a stick or other object that you use   N COUNT
to support something. EG *We need a clothes prop*
for the washing line.
4 The **props** in a play or film are all the objects   N COUNT :
and pieces of furniture that are used in it. EG *The*   USU PLURAL
sets, props, and costumes were all ready.

prop up. 1 If you **prop** an object **up**, you support   PHRASAL VB :
it in a particular position by putting something   V+O+ADV,
underneath it or by resting it against something. EG   USU+A
His feet were propped up on the coffee table.
2 If one organization or group of people **props up**   V+O+ADV
another, it helps the other one to survive. EG *The*
Government does not intend to prop up declining
industries.

propaganda /prɒpəgændə/ is information, often   N UNCOUNT
exaggerated or false information, which an organization publishes or broadcasts in order to influence
people. EG *...a campaign of anti-British propaganda.*

If you have a propensity to do something, are you
prone to do it?

propagandist /prɒpəgændɪst/, **propagandists.** N COUNT
A **propagandist** is a person who tries to persuade people to support a particular idea or group; often used showing disapproval. EG *...dedicated revolutionary activists and propagandists.*

propagate /prɒpəgeɪt/, **propagates, propagating, propagated. 1** If people **propagate** an idea or V+O piece of information, they spread it and try to Formal make people believe it or support it. EG *The group is doing what it can to propagate the rumour... They toured the principal cities to propagate her cause.*
2 If you **propagate** plants, you grow more of them V-ERG from the original ones.   Technical

propel /prəˈpel/, **propels, propelling, propelled.**
1 To **propel** something in a particular direction V+O:USU+A means to cause it to move in that direction. EG *The bullet is propelled out of the chamber.*
2 If something **propels** you into a particular ac- V+O+A tion, it causes you to do it. EG *...a sense of guilt strong enough to propel him into action.*

propeller /prəˈpelə/, **propellers.** A **propeller** is N COUNT a device with blades which is attached to a boat or aircraft. The engine makes the propeller spin round and causes the boat or aircraft to move.

propensity /prəˈpensɪtiˈ/, **propensities.** If you N COUNT: have a **propensity** to behave in a particular way, USU+for/to you have a natural tendency to do this. EG *...our* OR to-INF propensity to evil... ...their propensity for mass* Formal gatherings... There was no evidence of any propensity to act violently towards others.*

proper /prɒpə/. **1** You use **proper** to describe ADJ CLASSIF: things that you consider to be real and satisfactory ATTRIB rather than inadequate in some way. EG *He's never had a proper job... Lack of proper funding is making our job more difficult.*
2 The **proper** thing is the one that is correct or ADJ CLASSIF: most suitable. EG *Everything was in its proper* ATTRIB place... What's the proper word for those things?*
3 If you say that a way of behaving is **proper**, you ADJ CLASSIF mean that it is considered socially acceptable and right. EG *It wasn't proper for a man to cry.*
4 You can add **proper** after a word or name that ADJ AFTER N refers to a place to emphasize that you are referring to the main or central part of the place and not to its edges or outer parts. EG *By the time I got to the village proper everyone was out to meet me.*

properly /prɒpəliˈ/. **1** If something is done **prop-** ADV **erly**, it is done correctly and satisfactorily. EG *We must see that the children are properly fed... The reviewers aren't doing their job properly.*
2 If someone behaves **properly**, they behave in a ADV way that is considered acceptable and not rude.

proper noun, proper nouns. In grammar, a N COUNT **proper noun** is a noun which is the name of a person, place, or institution. Proper nouns are usually spelled with a capital letter at the beginning. Words that are proper nouns have N PROP in the Extra Column. See the entry headed NOUNS for more information.

property /prɒpətiˈ/, **properties. 1** Someone's N UNCOUNT **property** is all the things that belong to them or something that belongs to them. EG *Their job is to protect private property... Her property passes to her nephew.*
2 A **property** is a building and the land belonging N COUNT to it. EG *He arranged to rent the property.* Formal
3 The **properties** of a substance or object are the N COUNT: ways in which it behaves in particular conditions. OFT PLURAL EG *...the physical properties of substances.*

prophecy /prɒfɪsiˈ/, **prophecies.** A **prophecy** is N COUNT OR a statement in which someone says something that N UNCOUNT they believe will happen. EG *The prophecy was fulfilled... ...a prophecy which was greeted with ridicule.*

prophesy /prɒfɪsaɪ/, **prophesies, prophesying,** V-SPEECH **prophesied.** If you **prophesy** that something will happen, you say that you strongly believe that it will happen. EG *He has prophesied that the State*

will be destroyed... *He prophesied a violent uprising.*

prophet /prɒfɪt/, **prophets.** A **prophet** is **1** a N COUNT person who is believed to be chosen by God to say the things that God wants to tell people. **2** someone Literary who predicts that something will happen in the future. EG *The prophets of doom have been proved wrong before.*

prophetic /prəˈfetɪk/. If something was **prophet-** ADJ QUALIT **ic**, it described or suggested something that did happen later. EG *...now, more than fifty years after she wrote those prophetic words.*

propitious /prəˈpɪʃəs/. If something is **propi-** ADJ QUALIT **tious**, it is likely to lead to success. EG *It was hardly* Formal *a propitious time to join one of those newspapers.*

proponent /prəˈpəʊnənt/, **proponents.** If you are N COUNT: a **proponent** of a particular idea or course of USU+POSS action, you actively support it. EG *...the proponents* Formal *of conservation.*

proportion /prəˈpɔːʃən/, **proportions. 1** A **pro-** N PART **portion** of an amount or group is a part of it. EG *Courts are now sending a smaller proportion of offenders to prison... There is always a proportion of the crowd which wants to make trouble.*
2 The **proportion** of one kind of thing in a group is N PART the number of things of that kind compared to the total number of things in the group. EG *The proportion of women in the total work-force has risen.*
3 The **proportion** of one amount to another is how N COUNT much greater one is than the other. EG *The proportion of workers to employers was large... Usually men outnumber women, but we have about equal proportions at Sussex.*
4 You can refer to the size of something as its N PLURAL: **proportions**. EG *...a gin and tonic of giant propor-* USU+SUPP *tions... We are trying to reduce the problem to manageable proportions.*
5 If one thing increases or decreases **in propor-** PHRASE **tion to** another thing, it increases or decreases to the same degree as that thing. EG *Reliability has increased in proportion to the number of switching units.*
6 If one thing is small **in proportion** to another PHRASE thing, it is small when you compare it with the other thing. EG *Babies have big heads in proportion to their bodies.*
7 If you say that something is **out of all propor-** PHRASE **tion** to something else, you mean that it is far greater or more serious than it should be. EG *These buildings were built out of all proportion to any human scale.*
8 If you say that someone has **got** something **out** PHRASE **of proportion**, you mean that they think it is more important or worrying than it really is. EG *Haven't you got things just a little bit out of proportion, Captain?*
9 If someone has a **sense of proportion**, they PHRASE know what is really important and what is not. EG *Remember where you are and who you are, keep a sense of proportion.*

proportional /prəˈpɔːʃənəl, -ʃənəˈl/. If one amount ADJ CLASSIF: is **proportional** to another, it always remains the OFT+to same fraction of the other. EG *As a rule the suicide rates are proportional to the size of the city.*
◊ **proportionally.** EG *Males have proportionally* ◊ ADV *longer legs and larger feet than females.*

proportionate /prəˈpɔːʃənəˈt/ means the same as ADJ CLASSIF: proportional. EG *After a run, your recovery time is* OFT+to *proportionate to your fitness.* ◊ **proportionately.** ◊ ADV EG *Britain spent proportionately more on research than its competitors... Poorer people are losing proportionately more through these tax changes.*

proposal /prəˈpəʊzəˈl/, **proposals.** A **proposal** is N COUNT **1** a plan which is suggested for people to think about and decide upon. EG *There is controversy about a proposal to build a new nuclear power station... ...proposals for cheaper flights to the United States.* **2** a request that someone makes to a person to marry them. EG *She told me that the* *second proposal of marriage which she received came from an Italian prince.*

propose /prəpˈəʊz/, **proposes, proposing, proposed.** 1 If you **propose** a plan or idea, you suggest it for people to think about and decide upon. EG *He proposed a bargain... I proposed that the culprits should be fined.* ◊ **proposed.** EG *...the proposed alliance.* V+O OR V+REPORT ONLY *that* ◊ ADJ CLASSIF : ATTRIB

2 If you **propose** to do something, you intend to do it. EG *I do not propose to discuss this matter.* ◊ **proposed.** EG *...my proposed trip to America... The proposed tests should be interesting.* V+*to*-INF ◊ ADJ CLASSIF : ATTRIB

3 If someone **proposes** a motion in a debate, they introduce it and speak about why they agree with it. EG *Webb proposed the motion 'That this House has no confidence in the Government'.* V+O

4 If you **propose** a toast to someone or something, you ask people to drink a toast to them. V+O

5 If you **propose** to someone, you ask them to marry you. EG *He had known her for two years before he proposed... Was he proposing marriage?* V:OFT+*to*; ALSO V+O

proposition /prɒpəzˈɪʃəʰn/, **propositions, propositioning, propositioned.** 1 A **proposition** is 1.1 a statement expressing a theory or opinion. EG *I had plenty of evidence to support the proposition that man was basically selfish.* 1.2 an offer or arrangement that someone suggests. EG *He came to me one day with an extraordinary proposition.* N COUNT

2 If someone **propositions** you, they ask you to have sex with them. V+O Formal

proprietary /prəˈpraɪətəʰriˈ/. **Proprietary** substances are ones that are sold under a trade name. EG *For grease marks try a proprietary dry cleaner.* ADJ CLASSIF : ATTRIB Formal

proprietor /prəˈpraɪətə/, **proprietors.** The **proprietor** of a hotel, shop, or newspaper is the person who owns it. N COUNT

proprietress /prəˈpraɪətrɪˀs/, **proprietresses.** The **proprietress** of a hotel, shop, or newspaper is the woman who owns it. N COUNT

propriety /prəˈpraɪətiˈ/ is the quality of being socially or morally acceptable. EG *I doubt the propriety of receiving a lady this late at night.* N UNCOUNT Formal

prosaic /prəʊzˈeɪɪk/. Something that is **prosaic** is dull and uninteresting. EG *...a prosaic building... ...a prosaic existence... His methods were so prosaic.* ADJ QUALIT

prose /prəʊz/ is ordinary written language, in contrast to poetry. EG *...descriptive prose... ...a fancy prose style... ...a piece of continuous prose.* N UNCOUNT

prosecute /prɒsɪkjuːt/, **prosecutes, prosecuting, prosecuted.** 1 If someone **is prosecuted,** they are charged with a crime and put on trial. EG *He was prosecuted for drunken driving.* V+O OR V

2 The **prosecuting** lawyer in a trial tries to prove that the person who is on trial is guilty. ADJ CLASSIF : ATTRIB

prosecution /prɒsɪkjuːʃəʰn/, **prosecutions.** 1 **Prosecution** is the action of charging someone with a crime and putting them on trial. EG *He could face criminal prosecution... The Smiths brought a prosecution against the organizers.* N UNCOUNT OR N COUNT

2 The lawyers who try to prove that a person on trial is guilty are called the **prosecution.** EG *Today he will be questioned by the prosecution.* N SING : *the*+N

prosecutor /prɒsɪkjuːtə/, **prosecutors.** A **prosecutor** is a lawyer or official who brings charges against someone or tries to prove in a trial that they are guilty. N COUNT American

prospect, prospects, prospecting, prospected; pronounced /prɒspekt/ when it is a noun, and /prəˈspekt/ when it is a verb.

1 If there is some **prospect** of something happening, there is a possibility that it will happen. EG *There was little prospect of significant military aid... ...the prospects for peace... ...the prospect that the skills learnt might have to be unlearnt.* N UNCOUNT : OFT+*of/for* OR REPORT

2 A particular **prospect** is something that you expect or know is going to happen. EG *She did not relish the prospect of climbing another flight of stairs... You may be daunted by this bleak prospect.* N COUNT OR N UNCOUNT : USU+*of*

3 Someone's **prospects** are their chances of being N PLURAL : USU+POSS

successful in their career, especially by being promoted quickly. EG *Success or failure here would be crucial to his future prospects.*

4 If people **prospect** for oil, gold, or some other valuable substance, they look for it in the rock or under the sea. V:OFT+*for*

prospective /prəˈspektɪv/. You use **prospective** to refer to something that someone wants to do or be. For example, a **prospective** tenant wants to be a tenant somewhere. EG *Godalming College has been forced to turn away 300 prospective students... ...prospective buyers.* ADJ CLASSIF : ATTRIB

prospectus /prəˈspektəs/, **prospectuses.** A **prospectus** is a document produced by a college, school, or company, which gives details about it. N COUNT

prosper /prɒspə/, **prospers, prospering, prospered.** If people or businesses **prosper,** they are successful and do well financially. EG *The farmers prospered.* V

prosperity /prɒspeˈrɪʲtiˈ/ is a condition in which a person or community is doing well financially. EG *...a period of wealth and prosperity.* N UNCOUNT

prosperous /prɒspəʰrəs/. Someone who is **prosperous** is wealthy and successful. ADJ QUALIT

prostitute /prɒstɪtjuːt/, **prostitutes, prostituting, prostituted.** 1 A **prostitute** is a person, usually a woman, who has sex with men in exchange for money. N COUNT

2 If you **prostitute** yourself or your talents, you use your talents for unworthy purposes, usually for money. V-REFL OR V+O

prostitution /prɒstɪtjuːʃəʰn/ is the work of people who have sex with men in exchange for money. N UNCOUNT

prostrate, prostrates, prostrating, prostrated; pronounced /prɒstreɪt/ when it is a verb, and /prɒstreɪt/ when it is an adjective.

1 If you **prostrate** yourself, you lie flat on the ground with your face downwards. EG *I wanted to throw my arms about him, prostrate myself before him.* V-REFL

2 If you are **prostrate,** you are lying flat on the ground with your face downwards. EG *...the prostrate figure of Mr Green.* ADJ CLASSIF

protagonist /prəˈtægənɪst/, **protagonists.** 1 Someone who is a **protagonist** of an idea or movement is a supporter of it. EG *She was a vehement protagonist of sexual equality.* N COUNT : USU+SUPP Formal

2 A **protagonist** in a play or event is one of the main people in it. N COUNT Formal

protect /prəˈtekt/, **protects, protecting, protected.** To **protect** someone or something means to prevent them from being harmed or damaged. EG *She had his umbrella to protect her from the rain... Babies are protected against diseases like measles by their mothers' milk... The Common Law has always protected individual rights.* V+O : USU+A ◊ **protector** /prəˈtektə/, **protectors.** EG *...ecologists and protectors of wildlife.* ◊ N COUNT

protection /prəˈtekʃəʰn/. If something gives **protection** against something unpleasant, it prevents people or things from being harmed or damaged by it. EG *The mud walls of these huts offer little protection against rats... We need protection from the sun's rays... She put on dark glasses as a protection against the strong light.* N UNCOUNT

protective /prəˈtektɪv/. 1 A **protective** object or action is intended to protect something or someone from harm. EG *...protective clothing and equipment.* ADJ CLASSIF : ATTRIB

2 If someone is **protective** towards you, they show a strong desire to keep you safe. EG *She felt very protective towards her sister.* ◊ **protectively.** EG *Rudolph sat up, an arm tightening protectively around Julie's shoulder.* ADJ QUALIT : OFT+*towards* ◊ ADV

protégé /prɒtɪʒeɪ/, **protégés;** also spelled **protégée** when referring to a woman. N COUNT+POSS

If there is a prospect of rain, will it definitely rain?

If you are the **protégé** of an older and more ◊ ADJ CLASSIF : experienced person, that person helps you and ATTRIB guides you over a period of time. EG *She was a painter and a protégée of Duncan Grant.*

protein /prəʊtiːn/, **proteins. Protein** is a sub- N COUNT OR stance found, for example, in meat, eggs, and milk. N UNCOUNT You need protein in order to grow and be healthy.

protest, protests, protesting, protested; pro- nounced /prətest/ when it is a verb, and /prəʊtest/ when it is a noun.

1 If you **protest** about something or against some- v : USU thing, you say or show publicly that you object to it. +about/ EG *Labour MPs took to the streets to protest against* against/at *government economic policy... ...a group protesting at official inaction... I was shoved, protesting, into a side room.* ◊ **protester, protesters.** EG *The pro-* ◊ N COUNT *testers surrendered to the police after about an hour.*

2 If you **protest** something, you protest about it. EG v+o *He protested the action in a phone call to the* American *mayor.*

3 If you **protest** that something is the case, you v-SPEECH : insist that it is the case, when other people think ONLY *that* that it may not be. EG *They protested that they had never heard of him... 'You're wrong,' I protested... The mother protested her innocence.*

4 A **protest** is the act of saying or showing publicly N COUNT OR that you object to something. EG *They joined in the* N UNCOUNT *protests against the government's proposals... There was a wave of student riots, in protest at university conditions.*

Protestant /prɒtɪstənt/, **Protestants.** A **Pro-** N COUNT **testant** is someone who belongs to the branch of the Christian church which separated from the Catholic church in the sixteenth century. EG *Most of them were Protestants... ...Protestant groups.*

protestation /prɒtesteɪʃəⁿn/, pro-/, **protestations.** N COUNT A **protestation** is a strong declaration that some- Formal thing is true or not true. EG *...Meehan's vehement protestations of innocence.*

protocol /prəʊtəkɒl/ is a system of rules about the N UNCOUNT correct way to act in formal situations. EG *She was ignorant of protocol... Beaton had to face a tricky problem of protocol.*

proton /prəʊtɒn/, **protons.** A **proton** is an atomic N COUNT particle that has an electrical charge. Technical

prototype /prəʊtətaɪp/, **prototypes.** A **proto-** N COUNT **type** is the first model that is made of something new. EG *Funds for testing of the prototypes ran out... ...a prototype plane.*

protracted /prətræktɪ²d/. Something that is **pro-** ADJ QUALIT **tracted** lasts a long time, especially longer than usual. EG *She was late returning to the office after a protracted lunch... ...Tim's protracted absence.*

protrude /prətruːd/, **protrudes, protruding,** v : USU+A **protruded.** If something **protrudes** from some- Formal where, it sticks out. EG *He tripped over a pair of boots protruding from under the table... ...his pro-truding ribs... A steel stud protruded upwards.*

proud /praʊd/, **prouder, proudest. 1** If you feel ADJ QUALIT : **proud**, you feel glad about something good that OFT+*of* you or someone close to you owns or has done. EG OR *to*-INF *They seemed proud of what they had accom-plished... Their country should be proud of them... It makes me proud to be an American.* ◊ **proudly.** ◊ ADV EG *He was grinning proudly, delighted with his achievement.... 'I was a cop,' said Mac proudly.*

2 Someone who is **proud 2.1** has dignity and self- ADJ QUALIT respect. EG *He was a poor but very proud old man.* **2.2** feels that they are superior to other people. EG *She was too proud to apologize.*

prove /pruːv/, **proves, proving, proved, proven** /pruːvⁿn/. **Proved** and **proven** are both used as the past participle.

1 To **prove** that something is true means to show v+REPORT, definitely that it is true. EG *He was able to prove* v+O, OR V+C *that he was an American... He is going to have to prove his innocence... She has to be proved wrong.*

◊ **proven.** EG *This man is a proven liar... ...based on proven fact.*

2 If someone or something **proves** to have a v+to-INF particular quality, they are found to have that OR V+C quality. EG *I proved to be hopeless as a teacher... This information has proved useful to many people.*

proverb /prɒvɜːb/, **proverbs.** A **proverb** is a N COUNT short sentence that people often quote, which gives advice or tells you something about life. EG *...the old Jewish proverb 'A man is not a man until he has a son.'*

proverbial /prəvɜːbɪəl/. You use **proverbial** ADJ CLASSIF : when you want to emphasize that what you are ATTRIB saying is part of a well-known proverb or expres-sion. EG *It is rather like looking for the needle in the proverbial haystack.*

provide /prəvaɪd/, **provides, providing, provid-** v+O : OFT **ed.** If you **provide** something that someone needs +*for/with* or wants, you give it to them or make it available to them. EG *Most animals provide food for their young... The government cannot provide all young people with a job... A victory next Sunday could provide the opportunity he needs.* ◊ **provider,** ◊ N COUNT **providers.** EG *...her duties as a provider of food.* ● See also **provided, providing.**

provide for. 1 If you **provide for** someone, you PHRASAL VB : support them and give them the things that they V+PREP, need. EG *Parents are expected to provide for their* HAS PASS *children... Each of us would be provided for.*

2 If you **provide for** a possible future event, you V+PREP, make arrangements to deal with it. EG *Should the* HAS PASS *law provide for these cases?* Formal

provided /prəvaɪdɪ²d/. If you say that something CONJ will happen **provided** or **provided that** something else happens, you mean that the first thing will happen only if the second thing also happens. EG *Children were permitted into the hall, provided they sat at the back... She was prepared to come, provided that she might bring her daughter.*

providence /prɒvɪdəns/ is God or a force which N UNCOUNT is believed by some people to arrange the things Literary that happen to us. EG *The money lender proposed that they let providence decide the matter.*

providential /prɒvɪdenʃəl/. An event that is ADJ CLASSIF : **providential** is lucky. EG *...his providential deliver-* Formal *ance from danger.*

providing /prəvaɪdɪŋ/. If you say that something CONJ will happen **providing** or **providing that** some-thing else happens, you mean that the first thing will happen only if the second thing also happens. EG *It would be pleasant living in Glasgow providing you were living in a nice flat.*

province /prɒvɪns/, **provinces. 1** A **province** is a N COUNT large section of a country, which has its own administration. EG *...rallies in Zimbabwe's five prov-inces... ...the authorities in Guangdong province.*

2 The **provinces** are all the parts of a country N PLURAL : except the part where the capital is situated. EG *the*+N *...teenage life in the provinces.*

3 If you say that a subject or activity is a particular N SING+POSS person's **province**, you mean that this person has Formal special knowledge about it or special responsibility for it. EG *Dating fossils will always remain the province of the specialist.*

provincial /prəvɪnʃəl/. **1 Provincial** means con- ADJ CLASSIF : nected with the parts of a country outside the ATTRIB capital. EG *...provincial newspapers... ...provincial towns... ...the provincial police.*

2 Someone or something that is **provincial** is ADJ QUALIT narrow-minded and unsophisticated. EG *His art is primitive and provincial.*

provision /prəvɪʒəⁿn/, **provisions. 1** The **provi-** N UNCOUNT : **sion** of something is the act of giving it or making OFT+*of* it available to people who need it. EG *...helping needy people by the provision of food, clothing, and shelter... ...the provision of credit.*

2 If you make **provision** for a future need, you N UNCOUNT : make arrangements to ensure that it is dealt with. OFT+*for* EG *She did not make any provision for her chil-*

dren... They made provision for the defence of Britain... He failed to make provision for this threat.

3 A **provision** in an agreement or law is an arrangement which is included in it. EG *The Act excluded from its provisions death by murder.* N COUNT

4 Provisions are supplies of food. EG *We set out with enough provisions for the long trip.* N PLURAL

provisional /prəvɪʒəⁿnəl, -ʒənəⁿl/. Something that is **provisional** may be changed in the future. EG ...*a provisional government... ...a provisional diagnosis of schizophrenia... ...the provisional cost.* ADJ CLASSIF

proviso /prəvaɪzəʊ/, **provisos**. A **proviso** is a condition in an agreement. You agree to do something if this condition is fulfilled. EG *At last she consented, with the proviso that he should repay her as soon as he could.* N COUNT : OFT+REPORT

provocation /prɒvəkeɪʃəⁿn/, **provocations**. If you describe something that someone does as **provocation**, you mean that they did it deliberately in order to make someone react angrily or violently. EG *They must not react to this provocation... She has a tantrum at the least provocation.* N UNCOUNT OR N COUNT

provocative /prəvɒkətɪv/. Something that is **provocative** is **1** intended to make people react angrily or argue against it. EG *He wrote a provocative article on 'Anti-racialism'.* **2** intended to make someone feel sexual desire. EG ...*a provocative dance... ...exposing her leg in a provocative way.* ADJ QUALIT

provoke /prəvəʊk/, **provokes, provoking, provoked**. **1** If you **provoke** someone, you deliberately annoy them and try to make them behave aggressively. EG *Ray was trying to provoke them into fighting... They are armed and ready to shoot if provoked in the slightest way.* V+O

2 If something **provokes** a violent or unpleasant reaction, it causes it. EG *The petition provoked a storm of criticism.* V+O

prow /praʊ/, **prows**. The **prow** of a ship or boat is the front part of it. N COUNT

prowess /praʊⁱs/. Someone's **prowess** is their outstanding ability at doing a particular thing. EG *There are legends about his prowess as a jockey... ...her conversational prowess.* N UNCOUNT Formal

prowl /praʊl/, **prowls, prowling, prowled**. **1** When animals or people **prowl** around, they move around quietly, for example when they are hunting. EG *I found four foxes prowling round my flock one night... Gangs of youths prowl the streets.* V : OFT+A, OR V+O

2 An animal or person that is **on the prowl** is prowling around. PHRASE

proximity /prɒksɪmɪⁱtiⁱ/. **Proximity** to a place is nearness to that place. EG ...*the town's proximity to the northern cape of Japan.* N UNCOUNT +SUPP Formal

proxy /prɒksiⁱ/. If you do something **by proxy**, you arrange for someone else to do it for you. EG *Soviet support, direct or by proxy, ended any further threats.* PHRASE

prude /pruːd/, **prudes**. If you call someone a **prude**, you mean that they are easily shocked by things relating to nudity or sex; used showing disapproval. EG *Don't be such a prude.* N COUNT

prudent /pruːdənt/. Someone who is **prudent** is sensible and careful. EG *He now considered it prudent to carry a revolver.* ◊ **prudently**. EG ◊ ADV *Fanny prudently resolved to keep silent.* ADJ QUALIT

◊ **prudence** /pruːdəns/. EG *I consider that I have acted with proper diligence and prudence.* ◊ N UNCOUNT Formal

prudish /pruːdɪʃ/. If you describe someone as **prudish**, you mean that they are easily shocked by things relating to nudity or sex; used showing disapproval. EG ...*four aunts, religious and prudish.* ADJ QUALIT

prune /pruːn/, **prunes, pruning, pruned**. **1** A **prune** is a dried plum. N COUNT

2 When you **prune** a tree or bush, you cut off some of the branches. EG *He went to prune the roses.* V+O

pry /praɪ/, **pries, prying, pried**. When someone **pries**, they try to find out about someone else's private affairs, often secretly. EG *Look, I'm not* V : OFT+*into*

trying to pry... So don't go prying into my affairs or you'll get hurt.

PS /piː ɛs/. You write **PS** to introduce a further message at the end of a letter after you have signed it. EG *With love from us both, Dad. PS Mum asks me to remind you to bring back her duvet.*

psalm /sɑːm/, **psalms**. The **Psalms** are the 150 songs, poems, and prayers which together form the Book of Psalms in the Bible. EG *The reading of the Psalm was ended... ...the 24th Psalm.* N COUNT

pseud /sjuːd/, **pseuds**. If you say that someone is a **pseud**, you mean that they are trying to appear very well-educated or artistic, in a pretentious way. N COUNT Informal

pseudo- is used to form adjectives and nouns that describe something as not being the thing that it is claimed to be. For example, if you describe a country as a pseudo-democracy, you mean that it is not really a democracy, although its government claims that it is. EG ...*pseudo-scientific ideas... ...pseudo-liberals.* PREFIX

pseudonym /sjuːdənɪm/, **pseudonyms**. A **pseudonym** is a name which a writer uses instead of his or her real name. EG *Many journalists wrote under pseudonyms.* N COUNT

psych /saɪk/, **psychs, psyching, psyched**. The spellings **psyche, psyches** are also used. If you **psych** yourself **up** before a contest or a difficult task, you prepare yourself for it mentally, especially by telling yourself that you can win or succeed. EG *He had to psych himself into writing the book.* PHRASAL VB : V-REFL+ADV Informal

psyche /saɪkiⁱ/, **psyches**. **1** Your **psyche** is your mind and your deepest feelings and attitudes. EG *It is easy to understand how a person's psyche can be damaged by such experiences.* N COUNT : USU+SUPP

2 See also **psych**.

psychedelic /saɪkədɛlɪk/. **1 Psychedelic** drugs are drugs such as LSD, which affect your mind and make you imagine that you are seeing strange things. EG ...*the use of drugs in the pursuit of psychedelic experience.* ADJ CLASSIF ATTRIB

2 Psychedelic art has bright colours and strange patterns. EG ...*psychedelic posters.* ADJ CLASSIF

psychiatric /saɪkiætrɪk/ means **1** relating to psychiatry. EG ...*a psychiatric hospital... ...the psychiatric profession.* **2** involving mental illness. EG ...*psychiatric disorders... ...a mother with psychiatric problems.* ADJ CLASSIF ATTRIB

psychiatrist /saɪkaɪətrɪst/, **psychiatrists**. A **psychiatrist** is a doctor who treats people suffering from mental illness. EG *It was arranged that I should see a psychiatrist.* N COUNT

psychiatry /saɪkaɪətriⁱ/ is the branch of medicine concerned with the treatment of mental illness. EG ...*a Professor of Psychiatry.* N UNCOUNT

psychic /saɪkɪk/. **1** Someone who is **psychic** or who has **psychic** powers has strange mental powers, such as being able to read the minds of other people or to see into the future. ADJ CLASSIF

2 Psychic means relating to the mind rather than the body. EG *Most of the psychic damage to a child is done in the first five years of its life.* ADJ CLASSIF Formal

psychical /saɪkɪkəⁿl/ means the same as psychic. EG ...*the Society for Psychical Research.* ADJ CLASSIF Formal

psycho /saɪkəʊ/, **psychos**. A **psycho** is someone who is mad and who does violent things, such as killing people. EG ...*a raving psycho who kills just for kicks.* ▸ used as an adjective. EG *He was practically psycho.* N COUNT Informal ▸ ADJ PRED

psychoanalyse /saɪkəʊænəlaɪz/, **psychoanalyses, psychoanalysing, psychoanalysed**; also spelled **psychoanalyze** in American English. When a psychotherapist or psychiatrist **psychoanalyses** someone who is mentally ill, he or she V+O

Name four jobs on these pages.

examines or treats them using the method of psychoanalysis.

psychoanalysis /saɪkəʊənælɪsɪs/ is the examination or treatment of someone who is mentally ill by asking them about their feelings and their past in order to try to discover what may be causing their condition. EG *He sought help through psychoanalysis.* — N UNCOUNT

psychoanalyst /saɪkəʊænəlɪst/, **psychoanalysts.** A **psychoanalyst** is someone who treats people who are mentally ill using the method of psychoanalysis. — N COUNT

psychoanalyze /saɪkəʊænəlaɪz/. See **psychoanalyse.**

psychological /saɪkəˈlɒdʒɪkəl/. 1 **Psychological** means concerned with a person's mind and thoughts. EG *Are there important psychological differences between the two sexes?* — ADJ CLASSIF
◊ **psychologically.** EG *She was tough, both physically and psychologically.* — ◊ ADV
2 **Psychological** also means relating to psychology. EG *...psychological tests.* — ADJ CLASSIF : ATTRIB

psychologist /saɪkɒlədʒɪst/, **psychologists.** A **psychologist** is a person who studies the human mind and tries to explain why people behave in the way that they do. — N COUNT

psychology /saɪkɒlədʒi¹/. 1 **Psychology** is the scientific study of the human mind and the reasons for people's behaviour. — N UNCOUNT
2 The **psychology** of a person is the kind of mind that they have, which makes them think or behave in the way that they do. EG *...the psychology of the travelling salesman.* — N UNCOUNT +SUPP

psychopath /saɪkəˈpæθ/, **psychopaths.** A **psychopath** is someone who is mad and does violent things, such as killing people. — N COUNT
◊ **psychopathic** /saɪkəˈpæθɪk/. EG *...a film about a psychopathic murderer.* — ◊ ADJ CLASSIF : ATTRIB

psychosis /saɪkəʊsɪs/ is a kind of severe mental illness. EG *...acute psychosis following the birth of her first child.* — N UNCOUNT Medical

psychosomatic /saɪkəˈsəˈmætɪk/. A **psychosomatic** illness is a physical illness which someone has because they are very worried or unhappy. — ADJ CLASSIF

psychotherapist /saɪkəʊθerəpɪst/, **psychotherapists.** A **psychotherapist** is a person who treats people who are mentally ill using psychotherapy. — N COUNT

psychotherapy /saɪkəʊθerəpi¹/ is the use of psychological methods to treat people who are mentally ill, rather than using physical methods such as drugs or surgery. EG *Psychotherapy has helped me enormously... ...psychotherapy sessions.* — N UNCOUNT

psychotic /saɪkɒtɪk/, **psychotics.** Someone who is **psychotic** has a type of severe mental illness. EG *...a psychotic patient... ...the treatment of psychotic conditions.* ▸ used as a noun. EG *Do you want to turn the children into a bunch of psychotics?* — ADJ CLASSIF Medical ▸ N COUNT

pt, pts. pt is a written abbreviation for 'pint'. The plural is either 'pt' or 'pts'. EG *...1 pt warm water.*

PTO /piː tiː əʊ/ is a written abbreviation for 'please turn over'. You write it at the bottom of a page to indicate that there is more writing on the other side.

pub /pʌb/, **pubs.** A **pub** is a building where people can have drinks, especially alcoholic drinks, and talk to their friends. EG *We used to go drinking in a pub called the Soldier's Arms.* — N COUNT

puberty /pjuːbəti¹/ is the stage in someone's life when they start to become physically like an adult. EG *...a boy who has reached the age of puberty.* — N UNCOUNT

public /pʌblɪk/. 1 You can refer to people in general, or to all the people in a particular country or community, as the **public.** EG *...appeals to the public... All members of the public are welcome... The gardens are open to the public.* — N COLL : SING, the+N
2 You can refer to a set of people in a country who share a common interest, activity, or characteris- — N COLL : SING, the+N

tic as a particular kind of **public.** EG *...literature available to the general reading public.*
3 **Public** means relating to all the people in a country or community. EG *The campaigners have attracted significant public support... The politicians have to respond to public opinion... The problem was how to sustain public interest... These fumes are a hazard to public health.* — ADJ CLASSIF : ATTRIB
4 **Public** spending is money spent by the government of a country to provide services for its people. EG *The government is reducing public spending.* — ADJ CLASSIF : ATTRIB
5 **Public** buildings and services are provided for everyone to use. EG *Both of these books can be obtained from the Public Library... ...public transport... ...public telephones.* — ADJ CLASSIF : ATTRIB
6 If someone is a **public** figure or in **public** life, they are known about by many people because they are often mentioned in newspapers and on television. EG *...famous and highly respected public figures... Well-known people from all sections of public life gave the scheme their support.* — ADJ CLASSIF : ATTRIB
7 **Public** is used to describe statements, actions, and events that are made or done in such a way that any member of the public can see them or be aware of them. EG *No public announcement had yet been made... We hold weekly public meetings... ...public speakers addressing large groups of people.* ◊ **publicly.** EG *I am going to say what I think of him openly and publicly.* ● If you say or do something **in public,** you say or do it when a group of other people are present. EG *He repeated in public what he had said in private.* — ADJ CLASSIF : ATTRIB ◊ ADV ● PHRASE
8 If a fact is made **public,** it becomes known to everyone rather than being kept secret. EG *The cause of death was not made public.* — ADJ PRED
9 A **public** place is one where people can go about freely and where you can easily be seen and heard. EG *This is a very public place. Can we talk somewhere else?* — ADJ QUALIT

publican /pʌblɪkən/, **publicans.** A **publican** is a person who owns or manages a pub. EG *He was born in 1871, the son of a publican.* — N COUNT British Formal

publication /pʌblɪkeɪʃə⁰n/, **publications.** 1 The **publication** of a book or magazine is the act of printing it and sending it to shops to be sold. EG *Several of her articles have already been accepted for publication.* — N UNCOUNT
2 A **publication** is a book or magazine that has been published. EG *...a respected scholar with a long list of publications to his name.* — N COUNT

public bar, public bars. A **public bar** is a room in a British pub where the furniture is plain and the drinks are cheaper than in the other bars. — N COUNT

public company, public companies. A **public company** is a company whose shares can be bought by the general public. — N COUNT

public convenience, public conveniences. A **public convenience** is a toilet that is provided in a public place for everyone to use. — N COUNT British

public house, public houses. A **public house** is the same as a pub. EG *...the customers of a local public house... The best place to talk was the public house.* — N COUNT British

publicise /pʌblɪsaɪz/. See **publicize.**

publicist /pʌblɪsɪst/, **publicists.** A **publicist** is a person who publicizes things, especially as part of a job in advertising or journalism. — N COUNT

publicity /pʌblɪsɪ¹ti¹/. 1 **Publicity** is information or actions intended to attract the public's attention to someone or something. EG *There was some advance publicity for the book.* — N UNCOUNT
2 When newspapers and television pay a lot of attention to something, you can say that it is receiving **publicity.** EG *Feminism has attracted a lot of publicity... She sought out publicity.* — N UNCOUNT

publicize /pʌblɪsaɪz/, **publicizes, publicizing, publicized;** also spelled **publicise.** If you **publicize** a fact or event, you make it widely known to — V+O the public. EG *His programme for reform was well publicised in his newspapers.*

public relations is **1** the part of an organization's work that is concerned with obtaining the public's approval for what it does. EG *...running a large public relations department.* **2** the state of the relationship between an organization and the public. EG *It's good for public relations.* N UNCOUNT / N PLURAL

public school, public schools. **1** In Britain, a **public school** is a private school that provides secondary education which parents have to pay special fees for. The pupils often live at the school during the school term. EG *...a public school education.* N COUNT OR N UNCOUNT

2 In the USA, Australia, and some other parts of the world, a **public school** is a school that is supported financially by the government from the taxes that all working people pay. N COUNT OR N UNCOUNT

public-spirited. Someone who is **public-spirited** tries to help the community that they belong to. EG *She's a public-spirited woman who takes part in politics.* ADJ QUALIT

publish /pʌblɪʃ/, **publishes, publishing, published.** **1** When a company **publishes** a book or magazine, it prints copies of it, which are sent to shops and sold. EG *The Collins Cobuild dictionary was published in 1987.* V+O

2 When the people in charge of a newspaper or magazine **publish** a piece of writing, they print it in their newspaper or magazine. EG *The Times would never publish any letter I sent in.* V+O

3 If someone **publishes** a book or an article that they have written, they arrange to have it published. EG *He has published quite a lot of articles.* V+O

4 If you **publish** information or an opinion, you make it known to the public by having it printed in a newspaper or magazine. EG *He received a long prison term for publishing his views.* V+O

publisher /pʌblɪʃə/, **publishers.** A **publisher** is a person or a company that publishes books. EG *The publishers of the book are Collins.* N COUNT

publishing /pʌblɪʃɪŋ/ is the profession of publishing books. EG *I'd like a career in publishing.* N UNCOUNT

puce /pjuːs/. Something that is **puce** is a dark purple colour. EG *...his puce complexion.* ADJ COLOUR

pucker /pʌkə/, **puckers, puckering, puckered.**
1 When a part of your face **puckers** or when you **pucker** it, it becomes wrinkled because you are frowning or trying not to cry. EG *His face puckered, the tears leapt from his eyes.* V-ERG

2 If fabric or other material **puckers**, it becomes wrinkled or creased. V-ERG

pudding /pudɪŋ/, **puddings.** **1** A **pudding** is a cooked sweet food made with flour, fat, and eggs, and usually served hot. EG *They want vanilla pudding... ...steamed puddings.* N COUNT OR N UNCOUNT

2 Some people refer to the sweet course of a meal as the **pudding.** EG *Can they have second helpings of pudding?* N UNCOUNT Informal British

3 See also **Yorkshire pudding.**

puddle /pʌdəl/, **puddles.** A **puddle** is a small, shallow pool of liquid that has spread on the ground. EG *The road was filled with puddles from the rain... ...a puddle of blood.* N COUNT

puff /pʌf/, **puffs, puffing, puffed.** **1** If someone **puffs** a cigarette or pipe or if they **puff** at it, they smoke it. EG *He puffed his pipe for several moments... He sat at the desk and puffed at his cigar... She puffed on the cigarette and sipped her drink.* V+O OR V+at/on
▸ used as a noun. EG *She raised the cigarette to her lips, intending to take a puff.* ▸ N COUNT : IF SING OFT a+N

2 If you **are puffing,** you are breathing loudly and quickly with your mouth open because you are out of breath after a lot of physical effort. EG *We lugged the branch underneath, panting and puffing.* ▸ used as a noun. EG *Her breath came in puffs and gasps.* V : USU CONT / ▸ N COUNT

3 A **puff** of air or smoke is a small amount of it that is blown out from somewhere. EG *The stove let out a puff of smoke.* N PART

4 See also **puffed.**

puff out. To **puff** something **out** means to make it larger and rounder, usually by filling it with air. EG *Their chests were puffed out like angry swans... They puffed out their cheeks.* PHRASAL VB : V-ERG+ADV

puff up. If part of your body **puffs up** as a result of an injury, it becomes swollen. EG *Small areas on their arms or legs would puff up.* PHRASAL VB : V+ADV

puffed /pʌft/. **1** If a part of your body is **puffed** or **puffed up,** it is swollen because of an injury. EG *Her left eye is all puffed up.* ADJ PRED

2 If you are **puffed** or **puffed out,** you are breathing with difficulty because you have been using a lot of energy. EG *By the time I got to the top I was pretty well puffed out.* ADJ PRED Informal

puffin /pʌfɪn/, **puffins.** A **puffin** is a black and white bird with a large, brightly-coloured beak. Puffins live by the sea. N COUNT

puff pastry is a type of pastry which is very light and flaky. N UNCOUNT

puffy /pʌfɪ/. Something that is **puffy** has a round, swollen appearance. EG *One eye was a slit in his puffy cheek.* ADJ QUALIT

pugnacious /pʌgneɪʃəs/. Someone who is **pugnacious** is always ready to quarrel or start a fight. EG *I got punched in the face by a pugnacious apprentice.* ADJ QUALIT Formal

puke /pjuːk/, **pukes, puking, puked.** When someone **pukes,** they vomit. EG *The baby puked a couple more times.* V Informal

pull /pul/, **pulls, pulling, pulled.** **1** When you **pull** something, you hold it firmly and use force in order to move it towards you. EG *The women's job was to pull the grass and weeds out of the corn... She pulled Paul's hair so hard that he yelled... He hoisted the rope over the branch and pulled with all his strength... He got back into bed and pulled the blankets around him... He pulled forward a chair... They started pulling up the floorboards... I shut my eyes when I pulled the trigger.* V+O : USU+A; ALSO V

2 When a vehicle, animal, or person **pulls** a cart or piece of machinery, they are attached to it or hold it, so that it moves along behind them when they move forward. EG *Farmers were driving open carts pulled by donkeys.* V+O

3 If you **pull** a part of your body in a particular direction, or if you **pull away,** you move a part of your body with force. EG *'Let go of me,' she said, and pulled her arm savagely out of his grasp... He tried to kiss her, but she pulled away fiercely.* V+O+A OR V+A

4 If you **pull** yourself out of a place, you hold onto something and use effort to move your body out of the place. EG *Ralph pulled himself out of the water.* V-REFL+A

5 If you **pull** at something, you hold it and move it towards you and then let it go again. EG *'Come home now, Jim,' she said, pulling at his sleeve.* V+at

6 When you **pull** a curtain or blind, you move it across a window in order to cover or uncover it. EG *She closed the window and pulled the blind.* V+O

7 If you **pull** something apart or **pull** it to pieces, you break it or take it apart without much care. EG *If you pull apart one of the calculators, you won't get it back together again... Try and stop the cat pulling the Christmas tree to bits.* V+O+A

8 To **pull** people means to attract their support or interest. EG *He was interested in the number of voters she would pull.* V+O Informal

9 If you **pull** a muscle, you injure it by stretching it. EG *Despite pulling a muscle, he managed to finish third in the race.* V+O

10 to **pull** your **socks up:** see **sock.**

pull apart. If you **pull** fighting people or animals **apart,** you separate them using force. EG *I rushed in and tried to pull the dogs apart.* PHRASAL VB : V+O+ADV

pull away. When a vehicle **pulls away,** it starts PHRASAL VB :

When a bus pulls up, does it pull in?

moving forward. EG *The bus pulled away... As the* V+ADV
lights changed, I pulled away and drove past him.

pull down. If a building **is pulled down**, it is PHRASAL VB:
deliberately destroyed, often in order to build a V+O+ADV
new one. EG *Why did they pull those houses down?*

pull in. When a vehicle **pulls in** somewhere, it PHRASAL VB:
stops there. EG *I pulled in for petrol... The London* V+ADV, OFT+A
train pulled in to the station.

pull off. 1 If you **pull** clothes **off**, you take them PHRASAL VB:
off quickly. EG *He pulled off his shirt... She pulled off* V+O+ADV
her shoes and stockings. 2 If someone has suc- V+O+ADV
ceeded in doing something very difficult, you can Informal
say that they **have pulled** it **off.** EG *She had
succeeded, triumphantly: she had pulled it off.*

pull on. If you **pull** clothes **on**, you put them on PHRASAL VB:
quickly. EG *He started to pull on his tattered shorts.* V+O+ADV

pull out. 1 When a vehicle **pulls out** from a PHRASAL VB:
place, it moves out of the place. EG *The train pulled* V+ADV
out of the station. 2 If you **pull out** of a difficult V-ERG+ADV
situation, you succeed in getting out of it. EG *It's
going to take us even longer to pull out of this
recession.* 3 If you **pull out** of an agreement or V-ERG+ADV
business deal, you withdraw from it. EG *You pay a
10% deposit which you lose if you pull out before
completion... He pulled his party out of the coali-
tion.* 4 If an army **pulls out** of a place, it leaves it. V-ERG+ADV
EG *Troops had begun to pull out of the area... The
Prime Minister intended to pull them out soon.*

pull over. 1 When a vehicle **pulls over**, it moves PHRASAL VB:
closer to the side of the road. EG *Pull over, Oliver.* V+ADV
Stop the car. 2 See also **pullover**.

pull through. If you **pull through** a serious PHRASAL VB:
illness or if the doctor **pulls** you **through**, you V-ERG+ADV/
recover from it. EG *I think she'll pull through.* PREP

pull together. 1 If people **pull together**, they PHRASAL VB:
co-operate with each other. EG *We all pulled togeth-* V+ADV
er during the war. 2 If you are upset or excited and PHRASE
someone tells you to **pull** yourself **together**, they
are telling you to control your feelings and behave
calmly again. EG *That's quite enough of that. Pull
yourself together now.*

pull up. 1 When a vehicle **pulls up**, it slows down PHRASAL VB:
and stops. EG *The rain stopped as we pulled up at* V+ADV
the hotel. 2 If you **pull up** a chair, you move it V+O+ADV
closer to something or someone. EG *I pulled up a
chair and sat down to watch the news.* 3 If PHRASE
something **pulls** you **up short**, it makes you stop
what you are doing. EG *The man's evident surprise
pulled him up short.*

pulley /pʊlɪ/, **pulleys.** A **pulley** is a device which N COUNT
is used for lifting or lowering heavy weights. It
consists of a wheel with a hollow rim which is fixed
above the ground. You pass a rope over the rim,
attach one end of the rope to the weight, and pull
or gradually release the other end.

pullover /pʊləʊvə/, **pullovers.** A **pullover** is a N COUNT
woollen piece of clothing that covers the upper
part of your body and your arms. You put it on by
pulling it over your head. See picture at CLOTHES.

pulp /pʌlp/, **pulps, pulping, pulped.** 1 If an object N UNCOUNT
is turned into a **pulp**, it is crushed or beaten until it OR N SING
is soft, smooth, and wet. EG *We squashed the berries
into a pulp.*
2 The **pulp** of a fruit or vegetable is the soft inner N UNCOUNT
part. EG *Fill the bowl with the fruit pulp.*
3 Wood **pulp** is material made from crushed wood. N UNCOUNT
It is used to make paper. EG *...supplies of wood pulp
needed for the newsprint.*
4 People sometimes refer to books or magazines as N UNCOUNT:
pulp when they consider them to be of poor USU N MOD
quality. EG *They seem satisfied with cheap tabloids,
trite films, and the pulp library of crime.*
5 To **pulp** something means to crush it. EG *Once* V+O
*gnawed, ground, and pulped, the food has to be
digested.*

pulpit /pʊlpɪt/, **pulpits.** A **pulpit** is a small raised N COUNT
platform in a church with a rail or barrier around
it, where a member of the clergy stands to preach.
EG *The vicar descended from the pulpit.*

pulpy /pʌlpɪ/. Something that is **pulpy** is soft, ADJ QUALIT
smooth, and wet, often because it has been crushed
or beaten. EG *Her lips felt pulpy and tender.*

pulsate /pʌlseɪt/, **pulsates, pulsating, pulsated.** V
If something **pulsates**, it moves or shakes with
strong, regular movements. EG *The creature has no
heart, only a number of pulsating arteries... Her
final top note pulsated with triumph.*

pulse /pʌls/, **pulses, pulsing, pulsed.** 1 Your N COUNT:
pulse is the regular beating of blood through your USU SING
body, which you can feel when you touch particu-
lar parts of your body, especially your wrist. EG *Her
pulse started to race.* ● When a doctor or nurse ● PHRASE
takes your **pulse**, he or she finds out the speed of
your heartbeat by feeling the pulse in your wrist. EG
He was busy taking her pulse.
2 A **pulse** is also a regular beat in music, which is N SING
often produced by a drum. EG *...a rhythm which
contains a basic pulse.*
3 Some seeds which can be cooked and eaten are N COUNT:
called **pulses**, for example the seeds of peas, USU PLURAL
beans, and lentils. EG *...protein foods such as fish,
pulses, and wholemeal bread... ...a range of cereals,
pulses and vegetables.*
4 If something **pulses**, it moves or shakes with V
strong, regular movements. EG *...a soft rhythmic
pulsing sound.*

pulverize /pʌlvəraɪz/, **pulverizes, pulverizing,
pulverized;** also spelled **pulverise.** 1 To **pulver-** V+O
ize something means to make it into a powder by
crushing it. EG *The processes involved pulverising
the nuts.*
2 When guns or bombs **pulverize** a place, they V+O
destroy it completely. EG *Vast areas were pulverized by enemy tanks.*

pumice /pʌmɪs/ or **pumice stone** is a kind of N UNCOUNT
grey stone that is very light in weight. You can use
it to clean surfaces, or you can rub it on your skin
in order to soften it.

pummel /pʌmə⁰l/, **pummels, pummelling,** V+O
pummelled; spelled **pummeling, pummeled** in
American English.
If you **pummel** someone or something, you beat
them again and again using your fists. EG *She tipped
some water into the bowl of flour and fat, and
pummelled it fiercely.*

pump /pʌmp/, **pumps, pumping, pumped.** 1 A N COUNT
pump is a machine which is used to force a liquid
or gas to flow in strong, regular movements in a
particular direction.
2 A **pump** is also 2.1 a device for bringing water to N COUNT
the surface from below the ground. Pumps often
have a handle that you push in order to force the
water upwards. EG *...the village pump... We
scrubbed ourselves under the pump.* 2.2 a device
that you use in order to force air into something,
especially into the tyre of a vehicle. EG *...a bicycle
pump.*
3 A petrol **pump** is a machine with a hose attached N COUNT
to it from which you can fill a car with petrol.
4 **Pumps** are canvas shoes with flat rubber soles N COUNT:
which people wear for sports and leisure. USU PLURAL
5 To **pump** a liquid or gas in a particular direction V+O+A
means to force it to flow in that direction, using a
pump. EG *We can use the electricity to pump water
back into a dam or a reservoir.*
6 To **pump** water, oil, or gas means to get a supply V+O
of it from below the surface of the ground, using a
pump. EG *John went to a cast-iron pump and started
pumping water to drink.*
7 If you **pump** money or energy into something, V+O+into
you put a lot of money or energy into it. EG *Most* Informal
*governments have pumped all available funds into
large-scale modern technological projects.*
8 If you **pump** someone about something, you keep V+O
asking them questions in order to get information. Informal
EG *I pumped him discreetly about his past.*

pumpkin /pʌmpᵒkɪn/, **pumpkins.** A **pumpkin** is N COUNT OR
a large, round, orange-coloured vegetable with a N UNCOUNT
thick skin. EG ...*pumpkin pie.*

pun /pʌn/, **puns.** A **pun** is a clever and amusing N COUNT
use of words that have more than one meaning, or
words that have the same sound, so that what you
say has two different meanings. For example, if
you say 'Schmidt copied out scores of symphonies',
this could mean either that Schmidt copied out the
written versions of symphonies or that he copied
out a very large number of symphonies, because
'scores of' has these two different meanings.

punch /pʌntʃ/, **punches, punching, punched. 1** V+O
If you **punch** someone, you hit them hard with
your fist. EG *Boylan punched him hard on the nose...
I was punched in the stomach.*
2 A **punch** is a hard blow with your fist. EG *I landed* N COUNT
*a number of punches... Ringbaum, swaying with
the punch, kept his balance.*
3 A **punch** is also a tool that you use for pushing N COUNT
holes in something. EG *He made a small hole in the
belt with a leather punch.*
4 If you **punch** holes in something, you make holes V+O
in it by pushing or pressing it with something
sharp. EG *Edward was punching holes in a can.*
5 Punch is a drink usually made from wine or N MASS
spirits mixed with sugar, lemons, and spices. EG
...*hot rum punch.*

punch-line, punch-lines. The **punch-line** of a N COUNT
joke or funny story is its last sentence or phrase,
which gives it its humour.

punch-up, punch-ups. A **punch-up** is a fight in N COUNT
which people hit each other. EG *'Looks as though* Informal
you've been in a real punch-up,' says the barmaid. British

punchy /pʌntʃiⁱ/, **punchier, punchiest.** If you ADJ QUALIT
describe a piece of writing as **punchy**, you mean
that it is effective and forceful, because points are
made clearly, briefly, and decisively. EG ...*a punchy
little leaflet.*

punctual /pʌŋktjʊᵒəl/. Someone who is **punctual** ADJ PRED
arrives somewhere or does something at the right
time and is not late. EG *I expect my guests to be
punctual for breakfast.* ◇ **punctually.** EG *Mary* ◇ ADV
arrived at the New Inn punctually at ten o'clock.

punctuate /pʌŋktjʊeɪt/, **punctuates, punctuat-
ing, punctuated. 1** If an activity is **punctuated** V+O : USU PASS
by things, it is interrupted by them at intervals. EG +by/with
The old lady's words were punctuated by noise Formal
*from outside... They had a jolly conversation, punc-
tuated with bursts of laughter.*
2 When you **punctuate** a piece of writing, you put V+O
punctuation in it. Formal

punctuation /pʌŋktjʊeɪʃᵃn/ is the marks such as N UNCOUNT
full stops, commas, and question marks that you
use in writing to divide words into sentences and
clauses. EG *The punctuation needs putting right.*

punctuation mark, punctuation marks. A N COUNT
punctuation mark is a sign such as a full stop,
comma, or question mark that you use in writing to
divide words into sentences and clauses.

puncture /pʌŋktʃə/, **punctures, puncturing,
punctured. 1** A **puncture** is a small hole in a car N COUNT
tyre or bicycle tyre that has been made by a sharp
object. EG *One of the wheels has a puncture.*
2 To **puncture** something means to make a small V+O
hole in it. EG *The shrapnel may puncture tyres, fuel
tanks and radiators.*

pundit /pʌndɪt/, **pundits.** A **pundit** is a person N COUNT
who knows a lot about a subject and is often asked Informal
to give information or opinions about it. EG *John
Lowerson is one of our pundits on local history.*

pungent /pʌndʒənt/. **1** Something that is **pungent** ADJ QUALIT
has a strong, unpleasant smell or taste. EG *The
pungent, choking smell of sulphur filled the air.*
2 Speech or writing that is **pungent** has a direct, ADJ QUALIT
powerful effect and often cleverly criticizes some- Formal
thing. EG *This is the pungent and original argument.*

punish /pʌnɪʃ/, **punishes, punishing, punished.**
1 To **punish** someone means to make them suffer V+O : OFT+for

in some way because they have done something
wrong. EG *They discovered his crime and punished
him for it.*
2 To **punish** a crime means to punish anyone who V+O
commits that crime. EG *They punished adultery
with death.*

punishable /pʌnɪʃəbᵒl/. If a crime is **punishable** ADJ CLASSIF :
in a particular way, anyone who commits it is OFT+by
punished in that way. EG *Possession of drugs is
punishable by prison.*

punishing /pʌnɪʃɪŋ/. A **punishing** experience ADJ QUALIT :
makes you very weak or helpless. EG *The purpose* ATTRIB
was to inflict a punishing defeat on the enemy.

punishment /pʌnɪʃmᵃnt/, **punishments. 1 Pun- N UNCOUNT
ishment** is the act of punishing someone. EG *Punishment and prison sentences cannot reform the
hardened criminal.*
2 A **punishment** is a particular way of punishing N COUNT
someone. *He maintained that the only true punishment for murder was death.*
3 Punishment is also severe physical treatment of N UNCOUNT
any kind. EG *The crew were in no condition to
withstand any further punishment from the sea.*
4 See also **capital punishment**, **corporal punishment.**

punitive /pjuːnɪᵗtɪv/. **Punitive** actions are intend- ADJ CLASSIF :
ed to punish people and are therefore harsh. EG *We* USU ATTRIB
*will take no punitive action against those who have
broken the rules.*

punk /pʌŋk/, **punks. 1 Punk** or **punk rock** is rock N UNCOUNT
music that is played in a fast, loud, and aggressive
way and is often a protest against conventional
attitudes and behaviour. EG ...*a punk rock concert.*
2 Punk clothes or styles are associated with punk ADJ CLASSIF :
music and are very noticeable and unconventional. ATTRIB
EG ...*punk haircuts.*
3 A **punk** or a **punk rocker** is a young person who N COUNT
likes punk music and dresses in a very noticeable
and unconventional way, for example by having
brightly coloured hair and wearing metal chains.
EG ...*punk rockers with safety pins in their ears.*

punnet /pʌnɪt/, **punnets.** A **punnet** is a small, N COUNT
light, square box in which soft fruits such as OR N PART
strawberries or raspberries are often sold. EG ...*punnets of strawberries.*

punt /pʌnt/, **punts, punting, punted. 1** A **punt** is N COUNT
a long boat with a flat bottom. You move the boat
along by standing at one end and pushing a long
pole down against the bottom of the river.
2 When you **punt**, you travel along a river in a V : OFT+A
punt. EG *I punted slowly on.*

punter /pʌntə/, **punters. 1** A **punter** is a person N COUNT
who bets money on horse races. EG *Favourites, as* Informal
any punter will tell you, do not always win. British
2 People sometimes refer to their customers or N COUNT :
clients as the **punters.** EG *What was the punters'* USU PLURAL
reaction to it? Informal
British

puny /pjuːni¹/, **punier, puniest.** Someone or ADJ QUALIT
something that is **puny** is very small or weak. EG
...*a puny old man... ...her puny efforts.*

pup /pʌp/, **pups. 1** A **pup** is a young dog. EG ...*a* N COUNT
cocker spaniel pup.
2 Some other young animals are also called **pups.** N COUNT
EG ...*a seal pup.*

pupil /pjuːpɪᵒl/, **pupils. 1** The **pupils** of a school N COUNT
are the children who go to it. EG ...*a school with
more than 1300 pupils.*
2 A **pupil** of a painter, musician, or other expert is N COUNT+POSS
someone who studies under that expert and learns
his or her skills. EG *Auerbach and Kossoff were
pupils of David Bomberg.*
3 The **pupils** of your eyes are the small, round, N COUNT
black holes in the centre of them.

puppet /pʌpɪt/, **puppets. 1** A **puppet** is a doll that N COUNT
you can move, either by pulling strings which are

Does a punter punt?

attached to it or by putting your hand inside its body and moving your fingers.

2 You can refer to people or countries as **puppets** N COUNT when their actions are controlled by more powerful people or countries, although they may appear to be independent. EG ...*puppet governments.*

puppy /pʌpiˈ/, **puppies.** A **puppy** is a young dog. N COUNT EG *Don't buy a puppy less than seven weeks old.*

purchase /pɜːtʃəˈs/, **purchases, purchasing, purchased. 1** When you **purchase** something, you v+o buy it. EG *He sold the house he had purchased only* Formal *two years before.*

2 Purchase is the buying of something. EG *We need* N UNCOUNT *to know the exact day of purchase.* Formal

3 A **purchase** is something that you buy. EG *Among* N COUNT *his purchases were several books.* Formal

purchaser /pɜːtʃəˈsə/, **purchasers.** The **pur-** N COUNT **chaser** of something is the person who buys it. EG Formal *The house becomes the permanent property of the purchaser.... ...purchasers of paintings.*

pure /pjʊə/, **purer, purest. 1** Pure means not ADJ CLASSIF: mixed with anything else. EG ...*a dress of pure silk...* ATTRIB ...*pure white... ...pure happiness.*

2 Something that is **pure** is clean, healthy, and ADJ QUALIT does not contain any harmful substances. EG *An advantage of breast feeding is that the milk is always pure... ...the pure, dry desert air.* ◊ **purity** ◊ N UNCOUNT /pjʊərɪtiˈ/. EG ...*the importance of purity in the water supply.*

3 If people describe a woman or girl as **pure**, they ADJ QUALIT mean that she does not do the things that they Literary consider to be sinful, such as having sex. EG *Teddy Boylan's not fit for your pure, beautiful little sister to marry... ...pure in mind and body.* ◊ **purity.** EG ◊ N UNCOUNT ...*secret thoughts which defiled her purity.*

4 A **pure** sound is very clear and pleasant to hear. ADJ CLASSIF EG *The singer's voice remained pure and clear throughout the evening.* ◊ **purity.** EG ...*a tonal* ◊ N UNCOUNT *purity that no human soprano could challenge.*

5 Pure science or **pure** research is concerned ADJ CLASSIF: only with theory and not with how this theory can ATTRIB be used in practical ways. EG ...*chemistry, both pure and applied... ...pure maths.*

6 Pure also means complete and total. EG *I came* ADJ CLASSIF: *on the idea by pure chance... He shut his eyes in* ATTRIB *pure bliss.*

puree /pjʊreɪ/, **purees, pureeing, pureed. 1** A N MASS **puree** is food which has been mashed or blended so that it forms a thick, smooth sauce. EG ...*tomato puree... ...chestnut puree.*

2 If you **puree** food, you make it into a puree. EG *I* v+o *use a blender to puree cooked vegetables.*

purely /pjʊəliˈ/. **1 Purely** means involving only ADV one feature or characteristic and not including anything else. EG ...*something purely practical like mending a washing machine... There's nothing personal in this. Purely a routine check.*

2 You use **purely and simply** to emphasize that a ADV SEN particular thing is the only thing involved and no others are considered. EG *It is done through ignorance purely and simply.*

purgatory /pɜːgətəˈriˈ/. **1 Purgatory** is the place N PROPER where Roman Catholics believe the spirits of dead people are sent to suffer for their sins before they go to heaven.

2 You can refer to a very unpleasant experience as N UNCOUNT **purgatory.** EG *It was a sort of purgatory that had to be endured.*

purge /pɜːdʒ/, **purges, purging, purged. 1** When v+o: people **purge** an organization, they remove from it OFT+of/from all the members who are no longer thought to be acceptable. EG ...*to purge the government of Latimer's supporters... They had done their best to purge extremists from the party.* ▶ used as a noun. ▶ N COUNT EG *They discovered that there were infiltrators inside the party. A purge began.*

2 If you **purge** your mind of an undesirable feeling v+o OR such as envy, you stop yourself from having this V-REFL: OFT+of

feeling. EG *I tried desperately to purge myself of these dangerous desires.*

purify /pjʊərɪfaɪ/, **purifies, purifying, purified.** v+o If you **purify** a substance, you make it pure by removing any harmful, dirty, or inferior substances from it. EG ...*specially purified water.*

purist /pjʊərɪst/, **purists.** A **purist** is a person N COUNT who believes in absolute correctness, especially concerning a particular subject which they know a lot about. EG *Musical purists were outraged at this innovation.*

puritan /pjʊərɪtəˈn/, **puritans.** You refer to some- N COUNT one as a **puritan** when they live according to strict moral or religious principles, especially by avoiding physical pleasures. EG ...*an austere old puritan.* ▶ used as an adjective. EG ...*puritan morality... Their* ▶ ADJ QUALIT *attitude is puritan in such matters.*

puritanical /pjʊərɪtænɪkəˈl/. Someone who is pu- ADJ QUALIT **ritanical** behaves according to strict moral or religious principles, especially by avoiding physical pleasures. EG ...*a puritanical distaste for alcohol.*

purple /pɜːpəˈl/, **purples.** Something that is pur- ADJ COLOUR **ple** is of a reddish-blue colour.

purplish /pɜːplɪʃ/ means slightly purple in colour. ADJ COLOUR EG *What's that purplish spot on your neck?*

purport /pɜˈpɔːt/, **purports, purporting, pur-** v+to-INF **ported.** If you say that something **purports** to do Formal or be a particular thing, you mean that it is claimed to do or be that thing. EG ...*advertisements for cosmetics purporting to delay the development of wrinkles.*

purpose /pɜːpəs/, **purposes. 1** The **purpose** of N COUNT something is the reason for which it is made or done. EG *The purpose of the meeting was to discuss the committee's report... The prisoners did not know what the purpose of the robberies was... The buildings are now used as a prison, but they weren't built for that purpose.*

2 Your **purpose** is the thing that you want to N COUNT achieve. EG *Her only purpose in life was to get rich.*

3 Purpose is the feeling of having a definite aim N UNCOUNT and of being determined to achieve it. EG *She has given them a sense of purpose.*

4 Purpose is used in these phrases. **4.1** If you do PHRASES something **on purpose**, you do it deliberately. EG *He had gone there on purpose, to see what happened.* **4.2** You use the phrase **for all practical purposes** to suggest that a situation is not exactly as you describe it but the effect is the same as if it were. EG *The rest are now, for all practical purposes, useless.* **4.3** If something **serves a purpose**, it is useful. EG *I knew it would serve no purpose to argue with her.* **4.4** If you say that something was **to no purpose**, you mean that no good result came from it. If you say that it was **to good purpose**, you mean that it was useful. EG *He used his past experience to good purpose.* **4.5 to all intents and purposes:** see intent.

purpose-built. A **purpose-built** building has ADJ CLASSIF: been specially designed and built for a particular USU ATTRIB use. EG ...*a purpose-built nursery school.*

purposeful /pɜːpəsful/. If someone is **purpose-** ADJ QUALIT **ful**, they show that they have a definite aim and a strong desire to achieve it. EG *They were striving to bring about change in a purposeful way.* ◊ **purposefully.** EG *She began walking slowly but* ◊ ADV *purposefully towards the bridge.*

purposeless /pɜːpəsliˈs/. If an action is **purpose-** ADJ QUALIT **less**, it does not seem to have a sensible purpose. EG ...*casual, unprovoked and purposeless violence.*

purposely /pɜːpəsliˈ/. If you do something **pur-** ADV **posely**, you do it deliberately. EG *She purposely sat in the outside seat.*

purr /pɜː/, **purrs, purring, purred. 1** When a cat v **purrs**, it makes a low vibrating sound with its throat because it is contented.

2 When an engine or machine **purrs**, it makes a v quiet, continuous, vibrating sound. EG *I heard cars*

purr in the distance. ▶ used as a noun. EG *I could* ▶ N SING
hear the gentle purr of a movie projector.

3 When someone **purrs**, they speak in a soft, V+QUOTE
gentle voice because they are pleased about something. EG *'It's wonderful,' she purred delightedly.*

purse /pɜːs/, **purses, pursing, pursed. 1** A **purse** N COUNT
is a very small bag that people, especially women, British
keep their money in. EG *She began hunting in her
purse for some coins.*

2 A **purse** is also the same as a handbag. EG *She* N COUNT
strolled along, swinging her old white purse. American

3 If you **purse** your lips, you move them into a V+O
small, rounded shape. EG *He pursed his lips in
distaste.*

purser /pɜːsə/, **pursers.** The **purser** on a ship is N COUNT
an officer who deals with the accounts and official
papers. On a passenger ship, the purser is also
responsible for the welfare of the passengers.

pursue /pəsjuː/, **pursues, pursuing, pursued. 1** V+O
If you **pursue** an activity, interest, or plan, you do Formal
it or carry it out. EG *Lyttleton pursued a policy of
peace and order... His wealth enabled him to
pursue his passionate interest in art.*

2 If you **pursue** a particular aim or result, you V+O
make efforts to achieve it, often over a long period Formal
of time. EG *Economic growth must not be pursued
at the expense of environmental pollution.*

3 If you **pursue** a particular topic, you try to find V+O
out more about it. EG *I don't want to pursue that* Formal
question now.

4 If you **pursue** someone or something, you follow V+O
them, usually in order to catch them. EG *Weasels* Formal
*pursue rats and mice as well as birds... The police
pursued the wrong car.* ◊ **pursuer, pursuers.** EG ◊ N COUNT
He managed to lose his pursuers the slip.

pursuit /pəsjuːt/, **pursuits. 1** Your **pursuit** of N UNCOUNT+of
something that you want consists of your attempts Formal
at achieving it. EG *...the pursuit of happiness... How
far should any of us go in pursuit of what we want?*

2 The **pursuit** of an activity, interest, or plan N UNCOUNT+of
consists of all the things that you do when you are Formal
carrying it out. EG *He spent the summer in the
vigorous pursuit of sport.*

3 The **pursuit** of someone or something is the act N UNCOUNT
of chasing them. EG *...a gamekeeper in pursuit of a* Formal
poacher. ● If you are **in hot pursuit** of someone, ● PHRASE
you are chasing after them with great determination. EG *He started running – with all the others in
hot pursuit.*

4 Pursuits are activities, especially activities that N COUNT :
you enjoy doing when you are not working. EG USU+SUPP
Games like chess are rather intellectual pursuits. Formal

pus /pʌs/ is a thick yellowish liquid that forms in N UNCOUNT
wounds when they are infected.

push /pʊʃ/, **pushes, pushing, pushed. 1** When V+O :OFT+A;
you **push** something, you press it using force, often ALSO V
in order to move it. EG *She pushed the button that
locked the door... She pushed the drawing across
the desk... I pushed open the door... Castle pushed
his bicycle up King's Road.* ▶ used as a noun. EG ▶ N COUNT :
The gate slid open at the push of a button... My USU SING
car's broken down – would you give me a push?

2 If you **push** through things that are blocking your V+A, OR
way or **push** your **way** through them, you use PHRASE
force in order to be able to move past them. EG
*Ralph pushed between them to get a better view...
I pushed my way through the people.*

3 To **push** a value or amount up or down means to V+O+A
cause it to increase or decrease. EG *The oil boom
will push the inflation rate up to higher levels.*

4 If you **push** someone into doing something, you V+O :OFT+A
urge or force them to do it. EG *No one pushed me* Informal
*into this; I decided to do it of my own accord... The
government was pushed to desperate extremes.*

5 If you **push** for something, you try very hard to V+for
achieve it. EG *He is pushing for secret balloting in
Party elections.* ▶ used as a noun. EG *India led the* ▶ N SING+for
non-aligned nations in a push for sanctions.

6 To **push** something also means to try to increase V+O
Informal

its popularity or to attract people to it. EG *...huge
adverts pushing slimming drugs.*

7 When someone **pushes** drugs, they sell them V+O
illegally. Informal

8 If someone **gives** you **the push**, they end their PHRASE
relationship with you. EG *He gave me the push last* Informal
week. British

9 If your employer **gives** you **the push**, he or she PHRASE
dismisses you from your job. EG *Another forty* Informal
workers have been given the push. British

10 to **push** your **luck**: see **luck.** ● See also **pushed,
pushing.**

push ahead. If you **push ahead** with something, PHRASAL VB :
you make progress with it. EG *They have pushed* V+ADV
ahead with an optimistic development strategy.

push around. If someone **pushes** you **around**, PHRASAL VB :
they give you orders in a rude and insulting way. EG V+O+ADV
We're not going to let them push us around. Informal

push in. When someone **pushes in**, they come PHRASAL VB :
into a queue in front of other people; used showing V+ADV
disapproval. EG *Felicity pushed in next to Howard.*

push off. When you **push off**, you leave a place. PHRASAL VB :
EG *It's time I was pushing off... Push off. You're not* V+ADV
wanted. Informal

push on. When you **push on**, you continue travel- PHRASAL VB :
ling somewhere. EG *I wanted to push on.* V+ADV

push over. If you **push** someone or something PHRASAL VB :
over, you push them so that they fall onto the V+O+ADV
ground. EG *The children were pushing each other
over on the sand.* ● See also **pushover.**

push through. If you **push** something **through**, PHRASAL VB :
you succeed in getting it accepted, often with V+O+ADV
difficulty. EG *I'll see that the scheme is pushed
through at the earliest date.*

push bike, push bikes. People sometimes refer N COUNT
to a bicycle as a **push bike.** EG *She used to do her* Informal
rounds on an old push bike.

push-button. A **push-button** machine or process ADJ CLASSIF :
is controlled by means of buttons or switches. EG ATTRIB
...push-button telephones.

pushchair /pʊʃtʃeə/, **pushchairs.** A **pushchair** is N COUNT
a small chair on wheels, in which a baby or small British
child can sit and be wheeled around.

pushed /pʊʃt/. **1** If you are **pushed** for something ADJ PRED :
such as time or money, you do not have enough of USU+for
it. EG *Sorry – can't stop – I'm a bit pushed for time.* Informal

2 If you **are hard pushed** to do something, you PHRASE
find it very difficult to do it. EG *Most of us are hard* Informal
pushed to understand where all the money goes.

pusher /pʊʃə/, **pushers.** A **pusher** is a person N COUNT
who sells illegal drugs. EG *...professional dope push-* Informal
ers... Most of the pushers were addicts themselves.

pushing /pʊʃɪŋ/. If you say that someone is **push-** PREP
ing a particular age, you mean that they are Informal
nearly that age. EG *Until a man is pushing sixty-five,
he doesn't usually think about retirement.*

pushover /pʊʃəʊvə/. You say that something is a N SING :a
pushover when it is easy to do or easy to get. EG +N
From a British point of view, it sounds like a Informal
pushover.

pushy /pʊʃɪ/, **pushier, pushiest.** Someone who is ADJ QUALIT
pushy behaves in a forceful way to get things Informal
done, often because they want to do better or get
more than anyone else. EG *I have to be pushy in my
job or I get nowhere at all.*

puss /pʊs/. People sometimes call a cat by saying VOCATIVE
'**Puss**'. EG *'Puss! Puss!' he called.*

pussy /pʊsɪ/, **pussies.** You can refer to a cat as a N COUNT
pussy or a **pussy cat.** EG *I'll show you the pussy* Informal
cats... How are the pussies getting on?

put /pʊt/, **puts, putting.** The form **put** is used in
the present tense and is the past tense and past
participle of the verb.

1 When you **put** something in a particular place or V+O+A
position, you move it into that place or position. EG

She put her hand on his arm... I put her suitcase on the table... Marsha put her cup down... The women put a garland round her neck.

2 If you **put** someone somewhere, you cause them to go there and to stay there for a period of time. EG *They had to put him into an asylum... I have to put the kids to bed.* v+o+A

3 When you **put** an idea or remark in a particular way, you express it in that way. EG *He didn't put it quite as crudely as that... They cannot put their feelings into words... To put it briefly, the man is mad and may become dangerous.* v+o : USU+A

4 When you **put** a question to someone, you ask them the question. EG *I put this question to Dr Leslie Cook.* v+o : OFT+*to*

5 If you **put it to** someone that something is true, you suggest that it is true, especially when you think that they will be unwilling to admit this. EG *I put it to him that, in fact, he was losing a good worker.* PHRASE

6 To **put** someone or something in a particular state or situation means to cause them to be in that state or situation. EG *It puts me in a rather difficult position... The company closed several months ago, putting 120 people out of a job... This would put the party into power.* v+o+A

7 You can use **put** when you are expressing someone's estimate of the size or importance of something. EG *The pipeline's cost is now put at 2.7 billion pounds... He always put duty before pleasure... I wouldn't put him in the same class as Verdi.* v+o+A

8 If you **put** time, strength, or energy into an activity, you use it in doing that activity. EG *She put all her energy into tidying the place up.* v+o+*into*

9 If you **put** money into a business or project, you invest the money in it. EG *Capitalists are encouraged to put their wealth into productive enterprises.* v+o+*into*

10 To **put** something on people or things means to cause them to have it, or to cause them to be affected by it. EG *It puts a tremendous responsibility on us... We put pressure on our children to learn to read... ...a plan to put a tax on children's clothes.* v+o+*on/upon*

11 If you **put** written information somewhere, you write or type it there. EG *Put all the details on the card... He couldn't read what Ken had put for his address... For profession he put down simply 'businessman'.* v+o : USU+A

12 to be **hard put** to do something: see **hard**. ● to **stay put**: see **stay**.

put across or **put over.** When you **put** something **across** or **put** it **over**, you succeed in describing or explaining it to someone. EG *You need the skill to put your ideas across... It is difficult for her to put over her own thoughts.* PHRASAL VB : V+O+ADV

put aside. If you **put** something **aside**, you keep it to be dealt with or used at a later time. EG *My aunt put aside her sewing and chatted to me... Your best plan is to put aside funds to cover these bills.* PHRASAL VB : V+O+ADV

put away. 1 If you **put** something **away**, you put it into the place where it is normally kept, for example in a cupboard or a drawer. EG *Right – put your books away.* **2** If someone **is put away**, they are sent to prison or to a mental hospital for a long time. EG *The doctor wanted to have him put away.* PHRASAL VB : V+O+ADV ... Informal

put back. To **put** something **back** means to delay it or postpone it. EG *The meeting's been put back till Monday... This will put production back at least a month.* PHRASAL VB : V+O+ADV, USU+A

put by. If you **put by** a sum of money, you keep it so that you can use it at a later time. EG *I've got a bit put by.* PHRASAL VB : V+O+ADV

put down. 1 When soldiers, police, or the government **put down** a riot or rebellion, they stop it by using force. EG *These riots were put down by the local police.* **2** If you **put** someone **down**, you criticize them or make them appear foolish. EG *...her infuriating habit of putting people down in small ways.* ● See also **put-down. 3** When an PHRASAL VB : V+O+ADV ... Informal ... V+O+ADV, USU PASS

animal **is put down**, it is killed because it is dangerous or very ill. EG *We had to have the cat put down.*

put down to. If you **put** something **down to** a particular thing, you believe that it is caused by that thing. EG *I put it down to arthritis.* PHRASAL VB : V+O+ADV +PREP

put forward. If you **put forward** something or someone, you suggest that they should be considered or chosen for a particular purpose or job. EG *They rejected every proposal put forward... Too few women's names are put forward.* PHRASAL VB : V+O+ADV

put in. 1 If you **put in** an amount of time or effort doing something, you spend that time or effort doing it. EG *I put in fifteen hours of work daily... You've put in a lot of work.* **2** If you **put in** a request or **put in** for something, you make a formal request or application. EG *I put in a request for an interview... After the gamekeeper died, Father put in for his job.* **3** to **put in a good word** for someone: see **word**. PHRASAL VB : V+O+ADV ... V+O+ADV OR V+ADV+*for*

put off. 1 If you **put** something **off**, you delay doing it. EG *Don't put it off till tomorrow.* **2** If you **put** someone **off, 2.1** you make them wait for something that they want. EG *I'm sorry, but I can't put him off any longer.* **2.2** you make them give up trying to get or do something. EG *Nothing would put her off once she had made up her mind.* **3** To **put** someone **off** something means to cause them to dislike it. EG *I had seen enough to put me off farm work.* PHRASAL VB : V+O+ADV ... V+O+ADV ... V+O+ADV/ PREP

put on. 1 When you **put on** a piece of clothing, you place it on your body in order to wear it. EG *I put on my jacket.* **2** When people **put on** a show, exhibition, or service, they perform it, arrange it, or organize it. EG *A French company has put on 'Peter Grimes'... They're putting on a special train service.* **3** If someone **puts on** weight, they become heavier. EG *She had put on over a stone since I last saw her.* **4** If you **put on** a piece of equipment or a device, you make it start working. EG *He put on the light... She put the radio on... Put the brake on and leave the car in gear.* **5** If you **put on** a record or tape, you place it on a record player or in a tape machine and listen to it. **6** If you **put** food **on**, you begin to cook it. EG *She often forgets to put the dinner on before she goes to collect the children.* **7** If you **put** a sum of money **on** something, you make a bet about it. For example, if you put £10 on a racehorse, you bet £10 that it will win. **8** To **put** a particular amount **on** the cost or value of something means to add that amount to it. EG *This will put another 5p a gallon on petrol.* **9** If you **put on** a way of behaving, you behave in a way that is not natural to you or that does not express your real feelings. EG *She put on that look of not caring... I don't see why you have to put on a phoney English accent.* **10** If someone is putting you **on**, they are teasing you by trying to make you believe something that is not true. EG *'You're putting me on,' said Deirdre.* PHRASAL VB : V+O+ADV ... V+O+ADV ... V+O+ADV ... V+O+ADV ... V+O+ADV ... V+O+ADV/ PREP ... V+O+PREP ... V+O+ADV ... V+O+ADV, ONLY CONT Informal

put onto. If you **put** someone **onto** something useful, you tell them about it. EG *One of his friends put him on to Voluntary Service Overseas.* PHRASAL VB : V+O+PREP

put out. 1 If you **put out** an announcement or story, you make it known to a lot of people. EG *He put out a statement denouncing the commission's conclusions.* **2** If you **put out** a fire, a candle, or a cigarette, you make it stop burning. EG *He helped to put the fire out... Sheldon put out his cigar.* **3** If you **put out** an electric light, you make it stop shining by pressing a switch. EG *She put out the light.* **4** If you **put out** things that will be needed, you place them somewhere ready to be used. EG *I put clean clothes out for you on the bed.* **5** If you **put out** your hand, you move it forward, away from your body. EG *I walked over to one young woman and put out my hand.* **6** If you **put** your back, hip, or shoulder **out**, you injure yourself so that one of your bones is no longer in its normal position. **7** If PHRASAL VB : V+O+ADV ... V+O+ADV ... V+O+ADV ... V+O+ADV ... V+O+ADV ... V+O+ADV Informal ... V-PASS+ADV

you **are put out**, you are rather annoyed or upset by something. EG *I was somewhat put out when the audience laughed loudly.* **8** If you **put yourself out**, V-REFL+ADV you do something for someone even though it requires a lot of effort or causes you problems. EG *He was putting himself out to please her.*
put over. See **put across.**
put through. 1 When someone **puts through** a PHRASAL VB: telephone call or a caller, they make the connec- V+O+ADV tion that allows the caller to speak to the person they are phoning. EG *'Data Room, please.' – 'I'll put you through.'* **2** If someone **puts** you **through** an V+O+PREP unpleasant experience, they make you experience it. EG *I'm sorry to put you through this again.*
put together. 1 If you **put** something **together**, PHRASAL VB: you join its different parts to each other so that it V+O+ADV can be used. EG *He started to put his fishing rod together.* **2** If you **put** an event **together**, you V+O+ADV organize or arrange it. EG *The agency has put together the biggest ever campaign for a new car.*
3 If you say that something is bigger or better than PHRASE several things **put together**, you mean that it is bigger or has more good qualities than all of these things together. EG *He is smarter than all your colonels put together.*
put up. 1 If people **put up** a wall or a building, PHRASAL VB: they construct it. EG *We shall have to put up a* V+O+ADV *fence.* **2** If you **put up** an umbrella or a hood, you V+O+ADV unfold it or raise it so that it covers you. EG *I should put your umbrella up.* **3** If you **put up** a poster or V+O+ADV notice, you fix it to a wall or board. EG *These posters were put up all over the place.* **4** If you **put** V+ADV+O **up** resistance to something, you resist it. EG *America has put up so much resistance to Concorde... We had put up a fierce struggle.* **5** If you **put up** money V+ADV+O for something, you provide the money that is needed to pay for it. EG *The National Council for the Arts put up half the cost.* **6** To **put up** the price of V+O+ADV something means to cause it to increase. EG *This is what happens when they put up prices too far.* **7** If V-ERG+ADV someone **puts** you **up**, you stay at their home for one or more nights. EG *I offered to put him up for the night.* **8** to **put up a fight**: see **fight.** ● a **put-up job**: see **put-up.**
put up to. If you **put** someone **up to** something PHRASAL VB: wrong or foolish, you suggest that they do it and V+O+ADV you encourage them to do it. EG *Julie herself had* +PREP *probably put them up to it.*
put up with. If you **put up with** something, you PHRASAL VB: tolerate or accept it, even though you find it V+ADV+PREP unpleasant or unsatisfactory. EG *The natives have to put up with gaping tourists... I can't think why I put up with it.*
put-down, put-downs. A **put-down** is something N COUNT that you say or do which criticizes someone or Informal makes them appear foolish. EG *The ultimate put-down is to be given a pat on the head.*
putrefy /pjuːtrɪfaɪ/, **putrefies, putrefying, pu-** V **trefied.** When something **putrefies**, it rots and Formal produces a disgusting smell. EG *Thousands of bodies were decomposing and putrefying.*

putrid /pjuːtrɪd/. Something that is **putrid** is rot- ADJ CLASSIF ten and beginning to smell disgusting. EG *...a rotted* Formal *and putrid mess.*
putty /pʌti¹/ is a stiff paste used to fix glass panes N UNCOUNT into frames and to fill cracks or holes in woodwork.
put-up. If something is a **put-up job**, it has been PHRASE arranged beforehand in order to deceive someone. Informal
put-upon. If you are **put-upon**, you have been ADJ QUALIT treated badly by someone who has taken advan- Informal tage of your willingness to help them. EG *I felt cheated and put-upon.*
puzzle /pʌzə⁰l/, **puzzles, puzzling, puzzled. 1** If V+O something **puzzles** you, it makes you feel confused because you do not understand it. EG *There was one sentence which puzzled me deeply.* ◊ **puzzling.** EG ◊ ADJ QUALIT *I find this rather puzzling.*
2 If you **puzzle** over something, you try hard to V+A think of the answer to it or the explanation for it. EG *Astronomers had puzzled over these white ovals for some time.*
3 A **puzzle** is a question, game, or toy which you N COUNT have to think about carefully in order to answer it correctly or put it together properly.
4 You can describe anything that is hard to under- N SING stand as a **puzzle**. EG *The motives of the film- makers remain a puzzle.*
puzzle out. If you **puzzle out** a problem, you find PHRASAL VB: the answer to it by thinking hard about it. EG *She sat* V+O+ADV *down and tried to puzzle out the reports.*
puzzled /pʌzə⁰ld/. Someone who is **puzzled** is ADJ QUALIT confused because they do not understand some- thing. EG *Madeleine looked puzzled.*
puzzlement /pʌzə⁰lmənt/ is confusion that you N UNCOUNT feel when you do not understand something. EG *I looked at him in puzzlement.*
pyjamas /pədʒɑːməz/; spelled **pajamas** in Ameri- N PLURAL can English. The forms **pyjama** and **pajama** are used before another noun.
A pair of **pyjamas** consists of loose trousers and a loose jacket that people, especially men, wear in bed. EG *...pyjama trousers.*
pylon /paɪlə⁰n/, **pylons. Pylons** are very tall N COUNT metal structures which hold electric cables high above the ground so that electricity can be trans- mitted over long distances. EG *...electricity pylons.*
pyramid /pɪrəmɪd/, **pyramids. 1** The **Pyramids** N COUNT are ancient stone buildings built over the tombs of dead kings and queens in Egypt. They have trian- gular walls that slope upwards and inwards to a single point.
2 A **pyramid** is a shape, object, or pile of things N COUNT with a flat base and flat triangular sides that slope upwards and inwards to a point. EG *She made a pyramid of cans... ...pyramids of skulls.* See picture at SHAPES.
Pyrex /paɪrɛks/ is a type of strong glass which is N UNCOUNT used for making bowls and dishes that do not break Trademark when you cook things in them. EG *...Pyrex dishes.*
python /paɪθə⁰n/, **pythons.** A **python** is a large, N COUNT long snake that kills animals by squeezing them with its body.

Q q

Q, q /kjuː/, **Qs, q's. Q** is the seventeenth letter of the English alphabet. N COUNT

quack /kwæk/, **quacks, quacking, quacked. 1** If a duck **quacks**, it makes the noise that ducks typically make. ▶ used as a noun. EG *A feeble quack was heard from beyond the pond.* V ▶ N COUNT

2 If you call a doctor or an unqualified person a **quack**, you mean that they claim to be skilled in medicine but they are not. N COUNT

quad /kwɒd/, **quads. Quads** are the same as quadruplets. N COUNT

quadrangle /kwɒdræŋgəˀl/, **quadrangles.** A **quadrangle** is an open square area with buildings round it. N COUNT

quadruped /kwɒdruped/, **quadrupeds.** Any four-legged animal can be referred to as a **quadruped.** N COUNT Formal

quadruple /kwɒdrupəˀl/, **quadruples, quadrupling, quadrupled.** When an amount or number **quadruples**, it becomes four times as large. EG *In the last twenty years wheat production has almost quadrupled... We could quadruple output to around 10 million tons.* V·ERG

quadruplet /kwɒdruplɪˀt, kwɒdruːplɪˀt/, **quadruplets. Quadruplets** are four children who are born to the same mother at the same time. N COUNT

quail /kweɪl/, **quails, quailing, quailed. 1** A **quail** is a small bird which is often shot and eaten. The plural is either 'quail' or 'quails'. N COUNT OR N UNCOUNT

2 If you **quail**, you feel very afraid. EG *She quailed before his angry bitterness.* V Formal

quaint /kweɪnt/, **quainter, quaintest.** Something that is **quaint** is attractive because it is strange and rather old-fashioned. EG *...quaint little houses... ...a quaint fishing village... ...quaint ideas.* ADJ QUALIT

quake /kweɪk/, **quakes, quaking, quaked. 1** If you **quake**, you tremble or shake because you are very afraid. EG *I stood there quaking with fear.* V

2 A **quake** is the same as an earthquake. EG *On average, there are four major quakes in a century.* N COUNT Informal

qualification /kwɒlɪfɪkeɪʃəˀn/, **qualifications. 1** Your **qualifications** are the examinations that you have passed. EG *I haven't got any qualifications in English Literature.* ● See also **qualify.** N COUNT

2 The **qualifications** needed for a particular activity or task are the qualities and skills that you need in order to do it. EG *One of the qualifications you need in advertising is a fertile mind.* N COUNT

3 A **qualification** is also a detail or explanation that you add to a statement to make it less strong or less generalized. EG *Two qualifications need to be made... Few people praised him without qualification.* N COUNT OR N UNCOUNT

qualified /kwɒlɪfaɪd/. **1** Someone who is **qualified** has passed the examinations that they need to pass in order to work in a particular profession. EG *These tests have to be carried out by a qualified doctor... She is qualified to teach.* ADJ CLASSIF

2 If you are **qualified** to do something, you have the qualities or skills necessary to do it. EG *She did not feel qualified to discuss it... They were better qualified to suggest improvements.* ADJ PRED : OFT + to-INF

3 Qualified agreement or praise is not total and suggests that you have doubts. EG *The reaction was one of qualified praise.* ADJ QUALIT

qualify /kwɒlɪfaɪ/, **qualifies, qualifying, qualified. 1** When someone **qualifies**, they pass the examinations that they need to pass in order to work in a particular profession. EG *I was thirty-three before I qualified as a doctor.* V

◊ **qualification.** EG *Even after qualification, jobs were hard to find.* ◊ N UNCOUNT

2 If you **qualify** a statement, you add a detail or V+O

explanation to it to make it less strong or less generalized. EG *If I said that Warsaw was grim and grey, that statement has to be qualified.*

3 If someone **qualifies** for something, they have the right to have it or to do it. EG *By working all their lives, people qualify automatically for their pensions.* V+for

4 If you **qualify** in a competition, you are successful in one part of it and go on to the next stage. EG *He worked all season to qualify for the match.* V

qualitative /kwɒlɪtətɪv, -teɪt-/ means relating to the quality of something. EG *...qualitative improvements... ...a qualitative change.* ADJ CLASSIF : ATTRIB

quality /kwɒlɪtiˀ/, **qualities. 1** The **quality** of something is how good or bad it is. EG *The quality of the photograph was poor... I've got some good quality paper.* N UNCOUNT : USU + SUPP

2 Something of **quality** is of a high standard. EG *...a programme of quality... The employers don't want quality work any more.* N UNCOUNT

3 A person's **qualities** are their good characteristics, such as kindness or honesty. EG *Asquith paid tribute to his personal qualities... ...the qualities they look for in a teacher.* N COUNT + SUPP

4 The **qualities** of a substance or an object are its physical characteristics. EG *...the abstract qualities of the painting... The skin on the baby's face had a pearly translucent quality.* N COUNT + SUPP

qualm /kwɑːm/, **qualms.** If you have **qualms** about something that you are doing, you are worried that it may not be right. EG *I sometimes have qualms about our teaching methods.* N COUNT : USU PLURAL

quandary /kwɒndəˀriˀ/, **quandaries.** If you are in a **quandary**, you cannot decide what to do. EG *He found himself in a quandary... I couldn't offer any resolutions of this quandary.* N COUNT

QUANTIF stands for quantifier

Words which have the label QUANTIF in the Extra Column are words such as 'most', 'least', and 'several' which tell you about the amount or quantity of something.

See the entry headed QUANTIFIERS for more information.

---

quantitative /kwɒntɪtətɪv, -teɪt-/ means relating to the size or amount of something. EG *It is not yet possible to make a quantitative assessment of the effectiveness of our investment.* ADJ CLASSIF : USU ATTRIB

quantity /kwɒntɪtiˀ/, **quantities. 1** A **quantity** is an amount that you can measure or count. EG *You only need a very small quantity... Natural gas was discovered in large quantities beneath the North Sea... ...a quantity of leaves.* N COUNT OR N PART

2 Things that are produced **in quantity** are produced in large amounts. EG *The meat is produced in quantity and sold in Eastern Europe.* PHRASE

3 Quantity is the amount of something that there is; often used in contrast to its quality and how good it is. EG *Materials are being seen in terms simply of quantity rather than quality... The food supply has grown less, in quantity and quality.* N UNCOUNT

4 If you say that someone or something is an **unknown quantity**, you mean that you do not know anything about them. EG *To Shanti the outside world was a totally unknown quantity.* PHRASE

quantum /kwɒntəˀm/. **1 Quantum** is used to describe various theories in physics and mathematics which are concerned with the properties and N MOD Technical

QUANTIFIERS

Quantifiers (labelled QUANTIF in the Extra Column) are used to say how much of something there is. The main quantifiers are: **both**, **few**, **least**, **less**, **little**, **many**, **more**, **most**, **much**, **plenty**, **several**, **some**, and **a little**.

1 Quantifiers come in front of a noun: *many miles away* ... ... *less sugar*.

2 Some quantifiers are used with countable nouns in the plural: *few books* ... ... *several girls*. Others are used with uncountable nouns: *much money*.

3 They can be used in front of the preposition **of**: *Most of my work is political*.

4 They can be used as a complete group in the same way as pronouns: *Little can be seen of the Roman remains* ... *There is little to say about him*.

---

behaviour of atomic particles. EG ...*quantum mechanics*... ...*quantum physics*.

2 A **quantum** leap or jump is a very great change, increase, or advance. EG ...*a quantum leap in growth*... ...*sudden quantum jumps in values*.   ADJ CLASSIF: ATTRIB Formal

quarantine /kwɒrəntiːn/, **quarantines, quarantining, quarantined**. If a person or animal is in **quarantine**, they may have a disease and they are being kept separate from other people or animals to prevent the disease from spreading. EG *Her dog was in quarantine*. ▶ used as a verb. EG *He was quarantined in the hope of containing the infection*.   N SING : *the* + N, OR N UNCOUNT   ▶ V + O

quarrel /kwɒrəⁿl/, **quarrels, quarrelling, quarrelled**; spelled **quarreling, quarreled** in American English.

1 A **quarrel** is an angry argument between two or more people. EG *I don't think we should enter into a family quarrel*... *There wasn't any evidence of quarrels between them*. ▶ used as a verb. EG *They quarrelled quite often*... *I don't want to quarrel with you*... *It was not worth quarrelling about*.   N COUNT   ▶ V OR V + with : RECIP

2 If you say that you have no **quarrel** with something, you mean that you do not object to it. EG *I wouldn't have any quarrel with this proposal myself*.   N COUNT + with

3 If you say that you would **quarrel** with something that someone has said, you mean that you disagree with it. EG *One thing I would quarrel with in your introduction is the suggestion that people do not care*.   V + with Formal

quarrelsome /kwɒrəlsəm/. People who are **quarrelsome** are always having angry arguments. EG *His brothers were greedy and quarrelsome*.   ADJ QUALIT

quarry /kwɒri¹/, **quarries, quarrying, quarried**. **1** A **quarry** is a place that is dug out in order to extract stone, slate, or minerals. EG ...*sandstone quarries*.   N COUNT

2 To **quarry** a stone or mineral means to remove it from a quarry by digging, drilling, or blasting. EG *These limestones have been quarried for centuries*.   V + O OR V

3 A person's or animal's **quarry** is the animal that they are hunting. The plural form is also 'quarry'. EG *Move slowly, or you will startle your quarry*.   N COUNT : USU + POSS

quart /kwɔːt/, **quarts**. A **quart** is a unit of volume that is equal to two pints. EG ...*a quart of milk*.   N PART

quarter /kwɔːtə/, **quarters**. **1** A **quarter** is one of four equal parts of something. EG ...*a quarter of a century*... *It took me an hour and a quarter to make a phone call*. ▶ used as an adjective. EG ...*the quarter century following the Second World War*. ● See also **three-quarters**.   N COUNT   ▶ ADJ CLASSIF : ATTRIB

2 If it is a **quarter** to a particular hour, it is fifteen minutes before that hour. In American English, you say that it is a **quarter** of a particular hour. See the

entry headed TIME. EG *It's quarter to five*... *They allowed you to go at a quarter to eight*.

3 If it is a **quarter** past a particular hour, it is fifteen minutes past that hour. See the entry headed TIME. EG *We're due at Janet's at quarter past eleven*... ...*a quarter past three in the afternoon*.

4 A **quarter** is also **4.1** a period of three months. EG *In the last quarter of 1980 inflation rose by 1%*. **4.2** an American or Canadian coin that is worth 25 cents. **4.3** four ounces of something. EG *A quarter of walnuts, please*.   N COUNT   N COUNT   N PART : USU SING

5 You can refer to an area in a town or city where a particular group of people live or work as a particular **quarter**. EG ...*the Black quarters of New York, Detroit or Washington*.   N COUNT : USU + SUPP

6 If you refer to the feeling or reaction in certain **quarters** or from a particular **quarter**, you are referring rather vaguely to the feeling or reaction of a particular person or group of people. EG *Male prejudice still exists in certain quarters*.   N COUNT + SUPP : USU PLURAL

7 You can refer to the room or rooms provided for a person such as a soldier to live in as that person's **quarters**. EG ...*servants' quarters*.   N PLURAL

8 If you see someone at **close quarters**, you see them from a place that is very close to them. EG *It was a privilege to observe her at such close quarters*.   PHRASE

quarter-final /kwɔːtəfaɪnəⁿl/, **quarter-finals**. A **quarter-final** is one of the four matches in a competition which decides which four players or teams will compete in the semi-final. EG *A win by Leicestershire would give them a chance of qualifying for the quarter-finals*.   N COUNT

quarterly /kwɔːtəli¹/, **quarterlies**. **1** If something happens **quarterly**, it happens regularly four times a year, at intervals of three months. EG ...*an annual salary paid monthly or quarterly*... *We meet quarterly*... ...*a quarterly conference*.   ADV AFTER VB OR ADJ CLASSIF : ATTRIB

2 A **quarterly** or a **quarterly** publication is a magazine or journal that is published regularly four times a year, at intervals of three months.   N COUNT OR ADJ CLASSIF : ATTRIB

quartet /kwɔːtet/, **quartets**. A **quartet** is **1** a group of four people who play musical instruments or sing together. EG ...*the Amadeus String Quartet*. **2** a piece of music for four instruments or four singers. EG ...*a Beethoven quartet*.   N COUNT

quartz /kwɔːts/ is a kind of hard, shiny crystal. It is used in making electronic equipment and very accurate watches and clocks. EG ...*a quartz clock*.   N UNCOUNT

If you do something without question, do you quibble about it?

quash /kwɒʃ/, **quashes, quashing, quashed.** If v+o someone in authority **quashes** a decision or judgement, they officially reject it and make it no longer legally valid. EG *Their prison sentences were quashed on appeal.*

quasi- /kweɪzaɪ/ is used to form adjectives and PREFIX nouns that describe something as being in many ways like something else, without actually being that thing. EG *...a quasi-religious experience... They have turned their countries into quasi-republics.*

quaver /kweɪvə/, **quavers, quavering, qua-** V OR V+QUOTE **vered.** If someone's voice **quavers**, it sounds unsteady, for example because they are nervous or uncertain. EG *Ginny's voice was quavering... 'Am I safe?' he quavered.*

quay /kiː/, **quays.** A **quay** is a long platform N COUNT beside the sea or a river where boats can be tied up and loaded or unloaded.

quayside /kiːsaɪd/. The **quayside** is the area at N SING the edge of a quay.

queasy /kwiːzi¹/, **queasier, queasiest.** If you feel ADJ QUALIT **queasy**, you feel rather ill, as if you are going to be sick. EG *She felt a little queasy on the boat.*

queen /kwiːn/, **queens.** 1 A **queen** is 1.1 a woman N COUNT who rules a country as its monarch. EG *...Queen Victoria.* 1.2 a woman who is married to a king. EG *Henry VIII married his first Queen in the Tower of London.*

2 A **queen** or a **queen bee** is a large female bee N COUNT which can lay eggs.

3 In chess, the **queen** is the most powerful piece. It N COUNT can be moved backwards, forwards, sideways, or diagonally.

4 A **queen** is also a playing card with a picture of a N COUNT queen on it. EG *...the queen of spades.*

queer /kwɪə/, **queerer, queerest; queers.** 1 ADJ QUALIT Something that is **queer** is strange. EG *He's a queer character, my friend Evans... It gave her a queer sensation to shake hands with a murderer.*

2 People sometimes call a homosexual man a N COUNT **queer**; a very offensive use.

quell /kwel/, **quells, quelling, quelled.** 1 To v+o **quell** opposition or violent behaviour means to put an end to it using persuasion or force. EG *The police had been called in to quell a minor disturbance.*

2 If you **quell** unpleasant feelings such as fear or v+o grief, you stop yourself having these feelings. EG *I was trying to quell a growing unease.*

quench /kwentʃ/, **quenches, quenching,** v+o **quenched.** When you are thirsty, you can **quench** your thirst by having a drink.

querulous /kwerjʊˈləs/. Someone who is **queru-** ADJ QUALIT **lous** often complains about things; used showing Formal disapproval. EG *...querulous children... Otto spoke in a weakly querulous voice.*

query /kwɪəri¹/, **queries, querying, queried.** 1 A N COUNT OR **query** is a question. EG *If you have any queries,* N UNCOUNT *please don't hesitate to write... The assistant accepted my cheque without query.* ▶ used as a verb. ▶ V+QUOTE EG *'How much do I owe you?' I queried.*

2 If you **query** something, you check it by asking v+o about it because you are not sure if it is correct. EG *Your expenses have been queried by someone in the finance department.*

quest /kwest/, **quests.** A **quest** is a long and N COUNT: difficult search for something. EG *Little did I know* OFT+for *when I embarked on this quest how futile it would* Literary *be... ...the quest for truth.*

question /kwestʃə⁰n/, **questions, questioning, questioned.** 1 A **question** is something which you N COUNT say or write in order to ask someone about something. EG *Jill began to ask Fred a lot of questions about his childhood... A panel of experts will answer questions on education.*

2 If you **question** someone, you ask them a lot of v+o: questions about something. EG *I started questioning* OFT+about *her about Jane and Anthony.* ◇ **questioning.** EG ◇ N UNCOUNT *The three men were taken to the police station for questioning.*

3 If you **question** something, you express your v+o doubts about whether it is true, reasonable, or worthwhile. EG *Women are questioning their traditional role in society... No one ever questioned the necessity of the visit.*

4 If you say that there is some **question** about N UNCOUNT something, you mean that there is doubt or uncer- +SUPP tainty about it. EG *There has been some question as to whether or not the President will resign.*

5 A **question** is also 5.1 a problem or a point which N COUNT+SUPP needs to be discussed. EG *His resignation raised the question of his successor... It is difficult for them to admit there is another side to the missile question.* 5.2 a problem which is set in an examination in N COUNT order to test your knowledge or ability. EG *You have to answer four questions in two hours.*

6 **Question** is also used in these phrases. 6.1 If PHRASES something is **beyond question**, there is no doubt at all about it. EG *She knew beyond question that I was a person who could be trusted.* 6.2 To **bring** something **into question** means to make people think more seriously about it. EG *Unemployment has brought into question the right of married women to work.* 6.3 If you **call** something **into question**, you express serious doubts about it. EG *Are you calling my professional competence into question?* 6.4 If you say that something is **open to question**, you mean that it is not yet certain and people might disagree about it. 6.5 If you say that something is **out of the question**, you mean that it is impossible. EG *She knew that a holiday this year was out of the question.* 6.6 If you say **there is no question of** doing something, you mean that it is impossible to do it. EG *With so much happening there was no question of getting a full night's sleep.* 6.7 If you do something **without question**, you do it without arguing or asking why it is necessary. EG *They obeyed me without question.* 6.8 The time **in question** or the place **in question** is the time or place which you have just been talking about. EG *Did James have dinner with you on the night in question?... He was surprised to see the woman in question enter the shop.*

questionable /kwestʃənəb⁰l/. If you say that ADJ QUALIT something is **questionable**, you mean that it may be wrong or not suitable. EG *It is questionable whether the rat is a suitable test model... ...questionable projects like convention centres.*

question mark, question marks. 1 A **question** N COUNT **mark** is the punctuation mark (?) which is used in writing at the end of a question.

2 If there is doubt or uncertainty about something, N COUNT you can say that there is a **question mark** over it. EG *A question mark hangs over the Party's recent success.*

questionnaire /kwe⁰stʃəneə/, **questionnaires.** N COUNT A **questionnaire** is a written list of questions which are answered by a lot of people in order to provide information for a report or a survey.

question tag, question tags. A **question tag** is N COUNT a very short clause at the end of a statement which changes the statement into a question. In *'She said half price, didn't she?'*, the words *'didn't she'* are a question tag.

queue /kjuː/, **queues, queueing, queued.** The present participle is also spelled **queuing.**

1 A **queue** is a line of people or vehicles that are N COUNT waiting for something. EG *She was in the queue for coffee... I had to wait in a long, slow queue.*

2 When people **queue** or **queue up**, they stand in a v:OFT+up line waiting for something. EG *People were queueing up for his autograph... They had queued for hours to get in.*

quibble /kwɪbə⁰l/, **quibbles, quibbling, quib-** V:USU+a **bled.** 1 When people **quibble**, they argue about a small matter which is not important. EG *He had become more difficult, quibbling about minor points.*

2 A **quibble** is a minor objection to something. N COUNT

quiche /kiːʃ/, **quiches**. A **quiche** is a tart filled N COUNT
with a savoury mixture of eggs, cheese, and other
things. Quiches can be eaten either hot or cold.

quick /kwɪk/, **quicker, quickest. 1** Someone or ADJ QUALIT
something that is **quick** moves or does things with
great speed. EG *She was precise and quick in her
movements... Her hands were quick and strong.*
◇ **quickly.** EG *I walked quickly up the passage.* ◇ ADV
2 Something that is **quick 2.1** takes or lasts only a ADJ QUALIT
short time. EG *Let's just have a quick look at that...
...a quick visit.* ◇ **quickly.** EG *They embraced* ◇ ADV
quickly. **2.2** happens without any delay or with ADJ QUALIT
very little delay. EG *You're likely to get a quicker
reply if you telephone... John was quick to help
him.* ◇ **quickly.** EG *She wants to get the whole* ◇ ADV
thing over with as quickly as possible.
3 quick as a flash: see **flash**. ● **quick off the**
mark: see **mark**. ● **quick on the uptake**: see
uptake.

quicken /kwɪkəⁿn/, **quickens, quickening,** V-ERG
quickened. If something **quickens** or if you
quicken it, it moves at a greater speed. EG *This
thought made him quicken his pace... His voice
quickened.*

quicksand /kwɪksænd/, **quicksands.** Quicksand N UNCOUNT
is deep, wet sand that you sink into when you try to OR N COUNT
walk on it.

quickstep /kwɪkstep/. The **quickstep** is a ball- N SING : the+N
room dance with a lot of quick steps.

quid /kwɪd/. A **quid** is the same amount of money N COUNT
as a pound. The plural form is also 'quid'. EG *It cost* Informal
45 quid.   British

quiet /kwaɪət/, **quieter, quietest; quiets, quiet-**
ing, quieted. 1 Something or someone that is ADJ QUALIT
quiet makes only a small amount of noise. EG *Bal
said in a quiet voice, 'I have resigned.'... The music
had gone very quiet.* ◇ **quietly.** EG *'I'm going to do* ◇ ADV
it,' I said quietly.
2 If a place is **quiet**, there is very little noise there. ADJ QUALIT
EG *It was very quiet in there; you could just hear the
wind moving the trees.*
3 You also say that a place is **quiet** when nothing ADJ QUALIT
very exciting or important happens there. EG *The
village is so quiet now.*
4 Quiet is silence. EG *Ralph was on his feet too,* N UNCOUNT
shouting for quiet.
5 If you are **quiet**, you do not say anything. EG ADJ PRED
*There was nothing to say so she kept quiet... Be
quiet and listen.* ◇ **quietly.** EG *We lay quietly.* ◇ ADV
6 A **quiet** person behaves in a calm way and is not ADJ QUALIT
easily made angry or upset. EG *She is thoughtful,
quiet and controlled.*
7 You describe activities as **quiet** when they ADJ QUALIT
happen in secret or in such a way that people do
not notice. EG *He conducted some quiet diplomacy
during his world tour... The funeral was as quiet as
the marriage had been.* ◇ **quietly.** EG *She quietly* ◇ ADV
took a flat in a suburb of Paris. ● If something is ● PHRASE
done **on the quiet**, it is done secretly or in such a
way that people do not notice. ● If you **keep quiet** ● PHRASE
about something, you do not say anything about it.
EG *You must keep quiet about what you saw.*
8 You describe colours or clothes as **quiet** when ADJ QUALIT
they are not bright or not too noticeable.

quiet down. If someone **quiets down** or if you PHRASAL VB :
quiet them **down**, they become less noisy or less V-ERG+ADV
active. EG *When he quieted down, I began to tell* American
him the truth.

quieten /kwaɪətəⁿn/, **quietens, quietening, qui-** V+O
etened. If you **quieten** a person or an animal, you
make them become less noisy. EG *To quieten her I
had to tie her to a tree.*

quieten down. If someone or something **quiet-** PHRASAL VB :
ens down, they become less noisy, less active, and V+ADV
more calm. EG *We quietened down to think.*   British

quill /kwɪl/, **quills. 1** A **quill** is a pen made from a N COUNT
bird's feather.
2 A bird's **quills** are large, stiff feathers on its N COUNT
wings and tail.

3 The **quills** of an animal such as a porcupine are N COUNT
the stiff, sharp points on its body.

quilt /kwɪlt/, **quilts.** A **quilt** is a cover filled with N COUNT
feathers or some other warm, soft material, which
you put over yourself when you are in bed.

quilted /kwɪltɪ³d/. Something that is **quilted** con- ADJ CLASSIF
sists of two layers of fabric with a layer of soft
thick material between them. EG *She was wearing a
pink quilted jacket.*

quinine /kwɪniːn/ is a drug that is used to treat N UNCOUNT
fevers such as malaria.

quintet /kwɪntet/, **quintets.** A **quintet** is **1** a N COUNT
group of five singers or musicians singing or play-
ing together. **2** a piece of music written for five
instruments or five singers. EG *...Schubert's 'Trout'
quintet.*

quip /kwɪp/, **quips, quipping, quipped.** A **quip** is N COUNT
an amusing or clever remark. EG *I remember your* Outdated
quips and jokes. ▸ used as a verb. EG *'I've read so* ▸ V+QUOTE
much about him,' Philip quipped.

quirk /kwɜːk/, **quirks.** A **quirk** is **1** a habit or N COUNT :
aspect of a person's character which is odd or USU+SUPP
unusual. EG *Everyone has his little quirks.* **2** a
strange occurrence that is difficult to explain. EG *By
one of those strange quirks of fate, both had died
within a few days of each other.*

quit /kwɪt/, **quits, quitting.** The form **quit** is used
in the present tense and past tense, and is also the
past participle.
1 If you **quit** doing something, you stop doing it. EG V : OFT+-ING,
Jack wants to quit smoking... I had never quit OR V+O
feeling that way about him.   American
2 If you **quit**, or **quit** a job, you resign from it. EG V OR V+O
*I'm going to quit psychiatry... A week later he quit
and went home to America.*
3 If you say to someone 'We **are quits**', you mean PHRASE
that neither of you owes the other one anything. Informal
4 If people **call it quits**, they agree that an PHRASE
argument or fight should be ended. EG *We decided* Informal
to call it quits.

quite /kwaɪt/. **1** You use **quite 1.1** to indicate that SUBMOD OR ADV
something is the case to a fairly great extent but
not to a very great extent. EG *He was quite young...
It seemed quite a long time... I could save quite a
lot of money... He calls quite often... I quite enjoy
looking round museums.* **1.2** to emphasize that
something is completely the case or very much the
case. EG *I stood quite still... You're quite sure you
don't mind?... Oh I quite agree... Quite frankly, I'm
too miserable to care... The matter is quite simple.*
2 You use **quite** after a negative **2.1** to indicate ADV : WITH
that something is almost true. EG *It's not quite big* BROAD NEG
*enough... I didn't quite understand what it was all
about.* **2.2** to indicate that you do not know something exactly. EG *I don't know quite where to go.*
3 You use **quite a** to emphasize that something is PHRASE
very unusual, impressive, or significant. EG *It was
quite a sight... They have quite a problem.*
4 You can say **'quite'** or **'quite so'** to express your CONVENTION
agreement with someone. EG *'It does a lot for public* Formal
relations.'–'Quite.'

quiver /kwɪvə/, **quivers, quivering, quivered.** If V
something **quivers**, it shakes or trembles. EG *His
fingers quivered uncontrollably.* ▸ used as a noun. ▸ N SING : a+N
EG *Her whole body gave a slight quiver.*

quiz /kwɪz/, **quizzes, quizzing, quizzed. 1** A **quiz** N COUNT
is a game or competition in which someone tests
your knowledge by asking you questions. EG *...musi-
cal quizzes on TV... ...a quiz programme.*
2 If you **quiz** someone, you ask them questions V+O
because you want to obtain information from them.
EG *She couldn't be sure why he was quizzing her.*

quizzical /kwɪzɪkə³l/. If you give someone a **quiz-** ADJ QUALIT
zical look, you look at them with a slight smile,
because you know them well and are suspicious of

their behaviour or are amused by it. EG *I could see from Clare's quizzical glance that she knew that.*

quota /kwəʊtə/, **quotas.** A **quota** is a limited number or quantity of something which is officially allowed. EG *...an import quota of 1.6m cars... ...a daily food quota.*   N COUNT

quotation /kwəʊteɪʃ°n/, **quotations.** 1 A **quotation** is a sentence or phrase from a book, poem, or play. EG *...a quotation from a novel by Somerset Maugham... He recited a long bible quotation.*   N COUNT : OFT + *from*

2 When someone gives you a **quotation**, they tell you how much they will charge to do a particular piece of work. EG *They submitted quotations and agreed prices... Get a free quotation for the job.*   N COUNT

quotation mark, quotation marks. Quotation marks are punctuation marks that are used in writing to show where speech or a quotation begins and ends. They are usually written or printed as ' and '.   N COUNT : USU PLURAL

quote /kwəʊt/, **quotes, quoting, quoted.** 1 If you **quote** someone or something, you repeat the exact words that they have written or said. EG *He was quoted in the paper as saying: 'This strike is evil.'... She quoted the Chinese proverb about lighting candles... 'Change and decay in all round I see,' Castle quoted... ...quoting from a film he'd seen.*   V+O, V+QUOTE, OR V+A

2 If you **quote** something such as a law or a fact, you state it because it supports what you are   V+O

saying. EG *They quote figures to compare the costs of adult education in different countries... I will quote only one or two examples.*

3 If you **quote** a price, you suggest a price for which you are willing to do a particular piece of work. EG *Ask the refuse department to come and quote for removing the stuff... They quoted a price of twenty thousand dollars.*   V+O, V+O+O, OR V+*for*

4 A **quote** from a book, poem, or play is a sentence or phrase from it. EG *...a short quote from the Oration.*   N COUNT : OFT + *from*

5 A **quote** for a piece of work is the price that someone says they will charge you to do the work. EG *Try getting a quote from a caterer for a really big party.*   N COUNT

6 **Quotes** are the same as quotation marks. EG *Her comments are placed in quotes.*   N PLURAL, Informal

---

QUOTE stands for **direct speech**
+QUOTE is used in the Extra Column after verbs which can be used to describe direct speech, as in *'Your father was a good friend to me,' he remarked.*
See the entry headed VERBS for more information.

R r

R, r /ɑː/, **Rs, r's. R** is the eighteenth letter of the English alphabet.   N COUNT

rabbi /ræbaɪ/, **rabbis.** A **rabbi** is a Jewish religious leader, usually one who is in charge of a synagogue, one who is qualified to teach Judaism, or one who is an expert on Jewish law.   N COUNT

rabbit /ræbɪt/, **rabbits.** A **rabbit** is a small furry animal with long ears. Rabbits live in holes in the ground.   N COUNT

rabble /ræbə°l/. A **rabble** is a crowd of noisy, disorderly people. EG *...a rabble of boys and girls of all ages.*   N SING

rabid /ræbɪd, reɪ-/. 1 You use **rabid** to describe someone who has very strong and unreasonable opinions on a subject, especially in politics. EG *...a rabid feminist... ...rabid Republicans who worshipped Genet.*   ADJ QUALIT : ATTRIB

2 A dog or other animal that is **rabid** is infected with rabies. EG *...a rabid dog.*   ADJ CLASSIF

rabies /reɪbiˈz/ is a serious disease which causes people and animals, especially dogs, to go mad and die.   N UNCOUNT

race /reɪs/, **races, racing, raced.** 1 A **race** is a competition to see who is the fastest, for example in running, swimming, or driving. EG *She came second in the race... The race is run through the streets of London... ...a horse race.*   N COUNT

2 A **race** for power or control is a situation in which people or organizations compete with each other for power or control. EG *The race for the White House is now on.... ...the arms race.* ● See also **rat race.**   N SING+SUPP

3 If you **race** someone or **race** against them, you compete with them in a race. EG *They would often race one another to the bus stop... She has raced against some of the best runners in the country.*   V+O OR V+A

4 If you **race** an animal or vehicle, you prepare it for races and make it take part in races. EG *The Australians race camels... He races pigeons... They race vintage cars.*   V+O : NO PASS

5 If you **race** somewhere, you go there as quickly   V+A

as possible. EG *He turned and raced after the others... She raced down the stairs... We had to race across London to get the train.*

6 If your heart **races**, it beats very quickly because you are excited or afraid. EG *His heart raced as he saw the plane coming in to land.*   V

7 You describe a situation as a **race against time** when you have to work very fast in order to do something before a particular time.   PHRASE

8 A **race** is also one of the major groups which human beings can be divided into according to their physical features, such as colour of their skin. EG *The law prohibits discrimination on the grounds of colour or race.* ● See also **human race.**   N COUNT OR N UNCOUNT

9 See also **racing.**

racecourse /reɪskɔːs/, **racecourses.** A **racecourse** is a track on which horses race.   N COUNT, British

racehorse /reɪshɔːs/, **racehorses.** A **racehorse** is a horse that is trained to run in races.   N COUNT

race relations are the ways in which people of different races behave towards each other. EG *...efforts to improve race relations.*   N PLURAL

racial /reɪʃə°l/ describes things relating to people's race. EG *...racial discrimination... ...racial prejudice... ...racial equality... ...racial harmony.*   ADJ CLASSIF : USU ATTRIB
◊ **racially.** EG *...children of racially mixed parentage.*   ◊ ADV

racialism /reɪʃəlɪzə°m/ is the same as racism.   N UNCOUNT
◊ **racialist** /reɪʃəlɪst/, **racialists.** EG *...racialist brutality... ...racialist attitudes.*   ◊ ADJ QUALIT OR N COUNT

racing /reɪsɪŋ/ refers to races between animals, especially horses, or between vehicles. EG *...racing stables... ...motor racing... ...a racing car.*   N UNCOUNT

racism /reɪsɪzə°m/ is the belief that some races are inferior to others. It also refers to the treatment of certain people as inferior because they belong to a particular race; used showing disapproval. EG *...subtle forms of racism... ...a struggle against racism.* ◊ **racist** /reɪsɪst/, **racists.** EG *...racist posters... He's a racist and a sexist.*   N UNCOUNT, ◊ ADJ QUALIT OR N COUNT

rack /ræk/, **racks, racking, racked.** The verb is also spelled **wrack** in American English.

1 A **rack** is a piece of equipment that is used for N COUNT holding things or for hanging things on. EG *He rinsed the plates and put them on the rack to drain... He counted the bits of luggage on the racks.*

2 If someone **is racked** by something, it causes V+O: USU PASS them great suffering or pain. EG *She stood there, +by/with racked by indecision, and began to cry.* Literary

3 If you **rack** your **brains**, you try very hard to PHRASE think of something. EG *Even racking his brains he* Informal *couldn't think of a single example.*

racket /ræˈkɪt/, **rackets**; also spelled **racquet** in paragraph 3. **1** If someone is making a **racket**, N SING they are making a loud unpleasant noise. EG *...the non-stop racket that a healthy baby makes.*

2 A **racket** is an illegal activity that is used to N COUNT make money. EG *He was involved in an insurance racket.*

3 A **racket** is also an oval-shaped bat with strings N COUNT across it. Rackets are used in tennis, squash, and badminton. EG *...a tennis racket.*

racy /reɪsiˈ/, **racier, raciest. Racy** writing or ADJ QUALIT behaviour is lively, amusing, and slightly shocking. EG *...a racy, romantic historical novel.*

radar /reɪdɑː/ is a way of discovering the position N UNCOUNT or speed of things that cannot be seen, by using radio signals. EG *His speed was checked by radar.*

radiant /reɪdɪənt/. **1** Someone who is **radiant** is ADJ QUALIT so happy that their joy shows in their face. EG *Charlotte, you look radiant... ...Haig's radiant optimism.* ◇ **radiantly**. EG *Jane smiled radiantly.* ◇ ADV ◇ **radiance** /reɪdɪəns/. EG *...the radiance of her* ◇ N UNCOUNT *features... Hilary lost a little of her radiance.*

2 Something that is **radiant** glows brightly. EG *...a* ADJ QUALIT *morning of radiant light.* ◇ **radiance.** EG *The* ◇ N UNCOUNT *candle's light threw a faint radiance on the sleep-* Literary *ing girl.*

radiate /reɪdiˈeɪt/, **radiates, radiating, radi-** **ated. 1** If things **radiate** out from a place, they V: USU+A form a pattern that is like lines drawn from the centre of a circle to various points on its edge. EG *...roads that radiated before us... Rods radiate outwards from the centre.*

2 If you **radiate** an emotion or quality or if it V+O **radiates** from you, people can see it very clearly OR V+from in your face and in your behaviour. EG *In the evening Val was back, radiating confidence... There was a tenderness that radiated from her.*

radiation /reɪdiˈeɪʃəⁿn/ is **1** very small particles N UNCOUNT of a radioactive substance that can cause illness and death. EG *Those exposed to a very large amount of radiation experience internal bleeding.* **2** energy that comes from a particular source, for example the sun. EG *...heat radiation.*

radiator /reɪdieɪtə/, **radiators. 1** A **radiator** is a N COUNT hollow metal device, usually connected by pipes to a central heating system, that is used to heat a room.

2 The **radiator** in a car is the part of the engine N COUNT which is filled with water in order to cool the engine.

radical /rædɪkəⁿl/, **radicals. 1** A **radical** is some- N COUNT one who believes that there should be great changes in society and tries to bring about these changes. EG *...a new group of radicals who turned against the established social order.* ▸ used as an ▸ ADJ QUALIT adjective. EG *...a radical barrister... The League had become too radical.*

2 You use **radical** to describe things that relate to ADJ QUALIT: the basic nature of something. EG *...a radical dis-* USU ATTRIB *agreement over fundamentals... ...radical advances in computer design.* ◇ **radically.** EG *Attitudes* ◇ ADV *towards education will have to change radically.*

radii /reɪdiaɪ/ is the plural of **radius**.

radio /reɪdiəʊ/, **radios, radioing, radioed. 1 Ra-** **dio** is **1.1** a system of sending sound over a distance N UNCOUNT by transmitting electrical signals. EG *...radio waves... We managed to establish radio communi-*

cation with them. **1.2** the broadcasting of pro- N SING: the+N, grammes for the public to listen to, by sending out OR N UNCOUNT signals from a transmitter. EG *...a song that had been on the radio a lot... ...a local radio station.*

2 A **radio** or a **radio set** is the piece of equipment N COUNT, that you use when you listen to radio programmes. OR on+N EG *She switched on the radio... ...advertisements on radio and television.*

3 If you **radio** someone, you send a message to V+O OR V them by radio. EG *I had radioed Rick and arranged to have a car waiting for me.*

radioactive /reɪdɪəʊˈæktɪv/. Something that is ADJ QUALIT **radioactive** contains a substance that produces energy in the form of powerful and harmful rays. EG *...radioactive waste.*

radioactivity /reɪdɪəʊækˈtɪvˈtiˈ/ is radioactive N UNCOUNT energy. EG *...a serious leak of radioactivity.*

radiographer /reɪdiˈɒɡrəfə/, **radiographers.** A N COUNT **radiographer** is a person who is trained to take X-rays.

radiography /reɪdiˈɒɡrəfiˈ/ is the process of tak- N UNCOUNT ing X-rays, usually for medical examinations.

radiologist /reɪdiˈɒlədʒɪst/, **radiologists.** A radi- N COUNT **ologist** is a doctor who is trained in radiology.

radiology /reɪdiˈɒlədʒiˈ/ is the branch of medical N UNCOUNT science that uses radioactivity.

radiotherapy /reɪdiəʊˈθerəpiˈ/ is the treatment of N UNCOUNT diseases such as cancer by using radiation.

radish /rædɪʃ/, **radishes.** A **radish** is a small red N COUNT or white root vegetable with a fairly strong taste, which you can eat raw in salads.

radius /reɪdɪəs/, **radii** /reɪdiaɪ/. **1** The **radius** of a N COUNT circle is the distance from its centre to its outside edge.

2 You use **radius** to refer to the distance from a N SING+SUPP particular place that something happens or exists. EG *The missile landed within a half-mile radius of its target.*

raffle /ræfəⁿl/, **raffles.** A **raffle** is a competition N COUNT in which you buy tickets with numbers on them. Afterwards some numbers are chosen, and if your ticket has one of these numbers on it, you win a prize. EG *...organizing a raffle... ...raffle tickets.*

raft /rɑːft/, **rafts.** A **raft** is **1** a floating platform N COUNT made from large pieces of wood tied together. **2** an inflatable rubber or plastic mattress that floats on water.

rafter /rɑːftə/, **rafters. Rafters** are the sloping N COUNT pieces of wood that support a roof.

rag /ræg/, **rags. 1** A **rag** is a piece of old cloth N COUNT OR which you can use to clean or wipe things. EG N UNCOUNT *Wiping his hands on a rag, he went out to the car... ...a crumpled piece of rag.*

2 Rags are old, torn clothes. EG *They were thin and* N PLURAL *hungry, dressed in rags... ...beggars in dirty rags.*

3 People refer to a newspaper as a **rag** when they N COUNT do not have a high opinion of it. EG *...the local rag.* Informal

4 You use **rags to riches** to describe the way in PHRASE which someone quickly becomes very rich after Informal they have been quite poor. EG *...his kind of over-night rags-to-riches story.*

5 If you describe something as **a red rag to a bull,** PHRASE you mean that it is certain to make someone very Informal angry. EG *...a retired colonel to whom anything modern was a red rag to a bull.*

6 See also **ragged.**

rage /reɪdʒ/, **rages, raging, raged. 1 Rage** is N UNCOUNT strong anger that is difficult to control. EG *She was* OR N COUNT *trembling with rage... I stormed out of the room in a rage.*

2 If you **rage** about something, you speak or think V: USU+A, very angrily about it. EG *'How do you mean, you* OR V+QUOTE *can't tell me?' he raged... ...raging at his own weakness.*

3 You say that something powerful or unpleasant V: USU+A

If you are making a racket, are you intending to play tennis?

rages when it continues with great force or violence. EG *There was a monsoon raging outside... The debate raged throughout the whole day.*
◊ **raging**. EG *...the season of bitter cold and raging blizzards.* ◊ ADJ CLASSIF: ATTRIB

4 Raging feelings or desires are very intense and severe. EG *...a raging thirst.* ADJ CLASSIF: ATTRIB

5 When something is popular and fashionable, you can say that it is the **rage**. EG *Jogging and aerobics were all the rage that year.* N SING Informal

ragged /rægɪd/. **1** Someone who is **ragged** is wearing clothes that are old and torn. EG *...a ragged, skinny man of about fifty.* ADJ QUALIT

2 Ragged clothes are old and torn. ADJ QUALIT

3 You can say that something is **ragged** when it is untidy and uneven. EG *They were herded into a ragged line... ...ragged allotments.* ADJ QUALIT

ragtime /rægtaɪm/ is a kind of jazz music that became popular in America in the early 1900s. N UNCOUNT

raid /reɪd/, **raids, raiding, raided. 1** When soldiers **raid** a place, they make a sudden armed attack against it. EG *Blanco's supporters are still raiding villages along the border.* ► used as a noun. EG *Both the bridges were destroyed in bombing raids.* ◊ **raider, raiders**. EG *...a band of raiders.* V+O ► N COUNT ◊ N COUNT

2 If people **raid** a building, they enter it by force, usually in order to steal something. The police might raid a place to look for dangerous criminals or illegal drugs. EG *They shot him and raided his laboratory to seize his papers... Their headquarters in London were raided by the police.* ► used as a noun. EG *...police raids... The gang had carried out a series of bank raids.* ◊ **raider**. EG *It was clear that the raiders had been in the house much longer.* V+O ► N COUNT ◊ N COUNT

rail /reɪl/, **rails. 1** A **rail** is **1.1** a horizontal bar attached to posts or fixed round the edge of something and used as a fence or support. EG *Holding on to the rail with one hand, he pulled himself up.* **1.2** a horizontal bar that you hang things on. EG *...picture rails... ...a towel rail.* N COUNT

2 The steel bars which trains run on are called **rails**. N COUNT

3 If you travel somewhere by **rail**, you travel there in a train. If you send something by **rail**, you send it in a train. EG *I usually go by rail... ...rail travel.* N UNCOUNT

railcard /reɪlkɑːd/, **railcards**. A **railcard** is an identity card that allows people to buy train tickets cheaply. EG *...a Senior Citizens Railcard.* N COUNT

railing /reɪlɪŋ/, **railings**. A **railing** is a fence made from metal bars. EG *I peered through the railings into the courtyard.* N COUNT

railroad /reɪlrəʊd/, **railroads**. A **railroad** is the same as a railway. EG *...railroad tracks.* N COUNT American

railway /reɪlweɪ/, **railways**. A **railway** is **1** a route between two places along which trains travel on steel rails. EG *...the railway to Addis Ababa... ...the early days of railways... ...a railway station.* **2** a company or organization that operates railway routes. EG *...the Western Australian Government Railways.* N COUNT British

British

railway line, railway lines. A **railway line** is a route between two places along which trains travel on steel rails. EG *...the railway line from London to Brighton.* N COUNT

rain /reɪn/, **rains, raining, rained. 1** Rain is water that falls from the clouds in small drops. EG *You can't go home in this rain... A light rain had begun to fall.* N UNCOUNT

2 When rain falls, you can say that it **is raining**. EG *It had started to rain... Is it raining?* V

3 If something **rains** from above, it falls rapidly and in large quantities. EG *Ash rained from the sky.* V+A

rain down. If something **rains down**, it falls rapidly and in large quantities. EG *Mortar shells rained down... ...raining down arrows from both sides.* PHRASAL VB : V-ERG+ADV

rain off. If a sports match **is rained off**, it has to stop, or it is not able to start, because of rain. PHRASAL VB : V-PASS+ADV

rainbow /reɪnbəʊ/, **rainbows**. A **rainbow** is an arch of different colours that you can sometimes see in the sky when it is raining. N COUNT

raincoat /reɪnkəʊt/, **raincoats**. A **raincoat** is a waterproof coat that you wear when it is raining. N COUNT

raindrop /reɪndrɒp/, **raindrops**. A **raindrop** is a single drop of rain. N COUNT

rainfall /reɪnfɔːl/ is the amount of rain that falls in a place during a particular period. EG *...the average monthly rainfall of London.* N UNCOUNT

rainforest /reɪnfɒrɪst/, **rainforests**. A **rainforest** is a thick forest of tall trees which is found in tropical areas where there is a lot of rain. N COUNT OR N UNCOUNT

rainstorm /reɪnstɔːm/, **rainstorms**. A **rainstorm** is a fall of very heavy rain. N COUNT

rainwater /reɪnwɔːtə/ is rain that has been stored in a tank or bucket. N UNCOUNT

rainy /reɪni/. **1** If it is **rainy**, it is raining a lot. EG *Most tropical areas have rainy and dry seasons... ...a rainy Sunday afternoon.* ADJ QUALIT

2 If you say that you are saving something **for a rainy day**, you mean that you are saving it until a time in the future when you might need it. EG *They put part of the money in the bank for a rainy day.* PHRASE

raise /reɪz/, **raises, raising, raised. 1** If you **raise** something, you move it so that it is in a higher position. EG *He tried to raise the window, but the sash cord was broken... Ralph raised a hand for silence.* ● If you **raise** your **eyebrows**, you show surprise by moving your eyebrows upwards. V+O ● PHRASE

2 If you **raise** yourself, you stretch your body so that you are standing up straight, or so that you are no longer lying flat. EG *Slowly she raised herself to her full height.* V-REFL Literary

3 If you **raise** the rate or level of something, you increase it. EG *The maximum speed was raised to seventy miles per hour.* V+O

4 To **raise** the standard of something means to improve it. EG *Putting teachers in day nurseries would raise standards.* V+O

5 If you **raise** your voice, you speak more loudly, usually because you are angry. V+O

6 A **raise** is an increase in your wages or salary. EG *He thought about asking his boss for a raise.* N COUNT American

7 If you **raise** money for a charity or an institution, you get people to give you money for it. V+O

8 If you **raise** money that you need, you manage to get it, for example by selling your property or by borrowing. EG *He raised £300 to finance it.* V+O

9 If someone or something **raises** a particular emotion or memory in you, they cause you to feel it or remember it. EG *For me it always raises fond memories of broad main streets.* V+O

10 Someone who **raises** a child looks after it until it is grown up. EG *It was no place to raise a child.* V+O

11 If someone **raises** a particular type of animal or crop, they breed that type of animal or grow that type of crop. EG *He moved to Petaluma to raise chickens.* V+O

12 If you **raise** a subject, an objection, or a question, you mention it or bring it to someone's attention. EG *You would have to raise that with Mr Gerran personally... The Foreign Office raised no objection... ...questions raised by Senators.* V+O

13 to **raise a finger**: see **finger**.

raised /reɪzd/. A **raised** object or area is higher than the area that surrounds it. EG *He stood on a raised platform.* ADJ CLASSIF

raisin /reɪzⁿn/, **raisins**. **Raisins** are dried grapes. N COUNT

rake /reɪk/, **rakes, raking, raked. 1** A **rake** is a garden tool consisting of a row of metal teeth attached to a long handle. See picture at TOOLS. N COUNT

2 If you **rake** a surface, you move a rake across it in order to make it smooth and level. EG *The field had been raked.* V+O OR V

3 If you **rake** leaves or weeds, you move them somewhere using a rake. EG *Jeremy had raked the fallen leaves into a pile.* V+O+A

4 If you call a man a **rake**, you mean that he is rather immoral, because he has sexual relationships with many women. N COUNT Outdated Literary

rake in. If you say that someone **is raking in** money, you mean that they are earning a lot of it fairly easily. EG *They're raking it in!* PHRASAL VB: V+O+ADV, USU CONT Informal

rake up. If you **rake up** something unpleasant or embarrassing that happened in the past, you talk about it or remind someone about it. EG *Don't go raking up what happened thirteen years ago.* PHRASAL VB: V+O+ADV

rally /ræli¹/, **rallies, rallying, rallied. 1** A **rally** is **1.1** a large public meeting that is held in order to show support for something such as a political party. EG *...a big anti-government rally in Hyde Park.* **1.2** a competition in which vehicles are driven over public roads. EG *...the Monte Carlo Rally.* N COUNT

2 A **rally** in tennis, badminton, or squash is a continuous series of shots that the players exchange without stopping. N COUNT

3 When people **rally** to something, they unite to support it. EG *She believed that the voters would rally to the Conservatives... They made a final effort to rally their supporters.* V-ERG : IF V THEN+A

4 When a sick person **rallies**, he or she begins to become stronger again. V

rally round. When people **rally round**, they work as a group in order to support someone or something at a difficult time. EG *I'm very lucky. Everyone has rallied round... The party rallied round him after his election defeat.* PHRASAL VB: V+ADV/PREP

ram /ræm/, **rams, ramming, rammed. 1** If one vehicle **rams** another, it crashes into it with a lot of force. EG *The ship had been rammed by a British destroyer.* V+O

2 If you **ram** something somewhere, you push it there with great force. EG *I rammed the bolt back across the door... He rammed the tobacco into his pipe.* V+O+A

3 A **ram** is an adult male sheep. N COUNT

4 If something **rams home** a fact or idea, it makes you fully understand it or accept it. EG *The First World War rammed home the same lesson.* PHRASE

ramble /ræmbə⁰l/, **rambles, rambling, rambled. 1** A **ramble** is a long walk in the countryside. EG *We were out on a country ramble.* ▶ used as a verb. EG *...rambling over the Yorkshire hills.* N COUNT ▶ V+A

2 When someone **rambles**, they talk in a confused way. EG *He often rambled and said strange things.* V : NO IMPER

ramble on. You say that someone **rambles on** when they talk for a long time in a confused way. EG *...listening to Miriam as she rambled on.* PHRASAL VB: V+ADV

rambling /ræmblɪŋ/. **1** A **rambling** building has no regular shape and spreads out in many directions. EG *We bought a rambling old house near the village.* ADJ QUALIT

2 Rambling speech or writing is very confused. EG *She wrote me a long rambling letter.* ADJ QUALIT

ramification /ræmɪfɪkeɪʃə⁰n/, **ramifications.** The **ramifications** of a decision, idea, or plan are all the aspects of it that make it more complicated, especially when they are not obvious at first. EG *Not many people actually understand the ramifications of these guidelines.* N COUNT : USU PLURAL+SUPP Formal

ramp /ræmp/, **ramps.** A **ramp** is a sloping surface between two places that are at different levels. EG *It was driven up a ramp and straight on to the train.* N COUNT

rampage /ræmpeɪdʒ/, **rampages, rampaging, rampaged. 1** When people or animals **rampage**, they rush about in a wild or violent way, usually causing damage or destruction. EG *...elephants rampaging through the bush.* V : OFT+A

2 If people **go on the rampage**, they rush about in a wild or violent way. EG *A section of the crowd broke loose and went on the rampage.* PHRASE

rampant /ræmpənt/. If you describe something such as a crime or disease as **rampant**, you mean ADJ QUALIT

that it is growing or spreading in an uncontrolled way. EG *Political apathy is rampant.*

rampart /ræmpɑːt/, **ramparts.** A **rampart** is an earth bank, often with a wall on it, that is built to protect a fort, castle, or city. N COUNT : USU PLURAL Outdated

ramshackle /ræmʃækə⁰l/. A **ramshackle** building is badly made or in bad condition, and likely to fall down. EG *...a ramshackle cottage.* ADJ QUALIT : ATTRIB

ran /ræn/ is the past tense of **run.**

ranch /rɑːntʃ/, **ranches.** A **ranch** is a large farm in the United States, especially one used for raising cattle, sheep, or horses. EG *...cattle ranches.* N COUNT

rancher /rɑːntʃə/, **ranchers.** A **rancher** is someone who owns or manages a ranch. N COUNT

rancid /rænsɪd/. If butter, bacon, or other fatty foods are **rancid**, they have gone bad and taste stale and unpleasant. ADJ QUALIT

rancour /ræŋkə/; spelled **rancor** in American English. **Rancour** is a feeling of deep and bitter hatred. EG *He was shaken by rage and rancour.* N UNCOUNT Formal

random /rændə⁰m/. **1** If you do something in a **random** way, you do it without a definite plan or pattern. EG *The way the books were arranged seemed completely random... This is just a random selection of the complaints we have received.* ADJ QUALIT : USU ATTRIB

◇ **randomly.** EG *Ink had been randomly squirted on the floor and the walls.* ◇ ADV

2 If something is done **at random**, it is done without a definite plan or pattern. EG *He opened the book at random... I let my thoughts come at random.* PHRASE

randy /rændi¹/, **randier, randiest.** Someone who is **randy** is eager to have sexual intercourse. EG *The heat made them both randy.* ADJ QUALIT Informal

rang /ræŋ/ is the past tense of **ring.**

range /reɪndʒ/, **ranges, ranging, ranged. 1** The **range** of something is the maximum area within which it can reach things or detect things. EG *What is the range of their transmitters?... Their tanks stayed just beyond the range of our big guns... ...medium range ballistic missiles.* ● If something is **within range**, it is near enough to be reached or detected. If it is **out of range**, it is too far away to be reached or detected. EG *We managed to keep out of range.* N COUNT+SUPP ● PHRASE

2 If you shoot something **at close range**, you are very close to it when you shoot it. If you shoot something **at a range** of, for example, half a mile, you are half a mile away from it when you shoot it. PHRASE

3 A **range** of things is a number of different things of the same general kind. EG *They were questioned on a range of subjects from politics to astrology... ...a wide range of electrical goods... ...the range of research activities in the university.* N SING+SUPP

4 A **range** is the complete group that is included between two points on a scale of measurement or quality. EG *There are three price ranges... The age range is from six months to forty-seven years.* N COUNT+SUPP

5 When things **range** between two points or **range** from one point to another, they vary within these points on a scale of measurement or quality. EG *Their politics ranged from liberal to radical... They were offered increases ranging from £6.71 to £16.31 a week.* V+A

6 If a piece of writing or speech **ranges** over a group of topics, it includes all those topics. EG *The book ranges historically as far back as the Renaissance... The conversation ranged widely.* V+A

7 If you **range** people or things somewhere, you arrange them in a line or in lines. EG *Books were ranged on shelves on the walls.* V+O+A Formal

8 A **range** of mountains or hills is a line of mountains or hills. EG *...a splendid mountain range.* N COUNT+SUPP

9 A rifle **range** or a firing **range** is a place where people can practise shooting at targets. N COUNT : USU+SUPP

Would you like to live in a ramshackle building?

ranger /reɪndʒə/, **rangers.** A **ranger** is a person N COUNT whose job is to look after a forest or park. EG ...*the head ranger of a vast national park.*

rank /ræŋk/, **ranks, ranking, ranked. 1** Some- N COUNT OR one's **rank** is the position or grade that they have N UNCOUNT in an organization. EG *A prisoner of war must only reveal his name, rank, and number... She achieved the rank of professor at the age of 31... He wasn't getting the salary to which he was entitled by rank.*
● If someone **pulls rank**, they make unfair use of ● PHRASE the authority that they have in an organization. EG *She usually gets her way without needing to pull rank.*
2 When you say what something **ranks**, you say V-ERG+A : what position it has on a scale. EG *The island ranks* NO CONT *as one of the poorest of the whole region... Philips was ranked third in size among the industrial corporations.*
3 The **ranks** are the ordinary members of an N PLURAL : organization, especially of the armed forces. EG ...*a* the+N *senior officer who had risen from the ranks.*
4 When you become a member of a large group of N PLURAL people, you can say that you are joining its **ranks**. +SUPP EG ...*the growing ranks of the unemployed.*
5 When the members of a group **close ranks**, they PHRASE support each other in a united way and oppose any attack or criticism.
6 Your **rank** is the social class that you belong to. N COUNT OR EG ...*people from the upper and middle ranks of* N UNCOUNT *society... We cater for everyone, regardless of age* Outdated *or social rank.*
7 A **rank** is also a row of people or things. EG *Ralph* N COUNT : *examined the ranks of boys.* USU PLURAL
8 You use **rank** to describe a bad or undesirable ADJ CLASSIF : quality that exists in an extreme form. EG ...*rank* ATTRIB *corruption... ...rank favouritism.*
9 You can describe something as **rank** when it has ADJ QUALIT a strong and unpleasant smell.

rank and file. The **rank and file** are the ordi- N COLL : SING , nary members of an organization as opposed to the the+N leaders or officers. EG *There are now considerable political differences between the leadership and the rank and file.*

rankle /ræŋkəˀl/, **rankles, rankling, rankled.** V Something that **rankles** makes you feel angry or bitter. EG *The argument with Sam earlier on still rankled.*

ransack /rænsæk/, **ransacks, ransacking, ran-** V+O **sacked.** If you **ransack** a building or a room, you disturb everything in it and leave it in a mess, because you are looking for something. EG *Detectives ransacked the house.*

ransom /rænsəˀm/, **ransoms. 1** A **ransom** is an N COUNT amount of money that you must pay in order to set free a person who has been kidnapped. EG *The family paid a ransom of £50,000 for the child's release.*
2 If someone **holds** you **to ransom**, **2.1** they keep PHRASE you as a prisoner until money is paid for you to be set free. EG *The minister's daughter was held to ransom.* **2.2** they put you in a position in which you are forced to agree to unreasonable demands. EG *She accused them of holding the nation to ransom.*

rant /rænt/, **rants, ranting, ranted.** You say that V : USU+A someone **rants** when they talk in a loud, excited, and angry way. EG *He would rant like this till she could not bear it any more.* ◊ **ranting, rantings.** ◊ N COUNT EG ...*the rantings and ravings of these lunatics.*

rap /ræp/, **raps, rapping, rapped. 1** If you **rap** on V+A OR V+O+ something or if you **rap** it, you hit it with a series of A quick blows. EG *He rapped on the table and called for silence.*
2 A **rap** is a quick hit or knock against something. N COUNT EG *A light rap sounded at the door.*
3 If you receive a **rap over the knuckles**, you PHRASE receive a warning or criticism.
4 If you **take the rap**, you are blamed or punished PHRASE for something, even if it is not your fault. EG *Lloyd* Informal *will have to take the rap.*

rap out. If you **rap out** an order or a question, PHRASAL VB : you say it quickly and sharply. EG *'Is that the truth?'* V+ADV+O OR *he suddenly rapped out.* V+ADV+ QUOTE

rapacious /rəpeɪʃəs/. Someone who is **rapacious** ADJ QUALIT is extremely greedy for money. EG ...*rapacious* Formal *businessmen.*

rape /reɪp/, **rapes, raping, raped. 1** When a man V+O **rapes** a woman, he violently forces her to have sex with him when she does not want to. EG ...*an organization to help women who have been raped.*
▸ used as a noun. EG *She had to testify to his* ▸ N UNCOUNT *attempts at rape... ...a rape victim.* OR N COUNT
2 The **rape** of the countryside or the earth is the N SING+of destruction or spoiling of it. EG ...*the rape of their* Formal *beautiful landscape by developers.*

rapid /ræpɪd/, **rapids. 1** Something that is **rapid**
1.1 happens very fast. EG ...*a time of rapid economic* ADJ QUALIT *growth... ...the rapid development of British indus-* *try.* ◊ **rapidly.** EG *The situation had rapidly* ◊ ADV *deteriorated.* ◊ **rapidity** /rəpɪdɪˀtiˀ/. EG *The film* ◊ N UNCOUNT *shows the rapidity of the changes in this area of medicine.* **1.2** moves with great speed. EG *He took a* ADJ QUALIT *few rapid steps towards the beach.* ◊ **rapidly.** EG ◊ ADV *They walked rapidly past the churchyard.*
2 Rapids are parts of a river where the water N PLURAL moves very fast, often over rocks. EG *Further down the river there is another stretch of rapids.*

rapist /reɪpɪst/, **rapists.** A **rapist** is a man who N COUNT has raped a woman.

rapport /ræpɔː/. If people have a **rapport** with N UNCOUNT each other, they have a relationship in which they are able to understand each other very well. EG *There is insufficient rapport between hospitals and family doctors.*

rapt /ræpt/. Someone who is **rapt** is so interested ADJ QUALIT or fascinated by something that they cannot stop looking at it or cannot think about anything else. EG *Claud was staring at me, rapt... My audience lis-tened in rapt silence.*

rapture /ræptʃə/, **raptures. 1 Rapture** is is an N UNCOUNT overpowering feeling of delight. EG ...*his face shin-* OR N PLURAL *ing with rapture... ...the first raptures of their* Literary *honeymoon.*
2 If you **go into raptures** about something, you PHRASE express strong enthusiasm for it. EG *I had gone into raptures over the country I had been through.*

rapturous /ræptʃərəs/. A **rapturous** feeling or ADJ QUALIT reaction is one which in which you feel very great Literary happiness or enthusiasm. EG *They went out to a rapturous reception from their supporters.*

rare /reə/, **rarer, rarest. 1** Something that is ADJ QUALIT **rare 1.1** is not common and is therefore interest-ing or valuable. EG *These wild flowers are so rare that I want to do whatever I can to save them... Diane's hobby is collecting rare books.* **1.2** does not happen very often. EG *Cases of smallpox are ex-tremely rare... It's rare to come across any book which makes you laugh out loud.*
2 You use **rare** to describe an extremely good or ADJ QUALIT : remarkable quality. EG ...*her rare gift for comedy.* ATTRIB
3 Meat that is **rare** is cooked very lightly so that ADJ QUALIT the inside is still red.
4 See also **rarely, rarity.**

rarefied /reərɪfaɪd/; also spelled **rarified.** You ADJ QUALIT : use **rarefied** to describe people or things that USU ATTRIB seem not to be connected with ordinary life, be-cause of their high social or academic standards; used showing disapproval. EG ...*the rather rarefied atmosphere of university life... ...the rarefied world of the very rich.*

rarely /reəliˀ/ means not very often. EG *We very* ADV BRD NEG *rarely quarrel... I'd rarely seen a man look so unhappy... Rarely has so much time been wasted by so many people.*

rarity /reərɪˀtiˀ/, **rarities. 1** A **rarity** is some- N COUNT thing that is interesting or valuable because it is so unusual. EG *Bat twins are a rarity... ...six bags of gold coins, many of which were rarities.*
2 The **rarity** of something is the fact that it is very N UNCOUNT

uncommon. EG *Many animals are endangered by their rarity and beauty.*

rascal /rɑːskəl/, **rascals.** If you refer to a man or N COUNT a child as a **rascal**, you mean that he or she does Outdated bad or dishonest things.

rash /ræʃ/, **rashes. 1** Someone who is **rash** does ADJ QUALIT foolish things, because they act without thinking carefully first. EG *Don't be rash... Don't do anything rash... Some rash promises were made.* ◊ **rashly.** ◊ ADV EG *I'm not a man who does things rashly.*

2 A **rash** is an area of red spots that appear on N COUNT your skin when you are ill or have an allergy. EG *...a man with a rash on one side of his neck.*

3 A **rash** of events is a large number of them that N PART all happen in a short period of time. EG *A rash of robberies had suddenly struck the country.*

rasher /ræʃə/, **rashers.** A **rasher** of bacon is a N COUNT thin slice of it.

rasp /rɑːsp/, **rasps, rasping, rasped.** To **rasp** V OR V+QUOTE means to make a harsh unpleasant sound. EG *Crickets rasped loudly... 'It's frightful,' she rasped.*
▸ used as a noun. EG *...the rasp of sandpaper on* ▸ N SING *wood.* ◊ **rasping.** EG *...a dry rasping voice.* ◊ ADJ QUALIT

raspberry /rɑːzbəˈriː/, **raspberries. 1** A **rasp-** N COUNT **berry** is a small, soft, red fruit that grows on bushes. EG *...raspberry jam.*

2 If you blow a **raspberry**, you make an insulting N COUNT sound by putting your tongue out and blowing. EG *He blew a loud and lengthy raspberry.*

rat /ræt/, **rats. 1** A **rat** is an animal with a long tail N COUNT which looks like a large mouse.

2 If you call someone a **rat**, you mean that you are N COUNT angry with them or dislike them because they have Informal deceived you or done something unpleasant. EG *Oh, you rat... They're all rats in our business.*

rate /reɪt/, **rates, rating, rated. 1** The **rate** at which something happens is **1.1** the speed at which N COUNT+SUPP it happens over a period of time. EG *...the rapid rate of change which the industrial world is facing... ...an 8% inflation rate.* **1.2** the number of times that N COUNT+SUPP it happens during a period of time. EG *The divorce rate is fantastically high... ...a rising rate of unemployment.*

2 The **rate** of taxation or interest is its level, N COUNT : expressed as a percentage. EG *This money is taxed* USU+SUPP *at the rate of 59%... ...a good rate of interest.*

3 If you say that **at this rate** something will PHRASE happen, you mean that it will happen if things continue to develop as they have been developing. EG *At this rate we'll be millionaires by Christmas!*

4 You use **at any rate 4.1** to indicate that what ADV SEN you have just said might be exaggerated or too general, and that you want to be more precise. EG *They felt, or at any rate Dan felt, both relieved and frightened.* **4.2** to indicate that the important thing is what you are going to say now and not what has just been said. EG *I don't think there's been an edition since 1977; at any rate that's the one I'll be referring to.*

5 Rates are a local tax in Britain which has to be N PLURAL paid by people who own buildings or rent unfurnished buildings. EG *They find it hard to pay their rates... For a while fares in London were subsidised by the rates.*

6 You use **rate** to talk about people's opinion of V+O+A, V+A, someone or something. For example, if someone is V+O+C, **rated** as brilliant, people consider them to be OR V+C : brilliant. If you **rate** something as good, you consid- NO CONT er it to be good. EG *She was a self-taught geologist, rated as one of the best... Leontiev rated socialism highly... He was rated a successful man... She rated herself below average.*

7 If you **rate** something, you deserve it. EG *Who was* V+O : NO CONT *this man who rated such a long obituary in the Times?*

8 See also **rating**.

ratepayer /reɪtpeɪə/, **ratepayers.** In Britain, a N COUNT **ratepayer** is a person who has to pay rates.

rather /rɑːðə/. **1** You use **rather** to say that ADV OR SUBMOD something is the case to a slight extent or to quite a large extent. EG *I'm rather puzzled by this question... He looked rather pathetic standing in the rain outside... The company thought I did rather well... I rather think it was fifty pounds... I'm in rather a hurry. I've got to go.*

2 If you say that you **would rather** do a particular PHRASE thing, you mean that you would prefer to do that thing. If you **would rather** someone did a particular thing, you would prefer them to do that thing. EG *He'd rather be out playing golf... 'What was all that about?' – 'I'm sorry, I'd rather not say.'... Would you rather she came to see me?*

3 You use **rather than** to say what someone does PREP OR CONJ not do, in contrast to what they actually do. EG *I have used familiar English names rather than scientific Latin ones... She likes to keep things rather than throw them away.*

4 You also use **rather 4.1** to introduce a correction ADV SEN to something that you have said. EG *Suddenly there stood before him, or rather above him, a gigantic woman.* **4.2** when stating what you think is true, after you have stated what you think is not true. EG *This was no matter for congratulation, but rather a matter for vengeance.*

ratify /rætɪfaɪ/, **ratifies, ratifying, ratified.** V+O When people **ratify** a written agreement or docu- Formal ment, they give their formal approval to it, usually by signing it. EG *Over 90 countries ratified an agreement to ban the use of these chemicals.* ◊ **ratification** /rætɪfɪkeɪʃəⁿn/. EG *Opposition objec-* ◊ N UNCOUNT *tions prevented ratification of the proposals.*

rating /reɪtɪŋ/, **ratings. 1** A **rating** is a score or N COUNT : assessment based on how much of a particular USU+SUPP quality something has. EG *...jobs which are assigned a low rating on the economic scale.*

2 The **ratings** are the statistics published each N PLURAL week which show how popular each television programme is. EG *The ratings are a disaster and the reviews are worse.*

ratio /reɪʃɪəʊ/, **ratios.** A **ratio** is a relationship N COUNT : between two numbers, amounts, or measurements, USU+SUPP which shows how much greater one is than the other. For example, if there are two boys and six girls in a room, the ratio of boys to girls is one to three. EG *...a high teacher/pupil ratio... ...a ratio of one tutor to five students.*

ration /ræʃəⁿn/, **rations, rationing, rationed. 1** N COUNT When something is scarce, your **ration** of it is the amount that you are allowed to have. EG *...a 20 percent reduction in monthly meat rations.*

2 When something is **rationed**, you are only V+O : USU PASS allowed to have a limited amount of it, usually because there is a shortage. EG *Meat, flour and sugar were all rationed.* ◊ **rationing.** EG *...food and* ◊ N UNCOUNT *petrol rationing during the war.*

3 Rations are the food which is supplied to a N PLURAL soldier or a member of an expedition each day. EG *They had two days' rations and a couple of tents.*

rational /ræʃəⁿnəl, -ʃənⁿl/. Someone who is **ra-** ADJ QUALIT **tional** is able to make decisions and judgements that are based on reason rather than on emotion. EG *Let's talk about this like two rational people... Panic destroys rational thought.* ◊ **rationally.** EG ◊ ADV *Let's discuss this rationally.* ◊ **rationality** ◊ N UNCOUNT /ræʃənælɪˈtiː/. EG *The debate soon lost all semblance of rationality.*

rationale /ræʃənɑːl/. The **rationale** for a course N SING : of action, practice, or belief is the set of reasons on OFT+for/of which it is based. EG *We discussed the rationale for taking city kids into the country.*

rationalism /ræʃəⁿnəlɪzⁿm/ is the belief that N UNCOUNT your life should be based on reason and not on emotions or religious beliefs. ◊ **rationalist** ◊ N COUNT

Is the rat race a race between rats?

/ræʃəⁿnəlɪst/, **rationalists.** EG *Lavrov was a thorough rationalist.*

rationalize /ræʃəⁿnəlaɪz/, **rationalizes, rationalizing, rationalized;** also spelled **rationalise.** 1 If you **rationalize** something that you are unhappy or unsure about, you think of reasons to justify it or explain it. EG *I rationalise my decision by saying that I need the money.* ◇ **rationalization** /ræʃəⁿnəlaɪzeɪʃəⁿn/, **rationalizations.** EG *They devise elaborate rationalizations for their behaviour.* ◇ N COUNT OR N UNCOUNT

2 When a company, system, or industry **is rationalized**, it is made more efficient, especially by getting rid of staff and equipment that are not needed. EG *Society and industry had been rationalized and modernized.* ◇ **rationalization.** EG *...the continuing rationalization of the armed forces.* ◇ N UNCOUNT V+O

rat race. If you refer to a type of work or way of life as a **rat race**, you mean that the people in it are all competing fiercely with each other. EG *I was determined to get out of the rat race.* N SING : USU the+N

rattle /rætəⁿl/, **rattles, rattling, rattled.** 1 When something **rattles** or when you **rattle** it, it makes a series of short, regular knocking sounds because it is being shaken or it is hitting against something hard. EG *A cold November wind rattled the windows... The chains of playground swings rattled in the dark.* ► used as a noun. EG *The rattle of the engine became louder.* V-ERG ► N COUNT

2 A **rattle** is a baby's toy with loose bits inside which make a noise when the baby shakes it. N COUNT

3 If something **rattles** you, it makes you worried or annoyed. EG *It was an attempt to get him rattled... His questions obviously rattled her.* V+O

rattle off. If you **rattle** something **off**, you say it or do it very quickly and without much effort. EG *She rattled off a few names that I tried to write down... ...a machine capable of rattling off thousands of calculations in a few minutes.* PHRASAL VB : V+O+ADV

rattle on. When someone **rattles on** about something, they talk about it for a long time in a way that annoys you. EG *Some of the women would rattle on about sex.* PHRASAL VB : V+ADV, OFT+about

rattle through. If you **rattle through** something, you deal with it quickly in order to finish it. EG *They rattled through the rest of the meeting.* PHRASAL VB : V+PREP, HAS PASS

rattlesnake /rætəⁿlsneɪk/, **rattlesnakes.** A **rattlesnake** is a poisonous American snake. N COUNT

ratty /ræti¹/, **rattier, rattiest.** If someone is **ratty**, they are very irritable. EG *All right, don't get ratty... The pain makes you ratty.* ADJ QUALIT British Informal

raucous /rɔːkəs/. You describe someone's voice as **raucous** when it is loud and rough. EG *...the sound of her raucous voice... ...raucous laughter.* ADJ QUALIT

ravage /rævɪdʒ/, **ravages, ravaging, ravaged.** 1 To **ravage** something means to harm it or damage it so much that it is almost destroyed. EG *...the diseases which ravage Aboriginal populations... ...a country ravaged by war.* V+O

2 The **ravages** of the weather, time, or war are the damaging effects that it has. EG *...the ravages of rain and sun.* N PLURAL : USU+of

rave /reɪv/, **raves, raving, raved.** 1 If someone **raves**, they talk in an excited and uncontrolled way because they are very angry. EG *He sat and raved at me for half an hour... He started raving about the horror and brutality of war.* V : OFT+A

2 If you **rave** about something, you speak or write about it with great enthusiasm. EG *One newspaper raved: 'the most exciting play I have ever seen.'... People were raving about his fantastic course.* V+about OR V+QUOTE Informal

3 When someone writes a **rave** notice or review, they praise something such as a play or book in a very enthusiastic way. EG *Stoppard's new play has received rave reviews.* N COUNT Informal

4 When people **rave it up**, they enjoy themselves in a lively way, for example by drinking and dancing a lot at a party. EG *...a huge crowd raving it up in Trafalgar Square.* ● See also **rave-up.** PHRASE Informal

5 See also **raving.**

raven /reɪvəⁿn/, **ravens.** 1 A **raven** is a large bird with shiny black feathers and a deep harsh call. N COUNT

2 **Raven** hair is a shiny black colour. EG *...a raven-haired girl.* ADJ COLOUR : ATTRIB

ravenous /rævənəs/. If you are **ravenous**, you are very hungry indeed. EG *By that time I was ravenous... Most infants have a ravenous appetite.* ADJ QUALIT

◇ **ravenously.** EG *I was ravenously hungry.* ◇ ADV

rave-up, rave-ups. A **rave-up** is a very lively party. EG *We are looking for more friends to have a rave-up with tonight.* N COUNT British Informal

ravine /rəviːn/, **ravines.** A **ravine** is a very deep narrow valley with steep sides. N COUNT

raving /reɪvɪŋ/, **ravings.** 1 If you say that someone is **raving**, you mean that they are mad. EG *You're all raving lunatics... He went raving mad.* ADJ CLASSIF : ATTRIB, OR ADV+ADJ Informal

2 If you refer to the things that someone says or writes as their **ravings**, you mean that they are talking or writing like a mad person. EG *...the ravings of an obsessed anarchist.* N PLURAL

ravish /rævɪʃ/, **ravishes, ravishing, ravished.** If you **are ravished** by something, it gives you great pleasure and delight, because it is very beautiful. EG *He was ravished by the beauty of the language.* V+O : OFT PASS Literary

ravishing /rævɪʃɪŋ/. Someone or something that is **ravishing** is very beautiful. EG *I'd forgotten how ravishing you looked... ...a ravishing blonde.* ADJ QUALIT

raw /rɔː/. 1 Food that is **raw** is not cooked. EG *...a piece of raw meat... ...a raw carrot.* ADJ CLASSIF

2 A **raw** substance is in its natural state before being used in a manufacturing process. EG *...exports of raw cotton... ...raw rubber from Malaysia.* ADJ CLASSIF : ATTRIB

3 If a part of your body is **raw**, the skin has come off or been burnt, so it is sore. EG *Every boy's feet had big raw blisters on them.* ADJ QUALIT

4 If you describe someone as **raw**, you mean that they are too young or too new in a job to know how to behave properly. EG *He's just a raw kid... ...raw newcomers.* ADJ QUALIT

5 **Raw** weather is unpleasantly cold and wet. EG *...a raw day in Sunderland.* ADJ QUALIT

6 If you say that you have been given **a raw deal**, you mean that you have been treated unfairly. EG *He thinks he's got a raw deal from life.* PHRASE Informal

raw material, raw materials. 1 **Raw materials** are the natural substances that are used in making something, for example in an industrial process. EG *...coal, oil, gas, and other raw materials.* N COUNT OR N UNCOUNT

2 If you describe something as **raw material** for a particular thing, you mean that you can make this thing from it. EG *She makes use of people she meets as raw material for her fiction.* N UNCOUNT : USU+SUPP

ray /reɪ/, **rays.** 1 A **ray** is a beam of heat or light. EG *...the rays of the sun... ...ultraviolet rays.* N COUNT : USU PLURAL+SUPP

2 A **ray** of hope or comfort is a small amount of it that makes a bad situation seem less bad. EG *She let a ray of originality into his life.* N PART

rayon /reɪɒn/ is a smooth fabric made from cotton, wool, or synthetic fibres. N UNCOUNT

raze /reɪz/, **razes, razing, razed.** If people **raze** building, town, or forest, they completely destroy it. EG *Many villages were razed to the ground.* V+O

razor /reɪzə/, **razors.** A **razor** is a tool that people use for shaving. EG *...an electric razor.* N COUNT

razor blade, razor blades. A **razor blade** is a small, thin, flat piece of metal with a very sharp edge, that you fasten to a razor and use for shaving. N COUNT

Rd is a written abbreviation for 'road'. EG *49 St Johns Rd.*

-rd. You add **-rd** to most numbers written in figures and ending in 3 in order to form ordinal numbers. 3rd is pronounced the same as 'third'. EG *...3rd November 1972... ...23rd Street... ...the 143rd Psalm.* SUFFIX

re- is used to form verbs and nouns that refer to the repeating of an action or process. For example, to re-read something means to read it again, and to re-marry means to marry again. EG *He re-lit his* PREFIX pipe... ...*the re-introduction of an incomes policy by the government.*

-'re is a shortened form of 'are'. In spoken English it is added to the end of the pronoun or noun which is the subject of the verb. For example, 'we are' can be shortened to 'we're'. EG *You're quite right... They're lovely... What're you waiting for?*

reach /riːtʃ/, **reaches, reaching, reached.** 1 v+o When you **reach** a place, you arrive there. EG *It was dark by the time I reached their house... It took three days for the letter to reach me.*

2 If you **reach** in a particular direction, you stretch v+a or out your arm in order to do something or to get v+o+a something. EG *He reached into his inside pocket and produced a pen... She reached across the desk and shook my hand... I reached out my hand to touch him.*

3 If you say that you can **reach** something, you v+o mean that you can touch it by stretching out your arm and hand. EG *I can't reach that shelf unless I stand on a chair.*

4 You can say that you **reach** someone when you v+o succeed in contacting them by telephone. EG *I tried to reach you at home several times... Where can I reach you?*

5 If something **reaches** a place, point or level, it v+o or v+a extends as far as that place, point, or level. EG *When the water reached his waist, he had to start swimming... She wore a long blue skirt reaching down to the ground... Rumours of an enemy invasion began to reach the capital.*

6 If someone or something **reaches** a particular v+o stage, condition, or level, they get to it. EG *Unemployment has reached a very high level... Kangaroos can reach speeds of 60 kph... Most children stay at home until they reach school age.*

7 When people **reach** an agreement, decision, or v+o result, they succeed in achieving it. EG *They managed to reach an agreement on rates of pay.*

8 If something is within **reach**, you can touch it by N UNCOUNT stretching out your arm and hand. If it is **beyond** +SUPP your **reach** or **out of reach**, you cannot touch it. EG *Keep all medicines out of reach of children.*

9 If a place is within **reach**, you can get there. EG N UNCOUNT *The flat is within easy reach of the shops.* +SUPP

10 If you refer to the upper or lower **reaches** of a N PLURAL place, you are referring to the upper or lower parts +SUPP of it. EG *...the upper reaches of the Amazon... ...the most inaccessible reaches of the jungle.*

react /riˈækt/, **reacts, reacting, reacted.** 1 v : OFT+*to* When you **react** to something that has happened to you, you behave in a particular way because of it. EG *She tends to react strongly if he lights a cigarette... I wondered how he'd react to such a blunt question.*

2 If you **react** against the way other people v+*against* behave, you deliberately behave in a different way. EG *They reacted against the formality of their predecessors.*

3 When someone **reacts** to a drug, they are made v : OFT+*to* ill by it.

4 When one chemical substance **reacts** with an- v or v+*with* : other, it combines with it chemically to form RECIP another substance.

reaction /riˈækʃ⁰n/, **reactions.** 1 Your **reaction** N COUNT OR to something is what you feel, say, or do because of N UNCOUNT it. EG *My immediate reaction was one of revulsion...* +SUPP *What was the reaction to these proposals?*

2 A **reaction** against something is a way of behav- N COUNT+ ing or doing something that is deliberately differ- *against* ent from what has been done before. EG *My work has never been a reaction against Abstract Expressionism.*

3 A **reaction** against something that is popular or N COUNT+ accepted is a change of public opinion in which it *against* becomes unpopular. EG *This led to a reaction against public expenditure.*

4 You refer to your ability to move quickly in N PLURAL response to something, for example when you are

in danger, as your **reactions**. EG *...a computer game designed to time their reactions.*

5 **Reaction** is the belief that the political or social N UNCOUNT system of your country should not change; used Formal showing disapproval. EG *Once again the forces of reaction prevailed.*

6 A chemical **reaction** is a process in which two N COUNT substances combine together chemically to form another substance.

reactionary /riˈækʃ⁰n⁰riˈ/, **reactionaries.** ADJ QUALIT Someone who is **reactionary** tries to prevent changes in the political or social system of their country; used showing disapproval. EG *...reactionary forces.* ▸ used as a noun. EG *...political reaction-* ▸ N COUNT *aries.*

reactor /riˈæktə/, **reactors.** A **reactor** is the N COUNT same as a nuclear reactor. EG *They are making the reactors as safe as they possibly can.*

read, reads, reading. Read is used in the present tense, when it is pronounced /riːd/, and is also the past tense and past participle, when it is pronounced /red/.

1 When you **read** or when you **read** something written, 1.1 you look at written words or symbols v+o or v : on a page and understand them. EG *Have you read* usu+a *that article?... I remember reading about it in the paper... I have never been able to read music.* 1.2 v+o or v+*to* you say aloud the words that are written. EG *Shall I read to you?*

2 If you **read between the lines**, you understand PHRASE what someone really means, even though they do not say it openly. EG *Reading between the lines it is easy to see that she was desperately unhappy.*

3 If you say that a book or magazine is **a good** PHRASE **read**, you mean that it is very enjoyable to read.

4 If you refer to how a piece of writing **reads**, you v+a are referring to its style. EG *It read like a translation from the Latin.*

5 You can use **read** when saying what is written on v+c something or in something. For example, if a notice **reads** 'Exit', the word 'Exit' is written on it.

6 If you can **read** someone's moods or mind, you v+o can judge how they are feeling or what they are thinking. EG *He so often reads my thoughts.*

7 When you **read** a meter or gauge, you look at it v+o and record the figure on it.

8 If a measuring device **reads** a particular amount, v+c it shows that amount. EG *The thermometers are reading 108 degrees in the shade.*

9 If you **read** a subject at university, you study it. v+o EG *He went up to Oxford to read history.*

10 See also **reading**.

read into. If you **read** a meaning **into** some- PHRASAL VB : thing, you think it is there although it may not v+o+PREP actually be there. EG *Some people read sex into the most innocent story.*

read out. If you **read** a piece of writing **out**, you PHRASAL VB : say it aloud. EG *Could you just read out this next* v+o+ADV *paragraph?*

read up on. If you **read up on** a subject, you PHRASAL VB : read a lot about it so that you become informed on v+ADV+PREP it. EG *You can read up on the theory later.*

readable /riːdəb⁰l/. If you say that a book or ADJ QUALIT article is **readable**, you mean that it is interesting and worth reading. EG *It's a very readable book.*

reader /riːdə/, **readers.** A **reader** of a book, N COUNT : newspaper, or magazine is a person who reads it. OFT+SUPP EG *All of them were keen readers of detective stories... The paper is gathering one thousand new readers a week.*

readership /riːdəʃɪp/. The **readership** of a book, N SING+SUPP newspaper, or magazine is all the people who read it. EG *...a readership of about ten million people.*

readily /redɪliˈ/. 1 If you do something **readily**, ADV you do it in a way which shows that you are very

What two ways can 'read' be pronounced?

willing to do it. EG *He readily accepted an invitation to dinner.*

2 You also use **readily** to say that something can be done or obtained quickly and easily. For example, if you say that something can be readily understood, you mean that people can understand it quickly and easily. EG *Personal computers are readily available these days.* ADV

readiness /rɛdɪnɪ²s/. **1 Readiness** is the state of being prepared for something. EG *He faces it with calm readiness and resolute determination.* N UNCOUNT

2 Your **readiness** to do something is your willingness or eagerness to do it. EG *I restated our readiness to resume negotiations.* N UNCOUNT +to-INF

reading /riːdɪŋ/, **readings**. **1 Reading** is the activity of reading books. EG *I don't do a lot of reading.* N UNCOUNT

2 A **reading** is a text that is read aloud to an audience, for example in church. EG *We all said 'Amen!' when the readings were done.* N COUNT

3 A poetry **reading** is an entertainment in which poetry is read to an audience. N COUNT+SUPP

4 The **reading** on a meter or gauge is the figure or measurement that it shows. N COUNT

readjust /riːədʒʌst/, **readjusts, readjusting, readjusted. 1** If you **readjust** or **readjust** yourself, you adapt to a new situation. EG *It is difficult to readjust to changing environments.* V OR V-REFL : OFT+to

◊ **readjustment** /riːədʒʌstmə²nt/, **readjustments.** EG *...a period of readjustment.* ◊ N UNCOUNT OR N COUNT

2 If you **readjust** something, you alter it so that it is in a better position. EG *He readjusted the saddle before getting on... ...peering through a microscope, continually readjusting the focus.* V+O

ready /rɛdɪ¹/, **readies, readying, readied. 1** If someone or something is **ready**, they have prepared themselves or have been prepared for something, or they now have the right qualities for something. EG *We were getting ready for bed... By eight she was ready to leave... You're nowhere near ready for such a job... Lunch is ready... Their crops would soon be ready for harvesting.* ADJ PRED : OFT+for OR to-INF

2 If you are **ready** to do something, you are willing to do it. EG *...couples who are ready to move house in order to get work.* ADJ PRED +to-INF

3 If you are **ready** for something, you need it or want it. EG *We were all ready for sleep.* ADJ PRED+for

4 If something is **ready** to do something, it is about to do it or likely to do it. EG *...an over-ripe plum, ready to fall... I was ready to cry.* ADJ PRED +to-INF

5 You use **ready** to describe things that are able to appear or be used very quickly and easily. EG *He had a ready, engaging smile... ...ready cash.* ADJ CLASSIF : ATTRIB

6 When you **ready** something, you prepare it for a particular purpose. EG *The satellite would be readied with all possible haste... Standard Oil are readying themselves for a monumental struggle.* V+O OR V-REFL Formal

7 See also **readily, readiness.**

ready-made. 1 If something that you buy is **ready-made**, you can use it immediately. EG *...ready-made products such as baked beans... You can buy your greenhouse ready-made.* ADJ CLASSIF : ATTRIB OR ADV

2 If you have a **ready-made** reply to a question, you can answer it immediately. EG *He had no ready-made answers.* ADJ CLASSIF

reaffirm /riːəfɜːm/, **reaffirms, reaffirming, reaffirmed.** If you **reaffirm** something, you state it again. EG *The ministers reaffirmed their intention not to surrender.* V+O OR V+REPORT Formal

real /rɪəl/. **1** Something that is **real 1.1** actually exists and is not imagined, invented, or theoretical. EG *You must know the difference between what's real and make-believe... ...real or imagined feelings of inferiority.* **1.2** is natural or traditional, and not artificial or an imitation. EG *...real leather... ...fancy chocolates, with real liqueurs inside.* ADJ CLASSIF

2 You also use **real** to say that something **2.1** has all the characteristics or qualities that such a thing typically has. EG *...the only real accident that I've* ADJ CLASSIF : ATTRIB

ever had... I used to tell him he wasn't a real Christian. **2.2** is the true or original thing of its kind, in contrast to one that people may wrongly believe to be true. EG *That is the real reason for the muddle... My real home is in Tshabo.*

3 If you say that a thing or event is **the real thing**, you mean that it is the actual thing or event, and not an imitation or rehearsal. EG *'You're being recorded now.' – 'Is this the real thing?'* PHRASE

4 You can use **real** to emphasize that something exists, especially something unpleasant. EG *The threat of attack was a very real one... Everyone knew that Ray had no real chance of winning.* ADJ QUALIT

5 If you say that something is **for real**, you mean that it is actually happening or being done. EG *It was done. I was on my own. For real.* PHRASE Informal

6 You use **in real terms** when you are talking about the actual value or cost of something. For example, if your salary rises by 5% but prices rise by 10% in the same period, you can say that **in real terms** your salary has fallen. EG *Government spending this year is 12% up in real terms.* PHRASE

7 Real is sometimes used instead of 'very'. EG *I was getting some real good stories... You and I must have lunch together real soon.* SUBMOD American

8 See also **really.**

real estate is property in the form of buildings and land. EG *He acquired a bit of real estate... ...real estate agents.* N UNCOUNT American

realise /rɪəlaɪz/. See **realize.**

realism /rɪəlɪzə⁰m/. **1** When people show **realism** in their behaviour, they recognize and accept the true nature of a situation and try to deal with it in a practical way. EG *He marvelled at his father's lack of realism... There is a new mood of realism in Britain... ...economic realism.* N UNCOUNT

2 In painting, novels, and films, **realism** is the representing of things and people in a way that is like real life. EG *...the awesome realism of Aztec sculptures... Extraordinary degrees of realism are reached in the film.* N UNCOUNT

realist /rɪəlɪst/, **realists.** A **realist** is someone who recognizes and accepts the true nature of a situation and tries to deal with it in a practical way. EG *I am a realist and know that all this cannot last.* N COUNT

realistic /rɪəlɪstɪk/. **1** If you are **realistic** about a situation, you recognize and accept its true nature and try to deal with it in a practical way. EG *They were more realistic about its long term commercial prospects... ...a realistic attempt to solve problems.* ◊ **realistically.** EG *She accepted the position realistically... ...looking at it realistically.* ADJ QUALIT ◊ ADV

2 You say that a painting, story, or film is **realistic** when the people and things in it are like people and things in real life. EG *...a 19th century realistic novel... ...would make any new film surprisingly realistic.* ADJ QUALIT

reality /rɪ¹ælɪ¹ti¹/, **realities. 1 Reality** is the real nature of everything, rather than the way someone imagines it to be. EG *He is out of touch with reality... She had never seemed able to face reality... He cannot change reality.* N UNCOUNT

2 The **reality** of a situation is the truth about it, especially when it is unpleasant or unwelcome. EG *...the harsh reality of daily life... ...the realities of politics and diplomacy.* N COUNT+SUPP

3 You say that something has become a **reality** when it actually exists or is actually happening. EG *The Popular Front was already a reality... Daydreams had become realities.* N COUNT OR N UNCOUNT

4 You can use **in reality 4.1** to introduce a statement about the real nature of something, when it contrasts with something incorrect that has just been described. EG *They imagined that they made the rules but, in reality, they were mere puppets.* **4.2** to say that something exists or happens in real life rather than in stories or films. EG *The sound was far more menacing in reality than in the movies.* ADV SEN

realize /rɪəlaɪz/, **realizes, realizing, realized;** also spelled **realise. 1** If you **realize** something, you become aware of it. EG *She realized the significance of what he was trying to do... I realized that this man wasn't going to hurt me... He is much more remarkable than many people realized.* ◊ **realization** /rɪəlaɪzeɪʃə⁰n/. EG *This realization was shattering for all of us.*   V+O OR V+REPORT   ◊ N UNCOUNT

2 When someone **realizes** a design or an idea, they put it into a physical form, for example by painting a picture or building a machine. EG *No design is too sophisticated for him to realize.*   V+O Formal

3 If your hopes, desires, or fears **are realized**, the things that you hope for, desire, or fear actually happen. EG *Our national aspirations could be realised... My worst fears were realized.* ◊ **realization**. EG *...the realization of a lifelong dream.*   V+O : USU PASS Formal   ◊ N UNCOUNT

really /rɪəli¹/. **1** You can use **really** to emphasize what you are saying. EG *It is really very difficult... I really ought to go... I really think I've had enough.*   ADV Spoken

2 You can also use **really** to give emphasis to an adjective or adverb. EG *It was really good... These fires produce really obnoxious fumes... We're doing really well.*   SUBMOD Spoken

3 You use **really** when you are talking about the real facts about something, as opposed to something incorrect which has just been said. EG *I want to know what really happened... What I'm really saying is, I'm delighted... He's not really going for a bath; he's going to sit in the garden.*   ADV

4 People use **really** in questions when they want you to answer 'no'. EG *Do you really think they bother to listen to us?... Is there really anything new to say about him?*   ADV Spoken

5 People sometimes add **really** to negative statements to avoid seeming impolite. EG *I'm not really in favour of that... 'Any more problems?' – 'Not really, no.'*   ADV : WITH BROAD NEG

6 You can say **'Really?' 6.1** to indicate that you are listening with interest to what someone is telling you. EG *'It was quite close to the airport.' – 'Really?'* **6.2** to express surprise or disbelief at what someone has said, or to check that you have understood them properly. EG *'Nobody was allowed inside unless he'd been injected by Doc Murray.' – 'Really?'... 'Inflation's dropped faster than it did under Labour.' – 'Has it really?'*   CONVENTION

7 Some people say **'Really!'** or **'Well, really!'** when they are very annoyed.   EXCLAM

realm /relm/, **realms. 1** You can refer to any area of activity or thought as a **realm**. EG *Changes would not be confined to the technical realm... Clearly, we are in the realm of imagination rather than historical fact.*   N COUNT+SUPP Formal

2 A **realm** is also a country that has a king or queen. EG *...the established church of the realm.*   N COUNT Formal

reap /riːp/, **reaps, reaping, reaped. 1** When people **reap** a crop such as corn, they cut it down and gather it.   V+O

2 When people **reap** benefits or rewards, they obtain them as a result of hard work or careful planning. EG *One day we will reap the full benefits of North Sea oil.*   V+O

reappear /riːəpɪə/, **reappears, reappearing, reappeared.** When people or things **reappear**, you can see them again, because they have returned from another place or because they are being used again. EG *The waiter reappeared with a loaded tray... From time to time 'Gypsy' clothes reappear as a fashion.* ◊ **reappearance** /riːəpɪərəns/, **reappearances.** EG *He wanted to know the reason for my sudden reappearance.*   V : USU+A   ◊ N UNCOUNT OR N COUNT

reappraisal /riːəpreɪzə⁰l/, **reappraisals.** If there is a **reappraisal** of something such as a policy, people think about it carefully and decide whether they want to change it. EG *...a reappraisal of U.S. policy toward South Asia.*   N COUNT OR N UNCOUNT Formal

rear /rɪə/, **rears, rearing, reared. 1** The **rear** of something such as a building or vehicle is the part that is at the back of it. EG *He walked toward the rear of the house.* ▸ used as an adjective. EG *I got out and examined the right rear wheel.*   N SING : the+N, USU+of   ▸ ADJ CLASSIF: ATTRIB

2 If you are at the **rear** of a queue or of a moving line of people, you are the last person in it. EG *The motorcycles dropped back to a position at the rear of the convoy.* ● If you **bring up the rear**, you are the last person in a moving line of people.   N SING : the+N, USU+of   ● PHRASE

3 Your **rear** is the part of your body that you sit on. EG *She slapped him on the rear.*   N COUNT Informal

4 If you **rear** children, you bring them up until they are old enough to look after themselves. If you say that someone **was reared** in a particular way or in a particular place, you are describing how or where they were brought up. EG *Geraldo has adopted and reared four children... ...girls reared in country houses... ...a child reared without love.*   V+O

5 When a horse **rears** or **rears up**, it moves the front part of its body upwards, so that its front legs are high in the air and it is standing on its back legs. EG *...rearing up on his hind legs.*   V : OFT+up

6 When something unpleasant happens, you can say that it **rears** its **ugly head**. EG *Dissension might so easily have reared its ugly head.*   PHRASE

rearrange /riːəreɪndʒ/, **rearranges, rearranging, rearranged.** If you **rearrange** something, you organize or arrange it in a different way. EG *She rearranged the furniture.*   V+O

rearrangement /riːəreɪndʒmə⁰nt/, **rearrangements.** A **rearrangement** is a change in the way that something is arranged or organized. EG *...the rearrangement of the examination system.*   N COUNT OR N UNCOUNT

reason /riːzⁿn/, **reasons, reasoning, reasoned. 1** The **reason** for something is the fact or situation which explains why it happens or exists. EG *I asked the reason for the decision... There is a good reason why these committees are secret... Public pressure is towards more street lighting: the reason is that people feel safer in well-lit streets.*   N COUNT : USU+SUPP

2 If you say that you have **reason** to believe something or **reason** to feel something, you mean that there are definite reasons why you believe it or feel it. EG *I have reason to believe that you are concealing something... You had good reason to be distressed... I'm getting annoyed, and with reason.*   N UNCOUNT : USU+to-INF

3 **Reason** is also the ability that people have to think and make judgements. EG *He had to rely less on reason than on the rousing of emotion.*   N UNCOUNT

4 **Reason** is used in these phrases. **4.1** If something happens **by reason of** something else, it happens because of it. EG *I enjoyed a measure of protection by reason of my age.* **4.2** If you say that **for some reason** a particular thing happened, you mean that it happened and you do not know why. EG *For some reason he talked about death.* **4.3** If you get someone to **listen to reason**, you persuade them to listen to sensible arguments and be influenced by them. EG *The man refused to listen to reason.*   PREP Formal   PHRASE   PHRASE

5 If you **reason** that something is the case, you decide that it is the case after thinking carefully about all the facts. EG *Copernicus reasoned that the earth revolved around the sun... 'Very few Americans,' I reasoned, 'would know that.'* ● See also **reasoned, reasoning.**   V+REPORT ONLY that, OR V+QUOTE

reason with. If you **reason with** someone, you argue with them in order to try to persuade them to do something or to accept something. EG *We all know how difficult it is to reason with a prejudiced person.*   PHRASAL VB : V+PREP, HAS PASS

reasonable /riːzⁿnəbⁿl/. **1** If you say that someone is being **reasonable**, you mean that they are behaving in a fair and sensible way. EG *Our mother was always very reasonable... I can't do that,*   ADJ QUALIT

Morris. *Be reasonable.* ◊ **reasonableness**. EG *The*   ◊ N UNCOUNT
landlords responded with great reasonableness.

2 You describe a decision or explanation as **rea-**   ADJ QUALIT
sonable when there are good reasons for thinking
that it is correct. EG *There was no reasonable
explanation for her decision... It was quite reasonable to suppose that he wanted the money too.*

3 A **reasonable** amount of something is a fairly   ADJ QUALIT
large amount. EG *...a reasonable amount of luck... A
reasonable number of students are involved.*

4 If the price of something is **reasonable**, it is fair   ADJ QUALIT
and not too high. EG *...a good range of wines at
reasonable prices... The tickets cost a very reasonable £30.*

reasonably /ˈriːzəⁿnəblɪ/. 1 If you say that some-   SUBMOD
thing is **reasonably** large or **reasonably** good,
you mean that it is fairly large or fairly good. EG *I'm
reasonably broad across the shoulders... ...a reasonably well-known writer.*

2 If you say that someone is behaving **reasonably**,   ADV
you mean that they are behaving in a fair and
sensible way.

reasoned /ˈriːzəⁿnd/. A **reasoned** argument or   ADJ CLASSIF :
explanation is based on sensible reasons, rather   ATTRIB
than on an appeal to people's emotions. EG *We must
counter their propaganda with reasoned argument... They had been offered a reasoned explanation of the phenomena.*

reasoning /ˈriːzəⁿnɪŋ/ is the process by which you   N UNCOUNT
reach a conclusion after thinking about all the
facts. EG *I'm puzzled by his reasoning... What is the
reasoning behind that decision?*

reassemble /ˌriːəˈsembəⁿl/, **reassembles, reas-**   V+O
sembling, reassembled. If you **reassemble**
something, you put it back together after it has
been taken apart. EG *He reassembled an entire
engine.*

reassert /ˌriːəˈsɜːt/, **reasserts, reasserting, reas-**
serted. 1 If you **reassert** something such as power   V+O
or authority, you make it clear that you have it
again. EG *He made efforts to reassert his authority
over them.*

2 If something such as an idea or habit **reasserts**   V-REFL
itself, it becomes noticeable again. EG *The urge to
survive reasserted itself.*

reassess /ˌriːəˈses/, **reassesses, reassessing, re-**   V+O
assessed. If you **reassess** something, you think
about it and decide whether it still has the same
value or importance. EG *He was reassessing his
political position.*

reassessment /ˌriːəˈsesmənt/, **reassessments.** If   N COUNT OR
you make a **reassessment** of something, you think   N UNCOUNT
about it and decide whether it still has the same
value or importance. EG *...a reassessment of the
effect of family and schooling.*

reassurance /ˌriːəˈʃʊərəns/, **reassurances.** 1 If   N UNCOUNT
you give someone **reassurance**, you say things to
them that help them to stop worrying. EG *She wants
reassurance, that is all... Men came to her for
comfort and reassurance.*

2 **Reassurances** are things that you say to help   N COUNT
people stop worrying. EG *Reassurances were given
that investigations would proceed.*

reassure /ˌriːəˈʃʊə/, **reassures, reassuring, re-**   V+O :
assured. If you **reassure** someone, you say or do   OFT+REPORT :
things that help them to stop worrying. EG *I was*   ONLY that
*trying to reassure her that things weren't as bad as
she thought.* ◊ **reassuring**. EG *The woman smiled*   ◊ ADJ QUALIT
at him in a reassuring manner. ◊ **reassuringly.**   ◊ ADV
EG *She looked at me reassuringly.*

rebate /ˈriːbeɪt/, **rebates.** A **rebate** is an amount   N COUNT
of money which is paid back to you because you
have paid more tax, rent, or rates than you needed
to. EG *You should get a tax rebate.*

rebel, rebels, rebelling, rebelled; pronounced
/ˈrebəⁿl/ when it is a noun, and /rɪˈbel/ when it is a
verb. 1 **Rebels** are people who are fighting against   N COUNT
their own country's army in order to change the
political system there. EG *The rebels made regular*

attacks on the railways... *Rebel groups controlled
the centre of the city.*

2 You also describe someone as a **rebel** when they   N COUNT
reject their society's values and behave differently
from other people.

3 When people **rebel**, **3.1** they fight against their   V : OFT+
own country's army in order to change the political   against
system there. EG *The Duke of Monmouth rebelled
against James II in 1685.* **3.2** they behave differently from other people because they have rejected
their society's or parents' values. EG *...adolescents
who rebel and demand freedom and independence.*

rebellion /rɪˈbeljən/, **rebellions.** 1 A **rebellion** is   N COUNT OR
a violent, organized action by a large group of   N UNCOUNT
people who are trying to change their country's
political system.

2 Opposition to the leaders of an organization can   N UNCOUNT
also be referred to as a **rebellion**. EG *He faces a*   OR N COUNT
growing rebellion from the left wing of his party.

rebellious /rɪˈbeljəs/. Someone who is **rebellious**   ADJ QUALIT
does not do what someone in authority wants them
to do. EG *...an obstinate, rebellious child with a
violent temper.* ◊ **rebelliously.** EG *'Nonsense,' said*   ◊ ADV
my assistant rebelliously.

rebuff /rɪˈbʌf/, **rebuffs, rebuffing, rebuffed.** If   V+O : USU PASS
you **rebuff** someone, you refuse to cooperate with
them or to agree to what they are suggesting. EG *He
tried to question the girl and got rebuffed.* ▸ used   ▸ N COUNT
as a noun. EG *She didn't understand that her rebuff
had hurt him.*

rebuild /riːˈbɪld/, **rebuilds, rebuilding, rebuilt**
/riːˈbɪlt/. 1 When a town or building **is rebuilt**, it is   V+O
built again after it has been damaged or destroyed.
EG *They will be allowed to rebuild the bridges.*

2 When an organization **is rebuilt**, it is developed   V+O
again after it has stopped or become ineffective. EG
*...help him to rebuild his nation's shattered econo-
my.*

rebuke /rɪˈbjuːk/, **rebukes, rebuking, rebuked.**   V+O : OFT+for
If you **rebuke** someone, you speak severely to
them because they have said or done something
that you do not approve of. EG *She often rebuked
David for his authoritarian attitude.* ▸ used as a   ▸ N COUNT OR
noun. EG *He received a stern rebuke from his*   N UNCOUNT
superiors.

recall /rɪˈkɔːl/, **recalls, recalling, recalled.** 1   V+O; ALSO
When you **recall** something, you remember it. EG *I*   V+-ING, QUOTE,
started to recall the years after the War... Deirdre   OR REPORT
*recalled seeing a poster on his wall... 'I ran outside
to look for my children,' recalled Miriam... I recalled that my blankets had been taken away.*
▸ used as a noun. EG *Why are some memories more*   ▸ N UNCOUNT
available for recall than others?

2 If you **are recalled** to a place, you are ordered to   V+O : USU+A
return there. EG *Eighteen months ago they recalled
him to Mozambique... Parliament was hastily recalled from recess.*

recapture /riːˈkæptʃə/, **recaptures, recapturing,**
recaptured. 1 When you **recapture** a pleasant   V+O
feeling, you feel it again. EG *She failed to recapture
her earlier mood.*

2 When soldiers **recapture** a place, they capture it   V+O
from the people who had taken it from them. EG
*The Turks had returned and recaptured their
trench.* ▸ used as a noun. EG *...the recapture of the*   ▸ N SING
lost territories.

3 When animals or prisoners **are recaptured**,   V+O
they are caught after they have escaped.

recede /rɪˈsiːd/, **recedes, receding, receded.** 1 If   V
something **recedes**, it moves away into the distance. EG *Now and then cars passed me, their tail-
lights receding.*

2 You also say that something **recedes** when it   V
becomes less clear or less bright. EG *Already the
memory was receding.*

3 If you say that a man's hair **is receding**, you   V
mean that he is starting to go bald by losing hair at
the front of his head.

receipt /rɪˈsiːt/, **receipts.** 1 A **receipt** is a piece N COUNT of paper that you give or send to someone to confirm that you have received money or goods from them. EG *Give students a written receipt for each payment.*

2 Money received in a shop or a theatre is often N PLURAL referred to as the **receipts.** EG *The receipts from admission fees fell sharply.*

3 The **receipt** of something is the act of receiving N UNCOUNT it. EG *You have to sign here and acknowledge* Formal *receipt... We are awaiting the receipt of further information.*

receive /rɪˈsiːv/, **receives, receiving, received.** V+O

1 When you **receive** something, **1.1** someone gives it to you. EG *Did they receive money for their work?* **1.2** you get it after it has been sent to you. EG *Northcliffe received a letter from his brother.*

2 You can use **receive** to say that certain kinds of V+O thing happen to you. For example if you are injured, you can say that you **received** an injury. EG *...the criticism he received in England... She received a tremendous ovation.* ● If you **are on** ● PHRASE **the receiving end** of something unpleasant, you are the person that it happens to. EG *You may find yourself on the receiving end of my father's temper.*

3 When you **receive** a visitor or a guest, you V+O welcome them. EG *Tell her I shall be delighted to receive her... Fass received Lieber in his office.*

4 If you say that something **is received** in a V+O+A: particular way, you mean that people react to it in USU PASS that way. EG *Her latest novel has been very well received... This news was received with contempt.*

received /rɪˈsiːvd/. The **received** opinion about ADJ CLASSIF: something or the **received** way of doing some- ATTRIB thing is the one that is generally accepted as Formal correct. EG *...received ideas... ...received religion.*

receiver /rɪˈsiːvə/, **receivers.** A **receiver** is 1 N COUNT the part of a telephone that you hold near to your ear and speak into. EG *He replaced the receiver.* 2 a radio or television set. 3 a person who receives something. EG *...receivers of stolen goods.*

recent /ˈriːsənt/. A **recent** event or period of time ADJ QUALIT: happened only a short while ago. EG *They talked* USU ATTRIB *about their recent trip to Africa... Few sights have become more familiar in recent times.*

recently /ˈriːsəntli/. If something happened **re-** ADV **cently,** it happened only a short time ago. EG *Recently, I lectured to seven hundred Swedes... The problem has been ignored until very recently... This flower was discovered as recently as 1903.*

receptacle /rɪˈsɛptəkəl/, **receptacles.** A **recep-** N COUNT **tacle** is an object which you use to put or keep Formal things in. EG *Please put your cigarette ends into the receptacle provided... ...receptacles for ink.*

reception /rɪˈsɛpʃən/, **receptions.** 1 In a hotel, N UNCOUNT office, or hospital, **reception** is the place where reservations, appointments, and enquiries are dealt with. EG *...the young man at the reception desk.*

2 A **reception** is a formal party which is given to N COUNT welcome someone or to celebrate a special event. EG *The reception was held in the Albany.*

3 If something or someone has a particular kind of N COUNT+SUPP **reception,** that is the way people react to them. EG *I wrote to George about the enthusiastic reception of his book... Butler received a hostile reception in Bristol.*

4 The **reception** of guests is the act of formally N SING welcoming them. EG *...a room which was kept for* Formal *the reception of visitors.*

5 If you get good **reception** from your radio or N UNCOUNT television, the sound or picture is clear. EG *I'm getting perfect reception now... Radio reception kept fading.*

receptionist /rɪˈsɛpʃənɪst/, **receptionists.** The N COUNT **receptionist** in a hotel, office, or doctor's surgery is the person whose job is to deal with guests or clients when they first arrive, answer the tele-

phone, and arrange reservations or appointments. EG *He handed back his key to the receptionist.*

receptive /rɪˈsɛptɪv/. Someone who is **receptive** ADJ QUALIT: to new ideas or suggestions is willing to consider OFT+to and accept them. EG *We need people who are receptive to new ideas... The public began to develop a more receptive attitude.*

recess, recesses; pronounced /rɪˈsɛs/ in para- graph 1 and /ˈriːsɛs/ in paragraphs 2 and 3.

1 A **recess** is a period of holiday between the N UNCOUNT sessions of work of a committee or parliament. EG OR N COUNT *The committee is going into recess for a couple of weeks.*

2 In a room, a **recess** is a small extra area that is N COUNT created when one part of a wall is built further back than the rest. EG *...the arched window recess.*

3 The **recesses** of something are its deep or N COUNT hidden parts. EG *I pushed the problem down into* +SUPP: *the dim recesses of my mind.* USU PLURAL

recession /rɪˈsɛʃən/, **recessions.** A **recession** is N COUNT OR a period when the economy of a country is less N UNCOUNT successful, for example because industry is produc- ing less and more people are becoming unem- ployed.

RECIP stands for **reciprocal**

A number of verbs have the additional label RECIP in the Extra Column. This is used to indicate a particular pattern that the verb makes with two noun groups. A typical example is **meet**. If we know that 'John met Mary', then we also know that 'Mary met John', that 'John and Mary met', and that 'John and Mary met each other'. EG *When he was at university he **met** Barbara... Barbara **met** him in London... The couple **met** a week before the wedding... They **met** each other at a party.*

From this it can be seen that either of the two noun groups can be the subject or the object of the verb without changing the meaning of the sen- tence. 'He met Barbara' means that 'Barbara met him'.

Also, the two noun groups can be joined by 'and' to make the subject of the verb. In that case there is no object, except for the phrase 'each other', which is sometimes used. So that 'Barbara and Howard met at university' means the same as 'Barbara and Howard met each other at univer- sity'.

Many verbs use the preposition 'with' to make a reciprocal pattern. For example, the verb **argue**, as in EG *I was arguing with him about the miners' strike... He was arguing with me... Why do we always argue about money?*

Here, too, either of the noun groups can be the subject or the prepositional object without chang- ing the meaning of the sentence. When they are both the subject, there is no prepositional object, except for the phrase 'with each other', which is sometimes used.

---

recipe /ˈrɛsɪpi/, **recipes.** 1 A **recipe** is a list of N COUNT ingredients and a set of instructions that tell you how to cook something. EG *...a recipe for beetroot soup... It's one of Aunt Jane's recipes.*

2 If you say that something is a **recipe** for disaster N SING+for or a **recipe** for success, you mean that it is likely

Is a recluse happy to receive visitors?

to result in disaster or success. EG *This policy appeared to be a recipe for disaster.*

recipient /rɪ'sɪpɪənt/, **recipients**. The **recipient** N COUNT of something is the person who receives it. EG Formal *...letters kept by the recipients.*

reciprocal /rɪ'sɪprəkə⁰l/ A **reciprocal** arrange- ADJ CLASSIF ment or agreement is one in which two people or Formal two groups of people agree to help another in a similar way. EG *Their social security system is linked to Britain's by a reciprocal agreement.*

reciprocate /rɪ'sɪprəkeɪt/, **reciprocates, recip-** V+O OR V **rocating, reciprocated.** If you **reciprocate** Formal someone's feelings or behaviour towards you, you have the same feelings about them or behave the same way towards them. EG *This hostile attitude is reciprocated by potential employers... Invitations to the home of a subordinate may be accepted, but not reciprocated.*

recital /rɪ'saɪtə⁰l/, **recitals**. A **recital** is a perfor- N COUNT mance of music or poetry, usually given by one person. EG *She had been asked to give a piano recital.*

recitation /resɪteɪʃə⁰n/, **recitations**. When some- N UNCOUNT one does a **recitation**, they say aloud a piece of OR N COUNT poetry or other writing that they have learned.

recite /rɪ'saɪt/, **recites, reciting, recited.** 1 V+O OR When someone **recites** a poem or other piece of V+QUOTE writing, they say it aloud after they have learned it. EG *She recited a speech from 'As You Like It'.*

2 If you **recite** a list of things, you say it aloud. EG V+O *Mrs Zapp recited a catalogue of her husband's sins.*

reckless /reklɪ⁰s/. Someone who is **reckless** ADJ QUALIT shows a lack of care about danger or about the results of their actions. EG *I don't like the way he drives. He's reckless... They denounced the government for its reckless squandering of public funds.*
◊ **recklessly.** EG *He accelerated recklessly round* ◊ ADV *a blind corner.* ◊ **recklessness.** EG *...the reckless-* ◊ N UNCOUNT *ness of the attack.*

reckon /rekə⁰n/, **reckons, reckoning, reckoned.**
1 If you say that you **reckon** that something is true, V+REPORT : you mean that you think that it is true. EG *She* ONLY *that reckoned that there was a risk... I reckon he's* Informal *stupid... What do you reckon?*

2 If you say that something **is reckoned** to be true, V+O+to-INF you mean that people think that it is true. EG *About* OR V+O+C : *40 per cent of the country is reckoned to be* USU PASS *illiterate... It was reckoned a fine job but the money wasn't great.*

3 If you say that someone **reckons** to do some- V+to-INF thing, you mean that they claim or expect to do it. EG *They reckon to sell the same amount each year.*

4 When you **reckon** an amount, you calculate it. EG V+O OR V *The number of days lost through unemployment in 1968 can be reckoned at 146 million.*

reckon on. If you **reckon on** something, you feel PHRASAL VB : certain that it will happen and therefore make V+PREP, your plans believing that it will happen. EG *He* HAS PASS *reckoned on a large reward if he succeeded.*

reckon with. 1 If you say that you had not PHRASAL VB : **reckoned with** something, you mean that you had V+PREP, not expected it and so were not prepared for it. EG HAS PASS *She had not reckoned with a surprise of this sort.*
2 If you say that someone or something is **to be** PHRASE **reckoned with**, you mean that they must be dealt with and it will be difficult. EG *There was also Gertrude to be reckoned with... The Union has always been a force to be reckoned with.*

reckon without. If you say that you had reck- PHRASAL VB : **oned without** something, you mean that you had V+PREP not expected it and so were not prepared for it. EG *They reckoned without Margaret's determination.*

reckoning /rekə⁰nɪŋ/, **reckonings**. 1 A **reckon-** N COUNT OR **ing** is a calculation. EG *It's only a rough reckoning...* N UNCOUNT *By his own reckoning, he had taken five hours to get there.*

2 The **day of reckoning** for someone is the time PHRASE when they are eventually punished for things that

they have done wrong. EG *The day of reckoning had not yet come for Harold.*

reclaim /rɪ'kleɪm/, **reclaims, reclaiming, re-** **claimed.** 1 If you **reclaim** something that you V+O have lost or something that has been taken away from you, you succeed in getting it back. EG *You must present this ticket when you reclaim your luggage.*

2 When people **reclaim** land, they make it suitable V+O for use, for example by draining it or irrigating it. EG *Lowland bogs have been reclaimed.*
◊ **reclaimed.** EG *...reclaimed land.* ◊ ADJ CLASSIF

recline /rɪ'klaɪn/, **reclines, reclining, reclined.** V : USU+A If you **recline**, you sit or lie with the upper part of your body supported at an angle. EG *She was reclining comfortably in her chair.*

reclining /rɪ'klaɪnɪŋ/. A **reclining** chair or seat ADJ CLASSIF : has a back which can be adjusted so that you can ATTRIB lie down or sit with the upper part of your body supported at an angle.

recluse /rɪ'kluːs/, **recluses**. A **recluse** is a person N COUNT who lives alone and deliberately avoids other people.

recognise /rekəg⁰naɪz/. See **recognize**.

recognition /rekəg⁰nɪʃə⁰n/. 1 Recognition is the N UNCOUNT experience of recognizing someone or something. EG *She walked past me without so much as a glance of recognition.*

2 If something has changed **beyond recognition** PHRASE or **out of all recognition**, it has changed so much that you can no longer recognize it. EG *The social structure has changed beyond recognition.*

3 When there is **recognition** of something, people N UNCOUNT realize or accept that it exists or that it is true. EG +SUPP *There has been insufficient recognition of the magnitude of the problem... This might lead to a recognition by both the superpowers that arms talks must continue.*

4 If something is done **in recognition of** some- PHRASE one's achievements, it is done as a way of showing official appreciation of them. EG *He was awarded a knighthood in recognition of his great contribution to the British cinema.*

recognizable /rekəg⁰naɪzəbə⁰l/; also spelled rec- ADJ QUALIT **ognisable**. Something that is **recognizable** is easy to recognize or identify. EG *...a recognizable voice... There was an old statue barely recognisable as Charles II.* ◊ **recognizably.** EG *Its arrangement is* ◊ ADV *recognizably based on what existed before.*

recognize /rekəg⁰naɪz/, **recognizes, recogniz-** **ing, recognized**; also spelled **recognise**. 1 If you V+O OR **recognize** someone or something, you know who V+O+as : or what they are, because you have seen or heard NO CONT them before or because someone has described them to you. EG *She didn't recognise me at first... The postmistress recognised her as Mrs Pennington's daughter... They are trained to recognize the symptoms of radiation-sickness.*

2 You also say that you **recognize** something V+O, V+O+as, when you realize or accept that it exists or that it is OR V+REPORT true. EG *Governments are beginning to recognize the problem... We recognise this as a genuine need... They refused to recognise that a wrong decision had been made.*

3 You say that something **is recognized** when it is V+O accepted or approved. EG *Are qualifications gained in Britain recognized in other European countries?*
◊ **recognized.** EG *There are several recognized* ◊ ADJ CLASSIF *techniques for dealing with this.*

4 When a new government **is recognized**, it is V+O accepted as the legal government of a country. EG *The new regime was at once recognized by China.*

5 When an achievement **is recognized**, people V+O officially show their appreciation of it. EG *The nation recognized her efforts by making her home a historical monument.*

recoil /rɪ'kɔɪl/, **recoils, recoiling, recoiled.** 1 V : OFT+*from*/ You say that someone **recoils** from something *at* when it gives them an immediate feeling of fear, dislike, or horror. EG *He recoiled in horror from the savagery which he witnessed... Parents may recoil at this kind of behaviour.*

2 You also say that someone **recoils** from some-   V:USU+A
thing when they move their body, or part of their body, quickly away from it because it gives them a painful or unpleasant feeling. EG *When he touched the man's arm, he recoiled in horror, for it was cold and rigid.*

recollect /rɛkəlɛkt/, **recollects, recollecting,**   V+O OR
recollected. If you **recollect** something, you re-   V+REPORT
member it. EG *He was unable to recollect the names... He does not recollect how long they were in the house.*

recollection /rɛkəlɛkʃəⁿn/, **recollections. 1** If   N COUNT
you have a **recollection** of something, you remember it. EG *I have a vivid recollection of the house where I was born... ...my recollections of Australia.*

2 Recollection is the experience of remembering   N UNCOUNT
something. EG *She had a flash of recollection.*

recommend /rɛkəmɛnd/, **recommends, recommending, recommended. 1** If someone **rec-**   V+O:OFT+*for,*
ommends something to you, they suggest that you   OR V+O+O
should have it or use it, because it is good or useful.
EG *...a fine novel which I'd strongly recommend... ...the diet recommended for old people... Perhaps you could recommend me a solicitor.*

2 If you **recommend** an action, you suggest that it   V+O:
should be done. EG *They recommended a merger of*   OFT+*to*-INF;
the two biggest supermarket groups... The Harveys   ALSO
do not recommend other couples to have families   V+REPORT
of this size... He would strongly recommend that I   OR-ING
had it next year... Mr Tebbit recommends cycling as a good form of exercise.

recommendation /rɛkəmɛndeɪʃəⁿn/, **recommendations.** If you make a **recommendation,** **1**   N COUNT OR
you suggest that someone should have something   N UNCOUNT
or use something, because it is good or useful. EG
The best way to find a gardener is through personal recommendation. **2** you advise someone what is   N COUNT
the best thing to do. EG *The final choice will depend largely on what recommendation they make to the Prime Minister... ...recommendations for training.*

reconcile /rɛkənsaɪl/, **reconciles, reconciling, reconciled. 1** If you **reconcile** two beliefs that   V+O:OFT+*to/*
seem to be opposed to each other, you find a way   *with*
in which both of them can be held by the same person at the same time. EG *I cannot reconcile the two points of view... I asked how he would reconcile apartheid with Christianity.*

2 If you **are reconciled** with someone, you be-   V+O:
come friendly with them again after a quarrel or   OFT+*with/to,*
disagreement. EG *They had been reconciled with*   USU PASS
their families. ◇ **reconciliation** ◇ N UNCOUNT
/rɛkəⁿnsɪliˈeɪʃəⁿn/. EG *...hopes of reconciliation in Western Europe.*

3 If you **reconcile** yourself to an unpleasant situa-   V-REFL+*to*
tion, you accept it. EG *He told them to reconcile themselves to their misery on earth.*
◇ **reconciled.** EG *After a while he grew reconciled* ◇ ADJ PRED
to the situation.   +*to*

reconnaissance /rɪˈkɒnɪsəns/ is the process of   N UNCOUNT
obtaining military information about a place by sending soldiers, planes, or satellites there. EG *They decided to step up reconnaissance of enemy naval movements... ...reconnaissance planes.*

reconsider /riːkəⁿnsɪdə/, **reconsiders, recon-**   V+O OR V:
sidering, reconsidered. If you **reconsider** a deci-   OFT+REPORT,
sion or a way of doing something, you think about it   ONLY WH
and try to decide whether it should be changed. EG
He asked me to reconsider my decision... They have had to reconsider how modern warfare should be waged. ◇ **reconsideration** ◇ N UNCOUNT
/riːkəⁿnsɪdəreɪʃəⁿn/. EG *This would allow time for reconsideration.*

reconstruct /riːkəⁿnstrʌkt/, **reconstructs, reconstructing, reconstructed. 1** If you **recon-**   V+O
struct a building that has been destroyed or badly damaged, you build it again.

2 When a system or policy **is reconstructed**, it is   V+O
replaced with one that works in a different way. EG
...an attempt to reconstruct race relations policy.

3 If you **reconstruct** an event that happened in   V+O
the past, you obtain a complete description of it by combining a lot of small pieces of information.

reconstruction /riːkəⁿnstrʌkʃəⁿn/, **reconstruc-**
tions. 1 Reconstruction is the process of making   N UNCOUNT
a country normal again after a war, for example by replacing buildings that have been damaged or destroyed. EG *They played an active role in the reconstruction of post-war Britain.*

2 When the **reconstruction** of a building takes   N UNCOUNT
place, it is built again after it has been damaged or destroyed.

record, records, recording, recorded; pronounced /rɛkɔːd/ when it is a noun or adjective and /rɪˈkɔːd/ when it is a verb.

1 If you keep a **record** of something, you keep a   N COUNT
written account of it or store information about it in a computer so that it can be referred to later. EG
Keep a record of any repair bills... ...medical records.

2 If you **record** something, you write it down, film   V+O
it, or put it into a computer so that it can be referred to later. EG *All personnel details could be recorded on a computer... Their every action was recorded by concealed cameras.*

3 A **record** is a round, flat piece of black plastic on   N COUNT
which sound, especially music, is stored. You listen to the sound by playing the record on a record player. EG *...jazz records.*

4 When music or speech **is recorded**, it is put onto   V+O
a tape or a record, so that it can be heard again later. EG *We had better be careful what we say since it's being recorded.*

5 A **record** is also the shortest time or the longest   N COUNT
distance that has ever been achieved in a particular sport. EG *He held the record for the mile... ...world records.*

6 You use **record** to say that something is higher,   ADJ CLASSIF:
lower, or better than has ever been achieved   ATTRIB
before. EG *Unemployment was at a record high.*

7 Your **record** is all the facts that are known about   N COUNT+SUPP
your achievements or character. EG *Mr Gerran has a very distinguished record.*

8 If someone has a **record** of behaviour of a   N COUNT+SUPP
particular kind, they are known to have behaved in that way. EG *...a man with a record of instability.*

9 Record is also used in these phrases. **9.1** If   PHRASES
something that you say is **off the record**, it is not official and not intended to be published or made known. EG *Now that remark was off the record, understand?* **9.2** If you are **on record** as saying something, you have said it publicly and it has been written down. EG *You're on record as saying that you will retire at the end of the year.* **9.3** If you keep information **on record**, you write it down or store it in a computer so that it can be referred to later. **9.4** You use **on record** to say that something is, for example, the best or largest thing of its kind that has been noticed and recorded in writing. EG
...the highest monthly figures on record. **9.5** If you **set** or **put the record straight**, you show that something which has been regarded as true is in fact not true. EG *Harold Begbie wrote a book to put the record straight.*

10 See also **recording, track record.**

recorded delivery. If you send a letter or parcel   N UNCOUNT
by **recorded delivery**, you receive an official note   British
telling you that it has been received.

recorder /rɪˈkɔːdə/, **recorders. 1** You can refer   N COUNT
to a cassette recorder, a tape recorder, or a video recorder as a **recorder**. EG *He switched off the recorder.*

Where does a rector live?

2 A **recorder** is also a hollow musical instrument N COUNT
that you play by blowing down one end and putting
your fingers over a series of holes. See picture at
MUSICAL INSTRUMENTS.

recording /rɪˈkɔːdɪŋ/, **recordings. 1** A **record-** N COUNT
ing of something is a record, tape, or video of it. EG
...*a new recording of the Second Symphony... Very
few recordings of Picasso's voice exist.*

2 Recording is the process of making records, N UNCOUNT :
tapes, or videos. EG ...*a recording engineer... ...re-* USU N MOD
cording equipment.

record player, record players. A **record play-** N COUNT
er is a machine on which you play records.

recount, recounts, recounting, recounted; pronounced /rɪˈkaʊnt/ in paragraphs 1 and 2 and
/riːkaʊnt/ in paragraph 3.
1 If you **recount** a story, you tell it. EG *I'll just* V+O
recount one anecdote. Formal

2 If you **recount** an event, you describe what V+O
happened. EG *I let Henry recount the incident in his* Formal
own words.

3 A **recount** is a second count of votes in an N COUNT
election when the result is very close. EG *I'm
demanding a recount.*

recourse /rɪˈkɔːs/. If you have **recourse** to some- N UNCOUNT :
thing, you use it in order to help you in a difficult USU+*to*
situation. EG *We need never have recourse to* Formal
*violence... Industrial action is the only recourse we
have.*

recover /rɪˈkʌvə/, **recovers, recovering, recov-**
ered. 1 When you **recover** from an illness or an V : OFT+*from*
injury, you become well again. EG *It was weeks
before he fully recovered... ...a wound from which
he did not recover.* ◇ **recovered.** EG *Stay at home* ◇ ADJ PRED
until you are fully recovered.

2 If you **recover** from an unhappy or unpleasant V : OFT+*from*
experience, you stop being upset by it. EG *They took
a long time to recover from this shock.*

3 If you **recover** something that has been lost or V+O :
stolen, you get it back. EG *I would do my best to* OFT+*from*
*recover these documents... They recovered her
body from the old mine-shaft.*

4 If you **recover** your former mental or physical V+O
state or **recover** the ability to do something, you
get it back again. EG *She quickly recovered her
composure... He died without recovering consciousness... He was beginning to recover the use of his
voice.*

5 If you **recover** money that you have spent or V+O
invested, you get the same amount back. EG *We
recovered our purchase price in the first year.*

recovery /rɪˈkʌvəri/, **recoveries. 1** If a sick N UNCOUNT
person makes a **recovery**, he or she becomes well OR N COUNT
again. EG *He made a good recovery from his
stroke... The shock of the operation delayed his
recovery.*

2 When there is a **recovery** in a country's econo- N UNCOUNT
my, it improves after it has been in a bad state. EG OR N COUNT
*His advisers insisted that economic recovery was
in sight.*

3 You talk about the **recovery** of something when N UNCOUNT :
you get it back after it has been lost or stolen. EG USU+SUPP
...*the recovery of the treasure.* Formal

4 You talk about the **recovery** of someone's physi- N UNCOUNT :
cal or mental state when they return to this state. USU+SUPP
EG *The news was sufficient to bring about the* Formal
recovery of his equanimity.

recreate /riːkriˈeɪt/, **recreates, recreating, rec-** V+O
reated. If you **recreate** something, you succeed in
making it happen or exist again. EG *This country
can no longer hope to recreate its past... The
opportunity could not be recreated.*

recreation /rɛkriˈeɪʃ⁰n/, **recreations. Recrea-** N UNCOUNT
tion consists of things that you do to exercise your OR N COUNT
body and mind when you are not working or study-
ing. EG *Sport and recreation have always been part
of university life... The library was reserved for
quieter recreations.* ◇ **recreational** ◇ ADJ CLASSIF :
USU ATTRIB

/rɛkriˈeɪʃ⁰n/. EG ...*the recreational use of forests... ...recreational facilities.*

recreation ground, recreation grounds. A N COUNT
recreation ground is a piece of public land,
usually in a town, where people can go to play
sport and games.

recrimination /rɪˌkrɪmɪˈneɪʃ⁰n/, **recrimina-** N PLURAL
tions. Recriminations are accusations that two
people or two groups of people make about each
other. EG *There will be recriminations, no doubt.*
▸ used as an uncount noun. EG ...*prolonged bouts of* ▸ N UNCOUNT
recrimination.

recruit /rɪˈkruːt/, **recruits, recruiting, recruit-**
ed. 1 If you **recruit** people for an organization, you V+O OR V :
get them to join it or work for it. EG *It is becoming* OFT+A
*harder to recruit youngsters for the farms... I am
recruiting for the Union.* ◇ **recruiting.** EG *Other* ◇ N UNCOUNT
*organizations reported sharp rises in recruiting...
...a recruiting centre.*

2 A **recruit** is a person who has recently joined an N COUNT
organization or an army. EG *He joined the firm as a
young recruit more than thirty years ago... ...the
army, with its ranks swollen by these new recruits.*

3 If you **recruit** someone for a particular purpose, V+O : OFT+*for*
you get them to do something for you. EG *Men from* OR *to*-INF
*the villages were recruited to carry stores... Moth-
ers and fathers could be recruited to help.*

recruitment /rɪˈkruːtmənt/. When **recruitment** N UNCOUNT
takes place, people are persuaded to join an organization or an army. EG ...*the mass recruitment of
volunteer teachers... ...a recruitment scheme.*

rectangle /ˈrɛktæŋgəl/, **rectangles.** A **rectangle** N COUNT
is a four-sided shape whose angles are all right
angles. Each side of a rectangle is the same length
as the one opposite to it. See picture at SHAPES.
◇ **rectangular** /rɛkˈtæŋgjələ/. EG ...*a rectangular* ◇ ADJ CLASSIF
flower-bed.

rectify /ˈrɛktɪfaɪ/, **rectifies, rectifying, recti-** V+O
fied. If you **rectify** something which is wrong, you
change it so that it becomes correct or satisfactory. EG *Armed forces were sent in to rectify the
situation... The tenant will be held responsible for
rectifying any damage.*

rector /ˈrɛktə/, **rectors.** A **rector** is a Church of N COUNT
England priest who is in charge of a parish.

rectory /ˈrɛktəri/, **rectories.** A **rectory** is a N COUNT
house in which a rector and his family live.

recuperate /rɪˈkjuːpəreɪt/, **recuperates, recu-** V : OFT+*from*
perating, recuperated. When you **recuperate,** Formal
you recover your health or strength after you have
been ill or injured. EG *I was recuperating from an
accident in the gym.* ◇ **recuperation** ◇ N UNCOUNT
/rɪˌkjuːpəˈreɪʃ⁰n/. EG *My mother has gone to Bath
for rest and recuperation.*

recur /rɪˈkɜː/, **recurs, recurring, recurred.** If V : USU+A
something **recurs**, it happens again, either once or
many times. EG *It was probable that the same
circumstances would now recur... It was a phrase
that was to recur again and again.*

recurrence /rɪˈkʌrəns/, **recurrences.** If there is N COUNT OR
a **recurrence** of something, it happens again. EG N UNCOUNT
There were minor recurrences of her eye trouble. Formal

recurrent /rɪˈkʌrənt/ means the same as **recur-** ADJ CLASSIF :
ring. EG ...*a recurrent feeling of illness... ...his recur-* ATTRIB
rent successes... ...recurrent dreams. Formal

recurring /rɪˈkɜːrɪŋ/. **Recurring** things happen ADJ CLASSIF :
many times. EG *Food scarcity will be a recurring* ATTRIB
problem in the future.

recycle /riːˈsaɪk⁰l/, **recycles, recycling, recy-** V+O
cled. If you **recycle** things that have already been
used, such as bottles or sheets of paper, you
process them so that they can be used again.
◇ **recycled.** EG ...*recycled paper.* ◇ ADJ CLASSIF

red /rɛd/, **redder, reddest; reds. 1** Something ADJ COLOUR
that is **red** is the colour of blood or of a ripe
tomato. EG ...*a bunch of red roses... ...brilliant paintings in reds and greens.*

2 If you say that someone's face is **red**, you mean ADJ COLOUR
that it is redder than its normal colour, because

they are embarrassed or angry. EG *Jack turned, red in the face... Ralph clenched his fist and went very red.*

3 You describe someone's hair as **red** when it is ADJ COLOUR between red and brown in colour.

4 If you are **in the red** or if your bank account is PHRASE **in the red**, you have spent more money than you Informal have in your account and therefore you owe money to the bank.

5 If you **see red**, you become very angry. PHRASE

6 If you call someone a **red**, you mean that they N COUNT support communism, socialism, or left-wing ideas in general; used showing disapproval.

reddish /ˈrɛdɪʃ/. Something that is **reddish** is ADJ COLOUR slightly red in colour.

redeem /rɪˈdiːm/, **redeems, redeeming, redeemed. 1** When something **redeems** an unpleas- V+O ant thing or situation, it prevents it from being completely bad. ◊ **redeeming.** EG *...a book with no* ◊ ADJ CLASSIF: *redeeming qualities.* ATTRIB

2 If you **redeem** yourself, you do something that V:REFL makes people have a good opinion of you again after you have behaved badly. EG *He was trying to redeem himself for his earlier failure.*

3 If you **redeem** something, you get it back from V+O someone by repaying them money that you have Technical borrowed from them. EG *They came to redeem their jewellery.*

redemption /rɪˈdɛmpʃən/ is freedom from the N UNCOUNT consequences of sin and evil which Christians Formal believe was made possible by Jesus Christ's death on the cross.

redevelopment /ˌriːdɪˈvɛləpmənt/. When **re-** N UNCOUNT **development** takes place, the buildings in a part of a town are knocked down and new buildings are built in their place. EG *The area is undergoing redevelopment.*

red herring, red herrings. If you say that some- N COUNT thing is a **red herring**, you mean that it is irrelevant and takes people's attention away from what is important. EG *They were using the issue as a red herring.*

red-hot. 1 You say that metal is **red-hot** when it ADJ CLASSIF has been heated to such a high temperature that it has turned red.

2 You also use **red-hot** to describe people or Informal situations that are full of very strong feelings. EG *...a red-hot revolutionary... ...red-hot patriotism.*

redistribute /ˌriːdɪˈstrɪbjuːt/, **redistributes, re-** V+O **distributing, redistributed.** When something such as money **is redistributed**, it is shared among people or organizations in a different way from the way that it was previously shared. EG *Money would be redistributed from the traditional arts institutions.* ◊ **redistribution** ◊ N UNCOUNT /ˌriːdɪstrɪˈbjuːʃən/. EG *We do not envisage any redistribution of wealth and power.*

redouble /ˌriːˈdʌbəl/, **redoubles, redoubling, re-** V+O **doubled.** If you **redouble** your efforts, you try much harder to achieve something. EG *She redoubled her efforts to attract his curiosity.*

redress, redresses, redressing, redressed; pronounced /rɪˈdrɛs/ when it is a verb and either /rɪˈdrɛs/ or /ˈriːdrɛs/ when it is a noun.

1 If you **redress** something such as a wrong or a V+O grievance, you do something to correct it or to Formal improve things for the person who has been badly treated. EG *He did all that he could to redress these wrongs.* ● If you **redress the balance** between ● PHRASE two things that have become unequal, you make Formal them equal again. EG *We were refused the pay increase needed to redress the balance.*

2 Redress is compensation for something wrong N UNCOUNT that has been done. EG *Your claims for redress may* Formal *yet succeed.*

red tape. You refer to official rules and pro- N UNCOUNT cedures as **red tape** when they seem unnecessary and cause delay. EG *Applying for the grant involves a great deal of red tape.*

reduce /rɪˈdjuːs/, **reduces, reducing, reduced. 1** V+O:OFT+ If you **reduce** something, you make it smaller. EG *from/to They have promised to reduce public expenditure... The work-force would have to be reduced from 13,000 to 7,500.* ◊ **reduced.** EG *...a reduced rate of* ◊ ADJ CLASSIF *production.*

2 If you say that someone **is reduced** to a weaker V+O+to: or inferior state, you mean that they change to this USU PASS state as a result of something that happens to them. EG *He was reduced to tears... Her mother was reduced to infantile dependence.*

3 If you say that someone **is reduced** to doing V+O+to:USU something, you mean that they have to do it, PASS although it is unpleasant or humiliating. EG *They are reduced to begging in the streets... We were reduced to desperate measures to get an interview with her.*

reduction /rɪˈdʌkʃən/, **reductions.** When there N UNCOUNT is a **reduction** in something, it is made smaller. EG OR N COUNT: *The unions will be demanding a reduction in* OFT+in/of *working hours... ...a 6 per cent reduction in industrial investment.*

redundancy /rɪˈdʌndənsi/, **redundancies. 1** N COUNT: When there are **redundancies**, an organization USU PLURAL dismisses some of its employees because their jobs are no longer necessary or because the organization can no longer afford to pay them. EG *The trade unions accepted 3500 redundancies.*

2 Redundancy is the state of no longer having a N UNCOUNT job because you have been made redundant. EG *The possibility of redundancy was present in their minds... You should get a redundancy payment.*

redundant /rɪˈdʌndənt/. **1** If you are made **re-** ADJ CLASSIF **dundant**, you are dismissed by your employer because your job is no longer necessary or because your employer cannot afford to keep paying you. EG *Alumetal Ltd will be making 250 workers redundant next year.*

2 Something that is **redundant** is no longer needed ADJ QUALIT because it has been replaced by something else. EG *...skills which have been made redundant by technological advance... ...a large warehouse which faces onto three redundant docks.*

reed /riːd/, **reeds.** Reeds are tall plants that grow N COUNT: in large groups in shallow water or marshy ground. USU PLURAL, They have strong, hollow stems that can be used OR N UNCOUNT for making things such as baskets.

reef /riːf/, **reefs.** A **reef** is a long line of rocks or N COUNT sand that is just above or just below the surface of the sea.

reek /riːk/, **reeks, reeking, reeked. 1** If some- V:OFT+of/ thing **reeks** of a particular thing, it smells very with strongly of it. EG *Thomas appeared, reeking powerfully of brandy.*

2 If there is a **reek** of something, there is a very N SING+SUPP strong, unpleasant smell of it. EG *...the sickening reek of blood.*

reel /riːl/, **reels, reeling, reeled. 1** A **reel** is a N COUNT cylindrical object around which you wrap some- OR N PART thing such as thread or cinema film. EG *...a reel of white string.*

2 The **reel** on a fishing-rod is a round device that N COUNT you use to control the length of the fishing line. For example, when you have caught a fish, you shorten the line by turning the handle on the reel, and so pull the fish towards you.

3 When someone **reels** somewhere, they move V:USU+A there unsteadily as if they were going to fall. EG *I reeled back into the room.*

4 If you say that your brain or your mind **is** V **reeling**, you mean that you are very confused because you have too many things to think about. EG *His mind was reeling with all that he had seen and heard.*

5 A **reel** is also a type of fast Scottish dance. N COUNT

If people are made redundant, is there a reduction in the number of jobs?

reel in. If you **reel in** a fish, you pull it towards you by turning the handle on the reel and shortening the line. PHRASAL VB: V+O+ADV

reel off. If you **reel off** information, you repeat it from memory quickly and easily. EG *He could reel off the names of all the capitals of Europe.* PHRASAL VB: V+O+ADV

re-elect, re-elects, re-electing, re-elected. When someone such as an MP or a trade union official **is re-elected**, they win a new election and are therefore able to continue in their position as MP or union official. EG *I was re-elected with a majority of over 4,300... The Council re-elected him President.* ◊ **re-election.** EG *He stood for re-election.* V+O: OFT PASS, OR V+O+C ◊ N UNCOUNT

re-examine, re-examines, re-examining, re-examined. If you **re-examine** your ideas or beliefs, you think about them carefully because you are no longer sure if they are correct. EG *This forced researchers to re-examine their assumptions about man's early evolution.* ◊ **re-examination.** EG *This has prompted a re-examination of the purposes of education in modern Britain.* V+O ◊ N COUNT OR N UNCOUNT

ref. is written in front of a code at the top of business letters. The code refers to a file in which correspondence is kept. EG *Ref. ESB/33593/64.*

refectory /rɪfektərɪ¹/, **refectories.** In a university or a monastery, the **refectory** is the dining hall. N COUNT

refer /rɪ'fɜː/, **refers, referring, referred. 1** If you **refer to** a particular subject or person, you talk about them or mention them. EG *In his letters he rarely referred to political events... I am not allowed to describe the officers or refer to them by name.* V+to: HAS PASS

2 If you **refer** to someone or something by a particular expression, you use it as their name when you are talking about them. EG *This kind of art is often referred to as 'minimal art'... ...the decline of what I refer to as the industrial working class.* V+to+as: HAS PASS

3 If a word or expression **refers** to something, it is used as a name for it. EG *In the 18th century, 'antique' referred specifically to Greek and Roman antiquities.* V+to: HAS PASS

4 If you **refer to** a source of information such as a reference book, you look at it in order to find something out. EG *She could make a new dish without referring to a cookery book.* V+to: HAS PASS

5 If you **refer** someone to a source of information, you tell them to look for something there. EG *I refer you to a paper by Sutherland.* V+O+to

6 If you **refer** a task or problem to a person or an organization, you formally tell them about it, so that they can deal with it. EG *She referred the matter to the European Court of Justice.* V+O+to

referee /refəriː/, **referees.** The **referee** is the official who controls a football game or a boxing or wrestling match. N UNCOUNT

reference /refə⁰rəns/, **references. 1** If you make **reference** to someone or something or make a **reference** to them, you talk about them or mention them. EG *...the person to whom Philip had made such contemptuous reference... There is no further reference to him in her diary.* N UNCOUNT OR N COUNT: USU+to Formal

2 Reference is also the act of referring to someone or something for information or advice. EG *They acted without reference to the police committee... ...a wrist-size computer for quick reference and portability.* ● If you keep information for **future reference**, you keep it because it might be useful in the future. N UNCOUNT: OFT+to ● PHRASE

3 You use **'with reference to'** to indicate who or what you are talking or writing about. EG *Dear Sir, With reference to your recent communication, the matter is being dealt with as speedily as possible.* PREP Formal

4 A **reference** is also something such as a number or a name that tells you where you can obtain N COUNT

information. EG *...the two page references that I gave you.*

5 If someone gives you a **reference** when you are applying for a job, they write a letter to the employer describing your character and abilities. EG *I've got to get a reference from the University... I've given you a marvellous reference.* N COUNT

6 You look at **reference** books or visit a **reference** library in order to obtain information. EG *...a valuable reference document... He returned to the Reference Room and put the volume back.* N MOD

referendum /refərendəm/, **referenda** /refərendə/ or **referendums.** A **referendum** is a vote in which all the people in a country or region are asked whether they agree or disagree with a particular policy. N COUNT

refill /riːfɪl/, **refills, refilling, refilled.** If you **refill** something, you fill it again after it has been emptied. EG *Sue refilled Jennifer's glass... He went off to refill the aquarium.* ▸ used as a noun. EG *I handed her my cup for a refill.* V+O ▸ N COUNT Informal

refine /rɪ'faɪn/, **refines, refining, refined. 1** When a substance **is refined**, it is made pure by having all other substances removed from it. EG *...men who tested and refined gold.* ◊ **refining.** EG *...the refining of petroleum.* V+O ◊ N UNCOUNT

2 If you **refine** something such as a theory or an idea, you improve it by making small alterations to it. EG *I used these meetings to refine my ideas.* V+O

refined /rɪ'faɪnd/. **1 Refined** people are very polite and well-mannered. EG *...a thin, refined man in a bow tie.* ADJ QUALIT

2 If you describe a machine or process as **refined**, you mean that it has been carefully developed and is therefore very efficient. EG *The new model was larger, faster, and more refined than its predecessor.* ADJ QUALIT

3 A **refined** substance has been made pure by having other substances removed from it. EG *...refined oil.* ADJ CLASSIF

refinement /rɪ'faɪnmə²nt/, **refinements. 1 Refinements** are small alterations that you make to something in order to improve it. EG *...refinements of the system.* N COUNT OR N UNCOUNT

2 Refinement in someone's behaviour is politeness and good manners and a dislike of anything vulgar. EG *Mr Willet's tone changed to one of genteel refinement.* N UNCOUNT

refinery /rɪ'faɪnə⁰rɪ¹/, **refineries.** A **refinery** is a factory where substances such as oil or sugar are refined. EG *...oil refineries.* N COUNT

reflect /rɪ'flekt/, **reflects, reflecting, reflected. 1** If you say that something **reflects** a person's attitude or **reflects** a situation, you mean that it is a consequence of this attitude or situation. EG *The choice of school reflected Dad's hopes for us... Relative profits reflected relative efficiency in performance.* V+O

2 When something **reflects** light or heat, the light or heat is sent back from it and does not pass through it. EG *Although it feels like a normal fabric it reflects heat back into the room.* V+O

3 When something **is reflected** in a mirror or in water, you can see its image in the mirror or water. EG *I saw street lamps mistily reflected in black water.* V+O

4 When you **reflect** on something or **reflect** over it, you think deeply about it. EG *Rodin reflected long over Casson's argument.* V: OFT+on/over

5 If you **reflect** that something is the case, you are aware that it is the case and think about it. EG *Well, I reflected, I couldn't say I hadn't been warned.* V+REPORT, ONLY that, OR V+QUOTE

reflection /rɪ'flekʃə⁰n/, **reflections. 1** If you say, for example, that something is a **reflection** of a person's attitude or a situation, you mean that it is a consequence of it. EG *Their behaviour was a reflection of their very different personalities.* N COUNT+of

2 If you say that something is a **reflection** or a sad **reflection** on something else, you mean that it N SING+on/upon gives a bad impression of it. EG *This is a very sad reflection on the state of the Labour Party.*

3 A **reflection** is an image that you can see in a N COUNT mirror or in water. EG *She was standing there looking at her reflection in the mirror... The reflections from the fireworks twinkled in the river.*

4 Reflection is the process by which light and N UNCOUNT heat are sent back from a surface and do not pass Technical through it.

5 Reflection is thought. You can refer to your N UNCOUNT thoughts about something as your **reflections**. EG OR N COUNT *'You ought to take it,' she said, after a moment's reflection... Furious flashes of light jolted me out of my reflections.* ● You say **on reflection** to indi- ● ADV SEN cate that you have thought very carefully about something. EG *I suppose, on reflection, there is something immoral about it.*

reflective /rɪˈflɛktɪv/. If you are **reflective**, you ADJ QUALIT are thinking deeply about something. EG *He studied the statement in the same reflective way he always studied things... There was a long reflective silence.* ◇ **reflectively**. EG *Barney scratched his* ◇ ADV *chin reflectively.*

reflex /ˈriːflɛks/, **reflexes**. **1** A **reflex** or a **reflex** N COUNT action is a sudden, uncontrollable movement made by a part of your body as a result of pressure or a blow. EG *...the reflex that makes the baby kick.*

2 If you have good **reflexes**, you have the ability to N PLURAL act quickly when something unexpected happens, for example while you are driving a car. EG *She had incredible reflexes.*

reflexive pronoun /rɪˈflɛksɪv prəʊnaʊn/, **re-** N COUNT **flexive pronouns.** In grammar, a **reflexive pronoun** is one which refers back to the subject of a sentence or clause. For example, in the sentence 'you'll just have to do it yourself', the reflexive pronoun 'yourself' refers back to 'you'.

reflexive verb /rɪˈflɛksɪv vɜːb/, **reflexive** N COUNT **verbs.** In grammar, a **reflexive verb** is a transitive verb in which the subject and object refer to the same person or thing. The object is always a reflexive pronoun. For example in the sentence 'He introduced himself', the object of the verb, 'himself', refers to the subject of the verb, 'he'.

reform /rɪˈfɔːm/, **reforms**, **reforming**, **re-** **formed.** **1 Reform** consists of changes and im- N UNCOUNT provements to a law, social system, or institution. OR N COUNT EG *He called for the reform of the divorce laws... ...the task of carrying through the necessary reforms.* ▸ used as a verb. EG *...proposals to reform* ▸ V+O *the Labour Party.*

2 When someone **reforms** or **is reformed**, they V-ERG stop doing something that society does not approve of, such as stealing things or drinking too much alcohol. EG *You have had every chance to reform... Prison sentences cannot reform the criminal.* ◇ **reformed**. EG *...a reformed alcoholic.* ◇ ADJ CLASSIF

reformer /rɪˈfɔːmə/, **reformers.** A **reformer** is N COUNT someone who tries to improve something such as a law or a social system. EG *His early experiences turned him into a passionate social reformer.*

refrain /rɪˈfreɪn/, **refrains**, **refraining**, **re-** **frained.** **1** If you **refrain** from doing something, V : OFT+*from* you deliberately do not do it. EG *I carefully re-* Formal *frained from looking at him.*

2 A **refrain** is a short, simple part of a song, which N COUNT you repeat many times.

refresh /rɪˈfrɛʃ/, **refreshes**, **refreshing**, **re-** **freshed.** **1** If something **refreshes** you when you V+O have become hot or tired, it makes you feel cooler or more energetic. EG *I hoped that sleep would refresh me enough to remain civil.* ◇ **refreshed**. ◇ ADJ QUALIT : EG *These trains are so luxurious that you can end a* USU PRED *long journey feeling positively refreshed.*

2 If someone **refreshes** your **memory**, they tell PHRASE you something that you have forgotten.

refreshing /rɪˈfrɛʃɪŋ/. **1** You say that something ADJ QUALIT is **refreshing** when it is pleasantly different from what you are used to. EG *It was a refreshing change*

for her to meet a woman executive... I found a refreshing absence of industrial sprawl. ◇ **refreshingly**. EG *The plot is refreshingly intelli-* ◇ ADV *gent and original.*

2 A **refreshing** bath or drink makes you feel ADJ QUALIT energetic or cool again after you have been uncomfortably tired or hot. EG *He enjoyed the refreshing swims in the nearby creek.*

refreshment /rɪˈfrɛʃmə³nt/, **refreshments.** **1** N PLURAL **Refreshments** are drinks and small amounts of food that are provided, for example, during a meeting or a journey. EG *There was a stop for refreshments between Coalmont and Ramsdale.*

2 You can refer to food and drink as **refreshment**. N UNCOUNT EG *Come into the house for some refreshment.* Formal

refrigerator /rɪˈfrɪdʒəreɪtə/, **refrigerators.** A N COUNT **refrigerator** is a large container which is kept cool inside, usually by electricity, so that the food and drink in it stays fresh.

refuge /ˈrɛfjuːdʒ/, **refuges.** **1** When you take **ref-** N UNCOUNT **uge**, **1.1** you try to protect yourself from unhappiness or unpleasantness by behaving or thinking in a particular way. EG *He seeks refuge in silence... One must be careful not to take refuge in delusion.* **1.2** you try to protect yourself from physical harm by going to a particular place. EG *Whole families had taken refuge down the tunnels.*

2 A **refuge** is a place where you go for safety and N COUNT protection. EG *A small cave was the only refuge from the cold.*

refugee /ˌrɛfjuˈdʒiː/, **refugees.** **Refugees** are N COUNT people who have been forced to leave their country because there is a war there or because of their political or religious beliefs. EG *...a massive influx of refugees... ...a refugee camp.*

refund, **refunds**, **refunding**, **refunded;** pro- N COUNT nounced /ˈriːfʌnd/ when it is a noun and /rɪˈfʌnd/ when it is a verb.

A **refund** is a sum of money which is returned to you, for example because you have paid someone too much money or because you have returned goods to a shop. ▸ used as a verb. EG *I used to* ▸ V+O OR *refund people their money.* V+O+O

refusal /rɪˈfjuːzə³l/, **refusals.** **1** You describe someone's behaviour as a **refusal** to do something **1.1** when they deliberately do not do it. EG *In all his* N UNCOUNT *films we see his refusal to create outright villains.* +*to*-INF **1.2** when they say firmly that they will not do it. EG N COUNT OR *...the refusal of the workers to use forklift trucks.* N UNCOUNT

2 You also talk about someone's behaviour as a **refusal 2.1** when they do not give you something, N COUNT OR or do not allow you to have it. EG *All appeals met* N UNCOUNT *with bureaucratic refusal... I made many applications and had many refusals.* **2.2** when they do not N UNCOUNT : accept something that has been offered to them. EG OFT+*of* *...this refusal of a gift offered to us.*

refuse, **refuses**, **refusing**, **refused;** pronounced V : OFT+*to*-INF /rɪˈfjuːz/ when it is a verb, and /ˈrɛfjuːs/ or /ˈrɛfjuːz/ when it is a noun.

1 If you **refuse** to do something, **1.1** you deliberately do not do it. EG *He refused to accept this advice... Their bosses refuse to allow them any responsibility.* **1.2** you say firmly that you will not do it. EG *I refuse to believe that it can't be done... He was dismissed for refusing to join a union.*

2 If someone **refuses** you something, they do not V+O+O give it to you or do not allow you to have it. EG *Only* OR V+O+A *the president could refuse him a loan... The Council refused permission for them to live together.*

3 If you **refuse** something that is offered to you, V+O you do not accept it. EG *I offered him wine but he refused it.*

4 Refuse consists of the rubbish and all the things N UNCOUNT that are not wanted in a house, shop, or factory, Formal

What kind of register does a registrar keep?

and that are regularly thrown away. EG ...*a dump for refuse*... ...*refuse collection.*

regain /rɪˈgeɪn/, **regains, regaining, regained.** v+o
If you **regain** something that you have lost, you get it back again. EG *He might be able to regain his old job*... *He never regained political power.*

regal /ˈriːgəl/. If you describe something as **regal**, ADJ QUALIT you mean that it is suitable for a king or queen, because it is very splendid. EG ...*a regal staircase leading into a vast reception hall.*

regale /rɪˈgeɪl/, **regales, regaling, regaled.** If v+o+*with* someone **regales** you with stories or jokes, they tell you a lot of them, whether you want to hear them or not. EG *I used to have a dentist who regaled me with extraordinary stories.*

regard /rɪˈgɑːd/, **regards, regarding, regarded.**
1 If you **regard** someone or something as being a v+o+*as* particular thing or as having a particular quality, OR V-REFL+*as* you believe that they are that thing or have that quality. EG *I regard it as one of my masterpieces... Parents were still regarded as being responsible for the control of their children... She now regarded herself as a woman.*
2 If you **regard** something or someone with a v+o: feeling such as dislike or respect, you have that OFT+*with* feeling about them. EG *He is regarded with some suspicion by the country's leaders... His visitors regarded him with envy.*
3 If someone is highly **regarded**, people have a lot ADJ QUALIT of respect for them. EG *The more highly regarded* AFTER ADV *cameramen were kept very busy.*
4 If you have a high **regard** for someone, you have N UNCOUNT : a lot of respect for them. EG *I have a high regard* USU+*for* *for Mike... My regard for him grew day by day.*
5 Regards is used in expressions like 'best re- N PLURAL gards' and 'with warm regards' as a way of ex- pressing friendly feelings towards someone. EG *Give my regards to your daughter.*
6 Some people say **as regards, with regard to,** or PREP **in regard to** when indicating what they are talk- Formal ing or writing about. EG *As regards the car, I put an advertisement in the paper... With regard to the gas fire, we hardly use it... My upbringing was fairly strict in regard to obedience and truthful- ness.*
7 Some people say **in this regard** or **in that** PHRASE **regard** to indicate that what they are about to say Formal is connected with what they have just said. EG *In this regard, the child may be thought of as having two homes.*

regarding /rɪˈgɑːdɪŋ/. You can use **regarding** to PREP indicate what you are talking or writing about. EG *There was always some question regarding educa- tion.*

regardless /rɪˈgɑːdlɪ²s/. **1** If something happens PREP **regardless of** something else, it happens in spite of it. EG *If they are determined to strike, they will do so regardless of what the law says.*
2 If you say that someone did something **regard-** ADV AFTER VB **less,** you mean that they did it even though there were problems or factors that could have stopped them. EG *Mrs Hochstadt walked on regardless.*

regatta /rɪˈgætə/, **regattas.** A **regatta** is a sports N COUNT event consisting of races between yachts or rowing boats.

reggae /ˈregeɪ/ is a kind of West Indian popular N UNCOUNT music with a very strong beat.

regime /reɪˈʒiːm/, **regimes;** also spelled **régime.** N COUNT : A **regime** is **1** a system or method of government. USU+SUPP EG ...*a socialist regime... ...a regime where decision making is shared by all.* **2** a group of people who rule a country. EG ...*the corrupt regime that had ruled since 1921.*

regiment /ˈredʒɪmə²nt/, **regiments.** A **regiment** N COUNT is a large group of soldiers that is commanded by a colonel.

regimental /redʒɪˈmentə²l/ means belonging to a ADJ CLASSIF : particular regiment. EG *They took their orders* ATTRIB *from the regimental commander.*

regimentation /redʒɪmenteɪˈʃə²n/ is very strict N UNCOUNT control over a group of people. EG *He detested* Formal *every aspect of public school: the regimentation, the monotony, and the lack of privacy.*

regimented /ˈredʒɪmentɪ²d/. Something that is ADJ QUALIT **regimented** is very strictly controlled; used show- Formal ing disapproval. EG ...*the tightly regimented life of the prison.*

region /ˈriːdʒə²n/, **regions. 1** A **region** is a large N COUNT area of land that is different from other areas of land, for example because it is one of the different parts of a country or because it has a particular geographical feature. EG *The country has nine autonomous regions... ...fighting in the Central Re- gion... ...desert regions.*
2 You can refer to a part of your body as a **region.** N COUNT+SUPP EG *He was complaining of pains in the shoulder region.*
3 You say **in the region of** to indicate that an PREP amount that you are stating is only approximate. EG *Temperatures would be in the region of 500 de- grees centigrade.*

regional /ˈriːdʒə²nəl, -dʒə²nə²l/. **Regional** organiza- ADJ CLASSIF tions and activities relate to a particular area of a country. EG *Most regional committees meet four times a year... Apply to your local Regional Hospi- tal Board for details.*

register /ˈredʒɪstə/, **registers, registering, reg-** **istered. 1** A **register** is an official list or record of N COUNT things. EG ...*the electoral register... ...the register of births, marriages, and deaths.*
2 If you **register** for something, you put your name v : USU+A on an official list, for example to enable you to receive a service. EG *You must register for work at the employment agency... They're coming to regis- ter as students on the English course.*
◊ **registered.** EG *They are registered with the* ◊ ADJ CLASSIF *University Health Service... ...a registered drug addict.*
3 If you **register** something, such as the name of v+o : USU+A someone who has just died, or the details of ownership of your car, you have these facts record- ed on an official list. EG *One of the cars was registered in my name.*
4 When an amount **registers** or **is registered**, it V-ERG is shown on a scale or measuring instrument. EG *The inflation index registered a modest 7.8% an- nual rate.*
5 If you **register** your feelings or opinions about v+o something, you make them clear to other people, often by the expression on your face. EG *He stared at me for a moment, his face registering disbelief... Thousands joined the march to register their oppo- sition to cuts in education.*

registered /ˈredʒɪstəd/. A **registered** letter or ADJ CLASSIF : parcel is sent by a special postal service, for which ATTRIB you have to pay extra money to insure it in case it is lost. EG ...*a registered letter.*

registrar /redʒɪˈstrɑː/, **registrars.** A **registrar** is N COUNT **1** a person whose job is to keep official records, especially of births, marriages, and deaths. **2** a senior administrative official in a college or univer- sity.

registration /redʒɪˈstreɪʃə²n/. The **registration** N UNCOUNT of something such as a person's name or the details of an event is the recording of it in an official list. EG ...*a certificate of registration of death.*

registration number, registration numbers. N COUNT The **registration number** of a car or other road vehicle is the series of letters and numbers that are shown at the front and back of it.

registry /ˈredʒɪstri/, **registries.** A **registry** is a N COUNT place where official records are kept.

registry office, registry offices. A **registry** N COUNT **office** is a place where births, marriages, and deaths are officially recorded, and where people can get married without a religious ceremony.

regress /rɪˈgres/, **regresses, regressing, re-** v : OFT+*to* **gressed.** When people or things **regress,** they Formal return to a worse condition or way of life. EG *Since 1976 many rivers have regressed from being clean to being grossly polluted.* ◊ **regression** /rɪˈɡreʃəⁿ/. EG *...technological progress combined with moral and social regression.* ◊ N UNCOUNT: OFT+to

regressive /rɪˈɡresɪv/. Behaviour, activities, or processes that are **regressive** involve a return to a worse condition or way of life. EG *This fee has been criticized as a regressive tax.* ADJ QUALIT Formal

regret /rɪˈɡret/, **regrets, regretting, regretted.**
1 If you **regret** something that you have done, you wish that you had not done it. EG *I immediately regretted my decision... It made me regret that I had left home... Afterwards he regretted having spoken to them.* ▸ used as a noun. EG *Linda has no regrets at having become a banker.* V+O; ALSO V+REPORT OR -ING ▸ N UNCOUNT OR N COUNT

2 You can say that you **regret** something as a polite way of saying that you are sorry about it. EG *London Transport regrets any inconvenience caused by these delays... The Prime Minister regrets that he is unable to reconsider your case.* ▸ used as a noun. EG *We informed them with regret of our decision.* V+O; ALSO V+REPORT OR to-INF: NO CONT Formal ▸ N UNCOUNT

regretful /rɪˈɡretfʊl/. If you are **regretful**, you feel sorry about something. EG *Michael gave me a sad regretful smile.* ◊ **regretfully**. EG *He shook his head regretfully.* ADJ QUALIT ◊ ADV

regrettable /rɪˈɡretəbəⁱl/. You describe something as **regrettable** when you think that it is unfortunate and that it should not happen. EG *...the regrettable manifestations of cruelty to children... His tiredness caused him to make a regrettable error.* ◊ **regrettably** /rɪˈɡretəblⁱ/. EG *Regrettably few of them have gone to university... Regrettably, it is not an easy plant to grow in this country.* ADJ QUALIT ◊ SUBMOD OR ADV SEN

regroup /riːˈɡruːp/, **regroups, regrouping, regrouped.** When soldiers **regroup**, they form an organized group again, in order to continue fighting. EG *They regrouped and were ordered to open fire.* V

regular /ˈreɡjʊlə/, **regulars.** 1 You say that things are **regular** when they have equal amounts of time or space between them. EG *He could hear her deep, regular breathing... The doctor examined the baby at regular intervals... There were regular lines of holes between the windows.* ◊ **regularly**. EG *...regularly spaced cabbages.* ADJ QUALIT ◊ ADV

2 You also say that something is **regular** when it has a well-balanced appearance. EG *His face was sun-tanned, with regular features... It's easy to draw because it's such a regular shape.* ADJ QUALIT

3 **Regular** events or activities continue to happen according to a definite arrangement or plan, so that they happen, for example, at the same time each day or each week. EG *They give regular Sunday afternoon concerts... You need to take regular exercise.* ◊ **regularly**. EG *The members meet regularly in one another's homes.* ADJ QUALIT ◊ ADV

4 A **regular** event is also one that happens often. EG *...one of the regular bombings.* ◊ **regularly**. EG *Children are regularly abandoned.* ADJ QUALIT ◊ ADV

5 If you are a **regular** customer at a shop or a **regular** visitor to a place, you go there often. EG *...our regular customers... Gerald and I are regular churchgoers.* ▸ used as a noun. EG *He's one of the regulars at the village pub.* ADJ QUALIT: ATTRIB ▸ N COUNT

6 Your **regular** way of doing something is the way that you normally do it. Your **regular** time for doing something is the time when you normally do it. EG *It's past his regular bedtime... You can get in touch with a psychiatrist through your regular doctor.* ADJ CLASSIF: ATTRIB

7 A **regular** verb, noun, or adjective inflects in the same way as most verbs, nouns, or adjectives in the language. ADJ CLASSIF

regularity /ˌreɡjʊˈlærⁱtⁱ/. If something happens with **regularity**, it happens often. EG *The same exam questions cropped up with unfailing regularity.* N UNCOUNT

regulate /ˈreɡjʊleɪt/, **regulates, regulating, regulated.** 1 To **regulate** an activity or process means to control it, usually by means of rules. EG *Economic activity was regulated by the supply of money... ...rigid rules regulating all aspects of life.* ◊ **regulated**. EG *His life was too well regulated to be affected by affairs of the heart.* V+O ◊ ADJ QUALIT

2 If you **regulate** a machine or device, you adjust it to control the way it operates. EG *Do you know how to regulate the boiler?* V+O

regulation /ˌreɡjʊˈleɪʃəⁿ/, **regulations.** 1 **Regulations** are rules made by a government or other authority in order to control the way something is done or the way people behave. EG *There are specific regulations governing these types of machines... You can't do that. It's against the regulations.* ▸ used as an adjective. EG *He had the short regulation haircut of a policeman.* N COUNT: USU PLURAL ▸ ADJ CLASSIF: ATTRIB

2 **Regulation** is the controlling of an activity or process, usually by means of rules. EG *...strict regulation over toxic waste disposal.* N UNCOUNT

regurgitate /rɪˈɡɜːdʒɪteɪt/, **regurgitates, regurgitating, regurgitated.** 1 If you **regurgitate** food, you bring it back up from your stomach before it is digested. EG *The young feed on regurgitated food from the parent birds.* V+O Technical

2 If you **regurgitate** ideas or facts, you repeat them without understanding them properly. EG *The student is expected to regurgitate an answer to the teacher.* V+O Formal

rehabilitate /ˌriːhəˈbɪlɪteɪt/, **rehabilitates, rehabilitating, rehabilitated.** To **rehabilitate** someone who has been ill or in prison means to help them to live a normal life again. EG *He used exercise programmes to rehabilitate heart-attack victims.* ◊ **rehabilitation** /ˌriːhəbɪlɪˈteɪʃəⁿ/. EG *...the rehabilitation of drug addicts.* V+O ◊ N UNCOUNT

rehearsal /rɪˈhɜːsəⁱl/, **rehearsals.** A **rehearsal** of a play, dance, or piece of music is a practice, in which it is prepared for a performance. N COUNT OR N UNCOUNT

rehearse /rɪˈhɜːs/, **rehearses, rehearsing, rehearsed.** 1 If people **rehearse** a play, dance, or piece of music, they practise it in order to prepare for a performance. EG *The actors began to rehearse a few scenes... Stay and hear the orchestra rehearse.* V+O OR V

2 If you **rehearse** something that you are going to say, you silently practise it by imagining that you are saying it. EG *She was secretly rehearsing various amusing ways of telling what had happened.* V+O Formal

rehouse /riːˈhaʊz/, **rehouses, rehousing, rehoused.** If someone **is rehoused**, they are provided with a different house to live in, usually a better one than their previous one. EG *Young families are being rehoused in New Towns.* V+O: USU PASS

reign /reɪn/, **reigns, reigning, reigned.** 1 You can say that something **reigns** when it is the strongest or most noticeable feature of a situation or period of time. EG *Peace has reigned in Europe... ...the sense of comfort which reigned over the town.* ▸ used as a noun. EG *...a reign of terror... The reign of love has begun.* V: USU+A Literary ▸ N SING+of

2 When a king or queen **reigns**, he or she rules a country. EG *The emperor Chia Ching reigned from 1522 to 1566... ...the reigning monarch.* V: USU+A

3 The **reign** of a king or queen is the period during which he or she rules. EG *...George III's long reign.* N COUNT+POSS

reimburse /ˌriːɪmˈbɜːs/, **reimburses, reimbursing, reimbursed.** If you **reimburse** someone for something, you pay them back the money that they have spent or lost. EG *I promised to reimburse her for the damage to her car.* V+O: OFT+for, OR V+O+O Formal

rein /reɪn/, **reins.** 1 **Reins** are the thin leather straps attached to a horse's bridle, which you hold and use for controlling the horse when you are N PLURAL

What two words on these pages are pronounced in the same way?

riding it or when it is pulling a vehicle. EG *He pulled at the reins.*

2 If you **give a free rein to** someone, you give PHRASE them a lot of freedom to do what they want. If you **keep a tight rein on** them, you control them firmly. EG *He has given a free rein to the Security Service in their investigations.*

reincarnate /riːɪŋˈkɑːneɪt/, **reincarnates, re-** V+O : USU PASS **incarnating, reincarnated.** If people believe that they will be **reincarnated** when they die, they believe that their spirit will be born again and will live in the body of another person or animal.

reincarnation /riːɪŋkɑːˈneɪʃəʰn/, **reincarna-** **tions. 1 Reincarnation** is supposed to happen N UNCOUNT when someone is born again after death and lives again in the body of another creature. EG *I believe in reincarnation.*

2 A **reincarnation** is a person or animal in whose N COUNT body a dead person is believed to have been born again. EG *They all regarded us as reincarnations of their ancestors.*

reindeer /ˈreɪndɪə/. A **reindeer** is a deer with N COUNT large antlers that lives in northern areas of Europe, Asia, and America. The plural form is also **reindeer.**

reinforce /riːɪnˈfɔːs/, **reinforces, reinforcing, reinforced. 1** If something **reinforces** a feeling, V+O situation, or process, it strengthens it. EG *This sort of experience reinforces their feelings of worthlessness... They hope to reinforce their domination in these countries.*

2 If something **reinforces** an idea or point of view, V+O it provides more evidence or support for it. EG *This report reinforces practically everything that has been said.*

3 To **reinforce** an object means to make it strong- V+O : er or harder. EG *I had not thought of reinforcing the* OFT+*with* *handles with leather.* ◊ **reinforced.** *...reinforced* ◊ ADJ CLASSIF *helmets.*

reinforcement /riːɪnˈfɔːsməʰnt/, **reinforce-** **ments. 1 Reinforcements** are soldiers who are N PLURAL sent to join an army in order to make it stronger. EG *News reached them of the safe arrival of reinforcements.*

2 Reinforcement is **2.1** the strengthening of some- N UNCOUNT thing. EG *...the reinforcement of existing systems.* **2.2** something that is added to a material or an N UNCOUNT object in order to make it harder or stronger. EG OR N COUNT *...barges with fibreglass reinforcement.*

reinstate /riːɪnˈsteɪt/, **reinstates, reinstating, reinstated. 1** If you **reinstate** someone, you give V+O them back a job or position which had been taken from them. EG *He was four times sacked and four times reinstated.*

2 To **reinstate** something means to make it exist V+O again. EG *...threats to reinstate this tax... The trip reinstated my faith in myself.*

reiterate /riːˈɪtəreɪt/, **reiterates, reiterating, re-** V·SPEECH **iterated.** If you **reiterate** something, you say it Formal again. EG *He reiterated this advice several more times during the meeting.*

reject, rejects, rejecting, rejected; pronounced /rɪˈdʒekt/ when it is a verb and /ˈriːdʒekt/ when it is a noun.

1 If you **reject** something such as a proposal or V+O request, you do not accept it or you do not agree to it. EG *The Labour Party rejected offers to discuss the reform of the House of Lords... The amendment was rejected by 207 votes to 143.* ◊ **rejection** ◊ N UNCOUNT /rɪˈdʒekʃəʰn/, **rejections.** EG *...his rejection of re-* OR N COUNT *peated requests for military action.*

2 If you **reject** a belief or a political system, you V+O decide that you do not believe in it and do not want to live by its rules. EG *It was hard for me to reject my family's religious beliefs... Some people reject the idea of a mixed economy.* ◊ **rejection.** EG ◊ N UNCOUNT *There had been a widespread rejection of many of the traditional processes of political participation.*

3 If an employer **rejects** a person who has applied V+O

for a job, he or she does not offer that person the job. EG *Many candidates were rejected.*

◊ **rejection.** EG *After a week he received his* ◊ N UNCOUNT *rejection letter.* OR N COUNT

4 If a machine **rejects** a coin that you put in it, the V+O coin comes out and the machine does not work. EG *The phone-box often jammed, or rejected perfectly good coins.*

5 A **reject** is a product that has not been accepted N COUNT for use, because something is wrong with it. EG *We got the rejects half price.*

rejoice /rɪˈdʒɔɪs/, **rejoices, rejoicing, rejoiced.** V : OFT+*in* If you **rejoice**, you are very pleased about some- OR *to*-INF thing. EG *All his friends gathered to rejoice in his* Literary *freedom... I rejoice to hear it.*

rejuvenate /rɪˈdʒuːvɪneɪt/, **rejuvenates, reju-** **venating, rejuvenated. 1** If something **reju-** V+O **venates** you, it makes you feel or look young again. EG *I think we were rejuvenated by the experience.* ◊ **rejuvenating.** EG *...rejuvenating* ◊ ADJ QUALIT *cosmetics.*

2 If you **rejuvenate** an organization or system, you V+O make it more lively and more efficient, for example by introducing new ideas. EG *He resolved to rejuvenate the party.*

relaid /riːˈleɪd/ is a past tense and past participle of **relay.**

relapse, relapses, relapsing, relapsed; pronounced /rɪˈlæps/ when it is a verb and either /rɪˈlæps/ or /ˈriːlæps/ when it is a noun.

1 You say that someone **relapses** into an undesir- V : USU+*into* able way of behaving when they start to behave that way again. EG *She relapsed into depression... Cameron relapsed into silence again.* ▸ used as a ▸ N COUNT : noun. EG *...her relapses into alcoholism.* OFT+*into*

2 If a sick person has a **relapse**, their health N COUNT suddenly gets worse after it had been improving.

relate /rɪˈleɪt/, **relates, relating, related. 1** If V·ERG OR you say that one thing **relates** to another or if you V·ERG+*to* : **relate** one thing to another, you are saying that RECIP there is a connection between the two things. EG *Let us examine the way that the words in a sentence relate to each other... They were very religious and related everything to a dependence on God.* ◊ **related.** EG *...two important and closely* ◊ ADJ CLASSIF *related questions.*

2 If you say that something **relates** to a particular V+*to* subject, you mean that it concerns that subject. EG *I want to ask you a question that relates to electricity... ...discussion on matters relating to home-making in all its aspects.*

3 If you can **relate** to someone, you can under- V OR V+*to* : stand how they feel or behave and so are able to RECIP communicate with them or deal with them easily. EG *Children need to learn to relate to other children.*

4 If you **relate** a story, you tell it. EG *Davis related* V+O *the experience of three Cuban girls.* Literary

related /rɪˈleɪtɪʰd/. **1** People who are **related** ADJ CLASSIF belong to the same family. EG *...four people closely* OFT+*to* *related to each other.*

2 If you say that different types of animal or ADJ CLASSIF : different languages are **related**, you mean that OFT+*to* they have developed from the same type of animal or language. EG *Termites are closely related to cockroaches... French and Spanish are related languages.*

relation /rɪˈleɪʃəʰn/, **relations. 1** You use **in rela-** PREP **tion to 1.1** when you are talking about the state or size of something compared to other things. EG *Wages are very low in relation to the cost of living.* **1.2** when you are talking about where something is compared to other things. EG *Using this portable communications system, everybody knows exactly where they are in relation to everybody else.*

2 If you talk about the **relation** of one thing to N UNCOUNT another, you are talking about the connection or USU+*of/to* similarity between them. EG *She argued that literature has no relation to reality.*

3 Your **relations** are the members of your family. N COUNT:
EG *I was a distant relation of her husband.* OFT+POSS

4 Relations between people or groups are con- N PLURAL:
tacts between them and the way in which they USU+SUPP
behave towards each other. EG *This fear is causing
East-West relations to deteriorate... The unions
should have close relations with management.*

relationship /rɪ'leɪʃəⁿʃɪp/, **relationships. 1** The N COUNT: OFT
relationship between two people or groups is the +*between*/
way in which they feel and behave towards each *with*
other. EG *Pakistan's relationship with India has
changed dramatically.*

2 A **relationship** is also a close friendship between N COUNT: OFT
two people, especially one involving romantic or +*between*/
sexual feelings. EG *When the relationship ended two *with*
months ago he said he wanted to die... ...a sexual
relationship.*

3 The **relationship** between two things is the way N COUNT
in which they are connected. EG *What is the relationship between language and thought?*

relative /'relətɪv/, **relatives. 1** You use **relative** ADJ CLASSIF:
1.1 to say that something is true to a certain degree ATTRIB
or extent, especially when compared with other
things of the same kind. EG *The head of the
department is a relative newcomer... He chose to
return to the relative peace of his childhood village.* **1.2** when you are comparing the size or
quality of two things. EG *There was a discussion on
the relative naval strengths of the two countries.*

2 Relative to something means with reference to PREP
it or in comparison with it. EG *There is a shortage of* Formal
labour relative to the demand for it.

3 Your **relatives** are the members of your family. N COUNT:
EG *His wife had gone to visit some of her relatives* USU+POSS
for a few days.

4 If you say that something is **relative**, you mean ADJ CLASSIF
that it needs to be considered and judged in Formal
relation to other things. EG *All human values are
relative.*

relative clause, relative clauses. In grammar, N COUNT
a **relative clause** is a subordinate clause that is
introduced by a relative conjunction or a relative
pronoun, such as 'where' or 'who'.

relatively /'relətɪvli¹/ means to a fairly large SUBMOD
extent or degree. EG *It was relatively easy to find
her house... A relatively small number of people
disagreed.*

relative pronoun, relative pronouns. In gram- N COUNT
mar, a **relative pronoun** is a pronoun such as
'who' that is used to introduce a relative clause.

relax /rɪ'læks/, **relaxes, relaxing, relaxed. 1** If V-ERG
you **relax** or if something **relaxes** you, you feel
more calm and less worried or tense. EG *He saw
that nothing was wrong, and relaxed... Just lie back
and relax... Running relaxes you.*

2 When a part of your body **relaxes**, it becomes V-ERG
less stiff or firm. EG *She watched the muscles of his
arms hardening and relaxing.*

3 If you **relax** your grip or hold on something, you V-ERG
hold it less tightly than before.

4 If you **relax** a rule or **relax** your control over V+O
something, you make it less strict. EG *He had no
intention of relaxing his policies.*

relaxation /riːlæksˈeɪʃəⁿn/. **1 Relaxation** refers to N UNCOUNT
ways of spending time that are pleasant and rest-
ful. EG *It is so necessary for the mother to have
some rest and relaxation.*

2 If there is **relaxation** of a rule or control, it is N UNCOUNT:
made less strict. EG *The authorities encouraged a* OFT+*of/in*
general relaxation in child discipline.

relaxed /rɪ'lækst/. If you are **relaxed**, you are ADJ QUALIT
calm and not worried or tense. EG *It was a relaxed
and informal discussion... The children benefit
from the relaxed atmosphere.*

relaxing /rɪ'læksɪŋ/. Something that is **relaxing** ADJ QUALIT
is pleasant and helps you to relax. EG *It is a
delightful, relaxing place for a holiday.*

relay, relays, relaying, relayed, relaid; pronounced /riːleɪ/ in paragraphs 1, 2, and 3, /rɪ'leɪ/ in

paragraph 4, and /riːleɪ/ in paragraph 5. The past
tense and past participle of the verb are **relayed**
in paragraphs 3 and 4, and **relaid** in paragraph 5.

1 A **relay** or a **relay race** is a race between two or N COUNT
more teams, for example teams of runners or
swimmers. Each member of the team runs or
swims one section of the race. ● If people do ● PHRASE
something **in relays**, they do it in small groups at
different times. EG *The children at our school have
to be fed in two relays.*

2 A **relay** is a piece of equipment that receives N COUNT
television or radio signals from one place and
sends them on to another place. EG *...relay stations
in space.*

3 To **relay** television or radio signals means to V+O
send them on or broadcast them. EG *The Sunday
Concert will be relayed live on Radio Three.*

4 If you **relay** something that has been said to you, V+O: OFT+*to*
you repeat it to another person. EG *McKenzie
relayed the question to me.*

5 If you **relay** something such as a carpet or a road V+O
surface, you lay it again. EG *She wanted to relay the
carpet in her new home.*

release /rɪ'liːs/, **releases, releasing, released. 1** V+O:
If you **release** a person or animal that has been in OFT+*from*
captivity, you set them free. EG *They had just been
released from prison.* ► used as a noun. EG *Nearly a* ► N UNCOUNT
*year after his release he was still unable to sleep
properly.*

2 If something **releases** you from an unpleasant V+O:
situation or feeling, it frees you from it. EG *This* OFT+*from*
releases them from personal responsibility... This Formal
*failure released him from any obligation to take
further exams.* ► used as a noun. EG *...a feeling of* ► N UNCOUNT
release... ...a release from tension. OR N SING

3 If someone in authority **releases** something, V+O
they make it available or issue it. EG *Their aim was* Formal
*to release money for the schools... ...in a statement
released at 8 a.m.*

4 A press **release** or a publicity **release** is an N COUNT: SUPP
official written statement that is given to reporters.

5 If you **release** something, you stop holding it. EG V+O
He quickly released her hand. Formal

6 If you **release** a device, you move it so that it V+O
stops holding something. EG *I ran to the door and
released the catch.*

7 If something such as gas or water **is released**, it V+O
is let out of an enclosed space. EG *...releasing
radioactivity into the environment.* ► used as a ► N UNCOUNT:
noun. EG *...the controlled release of water from* USU+SUPP
reservoirs.

8 When a new film, record, or video **is released**, V+O
people can see it or buy it.

9 A new **release** is a new record or video that has N COUNT
just become available for people to buy.

10 If a film is **on release**, it is available for PHRASE
showing in public cinemas.

relegate /'relɪ²geɪt/, **relegates, relegating, rel-** V+O: USU+A
egated. If you **relegate** someone or something,
you give them a less important position or status.
EG *These old bits of furniture were relegated to the
attics... The management had relegated Mr Pelker
to the role of part-time consultant.*

relent /rɪ'lent/, **relents, relenting, relented.** If V
you **relent**, you allow someone to do something
that you did not allow them to do before. EG
*Sometimes our parents would relent and permit us
to meet... He relented somewhat and smiled at her.*

relentless /rɪ'lentⁿləs/. **1** Something that is **re-** ADJ CLASSIF
lentless never stops or never becomes less in-
tense. EG *...the relentless beating of the sun on the
roofs... ...the relentless population increase... You
get tired of relentless cynicism.* ◊ **relentlessly.** EG ◊ ADV
The chase relentlessly continues. Literary

2 Someone who is **relentless** is determined to do ADJ QUALIT

What grammatical words are explained on these
pages?

something and refuses to give up. ◇ **relentlessly.** ◇ ADV
EG ...*a relentlessly ambitious politician.* Literary

relevant /ˈrɛləvənt/. 1 If something is **relevant**, it ADJ QUALIT:
is connected with what is being talked or written OFT+*to*
about. EG ...*highly relevant information... This is not
strictly relevant to what I'll be saying.*
◇ **relevance** /ˈrɛləvəns/. EG *She did not understand* ◇ N UNCOUNT:
the relevance of his remarks. OFT+*to*
2 Something that is **relevant** to people is impor- ADJ QUALIT:
tant to them. EG *They accept that what you are* OFT+*to*
doing is relevant to their problems. ◇ **relevance.** ◇ N UNCOUNT:
EG *He spoke about the religion of Islam and its* OFT+*to*
relevance to people there.
3 The **relevant** thing of a particular kind is the one ADJ CLASSIF:
that is appropriate. EG *They are made to conform* ATTRIB
*with the relevant British Standards... Members are
drawn from people living in the relevant area.*

reliable /rɪˈlaɪəbᵊl/. 1 People or things that are ADJ QUALIT
reliable can be trusted to work well or to behave
in the way that you want them to. EG *She is a
charming and reliable person... The diesel engine
is long-lasting and extremely reliable.* ◇ **reliably.** ◇ ADV
EG *They worked reliably under battle conditions.*
◇ **reliability** /rɪˌlaɪəbɪˈlɪtiˈ/. EG *These machines* ◇ N UNCOUNT
have always been noted for reliability.
2 Information that is **reliable** is very likely to be ADJ QUALIT
correct. EG *The telegram was based on information
from a reliable source.* ◇ **reliably.** EG *We are* ◇ ADV
*reliably informed that her new record will be
released in the autumn.*

reliant /rɪˈlaɪənt/. Someone who is **reliant** on ADJ PRED+*on/*
something needs it and often cannot live or work *upon*
without it. EG *They are reliant on government
funds... We have become reliant on mechanical
equipment.* ◇ **reliance** /rɪˈlaɪəns/. EG ...*the stu-* ◇ N UNCOUNT:
dent's reliance on the teacher... ...complete reli- USU+*on/upon*
ance on drugs.

relic /ˈrɛlɪk/, **relics.** 1 When very old things or N COUNT:
customs are still used or practised, you can refer to USU+SUPP
them as **relics** of an earlier time. EG *These ideas
are relics of Victorian discipline.*
2 A **relic** is also something which was made or N COUNT:
used a long time ago but is no longer used. EG *We* USU+SUPP
visited a museum with relics of great explorers.
3 In a church, a **relic** is the body of a saint or N COUNT
something else associated with a saint, which some
people regard as holy.

relief /rɪˈliːf/. 1 If you feel **relief**, you feel glad N UNCOUNT OR
because something unpleasant has not happened N SING
or is no longer happening. EG *I breathed a sigh of
relief... To my relief, he found the suggestion
acceptable.*
2 **Relief** is also money, food, or clothing that is N UNCOUNT
provided for people who are very poor or hungry.
EG *She outlined what was being done to provide
relief... ...Christmas relief funds.*

relieve /rɪˈliːv/, **relieves, relieving, relieved.** 1 v+o
If something **relieves** an unpleasant feeling, it
makes it less unpleasant. EG *Anxiety may be relieved by talking to a friend... The passengers in
the plane swallow to relieve the pressure on their
eardrums.*
2 If someone or something **relieves** you of an v+o+*of*
unpleasant feeling or difficulty, they cause you to
no longer have it. EG *The news relieved him of
some of his embarrassment.*

relieved /rɪˈliːvd/. If you are **relieved**, you feel ADJ QUALIT:
glad because something unpleasant has not hap- USU PRED
pened or is no longer happening. EG *I am relieved
to hear that this isn't true... He felt enormously
relieved that they had taken the matter so calmly.*

religion /rɪˈlɪdʒən/, **religions.** 1 **Religion** is the N UNCOUNT
belief in a god or gods and the activities that are
connected with this belief, such as prayer or worship in a church or temple. EG *Politics and religion
were daily topics of conversation... The school
placed strong emphasis on religion.*
2 A **religion** is a particular system of belief in a N COUNT
god or gods and the activities that are connected

with this system. EG ...*the Christian religion... What
is your religion?*

religious /rɪˈlɪdʒəs/. 1 You use **religious** to de- ADJ CLASSIF:
scribe things connected with religion or with one ATTRIB
particular religion. EG *All religious activities were
suppressed... ...people who have no religious faith.*
2 Someone who is **religious** has a strong belief in a ADJ QUALIT
god or gods. EG *Our parents were very religious.*

religiously /rɪˈlɪdʒəsliˈ/. If you do something re- ADV
ligiously, you do it very regularly because you
regard it as a duty. EG *The ornaments were all
religiously dusted by Gertrude.*

relinquish /rɪˈlɪŋkwɪʃ/, **relinquishes, relin-** V+O
quishing, relinquished. If you **relinquish** some- Formal
thing such as authority or responsibility, you give it
up. EG *She relinquished the editorship of the newspaper.*

relish /ˈrɛlɪʃ/, **relishes, relishing, relished.** 1 If V+O
you **relish** something, you get a lot of enjoyment
from it. EG *He relishes the challenge of competition.*
► used as a noun. EG *In his book he exposed with* ► N UNCOUNT
relish all the evils of our present day.
2 If you **relish** the idea, thought, or prospect of V+O
something, you are looking forward to it very
much. EG ...*rebels who relish the prospect of conflict and violence... She didn't relish the idea of
going on her own.*
3 **Relish** is a sauce or a pickle that you add to food N MASS
in order to give it more flavour.

relive /riːˈlɪv/, **relives, reliving, relived.** If you V+O
relive something that has happened to you in the
past, you remember it and imagine that you are
experiencing it again. EG *You spend too much time
reliving old joys.*

relocate /riːˈləʊkeɪt/, **relocates, relocating, re-** V-ERG
located. If people or businesses **relocate** or are
relocated, they move to a different place. EG *Semi-
skilled workers find themselves compelled to relocate... They relocated me in another building.*
◇ **relocation** /riːləʊˈkeɪʃᵊn/. EG *Priority must be* ◇ N UNCOUNT
given to the relocation of industry.

reluctant /rɪˈlʌktənt/. If you are **reluctant** to do ADJ QUALIT:
something, you are unwilling to do it. EG *He is* OFT+*to*-INF
*reluctant to be photographed... The reluctant bride-
groom smiled for the first time.* ◇ **reluctantly.** EG ◇ ADV
A wage increase of 21% was reluctantly conceded.
◇ **reluctance** /rɪˈlʌktəns/. EG *They showed reluc-* ◇ N UNCOUNT
*tance to support these measures... They released
her with reluctance.*

rely /rɪˈlaɪ/, **relies, relying, relied.** 1 If you **rely** V+*on/upon*
on someone or something, you need them and
depend on them in order to live or work properly.
EG *He's relying on me completely... She is forced to
rely on social security money... Hong Kong's prosperity relies heavily on foreign businesses.*
2 If you can **rely** on someone to work well or to V+*on/upon*
behave as you want them to, you can trust them to
do this. EG *One could always rely on him to be polite
and do the right thing... They cannot be relied upon
to offer much support.*

remain /rɪˈmeɪn/, **remains, remaining, re-**
mained. 1 To **remain** in a particular state or V+C
condition means to stay in that state or condition
and not change. EG *Oliver remained silent... He
remained standing... The results of these experiments remain a secret.*
2 If you **remain** in a place, you stay there and do V : USU+A
not move away. EG *I was allowed to remain at
home... Otto was having difficulty in remaining in
his seat.*
3 You can say that something **remains** when it V
still exists. EG *Even today remnants of this practice
remain... He was cut off from what remained of his
family... The fact remains that they mean to de-
stroy us.* ◇ **remaining.** EG ...*the demise of her last* ◇ ADJ CLASSIF:
remaining relatives. ATTRIB
4 If something **remains** to be done, it has not yet V+*to*-INF
been done and still needs to be done. EG *One hazard
remained to be overcome.*

5 If you say that something **remains to be seen**, you mean that nobody is certain what will happen. EG *It remains to be seen what the long term effects will be.*   PHRASE

6 The **remains** of something are the parts of it that are left after most of it has been taken away or destroyed. EG *I searched through the bombed remains of the house... The remains of the meat sat on the kitchen table.*   N PLURAL USU+*of*

7 The **remains** of a person or animal are the parts of their body that are left after they have died, sometimes when they have been dead for a long time. EG *They discovered the remains of a huge dinosaur.*   N PLURAL +POSS

8 Remains are things that have been found from an earlier period of history, usually buried in the ground, for example parts of buildings and pieces of pottery. EG *...Roman remains.*   N PLURAL

remainder /rɪˈmeɪndə/. The **remainder** of something is the part of it that remains after the other parts have gone or been dealt with. EG *She went to Brighton where she lived for the remainder of her life... I will pay you a hundred pounds deposit and the remainder on delivery.*   N SING : *the*+N

remake, remakes, remaking, remade /riːˈmeɪd/. **Remake** is pronounced /riːˈmeɪk/ when it is a verb, and /ˈriːmeɪk/ when it is a noun.
1 If you **remake** something, you make it again, especially in a way that is better than before. EG *Ask what the price is for remaking old mattresses.*   V+O
2 A **remake** is a film that has the same story, and often the same title, as a film that was made earlier. EG *...the 1934 remake of 'Young Men in Spats'.*   N COUNT

remand /rɪˈmɑːnd/, **remands, remanding, remanded.**
1 If a judge **remands** a person who is accused of a crime, the trial does not take place immediately, and the person is ordered to come back to court at a later date. EG *He was remanded for trial at the central criminal court.*   V+O : OFT PASS
2 If someone accused of a crime is **on remand**, they have appeared in court and are waiting for their trial to begin.   PHRASE

remark /rɪˈmɑːk/, **remarks, remarking, remarked.**
1 If you **remark** that something is the case, you say that it is the case. EG *'Your father was a good friend to me,' he remarked... Mary's friends remarked that she could hate as passionately as she could love... His friends remarked on his failure to arrive.*   V+QUOTE OR REPORT : ONLY *that*; ALSO V+*on*
2 A **remark** is something that you say, often in a casual way. EG *At school some of the children used to make unkind remarks about my clothes... He closed the discussion with the remark that 'the economy shows signs of improving'.*   N COUNT : OFT+REPORT

remarkable /rɪˈmɑːkəbəl/. When you are very impressed by something that someone does, you can say that they are **remarkable** or that what they do is **remarkable**. EG *She was a remarkable woman... He prepared the dinner with remarkable speed and efficiency.* ◊ **remarkably.** EG *He has recovered from the accident remarkably well.*   ADJ QUALIT ◊ SUBMOD OR ADV SEN

remedial /rɪˈmiːdɪəl/. **Remedial** activities **1** are intended to improve someone's health when they are ill. EG *...remedial exercises for handicapped children.* **2** are intended to improve someone's ability to read, write, or do maths. EG *...a remedial English course.*   ADJ CLASSIF : ATTRIB Formal

remedy /ˈremɪdɪ/, **remedies, remedying, remedied.**
1 A **remedy** is **1.1** a successful way of dealing with a problem. EG *...a drastic remedy for lawlessness and disorder.* **1.2** something that is intended to cure you when you are ill or in pain. EG *...a remedy for skin and ear trouble... ...home-made remedies can often lessen the pain.*   N COUNT : OFT+*for* / N COUNT
2 If you **remedy** something that is wrong or harmful, you correct it or improve it. EG *Technicians laboriously tried to find and remedy faults... Can we remedy this at a later stage?*   V+O

remember /rɪˈmembə/, **remembers, remembering, remembered. 1** If you **remember** people or events from the past, your mind still has an impression of them and you are able to think about them. EG *He remembered the man well... I remember him falling down the steps... I remembered that the shop was on the way to Muswell Hill... I fell silent, remembering what I had heard.*   V+O OR V : OFT +ING; ALSO V+REPORT
2 If you can **remember** something, you are able to bring it back into your mind by making an effort to do so. EG *I'm trying to remember the things I have to do... There was something else, but she could not remember what it was.*   V+O OR V : OFT+-ING; ALSO V+REPORT
3 If you **remember** to do something, you do it when you intend to. EG *Remember to go to the bank.*   V : USU+*to*-INF
4 You say **remember** when you are reminding someone of something. EG *Remember that women did not gain the vote until 1918.*   V OR V+REPORT : ONLY *that*
5 If you ask someone to **remember** you to a person who you have not seen for a long time, you are asking them to pass your greetings to that person. EG *Remember me to your Grandma.*   V+O+*to* : NO CONT

remembrance /rɪˈmembrəns/. If you do something in **remembrance** of a dead person, you do it as a way of showing that you remember them and respect them. EG *We stood in silence for two minutes in remembrance of the dead.*   N UNCOUNT Formal

remind /rɪˈmaɪnd/, **reminds, reminding, reminded. 1** If someone **reminds** you of a fact or event that you already know about, they deliberately say something which makes you think about it. EG *She had to remind him that he had a wife... Remind me to speak to you about Davis... Miss Lemon reminded him of two appointments.*   V+O +*of/about*, REPORT, OR *to*-INF
2 If you say that someone or something **reminds** you of another person or thing, you mean that they are similar to the other person or thing and that they make you think about them. EG *Your son reminds me of you at his age... What does that remind you of?*   V+O+*of*

reminder /rɪˈmaɪndə/, **reminders. 1** You say that one thing is a **reminder** of another when the first thing makes you think about the second thing. EG *Seeing her again was a painful reminder of how different things had been five years ago.*   N COUNT : USU+SUPP
2 A **reminder** is also a letter or note that is sent to tell you that you have not done something such as pay a bill or return library books. EG *I've had another reminder from the library.*   N COUNT

reminisce /ˌremɪˈnɪs/, **reminisces, reminiscing, reminisced.** If you **reminisce** about something from your past, you write or talk about it, often with pleasure. EG *He reminisced about the 'old days' and how times had changed.*   V : OFT+*about* Formal

reminiscence /ˌremɪˈnɪsəns/, **reminiscences.** Someone's **reminiscences** are things that they remember from the past, and which they talk or write about. EG *She continued with fascinating reminiscences of their marriage.*   N COUNT : USU PLURAL

reminiscent /ˌremɪˈnɪsənt/. If you say that something is **reminiscent** of something else, you mean that it reminds you of it. EG *The atmosphere was reminiscent of spy movies... There was a sweet smell, vaguely reminiscent of coffee.*   ADJ PRED+*of* Formal

remission /rɪˈmɪʃəⁿn/. If someone in prison gets **remission**, their prison sentence is reduced, usually because they have behaved well. EG *I got four months' remission for good conduct.*   N UNCOUNT

remnant /ˈremnənt/, **remnants.** A **remnant** of something is a small part of it that is left over when the main part has disappeared or been destroyed. EG *Even today remnants of this practice remain.*   N COUNT : USU+*of*

What is the difference between 'remind' and 'remember'?

remorse /rɪˈmɔːs/ is a strong feeling of guilt about N UNCOUNT
something that you have done. EG *I had been filled* Formal
with remorse over hurting her.

remote /rɪˈməʊt/, **remoter, remotest. 1** Remote ADJ QUALIT
areas are far away from places where people live,
and are therefore difficult to get to. EG *Television
has begun to penetrate even the remote areas of
Java... Many children living in remote places cannot get to the playgroup.*

2 If something happened in the **remote** past, it ADJ QUALIT
happened a very long time ago. EG *...research into
the remote past.*

3 If something is **remote** from a particular subject ADJ QUALIT :
or area of experience, it is not relevant to it USU PRED +
because it is very different. EG *Much new knowl-* from
*edge is remote from the immediate interests of the
ordinary person... His stories are too remote from
everyday life.*

4 If you describe someone as **remote**, you mean ADJ QUALIT
that they behave as if they do not want to be
friendly or closely involved with other people. EG
*She was a silent girl, cool and remote... The union
leaders have to beware of getting too remote from
their members.* ◊ **remoteness.** EG *He criticised* ◊ N UNCOUNT
the remoteness of public authorities.

5 If the possibility of something happening is ADJ QUALIT
remote, it is very unlikely that it will happen. EG
*Winning is only a remote possibility at the mo-
ment.*

remote control is a system of controlling a N UNCOUNT
machine or a vehicle from a distance by using
radio or electronic signals. EG *The missile is guided
by remote control.*

remotely /rɪˈməʊtlɪ/. **1** You use **remotely** with a SUBMOD :
negative statement to emphasize the statement. EG USU WITH
Agreement did not seem remotely possible at the BROAD NEG
time... I've never seen anything remotely like it.

2 If someone or something is **remotely** placed or ADV
situated, they are a long way from other people or
places. EG *Living as remotely situated as she did, it
was very difficult to get to see her.*

removal /rɪˈmuːvəl/. **1** The **removal** of some- N UNCOUNT :
thing is the act of removing it. EG *He consented to* USU + SUPP
*the removal of the flags... ...a stain removal kit...
...the removal of the threat of intervention.*

2 A **removal** company transports furniture from N MOD
one building to another, for example when people
move house. EG *...removal men.*

remove /rɪˈmuːv/, **removes, removing, removed. 1** If you **remove** something from a place, V+O :
you take it away. EG *The servants came in to* OFT + from
*remove the cups... He removed his hand from the
man's collar.*

2 If you **remove** clothing, you take it off. EG *Will* V+O
you remove your shoes before you go in, please?

3 If you **remove** a stain from something, you treat V+O :
it with a chemical or wash it and make the stain OFT + from
disappear. EG *This mixture can remove stains from
metal and china.*

4 If you **are removed** from something such as a V+O :
committee, you are not allowed to continue as a OFT + from
member of it. EG *They made an attempt to remove
her from the General Council.*

5 If you **remove** an undesirable situation or atti- V+O
tude, you get rid of it. EG *The situation can be
helped by removing those inequalities... Instant
publication would have removed suspicion.*

removed /rɪˈmuːvd/. If you say that an idea or ADJ PRED
situation is far **removed** from something, you + from
mean that it is very different from it. EG *His ideas
on foreign policy were far removed from those of
the Government.*

rename /riːˈneɪm/, **renames, renaming, re- V+O : OFT + C
named.** If you **rename** something, you give it a
new name instead of the name it had before. EG *Mr
Haq has taken over the Carousel Cafe and re-
named it The Pearl of India.*

render /ˈrendə/, **renders, rendering, rendered.
1** You can use **render** to say that someone or V+O+C
Formal

something is changed into a particular state. For
example, if you **render** something harmless, you
do something to it that makes it harmless. EG
*...equipment which has been rendered obsolete... It
rendered him unconscious for a considerable period... Frank was rendered speechless by her reply.*

2 If you **render** someone help or assistance, you V+O, V+O+O,
help them. EG *Dr Lister Smith rendered vital first* OR V+O+ to
aid to Commander Bond. Formal

rendering /ˈrendərɪŋ/, **renderings.** A **rendering** N COUNT :
of a play, poem, or piece of music is a performance USU + of
of it. EG *They began with a loud rendering of the* Formal
hymn 'Onward Christian Soldiers'.

rendezvous /ˈrɒndeɪvuː/. **Rendezvous** is both the
singular and the plural form. It is pronounced
/ˈrɒndeɪvuːz/ when it is the plural.
A **rendezvous** is **1** a meeting, often a secret one, N COUNT
that you have arranged with someone for a particular time and place. EG *We made a dawn rendezvous.* **2** a place where you have arranged to meet
someone, often secretly. EG *I met him at a secret
rendezvous outside the city.*

rendition /rɛnˈdɪʃən/, **renditions.** A **rendition** of N COUNT :
a play, poem, or piece of music is a performance of USU + of
it. EG *...a rendition of 'The Four Seasons'.* Formal

renegade /ˈrenɪɡeɪd/, **renegades.** A **renegade** is N COUNT
a person who abandons the religious, political, or Formal
philosophical beliefs that he or she used to have,
and accepts opposing or different beliefs. EG *He was
a traitor and renegade... Renegade supporters of
the deposed King are still raiding villages.*

renew /rɪˈnjuː/, **renews, renewing, renewed. 1** V+O
If you **renew** an activity, you begin it again. EG *He
renewed his threat to resign... She at once renewed
her attack on Judy.* ◊ **renewed.** EG *We must* ◊ ADJ CLASSIF :
prepare for renewed efforts to recruit more mem- ATTRIB
bers.

2 If you **renew** a relationship with someone, you V+O :
start it again after you have not seen them for OFT + with
some time. EG *I hoped that we might renew our
friendship.*

3 When you **renew** something such as a licence or V+O
a contract, you extend the period of time for which
it is valid. EG *The studio did not renew his contract.*

4 You can say that something **is renewed** when it V+O : USU PASS
grows again or is replaced after it has been de-
stroyed or lost. ◊ **renewed.** EG *He looked at me* ◊ ADJ CLASSIF :
with renewed interest. ATTRIB

renewal /rɪˈnjuːəl/, **renewals. 1** If there is a N UNCOUNT :
renewal of an activity or situation, it starts again. USU + of
EG *Renewal of hostility with neighbouring countries
seemed likely... ...a renewal of civil disorder in U.S.
cities.*

2 The **renewal** of a document such as a licence or N UNCOUNT
a contract is an official extension of the time for OR N COUNT
which it remains valid. EG *Some licences need
yearly renewal... ...visa renewals.*

renounce /rɪˈnaʊns/, **renounces, renouncing,
renounced. 1** If you **renounce** a belief or a way of V+O
behaving, you decide to stop believing in it or Formal
behaving in that way. EG *...their determination to
renounce the materialism of society... We have
renounced the use of force to settle our disputes.*

2 If you **renounce** an official post, rank, or title, V+O
you formally give it up. EG *The Earl wanted to* Formal
renounce his peerage.

renovate /ˈrenəveɪt/, **renovates, renovating,** V+O
renovated. If someone **renovates** an old building
or a machine, they repair and improve it and get it
back into good condition. EG *The house had been
renovated three years earlier.* ◊ **renovation** ◊ N UNCOUNT
/ˌrenəˈveɪʃən/, **renovations.** EG *...the renovation of* OR N COUNT
old buildings.

renown /rɪˈnaʊn/. A person of **renown** is well N UNCOUNT
known, usually for something good. EG *His renown* Literary
as a soldier spread throughout the country.

renowned /rɪˈnaʊnd/. A person who is **renowned** ADJ QUALIT
for something, usually something good, is well OFT + for

known because of it. EG *The locals are renowned for their hospitality.*

rent /rɛnt/, **rents, renting, rented. 1** If you **rent** something, you pay its owner a sum of money every week or every month in order to be able to have it and use it yourself. EG *They rented a villa not far from Rome... He rented a colour TV soon after moving in.* ◊ **rented**. EG *...a rented flat.*   ◊ ADJ CLASSIF   V+O

2 Rent is the amount of money that you pay regularly to rent a house, flat, or piece of land. EG *He made enough money to pay the monthly rent punctually.*   N SING OR N UNCOUNT

rent out. If you **rent out** something such as a room or a car, you allow it to be used in return for payment. EG *They had to rent out the upstairs room for years.*   PHRASAL VB : V+O+ADV

rental /rɛntəᵊl/, **rentals. 1** You use **rental** to describe things that are connected with the renting out of goods and services. EG *...a computer rental service.*   ADJ CLASSIF : ATTRIB

2 The **rental** is the amount of money that you have to pay when you rent something such as a television or a car. EG *The quarterly rental will be £35.*   N COUNT : USU SING

reorganize /riˈɔːgənaɪz/, **reorganizes, reorganizing, reorganized;** also spelled **reorganise.**
If you **reorganize** something, you organize it in a new way that is intended to make it more efficient or acceptable. EG *The manufacturers were reorganising the soap industry.* ◊ **reorganization** /riːˌɔːgənaɪzˈeɪʃəᵊn/, **reorganizations.** EG *Recently there has been a reorganisation of the Health Service.*   V+O OR V   ◊ N UNCOUNT OR N COUNT

rep /rɛp/, **reps.** A **rep** is a person whose job is to sell a company's products or services, especially by travelling round and visiting other companies. EG *I've been working as a sales rep.*   N COUNT : USU+SUPP Informal

repaid /riˈpeɪd/ is the past tense and past participle of **repay.**

repair /rɪˈpɛə/, **repairs, repairing, repaired. 1** A **repair** is something that you do to mend a machine, piece of clothing, or other thing that has been damaged or is not working properly. EG *He had left his car for repairs in the garage.*   N COUNT OR N UNCOUNT

2 If something such as a building is **in good repair**, it is in good condition. If it is **in bad repair**, it is in bad condition. EG *...a small wooden shed in poor repair.*   PHRASE Formal

3 If you **repair** something that has been damaged or is not working properly, you mend it. EG *No one knew how to repair the engine.*   V+O

4 If you **repair** something wrong or harmful that someone has done, you do something to correct it or make it less serious. EG *Can you see any way in which we can repair these two very major omissions?*   V+O Formal

repartee /rɛpɑːˈtiː/ is conversation that consists of quick, witty comments and replies. EG *...his constant chatter and repartee with the spectators.*   N UNCOUNT

repay /rɪˈpeɪ/, **repays, repaying, repaid** /rɪˈpeɪd/. **1** If you **repay** money, you give it back to the person who borrowed or took it from. EG *He plans to repay most of that debt... He ordered the President to repay the money to the State.*   V+O, V+O+O, OR V+O+to

2 If you **repay** a favour that someone did for you, you do something or give them something in return. EG *We hope we can repay you for the pleasure you have given us.*   V+O : OFT+for

repayment /rɪˈpeɪmənt/, **repayments. 1** Repayments are amounts of money which you pay at regular intervals to a person or organization in order to repay a debt over a period of time. EG *They faced the burden of loan repayments.*   N COUNT : USU PLURAL

2 The **repayment** of money is the process of paying it back to the person you owe it to. EG *...repayment of international debts.*   N UNCOUNT : USU+SUPP

repeal /rɪˈpiːl/, **repeals, repealing, repealed.** If the government **repeals** a law, it officially ends it, so that it is no longer valid. EG *Nine countries repealed their anti-discrimination laws last year.*   V+O Legal

▸ used as a noun. EG *...a campaign for the repeal of incomes legislation.*   ▸ N UNCOUNT : USU+of

repeat /rɪˈpiːt/, **repeats, repeating, repeated. 1** If you **repeat** something, you say or write it again. EG *Haldane repeated his statement in the presence of the Prime Minister... 'We need half a million dollars,' Monty kept repeating. 'Half a million dollars.'*   V.SPEECH

2 If you **repeat** something that someone else has said or written, you say or write the same thing. EG *Ballin repeated what he had been told by Haldane.*   V+O OR V+QUOTE

3 If you **repeat** an action, you do it again. EG *I decided not to repeat the mistake of my first marriage.*   V+O

4 If you **repeat** yourself, you say or do something which you have said or done before. EG *People tend to repeat themselves a lot in conversation... History often repeats itself.*   V.REFL

5 If a television or radio programme **is repeated**, it is broadcast again. EG *'How Many Miles to Babylon' is being repeated on Radio 4 next Sunday afternoon.*   V+O : USU PASS

6 A **repeat** is something which is done again or which happens again. EG *'Any Answers' can first be heard tomorrow night at 8, with a repeat on Monday afternoon... ...a repeat performance of the play.*   N COUNT

repeated /rɪˈpiːtɪd/. **Repeated** actions or events are ones which happen many times. EG *After repeated attempts, the manager finally managed to call the police... Anxious patients require repeated reassurance that they are getting better.*   ADJ CLASSIF : ATTRIB

repeatedly /rɪˈpiːtɪdliᵊ/. If you do something **repeatedly**, you do it many times. EG *The child learns to read by seeing the words repeatedly.*   ADV

repel /rɪˈpɛl/, **repels, repelling, repelled.** If something **repels** you, you find it horrible and disgusting. EG *Any deformity frightened and repelled her.*   V+O

repellent /rɪˈpɛlənt/, **repellents. 1** If you find something **repellent**, you find it horrible and disgusting. EG *The idea of eating meat has become repellent to me.*   ADJ QUALIT : OFT+to Formal

2 Repellent is a chemical which is used to keep insects or other creatures away from an area. EG *...a bottle of insect repellent.*   N MASS

repent /rɪˈpɛnt/, **repents, repenting, repented.** If you **repent**, you feel sorry for something bad that you have done in the past. EG *He may repent of his sins... He lived to repent his early love.*   V : OFT+of/for, OR V+O Formal

repentance /rɪˈpɛntəns/ is sorrow and regret that you feel for something bad that you have done in the past. EG *...prayers of repentance.*   N UNCOUNT Formal

repentant /rɪˈpɛntənt/. Someone who is **repentant** feels sorrow and regret for something bad that they have done in the past. EG *...repentant sinners.*   ADJ QUALIT Formal

repercussion /riːpəkʌˈʃəᵊn/, **repercussions.** The **repercussions** of an event or action are the effects that it has at a later time. EG *They cannot foresee the complex repercussions of these changes... What happened had enormous repercussions on my family.*   N COUNT : USU PLURAL Formal

repertoire /rɛpətwɑː/. A musician's **repertoire** consists of all the music that he or she has learned and can perform. Similarly, an actor's or actress's **repertoire** consists of all the parts he or she has learned and can perform. EG *It was wonderful to be able to extend my song repertoire.*   N SING+SUPP

repertory /rɛpətəᵊriᵊ/ is the practice of performing a small number of plays in a theatre for a fairly short time, using the same actors in every play. EG *After leaving drama school I joined a repertory company.*   N UNCOUNT Formal

repetition /rɛpɪtˈɪʃəᵊn/, **repetitions.** When there is a **repetition** of something that has happened   N COUNT OR N UNCOUNT

Why might you rephrase a question?

before, it happens again. EG *He didn't want a repetition of the scene with his mother.*

repetitious /rɪpɪˈtɪʃəs/ means the same as repetitive. EG *...endlessly repetitious jobs.*   ADJ QUALIT

repetitive /rɪˈpɛtɪtɪv/. Something that is **repetitive** contains unnecessary repetition, and is therefore boring. EG *His job consists of dull, repetitive work... ...a shrill, repetitive sound.*   ADJ QUALIT

rephrase /riːˈfreɪz/, **rephrases, rephrasing, rephrased.** If you **rephrase** a question or statement, you ask it or say it again in a different way.   V+O

replace /rɪˈpleɪs/, **replaces, replacing, replaced.** 1 When one thing **replaces** another, the first thing takes the place of the second thing. EG *Thomas bought a new sweater to replace the one he lost... Arabic script was replaced with the Roman alphabet.*   V+O: OFT+with

2 If you **replace** one thing with another, you use the second thing in place of the first one. EG *The airline is currently replacing its DC10s with Boeing 747s.*   V+O: OFT+with

3 If you **replace** something that is damaged or lost, you get a new thing which will perform the same function. EG *The books that have been stolen will have to be replaced.*   V+O

4 To **replace** something also means to put it back in the place where it was before. EG *She replaced the receiver.*   V+O

replacement /rɪˈpleɪsmənt/, **replacements.** 1 The **replacement** of someone or something happens when they are replaced by another person or thing. EG *...the resignation of Jo Grimond and his replacement by Jeremy Thorpe... ...the replacement of steam by diesel.*   N UNCOUNT

2 A **replacement** for someone or something is another person or thing that takes their place. EG *The Colonel's replacement was due any day now.*   N COUNT

replay, replays, replaying, replayed; pronounced /riːˈpleɪ/ when it is a verb and /ˈriːpleɪ/ when it is a noun.

1 If two sports teams **replay** a match in a competition, they play it again because the previous match between them was a draw. ▸ used as a noun. EG *Who won the replay?*   V+O   ▸ N COUNT

2 If you **replay** something that you have recorded on tape or film, you play it again in order to listen to it or look at it. EG *He rewound the tape and replayed a few bits and pieces.*   V+O

replenish /rɪˈplɛnɪʃ/, **replenishes, replenishing, replenished.** To **replenish** something means to make it full or complete again by adding a quantity of the substance or material that has been lost or removed. EG *We have to import an extra 4 million tons of wheat to replenish our reserves... Mr Jones replenished his glass.*   V+O   Formal

replica /ˈrɛplɪkə/, **replicas.** A **replica** of a statue, machine, or building is an accurate copy of it, EG *...a plaster replica of the Venus di Milo.*   N COUNT

reply /rɪˈplaɪ/, **replies, replying, replied.** 1 When you **reply** to something that someone has said or written to you, you say or write something as an answer. EG *'Did you have a nice journey?' – 'Yes,' Jenny replied, 'nice and quick.'... He gave me no chance to reply to his question... I sent you a letter, and you never replied.*   V: USU +QUOTE OR REPORT: ONLY that; ALSO V+to

2 A **reply** is something that you say or write when you reply to someone. EG *He called 'Sarah', but there was no reply... I received about a dozen replies to my enquiry.*   N COUNT: OFT+to

3 If you say or do something **in reply** to something that someone else has said or done, you say or do it as an answer to them. EG *I have nothing to say in reply to your question.*   PHRASE

report /rɪˈpɔːt/, **reports, reporting, reported.** 1 If you **report** something that has happened, you tell people about it. EG *The papers reported that Southern England was 'paralysed' by snow... Accidents must be reported to the police within twenty-*   V:SPEECH: ONLY that; ALSO V+O: OFT+to

four hours. ◊ **reported**. *...the last reported position of the hurricane.*   ◊ ADJ CLASSIF: ATTRIB

2 If you **report** on an event or subject, you tell people about it, because it is your job or duty to do so. EG *He was summoned to report on the accident to his supervisor... On his return from the Summit the Prime Minister reported to the Cabinet.*   V: OFT+on OR to

3 If someone **reports** you to a person in authority, they tell the person about something wrong that you have done. EG *You should have reported them to the police.*   V+O: OFT+to

4 If you **report** to a person or place, you go to that person or place and say that you are ready to start work. EG *The next morning he reported for duty at Jack Starke's office... I told him to report to me after the job was completed.*   V: OFT+to/for

5 A **report** is a written or spoken account of an event or situation. EG *Write a report on the visit... There have been no reports of bomb attacks... ...a newspaper report that he had been killed.*   N COUNT: OFT +REPORT

6 A school **report** is an official written account of how well or how badly a pupil has done during the term that has just finished.   N COUNT British

7 See also **reporting**.

report back. If you **report back** to someone, you tell them about something that it was your job to find out about. EG *She was sent to attend the meeting and then to report back on its discussions.*   PHRASAL VB: V+ADV

REPORT stands for **report clause**

REPORT is used in the Extra Column to say that the word being described is followed by a report clause. Verbs, nouns, and adjectives can be followed by report clauses. Report clauses tell you what someone has said or what they have thought, and they come after words which refer to speaking or thinking.

The most typical report clauses come after verbs and begin with 'that', as in EG *He thought **that he had missed the train**.* It is, however, usually possible to omit the 'that', so you can say EG *He thought **he had missed the train**.*

Report clauses can also begin with a WH word such as 'why, where', or 'how', as in EG *They asked me **why I changed my mind**.*

When the label in the Extra Column says V+REPORT or V+O+REPORT, it means that the report clause can begin with 'that', with no 'that', or with a WH word.

When there are restrictions on the kind of report clause that is possible, the labels in the Extra Column say what they are. For example, the Extra Column label for **think** 1 says V+REPORT: ONLY *that*; and for **wonder** 1 and **describe** it says V+REPORT: ONLY WH. EG *I think **that you should go**... I think a **woman has as much right to work as a man**... I'm beginning to wonder **why we ever invited them**... He described **how he was kidnapped**.*

Verbs with +REPORT can usually have the report clause, without 'that', in front of them, as in EG *You should go, I think.*

When nouns or adjectives have the label +REPORT, they can be followed by a report clause with 'that'. The 'that' cannot usually be omitted, and it is not usually possible to have a report clause that begins with a WH word. EG *He felt certain **that she would disapprove**... I was conscious **that he had changed his tactics**... ...his conviction **that he could run a newspaper**.*

reportedly /rɪˈpɔːtɪdliˈ/. If something is report- ADV
edly true, someone has said that it is true. EG *He* Formal
has reportedly instructed his family not to inter-
fere if he tries to kill himself... Tests reportedly
showed that the substance was harmless.

reported speech is speech that gives an account N UNCOUNT
of something that someone has said, but without
quoting the actual words that are used. **Reported**
speech is usually introduced by a verb such as
'say' or 'tell' followed by the word 'that'. See entry
headed REPORT.

reporter /rɪˈpɔːtə/, **reporters.** A **reporter** is N COUNT
someone who writes news articles or who broad-
casts news reports. EG *He told his story to a*
reporter from a Chicago newspaper... ...a television
reporter.

reporting /rɪˈpɔːtɪŋ/ is the presenting of news in N UNCOUNT
newspapers or on radio or television. EG *The maga-*
zine was asked to be much less selective in its
reporting.

repose /rɪˈpəʊz/ is a state in which you are resting N UNCOUNT
and feel calm. EG *He thought her face was lovely in* Literary
repose.

repository /rɪˈpɒzɪtəˈriˈ/, **repositories.** A **re-** N COUNT+SUPP
pository is a place where something is kept safely. Formal
EG *The Foreign Office was regarded as the reposi-*
tory of all relevant information.

reprehensible /reprɪˈhensəˈbəˈl/. If you describe ADJ QUALIT
behaviour as **reprehensible**, you mean that it is Formal
very bad and morally wrong. EG *It is reprehensible*
to cheat other people.

represent /reprɪˈzent/, **represents, represent-**
ing, represented. 1 If you **represent** someone or V+O
their views, you act on their behalf, for example by
expressing their views in a parliament or meeting.
EG *Thirty one nations are now represented at the*
Disarmament Conference... ...lawyers representing
relatives of the victims.

2 If a group of people is **well represented** or PHRASE
strongly represented at a particular place, there
are a lot of them there, or a lot of examples of their
work. EG *All these artists are well represented at*
the exhibition.

3 If a sign or symbol **represents** something, it is V+O
accepted as meaning that thing, in the same way
that a word is accepted as meaning something. EG
The word 'love' was represented by a small red
heart.

4 If an object **represents** an idea to people, they V+O : NO PASS,
think of it as a symbol or expression of that idea. EG NO CONT
To many of the local people these castles repre-
sent a hundred years of domination by the aristoc-
racy.

5 You can say that something **represents** a par- V+C : NO CONT
ticular thing when it is an example of that type of Formal
thing. EG *Does the budget represent a departure*
from stated government policy?... Universities rep-
resent a very sizeable resource.

6 If you **represent** something in a particular way, V+O : USU+A
you describe it in that way. EG *The evacuation of*
our forces was represented as a triumphant suc-
cess.

representation /reprɪˈzenteɪʃəˈn/, **representa-**
tions. 1 Representation is the state of being N UNCOUNT
represented by someone in a parliament or on a
committee. EG *They're campaigning for student*
representation on the university's governing
bodies.

2 You can describe a picture or statue of someone N COUNT :
as a **representation** of them. EG *...crude represen-* OFT+of
tations of angels. Formal

3 Representations are formal requests, com- N PLURAL
plaints, or statements made to a government or Formal
another official group. EG *The committee's enquiry*
arose from representations made by a group of
local residents.

representative /reprɪˈzentətɪv/, **representa-**
tives. 1 A **representative** is a person who has N COUNT
been chosen to act on behalf of another person or a

group of people. EG *The Consumer Congress is*
made up of representatives of a wide range of
organizations... ...representatives from the police...
...union representatives.

2 A **representative** group consists of a small ADJ CLASSIF :
number of people who have been chosen to make ATTRIB
decisions on behalf of a larger group. EG *The*
government consists of two representative assem-
blies.

3 Something that is **representative** is typical of ADJ QUALIT
the group to which it belongs. EG *We questioned a* OFT+of
representative cross-section of the public... Are
these incidents representative of the way things
have gone?

repress /rɪˈpres/, **represses, repressing, re-**
pressed. 1 If you **repress** a feeling, you succeed in V+O
not showing it or not feeling it. EG *It was all I could*
do to repress my laughter.

2 If a group of people **repress** the people they V+O
have authority over, they restrict their freedom
and control them by force. EG *The military officers*
would help to exploit and repress their own people.

repressed /rɪˈprest/. You use **repressed** to describe **1** people who do not allow themselves to ADJ QUALIT
have natural feelings and desires, especially sexual
ones. **2** feelings that people do not allow them- ADJ QUALIT
selves to have. *...the child's repressed hate of his*
mother.

repression /rɪˈpreʃəˈn/. **1 Repression** is the use N UNCOUNT
of force to restrict and control a group of people,
especially the people of a country. EG *They wanted*
to fight all forms of injustice and repression.

2 Repression also refers to the way that people do N UNCOUNT
not allow themselves to have natural feelings and
desires, especially sexual ones.

repressive /rɪˈpresɪv/. **Repressive** governments ADJ QUALIT
use force and unjust laws to restrict and control
their people. EG *...a repressive society.*

reprieve /rɪˈpriːv/, **reprieves, reprieving, re-**
prieved. 1 If someone who has been sentenced to V+O : USU PASS
death **is reprieved**, their sentence is changed and
they are not executed.

2 A **reprieve** is **2.1** a delay before something very N COUNT
unpleasant happens. EG *The finding of oil repre-*
sents a colossal reprieve for the islanders. **2.2** an
official order cancelling a death sentence.

reprimand /ˈreprɪmɑːnd/, **reprimands, repri-** V+O
manding, reprimanded. If you **reprimand** someone, you officially tell them that they should not
have done a particular thing. EG *He was called to*
the office of a superior to be reprimanded. ▸ used ▸ N COUNT
as a noun. EG *...a gentle reprimand.*

reprint, reprints, reprinting, reprinted; pronounced /riːˈprɪnt/ when it is a verb and /ˈriːprɪnt/
when it is a noun.

1 If a book **is reprinted**, further copies of it are V+O : USU PASS
printed when all the other ones have been sold.

2 A **reprint** is a copy of a book which has been N COUNT
reprinted. EG *...the 1959 reprint of his book.*

reprisal /rɪˈpraɪzəˈl/, **reprisals. 1 Reprisals** are N COUNT :
violent actions that are taken by a group of people USU PLURAL
against another group who have harmed them. EG
They engaged in brutal reprisals against those who
had fought them.

2 Reprisal is the act of carrying out reprisals. EG N UNCOUNT
There have been threats of reprisal. Formal

reproach /rɪˈprəʊtʃ/, **reproaches, reproaching,**
reproached. 1 If you express **reproach**, you show N UNCOUNT
that you feel sad and rather angry about something Formal
that someone has done. EG *She was still staring at*
him in shocked and silent reproach... ...a long letter
of reproach.

2 If you **reproach** someone, you tell them, rather V+O OR V-
sadly, that they have done something wrong. EG *He* REFL : OFT+
used to reproach her mother for not being nice for/with
Formal

enough to her... He had bitterly reproached himself for his complacency. ▸ used as a noun. EG *She responded submissively to his reproaches.* ▸ N COUNT

reproachful /rɪˈprəʊtʃful/. **Reproachful** looks or remarks show that you feel sad and rather angry about something that someone has done. EG *She was looking at me with rather reproachful brown eyes.* ◊ **reproachfully.** EG *Morris looked at her reproachfully.* ◊ ADV

reproduce /riːprəˈdjuːs/, **reproduces, reproducing, reproduced. 1** If you **reproduce** something, v+o you produce a copy of it. EG *This painting has never been reproduced anywhere... She tried to reproduce his accent.*
2 When people, animals, or plants **reproduce**, they v or v-refl produce more of their own kind. EG *Bacteria reproduce by splitting into two.*

reproduction /riːprəˈdʌkʃən/, **reproductions. 1** N COUNT A **reproduction** is a modern copy of a painting or piece of furniture. EG *...reproductions of Impressionist paintings... ...reproduction Colonial furniture.*
2 The **reproduction** of sound, art, or writing is the N UNCOUNT copying of it. EG *The Controller has no objection to the reproduction of the Report.*
3 Reproduction is the process by which a living N UNCOUNT thing produces more of its own kind. EG *Today's lesson is about plant reproduction.*

reproductive /riːprəˈdʌktɪv/ means relating to ADJ CLASSIF : the reproduction of living things. EG *...a worm's* ATTRIB *digestive and reproductive systems.*

reproof /rɪˈpruːf/, **reproofs. 1** A **reproof** is some- N COUNT thing that you say to someone to show that you Formal disapprove of what they have done. EG *This reproof was ignored.*
2 If you say or do something as **reproof**, you say or N UNCOUNT do it to show that you disapprove of what someone Formal has done. EG *Discipline and reproof are out of fashion.*

reprove /rɪˈpruːv/, **reproves, reproving, re-** v+o : oft+for **proved.** If you **reprove** someone, you tell them Formal that they have behaved wrongly or foolishly. ◊ **reproving.** EG *She received a reproving look* ◊ ADJ CLASSIF *from her Aunt Agnes.*

reptile /ˈreptaɪl/, **reptiles.** A **reptile** is an animal N COUNT which has a scaly skin and lays eggs. Snakes and lizards are reptiles.

republic /rɪˈpʌblɪk/, **republics.** A **republic** is a N COUNT country which has a president rather than a king or queen and is governed by elected representatives. EG *Cuba became an independent republic... ...the Republic of Ireland.*

repudiate /rɪˈpjuːdɪeɪt/, **repudiates, repudiat-** v+o **ing, repudiated.** If you **repudiate** something, you Formal say that you will not accept it or have anything to do with it. EG *He repudiated the authority of the Church.* ◊ **repudiation** /rɪˈpjuːdɪeɪʃən/. EG *...his* ◊ N UNCOUNT : *repudiation of the evidence.* oft+of

repugnant /rɪˈpʌgnənt/. If something is **repug-** ADJ QUALIT : **nant** to you, you think it is horrible and disgusting. oft+to EG *The majority of British people find this sort of* Formal *souvenir repugnant... The idea was repugnant to him.*

repulsion /rɪˈpʌlʃən/ is a strong feeling of dislike N UNCOUNT and disgust. EG *She shivered with repulsion... I can't* Formal *help feeling repulsion.*

repulsive /rɪˈpʌlsɪv/. Something that is **repulsive** ADJ QUALIT is horrible and disgusting. EG *...his repulsive appearance... It's a repulsive idea... His behaviour was absolutely repulsive.*

reputable /ˈrepjətəbəl/. A **reputable** company ADJ QUALIT or person is known to be good and reliable. EG *All reputable companies give a guarantee.*

reputation /repjəˈteɪʃən/, **reputations.** The N COUNT : **reputation** of someone or something is the opinion USU+SUPP that people have about what they are like, especially about how good they are. EG *She had a reputation as a very good writer... ...his reputation for integrity... He had earned the reputation of being a formidable opponent.*

reputed /rɪˈpjuːtɪd/. If something is **reputed** to be ADJ PRED true or to exist, some people say that it is true or +to-INF OR that it exists. EG *The buildings were reputed to be* ADJ CLASSIF : *haunted... ...their reputed beauty.* ATTRIB

reputedly /rɪˈpjuːtɪdlɪ/. If something is **reputed-** ADV **ly** true, it is said to be true. EG *...events that reputedly took place thousands of years ago.*

request /rɪˈkwest/, **requests, requesting, re-** v+o : **quested. 1** If you **request** something, you ask for oft+to-INF, it politely or formally. EG *The President requested* OR V+REPORT, *an emergency session of the United Nations...* ONLY that *Visitors are requested not to pick the flowers.* Formal
2 If you make a **request** for something, you ask for N COUNT it politely. EG *I made repeated requests for money... ...an urgent request to devise some games.*
3 If something is given or done **on request**, it is PHRASE given or done whenever you ask for it. EG *A booklet on this subject will be sent on request.*
4 If you do something **at someone's request**, you PHRASE do it because they have asked you to. EG *We went into Afghanistan at the request of the Afghan government.*

require /rɪˈkwaɪə/, **requires, requiring, re-** v+o : oft+for **quired. 1** If you **require** something or if some- Formal thing is **required**, you need it or it is necessary. EG *Is there anything you require, Mr Heissman?... Parliamentary approval would be required for it.*
2 If you **are required** to do something, you have to v+o : USU PASS do it because someone says you must do it. EG *All* +to-INF, of, *the boys were required to study religion... He was* OR REPORT, *doing what was required of him... The course* ONLY that *requires you to be bilingual.* ◊ **required.** EG *Check* ◊ ADJ CLASSIF *that the machines meet required standards.* OR ADJ AFTER N

requirement /rɪˈkwaɪəmənt/, **requirements. 1** N COUNT : A **requirement** is something that you must have USU+SUPP or do in order to do something that you want to do. EG *Maths is no longer the most important requirement for a career in accounting... The applicant meets our general entrance requirements.*
2 Your **requirements** are things that you need. EG N COUNT : *Mexico imported half her grain requirements in* USU+SUPP *1940.* Formal

requisite /ˈrekwɪzɪt/ means necessary for a par- ADJ CLASSIF : ticular purpose. EG *They needed time to establish* ATTRIB *the requisite number of prisons.* Formal

requisition /rekwɪˈzɪʃən/, **requisitions, requisi-** v+o **tioning, requisitioned.** If people, especially sol- Formal diers, **requisition** something, they formally demand it and take it for their own use. EG *Transport was being requisitioned by the army.*

re-route /riːˈruːt/, **re-routes, re-routing, re-** v+o : USU+A **routed.** If traffic **is re-routed**, it is directed along different roads, for example because a road is blocked.

rescue /ˈreskjuː/, **rescues, rescuing, rescued. 1** v+o If you **rescue** someone, you get them out of a dangerous or unpleasant situation. EG *He was rescued from the sinking aircraft by a passing ship... The Cabinet decided not to rescue the company.* ◊ **rescuer, rescuers.** EG *The man's shouts could* ◊ N COUNT *not be heard by the rescuers.*
2 Rescue is help which gets someone out of a N UNCOUNT dangerous or unpleasant situation. EG *Rescue was at hand... ...the size of the rescue operation.*
3 If you **go** or **come to** someone's **rescue**, you help PHRASE them when they are in danger or difficulty. EG *Toby came to my rescue... It was William who came to the rescue.*
4 A **rescue** is a successful attempt to save some- N COUNT one from a dangerous or unpleasant situation. EG *The coastguard may be working on as many as 20 rescues at any one time.*

research /rɪˈsɜːtʃ/, **researches, researching, researched. 1 Research** is work that involves N UNCOUNT studying something and trying to discover facts OR N PLURAL about it. EG *...scientific research... I was doing some research on Indian literature... Soon after, Faraday began his researches into electricity.*
2 If you **research** something, you try to discover v+o or v

facts about it. EG *The historical background to the play had been very carefully researched... I spent some time researching abroad.* ◊ **researcher,** ◊ N COUNT **researchers.** EG *...a team of researchers.*

resemblance /rɪˈzɛmblᵊns/. If there is a **resem-** N SING OR N **blance** between two people or things, they are UNCOUNT similar to each other. EG *She bore a striking resemblance to his wife.*

resemble /rɪˈzɛmbᵊl/, **resembles, resembling,** V+O : NO CONT, **resembled.** If one thing or person **resembles** NO IMPER another, they are similar to each other. EG *You resemble him very much physically... The situation closely resembles that of Europe in 1940.*

resent /rɪˈzɛnt/, **resents, resenting, resented.** If V+O you **resent** something, you feel bitter and angry about it. EG *I resented his attitude... They resent being treated as common criminals.*

resentful /rɪˈzɛntful/. If you are **resentful,** you ADJ QUALIT feel resentment. EG *He was resentful at the way he had been treated... I felt resentful about having to see him again.*

resentment /rɪˈzɛntməⁿt/ is bitterness and an- N UNCOUNT ger. EG *He was filled with resentment... I felt no resentment against Keith.*

reservation /rɛzəveɪʃᵊn/, **reservations.** 1 If you N COUNT have **reservations** about something, you are not sure that it is entirely good or right. EG *I have reservations about the desirability of such a change... He shared his assistant's reservations.* 2 If you do something without **reservation,** you do N UNCOUNT it without any doubts at all. EG *They accepted the plan without reservation... With a little more reservation, I would recommend the second film.* 3 If you make a **reservation,** you arrange for N COUNT something such as a table in a restaurant or a room in a hotel to be kept for you. EG *I will make the reservation for seven thirty.*

reserve /rɪˈzɜːv/, **reserves, reserving, re-** **served.** 1 If something **is reserved** for a particu- V+O : USU PASS lar person or purpose, it is kept specially for that person or purpose. EG *The garden is reserved for those who work in the museum... I had a place reserved at the Youth Hostel... He gave me a look of the sort usually reserved for naughty schoolchildren.* 2 If you say that you **reserve the right** to do PHRASE something, you mean that you will do it if you feel Formal that it is necessary. EG *The French reserved the right to decide their own agricultural policy.* 3 A **reserve** is a supply of something that is N COUNT : available for use when it is needed. EG *We have* USU+SUPP *large coal reserves... ...the mobilization of reserve forces... He was able to draw on vast reserves of talent and enthusiasm.* 4 If you have something **in reserve,** you have it PHRASE available for use when it is needed. EG *I kept some tranquillizers in reserve in case I became agitated.* 5 In sport, a **reserve** is someone who is available N COUNT to play as part of a team if one of the members cannot play on a particular occasion. 6 A nature **reserve** is an area of land where the N COUNT : animals, birds, and plants are officially protected. USU+SUPP 7 If someone shows **reserve,** they keep their N UNCOUNT feelings hidden. EG *His tone had lost the cautious reserve it had previously had.*

reserved /rɪˈzɜːvd/. Someone who is **reserved** ADJ QUALIT keeps their feelings hidden. *He is reserved and cautious, never making a swift decision.*

reservoir /rɛzəvwɑː/, **reservoirs.** 1 A **reservoir** N COUNT is a lake that is used for storing water before it is supplied to people. 2 A **reservoir** of something is a large quantity of it N PART that is available to be used. EG *Industry must have a reservoir of cheap labour.*

reside /rɪˈzaɪd/, **resides, residing, resided.** If a V : USU+*in,* quality **resides** in something, it is in that thing. EG NO CONT, *Real power now resides in the workshop... The* NO IMPER *value of his sculptures resides in their simplicity.* Formal

residence /ˈrɛzɪdᵊns/, **residences.** 1 A **residence** N COUNT is a house where people live. EG *...the Prime* Formal *Minister's official residence.* 2 Your place of **residence** is the place where you N UNCOUNT live. EG *What is your place of residence?... ...lifelong* Formal *residence in one place.* 3 If you **take up residence** somewhere, you go PHRASE and live there. EG *They had taken up residence on* Formal *the top floor of a hotel.* 4 If an important person is **in residence** in a PHRASE particular place, they are living there. EG *None of* Formal *the royal family are in residence at the palace at the moment.* 5 See also **hall of residence.**

resident /ˈrɛzɪdᵊnt/, **residents.** 1 The **residents** N COUNT of a house or area are the people who live there. EG *The local residents complained... She became a permanent resident of California.* 2 Someone who is **resident** in a country or a town ADJ CLASSIF : lives there. EG *...students resident in England...* USU PRED+*in* *Since 1947 she has been resident abroad.* Formal 3 A **resident** doctor or tutor lives in the place ADJ CLASSIF where he or she works.

residential /rɛzɪˈdɛnʃᵊl/. 1 A **residential** area ADJ CLASSIF : contains mainly houses rather than offices or facto- ATTRIB ries. EG *...fashionable residential suburbs.* 2 A **residential** institution is an institution in ADJ CLASSIF : which you can live while you are studying there or ATTRIB being cared for there. EG *...residential colleges... ...residential courses... ...children living in residential care.*

residual /rɪˈzɪdjuᵊl/ is used to describe what ADJ CLASSIF : remains of something when most of it has gone. EG ATTRIB *...a prehistoric fish with residual limbs... ...the resid-* Formal *ual prejudices of the past.*

residue /ˈrɛzɪdjuː/, **residues.** A **residue** of some- N COUNT : thing is a small amount that remains after most of USU+SUPP it has gone. EG *Residues of pesticides can build up* Formal *in the soil.*

resign /rɪˈzaɪn/, **resigns, resigning, resigned.** 1 V : OFT+FROM, If you **resign** from a job or position, you formally OR V+O announce that you are leaving it, usually because of something that has happened. EG *She resigned from the Government... Lloyd George was threatening to resign.* 2 If you **resign** yourself to an unpleasant situation V-REFL+*to* or fact, you accept it because you realize that you cannot change it. EG *You're a widow now, Mrs Pearl. I think you must resign yourself to that fact.* 3 See also **resigned.**

resignation /rɛzɪgˈneɪʃᵊn/, **resignations.** 1 Your N COUNT OR **resignation** is a formal statement of your inten- N UNCOUNT tion to leave a job or position. EG *Mr McPherson has accepted my resignation... ...her letter of resignation.* 2 **Resignation** is the acceptance of an unpleasant N UNCOUNT situation or fact because you realize that you cannot change it. EG *She spoke with quiet resignation.*

resigned /rɪˈzaɪnd/. If you are **resigned** to an ADJ CLASSIF unpleasant situation or fact, you accept it without OFT+*to* complaining because you realize that you cannot change it. EG *They feel resigned to losing their money.* ◊ **resignedly** /rɪˈzaɪnədlɪ/. EG *'He will* ◊ ADV *come,' said Joe resignedly.*

resilient /rɪˈzɪljᵊnt/. People and things that are ADJ QUALIT **resilient** are able to recover quickly from unpleasant or damaging events. EG *He's bright, resilient, and ambitious.* ◊ **resilience** /rɪˈzɪljᵊns/. EG *The* ◊ N UNCOUNT *chairman has shown remarkable resilience.*

resin /ˈrɛzɪn/, **resins. Resin** is 1 a sticky sub- N MASS stance that is produced by some trees. 2 a substance that is produced chemically and used to make plastics.

If you resign from your job, are you resigned to it?

resist /rɪˈzɪst/, **resists, resisting, resisted. 1** If v+o
you **resist** something such as a change, you refuse
to accept it and try to prevent it. EG *Our trade union
has resisted the introduction of automation... He
resisted demands for a public enquiry.*
2 If you **resist** someone or **resist** an attack by v+o
them, you fight back against them. EG *Any attack
will be resisted with force if necessary.*
3 If you **resist** the temptation to do something, you v+o OR v+-ING
stop yourself from doing it although you would like
to do it. EG *I can't resist teasing him... I resisted the
temptation to get very drunk.*

resistance /rɪˈzɪstəns/, **resistances. 1 Resis-** N UNCOUNT :
tance to something such as a change or a new idea OFT+to
is a refusal to accept it. EG *There will be fierce
resistance if this is attempted... ...resistance to
bureaucratic controls.*
2 Resistance to an attack consists of fighting back N UNCOUNT
against the people who have attacked you. EG *The
advancing army met with no resistance... ...a group
of resistance fighters.*
3 The **resistance** of your body to germs or diseas- N UNCOUNT :
es is its power to remain unharmed or unaffected OFT+to
by them. EG *...resistance to infection.*

resistant /rɪˈzɪstənt/. **1** Someone who is **resistant** ADJ PRED :
to something is opposed to it and wants to prevent OFT+to
it. EG *They are extremely resistant to change.* Formal
2 If something is **resistant** to a particular thing, it ADJ QUALIT :
is not harmed by it. EG *This type of plastic is highly* OFT+to
*resistant to steam... Many pests are now resistant
to the commoner insecticides.*

-resistant is used to form adjectives that describe
something as not harmed or not affected by a
particular substance. EG *...penicillin-resistant
strains of bacteria... ...water-resistant make-up.*

resolute /ˈrezəljuːt/. Someone who is **resolute** ADJ QUALIT
shows great determination not to change their Formal
mind or not to give up a course of action. EG *We
urged him to be resolute... ...their resolute refusal
to make any real concessions.* ◊ **resolutely.** EG ◊ ADV
She resolutely refused to speak to me.

resolution /ˌrezəljuːʃən/, **resolutions. 1** A **reso-** N COUNT
lution is a formal decision taken at a meeting by
means of a vote. EG *Congress passed a resolution
accepting his services.*
2 If you make a **resolution**, you decide to try very N COUNT
hard to do something. EG *I'm always making resolutions, like giving up smoking.*
3 Resolution is determination to do something or N UNCOUNT
not do something. EG *A note of resolution entered
his voice.*
4 The **resolution** of a problem or difficulty is the N UNCOUNT :
final solving of it. EG *I longed for the resolution of* USU+SUPP
the agonizing dilemma. Formal

resolve /rɪˈzɒlv/, **resolves, resolving, resolved.**
1 If you **resolve** to do something, you make a firm v+to-INF
decision to do it. EG *I resolved to tell the truth... He* OR REPORT :
had already resolved that Kitchener should be ONLY that
appointed. Formal
2 Resolve is absolute determination to do what N UNCOUNT
you have decided to do. EG *We must be firm in our* Formal
resolve to oppose them.
3 To **resolve** a problem, argument, or difficulty v+o
means to find or provide a solution to it. EG *There* Formal
*are a number of ways of resolving the problem...
The Cabinet met to resolve the crisis.*

resonant /ˈrezənənt/. A sound that is **resonant** is ADJ QUALIT
deep and strong. EG *She could hear her father's
resonant voice.* ◊ **resonance** /ˈrezənəns/. EG *His* ◊ N UNCOUNT
voice suddenly took on a new resonance.

resonate /ˈrezəneɪt/, **resonates, resonating,** v
resonated. If something **resonates**, it vibrates Formal
and produces a deep, strong sound. EG *His laughter
resonated among the rocks.*

resort /rɪˈzɔːt/, **resorts, resorting, resorted. 1** If v+to
you **resort** to a course of action that you do not
really approve of, you adopt it because you cannot
see any other way of achieving what you want to

achieve. EG *They had not so far chosen to resort to
violence... Some groups have resorted to terrorism.*
2 If you do something **as a last resort**, you do it PHRASE
because you can find no other way of getting out of
a difficult situation or of solving a problem. EG *As a
last resort he went to the British Library.*
3 You use **in the last resort** when giving the basic PHRASE
truth or the most important fact about something. Formal
EG *We must have prisons in the last resort to
contain people who break the law frequently... The
difference was in the last resort no more than a
matter of emphasis.*
4 A **resort** is a place where a lot of people spend N COUNT :
their holidays. EG *...a seaside resort.* USU+SUPP

resound /rɪˈzaʊnd/, **resounds, resounding, re-**
sounded. 1 When a noise **resounds**, it is heard v
very loudly and clearly. EG *His steps resounded in* Literary
the courtyard.
2 If a place **resounds** with noise, it is filled with it. v : OFT+with
EG *The room began to resound with that powerful* Literary
voice.

resounding /rɪˈzaʊndɪŋ/. **1** A **resounding** sound ADJ CLASSIF :
is loud and echoing. EG *The tile sprang from the* ATTRIB
wall with a resounding crack.
2 You can refer to a very great success as a ADJ CLASSIF :
resounding success. EG *It was a resounding victory* ATTRIB
for the party.

resource /rɪˈzɔːs, -sɔːs/, **resources.** The **re-** N COUNT :
sources of a country, organization, or person are USU PLURAL
the things that they have and can use. EG *...Britain's
energy resources... Julius had invested all his resources in an unsuccessful restaurant.*

resourceful /rɪˈzɔːsfʊl, -sɔːs-/. Someone who is ADJ QUALIT
resourceful is good at finding ways of dealing
with problems. EG *...an able, resourceful politician.*
◊ **resourcefulness.** EG *They faced misfortune with* ◊ N UNCOUNT
resourcefulness and courage.

respect /rɪˈspekt/, **respects, respecting, re-**
spected. 1 If you **respect** someone, you have a v+o
good opinion of their character or ideas. EG *He was
particularly respected for his integrity.*
◊ **respected.** EG *...a highly respected scholar.* ◊ ADJ QUALIT
2 If you have **respect** for someone, you have a N UNCOUNT
good opinion of them. EG *I had an enormous respect* OFT+for
*and admiration for him... It is up to you to gain her
respect.* ● See also **self-respect.**
3 You can say **with respect** when you are politely PHRASE
disagreeing with someone or criticizing them. EG Formal
But Mr Hume, with respect, that wouldn't work.
4 If you **respect** someone's wishes, rights, or v+o
customs, you do not do anything that they would
dislike or regard as wrong. EG *She respected his
need for peace and quiet... We must respect the
practices of cultures different from our own.*
▶ used as a noun. EG *...respect for the rights of the* ▶ N UNCOUNT :
minority. OFT+for
5 If you **pay** your **last respects** to someone who PHRASE
has just died, you express your respect or affection
for them by coming to see their body or their
grave. EG *His family came to pay their last respects.*
6 You use expressions like **in this respect** and **in** PHRASE
many respects to indicate that what you are
saying applies to the feature you have just mentioned or to many features of something. EG *We are
lagging behind in this respect... He is different from
the people around him in many respects.*
7 You use **with respect to** to say what something PREP
relates to. EG *He informed me about my rights with* Formal
respect to the forthcoming extradition.

respectable /rɪˈspektəbəl/. **1** Someone or some- ADJ QUALIT
thing that is **respectable** is approved of by society
and considered to be morally correct. EG *He looked
like a respectable American businessman...
...young people from respectable homes... This
change had made it respectable to be on the Left.*
◊ **respectability** /rɪˌspektəˈbɪlɪti/. EG *...a states-* ◊ N UNCOUNT
man of great eminence and respectability.
2 You can also say that something is **respectable** ADJ QUALIT

when you mean that it is adequate or acceptable. EG *He had begun to earn a very respectable income... He came a respectable fourth in the race.*

respectful /rɪ'spektᵉful/. If you are **respectful** if your behaviour is **respectful**, you show respect for someone. EG *The woman kept a respectful silence.* ◇ **respectfully.** EG *He expected them to stand respectfully when he entered the room.* ◇ ADV

respective /rɪ'spektɪv/ means relating separately or belonging separately to the people you have just mentioned. EG *He drove them both to their respective homes.* ADJ CLASSIF : ATTRIB

respectively /rɪ'spektɪvli/ means in the same order as the items that have just been mentioned. EG *Harvard University and MIT are respectively the fourth and fifth largest employers in the area.* ADV

respiration /ˌrespəreɪʃᵃn/. Your **respiration** is your breathing. EG *His respiration was quick and shallow.* N UNCOUNT Technical

respiratory /ˌrespᵉrətri/ means relating to your breathing or to the parts of your body involved in breathing. EG *...respiratory infections.* ADJ CLASSIF : ATTRIB Technical

respite /respɪ't/. A **respite** is a short period of rest from something unpleasant. EG *She had got a job in town primarily as a respite from her husband... She was interrogated without respite for twenty-four hours.* N UNCOUNT, OR N SING : a+N Formal

resplendent /rɪ'splendənt/. If you describe someone as **resplendent**, you mean that their appearance is very impressive. EG *Miss Jackson, resplendent in a new red suit, watched the ceremony.* ADJ QUALIT : OFT+in Formal

respond /rɪ'spɒnd/, **responds, responding, responded.** When you **respond** to something that is done or said, you react to it by doing or saying something yourself. EG *The crowd waved and the liner responded with a blast on its siren... The government has responded to pressure by moving towards reform... The council responded by calling the raid 'deplorable'.* V : OFT+to/ with, V+by+-ING, OR V+QUOTE

response /rɪ'spɒns/, **responses.** 1 Your **response** to an event or to something that is said is what you do or say as a reaction or reply to it. EG *The Government response to the riots was firm... As an immediate response the university has cut admissions by 20 per cent... The proposal has produced a united response from the French people.* N COUNT

2 If you do or say something **in response** to an event, action, or question, you do it or say it as a reaction or reply to it. EG *Clearly, they did it in response to external pressures... Will waved his hand in response.* PHRASE

responsibility /rɪˌspɒnsəbɪlɪ'ti¹/, **responsibilities.** 1 If you have **responsibility** for something or if something is your **responsibility**, it is your duty to deal with it and make decisions relating to it. EG *She took over the responsibility for the project... The handling of the vessel remained his responsibility.* N UNCOUNT : OFT+for

2 If you accept **responsibility** for something that has happened, you agree that you were to blame for it or caused it. EG *I made a mistake and I will assume responsibility for it.* N UNCOUNT : OFT+for

3 Your **responsibilities** are duties that you have because of your job or position. EG *...the responsibilities of citizenship.* N COUNT : USU PLURAL

4 If you have a **responsibility** to someone, you have a duty to help them or to look after them. EG *I presume you take your responsibility to your students seriously?* N COUNT

responsible /rɪ'spɒnsəbᵉl/. 1 If you are **responsible** for something, it is your job or duty to deal with it and make decisions relating to it. EG *...the minister responsible for civil defence... The children were responsible for cleaning their own rooms.* ADJ PRED : OFT+for

2 If you are **responsible** for something bad that has happened, you caused it or could have pre- ADJ PRED : OFT+for

vented it. EG *I hold you personally responsible for all this.*

3 If you are **responsible** to a person or group, you are controlled by them and have to report to them about what you have done. EG *We're responsible to a development committee.* ADJ PRED : OFT+to

4 You describe someone as **responsible** when they behave properly without needing to be controlled by anyone else. EG *...responsible members of the local community.* ◇ **responsibly.** EG *You are doing your job conscientiously and responsibly.* ADJ QUALIT ◇ ADV

5 **Responsible** jobs involve making important decisions or carrying out important actions. EG *A lot of women didn't want responsible jobs.* ADJ QUALIT : ATTRIB

responsive /rɪ'spɒnsɪv/. 1 Someone who is **responsive** is quick to show emotions such as pleasure and affection. EG *The children were the most responsive members of the audience.* ADJ QUALIT

2 If you are **responsive** to things that happen, you take notice of them and react to them in an appropriate way. EG *Broadcasters should be responsive to public opinion... Industry is highly responsive to consumer demand.* ADJ PRED : OFT+to

rest /rest/, **rests, resting, rested.** 1 You refer to all the remaining parts of something or to all the other parts of something as the **rest** of it. EG *He spent the rest of his life in prison... It was happening not only in America but also throughout the rest of the world... It was just another grave like all the rest... The rest of us were allowed to go home.* N SING : the+N, OFT+of

2 If you **rest** or if you **rest** your body, you do not do anything active for a period of time. EG *Go back to bed and rest... The boy stopped for a moment to rest... Stop to relax and rest your muscles.* V OR V+O

3 If you get some **rest** or have a **rest**, you sit or lie quietly, not doing anything active, and relax. EG *It was weeks before I got a decent night's rest... They wanted a rest.* N UNCOUNT OR N COUNT : USU SING

4 If something such as an idea **rests** on a particular thing, it depends on that thing. EG *I believe that the future of civilisation rests on that decision.* V+on/upon

5 If a responsibility or duty **rests** with you, you have that responsibility or duty. V+with Formal

6 If something **rests** somewhere or if you **rest** it there, its weight is supported by something. EG *He let her shoulders rest against his knees... ...a tub with a wide edge to rest your arm on.* V-ERG+A

7 If your eyes **rest** on a particular object or person, you stop looking round you and look at that object or person. EG *Her eyes travelled slowly upward and rested on his hands.* V+on/upon Literary

8 A **rest** is also an object that is used to support something, especially your head or feet. EG *...a foot rest... ...a head rest.* N COUNT : USU+SUPP

9 When an object that has been moving **comes to rest**, it finally stops. EG *It would drop thousands of feet before coming to rest.* PHRASE Formal

10 If you **put** or **set** someone's **mind at rest**, you say something to them that stops them worrying about something. EG *Let me set your mind at rest. There is nothing to worry about.* PHRASE

11 If someone **lays** or **puts** an idea **to rest**, they succeed in proving that it is not true. EG *Mr Casey vowed to lay to rest allegations of improper business dealings.* PHRASE Formal

12 If you tell someone to **rest** assured that something is the case, you are reassuring them that it is the case. EG *Rest assured that everything's under control.* V+C : OFT+REPORT, ONLY that

restaurant /restᵉrɒnt, -rɒŋ/, **restaurants.** A **restaurant** is a place where you can buy and eat a meal. EG *...a splendid Hungarian restaurant.* N COUNT

rested /restɪ²d/. If you feel **rested**, you feel more energetic because you have just had a rest. ADJ QUALIT

If you are restrained, are you responsive?

restful /rɛstful/. Something that is **restful** helps ADJ QUALIT
you to feel calm and relaxed. EG *The lighting is
restful... ...a restful town.*

restive /rɛstɪv/. If you are **restive**, you are impa- ADJ QUALIT
tient, bored, or dissatisfied. EG *The crew were* Formal
restive and mutinous.

restless /rɛstlɪ²s/. If you are **restless**, 1 you are ADJ QUALIT
bored, impatient, or dissatisfied, and you want to do
something else. EG *I knew that within a fortnight I
should feel restless again.* ◊ **restlessness.** EG *They* ◊ N UNCOUNT
are showing some signs of restlessness. 2 you are ADJ QUALIT
always moving, because you find it difficult to stay
still. EG *She was restless and fidgety.* ◊ **restlessly.** ◊ ADV
EG *He walked restlessly around the room.*

restore /rɪ'stɔ:/, **restores, restoring, restored.** 1 V+O
To **restore** something means to cause it to exist
again. EG *...the task of restoring order... This generous action restored my faith in human beings.*
◊ **restoration** /rɛstəreɪʃⁿ/. EG *...the restoration* ◊ N UNCOUNT
of law and order.
2 To **restore** someone or something to a previous V+O+to
state or condition means to cause them to return to
that state or condition. EG *...a Charter which will
restore pensioners to a position of equality... The
Tories were restored to power.*
3 When someone **restores** an old building, paint- V+O
ing, or piece of furniture, they repair it and clean
it, so that it returns to its original condition.
◊ **restoration.** EG *...the restoration of ancient halls* ◊ N UNCOUNT
and manors.
4 If you **restore** something that was lost or stolen V+O:OFT+to
to someone, you return it to them. EG *The terri-* Formal
tories were restored to their former owners.

restrain /rɪ'streɪn/, **restrains, restraining, restrained.** 1 If someone or something **restrains** V+O OR
you, they stop you from doing what you were going V-REFL:
to do. EG *She raised a finger as if to restrain Morris* OFT+from
*from speaking... He had been unable to restrain
himself from telling Gertrude.*
2 If you **restrain** something that is growing or V+O
increasing, you prevent it from getting too large. EG
...the efforts of governments to restrain inflation.

restrained /rɪ'streɪnd/. Someone or something ADJ QUALIT
that is **restrained** is very calm and unemotional.
EG *He was polite and restrained... It is written in
restrained and formal language.*

restraint /rɪ'streɪnt/, **restraints.** 1 **Restraints** N COUNT OR
are rules or conditions that limit or restrict some- N UNCOUNT
one or something. EG *The king suffered few restraints on his freedom of action... ...an agreed
policy of income and price restraint.*
2 **Restraint** is calm, controlled, and unemotional N UNCOUNT
behaviour. EG *'Dear me,' he said with splendid
restraint.*

restrict /rɪ'strɪkt/, **restricts, restricting, restricted.** 1 If you **restrict** something, you put a V+O
limit on it in order to prevent it becoming too
large. EG *They restricted the number of students
joining these faculties... A third possibility would be
to restrict wage increases.* ◊ **restricted.** EG *...the* ◊ ADJ QUALIT
restricted field of vision provided by the camera.
2 To **restrict** people or animals means to limit V+O OR V-REFL
their movements or actions. EG *Some manufactur-
ers were not prepared to restrict themselves voluntarily.*
3 If you **restrict** someone or their activities to one V+O+to OR
thing, they can only do or deal with that thing. EG V-REFL+to
*The State should restrict its activities to the main-
tenance of law and order... I will restrict myself to
countries where English is the main language.*
4 If something **is restricted** to a particular group, V+O+to
only that group can have it or do it. EG *Membership
is restricted to men.*

restricted /rɪ'strɪktɪ²d/. 1 Something that is **re-** ADJ QUALIT
stricted is quite small or limited. EG *Many of these
are of restricted importance... The range of
choices, fortunately, is not as restricted as this.*
2 A **restricted** document is one that only people ADJ CLASSIF
with special permission can read.

3 A **restricted** area is one that only people with ADJ CLASSIF
special permission can enter.

restriction /rɪ'strɪkʃⁿ/, **restrictions.** 1 A **re-** N COUNT:
striction is an official rule that limits what you OFT+on/of
can do or that limits the amount or size of something. EG *The government placed restrictions on
sales of weapons... ...traffic restrictions.*
2 You can refer to anything that limits what you N COUNT:OFT
can do as a **restriction.** EG *...small salaries which* +on/of
*placed restrictions on our social life... ...the restric-
tions of ageing.*
3 When there is **restriction** of something that N UNCOUNT
might grow, it is prevented from becoming too
large. EG *...profit restriction.*
4 When there is **restriction** of people or **restric-** N UNCOUNT
tion of their movements or actions, they are
limited in their movements or actions. EG *Tight
clothing causes restriction of free movement...
There is no restriction on filming in the area.*

restrictive /rɪ'strɪktɪv/. Something that is **re-** ADJ QUALIT
strictive prevents you from doing what you want
to. EG *...teenagers eager to escape restrictive home
environments.*

restructure /ri:'strʌktʃə/, **restructures, re-** V+O
structuring, restructured. To **restructure** an
organization or system means to change the way it
is organized, usually in order to make it work more
effectively. EG *...proposals for restructuring the
industry.*

result /rɪzʌlt/, **results, resulting, resulted.** 1 A N COUNT
result is something that happens or exists because
of something else that has happened. EG *I nearly
missed the flight as a result of going to Havana...
The result was further victimisation... Twice he
followed his own advice, with disastrous results.*
2 If something **results** in a particular situation or V+in
event, it causes that situation or event to happen.
EG *The use of such techniques could result in
disastrous ecological changes... This will result in
consumers paying higher prices.*
3 If something **results** from a particular event or V:OFT+from
action, it is caused by that event or action. EG *Four-
fifths of the damage resulted from bombing... A
saving in cost would result.*
4 A **result** is also **4.1** the final situation that exists N COUNT
at the end of a contest. EG *...the result of the
Warrington by-election... ...the football results.* **4.2**
the number that you get when you do a calculation.
EG *The result should be calculated to three decimal
places.*
5 Your **results** are the marks or grades that you N COUNT:
get for examinations you have taken. EG *You need* USU PLURAL
good A-level results.

resultant /rɪzʌltənt/. When you refer to the **re-** ADJ CLASSIF:
sultant situation or thing, you are referring to the ATTRIB
situation or thing that was caused by the event you Formal
have just mentioned. EG *The resultant improvement in health totally justified the treatment.*

resume /rɪ'zju:m/, **resumes, resuming, re-** V-ERG
sumed. 1 If you **resume** an activity or if it
resumes, it begins again. EG *She was ready to
resume her duties... He resumed reading... The
music would stop at intervals, then resume after a
while.*
2 If you **resume** your former place or position, you V+O
return to it. EG *He resumed his seat.*

resumption /rɪ'zʌmpⁿʃⁿ/. When there is a **re-** N UNCOUNT
sumption of an activity, it begins again after it has Formal
stopped for a while. EG *They are pressing for a
quick resumption of arms negotiations.*

resurgence /rɪ'sɜ:dʒəns/. If there is a **resur-** N UNCOUNT:
gence of an attitude or activity, it reappears and OFT+of
grows. EG *There has been a resurgence of small
scale guerrilla activity.*

resurrect /rɛzərɛkt/, **resurrects, resurrecting,** V+O
resurrected. When you **resurrect** something, you
cause it to exist again after it had disappeared or
ended. EG *There is not the remotest possibility of
the government ever resurrecting the Maplin proj-*

ect. ◊ **resurrection** /rɛzərɛkʃəᵇn/. EG ...*the resurrection of the Jazz Festival.*

resuscitate /rɪˈsʌsɪteɪt/, **resuscitates, resuscitating, resuscitated.** If you **resuscitate** someone who has lost consciousness, you cause them to become conscious again. V+O Formal

retail /ˈriːteɪl/ is the activity of selling goods to the public. EG *We have opened a retail department... The original retail price was $80.* N UNCOUNT : USU N MOD

retailer /ˈriːteɪlə/, **retailers.** A **retailer** is a person or business that sells goods to the public. N COUNT

retain /rɪˈteɪn/, **retains, retaining, retained. 1** If you **retain** something, you keep it. EG *We are fighting to retain some independence.* V+O Formal

2 If an object or substance **retains** heat or a liquid, it continues to contain it. EG *Water retains heat much longer than air.* V+O

retaliate /rɪˈtælɪeɪt/, **retaliates, retaliating, retaliated.** If you **retaliate** when someone harms or annoys you, you do something which harms or annoys them in return. EG ...*the ability to retaliate during an attack... They retaliated by changing the venue for the meeting.* ◊ **retaliation** /rɪˌtælɪˈeɪʃəᵇn/. EG *It was agreed that immediate retaliation was necessary... They staged these attacks in retaliation for attacks on their own civilians.* V : USU+A

◊ N UNCOUNT

retaliatory /rɪˈtælɪətəᵇrɪ/. If you take **retaliatory** action, you try to harm someone who has harmed you. EG ...*a retaliatory attack against an opponent's cities.* ADJ CLASSIF Formal

retarded /rɪˈtɑːdɪd/. If someone is **retarded**, their mental development is much less advanced than that of most people of their age. EG *Her younger daughter was mentally retarded.* ADJ CLASSIF

retch /rɛtʃ/, **retches, retching, retched.** If you **retch**, your stomach moves as if you are vomiting. EG *The stench almost made him retch.* V

retention /rɪˈtɛnʃəᵇn/. The **retention** of something is the keeping of it. EG *They voted in favour of the retention of capital punishment.* N UNCOUNT Formal

rethink /riːˈθɪŋk/, **rethinks, rethinking, rethought.** If you **rethink** something such as a plan or a policy, you think about it and change it. EG *This forced us to rethink all of our plans.* V+O OR V

reticent /ˈrɛtɪsənt/. Someone who is **reticent** does not tell people about things. EG *She was always extremely reticent about her colleagues.* ◊ **reticence** /ˈrɛtɪsəns/. EG ...*her reticence about her personal life.* ADJ QUALIT : OFT+*about*

◊ N UNCOUNT

retire /rɪˈtaɪə/, **retires, retiring, retired. 1** When older people **retire**, they leave their job and usually stop working altogether. EG *Women, unlike men, retire at sixty... They had decided to retire from farming.* V : OFT+A

2 If you **retire** to another room or place, you leave the people you are with so that you can be on your own. EG *I retired to my study upstairs.* V : USU+A Formal

3 When you **retire**, you go to bed. EG *She retired early with a good book.* V Formal

retired /rɪˈtaɪəd/. A **retired** person is an older person who has left his or her job and has usually stopped working altogether. EG ...*a retired Army officer.* ADJ CLASSIF

retirement /rɪˈtaɪəmənt/ is **1** the time when a worker retires. EG *Since my retirement, I have felt more energetic.* **2** the period in a person's life after they have retired. EG ...*the house that his father had bought for his retirement.* N UNCOUNT

retiring /rɪˈtaɪərɪŋ/. **1** Someone who is **retiring** is shy and avoids meeting other people. EG *She was a shy, retiring girl.* ADJ QUALIT

2 A **retiring** official or employee is one who is going to retire very soon. EG ...*Jim Dacre, the retiring Labour MP.* ADJ CLASSIF : ATTRIB

retort /rɪˈtɔːt/, **retorts, retorting, retorted.** To **retort** means to reply angrily to someone. EG *'I wish no such thing,' retorted Sarah... Lady Sackville* V+QUOTE OR REPORT : ONLY *that* Written

retorted that if they came, she would leave. ▸ used as a noun. EG ...*a sharp retort.* ▸ N COUNT

retrace /rɪˈtreɪs/, **retraces, retracing, retraced.** If you **retrace** your steps or **retrace** your way, you return to where you started from by going back along the same route. EG *Stella retraced her steps toward the entrance.* V+O : USU+A

retract /rɪˈtrækt/, **retracts, retracting, retracted. 1** If you **retract** something that you have said or written, you say that you did not mean it. EG *At his trial, he retracted his confession.* V+O Formal

2 When a part of a machine or animal **retracts** or **is retracted**, it moves inwards or back. EG *The frog's eyes retract when its tongue shoots out.* V-ERG Formal

retreat /rɪˈtriːt/, **retreats, retreating, retreated. 1** If you **retreat**, you move away from something or someone. EG *Betsy and I retreated to the edge of the field... She retreated from him, pressing her back against the door.* V : USU+A

2 When an army **retreats**, it moves away from enemy forces in order to avoid fighting them. EG *They retreated a few kilometres.* ▸ used as a noun. EG ...*the retreat of Napoleon's army... They can be starved into retreat.* V ▸ N COUNT OR N UNCOUNT

3 If you **retreat** from something such as a plan or a way of life, you give it up and do something safer or less extreme. EG *The Government was retreating from its commitments... The country retreated into neutrality.* ▸ used as a noun. EG *There has been a gradual retreat from the original principles.* V : OFT+*from/into* ▸ N COUNT OR N UNCOUNT

4 A **retreat** is a quiet, secluded place that you go to in order to rest or to do things in private. EG *They met at a woodland retreat near the Canadian capital... ...a weekend retreat.* N COUNT Written

5 If you **beat a retreat**, you run away from something. EG *He beat a hasty retreat.* PHRASE

retribution /rɛtrɪˈbjuːʃəᵇn/ is punishment for a crime. EG ...*the fear of retribution.* N UNCOUNT Literary

retrieval /rɪˈtriːvəᵇl/. The **retrieval** of information from a computer is the process of getting it back. EG ...*data retrieval.* N UNCOUNT

retrieve /rɪˈtriːv/, **retrieves, retrieving, retrieved. 1** If you **retrieve** something, you get it back from the place where you left it. EG *I ran back to my room and retrieved my bag.* V+O Formal

2 If you **retrieve** a situation, you bring it back into a more acceptable state. EG *Henry did his best to retrieve the situation.* V+O Formal

retrograde /ˈrɛtrəᵇgreɪd/. You describe an action as **retrograde** when you think that it makes a situation worse rather than better. EG *The move was held to be an economically retrograde step.* ADJ CLASSIF Formal

retrospect /ˈrɛtrəᵇspɛkt/. When you consider something **in retrospect**, you think about it afterwards, and often have a different opinion about it from the one that you had at the time. EG *There are some things that you only become totally conscious of in retrospect... In retrospect, what I had done was clearly unjustifiable.* PHRASE OR ADV SEN

retrospective /rɛtrəᵇˈspɛktɪv/. **1 Retrospective** feelings or opinions concern things that happened in the past. EG ...*his retrospective embarrassment over the incident.* ◊ **retrospectively**. EG *Her father was described retrospectively as 'reserved and taciturn'.* ADJ CLASSIF Formal

◊ ADV OR ADV SEN

2 Retrospective laws or legal actions take effect from a date before the date when they are officially approved. ◊ **retrospectively**. EG *They are going to retrospectively validate unlawful actions.* ADJ CLASSIF Formal

◊ ADV

return /rɪˈtɜːn/, **returns, returning, returned. 1** When you **return** to a place, you go back there after you have been away. EG *I returned from the Middle East in 1956... He returned home several hours later... Her husband left for work one morning and did not return.* V : USU+A

When would you say 'Many happy returns'?

2 Your **return** is your arrival back at a place N UNCOUNT where you had been before. EG *On his return* +POSS *Haldane reported to the Cabinet... Julie had been tired since her return from New York.*

3 If you **return** something that you have borrowed V+O : OFT+*to* or taken from someone else, you give it back to them. EG *He borrowed my best suit and didn't return it.* ▶ used as a noun. EG *Greece will be* ▶ N UNCOUNT *offered the return of these treasures as a goodwill gift.*

4 If you **return** something to its previous place, V+O+*to* you put it back there. EG *We returned the books to* Formal *the shelf.*

5 When you **return** the ball during a game, you hit V+O it back to your opponent. ▶ used as a noun. EG *Miss* ▶ N COUNT *Evert reached to lob a return of Miss Wade's.*

6 If you **return** someone's action, you do the same V+O thing to them that they have just done to you. If you **return** someone's feeling, you feel the same way towards them as they feel towards you. EG *He didn't return their greetings... She was looking for somebody to return her affection.*

7 If you do something **in return** for what someone PHRASE else has done for you, you do it because they did that thing for you. EG *They had nothing to give in return.*

8 If a feeling or situation **returns**, it comes back or V happens again after a period of absence. EG *If the pain returns, the treatment is repeated... After nine months, the rains returned.* ▶ used as a noun. EG ▶ N SING+SUPP *...the return of better times.*

9 If you **return** to a subject that you have men- V+*to* tioned before, you begin talking about it again. EG *We shall return to this theme in Chapter 7.*

10 If you **return** to an activity that you were doing V+*to* before, you start doing it again. EG *After lunch, Edward returned to his gardening.* ▶ used as a ▶ N SING+*to* noun. EG *There seems to be a return to the use of wood in furniture-making.*

11 If you **return** to a state that you were formerly V+*to* in, you are in that state again. EG *...the groans of wounded men returning to consciousness.* ▶ used ▶ N SING+*to* as a noun. EG *He referred to the Party's hopes for a return to power.*

12 When a judge or jury **returns** a verdict, they V+O announce whether they think the person on trial is Legal guilty or not.

13 A **return** or a **return ticket** is a ticket for a N COUNT train, bus, or aeroplane that allows you to travel to a particular place and then back again. EG *...a return ticket to Vienna.*

14 The **return** on an investment is the profit that N COUNT OR you get from it. EG *Companies seek higher returns* N UNCOUNT *by investing in other corporations.*

15 You say **many happy returns** or **many happy** CONVENTION **returns of the day** as a way of wishing someone a happy birthday.

16 If you say that you have reached **the point of** PHRASE **no return**, you mean that you now have to con- tinue with what you are doing and it is too late to stop.

reunion /ri:'ju:njən/, **reunions**. A **reunion** is 1 a N COUNT party attended by members of the same family, school, or other group who have not seen each other for a long time. EG *...a family reunion.* **2** a N COUNT OR meeting between two people who have been sepa- N UNCOUNT rated for some time. EG *...her hope of reunion with her father.*

reunite /ri:ju:'naɪt/, **reunites, reuniting, reunit- ed.** **1** If two people **are reunited**, they meet each V+O : USU PASS other again after they have been separated for some time. EG *It won't be long before you are reunited with your family.*

2 If someone **reunites** a divided organization or V+O country, they bring its parts together to make it united again. EG *During 1979-80 he worked to re- unite the Labour movement.*

rev /rev/, **revs, revving, revved.** When you **rev** V-ERG : the engine of a vehicle or **rev** it **up**, you increase OFT+*up*

the engine speed by pressing the accelerator. EG *He revved the motor and then roared off... I heard the sound of an engine revving up.*

Rev. Rev and **Revd** are written abbreviations for 'Reverend'. EG *...the Rev David Drew.*

reveal /rɪ'vi:l/, **reveals, revealing, revealed.** 1 V+O, To **reveal** something means to make people aware V+REPORT, of it. EG *They were not ready to reveal any details* OR V+A *of the arrest... A newspaper had once revealed that he'd wanted to marry his cousin... Howard now revealed a certain talent for fixing things.*

2 If you **reveal** something that has been out of V+O sight, you uncover it so that people can see it. EG *She drew the curtains aside to reveal beautiful gardens.*

revealing /rɪ'vi:lɪŋ/. **1** An action or statement ADJ QUALIT that is **revealing** tells you something that you did not know, especially about the person doing it or making it. EG *He had nothing very revealing to say.*

2 Women's clothes that are **revealing** allow more ADJ QUALIT of their body to be seen than is usual. EG *...revealing black nightdresses.*

revel /revəl/, **revels, revelling, revelled;** V : USU+*in* spelled **reveling** and **reveled** in American Eng- lish. If you **revel** in a situation or experience, you enjoy it very much. EG *She seemed to revel in her success.*

revelation /revə'leɪʃəⁿn/, **revelations.** **1** A **rev-** N COUNT : **elation** is a fact that is made known to people, USU PLURAL especially a surprising or interesting one. EG *His book offers no illuminating personal revelations.*

2 If you say that an experience was a **revelation**, N SING : a+N, you mean that it made you realize something very OFT+*to* surprising. EG *The whole episode was a revelation to him of how poor the family had been.*

revelry /revəⁿlrɪ/ is noisy and often drunken N UNCOUNT enjoyment. EG *The sound of good-natured revelry* Outdated *filled the hotel.*

revenge /rɪ'vendʒ/, **revenges, revenging, re- venged.** **1 Revenge** involves hurting someone N UNCOUNT who has hurt you. EG *They were eager for re- venge... They had taken their revenge by blowing up his house.*

2 If you **revenge** yourself on someone who has V-REFL : hurt you, you hurt them in return. EG *She will* OFT+*on* *revenge herself on those who helped him to es-* Formal *cape.*

revenue /revɪ²nju:/, **revenues. Revenue** is mon- N UNCOUNT ey that a company, organization, or government OR N PLURAL receives from people. EG *The editor was concerned at the drop in advertising revenue... A recession would reduce government tax revenues.*

reverberate /rɪ'vɜ:bəreɪt/, **reverberates, re- verberating, reverberated.** **1** When a loud sound V : USU+A **reverberates** through a place, it echoes and Literary seems to shake the place. EG *A clap of thunder reverberated throughout the room.*

2 You can say that an event or idea **reverberates** V : USU+A when it has a powerful effect which lasts a long Literary time. EG *This was a shock which was to reverberate through the whole of his married life.*

revere /rɪ'vɪə/, **reveres, revering, revered.** If V+O you **revere** someone, you respect and admire Formal them greatly. EG *...her dead mother, whose memory she revered.* ◊ **revered.** EG *He was a revered* ◊ ADJ QUALIT figure with a national reputation.

reverence /revəⁿrəns/ is a feeling of great re- N UNCOUNT spect for someone or something. EG *The sect teach- es reverence for all life.*

Reverend /revəⁿrənd/ is a title used before the name or rank of a member of the clergy. EG *...the Reverend John Lamb.*

reverent /revəⁿrənt/. If your behaviour is **rever-** ADJ QUALIT **ent,** you show great respect for someone or some- thing. EG *We filed past the tomb in a reverent manner.* ◊ **reverently.** EG *She laid the book* ◊ ADV *reverently on the desk.*

reversal /rɪ'vɜ:səⁿl/, **reversals.** **1** When there is a N COUNT : **reversal** of a process or policy, it is changed to the USU SING+SUPP opposite process or policy. EG *Fortunately there was a reversal of this suicidal tendency... They were pressing for a reversal of British policy.*

2 When there is a **reversal** of two things, each one acquires the position or function that the other one had. EG *Events in this present century have produced a complete reversal of roles.*   N COUNT : USU SING+SUPP

reverse /rɪ'vɜːs/, **reverses, reversing, reversed.** **1** When someone **reverses** a process, decision, or policy, they change it to the opposite process, decision, or policy. EG *The farmers want to see this trend reversed... On January 31, the party reversed its decision and agreed to the change.*   v+o

2 If you **reverse** the order of a set of things, you arrange them in the opposite order, so that the first thing comes last.   v+o

3 If you **reverse** the positions or functions of two things, you change them so that each thing has the position or function that the other one had. EG *In this play the traditional sex roles are reversed... The next stage was to reverse the positions of the two pictures.*   v+o

4 When a car **reverses** or when you **reverse** it, you drive it backwards. EG *The street was so narrow that cars which entered it had to reverse out again.*   v-ERG

5 If your car is in **reverse**, you have changed gear so that you can drive it backwards. EG *I threw the truck into reverse.*   N UNCOUNT

6 Reverse means opposite to what is usual or to what has just been described. EG *In the past ten years I think we've seen the reverse process.*   ADJ CLASSIF : ATTRIB

7 The **reverse** is the exact opposite of what has just been mentioned. EG *You may think we have been making a profit. In fact the reverse is true.*   N SING : the+N

8 If a process happens **in reverse** or goes **into reverse**, things happen in the opposite way to what usually happens or to what has been happening. EG *At this point the Party's fortunes went into reverse.*   PHRASE

9 If you **reverse the charges** when you make a telephone call, the person who you are calling receives the bill and not you.   PHRASE British

reversion /rɪ'vɜːʃəⁿn/. **Reversion** to a former state, system, or kind of behaviour is a change back to it. EG *...this reversion to pre-scientific attitudes.*   N UNCOUNT+to Formal

revert /rɪ'vɜːt/, **reverts, reverting, reverted.** When people or things **revert** to a former state, system, or type of behaviour, they go back to it. EG *He was reverting rapidly to adolescence... Areas that are cleared for farming sometimes revert to forest later.*   v+to Formal

review /rɪ'vjuː/, **reviews, reviewing, reviewed.** **1** A **review** is an article in a newspaper or magazine, or an item on television or radio, in which someone gives their opinion of something such as a new book or play. EG *...a review of Lord Harewood's autobiography... ...book reviews.*   N COUNT

2 When there is a **review** of a situation or system, it is formally examined in order to decide whether changes are needed. EG *A review of public expenditure began immediately.* ▸ used as a verb. EG *By law, state pensions must be reviewed once a year.*   N COUNT OR N UNCOUNT   ▸ v+o

3 When something **comes up for review**, the time arrives for it to be formally examined to see whether changes are needed. When it is **under review**, it is being examined in this way. EG *They had the situation under review.*   PHRASE

4 If you **review** a situation, you consider it carefully. EG *Dawdling over a cup of coffee, he reviewed his situation once more.*   v+o

5 If you **review** something such as a new book or play, you write an article or give a talk on television or radio in which you express your opinion of it. ◊ **reviewer, reviewers**. EG *Reviewers loved the book.*   v+o ◊ N COUNT

revise /rɪ'vaɪz/, **revises, revising, revised. 1** If you **revise** something, you alter it in order to make it better or more correct. EG *The judges may revise their selection process... This book has sold a half-million copies since it was revised last year.* ◊ **revised**. EG *...a revised estimate of $9,000,000.*   v+o ◊ ADJ CLASSIF

2 When you **revise** for an examination, you read things again in order to learn them thoroughly. EG *I've been revising for the last three days... I was revising Dickens last night.*   v OR v+o

revision /rɪ'vɪʒəⁿn/, **revisions. 1** A **revision** of something is an alteration that is made to it in order to improve it. EG *They're discussing a complete revision of the timetable... The Shops Act is in need of revision.*   N COUNT OR N UNCOUNT : OFT+of

2 When you do **revision**, you read things again in order to learn them for an examination. EG *I've got to do some revision.*   N UNCOUNT

revitalize /riː'vaɪtəlaɪz/, **revitalizes, revitalizing, revitalized;** also spelled **revitalise.** To **revitalize** something means to make it more active or lively. EG *...its plan to revitalise the American economy... ...the Liverpool poets who revitalized poetry in England in the 1960s.*   v+o

revival /rɪ'vaɪvəⁿl/, **revivals.** When there is a **revival** of something, it becomes active again. EG *Inflation may start to rise with the revival of trade... Why is there such a revival of interest in the supernatural?*   N UNCOUNT OR N COUNT : USU+SUPP

revive /rɪ'vaɪv/, **revives, reviving, revived. 1** When something such as a feeling or a practice **revives** or **is revived**, it becomes active, popular, or successful again. EG *My spirits revived as we drove out into the countryside... They failed to fulfil their promises to revive the economy.*   v-ERG

2 When you **revive** someone who has fainted or when they **revive**, they become conscious again. EG *They had difficulty in reviving him... He slowly began to revive.*   v-ERG

revoke /rɪ'vəʊk/, **revokes, revoking, revoked.** When someone in authority **revokes** something such as a licence or an order, they cancel it. EG *The permission was revoked.*   v+o Formal

revolt /rɪ'vəʊlt/, **revolts, revolting, revolted.** A **revolt** is a violent attempt by a group of people to change their country's political system. EG *...the Peasants' Revolt of 1381... The settlers rose in revolt.* ▸ used as a verb. EG *Large sections of the army revolted against the civil government.*   N COUNT OR N UNCOUNT   ▸ V : OFT +against

revolting /rɪ'vəʊltɪŋ/. You say that something is **revolting** when you think that it is horrible and disgusting. EG *The smell was quite revolting.*   ADJ QUALIT

revolution /ˌrevəljⁿuːʃəⁿn/, **revolutions. 1** A **revolution** is a successful attempt by a large group of people to change the political system of their country by force. EG *...the fiftieth anniversary of the Russian revolution... France seemed to be on the verge of revolution.*   N COUNT OR N UNCOUNT

2 A **revolution** is also an important change in a particular area of human activity. EG *...the Industrial Revolution... ...the Computer Revolution... ...the revolution in communications.*   N COUNT

revolutionary /ˌrevəljⁿuːʃəⁿri/, **revolutionaries. 1 Revolutionary** activities are intended to cause a political revolution. EG *They had fled as a result of their revolutionary activities.*   ADJ CLASSIF

2 A **revolutionary** is a person who tries to cause a revolution or who takes part in one. ▸ used as an adjective. EG *...a revolutionary leader.*   N COUNT ▸ ADJ CLASSIF

3 Revolutionary ideas and developments involve great changes in the way that something is done or made. EG *...a revolutionary change in the way cars are manufactured.*   ADJ QUALIT

revolutionize /ˌrevəljⁿuːʃənaɪz/, **revolutionizes, revolutionizing, revolutionized;** also spelled **revolutionise.** When something **revolutionizes** an activity, it causes great changes in the way that   v+o

What is ambiguous about 'The peasants are revolting'?

it is done. EG *Our ideas will revolutionize the film industry.*

revolve /rɪ'vɒlv/, **revolves, revolving, revolved. 1** If you say that someone's life **revolves** around something, you mean that it is the main feature of their life. EG *Rural life revolved around agriculture.* V+around/round

2 If a discussion **revolves** around a particular topic, it is mainly about that topic. EG *The discussion revolved round three topics.* V+around/round

3 When something **revolves**, it moves or turns in a circle around a central point or line. EG *...the discovery that the earth revolved around the sun.* V:OFT+around/round
◊ **revolving**. EG *They were watering the ground with big revolving sprinklers.* ◊ ADJ CLASSIF: ATTRIB

revolver /rɪ'vɒlvə/, **revolvers**. A **revolver** is a kind of gun that you hold in your hand. See picture at WEAPONS. N COUNT

revolving door

revolving door, revolving doors. A **revolving door** consists of four glass doors which turn together around a vertical post. N COUNT

revulsion /rɪ'vʌlʃə⁰n/ is a strong feeling of disgust or disapproval. EG *Germ warfare has always been regarded with revulsion.* N UNCOUNT

reward /rɪ'wɔːd/, **rewards, rewarding, rewarded. 1** A **reward** is something that you get or are given because you have done something useful or good. EG *...a reward for outstanding service... ...the emotional rewards of parenthood... They work with no thought of reward.* N COUNT OR N UNCOUNT

2 To **reward** someone means to give them something because they have done something useful or good. EG *People should be rewarded for special effort... They rewarded the winners with gifts of fruit and flowers.* V+O

rewarding /rɪ'wɔːdɪŋ/. Something that is **rewarding** gives you a lot of satisfaction. EG *...rewarding jobs... ...a rewarding novel.* ADJ QUALIT

rewind /riː'waɪnd/, **rewinds, rewinding, rewound** /riː'waʊnd/. When you **rewind** the tape on a tape recorder, you make the tape go backwards so that you can play it again. V+O OR V

rewrite /riː'raɪt/, **rewrites, rewriting, rewrote** /riː'rəʊt/, **rewritten** /riː'rɪtə⁰n/. If you **rewrite** a piece of writing, you write it in a different way in order to improve it. EG *Scenes 9 and 10 need rewriting.* V+O

rhetoric /'retərɪk/ is fine-sounding speech or writing that is meant to convince and impress people; often used showing disapproval. EG *I was expecting the usual fiery rhetoric from the Chairman... ...political rhetoric.* N UNCOUNT

rhetorical /rɪ'tɒrɪkə⁰l/. **1** A **rhetorical** question is one which is asked in order to make a statement rather than to get an answer. ADJ CLASSIF

2 Rhetorical language is intended to be grand and impressive. EG *...their rhetorical threats to 'crush the oppressors'.* ADJ CLASSIF

rheumatic /ruː'mætɪk/. **1 Rheumatic** pains are caused by rheumatism. ADJ CLASSIF

2 Someone who is **rheumatic** suffers from rheumatism. ADJ CLASSIF

rheumatism /'ruːmətɪzə⁰m/ is an illness that makes your joints or muscles stiff and painful. EG *They were crippled with rheumatism.* N UNCOUNT

rhino /'raɪnəʊ/, **rhinos**. A **rhino** is the same as a rhinoceros. N COUNT

rhinoceros /raɪ'nɒsə⁰rəs/, **rhinoceroses**. A **rhinoceros** is a large animal with one or two horns on its nose. Rhinoceroses live in Africa and Asia and eat plants. N COUNT

rhododendron /ˌrəʊdə'dendrən/, **rhododendrons**. A **rhododendron** is a bush with large pink or purple flowers. N COUNT

rhubarb /'ruːbɑːb/ is a plant with long red stems which people eat after cooking them with sugar. N UNCOUNT

rhyme /raɪm/, **rhymes, rhyming, rhymed. 1** If one word **rhymes** with another or if two words **rhyme**, they have a very similar sound. Words that rhyme with each other are often used in poems. EG *She called him Guppy, to rhyme with puppy.* V OR V+with: RECIP

2 A **rhyme** is **2.1** a word which rhymes with another word. EG *...two words he could not find a rhyme for.* **2.2** a short poem which has rhyming words at the ends of its lines. EG *...children's games and rhymes.* ● See also **nursery rhyme**. N COUNT

3 Rhyme is the use of rhyming words as a technique in poetry. EG *She had a gift for rhythm and rhyme.* ● If something is written **in rhyme**, it is written as a poem in which the lines rhyme. EG *Tennyson's work was mostly in rhyme.* N UNCOUNT / ● PHRASE

rhythm /'rɪðə⁰m/, **rhythms**. A **rhythm** is **1** a regular movement or beat. EG *...the rhythm of the drums... J J Cale uses rhythm for the opposite effect in his music.* **2** a regular pattern of changes, for example changes in your body, in the seasons, or in the tides. EG *...the rhythms of the sea.* N COUNT OR N UNCOUNT / N COUNT

rhythmic /'rɪðmɪk/. If a movement or sound is **rhythmic**, it is repeated at regular intervals, forming a regular pattern or beat. EG *The machine made a soft rhythmic sound.* ◊ **rhythmically**. EG *The cradle rocked rhythmically to and fro.* ADJ QUALIT / ◊ ADV

rib /rɪb/, **ribs**. Your **ribs** are the curved bones that go from your backbone to your chest. EG *He had a broken rib.* N COUNT

ribald /'rɪbə⁰ld/. **Ribald** remarks are rather rude and refer to sex in a humorous way. EG *...exclamations of ribald encouragement... ...ribald laughter.* ADJ QUALIT Outdated

ribbon /'rɪbə⁰n/, **ribbons. 1** A **ribbon** is a long, narrow piece of cloth that you use for tying things together or as a decoration. EG *There was a white ribbon in her hair... ...a length of silk ribbon.* N COUNT OR N UNCOUNT

2 A typewriter **ribbon** is a long, narrow piece of cloth containing a special ink that you put into a typewriter to make it work. N COUNT OR N UNCOUNT

rib-cage, rib-cages. Your **rib-cage** is the structure of ribs in your chest. N COUNT

rice /raɪs/ is a food consisting of white grains which you cook and eat, usually with meat or vegetables. The plant from which rice is taken is also called **rice**. EG *She cooked a dish of rice and chicken... ...a rice field.* N UNCOUNT

rich /rɪtʃ/, **richer, richest; riches. 1** Someone who is **rich** has a lot of money or valuable possessions. EG *She was extremely rich... Our father was a very rich man.* ADJ QUALIT

2 Riches are valuable possessions or large amounts of money. EG *...young men in search of adventure and riches.* N PLURAL

3 If you talk about the earth's **riches**, you are referring to things that exist naturally in large quantities and that are useful to people, for example minerals, wood, and oil. EG *...the exploitation of the earth's riches.* N PLURAL

4 If something is **rich** in a desirable substance or quality, it contains a lot of it. EG *The sea bed is rich in buried minerals... The story is rich in comic and dramatic detail.* ADJ PRED+in

5 A **rich** deposit of a mineral or other substance ADJ QUALIT: ATTRIB consists of a large amount of it. EG *...the world's richest vein of copper.*

6 Rich soil contains large amounts of substances ADJ QUALIT that make it good for growing crops or flowers in.

7 Rich food contains a lot of fat or oil. EG *He was* ADJ QUALIT *prone to indigestion after rich restaurant meals.*

8 Rich colours, smells, and sounds are strong and ADJ QUALIT pleasant. EG *The sea was a deep rich blue... ...the rich sound of the brass instruments.*

9 If you say that a place has a **rich** history, you ADJ QUALIT mean that its history is very interesting. EG *The town has a rich social history.*

richly /rɪtʃli'/. **1** If someone is **richly** rewarded ADV for something, they are rewarded well by being given something very valuable.

2 If you feel strongly that someone deserves some- ADV thing or has earned it, you can say that it is **richly** deserved or **richly** earned. EG *It was a richly deserved honour.*

3 If a place is **richly** provided with something, it ADV has a lot of it. EG *These libraries are richly equipped with games and books.*

4 If something is **richly** decorated, it has a lot of ADV elaborate and beautiful decoration on it. EG *...the richly carved wooden screen.*

rickety /rɪkɪ'ti'/. A **rickety** building or piece of ADJ QUALIT furniture has not been made strongly, and is there- fore likely to collapse or break. EG *She started off down the rickety stairs.*

rickshaw /rɪkʃɔː/, **rickshaws**. A **rickshaw** is a N COUNT simple vehicle that is used in Asia for carrying passengers. Some rickshaws are pulled by a man who walks or runs in front.

ricochet /rɪkəʃeɪ, rɪkəʃɛt/, **ricochets, ricochet-** V : USU+A **ing, ricocheted;** also spelled **ricochetting, rico- chetted.** When a bullet **ricochets**, it hits a surface and bounces away from it. EG *The bullet ricochet- ted off the ceiling.*

rid /rɪd/, **rids, ridding.** The form **rid** is used in the present tense and is the past tense and past participle of the verb.

1 When you **get rid of** something that you do not PHRASE want, you take action so that you no longer have it. EG *She bathed thoroughly to get rid of the last traces of make-up... How do they get rid of rats and mice?... We had to get rid of the director.*

2 If you **rid** a place of something unpleasant or V+O+*of* annoying, you succeed in removing it completely. Formal EG *We must rid the country of this wickedness.*

3 If you **rid** yourself of something undesirable, you V.REFL+*of* take action so that you no longer have it or are no Formal longer affected by it. EG *He had rid himself of his illusions.*

4 If you are **rid** of someone or something that had ADJ PRED+*of* been worrying or annoying you, they are no longer with you or affecting you. EG *Eric was glad to be rid of him.*

riddance /rɪdəns/. You say **good riddance** to CONVENTION indicate that you are glad that someone has left. Informal

ridden /rɪdə⁰n/ is the past participle of **ride.**

riddle /rɪdə⁰l/, **riddles. 1** A **riddle** is a puzzle in N COUNT which you ask a question that seems to be non- sense but which has a clever or amusing answer, for example 'When is a door not a door? When it's ajar.'

2 If you describe something as a **riddle**, you mean N COUNT that you are unable to understand it or find an answer to it. EG *I was trying to solve the perplexing riddle of how to help my people.*

riddled /rɪdə⁰ld/. **1** If something is **riddled** with ADJ PRED holes, it is full of them. EG *They had left the whole* +*with* *building riddled with holes.*

2 If something is **riddled** with undesirable qualities ADJ PRED or features, it is full of them. EG *...cities riddled with* +*with* *corruption.*

ride /raɪd/, **rides, riding, rode** /rəʊd/, **ridden** /rɪdə⁰n/. **1** When you **ride** a horse, you sit on it and V+O OR V+A control its movements. EG *Every morning he used*

to ride his mare across the fields... He arrived later, riding on his large white horse.*

2 When you **ride** a bicycle or a motorcycle, you sit V+O OR V+A on it, control it, and travel along on it. EG *He rode round the campus on a bicycle.*

3 When you **ride** in a vehicle such as a car, you V+A travel in it. EG *That afternoon he rode in a jeep to the village.*

4 A **ride** is a journey on a horse or bicycle, or in a N COUNT vehicle. EG *I'd like to go for a ride... ...the bus ride to Worcester... Like a ride to the village?*

5 If you say that someone **has taken** you **for a** PHRASE **ride**, you mean that they have deceived you or Informal cheated you.

ride up. If a skirt or dress **rides up**, it moves PHRASAL VB : upwards, out of its proper position. V+ADV

rider /raɪdə/, **riders.** A **rider** is someone who is N COUNT riding a horse, a bicycle, or a motorcycle. EG *The rider was thrown off... ...a motorcycle rider.*

ridge /rɪdʒ/, **ridges.** A **ridge** is **1** a long, narrow N COUNT piece of raised land. EG *We drove up a hillside and finally stopped on a high ridge.* **2** a raised line on a flat surface. EG *He was counting the ridges in the wet sand.*

ridicule /rɪdɪkjuːl/, **ridicules, ridiculing, ridi-** V+O **culed.** If you **ridicule** someone or something what they say or do, you make fun of them in an unkind way. EG *He is liable to be teased and ridiculed.*

▸ used as a noun. EG *His prophecy was greeted with* ▸ N UNCOUNT *a good deal of ridicule.*

ridiculous /rɪdɪkjə⁰ləs/. If you say that something ADJ QUALIT is **ridiculous**, you mean that it is very foolish. EG *It would be ridiculous to pretend that there were no difficulties... Don't be so ridiculous... They charge you a ridiculous price.* ◊ **ridiculously.** EG *He let* ◊ SUBMOD *out his house at a ridiculously low rent.*

rife /raɪf/. If you say that something bad or ADJ PRED unpleasant is **rife**, you mean that it is very com- Formal mon. EG *Bribery and corruption in the government service were rife.*

rifle /raɪfə⁰l/, **rifles, rifling, rifled. 1** A **rifle** is a N COUNT gun with a long barrel. See picture at WEAPONS.

2 When someone **rifles** something, they steal V+O everything they want from it. EG *He rifled the dead man's wallet... She found him rifling her fridge.*

3 If you **rifle** through things, you make a quick V+*through* search among them. EG *The doctor rifled through the papers.*

rift /rɪft/, **rifts. 1** A **rift** between people is a N COUNT : OFT serious quarrel that makes them stop being +*between/in* friends. EG *It had been nine years since she had seen her brother, as a result of a rift between them.*

2 A **rift** is also a split that appears in something N COUNT solid, especially in the ground. EG *The Jemez Moun- tains face Santa Fe across the rift.*

rig /rɪg/, **rigs, rigging, rigged. 1** If someone **rigs** V+O an election, a job appointment, or a game, they dishonestly arrange it so that they achieve the result that they want.

2 A **rig** is a large structure that is used for looking N COUNT for oil or gas and for taking it out of the ground or the sea bed. EG *...an oil rig... ...a drilling rig.*

rig up. If you **rig up** a device or structure, you PHRASAL VB : make it and fix it in place using any materials that V+O+ADV are available. EG *He had rigged up a listening device.*

rigging /rɪgɪŋ/. The ropes which support a ship's N UNCOUNT masts and sails are referred to as the **rigging.**

right /raɪt/, **rights, righting, righted. 1** If some- ADJ CLASSIF thing is **right**, it is correct and in accordance with OR ADV the facts. EG *You get full marks for getting the right answer... You are French, is that right?... I hope I'm pronouncing the name right.*

2 If someone is **right** about something, they are ADJ PRED

Does a right-hand man have to be right-handed?

correct in what they say or think about it. EG *Lally was right about the repairs which the cottage needed... You're absolutely right.* ◊ **rightly**. EG *The arts are, as Geoffrey rightly said, underfinanced.*   ◊ ADV

3 If something such as a choice, action, or decision is the **right** one, it is the best or most suitable one. EG *Are you sure that was the right decision?... I thought it was the right thing to do... Clare is obviously the right person to talk to about it.* ◊ **rightly**. EG *He can be very good at acting when he is rightly cast.*   ADJ CLASSIF   ◊ ADV

4 If something isn't **right**, there is something unsatisfactory about the situation or thing that you are talking about. EG *She sensed that things weren't right between us.*   ADJ PRED : WITH BROAD NEG

5 If you say that someone is **right** to do something, you mean that you think that they are morally justified in doing it. EG *We were right to insist on certain reforms... I don't think it's right to leave children alone in a house.* ◊ **rightly**. EG *Many people are rightly indignant.*   ADJ PRED : USU + *to*-INF   ◊ ADV

6 Right is used to refer to actions that are considered to be morally good and acceptable. EG *One must have some principles, some sense of right and wrong.*   N UNCOUNT

7 If you refer to the **right** people or the **right** places, you are referring to people and places that are socially admired. EG *He knew all the right people.*   ADJ CLASSIF : ATTRIB

8 The **right** side of a piece of material is the side that is intended to be seen and that faces outwards when it is made into clothes.   ADJ CLASSIF : ATTRIB

9 You say **'Right'** in order to attract someone's attention, especially when you want to begin something. EG *Right, open your mouth, let's have a look.*   ADV SEN

10 If you have a **right** to do or have something, you are morally or legally entitled to do it or have it. EG *...the right to strike... They will fight for their rights... ...basic civil and political rights.*   N COUNT

11 Right is one of two opposite directions, sides, or positions. If you are facing north and you turn to the right, you will be facing east. In the word 'to', the 'o' is to the right of the 't'. EG *On my left was Tony Heard and on my right Allister Sparks... They turned their heads from left to right.* ▶ used as an adverb or an adjective. EG *Turn right off Broadway into Caxton Street... Her right hand was covered in blood.*   N UNCOUNT OR N SING   ▶ ADV OR ADJ CLASSIF : ATTRIB

12 The **Right** is used to refer to the people or groups who support the political ideals of capitalism and conservatism rather than socialism.   N COLL : SING

13 Right is used **13.1** to emphasize the precise place that you are talking about. EG *Our hotel was right on the beach... Stay right here.* **13.2** to emphasize how far something moves or extends, or how long something continues. EG *We took the lift right down to the basement... This went on right up until 1975.* **13.3** to emphasize a noun referring to something bad. EG *They've made a right mess of that, haven't they?*   ADV + A   ADV + A   ADJ CLASSIF : ATTRIB Informal

14 Right also means immediately and without delay. EG *I'll be right back... The Music Hall is going to close down right after Easter.*   ADV + A

15 If you **right** something that has fallen or rolled over or if it **rights** itself, it returns to its normal upright position. EG *The ship righted itself.*   V + O OR V-REFL

16 To **right** a wrong means to correct it or compensate for it.   V + O

17 Right is also used in these phrases. **17.1** If you **get** something **right**, you do it correctly. EG *Get the spelling right this time.* **17.2** If you **put right** or **set right** a mistake or an unsatisfactory situation, you do something to make things satisfactory. EG *The only way we can put things right is by borrowing even more money.* **17.3 Right now** means at this moment. EG *I have no time right now to discuss your problems.* **17.4 Right away** means immediately and without any delay. EG *He had written down a list of things to do right away.* **17.5** If you   PHRASES   Informal   Formal

are **in the right**, what you are doing is morally or legally correct. **17.6** If you say that something should be true **by rights**, you are emphasizing that it should be true, although it isn't. EG *I should by rights speak German – my mother's German – but I only know a few words.* **17.7** If you have a position, title, or claim to something **in** your **own right**, you have it because of what you are yourself rather than because of other people. EG *He had emerged as a leader in his own right.* **17.8** to **reserve the right to** do something: see **reserve**. ● to **serve** someone **right**: see **serve**. ● **on the right side of** someone: see **side**. ● See also **all right**.

right angle, right angles. 1 A **right angle** is an angle of 90°. A square has four right angles.   N COUNT

2 If one thing is **at right angles** to another, or if two things are **at right angles**, they are situated so that they form an angle of 90° where they touch each other. EG *...four corridors at right angles to each other.*   PHRASE

righteous /raɪtʃəs/. **Righteous** people behave in a way that is morally good, religious, and praiseworthy. EG *...a righteous and wise man... ...righteous anger.* ◊ **righteousness**. EG *Some of us strive for righteousness.*   ADJ QUALIT Formal   ◊ N UNCOUNT

rightful /raɪtfʊl/. Someone's **rightful** possession, place, or role is one which they have a legal or moral right to have. EG *They had been deprived of their rightful share of the property... He can now take his rightful place as president.*   ADJ CLASSIF : ATTRIB Formal

right-hand is used to describe something which is on the right side. EG *...a biggish house on the right-hand side of the road.*   ADJ CLASSIF : ATTRIB

right-handed. Someone who is **right-handed** uses their right hand rather than their left hand for activities such as writing and painting.   ADJ CLASSIF

right-hand man, right-hand men. If you refer to a man as your **right-hand man**, you mean that he is the person who helps you most in your work. EG *I'm counting on you being my right-hand man.*   N COUNT : USU + POSS

right of way, rights of way. 1 When a car or other vehicle has **right of way**, it has the right to cross a road or continue round a roundabout, and other traffic must stop for it.   N UNCOUNT

2 A **right of way** is a public path across private land.   N COUNT

right-wing. 1 Right-wing people support conservatism and capitalism. EG *...the election of a right-wing government... They are very right-wing.*   ADJ QUALIT

2 The **right wing** of a political party consists of the members who are most in favour of conservatism and capitalism. EG *If he started to introduce reforms, his right wing would challenge him.*   N SING

right-winger, right-wingers. A **right-winger** is a person who supports conservatism and capitalism or whose political beliefs are closer to conservatism than those of most of the other people in the same party.   N COUNT

rigid /rɪdʒɪd/. **1** Laws or systems that are **rigid** cannot be changed or varied, and are therefore considered to be rather severe. EG *Some mothers resented the rigid controls.* ◊ **rigidity** /rɪdʒɪdɪti/. EG *...the rigidity of Victorian marriage.*   ADJ QUALIT   ◊ N UNCOUNT

2 You say that people are **rigid** when they are not able or not willing to change their way of thinking or behaving; used showing disapproval. EG *...the rigid attitude of the Foreign Secretary.*   ADJ QUALIT

3 A **rigid** substance or object is stiff and does not bend easily. EG *...with permed hair in rigid waves... I sat upright, rigid with nervousness.* ◊ **rigidity**. EG *The function of bones is largely to give rigidity.*   ADJ QUALIT   ◊ N UNCOUNT

rigidly /rɪdʒɪdli/. **1** If you stay **rigidly** in one position, you do not move. EG *I looked rigidly ahead... My features stayed rigidly fixed in the same expression.*   ADV

2 If you deal with something **rigidly**, you do it in a very strict way with no possibility of variation or   ADV change. EG *These suggestions must not be inter-preted too rigidly.*

rigorous /rɪgəˈrəs/. **Rigorous** is used to describe ADJ QUALIT things that are done or carried out in a very thorough and strict way. EG *...rigorous controls... ...a rigorous training schedule.* ◊ **rigorously.** EG *These* ◊ ADV *methods have been rigorously tested over many years.*

rigours /rɪgəz/; spelled **rigors** in American Eng- N PLURAL: lish. The **rigours** of a situation or way of life are the+N+of the features that make it unpleasant and hard to Formal bear. EG *...the rigours of a city winter.*

rim /rɪm/, **rims. 1** The **rim** of a container such as N COUNT a cup or glass is the edge that goes all the way round the top. EG *Whisky splashed over the rim of his glass... ...the rim of the bath.*

2 The **rim** of a circular object such as a wheel is its N COUNT outside edge. EG *Muller's glasses had gold rims.*

rind /raɪnd/, **rinds. 1** The **rind** of a fruit such as a N COUNT OR lemon is its thick outer skin. N UNCOUNT

2 The **rind** of cheese or bacon is the hard outer N COUNT OR edge which you do not usually eat. N UNCOUNT

ring /rɪŋ/, **rings, ringing, rang** /ræŋ/, **rung** /rʌŋ/. For paragraphs 13 and 14, the past tense and past participle is **ringed.**

1 If you **ring** someone, you phone them. EG *You* V+O OR V *must ring the hospital at once... He may ring again.*

2 If you **give** someone **a ring,** you phone them. EG PHRASE *Give me a ring if you need me.* Informal

3 When you **ring** a bell or when a bell **rings,** it V-ERG makes a sound. EG *In the distance a church bell was ringing... I waited for the phone to ring... He had to ring the bell several times before the door was opened.* ● to **ring a bell:** see **bell.**

4 If you **ring** for someone or something, you ring a V:OFT+for bell to call them or to have them brought. EG *He rang for Tracy and asked, 'What's wrong with Davis?'*

5 A **ring** is the sound made by a bell. EG *There was* N COUNT *a ring at the door.*

6 If a place **rings** with a sound, the sound there is V:OFT+with very loud. EG *We went into a barn that rang with* Literary *the cries of geese and turkeys.*

7 If a sound or statement **rings in** your **head** or PHRASE **rings in** your **ears,** you remember it vividly. EG *He* Literary *left with the cheers still ringing in his ears.*

8 If you say that a statement **rings true,** you mean PHRASE that it seems likely to be true. EG *The bishop's answers so often ring true.*

9 You can use **ring** to say what quality something N SING: seems to have. For example, if an argument has a a+N+SUPP plausible **ring,** it seems quite plausible. EG *The books he mentioned had a familiar ring about them... The name had an unpleasant ring to it.*

10 A **ring** is also **10.1** a small circle of metal that N COUNT you wear on your finger as an ornament or to show that you are engaged or married. See picture at JEWELLERY. EG *...a diamond ring.* **10.2** an object or group of things which has the shape of a circle. EG *I like to blow smoke rings... They formed a ring round him... ...a ring of excited faces.*

11 At a boxing match, show jumping contest, or N COUNT circus, the **ring** is the enclosed space with seats round it where the contest or performance takes place.

12 A **ring** is also a group of people who do N COUNT something illegal together over a period of time. EG *The police exposed a large drug ring operating in the area.*

13 If you **ring** something, you draw a circle round V+O it. EG *I got a map and ringed all the likely villages.*

14 If something **is ringed** with something else, it V-PASS has that thing all the way around it. EG *...a valley* USU+with *ringed with mountains.*

ring back. If you **ring** someone **back,** you phone PHRASAL VB: them, either because they phoned you earlier V+O+ADV when you were not there, or because you did not OR V+ADV finish an earlier conversation on the phone. EG *He asked if you'd ring him back when you got in.*

ring off. When you **ring off** at the end of a PHRASAL VB: telephone call, you put down your receiver. V+ADV

ring out. If something **rings out,** they are heard PHRASAL VB: loudly and clearly. EG *Her voice rang out.* V+ADV

ring up. If you **ring** someone **up,** you phone PHRASAL VB: them. EG *He rang me up to tell me that he had* V+O+ADV *found the letter.* OR V+ADV

ringing /rɪŋɪŋ/. A **ringing** sound can be heard ADJ CLASSIF: very clearly. EG *...clear ringing tones.* ATTRIB

ringleader /rɪŋliːdə/, **ringleaders.** The **ring-** N COUNT **leader** of a group of people who are causing trouble is the person who is leading them. EG *The six ringleaders were arrested and charged.*

ring road, ring roads. A **ring road** is a road that N COUNT goes all the way round the edge of a town so that traffic does not have to go through the town centre.

rink /rɪŋk/, **rinks.** A **rink** is a large area, usually N COUNT indoors, where people go to ice-skate or roller-skate. EG *There's a good ice rink in Leeds... ...a skating rink.*

rinse /rɪns/, **rinses, rinsing, rinsed. 1** When you V+O **rinse** something, you wash it without using soap. EG *He rinsed his hands under the tap.* ▸ used as a ▸ N COUNT noun. EG *Just give these a quick rinse.*

2 If you **rinse** your mouth or **rinse** it **out,** you V+O:OFT+out wash it by holding a mouthful of liquid in it, for example to get rid of an unpleasant taste.

riot /raɪət/, **riots, rioting, rioted. 1** When there is N COUNT a **riot,** a crowd of people behave violently in a public place. EG *In May 1968 there was a wave of student riots.*

2 When people **riot,** they behave violently in a V public place. EG *If food prices are put up too far, the people will riot.* ◊ **rioter, rioters.** EG *Courts dealt* ◊ N COUNT *with rioters quickly and harshly.*

3 If people **run riot,** they behave in a wild and PHRASE uncontrolled manner. EG *You shouldn't allow the children to run riot.*

riotous /raɪətəs/. **1 Riotous** behaviour is violent ADJ CLASSIF: and uncontrolled behaviour, for example damaging ATTRIB vehicles and buildings and fighting in public. EG *...a* Formal *riotous mob... He was found guilty of riotous behav-iour.*

2 You can also describe people's behaviour as ADJ QUALIT **riotous** when they do things in an enthusiastic and rather wild way. EG *Both children would come rushing out in a riotous welcome.*

rip /rɪp/, **rips, ripping, ripped. 1** When you **rip** V-ERG something or when it **rips,** it is torn violently. EG *The poster had been ripped to pieces... Two of the canvas bags had ripped.*

2 If you **rip** something away, you remove it quickly V+O+A and violently. EG *I ripped the phone from her hand... He ripped his shirt off.*

3 A **rip** is a long cut or split in something made of N COUNT cloth or paper. EG *He had seen the rip in the book.*

rip off. If someone **rips** you **off,** they cheat you PHRASAL VB: by charging you too much money for something. EG V+O+ADV *The local shopkeepers were all trying to rip off the* Informal *tourists.* ● See also **rip-off.**

rip up. If you **rip** something **up,** you tear it into PHRASAL VB: small pieces. EG *I wanted to rip up my schedule and* V+O+ADV *fill out a new one.*

ripe /raɪp/, **riper, ripest. 1** When fruit or grain is ADJ QUALIT **ripe,** it is fully grown and ready to be eaten. EG *The pears are heavy and ripe.*

2 If you say that something is **ripe** for a change of ADJ PRED+for some kind, you mean that it is ready for it or likely to experience it. EG *Our people are ripe for free-dom... The nation was ripe for collapse.*

3 If you say **the time is ripe,** you mean that a PHRASE suitable time has arrived for something to be done. EG *The time was ripe to break his silence.*

4 If someone lives to a **ripe old age,** they live to be PHRASE very old.

If you **rise** at 8 o'clock, do you stand up?

ripen /raɪpəⁿn/, **ripens, ripening, ripened.** When v-ERG crops **ripen** or when the sun **ripens** them, they become ripe. EG ...*fields of ripening wheat.*

rip-off, rip-offs. If you say that something that N COUNT you bought was a **rip-off**, you mean that you were Informal charged too much for it.

ripple /rɪpəⁿl/, **ripples, rippling, rippled. 1** Rip- N COUNT : **ples** are little waves on the surface of water USU PLURAL caused by the wind or by an object dropping into the water. EG *A twig made tiny ripples on the water*... ...*sending out patterns of ripples.*
2 When the surface of an area of water **ripples** or v-ERG when something **ripples** it, a number of little waves appear on it. EG *A gentle breeze rippled the surface of the sea.*
3 If there is a **ripple** of laughter or applause, N SING+of people laugh or applaud quietly for a short time. EG *There was a ripple of amused applause from the newsmen.*

rise /raɪz/, **rises, rising, rose** /rəʊz/, **risen** /rɪzəⁿn/. **1** If something **rises**, it moves upwards. EG v : OFT+A *Clouds of birds rose from the tree-tops*... *He could see the smoke from his bonfire rising up in a white column.*
2 When you **rise**, · **2.1** you stand up. EG *Dr* v : OFT+A *Willoughby rose to greet him.* **2.2** you get out of Formal bed. EG *They had risen at dawn.*
3 When the sun or moon **rises**, it appears from v below the horizon.
4 You can also say that something **rises** when it v : USU+A appears as a large, tall shape. EG *St Paul's rose* Literary *majestically from the trees.*
5 If land **rises**, it slopes upwards. EG *He followed* v *Jack towards the castle where the ground rose slightly.* ◊ **rising.** EG *The house was built on rising* ◊ ADJ CLASSIF : *ground.* ATTRIB
6 If a sound **rises**, it becomes louder or higher. EG v : USU+A *His voice rose to a shriek.*
7 If a sound **rises** from a group of people, it comes v : USU+from from them. EG *A loud gasp rose from the boys.*
8 If an amount **rises**, it increases. EG *Prices rose by* v *more than 10%*... *The temperature began to rise.*
◊ **rising.** EG ...*the rising rate of inflation.* ◊ ADJ CLASSIF
9 A **rise** in the amount of something is an increase N COUNT+SUPP in it. EG ...*the rise in crime*... ...*price rises.*
10 A **rise** is an increase in wages or salary. EG ...*a* N COUNT *pay rise of about £20 a week*... *I asked for a rise.*
11 If you **rise** to a challenge or remark, you v+to respond to it in some way, rather than ignoring it.
12 When the people in a country **rise** up, they start v : OFT+up fighting the people in authority there. EG *The settlers rose in revolt.* ◊ **rising, risings.** EG ...*a big* ◊ N COUNT *peasant rising in the West of France.*
13 If someone **rises** to a higher position or status, v+A they become more important, successful, or power- ful. EG *Bergson rose rapidly to fame.*
14 Someone's **rise** is the process by which they N SING become more important, successful, or powerful. EG ...*the decline of the Liberal Party and the rise of Labour*... ...*his rise to fame.*
15 If something **gives rise to** an event or situation, PHRASE it causes the event or situation to happen. EG *This breakthrough could give rise to ethical problems.*
16 to **rise to the occasion:** see **occasion.**

rise above. If you **rise above** a difficulty or PHRASAL VB : problem, you manage not to let it affect you. EG *She* v+PREP *was in continual pain, but rose above it.*

risk /rɪsk/, **risks, risking, risked. 1** If there is a N COUNT OR **risk** of something unpleasant, there is a possibility N UNCOUNT that it will happen. EG *There is very little risk of infection*... ...*the risk that their men might disap- pear without trace.*
2 If something that you do is a **risk**, it might have N SING unpleasant or undesirable results. EG *Such a re- sponse would be an irrational risk.*
3 You say that an object is a **risk** when it is likely N SING to cause danger. EG *Your television is a fire risk if left plugged in overnight.*
4 Risk is also used in these phrases. **4.1** If someone PHRASES

or something is **at risk**, they are in a situation where something unpleasant might happen to them. EG *The sick and lonely are most at risk*... *You're putting my career at risk.* **4.2** If you do something **at the risk of** something unpleasant happening, you do it although you know that the unpleasant thing might happen as a result. EG ...*ensuring short-term survival at the risk of long- term ruin.* **4.3** If you tell someone that they are doing something **at their own risk**, you are warn- ing them that, if they are harmed, it will be their own responsibility. **4.4** If you **run the risk** of doing or experiencing something undesirable, you do something knowing that the undesirable thing might happen as a result. EG *We run the risk of confusing the voters.* **4.5** If you **take a risk**, you do something which you know might be dangerous or have unpleasant consequences. EG *I am taking a tremendous risk.*
5 If you **risk** something unpleasant, you do some- v+O OR V+-ING thing knowing that the unpleasant thing might happen as a result. EG *They were willing to risk losing their jobs.*
6 If you **risk** an action, you do it, even though you v+O OR V+-ING know that it might have undesirable consequences. EG *If you have an expensive rug, don't risk washing it yourself.*
7 If you **risk** someone's life, you put them in a v+O dangerous position where they might be killed. EG *She had risked her life to help save mine.*

risky /rɪski¹/, **riskier, riskiest.** If you say that an ADJ QUALIT activity or action is **risky**, you mean that it is dangerous or likely to fail. EG *The whole thing has become too risky.*

risqué /rɪskeɪ, rɪskeɪ/. Jokes or stories that are ADJ QUALIT **risqué** are considered to be slightly rude or offen- sive because they refer to sex.

rite /raɪt/, **rites.** A **rite** is a traditional ceremony N COUNT : that is carried out by a particular group or within a USU+SUPP particular society. EG ...*the rite of circumcision*... ...*fertility rites.*

ritual /rɪtjuˈəl/, **rituals. 1** A **ritual** is a series of N COUNT OR actions which people regularly carry out in a N UNCOUNT particular situation, because it is the custom to do so. EG *Our society has many rituals of greeting, farewell, and celebration.*
2 Ritual activities happen as part of a ritual or ADJ CLASSIF : tradition. EG ...*the practice of ritual murder.* ATTRIB

rival /raɪvəⁿl/, **rivals, rivalling, rivalled;** spelled **rivaling, rivaled** in American English. **1** Your N COUNT **rival** is someone who you are competing with. EG *His newspaper outstripped its rivals in circulation.*
▸ used as an adjective. EG *Fighting broke out* ▸ ADJ CLASSIF : *between rival groups.* ATTRIB
2 If you say that something **rivals** something else, v+O you mean that it is of the same standard or quality as the other thing. EG *Of all the flowers in the garden few can rival the lily.*

rivalry /raɪvəlri¹/, **rivalries. Rivalry** is active N COUNT OR competition between people. EG *Burr's rivalry with* N UNCOUNT *Hamilton began in those days*... ...*the intense rival- ries between groups and personalities.*

river /rɪvə/, **rivers.** A **river** is a large amount of N COUNT fresh water flowing continuously in a long line across land. EG *We fished in the river after lunch*... ...*the River Thames.*

riverside /rɪvəsaɪd/. The **riverside** is the area of N SING : the+N land by the banks of a river. EG *They had reached the rocks by the riverside.*

rivet /rɪvɪt/, **rivets, riveting, riveted. 1** If you v+O : USU PASS are **riveted** by something, it fascinates you and holds your interest completely. EG *I was riveted by his presentation.*
2 A **rivet** is a short, thin bolt with a flat head which N COUNT is used to fasten flat pieces of metal together.

riveting /rɪvɪtɪŋ/. Something that is **riveting** is ADJ QUALIT extremely interesting and exciting. EG ...*a riveting television documentary.*

RN /ɑː ɛn/ is a written abbreviation for 'Royal Navy', the navy of the United Kingdom. EG ...*Captain Andrew Waugh, RN.*

road /rəʊd/, **roads. 1** A **road** is a long piece of hard ground which is built between two places so N COUNT OR by+N that people can drive or ride easily from one place to the other. EG ...*the road from Belfast to Londonderry... The ruins were accessible by road... ...Tottenham Court Road.*

2 If you are **on the road**, you are travelling in a PHRASE vehicle or going on a journey by road. EG *I did meet some lovely people on the road.*

3 If you say that someone is **on the road** to PHRASE something, you mean that they are likely to achieve it. EG *She was well on the road to recovery... This is the first step on the road to victory.*

roadblock /rəʊdblɒk/, **roadblocks.** When the po- N COUNT lice or the army put a **roadblock** across a road, they stop all the traffic going through, for example because they are looking for a criminal.

roadside /rəʊdsaɪd/, **roadsides.** The **roadside** is N COUNT : the area at the edge of a road. EG *I sat down by the* USU SING *roadside and cried... ...a roadside cafe.*

roadway /rəʊdweɪ/, **roadways.** A **roadway** is N COUNT the same as a road. EG *He began to cross the* Formal *roadway towards me.*

roam /rəʊm/, **roams, roaming, roamed.** If you V+O OR V+A **roam** an area or **roam** around it, you wander or travel around it without having a particular purpose. EG *He roamed the streets at night... They roam over the hills and plains.*

roar /rɔː/, **roars, roaring, roared. 1** If something V **roars**, it makes a very loud noise. EG *The wind roared in the forest.* ▶ used as a noun. EG *I could* ▶ N COUNT *hear the roar of traffic outside.*

2 If someone **roars with laughter**, they laugh in a PHRASE very noisy way. EG *He put back his head and roared with laughter.*

3 If someone **roars**, they shout something in a very V OR V+QUOTE loud voice. EG *'Forward with the Revolution,' the crowd roared back.*

4 When a lion **roars**, it makes the loud sound that V lions typically make. ▶ used as a noun. EG *The lion* ▶ N COUNT *let out one of its roars.*

roaring /rɔːrɪŋ/. **1 Roaring** means making a very ADJ CLASSIF loud noise. EG *He sat on the terrace a few feet from* ATTRIB *the roaring traffic.*

2 A **roaring** fire is one which is burning with large ADJ CLASSIF flames and sending out a lot of heat. ATTRIB

3 If someone **does a roaring trade** in a type of PHRASE goods, they sell a lot of them. EG *He was doing a* Informal *roaring trade in T-shirts.*

4 If something is a **roaring** success, it is very ADJ CLASSIF successful indeed. ATTRIB

roast /rəʊst/, **roasts, roasting, roasted. 1** When V-ERG you **roast** meat or when it **roasts**, you cook it by dry heat in an oven or over a fire. EG *We got ourselves two fine chickens and roasted them.*

2 If you **roast** things such as nuts or coffee beans, V+O you heat them. EG *He was roasting chestnuts.*

3 Roast meat is meat that has been cooked by ADJ CLASSIF roasting. EG *I ordered roast beef.* ATTRIB

4 A **roast** is a piece of meat that has been cooked N COUNT OR by roasting. EG ...*taking the roast out of the oven.* N UNCOUNT

rob /rɒb/, **robs, robbing, robbed. 1** If someone V+O : OFT+of **robs** you, they steal money or property from you. EG *The only way I can get the money is to rob a few banks... He tried to rob her of her share.*

2 If you **rob** someone of something that they V+O+of deserve, have, or need, you take it away from them. EG *You robbed me of my moment of glory... The joy of battle had robbed him of his discretion... As these trees grow tall, they rob the grass of light.*

robber /rɒbə/, **robbers.** Robbers are people who N COUNT steal a lot of money or property from a bank, a shop, or a vehicle, often by using force or threats. EG ...*bank robbers... Did they ever catch the robbers?*

robbery /rɒbəʳri/, **robberies. 1 Robbery** is the N UNCOUNT crime of stealing a lot of money or property from a bank, a shop, or a vehicle, often by using force or threats. EG *He was arrested on charges of armed robbery.*

2 When there is a **robbery**, someone steals a lot of N COUNT money or property from a bank, a shop, or a vehicle. EG ...*if he had committed the robbery.*

robe /rəʊb/, **robes.** A **robe** is a loose piece of N COUNT clothing which covers all of your body and reaches Formal the ground. EG ...*priests and archbishops in their ceremonial robes.*

robin /rɒbɪn/, **robins.** A **robin** is a small brown N COUNT bird with a red neck and breast.

robot /rəʊbɒt/, **robots.** A **robot** is a machine N COUNT which is programmed to move and perform certain tasks automatically. EG *Japanese industry is making increasing use of robots.*

robust /rəˈbʌst, rəʊbəˈst/. Someone or something ADJ QUALIT that is **robust** is very strong and healthy. EG *She has four robust daughters... The once robust economy now lies in ruins.*

rock /rɒk/, **rocks, rocking, rocked. 1 Rock** is the N UNCOUNT hard substance which the earth is made of. EG *Large masses of rock are constantly falling into the sea.*

2 A **rock** is **2.1** a piece of rock that sticks up out of N COUNT the ground or the sea, or that has broken away from a mountain or a cliff. EG *I sat down on a rock.* **2.2** a small stone that you can pick up. EG *She* American *started putting the rocks in his shirt pocket.*

3 When something **rocks** or when you **rock** it, it V-ERG moves slowly and regularly backwards and forwards or from side to side. EG *She sat there, rocking gently backwards and forwards... Our parents cuddle and hug us, and rock us gently back and forth.*
● **to rock the boat:** see **boat.**

4 If something **rocks** people, it shocks and horri- V+O fies them. EG *France was rocked by an outbreak of* Written *violent crime.*

5 Rock or **rock music** is music with simple tunes N UNCOUNT and a very strong beat that is played and sung, usually loudly, by a small group of people with electric guitars and drums. EG ...*a rock concert... ...rock groups.*

6 Rock is also a sweet made in long, hard sticks N UNCOUNT which are sold at tourist places. EG ...*a stick of rock.*

7 If you have an alcoholic drink such as whisky **on** PHRASE **the rocks,** you have it with lumps of ice.

8 If someone's marriage or relationship is **on the** PHRASE **rocks,** it is unsuccessful and is about to end.

rock and roll is a kind of music with a strong N UNCOUNT beat sung and played by small groups, especially in the 1950s.

rocker /rɒkə/, **rockers. 1** A **rocker** is the same N COUNT as a rocking-chair. American

2 If you say that someone is **off** their **rocker,** you PHRASE mean that they are mad. EG *His landlady appeared* Informal *to be slightly off her rocker.*

rockery /rɒkəʳri/, **rockeries.** A **rockery** is a N COUNT raised part of a garden which is built of stones and soil and on which small plants are grown.

rocket /rɒkɪt/, **rockets, rocketing, rocketed. 1** N COUNT A **rocket** is **1.1** a space vehicle that is shaped like a long tube. EG ...*a space rocket.* **1.2** a missile containing explosive that drives itself through the air by sending out burning gas. EG *Rebels fired anti-tank rockets for three consecutive nights.* **1.3** a firework that quickly goes high into the air and then explodes.

2 If things such as prices and profits **rocket,** they V increase very quickly and suddenly. EG *His profits* Informal *rocketed... Land sales rocketed.*

rock-hard. Something that is **rock-hard** is very ADJ CLASSIF hard indeed. EG ...*the rock-hard earth.*

If something is a roaring success, does it make a noise?

rocking-chair, rocking-chairs. A **rocking-chair** is a chair that is built on two curved pieces of wood so that you can rock yourself backwards and forwards when you are sitting in it.   N COUNT

rocking-horse, rocking-horses. A **rocking-horse** is a toy horse which a child can sit on and rock backwards and forwards.   N COUNT

rock pool, rock pools. A **rock pool** is a small pool between rocks on the seashore.   N COUNT

rocky /rɒki[1]/. A place that is **rocky** is covered with rocks. EG *She drives carefully up the rocky lane.*   ADJ QUALIT

rod /rɒd/, **rods.** A **rod** is a long, thin pole or bar, usually one made of metal or wood. EG *The aluminium rod that held the seats broke.*   N COUNT

rode /rəʊd/ is the past tense of **ride.**

rodent /rəʊdənt/, **rodents.** A **rodent** is a small mammal which has sharp front teeth. Rats, mice, rabbits, and squirrels are rodents. EG *Some of the crop may be eaten up by insects or rodents.*   N COUNT

roe /rəʊ/ is the eggs or sperm of a fish, which is eaten as food. EG *...fried cod's roe.*   N UNCOUNT

rogue /rəʊg/, **rogues.** A **rogue** is a man who behaves in a dishonest or criminal way. EG *You're all cheats and rogues.*   N COUNT / Outdated

role /rəʊl/, **roles.** 1 Someone's or something's **role** is their position and function in a situation or society. EG *What is the role of the University in modern society?... He had played a major role in the formation of the United Nations.*   N COUNT+SUPP

2 A **role** is one of the characters that an actor or singer can play in a film, play, or opera. EG *She played the leading role in The Winter's Tale.*   N COUNT : USU+SUPP

roll /rəʊl/, **rolls, rolling, rolled.** 1 When something **rolls** or when you **roll** it, it moves along a surface, turning over and over many times. EG *The bucket rolled and clattered down the path... He rolled a boulder down the slope... She rolled off the sofa.*   V-ERG : USU+A

2 When vehicles **roll** along, they move along. EG *Trucks with loudspeakers rolled through the streets... The bus rolled to a stop.*   V+A

3 If drops of liquid **roll** down a surface, they move quickly down it. EG *He stood in a corner with tears rolling down his face.*   V+A

4 If you **roll** your eyes or if your eyes **roll**, they turn up or turn from one side to another, for example because you are very frightened.   V-ERG / Written

5 If you **roll** something flexible into a cylinder or a ball, you form it into a cylinder or a ball by wrapping it several times around itself or by shaping it between your hands. EG *She went on sorting the socks, rolling them into neat little bundles.* ◆ **rolled.** EG *...a rolled newspaper... a rolled umbrella.*   V+O+A / ◊ ADJ CLASSIF : ATTRIB

6 A **roll** of paper or cloth is a long piece of it that has been wrapped many times around itself or around a tube. EG *...a roll of film.*   N COUNT : OFT+of

7 A **roll** is a small loaf of bread that is eaten by one person.   N COUNT

8 A **roll** is also an official list of people's names. EG *...the roll of members... He is on the parish roll.*   N COUNT+SUPP

9 A **roll** of drums is a long, rumbling sound made by drums.   N COUNT

10 You say that something is several things **rolled into one** to emphasize that it combines the best qualities of all those things. EG *A good musical is a new play, a new opera and a new ballet all rolled into one.*   PHRASE

11 to **start the ball rolling**: see **ball.** ● See also **rock and roll, sausage roll, toilet roll.** ● See also **rolling.**

roll in. If something is **rolling in**, it is being received in large quantities. EG *Once we get there the money will just start rolling in.*   PHRASAL VB : V+ADV / Informal

roll over. If someone who is lying down **rolls over**, they move so that a different part of them is facing upwards.   PHRASAL VB : V+ADV

roll up. 1 If you **roll up** something flexible, you   PHRASAL VB : V-ERG+ADV

wrap it several times around itself until it is shaped like a cylinder or a ball. EG *The mattress was rolled up... The map kept rolling up.* 2 If you **roll up** your sleeves or trouser legs, you fold the edges over several times, making them shorter. EG *His father had his sleeves rolled up.*   V+O+ADV

roll-call, roll-calls. If you take a **roll-call**, you check which of the members of a group are present by reading their names out. Each member has to answer when his or her name is read out.   N COUNT

roller /rəʊlə/, **rollers.** 1 A **roller** is a cylinder that turns round in a machine or device. EG *She pulled the sheet of paper out of the roller.*   N COUNT

2 **Rollers** are hollow tubes that women roll their hair round in order to make it curly.   N COUNT : USU PLURAL

roller-coaster /rəʊlə kəʊstə/, **roller-coasters.** A **roller-coaster** is a small railway that goes up and down steep slopes and that people ride on for pleasure at fairs.   N COUNT

roller-skate, roller-skates, roller-skating, roller-skated. 1 **Roller-skates** are shoes with four small wheels on them.   N COUNT : USU PLURAL

2 If you **roller-skate**, you move over a flat surface wearing roller-skates. EG *Christopher taught the children to roller skate.*   V

rolling /rəʊlɪŋ/. 1 **Rolling** hills are small hills with gentle slopes that extend a long way into the distance. EG *...the rolling countryside west of Detroit.*   ADJ CLASSIF : ATTRIB

2 A **rolling** walk is slow and swaying, usually because the person is drunk or very fat.   ADJ CLASSIF : ATTRIB

3 If you say that someone is **rolling in it**, you mean that they are very rich.   PHRASE / Informal

rolling pin, rolling pins. A **rolling pin** is a cylinder that you roll several times over uncooked pastry in order to spread it.   N COUNT

Roman Catholic /rəʊmən kæθəlɪk/, **Roman Catholics.** A **Roman Catholic** is the same as a Catholic.   N COUNT

Roman Catholicism /rəʊmən kəθɒlɪsɪzəm/ is the same as Catholicism.   N UNCOUNT

romance /rəʊmæns, rəmæns/, **romances.** 1 A **romance** is a relationship between two people who are in love with each other but who are not married to each other. EG *...a wartime romance... Young people are re-discovering romance and passion.*   N COUNT OR N UNCOUNT

2 **Romance** is the pleasure and excitement of doing something new or exciting. EG *There is romance to be found in life on the river.*   N UNCOUNT

3 A **romance** is also a novel about a love affair. EG *...historical romances.*   N COUNT

Roman numeral /rəʊmən nju:mərəl/, **Roman numerals.** **Roman numerals** are the letters used by Romans in ancient times to write numbers, for example I(=1), IV(=4), VIII(=8), XL(=40). Roman numerals are still used sometimes.   N COUNT : USU PLURAL

romantic /rə[6]mæntɪk/, **romantics.** 1 Someone who is **romantic** has a lot of ideas that are not based on real life, for example about love or about ways of changing society. EG *She's as romantic as a child of sixteen.* ▶ used as a noun. EG *Cedric's a great romantic.*   ADJ QUALIT / ▶ N COUNT

2 **Romantic** means connected with sexual love. EG *A woman needs a romantic attachment.*   ADJ CLASSIF : ATTRIB

3 A **romantic** play, film, or story describes or represents a love affair. EG *...a charming romantic comedy starring Audrey Hepburn.*   ADJ CLASSIF : ATTRIB

4 Something that is **romantic** is beautiful in a way that strongly affects your feelings. EG *...a romantic moonlight ride.* ◊ **romantically.** EG *Her long hair was spread romantically over the pillow.*   ADJ QUALIT / ◊ ADV

romanticism /rə[6]mæntɪsɪzəm/ refers to thoughts and feelings which are idealistic and romantic, rather than realistic. EG *...the romanticism of the women's magazines.*   N UNCOUNT

romanticize /rə[6]mæntɪsaɪz/, **romanticizes, romanticizing, romanticized;** also spelled **romanticise.** If you **romanticize** someone or something,   V+O you think or talk about them in a way that is not at all realistic and makes them seem better than they really are. ◊ **romanticized**. EG ...*romanticized* ◊ ADJ QUALIT *notions about marriage.*

romp /rɒmp/, **romps, romping, romped.** When V : USU+A children **romp** around, they play and move around in a noisy, happy way. EG *They romped with their dogs.* ▶ used as a noun. EG *It's an excuse for a great* ▶ N SING : a+N *romp.*

rompers /rɒmpəz/ are a piece of clothing worn N PLURAL by babies or young children. Rompers consist of loose trousers and a top that are joined together.

roof /ruːf/, **roofs** /ruːvz, ruːfs/. 1 The **roof** of a N COUNT building is the covering on top of it. See picture at HOUSE. EG ...*a yellow brick house with a slate roof... I fixed a leak in the roof of her shed.*

2 The **roof** of a car or other vehicle is the covering N COUNT on top of it. See picture at CAR.

3 The **roof** of your mouth or of a cave is the N COUNT highest part of it.

4 **Roof** is also used in these phrases. **4.1** If you PHRASES have a **roof over your head**, you have somewhere to live. EG *She was without money and with no real roof over her head.* **4.2** If you say that something happens **under** someone's **roof**, you mean that it happens in their home. EG *Are we prepared to let this happen under our own roofs?* **4.3** If you say Informal that someone **hit the roof** or **went through the roof**, you mean that they were very angry indeed.

roofed /ruːft/. You can use **roofed** to say what ADJ CLASSIF kind of roof a building has. EG ...*houses roofed with reddish-brown tiles... ...red-roofed farmhouses.*

roofing /ruːfɪŋ/ is material used for making or N UNCOUNT covering roofs. EG *He sells bundles of rushes for roofing... Slate is the very best roofing material.*

roof-rack, roof-racks. A **roof-rack** is a metal N COUNT frame that is fixed on top of a car and used for carrying large objects.

rooftop /ruːftɒp/, **rooftops. Rooftops** are the N COUNT : outside parts of roofs. EG ...*a bedroom with a view* USU PLURAL *over the roof-tops.*

rook /rʊk/, **rooks.** 1 A **rook** is a large black bird. N COUNT 2 In chess, a **rook** is a piece which can move N COUNT forwards, backwards, or sideways.

room /ruːm/, **rooms.** 1 A **room** is one of the N COUNT separate sections in a house or other building, which has its own walls, ceiling, floor, and door. EG *The room contained a couch and a glass cabinet... Boylan came back into the room... She's in the music room.*

2 If there is **room** for something, there is enough N UNCOUNT : space for it. EG *There wasn't enough room for* OFT+SUPP *everybody... Just keep the crowd back so I have room to move.*

3 If there is **room** for a particular kind of behav- N UNCOUNT : iour or action, people are able to behave in that USU+*for* way or to take that action. EG *There ought to be room for differences of opinion... There is room for much more research.*

roommate /ruːmmeɪt/, **roommates.** Your **room-** N COUNT **mate** is the person who you share a rented room with.

roomy /ruːmiˈ/, **roomier, roomiest.** A place that ADJ QUALIT is **roomy** is large inside, so that you can move around freely and comfortably. EG ...*a ground floor apartment which was roomy but sparsely furnished.*

roost /ruːst/, **roosts, roosting, roosted.** 1 A **roost** N COUNT is a place where birds rest or build their nests. EG *The gulls were returning to their roosts among the rocks.*

2 When birds **roost**, they settle in a particular V : OFT+A place for the night. EG *The chickens roost there all winter.*

3 If you talk about someone's **chickens coming** PHRASE **home to roost**, you are talking about the fact that they are now experiencing the consequences of their past actions.

4 Someone who **rules the roost** in a particular PHRASE

place has control and authority over the people there.

rooster /ruːstə/, **roosters.** A **rooster** is an adult N COUNT male chicken. American

root /ruːt/, **roots, rooting, rooted.** 1 The **roots** of N COUNT a plant are the parts that grow under the ground. EG *These trees have large, spreading roots.*

2 The **root** of a hair or tooth is the part beneath the N COUNT skin. EG *They pulled her hair out by the roots.*

3 Your **roots** are the place or culture that you or N PLURAL your family grew up in, which you have now left. EG *People are searching again for their roots... They are now utterly cut off from their peasant roots.*

● If you **put down roots** in a particular place, you ● PHRASE become connected with it, for example by taking part in activities there or by making a lot of friends.

4 If you talk about the **root** or the **roots** of N COUNT : something, you mean its original cause or its basis. USU+POSS EG *Perhaps the root of the tragedy was here... Unemployment and inflation were at the root of the community's frustration.*

5 The **root** cause of something is its basic cause. EG ADJ CLASSIF : ...*the root causes of poverty.* ATTRIB

6 If things **take root**, they start to grow or develop. PHRASE EG *The seedlings of bushes and trees might take root there... ...the ideas that were to take root in a new land.*

7 If people or animals **root** through things, they V+A search through them, pushing them aside. EG *Meadows rooted around in his bag and pulled out a map.*

8 See also **grass roots, square root.**

root out. If you **root** someone or something **out,** PHRASAL VB : you find them and force them from the place they V+O+ADV are in. EG *He's in there somewhere. Let's go and root him out.*

rooted /ruːtɪˈd/. 1 If you say that something is ADJ PRED+*in* **rooted** in something else, you mean that it is strongly influenced by it or has developed from it. EG *His methods are rooted in years of experience... ...attitudes deeply rooted in history.*

2 If you say that someone's feelings or opinions are ADJ QUALIT **rooted,** you mean that they are not likely to change, because the person feels them or believes in them very strongly. EG ...*deeply rooted impulses... He has no rooted objections to it.* ● See also **deep-rooted.**

3 If you are **rooted to the spot,** you are unable to PHRASE move, for example because you are very afraid.

rootless /ruːtlɪˈs/. Someone who is **rootless** does ADJ CLASSIF not belong to any particular place or country. EG ...*a rootless vagabond.*

rope /rəʊp/, **ropes, roping, roped.** 1 A **rope** is a N COUNT OR piece of very thick string, made by twisting togeth- N UNCOUNT er several thinner pieces. EG *They should be tied together with a rope... ...a piece of rope.*

2 If you **rope** one thing to another, you tie them V+O : OFT+*to*/ together with a rope. EG *The wagons were roped* *together* *together.*

3 If you say that someone **knows the ropes,** you PHRASE mean that they know how something should be Informal done. EG *My friend knows the ropes, she can show them around... I know the ropes. Let me handle this.*

rope in. If you **rope** someone **in** to do something, PHRASAL VB : you persuade them to help you to do it. EG *Some* V+O+ADV *amazing people were roped in to work on these projects... How did he get roped into that?*

rope off. If you **rope off** an area, you tie ropes PHRASAL VB : between posts all around its edges, to keep people V+O+ADV away from it. EG *The quay was roped off and the spectators were pushed back.*

rosary /rəʊzəriˈ/, **rosaries.** A **rosary** is a string N COUNT of beads that Catholics and Hindus use for counting

Is there any difference between a roster and a rota?

prayers. A series of prayers counted in this way is also called a **rosary**.

rose /rəʊz/, **roses. 1** A **rose** is a garden flower N COUNT with a pleasant smell that grows on a bush with thorny stems. EG *The soil here is so good for roses... Eleanor was holding an armful of red roses.*

2 If you tell someone that a situation is **not a bed** PHRASE **of roses**, you are warning them that it is not as pleasant or as easy as they might think. EG *Your life is unlikely to be a bed of roses.*

3 Something that is **rose** is reddish-pink in colour. ADJ COLOUR
4 Rose is also the past tense of **rise**.

rosé /ˈrəʊzeɪ/ is wine which is pink in colour. N UNCOUNT

rosette /rəʊˈzet/, **rosettes**. A **rosette** is a large, N COUNT circular badge made from coloured ribbons, which is worn as a prize in a competition or to show support for a sports team or political party.

roster /ˈrɒstə/, **rosters**. A **roster** is a list of people N COUNT who each take it in turn to do a particular job. EG *...the committee's roster of officials.*

rostrum /ˈrɒstrəm/, **rostrums** or **rostra** /ˈrɒstrə/. N COUNT A **rostrum** is a raised platform on which someone stands when they are speaking to an audience or conducting an orchestra.

rosy /ˈrəʊzɪ¹/, **rosier, rosiest. 1** Something that is ADJ COLOUR **rosy** is reddish-pink in colour. EG *...rosy clouds... ...the dim, rosy light.*

2 If you describe someone as **rosy**, you mean that ADJ QUALIT their face is pink and that they look healthy. EG *He had five children, all rosy and handsome... ...her bright eyes and rosy cheeks.*

3 If you say that a situation seems **rosy**, you mean ADJ QUALIT that it seems likely to be pleasing or successful. EG *Bal tried to give a rosy picture of his prospects... He had not made things seem too rosy.*

rot /rɒt/, **rots, rotting, rotted. 1** When food, wood, V or other substances **rot**, they decay and can no longer be used. EG *Her teeth were rotting... ...the smell of rotting vegetables.* ▸ used as a noun. EG ▸ N UNCOUNT *Destroy any bulbs with rot and buy healthy ones.*

2 When something **rots** an object or a substance, it V+O causes it to decay. EG *Bleach might rot the fibres.*

3 If you say that someone **is rotting**, you mean V : USU+A that their physical or mental condition is getting worse, because they have been in a bad situation for a long time. EG *You will rot in jail... You must leave him and get out. You're just rotting here.*

4 If you say that **the rot is setting in**, you mean PHRASE that a situation is beginning to get worse and that nothing can prevent this from happening.

5 If you say that what someone is saying is **rot**, you N UNCOUNT mean that they are saying very silly things. EG Outdated *You're talking absolute rot.* Informal

rot away. When something **rots away**, it decays PHRASAL VB : until it falls to pieces or none of it remains. EG *His* V+ADV *body is rotting away... The shack rotted away.*

rota /ˈrəʊtə/, **rotas**. A **rota** is a list of people who N COUNT take turns to do a particular job. EG *We have a cooking rota... The office work was shared on a rota system.*

rotary /ˈrəʊtə⁰rɪ¹/ means moving in a circular ADJ CLASSIF : direction. EG *...the rotary motion of the racket.* ATTRIB

rotate /rəʊˈteɪt/, **rotates, rotating, rotated. 1** V-ERG : USU+A When something **rotates** or when you **rotate** it, it turns with a circular movement. EG *...two drums rotating in opposite directions.*

2 If you **rotate** a group of things or people, or if V-ERG they **rotate**, you use each of them in turn, and, when you have used all of them, you begin with the first one again. EG *Weeds and diseases are controlled by rotating the crops... They rotate the jobs so that everyone gets a turn.*

rotation /rəʊˈteɪʃ⁰n/, **rotations. 1 Rotation** is N UNCOUNT circular movement. EG *...the earth's rotation... ...the* OR N COUNT *rotations of the ceiling fan.*

2 When there is **rotation** of a group of things or N UNCOUNT people, you use each of them in turn and, when you OR N COUNT have used all of them, you begin with the first one

again. EG *Crop rotations will help to minimize disease... She did everything in strict rotation.*

rotor /ˈrəʊtə/, **rotors**. The **rotors** or **rotor** blades N COUNT of a helicopter are the four long, flat, thin pieces of metal on top of it which go round and lift it off the ground. EG *The rotors turned more slowly.*

rotten /ˈrɒt⁰n/. **1** When food, wood, or other ADJ QUALIT substances are **rotten**, they have decayed and can no longer be used. EG *...rotten eggs... The wood was so rotten that when they pulled, it broke.*

2 If you describe something as **rotten**, you mean ADJ QUALIT that it is of very poor quality. EG *...a rotten novel... It* Informal *was a rotten school.*

3 If you say that a situation is **rotten**, you mean ADJ QUALIT that it is very unfair or unpleasant. EG *They're* Informal *having a rotten deal... Must be rotten, having your every movement watched.*

4 If you describe someone as **rotten**, you mean ADJ QUALIT that they are very unpleasant or unkind. EG *He was* Informal *a rotten bastard, like all men.*

5 If you feel **rotten**, you feel very ill. EG *I asked him* ADJ PRED *how he was. 'Rotten,' said the Duke.*

6 You use **rotten** to emphasize your dislike for ADJ CLASSIF : something or your anger or frustration about it. EG ATTRIB *She was mumbling away about her rotten old* Informal *sugar.*

rouge /ruːʒ/ is a red powder which women and N UNCOUNT actors put on their cheeks in order to give them more colour. EG *They wore lipstick and rouge.*

rouged /ruːʒd/. If a woman's or actor's cheeks are ADJ QUALIT **rouged**, they look red because they are covered in rouge. EG *...an elderly lady with rouged cheeks.*

rough /rʌf/, **rougher, roughest; roughs, rough-ing, roughed. 1** If a surface is **rough**, it is uneven ADJ QUALIT and not smooth. EG *They journeyed for several weeks over rough roads... ...the rough surface of the stone.* ◇ **roughness**. EG *Roughness of the skin* ◇ N UNCOUNT *can be caused by bad diet.*

2 You say that people are **rough** when they use too ADJ QUALIT much force and not enough care or gentleness. EG *There were complaints of rough handling, especially by younger policemen... I grabbed her by the shoulders. Maybe I was too rough.* ◇ **roughly**. EG ◇ ADV *He shoved the boy roughly aside.*

3 If you say that someone is having a **rough** time, ADJ QUALIT you mean that they are experiencing something difficult or unpleasant. EG *I knew they were having a rough time and I felt sorry for them.*

4 A **rough** calculation or guess is approximately ADJ QUALIT correct. EG *Multiply the weekly amount by fifty two to get the rough annual cost.* ◇ **roughly**. EG *...a* ◇ ADV *woman of roughly her own age.*

5 A **rough** description or drawing indicates only ADJ QUALIT the most important features of something, without much detail. EG *Mr Boggis drew a rough sketch... ...a rough outline of the proposals.* ◇ **roughly**. EG ◇ ADV *Could you tell us roughly what is required?*

6 You can say that something is **rough** when it is ADJ QUALIT not well made. EG *They built a rough shelter of branches and leaves.* ◇ **roughly**. EG *The pieces* ◇ ADV *were then roughly cobbled together.*

7 If the sea or a sea journey is **rough**, the weather ADJ QUALIT is windy or stormy and there are very big waves. EG *By now the sea was really rough... ...ninety rough minutes on a cross-Channel trip.*

8 You can say that a town or district is **rough** ADJ QUALIT when there is a lot of crime or violence there. EG *Abilene was one of the roughest towns in America.*

9 When people **sleep rough**, they sleep in unusual PHRASE places, often out of doors, usually because they have no home. EG *We had great fun sleeping rough on the beach.*

10 If you have to **rough it**, you have to live without the possessions and comforts that you normally have. EG *You may have to rough it for a while.*

rough out. If you **rough out** a drawing or an PHRASAL VB : idea, you draw or write the main features of it V+O+ADV before you do it in detail. EG *I've roughed out a scene for my new play.*

rough up. If someone **roughs** you **up**, they attack you and hit or beat you. EG *They roughed me up a bit and then left me.* PHRASAL VB : V+O+ADV Informal

rough and ready. If you describe something as **rough and ready**, you mean that it has been made, done, or arranged in a hurry and may not be totally satisfactory. EG *...a rough-and-ready calculation... ...rough and ready treatments... The accommodation was a bit rough and ready.* ADJ QUALIT

rough and tumble. If you refer to the **rough and tumble** of a situation, you mean that the people involved try hard to get what they want, and do not worry about upsetting or harming others. EG *...the rough and tumble of world politics.* N UNCOUNT

roulette /ruːˈlet/ is a gambling game in which a ball is dropped onto a revolving wheel with numbered holes in it. The players bet on which hole the ball will be in when the wheel stops spinning. N UNCOUNT

round /raʊnd/, **rounder, roundest; rounds, rounding, rounded.** The form **around** can be used instead of **round** when it is a preposition or an adverb. ADJ QUALIT

1 Something that is **round** is **1.1** shaped like a ball. EG *...heavy round stones.* **1.2** shaped like a circle. EG *Shanti had a round face.* **1.3** curved, like the letter 'c'. EG *...the round bulge of the girl's belly.*

2 If something or a group of things is **round** or **around** something else, it surrounds it. EG *She was wearing a scarf round her head... We were sitting round a table eating and drinking... There was a wall all the way round.* PREP OR ADV

3 The distance **round** or **around** something is the length of its boundary or circumference. EG *It measures fifteen feet round the trunk.* PREP OR ADV

4 You can refer to the area near a place as the area **round** or **around** it. EG *We were the first farmers round here to use the new fertilizers.* PREP OR ADV

5 If something happens or exists in many parts of a place, you can say that it happens or exists **round** or **around** that place. EG *Think of what's happening politically round the world... He now has five shops scattered around the town.* PREP

6 If something moves **round** or **around** you, it keeps moving in a circle and you are at the centre of the circle. EG *The earth moves round the sun... The youth danced around in his pyjamas.* PREP, OR ADV AFTER VB

7 If something is going **round and round**, it is spinning or moving in small circles. EG *He twirled round and round... A swallow flew frantically round and round.* PHRASE

8 When someone goes to the other side of something, you can say that they have gone **round** it or **around** it. EG *They sailed round the Cape... The boys had disappeared around a corner.* PREP, OR ADV AFTER VB

9 If you turn or look **round** or **around**, you turn so that you are facing in a different direction. EG *He swung round and faced the window.* ADV AFTER VB

10 If you go **round** or **around** a place, you go to several different parts of it. EG *I wandered around the orchard.* PREP, OR ADV AFTER VB

11 When someone comes **round** or comes **around**, they visit you. EG *Her friend Emily came round... I'd like to ask him round for dinner.* ADV AFTER VB

12 If there is a way **round** or **around** a problem or difficulty, there is a solution to it. PREP

13 **Round about** means **13.1** very near a place. EG *...the shepherds who live round about here... She knew all the people in the houses round about.* **13.2** approximately. EG *I've been here for round about ten years... The lads were round about eighteen.* PREP OR ADV ... PREP

14 When you **round** something, you move in a curve past the edge or corner of it. EG *...as he rounded the corner at the top of the stairs.* V+O

15 A **round** of events is a series of events that is part of a larger series. EG *Turkey is eager for a further round of talks... We were on our final round of visits.* N COUNT+SUPP

16 When people such as doctors go on their **rounds** N COUNT

or make their **rounds**, they make a series of visits as part of their job.

17 A competition usually consists of a series of **rounds**. Each round is a set of games. The winners of these games go on to play in the next round. N COUNT

18 A **round** of golf is one game. EG *She's playing a round of golf.* N COUNT

19 In a boxing or wrestling match, a **round** is one of the periods during which the boxers or wrestlers fight. N COUNT

20 If you buy a **round** of drinks, you buy a drink for each member of the group of people that you are with. EG *He would have liked to pay for a round himself... It's my round.* N COUNT

21 A **round** of ammunition is the bullet or bullets that are released when a gun is fired. N COUNT

round up. If you **round up** animals or people, you gather them together. EG *They had rounded up people at gunpoint.* ● See also **roundup.** PHRASAL VB : V+O+ADV

roundabout /ˈraʊndəbaʊt/, **roundabouts.** 1 At a funfair, a **roundabout** is a large, circular mechanical device with seats, often in the shape of animals or cars, on which children sit and go round and round. N COUNT British

2 In a playground, a **roundabout** is a circular platform that children sit or stand on. The platform is made to rotate by being pushed. N COUNT British

roundabouts

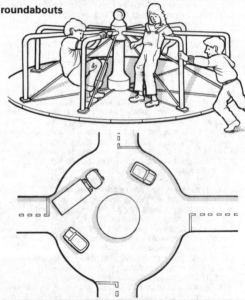

3 A **roundabout** is also a circle at a place where several roads meet. You drive round it until you come to the road that you want. EG *He got stuck in a traffic jam at the roundabout.* N COUNT British

4 If you do something in a **roundabout** way, you do not do it in the simplest or most direct way. EG *They drove back to Glasgow by a long roundabout route... He told me this in a rather gentle, roundabout way.* ADJ QUALIT : USU ATTRIB

rounded /ˈraʊndɪd/. Something that is **rounded** is curved in shape, without any points or sharp edges. EG *...rounded hills... Its teeth are small and rounded.* ADJ CLASSIF

rounders /ˈraʊndəz/ is a game played by two teams, in which a player scores points by hitting a ball thrown by a member of the other team and running round all four sides of a square. N UNCOUNT British

Who gets royalties?

roundly /raʊndli¹/. If you say something **roundly**,   ADV
you say it very forcefully. EG *Britain was roundly
condemned for selling arms to the rebels... 'What
utter rubbish!' declared Miss Clare roundly.*

round-the-clock activities happen all day and all   ADJ CLASSIF :
night. EG *...keeping the hotel under round-the-clock*   ATTRIB
*surveillance... They are offering free round-the-
clock legal advice.* ▶ used as an adverb. EG ▶ ADV
*Factories are working round the clock to keep
pace with the demand.*

round trip, round trips. If you make a **round**   N COUNT
trip, you travel to a place and then back again. EG
*He made the eighty mile round trip and was back
in time for dinner.*

roundup /raʊndʌp/, **roundups. 1** On television or   N COUNT :
radio, a **roundup** of news is a summary of it. EG   USU SING
...the news followed by the sports roundup.

2 When there is a **roundup** of people or animals,   N COUNT :
they are collected from different places and   USU SING
brought to one place. EG *In a massive roundup, they
arrested several hundred leaders.*

rouse /raʊz/, **rouses, rousing, roused. 1** If you   V-ERG
rouse or if someone **rouses** you, you wake up. EG *I*   Formal
was worried when I couldn't rouse her.

2 If you **rouse** yourself to do something, you make   V-REFL
yourself get up and do it. EG *After a moment he
roused himself to talk to Christine.*

3 If something **rouses** you, it makes you very   V+O
emotional or excited. EG *He roused the troops with
his oratory... He could move quickly when roused
to anger.* ◊ **rousing**. EG *...a rousing cheer.*   ◊ ADJ QUALIT

4 If something **rouses** an emotion in you, it causes   V+O : USU+A
you to feel it. EG *The proposal roused fears among
the public.*

rout /raʊt/, **routs, routing, routed.** If an army or   V+O
a sports team **routs** its opponents, it defeats them
completely and easily. EG *Spain could not muster
sufficient resources to rout the Cubans.* ▶ used as a ▶ N COUNT OR
noun. EG *The retreat turned into a rout... The*   N UNCOUNT
terrified army fled in rout.

route /ruːt/, **routes, routing, routed. 1** A **route** is   N COUNT :
a way from one place to another. EG *I took the*   USU+SUPP
*route through Beechwood... ...the main route out of
London to the west.* ● See also **en route**.

2 A bus **route** or train **route** is a way between two   N COUNT :
places which buses or trains travel along regularly.   USU+SUPP
EG *...shipping routes through the North Sea... ...bus
routes into the city centre.*

3 The **route** of a procession or a race is the way   N SING : the+N
that it is planned to go. EG *...the wedding procession
route... A million people were lining the route.*

4 You can refer to a way of achieving something as   N COUNT+SUPP
a **route**. EG *Another route is by active participation
in a trade union.*

5 When vehicles **are routed** past a place or   V+O :
through it, they are made to travel past it or   USU PASS+A
through it. EG *Flights were being routed around the
trouble area.*

routine /ruːtiːn/, **routines. 1** You describe activi-   ADJ CLASSIF
ties as **routine** when you do them as a normal part
of your job, rather than for a special reason. EG
They made a routine check on the whole section.
◊ **routinely**. EG *This information is routinely col-*   ◊ ADV
lected and published.

2 You can also describe activities as **routine** when   ADJ QUALIT
you do them so often that they have become
uninteresting. EG *We spend a lot of time performing
mindless routine tasks.*

3 A **routine** is **3.1** the usual way or order in which   N COUNT OR
you do something. EG *...his daily routine... Davis's*   N UNCOUNT
death has upset our routine. **3.2** the boring repeti-   N UNCOUNT
tion of a series of tasks. EG *...the dreary office*   +SUPP
routine... The routine was unbelievably tedious.

rove /raʊv/, **roves, roving, roved.** Someone who   V+A OR V+O
roves an area or **roves** around it wanders around   Literary
in it. EG *...the thugs who rove the streets at night...*   Outdated
We lived a roving life.

row, rows, rowing, rowed; pronounced /rəʊ/ for
paragraphs 1 to 5, and /raʊ/ for paragraphs 6 to 8.

1 A **row** of things or people is a number of them   N PART
arranged in a line. EG *...a large hall filled with rows
of desks... They were standing neatly in a row.*

2 In a theatre or cinema, each line of seats is called   N COUNT
a **row**. EG *...the young woman in the second row.*

3 If the same thing happens several times **in a**   PHRASE
row, it happens that number of times without
interruption. EG *...three bad summers in a row... He
was elected president three times in a row.*

4 When you **row**, you sit in a boat and make it   V : USU+A
move through the water by using oars. EG *We*   OR V+O
rowed slowly towards the centre of the river.
▶ used as a noun. EG *...a row on the lake.*   ▶ N SING

5 If you **row** people or goods somewhere, you take   V+O : USU+A
them there in a boat, using oars. EG *I rowed them
there and set them ashore.*

6 A **row** is a serious disagreement between politi-   N COUNT
cians or public institutions. EG *This row broke out*   Informal
on the eve of the Congress.

7 If two people have a **row**, they have a noisy   N COUNT
argument or quarrel. EG *They were always having*   Informal
terrible rows. ▶ used as a verb. EG *He never rowed*   ▶ V OR V+
with her mother.   with : RECIP

8 If you say that someone is making a **row**, you   N COUNT :
mean that they are making a loud, unpleasant   USU SING
noise. EG *'Little beasts!' said Anne. 'What a row they*   Informal
make!'

rowboat /rəʊbəʊt/, **rowboats.** A **rowboat** is the   N COUNT
same as a rowing boat.   American

rowdy /raʊdi¹/, **rowdier, rowdiest.** When people   ADJ QUALIT
are **rowdy**, they are noisy, rough, and likely to
cause trouble. EG *Not all teenage boys are rowdy.*

rowing /rəʊɪŋ/ is a sport in which people or   N UNCOUNT
teams race against each other in specially built
rowing boats. EG *...a rowing club.*

rowing boat, rowing boats. A **rowing boat** is a   N COUNT
small boat that you move through the water by   British
using oars. EG *He set off to sea alone in a rowing
boat.*

royal /rɔɪəl/, **royals. 1** Royal describes some-   ADJ CLASSIF :
thing that belongs to or involves a king, a queen, or   ATTRIB
members of their family. EG *...the royal wedding...
...a royal palace... ...the royal family.*

2 Royal also describes someone who is a king or   ADJ CLASSIF
queen or a member of their family. EG *...a royal*   ATTRIB
child.

3 Royal is used in the names of institutions or
organizations that are officially appointed or supported by a member of a royal family. EG *...the
Royal Navy... ...the Royal Opera House.*

4 Members of the royal family are sometimes   N COUNT :
referred to as the **royals**. EG *The royals hadn't put*   USU PLURAL
in an appearance yet.   Informal

royal blue. Something that is **royal blue** is deep   ADJ COLOUR
blue in colour.

Royal Highness, Royal Highnesses. You use
expressions such as **Your Royal Highness** and
Their Royal Highnesses when you are addressing or referring to members of royal families who
are not Kings or Queens; compare **Majesty**. EG
...Her Royal Highness Princess Alexandra.

royalist /rɔɪəlɪst/, **royalists.** A **royalist** is some-   N COUNT
one who supports their country's royal family or
who believes that their country should have a king
or queen. EG *They were both fervent royalists... He
belonged to a royalist family.*

royalty /rɔɪəlti¹/, **royalties. 1** The members of a   N UNCOUNT
royal family are sometimes referred to as **royalty**.
EG *...an official visit by royalty... ...generations of
English royalty.*

2 Royalties are payments made to authors and   N COUNT :
musicians which are linked to the sales of their   USU PLURAL
books or records, or to performance of their works.
EG *...all the royalties from my next play... There
should be a substantial income from royalties.*

RSVP /ɑː ɛs viː piː/ vi: means 'please reply'. It is   CONVENTION
written at the end of invitations.

rub /rʌb/, **rubs, rubbing, rubbed. 1** If you **rub**   V+O OR V+A
something, you move your hand or a cloth back-

wards and forwards over it while pressing firmly. EG *He groaned and rubbed his eyes... He rubbed at his throat... Peter rubbed his glasses slowly.*

2 If you **rub** a part of your body against a surface, you move it backwards and forwards while pressing it against the surface. EG *She rubbed her cheek against my temple.* v+o+a

3 If you **rub** a substance onto a surface, you spread it over the surface using your hand. EG *The ointment he rubbed into the wound made it feel better.* v+o+a

4 If two things **rub** together or if you **rub** them together, they move backwards and forwards, pressing against each other. EG *He rubbed his hands and laughed... His massive thighs rubbed together as he walked.* v-ERG : OFT +*together*

5 If someone draws attention to something that involves you and that you find embarrassing, you can say that they **are rubbing it in**. EG *'How old are you? Forty?' - 'All right, no need to rub it in.'* PHRASE Informal

6 If you **rub** someone **up the wrong way**, you unintentionally offend them or annoy them. PHRASE Informal

7 to **rub salt into** someone's **wounds**: see **salt**.

● to **rub shoulders with** someone: see **shoulder**.

rub off on. If someone's habits or characteristics **rub off on** you, you develop the same habits or characteristics after spending time with them. EG *They hoped that some of his prowess might rub off on them.* PHRASAL VB : V+ADV+PREP Informal

rub out. If you **rub out** something that someone has written on paper or on a blackboard, you remove it by rubbing it with a rubber or a cloth. PHRASAL VB : V+O+ADV

rubber /rʌbə/, **rubbers. 1 Rubber** is a strong, waterproof, elastic substance made from the sap of a tropical tree or produced chemically. N UNCOUNT

2 Rubber things are made of rubber. EG *...a rubber ball... ...rubber gloves.* ADJ CLASSIF

3 A **rubber** is a small piece of rubber that you use to rub out mistakes that you have made while writing, drawing, or typing. N COUNT

4 A **rubber** is also a series of games played between the same two people or teams, especially in cricket or bridge. N COUNT

rubber band, rubber bands. A **rubber band** is a thin circle of rubber that you put around things in order to hold them together. N COUNT

rubber stamp, rubber stamps, rubber-stamping, rubber-stamped. 1 A **rubber stamp** is a small device with something such as a name or a date on it. You press it on to an ink pad and then on to a document in order to show that the document has been officially dealt with. N COUNT

2 When someone in authority **rubber-stamps** something, they agree to it without thinking about it or discussing it; used showing disapproval. EG *The Council merely rubber-stamp decisions taken by him and his office.* v+o

rubbery /rʌbəri/. Something that is **rubbery** looks or feels soft or elastic like rubber. EG *...a long, rubbery piece of seaweed.* ADJ QUALIT

rubbish /rʌbɪʃ/. **1 Rubbish** consists of unwanted things or waste material. EG *That old shed is full of rubbish... ...a local rubbish dump.* N UNCOUNT

2 You can refer to something as **rubbish** when you think that it is of very poor quality. EG *There is so much rubbish on TV.* N UNCOUNT

3 You can refer to an idea or a statement as **rubbish** if you think that it is foolish or wrong. EG *Don't talk rubbish... How can you believe such rubbish?* N UNCOUNT OR CONVENTION Informal

rubble /rʌbəl/. **1** When a building is destroyed, the bits of brick, stone, or other materials that remain are referred to as **rubble**. EG *Every building was reduced to rubble... Injured people lay amongst the rubble.* N UNCOUNT

2 Rubble is also the small pieces of stone that are used to build the foundations for roads and houses.

rubric /ru:brɪk/, **rubrics.** A **rubric** is a set of rules or instructions, for example the instructions at the beginning of an examination paper. N COUNT Formal

ruby /ru:bɪ¹/, **rubies.** A **ruby** is a dark red jewel. EG *...a gift of rubies and diamonds.* N COUNT

rucksack

rucksack /rʌksæk/, **rucksacks.** A **rucksack** is a bag with straps that go over your shoulders, so that you can carry things on your back, for example when you are walking or climbing. N COUNT

rudder /rʌdə/, **rudders. 1** A **rudder** is a device for steering a boat. It consists of a vertical piece of wood or metal at the back of the boat. See picture at YACHT. N COUNT

2 An aeroplane's **rudder** is a vertical piece of metal at the back which is used to make the plane turn to the right or to the left.

ruddy /rʌdɪ¹/, **ruddier, ruddiest. 1** Something that is **ruddy** is reddish in colour. EG *His cheeks were ruddy... The craft still burned, throwing a ruddy glare into the night sky.* ADJ COLOUR Literary

2 Ruddy is used as a mild swear word to add emphasis or to express anger. EG *It's the biggest ruddy miracle of them all... Get on with the ruddy film!* ADJ CLASSIF OR ADV Outdated

rude /ru:d/, **ruder, rudest. 1** When people are **rude**, they behave in a way that is not polite. EG *I was rather rude to a young nurse... It's rude to stare... ...rude remarks.* ◊ **rudely**. EG *The President cannot rudely ignore a head of state.* ◊ **rudeness**. EG *He seemed not to notice their rudeness.* ADJ QUALIT ◊ ADV ◊ N UNCOUNT

2 Rude is used to describe words and behaviour that are likely to embarrass or offend people, because they relate to sex or other bodily functions. EG *...a rude gesture... ...a rude joke.* ADJ QUALIT USU ATTRIB

3 You use **rude** to describe events that are unexpected and unpleasant. EG *...a rude awakening to the realization that he had been robbed.* ◊ **rudely**. EG *My belief in the future was rudely shattered.* ADJ QUALIT ATTRIB ◊ ADV

4 Objects can be described as **rude** when they are very simply and roughly made. EG *I sat on the edge of one of the rude tables.* ADJ QUALIT ATTRIB Literary

rudimentary /ru:dɪmentə⁰ri¹/. **1** Something that is **rudimentary** is very basic or undeveloped and therefore unsatisfactory. EG *...a rather rudimentary planning system... ...rudimentary equipment.* ADJ QUALIT Formal

2 Knowledge that is **rudimentary** includes only the simplest and most important facts. EG *I had gathered only the most rudimentary information... ...rudimentary mathematics.* ADJ QUALIT Formal

rudiments /ru:dɪmə⁰nts/. When you learn the **rudiments** of something, you learn only the simplest and most important things about it. EG *I had time to pick up the rudiments of driving... He was teaching them the rudiments of Christianity.* N PLURAL : *the*+N, USU+*of*

rue /ru:/, **rues, ruing, rued.** If you **rue** something that you have done, you are sorry that you did it, because it has had unpleasant results. EG *I had ample cause to rue that decision.* v+o Literary Outdated

rueful /ru:fʊl/. If someone is **rueful**, they feel or express regret or sorrow in a quiet and gentle way. ADJ QUALIT Literary

On these pages, find two words that refer to the same game.

EG *She managed a rueful little smile.* ◊ **ruefully.** EG ◊ ADV
Rita said ruefully, 'You're too old for that.'

ruffian /rʌfɪən/, **ruffians.** A **ruffian** is a man N COUNT
who behaves violently and is involved in crime. EG Outdated
Some local ruffians are responsible for this.

ruffle /rʌfəʰl/, **ruffles, ruffling, ruffled. 1** If you V+O
ruffle someone's hair, you move your hand quickly
and fairly roughly over their head as a way of
showing affection.

2 Ruffles are small folds made in a piece of N COUNT
material or sewn onto it in order to decorate it. EG USU PLURAL
...a dress adorned with ruffles and ribbons.

ruffled /rʌfəʰld/. **1** Something that is **ruffled** is no ADJ QUALIT
longer smooth or neat. EG *...the ruffled bedclothes...*
She emerged, her hair ruffled and her face red.

2 Ruffled clothes are decorated with small folds of ADJ CLASSIF
material. EG *...a ruffled white blouse.*

3 You say that someone is **ruffled** when they are ADJ QUALIT
surprised, confused, or annoyed. EG *He was not*
easily ruffled... 'Why don't you come back later?'
said Alex, mildly ruffled.

rug /rʌg/, **rugs. 1** A **rug** is a piece of thick N COUNT
material like a carpet but covering only a small
area. EG *The floor was covered with rugs.*

2 A **rug** is also a small blanket which you use to N COUNT
cover your shoulders or your knees. EG *She took a*
tartan rug out of her case.

rugby /rʌgbiˡ/ is a game played by two teams, N UNCOUNT
who try to score points by carrying an oval ball to
their opponents' end of the pitch, or by kicking the
ball over a bar fixed between two goalposts.

rugged /rʌgɪˡd/. **1** A **rugged** area of land is rocky, ADJ QUALIT
uneven, and with few trees or plants. EG *The* Literary
coastline is wild and rugged.

2 If you describe a man as **rugged**, you mean that ADJ QUALIT
he has strong, rough features. EG *He was rugged* Literary
and handsome.

rugger /rʌgəʳ/ is the same as rugby. EG *I got badly* N UNCOUNT
hurt at rugger once... ...a rugger player... ...a rugger Informal
ball.

ruin /ruːɪn/, **ruins, ruining, ruined. 1** To **ruin** V+O
something means to severely harm, damage, or
spoil it. EG *You are ruining your health... India's*
textile industry was ruined... Villages had been
burned and ruined. ◊ **ruined.** EG *...the ruined patch* ◊ ADJ CLASSIF
of garden... ...my ruined career.

2 To **ruin** someone means to cause them to no V+O
longer have any money. EG *The contract would*
certainly have ruined him... We are all ruining
ourselves. ◊ **ruined.** EG *...a ruined man.* ◊ ADJ CLASSIF

3 Ruin is the state of no longer having any money. N UNCOUNT
EG *Crow was heading for ruin.*

4 The **ruins** of something are the parts of it that N COUNT :
remain after it has been severely damaged or USU PLURAL
weakened. EG *The Progressive Party was founded*
on the ruins of our Federal Party.

5 The **ruins** of a building are the parts of it that N COUNT :
remain after the rest has been destroyed. EG *...the* USU PLURAL
ruins of a castle... I walked around the ruins... It
was splendid once, but it is a ruin now.

6 If something is **in ruin** or **in ruins**, it is PHRASE
completely spoiled. EG *Their once robust economy*
lies in ruins... The regime collapsed in total ruin.

7 If a building or place is **in ruin** or **in ruins**, most PHRASE
of it has been destroyed and only parts of it
remain. EG *The castle, partly in ruins, stands on a*
crag... The villages are crumbling into ruin.

ruined /ruːɪnd/. A **ruined** building or place has ADJ CLASSIF :
been very badly damaged and is no longer used. EG ATTRIB
...a ruined castle... ...the ruined city of Tiahuanaco.

ruinous /ruːɪnəs/. If something that you are pay- ADJ CLASSIF
ing for is **ruinous**, it costs far more money than
you can afford. EG *The effects would be ruinous...*
...the ruinous expense of a funeral.

rule /ruːl/, **rules, ruling, ruled. 1 Rules** are N COUNT : OFT
instructions that tell you what you are allowed to PLURAL
do and what you are not allowed to do. EG *...the*
rules of chess... It is against the rules to keep pets...

This is forbidden under rule 7(c)... If she breaks the
rules, she will be punished.

2 The **rules** of something such as a language are N COUNT : OFT
statements that describe the way that things usual- PLURAL
ly happen in it. EG *There are rules for English*
spelling and pronunciation.

3 If something is the **rule**, it is the normal state of N SING : the+N
affairs. EG *Short haircuts became the rule.*

4 If you say that something happens **as a rule**, you PHRASE
mean that it usually happens. EG *Doctors are not as*
a rule trained in child rearing.

5 If someone in authority **bends the rules** or PHRASE
stretches the rules, they allow you to do something, even though it is against the rules.

6 When someone **rules** a country, they have the V+O OR
power to control its affairs, and they use this V+over
power. EG *...states ruled by kings... The military*
government went on ruling the country. ▶ used as ▶ N UNCOUNT
a noun. EG *...the dangers of one-party rule... ...the* +SUPP
days of British rule.

7 When someone in authority **rules** on a particular V+A OR
matter, they give an official decision about it. EG *I* V+REPORT :
was asked to rule on the case of a British seaman... ONLY that
The Supreme Court ruled that there was no federal Formal
offence involved.

8 See also **ground rules, ruling, work-to-rule.**

rule out. 1 If you **rule out** an idea, solution, or PHRASAL VB :
course of action, you reject it, because it is impos- V+O+ADV
sible or unsuitable. EG *Washington need not rule out*
military aid. **2** If one thing **rules out** another, it V+O+ADV
prevents it from happening or from being possible.
EG *The radio was on, effectively ruling out conver-*
sation... A search had ruled out that possibility.

ruler /ruːləʳ/, **rulers. 1** A **ruler** is a person who N COUNT
rules a country. EG *Caesar was then ruler of Per-*
sia... ...the world's rulers.

2 A **ruler** is also a long, narrow, flat piece of wood, N COUNT
metal, or plastic with straight edges marked in
inches or centimetres, which you use to measure
things or to draw straight lines. EG *Measure the*
holes with a ruler.

ruling /ruːlɪŋ/. **1** The **ruling** group of people in an ADJ CLASSIF :
organization or country is the group that controls ATTRIB
its affairs. EG *...the Church's ruling body... The*
ruling class will not surrender its power.

2 A **ruling** is an official decision made by a judge N COUNT
or court. EG *The judge gave his ruling... The Su-*
preme Court ruling still stands.

rum /rʌm/, **rums. 1 Rum** is an alcoholic drink N MASS
made from sugar cane juice. EG *He sipped his rum...*
...a bottle of rum.

2 If you describe people or things as **rum**, you ADJ QUALIT
mean that they are rather strange. EG *They were* Informal
rum old boys... ...rum ideas... In a rum sort of way, Outdated
Charles had helped enormously. British

rumble /rʌmbəʰl/, **rumbles, rumbling, rum-**
bled. 1 If something **rumbles**, it makes a low, V : OFT+A
continuous noise, often while moving slowly. EG
...the rumbling noise of barrels being rolled down
the ramp. ▶ used as a noun. EG *...a menacing* ▶ N COUNT :
rumble of distant thunder... ...the rumble of a USU+of
passing truck.

2 If you **rumble** someone or something, you find V+O
out the truth about them, which was being con- Informal
cealed. EG *You've rumbled that already, surely.*

rumbling /rʌmblɪŋ/, **rumblings. 1** A **rumbling** N COUNT
is a low, continuous noise. EG *There was a distant*
rumbling and the air-conditioning came on... ...the
rumbling of thunder.

2 Rumblings are signs that a bad situation is N COUNT :
developing. EG *There were rumblings of discon-* USU PLURAL
tent... ...the first rumblings of World War II.

ruminate /ruːmɪneɪt/, **ruminates, ruminating,** V : USU+A
ruminated. If you **ruminate** about something, you Formal
think about it very carefully. EG *George is now*
ruminating about the possibility... She ruminated a
bit longer and then said, 'Older, I think.'

rummage /rʌmɪdʒ/, **rummages, rummaging,** V+A
rummaged. If you **rummage** somewhere, you

search for something there by moving things in a careless way. EG *He rummaged around in his drawer... She was rummaging among the books and magazines.*

rummy /rʌmi¹/ is a card game in which players try to collect cards of the same value or cards in a sequence. EG *I had to play rummy with Dr Lutz.* N UNCOUNT

rumour /ruːmə/, **rumours, rumoured;** spelled **rumor** in American English. 1 A **rumour** is a story or piece of information that may or may not be true, but that people are talking about. EG *There's a rumour that Mangel is coming here to speak... ...rumours of street fighting and violence... Rumour has it that she's pregnant.* N COUNT

2 If something **is rumoured**, people are suggesting that it is true, but they do not know for certain. EG *It was rumoured that the body had been removed... He was rumored to be living in Detroit.* V-PASS +REPORT OR to-INF

rump /rʌmp/, **rumps.** 1 The **rump** of a group, organization, or political party consists of the members who remain in it after the rest have left it. EG *The party has dwindled to a disorganized rump.* N COUNT

2 An animal's **rump** is its rear end. EG *He sent the horse forward with a slap on its rump.* N COUNT

3 **Rump** or **rump steak** is meat cut from the rear end of a cow. N UNCOUNT

4 A person's **rump** is his or her buttocks. EG *He rubbed his rump.* N COUNT Informal

rumple /rʌmpə⁰l/, **rumples, rumpling, rumpled.** If you **rumple** something, you cause it to be untidy or creased. EG *...rumpling the papers on her desk... He rumpled her hair.* ◊ **rumpled.** EG *...a rumpled grey suit.* V+O ◊ ADJ QUALIT

rumpus /rʌmpəs/. A **rumpus** is a lot of noise or argument. EG *They caused a rumpus in the House of Commons... I never heard such a rumpus.* N SING

run /rʌn/, **runs, running, ran** /ræn/. The form **run** is used in the present tense of the verb and is also the past participle.

1 When you **run**, you move quickly, leaving the ground during each stride, because you are in a hurry to get somewhere or because you are taking part in a race. EG *I ran downstairs to open the door... She ran after me and coaxed me to come back... He ran the mile in just over four minutes.* V :OFT+A OR V+O

▸ used as a noun. EG *He found himself breaking into a run... We had to go for a cross-country run every weekend.* ▸ N COUNT : USU SING

2 If you say that something long, such as a road, **runs** in a particular direction, you are describing its course or position. EG *The reef runs parallel to the coast... ...a tunnel running from the Mediterranean into the Dead Sea.* V+A

3 If you **run** an object or your hand over something, you move the object or your hand over it. EG *He ran his hand over her hair... She ran her finger down a list of names.* V+O+A

4 If someone **runs** in an election, they take part as a candidate. EG *He ran for Governor.* V+A American

5 If you **run** something such as a business or an activity, you are in charge of it or you organize it. EG *She ran the office as a captain runs a ship... We run a course for local teachers.* V+O

6 If you **run** an experiment, computer program, or tape, you start it and let it continue. EG *Check everything and run the whole test again.* V+O

7 You can use **run** to say how something develops or progresses. EG *We tried to keep the business running smoothly.* V+A

8 If you **run** a car or piece of equipment, you have it and use it. EG *A freezer doesn't cost much to run... Its running costs were low.* V+O

9 When a machine **is running**, it is switched on and operating. EG *The engine was running.* V

10 If you **run** a machine on or off a particular source of energy, you use that source to make it work. EG *You can run the entire system off a mains plug... The heater ran on half-price electricity.* V-ERG+A

11 If a train or bus **runs** somewhere, it travels on a regular route at set times. EG *No buses have been running in the town for the past week.* V-ERG+A

12 If you **run** someone somewhere in a car, you drive them there. EG *Would you mind running me to the station?* V+O+A

13 If a liquid **runs** in a particular direction, it flows in that direction. EG *Tears were running down his face... The river ran past our house.* V+A OR V+C

14 If you **run** water or if you **run** a tap, you cause water to flow from the tap. EG *She was running hot water into the tub... Run my bath now!* V+O :USU+A

15 If a tap **is running**, water is coming out of it. V :USU CONT

16 If your nose **is running**, mucus is flowing out of it, usually because you have a cold. V :USU CONT

17 If the colour in something such as a piece of clothing **runs**, it comes out when the piece of clothing is washed. V

18 If a feeling **runs** through your body, it passes through it quickly and strongly. EG *A sharp tingling sensation ran through her.* V+A

19 If newspapers or magazines **run** a particular item or story, they publish it. EG *The local newspaper ran a feature on Liverpool.* V+O

20 You use **run** to indicate that you are quoting someone else's words or ideas. EG *'Attack on mother-to-be' ran the Evening News headline.* V+QUOTE

21 If an amount **is running** at a particular level, it is at that level. EG *Unemployment is running at 20 per cent.* V+O+at : USU CONT

22 If a play, event, or legal contract **runs** for a particular period of time, it lasts for that period of time. EG *'Chu-Chin-Chow' ran for years... The monsoons had six weeks more to run.* V+A

23 If someone or something **is running** late, they have taken more time than have been planned. EG *I'm running a bit over time, I'm afraid.* V+A

24 A **run** is also a journey somewhere. EG *It's a fair run up to Glasgow... ...planes which unload their bombs, on the home run, on innocent villages.* N COUNT USU+SUPP

25 In the theatre, a **run** is the period of time during which performances of a play are given. EG *The play ended its six-week run at the Regent.* N COUNT+SUPP

26 A **run** of success or failure is a series of successes or failures. EG *Leeds United had a run of wins in December.* N COUNT+SUPP

27 In cricket or baseball, a **run** is a score of one, which is made by players running between marked places on the pitch after hitting the ball. EG *They had beaten England by seventeen runs.* N COUNT

28 If you say that someone is different from the average **run** or common **run** of people, you mean that they are different from ordinary people. EG *Politicians seem to be more fallible than the average run of mankind.* N SING : the+N +SUPP Literary

29 If someone is **on the run, 29.1** they are trying to escape or hide from someone such as the police or an enemy. **29.2** they are being severely defeated in a contest or competition. EG *The Conservatives are on the run throughout Wales.* PHRASE

30 If you **make a run for it** or if you **run for it**, you go somewhere quickly in order to escape from something. EG *It was still raining hard, but we made a run for it... We'll just have to run for it.* PHRASE

31 If you talk about what will happen **in the long run**, you are saying what you think will happen over a long period of time in the future. If you talk about what will happen **in the short run**, you are saying what you think will happen in the near future. EG *Their policy would prove very costly in the long run.* PHRASE

32 If a river or well **runs dry**, it ceases to have any water in it. PHRASE

33 If people's feelings **are running high**, they are PHRASE

Has a runner-up been running?

very angry, concerned, or excited. EG *Public indignation was running high.*

34 to make your **blood run cold**: see **blood**. ● to **run its course**: see **course**. ● to **run** someone or something **to ground**: see **ground**. ● to **run riot**: see **riot**. ● to **run the risk**: see **risk**. ● to **run short**: see **short**. ● to **run wild**: see **wild**. ● See also **running, trial run**.

run across. If you **run across** someone, you   PHRASAL VB : meet them unexpectedly. EG *He ran across Tom*   V+PREP *and asked him what was happening.*

run along. If you tell a child to **run along**, you   PHRASAL VB : mean that you want them to go away. EG *Run along*   V+ADV *up to bed now, Sam.*   Informal

run away. 1 If you **run away** from a place, you   PHRASAL VB : leave it because you are unhappy there. EG *He had*   V+ADV, *run away from home at the age of thirteen... I ran*   OFT+*from* *away to Brighton.* **2** If you **run away** from   V+ADV, something unpleasant or new, you try to avoid   OFT+*from* dealing with it or thinking about it. EG *I can't run away from the horrors of the war.* **3** See also **runaway**.

run away with. If you let your emotions **run**   PHRASAL VB : **away with** you, you fail to control them and   V+ADV+PREP cannot think sensibly. EG *They did not allow their enthusiasm to run away with them.*

run down. 1 If you **run down** people or things,   PHRASAL VB : you criticize them strongly. EG *She was not used to*   V+O+ADV *people running down their own families.* **2** If   V+O+ADV people **run down** an industry or an organization, they deliberately reduce its size or activity. EG *The air force had been run down.* **3** See also **run-down**.

run into. 1 If you **run into** problems or difficul-   PHRASAL VB : ties, you unexpectedly begin to experience them.   V+PREP EG *The firm ran into foreign exchange problems.* **2**   V+PREP If you **run into** someone, you meet them unexpectedly. EG *You might run into him one of these days.* **3** If a vehicle **runs into** something, it accidentally   V+PREP, hits it. EG *She did not notice the driver's signal and*   HAS PASS *ran into the back of his bus... Taxis swerve round rickshaws, buses run into handcarts.* **4** You use   V+PREP **run into** to say that something costs a lot of money. EG *...exports running into billions of dollars.* **5** If one thing **runs into** another, it is difficult to   V+PREP see or hear the division between them. EG *The words run into each other.*

run off. 1 If you **run off** with someone, you   PHRASAL VB : secretly go away with them in order to live with   V+ADV OR them or marry them. EG *His wife ran off with*   V+ADV+*with* : *another man.* **2** If you **run off** copies of a piece of   V+O+ADV writing, you produce them using a machine.   RECIP

run on. If something **runs on**, it continues for   PHRASAL VB : longer than expected. EG *Donleavy tends to let his*   V+ADV *jokes run on too long.*

run out. 1 If you **run out** of something, you have   PHRASAL VB : no more of it left. EG *We were rapidly running out*   V+ADV,OFT+*of* *of money.* ● to **run out of steam**: see **steam**. **2** If   V+ADV something **runs out**, it becomes used up so that there is no more left. EG *Time is running out fast... My luck seemed to have run out.* **3** When a legal   V+ADV document **runs out**, it becomes no longer valid. EG *My passport's run out.*

run over. If a vehicle **runs over** someone or   PHRASAL VB : something, it knocks them down. EG *Rosamund*   V+PREP, *nearly got run over last night.*   HAS PASS

run through. 1 If something **runs through** a   PHRASAL VB : group of people or things, it is present in all of   V+PREP them, or spreads through all of them. EG *...the deep-rooted prejudice that runs through our society... A kind of shock-wave ran through the room.* **2** If you   V+PREP, **run through** something, you rehearse it or prac-   HAS PASS tise it. EG *You could hear the performers running through the whole programme in the background.* **3** If you **run through** a list of items, you read or   V+PREP mention all the items quickly. **4** See also **run-through.**

run to. 1 If you **run to** someone, you go to them   PHRASAL VB : for help or to tell them something. EG *I didn't think*   V+PREP *he'd run to you with the story.* **2** If something **runs**   V+PREP   Formal

to a particular amount or size, it is that amount or size. EG *The transcript runs to 1,200 pages.*

run up. 1 If someone **runs up** bills or debts, they   V+ADV+O acquire them by buying a lot of things or borrowing money. **2** See also **run-up.**

run up against. If you **run up against** prob-   PHRASAL VB : lems, you suddenly begin to experience them. EG   V+ADV+PREP *Sooner or later we would run up against major problems... You never know what you're liable to run up against.*

runaway /rʌnəweɪ/, **runaways. 1** A **runaway** is   N COUNT a child who leaves home without telling anyone where he or she is going. EG *They failed to find any trace of the runaways.* **2** A **runaway** vehicle is moving and its driver has   ADJ CLASSIF : lost control of it. EG *...a runaway bulldozer.*   ATTRIB **3** A **runaway** situation happens unexpectedly and   ADJ CLASSIF : cannot be controlled. EG *...the runaway success of*   ATTRIB *'Nicholas Nickleby'... ...the runaway inflation after the war.*

run-down, run-downs. 1 If someone is **run-**   ADJ PRED **down**, they are tired or ill. EG *'You're probably run*   Informal *down,' Clarissa said. 'You need a holiday.'* **2** A **run-down** building or area is in very poor   ADJ QUALIT condition. EG *...two small rooms in a run-down building.* **3** When the **run-down** of an industry or organiza-   N SING+SUPP tion takes place, it is reduced in size or activity. EG *...the run-down of the coal industry.* ▶ used as an   ▶ ADJ QUALIT adjective. EG *...run-down public services.* **4** If you give someone the **run-down** on a situation   N COUNT : USU or subject, you tell them the important facts about   SING+*on* it. EG *Let me give you the rundown on the Ritz*   Informal *Hotel situation.*

rung /rʌŋ/, **rungs. 1 Rung** is the past participle of **ring. 2** The **rungs** on a ladder are the wooden or metal   N COUNT bars that form the steps. EG *I had my foot on the first rung when she grabbed my arm.* **3** If you reach a particular **rung** in an organization,   N COUNT+SUPP you reach that level in it. EG *...the lower rungs of management.*

runner /rʌnə/, **runners. 1** A **runner** is a person   N COUNT who runs, especially for sport or pleasure. EG *...a long-distance runner... Not being a fast runner, I was glad I was close to the hall.* **2** A drugs **runner** or gun **runner** is someone who   N COUNT+SUPP illegally takes drugs or guns into a country. **3 Runners** are thin strips of wood or metal   N COUNT underneath something which help it to move smoothly. EG *Push the driving seat back on its runners... ...sledge runners.*

runner bean, runner beans. Runner beans are   N COUNT the long green pods of a climbing plant. You eat these pods as a vegetable.

runner-up, runners-up. A **runner-up** is some-   N COUNT one who finishes in second place in a race or competition. EG *...runner-up in the British Open.*

running /rʌnɪŋ/. **1 Running** is the activity of   N UNCOUNT running, especially as a sport. EG *He started professional running only eight years ago... ...running tracks... ...running techniques.* **2** The **running** of something such as a business is   N UNCOUNT the managing or organizing of it. EG *...the day-to-day*   +SUPP *running of the school.* **3** You use **running** to describe things that continue   ADJ CLASSIF : without stopping over a period of time. EG *...a*   ATTRIB *running battle between architects and planners... ...a running commentary.* **4** You also use **running** to describe things that   ADJ AFTER N keep happening regularly. For example, if something has happened every day for three days, you can say that it has happened for three days **running** or that it has happened for the third day **running**. EG *For three days running he had left the sandwiches at home... For the fourth year running, the weather was awful.* **5 Running** water is **5.1** water that is flowing   ADJ CLASSIF : rather than standing still. EG *...the sound of running*   ATTRIB *water*. **5.2** water that is supplied to a house through pipes and taps.

6 If someone **makes the running** in a situation, they are more active than the other people involved. EG *Women made all the running in demands for change.*   PHRASE

7 If someone is **in the running** for something, they have a good chance of winning or obtaining it. If they are **out of the running**, they have no chance of winning or obtaining it. EG *He's still in the running for the leadership of the Labour Party.*   PHRASE

runny /rʌniˈ/, **runnier, runniest. 1** Something that is **runny** is more liquid than usual or than was intended. EG *They had runny eggs for breakfast.*   ADJ QUALIT

2 If someone's nose or eyes are **runny**, liquid is flowing from them.   ADJ QUALIT

run-of-the-mill. A **run-of-the-mill** person or thing is very ordinary, with no special or interesting features. EG *...a run-of-the-mill customer.*   ADJ QUALIT

runt /rʌnt/, **runts.** If you call a small person a **runt**, you are expressing your dislike for them. EG *Pegler was a skinny little runt.*   N COUNT

run-through, run-throughs. A **run-through** for an event is a rehearsal or practice for it. EG *He agreed to come to a run-through.*   N COUNT

run-up. The **run-up** to an event is the period of time just before it. EG *...to reduce taxation in the run-up to the election.*   N SING : the+N

runway /rʌnweɪ/, **runways.** A **runway** is a long strip of ground with a hard surface which is used by aeroplanes when they are taking off or landing. EG *...the main runways at Heathrow Airport.*   N COUNT

rupee /ruːpiː/, **rupees.** A **rupee** is a unit of money that is used in India, Pakistan, and some other countries.   N COUNT

rupture /rʌptʃəˈ/, **ruptures, rupturing, ruptured. 1** A **rupture** is a severe injury in which a part of your body tears or bursts open. EG *See if you can open it without suffering a rupture.* ▸ used as a verb. EG *He ruptured himself playing football... ...the Mayor's ruptured appendix.*   N COUNT ▸ V+O, V-REFL, OR V

2 When there is a **rupture** between people, their relationship ends. EG *There has been a fundamental rupture between us.* ▸ used as a verb. EG *...at the risk of rupturing relations with the British.*   N COUNT Formal ▸ V+O

rural /rʊərəl/ means **1** existing far away from large towns or cities. EG *...a rural postmaster... ...poverty in the rural areas.* **2** typical of areas that are far away from large towns or cities. EG *India is still an overwhelmingly rural country... She spoke in a very rural accent.*   ADJ CLASSIF : ATTRIB   ADJ QUALIT

ruse /ruːz/, **ruses.** A **ruse** is an action which is intended to deceive someone. EG *The offer was just a ruse to gain time... His ruse had failed.*   N COUNT Formal

rush /rʌʃ/, **rushes, rushing, rushed. 1** If you **rush** somewhere, you go there quickly. EG *Please don't rush off... I'll rush over on Monday morning... When they saw us, they rushed forward.*   V : USU+A

2 When people **rush** to do something, they do it without delay, because they are very eager to do it. EG *People were rushing to buy the newspaper... Her friends rushed to her aid.*   V+to-INF OR to

3 If you **rush** something, you do it in a hurry. EG *I rushed my lunch.* ◊ **rushed.** EG *It'll be a bit of a rushed job, I'm afraid.*   V+O OR V+at ◊ ADJ CLASSIF : ATTRIB

4 If you **rush** someone or something to a place, you take them there quickly. EG *Barnett was rushed to hospital with a broken back.*   V+O+A

5 If you **rush** someone into doing something, you make them do it without allowing them enough time to think about it. EG *Do not be rushed into parting with goods before taking legal advice.*   V+O : USU+into

6 If you are **rushed off** your feet, you are very busy. EG *I've been rushed off my feet all day.*   PHRASE Informal

7 If there is **no rush** to do something, there is no need to do it quickly. EG *There is no rush to fill the vacancy... I'm not in any rush.*   PHRASE

8 You can refer to a part of the day that is usually busy as the **rush.** EG *...the five o'clock rush.*   N SING : the+N

9 If there is a **rush** for something or a **rush** to do something, there is a sudden increase in people's attempts to get it or do it. EG *There had been a rush for tickets... ...a rush to find the treasure.*   N SING+SUPP

10 If air or liquid **rushes** somewhere, it flows there suddenly and quickly. EG *The water rushed in over the top of his boots.* ▸ used as a noun. EG *There was a little rush of air... She shouted above the rush of water.* ◊ **rushing.** EG *They were carried along in the rushing stream... The rushing waters will carry them away.*   V : USU+A ▸ N SING : USU+SUPP ◊ ADJ CLASSIF : ATTRIB

11 If you experience a **rush** of a feeling, you suddenly experience it very strongly. EG *She felt a rush of pity for the boy... The memory came back with a painful rush.*   N SING : USU+SUPP

12 Rushes are plants that grow near water and have long, thin stems. EG *I hid in the rushes... ...baskets made from rushes.*   N COUNT : USU PLURAL

rush in or **rush into.** If you **rush in** or if you **rush into** a situation, you get involved in it without thinking about it carefully. EG *You wanted to rush in and protect him... Don't rush into marriage.*   PHRASAL VB : V+ADV/PREP

rush-hour. The **rush-hour** is one of the periods of the day when most people are travelling to or from work. EG *I had to start in the morning rush-hour... ...rush-hour traffic.*   N SING : the+N

Russian /rʌʃəⁿn/, **Russians. 1** Someone or something that is **Russian** belongs or relates to the Soviet Union. EG *...Russian dancers... ...the Russian Embassy.*   ADJ CLASSIF

2 A **Russian** is a person who comes from the Soviet Union. EG *His father is a Russian.*   N COUNT

3 Russian is the official language of the Soviet Union. EG *He had learnt to speak more Russian.*   N UNCOUNT

rust /rʌst/, **rusts, rusting, rusted. 1 Rust** is a brown substance that forms on iron or steel when it comes into contact with water. EG *The car looked free of rust.*   N UNCOUNT

2 When a metal object **rusts**, it becomes covered in rust. EG *The fittings had rusted.* ◊ **rusted.** EG *...kicking some rusted tins.*   V ◊ ADJ CLASSIF

rustic /rʌstɪk/. You use **rustic** to describe things that are simple in a way that is typical of places far away from large cities. EG *...rustic comfort and good food... ...rustic benches.*   ADJ CLASSIF : ATTRIB Formal

rustle /rʌsəⁿl/, **rustles, rustling, rustled. 1** When something **rustles** or when you **rustle** it, it makes soft sounds as it moves. EG *...mice rustling about... He rustled his papers.* ◊ **rustling, rustlings.** EG *Jim heard some furtive rustlings among the bushes.*   V-ERG ◊ N COUNT OR N UNCOUNT

2 A **rustle** is a soft sound made by something moving gently. EG *She heard a rustle behind her and turned... ...the rustle of chocolate wrappers.*   N COUNT OR N UNCOUNT

rustle up. If you **rustle up** a meal, you cook it quickly, using whatever food you have available. EG *I'll rustle something up... We could rustle up an omelette.*   PHRASAL VB : V+O+ADV

rusty /rʌstiˈ/, **rustier, rustiest. 1** Something that is **rusty** is affected by rust. EG *...a heap of rusty tins... ...a rusty old truck.*   ADJ QUALIT

2 If someone's skill or knowledge is **rusty**, it is not as good as it was before, because they have not used it for a long time. EG *My German's pretty rusty... Dilley looked rusty through lack of bowling.*   ADJ QUALIT

rut /rʌt/, **ruts. 1** A **rut** is a deep, narrow mark made in the ground by the wheels of vehicles. EG *We bumped over the ruts.*   N COUNT

2 If someone is in a **rut**, they have become fixed in their way of thinking and doing things, and find it difficult to change. EG *He is in a real rut... Some people never get out of their ruts.*   N COUNT

ruthless /ruːθlɪˈs/. **1** Someone who is **ruthless** is very harsh or cruel, and will do anything that is necessary to achieve what they want. EG *His adver-*   ADJ QUALIT

sary was ruthless... Political power was in the hands of a few ruthless men. ◊ **ruthlessly**. EG ◊ ADV Napoleon acted swiftly and ruthlessly. ◊ **ruthlessness**. EG He often operated with ex- ◊ N UNCOUNT treme ruthlessness.
2 A **ruthless** action is done forcefully and thor- ADJ QUALIT

oughly. EG ...a ruthless investigation... ...the ruthless suppression of the revolt.
rye /raɪ/ is a type of grass that is grown in cold N UNCOUNT countries for animals to eat. Bread and whisky are made from rye. EG ...rye bread.

S s

S, s /ɛs/, **S's, s's** /ɛsɪz/. **1 S** is the nineteenth letter N COUNT of the English alphabet.
2 s was a written form of 'shilling' or 'shillings' in Britain before decimal currency was introduced in 1971.
3 S is a written abbreviation for 'south'.
-s; also spelled **-es. 1 -s** and **-es** are added to nouns to form plurals. EG ...dogs, cats, and rabbits... ...ancient palaces... ...profits and losses... ...a sack of potatoes.
2 -s and **-es** are added to verbs to form the third person singular present tense. EG The lift stops at the fifth floor... He realizes what he has done... He pushes the button.
-'s. 1 -'s is added to singular nouns to form possessives. With a plural noun ending in '-s', you form the possessive by adding **-'**. EG ...Ralph's voice... ...the President's conduct... ...friends of the wife's... ...one's self-esteem... ...my colleagues' offices.
2 -'s is added to plural nouns that do not end in 's' to form possessives. EG ...women's rights... ...children's games.
3 -'s is the shortened form of 'is' in spoken English. For example, 'he is' can be shortened to 'he's'. EG He's a novelist... She's charming... It's fantastic... There's no hurry... Mary's going to look after you.
4 -'s is the shortened form of 'has' in spoken English, especially where 'has' is an auxiliary verb. For example, 'It has gone' can be shortened to 'It's gone'. EG He's got a problem... She's gone home... It's got to be done... Anne's got a scientific mind.
5 -'s is added to letters, numbers, abbreviations, and acronyms to form plurals. EG ...a row of q's... ...the 1870's.
Sabbath /sæbəθ/. The **Sabbath** is the day of the N PROPER: week when members of some religious groups, the+N especially Jews and Christians, do not work. EG No amount of arguing could make them break the Sabbath.
sabotage /sæbətɑːʒ/, **sabotages, sabotaging, sabotaged. 1** If a machine, railway line, or bridge V+O: USU PASS **is sabotaged**, it is deliberately damaged or destroyed, for example in a war or as a protest. EG The power station had been sabotaged by anti-government guerrillas. ▸ used as a noun. EG ▸ N UNCOUNT ...widespread sabotage and the disruption of rail communications.
2 If someone **sabotages** a plan or a meeting, they V+O deliberately prevent it from being successful. EG I don't wish to be accused of sabotaging the President's programme.
saccharine /sækəraɪn, -riːn/; also spelled **sac-** N UNCOUNT **charin. Saccharine** is a very sweet chemical substance that some people use instead of sugar.
sachet /sæʃeɪ/, **sachets**. A **sachet** is a small N COUNT closed plastic or paper packet, containing a very OR N PART small quantity of something.
sack /sæk/, **sacks, sacking, sacked. 1** A **sack** is N COUNT a large bag made of rough woven material. Sacks OR N PART are used to carry or store goods. EG ...a large sack containing oranges... ...sacks of flour.
2 If your employers **sack** you, they say that you V+O can no longer work for them, often because your

work is not good enough. EG Three railwaymen were sacked because they would not join a union.
● If you **get the sack** or **are given the sack**, your ● PHRASE employer sacks you. EG Years ago he would have got the sack for something like that.
sacking /sækɪŋ/ is rough woven material that is N UNCOUNT used to make sacks. EG ...a piece of old sacking.
sacrament /sækrəmə²nt/, **sacraments**. A **sacra-** N COUNT **ment** is an important Christian religious ceremony such as communion, baptism, or marriage.
sacred /seɪkrɪ²d/. **1** Something that is **sacred** is **1.1** believed to be holy and to have a special ADJ QUALIT connection with God. EG They entered the sacred mosque.... ...a group of sacred elephants.
◊ **sacredness**. EG ...the sacredness of the shrine ◊ N UNCOUNT had been violated. **1.2** connected with religion or ADJ CLASSIF used in religious ceremonies. EG ...sacred music.
2 You can describe something as **sacred** when it is ADJ QUALIT regarded as too important to be changed or interfered with. EG She saw motherhood as woman's sacred calling... In their search for a good news story, nothing was sacred. ◊ **sacredness**. EG ...the ◊ N UNCOUNT sacredness of private property.
sacrifice /sækrɪfaɪs/, **sacrifices, sacrificing, sacrificed. 1** To **sacrifice** an animal means to kill V+O it in a special religious ceremony as an offering to God. EG White animals were sacrificed by white-robed priests. ▸ used as a noun. EG ...a ritual ▸ N UNCOUNT sacrifice.   OR N COUNT
2 If you **sacrifice** something that is valuable or V+O important, you give it up, in order to be able to do something else. EG ...women who have sacrificed career and marriage to care for elderly relatives. ▸ used as a noun. EG ...a mother's ▸ N COUNT OR sacrifices for her children.   N UNCOUNT
sacrificial /sækrɪfɪʃə⁰l/ means connected with or ADJ CLASSIF: used in a religious sacrifice. EG ...sacrificial victims. ATTRIB
sacrilege /sækrɪlɪdʒ/. **1 Sacrilege** is behaviour N UNCOUNT that shows great disrespect for a holy place or object. EG He might have to be punished for his sacrilege.
2 You can use **sacrilege** to refer to disrespect that N UNCOUNT is shown for someone who is widely admired or for a belief that is widely accepted. EG Criticism of Woolley is sacrilege.
sacrilegious /sækrɪlɪdʒəs/. If your behaviour is ADJ QUALIT **sacrilegious**, you show great disrespect towards something holy or towards something that people think should be respected. EG It would have been sacrilegious to speak.
sacrosanct /sækrə⁶sæŋkt/. If you describe some- ADJ CLASSIF: thing as **sacrosanct**, you mean that people consid- USU PRED er it to be special and are unwilling to criticize or change it. EG ...the ruthlessness of leaders when their power was sacrosanct... He seems to think there's something sacrosanct about his annual fishing trip.
sad /sæd/, **sadder, saddest. 1** If you are **sad**, you ADJ QUALIT are not happy, usually because something has happened that you do not like. EG She looked sad... He was sad to see her go... The more he thought about it, the sadder he became... ...a sad face.
◊ **sadly**. EG He shook his head sadly... 'Not a cent,' ◊ ADV

she said sadly. ◊ **sadness.** EG *The news filled him*   N UNCOUNT
with sadness.

2 Sad stories and **sad** news make you feel sad. EG   ADJ QUALIT
She told Susan there was some sad news for her... It
seems rather sad that this should happen to you.
◊ **sadness.** EG *...the indescribable sadness of those*   ◊ N UNCOUNT
final pages.

3 You use **sad** to describe an unfortunate situation.   ADJ QUALIT :
EG *The sad fact is that full employment may never*   ATTRIB
be regained... This is a very sad comment on what
is happening to our cities. ◊ **sadly.** EG *One aspect*   ◊ ADV OR
of education today has been sadly neglected...   ADV SEN
Sadly, we don't appear to have much chance of
getting the contract.

sadden /sǽdə⁰n/, **saddens, saddening, sad-**   v+o
dened. If something **saddens** you, it makes you
feel sad. EG *I'm saddened by the fact that so many*
people died for nothing... This is one of the things
that saddens me most.

saddle /sǽdə⁰l/, **saddles, saddling, saddled. 1** A   N COUNT
saddle is **1.1** a leather seat that you put on the
back of an animal so that you can ride the animal.
EG *Jennifer swung herself into the saddle.* ● See also
side-saddle. 1.2 a seat on a bicycle or motorcycle.
See picture at BICYCLE.

2 If you **saddle** a horse or pony, you put a saddle   v+o
on it. EG *He saddled his horse and rode off.*

3 If you **saddle** someone with a problem or with   v+o+with OR
responsibility, you put them in the position where   v-REFL+with
they have to deal with it. EG *The last thing I want is*
to saddle myself with a second mortgage.

saddle up. If you **saddle up**, you put a saddle on   PHRASAL VB :
a horse or pony. EG *I saddled up and rode off... He*   v+ADV OR
went out to saddle up his horse.   v+o+ADV

saddlebag /sǽdə⁰lbæg/, **saddlebags.** A **saddle-**   N COUNT
bag is a bag fastened to the saddle of a horse,
bicycle, or motorcycle.

sadism /séɪdɪzə⁰m, sǽ-/ is a type of behaviour in   N UNCOUNT
which a person obtains pleasure from hurting
other people and making them suffer. EG *He teased*
her with malicious sadism. ◊ **sadist, sadists.** EG   ◊ N COUNT
...sadists and bullies.

sadistic /sədɪ́stɪk/. Someone who is **sadistic** ob-   ADJ QUALIT
tains pleasure from hurting other people and mak-
ing them suffer. EG *He was nothing but a sadistic*
drunkard... ...scenes of sadistic cruelty.
◊ **sadistically.** EG *He was sadistically cruel in his*   ◊ ADV
interrogations.

s.a.e. /és eɪ iː/, **s.a.e.s.** An **s.a.e.** is an envelope on   N COUNT
which you have stuck a stamp and written your
own name and address. You send it to someone so
that they can send you something such as information in it. **s.a.e.** is an abbreviation for 'stamped
addressed envelope'. EG *Please include s.a.e. for*
return of material.

safari /səfɑ́ːriː/, **safaris.** A **safari** is an expedition   N COUNT,
for hunting or observing wild animals, especially in   OR on+N
East Africa. EG *...a safari arranged by a travel*
agency... We're going on safari.

safe /seɪf/, **safer, safest; safes. 1** Something that   ADJ QUALIT
is **safe** does not cause physical harm or danger. EG
This powder is not safe for babies... He asked me if
it was safe to let my friend go out alone... Keep
your passport in a safe place. ◊ **safely.** EG *Most*   ◊ ADV
food can safely be frozen for months.

2 You are **safe** from something when you cannot   ADJ PRED :
be harmed by it. EG *We're safe now. They've gone...*   OFT+from
They were safe from attack. ● You say that   ● PHRASE
someone is **safe and sound** when they are still
alive or unharmed after being in danger. EG *I'm*
glad to see you home safe and sound.

3 A **safe** journey or arrival is one in which people   ADJ CLASSIF :
or things reach their destination without being   ATTRIB
harmed. EG *We are relying on the safe delivery of*
essential equipment. ◊ **safely.** EG *I sent a telegram*   ◊ ADV
to my mother saying I had arrived safely.

4 If it is **safe** to say something, you can say it with   ADJ QUALIT
very little risk of being wrong. EG *These practices,*
it is safe to say, are no longer common. ◊ **safely.**   ◊ ADV

EG *These creatures, we can safely say, have been*
dead a long time.

5 If a secret is **safe** with you, you will not tell it to   ADJ PRED :
anyone. EG *They knew their secrets would be safe*   OFT+with
with him.

6 Safe is also used in these phrases. **6.1** If you **play**   PHRASES
safe, you do not take unnecessary risks. EG *Play*   Informal
safe and always wear goggles. **6.2** If you are doing
something **to be on the safe side**, you are doing it
as a precaution, in case something unexpected
happens. EG *I'll take a few extra groceries, just to*
be on the safe side. **6.3** If someone or something is
in safe hands, they are being looked after by a
reliable person and will not be harmed. EG *Don't*
worry, she's in safe hands at the hospital.

7 A **safe** is a strong metal cupboard with special   N COUNT
locks, in which you keep money, jewellery, and
other valuable things.

safeguard /séɪfgɑːd/, **safeguards, safeguard-**
ing, safeguarded. 1 To **safeguard** something   v+o
means to prevent it from being harmed or de-   Formal
stroyed. EG *The Bureau's purpose was to safeguard*
human life... They have to fight to safeguard their
future.

2 A **safeguard** is a law or rule intended to prevent   N COUNT :
someone or something from being harmed. EG *This*   OFT+against
clause was inserted as a safeguard against possible   Formal
exploitation.

safekeeping /séɪfkiːpɪŋ/. If something is given to   N UNCOUNT
you for **safekeeping**, it is given to you so that you   Formal
will make sure that it is not harmed or stolen. EG *It*
had been placed in a Paris museum for safe-
keeping.

safety /séɪftiː/. **1 Safety** is **1.1** the state of being   N UNCOUNT
safe from harm or danger. EG *He was assured of his*
daughter's safety. **1.2** a place where you are safe
from danger. EG *They swam to the safety of a small,*
rocky island.

2 If you are concerned about the **safety** of some-   N UNCOUNT
thing, you are concerned that it might be harmful
or dangerous. EG *People worry about the safety of*
nuclear energy.

3 Safety features or measures are intended to   N MOD
make something less dangerous. EG *Every car will*
come with built-in safety features.

safety belt, safety belts. A **safety belt** is a strap   N COUNT
attached to a seat in a car or aeroplane. You fasten
it round your body when you are travelling in the
car or aeroplane.

safety catch, safety catches. The **safety catch**   N COUNT
on a gun is a catch that stops you firing the gun
accidentally.

safety net, safety nets. 1 In a circus, a **safety**   N COUNT
net is a large net that is placed below performers
on a high wire or trapeze in order to catch them
and prevent them being injured if they fall off.

2 A **safety net** is also something that you can rely   N COUNT
on to help you if you get into a difficult situation. EG
The Fund is our safety net if anything should go
wrong.

safety pin, safety pins. A **safety pin** is a bent   N COUNT
metal pin used for fastening things together. The
point of the pin has a cover so that it cannot hurt
anyone. See picture at PINS.

safety-valve, safety-valves. 1 A **safety-valve** is   N COUNT
a piece of equipment in a machine that allows
liquids or gases to escape when the pressure inside
the machine becomes too great.

2 You can use **safety-valve** to refer to anything   N COUNT
that allows you to express strong feelings without
harming other people. EG *...a safety-valve for the*
harmless release of rebellious feelings.

sag /sæg/, **sags, sagging, sagged.** When some-   v
thing **sags**, it hangs down loosely or sinks downwards in the middle. EG *The bed sagged in the*

Find two words on these pages with the same
pronunciation.

middle... His pocket sagged with the weight of the coins.

saga /sɑːgə/, **sagas.** A **saga** is a long story, N COUNT : account, or sequence of events. EG *I related some of* USU+SUPP *the episodes of my domestic saga... ...a saga of financial mismanagement.*

sage /seɪdʒ/, **sages. 1** A **sage** is a person who is N COUNT regarded as being very wise. EG *...the great sages* Literary *buried in the city.*

2 A **sage** person is wise and knowledgeable, usual- ADJ QUALIT ly because they are old and have had a lot of Literary experience. EG *...sage parents anxious to dispense their wisdom.* ◊ **sagely.** EG *He nodded his head* ◊ ADV *sagely.*

3 Sage is a herb used in cooking. N UNCOUNT

said /sɛd/ is the past tense and past participle of **say.**

sail /seɪl/, **sails, sailing, sailed. 1** A **sail** is a large N COUNT piece of material attached to the mast of a ship. The wind blows against the sail and pushes the ship along. See picture at YACHT. EG *...the white sails of the yacht.*

2 When a ship moves over the sea, it **sails.** EG *The* V+A *ship sailed down the east coast of South America... We were shortly to sail for New York.*

3 To **sail** a boat means to make it move across V+O OR V water using its sails. EG *I spent two weeks swimming and sailing in New Hampshire.*

4 When a ship **sets sail,** it leaves a port. EG *The* PHRASE *Beagle set sail on 27 December 1831.*

5 If someone or something **sails** somewhere, they V+A move there steadily and fairly quickly. EG *I watched the ball as it went sailing over the bushes.*

sail through. If you **sail through** a difficult PHRASAL VB : situation or experience, you deal with it very easily V+ADV/PREP and successfully. EG *She was expecting to sail through her exams.*

sailing /seɪlɪŋ/, **sailings. 1** A **sailing** is a voyage N COUNT made by a ship carrying passengers. EG *...regular sailings from Portsmouth.*

2 Sailing is the activity or sport of sailing boats. EG N UNCOUNT *...the traditional Royal sailing week in August.*

3 If you describe a task as **plain sailing,** you mean PHRASE that it is very easy. EG *Once we've fixed the computer, it will be plain sailing.*

sailor /seɪlə/, **sailors.** A **sailor** is a man who N COUNT works on a ship as a member of its crew. EG *He had been a sailor in the Italian navy.* ● If you are **a** ● PHRASE **good sailor,** you are able to travel on a boat in rough weather without being seasick.

saint /seɪnt/, **saints.** A **saint** is a dead person who N COUNT is officially recognized and honoured by the Christian church because his or her life was a perfect example of the way Christians should live. EG *...the church of Saint Francis.*

saintly /seɪntlɪ/. A **saintly** person behaves in a ADJ QUALIT very good or very holy way. EG *He was not at all a religious or saintly man... ...saintly virtues.*

sake /seɪk/, **sakes. 1** If you do something **for the** PHRASE **sake of** something, you do it for a particular purpose or in order to achieve a particular result. EG *I usually check from time to time, just for safety's sake... Let us assume, for the sake of argument, that the level of unemployment does not fall.*

2 If you do something **for** its **own sake,** you do it PHRASE because you enjoy it, and not for any other reason. EG *I'm studying the subject for its own sake.*

3 When you do something **for** someone's **sake,** you PHRASE do it in order to help them. EG *We moved out to the country for the children's sake... I must break the bonds for both our sakes... It is better for all our sakes that the trail should be lost.*

4 Some people say **for God's sake** or **for heav-** CONVENTION **en's sake** in order to express annoyance or impatience, or to add force to a question or request. EG *What are you staring at for heaven's sake?... For God's sake don't tell anyone.*

salad /sæləd/, **salads.** A **salad** is a mixture of N MASS uncooked vegetables. It is usually eaten with other foods as part of a meal. EG *I am not fond of salad... ...chicken salad.* ● See also **fruit salad.**

salami /səlɑːmiː/, **salamis. Salami** is a type of N MASS sausage made from chopped meat and spices.

salaried /sælərɪd/. **Salaried** people receive a ADJ CLASSIF : salary from their job. EG *The report listed the* USU ATTRIB *names of all salaried employees.*

salary /sælərɪ/, **salaries.** A **salary** is the money N COUNT OR that someone is paid for their job each month, N UNCOUNT especially when they have a professional job. EG *She earns a high salary as an accountant... ...the difference in salary between an instructor and a lecturer.*

sale /seɪl/, **sales. 1** The **sale** of goods is the selling N COUNT : of them for money. EG *...new laws to control the* USU+SUPP *sale of guns... We've just made our first sale.*

2 If something such as a house or a car is **for sale** PHRASE or **up for sale,** its owner is trying to sell it. EG *Their house is up for sale.*

3 Products that are **on sale** can be bought in shops. PHRASE EG *The only English newspaper on sale was the Morning Star.*

4 The **sales** of a product are the quantity that is N PLURAL sold. EG *Data General's sales grew by 140% a year... Car sales are 5 per cent down... Sales of the magazine are declining.*

5 The part of a company that deals with **sales** N PLURAL deals with selling the company's products. EG *...a sales executive.*

6 A **sale** is **6.1** an occasion when a shop sells things N COUNT at less than their normal price. EG *They're having a clearance sale.* **6.2** an event when goods are sold to the person who offers the highest price. EG *...the quarterly cattle sale.* ● See also **jumble sale.**

salesman /seɪlzmə³n/, **salesmen.** A **salesman** is N COUNT a man whose job is selling things, especially directly to shops or other businesses. EG *...a shoe salesman... ...chief salesman of Vickers... ...a travelling salesman.*

salient /seɪlɪənt/. The **salient** points or facts of a ADJ QUALIT : situation are the most important ones. EG *...the* USU ATTRIB *salient points of the prime minister's speech.* Formal

saline /seɪlaɪn/. A **saline** substance or liquid ADJ CLASSIF : contains salt. EG *She broke the crystals off into this* ATTRIB *water and made a saline solution.* Formal

saliva /səlaɪvə/ is the watery liquid that forms in N UNCOUNT your mouth and helps you to chew and digest food.

sallow /sæləʊ/. If a person's skin is **sallow,** it has ADJ QUALIT a pale yellowish colour and looks unhealthy. EG *...her sallow face.*

sally /sælɪ/, **sallies, sallying, sallied. Sallies** N COUNT : are clever and amusing remarks. EG *The laughter* USU PLURAL *with which his sallies were greeted excited him.* Literary

sally forth or **sally out.** If someone **sallies** PHRASAL VB : **forth** or **sallies out** somewhere, they go there V+ADV quickly or energetically. EG *He sallied out into the* Literary *raw London night... The animals sallied forth to meet them.*

salmon /sæmən/. **Salmon** is both the singular and N COUNT OR the plural form. A **salmon** is a large silver- N UNCOUNT coloured fish. EG *...smoked salmon.*

salmonella /sælmənelə/ is a kind of bacteria N UNCOUNT which can cause severe food poisoning.

salon /sælɒn/, **salons.** A **salon** is **1** a place where N COUNT hairdressers or beauticians work. EG *...a hairdressing salon.* **2** a shop where smart, expensive clothes are sold. EG *She is dressed by Dior, whose salon is located across the street.*

saloon /səluːn/, **saloons. 1** A **saloon** is a car with N COUNT seats for four or more people, a fixed roof, and a boot that is separated from the rear seats. EG *...Ford Cortina saloons.*

2 In the United States, a **saloon** is a place where N COUNT alcoholic drinks are sold and drunk. EG *There were nine saloons in those days, and they stayed open all the time.*

3 In Britain, the **saloon** or **saloon bar** in a pub or N COUNT hotel is a comfortable bar where the drinks are more expensive than in the other bars.

salt /sɒlt/, **salts, salting, salted. 1 Salt** is a N UNCOUNT strong-tasting substance, in the form of white powder or crystals, which is used to improve the flavour of food or to preserve it. Salt occurs naturally in sea water.

2 When you **salt** food, you add salt to it. EG *The* v+o *potatoes should be lightly salted.* ◊ **salted.** EG ◊ ADJ CLASSIF *...salted peanuts.*

3 Salt is used in these phrases. **3.1** If you describe PHRASES someone as **the salt of the earth**, you mean that you like and respect them very much because they always do what is required, deal with any problems, and never make a fuss. EG *Rodin worshipped soldiers as the true salt of the earth.* **3.2** If something **rubs salt into** your **wounds**, it makes the unpleasant situation that you are in even worse, often by reminding you of your failures or faults. EG *The proposed ten per cent cut in wages is really rubbing salt into the wound.* **3.3** If you **take** some- Informal thing **with a pinch of salt**, you do not believe that it is completely accurate or true. EG *This calculation has to be taken with a pinch of salt.*

salt cellar, salt cellars. A **salt cellar** is a small N COUNT container for salt which is used at mealtimes.

salty /sɒltɪ¹/, **saltier, saltiest.** Something that is ADJ QUALIT **salty** contains salt or tastes of salt. EG *We washed them in salty water.*

salubrious /səluːbrɪəs/. A place that is **salubri-** ADJ QUALIT **ous** is pleasant and healthy. EG *...one of the less* Formal *salubrious suburbs of London.*

salutary /sæljə¹tə⁰riː/. A **salutary** experience is ADJ QUALIT good for you, even though it may seem difficult or Formal unpleasant. EG *It is salutary to consider that in future we will not have such easy access to coal... The defeat was a deserved punishment, but also a salutary shock.*

salute /səluːt/, **salutes, saluting, saluted. 1** If v+o OR V you **salute** someone, you greet them or show your respect with a formal sign. Soldiers salute officers by raising their right hand so that their fingers touch their forehead. EG *He stood as if he were saluting the flag.* ▸ used as a noun. EG *He greeted* ▸ N COUNT *King Edward VIII with the customary salute.*

2 To **salute** a person or an achievement means to v+o publicly show or state your admiration for them. EG *...festivals in Spain that salute the independence of the Spanish character.* ▸ used as a noun. EG *...a* ▸ N COUNT *salute to America.*

salvage /sælvɪdʒ/, **salvages, salvaging, sal-** **vaged. 1** When you **salvage** things, you manage to v+o: save them, for example from a ship that has sunk, OFT+*from* or from a building that has been destroyed. EG *...a finely decorated window salvaged from an old chemist's shop.*

2 The **salvage** from wrecked ships or destroyed N UNCOUNT buildings consists of the things that are saved from them. EG *The insurers are entitled to take the wreck as salvage... ...a salvage operation.*

3 If you **salvage** something from a difficult situa- v+o: tion, you manage to get something useful from it so OFT+*from* that it is not a complete failure. EG *They were salvaging what they could from the present unhappy state of affairs.*

salvation /sælveɪʃⁿ/. **1** In Christianity, the **sal-** N UNCOUNT **vation** of a person is the fact that Christ has saved them from evil.

2 The **salvation** of someone or something is the N UNCOUNT act of saving them from harm. EG *The country's salvation was of immense importance to the British.*

3 If someone or something is your **salvation**, they N SING+POSS are responsible for saving you from harm or from an unpleasant situation. EG *Small industries will be the salvation of many areas now in decline... Their children were their only salvation.*

salve /sælv/, **salves, salving, salved.** If you PHRASE **salve** your **conscience** by doing something, it

makes you feel less guilty or worried. EG *We give money to charities, and thus salve our consciences.*

same /seɪm/. **1** If two things are the **same** or if N CLASSIF: one thing is the **same** as another, the two are ATTRIB, OR exactly like each other in some way. EG *They both* PRON : *the* wore the same overcoats... Look! They're exactly +ADJ/PRON the same... He did exactly the same as John did.

2 If two things have the **same** quality or if one ADJ CLASSIF : thing has the **same** quality as another, they both ATTRIB, have that quality. EG *He and Tom were exactly the* the+ADJ same age... It was the same colour as the wall.

3 You use **same 3.1** to indicate that you are ADJ CLASSIF : referring to only one thing, and not to different ATTRIB, ones. EG *We come from the same place... It was* the+ADJ possible to work while watching TV at the same time. **3.2** To refer to something that has already ADJ CLASSIF : been mentioned. EG *For the same reason, the* ATTRIB, OR United States lodged a formal protest... The same is PRON : *the* true of the arts... It's the same with teenage +ADJ/PRON fashions.

4 Something that is still the **same** has not changed ADJ CLASSIF : in any way. EG *The village stayed the same... He* ATTRIB, OR will never be the same again. PRON : *the*+ ADJ/PRON

5 Same is also used in these phrases. **5.1** You say ADV SEN **all the same** or **just the same** to indicate that a situation or your opinion has not changed, in spite of something that has happened or been said. EG *She knew he wasn't listening, but she went on all the same... All the same, the courses are very popular.* **5.2** If you say **'It's all the same to me'**, CONVENTION you mean that you do not care which of several things happens or is chosen. **5.3** You say **'Thanks** CONVENTION **all the same'** when you are thanking someone for an offer that you are refusing. EG *'Do you want a lift?' - 'No, but thanks all the same.'* **5.4** If PHRASE something **is not the same**, it is not as pleasant or as good as something that you would prefer. EG *We started out again by car. But it wasn't the same.*

sameness /seɪmnɪ²s/. The **sameness** of some- N UNCOUNT : thing is its lack of variety. EG *I was struck by the* USU+SUPP sameness of clothing among the villagers.

sample /sɑːmpə⁰l/, **samples, sampling, sam-** N COUNT **pled. 1** A **sample** of a substance or product is **1.1** a small quantity of it that shows you what it is like. EG *...free samples of shampoo.* **1.2** a small amount of it that is examined and analysed scientifically. EG *I'll take water samples here and in East Hampton... She took a sample of her urine to a clinic.*

2 A **sample** of people or things is a number of N COUNT them chosen out of a larger group and then used in tests or used to provide information about the whole group. EG *...a random sample of 10,000 adult civilians... ...a representative sample of viewers.*

3 If you **sample** food or drink, you taste a small v+o amount of it in order to find out if you like it. EG *Next he sampled the roast beef.*

4 If you **sample** a place or situation, you experi- v+o ence it for a short time in order to find out about it. EG *They can learn the language and sample the British way of life.*

sanatorium /sænətɔːrɪəm/, **sanatoriums** OR N COUNT **sanatoria** /sænətɔːrɪə/; spelled **sanitarium** /sænɪteərɪəm/ in American English. A **sanatorium** is an institution that provides medical treatment and rest for people who have been ill for a long time. EG *A dreadful breakdown sent me to a sanatorium for more than a year.*

sanctify /sæŋktɪfaɪ/, **sanctifies, sanctifying,** **sanctified. 1** If the Church or a holy person v+o **sanctifies** something, they officially bless it or approve it and declare that it should be treated or considered as holy. EG *St Francis wanted to sanctify poverty, not to abolish it... ...the silver of the sanctified coffin.*

2 If something **is sanctified** by someone or some- v+o : USU PASS

Is a sandwich course part of a meal?

thing, they approve of it, support it, and want it to remain exactly as it is. EG ...*the assumption, sanctified by the famous words of the Constitution... Teachers helped to protect and sanctify the power that was so ruthlessly being used.*

sanctimonious /sæŋktɪməʊnɪəs/. Someone who is **sanctimonious** tries to appear deeply religious and virtuous; used showing disapproval. EG ...*a sanctimonious hypocrite.* ADJ QUALIT

sanction /sæŋkᵏʃəᵘn/, **sanctions, sanctioning, sanctioned. 1** If someone in authority **sanctions** an action or practice, they officially approve of it and allow it to be done. EG ...*the law of 1856 which sanctioned the remarriage of widows.* ▸ used as a noun. EG *Some months later our proposal was given official sanction.* V+O ▸ N UNCOUNT +SUPP

2 A **sanction** is a severe course of action which is intended to make people obey the law. EG *The ultimate sanction of the government is the withdrawal of funds.* N COUNT

3 Sanctions are measures taken by countries to restrict trade and official contact with a country that has broken international law. EG *The UN would impose economic sanctions against the offending nation.* N PLURAL : OFT +against

sanctity /sæŋkᵏtɪʰtiʰ/. If you talk about the **sanctity** of something, you mean that it is very important and should always be respected. EG ...*the sanctity of marriage... ...the sanctity of human life.* N UNCOUNT : USU+of

sanctuary /sæŋkᵏtʃʊəriʰ/, **sanctuaries.** A **sanctuary** is **1** a place of safety for someone. EG *It was Clement's island and his sanctuary... I was glad to climb into the sanctuary of my bed.* **2** a place where birds or animals are protected and allowed to live freely. EG *She wants to turn her orchard into a bird sanctuary.* N COUNT OR N UNCOUNT ▸ N COUNT : USU+SUPP

sand /sænd/, **sands, sanding, sanded. 1 Sand** is a powdery substance that consists of extremely small pieces of stone. Most deserts and beaches are made of sand. EG *The children played in the sand at the water's edge... ...grains of sand.* N UNCOUNT

2 Sands are a large area of sand, for example a beach or a desert. EG ...*miles of empty sands.* N PLURAL

3 If you **sand** something, you rub sandpaper over it in order to make it smooth or clean. EG *A scratched item of furniture can be professionally sanded.* V+O

sandal /sændəl/, **sandals. Sandals** are light shoes that you wear in warm weather, which have straps instead of a solid part over the top of your foot. See picture at SHOES. N COUNT

sand castle, sand castles. A **sand castle** is a heap of sand which children make when they are playing on the beach. N COUNT

sandpaper /sændpeɪpə/ is strong paper that has a coating of sand on it. It is used for rubbing wooden or metal surfaces to make them smoother. N UNCOUNT

sandstone /sændstəʊn/ is a type of rock. EG ...*a long sandstone cliff.* N UNCOUNT

sandstorm /sændstɔːm/, **sandstorms.** A **sandstorm** is a strong wind in a desert area, which creates large moving clouds of sand. N COUNT

sandwich /sænwɪdʒ, -wɪtʃ/, **sandwiches, sandwiched. 1** A **sandwich** consists of two slices of bread with a layer of food such as cheese or meat between them. EG ...*eating sandwiches in the office for lunch... ...a bacon, lettuce, and tomato sandwich.* N COUNT

2 When one thing **is sandwiched** between two other things, it is in a very narrow space between them. EG *Wooden shacks are sandwiched between modern blocks of flats.* V-PASS+A

sandwich course, sandwich courses. A **sandwich course** is an educational course in which you have periods of study in between periods of work in industry or business. EG ...*a sandwich course in civil engineering.* N COUNT British

sandy /sændiʰ/. **1** A **sandy** area is covered with sand. EG ...*the long sandy beach.* ADJ QUALIT

2 Sandy hair is light orange-brown in colour. ADJ COLOUR

sane /seɪn/, **saner, sanest. 1** Someone who is **sane** is able to think and behave normally and reasonably, and is not mentally ill. EG *She appeared to be completely sane.* ADJ QUALIT

2 If you refer to a **sane** action or system, you mean one that you think is reasonable and sensible. EG *It is the only sane thing to do... ...a sane educational system.* ADJ QUALIT

sang /sæŋ/ is the past tense of **sing.**

sanguine /sæŋgwɪn/. If you are **sanguine** about something, you are cheerful and confident that things will happen as you want them to. EG *He was not sanguine about Bill's probable reactions.* ADJ QUALIT

sanitarium /sænɪteərɪəm/. See **sanatorium.**

sanitary /sænɪtəʰriʰ/. **1** If you say that a place is not **sanitary**, you mean that it is not very clean. EG *I sat in a small and not very sanitary café in Soho.* ADJ QUALIT

2 Sanitary also means concerned with keeping things clean and hygienic. EG *Sanitary conditions in the hospitals had deteriorated rapidly... ...a sanitary inspector.* ADJ CLASSIF : ATTRIB

sanitary napkin, sanitary napkins. A **sanitary napkin** is the same as a sanitary towel. N COUNT American

sanitary towel, sanitary towels. A **sanitary towel** is a pad of thick soft material which women wear during their periods. N COUNT

sanitation /sænɪteɪʃəⁿn/ is the process of keeping places clean and hygienic, especially by providing a sewage system and a clean water supply. EG *They live in conditions of appalling sanitation... ...the lack of sanitation and adequate health care.* N UNCOUNT

sanity /sænɪʰtiʰ/. **1** A person's **sanity** is their ability to think and behave normally and reasonably. EG ...*the doubts he had about Wilt's sanity... On this occasion they lost their sanity.* N UNCOUNT

2 Sanity is also the quality of having a purpose and a regular pattern, rather than being confusing and worrying. EG *They give some point and sanity to daily life.* N UNCOUNT

sank /sæŋk/ is the past tense of **sink.**

Santa Claus /sæntə klɔːz/ is another name for Father Christmas. N PROPER

sap /sæp/, **saps, sapping, sapped. 1** If something **saps** your strength or confidence, it gradually weakens or destroys it over a period of time. EG *The constant tension at work was sapping my energy.* V+O

2 Sap is the watery liquid in plants and trees. EG *The sap was rising in the maples.* N UNCOUNT

sapling /sæplɪŋ/, **saplings.** A **sapling** is a young tree. EG ...*a row of saplings.* N COUNT

sapphire /sæfaɪə/, **sapphires.** A **sapphire** is a precious stone which is blue in colour. EG ...*a sapphire and diamond ring.* N COUNT

sarcasm /sɑːkæzəᵘm/ is speech or writing which actually means the opposite of what it seems to say. Sarcasm is usually intended to mock or insult someone. EG *'Oh yeah,' said Jenny with broad sarcasm, 'I notice how you hate getting paid.'* N UNCOUNT

sarcastic /sɑːkæstɪk/. Someone who is **sarcastic** says or does the opposite of what they really mean in order to mock or insult someone. EG *She seemed her usual sarcastic self at dinner... He turned to me with a sarcastic smile.* ◇ **sarcastically.** EG *'Do you mind if I take notes?' said Stuart sarcastically.* ADJ QUALIT ◇ ADV

sardine /sɑːdiːn/, **sardines.** A **sardine** is a kind of small sea fish. EG ...*tins of sardines.* N COUNT

sardonic /sɑːdɒnɪk/. Someone who is **sardonic** is mocking or scornful in their behaviour. EG ...*a sardonic young man who never joined in the fun... ...a sardonic chuckle.* ◇ **sardonically.** EG *She smiled sardonically.* ADJ QUALIT ◇ ADV

sari /sɑːriʰ/, **saris.** A **sari** is a piece of clothing worn especially by Indian women. It consists of a long piece of thin material that is wrapped around the body. N COUNT

sartorial /sɑːtɔːrɪəl/ means relating to clothes and to the way they are made or worn. EG *People's sartorial habits have changed.* ADJ CLASSIF : ATTRIB Formal

sash /sæʃ/, **sashes**. A **sash** is a long piece of cloth N COUNT
which people wear round their waist or over one
shoulder, especially with formal or official clothes.

sash window, sash windows. A **sash window** is N COUNT
a window which consists of two frames placed one
above the other. The window can be opened by
sliding one frame over the other.

sat /sæt/ is the past tense and past participle of **sit**.

Satan /ˈseɪtəⁿn/. **Satan** is the Devil, considered to N PROPER
be the chief opponent of God.

satanic /səˈtænɪk/. Something that is **satanic** is ADJ QUALIT
considered to be caused by or influenced by Satan.
EG ...a satanic cult.

satchel /ˈsætʃəl/, **satchels**. A **satchel** is a bag N COUNT
with a long strap that schoolchildren use for carrying books.

sated /ˈseɪtɪ²d/. If you are **sated** with something, ADJ CLASSIF :
you have had more of it than you can enjoy at one USU PRED
time. EG They were sated with fresh air and hard Formal
exercise.

satellite /ˈsætəlaɪt/, **satellites**. 1 A **satellite** is 1.1 N COUNT
an object which has been sent into space in order OR by+N
to collect information or to be part of a communications system. Satellites move continually round
the earth or around another planet. EG ...communi-
cations satellites... The pictures were transmitted
by satellite. 1.2 a natural object in space that N COUNT
moves round a planet or star. EG Astronomers were
excited to discover a small, oddly shaped satellite,
Jupiter's 14th moon.

2 You can also use **satellite** to refer to a country N COUNT
or organization which has no real power of its own,
but which is dependent on a larger and more
powerful country or organization. EG The party
consolidates its power by building up satellite organizations.

satin /ˈsætɪn/ is a smooth and shiny kind of cloth, N UNCOUNT
usually made from silk. EG The bride was dressed in
white satin.

satire /ˈsætaɪə/, **satires**. 1 **Satire** is humour and N UNCOUNT
exaggeration that is used to show how foolish or
wicked some people's behaviour or ideas are. EG
...exquisite touches of irony and satire.

2 A **satire** is a play or novel that uses satire to N COUNT
criticize something. EG ...a brilliant political satire...
...a satire on existing society.

satirical /səˈtɪrɪkəⁿl/. A drawing or piece of writ- ADJ QUALIT
ing that is **satirical** uses satire to criticize something. EG ...a satirical fortnightly magazine... He
attacked the stupidity of women's trailing skirts in
satirical cartoons.

satisfaction /ˌsætɪsˈfækʃəⁿn/. 1 **Satisfaction** is the N UNCOUNT
pleasure that you feel when you do something that
you wanted or needed to do. EG She read what she
had written with satisfaction... ...a sigh which expressed her satisfaction at being there... ...a sense
of satisfaction.

2 If you get **satisfaction** from someone, you get N UNCOUNT
money or an apology from them because of some
harm or injustice which has been done to you. EG
Consumers who have been unable to get satisfaction from their local branch should write direct to
the Chairman.

3 If you do something to someone's **satisfaction**, PHRASE
they are happy with the way you have done it. EG
Every detail was worked out to everyone's satisfaction.

satisfactory /ˌsætɪsˈfæktəⁿriʲ/. Something that is ADJ QUALIT
satisfactory is acceptable to you or fulfils a
particular need or purpose. EG His doctor described
his general state of health as fairly satisfactory... It
will be much more satisfactory if you are given
more responsibility. ◊ **satisfactorily**. EG She was ◊ ADV
not recovering satisfactorily from the accident.

satisfied /ˈsætɪsfaɪd/. 1 If you are **satisfied** with ADJ QUALIT
something, you are happy because you have got
what you wanted. EG He was well satisfied with the
success of the aircraft... ...satisfied customers who
had bought the car.

2 If you are **satisfied** that something is true or has ADJ PRED
been done properly, you are convinced about this
after checking it. EG He turned to me and nodded,
satisfied... We can be satisfied that we've missed
nothing important.

satisfy /ˈsætɪsfaɪ/, **satisfies, satisfying, satisfied**. 1 If someone or something **satisfies** you, V+O
they give you enough of what you want to make
you pleased or contented. EG More frequent feeding
will usually help to satisfy a baby... He had not even
been able to satisfy her simple needs... The firm
has been unable to satisfy demand for its new
small car.

2 If someone or something **satisfies** you that V+O OR
something is true or has been done properly, they V+REFL :
convince you by giving you more information or by OFT+REPORT,
showing you what has been done. EG He would need ONLY that
to satisfy the authorities that he had paid tax for
the previous three years... I glanced around, satisfied myself that the last diner had left, and turned
off the lights.

3 If you **satisfy** the requirements for something, V+O
you are good enough or suitable to fulfil these
requirements. EG There is some doubt whether they
can satisfy our entrance requirements.

satisfying /ˈsætɪsfaɪɪŋ/. Something that is **satisfy- ADJ QUAL
ing** gives you a feeling of pleasure and fulfilment.
EG There's nothing more satisfying than doing the
work you love.

satsuma /sætˈsuːmə/, **satsumas**. A **satsuma** is a N COUNT
fruit that looks like a small orange.

saturate /ˈsætʃəreɪt/, **saturates, saturating,
saturated**. 1 If a place **is saturated** with things, it V+O : USU PASS
is so full of those things that no more can be added. +with/in
EG The next morning, teams saturated the community with literature about the attack... The area
where his brother was killed was saturated with
photographs of the wanted man. ◊ **saturation** ◊ N UNCOUNT
/ˌsætʃəˈreɪʃəⁿn/. EG Even when the market reaches
saturation, the process doesn't stop.

2 If someone or something **is saturated**, they V+O : USU PASS
become extremely wet. EG Philip was totally saturated.

Saturday /ˈsætədiʲ/, **Saturdays**. **Saturday** is one N UNCOUNT
of the seven days of the week. It is the day after OR N COUNT
Friday and before Sunday. EG What did you do on
Saturday?... I spent a Saturday being trained...
Fridays and Saturdays are more lively.

saturnine /ˈsætənaɪn/. Someone who is **saturnine** ADJ QUALIT
is gloomy and unfriendly. EG A saturnine customs Literary
officer looked through our baggage.

sauce /sɔːs/, **sauces**. A **sauce** is a thick liquid N MASS
which is served with other food. EG ...tomato sauce...
...chicken in walnut sauce... Make a sauce to go
with the fish.

saucepan /ˈsɔːspən/, **saucepans**. A **saucepan** is a N COUNT
deep metal cooking pot, usually with a long handle
and a lid.

saucer /ˈsɔːsə/, **saucers**. A **saucer** is a small N COUNT
curved plate on which you stand a cup. EG She OR N PART
offered me tea in her best cup and saucer... ...a
saucer of milk. ● See also **flying saucer**.

saucy /ˈsɔːsiʲ/, **saucier, sauciest**. Someone who is ADJ QUALIT
saucy is rather cheeky in a light-hearted, amusing Informal
way. EG Don't be saucy with me.

sauna /ˈsɔːnə/, **saunas**. A **sauna** is 1 a hot steam N COUNT
bath, after which you usually have a bath in cold
water. 2 the room or building where you have a
sauna.

saunter /ˈsɔːntə/, **saunters, sauntering, sauntered**. If you **saunter** somewhere, you walk there V+A
in a slow, casual way. EG He sauntered up and
down, looking at the shops and the people.

sausage /ˈsɒsɪdʒ/, **sausages**. 1 **Sausage** is finely N UNCOUNT
minced meat which is mixed with other ingredi-

Does sausage have a savoury flavour?

ents and put into a thin casing like a tube. EG *We lunched on garlic sausage and bread.*

2 A **sausage** is a tube-shaped piece of sausage meat. EG *...bacon, eggs, and sausages for breakfast.*   N COUNT

sausage roll, sausage rolls. A **sausage roll** is a small amount of sausage meat which is covered with pastry and cooked.   N COUNT

sauté /ˈsəʊteɪ/, **sautés, sautéing, sautéed.** When you **sauté** food, you fry it quickly in hot oil or butter. EG *Sauté the chicken breasts until they are golden brown.* ◊ **sautéed.** EG *...sautéed potatoes.*   V+O   ◊ ADJ CLASSIF

savage /ˈsævɪdʒ/, **savages, savaging, savaged. 1** Something that is **savage** is extremely cruel, violent, and uncontrolled. EG *His voice was loud and savage... ...two weeks of savage rioting... ...one of those savage remarks about the futility of life.* ◊ **savagely.** EG *The dog began to bark savagely.*   ADJ QUALIT   ◊ ADV

2 If you refer to someone as a **savage**, you mean that they are cruel, violent, or uncivilized. EG *You don't understand what savages these people are.*   N COUNT

3 If a dog **savages** you, it attacks you violently.   V+O

4 If you **savage** someone or **savage** something they have done, you criticize them severely. EG *An opposition spokesman savaged the Government's housing investment programme.*   V+O

savagery /ˈsævɪdʒri[1]/ is extremely cruel and violent behaviour. EG *I was appalled by the savagery of the attack.*   N UNCOUNT

save /seɪv/, **saves, saving, saved. 1** If you **save** someone or something, you help them to avoid harm or to escape from a dangerous or unpleasant situation. EG *An artificial heart could save his life... She saved him from drowning... Only love can save the world.*   V+O: OFT+*from*

2 If you **save** money, you gradually collect it by not spending it, usually so that you can buy something that you want. EG *They had managed to save enough to buy a house... She told him that she was saving with a building society.*   V+O OR V

3 If you **save** time or money, you prevent the loss or waste of it. EG *This measure would save the government £185 million... You could save up to 75 per cent of your heat loss by efficient insulation... The manufacturers save money on promotion... It's an attempt to save on labour costs.*   V+O: OFT+*on,* OR V+O+O, V+O+O

4 If you **save** something, you keep it because it will be needed later. EG *Always save business letters, bills, and receipts... Will you save him a place at your table?*   V+O OR V+O+O

5 If someone or something **saves** you from doing something or **saves** you the trouble of doing it, they do it for you or change the situation so that you do not have to do it. EG *Well, that saves me from denying it... A vote would save us a lot of trouble... You could save yourself a lot of work if you used a computer... Using electronic circuit boards saves wiring up thousands of individual transistors.*   V+O+*from,* V+O+O, V-REFL+O, OR V+-ING

6 If a goalkeeper **saves** or **saves** a shot, he or she succeeds in preventing the ball from going into the goal. EG *The shot was saved by Buller, who returned to Liverpool last week after three seasons with Barcelona.* ▶ used as a noun. EG *He made a brilliant save.*   V OR V+O   ▶ N COUNT

7 You can use **save** or **save for** to introduce the only things, people, or ideas that your main statement does not apply to. EG *No visitors are allowed save in the most exceptional cases... The curtained stage was empty save for a few pieces of furniture.*   PREP Formal

save up. If you **save up** money, you collect it by not spending it, usually so that you can buy something that you want. EG *It took me a year to save up for a new coat.*   PHRASAL VB: V+ADV

saving /ˈseɪvɪŋ/, **savings. 1** A **saving** is a reduction in the amount of time or money that is used or needed. EG *...a very great saving in cost as well as in manpower... The new management had achieved even bigger savings.*   N COUNT

2 Your **savings** are the money that you have   N PLURAL

saved, especially in a bank or a building society. EG *She drew out all her savings... ...a savings account.*

-saving combines with words like 'time' and 'labour' to describe something which prevents the wasting of time or labour. EG *...energy-saving gadgets.*

saviour /ˈseɪvjə/, **saviours. 1** A **saviour** is a person who saves people from danger. EG *Many people regarded Churchill as the saviour of the country.*   N COUNT

2 In Christianity, the **Saviour** is Jesus Christ.   N PROPER: *the*+N

savour /ˈseɪvə/, **savours, savouring, savoured;** spelled **savor** in American English. **1** If you **savour** food or drink, you eat or drink it slowly in order to taste its full flavour and to enjoy it properly. EG *Meadows took a bite of meat, savoured it, and said, 'Fantastic.'*   V+O

2 If you **savour** an experience, you take great pleasure and delight in it, enjoying it as much as you can. EG *He leaned back into his seat, savouring the comfort.*   V+O

savoury /ˈseɪvəri[1]/; spelled **savory** in American English. **1** **Savoury** food has a salty or spicy flavour rather than a sweet one.   ADJ QUALIT

2 If you describe something as not very **savoury**, you mean that it is not very pleasant, respectable, or morally acceptable. EG *...the less savoury episodes in her past.*   ADJ QUALIT: USU WITH BROAD NEG

saw /sɔː/, **saws, sawing, sawed, sawn** /sɔːn/. **1** **Saw** is the past tense of **see.**

2 A **saw** is a tool for cutting wood, which has a blade with sharp teeth along one edge. See picture at TOOLS.   N COUNT

3 If you **saw** something, you cut it with a saw. EG *I started sawing the branches off the main trunk.*   V+O: OFT+A

sawdust /ˈsɔːdʌst/ is very small pieces of wood which are produced when you saw wood.   N UNCOUNT

sax /sæks/, **saxes.** A **sax** is the same as a saxophone. EG *...a lovely sax... There was one kid who played sax.*   N COUNT OR N UNCOUNT Informal

saxophone /ˈsæksəfəʊn/, **saxophones.** A **saxophone** is a musical wind instrument. It is made of metal in a curved shape, and is often played in jazz bands. See picture at MUSICAL INSTRUMENTS. EG *...Kessler on the bass, Westerman on the saxophone, Dailey on the percussion... He revolutionised jazz saxophone playing.*   N COUNT OR N UNCOUNT

say /seɪ/, **says** /sez/, **saying** /ˈseɪɪŋ/, **said** /sed/. **1** When you **say** something, you speak words. EG *'Please come in,' she said... He said it was an accident... People kept coming up to us to say hello... He had said nothing to me about his meeting... He knelt down and said his prayers.*   V-SPEECH

2 You use **say** to introduce what you are actually saying, or to indicate that you are expressing an opinion or admitting a fact. EG *I just want to say how pleased I am to be here... I must say, it's a very sexist play... I think I can safely say that we have all learnt a great deal this evening... One thing you have to say about Americans: they love drama.*   V+REPORT OR V+O

3 If you **say** something **to** yourself, you think it. EG *I began to say to myself, 'What about becoming an actor?'*   PHRASE

4 If you **say** something in a letter or a book, for example, you express it in writing. EG *She wrote to say she wanted to meet me in London... There were stickers all over the crate saying: 'Glass – Handle with Care'.*   V+QUOTE OR REPORT

5 If something such as a clock or map **says** something, it gives you information when you look at it. EG *The clock says that it is six o'clock... The road was not where the map said it should be.*   V+O OR V+REPORT: ONLY *that*

6 If something **says** something about a person, situation, or thing, it reveals something about them. EG *The title says it all... Their glances seemed to be saying something about their relationship.*   V+O OR V+REPORT: ONLY *that*

7 If you state that you can't **say** something, you are indicating in a polite or indirect way that it is not   V: MODAL+V, WITH BROAD NEG the case or is not true. EG *I can't say I've heard of them... No one could say he was not practical.*

8 You use **say** in expressions such as 'just say' and 'let's say' when you want to discuss something that might possibly happen or be true. EG *Just say you found treasure in your garden. Would you sell it?*   V+REPORT: ONLY *that*

9 You also use **say 9.1** when you mention something as an example. EG *Compare, say, a Michelangelo painting with a Van Gogh.* **9.2** when you mention an approximate amount or time. EG *...in the next, say, ten years.*

10 If you have a **say** in something, you have the right to give your opinion and influence decisions. EG *People want a much greater say in how the country should be governed.* ● If you **have** your **say**, you give your opinion.   N SING   ● PHRASE

11 Say is also used in these phrases. **11.1** You use **to say the least** to suggest that a situation is actually much more serious, shocking, or extreme than you say it is. EG *She lacked tact (to say the least) in expressing her views.* **11.2** You use **that is to say** to indicate that you are about to express the same idea more clearly. EG *The Romans left Britain in 410 AD – that is to say, England was under Roman rule for nearly 500 years.* **11.3** You use **to say nothing of** when you add something which gives even more strength to the point you are making. EG *The effort required is immense, to say nothing of the cost.* **11.4** If something **goes without saying**, it is obvious or is bound to be true. EG *It goes without saying that I am grateful for all your help.* **11.5** You use **say** in expressions such as 'What would you say to a cup of tea?' as a way of making a suggestion or an offer. **11.6** You use **'I wouldn't say no'** to indicate that you would like something, especially something that has just been offered to you. EG *'Drink, Ted?' – 'I wouldn't say no, Brian.'* **11.7** You use the expression **'I'll say this for** him, her, or them', before you mention a quality that you admire in someone, especially when you have been criticizing them. EG *I will say this for the Suffolk farmers, they're loyal.* **11.8** If something **has a lot to be said for it**, it has a lot of good qualities. **11.9** If you **don't have much to say for** yourself, you do not speak much.   ADV SEN   ADV SEN Formal   PHRASE   PHRASE   PHRASE Informal   CONVENTION Informal   PHRASE   PHRASE   PHRASE Informal

saying /ˈseɪɪŋ/, **sayings**. A **saying** is a traditional sentence that people often say and that gives advice or information about human life and experience. EG *There is a saying that 'man shall not live by bread alone'.*   N COUNT

scab /skæb/, **scabs. 1** A **scab** is a hard, dry covering that forms over the surface of a wound. EG *A great scab had formed on his right knee.*   N COUNT

2 You can use **scab** to refer to someone who continues to work when the people that he or she works with are on strike; used showing disapproval.   N COUNT

scaffold /ˈskæfəʊld/, **scaffolds.** A **scaffold** is a platform on which criminals used to be executed. EG *Guy Fawkes died on the scaffold.*   N COUNT

scaffolding /ˈskæfəʊldɪŋ/ is a temporary framework of metal poles and wooden boards that is used by workmen to climb up and stand on while they are constructing, repairing, or painting the outside walls of a tall building.   N UNCOUNT

scald /skɔːld/, **scalds, scalding, scalded. 1** If you **scald** yourself, you burn yourself with very hot liquid or steam. EG *When it was cool enough not to scald my lips, I swallowed the coffee and asked for more.*   V-REFL OR V+O

2 A **scald** is a burn caused by very hot liquid or steam.   N COUNT

scalding /ˈskɔːldɪŋ/. Something that is **scalding** is extremely hot. EG *...scalding coffee.*   ADJ CLASSIF

scale /skeɪl/, **scales, scaling, scaled. 1** If you refer to the **scale** of something, you are referring to its size, especially when it is very big. EG *The scale of change is so enormous... ...the sheer scale of the United States.*   N SING+SUPP

2 You use **scale** in expressions such as **large scale** and **on a small scale** when you are indicating the size, extent, or degree of one thing when compared to other similar things. EG *The district grew peas on a large scale... The plan was never very grand in scale... ...small scale methods of getting energy.*   N UNCOUNT: OFT+SUPP

3 A **scale** is a set of levels or numbers which are used in a particular system of measuring things or are used in comparing things. EG *...the scale by which we measure the severity of earthquakes... ...a temperature scale... ...the pay scale... It happened everywhere, through the social scale.*   N COUNT: USU+SUPP

4 The **scale** of a map, plan, or model is the relationship between the measurements of something in the real world and the measurements of it in the map, plan, or model. EG *...a map with a scale of 1:50,000.* ▸ used as an adjective. EG *I used to collect scale models of ships.* ● If a map, plan, or model is **to scale**, it is accurately drawn or made according to the scale being used. EG *Draw it out to scale neatly on graph paper.*   N COUNT OR N UNCOUNT   ▸ ADJ CLASSIF   ● PHRASE

5 A **scale** is also a sequence of musical notes that are played or sung in an upward or downward order. EG *...the scale of C.*   N COUNT

6 The **scales** of fish or reptiles are the small, flat pieces of hard skin that cover their bodies.   N COUNT: USU PLURAL

7 Scales are a piece of equipment for weighing things, for example for weighing amounts of food that you need in order to make a particular dish. EG *...a pair of scales.*   N PLURAL

8 If you **scale** something high or steep, you climb up or over it. EG *She scaled the barrier like a Commando.*   V+O

scale down. If something **is scaled down**, it has been made smaller in size or amount than it used to be. EG *The operations were scaled down... ...a scaled-down version.*   PHRASAL VB: V+O+ADV, USU PASS

scalloped /ˈskɒləpt, skæl-/. **Scalloped** objects are decorated with a series of small curves along the edges. EG *...a blue and green scalloped design.*   ADJ CLASSIF: ATTRIB

scalp /skælp/, **scalps, scalping, scalped. 1** Your **scalp** is the skin under the hair on your head. EG *...rubbing his sore scalp.*   N COUNT

2 To **scalp** someone who has just been killed means to remove the skin and hair from the top of their head. EG *The whole family had been scalped.*   V+O

3 A **scalp** is also the piece of skin and hair that is removed when someone is scalped.   N COUNT

scalpel /ˈskælpəl/, **scalpels.** A **scalpel** is a knife with a short, thin, sharp blade. Scalpels are used by surgeons during operations.   N COUNT

scaly /ˈskeɪliː/. Something that is **scaly** is covered in small, stiff patches of hard skin. EG *...round patches of scaly skin.*   ADJ QUALIT

scamper /ˈskæmpə/, **scampers, scampering, scampered.** When people or small animals **scamper** somewhere, they move with small, quick, bouncing steps. EG *The squirrels scamper along the twigs.*   V+A

scampi /ˈskæmpiː/ are large prawns that are often fried in batter and eaten.   N PLURAL British

scan /skæn/, **scans, scanning, scanned. 1** When you **scan** an area, a group of things, or a piece of writing, you look at it very carefully, usually because you are looking for something in particular. EG *Anxiously Carol scanned their faces to see who she might know... ...lifeguards scanning the sea for shark fins.*   V+O

2 If a machine **scans** something, it examines it quickly, for example by moving a beam of light or X-rays over it. EG *The reconnaissance plane's job was to scan the oceans with its radar.* ▸ used as a noun. EG *A liver scan was performed.*   V+O   ▸ N COUNT

Is a scapegoat an animal?

scandal /skændəⁿl/, **scandals. 1** A **scandal** is a N COUNT
situation or event that a lot of people think is very
shocking and immoral. EG *We can't afford another
scandal in the firm... It became known as the
Marconi scandal.*

2 Scandal is talk about people's shocking and N UNCOUNT
immoral behaviour. EG *Someone must have been
spreading scandal.*

3 You can refer to something as a **scandal** when N SING : a+N
you are angry about it. EG *The defences were a
scandal.*

scandalize /skændəⁿlaɪz/, **scandalizes,** V+O : USU PASS
scandalizing, scandalized; also spelled **scandal-
ise.** If you **are scandalized,** you are shocked and
offended. EG *He was uncertain whether to laugh or
be scandalized.*

scandalous /skændəⁿləs/. **1** Something that is ADJ QUALIT
scandalous is considered immoral and shocking.
EG *There were some scandalous stories about her...
...scandalous scenes of ladies with bare breasts.*

2 You can describe something as **scandalous** ADJ QUALIT
when it makes you very angry. EG *It is scandalous
that the public should be treated in this way.*

◇ **scandalously.** EG *...schemes offering scandalous-* ◇ SUBMOD
ly large tax advantages.

scanner /skænə/, **scanners.** A **scanner** is a N COUNT
machine which is used to examine things, for
example by moving a beam of light or X-rays over
them. Scanners are used in places such as hospitals, airports, and research laboratories.

scant /skænt/. If you say that something receives ADJ QUALIT :
scant attention, you mean that it receives less ATTRIB
attention than you think it should receive. EG *The
campaign was conducted with scant regard for
truth.*

scanty /skænti¹/, **scantier, scantiest.** You de- ADJ QUALIT
scribe something as **scanty** when it is smaller in
quantity or size than you think it should be. EG *...a
rather scanty but enthusiastic audience... ...a waitress in her scanty nightclub costume... ...scanty
information about their pupils.* ◇ **scantily.** EG *The* ◇ ADV
bedroom was scantily furnished.

scapegoat /skeɪpgəʊt/, **scapegoats.** If someone N COUNT
is made a **scapegoat,** they are blamed for something that has happened, although it may not be
their fault, because other people are very angry
about it. EG *In their search for a scapegoat, the
government found an easy target in the unions.*

scar /skɑː/, **scars, scarring, scarred. 1** A **scar** is N COUNT
a mark on the skin which is left after a wound has
healed. EG *There was a scar on her arm.*

2 If your skin **is scarred,** it is badly marked as a V+O : USU PASS
result of a wound. EG *They will be scarred for life.*

3 If an object **is scarred,** it is damaged and there V+O : USU PASS
are ugly marks on it. EG *...the scarred tree trunk.*

4 A **scar** is also a permanent effect on someone's N COUNT
mind that results from a very unpleasant physical
or emotional experience. EG *The scars of poverty
have undoubtedly left their mark.*

5 If an unpleasant experience **scars** you, it has a V+O
permanent effect on you, and influences the way
you think and behave. EG *It wasn't the violence of
the attack that scarred my mind.*

scarce /skeəs/, **scarcer, scarcest. 1** If something ADJ QUALIT
is **scarce,** there is not very much of it. EG *...an
environment where water is scarce.*

2 If you **make** yourself **scarce,** you quickly leave PHRASE
the place you are in, usually in order to avoid a Informal
difficult or embarrassing situation.

scarcely /skeəsli¹/. **1** You use **scarcely** to say ADV BRD NEG
that something is only just true or is not quite true.
EG *I can scarcely remember what we ate... They
were scarcely ever apart... ...a very young man,
scarcely more than a boy.*

2 You can use **scarcely** in an ironic way to say ADV BRD NEG
that something is certainly not true. EG *There could
scarcely be a less promising environment for children.*

3 If you say **scarcely** had one thing happened ADV BRD NEG

when something else happened, you mean that the
first event was followed immediately by the second. EG *Scarcely had the car drawn to a halt when
armed police surrounded it.*

scarcity /skeəsɪ¹ti¹/. If there is a **scarcity** of N UNCOUNT
something, there is not enough of it. EG *...the* Formal
scarcity of food.

scare /skeə/, **scares, scaring, scared. 1** When V+O
people or things **scare** you, they frighten you. EG *I
didn't mean to scare you.* ● If something **scares** ● PHRASE
the life out of you or **scares the hell out of** you, Informal
it makes you very frightened.

2 If something gives you a **scare,** it frightens you. N COUNT
EG *The first attack gave me a scare... That night I
had an even worse scare.*

3 A **scare** is a situation in which many people are N COUNT :
afraid because they think that something danger- USU+SUPP
ous is happening. EG *Since none of the fragments
picked up was radioactive the scare died down...
...a rabies scare.*

scare away or **scare off.** If you **scare** animals PHRASAL VB :
or people **away** or **scare** them **off,** you frighten V+O+ADV
them so that they go away. EG *The least shadow or
movement would scare the fish away.*

scarecrow /skeəkrəʊ/, **scarecrows.** A **scare-** N COUNT
crow is an object in the shape of a person, which is
put in a field where crops are growing in order to
frighten birds away.

scared /skeəd/. **1** If you are **scared** of someone or ADJ PRED
something, you are frightened of them. EG *Every-
body's scared of him... He was terribly scared... She
was too shocked and scared to move.* ● If you are ● PHRASE
scared stiff or **scared to death,** you are extreme- Informal
ly frightened.

2 If you are **scared** that something unpleasant ADJ PRED
might happen, you are nervous and worried be- +REPORT
cause you think that it might happen. EG *I'm scared* OR +of
*that these will turn out to be the wrong ones...
They're scared of making a fool of themselves.*

scarf /skɑːf/, **scarfs** or **scarves** /skɑːvz/. A **scarf** N COUNT
is a piece of cloth that you wear round your neck
or head, usually to keep yourself warm. See picture
at CLOTHES. EG *The girl wrapped her black woollen
scarf tightly round her neck.*

scarlet /skɑːlə¹t/, **scarlets.** Something that is ADJ COLOUR
scarlet is bright red. EG *...a scarlet handkerchief...
...silky materials in scarlets, blues, and greens.*

scarlet fever is an infectious disease which N UNCOUNT
causes a painful throat, a high temperature, and a
red rash.

scarves /skɑːvz/ is a plural of **scarf.**

scary /skeəri¹/. Something that is **scary** is rather ADJ QUALIT
frightening. EG *It was a scary moment.* Informal

scathing /skeɪðɪŋ/. If you are **scathing** about ADJ QUALIT :
something, you criticize it harshly and scornfully. OFT+about
EG *Miss Jackson was scathing about our efforts... ...a
rather scathing article about lady novelists.*

◇ **scathingly.** EG *He refers scathingly to these* ◇ ADV
superstitions.

scatter /skætə/, **scatters, scattering, scat-**
tered. 1 If you **scatter** things over an area, you V+O : USU+A
throw or drop them so that they spread all over the
area. EG *Parrots scatter their food about and make
a mess... The papers had been scattered all over
the floor.*

2 If a group of people **scatter,** they suddenly V
separate and move in different directions. EG *The
boys scattered, squealing in horror.*

3 A **scatter** of things is a number of them spread N PART : SING
over an area in an irregular way. EG *My eye was* Literary
drawn to a small scatter of bone fragments.

scattered /skætə¹d/. **1** Things that are **scattered** ADJ CLASSIF
are spread over an area and are a long way from
each other. EG *We drove over the debris scattered
across the streets... The old people could not visit
their scattered families.*

2 If something is **scattered** with a lot of small ADJ PRED+
things, they are spread all over it. EG *Her hair was* with
scattered with pollen.

scattering /skǽtəⁿrɪŋ/. A **scattering** of things is N PART : SING a small number of them spread over a large area. Literary EG ...*the blue night sky with its scattering of stars.*

scavenge /skǽvɪndʒ/, **scavenges, scavenging,** V : OFT+*for* **scavenged**. If someone **scavenges** for food or OR V+O other things or **scavenges** things, they collect them by searching among waste and unwanted objects. EG *I had no resources at all, except what I could scavenge or beg.* ◇ **scavenger, scaven-** ◇ N COUNT **gers.** EG ...*a scavenger living from the dustbins behind restaurants.*

scenario /sɪnɑːrɪəʊ/, **scenarios. 1** If you talk N COUNT about a likely or possible **scenario**, you are talking about the way in which a situation may develop. EG *The death of democracy becomes quite a likely scenario.*

2 The **scenario** of a film is a piece of writing that N COUNT gives an outline of the story. Technical

scene /siːn/, **scenes. 1** A **scene** is one of the parts N COUNT of a play, film, or book in which a series of events happen in the same place. EG ...*the balcony scene from 'Romeo and Juliet'... It was like some scene from a Victorian novel.*

2 Paintings and drawings of places are sometimes N COUNT+SUPP called **scenes.** EG ...*the harbour scenes that he drew as a teenager.*

3 You can describe something that you see as a N COUNT+SUPP **scene** of a particular kind. EG *The moon rose over a scene of extraordinary destruction... ...a scene of domestic tranquillity.*

4 The **scene** of an event is the place where it N COUNT : happened. EG ...*the scene of the crime.* USU SING

5 If you have a **change of scene**, you go some- PHRASE where different after being in a particular place for a long time. EG *She was excited by the thought of a change of scene.*

6 You can refer to an area of activity as a N SING : *the*+N particular type of **scene.** EG ...*the business scene...* +SUPP ...*the German political scene.*

7 If you make a **scene**, you embarrass people by N COUNT publicly showing your anger about something. EG *There was a scene, and Father called Christopher a liar... Clarissa dear, please don't make a nasty scene.*

8 Scene is also used in these phrases. **8.1** If PHRASES something is done **behind the scenes**, it is done secretly. EG *Officials working behind the scenes urged them to avoid further confrontation.* **8.2** When someone appears **on the scene**, they arrive. **8.3** You also say that someone or something ap- pears **on the scene** when they become widely known or used. EG *The computer burst upon the scene around 1950.* **8.4** If you say that a place or Informal activity **is not** your **scene**, you mean that you do not like it. **8.5** If you **set the scene** for someone, you tell them what they need to know in order to understand what is going to happen or be said next. EG *First of all let's set the scene: in 1900 the population of the world was much smaller.*

scenery /siːnəⁿriː/. **1** When you are in the country- N SING OR side, you can refer to everything you see around N UNCOUNT you as the **scenery.** EG *As we neared the border the scenery became lush and spectacular... We had time to admire the scenery.*

2 In a theatre, the **scenery** is the painted cloth and N SING OR boards at the back of the stage. EG *Who designed* N UNCOUNT *the scenery?... The production uses a minimum of scenery.*

scenic /siːnɪk/. A **scenic** place or route is attrac- ADJ QUALIT tive and has nice views. EG *The island has a scenic coastline... ...a scenic railway.*

scent /sɛnt/, **scents, scenting, scented. 1** A N COUNT **scent** is a pleasant smell. EG ...*the overpowering scent of English garden flowers.*

2 Scent is a liquid that women put on their skin to N MASS make themselves smell nice. EG *She walked in smelling of French scent.*

3 An animal's **scent** is its smell. EG *The queen bee* N UNCOUNT *produces a scent which attracts the other bees.* OR N COUNT

4 When an animal **scents** something, it becomes V+O aware of it by smelling it. EG ...*when it scents its prey.*

5 If you **scent** something, you feel that it is going to V+O happen. EG *He scented danger.* Literary

scented /sɛntɪd/. Something that is **scented** has ADJ CLASSIF a pleasant smell. EG ...*scented soap... ...a sweet-scented variety of rose.*

sceptic /skɛptɪk/, **sceptics;** spelled **skeptic** in N COUNT American English. A **sceptic** is a person who has doubts about things that other people believe.

sceptical /skɛptɪkəⁿl/; spelled **skeptical** in ADJ QUALIT American English. If you are **sceptical** about something, you have doubts about it. EG *Robert's father was sceptical about hypnotism... Mrs Swal-low gave a sceptical grunt.* ◇ **sceptically.** EG *I had* ◇ ADV *listened sceptically to the broadcast.*

scepticism /skɛptɪsɪzəⁿm/; spelled **skepticism** in N UNCOUNT American English. **Scepticism** is great doubt about something. EG *He listened with growing scep-ticism... There was widespread scepticism about these proposals.*

schedule /ʃɛdjuːl/, **schedules, scheduling, scheduled;** also pronounced /skɛdjuːl/, especially in American English.

1 A **schedule** is a plan that gives a list of events or N COUNT tasks, together with the times at which each thing should happen or be done. EG ...*the next place on his busy schedule... ...the daily schedule of classes.*

2 If something is done **to schedule** or **according** PHRASE **to schedule**, it is done at the times that were planned in advance. EG *The operations have been carried out according to schedule.*

3 If something happens **on schedule**, it happens at PHRASE the time planned. EG *Simon showed up right on schedule.*

4 If something happens **ahead of schedule**, it PHRASE happens earlier than the time planned. EG *We arrived several hours ahead of schedule.*

5 If you are **behind schedule**, you are doing things PHRASE later than the times planned.

6 If something is **scheduled** to happen, arrange- V+O+*to*-INF ments have been made for it to happen. EG *He was* OR *for* : *scheduled to leave Plymouth yesterday... A meet-* USU PASS *ing had been scheduled for that day... ...a depart-ment store now scheduled for demolition.*

7 A **schedule** is also a written list of things, for N COUNT example a list of prices, details, or conditions. Formal

scheme /skiːm/, **schemes, scheming, schemed.**

1 A **scheme** is a large-scale plan or arrangement N COUNT produced by a government or other organization. EG ...*the State pension scheme... ...a scheme to build 63 houses.*

2 You can also refer to a person's plan for achiev- N COUNT ing something as a **scheme.** EG ...*an ambitious scheme... ...some scheme for perfecting the world.*

3 When people **scheme**, they make secret plans; V : OFT+A used showing disapproval. EG *He schemed against her... She schemed on her daughter's behalf.*

◇ **scheming.** EG ...*a ruthless, scheming man... ...his* ◇ ADJ CLASSIF *scheming old father.* ATTRIB

4 Someone's **scheme of things** is the way in which PHRASE they want things to be organized. EG *There was an important place for the State in their scheme of things.*

5 When people talk about **the scheme of things**, PHRASE they are referring to the way that everything in the world seems to be organized. EG *Man needed to understand his place in the scheme of things.*

schizophrenia /skɪtsəⁿfriːnɪə/ is a serious mental N UNCOUNT illness. People who suffer from it are unable to relate their thoughts and feelings to what is hap- pening around them.

schizophrenic /skɪtsəⁿfrɛnɪk/, **schizophrenics.** N COUNT A **schizophrenic** is a person who is suffering from

---

If you scoff at something, are you sceptical about it?

schizophrenia. EG ...a paranoid schizophrenic.
▸ used as an adjective. EG ...a schizophrenic patient. ▸ ADJ CLASSIF

scholar /skɒlə/, **scholars.** 1 A **scholar** is a per- N COUNT
son who studies an academic subject and knows a
lot about it. EG ...Benjamin Jowett, the theologian
and Greek scholar.

2 Someone who is a good **scholar** is good at N COUNT+SUPP
learning things at school or college, and someone Outdated
who is a bad **scholar** is bad at learning things. EG
Philpott was a poor scholar.

3 A **scholar** is also a pupil or student who has N COUNT
obtained a scholarship. EG ...an Eton scholar.

scholarly /skɒləli¹/. A **scholarly** person spends a ADJ QUALIT
lot of time studying and knows a lot about academ-
ic subjects.

scholarship /skɒləʃɪp/, **scholarships.** 1 If you N COUNT
get a **scholarship** to a school or university, your
studies are paid for by the school or university or
by some other organization. EG I applied for a
scholarship to study philosophy at Oxford.

2 **Scholarship** is serious academic study and the N UNCOUNT
knowledge that is obtained from it. EG ...the Islamic
tradition of scholarship.

scholastic /skə⁷læstɪk/. Your **scholastic** ability ADJ CLASSIF:
and achievements are your ability to study and ATTRIB
your achievements while you are at school. EG He Formal
was more involved in sports than in scholastic
achievements.

school /skuːl/, **schools.** 1 **School** or a **school** is a N UNCOUNT
place where children are educated. EG ...a school OR N COUNT
with more than 1300 pupils... I went to school
here... He was doing badly at school... What do you
want to do when you leave school?... ...the school
holidays... ...once their children reach school age.

2 If something happens before **school** or after N UNCOUNT
school, it happens before or after the part of the
day when you are at school. EG We met every day
after school.

3 University departments and colleges are some- N COUNT OR
times called **schools.** EG I went to an art school... N UNCOUNT
She had recently graduated from law school... +SUPP
...medical school.

4 In America, university is often referred to as N UNCOUNT
school. Informal

5 A particular **school of thought** is a particular PHRASE
theory or opinion that is shared by a group of
people. EG One school of thought argues that the
enterprise should be abandoned... There seemed to
be two schools of thought.

6 A large group of dolphins or fish can be referred N PART
to as a **school.** EG ...a school of dolphins.

7 See also **schooling, boarding school, finishing
school, first school, grammar school, high
school, infant school, junior school, middle
school, night school, nursery school, prep
school, primary school, private school, public
school, secondary school, summer school, Sunday school.**

schoolboy /skuːlbɔɪ/, **schoolboys.** A **schoolboy** is N COUNT
a boy who goes to school.

schoolchild /skuːltʃaɪld/, **schoolchildren.** N COUNT:
Schoolchildren are children who go to school. EG OFT PLURAL
The hall was rapidly filling with schoolchildren.

schooldays /skuːldeɪz/. Your **schooldays** are the N PLURAL:
period of your life when you are at school. EG I USU+POSS
enjoyed my schooldays.

schoolgirl /skuːlgɜːl/, **schoolgirls.** A **schoolgirl** N COUNT
is a girl who goes to school.

schooling /skuːlɪŋ/. Your **schooling** is the educa- N UNCOUNT
tion that you receive at school. EG Many of the Informal
workers had no schooling at all... Her schooling
had been highly irregular.

school-leaver, school-leavers. School-leavers N COUNT:
are young people who have just left school and who USU PLURAL
are looking for a job or are doing their first job. EG
...the growth of unemployment among school-
leavers.

schoolmaster /skuːlmɑːstə/, **schoolmasters.** A N COUNT
schoolmaster is a man who teaches children in a Outdated
school.

schoolmistress /skuːlmɪstrɪ²s/, **school-** N COUNT
mistresses. A **schoolmistress** is a woman who Outdated
teaches children in a school. EG ...the village schoolmistress.

schoolroom /skuːlruːm/, **schoolrooms.** A N COUNT
schoolroom is a classroom, especially the only Outdated
classroom in a small school.

schoolteacher /skuːltiːtʃə/, **schoolteachers.** A N COUNT
schoolteacher is a teacher in a school.

schoolteaching /skuːltiːtʃɪŋ/ is the work that N UNCOUNT
schoolteachers do. EG I was thinking of going in for Outdated
schoolteaching.

schoolwork /skuːlwɜːk/ is the work that a child N UNCOUNT
does at school or as homework.

science /saɪəns/, **sciences.** 1 **Science** is the N UNCOUNT
study of the nature and behaviour of natural things
and the knowledge that we obtain about them. EG
...the importance of mathematics to science... Why
don't many girls go into science?

2 A **science** is 2.1 a particular branch of science, N COUNT
for example physics or biology. 2.2 the study of
some aspect of human behaviour, for example
psychology or sociology. ● See also **social science.**

science fiction consists of stories and films N UNCOUNT
about events that take place in the future or in
other parts of the universe.

scientific /saɪəntɪfɪk/. 1 **Scientific** is used to ADJ CLASSIF
describe things that relate to science or to a
particular science. EG ...scientific research... ...sci-
entific instruments. ◇ **scientifically.** EG ...a scien- ◇ ADV
tifically advanced civilization.

2 If you do something in a **scientific** way, you do it ADJ QUALIT
systematically, using experiments or tests. EG ...a
scientific study of a language. ◇ **scientifically.** EG ◇ ADV
Our relationship to apes has been confirmed scientifically.

scientist /saɪəntɪst/, **scientists.** A **scientist** is an N COUNT
expert who does work in one of the sciences. EG ...a
distinguished medical scientist. ● See also **social
scientist.**

scissors

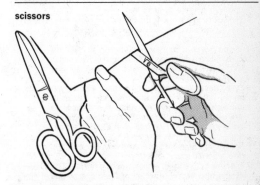

scissors /sɪzəz/ are a small tool with two sharp N PLURAL
blades which are screwed together. You use scissors for cutting things such as paper and cloth. EG
She took a pair of scissors and cut his hair... I wish
I'd brought some scissors.

scoff /skɒf/, **scoffs, scoffing, scoffed.** 1 If you V OR
scoff, you speak in a scornful, mocking way about V+QUOTE:
something. EG They scoff at the idea that he will OFT+at
retire next year... 'Women's movement!' they
scoffed. 'There isn't one.'... Let them scoff.

2 If you **scoff** food, you eat it quickly and greedily. V+O
EG They scoffed the lot. Informal

scold /skəʊld/, **scolds, scolding, scolded.** If you V+O OR
scold someone, you speak angrily to them because V+QUOTE
they have done something wrong. EG He scolded his
daughter for keeping them waiting.

scone /skəʊn, skɒn/, **scones**. Scones are small N COUNT cakes made from flour and fat. They are usually eaten with butter.

scoop /skuːp/, **scoops, scooping, scooped**. 1 If V+O : USU+A you **scoop** something up, 1.1 you put your hands under it and lift it in a quick movement. EG *The boys began to scoop up handfuls of water.* 1.2 you pick it up with something such as a spoon. EG *He scooped some instant coffee into a cup.*

2 A **scoop** is an object like a large spoon which is N COUNT used for picking up a quantity of a food such as ice cream or flour.

3 A **scoop** is also an exciting news story which is N COUNT reported in one newspaper before it appears anywhere else. EG *He got all the big scoops for the paper.*

scoop out. If you **scoop** part of something **out**, PHRASAL VB : you remove it using a spoon or other tool. EG *Scoop* V+O+ADV *out the flesh of the melon with a teaspoon.*

scooter /skuːtə/, **scooters**. A **scooter** is a small, N COUNT lightweight motorcycle with a low seat.

scope /skəʊp/. 1 If there is **scope** for a particular N UNCOUNT kind of behaviour, you have the opportunity to act USU+SUPP in this way. EG *There is not much scope for originality.*

2 The **scope** of an activity, topic, or piece of work N UNCOUNT is the whole area which it deals with or includes. EG USU+SUPP *Lack of time limited the scope of the course... It seemed out of place in a book so limited in scope.*

scorch /skɔːtʃ/, **scorches, scorching, scorched**. V+O If something **is scorched**, it is burned slightly or damaged by heat. EG *I once scorched a beautiful pink suit while ironing it... The lawn was scorched and the soil was baked hard... The sun scorched my face.*

scorching /skɔːtʃɪŋ/. If you use **scorching** to ADJ QUALIT describe the weather, you mean that it is very hot. Informal EG ...*a scorching day.*

score /skɔː/, **scores, scoring, scored**. 1 If some- V OR V+O one **scores** in a game, they get a goal, a run, or a point. EG *Barnes scored from a distance of twenty feet... Fowler scored 83.*

2 Someone's **score** is the total number of runs or N COUNT points they get in a game or test.

3 The **score** in a game is the number of goals, runs, N COUNT or points obtained by the two teams or players. EG *'What's the score?' – '2 – 0'.*

4 If you **score** a success, victory, or hit, you are V+O successful in what you are doing. EG *The Royal Shakespeare Company scored a runaway success with 'Richard III'.*

5 If you **score** over someone or **score** a point, you V+A OR V+O : gain an advantage over them or defeat them in OFT+*over* some way. EG *The Government was anxious to score over the opposition in the education debate... Gareth grinned, as if he had scored an important point.*

6 **Scores** of things means a large number of them. N PART : EG *We received scores of letters.* PLURAL

7 A **score** is twenty or approximately twenty. The N COUNT plural is also 'score'. EG *None of these groups had* OR N PART *more than a score of supporters... Even in my two* Outdated *score years the world has changed.*

8 If something sharp **scores** a surface, it cuts a line V+O into it. EG *Each stone is scored with very thin* Formal *grooves.*

9 The **score** of a piece of music is the written N COUNT version of it.

10 **On this score** or **on that score** means in PHRASE relation to the thing already mentioned. EG *There* Formal *was no need for concern on that score.*

scorn /skɔːn/, **scorns, scorning, scorned**. 1 If N UNCOUNT you treat someone or something with **scorn**, you show contempt for them. EG *This suggestion was greeted with scorn... She had nothing but scorn for those who got themselves into debt.* ● If you **heap** ● PHRASE **scorn** on something or **pour scorn on** it, you say that you think it is worthless. EG *Burgin heaped*

scorn on painting and sculpture... She poured scorn on my ideas.

2 If you **scorn** someone or something, you feel or V+O : OFT+*as* show contempt for them. EG *She scorned the girls who worshipped football heroes... What is now admired as art was then scorned as vulgar extravagance.*

3 If you **scorn** something, you refuse to have it or V+O accept it because you think it is not good enough or Formal suitable for you. EG *Although his hearing was not good, he scorned a deaf aid.*

scornful /skɔːnfʊl/. If you are **scornful**, you show ADJ QUALIT contempt for someone or something. EG *She is openly scornful of the idea that girls are weaker than men... ...scornful laughter.* ◊ **scornfully**. EG ◊ ADV *She looked at him scornfully.*

scorpion /skɔːpɪən/, **scorpions**. A **scorpion** is a N COUNT small tropical animal which looks like a large insect. It has a long tail with a poisonous sting on the end.

Scot /skɒt/, **Scots**. 1 A **Scot** is a person who comes N COUNT from Scotland.

2 **Scots** is a dialect of the English language that is N UNCOUNT spoken in Scotland. EG *He speaks broad Scots.*

3 **Scots** also means the same as Scottish. EG *He* ADJ CLASSIF : *spoke with a Scots accent.* ATTRIB

scotch /skɒtʃ/, **scotches**. 1 **Scotch** or **scotch** N UNCOUNT **whisky** is whisky made in Scotland. EG ...*a bottle of Scotch.*

2 A **scotch** is a glass of scotch. EG *He fixed two* N COUNT *more scotches.*

3 **Scotch** is sometimes used to mean Scottish. ADJ CLASSIF

Scotsman /skɒtsmən/, **Scotsmen**. A **Scotsman** N COUNT is a man who comes from Scotland.

Scotswoman /skɒtswʊmən/, **Scotswomen**. A N COUNT **Scotswoman** is a woman who comes from Scotland.

Scottish /skɒtɪʃ/. Something that is **Scottish** be- ADJ CLASSIF longs or relates to Scotland, its people, or its language. EG ...*the Scottish mountains... ...Scottish football... ...the Scottish legal system.*

scoundrel /skaʊndrəl/, **scoundrels**. People call N COUNT a man a **scoundrel** when he behaves very badly Outdated towards other people, especially by cheating them or deceiving them.

scour /skaʊə/, **scours, scouring, scoured**. If you V+O : USU+A **scour** a place for something or someone, you make a thorough search there for them. EG *Traders were scouring the villages for family treasures.*

scourge /skɜːdʒ/. When something causes a lot of N SING : OFT+*of* trouble or suffering to a group of people, you can refer to it as a **scourge**. EG *Smallpox was the scourge of the Western world.*

scout /skaʊt/, **scouts, scouting, scouted**. 1 A N COUNT **scout** or a **boy scout** is a boy who is a member of the Scout Association. Scouts go camping, learn how to look after themselves, and do things to help other people. EG *He joined the boy scouts... He was going away with the local scout troop.*

2 A **scout** is also a person who is sent to an area of N COUNT countryside to find out the position of an enemy army. EG *The scouts reported that the enemy was advancing.*

3 If you **scout** for something or **scout** around for it, V+A you search for it in different places. EG *We'll scout around to see if anyone is here.*

scowl /skaʊl/, **scowls, scowling, scowled**. When V : OFT+*at* someone **scowls**, they frown to show that they are angry or displeased. EG *I scowled at him.* ▶ used as ▶ N COUNT a noun. EG *Her grin changed to a scowl.*

scrabble /skræbəl/, **scrabbles, scrabbling, scrabbled**. 1 If you **scrabble** at something, you V+A scrape at it with your fingers or feet. EG *The woman scrabbled at the side of the boat... I hung there, scrabbling with my feet to find a foothold.*

Which is the odd one out - Scots, Scotch or Scottish?

2 If you **scrabble** around, you move your hands V+A about in order to find something that you cannot see. EG *I scrabbled around on the floor and eventually found my ring... She scrabbled in her handbag.*

3 Scrabble is a word game played with letters on a N PROPER board.   Trademark

scramble /skræmbə⁰l/, **scrambles, scrambling, scrambled. 1** If you **scramble** over rough or V : USU+A difficult ground, you move quickly over it using your hands to help you. EG *John scrambled up the bank.*

2 You also **scramble** when you move to a different V+A position or place in a hurried, undignified way. EG *He scrambled to his feet... The smaller boys were trying to scramble out of the way.* ▸ used as a ▸ N SING noun. EG *We had an awful scramble to get to the airport.*

scrambled egg, scrambled eggs. Scrambled N UNCOUNT **egg** or **scrambled eggs** is a food consisting of OR N PLURAL eggs mixed together and then cooked in a pan.

scrap /skræp/, **scraps, scrapping, scrapped. 1** N PART A **scrap** of something is a very small piece or amount of it. EG *He found a scrap of paper and a pencil... ...a rug made of scraps of old clothes... ...scraps of information.*

2 Scraps are pieces of unwanted food which are N PLURAL thrown away or given to animals. EG *...a tame puppy, begging for scraps.*

3 If there is **not a scrap** of something, there is PHRASE none of it at all. EG *There was not a scrap of evidence against him... It never made a scrap of difference to his feelings for her.*

4 If you **scrap** something, you get rid of it or V+O cancel it, for example because you no longer think it is suitable. EG *The existing system should be completely scrapped... Plans have now been scrapped for four nuclear power stations.*

5 Scrap or **scrap metal** is metal from old or N UNCOUNT damaged machinery or cars. EG *All he could do was sell it for scrap.*

6 You can refer to a fight or a quarrel as a **scrap**. N COUNT EG *Mr Roberts loved a scrap.*   Informal

scrapbook /skræpbʊk/, **scrapbooks.** A **scrap-** N COUNT **book** is a book with blank pages. People stick things such as pictures or newspaper articles into scrapbooks in order to make a collection.

scrape /skreɪp/, **scrapes, scraping, scraped. 1** V+O+A If you **scrape** something from a surface or **scrape** it off, you remove it by pulling a knife or other object over it. EG *She scraped the mud off her boots.*

2 If you **scrape** something, you remove its skin or V+O surface by pulling a knife over it. EG *The nuts can be eaten raw once they have been scraped.*

3 If you **scrape** one thing against another, you rub V+O+*against/* the first thing against the second, causing slight *on* damage. EG *He scraped his hand painfully on a rock.*

4 If something **scrapes** something else or **scrapes** V+O OR V+ against it, it rubs against it and damages it slightly *against/on* or makes a harsh noise. EG *In winter, the branches tapped and scraped the glass... His beard scraped against her skin.* ▸ used as a noun. EG *...the clink* ▸ N SING *and scrape of knives and forks.*

5 You say that people **scrape** when they spend as V : OFT+*to*-INF little money as possible, in order to have enough money to buy things that they want or need. EG *People scraped and saved to get their boys into private schools.*

6 If you are in a **scrape**, you are in a difficult N COUNT situation which you have caused yourself. EG *He got* Outdated *into several scrapes.*

7 to **scrape the barrel**: see **barrel**.

scrape through. If you **scrape through** an PHRASAL VB : examination, you just succeed in passing it. V+ADV/PREP

scrape together or **scrape up.** If you **scrape** PHRASAL VB : **together** or **scrape up** an amount of money or a V+O+ADV number of things, you succeed in obtaining them with difficulty. EG *He scraped up the money to start a restaurant.*

scratch /skrætʃ/, **scratches, scratching, scratched. 1** If a sharp object **scratches** you, it V+O rubs against your skin, cutting you slightly. EG *I got scratched by a rose bush... His knees were scratched by thorns.*

2 A **scratch** is a small cut on your body. EG *You're* N COUNT *not going to die. It's only a scratch.*

3 If you **scratch** yourself or **scratch**, you rub your V-REFL, V+O, fingernails against your skin because it is itching. OR V EG *Jackson was sleepily scratching himself.* ● If you ● PHRASE say that someone **is scratching** their **head**, you mean that they are thinking hard and trying to solve a problem or puzzle. EG *That will make him scratch his head.*

4 If you **scratch** an object, you accidentally make V+O small cuts on it which spoil its appearance.

5 Scratches are marks where something has been N COUNT scratched. EG *White shoe polish can hide scratches on white woodwork.*

6 If you say that an article or report only PHRASE **scratches the surface**, you mean that it deals with a subject in a superficial way.

7 If you do something **from scratch**, you do it PHRASE without making use of anything that has been done before. EG *Now we have to start again from scratch... We're building it from scratch.*

8 If you say that something is **up to scratch**, you PHRASE mean that it is good enough. EG *My Economics isn't likely to be up to scratch.*

scrawl /skrɔːl/, **scrawls, scrawling, scrawled. 1** V+O : OFT+A If you **scrawl** something, you write it in a careless and untidy way. EG *Someone had scrawled 'What does it all mean?' across the cover... I tried to read his notes scrawled on a piece of paper.*

2 You can refer to writing that looks careless and N COUNT untidy as a **scrawl**. EG *I did my best to write neatly instead of with my usual scrawl.*

scrawny /skrɔːnɪ¹/, **scrawnier, scrawniest.** A ADJ QUALIT **scrawny** person or animal is unpleasantly thin and bony. EG *...a scrawny youth... ...scrawny cattle.*

scream /skriːm/, **screams, screaming, screamed. 1** When someone **screams**, they make V a very loud, high-pitched cry, usually because they are in pain or are very frightened. EG *Kunta screamed as a whip struck his back.* ▸ used as a ▸ N COUNT noun. EG *He was awakened by the sound of screams.*

2 When anything makes a loud, high-pitched noise, V you can say that it **screams**. EG *The jets screamed overhead... The birds screamed in the trees.* ▸ used ▸ N SING as a noun. EG *The car roared round the corner with a scream of tyres.*

3 If you **scream** something, you shout it in a loud, V-SPEECH : high-pitched voice. EG *'Get out of there,' I* ONLY *that* *screamed... I screamed that I was all right.*

4 You can say that someone is a **scream** when you N SING : *a*+N think that they are very funny. EG *Do you know* Informal *Sheila? She's a scream.*

screech /skriːtʃ/, **screeches, screeching, screeched. 1** When a person or an animal V : OFT+QUOTE **screeches**, they make an unpleasant, loud, high- OR REPORT, pitched cry. EG *'You'll be sorry you did that!' she* ONLY *that* *screeched.* ▸ used as a noun. EG *The parrot gave a* ▸ N COUNT *loud screech.*

2 If a vehicle **screeches**, its tyres make an un- V : USU+A pleasant high-pitched noise on the road. EG *The bus came screeching to a stop.* ▸ used as a noun. EG *I* ▸ N SING *heard a screech of tyres.*

screen /skriːn/, **screens, screening, screened. 1** N COUNT A **screen** is a flat, vertical surface on which a picture is shown. Television sets and computer terminals have screens, and films are shown on a screen in cinemas. EG *A picture would flash onto the screen... The television screen remained the centre of attention.*

2 The films that are shown in cinemas are some- N SING : *the*+N times referred to as the **screen**. EG *...Greta Garbo and other stars of the screen.*

3 When a film or a television programme is V+O : USU PASS

screened, it is shown in the cinema or broadcast on television. EG *They tried to prevent the programme being screened.* ◊ **screening, screenings**. EG *There was an attempt to stop the screening.* ◊ N UNCOUNT OR N COUNT

4 A **screen** is also a vertical panel which can be moved around. It is used to keep cold air away from part of a room, or to create a smaller area within the room. EG *He got up and walked behind the screen.* N COUNT

5 If you **screen** someone, you stand in front of them or place something in front of them, in order to prevent them from being seen or hurt. EG *I moved in front of her trying to screen her.* V+O

6 When an organization **screens** people, **6.1** they investigate them to make sure that they are not likely to be dangerous or disloyal. EG *The Secret Service screens several hundred people every week.* **6.2** they examine them to make sure that they do not have a particular disease. EG *...a study of women who were screened for breast cancer.* ◊ **screening**. EG *...a screening at a London medical centre.* V+O ◊ N UNCOUNT OR N COUNT

screen off. If you **screen off** part of a room, you make it into a separate area, using a screen. PHRASAL VB : V+O+ADV

screenplay /skriːnpleɪ/, **screenplays**. The **screenplay** of a film is the script. EG *'The French Lieutenant's Woman' has a screenplay by Harold Pinter.* N COUNT

screw /skruː/, **screws, screwing, screwed. 1** A **screw** is a small, sharp piece of metal which you use to fix two things together. When you twist the screw with a screwdriver, it goes through one thing and into the other thing. See picture at TOOLS. N COUNT

2 If you **screw** something to something else, **2.1** you fix it there by means of a screw or screws. EG *Squeaking floorboards should be screwed down... I'm going to screw some handles onto the bathroom cabinet.* **2.2** you fasten it or fix it by twisting it round and round. EG *He screwed the lid tightly onto the top of the jar... ...hollow tubes which screw together.* V-ERG+A

screw up. 1 If you **screw up** your face or something flexible, you twist it or squeeze it so that it no longer has its natural shape. EG *She screwed up her eyes as she faced the sun... She screwed up the paper and tossed it in the bin.* **2** If you **screw** something up, you cause it to fail or be spoiled. EG *He can't do that; that screws up all my arrangements.* PHRASAL VB : V+O+ADV ◊ V+O+ADV Informal

screwdriver /skruːdraɪvə/, **screwdrivers**. A **screwdriver** is a tool that is used for turning screws. It consists of a metal rod with a thin end that fits into the top of the screw. See picture at TOOLS. N COUNT

scribble /skrɪbəl/, **scribbles, scribbling, scribbled. 1** If you **scribble** something, you write it quickly and roughly. EG *She was scribbling a letter to her mother... We were scribbling away furiously.* V+O OR V : OFT+A

2 To **scribble** also means to make meaningless marks or rough drawings using a pencil or pen. EG *Someone's scribbled all over the wall.* V+A

3 You can refer to something that has been written or drawn quickly and roughly as **scribble** or a **scribble**. EG *She was looking at my scribble, trying to work out what it said... There are scribbles on the lift wall.* N UNCOUNT OR N COUNT

scrimp /skrɪmp/, **scrimps, scrimping, scrimped.** If you **scrimp and save**, you live cheaply and spend as little money as possible. EG *I was scrimping and saving to buy necessities.* PHRASE

script /skrɪpt/, **scripts. 1** The **script** of a play, film, or television programme is the written version of it. EG *You can't have good acting without a decent script.* N COUNT

2 You can refer to a particular system of writing as a particular **script**. EG *...the Arabic script.* N COUNT OR N UNCOUNT

3 You can refer to handwriting as **script**. EG *Nobody could decipher my microscopic script.* N UNCOUNT Literary

scripture /skrɪptʃə/, **scriptures.** You use **scripture** or **scriptures** to refer to writings that are regarded as sacred in a particular religion, for example the Bible in Christianity. EG *They invoked Hindu scripture to justify their position... The scripture says, 'Man cannot live on bread alone.'* N UNCOUNT OR N COUNT

scriptwriter /skrɪptraɪtə/, **scriptwriters.** A **scriptwriter** is a person who writes scripts for films or for radio or television programmes. N COUNT

scroll /skrəʊl/, **scrolls.** A **scroll** is a long roll of paper, parchment, or other material with writing on it. EG *...an ancient Chinese scroll.* N COUNT

scrounge /skraʊndʒ/, **scrounges, scrounging, scrounged.** If you **scrounge** something such as food or money, you get it by asking someone for it, rather than by buying it or earning it. EG *He had come over to scrounge a few cans of food... She was always scrounging.* V+O OR V Informal

scrounger /skraʊndʒə/, **scroungers.** If you call someone a **scrounger**, you mean that they try to get things such as money or food without working for them. N COUNT Informal

scrub /skrʌb/, **scrubs, scrubbing, scrubbed. 1** If you **scrub** something, you rub it hard in order to clean it, using a stiff brush and water. EG *They scrub the kitchen floor every day... He scrubbed his hands at the sink.* ▸ used as a noun. EG *That floor needs a good scrub.* V+O OR V ▸ N SING

2 If you **scrub** dirt or stains off something, you remove them by rubbing hard. EG *There was a stain on the collar and he tried to scrub it off.* V+O+A

3 Scrub consists of low trees and bushes in an area that has very little rain. EG *The country is flat, grassy, and covered in scrub.* N UNCOUNT

scruff /skrʌf/, **scruffs.** If someone holds you **by the scruff** of your **neck**, they hold the back of your neck or collar. EG *Don't pick up a puppy by the scruff of its neck.* PHRASE

scruffy /skrʌfiˈ/, **scruffier, scruffiest.** Someone or something that is **scruffy** is dirty and untidy. EG *We looked scruffy... ...a scruffy child.* ADJ QUALIT

scrum /skrʌm/, **scrums.** A **scrum** in the game of rugby is a formation in which players from each side form a tight group and push against each other with their heads down in an attempt to get the ball. N COUNT

scruples /skruːpəʊlz/ are moral principles or beliefs that make you unwilling to do something that seems wrong. EG *He had no scruples about borrowing money... ...religious scruples.* N PLURAL

scrupulous /skruːpjəˈləs/. Someone who is **scrupulous 1** takes great care to do what is fair, honest, or morally right. EG *The paper was not entirely scrupulous in setting out its assumptions.* ◊ **scrupulously**. EG *...the pressure on manufacturers to behave scrupulously.* **2** is thorough, exact, and pays careful attention to detail. EG *...a historian with a reputation for scrupulous scholarship... They pay scrupulous attention to style.* ◊ **scrupulously**. EG *Everything was scrupulously clean.* ADJ QUALIT ◊ ADV ADJ QUALIT ◊ ADV

scrutinize /skruːtɪnaɪz/, **scrutinizes, scrutinizing, scrutinized;** also spelled **scrutinise.** If you **scrutinize** something, you look at it or examine it very carefully. EG *Bank examiners scrutinized the books of 600 financial institutions... He began to scrutinize the faces in the compartment.* V+O

scrutiny /skruːtɪniˈ/. If something is under **scrutiny**, it is being studied or observed very carefully. EG *At these visits the whole college comes under scrutiny... ...close scrutiny by explosives experts.* N UNCOUNT

scuff /skʌf/, **scuffs, scuffing, scuffed.** If you **scuff** your feet, you drag them along the ground by walking without lifting them. EG *My sister was scuffing her feet as we walked down the road.* V+O

Does a scruffy child have scuffed shoes?

scuffed /skʌft/. If shoes are **scuffed**, their surface ADJ QUALIT
has been damaged by rubbing and knocking
against things. EG ...*a man in a baggy suit and
scuffed shoes.*

scuffle /skʌfəl/, **scuffles, scuffling, scuffled.** A N COUNT
scuffle is a rough fight or struggle. EG *Two policemen were injured in the scuffle that followed.*
▸ used as a verb. EG *The girls scuffled for the best* ▸ V
seats.

scullery /skʌlərɪ/, **sculleries.** A **scullery** is a N COUNT
small room next to a kitchen where washing and
other domestic work is done.

sculpt /skʌlpt/, **sculpts, sculpting, sculpted.** V+O : USU PASS
When a sculpture is made, you can say that it **is** Formal
sculpted. EG ...*a nude woman, sculpted in marble.*

sculptor /skʌlptə/, **sculptors.** A **sculptor** is N COUNT
someone who makes sculptures.

sculpture /skʌlptʃə/, **sculptures. 1** A **sculpture** N COUNT OR
is a work of art that is produced by carving or N UNCOUNT
shaping stone, wood, or clay. EG ...*Aztec sculptures...
...an exhibition of 20th century sculpture.*

2 Sculpture is the art of making sculptures. EG *The* N UNCOUNT
college offers classes in sculpture.

sculptured /skʌlptʃəd/. **Sculptured** objects have ADJ CLASSIF
been carved or shaped from something. EG ...*sculptured heads of civic dignitaries.*

scum /skʌm/. **1 Scum** is a layer of a dirty or N SING OR N
unpleasant-looking substance on the surface of a UNCOUNT
liquid. EG *There was green scum over the pond.*

2 If you call people **scum**, you are expressing your N PLURAL
feelings of dislike and disgust for them. EG *I have to
mix with scum.*

scurrilous /skʌrɪləs/. If you say or write some- ADJ QUALIT
thing **scurrilous**, you criticize someone unfairly or
untruthfully in a way that is likely to damage their
reputation. EG ...*a scurrilous weekly magazine.*

scurry /skʌrɪ/, **scurries, scurrying, scurried.** V+A
When people or small animals **scurry** somewhere,
they run there quickly and hurriedly. EG *Everyone
scurried for cover... A mouse scurried across the
floor.*

scuttle /skʌtəl/, **scuttles, scuttling, scuttled. 1** V+A
When people or small animals **scuttle** somewhere,
they run there with short, quick steps. EG *A porcupine scuttled across the road.*

2 You can refer to a coal scuttle as a **scuttle**. EG *I* N COUNT
began to fill the scuttle with coal.

scythe /saɪð/, **scythes, scything, scythed. 1** A N COUNT
scythe is a tool with a long handle and a long
curved blade. You use it with a swinging movement to cut long grass or grain.

2 If you **scythe** grass or grain, you cut it with a V+O OR V
scythe. EG *Jem whistled as he scythed the grass.*

SE is an abbreviation for 'south-east'.

sea /siː/, **seas. 1** The **sea** is the salty water that N COUNT :
covers about three-quarters of the earth's surface. the+N; ALSO
EG *I watched the children running into the sea... ...a* N UNCOUNT
*wrecked ship at the bottom of the sea... ...calm
seas... ...sea travel... ...a bit of blue sea.*

2 A **sea** is a large area of salty water that is N COUNT
sometimes part of an ocean and sometimes surrounded by land. EG ...*the North Sea... ...the Caspian
Sea.*

3 Sea is used in these phrases. **3.1 At sea** means PHRASES
on or under the sea, far away from land. EG ...*a
storm at sea... Submarines can stay at sea for
weeks.* **3.2** You can say that someone is **at sea**
when they are in a state of confusion or uncertainty. **3.3** If you travel or send something **by sea**, you
travel or you send it in a ship. EG *They sent all the
heavy equipment by sea.* **3.4** If you spend some
time **by the sea**, you spend it at the seaside. EG ...*a
pleasant weekend by the sea.* **3.5** If something
floats **out to sea**, it floats away from the shore. If
you look **out to sea**, you look across the sea from
the shore. EG *The little boat was swept out to sea...
He stared out to sea.*

4 A **sea** of people or things is a very large number N PART : SING

of them. EG ...*a sea of white faces... ...a sea of
buttercups... ...a sea of troubles.*

seabed /siːbed/. The **seabed** is the ground under N SING : the+N
the sea. EG ...*pipelines on the sea-bed.*

seabird /siːbɜːd/, **seabirds. Seabirds** are birds N COUNT
that live near the sea and get their food from it.

seaboard /siːbɔːd/, **seaboards.** A **seaboard** is the N COUNT :
part of a country that is next to the sea. EG ...*the* USU SING
eastern seaboard of the United States.

seafaring /siːfeərɪŋ/. **Seafaring** people are peo- ADJ CLASSIF :
ple who work as sailors. EG *Britain has always been* ATTRIB
a seafaring nation.

seafood /siːfuːd/ refers to shellfish such as lob- N UNCOUNT
sters, mussels, and crabs, and to other sea creatures that you can eat. EG ...*fresh local seafood... ...a
seafood restaurant.*

seafront /siːfrʌnt/, **seafronts.** The **seafront** is N COUNT
the part of a seaside town that is next to the sea. It
usually consists of a road with buildings facing the
sea. EG *I walked along the seafront.*

sea-going. Sea-going boats and ships are de- ADJ CLASSIF :
signed for travelling on the sea, rather than on ATTRIB
lakes, rivers, or canals.

seagull /siːgʌl/, **seagulls.** A **seagull** is a common N COUNT
kind of seabird. EG *Our boat was followed by a flock
of seagulls.*

seal /siːl/, **seals, sealing, sealed. 1** A **seal** is **1.1** N COUNT
an official mark that is fixed to documents to show
that they are legal or genuine. **1.2** something fixed
to a container or letter that must be broken before
the container or letter can be opened. EG *I noticed
that the seals of the packet had been broken.*

2 If you **seal** an envelope, you stick down the flap V+O
so that the envelope cannot be opened without
being torn. ◊ **sealed**. EG *He took a sealed envelope* ◊ ADJ CLASSIF
from the folder on his desk.

3 If you **seal** an opening, you fill it or cover it with V+O : USU PASS
something in order to prevent air, gas, or a liquid
getting in or out. EG ...*a thin tube sealed at one end...
Small cracks can be sealed with this compound.*

4 If something **puts** or **sets the seal on** some- PHRASE
thing, it makes it definite or confirms how it is
going to be. EG *The recent floods put the seal on a
disappointing summer... The experience set the
seal on their friendship.*

5 If someone **gives** something their **seal of ap-** PHRASE
proval, they officially say that they approve of it.

6 A **seal** is also a large, shiny animal without legs, N COUNT
which eats fish and lives partly on land and partly
in the sea.

seal off. If you **seal** a place **off**, you prevent PHRASAL VB :
people from getting into it or out of it by blocking V+O+ADV
all the entrances.

sea level. If you are at **sea level**, you are at the N UNCOUNT
same level as the surface of the sea. EG ...*land below
sea level.*

sea lion, sea lions. A **sea lion** is a type of large N COUNT
seal.

seam /siːm/, **seams. 1** A **seam** is a line of stitches N COUNT
which joins two pieces of cloth together.

2 When something is very full, you can say that it is PHRASE
bursting or **bulging at the seams**. EG *Schools and
universities are bulging at the seams.*

3 A **seam** is also a long, narrow layer of coal N COUNT
beneath the ground.

seaman /siːmən/, **seamen.** A **seaman** is a sailor. N COUNT
EG ...*with a crew of experienced seamen.*

seamed /siːmd/. If something is **seamed**, it has ADJ QUALIT
long, thin lines on its surface. EG *His brown face
was seamed and wrinkled.*

séance /seɪɑːns/, **séances;** also spelled **seance.** A N COUNT
séance is a meeting in which people try to speak
to people who are dead.

search /sɜːtʃ/, **searches, searching, searched. 1** V+A OR V+O :
If you **search** for something, you look carefully for OFT+for
it. If you **search** a place, you look carefully for
something there. EG *He glanced around the room,
searching for a place to sit... He searched through*

a drawer and eventually found the photo... I searched the city for a room.

2 If the police **search** you, they examine your clothing because they think that you may have something hidden in it. EG *We were stopped by the police and searched.* `v+o`

3 A **search** is an attempt to find something by looking for it. EG *I found the keys after a long search... ...the search for oil.* ● If you go **in search** of something, you try to find it. EG *We went round the town in search of a place to stay.* `N COUNT` `● PHRASE`

4 When you are trying to think of something, you can say that you **are searching** for it or **are searching** your mind for it. EG *She searched her mind for some words of comfort.* `V OR V+O:` `OFT+for`

search out. If you **search** something **out**, you keep looking for it until you find it. EG *I have been searching out old sewing patterns.* `PHRASAL VB:` `V+O+ADV`

searching /sɜːtʃɪŋ/. A **searching** question or look is intended to discover the truth about something. EG *We had to answer the searching questions of the Social Security officials... He gave the girl a quick, searching look.* ◊ **searchingly.** EG *She was looking at me searchingly.* `ADJ QUALIT:` `USU ATTRIB` `◊ ADV`

search party, search parties. A **search party** is an organized group of people who are searching for someone who is lost or missing. `N COUNT`

searing /sɪərɪŋ/. **1** A **searing** pain is very sharp and causes a burning feeling. EG *He felt a searing pain in his left arm.* `ADJ QUALIT:` `ATTRIB`

2 A **searing** speech or piece of writing strongly criticizes something or someone. EG *...a searing exposure of modern America.* `ADJ QUALIT:` `ATTRIB`

seashell /siːʃel/, **seashells.** A **seashell** is the empty shell of a small sea creature. `N COUNT`

seashore /siːʃɔː/, **seashores.** The **seashore** is the part of a coast where the land slopes down into the sea. EG *...a walk along the seashore.* `N COUNT`

seasick /siːsɪk/. If someone is **seasick** when they are travelling in a boat, they vomit or feel sick because of the way the boat is moving. EG *He felt seasick.* ◊ **seasickness.** EG *He suffers from seasickness.* `ADJ QUALIT` `◊ N UNCOUNT`

seaside /siːsaɪd/. The **seaside** is a place next to the sea, especially one where people go for their holidays. EG *We spent the weekend at the seaside... ...a seaside resort.* `N SING: the+N`

season /siːzən/, **seasons, seasoning, seasoned.** **1** The **seasons** are the four periods into which a year is divided, because there is different weather in each period. They are called spring, summer, autumn, and winter. EG *...the endless cycle of the seasons.* `N COUNT`

2 A **season** is also the period during each year when something usually happens. EG *...the breeding season... ...the planting season... When does the football season end?* `N COUNT+SUPP`

3 The holiday **season** is the time when most people have their holiday. EG *Hotel rooms are available even at the height of the season.* ● If you go to a place **out of season**, you go there when it is not the busy holiday period. EG *We've often been there out of season, and it's much nicer.* `N COUNT` `● PHRASE`

4 If a fruit or vegetable is **in season**, it is the time of year when it is ready for eating and is widely available. If it is **out of season**, it is not widely available. `PHRASE`

5 A **season** of films is several of them shown as a series because they are connected in some way. EG *...a season of Clint Eastwood movies.* `N COUNT+SUPP`

6 If you **season** food, you add salt, pepper, or spices to it in order to improve its flavour. EG *...tuna fish seasoned with salt.* `v+o:` `OFT+with`

7 See also **seasoned, seasoning.**

seasonal /siːzənəl/. Something that is **seasonal** happens during one particular time of the year. EG *People found seasonal work on farms.* ◊ **seasonally.** EG *People there are employed seasonally.* `ADJ CLASSIF` `◊ ADV`

seasoned /siːzənd/ means having a lot of experience of something. For example, a **seasoned** traveller is someone who has travelled a lot. EG *...a seasoned election campaigner... ...seasoned troops.* `ADJ QUALIT:` `ATTRIB`

seasoning /siːzənɪŋ/ is salt, pepper, or spices that are added to food to improve its flavour. `N UNCOUNT`

season ticket, season tickets. A **season ticket** is a train or bus ticket that you can use continually during a certain period, without having to pay each time. `N COUNT`

seat /siːt/, **seats, seating, seated.** **1** A **seat** is an object that you can sit on, for example a chair. EG *Come in, take a seat... Roger sat down carefully, using the edge of the crate as a seat... There was some beer on the back seat of the car... I rang the theatre to see if I could get seats for the show.* `N COUNT`

2 The **seat** of a chair is the part that you sit on. `N COUNT`

3 If you **seat** yourself somewhere, you sit down. EG *'Thank you,' she said, seating herself on the sofa.* ◊ **seated.** EG *General Tomkins was seated behind his desk.* `V-REFL: OFT+A` `◊ ADJ PRED`

4 A building or vehicle that **seats** a particular number of people has enough seats for that number. EG *The hall seats four hundred.* `V+O: NO CONT`

5 The **seat** of a piece of clothing is the part that covers your bottom. EG *Her jeans had a gaping hole in the seat.* `N SING: the+N`

6 When someone is elected to parliament, you can say that they or their party have won a **seat**. EG *The Nationalists failed to win a single seat.* `N COUNT`

7 If you **take a back seat**, you allow other people to have all the power and to make all the decisions. `PHRASE`

seat-belt, seat-belts. A **seat-belt** is a strap attached to a seat in a car or an aeroplane. You fasten it across your body in order to prevent yourself being thrown out of the seat if there is a sudden movement. See picture at CAR. `N COUNT`

seating /siːtɪŋ/. **1** You can refer to the seats in a place as the **seating**. EG *The plastic seating was uncomfortable.* `N UNCOUNT`

2 A **seating** plan indicates how the seats are arranged in a theatre or where people will sit on a formal occasion. EG *Here's a seating plan of the concert hall.* `ADJ CLASSIF:` `ATTRIB`

seaweed /siːwiːd/, **seaweeds.** Seaweed is a plant that grows in the sea. `N MASS`

sec /sek/, **secs.** If you ask someone to wait a **sec**, you are asking them to wait for a very short time. EG *Hang on a sec. Let me have a look... I'll join you in a sec.* `N COUNT` `Informal` `British`

secluded /sɪˈkluːdɪd/. A **secluded** place is quiet, private, and undisturbed. EG *...secluded beaches... ...in a secluded corner of the garden.* `ADJ QUALIT`

seclusion /sɪˈkluːʒən/. If you are living in **seclusion**, you are in a quiet place away from other people. EG *You'd probably feel more at home in the seclusion of Flint Street.* `N UNCOUNT`

second, seconds, seconding, seconded; pronounced /sekənd/ except for paragraph 10, when it is pronounced /sɪˈkɒnd/.

1 A **second** is one of the sixty parts that a minute is divided into. EG *She looked at me for a few seconds... The rocket was rising at the rate of 300 feet per second.* `N COUNT`

2 A **second** is also used to mean a very short time. EG *Could I see your book for a second?* `N COUNT`

3 If you say that something happens in **seconds** or within **seconds**, you mean that it happens very quickly and suddenly. EG *In seconds the building had gone up in flames... Seconds later they were outside.* `N PLURAL`

4 The **second** item in a series is the one that you count as number two: see entry headed NUMBER. EG *...his father's second marriage... ...in the second week of August... ...the second of February.* `ORDINAL`

Would you choose a secluded place for doing things in secret?

5 You say **second** when you want to make a second point or give a second reason for something. EG *And second, this kind of policy doesn't help to create jobs.* ADV SEN

6 If you experience something **at second hand**, you are told about it by other people rather than experiencing it yourself. EG *I knew nothing about Judith except what I'd heard at second hand.* ● See also **second-hand**. PHRASE

7 If you say that something is **second only to** something else, you mean that the other thing is the only one that is better than it. EG *San Francisco is second only to New York as the tourist city of the States.* PHRASE

8 Seconds are goods that are sold cheaply in shops because they are slightly faulty. N COUNT : USU PLURAL

9 If you **second** a proposal in a meeting or debate, you formally agree with it so that it can then be discussed or voted on. EG *I seconded Gene's nomination.* V+O

10 If you **are seconded** somewhere, you are moved there temporarily in order to do special duties. EG *He was for a time seconded to the army.* V+O : USU PASS

11 second nature: see **nature**.

secondary /ˈsɛkəndəˈriː/. **1** Something that is **secondary** is less important than something else. EG *Many older people still believe that men's careers come first and women's careers are secondary.* ADJ QUALIT

2 Secondary education is given to pupils between the ages of 11 or 12 and 18. ADJ CLASSIF : ATTRIB

secondary school, secondary schools. A **secondary school** is a school for pupils between the ages of 11 or 12 and 18. N COUNT

second-best. Something that is **second-best** is not as good as the best thing of its kind but is better than all the other things of that kind. EG *...businessmen in their second-best suits... Hiring professionals is impractical, so as a second-best, we will use unpaid amateurs.* ADJ CLASSIF OR N SING

second-class. 1 Second-class things are things which are regarded as less valuable or less important than other things of the same kind. EG *There can be no second-class citizens in a free society.* ADJ CLASSIF : ATTRIB

2 A **second-class** ticket allows you to travel in the ordinary type of accommodation on a train, aircraft, or ship. EG *He sat in a second-class carriage reading a local newspaper.* N UNCOUNT : USU N MOD

3 Second-class postage is a cheaper and slower type of postage. EG *...a second-class stamp... There's no hurry – send it second-class.* ADJ CLASSIF OR ADV

4 A **second-class** degree is a good or average degree obtained from a British university. ADJ CLASSIF : ATTRIB

second cousin, second cousins. Your **second cousins** are the children of your parents' first cousins. N COUNT

second-hand. 1 Something that is **second-hand** is not new and has been owned by someone else. EG *...second-hand clothing... ...second-hand cars... It's a book he bought second-hand, years ago.* ADJ CLASSIF OR ADV

2 A **second-hand** shop sells second-hand goods. EG *He buys his clothes from a second-hand shop.* ADJ CLASSIF : ATTRIB

3 If you hear a story **second-hand**, you hear it from someone who has heard it from someone else. EG *...a second-hand report.* ADV OR ADJ CLASSIF

second language. Someone's **second language** is a language which is not their native language but which they use at work or at school. EG *...learners of English as a second language.* N SING

secondly /ˈsɛkəndliː/. You say **secondly** when you want to make a second point or give a second reason for something. EG *Firstly, the energy already exists in the ground. Secondly, there's plenty of it.* ADV SEN

second-rate. If you describe something as **second-rate**, you mean that it is of poor quality. EG *...a second-rate department store... ...second-rate ideas... ...second-rate students.* ADJ QUALIT

second thoughts. 1 If you **have second thoughts** about a decision that you have made, you PHRASE

have doubts about it and begin to wonder if it was wise.

2 You say **on second thoughts** when you suddenly change your mind about something that you are saying or something that you have decided to do. EG *Tell me more about America. No, on second thoughts, tell me more about your family.* PHRASE

secrecy /ˈsiːkrəsiː/ involves keeping something secret. EG *She stressed the necessity of absolute secrecy... The operation was conducted in secrecy.* N UNCOUNT

secret /ˈsiːkrɪt/, **secrets. 1** Something that is **secret** is known about by only a small number of people, and is not told or shown to anyone else. EG *The letter was marked 'secret'... We came through a secret back entrance... ...secret negotiations.* ◊ **secretly.** EG *Their work had to be done secretly.* ADJ QUALIT ◊ ADV

2 If you do something **in secret**, you do it without anyone else knowing. EG *I arranged to meet him in secret... He'll manufacture it in secret.* PHRASE

3 You use **secret** to describe someone who does something that they do not tell other people about. For example, if someone is your **secret** admirer, they admire you secretly. EG *She had become a secret drinker.* ◊ **secretly.** EG *He secretly hoped I would one day change my mind... Secretly, perhaps, some of them were also a little scared.* ADJ CLASSIF : ATTRIB ◊ ADV OR ADV SEN

4 A **secret** is a fact that is known by only a small number of people, and is not told to anyone else. EG *The results of these experiments remain a secret... I'll tell you a secret... She has made no secret of the fact that she wants a job.* N COUNT

5 If you describe a way of behaving as the **secret** of achieving something, you mean that it is the best way or the only way to achieve it. EG *The secret is not to involve too many other people... Think big! This is the secret of success.* N SING : the+N

secret agent, secret agents. A **secret agent** is a person who is employed by a government to find out the secrets of other governments. N COUNT

secretarial /ˌsɛkrəˈtɛəriəl/. **Secretarial** work or training involves the work of a secretary. EG *...a secretarial course... ...secretarial staff.* ADJ CLASSIF : ATTRIB

secretariat /ˌsɛkrəˈtɛəriət/, **secretariats.** A **secretariat** is a department that is responsible for the administration of an international political organization. EG *...a senior member of the U.N. Secretariat.* N COUNT

secretary /ˈsɛkrətəˈriː/, **secretaries. 1** A **secretary** is a person who is employed to do office work, such as typing letters, answering phone calls, and arranging meetings. N COUNT

2 The **secretary** of a club or other organization is the person whose job involves keeping records and writing letters. EG *If you want to join the cricket club, write to the secretary.* N COUNT

3 Secretary is used in the titles of ministers who are in charge of the main government departments. EG *...the Social Services Secretary... ...one of the best Foreign Secretaries since the war.* N COUNT+SUPP

secrete /sɪˈkriːt/, **secretes, secreting, secreted. 1** If part of a plant, animal, or human **secretes** a liquid, it produces it. EG *The skin pores enlarge and secrete more oil.* ◊ **secretion** /sɪˈkriːʃəˌn/. EG *Hormone secretion is controlled by the pituitary gland.* V+O ◊ N UNCOUNT

2 If you **secrete** something somewhere, you hide it there so that nobody will find it. EG *...clothes that she had secreted in her basket.* V+O : OFT+A Formal

secretive /ˈsiːkrɪtɪv, sɪˈkriːtɪv/. If you are **secretive**, you like to keep your knowledge, feelings, or intentions hidden from other people. EG *She's very secretive about money matters.* ADJ QUALIT

secret service, secret services. A country's **secret service** is a secret government department whose job is to find out enemy secrets and to prevent its own government's secrets from being discovered. N COUNT

sect /sɛkt/, **sects.** A **sect** is a group of people that has separated from a larger group and has a N COUNT

particular set of religious or political beliefs. EG
*Two religious sects came into being, one of which
was the Quakers... ...an extremist Protestant sect...
...the dictatorship of a socialist minority sect.*

sectarian /sɛktɛərɪən/. 1 **Sectarian** means re- ADJ CLASSIF :
sulting from the differences between sects. EG *The* ATTRIB
conference had collapsed in sectarian squabbles. Formal

2 Someone who is **sectarian** strongly supports a ADJ QUALIT
particular sect. EG *This group is frequently attacked* Formal
as sectarian and fanatical.

section /sɛkʃəⁿn/, **sections**. A **section** of some- N COUNT :
thing is one of the parts which the thing is divided USU+SUPP
into or is formed from. EG *I passed the written part
but failed the oral section... ...the first-class section
of the train... ...well-known people from all sections
of public life.* ● See also **cross-section**.

sector /sɛktə/, **sectors**. 1 A **sector** of a country's N COUNT :
economy is a particular part of it. EG *...the manufac-* USU+SUPP
*turing sector... ...Government support for the volun-
tary sector... ...the movement of weak firms from
the private sector to the public sector.*

2 A **sector** of a large group is a smaller group N COUNT+SUPP
which is part of it. EG *...a very narrow sector of the
Labour Party... ...resistance from all sectors of the
Black community.*

secular /sɛkjəⁿlə/. You use **secular** to describe ADJ CLASSIF
things that have no connection with religion. EG
*...secular education... The choir sings both sacred
and secular music... ...a new secular morality.*

secure /sɪˈkjuə/, **secures, securing, secured**. 1 V+O OR
If you **secure** something, you get it after a lot of V+O+O
effort. EG *He secured only 526 votes... We spent the* Formal
*morning securing their agreement... I did every-
thing possible to secure him a posting.*

2 If you **secure** a place, you make it safe from V+O : OFT+
harm or attack. EG *They endeavoured to secure the* from/against
bridge from the threat of attack. Formal

3 If a building is **secure**, it is tightly locked or well ADJ QUALIT :
protected, so that people cannot enter it or leave it. USU PRED
EG *Try and make your house as secure as you can.*

4 If you **secure** an object, you fasten it firmly to V+O
another object. EG *A plastic box was secured to the
wall by screws.*

5 If an object is **secure**, it is fixed firmly in ADJ QUALIT :
position. EG *Check that the leads to the battery are* USU PRED
in good condition and secure. ◊ **securely**. EG *The* ◊ ADV
chain seemed to be securely fastened.

6 If a position or power is **secure**, it is safe and ADJ QUALIT
certain not to be lost. EG *You've got a secure job... It
was a time when authority was secure and unchallenged.* ◊ **securely**. EG *The strike was securely* ◊ ADV
under the union's control.

7 A **secure** base or foundation is strong and ADJ QUALIT
reliable. EG *You need a secure base for the business.*

8 If you feel **secure**, you feel safe and happy and ADJ QUALIT :
are not worried about life. EG *We feel financially* USU PRED
secure.

security /sɪˈkjuərɪ¹tiː/, **securities**. 1 **Security** N UNCOUNT :
refers to all the precautions that are taken to USU N MOD
protect a country, for example from war, spying,
or violence. EG *...a possible threat to national security... Security forces were patrolling the streets...
...a top security prison.*

2 **Security** is legal protection against possible N UNCOUNT
harm or loss. EG *He hasn't got security of employment... The tenants are exploited and have no
security of tenure.*

3 A feeling of **security** is a feeling of being safe N UNCOUNT
and not having worries. EG *Children count on their
parents for love and security.*

4 **Securities** are stocks, shares, bonds, or other N COUNT :
certificates that you buy as a way of investing USU PLURAL
money, in order to earn regular interest from them Technical
or to sell them later for a profit.

5 See also **social security**.

sedate /sɪˈdeɪt/, **sedates, sedating, sedated**. 1 ADJ QUALIT
Someone who is **sedate** is quiet, calm, and rather
dignified. EG *Irene was graver and more sedate,*

though equally brilliant. ◊ **sedately**. EG *He walked* ◊ ADV
sedately down the lane.

2 If you **are sedated**, you are given a drug to calm V+O : USU PASS
you or to make you sleep.

sedation /sɪˈdeɪʃəⁿn/ is the use of drugs in order to N UNCOUNT
calm someone or to make them sleep. EG *Freddie
was still under sedation in his parents' house.*

sedative /sɛdətɪv/, **sedatives**. 1 A **sedative** is a N COUNT
drug that calms you or makes you sleep. EG *The
doctor may prescribe a sedative... Dolly had taken
a sedative.*

2 Something that is **sedative** has the effect of ADJ CLASSIF
calming you or making you sleep. EG *This drink has
been recognised to have sedative properties.*

sedentary /sɛdəntəⁿriː¹/. If you have a **sedentary** ADJ QUALIT
occupation or way of life, you sit down a lot of the
time and do not have much exercise. EG *I'm bored
with sedentary work... ...the sedentary lives we
lead.*

sediment /sɛdɪməⁿnt/, **sediments**. **Sediment** is 1 N UNCOUNT
solid material that settles at the bottom of a liquid. OR N COUNT
EG *Most of the sediment has sunk to the bottom.* 2
the material such as earth and rocks that has been
carried along and then left somewhere by water,
ice, or wind. EG *Rivers are bringing lots of sediment
down to the sea... The lake sediments preserved
evidence of an unusual hunting accident.*

seduce /sɪˈdjuːs/, **seduces, seducing, seduced**. 1 V+O :
If something **seduces** you, it is so attractive that it OFT+*into*
tempts you to do something that you would not
normally approve of. EG *He was seduced into saying
that he would do it... Both he and his partner had
been seduced by the grandeur of the scheme.*

2 If someone **seduces** another person, especially a V+O
young inexperienced person, they persuade that
person to have sex with them. EG *He used to seduce
all the maids up there in his house.* ◊ **seduction** ◊ N COUNT OR
/sɪˈdʌkʃəⁿn/, **seductions**. EG *The girl's seduction is* N UNCOUNT
an important part of the story.

seductive /sɪˈdʌktɪv/. 1 Something that is **seduc-** ADJ QUALIT
tive is very attractive or tempting. EG *These are
seductive arguments.* ◊ **seductively**. EG *...when* ◊ ADV
the music is played more seductively.

2 A person, especially a woman, who is **seductive** ADJ QUALIT
is very attractive sexually. EG *...the seductive softness of Mary's long limbs.* ◊ **seductively**. EG ◊ ADV
*Percival was leaning seductively forward and
speaking in a low voice.*

see /siː/, **sees, seeing, saw** /sɔː/, **seen** /siːn/. 1 V+O OR V :
When you **see** something, you notice it using your NO IMPER,
eyes, or you look at it. EG *We suddenly saw a boat* NO CONT
through a gap in the fog... I saw him glance at his
watch... He went to India to see the Taj Mahal...
Did you see 'The Doctor's Dilemma' on telly last
night?... Some animals have the ability to see in
very dim light.*

2 If you **see** someone, you visit them or meet them. V+O
EG *Perhaps she did not wish to come and see me...
It would be a good idea for you to see a doctor for a
checkup... They still saw quite a lot of Anthony.*

3 If you **see** someone to a particular place, you V+O+A
accompany them to make sure that they get there
safely. EG *I went down to see her safely to her car.*

4 If you **see** that something is true or exists, you V+REPORT
realise that it is true or exists, by carefully observ- OR V+O :
ing it or thinking about it. EG *Etta could see that he* NO IMPER,
wasn't listening... She begins to see that she has a NO CONT
choice... I was trying not to let the jailers see my
agitation.*

5 If you **see** what someone means or see why V+O OR
something happened, you understand what they V+REPORT :
mean or understand why it happened. EG *'Yes,' she* NO CONT,
said. 'I see what you mean.'... I can see why Mr NO IMPER
Smith is worried... Somebody got killed and I don't
see how.*

How many phrases are there with the word 'see'
in them?

6 You say '**I see**' to indicate that you understand CONVENTION what someone is telling you. EG *'Humbert is Dolly's real father.' – 'I see.'*

7 You say '**you see**' when you are telling someone ADV SEN something and you are very concerned that they should understand it. EG *That's very nice of you but, you see, Kurt, I have no money.*

8 If you ask what someone **sees** in a particular V+O+in: person or thing, you want to know what they find NO IMPER, attractive about that person or thing. EG *'What can* NO CONT *she see in him?' asked another friend.*

9 If you say that you will **see** what is happening or V+REPORT: what the situation is, you mean that you intend to NO CONT find out what is happening or what the situation is. EG *I'd better go and see what he wants... I must phone her up and see if she can come tonight.*

10 If you say that you will **see if** you can do PHRASE something, you mean that you will try to do it. EG *See if you can find my birthday book somewhere.*

● When someone asks you for help, if you say that ● PHRASE you will **see what you can do**, you mean that you will try to help them.

11 If you **see** that something is done or if you **see** V OR PHRASE **to it** that it is done, you make sure that it is done. +REPORT: EG *See that everything is marked with your ini-* ONLY *that* *tials... I'll see to it that there is some action.*

12 If you **see** one thing as another thing, you have V+O+A the opinion that it is that other thing. EG *I did not see his determination as a defect... The problem, as I see it, is not advice but direct help.*

13 If you say that a person or a period of time **sees** V+O a particular change or event, you mean that the change or event takes place while that person is alive or during that period of time. EG *In recent times we have seen a huge split develop between rich and poor nations... How would you like to see education changed?... Last week saw a drop in interest rates.*

14 If you **see** something happening in the future, V+O: USU+A, you imagine it, or predict that it will happen. EG *She* NO IMPER *saw herself seated behind the cash register, smil-ing... Can you see women going into combat carry-ing forty-pound guns?*

15 People say '**I'll see**' or '**We'll see**' to indicate CONVENTION that they do not intend to make a decision immedi-ately, and will decide later. EG *'Will you write to me?' she asked. 'I'll see,' he said.*

16 **See** is used in books to indicate to readers that V+O: they should look at another part of the book, or at ONLY IMPER another book, because more information is given there. EG *Reference to this problem is made else-where (see Chapter 14).*

17 People say '**let me see**' or '**let's see**' when they PHRASE are trying to remember something, or are trying to find something. EG *I think I've got her name somewhere. Now let me see.*

18 You can use '**seeing that**' or '**seeing as**' to CONJ introduce the reason for what you are doing or Informal saying. EG *Seeing that you're the guest on this little trip, you can decide where we're going.*

19 '**See you**' and '**see you later**' are informal ways CONVENTION of saying goodbye to someone when you expect to Informal meet them again soon.

see about. 1 When you **see about** something, PHRASAL VB: you arrange for it to be done or provided. EG V+PREP *Rudolph went into the station to see about Thom-as's ticket.* **2** If someone says that they will do CONVENTION something, and you say '**We'll see about that**', you mean that you intend to prevent them from doing it. EG *'We're not moving.' – 'We'll see about that.'*

see off. When you **see** someone **off**, you go with PHRASAL VB: them to the station, airport, or port that they are V+O+ADV leaving from, and say goodbye to them there.

see through. 1 If you **see through** someone or PHRASAL VB: **see through** what they are doing, you realize what V+PREP, their intentions are, even though they are trying to HAS PASS hide them. EG *She had learned to see through him... The jailers saw through my scheme.* **2** See also **see-through**.

see to. If you **see to** something that needs PHRASAL VB: attention, you deal with it. EG *Don't you worry about* V+PREP: *that. I'll see to that... He went out to see to the* HAS PASS *chickens.*

seed /siːd/, **seeds. 1** A **seed** is the small, hard part N COUNT OR of a plant from which a new plant grows. EG N UNCOUNT *...sunflower seeds... ...a packet of seed... There's something so satisfying about planting seeds.*

2 You can use **seeds** to refer to the cause or N PLURAL: beginning of a feeling or process that gradually *the+N+of* develops and becomes stronger or more important. Literary EG *The seeds of doubt had been sown... It contains the seeds of its own destruction... This protest contains the seeds of workers' control and social-ism.*

seedling /siːdlɪŋ/, **seedlings.** A **seedling** is a N COUNT young plant that has been grown from a seed.

seedy /siːdiˈ/. If you describe a person or place as ADJ QUALIT **seedy**, you mean that they look untidy or in bad condition. EG *...a seedy character with a cigarette between his lips... ...a seedy and rundown photogra-pher's studio.*

seek /siːk/, **seeks, seeking, sought** /sɔːt/. **1** If you V+O OR V+for **are seeking** something such as a job or a place to Formal live, you are trying to find one. EG *Thousands of people were seeking food and shelter... Books are eagerly sought for and sold on the streets.*

2 When someone **seeks** something such as peace, V+O revenge, or the answer to a problem, they try to Formal obtain it. EG *Both countries are seeking peace... They are seeking a 10 per cent reduction in their work force.*

3 If you **seek** someone's help or advice, you go to V+O OR V+for them and ask them for it. EG *I was seeking the help* Formal *of someone who spoke French.*

4 If you **seek** to do something, you try to do it. EG V+to-INF *Power stations are seeking to reduce their use of* Formal *oil... ...anybody who seeks to govern this country.*

seek out. If you **seek out** someone or something, PHRASAL VB: you keep looking for them until you find them. EG *It* V+O+ADV *was unusual for anyone to seek out her husband.*

seem /siːm/, **seems, seeming, seemed. 1** If V+C OR someone or something **seems** to have a particular V+to-INF quality or attitude, they give the impression of having that quality or attitude. EG *Even minor problems seem important... It seemed like a good idea... You seem to be very interested.*

2 If something **seems** to be the case, you get the V+to-INF, V+A, impression that it is the case. EG *There don't seem* V+C, OR to be many people here today... It seemed as V+REPORT: *though I had known them for a long time...* ONLY *Berger's thesis seems right... It seemed that every-* that *body smoked cigarettes.*

3 You use **seem 3.1** to indicate that you are not V+to-INF completely certain that what you are saying is OR V+C correct. EG *The experiments seem to prove that sugar is not good for you... For the time being, Thatcher seems politically secure.* **3.2** when you V+to-INF are describing something to indicate that you are not sure that you remember it correctly. EG *I seem to remember that he was a fiction writer.* **3.3** when V+C, V+to, you are giving your opinion about something or OR V+to-INF asking someone else's opinion. EG *Does that seem nonsense to you?... It did seem to me that she was far too romantic... That would seem a sensible thing to do.*

4 If you say that you cannot **seem** to do something, V: MODAL+ you mean that you have tried to do it and are BROAD NEG unable to do it. EG *I can't seem to get to sleep.* +V+to-INF

seeming /siːmɪŋ/. If you talk about someone's ADJ CLASSIF: **seeming** willingness or **seeming** interest, for ex- ATTRIB ample, you mean that they appear to you to be Formal willing or interested, but are not sure. EG *...his seeming willingness to participate... The old wom-an's seeming inattention provoked her.*

◊ **seemingly.** EG *...their seemingly limitless re-* ◊ SUBMOD OR *sources... Seemingly they don't have any problems.* ADV SEN

seen /siːn/ is the past participle of **see.**

seep /siːp/, **seeps, seeping, seeped.** If a liquid or V+A gas **seeps** through something, it flows through it very slowly and in small amounts. EG *I used to lie awake at night watching the rain seep through the cracks... The petrol fumes seeped into the cab.*

seethe /siːð/, **seethes, seething, seethed.** 1 V When you **are seething**, you are very angry about something but do not express your feelings about it. EG *I seethed with secret rage... By now David was seething.* 2 If a place **is seething** with people or things, it is V+*with* very full of them and they are all moving about. EG *The streets of London seethed with a marching, cheering crowd.* ◊ **seething.** EG *...a seething mass* ◊ ADJ CLASSIF : of maggots. ATTRIB

see-through. See-through clothes are made of ADJ CLASSIF : thin cloth, so that you can see a person's body or ATTRIB underclothes through them. EG *...a see-through blouse... ...the beige see-through dress.*

segment /segməⁿnt/, **segments.** 1 A **segment** of N PART something is one part of it, considered separately from the rest. EG *A much larger segment of the population might be affected... I did show her a segment of the eight-page letter.* 2 A **segment** of an orange or grapefruit is one of N COUNT the sections into which it is easily divided.

segregate /segrigeit/, **segregates, segregating,** V+O **segregated.** To **segregate** two groups of people or things means to keep them physically apart from each other. EG *They tried to segregate pedestrians and vehicles... Little effort was made to segregate the sexes.*

segregated /segrigeitɪⁿd/. A **segregated** group ADJ CLASSIF of people is kept apart from other people belonging to a different sex, race, or religion. EG *He refused to play before segregated audiences.*

segregation /segrigeiʃəⁿn/ is the practice of offi- N UNCOUNT cially keeping apart people of different sexes, or different racial or religious groups. EG *...segregation in the schools... ...articles on apartheid and segregation.*

seize /siːz/, **seizes, seizing, seized.** 1 If you **seize** V+O something, you take hold of it quickly and firmly. EG *Clarissa seized her arm and dragged her into the kitchen... I seized him by the collar... Seizing the bowl, he ran off.* 2 When a group of people **seize** a place or **seize** V+O control of it, they take control of it quickly and suddenly, using force. EG *The airfield had been seized by US troops... ...plots to seize power in Britain... ...seizing complete control of the Gulf.* 3 When someone is **seized**, they are arrested or V+O : USU PASS captured. EG *A university professor was seized on Wednesday by three armed men.* 4 If you **seize** an opportunity, you take advantage V+O of it, and do something that you want to do. EG *Derrick seized the chance and went to Spain.*

seize on or **seize upon.** If you **seize on** some- PHRASAL VB : thing or **seize upon** it, you show great interest in V+PREP, it, often because it is useful to you. EG *This was one HAS PASS of the points that I seized upon with some force... ...seizing on it as an excuse for a rest period.*

seize up. 1 If a part of your body **seizes up**, it PHRASAL VB : suddenly stops working, because you have strained V+ADV it. EG *Your back may seize up.* 2 If an engine **seizes** V+ADV **up**, it stops working, because of overheating or lack of oil.

seize upon. See **seize on.**

seizure /siːʒə/, **seizures.** 1 If someone has a N COUNT **seizure**, they have a sudden violent attack of an illness, especially a heart attack or an epileptic fit. 2 If there is a **seizure** of power in a place, a group N UNCOUNT of people suddenly take control of the place, using force. EG *...the seizure of factories by the workers.*

seldom /seldəⁿm/. If something **seldom** happens, ADV BRD NEG it happens only occasionally. EG *It seldom rains there... The waiting time was seldom less than four hours... He seldom feels confident.*

select /sɪˈlekt/, **selects, selecting, selected.** 1 If V+O you **select** something, you choose it from a number of things of the same kind. EG *They select books that seem to them important... There was a large number of people from whom she could select friends.* ◊ **selected.** EG *We were shown carefully* ◊ ADJ CLASSIF : *selected places during our visit.* ATTRIB 2 A **select** group is a small group of some of the ADJ CLASSIF : best people or things of their kind. EG *They are* ATTRIB *members of a select band of professional athletes.* 3 Something that is **select** has many desirable ADJ QUALIT features, and is available only to people who have a lot of money or who belong to a high social class. EG *He went to a select New England school.*

selection /sɪˈlekʃəⁿn/, **selections.** 1 **Selection** is N UNCOUNT the selecting of one or more people or things from a group. EG *She stood little chance of selection... ...the judges' selection process.* 2 A **selection** of people or things is a set of them N PART that have been selected from a larger group. EG *The orchestra was playing a selection of tunes from the Merry Widow.* 3 The **selection** of goods in a shop is the particular N PART range of goods that it has available and from which you can choose what you want. EG *We have London's largest selection of office furniture.*

selective /sɪˈlektɪv/. 1 A **selective** process ap- ADJ CLASSIF : plies only to a few things or people. EG *...the* ATTRIB *selective education of the most talented children.* ◊ **selectively.** EG *Trees are felled selectively.* ◊ ADV 2 When someone is **selective**, they choose things ADJ QUALIT carefully, for example the things that they buy or do. EG *They are particularly selective in their television watching.* ◊ **selectively.** EG *A film crew* ◊ ADV *was selectively filming broken windows of shops owned by white people.*

self /self/, **selves** /selvz/. Your **self** is your basic N COUNT+POSS personality or nature. EG *By evening she was her normal self again... He was his usual imperturbable self... ...when his wife reveals her real self to him.*

self- 1 combines with adjectives and nouns to refer to something that you do by yourself or do to yourself. For example, if you are self-admiring, you admire yourself. EG *...self-induced catastrophes... ...self-improvement... ...self-pity.* 2 combines with adjectives to describe something such as a device that does something automatically by itself. EG *...a self-locking door... ...self-fulfilling prophecies.*

self-assured. Someone who is **self-assured** ADJ QUALIT shows confidence in what they say and do. EG *His comments were firm and self-assured.*

self-centred. Someone who is **self-centred** is ADJ QUALIT only concerned with their own wants and needs and never thinks about other people. EG *He was much too self-centred to notice her.*

self-confessed is used to describe someone who ADJ CLASSIF : admits openly that they have a particular charac- ATTRIB teristic which is usually considered to be bad. EG *...a self-confessed racialist.*

self-confident. Someone who is **self-confident** ADJ QUALIT behaves confidently because they feel sure of their abilities or worth. EG *She was remarkably self-confident for her age.* ◊ **self-confidence.** EG *He* ◊ N UNCOUNT *can only develop self-confidence if he is told he is clever.*

self-conscious. Someone who is **self-conscious** ADJ QUALIT is easily embarrassed and nervous because they feel that everyone is looking at them and judging them. EG *I stood there, feeling self-conscious. Was my hair out of place?... Patrick is self-conscious about his baldness.*

self-contained. 1 Something that is **self-** ADJ CLASSIF **contained** is complete and separate and does not need help or resources from outside. EG *...a society*

If a shop has a good selection, are you likely to find what you want?

SEMI-MODALS

The verbs **need**, **dare**, and **used** are often called semi-modals. This is because they are similar to modals in some ways but not in all. You can also use **need** and **dare** as main verbs, and they then behave like any ordinary verb. See below, and also the entries in the dictionary for **need** and **dare**.

When **need**, **dare**, and **used** are semi-modals:

Followed by an infinitive

Need and **dare** are followed by an infinitive without 'to': *I didn't dare send it . . .   You needn't worry.*

Used is always followed by **to**: *I used to feel guilty about him.*

With or without inflections

Need and **used** do not inflect, so the form does not change: *He need not do anything . . .   Things are worse than they used to be.*

Note that the example with **need** could refer to either the present or the past, but the example with **used** refers only to the past.

Dare can inflect, although it does not always do so in the present tense: *She dare not express her feelings . . .   No one dares disturb him.* The form **dared** is used to express past time: *Nobody dared open his mouth.*

With negatives

Dare and **used** are frequently followed by **not** or **never**, and **need** is nearly always used with a negative. **Not** can be shortened to **n't** and attached to the verb: *You need never worry about money . . .   I needn't say any more . . .   She daren't go upstairs . . .   They used not to bother.*

In questions

Dare and **need** can also be used in questions, coming in front of the subject: *Dare I ask where you have been? . . .   Need I say more?*

Referring back

Need, **dare**, and **used** can all be used to refer back to a previous verbal group: *I won't go in by myself, I daren't . . .   "I'll tell you as much as I know" – "You needn't, I'm not interested" . . .   She still goes dancing, but not as often as she used to.*

As ordinary verbs

When **dare** and **need** are used as ordinary verbs, they have the normal range of auxiliaries and modals in front of them: *He doesn't dare tell her what he did . . .   They didn't dare go home . . .   Do you need any help? . . .   Don't you dare come here again!*

of immense power, self-contained and well organized.

2 A **self-contained** flat has all its own facilities, so ADJ CLASSIF that a person living there does not have to share rooms such as a kitchen or bathroom with other people.

self-control. Your **self-control** is your ability to N UNCOUNT control your feelings so that you appear calm, even when you feel angry or afraid. EG *He lost his self-control and cried aloud.*

self-defence. **1** **Self-defence** is the use of vio- N UNCOUNT lence or special physical skills and techniques to protect yourself against someone who is trying to hurt you. EG *He had struck her in self-defence... They carry knives as instruments of self-defence.*

2 If you say something **in self-defence**, you give PHRASE reasons for your behaviour to someone who thinks you have behaved wrongly. EG '*I didn't want to go anyway,' he grumbled in self-defence.*

self-employed. If you are **self-employed**, you ADJ CLASSIF organize your own work, pay, and taxes, rather than being employed by a person or firm and being paid regular wages or a salary. EG *...a self-employed builder and decorator.*

self-evident. A fact or situation that is **self-** ADJ CLASSIF **evident** is so obvious that there is no need for proof or explanation. EG *The need for reform was self-evident.*

self-government is government or control of a N UNCOUNT country or organization by its own people rather than by others. EG *In Parliament he called for the democratic self-government of the colonies.*

self-imposed. A **self-imposed** task, condition, or ADJ CLASSIF responsibility is one that you have deliberately accepted for yourself. EG *...troubles that were largely self-imposed... ...self-imposed restrictions.*

self-indulgent. If you are **self-indulgent**, you ADJ QUALIT allow yourself to have or do things that you enjoy very much. ◊ **self-indulgence**. EG *Temptations to* ◊ N UNCOUNT *self-indulgence should be resisted.*

self-interest is the attitude of always wanting to N UNCOUNT do what is best for yourself rather than for anyone else. EG *Are they influenced by duty or self-interest?*

selfish /sɛlfɪʃ/. If you are **selfish**, you care only ADJ QUALIT about yourself, and not about other people. EG *...a totally selfish attitude... That's a selfish argument... How mean and selfish you are!* ◊ **selfishly**. EG ◊ ADV *Why is he acting so selfishly?* ◊ **selfishness**. EG *He* ◊ N UNCOUNT *felt ashamed of his selfishness.*

selfless /sɛlflɪ's/. If you are **selfless**, you care ADJ QUALIT about other people and their needs rather than considering yourself and your own needs. EG *It was impossible to repay years of selfless devotion.*

self-made is used to describe people who have ADJ CLASSIF : become successful and rich through their own ATTRIB efforts. EG *My father was a self-made man... ...a self-made millionaire.*

self-respect is a feeling of confidence and pride N UNCOUNT that you have in your own ability and worth. EG *Billy needs to have his self-respect restored.*

self-righteous. Someone who is **self-righteous** ADJ QUALIT is convinced that they are right in their beliefs, attitudes, and behaviour and that other people are wrong. EG *...self-righteous indignation... ...the self-righteous assumption that this could never happen to him.* ◊ **self-righteousness**. EG *There was a* ◊ N UNCOUNT *strong note of self-righteousness in his voice.*

self-sacrifice is the giving up of what you want N UNCOUNT so that other people can have what they need. EG *The children's education demanded effort and self-sacrifice... I admired her self-sacrifice.*

self-satisfied. If you describe someone as **self-** ADJ QUALIT **satisfied**, you mean that they are so pleased about their achievements or their situation that they do not feel there is any need to do anything more; used showing disapproval.

self-service. A **self-service** shop, restaurant, or ADJ CLASSIF garage is one where you serve yourself rather than being served by another person.

self-sufficient. If a country or group is **self-** ADJ QUALIT : **sufficient**, it is able to produce or make every- OFT+ *in* thing that it needs. EG *This country is self-sufficient in energy supplies.*

sell /sɛl/, **sells, selling, sold** /səʊld/. **1** If you **sell** v+o, v+o+o, something, you let someone have it in return for OR v+o+ *to* money. EG *He is going to sell me his car... She sold the house to the local council... I hope to sell the house for £30,000.*

2 If a shop **sells** a particular thing, it has it v+o available for people to buy. EG *Do you sell flowers?*

3 If something **sells** for a particular price, it is v+ *for/at* offered for sale at that price. EG *These little books sell for 95p each... ...a pocket calculator selling at the same price.*

4 If something **sells**, it is bought by the public, v : usu+A usually in fairly large quantities. EG *Their revolutionary jet did not sell well... Our product sells in forty-seven countries.*

5 Something that **sells** a product makes people v+o want to buy the product. EG *Scandal and gossip is what sells newspapers.*

6 If you **sell** yourself, you present yourself in a way v-REFL which makes people have confidence in you and Informal your abilities. EG *You've got to sell yourself at the interview.*

sell off. If you **sell** something **off**, you sell it all, PHRASAL VB : usually because you need the money. EG *He was* V+O+ADV forced to sell off his land.*

sell out. **1** If a shop **is sold out** of something or PHRASAL VB : **has sold out** of it, it has sold it all and there is V+ADV, none of it left in the shop. EG *They've sold out of* OFT+ *of* bread.*

2 If a performance of a play, film, or other v+o+ADV, entertainment **is sold out**, all the tickets have USU PASS been sold.

sell up. If you **sell up**, you sell everything you PHRASAL VB : have, such as your house or your business, because V+ADV OR you need the money. V+O+ADV

seller /sɛlə/, **sellers**. A **seller** is a person or a N COUNT business that sells something. EG *Umbrella sellers went out of business.* ● See also **best-seller**.

Sellotape /sɛləteɪp/ is transparent sticky tape N UNCOUNT that is sold in rolls and is used for sticking together Trademark things such as paper and cardboard. EG *I tried to stick the sign back on with Sellotape.*

selves /sɛlvz/ is the plural of **self**.

semblance /sɛmbləns/. If there is a **semblance** N SING+ *of* of a particular condition or quality, it appears to Formal exist, even though this may be a false impression. EG *By this time some semblance of order had been established... This indifference helped him to regain a semblance of calm.*

semen /siːmɛn/ is the liquid containing sperm that N UNCOUNT is produced by the sex organs of men and male animals.

semi- is used to form adjectives and nouns that PREFIX describe someone or something as being partly, but not completely, in a particular state. For example, someone who is semi-conscious is not completely conscious. EG *...semi-skilled workers... He lived in semi-retirement... We sat in the semi-darkness.*

semicircle /sɛmiˈsɜːkəl/, **semicircles**. A **semi-** N COUNT circle is one half of a circle. EG *We sat in a big semicircle round Hunter's desk.*

semi-colon, semi-colons. A **semi-colon** is a N COUNT punctuation mark (;) which is used in writing to separate different parts of a sentence or list or to indicate a pause.

semi-detached. A **semi-detached** house is a ADJ CLASSIF house that is joined to another house on one side by a shared wall. ► used as a noun. EG *They have a* ► N SING *small semi-detached.* British

---

Does it make sense to stop a competition at the semi-finals?

semi-final, semi-finals. A **semi-final** is one of N COUNT the two matches in a competition that are played to decide which two players or teams will compete in the final. EG *We reached the semi-final of the World Cup.*

seminar /sɛmɪnɑː/, **seminars.** A **seminar** is a N COUNT class at a college or university in which the teacher and a small group of students discuss a topic.

semi-precious. **Semi-precious** stones are ADJ CLASSIF: stones such as opals or turquoises that are used in ATTRIB jewellery. They are less valuable than precious stones such as diamonds, rubies, and sapphires.

SEN /ɛs iː ɛn/, **SEN's.** An **SEN** is someone who N COUNT has successfully completed a two-year practical course in nursing in the United Kingdom. **SEN** is an abbreviation for 'State Enrolled Nurse'.

Senate /sɛnɪt/. The **Senate** is the smaller and N PROPER: more important of the two councils in the govern- the+N ment of some countries, for example in the U.S.A. EG *This proposal was approved by both the House and the Senate.*

senator /sɛnətə/, **senators.** A **senator** is a mem- N COUNT ber of a law-making senate. EG *...Senator Edward Kennedy.*

send /sɛnd/, **sends, sending, sent** /sɛnt/. 1 When V+O: OFT+*to* you **send** something to someone, you arrange for it OR V+O+O to be taken and delivered to them, for example by post. EG *I drafted a letter and sent it to the President... You will be sent a timetable of the election... Send it round in the morning.*

2 If you **send** a radio signal or message, you cause V+O: USU+A it to go to a place by means of radio waves. EG *Marconi succeeded in sending a signal across the Atlantic.*

3 If you **send** someone somewhere, **3.1** you tell V+O+A them to go there. EG *The doctor sent me to a specialist... Could you send someone round to help?* **3.2** you arrange for them to stay there for a period of time. EG *His parents couldn't afford to send him to university.*

4 If something **sends** things or people in a particu- V+O+A OR lar direction, it causes them to move in that V+O+-ING direction. EG *The stubble was burning in the fields, sending wisps of black smoke into the air... The noise sent them racing towards the bush.*

send for. 1 If you **send for** someone, you ask PHRASAL VB: them to come and see you, by sending them a V+PREP, message. EG *She sent for a doctor... We'd better* HAS PASS *send for the police.*

2 If you **send for** something or **send off for** it, you V+PREP OR write and ask for it to be sent to you. EG *Send for* V+ADV+PREP, *the nomination forms before it's too late... I'll send* HAS PASS *off for them next week.*

send in. If you **send in** a report or an application, PHRASAL VB: you send it to a place where it will be officially V+O+ADV dealt with. EG *Don't forget to send in your entries for the competition... I was expected to send in a written report every two months.*

send off. If you **send off** a letter or parcel, you PHRASAL VB: send it somewhere by post. EG *You fill in both parts* V+O+ADV *of the form, then send it off.*

send off for. See paragraph 2 of **send for.**

send up. If you **send** someone or something **up,** PHRASAL VB: you imitate them in a way that makes them appear V+O+ADV foolish. EG *Wodehouse sends up the world of* Informal *Buchan.*

senile /siːnaɪl/. If old people become **senile,** they ADJ CLASSIF become confused, can no longer remember things, and are unable to look after themselves. EG *The old lady was now half blind and nearly senile.*

◊ **senility** /sənɪlɪtiː/. EG *Sheila became increasing-* ◊ N UNCOUNT *ly affected by senility.*

senior /siːnjə/, **seniors.** 1 The **senior** people in an ADJ QUALIT organization or profession have the highest and most important jobs in it. EG *...senior officers... He held a very senior position in the British Foreign Service... ...a senior member of staff.*

2 If someone is **senior** to you in an organization or ADJ QUALIT: profession, they have a higher and more important OFT+*to*

job than you. EG *There are plenty of others senior to me: George and Jock for example.*

3 Someone who is your **senior** is older than you N SING+POSS are. EG *She was at least fifteen years his senior.*

4 At a school or college, the **seniors** are the pupils N COUNT or students who are older and have reached an advanced level in their studies.

senior citizen, senior citizens. A **senior citi-** N COUNT **zen** is a person who is old enough to receive an old-age pension. EG *...free bus travel for senior citizens.*

seniority /siːniˈɒrɪtiː/. A person's **seniority** in an N UNCOUNT organization is their degree of importance and power compared to other people who work there. EG *The size of office will vary according to your seniority... The report listed their names in order of seniority.*

sensation /sɛnseɪʃn/, **sensations.** 1 A **sensa-** N COUNT: **tion** is a physical feeling. EG *...a sharp tingling* USU+SUPP *sensation that ran through her whole body... It produces a mild burning sensation in the mouth.*

2 You can use **sensation** to refer to the general N COUNT: feeling or impression caused by a particular ex- USU+SUPP perience. EG *It was a strange sensation to return to the school again after so long... She had the sensation that she had done all this before.*

3 If an event or situation is a **sensation,** it causes N COUNT great excitement or interest. EG *The film was an overnight sensation... The discovery was hailed as the scientific sensation of the century.*

sensational /sɛnseɪʃənəl, -ʃənəl/. 1 Something ADJ QUALIT that is **sensational** is so remarkable that it causes great excitement and interest. EG *This is the most sensational result of any election since the war... ...sensational discoveries.*

2 You can describe something as **sensational** ADJ QUALIT when you think that it is extremely good. EG *I've discovered a sensational health-food store... That was a sensational evening.* ◊ **sensationally.** EG ◊ SUBMOD *Edith Evans was sensationally good.* Informal

sense /sɛns/, **senses, sensing, sensed.** 1 Your N COUNT **senses** are the physical abilities of sight, smell, hearing, touch, and taste. EG *They all have an excellent sense of smell.* ● See also **sixth sense.**

2 If you **sense** something, you become aware of it V+O OR or you realize it, although it is not very obvious. EG V+REPORT *Doctors often sense uneasiness in people... He sensed that she did not want to talk to him.*

3 If you have a **sense** of guilt or shame, for N SING+*of* example, you feel guilty or ashamed. EG *I was overcome by a sense of failure.*

4 If you have a **sense** of something such as duty or N SING+*of* justice, you can recognize it and you believe that it is important. EG *She has a strong sense of justice.*

5 Someone who has a **sense** of timing or style, for N SING+SUPP example, has a natural ability for timing or style. EG *A good sense of timing is important for an actor... He hasn't got much dress sense.*

6 Sense is the ability to make good judgements and N UNCOUNT to behave sensibly. EG *She had the good sense to realize that the plan would never work... Your friends have more money than sense.* ● See also **common sense.**

7 If you say that there is **no sense** or **little sense** PHRASE in doing something, you mean that nothing useful would be gained by doing it. EG *There's no sense in making people unhappy.*

8 The phrase **make sense** is used in these ways. PHRASE **8.1** If something **makes sense,** you can understand it. EG *I looked at the printed page but the words made no sense.* **8.2** When you **make sense** of something, you succeed in understanding it. EG *You had to read it six times to make any sense of it.* **8.3** If a course of action **makes sense,** it seems sensible. EG *Under these conditions it made sense to adopt labour-saving methods.*

9 If you say that someone **talks sense,** you mean PHRASE that what they say is sensible. EG *On defence matters he talked a great deal of sense.*

10 If you say that someone has **come to** their PHRASE

senses or has **been brought to** their **senses**, you mean that they have stopped being foolish and are being sensible again.

11 A **sense** of a word or expression is one of its possible meanings. EG *I don't like the Washington climate – in all senses of the word.* · N COUNT

12 If you say that something is true **in a sense**, you mean that it is partly true, or that it is true in one way. EG *In a sense, I still love him.* · ADV SEN

senseless /sɛnslɪˀs/. 1 You describe an action as **senseless** when it seems to have no meaning or purpose. EG *It was a senseless thing to do... He made senseless expeditions to India.* · ADJ QUALIT

2 If someone is **senseless**, they are unconscious. EG *A heavy blow with a club knocked him senseless.* · ADJ CLASSIF

sense of humour. 1 Someone who has a **sense of humour** often finds things amusing, rather than being serious all the time. EG *He lacked any sense of humour.* · N SING

2 Someone's **sense of humour** is the way that they are amused by certain things but not by others. EG *I see your sense of humour hasn't changed.* · N UNCOUNT

sensibility /sɛnsɪbɪlɪˈtiˀ/, **sensibilities.** Someone's **sensibility** is their ability to experience deep feelings. EG *...a writer of high sensibility and intelligence... These words touched his sensibilities.* · N UNCOUNT OR N COUNT

sensible /sɛnsɪbəˀl/. A **sensible** person is able to make good decisions and judgements based on reasons rather than emotions. EG *It seemed sensible to move to a bigger house... ...sensible decisions.* ◊ **sensibly.** EG *They sensibly concluded that this wouldn't be a good idea.* · ADJ QUALIT ◊ ADV

sensitive /sɛnsɪtɪv/. 1 If you are **sensitive** to other people's problems and feelings, you show understanding and awareness of them. EG *We're trying to make people more sensitive to the difficulties faced by working mothers... ...a sensitive story about the problems of growing up.* · ADJ QUALIT OFT+to
◊ **sensitively.** EG *...this well acted, sensitively directed play.* ◊ **sensitivity** /sɛnsɪtɪvɪˈtiˀ/. EG *Her remarks showed a lack of sensitivity.* ◊ ADV ◊ N UNCOUNT

2 If you are **sensitive** about something, it worries you or makes you upset or angry. EG *You really must stop being so sensitive about your accent... He's very sensitive to criticism.* · ADJ QUALIT OFT+about/to

3 A **sensitive** subject or issue needs to be dealt with carefully because it is likely to cause disagreement or make people angry or upset. EG *This is one of the most sensitive issues that the government faces.* · ADJ QUALIT

4 Something that is **sensitive** to a physical force, substance, or condition is easily affected by it and often harmed by it. EG *Children's bones are very sensitive to radiation... ...people with sensitive skin.* · ADJ QUALIT : OFT+to
◊ **sensitivity.** EG *...the sensitivity of the lining of the nasal cavity.* ◊ N UNCOUNT

5 A **sensitive** piece of scientific equipment is capable of measuring or recording very small changes. EG *...highly sensitive electronic cameras.* · ADJ QUALIT

sensory /sɛnsəˀriˀ/ means relating to the physical senses. EG *With these two highly developed sensory organs it hunts at night for insects.* · ADJ CLASSIF ATTRIB Formal

sensual /sɛnsjuˀəl/. 1 Someone or something that is **sensual** shows or suggests a great liking for physical pleasures, especially sexual pleasures. EG *...an extravagantly sensual woman... ...plump sensual lips.* ◊ **sensuality** /sɛnsjuˀælɪˈtiˀ/. EG *Her body shone through the cloth with sheer sensuality.* · ADJ QUALIT ◊ N UNCOUNT

2 Something that is **sensual** gives pleasure to your physical senses rather than to your mind. EG *...the subtle, sensual rhythms of the drums.* ◊ **sensuality.** EG *...the sensuality of English music.* · ADJ QUALIT ◊ N UNCOUNT

sensuous /sɛnsjuˀəs/. Something that is **sensuous** gives pleasure to the mind or body through the senses. EG *Sculpture is a sensuous art... ...a sensuous colour... ...fresh peaches, sweet, cool, and sensuous.* ◊ **sensuously.** EG *Her fingers sensuously stroked his neck.* · ADJ QUALIT ◊ ADV

sent /sɛnt/ is the past tense and past participle of **send.**

sentence /sɛntəns/, **sentences, sentencing, sentenced.** 1 A **sentence** is a group of words which, when they are written down, begin with a capital letter and end with a full stop. EG *Most of them could read a simple sentence in English... ...the opening sentence of the report... He put the phone down before she could finish the sentence.* · N COUNT

2 In a law court, a **sentence** is the punishment that a person receives after they have been found guilty of a crime. EG *If found guilty they will face a sentence of ten years in prison... He is serving a life sentence for murder.* · N COUNT OR N UNCOUNT

3 When a judge **sentences** someone, he or she states in court what their punishment will be. EG *Griffiths was sentenced to four years' imprisonment for robbery.* · V+O : OFT+to

sentence adverb, sentence adverbs. In grammar, a **sentence adverb** is an adverb which comments on the whole clause or sentence rather than on a single word. Sentence adverbs usually express the speaker's or writer's personal opinion. In this dictionary the label ADV SEN is used in the Extra Column to mean 'sentence adverb'. See the entry headed ADVERBS for more information. · N COUNT

sentiment /sɛntɪməˀnt/, **sentiments.** 1 A **sentiment** that people have is an attitude which is based on their thoughts and feelings. EG *These events led to a vast upsurge of anti-imperialist sentiment.* · N UNCOUNT OR N COUNT

2 Someone's **sentiment** is an idea or feeling that they express in words. EG *These sentiments were generally echoed by other speakers at the meeting.* · N COUNT

3 **Sentiment** is an emotion such as tenderness, romance, or sadness, which influences a person's behaviour. EG *I'm worried that you might be doing it out of sentiment. Out of affection for me.* · N UNCOUNT

sentimental /sɛntɪmɛntəˀl/. 1 Someone or something that is **sentimental** feels or arouses emotions such as tenderness, romance, or sadness, sometimes to an extent which is considered exaggerated. EG *...sentimental songs... People have become sentimental about the passing of ways and customs.* ◊ **sentimentally.** EG *Romantic love and motherhood are sentimentally idealized.* ◊ **sentimentality** /sɛntɪmɛntælɪˈtiˀ/. EG *...her sentimentality about animals.* · ADJ QUALIT ◊ ADV ◊ N UNCOUNT

2 You use **sentimental** to describe things relating to a person's emotions. EG *The ring had been her mother's and she wore it for sentimental reasons.* ◊ **sentimentally.** EG *He had become sentimentally attached to a postgraduate student.* · ADJ CLASSIF ◊ ADV

sentry /sɛntriˀ/, **sentries.** A **sentry** is a soldier who guards a camp or a building. EG *...look-out posts where sentries kept watch... Who is on sentry duty tonight?* · N COUNT

separate, separates, separating, separated; pronounced /sɛpəˀrəˀt/ when it is an adjective and /sɛpəreɪt/ when it is a verb. 1 If one thing is **separate** from another, the two things are apart from each other and are not connected. EG *Rosa had remained separate from us, asking for a room by herself... Two masses can be kept separate inside the bomb casing... They left the party in 1963 to form the first separate Maoist group in Britain.* · ADJ CLASSIF : OFT+from
◊ **separately.** EG *What we achieve together is more important than what we can do separately.* ◊ ADV

2 **Separate** things are individual and distinct from each other. EG *The sunlight caught each tiny separate hair and made it shine... Babies feed eagerly for two separate reasons.* ◊ **separately.** EG *Wash each pile separately.* · ADJ CLASSIF ◊ ADV

3 If you **separate** people or things, you move them or keep them apart so that they are not connected · V+O OR V+O+from : RECIP

Make a list of the things that you own that have serial numbers on them.

or cannot communicate. EG *Even at dinner time we were separated; she ate in one place, and I ate in another... In any angry discussion he would separate the opponents and soothe them.*

4 If you **separate** ideas from each other, you V+O OR consider them individually and show the distinction V+O+*from* : between them. EG *Faith and God to me are the* RECIP *same thing, I can't separate them.*

5 A detail that **separates** one thing from another V+O+*from* thing shows that the two things are different from each other. EG *Higher living standards separate the older generation from their children.*

6 If an object, period of time, or distance **sepa-** V+O : **rates** two people, groups, or things, it exists be- USU+*from* tween them and prevents them from having contact with each other. EG *A fence at the back of the garden separated us from the neighbours... ...the Great Lakes separating Canada from America.*

7 If you **separate** a group of things or if you V+O : OFT+*out* **separate** them out, you divide them so that each different part becomes separate. EG *Most schools decide to separate out their pupils into different groups according to age.*

8 If a group of people or things **separate**, they V OR V+*from* : move away from each other after being together RECIP or connected for a time. EG *They talked by the gate, unwilling to separate... The two pipes separated from each other.*

9 If a couple who are married or living together V : OFT+*from* **separate**, they decide to live apart. EG *Her parents separated when she was eleven.*

separated /sepəreɪtɪ²d/. Someone who is **sepa-** ADJ PRED **rated** from their wife or husband lives apart from them, but is not divorced. EG *My wife and I are separated.*

separation /sepəreɪʃə⁰n/, **separations. 1** The N UNCOUNT **separation** of two or more people, things, or groups is their movement away from each other or their state of being kept apart from each other. EG *...the separation of infant from mother.*

2 A **separation** between two or more people is a N COUNT OR period of time that they spend apart from each N UNCOUNT other. EG *Children recover remarkably quickly from a brief separation from their parents.*

3 If a couple who are married or living together N COUNT OR have a **separation**, they decide to live apart. EG N UNCOUNT *Last night we talked about a separation.*

September /septembə/ is the ninth month of the N UNCOUNT year in the Western calendar. EG *Gladys died on September 27th, 1976.*

septic /septɪk/. If a wound or a part of your body ADJ CLASSIF becomes **septic**, it becomes infected with poison.

sequel /si:kwə⁰l/, **sequels. 1** A book or film which N COUNT : is a **sequel** to an earlier one continues the story of OFT+*to* the earlier one. EG *He starred in 'The Godfather' and in its sequel, 'The Godfather II'.*

2 The **sequel** to something that happened is an N COUNT : event or situation that happened after it or as a OFT+*to* result of it. EG *There was an amusing sequel to this incident.*

sequence /si:kwə⁰ns/, **sequences. 1** A **sequence** N COUNT+*of* of events or things is a number of events or things that come one after another in a particular order. EG *...the strange sequence of events that led up to the murder.*

2 A particular **sequence** is a particular order in N COUNT OR which things happen or are arranged. EG *The* N UNCOUNT *paintings are exhibited in a chronological sequence... These recordings are in sequence and continuous.*

3 A film **sequence** is a part of a film that shows a N COUNT single set of actions. EG *What did you think of that ghastly sequence at the end?*

sequin /si:kwɪn/, **sequins. Sequins** are small, N COUNT : shiny discs that are sewn on clothes to decorate USU PLURAL them. EG *...a dress embroidered with thousands of tiny sequins.*

serene /sɪ²ri:n/. Someone or something that is ADJ QUALIT **serene** is calm and quiet. EG *She had a naturally*

cheerful and serene expression... ...a serene mountain landscape. ◇ **serenely**. EG *Her blue eyes* ◇ ADV *gazed serenely into space.* ◇ **serenity** /sɪ²reni¹ti¹/. ◇ N UNCOUNT EG *I was moved by her serenity and confidence.*

serf /sɜːf/, **serfs. Serfs** were a class of people in N COUNT medieval Europe who had to work on their master's land and could not leave without his permission.

sergeant /sɑːdʒənt/, **sergeants. A sergeant** is **1** N COUNT a non-commissioned officer of middle rank in the army or the air force. **2** an officer with the next to lowest rank in the police force.

sergeant major, sergeant majors. A sergeant N COUNT **major** is a non-commissioned army officer of the highest rank.

serial /sɪ²ərɪəl/, **serials. A serial** is a story which N COUNT is broadcast on television or radio or published in a magazine in a number of parts over a period of time. EG *The novel has recently been dramatized as a television serial.*

serialize /sɪ²ərɪəlaɪz/, **serializes, serializing, se-** V+O : USU PASS **rialized**; also spelled **serialise**. If a book **is se-** **rialized**, it is broadcast on the radio or television or published in a magazine in a number of parts. EG *His book 'Blood on the Snow' is currently being serialized on 'Woman's Hour'.*

serial number, serial numbers. The serial N COUNT **number** of an object is the number on that object which identifies it. EG *...the serial number of the cheque card.*

series /sɪ²ərɪ¹z/. **Series** is both the singular and the plural form.

1 A **series** of things or events is a number of them N COUNT : that come one after the other. EG *He was arrested* USU+*of* *in connection with a series of armed bank robberies... ...a series of lectures on American politics.*

2 A radio or television **series** is a set of pro- N COUNT grammes of a particular kind which have the same title. EG *...the popular television series, 'Yes, Minister'... ...a new 6 week series on Europe.*

serious /sɪ²ərɪəs/. **1** Problems or situations that ADJ QUALIT are **serious** are very bad and cause people to be worried. EG *Bad housing is one of the most serious problems in the inner cities... ...a serious illness... It is in a serious condition.* ◇ **seriously**. EG *She was* ◇ ADV *seriously ill.* ◇ **seriousness**. EG *...the seriousness of* ◇ N UNCOUNT *the problem.*

2 Serious matters are important and deserve ADJ QUALIT careful and thoughtful consideration. EG *It's time to get down to the serious business of the meeting... She is a serious candidate for the presidency.*

3 Serious work or consideration of something ADJ CLASSIF : involves thinking about things deeply and thought- ATTRIB fully because they are important. EG *The programme is a forum for serious political discussion... ...a serious newspaper.*

4 If someone is **serious** about something, they are ADJ QUALIT : sincere about what they are saying, doing, or OFT+*about* intending to do. EG *You can't be serious!... I knew that he was serious about the struggle.*

◇ **seriously**. EG *I'm seriously thinking of retiring.* ◇ ADV ◇ **seriousness**. EG *I see no reason, in all serious-* ◇ N UNCOUNT *ness, why women should not become priests.*

5 People who are **serious** are thoughtful, quiet, ADJ QUALIT and slightly humourless. EG *She was a rather serious girl... ...a serious manner.* ◇ **seriously**. EG *He* ◇ ADV *talked very seriously and solemnly about theoretical matters.*

seriously /sɪ²ərɪəsli¹/. **1** You say **seriously 1.1** to ADV SEN indicate that you really mean what you say. EG *What I do think is important, quite seriously, is that people should know the facts.* **1.2** when you are CONVENTION surprised by what someone has said, as a way of asking them if they really mean it. EG *'I've given up my job.' - 'Seriously?'*

2 If you **take** someone or something **seriously**, PHRASE you believe that they are important and deserve attention. EG *They take their responsibilities seriously... His work was not taken seriously.*

3 See also **serious**.

sermon /sɜːmən/, **sermons**. A **sermon** is a talk N COUNT
on a religious or moral subject that is given by a
member of the clergy as part of a church service.
EG ...the church where John Donne preached his
first sermon.

serpent /sɜːpənt/, **serpents**. A **serpent** is a N COUNT
snake. Literary

serrated /sɪˈreɪtɪᵈd/. A **serrated** object has a row ADJ CLASSIF:
of V-shaped points along the edge. EG ...serrated ATTRIB
scissors... ...huge serrated leaves.

serum /sɪərᵊm/, **serums**. A **serum** is a liquid N COUNT OR
that is injected into someone's blood to protect N UNCOUNT
them against a poison or disease. EG This serum
was most effective against snake poison.

servant /sɜːvᵊnt/, **servants**. A **servant** is some- N COUNT
one who is employed to work in another person's
house, for example as a cleaner or a gardener. EG
She worked all her life as a domestic servant. ● See
also **civil servant**.

serve /sɜːv/, **serves, serving, served**. 1 If you V+O OR V+A
serve your country, an organization, or a person,
you do useful work for them. EG For over thirty
years, she has served the company loyally and
well... He served with the army in France.

2 If something **serves** as a particular thing or V+A, V+to-INF,
serves a particular purpose, it performs a particu- OR V+O
lar function. EG There was a long, grey building that
served as a cafeteria... This will serve as a valuable
reminder of the dangers involved... His refusal to
answer only serves to increase our suspicions... I
failed to see what purpose this could serve.

3 If something **serves** people or an area, it pro- V+O
vides them with something that they need. EG
There were five water taps to serve all thirty
camps... ...work which will serve the community.

4 If you **serve** people or if you **serve** food and V+O
drink, you give people food and drink. EG When
everybody had been served, the meal began... A leg
of lamb came next, served with new potatoes... I
served the children their meal.

5 **Serve** is sometimes used in recipes. For exam- V+O : NO CONT
ple, a recipe that **serves** six provides enough food
for six people.

6 Someone who **serves** customers in a shop or a V+O OR V
bar helps them and provides them with what they
want to buy. EG The bartender refused to serve us...
She spent six months serving in a shop.

7 When a court **serves** a legal order on someone V+O+on OR
or **serves** them with it, it sends the legal order to V+O+with
them. EG The court served her with an enforcement Legal
notice.

8 If you **serve** something such as a prison sentence V+O
or an apprenticeship, you spend a period of time
doing it. EG He is now serving a life sentence in an
Italian jail.

9 When you **serve** in games such as tennis and V OR V+O
badminton, you throw up the ball or shuttlecock
and hit it to start play. EG He served an ace. ▸ used ▸ N COUNT
as a noun. EG Her second serve went into the net.

10 If you say it **serves** someone **right** when PHRASE
something unpleasant happens to them, you mean
that it is their own fault and you have no sympathy
for them. EG 'I feel terrible.' - 'Serves you right for
drinking so much.'

11 See also **serving**.

serve out or **serve up**. If you **serve out** food or PHRASAL VB :
serve it **up**, you give it to people as a meal. EG V+O+ADV
Army kitchens serve up better fare than some
hotels do.

service /sɜːvɪs/, **services, servicing, serviced**. N COUNT+SUPP
1 A **service** is 1.1 an organization or system that
provides something for the public, for example
transport or information. EG I think the train service is better than it used to be... ...the postal
service. 1.2 an official organization or government
department that does a particular job. EG ...the
diplomatic service.

2 A **service** is also a job that an organization can N COUNT+SUPP

do for you. EG The post office can forward your
letters; the fee for this service is £6... It boosts
demand for goods and services... ...taking people
out of factories into service industries.

3 The **services** are the army, the navy, and the air N PLURAL :
force. EG Young people are being encouraged to the+N
join the services.

4 Your **services** are the work that you can do for N PLURAL
people. EG They will be very happy to give their +POSS
services free of charge.

5 **Service** is the state or activity of working for a N UNCOUNT
particular person or organization. EG Conscription
would be limited to a maximum of six months'
service.

6 **Service** is also the process of being served in a N UNCOUNT
shop or restaurant. EG He hammered the table for
immediate service.

7 If someone or something is **of service** to you, PHRASE
they help you or are useful to you. EG In what way Formal
may I be of service to you?

8 If a machine or type of vehicle is in **service**, it is N UNCOUNT
being used or is able to be used. EG Most of the AFTER PREP
vehicles had been withdrawn from service.

9 When a machine is **serviced**, it is examined, V+O
adjusted, and cleaned so that it will keep working
efficiently and safely. EG Gas appliances should be
serviced regularly. ▸ used as a noun. EG The car ▸ N COUNT
needs a service.

10 A religious **service** is a religious ceremony. EG N COUNT
...the Sunday evening service.

11 A dinner **service** or a tea **service** is a complete N COUNT :
set of dishes, plates, and other pieces of china. USU+SUPP

12 A **services** is a place where you can stop on a N COUNT
motorway and where there is a garage, a restaurant, a shop, and toilets. The plural is also **services**.

13 See also **Civil Service, community service,
National Health Service, national service**.

serviceable /sɜːvɪsəbᵊl/. Something that is **ser-** ADJ QUALIT
viceable performs its function effectively. EG I Formal
wore serviceable boots.

service charge. A **service charge** is an amount N SING
that is added to your bill in a restaurant to pay for
the work of the waiter or waitress who serves you.
EG The service charge is 10 per cent.

serviceman /sɜːvɪsmᵊn/, **servicemen**. A **ser-** N COUNT
viceman is a man who is in the army, navy, or air
force.

serviette /sɜːvɪet/, **serviettes**. A **serviette** is a N COUNT
square of cloth or paper that you use to protect
your clothes or to wipe your mouth when you are
eating.

servile /sɜːvaɪl/. Someone who is **servile** is too ADJ QUALIT
eager to do things for someone and shows them too Formal
much respect. EG ...the incurably servile housekeeper.

serving /sɜːvɪŋ/, **servings**. 1 A **serving** is an N COUNT
amount of food that is given to one person at a
meal. EG His mother was spooning out servings of
tuna fish casserole.

2 A **serving** spoon or dish is used for giving out ADJ CLASSIF :
food at a meal. ATTRIB

session /seʃᵊn/, **sessions**. 1 A **session** is 1.1 a N COUNT
meeting of an official group. EG ...an emergency
session of the United Nations Security Council. 1.2 N COUNT
a period during which the meetings of an official
group are regularly held. EG ...the government's
programme for the 1966-67 parliamentary session.

2 When an official group is **in session**, it is PHRASE
formally holding a meeting. The court is still in
session.

3 A **session** of a particular activity is a period of N COUNT :
that activity. EG ...a tough bargaining session... ...an USU+SUPP
all-night drinking session.

What service do you use when you set the table?

set /sɛt/, **sets, setting.** The form **set** is used in the present tense and is the past tense and past participle of the verb.

1 A **set** of things is a number of things that belong together or that are thought of as a group. EG ...*a set of encyclopaedias... We soon encountered a new set of problems... ...a chess set.* `N COUNT+SUPP OR N PART`

2 If you **set** something somewhere, you put it there, especially in a careful or deliberate way. EG *He filled the kettle and set it on the stove.* `V+O+A`

3 If something **is set** in a particular place or position, it is in that place or position. EG *The house is set back from the road... His eyes were set close together.* `V-PASS+A`

4 If something **is set** into a surface, it is fixed there and does not stick out. EG *There was one tiny window set into the stone wall.* `V+O+into/in : USU PASS`

5 You can use **set** to say that a person or thing causes something to be in a particular condition or situation. EG *Let me set your mind at rest... The change was set in motion by President Carter... One prisoner had been set free... A gust of wind set all the candles spluttering.* `V+O+A, V+O+C, OR V+-ING`

6 When the sun **sets**, it goes below the horizon. `V`

7 When someone **sets** a trap, they prepare it. `V+O`

8 When someone **sets** the table, they prepare it for a meal by putting plates and cutlery on it. `V+O`

9 When someone **sets** a clock or control, they adjust it to a particular point or level. EG *His alarm clock was set for four a.m.* `V+O : OFT+A`

10 If you **set** a time, price, or level, you decide what it will be. EG *They haven't set a date for the wedding... The government set a minimum price of £1.15.* `V+O : OFT+A`

11 You use **set** to describe something which is fixed and does not change. EG *We paid a set amount for the course... There are no set rules laid down for dealing with this kind of emergency... Her day usually followed a set pattern.* `ADJ CLASSIF : ATTRIB`

12 If you **are set in** your **ways**, your habits and ideas are not likely to change. EG *She is too old and set in her ways ever to change.* `PHRASE`

13 If you **set** something such as a precedent or a standard, you establish it for other people to copy or to try to achieve. EG *Try and set the younger children a good example... They tended to follow the trend set by the other banks.* `V+O, V+O+O, OR V+O+for`

14 If someone **sets** you some work or **sets** you a target, they say that you must do the work or reach the target. EG *She had set a composition for her pupils... The new management set itself three aims.* `V+O, V+O+O, OR V+O+for`

15 A **set** book must be studied by students taking a particular course. `ADJ CLASSIF : ATTRIB`

16 If you are **set** to do something, you are ready to do it or are likely to do it. EG *The left-wing seem set to do very well in the general election.* `ADJ PRED : OFT +to-INF OR for`

17 If you are **set** on doing something, you are strongly determined to do it. EG *She is set on regaining her title.* `ADJ PRED+on`

18 If you **set** your face or jaw, you put on a fixed expression of determination. EG *I set my face into a grimace.* `V+O`

19 When something such as glue, jelly, or cement **sets**, it becomes firm or hard. EG *The cement had set hard.* `V OR V+C`

20 If someone **sets** a poem to music, they write music for it. `V+O+to : USU PASS`

21 A television **set** is a television. EG *We have a TV set in the living room.* `N COUNT : USU+SUPP`

22 The **set** for a play or film is the furniture or scenery on the stage or in the studio. `N COUNT`

23 If a play, film, or story **is set** at a particular time or in a particular place, the events in it take place at that time or in that place. EG *The play is set in a small Midlands village.* `V+O+A : USU PASS`

24 In tennis, a **set** is one of the groups of six or more games that form part of a match. `N COUNT`

25 to **set eyes on** someone: see **eye**. ● to **set fire to** something: see **fire**. ● to **set foot**: see **foot**. ● to

set your **heart on** something: see **heart**. ● to **set sail**: see **sail**. ● to **set the stage for**: see **stage**. ● to **set to work**: see **work**. ● See also **setting**.

set about. If you **set about** doing something, you start doing it. EG *The next morning they set about cleaning the house.* `PHRASAL VB : V+PREP, USU+-ING`

set against. 1 If you **set** one fact or argument **against** another, you consider the first one in relation to the second one. EG *This slight improvement has to be set against an enormous increase in crime.* **2** To **set** one person **against** another means to cause them to become enemies or rivals. `V+O+PREP`

set apart. If a characteristic **sets** you **apart** from other people, it makes you recognizably different from the others. EG *His exceptional height set him apart from the rest of the men.* `PHRASAL VB : V+O+ADV, OFT+from`

set aside. 1 If you **set** something **aside** for a special use or purpose, you keep it available for that use or purpose. EG *Try and set aside time to do some mending jobs.* **2** If you **set aside** a belief, principle, or feeling, you decide that you will not be influenced by it. EG *We must try and set aside our past hostilities.* `PHRASAL VB : V+O+ADV`

set back. 1 If something **sets** you **back** or **sets back** a project or scheme, it causes a delay. EG *This has set back the whole programme of nuclear power in America.* **2** If something **sets** you **back** a large amount of money, it costs you that much money. EG *The legal costs set him back something in the order of £10,000.* **3** See also **setback**. `PHRASAL VB : V+O+ADV` `V+O+ADV+O Informal`

set down. If you **set down** your thoughts or experiences, you write them all down. EG *They were asked to set down a summary of their views.* `PHRASAL VB : V+O+ADV`

set in. If something unpleasant **sets in**, it begins and seems likely to continue or develop. EG *A feeling of anti-climax set in... It must be treated quickly before infection sets in.* `PHRASAL VB : V+ADV`

set off. 1 When you **set off**, you start a journey. EG *Dan set off down the mountain to find help... He set off on a trip to Mexico.* **2** If something **sets off** an event or a series of events, it causes it to start happening. EG *Most analysts expected that Mobil's offer would set off a new round of bidding for Conoco.* `PHRASAL VB : V+ADV` `V+O+ADV+O`

set on. To **set** animals **on** someone means to cause the animals to attack them. EG *We were afraid they might set the dogs on us.* `PHRASAL VB : V+O+PREP`

set out. 1 When you **set out**, you start a journey. EG *We set out along the beach... They set out for Cuba on a two-day trip.* **2** If you **set out** to do something, you start trying to do it. EG *They had failed in what they had set out to do.* **3** If you **set** things **out**, you arrange or display them somewhere. EG *There were plenty of chairs set out for the guests.* **4** If you **set out** a number of facts, beliefs, or arguments, you give them in writing or speech in a clear, organized way. EG *Darwin set out his theory in detail in 'The Origin of Species'.* `PHRASAL VB : V+ADV, OFT+A` `V+ADV+to-INF` `PHRASAL VB : V+O+ADV` `V+O+ADV`

set up. 1 If you **set** something **up**, you make the preparations that are necessary for it to start. EG *It took a long time to set up the experiment... The government were setting up an inquiry into the affair... An anti-terrorist squad was set up.* ◇ **setting up.** EG *...the setting up of a Northern Seas Environmental Control Agency.* **2** If you **set up** a structure, you place it or build it somewhere. EG *A fund was launched to set up a monument in memory of the dead men.* **3** If you **set up** somewhere, you establish yourself in a new home or business. EG *She left her parents' home and set up on her own... He used the money to set himself up in business.* ● If you **set up home** or **set up house**, you buy a house or flat and start living in it. **4** If something **sets up** a process or series of events, it causes it to begin. EG *It may become possible to set up a nuclear chain reaction.* **5** If someone **sets** you **up**, they make it seem that you have done something wrong when you have not. EG *Those three women set him up.* **6** See also **set-up**. `PHRASAL VB : V+O+ADV` `◇ N SING` `PHRASAL VB : V+O+ADV` `PHRASAL VB : V+ADV+A, OR V-REFL+A` `● PHRASE` `PHRASAL VB : V+ADV+O` `PHRASAL VB : V+O+ADV Informal`

setback /sɛtbæk/, **setbacks.** A **setback** is an N COUNT event that delays your progress or makes your position worse than it was before. EG *The by-election result is a serious setback for the government... They had to face up to innumerable setbacks before they achieved their goal.*

settee /sɛtiː/, **settees.** A **settee** is a long comfort-N COUNT able seat with a back and arms, which two or three people can sit on.

setting /sɛtɪŋ/, **settings. 1** A particular **setting** is N COUNT+SUPP a particular place or type of surroundings which someone or something is in. EG *The castle provided the perfect setting for a horror story... Children should be cared for in a home setting.*

2 A **setting** is also one of the positions to which the N COUNT controls of a machine can be adjusted. EG *Set the control to the coldest setting.*

settle /sɛtəl/, **settles, settling, settled. 1** If V+O someone **settles** an argument, they end it by making a decision about who is right or about what to do. EG *The strike went on for over a year before it was finally settled.*

2 If something **is settled**, it has all been decided V+O : USU PASS and arranged. EG *Good, well, that's settled then.*

3 If you **settle** a bill, you pay the amount that you V+O owe.

4 When people **settle** in a new country or area, or V+A when they **settle** somewhere after moving around a lot, they start living there permanently. EG *He had settled in England.*

5 If you **settle** yourself somewhere or **settle** V:REFL OR V: somewhere, you sit down or make yourself com- USU+A fortable. EG *He settled himself beside her in the car... Casson took off his raincoat and settled before the fire.*

6 If something **settles**, it sinks slowly down and V : USU+A becomes still. EG *The dust was settling... The hull of the boat slowly settled in the mud.*

7 When birds or insects **settle** on something, they V+A land on it from above. EG *...flies and other insects that settle on plants growing on the banks.*

8 See also **settled.**

settle down. 1 If you **settle down** to something, PHRASAL VB : you prepare to do it and concentrate on it. EG V+ADV, *...before they settle down to university work... He* USU+to, to-INF, *had settled down to watch a sports programme...* OR for *He settled down for supper.* **2** When someone V+ADV **settles down**, they start living a quiet life in one place, especially when they get married or buy a house. EG *You should get a job and settle down.* **3** If V+ADV people who are upset or noisy **settle down**, they become calm or quiet. EG *Take it easy, she'll be all right, settle down.*

settle for. If you **settle for** something, you PHRASAL VB : choose or accept it, especially when it is not what V+PREP you really want but there is nothing else available. EG *When in doubt he settled for hamburgers.*

settle in. If you **are settling in**, you are becom- PHRASAL VB : ing used to living in a new place or doing a new job. V+ADV EG *And how are you settling in, Mr Swallow?*

settle on. If you **settle on** a particular thing, you PHRASAL VB : choose it after considering other possible choices. V+PREP, EG *Have you settled on a name for him yet?* HAS PASS

settle up. When you **settle up**, you pay a bill. EG PHRASAL VB : *As soon as the money arrived I was able to settle* V+ADV OR *up with him.* V+ADV+with : RECIP

settled /sɛtəld/. **1** If you have a **settled** way of ADJ CLASSIF life, you stay in one place rather than travelling around. EG *...the advent of settled civilization.*

2 A **settled** system stays the same all the time. EG ADJ QUALIT *...an easy, rich, peaceful and settled social order.*

3 If you feel **settled**, you have been living or ADJ QUALIT working in a place long enough to feel comfortable there.

settlement /sɛtəlmənt/, **settlements. 1** A **set-** N COUNT **tlement** is an official agreement between two sides who were involved in a conflict or argument. EG *The chance for a peaceful political settlement has disappeared... ...enormous wage settlements.*

2 A **settlement** is also a place where people have N COUNT come to live and have built homes. EG *He lives in the jungle, in a settlement by a river.*

settler /sɛtlə/, **settlers.** A **settler** is someone N COUNT who goes to live in a new country. EG *The first white settlers in South Africa were Dutch.*

set-up, set-ups. A particular **set-up** is a particular N COUNT : system or way of organizing something. EG *I've only* USU SING *been here a couple of days and I don't quite know* Informal *the set-up.*

seven /sɛvən/ **sevens. Seven** is the number 7: NUMBER see the entry headed NUMBER. EG *I am seven years older than Wendy.*

seventeen /sɛvəntiːn/ **seventeens. Seventeen** NUMBER is the number 17: see the entry headed NUMBER. EG *Buxhall is seventeen miles from Akenfield.*

seventeenth /sɛvəntiːnθ/ **seventeenths.** The ORDINAL **seventeenth** item in a series is the one that you count as number seventeen: see the entry headed NUMBER. EG *It was Rudolph's seventeenth birthday.*

seventh /sɛvənθ/, **sevenths. 1** The **seventh** item ORDINAL in a series is the one that you count as number seven: see the entry headed NUMBER. EG *She died giving birth to her seventh child.*

2 A **seventh** is one of seven equal parts of some- N COUNT : thing. USU+of

seventieth /sɛvəntiθ/ **seventieths.** The **seven-** ORDINAL **tieth** item in a series is the one that you count as number seventy: see the entry headed NUMBER.

seventy /sɛvənti/, **seventies. Seventy** is the NUMBER number 70: see the entry headed NUMBER. EG *...seventy per cent of the people.*

sever /sɛvə/, **severs, severing, severed. 1** To V+O **sever** something means to cut right through it so that one part is completely separated from the rest of it. EG *A bulldozer had severed a gas pipe... The boy's legs were severed at the hip.*

2 If you **sever** a relationship or connection that V+O you have with someone, you end it suddenly and completely. EG *She had to sever all ties with her parents... He severed his connection with the party.*

several /sɛvərəl/. **Several** people or things QUANTIF means a fairly small number of people or things. EG *He returned home several hours later... Several hundred people were killed... Several of us are married and have children.*

severe /sɪvɪə/, **severer, severest. 1** You use ADJ QUALIT **severe** to describe something that is very bad or undesirable. EG *The blast caused severe damage and heavy loss of life... ...a severe shortage of food.*

◇ **severely.** EG *A fire had severely damaged the* ◇ ADV *school... Bad weather severely hampered the emergency services.* ◇ **severity** /sɪvɛrɪti/. EG ◇ N UNCOUNT *...the severity of the world-wide recession.*

2 Someone who is **severe** is stern and treats ADJ QUALIT people rather harshly. EG *I hope the magistrate has not been too severe with him... I was his severest critic... ...her severe upbringing.* ◇ **severely.** EG ◇ ADV *'You didn't answer Mr Crow's question,' said the old lady severely.* ◇ **severity.** EG *...prison sen-* ◇ N UNCOUNT *tences of excessive severity.*

sew /səʊ/, **sews, sewing, sewed, sewn** /səʊn/. V OR V+O When someone **sews**, they join pieces of cloth together, or attach things such as buttons to cloth, by passing thread through them with a needle. EG *They teach the children to cook, sew, or knit... ...sewing buttons onto one of my shirts... We sewed military uniforms.* ● See also **sewing.**

sew up. 1 If you **sew up** two pieces of cloth, you PHRASAL VB : join them together using a needle and thread. V+O+ADV

2 If something such as a deal **is sewn up**, you have V+O+ADV, arranged things so that you are certain to be USU PASS successful. EG *Trask and Bass have it all sewn up.* Informal

sewage /suːɪdʒ/ is waste matter from homes and N UNCOUNT factories, which flows away through sewers.

sewer /suːə/, **sewers.** A **sewer** is a large under- N COUNT ground channel that carries waste matter and rain water away, usually to a place where it is treated and made harmless.

sewing /sɔʊɪŋ/ is **1** the activity of making or N UNCOUNT mending clothes or other things using a needle and thread. **2** clothes or other things that are being N UNCOUNT sewn. EG *My aunt put aside her sewing.*

sewing machine, sewing machines. A **sewing** N COUNT **machine** is a machine that you use for sewing.

sewn /sɔʊn/ is the past participle of **sew.**

sex /seks/, **sexes. 1** The two **sexes** are the two N COUNT groups, male and female, into which people and animals are divided according to the function they have in producing young. EG *...people of both sexes... ...a member of the opposite sex.*

2 The **sex** of a person or animal is their character- N UNCOUNT istic of being either male or female. EG *...tests to ascertain the sex of the baby before it was born... ...to prevent discrimination on the grounds of sex.*

3 Sex is the physical activity by which people and N UNCOUNT animals can produce young, or it is activities connected with this. EG *The film contains no explicit sex or violence.* ● If two people **have sex,** they ● PHRASE perform the act of sex.

sexism /seksɪz⁰m/ is the belief that the members N UNCOUNT of one sex, usually women, are less intelligent or less capable than those of the other sex and should be treated differently; used showing disapproval. EG *Their aims are to fight sexism in the world at large.*

sexist /seksɪst/, **sexists. 1** Something that is **sex-** ADJ QUALIT **ist** involves sexism; used showing disapproval. EG *...sexist attitudes... ...sexist advertising... ...sexist toys like guns and dolls.*

2 If you refer to a person, especially a man, as a N COUNT **sexist,** you mean that they have sexist attitudes; used showing disapproval.

sexless /sekslɪ²s/. If you describe a person as ADJ CLASSIF **sexless,** you mean that they have no sexual feel- ings. EG *...nondescript middle-aged sexless couples.*

sexual /seksjʊ⁰əl/. **1 Sexual** feelings or activities ADJ CLASSIF: are connected with the act of sex or with people's USU ATTRIB desire for sex. EG *...sexual attraction... They were not having a sexual relationship.* ◊ **sexually.** EG *I* ◊ ADV *find her sexually attractive.*

2 Sexual also means **2.1** relating to the differences ADJ CLASSIF: between male and female people or animals. EG ATTRIB *...campaigning for non-discrimination and sexual equality.* **2.2** relating to the biological process by ADJ CLASSIF: which people and animals produce young. EG *...sex-* ATTRIB *ual reproduction.*

sexual intercourse is the physical act of sex N UNCOUNT between a man and a woman. Formal

sexuality /seksjʊæli¹ti¹/. A person's **sexuality** is N UNCOUNT their ability to experience sexual feelings.

sexy /seksi¹/, **sexier, sexiest.** Someone or some- ADJ QUALIT thing that is **sexy** is sexually exciting or sexually attractive. EG *...her sexy brown eyes.*

sh /ʃ/ is a noise that you make in order to tell EXCLAM someone to be quiet. EG *Sh! The boys are in bed.*

shabby /ʃæbi¹/, **shabbier, shabbiest. 1** Some- ADJ QUALIT thing that is **shabby** looks old and is in bad condition. EG *...his shabby clothes... ...a shabby house with worn carpeting on the stairs.*
◊ **shabbily.** EG *They were shabbily dressed.* ◊ ADV
2 Someone who is **shabby** is wearing old, worn ADJ QUALIT clothes. EG *...shabby children in the streets.*
3 You describe someone's behaviour as **shabby** ADJ QUALIT when they behave in an unfair or unacceptable way. EG *...a series of shabby compromises.*
◊ **shabbily.** EG *Don't you think you've treated me a* ◊ ADV *little shabbily?*

shack /ʃæk/, **shacks.** A **shack** is a small hut built N COUNT from bits of wood or metal.

shackle /ʃækə⁰l/, **shackles, shackling, shack-** led. **1** If you **are shackled** by something, it V+O : USU PASS prevents you from doing what you want to do. EG Literary *He is shackled by domestic responsibilities.*

2 You can use **shackles** to refer to circumstances N PLURAL : that prevent you from doing what you want to do. USU+SUPP EG *There are a few who have managed to throw off* Literary *the shackles of the past.*

3 Shackles are two metal rings joined by a chain N PLURAL which are fastened around someone's wrists or ankles in order to prevent them from moving or escaping.

4 To **shackle** someone means to put shackles on v+o them. EG *The guards shackled his wrists and ankles.*

shade /ʃeɪd/, **shades, shading, shaded. 1 Shade** N UNCOUNT, OR is an area of darkness under or next to an object N SING : the+N such as a tree, where the sun cannot reach. EG *There are no trees or bushes to give shade... Right now the air is cool in the shade... He led the way to the shade of a large oak tree.*

2 If a place or person **is shaded** by something, that v+o : USU PASS thing prevents light from falling on the place or person. EG *The broad walks are shaded by chestnut trees.*

3 If you **shade** your **eyes,** you put your hand across PHRASE your forehead in order to prevent a bright light from shining into your eyes.

4 A **shade** is the same as a lampshade. EG *...a lamp* N COUNT *with a thick silk shade.*

5 The **shades** of a particular colour are its differ- N COUNT ent forms. For example, emerald green and olive green are shades of green. EG *They wore tight-fitting jackets in shades of pink, blue, and brown.*

6 The **shades** of something abstract are its differ- N COUNT+SUPP ent forms. EG *The phrase has many shades of meaning... ...various shades of socialist opinion.*

7 When something **shades** into something else, v+into there is no clear division between the two things. EG *...reds shading into pinks... ...innocence shading into ignorance.*

shadow /ʃædəʊ/, **shadows. 1** A **shadow** is a dark N COUNT shape on a surface that is made when something stands between a light and the surface. EG *...a car parked in the shadow of a tree... The smoky fires cast dancing shadows upon the wide circle of faces.*

2 Shadow is darkness in a place caused by some- N UNCOUNT thing preventing light from reaching it. EG *The whole canyon is in shadow.*

3 If you say that someone or something is **a** PHRASE **shadow** of their **former self,** you mean that they are much less strong or vigorous than they used to be. EG *The organization is now no more than a shadow of its former self.*

4 If there is no **shadow of a doubt** about some- N SING+of : thing, there is no doubt at all about it. EG *I never* WITH BROAD *had a shadow of a doubt that he was right.* NEG

5 A British Member of Parliament who is a mem- ADJ CLASSIF : ber of the **Shadow** Cabinet or who is a **Shadow** ATTRIB Cabinet minister belongs to the main opposition British party and takes a special interest in matters of a particular kind. EG *He is Shadow Secretary for Trade and Industry.*

shadowy /ʃædəʊi¹/. **1** A **shadowy** place is dark or ADJ CLASSIF full of shadows. EG *...a shadowy alcove.*

2 A **shadowy** figure or shape is someone or ADJ CLASSIF something that you can hardly see because it is ATTRIB dark or misty. EG *...the shadowy musicians in the background.*

3 You describe people and activities as **shadowy** ADJ QUALIT when very little is known about them. EG *...the shadowy world of espionage.*

shady /ʃeɪdi¹/, **shadier, shadiest. 1** A **shady** ADJ CLASSIF place is sheltered from bright sunlight by buildings or trees. EG *We found a shady spot in the park to have a rest.*

2 Shady trees produce a lot of shade. ADJ CLASSIF

3 You describe people and their activities as **shady** ADJ QUALIT when you think that their activities are dishonest Informal or illegal. EG *...shady dealings.*

shaft /ʃɑːft/, **shafts. 1** A **shaft** is a vertical pas- N COUNT sage, for example one for a lift. EG *...the lift shaft.*

2 A **shaft** in a machine is a rod that turns round N COUNT

shapes

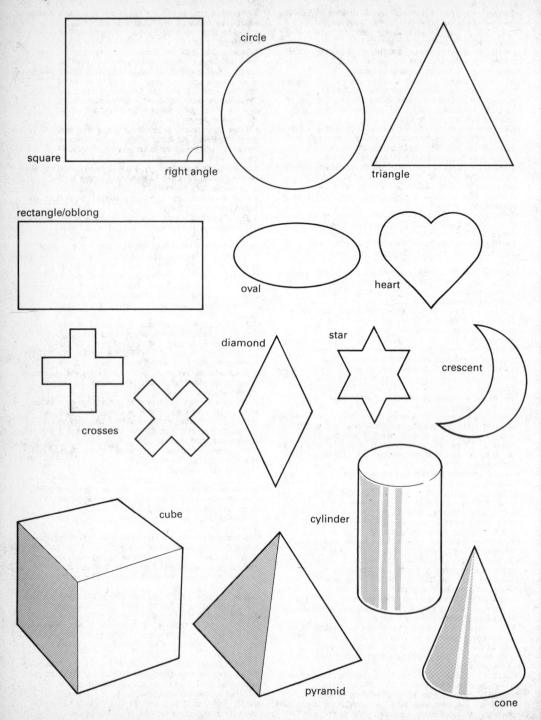

square

right angle

circle

triangle

rectangle/oblong

oval

heart

crosses

diamond

star

crescent

cube

cylinder

pyramid

cone

and round in order to transfer movement in the machine. EG ...the drive shaft.

3 A **shaft** of light is a beam of light. EG The hatch was opened, admitting a shaft of daylight. N COUNT: USU+of

shaggy /ʃægi¹/. **Shaggy** hair or fur is long and very untidy. EG ...his shaggy, unkempt beard... Shaggy sheep roamed on the higher slopes. ADJ QUALIT

shake /ʃeɪk/, **shakes**, **shaking**, **shook** /ʃʊk/, **shaken**. **1** If you **shake** someone or something, you hold them and move them quickly backwards and forwards or up and down. EG He awakened to find himself being shaken roughly by his father... He shook from a bag a heap of dried leaves... The wind shook white petals from the tree. ◊ used as a noun. EG She gave her skirts a vigorous shake. V+O: OFT+A ▸ N COUNT

2 If something **shakes**, it moves from side to side or up and down with quick, small movements. EG The earth shook and the sky darkened... He was shaking with laughter. V

3 If your voice **is shaking**, you cannot control it properly and it trembles, because you are nervous or angry. EG His eyes were wild and his voice shook. V

4 If something **shakes** you, it makes you feel shocked and upset. EG My mother's death had shaken him dreadfully. ◊ **shaken**. EG I was badly shaken. I had never had a crash before. V+O: NO CONT ◊ ADJ QUALIT

5 If something **shakes** your beliefs or ideas, it makes you feel less certain about them. EG The lecture did little to shake his convictions. V+O

6 If you **shake hands** with someone or **shake their hand**, you hold their right hand in your own when you are meeting them, saying goodbye to them, or congratulating them. EG Elijah and I shook hands and said good night. PHRASE

7 If you **shake your head**, you move it from side to side in order to say 'no' or to show disbelief or sadness. EG He offered her a cigarette. She shook her head. 'No thank you. I don't smoke.' PHRASE

shake off. If you **shake off** someone or something that you do not want, you manage to get away from them or get rid of them. EG It had taken Franklin several hours to shake off the police. PHRASAL VB: V+O+ADV

shake-up, **shake-ups**. A **shake-up** is a major set of changes in an organization or system. EG Many were eager for a shake-up in the two-party system. N COUNT

shaky /ʃeɪki¹/, **shakier**, **shakiest**. **1** If you are **shaky**, you are shaking or feeling weak because you are frightened, shocked, or ill. EG I was nervous and a bit shaky when he watched me. ◊ **shakily**. EG The man stood up shakily. ADJ QUALIT ◊ ADV

2 You can use **shaky** to describe something that is rather weak or not very good. EG After a shaky start the orchestra grew more confident... ...a company with very shaky financial prospects. ADJ QUALIT

shall /ʃəl¹/. **1** If someone says that they **shall** do something, they mean that they intend to do it. EG I shall get angry in a moment... We probably shan't sleep much... I shan't let you go. MODAL

2 If you say that something **shall** happen, you are emphasizing that it will definitely happen. EG It must be done and therefore it shall be done. MODAL Formal

3 If you say to someone that they **shall** do something, you are ordering them to do it. EG You're here to enjoy yourself, and enjoy yourself you shall... No more drink shall be drunk tonight. MODAL Formal

4 You use **shall** in questions **4.1** when you are asking someone for advice. EG Whatever shall I do?... Where shall we go for our drink? **4.2** when you are asking someone if they would like you to do something. EG Shall I shut the door? **4.3** when you are suggesting to someone that you should both do something together. EG Shall we go and see a film?... We'll go forward a little more, shall we? MODAL MODAL MODAL

shallow /ʃæləʊ/, **shallower**, **shallowest**; **shallows**. **1** A **shallow** hole, container, or layer of something measures only a short distance from the top to the bottom. EG When the fish comes into ADJ QUALIT

shallow water, grab it by the tail... ...a shallow bowl... ...a shallow valley.

2 A person, idea, or activity that is **shallow** does not show or involve any serious or careful thought; used showing disapproval. EG This kind of life is shallow and trivial... I was too young and shallow to understand love. ◊ **shallowness**. EG ...the shallowness of her social life. ADJ QUALIT ◊ N UNCOUNT

3 If your breathing is **shallow**, you take only a very small amount of air into your lungs at each breath. ADJ QUALIT

4 The **shallows** are the shallow part of an area of water. EG Thousands of little fish swim in the shallows. N PLURAL: the+N

sham /ʃæm/, **shams**. Something that is a **sham** is not real or not really what it seems to be; used showing disapproval. EG Their independence is a sham. ◊ used as an adjective. EG ...a sham fight... This is rather a sham enterprise. N COUNT ▸ ADJ CLASSIF: ATTRIB

shamble /ʃæmbə¹l/, **shambles**, **shambling**, **shambled**. **1** If a place, event, or situation is a **shambles**, everything is in disorder. EG The rehearsal was a shambles. N SING: a+N

2 If you **shamble** somewhere, you walk clumsily, dragging your feet. EG They got up and shambled out. V+A

shame /ʃeɪm/, **shames**, **shaming**, **shamed**. **1** **Shame** is an uncomfortable feeling that you have when you know that you have done something wrong or embarrassing, or when you know that someone close to you has. EG The memory fills me with shame... Simon lowered his face in shame. N UNCOUNT

2 If someone brings **shame** on you, they make other people lose their respect for you. EG Don't bring shame on the family. N UNCOUNT

3 If something **shames** you, it causes you to feel shame. EG It shamed him to know that his father had behaved in such a way. V+O

4 If you **shame** someone into doing something, you force them to do it by making them feel ashamed not to. EG Father was shamed into helping them. V+O+A

5 If you say that it is **a shame** that something happened, you are saying how sorry you are that it happened. EG It's a shame he didn't come too... What a shame. Never mind... It's a shame to waste all this food. N SING: a+N

shamefaced /ʃeɪmfeɪst/. If you are **shamefaced**, you feel embarrassed because you have done something that you know you should not have done. ADJ QUALIT

shameful /ʃeɪmfʊl/. If you describe a person's action or attitude as **shameful**, you mean that it is so bad that the person ought to be ashamed. EG It shows a shameful lack of concern. ◊ **shamefully**. EG The government have shamefully neglected this area. ADJ QUALIT ◊ ADV

shameless /ʃeɪmlɪ²s/. Someone who is **shameless** behaves in a way which is considered unacceptable, but is not at all ashamed of their behaviour. EG Her husband had run off with a shameless gipsy woman. ◊ **shamelessly**. EG Matty flatters me shamelessly. ADJ CLASSIF ◊ ADV

shampoo /ʃæmpuː/, **shampoos**. Shampoo is a soapy liquid that you use for washing your hair. N MASS

shandy /ʃændi¹/, **shandies**. Shandy is a drink which is made by mixing beer and lemonade. N MASS

shan't /ʃɑːnt/ is the usual spoken form of 'shall not'.

shanty town /ʃænti¹ taʊn/, **shanty towns**. A **shanty town** is a collection of rough huts which poor people live in. N COUNT

shape /ʃeɪp/, **shapes**, **shaping**, **shaped**. **1** The **shape** of an object or area is the appearance of its outside edges, for example whether it is round, square, curved, or wide. EG Bear Island is triangular in shape... ...a huge animal the size and shape of a rhinoceros... You can spin-dry this sweater and it will still retain its shape. N COUNT OR N UNCOUNT

2 A **shape** is **2.1** something which has a definite form, for example a circle, square, or triangle. EG N COUNT

...*patterns created from geometric shapes.* **2.2** an object or person that you cannot see clearly. EG *One could just distinguish a slim shape in a short white dress.*

3 The **shape** of something such as a plan or an organization is its structure and size. EG ...*developments which may alter the future course and shape of industry.* N SING+POSS

4 If you **shape** an object, you give it a particular shape, usually by using your hands. EG *He began to shape the dough into rolls.* V+O: OFT+*into*

5 Something or someone that **shapes** a thing or activity causes it to develop in a particular way. EG *It was the Greeks who shaped the thinking of Western man.* V+O

6 You use **in the shape of** before mentioning exactly what you are referring to, after referring to it in a general way. EG ...*large-scale enterprise in the shape of mines or plantations.* PREP

7 Shape is also used in these phrases. **7.1** If someone or something is **in good shape**, they are in a good condition or state of health. If they are **in bad shape**, they are in a bad condition or state of health. EG *He looked in good shape.* **7.2** If you say that you will not accept or tolerate something **in any shape or form**, you are emphasizing that you will not accept or tolerate it at all. EG *I'm strongly opposed to violence in any shape or form.* **7.3** If someone **licks** you **into shape** or **knocks** you **into shape**, they make you work or behave as they want you to. EG ...*knocking their children into shape.* **7.4** When something **takes shape**, it develops and starts to have a definite structure or shape. EG *The organization began to take shape.* PHRASES

shape up. The way that someone or something is **shaping up** is the way that they are developing. EG *This campaign is shaping up as one of the most intensive sales campaigns ever.* PHRASAL VB : V+ADV, USU+A

shaped /ʃeɪpt/. Something that is **shaped** like a particular object or in a particular way has the kind of shape indicated. EG ...*a chair shaped like a saddle*... ...*weirdly shaped trees.* ADJ CLASSIF

-shaped combines with nouns to form adjectives describing the shape of an object. EG ...*an egg-shaped face*... ...*a star-shaped card.*

shapeless /ʃeɪplɪˀs/. Something that is **shapeless** does not have a distinctive or attractive shape. EG ...*shapeless pyjamas.* ADJ QUALIT

shapely /ʃeɪplɪˀ/. A **shapely** person, especially a woman, has an attractive shape. EG *She had a slim waist and shapely legs.* ADJ QUALIT

share /ʃeə/, **shares, sharing, shared. 1** If you **share** something with another person, you both use it or do it. EG *Ralph went upstairs to the room he shared with his brother... We share the washing up... Let's share the petrol costs... Both partners share in rearing their family.* V+O OR V+O+*with* : RECIP; ALSO V+A

2 When you **share** an experience that someone else has, you are with them and so you experience it too. EG *Old age was something they would never be able to share.* V+O OR V+O+*with* : RECIP

3 If you **share** a thought or a piece of news with someone, you tell them about it. EG *He was so excited about his idea that he felt he had to share it with someone.* V+O OR V+O+*with* : RECIP

4 If two people or things **share** a particular quality, characteristic, or idea, they both have it. EG *I share your concern... ...people who share the same interests.* V+O

5 If you have or do a **share** of something, you have or do part of it. EG *An increasing share of the work is handed over to computers... ...a campaign for parents to have a share in discussing school policy.* N SING : OFT+ *of/in*

6 If you have or do your **share** of something, you have or do the amount that is fair for you. EG *It does help when a father does his share at home... ...if one man seizes more than his fair share of the food.* N SING+POSS

7 The **shares** of a company are the equal parts N COUNT : USU PLURAL

into which its ownership is divided. Shares can be bought by people as an investment. EG *A week ago, the firm's shares jumped 10p to 114p... I wonder how many companies he has shares in?*

share out. If you **share out** an amount of something, you give each person in a group an equal or fair part of it. EG *The fairest way to share things out is to distribute them equally.* PHRASAL VB : V+O+ADV

shareholder /ʃeəhoʊldə/, **shareholders.** A **shareholder** is a person who owns shares in a company. N COUNT

shark /ʃɑːk/, **sharks.** A **shark** is a very large fish with sharp teeth. Sharks sometimes attack people. N COUNT

sharp /ʃɑːp/, **sharper, sharpest; sharps. 1** A **sharp** object **1.1** has a very thin edge that is good for cutting things. EG *Cut it away with a sharp knife.* **1.2** has a very finely pointed end. EG ...*small, sharp teeth... He stepped on a sharp thorn.* ADJ QUALIT

2 A **sharp** picture, outline, or distinction is very clear and easy to see or understand. EG ...*sharp, fresh footprints in the snow... We try to draw a sharp dividing line between Civil Service and Government.* ◊ **sharply.** EG *The memory remains sharply engraved on my mind.* ADJ QUALIT ◊ ADV

3 Someone who is **sharp** is quick to notice, hear, or understand things; used showing approval. EG *You've got to be sharp to get ahead... His sharp eyes would never miss it.* ADJ QUALIT

4 A **sharp** change happens suddenly and is very big. EG ...*sharp food-price increases.* ◊ **sharply.** EG *Sales of the car have risen sharply in recent weeks.* ADJ QUALIT ◊ ADV

5 You also use **sharp** to describe an action that is done quickly and firmly. EG *She received a sharp clout on the head... With his finger and thumb he gave it a sharp turn.* ◊ **sharply.** EG *Both birds turned their heads sharply at the sound.* ADJ QUALIT ◊ ADV

6 If someone says something in a **sharp** way, they say it suddenly and rather firmly or angrily. EG *A sharp order came through his headphones.* ◊ **sharply.** EG *'Don't talk nonsense,' she said sharply.* ◊ ADV

7 A **sharp** sound is very short and sudden and quite loud. EG ...*the sharp crack of a twig.* ADJ QUALIT

8 Sharp pain or cold hurts a lot when it affects you. EG *His blistered foot at that moment caused him a sharp pang.* ADJ QUALIT

9 Food that has a **sharp** taste is slightly sour but also fresh. EG ...*the sharp, pure taste of gooseberries.* ADJ QUALIT

10 You can use **sharp** to indicate that something happens at exactly the time mentioned. EG *His train came in at eight sharp.* ADV

11 A **sharp** in music is a note that is a semitone higher than the note which is described by the same letter. It can be represented by the symbol (#). EG ...*the C sharp minor Prelude.* N COUNT, OR ADJ AFTER N

12 If a musical note is played or sung **sharp**, it is slightly higher in pitch than it should be. ADV OR ADJ QUALIT

sharpen /ʃɑːpˀn/, **sharpens, sharpening, sharpened. 1** If you **sharpen** an object, you make its edge very thin or you make its end pointed. EG *Roger sharpened a stick at both ends.* V+O

2 If your senses or abilities **sharpen** or **are sharpened**, you become quicker at noticing things or at thinking. EG *His eyes and instincts sharpened as he saw the fort in the distance... Generations of urban living had sharpened their wits.* V-ERG

3 If your voice **sharpens**, you speak more angrily and quickly than you did before. EG *'Who told you?' Her voice had sharpened a little... Fear and urgency sharpened Sarah's voice.* V-ERG

4 If something **sharpens** the disagreements or differences between people, it makes them fiercer or greater. EG *This sharpened the conflict between* V-ERG

Would you be upset if someone spoke to you sharply?

them... Tension in society has increased and sharpened.

sharpener /ˈʃɑːpəⁿnə/, **sharpeners.** A pencil N COUNT **sharpener** is an object or device used for sharpening pencils.

shatter /ˈʃætə/, **shatters, shattering, shattered.**
1 If something **shatters** or if you **shatter** it, it V-ERG breaks into a lot of small pieces. EG *The vase fell from her hand and shattered on the floor.*
2 If something **shatters** your beliefs or hopes, it V+O destroys them. EG *The trip completely shattered my ideas of what schools were supposed to do.*
3 If someone **is shattered** by an event, it shocks V-PASS and upsets them very much. EG *My father was shattered by the news.*

shattered /ˈʃætəd/. Someone who is **shattered** is ADJ PRED
1 very shocked and upset. EG *When Harris died, Dean was shattered.* 2 very tired. EG *I'm shattered* Informal *after a day's work.*

shattering /ˈʃætəⁿrɪŋ/. Something that is **shatter-** ADJ QUALIT **ing** 1 shocks and upsets you very much. EG *...a shattering experience.* 2 makes you very tired. EG *Sunday had been a shattering day.*

shave /ʃeɪv/, **shaves, shaving, shaved.** 1 When a V, V+O, OR man **shaves**, he cuts hair from his face using a V+O+*off* razor. EG *When he had shaved and dressed, he went down to the kitchen... He had shaved off his beard.*
▸ used as a noun. EG *He had a shave and a bath.* ▸ N COUNT
2 If someone **shaves** a part of their body, they cut V+O OR V+O+ all the hair from it using a razor. EG *She shaved her* *off* *legs and under her arms.*
3 If you **shave** off part of a piece of wood or other V+O+*off* material, you cut very thin pieces from it. EG *...shaving an inch off the inside.*
4 If you describe something as a **close shave**, you PHRASE mean that there was nearly an accident or a Outdated disaster but it was avoided.
5 See also **shaving.**

shaven /ˈʃeɪvəⁿn/. If a part of someone's body is ADJ CLASSIF **shaven**, it has been shaved. EG *His hair was very short, the back of his neck shaven.* ● See also **clean-shaven.**

shaver /ˈʃeɪvə/, **shavers.** A **shaver** is an electric N COUNT tool, used for shaving hair from the face and body.

shaving /ˈʃeɪvɪŋ/, **shavings.** 1 You use **shaving** to ADJ CLASSIF : describe something that people use when they ATTRIB shave. EG *...a shaving brush.*
2 **Shavings** are small, very thin pieces of some- N COUNT : thing such as wood which have been cut from a USU PLURAL larger piece.

shawl /ʃɔːl/, **shawls.** A **shawl** is a large piece of N COUNT woollen cloth which a woman wears over her shoulders or head, or which is wrapped around a baby to keep it warm.

she /ʃiː/ is used as the subject of a verb. 1 You use PRON : SING **she** to refer to a woman or girl who has already been mentioned, or whose identity is known. EG *'So long,' Mary said as she passed Miss Saunders... Ask her if she can do something with them.*
2 You also use **she** 2.1 to refer to a nation. EG PRON : SING *Britain is a poor nation now, and she would do well to remember this.* 2.2 to refer to a ship, car, or other vehicle. EG *She does 0 to 60 in 10 seconds.*

sheaf /ʃiːf/, **sheaves.** 1 A **sheaf** of papers is N PART OR N a bundle of papers. EG *...a thick sheaf of letters.* COUNT
2 A **sheaf** of corn is a bundle of ripe corn plants N PART OR N tied together. COUNT

shear /ʃɪə/, **shears, shearing, sheared, shorn.** /ʃɔːn/. The past participle can be either **sheared** or **shorn.**
1 To **shear** a sheep means to cut the wool off it. EG V+O *I sheared 500 ewes.*
2 A pair of **shears** is a tool like a very large pair of N PLURAL scissors, used especially for cutting garden hedges. See picture at TOOLS.
3 See also **shorn.**

shear off. If something such as a piece of metal PHRASAL VB : **shears off**, it breaks. EG *Another bolt has sheared* V-ERG+ADV *off.*

sheath /ʃiːθ/, **sheaths.** 1 A **sheath** is a covering N COUNT for the blade of a knife. EG *He wiped the knife and put it back in the sheath.*
2 A **sheath** is also a rubber covering for a man's N COUNT penis that is used as a contraceptive.

sheathe /ʃiːð/, **sheathes, sheathing, sheathed.** V+O When you **sheathe** a knife, you put it in its sheath.

sheaves /ʃiːvz/ is the plural of **sheaf.**

shed /ʃed/, **sheds, shedding.** The form **shed** is used in the present tense and is the past tense and past participle of the verb.
1 A **shed** is a small building that is used for N COUNT keeping things in. EG *She went to find her wellingtons in the shed... the coal shed.*
2 When an animal **sheds** hair or skin, some of its V+O hair or skin drops off. When a tree **sheds** its leaves, its leaves fall off in the autumn. EG *...like a snake shedding its skin.*
3 To **shed** something also means to get rid of it. EG V+O *2,600 workers are due to be shed by the company...* Formal *I shed all my restraint.*
4 If a lorry **sheds** its load, the goods that it is V+O carrying accidentally fall onto the road.
5 If you **shed** tears, you cry. EG *...a child shedding* V+O *tears over a broken toy.*
6 To **shed blood** means to kill people in a violent PHRASE way. EG *They called for an end to the shedding of blood.*
7 If something **sheds light on** a problem, it makes PHRASE it easier to understand by providing more information about it.

she'd /ʃiːd/. 1 **She'd** is the usual spoken form of 'she had', especially when 'had' is an auxiliary verb. EG *It was too late. She'd done it.*
2 **She'd** is also a spoken form of 'she would'. EG *She said she'd come by train.*

sheen /ʃiːn/. If something has a **sheen**, it has a N SING+SUPP smooth and gentle brightness on its surface. EG *...beautiful, long hair with a silky sheen.*

sheep /ʃiːp/. **Sheep** is both the singular and the plural form.
1 A **sheep** is a farm animal with a thick woolly N COUNT coat. Sheep are kept for their wool or for their meat. EG *...a flock of sheep.* ● See also **black sheep.**
2 If you say that a group of people are **like sheep**, PHRASE you mean that if one person does something, all the others copy that person.

sheepdog /ˈʃiːpdɒg/, **sheepdogs.** A **sheepdog** is a N COUNT breed of dog. Some sheepdogs are used for controlling sheep.

sheepish /ˈʃiːpɪʃ/. If you look **sheepish**, you look ADJ QUALIT slightly embarrassed because you feel foolish or you have done something silly. EG *He gave me a sheepish grin.* ◊ **sheepishly.** EG *Jo looked up at his* ◊ ADV *father sheepishly.*

sheepskin /ˈʃiːpskɪn/ is the skin and wool of a N UNCOUNT : sheep, used especially for coats and rugs. EG *...a* USU N MOD *sheepskin jacket.*

sheer /ʃɪə/. 1 **Sheer** means complete and not ADJ CLASSIF : involving or mixed with anything else; often used ATTRIB simply to emphasize the word it describes. EG *The eighth floor of the hotel was sheer luxury... Many of the audience walked out through sheer boredom.*
2 A **sheer** cliff or drop is a completely vertical one. ADJ QUALIT EG *...a gorge with sheer rock sides.*
3 **Sheer** is used to describe silk or other material ADJ QUALIT which is very thin, light, and delicate.

sheet /ʃiːt/, **sheets.** 1 A **sheet** is a large rectangu- N COUNT lar piece of cloth, usually made of cotton. Sheets are used with blankets or a duvet to make a bed. EG *It was bliss to sleep in a soft bed with clean sheets again.* ● **as white as a sheet:** see **white.**
2 A **sheet** of paper is a rectangular piece of paper. N COUNT EG *He handed a typewritten sheet to Karen.*
3 A **sheet** of glass, metal, or wood is a large, flat, N COUNT thin piece of it. EG *...a single sheet of glass.*

sheikh /ʃeɪk/, **sheikhs;** also spelled **sheik.** A N COUNT **sheikh** is an Arab chief or ruler.

shelf /ʃɛlf/, **shelves** /ʃɛlvz/. A **shelf** is a flat piece N COUNT of wood, metal, or glass which is attached to a wall or to the sides of a cupboard. Shelves are used for keeping things on. EG *There were a lot of books on the shelves along the walls.*

shelf life. The **shelf life** of a product, especially N SING+SUPP food, is the length of time that it can be kept in a shop before it becomes too old to sell. EG *This process should give butter a longer shelf life.*

shell /ʃɛl/, **shells, shelling, shelled.** 1 The **shell** N COUNT OR of an egg or nut is the hard covering which N UNCOUNT surrounds it. EG *...the blue shells of sparrows' eggs... ...coconut shells.*

2 The **shell** of a tortoise, snail, or crab is the hard, N COUNT OR protective covering that it has on its back. N UNCOUNT

3 A **shell** is the hard covering which surrounds, or N COUNT OR used to surround, a small, soft sea creature. EG *...a* N UNCOUNT *handkerchief full of shells which my sister had collected... ...oyster shells.*

4 If you **shell** peas or nuts, you remove the natural V+O covering from them. EG *I sat shelling some peas.*

5 You can refer to the frame of a building, boat, N COUNT car, or other structure as a **shell**. EG *...the burned-out shell of wood and mud that had once been their home.*

6 A **shell** is also a metal container filled with N COUNT explosives that can be fired from a large gun over long distances. EG *Arnold had his leg smashed when a shell hit the truck he was driving.*

7 To **shell** a place means to fire explosive shells at V+O it. EG *They continued to shell towns on the northern coast.*

shell out. If you **shell out** for something, you PHRASAL VB : spend money on it. EG *He will have to shell out* V+ADV OR *another three hundred dollars for the licence.* V+O+ADV Informal

she'll /ʃiːl/ is the usual spoken form of 'she will'. EG *I hope she'll be all right.*

shellfish /ʃɛlfɪʃ/. **Shellfish** is both the singular N COUNT and the plural form.
A **shellfish** is a small creature that lives in the sea and has a shell. EG *...edible shellfish.*

shelter /ʃɛltə/, **shelters, sheltering, sheltered.**
1 A **shelter** is a small building or covered place N COUNT which is made to protect people from bad weather or danger. EG *That shelter might fall down if the rain comes back.*

2 If a place provides **shelter**, it provides protection N UNCOUNT from bad weather or danger. EG *He found shelter in caves... We waited in the shelter of the trees.*

3 If you **shelter** in a place, you stay there and are V : USU+A protected from bad weather or danger. EG *It is natural to shelter from a storm.*

4 If a place or thing **is sheltered** by something, it V+O : USU PASS is protected by that thing from wind and rain. EG *This wide alley is sheltered by plane trees.*

5 If you **shelter** someone, 5.1 you provide them V+O with a place to stay or live. EG *Can those being sheltered be adequately fed?* 5.2 you help them by hiding them when other people are looking for them. EG *Some villagers are prepared to shelter wanted men.*

6 If you have **shelter**, you have a place where you N UNCOUNT can stay or live. EG *The basic necessities of life are food, shelter and clothing.*

sheltered /ʃɛltəd/. 1 A place that is **sheltered** is ADJ QUALIT protected from wind and rain. EG *I lay down in the warmest and most sheltered spot I could find.*

2 If you have a **sheltered** life, you do not experi- ADJ QUALIT ence things which other people experience, espe-cially unpleasant things. EG *We lived a sheltered life in our Irish village.*

3 **Sheltered** accommodation is designed for old or ADJ CLASSIF : handicapped people. It allows them to be independ- ATTRIB ent but also gives them supervision when they need it. EG *...a sheltered housing scheme.*

shelve /ʃɛlv/, **shelves, shelving, shelved.** 1 If V+O you **shelve** a plan, you decide not to continue with it for a while. EG *The project seems to have been shelved for the moment.*

2 If a seashore **shelves**, it slopes downwards. EG V *The beach shelved steeply... ...long, gently shelving sands.*

3 **Shelves** is the plural of **shelf**.

shelving /ʃɛlvɪŋ/ is a set of shelves. EG *Thousands* N UNCOUNT *of books are stocked on more than 8 miles of shelving in the library.*

shepherd /ʃɛpəd/, **shepherds, shepherding, shepherded.** 1 A **shepherd** is a person whose job N COUNT is to look after sheep.

2 If you **shepherd** someone somewhere, you ac- V+O : USU+A company them to make sure that they go to the right place. EG *I shepherded them towards the lobby.*

shepherd's pie is a dish consisting of minced N UNCOUNT meat covered with a layer of mashed potato.

sheriff /ʃɛrɪf/, **sheriffs.** A **sheriff** is a person who N COUNT is elected to make sure that the law is obeyed in a American particular county.

sherry /ʃɛri¹/, **sherries. Sherry** is a strong alco- N MASS holic drink made from grapes. It is usually drunk before a meal.

she's /ʃiːz/. 1 **She's** is the usual spoken form of 'she is'. EG *She's Swedish.*

2 **She's** is also a spoken form of 'she has', especial-ly when 'has' is an auxiliary verb. EG *She's gone back to Montrose.*

shield /ʃiːld/, **shields, shielding, shielded.** 1 A N COUNT **shield** is 1.1 a large piece of metal or leather which soldiers used to carry to protect their bodies while they were fighting. 1.2 a sports trophy or a badge that is shaped like a shield. EG *I shall remove her prefect's shield.*

2 Something which is a **shield** against a particular N COUNT : danger provides protection from it. EG *Dark pig-* OFT+against *ment in the skin provides an effective shield against the sun... ...a wind shield.*

3 Something or someone that **shields** you from a V+O OR danger protects you from it, by being or putting a V-REFL : barrier between you and it. EG *Her parasol was* USU+from *propped up behind her to shield her from the sun.*

shift /ʃɪft/, **shifts, shifting, shifted.** 1 If you **shift** V-ERG : OFT+A something or if it **shifts**, it moves. EG *He shifted the chair closer to the bed... Muller's eyes shifted to the telephone.*

2 A **shift** in opinion or in a situation is a slight N COUNT+SUPP change in it. EG *...a radical shift in public opinion... You may detect a shift of emphasis.*

3 If someone's opinion or a situation **shifts** or **is** V OR V-ERG : **shifted**, it changes slightly. EG *...shifting the bal-* OFT+A *ance of financial control... 'I don't know,' Margaret said, shifting from her earlier attitude.*

4 If you **shift** responsibility or blame onto someone V+O : USU+A else, you transfer it to them.

5 A **shift** is also a set period of time during which N COUNT people work in a factory. EG *He had chosen the midnight to 8 shift.*

shifty /ʃɪfti¹/. Someone who looks **shifty** gives the ADJ QUALIT impression of being deceitful and dishonest. EG *...a* Informal *man with small shifty eyes... He gave me a shifty look.*

shilling /ʃɪlɪŋ/, **shillings.** A **shilling** was a unit of N COUNT money used in Britain until 1971 which was the equivalent of 5p. There were twenty shillings in an English pound.

shimmer /ʃɪmə/, **shimmers, shimmering,** V **shimmered.** If something **shimmers**, it shines with a faint, unsteady light. EG *I sat looking at the sea shimmering in the moonlight.*

shin /ʃɪn/, **shins, shinning, shinned.** Your **shin** is N COUNT the front part of your leg between your knee and your ankle. EG *He kicked her shin.*

shin up. If you **shin up** a tree or a pole, you PHRASAL VB : climb it quickly and easily, using your hands and V+PREP/ADV

What do you find inside shells?

legs to grip it. EG *I shinned up a lamp post to get a better view.*

shine /ʃaɪn/, **shines, shining, shone** /ʃɒn/. 1 v When the sun or a light **shines**, it gives out bright light. EG *The sun shone all day.*

2 If you **shine** a torch or a lamp somewhere, you v+o+A point it there, so that you can see something when it is dark. EG *I asked him to shine the headlight on the door.*

3 Something that **shines** is very bright, usually v because it is reflecting light. EG *His eyes shone like stars.*

4 Something that has a **shine** is bright because it N SING reflects light. EG *...the shine of the handles on the doors.*

5 Someone who **shines** at a skill or activity does it v : OFT+at extremely well. EG *He shines at amateur theatricals.*

shingle /ʃɪŋgəl/. **Shingle** consists of small rough N UNCOUNT pieces of stone on the shore by a sea or a river. EG *The beach is a mixture of sand and shingle.*

shining /ʃaɪnɪŋ/. 1 **Shining** things are very bright, ADJ CLASSIF usually because they are reflecting light. EG *...rows of shining glasses... ...its shining feathers.*

2 A **shining** achievement or quality is a very good ADJ CLASSIF : one which should be greatly admired. EG *She was a* ATTRIB *shining example to people everywhere.*

shiny /ʃaɪnɪ/, **shinier, shiniest.** Something that is ADJ QUALIT **shiny** is bright and reflects light. EG *...shiny black shoes... ...shiny cars.*

ship /ʃɪp/, **ships, shipping, shipped.** 1 A **ship** is a N COUNT large boat which carries passengers or cargo. EG OR by+N *The ship was due to sail the following morning... They were sent home by ship.*

2 If people or things **are shipped** somewhere, they v+o : are sent there on a ship or by some other means of USU PASS+A transport. EG *They had their luggage shipped to Nigeria... The cattle were shipped out by rail.*

shipping /ʃɪpɪŋ/ is 1 the transport of cargo on N UNCOUNT ships. EG *It was sent at a cost, including shipping, of only £35.* 2 ships considered as a group. EG *Nearly a fifth of the shipping had been sunk.*

shipwreck /ʃɪprɛk/, **shipwrecks, shipwrecked.**
1 If there is a **shipwreck**, a ship is destroyed in an N COUNT OR accident at sea. EG *The whole family perished in a* N UNCOUNT *shipwreck.*

2 A **shipwreck** is a ship which has been destroyed N COUNT in an accident at sea. EG *Treasure has sometimes been found in shipwrecks.*

3 If someone **is shipwrecked**, their ship is de- V-PASS stroyed in an accident at sea but they survive and manage to reach land. EG *He was shipwrecked off the lonely island of Iona.*

shipyard /ʃɪpjɑːd/, **shipyards.** A **shipyard** is a N COUNT place where ships are built and repaired. EG *Many shipyards will have to close.*

shirk /ʃɜːk/, **shirks, shirking, shirked.** If some- v+o OR v one **shirks** a job or task, they avoid doing it; used showing disapproval. EG *It was a job everyone shirked whenever possible.*

shirt /ʃɜːt/, **shirts.** A **shirt** is a piece of clothing N COUNT that you wear on the upper part of your body. Shirts have a collar, sleeves, and buttons down the front. See picture at CLOTHES. EG *He was wearing a suit and a shirt and tie.*

shirtsleeves /ʃɜːtsliːvz/. If a man is **in shirt-** PHRASE **sleeves** or **in his shirtsleeves**, he is wearing a shirt but not a jacket. EG *I lay on the bed in my shirt-sleeves.*

shiver /ʃɪvə/, **shivers, shivering, shivered.** 1 v When you **shiver**, your body shakes slightly because you are cold or frightened. EG *I stood shivering with cold on the doorstep.* ► used as a noun. EG *I* ► N COUNT *could not repress a shiver whenever I thought of him.*

2 If something **gives** you **the shivers**, it makes PHRASE you feel very frightened. EG *That place gives me* Informal *the shivers.*

shivery /ʃɪvərɪ/. If you are **shivery**, you cannot ADJ QUALIT stop shivering, because you are cold or frightened. Informal

shoal /ʃəʊl/, **shoals.** A **shoal** of fish is a large N PART group of them swimming together.

shock /ʃɒk/, **shocks, shocking, shocked.** 1 If you N COUNT have a **shock**, you suddenly have an experience which is unpleasant, upsetting, or very surprising. EG *I slapped her hand and she got such a shock that she dropped the milk... It was a shock to discover that they were English... I recovered gradually from the shock of her death.*

2 **Shock** is a person's emotional and physical N UNCOUNT condition when something very frightening or upsetting has happened to them. EG *Numb with shock, she stood watching as they took his body away.*

3 In medicine, **shock** is a serious physical condi- N UNCOUNT tion in which your blood cannot circulate properly, for example because you have had a bad injury. EG *She was rushed to hospital suffering from shock.*

4 A **shock** is also 4.1 a slight movement in some- N COUNT OR thing when it is hit or jerked by something else. EG N UNCOUNT *This padding should absorb any sudden shocks.* 4.2 N COUNT the same as an electric shock. Informal

5 If something **shocks** you, 5.1 it makes you feel v+o : NO CONT very upset, because it involves death or suffering and because you had not expected it. EG *She was deeply shocked by her husband's death.*

◊ **shocked.** EG *I was shocked at the damage I had* ◊ ADJ QUALIT *done.* 5.2 it upsets or offends you because you think v+o OR v it is rude or morally wrong. EG *Are you easily shocked?* ◊ **shocked.** EG *Don't look so shocked.* ◊ ADJ QUALIT

6 A **shock** of hair is a very thick mass of hair on a N PART person's head. EG *He was tall and handsome with a* Written *shock of hair falling over his forehead.*

shocking /ʃɒkɪŋ/. Something that is **shocking** 1 ADJ QUALIT is very bad. EG *The paintwork was really shocking... I'm shocking at spelling.* 2 makes people feel upset or angry, because they think that it is morally wrong. EG *It was shocking how badly paid these young girls were... ...the most shocking book of its time.*

shoddy /ʃɒdɪ/. Something that is **shoddy** has been ADJ QUALIT done or made carelessly or badly. EG *It is up to the teacher not to accept shoddy work... ...tiny shoddy houses... ...shoddy goods.*

shoe /ʃuː/, **shoes, shoeing, shod** /ʃɒd/. 1 Shoes N COUNT are objects which you wear on your feet. They cover most of your foot and you wear them over socks or stockings. EG *I took off my shoes... She needs a new pair of shoes.*

2 When someone **shoes** a horse, they fix horse- v+o shoes onto its hooves.

shoelace /ʃuːleɪs/, **shoelaces.** Shoelaces are N COUNT : long, narrow pieces of material like pieces of USU PLURAL string that you use to fasten your shoes. EG *He stopped to tie up his shoelace.*

shoestring /ʃuːstrɪŋ/. 1 If you do something **on a** PHRASE **shoestring**, you do it using very little money. EG Informal *...cookery on a shoestring.*

2 A **shoestring** budget is one where you have very ADJ CLASSIF : little money to spend. EG *She made the film on a* ATTRIB *shoestring budget.*

shone /ʃɒn/ is the past tense and past participle of **shine.**

shoo /ʃuː/, **shoos, shooing, shooed.** 1 If you **shoo** v+o+A an animal or a person somewhere, you make them go there by waving your hands or arms at them. EG *She shooed the birds in the direction of the open window.*

2 You say or shout '**Shoo**' at an animal in order to EXCLAM make it go away. EG *'Go away!' we shouted. 'Shoo!'*

shook /ʃʊk/ is the past tense of **shake.**

shoot /ʃuːt/, **shoots, shooting, shot** /ʃɒt/. 1 To v : OFT+at **shoot** means to fire a bullet from a gun. EG *We were told to shoot first and ask questions later... ...troops that are being shot at.*

2 If someone **shoots** a person or an animal, they v+o OR V-REFL kill them or injure them by firing a gun at them. EG *He shot his wife and then shot himself.*

shoes and boots

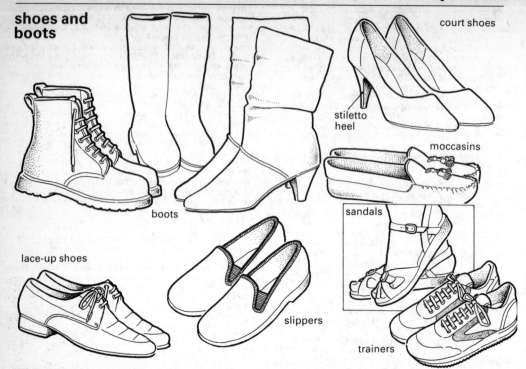

court shoes

stiletto heel

moccasins

boots

sandals

lace-up shoes

slippers

trainers

3 If people **shoot**, they hunt birds or animals with a gun as a form of sport. EG *He was too busy to fish or shoot.*   V OR V+O British

4 A **shoot** is an occasion when people hunt birds or animals with guns as a form of sport. EG *They often take part in the local shoot.*   N COUNT British

5 If you **shoot** an arrow, you fire it from a bow.   V+O

6 If someone or something **shoots** in a particular direction, they move in that direction quickly and suddenly. EG *She shot back into the room.*   V+A

7 If you **shoot** something somewhere, you send or move it there quickly and suddenly. EG *He shot out his hand and stopped the child from falling.*   V+O+A

8 If you **shoot** a glance at someone or something, you look at them quickly and briefly. EG *He shot a suspicious glare at me.*   V+O+*at* OR V+O+O

9 When a film **is shot**, it is photographed using film cameras. EG *Most of the film was shot in Spain.*   V+O OR V

10 A **shoot** is also a plant that is beginning to grow, or a new part growing from a plant or tree. EG *A few tender shoots of green had started to appear.*   N COUNT

11 See also **shot**.

shoot down. **1** If someone **shoots down** an aeroplane or helicopter, they make it fall to the ground by hitting it with a bullet or missile. **2** If someone **shoots down** someone else, they shoot them with a gun. **3** If you **shoot** someone **down** or **shoot down** their ideas, you show that their ideas are wrong or foolish.   PHRASAL VB : V+O+ADV / V+O+ADV / V+O+ADV

shoot up. If something **shoots up**, it grows or increases very quickly. EG *The inflation rate shot up from 30% to 48%.*   PHRASAL VB : V+ADV

shooting /ˈʃuːtɪŋ/, **shootings**. A **shooting** is an occasion when someone is killed or injured by being shot with a gun. EG *The police arrived fifteen minutes after the shooting.*   N COUNT OR N UNCOUNT

shoot-out, **shoot-outs**. A **shoot-out** is a fight in which people shoot at each other with guns. EG *He was wounded during a shoot-out with the police.*   N COUNT

shop /ʃɒp/, **shops, shopping, shopped**. **1** A **shop** is a building or part of a building where things are sold. EG *Two customers came into the shop... ...a shoe shop.*   N COUNT

2 When you **shop**, you go to shops and buy things. EG *We allow the older girls to shop in the village without an escort... They went shopping after lunch.* ◊ **shopper, shoppers**. EG *The city centre was crowded with shoppers.*   V : USU+A ◊ N COUNT : USU PLURAL

3 You can also refer to a place where things are made as a **shop**. EG *...metalwork shops.*   N COUNT+SUPP

4 See also **shopping**.

shop around. If you **shop around**, you go to different shops in order to compare the prices and quality of something before you decide to buy it.   PHRASAL VB : V+ADV

shop assistant, shop assistants. A **shop assistant** is a person who works in a shop selling things to customers.   N COUNT

shop floor. The **shop floor** is used to refer to all the workers in a factory, especially in contrast to the management. EG *There should be participation in decisions made on the shop floor.*   N SING : USU *the*+N

shopkeeper /ˈʃɒpkiːpə/, **shopkeepers**. A **shopkeeper** is a person who owns a small shop.   N COUNT

shoplifting /ˈʃɒplɪftɪŋ/ is stealing from a shop by walking round the shop and hiding things in a bag or in your clothes.   N ING

shopping /ˈʃɒpɪŋ/. Your **shopping** consists of the things that you have bought from shops, especially food and groceries. EG *She put her shopping away in the kitchen.*   N UNCOUNT

shopping centre, shopping centres. A **shopping centre** is an area in a town where a lot of shops have been built close together.   N COUNT

shop-soiled. Goods that are **shop-soiled** are slightly dirty or damaged, usually because they have been in a shop for a long time.   ADJ QUALIT British

shop steward, shop stewards. A **shop steward** is a trade union member who is elected by the other members in a factory or office to speak for them at official meetings.

shore /ʃɔː/, **shores, shoring, shored. 1** The **shore** N COUNT of a sea, lake, or wide river is the land along the edge of it. EG *We could see the trees on the other shore... ...swimming close to the shore.*

2 Someone who is **on shore** is on the land rather PHRASE than on a ship.

shore up. If you **shore** something **up**, you do PHRASAL VB : something in order to strengthen it. EG *Action is* V+O+ADV *needed to shore up economic links with American suppliers.*

shoreline /ʃɔːlaɪn/, **shorelines.** A **shoreline** is N COUNT the edge of a sea, lake, or wide river.

shorn /ʃɔːn/. **1** If grass or hair is **shorn**, it is cut ADJ CLASSIF very short. EG *...shorn blades of grass... ...his shorn head.*

2 Shorn is the past participle of **shear.**

short /ʃɔːt/, **shorter, shortest; shorts. 1** If some- ADJ QUALIT thing lasts for a **short** time, it does not last very long. EG *...a short holiday... The war was far shorter than they expected... He uttered a short cry of surprise.*

2 When you use **short** to describe a period of time, ADJ CLASSIF : you mean that it seems to have passed very ATTRIB quickly. EG *In a couple of short years she has destroyed all our hopes.*

3 Speeches, letters, or books that are **short** do not ADJ QUALIT have many words or pages in them. EG *She spoke in short sentences.*

4 Someone who is **short** is not as tall as most ADJ QUALIT people are. EG *...a short, fat man.*

5 Something that is **short** measures only a small ADJ QUALIT amount from one end to the other. EG *Her hair was cut short... She led the way down a short flight of steps... She showed us the shortest way home.*

6 If you are **short** with someone, you are rude to ADJ PRED them, because you are impatient or angry. EG *He* +with *was very short with her.*

7 If you have a **short** temper, you get angry very ADJ QUALIT easily.

8 Shorts are trousers with very short legs. See N PLURAL picture at CLOTHES.

9 If you are **short** of something or if it is **short**, you ADJ PRED : do not have enough of it. EG *We're dreadfully short* OFT+of *of staff at present... When money is short, we stick to a very careful budget.*

10 If something **is running short** or if you **are** PHRASE **running short** of it, you have almost used up your supply of it. EG *Water was running short... We were running short of food.*

11 If you are **short of breath**, you have difficulty PHRASE in breathing in enough air, for example after running or climbing stairs quickly.

12 If someone is **short on** a particular quality, they PHRASE do not have as much of it as you think they should Informal have. EG *She was intelligent but a bit short on wisdom.*

13 If someone or something is **short of** a place or PREP amount, they have not quite reached it. EG *He drove up the hill and stopped the car just short of the summit... He was only a year short of fifty.*

14 Short of a particular thing means except for CONJ that thing or without actually doing that thing. EG *Short of dynamiting his door open, how do I attract his attention?*

15 You use **nothing short of** to emphasize that the PHRASE thing that you are referring to is very great or extreme. For example, if you say that an action is **nothing short of** heroic, you are emphasizing that it is heroic.

16 If something **is cut short**, it is stopped before it PHRASE has finished. EG *The war cut short his education.*

17 If something **brings** you **up short** or **pulls** you PHRASE **up short**, it makes you suddenly stop what you are doing. EG *We were brought up short by the news.*

18 If you **stop short** or if something **stops** you PHRASE **short**, you suddenly stop what you are doing, for example because something has surprised you. EG

The soldier took a few steps and then stopped short... His disapproval stopped her short.

19 If someone **stops short of** doing something, PHRASE they come close to doing it but do not actually do it. EG *He just stopped short of calling her a murderer.*

20 If a person or thing is called something **for** PHRASE **short**, that is the short version of their name. EG *Her name was Madeleine but Celia always called her 'Maddy' for short.*

21 If a name **is short for** another name, it is the PHRASE short version of that name. EG *It's short for 'Madeleine'.*

22 You use the expression **in short** when you have ADV SEN been giving a lot of details and you want to give a conclusion or summary. EG *I was packing, arranging the trip, cleaning the house, and saying countless goodbyes. In short, it was a hectic week.*

23 at short notice: see **notice.** ● **to cut a long story short**: see **story.** ● **in short supply**: see **supply.**

shortage /ʃɔːtɪdʒ/, **shortages.** If there is a **short-** N COUNT **age** of something, there is not enough of it. EG USU+SUPP *There's a world shortage of fuel... ...the housing shortage after the last war.*

shortbread /ʃɔːtbred/ is a kind of biscuit made N UNCOUNT from flour, sugar, and butter.

shortcake /ʃɔːtkeɪk/ is the same as shortbread. N UNCOUNT

short-circuit, short-circuits. If there is a **short-** N COUNT **circuit** in an electrical system or device, there is a wrong connection or a damaged wire, so that electricity travels along the wrong route and damages the system or device. EG *The lamp-post was heating up from an electrical short-circuit inside.*

shortcoming /ʃɔːtkʌmɪŋ/, **shortcomings. Short-** N COUNT : **comings** are faults or weaknesses which a person USU PLURAL or thing has. EG *You've got to realize your own shortcomings... ...whatever shortcomings the airport might have.*

shortcrust /ʃɔːtkrʌst/. **Shortcrust** pastry is made ADJ CLASSIF : with a lot of fat and crumbles very easily. ATTRIB

short-cut, short-cuts. A **short-cut** is **1** a quicker N COUNT way of getting somewhere than the usual route. EG *Will you show me that short cut to Wirral Hill?* **2** a method of achieving something more quickly than if you use the usual methods. EG *Parents of twins simply have to find short-cuts in housework.*

shorten /ʃɔːtəⁿn/, **shortens, shortening, short-** **ened. 1** If you **shorten** an event or the length of V-ERG time that something lasts, or if it **shortens**, it does not last as long as it would otherwise do or as it used to do. EG *The colonel had a plan to shorten the war.*

2 If an object **shortens** or if you **shorten** it, it V-ERG becomes smaller in length. EG *She wondered if she could make the sleeves shortened... The back muscles contract and shorten as your leg lifts.*

shortfall /ʃɔːtfɔːl/, **shortfalls.** If there is a **short-** N COUNT : **fall** in something, there is less of it than you need. USU SING+SUPP EG *A shortfall of energy supplies seems inevitable in the near future.*

shorthand /ʃɔːthⁿænd/. **1 Shorthand** is a way of N UNCOUNT writing which uses signs to represent words or syllables. Shorthand is used especially by secretaries to quickly write down what someone is saying.

2 You can also use **shorthand** to mean a quick or N UNCOUNT simple way of referring to something. EG *All slogans are shorthand for something more complex.*

short-list, short-lists, short-listing, short- **listed. 1** If someone is on a **short-list**, for example N COUNT for a job or a prize, they are one of a small group of people that have been chosen from a larger group. The small group is judged again and a final decision is made about which of them is the best. EG *He produced a short-list of three MPs for the post.*

2 If someone or something is **short-listed** for a job V+O : USU PASS or a prize, they are put on a short-list. EG *Her novel has been short-listed for the Booker Prize.*

short-lived. Something that is **short-lived** does ADJ QUALIT not last very long. EG *His joy and relief were short-lived... He founded the shortlived Nationalist Party.*

shortly /ʃɔːtliʲ/. **1** If something is going to happen ADV **shortly**, it is going to happen soon. If something happened **shortly** after something else, it happened soon after it. EG *She's going to London shortly... She died in an accident shortly afterwards... Shortly before dawn he had an idea.*

2 If you say something **shortly**, you speak to ADV them in a cross or impatient way. EG *'You ought to be in bed,' I said shortly.*

short-sighted. 1 If you are **short-sighted**, you ADJ QUALIT cannot see things properly when they are far away, because there is something wrong with your eyes. EG *He finally realized that he was short-sighted and went to the optician.*

2 If you are **short-sighted** about something, or if ADJ QUALIT your ideas are **short-sighted**, you do not make proper or careful judgements about the future. EG *Until this short-sighted policy is reversed we shall never make any progress.*

short-staffed. A company that is **short-staffed** ADJ QUALIT : does not have enough people working for it. EG USU PRED *They're rather short-staffed at the moment.*

short-tempered. Someone who is **short-** ADJ QUALIT **tempered** gets angry very quickly. EG *Lebel was short-tempered with him, which was unusual.*

short-term. 1 Short-term effects or develop- ADJ QUALIT ments will happen soon, rather than happening more gradually over a longer period of time. EG *The effects of the Computer Revolution will be felt in the short-term future.*

2 A **short-term** problem or a solution lasts for only ADJ QUALIT a short time. EG *The artificial heart is designed only for short-term use.*

short wave is a range of radio waves which are ADJ CLASSIF used for broadcasting. EG *The only communication with the mainland was by short-wave radio.*

shot /ʃɒt/, **shots. 1 Shot** is the past tense and past participle of **shoot**.

2 A **shot** is an act of firing a gun. EG *One of them* N COUNT *fired several shots at Ward.*

3 Someone who is a good **shot** can shoot well. EG N COUNT : *He's an excellent shot.* ADJ+N

4 In sports such as football, golf, or tennis, a **shot** is N COUNT an act of kicking or hitting the ball, especially in an attempt to score a point. EG *Try to hit the green with your first shot... Oh, good shot.*

5 A **shot** is also a photograph or a picture seen in a N COUNT film. EG *I got some great shots of you... The film also contained some shots of the University.*

6 If you have a **shot** at something, you attempt to N COUNT do it. EG *I'd love to have a shot at hang-gliding.* Informal

7 A **shot** of a drug is an injection of it. EG *The* N COUNT *doctor gave her a shot of Librium.*

8 If you do something **like a shot**, you do it without PHRASE any delay or hesitation. EG *I told him to bring her at* Informal *once. He was off like a shot.*

shotgun /ʃɒtgʌn/, **shotguns.** A **shotgun** is a gun N COUNT used for shooting birds and animals which fires a lot of small metal balls at one time.

shot put. In athletics, the **shot put** is a competi- N SING : the+N tion in which the contestants throw a heavy metal ball as far as possible.

should /ʃəd/. **Should** is sometimes considered to be the past form of **shall**, but in this dictionary the two words are dealt with separately.

1 If you say that something **should** happen, you MODAL mean that you think it is right or a good idea. EG *Crimes should be punished... These birds shouldn't be in a cage... Should we remain in the Common Market?*

2 You use **should** in questions when you are asking MODAL someone for advice, permission, or information. EG *Where should I meet you tonight?... Should I turn the light on?*

3 You use **'I should'** when you are giving someone MODAL advice. EG *If you have anything really confidential I* Informal

should install a safe... I shouldn't bother to copy these down.

4 If you say that something **should** happen or MODAL **should** be true, you mean that you think it will probably happen or is probably true. EG *We should be there by dinner time... There shouldn't be any difficulties... She should be alone.*

5 If you say that something **should have** hap- MODAL pened, you mean that it did not happen, but you expected it to happen or you wish that it had happened. EG *Muskie should have won by a huge margin... You should have thought about that before you invited her.*

6 If you say that something **should have** happened MODAL by now, you mean that it has probably happened by now. EG *Dear Mom, you should have heard by now that I'm O.K.*

7 If you say that you **should** do something in a MODAL particular situation, you mean that you would do it Formal if you were in that situation. EG *And the first thing I should do would be to teach you how to cook.*

8 If you say that you **should** like to do something, MODAL you are saying politely that you want to do it. EG *I should be delighted to try it... I should like to give you a little practical advice.*

9 You can use **should** in conditional sentences MODAL when you are talking about things that might happen. EG *If we should be seen arriving together, they would get suspicious... Should you have an accident, synthetic quilts are quite easy to wash.*

10 You can use **should** in a 'that' clause after some MODAL verbs and adjectives. EG *It was arranged that Celia should come to Switzerland... It's strange you should come today.*

11 If you say that you **should** think something is MODAL true, you mean that you think it is true but you are not sure. EG *I should think it was about twelve years ago... He weighs, I should say, about 140 pounds.*

shoulder /ʃəʊldə/, **shoulders, shouldering, shouldered. 1** Your **shoulders** are the two parts N COUNT of your body between your neck and the tops of your arms. See picture at THE HUMAN BODY. EG *Sally patted me on the shoulder.*

2 If you look **over** your **shoulder**, you look behind PHRASE you by turning your neck. EG *He stopped and looked over his shoulder.*

3 If someone needs **a shoulder to cry on**, they PHRASE need a person who will listen sympathetically to all their troubles.

4 If you **rub shoulders with** famous people, you PHRASE meet them and talk to them. EG *...attend the royal* Informal *wedding, rub shoulders with world leaders.*

5 The **shoulders** of a piece of clothing are the N COUNT : parts that cover your shoulders. EG *...dust on the* USU PLURAL *shoulders of his expensive suit.*

6 If you **shoulder** something heavy, you put it V+O across one of your shoulders so that you can carry it more easily. EG *He shouldered his bundle again and set off.*

7 If you **shoulder** the responsibility or blame for V+O something, you accept it. EG *The government is expected to shoulder the responsibility for financing the project.*

8 You can say that a person's problems or respon- N PLURAL sibilities are on that person's **shoulders**. EG *The burden of decision is placed on the shoulders of the individual.*

9 A **shoulder** is also a joint of meat from the upper N COUNT OR part of the front leg of an animal. EG *...a shoulder of* N UNCOUNT *lamb.*

shoulder-bag, shoulder-bags. A **shoulder-bag** N COUNT is a bag that has a long strap so that it can be carried on a person's shoulder. See picture at BAGS.

shoulder blade, shoulder blades. Your **shoul-** N COUNT : **der blades** are the two large, flat, triangular bones USU PLURAL

If you tell someone to shove off, are you speaking to them shortly?

that you have in the upper part of your back, below your shoulders.

shouldn't /ʃʊdənt/ is the usual spoken form of 'should not'.

should've /ʃʊdəv/ is the usual spoken form of 'should have', especially when 'have' is an auxiliary verb.

shout /ʃaut/, **shouts, shouting, shouted.** 1 A N COUNT **shout** is a loud call or cry. EG *Excited shouts and laughter could be heard from the garden.*

2 If you **shout**, you say words as loudly as you can, V-SPEECH: so that you can be heard from a long distance ONLY *that;* away. EG *The children on the sand were shouting* ALSO V+*at* *with excitement... She shouted at us for spoiling her evening... 'Stop it!' he shouted.*

shout down. If people **shout** a person **down,** PHRASAL VB: they prevent the person from being heard by V+O+ADV shouting at them. EG *Mr Healey was shouted down at a meeting in Birmingham.*

shout out. If you **shout** something **out,** you PHRASAL VB: suddenly shout it. EG *I just had time to shout out and* V+ADV OR warn them not to cross the road. V-SPEECH+ADV

shove /ʃʌv/, **shoves, shoving, shoved.** If you V+O+A **shove** someone or something, you push them with a quick, violent movement. EG *He shoved the man through the door... He shoved the letter under her door.* ▶ used as a noun. EG *I gave him a shove in the* ▶ N COUNT: *direction of the street.* USU SING

shove off. If you tell someone to **shove off,** you PHRASAL VB: are telling them angrily to go away. EG *You shove* V+O+ADV, off, Eric. See? USU IMPER Informal

shovel /ʃʌvəl/, **shovels, shovelling, shovelled;** spelled **shoveling** and **shoveled** in American English.

1 A **shovel** is a tool like a spade, used for lifting N COUNT and moving earth, coal, or snow. EG *He was working with a pick and shovel... ...a coal shovel.*

2 If you **shovel** earth, coal, or snow, you lift and V+O move it with a shovel. EG *She helped us shovel the snow off the front path.*

3 If you **shovel** something somewhere, you push a V+O+A lot of it quickly into that place. EG *They were shovelling food into their mouths.*

show /ʃəu/, **shows, showing, showed, shown** /ʃəun/. 1 If something **shows** that a state of affairs V OR V+O: exists, it gives information that proves it or makes USU+REPORT it clear to people. EG *The post-mortem shows that death was due to natural causes... These figures show an 8.5% increase in exports.*

2 If a picture or piece of writing **shows** something, V+O OR it represents it or gives information about it. EG *The* V+REPORT *painting shows four athletes bathing... A statement showing how much you need to pay is sent each month.*

3 If you **show** someone something, you give it to V+O+O, them, take them to it, or point to it, so that they can V+O+REPORT, see it or know what you are referring to. EG *I* OR V+O+*to* *showed William what I had written... Let me show you the garden... She showed me where to park the car... Fetch that lovely drawing and show it to the vicar.*

4 If you **show** someone to a room or seat, you lead V+O+A them there. EG *I was shown into a large apartment.*

5 If you **show** someone how to do something, you V+O+*how,* do it yourself so that they can watch you and learn V+*how,* OR how to do it. EG *The woman took the gun and* V+O+O showed how the cylinder slotted into the barrel... Show us a card game.*

6 If something **shows** or if you **show** it, it is visible V OR V-ERG or noticeable. EG *The edge of the moon is just showing... The stitching is so fine that it doesn't show at all... He had a strange fierce way of grinning that showed his teeth.*

7 If you **show** yourself, you move into a position V-REFL where you can be seen by other people. EG *Come out from there and show yourself.*

8 If something **shows** a quality or characteristic, it V+O has this quality or characteristic in a noticeable

way. EG *Prices began to show some signs of decline in 1974... The sketch shows a lot of talent.*

9 If you **show** a particular attitude or quality, you V+O OR behave in a way that makes this attitude or quality V+REPORT: clear to other people. EG *This is a way in which* ONLY *that* Britain can show a readiness to help... He dared not show that he was pleased... She was feeling sad and didn't want to show it.*

10 If you **show** someone an emotion or reaction V+O+O, V+O such as affection or mercy, you behave towards +*to/towards,* them with affection or mercy. EG *She often showed* OR V+O *me kindness... I had been taught to show respect towards my elders.*

11 If you say **it just goes to show** that something PHRASE is the case, you mean that what you have just said proves that it is the case. EG *It all goes to show that people haven't changed.*

12 If you **have** something **to show for** your efforts, PHRASE you have achieved something as a result of what you have done. EG *Rodin's search was over and what he had to show for it was three slim dossiers.*

13 A **show** of a feeling or quality is an attempt that N COUNT: you make to appear to have that feeling or quality. USU+*of* EG *She put on a good show of looking interested... ...those who had made open shows of defiance.*

14 If something is done **for show,** it has no real PHRASE purpose and is done just to give a good impression. EG *These regulations are just for show.*

15 A **show** is a form of entertainment at the N COUNT theatre or on television that usually consists of several items. EG *Joy Leomine has been appearing in a show in London.*

16 To **show** a film or television programme means V-ERG: IF V to make it available for people to watch. EG *One* ONLY CONT evening the school showed a cowboy film.* ◇ **showing, showings.** EG *He had just been to a* ◇ N COUNT private showing of the film.*

17 A **show** is also an exhibition of things, often N COUNT: things that have been entered in a competition. EG USU+SUPP ...a flower show.*

18 If something is **on show,** it has been put in a PHRASE place where it can be seen by the public. EG *The photographs are on show at the Museum until October.*

19 A **show of hands** is a method of voting in which PHRASE people raise their hands and the number of hands is counted.

show around. See **show round.**

show off. 1 If someone **shows off,** they behave PHRASAL VB: in a way that makes their skills or good qualities V+ADV very obvious, in order to impress people. EG *...kids showing off on the diving board.* 2 If you **show off** V+O+ADV something that you own, you show it to a lot of people because you are proud of it. EG *He was eager to show off the new car.* 3 See also **show-off.**

show round. If you **show** someone **round** a PHRASAL VB: V place or **show** them **around** it, you go round it +O+ADV/PREP with them, pointing out all its interesting or important features.

show up. 1 If you **show up,** you appear at a place PHRASAL VB: where you are expected by someone. EG *Over a* V+ADV hundred people showed up at the meeting... He Informal showed up at ten o'clock the next morning.* 2 If something **shows up** or **is shown up,** it can be V-ERG+ADV clearly seen. EG *Dark colours will not show up against a similar background.* 3 If someone is with V+O+ADV you and they **show** you **up,** they behave in a way that makes you feel embarrassed and ashamed of them.

showbiz /ʃəubiz/ is the same as show business. EG N UNCOUNT *We do get some remarkable glimpses of showbiz* Informal *here.*

show business is the entertainment industry of N UNCOUNT film, theatre, and television. EG *Then he went into show business.*

showcase /ʃəukeis/, **showcases.** 1 A **showcase** N COUNT is a glass container with valuable objects inside it, for example at an exhibition or in a museum. EG ...showcases of gold artefacts.*

2 You use **showcase** to refer to a situation or setting in which something is displayed or presented to its best advantage. EG *This opera is a stunning showcase for the company.*   N COUNT+SUPP Formal

showdown /ˈʃəʊdaʊn/, **showdowns**. A **showdown** is a big argument or conflict which is intended to settle a dispute that has lasted for a long time. EG *It's time for a showdown with your boss.*   N COUNT : OFT SING+with

shower /ˈʃaʊə/, **showers, showering, showered.**
1 A **shower** is a device used for washing yourself. It consists of a pipe or hose which ends in a flat piece with a lot of holes in it so that water comes out in a spray. EG *All rooms have got a bath, shower and toilet.*   N COUNT

2 If you have a **shower**, you wash yourself by standing under a spray of water from a shower. EG *A hot shower and a change of clothes would be wonderful.* ▸ used as a verb. EG *I'll shave and shower and then have some coffee.*   N COUNT   ▸ V

3 A **shower** is also a short period of light rain. EG *...a week of scattered showers.*   N COUNT

4 You can refer to a lot of light things that are falling as a **shower** of them. EG *...a shower of falling leaves.*   N PART

5 If you **are showered** with a lot of small light things, they are scattered onto you from above. EG *Suddenly the lid came off and showered him with flakes of rust.*   V+O+A

6 If you **shower** a person with presents or kisses, you give them a lot of presents or kisses in a very generous and extravagant way. EG *They showered each other with gifts at Christmas.*   V+O+A

showery /ˈʃaʊəriˈ/. If the weather is **showery**, there are showers of rain but it does not rain all the time.   ADJ QUALIT

show jumping is a sport in which horses are ridden in competitions to demonstrate their skill in jumping over walls and fences.   N UNCOUNT

shown /ʃəʊn/ is the past participle of **show.**

show-off, show-offs. If you say that someone is a **show-off**, you mean that they behave in a way that shows their skills or abilities very obviously, in order to impress people; used showing disapproval.   N COUNT Informal

showroom /ˈʃəʊruˈm/, **showrooms**. A **showroom** is a shop in which goods are displayed for sale, especially goods such as cars or electrical or gas appliances. EG *The new model will be in the showrooms in a fortnight's time.*   N COUNT

showy /ˈʃəʊiˈ/. Something that is **showy** is very noticeable because it is large, colourful, or bright. EG *...a showy bracelet and earrings.*   ADJ QUALIT

shrank /ʃræŋk/ is the past tense of **shrink.**

shrapnel /ˈʃræpnəˈl/ consists of small pieces of metal which are scattered from exploding bombs and shells. EG *He'd been caught in the knee by a piece of shrapnel.*   N UNCOUNT

shred /ʃrɛd/, **shreds, shredding, shredded.** **1** If you **shred** something such as food or paper, you cut it or tear it into very small pieces. EG *Carrots taste delicious shredded in salad.*   V+O

2 A **shred** of material is a small narrow piece of it. EG *She took the letter and ripped it to shreds.*   N COUNT : USU PLURAL

3 If you say that there is no **shred** of something, you mean that there is not even a small amount of it. EG *There is no shred of evidence to support the theory that Emily was murdered.*   N PART

shrew /ʃruː/, **shrews**. A **shrew** is a small brown animal like a mouse with a long pointed nose.   N COUNT

shrewd /ʃruːd/, **shrewder, shrewdest.** Someone who is **shrewd** is able to understand and judge a situation quickly and to use this understanding to their own advantage. EG *He is a shrewd and sometimes ruthless adversary... It was a shrewd assessment.* ◊ **shrewdly.** EG *She looked at him shrewdly.*   ADJ QUALIT   ◊ ADV

shriek /ʃriːk/, **shrieks, shrieking, shrieked.** If you **shriek**, you give a sudden loud scream. EG *She shrieked in alarm... Ralph shrieked with laughter.* ▸ used as a noun. EG *She let out a shriek of laughter.*   V : OFT +with/in   ▸ N COUNT : OFT+of

shrill /ʃrɪl/, **shriller, shrillest.** A **shrill** sound is high-pitched, piercing, and unpleasant to listen to. EG *The boys broke into shrill, excited cheering... ...the shrill screaming of jet engines.* ◊ **shrilly.** EG *Lewis whistled shrilly.*   ADJ QUALIT   ◊ ADV

shrimp /ʃrɪmp/, **shrimps**. A **shrimp** is a small shellfish with a long tail and many legs.   N COUNT

shrine /ʃraɪn/, **shrines**. A **shrine** is a holy place of worship which is associated with a sacred person or object. EG *He went to the shrine of St Foy.*   N COUNT

shrink /ʃrɪŋk/, **shrinks, shrinking, shrank** /ʃræŋk/, **shrunk** /ʃrʌŋk/. **1** If cloth **shrinks** or if you **shrink** it, it becomes smaller in size, usually as a result of being washed. EG *You should dry-clean curtains if possible, as they are less likely to shrink.*   V-ERG

2 If something **shrinks**, it becomes smaller. EG *He commented on the amazing way in which computers have recently shrunk in size.*   V-ERG

3 If you **shrink** away from something, you move away from it because you are frightened or horrified by it. EG *The boys shrank away in horror... She shrank back, quivering.*   V+A

4 If you **shrink** from a task or duty, you are reluctant to do it because you find it unpleasant. EG *He shrank from giving Francis a direct answer.*   V+from

shrinkage /ˈʃrɪŋkɪdʒ/ is a decrease in the size or amount of something. EG *...the steady shrinkage of the tropical forests.*   N UNCOUNT

shrivel /ˈʃrɪvəˈl/, **shrivels, shrivelling, shrivelled;** spelled **shriveling** and **shriveled** in American English. When something **shrivels** or **shrivels up**, it becomes dry and wrinkled, usually because it loses moisture in the heat. EG *The seedlings had shrivelled up a bit in the hot sun... Every year we have a long dry season that shrivels and scorches plants.*   V-ERG : OFT+up

shroud /ʃraʊd/, **shrouds, shrouding, shrouded.**
1 A **shroud** is a cloth which is used for wrapping a dead body. EG *The doctor wanted to use the sheet for a shroud.*   N COUNT

2 If something **is shrouded** in darkness or fog, it is hidden by it. EG *Everything was shrouded in mist and raindrops.*   V+O : USU PASS+in

3 If something **is shrouded** in mystery, very little is known about it. EG *The precise sequence of events is shrouded in mystery.*   V+O : USU PASS+in

shrub /ʃrʌb/, **shrubs**. A **shrub** is a low plant like a small tree with several woody stems instead of a trunk. EG *...flowering shrubs.*   N COUNT

shrubbery /ˈʃrʌbəˈriˈ/, **shrubberies**. A **shrubbery** is the part of a garden where a lot of shrubs are growing.   N COUNT OR N UNCOUNT

shrug /ʃrʌg/, **shrugs, shrugging, shrugged.** If you **shrug** your shoulders, you raise them to show that you are not interested in something or that you do not know or care about it. EG *Don't just shrug your shoulders. Say something!... 'Do you mind if I want?' I asked. Melanie shrugged. 'Please yourself.'* ▸ used as a noun. EG *The man nodded with a faint shrug of his shoulders.*   V+O OR V   ▸ N COUNT : USU SING

shrug off. If you **shrug** something **off**, you ignore it or treat it as if it is not really important or serious. EG *The chairman shrugs off any criticism that their methods are not strictly legal.*   PHRASAL VB : V+O+ADV

shrunk /ʃrʌŋk/ is the past participle of **shrink.**

shrunken /ˈʃrʌŋkəˈn/. Something that is **shrunken** has become smaller than it used to be. EG *...a shrunken old man.*   ADJ QUALIT

shudder /ˈʃʌdə/, **shudders, shuddering, shuddered.** **1** If you **shudder**, you tremble with fear, horror, or disgust. EG *Robert shuddered with fear... The smell made her shudder.* ▸ used as a noun. EG *Max looked round him with a shudder.*   V : OFT+A   ▸ N COUNT : USU SING

2 If you say that you **shudder to think** of something, you mean that you expect to be so awful or   PHRASE disastrous that you do not really want to think about it. EG *I shudder to think of the consequences.*

3 If something such as a machine or vehicle **shudders**, it shakes suddenly in a very violent manner. EG *The tank braked and shuddered to a violent halt.* v

shuffle /ˈʃʌfəˀl/, **shuffles, shuffling, shuffled. 1** If you **shuffle**, **1.1** you walk without lifting your feet properly off the ground. EG *He slipped on his shoes and shuffled out of the room.* ▸ used as a noun. EG *We recognized him by his distinctive walk, a kind of shuffle.* **1.2** you move your feet about while standing or you move your bottom about while sitting, often because you feel uncomfortable or embarrassed. EG *I looked at the ground, shuffled my feet and mumbled something defensive... I was shuffling in my seat.* v : USU+A ▸ N SING v+o OR v

2 If you **shuffle** a pack of cards, you mix them up before you begin a game. EG *He took out the cards, shuffled them, and put them down on the table.* v+o OR v

shun /ʃʌn/, **shuns, shunning, shunned.** If you **shun** someone or something, you deliberately avoid them. EG *These people shun publicity.* v+o

shunt /ʃʌnt/, **shunts, shunting, shunted.** If you **shunt** objects or people somewhere, you move them to a different place. EG *...the sound of heavy desks being shunted across the room... He shunted me into a corner and looked over both shoulders before speaking.* v+o : USU+A Informal

shush /ʃʊʃ, ʃʌʃ/. You say **shush** when you are telling someone to be quiet. EXCLAM

shut /ʃʌt/, **shuts, shutting.** The form **shut** is used in the present tense and is the past tense and past participle of the verb.
1 If you **shut** something or if it **shuts**, its position is changed so that it fills a hole or gap. EG *I shut the door quietly... He goes in and the door shuts behind him.* ▸ used as an adjective. EG *The windows were all shut.* v-ERG ▸ ADJ PRED

2 If you **shut** your eyes, you lower your eyelids so that you cannot see anything. EG *Mrs Kaul shut her eyes for a moment.* ▸ used as an adjective. EG *He lay with his eyes shut.* v+o ▸ ADJ PRED

3 If you **shut** your mouth, you place your lips together so that nothing can get into your mouth or out of it. EG *Mr Boggis opened his mouth, then quickly shut it again.* ● If someone tells you to **shut your mouth** or **shut your face**, they are telling you very rudely to stop talking. ● If someone asks you to **keep your mouth shut** about something, they are asking you not to tell anyone else about it. EG *He warned me to keep my mouth shut about his visit.* v+o ● PHRASE Informal ● PHRASE Informal

4 When a shop or pub **shuts** or when someone **shuts** it, it is closed and you cannot go into it until the next time that it is open. EG *'What time do the shops shut?' – 'Half past five.'* ▸ used as an adjective. EG *I'm afraid all the pubs will be shut.* v-ERG ▸ ADJ PRED

shut away. If you **shut** something **away**, you keep it in a special room or cupboard where people cannot see it. EG *We have a small number of books which are shut away.* PHRASAL VB : v+o+ADV

shut down. If a factory or business **shuts down** or if someone **shuts** it **down**, it closes and stops working. EG *His department was shut down for lack of funds... That year my grandfather had to shut down the forge.* ● See also **shutdown.** PHRASAL VB : v-ERG+ADV

shut in. 1 If someone **shuts** you **in** a room, they close the door so that you cannot leave it. EG *He was shut in with an assortment of strangers.* **2** If you **shut** yourself **in** a room, you stay in there and make sure nobody else can get in. EG *She shut herself in the bathroom and wept.* PHRASAL VB : v+o+ADV/ PREP V-REFL+ADV/ PREP

shut out. 1 If you **shut** something or someone **out**, you prevent them from getting into a place, for example by closing the doors. EG *They had covered the holes to shut out the water.* **2** If you **shut out** a thought or a feeling, you prevent PHRASAL VB : v+o+ADV v+o+ADV

yourself from thinking or feeling it. EG *She found it impossible to shut out the pain.*

shut up. 1 If you **shut up**, you stop talking. EG *She was always telling him to shut up... Shut up and listen.* **2** If someone **shuts** you **up**, they prevent you from talking. EG *Turn the television on. That usually shuts them up.* PHRASAL VB : V+ADV V+O+ADV Informal

shutdown /ˈʃʌtdaʊn/, **shutdowns.** A **shutdown** is the closing of a factory, shop, or other business. EG *Refinery owners have already resorted to temporary shutdowns.* N COUNT

shutter /ˈʃʌtə/, **shutters. 1 Shutters** are wooden or metal covers fitted on the outside of a window. They can be opened to let in the light, or shut to keep out the sun or the cold or to protect the windows from damage. EG *...an old brick house with green shutters... ...closing the windows, fastening the shutters, and turning off all the lights.* N COUNT : USU PLURAL
2 The **shutter** in a camera is the part which opens to allow light through the lens when a photograph is taken. N COUNT

shuttered /ˈʃʌtəd/. A **shuttered** window has its shutters closed. EG *All doors were locked and the windows closed and shuttered.* ADJ CLASSIF

shuttle /ˈʃʌtəˀl/, **shuttles, shuttling, shuttled. 1** A **shuttle** service is an air, bus, or train service which makes frequent journeys between two places. ADJ CLASSIF : ATTRIB
2 A **shuttle** is a plane used in a shuttle service. EG *He caught the nine o'clock shuttle to New York.* N COUNT
3 See also **space shuttle.**

shy /ʃaɪ/, **shyer, shyest; shies, shying, shied. 1** A **shy** person is nervous and uncomfortable in the company of other people. EG *I've always been a bit shy... ...a shy smile.* ◊ **shyly.** EG *She smiled shyly at him.* ADJ QUALIT ◊ ADV
2 If you are **shy** of doing something, you are unwilling to do it because you are afraid of what might happen. EG *Don't be shy of telling them what you think.* ADJ PRED+OF
3 When a horse **shies**, it moves away suddenly, because something has frightened it. v
4 See also **work-shy.**

shy away from. If you **shy away from** doing something, you avoid doing it, often because you are afraid or not confident enough. EG *Are you going to grasp these opportunities or shy away from them?* PHRASAL VB : V+ADV+PREP

Siamese twins /ˌsaɪəmiːz ˈtwɪnz/ are twins who are born joined to each other by a part of their bodies. N PLURAL

sibling /ˈsɪblɪŋ/, **siblings.** Your **siblings** are your brothers and sisters. N COUNT Formal

sick /sɪk/, **sicker, sickest. 1** If you are **sick**, you are ill. EG *Your uncle is very sick.* ADJ QUALIT
2 If you feel **sick**, you feel ill in your stomach, and food that you have eaten is likely to be sent out through your mouth. EG *Flying always makes me feel sick.* ● If you **are sick**, food that you have eaten is sent out through your mouth. EG *I think I'm going to be sick.* ADJ PRED ● PHRASE
3 If you say that something **makes** you **sick**, you mean that you feel angry or disgusted about it. EG *It makes me sick the way they waste our money.* PHRASE
4 If you are **sick** of something, you are very annoyed by it and want it to stop. EG *We're sick of sitting around waiting for something to happen... Europe was sick of war.* ADJ PRED+OF
5 You describe acts, stories, or jokes as **sick** when they deal with death, cruelty, or suffering in a frivolous way. EG *She made a rather sick joke.* ADJ QUALIT
6 If you are **worried sick**, you are extremely worried. EG *He was worried sick that the factory might close.* PHRASE Informal

sickbed /ˈsɪkbed/, **sickbeds.** Your **sickbed** is the bed that you are lying in while you are ill. EG *I was able to watch television from my sickbed.* N COUNT

sicken /ˈsɪkəˀn/, **sickens, sickening, sickened. 1** If something **sickens** you, it makes you feel dis- v+o gusted. EG *The young officers were sickened by the greed of their generals.*

2 If you **sicken**, you become ill. EG *In these conditions a child could sicken and die in a year.*   V Outdated

sickening /sɪkəⁿnɪŋ/. You describe something as **sickening** **1** when it gives you feelings of horror or disgust. EG *The car crashed with a sickening crunch into a tree... The food smelled sickening.* **2** Informal when it annoys you very much. EG *Her mother's only concerned about the money. How sickening!*   ADJ QUALIT

sickle /sɪkəⁿl/, **sickles**. A **sickle** is a tool that is used for cutting grass and grain crops. It has a short handle and a long, curved blade.   N COUNT

sickly /sɪklɪ¹/, **sicklier, sickliest**. **1** A **sickly** person is weak, unhealthy, and often ill. EG *He was a sickly and ineffective man.*   ADJ QUALIT

2 Things that you describe as **sickly** are very unpleasant to smell or look at. EG *There was a musty, sickly smell... ...a sickly brown shirt.*   ADJ QUALIT

sickness /sɪknɪ²s/, **sicknesses**. **1** Sickness is **1.1** the state of being ill or unhealthy. EG *...people who are not working because of sickness or unemployment.* **1.2** a condition in which you feel ill in your stomach and in which food that you have eaten is sent out through your mouth. EG *The disease causes sickness and diarrhoea.* ● See also **morning sickness**.   N UNCOUNT

2 A **sickness** is a particular illness. EG *...the first signs of radiation sickness.*   N COUNT OR N UNCOUNT

side /saɪd/, **sides, siding, sided**. **1** The **side** of something is a position to the left or right of it, rather than in front of it or behind it. EG *A taxi bumped into us from the side... Standing on either side of him were two younger men... 'Get out of my way,' she cried, pushing Tom to one side... I sat down by her side.*   N COUNT

2 Side is used in these phrases referring to position or closeness. **2.1** If something is **on every side** or **on all sides** of you, you are surrounded by it. EG *The sea lay on every side.* **2.2** If you put something **to one side** or **on one side**, you keep it separate from other things, so that you can deal with it later. **2.3** If something moves **from side to side**, it moves repeatedly to the left and to the right. EG *The ship was swaying from side to side.* **2.4** If two people are **side by side**, they are sitting, standing, or walking next to each other. **2.5** If two people or things do something **side by side**, they do it together. EG *Student and tutor learn side by side... Two interdependent communities evolved side by side.* **2.6** If someone stays **at your side** or **by your side**, they stay near you and give you comfort or support. EG *He wanted to live forever by her side.*   PHRASES

3 Something that is on one **side** of a boundary or barrier is in one of the two areas that the boundary or barrier separates. EG *We were told of threatening developments on the other side of the border.*   N COUNT : USU SING+SUPP

4 Your **sides** are the parts of your body under your arms from your armpits down to your hips. EG *She lay on her side with her back to me.*   N COUNT

5 The **sides** of an area or surface are **5.1** its two halves. EG *Blood was streaming from one side of her face... She was driving on the wrong side of the road.* **5.2** its edges. EG *A hedge surrounds my garden on three sides... Mowbray's practically on the other side of the city.*   N COUNT : USU+SUPP   N COUNT

6 The **sides** of an object are its flat outside surfaces. EG *The box opens on this side.*   N COUNT

7 The **sides** of a building or a vehicle are the vertical outer parts which are not its front or its back. EG *Hogan walked round to the driver's side and unlocked the car door.* ▸ used as an adjective. EG *Smithy left the side door open.*   N COUNT ▸ ADJ CLASSIF : ATTRIB

8 The **sides** of a rectangular object are its two long edges. EG *She was kneeling by the side of the bed.*   N COUNT

9 The **sides** of a hill or valley are the sloping parts between its top and bottom. EG *We were driving up the side of a mountain.*   N COUNT

10 The **sides** of something flat, for example a   N COUNT

piece of paper, are its two flat surfaces. EG *What does the leaflet say on the other side?*

11 A **side** road or **side** street is a less important road or street leading off an important one. EG *I slipped away down a side street.*   ADJ CLASSIF : ATTRIB

12 The two **sides** in a war, argument, or game are the two groups of people who are fighting or arguing with each other, or playing against each other. EG *The argument was settled to the satisfaction of both sides.*   N COUNT

13 The two **sides** of an argument are the different points of view of the people who are arguing. EG *She only ever hears his side of things.*   N COUNT

14 The two **sides** in an agreement or a relationship are the two people or groups who are dealing with each other. EG *Both sides were confident that they would benefit from the partnership.*   N COUNT

15 Side is used in these phrases referring to supporting someone. **15.1** If you **take sides** or **take** someone's **side**, you support one of the two people who are involved in an argument. EG *I wouldn't want anyone to take my side against Tom.* **15.2** If you are **on** someone's **side**, you are supporting them in an argument or a war. EG *Whose side are you on?... Do everything you can to win people on to your side.* **15.3** If something is **on** your **side**, it helps you when you are trying to achieve something. EG *Luck was on our side.*   PHRASES

16 The two **sides** of your family are your mother's family and your father's family. EG *My grandparents on my father's side were both Polish.*   N COUNT

17 A particular **side** of something such as a situation or someone's character is one aspect of it. EG *The producers wanted to emphasize the political side of the play... There is something distasteful about this side of her character.*   N COUNT : USU+SUPP

18 Side is also used in these phrases. **18.1** If you do something **on the side**, you do it in addition to your main work. EG *If the farm prospers, we could start a little business on the side.* **18.2** If you say that something is **on the** large **side** or **on the** small **side**, for example, you mean that it is slightly too large or slightly too small. EG *The food is excellent though on the expensive side.* **18.3** If you keep **on the right side of** someone, you try to please them and avoid annoying them. If you get **on the wrong side of** someone, you annoy them and make them dislike you. **18.4** to be **on the safe side**: see **safe**. ● to **err on the side of** something: see **err**.   PHRASES

side with. If you **side with** someone, you support them in a quarrel or argument. EG *The daughters sided with their mothers.*   PHRASAL VB : V+PREP

sideboard /saɪdbɔːd/, **sideboards**. **1** A **sideboard** is a long, fairly low cupboard, normally kept in dining rooms to put plates and glasses in.   N COUNT

2 If a man has **sideboards**, he has a strip of hair growing down the side of each cheek.   N PLURAL British

sideburns /saɪdbɜːnz/ are the same as sideboards.   N PLURAL

side-effect, side-effects. **1** The **side-effects** of a drug are the effects that the drug has on you in addition to its function of curing illness or pain. EG *This type of aspirin can have appalling side-effects.*   N COUNT : USU PLURAL

2 The **side-effects** of a situation are the unplanned things that happen in addition to the main results or effects. EG *One side-effect of the crisis could be that she loses her job.*   N COUNT : USU PLURAL

sidelight /saɪdlaɪt/, **sidelights**. The **sidelights** on a vehicle are the small lights at the front that help other drivers to notice the vehicle and to judge its width.   N COUNT

sideline /saɪdlaɪn/, **sidelines**. **1** A **sideline** is something that you do in addition to your main job in order to earn extra money. EG *Fishing is both a relaxing hobby and a money-producing sideline.*   N COUNT

What is the opposite of keeping on the right side of someone?

2 The **sidelines** are the lines marking the long sides of the playing area, for example on a football pitch or tennis court. N COUNT: USU PLURAL

3 If you are on **the sidelines** in a situation, you are not personally involved in it. EG *I prefer to stand on the sidelines and watch... ...watching the drama from the sidelines.* N PLURAL Literary

sidelong /saɪdlɒŋ/. If you look at someone or something **sidelong** or if you give them **sidelong** looks, you look at them out of the corner of your eyes, because they are to one side of you. EG *Ralph looked at him sidelong and said nothing... Terry and I exchanged sidelong glances.* ADV OR ADJ CLASSIF: ATTRIB

side-saddle. When you ride a horse **side-saddle**, you sit on a special saddle with both your legs on one side rather than one leg on each side of the horse. ADV OR ADJ CLASSIF: ATTRIB

sideshow /saɪdʃəʊ/, **sideshows**. **Sideshows** are the stalls at a fairground or circus where you can do things such as shooting at moving targets and throwing darts. N COUNT

sidestep /saɪdstɛp/, **sidesteps, sidestepping, sidestepped.** If you **sidestep** a problem, you manage to avoid discussing it or dealing with it. EG *...a book that does not sidestep essential questions.* V+O

sidetracked /saɪdtrækt/. If you **are sidetracked**, you forget what you are supposed to be doing or saying and start doing or talking about something else. EG *I told him how I'd been sidetracked by Mr Starke.* V-PASS

sidewalk /saɪdwɔːk/, **sidewalks.** A **sidewalk** is the same as a pavement. EG *He avoided stepping on a crack in the sidewalk.* N COUNT American

sideways /saɪdweɪz/ means from or to the side of something or someone. EG *Flames blew out sideways from the fire... ...a sideways glance... She sat leaning sideways a little.* ADV OR ADJ CLASSIF: ATTRIB

siding /saɪdɪŋ/, **sidings.** A **siding** is a short railway track beside the main tracks, where engines and carriages are left when they are not being used. N COUNT

sidle /saɪdəl/, **sidles, sidling, sidled.** If you **sidle** somewhere, you walk there uncertainly or cautiously, as if you do not want anyone to notice you. EG *She stammered some apology as she sidled towards the door.* V+A

siege /siːdʒ/, **sieges.** A **siege** is **1** a military operation in which an army tries to capture a place by surrounding it and preventing food or help from reaching the people inside. EG *...the siege of Mafeking... Galilee had been under siege for months.* **2** a situation in which a place is surrounded for a long period of time, for example by police, in order to force the people inside to come out. EG *He had been in London to report on the Embassy siege in May 1980.* N COUNT OR N UNCOUNT

siesta /sɪˈɛstə/, **siestas.** A **siesta** is a short sleep or rest which people have in the early afternoon in hot countries. EG *She hadn't yet emerged from her siesta.* N COUNT OR N UNCOUNT

sieve

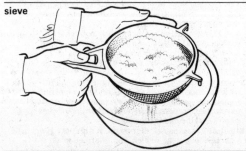

sieve /sɪv/, **sieves, sieving, sieved.** **1** A **sieve** is a tool used, especially in the kitchen, for separating liquids from solids or larger pieces of something N COUNT

from smaller pieces of it. It usually consists of a metal ring with a wire net attached underneath, which the liquids or smaller pieces pass through, leaving the solids or larger pieces in the net.

2 When you **sieve** a liquid or powdery substance, you put it through a sieve. EG *Sieve the flour into a basin to remove all the lumps.* V+O

3 If you say that someone has **a memory like a sieve**, you mean that they often forget things. PHRASE

sift /sɪft/, **sifts, sifting, sifted.** **1** If you **sift** a loose or powdery substance such as flour or sand, you put it through a sieve in order to remove large pieces or lumps. EG *Always sift icing sugar through a fine sieve.* V+O

2 If you **sift** through something such as evidence, you examine it thoroughly. EG *There are archives and documents to be sifted through... He was accustomed to sifting evidence and assessing the difference between fact and fiction.* V+through: HAS PASS OR V+O

sigh /saɪ/, **sighs, sighing, sighed.** **1** When you **sigh**, you let out a deep breath, as a way of expressing feelings such as disappointment, tiredness, or pleasure. EG *She sighed and shook her head sadly... Sighing with relief, she took the money.* V

2 A **sigh** is the action of sighing or the sound that someone makes when they sigh. EG *With a sigh, he rose and walked slowly away... They had breathed a great sigh of relief at the ending of the war.* • If you **heave a sigh**, you sigh. N COUNT ● PHRASE

sight /saɪt/, **sights, sighting, sighted.** **1** Sight is the ability to see. EG *Her sight is failing.* N UNCOUNT

2 The **sight** of something is the act of seeing it or an occasion on which you see it. EG *I had my first sight of home for two years... He was reduced to tears at the sight of the hundreds of dead bodies.* N SING: OFT+of

3 A **sight** is something that you see. EG *This was the most encouraging sight I'd seen all day... It was an awe-inspiring sight.* N COUNT+SUPP

4 The **sights** are the places that are interesting to see and that are often visited by tourists. EG *...the sights of London.* N PLURAL

5 If you say that something is **a sight** better or **a sight** worse, you mean that it is very much better or very much worse. EG *It's a damn sight better than most of the places we've stayed in.* PHRASE Informal

6 If you **sight** someone or something, you see them, often briefly or suddenly. EG *The missing woman has been sighted in the Birmingham area.* V+O

7 Sight is also used in these phrases. **7.1** If you say that something or someone seems to have certain characteristics **at first sight**, you mean that when you first see them that is how they appear. EG *The problem is not as simple as it might seem at first sight.* **7.2** If something is **in sight**, you can see it. If it is **out of sight**, you cannot see it. EG *As soon as the car was out of sight, we relaxed... At last a bus came into sight.* **7.3** If a result or a decision is **in sight**, it is likely to happen within a short time. EG *It seemed that an end to his agony was in sight.* **7.4** If someone is ordered to do something **on sight**, they have to do it without delay, as soon as a person or thing is seen. EG *They used to shoot on sight in those days.* **7.5** If you **catch sight of** someone, you see them suddenly or briefly. EG *She caught sight of her mother.* **7.6** If you **lose sight of** an important part of a situation, you no longer pay attention to it because you are worrying about less important things. EG *We mustn't get so bogged down by detail that we lose sight of our main objectives.* **7.7** If you **know** someone **by sight**, you can recognize them when you see them, but you have never met them and talked to them. **7.8** If you **set** your **sights on** something, you decide that you want it and try very hard to get it. EG *We have set our sights on a bigger house.* PHRASES

sighted /saɪtɪd/. People who are **sighted** are not blind. EG *...if you are blind or poorly sighted... ...partially sighted children.* ● See also **clear-** ADJ CLASSIF sighted, far-sighted, long-sighted, short-sighted.

sighting /saɪtɪŋ/, **sightings.** A **sighting** is an occasion on which something is seen, especially something unusual or unexpected. EG *There had been four reports of shark sightings.* N COUNT: USU+SUPP

sightless /saɪtlɪˀs/. Someone who is **sightless** is blind. EG *He covered his sightless eyes.* ADJ CLASSIF

sight-read, sight-reads, sight-reading. The form **sight-read** is used in the present tense and is also the past tense and past participle.
Someone who can **sight-read** can play or sing music from a printed sheet the first time they see it, without practising it beforehand. V OR V+O

sightseeing /saɪtsiːɪŋ/. If you go **sightseeing**, you travel around in order to see the interesting places that tourists usually visit. EG *Allow some time in all the major cities for sightseeing.* N ING

sightseer /saɪtsiːə/, **sightseers.** A **sightseer** is someone who is travelling around in order to visit places of interest. EG *The Changing of the Guard is normally watched by a large crowd of sightseers.* N COUNT

sign /saɪn/, **signs, signing, signed.** 1 A **sign** is 1.1 a mark or shape that always has a particular meaning, for example in mathematics or music. EG *...a minus sign... ...the equals sign.* 1.2 a movement of your arms, hands, or head which is intended to have a particular meaning. EG *Through signs she communicated that she wanted the women to hide.* N COUNT

2 A **sign** is also a piece of wood, metal, or plastic with words or pictures on it. Signs tell you where or what a particular place is, or give you a warning or an instruction. EG *The exit sign is marked with an arrow... A sign saying 'Women's Centre' hung over the door.* N COUNT

3 If there is a **sign** of something, a characteristic feature of it is present, which shows that it exists or is happening. EG *How pleasant to see a sign of summer once again... The Englishman showed no signs of his annoyance... His sores had begun to show signs of healing.* N COUNT+of

4 If you say that there is **no sign of** someone, you mean that they have not yet arrived, although you are expecting them to come. PHRASE

5 If you **sign** a document, you write your name on it, usually at the end or in a special space. EG *Sign your name in the book each time you use the photocopier... Sign here to acknowledge receipt.* V+O OR V

sign away. If you **sign** something **away**, you sign official documents that mean that you no longer own it or have a right to it. EG *Chiefs were encouraged to sign away land that appeared to be unoccupied.* PHRASAL VB: V+O+ADV

sign for. If you **sign for** something, 1 you officially state that you have received it, by signing a form or book. EG *When signing for any parcel, always add 'not inspected'.* 2 you officially agree to do a piece of work, by signing a legal contract. EG *He signed for his second film.* PHRASAL VB: V+PREP, HAS PASS; V+PREP, HAS PASS Informal

sign in. If you **sign in**, you officially indicate that you have arrived at a hotel or club, by signing a book or form. EG *They signed in at the reception desk.* PHRASAL VB: V+ADV

sign on. If you **sign on**, 1 you officially agree to work for an organization or do a course of study by signing a contract or form. EG *He signed on the next morning with the RAF... You could sign on for a course in word processing.* 2 you officially state that you are unemployed, so that you can receive money from the government in order to live. PHRASAL VB: V+ADV; V+ADV British

sign out. If you **sign out**, you officially state that you have left a hotel or club, by signing a book or form. PHRASAL VB: V+ADV

sign up. 1 If you **sign up**, you officially agree to do a job or course of study, by signing a contract or form. EG *He signed up as a painter on the Federal Art Project.* 2 If someone **signs** you **up**, you sign a contract stating that you will work for them. PHRASAL VB: V+ADV; V+O+ADV

signal /sɪgnəˀl/, **signals, signalling, signalled;** spelled **signaling** and **signaled** in American English. 1 A **signal** is a gesture, sound, or action which is intended to give a particular message to the person who sees or hears it. EG *My signal will be three knocks... He sat in the studio and waited for the signal to speak.* N COUNT

2 If you **signal** something or if you **signal** to someone, you make a gesture or sound in order to give a particular message to someone. EG *Don signalled his permission... Signal the driver to move off... ...a parent signalling to a child in the distance... The helpers signalled that all was ready.* V+O: OFT+to-INF; ALSO V: OFT+to OR REPORT

3 If an event or action is a **signal** of something, it suggests that this thing exists or is going to happen. EG *This was the first signal that an attack was brewing.* N COUNT+SUPP

4 If something **signals** an event, it suggests that the event is happening or likely to happen. EG *This decision seemed to signal a switch in the paper's editorial policy... ...the crisis signalling that the final moment was near.* V+O OR V+REPORT

5 A **signal** is also 5.1 a piece of equipment beside a railway, which indicates to train drivers whether they should stop the train or not. 5.2 a series of radio waves, light waves, or electrical impulses, which carry information. EG *Marconi finally succeeded in sending a signal across the Atlantic.* N COUNT

6 A **signal** triumph or failure is one that is especially important. EG *The year has seen one signal triumph for the Labour Party.* ADJ CLASSIF: ATTRIB Formal

signal box, signal boxes. A **signal box** is a small building near a railway, which contains the switches used to control the signals. N COUNT

signatory /sɪgnətəˀriː/, **signatories.** The **signatories** of an official document are the people who sign it. EG *...a signatory to the North Atlantic Treaty.* N COUNT: OFT+of/to Formal

signature /sɪgnəˀtʃə/, **signatures.** Your **signature** is your name, when you write it in your own characteristic way. EG *He underlined his signature with a little flourish... ...petitions bearing nearly half a million signatures.* N COUNT

signature tune, signature tunes. A **signature tune** is the tune which is always played at the beginning or end of a particular television or radio programme. N COUNT

significance /sɪgnɪfɪkəns/. The **significance** of something is its importance. EG *The meeting was of no significance... A year later I found out the true significance of the name.* N UNCOUNT

significant /sɪgnɪfɪkənt/. 1 A **significant** amount of something is a large amount of it. EG *Exports reached £232 million, making a significant contribution to the balance of payments... Lack of insulation can result in a significant amount of heat being lost.* ◊ **significantly.** EG *Prices were significantly reduced.* ADJ CLASSIF: ATTRIB; ◊ ADV

2 Something that is **significant** is important. EG *The incident was very significant... ...a significant discovery.* ◊ **significantly.** EG *Significantly, there was no reference to Iran.* ADJ QUALIT; ◊ ADV OR ADV SEN

3 A **significant** action or gesture is intended to have a special meaning. EG *With a significant look at her husband, Mrs Hochstadt went out.* ◊ **significantly.** EG *He cleared his throat significantly a few times.* ADJ QUALIT; ◊ ADV

signify /sɪgnɪfaɪ/, **signifies, signifying, signified.** A sign, symbol, or gesture that **signifies** something has a particular meaning. EG *Leggett gave a long wheeze, to signify disgust... Short pips signify that the phone is engaged.* V+O OR V+REPORT

signpost /saɪnpəʊst/, **signposts.** A **signpost** is a sign beside a road, which has information on it N COUNT

such as the name of a town and how far away it is.
EG ...a signpost marked 'Fairford 8 miles'.

signposted /saɪnpəʊstɪ²d/. A road or route that is ADJ PRED
signposted has signposts beside the road to show
the way. EG The route is well signposted.

Sikh /siːk/, **Sikhs**. 1 A **Sikh** is a person who N COUNT
believes in the Indian religion of Sikhism.
2 Something that is **Sikh** belongs or relates to the ADJ CLASSIF
Sikhs or to their religious beliefs and customs. EG
...a Sikh name... ...Sikh cavalry... ...Sikh ideals.

Sikhism /siːkɪzm/ is an Indian religion which N UNCOUNT
teaches that there is only one God.

silence /saɪləns/, **silences**, **silencing**, **silenced**.
1 If there is **silence**, it is quiet because nobody is N UNCOUNT
speaking. EG We walked on in silence... There was a OR N COUNT
shocked silence.
2 The **silence** of a place is the extreme quietness N SING : the+N
that normally exists there. EG ...the silence of the
mountains.
3 Someone's **silence** about something is their N UNCOUNT
failure or refusal to tell people anything about it. EG +SUPP
Levy's silence on the subject was unnerving.
4 If you **silence** someone or something, you stop V+O
them speaking or making a noise. EG Rodin silenced him with a gesture... Butler's firm speech
failed to silence opposition.

silencer /saɪlənsə/, **silencers**. A **silencer** is a N COUNT
device on a car exhaust or a gun which makes it
quieter.

silent /saɪlənt/. 1 Someone who is **silent** 1.1 is not ADJ CLASSIF
speaking. EG The woman was silent for a moment.
◊ **silently**. EG We finished breakfast silently. **1.2** ADJ QUALIT
does not talk to people very much. EG She was a
silent girl, cool and aloof.
2 If you are **silent** about something, you do not tell ADJ PRED
people anything about it. EG He remained absolute-
ly silent on his plans for using the money.
3 Something that is **silent** makes no sound at all. EG ADJ CLASSIF
The guns have fallen silent. ◊ **silently**. EG It ◊ ADV
appeared suddenly and silently out of the dusk.
4 A **silent** film has only pictures and no sound or ADJ CLASSIF :
speech. EG In 1924 I did my first silent film. ATTRIB
5 A **silent** letter in a word is written but not ADJ CLASSIF
pronounced. For example, the 'k' in the word
'know' is silent.

silhouette /sɪluːet/, **silhouettes**. A **silhouette** is N COUNT
the outline of a dark shape when it has a bright
light or pale background behind it. EG The figure
turned towards the sunrise, a tiny silhouette with
uplifted arms.

silhouetted /sɪluːetɪ²d/. If something is **silhou-** ADJ PRED :
etted against a background, you can see its silhou- USU+against
ette. EG ...hills silhouetted against a pale blue sky.

silicon /sɪlɪkən/ is an element that is used to make N UNCOUNT
parts of computers and other electronic equip-
ment. EG ...mini-computers on tiny silicon chips.

silk /sɪlk/, **silks**. **Silk** is a kind of smooth, fine cloth N MASS
which is made from a substance produced by
silkworms. EG ...a white silk scarf.

silken /sɪlkə⁰n/. You use **silken** to describe things ADJ CLASSIF
that are smooth and soft. EG ...silken hair. Literary

silkworm /sɪlkwɜːm/, **silkworms**. A **silkworm** is N COUNT
a type of caterpillar that produces a substance
used to make silk.

silky /sɪlki¹/, **silkier**, **silkiest**. Something that is ADJ QUALIT
silky is smooth and soft. EG ...fine silky skin.

sill /sɪl/, **sills**. A **sill** is a ledge at the bottom of a N COUNT
window, either inside or outside a building. EG She
sat with one elbow resting on the sill of the open
window... ...bending over the window sill.

silly /sɪli¹/, **sillier**, **silliest**. If you say that some- ADJ QUALIT
one is **silly**, you mean that they are behaving in a
foolish or childish way. EG You're a silly little boy...
You silly fool!... It was a silly thing to say... How
silly of me. I do apologise.

silt /sɪlt/, **silts**, **silting**, **silted**. **Silt** is fine sand, N UNCOUNT
soil, or mud which is carried along by a river. EG
The problem is keeping the harbours free of silt.

silt up. If a river or lake **silts up** or **is silted up**, PHRASAL VB :
it becomes blocked with silt. V-ERG+ADV

silver /sɪlvə/, **silvers**. **1 Silver** is a valuable N UNCOUNT
greyish-white metal that is used for making jewel-
lery and ornaments. EG ...a little box made of solid
silver... ...beautiful silver coffee pots.
2 Silver is also coins that are made from silver or N UNCOUNT
that look like silver. EG ...leaving five pounds in
silver in case somebody needed change.
3 In a house, the **silver** is the things there that are N UNCOUNT
made from silver, especially cutlery and dishes. EG
The silver sparkled in the candlelight.
4 You describe something as **silver** when it is ADJ COLOUR
greyish-white in colour. EG ...sparkling silver paint...
...a tall old man with long silver hair.
5 A **silver** is the same as a silver medal. N COUNT

silver birch, **silver birches**. A **silver birch** is a N COUNT
tree with a greyish-white trunk and branches.

silver jubilee, **silver jubilees**. A **silver jubilee** N COUNT
is the 25th anniversary of an important event. EG
It's the College's Silver Jubilee year.

silver medal, **silver medals**. If you win a **silver** N COUNT
medal, you come second in a competition, especially a sports contest, and are given a medal made
of silver as a prize.

silver-plated. Something that is **silver-plated** is ADJ CLASSIF
covered with a very thin layer of silver. EG ...silver-
plated forks.

silver wedding, **silver weddings**. A married N COUNT
couple's **silver wedding** is the 25th anniversary of
their wedding.

silvery /sɪlvə⁰ri¹/. Something that is **silvery** looks ADJ COLOUR
like silver. EG ...a silvery dress... His hair is silvery.

similar /sɪmɪlə/. If one thing is **similar** to anoth- ADJ QUALIT :
er, or if two things are **similar**, they have features OFT+to
that are the same. EG My problems are very similar
to yours... The four restaurants were all serving
similar food at similar prices.

similarity /sɪmɪlærɪ¹ti¹/, **similarities**. If there is N UNCOUNT OR
a **similarity** between two or more things, they are N COUNT : USU
similar to each other. EG There were points of +between/
similarity between them... ...the similarities and with
differences between British and American English... Many species have close similarities with one
another.

similarly /sɪmɪləli¹/. You use **similarly** to say ADV OR
that something is similar to something else that ADV SEN
you have just mentioned. EG Other guests sat under
similarly striped umbrellas... Similarly, savings certificates should be registered with the Post Office.

simile /sɪmɪli¹/, **similes**. A **simile** is an expres- N COUNT
sion which describes a person or thing as being
similar to someone or something else. For example, the sentences 'She runs like a deer' and 'He's
as white as a sheet' are similes.

simmer /sɪmə/, **simmers**, **simmering**, **sim-** V-ERG
mered. When you **simmer** food or when it **sim-**
mers, you cook it by keeping it at boiling point or
just below boiling point. EG Simmer the beans for
four hours until tender.

simmer down. If you **simmer down**, you stop PHRASAL VB :
being angry about something. EG I thought the trip V+ADV
might give me time to simmer down. Informal

simper /sɪmpə/, **simpers**, **simpering**, **sim-** V
pered. When someone **simpers**, they smile in a
rather silly way. EG The maid lowered her chin and
simpered. ▸ used as a noun. EG 'Thank you, doctor,' ▸ N COUNT
said the nurse with a simper.

simple /sɪmpə⁰l/, **simpler**, **simplest**. **1** If some- ADJ QUALIT
thing is **simple**, **1.1** it is not complicated, and is
therefore easy to understand. EG The point I am
making is a very simple one... ...a very simple
calculator. **1.2** it consists only of things that are
necessary, without any extra features. EG ...a tall
woman in a simple brown dress.
2 If a problem is **simple** or if its solution is **simple**, ADJ QUALIT
the problem can be solved easily. EG The solution is
very simple.

3 A **simple** task is easy to do. EG *It's a simple* ADJ QUALIT *operation, you can do it in a lunch hour.*

4 If you describe people or their way of life as ADJ QUALIT **simple**, you mean that they have an uncomplicated way of life. EG *They are only simple farmers... Nature, the simple life, that's what I need.*

5 A person who is **simple** is mentally retarded. EG ADJ QUALIT *Noreen despised Joyce and said she was simple.*

6 You use **simple** to emphasize that the thing you ADJ CLASSIF : are mentioning is the only important or relevant ATTRIB one. EG *Simple fear of death is often what turns people to religion.*

7 See also **simplicity, simply.**

simple-minded. Someone who is **simple-** ADJ QUALIT **minded** interprets everything in a way that is too simple, because they do not understand how complicated things are. EG *She was regarded by everyone as simple-minded.*

simplicity /sɪmplɪsɪ¹ti¹/. **1** The **simplicity** of N UNCOUNT something is the fact that it is uncomplicated and can be understood easily. EG *The advantage of the idea was its simplicity... The major considerations were simplicity and effectiveness.*

2 If you say that there is **simplicity** in the way that N UNCOUNT someone behaves or dresses, you mean that they behave or dress in a simple way that is very attractive. EG *He dressed with elegant simplicity.*

simplification /sɪmplɪfɪkeɪʃə⁰n/, **simplifica-** N COUNT OR **tions.** A **simplification** is the thing that you N UNCOUNT produce when you make something simpler. EG *I see this proposal as a long overdue simplification.*

simplify /sɪmplɪfaɪ/, **simplifies, simplifying,** V+O **simplified.** If you **simplify** something, you make it easier to understand or do. EG *The subject is immensely complex, and hard to simplify.* ◊ **simplified.** EG *The account given so far is a* ◊ ADJ QUALIT *simplified one... ...a simplified version of the model.*

simplistic /sɪmplɪstɪk/. A **simplistic** view or ADJ QUALIT interpretation of something makes it seem much simpler than it really is. EG *The Department has based its policies on a rather simplistic analysis of the situation... ...a simplistic attitude.*

simply /sɪmpli¹/. **1** You use **simply** to emphasize ADV that something consists of only one thing, happens for only one reason, or is done in only one way. EG *The job of a caterpillar is simply to eat... It's simply a question of hard work... A good deal can be done simply by suggestion.*

2 You also use **simply** to emphasize what you are ADV saying. EG *I simply can't believe it... I was happy, there is simply no other word for it.*

3 If you say or write something **simply**, you do it in ADV a way that makes it easy to understand. EG *'His life is finished,' he said simply.*

simulate /sɪmjʊ⁴leɪt/, **simulates, simulating,** **simulated.** **1** If you **simulate** a feeling or an V+O action, you pretend that you are feeling it or doing it. EG *We used this trick in the Army to simulate illness... Bomb tests can be simulated on computers.*

2 If you **simulate** an object, a substance, or a V+O noise, you produce something that looks or sounds like it. EG *The wood is carved to simulate hair... The body is simulated by packed straw... ...simulated silver.*

simulation /sɪmjʊ⁴leɪʃə⁰n/, **simulations.** **1** Simu- N UNCOUNT **lation** or a **simulation** is the process of simulating OR N COUNT something or the result of simulating it. EG *Spectators are entertained by the simulation of fighting... The viewer was unable to distinguish reality from simulation.*

2 A **simulation** is also an attempt to solve a N COUNT OR problem by representing the problem mathemati- N UNCOUNT cally, often using a computer. EG *Computer model* Technical *ling and simulation have been used as an aid to battle tactics.*

simultaneous /sɪmə⁴lteɪnɪəs/. Things which are ADJ CLASSIF **simultaneous** happen or exist at the same time. EG *...the simultaneous failure of all the lifts in the*

building. ◊ **simultaneously.** EG *His fear and his* ◊ ADV *hate grew simultaneously.*

sin /sɪn/, **sins, sinning, sinned. 1 Sin** is behaviour N UNCOUNT which is considered to be very bad and immoral. EG OR N COUNT *They believed they were being punished for their sins.* ● See also **cardinal sin.**

2 If you **sin**, you do something that is believed to be V : OFT very bad and immoral. EG *You have sinned against* +against *the Lord.* ◊ **sinner, sinners.** EG *Christ is inviting* ◊ N COUNT *sinners to repentance.*

3 If a man and a woman **are living in sin**, they PHRASE are living together as if they are married although Outdated they are not married.

since /sɪns/. **1** If something has happened **since** a PREP, CONJ, particular time or event, it has happened from that OR ADV time or event until now. EG *Since 1974, Marilyn has lived in Paris... I've been wearing glasses since I was three... For the first time since leaving home, she is without a boyfriend... I came here in 1972 and I have lived here ever since.*

2 Since also means at some time after a particular ADV time or event in the past. EG *He used to be an art student. He has since become a lawyer.*

3 If something has **long since** happened, it hap- PHRASE pened a long time ago. EG *The time for talking has* Formal *long since passed.*

4 You use **since** to introduce the reason for CONJ something. EG *Aircraft noise is a problem here since we're close to Heathrow Airport... Since it was Saturday, he stayed in bed an extra hour.*

sincere /sɪnsɪə/. If you are **sincere**, you say the ADJ QUALIT things that you really mean or believe. EG *He was decent, sincere, a good man... The apology was sincere.* ◊ **sincerity** /sɪnsɛrɪ¹ti¹/. EG *The Head* ◊ N UNCOUNT *Master is a man of deep conviction and sincerity.*

sincerely /sɪnsɪəli¹/. **1** If you say or feel some- ADV thing **sincerely**, you really mean it or feel it, and are not joking or being dishonest. EG *'I owe you an awful lot,' I said sincerely... He loves you very sincerely... I am sincerely delighted to hear that.*

2 You write **Yours sincerely** before your signa- CONVENTION ture at the end of a formal letter. EG *...Yours sincerely, Winston S. Churchill.*

sinew /sɪnju:/, **sinews.** A **sinew** is a cord in your N COUNT OR body that connects a muscle to a bone. EG *The* N UNCOUNT *sinews of his arm were tense.*

sinewy /sɪnju:i¹/. Someone who is **sinewy** has a ADJ QUALIT lean body with strong muscles. EG *...his sinewy brown arm... She was a tall, sinewy type.*

sinful /sɪnful/. **1** Someone who is **sinful** has a ADJ QUALIT tendency to commit sins. EG *Good women have always saved sinful men in stories.*

2 Something that is **sinful** is considered to be ADJ QUALIT wicked or immoral. EG *She believed that eyeshadow was sinful... ...a sinful desire... That is a sinful thing to say!*

sing /sɪŋ/, **sings, singing, sang** /sæŋ/, **sung** /sʌŋ/. **1** If you **sing**, or if you **sing** a song, you V, V+O, make musical sounds with your voice, usually OR V+QUOTE producing words that fit a tune. EG *I started to sing... The song is sung by Romy Blakeley.*

2 If you **sing** someone a song, you sing it to them V+O+O OR so that they can listen to it. EG *Would you like me to* V+O+to *sing you a song?*

3 If someone **sings** a particular type of music or a V+O particular musical role, they perform it as a singer, especially as a professional. EG *For five years I didn't sing opera on stage at all.*

4 If you **sing** someone's **praises**, you enthusiasti- PHRASE cally praise them. EG *I understand that he's now singing the praises of Mcleod.*

5 When birds or insects **sing**, they make pleasant V OR V+O sounds. EG *I could hear birds singing in the trees.*

6 See also **singing.**

Could your sister be called a sissy?

singe /sɪndʒ/, **singes, singeing, singed. 1** If you V-ERG **singe** something, or if it **singes**, you burn it very slightly so that it changes colour but does not catch fire. EG *She didn't notice that she had singed her gown.*

2 A **singe** is a slight burn, especially on cloth or N COUNT hair.

singer /sɪŋə/, **singers.** A **singer** is a person who N COUNT sings, especially as part of their job. EG *His mother was an actress and a singer.*

singing /sɪŋɪŋ/. **1 Singing** is **1.1** the activity of N UNCOUNT making musical sounds with your voice. EG *The dancing and singing ended at midnight.* **1.2** the art of being a singer. EG *I went to her for singing lessons.* **1.3** the pleasant sounds made by birds or insects. EG *...the singing of the blackbirds.*

2 Your **singing** voice is the quality of your voice ADJ CLASSIF : when you sing. EG *He had a fine singing voice.* ATTRIB

single /sɪŋgəl/, **singles, singling, singled. 1** If ADJ CLASSIF : you refer to a **single** thing, you mean only one, and ATTRIB not more. EG *We heard a single shot... I just couldn't think of a single thing to say.*

2 You use **single** to indicate that you are consider- ADJ CLASSIF : ing something on its own and separately from the ATTRIB other things like it. EG *This is the most important single invention since the wheel... We went to the house every single day for six months.*

3 If you are **single**, you are not married. ADJ CLASSIF

4 A **single** bed or room is intended to be used by ADJ CLASSIF only one person.

5 A **single** ticket is a ticket for a journey from one ADJ CLASSIF place to another but not back again. EG *How much* British *is the single fare to London?* ▸ used as a noun. EG *A* ▸ N COUNT *single to Edinburgh, please.*

6 A **single** is also a small gramophone record N COUNT which has one short song on each side.

7 Singles is a game of tennis or badminton in N UNCOUNT which one player plays another player. EG *The high serve is used a lot in singles.*

8 in single figures: see **figure.** ● **in single file:** see **file.**

single out. If you **single** someone **out** from a PHRASAL VB : group, you choose them and give them special V+O+ADV attention or treatment. EG *Three other people were singled out for special praise.*

single cream is thin cream that does not have a N UNCOUNT lot of fat in it. British

single-handed. If you do something **single-** ADV **handed**, you do it on your own, without help from anyone else. EG *He had rescued the girl single-handed.*

single-minded. Someone who is **single-minded** ADJ QUALIT has only one aim or purpose and is determined to achieve it. EG *...the single-minded pursuit of wealth.*

singly /sɪŋgli/. If people do something **singly**, ADV they do it on their own or one by one. EG *The children came out singly or in small groups.*

sing-song. 1 A **sing-song** voice repeatedly rises ADJ CLASSIF : and falls in pitch. EG *The dialect of the area has a* ATTRIB *sing-song intonation.*

2 A **sing-song** is an occasion when a group of N COUNT people sing songs together for pleasure. EG *We had a sing-song after the match.*

singular /sɪŋgjələ/. **1** In grammar, the **singular** N SING of a noun is the form of it that refers to one person or thing, and not more. EG *The singular of 'lice' is 'louse'... What is the singular form of 'media'?*

2 Something that is **singular** is unusual and re- ADJ QUALIT markable. EG *...a lady of singular beauty... ...a* Formal *singular ignorance of human nature.*

singularly /sɪŋgjələli/ means to a remarkable SUBMOD or extraordinary degree. EG *Then we did some* Formal *singularly boring experiments.*

sinister /sɪnɪstə/. Something that is **sinister** ADJ QUALIT makes you afraid that something evil or harmful will happen. EG *...a rather sinister figure walking behind the bushes... ...an evil and sinister place.*

sink /sɪŋk/, **sinks, sinking, sank** /sæŋk/, **sunk** N COUNT /sʌŋk/. **1** A **sink** is **1.1** a large basin in a kitchen,

with taps that supply water, used especially for washing dishes. EG *There was a stack of dirty dishes in the sink.* **1.2** the same as a washbasin.

2 If something **sinks**, it moves slowly downwards, V : USU+A especially below the surface of water. EG *The boat sank to the bottom of the lake... The sun had just sunk below the horizon.*

3 If people **sink** a ship, they cause it to sink by V+O attacking it with bombs or torpedoes.

4 If you **sink** back or down, you move into a lower V+A position. EG *She sank back in her chair and sipped her drink... She sank to her knees.*

5 If an amount or value **sinks**, it decreases. EG V+A *Wages have sunk so low in relation to the cost of living... ...if the energy input sinks or increases.*

6 If your voice **sinks**, it becomes quieter. EG *His* V *voice had sunk to a whisper.* Literary

7 If you **sink** into an unpleasant or less active state, V+into you pass gradually into it. EG *My father sank further into debt... I sank into a deep sleep.*

8 If your heart **sinks** or your spirits **sink**, you V become depressed or lose hope. EG *His heart sank at the thought that the exams were a week away.*

9 If you **sink** something sharp into something solid, V-ERG+into you make it go deeply into it. EG *He sank his teeth into the apple.*

10 See also **sunken.**

sink in. When a statement or fact **sinks in**, it PHRASAL VB : becomes fully understood or realized. EG *It took a* V+ADV *moment or two for her words to sink in.*

sinuous /sɪnjuəs/. Something that is **sinuous 1** ADJ QUALIT moves with smooth twists and turns, like a snake. Literary EG *Women danced sinuous dances in the middle of the room.* **2** has many smooth wavy turns and Literary curves. EG *...a sinuous trail of slime.*

sinus /saɪnəs/, **sinuses.** Your **sinuses** are the N COUNT : spaces in the bones of your skull just behind your USU PLURAL nose. EG *...blowing his nose noisily to clear the blocked sinuses... ...a sinus infection.*

sip /sɪp/, **sips, sipping, sipped. 1** If you **sip** a v+o drink, you drink by taking just a small amount at a time. EG *The guests were sipping their drinks.*

2 A **sip** is a small amount of drink that you take N COUNT into your mouth. EG *She took another sip from her* OR N PART *glass... Give them a few sips of water.*

siphon /saɪfən/, **siphons, siphoning, siphoned;** also spelled **syphon. 1** If you **siphon** a liquid or V+O : OFT+off **siphon** it off, you draw it out of a container through a tube by using atmospheric pressure. EG *Claude siphoned off a little petrol from his father's car.*

2 A **siphon** is a tube that you use for siphoning N COUNT liquid. ● See also **soda siphon.**

3 If you **siphon** money or resources or **siphon** V+O : OFT+off them off, you cause them to be used for a purpose for which they were not intended. EG *This scheme involved siphoning colossal sums of money into public transport.*

sir /sɜː/. **1** People sometimes call a man **sir** when they are being formal and polite. 'Dear Sir' is often used at the beginning of official letters. In spoken English, the plural of 'sir' is 'gentlemen'. EG *Dear Sir, I am writing in response to your letter of the 25th... What would you like, sir?... Brigadier Tomlinson wants to see you, sir.*

2 Sir is the title used in front of the name of a knight or baronet. EG *...Sir John Hargreaves.*

siren /saɪərən/, **sirens.** A **siren** is a warning N COUNT device which makes a long, loud, wailing noise. Most fire engines, ambulances, and police cars have sirens. EG *...the distant wail of police sirens.*

sissy /sɪsi/, **sissies;** also spelled **cissy.** A boy is N COUNT described as a **sissy**, especially by other boys, if he Informal does not like sport and is afraid to do things that are slightly dangerous. EG *You're a lot of cry-babies and sissies.*

sister /sɪstə/, **sisters. 1** Your **sister** is a girl or N COUNT woman who has the same parents as you. EG *My sister Jane married a farmer... Have you got any* brothers and sisters? ● See also **half-sister, step-sister**.

2 A **sister** is **2.1** a woman who is a member of a religious order. EG *The Sisters taught her a love of religion... ...Sister Catherine.* **2.2** a senior nurse who supervises a hospital ward. N COUNT / British

3 A woman sometimes refers to other women as her **sisters** when she feels very close to them because they work for the same organization or have the same aims or beliefs. EG *They would go to Paris and stay with feminist sisters there.* N COUNT

4 The **sister** of something is another thing of the same type that has the same function or that was built at the same time. EG *The city shows every sign of outgrowing its sister.* ▶ used as an adjective. EG *Her sister ship was sunk by a torpedo.* N COUNT+POSS / ▶ ADJ CLASSIF: ATTRIB

sister-in-law, sisters-in-law. Your **sister-in-law** is the sister of your husband or wife, or the wife of your brother. Some people also refer to a woman as their **sister-in-law** when she is married to their wife's or husband's brother. N COUNT

sisterly /sɪstəlɪ¹/. A woman's **sisterly** feelings are the feelings of warmth and affection that she has towards her sister or brother or towards a man who she likes very much but does not love. ADJ CLASSIF: ATTRIB

sit /sɪt/, **sits, sitting, sat** /sæt/. **1** If you **are sitting** somewhere, for example in a chair or on the floor, your weight is supported by your buttocks rather than your feet, and the upper part of your body is upright. EG *She was sitting on the edge of the bed... I was sitting at my desk reading.* V : USU+A

2 When you **sit** somewhere, you lower your body until you are sitting on something. EG *He came into the room and sat in his usual chair.* V : USU+A

3 If you **sit** an examination, you take it. EG *After the third term, we'll be sitting the exam.* V+O / British

4 If you **sit** on a committee, you are a member of it. EG *Representatives of the workers should sit on the board of directors.* V+on

5 When a parliament, law court, or other official body **sits**, it officially carries out its work. EG *Visitors are only allowed in on days when the Houses are not sitting.* V / Formal

6 If you say that a building or other object **sits** in a particular place, you mean that it is in that place. EG *The little parish church sits cosily in the middle of the village.* V+A / Literary

7 If you **sit tight**, you remain in the same place or situation and do not take any action. EG *All they have to do is sit tight until the Republic recognises their claims.* PHRASE

8 See also **sitting, baby-sit**. ● to **sit on the fence**: see **fence**.

sit about or **sit around**. If you **sit about** or **sit around**, you spend a lot of time doing nothing except sit. EG *We were tired of sitting about waiting for something to happen.* PHRASAL VB : V+ADV, OFT+-ING / Informal

sit back. If you **sit back** while something is happening, you relax and do not become involved in it. EG *He believes he has the right to sit back while others do the hard work.* PHRASAL VB : V+ADV / Informal

sit down. 1 When you **sit down** or **sit yourself down**, you lower your body until you are sitting on something. EG *He sat down on the edge of the bed... Sit down and ask yourself, 'What do I really want?'* PHRASAL VB : V+ADV OR V-REFL+ADV

2 If you **sit** someone **down**, you make them sit down. EG *I sat him down and gave him a drink.* **3** See also **sit-down**. V+O+ADV

sit in on. If you **sit in on** a meeting or discussion, you are present while it is taking place but do not take part in it. EG *I was allowed to sit in on the deliberations of the board.* PHRASAL VB : V+ADV+PREP

sit out. If you **sit** something **out**, you wait patiently for it to finish, without taking any action. EG *They would retire to their caves to sit out the winter.* PHRASAL VB : V+O+ADV

sit through. If you **sit through** something such as a concert or a lecture, you stay until it is finished although you are not enjoying it. PHRASAL VB : V+PREP, HAS PASS

sit up. If you **sit up, 1** you bring yourself into a PHRASAL VB : V+ADV

sitting position when you have been leaning back or lying down. EG *She sat up in bed when she saw him coming.* **2** you do not go to bed although it is very late. EG *Sometimes I sit up reading until three or four in the morning.* V+ADV

sitcom /sɪtkɒm/, **sitcoms**. A **sitcom** is a television comedy series which shows the same set of characters in each episode, in amusing situations that are similar to everyday life. N COUNT

sit-down. 1 If you have a **sit-down**, you sit down and rest for a short time. EG *When we got to the top we had a bit of a sit-down.* N SING : a+N / Informal

2 A **sit-down** meal is served to people sitting at tables. EG *...sit-down dinners.* ADJ CLASSIF : ATTRIB

site /saɪt/, **sites, siting, sited. 1** A **site** is a piece of ground that is used for a particular purpose or where a particular thing happens. EG *...dusty building sites... ...a caravan site... It is built on the site of the old Lion Tower... ...the site of the murder of the little princes in 1483.* N COUNT : USU+SUPP

2 If something **is sited** in a particular place or position, it is put there or built there. EG *They refused to have cruise missiles sited on their soil.* V+O+A : USU PASS

sit-in, sit-ins. A **sit-in** is a protest in which people go into a public place and stay sitting there for a long time. EG *The students voted to continue the sit-in.* N COUNT

sitting /sɪtɪŋ/, **sittings**. A **sitting** is **1** one of the times when a meal is served, for example in a school, when there is not enough space for everyone to eat at the same time. EG *The first sitting for breakfast is at 7.30.* **2** one of the occasions when an official body, such as a parliament or law court, meets in order to carry out its work. EG *It was the first sitting of the Senate since the election.* N COUNT

sitting-room, sitting-rooms. A **sitting-room** is a room in a house where people sit and relax. EG *Castle went back into the sitting-room.* N COUNT

sitting tenant, sitting tenants. A **sitting tenant** is a person who officially rents a house or flat as their home. EG *If you're a sitting tenant, then you're protected by a number of laws.* N COUNT

situate /sɪtjʊeɪt/, **situates, situating, situated.** If you **situate** something such as an idea or fact, you relate it to a particular context, especially in order to understand it better. EG *The dangers which press upon us must be situated in this context.* V+O+A / Formal

situated /sɪtjʊeɪt²d/. If something is **situated** in a particular place or position, it is in that place or position. EG *The control centre is situated many miles away... ...the building in which Morris's office was situated... Their flat was most conveniently situated.* ADJ PRED

situation /sɪtjʊeɪʃəᵇn/, **situations. 1** You use the word **situation** to refer generally to what is happening in a particular place at a particular time. EG *The situation was beginning to frighten me... It's an impossible situation... The situation in Georgia is radically different... ...the economic situation.* N COUNT : USU SING+SUPP

2 Your **situation** is the things that are happening to you or that are likely to happen to you at a particular time. EG *He knew a lot about my father's situation... ...the seriousness of his situation.* N COUNT : USU+POSS

3 The **situation** of a building or town is the kind of surroundings that it has. EG *The city is in a beautiful situation.* N COUNT : USU+SUPP / Formal

4 A **situation** is also a job, especially a professional job, a clerical job, or a job as a servant. EG *It's not so easy to find another situation.* ● **Situations Vacant** is the title of a column or page in a newspaper where jobs of all kinds are advertised. EG *She studied the 'Situations Vacant' columns in the newspapers.* N COUNT / Outdated / ● PHRASE

situation comedy, situation comedies. A **situation comedy** is a type of comedy, especially N COUNT OR N UNCOUNT

What can you put on your feet to move around on snow?

on television or radio, which shows the characters in amusing situations that are similar to everyday life.

six /sɪks/, sixes. 1 Six is the number 6: see entry NUMBER headed NUMBER. EG *He was about six feet tall... ...during the past six months.*

2 If a place or event is **at sixes and sevens**, it is PHRASE disorganized. EG *The household is at sixes and* Informal *sevens at the moment.*

sixteen /sɪksˈtiːn/, sixteens. Sixteen is the num- NUMBER ber 16: see entry headed NUMBER. EG *...a young woman of sixteen.*

sixteenth /sɪksˈtiːnθ/, sixteenths. 1 The six- ORDINAL teenth item in a series is the one that you count as number sixteen: see entry headed NUMBER. EG *...a furnished room on the sixteenth floor.*

2 A **sixteenth** is one of sixteen equal parts of N COUNT: something. USU+of

sixth /sɪksθ/, sixths. 1 The sixth item in a series ORDINAL is the one that you count as number six: see entry headed NUMBER. EG *On the sixth day we went on an excursion... ...the sixth of March.*

2 A **sixth** is one of six equal parts of something. EG N COUNT: *...one sixth of an acre of land.* USU+of

sixth form, sixth forms. The sixth form in a N COUNT British school consists of the classes that pupils go into at the age of about sixteen, usually in order to study for 'A' Levels. EG *...a group of sixth-form pupils.*

sixth former, sixth formers. A sixth former is N COUNT a pupil who is in the sixth form.

sixth sense. You say that someone has a sixth N SING: sense when they somehow know things although USU a+N they do not have any direct evidence of them. EG *He had a sort of sixth sense for tracking down burglary suspects.*

sixtieth /sɪkstiːˈəθ/, sixtieths. The sixtieth item ORDINAL in a series is the one that you count as number sixty: see entry headed NUMBER. EG *The dinner was in celebration of Mr Barrett's sixtieth birthday.*

sixty /sɪkstiː¹/, sixties. Sixty is the number 60: see NUMBER entry headed NUMBER. EG *She was being paid sixty dollars a week.*

sizable /saɪzəbəl/. See sizeable.

size /saɪz/, sizes, sizing, sized. 1 The size of N UNCOUNT something is 1.1 how big or small it is. EG *The company doubled its size in nine years... We saw butterflies the size of birds... ...a block of ice one cubic foot in size.* 1.2 the fact that it is very large. EG *The Grand was the only hotel of any size in the town... The world overwhelms us by its sheer size.*

2 A **size** is one of a series of graded measurements, N COUNT especially for things such as clothes or shoes. EG *'What size do you take?' – 'Ten.'... ...a jacket three sizes too big.*

3 If you **cut** someone **down to size**, you embarrass PHRASE or humiliate them in order to make them realize Informal that they are not as important as they think they are. EG *Your boss isn't just trying to cut you down to size, but actually to get rid of you.*

size up. If you size up a person or situation, you PHRASAL VB: carefully look at the person or think about the V+O+ADV situation, so that you can decide how to act. EG Informal *...people sizing each other up as if for a fight.*

sizeable /saɪzəbəl/; also spelled sizable. Some- ADJ QUALIT thing that is sizeable is fairly large. EG *...a sizeable sum of money... ...a sizeable number of students.*

sizzle /sɪzəl/, sizzles, sizzling, sizzled. If some- V thing sizzles, it makes a hissing sound like the sound made by frying food. EG *The steak and kidney pudding sizzled deliciously on the stove.*

skate /skeɪt/, skates, skating, skated. 1 A skate N COUNT is 1.1 an ice-skate. 1.2 a roller-skate.

2 If you **skate**, you move about on ice wearing ice- V skates. EG *I took her skating last week.* ◊ **skating** ◊ N UNCOUNT EG *There is skating in the winter.* ◊ **skater,** ◊ N COUNT **skaters.** EG *...skaters gliding along the frozen Thames.*

3 A **skate** is also a kind of flat sea fish. N COUNT

4 If you **skate** round or over a difficult subject, you V+A, HAS PASS avoid discussing it. EG *He skated round the subject once or twice... The book skates over the technicalities of adult life.*

skateboard /skeɪtbɔːd/, skateboards. A skate- N COUNT board is a narrow board with wheels at each end, which people stand on and ride for pleasure.

skateboarding /skeɪtbɔːdɪŋ/ is the activity of N ING riding on a skateboard.

skein /skeɪn/, skeins. A skein is a loosely coiled N COUNT length of thread, especially wool or silk. EG *...a skein of wool.*

skeletal /skelɪ²tə⁰l/. 1 You use skeletal to de- ADJ CLASSIF: scribe things that relate to skeletons. EG *...skeletal* ATTRIB *remains... ...their skeletal structure.*

2 A **skeletal** person is extremely thin. EG *...harrow-* ADJ CLASSIF *ing photographs of skeletal children in the desert.*

skeleton /skelɪ²tə⁰n/, skeletons. 1 Your skeleton N COUNT is the framework of bones which supports and protects your organs and muscles. EG *...the skeleton of a gigantic whale.*

2 If you say that someone has **a skeleton in the** PHRASE **cupboard,** you mean that they are keeping an unpleasant fact about their private life secret.

3 A **skeleton** staff is the smallest amount of staff N MOD necessary in order to run an organization or service. EG *They only employ a skeleton staff of fulltime workers at weekends.*

skeptic /skeptɪk/. See sceptic.

skeptical /skeptɪkə⁰l/. See sceptical.

sketch /sketʃ/, sketches, sketching, sketched. 1 N COUNT A sketch is a drawing that is done quickly without a lot of details. EG *...a rough sketch.* ▶ used as a ▶ V+O OR V verb. EG *These little drawings were sketched by a seventeenth century botanist... I sometimes sketched her.*

2 If you **sketch** a situation or incident, you give a V+O short description of it, including only the most important facts. EG *His rise to power is briefly sketched in the first two chapters.* ▶ used as a ▶ N COUNT noun. EG *...a brief sketch of the school's early history.*

3 A **sketch** is also a short humorous piece of N COUNT acting, usually forming part of a comedy show. EG *I loved the sketch about the dead parrot.*

sketch in. If you sketch in details about some- PHRASAL VB: thing, you tell them to people. EG *In this pro-* V+O+ADV *gramme I'm going to sketch in a bit of the background to the current crisis.*

sketch out. If you sketch out a situation or PHRASAL VB: incident, you give a short description of it, includ- V+ADV ing only the most important facts. EG *He sketched out his plan for the new sales campaign.*

sketchy /sketʃi¹/, sketchier, sketchiest. Some- ADJ QUALIT thing that is sketchy does not have many details. EG *...his sketchy lecture notes... I had only the sketchiest notion of what it was all about.*

skewer /skjuːə/, skewers, skewering, skew- ered. 1 A skewer is a long metal pin which is used N COUNT to hold pieces of food together during cooking.

2 If you **skewer** something, you push a long, thin, V+O pointed object through it. EG *They skewered bits of meat on branches and held them in the flames.*

ski /skiː/, skis, skiing, skied. 1 Skis are long, flat, N COUNT narrow pieces of wood, metal, or plastic that are fastened to boots so that you can move easily on snow. EG *...a pair of skis.*

2 When people **ski**, they move on snow wearing V skis, especially as a sport or a holiday activity. EG *They go skiing every winter.*

3 You use **ski** to describe things that are con- ADJ CLASSIF: cerned with skiing. EG *...ski boots... ...a Swiss ski* ATTRIB *instructor... ...a ski resort.*

skid /skɪd/, skids, skidding, skidded. If a vehicle V: USU+A **skids**, it slides sideways or forwards while moving, for example when you are trying to stop it suddenly on a wet road. EG *He slammed on his brakes and skidded into a wall... We skidded to a halt.* ▶ used ▶ N COUNT as a noun. EG *The car went into a skid.*

skilful /skɪlful/; spelled **skillful** in American English. Someone who is **skilful** at something does it very well. EG *The girl had grown more skilful with the sewing-machine... ...a skilful hunter... ...skilful political manoeuvres.* ◇ **skilfully.** EG *...a skilfully organized campaign.* ◇ ADV — ADJ QUALIT

skill /skɪl/, **skills. 1** Skill is the knowledge and ability that enables you to do something well. EG *Organized games involve skill, competition and teamwork... The carving shows remarkable technical skill.* — N UNCOUNT

2 A **skill** is a type of work or craft which requires special training and knowledge. EG *...the skills of painting and drawing... ...learning new skills.* — N COUNT

skilled /skɪld/. **1** Someone who is **skilled** has the knowledge and ability to do something well. EG *...hand-made items produced by skilled craftsmen.* — ADJ QUALIT

2 Skilled work can only be done by people who have had some training; used especially of manual and industrial work. — ADJ CLASSIF : ATTRIB

skillful /skɪlful/. See **skilful**.

skim /skɪm/, **skims, skimming, skimmed. 1** If you **skim** something from the surface of a liquid, you remove it. EG *Skim off the cream.* — V+O+A

2 If something **skims** a surface, it moves quickly along just above it. EG *The birds swoop in a breathtaking arc to skim the pond.* — V+O

3 If you **skim** a piece of writing, you read through it quickly. EG *I thought I would skim through a few of the letters.* — V+O OR V+through

skimmed milk is milk from which the cream has been removed. — N UNCOUNT

skimp /skɪmp/, **skimps, skimping, skimped.** If you **skimp** on something, you use less time, money, or material for it than you really need. EG *Don't skimp on stair carpet... When people get harassed work is skimped or rushed.* — V :OFT+on, OR V+O

skimpy /skɪmpi¹/. Something that is **skimpy** is too small in size or quantity. EG *...little girls in skimpy cotton frocks.* — ADJ QUALIT

skin /skɪn/, **skins, skinning, skinned. 1** Your **skin** is the natural covering of your body. EG *They had light skin and blue eyes... The poison may be absorbed through the skin... ...skin cancer.* — N UNCOUNT OR N COUNT

2 An animal **skin** is skin with fur on it which has been removed from a dead animal. Skins are used to make things such as coats or rugs. EG *There was a polar bear skin on the floor.* — N COUNT OR N UNCOUNT

3 The **skin** of a type of food is its outer layer or covering. EG *Cook the potatoes quickly with their skins on... ...sausage skins.* — N COUNT OR N UNCOUNT

4 If a **skin** forms on the surface of a liquid, a fairly solid layer forms on it. EG *The custard had a thick skin on it.* — N COUNT OR N UNCOUNT

5 If you **skin** a dead animal, you remove its skin. EG *The boys skinned and cleaned the day's game.* — V+O

6 If you **skin** part of your body, you injure it by accidentally scraping some of the skin off. EG *She skinned her knee.* — V+O

7 Skin is also used in these phrases. **7.1** If you do something **by the skin of** your **teeth**, you just manage to do it but very nearly fail. EG *I only passed by the skin of my teeth.* **7.2** If you say that something made you **jump out of** your **skin**, you mean that it surprised or shocked you very much. EG *He nearly jumped out of his skin when he saw her face at the window.* **7.3** If you try to **save** your own **skin** or to **protect** your own **skin**, you try to save yourself from something dangerous or unpleasant. EG *My first thought was to protect my own skin.* — PHRASES

skin-deep. If you say that beauty or glamour is only **skin-deep**, you mean that people or things that look attractive may really be bad or worthless. — ADJ CLASSIF

skinhead /skɪnhɛd/, **skinheads.** A **skinhead** is a young person whose hair is shaved or cut very short. Skinheads are usually regarded as violent and aggressive. — N COUNT

skinny /skɪni¹/. Someone who is **skinny** is very thin. EG *He's tall and skinny.* — ADJ QUALIT Informal

skint /skɪnt/. If you are **skint**, you have no money. EG *I could do with £10, I'm skint.* — ADJ PRED Informal

skin-tight. Skin-tight clothes fit very tightly so that they show the shape of a person's body. — ADJ CLASSIF

skip /skɪp/, **skips, skipping, skipped. 1** If you **skip** along, you move almost as if you are dancing, with a series of little jumps from one foot to the other. EG *He skipped around the room.* ▸ used as a noun. EG *...taking little skips as they walked.* — V :USU+A ▸ N COUNT

2 When someone **skips**, they jump up and down over a rope which they or two other people are holding at each end and turning round and round. EG *Three energetic little girls were skipping in the playground.* — V

3 If you **skip** something that you usually do, you deliberately do not do it. EG *I could skip every lecture for a month and still graduate... I decided to skip lunch.* — V+O Informal

4 A **skip** is a large metal container for holding rubbish and old bricks. EG *Debris was being loaded into skips.* — N COUNT British

skipper /skɪpə/, **skippers.** You can use **skipper** to refer to **1** the captain of a ship or boat. EG *I had to pass the signals to the skipper.* **2** the captain of a sports team. — N COUNT Informal / Informal

skirmish /skɜːmɪʃ/, **skirmishes, skirmishing, skirmished.** A **skirmish** is **1** a minor battle. EG *...a bitter skirmish in the half light of dawn.* ▸ used as a verb. EG *The expedition spent two years crossing deserts and skirmishing with tribesmen.* **2** a short, sharp argument. EG *She described the early skirmishes in the campaign for equality for women.* — N COUNT ▸ V / N COUNT

skirt /skɜːt/, **skirts, skirting, skirted. 1** A **skirt** is a piece of clothing worn by women and girls which fastens at the waist and hangs down to above or below the knees. See picture at CLOTHES. EG *...a very short skirt.* — N COUNT

2 Something that **skirts** an area is situated around the edge of it. EG *...the path which skirted the house.* — V+O

3 If you **skirt** something, you go around the edge of it. EG *As I walked through the lobby, I had to skirt a group of ladies... They skirted round a bus.* — V+O OR V+round/around

4 If you **skirt** a problem or question, you avoid dealing with it. EG *The President has skirted the issue.* — V+O OR V+round/around

skittle /skɪtə⁰l/, **skittles. 1** A **skittle** is a wooden object used as a target in the game of skittles. — N COUNT

2 Skittles is a game in which players try to knock over as many skittles as they can out of a group of nine by throwing a ball at them. — N UNCOUNT

skive /skaɪv/, **skives, skiving, skived.** If you **skive**, you avoid working, especially by staying away from a place. EG *Were you skiving or were you really ill?... He's always skiving off.* — V :OFT+off Informal British

skulk /skʌlk/, **skulks, skulking, skulked.** If you **skulk** somewhere, you stay there because you do not want to be seen or do not want to meet people. EG *There were half a dozen foxes skulking in the undergrowth.* — V+A

skull /skʌl/, **skulls.** Your **skull** is the bony part of your head which encloses your brain. EG *He had two broken ribs and a fractured skull.* — N COUNT

skunk /skʌŋk/, **skunks.** A **skunk** is a small black and white animal which gives off an unpleasant smell if it is frightened or attacked. — N COUNT

sky /skaɪ/, **skies.** The **sky** is the space around the earth which you can see when you stand outside and look upwards, and where you can see the sun, the moon, and the stars. EG *There were little white clouds high in the blue sky... ...the night skies of London.* ● **pie in the sky**: see **pie**. — N SING : the+N OR N COUNT +SUPP

sky-high. 1 If prices or wages go **sky-high**, they reach a very high level. EG *Land value has gone sky-high... ...sky-high property prices.* ADV OR ADJ CLASSIF

2 If you **blow** something **sky-high**, you destroy it completely. EG *His argument has just been blown sky-high.* PHRASE

skylight /skaɪlaɪt/, **skylights**. A **skylight** is a window in a roof. N COUNT

skyline /skaɪlaɪn/, **skylines**. The **skyline** is the line where the sky meets buildings or the land. EG *...the impressive Manhattan skyline.* N COUNT : USU SING+SUPP

skyscraper /skaɪskreɪpə/, **skyscrapers**. A **sky-scraper** is a very tall building in a city. EG *The view was blocked by new skyscrapers.* N COUNT

skyward /skaɪwəd/, **skywards**. If you look **sky-ward** or **skywards**, you look up towards the sky. EG *He had a habit of looking skyward each time he made a pronouncement.* ADV AFTER VB Literary

slab /slæb/, **slabs**. A **slab** of something is a thick, flat piece of it. EG *...a great slab of rock... ...a concrete slab... ...a slab of cheese.* N PART OR N COUNT

slack /slæk/, **slacker, slackest; slacks**. **1** Something that is **slack** is loose and not firmly stretched or tightly in position. EG *...a slack rope... ...his slack and wrinkled skin.* ADJ QUALIT

2 The **slack** in a rope, thread, or wire is the part of it that hangs loose. N UNCOUNT

3 A **slack** period is one in which there is not much work or activity. EG *Very few hotels offered work for the slack season.* ADJ QUALIT

4 If you are **slack** in your work, you do not do your work properly. EG *Security's got a bit slack.* ADJ QUALIT

◊ **slackness**. EG *She was dismissed for slackness.* ◊ N UNCOUNT

5 Slacks are casual trousers. EG *I put on a pair of golfing slacks and a blazer.* N PLURAL Outdated

slacken /slækəⁿn/, **slackens, slackening, slackened. 1** If something **slackens** or if you **slacken** it, it becomes slower, less active, or less intense. EG *She slackened her pace... The rain began to slacken.* V-ERG

2 If your grip or your body **slackens** or if you **slacken** it, it becomes looser or more relaxed. EG *The grip on Casson's right wrist did not slacken... Slacken your legs and slowly lie back.* V-ERG

slacken off. If something **slackens off**, it becomes slower, less active, or less intense. EG *The Depression slackened off and prosperity returned.* PHRASAL VB : V+ADV

slag /slæg/, **slags, slagging, slagged**. If you **slag** someone **off**, you criticize them in an unpleasant way. EG *Mark's always slagging off his friends behind their backs.* PHRASAL VB : V+O+ADV Informal

slag heap, slag heaps. A **slag heap** is a hill made of waste materials from mines and factories. N COUNT

slain /sleɪn/ is the past participle of **slay**.

slam /slæm/, **slams, slamming, slammed. 1** If you **slam** a door or window or if it **slams**, it shuts noisily and with great force. EG *She went out, slamming the door behind her... I waited for the gate behind me to slam shut.* V-ERG : OFT+A

2 If you **slam** something down, you put it there quickly and with great force. EG *He slammed the money on the table.* V+O+A

slander /slɑːndə/, **slanders, slandering, slandered**. A **slander** is an untrue spoken statement about someone which is intended to damage their reputation. EG *I'll sue her for slander.* ▸ used as a verb. EG *She slandered him behind his back.* N COUNT OR N UNCOUNT ▸ V+O

slang /slæŋ/. Words, expressions, and meanings which are very informal are referred to as **slang**. EG *...the Dictionary of American Slang... ...military slang.* ▸ used as an adjective. EG *'Porridge' is a slang term for 'prison'.* N UNCOUNT ▸ ADJ CLASSIF : ATTRIB

slanging match /slæŋɪŋ mætʃ/, **slanging matches**. A **slanging match** is an angry quarrel in which people insult each other. EG *We had a full-scale slanging match.* N COUNT British

slangy /slæŋiʲ/. **Slangy** speech or writing has a lot of slang in it. EG *...slangy colloquial passages.* ADJ QUALIT

slant /slɑːnt/, **slants, slanting, slanted. 1** Something that **slants** is sloping, rather than horizontal or vertical. EG *The old wooden floor slanted a little.* V

◊ **slanting**. EG *...a slanting roof... ...her slanting eyes.* ◊ ADJ CLASSIF : ATTRIB

2 A **slant** is a slanting position. EG *For some reason the shelf was set on a slant.* N SING

3 If news or information **is slanted**, it is presented in a way that shows favour towards a particular group or opinion. EG *Burger's report was obviously slanted.* V+O : USU PASS

4 A particular **slant** on a subject is a particular way of thinking about it, especially one that is unfair, biased, or prejudiced. EG *I was furious at the slant that had been put on the evidence... ...a leftist political slant... I don't know whether it's possible to get a new slant on it these days.* N SING+SUPP

slap /slæp/, **slaps, slapping, slapped. 1** If you **slap** someone, you hit them with the palm of your hand. EG *He slapped her across the face... I slapped her hand.* ▸ used as a noun. EG *Give him a slap if he is too much of a pest.* V+O ▸ N COUNT

2 If you **slap** someone on the back, you hit them in a friendly manner on their back. EG *I slapped him on the back and wished him the best of luck.* ▸ used as a noun. EG *...a hefty slap on the back.* V+O ▸ N COUNT

3 If you describe something that someone does as **a slap in the face**, you mean that it shocks and upsets you because it shows that they do not support you or respect you. EG *Their refusal was like a slap in the face.* PHRASE

4 If you **slap** something onto a surface, **4.1** you put it there quickly or carelessly. EG *All you have to do is slap a bit of Sellotape across it.* **4.2** you put it there with quite a lot of force. EG *He slapped the report down on the table.* V+O+A

5 If you walk or drive **slap** into something or **slap bang** into something, you walk or drive into it suddenly and with great force. EG *I walked slap into the wall.* ADV+PREP Informal

slapstick /slæpstɪk/ is a simple type of comedy in which the actors behave in a rough and foolish way. EG *...slapstick comics.* N UNCOUNT

slash /slæʃ/, **slashes, slashing, slashed. 1** If you **slash** something, you make a long, deep cut in it. EG *Jack's face had been slashed with broken glass.* V+O

2 If you **slash** at something, you quickly hit at it with something. EG *...slashing at each other with their swords.* V : OFT+at

3 To **slash** something such as money or time means to reduce it by a large amount. EG *...a plan to slash taxes... Disease slashes income.* V+O Informal

4 You say **slash** to refer to a diagonal line that separates letters, words, or numbers. For example, if you are giving the number 340/21/K, you say 'Three four zero, slash two one, slash K.' N COUNT OR N UNCOUNT Spoken

slat /slæt/, **slats**. **Slats** are the narrow pieces of wood, metal, or plastic in things such as Venetian blinds or cupboard doors. N COUNT : USU PLURAL

slate /sleɪt/, **slates, slating, slated. 1 Slate** is a dark grey rock that can be easily split into thin layers. Slate is often used for covering roofs. N UNCOUNT

2 A **slate** is one of the small flat pieces of slate that are used for covering roofs. N COUNT

slatted /slætɪʳd/. Something that is **slatted** is made with slats. EG *...white slatted Venetian blinds.* ADJ CLASSIF

slaughter /slɔːtə/, **slaughters, slaughtering, slaughtered. 1** To **slaughter** a large number of people means to kill them in a way that is cruel, unjust, or unnecessary. EG *Opponents of the regime were systematically slaughtered.* ▸ used as a noun. EG *Wholesale slaughter was carried out in the name of progress.* V+O ▸ N UNCOUNT

2 To **slaughter** animals such as cows and sheep means to kill them for their meat. EG *...a freshly slaughtered bullock.* ▸ used as a noun. EG *...animals going away to slaughter.* V+O ▸ N UNCOUNT

slaughterhouse /slɔːtəhaus/, **slaughterhouses.** N COUNT
A **slaughterhouse** is a place where animals are killed for their meat.

slave /sleɪv/, **slaves, slaving, slaved. 1** A **slave** N COUNT
is someone who is the property of another person and has to work for that person. EG ...a story about a slave who escapes and becomes a free man.

2 You can also describe someone as a **slave** when N COUNT + SUPP
they are completely under the control of another person or of a powerful influence. EG He's just become a slave to possessions and money.

3 If you **slave** for someone, you work very hard for V : USU + A
them. EG Why am I slaving away, running a house and family single-handed?

slave driver, slave drivers. If you call someone N COUNT
a **slave driver**, you mean that they make people Informal
work very hard.

slavery /sleɪvəⁿrɪ/. **1 Slavery** is the system by N UNCOUNT
which people are owned by other people as slaves. EG ...the abolition of slavery.

2 You also use **slavery** to refer to the state of not N UNCOUNT
being free because you have to work very hard or +SUPP
because you are strongly influenced by something. EG I had at last been freed from the slavery of a 9 to 5 job.

slavish /sleɪvɪʃ/. You use **slavish** to describe **1** ADJ QUALIT
things that copy or imitate something exactly, without any attempt to be original. EG ...a slavish adherence to things of the past. ◊ **slavishly.** EG I ◊ ADV
don't expect you to slavishly copy this. **2** someone ADJ QUALIT
who always obeys other people; used showing disapproval. EG ...a slavish figure, down on her knees polishing the floor.

slay /sleɪ/, **slays, slaying, slew** /sljuː/, **slain** V+O
/sleɪn/. If someone **slays** someone else, they kill Literary
them in a violent way. EG Two visitors were brutally slain yesterday.

sleazy /sliːzɪ¹/. A place that is **sleazy** looks dirty ADJ QUALIT
and badly cared for, and not respectable. EG ...a sleazy cafe... ...a sleazy area of town.

sled /sled/, **sleds.** A **sled** is the same as a sledge. N COUNT
EG ...a sled descending a snowy hill. American

sledge /sledʒ/, **sledges.** A **sledge** is a vehicle N COUNT
which can slide over snow. It consists of a framework which slides on two strips of wood or metal.

sledgehammer /sledʒhæmə/, **sledgehammers.** N COUNT
A **sledgehammer** is a large, heavy hammer with a long handle.

sleek /sliːk/, **sleeker, sleekest. 1** Hair or fur that ADJ QUALIT
is **sleek** is smooth, shiny, and healthy-looking. EG ...her sleek black hair.

2 Someone who is **sleek** looks very rich; usually ADJ QUALIT
used showing disapproval. EG They were all too fat and sleek and too pleased with themselves.

3 A vehicle that is **sleek** has a smooth, graceful ADJ QUALIT
shape. EG ...sleek, black cars.

sleep /sliːp/, **sleeps, sleeping, slept** /slept/. **1** N UNCOUNT
Sleep is the natural state of rest in which your eyes are closed and your mind and body are inactive and unconscious, usually for several hours every night. EG I haven't been getting enough sleep recently... She fell into a dreamless sleep... Now go to sleep and stop worrying... I didn't get to sleep until six in the morning.

2 When you **sleep**, you rest in a state of sleep. EG V
She slept till ten in the morning... He was so excited he could hardly sleep. ◊ **sleeping.** EG I glanced ◊ ADJ CLASSIF :
down at the sleeping figure. ATTRIB

3 A **sleep** is a period of sleeping. EG He hadn't had a N SING : a+N
proper night's sleep for a month... You'll feel better if you have a little sleep.

4 If a house **sleeps** a particular number of people, V+O : NO CONT,
it has beds for that number. EG Each apartment NO PASS
sleeps up to five adults.

5 If a part of your body **goes to sleep**, you lose the PHRASE
sense of feeling in it. EG His foot had gone to sleep.

6 If a sick or injured animal is **put to sleep**, it is PHRASE
painlessly killed. EG Sheba had to be put to sleep.

7 See also **sleeping.**

sleep around. If someone **sleeps around**, they PHRASAL VB :
have sex with several different people; used show- V+ADV
ing disapproval. EG I did everything I could to hurt Informal
her, including sleeping around.

sleep off. If you **sleep off** the effects of eating or PHRASAL VB :
drinking too much or the effects of a drug, you V+O+ADV
recover from them by sleeping. EG We went back to our room to sleep it off.

sleep through. If you **sleep through** a noise, it PHRASAL VB :
does not wake you up. EG The girl slept through V+PREP,
everything. HAS PASS

sleep together. If two people **sleep together**, PHRASAL VB :
they have a sexual relationship, but are not usually V+ADV
married to each other.

sleep with. If you **sleep with** someone, you have PHRASAL VB :
sex with them. EG Willie had slept with Mary Jane. V+PREP

sleeper /sliːpə/, **sleepers. 1** You use **sleeper** to N COUNT+SUPP
say how deeply someone sleeps. For example, someone who is a light **sleeper** is easily woken up. EG Eva was a sound sleeper.

2 A **sleeper** is also **2.1** a bed on a train. EG I booked N COUNT
a first-class sleeper. **2.2** a train with beds for N COUNT
passengers on overnight journeys. EG I usually go up to London on the sleeper.

3 Railway **sleepers** are the large, heavy beams N COUNT
that support the rails of a railway track. British

sleeping /sliːpɪŋ/. You use **sleeping** to describe ADJ CLASSIF :
places where people sleep. EG The sleeping accom- ATTRIB
modation is somewhat primitive. ● See also **sleep.**

sleeping bag, sleeping bags. A **sleeping bag** is N COUNT
a large deep bag with a warm lining which is used for sleeping in, especially when camping.

sleeping pill, sleeping pills. A **sleeping pill** or N COUNT
a **sleeping tablet** is a pill that you can take to help you sleep.

sleepless /sliːpləⁿs/. **1** A **sleepless** night is one ADJ QUALIT
during which you do not sleep. EG He'd had a sleepless night.

2 Someone who is **sleepless** is unable to sleep. EG ADJ QUALIT
Late in the night, sleepless and troubled, he went for a walk. ◊ **sleeplessness.** EG I began to suffer ◊ N UNCOUNT
from sleeplessness.

sleepwalk /sliːpwɔːk/, **sleepwalks, sleepwalk-** V : USU CONT
ing, sleepwalked. If someone **is sleepwalking**, they are walking around while they are asleep. EG She must have been sleepwalking.

sleepy /sliːpɪ¹/, **sleepier, sleepiest. 1** If you are ADJ QUALIT
sleepy, you are very tired and are ready to go to sleep. EG She suddenly started to feel very sleepy... ...a sleepy yawn. ◊ **sleepily.** EG 'Where have you ◊ ADV
been?' Rudolph asked sleepily.

2 A **sleepy** place is very quiet and does not have ADJ QUALIT :
much activity or excitement. EG ...sleepy villages. ATTRIB

sleet /sliːt/. **1 Sleet** is rain that is partly N UNCOUNT
frozen. EG An icy sleet was beginning to fall.

2 If it **is sleeting**, sleet is falling from the sky. EG It V : ONLY CONT
started to sleet. OR INF

sleeve /sliːv/, **sleeves. 1** The **sleeves** of a piece of N COUNT
clothing are the parts that cover your arms. EG ...a yellow dress with short sleeves.

2 A record **sleeve** is the stiff envelope in which a N COUNT
gramophone record is kept. EG ...the photograph of the conductor on the record sleeve.

3 If you **have** something **up your sleeve**, you have PHRASE
an idea or plan which you have not told anyone about. EG She thought the old man had some clever trick up his sleeve.

sleeveless /sliːvlɪⁿs/. A **sleeveless** piece of cloth- ADJ CLASSIF :
ing has no sleeves. EG ...a blue sleeveless dress. ATTRIB

sleigh /sleɪ/, **sleighs.** A **sleigh** is a vehicle which N COUNT
can slide over snow. Sleighs are usually pulled by horses.

sleight of hand /sleɪt əv hænd, slaɪt əv hænd/. **1** N UNCOUNT
If you do something by **sleight of hand**, you do it using quick skilful movements of your hands which

Find two words on these pages that mean the same as 'slim'.

other people cannot see. EG *He switched the watches by sleight of hand.*

2 Sleight of hand is also a skilful piece of deception. EG *With a little statistical sleight of hand we could make things look all right.*   N UNCOUNT

slender /slɛndə/. **1** A **slender** person is attractively thin and graceful. EG *...the girl's slender waist... She crossed her slender legs.*   ADJ QUALIT

2 You use **slender** to describe something that is small in amount or degree when you would like it to be greater. EG *With such slender resources they cannot hope to achieve their aims... ...slender prospects of promotion.*   ADJ QUALIT

slept /slɛpt/ is the past tense and past participle of **sleep.**

sleuth /sluːθ/, **sleuths.** A **sleuth** is a detective. EG *...a series about a lady sleuth.*   N COUNT   Outdated

slew /sljuː/ is the past tense of **slay.**

slice /slaɪs/, **slices, slicing, sliced. 1** A **slice** is a piece of food that has been cut from a larger piece. EG *She cut him three large slices of bread... ...slices of chicken pie.*   N COUNT OR N PART

2 If you **slice** food, you cut it into thin pieces. EG *I saw her slicing an apple.*   V+O

3 A **slice** of something is a part of it. EG *Rents provided a large slice of his income.*   N PART

4 If something **slices** a substance or **slices** through it, it cuts or moves through it quickly, like a knife. EG *They sliced the air with their knives... The shark's fin sliced through the water.*   V+O OR V+through

sliced /slaɪst/. **Sliced** bread is bread that has been cut into slices before being wrapped up and sold. EG *...a large sliced loaf.*   ADJ CLASSIF : ATTRIB

slick /slɪk/. **1** Something such as a book or film that is **slick** is well-made and attractive, but has little quality or sincerity; used showing disapproval. EG *Some people thought the broadcasts too slick.*   ADJ QUALIT

2 A **slick** action is done quickly and smoothly, and without any obvious effort. EG *...a relay race round London, with slick baton-changing.*   ADJ QUALIT

3 Someone who is **slick** speaks easily and persuasively but is not sincere; used showing disapproval. EG *...a slick, evasive answer.*   ADJ QUALIT

4 See also **oil slick.**

slide /slaɪd/, **slides, sliding, slid** /slɪd/. **1** When something **slides** or when you **slide** it, it moves smoothly over or against something else. EG *The gate slid open at the push of a button... She slid the key into the keyhole.*   V-ERG : USU+A

2 To **slide** somewhere means to move there smoothly and quietly. EG *An elderly lady slid into the seat... The black Mercedes slid away.*   V : USU+A

3 If you **slide** into a particular attitude, you change to it smoothly and gradually, and usually unintentionally. EG *He felt himself sliding into obsession.*   V+A

4 A **slide** is a small piece of photographic film which can be projected onto a screen so that you can see the picture. EG *...colour slides showing rice fields in Bangkok.*   N COUNT

5 A **slide** is also a piece of glass on which you put something that you want to examine through a microscope.   N COUNT

6 A **slide** in a playground is a structure that has a steep slope for children to slide down.   N COUNT

7 See also **hair slide.**

slight /slaɪt/, **slighter, slightest; slights, slighting, slighted. 1** Something that is **slight** is very small in degree or quantity. EG *He had a slight German accent... ...after a slight hesitation... He'd had a slight stroke... I haven't the slightest idea what you're talking about.* ◊ **slightly.** EG *White wine should be slightly chilled... 'Do you know him?' – 'Slightly.'* ● You use **in the slightest** to emphasize a negative statement. EG *My tennis hadn't improved in the slightest.*   ADJ QUALIT : USU ATTRIB   ◊ ADV   ● PHRASE : WITH BROAD NEG

2 Someone who is **slight** has a slim and delicate body. EG *I watched her slight figure cross the street.*   ADJ QUALIT

3 If you **slight** someone, you insult them by treating them as if they were unimportant. EG *His*   V+O

fear of being slighted made him avoid people.

▸ used as a noun. EG *It was a slight on a past award-winner, Stevenson.*   ▸ N COUNT

slim /slɪm/, **slimmer, slimmest; slims, slimming, slimmed. 1** Someone who is **slim** has an attractively thin and well-shaped body. EG *...a tall, slim girl with long, straight hair.*   ADJ QUALIT

2 If you **are slimming**, you are trying to make yourself thinner and lighter by eating less food or healthier food, or by taking exercise. EG *I may be slimming but I've no intentions of starving myself.* ◊ **slimmer, slimmers.** EG *...clubs for slimmers.*   V   ◊ N COUNT

3 You describe an object as **slim** when it is thinner than usual. EG *...a slim book.*   ADJ QUALIT

4 If the chance of something happening is **slim**, it is unlikely to happen. EG *The chance of American intervention is slim.*   ADJ QUALIT

slime /slaɪm/ is a thick, slippery substance which covers a surface or comes from the bodies of animals such as snails. EG *There was a green slime around the edges of the tub... ...a trail of slime.*   N UNCOUNT

slimy /slaɪmiˈ/. **1** Something that is **slimy** is covered in slime. EG *...a slimy pond... ...crawling, slimy creatures.*   ADJ QUALIT

2 You use **slimy** to describe people who are friendly and pleasant in an insincere way; used showing disapproval. EG *...a slimy politician.*   ADJ QUALIT Informal

sling /slɪŋ/, **slings, slinging, slung** /slʌŋ/. **1** If you **sling** something somewhere, you throw it there. EG *She slung the book across the room.*   V+O+A

2 If you **sling** something over your shoulder or over a chair, for example, you put it there quickly and carelessly so that it hangs down. EG *Patrick gets his camera bag and slings it over his shoulder.* ◊ **slung.** EG *His few bits of clothing were slung over a string on the wall.*   V+O+A   ◊ ADJ PRED

3 If you **sling** something such as a rope between two points, you attach it so that it hangs loosely between them. ◊ **slung.** EG *Pieces of meat were hanging to dry over a rope slung on the wall.*   V+O+A : USU PASS   ◊ ADJ PRED

4 A **sling** is **4.1** an object made of ropes, straps, or cloth that is used for carrying things. EG *Mothers carry their babies around with them in slings.* **4.2** a piece of cloth which supports someone's broken or injured arm and is tied round their neck. EG *His arm was in a sling.*   N COUNT

slink /slɪŋk/, **slinks, slinking, slunk** /slʌŋk/. If you **slink** somewhere, you move there in a slow and secretive way because you do not want to be seen. EG *I slunk away to my room, to brood in front of the fire.*   V+A

slip /slɪp/, **slips, slipping, slipped. 1** If you **slip**, you accidentally slide and lose your balance. EG *I slipped on the snow and sprained my ankle.*   V

2 If something **slips**, it slides out of place or out of your hands, especially accidentally. EG *It slipped from his fingers and fell with a bump... She pulled up her sock which had slipped down.*   V : USU+A

3 If you **slip** somewhere, you go there quickly and quietly. EG *I hope we can slip away before she notices.*   V+A

4 If you **slip** something somewhere, you put it there quickly in a way that does not attract attention. EG *He slipped it quickly into his pocket.*   V+O+A

5 If something **slips** your mind, you forget about it. EG *It must have slipped his mind.*   PHRASE

6 If you **let slip** information, you say it without intending to, especially when you had wanted to keep it secret. EG *He carelessly let slip this information in conversation with a journalist.*   PHRASE

7 If you **slip** into clothes or **slip** them on, you put them on quickly or easily. If you **slip** out of clothes or **slip** them off, you take them off quickly or easily. EG *I slipped into my pyjamas... He slipped on his shoes and went out... She slipped off her dress.*   V+A OR V+O+A

8 If you **give** someone **the slip**, you succeed in escaping from them. EG *I tried to follow her but she gave me the slip.*   PHRASE Informal

9 A **slip** is a small mistake. EG *I must have made a* N COUNT *slip somewhere.* ● **slip of the tongue**: see **tongue**.

10 A **slip** of paper is a small piece of paper. N COUNT

11 A **slip** is also a piece of clothing without sleeves N COUNT that a woman wears under her dress. EG *...a black nylon slip.*

slip up. If you **slip up**, you make a mistake. EG PHRASAL VB : *We must have slipped up somewhere.* ● See also V+ADV **slip-up.**

slipped disc, slipped discs. If you have a N COUNT **slipped disc**, one of the discs in your spine has moved out of its proper position.

slipper /slɪpə/, **slippers. Slippers** are loose, soft N COUNT : shoes that you wear in the house. See picture at USU PLURAL SHOES.

slippery /slɪpəⁱriⁱ/. **1** Something that is **slippery** ADJ QUALIT is smooth, wet, or greasy and is therefore difficult to hold or walk on. EG *The soap was smooth and slippery... ...a slippery pavement.*

2 If you say that someone is on **a slippery slope**, PHRASE you mean that they are becoming worse in a way Formal that is difficult to stop. EG *The economy is steadily sliding down the slippery slope.*

slip-up, slip-ups. A **slip-up** is a small or unimpor- N COUNT tant mistake. Informal

slit /slɪt/, **slits, slitting.** The form **slit** is used in the present tense and is the past tense and past participle of the verb.

1 If you **slit** something, you make a long narrow V+O:OFT+A cut in it. EG *She got a knife and slit the envelope... He slit open the packet with his thumb nail... He slit the fawn's throat.*

2 A **slit** is **2.1** a long narrow cut. EG *We make a tiny* N COUNT *slit in it with a razor blade.* **2.2** a long narrow opening in something. EG *...neon light came through the slits in the blind.*

slither /slɪðə/, **slithers, slithering, slithered.** If V:USU+A you **slither** somewhere, you slide along the ground in an uneven way. EG *We slithered down the steep slope... A huge snake was slithering under my bed.*

sliver /slɪvə/, **slivers.** A **sliver** of something is a N COUNT small thin piece of it. EG *...a sliver of soap.* OR N PART

slob /slɒb/, **slobs.** A **slob** is someone who is very N COUNT lazy and untidy. EG *You're a slob.* Informal

slobber /slɒbə/, **slobbers, slobbering, slob-** V **bered.** If someone **slobbers**, they let liquid fall from their mouth, like babies do. EG *Sally was happily slobbering in her pram.*

slog /slɒg/, **slogs, slogging, slogged. 1** If you V+A **slog** at something, you work hard and steadily at it. Informal EG *The children are slogging away at revision.*

2 If you **slog** somewhere, you make a long and V+A tiring journey there. EG *...slogging through the* Informal snow.

3 If you describe a task as a **slog**, you mean that it N SING is tiring and requires a lot of effort. EG *...the hard* Informal slog of trying to get views changed.

4 You can also refer to a long and tiring journey as N SING a **slog**. EG *...his long slog home.* Informal

slogan /sləʊgəⁿn/, **slogans.** A **slogan** is a short, N COUNT easily-remembered phrase. Slogans are used in advertisements and by political parties. EG *Racist slogans were scratched on walls throughout the city.*

slop /slɒp/, **slops, slopping, slopped.** If liquid V-ERG:USU+A **slops** or if you **slop** it, it spills over the edge of a container in a messy way. EG *We carried the buckets, slopping water, back to the kitchen.*

slope /sləʊp/, **slopes, sloping, sloped. 1** A **slope** N COUNT is a flat surface that is at an angle, so that one end is higher than the other. EG *She rode up a grassy slope.* ● **a slippery slope**: see **slippery.**

2 If a surface **slopes**, it is at an angle, so that one V:USU+A end is higher than the other. EG *The roof sloped down at the back.* ◊ **sloping.** EG *...gently sloping* ◊ ADJ CLASSIF hills. ATTRIB

3 If something **slopes**, it leans to the right or to the V:USU+A left rather than being upright. ◊ **sloping.** EG ◊ ADJ CLASSIF *...sloping handwriting.* ATTRIB

4 The **slope** of something is the angle at which it N SING+SUPP slopes. EG *...a slope of ten degrees.*

sloppy /slɒpiⁱ/. Something that is **sloppy** is messy, ADJ QUALIT careless, or muddled. EG *...sloppy workmanship.* Informal ◊ **sloppily.** EG *...a sloppily run hospital.* ◊ ADV

slosh /slɒʃ/, **sloshes, sloshing, sloshed.** If a V-ERG:USU+A liquid **sloshes** or if you **slosh** it, it splashes or moves around in a messy way. EG *The whiskey sloshed over from his glass on to his hand... They sat out on the decks laughing and sloshing water everywhere.*

sloshed /slɒʃt/. Someone who is **sloshed** is drunk. ADJ PRED EG *Everyone is totally sloshed.* Informal

slot /slɒt/, **slots, slotting, slotted. 1** A **slot** is a N COUNT narrow opening in a machine or container, for example a hole that you put coins in to make a machine work. EG *He put money in the slot and the music started again.*

2 When something **slots** into something else or V-ERG+in/into when you **slot** it in, you put it into a space where it fits. EG *The cylinder just slots into the barrel.*

3 A **slot** is also a place in a schedule, scheme, or N COUNT organization. EG *Students get only two slots in the week for private study.*

sloth /sləʊθ/ is laziness. EG *Mrs Humbert would* N UNCOUNT have to overcome her habitual sloth and write to Formal *Miss Phalen.*

slot machine, slot machines. A **slot machine** N COUNT is a machine from which you can get food or cigarettes or on which you can gamble. You work it by putting coins into a slot in the machine.

slouch /slaʊtʃ/, **slouches, slouching, slouched.** V If you **slouch**, you have your shoulders and head drooping down. EG *Many children slouch because of lack of self-confidence.* ▸ used as a noun. EG *Brad* ▸ N SING straightened out of his usual slouch.

slough /slʌf/, **sloughs, sloughing, sloughed. 1** PHRASAL VB : When an animal such as a snake **sloughs off** its V+O+ADV skin, its skin comes off naturally. **2** If you **slough** V+O+ADV **off** something that you no longer need, you get rid Literary of it. EG *Women are less willing than their husbands to slough off a friendship after a move.*

slovenly /slʌvənliⁱ/. Someone who is **slovenly** is ADJ QUALIT careless, untidy, or inefficient. EG *His appearance was even more slovenly than usual.*

slow /sləʊ/, **slower, slowest; slows, slowing, slowed. 1** Something or someone that is **slow 1.1** ADJ QUALIT moves, does something, or happens without very much speed. EG *His movements were all deliberate and slow... He is turned down for being too old and slow... ...slow music... ...the slow rate of growth.*

▸ used as an adverb. EG *You're going too slow.* ▸ ADV ◊ **slowly.** EG *He nodded slowly and walked very* ◊ ADV sadly out of the door ◊ **slowness.** EG *Time passed* ◊ N UNCOUNT with agonizing slowness. **1.2** takes a long time or is ADJ QUALIT done after a delay. EG *...slow changes in the family structure... They have slow reflexes... I was slow in reacting to her news.* ◊ **slowly.** EG *He slowly* ◊ ADV began to realize what she meant.* ● **slowly but surely**: see **surely.**

2 If something **slows** or if you **slow** it, it starts to V-ERG move or happen more slowly. EG *He slowed to a walk... ...ways of slowing population growth.*

3 Someone who is **slow** is not very clever. ADJ PRED

4 If you describe an activity, place, or story as ADJ PRED **slow**, you mean that it is not very busy or exciting. EG *Business will be slow in the shop for another hour.*

5 If a clock or watch is **slow**, it shows a time that is ADJ PRED earlier than the correct time. EG *That clock's half an hour slow.*

slow down. 1 If something **slows down** or if you PHRASAL VB : **slow** it **down**, it starts to move or happen more V-ERG+ADV slowly. EG *Economic growth has slowed down dra-* matically... Harold slowed the car down. **2** If V+ADV

Is a slum a smart place to live in?

someone **slows down**, they become less active. EG
He needs to slow down a little or he'll get an ulcer.

slow up. If something **slows up** or if you **slow** it PHRASAL VB :
up, it starts to move or happen more slowly. EG *The* V-ERG+ADV
extra weight would have slowed me up consider-
ably... She slowed up a little.

slow motion is movement which is much slower N UNCOUNT
than normal, especially in a film or on television.
EG *I dreamt I was falling off a cliff in slow motion.*
▸ used as an adjective. EG *...slow-motion film of* ▸ ADJ CLASSIF
people talking.

slow-witted. Someone who is **slow-witted** is not ADJ QUALIT
very clever.

sludge /slʌdʒ/ is thick mud. EG *I was covered in* N UNCOUNT
sludge and weeds.

slug /slʌg/, **slugs, slugging, slugged. 1** A **slug** is N COUNT
a small, slow-moving creature with a long, slimy
body, like a snail without a shell.
2 A **slug** of an alcoholic drink is a mouthful or a N PART
quantity of it. EG *Ken took a long slug of scotch.* Informal
3 If you **slug** someone, you hit them hard. EG *I* V+O
raised a fist to slug Eddie. Informal

sluggish /slʌgɪʃ/. Something that is **sluggish** ADJ QUALIT
moves or works very slowly, much slower than
normal. EG *I feel very sluggish... ...the black sluggish*
waters of East Canal.

slum /slʌm/, **slums.** A **slum** is an area of a city N COUNT
where living conditions are very bad. EG *I grew up*
in a slum... ...children from a slum area.

slumber /slʌmbə/, **slumbers, slumbering,** N UNCOUNT
slumbered. Slumber is sleep. EG *She fell into a* OR N COUNT
heavy slumber... Roused from his slumbers, O'Shea Literary
departed. ▸ used as a verb. EG *One old man* ▸ V
slumbered over his newspaper.

slump /slʌmp/, **slumps, slumping, slumped. 1** If V
something such as the value of something **slumps**,
it falls suddenly and by a large amount. EG *Profits*
last year slumped from $40 million to $26 million.
▸ used as a noun. EG *...the continuing slump in oil* ▸ N COUNT
demand.
2 A **slump** is also a time when there is a lot of N COUNT
unemployment and poverty in a country. EG *The*
slump set in during the summer of 1921.
3 If you **slump** somewhere, you fall or sit down V+A
there heavily. EG *Sarah slumped against the wall.*

slung /slʌŋ/ is the past tense and past participle of
sling.

slunk /slʌŋk/ is the past tense and past participle
of **slink.**

slur /slɜː/, **slurs, slurring, slurred. 1** A **slur** is an N COUNT
insulting remark which could damage someone's
reputation. EG *He got angry whenever anyone cast*
the slightest slur on the regiment.
2 If you **slur** your speech or if your speech **slurs**, V-ERG
you pronounce words in a way which is not clear
or distinct, often because you are drunk. EG *'I'll sing*
for you,' he said, his voice slurring so that he could
barely be understood. ◇ **slurred.** EG *His words* ◇ ADJ QUALIT
were slurred and his breath smelled of wine.

slurp /slɜːp/, **slurps, slurping, slurped.** If you V+O OR V
slurp a liquid, you drink it noisily. EG *He slurped*
the soup greedily.

slush /slʌʃ/ is snow which has begun to melt. N UNCOUNT

slushy /slʌʃi¹/. **1** Ground that is **slushy** is covered ADJ QUALIT
in wet snow. EG *A thaw had set in and the streets*
were slushy.
2 A **slushy** story or idea is extremely romantic and ADJ QUALIT
sentimental. EG *...a slushy film.*

sly /slaɪ/, **slyer, slyest.** The forms **slier** and
sliest are also used.
1 A **sly** look, expression, or remark shows that you ADJ QUALIT
know something that other people do not know or
that was meant to be a secret. EG *A slow sly smile*
was creeping around the corners of his mouth.
◇ **slyly.** EG *She glanced slyly at Madeleine.* ◇ ADV
2 Someone who is **sly** is clever at deceiving people. ADJ QUALIT
EG *They are suspicious and wary and sly.*

smack /smæk/, **smacks, smacking, smacked. 1** V+O
If you **smack** someone, you hit them with your

hand. EG *He smacked her on the bottom.* ▸ used as ▸ N COUNT
a noun. EG *I gave him a smack in the face.*
2 If you **smack** something somewhere, you put it V+O+A
or throw it there so that it makes a loud, sharp
noise. EG *He laughed, smacking the flat of his hand*
on the steering wheel. ▸ used as a noun. EG *She* ▸ N SING
gave out the books, dropping them with a satisfying
smack on each desk.
3 If you **smack** your **lips**, you open and close your PHRASE
mouth noisily, especially before or after eating. EG
He looked at the plate and smacked his lips.
4 If something **smacks** of something else, it re- V+OF
minds you of it or is like it. EG *Any literature other* Formal
than romantic novels smacked to her of school.
5 Something that is **smack** in a particular place is ADV+PREP
exactly in that place. EG *The office was right smack* Informal
in the middle of town.
6 If one thing runs **smack** into another thing, it hits ADV+PREP
it directly with a great deal of force. EG *The bus ran* Informal
smack into a car.

small /smɔːl/, **smaller, smallest. 1** Someone or ADJ QUALIT
something that is **small** is not large in physical
size. EG *She was rather small in stature... The male*
is smaller than the female... This is the smallest
church in England. ◇ **smallness.** EG *The smallness* ◇ N UNCOUNT
of the courtroom exaggerated its height.
2 A **small** group or amount consists of only a few ADJ QUALIT
things or not much of something. EG *...small fami-*
lies... ...a relatively small number of people... ...a
small amount of milk.
3 A **small** child is a very young child. EG *She had* ADJ QUALIT
two small children.
4 You also use **small** to describe something that is ADJ QUALIT
not significant or great in degree. EG *Certain small*
changes resulted from my report... Why did he
never make the smallest effort to reach my fa-
ther?... ...a matter of small importance.
5 If you say that something does something **in a** PHRASE
small way, you mean that it does it to a limited
extent. EG *...if, in their own small way, they had*
been able to help.
6 The **small of** your **back** is the narrow part of PHRASE
your back where it curves inwards slightly. EG *She*
had a pain in the small of her back.
7 the **small hours**: see **hour.** ● **small wonder**: see
wonder.

small ad, small ads. A **small ad** in a newspaper N COUNT :
is a short advertisement in which you can adver- USU PLURAL
tise something such as an object for sale or a room
to let.

small change is coins of low value. EG *I need* N UNCOUNT
some small change to make a phone call.

small fry is used to refer to people who are N UNCOUNT
considered to be unimportant. EG *Being small fry*
they had done what they were told.

smallish /smɔːlɪʃ/. Something that is **smallish** is ADJ QUALIT
fairly small. EG *He was a smallish man.*

smallpox /smɔːlpɒks/ is a serious infectious dis- N UNCOUNT
ease that causes a high fever and a rash.

small-scale. A **small-scale** activity or organiza- ADJ CLASSIF
tion is limited in extent. EG *...small-scale industry.* ATTRIB

small talk is conversation at social occasions N UNCOUNT
about unimportant things. EG *We stood around*
making small talk.

smarmy /smɑːmi¹/. Someone who is **smarmy** is ADJ QUALIT
unpleasantly polite and flattering. EG *...a nasty little* Informal
man, smarmy and obsequious.

smart /smɑːt/, **smarter, smartest; smarts,**
smarting, smarted. 1 Someone who is **smart** is ADJ QUALIT
pleasantly neat and clean in appearance. EG *The*
boys looked smart in their school uniforms.
◇ **smartly.** EG *...a smartly dressed executive.* ◇ ADV
2 You can also describe someone as **smart** when ADJ QUALIT
they are clever. EG *She's one of the smartest* American
students in the whole school... ...a smart idea.
3 A **smart** place or event is connected with ADJ QUALIT
wealthy and fashionable people. EG *We met at a*
very smart lunch party.
4 A **smart** movement or action is sharp and quick. ADJ QUALIT :
ATTRIB

EG *...the smart crack of a whip... ...moving along at a smart trot.* ◇ **smartly.** EG *Grabbing the bottle, she hit him smartly on the head.* ◇ ADV Written

5 If a part of your body or a wound **smarts**, you feel a sharp stinging pain in it. EG *His eyes smarted from the smoke of the fire.* V

6 If you **are smarting** from something such as criticism or unkindness, you feel upset about it. EG *Brody smarted under Quint's derision.* V : OFT+A

smarten /smɑːtəⁿn/, **smartens, smartening, smartened.** If you **smarten** yourself **up** or if you **smarten** a place **up**, you make yourself or the place look neater and tidier. EG *The New Electric Cinema has been smartened up.* PHRASAL VB : V-REFL+ADV OR V+O+ADV

smash /smæʃ/, **smashes, smashing, smashed. 1** If you **smash** something, you break it into many pieces by hitting it, throwing it, or dropping it. EG *Some windows have been smashed... I nearly smashed the TV set.* V+O

2 If something **smashes**, it breaks into many pieces when it falls and hits the ground. EG *A plate dropped from his fingers and smashed on the kitchen floor.* V : NO CONT

3 If you **smash** through something such as a wall, you move forwards by hitting it and breaking it. EG *The police smashed their way into eleven homes.* V+A OR V+O+A

4 If something **smashes** or **is smashed** against something solid, it moves very fast and with great force against it. EG *The waves smashed onto the shore... The sea smashed the boat against the rocks.* V-ERG+A

5 If people **smash** something such as a political system or a person's career, they deliberately ruin it. EG *We are interested in transforming the system rather than smashing it.* V+O

6 A play or film that is a **smash** or a **smash** hit is very successful and popular. EG *The show was a smash hit in London and New York.* N SING OR N MOD

7 A **smash** is also a car crash. EG *She had a serious motor smash on the way to Scotland.* N COUNT Informal

8 See also **smashed, smashing.**

smash up. If you **smash** something **up**, you completely destroy it by hitting it and breaking it into many pieces. EG *He started smashing up all the furniture.* PHRASAL VB : V+O+ADV

smashed /smæʃt/. Someone who is **smashed** is extremely drunk. ADJ PRED Informal

smashing /smæʃɪŋ/. If you describe something as **smashing**, you mean that you like it very much. EG *We had a smashing time.* ADJ QUALIT Informal

smattering /smætəⁿrɪŋ/. A **smattering** of knowledge or information is a very small amount of it. EG *Jane spoke Spanish, and a smattering of Greek.* N PART : SING

smear /smɪə/, **smears, smearing, smeared. 1** A **smear** is a dirty or greasy mark caused by something rubbing against a surface. EG *...a smear of blue paint.* N COUNT

2 To **smear** something means to make dirty or greasy marks on it. EG *Soot smeared our faces... The windows were all smeared.* V+O

3 If you **smear** a surface with a greasy or sticky substance or **smear** the substance onto the surface, you spread a layer of the substance over the surface. EG *Smear the baking tin with butter... She smeared this blood onto a slide.* V+O+A

4 A **smear** is also an unpleasant and untrue rumour or accusation that is intended to damage someone's reputation. EG *Party leaders denounced the allegation as a right-wing smear.* N COUNT

smell /smɛl/, **smells, smelling, smelled, smelt** /smɛlt/. The forms **smelled** and **smelt** are both used as the past tense and past participle of the verb.

1 The **smell** of something is the effect that it has on your nose; used especially when the effect is unpleasant. EG *What's that smell?... ...the smell of fresh bread... The air had a sweet smell... ...cooking smells.* N COUNT

2 If something **smells**, it has an effect on your V : OFT+*of/ like* OR V+C

nose. EG *The room smelled of cigars... Our kitchen smelt like a rubber factory... The papers smelt musty and stale... Dinner smells good.*

3 If you **smell** something, **3.1** you become aware of it because of the effect it has on your nose. EG *Don't strike a match if you smell gas.* **3.2** you put your nose near it and breathe in, in order to discover its smell. EG *She picked up the soap and smelled it.* V+O

4 Smell is the ability that your nose has. EG *They all have an excellent sense of smell.* N UNCOUNT

5 If you **smell** something such as danger or trouble, you feel instinctively that it is likely to happen. EG *He's shrewd and can smell a successful project.* ● If you **smell a rat**, you become suspicious that there is something wrong. EG *I accepted with suspicious gratitude. I could smell a rat.* V+O : NO CONT ● PHRASE

smelly /smɛlɪ¹/. Something that is **smelly** has an unpleasant smell. EG *...some rather smelly cheese.* ADJ QUALIT

smile /smaɪl/, **smiles, smiling, smiled. 1** When you **smile** because you are pleased or amused or are being friendly, the corners of your mouth curve upwards and you sometimes show your teeth. EG *Hooper smiled and leaned back in his chair... The girl was smiling at me.* V

2 A **smile** is the expression that you have on your face when you smile. EG *Barber welcomed me with a smile... ...a mocking, unpleasant smile.* N COUNT

3 If you **smile** something, you say it with a smile or express it by a smile. EG *'That remains to be seen,' smiled Mrs Barrett... She smiled her approval.* V+O OR V+QUOTE

smirk /smɜːk/, **smirks, smirking, smirked.** If you **smirk**, you smile in an unpleasant way. EG *'That's where you're wrong,' Ellen said, smirking.* ▸ used as a noun. EG *Mark detected a smirk on the clerk's face.* V ▸ N COUNT

smock /smɒk/, **smocks.** A **smock** is a loose garment, rather like a long blouse, usually worn by women. N COUNT

smog /smɒg/ is a mixture of fog and smoke which occurs in some busy industrial cities. EG *Black smog reduced visibility to about fifty yards.* N UNCOUNT

smoke /sməʊk/, **smokes, smoking, smoked. 1 Smoke** consists of gas and small bits of solid material that are sent into the air when something burns. EG *The room was full of smoke... ...cigarette smoke.* N UNCOUNT

2 If something **is smoking**, smoke is coming from it. EG *Down below in the valleys the chimneys were smoking.* V

3 When someone **smokes** a cigarette, pipe, or cigar, they have it in their mouth, sucking the smoke into their mouth and blowing it out again. EG *He was sitting quietly in his armchair, smoking a pipe... He sat and smoked and stared out of the window.* V+O OR V

4 If you **smoke**, you have the habit of smoking cigarettes, or perhaps a pipe. EG *Do you smoke?* ◇ **smoker, smokers.** EG *One smoker in 20 will give up the habit permanently... ...a pipe smoker.* V ◇ N COUNT

5 To **smoke** fish or meat means to hang it over burning wood so that the smoke will preserve it and give it a special flavour. ◇ **smoked.** EG *...smoked salmon.* V+O ◇ ADJ CLASSIF : ATTRIB

smokeless /sməʊklɪ²s/. **Smokeless** fuel burns without producing smoke. ADJ CLASSIF : ATTRIB

smoking /sməʊkɪŋ/. **1 Smoking** is the act or habit of smoking cigarettes or other forms of tobacco. EG *Does smoking cause cancer?... I'm trying to give up smoking.* N UNCOUNT

2 A **smoking** section or compartment is intended for people who want to smoke. EG *Do you want to go in the smoking or non-smoking section?* ADJ CLASSIF : ATTRIB

What is the difference between smirk and smile?

smoky /sməʊki[1]/. **1** A place that is **smoky** has a ADJ QUALIT lot of smoke in the air. EG *...a smoky industrial scene of the 1930's.*

2 You can also use **smoky** to describe something ADJ CLASSIF: that looks like smoke, for example because it is ATTRIB slightly blue or grey or because it appears cloudy. EG *...the smoky twilight.*

smolder /sməʊldə/. See **smoulder**.

smooth /smuːð/, **smoother**, **smoothest**; **smooths**, **smoothing**, **smoothed**. **1** A **smooth** ADJ QUALIT surface has no roughness, lumps, or holes. EG *Your skin looks so smooth... The boulders were so smooth and slippery I couldn't get a grip.*

2 A **smooth** liquid or mixture has been mixed well ADJ QUALIT so that it is without lumps. EG *...a smooth paste.*

3 If you **smooth** something, you move your hands V+O over its surface to make it smooth and flat. EG *Don't iron pyjamas. Just smooth and fold them... He turned his head and smoothed back the hair over one temple.*

4 A **smooth** movement or process happens or is ADJ QUALIT done evenly and steadily with no sudden changes or breaks. EG *He walked with a long, smooth stride.*

◊ **smoothly**. EG *The snake glides smoothly towards* ◊ ADV *it.*

5 A **smooth** ride, flight, or sea crossing is very ADJ QUALIT comfortable because there are no bumps or jolts.

6 You use **smooth** to describe something that is ADJ QUALIT going well and is free of problems or trouble. EG *Cooperation is essential if you are going to lead a smooth existence in the office.* ◊ **smoothly**. EG *Life* ◊ ADV *is running smoothly for them.*

7 A man who is **smooth** is extremely smart, ADJ QUALIT confident, and polite, especially in a way that you find rather unpleasant.

8 If you **smooth the path** or **smooth the way** of PHRASE something, you make it easier or more likely to happen. EG *Goodwill and cooperation can go a long way towards smoothing your way to the top.*

smooth out. If you **smooth** something **out**, you PHRASAL VB: move your hands over its surface to make it V+O+ADV smooth and flat. EG *I started smoothing out the tablecloth.*

smooth over. If you **smooth over** a problem or PHRASAL VB: difficulty, you make it less serious and easier to V+ADV+O deal with, especially by talking to the people concerned. EG *I tried to smooth over the awkwardness of this first meeting.*

smother /smʌðə/, **smothers**, **smothering**, **smothered**. **1** If you **smother** a fire, you cover it V+O with something in order to put it out. EG *She grabbed a blanket to smother the flames.*

2 To **smother** someone means to kill them by V+O covering their face with something so that they cannot breathe.

3 Things that **smother** something cover it com- V+O: pletely. EG *White roses smothered the apple tree...* OFT+with/in *She smothered him with kisses.* ◊ **smothered**. EG ◊ ADJ PRED: *The pear tree was smothered in ivy... ...bonnets* OFT+with/in *smothered with sequins.*

4 If you **smother** someone, you show your love for V+O: them too much and protect them too much. EG *She* OFT+with *should love them without smothering them with attention.*

5 If you **smother** an emotion or emotional reac- V+O tion, you control it so that people do not notice it. EG *I turned away and tried to smother my sobs.*

smoulder /sməʊldə/, **smoulders**, **smouldering**, **smouldered**; spelled **smolder** in American English. **1** If something **smoulders**, it burns slowly, V producing smoke but not flames. EG *The ruins are still smouldering.*

2 If anger or hatred **is smouldering** within you, V you continue to feel it but rarely show it. EG *Inside* Literary *me was a smouldering anger at what he had done.*

smudge /smʌdʒ/, **smudges**, **smudging**, **smudged**. **1** A **smudge** is a dirty mark caused by N COUNT rubbing a powder or a wet substance onto some-

thing. EG *He had a smudge of flour on his face... The wallpaper had smudges all over it.*

2 If you **smudge** something, you make it dirty or V+O: OFT+O messy by touching it or putting a mark on it. EG *I'm not allowed to kiss her in case I smudge her lipstick... Her cheeks were smudged with tears.*

smug /smʌg/. Someone who is **smug** is very ADJ QUALIT pleased with how good or clever they are; used showing disapproval. EG *...looks of smug satisfaction.* ◊ **smugly**. EG *'I know all that,' I said smugly.* ◊ ADV ◊ **smugness**. EG *'That,' I said with pardonable* ◊ N UNCOUNT *smugness, 'happens to be mine.'*

smuggle /smʌgə[0]l/, **smuggles**, **smuggling**, V+O: USU+A **smuggled**. If someone **smuggles** things or people into a country or place or out of it, they take them there illegally or secretly. EG *She smuggled these diamond bracelets out... ...smuggling refugees into the country.* ◊ **smuggler**, **smugglers**. EG *...hunt-* ◊ N COUNT *ing drug smugglers.*

snack /snæk/, **snacks**. A **snack** is a small, quick N COUNT meal, or something which you eat between meals. EG *Sardines can be served on toast as a delicious snack... We ate a snack supper in a pub.*

snack bar, **snack bars**. A **snack bar** is a place N COUNT where you can buy small meals such as sandwiches, and also drinks.

snag /snæg/, **snags**, **snagging**, **snagged**. **1** A N COUNT **snag** is a small problem or disadvantage. EG *It cleans very effectively. The only snag is that it dissolves plastics.*

2 If you **snag** part of your clothing on a sharp or V+O: rough object, it gets caught on the object and tears. OFT+on/with EG *I snagged my best skirt on a bramble.*

snail /sneɪl/, **snails**. A **snail** is a small animal N COUNT with a long, slimy body and a spiral-shaped shell. Snails move very slowly.

snake /sneɪk/, **snakes**, **snaking**, **snaked**. **1** A N COUNT **snake** is a long, thin reptile with no legs. EG *He was bitten by a poisonous snake.*

2 Something that **snakes** in a particular direction V+A goes in that direction in a line with a lot of bends. Literary EG *The procession snaked round the houses.*

snap /snæp/, **snaps**, **snapping**, **snapped**. **1** If V-ERG something **snaps** or if you **snap** it, it breaks suddenly, usually with a sharp cracking noise. EG *The rope snapped... One of those kicks could snap you in half like a dry twig.* ▶ used as a noun. EG *The* ▶ N SING *snap of a twig broke the silence.*

2 If you **snap** something into a particular position V-ERG+A or if it **snaps** into that position, it moves quickly into that position, with a sharp sound. EG *She snapped the silver chain around her neck... The jaws snapped shut around her arm.* ▶ used as a ▶ N SING noun. EG *The trap closes with a sudden snap.*

3 If you **snap** your **fingers**, you make a sharp PHRASE sound by moving your middle finger quickly across your thumb, for example in order to attract someone's attention. EG *He snapped his fingers in the air and cried, 'Waiter!'*

4 If a dog or other animal **snaps** at you, it shuts its V: OFT+at jaws quickly near you. EG *The dogs ran snapping and barking at his heels.*

5 If someone **snaps** at you, they speak to you in a V+at OR sharp, unfriendly way. EG *'Don't do that!' she* V+QUOTE *snapped.*

6 A **snap** decision or action is one that you take ADJ CLASSIF: suddenly, without thinking about it carefully. EG ATTRIB *The snap reaction of the press was to welcome the change... The strike led to a snap election.*

7 A **snap** is a photograph that is taken quickly and N COUNT casually. EG *I had taken dozens of snaps of Daisy.* Informal

8 If someone who is depressed **snaps out of it**, PHRASE they suddenly become more cheerful, especially by making an effort. EG *Come on, snap out of it!*

snap up. If you **snap** something **up**, you buy it PHRASAL VB: quickly because it is a bargain or because it is just V+O+ADV what you want. EG *All these houses were snapped up as soon as they were offered for sale.*

snapshot /ˈsnæpʃɒt/, **snapshots.** A **snapshot** is a N COUNT photograph that is taken quickly and casually. EG ...*family snapshots.*

snare /sneə/, **snares.** A **snare** is a trap for N COUNT catching birds or small animals. It consists of a loop of wire or rope which pulls tight around the animal. EG ...*a rabbit snare.*

snarl /snɑːl/, **snarls, snarling, snarled. 1** When V an animal **snarls**, it makes a fierce, rough sound in its throat while showing its teeth. EG ...*dogs snarling and snapping at the heels of sheep.* ▸ used as a ▸ N COUNT noun. EG *The leopard gave a snarl of fury.*
2 If you **snarl**, you say something in a fierce, angry V : OFT+QUOTE way. EG '*Let me alone,*' *I snarled.*

snatch /snætʃ/, **snatches, snatching, snatched.**
1 If you **snatch** something or **snatch** at it, you take V+O OR V+at it or pull it away quickly. EG *He snatched the letter from the man's hand... He remembered snatching at his gun.*
2 If you **snatch** a small amount of time or an V+O opportunity, you quickly make use of it. EG *I packed, then snatched four hours' sleep... She snatched a brief time alone with him... I snatched the opportunity to tell them that I was leaving.*
3 A **snatch** of a conversation or a song is a very N COUNT small piece of it. EG ...*listening to snatches of* OR N PART *overheard conversation.*

sneak /sniːk/, **sneaks, sneaking, sneaked. 1** If V+A you **sneak** somewhere, you go there very quietly on foot, trying to avoid being seen or heard. EG *I didn't notice Bob sneaking up behind me.*
2 If you **sneak** something somewhere, you take it V+O+A there secretly. EG *Eugene would sneak food down to his room... I tried to sneak a blanket away.*
3 If you **sneak** a look at someone or something, V+O+A you secretly have a quick look at them.
4 A **sneak** preview of something is an unofficial N COUNT opportunity to look at it before it is officially shown to the public. EG *We were shown his latest master-piece in a sneak preview.*
5 A **sneak** is someone who tells people in authority N COUNT that someone else has done something naughty or Informal wrong; used showing disapproval. EG *He has ac-quired a reputation as a sneak.*

sneaker /ˈsniːkə/, **sneakers. Sneakers** are casual N COUNT : shoes with rubber soles. USU PLURAL

sneaking /ˈsniːkɪŋ/. If you have a **sneaking** feel- ADJ CLASSIF : ing about something or someone, you are rather ATTRIB ashamed or unwilling to have this feeling. EG *His book leaves one with a sneaking admiration for his shameless commercialism... I have a sneaking suspicion you're right.*

sneaky /ˈsniːkiˈ/. Someone who is **sneaky** does ADJ QUALIT things secretly rather than openly; used showing Informal disapproval. EG *I had a sneaky glimpse at the list.*

sneer /snɪə/, **sneers, sneering, sneered.** If you V : OFT+at **sneer** at someone or something, you express your OR QUOTE contempt for them by the expression on your face or by what you say. EG *She was afraid he would sneer at the idea.* ▸ used as a noun. EG '*Oh yes,*' *said* ▸ N COUNT *McFee, a sneer flitting over his face.*

sneeze /sniːz/, **sneezes, sneezing, sneezed. 1** V When you **sneeze**, you suddenly take in your breath and then blow it down your nose noisily. People sneeze a lot when they have a cold. ▸ used ▸ N COUNT as a noun. EG ...*the sound of coughs and sneezes.*
2 If you say that something **is not to be sneezed** PHRASE **at**, you mean that it is worth having. EG *The* Informal *pension from the university was small but not to be sneezed at.*

snide /snaɪd/. A **snide** comment or remark is one ADJ QUALIT which criticizes someone nastily, often in an indi-rect, sarcastic way. EG *There were one or two snide comments about my family.*

sniff /snɪf/, **sniffs, sniffing, sniffed. 1** When you V **sniff**, you breathe in air through your nose hard enough to make a sound, for example when you are trying not to cry, or in order to show disapprov-al or scorn. EG *Felicity said, sniffing, 'When will you*

see me again?' ▸ used as a noun. EG *She gave a* ▸ N COUNT *bitter sniff... The classroom rang with coughs, sniffs, and sneezes.*
2 If you **sniff** something, you smell it by sniffing. EG V+O OR V+A '*What a revolting smell,*' *he said, sniffing the air... The dog sniffed at Marsha's bags.* ▸ used as a noun. ▸ N COUNT EG *He cracked the seal on the bottle and took a cautious sniff.*
3 If you **sniff** something such as glue, you deliber- V+O ately breathe it in as a drug. EG ...*glue sniffing.*

sniff out. If you **sniff** something **out**, you discov- PHRASAL VB : er it after some searching. EG *I ordered the Central* V+O+ADV *Office to sniff out a suitable job for him.* Informal

sniffle /ˈsnɪfəl/, **sniffles, sniffling, sniffled.** If V you **are sniffling**, you keep sniffing, for example because you have a cold.

snigger /ˈsnɪgə/, **sniggers, sniggering, snig-** V **gered.** If you **snigger**, you laugh quietly and disrespectfully, for example at something rude. EG *What are you sniggering at?* ▸ used as a noun. EG ▸ N COUNT *His sniggers became uncontrollable.*

snip /snɪp/, **snips, snipping, snipped.** If you **snip** V : OFT+A, off part of something, you cut it off with scissors or OR V+O shears in a single quick action. EG *Brian snipped energetically at the hedge... He took out a cigar and, after snipping off the end, lit it.*

snipe /snaɪp/, **snipes, sniping, sniped. 1** If some- V : OFT+at one **snipes** at you, they criticize you. EG *The unions are an easy target to snipe at.*
2 To **snipe** at someone also means to shoot at V : OFT+at them from a hidden position. EG *Just then someone started sniping at us.* ◇ **sniper, snipers.** EG *A* ◇ N COUNT *sniper's bullet tore up a wall two inches above his head.*

snippet /ˈsnɪpɪt/, **snippets.** A **snippet** of informa- N PART OR tion, news, or gossip is a small piece of it. EG N COUNT *Occasionally children come out with absolutely fascinating snippets of information.*

snivel /ˈsnɪvəl/, **snivels, snivelling, snivelled;** V spelled **sniveling, sniveled** in American English. If someone **is snivelling**, they are crying and sniffing in a way that irritates you.

snob /snɒb/, **snobs.** A **snob** is **1** someone who N COUNT admires upper-class people and despises lower-class people; used showing disapproval. **2** someone N COUNT+SUPP who believes that they are superior to other people because of their intelligence or taste; used showing disapproval. EG *You were always an intellectual snob.*

snobbery /ˈsnɒbəriˈ/ is the attitude of a snob; N UNCOUNT used showing disapproval. EG *Social snobbery reached a peak in the last century... There used to be a kind of snobbery in England about Central European writing.*

snobbish /ˈsnɒbɪʃ/. Someone who is **snobbish** is ADJ QUALIT too proud of their social status, intelligence, or taste. EG *She was too snobbish to mix with her neighbours... She had a snobbish attitude towards the theatre.*

snog /snɒg/, **snogs, snogging, snogged.** When V OR V+with : two people **snog**, they kiss and cuddle each other RECIP for a period of time. EG ...*snogging in the dark.* Informal ▸ used as a noun. EG *They went outside for a quiet* ▸ N SING *snog.*

snooker /ˈsnuːkə/ is a game involving balls on a N UNCOUNT large table. The players use a long stick to hit a white ball, and score points by knocking coloured balls into the pockets at the sides of the table.

snoop /snuːp/, **snoops, snooping, snooped.** Some- V : USU+A one who **is snooping** is secretly looking round a place in order to find out things. EG *He might have been killed simply for snooping around where he wasn't welcome.*

snooty /ˈsnuːtiˈ/. Someone who is **snooty** behaves ADJ QUALIT as if they are superior to other people; used

> Which words on these pages name noises you can make with your nose and mouth?

showing disapproval. EG *She is beautiful but snooty... I got a very snooty letter from them rejecting my application.*

snooze /snuːz/, **snoozes, snoozing, snoozed.** A **snooze** is a short, light sleep, especially during the day. EG *I've just had a nice snooze.* ▸ used as a verb. ▸ v EG *I lay on the sofa, snoozing.*   N SING : a+N Informal

snore /snɔː/, **snores, snoring, snored.** When v someone who is asleep **snores**, they make a loud noise each time they breathe. EG *He snored loudly on the camp-bed.* ▸ used as a noun. EG *I could hear* ▸ N COUNT *heavy snores coming from the bedroom.*

snorkel /snɔːkəⁱl/, **snorkels.** A **snorkel** is a tube N COUNT through which a person swimming just under the surface of the sea can breathe.

snorkelling /snɔːkəⁱlɪŋ/; spelled **snorkeling** in N ING American English. If you go **snorkelling**, you swim underwater using a snorkel.

snort /snɔːt/, **snorts, snorting, snorted. 1** When v people or animals **snort**, they breathe air noisily out through their noses. People snort in order to express contempt, disapproval, or amusement. EG *The pigs grunted and snorted... My sister snorted with laughter.* ▸ used as a noun. EG *Clarissa gave a* ▸ N COUNT *snort of disgust.*

2 If someone **snorts** something, they say it with a v+QUOTE snort. EG *'Garbage!' Eddie snorted.*

snout /snaʊt/, **snouts.** The **snout** of an animal N COUNT such as a pig is its long nose.

snow /snəʊ/, **snows, snowing, snowed. 1 Snow** N UNCOUNT consists of a lot of soft white bits of frozen water that fall from the sky in cold weather. EG *Outside the snow lay thick on the ground... Two inches of snow fell in London.* ▸ used as a plural noun. EG ▸ N PLURAL : *...driving down from the snows of the Alps... ...the* the+N *winter snows.*   Literary

2 When it **snows**, snow falls from the sky. EG *It was* v *snowing quite heavily.* ● See also **snowed in**, **snowed under**.

snowball /snəʊbɔːl/, **snowballs, snowballing, snowballed. 1** A **snowball** is a ball of snow. N COUNT Children often throw snowballs at each other.

2 If something such as a project or campaign v **snowballs**, it rapidly increases and grows. EG *The strike movement snowballed into a nationwide general strike.*

snowbound /snəʊbaʊnd/. If people or vehicles ADJ CLASSIF are **snowbound**, they cannot go anywhere because of heavy snow.

snowdrift /snəʊdrɪft/, **snowdrifts.** A **snowdrift** N COUNT is a deep pile of snow formed by the wind.

snowdrop /snəʊdrɒp/, **snowdrops.** A **snowdrop** N COUNT is a small white flower which appears in the early spring.

snowed in. If you are **snowed in** or **snowed up**, ADJ PRED you cannot go anywhere because of heavy snow. EG *Perhaps we'll be snowed in for a week.*

snowed under. If you are **snowed under**, you ADJ PRED have a large amount of work to deal with, especially paperwork. EG *At present we are snowed under with work.*

snowflake /snəʊfleɪk/, **snowflakes.** A **snow-** N COUNT **flake** is one of the soft, white bits of frozen water that fall as snow. EG *...snowflakes melting in her hair.*

snowman /snəʊmæn/, **snowmen.** A **snowman** is N COUNT a large shape made out of snow, especially by children, which is supposed to look like a person.

snowplough /snəʊplaʊ/, **snowploughs;** spelled N COUNT **snowplow** in American English. A **snowplough** is a vehicle which is used to push snow off roads or railway lines.

snowy /snəʊiⁱ/. Something that is **snowy** has a lot ADJ QUALIT of snow. EG *...two high snowy peaks... ...snowy streets... I went to see him one snowy day in London.*

snub /snʌb/, **snubs, snubbing, snubbed.** If you v+o **snub** someone, you deliberately insult them by ignoring them or by behaving rudely towards

them. EG *Both she and her husband were snubbed by the intellectuals they knew.* ▸ used as a noun. EG ▸ N COUNT *But George was impervious to snubs.*

snub-nosed. Someone who is **snub-nosed** has a ADJ CLASSIF short nose which points slightly upwards.

snuff /snʌf/ is powdered tobacco which people N UNCOUNT take by sniffing it up their nose. EG *...a snuff box.*

snuffle /snʌfəⁱl/, **snuffles, snuffling, snuffled.** If v people or animals **snuffle**, they make sniffing noises. EG *Brian snuffled into his handkerchief... ...snuffling pigs.*

snug /snʌg/. **1** If you are **snug**, you feel warm and ADJ QUALIT comfortable. EG *We lit a big fire which made us feel very snug and safe.* ◊ **snugly.** EG *Jamie was snugly* ◊ ADV *wrapped in a white woollen scarf.*

2 If a place is **snug**, it is warm and comfortable. EG ADJ QUALIT *It was warm and dry in his snug studio.*

3 Something that is **snug** fits very closely or ADJ QUALIT tightly. EG *...snug overcoats.* ◊ **snugly.** EG *The* ◊ ADV *metal box fitted snugly into the bottom.*

snuggle /snʌgəⁱl/, **snuggles, snuggling, snug-** v+A **gled.** If you **snuggle** somewhere, you settle yourself into a warm, comfortable position, especially by moving closer to another person. EG *He turned over to snuggle close to her.*

so /səʊ/. **1** You use **so 1.1** when you are referring ADV back to something that has just been mentioned. EG *Do you enjoy romantic films? If so, you should watch the film on ITV tonight... 'Is there anything else you want to tell me about?' – 'I don't think so.'... The issue is unresolved, and will remain so until the next SDP Congress.* **1.2** when you are ADV SEN agreeing with a statement that has just been made. EG *'The phone isn't working.' – 'So I see.'*

2 If you say that a state of affairs **is so**, you mean PHRASE that it is the way that it has been described. EG *It is worth knowing just why this is so.*

3 If you say that one person or thing does some- ADV SEN thing and **so** does another one, you mean that the second person or thing does it too. EG *Etta laughed heartily and so did he... His shoes are brightly polished; so is his briefcase.*

4 You use **so** and **so that** to introduce something CONJ that happens because of the situation you have just mentioned. EG *He speaks very little English, so I talked to him through an interpreter... The door was open, so that anyone passing could look in.*

5 You use **so that** and **so as** to introduce the CONJ reason for doing the thing that you have just mentioned. EG *He has to earn lots of money so that he can buy his children nice food and clothes... They went on foot, so as not to be heard.*

6 You say **'So?'** and **'So what?'** to indicate that you CONVENTION think that something that someone has said is Informal unimportant. EG *'Someone will see us.' – 'So what?'*

7 You can use **so** in a discussion or talk when you ADV SEN are checking that you have correctly understood something, when you are summarizing something, or when you are moving on to a new stage. EG *So it wasn't just an accident?... And so for now, good-night... So what are the advantages of nuclear energy?*

8 You can also use **so** when you are saying that ADV something is done or arranged in the way that you describe. EG *They have the eyes so located as to give a wide field of vision... The others are moving right to left, like so.*

9 You use the structures **as...so** and **just as...so** when you want to indicate that two events or situations are alike in some way. EG *Just as one gesture can have many different meanings, so many different gestures can have the same mean-ing... As with the railways, so with coal.*

10 You use **and so on** or **and so forth** at the end PHRASE of a list to indicate that there are other items that you could also mention. EG *You can program a computer to paint, play chess and so on.*

11 You use **or so** when you are giving an approxi- PHRASE mate amount. EG *We arrived a month or so ago.*

12 You can also use **so** to describe or emphasize ADV the degree or extent of something. EG *I'm so glad you could come... Don't go so fast... The objection is so fundamental and so widely accepted that it needs to be answered in detail... Carrying the weight was not so difficult.*

13 You can use **so** before words such as 'much' and 'many' when you are saying that there is a definite limit to something but you are not saying what this limit is. EG *We will only pay so much, no more... ...an old friend with only so long to live.*

14 You use the structures **not so much** and **not so** PHRASE **much...as** to say that something is one kind of thing rather than another kind. EG *...a cry not so much of pain as of amazement.*

15 ever so: see **ever**. ● **so far**, **so far as**: see **far**. ● **so long**, **so long as**: see **long**. ● **so much for**: see **much**. ● **every so often**: see **often**. ● **so there**: see **there**.

soak /səʊk/, **soaks, soaking, soaked. 1** When you V-ERG **soak** something or leave it to **soak**, you put it into a liquid and leave it there. EG *'Can I help you with the dishes?' – 'Oh, I'll just leave them to soak.'... Soak the material for several hours in cold water... ...breadcrumbs soaked in red wine.*

2 When a liquid **soaks** something, it makes it very V+O wet. EG *A stream of water came in and soaked both sleeping bags.*

3 When a liquid **soaks** through something, it passes V+A through it. EG *The blood had soaked through the handkerchief.*

soak up. When a soft or dry substance **soaks up** PHRASAL VB : a liquid, the liquid goes into the substance. EG *The* V+O+ADV *soil soaked up a huge volume of water.*

soaked /səʊkt/. If someone or something gets ADJ PRED **soaked**, they get extremely wet. EG *It was pouring down and we all got soaked... His beret was soaked.*

soaking /səʊkɪŋ/. If something is **soaking** or ADJ CLASSIF **soaking wet**, it is very wet. EG *My boots were soaking wet inside.*

so-and-so, so-and-sos. 1 You use **so-and-so** in- N UNCOUNT stead of a name or word when you are indicating Informal the sort of thing that is usually said or done and are not bothering to give a specific name or example. EG *What happens is that somebody will phone me and say, 'Mrs So-and-So would like a visit.'*

2 You call someone a **so-and-so** when you are N COUNT annoyed with them. Informal

soap /səʊp/, **soaps, soaping, soaped. 1 Soap** is a N MASS substance that you use with water for washing yourself or sometimes for washing clothes. EG *...a bar of yellow soap... Soap and towels were provided.*

2 If you **soap** yourself, you rub soap on your body V.REFL in order to wash yourself. EG *She soaped herself all over.*

3 A **soap** is the same as a soap opera. N COUNT

soap opera, soap operas. A **soap opera** is a N COUNT popular television drama serial about the daily lives and problems of a group of people.

soapy /səʊpɪ/. Something that is **soapy** is full of ADJ QUALIT soap or covered with soap. EG *Wash your brushes in warm soapy water.*

soar /sɔː/, **soars, soaring, soared. 1** If an amount V : OFT **soars**, it quickly increases by a great deal. EG +from/to *Property prices have soared... Rice production soared from 694,000 tons to 913,000.*

2 If something **soars** into the air, it goes quickly up V : USU+A into the air. EG *Flames were soaring into the sky.*

3 Trees or buildings that **soar** upwards are very V+A tall. ◊ **soaring**. EG *...the soaring spire of St* ◊ ADJ CLASSIF : *Patrick's... ...soaring tree trunks.* ATTRIB

4 If music **soars**, it rises greatly in volume or pitch. V EG *Her voice soared into a girlish treble.*

◊ **soaring**. EG *...the soaring, triumphant horn notes.* ◊ ADJ CLASSIF

sob /sɒb/, **sobs, sobbing, sobbed. 1** When some- V one **sobs**, they cry in a noisy way, breathing in short breaths. EG *She was sobbing bitterly.*

◊ **sobbing**. EG *The sobbing began again.* ◊ N UNCOUNT

2 If you **sob** something, you say it at the same time V+QUOTE as you are crying. EG *'It hurts!' sobbed Patty.*

3 A **sob** is one of the noises that you make when N COUNT you are crying. EG *She began to weep in gasping, choking sobs.*

sober /səʊbə/, **soberer, soberest; sobers, so- bering, sobered. 1** When you are **sober**, you are ADJ QUALIT not drunk. EG *Rudolph knew he had to stay sober to drive home.*

2 A **sober** person is serious and thoughtful. EG ADJ QUALIT *...sober and sensible attitudes.* ◊ **soberly**. EG ◊ ADV *'That's true,' Andy said soberly.*

3 Sober colours and clothes are plain and rather ADJ QUALIT : dull. EG *...a pair of sober black walking shoes.* ATTRIB ◊ **soberly**. EG *...a soberly dressed office employee.* ◊ ADV

sober up. When someone **sobers up**, they stop PHRASAL VB : being drunk. EG *When you sober up you may be* V+ADV ashamed of what you've done.

sobering /səʊbərɪŋ/. **Sobering** words, actions, or ADJ QUALIT ideas make you become serious. EG *His words had a sobering effect on Freddie... There was a more sobering thought: perhaps we should not succeed.*

sobriety /səˈbraɪɪti/ is serious and thoughtful N UNCOUNT behaviour. EG *...his mood of sobriety.* Formal

so-called. You use **so-called 1** to indicate that ADJ CLASSIF : you think that a particular word is incorrect or USU ATTRIB misleading. EG *...her so-called friends... ...the so- called 'developed' countries.* **2** to indicate that Formal something is generally referred to by the name that you have used. EG *Why did the so-called Agricultural Revolution occur?*

soccer /sɒkə/ is the same as football. **Soccer** is N UNCOUNT not used to refer to American football.

sociable /səʊʃəbəl/. **Sociable** people are friendly ADJ QUALIT and enjoy talking to other people. EG *Adler was an outgoing, sociable kind of man.* ◊ **sociability** ◊ N UNCOUNT /səʊʃəbɪlɪti/. EG *There was no doubt about his sociability.*

social /səʊʃəl/. **1 Social** means **1.1** relating to ADJ CLASSIF : society or to the way society is organized. EG *...a* ATTRIB *particular culture and social structure... ...govern- ment social and economic policy... ...demands for modernisation and social change.* ◊ **socially**. EG ◊ ADV *...socially useful activities.* **1.2** relating to the status ADJ CLASSIF : or rank that someone has in society. EG *...children* ATTRIB *from different social backgrounds... He is com- pelled by social pressures to seek advancement.* ◊ **socially**. EG *They must behave in a way which* ◊ ADV *will be socially acceptable.* **1.3** relating to leisure ADJ CLASSIF : activities that involve meeting other people. EG USU ATTRIB *We've met at social and business functions... ...their circle of social contacts.* ◊ **socially**. EG *...the only* ◊ ADV *people my father ever visited socially.*

2 Social animals live in groups and do things ADJ CLASSIF : together. EG *...social animals such as hyenas and* ATTRIB *wolves.*

socialise /səʊʃəlaɪz/. See **socialize**.

socialism /səʊʃəlɪzəm/ is a set of left-wing politi- N UNCOUNT cal principles based on the belief that the state should own industries on behalf of the people and that everyone should be equal.

socialist /səʊʃəlɪst/, **socialists. 1 Socialist** ADJ CLASSIF means based on socialism or relating to socialism. EG *...a Labour government with socialist policies... ...the French Socialist Party.*

2 A **socialist** is a person who believes in socialism N COUNT or who is a member of a socialist party.

socialize /səʊʃəlaɪz/, **socializes, socializing, so-** V : OFT+*with* **cialized**; also spelled **socialise**. If you **socialize**, you meet other people socially, for example at parties. EG *I socialized with the philosophy students.*

◊ **socializing**. EG *...people who do all their* ◊ N UNCOUNT *socialising in pubs.*

If you socialize, are you sociable or a socialist?

social life, social lives. Your **social life** consists N COUNT OR
of the activities in which you meet your friends and N UNCOUNT
acquaintances, for example at parties. EG ...busy,
competent people, with active social lives.

social science, social sciences. 1 Social sci- N UNCOUNT
ence is the scientific study of society.

2 The **social sciences** are the various branches of N COUNT :
social science. EG Economics is the oldest of the USU PLURAL
social sciences.

social scientist, social scientists. A **social** N COUNT
scientist is a person who studies or teaches social
science.

social security is a system by which the govern- N UNCOUNT
ment pays money regularly to people who have no
other income or only a very small income. EG
...social security benefits.

social services. The **social services** in a dis- N PLURAL
trict are the services provided by the local authority to help people who have social and financial
problems or needs. EG ...major cuts in social services... ...the local social services department.

social work is work which involves giving help N UNCOUNT
and advice to people with serious financial problems or family problems.

social worker, social workers. A **social work-** N COUNT
er is a person whose job is to do social work.

society /səsaɪətɪ¹/, **societies. 1** Society is the N UNCOUNT
people in a country, who have a particular way of OR N COUNT
life. EG ...society's attitude towards the elderly...
...the role of women in Western society... We live in
a multi-racial society.

2 A **society** is also an organization for people who N COUNT
have the same interest or aim. EG I'm on the
committee of the local film society... ...the Royal
Horticultural Society.

sociology /səʊsɪɒlədʒi¹/ is the study of human N UNCOUNT
societies. EG ...sociology students. ◊ **sociological.** ◊ ADJ CLASSIF :
EG ...sociological studies of criminals... ...sociological ATTRIB
issues. ◊ **sociologist** /səʊsɪɒlədʒɪst/, **sociologists.** ◊ N COUNT
EG This is what sociologists have been saying for
years.

sock /sɒk/, **socks. 1** Socks are pieces of clothing N COUNT
which cover your foot and ankle and are worn
inside shoes. See picture at CLOTHES. EG ...a pair of
light-blue wool socks.

2 If you tell someone to **pull** their **socks up**, you PHRASE
mean that they should start working or studying Informal
harder, because they have been lazy or careless British
recently.

socket /sɒkɪt/, **sockets. 1** A socket is a place on a N COUNT
wall or on a piece of electrical equipment into
which you can put a plug or bulb. EG I put a bulb in
the lamp socket.

2 You can refer to any hollow part or opening in a N COUNT :
structure which another part fits into as a **socket**. USU+SUPP
EG ...deep eye sockets... ...the hip socket.

soda /səʊdə/, **sodas. Soda** is the same as soda N MASS
water. EG ...a whisky and soda.

soda siphon, soda siphons; also spelled **soda** N COUNT
syphon. A **soda siphon** is a special bottle from
which you can squirt soda water into a drink.

soda water is fizzy water used for mixing with N UNCOUNT
alcoholic drinks and fruit juice.

sodden /sɒdə⁰n/. Something that is **sodden** is ADJ QUALIT
extremely wet. EG Her slippers were sodden.

sofa /səʊfə/, **sofas.** A **sofa** is a long, comfortable N COUNT
seat with a back and usually with arms, which two
or three people can sit on.

soft /sɒft/, **softer, softest. 1** Something that is
soft 1.1 changes shape or bends easily when you ADJ QUALIT
press it. EG ...a soft bed... His feet left prints in the
soft soil. **1.2** is pleasant to touch, and not rough or ADJ QUALIT
hard. EG ...soft black fur... Her skin was soft and
white. ◊ **softness.** EG ...the softness of her arms.

1.3 is very gentle and has no force. EG ...a soft ADJ QUALIT
breeze. ◊ **softly.** EG Mike softly placed his hand on ◊ ADV
her shoulder.

2 A **soft** sound or voice is quiet and not harsh. EG ADJ QUALIT

She had a soft South German accent. ◊ **softly.** EG ◊ ADV
'Listen,' she said softly.

3 A **soft** light or colour is pleasant and restful to ADJ QUALIT
look at because it is not bright. EG ...the soft glow of
the evening light... ...walls in soft pink stone.

4 Someone who is **soft 4.1** is kind and cares about ADJ QUALIT
other people's feelings. EG He's got a very soft
heart. **4.2** is not strict enough or severe enough. EG
...the 'soft' approach to juvenile offenders... She's
kind to everyone without ever being soft about it.

5 Soft drugs are illegal drugs, such as marijuana, ADJ CLASSIF
which are not considered to be very strong or
harmful.

6 Soft is also used in these phrases. **6.1** If you **have** PHRASES
a soft spot for someone, you are especially fond Informal
of them. **6.2** If you describe someone as a **soft** Informal
touch, you mean that they can easily be persuaded
to lend you money or to do things for you. **6.3** If Informal
you say that someone is **soft in the head**, you
mean that they are silly.

soft drink, soft drinks. A **soft drink** is a cold, N COUNT
non-alcoholic drink such as lemonade or fruit juice.

soften /sɒfə⁰n/, **softens, softening, softened. 1** If V-ERG
something **is softened** or **softens**, it becomes less
hard, stiff, or firm. EG Fry the onions for about 10
minutes to soften them... ...the softened leather.

2 If something **softens** a shock or a damaging V+O
effect, it makes it seem less severe. EG He had
alcohol to soften the blow... ...the softening effect of
music.

3 If you **soften**, you become more sympathetic and V-ERG
less hostile or critical. EG 'I'm sorry about your
mother,' Ira said, softening... She gradually softened towards me... I refused to be softened.

4 If your expression **softens** or if something **sof-** V-ERG
tens it, it becomes much more gentle and friendly.
EG His mother's face softened a little.

soften up. If you **soften** someone **up**, you put PHRASAL VB :
them into a good mood before asking them to do V+O+ADV
something. EG I wondered if there was any hope of Informal
softening him up.

soft-hearted. Someone who is **soft-hearted** has ADJ QUALIT
a very sympathetic and kind nature.

soft-spoken. Someone who is **soft-spoken** has a ADJ QUALIT
quiet, gentle voice.

software /sɒftwɛə/. Computer programs are re- N UNCOUNT
ferred to as **software**. EG My job is writing the
software.

soggy /sɒgi¹/. Something that is **soggy** is unpleas- ADJ QUALIT
antly wet. EG ...a soggy dishcloth... ...soggy biscuits.

soil /sɔɪl/, **soils, soiling, soiled. 1** Soil is the N UNCOUNT
substance on the land surface of the earth in which
plants grow. EG The soil here is very fertile.

2 You use **soil** in expressions like 'British soil' to N UNCOUNT
refer to a country's territory. EG ...if no foreign +SUPP
armies had invaded Russian soil.

3 If you **soil** something, you make it dirty. EG She V+O
never soils her dainty fingers with a washing up
mop. ◊ **soiled.** EG ...a soiled handkerchief. ◊ ADJ QUALIT

solace /sɒlə³s/. **1** Solace is a feeling of comfort N UNCOUNT
that makes you feel less sad. EG He began to find Formal
solace in the Bible.

2 If something is a **solace** to you, it makes you feel N SING
less sad. EG Her poetry has always been a solace to Formal
me in times of stress.

solar /səʊlə/. **1** Solar is used to describe things ADJ CLASSIF :
relating to the sun. EG They accurately predicted ATTRIB
solar eclipses.

2 Solar power is obtained from the sun's light and ADJ CLASSIF :
heat. EG ...the potential of solar energy. ATTRIB

solar system. The **solar system** is the sun and N PROPER :
all the planets and comets that go round it. the+N

sold /səʊld/ is the past tense and past participle of
sell.

soldier /səʊldʒə/, **soldiers.** A **soldier** is a person N COUNT
in an army. EG These exits are guarded by soldiers.

sole /səʊl/, **soles. 1** The **sole** thing or person of a ADJ CLASSIF
particular type is the only one of that type. EG In ATTRIB
some families, the woman is the sole wage earn-

er... They went with the sole purpose of making a nuisance of themselves.

2 If you have **sole** charge or ownership of something, you are the only person in charge of it or who owns it. EG *She has the sole responsibility for bringing up the child... He acquired sole control of the newspaper in 1914.* ADJ CLASSIF: ATTRIB

3 The **sole** of your foot or of a shoe or sock is the underneath surface of it. EG *...holes in the soles of my shoes.* N COUNT

4 A **sole** is a kind of flat fish that you can eat. The plural can also be **sole**. N COUNT OR N UNCOUNT

solely /ˈsəʊllɪ/. If something involves **solely** one thing, it involves only this thing and no others. EG *This is solely a matter of money... The blame for this situation lies solely with the government.* ADV

solemn /ˈsɒləm/. **1** Someone or something that is **solemn** is very serious rather than cheerful or humorous. EG *The service of burial is one with solemn and mournful music... ...the solemn tones of Winston Churchill.* ◇ **solemnly.** EG *Ralph nodded solemnly.* ◇ **solemnity** /səˈlɛmnɪtɪ/. EG *...the solemnity of the occasion.* ADJ QUALIT ◇ ADV ◇ N UNCOUNT

2 A **solemn** promise or agreement is one that you make in a very formal, sincere way. EG *The government has solemn commitments and must honour them.* ◇ **solemnly.** EG *Jacob solemnly vowed to keep this promise.* ADJ CLASSIF: ATTRIB ◇ ADV

solicit /səˈlɪsɪt/, **solicits, soliciting, solicited. 1** If you **solicit** money, help, or an opinion from someone, you ask them for it. EG *We had to solicit contributions to pay off her debts... Roy solicited aid from a number of influential members.* V+O Formal

2 When prostitutes **solicit**, they offer to have sex with people in return for money. ◇ **soliciting.** EG *She's been fined £35 for soliciting.* V ◇ N UNCOUNT

solicitor /səˈlɪsɪtə/, **solicitors.** A **solicitor** is a lawyer who gives legal advice and prepares legal documents and cases. EG *I was advised to put the matter into the hands of a solicitor.* N COUNT

solicitous /səˈlɪsɪtəs/. A person who is **solicitous** shows anxious concern for someone. EG *The hotel personnel could not have been more solicitous.* ◇ **solicitously.** EG *'Now, Mr Gerran, you must take it easy,' I said solicitously.* ADJ QUALIT Formal ◇ ADV

solicitude /səˈlɪsɪtjuːd/. The **solicitude** that someone shows is their anxious concern for someone. EG *I was moved by their genuine kindness and solicitude for Karin.* N UNCOUNT Formal

solid /ˈsɒlɪd/, **solids. 1** A **solid** substance or object stays the same shape whether it is in a container or not, and is hard or firm. EG *The basic choice is gas, electricity, or solid fuel... ...a solid layer of earth... Even the sea around them is frozen solid.* ADJ CLASSIF

2 A **solid** is a substance that stays the same shape whether it is in a container or not. EG *You must at least know whether it's a solid or a liquid or a gas.* N COUNT

3 A **solid** object or mass does not have a space inside it, or holes or gaps in it. EG *...a solid-tyred bus... ...steps carved into the solid rock... The car park was packed solid.* ADJ CLASSIF

4 If an object is made of **solid** gold or **solid** oak, for example, it is made of gold or oak all the way through. EG *Is that bracelet really solid gold?* ADJ CLASSIF: ATTRIB

5 A structure that is **solid** is strong and is not likely to collapse or fall over. EG *...solid Victorian houses.* ◇ **solidly.** EG *...large houses built solidly of wooden planks.* ◇ **solidity** /səˈlɪdɪtɪ/. EG *...their appearance of massive solidity.* ADJ QUALIT ◇ ADV ◇ N UNCOUNT

6 If you describe someone as **solid**, you mean that they are very respectable and reliable. EG *She regarded them as solid, good, dull people.* ◇ **solidly.** EG *...a solidly respectable family.* ADJ QUALIT ◇ ADV

7 If something is **solid**, it is reliable, strong, and large in amount. EG *...a veteran British Council worker, with solid experience in Asia and Africa... Solid evidence is needed... It is important that he has a firm, solid foundation of scientific knowledge on which to build.* ◇ **solidly.** EG *They are solidly* ADJ QUALIT ◇ ADV

behind the proposal. ◇ **solidity.** EG *...giving an added strength and solidity to the state.* ◇ N UNCOUNT

8 If you do something for a **solid** period of time, you do it without any pause or interruption throughout that time. EG *I waited a solid hour... ...fifteen minutes' solid conversation... I read for two hours solid.* ◇ **solidly.** EG *If you work for ten weeks solidly you might stand more of a chance.* ADJ CLASSIF: ATTRIB OR ADV ◇ ADV

solidarity /ˌsɒlɪˈdærɪtɪ/. If a group of people show **solidarity**, they show complete unity and support for each other. EG *...working-class solidarity... ...a great international gesture of women's solidarity with women.* N UNCOUNT

solidify /səˈlɪdɪfaɪ/, **solidifies, solidifying, solidified.** When a liquid **solidifies**, it changes into a solid. EG *Pour the fat into a basin and when it has solidified take it out.* V

solitary /ˈsɒlɪtərɪ/. **1** A **solitary** activity is one that you do alone. EG *He formed the habit of taking long solitary walks.* ADJ CLASSIF: ATTRIB

2 A person or animal that is **solitary** spends a lot of time alone. EG *Tigers are solitary creatures.* ADJ QUALIT

3 A **solitary** person or object is alone and has no others nearby. EG *Madeleine walked over to the solitary figure.* ADJ CLASSIF: ATTRIB

solitary confinement. A prisoner who is in **solitary confinement** is being kept alone in a prison cell. N UNCOUNT

solitude /ˈsɒlɪtjuːd/ is the state of being alone. EG *He preferred solitude... One can study far better in solitude.* N UNCOUNT

solo /ˈsəʊləʊ/, **solos. 1** A **solo** is a piece of music that is played or sung by one person alone. EG *...a clarinet solo by Donizetti.* N COUNT

2 A **solo** performance or activity is done by one person alone. EG *The morning of Will Kent's solo flight was fine and clear.* ▶ used as an adverb. EG *...the boat in which he sailed solo round the world.* ADJ CLASSIF: ATTRIB ▶ ADV AFTER VB

soloist /ˈsəʊləʊɪst/, **soloists.** A **soloist** is a person who plays a musical instrument alone or sings alone. EG *They have professional soloists and an amateur chorus.* N COUNT

soluble /ˈsɒljəbəl/. A substance that is **soluble** will dissolve in a liquid. EG *...soluble tablets... The powder is soluble in water.* ADJ CLASSIF

solution /səˈluːʃən/, **solutions. 1** A **solution** is a way of dealing with a difficult situation so that the difficulty is removed. EG *It's a very neat little solution to our problem... The only solution is to create an entirely new system.* N COUNT: OFT+to

2 The **solution** to a riddle or a puzzle is the answer to it. EG *...the crossword solution.* N COUNT: OFT+to

3 A **solution** is also a liquid in which a solid substance has been dissolved. EG *Immerse it in a solution of detergent and water.* N COUNT OR N UNCOUNT Technical

solve /sɒlv/, **solves, solving, solved.** If you **solve** a problem or a question, you find a solution or an answer to it. EG *...the failure of successive Government policies to solve Britain's economic problems... ...solving crossword puzzles.* V+O

solvent /ˈsɒlvənt/, **solvents. 1** If a person or a company is **solvent**, they have enough money to pay all their debts. EG *He behaved as if he alone kept the airport solvent.* ADJ QUALIT Formal

2 A **solvent** is a liquid that can dissolve other substances. EG *...rubber solvents.* N COUNT OR N UNCOUNT Formal

sombre /ˈsɒmbə/; spelled **somber** in American English. **1 Sombre** colours and places are dark and dull. EG *...two women dressed in sombre black... ...the sombre oak-panelled room.* ADJ QUALIT

2 If someone is **sombre**, they are serious, sad, or pessimistic. EG *Her face grew sombre... Mr Morris took a more sombre view.* ◇ **sombrely.** EG *Mercer shook his head sombrely.* ADJ QUALIT ◇ ADV

How many words are there on these pages that talk about people doing things alone?

some /sʌm/. **1** You use **some** to refer to a quantity QUANTIF of something or to a number of people or things, when you are not stating the quantity or number precisely. EG *She had a piece of pie and some coffee... I've got some friends coming over... 'You'll need graph paper.' - 'Yeah, I've got some at home.'*

2 You also use **some** to emphasize that a quantity DET or number is fairly large. EG *I did not meet her again for some years... They were having some difficulty in following the plot.*

3 If you refer to **some** of the people or things in a QUANTIF group, you mean a few of them but not all of them. If you refer to **some** of a particular thing, you mean a part of it but not all of it. EG *Some sports are very dangerous... She took some of the meat out.*

4 If you refer to **some** person or thing, you are DET referring to that person or thing vaguely, without stating precisely which one you mean. EG *We found it lying in some ditch in the middle of the desert... At some stage in your career you may need my help.*

5 You can also use **some** in front of a number to ADV+NUMBER indicate that it is approximate. EG *...a single layer of* Formal *stone, some four metres thick.*

6 You can also use **some** to indicate that a word DET being used to refer to something is not in fact Informal accurate. EG *Some holiday that turned out to be!*

somebody /sʌmbɔ'di¹/. See **someone**.

some day means at a date in the future that is ADV unknown or that has not yet been decided. EG *I'd like to see it some day... I hope someday we'll have enough money to get those pictures.*

somehow /sʌmhaʊ/. **1** You use **somehow** to say ADV that you do not know how something was done or will be done. EG *...a boy who'd somehow broken his thumb... We'll manage somehow.*

2 You also use **somehow** to indicate that you do ADV SEN OR not know the reason for something you are saying. ADV+ADJ EG *Somehow it didn't seem important to him any more... To hear her talking this way was somehow shocking.*

someone /sʌmwɔ³n/. You use **someone** or **some-** PRON INDEF : **body** to refer to a person without saying exactly SING who you mean. EG *There's someone coming upstairs... She wrote a book on somebody famous... It belongs to somebody else.*

someplace /sʌmpleɪs/ means the same as some- ADV where. EG *Why don't you boys go and sit someplace* American *else?* Informal

somersault /sʌmɔsɔːlt/, **somersaults**. A **somer-** N COUNT **sault** is a rolling or turning movement which you do by turning upside down and bringing your legs over your head. EG *My sister turned a somersault.*

something /sʌmθɪŋ/. **1** You use **something** to PRON INDEF : refer in a vague way to anything that is not a SING person, for example an object, action, or quality. EG *Hendricks saw something ahead of him... I've got something to do tonight... Something terrible has happened... There's something peculiar about him... His name is Victor something.*

2 If you say that what you have or what has been PRON INDEF : done is **something**, you mean that it is useful, even SING if only in a small way. EG *Of course I've got my savings now, that's something.*

3 You can use **something** to say that the descrip- ADV+PREP tion or amount that you are giving is not exact. EG *I can't remember the details, but it was something like this... Profits have fallen by something over 35%... ...a tax cut at something near 10 per cent.*

4 If you say that a person or thing is **something of** PHRASE a particular thing, you mean that they are that thing to a limited extent. EG *Their size does seem to be something of a handicap... It is something of a mystery why the party should continue to support this policy.*

5 You use the expression **or something** to indicate PHRASE that you are uncertain about what you have just Informal said. EG *She had cancer or something.*

6 If you say that **there is something in** an idea or PHRASE

suggestion, you mean that it is quite good and should be considered seriously. EG *I believe there is something in having ballots in trade unions.*

7 If you say that a person or thing **is really** PHRASE **something**, you mean that you are very impressed Informal by them.

8 something like: see **like**.

sometime /sʌmtaɪm/. **1 Sometime** means at a ADV time in the future or the past that is unknown or that has not yet been decided. EG *Can I come and see you sometime?... He saw Frieda Maloney sometime last week.*

2 You also use **sometime** to refer to a job or role ADJ CLASSIF : that a person used to have. EG *...Sir Alfred* ATTRIB *Munnings, sometime President of the Royal Acad-* Formal *emy.*

sometimes /sʌmtaɪmz/. You use **sometimes** to ADV say that something happens on some occasions. EG *Sometimes I wish I was back in Africa... Sometimes they just come for a term, sometimes six months.*

somewhat /sʌmwɒt/ means to some extent or ADV degree. EG *...a fine, though somewhat daunting,* Formal *director... Communication has altered things somewhat... I found, somewhat to my surprise, that I enjoyed myself.*

somewhere /sʌmwɛə/. **1** You use **somewhere** ADV **1.1** to refer to a place without saying exactly where you mean. EG *They lived somewhere near Bournemouth... There's an ashtray somewhere.* **1.2** when giving an approximate amount, number, or time. EG *This part of the church was built somewhere around 700 AD... ...somewhere between 55,000 and 60,000 men.*

2 If you say that you **are getting somewhere**, you PHRASE mean that you are making progress towards achieving something.

son /sʌn/, **sons**. Someone's **son** is their male child. N COUNT EG *Don Culver is the son of an engineer... ...photographs of their sons and daughters.*

sonar /sɔʊnɑː/ is equipment on a ship which can N UNCOUNT calculate the depth of the sea or the position of an underwater object using sound waves. EG *Sonar has a limited range... ...sonar apparatus.*

sonata /sɔnɑːtɔ/, **sonatas**. A **sonata** is a piece of N COUNT classical music written for the piano or for a piano and one other instrument. EG *...Beethoven piano sonatas.*

song /sɒŋ/, **songs**. **1** A **song** consists of words and N COUNT OR music that are sung together. EG *...a love song... I* N UNCOUNT *heard somebody singing a song... We all burst into song.*

2 A bird's **song** is the pleasant, musical sounds that N COUNT OR it makes. EG *...the sweet song of the skylark.* N UNCOUNT

3 If you buy something **for a song**, you buy it for PHRASE much less than its real value. EG *I was wearing a* Informal *dress that I had bought for a song in India.*

4 If you say that someone is making a **song and** PHRASE **dance** about something, you mean that they are Informal making an unnecessary fuss about it.

son-in-law, **sons-in-law**. Someone's **son-in-law** N COUNT is the husband of their daughter.

sonnet /sɒnɪt/, **sonnets**. A **sonnet** is a poem with N COUNT 14 lines, in which some lines rhyme with others according to certain fixed patterns.

soon /suːn/, **sooner**, **soonest**. **1** If something is ADV OR going to happen **soon**, it will happen in a very short ADV+PREP time from now. If something happened **soon** after a particular time or event, it happened a short time after it. EG *It will soon be Christmas... I shall soon be in a few years, perhaps sooner... He rented a TV soon after moving into his apartment... Contact the police as soon as possible.*

2 You say **the sooner the better** when you think CONVENTION something should be done as soon as possible. EG *The sooner we get out the better.*

3 If you say that something will happen **sooner or** PHRASE **later**, you mean that it will happen at some time in the future, even though it might take a long time.

EG *If you do not look after it carefully, sooner or later your car will fall to bits.*

4 If you say that something will happen **as soon as** CONJ something else happens, you mean that it will happen immediately after the other thing happens. EG *As soon as we get the tickets we'll send them to you... As soon as she got out of bed the telephone stopped ringing.*

5 If you say that **no sooner** has one thing hap- PHRASE pened **than** another thing happens, you mean that the second thing happens immediately after the first thing. EG *No sooner had he closed his eyes than he fell asleep.*

6 If you say that you **would just as soon** do PHRASE something, you mean that you would be equally willing to do it as to do something else. EG *I'd just as soon turn around and go back.*

7 If you say that you **would sooner** do something, PHRASE you mean that you would prefer to do it. EG *I would sooner read than watch television.*

soot /sʊt/ is black powder which rises in the N UNCOUNT smoke from a fire and collects on the inside of chimneys.

soothe /suːð/, **soothes, soothing, soothed. 1** If V+O you **soothe** someone who is angry or upset, you make them feel calmer. EG *He tried to soothe her by making conversation... She was soothed by his detachment from her troubles.* ◊ **soothing.** EG ◊ ADJ QUALIT *...soothing music... a soothing voice... a few soothing words.*

2 Something such as ointment that **soothes** pain V+O makes the pain less severe. EG *...cream she put on to soothe her sunburn.*

sooty /sʊtɪ¹/. Something that is **sooty** is covered ADJ QUALIT with soot. EG *...sooty windows... his sooty hands.*

sophisticated /səfɪstɪkeɪtɪ³d/. **1** A **sophisticated** ADJ QUALIT person **1.1** shows experience in social situations and knows about culture, fashion, and other matters that are considered socially important. EG *...a glossy magazine for today's sophisticated woman... ...a sophisticated lifestyle.* **1.2** is knowledgeable and able to understand complicated matters. EG *...a politically sophisticated electorate.*

2 A **sophisticated** machine or device is made ADJ QUALIT using advanced and complex methods. EG *These planes are among the most sophisticated aircraft now being manufactured.*

sophistication /səfɪstɪkeɪʃə³n/. The **sophistica-** N UNCOUNT **tion** of people, methods, or machines, is their quality of being sophisticated. EG *Their elegantly cut suits projected sophistication... The machinery will grow in sophistication and power.*

soppy /sɒpɪ¹/. If you describe someone or some- ADJ QUALIT thing as **soppy**, you mean that they are silly or Informal foolishly sentimental. EG *...the soppy expressions on their faces... Don't be soppy, Manfred.*

soprano /səpraːnəʊ/, **sopranos.** A **soprano** is a N COUNT woman, girl, or boy with a high singing voice.

sordid /sɔːdɪd/. Something that is **sordid 1** in- ADJ QUALIT volves dishonest or immoral behaviour. EG *...a rather sordid affair.* **2** is dirty, unpleasant, or depressing. EG *...a sordid street.*

sore /sɔː/, **sores. 1** If part of your body is **sore**, it ADJ QUALIT causes you pain and discomfort. EG *Her throat was so sore she could not talk... I've got sore feet after all that walking.*

2 A **sore** is a painful place on the body where the N COUNT skin is infected. EG *She had a big sore on her leg.*

3 If you are **sore** about something, you are angry ADJ PRED : and upset about it. EG *Nobody believed him, and* OFT+about this made him sore as hell. American

4 People sometimes use **sore** to describe some- ADJ CLASSIF : thing that is causing great difficulty, worry, or ATTRIB suffering. EG *Man is in sore need of new standards.* Literary ◊ **sorely.** EG *They were sorely in need of rest.* ◊ ADV

5 If something is a **sore point** with someone, it is PHRASE likely to make them angry or embarrassed if you try to discuss it. EG *'Have you got any children, Lynn?' – 'Hm. Sore point.' – 'Oh, sorry.'*

sorrow /sɒrəʊ/, **sorrows. 1 Sorrow** is a feeling of N UNCOUNT deep sadness or regret. EG *She wrote to express her sorrow at the tragic death of their son.*

2 Sorrows are events or situations that cause deep N COUNT sadness. EG *...suffering the sorrows that life brings.*

sorrowful /sɒrə⁶fʊl/. Someone or something that ADJ QUALIT is **sorrowful** shows or causes deep sadness. EG *It* Literary *was a sorrowful day in that town when the orders came to close down the mine.*

sorry /sɒrɪ¹/, **sorrier, sorriest. 1** You say **'Sorry'** ADJ PRED : or **'I'm sorry'** as a way of apologizing to someone OFT+REPORT, for something that you have done which has upset about/for, them or caused them difficulties. EG *I'm sorry I'm* OR to-INF *late... Sorry about the coffee on your bedspread... 'You're giving me a headache with all that noise.' – 'Sorry,' Thomas said... I'm sorry if I worried you.*

2 If you are **sorry** about a situation, you feel ADJ PRED : OFT sadness, regret, or disappointment about it. EG *He* +about/for, *was sorry he had agreed to stay... No one seemed* REPORT, *very sorry to see me go.* OR to-INF

3 You use **sorry** as a polite introduction when you CONVENTION are saying that you are unable to help someone or OR ADJ PRED when you are giving someone bad news. EG *I'm* +to-INF *sorry but there's no-one here called Nikki... I'm sorry to say that the experiment has failed.*

4 You also say **'I'm sorry'** to express your regret CONVENTION and sadness when you hear sad or unpleasant news. EG *'Jenny's dead,' I told him. 'I'm sorry,' he said in a stunned whisper.*

5 If you are or feel **sorry** for someone who is ADJ PRED+for unhappy or in an unpleasant situation, you feel sympathy and sadness for them. EG *I knew they were having a rough time and I felt sorry for them.*

6 If you are or feel **sorry** for yourself, you are ADJ PRED+for miserable and feel pity for yourself. EG *How dare* +REFL *you feel sorry for yourself? It was your own fault!*

7 You also say **sorry 7.1** when you haven't heard CONVENTION something that someone has said and you want them to repeat it. EG *'Have you seen the health guide book anywhere?' – 'Sorry?' – 'Seen the health guide book?'* **7.2** as a polite introduction when you CONVENTION are disagreeing with someone or refusing to do OR ADJ PRED something for them. EG *I'm sorry, I wouldn't agree with that at all, Brian.* **7.3** to correct yourself when ADV SEN you have said something incorrect. EG *It's in the southeast, sorry, southwest corner of the USA.*

8 You also use **sorry** to describe people and things ADJ QUALIT : that are in a bad physical or mental state. EG *He* ATTRIB *had never seen such a sorry lot... 'We are in a sorry state,' she lamented.*

sort /sɔːt/, **sorts, sorting, sorted. 1** If you talk N COUNT+SUPP about a particular **sort** of something, you are talking about one of the different types of that thing. EG *'What sort of iron did she get?' – 'A steam iron.'... ...a rock plant of some sort... There were five different sorts of biscuits... There are all sorts of reasons why this is true.*

2 You use **sort** of when you want to say that PHRASE something can roughly be described in a particular Informal way. EG *She was wearing a sort of velvet dress... I heard a strangling sort of noise.*

3 If you describe something as a thing **of sorts**, you PHRASE mean that it belongs to this class of things but is not of very good quality. EG *...cleaning a carpet of sorts... Farlow was a lawyer of sorts.*

4 You describe someone as a particular **sort** when N SING+SUPP you are describing their character. EG *She was a good sort... He's not the marrying sort.*

5 If you feel **out of sorts**, you feel slightly unwell, PHRASE discontented, or annoyed. EG *She complained of being out of sorts... ...when you are out of sorts with the group.*

6 If you **sort** things, you separate them into V+O or V+A different classes, groups, or places, so that you can arrange them in a useful or sensible order. EG

If someone is in a sorry state, are they apologising?

Minnie was in the office, sorting mail... They had got mixed up and needed to be sorted into three sets... He was sorting through a pile of socks.

sort out. 1 If you **sort out** a group of things, you organize them or tidy them. EG *It took a while to sort out all our luggage.* 2 If you **sort out** a problem, you deal with it and find a solution to it. EG *I need to get my own problems sorted out... We have to sort things out between us.* `PHRASAL VB: V+O+ADV` `V+O+ADV`

SOS /ɛs əu ɛs/. An **SOS** is a signal which indicates to other people that you are in danger and need help quickly. EG *...an SOS from a private plane proceeding to Nassau... No SOS messages were received.* `N SING`

so-so. If you say that something is **so-so**, you mean that it is average in quality, rather than being very good or very bad. EG *Some of the food is very good, some of it's so-so.* `ADJ CLASSIF OR ADV Informal`

souffle /suːfleɪ/, **souffles**; also spelled **soufflé**. A **souffle** is a light food made from a mixture of beaten egg whites and other ingredients that is baked in the oven. EG *...a cheese souffle.* `N COUNT OR N UNCOUNT`

sought /sɔːt/ is the past tense and past participle of **seek.**

sought-after. Something that is **sought-after** is in great demand, usually because it is rare or of very good quality. EG *The most sought-after item was an early painting by Picasso.* `ADJ QUALIT`

soul /səul/, **souls.** 1 A person's **soul** is 1.1 the spiritual part of them which is believed to continue existing after their body is dead. EG *They said a prayer for the souls of the men who had been drowned.* 1.2 their mind, character, thoughts, and feelings. EG *Only someone with the soul of a poet can understand this... His soul was in turmoil.* `N COUNT USU+POSS`

2 The **soul** of a nation or a political movement is the special quality it has that represents its basic nature. EG *...the soul of the American people.* `N SING`

3 You can refer to someone as a particular kind of **soul** when you are describing their character or condition. EG *She was a kind soul... Poor soul!* `N SING+SUPP`

4 You use **soul** in negative statements like 'not a soul' to mean nobody at all. EG *When I first went there I didn't know a single soul... I swear I will never tell a soul.* `N SING: a+N, WITH BROAD NEG`

5 **Soul** or **soul music** is a type of pop music performed mainly by black American musicians. EG *...a new soul band from Chicago.* `N UNCOUNT`

6 If you **keep body and soul together**, you have enough money to provide what you need to live. EG *I was earning just enough to keep body and soul together.* `PHRASE`

soul-destroying. Something that is **soul-destroying** makes you depressed, often because it is so boring. EG *The job has soul-destroying aspects.* `ADJ QUALIT`

soulful /səulful/. Something that is **soulful** expresses deep feelings. EG *...big, soulful eyes.* `ADJ QUALIT`

soulless /səullɪˈs/. Something that is **soulless** lacks human qualities and the ability to feel or produce deep feelings. EG *The place seemed soulless... ...a soulless routine job.* `ADJ QUALIT`

sound /saund/, **sounds, sounding, sounded; sounder, soundest.** 1 A **sound** is something that you hear. EG *He heard the sound of footsteps in the hall... He opened the door without a sound... The bells were making a gentle, tinkling sound.* `N COUNT`

2 **Sound** is what you hear. EG *Sound travels better in water than in air.* `N UNCOUNT`

3 The **sound** on a television is what you hear coming from the television set. Its loudness can be controlled. EG *When the news had finished Morris turned down the sound.* `N SING: the+N`

4 If something such as a horn **sounds** or if you **sound** it, it makes a noise. EG *A car passed him at top speed, sounding its horn.* ● to **sound the alarm**: see **alarm.** `V-ERG`

5 You can use **sound** 5.1 to say what quality a noise has. EG *The rustling of the woman's dress sounded alarmingly loud... Her footsteps sounded* `V+C OR V+as/like`

like pistol shots. 5.2 to say what emotion or quality someone seems to have when they speak. EG *'Ah,' Piper said. He sounded a little discouraged... You know, you sound just like an insurance salesman.* 5.3 to say what quality you think something has, when you have just heard about it or read about it. EG *'They've got a small farm down in Devon.' – 'That sounds nice.'... It all sounded so crazy that I laughed out loud... It sounds to me as though he's just doing it to be awkward.*

6 The **sound** of something that you have heard about or read about is the impression you have of what it is like. EG *I don't like the sound of linguistics... She had a rather off-putting manner by the sound of it.* `N SING: the+N`

7 If a structure, part of someone's body, or someone's mind is **sound**, it is in good condition or healthy. EG *My heart is basically sound.* ● **safe and sound**: see **safe.** `ADJ QUALIT`

8 Something or someone that is **sound** is reliable and sensible. EG *Adam met every objection with sound arguments... Is this sound advice?* `ADJ QUALIT`

9 If you are **sound asleep**, you are sleeping deeply. `PHRASE`

10 See also **soundly.**

sound out. If you **sound** someone **out**, you question them in order to find out what their opinion is about something. `PHRASAL VB: V+O+ADV`

sound effect, sound effects. Sound effects are the sounds that are created artificially to make a play more realistic, especially a radio play. `N COUNT: USU PLURAL`

soundly. 1 If someone is **soundly** defeated or beaten, they are defeated or beaten thoroughly. EG *He was grabbed and soundly whipped.* `ADV`

2 If you sleep **soundly**, you sleep deeply and do not wake during your sleep. EG *I slept soundly that night.* `ADV`

soundproof /saundˈpruːf/. Something such as a room that is **soundproof** is able to stop all sound from getting in or out. EG *The studio was soundproof.* `ADJ CLASSIF`

soundtrack /saundˈtræk/, **soundtracks.** The **soundtrack** of a film is its sound, speech, and music. `N COUNT`

soup /suːp/, **soups.** Soup is liquid food made by boiling meat, fish, or vegetables in water. EG *...a bowl of soup... ...chicken soup.* `N MASS`

sour /sauə/, **sours, souring, soured.** 1 Something that is **sour** has a sharp taste like the taste of a lemon or an unripe apple. EG *Add enough sugar to keep it from tasting sour.* `ADJ QUALIT`

2 **Sour** milk has an unpleasant taste because it is no longer fresh. `ADJ CLASSIF`

3 Someone who is **sour** is bad-tempered and unfriendly. EG *I received a sour look every time I passed her house.* `ADJ QUALIT`

4 If something **goes sour** or **turns sour**, it becomes less enjoyable or less satisfactory. EG *The evening had turned sour.* `PHRASE`

5 If a friendship, situation, or attitude **sours** or if something **sours** it, it becomes less friendly, enjoyable, or hopeful. EG *These latest cuts might sour relations between the government and the military.* `V-ERG`

source /sɔːs/, **sources.** 1 The **source** of something is 1.1 the person, place, or thing which you get it from. EG *...one of the world's main sources of uranium... Candidates are required to publish the sources of their campaign funds... ...the development of new energy sources.* 1.2 the place where it starts from or the thing which causes it. EG *They're trying to trace the source of the trouble... Bad housing is their main source of worry.* `N COUNT: USU+SUPP`

2 A **source** is a person or book that provides information for a news story or for a piece of research. EG *Western diplomatic sources confirmed reports of fighting in the capital... The story was based on information from a 'reliable source'.* `N COUNT`

3 The **source** of a river or stream is the place `N SING`

where it begins. EG *We are following the creek to its source.*

south /saʊθ/; often spelled with a capital letter. **1** The **south** is **1.1** the direction which is on your right when you are looking towards the direction where the sun rises. EG *We want to find a quiet place in the hills to the south of the little town... The island is a mile in length from north to south.* **1.2** the part of a place or country which is towards the south. EG *...the South of France... She's from the South.* N SING : *the*+N OR N UNCOUNT

N SING : *the*+N

2 South means towards the south or to the south of a place or thing. EG *I travelled by bus through Philadelphia... I was living in a house just south of Market Street.* ADV

3 The **south** part of a place or country is the part which is towards the south. EG *...South Wales... She owned a boarding house on the south coast.* ADJ CLASSIF : ATTRIB

4 A **south** wind blows from the south. ADJ CLASSIF

south-east; often spelled with a capital letter or capital letters. **1** The **south-east** is **1.1** the direction which is halfway between south and east. EG *To the south-east there is a dense date plantation.* **1.2** the part of a place or country which is towards the south-east. EG *...the south-east of England.* N SING : *the*+N, OR N UNCOUNT

N SING : *the*+N, OFT+*of*

2 South-east means towards the south-east or to the south-east of a place or thing. EG *...a forest somewhere south-east of Berlin.* ADV

3 The **south-east** part of a place or country is the part which is towards the south-east. EG *...a book-shop in south-east London.* ADJ CLASSIF : ATTRIB

4 A **south-east** wind blows from the south-east. ADJ CLASSIF

south-eastern means in or from the south-east of a region or country. EG *We were staying in Beaumont, in southeastern Kansas.* ADJ CLASSIF : ATTRIB

southerly /sʌðəlɪ¹/. **1** A **southerly** point, area, or direction is to the south or towards the south. EG *They headed in a southerly direction... ...the most southerly tip of Bear Island.* ADJ QUALIT

2 A **southerly** wind blows from the south. ADJ CLASSIF

southern /sʌðən/ means in or from the south of a region or country. EG *...the southern edge of the Sahara... ...a Southern English accent.* ADJ CLASSIF : ATTRIB

South Pole. The **South Pole** is the place on the surface of the earth which is farthest towards the south. N PROPER : *the*+N

southward /saʊθwəd/ or **southwards** means towards the south. EG *A level expanse of low-lying country extended southward.* ▸ **Southward** is also used as an adjective. EG *The shore was badly eaten away on its southward side.* ADV

▸ ADJ CLASSIF

south-west; often spelled with a capital letter or capital letters. **1** The **south-west** is **1.1** the direction which is halfway between south and west. EG *To the south-west lay the city.* **1.2** the part of a place or country which is towards the south-west. EG *...the south-west of England... We moved on to Dallas in the South-West.* N SING : *the*+N, OR N UNCOUNT

N SING : *the*+N

2 South-west means towards the south-west or to the south-west of a place or thing. EG *It flows south-west to the Atlantic Ocean... ...the mountain road southwest of Sapporo.* ADV

3 The **south-west** part of a place or country is the part which is towards the south-west. EG *...Conservative Party agent for Southwest Staffordshire.* ADJ CLASSIF : ATTRIB

4 A **south-west** wind blows from the south-west. ADJ CLASSIF

south-western means in or from the south-west of a region or country. EG *...the mountains of the southwestern United States.* ADJ CLASSIF

souvenir /suːvənɪə, suːvənɪə/, **souvenirs**. A **souvenir** is something which you buy or keep to remind you of a holiday, place, or event. EG *He kept a spoon as a souvenir of his journey... ...a souvenir shop.* N COUNT

sovereign /sɒvrɪn/, **sovereigns**. **1** A **sovereign** is a king, queen, or other royal ruler of a country. **2** A **sovereign** state or country is independent and not under the authority of any other country. EG N COUNT

ADJ CLASSIF : ATTRIB

The Punjab was the last sovereign independent Indian state.

3 Sovereign is used to describe someone who has the highest power in a country. EG *Parliament is sovereign... He will be given sovereign powers.* ADJ CLASSIF

sovereignty /sɒvrɪnti¹/ is complete political power that a country has to govern itself or another country or state. EG *...a threat to national sovereignty... ...the abandonment of British sovereignty over Africa.* N UNCOUNT

sow, sows, sowing, sowed, sown; pronounced /saʊ/ when it is a verb, and /saʊ/ when it is a noun. **1** If you **sow** seeds or **sow** an area of land with seeds, you plant the seeds in the ground. EG *You can sow winter wheat in October... The land was cleared of weeds and sown with grass.* V+O OR V+O+*with*

2 If someone **sows** an undesirable feeling or situation, they cause it to begin and develop. EG *She attacked those who sow dismay and division in the party... ...sowing doubt and uncertainty.* V+O Literary

3 A **sow** is an adult female pig. N COUNT

soya /sɔɪə/. **Soya** flour, butter, or other food is made from soya beans. N UNCOUNT : USU N MOD

soya bean, soya beans. Soya beans are a type of bean that can be eaten or used to make flour, oil, or soy sauce. N COUNT

soy sauce /sɔɪ sɔːs/ is a dark brown liquid made from soya beans and used as a flavouring, especially in Chinese cooking. N UNCOUNT

spa /spɑː/, **spas.** A **spa** is a place where water with minerals in it bubbles out of the ground. People drink the water or bathe in it in order to improve their health. N COUNT

space /speɪs/, **spaces, spacing, spaced. 1 Space** is **1.1** the area that is empty or available in a place, building, or container. EG *There was just enough space for a bed... Belongings take up space... I did not have the space to store the bricks... ...the luggage space at the back of the car.* **1.2** the vast area that lies beyond the Earth's atmosphere and surrounds the stars and planets. EG *...the first human being to travel in space... ...space research.* N UNCOUNT

2 Space in a talk or piece of writing is the amount of the talk or writing that is available for a particular thing to be discussed. EG *There is no space in this book to argue the alternative viewpoint... I shall devote some space to describing my own experiences.* N UNCOUNT

3 If a place gives a feeling of **space**, it gives an impression of being large and open. EG *The low hills give a feeling of great, intense space... A mirror can add space to a room.* N UNCOUNT

4 If you are looking or staring **into space**, you are looking straight in front of you, without actually looking at anything in particular. PHRASE

5 A **space** is **5.1** a gap or empty place in something solid or crowded. EG *The door had spaces at the top and bottom... ...an open space in the jungle.* **5.2** a place or area that is empty and available for people to use or fill. EG *There were two spaces on the morning plane to Canton... We spent half an hour looking for a parking space... There is no official space for it on the form.* N COUNT

6 A **space** of time is a period of time. EG *It happened three times in the space of five months... He should arrive in a very short space of time.* N SING+*of*

7 If you **space** a series of things, you arrange them so that they are not all together but have gaps between them. EG *The lines were spaced well apart... I had to space my inquiries carefully.* V+O OFT PASS+A

8 See also **outer space.**

space out. If you **space** things **out**, you arrange them so that they are not all together but have PHRASAL VB V+O+ADV gaps between them. EG *These books should have large print well spaced out on the page.*

spacecraft /ˈspeɪskrɑːft/. **Spacecraft** is both the N COUNT singular and the plural form.

A **spacecraft** is a rocket or other vehicle that can travel in space.

Space Invaders is the name of a computer game N UNCOUNT in which players use control buttons and levers to try to shoot and destroy spaceships that move and attack them on a computer screen.

spaceship /ˈspeɪsʃɪp/, **spaceships**. A **spaceship** N COUNT is a spacecraft that carries people through space.

space shuttle, **space shuttles**. A **space shuttle** N COUNT is a spacecraft that is designed to travel into space and back to earth many times.

spacious /ˈspeɪʃəs/. A room or other place that is ADJ QUALIT **spacious** is large in size or area inside. EG *...a spacious dining-room... ...spacious parks.*

spade /speɪd/, **spades**. 1 A **spade** is a tool used for N COUNT digging, with a flat metal blade and a long handle. See picture at TOOLS. EG *...a garden spade.*

2 **Spades** is one of the four suits in a pack of N UNCOUNT playing cards. Each card in the suit is marked with one or more black symbols in the shape of a heart-shaped leaf with a stem.

spades

3 A **spade** is also one of the thirteen playing cards N COUNT in the suit of spades.

spaghetti /spəˈgeti/ is a type of food made from N UNCOUNT pasta. It looks like long pieces of string and is usually served with a sauce.

span /spæn/, **spans**, **spanning**, **spanned**. 1 A N COUNT : **span** is 1.1 the period of time between two dates or USU+SUPP events, or the period during which something exists or functions. EG *...during the forty-year span from 1913 to 1953... ...in the short span that man has been on earth.* 1.2 the range of things that are N SING : included in a subject or task. EG *Each manager has* USU+SUPP *a fixed span of responsibility.*

2 If something **spans** a particular length of time, it V+O lasts throughout that time. EG *At 79, Dame Flora can look back at a career spanning more than half a century.*

3 The **span** of something is the total length of it N COUNT : from one end to the other, especially when it is OFT+SUPP stretched out as far as possible. EG *Some eagles have a wing span of one and a half metres.*

4 A bridge that **spans** something such as a river or V+O a valley stretches right across it. EG *...a long lake spanned by a high, arching iron bridge.*

spangle /ˈspæŋgəl/, **spangles**. **Spangles** are N COUNT small pieces of metal or plastic which sparkle brightly and are used to decorate clothing or hair.

spangled /ˈspæŋgəld/. Something that is **span-** ADJ CLASSIF : **gled** with small bright objects is covered with OFT+*with* them so that it sparkles. EG *...a crown spangled with glitter... ...the star-spangled night sky.*

spaniel /ˈspænjəl/, **spaniels**. A **spaniel** is a type N COUNT of dog with long ears that hang down.

spank /spæŋk/, **spanks**, **spanking**, **spanked**. If V+O you **spank** a child, you punish it by hitting its bottom several times with your hand.

spanner /ˈspænə/, **spanners**. A **spanner** is a N COUNT metal tool with a specially shaped end that fits round a nut so that you can loosen or tighten the nut. See picture at TOOLS.

spare /speə/, **spares**, **sparing**, **spared**. 1 You use **spare** 1.1 to describe something that is the same ADJ CLASSIF as things that you are already using, but that you

do not need yet and are keeping ready. EG *Keep a spare fuse handy by the fuse box... Take a spare shirt and a spare set of underwear.* ▸ used as a ▸ N COUNT noun. EG *There are some spares at the back if anyone wants more.* 1.2 to describe something that ADJ CLASSIF is not being used by anyone, and is therefore available for you to use. EG *We found a spare parking meter... There were no chairs spare.*

2 Time or money **to spare** is extra time or money PHRASE that is not needed for a particular purpose. EG *He often had money to spare nowadays... She caught her plane with a few minutes to spare.*

3 If you **spare** something for a particular purpose, V+O : USU+*for* you make it available for that purpose. EG *I got to* OR *to*-INF *my feet, thanking him for sparing time to see me... Nowadays more land is needed to grow food and less can be spared to graze cattle.*

4 If a person or a place **is spared**, they are not V+O : OFT PASS harmed, although someone threatened them or harmed other people or places. EG *The great cities of the Rhineland had not been spared... Thank God we were spared.*

5 If you **spare** someone an unpleasant experience, V+O+O you prevent them from suffering it. EG *We telephoned, wishing to spare poor Charlotte two or three hours of suspense... At least I am spared the shame of the children knowing.*

6 If you **spare no expense** in doing something, you PHRASE do it as well as possible, without trying to save money. EG *The Agency has spared no expense with the system for storage.*

spare part, **spare parts**. **Spare parts** are parts N COUNT : that you can buy separately to replace old or USU PLURAL broken parts in a piece of equipment, usually parts that are designed to be easily removed or fitted. EG *The tractors are out of order and there are no spare parts to get them working again... The guarantee includes the cost of spare parts and labour.*

sparing /ˈspeərɪŋ/. Someone who is **sparing** uses ADJ QUALIT : or gives something only in very small quantities. EG USU+*with* *She was sparing with heat and light.* ◇ **sparingly**. ◇ ADV EG *Use hot water sparingly.*

spark /spɑːk/, **sparks**, **sparking**, **sparked**. 1 A N COUNT **spark** is 1.1 a tiny, bright piece of burning material that flies up from something that is burning. EG *The fire sent smoke and sparks over the top of the fence.* 1.2 a flash of light that is caused by EG electricity and often makes a crackling sound. EG *Watch the gap for a blue spark. If there isn't one, check the circuit.*

2 A **spark** of a particular quality is a small but N COUNT+*of* noticeable amount of the quality. EG *A faint spark of pleasure came into his eyes.*

3 If one thing **sparks** another thing or **sparks** it V+O : OFT+*off* off, it causes the second thing to start happening. EG *The crisis was sparked by the assassination of the duke... The letter sparked off a friendship between the two men.*

sparkle /ˈspɑːkəl/, **sparkles**, **sparkling**, **spar-** **kled**. 1 If something **sparkles**, it is clear and V bright and shines with a lot of very small points of light. EG *They looked down to the sea, sparkling in the sun... The lawn was sparkling with frost.* ▸ used ▸ N UNCOUNT as a noun. EG *Her eyes had lost their sparkle.*

2 Someone who **sparkles** is lively, intelligent, and V witty. EG *It was years since he'd tried to sparkle.* ◇ **sparkling**. EG *She felt electric, sparkling, and* ◇ ADJ CLASSIF *irresistible.*

spark plug, **spark plugs**. A **spark plug** is a N COUNT device in the engine of a motor vehicle, which causes the electric sparks that ignite the fuel.

sparrow /ˈspærəʊ/, **sparrows**. A **sparrow** is a N COUNT very common, small brown bird.

sparse /spɑːs/, **sparser**, **sparsest**. Something ADJ QUALIT that is **sparse** is small in number or amount and spread out over an area. EG *The population was sparse... ...his sparse white hair... ...the sparse rain-*

fall. ◊ **sparsely**. EG ...*a sparsely populated region...* ◊ ADV
...*his sparsely furnished room.*

spartan /spɑːtəⁿn/. A **spartan** way of life is very ADJ QUALIT
simple with no luxuries. EG ...*the spartan lives of the*
islanders... ...spartan accommodation.

spasm /spæzəⁿm/, **spasms**. A **spasm** is 1 a sud- N COUNT OR
den tightening of your muscles. EG *Spasms shook* N UNCOUNT
her lungs and chest. 2 a sudden strong pain or N SING+*of*
unpleasant emotion which lasts for a short period
of time. EG ...*a spasm of anger.*

spasmodic /spæzmɒdɪk/. Something that is **spas-** ADJ QUALIT
modic happens suddenly for short periods of time
at irregular intervals. EG *As she talked, she kept*
making spasmodic dashes to the window.
◊ **spasmodically**. EG *The orchestra continued to* ◊ ADV
play spasmodically.

spastic /spæstɪk/, **spastics**. Someone who is ADJ CLASSIF
spastic is born with a disability which makes it
difficult for them to control their muscles, especially their arm and leg muscles. ► used as a noun. ► N COUNT
...*the Spastics Society.*

spat /spæt/ is the past tense and past participle of
spit.

spate /speɪt/. A **spate** of things is a large number N PART : SING
of them that happen or appear within a short
period of time. EG *The incident caused another*
spate of protests... ...a spate of new books about the
man.

spatial /speɪʃ³l/ is used to describe things relat- ADJ CLASSIF :
ing to size, area, or position. EG ...*spatial and* ATTRIB
temporal variations... ...spatial perception. Formal

spatter /spætə/, **spatters**, **spattering**, **spat-** V+O : OFT+A
tered. If something **spatters** a surface or **spat-**
ters a liquid over it, it covers the surface with
drops of the liquid. EG *He picked up his spoon so*
hurriedly that it spattered milk over his cardigan...
Beer spattered the bedspread. ◊ **spattered**. EG *My* ◊ ADJ CLASSIF
goggles were spattered with mud.

spawn /spɔːn/, **spawns**, **spawning**, **spawned**. 1 N UNCOUNT
Spawn is a soft, jelly-like substance containing the
eggs of fish, frogs, or other amphibians.
2 When fish, frogs, and other amphibians **spawn**, v
they lay their eggs.
3 If something **spawns** something else, it causes it v+o
to happen or to be created. EG *Poverty had* Literary
spawned numerous religious movements.

speak /spiːk/, **speaks**, **speaking**, **spoke** /spəʊk/,
spoken /spəʊkəⁿn/. 1 When you **speak**, you use v
your voice in order to say words. EG *Simon opened*
his mouth to speak... She spoke with an Irish
accent... Mary turned her head to speak to him...
He hadn't been able to speak of what had hap-
pened. ◊ **spoken**. EG ...*a robot capable of under-* ◊ ADJ CLASSIF :
standing spoken commands. ATTRIB
2 If you **speak** a foreign language, you know the v+o
language and are able to have a conversation in it.
EG *The men at the airport spoke fluent English.*
3 If you **speak** for a group of people, you give their v+*for*
opinion on their behalf. EG *I'm only speaking for*
myself, not for my colleagues.
4 When someone **speaks** to a group of people, they v : USU+A
make a speech. EG *It was announced that the Prime*
Minister would speak to the nation on television.
5 **Speak** is also used in these phrases. 5.1 You say ADV SEN
so to speak to draw attention to the fact that what
you are saying is not literally true, but is a colourful way of describing a situation. EG *He goes to*
work early; before the office is awake, so to speak.
5.2 **Nobody to speak of** or **nothing to speak of** PHRASE
means hardly anyone or anything, or only unimportant people or things. EG *'Did you find anything?'*
- 'No, nothing to speak of.' 5.3 If you say **'speak** CONVENTION
for yourself' when someone has said something, Informal
you mean that what they have said is only their
opinion or applies only to them. EG *'Posy, we're*
ridiculous.' - 'Speak for yourself.' 5.4 If you are on PHRASE
speaking terms with someone, you are quite
friendly with them and often talk to them. EG *They*
were rarely on speaking terms. 5.5 If you **speak** PHRASE

well or **speak highly** of someone, you say good
things about them. If you **speak ill** of someone,
you criticize them. EG *The students spoke highly of*
their history lecturer. 5.6 If you **speak** your **mind** PHRASE
about something, you say exactly what you think
about it. 5.7 If you say that something **speaks for** PHRASE
itself, you mean that its meaning or quality is so
obvious that it does not need any special explanation. EG *His writing speaks for itself.*
6 See also **speaking**.

speak out. If you **speak out** in favour of some- PHRASAL VB :
thing or against something, you say publicly that V+ADV, USU+A
you think it is a good thing or a bad thing. EG *He*
spoke out against racial discrimination many
times... We lose the courage to speak out.

speak up. 1 To **speak up** means the same as to PHRASAL VB :
speak out. EG *Never be frightened of speaking up* V+ADV, USU+A
for your beliefs... The cricketers themselves should
speak up in favour of it. 2 If you ask someone to v+ADV
speak up, you are asking them to speak more
loudly.

speaker /spiːkə/, **speakers**. 1 A **speaker** is 1.1 a N COUNT
person who is speaking. 1.2 a person who is making
a speech to a group of people. EG *The chairman got*
up to introduce the speaker.
2 A **speaker** of a particular language is a person N COUNT :
who can speak that language. EG *Some sounds are* USU+SUPP
very difficult for French speakers of English.
3 A **speaker** is also a piece of equipment on a N COUNT
radio or record-player, through which the sound
comes out.

speaking /spiːkɪŋ/. 1 You use expressions such as ADV SEN
generally speaking and **technically speaking**
to indicate the kind of statement you are making.
EG *America is still, generally speaking, the most*
technologically advanced... Roughly speaking,
there are two possibilities.
2 You can say **'speaking as** a parent' or **'speak-** ADV SEN
ing as a teacher', for example, to indicate that the
opinion you are giving is based on your experience
as a parent or as a teacher. EG *Speaking as a*
married woman, I consider it important to provide
nursery schools for all children who need them.
3 You can say **speaking of** a thing that has just v+*of*
been mentioned as a way of introducing a new
topic which has some connection with that thing.
EG *It's nice to have an admirer who gives nothing*
away. Speaking of giving away, I have brought you
a present.
4 **Speaking** is the activity of giving speeches and N UNCOUNT :
talks. EG ...*public speaking.* USU+SUPP

spear /spɪə/, **spears**, **spearing**, **speared**. 1 A N COUNT
spear is a weapon consisting of a long pole with a
sharp point. See picture at WEAPONS.
2 If you **spear** something, you push or throw a v+o
spear or other pointed object into it. EG *Lally took*
her fork and speared an oyster from its shell.

spearhead /spɪəhɛd/, **spearheads**, **spear-**
heading, **spearheaded**. 1 If someone **spearheads** v+o
a campaign, they lead it. EG *In India, Mrs Gandhi's* Literary
son Sanjay spearheaded a 'moral crusade' against
slums.
2 The **spearhead** of a campaign is the person or N COUNT
group that leads it. EG ...*the spearhead of a national-* Literary
ist movement.

special /speʃ³l/, **specials**. 1 Something that is ADJ QUALIT
special is more important or better than other
things of its kind. EG ...*china that was reserved for*
special occasions... Is there anything special you
would like for dinner, dear?
2 You use **special** 2.1 to describe someone who is ADJ CLASSIF :
officially appointed, or something that is needed or ATTRIB
intended for a particular purpose. EG *He was a*
special adviser to Mrs Judith Hart at the Ministry...
To marry a foreigner, special permission had to be

If you have specks on your specs, can you see
clearly?

obtained... *My Hoover has special attachments for upholstery...* *...special schools for maladjusted children.* **2.2** to describe something that belongs or relates to only one particular person, group, or place. EG *He spoke his own special variety of German... Hospital food seldom caters for the special needs of the aged.* **2.3** to describe something that is not ordinary but is better than usual or of a high quality or standard. EG *She made a special effort to be polite... Some places do special offers in May.*

3 A **special** is a product or programme which is N COUNT only available or shown at a certain time, or which is made for a special purpose. EG *Monday's special was chicken... I had seen his production of a TV special called 'The Male of the Species.'*

4 See also **speciality**, **specially**.

specialise /spɛʃəlaɪz/. See **specialize**.

specialist /spɛʃəlɪst/, **specialists**. A **specialist** is N COUNT a person who studies a particular subject or skill and knows a lot about it. EG *She is a specialist in Eastern European affairs... an eye specialist.* ▸ used as an adjective. EG *...a specialist teacher of* ▸ ADJ CLASSIF: *mathematics... ...specialist committees.* ATTRIB

speciality /spɛʃiˈælɪtiˈ/, **specialities**. **1** Someone's **speciality** is a particular type of work that they do or a subject that they know a lot about. EG *Work with children is their speciality... They enjoy talking about their own specialities.*

2 A **speciality** of a particular place is a special N COUNT+SUPP product that is always very good there. EG *Chocolate gateau was a speciality of the Café de Rome.*

specialize /spɛʃəlaɪz/, **specializes**, **specializing**, V : OFT+*in* **specialized**; also spelled **specialise**. If you **specialize** in a thing, you make this thing your speciality, for example in your work or when you are studying. EG *...a shop specializing in camping equipment.* ◇ **specialization** /spɛʃəlaɪzeɪʃəˈn/. EG *...the* ◇ N UNCOUNT *increasing specialisation of working life.*

specialized /spɛʃəlaɪzd/; also spelled **special-** ADJ QUALIT **ised**. Someone or something that is **specialized** is trained or developed for a particular purpose or area of knowledge. EG *...highly specialised staff... ...radar and specialised television systems.*

specially /spɛʃəliˈ/. **1** If something has been done ADV **specially** for a particular person or purpose, it has been done only for that person or purpose. EG *...free hotels run by the state specially for tourists... The rules were specially designed to protect travellers.*

2 You also use **specially** to say that something has SUBMOD a particular quality more than average. EG *...a pub* Informal *where the beer was specially good.*

specialty /spɛʃəltiˈ/, **specialties**. A **specialty** is N COUNT the same as a speciality. EG *...suitable people to* American *practise a specialty in a hospital.*

species /spiːʃiːz/. **Species** is both the singular and N COUNT the plural form.

A **species** is a class of plants or animals whose members have the same main characteristics and are able to breed with each other. EG *There are more than two hundred and fifty species of shark.*

specific /spɪˈsɪfɪk/, **specifics**. **1** You use **specific** ADJ CLASSIF: to refer to a particular fixed area or subject. EG ATTRIB *Education should not be restricted to any one specific age group... On certain specific issues there may be changes of emphasis.*

2 If a description is **specific**, it is precise and ADJ QUALIT exact. EG *It was a tooth, a tiger-shark tooth, to be more specific.*

3 Something that is **specific** to a particular thing is ADJ PRED connected with that thing only. EG *It's the program that's specific to this problem.*

4 The **specifics** of a subject are the particular N PLURAL details of it that need to be considered. EG *Let us focus on the specifics of Bengal's life.*

specifically /spɪˈsɪfɪkəliˈ/. You use **specifically 1** to emphasize that a particular subject is being ADV considered individually and separately from other things. EG *It is Christianity with which we are*

specifically concerned. **2** to indicate that you are ADV stating or describing something precisely and clearly. EG *...the peasant rising in the West of France, in Brittany specifically... The point is specifically made in the following passage.* **3** to ADV+ADJ emphasize a particular way of describing something. EG *It's a specifically medical problem.*

specification /spɛsɪfɪkeɪʃəˈn/, **specifications**. A N COUNT **specification** is a requirement which is clearly stated, for example about the necessary features in the design of something. EG *...ships built to merchant ship specifications.*

specify /spɛsɪfaɪ/, **specifies**, **specifying**, **specified**. If you **specify** something, **1** you state it or V+O describe it precisely. EG *The report specified seven areas where the Government had a responsibility.* **2** you clearly state it as a requirement. EG *The* V+REPORT *landlord can specify that rent be paid in cash.* OR V+O

specimen /spɛsɪmɪˈn/, **specimens**. **1** A **speci-** N COUNT **men** is a single plant or animal which is an example of a particular species or type and is examined by scientists. EG *The fins of fossil specimens are carefully dissected.*

2 A **specimen** of something is an example or small N COUNT amount of it which gives an idea of what the whole of it is like. EG *...an authentic specimen of the work of Carl Andre.*

speck /spɛk/, **specks**. A **speck** is **1** a very small N COUNT stain, spot, or shape. EG *There was a speck of blood on his collar.* **2** a very small piece of a N PART powdery substance. EG *...a tiny speck of dust.*

speckled /spɛkəˈld/. A surface that is **speckled** is ADJ CLASSIF: covered with small marks, spots, or shapes. EG *...a* OFT+*with blouse speckled with daisies... ...a speckled thrush.*

specs /spɛks/. Someone's **specs** are their glasses. N PLURAL EG *I've been wearing specs since I was three.* Informal

spectacle /spɛktəkəˈl/, **spectacles**. **1** Someone's N PLURAL **spectacles** are their glasses. Formal

2 A **spectacle** is **2.1** a strange or interesting sight N COUNT or scene. EG *She stood at the head of the stairs and surveyed the spectacle.* **2.2** a grand and impressive N COUNT OR event or performance. EG *It was a grand seven-hour* N UNCOUNT *spectacle consisting of songs, comedy acts, and acrobatics.*

spectacular /spɛktækjəˈlə/, **spectaculars**. **1** ADJ QUALIT Something that is **spectacular** is very impressive or dramatic. EG *The most spectacular of these extraordinary fossils can be seen in the museum... It was a spectacular jump.*

2 A **spectacular** is a show or a performance N COUNT+SUPP which is very grand and impressive. EG *They are to hold a fashion spectacular on Friday with 100 models.*

spectator /spɛkteɪtə/, **spectators**. A **spectator** N COUNT is a person who watches something, especially a sporting event. EG *The spectators rose to their feet to pay tribute to an outstanding performance.*

spectra /spɛktrə/ is a plural of **spectrum**.

spectre /spɛktə/, **spectres**; spelled **specter** in American English. A **spectre** is **1** a ghost. EG *...dim* N COUNT *red spectres with purple eyes.* **2** a frightening N SING: image or idea which you have in your mind. EG *the+N+of ...the spectre of another world war.* Literary

spectrum /spɛktrəm/, **spectra** /spɛktrə/ or **spectrums**. **1** The **spectrum** is the range of N SING: the+N different colours which is produced when light passes through a prism or through a drop of water. A rainbow shows the colours in the spectrum.

2 A **spectrum** is a range of light waves or radio N COUNT waves within particular frequencies. EG *...the electro-magnetic spectrum... ...the higher energy X-ray spectrum.*

3 A **spectrum** of opinions or emotions is a range of N COUNT: different opinions or emotions, especially when USU SING+SUPP one end of the range is considered to be opposite to the other end. EG *They have support at both ends of the political spectrum... We have experienced together the whole spectrum of emotion.*

speculate /spɛkjəˈleɪt/, **speculates, speculating, speculated. 1** If you **speculate** about something, you think about it together with all its possible aspects or effects. EG *It is natural for us to speculate about the reasons for their visits... Industry sources speculated that the least expensive model will be priced at £7000.* ◊ **speculation** /spɛkjəˈleɪʃən/, **speculations.** EG *The papers are full of speculation about who is likely to be the next prime minister.*
V : USU +about/on OR REPORT
◊ N UNCOUNT OR N COUNT

2 If someone **speculates** financially, they buy property, stocks, or shares, in the hope of being able to sell them again at a higher price and make a profit. EG *She speculated successfully on the stock exchange.*
V

speculative /spɛkjəˈlətɪv/. **1** A piece of information that is **speculative** is based on speculation rather than knowledge. EG *Budgets and profit forecasts are equally speculative.*
ADJ QUALIT

2 Someone who has a **speculative** expression seems to be trying to guess what someone or something is like. EG *He looked at me with an oddly speculative glint in his eyes.*
ADJ QUALIT : ATTRIB

3 Speculative is used to describe activities which involve buying goods or shares in the hope of being able to sell them again at a higher price and make a profit. EG *...speculative aircraft projects... ...speculative builders.*
ADJ CLASSIF : ATTRIB

speculator /spɛkjəˈleɪtə/, **speculators.** A **speculator** is a person who speculates financially.
N COUNT

sped /spɛd/ is a past tense and past participle of **speed.**

speech /spiːtʃ/, **speeches. 1 Speech** is **1.1** the ability to speak or the act of speaking. EG *She was so shocked that she lost her powers of speech.* **1.2** spoken language. EG *In ordinary speech we often shorten the word 'cannot' to 'can't'. ...communication through writing and speech.*
N UNCOUNT

2 A **speech** is **2.1** a formal talk which someone gives to an audience. EG *Mr Macmillan presented the prizes and made a speech on the importance of education.* **2.2** a group of lines spoken by a character in a play. EG *She recited a speech from 'As You Like It'.*
N COUNT

3 Your **speech** is the way in which you speak. EG *I detected a slight Brooklyn accent in her speech.*
N SING+POSS

4 The **speech** of a particular country or region is the language or dialect spoken in that country or region. EG *He can mimic Cockney speech quite well.*
N UNCOUNT +SUPP

speechless /spiːtʃlɪˈs/. If you are **speechless**, you are temporarily unable to speak, usually because something has shocked you. EG *She was speechless with astonishment.*
ADJ CLASSIF

speed /spiːd/, **speeds, speeding, sped** /spɛd/, **speeded.** The past tense and past participle is **sped** in paragraph 3, but **speeded** for the phrasal verb.

1 The **speed** of something is **1.1** the rate at which it moves or travels. EG *I drove at great speed to West Bank... ...capable of reaching speeds of over 110kph.* **1.2** the rate at which it happens or is done. EG *None of us grows at the same speed.*
N UNCOUNT +SUPP OR N COUNT
N UNCOUNT OR N COUNT

2 Speed is **2.1** very fast movement or travel. EG *The train gathered speed... The car is travelling at speed.* **2.2** a very fast rate at which something happens or is done. EG *...a room of busy journalists typing at speed.*
N UNCOUNT

3 If you **speed** somewhere, you move or travel there quickly, usually in a vehicle. EG *They sped along Main Street towards the highway.*
V+A

4 Someone who **is speeding** is driving a car or other vehicle faster than the legal speed limit. EG *They said you were speeding.* ◊ **speeding.** EG *His driver's licence was suspended for speeding.*
V : ONLY CONT
◊ N UNCOUNT

speed up. 1 When something **speeds up** or when you **speed** it **up**, its speed increases so that it moves or travels faster. EG *They're way ahead of us. Speed up!* **2** When a process or activity **speeds**
PHRASAL VB : V-ERG+ADV
V-ERG+ADV

up or when something **speeds** it **up**, it happens at a faster rate. EG *Africa's population growth speeded up... Warmth speeds up chemical reactions.*

speed limit, speed limits. The **speed limit** on a road is the maximum speed at which you are legally allowed to drive a vehicle on that road.
N COUNT : USU SING

speedometer /spɪˈdɒmɪtə/, **speedometers.** A **speedometer** is an instrument in a vehicle which shows how fast the vehicle is moving. See picture at CAR.
N COUNT

speedy /spiːdiˈ/. A **speedy** action happens or is done very quickly. EG *A speedy settlement of the strike is essential.* ◊ **speedily.** EG *Such doubts were now speedily removed.*
ADJ QUALIT
◊ ADV

spell /spɛl/, **spells, spelling, spelled, spelt** /spɛlt/. The forms **spelled** and **spelt** are both used as the past tense and past participle of the verb.

1 When you **spell** a word, you write or speak each letter in the word in the correct order. EG *'My name is Khulaifi. Shall I spell that for you?'... Bauxite is spelt B A U X I T E... Ninety per cent of the words were spelt wrong.*
V+O

2 Someone who can **spell** knows the correct order of letters in most words.
V

3 If something **spells** a particular result, often an unpleasant one, it suggests that this will be the result. EG *Nuclear conflict would spell the end of life as we know it... Any discussion of politics would spell disaster.*
V+C : NO CONT

4 A **spell** of a particular activity or type of weather is a short period of time during which this activity or type of weather occurs. EG *...a spell of good summer weather... She had a spell as editor.*
N COUNT : USU+SUPP

5 A **spell** is also **5.1** a situation in which events are controlled by a magical power. EG *The spell of the wicked fairy was broken.* **5.2** a sequence of words used to perform magic.
N COUNT

6 If you are **under** someone's **spell**, you are so fascinated by them that you cannot think about anything else. EG *The people on the stage were completely under his spell.*
SO PHRASE

7 See also **spelling.**

spell out. 1 If you **spell** something **out**, you explain it in detail or in a very clear way. EG *Let me try and spell out what I mean by that.* **2** If you **spell out** a word, you write or speak each letter in the word in the correct order. EG *We had to spell out the words we heard.*
PHRASAL VB : V+O+ADV
V+O+ADV

spellbound /spɛlbaʊnd/. If you are **spellbound**, you are so fascinated by something that you cannot think about anything else. EG *We were all spellbound as we listened to her.*
ADJ CLASSIF : USU PRED

spelling /spɛlɪŋ/, **spellings. 1** A **spelling** is the correct order of the letters in a word. EG *They were given twenty spellings to learn.*
N COUNT

2 Spelling is the ability to spell words in the correct way, or the way that words are spelt. EG *I'm terrible at spelling... In this language the pronunciation has changed over the centuries but the spelling has not.*
N UNCOUNT

spelt /spɛlt/ is a past tense and past participle of **spell.**

spend /spɛnd/, **spends, spending, spent** /spɛnt/.
1 When you **spend** money, you pay money for things that you want. EG *We always spend a lot of money on parties... The buildings need a lot of money spent on them.* ● to **spend a penny**: see **penny.**
V+O : OFT+on, OR V

2 If you **spend** time somewhere or energy doing something, you pass the time there or use your energy doing it. EG *He spent most of his time in the library... She woke early, meaning to spend all day writing.*
V+O+A

3 See also **spent.**

Where would you find a spine?

spending /spendɪŋ/ is payment of large amounts N UNCOUNT of money for public services by a government or other organization. EG *City departments must reduce their spending by £35 million before July 1st... ...government spending cuts.*

spent /spent/. 1 Spent is the past tense and past participle of **spend**.

2 **Spent** is used to describe something that has ADJ CLASSIF: already been used and cannot be used again. EG *It* USU ATTRIB *will take several seconds to extract the spent cartridge and insert a fresh one... ...spent matches.*

sperm /spɜːm/, **sperms**. Sperm can also be used N COUNT as the plural form.

A **sperm** is a cell which is produced in the sex organs of a male animal and can enter a female animal's egg and fertilize it.

spew /spjuː/, **spews**, **spewing**, **spewed**. When V-ERG : OFT+A things **spew** from something or when it **spews** them out, the things come out of it in large quantities. EG *Its cargo of canned goods had spewed out... Coal-burning factories spewed dense dirty smoke.*

sphere /sfɪə/, **spheres**. 1 A **sphere** is an object N COUNT that is perfectly round in shape like a ball.

2 A **sphere** of activity or interest is a particular N COUNT+SUPP area of activity or interest. EG *Apart from photography, he has several other spheres of interest... He works in the sphere of race relations.*

3 A **sphere** of people is a group of them who are N COUNT similar in social status or who have the same interests. EG *...mixing in the academic sphere.*

spherical /sferɪkᵊl/. Something that is **spherical** ADJ CLASSIF has the shape of a sphere. EG *The world is spherical... ...the red, spherical berries.*

spice /spaɪs/, **spices**, **spicing**, **spiced**. 1 Spice is N COUNT OR powder or seeds from a plant, which you put in N UNCOUNT food to give it flavour. Cinnamon, ginger, and paprika are spices.

2 When you **spice** food, you add spice to it. EG *Take* V+O : *the peas and butter and spice them with nutmeg.* OFT+ *with*
◊ **spiced**. EG *The soup was heavily spiced.* ◊ ADJ CLASSIF

3 If you **spice** something that you do or say, or if V+O OR you **spice** it **up**, you add excitement or liveliness to V+O+ *up* it. EG *His speech was spiced with anti-imperialist sentiment.*

4 **Spice** is something which makes life more N UNCOUNT exciting. EG *Variety is the spice of life.*

spicy /spaɪsi¹/, **spicier**, **spiciest**. Spicy food is ADJ QUALIT strongly flavoured with spices. EG *...a spicy sauce.*

spider /spaɪdə/, **spiders**. A **spider** is a small N COUNT creature with eight legs. Some types of spider make webs. EG *She had a spider on her leg.*

spidery /spaɪdəri¹/. Spidery handwriting consists ADJ QUALIT : of thin, angular lines and is hard to read. EG *...faded,* ATTRIB *spidery writing that he could not read.*

spike /spaɪk/, **spikes**. 1 A **spike** is a long piece of N COUNT metal with a sharp point. EG *Their heads were cut off and impaled on spikes.* ◊ **spiked** /spaɪkt/. EG ◊ ADJ CLASSIF *...spiked shoes.*

2 Any long, pointed object can be referred to as a N COUNT **spike**. EG *The plant bears spikes of greenish flowers.*

spiky /spaɪki¹/. Something that is **spiky** has sharp ADJ QUALIT : points. EG *...a tiny man with spiky hair... The shrub* ATTRIB *has spiky green leaves.*

spill /spɪl/, **spills**, **spilling**, **spilled**, **spilt** /spɪlt/. The forms **spilled** and **spilt** are both used as the past participle and past tense of the verb.

1 If you **spill** a liquid or if it **spills**, it accidentally V-ERG flows over the edge of a container. EG *She carried the bucket without spilling a drop... Make sure the water doesn't spill over the floor.*

2 If people or things **spill** out of a place, they come V+A out of it in large numbers. EG *Crowds started spilling out of bars.*

3 to **spill the beans**: see **bean**.

spin /spɪn/, **spins**, **spinning**, **spun** /spʌn/. 1 If V-ERG : USU+A something **spins** or if you **spin** it, it turns quickly around a central point. EG *The football went spin-*

---

ning into the canal... He spun the chair round to face the desk.

2 When you **spin** washing, it is turned round and V+O round quickly in a spin drier or a washing machine to get the water out.

3 If your head **is spinning**, you feel dizzy because V : USU CONT you are excited, ill, or drunk. EG *His head was spinning from wine and liqueurs.*

4 When people **spin**, they make thread by twisting V OR V+O together pieces of fibre using a device or machine. EG *My mother taught me to spin.*

spin out. If you **spin** something **out**, you make it PHRASAL VB : last longer than it otherwise would. EG *I might be* V+O+ADV *able to spin my talk out to three-quarters of an hour.*

spinach /spɪnɪdʒ, -ɪtʃ/ is a kind of vegetable with N UNCOUNT large green leaves.

spinal /spaɪnᵊl/ means relating to your spine. EG ADJ CLASSIF *...the spinal joints... ...a spinal injury.* ATTRIB

spinal column, **spinal columns**. Your **spinal** N COUNT **column** is your spine. Formal

spinal cord, **spinal cords**. Your **spinal cord** is a N COUNT bundle of nerves inside your spine which connects your brain to nerves in all parts of your body.

spindly /spɪndli¹/. Something that is **spindly** is ADJ QUALIT long and thin and looks very weak. EG *...spindly legs... ...spindly trees.*

spin drier, **spin driers**; also spelled **spin dryer**. N COUNT A **spin drier** is a machine that is used to spin washing to get the water out.

spin-dry, **spin-dries**, **spin-drying**, **spin-dried**. V+O When you **spin-dry** washing, you get the water out of it using a spin drier or a washing machine.

spine /spaɪn/, **spines**. 1 Your **spine** is the row of N COUNT bones down your back. EG *...pressure on the spine... A bullet penetrated his spine.*

2 The **spine** of a book is the narrow stiff part N COUNT which the pages and covers are attached to.

3 **Spines** are also long, sharp points on an animal's N COUNT body or on a plant. EG *...a cactus with red spines.*

spineless /spaɪnlɪ²s/. If you say that someone is ADJ QUALIT **spineless**, you mean that they are cowardly. EG *I think they're a spineless pair... Oh, you're so spineless.*

spin-off, **spin-offs**. A **spin-off** is something useful N COUNT OR that unexpectedly results from an activity that was N UNCOUNT designed to achieve something else. EG *The search for knowledge frequently has beneficial spin-offs for mankind.*

spinster /spɪnstə/, **spinsters**. A **spinster** is a N COUNT woman who has never been married, especially an Outdated old or middle-aged woman. Formal

spiral /spaɪərᵊl/, **spirals**, **spiralling**, **spiralled**; spelled **spiraling** and **spiraled** in American English. 1 A **spiral** is a curved shape which winds N COUNT round and round, with each curve above the previous one or outside it. ▸ used as an adjective. EG *We* ▸ ADJ CLASSIF : *followed him up the spiral staircase... ...an antelope* ATTRIB *with spiral horns.*

2 If something **spirals**, it moves up or down in a V+A spiral curve. EG *The swans came spiralling down... A small bird shot up, spiralling into the sky.*

3 If an amount or level **spirals**, it rises quickly and V at an increasing rate. EG *Military budgets had continued to spiral.* ▸ used as a noun. EG *...a wage* ▸ N SING *and price spiral.*

4 If an amount or level **spirals** downwards, it falls V+A quickly and at an increasing rate. EG *Costs started to spiral downwards.* ▸ used as a noun. EG *Industry* ▸ N SING+SUPP *entered a spiral of decline.*

spire /spaɪə/, **spires**. The **spire** of a church is the N COUNT tall cone-shaped structure on the top.

spirit /spɪrɪt/, **spirits**, **spiriting**, **spirited**. 1 Your N SING **spirit** is the part of you that is not physical and that is connected with your deepest thoughts and feelings. EG *Fulfilment must be sought through the spirit, not the body or the mind.*

2 The **spirit** of a dead person is a non-physical part N COUNT

of them that is believed to remain alive after their death. EG *We pray to our dead ancestors' spirits.*

3 A **spirit** is also a supernatural being. EG *The charm is worn to ward off evil spirits.* N COUNT

4 Spirit is liveliness, energy, and self-confidence. N UNCOUNT EG *...a performance full of spirit and originality.*

5 You can use **spirit** to refer to a particular kind of N SING+SUPP attitude. EG *...the pioneering spirit... He made the proposal in a spirit of rebellion... Governments must approach this subject in a new spirit.*

6 If you **enter into the spirit** of an activity or PHRASE event, you take part in it in an enthusiastic way. EG *Try to enter into the spirit of the thing.*

7 You can refer to your **spirits** when saying how N PLURAL happy or unhappy you are. For example, if your +SUPP spirits are high, you are happy. EG *The children lifted my spirits with their laughter.*

8 The **spirit** of a law or an agreement is the way N SING: that it was intended to be interpreted or applied. EG the+N+of *I think we'd be breaking the spirit of the agreement if we went ahead.*

9 Spirits are strong alcoholic drinks such as N PLURAL whisky and gin. EG *They brought with them several bottles of spirits.*

10 If you **spirit** someone out of a place or **spirit** V+O+A them into it, you get them out of it or into it quickly and secretly. EG *Somehow the Action Service had spirited him across the frontier.*

11 See also **white spirit**.

spirited /spɪrɪtɪ¹d/. A **spirited** action shows great ADJ QUALIT energy and courage. EG *Despite spirited resistance by Republican forces, the town fell to the Nationalists... ...spirited discussions.* ● See also **high-spirited**, **public-spirited**.

spiritual /spɪrɪtʃʊ⁰əl/ means **1** relating to people's ADJ CLASSIF deepest thoughts and beliefs, rather than to their bodies and physical surroundings. EG *...people's pursuit of material ends to the neglect of their spiritual needs.* ◇ **spiritually**. EG *...a spiritually* ◇ ADV sick society. ◇ **spirituality** /spɪrɪtjuælɪ¹tɪ¹/. EG ◇ N UNCOUNT *...the decline of spirituality in our time.* **2** relating ADJ CLASSIF to people's religious beliefs. EG *...the spiritual authority of the Christian Church.*

spit /spɪt/, **spits**, **spitting**, **spat** /spæt/. **Spit** is used as the past tense of the verb in American English.

1 Spit is the watery liquid produced in your mouth. N UNCOUNT You usually use **spit** to refer to an amount of it that has been forced out of someone's mouth.

2 When people say someone **spits**, they force an amount of spit V out of their mouth, sometimes in order to show hatred or scorn. EG *The driver spat contemptuously.*

3 If you **spit** liquid or food somewhere, you force a V+O: USU+A small amount of it out of your mouth. EG *If I don't like it I can always spit it out.*

4 When people say someone **spits** in an angry or V+O: hostile way, you can say that they **spit** it out. EG *He* OFT+QUOTE *spat out his answer.* OR V+O+out

5 If it is raining very lightly, you can say that it **is** V: ONLY CONT **spitting**. EG *'Is it raining?' – 'Only spitting.'*

6 A **spit** is a long rod which is pushed through a N COUNT piece of meat and hung over an open fire while the meat is roasted. EG *There was still food left on the wooden spits.*

7 If you say that someone is **the spitting image of** PHRASE another person, you mean that they look very like that other person. EG *She was the spitting image of his mother.*

spite /spaɪt/. **1** You use **in spite of** to introduce a PREP statement which makes what you have just said seem surprising. EG *The morning air was still clear and fresh, in spite of all the traffic... In spite of poor health, my father was always cheerful.*

2 If you do something **in spite of** yourself, you do it PREP although you did not really intend to or expect to. EG *Jane became edgy in spite of herself.*

3 If you do something nasty because of **spite**, you N UNCOUNT

do it deliberately because you want to hurt or upset someone. EG *He wrote that review out of pure spite.*

4 If you do something nasty to **spite** someone, you V+O: ONLY INF do it deliberately in order to hurt or annoy them. EG *They are being controversial just to spite us.*

5 If you **cut off** your **nose to spite** your **face**, you PHRASE deliberately do something that you think will hurt someone, without realizing or caring that it will hurt you as well.

spiteful /spaɪtful/. Someone who is **spiteful** does ADJ QUALIT nasty things to people they dislike. EG *Thomas could be so spiteful to his little brother... They told spiteful stories about her.*

spittle /spɪtə⁰l/ is the watery liquid which is N UNCOUNT produced in your mouth. Outdated

splash /splæʃ/, **splashes**, **splashing**, **splashed**. **1** V+A OR V+O If you **splash** around in water, you hit or disturb the water in a noisy way, causing some of it to fly up into the air. EG *Ralph started to run, splashing through the shallow water... They proceeded to hurl themselves about, splashing everybody within sight.*

2 If water **splashes** on something or **splashes** V+A OR V+O something, it hits it and scatters in a lot of small drops. EG *Drenching spray splashed over the deck... They flinched as the cold rain splashed them.*

3 If you **splash** a liquid somewhere, you pour or V+O+A throw it there rather carelessly. EG *He splashed his face with water... Otto splashed some brandy into a glass.*

4 A **splash** is the sound made when something hits N COUNT water or falls into it. EG *She disappeared into the water with a splash.*

5 A **splash** of a liquid is a small quantity of it that N PART OR has been spilt on something. EG *He wiped away the* N COUNT *splash of gasoline on the near fender.*

6 A **splash** of colour is an area of a bright colour N PART which contrasts strongly with the colours around it. EG *A large bouquet of tulips made a brilliant splash of yellow on the table.*

splash out. If you **splash out** on something, PHRASAL VB: especially on a luxury, you buy it even though it V+ADV, costs a lot of money. EG *We splashed out on a colour* OFT+on television. Informal

splatter /splætə/, **splatters**, **splattering**, **splat-** V-ERG: USU+A **tered.** If a thick wet substance **is splattered** on something or **splatters** on it, it is splashed or thrown over it. EG *Food was splattered all over the kitchen walls... She was wearing an apron splattered with blood.*

splay /spleɪ/, **splays**, **splaying**, **splayed.** If two V-ERG: or more things **are splayed** or **splay** out, their OFT+out ends are spread out away from each other. EG *He pressed the mattress with splayed fingers... The brush's bristles were beginning to splay out.*

splendid /splendɪd/. **1** If you say that something is ADJ QUALIT **splendid**, you mean that it is excellent. EG *She wrote splendid detective novels... I think it's a splendid idea... I thought life was simply splendid.* ◇ **splendidly**. EG *She was caring for him splendid-* ◇ ADV *ly.*

2 If you say that a building or work of art is ADJ QUALIT **splendid**, you mean that it is beautiful and impressive. EG *...splendid seventeenth-century paintings... In the middle of Hull stands a splendid Victorian building.* ◇ **splendidly**. EG *...a splendidly furnished* ◇ ADV *room.*

splendour /splendə/, **splendours**; spelled **splen-dor** in American English. **1** If you talk about the N UNCOUNT **splendour** of something, you are referring to the fact that it is beautiful and impressive. EG *...the splendour of Urbino... The room was decorated with great splendour.*

2 The **splendours** of something are its beautiful N PLURAL

If you splash out on a new coat, do you get it wet?

and impressive features. EG ...*the Elizabethan splendours of Watermouth Hall.*

splint /splɪnt/, **splints**. A **splint** is a long piece of N COUNT wood or metal that is fastened to a broken arm, leg, or back.

splinter /splɪntə/, **splinters, splintering, splintered.** 1 A **splinter** is a very thin, sharp piece of N COUNT wood, glass, or other hard substance, which has broken off from a larger piece. EG ...*splinters of coloured glass... Sue was worried about splinters in her bare feet.*
2 If something **splinters** or **is splintered**, it V-ERG breaks into thin, sharp pieces. EG *When feeding dogs, avoid chicken, rabbit or fish bones which can splinter... ...the splintered wood of a snapped plank.*
3 A **splinter** group or organization is a group of ADJ CLASSIF: people who break away from a larger group and ATTRIB form a separate organization.

split /splɪt/, **splits, splitting.** The form **split** is used in the present tense and is the past tense and past participle of the verb.
1 If something **splits** or if you **split** it, it is divided V-ERG into two or more parts. EG *Three people died when their car split in two after hitting a tree... Main roads like motorways can split communities in half... The children were split into two groups.*
2 If an organization **splits** or **is split**, one group of V-ERG members disagree strongly with the other members. EG *The council split down the middle over the issue... The government is split on how to deal with the situation.* ▸ used as a noun. EG *The last thing he* ▸ N COUNT: *wanted was a split in the party.* USU + *in*
3 A **split** between two things is a division or N COUNT: difference between them. EG *He experiences a split* USU SING- *between his thoughts and his actions... ...the split* *between* *between reality and the perception of it.*
4 If something such as wood or a piece of clothing V-ERG **splits** or **is split**, a long crack or tear appears in it. EG *It was a very poor quality wood which had already split in many places.* ▸ used as an adjec- ▸ ADJ CLASSIF tive. EG *Eric fingered his split lip.*
5 A **split** is also a long crack or tear. EG *There's a* N COUNT *split down the page of the atlas.*
6 If two or more people **split** something, they V+O share it between them. EG *The profits are to be split fifty-fifty between the two of them.*
7 If you **split the difference**, you agree on a PHRASE figure which is halfway between the two different figures that have been mentioned. EG *Okay, we'll split the difference and call it £10.*
8 to **split hairs**: see **hair**. ● See also **splitting**.

split off. If part of something **splits off** or **is** PHRASAL VB: **split off** from the main part of it, it breaks off or is V-ERG+ADV broken or cut off. EG *A particle splits off from the nucleus... A block had been split off from the rock.*

split up. 1 If two people **split up**, they end their PHRASAL VB: relationship or marriage. EG *Howard and I have* V+ADV OR *split up... They are more likely to split up and less* V+ADV+*with*: *likely to remarry... After he split up with his wife* RECIP *he went to Arizona.* 2 If a group of people **split up**, V+ADV *they go away in different directions.* EG *In Hamburg the girls split up.* 3 If you **split** something **up**, you V+O+ADV, *divide it so that it is in a number of smaller* USU+*into* *separate sections.* EG *You might achieve more by splitting them up into small groups.*

split second. You can refer to a very short N SING period of time as a **split second**. EG *For a split second nothing happened... She has to make split-second decisions.*

splitting /splɪtɪŋ/. A **splitting** headache is a very ADJ CLASSIF: severe one. ATTRIB

splutter /splʌtə/, **splutters, spluttering, spluttered.** 1 If someone **splutters**, they make spitting V OR V+QUOTE sounds and have difficulty speaking clearly. EG *The fumes make you cough and splutter... 'I know them. They're my friends,' I was spluttering.* ▸ used as a ▸ N COUNT: noun. EG *'Of course not,' she said with a splutter of* USU SING *mirth.*
2 If something **splutters**, it makes a series of V

short, sharp sounds. EG ...*the roaring and spluttering of motorbikes.*

spoil /spɔɪl/, **spoils, spoiling, spoiled, spoilt** /spɔɪlt/. The past participle can be either **spoiled** or **spoilt.**
1 If you **spoil** something, you prevent it from being V+O successful or satisfactory. EG *She shouted at him for spoiling her lovely evening... The presence of the woman spoiled his enjoyment of the view.*
2 If you **spoil** children, you give them everything V+O they want or ask for, which has a bad effect on their character. EG *You're spoiling him, Frieda.*
◇ **spoilt** or **spoiled**. EG ...*a spoilt brat.* ◇ ADJ QUALIT
3 If you **spoil** yourself or **spoil** someone you love, V-REFL OR V+O you give yourself or them something nice as a treat. EG *During the first week of the diet, you can spoil yourself a little.*
4 **Spoils** are things that people get as a result of N PLURAL: winning a battle or of doing something else suc- *the*+N cessfully. EG ...*the spoils of war.* Literary

spoil for. If you **are spoiling for** trouble or a PHRASAL VB: fight, you are very eager for it to happen. EG *The* V+PREP, *unions are spoiling for a fight about pay and* ONLY CONT *conditions once again.*

spoke /spəʊk/, **spokes.** 1 **Spoke** is the past tense of **speak.**
2 The **spokes** of a wheel are the bars that connect N COUNT: the outer ring to the centre. See picture at BICYCLE. USU PLURAL EG *Her baby caught his fingers in the spokes of the pram wheel.*

spoken /spəʊkə⁰n/ is the past participle of **speak.**
● See also **well-spoken.**

spokesman /spəʊksmə⁰n/, **spokesmen.** A N COUNT **spokesman** is a person who speaks as the representative of a group or organization. EG *Common Market spokesmen claim that more than 800,000 jobs have been lost recently.*

spokesperson /spəʊkspɜːsə⁰n/, **spokespersons.** N COUNT A **spokesperson** is the same as a spokesman. EG ...*the spokesperson for the delegation.*

spokeswoman /spəʊkswʊmən/, **spokeswomen.** N COUNT A **spokeswoman** is a female spokesman. EG *'They are staying here as guests of the Queen,' said a Palace spokeswoman.*

sponge /spʌndʒ/, **sponges, sponging, sponged.** 1 N COUNT OR A **sponge** is a piece of a squashy, absorbent N UNCOUNT substance with lots of little holes in it that you use for cleaning things or washing your body. EG *Wipe the surface with a clean sponge.*
2 If you **sponge** something, you clean it by wiping V+O it with a wet sponge. EG *Don't immerse it in water; just sponge it lightly.*
3 A **sponge** is also a light cake or pudding made N COUNT OR from flour, eggs, sugar, and sometimes fat. EG N UNCOUNT ...*baked apple with a layer of sponge on top.*

sponge off or **sponge on.** Someone who PHRASAL VB: **sponges off** other people or **sponges on** them V+PREP regularly gets money from them without giving Informal anything in return; used showing disapproval. EG *He sponged on his friends.*

spongebag /spʌndʒbæg/, **spongebags.** A N COUNT **spongebag** is a small bag in which you keep things British such as soap, a flannel, and a toothbrush when you are travelling.

spongy /spʌndʒi/. Something that is **spongy** is ADJ QUALIT soft and squashy, like a sponge. EG ...*spongy bread.*

sponsor /spɒnsə/, **sponsors, sponsoring, sponsored.** 1 If people or organizations **sponsor** some- V+O thing such as an event or someone's training, they pay some or all of the expenses connected with it, often in order to get publicity for themselves. EG *The Administration is sponsoring a research programme... The conference was sponsored by the Guardian.*
2 If you **sponsor** someone who is doing something V+O to raise money for charity, for example running a marathon, you agree to give them a sum of money for the charity if they succeed in doing it. EG *Would*

you mind sponsoring me in this swim for cancer research... A sponsored walk brought in £16000.

3 If you **sponsor** a proposal or suggestion, you v+o officially put it forward and support it. EG Two Liberal MPs sponsored the Bill.

4 A **sponsor** is a person or organization that N COUNT sponsors something or someone. EG ...the sponsor of the lectures... ...Virginia Slims, sponsors of the first professional women's tennis tour.

sponsorship /spɒnsəʃɪp/ is financial support that N UNCOUNT is given to someone by a sponsor. EG ...industrial sponsorship of the arts.

spontaneity /spɒntəniːˈɪtiˈ, -neɪ-/ is spontaneous, N UNCOUNT natural behaviour. EG ...a child's spontaneity.

spontaneous /spɒnteɪnɪəs/. **1 Spontaneous** acts ADJ QUALIT are not planned or arranged, but are done because someone suddenly wants to do them. EG ...a spontaneous display of friendship and affection.

◊ **spontaneously**. EG Flo and I decided sponta- ◊ ADV neously to board a train for Geneva.

2 A **spontaneous** event happens because of pro- ADJ QUALIT cesses within something rather than being caused by things outside it. EG ...spontaneous explosions.

◊ **spontaneously**. EG The fuel ignites spontaneous- ◊ ADV ly from the heat created by the compression.

spoof /spuːf/, **spoofs**. A **spoof** is something such N COUNT as an article or television programme that seems to be about a serious matter but is actually a joke. EG The weather forecast seemed to be some kind of spoof, predicting every possible combination of weather.

spooky /spuːkiˈ/, **spookier, spookiest**. A place ADJ QUALIT that is **spooky** has a frightening atmosphere, and Informal makes you feel that there are ghosts around. EG The Highlands are unbearably spooky... The whole place had a slightly spooky atmosphere.

spool /spuːl/, **spools**. A **spool** is a round object N COUNT onto which thread, tape, or film can be wound, especially before it is put in a sewing machine, tape recorder, or projector. EG She re-wound the tape back on to the spool.

spoon /spuːn/, **spoons, spooning, spooned**. **1** A N COUNT **spoon** is an object used for eating, stirring, and serving food. It is shaped like a small shallow bowl with a long handle. EG ...a knife, fork, and spoon.

2 You can use **spoon** to refer to the amount of a N PART substance that a spoon can hold, as in a **spoon** of sugar or a **spoon** of salt. EG He takes six spoons of sugar in his tea.

3 If you **spoon** food somewhere, you pick the food v+o : USU+A up in a spoon and put it there. EG He spooned the vegetables onto the plates.

spoonful /spuːnfʊl/, **spoonfuls**. A **spoonful** of a N PART substance is the amount that a spoon can hold. EG She put a spoonful of milk in each of the two cups.

sporadic /spəˈrædɪk/. **Sporadic** occurrences of ADJ QUALIT something happen at irregular intervals. EG ...spo- radic glimpses of truth... Sporadic attacks con- tinued throughout the night. ◊ **sporadically**. EG ◊ ADV Most families watch television sporadically.

spore /spɔː/, **spores**. **Spores** are cells produced N COUNT by bacteria and non-flowering plants such as fungi Technical which can develop into new bacteria and plants.

sport /spɔːt/, **sports, sporting, sported**. **1** Sports N UNCOUNT are games such as football and cricket and other OR N COUNT enjoyable activities which need physical effort and skill. EG My favourite sport is football... I was bad at sport... ...a sports reporter.

2 If you say that someone is a **sport** or a good N COUNT **sport**, you mean that they accept defeat or teasing Outdated in a cheerful way. EG Be a sport, Madeleine.

3 If you **sport** something noticeable or unusual, v+o you wear it. EG He sported a beard... One of them even sported an earring.

sporting /spɔːtɪŋ/ means relating to sport or used ADJ CLASSIF : for sport. EG It was his 29th international sporting ATTRIB event... ...a new sporting gun.

sports car, sports cars. A **sports car** is a low, N COUNT fast car, usually with room for only two people.

sports jacket, sports jackets. A **sports jacket** N COUNT is a man's jacket, usually made of tweed.

sportsman /spɔːtsməˈn/, **sportsmen**. A **sports-** N COUNT **man** is a man who takes part in sports.

sportswoman /spɔːtswʊmən/, **sportswomen**. A N COUNT **sportswoman** is a woman who takes part in sports. EG She is an enthusiastic sportswoman.

spot /spɒt/, **spots, spotting, spotted**. **1 Spots** are N COUNT small, round, coloured areas on a surface. EG She was wearing a white blouse with red spots.

2 Spots on a person's skin are small lumps or N COUNT marks, caused, for example, by a disease. EG Their bites leave itching red spots on the skin.

3 A **spot** of a substance is a small amount of it. EG I N COUNT think there's a spot of ketchup on the tablecloth... I OR N PART felt a few spots of rain.

4 If you have a **spot** of something, you have a small N PART amount of it. EG He invited them down for a spot of Informal grouse-shooting... What about a spot of lunch?

5 You can refer to a particular place as a **spot**. EG N COUNT : It's a lovely spot for a picnic... Four brass plates in USU+SUPP the floor mark the spot where the throne stood.

6 A **spot** in a television or radio show is a part of it N COUNT : that is regularly reserved for a particular perform- USU+SUPP er or type of entertainment. EG She's going to do a guest spot on the Muppet Show.

7 If you **spot** something, you notice it. EG I spotted v+o you standing by your car at the gas station.

8 On the spot is used in these ways. **8.1** If you are PHRASES **on the spot**, you are at the actual place where something is happening. EG Certain decisions had to be taken by the man on the spot. **8.2** If you do something **on the spot**, you do it immediately. EG They dismissed him on the spot. **8.3** If you **put** someone **on the spot**, you cause them to have to answer a difficult question or make a difficult decision. EG I think you've put him on the spot there.

9 to **have a soft spot for** someone: see **soft**. ● See also **blind spot**, **spotted**.

spot check, spot checks. A **spot check** is a N COUNT random inspection of one thing among a group of things.

spotless /spɒtlɪˈs/. Something that is **spotless** is ADJ QUALIT perfectly clean. EG ...a spotless white shirt.

spotlight /spɒtlaɪt/, **spotlights, spotlighting, spotlighted**. **1** A **spotlight** is a powerful light, N COUNT often in a theatre, which can be directed so that it lights up a small area. EG A spotlight threw a pool of light onto the stage.

2 Someone or something that is in the **spotlight** is N SING : the+N getting a great deal of public attention. EG I was inevitably the man in the spotlight... This incident turned the spotlight on Trent's discoveries.

spot-on means exactly correct or accurate. EG You ADJ CLASSIF can use this weapon at 130 metres with spot-on Informal accuracy.

spotted /spɒtɪd/. Something that is **spotted** has a ADJ CLASSIF pattern of spots on it. EG ...a red and white spotted handkerchief.

spotty /spɒtiˈ/. Someone who is **spotty** has spots ADJ QUALIT or pimples on their skin, especially on their face. EG ...spotty adolescents.

spouse /spaʊs, spaʊz/, **spouses**. Someone's N COUNT **spouse** is the person they are married to. EG They Formal receive free membership for themselves and their spouses.

spout /spaʊt/, **spouts, spouting, spouted**. **1** V-ERG : USU+A When liquid or flame **spouts** out of something, it comes out very fast in a long stream. EG ...jets of water spouting up from the basins below... Their tanks came on in hordes, spouting flames.

2 If you say that someone **is spouting** something, v+o OR you mean that they are saying something that they v+about have learned and that they are saying it in a boring

What is the difference between spotted and spotty?

way. EG *You were always spouting some theory to us at the table.*

3 The **spout** of a kettle or teapot is the tube that N COUNT the liquid comes out of when you pour it.

sprain /spreɪn/, **sprains, spraining, sprained.** **1** V+O If you **sprain** a joint such as your ankle or wrist, you accidentally damage it by twisting it or bending it violently. EG *Rosa fell and sprained her ankle.*

2 A **sprain** is the injury caused by spraining a joint. N COUNT

sprang /spræŋ/ is the past tense of **spring.**

sprawl /sprɔːl/, **sprawls, sprawling, sprawled.**
1 If you **sprawl** somewhere, you sit or lie down V : OFT+*out* with your legs and arms spread out in a careless way. EG *Segal sprawled out on the couch... I tried to pick it up, but I overbalanced and fell sprawling.*

2 If you say that a place **sprawls**, you mean that it V+A covers a large area of land. EG *The village sprawls along the coastline... The university sprawls across the Lenin Hills.* ◊ **sprawling.** EG *...a large, sprawl-* ◊ ADJ QUALIT *ing villa... ...a sprawling city.*

3 You can use **sprawl** to refer to an area where a N UNCOUNT city has expanded in an untidy and uncontrolled +SUPP way. EG *The new towns were to bring an end to London's urban sprawl.*

sprawled /sprɔːld/. If you are **sprawled** some- ADJ PRED+A where, you are sitting or lying with your legs and arms spread out in a careless way. EG *He lay sprawled in the chair with his legs stretched out.*

spray /spreɪ/, **sprays, spraying, sprayed.**
1 **Spray** is a lot of small drops of water which are N UNCOUNT being splashed or forced into the air. EG *Drenching* OR PART *spray splashed over the deck... A spray of salt water hit her in the face... ...clouds of spray.*

2 A **spray** is a liquid kept under pressure in a can N MASS or other container, which you can force out in very small drops. EG *...chemical sprays... ...hair spray... ...a spray insecticide.*

3 If you **spray** a liquid over something or if you V+O : USU+A **spray** something with a liquid, you cover it with drops of the liquid, for example using a hose or an aerosol. EG *He sprayed a little eau-de-cologne over himself... Spray the shelves with insecticide.*

4 If a lot of small things **spray** somewhere or if you V+A ; ALSO **spray** something with them, they are scattered V+O : USU+A with a lot of force. EG *A fine red dust sprayed out from the edge of the saw... He was spraying the street with bullets.*

5 A **spray** is a piece of equipment for spraying N COUNT water or another liquid, especially over growing plants. EG *...an ordinary garden spray.*

6 A **spray** of flowers or leaves is a number of N PART flowers or leaves on one stem or branch. EG *...great sprays of lilies.*

spray can, spray cans. A **spray can** is a can N COUNT containing liquid under pressure which can be sprayed out.

spread /spred/, **spreads, spreading.** The form **spread** is used in the present tense and is the past tense and past participle of the verb.

1 If you **spread** something, you open it out or V+O : USU+A arrange it over a place or surface, so that all of it can be seen or used easily. EG *He took the envelope, tipped it open and spread the contents on the table.*

2 If you **spread** a part of your body, for example V+O your fingers or arms, you stretch them out until they are far apart. EG *He just shrugged and spread his hands.*

3 If you **spread** a substance on a surface or V+O : USU+A **spread** the surface with the substance, you put a thin layer of the substance over the surface. EG *Liz was spreading marmalade on a piece of toast... I love biscuits spread with butter.*

4 A **spread** is a soft food which is put on bread. EG N MASS *...cheese spread.*

5 If something **spreads** or **is spread** by people, it V-ERG : USU+A gradually reaches or affects a larger and larger area or more and more people. EG *A stain was spreading on the bathroom ceiling... News of the wreck spread quickly... Disease might be spread*

very easily. ▶ used as a noun. EG *Girls have* ▶ N SING *benefited more than boys from the spread of higher education.*

6 If something **spreads** over a period of time, it V+*over* OR takes place regularly or continuously over that V+O+*over* period. EG *They had experience spreading over twenty years... The breeding season is spread over five months.*

7 If you **spread** something such as wealth or work, V+O you distribute it evenly or equally. EG *You are advised to spread the workload.*

8 A **spread** of ideas, interests, or other things is a N SING : USU+*of* wide variety of them. EG *The IBA wants to have a broad spread of opinion represented on its board.*

spread out. 1 If people, animals, or vehicles PHRASAL VB : **spread out** or **are spread out**, they are far apart. V-ERG+ADV EG *They followed him and spread out, nervously, in the forest... My family were spread out all over the countryside.* **2** If something such as a city or forest V-ERG+ADV **spreads out** or **is spread out**, it covers a large area. EG *Through the window, you can see the town spread out below.* **3** If you **spread** something **out**, V+O+ADV you open it out or arrange it over a place or surface, so that all of it can be seen or used easily. EG *I removed the tool kit and spread it out on the seat.* **4** If you **spread out** a part of your body, for V+O+ADV example your fingers or arms, you stretch them out until they are far apart. EG *He lifted up a hand and held it there, the fingers spread out.*

spread-eagled /spred iːgəˈld/. Someone who is ADJ CLASSIF **spread-eagled** is lying with their arms and legs spread out. EG *Stephanie found him spreadeagled on the stairs.*

spree /spriː/, **sprees.** If you spend a long time N COUNT : doing something that you enjoy, you can say that USU+SUPP you are going on a particular kind of **spree.** EG *Tim was away on a shopping spree... He went on a drinking spree.*

sprig /sprɪg/, **sprigs.** A **sprig** of a plant is a small N COUNT : twig or stem with leaves on it which someone has USU+*of* picked. EG *...a sprig of holly.*

sprightly /spraɪtliˈ/. Someone, especially an old ADJ QUALIT person, who is **sprightly** is lively and active. EG *Jimmy McGregor is a sprightly 71-year old.*

spring /sprɪŋ/, **springs, springing, sprang** /spræŋ/, **sprung** /sprʌŋ/. **Sprung** is the past participle of the verb and is sometimes used in American English as the past tense.

1 **Spring** is the season between winter and sum- N UNCOUNT mer. In the spring the weather begins to get OR N COUNT warmer and leaves and plants start to grow again. EG *It would have been better to have waited until the spring... He left in the spring of 1956.*

2 A **spring** is a coil of wire which returns to its N COUNT original shape after it is pressed or pulled. EG *One day they would get a real sofa, with springs.*

3 A **spring** is also a place where water comes up N COUNT through the ground. EG *...hot volcanic springs.*

4 When a person or animal **springs**, they jump V : USU+A upwards or forwards. EG *She sprang to her feet and faced him... The panther crouched, ready to spring.*

5 If something **springs** in a particular direction, it V+A moves suddenly and quickly. EG *Hands sprang up... The door of the safe had sprung open.*

6 If things or people **spring** into action or **spring** V+A to life, they suddenly start being active or suddenly come into existence. EG *A computer will not spring into action without something powering it... At last factories sprang to life again.*

7 If one thing **springs** from another thing, it is the V+*from*/ result of it. EG *These problems spring from differ-* *out of* *ent causes... Her hostility to him sprang out of sheer envy.*

8 If a boat or container **springs a leak**, water or PHRASE some other liquid starts coming in or out through a hole or crack.

9 If you **spring** some news or a surprise on V+O : OFT+*on* someone, you tell them something unexpected, without warning them. EG *It was then that I sprang* *my surprise... He wondered why this story should be sprung on him.*

spring up. If something **springs up**, it suddenly appears or comes into existence. EG *Computer stores are springing up all over the place.* PHRASAL VB : V+ADV

springboard /sprɪŋbɔːd/, **springboards.** 1 If something is a **springboard** for an action or enterprise, it makes it possible for the action or enterprise to begin. EG *The campaign might well be the springboard for the launching of a new party.* N COUNT : USU+for/to

2 A **springboard** is also a flexible board which you jump on before performing a dive or a gymnastic movement. N COUNT

spring-clean, spring-cleans, spring-cleaning, spring-cleaned. When you **spring-clean** a house, you thoroughly clean everything in it. ◊ **spring-cleaning.** EG *Mrs Pringle came to give me a hand with the spring-cleaning.* V OR V+O ◊ N UNCOUNT

spring onion, spring onions. A **spring onion** is a small onion with long green leaves that is often eaten raw in salads. N COUNT

springtime /sprɪŋtaɪm/ is the period of time during which spring lasts. EG *In the springtime the mountains take on a purple hue.* N UNCOUNT

springy /sprɪŋiˈ/. If something is **springy**, it returns quickly to its original shape after you press it. EG *...a springy mattress... The grass was short and springy.* ADJ QUALIT

sprinkle /sprɪŋkəˈl/, **sprinkles, sprinkling, sprinkled.** If you **sprinkle** something such as a liquid or powder over something, you scatter it over it. EG *Sprinkle the oil over the courgettes... She sprinkled the cakes with sugar.* V+O : USU+A

sprinkler /sprɪŋklə/, **sprinklers.** A **sprinkler** is a device used to spray water. Sprinklers are used to water plants or lawns or to put out a fire in a building. N COUNT

sprinkling /sprɪŋklɪŋ/. A **sprinkling** of something is a small quantity of it, especially one that is spread over a large area. EG *There is always a sprinkling of sightseers outside the palace... ...a sprinkling of grey hairs.* N PART : USU SING

sprint /sprɪnt/, **sprints, sprinting, sprinted.** 1 A **sprint** is 1.1 a short race in which the runners run very fast. EG *...a 100 metre sprint.* 1.2 a fast run. EG *Bessie had suddenly broken into a sprint.* N COUNT N SING

2 If you **sprint**, you run as fast as you can over a short distance. EG *She sprinted to her car.* V : USU+A

sprinter /sprɪntə/, **sprinters.** A **sprinter** is a person who takes part in short, fast races. N COUNT

sprout /spraʊt/, **sprouts, sprouting, sprouted.** 1 When plants or vegetables **sprout**, they produce new leaves or shoots. V OR V+O

2 When leaves or shoots **sprout** somewhere, they grow there. EG *Greenery sprouted between the white gravestones.* V

3 When hairs, feathers, or horns **sprout** or when a person or animal **sprouts** them, they grow. EG *...the hairs sprouting from a mole on her cheek... Some of the young men sprouted moustaches.* V-ERG

4 If things **sprout** up or if something **sprouts** them, they appear or spread rapidly. EG *Caravans had suddenly sprouted up in the fields... San Francisco has sprouted a rash of little theatres.* V-ERG

5 **Sprouts** or **Brussels sprouts** are vegetables like very small cabbages. N COUNT : OFT PLURAL

6 A **sprout** is a new shoot on a plant. EG *They produce new sprouts almost immediately.* N COUNT

spruce /spruːs/. **Spruce** is both the singular and the plural form.

1 A **spruce** is a kind of evergreen tree. N COUNT

2 Someone who is **spruce** is very neat and smart in appearance. EG *Miss Jackson arrived looking very spruce in a new linen suit.* ADJ QUALIT

sprung /sprʌŋ/ is the past participle or a past tense of **spring**.

spry /spraɪ/, **spryer, spryest.** Someone, especially an old person, who is **spry** is lively and active. EG *Now, at eighty, he was as spry as ever.* ADJ QUALIT

spud /spʌd/, **spuds. Spuds** are potatoes. EG *Are the spuds cooked yet?* N COUNT Informal

spun /spʌn/ is the past tense and past participle of **spin**.

spur /spɜː/, **spurs, spurring, spurred.** 1 If something **spurs** you to do something or **spurs** you on, it encourages you to do it. EG *I am not conceited about my achievement but I am spurred on by it... Martin's job offer spurred the others to do something themselves.* V+O+to-INF OR on

2 If something **spurs** a change or event, it makes it happen faster or sooner. EG *...a period of extremely rapid growth, spurred by the advent of the microprocessor.* V+O

3 Something that acts as a **spur** encourages a person to do something or makes something happen faster or sooner. EG *International competition was a spur to modernisation.* N SING+to

4 If you do something **on the spur of the moment**, you do it suddenly, without planning it beforehand. EG *I just took the bus on the spur of the moment.* ● See also **spur-of-the-moment.** PHRASE

5 **Spurs** are small metal wheels with sharp points attached to the heels of a rider's boots. The rider uses them to urge a horse to go faster. N COUNT

spurious /spjʊərɪəs/. Something that is **spurious** is not genuine or real. EG *I felt a moment's spurious comfort... ...the spurious attractions of modernity.* ADJ QUALIT

spurn /spɜːn/, **spurns, spurning, spurned.** If you **spurn** something, you refuse to accept it. EG *You spurned my friendship.* V+O Formal

spur-of-the-moment. A **spur-of-the-moment** action or decision is sudden and has not been planned. EG *...spur-of-the-moment impulses.* ADJ CLASSIF : ATTRIB

spurt /spɜːt/, **spurts, spurting, spurted.** 1 When a liquid or flame **spurts** out of something, it comes out quickly in a thin, powerful stream. EG *...a blow that sent blood spurting from his mouth... My arm began to spurt blood.* ▸ used as a noun. EG *...a small, clear spurt of flame.* V-ERG : USU+A ▸ N COUNT

2 A **spurt** of activity, effort, or emotion is a sudden, brief period of it. EG *Her feelings varied from tenderness to sudden spurts of genuine love.* N COUNT : USU+SUPP

3 If you **spurt** somewhere, you suddenly increase your speed for a short while. EG *With Claude driving they spurted through back streets.* ▸ used as a noun. EG *He drove past cars in fast spurts.* V : USU+A ▸ N COUNT

sputter /spʌtə/, **sputters, sputtering, sputtered.** If something **sputters**, it makes soft hissing and popping sounds. EG *The engine began coughing and sputtering.* V

spy /spaɪ/, **spies, spying, spied.** 1 A **spy** is a person whose job is to find out secret information about another country or organization. EG *A member of his staff was discovered to be a foreign spy.* N COUNT

2 Someone who **spies** for a country or organization tries to find out secret information about another country or organization. EG *He was convicted of spying for Russia.* V

3 If you **spy** on someone, you watch them secretly. EG *...girls spying on their unfaithful lovers.* V+on

4 If you **spy** something, you notice it. EG *Suddenly Quint spied the triangular fin of a shark coming towards them.* V+O Written

sq is a written abbreviation for 'square'. You write **sq** when you are giving the measurement of an area. EG *...280,000 sq ft of office space.*

squabble /skwɒbəˈl/, **squabbles, squabbling, squabbled.** When people **squabble**, they quarrel noisily, usually about something that is not really important. EG *They're always squabbling over details.* ▸ used as a noun. EG *...squabbles between the children.... The bitter squabble raged on.* V ▸ N COUNT

Which are the noisy words on these pages?

squad /skwɒd/, **squads**. 1 A **squad** is a section of N COUNT+SUPP
a police force that is responsible for dealing with a
particular type of crime. EG ...*the drugs squad*.
2 A **squad** of soldiers is a small group of them. N COUNT
squad car, **squad cars**. A **squad car** is a car N COUNT
used by the police.
squadron /skwɒdrən/, **squadrons**. A **squadron** N COUNT
is a section of one of the armed forces, especially
the air force. EG ...*a squadron of fighter planes*...
...*the commander of C Squadron*.
squalid /skwɒlɪd/. 1 A place that is **squalid** is ADJ QUALIT
dirty, untidy, and in bad condition. EG *The kitchen
was squalid*... ...*our small, squalid flat*.
2 **Squalid** activities are unpleasant and often dis- ADJ QUALIT
honest. EG *They're involved in a rather squalid
battle as to who controls the party*.
squall /skwɔːl/, **squalls**. A **squall** is a brief, N COUNT
violent storm. EG *A sudden squall overturned the
boat*.
squalor /skwɒlə/. You can refer to squalid condi- N UNCOUNT
tions or surroundings as **squalor**. EG ...*poor people
living in conditions of squalor*.
squander /skwɒndə/, **squanders**, **squandering**, V+O
squandered. If you **squander** money or resources, you use it all up in a foolish and wasteful
way. EG *If we squander our fossil fuels, we threaten
civilisation*... *He squandered large quantities of
cash on overpriced clothes*.
square /skweə/, **squares**, **squaring**, **squared**. 1 N COUNT
A **square** is a shape with four sides of the same
length and four corners that are all right angles.
See picture at SHAPES. EG *I folded the newspaper
neatly into a square*.
2 In a town or city, a **square** is a flat open place, N COUNT
often in the shape of a square. EG ...*the town
square*... ...*Trafalgar Square*.
3 Something that is **square** has a shape the same ADJ QUALIT
as a square or similar to a square. EG *The post
office was a small, square building*... *He had a
square ruddy face*.
4 **Square** is used before units of length when ADJ CLASSIF
mentioning the area of something. For example, if ATTRIB
a rectangle is three metres long and two metres
wide, its area is six square metres. EG ...*hundreds of
square miles of pine forest*.
5 **Square** is also used after units of length when ADJ AFTER N
you are giving the length of each side of something
that is square in shape. EG ...*a silicon chip less than
a centimetre square*.
6 If you **square** a number, you multiply it by itself. V+O
For example, 3 squared is 3 x 3, or 9. 3 squared is
usually written as 3².
7 When two people no longer owe each other any ADJ PRED
money, you can say that they are **square**. Informal
8 When you **square** two different situations or V-ERG OR
ideas with each other or when they **square** with V-ERG+with :
each other, they can be accepted together or they RECIP
seem compatible. EG *How do you square being a
Lord with being a Marxist?*
9 A **square** meal is a meal that is large and N COUNT
satisfying. EG *He had gone without a square meal
for nearly three days*.
10 If you are **back to square one**, you have to PHRASE
start dealing with something from the beginning Informal
again because one course of action has failed. EG *If
he says 'No', you are back to square one*.
squarely /skweəlɪ¹/. 1 **Squarely** means directly ADV :
and in the middle, rather than indirectly or at an USU+PREP
angle. EG *The television mast fell squarely onto a
Methodist chapel*.
2 If you face something **squarely**, you face it ADV
directly, without trying to avoid it. EG *This difficulty
will have to be squarely faced*.
square root, **square roots**. The **square root** of a N COUNT
number is a number which produces that number
when it is multiplied by itself. For example, 4 is the
square root of 16.
squash /skwɒʃ/, **squashes**, **squashing**,
squashed. 1 If you **squash** something, you press it, V+O : USU PASS

so that it becomes flat or loses its shape. EG *I saw a
dead cat. It had been squashed by a bus*.
2 **Squash** is a game in which two players hit a N UNCOUNT
small rubber ball against the walls of a court using
rackets. EG *I spent the afternoon playing squash*.
3 **Squash** is also a drink made from fruit juice, N MASS
sugar, and water. EG *We gave all the children a* British
glass of lemon squash.
squat /skwɒt/, **squats**, **squatting**, **squatted**. 1 If V : OFT+down
you **squat** or **squat** down, you crouch, balancing
on your feet with your legs bent. EG *He told the boys
to squat in a semicircle around him*.
2 Someone or something that is **squat** is short and ADJ QUALIT
thick, often in an unattractive way. EG ...*a squat,
bald, plump man*... ...*squat wooden churches*.
3 A person who **squats** in an unused building lives V
there without having a legal right to do so. EG *We
were squatting in an empty house*. ◊ **squatter**, ◊ N COUNT
squatters. EG ...*the subject of squatters' rights*.
squawk /skwɔːk/, **squawks**, **squawking**, V
squawked. When a bird **squawks**, it makes a loud
sharp noise. ► used as a noun. EG ...*the sad squawks* ► N COUNT
of the peacocks.
squeak /skwiːk/, **squeaks**, **squeaking**, V
squeaked. If something **squeaks**, it makes a short,
high-pitched sound. EG *A door squeaked open nearby*... *As the dusk deepened, small black bats began
squeaking*. ► used as a noun. EG *She let out a* ► N COUNT
squeak.
squeaky /skwiːkɪ¹/. Something that is **squeaky** ADJ QUALIT
makes squeaking noises. EG ...*a squeaky iron gate*...
...*a high, squeaky voice*.
squeal /skwiːl/, **squeals**, **squealing**, **squealed**. V
When people or things **squeal**, they make long,
high-pitched sounds. EG *The boys scattered, squealing in horror*. ► used as a noun. EG *There was a* ► N COUNT
squeal of brakes.
squeamish /skwiːmɪʃ/. If you are **squeamish**, ADJ QUALIT
you are easily upset by unpleasant sights or situations. EG *I'm squeamish about surgery*.
squeeze /skwiːz/, **squeezes**, **squeezing**,
squeezed. 1 When you **squeeze** something soft or V+O
flexible, you press it firmly from two sides. EG *The
children were squeezing the packets to find out
what was inside*... *He was holding her hands and
squeezing them between his*. ► used as a noun. EG ► N COUNT
He gave her hand a squeeze.
2 When you **squeeze** a liquid or a soft substance V+O+A
out of an object, you get the liquid or substance out
by pressing the object. EG *Squeeze all the surplus
water out of the cloth*.
3 If you **squeeze** through or into a small space, you V+A
manage to get through it or into it. EG *We squeezed
under the wire and into the garden*... *The inhabitants have to squeeze into a tiny area of living
space*.
4 If you say that getting a number of people into a N SING : a+N
small space is a **squeeze**, you mean that it is only Informal
just possible for them all to get into it. EG *We all got
in the lift but it was a bit of a squeeze*.
5 If you **squeeze** something into a small amount of V+O+A
time or space, you manage to fit it in. EG *Do you
think you can squeeze in your lunch break between
the two meetings?*
6 If you **squeeze** something out of someone, you V+O+A
persuade them to give it to you. EG *He's hoping to
squeeze the extra cash out of his bank manager*.
squelch /skweltʃ/, **squelches**, **squelching**, V : USU+A
squelched. To **squelch** means to make a wet,
sucking sound, like the sound you make when you
are walking on wet, muddy ground. EG *I squelched
along by the water's edge*.
squid /skwɪd/, **squids**. A **squid** is a sea creature N COUNT
with a long soft body and many tentacles. The
plural of 'squid' is either 'squid' or 'squids'.
squiggle /skwɪgəl/, **squiggles**. A **squiggle** is a N COUNT
line that bends and curls in an irregular way. EG
Her signature was a series of inky squiggles.

squint /skwɪnt/, **squints, squinting, squinted. 1** v : usu+*at*
If you **squint** at something, you look at it with your
eyes partly closed. eg *He squinted at the brightly
coloured figures.*

2 If someone has a **squint**, their eyes look in N count :
different directions from each other. usu sing

squire /skwaɪə/, **squires.** In former times, the N count
squire of an English village was the man who
owned most of the land in it.

squirm /skwɜːm/, **squirms, squirming,**
squirmed. 1 If you **squirm**, you move your body v : usu+A
from side to side, because you are nervous or
uncomfortable. eg *The girls squirmed in their
chairs and began giggling.*

2 You can also say that someone **squirms** when v : oft+*with*
they are very embarrassed or ashamed. eg *He
squirmed with embarrassment.*

squirrel /skwɪrəl/, **squirrels.** A **squirrel** is a N count
small furry animal with a long bushy tail. Squirrels
live mainly in trees.

squirt /skwɜːt/, **squirts, squirting, squirted. 1** If v-erg : usu+A
you **squirt** a liquid somewhere, the liquid comes
out of a narrow opening in a thin fast stream. eg
*Squirt a little oil into the keyhole... Water squirted
out of a hole in the pipe.*

2 If you **squirt** something with a liquid, you squirt v+o :
the liquid at it. eg *One woman was running ahead* usu+*with*
squirting windows with water.

SRN /ɛs ɑː ɛn/, **SRNs.** An **SRN** is someone who is N count
fully qualified as a nurse in the United Kingdom.
SRN is an abbreviation for 'State Registered
Nurse'. eg *...Jane Wilson SRN.*

SS. See **St.**

St. 1 St is a written abbreviation for 'Street'. eg *...22
Harley St, London W1.*

2 St is also a written abbreviation for 'Saint'. The
plural is **SS.** eg *...St Anselm... ...SS Peter and Paul.*

-st You add **-st** to most numbers written in figures suffix
and ending in 1 in order to form ordinal numbers.
1st is pronounced the same as 'first'. eg *...1st April
1982... ...21st Street... ...the 101st Psalm.*

stab /stæb/, **stabs, stabbing, stabbed. 1** If some- v+o
one **stabs** you, they push a knife into your body. eg
*A man was stabbed to death as he left a London
library.*

2 If you say that someone **has stabbed** you **in the** phrase
back, you mean that they have done something
very harmful to you when you thought that you
could trust them.

3 If you **stab** something or **stab** at it, you push at it v+o or v+A
with your finger or with something pointed that
you are holding. eg *He stabbed the air with his
index finger... She was typing in a fury, her fingers
stabbing at the keys.*

4 If you have a **stab** at something, you try to do it. N count :
eg *I'd like to have a stab at tap dancing... You've* oft+*at*
had a pretty good stab at it. Informal

5 You can refer to a sudden, unpleasant feeling as N count+*of*
a **stab** of that feeling. eg *Kitty felt a stab of dismay.* Literary

stabbing /stæbɪŋ/, **stabbings. 1** A **stabbing** is an N count
incident in which someone stabs someone else.

2 A **stabbing** pain is a sudden sharp pain. eg *I felt a* adj classif :
stabbing pain behind one of my eyes. attrib

stability /stəbɪlɪtiˈ/ is the state of being stable. eg N uncount
...a period of economic growth and stability.

stabilize /steɪbɪˈlaɪz/, **stabilizes, stabilizing,** v-erg
stabilized; also spelled **stabilise.** If something
stabilizes or **is stabilized**, it becomes stable. eg
*Eventually your weight will stabilise... The family
is one of the great stabilizing elements in society.*

stable /steɪbəl/, **stables. 1** If something is **stable,** adj qualit
it is not likely to change or come to an end
suddenly. eg *Oil prices are stable for the first time
in years... ...a stable marriage... ...politically stable
countries.*

2 If an object is **stable**, it is firmly fixed in position adj qualit
and is not likely to move or fall. eg *Eventually they
managed to get a more stable structure.*

3 A **stable** is a building in which horses are kept. N count
eg *He went to the stables to fetch his horse.*

staccato /stəkɑːtəʊ/. A **staccato** noise consists of adj classif :
a series of short, sharp, separate sounds. eg *...the* attrib
man's staccato Berlin accent. Literary

stack /stæk/, **stacks, stacking, stacked. 1** A N part
stack of things is a neat pile of them. eg *On the
sideboard was a stack of plates.*

2 If you **stack** a number of things or **stack** them v+o : oft+*up*
up, you arrange them in neat piles. eg *I started
stacking the chairs... We stacked up the plates and
carried them to the sink.*

3 If a place or surface **is stacked** with objects, it is v+o : usu
filled with piles of them. eg *The shed was stacked* pass+*with*
with old boxes.

4 If you say that someone has **stacks** of something, N part
you mean that they have a lot of it. eg *They've got* Informal
stacks of money... I've got stacks of socks.

stadium /steɪdɪəm/, **stadiums.** A **stadium** is a N count
large sports ground with rows of seats all round it.
eg *...football stadiums.*

staff /stɑːf/, **staffs, staffed. 1** The **staff** of an N coll or
organization are the people who work for it. eg *She* N uncount
*was invited to join the staff of the BBC... There are
two students to every member of staff.*

2 If an organization **is staffed** by particular peo- v+o : usu pass
ple, they are the people who work for it. eg *It was
staffed and run by engineers... ...a sports shop
staffed by runners.* ● See also **short-staffed.**

staffing /stɑːfɪŋ/ refers to the number of workers N uncount
employed to work in a particular organization or
building. eg *...inadequate staffing... ...the urgency of
securing additional staffing... ...staffing problems.*

stag /stæg/, **stags.** A **stag** is an adult male deer. N count

stage /steɪdʒ/, **stages, staging, staged. 1** A N count :
stage is **1.1** a part of a process. eg *In the early* usu+supp
*stages of learning to read, a child will usually need
a lot of help... Agriculture is the first stage of
economic development.* **1.2** a period that is part of
a longer period. eg *...at this stage in my life.*

2 In a theatre, the **stage** is a raised platform where N count
actors or other entertainers perform. eg *She stood
alone on the enormous stage.* ● When an actor or ● phrase
singer is **on stage**, he or she is performing on the Technical
stage. eg *She has been accused of being too flamboyant on stage... I didn't sing opera on stage.*

3 You can refer to acting and the production of N sing : *the*+N
plays in a theatre as the **stage**. eg *She retired from
the stage some years ago... He's adapted one of his
novels for the stage... ...stage productions.*

4 If someone **stages** a play or other show, they v+o
organize and present a performance of it.

5 If you **stage** an event or ceremony, you organize v+o
it. eg *The women staged a demonstration.*

6 To **set the stage** for something means to make phrase
preparations so that it can happen. eg *The stage
was now set for a massive publicity drive.*

stagecoach /steɪdʒkəʊtʃ/, **stagecoaches.** Stage- N count
coaches were large carriages pulled by horses
which carried passengers and mail.

stage-manage, stage-manages, stage- v+o
managing, stage-managed. If someone **stage-
manages** an event, they organize it, especially
secretly. eg *Could we be sure that the attacks were
not stage-managed?*

stagger /stægə/, **staggers, staggering, stag-**
gered. 1 If you **stagger**, you walk very unsteadily, v : usu+A
for example because you are ill or drunk. eg *I
staggered to the nearest chair.*

2 If something **staggers** you, it surprises you very v+o
much. ◊ **staggered.** eg *She was absolutely stag-* ◊ adj qualit :
gered... We were staggered to learn they would not usu pred
*be returning... I was staggered at how unpleasant
the country had become.* ◊ **staggering.** eg *Its* ◊ adj qualit

Is stained glass dirty?

estimated cost has climbed to a staggering £35 billion.

3 If things such as people's holidays or hours of work **are staggered**, they are arranged so that they do not all happen at the same time. `v+o : usu pass`

stagnant /stægnənt/. **1** If something such as a business or society is **stagnant**, there is little activity or little change; used showing disapproval. `EG ...stagnant economies.` `ADJ CLASSIF`

2 Stagnant water is not flowing, and is often dirty and unhealthy. `EG ...stagnant pools.` `ADJ CLASSIF`

stagnate /stægneɪt, stægneɪt/, **stagnates, stagnating, stagnated.** If something such as a business or society **stagnates**, it becomes inactive or unchanging; used showing disapproval. `EG The economy stagnated as a result of these tax measures.` ◊ **stagnation** /stægneɪʃəⁿn/. `EG Industrial stagnation inevitably leads to the loss of jobs.` `v` ◊ `N UNCOUNT`

stag night, stag nights. A **stag night** or a **stag party** is a party for a man who is getting married the next day, to which only men are invited. `N COUNT`

staid /steɪd/. Someone who is **staid** is serious, dull, and rather old-fashioned. `EG ...a staid elderly gentleman... I must have seemed rather staid.` `ADJ QUALIT`

stain /steɪn/, **stains, staining, stained.** **1** A **stain** is a mark on something that is difficult to remove. `EG There was a dark oval stain on the chair where his head had rested... ...grease stains.` `N COUNT`

2 If a liquid **stains** something, the thing becomes coloured or marked by the liquid. `EG Already the beast's blood was staining the sand.` ◊ **stained.** `EG ...a little man with stained teeth... His shirt was stained with blood.` `v+o` ◊ `ADJ CLASSIF`

stained glass consists of pieces of glass of different colours which are fixed together to make decorative windows or other objects. `EG St Nicholas's has fine Victorian stained-glass windows.` `N UNCOUNT`

stainless steel /steɪnlⁱs stiːl/ is a metal made from steel and chromium which does not rust. `EG ...a stainless steel sink.` `N UNCOUNT`

stair /steə/, **stairs.** **1 Stairs** are a set of steps inside a building which go from one floor to another. `EG He ran up the stairs... ...another flight of stairs... Bill stood at the foot of the stairs.` `N PLURAL`

2 A **stair** is one of the steps in a set of stairs. `EG A stair creaked as she made her way downstairs.` `N COUNT`

staircase /steəkeɪs/, **staircases.** A **staircase** is a set of stairs inside a house. See picture at HOUSE. `EG ...a white marble staircase.` `N COUNT`

stairway /steəweɪ/, **stairways.** A **stairway** is a set of steps, inside or outside of a building. `EG He stood halfway up the wooden stairway.` `N COUNT`

stake /steɪk/, **stakes, staking, staked.** **1** If something is **at stake**, it is being risked and might be lost or damaged if you are not successful. `EG There's a great deal of money at stake... He admits that his political life is at stake.` `PHRASE`

2 The **stakes** involved in a risky action or a contest are the things that can be gained or lost. `EG I'm playing for high stakes.` `N PLURAL`

3 If you **stake** something such as your money or your reputation on the result of something, you risk your money or reputation on it. `EG He staked his reputation as a prophet on this assertion.` `v+o : OFT + on/upon`

4 If you have a **stake** in something such as a business, its success matters to you, for example because you own part of it. `EG They soon had a substantial stake in the British textile industry.` `N COUNT`

5 You can use **stakes** to refer to something that is like a contest. For example, you can refer to the choosing of a leader as the leadership **stakes**. `EG ...the Presidential stakes... This gives you an advantage in the promotion stakes.` `N PLURAL : the+N`

6 A **stake** is a pointed wooden post which is pushed into the ground, for example in order to support a young tree. `EG His boat was fastened by a chain to a stake in the ground.` `N COUNT`

7 If you **stake a claim**, you say that something is `PHRASE`

yours or that you have a right to it. `EG Each group had staked its claim to its own territory.`

stale /steɪl/. **1 Stale** food or air is old and no longer fresh. `EG They had nothing to eat but stale bread... The box smelled of stale tobacco... Inside the flat was a musty smell of stale air.` `ADJ QUALIT`

2 If you feel **stale**, you are no longer enthusiastic or full of interesting ideas because you are tired or bored. `EG You need a break, a change. You're getting stale here.` `ADJ QUALIT`

stalemate /steɪlmeɪt/. **1 Stalemate** is a situation in which neither side in an argument or contest can win. `EG He hoped that the nuclear stalemate would lead to disarmament... A stalemate had been reached.` `N UNCOUNT`

2 In chess, **stalemate** is a position in which a player cannot make any move which is permitted by the rules, so that the game ends and no one wins. `N UNCOUNT`

stalk /stɔːk/, **stalks, stalking, stalked.** **1** The **stalk** of a flower or other plant is its main stem. `N COUNT`

2 The **stalk** of a fruit or leaf is the thin part that joins it to the plant or tree that it grows on. `N COUNT`

3 If you **stalk** a person or a wild animal, you follow them quietly in order to kill them, catch them, or observe them. `EG We stalked rabbits... He moved like a tiger stalking its prey.` `v+o`

4 If you **stalk** somewhere, you walk there in a stiff, proud, or angry way. `EG She stalked into the living room... Florrie stalked out, her head high.` `v+A`

stall /stɔːl/, **stalls, stalling, stalled.** **1** A **stall** is a large table on which you put goods that you want to sell or information that you want to give to people. `EG Never buy a dog from a market stall.` `N COUNT`

2 The **stalls** in a theatre or concert hall are the seats on the ground floor directly in front of the stage. `EG We got seats in the stalls.` `N PLURAL : the+N`

3 When a vehicle **stalls** or when you accidentally **stall** it, the engine stops suddenly. `v-ERG`

4 If you **stall**, you try to avoid doing something until a later time. `EG 'Well?' she said. Tom grinned at her, stalling for time.` `v`

5 If you **stall** someone, you prevent them from doing something until a later time. `EG Perhaps I can stall him till Thursday or Friday.` `v+o`

stallion /stæljən/, **stallions.** A **stallion** is a male horse, especially one kept for breeding. `N COUNT`

stalwart /stɔːlwət/, **stalwarts.** A **stalwart** worker or supporter of an organization is loyal and hard-working. `EG ...the proprietor and his three stalwart sons.` ► used as a noun. `EG ...a stalwart of the Trades Council... They were all Government stalwarts.` `ADJ QUALIT` ► `N COUNT`

stamina /stæmɪnə/ is the physical or mental energy needed to do a tiring activity for a long time. `EG I did not have the physical stamina needed for digging.` `N UNCOUNT`

stammer /stæmə/, **stammers, stammering, stammered.** **1** If you **stammer**, you speak with difficulty, hesitating and repeating words or sounds, for example because you are nervous. `EG I used to stammer quite badly... 'But...but...that's impossible,' the youth stammered.` `v, v+o OR v+QUOTE`

2 Someone who has a **stammer** tends to stammer when they speak. `N COUNT : USU SING`

stammer out. If you **stammer** something **out**, you stammer as you say it. `EG Before he could stammer out his thanks, she walked away.` `PHRASAL VB : V+O+ADV OR V+ADV+ QUOTE`

stamp /stæmp/, **stamps, stamping, stamped.** **1** A **stamp** or a **postage stamp** is a small piece of gummed paper which you stick on an envelope or parcel before you post it. `EG His interests were drawing and stamp collecting.` `N COUNT`

2 A **stamp** is also a small block of wood or metal which has a pattern or a group of letters on one side. You press it onto an inky pad and then onto a piece of paper in order to produce a mark on the paper. The mark that you produce is also called a `N COUNT` stamp. EG *They had German passports with Brazilian entrance stamps.*

3 If you **stamp** a mark or word on an object, you press the mark or word onto the object using a stamp or other device. EG *Articles that conform with the relevant British Standards are stamped with a kite-shaped mark... Unless they are stamped 'ovenproof' assume they are not.* `v+o+a OR v+o+c`

4 If you **stamp** your foot, you lift your foot and put it down very hard on the ground, for example because you are angry. EG *'Damn you, Edward!' she shouted, stamping her foot.* `v+o`

5 If you **stamp** somewhere, you walk there putting your feet down very hard on the ground because you are angry. EG *We reluctantly stamped into the principal's office.* `v+a`

6 If you **stamp** on something, you put your foot down on it very hard. EG *I stamped heavily on her foot and muttered, 'Shut up.'* `v+on`

7 If something bears the **stamp** of a particular quality or person, it clearly has that quality or was done by that person. EG *His work hardly bore the stamp of maturity... ...a designer who has left his stamp on 20th century industry.* `N SING+SUPP`

8 A quality, feature, or action that **stamps** someone or something as a particular thing shows clearly that they are this thing. EG *His achievement stamps him as one of the masterminds of our era.* `v+o+as`

stamp out. If you **stamp** something **out**, you put an end to it. EG *They are determined to stamp out political extremism.* `PHRASAL VB : v+o+ADV`

stamped /stæmpt/. A **stamped** envelope or parcel has a stamp stuck on it. EG *Two letters in stamped envelopes were already laid out on the desk.* `ADJ CLASSIF`

stampede /stæmpiːd/, **stampedes, stampeding, stampeded. 1** When a group of animals **stampede** or **are stampeded**, they rush away wildly because something has frightened them. EG *Outside the goats stampeded.* `V-ERG`

2 When there is a **stampede**, a group of animals rush away because something has frightened them. EG *...a stampede of elephants.* `N COUNT`

3 You can also say that there is a **stampede** when a group of people rush somewhere in an uncontrolled way. EG *Her foot got trodden on in the general stampede to the exit.* `N COUNT`

stance /stæns, stɑːns/, **stances. 1** Your **stance** on a particular matter is your attitude about it. EG *They criticized Martin Luther King for his rigid stance on non-violence.* `+SUPP : OFT+on`

2 Your **stance** is also the way that you are standing. EG *He altered his stance slightly and leaned against a tree.* `N COUNT : USU+SUPP Formal`

stand /stænd/, **stands, standing, stood** /stʊd/. **1** When you **are standing**, your body is upright, your legs are straight, and your weight is supported by your feet. EG *She was standing at the bus stop... Stand quietly behind your desks... I stood very still, hoping they wouldn't see me.* `v : USU+A`

2 When you **stand**, you change your position so that you are standing, rather than sitting. EG *One by one, he asked each graduate to stand.* `v Formal`

3 If you **stand** aside or **stand** back, you move a short distance sideways or backwards, so that you are standing in a different place. EG *Miss Darke told the girls to stand aside... He stood back and surveyed his handiwork.* `v+a`

4 If something **stands** somewhere, it is in an upright position in that place. EG *In the middle of the town stands a splendid Victorian building... The empty wine bottles stand in a neat row against the wall... Only one of the houses is still standing.* `v : USU+A`

5 If you **stand** something somewhere, you put it there in an upright position. EG *He stood the bottle on the bench beside him.* `v+o+a`

6 If a decision or offer **stands**, it is still valid. EG *Fifty years later, this Supreme Court ruling still stands.* `v : NO CONT`

7 If something that can be measured **stands** at a particular level, it is at that level. EG *Unemployment in North Wales now stands at 38 per cent.* `v+at`

8 You can use **stand** instead of 'is' when you are describing the state or condition of something. EG *Their honesty stands in total contrast to the deceitfulness of their opponents... His real intentions now stand revealed... They are dissatisfied with the law as it stands.* `v+a OR v+c : NO CONT`

9 If you ask someone **how** or **where** they **stand** on a particular issue, you are asking them what their attitude or view is. EG *There was never any doubt about where he stood on the racial issue.* `PHRASE`

10 If something can **stand** a situation or a test, it is good enough or strong enough to withstand it. EG *In its present state, the economy couldn't stand another rise in interest rates... Her arguments could hardly stand close inspection.* `v+o : OFT WITH MODAL +BROAD NEG`

11 If you cannot **stand** something, **11.1** you cannot bear it or tolerate it. EG *He kept on nagging until I couldn't stand it any longer.* **11.2** you dislike it very strongly. EG *She can't stand children.* `v+o : OFT WITH MODAL +BROAD NEG`

12 If you **stand** to gain something, you are likely to gain it. If you **stand** to lose something, you are likely to lose it. EG *Other groups stand to make a profit out of it... Few people are yet aware of how much we stand to lose by this agreement.* `v+to-INF`

13 If you **stand** in an election, you are a candidate. EG *She was invited to stand as the Liberal candidate... He has stood for Parliament 21 times.* `v : USU+A`

14 If you **stand** someone a meal or a drink, you buy it for them. `v+o+o`

15 If you say **it stands to reason** that something is true or likely to happen, you mean that it is obvious. EG *If they keep doing that, it stands to reason that the police are going to get suspicious.* `PHRASE Informal`

16 When someone **stands trial**, they are tried in a court of law. EG *He has come back to stand trial on a murder charge.* `PHRASE`

17 A **stand** is a small shop or stall, outdoors or in a large public building. EG *...a hamburger stand... ...an information stand.* `N COUNT+SUPP`

18 A **stand** is also an object or piece of furniture that is designed for holding a particular kind of thing. EG *...an umbrella stand... ...a music stand.* `N COUNT`

19 If you take a **stand** or make a **stand**, you resist attempts to defeat you or to make you change your mind. EG *...a heroic national stand against the invader... It's an important issue and you must be prepared to take a stand on it.* `N SING`

20 When a witness **takes the stand** in a court of law, he or she answers questions. EG *Hearne had not yet taken the stand.* `PHRASE American`

21 to stand a chance: see **chance.** ● **to stand on your own two feet**: see **ground.** ● See also **standing.**

stand by. 1 If you **stand by**, you are ready to provide help or to take action if it becomes necessary. EG *Stand by with lots of water in case a fire breaks out.* **2** If you **stand by** and let something bad happen, you do not do anything to stop it. EG *We cannot stand by and watch while our allies are attacked.* **3** If you **stand by** someone, you continue to give them support, especially when they are in trouble. EG *If they try to make you resign, we'll stand by you.* **4** If you **stand by** an earlier decision, promise, or agreement, you continue to support it or keep it. EG *I said I would do it and I stand by my promise.* **5** See also **standby.** `PHRASAL VB : v+ADV / v+ADV / v+PREP / v+PREP`

stand down. If someone **stands down**, they resign, often in order to let someone else take their place. EG *She was asked if she was prepared to stand down in favour of a younger candidate.* `PHRASAL VB : v+ADV`

stand for. 1 If you say that a letter **stands for** a particular word, you mean that it is an abbrevia- `PHRASAL VB : v+PREP`

If you cannot stand someone, would you be likely to stand them a meal?

tion for that word. EG *T.E.C. stands for Technical Education Certificate.* **2** The ideas or attitudes that someone or something **stands for** are the ones that they support or represent. EG *I disagreed fundamentally with what the party stood for.* **3** If you will not **stand for** something, you will not allow it to happen or continue. EG *He warned that the Army would not stand for it much longer.* `V+PREP` `V+PREP WITH BROAD NEG`

stand in. If you **stand in** for someone, you take their place or do their job, because they are ill or away. EG *He was standing in for his younger brother... You will stand in for me, John?* ● See also **stand-in.** `PHRASAL VB: V+ADV, USU+for`

stand out. If something **stands out**, **1** it can be seen very clearly. EG *The name on the van stood out clearly.* **2** it is much better or much more important than other things of the same kind. EG *One issue stood out as especially important... One article in this collection stands out from all the others.* `PHRASAL VB: V+ADV, NO CONT V+ADV, NO CONT`

stand up. **1** When you **stand up**, you change your position so that you are standing, rather than sitting. EG *I put down my glass and stood up.* **2** If something **stands up** to rough treatment, it remains almost undamaged or unharmed. EG *This carpet stands up to the wear and tear of continual use.* **3** If you **stand up** to someone, especially someone more powerful than you are, you defend yourself against their attacks or demands. EG *Maybe if I stood up to him, he'd back down.* **4** If you **stand up** for someone or something that is being attacked or criticized, you defend them vigorously. EG *...people who stood up for human rights... I'm glad to see that he's standing up for himself.* **5** If something such as a claim or a piece of evidence **stands up**, it is accepted as true or satisfactory after being carefully examined. EG *The prosecution had no evidence which would stand up in a court of law.* **6** If you **are stood up** by a boyfriend or girlfriend, they fail to keep an arrangement to meet you. `PHRASAL VB: V+ADV` `V+ADV, OFT+to/under` `V+ADV+A` `V+ADV+A` `V+ADV` `V+O+ADV Informal`

standard /stǽndəd/, **standards.** **1** A **standard** is a level of quality or achievement, especially a level that is thought to be acceptable. EG *The acting ability of the pupils is of a high standard... You're way below the standard required... We place emphasis on excellence and high standards.* `N COUNT OR N UNCOUNT +SUPP`

2 A **standard** is also something that you use in order to judge the quality of something else. EG *These families would be classified as rich by Asian standards... By any standard the work was good.* `N COUNT+SUPP`

3 **Standards** are moral principles which affect people's attitudes and behaviour. EG *There has been a corruption of moral standards.* `N COUNT: USU PLURAL +SUPP`

4 You use **standard** to describe things which are usual and normal, rather than being special or extra. EG *There is a standard procedure for recording drugs given to patients.* `ADJ CLASSIF`

5 **Standard** spelling, pronunciation, and grammar are generally regarded as correct or acceptable. `ADJ CLASSIF`

6 If a book is described as a **standard** work or text, it is the one most widely read and recommended about a particular subject. EG *This is the standard work on British moths.* `ADJ CLASSIF: ATTRIB`

standardize /stǽndədaɪz/, **standardizes, standardizing, standardized;** also spelled **standardise.** To **standardize** things means to change them so that they all have the same features. EG *Some people have criticized television for standardizing speech, habits, and tastes.* ◊ **standardized.** EG *Equipment is going to become standardized.* `V+O` `◊ ADJ QUALIT`

standard lamp, standard lamps. A **standard lamp** is a tall electric light which stands on the floor in a living-room. `N COUNT`

standard of living, standards of living. Your **standard of living** is the level of comfort and wealth which you have. EG *There will have to be an adjustment to a lower standard of living.* `N COUNT: USU SING+SUPP`

standby /stǽndᵇbaɪ/, **standbys.** **1** A **standby** is something that is always ready to be used if it is needed. EG *Eggs are a great standby in the kitchen.* **2** If someone or something is **on standby**, they are ready to be used if they are needed. EG *We have a crew on stand-by.* **3** A **standby** ticket for something such as the theatre or a plane journey is a cheap ticket that you buy just before the performance starts or the plane takes off, if there are still some seats left. `N COUNT` `PHRASE` `N MOD`

stand-in, stand-ins. A **stand-in** is a person who takes someone else's place or does someone else's job, because the other person is ill or away. EG *Make sure that your stand-in is available... He was trying to arrange stand-in lecturers for Wilt's classes.* `N COUNT`

standing /stǽndɪŋ/. **1** You use **standing** to describe something which is permanently in existence. EG *...a standing committee... This is a standing joke amongst psychologists.* **2** Someone's **standing** is their status or reputation. EG *His success was based on his popular standing... She was an economist of considerable standing.* **3** You use **standing** to say how long something has existed or how long it has had a particular function. For example, if a place is your home of ten years' standing, it has been your home for ten years. EG *...a member of twenty-five years' standing... The present unrest has its origins in social ills of long standing.* `ADJ CLASSIF: ATTRIB` `N UNCOUNT +SUPP Formal` `PHRASE Formal`

standing order, standing orders. A **standing order** is an instruction to your bank to pay a fixed amount of money to someone at regular times. EG *I pay their allowance by standing order.* `N COUNT OR by+N`

standing room is space in a room or bus, where people can stand when all the seats have been taken. EG *Inside there was standing room only.* `N UNCOUNT`

stand-offish /stǽndɒfɪʃ/. If you say that someone is **stand-offish**, you mean that they behave in a formal and rather unfriendly way. `ADJ QUALIT`

standpipe /stǽndpaɪp/, **standpipes.** A **standpipe** is a vertical pipe that is connected to a water supply and stands in a street or other public place. `N COUNT`

standpoint /stǽndpɔɪnt/, **standpoints.** Your **standpoint** is your attitude or opinion about an event, situation, or idea. EG *Up to now, we have only discussed the issue from a western standpoint.* `N COUNT+SUPP`

standstill /stǽndstɪl/. If movement or activity comes to a **standstill**, it stops completely. EG *The traffic had come to a standstill... The negotiations are at a standstill.* `N SING: a+N`

stank /stǽŋk/ is the past tense of **stink.**

staple /stéɪpᵊl/, **staples, stapling, stapled.** **1** **Staples** are small pieces of wire that are used for holding sheets of paper together firmly. You push the staples through the paper using a special device called a stapler. **2** If you **staple** something, you fasten it to something else or fix it in place using staples. EG *The letter was stapled to the other documents in the file.* **3** A **staple** meal or food is one that forms a regular and basic part of your everyday food. EG *...the dry bread which is their staple diet.* `N COUNT` `V+O+A` `ADJ CLASSIF: ATTRIB`

stapler /stéɪplə/, **staplers.** A **stapler** is a special device used for putting staples into sheets of paper. `N COUNT`

star /stɑː/, **stars, starring, starred.** **1** A **star** is a large ball of burning gas in space. Stars appear to us as small points of light in the sky on clear nights. **2** You can refer to a shape or an object as a **star** when it has four, five, or more points sticking out of it in a regular pattern. See picture at SHAPES. EG *...little star-shaped flowers.* **3** **Stars** are star-shaped marks that are printed against the name of something to indicate that it is of high quality. EG *...a four-star hotel.* **4** Famous actors, musicians, and sports players are often referred to as **stars**. EG *...a tennis star... ...film stars.* `N COUNT` `N COUNT` `N COUNT` `N COUNT`

5 If an actor or actress **stars** in a play or film, he v : usu+a
or she has one of the most important parts in it. eg
She'll be starring in a new play by Alan Bleasdale.

6 If a play or film **stars** a famous actor or actress, v+o
he or she has one of the most important parts in it.
eg *The last version of the movie starred John
Garfield and Lana Turner.*

7 The horoscope in a newspaper or magazine is n plural
sometimes referred to as the **stars**. eg *What do the* Informal
stars say for today?

starboard /stɑːbəᵈd/. The **starboard** side of a adj classif
ship is the right side when you are facing towards Technical
the front of it. eg *White, icy-cold water foamed over
the starboard side.* ▶ used as a noun. eg *...a few* ▶ n uncount
hundred yards to starboard.

starch /stɑːtʃ/, **starches. 1** Starch is a substance n uncount
that is used for stiffening cloth, especially cotton
and linen.

2 Starch is also a white substance in foods such as n mass
bread, potatoes, pasta, and rice. eg *Your doctor
may recommend limiting the amount of starch in
your diet.... Cut down on the starches.*

starched /stɑːtʃt/. **Starched** cloth has been stiff- adj classif
ened using starch. eg *They wore starched caps and
white gloves.*

starchy /stɑːtʃiˈ/. **Starchy** food contains a lot of adj qualit
starch. eg *Avoid starchy vegetables such as potato.*

stare /steə/, **stares, staring, stared. 1** If you v : usu+a
stare at something, you look at it for a long time.
eg *He stared at us in disbelief... He sat there quietly,
staring out of the window.* ▶ used as a noun. eg *She* ▶ n count
gave him a dreamy stare.

2 If an answer or solution **is staring** you **in the** phrase
face, it is very obvious.

starfish /stɑːfɪʃ/. A **starfish** is a flat, star-shaped n count
creature with five arms that lives in the sea. The
plural form is also 'starfish'.

stark /stɑːk/, **starker, starkest. 1** Something that adj qualit
is **stark** is very bare and plain in appearance. eg
*...the stark black rocks and deserted beaches... The
names were written in stark black print.*

2 Stark means harsh and unpleasant. eg *Those are* adj qualit :
the stark facts of the matter... ...grim stark poverty. attrib

3 Someone who is **stark naked** is completely phrase
naked. eg *He came out of the bathroom stark
naked.*

starlight /stɑːlaɪt/ is the light that comes from n uncount
the stars at night. eg *I enjoyed the view of the bay
in the starlight.*

starling /stɑːlɪŋ/, **starlings.** A **starling** is a very n count
common European bird with greenish-black feath-
ers. eg *...children chattering like starlings.*

starry /stɑːriˈ/. A **starry** night or sky is full of adj classif :
stars. eg *It was a cold, starry night.* attrib

starry-eyed. If you are **starry-eyed**, you are so adj qualit
full of dreams or hopes that you do not see how
things really are. eg *We were all starry-eyed about
visiting London.*

start /stɑːt/, **starts, starting, started. 1** If you v+to-inf,
start to do something, you do something that you v+-ing,
were not doing before and you continue doing it. eg v+o, or v
*Ralph started to run... He started laughing... My
father started work when he was ten.* ▶ used as a ▶ n sing
noun. eg *We must make a start now... We've not
made a bad start.*

2 When something **starts** or when you **start** it, it v-erg
takes place from a particular time. eg *The meeting
starts at 7... We didn't want to start a panic.* ▶ used ▶ n count :
as a noun. eg *...the start of negotiations... ...at the* usu sing
*start of the tax year... The project was doomed to
failure from the start.*

3 If you **get off to a good start**, you are successful phrase
in the early stages of doing something. If you **get
off to a bad start**, you are not successful in the
early stages. eg *Treatment sometimes gets off to a
bad start.* ● **to get off to a flying start**: see **flying.**

4 You use **start** to say what someone's first job v : usu+a
was. For example, if their first job was that of a

porter, you can say that they **started** as a porter.
eg *She started as a secretary.*

5 When someone **starts** something such as a new v+o
business, they create it or cause it to start. eg *He
scraped up the money to start a restaurant.*

6 If you **start** an engine or car, or if it **starts**, it v-erg
starts to work. eg *He couldn't get his engine started.*

7 If you **start**, your body jerks as a result of v
surprise or fear. eg *I sat down so quietly that she
started.* ▶ used as a noun. eg *He awakened with a* ▶ n count :
start. usu sing

8 You use **to start with** or **for a start** to introduce adv sen
the first of a number of things or reasons that you
want to mention or could mention. eg *'Why do you
call her a witch?' – 'Well, she looks like a witch to
start with.'... We can't afford this house for a start.*

9 **To start with** also means at the very first stage adv sen
of an event or process. eg *He was an engineer to
start with, then a designer.*

10 See also **head start.** ● **in fits and starts**: see
fit.

start off. 1 You can use **start off** to say what phrasal vb :
someone's first job was. For example, if their first v+adv,
job was that of a taxi driver, you can say that they oft+as
started off as a taxi driver. eg *I started off as a
bookseller.* **2** If you **start off** by doing something, v+adv,
you do it as the first part of an activity. eg *I started* oft+by
*off by showing a slide of the diseased cell... I
started off with a Chopin prelude.* **3** To **start** v+o+adv
someone **off** means to cause them to start doing
something. eg *It was doing 'Measure for Measure'
with him that started me off on this new work.* **4** v+o+adv
To **start** something **off** means to cause it to start.
eg *I know what started it all off.*

start on. If you **start on** something that needs to phrasal vb :
be done, you start dealing with it. eg *She put the* v+prep,
forks in a neat pile and started on the knives. has pass

start out. 1 If someone or something **starts out** phrasal vb :
as a particular thing, they are that thing at the v+adv
beginning although they change later. eg *These
areas started out as the private lands of settlers.* **2** v+adv
If you **start out** doing something, you do it at the
beginning of an activity. eg *You started out by
saying that this was the weapon they used.*

start up. 1 If you **start up** something such as a phrasal vb :
new business, you create it or cause it to start. eg v+o+adv
She wanted to start up a little country pub. **2** If you v+o+adv
start up an engine or a car, you make it start to
work. eg *The driver started up the car.*

starter /stɑːtə/, **starters. 1** A **starter** is a small n count
quantity of food that is served as the first part of a
meal. eg *Serve noodles tossed in butter or cream as
a starter.*

2 The **starter** of a car is a device that starts the n count
engine.

starting point, starting points. 1 A **starting** n count :
point is an idea or statement that can be used to oft+of/for
begin a conversation or argument. eg *The starting
point of the discussion is inflation.*

2 When you make a journey, your **starting point** n count :
is the place from which you start. eg *This is a good* oft+of/for
starting point for a car tour.

startle /stɑːtəˀl/, **startles, startling, startled.** If v+o
something such as a sudden noise **startles** you, it
surprises and frightens you slightly. eg *Goodness,
you startled me – I thought you were in the
garden... He was startled by the fevered look of his
patient.* ◊ **startled.** eg *We laughed at the startled* ◊ adj qualit
expressions on their faces.

startling /stɑːtlɪŋ/. Something that is **startling** is adj qualit
so different or unexpected that people react with
surprise. eg *The results were quite startling – a 77%
increase in six months.*

Is a stationer in charge of a railway station? If
not, who is?

starvation /staːˈveɪʃəˀn/ is extreme suffering or N UNCOUNT death, caused by lack of food. EG *Many thousands of people die from starvation every year.*

starve /staːv/, **starves, starving, starved.** 1 v When people **starve**, they suffer greatly from lack of food and sometimes die. EG *People are starving because of inefficient farming methods.*

2 To **starve** someone means to not give them any v+o OR V-REFL food. EG *You should starve him for twelve hours... Ten men starved themselves to death in the prison.*

3 If you say that you **are starving**, you mean that v : ONLY CONT you are very hungry. EG *I've got to have something Informal to eat. I'm starving.*

4 If someone or something **is starved** of some- v+o : USU PASS thing that they need, they are suffering because they are not getting enough of it. EG *They seem to be starved of attention from adults... The plant was starved of light and died.*

stash /stæʃ/, **stashes, stashing, stashed.** If you v+o+A **stash** something valuable in a secret place, you Informal store it there to keep it safe. EG *They had all that money stashed away in the loft.*

state /steɪt/, **states, stating, stated.** 1 When you N COUNT : talk about the **state** of someone or something, you USU SING+SUPP are referring to what they are like or what they are experiencing at a particular time. EG *They are very concerned about the state of the churchyard... His general state of health is fairly satisfactory... She seemed in a very queer and nervous state... People wandered about in a state of shock.*

2 If you are **in a state**, you are very upset or PHRASE nervous about something. EG *He used to get into an Informal awful state as exams approached.*

3 If you say that someone **is not in a fit state** to PHRASE do something, you mean that they are too upset or ill to do it. EG *The parent is often in no fit state to help the children at the time of crisis.*

4 Countries are often referred to as **states**. EG *The N COUNT Latin American states maintained their independence... Their country is now a one-party state.* ● See also **head of state**, **welfare state**.

5 Some large countries are divided into regions N COUNT called **states**. These states can make some of their own laws. EG *Haryana and Punjab were the fastest-developing states in India... ...New York State.*

6 You can refer to the government of a country as N SING : the+N the **state** when you are contrasting it with the ordinary people of the country. EG *...the conflict between the freedom of the individual and the security of the state.*

7 A **state** ceremony or event is a formal one N MOD involving the ruler or head of a country. EG *...the state visit of a European monarch.*

8 If you **state** something, you make it known by V-SPEECH saying or writing it, especially in a formal way. EG *The government have stated quite categorically that we're going to see changes... The police were called, but the man refused to state his business... He stated, 'I have passed the stage where such things matter.'*

stately /ˈsteɪtli/. Something that is **stately** is ADJ QUALIT impressive because it looks very graceful and dignified. EG *...strong and stately towers.*

stately home, stately homes. A **stately home** N COUNT is a large old house which has belonged to an aristocratic family for a long time and which can be visited by the public.

statement /ˈsteɪtməˀnt/, **statements.** 1 A state- N COUNT ment is something that you say, especially when you give facts or information in a formal way. EG *I could not deny the truth of this statement... The announcement was made in a statement immediately after the meeting... Soon afterwards he made his first public statement about the affair.*

2 The **statement** of a policy or theory is the N SING+of expression of it in words in a fairly formal and definite way. EG *This isn't a list of complaints, merely a statement of fact.*

3 A **statement** is also a printed document that N COUNT

your bank sends you, which lists all the money that you have paid in or taken out, and also shows how much money you have in your account.

state of affairs. A **state of affairs** is the general N SING situation and circumstances connected with a particular thing, person, or event. EG *What our present state of affairs demands is a firm leader... Any relief to this unjust state of affairs is welcome.*

state of mind, states of mind. Your **state of** N COUNT : **mind** is your mood at a particular time. EG *My USU SING sister was in a happier state of mind... ...words that in no way reflected my state of mind.*

statesman /ˈsteɪtsməˀn/, **statesmen.** A states- N COUNT **man** is an important and experienced politician who is widely known and respected. EG *Terrorism could threaten any visiting statesman.*

static /ˈstætɪk/. 1 Something that is **static** does not ADJ QUALIT move or change at all. EG *...a series of static images... ...the static quality in all village life.*

2 **Static** or **static electricity** is electricity which N UNCOUNT is caused by friction and which collects in things such as your body or metal objects.

3 If there is **static** on the radio or television, you N UNCOUNT hear a series of loud crackling noises. EG *I switched on and got nothing but static.*

station /ˈsteɪʃəˀn/, **stations, stationing, sta-** **tioned.** 1 A **station** is a building by a railway line N COUNT where a train stops to pick up passengers and goods. EG *The train stopped at a small station.*

2 A bus **station** or coach **station** is a place from N COUNT+SUPP which buses or coaches begin a journey.

3 If you talk about a particular radio **station**, you N COUNT are referring to the programmes broadcast on a particular frequency by a particular radio company. EG *The radio was tuned permanently to his favourite station.*

4 If you refer to someone's **station**, you are N SING+POSS referring to their position or rank in society. EG *She Outdated had been educated above her station.*

5 If people **are stationed** somewhere, they are v+o+A told to stay there, usually so that they can watch USU PASS someone or be ready to prevent trouble. EG *Two guards were stationed at the top of the stairs.*

6 If soldiers **are stationed** in a place, they are sent v+o+A : there to work for a period of time. EG *...the British USU PASS forces stationed in Germany.*

7 See also **fire station, gas station, petrol sta-** **tion, police station**.

stationary /ˈsteɪʃənəˀri/. Something that is **sta-** ADJ CLASSIF **tionary** is not moving. EG *...a stationary boat... The vehicle remained stationary.*

stationer /ˈsteɪʃənə/, **stationers.** A **stationer** is a N COUNT person who sells paper, envelopes, pens, and other equipment used for writing.

stationery /ˈsteɪʃənəˀri/ is paper, envelopes, pens, N UNCOUNT and other equipment used for writing.

stationmaster /ˈsteɪʃəˀnmɑːstə/, **station-** N COUNT **masters.** A **stationmaster** is the official who is in charge of a railway station.

station wagon, station wagons. A station wag- N COUNT **on** is the same as an estate car. American

statistic /stəˈtɪstɪk/, **statistics.** 1 Statistics are N COUNT : facts which are obtained from analysing informa- USU PLURAL tion expressed in numbers, for example information about the number of times that something happens. EG *...divorce statistics... I happen to have the official statistics with me.*

2 **Statistics** is a branch of mathematics concerned N UNCOUNT with the study of information that is expressed in numbers. EG *I teach statistics.*

statistical /stəˈtɪstɪkəˀl/ means relating to the use ADJ CLASSIF of statistics. EG *Statistical techniques are regularly employed.* ◊ **statistically.** EG *Statistically you ◊ ADV SEN have a one in six chance of succeeding.* OR ADV

statistician /ˌstætɪˈstɪʃəˀn/, **statisticians.** A stat- N COUNT **istician** is a person who studies statistics or who works using statistics. EG *...a statistician in the Civil Service.*

statue /stætjuː/, **statues.** A **statue** is a large N COUNT sculpture of a person or an animal, made of stone or metal. EG ...a bronze statue of Charles I.

statuette /stætjuɛt/, **statuettes.** A **statuette** is a N COUNT very small statue which is often displayed on a shelf. EG ...a statuette of a little girl.

stature /stætʃə/. Someone's **stature** is 1 their N UNCOUNT: height and general size. EG She was rather small in USU+SUPP stature. 2 the importance and reputation that they have. EG I can't tell you how pleased we are to have someone of your stature here.

status /steɪtəs/. 1 Your **status** is 1.1 your position N UNCOUNT in society. EG ...the changing status of women. 1.2 the prestige and importance that you have in the eyes of other people. EG He came in search of wealth, status, and power.

2 Status is also an official classification that a N UNCOUNT person, organization, or country receives, which +SUPP gives them particular rights or advantages. EG They appeared to have dropped their demand for status as political prisoners.

3 The **status** of something such as a dispute or a N UNCOUNT discussion is how important it is. EG They are +SUPP meeting to discuss the status of the dispute with club-owners over free membership.

status quo /steɪtəs kwəʊ/. The **status quo** is the N SING situation that exists at a particular time.

status symbol, status symbols. A **status sym-** N COUNT **bol** is something that a person has or owns that shows they have prestige and importance in society. EG A personal chauffeur is undoubtedly a status symbol.

statute /stætjuːt/, **statutes.** A **statute** is a formal N COUNT rule or law. EG There have been more than twenty statutes governing what can be published in newspapers.

statutory /stætjʊˈtəˀriˀ/ means relating to rules or ADJ CLASSIF: laws which have been formally written down. EG USU ATTRIB ...the IBA's statutory code of advertising standards. Formal

staunch /stɔːntʃ/, **staunchest; staunches,** **staunching, staunched. 1** A **staunch** supporter ADJ QUALIT: of someone or something is very loyal to them. EG USU ATTRIB Both are staunch supporters of Manchester United... ...Benny's staunchest ally.

2 If you **staunch** blood, you stop it from flowing out V+O of someone's body. EG Sophia staunched the blood Formal with a cloth.

stave /steɪv/, **staves, staving, staved.** If you PHRASAL VB: **stave** something **off**, you delay it happening. EG V+O+ADV They want to stave off any attempt to intervene.

stay /steɪ/, **stays, staying, stayed.** If you **stay** V+A somewhere, **1.1** you continue to be there and do not move away. EG Fewer women these days stay at home to look after their children. **1.2** you live there for a short time as a guest or a visitor. EG She was staying in the same hotel as I was.

2 If someone or something **stays** in a particular V+C OR V+A condition or situation, they continue to be in it. EG Last night I stayed awake until the whole house was sleeping... We'll work till eight if it stays light.

3 If you **stay** away from a place, you do not go V+A there. EG This town is unsafe: stay away from here.

4 If you **stay** out of something, you do not get V+A involved in it. EG I stayed out of the social life of the school... We try to stay out of politics.

5 If you **stay put**, you remain somewhere. EG Those PHRASE kinds of people stay put in one job all their lives.

6 A **stay** is a short time that you spend somewhere N COUNT: as a guest or visitor. EG We were good friends USU+SUPP throughout my stay in Germany.

stay in. If you **stay in**, you remain at home and PHRASAL VB: do not go out. EG She had to stay in and do the V+ADV dishes... We ought to have stayed in tonight.

stay on. If you **stay on** somewhere, you remain PHRASAL VB: there. EG He had stayed on to have a drink... Pupils V+ADV have to stay on at school till they are 16.

stay out. 1 If you **stay out**, you remain away PHRASAL VB: from home, especially when you are expected to V+ADV be there. EG She stayed out all night. **2** If workers V+ADV

stay out, they remain on strike. EG The men stayed out for nearly a year.

stay up. If you **stay up**, you remain out of bed at PHRASAL VB: a time when most people have gone to bed or at a V+ADV time when you are normally in bed yourself. EG Willie liked to eat out in restaurants and stay up late.

stead /stɛd/. If you say that something will **stand** PHRASE someone **in good stead**, you mean that it will be very useful to them in the future. EG My school theatrical performances stood me in good stead in later years.

steadfast /stɛdfəst, -fɑːst/. If you are **steadfast** in ADJ QUALIT something that you do, you are convinced that what you are doing is right and you refuse to change it or to give up; used showing approval. EG The refugees remained steadfast... ...steadfast loyalty. ◇ **steadfastly**. EG Her father has steadfastly ◇ ADV refused to take part in such activities.

steady /stɛdiˀ/, **steadier, steadiest; steadies,** **steadying, steadied. 1** Something that is **steady 1.1** continues or develops gradually and without ADJ QUALIT any interruptions. EG This year we've seen a steady rise in prices. ◇ **steadily**. EG Unemployment has ◇ ADV risen steadily. **1.2** stays at about the same level or ADJ QUALIT value with not much change or variation. EG These vehicles are reasonably economical at a steady 56 mph. ◇ **steadily**. EG He could hear Rudolph ◇ ADV breathing steadily.

2 If an object is **steady**, it is firm and does not ADJ QUALIT shake or move about. EG His hand was not quite steady... Try to hold the tray steady.

3 If you look at someone or speak to them in a ADJ QUALIT **steady** way, you look or speak in a calm, controlled way. EG Her voice was faint but steady. ◇ **steadily**. EG Foster looked steadily at me for ◇ ADV some moments.

4 Work that is **steady** is certain to continue for a ADJ CLASSIF long period of time. EG My son has a steady job.

5 If you describe a person as **steady**, you mean ADJ QUALIT that they are sensible and reliable. EG I like Simon very much – he's a very steady boy.

6 When you **steady** something or when it **stead-** V-ERG OR **ies**, you stop it shaking or moving about. EG His V-REFL elbows were resting on his knees to steady the binoculars... The boat moved slightly, and he steadied himself with his right hand.

7 When you **steady** yourself, you control your V-ERG OR voice or expression, so that people will think that V-REFL you are calm and not nervous. EG He drew a deep breath to steady himself.

steak /steɪk/, **steaks. 1 Steak** is beef without N MASS much fat on it. EG ...steak-and-kidney pie.

2 A fish **steak** is a large piece of fish. EG ...four N COUNT halibut steaks.

steal /stiːl/, **steals, stealing, stole** /stəʊl/, **stolen** /stəʊlɑˀn/. **1** If you **steal** something from someone, V+O OR V you take it away from them without their permission and without intending to return it. EG He stole knives and a gun... My first offence was stealing a pair of binoculars. ◇ **stealing**. EG He had been ◇ N UNCOUNT expelled from his previous school for stealing. ◇ **stolen**. EG ...stolen credit cards. ◇ ADJ CLASSIF

2 If you **steal** somewhere, you move there quietly V+A and cautiously so that nobody notices you. EG Simon Literary came stealing out of the shadows.

stealth /stɛlθ/. If you use **stealth** when you do N UNCOUNT something, you do it in such a slow, quiet, and secretive way that other people do not notice what you are doing. EG Sometimes tigers rely on stealth, creeping towards their victims.

stealthy /stɛlθiˀ/. **Stealthy** actions or movements ADJ QUALIT are performed quietly and secretively, so that no one will notice what you are doing. EG I managed to get there by a series of stealthy movements.

What things on these pages might be made of metal?

◊ **stealthily.** EG *I heard my landlady creeping* ◊ ADV
stealthily up to my door.

steam /stiːm/, **steams, steaming, steamed. 1** N UNCOUNT
Steam is the hot mist that water turns into when it
boils. EG *The room was filled with steam... Steam
hissed between the blocks of lava.*

2 Steam vehicles and machines are operated using ADJ CLASSIF :
steam as a means of power. EG *The first steam* ATTRIB
locomotive was introduced in 1825.

3 If something **steams,** it gives off steam. EG *The* V
*kettle was steaming away on the stove... Lynn
brought her a steaming cup of tea.*

4 If a vehicle **steams** somewhere, it moves along, V+A
giving out steam. EG *A British ship was steaming
into Valetta Harbour.*

5 If you **steam** food, you cook it in steam rather V+A
than in water. EG *...steamed rice.*

6 If you **let off steam,** you get rid of your energy, PHRASE
anger, or strong emotions by behaving in a noisy or Informal
violent way. EG *They can let off steam in pubs
where nobody knows them.*

7 If you **run out of steam,** you stop doing some- PHRASE
thing because you have no more energy or enthusi- Informal
asm left. EG *She would let me ramble on until I ran
out of steam.*

steam up. 1 If you are **steamed up** about PHRASE
something, you are very annoyed about it. EG *What* Informal
was she getting so steamed up about?

2 When a window or piece of glass **steams up,** it PHRASAL VB :
becomes covered with steam or mist. V+ADV

steamer /stiːmə/, **steamers.** A **steamer** is a ship N COUNT
that has an engine powered by steam.

steamroller /stiːmrəʊlə/, **steamrollers.** A N COUNT
steamroller is a large, heavy vehicle with wide
solid wheels. Steamrollers are used to flatten the
surfaces of roads.

steamy /stiːmiˈ/. A place that is **steamy** is very ADJ QUALIT
hot and humid because it is full of steam. EG *The
corridor opened onto a steamy and noisy kitchen.*

steel /stiːl/, **steels, steeling, steeled. 1** Steel is a N UNCOUNT :
very strong metal which is made mainly from iron. USU N MOD
Steel is used for making many things, for example
bridges, buildings, vehicles, and cutlery. EG *...a
modern tower made of concrete and steel.* ● See
also **stainless steel.**

2 If you **steel** yourself, you prepare to deal with V-REFL :
something unpleasant. EG *You had better steel* USU+*for*
yourself for a shock. OR *to*-INF

steel band, steel bands. A **steel band** is a band N COUNT
of people who play music on special metal drums.

steel wool is a mass of fine steel threads twisted N UNCOUNT
together into a small ball and used for cleaning
surfaces.

steelworker /stiːlwɜːkə/, **steelworkers.** A **steel-** N COUNT
worker is a person who works in a steelworks. EG
Steelworkers formed local committees.

steelworks /stiːlwɜːks/. A **steelworks** is a facto- N COUNT
ry where steel is made. The plural form is also
'steelworks'. EG *The flames from the steelworks
shot skywards.*

steely /stiːliˈ/. You use **steely 1** to describe some- ADJ QUALIT
thing that has a hard, greyish colour like steel. EG
The blue sky had changed to a steely grey. **2** to ADJ CLASSIF :
emphasize that a person is hard, strong, and deter- ATTRIB
mined. EG *There was shy modesty behind that
steely determination.*

steep /stiːp/, **steeper, steepest. 1** A **steep** slope ADJ QUALIT
forms a large angle with the horizontal, and is
difficult to go up. EG *...a steep little street... He
reached the steepest part of the mountain.*

◊ **steeply.** EG *...mountains rising steeply on three* ◊ ADV
sides.

2 A **steep** increase in something is a very big ADJ QUALIT
increase. EG *There's likely to be a steep increase in
unemployment.* ◊ **steeply.** EG *The costs of public* ◊ ADV
services have risen steeply.

3 If you say that the price of something is **steep,** ADJ PRED
you mean that it is expensive. Informal

steeped /stiːpt/. If a place or person is **steeped** in ADJ PRED+*in*
a quality or characteristic, they are surrounded by
it or deeply influenced by it. EG *The house is
centuries old and steeped in history.*

steeple /stiːpəˈl/, **steeples.** A **steeple** is a tall N COUNT
pointed structure on top of the tower of a church.

steer /stɪə/, **steers, steering, steered. 1** When V-ERG OR V
you **steer** a car, boat, or plane, you control it so
that it goes in the direction that you want. EG *He
steered the car through the broad entrance... The
freighter steered out of Santiago Bay that evening.*

2 If you **steer** someone in a particular direction, V+O : USU+A
you guide them there. EG *He steered me to a table
and sat me down in a chair.*

3 If you **steer** people towards a particular way of V+O : USU+A
behaving, you change their behaviour, especially
without them noticing, and make them behave in
that way. EG *He steers the conversation towards
more general topics.*

steering wheel, steering wheels. The **steering** N COUNT
wheel in a car or lorry is the wheel which the
driver holds when he or she is steering the vehicle.
See picture at CAR.

stem /stem/, **stems, stemming, stemmed. 1** The N COUNT
stem of a plant is the long, thin, central part of it
which is above the ground.

2 The **stem** of a glass or vase is the long thin part N COUNT
of it which connects the bowl to the base.

3 The **stem** of a pipe is the long thin part of it N COUNT
through which smoke is sucked.

4 If you **stem** something that is spreading from one V+O
place to another, you stop it spreading. EG *...stem-
ming the flow of illegal drugs.*

5 If a condition or problem **stems** from something, V+*from*
it started originally because of it. EG *Their aggres-
siveness stemmed from fear.*

stench /stentʃ/, **stenches.** A **stench** is a strong N COUNT :
and very unpleasant smell. EG *...the unmistakable* USU+*of*
stench of rotting eggs.

stencil /stensəˈl/, **stencils, stencilling, sten-**
cilled; spelled **stenciling, stenciled** in American
English. **1** A **stencil** is a piece of paper, plastic, or N COUNT
metal which has a design cut out of it. You place
the stencil on a surface and use it to create a
design, by allowing ink or paint to go through the
holes in the stencil onto the surface below.

2 If you **stencil** letters or designs, you print them V OR V+O
using a stencil. EG *...large dustbins bearing the
stencilled word LITTER.*

step /step/, **steps, stepping, stepped. 1** A **step** is N COUNT
the movement that you make when you lift your
foot and put it down in a different place, for
example when you are walking. EG *She took a step
back... I walked on with quick steps.*

2 If you **step** on something or **step** in a particular V+A
direction, you put your foot on the thing or move
your foot in that direction. EG *He had stepped on a
thorn... Step over the wire... Tom stepped back.*

3 If someone tells you to **watch** your **step,** they are PHRASE
telling you to be careful about how you behave or
what you say so that you don't get into trouble. EG
I'm cleverer than you are, so watch your step.

4 A **step** is also one of a series of actions that you N COUNT :
take in order to achieve something. EG *Today's* USU+SUPP
*announcement is a step in the right direction...
...the first step on the road to victory.*

5 A **step** in a process is one of a series of stages. EG N COUNT
*Simmel carried this idea one step further... Brody
was several steps ahead of Cassidy.* ● If you do ● PHRASE
something **step by step,** you do it by progressing
gradually from one stage to the next. EG *The proof
is set out, step by step, on page 6.*

6 A **step** is also a raised flat surface, often one of a N COUNT
series of surfaces at different heights, on which you
put your feet in order to walk up or down to a
different level. EG *She was sitting on the top step...
...a flight of concrete steps.*

7 People sometimes refer to a stepladder as **steps.** N PLURAL

8 If a group of people are walking **in step,** they are PHRASE moving their feet forward at exactly the same time as each other. EG ...*a party of boys marching in step.*

step aside. To **step aside** means the same as to step down. EG *The committee wanted Mr Casey to step aside.*   PHRASAL VB : V+ADV

step back. If you **step back** and think about a situation, you think about it in a fresh way as if you were not involved in it. EG *It is tempting to step back and ask whether it is worth all the trouble.*   PHRASAL VB : V+ADV

step down. If you **step down** or **step aside** from an important job or position, you resign from it. EG *He stepped down last month because of illness.*   PHRASAL VB : V+ADV

step in. If you **step in**, you get involved in a difficult situation, in order to help to find a solution. EG *She really appreciates the way you stepped in and saw to things.*   PHRASAL VB : V+ADV

step up. If you **step up** something, you increase it. EG *The government is stepping up its efforts... The pace of exploration for fossil fuels has been stepped up enormously.*   PHRASAL VB : V+O+ADV

stepbrother /stɛpbrʌðə/, **stepbrothers.** Someone's **stepbrother** is the son of their stepfather or stepmother.   N COUNT

stepchild /stɛptʃaɪld/, **stepchildren.** Someone's **stepchild** is the child of their husband or wife by an earlier marriage.   N COUNT

stepdaughter /stɛpdɔːtə/, **stepdaughters.** Someone's **stepdaughter** is the daughter of their husband or wife by an earlier marriage.   N COUNT

stepfather /stɛpfɑːðə/, **stepfathers.** Someone's **stepfather** is the man who has married their mother after the death or divorce of their father.   N COUNT

stepladder /stɛplædə/, **stepladders.** A **stepladder** is a ladder which you can carry around, consisting of two sloping parts that are hinged together at the top so that it will stand up on its own. EG *He got down off the stepladder.*   N COUNT

stepmother /stɛpmʌðə/, **stepmothers.** Someone's **stepmother** is the woman who has married their father after the death or divorce of their mother.   N COUNT

stepping stone, stepping stones. 1 A **stepping stone** is a job or event that helps you to make progress, often in your career. EG *That film was a big stepping-stone in my career.*   N COUNT

2 Stepping stones are a line of large stones which you can walk on in order to cross a shallow stream or river.   N COUNT : USU PLURAL

stepsister /stɛpsɪstə/, **stepsisters.** Someone's **stepsister** is the daughter of their stepfather or stepmother.   N COUNT

stepson /stɛpsʌn/, **stepsons.** Someone's **stepson** is the son of their husband or wife by an earlier marriage.   N COUNT

stereo /stɛriˡəʊ/, **stereos. 1 Stereo** is used to describe a record or a system of playing music in which the sound is directed through two different speakers. EG ...*buying stereo equipment... It sounds much better in stereo.*   ADJ CLASSIF OR N UNCOUNT

2 A **stereo** is a record player with two speakers. EG *He turned on the stereo.*   N COUNT Informal

stereotype /stɛriˡəˡtaɪp/, **stereotypes, stereotyping, stereotyped. 1** A **stereotype** is a fixed general image or set of characteristics that a lot of people believe represent a particular type of person or thing. EG *The song perpetuates two racist stereotypes.*   N COUNT

2 If you **stereotype** someone, you form a fixed general idea or image of them, so that you assume that they will behave in a particular way. EG *These images confine women to stereotyped roles.*   V+O

sterile /stɛraɪl/. **1** Something that is **sterile** is completely clean and free from germs. EG ...*rolls of sterile bandage.*   ADJ CLASSIF

2 A person or animal that is **sterile** is unable to have or produce babies. EG *He had learnt early in his marriage that he was sterile.*   ADJ CLASSIF

3 A situation that is **sterile** is lacking in energy   ADJ QUALIT

and new ideas. EG *The meeting degenerated into a sterile debate.*

sterilize /stɛrɪˡlaɪz/, **sterilizes, sterilizing, sterilized;** also spelled **sterilise. 1** If you **sterilize** a thing or a place, you make it completely clean and free from germs. EG *All nearby brickwork must be sterilized with a blowlamp, then treated with fungicide.*   V+O

2 If a person or an animal **is sterilized**, they have a medical operation that makes it impossible for them to have or produce babies. EG *By 1950, 16 per cent of women over twenty had been sterilized.*   V+O : USU PASS

sterling /stɜːlɪŋ/ is the money system of Great Britain. EG *Sterling has once again become one of the stronger currencies... ...a hundred and fifty pounds sterling.*   N UNCOUNT OR ADJ AFTER N

stern /stɜːn/, **sterner, sternest; sterns. 1** Someone who is **stern** is very serious and strict. EG *Sylvia had a stern father who never praised her... ...a stern warning.* ◇ **sternly** EG *He walked over to the boy and said to him sternly, 'Give that to me'.*   ADJ QUALIT ◇ ADV

2 The **stern** of a boat is the back part of it. EG *She seated herself in the stern.*   N COUNT

stethoscope

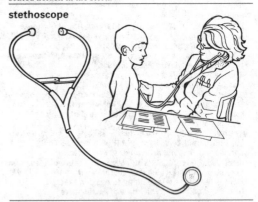

stethoscope /stɛθəskəʊp/, **stethoscopes.** A **stethoscope** is an instrument that a doctor uses to listen to your heart and breathing. It consists of a small disc that the doctor places on your body and a hollow tube that connects the disc to earpieces.   N COUNT

stew /stjuː/, **stews, stewing, stewed. 1** A **stew** is a meal which you make by cooking meat and vegetables in liquid at a low temperature. EG *We've got lamb stew tonight.*   N MASS

2 When you **stew** meat, vegetables, or fruit, you cook them slowly in liquid in a closed dish. EG ...*stewed fruit.*   V+O

3 If you **let** someone **stew**, you deliberately leave them to worry about something for a while, rather than telling them something which would make them feel better. EG *Let him stew... He let her stew for a day or two.*   PHRASE Informal

steward /stjuəd/, **stewards. 1** A **steward** is a man who works on a ship, plane, or train, looking after passengers and serving meals to them.   N COUNT

2 A **steward** is also a man or woman who helps to organize a race, march, or other public event. ● See also **shop steward.**   N COUNT

stewardess /stjuədɛs/, **stewardesses.** A **stewardess** is a woman who works on a ship, plane, or train, looking after passengers and serving meals to them. EG *The stewardess brought more drinks.*   N COUNT

stick /stɪk/, **sticks, sticking, stuck** /stʌk/. **1** A **stick** is a long, thin piece of wood, for example dead wood from a tree. EG *I gathered some sticks to*   N COUNT

If you stick your stereo on the table, is it sticky?

start the fire... ...a circle drawn in the dirt with a stick... ...boys armed with sticks... ...hockey sticks.

2 A **stick** of something is a long thin piece of it. EG N PART *...sticks of dynamite.*

3 If you **stick** a pointed object in something, you V-ERG+A push it in. EG *He stuck the knife right in... He stuck a cigar in his mouth... The pig had two spears sticking in her side.*

4 If you **stick** something to something else, you V+O+A attach it using glue, sticky tape, or another sticky substance. EG *They went round sticking posters on walls... Someone has stuck a label on the crate.*

5 If one thing **sticks** to another, it becomes V : USU+*to* attached to it and is difficult to remove. EG *...sand that sticks to your hair and skin.*

6 If something which can usually be moved **sticks**, V it becomes fixed in one position and can no longer be moved. EG *If your zip sticks, it might be because a thread has caught in it.*

7 If something **sticks** in your mind, you remember V : USU+A it for a long time. EG *One lecture stuck in my mind.*

8 If you **stick** something somewhere, you put it V+O+A there in a rather casual way. EG *She closed the bag* Informal *and stuck it back on the shelf.*

9 If you **stick it** in a difficult situation, you do not PHRASE leave or give up. EG *I don't know how I've stuck it.* Informal *It's been hell.*

10 If someone **gets the wrong end of the stick,** PHRASE they completely misunderstand something. Informal

11 to **stick** your **neck** out: see **neck.** ● to **stick in** your **throat**: see **throat.** ● See also **stuck.**

stick around. If you **stick around,** you stay PHRASAL VB : where you are, often because you are waiting for V+ADV something. EG *I'll stick around and keep an eye on* Informal *the food.*

stick at. If you **stick at** a task or activity, you PHRASAL VB : continue doing it, even if it is difficult. EG *You must* V+PREP *stick at it if you want to succeed.*

stick by. If you **stick by** someone, you continue PHRASAL VB : to give them help or support. EG *...a good command-* V+PREP *ing officer who stuck by his men when they got into trouble.*

stick out. 1 If you **stick** something **out,** you PHRASAL VB : make it appear from inside or behind something V+O+ADV else. EG *Lally stuck her head out of a window... Lynn stuck out her tongue.* **2** If something **sticks out, 2.1** it extends beyond something else. EG *There* V+ADV, USU+A *was a little chimney sticking out of the roof... A few grey hairs stuck out from under her hat.* **2.2** it is V+ADV very noticeable because it is unusual. EG *His accent made him stick out... a home that would not stick out in an English village.* **3** If someone in a difficult V+O+ADV situation **sticks** it **out,** they do not leave or give up. EG *I stuck it out as long as I could.*

stick out for. If you **stick out for** something, PHRASAL VB : you keep demanding it and do not accept anything V+ADV+PREP different or less. EG *He stuck out for twice the usual salary, and got it.*

stick to. 1 If you **stick to** someone or something PHRASAL VB : when you are travelling, you stay close to them. EG V+PREP *I went over the hill instead of sticking to the river.*

2 If you **stick to** something, you do not change to V+PREP, something else. EG *They are sticking to their pres-* HAS PASS *ent policy... I think I'll just stick to painting from now on.* **3** If you **stick to** a promise or agreement, V+PREP, you do what you said you would do. EG *They stuck* HAS PASS *to the bargain.*

stick together. If people **stick together,** they PHRASAL VB : stay with each other and support each other. EG V+ADV *The boys learned to stick together.*

stick up. 1 If you **stick up** a picture or a notice, PHRASAL VB : you attach it to a wall so that it can be seen. EG *We* V+O+ADV *have a painting stuck up on the wall.* **2** If some- V+ADV thing long **sticks up,** it points upwards. EG *These plants stick up vertically from the seabed.*

stick up for. If you **stick up for** a person or a PHRASAL VB : principle, you support or defend them forcefully. EG V+ADV+PREP *He thanked his father for sticking up for him... I was too scared to stick up for my rights.*

stick with. 1 If you **stick with** something, you PHRASAL VB : do not change to something else. EG *I stuck with my* V+PREP *staple diet: brown rice.* **2** If you **stick with** V+PREP someone, you stay close to them. EG *Stick with me and you'll be okay.*

sticker /stɪkə/, **stickers.** A **sticker** is a small N COUNT piece of paper or plastic, with writing or a picture on one side, which you can stick onto a surface. EG *They sell stickers and badges... On the rear window was a sticker saying 'Save the Whales'.*

sticking plaster is material that you can stick N UNCOUNT over a cut or blister in order to protect it.

stick-in-the-mud, stick-in-the-muds. If you de- N COUNT : scribe someone as a **stick-in-the-mud,** you mean USU SING that they do not like doing anything new. Informal

stickler /stɪklə/, **sticklers.** If you are a **stickler** N COUNT : for something, you always insist on it. EG *Kitty was* USU+*for* *a stickler for routine.*

sticky /stɪkiˈ/, **stickier, stickiest. 1** Something ADJ QUALIT that is **sticky** is covered with a substance that can stick to other things and leave unpleasant marks. EG *Her hands were sticky from the ice cream... ...a sticky bottle of fruit juice.*

2 Sticky paper has glue on one side so that you can ADJ CLASSIF stick it to surfaces. EG *...sticky labels... ...sticky tape.* ATTRIB

3 If you describe a situation as **sticky,** you mean ADJ QUALIT that it is difficult or embarrassing. EG *We had a* Informal *very sticky first day together in London.*

4 Sticky weather is unpleasantly hot and damp. EG ADJ QUALIT *...a hot, sticky, July afternoon.*

5 If someone **comes to a sticky end** or **meets a** PHRASE **sticky end,** they suffer very badly or die in an Informal unpleasant way. EG *...a disappointed man who had come to an exceptionally sticky end.*

stiff /stɪf/, **stiffer, stiffest. 1** Something that is ADJ QUALIT **stiff** is firm and does not bend easily. EG *Use a stiff brush... ...a new pair of stiff climbing boots... ...stiff brown paper.*

2 Something such as a door or drawer that is **stiff** ADJ QUALIT does not move as easily as it should. EG *The door was rather stiff... ...a stiff latch.*

3 If you are **stiff,** your muscles or joints ache when ADJ QUALIT you move, because of illness or because of too much exercise. EG *My arms were stiff.*

4 Stiff behaviour is rather formal and not very ADJ QUALIT friendly or relaxed. EG *...a stiff smile... The letter was stiff and formal.* ◊ **stiffly.** EG *'No, I haven't,'* ◊ ADV *Rudolph said stiffly.*

5 Stiff also means difficult or severe. EG *Competi-* ADJ QUALIT *tion is so stiff that he'll be lucky to get a place at all... ...a stiff tax... There will be stiffer penalties for drunken drivers.*

6 A **stiff** drink is a large amount of a strong ADJ QUALIT : alcoholic drink such as gin or whisky. EG *Morris* ATTRIB *fixed himself a stiff drink.*

7 A **stiff** breeze is blowing quite strongly. ADJ QUALIT

8 If you are bored **stiff,** worried **stiff,** or scared ADV AFTER ADJ **stiff,** you are extremely bored, worried, or scared. Informal EG *We were scared stiff of meeting him... The subject bores them stiff.*

stiffen /stɪfə°n/, **stiffens, stiffening, stiffened. 1** V If you **stiffen,** you stop moving and stand or sit with muscles that are suddenly tense, for example because you feel afraid or angry. EG *Tom suddenly stiffened with alarm... Her whole body stiffened.*

2 If your muscles or joints **stiffen,** they become V-ERG difficult to bend or move. EG *You are unlikely to be troubled with stiffening joints.*

3 If attitudes or behaviour **stiffen,** they become V-ERG stronger or more severe, and less likely to be changed. EG *Resistance stiffened even further last week... You will only stiffen his resolve.*

4 When something such as cloth is **stiffened,** it is V+O : USU PASS made firm so that it does not bend easily. ◊ **stiffened.** EG *...a dress of stiffened satin.* ◊ ADJ CLASSIF

stifle /staɪfə°l/, **stifles, stifling, stifled. 1** If some- V+O one **stifles** something that is happening, they stop it from continuing. EG *An authoritarian leadership stifled internal debate.*

2 If you **stifle** a cry or a yawn, you prevent v+o
yourself from crying out or yawning. EG *She placed
a hand over her mouth to stifle a shriek of laughter.*

3 If the air or the atmosphere **stifles** you, it makes v+o
you feel as if you cannot breathe properly. EG *She
was stifled with its scent.* ◊ **stifling**. EG *...a stifling* ◊ ADJ QUALIT
night... It was stifling inside.

stigma /ˈstɪgmə/. If something has a **stigma** at- N SING OR
tached to it, it has a bad reputation and a lot of N UNCOUNT
people disapprove of it. EG *...the stigma of failure...
Some of the stigma attached to mental illness will
be removed in future years.*

stile /staɪl/, **stiles**. A **stile** is an entrance to a field N COUNT
or path that consists of a step on either side of a
fence or wall. EG *I set off again along the path, over
the stile, and up the lane.*

stiletto /stɪˈletəʊ/, **stilettos**. **Stilettos** or **stiletto** N COUNT :
heels are women's shoes that have high, very USU PLURAL
narrow heels. See picture at SHOES.

still /stɪl/, **stiller, stillest; stills.** **1** If a situation ADV
that used to exist **still** exists, it has continued and
exists now. EG *She still lives in London... She was
still beautiful... I was still a schoolboy.*

2 If something that has not yet happened could ADV
still happen, it is possible that it will happen in the
future. EG *She could still change her mind... There is
still a chance that a few might survive.*

3 If you say that there is **still** an amount of ADV
something left, you are emphasizing that there is
that amount left. EG *There are ten weeks still to
go... I've still got three left.*

4 You use **still 4.1** to emphasize that something is ADV OR
the case in spite of what you have just said. EG ADV SEN
*Whatever they have done, they are still your
parents.* **4.2** when you are dismissing a problem or ADV SEN
difficulty as not really worth worrying about. EG
*...and that made me miss the last bus. Still, that's
life, isn't it?*

5 You also use **still** with 'better' or 'more' to ADV :
indicate that something has even more of a quality WITH COMPAR
than something else. EG *How about some Bach to
begin with? Or, better still, Vivaldi... To the astonishment of his friends, he ran for Governor of New
York. More astonishing still, he won.*

6 If you stay **still**, you stay in the same position and ADJ PRED OR
do not move. EG *Stand still!... We had to keep still* ADV AFTER VB
for about four minutes.

7 When air or water is **still**, it is not moving. EG ADJ QUALIT
...the still water of the lagoon.

8 If a place is **still**, it is quiet and shows no sign of ADJ QUALIT :
activity. EG *Around them the forest was very still.* USU PRED
◊ **stillness**. EG *The stillness of the fields was* ◊ N UNCOUNT
broken by the sound of a gunshot.

9 A **still** is a photograph taken from a cinema film N COUNT
which is used for publicity purposes.

stillborn /ˈstɪlbɔːn/. A **stillborn** baby is dead when ADJ CLASSIF
it is born.

stilt /stɪlt/, **stilts.** **1** **Stilts** are long upright pieces N COUNT :
of wood or metal which are used to support some USU PLURAL
buildings. EG *Thatched huts were raised high above
the paddy fields on stilts.*

2 **Stilts** are also two long pieces of wood that N COUNT :
circus clowns stand on in order to walk high up USU PLURAL
above the ground. EG *He is walking on stilts.*

stilted /ˈstɪltɪd/. If someone's behaviour or conver- ADJ QUALIT
sation is **stilted**, they behave or speak in a formal
and unnatural way. EG *After some stilted efforts at
conversation, he gave up and left.*

stimulant /ˈstɪmjʊlənt/, **stimulants.** A **stimu-** N COUNT
lant is a drug that makes your body work faster,
often increasing your heart rate and making you
less likely to sleep. EG *...coffee in which the drug
caffeine acts as a stimulant.*

stimulate /ˈstɪmjʊleɪt/, **stimulates, stimulating,
stimulated.** **1** To **stimulate** something means to v+o
encourage it to begin or develop further. EG *Rising
prices will stimulate demands for higher incomes...*

*An outsider who can offer a fresh point of view
may stimulate new ideas.*

2 If something **stimulates** you, it makes you feel v+o
full of ideas and enthusiasm. EG *The art course
stimulated me.* ◊ **stimulating**. EG *...a conversation* ◊ ADJ QUALIT
which I found both stimulating and exciting.
◊ **stimulation** /ˌstɪmjʊˈleɪʃən/. EG *I find great* ◊ N UNCOUNT
intellectual stimulation in these surroundings.

3 If something **stimulates** a part of a person's v+o
body, it causes it to move or function, usually Technical
automatically by a natural reflex. EG *The optical
system of the eye stimulates cells in the retina.*

stimulus /ˈstɪmjʊləs/, **stimuli** /ˈstɪmjʊlaɪ/. **1** If N COUNT
something acts as a **stimulus**, it makes a process
develop further or more quickly. EG *There would
not have been the same stimulus to mechanize
production so rapidly.*

2 **Stimulus** is something which causes people to N UNCOUNT
feel energetic and enthusiastic. EG *...all the stimulus
and excitement that battle brought.*

3 A **stimulus** is something that causes a part of a N COUNT
person's body to move or function, usually auto- Technical
matically by a natural reflex. EG *They change
automatically in response to stimuli.*

sting /stɪŋ/, **stings, stinging, stung** /stʌŋ/. **1** If v+o OR v
an insect, animal, or plant **stings** you, it causes you
to feel a sharp pain by pricking your skin, usually
with poison. EG *Bees do not normally sting without
being provoked.*

2 The **sting** of an insect or animal is the part that N SING
stings you. EG *They paralyse their victims with a
sting... This is not a worker bee, it has no sting.*

3 If you feel a **sting**, you feel a sharp pain in your N COUNT
skin or in another part of your body. EG *...the sting
of ashes in his eyes.*

4 If a part of your body **stings** or if something that v-ERG
you put on it **stings**, you feel a sharp pain there. EG
My eyes were stinging.

5 If someone's remarks **sting** you, they make you v+o : NO CONT
feel hurt and annoyed. EG *I wondered why I'd said
it, knowing it would really sting him.* ◊ **stinging**. ◊ ADJ QUALIT
EG *He made a stinging attack on Taverne.*

6 If something **takes the sting out** of a situation, it PHRASE
removes the painful or unpleasant aspect of it. EG
He smiled to take the sting out of his words.

stingy /ˈstɪndʒɪ/. Someone who is **stingy** is very ADJ QUALIT
mean. EG *The government was stingy and his salary
was miserable.*

stink /stɪŋk/, **stinks, stinking, stank** /stæŋk/,
stunk /stʌŋk/. **1** Something that **stinks** smells v
extremely unpleasant. EG *The butcher's shop stank
in hot weather... ...a foul, stinking lavatory.* ► used ► N SING
as a noun. EG *The stink of vomit reached Brody
almost instantly.*

2 If you say that a place or situation **stinks**, you v : NO CONT
mean that you think it is extremely bad or unpleas- Informal
ant. EG *'What do you think of the town?' she asked.
'I think it stinks,' I replied.*

stinking /ˈstɪŋkɪŋ/. You use **stinking** to describe ADJ CLASSIF
something that is extremely unpleasant. EG *I've got* ATTRIB
a stinking cold... You couldn't hide anything in this Informal
stinking little town.

stint /stɪnt/, **stints.** A **stint** is a period of time N COUNT+SUPP
which you spend doing a particular job or activity.
EG *I arrived at the University for a three month
stint as a lecturer.*

stipulate /ˈstɪpjʊleɪt/, **stipulates, stipulating,** v+o
stipulated. If you **stipulate** that something must OR V+REPORT
be done, you say clearly that it must be done. EG
*The document stipulated nine criteria as the basis
for any reform... I won't stipulate that it must be a
story, just that it should be a written piece.*

stir /stɜː/, **stirs, stirring, stirred.** **1** When you v+o
stir a liquid, you mix it inside a container by using

If a shop stocks stockings, what does it sell?

something such as a spoon. EG *The tourist was stirring his coffee and gazing at the buildings.*

2 If you **stir**, you move slightly, for example v because you are uncomfortable. EG *The boys stirred uneasily... Etta didn't stir, pretending to be asleep.*

3 If the wind **stirs** an object, it makes it move v+o gently. EG *A stray breath of wind stirred the stillness of the robes.*

4 If you **stir** yourself, you move yourself in order to v-REFL do something. EG *Finally, one of the males stirred himself and took a step forward, hesitantly.*

5 If something beautiful or terrible **stirs** you, it v+o makes you react with a strong emotion. EG *There was a particular passage which always stirred him profoundly.*

6 If an event causes a **stir**, it causes great excite- N SING ment, shock, or anger among a number of people. EG *Her speech created a huge stir.*

7 If a particular mood, feeling, or idea **stirs** in v:USU+A someone, they begin to feel it or think about it. EG *The political debate was reopened and a new mood was stirring... Something seemed to stir within her.*

stir up. 1 If something **stirs up** dust or mud, it PHRASAL VB: causes it to rise up and move around. EG *Some* V+O+ADV *gentle winds stirred up the dust.* **2** If you **stir up** v+O+ADV trouble or **stir up** a feeling, you cause trouble or cause people to have the feeling. EG *He was prevented from speaking on the grounds that it would 'stir up trouble'... ...a rally called to stir up popular support for nuclear disarmament.*

stirring /stɜːrɪŋ/, **stirrings. 1** You use **stirring** to ADJ QUALIT describe something such as a speech when it makes people very excited or enthusiastic. EG *...one of the most stirring shots of the whole film... They must have been stirring times.*

2 When there is a **stirring** of something such as a N COUNT: feeling, people begin to feel it. EG *There was a slight* USU+of *stirring of interest among them... ...the first stirrings of student protest.*

stirrup /stɪrəp/, **stirrups. Stirrups** are the two N COUNT metal loops attached to a horse's saddle, which you place your feet in when you are riding.

stitch /stɪtʃ/, **stitches, stitching, stitched. 1** V OR V+O When people **stitch** material, they use a needle and thread to join two pieces together or to make a decoration. EG *They were cut out and stitched together... ...finely stitched collars.*

2 A **stitch** is one of the short pieces of thread that N COUNT can be seen on a piece of material when it has been stitched. EG *...the little stitches in the canvas she was embroidering.*

3 When doctors **stitch** a wound or **stitch** it up, v+O:OFT+up they use a special needle and thread to tie the skin together. EG *The doctor who stitched it should have another look at it tomorrow.*

4 A **stitch** is also a piece of thread that has been N COUNT used to tie the skin round a wound. EG *His wound required five stitches.*

5 If you have a **stitch**, you feel a sharp pain at the N SING: side of your stomach, usually after running fast or USU a+N laughing a lot. EG *I began to have a bad stitch.*

6 If you are **in stitches**, you are laughing and PHRASE cannot stop. EG *I then fell down the stairs, which* Informal *sent everyone into stitches.*

stock /stɒk/, **stocks, stocking, stocked. 1** Stocks N COUNT:USU are shares in the ownership of a company, or PLURAL OR investments on which a fixed amount of interest N UNCOUNT will be paid. EG *Heavy bidding for oil company stocks may be just beginning... ...if they succeed in buying big blocks of stock.*

2 A shop or factory that **stocks** particular goods v+O:NO CONT keeps a supply of them to sell. EG *Several shops in London stock large fittings.*

3 A shop's **stock** is the total amount of goods which N UNCOUNT it has available to sell. EG *...selling a week's worth of stock in a single day.* ● If particular goods are **in** ● PHRASE **stock** in a shop, they are available to be sold. If they are **out of stock**, they have all been sold and have not yet been replaced.

4 If you **stock** a container or shelf, you fill it with v+o food or other things. EG *His locker was always stocked with screws... I found part-time work, stocking shelves in supermarkets.*

5 If you have a **stock** of things, you have a supply N COUNT+SUPP of them ready to be used. EG *Keep a stock of fuses... They want to conserve coal stocks during the miners' strike.*

6 The **stock** that a person or animal comes from is N UNCOUNT the original type of people or animals from which they are descended. EG *They were of European stock... He came from sturdy, peasant stock.*

7 Stock is a liquid that is used to give soups and N MASS sauces a stronger flavour. You can make stock by boiling meat, bones, or vegetables in water.

8 A **stock** expression, character, or way of doing ADJ CLASSIF: something is one that is very commonly used. EG ATTRIB *'Wild and wanton' was a stock phrase of the time.*

9 If you **take stock**, you pause and think about all PHRASE the aspects of a situation or event, before deciding what to do next. EG *The emergency committee had a chance to take stock of the situation.*

10 lock, stock, and barrel: see **lock.** ● See also **laughing stock.**

stock up. If you **stock up** with things, you buy a PHRASAL VB: lot of them, in case you cannot get them later. EG V+ADV *Stock up with groceries and canned foods.*

stockbroker /stɒkbrəʊkə/, **stockbrokers.** A N COUNT **stockbroker** is a person whose job is to buy and sell stocks and shares for people who want to invest money.

stock exchange, stock exchanges. A **stock** N COUNT: **exchange** is a place where people buy and sell USU the+N stocks and shares. EG *...the Tokyo Stock Exchange.*

stocking /stɒkɪŋ/, **stockings. Stockings** are N COUNT: pieces of clothing which fit closely over your feet USU PLURAL and legs. Stockings are usually made of nylon or silk and worn by women. EG *...a woman in a flowered skirt and black stockings and shoes.*

stockinged /stɒkɪŋd/. If someone is in their ADJ CLASSIF: **stockinged** feet, they are wearing socks or stock- ATTRIB ings, but no shoes.

stock-in-trade. Someone's **stock-in-trade** is a N SING+POSS usual part of their behaviour or work. EG *Cynicism was his stock-in-trade.*

stock market, stock markets. The **stock mar-** N COUNT: **ket** is the business organization and activity in- USU the+N volved in buying and selling stocks and shares. EG *Prices have risen sharply on the stock market.*

stockpile /stɒkpaɪl/, **stockpiles, stockpiling, stockpiled. 1** If people **stockpile** things, they v+o store large quantities of them for future use. EG *...a nation that stockpiled reserves of food.*

2 A **stockpile** of things is a large quantity of them N COUNT: that have been stored for future use. EG *...a stock-* USU+SUPP *pile of nuclear weapons.*

stock-still. If someone stands or sits **stock-still,** ADV AFTER VB they do not move at all. EG *She stood stock-still, staring at him.*

stocktaking /stɒkteɪkɪŋ/ is the activity of count- N UNCOUNT ing and checking all the goods that a shop or business has.

stocky /stɒki/, **stockier, stockiest. Stocky** peo- ADJ QUALIT ple look slightly fat, but strong and solid. EG *...a short, stocky man with dark hair.*

stodgy /stɒdʒi/, **stodgier, stodgiest. 1 Stodgy** ADJ QUALIT food is very solid, makes you feel very full, and is difficult to digest. EG *...a stodgy meal.*

2 Stodgy people and things are very dull and ADJ QUALIT uninteresting. EG *His friend Beale was stodgy and solemn... Can you imagine anything more stodgy?*

stoic /stəʊɪk/ or **stoical** /stəʊɪkəl/. If you behave ADJ QUALIT in a **stoic** or **stoical** way, you accept difficulties Formal and suffering without complaining or getting angry or upset. EG *I admired her stoic patience... He knew how brave and stoical they had to be.* ◊ **stoically.** ◊ ADV EG *Accept your punishment stoically.*

stoicism /stəʊɪsɪzəm/ is stoical behaviour. EG *He* N UNCOUNT *endured this treatment with stoicism.* Formal

stoke /stəʊk/, **stokes, stoking, stoked. 1** If you stoke a fire or stoke it up, you add coal or wood to it to keep it burning. EG *Willet was stoking up the stove again.* `V+O : OFT+up`

2 If you **stoke** or **stoke** up something such as a feeling, you cause it to be felt more strongly. EG *Similar schemes will only stoke the conflict... He stoked up their disgust.* `V+O : OFT+up`

stole /stəʊl/ is the past tense of **steal.**

stolen /ˈstəʊlᵊn/ is the past participle of **steal.**

stolid /ˈstɒlɪd/. **Stolid** people do not show much emotion. EG *He was slow to move, stolid, and dependable.* ◊ **stolidly.** EG *He looked thoughtful,* ◊ ADV *puffing stolidly at his pipe.* `ADJ QUALIT`

stomach /ˈstʌmək/, **stomachs, stomaching, stomached. 1** Your **stomach** is the organ inside your body where food is digested. EG *Foxes have small stomachs... His stomach was rumbling for breakfast... His stomach knotted with fright.* `N COUNT`

2 You can also refer to the front part of your body below your waist as your **stomach.** See picture at THE HUMAN BODY. EG *He folded his arms on his rather large stomach... He lay down on his stomach.* `N COUNT`

3 If you cannot **stomach** something, you cannot accept it because you dislike it or disapprove of it. EG *Rothermere was unable to stomach the idea.* `V+O : WITH BROAD NEG`

stomach-ache, stomach-aches. If you have a **stomach-ache**, you have a pain in your stomach. `N COUNT OR N UNCOUNT`

stomp /stɒmp/, **stomps, stomping, stomped.** If you **stomp** somewhere, you walk there with very heavy steps, often because you are angry. EG *I stomped back to the hotel.* `V+A`

stone /stəʊn/, **stones, stoning, stoned. 1 Stone** is a hard, solid substance found in the ground and often used for building houses. EG *The bits of stone are joined together with cement... ...the little stone bridge... ...a low stone wall.* `N UNCOUNT`

2 A **stone** is a small piece of rock. EG *Roger picked up a stone and threw it at Henry.* `N COUNT`

3 You can refer to a jewel as a **stone.** EG *...a ring with a white stone in it.* `N COUNT`

4 The **stone** in a plum or cherry is the large seed in the middle of it. EG *...plum stones.* `N COUNT`

5 If you **stone** someone or something, you throw stones at them. EG *Rioters had been stoning the Embassy... They took the man outside and stoned him to death.* `V+O`

6 A **stone** is also a measurement of weight which is equal to 14 pounds, or 6.35 kilograms. The plural form is 'stone' or 'stones'. EG *She weighed twelve stone.* `N COUNT OR N PART`

7 If you say that one place is a **stone's throw** from another, you mean that the places are close to each other. EG *They live within a stone's throw of the school.* `PHRASE`

8 to **kill two birds with one stone:** see **bird.** ● See also **stoned, cornerstone, paving stone, precious stone, stepping stone.**

Stone Age. The **Stone Age** is the earliest known period of human history, when people used tools and weapons made of stone. `N PROPER : the+N`

stone-cold. Something that is **stone-cold** is very cold indeed. EG *...cups of stone-cold coffee.* `ADJ CLASSIF`

stoned /stəʊnd/. Someone who is **stoned** is very drunk or is very affected by drugs. `ADJ QUALIT Informal`

stone deaf. Someone who is **stone deaf** is completely deaf. `ADJ CLASSIF`

stonework /ˈstəʊnwɜːk/ consists of objects or parts of a building that are made of stone. EG *...figures carved into the stonework.* `N UNCOUNT : OFT the+N`

stony /ˈstəʊnɪ¹/. **1 Stony** ground is rough and contains a lot of stones. EG *...a stony plain between low, barren hills.* `ADJ QUALIT`

2 If someone's voice, expression, or attitude is **stony,** they do not show any sympathy or friendliness. EG *She turned a stony face on Lucas... Her voice was stony... The announcement was received in stony silence.* `ADJ QUALIT`

stood /stʊd/ is the past tense and past participle of **stand.**

stooge /stuːdʒ/, **stooges.** A **stooge** is someone who is used by a powerful person to do unpleasant or dishonest tasks. EG *With the help of his stooges, he awarded contracts to favoured firms.* `N COUNT Informal`

stool

stool /stuːl/, **stools.** A **stool** is a seat with legs but no support for your arms or back. EG *He was sitting on a stool in the kitchen.* `N COUNT`

stoop /stuːp/, **stoops, stooping, stooped. 1** If you **stoop,** you stand or walk with your shoulders bent forwards. EG *If your ironing board is too low you have to stoop over it.* ▸ used as a noun. EG *He walks with a stoop.* `V : OFT+over` ▸ `N COUNT : USU SING`

2 If you **stoop** or **stoop** down, you bend your body forwards and downwards. EG *She stooped to feel the carpet... Bert stooped down and arranged them in a row.* `V : OFT+down`

3 When someone does something wrong or immoral that they would not normally do, you can say that they **stoop** to it. EG *They never stooped to spiteful tormenting... Only once did he stoop to the tactics of his opponents.* `V+to+-ING, V+to-INF, OR V+O`

stop /stɒp/, **stops, stopping, stopped. 1** If you have been doing something and then you **stop** doing it, you no longer do it. EG *We all stopped talking... He couldn't stop crying... She stopped work to have her baby... Stop it! You're hurting!* `V, V+-ING OR V+O`

2 If you **stop** something happening, you prevent it from happening or continuing. EG *You're trying to stop my trip to London... How do I stop a tap dripping?... Nothing was going to stop Sandy from being a writer.* `V+O : OFT+-ING OR from`

3 If you **put a stop to** something, you prevent it from happening or continuing. EG *We must put a stop to all this nonsense.* `PHRASE`

4 If an activity or process **stops,** it comes to an end. EG *The music stopped abruptly... They were waiting for the rain to stop.* `V`

5 If a machine or device **stops** or if you **stop** it, it no longer works or it is switched off. EG *My watch has stopped... Stop the recording now.* `V-ERG`

6 When people or things that are moving **stop** or **are stopped,** they no longer move. EG *He followed them for a few yards, and then stopped... Stop people in Oxford Street and ask them to answer these questions... The train stopped at Watford... Stop the car and let me out.* `V-ERG`

7 A **stop** is **7.1** a place where buses or trains regularly stop so that people can get on and off. EG *We'll get off at the next stop.* **7.2** a time or place at which you stop during a journey. EG *The first stop was a hotel outside Paris.* `N COUNT`

8 If something that is moving comes to a **stop,** it slows down and no longer moves. EG *The elevator came to a stop on the main floor... Harris brought the plane to a stop.* `N SING : a+N`

9 If you **stop** somewhere on a journey, you stay there for a short while. EG *On my way home I stopped at the shop.* `V : USU+A`

10 If you **stop** someone's pay or a cheque, you prevent the money from being paid. `V+O`

11 If you will **stop at nothing** to get or achieve `PHRASE`

Find two words on these pages that are pronounced the same.

something, you are prepared to do anything, even if it is wrong or dangerous, in order to get it or achieve it.

12 to **stop short**: see **short**.

stop off. If you **stop off** somewhere, you stop there for a short time in the middle of a journey. EG *On the way home I stopped off in London.*   PHRASAL VB: V+ADV

stopgap /stɒpgæp/, **stopgaps**. When something acts as a **stopgap**, it serves a purpose for a short time, but is replaced as soon as possible. EG *It can be used as a stopgap with patients who have lost a lot of blood... Pan Am must repay the stopgap loan it received earlier this year.*   N COUNT

stopover /stɒpəʊvə/, **stopovers**. A **stopover** is a short stay in a place in between parts of a journey. EG *...a five-week tour abroad with a three-day stopover in the United States.*   N COUNT

stoppage /stɒpɪdʒ/, **stoppages**. When there is a **stoppage**, people stop working because of a disagreement with their employers. EG *The stoppage had the full support of both unions.*   N COUNT

stopper /stɒpə/, **stoppers**. A **stopper** is a piece of glass, plastic, or cork that fits into the top of a bottle or jar. EG *I put the stopper in the bottle.*   N COUNT

stopwatch /stɒpwɒtʃ/, **stopwatches**. A **stopwatch** is a watch with buttons which you press at the beginning and end of an event, so that you can measure exactly how long it takes.   N COUNT

storage /stɔːrɪdʒ/ is 1 the keeping of something in a special place until it is needed. EG *A quarter of the crop may be lost in storage... You haven't got much storage space.* 2 the process of storing data in a computer. EG *...computer-based information storage and retrieval systems.*   N UNCOUNT

store /stɔː/, **stores, storing, stored.** 1 A **store** is a shop. EG *She came out of the store and sat down on the bench... ...smart stores like Harrods... ...a health-food store.* ● See also **chain store**.   N COUNT

2 When you **store** things, you put them in a container or other place and leave them there until they are needed. EG *The tool kit is stored under the seat... ...storing water for use in the dry season... ...storing and transmitting electricity.*   V+O

3 When you **store** information, you keep it in your memory, in a file, or in a computer. EG *...stored as images in the minds of people... ...pocket calculators which can store telephone numbers.*   V+O

4 A **store** is also 4.1 a supply of something that you keep somewhere until you need it. EG *...the village's store of grain... ...emergency stores of food and medical equipment.* 4.2 a place where things are kept while they are not being used. EG *...weapon stores in which nuclear warheads were kept... Goods in store will be insured for loss or damage.*   N COUNT OR N PART; N COUNT OR N UNCOUNT

5 If something is **in store** for you, it is going to happen at some time in the future. EG *Think of all the adventures in store for her... You never know what the next few months have got in store.*   PHRASE

6 If you **set great store** on or by something, you think that it is extremely important or necessary. EG *He set the greatest store on carrying out his decision... ...a mother who has set great store by breast-feeding.*   PHRASE

store up. If you **store** something **up**, you keep it until you think that the time is right to use it. EG *She had some sausage carefully stored up for the occasion.*   PHRASAL VB: V+O+ADV

storehouse /stɔːhaʊs/, **storehouses**. 1 A **storehouse** is a warehouse. EG *Food was still plentiful in the storehouses.*   N COUNT American

2 When a lot of things can be found together in one place, you can refer to this place as a **storehouse**. EG *...Egypt, the great storehouse of archaeology.*   N PART

storekeeper /stɔːkiːpə/, **storekeepers**. A **storekeeper** is a shopkeeper.   N COUNT American

storeroom /stɔːruːm/, **storerooms**. A **storeroom** is a room in which you keep things until they are needed. EG *...a storeroom for coffins.*   N COUNT

storey /stɔːriʰ/, **storeys**; spelled **story**, **stories** in American English. The **storeys** of a building are its different floors or levels. EG *The house was three storeys high... ...a multi-storey car park.*   N COUNT

stork /stɔːk/, **storks**. A **stork** is a large bird with a long beak and long legs, which lives near water.   N COUNT

storm /stɔːm/, **storms, storming, stormed.** 1 A **storm** is very bad weather, with heavy rain, strong winds, and often thunder and lightning. EG *Wait until the storm passes over.*   N COUNT

2 A **storm** is also an angry or excited reaction from a large number of people. EG *The decision provoked a storm of criticism from Conservative MPs... ...the storm of applause.*   N COUNT: USU+SUPP

3 If you **storm** into or out of a place, you enter or leave it quickly and noisily, because you are angry. EG *I stormed into the room in a rage.*   V+A

4 If you **storm**, you say something in a very loud voice, because you are extremely angry. EG *'You misled us,' the professor stormed.*   V OR V+QUOTE Literary

5 If people **storm** a place, they attack it. EG *The mob stormed the church.*   V+O OR V+A

stormy /stɔːmiʰ/, **stormier, stormiest.** 1 If the weather is **stormy**, there are strong winds and heavy rain. EG *...that stormy autumn evening.*   ADJ QUALIT

2 If a situation is **stormy**, it involves a lot of angry argument or criticism. EG *There was a stormy debate over it... ...the stormy relations between George and his mother.*   ADJ QUALIT

story /stɔːriʰ/, **stories.** 1 A **story** is a description of imaginary people and events, which is written or told in order to entertain people. EG *Tell me a story... ...a story about a foolish hunter... ...ghost stories.*   N COUNT

2 The **story** of something is a description of all the important things that have happened to it since it began. EG *The story of the firm begins in 1820... ...her life story.*   N COUNT: USU+SUPP

3 A news **story** is a piece of news in a newspaper or in a news broadcast. EG *What is your opinion of the front page story?*   N COUNT

4 If someone gives a false explanation or account of something, you can say that they are telling a **story**. EG *I hear that he told you some story about it being a practical joke.* ● **tall story**: see **tall**.   N COUNT

5 If you say **'It's the same old story'** or **'It's the old story'**, you mean that the same unfortunate situation seems to happen again and again. EG *It's the old story. When I'm happy, Barbara's not.*   PHRASE

6 If you say that something is **only part of the story** or is **not the whole story**, you mean that a situation cannot be fully understood because not enough is known about it. EG *One suspects this was only part of the story.*   PHRASE

7 You say **to cut a long story short** to indicate that you are going to state the final result of an event and not give any more details. EG *To cut a long story short, you have to go back.*   ADV SEN

8 See also **storey**.

stout /staʊt/, **stouter, stoutest.** 1 Someone who is **stout** is rather fat. EG *She was becoming stout... With him was a short, stout man.*   ADJ QUALIT

2 Something that is **stout** is thick and strong. EG *He broke a stout branch from a bush... ...stout black shoes... A stout cable connected the chains.*   ADJ QUALIT

3 **Stout** actions, attitudes, or beliefs are firm and strong. EG *...the stoutest possible resistance... ...its stoutest Republican allies.* ◊ **stoutly**. EG *Chris stoutly denied Eva's accusations.*   ADJ QUALIT: ATTRIB ◊ ADV

stove /staʊv/, **stoves**. A **stove** is an apparatus which provides heat for heating a room or for cooking. EG *...a gas stove... She left the sausages on the stove.*   N COUNT

stow /staʊ/, **stows, stowing, stowed.** If you **stow** something somewhere or **stow** it **away**, you put it carefully somewhere until it is needed. EG *She stowed the bags in two baskets... His baggage was safely stowed away in the plane.*   V+O+A OR V+O+away

stowaway /ˈstəʊəweɪ/, **stowaways**. A **stowaway** N COUNT
is a person who hides in a ship, aeroplane, or other
vehicle in order to make a journey secretly or
without paying the fare.

straddle /ˈstrædəl/, **straddles**, **straddling**,
straddled. 1 If you **straddle** someone or some- V+O
thing, you sit or stand with one leg on each side of
them. EG *He straddled a chair and began fiddling
with the keys.*

2 If something **straddles** a place, it crosses it or V+O
links different parts of it together. EG *A viaduct
straddles the river Wye.*

straggle /ˈstrægəl/, **straggles**, **straggling**,
straggled. 1 If a group of people **straggle** some- V
where, they move there slowly and with large,
irregular gaps between them. EG *The players straggled across the field.* ◊ **straggler** /ˈstræglə/, ◊ N COUNT
stragglers. EG *...waiting until the last straggler
came in.*

2 When things **straggle** over an area, they cover it V+A
in an uneven or untidy way. EG *The shacks straggle
along the dirt road... ...her hair straggling down
over her eyes.*

straggly /ˈstrægliː/. Something that is **straggly** ADJ QUALIT
grows or spreads out untidily in different direc-
tions. EG *...a straggly beard... ...a few straggly trees.*

straight /streɪt/, **straighter**, **straightest**. 1 If ADJ QUALIT
something such as a line is **straight**, it continues in OR ADV
the same direction and does not bend or curve. EG
*...a straight line... ...a long straight road... I saw the
car coming straight at me... She was staring
straight ahead.*

2 If the position of something is **straight**, it is ADJ CLASSIF
upright or level, rather than sloping or bent. EG OR ADV
*Keep your knees bent and your back straight...
Check that all the pictures hang straight.*

3 If someone's hair is **straight**, it has no curls or ADJ QUALIT
waves in it. EG *...a tall slim girl with long straight
hair.*

4 If you go **straight** to a place, you go there ADV+A
immediately. EG *The doctor told me to go straight
to bed... ...youngsters who move straight from
school onto the dole queue.*

5 If you **get** something **straight**, you make sure PHRASE
that you understand it properly. EG *Let me get this* Informal
straight - you claim that he hit you first?

6 If you give someone a **straight** answer, you ADJ CLASSIF
speak honestly and frankly to them. EG *I just want a
straight answer to the question.*

7 A **straight** choice or a **straight** fight involves ADJ CLASSIF:
only two people or things. EG *The voters have a* ATTRIB
straight choice between the two candidates.

8 If a criminal **is going straight**, he or she is no PHRASE
longer involved in crime and is living an honest
life. EG *I'm going straight from now on.*

9 If you keep **a straight face**, you manage to look PHRASE
serious, although you want to laugh. EG *I found it
hard to keep a straight face.*

straight away /streɪt əˈweɪ/. If you do something ADV
straight away, you do it immediately and without
any delay. EG *You might not recognize it straight
away... We went to work straightaway.*

straighten /ˈstreɪtən/, **straightens**, **straightening**, **straightened**. 1 If you **straighten** something, V+O
you make it tidy or put it in its proper position. EG
*I'll just straighten the bed... Straightening his tie, he
knocked on the door.*

2 If you are bending and you then **straighten** or V:OFT+*up*
straighten up, you make your back or body
straight and upright. EG *The man straightened and
looked him in the face... He straightens up, combs
his hair, and walks into the meeting.*

straighten out. If you **straighten out** a con- PHRASAL VB:
fused situation, you succeed in getting it organized V+O+ADV
and tidied up. EG *It'll take six weeks to get things
straightened out.*

straightforward /streɪtˈfɔːwəd/. 1 Something ADJ QUALIT
that is **straightforward** is easy to do or to under-

stand. EG *...a very straightforward set of instructions in simple English.*

2 If your behaviour is **straightforward**, you are ADJ QUALIT
honest and frank and do not try to hide your
feelings. EG *...the only Senator to speak with
straightforward contempt.*

strain /streɪn/, **strains**, **straining**, **strained**. 1 If
strain is put on something, 1.1 it is pulled or N UNCOUNT
stretched in a way that may damage it. EG *You
overloaded the floor and put strain on the pipes.*
1.2 it has to do more than it is able to do. EG *This* N UNCOUNT
policy puts a greater strain on the economic sys- OR N COUNT
tem than it can bear.

2 **Strain** is 2.1 a state of worry and tension caused N UNCOUNT
by a difficult situation. EG *...nervous strain... Over-* OR N COUNT
crowding imposes severe mental strains. 2.2 an N UNCOUNT:
injury to a muscle in your body. EG *...back strain.* OFT+SUPP

3 If you say that a situation is a **strain**, you mean N SING:a+N
that it causes you to feel worried and tense. EG *I
found it a strain being totally responsible for her.*

4 You can use **strain** to refer to a particular N SING+SUPP
quality in someone's character. EG *It was the romantic strain in me which made me do it.*

5 A **strain** of a plant is a particular type of it. EG N COUNT+SUPP
...high-yielding strains of wheat.

6 When you hear the **strains** of music, you hear N PLURAL
music being played. EG *The strains of Chopin* +SUPP
drifted in from the music room. Literary

7 To **strain** something means to use it beyond V+O
normal or reasonable limits. EG *The oil-price increases have strained the resources of the poorer
countries.*

8 If you **strain** to do something, you make a great V+to-INF OR
effort to do it. EG *He was straining to hear what the* V+O+to-INF
*speaker was saying... He strained his eyes to catch
a glimpse of the President.*

9 If you **strain** a muscle, you injure it by moving V+O
suddenly and awkwardly or by doing too much
exercise.

10 When you **strain** food, you remove the liquid V+O
from it. EG *I'll just strain the potatoes.*

strained /streɪnd/. 1 If you are **strained**, you ADJ QUALIT
seem worried and nervous. EG *She looked strained
and tired... Her voice was strained.*

2 If relations between people are **strained**, they ADJ QUALIT
are unfriendly and do not trust each other. EG
*Relations between the two families had become
increasingly strained.*

strait /streɪt/, **straits**. 1 You can refer to a N COUNT
narrow strip of sea which joins two large areas of
sea as a **strait** or the **straits**. EG *...the Strait of
Hormuz... ...the Straits of Gibraltar.*

2 You can use **straits** to refer to the situation that N PLURAL
someone is in when they do not have enough
money. EG *The family was in difficult straits... The
company was now in dire financial straits.*

strait jacket, **strait jackets**. A **strait jacket** is a N COUNT
special piece of clothing which is used to tie the
arms of a mental patient or a violent criminal and
prevent them from hurting themselves or other
people. EG *The cops put me in a strait jacket.*

strand /strænd/, **strands**, **stranding**, **stranded**.
1 A **strand** of thread, wire, or hair is a single, thin N PART
piece of it. EG *...a strand of silk... Make sure that
there are no loose strands of wire... A strand of hair
fell over her eyes.*

2 A **strand** of a situation or idea is a part of it. EG N COUNT
*...these two strands of industrial policy... Several
strands in Kate's life seemed to be pulled together.*

3 If a ship, whale, or fish **is stranded**, it is stuck on V+O:USU PASS
the shore. EG *The boat was stranded in the mud.*

4 If you **are stranded** in a place, you cannot leave V+O:
it, for example because you have no money or no USU PASS+A
transport. EG *He was stranded in Paris.*
◊ **stranded**. EG *...the stranded holidaymakers.* ◊ ADJ CLASSIF

If you go straight home, can you turn any
corners?

strange /streɪndʒ/, **stranger, strangest. 1** ADJ QUALIT
Something that is **strange** is unusual or unexpected, and may make you feel uneasy or afraid. EG *I had a strange dream last night... It was strange to hear her voice again... The strange thing is that this teacher didn't even know us.*

2 A **strange** place is one that you have never been ADJ QUALIT
to before. A **strange** person is one that you have never met before. EG *I don't like strange people coming into my house... Ipswich is really quite strange to me.*

strangely /streɪndʒliɪ/. **1** If you do something ADV
strangely, you do it in an unusual or unexpected way. EG *They had acted strangely as he went by... He laughed strangely.*

2 You can use **strangely** to say that something has SUBMOD
a particular quality, although you did not expect it to have this quality or cannot explain why it has it. EG *He answered in a strangely calm voice.*

3 You can also use **strangely** or **strangely** ADV SEN
enough to emphasize that what you are saying is surprising. EG *'Are students interested in religion these days?' – 'Strangely enough, they are.'*

stranger /streɪndʒə/, **strangers. 1** A **stranger** N COUNT
is someone who you have never met before. EG *A stranger appeared... Antonio was a stranger to all of us.*

2 If you are a **stranger** in a place, you do not know N COUNT
the place well. EG *They are strangers in the village and lost their way in the fog.*

3 If you are a **stranger** to something, you do not N COUNT :
understand it or have not had any experience of it. OFT+*to*
EG *I was a stranger to this kind of gathering.*

strangle /stræŋgəl/, **strangles, strangling,**
strangled. 1 To **strangle** someone means to kill V+O
them by squeezing their throat. EG *He was strangled in his bed.*

2 To **strangle** something means to prevent it from V+O
succeeding or developing. EG *Such policies were strangling economic development.*

strangled /stræŋgəld/. A **strangled** voice or ADJ CLASSIF :
laugh sounds unclear and muffled. EG *...a strangled* ATTRIB
cry of amazement.

stranglehold /stræŋgəlhəʊld/, **strangleholds.** If N COUNT :
people have a **stranglehold** on something, they USU SING
have control over it and are preventing it from being free or from developing. EG *The unions have a stranglehold on the country.*

strap /stræp/, **straps, strapping, strapped. 1** A N COUNT
strap is a narrow piece of leather, cloth, or other material. Straps are used to carry things or to fasten things together. EG *I undid the straps, and opened the case... ...high-heeled shoes, with straps above the ankle.*

2 If you **strap** something somewhere, you fasten it V+O+A
there with a strap. EG *Children should be strapped into a special car seat... He straps on his watch.*

strapping /stræpɪŋ/. You use **strapping** to de- ADJ QUALIT
scribe someone who is tall, strong, and healthy-looking. EG *...a strapping boy of eighteen.*

strata /strɑːtə/ is the plural of **stratum.**

stratagem /strætədʒəm/, **stratagems.** A N COUNT :
stratagem is a clever plan that you use to achieve USU+SUPP
something. EG *...a cunning stratagem to quieten the rebellious peasants.*

strategic /strətiːdʒɪk/. **1** A **strategic** plan or ADJ CLASSIF
action is intended to help you to achieve something or gain an advantage. EG *I took up a strategic position near the exit... The police made a strategic withdrawal against overwhelming odds.*

2 A country's **strategic** weapons and policies are ADJ CLASSIF
part of the general organization of its defence systems or its organization of a war. EG *His country had made the same strategic error... ...areas occupied for strategic reasons... ...strategic nuclear weapons.* ◊ **strategically.** EG *The islands were* ◊ ADV
strategically important to Venice.

strategist /strætədʒɪst/, **strategists.** A **strat-** N COUNT
egist is a person who is skilled in planning the best

way to gain an advantage or to achieve success, especially in war. EG *...military strategists.*

strategy /strætədʒiɪ/, **strategies. 1** A **strategy** N COUNT :
is a plan you use in order to achieve something. EG USU+SUPP
...Britain's defence strategy... He adopted a strategy of massive deflation.

2 Strategy is the art of planning the best way to N UNCOUNT
gain an advantage or to achieve success, especially in war. EG *...a major exercise in military strategy... ...the debate over strategy.*

stratum /strɑːtəm/, **strata** /strɑːtə/. **1** A **stratum** N COUNT :
of society is a group of people in it who are similar USU+SUPP
in their education, income, or social class. EG *Our* Formal
military leaders have always been drawn from the upper strata of society... Let us examine a particular social stratum.

2 The **strata** in the earth's surface are the layers N COUNT
of different types of rock or other material. EG *...the* Technical
underlying rock strata.

straw /strɔː/, **straws. 1 Straw** consists of the N UNCOUNT
dried, yellowish stalks from crops such as wheat or barley. EG *They make the roofs out of straw... ...a straw hat... The eggs were packed in straw.*

2 A **straw** is **2.1** a single stalk of straw. **2.2** a thin N COUNT
tube of paper or plastic, which you use to suck a drink into your mouth. EG *Fiona was drinking a milk shake through a straw.*

3 If you **are clutching at straws**, you are trying PHRASE
unusual or extreme ideas or methods because other ideas or methods have failed.

4 If an event is **the last straw**, it is the latest in a PHRASE
series of unpleasant or unfavourable events, and makes you feel that you cannot tolerate a situation any longer. EG *Colley refused. This was the last straw and a row broke out.*

strawberry /strɔːbəriɪ/, **strawberries.** A N COUNT
strawberry is a small red fruit which is soft and juicy. It has a thin, slightly rough skin. EG *...strawberry jam... ...strawberries and cream.*

stray /streɪ/, **strays, straying, strayed. 1** If V : USU+A
someone **strays**, they wander away from where they are supposed to be. EG *Children had strayed on to an airport runway... I hoped my animals wouldn't stray too far.*

2 A **stray** animal has wandered away from its ADJ CLASSIF :
owner's home. EG *...stray cats.* ATTRIB

3 If your thoughts **stray**, you do not concentrate on V
one particular subject, but start thinking or talking about other things. EG *He let his thoughts stray for five minutes... He does not stray from facts.*

4 Stray things exist separated from other similar ADJ CLASSIF :
things. EG *A hen was pecking around for stray* ATTRIB
grains of corn.

streak /striːk/, **streaks, streaking, streaked. 1** A N COUNT :
streak is a long stripe or mark on a surface. EG *The* OFT+*of*
table was smeared with streaks of paint... Her hair had a grey streak in it.

2 If something **streaks** a surface, it makes long V+O :
stripes or marks of a different colour on the OFT+*with*
surface. EG *His moustache was streaked with grey... The sun is streaking the sea with long lines of gold.*

3 If someone has a **streak** of a particular quality, N COUNT+SUPP
that quality sometimes shows in their behaviour. EG *Children have a streak of cruelty... ...the possessive streak in her.*

4 If something **streaks** somewhere, it moves there V+A
very quickly. EG *The fish streaked away.*

5 A lucky **streak** or a winning **streak** is a continu- N COUNT
ous series of successes, for example in gambling or sport. An unlucky **streak** is a series of failures or losses. EG *I was on a winning streak tonight.*

stream /striːm/, **streams, streaming,**
streamed. 1 A **stream** is a small, narrow river. EG N COUNT
He led us along the bank of the stream.

2 You can also refer to a narrow moving mass of N COUNT
liquid, gas, or smoke as a **stream**. EG *Horace blew out a stream of smoke.* ● See also **bloodstream.**

3 A **stream** of people or vehicles is a long moving N PART
OR N COUNT

line of them. EG *A steady stream of workers left the factory... ...the stream of cars.*

4 A **stream** of things is a large number of them occurring one after another. EG *...a steady stream of questions... The stream of insults continues.* `N PART OR N COUNT`

5 If a liquid **streams** somewhere, it flows or comes out in large amounts. EG *She stood in the doorway, tears streaming down her face... His back was streaming with sweat.* `V-ERG : USU+A`

6 If people or vehicles **stream** somewhere, they move there quickly and in large numbers. EG *The doors opened and the audience began to stream out... The cars are streaming by at sixty miles an hour.* `V+A`

7 When light **streams** somewhere, it shines strongly there after passing through or between things. EG *The sun was streaming in through the windows.* `V+A`

8 A **stream** in a school is a group of children of the same age and ability who are taught together. EG *...pupils in the top streams.* `N COUNT+SUPP`

9 To **stream** pupils means to teach them in groups according to their ability. ◊ **streaming**. EG *Our new headmaster says he's going to end streaming.* `V+O` `◊ N UNCOUNT`

streamer /striːmə/, **streamers**. A **streamer** is a long roll of coloured paper. Streamers are used for decorating rooms that parties are held in. EG *The gym was decorated with maroon streamers.* `N COUNT`

streamline /striːmlaɪn/, **streamlines**, **streamlining**, **streamlined**. 1 To **streamline** an object or a vehicle means to give it a long, narrow shape that allows it to move faster through air or water. ◊ **streamlined**. EG *Their new cars have lighter and more streamlined bodywork.* `V+O` `◊ ADJ QUALIT`

2 To **streamline** an organization or process means to make it more efficient by removing unnecessary parts of it. EG *He aimed to streamline the Post Office... ...an attempt to streamline timber production.* `V+O`

street /striːt/, **streets**. 1 A **street** is a road in a town or village, usually one with houses along it. EG *The two men walked slowly down the street... ...a street map of Paris... She lives in Seyer Street.* `N COUNT`

2 You can use **street** when talking about activities that happen out of doors in a town rather than inside a building. EG *We've got to keep youngsters off the streets... We don't usually embrace friends in the street... ...street theatre.* `N COUNT : the+N`

3 If you talk about **the man in the street**, you mean ordinary people in general. EG *The man in the street was unlikely ever to have seen a ghost.* `PHRASE`

4 If someone is **streets ahead** of you, they have made much more progress than you. EG *They are streets ahead of us in metal designing.* `PHRASE Informal`

5 If a subject or activity is **right up** your **street**, you are very interested in it or know a lot about it. `PHRASE Informal`

6 See also **high street**.

streetcar /striːtkɑː/, **streetcars**. A **streetcar** is a tram. EG *He caught the next streetcar home.* `N COUNT American`

strength /streŋθ/, **strengths**. 1 Your **strength** is the physical energy that you have, which gives you the ability to perform various actions, such as lifting or moving things. EG *I admired his immense physical strength... ...recovering their strength before trying again... He pulled with all his strength.* `N UNCOUNT`

2 You can use **strength** to refer to someone's confidence or courage in a difficult situation. EG *This gave us the strength to resist further temptation... With unshakable strength of character she stayed on after the crisis.* `N UNCOUNT`

3 You can refer to the power or influence that someone has as their **strength**. EG *...the enormous strength and influence of the unions... IBM's economic strength is phenomenal... Pacifist movements gathered strength in Norway.* ● If a person or organization **goes from strength to strength**, they gradually become more confident or successful. EG *His company went from strength to strength, and in 1911 merged with a number of other companies.* `N UNCOUNT` `● PHRASE`

4 Your **strengths** are the qualities and abilities that you have which are an advantage to you. EG *Each firm has its particular strengths and weaknesses.* `N COUNT OR N UNCOUNT`

5 The **strength** of an object is its ability to be treated roughly, or to support or carry heavy weights, without being damaged or destroyed. EG *It is these rigid struts that give the wing its strength.* `N SING`

6 The **strength** of a feeling or opinion is the degree to which people have it. EG *The Government had clearly underestimated the strength of popular feeling about this.* `N SING : USU+of`

7 The **strength** of an opinion, argument, or story is the extent to which it influences people or is likely to be true. EG *He continued to deny it, despite the growing strength of the argument... This lent some strength to the complaint.* ● If you do one thing **on the strength of** another, the second thing influences you and makes you decide to do the first. EG *The Cabinet agreed to a grant of £4m on the strength of the Company's projections of sales.* `N UNCOUNT` `● PREP`

8 The **strength** of a relationship is its degree of closeness. EG *This leads to bonds of deceptive strength being formed with the company.* `N UNCOUNT`

9 The **strength** of a group of people is the total number of people in it. EG *Their forces in the south were growing in strength.* `N UNCOUNT`

10 **Strength** is used in these phrases. **10.1** If a group exists **in strength**, it consists of many people. EG *By Easter, the tourists were arriving in strength.* **10.2** If a group is **at full strength**, it has all its members present. EG *Troops were now up to full strength.* **10.3** If a group is **below strength**, it does not have enough people. `PHRASES`

strengthen /streŋθən/, **strengthens**, **strengthening**, **strengthened**. 1 If a number of people **strengthen** a group, they make it more powerful by joining it. EG *The new peers will strengthen the Labour Party in the Upper House.* `V+O`

2 If something **strengthens** an argument or opinion, it supports it by providing more reasons or evidence for it. EG *The uncertainty about the railways strengthened the argument for planning.* `V+O`

3 If a feeling or attitude **strengthens** or if someone **strengthens** it, more people feel it or are influenced by it. EG *During the prolonged depression of the seventies, racialism strengthened.* `V-ERG`

4 If a relationship **strengthens** or if you **strengthen** it, it becomes closer and more successful. EG *We want to strengthen our ties with the United States.* `V-ERG`

5 If something **strengthens** you, it increases your confidence and determination. EG *It is designed to strengthen you against the hostile world.* `V+O`

6 If something **strengthens** an object or structure, it makes it able to be treated roughly or able to support heavy weights, without being damaged or destroyed. EG *...struts designed to strengthen the wings of aeroplanes.* `V+O`

strenuous /strenjuːəs/. A **strenuous** activity involves a lot of effort or energy. EG *...a strenuous twenty minute walk... Alf made strenuous efforts to improve his reading.* ◊ **strenuously**. EG *He strenuously denied that his airline was in any danger.* `ADJ QUALIT` `◊ ADV`

stress /stres/, **stresses**, **stressing**, **stressed**. 1 If you **stress** a point in a discussion, you put extra emphasis on it because you think it is important. EG *I ought to stress that this was not a trial but an enquiry... He stressed the importance of better public relations.* ▸ used as a noun. EG *...this stress on community values.* `V SPEECH` `▸ N UNCOUNT +on`

2 If you feel or are under **stress**, you feel worried and tense because of difficulties in your life. EG *...parents under stress... ...the stress of examinations... Too many stresses are being placed on the family.* `N UNCOUNT OR N COUNT`

Find two informal phrases on these pages.

3 Stresses are strong physical pressures applied to an object. EG *Earthquakes can result from stresses in the earth's crust.* N COUNT OR N UNCOUNT

4 Stress is emphasis that you put on a word or on part of a word when you pronounce it, so that it sounds slightly louder. EG *...the importance of stress and intonation.* ▸ used as a verb. EG *You should stress the second syllable in 'computer'.* N UNCOUNT ▸ V+O

stressful /ˈstresful/. If a situation or experience is stressful, it causes someone to feel stress. EG *Life with several children is hard and stressful.* ADJ QUALIT

stretch /stretʃ/, **stretches, stretching, stretched. 1** Something that **stretches** over an area or distance extends over this area or distance. EG *...the belt of flat land which stretches from the capital up to York.* V+A

2 A **stretch** of land or water is an area of land or water. EG *...the stretch of water that separates Asia from Europe.* N COUNT+SUPP

3 When you **stretch**, or when you **stretch** yourself, you hold your arms or legs out straight and tighten your muscles. EG *Thomas yawned and stretched.* V, V+O, OR V-REFL

4 A **stretch** of time is a period of time. EG *Any job carries with it daily stretches of boredom.* ● If you do an activity for a particular length of time **at a stretch**, you do it for this length of time without stopping. EG *It was impossible to work for more than an hour or so at a stretch.* N COUNT ● PHRASE

5 When something soft or elastic **stretches** or **is stretched**, it is pulled until it becomes very tight. EG *The skin of her face was stretched very tightly over the bones... Nylon stretches.* V-ERG

6 Stretch material can be stretched. EG *...stretch covers on armchairs.* ADJ CLASSIF: ATTRIB

7 If someone's money or resources **are stretched**, they have hardly enough money or resources for their needs. EG *The nation's resources were already stretched to their limits.* V+O: USU PASS

8 If a job or task **stretches** you, it makes you work hard and use all your energy or skills. V+O

9 If you say that something is not true or possible **by any stretch of the imagination**, you are emphasizing that you think it is completely untrue or absolutely impossible. EG *It could by no stretch of the imagination be seen as a victory.* PHRASE

stretch out. 1 If you **stretch out** or if you **stretch** yourself **out** somewhere, you lie there with your legs and body in a straight line. EG *I just want to stretch out in my own bed.* **2** If you **stretch out** a part of your body, you hold it out straight. EG *He stretched out a thin arm and took our hands.* PHRASAL VB : V+ADV OR V-REFL+ADV / V+O+ADV

stretcher /ˈstretʃə/, **stretchers.** A **stretcher** is a long piece of canvas with a pole along each side, which is used to carry an injured or sick person. N COUNT

strew /struː/, **strews, strewing, strewed, strewn** /struːn/. **1** If things **are strewn** somewhere, they are scattered there untidily. EG *His clothes were strewn all over the room... Tourists strew cans and wrappers all across the grass.* V+O: USU PASS+A

2 If things **strew** a place, they lie scattered there. EG *Books and cushions strewed the floor... The carpet is strewn with broken glass.* V+O

stricken /ˈstrɪkə⁰n/. If someone is **stricken** by something unpleasant, they are severely affected by it. EG *Madeleine was stricken by fear... Stricken with arthritis, she lay in bed for many years.* ADJ QUALIT OFT+with/by

strict /strɪkt/, **stricter, strictest. 1** Someone who is **strict** does not tolerate impolite or disobedient behaviour, especially from children. EG *Parents were strict in Victorian times... ...a school with strict discipline.* ◊ **strictly**. EG *The curfew was strictly enforced.* ADJ QUALIT ◊ ADV

2 A **strict** rule or order must be obeyed absolutely. EG *Strict instructions were issued... The Opposition demanded stricter control of prices.* ◊ **strictly**. EG *This is strictly confidential.* ADJ QUALIT ◊ ADV

3 If you talk about the **strict** meaning or truth of something, you mean the precise meaning or the ADJ CLASSIF: ATTRIB

absolute truth. EG *He may not be lying in the strict sense of the word, but he has not told the whole truth.* ◊ **strictly**. EG *That's not strictly true.* ◊ SUBMOD

4 You use **strict** to describe someone who never does things that are against their beliefs. For example, a strict vegetarian never eats meat. EG *His family were strict Methodists.* ADJ QUALIT: ATTRIB

strictly /ˈstrɪktli/. **1** If something is **strictly** for a particular thing or person, it is intended to be used or done only by them. EG *The discussion was strictly for members.* ADV+for

2 If someone keeps **strictly** to a particular subject or relationship, they do not try to change it. EG *This is a strictly doctor-patient relationship... Everything he said was strictly to the point.* SUBMOD

3 You say **strictly speaking** when you want to correct a statement or add more precise information about it. EG *Paul's a friend of mine. Well, strictly speaking my sister's friend... I think, strictly speaking, you are wrong there.* ADV SEN

stride /straɪd/, **strides, striding, strode** /strəʊd/, **stridden** /ˈstrɪdə⁰n/. **1** If you **stride** somewhere, you walk there with quick, long steps. EG *Louisa watched him striding across the lawn... He was striding out of the entrance.* V: USU+A

2 A **stride** is **2.1** a long step which you take when you are walking or running. EG *...the length of each stride.* **2.2** a way of walking with long steps. EG *She walked ahead with her purposeful stride.* N COUNT / N SING

3 If you make **strides** in something that you are doing, you make rapid progress in it. EG *On the question of pay, giant strides have been made.* N COUNT: USU PLURAL

4 If you **take** a problem or difficulty **in** your **stride**, you deal with it calmly and easily. EG *She takes examinations in her stride.* PHRASE

strident /ˈstraɪdə⁰nt/. **1** A **strident** sound is loud and unpleasant to listen to. EG *His voice was strident and triumphant.* ADJ QUALIT

2 If someone is **strident**, they state their feelings or opinions very strongly; used showing disapproval. EG *...a strident demand for rearmament... ...strident, hostile women.* ADJ QUALIT

strife /straɪf/ is strong disagreement or fighting. EG *...the basis of family strife... The Empire was torn by racial strife.* N UNCOUNT Formal

strike /straɪk/, **strikes, striking, struck** /strʌk/. **1** When there is a **strike**, workers stop doing their work for a period of time, usually to try to get better pay or conditions for themselves. EG *...the miners' strike.* ▸ used as a verb. EG *Airline pilots are threatening to strike.* ● Workers who are on **strike** are refusing to work. EG *I would never go on strike for more money.* N COUNT ▸ V ● PHRASE

2 A hunger **strike** is a refusal to eat anything as a protest about something. A rent **strike** is a refusal to pay your rent. N COUNT+SUPP

3 If you **strike** someone or something, you deliberately hit them. EG *The young man struck his father... He struck the ball beautifully.* V+O Literary

4 If something **strikes** something else or **strikes** against it, it hits it. EG *The house was struck by lightning... The trawler struck against the jetty.* V+O OR V+A

5 If something such as an illness or disaster **strikes**, it suddenly happens. EG *When disaster strikes, you need sympathy and practical advice... ...the earthquake that struck Japan last Tuesday.* V OR V+O

6 To **strike** means to attack someone or something quickly and violently. EG *Raising herself slightly, the snake strikes.* ▸ used as a noun. EG *The Air Force carried out air strikes as a result of the information received.* V: OFT+at ▸ N COUNT: OFT+SUPP

7 If an idea or thought **strikes** you, it comes into your mind suddenly. EG *It struck him how foolish his behaviour had been.* V+O: OFT+REPORT ONLY that

8 If something **strikes** you as being a particular thing, it gives you the impression of being that thing. EG *Gertie strikes me as a very silly girl.* V+O: USU+as

9 If you **are struck** by something, you are very V+O: USU PASS +with/by impressed by it. EG *He had been struck by what he saw... I was very much struck by London.*

10 When a clock **strikes**, its bells make a sound to indicate what the time is. EG *The church clock struck eleven.* V OR V+O

11 If something that someone says **strikes a** **note**, it produces a particular impression or atmosphere. EG *His words struck a slightly false note for me.* PHRASE

12 If something that someone says **strikes a** **chord**, it makes you feel sympathy or enthusiasm. PHRASE

13 If you **strike** a bargain or a deal with someone, you come to an agreement with them. EG *The council hoped to strike a deal that would give it more power.* V+O

14 If you **strike a balance**, you do something that is halfway between two extremes. EG *It is not easy to strike a balance between too much and too little freedom.* PHRASE

15 If something **strikes fear** or **strikes terror** into people, it causes them to be suddenly very frightened. EG *The tanks struck terror into the hearts of the peasants.* PHRASE

16 If you **are struck dumb** or **are struck blind**, you suddenly become unable to speak or to see. EG *We were struck dumb with horror.* PHRASE

17 If you **strike** a match, you make it produce a flame. EG *He struck a match and put it to his pipe.* V+O

18 If someone **strikes** oil or gold, they discover it in the ground as a result of mining or drilling. V+O

19 If you **strike lucky**, you have good luck. EG *He had struck lucky in having someone who was so sensitive to look after him.* PHRASE

20 See also **striking**.

strike back. If you **strike back**, you attempt to harm someone, because they have harmed you. PHRASAL VB : V+ADV

strike down. If something **strikes** someone **down**, it kills them or severely harms them. EG *Kennedy was struck down by an assassin's bullet.* PHRASAL VB : V+O+ADV

strike off. If someone such as a doctor or lawyer **is struck off**, their name is removed from the official register and they are not allowed to do medical or legal work any more. PHRASAL VB : V+O+ADV, USU PASS

strike out. If you **strike out**, you begin to do something different, often because you want to become more independent. EG *He decided to strike out on his own.* PHRASAL VB : V+ADV, USU+A

strike up. **1** When you **strike up** a conversation or friendship with someone, you begin it. EG *Alice and I struck up a friendship immediately.* **2** When musicians **strike up**, they begin to play music. EG *The band had just struck up Ellington's 'Satin Doll'.* PHRASAL VB : V+ADV+O

V+ADV+O

striker /stra͟ɪkə/, **strikers**. **1** Strikers are people who refuse to continue working, usually because they want more pay or better conditions. N COUNT

2 In football, a **striker** is a player whose main function is to attack rather than defend. N COUNT

striking /stra͟ɪkɪŋ/. **1** Something that is **striking** is so noticeable or unusual that it cannot be ignored. EG *The most striking thing about Piccadilly Circus is the statue of Eros in the centre.* ADJ QUALIT

◇ **strikingly.** EG *The two women appeared strikingly different.* ◇ SUBMOD

2 Someone who is **striking** is very attractive. EG ...*a striking redhead... ...his striking good looks.* ADJ QUALIT

◇ **strikingly.** EG ...*a strikingly beautiful child.* ◇ SUBMOD

string /strɪŋ/, **strings, stringing, strung** /strʌŋ/.

1 String is thin rope made of twisted threads. EG *She took the parcel and started to undo the string... ...a bunch of balloons on a string.* N UNCOUNT OR N COUNT

2 A **string** of things is a number of them on the same piece of thread or wire. EG ...*a string of beads round her neck.* N COUNT OR N PART

3 You can refer to a row of similar things as a **string**. EG ...*a string of islands.* N COUNT OR N PART

4 A **string** of similar events is a series of them happening one after the other. EG *It was the latest in a string of hotel disasters.* N COUNT OR N PART

5 The **strings** on a musical instrument such as a N COUNT

violin or guitar are thin pieces of tightly-stretched wire or nylon. You make sounds by plucking the strings or by passing a bow across them.

6 The section of an orchestra which consists of stringed instruments played with a bow is called the **strings**. N PLURAL

7 If you **pull strings** to get something done, you use your influence with other people in order to get it done; often used showing disapproval. EG *Derek offered to pull a few strings and get her a place at the university.* PHRASE

8 If something is offered to you with **no strings attached**, it is offered without any special conditions. EG *We will pay you ten per cent with no strings attached.* PHRASE

string out. If things **are strung out** somewhere, they are spread out in a long line. EG ...*small towns strung out along the dirt roads.* PHRASAL VB : V-ERG+ADV

string together. If you **string** things **together**, you make them into one thing by adding them to each other, one at a time. EG *I strung together some rhymes to amuse her.* PHRASAL VB : V+O+ADV

string up. To **string** someone **up** means to kill them by hanging them. EG *We will all be strung up from lamp-posts.* PHRASAL VB : V+O+ADV Informal

stringed /strɪŋd/. A **stringed** instrument is a musical instrument which has strings, such as a violin or a guitar. See picture at MUSICAL INSTRUMENTS. ADJ CLASSIF : ATTRIB

stringent /strɪ͟ndʒənt/. **Stringent** laws, rules, or conditions are very severe or are strictly controlled. EG *His budget proposal is even more stringent than the President's... These requirements are often very stringent.* ADJ QUALIT Formal

stringy /strɪŋi/, **stringier, stringiest**. **1** If food is **stringy**, it is tough and difficult to chew. EG *The meat was grey and stringy.* ADJ QUALIT

2 Stringy hair is thin and rough. ADJ QUALIT

strip /strɪp/, **strips, stripping, stripped**. **1** A **strip** of paper, cloth, or other material is a long, narrow piece of it. EG ...*a thin strip of paper... The room was bare, apart from a strip of carpet.* N COUNT OR N PART

2 A **strip** of land or water is a long narrow area of it. EG *There was only a narrow strip of beach.* N COUNT OR N PART

3 If you **strip**, you take off your clothes. EG *They told her to strip.* V

4 If someone **strips** you, they take off your clothes, for example in order to search for hidden or illegal things. EG *Before the ship sailed they were stripped and searched.* V+O

5 To **strip** something means to remove everything that is covering its surface. EG *The wind stripped the tree of all its leaves... The paint could easily be stripped off.* V+O : USU+A

6 To **strip** someone of their property, rights, or titles means to take them away from them. EG *She was automatically stripped of all her property and possessions... They were stripping away my remaining pension rights.* V+O+A

7 In a newspaper or magazine, a comic **strip** or a **strip** cartoon is a series of drawings which tell a story. The words spoken by the characters are often written on the drawings. N COUNT

8 If you **tear a strip off** someone or if you **tear** them **off a strip**, you scold them angrily and severely. PHRASE Informal

strip off. **1** If you **strip off** your clothes, you take them off. EG *She hurried into the bathroom, stripping off her clothes... Casson stripped off his raincoat.* **2** If someone **strips off** your clothes, they undress you in order to search you. EG *The other officer stripped off my waistcoat and threw it in the corner.* PHRASAL VB : V+ADV OR V+O+ADV

V+O+ADV

strip club, strip clubs. A **strip club** is a club which people go to in order to see striptease. N COUNT

If someone pulls strings, are they playing a stringed instrument?

stripe /straɪp/, **stripes.** 1 A **stripe** is a long line N COUNT
which is usually a different colour or texture from
the areas next to it. EG ...*a shirt with blue and white
stripes.* ◊ **striped** /straɪpt/. EG ...*a gentleman in a* ◊ ADJ CLASSIF
black coat and striped trousers.

2 In the police or the armed forces, **stripes** are N COUNT
narrow bands of material sewn onto a uniform to
indicate someone's rank. EG ...*a red uniform with
sergeant's stripes.*

strip lighting is a method of lighting which uses N UNCOUNT
long tubes rather than light bulbs.

stripper /strɪpə/, **strippers.** A **stripper** is a N COUNT
person who earns money by doing striptease. Informal

striptease /strɪptiːz/ is a form of entertainment N UNCOUNT
in which someone takes off their clothes slowly
and in a sexy way to music.

strive /straɪv/, **strives, striving,** **strove** V+for
/strəʊv/, **striven** /strɪvᵊn/. If you **strive** for OR to-INF
something or **strive** to do something, you make a Formal
great effort to get it or to do it. EG *They strove to
give the impression that they were leaving... They
have striven for freedom for many years.*

strode /strəʊd/ is the past tense of **stride.**

stroke /strəʊk/, **strokes, stroking, stroked.** 1 If V+O
you **stroke** someone or something, you move your
hand slowly and gently over them. EG *She put out a
hand and stroked the cat... He stroked her hair
affectionately.*

2 A **stroke** is a sudden and severe illness which N COUNT
affects your brain, and which often kills people or
causes them to be paralysed in one side of their
body. EG *Wilson was crippled by a stroke... She had
a stroke and was unable to walk again.*

3 The **strokes** of a pen or brush are the move- N COUNT
ments or marks you make with it when you are
writing or painting. EG *She began to paint with bold,
defiant strokes.*

4 When you are swimming or rowing, your **strokes** N COUNT
are the repeated movements you make with your
arms or the oars. EG *She swam with steady strokes.*

5 A swimming **stroke** is a particular style or N COUNT
method of swimming. See picture at SWIMMING.

6 The **strokes** of a clock are the sounds that N COUNT
indicate each hour. EG *At the twelfth stroke, we
welcomed in the New Year.*

7 If you describe something that happens as a PHRASE
stroke of luck, you mean that it is lucky that it
happened. EG *We had a real stroke of good luck...
Then it came, my stroke of great good fortune.*

8 If you describe a thought or idea as a **stroke of** PHRASE
genius, you mean that it is very clever.

9 If something happens **at a stroke** or **in one** PHRASE
stroke, it happens suddenly and completely because of one single action. EG *He was determined at
a stroke to remove those distinctions.*

10 If someone **does not do a stroke** of work, they PHRASE
are very lazy and do no work at all. Informal

stroll /strəʊl/, **strolls, strolling, strolled.** If you V+A
stroll somewhere, you walk in a slow, relaxed
way. EG *They strolled along the beach.* ▶ used as a ▶ N COUNT
noun. EG *She decided to take a stroll in the garden.*

strong /strɒŋ/, **stronger, strongest.** 1 Someone ADJ QUALIT
who is **strong** **1.1** has powerful muscles and can
move or carry heavy things, or hold things very
tightly. EG *His strong arms were around me, pinning me down.* **1.2** is very confident and not easily
influenced or worried by other people. EG *I felt very
strong in the knowledge of my own innocence... ...a
strong personality.*

2 **Strong** objects are not easily broken. EG ...*steel* ADJ QUALIT
*cylinders strong enough to survive even a nuclear
catastrophe.* ◊ **strongly.** EG ...*strongly constructed* ◊ ADV
buildings.

3 You use **strong** to describe things that are great ADJ QUALIT
in degree or intensity. EG *His teachings still exert a
strong influence... ...a strong incentive to buy more
machines... ...a strong sense of identity... The strong
possibility is that he will be told tomorrow... ...the
strong wind... The smell of the gas grew stronger...*

They still spoke with a strong German accent.
 ◊ **strongly.** EG *His mother will strongly influence* ◊ ADV
his choice of a wife.

4 If you have **strong** views on something or ADJ QUALIT :
express your views using **strong** words, you have USU ATTRIB
very definite views or express them in a very
definite way. EG *There is strong criticism of certain
aspects of the case... He has condemned the present sit-in by students in strong terms... ...a strong
Labour supporter.* ◊ **strongly.** EG *I feel very* ◊ ADV
*strongly about drugs... I would strongly advise you
against such an action... He is remembered for his
strongly anti-war attitude.*

5 If someone in authority takes **strong** action, they ADJ QUALIT
act firmly and severely. EG *They introduced a
strong anti-inflation programme.*

6 If the arguments for something are **strong,** they ADJ QUALIT
are supported by a lot of evidence. EG *There is a
strong case for an Act of Parliament.*

7 If a group is **strong,** it has many members or ADJ QUALIT
great power. EG *It was essential to build a strong
organization.*

8 You can also use **strong** when you are saying ADJ CLASSIF :
how many people there are in a group. For exam- AFTER NUMBER
ple, if a group is twenty **strong,** there are twenty
people in it.

9 Your **strong** points or your **strong** subjects are ADJ QUALIT :
things which you are good at. EG *Maths was always* ATTRIB
his strong subject.

10 A **strong** competitor or candidate is likely to ADJ QUALIT :
win in a contest. EG *She was a very strong candi-* ATTRIB
date.

11 If someone has **strong** nerves or a **strong** ADJ QUALIT
stomach, they are not easily frightened or upset.

12 If a relationship is **strong,** it is firm and likely to ADJ QUALIT
last for a long time. EG *Links with the trade unions
were strong.*

13 Industries, economies, or currencies that are ADJ QUALIT
strong are financially successful. EG *Sterling has
once again become one of the stronger currencies.*

14 Drinks, chemicals, or drugs that are **strong** ADJ QUALIT
contain a lot of a particular substance. EG *She made
him a cup of tea so strong that he could not drink
it... ...a strong household bleach.*

15 If someone or something is still **going strong,** PHRASE
they are still living or still working well after a long
time. EG *The society started in 1904 and is still going
strong.*

stronghold /strɒŋhəʊld/, **strongholds.** If a place N COUNT+SUPP
is a **stronghold** of an attitude or belief, many
people there have this attitude or belief. EG *It is a
solid Labour stronghold.*

stroppy /strɒpiˈ/. Someone who is **stroppy** is bad- ADJ QUALIT
tempered and obstinate. EG *She threatened to get* Informal
stroppy. British

strove /strəʊv/ is the past tense of **strive.**

struck /strʌk/ is the past tense and past participle
of **strike.**

structural /strʌktʃᵊrəl/ is used to describe an ADJ CLASSIF
aspect of the structure of something. EG *We plastered over the major structural faults in the walls...
I was shocked at the structural damage.*

structure /strʌktʃə/, **structures, structuring,**
structured. 1 The **structure** of something is the N UNCOUNT
way in which it is made, built, or organized. EG *She* USU+SUPP,
analysed the structure of its skull in great detail... OR N COUNT
The whole structure of the film was rather simplistic... The class structures of England and America
are quite different.*

2 A **structure** is something that has been built or N COUNT :
formed in a particular way. EG *We visited the* USU+SUPP
Children's Palace, a great sprawling structure.

3 A system or activity that has **structure** is well N UNCOUNT
arranged and organized and is therefore efficient.
EG *She loved the sense of structure, organization
and enthusiasm.*

4 If you **structure** something, you arrange it in a V+O
careful, organized pattern or system. EG *They structure their communication to meet the needs of the*

client... They could never achieve anything because they wouldn't structure the group and have effective leadership.

struggle /strʌgⁿl/, **struggles, struggling, struggled.** 1 If you **struggle** to do something, you try very hard to do it, although it is difficult for you. EG *We should give moral support to them as they struggle to build a more democratic society... ...a nationalist movement that has had to struggle for independence.* ▸ used as a noun. EG *...the day-to-day struggle for survival.* `V: USU+to-INF OR for` `▸ N COUNT USU SING`

2 If you **struggle** when you are being held, you twist, kick, and move violently in order to get free. EG *She struggled in his embrace.* `V: OFT+to-INF OR A`

3 If two people **struggle** with each other, they fight. EG *We struggled for the gun, until at last it went off.* ▸ used as a noun. EG *There was a moment's struggle and the gun fell to the ground.* `V OR V+with: RECIP` `▸ N COUNT`

4 If you **struggle** to move yourself, you manage to do it with great difficulty. EG *He struggled to his feet... He struggled forward for about half a mile.* `V+to-INF OR A`

5 An action or activity that is a **struggle** is very difficult for you to do. EG *Reading was a struggle for him.* `N SING: a+N`

struggle on. If you **struggle on**, you manage with great difficulty to continue doing something. EG *Some struggled on, but those who couldn't were left behind.* `PHRASAL VB: V+ADV`

strum /strʌm/, **strums, strumming, strummed.** If you **strum** a guitar, you play it by moving your hand quickly up and down across the strings. EG *The guitar player started strumming softly.* `V OR V+O`

strung /strʌŋ/ is the past tense and past participle of **string.**

strut /strʌt/, **struts, strutting, strutted.** 1 Someone who **struts** walks in a proud way, with their head held high and their chest out. EG *Eddie turned around and strutted back to them... ...a peacock strutting on the lawn.* `V: USU+A`

2 A **strut** is a piece of wood or metal which holds the weight of other pieces in a building. `N COUNT`

stub /stʌb/, **stubs, stubbing, stubbed.** 1 The **stub** of a cigarette or a pencil is the last short piece of it which remains when the rest has been used. EG *...an ashtray full of old cigarette stubs.* `N COUNT+SUPP`

2 The **stub** of a cheque or ticket is the small part that you keep. `N COUNT`

3 If you **stub** your toe, you hurt your toe by accidentally kicking something. EG *I stubbed my toe against a stone.* `V+O`

stub out. When someone **stubs out** a cigarette, they put it out by pressing it against something hard. EG *He stubbed his cigarette out in an ash tray.* `PHRASAL VB: V+O+ADV`

stubble /stʌbⁿl/. 1 The short stalks which are left standing in fields after corn or wheat has been harvested are referred to as **stubble.** EG *The stubble was burning on the harvested fields.* `N UNCOUNT`

2 The very short hairs on a man's face when he has not shaved recently are also referred to as **stubble.** EG *...a hint of stubble round the chin.* `N UNCOUNT`

stubborn /stʌbⁿn/. 1 Someone who is **stubborn** is determined to do what they want and is very unwilling to change their mind. EG *Our son is stubborn and rebellious... ...his stubborn determination.* ◇ **stubbornly.** EG *'It was an accident,' he said stubbornly, 'and that's that.'* `ADJ QUALIT` `◇ ADV`

2 A **stubborn** stain is difficult to remove. EG *Remove stubborn marks on tiles with a wire brush.* `ADJ QUALIT`

stubby /stʌbiʰ/. A **stubby** object is short and thick. EG *His stubby fingers were strong and mobile.* `ADJ QUALIT`

stuck /stʌk/. 1 **Stuck** is the past tense and past participle of **stick.**

2 If something is **stuck** in a particular position, it is fixed tightly in this position and unable to move. EG *The lift seems to be stuck between the second and third floors.* `ADJ PRED: USU+A`

3 If you are **stuck** when you are trying to do something, you are unable to continue doing it because it is too difficult. EG *Ask for help the minute* `ADJ PRED`

you're stuck... They used the dictionary when they got stuck on words.

4 If you are **stuck** in a place, you are unable to get away from it. EG *The boss rang to explain that he was stuck in Milan.* `ADJ PRED: USU+A`

5 If you are **stuck** in an unpleasant situation, you are unable to change it. EG *They are stuck in boring jobs.* `ADJ PRED: USU+A`

stud /stʌd/, **studs.** 1 A **stud** is 1.1 a small piece of metal which is attached to a surface. EG *...black leather with gold studs.* 1.2 a kind of small earring which goes straight through your ear. EG *Some women wore jade studs in their ears.* `N COUNT`

2 Male horses or other animals that are kept for **stud** are kept to be used for breeding. EG *I'm not going to race him, I'm going to put him to stud... ...stud horses.* `N UNCOUNT`

3 A **stud** or a **stud farm** is a place where horses are bred. `N COUNT`

studded /stʌdɪ²d/. Something that is **studded** is decorated with studs or things that look like studs. EG *...enamel bracelets studded with precious stones.* `ADJ CLASSIF: OFT+with`

student /stjuːdənt/, **students.** 1 A **student** is 1.1 a person who is studying at a university or college. EG *...a part-time student at King's College, London... ...student nurses.* ● See also **mature student.** 1.2 a person who is studying in a secondary school. `N COUNT` `American`

2 Someone who is a **student** of a particular subject is interested in the subject and is trying to learn about it. EG *It is our treatment of old people which most shocks students of our culture.* `N COUNT+of`

studied /stʌdɪd/. 1 A **studied** action has been carefully thought about or planned and is not spontaneous or natural. EG *With studied casualness he mentioned his departure to Hilary... ...a studied gesture of impatience.* `ADJ CLASSIF: ATTRIB`

2 See also **study.**

studio /stjuːdɪəʊ/, **studios.** A **studio** is 1 a room where a painter or photographer works. EG *Upstairs he had a studio where he painted a little.* 2 a room where radio or television programmes are recorded, records are produced, or films are made. EG *I went up to the big recording studio in Maida Vale.* `N COUNT`

studious /stjuːdɪəs/. Someone who is **studious** spends a lot of time reading and studying books. `ADJ QUALIT`

studiously /stjuːdɪəsliʰ/. If you **studiously** do something, you do it carefully and deliberately. EG *The Colonel studiously examined his folders.* `ADV`

study /stʌdiʰ/, **studies, studying, studied.** 1 If you **study** a particular subject, you spend time learning about it. EG *He studied chemistry at university... She's studying for a law degree.* `V+O OR V`

2 **Study** is the activity of studying a subject. EG *There are no rooms specifically set aside for quiet study.* `N UNCOUNT`

3 **Studies** are subjects which are studied. EG *...the School of European Studies... ...the introduction of new studies into the curriculum.* `N PLURAL`

4 If you **study** something, you look at it or watch it very carefully. EG *He looked at her hard, studying her face... I studied a map.* `V+O`

5 A **study** of a subject is a piece of research on it. EG *She has made a close study of male executives and their drinking habits.* `N COUNT`

6 A **study** by an artist is a drawing which is done in preparation for a larger picture. `N COUNT`

7 A **study** in a house is a room which you use for reading, writing, and studying. `N COUNT`

8 See also **studied.**

stuff /stʌf/, **stuffs, stuffing, stuffed.** 1 You can refer to a substance, a thing, or a group of things as **stuff.** EG *What's that stuff in the bucket?... Quite a lot of stuff had been stolen... She was reading the travel stuff in the colour supplement.* `N UNCOUNT: USU+SUPP`

Does a stunt man sometimes work in a studio?

2 If you **stuff** something somewhere, you push it there quickly and roughly. EG *Willie gathered up the bills and stuffed them carelessly into his pocket... Nora stuffed a cigarette into her mouth.*   V+O+A

3 If you **stuff** a place or container, you fill it with material or other things until it is full. EG *...stuffing a toy dog.* ◊ **stuffed**. EG *He'd got a big rucksack, stuffed with notes, on his back.*   V+O: OFT+*with* ◊ ADJ CLASSIF

4 If you **stuff** yourself, you eat a lot of food. EG *Karin was stuffing herself with eggs and toast.*   V-REFL OR V+O Informal

5 If you **stuff** a bird such as a chicken or a vegetable such as a pepper, you put a mixture of food inside it before cooking it. ◊ **stuffed**. EG *...stuffed olives.*   V+O ◊ ADJ CLASSIF

6 If a dead animal **is stuffed**, it is filled with material so that it can be preserved and displayed. ◊ **stuffed**. EG *...a stuffed parrot.*   V+O: USU PASS ◊ ADJ CLASSIF

7 If you say that someone **knows** their **stuff**, you mean that they are good at doing something because they are experienced at it and know a lot about it. EG *These union negotiators know their stuff.*   PHRASE Informal

8 If you are angry with someone for something that they have said or done, you might say '**Get stuffed!**' to them; a rude expression.   EXCLAM Informal

stuffing /stʌfɪŋ/ is **1** a mixture of food that is put inside a bird such as a chicken, or a vegetable such as a pepper, before it is cooked. EG *We had chicken with stuffing and new potatoes.* **2** material that is put inside pillows, cushions, or toys, in order to fill them and make them firm or solid.   N MASS   N UNCOUNT

stuffy /stʌfiː/, **stuffier, stuffiest. 1 Stuffy** people or institutions are formal and old-fashioned.   ADJ QUALIT

2 If it is **stuffy** in a place, it is unpleasantly warm and there is not enough fresh air. EG *...a stuffy room.*   ADJ QUALIT

stultify /stʌltɪfaɪ/, **stultifies, stultifying, stultified.** If something **stultifies** you, it makes you feel dull and stop thinking, because it is so boring or repetitive. EG *The regular use of calculators can stultify a child's capacity to do mental arithmetic.* ◊ **stultifying**. EG *...the stultifying rituals of court procedure.*   V+O ◊ ADJ QUALIT

stumble /stʌmbəl/, **stumbles, stumbling, stumbled. 1** If you **stumble**, you put your foot down awkwardly while you are walking or running and nearly fall over. EG *The man was drunk and he stumbled on the bottom step.*   V: NO IMPER

2 If you **stumble** while you are reading aloud or speaking, you make a mistake, and have to pause and read it or say it again. EG *She stumbled over the foreign words.*   V: NO IMPER

stumble across or **stumble on.** If you **stumble across** something or **stumble on** it, you find it or discover it unexpectedly. EG *In the course of their search they may stumble across something quite different... Sir Alexander Fleming stumbled on his great discovery of penicillin quite by accident.*   PHRASAL VB: V+PREP, HAS PASS

stumbling block, stumbling blocks. A **stumbling block** is something which stops you from doing or getting what you want. EG *Perhaps the biggest stumbling block to disarmament is the deterrent theory.*   N COUNT

stump /stʌmp/, **stumps, stumping, stumped. 1** A **stump** is a small part of something that remains when the rest of it has been removed or broken off. EG *We left him sitting on the stump of an old oak tree.*   N COUNT

2 The **stumps** in cricket are the three wooden sticks that are placed upright in the ground to form the wicket.   N COUNT

3 If a question or problem **stumps** you, you cannot think of any solution or answer to it. EG *...the question that has stumped philosophers since the beginning of time.*   V+O

4 If you **stump** somewhere, you walk there with heavy steps. EG *She stumped back into the house.*   V+A

stump up. If you **stump up** a sum of money, you pay the money that is required for something,   PHRASAL VB: V+ADV+O

often reluctantly. EG *The government is being asked to stump up the balance.*

stumpy /stʌmpiː/. **Stumpy** things are short and thick. EG *...a short stumpy tail.*   ADJ QUALIT

stun /stʌn/, **stuns, stunning, stunned. 1** If you **are stunned** by something, you are very shocked by it. EG *We were all stunned by the news.* ◊ **stunned**. EG *I sat in stunned silence.*   V+O: USU PASS ◊ ADJ QUALIT

2 If something such as a blow on the head **stuns** you, it makes you unconscious or confused and unsteady. EG *He was stunned by a blow from the rifle.*   V+O

3 See also **stunning**.

stung /stʌŋ/ is the past tense and past participle of **sting**.

stunk /stʌŋk/ is the past participle of **stink**.

stunning /stʌnɪŋ/. Something that is **stunning** is **1** extremely beautiful or impressive. EG *The film is visually stunning... Her dress was simply stunning.* **2** so unusual or unexpected that people are astonished by it. EG *...a stunning victory in the general election.*   ADJ QUALIT

stunt /stʌnt/, **stunts, stunting, stunted. 1** A **stunt** is **1.1** something that someone does in order to get publicity. EG *Climbing up the church tower was a fine publicity stunt.* **1.2** a dangerous and exciting action that someone does in a film. EG *Steve McQueen did most of his own stunts.*   N COUNT

2 If one thing **stunts** the growth or development of another, it prevents it from growing or developing as much as it should. EG *These insecticides can stunt plant growth.* ◊ **stunted**. EG *...old, stunted thorn trees.*   V+O ◊ ADJ QUALIT

stunt man, stunt men. A **stunt man** is a man whose job is to do dangerous things in films instead of the actors.   N COUNT

stupefied /stjuːpɪfaɪd/. If you are **stupefied**, **1** you feel so tired or bored that you are unable to think clearly. EG *I felt stupefied by the heavy meal.* **2** you are very surprised. EG *He was too stupefied to answer her.*   ADJ QUALIT: USU PRED

stupendous /stjuːpɛndəs/. Something that is **stupendous** is extremely large or impressive. EG *The roar of the explosion was stupendous... ...stupendous sums of money.*   ADJ QUALIT

stupid /stjuːpɪd/, **stupider, stupidest. 1** Someone who is **stupid** shows a lack of good judgement or intelligence and is not at all sensible. EG *I have been extremely stupid... ...a stupid question.* ◊ **stupidly**. EG *I once stupidly asked him why he smiled so often.*   ADJ QUALIT ◊ ADV

2 You say that something is **stupid** to indicate that you do not like it or that it annoys you. EG *I hate these stupid black shoes.*   ADJ CLASSIF Informal

stupidity /stjuːpɪdɪtiː/, **stupidities. Stupidity** is **1** behaviour that is not at all sensible. EG *I used to find her occasional stupidities amusing... He is paying a big price for his stupidity.* **2** the quality of being stupid. EG *...the stupidity of their error.*   N COUNT OR N UNCOUNT   N UNCOUNT

stupor /stjuːpə/, **stupors.** Someone who is in a **stupor** is almost unconscious. EG *He collapsed in a drunken stupor.*   N COUNT

sturdy /stɜːdiː/, **sturdier, sturdiest.** Someone or something that is **sturdy** looks strong and is unlikely to be easily damaged or injured. EG *He is short and sturdy... ...sturdy oak tables.* ◊ **sturdily**. EG *...a sturdily built little boy.*   ADJ QUALIT ◊ ADV

stutter /stʌtə/, **stutters, stuttering, stuttered. 1** If someone has a **stutter**, they find it difficult to say the first sound of a word, and so they often hesitate or repeat it two or three times.   N COUNT

2 If someone **stutters**, they have difficulty speaking because they find it hard to say the first sound of a word. EG *'I...I want to do it,' she stuttered.*   V, V+O, OR V+QUOTE

sty /staɪ/, **sties.** A **sty** is the same as a pigsty.   N COUNT

style /staɪl/, **styles, styling, styled. 1** The **style** of something is the general way in which it is done or presented, which often shows the attitudes of the people involved. EG *Some people find our lei-*   N COUNT+SUPP

surely style of decision-making rather frustrating...
...western styles of education.

2 Someone's **style** is all their general attitudes and   N COUNT OR
usual ways of behaving. EG *In characteristic style,*   N UNCOUNT :
he peered over his glasses... Purple is not my style.   +SUPP
● to **cramp** someone's **style**: see **cramp**.

3 If people or places have **style**, they are smart   N UNCOUNT
and elegant. EG *Both were rather short and plump,*
but they had style... Here you can eat in style.

4 The **style** of a product is its design. EG *These*   N UNCOUNT
pants come in several styles... The clothes I wore   OR N COUNT :
weren't different in style or appearance from those   OFT + SUPP
of the other children. ● See also **hairstyle**.

5 If you **style** a piece of clothing or someone's hair,   V+O : USU PASS
you design the clothing or do their hair. EG *Her hair*
was styled in a short cropped pony tail.

stylish /ˈstaɪlɪʃ/. Someone or something that is   ADJ QUALIT
stylish is smart, elegant, and fashionable. EG *...the*
stylish Swiss resort of Gstaad.

stylistic /staɪˈlɪstɪk/ describes things relating to   ADJ CLASSIF :
the methods and techniques used in creating a   ATTRIB
piece of writing, music, or art. EG *Such work lacks*
any development of stylistic features.

suave /swɑːv/. Someone who is **suave** is charming   ADJ QUALIT
and polite. EG *...a suave young man... They had*
suave manners.

sub-. 1 sub- is used at the beginning of words such   PREFIX
as 'submerge', 'subway', and 'submarine' that have
'under' as part of their meaning.

2 sub- is also used to form nouns that refer to the   PREFIX
parts or divisions of something. For example, a
category may be divided into subcategories, and a
species may consist of subspecies. EG *...subsection*
1(b) of the report... ...the sub-groups of society.

subconscious /sʌbˈkɒnʃəs/. **1** Your **subcon-**   N SING
scious is the part of your mind that can influence
you or affect your behaviour even though you are
not aware of it. EG *The knowledge was there*
somewhere in the depths of his subconscious.

2 Something that is **subconscious** happens or   ADJ CLASSIF
exists in your subconscious. EG *...a subconscious*
desire to punish himself.

subcontract, subcontracts, subcontracting,
subcontracted; pronounced /sʌbkəˈntrækt/ when
it is a verb, and /sʌbˈkɒntrækt/ when it is a noun.

1 If one firm **subcontracts** a part of its work to   V+O : OFT+to
another firm, it pays the other firm to do that part.
EG *They had subcontracted some of the work to an*
electrician.

2 A **subcontract** is a contract between two firms   N COUNT
in which one firm agrees to do a part of the other
firm's work. EG *We managed to get the subcontract*
for that job in Edinburgh.

subculture /ˈsʌbkʌltʃə/, **subcultures.** A **subcul-**   N COUNT
ture is the ideas, art, and way of life of a group of
people within a society, which are different from
the ideas, art, and way of life of the rest of the
society. EG *...an extremist political subculture.*

subdivide /sʌbdɪˈvaɪd/, **subdivides, subdividing,**   V+O : USU PASS
subdivided. If something **is subdivided**, it is   +into
made into several smaller areas, parts, or sections.
EG *Our office was subdivided into departments.*

subdivision /ˈsʌbdɪvɪʒən/, **subdivisions.** A **sub-**   N COUNT
division is an area or section which is a part of a
larger area or section of something.

subdue /səbˈdjuː/, **subdues, subduing, subdued.**

1 If soldiers **subdue** a group of people, they defeat   V+O
them or bring them under control by using force.
EG *Troops were sent to subdue the rebels.*

2 If something **subdues** your feelings, it makes   V+O
them less strong. EG *This thought subdued my*
delight at the news.

3 If something **subdues** a light or a colour, it   V+O
makes it less bright.

subdued /səbˈdjuːd/. **1** Someone who is **subdued** is   ADJ QUALIT
very quiet, often because they are sad. EG *They*
were subdued and silent.

2 Subdued feelings, sounds, or qualities are not   ADJ QUALIT

very noticeable. EG *The assembly murmured in*
subdued agreement.

3 Subdued lights or colours are not very bright.   ADJ QUALIT

subhuman /sʌbˈhjuːmən/. If you describe some-   ADJ CLASSIF
one as **subhuman**, you mean that their behaviour
is disgusting.

subject, subjects, subjecting, subjected; pronounced /ˈsʌbdʒɪkt/ when it is a noun or adjective,
and /səbˈdʒɛkt/ when it is a verb.

1 The **subject** of a conversation, letter, or book is   N COUNT
the thing, person, or idea that is being discussed or
written about. EG *I don't have any strong views on*
the subject... I simply did not know which subjects I
could talk about... However much you try to
change the subject, the conversation invariably
returns to politics.

2 In grammar, the **subject** of a sentence or clause   N COUNT
is the word or words that represent the person or
thing that is doing the action expressed by the
verb. For example, in the sentence 'My cat keeps
catching birds', 'my cat' is the subject.

3 A **subject** is also something such as maths,   N COUNT
chemistry, or English, that you study at school,
college, or university. EG *Maths was my best subject*
at school.

4 The **subjects** of a country are the people who   N COUNT
live there. EG *...British subjects.*   Formal

5 Subject peoples and countries are being ruled or   ADJ CLASSIF :
controlled by the government of another country.   ATTRIB
EG *...freedom for the subject peoples of the world.*

6 If rulers or governments **subject** their people or   V+O
their country, they control them strictly and take
away their freedom. EG *He began to pass laws to*
subject every area of the country.

7 If you are **subject** to something, you are affected   ADJ PRED+to
by it or likely to be affected by it. EG *Your profit*
will be subject to tax... He is highly strung and,
therefore, subject to heart attacks.

8 If you say that one thing will happen **subject to**   PREP
another, you mean that it will happen only if the
other thing happens. EG *The property will be sold*
subject to the following conditions.

9 If you **subject** someone to something unpleasant,   V+O+to
you make them experience it. EG *He was subjected*
to the harshest possible punishment.

subjective /səbˈdʒɛktɪv/. Something that is **sub-**   ADJ QUALIT
jective is strongly influenced by personal opinions
and feelings. EG *He knew his arguments were*
subjective, based on intuition.

subject matter. The **subject matter** of a con-   N UNCOUNT
versation, book, or film is the thing, person, or idea
that is being discussed, written about, or shown.

subjugate /ˈsʌbdʒəˌɡeɪt/, **subjugates, subjugat-**
ing, subjugated. 1 If someone **subjugates** a   V+O
group of people, they take complete control of   Formal
them, especially by defeating them in a war. EG
They wondered where Hitler would turn when he
had subjugated Europe. ◊ **subjugation**   ◊ N UNCOUNT
/sʌbdʒəˈɡeɪʃən/. EG *These people are resisting*
attempted subjugation by armed minorities.

2 If your wishes or desires **are subjugated** to   V+O : USU PASS
something, they are treated as less important than   Formal
that thing. EG *She has subjugated her own desires to*
those of her husband.

subjunctive /səbˈdʒʌŋktɪv/. The **subjunctive** or   N SING : the+N
subjunctive mood is one of the moods that a verb
can take in some languages such as French and
Latin. In contrast with the indicative and imperative moods, the subjunctive is usually used to
express attitudes such as wishing, hoping, and
doubting.

sublime /səˈblaɪm/. **1** If you describe something as   ADJ QUALIT
sublime, you mean that it has a wonderful quality   Literary
that affects you deeply. EG *She paid me a sublime*

Is it a good idea to use subdued lighting when you
are reading?

SUBMODIFIERS

Submodifiers (SUBMOD) are adverbs such as **very**, **quite**, and **surprisingly**. An adjective such as 'happy' can have one of these words in front of it, so that you can vary from being *exceptionally happy* to *quite happy*. Submodifiers come in front of adjectives or other adverbs, but are not used with verbs.

Typically, submodifiers are used in front of qualitative adjectives, such as 'ugly', 'big', 'small', 'nice', and so on. For example: *He is rather ugly, but very nice.*

Submodifiers are used to strengthen or weaken the adjective, rather than to add new meaning. So if you want to say that someone has ideas that are more interesting than most people's ideas, you can say: *His ideas are very interesting . . .   His ideas are extremely interesting . . .   His ideas are terribly interesting.*

There are a number of submodifiers, such as **absolutely**, **utterly**, and **totally**, which can be used with adjectives that are not usually graded: *He became totally blind . . .   . . . two totally opposed ideas.*

Submodifiers are often used after **not** to lessen the negative effect of what you are saying. So that instead of using an adjective such as 'boring', 'wrong', or 'stupid' that has a very strong negative feel to it, you can use the corresponding positive adjective, with a negative and with a submodifier, as in: *It wasn't terribly interesting . . .   I don't think that's quite right . . .   He's not very clever.*

---

compliment which I shall always cherish... ...the author of this sublime document.

2 You describe something as going **from the** PHRASE **sublime to the ridiculous** when it changes from being of high quality to being silly or trivial. EG *The film goes from the sublime to the ridiculous.*

subliminal /sʌblɪmɪnəl/. Something that is sub- ADJ CLASSIF liminal affects your mind without you being aware of it. EG *...subliminal advertising.*

sub-machine gun, sub-machine guns. A sub- N COUNT machine gun is a light, portable type of machine-gun.

submarine /sʌbməriːn/, **submarines.** A subma- N COUNT rine is a type of ship that can travel below the surface of the sea.

submerge /səbmɜːdʒ/, **submerges, submerg-ing, submerged.** **1** If something **submerges** or if V-ERG : OFT+A you **submerge** it, it goes below the surface of the water. EG *The alligator showed its snout before submerging.*

2 If you **submerge** yourself in an activity, you give V-REFL+in all your attention to it and do not think about anything else. EG *I was eager to submerge myself in the feminist movement.*

submerged /səbmɜːdʒd/. If something is sub- ADJ CLASSIF merged, it is below the surface of the water. EG *...a line of submerged rocks... The submarine can remain submerged for eight weeks.*

submission /səbmɪʃəⁿn/. **1** Submission is a state N UNCOUNT in which people can no longer do what they want to do because they are under the control of some-one else. EG *The trade unions were brought into submission.*

2 The **submission** of a proposal or application is N UNCOUNT the act of sending it to someone, so that they can Formal decide whether to accept it or not. EG *...the submis-sion of these plans to the local authority.*

submissive /səbmɪsɪv/. If you are **submissive**, ADJ QUALIT you behave in a quiet, obedient way. EG *She became submissive and subservient.*

submit /səbmɪt/, **submits, submitting, submit-ted.** **1** If you **submit** to something, you accept it, V : OFT+to because you are not powerful enough to resist it. EG *They were forced to submit to military discipline... Liang submitted to his beatings... They had to submit to a thorough search at the airport.*

2 If you **submit** a proposal or application to V+O someone, you send it to them so that they can decide whether to accept it or not. EG *I submitted my resignation.*

SUBMOD stands for **submodifier**
Adverbs which have the label SUBMOD in the Extra Column are used in front of adjectives and other adverbs.
See the entry headed SUBMODIFIERS for more infor-mation.

---

subnormal /sʌbnɔːməⁿl/. If someone is **subnor-** ADJ CLASSIF mal, they have less ability or intelligence than a normal person of their age. EG *...a woman who was clearly educationally subnormal... ...homes for sub-normal children.*

subordinate, subordinates, subordinating, subordinated; pronounced /səbɔːdɪnəⁱt/ when it is a noun or adjective, and /səbɔːdɪneɪt/ when it is a verb. **1** If someone is your **subordinate**, they have N COUNT a less important position than you in the organiza- WITH POSS tion that you both work for. EG *He humiliated his senior staff before their subordinates.*

2 If one thing is **subordinate** to another, it is less ADJ CLASSIF : important than the other thing. EG *All other ques-* OFT+to *tions are subordinate to this one.* Formal

3 If you **subordinate** one thing to another, you V+O+to regard it or treat it as less important than the other Formal thing. EG *To keep his job, he subordinated his own interests to the objectives of the company.*

subordinate clause, subordinate clauses. A N COUNT **subordinate clause** is a clause which adds some details to the main clause of a sentence.

subscribe /səbskraɪb/, **subscribes, subscribing, subscribed.** 1 If you **subscribe** to an opinion or v : usu+to belief, you are one of a number of people who have this opinion or belief. EG *The rest of us do not subscribe to this theory.*

2 If you **subscribe** to a magazine or a newspaper, v : usu+to you pay to receive copies of it regularly. EG *I started subscribing to a morning newspaper.*

3 If you **subscribe** money to a charity or a v+o+a campaign, you send money to it regularly. EG *They subscribed to local charities... Substantial sums were subscribed towards the work.*

subscriber /səbskraɪbə/, **subscribers.** 1 A maga- N COUNT zine's or a newspaper's **subscribers** are the people who pay to receive copies of it regularly.

2 **Subscribers** to a service are the people who pay N COUNT to receive the service. EG *...telephone subscribers.*

3 The **subscribers** to a charity or campaign are N COUNT the people who support it by sending money regularly to it.

subscription /səbskrɪpʃəᵘn/, **subscriptions.** A N COUNT **subscription** is an amount of money that you pay regularly in order to belong to a society, to help a charity or campaign, or to receive copies of a magazine or newspaper. EG *...my first year's subscription to the National Union of Agricultural Workers... He could not afford to renew his magazine subscriptions.*

subsequent /sʌbsɪkwənt/. You use **subsequent** ADJ CLASSIF : to describe something that happens or exists at a ATTRIB later time than something else. EG *Subsequent research has produced even better results.*

◊ **subsequently.** EG *Brooke was arrested and* ◊ ADV *subsequently sentenced to five years' imprisonment.*

subservient /səbsɜːvɪənt/. 1 If you are **subservi-** ADJ QUALIT : **ent**, you do whatever someone wants you to do. EG OFT+to *She was subservient and eager to please.*

◊ **subservience** /səbsɜːvɪəns/. EG *How long would* ◊ N UNCOUNT *they keep us in subservience?*

2 If you treat one thing as **subservient** to another, ADJ PRED+to you treat it as less important than the other thing. EG *Economic systems became subservient to social objectives.*

subside /səbsaɪd/, **subsides, subsiding, subsided.** 1 If a feeling **subsides**, it becomes less violent v or intense. EG *She stopped and waited until the pain subsided.*

2 If a noise **subsides**, it becomes much quieter. EG v *His voice subsided to a mutter.*

3 If water **subsides** or if the ground **subsides**, it v sinks to a lower level. EG *The flooded river was subsiding rapidly.*

subsidence /səbsaɪdəns, sʌbsɪdəns/. When there N UNCOUNT is **subsidence** in a place, the ground there sinks to a lower level. EG *The cracks in your house are due to subsidence.*

subsidiary /səbsɪdjəri¹/, **subsidiaries.** 1 If some- ADJ CLASSIF : thing is **subsidiary**, it is less important than some- USU ATTRIB thing else with which it is connected. EG *I tried to discuss this and some subsidiary questions... The Department offers a course in Opera Studies as a subsidiary subject.*

2 A **subsidiary** or **subsidiary company** is a N COUNT company which is part of a larger and more important company. EG *The British company is a subsidiary of Racal Electronics.*

subsidize /sʌbsɪdaɪz/, **subsidizes, subsidizing, subsidized;** also spelled **subsidise.** 1 If a govern- v+o ment or other authority **subsidizes** a public service, they pay part of the cost of it. EG *In this country the State subsidizes education, housing and health care.* ◊ **subsidized.** EG *...subsidized housing.* ◊ ADJ CLASSIF

2 If a government **subsidizes** an industry, they v+o provide money in order to enable the industry to

continue. EG *Every government since the last war has subsidized upland farming.*

subsidy /sʌbsɪdi¹/, **subsidies.** A **subsidy** is mon- N COUNT OR ey that is paid by a government or other authority N UNCOUNT in order to help a company financially or to pay for a public service.

subsist /səbsɪst/, **subsists, subsisting, sub-** v : OFT+on **sisted.** If people **subsist**, they are just able to obtain the food that they need in order to stay alive. EG *In some places, the settlers were subsisting on potato peelings.*

subsistence /səbsɪstəns/ is the condition of just N UNCOUNT having enough food to stay alive. EG *Thousands of pensioners live out their lives at subsistence level.*

substance /sʌbstəns/, **substances.** 1 A **sub-** N COUNT **stance** is a solid, a powder, or a liquid. EG *He discovered a substance called phosphotase... We try to remove the harmful substances from cigarettes.*

2 **Substance** is something that you can touch, N UNCOUNT rather than something that you can only see, hear, or imagine. EG *They had no more substance than shadows.*

3 The **substance** of what someone says or writes N SING : is the main thing that they are trying to say. EG *The* the+N+of *substance of their talk is condensed into a paragraph.*

4 **Substance** is also the quality of being important N UNCOUNT or significant. EG *There isn't anything of real substance in her book... There is some substance to this criticism.*

substandard /sʌbstændəd/. If something is **sub-** ADJ CLASSIF **standard**, it is unacceptable because it is below a required standard. EG *...substandard housing.*

substantial /səbstænʃəᵘl/. 1 **Substantial** means ADJ QUALIT very large in amount or degree. EG *She will receive a substantial amount of money... Many factories suffered substantial damage.*

2 A **substantial** building is large and strongly built. ADJ CLASSIF EG *On the site were a number of substantial timber buildings.*

substantially /səbstænʃəli¹/. 1 If something in- ADV creases or decreases **substantially**, it increases or decreases by a large amount. EG *The price may go up quite substantially.*

2 If you say that something is **substantially** true, SUBMOD you mean that it is generally true. EG *Steed always maintained that the story was substantially true.*

substantiate /səbstænʃɪeɪt/, **substantiates, sub-** v+o **stantiating, substantiated.** To **substantiate** a Formal statement or a story means to supply evidence which proves that it is true. EG *Your report might be difficult to substantiate.*

substitute /sʌbstɪtjuːt/, **substitutes, substitut-** v+o : OFT+for **ing, substituted.** 1 If you **substitute** one thing for another, you use it instead of the other thing. EG *Force was substituted for argument.*

◊ **substitution** /sʌbstɪtjuːʃəᵘn/, **substitutions.** EG ◊ N UNCOUNT *...the substitution of local goods for those previous-* OR N COUNT *ly imported... Some of these substitutions were successful.*

2 If one thing **substitutes** for another, it takes the v : OFT+for place or performs the function of the other thing. EG *In the past, oil has substituted for certain natural materials.*

3 A **substitute** is something that you have or use N COUNT : instead of something else. EG *Their dog was a* OFT+for *substitute for the children they never had... She had become attached to her substitute parents.*

4 If you say that one thing is **no substitute** for PHRASE another, you mean that it does not have certain desirable features that the other thing has, and is therefore unsatisfactory. EG *The pub was no substitute for a luxury hotel.*

subsume /səbsjuːm/, **subsumes, subsuming, subsumed.** If something **is subsumed** within a larger group or class, it is included within it, rather than being considered as something separate.   v+o : usu pass   Formal

subterfuge /sʌbtəfjuːdʒ/, **subterfuges.** A **subterfuge** is a trick or a dishonest way of getting what you want. EG *Resistance will be possible only through cheating, subterfuge and sabotage.*   N COUNT OR N UNCOUNT

subterranean /sʌbtəreɪnɪən/. A **subterranean** river or tunnel is underground. EG *We wandered through winding subterranean passages.*   ADJ CLASSIF : ATTRIB

subtitles /sʌbtaɪtəlz/ are the printed translation that you can read at the bottom of the screen when you are watching a foreign film. EG *...an Italian film with English subtitles.*   N PLURAL

subtle /sʌtəl/, **subtler, subtlest. 1** Something that is **subtle** is not immediately obvious or noticeable, and is therefore a little difficult to explain or describe. EG *His whole attitude had undergone a subtle change... ...subtle forms of racism.* ◊ **subtly.** EG *The tastes are subtly different.*   ADJ QUALIT   ◊ ADV

2 Someone who is **subtle** uses indirect and clever methods to achieve something, rather than doing something that is obvious. EG *You must be more subtle... ...the subtlest of our politicians... My plan was subtler.* ◊ **subtly.** EG *He subtly criticized me.*   ADJ QUALIT   ◊ ADV

subtlety /sʌtəltiː/, **subtleties. 1** A **subtlety** is a very small detail or difference which is difficult to notice. EG *...the subtleties of English intonation... He was aware of the subtleties of Elaine's moods.*   N COUNT : USU+of

2 Subtlety is **2.1** the quality of being not immediately obvious or noticeable, and therefore difficult to explain or describe. EG *In your cooking remember that subtlety is everything... The subtlety of this process is extraordinary.* **2.2** the ability to notice and recognize things which are not obvious, especially small differences between things. EG *They can sense each other's intentions with great subtlety.* **2.3** the ability to use indirect and clever methods to achieve something, rather than doing something that is obvious. EG *...their subtlety of mind.*   N UNCOUNT   Formal

subtract /səbtrækt/, **subtracts, subtracting, subtracted.** If you **subtract** one number from another, you do a calculation in which you take it away from the other number. For example, if you subtract 3 from 5, you get 2. ◊ **subtraction** /səbtrækʃən/, **subtractions.** EG *...simple techniques for handling subtraction and multiplication.*   v+o : OFT+from   ◊ N UNCOUNT OR N COUNT

subtropical /sʌbtrɒpɪkəl/ describes things relating to the areas of the world that lie between the tropical and temperate regions. EG *...sub-tropical forests.*   ADJ CLASSIF : ATTRIB

suburb /sʌbɜːb/, **suburbs.** A **suburb** of a town or city is an area of it which is not close to the centre. People who work in the town or city often live in the **suburbs.**   N COUNT

suburban /səbɜːbən/. **1 Suburban** means relating to a suburb. EG *...suburban areas.*   ADJ CLASSIF

2 If you describe something as **suburban**, you mean that it is dull and conventional, and lacks change or excitement. EG *...a suburban lifestyle.*   ADJ QUALIT

suburbia /səbɜːbɪə/ refers to the suburbs of towns and cities considered as a whole. EG *...the gardens of London suburbia.*   N UNCOUNT

subversion /səbvɜːʃən/ is the attempt to weaken or destroy a political system or a government. EG *She was arrested for subversion.*   N UNCOUNT   Formal

subversive /səbvɜːsɪv/, **subversives. 1** Something that is **subversive** is intended to weaken or destroy a political system or government. EG *...subversive literature.*   ADJ QUALIT   Formal

2 Subversives are people who attempt to weaken or destroy a political system or government.   N COUNT   Formal

subvert /səbvɜːt/, **subverts, subverting, subverted.** To **subvert** something means to destroy its power and influence. EG *Conflict and division subvert the foundations of society.*   v+o   Formal   N COUNT

subway /sʌbweɪ/, **subways.** A **subway** is **1** a passage for pedestrians that goes underneath a busy road. **2** an underground railway. EG *...a subway station.*   American

succeed /səksiːd/, **succeeds, succeeding, succeeded. 1** If you **succeed** in doing something, you manage to do it. EG *I succeeded in getting the job... She tried to smile but did not succeed.*   v : OFT+in

2 If something **succeeds, 2.1** it has the result that is intended. EG *Nobody expected that strike to succeed.* **2.2** it works in a satisfactory way. EG *They had a marriage which succeeded beyond their dreams.*   v

3 Someone who **succeeds** gains a high position in what they do, for example in business or politics. EG *She is eager to succeed.*   v : OFT+in

4 If you **succeed** another person, you are the next person to have their job or position. EG *Somebody's got to succeed Murray as editor.*   v+o OR v

5 If one thing **succeeds** another, it comes after it in time. EG *The first demand would be succeeded by others.* ◊ **succeeding.** EG *In the succeeding months, little was heard about him.*   v+o   ◊ ADJ CLASSIF : ATTRIB

success /səkses/, **successes. 1 Success** is **1.1** the achievement of something that you have been trying to do. EG *His attempt to shoot the president came very close to success.* **1.2** the achievement of a high position in a particular field, for example in business or politics. EG *Confidence is the key to success... The firm is assured of success in the coming year.*   N UNCOUNT

2 Someone or something that is a **success** achieves a high position, makes a lot of money, or becomes very popular. EG *His next film - 'Jaws' - was a tremendous success.*   N COUNT

successful /səksesful/. **1** Something that is **successful 1.1** achieves what it was intended to achieve. EG *...a successful attempt to land on the moon.* ◊ **successfully.** EG *The operation had been completed successfully.* **1.2** is popular or makes a lot of money. EG *...a very successful film.*   ADJ QUALIT   ◊ ADV   ADJ QUALIT

2 Someone who is **successful** achieves a high position in what they do, for example in business or politics. EG *...a successful writer.*   ADJ QUALIT

succession /səkseʃən/, **successions. 1** A **succession** of things of the same kind is a number of them that exist or happen one after the other. EG *My life is a succession of failures.*   N COUNT+of

2 Succession is the act or right of being the next person to have an important job or position. EG *...his succession to the peerage.*   N UNCOUNT : OFT+to

3 If something happens for a number of weeks or years **in succession**, it happens in each of those weeks or years, without a break. EG *Vita went to Florence for the third year in succession.*   PHRASE

successive /səksesɪv/ means happening or existing one after another without a break. EG *On two successive Saturdays, the car broke down... ...the actions of successive British governments.*   ADJ CLASSIF : ATTRIB

successor /səksesə/, **successors.** Someone's **successor** is the person who takes their job after they have left. EG *Who will be Brearley's successor?*   N COUNT : USU+POSS

success story, success stories. Someone or something that is a **success story** is very successful, often unexpectedly or in spite of unfavourable conditions. EG *One of the greatest success stories in rapid industrialization was Singapore.*   N COUNT

succinct /səksɪŋkt/. Something that is **succinct** expresses facts or ideas clearly and in few words. EG *...an accurate and succinct account of their policies.*   ADJ QUALIT

succour /sʌkə/; spelled **succor** in American English. **Succour** is help that is given to someone who is suffering or in difficulties. EG *They were busy providing succour to the injured.*   N UNCOUNT   Formal

succulent /sʌkjələnt/. Food that is **succulent** is juicy and delicious. EG *...a succulent mango.*   ADJ QUALIT

succumb /səkʌm/, **succumbs, succumbing, succumbed. 1** If you **succumb** to persuasion or   v : OFT+to desire, you are unable to resist it. EG *He finally succumbed to the temptation to have another drink.*

2 If you **succumb** to an illness, you become V : OFT + *to* affected by it. EG *...those who succumb to ulcers.* Formal

such /sʌtʃ/. **1 Such** a thing or person means the PREDET, DET, thing or person that you have just mentioned, or a OR PRON thing or person like the one that you have just mentioned. EG *They lasted for hundreds of thousands of years. On a human time scale, such a period seems an eternity... The nobility held tournaments, but peasants had no time to spare for such frivolity... I don't believe in magic, there is no such thing... It was in Brighton or Bournemouth or some such place.*

2 You use **such as** or **such...as** to introduce one or more examples of something. EG *...a game of chance such as roulette... ...a prolonged rise in prices such as occurred in the late 1960s... ...such things as pork pies, sausage rolls, and plum cake.*

3 You also use **such** to emphasize the degree or PREDET OR DET extent of something. EG *It was such a lovely day... It was strange that such elegant creatures made such ugly sounds... There was such a crowd of people.*

4 You use **such...that** or **such...as** when saying PREDET, DET, what the result or consequence of a particular kind OR PRON of thing is. EG *They have to charge in such a way that they don't make a loss.*

5 You use **such as it is** or **such as there is** to PHRASE indicate that something is not very good, important, or useful. EG *Dinner's on the table, such as it is.*

6 You use **as such** to indicate that you are PHRASE considering something by itself and only as an idea, and are not considering any connected things or practical situations. EG *He is not terribly interested in politics as such.*

7 You use **such and such** to refer to a thing or person when you do not want to be exact or precise. EG *John always tells me that I have not taken such and such into account.*

suchlike /sʌtʃlaɪk/. You use **suchlike** to refer to DET OR PRON things like the ones already mentioned. EG *...artichokes, smoked fish, and suchlike delicacies... ...mills, threshing machines and such like.*

suck /sʌk/, **sucks, sucking, sucked. 1** If you V+O OR V+A **suck** something, you hold it in your mouth and pull at it with the muscles in your cheeks and tongue, for example in order to get liquid out of it. EG *The baby went on sucking the bottle... Bite open the fruit and suck out the flesh.*

2 If something **sucks** an object or liquid in a V+O+A particular direction, it draws it there with a powerful force. EG *The water is sucked upwards through the roots.*

3 If you **are sucked** into a situation, you are V+O : unable to prevent yourself from becoming involved USU PASS + *into* in it. EG *They found themselves sucked into the quarrel.*

suck up. If you **suck up** to someone in authority, PHRASAL VB : you try to please them; used showing disapproval. V + ADV, EG *He's been sucking up like mad to the boss.* OFT + *to* Informal

sucker /sʌkə/, **suckers. 1** If you call someone a N COUNT **sucker**, you mean that it is very easy to cheat them. EG *He was no sucker.*

2 The **suckers** on some animals and insects are N COUNT the parts on the outside of their body which they use in order to stick to a surface.

suckle /sʌkəl/, **suckles, suckling, suckled. 1** V+O When a mother **suckles** her baby, she feeds it by letting it suck milk from her breast.

2 When a baby **suckles**, it sucks milk from its V mother's breast.

suction /sʌkʃən/ is **1** the process by which N UNCOUNT liquids, gases, or other substances are drawn from one space to another. EG *The draining process was assisted by suction.* **2** the process by which two surfaces stick together when the air between them is removed. EG *...stuck on to the bath by suction pads.*

sudden /sʌdən/. **1** Something that is **sudden** ADJ QUALIT happens quickly and unexpectedly. EG *...a sudden drop in the temperature... I felt a sudden twinge of regret.* ◊ **suddenly.** EG *Suddenly, the door opened* ◊ ADV OR *and in walked the boss.* ADV SEN

2 If something happens **all of a sudden**, it happens PHRASE so quickly and unexpectedly that you are surprised by it. EG *All of a sudden I noticed that someone was following me.*

suds /sʌdz/ are the bubbles that are produced N PLURAL when soap is mixed with water.

sue /su:/, **sues, suing, sued.** If you **sue** someone, V+O OR you start a legal case against them, usually in order V : OFT + *for* to claim money from them because they have harmed you in some way. EG *He couldn't even sue them for wrongful arrest.*

suede /sweɪd/ is thin, soft leather with a slightly N UNCOUNT rough surface. EG *...boots of light brown suede... ...a suede jacket.*

suet /sjuːɪt/ is hard animal fat that is used in N UNCOUNT cooking.

suffer /sʌfə/, **suffers, suffering, suffered. 1** If V+O OR V you **suffer** pain, you feel it in your body or in your mind. EG *She was suffering violent abdominal pains... They had suffered a lot of nervous strain.*

2 If you **suffer** from an illness, you are badly V + *from* affected by it. EG *Seventy-five percent of its population suffers from malnutrition.*

3 If you **suffer** something bad, you are in a V+O situation in which something painful, harmful, or very unpleasant happens to you. EG *We were warned to support the government or suffer the consequences.*

4 If you **suffer**, you are badly affected by an V unfavourable event or situation. EG *They would be the first to suffer if these proposals were ever carried out.*

5 If something **suffers**, it becomes worse in quality V or condition because it has been neglected or because of an unfavourable situation. EG *I'm not surprised that your studies are suffering.*

sufferer /sʌfərə/, **sufferers.** A **sufferer** of an N COUNT + SUPP illness is a person who is affected by the illness. EG *...sufferers of chronic disease.*

suffering /sʌfərɪŋ/, **sufferings. Suffering** is se- N UNCOUNT rious pain which someone feels in their body or OR N COUNT their mind. EG *This would cause great hardship and suffering... This might alleviate their sufferings.*

suffice /səfaɪs/, **suffices, sufficing, sufficed.** If V : NO CONT something **suffices**, it is enough to achieve a Formal purpose or to fulfil a need. EG *A very few drains will suffice to drain light or sandy soil.*

sufficiency /səfɪʃənsi/. If there is a **sufficiency** N SING : USU + *of* of something, there is enough of it to achieve a Formal purpose or to fulfil a need. EG *We had 600 jet fighters and a sufficiency of airfields to support them.*

sufficient /səfɪʃənt/. If something is **sufficient** ADJ CLASSIF for a particular purpose, there is as much of it as is necessary. EG *Japan had a reserve of oil sufficient for its needs.* ◊ **sufficiently.** EG *He had not insured* ◊ ADV *the house sufficiently.*

suffix /sʌfɪks/, **suffixes.** A **suffix** is a letter or N COUNT group of letters which is added to the end of a word in order to form a new word, often of a different word class.

SUFFIX

Some groups of letters have the label SUFFIX in the Extra Column. This means that they are not used by themselves as words, but are added to the end of existing words. By adding a suffix to a word, you create a new word which belongs to a different

---

Are there any words with suffixes on these pages? If so, what are they?

word class. For example, you can add 'ly' to the adjective 'sad' and create the adverb 'sadly'. To change 'sad' into a noun, you can add 'ness', making the word 'sadness'.

It is worth noting that there are sometimes spelling changes to a word when you add a suffix to it. For example, 'happy' becomes 'happily' and 'happiness', and 'recite' becomes 'recitation'.

You will find many of the words with suffixes *inside* the entry of the same word without a suffix. For example, **sadly** and **sadness** are in the entry for **sad**. This tells you that there is no change in meaning, and that an example is sufficient to show its use. You can always find the words with suffixes by looking for the lozenge (◊) sign.

Here is a list of all the suffixes defined in this dictionary:

-ability, -able, -al, -ance, -ancy, -ation, -ed, -ence, -ency, -er, -est, -ful, -ibility, -ing, -ion, -ise, -ish, -ism, -ist, -ity, -ize, -less, -ly, -ment, -most, -nd, -ness, -ological, -ologist, -or, -ous, -person, -rd, -st, -th, -tion, -ward, -wise.

suffocate /ˈsʌfəkeɪt/, **suffocates, suffocating,** v-ERG **suffocated.** If someone **suffocates** or if something **suffocates** them, they die because there is no air for them to breathe. EG *The smoke and fumes almost suffocated me... Sir, we are suffocating. We must surrender.* ◊ **suffocation** ◊ N UNCOUNT /ˌsʌfəˈkeɪʃəᵒn/. EG *Many slaves died of heat and suffocation.*

suffrage /ˈsʌfrɪdʒ/ is the right that people have to N UNCOUNT vote for a government or national leader. EG *...the introduction of universal adult suffrage.*

sugar /ˈʃʊɡə/, **sugars, sugaring, sugared. 1** Sug- N MASS **ar** is a sweet substance, often in the form of white or brown crystals, which is used to sweeten food and drink. EG *Lally poured us all a cup of tea and helped herself to sugar... I take my coffee black with no sugar.* **2** When you **sugar** food or drink, you add sugar to v+o it.

sugar beet is a plant which is cultivated for the N UNCOUNT sugar that can be obtained from its root.

sugar cane is a tall tropical plant which is N UNCOUNT cultivated because of the sugar that can be obtained from its thick stems.

sugar lump, sugar lumps. A **sugar lump** is a N COUNT small cube of sugar.

suggest /səˈdʒest/, **suggests, suggesting, sug- gested. 1** If you **suggest** something, you put v-SPEECH forward a plan or idea for someone to think about. EG *We have to suggest a list of possible topics for next term's seminars.* **2** If you **suggest** the name of a person or place, v+o : USU+A you recommend them to someone. EG *Can you suggest somewhere for a short holiday?* **3** If you **suggest** something to someone, you say v+o OR something to them which puts an idea into their v+REPORT mind. EG *I'm not suggesting that the accident was your fault... It would be foolish to suggest that everyone in Britain is rich.* **4** If one thing **suggests** another, it implies it or v+o OR makes you think that it is the case. EG *His expres- v+REPORT sion suggested some pleasure at the fact that I had come... The forecasts suggest that there will be higher unemployment.*

suggestion /səˈdʒestʃəᵒn/, **suggestions. 1** A sug- N COUNT **gestion** is an idea or plan which is put forward for people to think about. EG *I made a few suggestions about how we could spend the afternoon.* **2** If there is a **suggestion** of something, there is a N SING+*of* slight indication or sign of it. EG *He replied to her question with the merest suggestion of a smile.*

3 Suggestion is giving people a particular idea by N UNCOUNT associating it with other ideas. EG *Such is the power of suggestion that within two minutes the patient is asleep.*

suggestive /səˈdʒestɪv/. **1** Something that is **sug-** ADJ PRED+*of* **gestive** of something else gives a hint of it or reminds you of it. EG *His behaviour was suggestive of a cultured man.* **2** Remarks or looks that are **suggestive** cause ADJ QUALIT people to think about sex. EG *The girls stood around, exchanging gossip and calling out sugges- tive remarks.*

suicidal /ˌsjuːɪˈsaɪdᵒl/. **1** People who are **suicidal** ADJ CLASSIF want to kill themselves. EG *What should you do if your friend feels suicidal?* **2** Behaviour that is **suicidal** leads to great danger ADJ CLASSIF or death. EG *They would not risk a suicidal attack on the American fleet.*

suicide /ˈsjuːɪsaɪd/, **suicides. 1** People who com- N UNCOUNT mit **suicide** deliberately kill themselves because OR N COUNT they do not want to continue living. EG *The founder of British history, Clive, committed suicide in 1774.* **2** You also say that people commit **suicide** when N UNCOUNT they deliberately do something which ruins their career or position in society. EG *People had told me it was suicide to admit my mistake.*

suit /sjuːt/, **suits, suiting, suited. 1** A man's **suit** N COUNT consists of a jacket, trousers, and sometimes a waistcoat, all made from the same fabric. EG *He arrived at the office in a suit and tie.* **2** A woman's **suit** consists of a jacket and skirt, or N COUNT sometimes trousers, all made from the same fab- ric. EG *She wore a black suit and a tiny black hat.* **3** A **suit** can also be a piece of clothing that you N COUNT : wear for a particular activity. EG *She was wearing a* USU+SUPP *short robe over her bathing suit.* **4** If something **suits** you, it is the best thing for you v+o : NO CONT in the circumstances. EG *All this suits my purpose very well.* **5** If a piece of clothing or a particular style or v+o : NO CONT colour **suits** you, it makes you look attractive. EG *That colour will suit you... That coat really suits you.* **6** If you say that something **suits** you, you mean v+o : NO CONT that **6.1** it is convenient for you. EG *Would Monday suit you?... It suits me to be registered here.* **6.2** you like it. EG *A job where I was indoors all day wouldn't suit me.* **7** If you **suit** yourself, you do something just v-REFL : because you want to do it, and do not bother to USU IMPER consider other people. EG *Casual people arrive, at times to suit themselves... If later is more conveni- ent, suit yourself.* **8** If people **follow suit**, they do the same thing that PHRASE someone else has just done. EG *He bowed his head. Mother and Jenny followed suit.* **9** In a court of law, a **suit** is a case in which a N COUNT person tries to get justice for some wrong that has been done to them. **10** A **suit** is also one of the four types of card in a N COUNT set of playing cards. These are hearts, diamonds, clubs, and spades.

suitable /ˈsjuːtəbᵒl/. Someone or something that ADJ QUALIT : is **suitable** for a particular purpose or occasion is OFT+*for* right or acceptable for that purpose or occasion. EG *These flats are not really suitable for families with children... It takes years to turn suitable young men into fighter-pilots.* ◊ **suitability** ◊ N UNCOUNT /ˌsjuːtəbɪlˈtiʲ/. EG *...the candidate's intellectual abil- ity and suitability for admission.* ◊ **suitably.** EG *See* ◊ ADV *that you are suitably dressed for the weather... ...suitably trained teachers.*

suitcase /ˈsjuːtkeɪs/, **suitcases.** A **suitcase** is a N COUNT case in which you carry your clothes when you are travelling.

suite /swiːt/, **suites.** A **suite** is **1** a set of rooms in N COUNT a hotel. EG *They always stayed in a suite at the Ritz.* **2** a set of matching furniture for a sitting-room or bathroom. EG *...a three-piece suite for the lounge.*

suited /sjᵘuːtɪ²d/. **1** If something is **suited** to a ADJ PRED: particular purpose or person, it is right or appro- OFT+to/for priate for that purpose or person. EG *They were* *ferred to join clubs more suited to their tastes... He* *considered himself ideally suited for the job of* *Prime Minister.*
2 If a man and a woman are well **suited**, they are ADJ PRED likely to have a successful relationship because they have similar personalities or interests.

suitor /sjᵘuːtə/, **suitors**. A woman's **suitor** is a N COUNT man who wants to marry her. EG *She had many* Outdated *suitors.*

sulfur /sʌlfə/. See **sulphur**.

sulk /sʌlk/, **sulks, sulking, sulked**. If you **sulk**, v you are silent and bad-tempered for a while be- cause you are annoyed about something. EG *He* *sulked and behaved badly for weeks after I refused.*
▸ used as a noun. EG *I thought you were in one of* ▸ N COUNT *your sulks.*

sulky /sʌlkɪ¹/, **sulkier, sulkiest**. Someone who is ADJ QUALIT **sulky** is sulking about something. EG *Sam glowered* *at him in sulky silence.* ◊ **sulkily**. EG *'I don't want* ◊ ADV *anything,' the boy answered sulkily.*

sullen /sʌlən/. Someone who is **sullen** is bad- ADJ QUALIT tempered and does not speak much. EG *...a sullen* *boy... She looked at the Duke with sullen hatred.*
◊ **sullenly**. EG *'So what?' Thomas said sullenly.* ◊ ADV

sulphur /sʌlfə/; spelled **sulfur** in American Eng- N UNCOUNT lish. **Sulphur** is a yellow substance which has a strong unpleasant smell.

sultan /sʌltə⁰n/, **sultans**. A **sultan** is a ruler in N COUNT some Muslim countries. EG *...the Sultan of Oman.*

sultana /sʌltɑːnə/, **sultanas**. Sultanas are dried N COUNT grapes.

sultry /sʌltrɪ¹/. **1** **Sultry** weather is unpleasantly ADJ QUALIT hot and humid. EG *It was hot and sultry.*
2 A **sultry** woman is attractive in a way that ADJ QUALIT suggests hidden passion.

sum /sʌm/, **sums, summing, summed**. **1** A **sum** N PART of money is an amount of money. EG *...the stagger-* *ing sum of 212,000 million pounds... Manufacturers* *spend huge sums of money on advertising their* *product.* ● See also **lump sum**.
2 A **sum** is a simple calculation in arithmetic. EG N COUNT *He couldn't do his sums.*

sum up. 1 If you **sum** something **up**, you describe PHRASAL VB: it as briefly as possible. EG *My mood could be* V+O+ADV *summed up by the single word 'boredom'.* **2** If you V+ADV **sum up** after saying something or **sum up** what has been said, you briefly state the main points again. EG *To sum up: within our society there still* *exist rampant inequalities.* **3** See also **summing** **up**.

summarize /sʌməraɪz/, **summarizes, summa-** V+O OR V **rizing, summarized**; also spelled **summarise**. If you **summarize** something, you give a summary of it. EG *The seven categories can be briefly sum-* *marized as follows.*

summary /sʌmərɪ¹/, **summaries**. **1** A **summary** N COUNT is a short account of something, which gives the main points but not the details. EG *Here is a* *summary of the plot.*
2 You use **in summary** to indicate that what you ADV SEN are about to say is a summary of what has just been said. EG *In summary, all government depart-* *ments are administered rather differently.*
3 Summary actions are done without delay, often ADJ CLASSIF: when something else should have been done first ATTRIB or done instead. EG *...mass arrests and summary* *executions.* ◊ **summarily**. EG *He summarily dis-* ◊ ADV *missed our problem as unimportant... They were* Formal *summarily evicted.*

summer /sʌmə/, **summers**. Summer is the sea- N COUNT OR son between spring and autumn. In the summer N UNCOUNT the weather is usually warm or hot. EG *I am going* *to Greece this summer... ...summer holidays.*

summer school, summer schools. A **summer** N COUNT OR **school** is an educational course on a particular N UNCOUNT subject that is run during the summer.

summertime /sʌmətaɪm/ is the period of time N UNCOUNT during which summer lasts. EG *The dust from the* *roads in the summertime was enough to blind you.*

summery /sʌmərɪ¹/. Something that is **summery** ADJ CLASSIF is suitable for summer or characteristic of sum- mer. EG *...a summery dress... ...a summery fra-* *grance.*

summing up, summings up. A **summing up** is N COUNT a summary of something, especially of the evi- dence presented in a trial. EG *In his summing up,* *the judge again returned to this point.*

summit /sʌmɪt/, **summits**. **1** A **summit** is a N COUNT meeting at which the leaders of two or more countries discuss important matters. EG *Western* *leaders are gathering for this week's Ottawa sum-* *mit... ...a summit meeting.*
2 The **summit** of a mountain is the top of it. N COUNT

summon /sʌmən/, **summons, summoning,** V+O **summoned**. If you **summon** someone, you order them to come to you. EG *He summoned his secre-* *tary... He was summoned to report on the accident.*

summon up. If you **summon up** your strength, PHRASAL VB: energy, or courage, you make a great effort to be V+O+ADV strong, energetic, or brave. EG *...if you can't sum-* *mon up enough energy to get up early... He eventu-* *ally summoned up the courage to ask them if* *Melanie was all right.*

summons /sʌmənz/, **summonses, summonsing,** N COUNT **summonsed**. **1** A **summons** is **1.1** an order to come and see someone. EG *I waited in my office for* *a summons from the boss.* **1.2** an official order to appear in court.
2 If someone **is summonsed**, they are officially V+O: USU PASS ordered to appear in court.

sumptuous /sʌmptjʊəs/. Something that is **sump-** ADJ QUALIT **tuous** is magnificent and obviously very expen- sive. EG *...sumptuous furnishings.*

sum total. The **sum total** of a number of things is N SING: *the*+N all the things added or considered together.

sun /sʌn/, **suns, sunning, sunned**. **1** The **sun** is N SING: *the*+N the ball of fire in the sky that the Earth goes round, and that gives us heat and light.
2 You also refer to the light and heat that reach us N UNCOUNT. from the sun as **sun**. EG *You need plenty of sun and* OR N SING *fresh air... We all sat in the sun.* +SUPP
3 If you **sun** yourself, you sit or lie in a place where V-REFL: OFT+A the sun shines on you. EG *He spent Saturday sunning* *himself on the beach.*

sunbathe /sʌnbeɪθ/, **sunbathes, sunbathing,** v **sunbathed**. When people **sunbathe**, they sit or lie in a place where the sun shines strongly on them, so that they get a suntan. EG *I spent my afternoons* *sunbathing instead of doing my work.*

sunburn /sʌnbɜːn/. If someone has **sunburn**, N UNCOUNT their skin is bright pink and sore because they have spent too much time in hot sunshine.

sunburnt /sʌnbɜːnt/; also spelled **sunburned**. ADJ QUALIT Someone who is **sunburnt 1** has sore, bright pink skin because they have spent too much time in hot sunshine. EG *His neck was badly sunburnt.* **2** has very brown skin because they have spent a lot of time in the sunshine. EG *Carlo was handsomely* *sunburned.*

sundae /sʌndiː, -deɪ/, **sundaes**. A **sundae** is a dish N COUNT of ice cream with cream and nuts or fruit on top.

Sunday /sʌndɪ¹/, **Sundays**. Sunday is one of the N UNCOUNT seven days of the week. It is the day after Saturday OR N COUNT and before Monday. Christians go to church on Sunday. EG *I never eat breakfast on Sundays.*

Sunday school, Sunday schools. If children go N UNCOUNT to **Sunday school**, they go to a special class on OR N COUNT Sundays in order to learn about Christianity.

sundial /sʌndaɪəl/, **sundials**. A **sundial** is a de- N COUNT vice used for telling the time when the sun is shining. The shadow of a pointer falls on a flat

Find another word for sunset.

surface that is marked with the hours, and points to the correct hour.

sundown /sʌndaun/ is the same as sunset. EG *It was about an hour before sundown.* N UNCOUNT American

sundry /sʌndri¹/. 1 If you refer to **sundry** things or people, you mean several things or people of various sorts. EG *...stools, wicker mats, food bowls, and sundry other objects.* ADJ CLASSIF: ATTRIB Formal

2 **All and sundry** means everyone. EG *She was fondly known to all and sundry as 'Little Madge'.* PHRASE Informal

sunflower /sʌnflauə/, **sunflowers.** A **sunflower** is a very tall plant with large yellow flowers. N COUNT

sung /sʌŋ/ is the past participle of **sing.**

sunglasses /sʌnglɑ:sɪz/ are spectacles with dark lenses which you wear to protect your eyes from bright sunlight. N PLURAL

sunk /sʌŋk/ is the past participle of **sink.**

sunken /sʌŋkə⁰n/. 1 **Sunken** is used to describe 1.1 things that have sunk to the bottom of the sea or a lake. EG *...the remains of a sunken battleship.* ADJ CLASSIF: ATTRIB

1.2 things that are constructed below the level of the surrounding area. EG *...a sunken garden.*

2 If you have **sunken** cheeks or eyes or a **sunken** chest, they curve inwards and make you look thin and unwell. ADJ CLASSIF

sun lamp, sun lamps. A **sun lamp** is a lamp that produces rays which can make people's skin suntanned. N COUNT

sunlight /sʌnlaɪt/ is the light that comes from the sun. EG *The sea sparkled in the brilliant sunlight.* N UNCOUNT

sunlit /sʌnlɪt/. **Sunlit** places are brightly lit by the sun. EG *...the sunlit slopes of the valley.* ADJ CLASSIF

sunny /sʌni¹/, **sunnier, sunniest.** 1 When it is **sunny**, the sun is shining brightly. ADJ QUALIT

2 **Sunny** places are brightly lit by the sun. EG *...a lovely sunny region of green hills and valleys.* ADJ QUALIT

sunrise /sʌnraɪz/, **sunrises.** 1 **Sunrise** is the time in the morning when the sun first appears in the sky. EG *They left their camp at sunrise.* N UNCOUNT

2 A **sunrise** is the colours and light that you see in the eastern part of the sky when the sun first appears. EG *...the beautiful sunrise over the sea.* N COUNT OR N UNCOUNT

sunset /sʌnsɛt/, **sunsets.** 1 **Sunset** is the time in the evening when the sun disappears out of sight. EG *We'll leave just before sunset.* N UNCOUNT

2 A **sunset** is the colours and light that you see in the western part of the sky when the sun disappears in the evening. EG *You must see some beautiful sunsets here.* N COUNT OR N UNCOUNT

sunshine /sʌnʃaɪn/ is the light that comes from the sun. EG *Families were scattered along the beach enjoying the sunshine.* N UNCOUNT

sunstroke /sʌnstrəuk/ is an illness caused by spending too much time in hot sunshine. N UNCOUNT

suntan /sʌntæn/, **suntans.** If you have a **suntan**, the sun has turned your skin an attractive brown colour. N COUNT

sun-tanned. Someone who is **sun-tanned** has attractively brown skin because they have been in the sunshine. ADJ QUALIT

super /sj⁰u:pə/. 1 If you say that someone or something is **super**, you mean that they are very nice or good. EG *I've got a super secretary.* ADJ CLASSIF Informal

2 **Super** is also used to describe things that are larger or better than similar things. EG *...a super plastic that is resistant to high temperatures... ...the building of new super warships.* ADJ CLASSIF: ATTRIB

superb /sj⁰upɜ:b/. If something is **superb**, its quality is very good indeed. EG *The children's library is superb.* ◊ **superbly**. EG *...a small but superbly equipped workshop.* ADJ CLASSIF ◊ ADV

supercilious /sj⁰u:pəsɪlɪəs/. If you are **supercilious**, you behave in a scornful way towards other people because you think they are inferior to you; used showing disapproval. EG *A slow supercilious smile crossed her face.* ADJ QUALIT

superficial /sj⁰u:pəfɪʃə⁰l/. 1 Something that is **superficial** involves only the most obvious or most easily understood aspects of something. EG *They've only got a superficial knowledge of linguistics... The new scheme has superficial similarities with the old one.* ◊ **superficially**. EG *Superficially it looks rather harmless.* ADJ QUALIT ◊ ADV OR ADV SEN

2 People who are **superficial** do not care very deeply about anything or are not interested in anything serious or important. ADJ QUALIT

3 **Superficial** wounds are not very deep or severe. ADJ QUALIT

superfluous /sj⁰u:pɜ:fluəs/. Something that is **superfluous** is unnecessary or is no longer needed. EG *Certain parts of our religion have become superfluous... I had not been using maps at all. They were superfluous with Eddie around.* ADJ CLASSIF

superhuman /sj⁰u:pəhju:mən/. If you describe a quality that someone has as **superhuman**, you mean that it seems to be much greater than that of ordinary people. EG *You must have superhuman strength... I controlled myself with a superhuman effort.* ADJ CLASSIF

superimpose /sj⁰u:pə⁰rɪmpəuz/, **superimposes, superimposing, superimposed.** If you **superimpose** one image on another, you put one image on top of another one. EG *Three photos were superimposed one on top of the other.* V+O: OFT +on/with

superintendent /sj⁰u:pə⁰rɪntɛndənt/, **superintendents.** A **superintendent** is 1 a person who has a high rank in the police force. EG *...Superintendent Spence.* 2 a person who is responsible for a particular thing or department. EG *He was attached to the College as Superintendent of Buildings.* N COUNT

superior /sj⁰u:pɪərɪə/, **superiors.** 1 Something or someone that is **superior** to something or someone else is better than them. EG *The computer is vastly superior to the book... I secretly feel superior to him... The school prided itself upon its policy of providing a superior education.* ◊ **superiority** /sj⁰u:pɪərɪɒrɪ¹ti¹/. EG *...the great superiority of Hoyland over younger abstract painters.* ADJ QUALIT: OFT+to ◊ N UNCOUNT

2 Someone who is **superior** to someone else is more important or has more authority. EG *These matters are better left to someone superior to you.* ADJ CLASSIF: OFT+to

3 Someone who is **superior** behaves in a way which shows that they believe they are better than other people. EG *'You wouldn't understand,' Clarissa said in a superior way.* ADJ QUALIT

4 Your **superior** is a person who has a higher rank in an organization or a higher social position than you. EG *He was called to the office of a superior to be reprimanded... Myra was his social superior.* N COUNT

> **SUPERL** stands for **superlative**
> Some adjectives, and a few adverbs, have the label SUPERL in the Extra Column. This tells you that they are in the superlative form. Therefore, words like *best, worst,* and *most* have this label.
> See the entry headed ADJECTIVES for more information.

superlative /sj⁰u:pɜ:lətɪv/, **superlatives.** In grammar, a **superlative** is the form of an adjective which indicates that the person or object being described has more of a particular quality or character than anyone or anything else in a group. N COUNT

supermarket /sj⁰u:pəmɑ:kɪt/, **supermarkets.** A **supermarket** is a large shop which sells all kinds of food and household goods. N COUNT

supernatural /sj⁰u:pənætʃrəl/. 1 **Supernatural** creatures, forces, and events are believed by some people to exist or happen, although they are impossible according to scientific laws. EG *...witchcraft, the supernatural power to cure or control.* ADJ CLASSIF

2 Supernatural things and events are referred to as the **supernatural**. EG *Do you believe in the supernatural?* N SING: the+N

superpower /sj⁰u:pəpauə/, **superpowers.** A **superpower** is a very powerful country. When N COUNT people talk about 'the superpowers', they usually mean the USA and the USSR.

supersede /sjˈuːpəsiːd/, **supersedes, superseding, superseded.** If something **supersedes** something else, it replaces it, often because the other thing has become old-fashioned. EG *Steam locomotives were superseded by diesel... New ways of thinking superseded older ones... This system is already being superseded.*   v+o : USU PASS

supersonic /sjˈuːpəsɒnɪk/. **Supersonic** aircraft travel faster than the speed of sound. EG *...the demand for supersonic travel.*   ADJ CLASSIF

superstar /sjˈuːpəstɑː/, **superstars.** A **superstar** is a very famous entertainer or sports player. EG *The press built me up into a superstar.*   N COUNT Informal

superstition /sjˈuːpəstɪʃəⁿn/, **superstitions.** **Superstition** is belief in things that are not real or possible, for example magic. EG *They were peasants filled with ignorance and superstition... ...old prejudices and superstitions.*   N UNCOUNT OR N COUNT

superstitious /sjˈuːpəstɪʃəs/. People who are **superstitious** believe in things that are not real or possible, for example magic. EG *...a superstitious man with an unnatural fear of the dark... ...superstitious practices.*   ADJ QUALIT

supervise /sjˈuːpəvaɪz/, **supervises, supervising, supervised.** If you **supervise** an activity or a person, you make sure that the activity is done correctly or that the person is behaving correctly. EG *Miss Young had three netball games to supervise... One evening, when there were no staff to supervise her, she walked out of the hospital.*   v+o OR V
◊ **supervision** /sjˈuːpəvɪʒəⁿn/. EG *They are under the supervision of qualified social workers.*   ◊ N UNCOUNT

supervisor /sjˈuːpəvaɪzə/, **supervisors.** A **supervisor** is a person who supervises activities or people, especially workers or students. EG *The maintenance supervisor dispatched a crew to repair the damage... My supervisor said he would strongly recommend me for the course.*   N COUNT

SUPP stands for **supporting word or words**
Many nouns have the label +SUPP in the Extra Column. This means that the noun is not usually used on its own in this sense, but is used with other words, phrases, or clauses which give extra information about it or which add to its meaning in some way.
See the entry headed NOUNS for more information.

---

supper /sʌpə/, **suppers. Supper** is **1** a meal eaten in the early part of the evening. EG *He insisted on staying for supper.* **2** a small meal eaten just before you go to bed at night.   N UNCOUNT OR N COUNT

supplant /səplɑːnt/, **supplants, supplanting, supplanted.** To **supplant** something or someone means to take their place. EG *Electric cars may one day supplant petrol-driven ones... He began his campaign to supplant Gaitskell as party leader.*   v+o Formal

supple /sʌpəⁿl/. **1** Someone who is **supple** moves and bends easily. EG *She had once been slim and supple... He keeps his fingers supple with regular exercises.*   ADJ QUALIT

2 If an object or material is **supple**, it is soft and bends easily without cracking or breaking. EG *The leather straps were worn supple with use.*   ADJ QUALIT

supplement /sʌplɪməⁿnt/, **supplements, supplementing, supplemented.** **1** If you **supplement** something, you add something to it, especially in order to make it more adequate. EG *They had to get a job to supplement the family income... I supplemented my diet with vitamin pills.*   v+o : OFT +with/by

2 A **supplement** is something that is added to something else, especially in order to make it more adequate. EG *They will sometimes eat fish as a supplement to their natural diet.*   N COUNT : OFT +to

3 A magazine or newspaper **supplement** is a separate part of a magazine or newspaper. EG *...the Times Literary Supplement.* ● See also **colour supplement.**   N COUNT

supplementary /sʌplɪməⁿntəⁿriː/ is used to describe something that is added to another thing in order to make it more adequate. EG *You can claim a supplementary pension.*   ADJ CLASSIF : ATTRIB

supplementary benefit is an amount of money that the government in Britain gives regularly to people with no income or very low incomes. EG *They asked if I was on supplementary benefit.*   N UNCOUNT

supplier /səplaɪə/, **suppliers.** A **supplier** is a person or firm that provides you with something such as goods or equipment. EG *...textile suppliers.*   N COUNT

supply /səplaɪ/, **supplies, supplying, supplied. 1** If you **supply** someone with something, you provide them with it. EG *I can supply you with food and drink... Germany is supplying the steel for the new pipeline... Most large towns there are supplied with electricity.*   v+o : OFT +for/with

2 A **supply** of something is an amount of it which someone has or which is available for them to use. EG *Bill had his own supply of whisky... Most houses now have lavatories and a hot water supply.*   N COUNT

3 Supplies are food, equipment, and other things needed by a group of people, for example by an army or by people going on an expedition. EG *The plane had been ferrying military supplies over the border.*   N PLURAL

4 Supply is the amount of something that can be produced and made available for people to buy. EG *Economic stability can only be reached if demand and supply are in approximate balance.*   N UNCOUNT

5 If something is **in short supply**, there is very little of it available. EG *Petrol is in desperately short supply.*   PHRASE

support /səpɔːt/, **supports, supporting, supported. 1** If you **support** someone or their ideas or aims, you agree with them, want them to succeed, and perhaps help them. EG *A lot of building workers supported the campaign... His work colleagues refused to support him.* ▸ used as a noun. EG *The party declared its support for the campaign... The group drew some support from the idealistic young.*   v+o ▸ N UNCOUNT

2 If you **support** a sports team, especially a football team, you want them to win and perhaps go regularly to their games.   v+o

3 If you give **support** to someone during a difficult or unhappy time, you are kind to them and help them. EG *They find it hard to give their children emotional support.*   N UNCOUNT

4 If something **supports** an object, it is underneath the object and holding it up. EG *...the steel girders that supported the walkway... ...a horizontal bar supported by two vertical pillars.*   v+o

5 A **support** is a bar or other object that supports something. EG *Most large scale buildings now have steel supports.*   N COUNT

6 If you **support** yourself, you prevent yourself from falling by holding onto something or by leaning on something. EG *I clung to the outside edge of the door to support myself.* ▸ used as a noun. EG *She was standing behind the ladder and holding on to it for support.*   V-REFL ▸ N UNCOUNT

7 Financial **support** is money provided to enable a firm or organization to continue, usually by the government. EG *These industries were dependent on state support.*   N UNCOUNT

8 If you **support** someone, you provide them with money or the things that they need. EG *He has a wife and three children to support.*   v+o

9 If a fact **supports** a statement or a theory, it helps to show that it is true or correct. EG *There*   v+o

---

On these pages find an informal way of saying 'yes'.

was simply no visible evidence to support such a theory. ▸ used as a noun. EG *Scholars have found* ▸ N UNCOUNT *little support for this interpretation... In support of this view, Rose cites Pollock's own evidence.*

supporter /sə⁰pɔːtə/, **supporters.** A **supporter** is N COUNT + SUPP a person who supports someone or something, for example a political leader or a sports team. EG *The Minister's supporters did not desert him in his hour of need... He's an Everton supporter.*

supportive /sə⁰pɔːtɪv/. If you are **supportive**, you ADJ QUALIT are kind and helpful to someone at a difficult or unhappy time in their life. EG *When I became a widow he was supportive.*

suppose /sə⁰pəʊz/, **supposes, supposing, supposed.** 1 If you **suppose** that something is true, V + REPORT : you think that it is likely to be true. EG *He supposed* ONLY *that;* *that MPs were unaware of the danger... It was* ALSO V + O + C *quite reasonable to suppose that he wanted the money too... The situation was even worse than was supposed.*

2 You say **I suppose** when you are not entirely PHRASE certain or enthusiastic about what you are saying. EG *I suppose he wasn't trying hard enough... I don't suppose you would be prepared to stay in Edinburgh?... We could take Davis with us, I suppose... 'So it was worth doing?' - 'I suppose so.'*

3 You say **you don't suppose** to introduce a PHRASE possibility which you want someone else to give their opinion about. EG *You don't suppose he'll get lost out there?*

4 You use **suppose** or **supposing** when you are CONJ considering a possible situation or action and trying to think what effects it would have. EG *Suppose we don't say a word, and somebody else finds out about it... Supposing something should go wrong, what would you do then?*

supposed /sə⁰pəʊzd/. 1 The phrase **be supposed** PHRASE is used in these ways. **1.1** If you say that something **is supposed** to be done, you mean that it should be done because of a rule, instruction, or custom. EG *You are supposed to report it to the police as soon as possible... I'm not supposed to talk to you about this.* **1.2** If you say that something **is supposed** to happen, especially when it does not in fact happen, you mean that it is planned or intended to happen. EG *I was supposed to go last summer... A machine at the entrance is supposed to check the tickets.* **1.3** You say that something **is supposed** to be true when people think that it is true but you do not know for certain that it is true. EG *They are supposed to be the best in London... The hill was supposed to be haunted by the ghost of a leper.*

2 You also use **supposed** to express doubt about a ADJ CLASSIF : way of describing someone or something that is ATTRIB generally believed or stated. EG *...his supposed ancestor, the pirate Henry Morgan... the supposed benefits of a progressive welfare state.*

◊ **supposedly.** EG *...a robot supposedly capable of* ◊ ADV *understanding spoken commands.*

supposition /sʌpəzɪʃⁿn/, **suppositions.** A **sup-** N COUNT **position** is an idea or statement which is thought Formal or assumed to be true. EG *The supposition is that the infiltrators knew the raids were to take place... That is a most unlikely supposition.*

suppress /səpres/, **suppresses, suppressing, suppressed.** 1 If an army or government **sup-** V + O **presses** an activity, they prevent it from continuing. EG *The army soon suppressed the revolt.*

◊ **suppression** /səpreʃⁿn/. EG *...the suppression of* ◊ N UNCOUNT : *freedom... ...the suppression of rebellions.* USU + SUPP

2 If someone **suppresses** a piece of information, V + O they prevent it from becoming known to the general public. EG *The committee's report has been suppressed.* ◊ **suppression.** EG *...the deliberate* ◊ N UNCOUNT : *suppression of information.* USU + SUPP

3 If you **suppress** your feelings, you prevent V + O yourself from expressing them. EG *Suppressing her annoyance, she smiled at him... She was struggling*

to suppress her sobs. ◊ **suppression.** EG *...the* ◊ N UNCOUNT : *polite suppression of a yawn.* USU + SUPP

supremacy /sjⁿuːpreməsɪ/. If one group of people N UNCOUNT has **supremacy** over another group, they are more powerful than the other group. EG *...the supremacy of the House of Commons... Their political supremacy continued.*

supreme /sjuːpriːm/. 1 **Supreme** is used in the ADJ CLASSIF : title of a person or an official group to indicate that ATTRIB they are at the highest level in a particular organization or system. EG *The Supreme Commander ordered their release... ...the Supreme Court.*

2 You also use **supreme** to emphasize the great- ADJ CLASSIF : ness of something. EG *...one of this century's su-* USU ATTRIB *preme achievements... ...tasks of supreme importance.* ◊ **supremely.** EG *...a supremely important* ◊ SUBMOD *moment... The only thing he had ever been able to do supremely well was to fly airplanes.*

sure /ʃʊə, ʃɔː/, **surer, surest.** 1 If you are **sure** ADJ PRED that something is true, you are certain that it is OFT + REPORT true. EG *I'm sure she's right... Something had gone* OR *of* *wrong, he was sure of it... I'm not quite sure but I think it's half past five.*

2 If you are **sure** about your feelings or wishes, you ADJ PRED : know exactly what you feel or what you want to do. OFT + REPORT EG *Jane wasn't sure how she felt about being married... Are you sure you won't have another drink?*

3 If you are **sure** of yourself, you are very confi- ADJ PRED + *of* dent about your own abilities or opinions.

4 If you say that someone is **sure** of getting ADJ PRED + *of* something, you mean that they will certainly get it. EG *We can be sure of success... You could not always be sure of winning.*

5 If you say that something is **sure** to happen, you ADJ PRED mean that it will certainly happen. EG *He was sure* + *to*-INF *to see her again... We're sure to get a place.*

6 If you **make sure** that something is the way that PHRASE you want or expect it to be, you check that it is that way. EG *He glanced over his shoulder to make sure that there was nobody listening... Make sure the brake has been fully released.*

7 If you **make sure** that something is done, you PHRASE take action so that it is done. EG *Ask for a receipt and make sure that you get it... I did it to make sure you noticed.*

8 If you tell someone to **be sure** to do something, PHRASE you mean that they must not forget to do it. EG *Be sure to remind your uncle.*

9 You use **sure** to describe something such as a ADJ QUALIT : method or a sign when it is reliable or accurate. EG USU ATTRIB *Going to places is a sure way of getting to know them... Wood dust beneath a piece of furniture is a sure sign of woodworm... She had a sure grasp of the subject.*

10 **Sure** is an informal way of saying 'yes'. EG *'Can I* CONVENTION *go with you?' - 'Sure.'* Informal

11 You can also use **sure** in order to emphasize ADV what you are saying. EG *He sure is cute... You sure* Informal *do have an interesting job.* American

12 If you say that something is **for sure** or that you PHRASE know it **for sure**, you mean that it is definitely true Informal or will definitely happen. EG *One thing was for sure, there was nothing wrong with Allen's eyesight.*

13 You say **sure enough** to confirm that some- ADV SEN thing is really true or is actually happening. EG *'The baby's crying,' she said. Sure enough, a yelling noise was coming from upstairs.*

surely /ʃʊəliˈ ʃɔː-/. 1 You use **surely** to emphasize ADV SEN that you think something is true, and often to express surprise that other people do not agree with you. EG *He surely knew the danger... She was surely one of the rarest women of our time... You don't mind that surely?... Good heavens! Surely you are not suggesting she did it on purpose?*

2 If you say that something is happening **slowly** PHRASE **but surely**, you mean that it is happening gradually and cannot be stopped. EG *Slowly but surely we're becoming a computer-centred society.*

surf /sɜːf/ is the mass of white foam that is formed N UNCOUNT : by waves as they fall upon the shore. EG *We* OFT *the*+N *watched the children play in the surf.*

surface /ˈsɜːfɪs/. **surfaces, surfacing, surfaced.**
1 The **surface** of something is the top part of it or N COUNT : the outside of it. EG *...the jumble which covers the* USU+SUPP *surface of my desk... A gentle breeze rippled the surface of the sea... ...the surface of the moon... ...holes in the road surface.*
2 The **surface** of a situation is what can be seen N COUNT easily rather than what is hidden or not immediate- ly obvious. EG *His job was not as enviable as it appeared on the surface... This dispute first came to the surface in 1962.* ● If a quality or feeling is ● PHRASE **below** or **beneath the surface** of something such as a society or a play, it is not obvious when you first consider the thing. EG *You don't have to look far to encounter the tensions beneath the surface.*
3 If someone or something under water **surfaces**, V : OFT+A they come up to the surface of the water. EG *Bobby surfaced twenty feet in front of the boat.*
4 When a piece of news or a feeling **surfaces**, it V becomes known or becomes obvious. EG *Such ru- mours have surfaced several times over the past ten years... Concern for the children never took long to surface.*
5 When someone **surfaces** after sleeping, they V : OFT+A appear, usually later than expected. EG *He didn't* Informal *surface today until after eleven.*

surfboard /ˈsɜːfbɔːd/, **surfboards.** A **surfboard** is N COUNT a long narrow board that is used in surfing.

surfeit /ˈsɜːfɪt/. A **surfeit** of something is an N SING : amount which is too large. EG *Recently there has* a+N+*of* *been a surfeit of cricket on the television.* Formal

surfing /ˈsɜːfɪŋ/. When someone goes **surfing**, N ING they ride towards the seashore on the top of a big wave while standing or lying on a surfboard.

surge /sɜːdʒ/, **surges, surging, surged. 1** A N COUNT : **surge** is a sudden great increase in something. EG USU SING *A surge of activity spread through the party...* +in/of *There has been a surge in sales of Waugh's novels.*
2 A **surge** of an emotion such as pity or anger is a N COUNT : sudden strong feeling of it. EG *She felt a surge of* USU SING+*of* *affection for him... ...a surge of jealousy.*
3 If an emotion or sensation **surges** in you, you V+A feel it suddenly and powerfully. EG *Hope surged in* Literary *Peter... Relief surged through him.*
4 If people or vehicles **surge** forward, they move V+A forward suddenly in a mass. EG *When the doors were flung open, a crowd surged in.* ◊ **surging**. EG ◊ ADJ CLASSIF : *...surging crowds of demonstrators... ...a surging* ATTRIB *swarm of people.*
5 If water **surges**, it moves forward suddenly and V : USU+A powerfully. EG *...the tides surging over the rocks.*

surgeon /ˈsɜːdʒən/, **surgeons.** A **surgeon** is a N COUNT doctor who performs surgery. EG *...a brain surgeon.*

surgery /ˈsɜːdʒəriː/, **surgeries. 1 Surgery** is N UNCOUNT medical treatment in which someone's body is cut open so that a doctor can repair or remove a diseased or damaged part. EG *He has had major abdominal surgery.* ● See also **plastic surgery.**
2 A **surgery** is the room or house where a doctor N COUNT or dentist works. British
3 A doctor's **surgery** is also the period of time N COUNT OR each day when he or she sees patients at the N UNCOUNT surgery. EG *I'll be in for morning surgery at ten.* British

surgical /ˈsɜːdʒɪkəl/. **1 Surgical** equipment and ADJ CLASSIF : clothing is used in surgery. EG *...surgical instru-* ATTRIB *ments... ...a surgical mask.*
2 Surgical treatment involves surgery. EG *Some* ADJ CLASSIF : *people can have their vision restored by a surgical* ATTRIB *operation.* ◊ **surgically**. EG *The cataract can then* ◊ ADV *be removed surgically.*

surly /ˈsɜːliː/. Someone who is **surly** behaves in a ADJ QUALIT rude, bad-tempered way. EG *His voice was surly.*

surmise /səˈmaɪz/, **surmises, surmising, sur-** V+REPORT, **mised.** If you **surmise** that something is true, you OR V+O guess that it is true, although it may not be. EG *The* Formal *last question, Turing surmised, was the key one...*

The French, for reasons which could only be surmised, opposed the idea.

surmount /səˈmaʊnt/, **surmounts, sur- mounting, surmounted. 1** If you **surmount** a V+O problem or difficulty, you deal successfully with it. EG *She managed to surmount this obstacle.*
2 If something **is surmounted** by a particular V+O : USU PASS thing, that thing is on top of it. EG *The column is* Formal *surmounted by a statue.*

surname /ˈsɜːneɪm/, **surnames.** Your **surname** N COUNT : is the name that you share with other members of USU+POSS your family. It is usually your last name. EG *'What's your surname?' – 'Barker.'*

surpass /səˈpɑːs/, **surpasses, surpassing, sur-** V+O **passed.** To **surpass** someone or something means Formal to be better than them, to do better than them, or to have more of a particular quality than them. EG *The women were able to equal or surpass the men who worked beside them... Your excellent perfor- mance surpassed all expectations... In my opinion the jewel is surpassed in beauty by the other ornaments.*

surplus /ˈsɜːpləs/, **surpluses.** A **surplus** is a quan- N COUNT OR tity of something that is extra or more than is N UNCOUNT needed. EG *...the recent worldwide surplus of crude oil... In this continent there is a vast surplus of workers.* ▶ used as an adjective. EG *...surplus grain.* ▶ ADJ CLASSIF

surprise /səˈpraɪz/, **surprises, surprising, sur- prised. 1** A **surprise** is an unexpected event. EG N COUNT *This ruling came as a surprise to everyone... 'Why don't you tell me?' – 'Because I want it to be a surprise.'* ▶ used before a noun. EG *The minister* ▶ N MOD *made the surprise announcement in a statement earlier today... ...a surprise attack.*
2 Surprise is the feeling that you have when N UNCOUNT something unexpected happens. EG *Boylan looked at her in surprise... To my surprise, he nodded and agreed.*
3 If something **takes** you **by surprise**, it happens PHRASE to you suddenly or unexpectedly. EG *The storm, when it broke, took them entirely by surprise.*
4 If something **surprises** you, it gives you a feeling V+O of surprise. EG *I surprised everyone by gobbling an enormous lunch... It would not surprise me if he ends up in jail.*
5 If you **surprise** someone, you attack them or V+O find them when they are not expecting it. EG *They were surprised by a unit of US marines during the night... She feared her parents would return and surprise them.*

surprised /səˈpraɪzd/. If you are **surprised** by ADJ QUALIT : something, you have a feeling of surprise, because USU PRED it is unexpected or unusual. EG *The twins were very surprised to see Ralph... I was surprised at the number of bicycles... Gretchen stood up, surprised that Miss Saunders remembered her name.*

surprising /səˈpraɪzɪŋ/. Something that is **sur-** ADJ QUALIT **prising** is unexpected or unusual and makes you feel surprised. EG *He leapt out of the car with surprising agility... It was surprising how much money she managed to earn.* ◊ **surprisingly.** EG *It* ◊ SUBMOD *was surprisingly cheap... Not surprisingly the pro-* OR ADV SEN *posal met with hostile reactions.*

surreal /səˈrɪəl/ means the same as surrealistic. ADJ QUALIT

surrealist /səˈrɪəlɪst/. **Surrealist** paintings show ADJ CLASSIF : strange objects or strange combinations of objects. ATTRIB

surrealistic /səˌrɪəˈlɪstɪk/. If you describe a situa- ADJ QUALIT tion as **surrealistic**, you mean that it is very strange and like a dream. EG *The search had a kind of mad, surrealistic quality.*

surrender /səˈrɛndə/, **surrenders, surrender- ing, surrendered. 1** If you **surrender**, you stop V fighting or resisting someone and agree that you have been beaten. EG *All the British forces surren- dered... The protesters surrendered to the police*

If someone is called James Watt, what is his surname?

after about an hour. ▸ used as a noun. EG *They tried* ▸ N UNCOUNT
to starve us into surrender.

2 If you **surrender** to a force, temptation, or V : OFT+*to*
feeling, you allow it to gain control over you or to
influence you. EG *A nation of nature-lovers seemed
to have surrendered to technology... ...surrendering
to a sense of apathy.*

3 If you **surrender** something, you give it up or let V+O : OFT+*to*
someone else have it. EG *The United States would
never surrender this territory.* ▸ used as a noun. EG ▸ N UNCOUNT
The surrender of liberties is irrevocable.

surreptitious /sʌrəˈptɪʃəs/. A **surreptitious** ac- ADJ QUALIT
tion is done secretly. EG *He began paying surreptitious visits to betting shops.* ◊ **surreptitiously.** EG ◊ ADV
Rudolph looked surreptitiously at his watch.

surrogate /ˈsʌrəgeɪt, -gət/, **surrogates.** You use ADJ CLASSIF :
surrogate to describe a person or thing that acts ATTRIB
as a substitute for someone or something else. EG Formal
Uncle Paul has become a surrogate father to me.
▸ used as a noun. EG *...a surrogate for another* ▸ N COUNT
person.

surrogate mother, surrogate mothers. A **sur-** N COUNT
rogate mother is a woman who has agreed to give
birth to a baby on behalf of another woman.

surround /səˈraʊnd/, **surrounds, surrounding,**
surrounded. 1 If something **surrounds** something V+O : OFT PASS
else, it is situated all around it. EG *Muscles surround
blood vessels in the body... The house was surrounded by high walls.*

2 If people **surround** a person or place, they V+O
spread out so that they are positioned all the way
round. EG *Don't get near him. Just surround him
and keep him there.*

3 If problems or dangers **surround** something, V+O
they exist all around it or are closely associated
with it. EG *...the dangers which surround us... ...the
uncertainty surrounding the future of the railways.*

4 If you **surround** yourself with things, you make V-REFL+*with*
sure that you have a lot of them near you all the
time. EG *Get involved in social activities and surround yourself with friends.*

surrounding /səˈraʊndɪŋ/, **surroundings.** 1 You ADJ CLASSIF :
use **surrounding** to describe the area which is all ATTRIB
around a particular place. EG *Foxes started coming
in from the surrounding countryside... They could
see into the courtyard from the roofs of the surrounding buildings.*

2 You can refer to the place where you live or N PLURAL
where you are at the moment as your **surroundings.** EG *We used to live in nice surroundings.*

surveillance /səˈveɪləns/ is the careful watching N UNCOUNT
of someone, especially by an organization such as Formal
the police or the army. EG *Everyone we knew was
under surveillance... They intensified their surveillance of her home.*

survey, surveys, surveying, surveyed; pronounced /səˈveɪ/ when it is a verb, and /ˈsɜːveɪ/
when it is a noun.

1 If you **survey** something, you look carefully at V+O
the whole of it. EG *He drove to a point from which
he could survey the beach... She stepped back and
surveyed her work.*

2 When people **survey** an area of land, they V+O
examine it and measure it, usually in order to
make a map of it. EG *He had the land surveyed from
a helicopter.*

3 When someone **surveys** a house, they examine it V+O
carefully and report on its structure, usually in
order to give advice to a person who is buying it.

4 A **survey** is 4.1 a detailed investigation of N COUNT
something, for example people's behaviour or opinions. EG *This book was based on a survey of a
thousand male and female graduates... ...a national
survey of eye diseases among children.* 4.2 an
examination of an area of land. EG *...aerial surveys.*
4.3 a careful examination of a house in order to
report on its condition.

surveyor /səˈveɪə/, **surveyors.** A **surveyor** is a N COUNT
person whose job is to survey houses or land.

survival /səˈvaɪvəl/, **survivals.** 1 **Survival** is N UNCOUNT
continuing to live in spite of nearly dying or being
in great difficulty. EG *What are their chances of
survival?... ...the day-to-day struggle for survival.*

2 Something that is a **survival** from an earlier N COUNT
time has continued to exist from that time. EG *The* Formal
*royal house is full of survivals from many centu-
ries.*

survive /səˈvaɪv/, **survives, surviving, survived.**
1 If someone **survives** or if they **survive** a V OR V+O :
disaster or illness, they continue to live in spite of NO PASS,
coming close to death. EG *Four of his brothers died:* NO IMPER
*the fifth survived... Very few people survived the
immediate effects of the explosion... She is Britain's
longest surviving transplant patient.*

2 If you **survive** someone, you continue to live V+O :
after they have died. EG *She will probably survive* NO IMPER
me by many years.

3 If something **survives**, it continues to exist from V OR V+O :
an earlier time. EG *I doubt whether the National* NO PASS,
Health Service will survive to the end of the NO IMPER
*century... The project survived three changes of
government.*

4 If you **survive** a difficult experience, you man- V+O OR V :
age to cope with it and do not let it affect you too NO PASS,
badly. EG *She seems to have survived the divorce* NO IMPER
*pretty well... You have to make difficult decisions
to survive in business.*

survive on. If you **survive on** a particular PHRASAL VB :
amount of money or food, you earn just enough V+PREP
money to buy essential things to live, or you have
just enough food to live. EG *My salary's only just
enough to survive on... They store water to survive
on during the drought.*

survivor /səˈvaɪvə/, **survivors.** 1 A **survivor** of a N COUNT :
disaster or illness is someone who continues to live OFT+SUPP
afterwards in spite of coming close to death. EG *I
talked to one of the survivors of the crash.*

2 If you describe someone as a **survivor**, you N COUNT
mean that they are able to carry on with their life
even though they experience many difficulties. EG
He sounds like one of life's survivors.

susceptible /səˈseptɪbəl/. 1 If you are **suscep-** ADJ PRED :
tible to something, you are likely to be influenced USU+*to*
by it. EG *We are all susceptible to advertising...
These organizations are susceptible to Government pressure.*

2 If you are **susceptible** to a disease or injury, you ADJ QUALIT :
are likely to be affected by it. EG *Many people were* USU+*to*
lightly dressed and therefore susceptible to burns
on their skin.* ◊ **susceptibility** /səˌseptəˈbɪlɪtiˈ/. ◊ N UNCOUNT :
EG *...his susceptibility to infection.* OFT+*to*

suspect, suspects, suspecting, suspected; pronounced /səˈspekt/ when it is a verb, and /ˈsʌspekt/
when it is a noun or adjective.

1 If you **suspect** something, 1.1 you think that it is V+O OR
likely or is probably true. EG *People suspected that* V+REPORT :
a secret deal had been made... He suspected mur- ONLY *that*
der... I suspect the boy is in love. 1.2 you doubt that V+O
it can be trusted or that it is reliable. EG *I had many
reasons for suspecting this approach.*

2 If you **suspect** someone of a crime, you think V+O : OFT+*of*
that they are guilty of it. EG *He was suspected of
treason.*

3 A **suspect** is a person who is thought to be guilty N COUNT
of a crime. EG *Last week police finally had a
suspect for the murder.*

4 If something is **suspect**, it cannot be trusted or ADJ QUALIT
regarded as genuine. EG *My friendliness was
viewed as suspect by some people... Their military
titles were a little suspect.*

suspend /səˈspend/, **suspends, suspending, suspended.** 1 If something is **suspended** from a high V+O+A :
place, it is hanging from that place. EG *A model* USU PASS
aeroplane was suspended above the stage.

2 If you **suspend** something, you delay it or stop it V+O
from happening for a while. EG *There were demands that the trial be temporarily suspended...
The builders suspended their work.*

3 If someone **is suspended**, they are prevented V+O:USU PASS from holding a particular job or position for a fixed length of time, usually as a punishment. EG *The people involved in the incident have been suspended from their duties... He was the third member to be suspended from the party.*

suspender /səspɛndə/, **suspenders. Suspenders** N COUNT: are fastenings hanging down from a belt or girdle USU PLURAL which hold a woman's stockings up.

suspense /səspɛns/. **1 Suspense** is a state of N UNCOUNT excitement or anxiety about something that is going to happen very soon, for example when you are waiting for some news. EG *I try to add an element of suspense and mystery to my novels.*

2 If you **keep** someone **in suspense**, you delay PHRASE telling them something that they are very eager to know about. EG *I did not leave him in suspense, but quickly informed him that he had passed.*

suspension /səspɛnʃəᵊn/, **suspensions. 1 Sus-** N UNCOUNT: **pension** of something is delaying it or stopping it OFT+*of* from happening for a while. EG *...the suspension of all social security payments.*

2 Someone's **suspension** is their removal from a N UNCOUNT job or position for a period of time, usually as a OR N COUNT punishment.

3 A vehicle's **suspension** consists of the springs N UNCOUNT and shock absorbers attached to the wheels, which give a smooth ride in spite of bumps in the road.

suspension bridge, suspension bridges. A N COUNT **suspension bridge** is a type of bridge that is supported from above by cables.

suspicion /səspɪʃᵊn/, **suspicions. 1 Suspicion** is N UNCOUNT the feeling that you do not trust someone or that OR N COUNT something is wrong in some way. EG *Derek shared Lynn's suspicion of Michael... I had aroused his suspicions last week... Their friendship is regarded with suspicion by their teachers.*

2 If someone is **under suspicion**, they are suspect- PHRASE ed of being guilty of something such as a crime. EG *He felt that he was possibly under suspicion.*

3 A **suspicion** is a feeling that something is N COUNT probably true or is likely to happen. EG *Investigators have strong suspicions of a clandestine trade.*

4 A **suspicion** of a quality or feeling is a very small N SING+*of* amount of it. EG *My dog barks at the slightest suspicion of danger.*

suspicious /səspɪʃəs/. **1** If you are **suspicious** of ADJ QUALIT: someone, you do not trust them. EG *The policeman* OFT+*of* *on duty became suspicious of the youth and asked him why he was standing there... He shot a suspicious glance at me.* ◊ **suspiciously.** EG *'Why are* ◊ ADV *you laughing?' Rachel asked suspiciously.*

2 You can use **suspicious** to describe things that ADJ QUALIT make you think that something is wrong with a situation. EG *There were suspicious circumstances about his death... Several suspicious aircraft were spotted.* ◊ **suspiciously.** EG *The lump was suspi-* ◊ SUBMOD *ciously big.*

sustain /səsteɪn/, **sustains, sustaining, sus-** **tained. 1** If you **sustain** something, you continue it V+O or maintain it for a period of time. EG *They do not have enough money to sustain a strike... The problem was how to sustain public interest.*

2 If food or drink **sustains** you, it gives you energy V+O and strength. EG *They had nothing to sustain them all day except two cups of coffee.*

3 If something **sustains** you, it supports you by V+O giving you help, strength, or encouragement. EG *It is his belief in God that sustains him.*

sustained /səsteɪnd/. An activity that is **sus-** ADJ QUALIT **tained** is continued for a long time. EG *The enemy mounted a sustained attack on the castle.*

sustenance /sʌstənəns/ is food and drink which N UNCOUNT helps to keep a person, animal, or plant strong and Formal healthy. EG *We derive our sustenance from the land... Minerals provide sustenance for their roots.*

SW is an abbreviation for 'south-west'.

swab /swɒb/, **swabs.** A **swab** is a small piece of N COUNT cotton wool used by a doctor or nurse for cleaning a wound or for applying ointment or disinfectant.

swagger /swægə/, **swaggers, swaggering,** V:USU+A **swaggered.** If you **swagger**, you walk in a proud way, holding your body upright and swinging your hips. EG *She swaggered back to her place by the window.* ▸ used as a noun. EG *Bernard left the room* ▸ N SING *with a swagger.*

swallow /swɒləʊ/, **swallows, swallowing, swal-** **lowed. 1** If you **swallow** something, you cause it to V+O go from your mouth down into your stomach. EG *He swallowed more pills.* ▸ used as a noun. EG *Brody* ▸ N COUNT *took a long swallow of his drink.*

2 If you **swallow**, you make a movement in your V throat as if you are swallowing something, often because you are nervous or frightened. EG *He swallowed and closed his eyes.*

3 If someone **swallows** a story or a statement, V+O they believe it completely. EG *I sometimes think that crowds will swallow whole any political speech whatsoever.*

4 If you **swallow** an insult or an unkind remark, V+O you accept it and do not protest. EG *She swallowed the sarcasm and got on with her work.* ● to **swallow** your **pride**: see **pride.**

5 A **swallow** is also a kind of small bird with N COUNT pointed wings and a forked tail.

swam /swæm/ is the past tense of **swim.**

swamp /swɒmp/, **swamps, swamping,** **swamped. 1** A **swamp** is an area of very wet land N COUNT OR with wild plants growing in it. N UNCOUNT

2 If something **swamps** a ship or boat, it fills it V+O with water and causes it to sink. EG *Sudden heavy seas swamped the ship.*

3 If you **are swamped** by things or people, you V+O:USU PASS have more of them than you can deal with. EG *Pubs were suddenly swamped by a flood of troops... We've been swamped with applicants.*

swampy /swɒmpiᵊ/. A **swampy** area of land ADJ QUALIT consists mainly of swamps. EG *...swampy river banks.*

swan /swɒn/, **swans.** A **swan** is a large bird with N COUNT a very long neck. Swans live on rivers and lakes and are usually white.

swan song. Someone's **swan song** is the last time N SING+POSS that they do something for which they are famous, for example the last time that an actor gives a performance in the theatre.

swap /swɒp/, **swaps, swapping, swapped;** also spelled **swop. 1** If you **swap** one thing for another, **1.1** you give the first thing to someone and receive V+O:OFT the other thing in exchange. EG *He swapped a* +*for/with* *dozen goats for a female calf... Try swapping homes with a friend.* ▸ used as a noun. EG *Let's do a* ▸ N COUNT *swap.* **1.2** you remove the first thing and replace it V+O+*for* with something else. EG *I swapped my cap for a large black waterproof one.*

2 If you **swap** stories or opinions with someone, V+O: you tell each other stories or give each other your OFT+*with* opinions. EG *They swap amusing stories about the place... ...swopping views with the other people.*

swarm /swɔːm/, **swarms, swarming, swarmed.** **1** A **swarm** of bees or other insects is a large N PART group of them flying together. EG *The showers brought swarms of flying insects to torment them.*

2 When bees or other insects **swarm**, they move or V fly in a large group. EG *When the bees swarmed we all rushed out into the garden.*

3 When people **swarm** somewhere, they move V+A there quickly in a large group. EG *They swarmed across the bridge and began climbing up the bank.*

4 A **swarm** of people is a large group of them N PART moving about quickly. EG *She left amid a swarm of photographers.*

Is a swan song ever a song?

5 If a place **is swarming** with people, it is full of v+with people moving about in a busy way. EG *The White House garden was swarming with security men.*

swarthy /swɔːðɪ¹/. A **swarthy** person has a dark ADJ QUALIT complexion. EG *...his swarthy face.*

swat /swɒt/, **swats, swatting, swatted.** If you v+o **swat** something such as an insect, you hit it with a quick, swinging movement, using your hand or a flat object.

swathe /sweɪð/, **swathes. 1** A **swathe** is a long N COUNT strip of cloth, especially when it is wrapped round someone or something. EG *...balconies strewn with swathes of silk.*

2 A **swathe** of land is a long strip of land that is N COUNT different from the land on either side of it, for Literary example because it is higher, or has no vegetation. EG *...new roads cutting swathes through our countryside.*

swathed /sweɪðd/. If someone is **swathed** in ADJ PRED+in something, they are completely wrapped in it. EG *She was swathed in bandages from head to foot.*

sway /sweɪ/, **sways, swaying, swayed. 1** When v:OFT+A people or things **sway**, they lean or swing slowly from one side to the other. EG *He didn't fall, but swayed a little... She sang and swayed from side to side... ...trees swaying in the wind.*

2 If you **are swayed** by something that you hear or v+o:USU PASS read, it influences you. EG *Do not be swayed by glamorous advertisements.*

3 Sway is the power that someone or something N UNCOUNT has to influence people. EG *Laing was coming* Literary *increasingly under the sway of new ideas.* ● If ● PHRASE someone or something **holds sway**, they have Formal great power or influence over a particular place or activity. EG *The beliefs which now hold sway may one day be rejected.*

swear /sweə/, **swears, swearing, swore** /swɔː/, **sworn** /swɔːn/. **1** If someone **swears**, they use v:OFT+at language that is considered to be rude or blasphemous. Some people often swear when they are angry. EG *Glenys leant out of the car window and swore at the other driver.*

2 If you **swear** to do something, you solemnly v+to-INF promise that you will do it. EG *I swear I will never* OR REPORT: *tell anyone.* ONLY that

3 If you say that you **swear** that something is true v+to or that you can **swear** to it, you are saying very OR REPORT: firmly that it is true. EG *She did not know a thing,* ONLY that *she swore... I swear that he never consulted me.*

4 See also **sworn.**

swear by. If you say that you **swear by** some- PHRASAL VB: thing, you mean that you believe that it can be V+PREP relied on to have a particular effect. EG *He swears* Informal *by my herbal tea to make him sleep.*

swear in. When someone **is sworn in**, they PHRASAL VB: solemnly promise to fulfil the duties of a new job or V+O+ADV, appointment. EG *The jury was sworn in on May 4.* USU PASS

swear-word, swear-words. A **swear-word** is a N COUNT word which is considered to be rude or blasphemous, which people use when they are angry.

sweat /swet/, **sweats, sweating, sweated. 1** N UNCOUNT **Sweat** is the salty, colourless liquid which comes through your skin when you are hot, ill, or afraid. EG *Jack paused, wiping the sweat from his face.*

2 When you **sweat**, sweat comes through your v skin. EG *I lay and sweated in bed... The heat was nearly unbearable, but the sweating people danced.*

3 If someone is **in a sweat** or **in a cold sweat**, PHRASE they are sweating a lot, especially because they are afraid or ill. EG *He awoke trembling and in a cold sweat.*

4 You can refer to hard work or effort as **sweat**. EG N UNCOUNT *...the money he makes out of the labouring man's* Literary *sweat.*

sweater /swetə/, **sweaters.** A **sweater** is a warm N COUNT knitted piece of clothing which covers the upper part of your body and your arms. You put it on by pulling it over your head. EG *The girl had come out wearing jeans and a sweater.*

sweatshirt /swetʃɜːt/, **sweatshirts.** A N COUNT **sweatshirt** is a piece of casual clothing, usually made from thick cotton, which covers the upper part of your body and your arms. You put it on by pulling it over your head.

sweaty /swetɪ¹/. **1** A **sweaty** place or activity ADJ QUALIT makes you sweat because it is hot or tiring. EG *...the sweaty march along the blazing beach.*

2 If your clothes or parts of your body are **sweaty**, ADJ QUALIT they are soaked or covered with sweat. EG *...students in sweaty sports shirts... ...cold sweaty hands.*

swede /swiːd/, **swedes.** A **swede** is a round yellow N COUNT root vegetable with a brown or purple skin.

sweep /swiːp/, **sweeps, sweeping, swept** /swept/. **1** If you **sweep** an area of ground, you v+o OR V+A push dirt or rubbish off it with a long-handled brush. EG *I must sweep the kitchen floor... ...men sweeping streets... He swept away the broken glass.*

2 If you **sweep** things off something, you push v+o+A them off with a quick, smooth movement of your arm. EG *He went into the study and swept some books and papers off the couch.*

3 If your hand or arm **sweeps** in a particular v+A direction, it moves in a quick, smooth curve. EG *The dog was flung aside by the panther's sweeping paw.* ▸ used as a noun. EG *With a great sweep of the arm* ▸ N COUNT *he flung the whole handful high in the air.*

4 If a strong force **sweeps** you along, it moves you v+o+A quickly along. EG *She was swept out to sea by the currents.*

5 If something **sweeps** from one place to another, v+A it moves very quickly. EG *Cold winds sweep over the barren, treeless plains... He stared out at the traffic sweeping along the road.*

6 If ideas, beliefs, or statements **sweep** a place or v+o OR V+A **sweep** through it, they spread quickly through it. EG *...the camping craze that is currently sweeping America... Change sweeps through the highly industrialized countries.*

7 If something **sweeps** something else away or v+o+A aside, it removes it quickly and completely. EG *The matter was soon swept from his mind... ...sweeping away restrictions on publication.*

8 If someone's gaze or a light **sweeps** an area, it v+o moves over it. EG *We began rushing around in the dark, sweeping the ground with our flashlights.*

9 If you **sweep** something **under the carpet**, you PHRASE try to prevent people from hearing about it, usually because you are rather ashamed of it. EG *This fact has been swept under the carpet for years.*

sweep up. If you **sweep up** dirt or rubbish, you PHRASAL VB: push it together with a brush and then remove it. V+O+ADV

sweeping /swiːpɪŋ/. **1** A **sweeping** curve is long, ADJ QUALIT: wide, and stretched out. EG *...a place where the* ATTRIB *stream made a sweeping curve.*

2 A **sweeping** statement or generalization is a ADJ QUALIT: very general one that you assume is true, without USU ATTRIB considering facts or details carefully; used showing disapproval. EG *It is too easy to make sweeping generalizations about someone else's problems.*

3 Sweeping effects or consequences are very ADJ QUALIT: great. EG *...sweeping public expenditure cuts... They* ATTRIB *had embarked on a course which might have quite sweeping effects.*

sweet /swiːt/, **sweets; sweeter, sweetest. 1** Food ADJ QUALIT or drink that is **sweet** contains a lot of sugar. EG *I had some horribly sweet chocolate gateau... ...a cup of sweet tea.*

2 Sweets are sweet things such as toffees, choco- N COUNT: lates, and mints. EG *She urged her children not to* USU PLURAL *eat too many sweets.* British

3 A **sweet** is the same as a dessert. EG *We get a* N COUNT *good meal in our canteen; soup and a main meal* British *and a sweet.*

4 If you describe a feeling as **sweet**, you mean that ADJ QUALIT it gives you great pleasure and satisfaction. EG

However sweet love is, when it goes there is always bitterness. ◊ **sweetness**. EG *...the sweetness of freedom.*

5 A **sweet** smell is pleasant and fragrant. EG *...the sweet smell of ripe blackberry bushes.* ADJ QUALIT

6 A **sweet** sound is pleasant, smooth, and gentle. EG *...the sweet song of the skylark.* ◊ **sweetly**. EG *...a piper who played sweetly on his pipes.* ADJ QUALIT ◊ ADV

7 If you describe someone as **sweet**, you mean that they are pleasant, kind, and gentle towards other people. EG *My grandparents were very sweet to me... She's a sweet person.* ADJ QUALIT

8 You can also describe someone or something as **sweet** when you think that they are attractive and delightful. EG *Oh! Look at that kitten! How sweet!... She has a really sweet face.* ◊ **sweetly**. EG *She remembered him sitting so sweetly on the cot, looking up at her.* ADJ QUALIT ◊ ADV

9 If someone has a **sweet tooth**, they have a great liking for food that tastes sweet. PHRASE

sweet corn is a vegetable which comes from the maize plant. It is like a long hard stalk covered with small round yellow seeds which taste fairly sweet. N UNCOUNT

sweeten /swiːtəⁿn/, **sweetens**, **sweetening**, **sweetened**. If you **sweeten** food or drink, you add sugar, honey, or another sweet substance to it. EG *...tea sweetened with honey.* V+O

sweetener /swiːtəⁿnə/, **sweeteners**. A **sweetener** is an artificial substance that can be used in drinks instead of sugar and is usually less fattening. N MASS

sweetheart /swiːthɑːt/, **sweethearts**. **1** You call someone **sweetheart** if you are very fond of them. VOCATIVE

2 Your **sweetheart** is your boyfriend or your girlfriend. This word is used especially for young people. EG *He married his childhood sweetheart.* N COUNT

swell /swel/, **swells**, **swelling**, **swelled**, **swollen** /swəʊləⁿn/. The past participle can be either **swelled** or **swollen**.

1 If part of your body **swells** or **swells** up, it becomes larger and rounder than normal, usually as a result of an injury or an illness. EG *A mosquito had bitten her and her whole arm had swollen up.* V : OFT+*up*

2 When something **swells** or **swells** up, it becomes larger and rounder by being filled with air or liquid. EG *The insect inflates her lungs so that they swell into her abdomen.* V : OFT+*up*

3 If numbers or amounts **swell**, they increase in amount. EG *It took another twenty years for the population to swell to twice its size... The army had its ranks swollen by new recruits.* V-ERG

4 If feelings or sounds **swell**, they suddenly get stronger or louder. EG *His guilt swelled, but he quashed it... The murmur swelled and then died away.* V Literary

5 A **swell** is the regular movement of waves up and down in the open sea. EG *...the gentle, monotonous swell of the ocean.* N COUNT

6 See also **swollen**.

swelling /swelɪŋ/, **swellings**. A **swelling** is a raised, curved shape on the surface of your body, that appears as a result of an injury or an illness. EG *He had a painful swelling on his neck.* N COUNT OR N UNCOUNT

sweltering /sweltəⁿrɪŋ/. **1** If you describe the weather as **sweltering**, you mean that it is extremely hot and makes you feel uncomfortable. EG *...a good place to go on a sweltering August day.* ADJ CLASSIF

2 If you are **sweltering**, you are so hot that you feel uncomfortable. EG *On the deck everyone was sweltering in the still air.* ADJ CLASSIF

swept /swept/ is the past tense and past participle of **sweep**.

swerve /swɜːv/, **swerves**, **swerving**, **swerved**. If a vehicle or other moving thing **swerves**, it suddenly changes direction, often in order to avoid colliding with something else. EG *The car swerved off the road and into the river... I swerved to avoid a lorry that was in my way... A charging shark cannot stop, it can only swerve away to one side.* V : USU+A

swift /swɪft/, **swifter**, **swiftest**; **swifts**. **1** A **swift** event or process happens very quickly. EG *I made a swift and complete recovery... never making a swift decision about anything.* ◊ **swiftly**. EG *No one volunteered very swiftly.* ◊ **swiftness**. EG *...stunned by the swiftness of the assault.* ADJ QUALIT ◊ ADV ◊ N UNCOUNT

2 Something that is **swift** moves very quickly. EG *The president's swift fleet reached Dover around 10 a.m... ...a swift stream... ...a swift glance.* ◊ **swiftly**. EG *He walked swiftly down the dark street.* ◊ **swiftness**. EG *He moved with remarkable swiftness to one side.* ADJ QUALIT ◊ ADV ◊ N UNCOUNT

3 A **swift** is a small bird with crescent-shaped wings. N COUNT

swig /swɪg/, **swigs**, **swigging**, **swigged**. If you **swig** a drink, you drink it from a bottle or cup quickly and in large amounts. EG *When her back was turned I swigged two cupfuls from the tub.* ▸ used as a noun. EG *She took a swig of brandy.* V+O OR V+A Informal ▸ N COUNT

swim /swɪm/, **swims**, **swimming**, **swam** /swæm/, **swum** /swʌm/. **1** When you **swim**, you move through water by making movements with your arms and legs. EG *The children are learning to swim... We managed to swim ashore... I go swimming twice a week.* ▸ used as a noun. EG *Let's go for a swim.* ◊ **swimmer** /swɪmə/, **swimmers**. EG *He went to the aid of a swimmer in difficulty... Are they good swimmers?* ◊ **swimming**. EG *Her father encouraged her to take up swimming again.* V ▸ N SING ◊ N COUNT ◊ N UNCOUNT

2 If objects seem to you to **swim**, they seem to be moving backwards and forwards, usually because you are ill. EG *The room swam and darkened before his eyes.* V

3 If your head **is swimming**, you feel dizzy. V

swimming bath, **swimming baths**. A **swimming bath** is a public swimming pool, especially an indoor one. N COUNT British

swimming costume, **swimming costumes**. A **swimming costume** is the same as a swimsuit. N COUNT British

swimming pool, **swimming pools**. A **swimming pool** is a place built for people to swim in, usually consisting of a large hole in the ground that has been tiled and filled with water. N COUNT

swimming trunks are the shorts that a man wears when he goes swimming. EG *He put on a pair of swimming trunks and lay out in the sun.* N PLURAL

swimsuit /swɪmsjⁿuːt/, **swimsuits**. A **swimsuit** is a tight-fitting piece of clothing that a woman wears when she goes swimming. N COUNT

swindle /swɪndəⁿl/, **swindles**, **swindling**, **swindled**. If someone **swindles** you, they deceive you in order to get something valuable from you, especially money. EG *I'm sure they swindled you out of that money.* ▸ used as a noun. EG *I'm afraid we have been the victims of a monumental swindle.* ◊ **swindler** /swɪndlə/, **swindlers**. EG *They are the biggest swindlers on earth.* V+O : OFT+A ▸ N COUNT ◊ N COUNT

swine /swaɪn/, **swines**. If you call someone a **swine**, you mean that you think they are very unpleasant, especially because they have caused you trouble; an offensive word. N COUNT Informal

swing /swɪŋ/, **swings**, **swinging**, **swung** /swʌŋ/. **1** If something **swings** or if you **swing** it, it moves repeatedly backwards and forwards or from side to side from a fixed point. EG *The chandelier started to swing... He sat there swinging his legs... Jane walked ahead, swinging the shopping bag.* ▸ used as a noun. EG *She walked with an exaggerated swing of the hips.* V-ERG ▸ N SING

2 If something **swings** in a particular direction or if you **swing** it in that direction, it moves in that direction with a smooth, curving movement. EG *I pushed the door and it swung open... Boylan swung the bag on to the back seat.* ▸ used as a noun. EG *...a grand, impatient swing of his arm.* V-ERG+A ▸ N COUNT

Can a man wear a swimsuit?

swimming

front crawl

butterfly

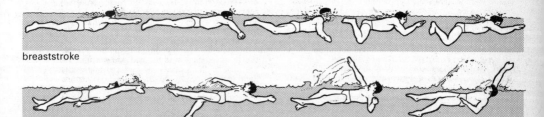

breaststroke

backstroke

3 If a person or a vehicle **swings** in a particular direction, they turn suddenly in that direction. EG *He swung round and faced the window... The taxi turned left and swung in through the gates.*   V·ERG+A

4 If you **swing** at someone or something, you try to hit them with your arm. EG *I swung at him and hit him forcefully... The soldier swung a slow, heavy right hand at Tom.*   V+A OR V+O+A

5 A **swing** is a seat hanging by two ropes or chains from a metal frame or from the branch of a tree. You can sit on the seat and move forwards and backwards through the air.   N COUNT

6 A **swing** in people's opinions or attitudes is a significant change in them. EG *There was a 16.2% swing to the Social Democrats.* ▸ used as a verb. EG *The balance of power had swung decisively in favour of the moderates.*   N COUNT+SUPP   ▸ V+A

7 If something is **in full swing**, it is operating fully and is no longer in its early stages. EG *By the 1980's the Computer Revolution was in full swing.*   PHRASE

8 If you **get into the swing** of something, you become very involved in it and enjoy what you are doing. EG *Dr Stein had got into the swing of his speech and was enthusiastically quoting authors.*   PHRASE *Informal*

swipe /swaɪp/, **swipes, swiping, swiped. 1** If you **swipe** at something, you try to hit it with a stick or other object, making a swinging movement with your arm. EG *The batsman swiped at the ball and missed it.* ▸ used as a noun. EG *She took a casual swipe at the nettles.*   V+at   ▸ N COUNT: OFT+at

2 If you **swipe** something, you steal it quickly. EG *I swiped somebody else's apple.*   V+O *Informal*

swirl /swɜːl/, **swirls, swirling, swirled.** If something **swirls**, it moves round and round quickly. EG *Dust swirled in small circles around me... He swirled his drink round his glass.* ▸ used as a noun. EG *...the slow swirl of the stream.*   V·ERG+A   ▸ N COUNT

swish /swɪʃ/, **swishes, swishing, swished.** If something **swishes** or if you **swish** it, it moves quickly through the air, making a soft sound. EG

The curtains swished open... ...swishing his long black tail against his sides. ▸ used as a noun. EG *...the swish of a horse's tail.*   ▸ N COUNT

switch /swɪtʃ/, **switches, switching, switched. 1** A **switch** is a small control for an electrical device such as a light, a radio, or a heater. You press the switch or move it up or down in order to turn the device on or off. EG *...electric light switches... Somebody pressed the wrong switch.*   N COUNT

2 If you **switch** to something different, for example to a different task or a different subject of conversation, you change to it from what you were doing or saying before. EG *I would like now to switch to quite a different topic... He switched his attention back to the magazine.* ▸ used as a noun. EG *...the switch from planned to impromptu tactics... ...a switch in policy.*   V OR V+O: OFT+to/from   ▸ N COUNT

3 If you **switch** something, you remove it and replace it with something else. EG *The plane switched loads and took off.*   V+O

switch off. 1 If you **switch off** a light or other electrical device, you stop it working by pressing a switch. EG *He switched the radio off.* **2** If you **switch off**, you stop paying attention to something, because you are no longer interested in it. EG *I just switched off after the first speech.*   PHRASAL VB: V+O+ADV   V+ADV *Informal*

switch on. If you **switch on** a light or other electrical device, you make it start working by pressing a switch. EG *He switched on the TV... Would you switch on the light, please?*   PHRASAL VB: V+O+ADV

switchboard /swɪtʃbɔːd/, **switchboards.** A **switchboard** is a place in a large office or business where all the telephone calls are connected. EG *The girl on the switchboard told me there was a phone call for me.*   N COUNT

swivel /swɪvəl/, **swivels, swivelling, swivelled;** spelled **swiveling** and **swiveled** in American English. If something **swivels** or if you **swivel** it, it turns around a central point so that it is facing in a different direction. EG *I swivelled right round in my*   V·ERG: USU+A

chair... Mellors slowly swivelled his chair round...
His head swivelled toward her.

swollen /swəʊlə⁰n/. **1 Swollen** is the past participle of **swell**.

2 Something that is **swollen** has grown outwards ADJ QUALIT
until it is broader or wider than usual. EG *Her*
fingers were badly swollen with arthritis.

swoon /swuːn/, **swoons, swooning, swooned.** If v
you **swoon**, you are strongly affected by your
feelings for someone you love or admire very
much. EG *We fell in love, and swooned in each*
other's arms.

swoop /swuːp/, **swoops, swooping, swooped. 1** V : USU+A
When a bird or aeroplane **swoops**, it suddenly
moves downwards through the air in a smooth,
curving movement. EG *We saw a distant eagle*
swoop down from the sky. ▸ used as a noun. EG *The* ▸ N COUNT
swallow made a dazzling swoop through the air.

2 If soldiers or police **swoop** on a place, they move v+A
towards it suddenly and quickly, usually in order to
attack it or to arrest the people there. EG *British*
troops swooped down twice in dawn raids. ▸ used ▸ N COUNT
as a noun. EG *The police made a swoop on the*
headquarters.

3 If you achieve something **in one fell swoop**, you PHRASE
do it on a single occasion or by a single action. EG
All our problems were solved in one fell swoop.

swop /swɒp/. See **swap**.

sword /sɔːd/, **swords. 1** A **sword** is a weapon with N COUNT
a handle and a long blade. See picture at WEAPONS.

2 If you **cross swords** with someone, you disagree PHRASE
and argue with them about something. EG *It was*
over this that Clare and Arthur crossed swords.

swore /swɔː/ is the past tense of **swear**.

sworn /swɔːn/. **1 Sworn** is the past participle of
swear.

2 If two people are **sworn enemies**, they dislike PHRASE
each other very much.

3 If you make a **sworn** statement or declaration, ADJ CLASSIF :
you swear that everything that you have said in it ATTRIB
is true. EG *The American made a sworn statement*
to the police.

swot /swɒt/, **swots, swotting, swotted. 1** If you v
swot, you study very hard, especially when you are Informal
preparing for an examination. EG *How do you find*
time to swot for exams?

2 If you call someone a **swot**, you mean that they N COUNT
study extremely hard and are not interested in Informal
other things; used showing disapproval.

swot up. If you **swot up** a subject or **swot up** on PHRASAL VB :
it, you read as much as you can about it, usually V+O+ADV
because you are going to be asked questions about OR V+ADV+A
it. EG *She swotted up American history.* Informal

swum /swʌm/ is the past participle of **swim.**

swung /swʌŋ/ is the past tense and past participle
of **swing**.

sycamore /sɪkəmɔː/, **sycamores.** A **sycamore** is N COUNT
a tree that has leaves with five points.

syllable /sɪləbə⁰l/, **syllables.** A **syllable** is a part N COUNT
of a word that contains a single vowel-sound and
that is pronounced as a unit. So, for example, 'book'
has one syllable, and 'reading' has two syllables.

syllabus /sɪləbəs/, **syllabuses.** You can refer to N COUNT
the subjects that are studied in a particular course
as the **syllabus**. EG *They've got to cover a very*
wide syllabus... ...the new physics syllabus.

symbol /sɪmbə⁰l/, **symbols. 1** A **symbol** of some- N COUNT+SUPP
thing such as an idea is a shape or design that is
used to represent it. EG *Picasso painted a red circle*
as a symbol of the Revolution... ...a peace symbol.

2 Something that is a **symbol** of a society or aspect N COUNT :
of life seems to represent it because it is very USU+of
typical of it. EG *Perhaps the most glittering symbol*
of the new Britain was London's Post Office Tower.

3 A **symbol** for an item in a calculation or formula N COUNT
is a number, letter, or shape that represents the
item. EG *I use my own symbol for 'approximately'.*

symbolic /sɪmbɒlɪk/. **1** Something that is **sym-** ADJ CLASSIF :
bolic of someone or something else is regarded or USU+of

used as a symbol of them. EG *The crescent moon is*
symbolic of Allah... ...gold, with its rich symbolic
significance. ◊ **symbolically.** EG *To put on some-* ◊ ADV
one else's clothes is symbolically to take on their
personality.

2 Symbolic is also used to describe things involv- ADJ QUALIT
ing or relating to symbols. EG *Water is full of*
symbolic associations... ...a symbolic play.

symbolism /sɪmbəlɪzə⁰m/ is the use of symbols in N UNCOUNT
order to represent something. EG *...messages con-*
veyed by symbolism in the architecture.

symbolize /sɪmbəlaɪz/, **symbolizes, symboliz-** V+O
ing, symbolized; also spelled **symbolise.** If something **symbolizes** something else, it is used or
regarded as a symbol of it. EG *...a dancer in a flame-*
red robe symbolizing the sun.

symmetrical /sɪmetrɪkə⁰l/. If something is **sym-** ADJ CLASSIF
metrical, it has two halves which are exactly the
same, except that one half is the mirror image of
the other. EG *...pleasingly symmetrical designs.*
◊ **symmetrically.** EG *Smaller rooms were ar-* ◊ ADV
ranged symmetrically to either side.

symmetry /sɪmɪ²tri¹/. Something that has **sym-** N UNCOUNT
metry is symmetrical in shape or design. EG *...the*
symmetry of the Square.

sympathetic /sɪmpəθetɪk/. **1** If you are **sympa-** ADJ QUALIT
thetic to someone who has had a misfortune, you
are kind to them and show that you understand
their feelings. EG *My boyfriend was very sympa-*
thetic and it did make me feel better.
◊ **sympathetically.** EG *She put a hand sympatheti-* ◊ ADV
cally on his arm.

2 If you are **sympathetic** to a proposal or action, ADJ PRED :
you approve of it and are willing to support it. EG OFT+to
He is sympathetic to our cause... The university is
not particularly sympathetic to this problem.

3 You describe someone as **sympathetic** when ADJ QUALIT
you like them and approve of the way that they
behave. EG *I found him a very sympathetic charac-*
ter.

sympathize /sɪmpəθaɪz/, **sympathizes, sympa-**
thizing, sympathized; also spelled **sympathise. 1** V : OFT+with
If you **sympathize** with someone who has had a
misfortune, you are sorry for them, and show this
in the way you behave towards them. EG *I sympa-*
thized with her and tried to help.

2 If you **sympathize** with someone's feelings, you V+with
understand them and are not critical of them,
because you think that you would have the same
feelings in the same circumstances. EG *I can sym-*
pathize with your hesitations... He could neither
understand nor sympathize with Isobel's eagerness.

3 If you **sympathize** with a proposal or action, you V+with
approve of it and are willing to support it. EG
Everyone sympathised with the anti-colonial cause.

sympathizer /sɪmpəθaɪzə/, **sympathizers;** also N COUNT
spelled **sympathiser.** The **sympathizers** of an
organization or cause are the people who approve
of it and support it. EG *White was an ardent*
Communist sympathiser.

sympathy /sɪmpəθi¹/, **sympathies. 1** If you have N UNCOUNT :
sympathy for someone who has had a misfortune, OFT+for
you are sorry for them, and show this in the way
you behave towards them. EG *People feel immedi-*
ate sympathy for a man left alone with his chil-
dren.

2 If you have **sympathy** with someone's ideas or N UNCOUNT
opinions, you agree with them. EG *On that point I'm* +with
in sympathy with Mr McCabe.

3 Your **sympathies** are your feelings of approval N PLURAL
and support for a particular proposal or action. EG
Her sympathies lay with what we were doing... He
knows I have strong left-wing sympathies.

4 If you take some action **in sympathy** with PHRASE
someone else, you do it in order to show that you

Find a synonym for 'grammar' on these pages.

support them. EG *They were carrying out a hunger strike in sympathy with mine.*

symphony /sɪmfəniː/, **symphonies**. A symphony is a piece of music written to be played by an orchestra, usually in four parts called movements. EG *...Sibelius's Second Symphony.* N COUNT

symptom /sɪmpᵗəm/, **symptoms**. 1 A symptom of an illness is something wrong with your body that is a sign of the illness. EG *Most infections are contagious before any symptoms are noticed... The first symptom of a cold is often a sore throat.* N COUNT

2 A **symptom** of a bad condition, for example in a society, is something that happens and that is taken as a sign of this condition. EG *Migration is a symptom of rural poverty.* N COUNT : USU+SUPP

symptomatic /sɪmpᵗəmætɪk/. If something is **symptomatic** of something else, it is a sign of it. EG *The irritation seems symptomatic of something deeper.* ADJ PRED : USU+of Formal

synagogue /sɪnəgog/, **synagogues**. A synagogue is a building where Jewish people meet to worship or to study their religion. N COUNT

synchronize /sɪŋkrənaɪz/, **synchronizes, synchronizing, synchronized**; also spelled **synchronise**. 1 If two people **synchronize** something that they do, they do it at the same time and speed as each other. EG *They frequently synchronize their movements as they talk.* V+O OR V+O+with : RECIP

2 If you **synchronize** two watches or clocks, you adjust them so that they say exactly the same time. EG *His watch has been accurately synchronized with the church clock.* V+O OR V+O+with : RECIP

syndicate /sɪndɪkᵊt/, **syndicates**. A syndicate is an association of people or organizations that is formed for business purposes or in order to carry out a project together. EG *...a syndicate of German industrialists.* N COUNT

syndrome /sɪndrəʊm/, **syndromes**. A syndrome is 1 a medical condition that is characterized by a particular group of signs and symptoms. EG *...Down's syndrome.* 2 a condition that is characterized by a particular type of activity, behaviour, or feeling. EG *...the capitalist syndrome of growth, profits, competition.* N COUNT+SUPP

synonym /sɪnənɪm/, **synonyms**. A synonym is a word or expression which means the same as another word or expression. EG *'Totalitarian' is not a synonym for 'communist'.* N COUNT : OFT+for/of

synonymous /sɪnɒnɪməs/. 1 Two words or expressions that are **synonymous** have the same meaning as each other. EG *For these economists 'development' seems to be synonymous with 'growth'.* ADJ CLASSIF : OFT+with

2 If you say that one thing is **synonymous** with another, you suggest that the two things are very closely associated with each other so that one implies the other. EG *His name became synonymous with wild fearlessness... Socialism became to him synonymous with peace.* ADJ PRED : OFT+with

syntax /sɪntæks/ is the grammatical arrangement of words in a language or the grammatical rules in a language. N UNCOUNT Technical

synthesis /sɪnθəˈsɪs/, **syntheses** /sɪnθəˈsiːz/. 1 A synthesis of different ideas or styles is a mixture or combination of these ideas or styles, in which they blend together. EG *...a synthesis of Jewish theology and Greek philosophy.* N COUNT : OFT+of

2 The **synthesis** of a substance is the production of it by means of chemical or biological reactions. EG *We need sunlight for the synthesis of vitamin D.* N UNCOUNT +SUPP

synthesize /sɪnθɪsaɪz/, **synthesizes, synthesizing, synthesized**; also spelled **synthesise**. 1 If you **synthesize** a substance, you produce it by means of chemical or biological reactions. EG *...proteins which the body is unable to synthesise for itself.* V+O

2 If you **synthesize** different ideas, facts, or experiences, you combine them to develop a single idea or impression. EG *He synthesizes data from a* V+O : OFT+A Formal

variety of sources... They synthesise their experience into principles and theories.

synthetic /sɪnθɛtɪk/. 1 A **synthetic** material is made from chemicals or artificial substances rather than from natural ones. EG *...curtains made of synthetic fibres... ...synthetic rubber as a substitute for natural rubber.* ADJ CLASSIF : USU ATTRIB

2 If you describe someone's behaviour as **synthetic**, you mean that it is not sincere or genuine. EG *...a synthetic skin-deep smile.* ADJ QUALIT

3 If you describe food as **synthetic**, you mean that it does not have a natural taste or appearance and is therefore unpleasant. EG *...a frightful synthetic omelette.* ADJ QUALIT

syphilis /sɪfɪlɪs/ is a type of venereal disease. N UNCOUNT

syphon /saɪfᵊn/, **syphons**. See **siphon**.

syringe /sɪrɪndʒ, sɪrɪndʒ/, **syringes, syringing, syringed**. 1 A **syringe** is a small tube with a plunger and a fine hollow needle or pointed end. Syringes are used for putting liquids into something and for taking liquids out, for example for injecting drugs into a person's body or for taking blood samples from them. EG *I attached the syringe and injected 10cc of the drug.* N COUNT

2 If a doctor **syringes** your ear or a wound, he or she cleans it using a syringe to suck substances out. V+O

syrup /sɪrəp/, **syrups**. **Syrup** is 1 a sweet liquid made by cooking sugar with water, sometimes with fruit juice as well. EG *...cherry syrup.* 2 a very sweet thick liquid food made from sugar. EG *...bread spread with golden syrup.* N MASS / N UNCOUNT

syrupy /sɪrəpiː/. 1 Liquid that is **syrupy** is sweet or thick like syrup. ADJ QUALIT

2 You can describe behaviour as **syrupy** when it is sentimental in an irritating way. EG *She admired everything she saw in a tone of syrupy earnestness.* ADJ QUALIT

system /sɪstᵊm/, **systems**. 1 A system is 1.1 a way of working, organizing, or doing something in which you follow a fixed plan or set of rules. EG *The new system has been running now for a number of years... They have developed a remarkably efficient system for gathering food.* 1.2 a particular set of rules, especially one in mathematics or science which is used to count or measure things. EG *...Egyptian or Roman number systems.* N COUNT : USU+SUPP

2 A **system** is also the way that a whole institution or aspect of society has been organized and arranged. EG *There's a difference between the Scottish legal system and the English one... ...the need to modernise Britain's transport system.* N COUNT+SUPP

3 People sometimes refer to the government or administration of a country as the **system**. EG *...the revolutionary overthrow of the system.* N SING : the+N

4 A **system** of a particular kind is 4.1 a set of equipment or parts such as water pipes or electrical wiring, which is used to supply water, heat, or electricity. EG *Have you thought of installing your own central heating system?* 4.2 a device or set of devices powered by electricity, for example a hi-fi or a computer. EG *They stole the stereo system and the television set.* N COUNT+SUPP

5 A **system** of a particular kind in your body is the set of organs or other parts in your body that together perform a particular function. EG *...a diagram of the digestive system... He has a very delicate nervous system.* N COUNT+SUPP

6 If you **get** something **out of** your **system**, you express the anger or other strong feeling that you have about something, so that you feel better afterwards. EG *Getting it out of my system made me relax a bit.* PHRASE Informal

systematic /sɪstɪmætɪk/. Activity or behaviour that is **systematic** follows a fixed plan, so that things are done in an efficient way. EG *These skills are developed in a formal and systematic way.* ADJ QUALIT

◊ **systematically**. EG *I wish they'd organise themselves more systematically.* ◊ ADV

T t

T, t /tiː/ **Ts, t's. T** is the twentieth letter of the N COUNT
English alphabet.

ta /tɑː/ means thank you. EG *He passed it over to* CONVENTION
Myra, who smiled at him and said 'Ta'. Informal

tab /tæb/, **tabs. 1** A **tab** is a small piece of cloth or N COUNT
paper that is attached to something. EG *It had the*
maker's name on a small cloth tab inside.
2 If you **keep tabs on** someone, you make sure PHRASE
that you always know where they are and what Informal
they are doing.

tabby /tæbɪ¹/, **tabbies.** A **tabby** is a cat whose fur N COUNT
has grey, brown, or orange stripes. ▸ used as an ▸ ADJ CLASSIF :
adjective. EG *...a tabby cat.* ATTRIB

table /teɪbə⁰l/, **tables, tabling, tabled. 1** A **table** N COUNT
is a piece of furniture with a flat top that you put
things on. EG *The book is there on the table... ...her*
bedside table.
2 A **table** is also a set of facts or figures arranged N COUNT
in columns or rows on a piece of paper.
3 If you **turn the tables on** someone, you change PHRASE
the situation completely, so that they have the
problems that they were trying to cause for you.
4 If you **table** something such as a proposal, you V+O
say formally that you want it to be discussed at a
meeting. EG *...a set of parliamentary questions*
tabled by Frank Field.

tableau /tæbləʊ/, **tableaux** or **tableaus.** A tab- N COUNT
leau is a scene from history or a legend, represented by people standing on a stage wearing costumes.

tablecloth /teɪbə⁰lklɒθ/, **tablecloths.** A table- N COUNT
cloth is a cloth used to cover a table and keep it
clean, especially while you are eating a meal.

table manners. Your **table manners** are the N PLURAL
way you behave when you are eating a meal. EG *He*
had to be careful about his table manners.

tablespoon /teɪbə⁰lspuːn/, **tablespoons. 1** A N COUNT
tablespoon is a large spoon used for serving food.
2 You can use **tablespoon** to refer to the amount N PART
that a tablespoon contains. EG *Use 1 tablespoon of*
vinegar to 1 pint of warm water.

tablespoonful /teɪbə⁰lspuːnful/, **tablespoonfuls** N PART
or **tablespoonsful.** A **tablespoonful** is the amount
that a tablespoon contains. EG *...two level table-*
spoonfuls of sugar.

tablet /tæblɪ²t/, **tablets. 1** A **tablet** is a small, N COUNT
hard piece of medicine, which you swallow. EG
Take three tablets after each meal... The drug is
available in tablet form.
2 A **tablet** is also a flat piece of stone or wood with N COUNT
words cut into it. Tablets are usually fixed to a wall
so that a person or event will be remembered for a
long time. EG *There is a tablet in memory of those*
who died.

table tennis is a game played indoors by two or N UNCOUNT
four people. They stand at each end of a long table
which has a low net across the middle and hit a
small, light ball to each other, using small bats.

tabloid /tæblɔɪd/, **tabloids.** A **tabloid** is a news- N COUNT
paper with small pages, short news stories and
articles, and a lot of photographs.

taboo /təbuː/, **taboos.** A **taboo** is **1** a religious N COUNT
custom that forbids people to do something. EG
...religious taboos against marrying people from
another religion. **2** a social custom that some N COUNT
words, subjects, or actions must be avoided because they are considered to be embarrassing or
offensive. EG *...the old taboo on kissing in public.*
▸ used as an adjective. EG *Birth control is no longer* ▸ ADJ CLASSIF
a taboo subject.

tabulate /tæbjʊ⁴leɪt/, **tabulates, tabulating,** V+O
tabulated. If you **tabulate** information, you ar-

range it in columns on a page. EG *It took twenty*
hours to tabulate the results.

tacit /tæsɪt/ means understood or implied without ADJ CLASSIF :
actually being said or written. EG *They had by tacit* USU ATTRIB
agreement not renewed the contract... ...a tacit Formal
admission of guilt. ◇ **tacitly.** EG *Is she tacitly* ◇ ADV
admitting that her place is in the home?

taciturn /tæsɪtɜːn/. Someone who is **taciturn** ADJ QUALIT
does not usually talk very much and so sometimes
seems unfriendly or depressed. EG *He was a*
gloomy, taciturn man who never had anything to
say.

tack /tæk/, **tacks, tacking, tacked. 1** A **tack** is a N COUNT
short nail with a broad, flat head, used especially
for fixing carpets to the floor. ● **to get down to**
brass tacks: see **brass.**
2 If you **tack** something to a surface, you nail it V+O : OFT+A
there with tacks. EG *Gretchen had tacked some*
travel posters on the wall.
3 If you change **tack**, you try to achieve something N UNCOUNT
using a different method from the one you were
using before. EG *They didn't seem convinced so I*
tried another tack.

tack on. If you **tack** something **on** to something PHRASAL VB :
else, you add it to it hurriedly and in an unsatisfac- V+O+ADV
tory way. EG *They've tacked a couple of new*
clauses on to the end of the contract.

tackle /tækə⁰l/, **tackles, tackling, tackled. 1** If V+O
you **tackle** a difficult task, you start dealing with it
in a determined way. EG *...a means of tackling the*
growing housing problem.
2 If you **tackle** someone in a game such as football, V+O
you try to take the ball away from them. EG *He was*
tackled before he had a chance to shoot. ▸ used as ▸ N COUNT
a noun. EG *The tackle looked fair but a free kick*
was awarded.
3 To **tackle** a person or an animal also means to V+O
attack and fight them. EG *Some pythons can tackle*
creatures as big as goats.
4 If you **tackle** someone about something that you V+O : OFT
are not satisfied with, you talk to them about it in +about/on
order to get something changed or done. EG *He*
tackled me about several editorials I had written.
5 **Tackle** is the equipment that you need for a N UNCOUNT
sport or activity. EG *...fishing tackle.*

tacky /tækɪ¹/. Something that is **tacky** is badly ADJ QUALIT
made and unpleasant. EG *...tacky jewellery... It's a* Informal
tacky, nasty little movie.

tact /tækt/ is behaviour in which you are careful N UNCOUNT
to avoid upsetting or offending people. EG *I tried to*
behave with the utmost tact.

tactful /tæktful/. If you are **tactful**, you are ADJ QUALIT
careful not to upset or offend people. EG *Nick was*
tactful enough not to shatter this illusion... The
tactful thing would have been not to say anything.
◇ **tactfully.** EG *The topic was tactfully dropped.* ◇ ADV

tactic /tæktɪk/, **tactics. Tactics** are **1** the meth- N COUNT :
ods that you use to achieve what you want. EG *They* USU PLURAL
use delaying tactics... Different circumstances in-
volve adopting different tactics. **2** the ways in
which troops and equipment are used in order to
win a battle. EG *...a general with a sound grasp of*
tactics.

tactical /tæktɪkə⁰l/. **1** If an action is **tactical**, it is ADJ CLASSIF
intended to gain an advantage in the future, rather
than immediately. EG *This was simply a tactical*
move by De Gaulle. ◇ **tactically.** EG *Tactically, I* ◇ ADV SEN
think we can be faulted for not voting against the OR ADV
strike.
2 Tactical weapons are used over fairly short ADJ CLASSIF :
distances. EG *...a vast arsenal of tactical nuclear* ATTRIB
weapons.

3 Anything related to military tactics can be described as **tactical**. EG ...a tactical advance. `ADJ CLASSIF ATTRIB`

tactile /tǽktaɪl/ means relating to the feelings that you experience when you touch things. EG ...the tactile qualities of the physical world. `ADJ CLASSIF Formal`

tactless /tǽktlɪ²s/. If someone is **tactless**, they behave in a way that is likely to upset or offend people. EG I suppose it was rather tactless of me to ask... Tilly's tactless outburst had really upset her. `ADJ QUALIT`

◊ **tactlessly**. EG She behaved very tactlessly in reminding him of his failure on the Stock Exchange. `◊ ADV`

tadpole /tǽdpəʊl/, **tadpoles**. **Tadpoles** are small water creatures which grow into frogs or toads. They have round black heads and long tails. `N COUNT`

tag /tǽg/, **tags**, **tagging**, **tagged**. **1** A **tag** is a small piece of cloth or paper which is attached to an object and which has information on it about the object or its owner. EG Have you tied the airline tags on the luggage?... Where's the price tag? `N COUNT`

2 Tag is a children's game in which one child chases the others and tries to touch them. `N UNCOUNT`

tag along. If you **tag along** with someone, you go with them, especially when they have not asked you to. EG Our younger sisters always wanted to tag along. `PHRASAL VB : V+ADV`

tail /teɪl/, **tails**, **tailing**, **tailed**. **1** The **tail** of an animal, bird, or fish is the part of its body that is at the opposite end to its head. Tails are usually long and thin. EG The dog was wagging his tail. `N COUNT`

2 You can refer to the long thin part at the back of an object as its **tail**. EG He ran into the street, the tails of his shirt flying... ...the stairway descending from the tail of the plane. `N COUNT : USU+SUPP`

3 If a man is wearing **tails**, he is wearing a formal jacket which has two long pieces hanging down at the back. `N PLURAL`

4 If you **tail** someone, you follow them in order to find out where they go and what they do. EG All day he was tailed by police cars. `V+O Informal`

5 If you toss a coin and it comes down **tails**, the side of it that you can see does not have a person's head on it. `ADV AFTER VB`

6 If you say that someone has their **tail between their legs**, you mean that they are feeling defeated and humiliated. EG She left the kitchen with her tail between her legs. `PHRASE`

7 to not **make head nor tail** of something: see **head**.

tail off. **1** If something **tails off**, it gradually becomes less, and often ends completely. EG The rains tail off in September... The average figure has tailed off in the last few years. **2** When someone's voice **tails off**, it gradually becomes quieter as they stop speaking. `PHRASAL VB : V+ADV` `V+ADV`

tailor /teɪlə/, **tailors**, **tailored**. **1** A **tailor** is a person who makes clothes, especially for men. EG In this street there were gentlemen's tailors of the highest quality. `N COUNT`

2 Tailored clothes are made to fit close to your body. EG ...a tight-fitting tailored dress. `ADJ CLASSIF : ATTRIB`

3 If something **is tailored** for a particular purpose, it is specially designed to be suitable for that purpose. EG ...factories and equipment tailored to meet the needs of the 20th century. `V+O : USU PASS`

tailor-made. Something that is **tailor-made** is very suitable for a particular person or purpose or was specially designed for them. EG Both the play and the role were tailor-made for her. `ADJ CLASSIF : OFT+for`

taint /teɪnt/, **taints**, **tainting**, **tainted**. **1** If you **taint** something, you spoil it by adding an undesirable quality to it. EG He feared that this would taint the scheme with some element of commercialism. `V+O Formal`

◊ **tainted**. EG The report was heavily tainted with racism... ...the tainted profits of conquest in South America. `◊ ADJ QUALIT : OFT+with`

2 A **taint** is an undesirable quality in something which spoils it. EG His career was never free of the taint of corruption. `N SING+SUPP Formal`

take /teɪk/, **takes**, **taking**, **took** /tʊk/, **taken** /teɪkə²n/. **1** You can use **take** to say that someone performs an action. For example, if you say that someone **takes** a look at something, you mean that they look at it. EG He took a step towards Jack... I took a magnificent photo of him... She took a shower... Certain decisions had to be taken... He formed the habit of taking long solitary walks... She's not yet taken her driving test. `V+O`

2 If someone **takes** office or **takes** power, they start being in control of something. EG He asked me to take charge... She showed no sign of taking command. `V+O`

3 If you **take** a particular attitude or view, you have it. EG The public was beginning to take a positive interest in defence. `V+O`

4 If something **takes** a certain amount of time, you need that amount of time in order to do it. EG How long will it take?... It may take them several weeks to get back. `V+O OR V+O+O`

5 If something **takes** a particular quality or thing, it requires it. EG It took a lot of courage to admit his mistake... It took three men to hold him down. `V+O`

6 If you **take** something, especially when someone is offering it to you, you put your hand round it and hold it. EG Let me take your coat... She took the menu from him... He took Sam by the hand. `V+O OR V+O+A`

7 If you **take** something from one place to another, you carry it there. EG She gave me some books to take home... He took a cigarette from the box on the table... A maid came to take away the tray... Emma opened her bag and took out her comb. `V+O : USU+A`

8 If you **take** someone somewhere, you drive them there in your car or lead them there. EG It's his turn to take the children to school. `V+O : USU+A`

9 If you **take** something that is offered to you, you accept it. EG She took a job in publishing... We've just had to take a pay cut. `V+O`

10 If you **take** the responsibilty or blame for something, you accept the responsibilty or blame for it. EG She doesn't expect you to take the blame... I would be perfectly willing to take the consequences. `V+O`

11 If you are in a shop and you say that you will **take** something, you mean that you will buy it. EG I'll take a dozen eggs. `V+O`

12 If someone **takes** something that belongs to you, they steal it or go away with it without your permission. EG A pickpocket took Barry's wallet... Someone's taken my pen. `V+O`

13 If you **take** pills, medicine, or drugs, you swallow them. EG I took a couple of aspirins. `V+O`

14 If you **take** a house or flat, you start renting it. EG He had taken a small flat in Brussels. `V+O`

15 If soldiers or terrorists **take** people or places, they capture them. EG We took the village without a shot being fired. `V+O : OFT+A OR C`

16 If you can **take** something such as pain or loneliness, you can bear it or endure it. EG I can't take pain... I can't take any more... Ordinary people find his arrogance hard to take. `V+O : NO CONT`

17 If you **take** an event or piece of news well or badly, you react to it well or badly. EG He would never take her fears seriously. `V+O+A`

18 If you **take** students for a subject, you give them lessons in it. EG She took them for geography. `V+O : USU+A`

19 If you **take** a person's temperature or pulse, you measure it. EG I took her temperature. `V+O`

20 If you **take** a particular size in shoes or clothes, you wear that size. EG She asked what size of shoes he took. `V+O`

21 If you **take** a car or train, for example, you use it to go from one place to another. EG She said she'd take a taxi... I think we ought to take the car. `V+O : USU+A`

22 If you **take** a road or route, you travel along it. EG He took the road southwards into the hills. `V+O : OFT+A`

23 If you **take** someone's advice or orders, you do what they say you should do. EG They have to take `V+O` *instructions from her... Take my advice, don't buy a house.*

24 To **take** something means to consider it. EG *Let's take one thing at a time... Some men change the world. Take Albert Einstein, for instance.* v+o: OFT IMPER

25 If you **take** someone's meaning, you understand v+o+A what they are saying. EG *He took my meaning perfectly... They took what I said as a kind of rebuke.*

26 Take is also used in these phrases. **26.1** You PHRASES can say **'I take it'** to check that the person you are talking to knows or understands something, or is giving you correct information. EG *I take it you know what a stethoscope is?... I take it that you've been quite candid with me.* **26.2** If something **takes a lot out of** you or **takes it out of** you, it makes you feel very tired. EG *Talking in a foreign language all day takes a lot out of you.*

take aback. If you **are taken aback**, you are PHRASAL VB: surprised or shocked. EG *I was a bit taken aback by* v+o+ADV *this sudden reversal.*

take after. If you **take after** someone in your PHRASAL VB: family, you look like them or behave like them. EG v+PREP *You don't take after your sister.*

take apart. If you **take** something **apart**, you PHRASAL VB: separate it into the different parts that it is made v+o+ADV of. EG *We encouraged them to explore, invent, take things apart, and put them together.*

take away. If you **take away** one number or PHRASAL VB: amount from another, you subtract it or deduct it. v+o+ADV For example, if you take 3 away from 5, you get 2. ● See also **takeaway**.

take back. **1** If you **take** something **back**, **1.1** you PHRASAL VB: return it to the place where you got it from. EG v+o+ADV *Don't forget to take your books back to the library.* **1.2** you agree to accept it again after you have sold v+o+ADV it or got rid of it. EG *Shopkeepers are often reluctant to take back unsatisfactory goods.* **2** If you v+o+ADV **take back** something that you said, you admit that it was wrong. EG *I'm going to have to take back all those things I said about you.*

take down. **1** When people **take down** a tempo- PHRASAL VB: rary structure, they separate it into pieces and v+o+ADV remove it. EG *The scaffolding won't be taken down until next year.* **2** If you **take down** what someone v+o+ADV is saying, you write it down. EG *The postmistress began to take down the message.*

take in. **1** If someone **is taken in**, they are PHRASAL VB: deceived. EG *I wasn't going to be taken in by this* v+o+ADV, kind of sentimentality... I completely took them in* OFT PASS *by telling them I'd been given a week's holiday.* **2** v+o+ADV If you **take** something **in**, you understand it when you hear it or read it. EG *People never take in new facts very easily when they're unhappy.* **3** If v+o+ADV something **takes in** something else, the first thing includes the second. EG *The area was stretched to take in some parts of Wales.*

take off. **1** When an aeroplane **takes off**, it PHRASAL VB: leaves the ground and starts flying. ● See also v+ADV. **takeoff.** **2** If you **take off** or **take** yourself **off**, you v+ADV OR go away suddenly. EG *They took off for a weekend* v+REFL+ADV, *in the country... She took herself off to Amsterdam.* USU+A **3** If you **take off** something that you are wearing, v+o+ADV you remove it. EG *He took off his glasses and blinked.* **4** If you **take** time **off**, you do not go to v+o+ADV work for one or more days. EG *She's taken the day off.*

take on. **1** If you **take on** a job or responsibility, PHRASAL VB: you accept it. EG *She takes on more work than is* v+o+ADV *good for her.* **2** If something **takes on** a new v+ADV+o quality, it begins to have that quality. EG *His voice took on a new note of uncertainty... The word 'profession' is taking on a new meaning.* **3** If you v+o+ADV **take** someone **on**, you employ them. EG *They took me on because I was a good mathematician.* **4** If v+o+ADV you **take on** a person or organization that is more powerful than you, you fight them or compete against them. EG *British Leyland plans to take on the competition at home and abroad.*

take out. If you **take** someone **out**, you invite PHRASAL VB: them to go with you to a restaurant or cinema, for v+o+ADV example, and you pay for both of you. EG *He offered to take her out for a meal.*

take out on. If you **take** your unhappiness or PHRASAL VB: anger **out on** someone, you behave in an unpleas- v+o+ADV ant way towards them, even though it is not their +PREP fault that you feel so upset. EG *She took out most of her unhappiness on her husband.*

take over. **1** If you **take over** something such as PHRASAL VB: a company or country, you gain control of it. EG *The* v+o+ADV agency tried to take over another company... Once* OR V+ADV *again the military had taken over.* ● See also **takeover.** **2** If you **take over** a job or if you **take** v+o+ADV **over**, you start doing the job after someone else OR V+ADV has stopped doing it. EG *They want me to take over as editor when Harold leaves.*

take to. **1** If you **take to** someone or something, PHRASAL VB: you like them immediately. EG *She immediately* v+PREP *took to him... We asked him if the Russians would take to golf.* **2** If you **take to** doing something, you v+PREP+-ING begin to do it regularly. EG *He took to wearing black leather jackets.*

take up. **1** If you **take up** an activity or job, you PHRASAL VB: start doing it. EG *I thought I'd take up fishing... My* v+o+ADV *assistant left to take up another post.* **2** If you **take** OR V+ADV **up** an activity that was interrupted, you continue doing it from the point where it had stopped. EG *Sam took up the story... David was taking up where he had left off.* **3** If you **take up** an idea or v+o+ADV suggestion, you discuss it further. EG *The committee is expected to take up the question of government grants.* **4** If something **takes up** an amount of v+ADV+o time, space, or effort, it uses that amount. EG *I won't take up any more of your time... Much of the day was taken up with classes or study.*

take up on. **1** If you **take** someone **up on** an PHRASAL VB: offer that they have made, you accept their offer. v+o+ADV EG *I really think you ought to take him up on his* +PREP *offer... I didn't expect her to take me up on my invitation.* **2** If you **take** someone **up on** what they v+o+ADV have just said, you ask them to explain or justify it. +PREP EG *I think I would like to take Tony up on that.*

take upon. If you **take** it **upon** yourself to do PHRASAL VB: something, you do it even though it is not your duty v+o+PREP or your job. EG *Mrs Kaul took it upon herself to turn round and say 'Sh'.*

takeaway /teɪkəweɪ/, **takeaways.** A **takeaway** N COUNT is **1** a shop or restaurant which sells hot cooked British food that you eat somewhere else. **2** a hot cooked British meal that is sold to be eaten somewhere else. EG *I fancy an Indian takeaway.*

taken /teɪkəᵊn/. **1 Taken** is the past participle of **take.**

2 If you are **taken** with something, you find it ADJ PRED attractive and interesting. EG *Philip had been ra-* +with *ther taken with the idea... We were all very taken with Mrs Wilkins.*

takeoff /teɪkɒf/, **takeoffs. Takeoff** is the begin- N UNCOUNT ning of a flight, when an aircraft leaves the ground. OR N COUNT EG *...fifty minutes after takeoff.*

takeover /teɪkəʊvə/, **takeovers. 1** When some- N COUNT OR one buys enough shares in a company to gain N UNCOUNT control of it, you describe this process as a **take- over.** EG *The trend towards takeovers has intensi- fied... ...another oil company ripe for takeover.*

2 When someone takes control of a country by N COUNT OR force, this is also described as a **takeover.** EG *He* N UNCOUNT *may be ousted by a military takeover.*

taker /teɪkə/, **takers.** If you say that there are no N COUNT **takers** or few **takers**, you mean that nobody, or hardly anybody, is willing to accept a bet or a challenge. EG *The bookmakers were offering 4 to 1 on, but there were no takers.*

If someone talks down to you, are they taller than you?

takings /teɪkɪŋz/. The **takings** are the money N PLURAL that a shop, theatre, or cinema gets from selling its goods or tickets. EG *The manager said that takings were as high as ever.*

talcum powder /tælkəm paʊdə/ is a soft, per- N UNCOUNT fumed powder which people put on their bodies after they have had a bath.

tale /teɪl/, **tales. 1** A **tale** is a story, especially one N COUNT involving adventure or magic. EG *They acted out tales of princes and magic birds.*

2 You can refer to an account of a real event as a N COUNT **tale**, especially when it is interesting or exciting. EG *Everyone had some tale to tell about the very cold winter.* ● See also **old wives' tale.**

talent /tælənt/, **talents. Talent** is the natural N UNCOUNT ability to do something well. EG *Does she have* OR N COUNT *talent?... Your work shows a lot of talent... Rudolph had a talent for music... ...my artistic talents.*

talented /tæləntɪd/. Someone who is **talented** ADJ QUALIT has a natural ability to do something well. EG *...a young and very talented writer... ...talented children.*

talisman /tælɪzmən/, **talismans.** A **talisman** is N COUNT an object which you believe has magic powers to Formal protect you or bring you luck.

talk /tɔːk/, **talks, talking, talked. 1** When you V : OFT+A **talk**, you say things to someone. EG *All the boys were talking at once... They talked about old times... He was the only one in the family she could talk to.* ▸ used as a noun. EG *I must have a long talk* ▸ N UNCOUNT *with him.* ● See also **small talk.** OR N COUNT

2 If people **are talking**, they are discussing inter- V esting things that they think are happening, especially other people's private affairs. EG *The neighbours will soon be talking.* ▸ used as a noun. EG ▸ N UNCOUNT *There was a lot of talk about his divorce.*

3 If you **talk** something such as politics or sport, V+O you discuss it. EG *They won't talk politics in the pub... Let's talk a little business, shall we?*

4 If you **talk** on or about something, you make an V+on/about informal speech about it. EG *I talked yesterday about the history of the project.* ▸ used as a noun. ▸ N COUNT EG *I used to give the staff a talk on psychology every week.*

5 If someone **talks**, they give other people secret V information. EG *Start talking, Castle. Or I'll shoot.*

6 You say **talking of** something that has just been PHRASE mentioned to introduce a new topic which has some connection with that thing. EG *Talking of marriage, isn't it lovely about Claire getting married?*

7 Talks are formal discussions, especially between N PLURAL two countries or two sides in a dispute. EG *Talks in London last week produced no hint of a settlement... ...peace talks.*

8 If you say to someone **'You can talk'**, you are CONVENTION telling them that they have the same fault that they have just criticized in someone else. EG *'She's so untidy.' – 'You can talk!'*

talk down to. If someone **talks down to** you, PHRASAL VB : they talk to you in a way that shows that they think V+ADV+PREP they are more important or more clever than you. EG *I think some of the teachers felt they were being talked down to.*

talk into. If you **talk** someone **into** doing some- PHRASAL VB : thing, you persuade them to do it. EG *She talked me* V+O+PREP *into taking a week's holiday.*

talk out of. If you **talk** someone **out of** doing PHRASAL VB : something, you persuade them not to do it. EG *He* V+O+ADV *tried to talk me out of buying such a big car.* +PREP

talk over. If you **talk** something **over**, you PHRASAL VB : discuss it with someone. EG *I agreed to go home and* V+O+ADV *talk things over with my father.*

talkative /tɔːkətɪv/. Someone who is **talkative** ADJ QUALIT talks a lot. EG *She was one of the more talkative members of the class... After the third whisky, he became lively and talkative.*

tall /tɔːl/, **taller, tallest. 1** Someone or something ADJ QUALIT that is **tall** has a greater height than most other people or things. EG *He was a tall, dark man... ...a tall cypress tree.*

2 You use **tall** when you refer to people's height. ADJ QUALIT OR For example, if you are six feet **tall**, your height is ADJ AFTER N six feet. If you are **taller** than someone else, your height is greater than theirs. EG *How tall is he?... ...a six-foot tall fifteen-year-old... She is starting to grow taller.*

3 If you say that a task is a **tall order**, you mean PHRASE that it will be difficult to do.

4 If you describe someone's account of an event as PHRASE a **tall story**, you mean that it is difficult to believe, because it is so unlikely. EG *He was full of tall stories.*

tally /tæliː/, **tallies, tallying, tallied. 1** A **tally** is N COUNT an informal record of amounts, such as money that you spend or points that you score in a game, which you keep adding to as you go along. EG *Can you keep a tally of your own marks, please?... The tally had now reached thirty-six.*

2 If numbers or statements **tally**, they are exactly V OR V+with : the same or they give the same results or conclu- RECIP sions. EG *We've checked their stories and they don't quite tally... The amount she mentioned failed to tally with the figure shown in the records.*

talon /tælən/, **talons.** The **talons** of a bird of prey, N COUNT : such as an eagle, are its hooked claws. USU PLURAL

tambourine /tæmbəriːn/, **tambourines.** A **tam-** N COUNT **bourine** is a musical instrument which you shake or hit with your hand. It consists of a drum skin on a circular frame and small round pieces of metal all around the edge. See picture at MUSICAL INSTRU-MENTS.

tame /teɪm/, **tamer, tamest; tames, taming, tamed. 1** A **tame** animal or bird is not afraid of ADJ QUALIT people and is not violent towards them. EG *...a tame monkey.* ◇ **tameness.** EG *We were amazed at their* ◇ N UNCOUNT *tameness.*

2 If you describe people as **tame**, you mean that ADJ QUALIT they do what they are told to do without questioning it; used showing disapproval. EG *...a tame family doctor.* ◇ **tamely.** EG *These measures are unlikely* ◇ ADV *to be accepted as tamely as the government hopes.*

3 You describe an activity as **tame** when you think ADJ QUALIT that it is uninteresting because it does not involve any excitement or risk. EG *It sounded like a rather tame party.*

4 If you **tame** people or things that are dangerous V+O or likely to cause trouble, you bring them under control. EG *...savages to be tamed and civilized... Governments have found it necessary to tame large concentrations of economic power.*

5 If you **tame** a wild animal or bird, you train it to V+O be obedient and not to be afraid of people. EG *She was a wild owl and I had no intention of taming her.*

tamper /tæmpə/, **tampers, tampering, tampe-** PHRASAL VB : **red.** If you **tamper with** something, you interfere V+PREP, with it when you have no right to do so. EG *Someone* HAS PASS *had tampered with the register and changed the records... He claimed that his briefcase had been tampered with.*

tampon /tæmpɒn/, **tampons.** A **tampon** is a firm, N COUNT specially shaped piece of cotton wool that a woman puts inside her vagina to absorb the blood when she has a period.

tan /tæn/. **1** If you have a **tan**, your skin has N SING : a+N become darker than usual because you have spent a lot of time in the sun. EG *She had a beautiful golden tan.*

2 Something that is **tan** is of a light yellowish- ADJ COLOUR brown colour. EG *...tan shoes.*

tandem /tændəm/, **tandems. 1** A **tandem** is a N COUNT bicycle designed for two riders sitting one behind the other.

2 If two people do something **in tandem**, they do it PHRASE working together. EG *...a new play we had written in tandem.*

tandoori /tænˈdʊəriː/ is an Indian method of cook- N UNCOUNT
ing meat in a clay oven.

tang /tæŋ/, **tangs.** A **tang** is a strong, sharp smell N COUNT :
or taste. EG ...*the tang of an expensive perfume.* USU SING

tangent /ˈtændʒənt/, **tangents.** 1 A **tangent** is a N COUNT
straight line that touches a curve at one point but
does not cross it.

2 If you **go off at a tangent**, you start talking or PHRASE
thinking about something that is not directly connected with what you were talking or thinking
about before. EG *His scientific mind immediately
went off at a tangent.*

tangerine /ˌtændʒəˈriːn/, **tangerines.** A **tange-** N COUNT
rine is a small, sweet orange.

tangible /ˈtændʒəbəl/. Something that is **tan-** ADJ QUALIT
gible is clear enough or definite enough to be
easily seen, felt, or noticed. EG *His rule as Prime
Minister brought few tangible benefits to the poor...
Politicians always want tangible results.*
◊ **tangibly.** EG *The evidence tangibly supports his* ◊ ADV
claim.

tangle /ˈtæŋgəl/, **tangles, tangling, tangled.** 1 A N COUNT :
tangle is a mass of things such as string, wire, or OFT+*of*
hair twisted together in an untidy way so that they
are difficult to separate. EG ...*an impenetrable tangle of creepers and trees.*

2 Something that is **tangled** is twisted together in ADJ QUALIT
an untidy way. EG *She pushed the tangled hair back
from her face... The wires got all tangled.*

3 If you **are tangled** in wires or ropes or **are** V-PASS+A :
tangled up in them, you are caught or trapped in OFT+*up*
them so that it is difficult to get free. EG *His leg got
tangled in a harpoon line.*

4 You can refer to a state of disorder and confusion N SING
as a **tangle.** EG *My tax affairs were in a complete
tangle.*

tangle with. If you **tangle with** someone, you PHRASAL VB :
get involved in a fight or quarrel with them. EG *I* V+PREP,
wouldn't tangle with him if I were you. HAS PASS

tank /tæŋk/, **tanks.** 1 A **tank** is a large container, N COUNT
usually made of metal, for holding liquid or gas. EG
*The tank will only hold three gallons... ...a petrol
tank... ...the cold water tank.*

2 A **tank** is also a military vehicle covered with N COUNT
armour and equipped with guns or rockets.

tankard /ˈtæŋkəd/, **tankards.** A **tankard** is a N COUNT
large metal mug with a handle that people drink
beer from.

tanker /ˈtæŋkə/, **tankers.** A **tanker** is a ship, N COUNT
truck, or railway vehicle used for transporting
large quantities of gas or liquid. EG ...*an oil tanker.*

tanned /tænd/. If you are **tanned**, your skin is ADJ QUALIT
darker than usual because you have spent a lot of
time in the sun. EG ...*tanned, slim young men.*

tannery /ˈtænəriː/, **tanneries.** A **tannery** is a N COUNT
place where animal skins are made into leather.

tantalize /ˈtæntəlaɪz/, **tantalizes, tantalizing,** V+O
tantalized; also spelled **tantalise.** If something or
someone **tantalizes** you, they make you feel hopeful and excited, and then do not allow you to have
what you want. ◊ **tantalizing.** EG *This raises the* ◊ ADJ QUALIT
*tantalizing possibility that there may be life on
other stars.* ◊ **tantalizingly.** EG *Sometimes a new* ◊ ADV
idea may be tantalizingly close.*

tantamount /ˈtæntəmaʊnt/. If you say that some- ADJ PRED+*to*
thing is **tantamount** to something else, you mean
that it is almost the same as it. EG *His statement
was tantamount to an admission of responsibility.*

tantrum /ˈtæntrəm/, **tantrums.** A **tantrum** is a N COUNT
noisy outburst of bad temper, especially by a child.
EG ...*a spoiled child who throws tantrums when she
doesn't get her own way.*

tap /tæp/, **taps, tapping, tapped.** 1 A **tap** is a N COUNT
device that you turn in order to control the flow of
a liquid or gas from a pipe or container. Sinks and
baths have taps attached to them. EG *Someone left
the tap running... Turn on the hot tap... ...a gas tap.*

2 If you **tap** something or **tap** on it, you hit it V+O OR V+A
lightly with your fingers or with something else. EG

*It will come loose if you tap it with a hammer... She
tapped on the glass partition.* ▸ used as a noun. EG *I* ▸ N COUNT
heard a soft tap at the front door.

3 If you **tap** a resource or situation, you make use V+O
of it by getting something that you want from it. EG
...*a new way of tapping the sun's energy.*

tape /teɪp/, **tapes, taping, taped.** 1 **Tape** is N UNCOUNT
plastic made in long strips and covered with a
magnetic substance. It is used to record sounds,
pictures, and computer information. EG ...*a conversation recorded on tape.* ● See also **magnetic tape,
video tape.**

2 A **tape** is a cassette or spool with magnetic tape N COUNT
wound round it. It is used for recording or replaying sounds, pictures, or computer information. EG
*Do you want to put on a tape?... His manager
persuaded him to make a tape of the song.*

3 If you **tape** music, sounds, or television pictures, V+O
you record them using a tape recorder or a video
recorder. EG *I'm having to tape this talk several
days in advance... ...a taped commentary.*

4 A **tape** is also a strip of cloth sewn onto a piece of N COUNT OR
clothing or other material. Tapes are used to tie N UNCOUNT
things together or to identify who a piece of
clothing belongs to. EG ...*three metres of white
tape... You have to sew name tapes into everything.*

5 In a race, the **tape** is a ribbon stretched across N COUNT
the finishing line.

6 **Tape** is also sticky strips of plastic which you use N UNCOUNT
for sticking things together. EG ...*a bit of adhesive
tape.*

7 If you **tape** one thing to another, you attach them V+O+A
together using sticky tape.

8 See also **red tape.**

tape deck, tape decks. A **tape deck** is a ma- N COUNT
chine on which you can play or record tapes.

tape measure, tape measures. A **tape meas-** N COUNT
ure is a strip of plastic or cloth with centimetres or
inches marked on it. You use it for measuring
things.

taper /ˈteɪpə/, **tapers, tapering, tapered.** 1 You V
say that something **tapers** when it gradually becomes thinner at one end. EG *Eventually the gallery
tapered to a long, narrow corridor.* ◊ **tapered.** EG ◊ ADJ QUALIT
The trousers should have tapered legs.
◊ **tapering.** EG ...*long tapering fingers.* ◊ ADJ QUALIT

2 A **taper** is a long, thin candle. N COUNT

taper off. If something **tapers off**, it gradually PHRASAL VB :
becomes much smaller. EG *The economic boom* V+ADV
tapered off.

tape recorder, tape recorders. A **tape record-** N COUNT
er is a machine used for recording and playing
music, speech, and other sounds.

tape recording, tape recordings. A **tape re-** N COUNT
cording is a recording of speech or other sounds
that has been made on a tape.

tapestry /ˈtæpɪstriː/, **tapestries.** 1 A **tapestry** is N COUNT OR
a piece of heavy cloth with a picture or pattern N UNCOUNT
sewn on it. EG ...*the Bayeux tapestry.*

2 You can refer to something as a **tapestry** when N COUNT+*of*
it is made up of many interesting and different Literary
things or people. EG *The book presents a tapestry of
teenage life in the provinces.*

tar /tɑː/ is a thick, black, sticky substance that N UNCOUNT
becomes hard when it is cold. It is used in making
roads.

target /ˈtɑːgɪt/, **targets.** 1 A **target** is **1.1** a town, N COUNT
building, or other place at which a weapon such as
a missile or bomb is aimed. EG *The missile can land
within a half-mile radius of its target... The station
was an easy target for an air attack.* **1.2** an object
at which you fire arrows or bullets when you are
shooting for sport or practice. A target often
consists of a large circle with smaller circles inside

If you tangle with someone, do you get tangled
up?

it, marked on a board or piece of paper. EG *My first two shots missed the target.*

2 When someone or something is being criticized or blamed, you can refer to them as a **target**. EG *In their search for a scapegoat, the Government found an easy target in the unions.* N COUNT : OFT+SUPP

3 A **target** is also a result that you are trying to achieve. EG *It set a target for economic growth in excess of 4% a year.* ● If you are **on target**, you are making good progress and are likely to achieve the result you want. EG *The latest sales figures are on target.* N COUNT ● PHRASE

tariff /tǽrɪf/, **tariffs**. A **tariff** is a tax that a government collects on goods coming into a country. EG *...a high tariff on all imports.* N COUNT

tarmac /tɑ́ːmæk/. **1 Tarmac** is a material used for making road surfaces. It consists of crushed stones mixed with tar. EG *...a tarmac road.* N UNCOUNT Trademark

2 You can refer to any area with a tarmac surface as the **tarmac**. EG *He went out onto the tarmac where the jet was waiting.* N SING : the+N

tarnish /tɑ́ːnɪʃ/, **tarnishes, tarnishing, tarnished**. **1** If metal **tarnishes**, it becomes stained and loses its brightness. EG *Chrome doesn't tarnish easily... The damp atmosphere tends to tarnish the brass taps.* ◊ **tarnished**. EG *There was a photo in a silver frame, by now rather tarnished.* V-ERG ◊ ADJ QUALIT

2 If something **tarnishes** your reputation, it damages it and causes people to lose their respect for you. EG *...a trial that tarnished the names of many intellectuals.* ◊ **tarnished**. EG *...an attempt to restore some of their tarnished popularity.* V+O ◊ ADJ QUALIT

tarpaulin /tɑːpɔ́ːlɪn/, **tarpaulins**. A **tarpaulin** is a sheet of heavy, waterproof material that is used to cover things and protect them from rain. N COUNT

tarred /tɑːd/. A **tarred** road has a surface of tar. ADJ CLASSIF

tart /tɑːt/, **tarts; tarter, tartest**. **1** A **tart** is a piece of pastry with something sweet, such as jam or cooked fruit, inside. EG *...jam tarts... Have another slice of tart.* N COUNT OR N UNCOUNT

2 A **tart** remark is unpleasant and rather cruel. EG *She spoke with tart contempt.* ◊ **tartly**. EG *She tartly pointed out that he owed her some money.* ADJ QUALIT ◊ ADV

3 Prostitutes are sometimes referred to as **tarts**. EG *Only tarts wore make-up in those days.* N COUNT Informal

tartan /tɑ́ːtəⁿn/, **tartans**. **Tartan** is woollen cloth from Scotland that has patterns of different coloured stripes crossing each other. EG *...a skirt made of tartan... ...the tartans of the Gordon and Wallace clans... ...a tartan rug.* N UNCOUNT OR N COUNT

task /tɑːsk/, **tasks**. A **task** is a piece of work that must be done. EG *...the endless task of classifying the samples... Computers can be applied to a wide range of tasks.* N COUNT

tassel /tǽsəⁿl/, **tassels**. A **tassel** is a bunch of short pieces of material tied together at one end and attached to something as a decoration. EG *...the tassels on their cloaks.* N COUNT

taste /teɪst/, **tastes, tasting, tasted**. **1** Your sense of **taste** is your ability to recognize things when you touch them with your tongue. EG *Some animals have a better sense of taste than others.* N UNCOUNT

2 The **taste** of something is the special flavour that it has, for example whether it is sweet or salty. EG *I don't like the taste of fresh fish... The soup was peppered and spiced to improve the taste.* N SING : USU+SUPP

3 If you have a **taste** of food or drink, you try a small amount in order to see what its taste is like. EG *I opened one of the bottles and had a taste of the contents.* N SING

4 When you can **taste** something that you are eating or drinking, you are aware of its flavour. EG *Roger chewed and swallowed so fast that he hardly tasted the meat.* V+O

5 If you **taste** food or drink, you try a small amount in order to decide whether you like it or not. EG *He insisted on pouring the wine for a guest to taste.* V+O

6 If food or drink **tastes** of something, it has a particular flavour, which you notice when you eat V+A OR C : NO CONT

or drink it. EG *The tea tasted faintly of bitter almonds.*

7 If you have a **taste** for something, you enjoy it. EG *He had not lost the taste for power... He has little taste for politics... Ben suddenly lost his taste for publicity.* N SING+for

8 If you have a **taste** of something such as a way of life or a pleasure, you experience it for a short time. EG *The child may already have had a taste of street life.* N SING+of

9 A person's **taste** is their choice in the things that they like or buy. You can show your opinion of their choice by talking about their 'good taste' or their 'bad taste'. EG *She has very good taste in clothes... Her novels are too violent for my taste.* N UNCOUNT : USU+SUPP

10 If you say that something that someone has said or done is **in bad taste**, you mean that it is offensive. If it is **in good taste**, it is not offensive. EG *That remark was in rather poor taste... Her jokes are always in the best possible taste.* PHRASE

tasteful /teɪstfʊl/. If you describe something as **tasteful**, you mean that it is attractive and elegant. EG *The bedroom was simple but tasteful.* ◊ **tastefully** EG *Their house was tastefully furnished.* ADJ QUALIT ◊ ADV

tasteless /teɪstlɪ²s/. **1** If you say that something is **tasteless**, you mean that it is vulgar and unattractive. EG *The room was full of tasteless ornaments.* ADJ QUALIT

2 If you describe a remark or joke as **tasteless**, you mean that it is offensive. EG *Apart from a few tasteless remarks, he was reasonably well-behaved... ...tasteless jokes.* ADJ QUALIT

3 If you describe food as **tasteless**, you mean that it is not enjoyable, because it has very little flavour. EG *The cafeteria serves cold, tasteless pizzas.* ADJ QUALIT

tasty /teɪsti/, **tastier, tastiest**. If you describe food as **tasty**, you mean that it is enjoyable, because it has a pleasant flavour. EG *Sunflower seeds are tasty and nutritious.* ADJ QUALIT

tattered /tǽtəd/. **Tattered** clothing or paper is torn or crumpled. EG *...a man in a tattered shirt... ...paintings tied up in tattered brown paper.* ADJ QUALIT

tatters /tǽtəz/. **1** Clothes that are **in tatters** are badly torn. EG *He arrived with his garments in tatters.* PHRASE

2 You can say that something is **in tatters** when it has been severely damaged or ruined. EG *Peter was dejected, his confidence in tatters.* PHRASE

tattoo /tætúː/, **tattoos, tattooing, tattooed**. **1** If someone **tattoos** you or **tattoos** a picture or design on you, they draw it on your skin by pricking little holes and filling them with coloured dye. EG *He had tattooed the name 'Marlene' on his upper arm.* ◊ **tattooed**. EG *...a tattooed sailor.* V+O ◊ ADJ CLASSIF

2 A **tattoo** is a picture or design tattooed on someone's body. EG *He had a tattoo on the back of his hand.* N COUNT

3 If you beat a **tattoo**, you hit something quickly and repeatedly. EG *He beat a frantic tattoo with his hands on the door.* N COUNT : USU SING

4 A **tattoo** is also a public display of exercises and music given by the army, navy, or air force. N COUNT

tatty /tǽti/. If you describe something as **tatty**, you mean that it is untidy and rather dirty. EG *...a tatty old skirt... ...this pleasantly tatty seaside resort.* ADJ QUALIT Informal

taught /tɔːt/ is the past tense and past participle of **teach**.

taunt /tɔːnt/, **taunts, taunting, taunted**. If you **taunt** someone, you speak offensively to them about their weaknesses or failures in order to upset or annoy them. EG *...street marchers taunting the police.* ▸ used as a noun. EG *The children had to put up with taunts like 'You haven't got a Dad.'* V+O ▸ N COUNT

taut /tɔːt/. Something that is **taut** is stretched very tight. EG *...a taut wire.* ADJ QUALIT

tavern /tǽvəⁿn/, **taverns**. A **tavern** is a pub. EG *I opened the door of the Shakespeare Tavern.* N COUNT Outdated

tax /tæks/, **taxes, taxing, taxed. 1 Tax** is an N UNCOUNT amount of money that you have to pay to the OR N COUNT government so that it can pay for public services. EG *...a tax on pensions... The tax cuts take effect on July 1st... ...a reduction in taxes.*

2 If a sum of money **is taxed**, a part of it has to be V+O : OFT PASS paid to the government. EG *Any money earned over that level is taxed at the rate of 59%.*

3 If goods **are taxed**, a part of their price has to be V+O : OFT PASS paid to the government. EG *Crops were taxed very heavily.*

4 If a person or company **is taxed**, they have to V+O : OFT PASS pay a part of their income or profits to the government. EG *She was not taxed separately from her husband.*

5 See also **taxing.**

taxable /tæksəbªl/. If something is **taxable**, you ADJ CLASSIF have to pay tax on it. EG *...taxable income.*

taxation /tækseɪʃªn/ is **1** the system by which a N UNCOUNT government takes some money from the people and spends it on such things as education, health, and defence. **2** the amount of money that people have to pay in taxes. EG *The government is hoping to reduce taxation.*

tax-free. When goods or services are **tax-free**, ADJ CLASSIF you do not have to pay tax on them.

taxi /tæksiˈ/, **taxis, taxiing, taxied. 1** A **taxi** is a N COUNT car driven by someone whose job is to take you OR by+N where you want to go in return for money.

2 When an aircraft **taxis**, it moves slowly along the V : USU+A runway before taking off or after landing. EG *The Boeing taxied down the runway.*

taxing /tæksɪŋ/. A **taxing** task requires a lot of ADJ QUALIT mental or physical effort. EG *They faced new and taxing problems.*

taxpayer /tækspeɪə/, **taxpayers. Taxpayers** are N COUNT people who pay a percentage of their income to the government as tax.

TB /tiː biː/ is an abbreviation for 'tuberculosis'. N UNCOUNT

tea /tiː/, **teas. 1 Tea** is a drink made with hot N MASS water and the chopped, dried leaves of a particular bush. Milk and sugar are often added to the drink. EG *She poured herself another cup of tea... She went into the kitchen to make a fresh pot of tea.*

2 Tea is also **2.1** the bush whose leaves are used to N UNCOUNT make tea. EG *He wanted to go to Ceylon and plant tea.* **2.2** the chopped, dried leaves of the bush that N MASS you use to make tea. EG *...a packet of tea.*

3 A **tea** is a cup of tea. EG *Two teas, please.* N COUNT

4 Other drinks made with hot water and leaves or N MASS+SUPP flowers are also called **tea.** EG *...mint tea.*

5 Tea is also a light meal that is eaten in the N UNCOUNT afternoon. Some British people refer to the main OR N COUNT meal that they eat in the early evening as **tea.** EG *I always come back from work to find the tea ready... At tea we talked about the day's events... Mr Evans is coming to tea.*

6 If you say that something is **not** your **cup of tea,** PHRASE you mean that you do not like it and would not choose to do it or to have it. EG *Ballet isn't really my cup of tea.*

tea bag, tea bags. A **tea bag** is a small paper bag N COUNT with tea leaves in it. You put the tea bag into hot water to make tea and then throw the tea bag away.

teach /tiːtʃ/, **teaches, teaching, taught** /tɔːt/. **1** If V+O+O; ALSO you **teach** someone something, you give them V+O+REPORT, instructions so that they know about it or know to-INF, OR how to do it. EG *Mother taught me how to read...* to *Boylan had taught him to drive... Johnny taught me everything I know.*

2 If you **teach** someone to think or to behave in a V+O+O; ALSO particular way, you persuade them to think or to V+O+REPORT, behave in that way. EG *Gandhi taught the world* to-INF, OR *passive resistance... Boys are often taught that they* to *mustn't show their feelings... We've been taught to believe in the wisdom of those who govern us.*

3 If you **teach** a subject or **teach**, your job is to V+O, V+O+to, help students to learn about something at a school, OR V

college, or university. EG *I taught history for many years... I found a job teaching English to a group of adults in Paris... Mrs Barton teaches in a secondary modern school.*

teacher /tiːtʃə/, **teachers.** A **teacher** is someone N COUNT who teaches, especially at a school. EG *...a French teacher... ...a teacher of English Literature.*

teaching /tiːtʃɪŋ/, **teachings. 1 Teaching** is the N UNCOUNT work that a teacher does. EG *Have you done any teaching lately?*

2 A person's **teachings** are the principles that they N COUNT : teach to other people. EG *His teachings still exert a* USU PLURAL *strong influence.*

teacup /tiːkʌp/, **teacups. 1** A **teacup** is a cup that N COUNT you drink tea from.

2 If you describe a situation as a **storm in a** PHRASE **teacup,** you mean that a lot of fuss is being made about something that is not important.

teak /tiːk/ is a kind of very hard wood. EG *The* N UNCOUNT *chairs were of black teak... ...teak furniture.*

tea leaf, tea leaves. Tea leaves are the small N COUNT : pieces of dried leaves that are left in a teapot or a USU PLURAL cup after you have drunk the tea.

team /tiːm/, **teams, teaming, teamed. 1** A **team** N COLL is a group of people who play together against another group in a sport or game. EG *...the New Zealand rugby team.*

2 You can refer to any group of people who work N COLL together as a **team.** EG *...a team of scientists.*

team up. If you **team up** with someone, you join PHRASAL VB : them so that you can do something together. EG *He* V+ADV OR *teamed up with a friend and set up a business doing* V+ADV+with : *interior decorating.* RECIP

teamwork /tiːmwɜːk/ is the ability of a group of N UNCOUNT people to work well together. EG *Teamwork was even more important in the later stages of the project.*

tea party, tea parties. A **tea party** is a social N COUNT gathering in the afternoon at which you drink tea and eat food such as sandwiches and cakes.

teapot /tiːpɒt/, **teapots.** A **teapot** is a container N COUNT with a lid, a handle, and a spout. You use it for making and serving tea.

tear, tears, tearing, tore /tɔː/, **torn** /tɔːn/. **Tear** is pronounced /tɪə/ for paragraph 1, and /teə/ for paragraphs 2 to 8 and the phrasal verbs.

1 Tears are the drops of liquid that come out of N COUNT : your eyes when you cry. EG *He was sitting there* USU PLURAL *with tears in his eyes... Tears were streaming down her face... Tears fell from Mother's eyes.* ● If ● PHRASE someone is **in tears,** they are crying. EG *When Curzon heard the news, he burst into tears.*

2 If you **tear** something made of cloth or paper, V-ERG : OFT+A you pull it into two pieces or pull it so that a hole appears in it. EG *He tore my coat in the struggle... Regretfully, he tore both letters into small pieces... I tugged at the sleeve to get it free. It tore.* ◊ **torn.** ◊ ADJ CLASSIF EG *...my torn sweater.*

3 A **tear** in something such as a piece of clothing is N COUNT a hole that has been made in it. EG *There was a triangular tear at the knee of his trousers.* ● See also **wear and tear.**

4 To **tear** something from somewhere means to V+O+A remove it roughly and violently. EG *She tore several sheets of paper out of the back of the book... Boats were torn from their moorings by the storm.*

5 If you **tear** somewhere, you move very quickly. V+A EG *She came tearing out of the house... He tore off home... They tore down the street after the dog.*

6 If you **are torn** between two or more things, you V+O : cannot decide which one to choose, and this makes USU PASS+A you feel unhappy. EG *Charles is torn between Susan and his fiancee, Tina.*

7 If you **tear loose** or **tear** yourself **loose,** you PHRASE suddenly and violently escape from someone or something that is holding you. EG *The piglet tore loose from the creepers.*

8 If you **tear** something **open**, you open it roughly and quickly, by tearing it. EG *He tore open the envelope... I watched her tearing open a packet of sugar.* PHRASE

tear apart. **1** If you **tear** something **apart**, you pull it into pieces violently. EG *I tore the parcel apart.* **2** If something **tears** an organization or country **apart**, it causes great quarrels or disturbances. EG *He was fighting against the 'anarchy' which he insisted was tearing the Church apart.* **3** If something **tears** you **apart**, it makes you feel very upset. EG *She is torn apart by conflicting pressures.* PHRASAL VB : V+O+ADV

tear at. If you **tear at** something, you violently try to pull pieces off it. EG *The boys tore at the meat like wolves.* PHRASAL VB : V+PREP

tear away. If you **tear** someone **away** from a place or activity, you force them to leave the place or stop doing the activity. EG *Mourners often find it difficult to tear themselves away from the grave.* PHRASAL VB : V+O+ADV, OFT+*from*

tear down. If you **tear down** a building, you destroy it. EG *It is often cheaper to tear down the buildings than to modify them.* PHRASAL VB : V+O+ADV

tear off. If you **tear** your clothes **off**, you take them off quickly in a rough way. EG *I tore off my shirt.* PHRASAL VB : V+O+ADV

tear up. If you **tear up** a piece of paper, you pull it into a lot of small pieces. EG *She wrote a suicide note. Then she tore it up.* PHRASAL VB : V+O+ADV

tearful /tɪəful/. If you are **tearful**, you are crying. EG *His tearful family came to pay their last respects.* ◊ **tearfully.** EG *He looked at her tearfully.* ADJ QUALIT ◊ ADV

tear gas /tɪə gæs/ is a gas that causes your eyes to sting and fill with tears. It is sometimes used by the police to control violent crowds. N UNCOUNT

tease /tiːz/, **teases, teasing, teased.** **1** If you **tease** someone, you deliberately embarrass them, trick them, or make fun of them, because this amuses you. EG *She teased him about his girlfriends... 'Ah hah,' the old man teased, 'perhaps you already have a child?'* V+O, V+O+A, OR V+QUOTE

2 A **tease** is someone who makes fun of people in a gentle but slightly cruel way. EG *You're a terrible tease. I never know when you're serious.* N SING : a+N

tea shop, tea shops. A **tea shop** is a small restaurant or café where tea, coffee, cakes, and light meals are served. N COUNT British

teaspoon /tiːspuːn/, **teaspoons.** **1** A **teaspoon** is a small spoon that you use to put sugar into tea or coffee. N COUNT

2 A **teaspoon** of food or liquid is the amount that a teaspoon will hold. EG *Add one teaspoon of salt.* N PART

teaspoonful /tiːspuːnful/, **teaspoonfuls** or **teaspoonsful.** A **teaspoonful** is the amount that a teaspoon will hold. EG *...two teaspoonfuls of sugar.* N PART

tea strainer /tiː streɪnə/, **tea strainers.** A **tea strainer** is a small metal or plastic object with a lot of small holes in it. It is used to stop tea leaves going into the cup when you are pouring tea. N COUNT

teat /tiːt/, **teats.** A **teat** is **1** one of the pieces of flesh that stick out on the chest or stomach of a female animal and from which its babies suck milk: compare **nipple.** EG *...tiny naked pink creatures clinging to the teats with their mouths.* **2** a piece of rubber or plastic that is shaped like a teat and is fitted to a bottle so that a baby can suck liquids from it. EG *The baby grabbed the teat and began to suck.* N COUNT

teatime /tiːtaɪm/ is the time in the afternoon when people often have tea. EG *At teatime there was much excited chatter around the table.* N UNCOUNT British

tea-towel, tea-towels. A **tea-towel** is a cloth which you use to dry dishes and cutlery after they have been washed. N COUNT British

tech /tek/, **techs.** A **tech** is the same as a technical college. EG *Actually I teach at the Tech... The* N COUNT Informal British

woman felt strongly that Techs served a valuable function.

technical /teknɪkəl/. **1 Technical** means involving details about machines, processes, and materials that are used, especially in industry, transport, and communications. EG *...scientific and technical knowledge... ...technical advances that improve productivity.* ADJ QUALIT : USU ATTRIB

2 You also use **technical** to describe the practical skills and methods a person uses to do an activity such as an art, a craft, or a sport. EG *...wood carving of remarkable technical skill.* ADJ QUALIT : USU ATTRIB

3 Technical language involves using special words, or using ordinary words in a special way, in order to describe the details of a subject or activity. In this dictionary, language of this kind is indicated by the word 'Technical' in the Extra Column. ADJ QUALIT : ATTRIB

technical college, technical colleges. A **technical college** is a college in Britain where you can study subjects to 'O' or 'A' level, usually as part of the qualifications and training required for a particular job. N COUNT

technicality /teknɪkælɪtiː/, **technicalities.** **1** The **technicalities** of a process or activity are the detailed methods used to do it. EG *I was quite interested in the technicalities of the recording.* N PLURAL

2 A **technicality** is a point that is based on a strict interpretation of a law or a set of rules. EG *On a technicality, the judge dismissed the case.* N COUNT

technically /teknɪkəliː/. **1** If something is **technically** true or correct, it is true or correct when you consider only the facts, laws, or rules but may not be important or relevant in a particular situation. EG *He was technically in breach of contract.* ADV SEN OR ADV

2 You use **technically** when discussing details about machines, processes, and materials used, especially in industry, transport, and communications. EG *It's quite clear that the electric car is technically feasible.* ADV

3 You also use **technically** when discussing the practical skills and methods a person uses to do an activity such as an art, a craft, or a sport. EG *Pollock was certainly a skilful artist technically.* ADV

technician /teknɪʃən/, **technicians.** A **technician** is someone whose job involves skilled practical work with scientific equipment, for example in a laboratory. N COUNT

Technicolor /teknɪkʌlə/ is a system of colour photography used in making cinema films. N UNCOUNT Trademark

technique /teknɪːk/, **techniques.** **1** A **technique** is a particular method of doing something. EG *...the techniques of film-making.* N COUNT

2 Technique is skill and ability in an artistic, sporting, or other practical activity that you develop through training and practice. EG *She owed her technique entirely to his teaching.* N UNCOUNT

technological /teknəlɒdʒɪkəl/ means relating to, resulting from, or associated with technology. EG *...modern scientific and technological knowledge.* ◊ **technologically.** EG *...the world's richest and most technologically advanced nations.* ADJ CLASSIF : ATTRIB ◊ ADV

technology /teknɒlədʒiː/, **technologies.** **1 Technology** is the activity or study of using scientific knowledge for practical purposes in industry, farming, medicine, or business. EG *...advances in technology and science.* ◊ **technologist** /teknɒlədʒɪst/, **technologists.** EG *...a small group of distinguished scientists and technologists.* N UNCOUNT ◊ N COUNT

2 A **technology** is a particular area of activity that requires scientific methods and knowledge. EG *...computer technology.* N COUNT OR N UNCOUNT +SUPP

teddy /tediː/, **teddies.** A **teddy** or a **teddy bear** is a soft toy that looks like a bear. N COUNT

tedious /tiːdɪəs/. Something that is **tedious** is boring and lasts for a long time. EG *The arguments were tedious and complicated... ...rather tedious lunch parties... ...four weeks of remarkably tedious work.* ADJ QUALIT

tedium /tiːdɪəm/. The **tedium** of a situation is its N UNCOUNT quality of being boring and seeming to last for a Formal long time. EG ...*the tedium of being young and poor*... ...*a cricket match of unspeakable tedium.*

teem /tiːm/, **teems, teeming, teemed.** If a place V+with : **is teeming** with people, there are a lot of people USU CONT moving around in it. EG ...*a large, busy capital teeming with people.* ◊ **teeming.** EG *She walked* ◊ ADJ CLASSIF : *home through the teeming streets*... ...*separating it* ATTRIB *from the teeming jungle to the east.*

teenage /tiːneɪdʒ/. **1 Teenage** people are aged ADJ CLASSIF : between thirteen and nineteen. EG ...*a divorced* ATTRIB *woman with two teenage children.*
2 Teenage fashions and activities are considered ADJ CLASSIF : to be typical of young people aged between thir- ATTRIB teen and nineteen or to be suitable for them. EG ...*the teenage culture of pop music and magazines.*

teenager /tiːneɪdʒə/, **teenagers.** A **teenager** is N COUNT someone aged between thirteen and nineteen. EG ...*a highly intelligent teenager.*

teens /tiːnz/. Your **teens** are the period of your N PLURAL life when you are between thirteen and nineteen years old. EG *She was young, maybe still in her teens*... ...*her first serious run since her teens.*

teeter /tiːtə/, **teeters, teetering, teetered. 1** If V : USU+A someone or something **teeters**, they move or shake unsteadily and seem about to fall over. EG *My last penny wobbled across the board, teetered about for a second, and then fell over.*
2 If something **teeters** on the brink of disaster, it is V+on very close to disaster. EG *British theatre is in a perilous state, teetering on the brink of ruin.*

teeth /tiːθ/ is the plural of **tooth.**

teethe /tiːð/, **teethes, teething, teethed.** When V : USU CONT babies **are teething,** their teeth are starting to appear through their gums, usually causing them pain.

teething troubles are difficulties which arise N PLURAL when a project has just begun or when something is new. EG *They had terrible teething troubles with the steering on the new model.*

teetotal /tiːtəʊtəl/. Someone who is **teetotal** nev- ADJ CLASSIF er drinks alcohol.

teetotaller /tiːtəʊtələ/, **teetotallers.** A **teetotal-** N COUNT **ler** is someone who never drinks alcohol.

TEFL /tefəl/ is the teaching of English to stu- N UNCOUNT dents from countries where English is not the main language and where it is not essential for education or jobs. **TEFL** is an abbreviation for 'teaching English as a foreign language'.

telecommunications /telɪkəmjuːnɪkeɪʃənz/ is N UNCOUNT : the science and activity of sending signals and OFT N MOD messages over long distances using electronic equipment, such as radio or telephone.

telegram /telɪgræm/, **telegrams.** A **telegram** is N COUNT a message that is sent by telegraph and then printed and delivered to someone. EG *I sent a telegram to my mother saying I had arrived safely.*

telegraph /telɪgræf, -grɑːf/, **telegraphs, tele-** N SING : the+N **graphing, telegraphed. 1** The **telegraph** is a system of sending messages over long distances by means of electrical or radio signals, and printing them at the other end.
2 If you **telegraph** someone, you send them a V OR V+O : message using the telegraph system. EG *Harold had* OFT+REPORT *telegraphed him in France.* OR to
Outdated

telepathic /telɪpæθɪk/. If someone claims to be ADJ CLASSIF **telepathic** or to have **telepathic** powers, they claim to be able to communicate directly with other people using only their minds.

telepathy /tɪˈlepəθɪ/ is direct communication be- N UNCOUNT tween people's minds. EG *We are particularly inter- ested in phenomena such as telepathy.*

telephone /telɪfəʊn/, **telephones, telephoning, telephoned. 1** The **telephone** is an electrical N SING : the+N, system that you use to talk to someone in another OR by+N place by dialling a number on a piece of equipment and speaking into it. EG *Reports came in by tele- phone*... *I have to make a telephone call.*

2 A **telephone** is the piece of equipment that you N COUNT use when you talk to someone by telephone. EG *He put down the telephone.*
3 If you **telephone** someone, you dial their tele- V OR V+O phone number and speak to them by telephone. EG Formal *I'll telephone her this evening*... *Brody telephoned to thank her.*
4 If you are **on the telephone, 4.1** you are PHRASE speaking to someone by telephone. **4.2** you have a telephone in your home or place of work, so that you can be contacted by telephone.

telephone book, telephone books. A **telephone** N COUNT **book** is a book that contains an alphabetical list of names, addresses, and telephone numbers of the people in a town or area.

telephone booth, telephone booths. A **tele-** N COUNT **phone booth** is a place in a station, hotel, or other British public building where there is a public telephone.

telephone box, telephone boxes. A **telephone** N COUNT **box** is a small shelter in the street in which there is British a public telephone.

telephone directory, telephone directories. N COUNT A **telephone directory** is the same as a telephone book.

telephone exchange, telephone exchanges. A N COUNT **telephone exchange** is a building belonging to a telephone company or system, where the tele- phone lines are connected when someone in the area makes or receives a telephone call.

telephone number, telephone numbers. Your N COUNT **telephone number** is the number that other peo- ple dial when they want to talk to you on the telephone. EG *He gave her his telephone number.*

telephonist /tɪˈlefənɪst/, **telephonists.** A **tele-** N COUNT **phonist** is someone who works in a telephone British exchange or whose job is to answer the telephone for a business or other organization.

telephoto lens /telɪfəʊtəʊ lenz/, **telephoto** N COUNT **lenses.** A **telephoto lens** is a lens which you can attach to a camera and which makes far away things larger and clearer in the photographs.

telescope /telɪskəʊp/, **telescopes.** A **telescope** is N COUNT a long tube-shaped instrument with lenses inside it. You look through a telescope in order to make distant things appear larger and nearer. EG *They peered at the targets through the telescope.*

telescopic /telɪskɒpɪk/. **1 Telescopic** instru- ADJ CLASSIF ments and lenses make things seem larger and ATTRIB nearer. EG *The telescopic sight fitted snugly along the top of the gun*... ...*a 400 mm telescopic lens.*
2 A **telescopic** piece of equipment is made of ADJ CLASSIF : sections that fit or slide into each other so that it ATTRIB can be made shorter when it is not being used. EG *I pulled out the telescopic aerial to its fullest extent.*

televise /telɪvaɪz/, **televises, televising, tele-** V+O : USU PASS **vised.** If an event **is televised,** it is filmed and shown on television. EG *The ceremony would be televised nationally*... *The BBC agreed to televise the debate.*

television /telɪvɪʒən/, **televisions. 1** A **televi-** N COUNT **sion** or a **television set** is a piece of electrical equipment consisting of a box with a glass screen. You use a television to watch programmes with pictures and sounds. EG *You don't have a television, do you?*... *I turned on the television to watch the news.* ● If something is **on television,** you can ● PHRASE watch it by using a television set. EG *His first film was shown on television this weekend.*
2 Television 2.1 is the system of sending pictures N UNCOUNT and sounds by electrical signals over a distance so that people can receive them on a television set. EG ...*television pictures transmitted from a camera on the other side of the world.* **2.2** refers to all the programmes, such as plays, films, and news, that are broadcast and that you can watch on a televi-

If you have teething troubles, does your mouth hurt?

sion set. EG *The boys were watching television.* **2.3** is the business or industry concerned with making programmes and broadcasting them on television. EG *...the most exciting job in television.*

telex /tɛlɛks/, **telexes, telexing, telexed. 1** Tel- N UNCOUNT ex is an international system of sending written messages. The message is typed on a machine in one place and is immediately printed out by a machine in another place.

2 A **telex** is **2.1** a machine that sends and receives N COUNT telex messages. **2.2** a message that is sent by telex. EG *He burst in with an urgent telex.*

3 If you **telex** a message, you send it by using a V+O : OFT+*to* telex machine. EG *The file on this man had been telexed to Paris.*

tell /tɛl/, **tells, telling, told** /təʊld/. **1** If you **tell** V+O+O; ALSO someone something, you give them information. EG V+O : *John refused to tell me her name... He told me that* USU+REPORT, *he was a farmer... I told her what the doctor had* QUOTE, OR *said... 'Jenny's dead,' I told him... My aunt wrote* A *and told me all about it... She told me the story of her life... 'We told a lot of lies,' said Bill.*

2 If you **tell** someone to do something, you order, V+O+*to*-INF, instruct, or advise them to do it. EG *I was furious* QUOTE OR *and told them to get out of my house... Just do as* REPORT *you're told... My uncle smiled and told me not to worry.*

3 If you can **tell** what is happening or what is true, V+O OR you are able to judge correctly what is happening V+REPORT or what is true. EG *You can't tell the difference* WITH MODAL, *between truth and fiction... I couldn't tell what they* NO CONT *were thinking... So far as we can tell, it is still in perfect condition.*

4 If a child can **tell the time**, he or she is able to PHRASE look at a watch or clock and say what time it is.

5 If something **tells** you something, it reveals a V+O+O; ALSO fact to you or indicates what you should do. EG *The* V+O : *design of the computer tells us nothing about such* OFT+REPORT *things... Every movement they make tells you that* OR *to*-INF *they are real... My intuition told me to stay away.*

6 If an unpleasant or tiring experience begins to V : OFT+*on* **tell**, it begins to have a serious effect. EG *The strain was beginning to tell... All these late nights were beginning to tell on my health.*

7 You say **'I can tell you'**, or **'I can't tell you'** to CONVENTION emphasize what you are saying. EG *Some of your friends have some very funny ideas, I can tell you... I can't tell you how pleased we are to have you here today, Professor.*

8 If someone did not accept something you said or CONVENTION suggested and finds out later that you were right, Informal you can say **'I told you so'** if you want to be slightly cruel and rude.

9 If you say **'Time will tell'**, you mean that the CONVENTION truth about something will not be known until some time in the future.

tell apart. If you can **tell** similar people or PHRASAL VB : things **apart**, you are able to recognize the differ- V+O+ADV, ences between them and can identify each one. EG WITH MODAL, *He couldn't tell them apart.* NO CONT

tell off. If you **tell** someone **off**, you speak to PHRASAL VB : them angrily or seriously because they have done V+O+ADV something wrong. EG *We don't want to get told off, do we?... ...and a cop would tell the noisy kids off.*

telling /tɛlɪŋ/. If something that you say is **telling**, ADJ QUALIT **1** it is very important or relevant. EG *The lawyer made a brief, telling speech to the magistrate.* **2** it reveals thoughts or feelings that you were trying to hide. EG *He let slip a particularly telling remark.*

telling-off, tellings-off. If you give someone a N COUNT **telling-off**, you speak to them angrily about some- thing foolish or wrong that they have done. EG *When she got back she would give him such a telling-off about that doll.*

telltale /tɛlteɪl/. A **telltale** sign reveals informa- ADJ CLASSIF : tion, often about something that is meant to be USU ATTRIB secret. EG *I was beginning to recognize the first tell- tale signs of panic.*

telly /tɛli[1]/, **tellies.** A **telly** is the same as a N COUNT OR television. EG *Dad was half asleep in front of a* N UNCOUNT *flickering telly... Did you see it on telly last night?* Informal

temerity /tɪˈmɛrɪti[1]/. If someone has the temer- N UNCOUNT **ity** to do something, they do it boldly and upset +SUPP people who think that they should not have done it at all. EG *He had the temerity to suggest that a few of us should leave.*

temp /tɛmp/, **temps.** A **temp** is a secretary who is N COUNT employed by an agency that sends him or her to work for short periods of time in different offices, replacing secretaries who are ill or on holiday.

temper /tɛmpə/, **tempers, tempering, tem- pered. 1** Your **temper** is **1.1** the tendency you N COUNT OR have to become angry or to stay calm. EG *He had a* N UNCOUNT *most violent temper.* **1.2** the way you are feeling at N COUNT OR a particular time, especially how cheerful or how N UNCOUNT angry you are. EG *She might come home in a better* +SUPP *temper.*

2 If you are in a **temper**, you are extremely angry N SING : *a*+N and cannot control your behaviour. EG *One day the* OR N UNCOUNT *man attacked me in a temper.*

3 If you **lose** your **temper**, you become very PHRASE angry. EG *She suddenly lost her temper and left the room.*

4 If someone or something **tempers** something, V+O they make it less extreme or more acceptable. EG Formal *Our delight was tempered by surprise... She tem- pered her approach to each child... Justice needs to be tempered with efficiency.*

temperament /tɛmpəˈrəməˀnt/, **tempera-** N UNCOUNT **ments.** Your **temperament** is your character, OR N COUNT which you show in your usual way of behaving or reacting in situations, for example whether you are calm, energetic, or violent. EG *He had a cheerful temperament... She was placid in temperament... They were gamblers by temperament.*

temperamental /tɛmpəˈrəmɛntᵊl/. **1** Someone ADJ QUALIT who is **temperamental** has moods that change often and suddenly. EG *...a temperamental Polish actress... The old men are pretty temperamental.*

2 **Temperamental** features relate to the tempera- ADJ CLASSIF ment a person has. EG *Many political and tempera- mental differences exist between them.*

◊ **temperamentally.** EG *My father wasn't tem-* ◊ ADV *peramentally suited for business.*

temperate /tɛmpəˈrət/. A **temperate** place has ADJ QUALIT weather that is never extremely hot or extremely cold. EG *...the temperate woodlands of Tasmania.*

temperature /tɛmprᵊtʃə/, **temperatures. 1** The N COUNT OR **temperature** of something or the **temperature** in N UNCOUNT a place is how hot or cold it is. EG *...a sudden drop in temperature... ...a temperature of 10°C.*

2 Your **temperature** is the temperature of your N COUNT body. ● If someone **takes** your **temperature**, they ● PHRASE use a thermometer to measure your temperature in order to see if you are ill. EG *I took her temperature and it was 40°C.*

3 If you **have a temperature**, you are ill and your PHRASE temperature is higher than it usually is.

tempestuous /tɛmˈpɛstjʊəs/. Something or some- ADJ QUALIT one that is **tempestuous** is full of very strong emotions. EG *...a tempestuous love affair... He is such a wild and tempestuous character.*

temple /tɛmpᵊl/, **temples. 1** A **temple** is a N COUNT building used for the worship of god in some religions.

2 Your **temples** are the flat parts on each side of N COUNT your forehead. EG *He felt the vein throb in his temple where Thomas had hit him.*

tempo /tɛmpəʊ/, **tempos. 1** The **tempo** of an N SING OR event is the speed at which it happens. EG *Events* N UNCOUNT : *had been moving at an equally dramatic tempo.* USU+SUPP Formal

2 The **tempo** of a piece of music is the speed at N UNCOUNT which it is played. EG *In fact, considerable fluctua-* Technical *tions of tempo are possible in a romantic piece.*

temporary /tɛmpəˈrəri[1]/. Something that is **tem-** ADJ CLASSIF **porary** lasts for only a short time. EG *...my tempo- rary absence from the saloon... There might be*

some temporary advantage... ...temporary jobs.
◊ **temporarily**. EG She is temporarily in charge.   ◊ ADV

tempt /tɛmpᵗt/, **tempts, tempting, tempted. 1** If V+O
you **tempt** someone, you offer them something
that they want in order to encourage them to do
something that you want them to do. EG She tried to
tempt him into eating some more... The building
societies are offering higher rates of interest to
tempt new savers.

2 If you say that you **are tempted** or **feel tempt-** PHRASE
ed to do something, you mean that you want to do
it, but you think it might be wrong or harmful. EG I
was tempted to call you last night, but I thought
you'd probably be asleep.

3 If you say that someone **is tempting fate**, you PHRASE
mean that they are taking a foolish and unnecessary risk.

temptation /tɛmpᵗteɪʃᵊn/, **temptations. 1** N UNCOUNT
Temptation is the state you are in when you want
to do or have something, although you know it
might be wrong or harmful. EG He had the strength
to resist further temptation.

2 A **temptation** is something that makes you want N COUNT
to do or have something, although you know it
might be wrong or harmful. EG ...the temptations to
which he was continually exposed.

tempting /tɛmpᵗtɪŋ/. Something that is **tempting** ADJ QUALIT
makes you want to do or have something, although
you know it might be wrong or harmful. EG ...an
extremely tempting price... ...spicy vegetable cutlets, the smell of which was so tempting that they
became hungry again.

ten /tɛn/ **tens. Ten** is the number 10: see the entry NUMBER
headed NUMBER. EG It had been ten years since I
left school.

tenacious /tɪˈneɪʃəs/. If you are **tenacious**, you ADJ QUALIT
are very determined and do not give up easily. EG
They kept a tenacious grip on their possessions...
The working classes struggle in the most energetic,
most tenacious way. ◊ **tenacity** /tɪˈnæsɪˈtiⁱ/. EG ◊ N UNCOUNT
We respect their tenacity and courage.

tenancy /tɛnənsiⁱ/, **tenancies. Tenancy** is the N UNCOUNT
use of land or property belonging to someone else, OR N COUNT
for which you pay rent. EG Once they took up the
tenancy they couldn't be evicted... ...a three-year
tenancy.

tenant /tɛnənt/, **tenants.** A **tenant** is someone N COUNT
who pays rent for the place they live in, or for land
or buildings that they use. EG ...a tenant who pays
rent direct to the landlord.

tend /tɛnd/, **tends, tending, tended. 1** If some- V+to-INF
thing **tends** to happen, it happens usually or often.
EG I tend to wake up early in the morning...
Shopping lists on old envelopes tend to get lost.

2 If you say that you **tend** to think something, you V+to-INF
are giving your opinion in a hesitant or polite way.
EG I tend to think that's not a good solution.

3 If you **tend** someone or something, you look after V+O
them very carefully. EG She'd tended four very sick Formal
men... ...a young man who tended his crops well.

tendency /tɛndənsiⁱ/, **tendencies. 1** If there is a N COUNT+SUPP
tendency for something, it starts happening more
often or increases in intensity. EG There is a
growing tendency for people to opt out... ...a permanent tendency towards inflation.

2 If you have a particular **tendency**, you often N COUNT+SUPP
behave in a particular way because of your charac-
ter. EG I have a tendency to tease... The girl might
have murderous tendencies.

tender /tɛndə/, **tenderest; tenders, tendering,
tendered. 1** Someone who is **tender** expresses ADJ QUALIT
gentle and caring feelings. EG He gave her a tender
smile. ◊ **tenderly**. EG She cradled the baby tender- ◊ ADV
ly. ◊ **tenderness**. EG I have a feeling of great ◊ N UNCOUNT
tenderness for you.

2 If someone is at a **tender** age, they are young ADJ QUALIT:
and inexperienced. ATTRIB

3 Meat that is **tender** is soft and easy to cut or ADJ QUALIT
chew.

4 If a part of your body is **tender**, it hurts when you ADJ QUALIT
touch it, for example because it is injured. EG ...the
tender, swollen side of his jaw.

5 A **tender** is a formal offer to supply goods or do a N COUNT
job for a particular price. EG Tenders are to be Technical
submitted on 15 December at 10 a.m.

6 If you **tender** a suggestion, an apology, or your V+O
resignation, you formally offer it. EG Dr Mayfield Formal
has tendered his resignation.

tendon /tɛndə⁰n/, **tendons.** A **tendon** is a strong N COUNT
cord in your body which joins a muscle to a bone.

tendril /tɛndrɪ⁰l/, **tendrils. Tendrils** are short, N COUNT:
thin stems which grow on some plants and attach USU PLURAL
themselves to walls, trees, or other plants.

tenement /tɛnəmənt/, **tenements.** A **tenement** N COUNT
is a large building that is divided into a lot of small
flats. Tenements are situated in a poor area of a
city.

tenet /tɛnɪⁱt/, **tenets.** The **tenets** of a theory or N COUNT:
belief are the principles on which it is based. EG OFT+of
...one of the central tenets of capitalism... ...the Formal
basic tenets on which this chapter is based.

tenner /tɛnə/, **tenners.** A **tenner** is ten pounds or N COUNT
a ten-pound note. EG He's earning a tenner an hour. Informal

tennis /tɛnɪs/ is a game played by two or four N UNCOUNT
players on a rectangular court. They use rackets to
hit a ball over a net which is between them. EG
They've gone to play tennis in the park... ...a tennis
court.

tenor /tɛnə/, **tenors. 1** A **tenor** is a male singer N COUNT
whose voice is fairly high. EG ...'Roses of Picardy'
sung by an Irish tenor. ▶ used as an adjective. EG ▶ ADJ CLASSIF
...his pleasant tenor voice.

2 A **tenor** recorder, saxophone, or other musical ADJ CLASSIF:
instrument has a range of notes that are of a fairly ATTRIB
low pitch.

3 The **tenor** of something is the general meaning N SING+SUPP
or mood that it expresses. EG I forget the tenor of Formal
her reply... The whole tenor of his work was
socialist.

tenpin bowling /tɛnpɪn bəʊlɪŋ/ is a game in N UNCOUNT
which you try to knock down ten objects, called
tenpins, by rolling a heavy ball towards them.

tense /tɛns/, **tenser, tensest; tenses, tensing,
tensed. 1** If you are **tense**, you are worried and ADJ QUALIT
nervous and cannot relax. EG They began to grow
tense over the likelihood of a long delay.

2 If your body is **tense**, your muscles are tight and ADJ QUALIT
not relaxed. EG Your neck is tense.

3 If you **tense**, or if your muscles **tense**, your V-ERG:
muscles become tight and stiff. EG The man on the OFT+up
terrace tensed slightly... 'What are you talking
about?' I asked, the skin of my cheek-bones tensing
up.

4 A **tense** situation or period of time is one that ADJ QUALIT
makes people anxious. EG After a long, tense si-
lence, he asked: 'What is your name?'... The situation was very tense; anything might happen.

5 The **tense** of a verb is the form which shows N COUNT OR
whether you are referring to the past, the present, N UNCOUNT
or the future. EG The present tense is 'I swim' or 'I
am swimming'.

tensed up. If you are **tensed up**, you are nervous ADJ PRED
and unable to relax. EG You've been so tensed up,
you're ready to explode.

tension /tɛnʃᵊn/, **tensions. 1 Tension** is the N UNCOUNT
feeling of fear or nervousness that is produced OR N PLURAL
when something difficult, dangerous, or important
is happening. EG ...the tension between the two
countries... Family tensions are increasing... With
tension in his voice he said he wanted to tell me
something.

2 The **tension** in a rope or wire is how tightly it is N UNCOUNT
stretched, for example between two poles. EG The
loss of tension in the cables is a problem.

Write down the two games that appear on these
pages.

tent /tent/, **tents**. A **tent** is a shelter made of canvas or nylon, which you sleep in when you are camping. It is held up by poles and ropes. EG *She pitched her tent in a field.* N COUNT

tentacle /tentəkəⁿl/, **tentacles**. The **tentacles** of an animal such as an octopus are the long, thin parts that it uses to feel and hold things, to catch food, and to move. EG *The jellyfish is fringed with stinging tentacles.* N COUNT : USU PLURAL

tentative /tentətɪv/. If you are **tentative**, you act or speak slowly and carefully because you are uncertain or afraid. EG *We are tentative about tackling these issues... Each step he took was slightly tentative.* ADJ QUALIT

tenterhooks /tentəhʊks/. If you are **on tenterhooks**, you are nervous and excited about something that is going to happen. EG *I was on tenterhooks to see who his passenger was... I will keep him on tenterhooks for just a little longer.* PHRASE

tenth /tenθ/, **tenths**. 1 The **tenth** item in a series is the one that you count as number ten: see the entry headed NUMBER. EG *...the tenth day of the strike... ...the tenth programme in our series.* ORDINAL

2 A **tenth** is one of ten equal parts of something. EG *...a tenth of a second... The jar was about nine tenths full of leaves... His income is eight tenths of the average wage.* N COUNT : USU+*of*

tenuous /tenjʊəs/. If an idea, connection, or reason is **tenuous**, it is so slight or weak that it may not really exist or may easily cease to exist. EG *There is only the most tenuous evidence for it... Their links with the school were tenuous... He struggled to maintain his tenuous hold on her.* ADJ QUALIT

tenure /tenjʊ³ə/ is 1 the legal right to live in a place or to use land or buildings for a period of time. EG *They get tenure under the Rent Act.* 2 the period of time during which someone holds an important job in a government or other organization. EG *...the first week of his tenure of the Home Office.* N UNCOUNT / N UNCOUNT : OFT+*of*

tepid /tepɪd/. 1 A liquid that is **tepid** is slightly warm. EG *...drinking tepid coffee... They lay their eggs in the shallow tepid pools.* ADJ CLASSIF

2 A feeling or reaction that is **tepid** lacks enthusiasm or liveliness. EG *Tepid applause greeted her efforts.* ADJ QUALIT

term /tɜːm/, **terms, terming, termed**. 1 If you talk about something in particular **terms**, or in **terms of** a particular thing, you are specifying which aspect of it or whose view of it you are discussing. EG *Life is going to be a little easier in economic terms... He was talking in international terms... In Marxist terms, nationalism of this kind cannot last... In your terms the situation's got worse... A computer is powerful in terms of capacity and speed... These losses are not to be explained in terms of what happened last week.* PHRASE

2 If you are **thinking in terms of** doing something or **talking in terms of** doing it, you are considering doing it. EG *You should be thinking in terms of paying off your debts.* PHRASE

3 If you express something in particular **terms**, you express it using a particular type of language or in a way that shows clearly your attitude or feelings. EG *She condemned the decision in strong terms... Try to explain it in terms a small boy might understand.* PHRASE

4 A **term** is a word or expression that is used in relation to a particular subject. EG *He asked them what they understood by the term 'radical'... 'Habeas corpus' is a legal term.* ● **contradiction in terms**: see **contradiction**. N COUNT : USU+SUPP

5 You can use **term** to say what someone calls something or what their opinion of it is. EG *...recent breakthroughs in what might be termed 'birth technology'... The press termed the visit a triumph.* V+O+C

6 A **term** is also **6.1** one of the periods of time that each year is divided into at a school or college. EG *...the spring term... It was the first week of term.* N COUNT OR N UNCOUNT

6.2 a period of time during which a particular political party, prime minister, or president is in power. EG *...Baldwin's second term of office as Premier.* **6.3** a period of time spent doing a particular job or in a particular place. EG *He has just been sentenced to a long prison term.* N COUNT+SUPP / N COUNT+SUPP

7 If you talk about 'the **long term**' or 'the **short term**', you are talking about what will happen over a long or short period of time in the future. EG *Such a policy would be economically disastrous in the long term... These are only short-term solutions.* PHRASE

8 The **terms** of an agreement or arrangement are the conditions that have been accepted by the people involved in it. EG *We will not accept these terms... They finally agreed to the Bill on the President's terms.* N PLURAL

9 If two people are treated **on the same terms** or **on equal terms**, they are treated in exactly the same way. EG *They decided to let women be conscripted on the same terms as men.* PHRASE

10 If two people are **on** good **terms** or **on** friendly **terms**, they are friendly towards each other. EG *You need to be on friendly terms with him... They were on Christian-name terms.* ● **on speaking terms**: see **speak**. PHRASE

11 If you **come to terms with** something difficult or unpleasant, you learn to accept it. EG *He has come to terms with death.* PHRASE

terminal /tɜːmɪnəⁿl/, **terminals**. 1 A **terminal** illness or disease causes death gradually and cannot be cured. ADJ CLASSIF

2 A **terminal** patient is dying of a terminal illness or disease. ADJ CLASSIF : ATTRIB

3 A **terminal** is a place where vehicles, passengers, or goods begin or end a journey. EG *...a bus terminal... ...oil terminals.* N COUNT : USU+SUPP

4 A computer **terminal** is a piece of equipment, usually a keyboard and a VDU, that you use to put information into a computer or to obtain information from it. EG *...terminals giving access to larger computers.* N COUNT

terminate /tɜːmɪneɪt/, **terminates, terminating, terminated**. 1 When you **terminate** something or when it **terminates**, it ends completely. EG *I thought that he would terminate the discussion then and there... We are confident that the case will terminate with two words: 'Not guilty.'* V-ERG Formal

◊ **termination** /tɜːmɪneɪʃ³ⁿn/. EG *...the termination of their romance.* ◊ N UNCOUNT

2 When a train or bus **terminates** somewhere, it ends its journey there. V+A Formal

terminology /tɜːmɪnɒlədʒiⁱ/, **terminologies**. The **terminology** of a subject is the set of special words and expressions used in connection with it. EG *The author uses Marxist terminology.* N UNCOUNT OR N COUNT

terminus /tɜːmɪnəs/, **terminuses**. A **terminus** is a large railway station or bus station where several routes begin and end. EG *He had waited near the terminus until the last bus had come in.* N COUNT

termite /tɜːmaɪt/, **termites**. Termites are small white insects that eat wood. They live in hot countries in nests made of earth. N COUNT : USU PLURAL

terrace /terəˀs/, **terraces**. 1 A **terrace** is a row of similar houses joined together by their side walls. EG *...a house in a fashionable terrace.* N COUNT British

2 A **terrace** is also **2.1** a flat area of stone or grass next to a building, where people can sit or eat meals. EG *He wandered out onto the terrace.* **2.2** one of a series of flat areas of ground built like steps on a hillside so that crops can be grown there. EG *...the landscape with its terraces of vines and olives.* N COUNT / N COUNT : USU PLURAL

3 The **terraces** at a football ground are wide steps that people stand on when they are watching a game. EG *...on the terraces of football clubs.* N PLURAL : the+N

terraced /terəˀst/. 1 A **terraced** hillside has flat areas of ground like steps built on it so that people can grow crops there. EG *...the forests and terraced vineyards.* ADJ CLASSIF

2 A **terraced** house is one of a row of similar ADJ CLASSIF
houses that are joined together by their side walls. British
EG ...*an ordinary terraced house in the East End of
London.*

terrain /tɛreɪn/. The **terrain** in an area is the N UNCOUNT
type of land there, especially the physical features +SUPP
of the land. EG *The commander made a detailed
study of the terrain... The terrain was bare and
flat... ...hilly terrain.*

terrapin /tɛrəpɪn/, **terrapins.** A **terrapin** is a N COUNT
small turtle.

terrible /tɛrəˈbᵊl/. **1** A **terrible** experience or ADJ QUALIT
situation is very serious and unpleasant. EG *It was a
terrible accident, but we did not panic.*
2 If you feel **terrible**, you feel very ill, or feel a ADJ QUALIT
very strong and unpleasant emotion. EG ...*a terrible
sense of guilt.*
3 You describe something as **terrible** when you ADJ QUALIT
think that it is very bad or poor quality. EG *I've had
a terrible day at the office... ...terrible weather...
The food was terrible.*
4 You also use **terrible** to emphasize the great ADJ CLASSIF :
degree or extent of something. EG *I've been a* ATTRIB
terrible fool... It's a terrible waste of their talents.

terribly /tɛrəˈblɪ/. You use **terribly** to empha- SUBMOD
size the extent or degree of something. EG *I'm* Informal
*terribly sorry... It's terribly important... It gets
terribly cold at night.*

terrier /tɛrɪə/, **terriers.** A **terrier** is a type of N COUNT
small dog.

terrific /tərɪfɪk/. **1** If you say that something is ADJ CLASSIF
terrific, you mean that you are very pleased with Informal
it or are very impressed by it. EG *Our new carpet
looks terrific.*
2 Terrific also means very great in amount, ADJ CLASSIF :
degree, or intensity. EG ...*a terrific thunderstorm...* ATTRIB
...*a terrific amount of money.*

terrify /tɛrɪfaɪ/, **terrifies, terrifying, terrified.** V+O
If something **terrifies** you, it makes you feel
extremely frightened. EG *Rats terrify me.*
◇ **terrifying.** EG *The most terrifying aspect of* ◇ ADJ QUALIT
nuclear bombing is radiation. ◇ **terrified.** EG *My* ◇ ADJ QUALIT
sister was too terrified to cry.

territorial /tɛrɪtɔːrɪəl/ means concerned with the ADJ CLASSIF
ownership of a particular area of land or water. EG ATTRIB
...*territorial boundaries.*

territory /tɛrɪtᵊrɪ/, **territories. 1** The **territory** N UNCOUNT
of a country is the land that it controls. EG *This* OR N COUNT :
meeting is to be held on neutral territory... ...the OFT+SUPP
French territories on the East coast.
2 Territory is land that has a particular character. N UNCOUNT
EG *We were passing through mountainous territory.* +SUPP
3 You can use **territory** to refer to an area of N UNCOUNT
knowledge or experience. EG *All this is familiar* +SUPP
territory to readers of her recent novels.

terror /tɛrə/, **terrors. 1 Terror** is very great N UNCOUNT
fear. EG *She awakened in terror as the flaming roof
came crashing down.*
2 A **terror** is something that makes you very N COUNT
frightened. EG *They suffered untold terrors in the
dark.*

terrorise /tɛrəraɪz/. See **terrorize.**

terrorism /tɛrərɪzᵊm/ is the use of violence, N UNCOUNT
especially murder, kidnapping, and bombing, in
order to achieve political aims or to influence a
government. EG *These measures failed to bring acts
of terrorism to an end.* ◇ **terrorist** /tɛrərɪst/, ◇ N COUNT
terrorists. EG *They have given aid to terrorists...
She is in prison for terrorist activities.*

terrorize /tɛrəraɪz/, **terrorizes, terrorizing,** V+O
terrorized; also spelled **terrorise.** If someone
terrorizes you, they keep you in a state of fear by
using threats or violence. EG *Lee was a bully who
terrorized us all.*

terror-stricken. If you are **terror-stricken** or ADJ CLASSIF
terror-struck, you are extremely frightened. EG
...*terror-stricken women and children.*

terse /tɜːs/, **terser, tersest.** A **terse** comment or ADJ QUALIT
statement is brief and rather unfriendly. EG *I re-*

ceived a terse and unsympathetic reply... ...the
terse message: 'Do not touch'.

TESL /tɛsᵊl/ is the teaching of English to students N UNCOUNT
whose first language is not English, but who live in
an English-speaking country or need to use English
for their education or job. **TESL** is an abbreviation
for 'teaching English as a second language'.

test /tɛst/, **tests, testing, tested. 1** When you **test** V+O
something, you try it, for example by touching it or
using it for a short time, in order to find out what it
is, what condition it is in, or how well it works. EG
*He tested the water with one toe. 'It's hot!'... The
BBC in Scotland wanted to test the range of their
transmitters... A number of new techniques were
tested.*
2 If you **test** someone, you ask them questions to V+O : OFT+on
find out how much they know about something. EG *I
will test you on your knowledge of French.*
3 A **test** is a deliberate action or experiment to N COUNT
find out whether something works. EG *They proved
it by several tests... ...an underground nuclear test.*
4 If an event or situation is a **test** of a person or N COUNT :
thing, it reveals their qualities or effectiveness. EG OFT+of
...*the first major test of the President's policies.*
5 A **test** is also an examination consisting of a set N COUNT
of questions or tasks, which is intended to measure
your knowledge or skill. EG ...*a mathematics test...
He hadn't passed the test.*
6 A medical **test** is an examination of a part of N COUNT
your body in order to make sure that it is healthy
or to find out what is making you ill. EG ...*a blood
test... They rushed her to a hospital for tests.*
7 If you **put** something **to the test,** you find out PHRASE
how useful or effective it is by using it. EG *The idea
is being put to the test in a theatre in Paris.*
8 an acid test: see **acid.**

testament /tɛstəməᵊnt/, **testaments.** If one thing N COUNT :
is a **testament** to another thing, it shows clearly OFT+to
that the other thing exists or is true. EG *The* Formal
building is a testament to their success. ● See also
New Testament, Old Testament.

test case, test cases. A **test case** is a legal case N COUNT
in a court of law which establishes an important
principle that can then be used in other cases.

testicle /tɛstɪkᵊl/, **testicles.** A man's **testicles** N COUNT
are the two sex glands that produce sperm.

testify /tɛstɪfaɪ/, **testifies, testifying, testified.**
1 When someone **testifies,** they make a formal V : OFT+A OR
statement, especially a statement in a court of law. V+REPORT :
EG *None of the victims would appear in court to* ONLY that
testify against him... Witnesses testify to his at- Formal
tempts at rape.
2 If something **testifies** to an idea, it shows that V : OFT+to
the idea is likely to be true. EG *All kinds of human* Formal
*experience testify to the close link between love
and fear.*

testimonial /tɛstɪməʊnɪəl/, **testimonials.** A tes- N COUNT
timonial is a statement saying how good someone
or something is, usually a statement made by
someone in authority.

testimony /tɛstɪmənɪ/, **testimonies. 1** A per- N UNCOUNT
son's **testimony** is a formal statement that they OR N COUNT
make, especially in a court of law. EG ...*the angry
testimony of injured wives.*
2 If one thing is a **testimony** to another thing, it N UNCOUNT+to
shows clearly that the other thing exists or is true. Formal
EG *This is spectacular testimony to the computer's
creative powers.*

Test match, Test matches. A **Test match** is a N COUNT
cricket or rugby match that is one of a series
played between the same two countries. EG ...*the
fourth Test match between England and Australia.*

If something is terrific, does it terrify you?

test tube

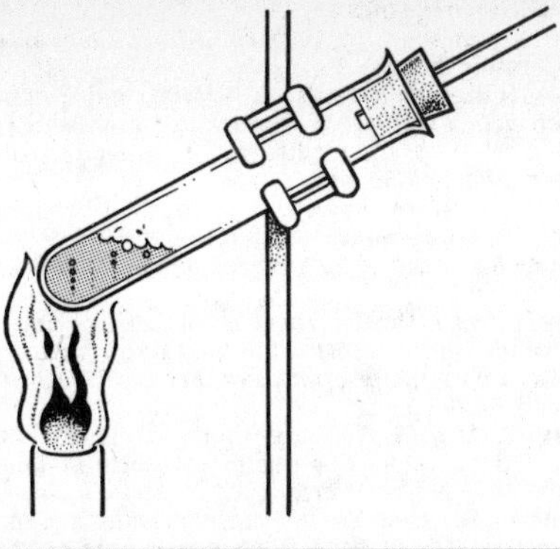

test tube, test tubes. A **test tube** is a small glass container that is used in chemical experiments. N COUNT

test-tube baby, test-tube babies. A **test-tube baby** is a baby that develops from an egg which has been removed from the mother's body, fertilized, and then replaced in her womb. N COUNT

tetanus /tetəⁿnəs/ is a serious and painful disease caused by germs getting into wounds. It makes your muscles, especially your jaw muscles, go stiff. N UNCOUNT

tether /teðə/, **tethers, tethering, tethered. 1** If you **tether** an animal, you tie it to a post. V+O

2 If you say that you are **at the end of** your **tether**, you mean that you are extremely tired or unhappy and cannot cope with your problems or make any more effort. PHRASE

text /tekst/, **texts. 1** The **text** of a book is the main written part of it, rather than the introduction, pictures, or index. EG *The excellent photographs in this book did a lot to amplify the text.* N SING : *the*+N

2 Text is any written material. EG *These machines have the capacity to 'read' printed text.* N UNCOUNT

3 The **text** of a speech or interview is the written version of it. N COUNT : OFT+*of*

4 A **text** is a book or other piece of writing connected with an academic subject or used for a school or college examination. EG *...a text on Oriental philosophy... We're supposed to discuss a text we've been assigned.* N COUNT

textbook /tekstbuk/, **textbooks.** A **textbook** is a book about a particular subject that is intended for students to use. EG *...a history textbook.* N COUNT

textile /tekstaɪl/, **textiles. 1** A **textile** is a woven cloth or fabric. EG *The designers have created a new textile... ...a textile factory.* N COUNT

2 Textiles are the industries concerned with making cloth. EG *There are still more people employed in textiles than in computers.* N PLURAL

texture /tekstʃə/, **textures.** The **texture** of something is the way that it feels when you touch it, for example how smooth or rough it is. EG *...the slightly rough texture of the cloth.* N UNCOUNT OR N COUNT

-th. You add **-th** to numbers written in figures and ending in 4, 5, 6, 7, 8, 9, 0, 11, 12, or 13 in order to form ordinal numbers. These numbers are pronounced as if they were written as words. For example, 7th is pronounced the same as 'seventh'. EG *...6th June 1982... ...48th Street... ...the 124th Psalm.* SUFFIX

than; usually pronounced /ðən/, but pronounced /ðæn/when you are emphasizing it. **1** You use **than** to link two parts of a comparison. EG *You've got more money than me... She was older than I was... She was fatter than when he last saw her... We talked for more than an hour... ...temperatures lower than 25 degrees.* PREP OR CONJ : AFTER COMPAR

2 You also use **than** in order to link two parts of a contrast. EG *He chose the stairs rather than the lift... She likes to keep things rather than throw them away... I'd rather starve than ask for a penny... I would sooner read than watch television.* PREP OR CONJ

thank /θæŋk/, **thanks, thanking, thanked. 1** You say **thanks** or **thank you** to express your gratitude to someone for something they have done, said, or given you. EG *Thank you very much indeed for coming to see me... Many thanks for your long and interesting letter... 'What'll you have, Castle? A whisky?' – 'A small one, thank you.'... 'Do you want a biscuit?' – 'No thanks.'... 'How are you?' – 'Fine, thanks.'* CONVENTION

2 When you **thank** someone, you express your gratitude to them for something. EG *He thanked me for bringing the books... 'Have a good time,' he said. She smiled at him, thanked him, and drove off.* V+O

3 When you express your **thanks** to someone, you express your gratitude to them for something. EG *He sent a letter of thanks to Haldane.* N PLURAL

4 Thank is used in these phrases. **4.1** You say **thank God**, **thank goodness** or **thank heavens** when you are very relieved about something. EG *Thank goodness it only lasts an hour.* CONVENTION **4.2** If you say that something happens **thanks to** someone or something, you mean that they caused it to happen. EG *Thanks to him I began to learn to trust my feelings... The building became very well known, thanks to detective films.* PREP

thankful /θæŋkful/. When you are **thankful**, you are very happy and relieved that something has happened. EG *We were thankful that it was all over.* ADJ PRED

thankless /θæŋklɪ²s/. A **thankless** job or task involves doing a lot of hard work that other people do not notice or appreciate. EG *She used to take on thankless jobs like running school dances.* ADJ QUALIT : ATTRIB

Thanksgiving /θæŋksgɪvɪŋ/. **Thanksgiving** or **Thanksgiving Day** is a public holiday in the United States and Canada in the autumn. It was originally a day when people celebrated the end of the harvest and thanked God for it. EG *...the week after Thanksgiving... We always had turkey for our Thanksgiving meal.* N UNCOUNT

that /ðæt, ðə³t/, **those** /ðəuz/. The pronunciation /ðə³t/ can only be used for paragraphs 3 and 4.

1 You use **that** or **those** to refer to things or people already mentioned or known about. EG *That old woman saved my life... Not all crimes are committed for those reasons... Who are those men?... 'Did you see him?' – 'No.' – 'That's a pity.'... Hello. Is that Mrs Vass? I'm phoning about your car.* DET OR PRON

2 You can use **those** to refer to people or things that you are going to give details about. EG *I want to thank those of you who've offered to help... The scheme was set up to help those concerned with the teaching of reading... Students should write off to those bodies which provide awards.* PRON OR DET

3 You use **that** after some verbs, nouns, and adjectives in order to introduce a clause. EG *She suggested that I telephoned you... He was motivated by the conviction that these tendencies would increase... It is important that you should know precisely what is needed.* CONJ

4 You also use **that** to introduce a relative clause. EG *I reached the gate that opened onto the lake... For dessert there was ice cream that Mum had made herself.* PRON REL

5 If you say that something is not **that** bad or not **that** funny, for example, you mean that it is not as bad or as funny as other people think. EG *It isn't quite that bad.* SUBMOD : WITH BROAD NEG

6 You use **at that** when you are modifying or limiting what you have previously said. EG *There is work for only 250 people, and a very specialized 250 at that.* PHRASE

7 You use **that is** or **that is to say** when you are giving further details about something. EG *It deals with matters of social policy; that is to say, everything from housing to education.* PHRASE

8 You use **that's it** to indicate that nothing more PHRASE

needs to be done or that the end has been reached. EG *They get a direct grant of a sum of money and that's it... 'I quit,' I said. 'That's it. Finish.'*
9 You use **that's that** to say there is nothing more PHRASE you can do or say about a particular matter. EG *It was an accident, and that's that... The Ravenscrofts refused and that was that.*
10 this and that: see **this.**

thatched /θætʃt/. A **thatched** house or one with a ADJ CLASSIF : **thatched** roof has a roof made of straw or reeds. ATTRIB EG *...a three-hundred-year old thatched cottage... ...mud huts with thatched roofs.*

that's /ðæts/ is a spoken form of 'that is'.

thaw /θɔː/, **thaws, thawing, thawed. 1** When ice V-ERG or snow **thaws**, it melts. EG *The snow soon thawed and they all went out for a walk... The ice was thawed by the warm wind.*
2 A **thaw** is a period of warmer weather, usually at N COUNT : the end of winter, when the snow and ice melts. EG USU SING *A thaw had set in and the streets were slushy.*
3 When you **thaw** frozen food, you take it out of a V+O freezer and leave it in a place where it can warm up so that it is ready for cooking or eating. EG *Unwrap the pastry and then thaw it overnight.*
4 When unfriendly people or unfriendly relation- V-ERG ships **thaw**, they start to be more friendly. EG *The Vatican indicated that it might be thawing and accepting the critics' argument.*

the; usually pronounced /ðə/ before a consonant and /ði¹/ before a vowel, but pronounced /ðiː/ when you are emphasizing it.
1 You use **the** at the beginning of noun groups to DET refer to a person or thing that is known about, that has just been mentioned, or that you are going to give details about. EG *The sea was really rough... ...Her Majesty the Queen... He said that she ought to see the doctor... He took Sam by the hand... Do you play the violin?... ...the waiter with the droopy moustache... I think I'll keep the information to myself... They continued walking on the opposite pavement... Another mineral was named by the scientist who first examined it.*
2 You can also use **the** in front of a singular noun DET to refer to all the people or things of that type. EG *The koala bear is a medium-sized creature that lives in trees.*
3 You can use **the** in front of a surname in the DET plural to refer to a married couple or to a whole family who have that surname. EG *...some friends of hers called the Hochstadts.*
4 You use **the** in front of an adjective to make it a DET noun that refers to someone or something that the adjective describes. EG *...institutions for the mentally handicapped... ...the British and the French... The wounded were given first aid... Don't you think that perhaps you're wanting the impossible?*
5 You can use **the** in front of ordinal numbers, DET especially in dates. EG *...Tuesday, May the thirteenth.*
6 You use **the** in front of numbers when they refer DET to decades. EG *...in Stockholm in the thirties.*
7 You use **the** in front of two comparative adjec- DET tives or adverbs when you are describing how one amount or quality changes in relation to another. EG *The more I hear about him, the less I like him... The longer we look at it the more interesting we find it.*
8 You can emphasize **the** to indicate that some- DET thing or someone is the most famous, most important, or best thing of their kind. EG *It's the club in town.*

theatre /θɪətə/, **theatres;** also spelled **theater** in American English. **1** A **theatre** is a building with a N COUNT stage on which plays and other entertainments are performed. EG *...the new Arnold Wesker play at the National Theatre... Her mother never went to the theatre.*
2 You can use the **theatre** to refer to work in the N SING : *the*+N theatre, including acting in, producing, and writing

plays. EG *She was only really happy when she was working in the theatre.*
3 In a hospital, a **theatre** is the same as an N COUNT operating theatre.

theatrical /θɪ'ætrɪkə⁰l/. **1** A **theatrical** event or ADJ CLASSIF : production is one that is performed in a theatre or ATTRIB that relates to the theatre. EG *...posters advertising theatrical productions.*
2 You can use **theatrical** to describe behaviour ADJ QUALIT : that is exaggerated, unnatural, and done deliber- ATTRIB ately for effect. EG *Jack moved forward with theatrical caution.*

theft /θeft/, **thefts.** Theft is the act or crime of N COUNT OR stealing. EG *He reported the theft of his passport...* N UNCOUNT *The drop in petty crime and theft will mean less work for the police.*

their /ðeə/. **1** You use **their** to indicate that DET POSS something belongs or relates to people or things that have just been mentioned or whose identity is known. See **they.** EG *...the car companies and their workers... Don't hope to change anyone or their attitudes.*
2 You also use **their** with some titles when you are DET referring to people with that title. EG *Their Lordships were already late for dinner.*

theirs /ðeəz/. You use **theirs** to indicate that PRON POSS something belongs or relates to people or things that have just been mentioned or whose identity is known. EG *It was his fault, not theirs... They were off to visit a friend of theirs.*

them /ðem, ðəm/ is used as the object of a verb or PRON preposition. You use **them** to refer to people or things that have just been mentioned or whose identity is known. EG *He took off his glasses and put them in his pocket... Smith harangued his fellow students and persuaded them that they must support the strike... If I think someone may attempt to take an overdose, I will spend hours talking to them.*

theme /θiːm/, **themes. 1** A **theme** in a discussion N COUNT or lecture is a main idea or subject in it. EG *...organised public meetings on the theme: 'Law not War'... We shall return to this theme in chapter 7.*
2 A **theme** in an artist's work or in a work of N COUNT literature is an idea in it that an artist or writer develops or repeats. EG *The main theme of the play was clear.*
3 In music, a **theme** is a short simple tune on N COUNT which a piece of music is based. EG *...variations on a theme.*
4 A **theme** is also a tune that is played at the N COUNT beginning and end of a television or radio programme.
5 A **theme** song or **theme** tune is a song or tune ADJ CLASSIF : which is played several times in a film or a musical ATTRIB and which expresses its general mood or is associated with a particular character in it.

themselves /ðə⁰mselvz/. **1** You use **themselves** PRON REFL as the object of a verb or preposition when it refers PLURAL to the same people or things as the subject of the clause or a previous object in the clause. EG *They are trying to educate themselves... They had ceased to think of themselves as rebels.*
2 You also use **themselves** to emphasize the PRON REFL : subject or object of a clause, and to make it clear PLURAL who or what you are referring to. EG *Let's turn to the books themselves... ...a cultural preference on the part of the Chinese themselves.*
3 If people do something **themselves**, they do it PRON REFL without any help from anyone else. EG *They must PLURAL settle it themselves and get their own solutions.*

then /ðen/. **1 Then** means at a particular time in ADV the past or in the future. EG *I didn't have it then... The situation's changed since then... I'm going to see him at lunchtime. He's busy till then.*

What phrase on these pages means 'approximately'?

2 You use **then** to say that one thing happens after ADV another, or is after another in a list. EG *He went to the village school, then to the grammar school, and then to the university... It didn't hurt at first, but then I realized you could die from a cut like that.*

3 You use **then** in conversation **3.1** to link what ADV SEN you say to something that has just been said. EG *'Have some more cake.' - 'Oh all right then.'.. 'Are you a student?' - 'No, I'm not' - 'What do you do then?'* **3.2** at the end of a topic or at the end of a conversation. EG *Well, that's settled, then... Bye then.* **3.3** after words like 'now', 'well' and 'okay', to draw attention to what you are about to say. EG *Now then, it's time you went to bed.*

4 You use **then** to introduce a summary of what ADV SEN you have said or the conclusion that you are drawing from it. EG *These then are some of the feelings which may occur... Democracy, then, is a form of government.*

5 You can use **then** to introduce the second part of ADV SEN a sentence which begins with 'if'. EG *If any questions do occur to you, then don't hesitate to write.*

6 You use **then** at the beginning of a sentence or ADV SEN after 'and' or 'but' to introduce a comment or an extra piece of information to what you have already said. EG *Then there could be a tax problem... Iron would do the job much better. But then you can't weld iron so easily.*

7 now and then: see now. • there and then: see there.

thence /ðɛns/ means from the place that has just ADV been mentioned. EG *He hitched south towards Italy,* Formal *and thence into France.* Outdated

theologian /θɪəˈləʊdʒɪən/, **theologians.** A theolo- N COUNT gian is someone who studies religion and God.

theology /θɪˈɒlədʒɪ/ is the study of religion and N UNCOUNT God. EG *...a diploma in theology.* ◊ **theological** ◊ ADJ CLASSIF /θɪəˈlɒdʒɪkəˀl/. EG *...a theological college.*

theorem /ˈθɪərəˀm/, **theorems.** A theorem is a N COUNT statement in mathematics that can be proved to be true by reasoning. EG *...the theorem of Pythagoras... ...a book about the attempts to prove Fermat's last theorem.*

theoretical /θɪəˈrɛtɪkəˀl/ means based on or con- ADJ CLASSIF : cerning the ideas and abstract principles of a ATTRIB subject, rather than the practical aspects of it. EG *...theoretical biology... ...theoretical ideas which, in practice, may not work.*

theoretically /θɪəˈrɛtɪkəˀliˀ/. You use theoreti- ADV OR cally to say that although something is supposed to ADV SEN happen or to be the case, it may not in fact happen or be the case. EG *Laws still theoretically controlled the availability of alcohol... It was theoretically possible to get permission from the council.*

theorize /ˈθɪəraɪz/, **theorizes, theorizing, theo-** V : USU+about rized; also spelled **theorise.** If you **theorize** about something, you develop ideas about it in order to try and explain it. EG *...people who theorize about teaching methods... As leisure increases, they theorized, families will spend more time together.*

theory /ˈθɪərɪˀ/, **theories.** **1** A theory is an idea or N COUNT : set of ideas that is intended to explain something. OFT+SUPP EG *Darwin spent more than twenty years working on his theory of evolution... Mary is full of fascinating theories about men and women.*

2 Theory is **2.1** the set of ideas that relate to a N UNCOUNT : particular subject. EG *...Marxist economic theory.* OFT+SUPP **2.2** the set of rules and principles that a practical method or skill is based on. EG *...the theory and practice of inoculation.*

3 You use **in theory** to say that although some- ADV SEN thing is supposed to happen or to be the case, it may not in fact happen or be the case. EG *In theory all British citizens are eligible for this.*

therapeutic /θɛrəˈpjuːtɪk/. **1** If something is ADJ QUALIT **therapeutic,** it helps you to feel happier and more relaxed. EG *All that fresh air is very therapeutic.*

2 In medicine, **therapeutic** treatment is designed ADJ CLASSIF to treat a disease or to improve a person's health.

therapist /ˈθɛrəpɪst/, **therapists.** A **therapist** is a N COUNT person skilled in a particular type of therapy, especially psychotherapy. EG *...a speech therapist.*

therapy /ˈθɛrəpiˀ/ is the treatment of mental or N UNCOUNT physical illness, often without the use of drugs or operations. EG *...a short course of heat therapy.*

there /ðɛə/. **1** You use **there** as the subject of the PRON verb 'be' to say that something exists or does not exist, or to draw attention to it. EG *There was a new cushion on one of the settees... There must be a reason... There's no inspection service, is there?*

2 You use **there** in front of a verb to emphasize its PRON meaning. The subject of the verb is placed after Literary the verb. EG *Beside them there curls up a twist of* Formal *blue smoke... There still remains the point about creativity.*

3 If something is **there,** it exists or is available. EG ADV : USU *We talked about reality, about whether things are* AFTER be *really there... The problem is still there... The play group is there for the children of staff and students.*

4 You use **there** to refer to a place that has ADV AFTER VB already been mentioned. EG *I must get home. Bill's there on his own... I walked two miles there and back.*

5 You say **there** to indicate a place that you are ADV pointing to or looking at. EG *'Over there,' she said and pointed to the door... Where's the ball? Oh, there it is.*

6 You use **there** when speaking on the telephone ADV to ask if someone is available to speak to you. EG *Is Jane there, please?*

7 You use **there** to refer to **7.1** a point in a ADV conversation, or an idea that someone has put forward. EG *Could I interrupt you just there?... You're right there Howard.* **7.2** a stage reached in an activity or process. EG *I'll write to the headmaster and then take the matter from there... The man who wants to be president will do anything to get there.*

8 If you say that someone is **not all there,** you PHRASE mean that they are stupid or not mentally alert. Informal

9 If something happens **there and then** or **then** PHRASE **and there,** it happens immediately. EG *He terminated the discussion then and there.*

10 You say **'There you are'** or **'There you go'** CONVENTION **10.1** when accepting that an unsatisfactory situation cannot be changed. EG *It wasn't a very good reason for refusing, but there you are.* **10.2** when emphasizing that something proves that you were right. EG *There you are, Mabel! What did I tell you?* **10.3** when offering something to someone. EG *'There you are' he said, handing the screws to me.*

11 You can add **'so there'** to what you are saying CONVENTION to show that you have made a firm decision and Informal will not change your mind. EG *Well, I won't apologize, so there.*

12 You can say **'There there'** when comforting a CONVENTION child who is very upset. EG *There, there, it's not your fault.*

thereabouts /ðɛərəˈbaʊts/. You can add **or** PHRASE **thereabouts** after a number to indicate that it is only approximate. EG *Inflation could be down to 8 per cent or thereabouts... It was in 1982 or thereabouts.*

thereafter /ðɛərˈɑːftə/ means after the event or ADV date mentioned. EG *We first met in 1966 and I saw* Formal *him quite often thereafter.*

thereby /ðɛəˈbaɪ/ means as an inevitable result of ADV SEN the event or action mentioned. EG *The President* Formal *had lied and thereby obstructed justice.*

therefore /ˈðɛəfɔː/. You use **therefore** to intro- ADV SEN duce a conclusion that you are making. EG *We have a growing population and therefore we need more food... The new car is smaller and therefore cheaper.*

therein /ðɛərˈɪn/ means in the place or because of ADV the situation just mentioned. EG *...the lakes and the* Formal *fish therein... He was not a snob, you see. And therein lay his downfall.*

thereupon /ðɛərəpɒn/ means immediately after an event and usually as a result of it. EG *I flung a few copies of the report in his lap, which thereupon fell to the floor.* ADV Formal

thermal /θɜːməˀl/. **1 Thermal** means relating to heat or caused by heat. EG *...the thermal efficiency of an engine... ...thermal energy.* ADJ CLASSIF : ATTRIB

2 Thermal clothes are specially designed to keep you warm in cold weather. EG *...thermal underwear.* ADJ CLASSIF : ATTRIB

thermometer /θəmɒmɪtə/, **thermometers.** A **thermometer** is an instrument for measuring the temperature of a room or of a person's body. It usually consists of a narrow glass tube containing a thin column of mercury which rises and falls as the temperature rises and falls. EG *The thermometer reads 92 degrees... ...a clinical thermometer.* N COUNT

Thermos /θɜːmɒs/, **Thermoses.** A **Thermos** or a **Thermos flask** is a container which is used to keep hot drinks hot and cold drinks cold. N COUNT Trademark

thermostat /θɜːməstæt/, **thermostats.** A **thermostat** is a device that controls the temperature of a car engine or a house, for example, by switching the cooling or heating system on and off. N COUNT

thesaurus /θɪˀsɔːrəs/, **thesauruses.** A **thesaurus** is a reference book in which words with similar meanings are grouped together. EG *...the new Collins School Thesaurus.* N COUNT

these /ðiːz/ is the plural of **this.**

thesis /θiːsɪs/, **theses** /θiːsiːz/. **1** A **thesis** is an idea or theory that is expressed as a statement and is discussed in a logical way. EG *It is my thesis that Australia underwent fundamental changes in the 1920s.* N COUNT

2 A **thesis** is also a long piece of writing, based on your own research, that you do as part of a university degree, especially a Ph.D. EG *He is writing a thesis on the novels of Jane Austen.* N COUNT

they /ðeɪ/ is used as the subject of a verb. You use **they 1** to refer to people or things that have just been mentioned or whose identity is known. EG *All universities have chancellors. They are always rather senior people.* **2** to refer to people in general, or to a group of people whose identity is not actually stated. EG *They found the body in a dustbin.* **3** instead of 'he' or 'she' to refer to a person whose sex is not known or not stated. Some people consider this use to be incorrect. EG *Nearly everybody thinks they're middle class... I was going to stay with a friend, but they were ill.* PRON : PLURAL

they'd /ðeɪd/. **1 They'd** is a spoken form of 'they had', especially when 'had' is an auxiliary verb. EG *They said they'd read it all before.*

2 They'd is also a spoken form of 'they would'. EG *I wish they'd publish more books like this.*

they'll /ðeɪəˀl/ is the usual spoken form of 'they will'. EG *They'll probably sell it cheaper.*

they're /ðɛə, ðeɪə/ is the usual spoken form of 'they are'. EG *They're not interested.*

they've /ðeɪv/ is the usual spoken form of 'they have', especially when 'have' is an auxiliary verb. EG *They've been studying very hard.*

thick /θɪk/, **thicker, thickest. 1** Something that is **thick** has a large distance between its two opposite surfaces. EG *...thick slices of bread... We were separated by thick concrete walls... ...a thick sweater... Last winter the snow lay thick on the ground.* ADJ QUALIT OR ADV
◊ **thickly.** EG *She buttered my bread thickly.* ◊ ADV

2 If something that consists of several things is **thick**, the things in it are present in large quantities and are grouped very closely together. EG *She had a lot of thick black hair... They were on the edge of the thick forest... She came out of the thickest part of the crowd.* ◊ **thickly.** EG *Plants and trees grew thickly on both sides of the river.* ADJ QUALIT ◊ ADV

3 You use **thick** to say what the width or depth of something is. EG *The tree was one foot thick at the base... Her arms and legs were as thick as trees.* ADJ QUALIT
◊ **thickness.** EG *Insert a new wire of the same thickness and wind it round the screws.* ◊ N UNCOUNT

4 If you say that someone is **thick**, you mean that they are stupid or slow to understand things. EG *He's a bit thick... They were too thick to notice it.* ADJ QUALIT Informal

5 Liquids that are **thick** contain very little water and do not flow easily. EG *The chef has made the sauce too thick... ...thick cream.* ADJ QUALIT

6 Smoke or fog that is **thick** is difficult to see through. EG *The fog seemed to be getting thicker.* ADJ QUALIT

7 If someone's voice is **thick**, they are not speaking clearly, for example because they are ill, upset, or drunk. EG *His voice sounded blurred and thick.* ADJ QUALIT
◊ **thickly.** EG *'Let's get out of here,' Tom said thickly.* ◊ ADV

8 If things happen **thick and fast**, they happen very quickly and in large numbers. EG *More discoveries followed thick and fast.* PHRASE

9 To be **thick with** something means to be full of it or be covered with it. EG *The windows were thick with grime... The air was thick with butterflies.* PHRASE

10 If you are **in the thick of** an activity or situation, you are very involved in it. EG *It won't be long before Amanda is in the thick of O levels.* PHRASE

11 If you continue to do something **through thick and thin**, you do it even though the conditions or circumstances have become very bad. EG *She stayed with her husband through thick and thin.* PHRASE

thicken /θɪkəˀn/, **thickens, thickening, thickened. 1** If something **thickens**, it becomes more closely grouped together than it has previously been. EG *Here the vegetation thickens into a jungle.* V

2 If fog or smoke **thickens**, it becomes denser or darker and more difficult to see through. V

3 When you **thicken** a liquid or when it **thickens**, you make it stiffer and more solid. EG *You can use flour to thicken sauces.* V-ERG

4 You say **'The plot thickens'** when a situation or series of events is getting more and more complicated and mysterious. CONVENTION

thicket /θɪkɪt/, **thickets.** A **thicket** is a small group of trees or bushes which are growing closely together. EG *They live in hidden valleys or dense thickets.* N COUNT

thickset /θɪksɛt/. Someone who is **thickset** is broad and heavy, with a solid-looking body. EG *...a big, thickset man with heavy shoulders.* ADJ QUALIT

thick-skinned. Someone who is **thick-skinned** is not easily hurt by what other people say to them or say about them. EG *...a thick-skinned, brutal person.* ADJ QUALIT

thief /θiːf/, **thieves.** A **thief** is a person who steals something from another person, especially without using violence. EG *...jewel thieves.* N COUNT

thieving /θiːvɪŋ/ means involved in stealing things. EG *...those thieving village kids.* ADJ CLASSIF : ATTRIB

thigh /θaɪ/, **thighs.** Your **thighs** are the top parts of your legs, between your knees and your hips. See picture at THE HUMAN BODY. EG *I walked the last six miles in water up to my thighs.* N COUNT

thimble /θɪmbəˀl/, **thimbles.** A **thimble** is a small metal or plastic object that you put on the end of your finger to protect it from being pricked by a needle when you are sewing. N COUNT

thin /θɪn/, **thinner, thinnest; thins, thinning, thinned. 1** Something that is **thin** has a small distance between its two opposite surfaces. EG *His nose was long and thin... ...their tall, thin house... ...thin slices of bread... ...thin cotton cloth.* ADJ QUALIT
◊ **thinly.** EG *...fresh, thinly cut bread.* ◊ ADV

2 A person or animal that is **thin** has very little fat on their body. EG *Angela was dreadfully thin.* ADJ QUALIT

3 Liquids that are **thin** contain a lot of water. EG *The liquid was thin and greyish brown.* ADJ QUALIT

4 A crowd or other group of people that is **thin** has very few people in it. EG *The crowd seemed suddenly thinner.* ◊ **thinly.** EG *...a thinly populated region.* ADJ QUALIT ◊ ADV

Is a thesaurus useful for language students?

5 If your hair **is thinning** or if you are getting **thin on top**, you are beginning to go bald. V: ONLY CONT OR PHRASE

6 When you say that people or things are **thin on the ground**, you mean that there are not very many of them and so they are hard to find. EG *Good new plays are still rather thin on the ground.* PHRASE

7 When a joke or a story **is wearing thin**, it is beginning to lose its interest because it has been repeated too many times. PHRASE

8 When your patience or your temper **is wearing thin**, you are beginning to get impatient or angry. PHRASE

9 to disappear **into thin air**: see **air**.

thin down. When you **thin** a liquid **down**, you add more water or other liquid to it. EG *The paint has been thinned down too much.* PHRASAL VB: V+O+ADV

thing /θɪŋ/, **things. 1** You use **thing** as a substitute for another word when you do not want to be more precise, when you are referring to something that has already been mentioned, or when you are going to give more details about it. EG *He needed a few things so we went to the store to purchase them... It's silly to train a group of people just to do one thing... A terrible thing happened to me on my way to work... Do you know how to drive this thing?... The fourth drawer holds family things such as photographs and letters... I've seen this sort of thing so many times before... Education isn't the same thing as intelligence... The first thing I did when I came back was clean the bathroom... She sobbed last night, a thing she rarely does.* N COUNT+SUPP

2 You can use **thing** instead of 'anything' to emphasize what you are saying. EG *I just couldn't think of a thing to say... Don't worry about a thing.* N SING: a+N

3 You can say **'The thing is'** to introduce an explanation or opinion relating to something that has just been said. EG *I can't come on Thursday. The thing is, I've already arranged to do something on Thursday.* PHRASE Spoken

4 A **thing** is a physical object, rather than plants, animals, or human beings. EG *He's only interested in things and not people.* N COUNT

5 Your **things** are your clothes or possessions. EG *She changed into her bathing things... I like my own things around me: my photos and books.* N PLURAL +POSS

6 You can use **things** to refer to life in general and the way it is changing or affecting you. EG *Things are going very well for us at the moment... I hope I've not spoiled things... How are things?* N PLURAL

7 You can call a person or an animal a **thing** when you are expressing your feelings towards them. EG *She was very cold, poor thing... You lucky thing!* N COUNT+SUPP

8 If you say that something is **the thing**, you mean that it is fashionable or popular. EG *Ambivalence is the thing nowadays.* N SING: the+N

9 You say **with one thing and another** when you mean that there are several reasons for something, but you are not going to explain what they are. EG *He sees a lot of her, you know, with one thing and another.* PHRASE

10 You say **for one thing** when you give only one reason for something, but want to indicate that there are other reasons that you are not bothering to give. EG *I prefer badminton to squash. It's not so tiring for one thing.* PHRASE

11 Thing is also used in these phrases. **11.1** If you say **it is just one of those things**, you mean that you cannot explain why something happens. **11.2** If you **have a thing** about someone or something, you have very strong feelings about them. EG *I've got a thing about drinking.* **11.3** If you **make a thing** of or out of something, you make it much more important than it really is. EG *He made a big thing of not eating chilli.* PHRASES Informal

thingamabob /θɪŋəməbɒb/, **thingamabobs.** You can refer to something or someone as **thingamabob** or **thingummy** when you cannot remember or do not know the proper word or name for them. EG *Her phone is out of order. She's getting a new thingamabob.* N COUNT Informal

thingummy /θɪŋəmiː/, **thingummies.** See **thingamabob.** N COUNT

think /θɪŋk/, **thinks, thinking, thought** /θɔːt/. **1** If you **think** that something is the case, you have the opinion that it is the case. EG *I think a woman has as much right to work as a man... You expect everyone to think like you... She thought of Deirdre simply as an old chum... She's cleverer than I thought... He was thought by the Conservatives to be an extreme radical.* V+REPORT: ONLY that, V+A, OR V+of+as; ALSO V+O+C OR V+O+to-INF

2 If you **think** that something is true, you judge or believe it to be true, but you are not sure. EG *I think it's at six thirty on Sundays... At first I thought he was asleep.* V+REPORT: ONLY that

3 When you **think** about ideas or problems, you make a mental effort to consider them. EG *That ought to make us think hard about how we can make a safer product... He thought for a moment.* V: OFT+about
▸ used as a noun. EG *We'll be in touch when we've had a think about what to do.* ▸ N SING: a+N, OFT+about

4 If you **think** of something, **4.1** you remember it or it comes into your mind. EG *I can never think of her name... I can think of at least two examples of his stupidity... He can think of no reason for going... I'm trying to think which other companies I can try for you.* **4.2** you create it in your mind using your intelligence and imagination. EG *...a method which had never even been thought of before.* V: USU+of, USU WITH MODAL; ALSO V+REPORT: ONLY WH; V+of

5 If you **are thinking** something at a particular moment, you have ideas in your mind that you do not say out loud. EG *All the while I was thinking, 'What's happening here?'... I lay there thinking how funny it was.* V+QUOTE OR REPORT

6 If you **are thinking** of doing something, you are considering doing it in the future. EG *Is he still thinking of going away to Italy for a month?... I thought about being a reporter.* V+of/about

7 If you **think** of someone, you show consideration for them, their needs, and their problems. EG *It was very kind of you to think of him... You never think about anybody but yourself!* V+of/about

8 You use **think** in questions and exclamations to express your anger, shock, or surprise at someone's behaviour. EG *Who do you think you are?... Whatever could I have been thinking about?... To think that I trusted him!* V+REPORT OR V+A

9 If you **think** a lot of someone or something, you admire them very much or think they are very good. EG *She thinks a lot of you... I didn't think much of his letter... What did you think of her? What did your husband think about it?* V+QUANTIF +of/about

10 Think is also used in these phrases. **10.1** You say **'I think'** to add politeness to what you are saying, or to make it sound less forceful or rude. EG *I think I ought to go... Thank you, I don't think I will, if you don't mind... I think that you will find my figures are correct.* **10.2** If you **think the best of** people, you expect that they will behave well. If you **think the worst of** people, you expect them to behave badly. EG *You always think the best of everyone... I must say I thought better of you.* **10.3** If you are intending to do something but you **think better of it**, you decide not to do it. EG *She was on the point of waking Ben again, but then thought better of it.* **10.4** If you **think nothing of** doing something that other people consider difficult or strange, you consider it to be easy or normal. EG *We would think nothing of walking six miles just to post a letter.* **10.5** If you **think twice** or **think again** about doing something, you consider it very carefully before you do it and sometimes decide not to do it. EG *You've got to think twice before you spend ten pounds on a book... He may have to think again.* **10.6** If you say **anybody would think** that a particular thing was true, you are expressing your surprise or disapproval at someone's behaviour. EG *Anybody'd think you were our nanny... You would have thought they had never seen a man before.* **10.7** You say **just think** when you feel excited, PHRASES fascinated, or shocked by something. EG *Judy, just think, what an opportunity!... Just think how much it's going to cost us.*

11 come to think of it: see **come**. ● **to think the world of** someone: see **world**. ● See also **thinking**, **thought**.

think back. If you **think back**, you make an effort to remember things that happened to you in the past. EG *I'm thinking back to my own experience as a teacher... ...an opportunity to think back over the year.* PHRASAL VB : V+ADV, OFT+to/over

think over. If you **think** something **over**, you consider it carefully before making a decision. EG *I wanted to think over one or two business problems.* PHRASAL VB : V+O+ADV

think through. If you **think** a problem or situation **through**, you consider it thoroughly. EG *I haven't really thought the whole business through in my own mind.* PHRASAL VB : V+O+ADV

think up. If you **think up** something clever or unusual, you create it in your mind. EG *...a new financial agreement he had thought up... ...examples that mathematicians think up.* PHRASAL VB : V+O+ADV

thinker /θɪŋkə/, **thinkers**. A **thinker** is someone who is famous for their ideas on a particular subject, especially someone who is a philosopher. EG *...such thinkers as Plato, Rousseau, and Freud.* N COUNT

thinking /θɪŋkɪŋ/. **1** The general ideas or opinions of a person or group can be referred to as their **thinking**. EG *We are so alike in our thinking... ...a reluctance which dominated the thinking of a whole generation.* N UNCOUNT +SUPP

2 You add **to my way of thinking** to a statement to emphasize that it is your opinion and not a fact. EG *...issues which, to my way of thinking, are some of the fundamental human issues.* ADV SEN

3 Thinking is the activity of using your brain to consider a problem or to create an idea. EG *I've done some thinking... That requires a great deal of serious thinking.* ● See also **wishful thinking**. N UNCOUNT

4 You use **thinking** to describe intelligent people who take an interest in important events and issues. EG *...conditions which forced the thinking man to decide that changes must be made.* ADJ CLASSIF : ATTRIB

third /θɜːd/, **thirds. 1** The **third** item in a series is the one that you count as number three: see the entry headed NUMBER. EG *This room was on the third floor.* ORDINAL

2 A **third** is one of three equal parts of something. EG *It covers a third of the world's surface.* N COUNT : USU+of

3 A **third** at a British university is the lowest class of honours degree that you can get. N COUNT

thirdly /θɜːdliˈ/. You use **thirdly** when you want to make a third point or give a third reason for something. EG *And thirdly, remember that they have supported you in the past.* ADV SEN

third party, third parties. 1 A **third party** is a person who is not directly involved in a business agreement or legal case, but is affected by it or is asked to take part in a minor way. EG *A third party from outside the village was brought in as a witness.* N COUNT

2 If you have **third-party** insurance and cause an accident, your insurance company will pay money only to other people who are hurt or whose property is damaged, and not to you. ADJ CLASSIF

third person. In grammar, a statement in the **third person** is a statement about another person or thing, and not directly about yourself or about the person you are talking to. The **third person** is expressed as 'he', 'she', 'it', or 'they' with the appropriate form of a verb. N SING : the+N

third-rate. Something that is **third-rate** is of a very poor quality or standard. EG *...the seedy world of third-rate theatricals.* ADJ QUALIT

Third World. The poorer countries of Africa, Asia, and South America are sometimes referred to as the **Third World**. EG *I had seen a good deal of the Third World before I visited Calcutta.* N PROPER : the+N

thirst /θɜːst/. **1** If you have a **thirst**, you feel a need to drink something. EG *He woke up in the night with a terrible thirst.* N SING

2 Thirst is the condition of not having enough to drink. EG *She was dying of thirst.* N UNCOUNT

3 A **thirst** for something is a very strong desire for it. EG *...his thirst for knowledge.* N SING+for

thirsty /θɜːstiˈ/. **1** If you are **thirsty**, you feel that you need to drink something. EG *Have you got any water? I'm thirsty.* ◊ **thirstily**. EG *Jane drank thirstily.* ADJ QUALIT ◊ ADV

2 Thirsty is also used to describe things that make you feel thirsty. EG *Gardening is really thirsty work.* ADJ QUALIT : ATTRIB

thirteen /θɜːtiːn/ **thirteens. Thirteen** is the number 13: see the entry headed NUMBER. EG *He hadn't appeared in a film for thirteen years.* NUMBER

thirteenth /θɜːtiːnθ/ **thirteenths. The thirteenth** item in a series is the one that you count as number thirteen: see the entry headed NUMBER. EG *...my thirteenth birthday.* ORDINAL

thirtieth /θɜːtiˈəθ/ **thirtieths. The thirtieth** item in a series is the one that you count as number thirty: see the entry headed NUMBER. EG *...a parade to celebrate the thirtieth year of Independence.* ORDINAL

thirty /θɜːtiˈ/ **thirties. Thirty** is the number 30: see the entry headed NUMBER. EG *...thirty years of marriage.* NUMBER

this /ðɪs/, **these** /ðiːz/. **1** You use **this** to refer to a person or thing that has been mentioned, or to introduce a person or thing that you are going to talk about. EG *The colonel handed him the bag. 'This is for you.'... 'My God,' I said. 'This is awful.'... This is Desiree, my father's second wife... These particular students are extremely bright... So, for all these reasons, my advice is to be very, very careful... Get these kids out of here.* DET OR PRON

2 You also use **this** to introduce a person or thing into a story. EG *I stopped at a junction and this bowler-hatted gent comes up.* DET Spoken Informal

3 You also use **this** when you refer to the present time or place. EG *...the prime minister of this country... Could I make an appointment to see the doctor this morning please?* DET

4 If you say that something will happen **this** Friday or **this** summer, for example, you mean that it will happen on the next Friday or during the next summer. EG *Let's fix a time. This Sunday. Four o'clock.* DET

5 You also use **this** when you are indicating the size or shape of something with your hands. EG *It was about this big.* SUBMOD

6 You say **this is** in order to introduce yourself on the telephone. EG *He looked for her number, and dialled it. 'Sally? This is Martin Brody.'* PHRASE

7 If you say that you are doing or talking about **this and that**, you mean that you are doing or talking about a variety of things that you do not want to specify. EG *'What have you been up to?' - 'This and that.'* PHRASE

thistle /θɪsəl/, **thistles.** A **thistle** is a wild plant with prickly leaves and purple flowers. N COUNT

thong /θɒŋ/, **thongs.** A **thong** is a long, thin strip of leather, plastic, or rubber. N COUNT

thorn /θɔːn/, **thorns. 1** A **thorn** is **1.1** one of the many sharp points on some plants and trees, for example on rose bushes. EG *He stepped on a sharp thorn.* **1.2** a tree or bush such as a hawthorn. EG *...dragging branches of thorn across the entrance.* N COUNT / N COUNT OR PLURAL / N UNCOUNT

2 If you describe someone as a **thorn in** your **flesh** or a **thorn in** your **side**, you mean that they are a constant problem or annoyance to you. EG *Howard is a well-known activist, a thorn in the flesh of the council.* PHRASE

thorny /θɔːniˈ/. **1** A **thorny** plant or tree is covered with thorns. EG *...a long thorny stem.* ADJ QUALIT

How many numbers are there on these pages? Include ordinals.

2 A **thorny** subject or question is difficult to discuss ADJ QUALIT or answer. EG ...*the thorny problem of what happens when the boss is absent.*

thorough /θʌrə/. 1 An action that is **thorough** is ADJ QUALIT done very carefully and completely. EG ...*a thorough search... These drugs have been subject to very thorough testing.* ◊ **thoroughly.** EG *They had* ◊ ADV *not studied the language thoroughly.* ◊ **thoroughness.** EG ...*the thoroughness of the* ◊ N UNCOUNT *training programme.*

2 Someone who is **thorough** is very careful and ADJ QUALIT methodical in their work. EG *He is enormously thorough and full of inspiration.* ◊ **thoroughness.** ◊ N UNCOUNT EG *The President was impressed by his speed and thoroughness.*

3 You can use **thorough** to emphasize what you ADJ QUALIT: are saying. EG *I'd enjoy giving him a thorough* ATTRIB *beating.* ◊ **thoroughly.** EG ...*a thoroughly unrea-* ◊ ADV *sonable person... Yes, I thoroughly agree.*

thoroughfare /θʌrəfɛə/, **thoroughfares.** A N COUNT **thoroughfare** is a main road in a town or city. EG Formal *We went back towards the main thoroughfare.*

those /ðəʊz/ is the plural of **that.**

though /ðəʊ/. 1 You use **though** to introduce and CONJ emphasize a fact or comment which makes another part of the sentence rather surprising. EG *She wore a fur coat, even though it was a very hot day.... Though he hadn't stopped working all day, he wasn't tired.*

2 You also use **though** to add information that CONJ OR makes a statement less forceful, or points out ADV SEN exceptions to it. EG *It wasn't my decision, though I think I agree with it... She resembled her mother physically, though not mentally... 'It's not very useful.' – 'It's pretty, though, isn't it ?'*

3 as **though**: see **as.**

thought /θɔːt/, **thoughts.** 1 **Thought** is the past tense and past participle of **think.**

2 A **thought** is an idea that you have in your mind. N COUNT : EG *The thought never crossed my mind... He* USU SING+SUPP *couldn't bear the thought of going home... I had vague thoughts of emigrating.*

3 **Thought** is 3.1 the activity of thinking. EG *She* N UNCOUNT *frowned as though deep in thought... After giving our predicament some thought, he said he had a proposal.* 3.2 a particular way of thinking or a N UNCOUNT particular set of ideas. EG ...*two schools of socialist* +SUPP *thought.*

4 Your **thoughts** are 4.1 all the ideas in your mind N PLURAL : when you are concentrating on something. EG *They* USU+POSS *walked back, each deep in his own private thoughts... His mind was empty except for thoughts of her.* 4.2 your opinions on something. EG *Rothermere disclosed his thoughts on Britain.*

5 You use **thought** to refer to an act of kindness, N SING+SUPP especially when you are thanking someone. EG *It's a kind thought, sir. I'll tell him you called.*

6 a penny for your **thoughts**: see **penny.** ● See also **second thoughts.**

thoughtful /θɔːtful/. 1 If you are **thoughtful**, you ADJ QUALIT are quiet and serious because you are thinking about something. EG *He looked thoughtful for a moment.* ◊ **thoughtfully.** EG *Tom closed the book* ◊ ADV *thoughtfully.*

2 A **thoughtful** person remembers what other ADJ QUALIT people want or need, and tries to be kind to them. EG *That's very kind of you, Mr Zapp, very thoughtful... I thanked him for his thoughtful gesture.* ◊ **thoughtfully.** EG *The book thoughtfully provides* ◊ ADV *a clue on how to do this.*

thoughtless /θɔːtl²s/. If you are **thoughtless**, you ADJ QUALIT forget or ignore what other people want, need, or feel. EG *I had to scold Vita severely for being so thoughtless... How thoughtless of you!* ◊ **thoughtlessly.** EG *Traditional sources of employ-* ◊ ADV *ment are thoughtlessly destroyed.*

thousand /θaʊzənd/, **thousands.** 1 A **thousand** NUMBER or one **thousand** is the number 1,000: see the entry

headed NUMBER. EG ...*an annual income of twenty thousand dollars.* ● **a thousand and one**: see **one.**

2 You can say '**a thousand**' or '**thousands**' when N PART : you mean a large number or quantity. EG *I've told* USU PLURAL *him thousands of times.*

thousandth /θaʊzənθ/, **thousandths.** 1 The **thou-** ORDINAL **sandth** item in a series is the one that you count as number one thousand: see the entry headed NUMBER.

2 A **thousandth** is one of a thousand equal parts of N COUNT : something. EG ...*a thousandth of a second.* USU+of

thrash /θræʃ/, **thrashes, thrashing, thrashed.** 1 v+o If someone **thrashes** you, they hit you several times. EG *We were thrashed a lot at school.* ◊ **thrashing, thrashings.** EG *He got a thrashing* ◊ N COUNT *from his father.*

2 If someone **thrashes** you in a game, contest, or v+o fight, they defeat you completely. EG *They had challenged and thrashed the enemy's navy.* ◊ **thrashing.** EG ...*the thrashing our team got at* ◊ N COUNT *Southampton last week.*

3 If you **thrash** around, you twist and turn your v : OFT+A body quickly and violently because you are afraid or are·in pain. EG *The boy was thrashing around, trying to get free.*

thrash out. If you **thrash out** a problem or an PHRASAL VB : idea, you discuss it in detail until you arrive at a V+O+ADV solution. EG ...*an agreement that we had already thrashed out.*

thread /θrɛd/, **threads, threading, threaded.** 1 N COUNT OR A **thread** is a long, very thin piece of cotton, silk, N UNCOUNT nylon, or wool. Thread is used in sewing. EG ...*cotton thread.*

2 The **thread** on something such as a screw or the N COUNT top of a container is the raised spiral line of metal or plastic around it.

3 The **thread** in an argument or story is an idea or N COUNT theme that connects the different parts of it together. EG *He had lost his thread and didn't know what to say next.*

4 When you **thread** a needle, you put a piece of v+o thread through the hole at the end of the needle.

5 If you **thread** your way through people or things, v+o+a you go forwards slowly, using the spaces between OR V+A them. EG *We turned and threaded our way through the fairground.*

threadbare /θrɛdbɛə/. **Threadbare** clothes, car- ADJ QUALIT pets, and other pieces of cloth are old and very thin. EG *O'Shea's suit was baggy and threadbare.*

threat /θrɛt/, **threats.** 1 A **threat** is a statement N COUNT OR that someone will harm you, especially if you do N UNCOUNT not do what they want. EG *We mustn't give in to threats... Under threat of death, he confessed.*

2 You can refer to anything or anyone that seems N COUNT : likely to harm you as a **threat.** EG *He felt that I was* OFT+to *becoming a real threat to his plans.*

3 If there is a **threat** of something unpleasant N COUNT OR happening, it is very possible that it will happen. EG N UNCOUNT ...*the ever-growing threat of flooding.*

threaten /θrɛtə⁰n/, **threatens, threatening, threatened.** 1 If you **threaten** to harm someone V+to-INF; or **threaten** to do something that will upset them, ALSO V+O : you say that you will do it. EG *He threatened to* OFT+with *resign... They were threatened with imprisonment.*

2 If someone or something **threatens** a person or v+o thing, they are likely to harm that person or thing. EG *He said that the war threatened the peace of the whole world.* ◊ **threatened.** EG *He felt threatened.* ◊ ADJ PRED

3 If something **threatens** to do something unpleas- V+to-INF ant, it seems likely to do it. EG *The riots threatened to get out of hand.*

4 If something unpleasant **threatens** or if someone V; ALSO V+O : or something **is threatened** with it, it seems likely USU PASS+with to happen. EG *The whole country is threatened with starvation.*

threatening /θrɛtə⁰nɪŋ/. Something or someone ADJ QUALIT that is **threatening** seems likely to cause harm. EG ...*a threatening environment... He became angry*

and threatening. ◊ **threateningly.** EG He ad- ◊ ADV
vanced threateningly on the boy.

three /θriː/, **threes. Three** is the number 3: see NUMBER
entry headed NUMBER. EG We agreed to meet three
days later.

three-dimensional. 1 A **three-dimensional** ADJ CLASSIF
picture, film, or image looks as if it is deep or solid
rather than flat.

2 A **three-dimensional** object is solid rather than ADJ CLASSIF
flat. EG ...a three-dimensional model of the theatre.

three-quarters. Three-quarters of something QUANTIF
is a half of it plus a quarter of it. EG Three-quarters
of the world's surface is covered by water... ...a
play lasting one and three-quarter hours. ▶ used as ▶ ADV OR
an adverb or adjective. EG The tank is three- ADJ CLASSIF
quarters full... ...a bright three-quarter moon.

thresh /θrɛʃ/, **threshes, threshing, threshed.** V+O
When people **thresh** corn, wheat, or rice, they
beat it in order to separate the grains from the rest
of the plant.

threshold /θrɛʃhˀəʊld/, **thresholds.** 1 The N COUNT:
threshold of a building or room is the floor in the USU SING
doorway, or the doorway itself. EG Suddenly the Formal
door opened and Madame stood on the threshold...
Morris had never crossed the threshold of a public
house before.

2 A **threshold** is an amount, level, or limit on a N COUNT+SUPP
scale. When the **threshold** is reached, something Formal
else happens or changes. EG The tax threshold for a
single pensioner is £445.

3 Someone who is **on the threshold of** an action, PHRASE
activity, or state is about to do it or experience it. Formal
EG He was on the threshold of public life.

threw /θruː/ is the past tense of **throw.**

thrift /θrɪft/ is the quality and practice of being N UNCOUNT
thrifty. EG ...the virtues of thrift, hard work, and
punctuality.

thrifty /θrɪftiˀ/, **thriftier, thriftiest.** Someone ADJ QUALIT
who is **thrifty** saves money and does not waste
things. EG She was a thrifty housekeeper.

thrill /θrɪl/, **thrills, thrilling, thrilled.** 1 A **thrill** N COUNT
is **1.1** a sudden feeling of great excitement, pleas-
ure, or fear. EG The sound of the bell sent a thrill of
anticipation through her... They get a considerable
thrill out of it. **1.2** an event or experience that gives
you a thrill. EG The thrill for me was finding the
rare specimens.

2 If something **thrills** you, or if you **thrill** to it, it V·ERG : IF V
gives you a feeling of great pleasure and excite- THEN+to
ment. EG It's a sight that never fails to thrill me...
...those who thrill to the taste of smoked salmon.

thrilled /θrɪld/. If someone is **thrilled**, they are ADJ PRED :
extremely pleased about something. EG I was OFT+to·INF
thrilled to be sitting next to such a distinguished
author.

thriller /θrɪlə/, **thrillers.** A **thriller** is a book, N COUNT
film, or play that tells an exciting story about
dangerous, frightening, or mysterious events. EG ...a
spy thriller... ...a thriller writer.

thrilling /θrɪlɪŋ/. Something that is **thrilling** is ADJ QUALIT
very exciting and enjoyable. EG ...a thrilling adventure.. She gave a thrilling performance.

thrive /θraɪv/, **thrives, thriving, thrived.** V : USU+A
Throve /θrəʊv/ is sometimes used for the past
tense. When people or things **thrive**, they are
healthy, happy, successful, or strong. EG Are you the
type of person who thrives on activity?... My business was thriving. ◊ **thriving.** EG ...a thriving ◊ ADJ CLASSIF
community.

throat /θrəʊt/, **throats.** 1 Your **throat** is **1.1** the N COUNT
back of your mouth and the top part of the tubes
inside your neck that go down into your stomach
and your lungs. EG His throat was so dry that he
could hardly swallow. **1.2** the front part of your
neck. EG He grabbed the man by the throat.

2 **Throat** is used in these phrases. **2.1** If two people PHRASES
are **at each other's throats**, they are quarrelling
or fighting violently with each other. EG When the
danger had passed they would again be at each

other's throats. **2.2** If you **ram** or **force** something
down someone's **throat**, you mention it very often
and very emphatically in order to make them
accept it, believe it, or learn it. EG They have this
viewpoint rammed down their throats every day.
2.3 If something **sticks in** your **throat**, you find it Informal
unacceptable. EG It was his arrogance which stuck
in my throat. **2.4** to **clear** your **throat**: see **clear.**

throb /θrɒb/, **throbs, throbbing, throbbed.** 1 If a V
part of your body **throbs**, you feel a series of
strong beats or dull pains. EG His head was throbbing. ▶ used as a noun. EG She felt her heart give a ▶ N COUNT
great throb.

2 If something **throbs**, it vibrates and makes a V
loud, rhythmic noise. EG The drums seemed to
throb in his ears. ▶ used as a noun. EG ...the throb of ▶ N COUNT
the engine.

throes /θrəʊz/. If you are **in the throes of** PHRASE
something, you are deeply involved in it. EG The
British Army was in the throes of reorganization.

throne /θrəʊn/, **thrones.** 1 A **throne** is a special N COUNT
chair used by a king or queen on important official
occasions. EG ...a picture of the Queen seated on a
rich throne.

2 The **throne** is a way of referring to the position N SING : the+N
of being king or queen. EG ...when Queen Victoria
was on the throne... ...the heir to the throne.

throng /θrɒŋ/, **throngs, thronging, thronged.** 1 N COUNT
A **throng** is a large crowd of people. EG A patient OR N PART
throng was waiting in silence.... The throng of Literary
guests roared its approval.

2 If people **throng** somewhere or **throng** a place, V+A OR V+O
they go there in great numbers. EG Mourners Literary
thronged to the funeral... The lane was thronged
with shoppers.

throttle /θrɒtˀl/, **throttles, throttling, throt-** V+O
tled. To **throttle** someone means to hold them
tightly by the throat so that they cannot breathe,
usually in order to kill them. EG He wanted to put
his hands around her throat and throttle her.

through /θruː/. 1 To move **through** a hole or PREP, OR
opening means to move directly from one side or ADV AFTER VB
end of it to the other. EG Go straight through that
door and then turn right... The rain poured through
a hole in the roof.

2 If you cut **through** something such as a rope, you PREP, OR
cut it into two pieces. EG The fish must have ADV AFTER VB
chewed right through it.

3 If someone or something travels or moves PREP, OR
through a place or area, they travel or move ADV AFTER VB
across it or in it. EG We drove through London... We
decided to drive straight through to Birmingham...
The fish swims through the water... They drove
home through the darkness... A chill shot through
him.

4 If you get **through** a barrier or obstruction, you PREP, OR
get from one side of it to the other. EG The traffic ADV AFTER VB
couldn't get through.

5 If an object or hole extends from one side of PREP, OR
something to another, you can say that it goes or ADV AFTER VB
passes **through** it. EG The heating pipes pass
through tunnels... ...a hat with a feather stuck
through it.

6 If you can see, hear, or feel something **through** PREP
an object, the object is between you and the thing
you can see, hear, or feel. EG Lonnie gazed out
through a side window... He's looking at them
through a magnifying glass... I can hear John
snoring right through the partition... She could feel
the gravel through the soles of her slippers.

7 If something happens or exists **through** a period PREP, OR ADV+
of time, it happens or exists from the beginning PREP
until the end. EG I wished that I could stay through
the winter... We had no rain from March right
through to October.

8 If you go **through** an experience, it happens to PREP, OR you. EG *He didn't want to go through all that divorce* ADV AFTER VB *business again.*

9 If you live **through** a historical event, it takes PREP place while you are alive. EG *He lived through the decline of the Liberal Party.*

10 If you are **through** with something, you have ADJ PRED : finished doing it or using it. EG *He was through with* USU + *with seminars and tutorials.*

11 You use **through** in expressions such as 'half- PREP, OR way through' and 'all the way through' to indicate ADV AFTER VB to what extent an action or task is completed. EG *Harris tried to stop the operation halfway through... I do not think she ever saw a play right through.*

12 If something happens because of something PREP else, you can say that it happens **through** it. EG *Many people have difficulty in walking, for example through age or frailty... The discovery of adrenalin came about through a mistake.*

13 If you achieve something **through** particular PREP methods, you use those methods to achieve it. EG *They were opposed to change through violence.*

14 If you go **through** or look **through** a lot of PREP, OR things, you look at them one after another. EG *I* ADV AFTER VB *wanted to read through as much information as possible... She was sorting through a pile of socks.*

15 Through and through means thoroughly or PHRASE completely. EG *Those boards are rotten through and through... She knew Mr Evans through and through.*

throughout /θru:ˈaʊt/. **1** If something happens PREP, OR **throughout** an event or period of time, it happens ADV AFTER VB during the whole of it. EG *This dream recurred throughout her life... We co-operated throughout with trade unionists.*

2 If something happens or exists **throughout** a PREP, OR place, it happens or exists in all parts of it. EG *The* ADV AFTER VB *pictures can be transmitted by satellite throughout the world... The house was carpeted throughout.*

throve /θrəʊv/ is a past tense of **thrive**.

throw /θrəʊ/, **throws, throwing, threw** /θru:/, **thrown** /θrəʊn/. **1** When you **throw** an object that V+O : USU+A you are holding, you move your hand quickly and let go of the object, so that it moves through the air. EG *Roger picked up a stone and threw it at Henry... He threw the book in the air.*

2 To **throw** someone or something into a place or V+O+A position means to put or force them there quickly or carelessly. EG *Tom undressed in the dark, throwing his clothes carelessly over a chair... She threw both letters in the bin... The train braked violently, throwing everyone to the floor.*

3 If you **throw** a part of your body in a particular V+O+A direction, you move it suddenly and with a lot of force. EG *She threw her arms around his neck.*

4 If you **throw** yourself somewhere, you move or V-REFL+A jump there suddenly and with a lot of force. EG *He threw himself on his bed.*

5 If a horse **throws** its rider, it makes the rider fall V+O off.

6 If one person or thing **throws** another into an V+O+A unpleasant situation, it suddenly causes the other person or thing to be in that situation. EG *The thought of being late on occasions like these would throw her into a state of panic... The cop threatened to throw all of us in jail... The Depression had thrown almost everybody out of work.*

7 If something **throws** light or shadow on some- V+O+A thing else, it causes that thing to have light or shadow on it. EG *A spotlight threw a pool of violet light onto the stage.*

8 If you **throw** yourself, your energy, or your V-REFL+*into* money into an activity, you become involved in it OR V+O+*into* very actively and enthusiastically. EG *Mrs Kaul threw herself into her work heart and soul... Many women throw all of their energies into a career.*

9 If you **throw** a fit or a tantrum, you suddenly V+O

start to behave in an uncontrolled way. EG *She threw a fit of hysterics.*

10 If something such as a remark or an experience V+O **throws** you, it confuses you or surprises you be- Informal cause it is unexpected. EG *It was the fact that she was married that threw me.*

11 a **stone's throw**: see **stone**. ● to **throw light on** something: see **light**. ● to **throw** your **weight about**: see **weight**.

throw away. 1 When you **throw away** some- PHRASAL VB : thing that you do not want, you get rid of it, for V+O+ADV example by putting it in a dustbin. EG *She likes to keep things, even old things, rather than throw them away.* **2** If you **throw away** something good V+O+ADV or useful that you have, you waste it rather than using it sensibly. EG *He is evidently prepared to throw his money away... They threw away their advantage.* **3** See also **throwaway**.

throw in. If someone who is selling you one thing PHRASAL VB : **throws in** another, they give you both things but V+O+ADV only ask you to pay for the first thing. EG *We only had to pay £9 for bed and breakfast, with lunch thrown in.*

throw out. 1 If you **throw** something **out**, **1.1** you PHRASAL VB : get rid of it, for example by putting it in a dustbin. V+O+ADV EG *The broken cooking pots were thrown out.* **1.2** V+O+ADV you reject it because it is unsatisfactory. EG *He threw out the scripts for the next six episodes.* **2** If V+O+ADV you **throw** someone **out**, you force them to leave a job or a place such as a house or club. EG *Her parents threw her out when they found she was pregnant.*

throw up. 1 If someone **throws up**, food or drink PHRASAL VB : from their stomach comes out of their mouth V+O+ADV OR because they are ill. EG *She got out of the car and* Informal *threw up by the side of the road.* **2** If something V+O+ADV **throws up** dust or water, it causes dust or water to rise up into the air. EG *Each passing car threw up a cloud of white dust.*

throwaway /ˈθrəʊəweɪ/. **1** A **throwaway** product ADJ CLASSIF : is intended to be used only for a short time, and ATTRIB then to be thrown away. EG *...a throwaway toothbrush.*

2 A **throwaway** remark or gesture is made in a ADJ CLASSIF : casual way, although it is important, in order to ATTRIB have a humorous or strong emotional effect.

throwback /ˈθrəʊbæk/, **throwbacks.** Something N COUNT : that is a **throwback** is like something that existed USU SING + *to* a long time ago. EG *His sentiments were a throwback to the old colonial days.*

thrown /θrəʊn/ is the past participle of **throw**.

thrush /θrʌʃ/, **thrushes.** A **thrush** is a type of N COUNT fairly small bird.

thrust /θrʌst/, **thrusts, thrusting.** The form **thrust** is used in the present tense and is the past tense and past participle of the verb.

1 If you **thrust** something somewhere, you push or V+O+A move it there quickly with a lot of force. EG *The captain thrust his hands into his pockets... He thrust the bag at Buddy.*

2 A **thrust** is a sudden forceful movement. EG N COUNT *...repeated sword thrusts.*

3 If you **thrust** your way somewhere, you move V+O+A along, pushing between people or things. EG *Ed-* OR V+A *ward thrust his way towards them.*

4 The main **thrust** of an activity or idea is the N SING most important part or aspect of it. EG *The main thrust of robot research in the '80s has been towards improving vision techniques.*

thrust upon. If you **thrust** something **upon** PHRASAL VB : someone, you force them to have it. EG *The new* V+O+PREP, *religion was thrust upon the population by force.* HAS PASS

thud /θʌd/, **thuds, thudding, thudded. 1** A **thud** N COUNT is a dull sound, usually made by a solid, heavy object hitting something soft. EG *He fell on the floor with a thud.*

2 If something **thuds** somewhere, it makes a dull V : USU+A sound, usually by hitting something else. EG *The mail bags thudded onto the platform.*

thug /θʌg/, **thugs**. A **thug** is a very rough and violent person. EG ...*a gang of thugs.* N COUNT

thumb /θʌm/, **thumbs**, **thumbing**, **thumbed**. **1** Your **thumb** is the short, thick finger on the side of your hand. EG *I took her ear between my thumb and forefinger, and tugged it playfully.* N COUNT

2 If you **thumb** a lift, you stand next to a road and stick out your thumb until a driver stops and gives you a lift. EG *Jackie is a confirmed hitch-hiker, thumbing her way all over Europe.* V+O OR V+O+A

thumb through. If you **thumb through** a book or magazine, you turn over the pages quickly rather than reading each page carefully. PHRASAL VB : V+PREP

thumbnail /θʌmneɪl/, **thumbnails**. **1** Your **thumbnail** is the nail on your thumb. N COUNT

2 A **thumbnail** sketch or account of something is very brief and gives only the main features of it. ADJ CLASSIF : ATTRIB

thump /θʌmp/, **thumps**, **thumping**, **thumped**. **1** If you **thump** someone or something, you hit them hard with your fist. EG *I'll thump you, Tommy, if you don't get out of my way... She thumped the table.* V+O

2 If something **thumps** somewhere, it makes a fairly loud, dull sound, usually when it hits something else. EG *The kitchen door opened, feet thumped up the stairs... Two rockets thumped into the ground by the roadside.* V : USU+A

3 When your heart **thumps**, it beats strongly and quickly. EG *My heart was thumping with happiness.* V

4 A **thump** is **4.1** a hard blow that you give with your fist. EG *Ralph pushed between them and got a thump on the chest.* **4.2** a fairly loud but dull sound. EG *He sat down with a thump.* N COUNT

thunder /θʌndə/, **thunders**, **thundering**, **thundered**. **1** **Thunder** is the loud noise that you hear in the sky after a flash of lightning. EG *There's going to be thunder tonight... ...a clap of thunder.* N UNCOUNT

2 When it **thunders**, a loud noise occurs in the sky after a flash of lightning. V

3 If you refer to the **thunder** of something such as traffic or a drum, you are referring to the loud, deep noise it makes. N UNCOUNT+of

4 If something **thunders**, it makes a very loud continuous noise. EG *A truck thundered by.* V : USU+A

5 If you **thunder**, you say something loudly and often angrily. EG *'It's not your bed!' thundered Edwin.* V : USU+QUOTE Literary

thunderbolt /θʌndəbəʊlt/, **thunderbolts**. A **thunderbolt** is a flash of lightning, accompanied by thunder, which strikes something such as a building or a tree. N COUNT

thunderous /θʌndərəs/. A **thunderous** noise is very loud and deep. EG *The tree fell with a thunderous crash... ...thunderous applause.* ADJ CLASSIF

thunderstorm /θʌndəstɔːm/, **thunderstorms**. A **thunderstorm** is a storm in which there is thunder and lightning. N COUNT

Thursday /θɜːzdi/, **Thursdays**. **Thursday** is one of the seven days of the week. It is the day after Wednesday and before Friday. EG *I got your postcard on Thursday... The question was raised at the meeting last Thursday.* N UNCOUNT OR N COUNT

thus /ðʌs/. **1** You use **thus** to introduce the consequence or conclusion of something that you have just said. EG *They are now down to their last 2,000 pounds and thus qualify for social security benefits... Thus, an incomes policy has to be controlled if it is to be effective.* ADV SEN Formal

2 If you say that something is or happens **thus**, you mean that it is or happens in the way you are describing. EG *She lay down. Her eyelids closed. It was thus that Robert saw her... Thus encouraged, Lexington walked through the gate... It has always been thus and will continue to be so.* ADV

thwart /θwɔːt/, **thwarts**, **thwarting**, **thwarted**. To **thwart** someone or their plans means to prevent them from doing or getting what they want. EG *The big man's hopes were thwarted by Taylor... She had never tried to thwart him in any way... ...the only factor likely to thwart land reforms.* V+O Formal

thyme /taɪm/ is a type of herb used in cooking. N UNCOUNT

tiara /tiˈɑːrə/, **tiaras**. A **tiara** is a small crown worn by a woman of high social rank on formal occasions. N COUNT

tic /tɪk/, **tics**. If someone has a **tic**, a part of their face or body keeps moving suddenly and they cannot control it. EG *She seemed to have developed a tic in her neck.* N COUNT

tick /tɪk/, **ticks**, **ticking**, **ticked**. **1** A **tick** is a written mark like a V with the right hand line extended upwards. You use it to show that something is correct or has been dealt with. EG *There was a nice red tick in the margin.* N COUNT

2 If you **tick** something that is written on a piece of paper, you put a tick next to it. V+O

3 When a clock or watch **ticks**, it makes a regular series of short sounds as it works. EG *It was so quiet I could hear my wristwatch ticking away.* V

◊ **ticking**. EG *She could hear a faint ticking.* ◊ N UNCOUNT

4 The **tick** of a clock or watch is the series of short sounds it makes when it is working. EG *The clock in the kitchen had a noisy tick.* N COUNT

5 If you talk about what makes someone **tick**, you are talking about the reasons for their character and behaviour. EG *What makes Patrick tick?* V

tick away or **tick by**. If you say that the seconds, minutes, or hours **tick away** or **tick by**, you are emphasizing the fact that time is passing. EG *The seconds ticked by and still they heard no explosion.* PHRASAL VB : V+ADV

tick off. **1** If you **tick off** an item on a list, you put a tick by it in order to show that it has been dealt with. **2** If you **tick** someone **off**, you speak angrily to them because they have done something wrong. EG *David had ticked her off for being careless.* PHRASAL VB : V+O+ADV V+O+ADV Informal

tick over. Something that **is ticking over** is working or operating steadily but not as hard or well as it can do. EG *...enough to keep the essential processes ticking over for a few months.* PHRASAL VB : V+ADV, USU CONT

ticket /tɪkɪt/, **tickets**. **1** A **ticket** is an official piece of paper or card which shows that you have paid for a journey or have paid to enter a place of entertainment such as a sports ground or cinema. EG *She bought two tickets for the opera... ...bus tickets... I'd like a return ticket to Vienna, please.* ● See also **season ticket**. N COUNT

2 When drivers of road vehicles get a **ticket**, they are given an official piece of paper which says that they have committed a minor driving or parking offence and must pay a fine or appear in court. EG *There was a parking ticket under the windshield wiper.* N COUNT

3 The particular **ticket** on which a candidate fights an election is the set of political policies which he or she supports. EG *He ran as Vice-President on the Republican ticket.* N SING : the+N+SUPP

tickle /tɪkəl/, **tickles**, **tickling**, **tickled**. **1** When you **tickle** someone, you move your fingers lightly over their body, often in order to make them laugh. EG *Babies want to be tickled and hugged.* V+O

2 If something **tickles** you or if it **tickles**, it causes an irritating feeling by touching a part of your body lightly. EG *He flicked away a strand of hair that was tickling Ellen's nose.* V+O OR V

3 If a fact or a situation **tickles** you, it amuses you or gives you pleasure. EG *'Yes, sir,' she answered. The Colonel was tickled by that.* V+O

ticklish /tɪklɪʃ/. **1** A **ticklish** problem or situation is difficult and needs to be dealt with carefully. EG *It was a ticklish moment in the discussion.* ADJ QUALIT : USU ATTRIB

2 If someone is **ticklish**, you can make them laugh very easily by tickling them, because they have very sensitive bodies. ADJ QUALIT : USU PRED

tidal /taɪdəl/ means relating to or produced by tides. EG *...tidal estuaries... ...tidal energy.* ADJ CLASSIF : ATTRIB

What day comes before Friday?

tidal wave, tidal waves. A **tidal wave** is a very N COUNT large wave, often caused by an earthquake, that comes over the land and destroys things.

tide /taɪd/, **tides, tiding, tided. 1** The **tide** is the N SING: the+N, regular change in the level of the sea on the shore. OR N UNCOUNT When the tide is high, full, or in, it is at its highest +SUPP level, and when it is low or out, it is at its lowest level. EG *The tide was coming in... The rocks were exposed at low tide.*

2 The **tide** of opinion or fashion is what the N SING+of majority of people think or do at a particular time. EG *He's always gone against the tide of fashion.*

3 A **tide** of things is a large quantity of them. EG N PART *...the tide of highly qualified academics who come looking for work... ...a rising tide of alcoholism.*

tide over. If something will **tide** someone **over,** PHRASAL VB: it will help them through a difficult period of time. V+O+ADV/ EG *I only want to borrow enough to tide me over till* PREP *Monday.*

tidings /taɪdɪŋz/ are news that someone tells you. N PLURAL EG *He kissed her and told her the good tidings...* +SUPP *Pigeons were sent out to spread tidings of the* Formal *rebellion.*

tidy /taɪdi¹/, **tidier, tidiest; tidies, tidying, ti-** died. **1** Something that is **tidy** is neat and arranged ADJ QUALIT in an orderly way. EG *It is very difficult to keep a house tidy... ...a tidy desk.* ◊ **tidiness.** EG *...his* ◊ N UNCOUNT *parents' concern with tidiness and punctuality.*

2 Someone who is **tidy** always keeps their things ADJ QUALIT neat and arranged in an orderly way. EG *I wish you were a little bit tidier!*

3 When you **tidy** a place, you make it neat by V+O putting things in their proper places. EG *You can't tidy a bedroom until you've made the beds.*

4 A **tidy** amount of money is a fairly large amount ADJ QUALIT: of it. EG *He managed to make quite a tidy income* ATTRIB *every year.* Informal

tidy away. When you **tidy** something **away,** you PHRASAL VB: put it in a cupboard or drawer so that it is not in V+O+ADV the way. EG *Someone had tidied my papers away.*

tidy up. When you **tidy up** or **tidy** a place **up,** PHRASAL VB: you put things back in their proper places so that V+ADV OR everything is neat. EG *Then I made the beds and* V+O+ADV *tidied up.*

tie /taɪ/, **ties, tying, tied. 1** If you **tie** one thing to V+O+A another or if you **tie** it in a particular position, you fasten it to the other thing or fasten it in that position, often using string or rope. EG *...one of those labels you tie onto the handle of your suitcase.*

2 If you **tie** a piece of string or cloth round V+O+A something or **tie** something with the string or cloth, you put the string or cloth round it and fasten the ends together in a knot or bow. EG *...a little dog which had a ribbon tied round its neck... ...a parcel tied with string... The children spent the morning tying the straw into small bundles.*

3 If you **tie** a knot or a bow in a piece of string or V+O: USU+A cloth, you fasten the ends together and make a knot or bow.

4 When you **tie** your shoelaces, you fasten the ends V+O together in a bow. EG *He was still tying his laces.*

5 A **tie** is a long, narrow piece of cloth that is worn N COUNT around someone's neck under their shirt collar and tied in a knot at the front. Ties are worn mainly by men. EG *He took off his jacket and loosened his tie.* ● See also **bow tie.**

6 Something that **is tied** to or into something else V+O+to/into is connected to it or linked closely with it. EG USU PASS *Canada is more tightly tied into the American economy.*

7 A **tie** is also a connection or feeling that links you N COUNT: with a person, place, or organization. EG *Family ties* USU+SUPP *are often very strong... They want to loosen their ties with Britain.*

8 If you **tie** with someone in a competition V OR V+with: game, you have the same number of points or the RECIP same degree of success. EG *Two actresses tied for the Best Actress award.* ▶ used as a noun. EG *In the* ▶ N COUNT

event of a tie, the winner will be the contestant who took the shortest time.

tie down. A person or thing that **ties** you **down** PHRASAL VB: restricts your freedom, for example by making you V+O+ADV live, behave, or act in a particular way. EG *You're not tied down to a date.*

tie in with. An idea or fact that **ties in with** PHRASAL VB: something else fits in with it or agrees with it. EG V+ADV+PREP *His beliefs didn't seem to tie in at all with reality.*

tie up. 1 If you **tie** something **up,** you put string or PHRASAL VB: rope round it so that it is firm or secure. EG *Clarissa* V+O+ADV *came in, carrying some canvases tied up in brown paper.* **2** If someone **ties** you **up,** they fasten ropes V+O+ADV or chains around you so that you cannot move or escape. **3** When you **tie up** your shoelaces, you V+O+ADV fasten them in a bow. EG *Tie up your laces. Hurry!* **4** V+O+ADV When you **tie up** an animal, you fasten it to a fixed object with a piece of rope or chain so that it cannot run away. **5** If you **tie up** something such V+O+ADV as money or resources, you do something with it, so that it is not available for other people or for other purposes. EG *People don't want to tie their money up for long periods.* **6** Something that **is** V-ERG+ADV, **tied up** with something else or **ties up** with it is OFT+with closely linked with it. EG *It tied up with her interest in dance.*

tied up. If you are **tied up,** you are busy. EG *I'm* ADJ PRED *tied up right now, can you call me back later?* Informal

tier /tɪə/, **tiers.** A **tier** is a row or layer of N COUNT something that has other layers above or below it. EG *The theatre had semicircular tiers of seats.*

tiger /taɪgə/, **tigers.** A **tiger** is a large, fierce N COUNT animal that belongs to the cat family. Tigers are orange-coloured with black stripes.

tight /taɪt/, **tighter, tightest; tights. 1** Clothes or ADJ QUALIT shoes that are **tight** fit closely to your body. EG *He was wearing tight cream-coloured trousers.* ◊ **tightly.** EG *...a tightly fitting suit.* ◊ ADV

2 If you hold something or someone **tight,** you hold ADV AFTER VB them firmly and securely. EG *Ann was now clutching the letter tight in her hand.* ▶ used as an ▶ ADJ QUALIT adjective. EG *His fingers were tight on Thomas's arm.* ◊ **tightly.** EG *They clung together very* ◊ ADV *tightly.*

3 Something that is **tight** is firmly fastened, and ADJ QUALIT difficult to move. EG *...a tight knot.* ◊ **tightly.** EG *He* ◊ ADV *screwed the caps tightly onto the bottles.*

4 Something that is shut **tight** is shut very firmly. ADV AFTER VB EG *He closed his eyes tight.*

5 Skin, cloth, or string that is stretched **tight** is ADJ QUALIT stretched or pulled so that it is smooth or straight. EG *The skin was stretched tight over her fine facial bones.* ◊ **tightly.** EG *The skin on his face was* ◊ ADV *drawn back tightly like stretched leather.*

6 You use **tight** to describe things that are very ADJ QUALIT close together. EG *They stood in a tight group... Her hair was arranged in tight curls.* ◊ **tightly.** EG ◊ ADV *...houses tightly packed together.*

7 If your chest or stomach feels **tight,** it feels hard ADJ QUALIT and painful, because you are ill or anxious. ◊ **tightness.** EG *I went to the interview with the* ◊ N UNCOUNT *familiar tightness in my stomach.*

8 A **tight** plan or arrangement allows only the ADJ QUALIT minimum time or money needed to do something. EG *We have a tight schedule.*

9 A **tight** rule or system of control is very strict. EG ADJ QUALIT *Security has become visibly tighter over the last year.* ◊ **tightly.** EG *...a society which is very tightly* ◊ ADV *controlled.*

10 Someone who is **tight** is drunk. EG *Some of the* ADJ QUALIT *village lads tried to get him tight.* Informal

11 Tights are a thin piece of clothing made of N PLURAL stretchy material that fits closely round a person's hips, legs, and feet. They are usually worn by women, and sometimes by male dancers. EG *She had a ladder in her only pair of silk tights.*

12 to **keep a tight rein on** someone: see **rein.** ● to **sit tight:** see **sit.** ● See also **airtight, watertight.**

tighten /ˈtaɪtəᵊn/, **tightens, tightening, tight-** | V-ERG : OFT+A
ened. 1 If you **tighten** your hold on something or if
your hold **tightens**, you hold the thing more firmly.
EG *His fingers tightened around his rifle... He tightened his grip on the spear.*

2 If you **tighten** a rope or chain, or if it **tightens**, it | V-ERG
is stretched or pulled until it is straight. EG *The
chain tightened and the pig's leg was pulled back.*

3 When you **tighten** a fastening, you move it so | V+O
that it is more firmly in place or holds something
more firmly. EG *She bent down to tighten the strap
of her roller skate.* ● to **tighten** your **belt**: see **belt**.

4 If a part of your body **tightens**, it becomes tense | V
and stiff. EG *His face and eyes tightened with
hatred.*

5 If someone **tightens** a rule or system, they make | V+O
it stricter or more efficient. EG *The authorities
tightened security around the embassy.*

tighten up. 1 When you **tighten up** a fastening, | PHRASAL VB :
you move it so that it is more firmly in place or | V+O+ADV
holds something more firmly. EG *Tighten up the
axle nut.* **2** If someone **tightens up** a rule or | V+O+ADV
system, they make it stricter or more efficient. EG
*He said he would take steps to tighten up the
administration.*

tight-fisted /ˌtaɪt ˈfɪstɪd/. Someone who is **tight-** | ADJ QUALIT
fisted is unwilling to spend money. EG *He was | Informal
unable to squeeze the extra cash out of his tight-
fisted employers.*

tightrope /ˈtaɪtrəʊp/, **tightropes. 1** A **tightrope** | N COUNT
is a tightly-stretched piece of rope on which an
acrobat balances and performs tricks.

2 If you say that someone is **on a tightrope** or is | PHRASE
walking a tightrope, you mean that they are in a
very difficult or delicate situation and have to be
careful about what they say or do. EG *He recognized
that he was walking a tightrope: one slip would
mean political destruction.*

tile /taɪl/, **tiles.** A **tile** is a small, flat, square piece | N COUNT
of something such as slate, carpet, or cork. You use
tiles to cover surfaces such as floors, walls, or
roofs. EG *Polystyrene ceiling tiles help to insulate a
room... ...brick houses roofed in reddish-brown tiles.*

tiled /taɪld/. A **tiled** surface is covered with tiles. | ADJ CLASSIF
EG *He heard footsteps on the tiled floor... ...stone
houses with red tiled roofs.*

till /tɪl/, **tills. 1 Till** means the same as until. EG *He* | PREP OR CONJ
*wrote from morning till night... We didn't get back
till 2... Wait till I come back.*

2 A **till** is a drawer or box in a shop where money | N UNCOUNT
is kept. Usually it is part of a machine called a cash
register. EG *He put the money into the till.*

tilt /tɪlt/, **tilts, tilting, tilted.** If you **tilt** an object | V-ERG : USU+A
or if it **tilts**, it changes position so that one end or
side is higher than the other. EG *He tilted the flask
and two or three drops trickled out... Let your head
gently tilt forwards.* ▸ used as a noun. EG *He* | ▸ N COUNT
indicated, with a tilt of his head, a girl nearby.

timber /ˈtɪmbə/, **timbers. 1 Timber** is wood that | N UNCOUNT
is used for building houses and making furniture. EG
*Most of the region's timber is imported from the
south... We live in timber cabins.*

2 The **timbers** of a ship or house are the big pieces | N COUNT :
of wood that have been used to build it. EG *He could | USU PLURAL
hear the ship's timbers creaking.*

time /taɪm/, **times, timing, timed. 1 Time** is | N UNCOUNT
what we measure in hours, days, and years. EG *...a
period of time... Time passed, and finally he fell
asleep again... You're getting more and more depressed as time goes on.*

2 You use **time** to refer to **2.1** a specific point in | N COUNT :
time, which can be stated in hours and minutes and | USU *the/what*
is shown on clocks. EG *What's the time?... What | +N SING
time did you get back?... Ask the times of planes
from Rome to Vienna... I will see you at the same
time next week.* **2.2** the official system of time that | N UNCOUNT
is used in a particular place in the world. EG *It was | +SUPP
1035 hours Greenwich Mean Time... ...at 6 in the
evening, local time.*

3 You also use **time** to refer to **3.1** the period of | N UNCOUNT
time that someone spends doing something. EG *How | OR N SING :
do you find time to write these books?... I didn't | USU+SUPP
have time for tea... She spends most of her time
sunbathing... That would take a long time to discuss
in detail.* **3.2** a period of time or a point in time, | N UNCOUNT
when you are describing what is happening then. | OR N COUNT
EG *It seemed a good time to invite my sister to
stay... ...during my time in Toronto... Do you remember that time when Adrian phoned?... He
blushed each time she spoke to him... Ask for
something different next time... There were times
when I didn't know what to do.*

4 A particular **time** in history is a period in it. EG | N COUNT OR
*...the history of modern times... The film begins at | N UNCOUNT
the time of the Roman Empire... ...one of the great | +SUPP
unsolved mysteries of our time.*

5 If you say it is **time** for an action or it is **time** to | N UNCOUNT
do it, you mean that it ought to happen or be done | +SUPP
now. EG *It is time to go... It was time for tea... The
time has come to change things... It is time we
realized that we were wrong.*

6 If something happens for a **time**, it happens for a | N SING : a+N
fairly long period of time. EG *It's nice to be in
London for a time... It became clear after a time
that he was very ill.*

7 You use **time** after numbers **7.1** to say how often | N COUNT
something happens. EG *Ray and I play squash three
times a week... The telephone rang a second time.*
7.2 when you are saying how much bigger, smaller, | N PLURAL
better, or worse one thing is compared to another.
EG *It would cost me ten times as much... It has
become three times as difficult as it used to be.*

8 You use **times** in arithmetic to link numbers or
amounts that are multiplied together. EG *5 times 50
– that's 250.*

9 If you **time** something for a particular time, you | V+O+*for*
plan that it should happen at that time. EG *Their | OR to-INF
disruption was timed for 9.20.* ◊ **timed.** EG *His* | ◊ timed.
remarks were badly timed. ● See also **timing**. | ◊ ADJ CLASSIF
| AFTER ADV

10 If you **time** an action or activity, you measure | V+O
how long it lasts. EG *This was repeated at intervals
which he timed on his watch.*

11 You can use **time** when talking about how late | PHRASE
or how early you are for an appointment or event.
For example, if you are **in time**, you are not late. If
you are **in good time** or **ahead of time**, you are
earlier than necessary or expected. If you are **on
time**, you arrive at the correct time. EG *We're just
in time... We got there in plenty of time... She did
the exam two years ahead of time... We all got here
on time.*

12 Time is used with 'at' in these ways. **12.1** You | PHRASES
use **at a time** when saying how many things or
how much of something is involved in one place,
group, or action. EG *He used to abandon his work
for many months at a time... There was only room
for one person at a time.* **12.2** If something happens
at times, it happens sometimes but not always. EG
She's really rude at times. **12.3 At one time** or **at
any one time** means at a single point in time or
during a single period of time. EG *The library has
room for six hundred readers at any one time.* **12.4**
If you say that something existed or was true **at
one time**, you mean that it existed or was true in
the past. EG *You worked for them, didn't you, at one
time?* **12.5** If you say that something unpleasant is
the case **at the best of times**, you are emphasizing that it is the case even when everything else is
as pleasant as possible. EG *I find cleaning tedious at
the best of times.* **12.6** You use **at the same time**
to introduce a statement that contrasts with the
previous statement or modifies it. EG *It made us
cautious but at the same time it made us willing to
take a risk... Such a development would be wel-*

> What is two times three?

come. *At the same time, it is crucial to recognize the narrowness of the approach.*

13 Time is used with other prepositions in these PHRASES ways. **13.1** If you say it is **about time** that something was done, you are emphasizing that you think it should be done. EG *It's about time that Parliament concentrated on unemployment.* **13.2** If someone is **ahead of** their **time**, they have an idea long before other people start thinking in the same way. EG *Diaghilev was ahead of his time.* **13.3** If something was **before** your **time**, it happened or existed before you were born. **13.4** Someone who is **behind the times** is old-fashioned. EG *The law is behind the times on a number of important issues.* **13.5** If you do something **for the time being**, you do it for a short time until something else can be arranged. EG *For the time being, we ought to stay with him.* **13.6** If you do something **from time to time**, you do it occasionally. EG *From time to time she stopped and looked round.* **13.7** If you say that something will happen **in time**, you mean that it will happen eventually. EG *In time the arguments will straighten themselves out.* **13.8** If something will happen **in** a week's **time** or **in** a month's **time**, it will happen after one week or one month has passed. EG *Celia is coming along in about an hour's time... ...in three weeks' time.*

14 Time is also used in these phrases. **14.1** When PHRASES you talk about how well a watch or clock **keeps time**, you are talking about how accurately it measures time. EG *This has kept perfect time since I got it back.* **14.2** If you **have no time for** Informal someone or something, you do not like them or approve of them. EG *I haven't got a lot of time for politicians.* **14.3** If you say that you **made good time** on a journey, you mean that you completed the journey more quickly than you expected. EG *We made pretty good time on the journey up here.* **14.4** If you do something to **pass the time**, you do it because you are bored or are waiting for something else, and not because you really want to do it. EG *They read every page just to pass the time.* **14.5** If you say that something will **take time**, you mean that it will happen slowly or gradually and not immediately. EG *It would take time to get results.* **14.6** If you **take** your **time** doing something, you do it slowly. EG *The steamer took its time.* **14.7** If something happens **time after time** or **time and again**, it happens on many occasions. EG *She had threatened time after time to leave him... Thousands of people have proved it time and time again.*

TIME

This entry shows some of the ways in which you can refer to time in English.

There are a number of ways of asking the time or of saying what time it is. EG *'What time is it, Gordon?' – 'Just after five.'... 'What's the time now?' – 'It's quarter past nine.'... 'Can you tell me the time?' – 'It's twenty-five past twelve.'... 'Have you got the time?' – 'It is nearly one o'clock.'... 'What time does the boat leave from Weymouth?' – 'At a quarter past three in the afternoon.'... The time is six forty-five... My watch says six thirty... It's five to eight and breakfast's at eight o'clock... The time was 10.35 hours Greenwich Mean Time.*

Here are some other ways of talking about time. EG *I'll be back at quarter past one... By eleven o'clock Brody was back in his office... At two o'clock in the morning Castle was still awake... You should be there no later than nine thirty... Office hours are from 9 a.m. to 6 p.m.*

---

four o'clock	four in the morning	`04:00`
four	4 a.m.	
4 o'clock	four in the afternoon	`16:00`
	4 p.m.	
nine o'clock	nine in the morning	`09:00`
nine	9 a.m.	
9 o'clock	nine in the evening	`21:00`
	nine at night	
	9 p.m.	
	twelve in the morning	
twelve o'clock	12 a.m.	`12:00`
twelve	midday	
12 o'clock	noon	
	twelve at night	`00:00`
	12 p.m.	
	midnight	
	a quarter past twelve	`12:15`
	quarter past twelve	
	twelve fifteen	
	a quarter after twelve	`00:15`
	twenty-five past two	`02:25`
	twenty-five minutes past two	
	two twenty-five	
	twenty-five after two	`14:25`
	half past eleven	`11:30`
	eleven-thirty	
	half eleven	
	half after eleven	`23:30`
	a quarter to one	`12:45`
	quarter to one	
	twelve forty-five	
	a quarter of one	`00:45`
	ten to eight	`07:50`
	ten minutes to eight	
	seven-fifty	
	ten of eight	`19:50`

---

time-honoured. A **time-honoured** way of doing ADJ CLASSIF: something has been used for a very long time. EG ATTRIB *...a time-honoured practice.*

timeless /taɪmlɪ²s/. If you describe something as ADJ CLASSIF **timeless**, you mean that it is so good, beautiful, or Formal perfect that it cannot be affected by the passing of time or by changes in society or fashion. EG *His art has something universal, something timeless and enduring from age to age.*

time limit, time limits. A **time limit** is a period N COUNT of time during which a particular task must be completed. EG *I had set myself a time limit of two years.*

timely /taɪmli¹/. Something that is **timely** hap- ADJ QUALIT pens at just the right time, so that it is most effective or prevents possible problems or difficulties. EG *...the safe and timely arrival of reinforcements.*

time out. If you take **time out** to do something, N UNCOUNT you stop your normal activities for a while in order to do it. EG *He took time out to chair a meeting of local officials.*

timer /taɪmə/, **timers.** A **timer** is a device that N COUNT measures time, especially one that is part of a machine. EG *The timer on the stove started ringing.*
● See also **egg-timer**.

time scale, time scales. The **time scale** of an N COUNT event is the length of time during which it happens. EG *...the time scale of technological development.*

timetable /taɪmteɪbə⁰l/, **timetables.** A **time-** N COUNT **table** is 1 a plan of the times when particular activities or jobs should be done. EG *...a timetable of all events on Wednesday... ...the timetable of a* second year pupil at a comprehensive school. **2** a list of the times when particular trains, boats, buses, or aeroplanes arrive and depart. EG *...railway timetables.*

timid /tɪmɪd/. Someone who is **timid** is shy and ADJ QUALIT shows no courage or self-confidence. EG *...a timid young girl... ...a timid smile.* ◊ **timidly**. EG *I left the* ◊ ADV *car and timidly rang the doorbell.* ◊ **timidity** ◊ N UNCOUNT /tɪmɪdɪ'tɪ¹/. EG *He had a terrible time in overcoming his timidity.*

timing /taɪmɪŋ/. **1** Someone's **timing** is their skill N UNCOUNT in judging the right moment at which to do something in a situation or activity. EG *She displayed perfect timing and control.*
2 The **timing** of an event is **2.1** the act of deciding N UNCOUNT when it should happen. EG *They met to consider the timing of elections.* **2.2** the act of measuring how much time it takes.

tin /tɪn/, **tins**. **1 Tin** is a soft silvery-white metal. EG N UNCOUNT *...a tin can... ...a tin kettle.*
2 A **tin** is **2.1** a metal container which is filled with N COUNT OR food and sealed in order to preserve the food. EG *...a* N PART *tin of sardines... ...a tin of condensed milk.* **2.2** a British small metal container with a lid. EG *She put the biscuit tin back in the cupboard.*

tinge /tɪndʒ/, **tinges**. A **tinge** of something, espe- N COUNT+SUPP cially a colour or a feeling, is a small amount of it. EG *The sky had a greenish tinge... There was a tinge of envy in her voice... Other colonial systems lacked even that tinge of liberalism.*

tinged /tɪndʒd/. If something is **tinged** with some- ADJ PRED thing else, especially with a colour or a feeling, it +with has a small amount of that colour or feeling in it. EG *Her eyes were slightly tinged with red... ...joy tinged with bitterness.*

tingle /tɪŋɡ⁰l/, **tingles**, **tingling**, **tingled**. **1** v When a part of your body **tingles**, you feel a slight prickling feeling in it. EG *His fingertips tingled.* ◊ **tingling**. EG *...a sharp tingling in her fingers.* ◊ N UNCOUNT
2 When you **tingle** with excitement or shock, you v : USU+with feel it very strongly. EG *I was tingling with excitement.*

tinker /tɪŋkə/, **tinkers**, **tinkering**, **tinkered**. If v : USU+with you **tinker** with something, you make a lot of small Informal adjustments to it in order to repair it or improve it. EG *He's still tinkering with the motor.*

tinkle /tɪŋk⁰l/, **tinkles**, **tinkling**, **tinkled**. **1** If v something **tinkles**, it makes a sound like a small bell ringing. EG *I could hear bells tinkling.* ▸ used as ▸ N COUNT : a noun. EG *The telephone gave a tinkle.* OFT+of
2 If you **give** someone **a tinkle**, you call them on PHRASE the telephone. Informal

tinned /tɪnd/. **Tinned** food has been preserved by ADJ CLASSIF being sealed in a tin. EG *...tinned peas.*

tinny /tɪnɪ¹/, **tinnier**, **tinniest**. **1** A **tinny** sound ADJ QUALIT has an unpleasant high-pitched quality. EG *One hears bursts of tinny pop music from teenagers' handbags.*
2 If something such as a car is **tinny**, it is made of ADJ QUALIT thin metal and is of poor quality.

tin-opener /tɪn əʊpⁿnə/, **tin-openers**. A **tin-** N COUNT **opener** is a tool that you use to open tins of food.

tinsel /tɪnsⁿl/ consists of small pieces of sparkling, N UNCOUNT coloured paper attached to long pieces of thread. Tinsel is used to decorate rooms at Christmas. EG *...tinsel on a Christmas tree.*

tint /tɪnt/, **tints**, **tinted**, **tinting**. **1** A **tint** is a N COUNT colour. EG *His eyes had a yellow tint.*
2 If you **tint** your hair, you change its colour by v+o adding a weak dye to it. EG *He acquired a preparation for tinting his hair chestnut brown.*

tinted /tɪntɪ'd/. Something such as glass that is ADJ CLASSIF **tinted** is coloured, especially with pale colours. EG *He glanced through the tinted rear window.*

tiny /taɪnɪ¹/, **tinier**, **tiniest**. Something that is **tiny** ADJ QUALIT is extremely small. EG *...tiny shells, the size of your finger nail... ...the tiny little room at the end.*

-tion, **-tions**. See **-ation**.

tip /tɪp/, **tips**, **tipping**, **tipped**. **1** The **tip** of N COUNT : something long and thin is the end of it. EG *He was* OFT+of *hanging by his finger tips from a window frame... The animal plucks fruit from the tips of branches.*
2 If you **tip** an object, you move it so that it is no v+o+A longer horizontal or upright. EG *He tipped his soup bowl towards himself... He was sitting with his chair tipped back against the wall.*
3 If you **tip** something somewhere, you pour it v+o+A there quickly and carelessly. EG *He tipped the contents of the rucksack out on to the floor.*
4 A **tip** is a place where rubbish is dumped. EG *The* N COUNT *area was covered with wrecked cars and rubbish* British *tips.*
5 If you give someone such as a waiter or a taxi N COUNT driver a **tip**, you give them some money to thank them for their services. EG *The woman gave me a dollar tip.* ▸ used as a verb. EG *I tipped the* ▸ V+O OR V *chauffeur... People aren't tipping very much.*
6 A **tip** is also a useful piece of advice or informa- N COUNT tion, often one that is given privately or secretly. EG *He consulted books by well-known tennis players for tips on basic techniques.*
7 If you say that a word or name is **on the tip of** PHRASE your **tongue**, you mean that you cannot remember it just at the moment, but you are sure you will remember it very soon.
8 If you say that something is **the tip of the** PHRASE **iceberg**, you mean that it is only a very small part of a much larger problem.

tip off. If you **tip** someone **off**, you give them PHRASAL VB : information, often privately or secretly, about V+O+ADV something that has happened or that is going to happen. EG *The burglars were tipped off by a lookout and escaped.* ● See also **tip-off.**

tip over. If you **tip** something **over** or if it **tips** PHRASAL VB : **over**, it falls over or turns over. EG *She tipped the* V-ERG+ADV *pan over and a dozen fish flopped out... His chair was tipping over.*

tip-off, **tip-offs**. A **tip-off** is a piece of information N COUNT that you give to someone, often privately or secret- ly, usually as a warning that something is going to happen. EG *The building was evacuated as the result of a tip-off.*

tipped /tɪpt/. **1** Something that is **tipped** has a tip ADJ CLASSIF made of a different substance. EG *They hunted in* OFT+with *the woods with spears tipped with stone blades.*
2 A **tipped** cigarette has a filter at the end which ADJ CLASSIF the smoke passes through when you breathe it in.

tipsy /tɪpsɪ¹/. If you are **tipsy**, you are slightly ADJ QUALIT drunk. EG *The wine had made Barton a trifle tipsy.* Informal

tiptoe /tɪptəʊ/, **tiptoes**, **tiptoeing**, **tiptoed**. **1** If v : USU+A you **tiptoe** somewhere, you walk there very quietly on your toes. EG *He knocked softly on the door and tiptoed into the room.*
2 If you do something **on tiptoe**, you do it standing PHRASE or walking on your toes. EG *They stretched their arms and stood on tiptoe.*

tirade /taɪreɪd/, **tirades**. A **tirade** is a long, angry N COUNT speech in which you criticize someone or some- Formal thing. EG *He launched into a familiar tirade against the government.*

tire /taɪə/, **tires**, **tiring**, **tired**. **1** If something V-ERG **tires** you, it makes you use a lot of energy, with the result that you want to rest or sleep. EG *The run did not seem to tire them at all... The other men began to tire and fall.*
2 If you **tire** of something, you become bored with v+of it. EG *He tired of my questions... The modern businessman never tires of claiming and complaining.*
3 See also **tyre.**

tire out. If something **tires** you **out**, it makes you PHRASAL VB : exhausted. V+O+ADV

Name some activities that tire you out.

tired /taɪəd/. 1 If you are **tired**, you feel that you ADJ QUALIT want to rest or sleep. EG *I'm sure you must be tired after cycling all that distance.* ◇ **tiredness**. EG ◇ N UNCOUNT *Tiredness overwhelmed me.* ● If you are **tired out**, ● PHRASE you are exhausted. EG *Have a good trip? I expect you're tired out.*

2 If a person's voice or eyes are **tired**, they show ADJ QUALIT that the person needs rest or sleep. EG *'I'm hungry,' said the little boy in a tired voice.*

3 If you are **tired** of something, you are bored with ADJ PRED+*of* it. EG *Judy was tired of quarrelling with him.*

tireless /taɪəl²s/. Someone who is **tireless** has a ADJ CLASSIF lot of energy and never seems to need a rest. EG *Both of them were tireless workers.*

tiresome /taɪəsəm/. A person or thing that is ADJ QUALIT **tiresome** makes you feel irritated or bored. EG *...a tiresome obstacle to be overcome.*

tiring /taɪərɪŋ/. Something that is **tiring** makes ADJ QUALIT you tired so that you want to rest or sleep. EG *We should have an early night after such a tiring day.*

tissue /tɪsjuː, tɪʃuː/, **tissues.** 1 In animals and N MASS plants, **tissue** consists of cells that are similar in Technical appearance and function. EG *...the scar tissue left by a wound.*

2 Tissue or **tissue paper** is thin paper that is used N UNCOUNT for wrapping things that are easily damaged, such as glass or china.

3 A **tissue** is a small, square piece of soft paper N COUNT that you use as a handkerchief. EG *There was a box of tissues in the back window of the car.*

4 You can refer to a totally false story as a **tissue** PHRASE **of lies.** EG *Their allegations were a tissue of lies.*

titbit /tɪtbɪt/, **titbits.** A **titbit** is a small, tasty N COUNT piece of food. EG *...a dog begging for titbits.*

titillate /tɪtɪleɪt/, **titillates, titillating, titillated.** V+O OR V If something **titillates** someone, it pleases and excites them, especially in a sexual way. EG *...various other bits of scandal designed to titillate.*

title /taɪtªl/, **titles.** 1 The **title** of a book, play, or N COUNT piece of music is its name. EG *He wrote a book with the title 'The Castle'.*

2 Someone's **title** is **2.1** a word such as Lord, Lady, N COUNT Mr, or Mrs, that is used before their name in order to show their rank or status. **2.2** a word that describes their job or position in an organization. EG *The person in charge usually has a title of some sort like Administration Manager.*

3 A **title** in a sports competition is the position of N COUNT champion. Usually a person or team keeps a title until someone else defeats them. EG *We had beaten Cornell and taken the title.*

titled /taɪtªld/. Someone who is **titled** has a high ADJ CLASSIF social rank and has a word such as 'Princess', 'Lord', 'Lady', or 'Sir' before their own name to show this. EG *...titled ladies... ...a titled Englishman.*

title-holder, title-holders. The **title-holder** is N COUNT the winner of a competition that takes place regularly. They remain the title-holder until someone else wins it.

title role, title roles. If an actor or an actress has N COUNT the **title role** in a play or film, he or she plays the character referred to in its name. For example, if an actress has the title role in 'Hedda Gabler', she plays Hedda Gabler. EG *...an actor best known for the title role in 'The Eddie Cantor Story'.*

titter /tɪtə/, **titters, tittering, tittered.** If you v **titter**, you laugh in a way that shows that you are nervous or embarrassed. EG *Someone began to titter. 'What's the matter?' asked the Director.*

TNT /tiː ɛn tiː/ is a powerful explosive substance. N UNCOUNT

to /tə, tuː/. 1 You use **to** when indicating the place PREP that someone or something is moving towards or pointing at. EG *I'm going with her to Australia... We'll drive to the top of the next hill... The children have gone to school... He thought that he might go to a concert... He was pointing to an oil tanker somewhere on the horizon.*

2 You use **to** when indicating where something is PREP tied or attached, or what it is touching. EG *I was*

planning *to tie him to a tree... He clutched the parcel to his chest.*

3 You use **to** when indicating the position of PREP something. For example, if something is **to** your left, it is on your left. EG *To one side, he could see the block of luxury flats.*

4 You use **to** when indicating who or what an PREP action, a feeling, or your attention is directed towards. EG *He showed the letter to Barbara... She had given German lessons to a leading industrialist... We don't do repairs to farm machines... The answer to your question is unexpectedly simple... They were sympathetic to his ideas... She listened to a flute being played.*

5 You use **to** when indicating someone's reaction PREP to something. For example, if you say that something happens **to** someone's relief, you mean that they are relieved when it happens. EG *To his great surprise he was offered both jobs.*

6 You use **to** when indicating the effect that PREP something has on someone. For example, if something is **to** someone's liking, they are satisfied or pleased with it. EG *It's to your own advantage.*

7 You use **to** when indicating the person whose PREP opinion you are stating, especially when you know that other people may disagree with it. EG *To me it didn't seem necessary.*

8 You use **to** when indicating what something or PREP someone is becoming, or the state or situation that they are progressing towards. EG *It had almost turned to dust over the years... It drove me to distraction and despair... ...her rapid rise to fame... The danger is that a conventional conflict might escalate to a nuclear confrontation.*

9 You use **to** when indicating that something PREP happens until the time or amount mentioned is reached. EG *Breakfast was from 9 to 10 in the morning... The job will take anything from two to five weeks.*

10 You say **from** one thing **to** another when giving PHRASE two extreme examples of something which emphasize the scope or range of what you are saying. EG *I do everything, from washing up dishes to putting out the cat at night... We have branches in most of the cities of the world, from Yokohama to York.*

11 If someone goes **from** place **to** place or **from** PHRASE job **to** job, they go to several places, or work in several jobs, and spend only a short time in each one. EG *I've spent years going from town to town.*

12 If someone moves **to and fro**, they move PHRASE repeatedly from one place to another and back again, or from side to side. EG *All day, he rushed to and fro between his living quarters and his place of work... She rocked herself to and fro in amusement.* ● See also **to-ing and fro-ing**.

13 You use **to** in expressions of time that state the PREP number of minutes before a particular hour. For example, 'five **to** eight' means five minutes before eight o'clock: see the entry headed TIME.

14 You use **to** in ratios and rates when saying how PREP many units of one type there are for each unit of another. EG *My car does 35 miles to the gallon... The current exchange rate is $1.78 to the pound.*

15 If you push or shut a door **to**, you close it but do ADV AFTER VB not shut it completely.

16 You use **to** when indicating that two things PREP happen at the same time. For example, if something happens **to** music, it happens at the same time as music is being played. EG *To a chorus of laughter the President left the room.*

17 If you say **'There's nothing to it'**, **'There's not** PHRASE **much to it'**, or **'That's all there is to it'**, you are emphasizing how simple or easy you think something is.

18 You use **to** with the infinitive of a verb **18.1** *to*+INF when indicating the purpose or intention of an action. EG *People would stroll down the path to admire the garden.* ● **in order to**: see **order. 18.2** when commenting on a statement that you are making, for example when saying that you are being honest or brief, or that you are summing up or giving an example. EG *To be honest, we knew he was there... To tell you the truth, Phil, I don't want it... To sum up, my contention is that the law must be changed.* **18.3** in various other constructions. EG *She looked up to find Tony standing there... It costs about 150 pounds a week to keep someone in prison... They don't know who to ask... Some of us have got work to do... They were lovely to watch... This is difficult for us to accept... ...the first person to climb Everest... He was too proud to apologize... Sorry to keep you waiting.*

19 To is also used after verbs such as 'refer', 'relate', and 'attend', and in phrasal verbs such as 'see to' and 'come to'. See the individual verb and phrasal verb entries.

toad /təʊd/, **toads**. A **toad** is an animal that looks N COUNT like a frog but has a drier skin and lives less in the water. EG *I've been sitting here like a toad on a log.*

toadstool /təʊdstuːl/, **toadstools**. A **toadstool** is a N COUNT fungus that looks like a mushroom but is poisonous, so you cannot eat it.

toast /təʊst/, **toasts, toasting, toasted. 1 Toast** is N UNCOUNT bread which has been cut into slices and made brown and crisp by cooking at a high temperature. EG *Lally was spreading marmalade on a piece of toast... I like baked beans on toast.*

2 When you **toast** bread, you cook it at a high V+O temperature so that it becomes brown and crisp.

3 If you **toast** yourself or **toast** a part of your body, V-REFL OR V+O you sit in front of a fire so that you feel pleasantly warm. EG *He was toasting his toes at the fire.*

4 When you drink a **toast** to someone, you wish N COUNT : them success or good health, and then drink some USU A+N wine or other alcoholic drink. EG *It was an old fisherman's custom to drink a toast to the dead... Harold raised his glass in a toast: 'Welcome!'*

5 When you **toast** someone, you show your respect V+O for them or wish them success by saying their name, and then drinking some wine or other alcoholic drink. EG *I toasted the young hero and wished him luck.*

6 If someone is the **toast** of a place, they are very N SING : popular and are greatly admired there. EG *Joan was* the+N+of *the toast of the Senior Common Room.*

toaster /təʊstə/, **toasters**. A **toaster** is a piece of N COUNT electric equipment which you use to toast bread. EG *She put her slice of bread in the toaster.*

tobacco /təbækəʊ/ is **1** a substance which people N UNCOUNT smoke in pipes, cigars, and cigarettes. EG *He took out his pipe and filled it with tobacco and lit it.* **2** the plant from which tobacco is obtained. EG *...the cotton and tobacco fields.*

tobacconist /təbækənɪst/, **tobacconists**. A **to-** N COUNT **bacconist** is **1** a person who runs a shop that sells things such as tobacco, cigarettes, and cigars. **2** a shop that sells things such as tobacco, cigarettes, and cigars.

toboggan /təbɒgən/, **toboggans, tobogganing, tobogganed. 1** A **toboggan** is a vehicle for travel- N COUNT ling on snow. It consists of a flat seat with two narrow pieces of wood or metal underneath that slide easily over the snow.

2 If you **toboggan**, you ride on a toboggan. EG V : USU+A *...tobogganing down the long slope.*

today /tədeɪ/. **1 Today** means the day on which ADV OR N you are speaking or writing. EG *I hope you're* UNCOUNT *feeling better today... I had a letter today from my solicitor... Today is Thursday.*

2 You can refer to the present period of history as ADV OR N **today**. EG *Today we are threatened on all sides by* UNCOUNT *financial and political crises... ...differences be- tween the America of today and the America of thirty years ago.*

toddle /tɒdəl/, **toddles, toddling, toddled**. When V a child **toddles**, it walks unsteadily with short, quick steps. EG *You can see his grandson toddling around in the garden.*

toddler /tɒdlə/, **toddlers**. A **toddler** is a small N COUNT child who has just learned to walk. EG *...forty women, many of them with toddlers and young babies.*

to-do /tə duː/. When there is a **to-do**, people are N SING+SUPP very excited, confused, or angry about something. Informal EG *There was an awful to-do about the election result.*

toe /təʊ/, **toes, toeing, toed. 1** Your **toes** are the N COUNT : five movable parts at the end of your foot. See USU PLURAL picture at THE HUMAN BODY. EG *I stubbed my toe against a stone... I've got sand between my toes.*

2 The **toe** of a shoe or sock is the part that covers N COUNT the end of your foot. EG *Maria's shoes had holes in the toes.*

3 If you **toe the line**, you behave in the way that PHRASE people in authority expect you to. EG *She had always tried to toe the line in public.*

toenail /təʊneɪl/, **toenails**. Your **toenails** are the N COUNT : thin, hard coverings on the end of your toes. EG *Cut* USU PLURAL *their toenails once a fortnight.*

toffee /tɒfiː/, **toffees**. A **toffee** is a chewy sweet N COUNT OR that is made by boiling sugar and butter together N UNCOUNT with water. EG *...a few assorted toffees... ...a chunk of toffee.*

toffee apple, toffee apples. A **toffee apple** is an N COUNT apple covered with a thin, hard layer of toffee and mounted on a stick.

together /təgeðə/. **1** If people do something **to-** ADV **gether**, they do it with each other. EG *They flew back to London together... You all work together as a team in the office.*

2 If two things happen **together**, they happen at ADV AFTER VB the same time. EG *The reports will have to be seen and judged together before we decide.*

3 If things are joined or fixed **together**, they are ADV AFTER VB joined or fixed to each other. EG *Her hands were clasped tightly together... ...a series of hollow alu- minium tubes which screw together.*

4 If things or people are **together**, they are very ADV AFTER VB near to each other. EG *There were two metal plates lying close together on the floor... The fossils are packed densely together in display cases.*

5 Together with something else means as well as CONJ that other thing. EG *Lee handed over the key to his room, together with some pens and leaflets.*

6 If you say that things go **together**, you mean that ADV AFTER VB they fit or suit each other or can both exist or happen without causing any problems. EG *Nell feels marriage and studying don't go together.*

7 You use **together** when you are adding two or ADV more things to each other in order to consider the total as a whole. EG *The two companies together spend more on research than the whole of the rest of the industry.*

toil /tɔɪl/, **toils, toiling, toiled. 1** When people V : USU+A **toil**, they work hard doing unpleasant, difficult, or Formal tiring tasks or jobs. EG *...factories where men toiled all through the night.*

2 Toil is unpleasant, difficult, or tiring work. EG *The* N UNCOUNT *wealth of industrial society could only come from* Formal *the toil of the masses.*

toil away. If you **toil away**, you work hard for a PHRASAL VB : long time doing an unpleasant, difficult, or tiring V+ADV task or job. EG *...the coalminer toiling away in the deepest mines.*

toilet /tɔɪlɪ̩t/, **toilets. 1** A **toilet** is **1.1** a large N COUNT bowl with a seat which you use when you want to get rid of urine or faeces from your body. EG *She heard the toilet flush.* **1.2** a small room containing a toilet. EG *He opens the door of the toilet.*

2 When you **go to the toilet**, you get rid of urine or PHRASE faeces from your body in a toilet. EG *He wants to go to the toilet.*

Would you call this dictionary a tome?

toilet paper is paper that you use to clean yourself after getting rid of urine or faeces from your body. EG *On the wall was a roll of toilet paper.*   N UNCOUNT

toiletries /ˈtɔɪlɪˈtrɪz/ are the things that you use when cleaning or taking care of your body, such as soap, deodorant, and toothpaste. EG *Madeleine went across to buy some toiletries.*   N PLURAL

toilet roll, toilet rolls. A **toilet roll** is a long strip of toilet paper that is wound around a small cardboard tube.   N COUNT OR N UNCOUNT

to-ing and fro-ing /ˈtuːɪŋ ənd ˈfrəʊɪŋ/ is a situation in which the same action or the same movement between two places is repeated many times. EG *There was a lot of to-ing and fro-ing between London and Glasgow.*   PHRASE

token /ˈtəʊkəⁿn/, **tokens. 1** A **token** is a piece of paper or card that is worth a particular amount of money and that can be exchanged for goods. EG *...a record token... I got three book tokens for my birthday.*   N COUNT

2 Tokens are also round, flat pieces of metal that are sometimes used instead of money. EG *Some manufacturers minted their own wage tokens.*   N COUNT

3 If you give something to someone as a **token** of your feelings for them, you give it to them as a way of expressing those feelings. EG *He gave her a gold brooch as a token of his esteem.*   N COUNT

4 Token also means small or unimportant, but intended to show publicly what you think or feel. EG *The union wanted to go beyond one-day token strikes and marches... ...token resistance.*   ADJ CLASSIF : ATTRIB

5 You use **by the same token** to introduce a statement that you think is true or correct for the same reasons that were given for a previous statement. EG *We make people mentally old by retiring them, and we may even by the same token make them physically old.*   PHRASE

told /təʊld/. **1 Told** is the past tense and past participle of **tell.**

2 You use **all told** when you want to emphasize that everything has been counted. EG *There are only four characters all told in Pinter's new play.*   PHRASE

tolerable /ˈtɒlᵊrəbᵊl/. If something is **tolerable**, you are able to accept it, although it is not enjoyable or not pleasant. EG *I was given a tolerable meal... They never found the climate tolerable enough to settle there.*   ADJ QUALIT

tolerant /ˈtɒlərənt/. If you are **tolerant**, you let other people say and do what they think is right, even if you do not agree with it or approve of it. EG *Michael is a remarkably tolerant person... I think I've become more tolerant of other people's attitudes.* ◊ **tolerance** /ˈtɒlərəns/. EG *He has a sense of humour plus tolerance and patience.*   ADJ QUALIT   ◊ N UNCOUNT

tolerate /ˈtɒləreɪt/, **tolerates, tolerating, tolerated. 1** If you **tolerate** things that you do not approve of or agree with, you allow them to exist or to happen. EG *They happily tolerated the existence of opinions contrary to their own.* ◊ **toleration** /ˌtɒləˈreɪʃəⁿn/. EG *...her toleration of religious variety.*   V+O   ◊ N UNCOUNT

2 If you can **tolerate** something, you are able to accept it, although it is unsatisfactory or unpleasant. EG *I was wondering how much longer I could tolerate isolation... They couldn't tolerate the noise.*   V+O

toll /təʊl/, **tolls, tolling, tolled. 1** When someone **tolls** a bell or when it **tolls**, they ring it slowly and repeatedly, often as a sign that someone has died. EG *The bell tolled for him.*   V-ERG

2 The death **toll** in an accident is the number of people who have died in it. EG *By Wednesday the death toll had risen to more than 40.*   N COUNT+SUPP

3 If something **takes a toll** or **takes its toll**, it has a serious effect and causes a lot of suffering. EG *The walking was beginning to take its toll on all of us.*   PHRASE

4 A **toll** is a sum of money that you have to pay in order to use a particular bridge or road.   N COUNT

tomato /təˈmɑːtəʊ/, **tomatoes.** A **tomato** is a small, soft, red fruit that you can eat raw in salads,   N COUNT

or cooked as a vegetable or in a sauce. EG *...a lettuce and tomato sandwich.*

tomb /tuːm/, **tombs.** A **tomb** is a large grave that is above ground and that usually has a sculpture or other decoration on it.   N COUNT

tomboy /ˈtɒmbɔɪ/, **tomboys.** A **tomboy** is a young girl who likes playing rough or noisy games.   N COUNT

tombstone /ˈtuːmstəʊn/, **tombstones.** A **tombstone** is a large, flat piece of stone on someone's grave or tomb, on which their name is written.   N COUNT

tomcat /ˈtɒmkæt/, **tomcats.** A **tomcat** is a male cat.   N COUNT

tome /təʊm/, **tomes.** A **tome** is a large, heavy book. EG *I was attempting to read a weighty tome... ...bookshelves loaded with tomes.*   N COUNT Literary

tomorrow /təˈmɒrəʊ/. **1 Tomorrow** means the day after today. EG *They're coming tomorrow... See you tomorrow... Shall I come tomorrow night?... Tomorrow's concert has been cancelled.*   ADV OR N UNCOUNT

2 You can refer to the future, especially the near future, as **tomorrow.** EG *They live today as millions more will live tomorrow... You're always searching after a better tomorrow... ...a citizen of tomorrow's super-industrial world.*

ton /tʌn/, **tons. 1** A **ton** is **1.1** a unit of weight that is equal to 2240 pounds in Britain and to 2000 pounds in the United States. EG *It's made of steel and weighs ten tons... The Japanese extract ten million tons of coal each year from underwater mines.* **1.2** the same as a tonne.   N COUNT OR N PART

2 If you say that something **weighs a ton**, you mean that it is very heavy. EG *The batteries alone weighed a ton... It'll need six of us to lift that piano – it weighs a ton!*   PHRASE Informal

3 If you **come down on** someone **like a ton of bricks**, you speak very angrily to them or punish them very severely when they do something wrong. EG *The judges will come down on them like a ton of bricks... She came down on me like a ton of bricks when she found out.*   PHRASE Informal

4 If you have **tons** of something, you have a lot of it. EG *I've got tons of paper to draw on... He's making tons of money.*   N PART : PLURAL Informal British

tone /təʊn/, **tones, toning, toned. 1** Someone's **tone** is a quality in their voice which shows what they are feeling or thinking. EG *'Very good,' he said in an encouraging tone... Her tone was defiant... She was speaking now in cold, sarcastic tones.*   N COUNT+SUPP

2 A **tone** is one of the sounds that you hear when you are using a telephone, for example the sound that tells you that a number is engaged. EG *I'm getting the ringing tone, but there doesn't appear to be anyone at home... Don't put your money in until you hear the pay tone.*   N COUNT

3 The **tone** of a musical instrument or a singer's voice is the kind of sound it has, for example a rich sound or a thin sound. EG *I wish I had a piano with a better tone.*   N COUNT OR N UNCOUNT +SUPP

4 The **tone** of a piece of writing is its style and the opinions or ideas expressed in it. EG *I was greatly offended by the tone of the article.*   N UNCOUNT

5 If something **lowers the tone** of a place, it makes it seem less respectable. EG *He said the new people had lowered the tone of the neighbourhood.*   PHRASE

6 A **tone** is also one of the lighter, darker, or brighter shades of the same colour. EG *The colours of the pigeons matched the tones of the sky... You need a blue that is darker in tone.*   N COUNT OR N UNCOUNT

tone down. If you **tone down** something that you have written, you make it less forceful, severe, or offensive. EG *He advised me to tone down my letter.*   PHRASAL VB : V+O+ADV

tone in. If something **tones in** with something else, the two things look nice together because their colours are similar in quality or brightness. EG *The thick velvet toned in with the her dress.*   PHRASAL VB : V+ADV, OFT+with

tone-deaf. Someone who is **tone-deaf** cannot sing in tune or cannot recognize different tunes.   ADJ CLASSIF

tools

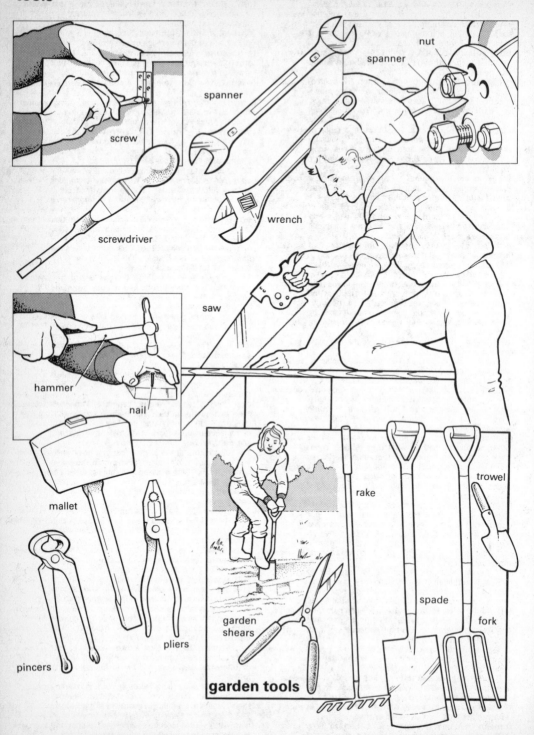

screw

spanner

nut

spanner

screwdriver

wrench

saw

hammer

nail

mallet

pliers

pincers

rake

trowel

spade

fork

garden shears

garden tools

tongs

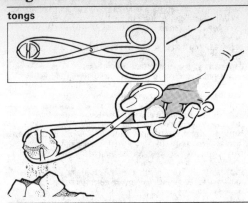

tongs /tɒŋz/. **Tongs** consist of two long narrow N PLURAL pieces of metal joined together at one end. You press the pieces together in order to grip an object and pick it up. EG *She was putting lumps of sugar into her tea with a pair of silver tongs.*

tongue /tʌŋ/, **tongues. 1** Your **tongue** is the soft N COUNT part inside your mouth that you can move and use for tasting, licking, and speaking. EG *Lynn stuck out her tongue... He ran his tongue over his lips.*

2 You can use **tongue** to refer to the kind of things N COUNT+SUPP that a person says. EG *...his eloquent tongue... She had a sharp and hurtful tongue.*

3 A **tongue** is a language. EG *...an alien tongue... I* N COUNT *answered her in her own tongue.* Literary

4 Tongue is the cooked tongue of an ox. N UNCOUNT

5 The **tongue** of a shoe or boot is the piece of N COUNT leather which is underneath the laces.

6 Tongue is used in these phrases. **6.1** If you **hold** PHRASES your **tongue**, you do not say anything. EG *I just held my tongue and followed them.* **6.2** If you **have** your **tongue in** your **cheek** when you say or do something, you are not being sincere or serious about it, although you may appear to be. EG *I suspect Dr Vidler had his tongue in his cheek when he wrote that.* ● See also **tongue-in-cheek**. **6.3** A **slip of the tongue** is a small mistake that you make when you are speaking, especially a mistake that is humorous or embarrassing. EG *If I did say that, it was just a slip of the tongue.* **6.4 on the tip of** your **tongue**: see **tip**.

tongue-in-cheek. A **tongue-in-cheek** remark is ADJ QUALIT made as a joke, and is not serious or sincere. EG *He offered some tongue-in-cheek advice about keeping out of the rain.*

tongue-tied. If you are **tongue-tied**, you are ADJ QUALIT unable to say anything because you feel shy or nervous. EG *He became completely tongue-tied.*

tongue-twister, tongue-twisters. A **tongue-** N COUNT **twister** is a sentence or expression which is very difficult to say properly, especially when you try saying it quickly. For example, 'She sells seashells on the seashore' is an English tongue-twister.

tonic /tɒnɪk/, **tonics. 1 Tonic** or **tonic water** is a N MASS colourless, fizzy drink that has a slightly bitter flavour and is often mixed with alcoholic drinks, especially gin. EG *A gin and tonic, please.*

2 A **tonic** is a medicine that makes you feel N MASS stronger, healthier, and less tired.

3 You can refer to anything that makes you feel N COUNT stronger or more cheerful as a **tonic**. EG *It was a tonic to talk to her.*

4 Skin **tonic** or hair **tonic** is a liquid that you put N MASS on your skin or hair in order to improve it.

tonight /tənaɪt/ means the evening or night that ADV OR N will come at the end of today. EG *I think I'll go to* UNCOUNT *bed early tonight... In tonight's programme we shall be explaining the history of the movement.*

tonnage /tʌnɪdʒ/. **1** The **tonnage** of a ship is its N UNCOUNT size or the amount of cargo that it can carry. Technical

2 Tonnage is also the total number of tons that N COUNT something weighs, or the total amount that there is OFT+*of* of something that is measured in tons. EG *...the total tonnage of TNT used during the last war.*

tonne /tʌn/, **tonnes.** A **tonne** is a metric unit of N COUNT weight that is equal to 1000 kilograms. EG *...500* OR N PART *million tonnes of crude oil.*

tonsil /tɒnsⁱəl/, **tonsils.** Your **tonsils** are the two N COUNT: small, soft lumps in your throat at the back of your USU PLURAL mouth.

tonsillitis /tɒnsɪ'laɪtɪs/ is a painful swelling of N UNCOUNT your tonsils caused by an infection.

too /tuː/. **1** You use **too** after adding another ADV SEN person, thing, or aspect that a previous statement applies to or includes. EG *I'm on your side. Seibert is too... There were carrots too... Physically, too, the peoples of the world are incredibly mixed.*

2 You use **too** after adding a piece of information ADV SEN or a comment to a statement, in order to emphasize that it is surprising or important. EG *It was a pretty play, and very sad too... He was always kind and helpful to me. But he could be alarming too... I remember that quite well. It was a Tuesday too... You ought to see a doctor. And quickly, too.*

3 You also use **too** to indicate that there is a ADV+QUANTIF greater amount or degree of something than is OR SUBMOD desirable, necessary, or acceptable. EG *Avoid using too much water... Philip decided it was not too far to walk... Don't leave it in too warm a place.*

4 You use **all too** or **only too** to emphasize that PHRASE something happens to a greater extent or degree than is pleasant or desirable. EG *I can remember only too well the disasters that followed... The suspicions had proved all too true... All too soon, we had to leave.*

5 You can use **too** with a negative when you really SUBMOD: WITH mean the opposite, but are being polite, sarcastic, BROAD NEG or cautious. EG *That's probably not too far from the truth... He wasn't too keen on it... It's not too bad.*

6 too bad: see **bad.** ● **too** clever, arrogant, etc **by half:** see **half.** ● **none too:** see **none.**

took /tʊk/ is the past tense of **take.**

tool /tuːl/, **tools. 1** A **tool** is any instrument or N COUNT piece of equipment that you hold in your hands in order to help you to do a particular kind of work. Spades, hammers, and knives are tools.

2 When workers **down tools**, they stop working PHRASE suddenly in order to make a protest or to go on British strike. EG *Workers downed tools in what soon became a general strike.*

3 The tools of your **trade** are the skills, instru- PHRASE ments, and other equipment that you need in order to do your job properly.

toot /tuːt/, **toots, tooting, tooted.** If you **toot** your V-ERG OR V car horn, you make it produce a short sound or series of sounds. EG *She tooted the horn... A car horn tooted.* ▸ used as a noun. EG *'Look,' she said* ▸ N COUNT *and gave a toot on the horn.*

tooth /tuːθ/, **teeth** /tiːθ/. **1** Your **teeth** are the N COUNT hard, white objects in your mouth that you use for biting and chewing food. EG *He had very white, even teeth.* ● See also **wisdom tooth.**

2 The **teeth** of a comb, saw, or zip are the parts N COUNT that stick out in a row on its edge.

3 If an official group or a law has **teeth**, it has N PLURAL power and is able to be effective. EG *The code will not have more teeth than the guidelines unless governments support it fully.*

4 Tooth and **teeth** are used in these phrases. **4.1** PHRASES Someone who is **long in the tooth** is old or getting Informal old. EG *She's getting a bit long in the tooth for this sort of thing.* **4.2** If you are **fed up to the back teeth** with something, you are extremely dissatisfied or bored with it. **4.3** If you say that someone is **lying through** their **teeth**, you mean that they are deliberately telling lies. **4.4 to grit** your **teeth**: see

grit. • by the skin of your teeth: see skin. • a
sweet tooth: see sweet.

toothache /tuːθeɪk/ is a feeling of pain in one of N UNCOUNT
your teeth.

toothbrush /tuːθbrʌʃ/, **toothbrushes.** A tooth- N COUNT
brush is a small brush with a long handle which
you use for cleaning your teeth. See picture at
BRUSHES.

toothless /tuːθlɪ²s/. If someone is **toothless**, they ADJ CLASSIF
have no teeth. EG ...a toothless old woman... ...a sly
toothless grin.

toothpaste /tuːθpeɪst/, **toothpastes. Toothpaste** N MASS
is a thick substance which you put on your toothbrush and use to clean your teeth.

toothpick /tuːθpɪk/, **toothpicks.** A **toothpick** is a N COUNT
small wooden, metal, or plastic stick with pointed
ends which you use to remove food from between
your teeth. EG ...picking his teeth with a gold
toothpick.

top /tɒp/, **tops, topping, topped. 1** The **top** of N COUNT
something is its highest point, part, or surface. EG +SUPP :
...at the top of the steps... He filled his glass to the USU the+N
top... ...hill tops... ...the wooden top of the bench.

2 The **top** thing of a series of things is the highest ADJ CLASSIF :
one. EG She was sitting on the top step... ...a room on ATTRIB
the top floor.

3 The **top** of a street or garden is one end of it, N SING : the+N
usually the end furthest away from you. EG ...a new
building at the top of Victoria Street. ▶ used as an ▶ ADJ CLASSIF :
adjective. EG The boy waved to her from the top ATTRIB
end of the field.

4 The **top** of a bottle, jar, or tube is a cap or lid that N COUNT
fits onto one end of it and closes it. EG He un-
screwed the top and put the bottle to his mouth.

5 A **top** is a piece of clothing such as a blouse, N COUNT
which a woman wears on the upper half of her
body. EG She wore denim jeans and a denim top.

6 A **top** is also a cone-shaped toy that can spin on N COUNT
its pointed end.

7 The **top** of an organization is its highest or most N SING : the+N
important level. EG Officials at the top make the
decisions. ▶ used as an adjective. ...top executives... ▶ ADJ CLASSIF :
...top level negotiations. ATTRIB

8 The **top** of a scale of measurement is the highest N SING : the+N
point on it. EG This group is already near the top of
the UK income scale. ▶ used as an adjective. EG ▶ ADJ CLASSIF :
The vehicle's top speed is about 100. ATTRIB

9 If someone **tops** a poll or popularity chart, they V+O
do better than anyone else in it. EG She topped a
nationwide poll for 1981's most outstanding sportswoman.

10 If something **tops** a particular amount, it be- V+O
comes greater than that amount. EG US investments topped fifty million dollars.

11 If you **top** a remark or action, you follow it with V+O :
a better or more impressive one. EG Sudhir topped OFT+ with
her story with one about an Indian princess.

12 You use **on top** in these ways. **12.1** If something PHRASES
is **on top** or **over the top** of something else, it is
placed over it or on its highest part. EG She laid her
hand on top of his... ...a tower with a little flag on
top... Something had been stamped over the top.
12.2 If something happens **on top** of other things, it
happens in addition to them. EG You don't want to
give the poor man ulcers on top of all the problems
he's already got. **12.3** If you are **on top of** what you
are doing, you are dealing with it successfully. EG
...jobs that they never really got on top of. **12.4**
When something **gets on top of** you, it makes you
feel depressed because you cannot cope with it. EG
You may find the housework is getting on top of
you.

13 If you say that something is **over the top**, you PHRASE
mean that it is unacceptable because it is too
extreme or exaggerated. EG Here I think Wenders
goes right over the top.

14 off the top of your head: see head. • at the
top of your voice: see voice. • See also topped,
topping.

top up. If you **top up** a container, you fill it again PHRASAL VB :
when it has been partly emptied. EG The radiator V+O+ADV
will have to be topped up because of evaporation.
• See also **top-up.**

top hat, top hats. A **top hat** is a tall hat with a N COUNT
narrow brim that men wear on formal occasions.

top-heavy. Something that is **top-heavy** is larger ADJ QUALIT
or heavier at the top than at the bottom, and is
therefore not stable. EG ...high-heeled shoes and
hats top-heavy with feathers and flowers.

topic /tɒpɪk/, **topics.** A **topic** is a particular N COUNT+SUPP
subject that you write about or discuss. EG The main
topic of conversation was food.

topical /tɒpɪkə⁰l/ means relating to events that ADJ QUALIT
are happening at the time you are speaking or
writing. EG They used to discuss topical issues... The
question you ask is very topical.

topless /tɒplɪ²s/. When a woman is **topless**, she is ADJ CLASSIF
not wearing anything that covers her breasts. EG ...a
topless dancer.

topmost /tɒpməʊst/. The **topmost** thing in a ADJ CLASSIF
group of things is the one that is highest or nearest ATTRIB
the top. EG ...the topmost branches of the lime trees.

topped /tɒpt/. If something is **topped** by or ADJ PRED+A
topped with another thing, the other thing covers
it or is on top of it. EG ...a heap of stones topped by a
wooden cross.

topping /tɒpɪŋ/, **toppings.** A **topping** is food, N MASS
such as cream or cheese, that is poured or put on
top of other food in order to decorate it or to add to
its flavour. EG ...a topping of whipped cream.

topple /tɒpə⁰l/, **topples, toppling, toppled. 1** If V
something **topples**, it becomes unsteady and falls
over. EG He caught the glass just as it began to
topple... She toppled from her chair.

2 To **topple** a government or leader means to V+O
cause them to be no longer in power. EG This action
threatens to topple the government... His regime
was toppled in a coup.

topple over. If something **topples over**, it be- PHRASAL VB :
comes unsteady and falls over. EG She looked at the V+ADV
tree nervously, as if expecting it to topple over.

top-secret. Something that is **top-secret** is in- ADJ CLASSIF
tended to be kept completely secret. EG ...a top-
secret experiment.

top-up, top-ups. A **top-up** is another serving of a N COUNT
drink in the same glass that you have just used. EG Informal
Anyone ready for a top-up?

torch /tɔːtʃ/, **torches.** A **torch** is **1** a small electric N COUNT
light which you can carry in your hand and which
gets its power from batteries inside it. EG He took
the torch and disappeared into the dark. **2** a long
stick with burning material at the end that was
used in former times to provide light.

torchlight /tɔːtʃlaɪt/ is **1** light that is produced by N UNCOUNT
an electric torch. EG ...the circle of torchlight. **2**
light that is produced by burning torches. EG ...a
torchlight procession from the station.

tore /tɔː/ is the past tense of **tear.**

torment, torments, tormenting, tormented;
pronounced /tɔːmə³nt/ when it is a noun, and
/tɔːment/ when it is a verb.

1 Torment is extreme pain or unhappiness. EG N UNCOUNT
...the scream of a man dying in torment.

2 A **torment** is something that causes extreme N COUNT
pain or unhappiness. EG He was subjected to various torments... His schooldays were a torment.

3 If something **torments** you, it causes you ex- V+O
treme unhappiness. EG His emotional turmoil continues to torment him.

4 If someone **torments** you, they annoy you in a V+O
playful and rather cruel way. EG She is forever
tormenting and teasing Tom.

tormentor /tɔːmentə/, **tormentors.** A **tormen-** N COUNT :
tor is someone who deliberately causes pain or USU+POSS

Name the things on these pages that you can use
to clean your teeth.

unhappiness to another person. EG *The child eventually turned on his tormentors.*

torn /tɔːn/ is the past participle of **tear**.

tornado /tɔːneɪdəʊ/, **tornadoes** or **tornados**. A N COUNT **tornado** is a violent storm with strong circular winds around a funnel-shaped cloud. Tornados move very quickly and cause a lot of damage.

torpedo /tɔːpiːdəʊ/, **torpedoes, torpedoing, torpedoed. 1** A **torpedo** is a tube-shaped bomb that N COUNT travels underwater and explodes when it hits its target. Torpedoes can be fired from ships, submarine, or aircraft. EG *His ship was blown up by a torpedo.*

2 If a ship **is torpedoed**, it is hit, and usually sunk, V+O : USU PASS by a torpedo.

torrent /tɒrənt/, **torrents. 1** When a lot of water N COUNT : is falling very rapidly, you can say that it is falling USU PLURAL in **torrents**. EG *The rain suddenly burst upon us in torrents... Valerie was now shedding torrents of tears.*

2 A **torrent** of speech is a lot of it directed N COUNT+SUPP continuously at someone. EG *She burst out in a torrent of speech... ...a torrent of questions... He was answered with a torrent of oaths.*

torrential /təˈrɛnʃəl/. **Torrential** rain pours ADJ CLASSIF : down very rapidly and in great quantities. EG ATTRIB *Before the meeting could end, torrential rain began to pour.*

torso /tɔːsəʊ/, **torsos.** Your **torso** is the main part N COUNT of your body, excluding your head, arms, and legs. EG *...a carving of a woman's torso.*

tortoise /tɔːtəs/, **tortoises.** A **tortoise** is a slow- N COUNT moving animal with a large, hard shell over its body. The tortoise can pull its head and legs into the shell in order to protect them.

tortoiseshell /tɔːtəsʃel/ is the hard, brown and N UNCOUNT yellow shell from a sea turtle. It is often polished and used to make jewellery and ornaments.

tortuous /tɔːtjʊəs/. **1** A **tortuous** road is full of ADJ QUALIT bends and twists. EG *They walked through the* Formal *narrow, tortuous streets of the old city.*

2 A **tortuous** piece of writing is long and compli- ADJ QUALIT cated. EG *I wrote tortuous essays for obscure jour-* Formal *nals... ...laws framed in tortuous jargon.*

torture /tɔːtʃə/, **tortures, torturing, tortured. 1** N UNCOUNT **Torture** is great pain that is deliberately caused to OR N COUNT someone in order to punish them or to get information from them. EG *...the constant threat of death and torture... Here floggings and tortures were carried out.*

2 If someone **tortures** another person, they delib- V+O erately cause that person great pain in order to punish them or get information from them. EG *...prisons where the inmates were tortured and murdered... He saw his relatives being tortured.*

Tory /tɔːriˈ/, **Tories.** A **Tory** is a member or N COUNT supporter of the Conservative Party in Britain. EG Informal *The Tories were restored to power... ...the Tory MP for Hornchurch.*

toss /tɒs/, **tosses, tossing, tossed. 1** If you **toss** V+O : USU+A something somewhere, you throw it there lightly and carelessly. EG *He took the bag and tossed it into some nearby bushes.*

2 If you **toss** your head, you move it suddenly V+O backwards. EG *'That's the main thing, isn't it?' said Frederica, tossing her head.* ▶ used as a noun. EG ▶ N COUNT *She gave a toss of her head.*

3 If you **toss** food while preparing it, you gently V+O : OFT+in shake pieces of it in a container with some liquid in order to cover the pieces with the liquid. EG *Serve noodles tossed in cream.*

4 If you **toss** a coin or **toss**, you decide something V OR V+O by throwing a coin into the air and guessing which side of it will be facing upwards after it falls. EG *They used the penny to toss for the first round of drinks.* ▶ used as a noun. EG *Business deals were* ▶ N COUNT *clinched by the toss of a coin.*

5 If something or someone **tosses** or **is tossed**, V-ERG

they move repeatedly from side to side. EG *I tossed and turned all night... Ships were tossed at sea.*

toss up. If you **toss up**, you decide something by PHRASAL VB : throwing a coin into the air and guessing which V+ADV, OFT+A side of the coin will be facing upwards after it falls.

toss-up. If you refer to a situation as a **toss-up**, N SING : a+N you mean that either of two results seems equally likely. EG *It was a toss-up who would get there first.*

tot /tɒt/, **tots, totting, totted. 1** A **tot** is a very N COUNT young child. EG *I've known her since she was a tot.* Informal

2 A **tot** of a strong alcoholic drink such as whisky is N PART a small amount of it in a glass. EG *...a tot of whisky.*

tot up. If you **tot up** numbers, you add them PHRASAL VB : together. EG *I was totting up the number of photo-* V+O+ADV *graphs... The machine totted up your score.* Informal

total /təʊtəˈl/, **totals, totalling, totalled. 1** A N COUNT **total** is the number that you get when you add several numbers together. EG *The factory employed a total of forty workers.* ▶ used as an ▶ ADJ CLASSIF : adjective. EG *...the total number of students on* ATTRIB *campus.* ● See also **sum total**.

2 If there are a number of things **in total**, there PHRASE are that many of them altogether. EG *...a force containing in total over half a million men.*

3 When you **total** a set of numbers or objects, you V+O add them all together. EG *Votes cast for each candidate will be totalled to get a result.*

4 If several numbers **total** a certain figure, that is V+C the figure you get when all the numbers are added together. EG *Conoco's 1980 revenues totalled £18.3 billion... They paid fines totalling 16,000 dollars.*

5 You use **total** to say that something is complete. ADJ CLASSIF : EG *...total secrecy... ...a total failure... ...a total* USU ATTRIB *eclipse of the sun.* ◇ **totally.** EG *He became almost* ◇ SUBMOD *totally blind... I totally disagree.* OR ADV

totalitarian /təʊtælɪˈteəriən/. A **totalitarian** po- ADJ CLASSIF litical system is one in which one political party controls everything and does not allow any other parties to exist. EG *...the brutalities of the totalitarian regimes.*

totality /təʊtælɪˈtiˈ/. The **totality** of something is N UNCOUNT the whole of it. EG *...the totality of life... ...the totality* USU+SUPP *of French culture.* Formal

totter /tɒtə/, **totters, tottering, tottered. 1** When V : USU+A someone **totters**, they walk in an unsteady way, for example because they are ill or drunk. EG *Thelma tottered from the stage in search of the gin bottle.*

2 If something such as a government **totters**, it V becomes weak and is likely to lose control. EG *The wartime Liberal Government was tottering.*

touch /tʌtʃ/, **touches, touching, touched. 1** If you V+O **touch** something, you gently put your fingers or hand on it. EG *The metal is so hot I can't touch it... Madeleine stretched out her hand to touch his.* ▶ used as a noun. EG *The wood is so rotten that it* ▶ N COUNT : *crumbles at the touch... He remembered the touch* OFT SING *of her hand.*

2 If you **are touched** by something, you are V+O : USU PASS emotionally affected by it and feel sad, sympathetic, or grateful. EG *The whole audience was touched... I was very touched by his thoughtfulness... They helped us get the harvest in and I was touched.*

3 When two things **touch**, their surfaces come into V OR V+O : contact with one other. EG *Make sure that the wires* RECIP *are not touching... He stood so close to me that our bodies touched... My feet touched the ground.*

4 Your sense of **touch** is the sense that tells you N UNCOUNT what the surface of something is like, for example when you put your fingers on it. EG *The skin was fleshy and slightly waxy to the touch.*

5 A **touch** is a detail which is added to something N COUNT+SUPP to improve it. EG *The final touches were put to their report.* ● **finishing touches**: see **finish**.

6 Someone's manner of doing something can be N SING+SUPP referred to as their **touch**. EG *In the play, religion is handled with quite a light, comic touch... She hasn't got your touch, Flora.*

7 A **touch** of something is a very small amount of N SING+SUPP it. EG *There was a touch of frost this morning.*

8 You can use **a touch** to mean slightly or to a PHRASE small extent. EG *Richard's voice suddenly became important and even a touch official.*

9 If you get **in touch** with someone, you contact PHRASE them by writing to them or telephoning them. If you are, stay, or keep **in touch** with them, you write, phone, or visit each other regularly. EG *A man from the Organization got in touch with me... I'll be in touch with you... Please drop in when you can. I'd like to keep in touch.*

10 If you are or keep **in touch** with a subject or PHRASE situation, you know the latest news or information about it. If you are **out of touch** with it, your knowledge of it is out-of-date. EG *I'm a bit out of touch with new developments.*

11 If you **lose touch** with someone, you gradually PHRASE stop writing, phoning, or visiting each other.

12 If you say that something is **touch and go**, you PHRASE mean that you are uncertain whether it will happen or succeed. EG *It is still touch and go but we managed to get this far.*

13 Some people say **'Touch wood'**, and often touch PHRASE a piece of wood, in order to prevent bad luck. EG *'Has anything gone wrong with your car recently?' – 'No, touch wood.'*

14 See also **touching**.

touch down. When an aircraft **touches down**, it PHRASAL VB : lands. EG *He watched the plane as it touched down.* V+ADV ● See also **touchdown**.

touch on. If you **touch on** something, you men- PHRASAL VB : tion it briefly. EG *...the topic which I touched on at* V+PREP, *the beginning of this chapter.* HAS PASS

touchdown /tʌtʃdaʊn/, **touchdowns. Touch-** N UNCOUNT **down** or a **touchdown** is the landing of an aircraft. OR N COUNT EG *Failure of any mechanical system to function after touchdown could destroy human lives.*

touching /tʌtʃɪŋ/. If something is **touching**, it ADJ QUALIT causes feelings of sadness and sympathy. EG *'I've seen the photographs.' – 'Touching, weren't they?'*

touchy /tʌtʃiˀ/, **touchier, touchiest. 1** If someone ADJ QUALIT is **touchy**, they are easily upset, offended, or irritated. EG *He always was a touchy and bad-tempered man.*

2 A **touchy** subject is one that needs to be dealt ADJ QUALIT with carefully, because it might upset or offend people. EG *I had to face the touchy question: could I really have him arrested?*

tough /tʌf/, **tougher, toughest. 1** Someone who is ADJ QUALIT **tough** has a strong, independent character and is able to tolerate a lot of pain or hardship. EG *...a tough reporter... He's not hard-hearted but resolute and tough.*

2 A **tough** substance is strong, and difficult to ADJ QUALIT break, cut, or tear. EG *Some plastics are as tough as metal... With a hoe you can tackle tougher weeds.*

3 Meat which is **tough** is difficult to cut and chew. ADJ QUALIT EG *The steak was smelly and a little tough.*

4 A **tough** task, problem, or way of life is difficult ADJ QUALIT or full of hardship. EG *The toughest problem is theft.*

5 Tough policies or actions are strict and firm, and ADJ QUALIT show determination. EG *We are convinced that her tough economic policies will succeed.*

toughen /tʌfˀn/, **toughens, toughening, tough-** **ened. 1** To **toughen** something means to make it V+O stronger so that it will not break easily. ◊ **toughened.** EG *...the use of toughened glass in* ◊ ADJ CLASSIF *windscreens.*

2 When someone **toughens** or when a difficult V-ERG experience **toughens** them, they become stronger and more independent in character. EG *She had been toughened by Guy's death.*

toupee /tuːpeɪ/, **toupees.** A **toupee** is a small wig N COUNT worn by a man to cover a bald patch on his head.

tour /tʊə, tɔː/, **tours, touring, toured. 1** A **tour** is N COUNT **1.1** a long journey during which you visit several places. EG *I made a five-month tour of India and the Far East.* **1.2** a short trip round a place such as a

city or a famous building. EG *Admission to a tour of Parliament is easier in summer... ...guided tours.*

2 If you **tour** a place, you go on a journey or trip V+O round it. EG *He spent his vacation touring the highlands of Scotland.*

tourism /tʊərɪzˀm, tɔː-/ is the business of provid- N UNCOUNT ing services for people on holiday, for example hotels, travel arrangements, sightseeing trips, and leisure activities.

tourist /tʊərɪst, tɔː-/, **tourists.** A **tourist** is a N COUNT person who visits places for pleasure and interest. EG *She showed a party of tourists round the mu-seum... You should visit the tourist attractions.*

tournament /tʊənəməˀnt, tɔː-/, **tournaments.** A N COUNT **tournament** is a sports competition in which players who win a match play further matches, until just one person or team is left. EG *...a table tennis tournament.*

tousled /taʊzˀld/. **Tousled** hair is untidy and ADJ QUALIT looks as if it has not been combed.

tout /taʊt/, **touts, touting, touted. 1** If someone V+O **touts** something, they try and sell it. EG *...an* Informal *exporter touting a range of plastic toys.*

2 If someone **touts** for business or custom, they try V+for to obtain it. EG *...porters touting for loads at a railway station.*

tow /təʊ/, **tows, towing, towed. 1** If a vehicle V+O **tows** another vehicle, it pulls it along behind it. EG *...a lorry towing a trailer of hay.* ► used as a noun. ► N SING : a+N EG *If you can't get a tow, you'll have to walk.*

2 If a vehicle is **on tow**, it is being towed by PHRASE another vehicle.

3 If you have someone **in tow**, they are with you PHRASE because you are looking after them. EG *He arrived* Informal *on Sunday with his children in tow.*

towards /təwɔːdz/; also **toward. 1** If you move, PREP look, or point **towards** something or someone, you move, look, or point in their direction. EG *He saw his mother running towards him... She turned towards John.*

2 If things develop **towards** a particular situation, PREP that situation becomes nearer in time or more likely to happen. EG *There is a tendency towards inflation... We are drifting towards disaster.*

3 If you have a particular attitude **towards** some- PREP thing or someone, you have that attitude when you think about them or deal with them. EG *He felt very friendly towards them.*

4 If something happens **towards** a particular time PREP or date, it happens just before that time or date. EG *Towards midnight the rain ceased... I went to London towards the end of 1977.*

5 Towards a place or area can also mean near to PREP it. EG *He was sitting towards the back of the room.*

6 If you give money **towards** something, you give PREP it to help pay for that thing. EG *British Rail contrib-uted 154,000 pounds towards improving safety... They may give you something towards your hous-ing costs.*

7 You can also use **towards** to indicate the result PREP that you are trying to achieve. EG *The twins did a lot towards making Tom willing to stay.*

towel /taʊˀl/, **towels.** A **towel** is a piece of thick, N COUNT soft cloth that you use to dry yourself with after a wash or bath. ● See also **sanitary towel, tea-towel**.

towelling /taʊəlɪŋ/ is thick, soft cloth that is used N UNCOUNT especially for making towels. EG *...a bit of old towelling... She was dressed in a towelling bath-robe.*

tower /taʊə/, **towers, towering, towered. 1** A N COUNT **tower** is a tall, narrow building, sometimes at-tached to a larger building such as a castle or church. EG *...London's Post Office Tower.*

2 If you refer to someone as a **tower of strength**, PHRASE

Where would you find a towpath?

you mean that they give you a lot of help, support, and encouragement.

3 Someone or something that **towers** over other V+A people or things is a lot taller than they are. EG *Jane stood up, towering over him.*

tower block, tower blocks. A **tower block** is a N COUNT tall building divided into flats or offices. British

towering /ˈtaʊərɪŋ/. A **towering** building or tree ADJ CLASSIF: is very tall and impressive. EG *...lush green mead-* ATTRIB *ows surrounded by towering trees.*

town /taʊn/, **towns. 1** A **town** is a place with N COUNT many streets and buildings where people live and work. EG *...the town of Pangbourne in England.*

2 People sometimes refer to the town they live in N UNCOUNT as **town**. EG *We packed our stuff and left town on a bus.*

3 Town is also used to refer to the central part of a N UNCOUNT city or town. EG *I had lunch in town.* ● If you go **out** ● PHRASE **on the town**, you enjoy yourself by visiting some of the places of entertainment in a city or town, especially at night.

4 If you **go to town** on an activity, you put a lot of PHRASE effort and enthusiasm into doing it. EG *Once they got permission, they could really go to town on it.*

5 See also **ghost town.**

town hall, town halls. The **town hall** is a large N COUNT building in a town that is owned by the town council and that is often used by them as their headquarters.

townspeople /ˈtaʊnziːpəᵊl/. The **townspeople** of N PLURAL: a town or city are the people who live there. EG *The* USU the+N *townspeople refused to buy anything from his shop.* Outdated

towpath /ˈtaʊpɑːθ/, **towpaths.** A **towpath** is a N COUNT path along the side of a canal or river.

towrope /ˈtaʊrəʊp/, **towropes.** A **towrope** is a N COUNT strong rope used for towing vehicles.

toxic /ˈtɒksɪk/. A **toxic** substance is poisonous. EG ADJ QUALIT *The water became contaminated by toxic chemi-* Formal *cals... Aluminium can be highly toxic to fish.*

toy /tɔɪ/, **toys, toying, toyed.** A **toy** is an object N COUNT that children play with, for example a doll or a model car. EG *The children could bring their own toys... ...a toy soldier... ...a toy theatre.*

toy with. 1 If you **toy with** an idea, you consider PHRASAL VB: it casually, without making any decisions about it. V+PREP, EG *I've been toying with the idea for some time.* **2** If V+PREP, you **toy with** an object, you keep moving it about HAS PASS with your fingers, usually while you are thinking about something else. EG *He withdrew the key from his pocket where he had been toying with it.*

trace /treɪs/, **traces, tracing, traced. 1** If you V+O **trace** something, you find it after looking for it. EG *I think I've traced the source of the poison... They were trying to trace her missing husband.*

2 If you **trace** the development of something, you V+O find out or describe how it developed. EG *Throughout the nineteenth century we can trace the gradual progress of this idea.*

3 If you **trace** a drawing or a map, you copy it by V+O covering it with a piece of transparent paper and drawing over the lines underneath.

4 A **trace** is a sign which shows you that someone N COUNT or something has been in a place. EG *No trace was found of either the bag or its contents.* ● If ● PHRASE someone disappears **without trace**, they disappear without leaving any signs of where they have gone. EG *Madeleine vanished without trace.*

5 A **trace** of something is a very small amount of N PART it. EG *I can still see traces of the paint on your hands... There wasn't the slightest trace of fear in my father.*

tracing /ˈtreɪsɪŋ/, **tracings.** A **tracing** is a copy N COUNT that has been made by covering a drawing or map with a piece of transparent paper and drawing over the lines underneath.

tracing paper is transparent paper that you use N UNCOUNT to make tracings.

track /træk/, **tracks, tracking, tracked. 1** A N COUNT **track** is a narrow road or path. EG *I remember riding along a dusty mountain track in Morocco.*

2 A **track** is also a piece of ground, often shaped N COUNT like a ring, which horses, cars, or athletes race around. EG *The recreation ground had a proper cinder track.*

3 A railway **track** is a strip of ground with rails on N COUNT it that a train travels along. EG *The train on the next track was moving.*

4 Tracks are marks left on the ground which show N PLURAL that someone or something has been there. EG *The fox didn't leave any tracks.*

5 If you **track** animals or people, you find them by V+O following their footprints or other signs that they have left behind. EG *I lost my camels, tracked them, and found them again.*

6 A **track** on a record or tape is one of the songs or N COUNT pieces of music on it. EG *That's Sonny Rollins singing on that track.*

7 Track is used in these phrases. **7.1** A place that PHRASES is **off the beaten track** is in a quiet and isolated area. **7.2** If you **hide** your **tracks** or **cover** your **tracks**, you are careful not to leave any signs or clues that might reveal what you have been doing. **7.3** If you **stop dead in** your **tracks** or if someone or something **stops** you **dead in** your **tracks**, you suddenly stop what you are doing, because something has surprised you. EG *He stopped dead in his tracks and gave a gasp of shock.* **7.4** If you **keep track of** things or people, you pay attention to them so that you know where they are or what is happening. If you **lose track of** them, you no longer know where they are or what is happening. EG *We would never be able to keep track of the luggage on such a long journey.* **7.5** If you are **on the right track**, you are thinking in a way that is likely to give you the right answer to a question or problem. If you are **on the wrong track**, you are thinking in a way that is mistaken and that will not give you the right answer.

track down. If you **track down** someone or PHRASAL VB: something, you find them by searching for them. EG V+O+ADV *They lost all hope of tracking down the submarine.*

tracker /ˈtrækə/, **trackers.** A **tracker** is someone N COUNT who is skilled at finding people or animals by following their footprints or other signs that they have left behind. EG *Peter was a brilliant tracker.*

track record, track records. The **track record** N COUNT+SUPP of a person or a company consists of their past achievements or failures in their job or business. EG *They have established a good track record of successful trading.*

tracksuit /ˈtræksjuːt/, **tracksuits.** A **tracksuit** is N COUNT a loose, warm suit consisting of trousers and a top. You wear a tracksuit when you are jogging or doing exercises.

tract /trækt/, **tracts. 1** A **tract** is a short article N COUNT expressing a strong opinion on a religious, moral, or political subject.

2 A **tract** of land or forest is a large area of it. EG N COUNT *...immense tracts of impenetrable jungle.*

traction engine /ˈtrækʃᵊn endʒɪn/, **traction en-** N COUNT **gines.** A **traction engine** is a large vehicle that was used in the past for pulling heavy loads.

tractor /ˈtræktə/, **tractors.** A **tractor** is a farm N COUNT vehicle with large rear wheels that is used for ploughing fields, sowing crops, and pulling trailers.

trade /treɪd/, **trades, trading, traded. 1 Trade** is N UNCOUNT the activity of buying, selling, or exchanging goods or services. EG *France is heavily dependent on foreign trade... A friend of mine went into the antique trade.*

2 When people, firms, or countries **trade**, they buy, V : USU+A sell, or exchange goods or services. EG *They specialized in trading with China.*

3 Someone's **trade** is the kind of work that they do, N COUNT especially when it requires special training in practical skills. EG *Settle down to learn your trade.*

● If you are, for example, a plumber or an electri- ● PHRASE
cian, you can say that you are a plumber or
electrician **by trade**. EG *By trade he was a dealer
in antique furniture.*

4 If you **trade** one thing for another, you exchange V+O:OFT+*for*
it for the other thing. EG *Leah traded a piece of her
jewellery for food.*

trade in. If you **trade in** something such as your PHRASAL VB:
old car or old TV set, you give it to a dealer when V+O+ADV,
you buy a new one so that you get a reduction on USU+A
the price. EG *You might trade the car in for a
smaller one.*

trademark /ˈtreɪdmɑːk/, **trademarks. 1** A **trade-** N COUNT
mark is a name or symbol that a company uses on
its products and that cannot legally be used by
another company.

2 If someone or something has a typical feature, N COUNT+SUPP
you can refer to this feature as their **trademark**.
EG *That's Mr Sedgwick's trademark. He's always
got a cigar in his mouth... Long hair had become
the trademark of rebellion among the young.*

trader /ˈtreɪdə/, **traders.** A **trader** is a person N COUNT
whose job is to trade in goods. EG *...a whisky
trader... ...a wealthy trader in tea.*

trade secret, trade secrets. A **trade secret** is N COUNT
information that is known and used by only one
firm, for example about the substances required to
produce something or about a particular method of
producing it.

tradesman /ˈtreɪdzmən/, **tradesmen.** A **trades-** N COUNT
man is a person, for example a shopkeeper, whose
job is to sell goods.

tradespeople /ˈtreɪdzpiːpl/ are people who sell N PLURAL
goods as their job.

trade union, trade unions. The form **trades** N COUNT
union is also used. A **trade union** is an organization of workers that tries to improve the pay and
working conditions of its members. EG *...a highly
organized trade union... The Secretary of State will
meet the trade union leaders tomorrow.*

trade unionist, trade unionists. A **trade un-** N COUNT
ionist is an active member of a trade union. EG
...militant trade unionists.

tradition /trəˈdɪʃən/, **traditions.** A **tradition** is a N COUNT OR
custom or belief that has existed for a long time N UNCOUNT
without changing. EG *...Britain's long tradition of
political independence... I was not going to keep up
the family tradition... We must have respect for
tradition.*

traditional /trəˈdɪʃənəl, -ʃənəl/. **Traditional** cus- ADJ CLASSIF
toms or beliefs have existed for a long time without
changing. EG *The bride is dressed in traditional
costume... Women are questioning their traditional
role in society, as wives and mothers.*
◊ **traditionally**. EG *Traditionally in this culture,* ◊ ADV OR
there is no figurative art. ADV SEN

traffic /ˈtræfɪk/, **traffics, trafficking, traf-**
ficked. 1 **Traffic** refers to all the cars and other N UNCOUNT
vehicles that are moving along a road at a particu-
lar time. EG *He eased the van out into the line of
rush-hour traffic.*

2 **Traffic** in something such as drugs is an illegal N UNCOUNT
trade in them. EG *...an operation designed to uncov-* +SUPP
er illegal traffic in protected animals.

3 Someone who **traffics** in drugs or other goods V+*in*
buys and sells them even though it is illegal to do
so. EG *...rumours that he trafficked in opium.*

traffic jam, traffic jams. A **traffic jam** is a long N COUNT
line of cars and other vehicles that cannot move
because the road is blocked.

traffic light, traffic lights. Traffic lights are N COUNT:
the set of red, amber, and green lights at a road USU PLURAL
junction which control the flow of traffic. The red
light means stop, amber means prepare to stop or
to move off, and green means go.

traffic warden, traffic wardens. A **traffic** N COUNT
warden is a person whose job is to make sure that
cars are not parked in the wrong place or for
longer than is allowed.

tragedy /ˈtrædʒɪdi/, **tragedies. 1** A **tragedy** is N COUNT OR
an event or situation that is very sad and serious. N UNCOUNT
EG *The change of flight plans was the principal
cause of the tragedy... I know something of Dolly,
the tragedy of her life.*

2 In the theatre, a **tragedy** is a play that has a very N COUNT
sad ending.

3 You refer to plays with sad endings as **tragedy**. N UNCOUNT
EG *She acted brilliantly in Greek tragedy.*

tragic /ˈtrædʒɪk/. **1** Something that is **tragic** is ADJ QUALIT
very sad. EG *...the tragic death of his elder brother
Michael.* ◊ **tragically**. EG *He was tragically killed* ◊ ADV OR
in a car crash. ADV SEN

2 **Tragic** plays, films, and books have sad endings. ADJ CLASSIF :
EG *...Scott Fitzgerald's tragic novel 'Tender is the* ATTRIB
Night'... ...the Greek tragic heroes.

trail /treɪl/, **trails, trailing, trailed. 1** A **trail** is a N COUNT
rough path across open country or through forests.
EG *...as they trudged along the seemingly endless
trail.*

2 If someone or something leaves a **trail** behind N COUNT
them, they leave marks or other signs behind them
as they move along, which tell you which way they
went. EG *Eventually we lost the trail... She didn't
want him to leave a trail of wet footprints all over
the house.*

3 If you are **on the trail of** a person or animal, you PHRASE
are following them or are trying to find them.

4 If you **trail** something or if it **trails**, it drags V-ERG : USU+A
along behind you as you move, or it hangs down
loosely. EG *She trails the fingers of her right hand
through the water... She went out with her dress
trailing behind her on the floor... He had left his
horse standing with the reins trailing in the dust.*

5 If someone **trails** along, they move slowly, V+A
without any energy or enthusiasm, often following
someone else. EG *I used to trail around after him
like a small child.*

6 If you **are trailing** in a game or contest, you V OR V+O :
have a lower score than your opponents. EG *Public* USU CONT
*opinion polls showed Giscard trailing Mitterand by
as much as 3 points... At half-time, England were
trailing 8-5.*

trail away or **trail off**. If a speaker's voice PHRASAL VB :
trails away or **trails off**, it gradually becomes V+ADV
quieter or more hesitant until it stops completely.
EG *'I have an appointment that's very...' His voice
trailed off unconvincingly.*

trailer /ˈtreɪlə/, **trailers. 1** A **trailer** is **1.1** a N COUNT
vehicle like a cart which can be loaded with things
and pulled behind a car. **1.2** a vehicle which people American
use as a home or an office and which can be pulled
behind a car.

2 A **trailer** for a film or a television or radio N COUNT
programme is a set of short extracts from it, which
are shown or broadcast in order to advertise it.

train /treɪn/, **trains, training, trained. 1** A **train** N COUNT
is a number of carriages or trucks which are pulled OR *by*+N
by an engine along a railway line. EG *I caught a
train to Oxford... We are planning to go by train...
...the long train journey from Leeds.*

2 A **train of thought** is a connected series of PHRASE
thoughts. EG *I felt annoyed with her for interrupting
my train of thought.*

3 The **train** of a formal dress is a long part at the N COUNT
back of it that rests on the ground.

4 If you **train** a person or animal to do something, V+O:OFT
you teach them how to do it. EG *The police are* +*to*-INF OR A
trained to keep calm. ◊ **trained**. EG *She's a trained* ◊ ADJ CLASSIF
nurse.

5 If you **train** as something, you learn how to do a V : OFT+*to*-INF
particular job. EG *She started to train as a nurse...* OR A
We trained together at art school.

6 If you **train** for a sports match or a race, you V-ERG

If you start a transatlantic journey in the USA,
where are you likely to finish it?

prepare for it by doing exercises and eating a special diet.

7 See also **training**.

trainee /treɪniː/, **trainees**. A **trainee** is someone who is being taught how to do a job. EG *The trainees are shown around each of the departments... ...a trainee chef.*   N COUNT

trainer /treɪnə/, **trainers**. **1** A **trainer** is a person who trains animals or sports players.   N COUNT

2 Trainers are special shoes that people wear for running or jogging. See picture at SHOES.   N COUNT : USU PLURAL

training /treɪnɪŋ/. **1 Training** for a particular job involves learning or teaching the skills that are needed for the job. EG *I had a great training as a gardener... ...giving people training in computer programming.*   N UNCOUNT

2 Training also involves doing physical exercises and eating a special diet in order to be fit for a sports match or a race. EG *Are you in training for a cross-country run?*   N UNCOUNT

traipse /treɪps/, **traipses, traipsing, traipsed**. If you **traipse** somewhere, you go there slowly, because you are tired or because it is a long journey. EG *For eighteen weeks we traipsed around southern England.*   V+A Informal

trait /treɪt⁰/, **traits**. A **trait** is a characteristic or tendency that someone has. EG *Certain personality traits had made her unpopular.*   N COUNT+SUPP

traitor /treɪtə/, **traitors**. A **traitor** is someone who betrays their country or the group which they belong to, or who stops supporting one group and starts supporting another. EG *He was denounced as a traitor to France.*   N COUNT

tram /træm/, **trams**. A **tram** is an electric vehicle for carrying people which travels on rails in the streets of a town.   N COUNT OR by+N

tramp /træmp/, **tramps, tramping, tramped**. **1** A **tramp** is a person who has no home, no job, and very little money.   N COUNT

2 If you **tramp** from one place to another, you walk with slow, heavy footsteps. EG *She tramped slowly up the beach... ...if you are tramping the streets all day as a postman.*   V+A OR V+O

trample /træmpⁿl/, **tramples, trampling, trampled**. **1** If you **trample** on something, you tread heavily on it so that it is damaged. EG *As soon as I came to, I stood up to avoid being trampled on... They had trampled his lovely rose garden... They led each other back, trampling through the undergrowth.*   V+A OR V+O

2 If you **trample** on someone or on their rights or feelings, you behave towards them in a cruel or unjust way. EG *Half the population trample on the rights of the other half... We will not allow ourselves to be trampled on.*   V+on

trampoline /træmpəˈliːn/, **trampolines**. A **trampoline** is an apparatus on which you can do acrobatic jumps. It consists of a large piece of strong cloth held by springs in a frame.   N COUNT

trance /trɑːns/, **trances**. A **trance** is a mental state in which your thoughts and actions are controlled by the person who put you in that state. EG *While in a trance a hypnotized person can be instructed to perform a variety of actions.*   N COUNT

tranquil /træŋkwɪl/. **1** Something that is **tranquil** is calm and peaceful. EG *...this tranquil island...*   ◊ **tranquillity** /træŋkwɪlɪtiⁱ/. EG *...a time of political tranquillity.*   ADJ QUALIT Literary   ◊ N UNCOUNT

2 If you feel **tranquil**, you feel calm and relaxed. EG *...the prospect of a tranquil old age... ...a long, deep, dreamless, tranquil sleep.*   ADJ QUALIT Literary

tranquillize /træŋkwɪlaɪz/, **tranquillizes, tranquillizing, tranquillized**; also spelled **tranquillise** and, in American English, **tranquillize**. If people or animals **are tranquillized**, they are given a drug to make them become calm, sleepy, or unconscious.   V+O : USU PASS

tranquillizer /træŋkwɪlaɪzə/, **tranquillizers**; also spelled **tranquilliser** and, in American Eng-   N COUNT

lish, **tranquilizer**. A **tranquillizer** is a drug that makes people feel less anxious or nervous.

trans- is used to form adjectives that describe something as happening or existing across a place, from one side to the other. For example, a transcontinental journey is a journey across a continent. EG *...the Trans-Alaska pipeline... ...the Trans-Siberian Railway.*   PREFIX

transaction /trænzækʃəⁿn/, **transactions**. A **transaction** is a piece of business that involves a deal or arrangement, especially the sale of something. EG *...a business transaction.*   N COUNT

transatlantic /trænzəˈtlæntɪk/. **1 Transatlantic** journeys or communications involve travelling or communicating across the Atlantic Ocean, especially between Europe and the USA. EG *...a transatlantic phone call... ...regular transatlantic crossings.*   ADJ CLASSIF : ATTRIB

2 Transatlantic is also used by Europeans to describe things that happen or exist in the USA, and by Americans to describe things in Europe. EG *...a transatlantic television soap opera.*   ADJ CLASSIF : ATTRIB

transcend /trænsend/, **transcends, transcending, transcended**. If one thing **transcends** another, it is not limited by the other thing or it makes the other thing seem unimportant. EG *...a vital national issue that transcended party loyalties... Drama transcends national boundaries.*   V+O Formal

transcribe /trænskraɪb/, **transcribes, transcribing, transcribed**. If you **transcribe** something that is spoken or written, you write it down, copy it, or change it into a different form of writing. EG *He transcribed recordings of schoolchildren.*   V+O : USU+A

transcript /trænskrɪpt/, **transcripts**. A **transcript** of something that is spoken is a written copy of it. EG *...transcripts of tapes.*   N COUNT : OFT+of

transfer, **transfers, transferring, transferred**; pronounced /trænsfɜː/ when it is a verb and /trænsfɜː/ when it is a noun. **1** If you **transfer** something from one place to another, you move it. EG *Perkins transferred the trout to a silver platter... Ten thousand pounds has been transferred into your account.* ▶ used as a noun. EG *...the electronic transfer of money.*   V+O : USU+A   ▶ N UNCOUNT OR N COUNT

2 If something **is transferred** from one person or group to another, the second one then has it instead of the first. EG *Responsibility is lifted from individual shoulders and transferred to the State... Ravenscroft transferred his affections to his secretary.* ▶ used as a noun. EG *...the transfer of power.*   V+O : USU+A   ▶ N UNCOUNT

◊ **transference** /trænsfəⁿrəns/. EG *There has been no genuine transference of authority to local level.*   ◊ N UNCOUNT : USU+SUPP

3 If you **transfer** to a different place or job, or **are transferred** to it, you move to a different place or job within the same organization. EG *She's been transferred to another department.* ▶ used as a noun. EG *He resisted his transfer to the political section.*   V-ERG : OFT+to   ▶ N COUNT OR N UNCOUNT

4 A **transfer** is also a piece of paper with a design on one side. The design can be ironed or pressed onto cloth, paper, or china.   N COUNT

transfixed /trænsfɪkst/. If you are **transfixed** by something, you are so impressed, fascinated, or frightened by it that you do not move. EG *I stood transfixed with terror.*   ADJ PRED : USU+by/with Literary

transform /trænsfɔːm/, **transforms, transforming, transformed**. If something **is transformed**, it is changed completely. EG *An area of pasture land can be transformed into a barren landscape in two or three years... They claimed to be able to transform the lives of millions of people.*   V+O : OFT +from/into

◊ **transformation** /trænsfəmeɪʃəⁿn/, **transformations**. EG *...the social and political transformation of society... After a few months, the creature undergoes a transformation.*   ◊ N COUNT OR N UNCOUNT

transfusion /trænsfjuːʒəⁿn/, **transfusions**. When a patient is given a blood **transfusion**, blood is put into his or her body.   N COUNT

transient /trænziˈənt/. Something that is **tran-** ADJ QUALIT
sient does not exist or stay in a place very long. EG Formal
In our fast-changing society even failure is tran-
sient... ...transient visitors.

transistor /trænzistə/, **transistors. 1** A **transis-** N COUNT
tor is a small electronic device in something such
as a television or a radio. It is used for amplification and switching.

2 A **transistor** or a **transistor radio** is a small N COUNT
portable radio.

transit /trænzit/. **1** If people or things are **in** PHRASE
transit, they are travelling or being taken from
one place to another. EG *The tablets had been lost*
in transit.

2 A **transit** area or building is where people wait ADJ CLASSIF :
or where goods are kept between different stages ATTRIB
of a journey. EG *...the transit lounge.*

transition /trænziʃəⁿn/, **transitions.** A **transi-** N COUNT OR
tion is a change from one form or state to another. N UNCOUNT :
EG *How do you think this made the transition from* OFT+*from/to*
book to stage?... The world was in transition from
the old-fashioned conflict situation to a new era of
co-operation.

transitional /trænziʃəⁿnəl, -ʃənəⁿl/. A **transition-** ADJ CLASSIF
al period or stage is one during which something
changes from one form or state to another. EG *...a*
transitional period of civil war.

transitive /trænzitiv/. In grammar, a **transitive** ADJ CLASSIF
verb is a verb which has an object. In this diction-
ary v+o is used in the Extra Column to indicate
that the verb is transitive.

transitory /trænzitəⁿriˈ/. If something is **transi-** ADJ QUALIT
tory, it lasts for only a short time. EG *Love is*
transitory, but art is eternal... ...the transitory na-
ture of human ties in urban society.

translate /trænsleɪt, trænz-/, **translates, trans-**
lating, translated. 1 If you **translate** something V+O OR V : OFT
that someone has said or written, you say it or +*from/into*
write it in a different language. EG *My books have*
been translated into many languages.

2 If you **translate** one thing into another, you V+O+*into*
change it or convert it into something else. EG *He*
started to translate into action the dreams of
African unity.

translation /trænsleɪʃəⁿn, trænz-/, **translations.** N COUNT
A **translation** is a piece of writing or speech that
has been translated from a different language. EG
...a new translation of the Bible... It reads like a
poor translation from Latin.

translator /trænsleɪtə, trænz-/, **translators.** A N COUNT
translator is a person whose job involves translating writing or speech from one language to another.

translucent /trænzluːsəⁿnt/. If something is ADJ QUALIT
translucent, light passes through it, so that it Literary
seems to glow. EG *The leaves of the beeches are*
translucent in the setting sun.

transmission /trænzmiʃəⁿn/, **transmissions. 1** N UNCOUNT
The **transmission** of something involves passing it
or sending it to a different place or person. EG *...the*
transmission of diseases... ...data transmission.

2 The **transmission** of television or radio pro- N UNCOUNT
grammes is the broadcasting of them. EG *...a unique*
film record that was destroyed after transmission.

3 A **transmission** is a broadcast. EG *Millions would* N COUNT
have heard that transmission.

transmit /trænzmit/, **transmits, transmitting,**
transmitted. 1 When a message or an electronic V+O : USU PASS
signal **is transmitted**, it is sent by means of radio
waves. EG *The material was transmitted by satellite*
throughout the world.

2 To **transmit** something to a different place or V+O : OFT+*to*
person means to pass it or send it to the place or Formal
person. EG *...a disease that is sometimes transmit-*
ted to humans... ...a superior way of storing and
transmitting energy.

transmitter /trænzmitə/, **transmitters.** A N COUNT
transmitter is a piece of equipment that is used

for sending radio signals or for broadcasting programmes.

transparency /trænspærənsiˈ/, **transparencies.**
1 A **transparency** is a small piece of photographic N COUNT
film in a frame which can be projected onto a Technical
screen.

2 Transparency is the quality that an object or N UNCOUNT
substance has if you can see through it. EG *The*
crystal lost its transparency.

transparent /trænspærənt/. **1** If an object or ADJ CLASSIF
substance is **transparent**, you can see through it.
EG *...a transparent plastic lid.*

2 If something such as a feeling is **transparent**, it ADJ QUALIT
is easily understood or recognized. EG *We wanted* Formal
our goals to be transparent. ◇ **transparently.** EG ◇ SUBMOD
...an attitude that was transparently false.

transpire /trænspaɪə/, **transpires, transpiring,**
transpired. 1 When it **transpires** that something V
is the case, people discover that it is the case. EG *It* Formal
finally transpired that he was a special investigator
for the CIA.

2 When something **transpires**, it happens. EG V
Nobody knows what transpired at the meeting. Formal

transplant, transplants, transplanting, trans-
planted; pronounced /trænsplɑːnt/ when it is a
noun and /trænsplɑːnt/ when it is a verb.

1 A **transplant** is a surgical operation in which a N COUNT OR
part of a person's body is replaced because it is N UNCOUNT
diseased. EG *...one of Britain's youngest heart trans-*
plant patients. ▶ used as a verb. EG *Doctors hope to* ▶ V+O
transplant a human heart into the patient within
the next few days.

2 When something **is transplanted**, it is moved to V-ERG : OFT+A
a different place. EG *...how an established technol-*
ogy can be transplanted to another region...
...transplanting seedlings.

transport, transports, transporting, trans-
ported; pronounced /trænspɔːt/ when it is a noun
and /trænspɔːt/ when it is a verb.

1 You can refer to things which you travel in such N UNCOUNT
as cars, aircraft, and boats as **transport**. EG *It is*
easier if you have your own transport... Why can't
he use public transport?

2 Transport involves moving goods or people N UNCOUNT
from one place to another. EG *The essential means*
of transport for heavy equipment remained the
railway... High transport costs make foreign goods
too expensive.

3 When goods or people **are transported** from V+O : USU+A
one place to another, they are moved from one
place to another. EG *The goods were transported to*
East Africa.

transportation /trænspɔːteɪʃəⁿn/ is the same as N UNCOUNT
transport. EG *The food is ready for transportation.* American

transvestite /trænzvestaɪt/, **transvestites.** A N COUNT
transvestite is a person, usually a man, who
enjoys wearing clothes normally worn by people of
the opposite sex.

trap /træp/, **traps, trapping, trapped. 1** A **trap** is N COUNT
1.1 something such as a piece of equipment or a
hole that is carefully positioned in order to catch
animals or birds. EG *...an otter trap.* **1.2** a trick that
is intended to catch or deceive someone. EG *I knew*
perfectly well it was a trap.

2 Someone who **traps** animals catches them using V+O
traps.

3 If you **trap** someone, you trick them so that they V+O
do or say something which they did not want to do.
EG *This wasn't the first time we had been trapped*
into a situation like this.

4 If you **are trapped** somewhere, you cannot V+O : USU PASS
move or escape because something is blocking
your way or is holding you down. EG *Many people*
trapped in buildings died before they could be
rescued.

Can you call a bad translation a travesty of the
original?

5 If you **are trapped**, you are in an unpleasant situation that you cannot easily change. EG *She felt trapped... Many women are trapped in loveless marriages.*

6 A **trap** is also an unpleasant situation that cannot easily be changed. EG *To break out of the poverty trap they need help from the government.*

7 When something **traps** gas, water, or energy, it stores it so that it can be used. EG *A building can be designed to trap and store radiation from the sun.*

8 See also **booby-trap**.

trapdoor /ˈtræpdɔː/, **trapdoors**. A **trapdoor** is a small horizontal door in a floor, ceiling, or stage.

trapeze /trəˈpiːz/, **trapezes**. A **trapeze** is a bar of wood or metal hanging from two ropes. Acrobats and gymnasts swing on trapezes and perform skilful movements on them.

trappings /ˈtræpɪŋz/. The **trappings** of a particular rank, position, or state are the things that you acquire as a result of having it. EG *...the trappings of power that have surrounded him since he took office.*

trash /træʃ/. **1 Trash** is rubbish. EG *The yards were filled with trash.*

2 If you say that something such as a book, painting, or film is **trash**, you mean that it is not very good. EG *'I've told you not to read that trash,' he said.*

trashcan /ˈtræʃkæn/, **trashcans**. A **trashcan** is a container you put rubbish in.

trashy /ˈtræʃɪ/, **trashier, trashiest. Trashy** books are not very good.

trauma /ˈtrɔːmə/, **traumas. 1** A **trauma** is a very upsetting experience. EG *I look at my daughter and think of what traumas lie in store for her... ...the trauma of having their parents arrested.*

2 Trauma is great stress and unhappiness. EG *This would impose unnecessary trauma and suffering.*

traumatic /trɔːˈmætɪk/. A **traumatic** experience is very upsetting. EG *...the traumatic ordeal of facing a firing squad.*

travel /ˈtrævəl/, **travels, travelling, travelled;** spelled **traveling** and **traveled** in American English.

1 When you **travel**, you go from one place to another or you go to several places, especially in a foreign country. EG *I travelled to work by train... Margaret travelled alone around the United States... I travelled sixty miles to buy those books.* ▶ used as a noun. EG *...air travel.*

2 Someone's **travels** are the journeys that they make to places a long way from their home. EG *...his extensive travels abroad.*

3 When something reaches one place from another, you say that it **travels** there. EG *Sound travels better in water than in air... News travels fast.*

travel agency, travel agencies. A travel agency is a business which makes arrangements for people's holidays and journeys.

travel agent, travel agents. A travel agent is a person who works in a travel agency.

traveller /ˈtrævələ/, **travellers;** spelled **traveler** in American English. A **traveller** is a person who is making a journey or who travels a lot.

traveller's cheque, traveller's cheques; spelled **traveler's check** in American English. **Traveller's cheques** are cheques that you buy at a bank and take abroad with you. You can exchange them for the local currency.

traverse /ˈtrævɜːs, trəˈvɜːs/, **traverses, traversing, traversed.** If you **traverse** an area of land or water, you go across it or over it. EG *I traversed the rest of the slope at a run.*

travesty /ˈtrævəstɪ/, **travesties.** If you say that something is a **travesty**, you mean that it is a very bad representation or imitation of something. EG *His account of my essay was a travesty... ...the travesties of justice played out in their courts.*

trawler /ˈtrɔːlə/, **trawlers.** A **trawler** is a fishing boat on which fish are caught in large nets.

tray /treɪ/, **trays.** A **tray** is a flat object with raised edges which is used for carrying food or drinks. EG *There were two champagne glasses on the tray... ...trays of tea and sandwiches.*

treacherous /ˈtretʃərəs/. **1** A **treacherous** person is likely to betray you. EG *...my treacherous fellow travellers.*

2 You describe the ground or the sea as **treacherous** when it is dangerous and unpredictable. EG *The tides are treacherous and only strong swimmers can make it.*

treachery /ˈtretʃərɪ/. If someone betrays their country or betrays a person who trusts them, you describe their action as **treachery**. EG *He could not believe that Clemenza was guilty of treachery.*

treacle /ˈtriːkəl/ is a sweet, sticky liquid used in making cakes and puddings. EG *...bread and black treacle... ...treacle tart.*

tread /tred/, **treads, treading, trod** /trɒd/, **trodden** /ˈtrɒdən/. **1** If you **tread** on something, you step on it. EG *Oh, do be careful, don't tread on the flowers... There is a squeak every time I tread on the pedal.*

2 If you **tread** something into the ground or into a carpet, you crush it into the ground or carpet by stepping on it. EG *Damp chips had been trodden into the carpet.*

3 If you **tread** in a particular way, you walk in that way. EG *She trod heavily out of the room.*

4 A person's **tread** is the sound that they make with their feet as they walk. EG *They could hear his heavy limping tread.*

5 If you **tread** carefully, you behave carefully or cautiously. EG *The government was treading warily.*

6 If someone who is in deep water **treads water**, they stay afloat in an upright position by moving their legs.

7 The **tread** of a tyre or shoe is the pattern of ridges on it that stops it slipping.

8 See also **trodden**.

treason /ˈtriːzən/ is the crime of betraying your country, for example by helping its enemies.

treasure /ˈtreʒə/, **treasures, treasuring, treasured. 1 Treasure** is a collection of gold or silver objects, or jewels, especially one that has been hidden. EG *...buried treasure.*

2 Treasures are valuable works of art. EG *...the sale of art treasures.*

3 If you **treasure** something, you are very pleased that you have it and you regard it as precious. EG *...one of the memories which they would treasure.*
◊ **treasured.** EG *The letters he wrote me are my most treasured possessions.*

4 If you say that someone is a **treasure**, you mean that they are very helpful and useful to you.

treasurer /ˈtreʒərə/, **treasurers.** The **treasurer** of an organization is in charge of its finances and keeps its accounts.

treat /triːt/, **treats, treating, treated. 1** If you **treat** someone in a particular way, you behave that way towards them. EG *We were treated with respect... Their parents continue to treat them as children.*

2 If you **treat** something in a particular way, you deal with it that way or you regard it in that way. EG *Electricity is potentially dangerous, so treat it with respect... Does he treat it as some sort of joke?*

3 When a doctor **treats** a patient or an illness, he or she tries to make the patient well again. EG *...a way to treat cancer.*

4 If you **treat** something such as wood or cloth, you put a special substance on it in order to protect it or to give it special properties. EG *New timber should be treated with a preservative.*

5 If you give someone a **treat**, you buy or arrange something special for them which they will enjoy.

EG *Granny took us for tea at Lyons Corner House as a special treat.* ▸ used as a verb. **EG** *Treat yourself to a new pair of shoes... I was treated to lunch by the vice-president.* ▸ V·REFL OR V+O

treatment /tri:tmə²nt/, **treatments. 1** Medical **treatment** consists of all the things that are done in order to make a sick or injured person well again. **EG** *...free dental treatment... I tried every treatment the doctor suggested.* N UNCOUNT OR N COUNT

2 Your **treatment** of someone is the way that you behave towards them or the way you deal with them. **EG** *Their treatment of women is unspeakable... I didn't want special treatment.* N UNCOUNT

treaty /tri:ti¹/, **treaties. A treaty** is a written agreement between countries. **EG** *...the Treaty of Versailles... The Government has signed a treaty with Moscow.* N COUNT

treble /trebə¹l/, **trebles, trebling, trebled.** If something **trebles** or **is trebled**, it becomes three times greater in number or amount than it was. **EG** *The population has nearly trebled since 1950.* V·ERG

tree /tri:/, **trees. A tree** is a tall plant with a hard trunk, branches, and leaves. **EG** *In the middle of the lawn was a great cedar tree.* ● See also **Christmas tree, family tree.** ● to **be barking up the wrong tree:** see **bark.** N COUNT

treetop /tri:tɒp/, **treetops.** The **treetops** are the top part of the trees in a forest. **EG** *Monkeys were bounding away through the treetops.* N COUNT : USU PLURAL

trek /trek/, **treks, trekking, trekked.** If you **trek** somewhere, you go on a long and difficult journey, especially on foot. **EG** *They trekked for three days along the banks of the Zambezi.* ▸ used as a noun. **EG** *We set off on a four hour trek through swamps and fields.* V+A ▸ N COUNT

trellis /trelɪs/, **trellises. A trellis** is a frame which is used to support climbing plants. N COUNT

tremble /trembə¹l/, **trembles, trembling, trembled. 1** If you **tremble,** you shake slightly, usually because you are frightened or cold. **EG** *Claude's hands trembled as he struck a match... 'What is this place?' asked Mother, trembling with fear.* V : OFT+A

2 If something **trembles,** it shakes slightly. **EG** *The wind made the branches shake and tremble.* V Written

3 If your voice **trembles,** it sounds unsteady, for example because you are upset. **EG** *'It does concern me.' Fanny's voice trembled a little.* V Written

tremendous /trɪ²mendəs/. **1** If you describe something as **tremendous,** you mean that it is very large or impressive. **EG** *The play became a tremendous hit... They cost a tremendous amount of money.* ◊ **tremendously.** **EG** *There is a tremendously difficult struggle ahead of us... She envied and admired Judy tremendously.* ADJ QUALIT ◊ ADV

2 You can also describe something as **tremendous** when you think it is very good or pleasing. **EG** *The view is tremendous... The holiday was tremendous.* ADJ QUALIT

tremor /tremə/, **tremors. 1** A **tremor** is **1.1** a shaking movement of your body which you cannot control. **EG** *Words cannot describe the tremor of pleasure that went through me.* **1.2** an unsteady quality in your voice, for example because you are upset. **EG** *Burton detected a tremor in the voice of the Controller.* N COUNT

2 A **tremor** is also a small earthquake. **EG** *These local volcanic tremors are usually not strong.* N COUNT

tremulous /tremjə¹ləs/. If someone's smile or voice is **tremulous,** it is unsteady because they are nervous, uncertain, or unhappy. **EG** *Jack's voice went on, tremulous yet determined.* ADJ QUALIT Literary

trench /trentʃ/, **trenches. A trench** is a long narrow channel dug in the ground, for example for drainage. N COUNT

trend /trend/, **trends. A trend** is a change towards doing or being something different. **EG** *There is a trend towards equal opportunities for men and women... The trend has been to stress the artistic side of education.* N COUNT : USU+SUPP

trendy /trendi¹/, **trendier, trendiest.** Trendy things or people are fashionable. **EG** *...trendy clothes... ...trendy intellectuals.* ADJ QUALIT Informal

trepidation /trepɪdeɪʃə²n/ is fear or anxiety. **EG** *'What do you mean?' I asked, with some trepidation... We approached with trepidation.* N UNCOUNT Formal

trespass /trespəs/, **trespasses, trespassing, trespassed.** If you **trespass** on someone's land, you go onto it without their permission. **EG** *...signs saying 'No trespassing'.* ◊ **trespasser, trespassers. EG** *Trespassers will be prosecuted.* V : OFT+on ◊ N COUNT

trial /traɪəl/, **trials. 1** A **trial** is the legal process in which a judge and jury decide whether a person is guilty of a particular crime after listening to evidence relating to it. **EG** *She won't get a fair trial... Huey was awaiting trial for murder.* ● If someone is **on trial,** they are being tried in a court of law. **EG** *We don't intend to put him on trial.* ● to **stand trial:** see **stand.** N COUNT OR N UNCOUNT ● PHRASE

2 A **trial** is also an experiment in which you test something. **EG** *We've completed a number of fairly successful trials with laboratory animals.* ● If something is **on trial,** it is being tested or closely examined to see if it is suitable. **EG** *The Parliamentary system is on trial.* N COUNT OR N UNCOUNT ● PHRASE

3 A **trial** period is a short period of time during which you employ a person or use a thing in order to find out if they are suitable. N MOD

4 If you do something by **trial and error,** you try different methods of doing it until you find one that works well. **EG** *The best solution can only be found by a process of trial and error.* PHRASE

5 If you talk about the **trials** that someone experiences, you mean the unpleasant things that they experience. **EG** *...the trials of pregnancy and childbirth.* N COUNT +SUPP : USU PLURAL

trial run, trial runs. A trial run is a first attempt at doing something, to make sure that you can do it properly when you need to. N COUNT

triangle /traɪæŋgə¹l/, **triangles. A triangle** is a flat shape or area which has three straight sides and three angles. See picture at SHAPES. **EG** *The place of assembly in which he stood was roughly a triangle.* N COUNT

triangular /traɪæŋgjə⁴lə/. Something that is **triangular** is in the shape of a triangle. **EG** *I punched two triangular holes in the tin.* ADJ CLASSIF

tribal /traɪbə¹l/ describes things relating or belonging to tribes. **EG** *...tribal leaders... ...a tribal war.* ADJ CLASSIF ATTRIB

tribe /traɪb/, **tribes. A tribe** is a small group of people with the same language and customs. **EG** *Mr Otunnu is a member of the Acholi tribe... ...primitive tribes in the heart of Africa.* N COUNT

tribesman /traɪbzmə³n/, **tribesmen. A tribesman** is a man who belongs to a particular tribe. N COUNT

tribulation /trɪbjə⁴leɪʃə²n/, **tribulations. Tribulation** is trouble or suffering. **EG** *Life is uncertain and full of tribulation... ...after many trials and tribulations during the war.* N UNCOUNT OR N PLURAL Formal

tribunal /traɪbju:nə¹l/, **tribunals. A tribunal** is a special court or committee that is appointed to deal with particular problems. **EG** *An industrial tribunal was hearing cases of unfair dismissal.* N COLL

tributary /trɪbjə⁴tə³ri¹/, **tributaries. A tributary** is a stream or river that flows into a larger river. **EG** *...the Neander River, a tributary of the Rhine.* N COUNT

tribute /trɪbju:t/, **tributes. 1** A **tribute** is something that you say or do in order to show your admiration and respect for someone. **EG** *On Johnson's death in 1922, Asquith paid tribute to his personal qualities... She accepted the tribute graciously.* N COUNT OR N UNCOUNT

2 If you say that one thing is a **tribute** to another, you mean that it is the result of the other thing and shows how good the other thing is. **EG** *The fact that* N SING : a+n

Which two words on these pages mean to become three times greater than before?

I survived is a tribute to the indestructibility of the human body.

trick /trɪk/, **tricks, tricking, tricked. 1** If some- V+O: one **tricks** you, they deceive you, often in order to OFT+*into* make you do something. EG *He realized that the visitors had tricked him... She felt she had been tricked into marriage.*

2 A **trick** is   **2.1** a clever or skilful action that N COUNT someone does in order to entertain people. EG *Mr Poliakin was performing his popular trick of playing the bow with the violin.* **2.2** a clever way of doing something. EG *An old campers' trick is to use three thin blankets instead of one thick one... These are standard tricks of the trade.*

3 A **trick** question is one where the obvious answer ADJ CLASSIF: is in fact wrong, or one which is intended to make ATTRIB you accidentally reveal something.

4 Trick devices and methods are intended to ADJ CLASSIF: deceive people for a joke or for entertainment. EG ATTRIB *...trick mirrors... ...trick photography.*

5 If you **play a trick** on someone, you do some- PHRASE thing that is intended to deceive them. EG *They played a dirty trick on us.*

6 If you say that something **does the trick**, you PHRASE mean that it achieves what you wanted. EG *They* Informal *thought that just one push would do the trick.*

7 See also **conjuring trick**.

trickery /trɪkəri¹/ is deception. EG *The old man* N UNCOUNT *suspected trickery.*

trickle /trɪkəⁿl/, **trickles, trickling, trickled. 1** V: USU+A When a liquid **trickles** somewhere, it flows slowly in a thin stream. EG *The tears were beginning to trickle down her cheeks.*

2 When people or things **trickle** somewhere, they V+A move there slowly in small groups or amounts. EG *The coach parties began trickling back to the car park.*

3 A **trickle** of liquid is a thin, slow stream of it. EG N PART: *...a thin trickle of blood.*   USU SING

4 A **trickle** of people or things is a small number N PART: or quantity of them. EG *A trickle of people were still* USU SING *coming in... Income is down to a trickle.*

tricky /trɪki¹/, **trickier, trickiest.** A **tricky** task ADJ QUALIT or problem is difficult to do or to deal with. EG *Dyeing patterned material is tricky... It had been a slow, tricky job.*

tricycle /traɪsɪkəⁿl/, **tricycles.** A **tricycle** is a N COUNT vehicle similar to a bicycle but with two wheels at the back instead of one.

tried /traɪd/. **1 Tried** is the past tense and past participle of **try**.

2 A product or method that is **tried and tested** has PHRASE often been used and has always worked well.

trifle /traɪfəⁿl/, **trifles, trifling, trifled. 1** You PHRASE use **a trifle** to describe a quality or manner that Formal exists to a small extent or degree. EG *She was a trifle breathless... 'They seemed very nice men,' she added, a trifle wistfully.*

2 Trifles are things that are considered to be not N COUNT: very important or not very valuable. EG *They worry* USU PLURAL *over trifles.*

3 A **trifle** is a cold pudding made of layers of N COUNT OR sponge cake, fruit, jelly, and custard.   N UNCOUNT

trifle with. If you **trifle with** someone or some- PHRASAL VB: thing, you treat them in a disrespectful way, rather V+PREP, than seriously. EG *Mitchell was not someone to be* HAS PASS *trifled with.*

trifling /traɪflɪŋ/. Something that is **trifling** is ADJ QUALIT small and unimportant. EG *There was no need for you to come out here on such a trifling matter.*

trigger /trɪgə/, **triggers, triggering, triggered. 1** The **trigger** of a gun is the small lever which you N COUNT pull in order to fire it. See picture at WEAPONS.

2 If something **triggers** an event or **triggers** it V+O: OFT+*off* **off**, it causes it to happen. EG *There had been disagreements between them, triggered by his work.*

trillion /trɪljən/, **trillions. 1** A **trillion** is a num- NUMBER ber representing a million million. EG *...with income now in excess of a trillion dollars.*

2 You can use **trillions** to mean an extremely N PART: USU large number. EG *There are trillions of places* PLURAL *where we could go.*   Informal

trilogy /trɪlədʒi¹/, **trilogies.** A **trilogy** is a series N COUNT of three books or plays that have the same characters or the same subject.

trim /trɪm/, **trimmer, trimmest; trims, trim- ming, trimmed. 1** Something that is **trim** is neat, ADJ QUALIT tidy, and attractive. EG *...the trim lawns and trees of suburbia... ...a man with a trim beard.*

2 If someone has a **trim** figure, they are slim. EG *...a* ADJ QUALIT *trim, balding man in his early sixties.*

3 If you **trim** your hair or **trim** a hedge, you cut off V+O small amounts of it in order to make it look neater. EG *His beard was freshly trimmed... The grass needed trimming.* ▸ used as a noun. EG *My hair* ▸ N SING *needs a trim.*

4 If a piece of clothing **is trimmed** with things V+O: USU PASS such as ribbons or feathers, these things are added +*with* to the edge in order to make it look nice.

◊ **trimmed**. EG *Her dress was trimmed with lace at* ◊ ADJ PRED *the neck... ...a hat trimmed with ribbons.*   +*with*

trim away or **trim off.** If you **trim away** parts PHRASAL VB: of something or **trim** them **off**, you cut them off V+O+ADV because they are not needed. EG *Most of the fat should be trimmed off meat.*

trimming /trɪmɪŋ/, **trimmings. 1** The **trimming** N MASS OR N or the **trimmings** on a piece of clothing are extra PLURAL parts added for decoration. EG *...a pink nightdress with nylon lace trimmings.*

2 Trimmings are also nice things that can be N PLURAL added to something or included in something. EG *Tonight it was turkey with all the trimmings.*

trinket /trɪŋkɪt/, **trinkets.** A **trinket** is a cheap N COUNT ornament or piece of jewellery.

trio /triːoʊ/, **trios.** A **trio** is a group of three N COUNT people, especially three musicians or singers who play or sing together. EG *...a trio of journalists... ...the Pump Room Trio.*

trip /trɪp/, **trips, tripping, tripped. 1** A **trip** is a N COUNT journey that you make to a place and back again. EG *Morris decided to take a trip to London... ...executives on business trips abroad.*

2 If you **trip**, you knock your foot against some- V: USU+A thing when you are walking, and you fall over or nearly fall over. EG *I tripped and fell... She tripped over a stone.*

3 If you **trip** someone who is walking along, you V+O put your foot or something else in front of them so that they knock their own foot against it and fall. EG *Somebody thrust out a foot and tripped him.*

4 You can also refer to a strange or unreal N COUNT experience that is caused by taking drugs as a **trip**. Informal EG *She had a bad trip.*

5 See also **round trip**.

trip up. If you **trip up** someone who is walking PHRASAL VB: along, you put your foot or something else in front V+O+ADV of them so that they knock their own foot against it and fall.

tripartite /traɪpɑːtaɪt/ means having three parts ADJ CLASSIF or involving three groups of people. EG *...the tripar-* ATTRIB *tite system of education... The unions called for* Formal *tripartite talks.*

tripe /traɪp/. **1 Tripe** is the stomach of a pig, cow, N UNCOUNT or ox, which is eaten as food.

2 If you say that something that someone has said N UNCOUNT or written is **tripe**, you mean that it is silly or not Informal very good.

triple /trɪpəⁿl/, **triples, tripling, tripled. 1 Tri-** ADJ CLASSIF: **ple** means consisting of three things or three parts. ATTRIB EG *...a triple alliance... ...a breath-taking triple som- ersault.*

2 If you **triple** something or if it **triples**, it V-ERG becomes three times greater in size or number than it was. EG *In three years the company had* *tripled its sales... During this period the Japanese national income has tripled.*

triplet /trɪplɪ²t/, **triplets. Triplets** are three chil- N COUNT : dren born at the same time to the same mother.   USU PLURAL

tripod /traɪpɒd/, **tripods.** A **tripod** is a stand with N COUNT three legs which you use to support something such as a camera or telescope.

trite /traɪt/. Ideas, remarks, and stories that are ADJ QUALIT **trite** are dull and not original. EG *...trite films... a trite piece of philosophy.*

triumph /traɪəmf/, **triumphs, triumphing, tri- umphed.** 1 A **triumph** is a great success or N COUNT achievement. EG *The election result was a personal triumph for the party leader... This machine is a triumph of advanced technology.*

2 **Triumph** is a feeling of great satisfaction when N UNCOUNT you win or achieve something. EG *He gave a cry of triumph... I saw a gleam of triumph in his eye.*

3 If you **triumph**, you win a victory or succeed in V : OFT+*over* overcoming something. EG *They had met the chal- lenge and triumphed... She learned to triumph over her disabilities.*

triumphant /traɪʌmfənt/. Someone who is **tri- umphant** feels very happy because they have won a victory or have achieved something. EG *...trium- phant soldiers... His parents looked on with a triumphant smile.* ◊ **triumphantly.** EG *Robert was* ◊ ADV *looking at me triumphantly.*

trivia /trɪvɪə/. If you refer to things as **trivia**, you N UNCOUNT mean that they are unimportant. EG *She takes a childish delight in remembering trivia... ...the trivia of everyday life.*

trivial /trɪvɪəl/. Something that is **trivial** is unim- ADJ QUALIT portant. EG *All those little details of organization seemed trivial.*

triviality /trɪvɪælɪ¹ti¹/, **trivialities.** 1 **Trivial- ities** are unimportant things. EG *...the daily trivial- ities which seem so important to men.*

2 The **triviality** of something is the fact that it is N UNCOUNT unimportant. EG *...conversations of unbelievable triviality.*

trivialize /trɪvɪəlaɪz/, **trivializes, trivializing,** V+O **trivialized;** also spelled **trivialise.** If you **trivial- ize** something, you make it seem unimportant, although it is actually important. EG *Their political role is often trivialized.*

trod /trɒd/ is the past tense of **tread.**

trodden /trɒdə⁰n/. 1 **Trodden** is the past partici- ple of **tread.**

2 Ground that is **trodden** has been walked over by ADJ CLASSIF a lot of people, and is therefore flattened or marked with footprints. EG *The grass was trodden and muddy.*

trolley /trɒli¹/, **trolleys.** 1 A **trolley** is 1.1 a small N COUNT cart that you use to carry heavy things, for exam- ple shopping or luggage. EG *...supermarket trolleys.* 1.2 a small table on wheels on which things, especially food and drinks, can be taken from one part of a building to another. EG *The room-service boy wheeled the trolley in.*

2 A **trolley** is also a tram. EG *Cars and trolleys* N COUNT *filled the street.*   American

trombone /trɒmbəʊn/, **trombones.** A **trombone** N COUNT is a brass musical instrument which you play by blowing into it and sliding part of it backwards and forwards to make different notes. See picture at MUSICAL INSTRUMENTS.

troop /tru:p/, **troops, trooping, trooped.** 1 N PLURAL **Troops** are soldiers, especially ones taking part in military action. EG *They have more than 11,000 troops in Northern Ireland... ...reports on troop movements.*

2 A **troop** of people or animals is a group of them. N PART EG *...a troop of monkeys.*

3 If people **troop** somewhere, they walk there in a V+A group. EG *The twelve men trooped downstairs.*

trophy /trəʊfi¹/, **trophies.** A **trophy** is a prize, for N COUNT example a silver cup or shield, that is given to the winner of a competition or race.

tropical /trɒpɪkə⁰l/. **Tropical** places or things are ADJ CLASSIF : in the tropics or come from the tropics. EG *Most* ATTRIB *tropical areas have rainy and dry seasons... ...tropi- cal rain forests.*

tropics /trɒpɪks/. The **tropics** are the hottest N PLURAL : parts of the world, near the equator.   the+N

trot /trɒt/, **trots, trotting, trotted.** 1 When an V : USU+A animal such as a horse **trots**, it moves fairly fast, lifting its feet quite high off the ground. EG *He made the beast turn aside and trot away.* ► used as a ► N SING noun. EG *She urged her pony into an energetic trot.*

2 If you **trot** somewhere, you move fairly fast, V+A taking small quick steps. EG *We trotted along behind him.* ► used as a noun. EG *Hobbs immediate-* ► N SING *ly went off at a trot.*

3 If you say that several things happen **on the trot**, PHRASE you mean that they happen one after the other, Informal without a break. EG *Try not to miss two lessons on the trot.*

trot out. If you **trot out** old ideas or pieces of PHRASAL VB : information, you repeat them in a boring way. EG V+O+ADV *They trot out all the old reasons for their failure.*

trouble /trʌbə⁰l/, **troubles, troubling, troubled.** 1 If you have **trouble** doing something, you have N UNCOUNT difficulties or problems doing it. EG *You shouldn't have any trouble locating them... This would save everyone a lot of trouble.*

2 If you say that one aspect of a situation is the N SING : **trouble**, you mean that it is that aspect which is USU the+N causing problems or making the situation unsatis- factory. EG *It's getting a bit expensive now, that's the trouble... The trouble with you is that you've forgotten what it's like to be young.*

3 Your **troubles** are the problems in your life. EG N PLURAL : *The old lady next door was telling me all her* USU+POSS *troubles... She thought that all her troubles were over.*

4 If you have kidney **trouble** or back **trouble**, for N UNCOUNT example, there is something wrong with your +SUPP kidneys or your back. EG *He has heart trouble.*

5 If you are **in trouble**, 5.1 you have a serious PHRASE problem. EG *Frank was still in deep financial trou- ble.* 5.2 someone in authority is angry with you because of something you have done. EG *...if a child is in trouble with the police... I don't want to get you into trouble.*

6 If there is **trouble**, people are quarrelling or N UNCOUNT fighting. EG *He's the sort of person who always makes trouble... The demonstration was cancelled because the police felt that it could lead to trouble.*

7 If you say that it is no **trouble** to do something N UNCOUNT : for someone, you mean that you do not mind doing WITH BROAD it. EG *'It wouldn't be any trouble.' - 'That's very kind* NEG *of you.'*

8 If you **take the trouble** to do something, you do PHRASE it although it requires some time or effort. EG *Many of them do not even take the trouble to answer letters.*

9 If something **troubles** you, it makes you feel V+O rather worried. EG *What's troubling you?... He was deeply troubled by the thought that she might leave him.* ◊ **troubling.** EG *It was a new and* ◊ ADJ QUALIT *troubling thought.*

10 If you say that you are sorry to **trouble** some- V+O one, you are apologizing for disturbing them in order to ask them something. EG *I'm sorry to trouble you, but I wondered if we could have a word some time.*

troubled /trʌbə⁰ld/. 1 Someone who is **troubled** is ADJ QUALIT worried because they have problems.

2 A **troubled** place, organization, or time has ADJ QUALIT many problems or conflicts. EG *We live in troubled times... ...Britain's troubled car industry.*

troublemaker /trʌbə⁰lmeɪkə/, **troublemakers.** N COUNT A **troublemaker** is someone who causes trouble

Find two musical instruments on these pages. What are they made of?

or arguments. EG *The trouble-makers are a tiny minority.*

troublesome /trʌbəˈlsəm/. Someone or some- ADJ QUALIT thing that is **troublesome** causes problems or difficulties. EG *...troublesome tenants.*

trough /trɒf/, **troughs**. 1 A **trough** is a long N COUNT narrow container from which farm animals drink or eat.

2 A **trough** in a system or process is a point at N COUNT which something is low in amount. EG *The trough in consumption of electricity occurs at night.*

troupe /truːp/, **troupes**. A **troupe** is a group of N COLL actors, singers, or dancers who work together. EG *...a troupe of travelling actors.*

trousers /traʊzəz/. The form **trouser** is usually N PLURAL used before another noun. **Trousers** are a piece of clothing that covers your body from the waist downwards, and covers each leg separately. See picture at CLOTHES. EG *Claud was dressed in a pair of black trousers... He slid it gently into his trouser pocket.*

trout /traʊt/. **Trout** is both the singular and the N COUNT OR plural form. A **trout** is a kind of fish that lives in N UNCOUNT rivers.

trowel /traʊəl/, **trowels**. A **trowel** is 1 a small N COUNT garden tool with a curved, pointed blade that you use for digging small holes or for removing weeds. See picture at TOOLS. 2 a small tool with a flat, diamond-shaped blade that you use for spreading cement or plaster onto walls.

truancy /truːənsɪ/ is the practice of children N UNCOUNT staying away from school without permission. EG *The longer the period of truancy, the harder it becomes to return to school.*

truant /truːənt/, **truants**. 1 A **truant** is a child N COUNT who stays away from school without permission. EG *His elder brother had been a habitual truant.*

2 If children **play truant**, they stay away from PHRASE school without permission. EG *In my last year I played truant a lot.*

truce /truːs/, **truces**. A **truce** is an agreement N COUNT between two people or groups to stop fighting for a short time. EG *The British called a truce.*

truck /trʌk/, **trucks**. A **truck** is 1 a lorry. EG N COUNT *There was a big truck parked on the side of the* American *road... ...a truck driver.* 2 a large motor vehicle which is open at the back and is used for carrying goods, animals, or people, often on rough roads. EG *The farmer drove them out to the orchard in a rusty old truck.* 3 an open vehicle used for carrying N COUNT goods on a railway. EG *...a long truck loaded with bricks.*

trudge /trʌdʒ/, **trudges**, **trudging**, **trudged**. If V+A you **trudge** somewhere, you walk there with slow, heavy steps. EG *Michael trudged up the hill.* ▶ used ▶ N SING as a noun. EG *They set off before dawn for the long trudge home.*

true /truː/, **truer**, **truest**. 1 A story or statement ADJ QUALIT that is **true** is based on facts and on things that really have happened and are not invented. EG *The story about the murder is true... Unfortunately it was true about the illness of little Sylvie.*

2 If a dream, wish, or prediction **comes true**, it PHRASE actually happens. EG *My wish had come true.*

3 You use **true** to describe people or things that ADJ QUALIT : have all the characteristics of a particular kind of ATTRIB thing. For example, if you describe someone as a **true** American, you mean that they have all the characteristics of a typical American. EG *I suppose it takes time for true democracy to work.*

4 **True** feelings are sincere and genuine. EG *We* ADJ QUALIT : *sometimes wish to hide our true feelings... She* ATTRIB *smiled with true amusement.*

5 If you are **true to** your **word**, you do what you PHRASE had promised to do.

6 If an object is **true**, it is perfectly straight and ADJ PRED level and has a regular and correct shape. EG *The window frame isn't quite true.*

truffle /trʌfəl/, **truffles**. A **truffle** is 1 a soft N COUNT round sweet flavoured with chocolate or rum. 2 a round mushroom-like fungus which grows underground and is considered very good to eat.

truly /truːlɪ/. 1 **Truly** means completely and ADV genuinely. EG *He was now truly American... He alone truly appreciates it.*

2 If you **truly** feel something, you feel it in a ADV sincere and genuine way. EG *She didn't say what she truly felt.*

3 **Truly** also means to a very great degree. EG *He* SUBMOD *possessed a truly remarkable talent.* ● **well and** Formal **truly**: see **well**.

4 You also use **truly** to emphasize that you are ADV SEN telling the truth and are not lying. EG *And truly, coming home was the nicest part of the trip.*

5 You can write **yours truly** before your signature PHRASE at the end of a formal letter. EG *Yours truly, Desmond Burton-Cox.*

trump /trʌmp/, **trumps**. 1 **Trumps** is the suit in a N PLURAL game of cards which is chosen to have the highest value in one particular game.

2 Your **trump card** is the most powerful thing that PHRASE you can use or do in order to gain an advantage over someone. EG *Spain has at last produced her trump card and sent on the field of battle her most deadly weapon.*

trumpet /trʌmpɪt/, **trumpets**, **trumpeting**, **trumpeted**. 1 A **trumpet** is a brass musical instru- N COUNT ment that you play by blowing into it. It has three buttons that you press to get different notes. See picture at MUSICAL INSTRUMENTS.

2 When an elephant makes a sound, it **trumpets**. V OR V+O

trumpeter /trʌmpɪtə/, **trumpeters**. A **trumpet- N COUNT er** is someone who plays a trumpet.

truncate /trʌŋkeɪt/, **truncates**, **truncating**, V+O : USU PASS **truncated**. If something **is truncated**, it is made shorter. EG *The lines were truncated... The truncated corpse was stuffed into a bag.*

truncheon /trʌntʃən/, **truncheons**. A **trun- N COUNT cheon** is a short, thick stick that British policemen carry as a weapon.

trundle /trʌndəl/, **trundles**, **trundling**, **trun- dled**. 1 If a vehicle **trundles** somewhere, it moves V+A slowly. EG *The lorry trundled up the hill.*

2 If you **trundle** something somewhere, you push V+O+A or pull it along slowly on its wheels. EG *She saw him trundling the push chair along in the nearby park.*

trunk /trʌŋk/, **trunks**. 1 The **trunk** of a tree is the N COUNT large main stem from which the branches grow.

2 Your **trunk** is the main central part of your body, N COUNT but not your neck, head, legs, or arms.

3 An elephant's **trunk** is its very long nose that it N COUNT uses to lift food and water.

4 A **trunk** is also a large, strong case or box used N COUNT for storing things or for taking them on a journey.

5 The **trunk** of a car is a covered space at the back N COUNT or front in which you put luggage or other belong- American ings.

trust /trʌst/, **trusts**, **trusting**, **trusted**. 1 If you V+O **trust** someone, you believe that they are honest and will not deliberately do anything to harm you. EG *Everybody liked and trusted him... You can trust me.* ▶ used as a noun. EG *Adam could feel his* ▶ N UNCOUNT : *father's trust in him.* OFT+*in*

2 If you **trust** someone to do something, you V+O+*to*-INF believe that they will do it successfully or properly. EG *I trust you to find them... She didn't trust anyone to look after her child properly.*

3 If you **trust** someone with something important V+O+*with* or valuable, you give it to them or tell it to them. EG *She's not a person I can trust with this sort of secret... Next year I hope the company will trust me with a bigger budget.*

4 If you do not **trust** something, you feel that it is V+O : WITH not safe or reliable. EG *I don't trust fancy gimmicks* BROAD NEG *in cars... He wanted to get up and walk, but he didn't trust his legs.*

5 If you **trust** your judgement or **trust** someone's V+O

advice, you believe that it is good or right. EG *Trust your own instincts... She seems to trust his advice about people.*

6 If you say you **trust** that something is true, you mean that you hope and expect that it is true. EG *They will give you a good pension, I trust?... I trust you all like coffee.* `V+REPORT: ONLY that` `Outdated`

7 If you say '**trust** someone **to do** something', you mean that it is typical of that person to do that foolish thing. EG *Trust Julia to get the name wrong.* `PHRASE`

8 Trust is also responsibility that you are given, for example in your job, to deal with or look after important, valuable, or secret things. EG *The judge took the view that to betray a position of trust in such a manner was disgraceful.* `N UNCOUNT`

9 If you **take** something that someone tells you **on trust**, you believe it completely without checking it. `PHRASE`

10 A **trust** is a financial arrangement in which an organization keeps and invests money for someone. EG *...a lifetime interest trust.* ● If money is kept **in trust**, it is kept and invested for someone by an organization. EG *His mother's money was left in trust for him to acquire at the age of twenty-five.* `N COUNT` ● `PHRASE`

11 See also **trusting**.

trustee /trʌstiː/, **trustees**. A **trustee** is someone who has legal control of money or property that they are keeping or investing for another person. EG *Her request for money was turned down by the trustees.* `N COUNT`

trusting /trʌstɪŋ/. If you are **trusting**, you tend to believe that people are honest and sincere and do not intend to harm you. EG *Judy had an open and trusting nature.* `ADJ QUALIT`

trustworthy /trʌstwɜːðiˈ/. Someone who is **trustworthy** is reliable and responsible so that you can trust them completely. EG *He was an experienced and trustworthy travelling companion.* `ADJ QUALIT`

trusty /trʌstiˈ/. **Trusty** things and animals are considered to be reliable because they have always worked well in the past. EG *I put on my trusty overcoat... I tied up my trusty horse.* `ADJ QUALIT ATTRIB`

truth /truːθ/, **truths**. **1** The **truth** is all the facts about something, rather than things that are imagined or invented. EG *He learned the truth about Sam... He's probably telling the truth... This is not the whole truth.* `N SING: the+N`

2 If you say that there is **truth** in a statement or story, you mean that it is true, or at least partly true. EG *There is an element of truth in this argument... I could not deny the truth of this statement.* `N UNCOUNT`

3 A **truth** is an idea or principle that is generally accepted to be true. EG *It's a book that contains important truths... ...a universal truth.* `N COUNT`

4 You say **in truth** or **in all truth** when you are giving your honest opinion about something. EG *In all truth, the British people deserved something better than this.* `PHRASE`

5 You say to **tell you the truth** when you are admitting something and emphasizing that you are being honest and not hiding anything. EG *I can't remember his name, to tell you the truth.* `ADV SEN`

truthful /truːθful/. **1** Someone who is **truthful** is honest and tells the truth. EG *Many patients are more truthful when they talk to the computer than when they talk to the doctor.* ◊ **truthfully**. EG *If I ask him a question he will answer it as truthfully as he can.* `ADJ QUALIT` ◊ `ADV`

2 A statement or account that is **truthful** is true rather than invented. EG *He gave a truthful answer.* `ADJ QUALIT`

try /traɪ/, **tries, trying, tried**. **1** If you **try** to do something, you make an effort to do it because you want to do it. EG *My sister tried to cheer me up... They tried but failed... You can do it if you try... I tried hard not to think about it.* ▶ used as a noun. EG *After a few tries they gave up... It's certainly worth a try.* `V: USU+to-INF` ▶ `N COUNT`

2 To **try** and do something means to try to do it. EG `V: ONLY INF OR IMPER`

We must try and understand... Try and finish that by next Friday.

3 If you **try** for something, you make an effort to get it or achieve it. EG *The school advised Mr Denby to let his son try for university.* `V+for`

4 If you **try** something, you use it or do it in order to find out how useful, effective, or enjoyable it is. EG *I tried a different approach to the problem... Have you ever tried painting?... The fourth key he tried opened the lid... He tried his wine.* ▶ used as a noun. EG *We can give it a try and see how it looks.* `V+O OR V+-ING` ▶ `N COUNT: USU SING`

5 If you **try** a particular place or person, you go to that place or person because you think that they may be able to provide you with something that you want. EG *We tried two or three hotels, but they were full.* `V+O`

6 If you **try** a door or window, you try to open it. EG *I tried the handle, but it was locked.* `V+O`

7 When a person **is tried**, he or she has to appear in a court of law and the judge and jury listen to the evidence about a crime, and decide if the person is guilty. EG *A youth was tried in the criminal courts for stealing.* `V+O: USU PASS`

8 to **try** your **hand** at something: see **hand** ● to **try** your **luck** at something: see **luck**.

try on. If you **try on** a piece of clothing, you put it on to see if it fits you or if it looks nice. EG *She tried on her new party dress.* `PHRASAL VB: V+O+ADV`

try out. If you **try** something **out**, you test it in order to find out how useful or effective it is. EG *Oxford is trying out an idea to help working parents... It's best to try this out first on a bit of spare fabric.* `PHRASAL VB: V+O+ADV`

trying /traɪɪŋ/. Something or someone that is **trying** is difficult to deal with and makes you feel impatient or annoyed. EG *It had been a most trying experience for them.* `ADJ QUALIT`

T-shirt, T-shirts. A **T-shirt** is a piece of clothing that you wear on the top half of your body. It has short sleeves, no collar, and no buttons down the front. See picture at CLOTHES. `N COUNT`

tub /tʌb/, **tubs**. **1** A **tub** is a wide, circular container of any size. EG *...a tub big enough to hold eighteen gallons... ...tubs of lard.* `N COUNT OR N PART`

2 A **tub** is also a bath. EG *I splashed around in the tub.* `N COUNT` `American`

tuba /tjuːbə/, **tubas**. A **tuba** is a very large brass musical instrument that produces very low notes. `N COUNT`

tubby /tʌbiˈ/. Someone who is **tubby** is rather fat. EG *She was a short, tubby woman.* `ADJ QUALIT` `Informal`

tube /tjuːb/, **tubes**. **1** A **tube** is a round, hollow pipe. Tubes are often used for liquids to move along. EG *...a rubber tube fixed to the tap... He slipped the telescope into the steel tube designed for it.* `N COUNT`

2 Some long, thin, hollow parts inside your body are referred to as **tubes**. EG *...a system of breathing tubes.* `N COUNT+SUPP`

3 A **tube** of paste is a long, thin container which you squeeze in order to force the paste out through a hole in one end. EG *...a tube of toothpaste... ...tubes of glue... ...antiseptic ointment in a tube or jar.* `N COUNT OR N PART`

4 The **tube** is an underground railway, especially the one in London. EG *When I come by tube it takes about an hour.* `N SING: the+N, OR by+N`

tuberculosis /tjʊbɜːkjəˈləʊsɪs/ is a serious infectious disease that affects people's lungs and other parts of their body. `N UNCOUNT`

tubing /tjuːbɪŋ/ is plastic, rubber, or another material in the shape of a tube. EG *The cooling system runs through 300 feet of copper tubing.* `N UNCOUNT`

tuck /tʌk/, **tucks, tucking, tucked**. **1** If you **tuck** one piece of clothing into another, you push the loose ends of it inside the other piece so that it is tidy. EG *I sat up and tucked my shirt into my shorts.* `V+O+A`

2 If you **tuck** something somewhere, you put it v+o+A there so that it is safe or comfortable. EG *He tucked the shell under his arm... He found the card and tucked it under the phone.*

tuck away. 1 If you **tuck away** something such PHRASAL VB: as money, you store it in a safe place. EG *She had a* v+o+ADV *bit of money tucked away.* **2** If something **is** v+o+ADV, **tucked away**, it is in a quiet place where very few OFT PASS people go. EG *The parish church is tucked away behind the cathedral.*

tuck in. 1 If you **tuck** a child or other person **in**, PHRASAL VB: you make them comfortable in bed by straighten- v+o ing their sheets and blankets and pushing the loose +ADV/PREP ends firmly under the mattress. EG *He was asleep before I tucked him in.* **2** If you **tuck in** your shirt v+o+ADV/ or blouse, you put the loose ends of it inside your PREP trousers or skirt. EG *She buttoned up her shirt and tucked it in.* **3** If you **tuck in**, you eat something v+ADV/PREP with a lot of pleasure. EG *By the end of the holiday* Informal *she was happily tucking into whatever dishes were put in front of her.*

tuck up. If you **tuck** a child or other person **up**, PHRASAL VB: you make them comfortable in bed by straighten- v+o+ADV ing their sheets and blankets and pushing the loose ends firmly under the mattress.

Tuesday /tjuːzdiˈ/, **Tuesdays. Tuesday** is one of N UNCOUNT the seven days of the week. It is the day after OR N COUNT Monday and before Wednesday. EG *Our rugby team goes to Swansea on Tuesday.*

tuft /tʌft/, **tufts.** A **tuft** of something such as hair N COUNT or grass is a bunch of it that grows closely togeth- OR N PART er. EG *Her tiny head was covered with tufts of fair hair.*

tug /tʌg/, **tugs, tugging, tugged. 1** If you **tug** v+o OR v+at something or **tug** at it, you give it a quick pull. EG *He tugged at the handle, and it came off in his hand.* ▸ used as a noun. EG *Tom felt a tug at his* ▸ N COUNT *sleeve.*

2 A **tug** is a small, powerful boat which pulls large N COUNT ships, usually when they come into a port.

tuition /tjuːɪʃəˈn/ is the teaching of a subject, N UNCOUNT especially to one person or to a small group. EG *Her father decided she ought to have private tuition.*

tulip /tjuːlɪp/, **tulips.** A **tulip** is a brightly-coloured N COUNT garden flower that is shaped like an upside-down bell and that grows in the spring.

tumble /tʌmbəˈl/, **tumbles, tumbling, tumbled.**

1 If you **tumble**, you fall with a rolling or bouncing v:USU+A movement. EG *She pushed him and sent him tum- bling downstairs.* ▸ used as a noun. EG *She suffered* ▸ N COUNT: *a tumble running after her kite.* USU SING

2 If water **tumbles**, it flows quickly over an v:USU+A uneven surface so that it splashes and swirls a lot. EG *He could hear the water tumbling over the rocks.*

3 If you **tumble** into a situation, you suddenly get v+A into that situation without being able to stop your- self. EG *She tumbled into love... The world tumbled into the atomic age.*

tumble to. If you **tumble to** something, you PHRASAL VB: suddenly understand it or realize what is happen- v+PREP, ing. EG *What if he tumbles to what's going on?* HAS PASS

tumble dryer, tumble dryers; also spelled **tum-** N COUNT **ble drier.** A **tumble dryer** is an electric machine that dries washing quickly. You put the wet clothes inside it and it turns them over slowly while blowing hot air onto them.

tumbler /tʌmblə/, **tumblers.** A **tumbler** is a N COUNT drinking glass with straight sides.

tummy /tʌmiˈ/, **tummies.** Your **tummy** is **1** the N COUNT part of the front of your body below your waist. EG Informal *She tickled their tummies.* **2** the parts inside your body where food is digested. EG *...the rumbling of empty tummies... ...tummy upsets.*

tumour /tjuːmə/, **tumours;** spelled **tumor** in N COUNT American English. A **tumour** is a mass of diseased or abnormal cells that has grown in a person's or animal's body. EG *He was suffering from a brain tumour.*

tumult /tjuːmʌˈlt/. A **tumult** is a lot of noise N COUNT OR caused by a crowd of people shouting or doing N UNCOUNT noisy things. EG *A tumult of shots and yells could be* Formal *heard... Presently the tumult died down.*

tumultuous /tjuːmʌltjʊəs/. A **tumultuous** event ADJ CLASSIF: is very noisy, because people are very happy or ATTRIB excited. EG *When the war was over, there was a* Formal *tumultuous parade in London.*

tuna /tjuːnə/. **Tuna** is both the singular and the N UNCOUNT plural form. **Tuna** or **tuna fish** are large fish that OR N COUNT live in warm seas and are caught for food.

tune /tjuːn/, **tunes, tuning, tuned. 1** A **tune** is a N COUNT series of musical notes that occurs repeatedly in a piece of music and forms a main part of it, usually one that is pleasant or memorable. EG *The orches- tra was playing a selection of tunes from The Merry Widow.*

2 When someone **tunes** a musical instrument, they v+o adjust it so that it produces the right notes.

3 When someone **tunes** an engine or machine, v+o they adjust it so that it works well. EG *I told her the car needed tuning.*

4 If your radio or television **is tuned** to a particu- v+o:OFT+to; lar broadcasting station, or if you **tune** to that ALSO v+to station, you are listening to or watching the pro- grammes being broadcast by that station. EG *Stay tuned to Radio Desland for a further announce- ment.*

5 If a musical instrument is **in tune**, it is adjusted PHRASE so that it produces the right notes exactly. If it is **out of tune**, it does not produce the right notes. If you sing or play an instrument **in tune**, you sing or play the right notes. If you sing or play **out of tune**, you sing or play the wrong notes.

6 If you are **in tune** with a group of people, you are PHRASE in agreement or sympathy with them. If you are **out of tune**, you are not in agreement or sympathy with them. EG *His ideas are in tune with the spirit of his age.*

7 If you **change** your **tune**, you say or do some- PHRASE thing different from what you previously said or did, because your opinion has changed. EG *He soon changed his tune and started working as hard as the others.*

8 To the tune of a particular amount means to the PHRASE extent of that amount. EG *The university subsidises* Formal *its students to the tune of £100,000 a year.*

tune in. If you **tune in** to a particular radio PHRASAL VB: station, you set the controls of your radio, so that v+ADV you can listen to it. EG *He turned the dial and tuned in to Radio Paris.*

tune up. When a group of musicians **tune up**, PHRASAL VB: they adjust their instruments so that they produce v+ADV the right notes. EG *The orchestra was tuning up for its regular Sunday afternoon broadcast.*

tuneful /tjuːnful/. A piece of music that is **tuneful** ADJ QUALIT has a pleasant tune.

tunic /tjuːnɪk/, **tunics.** A **tunic** is a piece of N COUNT clothing which covers the top part of your body and reaches to your hips, thighs, or knees.

tunnel /tʌnəˈl/, **tunnels, tunnelling, tunnelled;** spelled **tunneling** and **tunneled** in American Eng- lish.

1 A **tunnel** is a long passage which has been made N COUNT under the ground, usually through a hill or under the sea. EG *Suddenly the train roared into a tunnel and everything went black.* ● **the light at the end of the tunnel**: see **light**.

2 If someone or something **tunnels** somewhere, v+A OR they make a tunnel. EG *One person suggested* v+o+A *tunnelling under the walls.*

turban /tɜːbəˈn/, **turbans.** A **turban** is a head- N COUNT covering worn by a Hindu, Muslim, or Sikh man. It consists of a long piece of cloth wound round and round his head.

turbine /tɜːbɪˈn/, **turbines.** A **turbine** is a ma- N COUNT chine or engine in which power is produced when a stream of air, gas, water, or steam makes a wheel turn round.

turbulent /tɜːˈbjəˈlənt/. **1** A **turbulent** period of ADJ QUALIT
time is one in which there is a lot of confusion and
constant change. EG ...*a period of fierce and turbu-
lent struggle*. ◊ **turbulence** /tɜːˈbjəˈləns/. EG ...*peri-* ◊ N UNCOUNT
ods of social turbulence.

2 Turbulent water or air contains currents which ADJ QUALIT
suddenly change direction or make violent circular
movements. EG ...*in the midst of turbulent seas and
clashing rocks.* ◊ **turbulence**. EG *The turbulence* ◊ N SING:
caused the plane to turn over. USU *the*+N

turf /tɜːf/, **turfs, turfing, turfed. 1 Turf** is short, N UNCOUNT
thick, even grass. EG *He was busy levelling the
ground and laying turf.*

2 When someone **turfs** an area of ground, they V+O
cover it with turf. EG *The hole was padded with
earth and turfed with strips of moss.*

turf out. If you **turf** someone **out**, you force them PHRASAL VB:
to leave a place. EG *She was turfed out of her flat...* V+O+ADV
The chief can turf them out at any time. Informal

turkey /tɜːkiˈ/, **turkeys. 1** A **turkey** is a large N COUNT
bird that is kept on a farm for its meat.

2 Turkey is the meat of a turkey. N UNCOUNT

turmoil /tɜːmɔɪl/ is a state of confusion, disorder, N UNCOUNT
or great anxiety. EG ...*his emotional turmoil... The
city was in turmoil.*

turn /tɜːn/, **turns, turning, turned. 1** When you V OR V+O:
turn or when you **turn** your head, you move your USU+A
body or your head so that you are facing in a
different direction. EG *He turned to Jan and began
to explain... She turned and walked away... They
kept turning round to smile at friends... 'You're
crying.' – 'Nonsense,' Etta said, turning away.*
▸ used as a noun. EG *He made a smart military turn,* ▸ N COUNT
clicking his heels.

2 When you **turn** something or when it **turns**, it V-ERG: USU+A
moves and faces in a different direction, or keeps
changing the direction it faces in. EG *I have turned
the TV to the wall... The wheels started to turn... I
turned the saucer over to look at the markings
underneath... She idly turned the pages of a magazine... He turned the book upside down.* ▸ used as a ▸ N COUNT
noun. EG ...*with an agile turn of the wrist.*

3 When you **turn** something such as a knob, key, or V-ERG
switch, you hold it and twist your hand in order to
open, start, or adjust something. EG *He turned the
handle and pushed open the door... Turn the gas as
low as possible.*

4 When you **turn** in a particular direction or **turn** V OR V-ERG:
a corner, you change the direction in which you OFT+A
are moving or travelling. EG *You come over a
bridge and turn sharply to the right... He turns
down a side street... Howard turns the van towards
the exit.* ▸ used as a noun. EG *The cars were waiting* ▸ N COUNT
to make the turn into the campus.

5 If you **turn** to a particular page in a book, you V+*to*
find that page. EG *Turn to page 349.*

6 If you **turn** your attention or thoughts to some- V-ERG+*to*
one or something, you start thinking about them or
discussing them. EG *I wonder if we can turn our
attention to something you mentioned earlier... His
thoughts turned to Calcutta.*

7 If you **turn** to someone, you ask for their help or V+A
advice. EG *She'd turned to him for help.*

8 When something **turns** into something else or V-ERG+A
when you **turn** it into something else, it becomes
something different. EG *If you apply more heat, the
water turns into steam... Soon her glee turned to
fear... ...a dramatist turned scriptwriter.*

9 You can use **turn** to say that a particular quality V-ERG+C
in something changes. For example, if something
turns sour, or if something else **turns** it sour, it
changes and becomes sour. EG *My hair has turned
completely grey... It will turn the water blue...
Things were turning nasty... He had just turned
fifteen.*

10 A **turn** is also a change in the way that N COUNT+SUPP
something is happening or being done. EG *In that
year things took a sharp turn for the worse...
...every twist and turn in government economic*

*policy... Employers are not happy about this turn of
events.*

11 If you do someone **a good turn**, you do some- PHRASE
thing that helps or benefits them.

12 If you refer to the **turn** of the century, you N SING:
mean the period of time including the end of the *the*+N+*of*
previous century and the beginning of the century
you are talking about. EG *These issues have preoccupied sociology since the turn of the century.*

13 If it is your **turn** to do something, you now have N COUNT
the right, chance, or duty to do it, when other USU+POSS
people have done it before you or will do it after
you. EG *It is his turn to take the children to school...
He stood in the queue waiting his turn.*

14 You use **in turn** to refer to people, things, or PHRASE
actions that are in a sequence one after the other.
EG *She went round the ward, talking to each woman
in turn... It became in turn a stable, a chapel, and a
theatre.*

15 If two or more people **take turns** or **take it in** PHRASE
turns to do something, they do it one after the
other. EG *You can take turns paying... They took
turns at the same typewriter.*

16 If you **turn** something such as a dress or bag PHRASE
inside out, you pull the inside part until it faces
outwards.

17 If something such as a system or way of life **is** PHRASE
turned upside down or **turned inside out**, it is
changed completely, causing great confusion. EG *All
the old theories about child rearing were suddenly
turned upside down... Industrial life has been
turned inside out by the computer.*

18 See also **turning**.

19 to **turn** your **back on** someone or something:
see **back**. ● to **turn a blind eye**: see **blind**. ● to
turn the tables on someone: see **table**. ● See also
about-turn.

turn against. If someone **turns against** you or PHRASAL VB:
is turned against you, they start to dislike you or V-ERG+PREP
disapprove of you. EG *They might at any time turn
against their masters... You turn everyone against
me.*

turn around. See **turn round**.

turn away. If you **turn** someone **away**, you PHRASAL VB:
reject them or send them away. EG *The college has* V+O+ADV
been forced to turn away 300 prospective students.

turn back. 1 If you **turn back** when travelling PHRASAL VB:
somewhere, you stop and return to the place you V+ADV
started from. EG *The snow started to fall, so we
turned back.* **2** If you **turn** someone **back**, you stop V+O+ADV
them travelling any farther and make them return
in the direction they came from. EG *A lot of the
convoys had been turned back at the border.*

turn down. 1 If you **turn down** someone's PHRASAL VB:
request or offer, you refuse or reject it. EG *I was* V+O+ADV
*invited to be foreman but I turned it down... I
couldn't turn him down.* **2** If you **turn down** V+O+ADV
something such as a radio or a heater, you adjust
the controls and reduce the amount of sound or
heat being produced. EG *If you are hot you can turn
the heating down.*

turn in. When you **turn in**, you go to bed. EG PHRASAL VB:
Before turning in for the night he asked for an V+ADV
early morning call. Informal

turn off. 1 If you **turn off** the road or path you PHRASAL VB:
are going along, you start going along a different V+ADV/PREP
road or path which leads away from it. EG *They
turned off the main road... Don't turn off, just go
straight ahead.* ● See also **turn-off. 2** If you **turn** V+O+ADV
off something such as a radio, light, or heater, you
move the switch or knob that controls it so that it
stops working. EG *The switch was sticking and we
couldn't turn the heat off... She turned off the tap.*

turn on. 1 If you **turn on** something such as a PHRASAL VB:
radio, light, or heater, you move the switch or knob V+O+ADV

Where would you find turn-ups?

that controls it so that it starts working. EG *Shall I
turn the fire on low?... She turned on the shower.* V+O+ADV
If someone or something **turns** you **on**, they Informal
attract you and make you feel sexually excited. EG
...if you meet someone who really turns you on. **3** If V+PREP,
someone **turns on** you, they attack you or speak HAS PASS
angrily to you. EG *She turned on the men. 'How can
you treat your daughters like this!'*

turn out. **1** If something **turns out** a particular PHRASAL VB:
way, it happens in that way. EG *Nothing ever turned* V+ADV+A
out right... The transaction turned out badly for OR *to*-INF
them... It turned out to be a sensational evening. **2**
If something **turns out** to be a particular thing, it +*to*-INF OR
is discovered to be that thing. EG *The Marvins'* REPORT:
house turned out to be an old converted barn... It ONLY *that*
turned out that the message had been intercepted.
3 If you **turn out** a light or a gas fire, you move the V+O+ADV
switch or knob that controls it so that it stops
giving out light or heat. **4** If a business or other V+ADV+O
organization **turns out** something, it produces it.
EG *Salford was turning out the type of graduate they
wanted.* **5** If you **turn** someone **out** or **turn** them V+O+ADV OR
out of a place, you force them to leave the place. V+O+ADV+
EG *...a woman who had been turned out of the* PREP
community 20 years before. **6** If you **turn out** a V+O+ADV
container, you take all its contents out. EG *Come on
everyone, turn out your pockets!* **7** If people **turn** V+ADV
out for an event or activity, they go and take part
in it or watch it. EG *Voters turned out in extraordinary numbers for the election.* **8** See also **turned
out, turnout.**

turn over. **1** If you **turn** something **over** in your PHRASAL VB:
mind, you think carefully about it. EG *Going home* V+O+ADV
*that night, Dr Renshaw turned over the facts of the
case.* **2** If you **turn** something **over** to someone, V+O+ADV
you give it to them because they have a right to it.
EG *He had refused to turn over funds that belonged
to Potter.* **3** See also **turnover.**

turn round. If you **turn** something **round**, you PHRASAL VB:
change the way in which it is expressed. EG *I can* V+O+ADV
turn it round and make it sound funny.

turn up. **1** If someone or something **turns up**, PHRASAL VB:
they arrive or appear somewhere. EG *He turned up* V+ADV
at rehearsal the next day looking awful. **2** If V-ERG+ADV
something **turns up**, it is found or discovered. EG
*You must be willing to take a job as soon as one
turns up.* **3** If you **turn up** something such as a V+O+ADV
radio or heater, you adjust the controls and increase the amount of sound or heat being produced. EG *Turn the volume control up.* **4** See also
turn-up.

turned out. You use **turned out** to describe how ADJ CLASSIF
a person is dressed. For example, someone who is +SUPP
smartly **turned out** is dressed smartly. EG *...attrac-
tive girls, well turned out and smart.*

turning /tɜːnɪŋ/, **turnings.** A **turning** is a road N COUNT
which leads away from the side of another road. EG
It's the next turning on the left.

turning point, turning points. A **turning point** N COUNT
is a time at which an event or change occurs which
affects the future of a person or thing. EG *The
turning point for the business came in 1974 when I
bought the computer... It proved to be a turning
point in his life.*

turnip /tɜːnɪp/, **turnips.** A **turnip** is a round N COUNT
vegetable with a greenish-white skin, which grows
underneath the ground.

turn-off, turn-offs. A **turn-off** is a road which N COUNT
leads away from the side of another road.

turnout /tɜːnaʊt/, **turnouts.** The **turnout** at an N COUNT
event is the number of people who go to it. EG
There was a very large turnout at the trial.

turnover /tɜːnəʊvə/. **1** The **turnover** of people in N UNCOUNT
an organization is the rate at which people leave it
and are replaced by others. EG *The group has an
extremely high turnover of members.*

2 The **turnover** of a company is the value of the N UNCOUNT
goods or services that it has sold during a particu-

lar period of time. EG *Annual turnover is about
£9,000 million.*

turntable /tɜːnteɪbəl/, **turntables.** A **turntable** N COUNT
is the flat, round part of a record player that you
put a record on when you play it.

turn-up, turn-ups. **1** The **turn-ups** of a pair of N COUNT:
trousers are the ends of the trouser legs, which are USU PLURAL
folded upwards.

2 If you describe an event as **a turn-up for the** PHRASE
books, you mean that it is very surprising or Informal
unexpected.

turpentine /tɜːpəntaɪn/ is a strong-smelling, col- N UNCOUNT
ourless liquid which is used for cleaning and for
making paint thinner.

turps /tɜːps/ is turpentine. EG *...an awful smell of* N UNCOUNT
turps and paint. Informal

turquoise /tɜːkwɔɪz, -kwɑːz/, **turquoises.** **1** Some- ADJ COLOUR
thing that is **turquoise** has a light bluish-green
colour. EG *...the warm turquoise sea.*

2 Turquoise is a light bluish-green stone that is N COUNT OR
quite valuable and is often used in jewellery. N UNCOUNT

turret /tʌrɪt/, **turrets.** A **turret** is a small, narrow N COUNT
tower on top of a larger tower or other building.

turtle /tɜːtəl/, **turtles.** A **turtle** is a large reptile N COUNT
which has a thick shell covering its body and which
lives in the sea most of the time.

tusk /tʌsk/, **tusks.** The **tusks** of an elephant, wild N COUNT
boar, or walrus are the pair of very long, pointed
teeth that it has, which are often curved.

tussle /tʌsəl/, **tussles, tussling, tussled.** A **tus-** N COUNT
sle is an energetic fight, struggle, or argument
between two people, especially about something
that they both want. EG *He was still smarting from
the tussle over the bottle.* ▸ used as a verb. EG ▸ V OR V+
...directors tussling about levels of authority. with: RECIP

tut or **tut-tut** is used in written English to repre- EXCLAM
sent a sound that you make to show that you are Written
annoyed or disapprove of something. You make
the sound by putting your tongue behind your teeth
and sucking in air.

tutor /tjuːtə/, **tutors, tutoring, tutored.** **1** A **tutor** N COUNT
is **1.1** a member of staff at a British university or
college who teaches small groups of students or
gives individual students general help and advice.
1.2 a private teacher who teaches one pupil or a
very small group of pupils, usually at the pupil's
home.

2 If someone **tutors** a person or **tutors** a subject, V OR V+O
they teach that person or subject. EG *The majority
were tutored by parents... Next year I want to tutor
A level maths... I'm tutoring at a local college.*

tutorial /tjuːtɔːrɪəl/, **tutorials.** **1** A **tutorial** is a N COUNT
regular meeting in which a tutor and a small group
of students discuss a subject as part of the students'
course.

2 Tutorial means relating to a tutor, especially ADJ CLASSIF:
one at a university or college. EG *All undergradu-* ATTRIB
ates attend a tutorial group each week.

tuxedo /tʌksiːdəʊ/, **tuxedos.** A **tuxedo** is a black N COUNT
or white jacket that men wear with a bow tie at American
formal social events.

TV /tiː viː/, **TVs. TV** is television and a **TV** is a N UNCOUNT
television set. EG *I've just been watching a film on* OR N COUNT
TV... Nicola turned on the TV.

twaddle /twɒdəl/. If you describe something that N UNCOUNT
someone says as **twaddle,** you mean that it is silly Informal
or untrue. EG *Beata was talking a load of twaddle.*

twang /twæŋ/, **twangs, twanging, twanged.** **1** A N COUNT
twang is a sound like the one made by pulling and
then releasing a tight wire. EG *...the twang of tennis
balls bouncing off tightly-strung rackets.*

2 If you **twang** a tight wire or string, or if it V-ERG
twangs, it makes a sound as it is pulled and then
released. EG *He was sitting twanging a guitar... The
bed springs twanged.*

tweed /twiːd/ is a thick woollen cloth, often woven N UNCOUNT
from different coloured threads. EG *...seats upholstered in brown tweed... He wore a tweed jacket.*

tweet /twiːt/, **tweets, tweeting, tweeted.** When a small bird **tweets**, it makes short, high-pitched sounds. `V` `Informal`

tweezers /twiːzəz/ are a small tool consisting of two narrow strips of metal joined at one end. You use tweezers for things like pulling out hairs and picking up small objects. EG *She took the glass out of the back of Farnbach's head with a pair of tweezers.* `N PLURAL`

twelfth /twelfθ/, **twelfths. 1** The **twelfth** item in a series is the one that you count as number twelve: see the entry headed NUMBER. EG *...the end of the twelfth century.* `ORDINAL`

2 A **twelfth** is one of twelve equal parts of something. `N COUNT : USU+of`

twelve /twelv/ **twelves. Twelve** is the number 12: see the entry headed NUMBER. EG *They have been married for twelve years.* `NUMBER`

twentieth /twentiˈəθ/, **twentieths. 1** The **twentieth** item in a series is the one that you count as number twenty: see the entry headed NUMBER. EG *...in the latter half of the twentieth century.* `ORDINAL`

2 A **twentieth** is one of twenty equal parts of something. EG *He agreed to pay her a twentieth of their value.* `N COUNT : USU+of`

twenty /twentiˈ/, **twenties. Twenty** is the number 20: see the entry headed NUMBER. EG *Twenty minutes later he sighted two helicopters.* `NUMBER`

twice /twaɪs/. **1** Something that happens **twice** happens two times. EG *I knocked on the door twice... The committee meets twice a year.* `ADV`

2 If one thing is **twice** as big or old as another thing, or is **twice** the size or age of another thing, it is two times as big or old as the other thing. EG *This is twice as common in France as in England... He's twice my size.* `ADV OR PREDET`

3 once or twice: see **once.** ● **to think twice:** see **think.**

twiddle /twɪdəˀl/, **twiddles, twiddling, twiddled. 1** If you **twiddle** something or **twiddle** with it, you twist it or turn it quickly using small movements of your fingers. EG *Ella sat twiddling her long, dark hair... Frank twiddled with the knobs of the radio.* `V+O OR V+with`

2 People who are bored sometimes sit **twiddling** their **thumbs.** This means that they move their thumbs around each other while their fingers are linked together. `PHRASE`

twig /twɪg/, **twigs.** A **twig** is a very small, thin branch that grows out from a main branch of a tree or bush. EG *He was busy making a little fire from twigs.* `N COUNT`

twilight /twaɪlaɪt/ is the time after sunset when it is getting dark outside. EG *You'll most likely see these animals at twilight, when they begin the night's hunt.* `N UNCOUNT`

twin /twɪn/, **twins. 1** If two people are **twins**, they have the same mother and were born on the same day. EG *The two boys looked like twins... She went to stay with her twin sister.* ● See also **identical twin.** `N COUNT`

2 You use **twin** to describe a pair of things that look the same and are close together. EG *...the twin turrets of Tower Bridge... ...a room with twin beds.* `N MOD`

twine /twaɪn/, **twines, twining, twined. 1 Twine** is strong, smooth string. EG *...a ball of twine.* `N UNCOUNT`

2 If you **twine** one thing round another, you twist or wind the first thing around the second thing. EG *...twining the rope around his legs. ...a long scarf twined around her neck.* `V-ERG+A`

twinge /twɪndʒ/, **twinges. 1** If you feel a **twinge** of an unpleasant emotion, you suddenly feel this emotion. EG *Hugh felt a twinge of fear when he saw the officer approaching... ...a twinge of guilt.* `N COUNT+SUPP`

2 A **twinge** is a sudden, sharp pain. EG *I feel a twinge in my back now and again.* `N COUNT`

twinkle /twɪŋkəˀl/, **twinkles, twinkling, twinkled. 1** If a star or a light **twinkles**, it shines with `V`

an unsteady light. EG *He could see the flashing blue lights twinkling through the haze of rain.*

2 If your eyes **twinkle**, they show that you are amused, excited, or joking. EG *The Englishman's eyes twinkled and he grinned.* ▸ used as a noun. EG *She noticed a twinkle in his eye at the suggestion.* `V` `▸ N SING`

twirl /twɜːl/, **twirls, twirling, twirled. 1** When you **twirl** something, you make it spin or twist round and round. EG *In a bored way she twirled her parasol... He stood twirling his key on a chain.* `V-ERG`

2 If you **twirl**, you spin round and round, for example when you are dancing. EG *He twirled round on his toes.* `V`

twist /twɪst/, **twists, twisting, twisted. 1** When you **twist** something or when it **twists**, you turn one end of it in one direction while holding the other end or turning it in the opposite direction. EG *Never twist or wring woollen garments... Her fingers twisted the handle of her bag.* ▸ used as a noun. EG *He gave one short twist to its neck.* `V-ERG` `▸ N COUNT`

2 When something **twists** or **is twisted**, it moves or bends into a strange shape. EG *Her features twisted into a stare of disgusted incredulity.* `V-ERG`

◇ **twisted.** EG *Hundreds of people were trapped under the twisted steel girders.* `◇ ADJ CLASSIF`

3 If you **twist** part of your body such as your head or shoulders, you turn it while keeping the rest of your body still. EG *Swing your shoulders so that you twist from side to side... She twisted round on the couch to watch him.* `V+O OR V`

4 If you **twist** part of your body such as your ankle or wrist, you injure it by turning it too sharply or in an unusual direction. EG *I twisted my ankle doing a Mexican hat dance.* `V+O`

5 If you **twist** someone's **arm**, you persuade them to do something. `PHRASE` `Informal`

6 If you **twist** something, you turn it so that it moves around in a circular direction. EG *Brody grabbed the bottle and twisted off the cap.* ▸ used as a noun. EG *She gave a lazy little twist to her parasol.* `V+O` `▸ N COUNT`

7 If you say that you can **twist** someone **round** your **little finger**, you mean that they will do anything that you want them to do. `PHRASE` `Informal`

8 If a road or river **twists**, it has a lot of sharp bends. EG *The road began to twist up past the lower slopes of a pine forest.* `V : USU+A`

9 If you **twist** something that a person has said, you change the meaning slightly. EG *You're twisting my words around.* `V+O`

10 A **twist** is also the shape that something has when it has been twisted. EG *...a shell with a spiral twist.* `N COUNT`

11 A **twist** in a story, film, or situation is an unexpected development or event, especially at the end. EG *There was an odd twist to the plot.* `N COUNT`

twisted /twɪstɪˀd/. If someone's mind or behaviour is **twisted**, it is unpleasantly abnormal. EG *He has become bitter and twisted.* `ADJ QUALIT`

twit /twɪt/, **twits.** If you call someone a **twit**, you mean that they are silly or thoughtless. EG *Don't be a twit!* `N COUNT OR VOCATIVE` `Informal`

twitch /twɪtʃ/, **twitches, twitching, twitched. 1** If you **twitch**, you make little jerky movements which you cannot control. EG *Ralph felt his lips twitch... She trembled and twitched as I touched her... ...their jerking, twitching bodies.* `V`

2 If you **twitch** something, you give it a little jerk in order to move it. EG *She twitched the curtain into place.* `V-ERG`

3 A **twitch** is a little jerky movement. EG *...twitches of the muscles.* `N COUNT`

twitter /twɪtə/, **twitters, twittering, twittered. 1** When birds **twitter**, they make a lot of short, high-pitched sounds. `V`

If you twist someone's arm, do they need a bandage?

2 If someone **twitters**, they speak very fast in a v high-pitched voice. EG *They talked all the time in high, twittering voices.*

two /tuː/, **twos**. **1 Two** is the number 2: see the NUMBER entry headed NUMBER. EG *I have been away from London for two weeks... The two boys glared at each other... For a moment or two Simon was happy.*

2 If you cut or divide something **in two**, or if it PHRASE breaks **in two**, it becomes separated into two pieces or amounts. EG *The twig snapped in two.*

two-dimensional /tuː dəmenʃəˀnəl, -ʃənəˀl/. ADJ CLASSIF Something that is **two-dimensional** is flat and in two dimensions only. EG *...a two-dimensional sheet of paper.*

two-faced. If you describe someone as **two-** ADJ QUALIT **faced**, you mean that they are not honest in the way that they behave towards other people. EG *He is a two-faced liar and an opportunist... How could she be so two-faced?*

two-way. 1 Two-way means moving in two oppo- ADJ CLASSIF : site directions. EG *...a two-way channel of communi-* ATTRIB *cation... ...two-way traffic.*

2 Two-way radios and transmitters can both send ADJ CLASSIF : and receive signals. ATTRIB

tycoon /taɪkuːn/, **tycoons**. A **tycoon** is a person N COUNT who is successful in business and so has become rich and powerful. EG *...a newspaper tycoon.*

type /taɪp/, **types, typing, typed. 1** A **type** of N COUNT+SUPP something is a class of it that has particular features in common and that belongs to a larger group of related things. EG *What type of salt do you prefer?... There are several different types of accounts... They usually test your blood type during pregnancy.*

2 If you refer to a particular thing as a **type**, you N COUNT+SUPP are thinking of it in relation to other things that have similar qualities. EG *How much longer can you do this type of work?... ...other simple problems of this type... ...a standard type of question.*

3 You can refer to someone as a particular **type** N COUNT+SUPP when you are describing the appearance or quality that they have. EG *He was good-looking, if you like the strong, dark type... ...an eccentric painter type.*

4 If you say that someone is **not** your **type**, you PHRASE mean that they are not the sort of person who you Informal find interesting or attractive.

5 If you **type** something, you use a typewriter or V+O OR V word processor to write it. EG *I typed the reply.*

◊ **typing**. EG *I had to do some typing for him...* ◊ N UNCOUNT *...typing skills.*

6 If you **type** information into a computer or word V+O : USU+A processor, you put it in by pressing keys on the keyboard. EG *The letter was typed into a word processor.*

7 Type is the size or style of printing that is used, N UNCOUNT for example, in a book or newspaper. EG *The declaration was proclaimed in type four inches deep on the front page.*

type up. If you **type up** your ideas, notes, or PHRASAL VB : handwritten text, you produce a typed form of it. EG V+O+ADV *After thinking about it, she typed it up, then we both read it.*

typecast /taɪpkɑːst/, **typecasts, typecasting.** The form **typecast** is used in the present tense and is also the past tense and past participle.

If actors or actresses **are typecast**, they play the V+O : USU PASS same type of character in every play or film that they are in. EG *He refused to be typecast as the loser.*

typewriter /taɪpraɪtə/, **typewriters**. A **type-** N COUNT **writer** is a machine that you use to write things in print. It has a series of keys that you press in order to write the letters, numbers, or other characters on the paper.

typewritten /taɪprɪtəˀn/. Something that is **type-** ADJ CLASSIF **written** has been typed on a typewriter or a word processor. EG *His notes were typewritten.*

typhoid /taɪfɔɪd/ is an infectious disease that N UNCOUNT produces fever and can cause death.

typhoon /taɪfuːn/, **typhoons**. A **typhoon** is a very N COUNT violent storm in the western Pacific.

typical /tɪpɪkəˀl/. **1** Something that is **typical** of a ADJ QUALIT : particular type of thing shows the most usual OFT+*of* characteristics of that type. EG *It was typical tropical weather... Louisa is typical of many young women who attempt suicide.*

2 Behaviour that is **typical** of someone is their ADJ QUALIT : most usual behaviour. EG *He crushed the beetle* OFT+*of* *deliberately, which is very typical of him.*

typically /tɪpɪkəˀliˀ/. **1** You use **typically** to say ADV OR that something usually happens in the way that you ADV SEN are describing. EG *She typically handles less than a dozen accounts at a time.*

2 You also use **typically** to say that something SUBMOD shows all the most usual characteristics or behaviour of a particular type of thing. EG *...this group of typically American students.*

typify /tɪpɪfaɪ/, **typifies, typifying, typified. 1** If V+O something **typifies** a situation or a thing, it is characteristic of that situation or thing, and shows what it is like. EG *Modern industrial society is typified by these large-scale organizations.*

2 If someone **typifies** a particular type of person V+O or attitude, they show all the most usual characteristics of that person or attitude. EG *He typified the old Liberalism of Samuel Smiles.*

typist /taɪpɪst/, **typists**. A **typist** is someone N COUNT whose job is typing, usually in an office.

tyrannical /tɪrænɪkəˀl/. A ruler, government, or ADJ QUALIT organization that is **tyrannical** acts cruelly and unjustly towards the people who they control.

tyranny /tɪrəniˀ/ is cruel and unjust rule by a N UNCOUNT person or small group of people who have absolute power over everyone else in their country or state. EG *They came here to escape political tyranny.*

tyrant /taɪrənt/, **tyrants**. A **tyrant** is a ruler who N COUNT has absolute power over other people, and who uses this power cruelly and unjustly.

tyre /taɪə/, **tyres**; spelled **tire** in American Eng- N COUNT lish. A **tyre** is a thick ring of rubber which is fitted round each wheel of a vehicle such as a car or bicycle, and which is usually filled with air. See pictures at BICYCLE and CAR. EG *When he braked a tyre burst and the car swung off the road.*

typewriter

U u

U, u /juː/, **U's, u's.** U is the twenty-first letter of the English alphabet. · N COUNT

ubiquitous /juːbɪkwɪtəs/. You say that something is **ubiquitous** when it seems to be everywhere. EG ...the ubiquitous white dust of Athens... ...the ubiquitous intelligence service. · ADJ QUALIT · Formal

udder /ʌdə/, **udders.** A cow's **udder** is the part of its body that hangs loosely between its legs and produces milk. · N COUNT

UFO /juː ɛf əʊ, juːfəʊ/, **UFOs.** A UFO is an object seen in the sky or landing on earth which cannot be identified and which some people believe to be a spaceship from another planet. **UFO** is an abbreviation for 'unidentified flying object'. · N COUNT

ugh is used in writing to represent the sound that people make when they think that something is unpleasant, horrible, or disgusting. EG Your clothes are filthy and your hair too – ugh, you're awful. · EXCLAM

ugly /ʌglɪ/, **uglier, ugliest. 1** Someone or something that is **ugly** is very unattractive and unpleasant to look at. EG She really was frightfully ugly... This is the ugliest dress I've ever worn. · ADJ QUALIT

2 You describe a situation as **ugly** when it is very unpleasant, usually because it involves violence or aggression. EG A couple of ugly incidents occurred, and one man was killed. · ADJ QUALIT

uh huh is used in writing to represent a sound that people make when they are agreeing with you, or when they want to show that they understand what you are saying, or when they are answering 'yes'. EG 'Did you know he was rich?' – 'Uh huh. It said so in the paper.' · CONVENTION · Informal

UK /juː keɪ/. The UK consists of Great Britain and Northern Ireland. **UK** is an abbreviation for 'United Kingdom'. · N PROPER : the+N

ulcer /ʌlsə/, **ulcers.** An **ulcer** is a sore area on your skin or inside your body. Ulcers are painful and sometimes bleed. EG ...stomach ulcers. · N COUNT

ulterior /ʌltɪərɪə/. If someone has an **ulterior** motive for doing something, they do not show their real reason for doing it, because they think people would not approve of it. EG I assure you there was no ulterior motive in my suggestion. · ADJ CLASSIF : ATTRIB

ultimate /ʌltɪmə't/. **1** You use **ultimate** to describe **1.1** the final result of a long and complicated series of events. EG He knew this action was necessary for the ultimate success of the revolution. **1.2** the most important or powerful thing of a particular kind. EG Parliament retains the ultimate authority to dismiss the government... We must keep in mind the ultimate goal. · ADJ CLASSIF : ATTRIB

2 You use the expression **the ultimate in** to say that something is the best or most advanced thing of its kind. EG ...the ultimate in luxury. · PHRASE

ultimately /ʌltɪmə't lɪ/. **1 Ultimately** means finally, after a long and complicated series of events. EG Elections ultimately produced a Communist victory... Ultimately they did get the police to come. · ADV

2 You also use **ultimately** to emphasize that what you are saying is the most important point in a discussion or argument. EG Ultimately, the problems are not scientific but moral... Isn't it ultimately the fault of the universities? · ADV SEN

ultimatum /ʌltɪmeɪtəm/, **ultimatums.** An **ultimatum** is a warning that you give to someone which states that they must act in a particular way, otherwise you will take action against them. EG Belgium rejected the ultimatum and war was declared... He gave her an ultimatum to leave. · N COUNT · Formal

ultra- is used to form adjectives that describe someone or something as having a quality to an · PREFIX

extreme degree. For example, someone who is ultra-intelligent is extremely intelligent. EG ...ultra-sophisticated equipment... ...an ultra-modern building.

ultraviolet /ʌltrəvaɪələ't/. **Ultraviolet** light or radiation causes your skin to become darker in colour after you have been in sunlight. Large amounts of it can be harmful. EG ...the ultraviolet rays of the sun. · ADJ CLASSIF : ATTRIB

um /əm, ʌm/ is used in writing to represent a sound that people make when they are hesitating, usually because they have not decided what to say next. EG What can be done about it? Well, um, the first thing you can do is colour it.

umbilical cord /ʌmbɪlɪkə'l kɔːd/, **umbilical cords.** The **umbilical cord** is the tube which connects a baby to its mother before it is born and through which the baby receives oxygen and nutrients. · N COUNT

umbrella

umbrella /ʌmbrɛlə/, **umbrellas. 1** An **umbrella** is an object which you carry to protect yourself from the rain. It consists of a long stick with a folding frame covered in cloth. EG Put your umbrella up. It's going to rain. · N COUNT

2 An **umbrella** is also a device like a large umbrella that protects you from the hot sun when you are sitting or lying outdoors. EG Other hotel guests sat under striped umbrellas. · N COUNT

3 Umbrella describes a single organization or idea that contains or includes a lot of different organizations or ideas. EG Corn is an umbrella word for wheat, barley and oats. · ADJ CLASSIF : ATTRIB

umpire /ʌmpaɪə/, **umpires, umpiring, umpired. 1** In games such as cricket and tennis, the **umpire** is the person whose job is to make sure that the game is played fairly and that the rules are not broken. EG The umpires declared that play should start. · N COUNT

2 If you **umpire** a game, you are the umpire. · V+O OR V

umpteen /ʌmp'tiːn/ means very many. EG They recounted umpteen tales of unfair treatment. · NUMBER · Informal

umpteenth /ʌmp'tiːnθ/ describes something which has happened many times before. EG I went to the pictures and saw 'Hello Dolly' for the umpteenth time. · ORDINAL · Informal

UN /juː ɛn/. The UN is an organization which most countries in the world belong to, and which tries to encourage international peace, co-operation, and friendship. **UN** is an abbreviation for 'United Nations'. · N PROPER : the+N

un-. 1 un- is added to the beginning of many adjectives, adverbs, and nouns in order to form · PREFIX words with the opposite meaning. For example, if something is unavailable, it is not available. EG *...undemocratic regimes... ...an uncomfortable chair... She may unintentionally have caused suffering... He regretted his unkindness.*

2 When a verb describes a process, **2.1** you can add PREFIX un- to the beginning of it in order to form a verb describing the reverse process. EG *He unlocked the door... She untied the rope and rowed back to shore.* **2.2** you can add un- to the past participle in order to form an adjective indicating that the process has not been carried out. For example, if your hair is uncombed, it has not been combed. EG *Everywhere hedges remain uncut... ...unconvicted prisoners.*

unabashed /ʌnəbæʃt/. If you are **unabashed**, you ADJ CLASSIF are not ashamed, embarrassed, or discouraged by something that has been done or said. EG *The little old lady seemed unabashed.*

unabated /ʌnəbeɪtɪ²d/. If something continues ADV OR **unabated**, it continues without any reduction in ADJ CLASSIF intensity or amount. EG *The war at sea continued unabated... They continued with unabated enthusiasm.*

unable /ʌneɪbə⁰l/. If you are **unable** to do some- ADJ PRED thing, you cannot do it, for example because you do +to-INF not have the necessary skill or knowledge, or because you do not have enough time or money. EG *Many people were unable to read or write... He was unable to sleep at night because of his anxiety.*

unacceptable /ʌnə³ksɛptəbə⁰l/. If you describe ADJ QUALIT something as **unacceptable**, you mean that you strongly disapprove of it and feel that you cannot allow it to continue. EG *That sort of behaviour was completely unacceptable... ...an unacceptable violation of personal freedom.* ◊ **unacceptably.** EG ◊ ADV *Their standard of performance has been unacceptably poor on several recent occasions.*

unaccompanied /ʌnəkʌmpənɪd/. **1** If you are ADJ CLASSIF **unaccompanied**, you are alone. EG *I wouldn't leave him for a moment unaccompanied.*

2 An **unaccompanied** song is written to be sung ADJ CLASSIF by singers alone, without musical instruments.

unaccountable /ʌnəkaʊntəbə⁰l/. **1** Something ADJ QUALIT that is **unaccountable** does not seem to have any Formal sensible explanation. EG *For some unaccountable reason, I put the letter in the wrong envelope... I suffer every now and then from unaccountable headaches.* ◊ **unaccountably.** EG *Elaine felt unac-* ◊ ADV OR *countably shy.* ADV SEN

2 If you are **unaccountable**, you are not respon- ADJ PRED : sible to anyone for your actions and you do not OFT+*to* have to explain to anyone why you behave in the Formal way you do. EG *Many of our important decision-makers are unaccountable to the public.*

unaccounted /ʌnəkaʊntɪ²d/. If something, espe- PHRASE cially money, is **unaccounted for**, you do not know where it is or what has happened to it. EG *The remaining 30 per cent were unaccounted for.*

unaccustomed /ʌnəkʌstəmd/. **1** If you are unac- ADJ PRED+*to* **customed** to something, you are not used to it. EG *They were unaccustomed to wearing suits and ties.*

2 If you describe someone's behaviour or experi- ADJ CLASSIF : ences as **unaccustomed**, you mean that they do ATTRIB not usually behave like this or have experiences of this kind. EG *Judy cried with unaccustomed vehemence, 'Yes, I know!'... ...his unaccustomed and unwelcome leisure time.*

unacquainted /ʌnəkweɪntɪ²d/. If you are unac- ADJ PRED : **quainted** with something, you do not know about it OFT+*with* or you have not had much experience of it. EG *...people who are unacquainted with feminist ideas.*

unadulterated /ʌnədʌltəreɪtɪ²d/. **1** Something ADJ CLASSIF that is **unadulterated** is completely pure and has had nothing added to it. EG *...unadulterated spring water.*

2 You can also use **unadulterated** to emphasize a ADJ CLASSIF : quality, especially a bad quality. EG *It was going to* ATTRIB *be unadulterated misery from now on.*

unaffected /ʌnə³fɛktɪ²d/. **1** Something that is un- ADJ PRED **affected** by a particular thing is not changed in OFT+*by* any way by it. EG *Jobs have been largely unaffected by automation... This acid is unaffected by heat.*

2 Someone who is **unaffected** is natural and ADJ QUALIT genuine in their behaviour, and not pretentious. EG *He was simple and unaffected and obviously sincere.*

unaided /ʌneɪdɪ²d/. If you do something **unaided**, ADV AFTER VB, you do it without help from anyone or anything OR ADJ CLASSIF else. EG *He could not possibly have got through the window unaided... The baby was sitting up unaided.*

unalterable /ʌnɒltə⁰rəbə⁰l, ʌnɔːl- /. Something ADJ CLASSIF that is **unalterable** cannot be changed. EG *She had reached an unalterable decision to marry him.*

unaltered /ʌnɒltəd, ʌnɔːl-/. Something that is un- ADJ CLASSIF **altered** has not been changed and is therefore still in its original form. EG *The Great Hall survives relatively unaltered... In a few places conditions remain unaltered.*

unambiguous /ʌnæmbɪgjuː²əs/. If something spo- ADJ QUALIT ken or written is **unambiguous**, it can only be interpreted or understood in one way. EG *The rules are quite unambiguous... He made an unambiguous statement of his beliefs.*

unanimous /juːnænɪməs/. When a group of peo- ADJ CLASSIF ple are **unanimous**, they all agree about something. EG *The critics have been almost unanimous in their dislike of this film... We reached unanimous agreement.* ◊ **unanimously.** EG *The union voted* ◊ ADV *unanimously to boycott foreign imports.* ◊ **unanimity** /juːnə³nɪmɪ¹tiː/. EG *About this there is* ◊ N UNCOUNT *unanimity among the sociologists.*

unannounced /ʌnənaʊnst/. If an action or event ADJ CLASSIF, OR is **unannounced**, it happens unexpectedly and ADV AFTER VB without anyone having being told about it beforehand. EG *Forgive me for this unannounced intrusion... Churchill arrived unannounced.*

unanswered /ʌnɑːnsəd/. Something that is unan- ADJ CLASSIF **swered** has not been answered. EG *Many questions were left unanswered... ...unanswered letters.*

unarmed /ʌnɑːmd/. If you are **unarmed**, you are ADJ CLASSIF not carrying any weapons. EG *They were shooting* OR ADV *unarmed peasants... He walked alone and unarmed into the hills... Girls were practising unarmed combat.*

unashamed /ʌnəʃeɪmd/. If someone behaves in ADJ CLASSIF, an **unashamed** way, they openly do things that ATTRIB other people find rude or shocking. EG *He looked at her with unashamed curiosity... ...their unashamed pursuit of money.*

unassuming /ʌnəsjuː²mɪŋ/. An **unassuming** per- ADJ QUALIT son is modest and quiet and does not wish to be noticed by other people.

unattached /ʌnətætʃt/. **1** If something is unat- ADJ CLASSIF : **tached** to something else, it is not formally con- USU+*to* nected with it. EG *The centre is unattached to any hospital or clinic.*

2 An **unattached** person is not married and is not ADJ CLASSIF having a steady relationship. EG *A lot of unattached women seem to be very happy.*

unattended /ʌnətɛndɪ²d/. When people or things ADJ CLASSIF are **unattended**, they are not being watched or looked after. EG *Most of the casualties were lying unattended... ...unattended baggage.*

unattractive /ʌnətræktɪv/. **1** Unattractive peo- ADJ QUALIT ple and things are unpleasant in their appearance or behaviour and are therefore not liked or wanted. EG *He was physically unattractive... ...unattractive dwellings... ...her unattractive coyness.*

2 If you say that something such as an idea or ADJ QUALIT proposal is **unattractive**, you mean that people do not like it and do not want to be involved with it. EG *Being unemployed is a most unattractive prospect.*

unauthorized /ʌnɔːθəraɪzd/; also spelled un- ADJ CLASSIF **authorised**. If an action is **unauthorized**, it is done without official permission. EG *She made several unauthorized visits to the laboratory.*

unavoidable /ˌʌnəˈvɔɪdəbəl/. If something is **un-** ADJ CLASSIF
avoidable, it cannot be avoided or prevented. EG
This delay was unavoidable.

unaware /ˌʌnəˈweə/. If you are **unaware** of some- ADJ PRED :
thing, you do not know about it. EG *I was unaware* OFT+*of*
that he had any complaints... She seemed quite OR REPORT
unaware of the other people sitting around her.

unawares /ˌʌnəˈweəz/. If something **catches** you PHRASE
unawares or **takes** you **unawares**, it happens
when you are not expecting it and are not prepared for it. EG *It's a change like this that catches
you unawares.*

unbalanced /ˌʌmˈbælənst/. 1 If someone is **un-** ADJ QUALIT
balanced, they are slightly mad. EG *The strain of
the past few days has made you mentally unbalanced.*

2 If an account of something is **unbalanced**, it is ADJ QUALIT
unfair or inaccurate because it emphasizes some
things and ignores others. EG *She complained that
the magazine had published an unbalanced report.*

unbearable /ˌʌmˈbeərəbəl/. If something is **un-** ADJ QUALIT
bearable, it is so unpleasant, painful, or upsetting
that you feel unable to accept it or deal with it. EG
*The heat was unbearable... I found it unbearable to
be the centre of attention.* ◊ **unbearably**. EG *It was* ◊ SUBMOD
unbearably painful.

unbeatable /ˌʌmˈbiːtəbəl/. If you say that some- ADJ CLASSIF
thing is **unbeatable**, you mean that it is the best
thing of its kind. EG *The food here is absolutely
unbeatable.*

unbelievable /ˌʌmbɪˈliːvəbəl/. 1 If you say that ADJ QUALIT
something is **unbelievable**, you mean that it is
extremely good, large, or surprising. EG *They work
with unbelievable speed... I went to her house in
Henley: it was unbelievable.*

2 If you say that an idea or theory is **unbelievable**, ADJ CLASSIF
you mean that it is so unlikely or so illogical that
you cannot believe it. EG *There are many unbelievable aspects to this theory.*

unbelievably /ˌʌmbɪˈliːvəbli/. 1 You use **unbe-** ADV SEN
lievably when you are commenting on something
that you are describing, in order to say that it is
very surprising. EG *Unbelievably, the door in the
wall opened.*

2 You also use **unbelievably** to emphasize that SUBMOD
something is extremely good, large, or surprising.
EG *...unbelievably beautiful scenery... He has been
unbelievably successful.*

unbeliever /ˌʌmbɪˈliːvə/, **unbelievers**. People N COUNT
are referred to as **unbelievers** when they do not
believe in a particular religion.

unborn /ˌʌmˈbɔːn/. An **unborn** child has not yet ADJ CLASSIF
been born and is still inside its mother's womb. EG
*The doctor tried desperately to save her and her
unborn child.*

unbroken /ˌʌmˈbrəʊkən/. If something is **unbro-** ADJ CLASSIF
ken, it is continuous or complete and has not been
interrupted or broken. EG *The silence continued,
unbroken.*

unbutton /ˌʌmˈbʌtən/, **unbuttons, unbuttoning,** V+O
unbuttoned. When you **unbutton** something that
you are wearing, you unfasten the buttons on it. EG
He unbuttoned his coat.

uncalled-for. If you say that a remark was ADJ QUALIT
uncalled-for, you mean that it was unkind or
unfair and should not have been made. EG *That last
remark was uncalled-for.*

uncanny /ʌŋˈkæni/, **uncannier, uncanniest**. If ADJ QUALIT
you say that something is **uncanny**, you mean that
it is strange and hard to explain. EG *The owl strikes
at its prey with uncanny accuracy... The silence
was uncanny.*

uncaring /ʌŋˈkeərɪŋ/. If you say that someone is ADJ QUALIT
uncaring, you mean that they do not care about
other people's suffering. EG *We now know how
uncaring and selfish the landlords were.*

unceasing /ʌnˈsiːsɪŋ/. If something is **unceasing**, ADJ CLASSIF
it continues without stopping. EG *...a profound, un-*

ceasing misery... The noise of the traffic was loud
and unceasing.

unceremonious /ˌʌnsɛrɪˈməʊnɪəs/. If something
that you do is **unceremonious**, 1 you do it in a ADJ CLASSIF
relaxed and informal way. EG *She treated him with
unceremonious friendliness.* **2** you do it suddenly ADJ QUALIT
and rudely. ◊ **unceremoniously**. EG *The door was* ◊ ADV
unceremoniously pushed open.

uncertain /ʌnˈsɜːtən/. **1** If you are **uncertain** ADJ QUALIT
about something, you do not know what to do. EG
She hesitated, uncertain whether to continue.
◊ **uncertainly**. EG *They looked at each other* ◊ ADV
uncertainly.

2 If something in the future is **uncertain**, nobody ADJ QUALIT
knows what will happen. EG *The outcome of his
case was uncertain.*

3 If the cause of something is **uncertain**, nobody ADJ CLASSIF
knows what caused it. EG *The cause of death
remains uncertain.*

uncertainty /ʌnˈsɜːtənti/, **uncertainties**. **1** N UNCOUNT
When there is **uncertainty**, people do not know
what will happen or what they should do. EG *...the
continued uncertainty about the future of the aircraft industry.*

2 Uncertainties are things, especially future N COUNT :
events, which no one is certain about. EG *The* USU PLURAL
industry is still plagued by economic uncertainties.

unchallenged /ʌnˈtʃæləndʒd/. When something ADJ CLASSIF
is **unchallenged** or goes **unchallenged**, people OR ADV
accept it without asking questions about whether it
is right or wrong. EG *His authority was secure and
unchallenged... Her decisions on these matters
went unchallenged.*

uncharacteristic /ˌʌnkærəktəˈrɪstɪk/. Some- ADJ QUALIT
thing that is **uncharacteristic** of someone is not
typical of them. EG *He jumped out of the car with
uncharacteristic agility.*

uncharitable /ʌnˈtʃærɪtəbəl/. **Uncharitable** re- ADJ QUALIT
marks, thoughts, or behaviour are unkind or unfair.
EG *I hope I'm not being too uncharitable, but he
really is very boring.*

unchecked /ʌnˈtʃekt/. You say that something ADJ CLASSIF, OR
undesirable is **unchecked** when it keeps growing ADV AFTER VB
without anyone trying to stop it. EG *...the danger of
unchecked military expansion... Such horrors could
not be allowed to continue unchecked.*

uncivilized /ʌnˈsɪvɪlaɪzd/; also spelled **uncivi-**
lised. **1** You say that someone is **uncivilized** or ADJ QUALIT
that their behaviour is **uncivilized** when they
behave in an unacceptable way, for example by
being very cruel or very rude. EG *The conditions in
which we keep them are uncivilized and inhumane.*

2 If you do something at an **uncivilized** hour, you ADJ QUALIT
do it very early in the morning when most people Informal
are in bed and asleep. EG *We had to be at the
ground at a fairly uncivilized hour.*

uncle /ˈʌŋkəl/, **uncles**. Your **uncle** is the brother N COUNT
of your mother or father, or the husband of your
aunt. EG *...Uncle Harold.*

unclean /ʌnˈkliːn/. **1** Something that is **unclean** is ADJ QUALIT
dirty and likely to cause disease. EG *A major cause
of illness in the Third World is unclean water.*

2 People sometimes use **unclean** to describe prac- ADJ CLASSIF
tices which are unacceptable according to their
religion. EG *Pigs are considered unclean and must
not be eaten.*

unclear /ʌnˈklɪə/. **1** If something is **unclear**, **1.1** it ADJ PRED
is not obvious. EG *The reasons for this remained
unclear.* **1.2** it has been badly explained or written ADJ QUALIT
in a confusing way, so that you cannot understand
it properly. EG *The instruction books are badly
written, unclear, and boring.*

2 If you are **unclear** about something, you do not ADJ PRED
understand it properly. EG *I'm still very unclear* OFT+*about*
about what he has actually done.

What grammatical word is explained on these
pages?

uncomfortable /ʌŋˈkʌmftəbəˈl/. 1 If you are ADJ QUALIT **uncomfortable**, you are not physically content and relaxed, and feel slight pain or discomfort. EG *I was cramped and uncomfortable in the back seat.* ◊ **uncomfortably**. EG *...sitting uncomfortably on* ◊ ADV *the rock... My shirt was uncomfortably tight.*

2 You can also say that you are **uncomfortable** ADJ QUALIT when you are slightly worried or embarrassed and not relaxed and confident. EG *Her presence made him uncomfortable... He seemed uncomfortable with people who were aggressive.* ◊ **uncomfortably**. EG *She smiled across the room* ◊ ADV *at him uncomfortably.*

3 If a room or a piece of furniture is **uncomfort-** ADJ QUALIT **able**, you do not feel comfortable when you are in it or using it. EG *They were sitting on uncomfortable chairs.*

4 If a situation or fact is **uncomfortable**, it is ADJ QUALIT difficult to accept and causes problems. EG *This kind of life may prove disruptive and uncomfortable... ...the uncomfortable truth.*

uncommitted /ʌŋˈkəmɪtɪˈd/. 1 If you are **uncom-** ADJ CLASSIF **mitted**, you do not support either of the sides in a dispute. EG *...their uncommitted position in the war.*

2 If you are **uncommitted** to a particular group or ADJ PRED+to belief, you do not support it. EG *Maxwell was uncommitted to the Cooperative.*

uncommon /ʌŋˈkɒmən/. 1 If something is **un-** ADJ PRED **common**, it does not happen often, or it is not often seen. EG *...uncommon birds... Frost and snow are not uncommon during these months.*

2 You also use **uncommon** to describe a quality ADJ CLASSIF : that is unusually large in degree. EG *...a general of* ATTRIB *uncommon intelligence and subtlety.* ◊ **uncommonly**. EG *Marcus was uncommonly gift-* ◊ SUBMOD ed.

uncommunicative /ʌŋˈkəmjuːnɪkətɪv/. An **un-** ADJ QUALIT **communicative** person does not talk to other people very much and is unwilling to express opinions or give information. EG *Roger, uncommunicative by nature, said nothing.*

uncomplicated /ʌŋˈkɒmplɪkeɪtɪˈd/. **Uncompli-** ADJ QUALIT **cated** things are simple and straightforward. EG *The play had an uncomplicated plot.*

uncomprehending /ʌŋˈkɒmprɪhendɪŋ/. If some- ADJ CLASSIF one is **uncomprehending**, they do not understand what is happening or what someone else has said. EG *Bonasera turned to his uncomprehending wife and explained.*

uncompromising /ʌŋˈkɒmprəmaɪzɪŋ/. When ADJ QUALIT people are **uncompromising**, they are determined not to change their opinions or aims in any way. EG *He was an uncompromising opponent of the Great War... ...an uncompromising commitment to the equality of all races.*

unconcealed /ʌŋˈkəˈnsiːld/. If something such as ADJ CLASSIF an emotion is **unconcealed**, you make no attempt to hide it. EG *Mary gazed with unconcealed curiosity... ...her unconcealed dislike for me.*

unconcerned /ʌŋˈkənsɜːnd/. If someone is **un-** ADJ QUALIT **concerned** about something, they are not interested in it or not worried about it. EG *We have suddenly become an insular people, unconcerned with the underdeveloped countries... You seem remarkably unconcerned.*

unconditional /ʌŋˈkəndɪʃəˈnəl, -ʃənəˈl/. Some- ADJ CLASSIF thing that is **unconditional** has no conditions or limitations attached to it. EG *...unconditional surrender... They offered unconditional support.* ◊ **unconditionally**. EG *The laws of the State had to* ◊ ADV *be obeyed unconditionally.*

unconfirmed /ʌŋˈkəˈnfɜːmd/. If a report or a ADJ CLASSIF rumour is **unconfirmed**, there is not yet any definite proof that it is true.

unconnected /ʌŋˈkəˈnektɪˈd/. If one thing is **un-** ADJ CLASSIF **connected** with another, or if two things are **unconnected**, the two things are not related to each other in any way. EG *The two incidents were*

unconnected... *The allergy may be due to causes quite unconnected with food.*

unconscious /ʌŋˈkɒnʃəs/. 1 Someone who is **un-** ADJ CLASSIF **conscious** is in a state which is similar to sleep, as a result of something such as an accident or an injury. EG *The blow knocked him unconscious... She lay unconscious on the table.*

2 If you are **unconscious** of something that has ADJ PRED : been said or done, you are not aware of it. EG OFT+of *Dekker seemed totally unconscious of the insult.*

3 If feelings or attitudes are **unconscious**, you are ADJ CLASSIF not aware that you have them, but they show in the way that you behave. EG *...unconscious feelings of envy.* ◊ **unconsciously**. EG *They can't help re-* ◊ ADV *senting the baby unconsciously.*

4 Your **unconscious** is the part of your mind N SING which contains feelings and ideas that you do not know about or cannot control. EG *...images retrieved from the unconscious.*

unconstitutional /ʌŋˈkɒnstɪtjuːʃəˈnəl, -ʃənəˈl/. If ADJ CLASSIF something is **unconstitutional**, it is against the rules of an organization or political system. EG *They denied that a referendum would be unconstitutional... ...unconstitutional strikes.*

uncontrollable /ʌŋˈkəˈntrəʊləbəˈl/. If something ADJ CLASSIF such as an emotion is **uncontrollable**, you can do nothing to prevent it or control it. EG *...the sudden uncontrollable note of fear in her voice.* ◊ **uncontrollably**. EG *He found himself giggling* ◊ ADV *quite uncontrollably.*

uncontrolled /ʌŋˈkəˈntrəʊld/. 1 If someone's be- ADJ CLASSIF haviour is **uncontrolled**, they cannot prevent it or change it. EG *He was letting out loud uncontrolled shrieks... ...uncontrolled laughter.*

2 If a situation or activity is **uncontrolled**, nobody ADJ CLASSIF is responsible for controlling it and preventing it from becoming harmful. EG *...the uncontrolled use of pesticides... ...uncontrolled building development.*

unconventional /ʌŋˈkəˈnvenʃəˈnəl, -ʃənəˈl/. If ADJ QUALIT someone is **unconventional**, they do not behave in the same way as most other people in their society. EG *...an unconventional clergyman... ...her unconventional dress... ...unconventional ways of writing.*

unconvinced /ʌŋˈkənvɪnst/. If you are **uncon-** ADJ PRED **vinced** about something, you are not at all certain that it is true or right. EG *I remained unconvinced by what she had said.*

unconvincing /ʌŋˈkənvɪnsɪŋ/. If arguments or ADJ QUALIT reasons are **unconvincing**, you do not believe that they are true or valid. EG *I find this argument unconvincing... He offered an unconvincing excuse.*

uncooked /ʌŋˈkʊkt/. **Uncooked** meat or other ADJ CLASSIF food has not yet been cooked. EG *There were three uncooked chops on the kitchen table.*

uncooperative /ʌŋˈkəʊɒpəˈrətɪv/. If someone is ADJ QUALIT **uncooperative**, they make no effort at all to help other people. EG *He is deliberately being uncooperative.*

uncoordinated /ʌŋˈkəʊɒːdɪneɪtɪˈd/. If you are ADJ QUALIT **uncoordinated**, your movements are jerky and you cannot control them properly. EG *He's careless, clumsy, and uncoordinated... ...the baby's uncoordinated movements.*

uncork /ʌŋˈkɔːk/, **uncorks**, **uncorking**, **un-** V+O **corked**. When you **uncork** a bottle, you pull the cork out of it.

uncountable noun, **uncountable nouns**. In N COUNT grammar, an **uncountable noun** is a noun which cannot be treated as countable, and so has only one form. In this dictionary uncount nouns are labelled N UNCOUNT in the Extra Column. See the entry headed NOUNS for more information.

uncouth /ʌŋˈkuːθ/. Someone who is **uncouth** be- ADJ QUALIT haves in a bad-mannered, unpleasant, and unacceptable way. EG *...an uncouth soldier... She may embarrass you with her uncouth behaviour.*

uncover /ʌŋˈkʌvə/, **uncovers**, **uncovering**, **un-** V+O **covered**. 1 If you **uncover** something that has been secret, you find out about it. EG *...helping to uncover illegal activity... Another plot to assassinate General de Gaulle was uncovered.*

2 To **uncover** something also means to remove a v+o cover from it, so that it can be seen. EG *She uncovered her face.*

uncovered /ʌŋˈkʌvəd/. Something that is **uncov-** ADJ CLASSIF **ered** does not have a cover over it. EG *...uncovered food... ...their uncovered heads.*

uncritical /ʌŋˈkrɪtɪkəˀl/. If you are **uncritical**, ADJ CLASSIF you are unable or unwilling to judge whether someone or something is good or bad. EG *...uncritical acceptance of traditional values... ...an uncritical audience... ...their uncritical attitude.*

undaunted /ʌnˈdɔːntɪˀd/. If you are **undaunted**, ADJ CLASSIF you are not discouraged by disappointing things Formal that have happened to you. EG *Undaunted by his first setbacks, he decided to try once more to swim the Channel.*

undecided /ʌndɪˈsaɪdɪˀd/. If you are **undecided** ADJ CLASSIF about something, you have not yet made a decision about it. EG *She was still undecided whether she would or would not return home.*

undemanding /ʌndɪˈmɑːndɪŋ/. **1** If you do an ADJ QUALIT **undemanding** job, you are not required to work very hard or to think a great deal.

2 Someone who is **undemanding** is easy to be with ADJ QUALIT and does not ask other people to do a lot for them. EG *...an undemanding husband.*

undemocratic /ʌndɛməkrætɪk/. In an **undemo-** ADJ QUALIT **cratic** system or regime, decisions are made by a small number of powerful people, rather than by all the people who are affected.

undeniable /ʌndɪnaɪəbəˀl/. Something that is **un-** ADJ CLASSIF **deniable** is certainly true. EG *Both of these statements are undeniable facts... The evidence is undeniable.* ◊ **undeniably**. EG *He was a tall, dark, and* ◊ SUBMOD *undeniably handsome man.*

under /ʌndə/. **1** If something is **under** something PREP else, it is directly below or beneath it. EG *There was a cask of beer under the bench... He had no shirt on under his thin jumper... We squeezed under the wire and into the garden.*

2 If something happens **under** particular circum- PREP stances or conditions, it happens when those circumstances or conditions exist. EG *He travelled under difficult circumstances.*

3 If something happens **under** a law, agreement, PREP or system, it happens because that law, agreement, or system says that it shall happen. EG *Equal pay for men and women is guaranteed under English law.*

4 You can use **under** to say that a person or thing PREP is being affected by something. EG *There is a new film project under discussion... The company is under enormous pressure to act quickly... She was evidently under the impression that Morris was the doctor.*

5 If something happens **under** a particular person PREP or government, it happens when that person or government is in power. EG *...China under Chairman Mao.*

6 If you study or work **under** a particular person, PREP that person is your teacher or boss. EG *He studied under Thomas Hart Benton... He has a large number of executives under him.*

7 If you write a book or article **under** a name that PREP is not your real name, that name appears on the book or article as the name of the author. EG *He wrote an anti-war novel under an assumed name.*

8 You use **under** to say what section of a list, book, PREP or system of classification something is in. EG *You'll find it under O for Orwell.*

9 If something is **under** a particular amount, PREP number, or age, it is less than that amount, number, or age. EG *Expenditure this year should be just under 15 billion pounds... Tickets cost £2 for adults and 50p for children under 16.*

under- is used to form words that describe some- PREFIX thing as not being provided to a sufficient extent, or as not having happened to a sufficient extent. For example, if people are underfed, they are not receiving enough food. EG *The hospitals were seriously under-financed... ...under-ripe fruit... Under-employment is widespread.*

undercarriage /ʌndəkærɪdʒ/, **undercarriages.** N COUNT The **undercarriage** of an aeroplane is the part, including the wheels, which supports the aeroplane when it is on the ground and when it is landing or taking off.

underclothes /ʌndəkləʊðz/. Your **underclothes** N PLURAL are the clothes such as a vest, bra, or pants that you wear next to your skin under your other clothes. EG *Renata's underclothes were all over the floor... A man in his underclothes was reading his paper by the window.*

undercover /ʌndəkʌvə/. People who take part in ADJ CLASSIF : **undercover** work or who use **undercover** meth- ATTRIB ods work secretly in order to obtain information for their government or for the police. EG *...police on undercover duty... ...undercover agents.*

undercurrent /ʌndəkʌrənt/, **undercurrents.** If N COUNT : there is an **undercurrent** of a feeling, that feeling OFT+*of* exists in a weak form but may become powerful later. EG *He was aware of an increasing undercurrent of unease in his mind.*

undercut /ʌndəkʌt/, **undercuts, undercutting.** The form **undercut** is used in the present tense and is also the past tense and past participle.

1 If you **undercut** someone or **undercut** their v+o prices, you sell a product more cheaply than they do. EG *The large-scale producer can usually undercut smaller competitors.*

2 If something **undercuts** your attempts to v+o achieve something, it prevents your attempts from being effective. EG *The delay would surely undercut efforts to force modernization.*

underdeveloped /ʌndədɪˈvɛləpt/. An **underde-** ADJ CLASSIF **veloped** country or region does not have modern industries and usually has a low standard of living. EG *...the problem of underdeveloped rural areas.*

underdog /ʌndədɒg/, **underdogs.** The **underdog** N COUNT : in a competition or situation is the person who *the*+N seems least likely to succeed or win. EG *She took up the cause of the underdog.*

underdone /ʌndədʌn/. If food is **underdone**, it ADJ QUALIT has not been cooked for long enough.

underemployed /ʌndərɪmplɔɪd/. If someone is ADJ CLASSIF **underemployed**, they have not got enough work to do, or they have work to do that does not make full use of their skills or abilities. EG *Migrants are much more likely to be poor and underemployed.*

underestimate /ʌndərɛstɪmeɪt/, **underesti-** **mates, underestimating, underestimated. 1** If V+O OR you **underestimate** something, you do not realize V+REPORT : how large or great it is or will be. EG *The Ameri-* ONLY WH *cans underestimated the power of the explosion... It was easy to underestimate what she had endured.*

2 If you **underestimate** someone, you do not v+o realize what they are capable of doing. EG *He had underestimated Muller.*

underfed /ʌndəfɛd/. People who are **underfed** do ADJ CLASSIF not get enough food to eat. EG *Underfed children are more likely to catch diseases.*

underfoot /ʌndəfʊt/. **1** You describe something as ADJ AFTER N **underfoot** when it is under your feet, because you OR are walking on it. EG *The grass underfoot was short* ADV AFTER VB *and springy... The ground was hardening underfoot.*

2 If you trample or crush something **underfoot**, ADV AFTER VB you spoil or destroy it by treading on it. EG *The banner was accidentally trampled underfoot.*

Is an undergraduate underprivileged?

undergarment /ˈʌndəgɑːmənt/, **undergar-** N COUNT
ments. An **undergarment** is a piece of clothing Formal
that you wear next to your skin and under your
other clothes. EG ...ladies' undergarments.

undergo /ˌʌndəˈgəʊ/, **undergoes, undergoing,** V+O
underwent /ˌʌndəˈwent/, **undergone** /ˌʌndəˈgɒn/. If
you **undergo** something necessary or unpleasant,
it happens to you and you endure it. EG The United
States will have to undergo radical changes... Her
mother was about to undergo a major operation.

undergraduate /ˌʌndəˈgrædjʊət/, **undergradu-** N COUNT
ates. An **undergraduate** is a student at a university or college who has not yet taken his or her first
degree. EG He was a Cambridge undergraduate.
▸ used as an adjective. EG ...an undergraduate ▸ ADJ CLASSIF:
degree in Social Administration. ATTRIB

underground; pronounced /ˌʌndəˈgraʊnd/ when it
is an adverb, and /ˈʌndəgraʊnd/ when it is a noun
or adjective.
1 Something that is **underground** is below the ADJ CLASSIF, OR
surface of the ground. EG ...an underground car ADV AFTER VB
park... The larvae hatch and make their way
underground.
2 Underground activities are done secretly be- ADJ CLASSIF:
cause they are unofficial and illegal and are usually ATTRIB
directed against the government. EG ...an underground newspaper.
3 The **underground** in a country is an organized N SING : the+N
group of people who are engaged in illegal activi-
ties, often against the government in power.
4 If you go **underground**, you hide from the ADV AFTER VB
authorities or the police because your political
ideas or activities are illegal. EG Among those
forced underground was James Jackson.
5 The **Underground** in a city is a railway system N SING OR
in which electric trains travel below the ground in by+N
tunnels. EG We went by Underground to Trafalgar British
Square... She walked towards the Underground
station.

undergrowth /ˈʌndəgrəʊθ/ is bushes and plants N UNCOUNT OR
growing together under the trees in a forest or N SING : the+N
jungle. EG She went crashing through the undergrowth.

underhand /ˌʌndəˈhænd/. If an action is **under-** ADJ QUALIT
hand or if it is done in an **underhand** way, it is
done secretly and dishonestly. EG Did they ever do
anything which you regarded as underhand?

underlay /ˈʌndəleɪ/, **underlays. 1 Underlay** is a N MASS
thick material that you place between a carpet and
the floor for extra warmth and in order to protect
the carpet.
2 Underlay is also the past tense of **underlie**.

underlie /ˌʌndəˈlaɪ/, **underlies, underlying,** V+O
underlay /ˌʌndəˈleɪ/, **underlain** /ˌʌndəˈleɪn/. If
something **underlies** something else, it is the
cause or basis of it. EG The social problems underlying these crises are unsolved. ● See also **underlying**.

underline /ˌʌndəˈlaɪn/, **underlines, underlining,**
underlined. 1 If something **underlines** something V+O
such as a feeling or a problem, it emphasizes it. EG
An article in the Lancet underlined the same
problem.
2 If you **underline** something such as a word or a V+O
sentence, you draw a line underneath it in order to
make people notice it or to give it extra importance. EG He underlined his signature with a little
flourish.

underling /ˈʌndəlɪŋ/, **underlings.** You refer to N COUNT
someone as an **underling** when they are inferior
in rank or status to someone else and take orders
from them. EG He expected his underlings to stand
respectfully when he entered the room.

underlying /ˌʌndəˈlaɪɪŋ/. The **underlying** fea- ADJ CLASSIF :
tures of an object, event, or situation are not ATTRIB
obvious, and effort may be needed in order to
discover or reveal them. EG There are underlying
similarities between all human beings... The underlying theme of the novel is very serious.

undermine /ˌʌndəˈmaɪn/, **undermines, under-** V+O
mining, undermined. If you **undermine** something such as an idea, a feeling, or a system, you
make it less strong or less secure than it was
before, often by a gradual process or by repeated
efforts. EG Public confidence in the company had
now been completely undermined... The landowners resented government measures which
undermined their authority.

underneath /ˌʌndəˈniːθ/. **1** If one thing is under- PREP, OR
neath another, it is directly below or beneath it. EG ADV AFTER VB
The dog was underneath the table... There was a
portrait underneath.
2 The **underneath** part of something is the part ADJ CLASSIF :
which normally touches or faces the ground. EG ATTRIB, OR
The underneath part felt damp... I lifted the dog's ADV AFTER VB
foot and checked the soft pad underneath. ▸ used ▸ N SING
as a noun. EG The underneath of the car was
covered with rust.
3 You use **underneath** when talking about feelings ADV OR PREP
and emotions that people do not show in their
behaviour. EG Underneath, most of us are shy.

undernourished /ˌʌndəˈnʌrɪʃt/. If someone is ADJ QUALIT
undernourished, they are weak and unhealthy
because they have not been eating enough food. EG
He was badly undernourished.

underpaid /ˌʌndəˈpeɪd/. People who are **under-** ADJ QUALIT
paid are not paid enough money for the job that
they do. EG ...a great mass of underpaid workers.

underpants /ˈʌndəpænts/ are a piece of clothing N PLURAL
worn by men and boys under their trousers. EG
Morris was standing in the hall in his underpants.

underpass /ˈʌndəpɑːs/, **underpasses.** An under- N COUNT
pass is a road or footpath that goes underneath a
railway or another road. EG ...the Knightsbridge
Underpass.

underprivileged /ˌʌndəˈprɪvəlɪdʒd/. **Under-** ADJ QUALIT
privileged people have less money and fewer
possessions and opportunities than other people in
their society. EG ...an underprivileged family.

underrate /ˌʌndəˈreɪt/, **underrates, underrating,** V+O
underrated. If you **underrate** someone or something, you do not recognize how clever, important,
or significant they are. EG He soon discovered that
he had underrated Lucy... Frank had underrated
Sir James's knowledge of Africa.

underside /ˈʌndəsaɪd/, **undersides.** The **under-** N COUNT :
side of something is the part of it which normally USU the+N
faces towards the ground. EG He turned the rifle
over and examined the underside.

undersized /ˌʌndəˈsaɪzd/. **Undersized** people or ADJ CLASSIF
things are smaller than usual, or smaller than they
should be. EG ...rows of undersized babies.

understaffed /ˌʌndəˈstɑːft/. An **understaffed** or- ADJ QUALIT
ganization does not have enough employees to do
its work properly. EG The Department was understaffed and over-worked.

understand /ˌʌndəˈstænd/, **understands, under-**
standing, understood /ˌʌndəˈstʊd/. **1** If you under- V+O,
stand someone or understand what they are V+REPORT :
saying, you know what they mean. EG She under- ONLY WH,
stood him perfectly... I don't understand what you OR V : NO CONT
mean... Do you understand?
2 You can also say that you **understand** someone V+O, OR V :
when you know why they behave in the way that NO CONT
they do. EG His wife doesn't understand him.
3 If you **understand** what is happening or why it is V+REPORT :
happening, you know what is happening or why it ONLY WH,
is happening. EG I don't understand why the engine NO CONT
isn't working.
4 If you say that you **understand** that something is V+REPORT :
the case, you mean that you have been told that it NO CONT
is the case. EG I understand she has several aunts... Formal
You and Celia, I understand, are close friends.
5 If you **understand** a language, you know what V+O : NO CONT
someone is saying when they are speaking that
language. EG I don't understand English.
6 If you **make** yourself **understood**, you get some- PHRASE
one to understand what you are telling them. EG

They were all speaking at once in different dialects, trying to make themselves understood.

understandable /ʌndəstændəbəⁿl/. **1** If you say ADJ QUALIT that someone's behaviour is **understandable**, you mean that they have reacted to a situation in a natural or normal way. EG *His reaction was perfectly understandable.* ◊ **understandably**. EG *Under-* ◊ ADV SEN *standably, he was frightened.*
2 If something such as a statement or theory is ADJ QUALIT **understandable**, people can easily understand it. EG *...the storage of information in a form which is readily understandable.*

understanding /ʌndəstændɪŋ/, **understandings. 1** If you have an **understanding** of some- N UNCOUNT thing, you have some knowledge of it, know how it OFT+*of* works, or know what it means. EG *I doubt whether he had any real understanding of Shakespeare... The job requires an understanding of Spanish.*
2 If you are **understanding** towards someone, you ADJ QUALIT are kind and forgiving. EG *I have always thought you were an understanding person.*
3 If there is **understanding** between people, they N UNCOUNT are friendly towards each other and trust each other. EG *What is needed is greater understanding between management and workers.*
4 An **understanding** is an informal agreement N COUNT about something. EG *Tacit understandings had been reached.*
5 If you agree to do something **on the under-** CONJ **standing that** something else will be done, you do it because you have been told that the other thing will be done. EG *I signed the contract on the understanding that delivery would be this week.*

understate /ʌndəsteɪt/, **understates, under-** V+O **stating, understated.** If you **understate** something, you describe it in a way that suggests that it is smaller or less important than it really is. EG *They understate the magnitude of the problem.*

understatement /ʌndəsteɪtməⁿnt/, **understate-** **ments. 1** If you say that a statement is an **under-** N COUNT **statement**, you mean that it does not fully express the extent to which something is true. EG *To say it's been good is quite an understatement... 'You must be exhausted.' – 'That's an understatement.'*
2 Understatement is the practice of suggesting N UNCOUNT that things have much less of a particular quality than they really have. EG *That sounds like typical British understatement.*

understood /ʌndəstʊd/ is the past tense and past participle of **understand.**

understudy /ʌndəstʌdi¹/, **understudies.** An ac- N COUNT tor's or actress's **understudy** is a person who has learned their part in a play and can act the part if they are ill. EG *He was Bobby's understudy.*

undertake /ʌndəteɪk/, **undertakes, undertak-** **ing, undertook** /ʌndətʊk/, **undertaken. 1** When V+O you **undertake** a task or job, you start doing it and Formal accept responsibility for it. EG *Reluctantly, he undertook the mission.*
2 If you **undertake** to do something, you promise V+*to*-INF that you will do it. EG *Most shareholders have* Formal *undertaken to accept the offer.*

undertaker /ʌndəteɪkə/, **undertakers.** An N COUNT **undertaker** is a person whose job is to look after the bodies of people who have died and to arrange their funerals.

undertaking /ʌndəteɪkɪŋ/, **undertakings. 1** An N COUNT **undertaking** is a task or job that you start doing and that you accept responsibility for. EG *...a complex and expensive undertaking.*
2 If you give an **undertaking** to do something, you N COUNT formally promise to do it. EG *Jenkins gave an* Formal *undertaking not to stand again for election.*

undertone /ʌndətəʊn/, **undertones. 1** If you say N COUNT something in an **undertone**, you say it very quietly. EG *Marcus said in an undertone, 'It doesn't matter, Lucas.'*
2 If something has **undertones** of a particular N COUNT+ kind, it suggests ideas or attitudes of this kind SUPP : USU PLURAL

without expressing them directly. EG *The custom had religious undertones.*

undertook /ʌndətʊk/ is the past tense of **under-** **take.**

undervalue /ʌndəvælju¹/, **undervalues, under-** V+O **valuing, undervalued.** If you **undervalue** something or someone, you think that they are less valuable or important than they really are. EG *We tend to overvalue money and undervalue art.*

underwater /ʌndəwɔːtə/. **1** Something that exists ADV OR or happens **underwater** exists or happens below ADJ CLASSIF : the surface of the sea, a river, or a lake. EG *She* ATTRIB *swam underwater... ...underwater exploration... ...underwater vegetation.*
2 Underwater devices are specially made so that ADJ CLASSIF : they can work in water. EG *It was filmed with an* ATTRIB *underwater camera.*

underway /ʌndəweɪ/. If an activity is **underway**, ADJ PRED it has already started. EG *Preparations for the trial were underway.*

underwear /ʌndəweə/. Your **underwear** is N UNCOUNT clothing such as a vest, bra, or pants that you wear next to your skin under your other clothes.

underwent /ʌndəwent/ is the past tense of **undergo.**

underworld /ʌndəwɜːld/. The **underworld** in a N SING : *the*+N city is the organized crime there and the people who are involved in it. EG *...professional thugs from the underworld.*

undesirable /ʌndi¹zaɪərəbəⁿl/. You describe peo- ADJ QUALIT ple or things as **undesirable** when you disapprove of them and think that they will have harmful effects. EG *These cuts in education are very undesirable.*

undetected /ʌndi¹tektɪ²d/. If you are **undetected** ADJ CLASSIF or if you do something **undetected**, people do not OR ADV find out where you are or what you are doing. EG *It was important to my safety that I should remain undetected.*

undeveloped /ʌndi¹veləpt/. **Undeveloped** coun- ADJ CLASSIF tries are countries that are not industrialized and where modern methods of large-scale farming are not used.

undid /ʌndɪd/ is the past tense of **undo.**

undignified /ʌndɪgnɪfaɪd/. **Undignified** behav- ADJ QUALIT iour is foolish and embarrassing. EG *They had a somewhat undignified argument.*

undiscovered /ʌndɪskʌvəd/. Something that is ADJ CLASSIF **undiscovered** has not been discovered or found OR ADV out about. EG *These authors were undiscovered geniuses... Old people who are ill sometimes lie undiscovered in their homes for days.*

undisguised /ʌndɪsgaɪzd/. An **undisguised** qual- ADJ CLASSIF ity or feeling is one that you show openly and do not make any attempt to hide. EG *He looked at her with undisguised admiration.*

undisputed /ʌndɪspju¹tɪ²d/. **1** Something which is ADJ CLASSIF **undisputed** is definitely true or definitely exists and cannot be questioned or doubted. EG *The facts are undisputed... ...her undisputed good looks.*
2 If you describe someone as the **undisputed** ADJ CLASSIF leader or champion, you mean that they have proved that nobody else has more power or ability than they have. EG *Mao became undisputed leader in China.*

undistinguished /ʌndɪstɪŋgwɪʃt/. Someone or ADJ QUALIT something that is **undistinguished** has no especially good qualities or features. EG *His political career had been undistinguished.*

undisturbed /ʌndɪstɜːbd/. **1** A place that is **un-** ADJ QUALIT **disturbed** is peaceful and not spoiled by noise or people. EG *The village is changing but it is still very undisturbed... The ship's remains lay undisturbed until 1975.*
2 If you are **undisturbed** in something that you ADJ PRED

Is it undesirable to be a member of the underworld?

undivided /ˌʌndɪˈvaɪdɪd/. If you give something **ADJ CLASSIF:** your **undivided** attention, you concentrate on it **ATTRIB** fully. EG *I was listening with undivided attention.*

undo /ʌnˈduː/, **undoes** /ʌnˈdʌz/, **undoing** /ʌnˈduːɪŋ/, **undid** /ʌnˈdɪd/, **undone** /ʌnˈdʌn/. **1** If you **undo** v+o something that is tied together, you unfasten it or untie it. EG *He bent down and undid the laces of his shoes.*
2 If you **undo** something that has been done, you v+o prevent it from being effective. EG *He appeared to be undoing all their patient work.*

undoing /ʌnˈduːɪŋ/. If something is someone's **un-** N UNCOUNT **doing**, it is the cause of their failure. EG *Stress can* +POSS *be the undoing of so many fine players.* Formal

undone /ʌnˈdʌn/. Something that is **undone** is no ADJ PRED longer held or tied together. EG *His bow tie had come undone.*

undoubted /ʌnˈdaʊtɪd/. You use **undoubted** to ADJ CLASSIF emphasize that something exists or is true. EG *...her undoubted acting ability... The play was an undoubted success.* ◊ **undoubtedly**. EG *A chauffeur is* ◊ ADV SEN *undoubtedly a status symbol.*

undreamed of /ʌnˈdriːmd ɒv/ or **undreamt of** ADJ CLASSIF /ʌnˈdrɛmt ɒv/. Something that is **undreamed of** is much better, worse, or more unusual than you thought was possible. EG *...undreamed-of luxury.*

undress /ʌnˈdrɛs/, **undresses**, **undressing**, **un-** v **dressed**. **1** When you **undress**, you take off your clothes. EG *Tom undressed in the dark.*
2 If you **undress** someone, you take off their v+o clothes.

undressed /ʌnˈdrɛst/. If you are **undressed**, you ADJ PRED are wearing no clothes or very few clothes. EG *They had all seen each other undressed.* ● When you **get** ● PHRASE **undressed**, you take off your clothes. EG *He took ages getting undressed.*

undue /ʌnˈdjuː/. You use **undue** to say that some- ADJ CLASSIF: thing is greater or more extreme than you think is ATTRIB reasonable. EG *She was reprimanded for putting* Formal *undue pressure on her clients.*

undulate /ˈʌndjʊleɪt/, **undulates**, **undulating**, v **undulated**. Something that **undulates** has gentle Formal curves or slopes, or moves gently and slowly up and down. EG *The road undulates through pleasant scenery.*

unduly /ʌnˈdjuːlɪ/. You use **unduly** to say that ADV OR SUBMOD something happens to an excessive or unnecessary extent. EG *None of the women seemed unduly worried... This attitude seemed to me unduly fussy.*

undying /ʌnˈdaɪɪŋ/. If you describe a feeling or a ADJ CLASSIF belief as **undying**, you mean that it will last Literary forever. EG *...Daniel's undying love for his wife.*

unearth /ʌnˈɜːθ/, **unearths**, **unearthing**, **un-** v+o **earthed**. If you **unearth** something that is hidden or secret, you discover it. EG *These ruins had been unearthed six feet below the surface... This dossier was unearthed along with many others.*

unearthly /ʌnˈɜːθlɪ/. **1** Something that is **un-** ADJ CLASSIF **earthly** has a strange and unnatural sound or appearance. EG *The light was unearthly.*
2 If you do something at an **unearthly** hour, you do ADJ CLASSIF: it very early or very late when most people are in ATTRIB bed and asleep. EG *I wondered why he had risen at that unearthly hour.*

unease /ʌnˈiːz/. If you have a feeling of **unease**, N UNCOUNT you feel that something is wrong and you are anxious about it. EG *'He'll be alright,' I said to myself, trying to quell a growing unease.*

uneasy /ʌnˈiːzɪ/. If you are **uneasy**, you feel ADJ QUALIT anxious that something may be wrong or that there may be danger. EG *She had an uneasy feeling that they were following her... I felt increasingly uneasy about my answer.* ◊ **uneasily**. EG *Philip blushed* ◊ ADV *and laughed uneasily.* ◊ **uneasiness.** EG *Pat's* ◊ N UNCOUNT *uneasiness grew as each minute passed.*

uneconomic /ˌʌniːkəˈnɒmɪk, ˌʌnɛkə-/. Something ADJ QUALIT that is **uneconomic** does not produce enough profit or wastes time, energy, or money. EG *...uneconomic coal mines... ...a one-teacher school is uneconomic.*

uneconomical /ˌʌniːkəˈnɒmɪkəl, ˌʌnɛkə-/. Some- ADJ QUALIT thing that is **uneconomical** wastes time, energy, or money. EG *...current sources of coal may become exhausted or uneconomical.*

uneducated /ʌnˈɛdʒʊkeɪtɪd/. Someone who is ADJ QUALIT **uneducated** has not received much education.

unemotional /ˌʌnɪˈməʊʃənəl, -ʃənəl/. Someone ADJ QUALIT who is **unemotional** does not show any feelings; often used showing disapproval. EG *He was cold and unemotional.*

unemployable /ˌʌnɪmˈplɔɪəbəl/. Someone who is ADJ CLASSIF **unemployable** does not have a job and is unlikely to get a job, for example because of the way that they behave. EG *Owing to their low intelligence, they were unemployable.*

unemployed /ˌʌnɪmˈplɔɪd/. **1** Someone who is ADJ CLASSIF **unemployed** does not have a job. EG *The govern-ment ought to create more job vacancies for unemployed young people.*
2 People who want to work but cannot get a job are N PLURAL : USU often referred to as the **unemployed**. EG *They* the+N *were discussing the problem of the unemployed.*

unemployment /ˌʌnɪmˈplɔɪmənt/. You say that N UNCOUNT there is **unemployment** in a place when many people there cannot get jobs. EG *The government is concerned about the level of unemployment in Scotland.*

unending /ʌnˈɛndɪŋ/. You say that something is ADJ CLASSIF **unending** when it has continued for a long time and seems as though it will never stop. EG *...the unending debate about tobacco.*

unenviable /ʌnˈɛnvɪəbəl/. If you describe a task ADJ QUALIT: or situation as **unenviable**, you mean that you ATTRIB would not like to have it or to be in it, because it is difficult, dangerous, or unpleasant. EG *...the unenvi-able task of phoning the parents of the dead child.*

unequal /ʌnˈiːkwəl/. **1** If you say that a political or ADJ QUALIT social system is **unequal**, you mean that it treats people in different ways, for example by giving some people more money or privileges than oth-ers. EG *...the unequal distribution of wealth.*
2 Two things that are **unequal** are different in size, ADJ QUALIT strength, or ability. EG *Her feet are of unequal sizes.*

unequivocal /ˌʌnɪkwɪˈvɒkəl/. You say that a state- ADJ CLASSIF ment is **unequivocal** when its meaning is com- Formal pletely clear. EG *The reply was unequivocal.*
◊ **unequivocally.** EG *They have stated* ◊ ADV *uneqivocally what they stand for.*

unerring /ʌnˈɜːrɪŋ/. If someone has an **unerring** ADJ CLASSIF ability to do something, they can always manage to do it. EG *Sheila's unerring sense of direction helped them.*

unethical /ʌnˈɛθɪkəl/. Behaviour that is **unethi-** ADJ QUALIT **cal** is morally wrong. EG *He was accused of unethi-* Formal *cal conduct.*

uneven /ʌnˈiːvən/. **1** Something that is **uneven** is ADJ QUALIT not regular or consistent. EG *...uneven teeth... It was an uneven but inspired performance.*
2 An **uneven** surface is not level or smooth. EG *She* ADJ QUALIT *stumbled on the uneven ground.*

uneventful /ˌʌnɪˈvɛntful/. If you describe an occa- ADJ QUALIT sion or period of time as **uneventful**, you mean that nothing interesting, exciting, or important happened during it. EG *The day was quiet and uneventful.*

unexpected /ˌʌnɪkˈspɛktɪd/. Something that is ADJ QUALIT **unexpected** surprises you because you were not expecting it to happen. EG *My hostess greeted me with unexpected warmth... His death was hardly unexpected.* ◊ **unexpectedly**. EG *She died quite* ◊ ADV *unexpectedly.*

unfailing /ʌnˈfeɪlɪŋ/ is used to describe a quality ADJ CLASSIF that stays the same and does not get weaker as Formal time passes. EG *I could never have carried on without the unfailing support of the teaching staff.*

unfair /ʌnfeə/. 1 If you think that something is **unfair**, you think that it is not right or not just. EG *It would be quite unfair to expose him to publicity... I knew I was being unfair to him.* ◊ **unfairly.** EG ◊ ADV *Workers who have been unfairly dismissed may claim compensation.* ADJ QUALIT

2 A situation or system that is **unfair** does not give ADJ QUALIT equal treatment or the same chances to everyone involved. EG *The whole academic system is unfair.*

unfaithful /ʌnfeɪθful/. If someone is **unfaithful** ADJ CLASSIF to their lover or to the person they are married to, OFT+to they have a sexual relationship with someone else. EG *I swear I've never been unfaithful to you.*

unfamiliar /ʌnfəmɪliə/. 1 If something is **unfa-** ADJ QUALIT **miliar** to you, you have not seen or heard it before. EG *This name may be unfamiliar to most of you.*

2 If you are **unfamiliar** with something, you have ADJ PRED not seen or heard it before. EG *...a person unfamil-* +with *iar with the French railway system.*

unfashionable /ʌnfæʃənəbəl/. If something is ADJ QUALIT **unfashionable**, it is not fashionable or popular. EG *His ideas were unfashionable among his col-leagues... Daisy liked the place because it was quiet and unfashionable.*

unfasten /ʌnfɑːsən/, **unfastens, unfastening,** V+O **unfastened.** If you **unfasten** a piece of clothing or something such as a seat belt or a window, you undo the buttons, hooks, or straps on it so that it is no longer closed. EG *He unfastened the buttons of his shirt.*

unfavourable /ʌnfeɪvərəbəl/; spelled **unfavor-able** in American English. 1 **Unfavourable** condi- ADJ QUALIT tions or circumstances cause problems for you and reduce your chance of success. EG *...unfavourable weather conditions.*

2 If you have an **unfavourable** opinion of some- ADJ QUALIT thing, you do not like it or approve of it. EG *He had formed an unfavourable opinion of my work.*

unfeeling /ʌnfiːlɪŋ/. Someone who is **unfeeling** is ADJ QUALIT not sympathetic towards people who are suffering or unhappy. EG *How stupid and unfeeling I have been!... ...unfeeling journalists.*

unfettered /ʌnfetəd/. Something or someone that ADJ CLASSIF is **unfettered** is completely free and not controlled or limited by anything. EG *...the right of free speech, unfettered by the party system... They are young and still unfettered by families.*

unfinished /ʌnfɪnɪʃt/. If something is **unfinished**, ADJ CLASSIF it has not been completed. EG *The unfinished build-ing grew rusty and dilapidated... People shouldn't leave jobs unfinished.*

unfit /ʌnfɪt/. 1 If you are **unfit**, you have not been ADJ QUALIT taking regular exercise, so that, for example, you get tired quickly when you run.

2 If someone or something is **unfit** for a particular ADJ PRED : purpose, they are not suitable or not of a good OFT+for enough quality. EG *This meat is unfit for human* OR to-INF *consumption... Adams is clearly unfit to hold an administrative post.*

unfold /ʌnfəʊld/, **unfolds, unfolding, unfolded.** 1 V When a situation **unfolds**, it develops and becomes known or understood. EG *The great invasion plan was beginning to unfold.*

2 If you **unfold** your plans or intentions, you tell V+O someone what your plans or intentions are. EG *She had soon unfolded all her plans to him.*

3 If you **unfold** something which has been folded, V-ERG you open it so that it becomes flat.

unforeseen /ʌnfɔːsiːn/. An **unforeseen** event ADJ CLASSIF happens unexpectedly. EG *This was an unforeseen complication.*

unforgettable /ʌnfəgetəbəl/. You say that some- ADJ QUALIT thing is **unforgettable** when it is so good or so bad that you are unlikely to forget it. EG *It was an unforgettable experience.*

unforgivable /ʌnfəgɪvəbəl/. If something you do ADJ QUALIT is **unforgivable**, it is so bad or cruel that it can

never be forgiven or justified. EG *...an unforgivable error in judgement.*

unformed /ʌnfɔːmd/. Something that is **un-** ADJ CLASSIF **formed** is in an early stage of development and not yet fully formed. EG *...unformed ideas.*

unfortunate /ʌnfɔːtʃənət/. 1 Someone who is ADJ QUALIT **unfortunate** is unlucky. EG *He's been very unfortu-nate... We will do our utmost to help these unfortu-nate people.*

2 If you say that something that has happened is ADJ QUALIT **unfortunate**, you mean that it is a pity that it happened. EG *It is rather unfortunate that the Prime Minister should have said this... ...one of those unfortunate lulls in the conversation.*

unfortunately /ʌnfɔːtʃənətli/. You use **unfor-** ADV SEN **tunately** to express regret about what you are saying. EG *'Will you be here in the morning?' – 'No, unfortunately I won't.'*

unfounded /ʌnfaʊndɪd/. You say that a belief is ADJ CLASSIF **unfounded** when it is not based on facts or evi-dence. EG *Our worst fears have proved unfounded.*

unfriendly /ʌnfrendli/. Someone who is **un-** ADJ QUALIT **friendly** does not behave in a friendly way. EG *He looked unfriendly... ...a cold, unfriendly stare.*

unfulfilled /ʌnfulfɪld/. You say that something ADJ CLASSIF : such as a hope is **unfulfilled** when the thing that USU ATTRIB you hoped for has not happened. EG *...an unfulfilled wish... ...Leggett's unfulfilled ambition.*

unfurnished /ʌnfɜːnɪʃt/. If you rent an **unfur-** ADJ CLASSIF **nished** flat or house, no furniture is provided in it by the owner.

ungainly /ʌngeɪnli/. **Ungainly** people are awk- ADJ QUALIT ward or clumsy in the way that they move. EG *I* Written *thought him terribly ungainly.*

ungrateful /ʌngreɪtful/. If someone is **ungrate-** ADJ QUALIT **ful**, they do not seem to be thankful for something that has been given to them or done for them. EG *I hope I don't sound ungrateful.*

unguarded /ʌngɑːdɪd/. 1 If something is left ADJ CLASSIF **unguarded**, it is left without anyone to protect it or look after it. EG *I couldn't go without leaving my suitcase unguarded.*

2 An **unguarded** moment is one when you are ADJ CLASSIF : careless in what you say or do, with the result that ATTRIB someone discovers something that you did not want them to know. EG *I told him, in an unguarded moment, what I planned to do.*

unhappily /ʌnhæpɪli/. 1 If you do something ADV **unhappily**, you are not happy or contented while you do it. EG *He trudged unhappily towards the house.*

2 You use **unhappily** to say that you regret a ADV SEN situation or event. EG *Unhappily, George had died by the time Ralph got to America.*

unhappy /ʌnhæpi/, **unhappier, unhappiest.** 1 If ADJ QUALIT you are **unhappy**, you are sad and depressed. EG *She looked unhappy... I had an unhappy time at school.* ◊ **unhappiness.** EG *The quarrel caused her* ◊ N UNCOUNT *intense unhappiness.*

2 If you are **unhappy** about something, you are not ADJ PRED+A pleased about it or are not satisfied with it. EG *The residents of the area are unhappy about the crowds and the noise.*

3 If you describe a situation as an **unhappy** one, ADJ QUALIT : you are expressing regret that it exists. EG *This* ATTRIB *unhappy state of affairs would not exist if all Ministers acted in a responsible way.*

unharmed /ʌnhɑːmd/. If someone who has been ADJ CLASSIF attacked or involved in an accident is **unharmed**, they are not injured. EG *The four men managed to escape unharmed.*

unhealthy /ʌnhelθi/. 1 Something that is **un-** ADJ QUALIT **healthy** is likely to cause illness. EG *This is prob-ably the most unhealthy place in the world.*

If a place is uninhabited, is it also uninhabitable?

2 You say that a person is **unhealthy** when they ADJ QUALIT are often ill.

unheard of /ʌnhɜːd ɒv/. You say that an event or ADJ CLASSIF situation is **unheard of 1** when it never happens. EG *Contracts and written agreements are quite unheard of.* **2** when it has never happened before and so is very surprising or shocking. EG *This is an unheard-of outrage.*

unheeded /ʌnhiːdɪ²d/. If something goes **unheed-** ADJ PRED **ed**, it is ignored. EG *Their appeals for help went unheeded.*

unhelpful /ʌnhelpful/. You say that someone is ADJ QUALIT **unhelpful** when they do nothing to help you. EG *He came barging into the kitchen with unhelpful suggestions.*

unhesitating /ʌnhezɪteɪtɪŋ/. When you are **un-** ADJ CLASSIF **hesitating**, you do or say something immediately, because you are confident that it is the right thing to do or say. EG ...*her unhesitating readiness to help.* ◊ **unhesitatingly.** EG *McCalden replied unhesitatingly, 'Yes, certainly.'* ◊ ADV

unhinge /ʌnhɪndʒ/, **unhinges, unhinging, un-** V+O **hinged.** If an experience **unhinges** someone, it affects them so deeply that they become mentally ill. EG *It seemed to me the accident had unhinged her.* EG *According to Morris, Gordon* ◊ ADJ QUALIT *Masters is quite unhinged.*

unholy /ʌnhəʊliˈ/. Something that is **unholy** is ADJ QUALIT considered to be wicked or sinful. EG *I discovered the unholy pleasures of gossip and malice.*

unhurried /ʌnhʌrɪd/. If something that you do or ADJ CLASSIF say is **unhurried**, you do it or say it in a slow and relaxed way. EG *Her voice was calm and unhurried.* ◊ **unhurriedly.** EG *She walked unhurriedly out of* ◊ ADV *the building.*

unhurt /ʌnhɜːt/. If someone who has been at- ADJ PRED tacked or involved in an accident is **unhurt**, they are not injured. EG *Two men crawled out unhurt.*

unhygienic /ʌnhaɪdʒiːnɪk/. Something that is un- ADJ QUALIT **hygienic** is dirty and likely to cause infection or disease. EG ...*tiny unhygienic cages.*

unicorn /juːnɪkɔːn/, **unicorns.** In stories and leg- N COUNT ends, a **unicorn** is an imaginary animal that looks like a white horse and has a horn growing from its forehead.

unidentified /ʌnaɪdentɪfaɪd/. You say that some- ADJ CLASSIF : one or something is **unidentified** when nobody USU ATTRIB knows who or what they are. EG ...*the house of an unidentified Scottish merchant....* ...*unidentified flying objects.*

unification /juːnɪfɪkeɪʃəˈn/ is the act of unifying N UNCOUNT : something, or the result of doing this. EG ...*the* USU+SUPP *unification of Italy.*

uniform /juːnɪfɔːm/, **uniforms. 1** A **uniform** is a N COUNT OR special set of clothes which some people, for N UNCOUNT example soldiers or the police, wear at work, and which some children wear at school. EG ...*a man in the uniform of a captain in the Air Force....* *She wasn't in uniform.*

2 If something is **uniform**, it does not vary, but is ADJ CLASSIF even and regular throughout. EG ...*a structure of uniform width.*

uniformed /juːnɪfɔːmd/. **Uniformed** people are ADJ CLASSIF : wearing uniforms. EG ...*uniformed policemen.* ATTRIB

uniformity /juːnɪfɔːmɪtiˈ/ is a state in which N UNCOUNT everyone or everything behaves or looks the same as everyone or everything else. EG ...*the dreary uniformity of the housing estate.*

unify /juːnɪfaɪ/, **unifies, unifying, unified.** If you V+O **unify** a number of things or people, you join or bring them together. EG *Smaller tribes are unified into larger societies.* ◊ **unified.** ...*a unified labour* ◊ ADJ CLASSIF *movement.* ◊ **unifying.** EG ...*the importance of* ◊ ADJ CLASSIF *Hinduism as a unifying cultural force.*

unilateral /juːnɪlætəˈrəl/. A **unilateral** decision ADJ CLASSIF : or action is made or done by only one of the groups ATTRIB that are involved in a particular situation. EG *We will take unilateral action....* ...*unilateral disarmament.*

unilateralism /juːnɪlætəˈrəlɪzəˈm/ is belief in uni- N UNCOUNT lateral disarmament. EG *The party had reversed its* Formal support of unilateralism. ◊ **unilateralist** ◊ N COUNT /juːnɪlætəˈrəlɪst/, **unilateralists.** EG *I am not a unilateralist.*

unimaginable /ʌnɪmædʒɪnəbəˈl/. Something that ADJ CLASSIF is **unimaginable** is difficult to imagine or understand properly, because it is not part of people's normal experience. EG ...*the unimaginable vastness of space....* ...*experiments carried out under almost unimaginable conditions.*

unimaginative /ʌnɪmædʒɪnətɪv/. Someone who ADJ QUALIT is **unimaginative** does not use their imagination enough in what they do. EG ...*unimaginative teachers....* ...*unimaginative projects.*

unimpressive /ʌnɪmpresɪv/. You say that some- ADJ QUALIT one or something is **unimpressive** when they seem to have no good or interesting qualities. EG *Barney's wife was an unimpressive little woman.*

uninhabitable /ʌnɪnhæbɪtəbəˈl/. An **uninhabit-** ADJ CLASSIF **able** place is one where it is impossible for people to live. EG *Worldwide pollution threatens to make the planet uninhabitable.*

uninhabited /ʌnɪnhæbɪtɪˈd/. An **uninhabited** ADJ CLASSIF place is one where nobody lives. EG ...*an uninhabited island.*

uninhibited /ʌnɪnhɪbɪtɪˈd/. If you are **uninhibit-** ADJ QUALIT **ed**, you behave freely and naturally and show your real feelings. EG ...*a sound of uninhibited laughter.*

uninitiated /ʌnɪnɪʃieɪtɪˈd/. You can refer to the N PLURAL : people who have no knowledge or experience of the+N something as the **uninitiated.** EG *For the uninitiated, may I say that golf is one game that demands patience and concentration.*

unintelligible /ʌnɪntelɪdʒəˈbəˈl/. Something that ADJ QUALIT is **unintelligible** is impossible to understand. EG *He* Formal *answered in words unintelligible to her.*

unintended /ʌnɪntendɪˈd/. If something that hap- ADJ CLASSIF pens is **unintended**, it was not planned to happen. EG ...*the unintended consequences of advertising on television.*

unintentional /ʌnɪntenʃəˈnəl, -ʃənəˈl/. Something ADJ CLASSIF that is **unintentional** is not done deliberately, but happens by accident. EG ...*unintentional damage.*

uninterested /ʌnɪntəˈriˈstɪd/. If you are **unin-** ADJ QUALIT : **terested** in something, you are not interested in it. OFT+in EG *Lionel was uninterested in the house.*

uninteresting /ʌnɪntəˈriˈstɪŋ/. Someone or some- ADJ QUALIT thing that is **uninteresting** is dull and boring. EG *He found her uninteresting as a person.*

uninterrupted /ʌnɪntərʌptɪˈd/. If something is ADJ CLASSIF **uninterrupted**, it continues without any breaks or interruptions. EG *Lynn did some uninterrupted reading.*

uninvited /ʌnɪnvaɪtɪˈd/. You use **uninvited** to ADJ CLASSIF describe a person who arrives somewhere or does something without being asked. EG ...*uninvited guests....* *Henry sat down uninvited.*

union /juːnjən/, **unions. 1** A **union** is an organiza- N COUNT tion of workers that has the aim of improving such things as the working conditions, pay, and benefits of its members. EG ...*Mr Ray Buckton, leader of the train drivers' union.*

2 When the **union** of two or more things takes N UNCOUNT place, they are joined together and become one Formal thing. EG *We are working for the union of the two countries.*

unique /juːniːk/. **1** If something is **unique**, it is the ADJ CLASSIF only thing of its kind. EG ...*that unique human ability, speech.* ◊ **uniqueness.** EG ...*the uniqueness* ◊ N UNCOUNT *of the individual.*

2 If something is **unique** to one thing or person, it ADJ PRED+to concerns or belongs to that thing or person only. EG *These problems are not unique to nuclear power.*

3 Some people use **unique** to mean very unusual ADJ CLASSIF and special. EG *It was a unique and exquisite performance.* ◊ **uniquely.** EG *He had a fine singing* ◊ SUBMOD *voice, uniquely gentle and deep.*

unisex /ˈjuːnɪsɛks/ is used to describe things which ADJ CLASSIF are designed to be used by both men and women. EG *The women were dressed in nondescript unisex clothes.*

unison /ˈjuːnɪsən, -zən/. If a group of people do PHRASE something **in unison**, they all do it together at the same time. EG *'All of us,' they said in unison.*

unit /ˈjuːnɪt/, **units. 1** If you consider something as N COUNT a **unit**, you consider it as a single, complete thing. EG *It is not realistic to treat the world as a unit, because resources are very unevenly distributed... ...the decline of the family as a self-sufficient unit.*
2 A **unit** is also **2.1** a group of people who work N COUNT together at a specific job, often in a particular place. EG *I was working in that unit as the librarian... ...the science policy research unit at the university.* **2.2** a small machine which has a N COUNT : particular function, often part of a larger machine. USU + SUPP EG *...a power supply unit.*
3 A **unit** of measurement is a fixed, standard N COUNT quantity, length, or weight that is used for measur- OR N PART ing things. The metre, the litre, and the gram are all units. EG *...a unit of electricity... ...units of sound.*

unite /juːˈnaɪt/, **unites, uniting, united.** If a group V-ERG of people or things **unite** or if something **unites** them, they join together and act as a group. EG *They must unite to combat the enemy... This measure would unite all the provinces into a single state.*

united /juːˈnaɪtɪd/. **1** If a group of people are ADJ CLASSIF **united** about something, they agree with each other about it and act together. EG *They were united in their dislike of authority.*
2 If different areas or groups are **united**, they have ADJ CLASSIF been joined together to form a single country or organization. EG *Some people want a united Ireland... ...the United States.*

United Kingdom. The **United Kingdom** is the N PROPER : official name for Great Britain and Northern Ire- the + N land.

United Nations. The **United Nations** is an N PROPER : organization which most countries in the world the + N belong to and which tries to encourage peace, co-operation, and friendship.

unity /ˈjuːnɪti/. When there is **unity**, people are in N UNCOUNT agreement and act together for a particular purpose. EG *He failed to preserve his party's unity... They are discussing church unity.*

universal /ˌjuːnɪˈvɜːsəl/, **universals. 1** Something that is **universal 1.1** relates to everyone in the ADJ CLASSIF world or to everyone in a particular group or society. EG *They touched on various topics of universal interest.* ◊ **universally.** EG *This explanation* ◊ ADV *is not yet universally accepted.* **1.2** affects or ADJ CLASSIF relates to every part of the world or the universe. EG *The threat of universal extinction hangs over all the world.*
2 A **universal** is something that is the same or N COUNT equally true at all times and in all situations. ▸ used ▸ ADJ CLASSIF as an adjective. EG *...a universal truth.*
◊ **universally.** EG *One thing was universally true.* ◊ ADV + ADJ

universe /ˈjuːnɪvɜːs/, **universes.** The **universe** is N SING : the + N the whole of space, including all the stars and planets. EG *They thought the earth was the centre of the universe.*

university /ˌjuːnɪˈvɜːsɪti/, **universities.** A uni- N COUNT OR **versity** is an institution where students study for N UNCOUNT degrees and where academic research is done. EG *She is a student at Norwich University... Her one aim in life is to go to university.*

unjust /ʌnˈdʒʌst/. An **unjust** action, system, or law ADJ QUALIT is morally wrong because it treats a person or a group badly in a way that they do not deserve. EG *...a thoroughly unjust society.* ◊ **unjustly.** EG ◊ ADV *...schoolmates who had unjustly accused him of bullying.*

unjustifiable /ˌʌndʒʌstɪˈfaɪəbəl/. You say that an ADJ QUALIT action is **unjustifiable** when it harms someone and there is no good reason for doing it. EG *What I had done was clearly unjustifiable.*

unjustified /ʌnˈdʒʌstɪfaɪd/. You say that a belief ADJ QUALIT or action is **unjustified** when there is no good reason for having it or for doing it. EG *It was an unjustified attack.*

unkempt /ʌnˈkɛmpt/. Something that is **unkempt** ADJ QUALIT is untidy and not looked after carefully. EG *He had a shaggy, unkempt beard.*

unkind /ʌnˈkaɪnd/, **unkinder, unkindest.** Some- ADJ QUALIT one who is **unkind** to you behaves towards you in an unpleasant and rather cruel way. EG *Why are you so unkind to me when you know I'm unhappy?... ...a silly and unkind remark.*

unknown /ʌnˈnəʊn/. **1** If someone or something is ADJ CLASSIF **unknown**, people do not know about them, or do not know who or what they are. EG *She took me to another village where she was unknown... ...this man Boris, whose real name is unknown to me... She wouldn't be alone with an unknown male visitor.*
2 You can refer to the things that people do not N SING : the + N know about as the **unknown**. EG *...fear of the unknown.*

unlawful /ʌnˈlɔːfəl/. Something that is **unlawful** ADJ CLASSIF is not legal. EG *...unlawful business activities.* Formal

unleash /ʌnˈliːʃ/, **unleashes, unleashing, un-** V + O **leashed.** When someone or something **unleashes** Formal a powerful or violent force, they release it. EG *How could they have justified all the violence unleashed on the prisoners?... Strong feelings had been unleashed in me by the news of the bomb.*

unless /ʌnˈlɛs/. You use **unless** to introduce the CONJ only circumstances in which the event you are mentioning will not take place or in which the statement you are making is not true. EG *He phoned me to say that unless the paper stopped my articles he would withdraw his advertisements... I couldn't get a grant unless I had five years' teaching experience.*

unlike /ʌnˈlaɪk/. **1** If one thing is **unlike** another PREP thing, the two things have different features from each other. EG *Rodin was unlike his predecessor in every way.*
2 You can use **unlike** to contrast two people, PREP things, or situations, and show how they are different. EG *Mrs Hochstadt, unlike Etta, was a careful shopper.*
3 If you describe something that a particular PREP person has done as being **unlike** them, you mean that you are surprised by it because it is not typical of their character or normal behaviour. EG *It was unlike her to mention it.*

unlikely /ʌnˈlaɪkli/. **1** If you say that something is ADJ QUALIT : **unlikely** to happen or **unlikely** to be true, you OFT + to-INF mean that it will probably not happen, or that it is OR REPORT probably not true. EG *The dispute is unlikely to be settled for a long time... It is unlikely that you will get your own office... In the unlikely event that they give you any trouble, write to us.*
2 You can also use **unlikely** to describe a situation ADJ QUALIT : or event that actually occurs but that seems very ATTRIB strange because it is so unexpected. EG *Brody was startled by the unlikely sight of Hendricks in a bathing suit.*

unlimited /ʌnˈlɪmɪtɪd/. You say that something is ADJ CLASSIF **unlimited** when you can have as much of it as you want. EG *...a ticket that allows unlimited travel on buses... They were given unlimited amounts of food.*

unlit /ʌnˈlɪt/. **1** An **unlit** fire or cigarette has not ADJ CLASSIF yet been lit and is therefore not burning.
2 An **unlit** street or building is dark because it does ADJ CLASSIF not have any lights switched on to make it bright.

Why do you not talk about things that are unmentionable?

unload /ʌnlˈəʊd/, **unloads, unloading, unloaded.** v+o or v
1 If you **unload** goods from a container or vehicle, you remove them. EG *We began to unload the bricks from Philip's car.*

2 If you **unload** a problem onto someone, you tell v+o:OFT them about it because you need advice or sympa- +onto/on thy. EG *He wanted to unload some of the anguish onto someone else.*

unlock /ʌnlˈɒk/, **unlocks, unlocking, unlocked.** v+o
If you **unlock** something·such as a door or a container, you open it by means of a key.

unlocked /ʌnlˈɒkt/. If a door or container is **un-locked**, it has not been locked. ASSIF

unloving /ʌnlˈʌvɪŋ/. You say that people are **un-** ADJ QUALIT **loving** when they do not show love to other people, especially their own family. EG ...*unloving parents.*

unlucky /ʌnlˈʌkiˈ/. **1** Someone who is **unlucky** has ADJ QUALIT bad luck. EG *I was unlucky enough to miss the final episode... She had been unlucky in love.*

2 If something is **unlucky**, it is thought to cause bad luck. EG *13 is a very unlucky number.*

unmade /ʌmˈmeɪd/. An **unmade** bed has not had ADJ CLASSIF its sheets and blankets neatly arranged after it was last slept in.

unmanageable /ʌmˈmænɪdʒəbəˈl/. Something ADJ QUALIT that is **unmanageable** is difficult to use, deal with, or control, usually because it is too big. EG *The complete encyclopaedia is quite unmanageable.*

unmanly /ʌmˈmænliˈ/. **Unmanly** behaviour is ADJ QUALIT thought to be not suitable for a man. EG ...*the attitude that it is unmanly to be domesticated.*

unmanned /ʌmˈmænd/. **Unmanned** aircraft or ADJ CLASSIF spacecraft do not carry humans in them.

unmarked /ʌmˈmɑːkt/. Something that is **un-** ADJ CLASSIF **marked** **1** has no marks of damage or injury on it. EG *His face was unmarked.* **2** has no signs on it to identify it. EG ...*unmarked police cars.*

unmarried /ʌmˈmærɪd/. Someone who is **un-** ADJ CLASSIF **married** is not married. EG ...*an unmarried mother.*

unmentionable /ʌmˈmenʃənəbəˈl/. Something ADJ CLASSIF that is **unmentionable** is too embarrassing or unpleasant to talk about. EG *He's had all kinds of unmentionable operations.*

unmistakable /ʌmˈmɪsteɪkəbəˈl/; also spelled ADJ CLASSIF **unmistakeable.** Something that is **unmistakable** is so obvious that it cannot be mistaken for anything else. EG ...*the unmistakable stench of rotting eggs.* ◇ **unmistakably.** EG *He was unmistakably of* ◇ ADV OR *Italian descent.* ADV SEN

unmitigated /ʌmˈmɪtɪgeɪtˈd/. You use **unmiti-** ADJ CLASSIF: **gated** to describe bad situations or qualities that ATTRIB are totally and completely bad. EG *This govern-* Formal *ment's policy on education is an unmitigated disaster... ...his unmitigated selfishness.*

unmoved /ʌmˈmuːvd/. If someone is **unmoved** by ADJ PRED something, they are not emotionally affected by it. EG *No one can remain unmoved by this music.*

unnamed /ʌnneɪmd/. If someone or something is ADJ CLASSIF **unnamed**, their name is not mentioned. EG ...*an unnamed ministry spokesman.*

unnatural /ʌnnætʃəˈrəl/. **1** If you describe some- ADJ QUALIT thing as **unnatural**, you mean that it is strange and rather frightening, because it is different from what you normally expect. EG ...*the house's unnatural silence.* ◇ **unnaturally.** EG *Her arms felt* ◇ ADV *unnaturally hot.*

2 If someone's behaviour is **unnatural**, they are ADJ QUALIT behaving in a way that seems artificial and not typical of them. EG *Her voice was a little strained, a little unnatural.*

unnecessary /ʌnnesəˈsəˈriˈ/. Something that is ADJ QUALIT **unnecessary** is not necessary. EG *The reason behind this is to avoid unnecessary expenses.* ◇ **unnecessarily.** EG *Some parents worry unneces-* ◇ ADV *sarily about their children.*

unnerve /ʌnnɜːˈv/, **unnerves, unnerving, un-** v+o **nerved.** If something **unnerves** you, it frightens or startles you. EG *His touch unnerved her.*

unnerving /ʌnnɜːˈvɪŋ/. Something that is **unnerv-** ADJ QUALIT **ing** is frightening and startling. EG *This kind of experience can be quite unnerving.*

unnoticed /ʌnnəʊtɪst/. If something happens or ADJ PRED passes **unnoticed**, it is not seen or noticed by anyone. EG *We tried to get into the room unnoticed... He hoped his departure had passed unnoticed.*

unobserved /ʌnəˈbzɜːvd/. If you do something ADJ CLASSIF **unobserved**, you do it without being seen by anyone. EG *She was able to slip past the guard unobserved.*

unobtrusive /ʌnəˈbtruːsɪv/. Something that is **un-** ADJ QUALIT **obtrusive** does not draw attention to itself. EG *We'll* Formal *try to be as unobtrusive as possible.*

unoccupied /ʌnɒkjəˈpaɪd/. If a place is **unoccu-** ADJ CLASSIF **pied**, there is nobody in it. EG *The house was left unoccupied for fifteen years.*

unofficial /ʌnəˈfɪʃəˈl/. An **unofficial** action is not ADJ CLASSIF authorized, approved, or organized by a person in authority. EG ...*an unofficial strike... You will be sent unofficial notification of the results.*

unopened /ʌnəʊpəˈnd/. If something is **un-** ADJ CLASSIF **opened**, it has not been opened yet. EG ...*an unopened bottle of whisky.*

unorthodox /ʌnɔːθədɒks/. **Unorthodox** behav- ADJ QUALIT iour, beliefs, or customs are unusual and not generally accepted. EG *Many doctors don't approve of unorthodox medicine.*

unpack /ʌmˈpæk/, **unpacks, unpacking, un-** v or v+o **packed.** When you **unpack**, you take everything out of a suitcase, bag, or box. EG *I'll leave you now so that you can unpack... He began to unpack his briefcase.*

unpaid /ʌmˈpeɪd/. **1** If you are **unpaid**, you do a ADJ CLASSIF job without receiving any money or wages for it. EG *Carol was Pat's unpaid teacher.*

2 Unpaid work or leave is work or leave that you ADJ CLASSIF do not get paid for. EG ...*unpaid overtime.*

3 If something such as rent or a bill is **unpaid**, it ADJ CLASSIF has not yet been paid.

unpalatable /ʌmˈpæləˈtəbəˈl/. **1 Unpalatable** ADJ QUALIT food is so unpleasant that you can hardly eat it. EG Formal ...*an unpalatable breakfast.*

2 An **unpalatable** idea is one that you find un- ADJ QUALIT pleasant and difficult to accept. EG ...*the unpalat-* Formal *able truth.*

unparalleled /ʌmˈpærəleld/. If you say that ADJ CLASSIF something is **unparalleled**, you mean that it is bigger or better than anything else of its kind. EG *Our specialist library is unparalleled.*

unpleasant /ʌmˈplezənt/. **1** You say that some- ADJ QUALIT thing is **unpleasant** when it gives you bad feelings rather than good ones, for example by making you feel upset, uncomfortable, or frightened. EG *The only work available is dirty, unpleasant and dangerous... The smell was unpleasant.*

2 Someone who is **unpleasant** is very unfriendly ADJ QUALIT or rude. EG *Their son is even more ill-tempered, difficult, and unpleasant.*

unplug /ʌmˈplʌg/, **unplugs, unplugging, un-** v+o **plugged.** If you **unplug** a piece of electrical equipment, you take the plug out of the electric socket. EG *Will you unplug the iron?*

unpopular /ʌmˈpɒpjəˈlə/. Something or someone ADJ QUALIT that is **unpopular** is disliked by most of the people in a place or community. EG *The war was both costly and unpopular... ...an unpopular minister.*

unprecedented /ʌmˈpresɪdentɪˈd/. You use **un-** ADJ CLASSIF **precedented** to say that something has never Formal happened before, or that it is the best or largest thing of its kind that there has ever been. EG ...*a period of unprecedented wealth and prosperity.*

unpredictable /ʌmˈprɪdɪktəbəˈl/. If someone or ADJ QUALIT something is **unpredictable**, you never know how they will behave or what effects they will have. EG *She was totally unpredictable... Poisons are notoriously unpredictable.*

unprepared /ʌmˈprɪpɛəd/. If you are **unpre-** ADJ CLASSIF: **pared** for something, you are not ready for it, and OFT+*for* are therefore surprised or at a disadvantage when it happens. EG *Students from tropical countries are often unprepared for the British climate... We were pushed into battle unprepared.*

unproductive /ʌmˈprədʌktɪv/. Something that is ADJ QUALIT **unproductive** does not produce anything useful. EG *Their land is unproductive.*

unprofitable /ʌmˈprɒfɪtəbᵊl/. An **unprofitable** ADJ QUALIT company or product does not make any profit or does not make enough profit. EG *Agriculture remained unprofitable... ...unprofitable business contracts.*

unprotected /ʌmˈprətɛktɪ²d/. Someone or some- ADJ QUALIT thing that is **unprotected** is not protected in any way. EG *They feel quite naked and unprotected... Beware of the sun beating on unprotected fair skin.*

unprovoked /ʌmˈprəvəʊkt/. If you make an **un-** ADJ CLASSIF **provoked** attack, you attack someone who has not harmed you in any way. EG *...casual and unprovoked violence.*

unpublished /ʌmˈpʌblɪʃt/. **Unpublished** books, ADJ CLASSIF manuscripts, or letters have never been published.

unqualified /ʌnkwɒlɪfaɪd/. **1** If you are **unquali-** ADJ CLASSIF **fied**, you do not have any qualifications, or do not have the right qualifications for a particular job. EG *...an unqualified childminder.*

2 Unqualified also means total and complete. EG ADJ CLASSIF: *The party was an unqualified disaster... The Gov-* ATTRIB *ernment does not have unqualified control over the economy.*

unquestionable /ʌnkwɛstʃənəbᵊl/. Something ADJ CLASSIF that is **unquestionable** is so obviously true or real that nobody can doubt it. EG *These are unquestionable facts... His courage and commitment are unquestionable.* ◊ **unquestionably.** EG *The visit to* ◊ ADV SEN *Greenland was unquestionably the highlight of the* OR ADV *voyage.*

unquestioned /ʌnkwɛstʃənd/. Something that is ADJ CLASSIF **unquestioned** is accepted by everyone, without anyone doubting or disagreeing. EG *...a system in which obedience and fortitude were unquestioned virtues.*

unquestioning /ʌnkwɛstʃənɪŋ/ is used to de- ADJ CLASSIF scribe beliefs or attitudes that people have without thinking closely about them or doubting them in any way. EG *You were chosen for this operation on the basis of your unquestioning obedience.*

unravel /ʌnrævᵊl/, **unravels, unravelling, un- ravelled;** also spelled **unraveling, unraveled** in American English.

1 If you **unravel** something that is knotted or V-ERG twisted, or if it **unravels**, it becomes undone. EG *Her knitting was starting to unravel.*

2 If you **unravel** a mystery or puzzle, you explain V+O it or work out the answer to it. EG *...factors which only the experts could unravel.*

unreal /ʌnrɪəl/. If you describe something as ADJ QUALIT **unreal**, you mean that it is so strange that you find it difficult to believe that it is real. EG *I felt unreal, in a bad dream, still not properly awake... This conversation is getting more and more unreal.*

unrealistic /ʌnrɪəlɪstɪk/. Someone who is **unre-** ADJ QUALIT **alistic** or who has **unrealistic** ideas does not recognize the truth about a situation or does not deal with it in a practical way. EG *This demand proved unrealistic and unworkable... You have unrealistic expectations.*

unreasonable /ʌnriːznəbᵊl/. **1** People who are ADJ QUALIT **unreasonable** are difficult to deal with because they behave in an unfair or illogical way. EG *We think he is being unreasonable.*

2 You say that something such as a decision is ADJ QUALIT **unreasonable** when it seems unfair and difficult to justify. EG *The request didn't seem unreasonable.*

unrecognizable /ʌnrɛkəɡ⁰naɪzəbᵊl/; also spelled ADJ CLASSIF **unrecognisable.** Something that is **unrecogniz-**

able is impossible to recognize or identify. EG *His voice was almost unrecognizable.*

unrecognized /ʌnrɛkəɡ⁰naɪzd/; also spelled **un-** ADJ CLASSIF **recognised.** If someone or something is **unrecog- nized**, they are not recognized or are not known about. EG *Unrecognized by any of the women, he entered the house... These common defects are often unrecognized.*

unrelated /ʌnrɪˈleɪtɪ²d/. Things which are **unre-** ADJ CLASSIF: **lated** have no connection with each other. EG *...a* OFT+*to series of unrelated incidents... New issues may arise, unrelated to the original ones.*

unrelenting /ʌnrɪˈlɛntɪŋ/. If someone's behav- ADJ CLASSIF iour is **unrelenting**, they continue to do something in a very determined way, often without caring whether they hurt or embarrass other people. EG *They kept up a sustained, unrelenting barrage of questions... ...the unrelenting quest for knowledge.*

unreliable /ʌnrɪˈlaɪəbᵊl/. If people, machines, or ADJ QUALIT methods are **unreliable**, you cannot trust them or rely on them. EG *Godwin was a thoroughly unreliable man... ...an unreliable second-hand car.*

unremarkable /ʌnrɪˈmɑːkəbᵊl/. If you say that ADJ CLASSIF something is **unremarkable**, you mean that it is not beautiful, interesting, or exciting. EG *The view is unremarkable.*

unremitting /ʌnrɪˈmɪtɪŋ/. Something that is **un-** ADJ CLASSIF **remitting** continues without stopping. EG *...their* Formal *unremitting efforts to get him into college.*

unrepentant /ʌnrɪˈpɛntᵊnt/. If you are **unre-** ADJ QUALIT **pentant**, you are not ashamed of your beliefs or actions. EG *I am an unrepentant believer in free enterprise.*

unresolved /ʌnrɪˈzɒlvd/. If a problem or difficul- ADJ CLASSIF ty is **unresolved**, no satisfactory solution has been Formal found to it. EG *Several major technological problems remained unresolved.*

unresponsive /ʌnrɪˈspɒnsɪv/. If you are **unre-** ADJ QUALIT: **sponsive** to something, you do not react to it or let OFT+*to* it affect your behaviour. EG *The audience was unresponsive... ...a government that is unresponsive to our needs.*

unrest /ʌnrɛst/. If there is **unrest**, people are N UNCOUNT angry and dissatisfied. EG *...the causes of industrial unrest.*

unrestrained /ʌnrɪˈstreɪnd/. If something is **un-** ADJ CLASSIF **restrained**, it is not controlled or limited in any way. EG *...the dangers of unrestrained growth.*

unrestricted /ʌnrɪˈstrɪktɪ²d/. If something is **un-** ADJ CLASSIF **restricted**, it is not limited by any laws or rules. EG *...the unrestricted dumping of waste.*

unrewarding /ʌnrɪˈwɔːdɪŋ/. If a job or task is ADJ QUALIT **unrewarding**, it does not give you any feelings of achievement or pleasure. EG *Learning a language often seems unrewarding at the time.*

unripe /ʌnraɪp/. **Unripe** fruit is not yet ripe. EG ADJ CLASSIF *We ate unripe apples from the garden.*

unrivalled /ʌnraɪvᵊld/. If you say that something ADJ CLASSIF is **unrivalled**, you mean that it is better than anything else of the same kind. EG *The gallery has an unrivalled collection of modern art.*

unroll /ʌnrəʊl/, **unrolls, unrolling, unrolled.** If V-ERG you **unroll** something such as a sheet of paper or a roll of cloth, you open it up and make it flat when it was previously rolled in a cylindrical shape. EG *Someone unrolled a map of America.*

unruffled /ʌnrʌfᵊld/. If you are **unruffled**, you ADJ CLASSIF are calm and not affected by surprising or frightening events. EG *She remained singularly unruffled when confronted with my discovery.*

unruly /ʌnruːliˈ/. **1 Unruly** people are difficult to ADJ QUALIT control or organize. EG *...unruly children.*

2 Unruly hair is difficult to keep tidy. EG *He* ADJ QUALIT *smoothed his unruly hair.*

Is this an unpublished book?

unsafe /ʌnseɪf/. **1** If something is **unsafe**, it is ADJ QUALIT: dangerous. EG *The house was declared unsafe for* USU PRED *habitation.*
2 If you are **unsafe**, you are in danger of being ADJ PRED harmed. EG *I feel very unsafe.*

unsatisfactory /ʌnsætɪsfæktəˀriˀ/. Something ADJ QUALIT that is **unsatisfactory** is not good enough to be acceptable. EG *I had an unsatisfactory discussion with him about my job.*

unsatisfied /ʌnsætɪsfaɪd/. If you are **unsatisfied**, ADJ QUALIT: you are disappointed because you have not got OFT+*with* what you wanted. EG *He asked a lot of questions, and was unsatisfied with the answers.*

unsavoury /ʌnseɪvəˀriˀ/; spelled **unsavory** in ADJ QUALIT American English. You describe people, places, and things as **unsavoury** when you find them unpleasant. EG *He looks so unsavoury... Parts of Birmingham are pretty unsavoury.*

unscathed /ʌnskeɪðd/. If you are **unscathed** af- ADJ PRED ter a dangerous experience, you have not been injured or harmed by it. EG *We all escaped unscathed.*

unscheduled /ʌnʃedjuːld/, ʌnskɛd-/. An **unsched-** ADJ CLASSIF **uled** event is not planned to happen, but happens unexpectedly or because someone changes their plans at a late stage. EG *Grimes was about to make an unscheduled announcement.*

unscrew /ʌnskruː/, **unscrews**, **unscrewing**, **un-** V+O **screwed**. If you **unscrew** something, you remove it by turning it, or by removing the screws that fasten it to something else. EG *He unscrewed the top and put the bottle to his mouth... The mirrors had been unscrewed and removed.*

unscrupulous /ʌnskruːpjəˀləs/. **Unscrupulous** ADJ QUALIT people are prepared to act dishonestly in order to get what they want. EG *He was cruel, treacherous and unscrupulous.*

unseeing /ʌnsiːɪŋ/. You describe a person as ADJ CLASSIF **unseeing** or say that their eyes are **unseeing** Literary when they are not looking at anything, or not noticing something, although their eyes are open. EG *She stared ahead, unseeing... She was gazing with unseeing eyes at the harbour.*

unseemly /ʌnsiːmliˀ/. If someone's behaviour is ADJ QUALIT **unseemly**, it is not polite or not suitable for a Formal particular occasion or situation. EG *...an unseemly* Outdated *public squabble over his salary.*

unseen /ʌnsiːn/. You use **unseen** to describe ADJ CLASSIF things that you cannot see. EG *A large unseen orchestra was playing jazzy rhythms.*

unselfish /ʌnselfɪʃ/. If you are **unselfish**, you ADJ QUALIT think about other people's wishes and needs rather than your own. EG *He was a brave and unselfish man... ...her unselfish devotion to her children.*

unsettle /ʌnsetəˀl/, **unsettles**, **unsettling**, **un-** V+O **settled**. If something **unsettles** you, it causes you to feel restless, dissatisfied, or rather worried. EG *It unsettled him not to know where he was.*

unsettled /ʌnsetəˀld/. **1** In an **unsettled** situation, ADJ CLASSIF there is a lot of uncertainty about what will hap- pen. EG *...in the early days of 1968, when everything was unsettled.*
2 If you are **unsettled**, you cannot concentrate on ADJ PRED anything, because you are worried or excited about something. EG *I felt pretty unsettled all that week.*
3 An **unsettled** argument or dispute has not yet ADJ CLASSIF been resolved. EG *This argument remained unset-* Formal *tled until January 1975.*

unshakable /ʌnʃeɪkəˀbəˀl/; also spelled **unshake-** ADJ CLASSIF **able**. **Unshakable** beliefs are so strong that they cannot be destroyed or altered. EG *...her unshakable faith in progress... ...a man of unshakable convic- tions.*

unshaven /ʌnʃeɪvəˀn/. If a man is **unshaven**, he ADJ CLASSIF has not shaved recently and there are short hairs on his face or chin. EG *...his unshaven face.*

unsightly /ʌnsaɪtliˀ/. If something is **unsightly**, it ADJ QUALIT is ugly and unattractive to look at. EG *His skin was covered with unsightly blotches.*

unskilled /ʌnskɪld/. **Unskilled** workers do work ADJ CLASSIF that does not require any special training. EG *...unskilled labourers... They are all in low-paid, unskilled jobs.*

unsociable /ʌnsəʊʃəˀbəˀl/. **Unsociable** people do ADJ QUALIT not like talking to other people and try to avoid meeting them; used showing disapproval. EG *She was an awkward and unsociable girl.*

unsolicited /ʌnsəlɪsɪtɪˀd/. Something that is **un-** ADJ CLASSIF **solicited** is given or happens without being asked Formal for. EG *She was given much unsolicited advice from her companions... ...unsolicited letters from pub- lishers.*

unsolved /ʌnsɒlvd/. An **unsolved** problem or ADJ CLASSIF mystery has never been solved. EG *The mystery will probably remain forever unsolved.*

unsophisticated /ʌnsəfɪstɪkeɪtɪˀd/. **1** People who ADJ QUALIT are **unsophisticated** do not have a wide range of experience or knowledge and their tastes are simple. EG *It is easy to write because the readers are relatively unsophisticated.*
2 An **unsophisticated** method or device is very ADJ QUALIT simple. EG *These forecasts are based on rather unsophisticated economic analyses.*

unsound /ʌnsaʊnd/. **1** If you say that a conclusion ADJ QUALIT or method is **unsound**, you mean that it is based on ideas that are wrong. EG *The basic research seems unsound... These procedures are economically un- sound.*
2 An **unsound** building or other structure is in poor ADJ QUALIT condition and is likely to collapse.

unspeakable /ʌnspiːkəˀbəˀl/. If you say that some- ADJ QUALIT thing is **unspeakable**, you mean that it is extreme- ly unpleasant. EG *All I remember is the unspeak- able pain... Their treatment of women is unspeak- able.*

unspecified /ʌnspesɪfaɪd/. You say that some- ADJ CLASSIF thing is **unspecified** when you are not told exactly what it is. EG *She was dying of some unspecified disease.*

unspoiled /ʌnspɔɪld/; also spelled **unspoilt** /ʌnspɔɪlt/. **1** If something is **unspoiled**, it has not ADJ CLASSIF been damaged or harmed in any way. EG *The wine's flavour was unspoiled.*
2 You describe a place as **unspoiled** when it has ADJ CLASSIF not changed for a long time. EG *...areas of unspoiled countryside... ...a paradise of unspoilt beaches.*

unspoken /ʌnspəʊkəˀn/. If someone's thoughts, ADJ CLASSIF wishes, or feelings are **unspoken**, they do not tell other people about them. EG *I was full of unspoken fears... ...her unspoken criticism of him.*

unstable /ʌnsteɪbəˀl/. **1** If something is **unstable**, ADJ QUALIT **1.1** it is likely to change suddenly and to create difficulty or danger. EG *...unstable governments... ...the unstable political situation.* **1.2** it is not firm or not fixed properly, and is likely to move or fall. EG *...the unstable guttering on the house.*
2 If people are **unstable**, their emotions and ADJ QUALIT behaviour keep changing because their minds are disturbed or upset. EG *He was a neurotic and unstable man... She was always mentally unstable.*

unsteady /ʌnstediˀ/. **1** If you are **unsteady**, you ADJ QUALIT have difficulty standing or walking because you cannot completely control your legs or your body. EG *She seemed unsteady on her feet.* ◊ **unsteadily.** ◊ ADV EG *He rose unsteadily to his feet.*
2 If your hands are **unsteady**, you have difficulty ADJ QUALIT controlling them. EG *Stephen poured two brandies with an unsteady hand.*
3 **Unsteady** objects are not held, fixed, or bal- ADJ QUALIT anced securely. EG *She was balancing three boxes in an unsteady pile.*

unstructured /ʌnstrʌktʃəd/. If an activity is **un-** ADJ QUALIT **structured**, it is not organized in a complete or detailed way. EG *...an unstructured but effective method of education.*

unstuck /ʌnstʌk/. **1** If something **comes unstuck**, PHRASE it becomes separated from something else that it was attached to. EG *Some of the posters regularly came unstuck.*

2 If a plan or system **comes unstuck**, it fails. EG PHRASE *The system is not so likely to come unstuck in a* Informal *small organization.*

3 If someone **comes unstuck**, they fail badly in PHRASE something that they are trying to achieve. EG *I* Informal *always knew he'd come unstuck somewhere.*

unsubstantiated /ˌʌnsəbˈstænʃieitɪ²d/. A state- ADJ CLASSIF ment or story that is **unsubstantiated** has not been proved to be true. EG *There have been many unsubstantiated reports of gas used in war zones.*

unsuccessful /ˌʌnsəkˈsesful/. If you are **unsuc-** ADJ QUALIT **cessful**, you do not succeed in what you are trying to do. EG *Tom tried to hypnotize me but he was unsuccessful... ...an unsuccessful farmer... ...an unsuccessful attempt to kill him.* ◊ **unsuccessfully.** ◊ ADV EG *I tried unsuccessfully to talk to him.*

unsuitable /ˌʌnsuːˈtəbəl/. Someone or something ADJ QUALIT : that is **unsuitable** has qualities that are not right OFT+*for* or appropriate for a particular purpose. EG *...areas that are entirely unsuitable for agriculture.* ◊ **unsuitably.** EG *She was most unsuitably dressed.* ◊ ADV

unsuited /ˌʌnsjuːˈtɪ²d/. **1** Someone or something ADJ CLASSIF : that is **unsuited** to a particular situation, place, or USU+*to*/*for* task, has qualities that are not right or appropriate for that situation, place, or task. EG *...vehicles that are clearly unsuited for use in the desert.*

2 If two people, especially a man and a woman, are ADJ QUALIT : **unsuited** to each other, they have different per- OFT+*to* sonalities and interests, and so are unlikely to have a successful relationship.

unsung /ˌʌnˈsʌŋ/. You use **unsung** to describe ADJ CLASSIF : people who are not appreciated or praised, al- USU ATTRIB though you think they should be. EG *...research by* Literary *heroic but unsung volunteers.*

unsure /ˌʌnˈʃʊə/. **1** If you are **unsure** of yourself, ADJ QUALIT : you lack confidence. EG *His demands made the boy* OFT+*of* *nervous and unsure of himself.*

2 If you are **unsure** about something, you feel ADJ QUALIT : uncertain about it or about what to do. EG *She took* OFT+*about/of* *a step back, unsure of his reaction.*

unsuspected /ˌʌnsəsˈpektɪ²d/. If something is **un-** ADJ CLASSIF **suspected**, people are not aware of it. EG *As the project developed, unsuspected difficulties came to light.*

unsuspecting /ˌʌnsəsˈpektɪŋ/. Someone who is ADJ CLASSIF **unsuspecting** is not at all aware of something that is happening or going to happen. EG *...a survey conducted on 763 unsuspecting male students... ...leopards pouncing on unsuspecting young baboons.*

unsympathetic /ˌʌnsɪmpəˈθetɪk/. Someone who is ADJ QUALIT **unsympathetic** is unwilling to be friendly or helpful to a person who needs help or sympathy. EG *Posy had been utterly unsympathetic when she heard about it... ...a terse and unsympathetic reply.*

untangle /ˌʌnˈtæŋgəl/, **untangles, untangling,** V+O **untangled.** If you **untangle** something such as string that is twisted together, you undo the knots in it. EG *He untangled the cable carefully.*

untapped /ˌʌnˈtæpt/. An **untapped** supply or ADJ CLASSIF source of something has not yet been used. EG *...Britain's vast untapped reserves of coal... ...an abundant and largely untapped water source.*

untenable /ˌʌnˈtenəbəl/. An argument, theory, or ADJ CLASSIF position that is **untenable** cannot be defended Formal successfully against criticism or attack. EG *His position is morally untenable.*

unthinkable /ˌʌnˈθɪŋkəbəl/. If you describe some- ADJ CLASSIF : thing as **unthinkable**, you mean that it is so USU PRED shocking or awful that you cannot imagine it happening or being true. EG *War was unthinkable... I can't marry again so soon after Guy's death, it's unthinkable... It was unthinkable to defy his authority.*

unthinking /ˌʌnˈθɪŋkɪŋ/. Someone who is **unthink-** ADJ QUALIT **ing** does not think carefully about the effects of their behaviour and therefore does foolish things.

EG *Our society seems to be rushing ahead, unthinking, into ever greater mechanisation.*

untidy /ˌʌnˈtaidi¹/, **untidier, untidiest. 1** Some- ADJ QUALIT thing that is **untidy** is messy and disordered and not neat or well arranged. EG *It's a neglected, untidy park... The living-room was untidier than usual.*

2 Someone who is **untidy** leaves things in an ADJ QUALIT untidy state. EG *She is so careless and untidy.*

untie /ˌʌnˈtai/, **unties, untying, untied.** If you V+O **untie** someone or something, you remove the string or rope that has been tied round them by undoing the knots. EG *He quickly untied the captives... She tried to untie the knot.*

untied /ˌʌnˈtaid/. Something such as a tie, shoelace, ADJ CLASSIF or ribbon that is **untied** has its ends loose rather than tied together in a bow or knot.

until /ˌʌnˈtɪl/. **1** If something happens **until** a PREP OR CONJ particular time, it happens before that time and stops at that time. EG *We went on duty at six in the evening and worked until 2 a.m... You can get free prescriptions until you are 16.*

2 If something does not happen **until** a particular PREP OR CONJ time, it does not happen before that time and only WITH happens after it. EG *They didn't find her until the* BROAD NEG *next day... Women did not gain the vote until after the First World War.*

unto /ˈʌntu:/ means the same as to. EG *Do unto* PREP *others as you would have them do unto you.* Outdated

untold /ˌʌnˈtəʊld/. You use **untold** to emphasize ADJ CLASSIF : how great something is, especially something un- ATTRIB pleasant. EG *The war brought untold suffering upon* Formal *the population... It cost them untold millions of dollars... That idea did untold damage.*

untouched /ˌʌnˈtʌtʃt/. **1** Something that is **un-** ADJ CLASSIF **touched** has not been changed, moved, or damaged in any way. EG *The island has been untouched by tourism... ...an original Norman chapel untouched since the twelfth century.*

2 If a meal is **untouched**, none of it has been ADJ CLASSIF eaten. EG *She sent back her breakfast tray untouched.*

untoward /ˌʌntə²ˈwɔːd/. You use **untoward** to de- ADJ CLASSIF scribe something that happens unexpectedly and Formal causes difficulties. EG *Nothing untoward had happened... Should any untoward side-effects occur, consult a doctor.*

untrained /ˌʌnˈtreind/. **1** Someone who is **un-** ADJ CLASSIF **trained** has had no education in the skills that they need for a particular job or activity. EG *We do not expect untrained people to accept risky occupations... ...untrained assistants.*

2 An **untrained** voice or mind has not been ADJ CLASSIF developed through formal education or training. EG *He had a deep, untrained voice.*

untreated /ˌʌnˈtriːtɪ²d/. **1** If an injury or illness is ADJ CLASSIF left **untreated**, it is not given medical treatment. EG *...a period of time during which a brain tumour remained untreated.*

2 Harmful materials or chemicals that are **un-** ADJ CLASSIF **treated** have not been made safe. EG *Our rivers have been poisoned by untreated effluent.*

untried /ˌʌnˈtraid/. Something that is **untried** has ADJ CLASSIF not yet been used, done, or tested. EG *It is still an untried policy.*

untroubled /ˌʌnˈtrʌbəld/. If you are **untroubled** ADJ PRED+*by* by something, you are not affected or worried by it. EG *...nations that were untroubled by the presence of terrorists on their streets.*

untrue /ˌʌnˈtruː/. **1** Something that is **untrue** is not ADJ CLASSIF true. EG *The story was probably untrue.*

2 If someone is **untrue** to you, they are unfaithful ADJ PRED+*to* to you or lie to you. Literary

untrustworthy /ˌʌnˈtrʌstwɜːð1/. Someone who is ADJ QUALIT **untrustworthy** is unreliable and cannot be trust-

Is an unsubstantiated story untrue?

ed. EG *He has proved himself completely untrust-*
worthy.

untruth /ʌntruːθ/, **untruths** /ʌntruːðz/. An **un-** N COUNT
truth is a lie. EG *I hesitated rather than tell a* Formal
deliberate untruth.

untruthful /ʌntruːθful/. Someone who is **untruth-** ADJ QUALIT
ful is dishonest and says things that are not true. EG Formal
He was being untruthful when he claimed that he
had never seen her before.

untutored /ʌntjuːtəd/. Someone who is **untutored** ADJ CLASSIF
in a particular area of knowledge has not learnt Formal
about it from other people or from books. EG *...the*
natural ease that some untutored men bring to
horse-racing.

unusable /ʌnjuːzəbəl/. Something that is **unus-** ADJ CLASSIF
able is not in a good enough state or condition to
be used. EG *The living room was unusable.*

unused; pronounced /ʌnjuːzd/ in paragraph 1 and
/ʌnjuːst/ in paragraph 2.

1 Something that is **unused** has not been used. EG ADJ CLASSIF
...a pile of unused fuel.

2 If you are **unused** to something, you have not ADJ PRED+to
often done it or experienced it, so it is unfamiliar to
you. EG *She was unused to hardship.*

unusual /ʌnjuːʒuəl/. If something is **unusual**, it ADJ QUALIT
does not happen very often or you do not see it or
hear it very often. EG *He had an unusual name... It*
was not unusual for me to come home at two or
three in the morning.

unusually /ʌnjuːʒuəliː/. You use **unusually 1** to SUBMOD
emphasize that something is bigger than usual or
has more of a particular quality than usual. EG *...a*
clump of weed that seemed unusually large... Octo-
ber has been unusually wet and cold. **2** to say that ADV SEN
something you are describing is not what normally
happens. EG *The service charge, unusually, is 10 per*
cent.

unveil /ʌnveɪl/, **unveils**, **unveiling**, **unveiled**. **1** V+O
When someone **unveils** something such as a new
statue or painting, they draw back a curtain which
is covering it, in a special ceremony.

2 If you **unveil** something that has been a secret, V+O
you make it known. EG *The plan was unveiled with* Formal
approval from the Minister.

unwanted /ʌnwɒntɪd/. You say that something is ADJ CLASSIF
unwanted when a particular person does not want
it, or when nobody wants it. EG *...the appalling*
suffering caused by unwanted pregnancies... She
was starting to feel unwanted.

unwarranted /ʌnwɒrəntɪd/. Something that is ADJ CLASSIF
unwarranted is not justified or not deserved. EG *It* Formal
was a totally unwarranted waste of public money...
He saw himself as the victim of unwarranted
attacks... This concern proved unwarranted.

unwary /ʌnweəriː/. Someone who is **unwary** is ADJ QUALIT
not cautious, and is therefore likely to be harmed
or deceived. EG *...the shrieks of unwary animals*
taken by surprise.

unwelcome /ʌnwelkəm/. **1** An **unwelcome** ex- ADJ QUALIT
perience is one that you do not like and did not
want. EG *The move from London was entirely*
unwelcome to her... ...unwelcome publicity.

2 You say that a visitor is **unwelcome** when you ADJ QUALIT
did not want them to come. EG *...an unwelcome*
guest.

unwell /ʌnwel/. If you are **unwell**, you are ill. EG *I* ADJ PRED
informed her that I was unwell and could not
come... He complained of feeling unwell.

unwieldy /ʌnwiːldiː/. **1** An **unwieldy** object is ADJ QUALIT
difficult to move or carry because it is big or
heavy. EG *We set about the task of towing the*
unwieldy structure into the shelter.

2 A system that is **unwieldy** does not work well ADJ QUALIT
because it is too large or is badly organized. EG
...the country's unwieldy banking system.

unwilling /ʌnwɪlɪŋ/. If you are **unwilling** to do ADJ QUALIT:
something, you do not want to do it. EG *He's* OFT+to-INF
unwilling to accept advice. ◊ **unwillingly**. EG *He* ◊ ADV
submitted unwillingly to his mother.

◊ **unwillingness**. EG *...their unwillingness to dis-* ◊ N UNCOUNT
cuss common problems.

unwind /ʌnwaɪnd/, **unwinds**, **unwinding**, **un-**
wound. **1** When you **unwind**, you relax, especially V
after working hard. EG *Reading is a good way to*
unwind.

2 If you **unwind** something that is wrapped round V+O
something else or that is wound in a ball, you undo
it or straighten it out. EG *Francis was unwinding his*
bandage.

unwise /ʌnwaɪz/. Something that is **unwise** is ADJ QUALIT:
foolish. EG *It would be very unwise for the boy to* OFT PRED
marry her... It was an unwise choice.

unwitting /ʌnwɪtɪŋ/ is used to describe people or ADJ CLASSIF:
their actions when they do something or become ATTRIB
involved in something without realizing what is Formal
really happening. EG *I became the unwitting instru-*
ment of that unscrupulous man. ◊ **unwittingly**. EG ◊ ADV
Sometimes we ourselves unwittingly invite trouble.

unworkable /ʌnwɜːkəbəl/. If you say that an ADJ CLASSIF
idea or plan is **unworkable**, you mean that it
cannot be made to work. EG *His proposals for*
reform of the Trades Unions are unworkable.

unworldly /ʌnwɜːldliː/. Someone who is **un-** ADJ QUALIT
worldly is not interested in having a lot of money Formal
or possessions.

unworthy /ʌnwɜːðiː/. If someone is **unworthy** of ADJ QUALIT:
something, they do not deserve it. EG *I am unwor-* OFT+of
thy of this honour... I felt I was unworthy of her Formal
love.

unwrap /ʌnræp/, **unwraps**, **unwrapping**, **un-** V+O
wrapped. When you **unwrap** something, you take
off the paper or other covering that is around it. EG
I started to unwrap my sandwiches... Ellen careful-
ly unwrapped the parcel.

unwritten /ʌnrɪtən/. **Unwritten** things have not ADJ CLASSIF
been printed or written down. EG *Thoughts of my* USU ATTRIB
unwritten novel nagged me... ...unwritten laws.

unzip /ʌnzɪp/, **unzips**, **unzipping**, **unzipped**. V+O
When you **unzip** something which is fastened by a
zip, you unfasten it. EG *He unzipped his anorak.*

up /ʌp/, **ups**, **upping**, **upped**. **1** Up is used in
phrasal verbs such as 'get up' and 'add up'.

2 Up means towards a higher place, or in a higher PREP, OR
place. EG *I carried my suitcase up the stairs behind* ADV AFTER VB
her... Bill put up his hand... ...comfortable houses up
in the hills.

3 If someone stands **up**, they move so that they are ADV AFTER VB
standing. EG *She scrambled up from the floor... She*
helped Henry up from the bench.

4 Up also means in the north or towards the north. ADV+ADV/
EG *Why did you come up to Edinburgh?... We're* PREP
having brilliant sunshine up here.

5 If you go **up** a road or river, you go along it. EG *...a* PREP OR ADV
voyage up the Nile... There's a cafe just a hundred
yards further up.

6 You also use **up** to show that something is close ADV+ADV/
to something else. EG *It's only when you get right up* PREP
to them that you realise what they are... Ferdinand
ran up to his father-in-law.

7 If you move **up and down**, you move repeatedly PHRASE
in one direction and then in the opposite direction.
EG *I was so happy I jumped up and down... He*
started pacing up and down the office.

8 If you have **ups and downs**, you experience a PHRASE
mixture of good things and bad things. EG *We have*
had our ups and downs.

9 If you are **up**, you are not in bed. EG *They were up* ADJ PRED
early... He has begun to half the night.

10 If someone or something is **up** for election, ADV+PREP
review, or examination, they are about to be
considered or judged. EG *One of my colleagues*
comes up for election next week.

11 If a period of time is **up**, it has come to an end. ADJ PRED
EG *When the six weeks were up, everybody was sad*
that she had to leave.

12 You say that a road is **up** when it is being ADJ PRED
repaired.

13 If a number or an amount goes **up**, it increases. ADV AFTER VB EG *...when interest rates go up.*

14 You use **up to** to say how large something can PREP be or what level it has reached. EG *They might be up to a metre wide... Our total energy consumption is now up to about 40% and still rising... The work isn't up to the standard I require.*

15 If you feel **up to** doing something, you are well PREP : OFT + enough to do it. EG *Are you up to doing some work?* -ING

16 If you say that someone is **up to** something, you PREP mean that they are secretly doing something that Informal they should not be doing. EG *The neighbours think the Hochstadts are up to something.*

17 If you say that it is **up** to someone to do PREP something, you mean that it is their responsibility to do it. EG *It is up to the teacher not to accept shoddy work.*

18 If something happens **up to** or **up until** a PREP particular time, it happens until that time. EG *Up until the early sixties there was no shortage.*

19 If you say that something is **not up to much**, PHRASE you mean that it is of poor quality. EG *The dances* Informal *weren't up to much.*

20 If you are **up against** something, you have a PREP very difficult situation or problem to deal with. EG *They are up against the slowness of the system.*

21 If you say that something **is up**, you mean that PHRASE something is wrong or that something worrying is Informal happening. EG *I know something's up... What's up, Myra? You look sad.*

22 If you **up** an amount of money, you increase it. V+O EG *They upped the cost to the public.* Informal

up-and-coming. Up-and-coming people are ADJ CLASSIF likely to be successful in the future. EG *...up-and-coming Third World Exporters.*

upbringing /ˈʌpbrɪŋɪŋ/. Your **upbringing** is the N UNCOUNT : way your parents treat you and the things that they OFT + SUPP teach you. EG *Tony never rebelled against his upbringing... a strict upbringing.*

update /ʌpˈdeɪt/, **updates, updating, updated.** If V+O you **update** something, you make it more modern, usually by adding newer parts to it. EG *The information will need updating from time to time... ...regularly updated criminal records.*

upend /ʌpˈend/, **upends, upending, upended.** If V+O : USU PASS something **is upended**, it is turned upside down. EG *There the car stood, upended in the grass.*

upgrade /ʌpˈɡreɪd/, **upgrades, upgrading, up-** V+O **graded.** If you **upgrade** something such as a person's job or status, you change it, so that the person becomes more important or receives more money. EG *We need to upgrade the pay and status of doctors.*

upheaval /ʌpˈhiːvəl/, **upheavals.** An **upheaval** is N COUNT OR a big change which causes a lot of trouble, confu- N UNCOUNT sion, and worry. EG *Great upheavals were taking place in the States... They have brought social upheaval and conflict into the country.*

upheld /ʌpˈheld/ is the past tense and past partici- ple of **uphold.**

uphill /ʌpˈhɪl/. **1** If you go **uphill**, you go up a ADV OR slope. EG *She ran furiously uphill... ...the effort of* ADJ CLASSIF : *pushing the cart uphill.* ATTRIB

2 An **uphill** task requires a great deal of effort and ADJ CLASSIF : determination. EG *This is hard, uphill work.* ATTRIB

uphold /ʌpˈhəʊld/, **upholds, upholding, upheld** V+O /ʌpˈheld/. If you **uphold** something such as a law, a principle, or a decision, you support and maintain it. EG *He had sworn to uphold the law... His conviction was upheld on appeal.*

upholstered /ʌpˈhəʊlstəd/. **Upholstered** chairs ADJ CLASSIF and sofas have a soft covering that makes them comfortable to sit on. EG *...two handsome chairs, upholstered in black leather.*

upholstery /ʌpˈhəʊlstəˈriː/ is the soft covering on N UNCOUNT chairs and sofas that makes them more comfort- able to sit on.

upkeep /ˈʌpkiːp/. The **upkeep** of a building is the N UNCOUNT : continual process of keeping it in good condition. USU + of EG *We have to pay for the upkeep of the chapel.*

upland /ˈʌplənd/, **uplands. 1 Upland** places are ADJ CLASSIF : situated on high hills, plateaus, or mountains. EG ATTRIB *They move with their flocks to upland pastures.*

2 Uplands are areas of land on high hills, plateaus, N PLURAL or mountains. EG *...the chalk uplands of Wiltshire.*

uplifted /ʌpˈlɪftɪˈd/. If people's faces or arms are ADJ CLASSIF **uplifted**, they are pointing them upwards or are Literary holding them in a high position. EG *We could just see him, a tiny silhouette with uplifted arms.*

uplifting /ʌpˈlɪftɪŋ/. You describe something as ADJ QUALIT **uplifting** when it makes you feel very cheerful and happy. EG *My experience of love has hardly been uplifting... ...uplifting literature.*

upmarket /ʌpˈmɑːkɪt/. **Upmarket** places and ADJ QUALIT goods are visited or bought by people who have Informal sophisticated and expensive tastes. EG *Paleo is an upmarket resort... ...upmarket shops.*

upon /əˈpɒn/. **1 Upon** is used in phrasal verbs such as 'come upon' and 'look upon', and after some other verbs such as 'decide' and 'depend'.

2 If one thing is **upon** another, it is on it. EG *She was* PREP *sitting with a cat upon her knee... He lay down* Formal *upon the grass... He had a furtive look upon his face.*

3 You use **upon** when mentioning an event that is PREP followed immediately by another event. EG *Upon entering the cabin, she sat down.*

4 You also use **upon** between two occurrences of PREP the same noun in order to say that there are very large numbers of the thing referred to. EG *We drove through mile upon mile of brick villas... ...row upon row of red roofs.*

5 If an event is **upon** you, it is just about to happen. PREP EG *Suddenly the concert was upon us with me totally unprepared.*

upper /ˈʌpə/, **uppers. 1 Upper** describes **1.1** ADJ CLASSIF : something that is above something else, usually the ATTRIB top one of a pair of things. EG *I pulled down a book from an upper shelf.* **1.2** the higher part of some- thing. *Dark glasses masked the upper half of his face.*

2 If you have **the upper hand** in a situation, you PHRASE have more power than the other people involved and can make decisions about what happens. EG *The farmers had got the upper hand now.*

3 The **upper** of a shoe is the top part of it, which is N COUNT attached to the sole and the heel. EG *A lot of shoes now have nylon uppers.*

upper class, upper classes. The **upper classes** N COUNT : OFT are the people who belong to the social class above PLURAL the middle class. EG *The upper classes still send their children to Eton or Harrow... ...upper-class families.*

upper lip, upper lips. Your **upper lip** is the part N COUNT : of your face between your mouth and your nose. EG USU SING *His chin and upper lip were clean shaven.* ● to **keep a stiff upper lip**: see **lip.**

uppermost /ˈʌpəməʊst/. **1** You say that something ADJ CLASSIF OR is **uppermost** when it is higher than the rest of ADV something or when it is the highest one of a group of things. EG *He was pointing with the whole of his hand, thumb uppermost... He gently examined the uppermost leaves.*

2 If something is **uppermost** in a particular situa- ADJ PRED tion, it is the most important thing in that situation. EG *Political motives were uppermost... There were two thoughts uppermost in my mind.*

upright /ˈʌpraɪt/. **1** If you are **upright**, you are ADJ CLASSIF OR sitting or standing with your back straight, rather ADV AFTER VB than bending or lying down. EG *I cannot stand upright any more... He sat bolt upright.*

2 An **upright** vacuum cleaner or freezer stands ADJ CLASSIF

Is up-to-the-minute information up-to-date?

vertically and is taller than it is wide. EG ...*a small upright model light enough to carry upstairs.*

3 An **upright** chair has a straight back and no ADJ CLASSIF arms.

4 You can describe people as **upright** when they ADJ QUALIT are careful to follow acceptable rules of behaviour and behave in a moral way. EG ...*the upright and respectable Charles Smithson.*

uprising /ˈʌpraɪzɪŋ/, **uprisings.** When there is an N COUNT **uprising**, a group of people start fighting against the people who are in power in their country, usually because they want to bring about a political change. EG ...*the Sepoy uprising of 1857.*

uproar /ˈʌprɔː/. **1** If there is an **uproar**, there is a lot N SING OR of shouting and noise because people are very N UNCOUNT angry or shocked about something. EG *Soon all was uproar... She could hear the uproar in the prisoners' coaches.*

2 You can also use **uproar** to refer to a lot of N SING OR public criticism and debate about something. EG N UNCOUNT *The Parisian intellectuals were in an uproar.*

uproarious /ʌpˈrɔːrɪəs/. **Uproarious** laughter is ADJ CLASSIF very noisy. EG ...*an uproarious burst of laughter.* Literary
◊ **uproariously.** EG *He laughed uproariously.* ◊ ADV

uproot /ʌpˈruːt/, **uproots, uprooting, uprooted. 1** V-REFL; ALSO If you **uproot** yourself or if you **are uprooted**, you V+O : USU PASS leave, or are made to leave, a place where you have lived for a long time. EG *People were uprooted and rehoused.*

2 If someone **uproots** a tree or if the wind **uproots** V+O it, it is pulled out of the ground. EG *Windows were smashed and large trees uprooted.*

upset, **upsets, upsetting.** The form **upset** is used in the present tense and is the past tense and past participle of the verb. **Upset** is pronounced /ʌpˈsɛt/ when it is an adjective in predicative position or a verb, and /ˈʌpsɛt/ when it is an adjective in attributive position or a noun.

1 If you are **upset**, you are unhappy or disappoint- ADJ PRED ed because something unpleasant has happened to you. EG *I'm dreadfully upset about it all... They were upset by the poverty they saw in Dublin.*

2 If something **upsets** you, it makes you feel V+O worried or unhappy. EG *I didn't mean to upset you.*
◊ **upsetting.** EG *It was a very upsetting experience.* ◊ ADJ QUALIT

3 If you **upset** something such as a procedure or a V+O state of affairs, you cause it to go wrong. EG *Davis's death has upset the routine.*

4 To **upset** something also means to turn it over V+O accidentally. EG *He almost upset the canoe.*

5 If your stomach is **upset**, you have a slight illness ADJ QUALIT in your stomach caused by an infection or by something that you have eaten. EG *I've got an upset stomach.*

6 A stomach **upset** is a slight illness in your N COUNT stomach caused by an infection or by something that you have eaten.

upshot /ˈʌpʃɒt/. The **upshot** of a series of events or N SING : the+N, discussions is the final result. EG *The upshot was* OFT+*of that the agreement had to be re-negotiated.* Formal

upside down. 1 If something is **upside down**, it ADJ PRED OR has been turned round so that the part that is ADV AFTER VB usually lowest is above the part that is usually highest. EG *They were hanging upside down... You are holding it upside down.*

2 If you turn a place **upside down**, you create ADV AFTER VB disorder or untidiness in it. EG *I've turned the house upside down, but I still can't find his watch.*

upstage /ʌpˈsteɪdʒ/, **upstages, upstaging, up-** V+O **staged.** If you **upstage** someone, you take people's attention away from them by making them watch or listen to you instead. EG *He seems to be attempting to upstage the Prime Minister.*

upstairs /ʌpˈsteəz/. **1** If you go **upstairs** in a ADV AFTER VB building, you go up towards a higher floor, usually by a staircase. EG *I ran back upstairs.*

2 If something or someone is **upstairs** in a build- ADV ing, they are on an upper floor. EG *Upstairs, there were three little bedrooms.*

3 The **upstairs** of a building is its upper floor or N SING floors. EG *They had to rent out the upstairs to make* Informal *the mortgage payments.*

4 An **upstairs** room or object is one which is ADJ CLASSIF : situated on an upper floor of a building. EG *Neigh-* ATTRIB *bours watched from their upstairs windows.*

upstart /ˈʌpstɑːt/, **upstarts.** You refer to someone N COUNT as an **upstart** when they behave as if they are important, but you think that they are too new in a place or job to be treated as important. EG *He regarded me as a young upstart.*

upstream /ʌpˈstriːm/. **1** If something moves **up-** ADV AFTER VB **stream**, it moves along a river towards the source of the river. EG *He was making his way upstream.*

2 If something is **upstream** from a place, it is on ADJ PRED the same river but further towards the river's source. EG ...*the chemical plant upstream.*

upsurge /ˈʌpsɜːdʒ/. If there is an **upsurge** in N SING : something, there is a sudden, large increase in it. USU+SUPP EG ...*a massive upsurge of social unrest.* Formal

uptake /ˈʌpteɪk/. You say that someone is **quick** PHRASE **on the uptake** when they understand things quick- Informal ly. You say that someone is **slow on the uptake** when they have difficulty understanding simple or obvious things. EG *She was not very quick on the uptake.*

uptight /ʌpˈtaɪt/. You say that someone is **uptight** ADJ QUALIT when they are nervous or annoyed about some- Informal thing but are not saying so directly. EG *You get so uptight whenever I raise the subject.*

up-to-date. 1 If something is **up-to-date**, it is the ADJ QUALIT newest thing of its kind. EG ...*a fleet of up-to-date lorries... The industry is modern and up-to-date.*

2 If you are **up-to-date** about something, you have ADJ QUALIT the latest information about it. EG *Tony was more up-to-date than I.*

up-to-the-minute. Up-to-the-minute informa- ADJ CLASSIF tion is the latest information that you can get about something. EG ...*up-to-the-minute news.*

uptown /ʌpˈtaʊn/. If you go **uptown**, you go away ADV AFTER VB, from the centre of a town or city towards one of its OR ADJ CLASSIF outer parts. EG *He walked uptown... She met him at* American *his apartment uptown.*

upturn /ˈʌptɜːn/, **upturns.** If there is an **upturn** in N COUNT : something such as a country's economy, it starts to USU SING improve. EG *The economy is experiencing an upturn.*

upturned /ʌpˈtɜːnd/. Something that is **upturned** ADJ CLASSIF **1** points upwards. EG *She had a small upturned nose.*

2 is upside down. EG *She sat on an upturned bucket.*

upwards /ˈʌpwədz/; also **upward.** **1** If something ADV AFTER VB moves or looks **upwards** or **upward**, it moves or looks up towards a higher place. EG *He happened to look upwards.*

2 An **upward** movement or look is directed to- ADJ CLASSIF : wards a higher place. EG *He would steal upward* ATTRIB *glances at the clock.*

3 **Upwards** or **upward** is used to say that some- ADV AFTER VB thing rises to a higher level or point on a scale. EG *The world urban population is rocketing upward at a rate of 6.5 per cent per year.*

4 **Upwards of** or **upward of** a particular number PREP means more than that number. EG *The cyclone killed upwards of 200,000 people.*

uranium /jʊəˈreɪnɪəm/ is a radioactive metal that N UNCOUNT is used to produce nuclear energy and weapons.

urban /ˈɜːbən/ means belonging to or relating to a ADJ CLASSIF : town or city. EG ...*urban unemployment.* ATTRIB

urbane /ɜːˈbeɪn/. Someone who is **urbane** is well- ADJ QUALIT mannered, relaxed, and appears comfortable in Formal social situations. EG *He was composed, urbane, and affable... The professor was an urbane little man.*

urbanize /ˈɜːbənaɪz/, **urbanizes, urbanizing, ur-** V+O : USU PASS **banized;** also spelled **urbanise.** If a country area **is urbanized**, it is made more like a town, with more buildings, industry, and business. EG ...*highly urbanized and industrialized areas.*
◊ **urbanization** /ɜːbənaɪˈzeɪʃən/. EG ...*the urbaniza-* ◊ N UNCOUNT *tion of farmland.*

urchin /ˈɜːtʃɪn/, **urchins.** You can refer to a young child who is very poor, has no home or family, and lives in a town or city as an **urchin**. N COUNT Outdated

urge /ɜːdʒ/, **urges, urging, urged. 1** If you have an **urge** to do something or to have something, you strongly want to do it or to have it, often without being able to explain why. EG *They have a strong urge to communicate... ...our insane urge for greater and greater material wealth.* N COUNT : USU + to-INF

2 If you **urge** someone to do something, you try hard to persuade them to do it. EG *I urged him to take a year off to study drawing... 'At least stay for Christmas,' Pam urged.* V+O+to-INF OR QUOTE; ALSO V+REPORT : ONLY that

3 If you **urge** a course of action, you strongly advise that it should be taken. EG *US officials urged restraint.* V+O Formal

urgent /ˈɜːdʒənt/. **1** Something that is **urgent** needs to be dealt with as soon as possible. EG *Most of the motorway network is in urgent need of repair... ...urgent messages.* ◇ **urgently.** EG *Improved health and education are urgently needed.* ADJ QUALIT ◇ ADV

◇ **urgency** /ˈɜːdʒənsɪ/. EG *...matters of the greatest urgency.* ◇ N UNCOUNT

2 If you say something in an **urgent** way, you indicate that you are very anxious for people to notice something or do something. EG *She spoke to him in a low and urgent voice.* ◇ **urgently.** EG *'Do you see it?' he demanded urgently.* ◇ **urgency.** EG *There was a note of urgency in his voice.* ADJ QUALIT ◇ ADV ◇ N UNCOUNT

urinal /jʊˈraɪnəl, jʊərɪnəl/, **urinals.** A **urinal** is a bowl or trough fixed to the wall of men's public lavatories for men to urinate in. N COUNT

urinate /ˈjʊərɪneɪt/, **urinates, urinating, urinated.** When you **urinate**, you get rid of urine from your body. V Formal

urine /ˈjʊərɪn/ is the liquid that you get rid of from your body when you go to the toilet. N UNCOUNT

urn /ɜːn/, **urns. 1** An **urn** is a decorated container with handles and a lid that is used to hold the ashes of a person who has been cremated. N COUNT

2 A tea or coffee **urn** is a large container used for making a large quantity of tea or coffee and for keeping it warm. N COUNT

us /ʌs, əs/ is used as the object of a verb or preposition. **1** A speaker or writer uses **us** to refer both to himself or herself and to one or more other people as a group. See **we**. EG *Why didn't you tell us?... There wasn't room for us all.* PRON : PLURAL

2 A speaker sometimes says **us** instead of 'me'. EG *Give us a chance.* PRON Informal

US /juː es/is an abbreviation for 'United States'. EG *...a brief visit to the US... ...the US army.* N PROPER : the+N

USA /juː es eɪ/is an abbreviation for 'United States of America'. N PROPER : the+N

usable /ˈjuːzəbəl/. If something is **usable**, it is in a state or condition which makes it possible to use it. EG *He told me which wells were usable along the road... ...the least usable land areas in Africa.* ADJ CLASSIF

usage /ˈjuːsɪdʒ, -zɪdʒ/, **usages. 1** Usage is the way in which words are actually used in particular contexts, especially with regard to their meanings. EG *...a guide to English usage... Today the word has virtually dropped out of usage.* N UNCOUNT

2 A **usage** is a particular meaning that a word has or a particular way in which it can be used. EG *It's a curious usage, isn't it?* N COUNT

3 Usage is also the degree to which something is used or the way in which it is used. EG *...the environmental effects of energy usage.* N UNCOUNT

use, uses, using, used; pronounced /juːz/ when it is a verb and /juːs/ when it is a noun.

1 If you **use** something, you do something with it in order to do a job or to achieve something. EG *Use pins to keep it in place... He wants to use the phone... Wash this garment using a mild detergent... Use your imagination... No violence was used.* V+O

2 If you **use** a particular word or expression, you say or write it, because it has the meaning that you want to express. EG *It's a phrase I once heard him use in a sermon.* V+O

3 If you **use** people, you make them do things for you, without caring about them. EG *For the first time he felt used.* V+O

4 If you **make use of** something, you do something with it in order to do a job or to achieve something. EG *Industry is making increasing use of robots.* PHRASE

5 The **use** of something is the act or fact of using it. EG *...the large-scale use of fertilisers and insecticides... ...a pamphlet for use in schools.* N UNCOUNT : USU + POSS

6 If a device, machine, or technique is **in use**, it is being used regularly by people. If it has gone **out of use**, it is no longer used regularly by people. EG *Within the next decade industrial robots will be in widespread use.* PHRASE

7 If you have the **use** of something, you have the ability or the permission to use it. EG *He lost the use of his legs.* N SING : the+N+of

8 If something has a **use** or if you have a **use** for it, there is a purpose for which it can be used. EG *Possibly I could find some use for these drawers.* N COUNT OR N UNCOUNT

9 If something is **of use**, it is useful. If it is **no use**, it is not at all useful. EG *She kept in touch with friends who would be of use in later life... I don't know whether any of these things will be any use to you.* PHRASE

10 You say **it's no use** doing something or **what's the use** of doing something as a way of saying that the action is pointless and will not achieve anything. EG *It is no use arguing with you... There's no use having regrets... What is the use of sitting and waiting for success to come?* PHRASE

11 A **use** of a word is a particular meaning that it has or a particular way in which it is used. N COUNT+SUPP

use up. If you **use up** a supply of something, you finish it so that none of it is left. EG *He used up all the coins he had.* PHRASAL VB : V+O+ADV

used; pronounced /juːst/ in paragraphs 1, 2, and 3, and /juːzd/ in paragraphs 4 and 5.

1 If something **used** to be done or **used** to be true, it was done regularly in the past or was true in the past. EG *The two children used to send me a card at Christmas time... I used to be very mean.* SEMI-MODAL + to-INF

2 If you **are used** to something, you are familiar with it because you have done or seen it often. EG *San Diego was not used to such demonstrations... We are used to working together.* PHRASE

3 If you **get used** to something, you become familiar with it. EG *After a few days, I got used to it all... I was beginning to get used to the old iron bed.* PHRASE

4 A **used** handkerchief, towel, or glass is dirty because it has been used. ADJ CLASSIF : ATTRIB

5 A **used** car is no longer new but has already had an owner. ADJ CLASSIF : ATTRIB

useful /ˈjuːsfʊl/. **1** If something is **useful**, you can use it in order to do something or to help you in some way. EG *She gave us some useful information.* ◇ **usefulness.** EG *...the usefulness of the computer.* ADJ QUALIT ◇ N UNCOUNT

2 If you are being **useful**, you are doing things that help other people. EG *Make yourself useful and fry up some bacon.* ◇ **usefully.** EG *His time could be more usefully spent.* ADJ CLASSIF : USU PRED ◇ ADV

3 When a possession or a skill **comes in useful**, you are able to use it on a particular occasion. EG *This is where your sketch comes in useful.* PHRASE Informal

useless /ˈjuːslɪs/. **1** If something is **useless**, you cannot use it. EG *Land is useless without labour.* ADJ CLASSIF

2 If a course of action is **useless**, it does not achieve anything helpful. EG *I realized it was useless to pursue the subject... She underwent some twenty useless operations.* ADJ CLASSIF

3 If you describe someone or something as **useless**, you mean that they are no good at all. EG *I was always useless at maths.* ADJ QUALIT Informal

How many uses of the word 'useless' are explained in this dictionary?

user /juːzə/, **users**. The **users** of a product, ma- N COUNT+SUPP
chine, service, or place are the people who use it.
EG ...*vehicle users*... ...*electricity users*.

usher /ʌʃə/, **ushers**, **ushering**, **ushered**. 1 If you V+O+A
usher someone somewhere, you show them where
they should go, often politely letting them go in
front of you. EG *The hostess ushered me into the
room*... *I was ushered into the study*.
2 An **usher** is a person who shows people where to N COUNT
sit, for example at a wedding or a concert.

usherette /ʌʃərɛt/, **usherettes**. An **usherette** is N COUNT
a woman who shows people where to sit in a
cinema or theatre and who sells refreshments or
programmes.

USSR /juː ɛs ɛs ɑː/ is an abbreviation for 'Union of N PROPER :
Soviet Socialist Republics'. the+N

USU stands for **usually**
Words which have the label USU in the Extra
Column are usually used in the way mentioned.
For example, N COUNT: USU SING means that the
noun is usually used in the singular, although you
will occasionally find it used in the plural.

---

usual /juːʒuəl/. 1 **Usual** is used to describe the ADJ CLASSIF
thing that happens most often, or that is done or
used most often, in a particular situation. EG *He
asked the usual questions*... *He sat in his usual
chair*... *She got up earlier than usual*.
2 If you do something **as usual**, you do it in the PHRASE
way that you normally do it. EG *As usual, he spent
the night at home*... *He was dressed in a suit and
tie, as usual*... *She had to try and carry on as usual*.
3 You also use **as usual** to say that you are PHRASE
describing something that often happens or is often
the case. EG *The telephone box on the corner is
broken, as usual*.

usually /juːʒuəliː/. 1 If something **usually** hap- ADV OR
pens, it is the thing that most often happens in a ADV SEN
particular situation. EG *She usually found it easy to
go to sleep at night*.
2 You use **more than usually** to say that some- PHRASE
one's behaviour shows even more of a particular
quality than it normally does. EG *They had shown
themselves to be more than usually gullible*.

usurp /juːzɜːp/, **usurps**, **usurping**, **usurped**. If V+O
you **usurp** a job, role, title, or position, you take it Formal
from someone when you have no right to do so. EG
*Their position of control enables them to usurp
power and privilege*.

utensil /juːtɛnsəl/, **utensils**. **Utensils** are tools N COUNT :
or objects that you use when you are cooking or USU PLURAL
doing other tasks in your home. EG *The kitchen had* +SUPP
no cooker and no proper cooking utensils. Formal

uterus /juːtərəs/, **uteruses**. A woman's **uterus** is N COUNT
her womb. Medical

utilise /juːtɪlaɪz/. See **utilize**.

utilitarian /juːtɪlɪtɛərɪən/. Something that is
utilitarian 1 is intended to produce the greatest ADJ CLASSIF
benefit for the greatest number of people. EG *He* Formal
*had not entered science for ambitious or utilitarian
purposes*. 2 is designed to be useful rather than ADJ QUALIT
beautiful. EG *We toured a number of clean, utilitar-* Formal
ian flats.

utility /juːtɪlɪtiː/, **utilities**. 1 The **utility** of some- N UNCOUNT
thing is its usefulness. EG ...*the utility and potential
of computers*.
2 A **utility** is an important service such as water, N COUNT
electricity, or gas that is provided for everyone. EG
...*the development of roads and public utilities in
the area*.

utilize /juːtɪlaɪz/, **utilizes**, **utilizing**, **utilized**; also V+O
spelled **utilise**. If you **utilize** something, you use it. Formal
EG *He thought it impossible to utilize atomic ener-*
gy. ◊ **utilization** /juːtɪlaɪzeɪʃən/. EG ...*the utiliza-* ◊ N UNCOUNT
tion of things like wind energy and wave-power.

utmost /ʌtməʊst/. 1 You use **utmost** to emphasize ADJ CLASSIF :
a particular quality that you are mentioning. EG ATTRIB
Learning is of the utmost importance... *He had the
utmost respect for his children*.
2 If something is done to the **utmost**, it is done to N SING :
the greatest extent, amount, or degree possible. EG the/POSS+N
*We will do our utmost to help these unfortunate
people*.

Utopia /juːtəʊpɪə/, **Utopias**. A **Utopia** is a perfect N COUNT OR
social system in which everyone is satisfied and N UNCOUNT
happy. EG *Every so often someone invents a new
Utopia*.

utopian /juːtəʊpɪən/ is used to describe someone's ADJ CLASSIF
idea of a perfect social system in which everyone
is satisfied and happy. EG ...*this utopian dream*...
...*utopian experiments*... *This may sound impossibly
utopian*.

utter /ʌtə/, **utters**, **uttering**, **uttered**. 1 When V+O
you **utter** sounds or words, you say them. EG *Sam
opened his mouth, then quickly shut it again without uttering a sound*.
2 **Utter** also means complete or total. EG *To my* ADJ CLASSIF :
utter amazement I was made managing director... ATTRIB
Judith is a complete and utter fool. ◊ **utterly**. EG *I* ◊ SUBMOD
am utterly convinced of your loyalty... *She was* OR ADV
trying to look like a young lady but failing utterly.

utterance /ʌtərəns/, **utterances**. An **utterance** N COUNT
is something which is expressed in speech or in Formal
writing, such as a word or a sentence. EG *The
children watched and copied every act and utterance of the older men*.

U-turn, U-turns. 1 When a vehicle does a **U-turn**, N COUNT
it turns through a half circle and starts to move in
the opposite direction.
2 When a government does a **U-turn**, it abandons a N COUNT
policy and starts to do something completely different.

V v

V, v /viː/, **Vs, v's. 1** V is the twenty-second letter of the English alphabet. N COUNT

2 v is used in writing to say that two people or two teams are competing against each other in a sporting event. **v** is an abbreviation for 'versus'. EG ...*Arsenal v Liverpool.* PREP

V stands for **intransitive verb**
When V is used by itself in the Extra Column, it refers to an intransitive verb, which is a verb that does not have an object.
See the entry headed VERBS for more information.

V+A stands for **intransitive verb used with adjunct**
Verbs which have the label V+A in the Extra Column are intransitive verbs which need an adjunct to complete their meaning.
See the entry headed ADJUNCTS for more information about adjuncts. See the entry headed VERBS for more information about these verbs.

---

vacancy /veɪkənsi¹/, **vacancies. 1** A **vacancy** is a job which is not being done by anyone and which people can apply for. EG ...*an unexpected vacancy in the Department.* N COUNT

2 If there are **vacancies** at a hotel or guest house, some of the rooms are not occupied and are available for people to stay in. N COUNT : USU PLURAL

vacant /veɪkənt/. **1** If something such as a room, a chair, or a toilet is **vacant**, it is not being used by anyone. EG *I sat down in a vacant chair.* ADJ CLASSIF

2 If a job is **vacant**, no one is doing it at present and people can apply for it. EG *They keep a list of all vacant jobs in the area.* ADJ CLASSIF

3 A **vacant** look or expression suggests that someone does not understand something or that they are not very intelligent. EG *She looked round her with a rather vacant expression.* ADJ QUALIT

vacate /vəkeɪt/, **vacates, vacating, vacated. 1** If you **vacate** a job, you make it available for other people by leaving it or giving it up. EG *I got the job Allister was vacating.* V+O

2 If you **vacate** something such as a room, seat, or parking space, you leave it and so make it available for someone else to use. EG *He ordered her to vacate her apartment... He drove neatly into the vacated space.* V+O

vacation /vəkeɪʃə⁰n/, **vacations.** A **vacation** is **1** a period of the year when universities or colleges are officially closed. EG *I've a lot of reading to do over the vacation... ...the summer vacation.* **2** a holiday. EG *Harold used to take a vacation at that time... She plans to go on vacation for most of August.* N COUNT / N COUNT OR N UNCOUNT American

vaccinate /væksɪneɪt/, **vaccinates, vaccinating, vaccinated.** If you **are vaccinated** against a disease, you are given an injection to prevent you from getting it. EG *Most of them were vaccinated against hepatitis.* ◊ **vaccination** /væksɪneɪʃə⁰n/. EG ...*vaccination against smallpox.* V+O : USU PASS ◊ N UNCOUNT OR N COUNT

vaccine /væksiːn/, **vaccines.** A **vaccine** is a substance made from the germs that cause a disease. Vaccines are injected into people to prevent them from getting the disease. EG ...*the measles vaccine... ...polio vaccine.* N COUNT OR N UNCOUNT

vacillate /væsɪleɪt/, **vacillates, vacillating, vacillated.** If you **vacillate**, you keep changing your opinion or feelings, so that you cannot make a decision or people cannot rely on you. EG *He vacillated between periods of creative fever and nervous exhaustion... They are vacillating when the child needs firmness.* V : OFT + between Formal

vacuum /vækjuⁿəm/, **vacuums, vacuuming, vacuumed. 1** A **vacuum** is a space that contains no air or other gas, especially an enclosed space from which the air has been removed. N COUNT

2 If someone or something creates a **vacuum**, they leave a place or position in which they had an important role, so that the role needs to be filled by someone or something else. EG *Rival groups would seek to fill the power vacuum that the departing British would leave.* N COUNT : USU SING+SUPP

3 If you **vacuum** something, you clean it using a vacuum cleaner. EG *I'm going to vacuum the car.* V+O OR V

4 People sometimes refer to a vacuum cleaner as a **vacuum**. EG *I'll just turn off the vacuum.* N COUNT Informal

vacuum cleaner, vacuum cleaners. A **vacuum cleaner** is an electric machine which removes dust and dirt from carpets by sucking it up. N COUNT

vagina /vədʒaɪnə/, **vaginas.** A woman's **vagina** is the passage that connects her outer sex organs to her womb. N COUNT

vagrant /veɪgrənt/, **vagrants.** A **vagrant** is a person who has no home or money, and who lives by going from place to place and begging or stealing. ◊ **vagrancy** /veɪgrənsi¹/. EG *I don't want you to be arrested for vagrancy.* N COUNT ◊ N UNCOUNT

vague /veɪg/, **vaguer, vaguest. 1** If something written or spoken is **vague**, it does not explain or express things clearly. EG *The terms of the agreement were left deliberately vague... ...vague instructions.* ◊ **vaguely.** EG *'What happened?' – 'Oh, a lot of things,' she said vaguely.* ADJ QUALIT ◊ ADV

2 If you have a **vague** memory of something, you cannot remember it clearly. EG *I've got a vague recollection of going there once as a child.* ◊ **vaguely.** EG *I vaguely remember their house.* ADJ QUALIT ◊ ADV

3 If a feeling is **vague**, you experience it only slightly. EG *I realized with a vague feeling of surprise that he had gone.* ◊ **vaguely.** EG *They were vaguely amused.* ADJ QUALIT ◊ ADV

4 If you are **vague** about something, you deliberately do not tell people much about it. EG *They were vague and evasive about their backgrounds.* ADJ PRED : OFT +about

5 You say that someone looks or sounds **vague** when they do not seem to be thinking clearly. EG *Jones looked very vague.* ADJ QUALIT

6 If the shape or outline of something is **vague**, it is not clear and so the thing is not easy to see. EG *It appeared in vague form at first and then in sharper outline.* ADJ QUALIT

vain /veɪn/, **vainer, vainest. 1** If you do something **in vain**, you do not succeed in achieving what you intend. EG *We tried in vain to discover what had happened... Your son didn't die in vain.* PHRASE

2 A **vain** attempt or action fails to achieve what is intended. EG ...*the teacher's vain plea for silence.* ADJ CLASSIF : ATTRIB

3 Someone who is **vain** is extremely proud of their beauty, intelligence, or other good qualities; used showing disapproval. EG ...*a vain young aristocrat.* ADJ QUALIT

vale /veɪl/, **vales.** A **vale** is a valley. EG ...*a rich, lush vale of meadows and blossoms.* N COUNT Literary

valedictory /vælɪdɪktə⁰ri¹/. A **valedictory** speech or letter is one in which you say goodbye to someone. ADJ CLASSIF : ATTRIB Formal

valentine /ˈvæləntaɪn/, **valentines. 1** Your **val-** N SING : **entine** is someone who you love or are attracted to USU POSS+N and who you send a card to on St Valentine's Day, February 14th.
2 A **valentine** or a **valentine card** is the card that N COUNT you send to your valentine, usually without signing your name, on St Valentine's Day.

valet /ˈvælɪt, ˈvæleɪ/, **valets.** A **valet** is a male N COUNT servant who looks after his male employer by doing things such as caring for his clothes.

valiant /ˈvæljənt/ means very brave. EG *He made a* ADJ QUALIT *valiant attempt to rescue the struggling victim.*

valid /ˈvælɪd/. **1** Something that is **valid** is based on ADJ QUALIT sound reasoning. EG *This is a valid argument against economic growth... This was the real reason, and it was a valid reason... It was a valid protest.* ◊ **validity** /vəˈlɪdɪtiɪ/. EG *We should ques-* ◊ N UNCOUNT *tion the validity of those figures.*
2 If a ticket or document is **valid**, it can be used ADJ CLASSIF and will be accepted by people in authority. EG *It's valid for six months from the date of issue... This passport is no longer valid.*

validate /ˈvælɪdeɪt/, **validates, validating, vali-** V+O **dated.** If something **validates** a statement or claim, it proves that it is true or correct. EG *Their remarkable achievement seems to validate Bomberg's claim.*

Valium /ˈvælɪəm/ is a drug which is given to N UNCOUNT people to calm their nerves when they are worried Trademark or upset.

valley /ˈvæliɪ/, **valleys.** A **valley** is a long, narrow N COUNT area of land between hills, especially one that has a river flowing through it.

valour /ˈvælə/; spelled **valor** in American English. N UNCOUNT **Valour** is great bravery, especially in battle. EG Formal *...an act of epic valour.*

valuable /ˈvæljʊəbºlˀ/, **valuables. 1** Valuable ADJ QUALIT help or advice is very useful. EG *They could also give valuable help.*
2 When objects such as paintings or jewellery are ADJ QUALIT **valuable,** they are worth a lot of money.
3 Valuables are things that you own which are N PLURAL worth a lot of money, especially small objects such as jewellery. EG *They were robbed of money and valuables at gunpoint.*

valuation /ˌvæljʊeɪʃºˀn/, **valuations.** A **valuation** N COUNT OR is **1** a judgement about how much money some- N UNCOUNT thing is worth. EG *The land's valuation was £6,000.* **2** a judgement about how good or bad something is. EG *...his rather low valuation of the novel.*

value /ˈvælju:/, **values, valuing, valued. 1** The N UNCOUNT **value** of something such as a quality or a method is its importance or usefulness. EG *Everyone realizes the value of sincerity.*
2 The **value** of something that you can own, for N UNCOUNT example a house or a painting, is the amount of OR N COUNT money that it is worth. EG *What will happen to the value of my property?*
3 If you say that something is **good value** or is PHRASE **value for money,** you mean that it is worth the money it costs. EG *The set lunch is good value at £5.95.*
4 Something that is **of value** is useful or important. PHRASE EG *You may find them of value... ...information which would be of value to him... Nothing of value can be said about this matter.*
5 If you put or place **a high value** on something, PHRASE you think that it is very important. EG *He places a high value on educating his children.*
6 The **values** of a person or group are the moral N PLURAL principles and beliefs that they think are important. EG *...the traditional values of civility, moderation, and family... They have different values from the families they serve.*
7 If you **take** a remark or compliment **at face** PHRASE **value,** you accept it without thinking what its real meaning or purpose might be. EG *She took the praise at face value.*
8 Value is used after another noun to say that N UNCOUNT

something has a particular kind of importance or usefulness. For example, if you say that something has propaganda **value,** you mean that it is useful as propaganda. EG *It should have novelty value, if nothing else.*
9 If you **value** something, you think that it is V+O important and you appreciate it. EG *Which do you value most – wealth or health?* ◊ **valued.** EG *...one* ◊ ADJ QUALIT *of our valued customers.*
10 When experts **value** something such as a house V+O : USU PASS or a painting, they decide how much money it is worth. EG *They had gone to have their jewels valued... The table silver was valued at £20,000.*

value-added tax. See VAT.

value judgement, value judgements. A **value** N COUNT : **judgement** is an opinion about something that is USU PLURAL based on the principles and beliefs of the person expressing the opinion and not on facts which can be checked or proved. EG *It is difficult to answer that question without making a value judgement... ...an argument based on value judgements.*

valueless /ˈvæljuːlˀs/. Something that is **valueless** ADJ CLASSIF is not effective or useful. EG *...involvement in valueless activities.*

valuer /ˈvæljʊə/, **valuers.** A **valuer** is someone N COUNT whose job is to decide how much money things are worth.

valve /vælv/, **valves.** A **valve** is a part attached to N COUNT a pipe or a tube. When the valve is open, it lets air or liquid pass through. When it is closed, it stops the air or liquid passing through. EG *...a radiator valve.* ● See also **safety-valve.**

vampire /ˈvæmpaɪə/, **vampires.** In legends and N COUNT horror stories, **vampires** are people who come out of their graves at night and suck the blood of living people.

van /væn/, **vans.** A **van** is a vehicle like a large N COUNT car that is used for carrying goods.

vandal /ˈvændºl/, **vandals.** A **vandal** is someone N COUNT who deliberately damages things, especially public property, for no good reason. EG *The phone box is attacked by vandals from time to time.*

vandalise /ˈvændəlaɪz/. See **vandalize.**

vandalism /ˈvændəlɪzºm/ is the deliberate dam- N UNCOUNT aging of things, especially public property, for no good reason. EG *These housing estates suffer from widespread vandalism.*

vandalize /ˈvændəlaɪz/, **vandalizes, vandalizing,** V+O : USU PASS **vandalized;** also spelled **vandalise.** If someone **vandalizes** something, they damage it on purpose, for no good reason. EG *All our telephones were vandalized.*

vanguard /ˈvængɑːd/. If someone is in the **van-** N SING : **guard** of something such as a revolution or a USU+SUPP particular kind of research, they are involved in the most advanced part of it. EG *They are in the vanguard of technological advance.*

vanilla /vəˈnɪlə/ is a flavouring that comes from a N UNCOUNT : plant and that can be put into ice cream and other OFT N MOD sweet food. EG *...vanilla ice-cream... ...vanilla fudge.*

vanish /ˈvænɪʃ/, **vanishes, vanishing, vanished.** V If something **vanishes,** **1** it disappears suddenly. EG *The car had vanished from sight... Madeleine vanished without trace.* **2** it ceases to exist. EG *...laws to protect vanishing American species.*

vanity /ˈvænɪˀtiɪ/ is a feeling of pride about your N UNCOUNT appearance or abilities; used showing disapproval. EG *He refused to wear glasses. It was sheer vanity.*

vanquish /ˈvæŋkwɪʃ/, **vanquishes, vanquishing,** V+O **vanquished.** If you **vanquish** someone, you defeat Literary them completely in a battle or a competition. EG *All their enemies were vanquished.*

vantage point, vantage points. N COUNT A **vantage point** is a place from which you can see a lot of things. EG *From the vantage point on the hill, Port Philip shimmered beneath them.*

vapour /ˈveɪpə/; spelled **vapor** in American Eng- N UNCOUNT lish. **Vapour** is a mass of tiny drops of water or other liquids in the air, which appear as smoke, clouds, mist, or fumes. EG ...water vapour... ...a little cloud of exhaust vapour.

variability /vɛəriˈəbɪlɪˈtiˈ/. The **variability** of N UNCOUNT : something is the range of different forms that it USU+SUPP can take. EG ...the enormous variability you get in speech sounds.

variable /vɛəriˈəbəl/, **variables. 1** Something ADJ QUALIT that is **variable** is likely to change at any time. EG In the tropics, rainfall is notoriously variable.

2 A **variable** is a factor that can change in quality, N COUNT quantity, or size, which you have to take into account when looking at a situation as a whole. EG How long your shoes will last depends on a lot of variables, such as how much you weigh, how far you walk, and so on.

3 In mathematics, a **variable** is an expression that N COUNT can have any one of a set of values. Technical

variance /vɛəriˈəns/. If one thing is **at variance** PHRASE with another, the two things seem to contradict Formal each other. EG Nothing in the story was at variance with what he understood to be true.

variant /vɛəriˈənt/, **variants**. A **variant** of some- N COUNT : thing has a different form from the usual one. EG USU+of This American bird is a variant of the English buzzard. ▸ used as an adjective. EG ...a variant form ▸ ADJ CLASSIF : of the basic action. ATTRIB

variation /vɛəriˈeɪʃəˈn/, **variations. 1** A **vari-** N COUNT **ation** on something is the same thing presented in a different form. EG ...the same programme with only nightly variations... His books are all vari- ations on a basic theme.

2 A **variation** is also a change in a level, amount, N COUNT OR or quantity. EG The Boards have learned how to N UNCOUNT cope with a large variation in demand for electric- ity... ...variation in blood pressure.

varicose veins /værɪkəˈs veɪnz/ are veins in a N PLURAL person's legs which are very swollen and painful and which sometimes need to be operated on.

varied /vɛərɪd/. **1 Varied** is the past tense and past participle of **vary**.

2 Something that is **varied** consists of things that ADJ QUALIT are of different types, sizes, or qualities. EG Many varied motives prompt individuals to join a politi- cal party... The work of a JP is very varied.

variegated /vɛərɪgeɪtɪˈd/. A **variegated** plant or ADJ CLASSIF leaf has different coloured markings on it. EG ...a variegated holly.

variety /vɔrаɪˈtiˈ/, **varieties. 1** If something has N UNCOUNT **variety**, it consists of things which are different from each other. EG Those are the holiday bro- chures that give you the most variety.

2 If you have a **variety** of things, you have a N PART : SING number of them of different kinds. EG The college library had a wide variety of books.

3 A **variety** of something is a type of it. EG ...three N COUNT : varieties of whisky. USU+of

4 Variety is a type of theatre or television enter- N UNCOUNT : tainment which includes many different kinds of OFT N MOD performance in the same show, for example sing- ing, dancing, and comedy. EG ...a high-quality vari- ety show... ...a variety act.

various /vɛərɪəs/. **1** If you refer to **various** things, ADJ CLASSIF : you mean that there are several different things of ATTRIB the type mentioned. EG There were various ques- tions he wanted to ask... ...trying to piece together the various bits of information.

2 If a number of things are described as **various**, ADJ CLASSIF : they are very different from one another. EG His USU PRED excuses are many and various.

variously /vɛərɪəsliˈ/ is used to introduce a num- ADV ber of different ways in which something is de- scribed or a number of different opinions that people have about something. EG He married a Japanese lady who was variously described as a painter and a film maker.

varnish /vɑːnɪʃ/, **varnishes, varnishing, var-** **nished. 1 Varnish** is a liquid made from oil and N MASS other substances which is painted onto wood to

give it a hard, clear, shiny surface. ● See also **nail** **varnish**.

2 The **varnish** on an object is the hard, clear, shiny N SING surface that it has when it has been painted with varnish. EG The varnish was slightly chipped.

3 If you **varnish** something, you paint it with v+o varnish. EG He has varnished the table.

vary /vɛəriˈ/, **varies, varying, varied. 1** Things v that **vary** are different in size, amount, or degree. EG The fees vary a lot... The screens will vary in size depending upon what one wants. ◊ **varying**. ◊ ADJ QUALIT : EG Its members have widely varying views on ATTRIB foreign policy.

2 If one thing **varies** with another, it changes v+with when the other thing changes. EG The colour of the fruit varies with age.

3 If you **vary** something that you do, you keep v+o changing the way that you do it. EG He took special care to vary his daily routine.

4 See also **varied**.

vase /vɑːz/, **vases**. A **vase** is a jar, usually made of N COUNT glass or pottery, which is used for holding cut flowers or as an ornament.

vasectomy /vɔˈsɛktəmiˈ/, **vasectomies**. A **vas-** N COUNT OR **ectomy** is a surgical operation that is done in N UNCOUNT order to sterilize a man, by cutting the tube that carries the sperm to his penis.

vast /vɑːst/. Something that is **vast** is extremely ADJ QUALIT : large. EG He was responsible for running a vast OFT ATTRIB organization... ...the roads that they're building at vast expense.

vastly /vɑːstliˈ/ means very much or to a very SUBMOD large extent. EG Management of the factory could be vastly improved.

vat /væt/, **vats**. A **vat** is a large barrel or tank in N COUNT which liquids are stored. EG ...a vat of water. OR N PART

VAT /viː eɪ tiː, væt/ is a tax that is added to the N UNCOUNT price of goods or services. **VAT** is an abbreviation for 'value-added tax'.

vault /vɔːlt/, **vaults, vaulting, vaulted. 1** A **vault** N COUNT is **1.1** a room with thick walls, a strong door, and strong locks where money, important documents, and jewels can be kept safely. EG The money was deposited in the vaults of a firm of solicitors. **1.2** a room underneath a church or in a cemetery where people are buried.

2 A **vault** is also a roof or ceiling consisting of N COUNT several arches joined together at the top.

3 If you **vault** something or **vault** over it, you jump v+o OR v+A over it, putting one or both of your hands on it. EG They vaulted effortlessly over the wall.

VB stands for **verb**
VB is used in the Extra Column to mean 'verb', without indicating what type of verb it is, as in, for example ADV AFTER VB.

V+C stands for **intransitive verb followed by** **complement**
Verbs which have the label **V+C** in the Extra Column are verbs which need a complement, that is a noun or adjective group which refers to the subject, to complete their meaning.
See the entry headed COMPLEMENTS for more infor- mation about complements. See the entry headed VERBS for more information about these verbs.

VD /viː diː/ is an abbreviation for 'venereal dis- ease'.

Are you wearing a veil if you make a veiled comment?

VDU /viː diː juː/, **VDU's**. A **VDU** is a machine N COUNT which looks like a television set and which shows information from a computer on its screen. **VDU** is an abbreviation for 'visual display unit'.

veal /viːl/ is meat from a calf. N UNCOUNT

veer /vɪə/, **veers, veering, veered**. If something V+A that is moving **veers** in a particular direction, it suddenly starts moving in that direction. EG *He veered away from a tree... The plane seemed to veer off to one side.*

vegetable /ˈvedʒɪˈtəbəl/, **vegetables. 1 Vegeta-** N COUNT : **bles** are plants such as cabbages, potatoes, and USU PLURAL onions which you can cook and eat.

2 Vegetable is used to refer to plants in general. EG N UNCOUNT : *...vegetable matter.* USU MOD

vegetarian /ˌvedʒɪˈteərɪən/, **vegetarians**. Some- N COUNT one who is a **vegetarian** does not eat meat or fish. EG *She was a strict vegetarian.* ▶ used as an ▶ ADJ CLASSIF adjective. EG *...a vegetarian diet.*

vegetate /ˈvedʒɪteɪt/, **vegetates, vegetating,** V **vegetated**. If you **vegetate**, you have a very boring life, staying in the same place and doing very little. EG *Many elderly folk vegetate and die in loneliness.*

vegetation /ˌvedʒɪˈteɪʃən/ is plant life in general. N UNCOUNT EG *The forest floor is not rich in vegetation.*

vehemence /ˈviːəməns/ is intense and violent N UNCOUNT emotion, especially anger. EG *...the hate and vehemence in Hubert's eyes.*

vehement /ˈviːəmənt/. Someone who is **vehe-** ADJ QUALIT **ment** has very strong feelings or opinions and expresses them forcefully. EG *They are vehement in their praises of the new system... With a vehement gesture he flung away his chicken leg.*
◊ **vehemently**. EG *They were arguing vehemently.* ◊ ADV

vehicle /ˈviːɪkəl/, **vehicles. 1** A **vehicle** is a N COUNT machine such as a bus, car, or lorry, that carries people or things from place to place. EG *We saw a vehicle travelling across the bridge... ...the motor vehicle industry.*

2 If you use something as a **vehicle** for a particular N COUNT : thing, you use it in order to achieve that thing. EG USU+for/of *They saw education as a vehicle of liberation...* Formal *They support the Labour Party as a vehicle for socialism.*

veil /veɪl/, **veils. 1** A **veil** is a piece of thin, soft N COUNT material that women sometimes wear over their heads. EG *The bride's face was covered in a white veil... ...a hat with a veil.*

2 You can refer to something that you can partly N SING+of see through, for example a mist, as a **veil**. EG Literary *Everything was wrapped in a veil of evening light.*

3 You can also refer to something that hides or N SING+of partly hides an activity or situation as a **veil**. EG *The research centre shrouded its communications with every possible veil of secrecy.*

veiled /veɪld/. If you make a **veiled** comment or ADJ CLASSIF : **remark**, you express it in a disguised form, so that ATTRIB you do not actually say what you mean. EG *...thinly veiled criticism... ...veiled threats.*

vein /veɪn/, **veins. 1** Your **veins** are the tubes in N COUNT your body through which your blood flows. ● See also **varicose veins**.

2 The **veins** on a leaf are the thin lines on it. N COUNT

3 A **vein** of a metal or mineral is a layer of it in N COUNT+of rock. EG *...the world's richest vein of copper.*

4 Something that is written or spoken in a particu- N UNCOUNT lar **vein** is written or spoken in that style or mood. +SUPP EG *The letter continued in this vein for several pages.*

velocity /vɪˈlɒsɪtiː/, **velocities**. The **velocity** of N UNCOUNT something is the speed at which it moves in a OR N COUNT particular direction. EG *...the velocity of light.* Technical

velvet /ˈvelvɪt/ is soft material made from cotton, N UNCOUNT silk, or nylon, which has a thick layer of short, cut threads on one side. EG *...velvet curtains.*

velvety /ˈvelvɪtiː/. Something that is **velvety** is ADJ QUALIT soft to touch and has the appearance of velvet. EG *The spider has a velvety black body.*

vendetta /venˈdetə/, **vendettas**. A **vendetta** is a N COUNT long-lasting and bitter quarrel between people in which they attempt to harm each other. EG *He conducted a vendetta against Haldane behind the scenes.*

vending machine, vending machines. A **vend-** N COUNT **ing machine** is a machine from which you can get things such as cigarettes, chocolate, or coffee by putting in money and pressing a button.

vendor /ˈvendə/, **vendors. 1** A **vendor** is some- N COUNT : one who sells things such as newspapers, ciga- USU+SUPP rettes, or hamburgers from a small stall or cart. EG *...cigarette vendors.*

2 The **vendor** of a house or piece of land is the N COUNT person who owns it and is selling it. Technical

veneer /vɪˈnɪə/. **1** If you refer to the way that N SING : someone behaves as a **veneer**, you mean that they USU+SUPP are behaving in a way which hides their real character or feelings. EG *He hides his values beneath a veneer of scientific objectivity.*

2 Veneer is a thin layer of wood or plastic which is N UNCOUNT glued onto the outside of something made of cheaper material, in order to improve its appearance. EG *...a table whose veneer had come loose.*

venerable /ˈvenərəbəl/. **Venerable** people are ADJ QUALIT : entitled to respect because they are old and wise. USU ATTRIB EG *...a venerable elder for whom he had enormous* Formal *respect... ...the venerable head of the house.*

venerate /ˈvenəreɪt/, **venerates, venerating,** V+O **venerated**. If you **venerate** someone, you feel Formal great respect for them. EG *Lincoln was a lawyer and I always venerated him.*

venereal disease /vəˈnɪərɪəl dɪziːz/, **venereal** N COUNT OR **diseases**. A **venereal disease** is a disease that is N UNCOUNT passed on by sexual intercourse. There are several different venereal diseases, for example syphilis.

Venetian blind /vəniːʃən blaɪnd/, **Venetian** N COUNT **blinds**. A **Venetian blind** is a window blind made of thin horizontal strips of wood, plastic, or metal. The strips can be turned to a different angle in order to let in more or less light.

vengeance /ˈvendʒəns/. **1 Vengeance** is the act N UNCOUNT of killing, injuring, or harming someone because they have harmed you. EG *I want vengeance for the deaths of my parents and sisters.*

2 If something happens **with a vengeance**, it PHRASE happens to a much greater extent than was expected. EG *He now broke the rules with a vengeance.*

vengeful /ˈvendʒfʊl/. If you are **vengeful**, you feel ADJ QUALIT a great desire for revenge. EG *The whole episode* Literary *made me vengeful.*

venison /ˈvenɪˈzən, -sən/ is meat from a deer. N UNCOUNT

venom /ˈvenəm/. **1 Venom** is a feeling of great N UNCOUNT bitterness or anger that you show in the way that you say or do something. EG *'What a filthy trick,' she said with unexpected venom.*

2 The **venom** of a snake, scorpion, or spider is the N UNCOUNT poison that it injects into you when it bites you or stings you.

venomous /ˈvenəməs/. **1** A **venomous** snake, ADJ CLASSIF scorpion, or spider produces poison and uses it to attack its enemy or prey.

2 If your behaviour or appearance is **venomous**, it ADJ QUALIT shows great bitterness or anger. EG *Her beautiful green eyes were venomous... They shot each other venomous glances.*

vent /vent/, **vents, venting, vented. 1** A **vent** is a N COUNT hole in something such as the wall of a room, through which air can come in and smoke, gas, or smells can go out. EG *...the air vents of the bunkers.*

2 If you **give vent to** strong feelings, you express PHRASE them. EG *They gave vent to their rage.* Formal

3 If you **vent** your feelings, you express them. EG V+O:OFT+A *She vented her feelings in wails and screams... He* Formal *vented his rage on Bernard.*

ventilate /ˈventɪleɪt/, **ventilates, ventilating,** V+O **ventilated**. To **ventilate** a room or building means to allow fresh air to get into it, for example by means of windows. ◊ **ventilated**. EG *...badly* ◊ ADJ CLASSIF

VERBS

Verbs are words which describe actions, thought, speech, and other activities. Verbs can either present a complete action and so occur on their own, or they can be followed by objects, complements, or adjuncts. For more information about these, see the entries headed OBJECTS, COMPLEMENTS, and ADJUNCTS.

Verbs can be used in many different ways, and the most important ways are explained here, together with the labels that are used in the Extra Column. In addition to the patterns explained here, you can add more adverbs or other adjuncts. These are only shown in the Extra Column where the adjuncts are essential for the meaning.

V

The verb is intransitive; that is, it is not followed by an object. For example: *His leg ached ... She smiled.*

V+O

The verb is transitive; that is, it is followed by an object. Transitive verbs usually have a passive form, in which the object of the active form is used as the subject of the passive form. For example: *I arranged a meeting for 9 o'clock ... ...The meeting was arranged for 9 o'clock.*

Although all transitive verbs can be used in the active form, some are much more likely to be used in the passive (V-PASS). For example: *I was taken aback at the news ... He was orphaned at the age of six.*

Some verbs can be used either transitively or intransitively, as in: *The men saluted.* (v) *He stood as if he were saluting the flag.* (v+o) In this case, the Extra Column says V OR V+O.

V+C

The verb is intransitive, and must be followed by a complement, which refers back to the subject of the verb. For example: *It seems odd ... You seem young to be a policeman ... James is a teacher.*

V+A

The verb is intransitive, and must be followed by an adjunct, which is usually a prepositional phrase telling you about direction, manner, time, and so on. For example: *I strolled around the city centre ... He behaved disgracefully ... We waited for half an hour.*

Combinations of these

V+O+C: *He makes me very happy ... I thought him cruel and heartless.*

V+O+A: *She put her diary in her bag ... He threw the packet into the bin.*

V+O+O: *She made her mother a dress ... Give me that book ... He fixed himself a stiff drink.*

V-REFL

The verb is always used with a reflexive pronoun. Reflexive verbs describe actions in which the subject and the object of the verb are the same. For example: *I helped myself to more potatoes . . . She cut herself with the breadknife.*

V-ERG

Ergative verbs can describe an action from the point of view of the performer of the action or from the point of view of the object of the action.

Ergative verbs can be used transitively, as in *I'm baking a cake,* or they can be used intransitively, as in *The cake is baking in the oven.*

To use the verb intransitively, you use the object of the transitive verb as the subject of the intransitive verb.

RECIP

Reciprocal verbs describe actions that involve two people or two groups of people. For example: *Do you agree with him about this? . . . They agreed without argument.* See the entry headed RECIP.

+REPORT

Many verbs, especially verbs of speech such as **say**, **report**, and **tell**, are followed by a clause which tells you what the person said. These clauses usually start with **that** or with a **wh**- word such as **what** or **when**. In this dictionary, these clauses are called report clauses, and more information about them can be found in the entry headed REPORT. For example: *She hoped that she wasn't going to cry.* (V+REPORT)   *She told me where to leave the documents.* (V+O+REPORT)

V+QUOTE

Verbs with this label are used to report direct speech – the actual words that someone spoke. For example: *"You're wrong" she retorted . . . "Follow me," Claude whispered, "and keep quiet." . . . I said, "I'd never do that, and you know it."*

V-SPEECH

Verbs with this label can be used transitively (V+O), intransitively describing direct speech (V+QUOTE), and intransitively describing indirect speech (V+REPORT). For example: *We have to suggest a list of possible topics for next term's seminars . . .* (V+O)   *"Has it been thrown away?" suggested Miss Livingstone . . .* (V+QUOTE) *I suggested that it was time to leave.* (V+REPORT)

ventilated houses. ◊ **ventilation** /vɛntɪleɪʃəⁿn/. EG ◊ N UNCOUNT *The only ventilation was through a small door at the back.*

ventilator /vɛntɪleɪtə/, **ventilators.** A **ventilator** N COUNT is something such as a fan which lets fresh air into a room or building and lets stale air out.

ventriloquist /vɛntrɪləkwɪst/, **ventriloquists.** A N COUNT **ventriloquist** is someone who can speak without moving their lips and who entertains people by making their words appear to be spoken by a wooden dummy.

venture /vɛntʃə/, **ventures, venturing, ven-tured. 1** A **venture** is something you do that is N COUNT : new and difficult and so involves the risk of failure. USU+SUPP EG *...an interesting scientific venture... The number of successful new business ventures is dwindling.*

2 If you **venture** into something, you do something V+A that involves the risk of failure because it is new and different. EG *I might actually venture into advertising if I had enough money.*

3 If you **venture** something such as an opinion, you V+O; ALSO say it in a cautious, hesitant manner because you V+QUOTE are afraid it might be foolish or wrong. EG *'Any-* OR *to*-INF *way,' Marsha ventured, 'If we want to know what's going on, we'll have to do our own research.'... No one has ventured to suggest why this should be.*

4 If you **venture** somewhere that might be danger- V+A ous, you go there. EG *He wouldn't venture far from his mother's door.*

venue /vɛnjuː/, **venues.** The **venue** for an event N COUNT or activity is the place where it will happen. EG Formal *Where is the venue for the conference?*

veranda /vərændə/, **verandas;** also spelled **ve-** N COUNT **randah.** A **veranda** is a platform along one of the outside walls of a house, usually on ground level. It has a roof supported by pillars.

verb /vɜːb/, **verbs.** In grammar, a **verb** is a word N COUNT which is concerned with what people and things do, and what happens to them.

verbal /vɜːbəⁿl/. **1** You use **verbal** to describe **1.1** ADJ CLASSIF : things connected with words and the use of words. USU ATTRIB EG *It was a contest in verbal skills.* **1.2** things that ADJ CLASSIF : are spoken rather than written. EG *...a succession of* USU ATTRIB *verbal attacks on the chairman.* EG *I* ◊ ADV **verbally.** *will communicate your views verbally to the mem-bers of the committee.*

2 Verbal also describes something that consists of ADJ CLASSIF or relates to verbs. EG *...the structure of verbal groups in English.*

verbatim /vɜːbeɪtɪm/. If you repeat something ADV AFTER VB **verbatim,** you use exactly the same words that the OR ADJ CLASSIF original speaker or writer used. EG *It was almost a* Formal *verbatim quotation of the article.*

verbiage /vɜːbiˈɪdʒ/ is the use of too many words, N UNCOUNT which makes something difficult to understand. EG Formal *...a lot of meaningless verbiage.*

verdict /vɜːdɪkt/, **verdicts. 1** In a law court, a N COUNT **verdict** is the decision whether a prisoner is guilty or not guilty. EG *The jury gave a verdict of not guilty.*

2 If you give your **verdict** on something, you say N COUNT : what your opinion of it is, after thinking about it. EG USU+SUPP *The critics hated the film, but the public verdict was favourable.*

V-ERG stands for **ergative verb**
Verbs which have the label V-ERG in the Extra Column are both transitive and intransitive in the same meaning.
See the entry headed VERBS for more information.

---

verge /vɜːdʒ/, **verges, verging, verged. 1** If you PHRASE are **on the verge** of something, you are likely to do it very soon, or it is likely to happen to you very soon. EG *The unions are on the verge of settling their latest pay dispute... ...people living on the verge of starvation.*

2 The **verge** of a road is a narrow piece of ground N COUNT at the side, which is usually covered with grass. EG *We began walking together along the grass verge.*

verge on or **verge upon.** Something that **verges** PHRASAL VB : **on** or **verges upon** something else is almost the V+PREP same as it. EG *I had a feeling of distrust verging on panic... ...direct action verging on violence.*

verify /vɛrɪfaɪ/, **verifies, verifying, verified.** If you **verify** something, **1** you check that it is true by V+O careful investigation. EG *...evidence that could be tested and verified.* ◊ **verification** /vɛrɪfɪkeɪʃəⁿn/. ◊ N UNCOUNT EG *Any hypothesis must depend for its verification on observable evidence.* **2** you state or confirm V+O that it is true. EG *I was asked to verify or deny this suggestion.* ◊ **verification.** EG *He looked at his* ◊ N UNCOUNT *daughter for verification.*

veritable /vɛrɪtəbəⁿl/. You use **veritable** when ADJ CLASSIF : you are exaggerating, often humorously, in order ATTRIB to emphasize a feature that something has. EG *His toilet flushed like a veritable Niagara.*

vermilion /vəˈmɪljən/. Something that is **vermil-** ADJ COLOUR **ion** is bright red in colour. EG *...vermilion robes.* Formal

vermin /vɜːmɪn/ are small animals such as rats N PLURAL and mice, which carry disease and damage crops or food. EG *In Scotland, wild cats are treated as vermin, and are poisoned.*

vernacular /vənækjʊˈlə/, **vernaculars.** The **ver-** N COUNT : **nacular** of a country or region is the language that OFT *the*+N is most widely spoken there. EG *'Who is it?' asked Ash in the vernacular.*

versatile /vɜːsətaɪl/. **1** Someone who is **versatile** ADJ QUALIT has many different skills and can change quickly from using one to using another. EG *He's the most versatile of actors.*

2 Something such as a tool, machine, or material ADJ QUALIT that is **versatile** can be used for many different purposes. EG *...this extremely versatile new kitchen machine... Chestnuts are a highly versatile vegeta-ble.*

verse /vɜːs/, **verses. 1** Verse is writing arranged N UNCOUNT in lines which have a rhythm and which often rhyme at the end. EG *She used to write plays in verse.*

2 A **verse** is one of the parts into which a poem, a N COUNT song, or a chapter of the Bible is divided. EG *He sang a verse of 'Lili Marlene'.*

versed /vɜːst/. If you **are versed in** something, PHRASE you know a lot about it. EG *She is well versed in* Formal *French history.*

version /vɜːʃəⁿn, -zəⁿn/, **versions. 1** A **version** of N COUNT+SUPP something is a form of it in which some details are different from earlier or later forms. EG *She asked a different version of the question... ...from the first draft to the final printed version.*

2 The film or stage **version** of a story is a film or N COUNT+SUPP play based on the story. EG *...the 1939 film version of 'Wuthering Heights'.*

3 Someone's **version** of an event is their descrip- N COUNT+SUPP tion of what happened. EG *Each of the women had a different version of what actually happened.*

versus /vɜːsəs/. **1** You use **versus** to say that two PREP ideas or things are opposed, especially when a choice has to be made between them. EG *...the problem of determinism versus freedom.*

2 Versus is also used to say that two people or PREP teams are competing against each other in a sporting event. EG *The big match tonight is England versus Spain.*

vertebra /vɜːtɪbrə/, **vertebrae** /vɜːtɪbreɪ/. Your N COUNT : **vertebrae** are the small circular bones that form USU PLURAL your backbone.

vertebrate /vɜːtɪbreɪt, -brəˈt/, **vertebrates.** A N COUNT **vertebrate** is a creature which has a backbone. Technical Mammals, birds, and reptiles are all vertebrates.

What are the two other names for a vet?

vertical /vɜːtɪkəl/. **1** Something that is **vertical** ADJ CLASSIF
stands or points straight upwards. EG *The monu-*
ment consists of a horizontal slab supported by two
vertical pillars... A vertical line divides the page
into two halves. ◊ **vertically**. EG *The human brain* ◊ ADV
is divided vertically down the middle into two
hemispheres.

2 You use **vertical** to say that a cliff or slope is ADJ CLASSIF
very steep. EG *The cliff plunged in a vertical drop to*
the bottom.

vertigo /vɜːtɪɡəʊ/ is a feeling of dizziness and N UNCOUNT
sickness caused by looking down from a high place.
EG *Looking out of the window gives him vertigo.*

very /veri/. **1** You use **very** in order to emphasize SUBMOD
an adjective or adverb. EG *...a very small child... It's*
a very good idea... Think very carefully... I liked it
very much... ...the very latest techniques.

2 You use **not very** to say that something is the PHRASE
case only to a small degree. EG *He's not there very*
often... 'Is the work difficult?' - 'Not very, but it's
boring.'

3 You use **very** with nouns **3.1** to emphasize a ADJ CLASSIF :
point in space or time. EG *I walked up to the very* ATTRIB
top... We were there from the very beginning. **3.2**
to emphasize that something is exactly the right
one or exactly the same as something else. EG *Ah,*
there you are. The very man I've been looking
for!... Those are the very words he used. **3.3** to
emphasize the importance or seriousness of what
you are saying. EG *The theatre is fighting for its*
very life.

4 You say **very much so** as an emphatic way of CONVENTION
saying 'yes'. EG *'Did your father resist this?' - 'Very*
much so.'

5 Something **of** your **very own** belongs only to you PHRASE
and does not have to be shared with anyone else. EG
The town has its very own bus service.

6 You can say **very well** when you agree to do CONVENTION
something. EG *'Mr Brown wants to see you.' - 'Very* Formal
well. I'll be along in a moment.'

7 If you say that you **cannot very well** do some- PHRASE
thing, you mean that it would not be the right thing
to do. EG *I can't very well drag him out of the*
meeting, can I?

vessel /vesəl/, **vessels. 1** A **vessel** is a ship or N COUNT
large boat. EG *...fishing vessels.* Formal

2 A **vessel** is also a bowl or other container in N COUNT
which liquid is kept. EG *He began putting the sacred* Literary
vessels away.

3 See also **blood vessel.**

vest /vest/, **vests.** A **vest** is **1** a piece of clothing N COUNT
which you can wear on the top half of your body British
underneath a shirt, blouse, or dress in order to
keep warm. **2** a waistcoat. American

vested /vestɪ²d/. Something that is **vested** in ADJ PRED + in
someone is given to them as a right or responsibil- Formal
ity. EG *...the authority vested in him by the State of*
Massachusetts.

vested interest, vested interests. If you have a N COUNT :
vested interest in something, you have a strong USU PLURAL
reason for acting in a particular way, for example
you are trying to protect your own money, power,
or reputation. EG *They have vested interests in*
farming and forestry... They share a common
vested interest in a strong modern army.

vestige /vestɪdʒ/, **vestiges.** A **vestige** of some- N COUNT :
thing is a very small part of it, often a part that OFT + of
remains after all the rest has gone. EG *...a country* Formal
without any vestige of political freedom.

vet /vet/, **vets, vetting, vetted. 1** A **vet** is a doctor N COUNT
who is specially trained to look after animals. EG British
Get your kitten checked by the vet.

2 When someone or something **is vetted**, they are V + O : USU PASS
carefully checked to make sure that they are British
acceptable to the people in authority. EG *His*
speeches were vetted... He was thoroughly vetted.

◊ **vetting.** EG *He wanted to tighten the security* ◊ N UNCOUNT
vetting of civil servants.

veteran /vetərən/, **veterans. 1** A **veteran** is N COUNT
someone who has served in the armed forces of
their country, especially during a war. EG *...a World*
War Two veteran.

2 You also refer to someone as a **veteran** when N COUNT
they have been involved in a particular activity for
a long time. EG *...a veteran of the civil rights*
movement.

veterinarian /vetərɪneəriən/, **veterinarians.** A N COUNT
veterinarian is a doctor who is specially trained American
to look after animals.

veterinary /vetərɪnəri¹/ is used to describe the ADJ CLASSIF :
work of a vet and the medical treatment of ani- ATTRIB
mals. EG *They had a veterinary practice in Perth.*

veterinary surgeon, veterinary surgeons. A N COUNT
veterinary surgeon is the same as a vet. Formal
British

veto /viːtəʊ/, **vetoes, vetoing, vetoed. 1** If some- V + O
one in authority **vetoes** something, they forbid it.
EG *The government vetoed this proposal.* ▸ used as ▸ N COUNT
a noun. EG *The rest of the committee could not*
accept the veto.

2 Veto is the right that someone in authority has to N UNCOUNT
forbid something. EG *...the Sovereign's power of*
veto... They have a veto they are prepared to use.

vex /veks/, **vexes, vexing, vexed.** If something V + O
vexes you, it makes you feel annoyed. EG *It vexed* Formal
her to be ignored like this.

vexed /vekst/. **1** If you are **vexed**, you are an- ADJ QUALIT
noyed and puzzled. EG *Feeling vexed, I spoke up for*
myself... He sat with a vexed frown on his face.

2 A **vexed** problem or question is very difficult and ADJ QUALIT :
causes people a lot of trouble. EG *This leads to the* ATTRIB
vexed issue of priorities.

VHF /viː eɪtʃ ef/ is a range of very high radio N UNCOUNT
frequencies. **VHF** is an abbreviation for 'very high
frequency'.

via /vaɪə, viːə/. **1** You use **via** to say that someone PREP
or something goes through a particular place on
their way to somewhere else. EG *He booked a ticket*
to Washington via Frankfurt and New York... We
came home via a pub.

2 You also use **via** to say that you do something or PREP
achieve something by making use of a particular
thing or person. EG *...the transmission of television*
pictures via satellite... It was so kind of you to send
that message via Toby.

viable /vaɪəbəl/. Something that is **viable** is ADJ QUALIT
capable of doing what it is intended to do. EG *We*
should be doing everything in our power to develop
viable alternatives to petrol... ...a viable project.

◊ **viability** /vaɪəbɪlɪti¹/. EG *...the commercial vi-* ◊ N UNCOUNT
ability of the new product.

viaduct /vaɪədʌkt/, **viaducts.** A **viaduct** is a long, N COUNT
high bridge that carries a road or railway across a
valley.

vibrant /vaɪbrənt/. **1** Something that is **vibrant** is ADJ QUALIT :
full of life, energy, and enthusiasm. EG *His vibrant* OFT + with
talk fascinated and excited me.

2 A **vibrant** voice or sound is full of emotion and is ADJ QUALIT :
very exciting. EG *...the vibrant tones of Richard* USU ATTRIB
Burton... ...vibrant music.

3 Vibrant light and colours are very bright and ADJ QUALIT
clear. EG *...a flower bed vibrant with red tulips.*

vibrate /vaɪbreɪt/, **vibrates, vibrating, vi-** V
brated. When something **vibrates**, it shakes with
a slight, very quick movement. EG *The foundation*
of the city began to rumble and vibrate.

◊ **vibration** /vaɪbreɪʃə⁰n/, **vibrations.** EG *Your* ◊ N COUNT OR
fingers feel the vibration on the violin string. N UNCOUNT

vicar /vɪkə/, **vicars.** A **vicar** is a priest in the N COUNT
Church of England.

vicarage /vɪkərɪdʒ/, **vicarages.** A **vicarage** is a N COUNT
house in which a vicar lives.

vicarious /vɪkeəriəs, vaɪ-/. A **vicarious** pleasure ADJ CLASSIF
or feeling is one that you experience by watching, ATTRIB
listening to, or reading about other people doing
something, rather than by doing it yourself. EG *...a*
vicarious sense of power and adventure.

vice /vaɪs/, **vices.** 1 A **vice** is a moral fault in   N COUNT
someone's character or behaviour. EG ...*human
vices such as greed and envy... Her one small vice
was smoking... What are your vices?*

2 The criminal activities connected with pornogra-   N UNCOUNT
phy, prostitution, drugs, or gambling are referred
to as **vice.** EG ...*a campaign against vice and
violence... ...strict vice laws.*

3 A **vice** is also a tool with a pair of jaws that hold   N COUNT
an object tightly while you do work on it. For this
meaning, American English has the spelling **vise.**

vice-chancellor, vice-chancellors. The **vice-**   N COUNT :
chancellor of a British University is the person   OFT *the*+N
who is in charge of its academic and administra-
tive policies and activities.

vice versa /vaɪsə vɜːsə/ is used to indicate that   PHRASE
the reverse of what you have said is also true. For
example, 'Women may bring their husbands with
them, and vice versa' means that men may also
bring their wives with them.

vicinity /vɪsɪnɪˈtiⁱ/. If something is in the **vicinity**   N SING :
of a place, it is in the area immediately around that   USU *the*+N
place. EG *The hotels in the vicinity of the campus
were cheap and shabby.*

vicious /vɪʃəs/. Someone or something that is   ADJ QUALIT
vicious is cruel and violent. EG ...*a vicious killer...
...the most vicious totalitarian system in history.*
◊ **viciously.** EG *He twisted her wrist viciously.*   ◊ ADV

vicious circle. A **vicious circle** is a problem or   N SING
difficult situation that causes a new problem or
situation which then causes the original problem or
situation to occur again. EG *We've got to break out
of this vicious circle.*

victim /vɪktɪm/, **victims.** A **victim** is someone   N COUNT
who has been hurt or killed by someone or some-
thing. EG *Most of the victims were shot in the back
while trying to run away... ...a rape victim... ...a
victim of hypothermia.*

victimize /vɪktɪmaɪz/, **victimizes, victimizing,**   V+O : USU PASS
victimized; also spelled **victimise.** If someone **is
victimized,** they are treated unfairly, usually because of their beliefs. EG *Management insisted that
she was not being victimized.* ◊ **victimization**   ◊ N UNCOUNT
/vɪktɪmaɪzeɪʃəⁿn/. EG *There must be no victimization of workers.*

victor /vɪktə/, **victors.** The **victor** in a contest or   N COUNT
battle is the person who wins, or the person who   Outdated
commands the winning army. EG ...*the victor of
Waterloo... He emerged as the victor over Mulder.*

Victorian /vɪktɔːrɪən/, **Victorians.** 1 **Victorian**   ADJ CLASSIF
describes things that happened or were made in
Britain in the middle and last parts of the 19th
century, when Victoria was the Queen. EG ...*Victorian architecture.*

2 You say that someone is **Victorian** when they   ADJ QUALIT
have qualities which are thought to have been
common in the time of Queen Victoria, especially a
belief in strict discipline and morals. EG *His parents
were very Victorian and very domineering.*

3 A **Victorian** is a British person who was alive   N COUNT
when Victoria was Queen.

Victoriana /vɪktɔːrɪɑːnə/. Objects made during   N UNCOUNT
the reign of Queen Victoria are referred to as
Victoriana.

victorious /vɪktɔːrɪəs/. Someone who is **victori-**   ADJ CLASSIF
ous has won a victory, especially in a war. EG *The
army came home victorious.*

victory /vɪktəˈriⁱ/, **victories.** A **victory** is a situa-   N COUNT OR
tion in which you gain complete success, for exam-   N UNCOUNT
ple in a war or a competition. EG *In A.D. 636, an
Arab army won a famous victory over a much
larger Persian force... Nobody believed he had any
chance of victory... The final agreement was a
victory for common sense.*

video /vɪdɪəʊ/, **videos, videoing, videoed.** 1   N UNCOUNT
Video is the recording and showing of television
programmes, films, or actual events, using a video
recorder, video tapes, and a television set. EG *I*

know that you use video for teaching these students... The film's on video.*

2 A **video** is **2.1** a machine which can be used to   N COUNT
play video tapes on a television set and to record
television programmes onto video tape. EG *Turn off
the video.* **2.2** a film or television programme
recorded on video tape for people to watch on a
television set. EG *I've seen this video before.*

3 If you **video** something, you record it on magnet-   V+O
ic tape, either by using a television camera and
recording the actual events, or by using a video to
record a television programme as it is being transmitted, in order to watch it later.

video cassette, video cassettes. A **video cas-**   N COUNT
sette is a cassette containing a video tape.

video recorder, video recorders. A **video re-**   N COUNT
corder or a **video cassette recorder** is a machine that can be used to record television programmes and films onto video tapes, so that people
can play them back and watch them later on a
television set.

video tape, video tapes. Video tape is magnetic   N UNCOUNT
tape that is used to record pictures or films which   OR N COUNT
you can then play back and watch on a television
set. EG *The information can be printed, or put on
video tape... They saw the videotapes of Mr Frost's
interviews.*

vie /vaɪ/, **vies, vying, vied.** If you **vie** with   V OR V+*with* :
someone, you try hard to get something before   RECIP
they do, or to do something better than they do. EG   Formal
*The artists vied for the prime sites... ...vying with
each other to express their disgust.*

view /vjuː/, **views, viewing, viewed.** 1 Your   N COUNT :
view on a particular subject is your opinion about   USU+SUPP
it. EG *I've changed my view on this issue... He was
sent to jail for his political views... I have strong
views about the Church.*

2 Your **view** of something is your attitude to it and   N SING+SUPP
the way in which you understand it. EG *She has a
view of life which is deeply corrupt... He tends to
take a wider, more overall view of things than
most people.*

3 If you **view** something in a particular way, you   V+O+A
think of it in that way. EG *He viewed the future with
gloom... Their missiles are viewed as a defensive
and deterrent force.*

4 The **view** from a window or high place is   N COUNT :
everything that you can see from it. EG *The win-*   USU SING
*dows of her flat looked out on to a superb view of
London... From the top there is a fine view.*

5 If you have a **view** of something, you can see it.   N SING+SUPP
EG *The driver blocked his view... I had one last view
of the gorge.*

6 If you **view** something, you look at it. EG *A drop*   V+O
from a pond, viewed through a microscope,   Formal
swarms with tiny organisms.

7 You use **in my view** when you want to empha-   ADV SEN
size that you are stating your personal opinion. EG
*In my view, we have a long way to go before we
have a United States of Europe.*

8 **View** is also used in these phrases. **8.1** If you   PHRASES
take the view that something is true, your opinion is that it is true. EG *The civil servants generally
took the view that experts know best.* **8.2** You use
in view of to specify the main fact or event that
causes you to do, say, or think something. EG *In
view of the fact that all the other members of the
group are going, I think you should go too.* **8.3** If
you do something **with a view to** a particular
result, you do it in order to achieve that result. EG
*We have exchanged letters with a view to meeting
to discuss these problems.* **8.4** If something is **in
view**, you can see it from where you are. EG *We
crept around the cage to keep the monkey in
view... Marie turned her back on her rival in full*

Is a vicious circle really vicious?

view of the audience. **8.5** If you have something **in view**, you are aware of it and your actions are aimed towards it. EG *I don't teach with the exams in view.* **8.6** If something **comes into view**, you begin to be able to see it, either because it has moved or because you have moved. EG *The bridge suddenly came into view.* **8.7** If something is **on view**, it is being exhibited in public. EG *The Turner exhibition is on view at the Tate Gallery.*

viewer /vjuːə/, **viewers.** A **viewer** is someone N COUNT who watches television. EG *Many of these programmes are an insult to the viewer's intelligence.*

viewpoint /vjuːpɔɪnt/, **viewpoints. 1** Someone's N COUNT+SUPP **viewpoint** is the way that they think about things in general or about a particular thing. EG *I cannot make sense of it from my particular viewpoint as a Christian minister.*

2 A **viewpoint** is also a place from which you can N COUNT get a good view of something that is happening.

vigil /vɪdʒɪl/, **vigils.** A **vigil** is a period of time N COUNT when you remain quietly in a place, especially at night, for example because you are looking after a sick person or are making a political protest. EG *Last weekend a nun on a hunger strike held a vigil at the United Nations.*

vigilant /vɪdʒɪlənt/. If you are **vigilant**, you give ADJ QUALIT careful attention to a situation and try to notice Formal any danger or trouble that there might be. EG *This evening, I had to be especially vigilant.*
◊ **vigilance** /vɪdʒɪləns/. EG *Constant vigilance is* ◊ N UNCOUNT *required from all of us.*

vigilante /vɪdʒɪlænti[1]/, **vigilantes. Vigilantes** N COUNT : are people who unofficially organize themselves USU PLURAL into a group to protect their community and to catch and punish criminals.

vigorous /vɪgərəs/. **1** A **vigorous** action is done ADJ QUALIT with a lot of energy. EG *Mary gave her skirt a vigorous shake.* ◊ **vigorously.** EG *We shook hands* ◊ ADV *vigorously and he went off.*

2 If you make a **vigorous** attempt to achieve ADJ QUALIT something, you do it with a lot of energy and enthusiasm. EG *Their home has been saved by a vigorous campaign... He was one of the most vigorous advocates of workers' control.*
◊ **vigorously.** EG *Chomsky defended this view very* ◊ ADV *vigorously.*

3 Someone who is **vigorous** is strong and healthy ADJ QUALIT and full of energy. EG *...an elderly but vigorous man.*

vigour /vɪgə/; spelled **vigor** in American English. N UNCOUNT : **Vigour** is physical or mental energy and enthusi- USU+SUPP asm. EG *These problems were discussed with great vigour.*

vile /vaɪl/, **viler, vilest.** If you say that someone ADJ QUALIT or something is **vile**, you are emphasizing how unpleasant they are and how much you dislike them. EG *...England's vile weather... ...her vile language... ...rage against this vile, contemptible act.*

villa /vɪlə/, **villas.** A **villa** is an attractive house, N COUNT especially one in the country that is used for holidays. EG *They rented a villa not far from Pisa.*

village /vɪlɪdʒ/, **villages.** A **village** consists of a N COUNT large group of houses, together with other buildings such as a church and a school, situated in a country area. EG *...an Austrian village... ...the village school... I work among the village people.*

villager /vɪlɪdʒə/, **villagers. Villagers** are peo- N COUNT : ple who live in a village. EG *The villagers were* USU PLURAL *suspicious of anything new.*

villain /vɪlən/, **villains.** A **villain** is someone who N COUNT deliberately harms other people or breaks the law. EG *A villain named Thomson broke into the premises... ...the treacherous villain who had upset all his plans.*

villainous /vɪlənəs/. Someone who is **villainous** ADJ CLASSIF is very bad and willing to harm other people or break the law. EG *...villainous or wicked characters.*

villainy /vɪləni[1]/ is very bad or criminal behav- N UNCOUNT iour. EG *...the villainy of her landlord.*

vindicate /vɪndɪkeɪt/, **vindicates, vindicating,** V+O : OFT PASS **vindicated.** When someone is **vindicated**, their Formal ideas or actions are proved to be correct. EG *Benn was decisively vindicated at the polls, receiving 23,275 votes to 10,231... His gloomy forecasts have been vindicated.* ◊ **vindication** /vɪndɪkeɪʃə[n]n/, ◊ N COUNT OR **vindications.** EG *These changes to the law were* N UNCOUNT *widely regarded as a vindication of his long campaign.*

vindictive /vɪndɪktɪv/. Someone who is **vindic-** ADJ QUALIT **tive** tries deliberately to hurt someone, often because they think that they have been harmed by them. EG *...a vindictive and violent man.*
◊ **vindictively.** EG *Her dress had been vindictively* ◊ ADV *cut to shreds.*

vine /vaɪn/, **vines.** A **vine** is a climbing or trailing N COUNT plant, especially the climbing plant that produces grapes as its fruit.

vinegar /vɪnɪgə/ is a sharp-tasting liquid, usually N UNCOUNT made from sour wine or malt, which is used in making things such as salad dressing.

vineyard /vɪnjəd/, **vineyards.** A **vineyard** is an N COUNT area of land where grape vines are grown in order to produce wine. EG *...the vineyards of Bordeaux.*

vintage /vɪntɪdʒ/, **vintages. 1 Vintage** wine has ADJ CLASSIF : been stored for several years in order to improve ATTRIB its quality. EG *...vintage port.*

2 Vintage describes something which is the best ADJ CLASSIF : or most typical of its kind, especially because it ATTRIB was produced at a time when the thing was at its best. EG *...vintage Bob Dylan music... ...vintage cars.*

vinyl /vaɪn[o]l/ is a strong plastic used for making N UNCOUNT : things such as furniture and floor coverings. EG OFT N MOD *...white vinyl chairs.*

viola /viˈəʊlə/ **violas.** A **viola** is a musical instru- N COUNT ment played with a bow. It is like a violin, but is slightly larger.

violate /vaɪəleɪt/, **violates, violating, violated. 1** V+O If you **violate** an agreement, law, or promise, you break it. EG *Ancient property laws are openly violated... He is violating his contract.* ◊ **violation** ◊ N UNCOUNT /vaɪəleɪʃə[n]n/, **violations.** EG *They blockaded the* OR N COUNT *Suez Canal in violation of international agreements... ...violations of the Constitution.*

2 If you **violate** someone's privacy or peace, you V+O disturb it. EG *The calm of the press lounge was* Formal *suddenly violated.*

3 If someone **violates** a place, especially a tomb, V+O they treat it with no respect, for example by breaking into it and removing its treasures. EG *...a curse on those who violated the tomb of the king.*
◊ **violation, violations.** EG *...the violation of our* ◊ N UNCOUNT *homes.* OR N COUNT

violence /vaɪələns/. **1 Violence** is behaviour N UNCOUNT which is intended to hurt or kill people, for example hitting or kicking or using guns or bombs. EG *...threats of terrorist violence... ...acts of violence... ...robbery with violence.*

2 If you do or say something with **violence**, you N UNCOUNT use a lot of energy in doing or saying it, often because you are angry. EG *He flung open the door with unnecessary violence... I was surprised at the violence of his reaction.*

violent /vaɪələnt/. **1** If someone is **violent**, they ADJ QUALIT behave in a way that is intended to hurt or kill people, for example by hitting or kicking or using guns or bombs. EG *People in this society are prepared to be violent... ...violent clashes with the police.* ◊ **violently.** EG *They have come into* ◊ ADV *conflict, sometimes violently.*

2 A **violent** death is painful and unexpected, ADJ CLASSIF usually because the person who dies has been murdered. EG *...the constant threat of violent death.*
◊ **violently.** EG *...a poison that can kill violently* ◊ ADV *and quickly.*

3 Violent describes something that is said or ADJ QUALIT argued with a lot of force and energy, usually because people are angry. EG *At times the argument grew violent... Burt's work came under vio-*

lent attack. ◊ **violently**. EG *They violently dis-* ◊ ADV
agreed with their Commander-in-Chief.

4 Violent also describes something which happens ADJ QUALIT
suddenly and with a lot of force. EG *...a violent*
explosion... I gave it a violent tug. ◊ **violently**. EG ◊ ADV
The train braked violently.

5 A **violent** emotion or sensation is very powerful. ADJ QUALIT
EG *He had a violent urge to create... A violent*
impatience overcame him. ◊ **violently**. EG *This* ◊ ADV
drug can make some people violently ill.

6 Violent colours are unpleasantly bright. EG *...a* ADJ QUALIT :
shirt of violent red. ATTRIB

7 Violent weather is stormy. ADJ QUALIT

violin /ˌvaɪəˈlɪn/, **violins**. A **violin** is a musical N COUNT
instrument consisting of a shaped and polished
hollow wooden box, with four strings stretched
over it. You hold a violin under your chin and play
it with a bow. See picture at MUSICAL INSTRUMENTS.

violinist /ˌvaɪəˈlɪnɪst/, **violinists**. A **violinist** is N COUNT
someone who plays the violin.

VIP /ˌviː aɪ ˈpiː/, **VIPs**. A **VIP** is someone who is N COUNT
given better treatment than ordinary people be-
cause he or she is famous, influential, or important.
VIP is an abbreviation for 'very important person'.
EG *...a private lounge for VIPs... She gave us the full*
VIP treatment.

viper /ˈvaɪpə/, **vipers**. A **viper** is a small poison- N COUNT
ous snake found mainly in Britain and Europe.

virgin /ˈvɜːdʒɪn/, **virgins**. **1** A **virgin** is someone N COUNT
who has never had sex. EG *Men here still demand*
that the girls they marry should be virgins. ▶ used ▶ ADJ CLASSIF :
as an adjective. EG *...a spinster or a virgin lady.* ATTRIB
◊ **virginity** /vəˈdʒɪnɪtiˈ/. EG *His sister had lost her* ◊ N UNCOUNT
virginity many years before.

2 Something that is **virgin** is fresh and clean, and ADJ CLASSIF
its appearance shows that it has never been used
before. EG *There were piles and piles of books, all*
virgin, all untouched.

3 Virgin land has not been explored, cultivated, or ADJ CLASSIF :
spoiled by people. EG *...opening up virgin territory...* ATTRIB
...virgin rain forest.

virginal /ˈvɜːdʒɪnəl/. Someone who is **virginal** ADJ QUALIT
looks young and innocent, and has had no experi-
ence of sex. EG *The men have decreed that their*
women must be pure, virginal, innocent.

virile /ˈvɪraɪl/. A man who is **virile** has the qual- ADJ QUALIT
ities that a man is traditionally expected to have,
such as physical strength, forcefulness, and strong
sexuality; used showing approval. EG *...virile young*
male actors. ◊ **virility** /vɪˈrɪlɪtiˈ/. EG *The macho* ◊ N UNCOUNT
male wishes to prove his virility.

virtual /ˈvɜːtʃʊəl/ is used to say that something ADJ CLASSIF :
has all the characteristics of a particular thing, ATTRIB
although it is not formally recognized as being that
thing. EG *The peasants remain in a state of virtual*
slavery... ...a virtual revolution in organization.

virtually /ˈvɜːtʃʊəliˈ/ is used to say that something ADV
is so nearly true that for most purposes it can be
regarded as being true. EG *They are virtually*
impossible to detect... He virtually lived in his
office... This opinion was held by virtually all the
experts.

virtue /ˈvɜːtjuː, -tʃuː/, **virtues**. **1 Virtue** is thinking N UNCOUNT
and doing what is right and avoiding what is wrong.
EG *We accept certain principles of religion and*
traditional virtue.

2 A **virtue** is a good quality or a good way of N COUNT
behaving. EG *Charity is the greatest of Christian*
virtues.

3 A **virtue** of something is an advantage or benefit N COUNT OR
that it has. EG *He was extolling the virtues of* N UNCOUNT
female independence... There is no virtue in taking
this action.

4 You use **by virtue of** to explain why something PREP
happens or is true. EG *He was an object of interest* Formal
simply by virtue of being British.

virtuoso /ˌvɜːtjʊˈəʊzəʊ, -səʊ/, **virtuosos** or **virtuo-** N COUNT
si /ˌvɜːtjʊˈəʊziˈ/. A **virtuoso** is someone who is
exceptionally good at something, especially at

playing a musical instrument. EG *He was a virtuoso*
of the jazz guitar.

virtuous /ˈvɜːtʃʊəs, -tjʊəs/. Someone who is **virtu-** ADJ QUALIT
ous behaves correctly according to the moral code
of a particular religion or society. EG *People who*
lead virtuous lives in this world are assured of
paradise in the next.

virulent /ˈvɪrʊlənt/. **1** Feelings, actions, or ADJ QUALIT
speeches that are **virulent** are extremely bitter Formal
and hostile. EG *Nehru and Nasser were the objects*
of special hatred and virulent attack.
◊ **virulently**. EG *Fighting broke out again much* ◊ ADV
more virulently.

2 A **virulent** disease or poison is extremely power- ADJ QUALIT
ful and dangerous. EG *...a virulent virus.* Formal

virus /ˈvaɪrəs/, **viruses**. A **virus** is a germ that N COUNT
can cause disease in people, animals, or plants. EG
She had a flu virus... ...a virus infection.

visa /ˈviːzə/, **visas**. A **visa** is an official stamp N COUNT
which is put in your passport by the embassy or
consulate of a country that you want to visit, and
which allows you to enter or leave that country, or
to travel through it. EG *I obtained a visa to visit East*
Germany.

vis-à-vis /ˌviːz æ ˈviː/. You use **vis-à-vis** when you PREP
are considering one thing or quantity in compari- Formal
son with another. EG *One solution would be for us to*
lower our exchange rate vis-à-vis other countries.

viscount /ˈvaɪkaʊnt/, **viscounts**. A **viscount** is a N COUNT
British nobleman who is below an earl and above a
baron in rank.

viscountess /ˌvaɪkaʊnˈtəs/, **viscountesses**. A **vis-** N COUNT
countess is **1** the wife of a viscount. **2** a woman
who holds the same rank as a viscount.

vise /vaɪs/. See **vice**.

visibility /ˌvɪzɪˈbɪlɪtiˈ/. You use **visibility** to say N UNCOUNT
how far or how clearly you can see in particular
weather conditions. EG *Visibility was excellent that*
day... ...conditions of restricted visibility.

visible /ˈvɪzɪbəl/. **1** If an object is **visible**, it is ADJ QUALIT
large enough to be seen, or is in a position where it
can be seen. EG *These tiny creatures are hardly*
visible to the naked eye... The moon was fully
visible... It was just visible from the beach.

2 If a situation, a change, or the state of something ADJ QUALIT
is **visible**, it can be noticed or recognized. EG *The*
results are visible in the growth of the Conserva-
tive vote... ...a period of little visible advance.
◊ **visibly**. EG *She was visibly nervous.* ◊ ADV

vision /ˈvɪʒən/, **visions**. **1** If you have a **vision** of N COUNT :
a possible situation or state of affairs, you have a OFT + *of*
mental picture of it, in which you imagine how
things might be different from the way they are
now. EG *...fighting for the vision of the new China... I*
had nightmarish visions of what could go wrong.

2 Vision is the ability to see clearly. EG *He has very* N UNCOUNT
little vision in his left eye... ...children with poor
vision.

3 The **vision** on a television set is the picture that N UNCOUNT
is shown on it. EG *We apologize for the temporary*
loss of vision.

visionary /ˈvɪʒənəˈriˈ/, **visionaries**. A **visionary** N COUNT
is someone who has visions about how things might
be different in the future. EG *...left-wing visionaries.*
▶ used as an adjective. EG *...the greatest visionary* ▶ ADJ QUALIT
king in Ethiopian history.

visit /ˈvɪzɪt/, **visits**, **visiting**, **visited**. **1** If you **visit** V+O OR V
someone, you go to see them and to spend time
with them. EG *She visited some of her relatives for a*
few days... You might need to visit a solicitor.
▶ used as a noun. EG *It would be nice if you paid me* ▶ N COUNT
a visit... She made a visit to her mother in Suffolk.

2 If you **visit** a place, you go to see it because you V+O OR V
are interested in it. EG *This is the best museum*
we've visited... More than a million foreigners visit

Are there any visual aids in this dictionary?

the United States every year. ▸ used as a noun. EG ▸ N COUNT
He wrote to me after a brief visit to the U.S.

visitor /vɪzɪtə/, **visitors**. A **visitor** is someone N COUNT
who is visiting a person or place. EG Marsha was a
frequent visitor to our house... The Hall is open to
visitors on weekdays.

visor /vaɪzə/, **visors**. A **visor** is a movable part of N COUNT
a helmet, for example one worn by a motorcyclist,
which can be pulled down to protect a person's
eyes or face.

vista /vɪstə/, **vistas**. 1 A **vista** is the view that you N COUNT+SUPP
get from a particular place, especially a long view Literary
rather than a wide one. EG He could see through the
tall windows a vista of green fields.

2 You can also refer to a range of exciting or N COUNT+SUPP
worrying new ideas and possibilities as a **vista**. EG Literary
This turn of events opened up a whole new vista of
troubles for me.

visual /vɪʒʊəl, -zju-/ means relating to sight. EG ADJ CLASSIF
...visual jokes... ...exhibitions in the visual arts.
◊ **visually**. EG Visually, it is a very exciting film... ◊ ADV SEN OR
The island is visually stunning. ADV

visual aid, **visual aids**. **Visual aids** are things N COUNT+
that you can look at, such as films, models, maps, USU PLURAL
or slides, in order to help you understand, learn, or
remember information of some kind.

visualize /vɪʒʊəlaɪz/, **visualizes**, **visualizing**, V+O
visualized; also spelled **visualise**. If you **visual-**
ize something, you imagine what it is like by
forming a mental picture of it. EG He found he could
visualize her face quite clearly.

vital /vaɪtəl/. 1 Something that is **vital** is neces- ADJ QUALIT
sary or very important. EG It is vital to keep an
accurate record of every transaction... They
pressed on with their vital repair work. ◊ **vitally**. ◊ ADV+ADJ
EG The way we choose to bring up children is vitally
important.

2 You say that people or organizations are **vital** ADJ QUALIT
when they are energetic, exciting, and full of life.
EG The Chinese were trusting, open, and vital... We
want to have a modern vital parliament.

vitality /vaɪtælɪtɪ/. People who have **vitality** N UNCOUNT
have great energy and liveliness. EG ...the vitality
and eagerness of a normal toddler.

vital statistics. A woman's **vital statistics** are N PLURAL
the measurements of her bust, waist, and hips. +POSS
These are often used to indicate how attractive and
shapely her figure is.

vitamin /vɪtəmɪn/, **vitamins**. **Vitamins** are or- N COUNT
ganic substances which you need in order to re-
main healthy. They exist naturally in many kinds
of food and are also sold in the form of pills. EG She
needs extra vitamins and protein... One tiny berry
contained more vitamin C than an orange.

vitriolic /vɪtrɪɒlɪk/. **Vitriolic** language or behav- ADJ QUALIT :
iour is full of bitterness and hate. EG He was ATTRIB
subjected to the most vitriolic personal abuse. Formal

viva /vaɪvə/, **vivas**. A **viva** is an oral examination, N COUNT
especially one taken in a university.

vivacious /vɪveɪʃəs/. Someone who is **vivacious** ADJ QUALIT
is lively, exciting, and attractive. EG She was young
and vivacious.

vivacity /vɪvæsɪtɪ/ is the quality of being lively N UNCOUNT
in an attractive and exciting way. EG ...a man of Formal
great charm and vivacity.

vivid /vɪvɪd/. 1 Something that is **vivid** is very ADJ QUALIT
bright in colour. EG She was walking slowly across a
vivid green lawn. ◊ **vividly**. EG They are the most ◊ ADV
vividly coloured birds in Australia.

2 Memories or descriptions that are **vivid** are very ADJ QUALIT
clear and detailed. EG I have a vivid memory of an
excursion with my grandmother... She gave a vivid
account of her travels. ◊ **vividly**. EG 'You remem- ◊ ADV
ber Captain Donck?' - 'Oh, yes. Vividly.'

vivisection /vɪvɪsekʃən/ is the practice of cut- N UNCOUNT
ting open living animals in order to perform scientific or medical experiments on them.

V+O stands for **transitive verb**
Verbs which have the label V+O in the Extra
Column are transitive verbs, that is, they need an
object to complete their meaning.
See the entry headed VERBS for more information.

V+O+A stands for **transitive verb used with ad-**
junct
Verbs which have the label V+O+A in the Extra
Column are verbs which need both an object and
an adjunct to complete their meaning.
See the entry headed VERBS for more information.

V+O+C stands for **transitive verb followed by**
complement
Verbs which have the label V+O+C in the Extra
Column are verbs which have an object and also a
complement which refers back to the object.
See the entry headed VERBS for more information.

---

vocabulary /vəkæbjʊlərɪ/, **vocabularies**. 1 N COUNT OR
Your **vocabulary** is the total number of words that N UNCOUNT
you know in a particular language. EG By the age of
five, a child has a vocabulary of over 2,000 words.

2 The **vocabulary** of a language is the words in it. N SING
EG New words are constantly coming into use and
then dropping out of the vocabulary.

3 The **vocabulary** of a subject is the group of N COUNT OR
words that are typically used when discussing it. EG N UNCOUNT :
'Struggle' is a key word in the Marxist vocabulary. +SUPP

vocal /vəʊkəl/, **vocals**. 1 You say that people are ADJ QUALIT
vocal when they speak very loudly about some-
thing that they feel strongly about. EG The members had been quite vocal on issues of academic
freedom.

2 **Vocal** means involving the use of the human ADJ CLASSIF :
voice, especially in singing. EG She amazed her ATTRIB
audiences with her superb vocal range... ...Russian
vocal music.

3 When you refer to the **vocals** in a pop song, you N PLURAL
are referring to the singing. EG Lead vocals: Boy
George. Backing vocals: Helen Terry.

vocal cords; also spelled **vocal chords**. Your N PLURAL
vocal cords are the part of your larynx which can
be made to vibrate when you breathe out, making
the sounds which you use for speaking.

vocalist /vəʊkəlɪst/, **vocalists**. A **vocalist** is a N COUNT
singer who sings with a pop group.

vocation /vəʊkeɪʃən/, **vocations**. A **vocation** is a N COUNT OR
strong feeling that you want to do a particular job, N UNCOUNT
especially one which involves serving other people. EG By vocation I'm not a politician... Medicine
is my vocation.

vocational /vəʊkeɪʃənəl, -ʃənəl/ is used to de- ADJ CLASSIF
scribe the skills needed for a particular job or USU ATTRIB
profession. EG ...a college that does technical and
vocational training.

VOCATIVE
Some words have the label VOCATIVE in the Extra
Column. This shows that you use the word when
you are speaking to someone, just as if it were
their name. Examples of words labelled VOCATIVE
are **sir** and **honey**, as in EG Mr Hink to see you,
sir... Hello, **honey!**

vociferous /vəˈsɪfərəs/. Someone who is **vociferous** speaks very loudly, because they want to make sure that people hear what they are saying. EG *They were supported by a vociferous group in the actors' union.* ADJ QUALIT Formal

vodka /ˈvɒdkə/, **vodkas**. **Vodka** is a strong, clear alcoholic drink. N MASS

vogue /vəʊg/. **1** If something is the **vogue**, it is very popular and fashionable. EG *The current vogue is for decentralization... Flowery carpets became the vogue.* N SING

2 Something that is **in vogue** is very popular and fashionable. EG *At that time aftershave was not in vogue in France.* PHRASE

voice /vɔɪs/, **voices, voicing, voiced**. **1** When someone speaks, you hear their **voice**. EG *She heard a voice calling her name... He recognized me by my voice... 'I suppose we'd better go,' said John in a low voice.* N COUNT

2 You use **voice** to refer to someone's opinion on a particular topic and what they say about it. EG *Numerous voices were raised against the idea... The only dissenting voice was Mr Foot's.* N COUNT

3 If you have a **voice** in something, you have the right to express an opinion on it. EG *Students should have a voice in determining the way universities develop.* N SING : a+N

4 If you **voice** something such as an opinion or an emotion, you say what you think or feel. EG *The African delegates voiced their anger... Some fierce public criticism of it had been voiced.* V+O

5 In grammar, the active **voice** and the passive **voice** refer to the relation between a verb and its subject. N SING : the+N

6 **Voice** is also used in these phrases. **6.1** If you **raise** your **voice**, you speak more loudly. If you **lower** your **voice**, you speak more quietly. EG *Gregory began to raise his voice in protest... She lowered her voice to a discreet whisper.* **6.2** If someone tells you to **keep** your **voice down**, they are asking you to speak more quietly. EG *'Can't you keep your voice down?' Brody said in a hoarse whisper.* **6.3** If you say something **at the top of** your **voice**, you say it as loudly as possible. EG *'I am drenched,' she declared at the top of her voice.* PHRASES

void /vɔɪd/, **voids**. **1** A **void** is a situation or state of affairs which seems empty because it has no interest, excitement, or value. EG *Tending their mother had filled the void for a time... ...the need to fill the void of materialism with humane and spiritual values.* N COUNT : USU SING Literary

2 A **void** is also a big hole or space, especially one which is frightening. EG *He looked down into the gaping void at his feet.* N COUNT Literary

3 Something that is **void** or that is **null and void** has no official value or authority. EG *...declaring the contract null and void.* ADJ PRED Technical

volatile /ˈvɒlətaɪl/. **1** A situation that is **volatile** is liable to change suddenly and unexpectedly. EG *The situation in Lebanon was 'tense, dangerous and volatile'.* ADJ QUALIT

2 Someone who is **volatile** is liable to change their mood or behaviour suddenly and unexpectedly. EG *He was a very clever, volatile actor.* ADJ QUALIT

volcanic /vɒlˈkænɪk/. A place or region that is **volcanic** has a lot of volcanoes or was created by volcanoes. EG *The islands are volcanic.* ADJ CLASSIF

volcano /vɒlˈkeɪnəʊ/, **volcanoes**. A **volcano** is a mountain which hot melted rock, gas, steam, and ash sometimes burst out of, coming from inside the earth. EG *Six other volcanoes were still erupting.* N COUNT

volition /vəˈlɪʃən/. If you do something **of** your **own volition**, you do it because you have decided for yourself that you will do it. EG *She didn't go down there of her own volition.* PHRASE Formal

volley /ˈvɒli/, **volleys, volleying, volleyed**. **1** A **volley** of shots or gunfire is a lot of shots fired at the same time. EG *...a volley of automatic rifle fire.* N COUNT

2 In tennis, a **volley** is a shot in which the player N COUNT

hits the ball before it touches the ground. EG *He missed an easy cross-court volley.* ▸ used as a verb. EG *She ran to the other side and volleyed into the net.* ▸ V OR V+O

volleyball /ˈvɒlibɔːl/ is a game in which two teams hit a large ball with their hands, backwards and forwards over a high net. If you allow the ball to touch the ground within the court, your team loses a point. N UNCOUNT

volt /vəʊlt/, **volts**. A **volt** is a unit used to measure the force of an electrical current. N COUNT

voltage /ˈvəʊltɪdʒ/, **voltages**. The voltage of an electrical current is its force measured in volts. N UNCOUNT OR N COUNT

voluble /ˈvɒljəbəl/. Someone who is **voluble** talks a lot with great energy and enthusiasm. EG *He became very voluble and told her everything.* ADJ QUALIT Formal

volume /ˈvɒljuːm/, **volumes**. **1** A **volume** is **1.1** a book. EG *She took from the shelf a large green volume... ...a scholarly volume on Stonehenge.* **1.2** a book which is one of a series of books. EG *It was published in three volumes.* N COUNT : OFT+SUPP / N COUNT

2 The **volume** of something is **2.1** the amount of space that it contains or occupies. EG *The gas expanded to nine times its original volume.* **2.2** the amount of it that there is. EG *The volume of work is incredible... ...the growing volume of imports.* N SING : USU+POSS / N PART : SING

3 The **volume** of a radio, TV, or record player is the amount of sound that it produces. EG *She turned up the volume... They kept the radio playing at full volume.* N UNCOUNT

voluminous /vəˈljuːmɪnəs/. **1** **Voluminous** clothes are very large. EG *...a voluminous skirt.* ADJ QUALIT Literary

2 If written information is **voluminous**, there is a lot of it. EG *I took voluminous notes.* ADJ QUALIT Formal

voluntary /ˈvɒləntəri/, **voluntaries**. **1** **Voluntary** describes actions that you do because you choose to do them and not because you have been forced to do them. EG *Attendance at the parade was voluntary... He went into voluntary exile.* ADJ CLASSIF

◊ **voluntarily**. EG *They were said to have left their land voluntarily.* ◊ ADV

2 **Voluntary** work is done by people who are not paid for it. EG *...voluntary services... I do voluntary home tuition.* ADJ CLASSIF

3 A **voluntary** worker is someone who does work, especially social work, without being paid for it. EG *The group is run by voluntary helpers.* ADJ CLASSIF

volunteer /vɒlənˈtɪə/, **volunteers, volunteering, volunteered**. **1** A **volunteer** is **1.1** someone who does work, especially socially useful work, for which they are not paid. EG *Teaching literacy to adults using volunteers began in 1963... ...volunteer work at the hospital.* **1.2** someone who chooses to join the army, navy, or air force, especially in wartime, as opposed to someone who is forced to join by law. EG *Many Australians fought as volunteers on the Allied side.* N COUNT

2 If you **volunteer** to do something, you offer to do it, rather than being forced to do it. EG *He volunteered to do whatever he could for them... ...an extra payment to those who volunteer for redundancy.* V : OFT+to-INF OR for; ALSO V+O

3 If you **volunteer** for the army, navy, or air force, you offer to join it without being required to do so by law. V : OFT+for

4 If you **volunteer** information or an explanation, you tell it to someone without being asked. EG *I volunteered no explanation for our visit.* V+O Formal

voluptuous /vəˈlʌptjuəs/. A **voluptuous** woman has large breasts and hips and is considered to be sexually desirable. EG *She was a voluptuous creature with blonde hair.* ADJ QUALIT Formal

vomit /ˈvɒmɪt/, **vomits, vomiting, vomited**. **1** If you **vomit**, food and drink comes back up from your stomach and out through your mouth, usually V OR V+O

Do you vote when there is a vote of thanks?

because you are ill. EG *She vomited into a paper bag.*

2 Vomit is partly digested food and drink that has come back up from someone's stomach and out through their mouth. EG *The stink of vomit reached Brody almost instantly.* N UNCOUNT

V+O+O stands for **double object verb**

Verbs which have the label V+O+O in the Extra Column are verbs which can have two objects. See the entry headed VERBS for more information.

---

voracious /vəˈreɪʃəs/. If you say that someone is **voracious** or that they have a **voracious** appetite for something, you mean that they want a lot of it. EG *The Duke's voracious capacity for food was abnormal... Nearly all of them were voracious readers of detective stories.* ADJ CLASSIF Literary

vortex /ˈvɔːtɛks/, **vortexes** or **vortices** /ˈvɔːtəsiːz/.

1 A **vortex** is a mass of wind or water which spins round so fast that it pulls objects into its empty centre. N COUNT Formal

2 You can refer to a situation as a **vortex** when you feel that you are being forced into it without being able to prevent it. EG *They found themselves sucked into the revolutionary vortex.* N COUNT+SUPP Formal

vote /vəʊt/, **votes, voting, voted. 1** Your **vote** is your choice in an election, or at a meeting where decisions are taken. EG *...an increase in votes for the Conservative Party... He will get my vote... The motion was defeated by 221 votes to 152.* N COUNT

2 When a group of people have a **vote** or take a **vote**, they make a decision by allowing each person in the group to say what they would prefer. The final decision is the one that most people prefer. EG *Let's have a vote.* N COUNT

3 In an election, the **vote** is the total number of people who have indicated their choice. EG *They captured 13 per cent of the vote.* N SING : the+N

4 When you **vote**, you make your choice in an election or at a meeting, usually by writing on a piece of paper or by raising your hand. EG *We've always voted Conservative... 381 delegates voted for unilateral disarmament... They voted to continue the strike.* V : OFT+A OR to-INF; ALSO V+O

5 You say that people have the **vote** when they have the legal right to indicate in an election who they would like to represent them as their government. EG *Women have had the vote for over fifty years.* N SING : the+N

vote in. When people **vote** a political party or leader **in**, they give them enough votes in an election to allow them to start governing the country. PHRASAL VB : V+O+ADV

vote out. When people **vote** a political party or leader **out**, they do not give them enough votes in an election to allow them to continue governing the country. PHRASAL VB : V+O+ADV

vote of thanks, votes of thanks. A **vote of thanks** is an official speech, usually at a meeting or a formal dinner, in which the speaker formally thanks a person for doing something. EG *The chairman will be proposing the vote of thanks.* N COUNT

voter /ˈvəʊtə/, **voters.** A **voter** is someone who has the legal right to vote in an election. EG *Many of Britain's voters are looking for new answers.* N COUNT

vouch /vaʊtʃ/, **vouches, vouching, vouched. 1** If you say that you can or will **vouch for** someone, you mean that you are sure that they will behave correctly, and that you take responsibility for their good behaviour. EG *He said that he could vouch for your discretion... He said you'd vouch for him... I was vouched for by the Tattaglia family.* PHRASAL VB : V+PREP, HAS PASS

2 If you say that you can **vouch for** something, you mean that you have evidence from your own V+PREP, HAS PASS

personal experience that it is true or correct. EG *I can vouch for the accuracy of my information.*

voucher /ˈvaʊtʃə/, **vouchers.** A **voucher** is a ticket or a piece of paper that can be used instead of money to pay for a particular thing. EG *...meal vouchers worth 15p each.* N COUNT

vow /vaʊ/, **vows, vowing, vowed. 1** If you **vow** to do something, you make a solemn promise to do it. EG *He vowed never to let it happen again... He vowed that he would ride at my side.* V+to-INF OR REPORT : ONLY that

2 A **vow** is a solemn promise to do something. EG *She made a vow to give up smoking.* N COUNT

vowel /ˈvaʊəl/, **vowels.** A **vowel** is a sound such as the ones represented by the letters 'a' or 'o', which you pronounce with your mouth open. Most words are pronounced with a combination of consonants and vowels. N COUNT

voyage /ˈvɔɪɪdʒ/, **voyages.** A **voyage** is a long journey on a ship or in a spacecraft. EG *...the long sea voyage from London to Bombay.* N COUNT

voyager /ˈvɔɪɪdʒə/, **voyagers.** A **voyager** is someone who goes on a voyage, especially a difficult or dangerous one. EG *...our first voyagers to the stars... ...early ocean voyagers.* N COUNT

V-PASS stands for **passive verb**

Verbs which have the label V-PASS in the Extra Column are verbs which are more often used in the passive than in the active. So you are more likely to find *I was flattered by his courtesy* than *His courtesy flattered me*. And *I was taken aback by the price* is more frequent than *The price took me aback*.

See the entry headed VERBS for more information.

V-REFL stands for **reflexive verb**

Verbs which have the label V-REFL in the Extra Column are verbs where the object can be a reflexive pronoun which refers back to the subject. See the entry headed VERBS for more information.

---

vs. is an abbreviation for 'versus'. EG *The first match is England vs. South America.*

V-SPEECH stands for **speech verb**

Verbs which have the label V-SPEECH in the Extra Column can be used as a transitive verb (V+O), as an intransitive verb describing direct speech (V+QUOTE), and as an intransitive verb describing indirect speech (V+REPORT).

See the entry headed VERBS for more information.

---

vulgar /ˈvʌlgə/. Something that is **vulgar** is socially unacceptable or offensive. EG *The boys had scrawled some vulgar graffiti about him in the loo... ...vulgar remarks.* ADJ QUALIT

vulnerable /ˈvʌlnərəbəl/. Someone who is **vulnerable** is weak and easily hurt physically or emotionally. EG *Lack of employment outside the home tends to make women vulnerable to depression... Elderly people, living alone, are especially vulnerable.* ◊ **vulnerability** /ˌvʌlnərəˈbɪlɪtɪ/. EG *...Britain's extreme vulnerability to attack.* ADJ QUALIT OFT+to ◊ N UNCOUNT : OFT+to

vulture /ˈvʌltʃə/, **vultures.** A **vulture** is a large bird which eats the flesh of dead animals. Vultures live in hot countries. N COUNT

vying /ˈvaɪɪŋ/ is the present participle of **vie**.

W w

W, w /dʌbəˀljuː/, **Ws, w's.** 1 W is the twenty-third N COUNT letter of the English alphabet.

2 W is an abbreviation for 'west'.

wad /wɒd/, **wads.** 1 A **wad** of papers or bank N COUNT notes is a thick bundle of them. EG *She handed over* OR N PART *a wad of forms and leaflets.*

2 A **wad** of something is a lump of it. EG *...a wad of* N COUNT *tobacco... ...a small, loose wad of cotton wool.* OR N PART

waddle /wɒdəˀl/, **waddles, waddling, waddled.** V : USU+A When a fat person or a duck **waddles**, they walk with short, quick steps, swaying slightly from side to side. EG *A little squat man waddled out of the bathroom.*

wade /weɪd/, **wades, wading, waded.** If you V : USU+A **wade** through water, you walk slowly through it, with your legs or the lower part of your body in the water. EG *The children waded out into the lake.*

wade through. If you **wade through** a difficult PHRASAL VB : book or document, you spend a lot of time and V+PREP effort reading it. EG *Each evening, he had to wade through columns of Parliamentary reports.*

wafer /weɪfə/, **wafers.** A **wafer** is a thin crisp N COUNT biscuit which is usually eaten with ice cream.

waffle /wɒfəˀl/, **waffles, waffling, waffled.** 1 V When someone **waffles**, they talk or write a lot without saying anything clear or important. EG *He's still waffling away about economic recovery.*
▶ used as a noun. EG *I don't want waffle, I want the* ▶ N UNCOUNT *real figures.*

2 A **waffle** is a thick crisp pancake with squares N COUNT marked on it. Waffles are often eaten with syrup poured over them.

waft /wɑːft, wɒft/, **wafts, wafting, wafted.** If a V-ERG+A sound or scent **wafts** or **is wafted** through the air, it moves gently through the air. EG *A scent of lemon wafted up from the gardens below.*

wag /wæg/, **wags, wagging, wagged.** 1 When a V-ERG dog **wags** its tail or when its tail **wags**, the dog repeatedly waves its tail from side to side. EG *The dog waited, making happy little barks and wagging his tail.*

2 If **tongues wag**, people are gossiping about other PHRASE people and their behaviour. EG *He dared not give* Informal *her a scarf as a gift, because tongues might wag.*

wage /weɪdʒ/, **wages, waging, waged.** 1 A **wage** N COUNT is the amount of money that is regularly paid to someone for the work that they do, especially manual or unskilled work. EG *...the problems of families bringing up children on a low wage.*

2 Someone's **wages** are the money that they are N PLURAL paid each week for the work that they do, especially when they have a manual or unskilled job. EG *My wages had not increased for two years.*

3 If a person or country **wages** a campaign or war, V+O they start it and carry it on over a period of time. EG *He believes that they are plotting to wage a limited nuclear war in Europe.*

wager /weɪdʒə/, **wagers.** A **wager** is an agree- N COUNT ment that you make with someone in which you Outdated decide on an amount of money that you will pay them, or that they will pay you, depending on the result of a particular event. EG *...wagers on who will win the World Series.*

waggle /wægəˀl/, **waggles, waggling, waggled.** V-ERG If you **waggle** something or if it **waggles**, it moves up and down or from side to side with short, quick movements. EG *He waggled his eyebrows.*

wagon /wægəˀn/, **wagons;** also spelled **waggon** in N COUNT British English. A **wagon** is 1 a strong vehicle with four wheels, usually pulled by horses and used for carrying heavy loads. 2 a large container on British

wheels which is pulled by a train. EG *The cattle go by rail in wagons.*

wail /weɪl/, **wails, wailing, wailed.** If someone V : OFT+QUOTE **wails**, they cry loudly. EG *One of the children began to wail... He raised a red, wet face and wailed, 'I didn't start the fight, she did.'* ▶ used as a noun. EG *I* ▶ N COUNT *could hear the wail of a baby next door.*

waist /weɪst/, **waists.** 1 Your **waist** is the narrow N COUNT : part of your body above your hips. See picture at OFT+POSS THE HUMAN BODY. EG *She tied an apron around her waist.*

2 The **waist** of a piece of clothing is the part of it N COUNT which covers the middle part of your body. EG *...the waist of her skirt.*

waistband /weɪstˀbænd/, **waistbands.** A **waist-** N COUNT **band** is a narrow piece of material which is sewn on to a pair of trousers, a skirt, or another piece of clothing at the waist.

waistcoat /weɪstˀkəʊt/, **waistcoats.** A **waistcoat** N COUNT is a sleeveless piece of clothing with buttons, which you wear on the top part of your body. Men often wear waistcoats over their shirts and under their jackets. See picture at CLOTHES.

waistline /weɪstˀlaɪn/, **waistlines.** Your **waist-** N COUNT **line** is an imaginary line around your waist which you use as a way of measuring how fat you are. EG *...a 40-year-old lady with a large waistline.*

wait /weɪt/, **waits, waiting, waited.** 1 If you V : OFT+A OR **wait**, you spend some time, usually doing very to-INF little, before something happens. EG *He waited patiently for her... She had been waiting in the queue to buy some stamps... Wait until we sit down.*
◊ **waiting.** EG *There was a waiting period of one* ◊ ADJ CLASSIF : *month.* ATTRIB

2 A **wait** is a period of time in which you do very N COUNT : little, before something happens. EG *There was a* USU SING *long wait.*

3 If you **can't wait** to do something, you are very PHRASE excited about it and eager to do it. EG *He couldn't wait to tell Judy.*

4 If you say **'just you wait'** to someone, you are PHRASE OR threatening them or warning them. EG *You wait!* CONVENTION *You'll find Robinson isn't as gentle as he seems.*

5 You say **wait and see** to tell someone that they PHRASE must be patient or that they must not worry about what is going to happen. EG *All you can do is wait and see.*

6 You say **wait a minute, wait a second,** and PHRASE **wait a moment.** **6.1** to interrupt someone when Informal they are speaking, for example because you dis- agree with them. EG *Wait a minute, are you propos- ing to rewrite the entire play?* **6.2** to interrupt Informal yourself when you are speaking, for example be- cause you are trying to remember something. EG *Wait a minute. What did I do with the other one?*

7 If something **is waiting** for you, it is ready for V you to use or to do. EG *I have a lot of work waiting.*

8 If you say that something can **wait**, you mean V : USU that it is not important or urgent and so you will WITH MODAL deal with it later. EG *The dishes can wait.*

9 If you **wait** on people in a restaurant, you serve V+A people food as your job.

10 If you **wait** on someone **hand and foot**, you PHRASE provide everything that they need and do every- thing for them. EG *At the hospital, she had been waited on hand and foot.*

wait about or **wait around.** If you **wait about** PHRASAL VB : or **wait around**, you spend a lot of time, usually V+ADV doing very little, before something happens. EG *Don't keep him waiting about in the hotel.*

wait up. If you **wait up**, you deliberately do not PHRASAL VB : go to bed, usually because you are expecting V+ADV someone to return home late at night. EG *She said that you shouldn't bother to wait up for her.*

waiter /weɪtə/, **waiters.** A **waiter** is a man who works in a restaurant, serving people with food and drink. N COUNT

waiting list, waiting lists. A **waiting list** is a list of people who have asked for something which cannot be given to them immediately, for example medical treatment or a job, and who must therefore wait until it is available. EG *He's on the waiting list for a council house.* N COUNT

waiting-room, waiting-rooms. A **waiting-room** is a room in a place such as a railway station or a doctor's surgery, where people can sit and wait. N COUNT

waitress /weɪtrɪ²s/, **waitresses.** A **waitress** is a woman who works in a restaurant, serving people with food and drink. N COUNT

waive /weɪv/, **waives, waiving, waived.** If someone **waives** a rule, they decide not to enforce it in a particular situation. EG *Rules about proper dress may be waived.* V+O Formal

wake /weɪk/, **wakes, waking, woke** /wəʊk/, **woken** /wəʊkə⁰n/. American English also uses the form **waked** for the past tense and past participle.

1 When you **wake** or when someone **wakes** you, you become conscious again after being asleep. EG *I sometimes wake at four in the morning... He woke me early.* V-ERG • Your **waking hours** are the times when you are awake rather than asleep. EG *I spend most of my waking hours in the library.* • PHRASE

2 If you leave something **in** your **wake**, you leave it behind you as you go. EG *They left trails of sweet papers in their wake.* PHRASE

3 If one thing follows **in the wake of** another, it happens after the other thing is over, and often as a result of it. EG *Famine came in the wake of disastrous floods.* PHRASE

wake up. 1 When you **wake up** or when someone **wakes** you **up**, you become conscious again after being asleep. EG *Ralph, wake up!... I woke up to discover that he had gone.* PHRASAL VB : V-ERG+ADV **2** If you **wake up** to a dangerous situation, you become aware of it. EG *The West began to wake up to the danger it faced.* V+ADV+*to*

waken /weɪkə⁰n/, **wakens, wakening, wakened.** When you **waken** or when someone **wakens** you, you wake. EG *It is frightening to most children to waken and find a stranger in the room.* V-ERG Literary

walk /wɔːk/, **walks, walking, walked. 1** When you **walk**, you move along by putting one foot in front of the other on the ground. EG *Most children learn to walk when they are about one... We walked along in silence... They walk ten miles to school each day.* V : OFT+A OR V+O

2 A **walk** is **2.1** the action of walking rather than running. EG *He came in with his distinctive walk.* N SING

2.2 a journey which you make by walking. EG *He went out for a long walk... The station is a three minute walk from the park.* N COUNT **2.3** a path which is designed or used for people to walk along. EG *There are some beautiful walks along the coast.* N COUNT

3 If you **walk** someone somewhere, you walk there with them. EG *He walked her home.* V+O+A : NO PASS

4 If you **walk** your dog, you take it for a walk. V+O

5 See also **walking**.

walk away with. If you **walk away with** something such as a prize, you win it or achieve it very easily. PHRASAL VB : V+ADV+PREP

walk in on. If you **walk in on** someone, you go into a place and interrupt them without intending to, because you did not expect them to be there. PHRASAL VB : V+ADV+PREP

walk off. If you try to **walk off** a headache or other illness, you go for a walk in order to try to feel better. PHRASAL VB : V+O+ADV

walk off with. 1 If someone **walks off with** something that does not belong to them, they take it without asking the person who owns it. EG *Who's walked off with my pen?* PHRASAL VB : V+ADV+PREP Informal **2** If you **walk off with** something such as a prize, you win it or achieve it very easily. EG *She'll walk off with a first class degree.* V+ADV+PREP Informal

walk out. 1 If you **walk out** of a meeting, a performance, or an unpleasant situation, you leave it suddenly without explaining why, usually as a way of showing that you are angry. EG *Most of the audience walked out after the first half hour... He walked out of his job.* PHRASAL VB : V+ADV **2** If workers **walk out**, they go on strike. • See also **walkout**. V+ADV

walk out on. If you **walk out on** someone, you leave them suddenly. EG *His girlfriend walked out on him.* PHRASAL VB : V+ADV+PREP

walkabout /wɔːkəbaʊt/, **walkabouts.** When a king, queen, or other important person **goes walkabout** or **does a walkabout**, he or she walks through crowds in a public place in order to meet people in an informal way. EG *The Pope suddenly went walkabout.* PHRASE

walker /wɔːkə/, **walkers.** A **walker** is a person who walks, especially in the countryside for pleasure. EG *The woods are heavily visited by tourists and walkers.* N COUNT

walkie-talkie /wɔːki¹ tɔːki¹/, **walkie-talkies.** A **walkie-talkie** is a small radio that you can carry about and use to talk to and listen to someone far away. EG *There were hundreds of policemen around with walkie-talkies.* N COUNT

walking /wɔːkɪŋ/ is the activity of going for walks in the country. EG *Walking and mountaineering are very popular here... ...a walking holiday.* N UNCOUNT

walking stick, walking sticks. A **walking stick** is a long wooden stick which people can use to lean on while they are walking. N COUNT

Walkman /wɔːkmə³n/, **Walkmans.** A **Walkman** is a small cassette player with very light headphones, which people carry around so that they can listen to music while they are doing something such as walking or travelling on a bus. N COUNT Trademark

walk of life, walks of life. The **walk of life** that you come from is the position that you have in society and the kind of job you have. EG *Members of this club come from many different walks of life.* N COUNT : USU+SUPP

walk-on. A **walk-on** part in a play is a very small part which usually does not involve any speaking. ADJ CLASSIF : ATTRIB

walkout /wɔːkaʊt/, **walkouts.** A **walkout** is a strike. EG *The pay deal ended the 43-day-old walkout.* N COUNT

walkover /wɔːkəʊvə/, **walkovers.** If a competition or contest is a **walkover** for you, you win it very easily indeed. EG *It was a walkover for Tyson.* N COUNT

walkway /wɔːkweɪ/, **walkways.** A **walkway** is a passage or path between two buildings for pedestrians to use. N COUNT

wall /wɔːl/, **walls. 1** A **wall** is **1.1** one of the vertical sides of a building or room. EG *There was a picture on the wall.* **1.2** a long narrow vertical structure made of stone or brick that surrounds or divides an area of land. EG *We crouched behind the wall and waited.* N COUNT

2 The **wall** of something hollow is the side of it. EG *...cellulose, the material from which the cell walls of plants are built.* N COUNT+SUPP

3 Wall is used in these phrases. **3.1** If you **are banging** your **head against a brick wall**, you are not making any progress in something that you are trying to do. **3.2** If you **come up against a brick wall**, someone or something prevents you from making any further progress. EG *The latest talks about Northern Ireland have come up against a brick wall.* **3.3** If someone or something **drives** you **up the wall**, they make you very irritated or annoyed. EG *This drove him up the wall.* PHRASES Informal

walled /wɔːld/. If an area of land is **walled**, it is surrounded or enclosed by a wall. EG *...the old walled city of Jerusalem.* ADJ CLASSIF

wallet /wɒlɪt/, **wallets.** A **wallet** is a small flat case made of leather or plastic, which is used for keeping paper money in and other small things such as credit cards. N COUNT

wallop /ˈwɒləp/, **wallops, walloping, walloped.** v+o
If you **wallop** someone, you hit them very hard. EG Informal
*His mother would have walloped him if she'd
known what he was up to.*

wallow /ˈwɒləʊ/, **wallows, wallowing, wal-**
lowed. 1 If you **wallow** in an unpleasant situation v+in
or feeling, you allow it to continue longer than is
reasonable or necessary. EG *At first I just wanted to
wallow in misery... Her mother was wallowing in
widowhood.*

2 When an animal **wallows** in mud or water, it lies v : usu+in
or rolls about in it slowly for pleasure.

wallpaper /ˈwɔːlpeɪpə/, **wallpapers, wall-**
papering, wallpapered. 1 **Wallpaper** is thick N MASS
coloured or patterned paper that is used to decorate the walls of rooms.

2 If someone **wallpapers** a room, they cover the v+o
walls with wallpaper.

wall-to-wall. A **wall-to-wall** carpet covers the ADJ CLASSIF
floor of a room completely.

wally /ˈwɒlɪ/, **wallies.** If you call someone a N COUNT
wally, you mean that they are stupid or foolish. EG Informal
He looked a right wally in that hat. British

walnut /ˈwɔːlnʌt/, **walnuts.** A **walnut** is a nut N COUNT
which has a wrinkled shape and a hard, round,
light brown shell.

walrus /ˈwɔːlrəs, ˈwɒl-/, **walruses.** A **walrus** is an N COUNT
animal which lives in the sea and looks like a large
seal. It has long whiskers and two long teeth
pointing downwards.

waltz /wɔːls/, **waltzes, waltzing, waltzed.** 1 A N COUNT
waltz is **1.1** a piece of music with a rhythm of
three beats in each bar, which people can dance to.
1.2 a dance in which two people hold each other
and move around the floor in time to waltz music.

2 If you **waltz** with someone, you dance a waltz v OR v+with :
with them. EG *I dreamt of going to Hollywood to* RECIP
waltz with Ginger Rogers.

3 If you **waltz** somewhere, you walk there in a v+A
relaxed and confident way. EG *She waltzed across to* Informal
Helen and sat down beside her.

wan /wɒn/. Someone who is **wan** looks pale and ADJ QUALIT
tired. EG *She looked wan and fragile... ...a wan* Literary
smile.

wand /wɒnd/, **wands.** A **wand** is a long thin rod N COUNT
that magicians wave when they are performing
tricks and magic. In children's stories, fairies also
use wands when doing magic. EG *She seemed to
expect him to wave a magic wand and make the
problem disappear.*

wander /ˈwɒndə/, **wanders, wandering, wan-**
dered. 1 If you **wander** in a place, you walk v+A OR v+o
around in a casual way. EG *We wandered round the
little harbour town... A man was found wandering
in the hills... The children wandered the streets
after school.*

2 If your mind **wanders** or your thoughts **wander**, v
you stop concentrating on something and start
thinking about other things. EG *When she was alone,
she would let her mind wander... My thoughts kept
wandering back to that night.*

wane /weɪn/, **wanes, waning, waned.** 1 If a v
condition, attitude, or emotion **wanes**, it becomes
weaker, often disappearing completely in the end.
EG *Her enthusiasm for Harold was beginning to
wane... The influence of this group waned considerably.* ● to **wax and wane**: see **wax.**

2 If a condition, attitude, or emotion is **on the** PHRASE
wane, it is becoming weaker. EG *They could claim
that pollution for the first time was on the wane.*

wangle /ˈwæŋɡəl/, **wangles, wangling, wan-**
gled. If you **wangle** something that you want, you Informal
manage to get it by being clever or persuasive. EG
He always managed to wangle the easy jobs.

want /wɒnt/, **wants, wanting, wanted.** 1 If you v+o, v+to-INF,
want something, you have a desire to have it or you OR v+o+to-INF
feel a need for it. EG *Do you want a cup of coffee?...
All they want is a holiday... I want to be an
actress... I didn't want him to go.*

2 If something **wants** doing, there is a need for it v+-ING
to be done. EG *We've got a couple of jobs that want
doing in the garden.*

3 If you tell someone that they **want** to do a v+to-INF
particular thing, you are advising them to do it. EG
You want to book your holiday early this year.

4 If someone **is wanted**, the police are searching v+o : OFT PASS
for them. EG *He is wanted for the crimes of murder
and kidnapping.*

5 A **want** of something is a lack of it. EG *They had* N SING+of
to confess their complete want of foresight. Formal

6 If you do something **for want of** something else, PHRASE
you do it because the other thing is not available or Formal
not possible. EG *For want of anything better to do,
he continued to read.*

7 Your **wants** are the things that you want. EG *They* N PLURAL :
developed new wants: for bicycles, watches, and USU+POSS
radios.

wanting /ˈwɒntɪŋ/. If you find something **wanting** ADJ PRED
or if it proves **wanting**, it is not as good as you Formal
think it should be. EG *He judged the nation and
found it wanting.*

wanton /ˈwɒntən/. A **wanton** action deliberately ADJ CLASSIF
causes harm, damage, or waste without any rea- USU ATTRIB
son. EG *...senseless and wanton cruelty.* Formal

war /wɔː/, **wars, warring, warred.** 1 A **war** is a N COUNT OR
period of fighting between countries or states. EG N UNCOUNT
*They fought in the war against Britain... They did
not want to lose another war... There are no
winners in nuclear war... England and Germany
were at war.* ● If a country **goes to war**, it starts ● PHRASE
fighting a war with another country. ● See also
cold war.

2 If two countries or states **war** with each other, v OR v+with :
they fight a war with each other. EG *India and* RECIP
Pakistan warred in 1965 over Kashmir.
◊ **warring.** EG *...the warring nations.* ◊ ADJ CLASSIF

3 You also use **war** to refer to competition be- N COUNT OR
tween groups of people, or a campaign against a N UNCOUNT :
particular thing. EG *...a trade war... The administra-* USU+SUPP
tion is planning a new war on drugs.

4 If you say that someone **has been in the wars**, PHRASE
you mean that they have been injured, for example Informal
in a fight or an accident. EG *You look as if you've
been in the wars.*

warble /ˈwɔːbəl/, **warbles, warbling, warbled.** v OR v+o
When a bird **warbles**, it sings pleasantly with high Literary
notes and many variations.

ward /wɔːd/, **wards, warding, warded.** 1 A **ward** N COUNT
is **1.1** a room in a hospital which has beds for
several people who need similar treatment. EG *She
stayed five days in the emergency ward for observation.* **1.2** a district which forms part of a political British
constituency or local council. EG *We shall analyse
the votes ward by ward.*

2 A **ward** is a child who is officially put in the care N COUNT
of an adult because their parents are dead. A **ward
of court** is a child who is in the care of a court of
law because they need protection. EG *He recognized her at once as Mrs Pennington's ward.*

ward off. If you **ward off** a danger or an illness, PHRASAL VB :
you do something to prevent it from affecting you V+O+ADV
or harming you. EG *He wears a copper bracelet to
ward off rheumatism... He placed charms at the
head of his bed to ward off evil spirits.*

-ward. -ward or **-wards** can be added to nouns SUFFIX
that refer to places or directions in order to form
adverbs or adjectives. These adverbs and adjectives indicate the direction in which something is
moving or facing. EG *He was gazing skyward... He
led the group homewards... ...the westward trail.*

warden /ˈwɔːdən/, **wardens.** 1 A **warden** is an N COUNT+SUPP
official who makes sure that certain laws are being
obeyed. EG *...traffic wardens... ...game wardens.*

2 A **warden** in a building such as a youth hostel is N COUNT

If someone is on the warpath, are they going off
to war?

the person who is in charge of the building and the people in it.

3 The **warden** of a prison is the person who is in charge of the prison. N COUNT American

warder /wɔːdə/, **warders.** A **warder** is a person who works in a prison and is in charge of prisoners. N COUNT

wardrobe /wɔːdrəub/, **wardrobes. 1** A **wardrobe** is a tall cupboard in which you can hang your clothes. EG *The red dress hung in her wardrobe.* N COUNT

2 Someone's **wardrobe** is the total collection of clothes that they have. EG *He was familiar with her entire wardrobe.* N COUNT

-wards. See **-ward.**

ware /weə/, **wares. 1** You can refer to things that are made of a particular substance or that are used for a particular purpose as a particular type of ware. EG *...glass ware... ...kitchen ware.* N UNCOUNT +SUPP

2 Someone's **wares** are the things that they sell, usually in the street or in a market. EG *The market traders began to sell their wares at half-price.* N PLURAL : USU+POSS Outdated

warehouse /weəhaus/, **warehouses.** A **warehouse** is a large building where raw materials or manufactured goods are stored. N COUNT

warfare /wɔːfeə/ is the activity of fighting a war. EG *They are anxious to prevent this conflict from erupting into open warfare.* N UNCOUNT Formal

warhead /wɔːhed/, **warheads.** A **warhead** is the front end of a bomb or missile, where the explosives are carried. EG *...missiles with nuclear warheads.* N COUNT

warlike /wɔːlaɪk/. People who are **warlike** seem aggressive and eager to start a war. EG *...a warlike leader... ...a warlike nation.* ADJ QUALIT Formal

warm /wɔːm/, **warmer, warmest; warms, warming, warmed. 1** Something that is **warm** has some heat but not enough to be hot. EG *...a bowl of warm water... ...a warm summer evening.* ADJ QUALIT

2 If you **warm** a part of your body, you put it near a fire or heater so that it stops feeling cold. EG *I warmed my hand on the radiator... Come and warm yourself in front of the fire.* V+O OR V-REFL

3 Clothes and blankets that are **warm** are made of a material such as wool which protects you from the cold. EG *...a pair of nice warm socks.* ADJ QUALIT
◊ **warmly.** EG *I'll see that Chris dresses warmly.* ◊ ADV

4 Warm colours or sounds are pleasant and make you feel comfortable and relaxed. EG *...a room decorated in warm reds and browns.* ADJ QUALIT

5 A **warm** person is friendly and behaves with a lot of affection or enthusiasm. EG *She had a warm, generous heart... He was given a warm welcome.* ADJ QUALIT
◊ **warmly.** EG *He shook Tony warmly by the hand.* ◊ ADV

6 If you **warm** to a person, you become fonder of them. If you **warm** to an idea, you become more interested in it. EG *This makes you warm to Meadows... He warmed to the prospect of a new job.* V+to

warm up. 1 If you **warm** something **up** or if it **warms up,** it gets hotter. EG *Start warming up the soup now... When the weather warmed up mosquitoes began swarming.* **2** If you **warm up** for an event such as a race, you prepare yourself for it by doing exercises or by practising just before it starts. ● See also **warm-up. 3** When a machine or engine **warms up,** it becomes ready for use a little while after being switched on or started. EG *I turned on the radio. It warmed up and a radio announcer's voice came out.* PHRASAL VB : V-ERG+ADV / V+ADV / V+ADV

warm-blooded. An animal that is **warm-blooded,** for example a bird or a mammal, has a relatively high body temperature which remains constant and does not change according to the surrounding temperature. ADJ CLASSIF

warm-hearted. Someone who is **warm-hearted** is friendly and affectionate towards other people. ADJ QUALIT

warmonger /wɔːmʌŋgə/, **warmongers.** A **warmonger** is a person, for example a politician or a newspaper editor, who encourages people to start a war or to prepare for one. N COUNT

warmongering /wɔːmʌŋgə⁰rɪŋ/ is the activity of encouraging people to start a war or to prepare for one. N UNCOUNT

warmth /wɔːmθ/. **1 Warmth** is a moderate amount of heat that something has, for example enough heat to make you feel comfortable. EG *...the warmth of the sun... We huddled together for warmth.* N UNCOUNT

2 The **warmth** of clothes or blankets is their ability to protect you from the cold. EG *...blankets which have little warmth.* N UNCOUNT

3 Someone who has **warmth** is friendly and enthusiastic in their behaviour. EG *...my uncle's warmth and affection... 'How do you do, sir?' she said, without warmth.* N UNCOUNT

warm-up, warm-ups. A **warm-up** is preparation that you do just before an event such as a race, for example exercises or practising. EG *During the warm-up exercises, I was still shaking.* N COUNT

warn /wɔːn/, **warns, warning, warned. 1** If you **warn** someone about a possible danger or problem, you tell them about it so that they are aware of it. EG *The least I can do is warn them that there is a danger... I did warn you of possible failure... I warn you it's going to be expensive.* V+O : USU+A, REPORT, OR QUOTE; ALSO V+QUOTE

2 If you **warn** someone not to do something, you advise them not to do it in order to avoid possible danger or punishment. EG *I warned him not to lose his temper with her... I'm warning you, if you do that again there'll be trouble.* V+O USU+to-INF

warn off. If you **warn** someone **off,** you tell them to go away or to stop doing something because of possible danger or punishment. EG *Intruders are warned off by the sound.* PHRASAL VB : V+O+ADV/ PREP

warning /wɔːnɪŋ/, **warnings. 1** A **warning** is something which is said or written to tell people of a possible danger, problem, or other unpleasant thing that might happen. EG *The hospital issued warnings about drugs to be avoided... Dad gave a final warning to them not to look directly at the sun... Mary left her husband without any warning.* N COUNT OR N UNCOUNT

2 Warning actions or signs give a warning. EG *His wife made warning faces at him not to irritate their guest... Watch out for the warning signs of depression like insomnia.* ADJ CLASSIF : ATTRIB

warp /wɔːp/, **warps, warping, warped. 1** If something **warps** or **is warped,** it becomes damaged by bending or curving, often because of the effect of heat or water. EG *The cabinet doors began to warp soon after they were installed.* ◊ **warped.** EG *The wooden balconies were warped and weatherbeaten.* V-ERG : IF V+O THEN OFT PASS ◊ ADJ QUALIT

2 If something **warps** someone's character, it influences them and makes them abnormal or bad. EG *...a man whose whole character was warped by being bullied.* V+O

3 A **warp** in someone's character is a fault or abnormality that they have. EG *The same warp in my nature made me do it again.* N COUNT

4 A **warp** in time or space is an imaginary break or sudden change in the normal experience of time or space. EG *There's a kind of time warp in his education.* N COUNT

warpath /wɔːpɑːθ/. If someone is **on the warpath,** they are angry and are getting ready for a fight or argument. EG *He scares me to death when he's on the warpath.* PHRASE Informal

warrant /wɒrənt/, **warrants, warranting, warranted. 1** If something **warrants** a particular action, it makes the action seem necessary. EG *The situation is serious enough to warrant a special effort... The case warrants further investigation.* V+O Formal

2 A **warrant** is an official document signed by a judge or magistrate, which gives the police special permission to do something such as arrest someone or search their house. EG *A warrant was issued for his arrest.* N COUNT

warren /wɒrən/, **warrens.** A **warren** is a group N COUNT
of holes in the ground which are connected by
tunnels and which rabbits live in.

warrior /wɒrɪə/, **warriors. Warriors** were sol- N COUNT
diers or experienced fighting men in former times. Literary
EG ...*stories of ancient kings, warriors and great
battles.*

warship /wɔːʃɪp/, **warships.** A **warship** is a ship N COUNT
with guns that is used for fighting in wars.

wart /wɔːt/, **warts.** A **wart** is a small hard piece N COUNT
of skin which sometimes grows and sticks out on
part of your body, usually your face or hands. EG ...*a
large woman with a wart on her nose.*

wartime /wɔːtaɪm/ is a period of time when there N UNCOUNT
is a war. EG ...*the disruption of the environment in
wartime*... ...*wartime memories.*

wary /weəriʰ/. If you are **wary** about something, ADJ QUALIT
you are cautious about it, for example because it is
a new experience or because there may be dangers or problems. EG *People are understandably
wary of the new government... I'm very wary about
believing these stories.*

was /wɒˀz/ is the first and third person singular of
the past tense of **be.**

wash /wɒʃ/, **washes, washing, washed.** 1 If you V+O
wash something, you clean it using water and
soap. EG ...*the clatter of dishes being washed and
put away... She washes and irons his clothes.* ▸ used ▸ N COUNT :
as a noun. EG *Give it a good wash.* OFT SING

2 The **wash** is all the clothes that are washed N SING : the+N
together at one time, for example once a week. EG
...*the average weekly wash.*

3 If you **wash** or if you **wash** part of your body, V OR V+O
you clean part of your body using soap and water.
EG *First wash your hands. The children were
encouraged to wash and dress themselves.* ▸ used ▸ N COUNT :
as a noun. EG *He was having a wash.* OFT SING

4 If water **washes** somewhere, it flows there V+A OR
gently. If something **is washed** somewhere, it is V-ERG+A
carried there gently by water. EG *The surf washed
over her ankles... The body was washed ashore in
Norway.*

5 If you say that you **wash** your **hands** of some- PHRASE
thing, you mean that you refuse to be involved with
it any longer or that you refuse to accept responsibility for it. EG ...*a building that the authorities had
put up and then washed their hands of.*

6 See also **washing.**

wash away. If floods **wash away** buildings, they PHRASAL VB :
destroy the buildings and carry them away. EG *The V+O+ADV
flood washed the old bridge away.*

wash down. 1 If you **wash down** food, you drink PHRASAL VB :
something after you have eaten it or while you are V+O+ADV :
eating it. EG *We had smoked salmon and grouse,* USU +with
washed down with claret and vintage port. 2 If you V+O+ADV
wash an object **down**, you wash all of it thoroughly. EG *I spent the morning washing down paintwork.*

wash out. 1 If you **wash** a stain or colour **out** of PHRASAL VB :
something, you manage to remove it by using V-ERG+ADV
water and soap. 2 If you **wash out** a container, you V+O+ADV
wash the inside of it. 3 See also **washed-out,
washout.**

wash up. 1 If you **wash up**, 1.1 you wash the PHRASAL VB :
plates, cups, knives, and forks which have been V+ADV OR
used in cooking and eating a meal. EG *He insisted V+O+ADV
on helping me wash up.* 1.2 you clean part of your V+ADV
body with soap and water, especially your hands American
and face. EG *I washed up as best I could in the
adjacent bathroom.* 2 If something **is washed up** V+O+ADV,
on a piece of land, it is carried by a river or sea OFT PASS+A
and left there. EG *His body was washed up under
the bridge at Dakao.* 3 See also **washing-up.**

washable /wɒʃəbəʰl/. Clothes or materials that ADJ CLASSIF
are **washable** can be washed without being damaged. EG *Acrylic blankets are warm and washable.*

washbasin /wɒʃbeɪsəʰn/, **washbasins.** A **wash-** N COUNT
basin is a large basin for washing your hands and
face. Washbasins are usually fixed to a wall and
have taps for hot and cold water.

washed-out. 1 Something that is **washed-out** is ADJ QUALIT
pale in colour and dull. EG ...*eyes of washed-out
grey.*

2 If someone looks **washed-out**, they look very ADJ QUALIT
tired. EG *He had lots of children and a washed-out
wife.*

washer /wɒʃə/, **washers.** A **washer** is a thin flat N COUNT
ring of metal or plastic, which is placed over a bolt
before the nut is screwed on, in order to make a
tighter connection. EG *Unscrew the nut, remove
and replace the washer and reassemble the tap.*

washing /wɒʃɪŋ/ consists of clothes which need to N UNCOUNT
be washed or which are in the process of being
washed or dried. EG *Her husband comes home at
weekends bringing his washing with him... There
was nowhere to hang washing.*

washing machine, washing machines. A N COUNT
washing machine is a machine which you can
wash clothes in. EG ...*a fully automatic washing
machine.*

washing powder, washing powders. Washing N MASS
powder is powdered detergent that you use to
wash clothes.

washing-up. If you do the **washing-up**, you wash N UNCOUNT
the plates, cups, knives, and forks which have been
used in cooking and eating a meal. EG *We share the
cooking and the washing-up*... ...*a washing-up bowl.*

washing-up liquid, washing-up liquids. N MASS
Washing-up liquid is thick soapy liquid which you
add to hot water to clean dirty dishes after a meal.

washout /wɒʃaʊt/, **washouts.** If an event or proj- N COUNT
ect is a **washout**, it is a total failure. EG *Thanks to* Informal
you, today's been an appalling washout.

washroom /wɒʃruˀm/, **washrooms.** A **wash-** N COUNT
room is a room with toilets and washing facilities, American
situated in a large building such as an office block
or a hostel.

wasn't /wɒzəˀnt/ is the usual spoken form of 'was
not'. EG *I wasn't ready for it... He was first, wasn't
he?*

wasp /wɒsp/, **wasps.** A **wasp** is an insect with N COUNT
yellow and black stripes across its body, which can
sting like a bee but does not produce honey.

wastage /weɪstɪdʒ/. **Wastage** of something is a N UNCOUNT
waste of it. EG *The Government is to blame for this* USU +SUPP
serious wastage of talent among the young... ...*the* Formal
tremendous wastage from inefficient energy use.

waste /weɪst/, **wastes, wasting, wasted.** 1 If you V+O
waste time, money, or energy, you use too much of
it on something that is not important or necessary.
EG *You're wasting your time*... ...*fear of wasting
money on a new idea.*

2 If you **waste** an opportunity for something, you V+O
do not take advantage of it when it is available.

3 If you say that something **is wasted** on someone, V+O+on :
you mean that it is too good, clever, or sophisticat- USU PASS
ed for them. EG *Her parents were wealthy and did
not want her to be wasted on a poor university
lecturer.*

4 If you say that an action or activity is a **waste** of N SING :
time, money, or energy, you mean that it involves a+N+of
using too much time, money, or energy and it is not
important or necessary. EG *It's probably a waste of
time... It's a waste of money hiring skis.*

5 **Waste** is the use of too much money or other N UNCOUNT
resources on things that do not need it. EG *A
committee was set up to avoid future waste of
public money.*

6 **Waste** is also material which has been used and N UNCOUNT
is no longer wanted, for example because the
valuable or useful part of it has been taken out. EG
...*radioactive waste from nuclear power stations...
The river was thick with industrial waste.* ▸ used ▸ ADJ CLASSIF
as an adjective. EG ...*waste material from the oil* ATTRIB
industry... ...*waste paper.*

Do you use washing powder to do the washing
up?

7 Waste land is land which is not used or looked after by anyone, and so is covered by wild plants and rubbish. EG *The car was found abandoned on waste ground near Leeds.*   ADJ CLASSIF: ATTRIB

8 Wastes are large areas of land in which there are very few people, plants, or animals. EG ...*the polar wastes... ...the endless wastes of the desert.*   N PLURAL Formal

9 If something **goes to waste**, it remains unused, goes bad, or is thrown away.   PHRASE

10 See also **wasted.**

waste away. If someone **wastes away**, they become extremely thin and weak because they are ill or worried and they are not eating properly. EG *I don't want you to waste away.*   PHRASAL VB: V+ADV

wastebasket /ˈweɪstbɑːskɪt/, **wastebaskets.** A wastebasket is the same as a wastepaper basket.   N COUNT American

wasted /ˈweɪstɪ³d/. A **wasted** action is one that is unnecessary. EG *It was a wasted journey.*   ADJ CLASSIF

wasteful /ˈweɪstful/. An action that is **wasteful** causes waste, because it uses resources in a careless or inefficient way. EG ...*the wasteful use of scarce resources.*   ADJ QUALIT

wasteland /ˈweɪstlænd/, **wastelands.** A wasteland is an area of land which is of no use, for example because it is infertile or because it has been misused by people. EG *The highways cross endless wastelands.*   N COUNT OR N UNCOUNT

wastepaper basket, wastepaper baskets. A wastepaper basket or wastepaper bin is a container for rubbish, especially for waste paper, which is usually placed on the floor in the corner of a room or next to a desk. See picture at BASKETS. EG *He crumpled the note and tossed it into the wastepaper basket.*   N COUNT

watch /wɒtʃ/, **watches, watching, watched.** 1 A watch is a small clock which you wear on a strap on your wrist. EG *He looked at his watch... My watch has stopped.*   N COUNT

2 If you **watch** something, you look at it for a period of time, and pay attention to what is happening. EG *I used to sit and watch the boats moving down the river... I'm just watching television... A policeman stood watching... When did you last watch a football match?*   V+O OR V

3 If you **watch** someone, you follow them secretly or spy on them. EG *Liebermann's going to be watched from now on.*   V+O

4 If you **watch** a situation, you pay attention to it or you are aware of it. EG *The federation never ceases to watch events and fight injustices... She sits back and just watches a situation develop... Many companies have watched helplessly as their stock prices fell.*   V+O OR V+A

5 If you **keep watch** on a situation, you pay attention to what is happening, so that you can take action at the right moment. EG *The closest watch should be kept on any signs of industrial unrest.*   PHRASE

6 If someone **keeps watch**, they look around all the time, for example while other people are asleep, so that they can warn the others of danger. EG *A woman kept watch at the gate.*   PHRASE

7 A **watch** is also a group of guards or soldiers who have the job of carefully looking around so that they can warn others of danger. EG *The day watch had been on duty for a couple of hours.*   N COLL

8 If you **watch** someone or something, you take care that they do not get out of control or do something unpleasant. EG *You ought to watch Barbara – she's behaving very oddly.*   V+O

9 You say **'watch it'** in order to warn someone to be careful. EG *Watch it! There's a rotten floorboard somewhere just here.*   PHRASE Informal

10 If you tell someone to **watch** their **step**, you are warning them to be careful what they say and do. EG *I'm cleverer than you are, so watch your step.*   PHRASE Informal

watch out. If you **watch out**, you are very careful because something unpleasant might happen to you. EG *If you don't watch out, he might stick a knife into you.*   PHRASAL VB: V+ADV, ONLY INF

watch over. If you **watch over** someone or something, you care for them. EG *The wives took turns to watch over the children.*   PHRASAL VB: V+PREP, HAS PASS

watchband /ˈwɒtʃbænd/, **watchbands.** A watchband is the same as a watchstrap.   N COUNT American

watchdog /ˈwɒtʃdɒg/, **watchdogs.** You use watchdog to refer to a person or committee whose job is to make sure that companies do not act illegally or irresponsibly. EG *They established the Atomic Energy Commission to act as a watchdog.*   N COUNT

watcher /ˈwɒtʃə/, **watchers.** A **watcher** is a person who looks at something for a period of time, and who pays attention to what is happening. EG *Their behaviour baffled the watchers in the house.*   N COUNT

watchful /ˈwɒtʃful/. Someone who is **watchful** is careful to notice everything that is happening. EG *It is important that governments remain watchful... He spent his days under the watchful eyes of his grandmother.*   ADJ QUALIT

watchstrap /ˈwɒtʃstræp/, **watchstraps.** A watchstrap is a piece of leather, plastic, or metal which is attached to a watch so that you can wear it round your wrist.   N COUNT

watchword /ˈwɒtʃwɜːd/, **watchwords.** A watchword is a word or phrase that sums up the way that a particular group of people think or behave. EG *Today the watchword is 'Learn through playing'.*   N COUNT

water /ˈwɔːtə/, **waters, watering, watered.** 1 Water is the clear, thin liquid that has no colour and no taste when it is pure. It falls from clouds as rain and enters rivers and seas. All animals and people need to drink water in order to live. EG ...*a drink of water... Mammals can't breathe under water.*   N UNCOUNT

2 You use **water** or **waters** to refer to a large amount or area of water, for example a lake or sea. EG *The children played at the water's edge... ...the black waters of the Thames.*   N UNCOUNT OR N PLURAL

3 A country's **waters** consist of the area of sea which is near to that country and which is regarded as belonging to it. EG *The ship was in British waters.*   N PLURAL +SUPP

4 If you **water** plants, you pour water into the soil in order to help them to grow.   V+O

5 If your eyes **water**, you have tears in them because they are hurting. EG *The onions made his eyes water.*   V

6 If your mouth **waters**, it produces more saliva, usually because you can smell or see some appetizing food. EG *This should make your mouth water.*   V

7 When you **pass water**, you urinate.   PHRASE

8 Water is also used in these phrases. **8.1** If you say that an event is **water under the bridge**, you mean that it has happened and cannot now be changed, so there is no point in worrying about it any more. **8.2** If you **pour** or **throw cold water on** an idea or suggestion, you indicate that you do not think it is very good. **8.3** If you **keep** your **head above water**, you avoid getting into difficulties, especially in business. **8.4** to **take to** something **like a duck to water**: see **duck**.   PHRASES

water down. 1 If you **water down** food or drink, you add water to it to make it weaker. EG *The milk had been watered down.* 2 If a speech or plan is **watered down**, it is made much weaker and less forceful. EG *The whole article had been watered down.* ◊ **watered-down.** EG *The Equal Pay Act is so watered down as to be useless... ...a watered-down pay claim.*   PHRASAL VB: V+O+ADV   V+O+ADV, USU PASS   ◊ ADJ QUALIT

water-borne. Something that is **water-borne** is carried or passed on by water. EG ...*water-borne diseases.*   ADJ CLASSIF

water cannon, water cannons. A water cannon is a machine which shoots out a powerful jet of water. It is used by police to break up crowds of people.   N COUNT

watercolour /ˈwɔːtəkʌlə/, **watercolours;** spelled **watercolor** in American English. 1 **Watercolours**   N PLURAL are coloured paints used for painting pictures. You can mix them with water first, or put them on the paper with a wet brush.

2 A **watercolour** is a picture which has been painted using watercolours. EG *...an exhibition of watercolours.* N COUNT

watercress /wɔːtəkrɛs/ is a small plant with white flowers which grows in streams and pools. Its leaves taste hot and are eaten raw in salads. N UNCOUNT

waterfall /wɔːtəfɔːl/, **waterfalls.** A **waterfall** is water that flows over the edge of a steep cliff and falls to the ground below. N COUNT

waterfront /wɔːtəfrʌnt/, **waterfronts.** A **waterfront** is a street or piece of land which is next to an area of water, for example a river or the sea. EG *...a warehouse on the waterfront.* N COUNT : USU SING

waterhole /wɔːtəhəʊl/, **waterholes.** A **waterhole** is a pond or pool in a desert or other dry area where animals can find water to drink. N COUNT

watering can, **watering cans.** A **watering can** is a container shaped like a bucket with a long spout on one side, which you use to water plants. N COUNT

waterlogged /wɔːtəlɒgd/. **1** An area of land that is **waterlogged** is so wet that the soil cannot contain any more water, with the result that a layer of water remains on the surface of the ground. ADJ QUALIT

2 A **waterlogged** boat is so full of water that it may soon sink. ADJ QUALIT

watermelon /wɔːtəmɛlən/, **watermelons.** A **watermelon** is a large round fruit which has a green skin and is pink and juicy inside with a lot of black seeds. N COUNT

waterproof /wɔːtəpruːf/, **waterproofs**, **waterproofing**, **waterproofed.** **1** Something that is **waterproof** does not let water pass through it. EG *...a pair of waterproof trousers.* ADJ CLASSIF

2 A **waterproof** is a coat which does not let water pass through it. N COUNT

3 If you **waterproof** something, you make it waterproof. EG *...a system for waterproofing damp walls.* V+O

watershed /wɔːtəʃɛd/, **watersheds.** A **watershed** is an event or period which is important, because it marks the beginning of a new way of life or a new stage in a person's career. EG *The Vietnam war was one of the great watersheds of modern history.* N COUNT

waterside /wɔːtəsaɪd/. The **waterside** is a street or shore beside an area of water such as a river or lake. EG *I drove down to the waterside.* N SING : the+N

water-ski, **water-skis**, **water-skiing**, **water-skied.** If you **water-ski**, you ski on water while being pulled along by a boat. ◊ **water-skiing.** EG *...excellent facilities for sailing, water-skiing, and skin-diving.* V ◊ N UNCOUNT

watertight /wɔːtətaɪt/. **1** Something that is **watertight** does not allow water to pass through it because it is very tightly sealed. EG *...watertight doors.* ADJ CLASSIF

2 An agreement or argument that is **watertight** has been so carefully put together that nobody should be able to find a fault in it. EG *It sounded a good watertight story.* ADJ CLASSIF

waterway /wɔːtəweɪ/, **waterways.** A **waterway** is a canal, river, or narrow channel of sea which ships or boats can sail along. N COUNT

waterworks /wɔːtəwɜːks/. **Waterworks** is both the singular and the plural form.
A **waterworks** is a building where a supply of water is stored and cleaned before being distributed to the public. N COUNT

watery /wɔːtəri¹/. **1** Something that is **watery** is weak or pale. EG *...a watery smile... ...a watery April sun.* ADJ QUALIT

2 Food or drink that is **watery** contains a lot of water. EG *...watery cabbage.* ADJ QUALIT

watt /wɒt/, **watts.** A **watt** is a unit of measurement of electrical power. EG *...a 60 watt bulb.* N COUNT

wave /weɪv/, **waves**, **waving**, **waved.** **1** If you **wave** or **wave** your hand, you move your hand from side to side in the air, usually in order to say hello or goodbye to someone. EG *His mother waved to him... We waved at them from the train... Peter waved his hand towards the house.* ▶ used as a noun. EG *Jack gave his usual cheery wave.* V OR V+O : USU+A ▶ N COUNT

2 If you **wave** someone away or **wave** them on, you make a movement with your hand to indicate that they should move in a particular direction. EG *He waves on the traffic... I was waved through.* V+O+A

3 If you **wave** something, you hold it up and move it rapidly from side to side. EG *All along the route, people applauded and waved flags at them.* V+O

4 If something **waves**, it moves gently up and down or from side to side. EG *The grass was waving in the wind.* V

5 A **wave** is also a raised line of water on the surface of water, especially the sea, which is caused by the wind or by tides making the surface of the water rise and fall. EG *She could see the line of white foam where the waves broke on the beach.* ● See also **tidal wave**. N COUNT

6 **Wave** is used to refer to **6.1** the sudden increase in heat or energy that spreads out from an earthquake, eruption, or explosion. EG *...the shock wave from a one megaton bomb.* **6.2** the form in which some types of energy travel, for example light, sound, or radio signals. EG *Radar employs radio waves whereas sonar uses sound waves.* ● See also **long wave**, **medium wave** and **short wave**. N COUNT+SUPP

7 A **wave** in someone's hair is a part of the hair that forms a gentle curving shape. N COUNT

8 A **wave** of sympathy, alarm, or panic is a steady increase in that feeling which spreads through you or through a group of people. EG *A mounting wave of dislike and anger rose within me... In the general wave of panic, nobody thought of phoning for an ambulance.* N COUNT+SUPP

9 A **wave** is also **9.1** a sudden increase in a particular activity or type of behaviour. EG *In Paris in May 1968 there was a massive wave of student riots... ...a crime wave.* ● See also **new wave**. **9.2** a sudden increase in the number of people moving somewhere. EG *...the last great wave of migrants.* N COUNT+SUPP

wave aside. If you **wave aside** an idea or comment, you decide that it is not important enough to be used or considered. EG *The Chief waved his objection aside.* PHRASAL VB : V+ADV

wave down. If you **wave down** a vehicle, you wave your hand as a signal to the driver to stop the vehicle. PHRASAL VB : V+O+ADV

waveband /weɪvbænd/, **wavebands.** A **waveband** is a group of radio waves of similar length which are used for particular types of radio transmission. N COUNT

wavelength /weɪvlɛŋkθ/, **wavelengths.** **1** A **wavelength** is the size of radio wave which a particular radio station uses to broadcast its programmes. N COUNT

2 If two people are **on the same wavelength**, they share the same interests and attitudes and understand each other very well. PHRASE

waver /weɪvə/, **wavers**, **wavering**, **wavered.** **1** If you **waver** or if your confidence or beliefs **waver**, you are no longer firm or confident in your beliefs. EG *Meehan has never wavered in his assertions of innocence... Her love for him never wavered.* V

2 If you **waver**, you hesitate before making a decision. EG *If you're going to start wavering then the deal's off!* V

3 If something **wavers**, it moves or changes slightly. EG *The temperature wavered between freezing* V

What is the difference between a wave band and a wavelength?

and thawing... *I looked into his eyes. They didn't waver.*

wavy /ˈweɪviː/. 1 **Wavy** hair grows in loose curls. ADJ QUALIT EG *He had wavy grey hair.*

2 A **wavy** line has a series of regular curves along ADJ QUALIT it.

wax /wæks/, **waxes, waxing, waxed. 1 Wax** is N UNCOUNT 1.1 a solid, slightly shiny substance made of fat or oil and used especially to make candles and polish. Wax goes soft and melts when it is heated. EG *...wax candles... The packet was then sealed with wax.* 1.2 the sticky yellow substance found in your ears.

2 If you **wax** a surface, you put a thin layer of wax v+o onto it, usually in order to polish it. EG *I started waxing the floor.*

3 If something **waxes and wanes**, it first increases PHRASE and then decreases over a period of time. EG *The popularity of the film stars waxed and waned.*

4 If you **wax** eloquent or **wax** romantic, you start v+c to show that quality in the way you talk. EG *I can* Literary *just imagine David waxing lyrical about Ireland.*

waxwork /ˈwækswɜːk/, **waxworks.** In paragraph 2 **waxworks** is both the singular and the plural form.

1 A **waxwork** is a model of a famous person, made N COUNT out of wax.

2 A **waxworks** is a place where wax models of N COUNT famous people are displayed for the public to look at.

waxy /ˈwæksiː/. Something that is **waxy** looks or ADJ QUALIT feels like wax. EG *The skin was fleshy and slightly waxy to the touch.*

way /weɪ/, **ways. 1** If you refer to a **way** of doing N COUNT+SUPP something, you are referring to how you can do it. EG *...different ways of cooking fish... The only way to stop an accident is to remove the risk... You can qualify for a pension in two ways... I'm going to handle this my way.*

2 When you talk about the **way** someone does N SING+SUPP something, you are talking about the qualities which their action has. EG *He smiles in a superior way... He hated the way she talked.*

3 The **ways** of a particular person or group of N PLURAL people are their customs or their usual behaviour. +SUPP EG *We will not impose our ways on them... ...the difficulty of changing one's ways.*

4 If something is true or has an effect in a N COUNT+SUPP particular **way**, it is true with regard to some aspect of the thing involved or it has some sort of effect. EG *Breast feeding is valuable in a number of ways... In a way, these officers were prisoners themselves... The job was changing me in a way that I had not expected.*

5 The **way** you feel about something is your N SING+SUPP attitude to it or your opinion about it. EG *Do you still feel the same way?*

6 When you mention the **way** that something N SING: happens, you are mentioning the fact that it hap- the+N+SUPP pens. EG *Do you remember the way the boat leaked?*

7 If you have a **way** with people or things of a N SING+with particular type, you are very skilful at dealing with them. EG *...a village boy who had a way with horses.*

8 You also use **way** in expressions such as 'push N SING+POSS your way somewhere' or 'work your way some-where' which refer to movement or progress, especially difficult movement or progress. EG *You can't force your way into somebody's house... He started to work his way through the back copies of 'The Times'.*

9 The **way** to a particular place is the route that N SING: the+N you must take in order to get there. EG *A man asked me the way to Tower Bridge.* ● If you **have lost** ● PHRASE your **way**, you are lost and do not know which direction you should go in.

10 If you go or look a particular **way**, you go or N SING+SUPP look in that direction. EG *Will you come this way, please?... I waved but she was looking the other way.*

11 If something is the right **way** up or the right N SING+SUPP **way** round, it is facing in the right direction. EG *Have I got this the right way up?... Good heavens, it used to be the other way up.*

12 If someone or something is in the **way**, they N SING: the/ prevent you from moving freely or from seeing POSS+N clearly. EG *Why did you stand in the way?... Get out of my way... Judy barred Jim's way.*

13 In a building, the **way** in is the door or space N COUNT+SUPP through which you go in and the **way** out is the door or space through which you go out.

14 You also use **way** to emphasize that something ADV+ADV/ is a great distance away, or is very much below or PREP above a particular level or amount. EG *They're way* Informal *ahead of us... I'm way over thirty... You're way below the standard required.*

15 You use **way** in phrases such as 'all the way' PHRASE and 'most of the way' which refer to a particular amount of a journey or distance. EG *They drove all the way back without a word.*

16 You use **way** in phrases such as 'a long way' and PHRASE 'a little way' to say how far away something is or how near it is. EG *You could see them from a long way off... We're a long way away from Cuba.*

17 If you say that something **goes a long way** PHRASE towards doing a particular thing, you mean that it helps to achieve that thing. EG *Goodwill and co-operation can go a long way towards smoothing your way to the top.*

18 **Way** is used after 'have' in these phrases. 18.1 If PHRASE you say that someone or something **has a way** of doing a particular thing, you mean that they com-monly do it. EG *Ex-wives have a way of re-appearing.* 18.2 If you **get** or **have your way**, or if PHRASE you **have everything your own way**, what you want to happen happens. EG *If Baker has his way, the money will be paid to you.* 18.3 You say to CONVENTION someone **'You can't have it both ways'** to re-mind them that they have to choose between two things and cannot do or have them both.

19 **Way** is used after 'make' in these phrases. 19.1 PHRASES When you **make** your **way** somewhere, you walk or travel there. EG *I made my way back to my seat.* 19.2 If someone or something moves or is moved to **make way** for another person or thing, they move or are moved so that the other person or thing is able to stand there. EG *He refused to make way for anyone.*

20 **Way** is used after 'by' in these phrases. 20.1 You ADV SEN say **by the way** when you add something to what you are saying, especially something that you have just thought of. EG *By the way, this visit of Muller's is strictly secret.* 20.2 If you say or do something PREP **by way of** a particular thing, you say or do it as Formal that thing. EG *I'm going to sketch in a bit of the background by way of introduction.*

21 **Way** is used after 'in' in these phrases. 21.1 You PHRASE use **in the same way** when saying that a similar thing to the thing you have just mentioned happens or is true with something else. EG *Every baby's face is different from every other's. In the same way, every baby's pattern of development is different from every other's.* 21.2 You use **in a big way** and PHRASE **in a small way** to suggest the scale or importance of an activity. EG *They are going into the arms business in a big way.* 21.3 You use **in the way of** PREP in order to specify exactly what you are talking or asking about. EG *He received very little in the way of wages.*

22 **Way** is used after 'out' in these phrases. 22.1 If PHRASES a place is **out of** your **way**, you are not going to pass near it on your journey somewhere. EG *'Would you like a lift?' - 'Please, if it's not out of your way.'* 22.2 If you **go out of** your **way** to do something, you make a special effort to do it. EG *He didn't really go out of his way to help me.* 22.3 If you **keep out of** someone's **way**, you avoid them. 22.4 When something **is out of the way**, it is over or

you have dealt with it. EG *We'll be all right once this meeting is out of the way.*

23 Way is also used in these phrases. **23.1 Across** PHRASES **the way** or **over the way** means nearby, on the opposite side of a road or area. EG *...the derelict houses across the way.* **23.2 On the way** or **on your way** means in the course of the journey that you are making somewhere. EG *Lynn was on her way home.* **23.3** If an activity or plan is **under way**, it has begun and is now taking place. EG *Formal negotiations are under way.* **23.4** You use **that way** and **this way** to refer to a possible course of action that you have just mentioned, when you go on to mention the likely consequence or effect of it. EG *He could do it on Sundays. That way, it wouldn't interfere with his work at all.*

waylay /werleɪ/, **waylays, waylaying, waylaid.** V+O If you **waylay** someone, you stop them when they are going somewhere, for example in order to talk to them. EG *She lingered on the street to waylay him after the show.*

way of life, ways of life. Someone's **way of life** N COUNT: is the behaviour and habits that are typical of USU SING them, or that are chosen by them. EG *...the British way of life... I've had a rather curious way of life for the last few years.*

wayside /weɪsaɪd/. **1** The **wayside** is the side of N SING: the road. EG *...travellers who buy food from wayside* USU *the*+N stalls. Outdated

2 If someone or something **falls by the wayside**, PHRASE they become forgotten or ignored, or fail in what they are trying to do. EG *We must care for the weak who would otherwise fall by the wayside.*

wayward /weɪwəd/. Someone who is **wayward** is ADJ QUALIT difficult to control because they are likely to change suddenly and are often selfish or stubborn. EG *...a wayward and capricious lad.*

wc, wc's; also written **WC. A wc** is a toilet. N COUNT

we /wiː/ is used as the subject of a verb. A speaker PRON: PL or writer uses **we** to refer both to himself or herself and to one or more other people as a group. EG *We could hear the birds singing.*

weak /wiːk/, **weaker, weakest. 1** People who are ADJ QUALIT **weak** do not have very much strength or energy. EG *He was weak from hunger... His legs were weak... Internationally the movement has appeared weak and isolated.* ◊ **weakly**. EG *He* ◊ ADV *struggled weakly to his knees.* ◊ **weakness**. EG ◊ N UNCOUNT *...his worsening pain and physical weakness.*

2 If something is **weak**, it is likely to break, be ADJ QUALIT destroyed, or fail. EG *A fuse is a deliberately weak link in an electrical system... The small farmer is economically weak by himself.* ◊ **weakness,** ◊ N UNCOUNT **weaknesses.** EG *This would exploit a known weak-* OR N COUNT *ness on the enemy's Eastern Front.*

3 If you describe someone as **weak**, you mean that ADJ QUALIT they are easily influenced by other people. EG *She was so terribly weak and trusting... ...incompetent and weak leadership.* ◊ **weakness.** EG *...his appar-* ◊ N UNCOUNT *ent weakness under pressure.*

4 If an argument or reason is **weak**, it does not ADJ QUALIT convince you that it is right or logical. EG *That was an incredibly weak answer... The film had a weak plot.*

5 Sounds or lights that are **weak** are very faint and ADJ QUALIT difficult to distinguish clearly. EG *A weak sun shines on the promenade... In the weak light of the headlamp, I wrote down the number.*

6 Drinks such as tea or coffee that are **weak** are ADJ QUALIT made using a lot of water and therefore do not have a strong taste. EG *He sat sipping weak tea from a chipped mug.*

7 A **weak** reaction or response to something is ADJ QUALIT done without enthusiasm or emphasis. EG *He managed a weak smile.*

8 If someone or something is **weak** on a particular ADJ QUALIT: subject, they do not have much ability, skill, or USU PRED information in that subject. EG *The book was weak on fact and documentation... The course was very*

weak on traditional grammar. ◊ **weakness**. EG ◊ N UNCOUNT *...the strengths and weaknesses of international co-* OR N COUNT *operation.*

weaken /wiːkəⁿn/, **weakens, weakening, weak-** **ened. 1** If someone **weakens** something, they V-ERG make it less strong or less powerful. EG *Her armed forces had been weakened by the restriction on equipment supplies... Repeated pushing may weaken the catch and damage it.*

2 If someone **weakens** or if you **weaken** them, V-ERG they become less certain about something that they had previously decided. EG *His sense of duty never weakened... ...the government's weakening resolve.*

3 If something **weakens** you, it causes you to lose V+O some of your physical strength. EG *I was weakened by my exertions, and fell and broke my arm.*

weakling /wiːklɪŋ/, **weaklings.** If you call some- N COUNT one a **weakling**, you mean that they are physically Informal weak.

weakness /wiːknɪ²s/, **weaknesses.** If you have a N COUNT **weakness** for something, you like it so much that you want to have it or do it whenever you can. EG *Food was his weakness.* ● See also **weak**.

weal /wiːl/, **weals.** A **weal** is a mark made on N COUNT someone's skin by a blow, especially from something sharp or thin such as a sword or whip.

wealth /welθ/. **1 Wealth** is **1.1** the possession of a N UNCOUNT large amount of money, property, or other valuable things. EG *It was a period of wealth and prosperity.* **1.2** the money, property, and other valuable things that someone owns. EG *She was a woman of considerable wealth.*

2 If someone or something has a **wealth** of a N PART: SING particular thing, they have a very large amount of Formal that thing. EG *His air of confidence and his wealth of knowledge made him seem ageless.*

wealthy /welθi¹/, **wealthier, wealthiest.** Some- ADJ QUALIT one who is **wealthy** has a large amount of money, property, or valuable possessions. EG *He was the eldest son of a wealthy family.*

wean /wiːn/, **weans, weaning, weaned. 1** When a V+O mother **weans** her baby, she stops feeding it with milk from her breast and starts giving it other food. EG *The earlier a child is weaned, the greater risk he runs of serious illness.*

2 If you **wean** someone from something, you help V+O them to gradually stop doing it. EG *...trying to wean* +from/off *people from cigarettes by gradually reducing the nicotine content.*

weapon /wepən/, **weapons.** A **weapon** is an N COUNT object such as a gun, a knife, or a missile, which is used to kill or hurt people in a fight or a war. EG *...nuclear weapons.*

wear /weə/, **wears, wearing, wore** /wɔː/, **worn** /wɔːn/. **1** When you **wear** things such as clothes, V+O shoes, or jewellery, you have them on your body. EG *She was wearing a T-shirt and jeans... He didn't like wearing a hat... ...a girl who wore spectacles.*

2 If you **wear** your hair in a particular way, you V+O+A have it cut in that style or shape. EG *His face was framed by his curly hair which he wore too long.*

3 You can refer to clothes that are suitable for a N UNCOUNT particular time or occasion as a particular kind of +SUPP **wear**. For example, evening **wear** refers to clothes that are suitable for wearing in the evening.

4 If something **wears**, it becomes thinner or weak- V er because it is constantly being used over a long period of time. EG *Move the carpet up or down as it starts to wear.*

5 If something **wears** well, it can be used for a long V+ADV time without becoming weak or thin. If it **wears** badly, it is not very strong and will not last for a

---

If you are under the weather, are you outside?

weapons

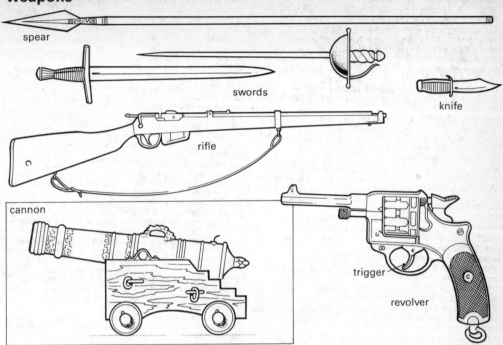

spear

swords

knife

rifle

cannon

trigger

revolver

long time. EG *Rayon blankets are less warm and don't wear as well as woollen ones.*

6 Wear is the amount of use that clothes or other N UNCOUNT things have over a period of time, which causes damage to them. EG *...a jumper, tatty from years of wear... These sheets are showing signs of wear.*

7 If you say that something **is wearing thin**, you PHRASE mean that it has been used too much and so is becoming less interesting or more annoying. EG *His excuses are beginning to wear thin.*

8 If you say that someone or something is **the** PHRASE **worse for wear**, you mean that they are in a poor Informal condition or are tired because they have been very active or have been used a lot. EG *Most of them were looking rather the worse for wear.*

wear away. If you **wear** something away or if it PHRASAL VB : **wears away**, it becomes thin and eventually disap- V·ERG+ADV pears because it is used a lot. EG *The grass was worn away where the children used to play.*

wear down. 1 If you **wear** something **down** or if PHRASAL VB : it **wears down**, it becomes shorter as a result of V·ERG+ADV constantly rubbing against something else. EG *As the teeth wear down, new ones start growing.* **2** If V+O+ADV you **wear** people **down**, you weaken them by being more persistent than they are. EG *We tried to wear them down gradually and make them agree.*

wear off. If a feeling such as pain **wears off**, it PHRASAL VB : disappears slowly. EG *By the next afternoon the* V+ADV *shock had worn off.*

wear on. If time **wears on**, it seems to pass very PHRASAL VB : slowly. EG *So the day wore on and still they sat,* V+ADV *drinking, smoking, talking.* Literary

wear out. 1 When something **wears out** or when PHRASAL VB : you **wear** it **out**, it is used so much that it becomes V·ERG+ADV thin or weak and cannot be used any more. EG *His shoes keep wearing out.* ● See also **worn-out**. **2** If V+O+ADV you **wear** someone **out**, you make them feel extremely tired. EG *They wore us out with their constant screaming and crying.*

wear and tear is the damage that is caused to N UNCOUNT something during normal use. EG *...good quality materials that stand up to the wear and tear of continual use.*

wearing /wɛərɪŋ/. An activity that is **wearing** ADJ QUALIT requires a lot of energy and makes you feel very tired. EG *It is a very wearing and demanding job.*

wearisome /wɪərɪsəm/. Something that is **weari-** ADJ QUALIT **some** is very tiring and boring or frustrating. EG *...a* Formal *wearisome meeting.*

weary /wɪəri¹/, **wearier, weariest; wearies, wearying, wearied. 1** If you are **weary**, you are ADJ QUALIT very tired. EG *He was now feeling pretty weary... He made a weary gesture... ...a weary sigh.*

◊ **wearily.** EG *The farmers trudged wearily to the* ◊ ADV *nearest stream.* Literary

2 If you **weary** of something, you become tired and V:OFT+*of* lose your enthusiasm for it. EG *He is beginning to* Formal *weary of sitting still.*

weather /wɛðə/, **weathers, weathering, weath- ered. 1** The **weather** is the condition of the N SING:*the*+N atmosphere, for example whether it is raining, OR N UNCOUNT sunny, hot, or windy in an area at a particular time. EG *The weather was good for the time of year... ...bad weather conditions.*

2 If you say that someone **is making heavy** PHRASE **weather** of a task, you mean that they are doing it very inefficiently and are making it more difficult than it needs to be.

3 If you say that you are **under the weather**, you PHRASE mean that you feel slightly ill. EG *You look a bit under the weather.*

4 If something such as rock or wood **weathers**, it V·ERG changes colour or shape as a result of the wind, Formal sun, rain, or other weather conditions. EG *The rocks weathered and turned to clay and mud.*

5 If you **weather** a problem or difficult time, you V+O survive it and are able to continue normally after it Formal is over. EG *Anyone who weathers the first four years seems to be all right.*

weatherbeaten /weðəbi:tə°n/. 1 If your face or ADJ QUALIT skin is **weatherbeaten**, it is brown and rough with deep lines because you have spent a lot of time outside in bad weather.

2 Something that is **weatherbeaten** has become ADJ QUALIT rough and slightly damaged after being outside for a long time. EG *The wooden balconies were warped and weatherbeaten.*

weathercock /weðəkɒk/, **weathercocks**. A N COUNT **weathercock** is a metal object in the shape of a cock which is fixed to the roof of a building. It turns round in the wind to show which way the wind is blowing.

weather forecast, **weather forecasts**. A N COUNT **weather forecast** is a statement that is broadcast on television or radio, or printed in a newspaper, saying what the weather will be like the next day or for the next few days.

weatherman /weðəmə°n/, **weathermen**. A N COUNT **weatherman** is a person whose job involves mak- Informal ing weather forecasts on the television or radio. EG *The day proved to be as bright as the weatherman had predicted.*

weather-vane, **weather-vanes**. A **weather-** N COUNT **vane** is a metal object on the roof of a building, which turns round in the wind to show which way the wind is blowing.

weave /wi:v/, **weaves**, **weaving**, **wove** /wəʊv/, **woven** /wəʊvə°n/. 1 If you **weave** cloth, you make V+O OR V it by crossing the threads over and under each other using a machine called a loom. EG *Let's weave a rug.* ◊ **woven**. EG ...*woven fabrics.*   ◊ ADJ CLASSIF

2 The **weave** of a cloth is the way in which the N COUNT+SUPP threads are arranged and the pattern that they form. EG ...*a tight, firm weave.*

3 If you **weave** your way somewhere, you go there V+O+A by moving through and around things and chang- OR V+A ing direction often in order to avoid hitting them. EG *He holds a tray aloft as he weaves his way through the crowd.*

weaver /wi:və/, **weavers**. A **weaver** is a person N COUNT who weaves cloth.

web

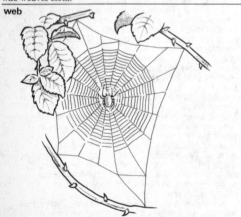

web /wεb/, **webs**. 1 A **web** is a fine net that a N COUNT spider makes from a sticky substance which it produces in its body. Insects stick to the web as they fly past and are eaten by the spider.

2 You use **web** to refer to a complicated pattern or N COUNT+SUPP structure, with many different connections and relationships, which is sometimes considered as an obstacle or a danger. EG ...*the complex web of reasons.*

webbed /wεbd/. **Webbed** feet have a piece of skin ADJ CLASSIF between the toes. Ducks and other water birds have webbed feet.

we'd /wi:d/. 1 **We'd** is the usual spoken form of 'we had', especially when 'had' is an auxiliary verb. EG *We'd done a good job.*

2 **We'd** is also the usual spoken form of 'we would'. EG *We'd have given them five if they'd asked.*

wedded /wεdr²d/. If you are **wedded** to an idea or ADJ PRED+ to system, you support it very strongly. EG ...*a party* Formal *wedded to unrestricted free enterprise.*

wedding /wεdɪŋ/, **weddings**. A **wedding** is a N COUNT marriage ceremony. EG ...*the wedding of Prince Charles and Lady Diana*... ...*a wedding dress.*

wedge /wεdʒ/, **wedges**, **wedging**, **wedged**. 1 If V+O : USU+A you **wedge** something, you force it to remain in a particular position by holding it there tightly or by fixing something next to it to prevent it from moving. EG *Open the door wide and wedge it with a wad of newspaper*... *She sat in a chair wedged between table and bunk.*

2 A **wedge** is 2.1 a piece of wood, rubber, metal, or N COUNT plastic which has one pointed edge and one thick edge. The pointed edge can be pushed into a gap, for example the gap between a door and the floor, and the thick edge then prevents any movement by either object. 2.2 a piece of something that has N COUNT a thick triangular shape, for example a slice of OR N PART cheese or pie. EG ...*a huge wedge of cherry pie.*

3 If someone **drives a wedge** between people or PHRASE groups, they cause bad feelings between them in Formal order to weaken their relationship. EG *They are trying to drive a wedge between us and the Arabs.*

4 If you describe something as **the thin end of the** PHRASE **wedge**, you mean that it appears to be unimpor- tant at the moment, but that you think it is the beginning of a harmful development.

Wednesday /wεnzdɪ³/, **Wednesdays**. **Wednes-** N UNCOUNT **day** is one of the seven days of the week. It is the OR N COUNT day after Tuesday and before Thursday. EG *Do they know you're coming next Wednesday?*

wee /wi:/. **Wee** means small or little. EG ...*wee bits* ADJ CLASSIF : *of stone*... *Can I ask you just one wee question?*... ATTRIB *It's a wee bit hot in here.* Scottish

weed /wi:d/, **weeds**, **weeding**, **weeded**. 1 A **weed** N COUNT is a wild plant that grows in gardens or fields of crops and prevents the cultivated plants from growing properly. EG ...*pulling out the weeds from among the tall, green rows of rice.*

2 If you **weed** a place, you remove the weeds from V OR V+O it. EG *I had weeded the garden.*

3 If you call someone a **weed**, you mean that they N COUNT are physically weak and that they have a weak Informal character. British

weed out. If you **weed out** things that are not PHRASAL VB : wanted in a group, you get rid of them. EG *Natural* V+O+ADV *selection had weeded out the weakest.*

weedy /wi:dɪ¹/. 1 A place that is **weedy** is full of ADJ QUALIT weeds. EG ...*the long weedy path.*

2 If you describe someone as **weedy**, you mean ADJ QUALIT that they are physically weak and thin. EG *He's tall* Informal *and weedy, with long hair.* British

week /wi:k/, **weeks**. 1 A **week** is 1.1 a period of N COUNT seven days, beginning on a Sunday and ending on a Saturday. Some people consider that a week starts on Monday and ends on Sunday. EG *That was a terrible air crash last week*... ...*once a week, on Tuesdays*... *He worked seven days a week*... *I've been wanting to ring you all week.* 1.2 the hours N COUNT+SUPP that you spend at work during a week. EG *I work a thirty-five hour week.* 1.3 the part of the week that N SING : the+N does not include Saturday and Sunday. EG *She never goes out during the week.*

2 You use **week** 2.1 in expressions such as 'a week on Monday', 'a week next Tuesday', and 'tomorrow week', to mean exactly one week after the day that you mention. EG *'When is it to open?' – 'Monday week.'*... *It's due a week tomorrow.* 2.2 in expres-

sions such as 'a week last Monday', 'a week ago this Tuesday', and 'a week ago yesterday', to mean exactly one week before the day that you mention. EG *She died a week last Thursday.*

weekday /wiːkdeɪ/, **weekdays.** A **weekday** is N COUNT any of the days of the week except Saturday and Sunday.

weekend /wiːkend/, **weekends.** A **weekend** is N COUNT Saturday and Sunday. EG *I spent the weekend at home... I know what I need. A weekend in London.*

weekly /wiːkliː/, **weeklies.** 1 **Weekly** is used to ADJ CLASSIF describe something that happens, appears, or is OR ADV done once a week or every week. EG *...a weekly newspaper... ...a weekly payment of seven shillings... We played chess two or three times weekly... Several groups meet weekly.*

2 A **weekly** is a newspaper or magazine that is N COUNT published once a week. EG *He controls two daily newspapers and four local weeklies.*

weep /wiːp/, **weeps, weeping, wept** /wept/. If V OR V+O someone **weeps**, they cry. EG *The girl was weeping* Literary *as she kissed him goodbye.* ▶ used as a noun. EG ▶ N SING : a+N *They had a little weep together.*

weeping willow, weeping willows. A **weeping** N COUNT **willow** is a willow tree with long, thin branches that hang down to the ground.

weepy /wiːpiː/. Someone who is **weepy** is sad and ADJ QUALIT likely to cry easily. EG *She came in very weepy. 'Dad's leaving home.'*

weigh /weɪ/, **weighs, weighing, weighed.** 1 If V+C something **weighs** a particular amount, that is how heavy it is. EG *It's made of steel and weighs ten tons.*

2 If you **weigh** something, you measure how heavy V+O it is, using scales. EG *She was weighing a parcel.*

3 If you **weigh** the facts about a situation, you V+O consider them very carefully before you make a decision. EG *She had weighed the risks and decided it wasn't worth it.*

4 If you **weigh** your **words**, you think very careful- PHRASE ly before you speak. EG *'I like Tom very much,' she said, scrupulously weighing her words.*

weigh down. 1 If a heavy load **weighs** you PHRASAL VB : **down**, it stops you moving easily by making you V+O+ADV heavier. EG *He was weighed down with weapons and equipment.* 2 If you **are weighed down** by a V+O+ADV, difficulty, it is making you very worried. EG *So* USU PASS *you're weighed down with problems.*

weigh on or **weigh upon.** If a problem **weighs** PHRASAL VB : **on** you or **weighs upon** you, it makes you worry. V+PREP EG *Her absence began to weigh upon me.*

weigh out. If you **weigh** something **out**, you PHRASAL VB : measure a certain weight of it in order to make V+O+ADV sure that you have the correct amount. EG *He weighed out a pound of tomatoes.*

weigh up. 1 If you **weigh** things **up**, you consider PHRASAL VB : their importance in relation to each other in order V+O+ADV to help you make a decision. EG *You have to weigh up in your mind whether to punish him or not.* 2 If V+O+ADV you **weigh** someone **up**, you try and find out what they are like and form an opinion of them. EG *We spoke for a while, weighing each other up.*

weight /weɪt/, **weights, weighting, weighted.** 1 N SING OR The **weight** of something is its heaviness, which N UNCOUNT can be measured in units such as kilos, pounds, and tons. EG *The weight of the load is too great... It was 25 metres long and 30 tons in weight.*

2 A **weight** is a metal object which weighs a N COUNT known amount. You use weights with sets of scales to weigh things, by balancing the thing that you are weighing against one or more weights. EG *...big brass scales with all the weights sparkling in a row.*

3 You can use **weight** to refer to an object that is N COUNT heavy. EG *I'm not allowed to do heavy work, nor can I carry heavy weights any more.*

4 If you **weight** something or **weight** it down, you V+O : OFT+ make it heavier, often so that it cannot move *down* easily. EG *...a plastic sheet weighted down with straw bales.*

5 The **weight** of something is its large amount or N SING+of its great power, which means that it is difficult to contradict it or fight against it. EG *The weight of the evidence convinces me that he was wrongly imprisoned... They had the weight of official support behind them.*

6 If you feel a **weight** of some kind on you, you N SING have a problem or a responsibility that you are very worried about. EG *This was a great weight lifted off my back... Without a producer, the weight of responsibility fell upon me.*

7 **Weight** is also used in these phrases. 7.1 If you PHRASES **put on weight** or **gain weight**, your body becomes fatter and heavier. If you **lose weight**, your body becomes thinner and lighter. EG *I think she might have lost a bit of weight.* 7.2 If you **pull** your **weight**, you work as hard as the other people who are involved in the same task or activity. EG *They'll refuse to fund anyone who is not pulling their weight.* 7.3 If you **take the weight off** your **feet**, Informal you sit down to have a rest. EG *Take the weight off your feet for an hour.* 7.4 If you **throw** your **weight about**, you act aggressively and use your authority over other people more than you need to. 7.5 a **weight off** your **mind**: see mind. ● See also **dead weight.**

weighted /weɪtɪd/. A system that is **weighted** in ADJ PRED+A favour of a particular person or group is organized so that this person or group has an advantage. EG *The law is weighted in favour of landlords.*

weightless /weɪtlɪs/. Something that is **weightless** seems to have very little weight or no weight ADJ CLASSIF at all. EG *These creatures may have been virtually weightless in water.* ◇ **weightlessness.** EG *...ex-* ◇ N UNCOUNT *periencing the weightlessness of space travel.*

weightlifter /weɪtlɪftə/, **weightlifters.** A N COUNT **weightlifter** is a person who does weightlifting.

weightlifting /weɪtlɪftɪŋ/ is a sport in which N ING competitors try to lift very heavy weights. The winner is the person who lifts the heaviest weight.

weighty /weɪtiː/, **weightier, weightiest.** You use ADJ QUALIT **weighty** to describe something that seems serious or important. EG *Let us turn to less weighty matters.*

weir /wɪə/, **weirs.** A **weir** is a low dam which is N COUNT built across a river in order to control the flow of water or to change its direction.

weird /wɪəd/, **weirder, weirdest.** Something or ADJ QUALIT someone that is **weird** seems strange and peculiar. EG *The markets sell all sorts of weird vegetables... He's a weird child.* ◇ **weirdly.** EG *...weirdly shaped* ◇ ADV *trees.*

weirdo /wɪədəʊ/, **weirdos.** If you call someone a N COUNT **weirdo**, you mean that they behave in a strange Informal and peculiar way. EG *When we started up, the locals thought we were weirdos.*

welcome /welkəm/, **welcomes, welcoming, welcomed.** 1 If you **welcome** someone, you greet V+O them in a friendly way when they arrive somewhere. EG *He moved eagerly towards the door to welcome his visitor.* ▶ used as a noun. EG *I was* ▶ N COUNT *given a warm welcome by the President.*

2 You can say **'Welcome'** to someone when you CONVENTION are greeting them. EG *Welcome to Peking... 'Welcome back,' said Howard.*

3 If you say that someone is **welcome** in a ADJ QUALIT : particular place, you mean that they will be ac- USU PRED cepted there gladly. EG *All members of the public are welcome... I was a welcome visitor in both camps.* ● If you **make** someone **welcome**, you ● PHRASE make them feel happy and accepted in a new place. EG *The women made her welcome.*

4 If you tell someone that they are **welcome** to do ADJ PRED something, you are encouraging them to do it. EG +to-INF *You will always be welcome to come back.*

5 If you say that you **welcome** something, you V+O mean that you approve of it and support it. EG *I warmly welcomed his proposal.*

6 You use **welcome** to describe something that ADJ QUALIT

someone does or gives you which you want and greatly appreciate. EG *A little drop of Scotch would be very welcome.*

7 If you say **'You're welcome'** to someone who has thanked you for something, you are acknowledging their thanks in a polite way. EG *'Thank you for the beautiful scarf.' – 'You're welcome. I'm glad you like it.'*   CONVENTION

welcoming /wɔlkəmɪŋ/. Someone who is **welcoming** is friendly to you when you arrive in a place so that you feel happy and accepted. EG *Should she be cool and withdrawn, or warm and welcoming?... She gave him a welcoming smile.*   ADJ QUALIT

weld /weld/, **welds, welding, welded. 1** If you **weld** two pieces of metal together, you join them by heating their edges and fixing them together so that they cool and harden into one piece. EG *It takes speed and skill to weld steel at this heat.*   V+O : OFT-OGETHER

2 A **weld** is a join where two pieces of metal have been welded together.   N COUNT

welfare /welfeə/. **1** The **welfare** of a person or group is their general state of health, comfort, and prosperity. EG *...a society in which all cooperate and work for the welfare of all its members... I would devote my life to the child's welfare.*   N UNCOUNT +POSS

2 Welfare is used to describe the activities of an organization, especially the government, which are concerned with the health, education, living conditions, and financial problems of the people in society. EG *...cut-backs in health and welfare services... ...welfare workers.*   N MOD

3 Welfare is money which is paid by the government to people who are unemployed, have poorly paid jobs, or cannot work because they are ill. EG *They were living off welfare.*   N UNCOUNT American

welfare state. The **welfare state** is a system in which the government uses the money from taxes to provide free social services such as health care and education and to give money to people when they are old, unemployed, or sick.   N SING : the+N

well /wel/, **wells, welling, welled.** The comparative and superlative of **well** when it is used as an adverb are **better** and **best**: see separate entries for these words.

1 You say **'Well' 1.1** when you are hesitating or about to say something. EG *'Is that right?' – 'Well, I think so.'... Well thank you Jim for talking to us about your work... I've told her that you are, well, helping me in this matter.* **1.2** when you are correcting something that you have just said. EG *It took me years, well months at least, to realise that he'd actually lied to me.* **1.3** in the expression 'oh well' to indicate that you accept that the situation cannot be changed, although you are not happy about it. EG *Oh well, you wouldn't understand.* **1.4** to indicate that you are surprised or amused by something that someone has said. EG *'Well, well,' said Flora, 'now we know why she came to see me.'... Twenty years since you've been home, eh? Well, well, well, what do you think of America?* ● **very well**: see **very.**

2 If you do something **well, 2.1** you do it to a high standard. EG *She speaks French well... He handled it well... I could see almost as well at night as I could in sunlight.* **2.2** you do it thoroughly and completely. EG *You say you don't know this man very well?... The roots of democracy are very well established there.*   ADV AFTER VB

3 You use **well** to give emphasis to a prepositional phrase or to an adjective. EG *I woke well before dawn... They stood well back from the heat... I was very well aware that my little boat was far too frail... The film is well worth seeing.*   ADV +PREP/ADJ

4 You also use **well** after adverbs such as 'perfectly' or 'jolly' in order to emphasize what you are saying. EG *We managed perfectly well without you.* ● **pretty well**: see **pretty.**   ADV AFTER ADV

5 If you say that something may **well** happen or   ADV AFTER MODAL

could **well** happen, you mean that it is likely to happen. EG *Your eyesight may well improve.*

6 If you are **well**, you are healthy and not ill. EG *She answered, 'I am very well.'... She looked well.*   ADJ QUALIT : USU PRED

7 Well is also used in these phrases. **7.1** If you say that things are **going well** or that **all is well**, you mean that the situation is satisfactory. EG *Things went well for John until the First World War... All well at the office I hope?* **7.2** If you say that you **are well in** with someone, you mean that you are very friendly with them. EG *She's well in with the people next door.* **7.3** If you say that you **are well out of** a situation, you mean that you are no longer involved in it and you are pleased about this. EG *I'm glad to be well out of it.* **7.4** You say **well and good** to indicate that you find a situation acceptable or satisfactory. EG *If the worker can do it in less time, well and good.* **7.5** You use **well and truly** to emphasize that something has happened completely or thoroughly. EG *Make sure your tyres are well and truly wet.* **7.6 all very well**: see **all.** ● **would do well to** do something: see **do.**   PHRASES

8 You use **as well** in the following ways. **8.1** You use **as well** when mentioning something which happens in the same way as something else already mentioned. EG *It brought him a good deal of local fame – money as well, obviously... Now she stretched out the other leg as well.* **8.2** If you refer to a second thing **as well as** a first thing, you refer to the second thing in addition to the first. EG *Women, as well as men, have a fundamental right to work.* **8.3** If you say that you **may as well** do something, or that you **might as well** do it, you mean that you will do it although you feel slightly reluctant or unenthusiastic. EG *I may as well admit that I knew the answer all along.* **8.4** If you say that something that has happened **is just as well**, you mean that it is fortunate that it happened in the way it did. EG *He didn't have to speak very often, which was just as well as he was a man who liked to keep words to himself.*   PHRASE / PREP / PHRASE / PHRASE

9 A **well** is **9.1** a hole in the ground from which a supply of water is extracted. EG *Everyone digs his own well, but in the dry season these dry up.* **9.2** an oil well.   N COUNT

well up. If tears **well up** in your eyes, they come to the surface. EG *Tears welled up in his eyes and he brushed them aside.*   PHRASAL VB : V+ADV+A

we'll /wiːl/ is the usual spoken form of 'we shall' or 'we will'. EG *Come on, then, we'll have to hurry.*

well-advised. If someone says that you would be **well-advised** to do something, they are advising you to do it. EG *She's leaving, and I think you'd be well-advised to do the same.*   ADJ PRED : OFT+to-INF

well-balanced. Someone who is **well-balanced** is sensible and does not have many emotional problems. EG *His children are sufficiently mature and well balanced to be able to live happily with their step-mother.*   ADJ QUALIT

well-behaved. A child who is **well-behaved** behaves in a way that adults like and think is correct. EG *She's a very well behaved little girl.*   ADJ QUALIT

well-being. If you refer to someone's **well-being**, you are referring to whether they are healthy and happy. EG *This new physical fitness will produce a general feeling of well-being.*   N UNCOUNT : USU+SUPP

well-bred. Someone who is **well-bred** is very polite and has good manners.   ADJ QUALIT

well-built. Someone, especially a man, who is **well-built** is strong and muscular.   ADJ QUALIT

well done. 1 You say **well done** to indicate how pleased you are that someone has got something right or has done something properly or successfully. EG *'Which sea is this?' – 'The Atlantic Ocean.' –*   CONVENTION

What is the difference between 'well-off' and 'well-to-do'?

'Atlantic Ocean. Well done.'... That's right. Well done.

2 If something has been **well done**, it has been ADJ PRED done or carried out successfully or properly. EG The adaptation of the play from TV to theatre was exceptionally well done... ...a good job well done.

3 If something that you have cooked is **well done**, ADJ QUALIT it has been cooked thoroughly. EG Pork has to be very well done, or you can't eat it.

well-dressed. Someone who is **well-dressed** is ADJ QUALIT wearing smart or elegant clothes. EG ...two dainty well-dressed women.

well-earned. If you describe something as **well- ADJ QUALIT earned**, you mean that someone deserves it, for example because they have been working very hard. EG Let us take a well-earned rest.

well-established. If something is **well- ADJ QUALIT established**, it has existed for a long time and is successful. EG Senegal already has a well-established film industry.

well-fed. Someone who is **well-fed** gets enough ADJ QUALIT good food regularly. EG The children are well-fed and happy.

well-founded. If an idea, opinion, or feeling is ADJ CLASSIF **well-founded**, it is based on facts and can there- Formal fore be justified. EG These warnings proved well-founded.

well-groomed. Someone who is **well-groomed** ADJ QUALIT is neat and tidy in appearance. EG ...a stout and Formal well-groomed man in his fifties.

well-heeled. If you say that someone is **well- ADJ QUALIT heeled**, you mean that they are wealthy. Informal

well-informed. Someone who is **well-informed** ADJ QUALIT knows a lot, usually about many different subjects. EG They become as well-informed as possible on the issues involved.

wellington /wɛlɪŋtən/, **wellingtons. Welling- N COUNT tons** or **wellington boots** are long rubber boots which you wear to keep your feet dry. See picture at SHOES.

well-intentioned. If someone is **well- ADJ QUALIT intentioned**, they are trying to be helpful or kind, but are unsuccessful or cause unfortunate results. EG A well-intentioned effort to obtain evidence failed abysmally.

well-kept. A **well-kept** building, room, or place is ADJ QUALIT looked after carefully, so that it is always neat and tidy. EG ...a mansion with a well-kept lawn.

well-known. Something or someone that is **well- ADJ QUALIT known** is known by a lot of people and is therefore famous or familiar. EG ...his two well-known books on modern art... It's well known that separating children from their mothers can lead to problems in later life.

well-mannered. Someone who is **well- ADJ QUALIT mannered** is polite and has good manners.

well-meaning. Someone who is **well-meaning** ADJ QUALIT tries to be helpful or kind, but is often unsuccessful. EG Well-meaning friends said, 'You cannot afford another baby.'... Their sympathy was well-meaning but ineffective.

well-meant. Something that is **well-meant** is ADJ CLASSIF intended to be helpful, useful, or kind, but is unsuccessful or has unfortunate results. EG I don't want anyone else's opinion, however well-meant.

well-nigh. You use **well-nigh** to say that some- ADV+ADJ thing is almost true. EG It's extremely difficult, well Formal nigh impossible to choose between them... The otter is well-nigh extinct in Britain.

well-off. 1 If you say that someone is **well-off**, you ADJ QUALIT : mean that they are quite rich. EG A lot of the USU PRED students were quite well-off.

2 Someone who is **well-off** for something has as ADJ PRED+for much of it as they want or need. EG You're well off Informal for coal, I hope?

3 If you say that someone **doesn't know when** PHRASE they **are well off**, you are criticizing them for not Informal appreciating how fortunate they are.

well-preserved. If you say that someone is **well- ADJ QUALIT preserved**, you mean that they do not look as old Formal as they really are. EG ...a well-preserved man in his late fifties.

well-read. Someone who is **well-read** has read a ADJ QUALIT lot of books and has learnt a lot from them. Formal

well-spoken. Someone who is **well-spoken** ADJ QUALIT speaks in a polite, correct way and with an accent Formal which is considered socially acceptable.

well-thought-of. Someone or something that is ADJ QUALIT **well-thought-of** is admired, respected, and has a good reputation.

well-thought-out. Something that is **well- ADJ QUALIT thought-out** is very carefully planned. EG ...a well written, entertaining, and well thought-out novel.

well-timed. An action or remark that is **well- ADJ CLASSIF timed** is said or done at the most suitable time. EG ...well-timed purchases of stock.

well-to-do. Someone who is **well-to-do** is rich. EG ADJ QUALIT He came from a well-to-do family. Outdated

well-tried. Something that is **well-tried** has been ADJ QUALIT used or done many times before and so is known to work well or to be successful. EG ...a well-tried technique.

wellwisher /wɛlwɪʃə/, **wellwishers.** A **well- N COUNT wisher** is someone who hopes that a particular Formal person or thing will be successful and who does something to show their feelings. EG Hundreds of telegrams arrived from wellwishers.

well-worn. 1 A **well-worn** expression or remark ADJ QUALIT has been used so often that it is boring. EG ...a well-worn joke... ...well-worn slogans.

2 A **well-worn** object or piece of clothing has been ADJ QUALIT used or worn so much that it looks old and untidy.

welly /wɛli[1]/, **wellies.** A **welly** is the same as a N COUNT wellington. EG I put on my wellies and we went off Informal into the rain. British

welter /wɛltə/. A **welter** of things is a large N PART : SING number of them which occur together. EG ...the Literary daily welter of details and little problems.

wend /wɛnd/, **wends, wending, wended.** If you PHRASE **wend** your **way** in a particular direction, you walk Literary slowly in that direction. EG We watched them wend their leisurely way up and down the street.

went /wɛnt/ is the past tense of **go.**

wept /wɛpt/ is the past tense and past participle of **weep.**

were /wə, wɜː/. **1 Were** is the plural form and the second person singular form of the past tense of **be.**

2 Were is sometimes used instead of 'was' in Formal conditional clauses or when you are wishing for something. EG He treated me as if I were crazy... He wished he were taking a bath. ● **as it were**: see **as.**

we're /wɪə/ is the usual spoken form of 'we are'. EG We're all here.

weren't /wɜːnt/ is the usual spoken form of 'were not'. EG We weren't asleep.

werewolf /wɛəwʊlf/, **werewolves.** In horror sto- N COUNT ries and films, a **werewolf** is a person who some-times changes into a wolf.

west /wɛst/; often spelled with a capital letter.

1 The **west** is **1.1** the direction which you look N SING : the+N towards in order to see the sun set. EG The next settlement is two hundred miles to the west... The hills behind Agadir in the west are built of blue limestone. **1.2** the part of a place or country which is towards the west. EG ...in remote rural areas of the west of Ireland.

2 West means towards the west or to the west of a ADV AFTER VB place or thing. EG I was accompanied by an English friend who had never been West.

3 The **west** part of a place or country is the part ADJ CLASSIF which is towards the west. EG ...West Africa... ...the Labour MP for Oldham West.

4 A **west** wind blows from the west. EG ...a pleasant- ADJ CLASSIF : ly warm west wind. ATTRIB

5 The **West** is also used to refer to the United N SING : the+N States, Canada, and the countries of Western and

Southern Europe. EG *...the capitalist West... The West exported wheat to the third world.*

westerly /wɛstəliˈ/. **1** A **westerly** point, area, or ADJ QUALIT direction is to the west or towards the west. EG *The harbour has a westerly outlook.*

2 A **westerly** wind blows from the west. EG *The* ADJ CLASSIF *ship was driven by the incessant westerly gales.*

western /wɛstᵊn/, **westerns;** often spelled with a capital letter.

1 Western means **1.1** in or from the west of a ADJ CLASSIF: region or country. EG *The sun began to turn crim-* ATTRIB *son on the western horizon... I've just been in Western Nigeria.* **1.2** coming from or associated with the people of Europe and North America, and the way in which they live, especially their attitudes, technology, or political and economic systems. EG *...the impact of western technology... ...western-style housing.*

2 A **western** is a book or film about life in the west N COUNT of America in the nineteenth century. The story usually involves a lot of fighting and shooting.

westerner /wɛstᵊnə/, **westerners.** A **westerner** N COUNT is **1** a person who was born in or lives in the West, especially in Europe or North America. **2** a person who was born in or who lives in the west of a place or country.

westernize /wɛstᵊnaɪz/, **westernizes, western-** V+O : USU PASS **izing, westernized;** also spelled **westernise.** If a society, place, or system **is westernized,** ideas and behaviour which are common in Europe and North America are introduced into it. EG *Westernized tastes spread and traditions weaken.*

westward /wɛstwəd/, **westwards. Westward** or ADV AFTER VB **westwards** means towards the west. EG *She suggested we continue westward... The reef stretches westwards from the tip of Florida.* ▸ **Westward** is ▸ ADJ CLASSIF also used as an adjective. EG *...the westward expansion of the city.*

wet /wɛt/, **wetter, wettest; wets, wetting, wetted.** The forms **wet** and **wetted** are both used as the past participle and past tense of the verb.

1 If something is **wet,** it is covered in water, rain, ADJ QUALIT sweat, or another liquid. EG *I don't want to get my feet wet... The grass is wet.*

2 If the weather is **wet,** it is raining. EG *Take a* ADJ QUALIT *raincoat if it's wet... It was a wet day.*

3 If something such as paint, ink, or cement is **wet,** ADJ CLASSIF it is not yet dry or solid. EG *...a fan-shaped pattern in the wet plaster... ...wet paint.*

4 If people's faces, cheeks, or eyes are **wet,** they ADJ QUALIT are covered in tears or filled with tears. EG *She raised a red, wet face to me and wailed.*

5 If you say that someone is **wet,** you mean that ADJ QUALIT they are weak and lack enthusiasm, energy, or Informal confidence. EG *'I don't see what I can do.' – 'Judy! Don't be so wet.'*

6 A **wet** is a person, especially a Conservative N COUNT politician, who supports moderate political policies Informal and opposes extreme ones. EG *...the Tory Wets.* British

7 To **wet** something means to get water or some V+O other liquid over it. EG *Uncle Ted wet his lips... A column of spray wetted them.*

8 If people, especially children, **wet** their beds or V+O OR V-REFL clothes or **wet** themselves, they urinate in their beds or clothes because they cannot control their bladder. EG *Martin's wet his pyjama trousers.*

wet blanket, wet blankets. If you call someone N COUNT a **wet blanket,** you mean that they refuse to join in Informal an activity with other people or that they speak or behave in such a way that they stop other people enjoying themselves.

wet suit, wet suits. A **wet suit** is a close-fitting N COUNT rubber suit which a diver or underwater swimmer wears in order to keep his or her body warm.

we've /wiːv/ is the usual spoken form of 'we have', especially when 'have' is an auxiliary verb. EG *We've had a very interesting discussion.*

WH stands for **words starting with 'wh'**
There are 14 words in the dictionary that are labelled WH in the Extra Column. These are: *what, whatever, when, whenever, where, wherever, which, whichever, who, whoever, whom, whose, why, how.* Notice that 'how' is regarded as a WH word.

Words that are labelled WH are always given a more precise grammatical label after a colon, as in the entry for **when,** where the first sense is labelled WH: ADV, and the third sense is labelled WH: CONJ OR PRON REL.

WH words have three main uses.

1. They often begin a report clause. When the report clause can only begin with a WH word, the label says V+REPORT: ONLY WH, or V+O+REPORT: ONLY WH. EG *Do we know where he went?... I can't tell you why I'm worried.*

2. They are used to begin a question. EG *Where are you going?... What are the dangers?*

3. Apart from 'what', they can all be used to begin a relative clause. EG *...my sister who lives in London... ...a place where they could go swimming... There are a number of reasons why this is important.*

See the entry headed VERBS for more information.

---

whack /wæk/, **whacks, whacking, whacked. 1** V+O If you **whack** someone or something, you hit them hard. EG *His father might whack him if he found out.*

2 If someone gets their **whack** of something, they N COUNT : USU receive their fair share of it. EG *Whatever happens,* SING+POSS *I've got to have my whack. That was in the* Informal *agreement.*

whacked /wækt/. If you are **whacked,** you are ADJ PRED extremely tired. EG *By 9 p.m. I was whacked. By* Informal *9.30 I was asleep in bed.*

whale /weɪl/, **whales. 1** A **whale** is a very large N COUNT animal that lives in the sea and looks like a huge fish.

2 If you say that you **had a whale of a time,** you PHRASE mean that you enjoyed yourself very much. EG *I* Informal *gather they've all been having a whale of a time these last few days.*

whaling /weɪlɪŋ/ is the activity of hunting and N UNCOUNT killing whales. EG *...the whaling industry.*

wharf /wɔːf/, **wharves.** A **wharf** is a platform N COUNT built of stone or wood along the side of a river or sea, where ships can be tied up.

what /wɒt/. **1** You use **what 1.1** in questions when WH : PRON you are asking for information about something. EG OR DET *What is your name?... What are you doing here?... What time is it?* **1.2** in indirect questions and WH : PRON indirect statements about knowing or telling OR DET things. EG *Do you know what a pendulum is?... I don't know what to do... We didn't know what bus to get... I find it difficult to understand what people are saying.*

2 You also use **what** at the beginning of a clause **2.1** to refer to something with a particular quality WH : PRON or nature. EG *He mixes what is real with what is* OR DET *unreal... A computer can only do what you have programmed it to do... What he really needs is a nice cup of tea.* **2.2** to indicate that you are talking WH : DET about the whole of an amount that is available to OR PRON you. EG *I've spent what money I had... The house consumed what little there was of my spare time.*

Who uses a wheelchair?

3 You say **'What'** **3.1** to show someone who has wh: CONVENTION spoken to you that you have heard them and want them to continue. EG *'Dad?' – 'What?' – 'Can I have the car tonight?'* **3.2** to ask someone to say wh: CONVENTION something again because you did not hear it properly. 'What' is not as polite as 'pardon'. EG *'Do you want another coffee?' – 'What?' – 'Do you want another coffee?'* **3.3** to express surprise or disbelief. EG *'Could I see you?' – 'What, right this minute?'* wh: CONVENTION **3.4** to emphasize an opinion or reaction, especially wh: PREDET OR DET in exclamations. EG *What a pity... What rubbish!* **3.5** wh: ADV SEN to indicate that you are making a guess about something such as an amount or value. EG *I've been an academic for, what, something like 18 years.*

4 You say **what about** at the beginning of a PHRASE question when you are making a suggestion or offer. EG *What about some lunch, Colonel?*

5 You say **what if** at the beginning of a question PHRASE when you ask about the consequences of something happening, especially something undesirable. EG *What if I miss the train?*

6 You say **what with** in order to introduce the CONJ reasons for a particular situation, especially an undesirable one. EG *What with paying for lunch and the theatre tickets, I'm very short of cash.*

7 What is also used in these phrases. **7.1** You say **'I** PHRASE **tell you what'** or **'I know what'** to introduce a Informal suggestion or offer. EG *Tell you what – let's go for a walk.* **7.2** You say **what have you** at the end of a PHRASE list in order to refer generally to other things of the Informal same kind. EG *...the needs, cultural, recreational, what have you, of this community.* **7.3** You can PHRASE refer to someone as **what's his name** or **what's** Informal **her name** when you cannot remember their name. EG *You're like what's his name... It was Mr – what's his name, you know, the new people.* **7.4** If PHRASE you know **what's what**, you know the important things that need to be known about a situation. EG *This is a meeting to find out what's what.* **7.5 what is more**: see **more**.

whatever /wɒˈtevə/. **1** You use **whatever 1.1** to wh: PRON OR DET refer to anything or everything of a particular type. EG *He volunteered to do whatever he could... She had to rely on whatever books were lying around.* **1.2** when you want to say that something is wh: CONJ the case in all possible circumstances. EG *I have to bring my family back whatever happens.* **1.3** after wh: a noun group in order to emphasize a negative ADV AFTER N, statement. EG *There is no scientific evidence what-* WITH BROAD NEG *ever to support such a view... He knew nothing whatever about it.* **1.4** to ask in an emphatic way wh: PRON about something which you are very surprised about. EG *Whatever is the matter?* **1.5** when you are wh: PRON indicating that you do not know the precise iden- OR DET tity, meaning, or value of something. EG *She offered us a bowl of chilli, whatever that is... Whatever the reason, Rudolph was glad that she had come back.*

2 You say **or whatever** to refer generally to PHRASE something else of the same kind as the thing or things that you have just mentioned. EG *You plug it into a computer or whatever and it does the rest.*

what's /wɒts/. **1 What's** is the usual spoken form of 'what is'. EG *What's your name?... What's the matter?... What's going on?*

2 What's is also a spoken form of 'what has', especially when 'has' is an auxiliary verb. EG *What's happened?*

whatsoever /wɒtsəʊevə/. You use **whatsoever** ADV AFTER N: after a noun group in order to emphasize a nega- WITH tive statement. EG *I don't think there's any evidence* BROAD NEG *of that whatsoever.*

wheat /wiːt/ is **1** a grain which people usually N UNCOUNT grind into flour and use to make bread. **2** the plant that produces this grain, which is grown for food.

wheedle /wiːdəⁿl/, **wheedles**, **wheedling**, **whee-** V+O+A OR V **dled**. If you **wheedle** someone into doing something, you gently and cleverly persuade them to do it. If you **wheedle** something out of someone, you gently and cleverly persuade them to give it to you.

EG *They tried to wheedle her into leaving the house... She wheedled money out of him.*

wheel /wiːl/, **wheels**, **wheeling**, **wheeled**. **1** A N COUNT **wheel** is a circular object which turns round on a rod attached to its centre. Wheels are fixed underneath things such as cars, bicycles, and trains, so that they can move along. EG *The train started, its wheels squealing against the metal tracks.*

2 A **wheel** is also the same as a steering wheel. EG N COUNT *Howard sits behind the wheel... After so many hours at the wheel, I was very tired.*

3 If you **wheel** something that has wheels, for v+O: USU+A example a bicycle or cart, you push it along. EG *My father was wheeling his bicycle up the hill... The equipment was so bulky that it had to be wheeled around on a large trolley.*

4 If a vehicle or a group of birds **wheels**, it moves v: USU+A round in the shape of a circle or part of a circle. EG *The sky becomes filled with birds wheeling back and forth... The plane banked and wheeled.*

5 If you **wheel** round, you turn round suddenly. EG *I* v+A *wheeled around and shook her hand.*

wheelbarrow /wiːlbærəʊ/, **wheelbarrows**. A N COUNT **wheelbarrow** is a small cart that is used in the garden for carrying things. It is usually shaped like an open box, with one wheel at the front, two legs at the back, and two handles to lift and push it with.

wheelchair /wiːltʃeə/, **wheelchairs**. A **wheel-** N COUNT **chair** is a chair with wheels that ill or injured people use in order to move about, when they cannot walk.

wheeling and dealing is the process of trying N ING to get what you want, especially in business, often by dishonest or unfair methods. EG *...complex business deals and financial wheeling and dealing... ...wheeling and dealing on the stock-exchange.*

wheeze /wiːz/, **wheezes**, **wheezing**, **wheezed**. If v you **wheeze**, you breathe with difficulty, making a hissing or whistling sound, usually because you are very old or have an illness such as asthma. EG *Coughing and wheezing, he climbed up the last few steps.* ▸ used as a noun. EG *All this was said very* ▸ N COUNT *slowly, between wheezes.*

when /wen/. **1** You use **when 1.1** to ask questions wh: ADV about the time at which things happen. EG *'I have to go to Germany.' – 'When?' – 'Now.'... When did you arrive?... When are you getting married?* **1.2** in wh: CONJ indirect questions and indirect statements about the time at which something happens. EG *He didn't know when he was coming back... Ask her when the trouble first started.* **1.3** to specify or refer to wh: CONJ the time at which something happens. EG *He left* OR PRON REL *school when he was eleven... When I have free time, I always spend it fishing... Do you remember that time when Adrian phoned up from Tunbridge?... Join us next week, when we shall be talking about solar energy.*

2 You also use **when** to introduce the reason for a wh: CONJ particular opinion, comment, or question. EG *How can I get a job when I can't even read or write?... How silly we are to sit around indoors when outside it is so lovely.*

3 When also means the same as although. EG *You* wh: CONJ *describe this policy as rigid and inflexible, when in fact it has been extremely flexible.*

whence /wens/ means from where. EG *He re-* ADV OR CONJ *turned hastily to the United States, whence he* Outdated *originally came.*

whenever /wenevə/. You use **whenever** to refer wh: CONJ to any time or every time that something happens or is true. EG *Come and see me whenever you feel depressed... I avoided conflict whenever possible.*

where /weə/. **1** You use **where 1.1** to ask ques- wh: ADV tions about the place something is in, or is coming from, or is going to. EG *Where's Jane?... Where are you going?* **1.2** to specify or refer to the place in wh: CONJ which something is situated or happens. EG *I think I* OR PRON REL *know where we are... How did you know where to* *find me?... She walked over to where Madeleine stood... The place where they landed was very wet.*

2 You also use **where** when you are referring to or asking about a situation, a stage in something, or an aspect of something. EG *Bryan wouldn't know where to start... ...a situation where unemployment is three million and rising fast... I wished, where possible, to avoid any mention of my family... This is where I profoundly disagree with you.* WH:CONJ, PRON REL, OR ADV

3 You also use **where** to introduce a clause that contrasts with the other part of the sentence. EG *Sometimes a teacher will be listened to, where a parent might not.* WH:CONJ

whereabouts /weərəbauts/. **1** If you refer to the **whereabouts** of a person or thing, you mean the place where that person or thing is. EG *I will not give anyone my whereabouts... We have discovered the whereabouts of one of the paintings.* N PLURAL +POSS

2 You use **whereabouts** in questions when you are asking where something is. EG *Whereabouts are you going in Yugoslavia?* ADV

whereas /weəræz/. You use **whereas** to introduce a comment that contrasts with the other part of the sentence. EG *Humans are capable of error whereas the computer is not.* CONJ

whereby /weəbaɪ/. A system or action **whereby** something happens is one that makes that thing happen. EG *I worked out an arrangement whereby each person would have a different roommate each term... ...a system whereby we work more overtime than any other country.* PRON REL Formal

wherein /weərɪn/ means **1** in which place. EG *...the box wherein she kept her wool... ...the room wherein we were to dine.* **2** in which part or respect. EG *Wherein lay her greatness?* PRON REL Outdated ADV OR CONJ Outdated

whereupon /weərəpɒn/. You use **whereupon** to say that one thing happens immediately after another thing and usually as a result of the other thing. EG *His department was shut down, whereupon he returned to Calcutta.* CONJ Formal

wherever /weərevə/. You use **wherever** **1** to say that something is true or happens in any place or situation. EG *In Bali, wherever you go you see these ceremonies... Wherever he was, he was happy... They have tried to restore the house wherever possible to its original state.* **2** to indicate that you do not know where a place or person is. EG *'Where does she live?' – 'Alten, wherever that is.'* WH:CONJ

wherewithal /weəwɪðɔːl/. If you have the **wherewithal** to do something, you have enough money to do it. EG *Where did they get the wherewithal to finance all those concerts?* N SING: the+N Formal

whet /wet/, **whets**, **whetting**, **whetted**. If you **whet** someone's **appetite** for something, you increase their desire for it. EG *The tutor at the college had whetted her appetite for more work.* PHRASE

whether /weðə/. You use **whether** **1** when you are talking about a choice or doubt between two or more alternatives. EG *I can't tell whether she loves me or she hates me... I wasn't sure whether I liked it or not.* **2** to say that something is true in any of the circumstances that you mention. EG *He's going to buy a house whether he gets married or not.* CONJ

whew /fjuː/ is used to represent a sound that you make when you breathe out very quickly, for example when you are very hot or when you are relieved. EG *Whew! It's nice to have that over with.* EXCLAM

which /wɪtʃ/. **1** You use **which** **1.1** to ask questions when there are two or more possible answers or alternatives. EG *Which department do you want?... Which is her room?* **1.2** to refer to a choice between two or more possible answers or alternatives. EG *I don't know which country he played for... The book says one thing and you say another. I don't know which to believe.* WH:DET OR PRON

2 You also use **which** at the beginning of a relative clause that specifies the thing that you are talking about or gives more information about it. EG *...the* WH:PRON REL

awful conditions which exist in British prisons... We sat on the carpet, which was pale green.

3 You also use **which** to refer back to what has just been said. EG *It takes me an hour from door to door, which is not bad... I usually enjoy these dinners, unless I have to make a speech, in which case I worry throughout the meal.* WH:PRON REL OR DET

whichever /wɪtʃevə/. You use **whichever** **1** to indicate that it does not matter which of the possible alternatives happens or is chosen. EG *The United States would be safe whichever side won... Then they have lunch, have a chat, have a sleep, whichever they like, up in the lounge.* **2** to specify which of a number of possibilities is the right one or the one you mean. EG *Use whichever soap powder is recommended by the manufacturer... Use whichever of the forms is appropriate.* WH:DET OR PRON

whiff /wɪf/, **whiffs**. **1** If there is a **whiff** of a smell, you smell it faintly or briefly. EG *...a little whiff of perfume as she passed... ...a whiff of petrol.* N COUNT+of

2 A **whiff** of a particular feeling or type of behaviour is a slight sign of it. EG *...a whiff of rebellion... ...the first whiff of danger.* N COUNT+of

while /waɪl/, **whiles**, **whiling**, **whiled**. **1** If something happens **while** something else is happening, the two things happen at the same time. EG *He stayed with me while Dad talked with Dr Leon... They wanted a place to stay while in Paris... While he was turning the key in the lock, someone opened the door from the other side.* CONJ

2 You also use **while** to introduce a clause that contrasts with the other part of the sentence. EG *Fred gambled his money away while Julia spent hers all on dresses... While I have some sympathy for these fellows, I think they went too far.* CONJ

3 A **while** is a period of time. EG *They talked for a short while... ...a little while ago... After a while, my eyes became accustomed to the darkness.* ● to be **worth** your **while**: see **worth**. ● **once in a while**: see **once**. N SING

while away. If you **while away** the time in a particular way, you spend time in that way because you are waiting for something or because you have nothing else to do. EG *How about whiling away the time by telling me a story?* PHRASAL VB: V+ADV+O

whilst /waɪlst/ means the same as **while**. EG *I didn't want to live at home whilst I was at university... Whilst these cars are economical at a steady 56 mph, they perform badly in traffic.* CONJ

whim /wɪm/, **whims**. A **whim** is a sudden wish to do or have something, which is not the result of any strong reason or purpose. EG *She might go, or might not, as the whim took her... ...his tendency to change his mind at whim.* N COUNT OR N UNCOUNT

whimper /wɪmpə/, **whimpers**, **whimpering**, **whimpered**. **1** If children or animals **whimper**, they make little, low, unhappy sounds. EG *You don't have to feed the baby the minute she whimpers.* ▸ used as a noun. EG *I was listening for a cry or a whimper from upstairs.* V ▸ N COUNT

2 If someone **whimpers** something, they say it in an unhappy or frightened way. EG *'I want to go home,' she whimpered.* V+QUOTE

whimsical /wɪmzɪkəl/. Something that is **whimsical** is unusual and slightly playful, and is done without any strong reason or purpose. EG *...a whimsical smile... ...whimsical images of birds and beasts.* ADJ QUALIT

whine /waɪn/, **whines**, **whining**, **whined**. **1** If someone or something **whines**, they make a long, high-pitched noise, especially one which sounds sad or unpleasant. EG *His dog was whining in pain... The clattering and whining elevator began to move slowly upwards.* ▸ used as a noun. EG *...the whine of the police sirens.* V ▸ N COUNT

Do white-collar workers wear white collars?

2 If someone **whines** about something, they complain about it in a way that annoys you. EG *My father never whined or complained about his work.*   V : OFT+about OR QUOTE

whinge /wɪndʒ/, **whinges, whinging, whinged.** The spelling **whingeing** is also used. If someone **whinges** about something, they complain about it in a way that annoys you. EG *I'm sick of hearing her whinge.*   V : OFT+about Informal

whip /wɪp/, **whips, whipping, whipped. 1** A **whip** is a piece of leather or rope fastened to a handle, which is used for hitting people or animals. EG *He was lashed with whips.*   N COUNT

2 If you **whip** a person or animal, you hit them with a whip. EG *I saw him whipping his mules.*   V+O

◊ **whipping, whippings.** EG *He could not possibly have endured a whipping.*   ◊ N COUNT

3 If the wind **whips** something, it strikes it sharply. EG *The wind whipped my face.*   V+O

4 If you **whip** something out or off, you take it out or off very quickly and suddenly. EG *Glenn whipped off the mask to reveal his identity.*   V+O+A

5 If you **whip** cream or eggs, you stir them very fast until they are thick and frothy or stiff.   V+O

◊ **whipped.** EG *...fruit flan with whipped cream.*   ◊ ADJ CLASSIF

whip up. If you **whip up** a strong emotion such as hatred or excitement in people, you deliberately make them feel that emotion. EG *The interview whipped up the Americans into a frenzy of rage.*   PHRASAL VB : V+O+ADV

whip-round, whip-rounds. When a group of people have a **whip-round**, money is collected from each person so that it can be used to buy something for all of them or for someone they all know.   N COUNT Informal

whir /wɜː/. See **whirr.**

whirl /wɜːl/, **whirls, whirling, whirled. 1** When something **whirls** or when you **whirl** it round, it moves round or turns round very fast. EG *...the whirling blades of a helicopter.* ▸ used as a noun. EG *...a whirl of dust.*   V-ERG : OFT+A ▸ N COUNT

2 You can refer to a lot of intense activity as a **whirl** of activity. EG *We flung ourselves into the mad whirl of pleasure.*   N COUNT+SUPP

3 If you say that your head or mind **is whirling,** you mean that you are very confused or excited by something. EG *My head's whirling with ideas.*   V : USU CONT

4 If someone or their mind is **in a whirl,** they are very confused or excited by something.   PHRASE Literary

5 If you say that you will **give it a whirl,** you mean that you will try doing something new for a while.   PHRASE Informal

whirlpool /wɜːlpuːl/, **whirlpools.** A **whirlpool** is a small area in a river or sea where the water is moving quickly round and round, so that objects floating near it are pulled into its centre.   N COUNT

whirlwind /wɜːlwɪnd/, **whirlwinds. 1** A **whirlwind** is a tall column of air which spins round and round very fast and moves across the land or sea.   N COUNT

2 A **whirlwind** event happens much more quickly than normal. EG *...a whirlwind romance.*   ADJ CLASSIF : ATTRIB

whirr /wɜː/, **whirrs, whirring, whirred;** also spelled **whir.** When something **whirrs,** it makes a series of low sounds so fast that they seem like one continuous sound. EG *Fans whirred on the ceiling... ...insects whirring and buzzing through the air.* ▸ used as a noun. EG *...the whirr of an engine.*   V ▸ N COUNT

whisk /wɪsk/, **whisks, whisking, whisked. 1** If you **whisk** someone or something somewhere, you take them there very quickly. EG *I was whisked into hospital with fierce abdominal pains.*   V+O+A

2 If you **whisk** eggs or cream, you stir air into them very fast. EG *Whisk the egg whites until stiff.*   V+O

3 A **whisk** is a kitchen tool used for stirring air into eggs or cream very fast.   N COUNT

whisker /wɪskə/, **whiskers. 1** The **whiskers** of an animal such as a cat or a mouse are the long, stiff hairs that grow near its mouth. EG *The animal's whiskers began to twitch.*   N COUNT : USU PLURAL

2 You can refer to the hair on a man's face, especially on the sides of his face, as his **whiskers.** EG *He tugged at his side whiskers.*   N PLURAL

whisky /wɪskiː/, **whiskies;** also spelled **whiskey** in American English and Irish English.

Whisky is a strong alcoholic drink made from grain such as barley or rye, especially in Scotland. EG *He had drunk too much whisky... ...a large whisky and soda.*   N MASS

whisper /wɪspə/, **whispers, whispering, whispered. 1** When you **whisper** something, you say something to someone very quietly, using only your breath and not your throat, so that other people cannot hear what you are saying. EG *'Follow me,' Claude whispered. 'And keep quiet.'... When we were washing I whispered the news to my sister... What are you two whispering about?*   V : OFT+QUOTE, REPORT, OR about; ALSO V+O

2 A **whisper** is a very quiet voice in which you use your breath and not your throat. EG *Hooper lowered his voice to a whisper... We spoke in whispers.*   N COUNT

whistle /wɪsᵊl/, **whistles, whistling, whistled. 1** When you **whistle** or when you **whistle** a tune, you make a sound by forcing your breath out between your lips. EG *He walked home whistling cheerfully... I was whistling little bits of the song.*   V OR V+O

2 If something **whistles,** it makes a loud, high sound as it moves quickly through the air. EG *The bullets whistled past his head.*   V : USU+A

3 When something such as a steam train or a kettle **whistles,** it produces a loud, high sound as steam is forced through a small opening. EG *The train whistled as it approached the tunnel.*   V

4 A **whistle** is a sound that you make when you whistle. EG *Sean let out a low whistle of surprise.*   N COUNT

5 A **whistle** is also a small metal tube which you blow in order to produce a loud sound and attract someone's attention. EG *The guard blew his whistle and waved his green flag.*   N COUNT

white /waɪt/, **whiter, whitest; whites. 1** Something that is **white** is of the lightest colour that there is, the colour of snow or milk. EG *There were little white clouds high in the blue sky... A woman dressed in white came up to me.*   ADJ COLOUR

2 Someone who is **white** has a pale skin and is of European origin. EG *They had never seen a white person before.* ▸ used as a noun. EG *The race riots had been caused by whites attacking blacks.*   ADJ CLASSIF ▸ N COUNT

3 If someone goes **white, 3.1** their hair becomes white in colour because they are getting old. EG *My grandfather went white at the age of fifty.* **3.2** they become very pale, for example because they are afraid or shocked. EG *My sister went white with rage.* ● If someone looks **as white as a sheet,** they look very frightened, shocked, or ill.   ADJ COLOUR ADJ PRED ● PHRASE

4 White coffee contains milk or cream.   ADJ CLASSIF

5 White wine is wine of a pale yellowish colour.   ADJ CLASSIF

6 The **white** of an egg is the transparent liquid that surrounds the yolk.   N COUNT

7 The **white** of someone's eye is the white part of their eyeball.   N COUNT

white Christmas, white Christmases. A **white Christmas** is a Christmas when it snows.   N COUNT

white-collar. White-collar workers work in offices rather than doing manual work in industry.   ADJ CLASSIF : ATTRIB

white elephant. If you refer to something as a **white elephant,** you mean that it is expensive but completely useless. EG *The new naval base has proved to be a white elephant.*   N SING : a+N

white-hot /waɪt hɒt/. If something is **white-hot,** it is extremely hot. EG *...the white-hot centre of the bonfire.*   ADJ CLASSIF

white lie, white lies. A **white lie** is a lie that is not very serious.   N COUNT

whiten /waɪtᵊn/, **whitens, whitening, whitened.** When something **whitens** or when you **whiten** it, it becomes whiter or paler in colour. EG *Use very mild bleach to whiten white nylon.*   V-ERG+A

white spirit is a colourless liquid that is made from petrol and is used, for example, to make paint thinner or to clean surfaces.   N UNCOUNT British

whitewash /waɪtwɒʃ/, **whitewashes, whitewashing, whitewashed. 1 Whitewash** is a mix-   N UNCOUNT ture of lime or chalk and water that is used for painting walls white.

2 If a wall or building **is whitewashed**, it is painted white with whitewash. `v+o`

3 Whitewash is also an attempt to hide the unpleasant facts about someone or something. EG ...*the refusal to accept official whitewash in police enquiries.* `N UNCOUNT OR N SING`

whiting /waɪtɪŋ/. Whiting is both the singular and the plural form. A **whiting** is a kind of fish. `N COUNT`

whittle /wɪtə⁰l/, **whittles**, **whittling**, **whittled**. To **whittle** something **away** or to **whittle** it **down** means to make it smaller or less effective over a period of time. EG *This may whittle away our liberties... Profits are whittled down by the ever-rising cost of energy.* `PHRASAL VB : V+O+ADV OR V+ADV+at`

whizz /wɪz/, **whizzes**, **whizzing**, **whizzed**; also spelled **whiz**. **1** If you **whizz** somewhere, you move there very fast. EG *We just stood there with the cars whizzing by.* `v+A Informal`

2 If you are a **whizz** at something, you are very good at it. EG *He might be a whiz at electronics... Renata was a perfect whiz at rhyming words.* `N COUNT : OFT+at Informal`

whizz-kid /wɪz kɪd/, **whizz-kids**; also spelled **whiz-kid**. A **whizz-kid** is someone who is very good at their job and achieves success quickly. EG ...*a multi-millionaire insurance whizz-kid.* `N COUNT Informal`

who /hu/. You can use **who** as the subject or object of a verb: see also **whom, whose**.

1 You use **who 1.1** when asking questions about someone's name or identity. EG *Who are you?... Who are you going to invite?* **1.2** in indirect questions and indirect statements about someone's name or identity. EG *She didn't know who I was.* `WH : PRON`

2 You also use **who** at the beginning of a relative clause when specifying the person you are talking about or when giving more information about them. EG *If you can't do it, we'll find someone who can... Joe, who was always early, was there already.* `WH : PRON REL`

who'd /hud/. **1 Who'd** is the usual spoken form of 'who had', especially when 'had' is an auxiliary verb. EG *It was the little girl who'd come to play with her that afternoon.*

2 Who'd is also a spoken form of 'who would'. EG *I don't think he's the sort of young man who'd be thinking of marriage.*

whodunit /hu:dʌnɪt/, **whodunits**; also spelled **whodunnit**. A **whodunit** is a book, film, or play which is about a murder and in which the identity of the murderer is kept a mystery until the end. `N COUNT Informal`

whoever /hu:evə/. **1** You use **whoever 1.1** to refer to the person who does something, when their identity does not matter or is not known. EG *If death occurs at home, whoever discovers the body should contact the family doctor... Whoever answered the telephone was a very charming woman.* **1.2** to indicate that the identity of the person who does something will not affect a situation. EG *Whoever wins the war, there will be little peace... Whoever you vote for, prices will go on rising.* `WH : PRON` `WH : CONJ`

2 You also use **whoever** in questions as an emphatic way of saying 'who'. EG *Whoever could that be at this time of night?* `WH : PRON`

whole /həʊl/. **1** If you refer to the **whole** of something, you mean all of it. EG ...*the whole of Europe... ...the whole of July.* ▸ used as an adjective. EG *They're the best in the whole world... I've never told this to anyone else in my whole life.* ● If you refer to something **as a whole**, you are referring to it generally and as a single unit. EG *Is that just in India, or in the world as a whole?* `N SING : the+N+of` `▸ ADJ CLASSIF : ATTRIB` `● PHRASE`

2 A **whole** is a single thing which contains several different parts. EG *The earth's weather system is an integrated whole.* `N SING`

3 You use **whole** to say that an action is done to something without dividing it up. For example, if you swallow something **whole**, you do not bite it into smaller bits. `ADV AFTER VB`

4 You also use **whole** to emphasize what you are saying. EG ...*a whole new way of life... Charles was a whole lot nicer than I had expected.* `SUBMOD OR ADJ CLASSIF : ATTRIB Informal`

5 You say **on the whole** to indicate that what you are saying is only true in general and may not be true in every case. EG *On the whole he is a very difficult character.* `ADV SEN`

wholefood /həʊlfuːd/, **wholefoods**. Wholefoods are foods which have not been refined very much and do not contain additives or artificial ingredients. EG *Wholefoods and fresh fruit are essential in your diet... ...a wholefood shop.* `N PLURAL OR N UNCOUNT`

wholehearted /həʊlhɑːtɪd/. If you support something in a **wholehearted** way, you support it enthusiastically and completely. EG *He had the wholehearted backing of the younger members.* `ADJ QUALIT`

◊ **wholeheartedly**. EG *I agree wholeheartedly.* `◊ ADV`

wholemeal /həʊlmiːl/. **Wholemeal** flour or bread is made from the complete grain of the wheat plant, including the husk. `ADJ CLASSIF : ATTRIB`

wholeness /həʊlnɪs/ is the quality of being complete or a single unit and not broken or divided into parts. EG *The peace, the wholeness, all that India promised, seemed fulfilled.* `N UNCOUNT Literary`

wholesale /həʊlseɪl/. **1** You use **wholesale** to refer to the activity of buying and selling goods in large quantities and therefore at cheaper prices, especially selling goods to shopkeepers who then sell them to the public. EG ...*a sharp rise in wholesale prices... Stein got the food for me wholesale.* `ADJ CLASSIF : ATTRIB, OR ADV AFTER VB`

2 You also use **wholesale** to describe something that is done to an excessive extent, for example because it has not been thought about carefully enough. EG *Wholesale slaughter was carried out in the name of progress.* `ADJ CLASSIF : ATTRIB, OR ADV AFTER VB`

wholesaler /həʊlseɪlə/, **wholesalers**. A **wholesaler** is a person whose business is buying large quantities of goods and selling them in smaller amounts, usually to shops. `N COUNT`

wholesome /həʊlsə⁰m/. **1** Something that is **wholesome** is good and morally acceptable. EG *Young people enter marriage nowadays with a much more wholesome attitude.* `ADJ QUALIT`

2 Wholesome food is good for your health. `ADJ QUALIT`

wholewheat /həʊlwiːt/ means the same as **wholemeal**. EG *Wholewheat spaghetti takes slightly longer to cook.* `ADJ CLASSIF : ATTRIB American`

who'll /hul/ is a spoken form of 'who will' or 'who shall'. EG *Who'll believe him?*

wholly /həʊllɪ¹/ means completely. EG *The idea was not a wholly new one... ...people whom we could not wholly trust.* `ADV`

whom /hu:m/. The word **whom** is used in formal or written English instead of 'who' when it is the object of a verb or preposition.

1 You use **whom** in questions, indirect questions, and other structures in which you refer to someone whose name or identity is unknown. EG '*I'm a reporter.' - 'Oh yes? For whom?'... Whom do you suggest I should ask?* `WH : PRON Formal`

2 You also use **whom** at the beginning of a relative clause in which you specify the person you are talking about or give more information about them. EG *She was engaged to a sailor named Raikes, whom she had met at Dartmouth.* `WH : PRON REL`

whoop, **whoops**, **whooping**, **whooped**; pronounced /wuːp/ for paragraph 1 and /wʊps/ for paragraph 2. **1** If you **whoop**, you shout loudly in a very happy or excited way. EG *Eddie whooped with delight.* ▸ used as a noun. EG *There were whoops of approval by the bar customers.* `v Written` `▸ N COUNT`

2 People say **whoops** when they have a slight accident or make a mistake. EG *Whoops. You nearly dropped it.* `EXCLAM Informal`

If you wholeheartedly agree with something, do you agree with it on the whole?

whoopee /wʊpiː/. People sometimes shout 'whoo-pee' when they are very happy or excited. EG *Whoopee! We've hit the jackpot.* EXCLAM Informal

whooping cough /huːpɪŋ kɒf/ is an illness which children get and which makes them cough and make a loud noise when they breathe in. N UNCOUNT

whoosh /wʊʃ/, **whooshes, whooshing, whooshed. 1** If something **whooshes** somewhere, it moves there very quickly or suddenly. EG *Thousands of rockets whooshed over our heads.* V+A Informal

2 A **whoosh** of air or water is a sudden rush of it. EG *The train came in with a whoosh of country dust.* N SING : OFT+of

whopping /wɒpɪŋ/ means much larger than usual. EG *Real growth was at a whopping six and a half per cent.* ADJ CLASSIF : ATTRIB Informal

whore /hɔː/, **whores.** A **whore** is a prostitute; an offensive word. N COUNT

who're /huːə/ is a spoken form of 'who are'. EG *...married couples who're waiting to be housed.*

who's /huːz/. **1 Who's** is the usual spoken form of 'who is'. EG *'Edward drove me up.' - 'Who's Edward?'*

2 Who's is also a spoken form of 'who has', especially when 'has' is an auxiliary verb. EG *...an American author who's settled in London.*

whose /huːz/. **1** You use **whose** at the beginning of a relative clause to indicate that something belongs to or is associated with the person or thing that you mentioned in the previous clause. EG *...a woman whose husband had deserted her.* WH : PRON REL

2 You also use **whose** in questions, indirect questions, and other structures in which you ask about or refer to the person that something belongs to or is associated with. EG *Whose fault is it?* WH : DET POSS OR PRON POSS

who've /huːv/ is the usual spoken form of 'who have,' especially when 'have' is an auxiliary verb. EG *...people who've gone to universities.*

why /waɪ/. **1** You use **why** when asking questions about the reason for something. EG *'I had to say no.' - 'Why?'... Why did you do it, Martin?* WH : ADV

2 You also use **why** at the beginning of a clause **2.1** to link clauses in which you talk about the reason for something. EG *He wondered why she had come... I did not know why, but I was afraid.* **2.2** to introduce a relative clause after the word 'reason'. EG *There are several good reasons why I have a freezer.* WH : CONJ / WH : PRON REL

3 You use **why** with 'not' to introduce a suggestion in the form of a question. EG *Why don't we all go?* WH : ADV

4 You say **why not** in order to agree with what someone has suggested. EG *'Can I come too?' - 'I don't see why not.'* PHRASE

5 People also say **'Why!'** to indicate their surprise, shock, or indignation. EG *Why, Dr Kirk, I do believe you are serious.* American

wick /wɪk/, **wicks. 1** The **wick** of a candle is the piece of string in it which burns when it is lit. N COUNT

2 The **wick** of a paraffin lamp or cigarette lighter is the part which supplies the fuel to the flame when it is lit. EG *It's very hard to turn the wick up and down.* N COUNT

3 If you say that someone **gets on** your **wick**, you mean that they irritate you. EG *The kids have been getting on my wick.* PHRASE Informal British

wicked /wɪkɪ²d/. **1** Someone or something that is **wicked** is very bad in a way that is deliberately immoral or harmful to other people. EG *It was clear to him that he had done something wicked.* ◇ **wickedness**. EG *...the wickedness of his crime.* ADJ QUALIT / ◇ N UNCOUNT

2 If you describe someone or something as **wicked**, you mean that they are rather mischievous or seem slightly immoral, but that you find them attractive or enjoyable. EG *He had a wicked grin... ...the wicked wit of the cartoonist.* ◇ **wickedly**. EG *She smiled wickedly.* ADJ QUALIT / ◇ ADV

wicker /wɪkə/. A **wicker** basket, chair, or mat is made of wickerwork. N UNCOUNT : OFT N MOD

wickerwork /wɪkəwɜːk/ is made by weaving twigs, canes, or reeds together. It is used to make baskets and furniture. EG *...wickerwork armchairs.* N UNCOUNT : OFT N MOD

wicket /wɪkɪt/, **wickets.** A **wicket** is **1** a set of three upright sticks with two small sticks on top of them, which the ball is bowled at in cricket. There is a wicket at each end of a cricket pitch. **2** the area of grass in between the two wickets on a cricket pitch. N COUNT

wide /waɪd/, **wider, widest. 1** Something that is **wide** measures a large distance from one side to the other. EG *...a wide bed... She looked across the wide, flat meadow... ...a wide grin.* ◇ **widely**. EG *'That's all right,' she said, smiling widely.* ADJ QUALIT / ◇ ADV

2 If you open or spread something **wide**, you open or spread it as far as possible or to the fullest extent. EG *Rudolph always opened the window wide at night... He left his office door wide open.* ADV : OFT BEFORE ADV

3 If your eyes are **wide** or **wide open**, they are open more than usual because you are surprised or frightened. EG *Lamin watched with wide eyes... She sat looking up at me, her eyes wide with pleasure.* ADJ CLASSIF

4 You use **wide** when you are talking about how much something measures from one side or edge to the other. EG *The bay is about thirty miles long and six miles wide... How wide is the bed?* ADJ CLASSIF

5 A **wide** variety, range, or selection is one that includes a lot of different things. EG *The college library had a wide variety of books.* ◇ **widely**. EG *Over the next twelve years, he travelled widely.* ADJ QUALIT / ◇ ADV

6 You also use **wide** when describing something which is found, believed, or known by many people. EG *The event received wide publicity in the press.* ◇ **widely**. EG *Your views on education are already widely known.* ADJ QUALIT / ◇ ADV

7 A **wide** difference or gap between two things is a large difference or gap. EG *The gap between the poor and the rich is very wide indeed.* ◇ **widely**. EG *Customs vary widely from one area to another.* ADJ QUALIT / ◇ ADV

8 Wide is used to describe something which relates to the most important or general parts of a situation, rather than to the smaller details. EG *...the wider context of world events.* ADJ QUALIT : USU COMPAR

9 If a shot or a punch is **wide**, it does not hit its target. ADJ PRED

10 far and wide: see **far**. ● **wide of the mark**: see **mark**.

wide-awake. If you are **wide-awake**, you are completely awake. ADJ PRED

wide-eyed. If you describe someone as **wide-eyed, 1** you mean that their eyes are more open than usual, especially because they are surprised or frightened. EG *Her face seemed frozen in an expression of wide-eyed alarm.* **2** you mean that they seem inexperienced, and perhaps lack common sense. EG *Part of me was still a wide-eyed American.* ADJ CLASSIF

widen /waɪdə⁰n/, **widens, widening, widened. 1** If something **widens** or if you **widen** it, **1.1** it becomes greater in measurement from one side or edge to the other. EG *The original trail had been widened... Below Wapping, the river widens.* **1.2** it becomes greater in range or variety or affects a larger number of people or things. EG *Labour had to widen its appeal if it was to win the election... They could widen their experience by going on a course.* V-ERG

2 If your eyes **widen**, they open more. EG *Sandy stared at me, his eyes widening.* V

3 If a difference or gap **widens**, it becomes more extreme. EG *The gap between the rich and poor regions widened... Society continues to widen the gulf between specialists and non-specialists.* V-ERG

wide-ranging. If something is **wide-ranging**, it includes or deals with a great variety of different things. EG *...a wide-ranging interview... This attack carried wide-ranging implications for the police.* ADJ QUALIT

widespread /waɪdspred/. If something is **widespread**, it exists or happens over a large area, or to a great extent. EG *These housing estates suffer* ADJ QUALIT *from widespread vandalism and neglect... There was a widespread belief that the newspapers had invented the story.*

widow /wɪdəʊ/, **widows**. A **widow** is a woman N COUNT whose husband has died.

widowed /wɪdəʊd/. If someone is **widowed**, their ADJ CLASSIF husband or wife has died. EG ...*his widowed mother.*

widower /wɪdəʊə/, **widowers**. A **widower** is a N COUNT man whose wife has died.

widowhood /wɪdəʊhʊd/ is the state of being a N UNCOUNT widow or the period of time during which a woman is a widow. EG *The shock of widowhood weakens resistance to illness... She continued to worship his memory throughout her long widowhood.*

width /wɪdθ/. The **width** of something is the N UNCOUNT distance that it measures from one side or edge to the other. EG *The area was just over a thousand yards in width... ...the width of a man's hand.*

wield /wiːld/, **wields, wielding, wielded**. 1 If you v+o **wield** a weapon, you carry it and use it. EG *They surrounded the Embassy, hurling stones and wielding sticks.*

2 If someone **wields** power, they have it and are v+o able to use it. EG *The union officials wielded enormous political power.*

wife /waɪf/, **wives** /waɪvz/. A man's **wife** is the N COUNT: woman that he is married to. EG *She is the wife of* OFT+POSS *an army colonel... Their wives were joining them for lunch.* ● See also **old wives' tale**.

wig /wɪg/, **wigs**. A **wig** is a mass of false hair N COUNT which you wear on your head, for example because you are bald or because you want to cover up your own hair.

wiggle /wɪgəl/, **wiggles, wiggling, wiggled**. 1 If v-ERG you **wiggle** something, you move it up and down or from side to side with small quick movements. EG *They wiggle their hips to the sound of pop music... Can you wiggle your ears?*

2 A **wiggle** is a small quick movement in which N COUNT something moves up and down or from side to side. EG *Give the wire a quick wiggle. I think it's stuck.*

3 A **wiggle** is also a line that has a lot of little N COUNT bumps in it. EG *He drew the sea as a series of wiggles.*

wigwam /wɪgwæm/, **wigwams**. A **wigwam** is a N COUNT kind of tent used by North American Indians.

wild /waɪld/, **wilder, wildest; wilds**. 1 Wild ani- ADJ CLASSIF: mals and plants live or grow in natural surround- ATTRIB ings and are not looked after by people. EG ...*wild pigs... He lived on berries and wild herbs.*

2 Animals living in the **wild** are living in their N SING: the+N natural surroundings and are not being looked after by people. EG *They couldn't survive in the wild.*

3 **Wild** land is natural and not cultivated at all. EG ADJ QUALIT ...*the wilder parts of Scotland.*

4 The **wilds** are remote areas, far away from N PLURAL: towns. EG *We live out in the whisks... ...the wilds of* the+N *Australia.*

5 **Wild** is used to describe the weather or the sea ADJ QUALIT when it is very stormy. EG ...*a wild night in February.*

6 People who behave in a **wild** way behave in a ADJ QUALIT very uncontrolled, excited, or energetic way. EG *The audience went wild... The men were wild with excitement... He made a wild dash for the door.* ◊ **wildly**. EG *The spectators applauded wildly.* ◊ ADV

7 If you have **wild** eyes or a **wild** look, your eyes ADJ QUALIT are wide open and staring, because you are frightened, angry, or mad.

8 If you **are not wild about** something, you do not PHRASE like it very much. EG *I'm not wild about the* Informal *wallpaper.*

9 If something **runs wild**, it behaves in a natural PHRASE or free way, without being controlled. EG *Early in the morning, dogs run wild in the park.*

10 A **wild** idea or scheme is very unusual and ADJ QUALIT rather silly.

11 If something is **beyond** your **wildest dreams**, it PHRASE

is much better than you hoped for or believed possible. EG *He's paying them a salary beyond their wildest dreams.*

12 A **wild** guess is one which is very unlikely and is ADJ QUALIT made without much thought. ◊ **wildly**. EG *I was* ◊ ADV *guessing wildly.*

13 See also **wildly**.

wilderness /wɪldənɪˀs/, **wildernesses**. 1 A wil- N COUNT: **derness** is 1.1 a desert or other area of land which USU SING has very few plants or animals. EG ...*the arctic wilderness.* 1.2 an area where grass or plants are growing thickly and without any control. EG *The garden's turned into a wilderness.*

2 If a politician spends time **in the wilderness**, he PHRASE or she is not in an important or influential position in politics for that time. EG *He is enjoying a revival after four years in the wilderness.*

wildfire /waɪldfaɪə/. If something **spreads like** PHRASE **wildfire**, it spreads very quickly. EG *The news spread like wildfire round the world... The infection spread like wildfire.*

wild-goose chase, wild-goose chases. If you N COUNT are on a **wild-goose chase**, you waste a lot of time Informal searching for something that you have little chance of finding. EG *He sent us on a wild-goose chase.*

wildlife /waɪldlaɪf/. You can refer to animals that N UNCOUNT live in the wild as **wildlife**. EG *These chemicals would destroy crops and all wildlife.*

wildly /waɪldliˀ/. You use **wildly** to emphasize ADV+ADJ that a quality is very great indeed. EG ...*wildly erratic behaviour... ...wildly impractical ideas.* ● See also **wild**.

wiles /waɪlz/ are clever tricks that people use to N PLURAL persuade other people to do something. EG *You* Formal *seem familiar with the wiles of children.*

wilful /wɪlfʊl/. 1 Wilful actions or attitudes are ADJ CLASSIF: done or expressed deliberately, especially with the ATTRIB intention of hurting someone. EG ...*wilful destruction... He displayed a wilful ignorance of their plight.* ◊ **wilfully**. EG *She had wilfully betrayed* ◊ ADV *him to his father.*

2 Someone who is **wilful** is determined to get what ADJ QUALIT they want and to do things in their own way. EG *She was a wilful child.*

will /wɪl/, **wills, willing, willed**. 1 If you say that MODAL something **will** happen, you mean that it is going to happen in the future. EG *Inflation is rising and will continue to rise... Perhaps this time it won't rain... Will I get paid?... Perhaps when I am fifty I will have forgotten.*

2 If you say that you **will** do something, you mean MODAL that you intend to do it or are willing to do it. EG *I will see you tomorrow... I will never betray you... We won't accept that.*

3 You can use **will** 3.1 when inviting someone to MODAL do something or when offering them something. EG *Will you have a whisky, Doctor?* 3.2 to ask or tell someone to do something. EG *Will you do me a favour?... Please keep an eye on him, will you?... Will you shut up!* 3.3 to give an order to someone. Formal EG *You will forget this conversation immediately.*

4 You can also use **will** 4.1 to say that someone or MODAL something is able to do something. EG *This will cure anything... The car won't go.* 4.2 to say that something usually happens. EG *The bonus will usually be paid automatically... When I get on a bus and I see an advert, I will read it.* 4.3 to say that you are assuming or guessing that something is true, because you have good reasons for thinking it. EG *You will probably already be a member of a union... That'll be young Christopher there... You will already have gathered that I don't like her.* 4.4 to say that someone insists on doing something that you think is unpleasant or silly. You emphasize the

---

What is the difference between a widow and a widower?

word **will** when you use it in this way. EG *He will leave his socks lying around.*

5 Will is the determination to do something. EG *She* N UNCOUNT *lost her will to live... Their marriage became a* OR N COUNT *fierce battle of wills.* ● See also **free will**.

6 If something is the **will** of someone with power N SING+POSS or authority, they want it to happen. EG *I must abide* Formal *by the will of the people... It is the will of Allah.*

7 If you can do something **at will**, you can do it PHRASE whenever you want. EG *Chang told us that we could wander around at will.*

8 If you **will** something to happen, you try to make V+O+to-INF it happen by using mental effort rather than physical means. EG *I willed my trembling legs to walk straight.*

9 A **will** is a legal document in which you state N COUNT what you want to happen to your money and property when you die. EG *Has Des made a will?*

willing /wɪlɪŋ/. **1** If you are **willing** to do some- ADJ PRED : thing, you do not object to doing it and you will do it USU+to-INF if someone asks or wants you to do it. EG *I was still willing to marry her... The patient becomes cheerful, relaxed, and willing to talk.* ◊ **willingness**. EG ◊ N UNCOUNT *You need initiative and a willingness to work.*

2 If you describe someone as **willing**, you mean ADJ QUALIT : that they do something enthusiastically rather than USU ATTRIB because they are forced to do it. EG *...a class of willing students.* ◊ **willingly**. EG *Many liberties* ◊ ADV *were given up willingly during the war.* ◊ **willingness**. EG *They showed great willingness.* ◊ N UNCOUNT

willow /wɪləʊ/, **willows**. A **willow** or a **willow** N COUNT **tree** is a kind of tree with long narrow leaves.

will-power. If you do something by **will-power**, N UNCOUNT you succeed in doing it because you are very determined to do it. EG *She stayed calm by sheer will-power... Removing this obstacle demanded all his will-power.*

willy-nilly /wɪli¹ nɪli¹/. If something happens to ADV you **willy-nilly**, you cannot prevent it happening. EG *All of them were taken willy-nilly on a guided tour of the town.*

wilt /wɪlt/, **wilts**, **wilting**, **wilted**. If a plant **wilts**, V it gradually bends downwards and becomes weak, because it needs more water or is dying.

wily /waɪli¹/, **wilier**, **wiliest**. **Wily** people are ADJ QUALIT clever at thinking of ways to get what they want, especially ways that involve deceiving people. EG *...a wily diplomat.*

win /wɪn/, **wins**, **winning**, **won** /wʌn/. **1** If you V+O OR V **win** a fight, a game, or an argument, you defeat the person who you are fighting, playing against, or arguing with. EG *Who's winning the war?... Their side was winning.* ▶ used as a noun. EG *...another* ▶ N COUNT *win for our team.*

2 To **win** an election or a competition means to do V+O OR V better than anyone else involved. EG *The Party won a convincing victory at the polls.*

3 If you **win** a prize or a medal, you get it because V+O you have been very successful at something. EG *Mum has just won a microwave cooker in a competition.*

4 If you **win** something that you want, for example V+O someone's approval or support, you succeed in getting it. EG *...the party's failure to win mass support among the working class... They are winning honour and glory.*

5 If you say that someone **can't win** in a particular PHRASE situation, you mean that they are certain to fail or Informal to suffer in some way whatever they do. EG *You pay the fine or you lose your job. You can't win.*

6 See also **winning**.

win over or **win round**. If you **win** someone PHRASAL VB : **over** or **win** them **round**, you persuade them to V+O+ADV support you or to agree with you.

wince /wɪns/, **winces**, **wincing**, **winced**. When V you **wince**, the muscles of your face tighten suddenly because you have felt a pain or because you have just seen, heard, or remembered something unpleasant. EG *He tried not to wince... The pressure*

made her wince with pain... He winces at the memory of that defeat. ▶ used as a noun. EG *His* ▶ N COUNT *smile soon modified to a wince.*

winch /wɪntʃ/, **winches**, **winching**, **winched**. **1** A N COUNT **winch** is a machine which is used to lift heavy objects. It consists of a cylinder around which a rope or chain is wound.

2 If you **winch** an object or person somewhere, V+O+A you lift or lower them using a winch. EG *...helicopters into which they could be winched.*

wind, winds, winding, winded, wound; pronounced /wɪnd/ for paragraphs 1-6 and /waɪnd/ for paragraphs 7-9 and the phrasal verbs. **Winded** is the past tense and past participle of the verb in paragraph 3. **Wound** /waʊnd/ is the past tense and past participle of the verbs in paragraphs 7-9 and the phrasal verbs.

1 A **wind** is a current of air moving across the N COUNT OR earth's surface. EG *...poppies fluttering in the wind...* N UNCOUNT *There was a fierce wind blowing... ...a gust of wind.*

2 Your **wind** is your ability to breathe easily. EG *I* N SING+POSS *had to stop and regain my wind.*

3 If you **are winded** by something such as a blow, V+O : OFT PASS the air is suddenly knocked out of your lungs so that you have difficulty breathing for a short time.

4 Wind is the air that you sometimes swallow with N UNCOUNT food or drink, or the gas that is produced in your stomach, which causes an uncomfortable feeling.

5 The **wind** section of an orchestra or band is the N MOD group of musicians who play instruments that they blow into. EG *...brilliant wind players.*

6 If you **get wind of** something, you hear about it, PHRASE especially when someone else did not want you to Informal know about it. EG *He somehow got wind of the party and managed to get himself invited.*

7 If a road or river **winds** in a particular direction, V+A it goes in that direction with a lot of bends in it. EG *The river winds through the town.* ◊ **winding**. EG ◊ ADJ CLASSIF *...the winding road leading to the Castle.* ● If you ● PHRASE **wind** your **way** somewhere, you do not go there quickly or directly. EG *The procession wound its way through the sunlit streets.*

8 When you **wind** something round something else, V+O+round/ you wrap it round it several times. EG *Wind the wire* around *round the screws.*

9 When you **wind** a clock or watch, you turn a V+O knob, key, or handle on it round and round in order to make it operate.

wind back. When you **wind back** the tape in a PHRASAL VB : tape recorder or the film in a camera, you make it V+O+ADV move back towards its starting position.

wind down. 1 When you **wind down** the window PHRASAL VB : of a car, you make it move downwards by turning a V+O+ADV handle. **2** If a clock or machine **winds down**, it V+ADV gradually works more slowly before stopping completely. **3** If someone **winds down** a business, they V-ERG+ADV gradually reduce the amount of work or the number of people involved in it, before closing it down completely.

wind forward. When you **wind forward** the PHRASAL VB : tape in a tape recorder, you make it move forward V+O+ADV to a new position.

wind up. 1 When you **wind up** an activity, you PHRASAL VB : finish it or stop doing it. EG *We were winding up this* V-ERG+ADV *conference... It was time to wind up the game.* **2** V+ADV, OR When someone **winds up** a business or other V-ERG+ADV organization, they close it down completely. EG *Four years later the company was wound up.* **3** If V+ADV+A you **wind up** in a particular place, you are in that Informal place at the end of a series of journeys or events. EG *We wound up at the Indian restaurant... It wouldn't surprise me if he winds up in jail.* **4** When V+O+ADV you **wind up** a clock or watch, you turn a knob, key, or handle on it round and round in order to make it operate. **5** When you **wind up** the window V+O+ADV of a car, you make it move upwards by turning a handle.

windbreak /wɪndbreɪk/, **windbreaks**. A **wind-** N COUNT **break** is a line of trees or a fence which gives protection against the wind. EG *The orchard serves as a windbreak.*

windfall /wɪndfɔːl/, **windfalls**. A windfall is a N COUNT sum of money that you receive unexpectedly or by luck. EG *He had a windfall from the football pools.*

wind instrument, **wind instruments**. A wind N COUNT **instrument** is a musical instrument that you blow into in order to produce sounds, for example a trumpet or a clarinet. See picture at MUSICAL INSTRUMENTS.

windmill /wɪndⁿmɪl/, **windmills**. A windmill is a N COUNT tall building with a cross-shaped structure on the outside which turns round as the wind blows. This provides energy, often for a machine which crushes grain.

window /wɪndəʊ/, **windows**. A window is a N COUNT space in a wall or roof or in the side of a vehicle, often with glass in it so that light can pass through it and people can see through it. See picture at HOUSE. EG *The kitchen windows were wide open... ...looking in a jeweller's window.*

window-box, **window-boxes**. A window-box is a N COUNT long, narrow container on a window-sill outside a house, in which plants are grown.

window-frame, **window-frames**. A window- N COUNT **frame** is a frame round the edges of a window, which the glass is fixed into.

window-pane, **window-panes**. A window-pane N COUNT is a piece of glass in the window of a building. EG *...the clatter of rain against the window-pane.*

window-shopping. If you go **window-shopping**, N ING you spend time looking at the things in the windows of shops without intending to buy anything. EG *I had been window-shopping on Madison Avenue.*

window-sill, **window-sills**. A window-sill is a N COUNT ledge along the bottom of a window, either inside or outside a building. EG *Pots of herbs stood on the window-sill.*

windpipe /wɪndpaɪp/, **windpipes**. Your wind- N COUNT **pipe** is the tube in your body that carries air into your lungs when you breathe.

windscreen /wɪndskriːn/, **windscreens**. The N COUNT **windscreen** of a car or other vehicle is the glass British window at the front which the driver looks through. See picture at CAR.

windscreen wiper, **windscreen wipers**. A N COUNT : **windscreen wiper** is a long thin piece of metal USU PLURAL with a rubber edge, which is electrically operated British and which wipes rain from the windscreen of a vehicle. See picture at CAR.

windshield /wɪndʃiːld/, **windshields**. A wind- N COUNT **shield** is **1** the same as a windscreen. EG *I wiped* American *my windshield... ...a windshield wiper.* **2** a glass or plastic screen that provides protection from the wind, for example on the front of a motorbike.

windsurfer

windsurfer /wɪndsɜːfə/, **windsurfers**. **1** A wind- N COUNT **surfer** is a long, narrow board with a sail attached, which you stand on in the sea or in a lake and which moves along as the wind blows it.
2 You can also refer to a person riding on a N COUNT windsurfer as a **windsurfer**.

windsurfing /wɪndsɜːfɪŋ/ is the activity of mov- N ING ing along the surface of the sea or a lake on a

windsurfer. EG *On the beach you can go windsurfing or sailing.*

windswept /wɪndswɛpt/. **1** A **windswept** place is ADJ CLASSIF open and not protected against strong winds. EG *...a* Literary *beautiful windswept hillside.*
2 Someone who looks **windswept** has untidy hair ADJ QUALIT because they have been out in the wind. Literary

windy /wɪndi¹/, **windier**, **windiest**. If it is **windy**, ADJ QUALIT the wind is blowing a lot. EG *The winter was cold, wet, and windy... It was a windy spring day.*

wine /waɪn/, **wines**. Wine is an alcoholic drink N MASS made from grapes. There are two main kinds, called red wine and white wine. Wine can also be made from other fruits or vegetables. EG *I was drinking white wine... Have you tried his turnip wine?*

wine bar, **wine bars**. A **wine bar** is a place N COUNT where people can buy and drink wine.

wing /wɪŋ/, **wings**, **winging**, **winged**. **1** The N COUNT **wings** of a bird or an insect are the two parts of its body that it uses for flying.
2 The **wings** of an aeroplane are the long flat parts N COUNT which stick out of either side and support it while it is flying.
3 A **wing** of a building is a part of it which sticks N COUNT : out from the main part or which has been built USU+SUPP later than the main part. EG *...the west wing of the museum... ...the hospital wing of the prison.*
4 A **wing** of an organization, especially a political N COUNT+SUPP organization, is a group within it which has a particular function or particular beliefs. EG *...the political wing of the IRA.* ● See also **left-wing**, **right-wing**.
5 The **wings** in a theatre are the sides of the stage N PLURAL : which are hidden from the audience by curtains or the+N scenery. EG *She dropped her cloak in the wings.*
6 The **wings** of a car are the parts of the body N COUNT which are around the wheels. See picture at CAR. British

winger /wɪŋə/, **wingers**. In football or hockey, a N COUNT **winger** is an attacking player who plays mainly on the far left or the far right of the pitch.

wingspan /wɪŋspæn/, **wingspans**. The **wing-** N COUNT : **span** of a bird, insect, or aeroplane is the distance USU+SUPP from the end of one wing to the end of the other wing. EG *...dragonflies with a wingspan of 70 centimetres.*

wink /wɪŋk/, **winks**, **winking**, **winked**. **1** When V : OFT+at you **wink**, you close one eye very briefly, often as a signal to someone that something is a joke or a secret. EG *Uncle John winked at me across the table.* ▸ used as a noun. EG *'What a hostess!' said* ▸ N COUNT *Clarissa with a big wink at George.*
2 If a light **winks**, it shines in short flashes. If a V surface **winks**, it reflects light in short flashes. EG Literary *Lights winked under the trees... ...the sea, sparkling and winking in the sun.*
3 If you have **forty winks**, you sleep for a short PHRASE while. Informal
4 If you **don't sleep a wink** or **don't get a wink** PHRASE **of sleep**, you stay awake and do not sleep at all. EG Informal *I never slept a wink that night.*

winner /wɪnə/, **winners**. The **winner** of a prize, N COUNT race, or competition is the person who wins it. EG *He was a worthy winner of the Nobel Prize.*

winning /wɪnɪŋ/, **winnings**. **1** The **winning** com- ADJ CLASSIF : petitor, team, or entry in a competition is the one ATTRIB that has won. EG *Here are some extracts from the five winning entries.*
2 **Winning** is also used to describe actions or ADJ CLASSIF : qualities that please other people and make them ATTRIB feel friendly towards you. EG *His chief asset is his* Literary *winning smile.*
3 The money that someone wins in a competition N PLURAL or by gambling is referred to as their **winnings**. EG *Mark laughed and went to collect his winnings.*

What do you buy when you go window-shopping?

winter /wɪntə/, **winters. Winter** is the coldest season of the year, between autumn and spring. In winter, many trees and plants do not have any leaves. EG *It was a terrible winter... ...a dark winter's night.* N UNCOUNT OR N COUNT

wintertime /wɪntətaɪm/ is the period of time during which winter lasts. EG *Where do they go in the wintertime?* N UNCOUNT

wintry /wɪntri¹/. Something that is **wintry** has features that are typical of winter. EG *...one wintry day early in March.* ADJ QUALIT

wipe /waɪp/, **wipes, wiping, wiped. 1** If you **wipe** something, you rub its surface lightly in order to remove dirt or liquid from it. EG *He wiped his mouth with the back of his hand.* ▸ used as a noun. EG *Give the table a wipe.* V+O : USU+A ▸ N COUNT

2 If you **wipe** dirt or liquid from something, you remove it, for example by using a cloth or your hand. EG *She wiped the tears from her eyes.* V+O+A

3 If you **wipe** the dishes, you dry plates, knives, forks, and other things with a cloth when they have been washed after a meal. V+O OR V

4 If you **wipe** the sounds or pictures recorded on a tape, you remove them, for example by recording different sounds or pictures on the tape. V+O

wipe out. To **wipe out** places or groups of people means to destroy them completely, especially suddenly or violently. EG *Epidemics wiped out the local population.* PHRASAL VB : V+ADV+O

wipe up. If you **wipe up** dirt or liquid from something, you remove it using a cloth. EG *He began to wipe up the mess.* PHRASAL VB : V+O+ADV

wire /waɪə/, **wires, wiring, wired. 1** A **wire** is a long thin piece of metal that is used to fasten or connect things. EG *You can mend it with a length of wire... ...overhead lights suspended from wires... ...a telephone wire.* ● See also **barbed wire.** N COUNT OR N UNCOUNT

2 A **wire** is also a telegram. EG *I decided to send a wire ordering a room with twin beds.* N COUNT American

3 If you **wire** one thing to another, you fasten the two things together using wire. EG *He wired one end of the chain to the hook.* V+O+to

4 If you **wire** something or **wire** it up, you connect it to something else with wire so that electricity or electrical signals can pass between them. EG *Wire one end of the cable to the plug... ...electrical fittings wired up to the mains.* V+O+A : OFT+ up

5 If you **wire** a person, you send them a telegram. EG *I wired Renata yesterday and asked her to marry me.* V+O : OFT+REPORT : ONLY that American

wireless /waɪəli²s/, **wirelesses.** A **wireless** is the same as a radio. EG *They always announce the results on the wireless.* N COUNT Outdated

wire wool consists of very thin pieces of wire twisted together, often in the form of small pads. Wire wool is used to clean metal objects, especially saucepans and other kitchen equipment. N UNCOUNT

wiring /waɪərɪŋ/. The **wiring** in a building is the system of wires that supply electricity to the rooms. EG *Will the cottage need new wiring?* N UNCOUNT

wiry /waɪəri¹/. **1** Someone who is **wiry** is rather thin but has strong muscles. EG *...a short, wiry man.* ADJ CLASSIF

2 Something that is **wiry** is stiff and rough to touch. EG *...her wiry, black hair.* ADJ CLASSIF

wisdom /wɪzdə⁰m/. **1 Wisdom** is the ability to use your experience and knowledge in order to make sensible decisions or judgements. EG *She spoke with authority as well as wisdom.* N UNCOUNT

2 If you talk about the **wisdom** of an action or decision, you are talking about how sensible it is. EG *Doubts were expressed about the wisdom of the visit.* N SING : the+N+of

wisdom tooth, wisdom teeth. Your **wisdom teeth** are the four teeth at the back of your mouth which grow much later than your other teeth. N COUNT

wise /waɪz/, **wiser, wisest. 1** Someone who is **wise** is able to use their experience and knowledge in order to make sensible decisions and judgements. EG *She has suddenly become wise... He's a* ADJ QUALIT *very wise man... Hugh made the wisest decision of all.* ◊ **wisely.** EG *You have chosen wisely.* ◊ ADV

2 Wise is used in these phrases. **2.1** If you say that a person **would be wise** to do something, you are advising them to do it. EG *It would be wise to give up now and try again later... I think you'd be very wise to accept it.* **2.2** If you **get wise to** something, you find out about it, especially when someone has been trying to keep it secret. EG *They tried to burn the evidence before the cops got wise.* **2.3** If you say that someone is **none the wiser** or **no wiser,** you mean that they have failed to understand something, or that they are not aware of something that has happened. EG *So we're none the wiser... No one outside would be any the wiser.* PHRASES American

-wise. You can add **-wise** to nouns to form adverbs when you want to indicate **1** that someone is behaving like a particular person or thing. EG *I edged my way crabwise along the row to my seat.* **2** that you are considering one particular aspect of something. EG *You're at a disadvantage status-wise.* SUFFIX

wisecrack /waɪzkræk/, **wisecracks.** A **wisecrack** is a clever remark that is intended to be amusing, but is often rather unkind. EG *I fought down the temptation to make a wisecrack about his clothes.* N COUNT

wish /wɪʃ/, **wishes, wishing, wished. 1** A **wish** is a longing or desire for something, often something that is difficult to obtain or achieve. EG *She told me of her wish to leave the convent.* N COUNT

2 If you send your good **wishes** to someone, you express the hope that they will be happy or successful. EG *My parents send their best wishes.* N PLURAL

3 If you **wish** to do something, you want to do it. EG *They are in love and wish to marry... We do not wish to waste our money.* V : USU+to-INF OR for Formal

4 If you **wish** that something were the case, you would like it to be the case, even though you know that it is impossible or unlikely. EG *I often wish that I were really wealthy.* V+REPORT : ONLY that

5 If you **wish** for something, you express your desire for it silently to yourself. In fairy stories, when someone wishes for something, it often happens by magic. EG *I blew out the candles on my cake and wished for a new bike.* ▸ used as a noun. EG *The fairy granted her three wishes.* V : USU+for ▸ N COUNT

6 If you **wish** someone good luck, you say 'Good luck' to them to indicate that you hope they will have good luck. If you **wish** someone a happy birthday, you say 'Happy Birthday' to them to indicate that you hope they will enjoy their birthday. EG *They wished each other luck before the exam.* V+O+O

7 If you say that you **would not wish** something **on** a particular person, you mean that the thing is so unpleasant that you would not want the person to be forced to experience it. EG *...an illness I would not wish on my worst enemy.* PHRASE

wishful thinking. If you say that someone's hope or wish is **wishful thinking,** you mean that it is very unlikely to come true. EG *It is wishful thinking to assume that the generals will agree to this.* N UNCOUNT

wishy-washy /wɪʃi¹ wɒʃi¹/. If you describe a person or their ideas as **wishy-washy,** you mean that their ideas are not firm or clear. EG *He's just a wishy-washy liberal... ...a wishy-washy concept.* ADJ QUALIT Informal

wisp /wɪsp/, **wisps. 1** A **wisp** of grass or hair is a small, thin, untidy bunch of it. EG *A wisp of grey hair stuck out from under her hat.* N COUNT OR N PART

2 A **wisp** of smoke or fog is a long thin amount of it. EG *...wisps of smoke from a small fire.* N PART

wispy /wɪspi¹/. Hair that is **wispy** is thin and grows in small, untidy bunches. ADJ QUALIT

wistful /wɪstfʊl/. If someone is **wistful,** they are rather sad because they want something and know that they cannot have it. EG *She had a last wistful look round the flat... ...a little wistful smile.* ADJ QUALIT

wit /wɪt/, **wits. 1 Wit** is the ability to use words or ideas in an amusing and clever way. EG *The girl laughed at his wit... ...the wit of the cartoonist.* `N UNCOUNT`

2 If someone does something sensible, you can say that they have the **wit** to do it. EG *No one had had the wit to bring a bottle-opener.* `N SING: the+N +to-INF`

3 You can refer to someone's ability to think quickly in a difficult situation as their **wits**. EG *Her only chance was to use her wits to bluff the enemy.* `N PLURAL: USU+POSS`

4 Wits is used in these phrases. **4.1** If you **have** or **keep** your **wits about** you, you are alert and ready to act in a difficult situation. EG *In this part of the city you have to keep your wits about you all the time.* **4.2** If something **scares** you **out of your wits** or if it **scares the wits out of** you, it scares you very much indeed. EG *We were frightened out of our wits by a banging at the door.* **4.3** If someone is **at** their **wits' end**, they are so worried and exhausted by problems or difficulties that they do not know what to do next. EG *I am at my wits' end to know what to do with my son.* **4.4** a **battle of wits**: see **battle**. ● to **pit** your **wits against** someone: see **pit**. `PHRASES`

witch /wɪtʃ/, **witches.** A **witch** is a woman who is believed to have magic powers, especially evil ones. EG *She looked like a dreadful old witch.* `N COUNT`

witchcraft /wɪtʃkrɑːft/ is the skill of using magic powers, especially evil ones. `N UNCOUNT`

witch doctor, witch doctors. A **witch doctor** is a person in some societies, especially in Africa, who heals people and is thought to have magic powers. EG *...one of the most eminent witch doctors.* `N COUNT`

witch-hunt, witch-hunts. A **witch-hunt** is a search for people who are thought to be responsible for things that have gone wrong, in order to punish them. The victims of a witch-hunt are often innocent people who have strong and independent opinions, but have not actually done any harm. EG *Hearst's campaign developed into a witch-hunt that terrorized the campuses.* `N COUNT`

with /wɪð, wɪθ/. **1** If one thing or person is **with** another, they are together in one place. EG *I stayed with her until dusk.* `PREP`

2 If you do something **with** someone else, you both do it together. EG *Boys do not generally play with girls... I discussed it with Phil... ...weekly meetings with junior ministers.* `PREP`

3 If you fight or argue **with** someone, you oppose them. EG *...a naval war with France... Judy was tired of quarrelling with Bal.* `PREP`

4 If you do something **with** a particular tool or object, you do it using that tool or object. EG *Clean mirrors with a mop... He brushed back his hair with his hand.* `PREP`

5 You use **with** when you mention a feature, characteristic, or possession that someone or something has. EG *...an old man with a beard... ...an old house with steep stairs and dark corridors.* `PREP`

6 Something that is filled or covered **with** things has those things in it or on it. EG *The building is decorated with bright banners.* `PREP`

7 You use **with** to indicate how someone does something or the feeling they have when they do it. For example, if you do something **with** care, you do it carefully. EG *These files can be inspected by the computer with great accuracy and speed... Jordache looked over at his son with genuine surprise... 'There is a blanket missing,' said Matron with a sigh.* `PREP`

8 You also use **with** to indicate the feeling that makes someone behave in a particular way. EG *This experience leaves him quaking with fear.* `PREP`

9 You can use **with** to indicate what something relates to. EG *Don't be inflexible with shopping... There was a particular problem with claims for maternity allowance.* `PREP`

10 You can also use **with** to say that something happens at the same time as something else. EG *He didn't have the courage to put his hat on with* `PREP`

Perkins watching him... With advancing age, reactions become slower.

11 You use **with** to introduce a factor that affects something. EG *With all the traffic jams, it wouldn't be economic.* `PREP`

12 If someone says that they are **with** you, **12.1** they mean that they understand what you are talking about. EG *Sorry, I'm not quite with you.* **12.2** they mean that they support or approve of what you are doing. EG *I'm with the government in this.* `PREP+PRON Informal` `PREP`

withdraw /wɪðˈdrɔː/, **withdraws, withdrawing, withdrew** /wɪðˈdruː/, **withdrawn. 1** If you **withdraw** something from a place, you remove it or take it away. EG *She withdrew the key from the door... You must present your cheque card when you withdraw any money.* `V+O: OFT+from Formal`

2 If you **withdraw** to another place, you leave the place where you are and go to the other place. EG *He breathed a sigh of relief and withdrew to his office to count the money.* `V: USU+A Formal`

3 When troops **withdraw** or **are withdrawn**, they leave the place where they are fighting or where they are based. EG *We could see the force withdrawing... They are willing to withdraw some troops.* `V-ERG: OFT+from`

4 If you **withdraw** from an activity, you decide that you will no longer take part in it. EG *Marsha withdrew from the argument.* `V OR V+O: OFT+from Formal`

5 If you **withdraw** a remark or statement, you say that you wish to change or deny it. EG *I want to withdraw a statement I made earlier on.* `V+O Formal`

withdrawal /wɪðˈdrɔːəl/, **withdrawals. 1** The **withdrawal** of something is the act or process of removing it or taking it away. EG *...major matters like the withdrawal of public services... They are trying to negotiate the withdrawal of 20,000 troops.* `N UNCOUNT OR N COUNT`

2 The **withdrawal** of a remark or statement is the act of saying formally that you wish to change or deny it. EG *...the withdrawal of invitations.* `N UNCOUNT`

3 Your **withdrawal** from an activity or an organization is your decision to stop taking part in it. EG *...withdrawal from the Common Market.* `N UNCOUNT`

4 Withdrawal is behaviour in which someone prefers to be alone and does not want to communicate with other people. EG *...spells of sulking, withdrawal and vindictiveness.* `N UNCOUNT`

5 When someone has **withdrawal** symptoms, they feel ill after they have stopped taking a drug which they were addicted to. `N UNCOUNT`

6 A **withdrawal** is an amount of money that you take from your bank account. EG *It is not the bank's policy to deduct interest on withdrawals.* `N COUNT`

withdrawn /wɪðˈdrɔːn/. **1 Withdrawn** is the past participle of **withdraw.**

2 Someone who is **withdrawn** is very shy or quiet, and finds it difficult to talk to other people. EG *The isolated life made them withdrawn.* `ADJ QUALIT`

withdrew /wɪðˈdruː/ is the past tense of **withdraw.**

wither /wɪðə/, **withers, withering, withered. 1** When something **withers** or **withers** away, it becomes weaker, often until it no longer exists. EG *Links with the outside community withered... His eagerness to fight back could not be permitted to wither away.* `V: OFT+away`

2 If a plant **withers** or if heat or drought **withers** it, it shrinks and dries up, and dies. EG *The leaves had withered and fallen.* `V-ERG`

withered /wɪðəd/. **1** A **withered** plant is shrunken, dried up, and dead. EG *...a pot of withered roses.* `ADJ CLASSIF`

2 If you describe a person or a part of their body as **withered**, you mean that their skin is very wrinkled and dry, and looks old. EG *...a withered old lady... ...her withered fingers.* `ADJ QUALIT`

Should a witness withhold evidence?

withering /wɪðəˈrɪŋ/. If someone gives you a ADJ CLASSIF
withering look or makes a **withering** remark,
their look or remark makes you feel ashamed or
stupid. EG *Scylla gave him a withering glare.*

withhold /wɪðˈhəʊld/, **withholds**, **withholding**, V+O
withheld /wɪðˈhɛld/. If you **withhold** something Formal
that someone wants, you do not let them have it. EG
*His salary was withheld... I decided to withhold the
information till later.*

within /wɪðˈɪn/. 1 If something is **within** some- PREP OR ADV
thing else, it is inside it. EG *The prisoners demanded
the freedom to congregate within the prison... ...the
dominant role of women within the family... She
cut open the fruit and began to suck out the soft
flesh within.*

2 If you have a feeling **within** you, you feel it. EG *A* PREP OR ADV
mounting wave of dislike and anger rose within Literary
me... ...the hatred he felt within.

3 If something is **within** a particular limit, it does PREP
not go beyond that limit or is not more than what is
allowed. EG *We must ask the schools to keep within
their budget.*

4 If you are **within** a particular distance of a place, PREP
you are less than that distance from it. EG *They
were within fifty miles of Chicago.*

5 If something is **within** sight, **within** earshot, or PREP
within reach, you can see it, hear it, or reach it. EG
They finally came within sight of the gates.

6 If **within** a particular length of time means before PREP
that length of time has passed. EG *Within minutes I
was called to his office... Sixteen houses were
vandalized within a few weeks.*

without /wɪðˈaʊt/. 1 If people or things are **with-** PREP
out something, they do not have it. EG *The chairs
were of black teak, without cushions... ...city slums
without lights, roads or water... She was without an
ambition in the world.*

2 If you do one thing **without** doing another thing, CONJ+-ING,
you do not do the other thing. EG *They drove into* OR PREP
*town without talking to each other... 'No,' she said,
without explanation.*

3 If you do something **without** a particular feeling, PREP
you do not have that feeling when you do it. EG
They greeted him without enthusiasm.

4 If one thing happens **without** another thing PREP
happening, the other thing does not happen. EG *The
rest of the press conference passed without incident... I knocked twice, without reply.*

5 **Without** someone means not in their company PREP
or not living or working with them. EG *You can go
without me... Her husband felt he couldn't face life
without her.*

6 to **do without**: see do. ● to **go without**: see go.

withstand /wɪðˈstænd/, **withstands**, **withstand-** V+O
ing, **withstood** /wɪðˈstʊd/. When something or Formal
someone **withstands** a force or action, they survive it or do not give in to it. EG *They have to make
the walls strong enough to withstand high winds...
He was in no condition to withstand any further
punishment.*

witness /wɪtnɪs/, **witnesses**, **witnessing**, **wit-**
nessed. 1 If you are a **witness** to an event, you see N COUNT :
it and can tell other people what happened. EG *They* OFT+to
*listened avidly as witnesses to the murder told
what they had seen.* ● If you **are witness to** ● PHRASE
something, you see it happen. EG *This was the first* Formal
time I was witness to one of his rages.

2 If you **witness** something, you see it happen. EG V+O
At least fifteen people witnessed the attack on Formal
Morris.

3 A **witness** is someone who appears in a court of N COUNT
law to tell what they know about a crime or other
event. EG *Other witnesses were called, and gave
similar evidence.*

4 A **witness** is also someone who writes their N COUNT
name on a document that another person has
signed, to confirm that it is really that person's
signature. ▶ used as a verb. EG *Now everything is* ▶V+O
signed and witnessed.

5 If something **is a witness** to something else or PHRASE
bears witness to it, it shows that it exists or Formal
happened. EG *His smile is a witness to his new
found happiness... This lack of action bears witness
to a complacency which has survived two World
Wars.*

witness-box, **witness-boxes**. The **witness-box** N COUNT
or **witness-stand** in a court of law is the place
where people stand or sit when they are giving
evidence. EG *He was shown into the witness-box.*

witter /wɪtə/, **witters**, **wittering**, **wittered**. If V : USU+A
you say that someone **is wittering** about some- Informal
thing, you mean that they are saying a lot of silly
and boring things. EG *He was wittering on as usual.*

witticism /wɪtɪsɪzəm/, **witticisms**. A **witticism** N COUNT
is a witty remark or joke. EG *Don smiled at this
witticism.*

witty /wɪtɪ/, **wittier**, **wittiest**. Someone or some- ADJ QUALIT
thing that is **witty** is amusing in a clever way. EG
It's a neat and witty play.

wives /waɪvz/ is the plural of **wife.**

wizard /wɪzəd/, **wizards**. A **wizard** is a man in a N COUNT
fairy story who has magic powers.

wizardry /wɪzədrɪ/. You can refer to a very N UNCOUNT
clever achievement or piece of work as **wizardry**, +SUPP
especially when you do not understand how it is
done. EG *...a sophisticated piece of computing wizardry... ...her reputation for financial wizardry.*

wizened /wɪzənd/. A **wizened** person, fruit, or ADJ QUALIT
vegetable is old and has wrinkled skin. EG *Mr* Literary
*Solomon was a wizened little man with frizzy grey
hair... ...a wizened pumpkin.*

wobble /wɒbəl/, **wobbles**, **wobbling**, **wobbled**. V
If something **wobbles**, it makes small movements
from side to side, because it is loose or unsteady. EG
*The old car wobbled back and forth on the road...
My legs were wobbling under me.*

wobbly /wɒblɪ/. Something that is **wobbly** moves ADJ QUALIT
unsteadily from side to side. EG *...a wobbly bed... My* Informal
legs still feel weak and wobbly.

wodge /wɒdʒ/, **wodges**. A **wodge** of something is N COUNT
a large amount of it or a large piece of it. EG OR N PART
Professor Marvin banged his wodge of files down Informal
hard on the desk. British

woe /wəʊ/, **woes**. 1 Woe is great unhappiness or N UNCOUNT
sorrow. EG *His distraught wife poured out her tale* Literary
of woe... ...an occasional bird cry like an exclama- Outdated
tion of woe.

2 You can refer to someone's problems or misfor- N PLURAL
tunes as their **woes**. EG *They listened sympatheti-* Literary
cally to his woes.

woebegone /wəʊbɪgɒn/. Someone who looks or ADJ QUALIT
feels **woebegone** looks or feels very sad. EG *...a* Formal
little woebegone face.

woeful /wəʊfʊl/. 1 Someone or something that is ADJ QUALIT
woeful is very sad. EG *...the lovers' long and woeful
farewell.* ◊ **woefully**. EG *She announced woefully,* ◊ ADV
'I've lost my job.'

2 You also describe something as **woeful** when it ADJ QUALIT
is very bad. EG *His work displays a woeful lack of
imagination.* ◊ **woefully**. EG *The quantities were* ◊ SUBMOD
generally woefully inadequate.

wok /wɒk/, **woks**. A **wok** is a large bowl-shaped N COUNT
pan which is used for Chinese-style cooking.

woke /wəʊk/ is the past tense of **wake.**

woken /wəʊkən/ is the past participle of **wake.**

wolf /wʊlf/, **wolves**; **wolfs**, **wolfing**, **wolfed**.
Wolves /wʊlvz/ is the plural of the noun. **Wolfs** is
the third person singular, present tense, of the
verb.

1 A **wolf** is a wild animal that looks like a large dog N COUNT
and that kills and eats other animals.

2 If you **wolf** food or **wolf** it down, you eat it up V+O :
quickly and greedily. EG *He wolfed the food down,* OFT+down
bones and all. Informal

woman /wʊmən/, **women** /wɪmɪn/. 1 A **woman** N COUNT
is an adult female human being. EG *There were
men and women working in the fields... We had
one woman teacher.*

2 You can refer to women in general as **woman**. EG N UNCOUNT
...*man's inhumanity to woman.*

3 A man's **woman** is his lover or his wife. EG *My* N COUNT
woman took a blanket out of the car. Informal

4 People sometimes address a woman as **'woman'** VOCATIVE
when they are angry or impatient with her. EG *Oh,*
for God's sake, woman, sit down!

5 If two women talk to each other **woman to** PHRASE
woman, they talk honestly and openly, treating
each other as equals.

womanhood /wʊmənhʊd/. **1 Womanhood** is the N UNCOUNT
state of being a woman rather than a girl. EG
...*when a girl is on the threshold of womanhood.*

2 You can refer to women in general as **woman-** N UNCOUNT
hood. You can also refer to the women of a
particular place as its **womanhood**. EG ...*a perfect*
specimen of English womanhood.

womanizer /wʊmənaɪzə/, **womanizers;** also N COUNT
spelled **womaniser.** A **womanizer** is a man who
likes to spend a lot of time in the company of
women, usually in order to have short sexual
relationships with them.

womankind /wʊmənkaɪnd/. You can refer to all N UNCOUNT
women as **womankind** when considering them as Formal
a group. EG *I spoke up on behalf of womankind.*

womanly /wʊmənlɪ¹/. You can describe a wom- ADJ QUALIT
an's behaviour or character as **womanly** when you
think that it is typical of a woman or suitable for a
woman. EG ...*the womanly virtues of gentleness and*
compassion.

womb /wuːm/, **wombs.** A woman's **womb** is the N COUNT
part inside her body where a baby grows before it
is born. EG ...*a baby in his mother's womb.*

women /wɪmɪn/ is the plural of **woman.**

Women's Lib is the same as Women's Liberation. N UNCOUNT
EG ...*a Women's Lib attitude.* Informal

Women's Liberation is the ideal that women N UNCOUNT
should have the same social and economic rights
and privileges as men. EG *I got interested in Wom-*
en's Liberation... ...the local Women's Liberation
Movement.

won /wʌn/ is the past tense and past participle of
win.

wonder /wʌndə/, **wonders, wondering, won-**
dered. 1 If you **wonder** about something you do V+about,
not know or understand, you think about it and try QUOTE,
to guess or understand more about it. EG *I wonder* OR REPORT:
what she'll look like... I keep wondering and worry- ONLY WH
ing about what you said... I am beginning to wonder
why we ever invited them.

2 You can begin a request by saying 'I **wonder** if' V+if/whether
when you are being very polite. EG *I wonder if you'd*
mind closing the window.

3 If you **wonder** at something, you are surprised V+at OR
and amazed about it. EG *I wondered at her* REPORT
strength... I used to wonder at their slowness.

4 If you say that it is a **wonder** that something N SING:
happened, you mean that it is very surprising. EG *It* a+N+that
was a wonder that she managed to come – she's
usually too busy.

5 Wonder is a feeling of surprise and amazement. N UNCOUNT
EG ...*exclamations of wonder.*

6 A **wonder** is something or someone that amazes N COUNT:
people and makes them feel great admiration. EG USU+SUPP
...*the wonders of modern technology.*

7 You can also use **wonder** to describe someone or N MOD
something that is extremely clever or skilful. EG
...*the wonder boy of American racing.*

8 Wonder is used in these phrases. **8.1** If you say CONVENTION
wonders will never cease, you mean that you Informal
are very surprised because something unexpected
has happened. **8.2** If you say **no wonder, little** PHRASE
wonder, or **small wonder**, you mean that you are
not surprised by something that happens. EG *Little*
wonder that today we are in such a mess... 'Any-
way, he didn't win.' - 'No wonder.' **8.3** If you say PHRASE
that something **works wonders** or **does wonders**,
you mean that it has a very good effect. EG *A*
whisky at the end of the day will sometimes work

wonders... The nurses tell me the doctors have
done wonders for your leg.

wonderful /wʌndəful/. If you describe something ADJ QUALIT
as **wonderful, 1** you mean that it makes you feel
very happy and pleased. EG *It was wonderful to be*
able to walk again. **2** you mean that it is very
impressive or successful. EG *I think the heart*
transplant is a wonderful thing.

wonderfully /wʌndəfulɪ¹/. You use **wonderfully**
1 to emphasize that something is much better than SUBMOD
you expected. EG *Both plays are wonderfully fun-*
ny... She was always wonderfully kind to me. **2** to ADV
say that something happens or is done extremely
well. EG *I had slept wonderfully.*

wonderment /wʌndəmə²nt/ is a feeling of amaze- N UNCOUNT
ment and admiration. EG *I stood shaking my head in*
wonderment.

wondrous /wʌndrəs/ means amazing and impres- ADJ QUALIT:
sive. EG *It was a wondrous victory... ...the wondrous* ATTRIB
inventions of the twentieth century. Outdated

wonky /wɒŋkɪ¹/. Something that is **wonky** is ADJ QUALIT
likely to shake or not work properly because it is Informal
unsteady or not in its proper position. EG *The legs* British
have gone a bit wonky.

wont /wəʊnt/. **1** If someone is **wont** to do some- ADJ PRED
thing, they do it regularly as a habit. EG *They were* +to-INF
wont to take long walks in the evening. Outdated

2 If you say that someone does something **as is** PHRASE
their **wont**, you mean that they do it regularly as a Outdated
habit. EG *They were all talking, as is their wont,*
about cars.

won't /wəʊnt/ is the usual spoken form of 'will
not'.

woo /wuː/, **woos, wooing, wooed. 1** If you **woo** V+O
people, you try to encourage them to help you or Literary
support you. EG *She hoped to woo the working-class*
voters of Warrington.

2 When a man **woos** a woman, he tries to make V+O
himself seem attractive to her, because he wants Outdated
to marry her.

wood /wʊd/, **woods. 1 Wood** is the material which N MASS
forms the trunks and branches of trees. EG *We*
gathered wood for the fire.

2 A **wood** is a large area of trees growing near N COUNT
each other. You can refer to a large wood as **the**
woods. EG ...*the big wood where the pheasants*
lived... They walked through the woods.

3 If you say that someone **can't see the wood for** PHRASE
the trees, you mean that they are so involved in
the details of a situation or activity that they forget
or cannot understand its general purpose or importance. ● **touch wood**: see **touch.**

wooded /wʊdɪ¹d/. A **wooded** area is covered in ADJ QUALIT
trees. EG ...*a narrow wooded valley.*

wooden /wʊdə⁰n/. **1** A **wooden** object is made of ADJ CLASSIF
wood. EG ...*a wooden box.*

2 If you say that someone such as an actor is ADJ QUALIT
wooden, you mean that they act without showing
any emotion in their face or movements. EG *His*
performances have become wooden and dull.

woodland /wʊdlə³nd/, **woodlands. Woodland** is N UNCOUNT
land which is mostly covered with trees. EG ...*a* OR N COUNT
patch of woodland in Malaysia.

woodpecker /wʊdpɛkə/, **woodpeckers.** A **wood-** N COUNT
pecker is a bird with a long sharp beak, which
makes holes in tree trunks in order to eat insects.
EG ...*a lesser spotted woodpecker.*

woodwind /wʊdwɪnd/. **Woodwind** instruments ADJ CLASSIF:
are musical instruments such as flutes, oboes, ATTRIB
clarinets, and bassoons, that are played by blowing
into them, usually by members of an orchestra.

woodwork /wʊdwɜːk/. **1** You can refer to the N UNCOUNT
doors, window-frames, and other parts of a house
that are made of wood as the **woodwork**. EG *The*
paint was peeling from the woodwork.

Should actors be word-perfect?

2 Woodwork is also the activity or skill of making things out of wood. N UNCOUNT

woodworm /ˈwʊdwɜːm/, **woodworms**. **Woodworm** is the usual plural form.
1 Woodworm are larvae of a particular type of beetle, which make holes in wood by feeding on it. N COUNT
2 Woodworm is damage caused to wood by woodworm making holes in it. EG *If your house has woodworm, get expert treatment.* N UNCOUNT

woody /ˈwʊdi¹/, **woodier**, **woodiest**. **1 Woody** plants have very hard stems. EG *The roots of woody plants grow deep.* ADJ QUALIT
2 A **woody** area has a lot of trees in it. EG *...a farm set amid woody valleys.* ADJ QUALIT

woof /wʊf/, **woofs**. A **woof** is the sound that a dog makes when it barks. N COUNT Informal

wool /wʊl/, **wools**. **1 Wool** is the hair that grows on sheep and on some other animals. N MASS
2 Wool is also a material made from animals' wool. It is used for making things such as clothes, blankets, and carpets. EG *...a hat made of wool.* N MASS
3 If you **pull the wool over** someone's **eyes**, you deliberately tell them something that is not true in order to have an advantage over them. PHRASE Informal
4 See also **cotton wool**, **steel wool**, **wire wool**.

woollen /ˈwʊlən/; spelled **woolen** in American English. **1 Woollen** clothes or materials are made from wool or from a mixture of wool and artificial fibres. EG *...woollen rugs... ...a woollen scarf... ...long woollen socks.* ADJ CLASSIF: ATTRIB
2 Woollens are clothes made of wool. EG *...a good fabric softener for woollens.* N PLURAL

woolly /ˈwʊli¹/, **woollies**; **woollier**, **woolliest**; spelled **wooly** in American English. **1** Something that is **woolly** is made of wool or looks like wool. EG *...a woolly cap.* ADJ CLASSIF
2 A **woolly** is a woollen piece of clothing, especially a pullover. EG *She wore a long woolly with a belt.* N COUNT Informal
3 If you describe people or their ideas as **woolly**, you mean that their ideas are very unclear. EG *They cannot afford to be vague and woolly.* ADJ QUALIT

woozy /ˈwuːzi¹/, **woozier**, **wooziest**. If you feel **woozy**, you feel rather weak and unsteady and cannot think clearly. EG *I smiled uncertainly, feeling woozy from the whisky.* ADJ QUALIT Informal

word /wɜːd/, **words**, **wording**, **worded**. **1** A **word** is a single unit of language that can be represented in writing or speech. In English, a word has a space on either side of it when it is written. A word can usually have one or more meanings. EG *...a short passage of about seventy words... His eye had been caught by the word 'scandal' in the headline... He was, in the words of his doctor, making satisfactory progress.* N COUNT
2 If you have a **word** or a few **words** with someone, you have a short conversation with them. EG *May I have a word with you please?* N COUNT : a+N Informal
3 A **word** of advice or warning is a short piece of advice or warning. N SING : a+N
4 If you say that you cannot hear, understand, or believe a **word** of what someone is saying, you mean that you cannot hear, understand, or believe what they are saying at all. EG *I did not understand one word of what she'd said... Have you heard a word I've said?* N SING : a+N, USU WITH BROAD NEG
5 You can use **word** to mean a message. EG *The young man brought them word of her visit... The word got out that he was leaving.* N UNCOUNT OR N SING
6 Your **word** is a sincere promise that you make to someone. EG *I give you my word I won't ask him... I apologized for having doubted his word.* N SING+POSS
7 If you give the **word** to do something, you give an order to do it. EG *The light was improving as he gave the word to move.* N SING : the+N
8 When you **word** something in a particular way, you carefully choose the words that you use in order to express your ideas in an accurate or acceptable way. EG *How would one word such an announcement?* ◊ **worded**. EG *He wrote a strongly* ◊ ADJ CLASSIF : ADV+ADJ V+O

worded report to the Secretary of the Interior... ...one of the most sharply worded attacks on EEC ministers.
9 Word is used in these phrases. **9.1** If you repeat something **word for word**, you repeat it exactly as it was originally said or written. EG *We had a long chat and he printed it more or less word for word.* PHRASES
9.2 A **word for word** translation is done by translating each word separately rather than by giving the general meaning of a group of words. **9.3** If you have **the last word** in an argument, you make the comment that finishes it and often makes the other person feel that they have been defeated. EG *Doctors always have the last word.* **9.4** If news or information passes **by word of mouth**, people tell it to each other rather than writing it down. **9.5** If you **put in a word** for someone or **put in a good word** for them, you speak favourably about them to a person who has influence. EG *I put in a word for her and she was forgiven.* **9.6** If someone **says the word**, they give their approval that something should start to happen. EG *You only have to say the word and they will do it.* **9.7** If you say to someone **'take my word for it'**, you mean that they should believe you because you are telling the truth. EG *You can take my word for it, she's not there.* **9.8** You say **in a word** to indicate that you are summarizing what you have just been saying. EG *The house is roomy, cool in summer, and in a word comfortable.* **9.9** to **not get a word in edgeways**: see **edgeways**. See also **four-letter word**.
10 The plural form **words** is used in these phrases. **10.1** If you **have words with** someone, you have an argument with them. **10.2** You say **in other words** when introducing a simpler or clearer explanation of something that has just been said. EG *Is there a cheaper solution? In other words, can you make a cheaper device?* **10.3** If you say something **in your own words**, you say it in your own way, without copying or repeating what someone else has said. EG *He was asked to tell the story in his own words.* **10.4** If you say that someone said something **in so many words**, you mean that they said it clearly and directly. If you say that they said it **not in so many words**, you mean that they expressed it in an indirect way. EG *This is what he claims, only he does not state it in so many words.* **10.5** You can use the expression **for words** when you are emphasizing a quality that someone or something has. For example, if you say that someone is too stupid **for words**, you mean that they are very stupid indeed. **10.6** to **not mince** your **words**: see **mince**. PHRASES Informal

wording /ˈwɜːdɪŋ/. The **wording** of a piece of writing or a speech is the words used in it, especially when these words have been chosen to have a particular effect. EG *For a full hour he argued over the wording of the editorial.* N UNCOUNT

word-perfect. If you are **word-perfect**, you are able to repeat from memory the exact words of something that you have learned. ADJ CLASSIF

word-play /ˈwɜːdpleɪ/. **Word-play** involves making jokes by using the meanings of words in an amusing or clever way. EG *...a fondness for word-play.* N UNCOUNT

word processing is the work of producing documents, letters, and other printed material using a word processor. N UNCOUNT

word processor, **word processors**. A **word processor** is an electronic machine which has a keyboard and a screen like a computer terminal, but which is used as a typewriter to produce documents, letters, and other printed material. N COUNT

wordy /ˈwɜːdi¹/, **wordier**, **wordiest**. Something that is **wordy** uses too many words, especially long or formal words. EG *...this very wordy book on biology... ...wordy writers.* ADJ QUALIT

wore /wɔː/ is the past tense of **wear**.

work /wɜːk/, **works, working, worked.** 1 People v:OFT+A
who **work** have a job which they are paid to do. EG
*He was working in a bank... Large numbers of
them now work as labourers... Some of my salesmen formerly worked for a rival firm.*

2 People who have **work** or who are in **work** have N UNCOUNT
a job which they are paid to do. EG *...people who
can't find work... ...the numbers out of work.*

3 When you **work**, 3.1 you do the tasks which your v:OFT+A
job involves. EG *I watched the people working at* OR V+O
the weaving looms... I used to work a ten-hour day.
3.2 you do a task that needs to be done or make an v:OFT+A
effort to achieve something. EG *All through the
winter, the Kirks worked on their house... She
works hard at keeping herself fit... He has been
working all season on his game... They work for
international peace.*

4 **Work** is also 4.1 the tasks which your job N UNCOUNT
involves. EG *I've got some work to do... I finish work
at 3.* 4.2 tasks which you do because they need to
be done. EG *A housewife's work can take ten or
twelve hours a day.* 4.3 something which you
produce as a result of an activity or as a result of
doing your job. EG *It is standard practice to put
remarks on their work... That's an absolutely fascinating piece of work.* 4.4 research on a particular
subject. EG *There has been considerable work done
in America on this subject.*

5 If you **work** someone hard, you make them work v+o+A
hard. EG *I was worked mercilessly.*

6 If you **work** the land, you cultivate it. EG *...peas-* v+o
ants working the land.

7 If you **work** a machine or piece of equipment, v+o
you use it or control it. EG *...the boy who worked the
milking machine.*

8 If a machine or piece of equipment **works**, it v
operates and performs its function. EG *The traffic
lights weren't working properly.*

9 If something such as an idea, method, or system v
works, it is successful. EG *That kind of democracy
will never work.*

10 If something **works** against you, it causes v+A
problems for you. If something **works** in your
favour, it helps you in some way. EG *The apathy of
the opposition is working in his favour.*

11 If you **work** on an assumption or idea, you make v+on
decisions relying on your belief that it is correct. EG
*Mr Reagan said he was working on the assumption
that formal negotiations would take place shortly.*

12 If something **works** into a particular position, it v+A OR V+C
gradually moves so that it is in that position. EG *The
ropes had worked loose.*

13 If you **work** yourself into a state of being very v-REFL+into
upset or angry, you make yourself become very
upset or angry. EG *She worked herself into a rage.*

14 If you **work** your way somewhere, you move or v+o+A
progress there slowly and with a lot of effort. EG *I
worked my way slowly out of the marsh.*

15 A **work** is something such as a painting, book, N COUNT+SUPP
or piece of music, produced by an artist, writer, or
composer. EG *...a large volume containing all of
Chopin's works... ...the collected works of Proust.*

16 A **works** is a place where something is made or N COLL
where an industrial process is carried out. EG *...the
metal works... ...the gas works.*

17 **Works** consist of large-scale digging or building, N PLURAL:
for example in order to install pipes, or to con- USU+SUPP
struct roads or bridges. EG *He was in charge of
planning the great plumbing and civic engineering
works of the city.*

18 **Work** is used in these phrases. 18.1 If someone PHRASES
is **at work**, they are doing their job or are busy
doing a particular task. EG *Aren't you supposed to
be at work?... Computers will be hard at work on
these problems.* 18.2 If you **go to work**, **set to
work**, or **get to work**, you start doing a particular
task. EG *Smithy set to work on the gardening.* 18.3 If
you say that you will **have** your **work cut out** to
do something, you mean that it will be very diffi-

cult for you to do it. EG *We'll have our work cut out
to finish on time.* 18.4 If a group of workers **work** British
to rule as a protest, they stop doing extra work
and just do the minimum that they are required to
do in their job. EG *The delivery men are working to
rule.* ● See also **work-to-rule.** 18.5 See also **social
work, working.**

work off. If you **work off** a feeling such as anger, PHRASAL VB:
you gradually overcome it by doing something V+O+ADV
energetic or violent.

work out. 1 If you **work out** a solution to a PHRASAL VB:
problem or mystery, you think about it and man- V+O+ADV OR
age to solve it or understand it. EG *We are always* V+ADV
hoping that a more peaceful solution can be +REPORT
*worked out... He couldn't work out why the room
seemed so strange.* 2 If you **work out** the answer v+o+ADV
to a mathematical problem, you calculate it. EG
Now you can work out the area of the triangle. 3 If v+ADV, USU+A
something **works out** at a particular amount, it is
found to be that amount when the necessary calculations have been made. EG *Petrol prices here are
among the cheapest in Europe, working out at
around £1.15 a gallon.* 4 If a situation **works out** in v+ADV, USU+A
a particular way, it happens or progresses in that
way. EG *It's funny how life worked out... Things
worked out well with Marian.* 5 If you **work out**, v+ADV
you do physical exercises in order to make your
body fit and strong. EG *She worked out in a ballet
class three hours a week.* 6 See also **workout.**

work up. 1 If you **work** yourself **up** into a state of PHRASAL VB:
being very upset or angry, you make yourself V-REFL+ADV
become very upset or angry. EG *He worked himself
up into a frenzy.* ● See also **worked up.** 2 If you v+o+ADV
work up a feeling, you make yourself start to have
it. EG *I can hardly work up enough energy to go to
the shops.* 3 If you **work up** to something impor- v+ADV+to
tant or difficult, you gradually progress towards it.
EG *Start slowly and work up to a faster time.*

workable /ˈwɜːkəbəl/. Something that is **work-** ADJ QUALIT
able can operate efficiently or can be used for a
particular purpose. EG *This doesn't seem to me to
be a workable system.*

workaholic /ˌwɜːkəˈhɒlɪk/, **workaholics.** If you N COUNT
say that someone is a **workaholic**, you mean that
they find it difficult to stop working in order to do
other things.

workbench /ˈwɜːkbentʃ/, **workbenches.** A N COUNT
workbench is a heavy wooden table on which
people use tools to make or repair things.

workbook /ˈwɜːkbʊk/, **workbooks.** A **workbook** N COUNT
is an exercise book or textbook that is used for
study, especially a book with questions in it and
spaces for you to fill in the answers.

workday /ˈwɜːkdeɪ/, **workdays.** A **workday** is 1 N COUNT
the amount of time during a day which you spend
doing your job. EG *I have a 9-to-5 workday.* 2 a day
on which people go to work.

worked up. If you are **worked up** about some- ADJ PRED
thing, you are very upset or angry about it. EG *Why
are you so worked up over that editorial?*

worker /ˈwɜːkə/, **workers.** 1 A **worker** is a person N COUNT
who is employed in an industry or business by
another person or by an organization, and who has
no responsibility for managing the industry or
business. EG *The dispute affected relations between
management and workers.*

2 You can use **worker** to say how well or badly N COUNT+SUPP
someone works. For example, a good **worker** is
someone who works well. EG *My husband was a
hard worker... You're a fast worker.*

3 A **worker** is also someone who does a particular N COUNT:
kind of job. EG *...a series of experiments by Ameri-* USU+SUPP
can research workers... ...charity workers. ● See
also **social worker.**

What are all the workers in a company called?

workforce /wɜːkfɔːs/. You can refer to all the N SING+SUPP people who work in a particular industry, company, or country as the **workforce**. EG *Asia's workforce will expand by 60 per cent... They agreed to reduce the workforce by 350.*

working /wɜːkɪŋ/, **workings. 1 Working** people ADJ CLASSIF have jobs which they are paid to do. EG *...children ATTRIB with working mothers.*

2 Your **working** day or week is the number of ADJ CLASSIF: hours that you work during a day or a week. EG *The ATTRIB unions will demand a reduction in working hours.*

3 Your **working** life is the period of your life in ADJ CLASSIF: which you have a job or you are of a suitable age to ATTRIB have a job. EG *Most of these people spend their entire working lives at General Motors.*

4 Working conditions or practices are ones which ADJ CLASSIF: you have in your job. EG *We want to achieve better ATTRIB working conditions for all women.*

5 Working clothes are designed for doing work in ADJ CLASSIF: and so are not intended to be attractive. EG *I didn't ATTRIB bring any working clothes.*

6 If you have a **working** knowledge of something ADJ CLASSIF: such as a foreign language, you do not know it very ATTRIB well but you know it well enough to be able to use it. EG *In the first week I picked up a tolerable working knowledge of Spanish.*

7 The **workings** of a piece of equipment, an N PLURAL organization, or a system are the ways in which it +SUPP operates and the processes which are involved in it. EG *The general workings of a Wall Street bank are discussed in the programme.*

8 in working order: see **order**.

working class, working classes. The **working** N COUNT **class** or **working classes** are the group of people in a society who do not own much property and who do jobs which involve using physical skills rather than intellectual skills. EG *...the urban working class... Eleven members were of working-class origins.*

workload /wɜːkləʊd/, **workloads.** Your **workload** N COUNT+SUPP is the amount of work that you have to do. EG *I have a terrible workload this year.*

workman /wɜːkmən/, **workmen.** A **workman** is N COUNT a man whose job involves doing work with his hands, for example building houses or plumbing. EG *The workmen arrived and put up a fence.*

workmanlike /wɜːkmənlaɪk/. A piece of work ADJ QUALIT that is **workmanlike** has been done well and skilfully.

workmanship /wɜːkmənʃɪp/ is the skill with N UNCOUNT which something is made. EG *...good materials and sound workmanship.*

work of art, works of art. 1 A **work of art** is a N COUNT painting or a piece of sculpture which is of high quality. EG *Some of the world's greatest works of art are on display here.*

2 You can refer to something that has been skilful- N COUNT ly produced and that is often very complex as a **work of art**. EG *His own papers were works of art on which he laboured with loving care.*

workout /wɜːkaʊt/, **workouts.** A **workout** is a N COUNT period of physical exercise or training. EG *They all had a good workout before lunch.*

workshop /wɜːkʃɒp/, **workshops. 1** A **workshop** N COUNT is a room or building that contains tools or machinery for making or repairing things. EG *...a small engineering workshop.*

2 A **workshop** on a particular subject is a period of N COUNT discussion or practical work in which a group of people learn about the subject by sharing their knowledge or experience. EG *...a theatre workshop... ...a workshop on child care.*

work-shy. If you say that someone is **work-shy**, ADJ QUALIT you mean that they do not want to have a job or they do not put any effort into their job.

work surface, work surfaces. A **work surface** N COUNT is the same as a worktop.

worktop /wɜːktɒp/, **worktops.** A **worktop** is a N COUNT flat surface on top of a fridge or low cupboard, on which you can prepare food.

work-to-rule. A **work-to-rule** is a protest by N SING workers in which they stop doing extra work and British just do the minimum that they are required to do in their job.

world /wɜːld/, **worlds. 1** The **world** is the planet N SING: the+N that we live on. EG *He attempted to sail round the world... ...one of the most famous artists in the world... ...the growth in world population.*

2 The **world** also refers to all the societies, institu- N SING+SUPP tions, and ways of life of people living on this planet. EG *We are now moving into a world which will be more and more dominated by energy crises.*

3 World is used to describe someone or something N MOD that is one of the best or most important of its kind in the world. EG *He argued that Britain was still a world power... This book is a world classic.*

4 Someone's **world** is the life they lead, the people N COUNT+SUPP they have contact with, and the things they experience. EG *Look, Howard, we're in different worlds now... They were letting me into their world.*

5 A particular **world** is a particular field of activ- N COUNT+SUPP ity, and the people involved in it. EG *They are well-known names in the film world... ...the world of art.*

6 You can refer to the state of being alive as this N SING: **world** and to a state of existence after death as the USU+SUPP next **world** or the **world** to come. EG *...the vision that people hold of the world to come.*

7 You can refer to a particular group of living N COUNT things such as the animal **world**, the plant **world**, or the +SUPP: insect **world**. USU the+N

8 A **world** is another planet. EG *...an alien world.* N COUNT

9 World is also used in these phrases. **9.1** You can PHRASES use **in the world** to emphasize what you are saying. EG *To them housework was the most important activity in the world... What in the world are you doing here?* **9.2 The world over** means everywhere, throughout the world. EG *Journalists the world over speculated on the assassination attempt.* **9.3** If you say that someone has or wants **the best of both worlds,** you mean that they have or want all the benefits from two different situations, without the disadvantages. **9.4** If you **think the world of** someone or something, you like or admire them very much. EG *They thought the world of Sam.* **9.5** If you say that something **does** some- Informal one **the world of good,** you mean that it makes them feel much better. EG *A bit of fresh air will do you the world of good.* **9.6** If you say that **there is a world of difference** between one thing and another, you mean that they are very different from each other.

world-class. Someone, especially a sports player, ADJ CLASSIF who is **world-class** is one of the best in the world at what they do. EG *...a world-class cricketer.*

world-famous. Someone or something that is ADJ CLASSIF **world-famous** is known about by people all over the world. EG *...a world-famous physicist.*

worldly /wɜːldliˈ/. **1 Worldly** is used to describe ADJ CLASSIF: things relating to the ordinary activities of life, USU ATTRIB rather than to spiritual things. EG *...worldly thoughts... Coleridge had experienced a conversion and put aside worldly things.*

2 You can refer to someone's possessions as their ADJ CLASSIF: **worldly** goods or possessions. EG *He made a will ATTRIB leaving all his worldly goods to his daughter.* Literary

3 Someone who is **worldly** is experienced, practi- ADJ QUALIT cal, and knowledgeable about life. EG *She was surprised at their educated, even worldly manner.*

worldly-wise. Someone who is **worldly-wise** is ADJ QUALIT experienced and knowledgeable about life, and is Literary not often shocked or impressed by anything.

world war, world wars. A **world war** is a war N COUNT OR that involves countries all over the world. EG *...the N UNCOUNT First World War.*

worldwide /wɜːldwaɪd/ means happening throughout the world. EG ...in 1930, during the world-wide economic depression... This move made headlines worldwide last year. ADJ CLASSIF OR ADV

worm /wɜːm/, **worms, worming, wormed. 1** A **worm** is a small animal with a long thin body, no bones, and no legs, which lives in the soil. N COUNT

2 If animals or people have **worms**, they have worms living as parasites in their intestines. These worms often enter their body when they eat food that is not clean, and may cause disease. EG He wiggled about like a dog with worms. N PLURAL

3 If you **worm** your **way** somewhere, you move there slowly and carefully or with difficulty. EG He wormed his way forward. PHRASE

4 If you **worm** your **way** into someone's confidence or affection, you gradually make them trust you or like you, often in order to gain some advantage. EG These aliens could worm their way into French society. PHRASE

worm out. If you **worm** information **out** of someone, you gradually find it out from them when they were trying to keep it secret. EG The truth had been wormed out of him by his lawyers. PHRASAL VB : V+O+ADV, USU+of

worm-eaten. Something that is **worm-eaten** has been damaged by insects which have made holes in it. EG ...an old, worm-eaten piece of furniture. ADJ QUALIT

worn /wɔːn/. **1 Worn** is the past participle of **wear**.

2 Something that is **worn** is damaged or thin because it is old and has been used a lot. EG ...the worn carpet... ...his worn suit. ADJ QUALIT

3 Someone who is **worn** looks old and tired, for example because of hard work or illness. ADJ QUALIT

worn-out. 1 Something that is **worn-out** is so old, damaged, or thin from use that it cannot be used any more. EG ...a worn-out sofa. ADJ CLASSIF

2 If you are **worn-out**, you are extremely tired. ADJ QUALIT

worried /wʌrɪd/. If you are **worried**, you are unhappy because you keep thinking about a problem or about something unpleasant that might happen. EG People are becoming increasingly worried about pollution... I was worried that she'd say no... He was worried about the danger of them falling. ADJ QUALIT

worrier /wʌrɪə/, **worriers.** Someone who is a **worrier** spends a lot of time thinking about problems or about unpleasant things that might happen. EG He was a worrier by nature. N COUNT

worry /wʌri/, **worries, worrying, worried. 1** If you **worry**, you keep thinking about a problem or about something unpleasant that might happen. EG Don't worry, Andrew, you can do it... People worry about the safety of nuclear energy... I worried that when I got back he wouldn't be there. V : OFT+about OR REPORT : ONLY that

2 If someone or something **worries** you, they cause you to worry. EG Terry was worried by the challenge... I'm sorry if I worried you... It worried him to think that Sylvie was alone. V+O

3 If you **worry** someone with a problem, you tell them about it in order to get their help or advice, often causing them trouble or irritation. EG Why worry her when it's all over? V+O

4 Worry is a feeling of anxiety and unhappiness caused by a problem that you have or by thinking about something unpleasant that might happen. EG She would be free from all financial worry... Bad housing is their main source of worry. N UNCOUNT

5 A **worry** is a problem that you keep thinking about and that makes you unhappy. EG My only worry was that my aunt would be upset... I don't have any worries. N COUNT

6 You say **'Not to worry'** to someone to indicate that you are not upset or angry when something has gone wrong. EG Not to worry. We'll find something. CONVENTION Informal

worrying /wʌriɪŋ/. Something that is **worrying** causes you a lot of worry. EG ...a very worrying situation... She asked me a worrying question. ADJ QUALIT

worse /wɜːs/. **1 Worse** is **1.1** the comparative of **bad**. EG I have even worse news for you... The noise is getting worse... Her marks are getting worse and worse. **1.2** the comparative of **badly**. EG Some people ski worse than others. ADJ QUALIT : COMPAR; ADV : COMPAR

2 If someone who is ill gets **worse**, they become more ill than before. EG You'll get worse if you don't take this medicine. ADJ QUALIT : COMPAR

3 If someone or something is **none the worse** for something, they have not been harmed by it. EG The children had gone to bed very late but they were none the worse for it. PHRASE

4 If something happens **for the worse**, the situation becomes more unpleasant or more difficult as a result. EG There were constant changes, usually for the worse. PHRASE

5 to **go from bad to worse**: see **bad**.

worsen /wɜːsən/, **worsens, worsening, worsened.** If a situation **worsens** or if something **worsens** it, it becomes more difficult, unpleasant, or unacceptable. EG Economic sanctions would only worsen the situation... The weather steadily worsened... Oil pollution seems to be worsening. V-ERG

worse off. 1 Someone who is **worse off** has less money than before or less than someone else. EG This budget would leave taxpayers far worse off... There are lots of people worse off than us. ADJ PRED : COMPAR

2 Someone or something that is **worse off** is in a more unpleasant situation than before or than someone else. EG You believe the world to be worse off because of Kennedy's death. ADJ PRED : COMPAR

worship /wɜːʃɪp/, **worships, worshipping, worshipped;** spelled **worshiping, worshiped** in American English.

1 If you **worship** a god, you show your respect to the god, for example by saying prayers. EG I knelt down and worshipped the Lord. ► used as a noun. EG ...places of worship. V+O OR V; N UNCOUNT

2 If you **worship** someone or something, you love or admire them very much. EG Vita worshipped her father. ► used as a noun. EG She became an object of worship. V+O; N UNCOUNT

3 Your Worship and **His Worship** are respectful ways of addressing or referring to a magistrate or a mayor. British

worshipper /wɜːʃɪpə/, **worshippers;** spelled **worshiper** in American English.

1 A **worshipper** is someone who believes in and worships a god. EG ...shoes left there by worshippers who had gone into the mosque. N COUNT

2 If you are a **worshipper** of someone or something, you love or admire them very much. EG ...a worshipper of the past. N COUNT+SUPP

worst /wɜːst/. **1 Worst** is **1.1** the superlative of **bad**. EG ...the worst thing which ever happened to me... The worst is over. **1.2** the superlative of **badly**. EG ...the worst affected areas. ADJ QUALIT : SUPERL; ADV SUPERL

2 You use **at worst** to indicate that you are considering a situation in the most unfavourable or most pessimistic way. EG At worst they are looked upon as an irritation... He was described as forceful at best, ruthless at worst. PHRASE

3 If you say that something might happen **if the worst comes to the worst**, you mean that it might happen if the situation develops in the most unfavourable way. EG If the worst comes to the worst we'll have to sell the house. PHRASE

worth /wɜːθ/. **1** If something is **worth** a particular amount of money, it can be sold for that amount or is considered to have that value in terms of money. EG ...a two-bedroom house worth 50,000 pounds. PREP

2 If you talk about a particular amount of money's **worth** of something, you mean the quantity of it that you can buy for that amount of money. EG They stole fifty thousand dollars' worth of equipment. N UNCOUNT

If you are a would-be actor, are you a real actor?

3 You can use **worth** when you are saying how N UNCOUNT long something will last. For example, a week's **worth** of food is the amount of food that will last you for a week.

4 If you say that something is **worth** doing, **worth** PREP OR having, or **worth it**, you mean that it is enjoyable PHRASE or useful, and therefore a good thing to do or have. EG *This film's really worth seeing... The building is well worth a visit... They're expensive, but they're worth it.*

5 If you add **for what it's worth** to something that PHRASE you say, you mean that you do not think that what you are saying is very valuable or helpful. EG *I've brought my notes, for what it's worth.*

6 If an action or activity is **worth** someone's PHRASE **while**, it will be helpful or useful to them if they do it. EG *It will be well worth your while to track down these treasures.*

7 Someone's **worth** is the value, usefulness, or N UNCOUNT importance that they are considered to have. EG OR ADJ PRED *This job has robbed me of all worth... No man can* Formal *say what another man is worth.*

worthless /wɜːθlɪs/. **1** Something that is **worth-** ADJ CLASSIF **less** is of no real value or use. EG *The goods are often worthless by the time they arrive... This made the treaty worthless.*

2 Someone who is described as **worthless** is ADJ CLASSIF considered to lack the qualities or skills that they should have. EG *His brother is a worthless fool.*

worthwhile /wɜːθwaɪl/. If something is **worth-** ADJ QUALIT **while**, it is enjoyable or useful, and worth the time, money, or effort that is spent on it. EG *A visit to London will always be worthwhile.*

worthy /wɜːðɪ/, **worthier, worthiest. 1** If some- ADJ QUALIT : one or something is **worthy** of something, they OFT+*of* deserve it because they have the qualities or Formal abilities required. EG *Their cause is worthy of our continued support... He was a worthy winner.*

2 A **worthy** person or thing deserves people's ADJ QUALIT respect or admiration. EG *...our worthy command-* Literary *ing officer.*

would /wəd/. **Would** is sometimes considered to be the past form of **will**, but in this dictionary the two words are dealt with separately.

1 If someone said or thought that something **would** MODAL happen, they said or thought that it was going to happen. EG *I felt confident that everything would be all right... He made me promise that I would never break the law.*

2 You say what **would** happen when you are MODAL referring to the result or effect of a possible situation. EG *If you can help me I would be very grateful... Without them life would not be the same.*

3 If you say that you **would** do something, you MODAL mean that you are willing to do it. EG *Some men would do more for a dog than they would for a wife.*

4 If you say that someone **would** not do something, MODAL : WITH you mean that they refused to do it. EG *Though we* BROAD NEG *were as rude as possible, she wouldn't go... He would not give up.*

5 If you say that you **would** like to do or have MODAL something, you mean that you want to do it or have it. EG *Posy said she'd love to stay... Would you like a drink?*

6 You use **would** in questions when you are MODAL politely asking someone to do something. EG *Would you tell her that Adrian phoned?... Put the light on, Bryan, would you?*

7 If you say that someone **would** do something, you MODAL mean that it is typical of them. EG *'Of course you would say that,' says Miss Callendar... 'He's backed out of it.' – 'He would.'*

8 You use **would** or **would have** when you are MODAL expressing your opinion about something. EG *I would think that in our climate we might have a few problems... I would have thought that his chief asset was his enthusiasm.*

9 You use **would** or **would have** when you are MODAL

saying something that you are assuming is true or was true. EG *We had a discussion on jazz, but you wouldn't remember that... She wouldn't have noticed. She was too far away.*

10 You use **I would** when you are giving someone PHRASE advice. EG *I would have a word with him about it... I* Informal *wouldn't worry too much, if I were you.*

11 If you say that you **wouldn't** know or guess PHRASE something, you mean that it is not at all obvious. EG *You wouldn't guess that from the film.*

12 If you say that someone **would** do something, MODAL you mean that they often used to do it. EG *I used to meet her and she would say 'Can't stop. I must get home.'... In the intervals she would talk to me.*

13 If you talk about what **would have** happened if MODAL a possible event had occurred, you are talking about the result or effect of that event. EG *If the bosses had known that he voted Liberal, he would have got the sack.*

14 If you say that someone **would have** liked or MODAL preferred something, you mean that they wanted to do it or have it but were unable to. EG *I would have liked a year more.*

would-be. You use **would-be** to describe what ADJ CLASSIF : someone wants to do or become. For example, if ATTRIB you say that someone is a **would-be** writer, you mean that they want to become a writer.

wouldn't /wʊdənt/ is the usual spoken form of 'would not'. EG *It wouldn't be safe... You'd like to see this, wouldn't you?*

would've /wʊdəv/ is a spoken form of 'would have', especially when 'have' is an auxiliary verb. EG *It would've meant leaving home.*

wound /wuːnd/, **wounds, wounding, wounded. 1** N COUNT A **wound** is damage to part of your body, especially a cut in your flesh, which is caused by a gun, knife, or other weapon. EG *He died from his wounds nine days after the shooting... The wound on his face was burning.*

2 If someone **wounds** you, they damage your body V+O : USU PASS using a gun, knife, or other weapon. EG *He had been badly wounded in the fighting.*

3 If you **are wounded** by what someone says or V+O : USU PASS does, your feelings are deeply hurt. EG *She had been* Literary *grievously wounded by his words.*

4 Wound is also a past tense and past participle of **wind**. In this sense it is pronounced /waʊnd/.

wove /wəʊv/ is the past tense of **weave**.

woven /wəʊvən/ is the past participle of **weave**.

wow /waʊ/. You can say **'wow'** when you are very EXCLAM impressed by something or very pleased about Informal something.

WPC /dʌbəljuː piː siː/, **WPCs.** A **WPC** is a female N COUNT police officer of the lowest rank in Britain. **WPC** is an abbreviation for 'woman police constable'. EG *I was put into the car with a WPC. ...WPC Morris.*

wrack /ræk/. See **rack**.

wrangle /ræŋgəl/, **wrangles, wrangling, wran-** V OR V+*with/* **gled.** If you **wrangle** with someone, you argue *over* : RECIP with them angrily, often about something unimportant. EG *They wrangled over what to do next.*

▸ used as a noun. EG *We avoided wrangles and got* ▸ N COUNT *down to business.*

wrap /ræp/, **wraps, wrapping, wrapped. 1** If you V+O : OFT+*in* **wrap** something, you fold a piece of paper or cloth tightly round it so that it is covered. EG *I wrapped the ring in my handkerchief... The book was wrapped in brown paper.*

2 If you **wrap** a piece of paper or cloth round V+O+*round/* something, you put it round it. EG *Wrap a cloth* around *round the tap... A handkerchief was wrapped around his left hand.*

3 If you **wrap** your arms or fingers around some- V+O+*round/* thing, you put them tightly around it. EG *He* around *wrapped his arms around me.*

4 See also **wrapping.**

wrap up. 1 If you **wrap** something **up**, you fold a PHRASAL VB : piece of paper or cloth tightly around it so that it is V+O+ADV covered. EG *Could you wrap the vase up?... ...a little* *box wrapped up in white paper.* **2** If you **wrap up,** V+ADV you put warm clothes on. EG *Wrap up well. It's a cold night tonight... I told her to wrap up warmly.* **3** V+O+ADV If you **wrap up** something such as a job or an Informal agreement, you complete it in a satisfactory way.

wrapped up. If you are **wrapped up** in a person ADJ PRED+*in* or thing, you spend most of your time thinking Informal about that person or thing. EG *He was always wrapped up in his work... All the household are completely wrapped up in the baby.*

wrapper /ræpə/, **wrappers.** A **wrapper** is a N COUNT piece of paper, plastic, or foil which covers and protects something that you buy. EG *...the rustle of chocolate wrappers.*

wrapping /ræpɪŋ/, **wrappings.** A **wrapping** is a N COUNT OR piece of paper or plastic which is used to cover and N UNCOUNT protect something. EG *He picked up the bottle and tore off its paper wrapping.*

wrapping paper is special pretty paper which is N UNCOUNT used for wrapping presents.

wrath /rɒθ/ is very great anger. EG *I wanted* N UNCOUNT *someone to protect me from the wrath of Miss* Literary *Templeman.*

wreak /riːk/, **wreaks, wreaking, wreaked. 1** If V+O:OFT+A something **wreaks** havoc or damage, it causes it. Formal EG *These chemicals can wreak havoc on crops.*

2 If you **wreak** revenge or vengeance on someone, V+O:OFT+A you do something that will harm them, because Literary you feel angry about the harm that they have done to you.

wreath /riːθ/, **wreaths.** A **wreath** is an arrange- N COUNT ment of flowers and leaves, usually in the shape of a circle, which is put onto a grave as a sign of remembrance for the dead person.

wreathed /riːðd/. If something is **wreathed** in ADJ PRED something else, it is surrounded by it. EG *The sun* +*in/with* *was wreathed in mist... Colonel Burr sat wreathed* Literary *in smoke.*

wreck /rek/, **wrecks, wrecking, wrecked. 1** If someone **wrecks** something, **1.1** they break it or V+O destroy it completely. EG *I wrecked a good stereo by not following the instructions properly.* ◊ **wrecked.** EG *Piles of wrecked cars took up most* ◊ ADJ CLASSIF *of the space.* **1.2** they spoil it completely. EG *I'm* V+O *sorry if I wrecked your weekend.* Informal

2 If a ship **is wrecked,** it is damaged so much that V+O:USU PASS it sinks or it can no longer sail, for example when it hits rocks. EG *...Spanish vessels that had been wrecked off the North American coast.*

3 A **wreck** is **3.1** a plane, car, or other vehicle N COUNT which has been very badly damaged in an acci- dent. EG *All around were the wrecks of previous crashes.* **3.2** a ship which has sunk or been de- stroyed at sea. EG *The seabed where the wreck lies is level and rocky.*

4 If you say that someone is a **wreck,** you mean N COUNT: that they are very unhealthy or exhausted. EG *If you* USU SING *work like this you'll end up a wreck.* ● See also Informal **nervous wreck.**

wreckage /rekɪdʒ/. When a plane, car, or build- N UNCOUNT ing has been very badly damaged, you can refer to what remains as **wreckage.** EG *Experts arrived to examine the wreckage of a cargo plane.*

wren /ren/, **wrens.** A **wren** is a type of very small N COUNT brown bird.

wrench /rentʃ/, **wrenches, wrenching, wrenched. 1** If you **wrench** something into a V+O+A particular position, you pull it or twist it violently, OR V+O+C especially in order to move it from a fixed or firm position. EG *He was trying to wrench my button off... I wrenched the door open.*

2 If you **wrench** your arm or leg, or one of your V+O joints, you twist it and injure it.

3 If you **wrench** your eyes or your mind away V+O+A from something, you make a great effort to stop looking at it or thinking about it. EG *I tried to wrench my gaze away from the appalling sight.*

4 A **wrench** is a metal tool with parts which can be N COUNT adjusted to fit round nuts or bolts of various sizes,

so that the nut or bolt can be loosened or tightened. See picture at TOOLS.

5 If you feel that leaving someone or something is N SING:*a*+N a **wrench,** you feel very sad about it. EG *It was a wrench when the time came for me to go to boarding school.*

wrest /rest/, **wrests, wresting, wrested.** If you V+O+A **wrest** something away from someone who is hold- Literary ing it, you take it from them by pulling it violently. EG *He wrested the knife from her.*

wrestle /resəl/, **wrestles, wrestling, wrestled.**

1 If you **wrestle** with someone, you fight them by V OR V+*with*: forcing them into painful positions or throwing RECIP; them to the ground, rather than by hitting them. ALSO V+O Some people wrestle as a sport. EG *John wrestled with the intruder.* ● See also **wrestling.**

2 When you **wrestle** with a problem, you try to V+*with* deal with it. EG *For decades, mathematicians have wrestled with this problem.*

wrestler /reslə/, **wrestlers.** A **wrestler** is some- N COUNT one who wrestles as a sport.

wrestling /reslɪŋ/ is a sport in which two people N UNCOUNT wrestle and try to throw each other to the ground.

wretch /retʃ/, **wretches.** You can refer to some- N COUNT one as a **wretch** when you think that they are Outdated wicked or unfortunate. EG *...the wretch who shot the President... The poor wretch groaned.*

wretched /retʃɪ²d/. **1** Someone who is **wretched** ADJ CLASSIF: is very unhappy or unfortunate. EG *She spent the* USU PRED *day in her room lying down and feeling wretched.* Formal

2 You use **wretched** to describe something or ADJ CLASSIF: someone that you dislike or feel angry about. EG *I* ATTRIB *had to drag the wretched animal all the way... I* Informal *hate this wretched system.*

wriggle /rɪgəl/, **wriggles, wriggling, wriggled.**

1 If you **wriggle** a part of your body, you twist it V OR V+O and turn it with quick movements. EG *The children were wriggling in anticipation... She wriggled her toes.*

2 If you **wriggle** somewhere, you move there by V+A OR twisting and turning your body. EG *We had to* V+O+A *wriggle under the fence.*

wriggle out of. If you **wriggle out of** doing PHRASAL VB: something that you do not want to do, you manage V+ADV+PREP to avoid doing it. EG *I can't wriggle out of accompa-* Informal *nying my parents to Europe.*

wring /rɪŋ/, **wrings, wringing, wrung** /rʌŋ/. **1** V+O:OFT+*out* When you **wring** a wet cloth or **wring** it out, you squeeze the water out of it by twisting it strongly.

2 When someone **wrings** their hands, they hold V+O them together and twist and turn them, usually Literary because they are very worried or upset. EG *He looked dazed and wrung his hands.*

3 If someone **wrings** a bird's neck, they kill the V+O bird by twisting its neck.

wringing wet. If a piece of clothing is **wringing** ADJ CLASSIF: **wet,** it is extremely wet. USU PRED

wrinkle /rɪŋkəl/, **wrinkles, wrinkling, wrin- kled. 1 Wrinkles** are lines in someone's skin, N COUNT: especially on their face, which form as they grow USU PLURAL old. EG *His small eyes were surrounded by many wrinkles.*

2 If something **wrinkles** or if something **wrinkles** V-ERG it, it gets folds or lines in it. EG *Clean the surface well or the paint might wrinkle and peel.*

3 When you **wrinkle** your nose, forehead, or eyes, V+O you tighten the muscles in your face so that the skin folds into several lines. EG *He wrinkled his nose. 'What an awful smell.'*

wrinkled /rɪŋkəld/. **1** If your skin is **wrinkled,** it ADJ QUALIT has wrinkles as a result of old age. EG *...a very old woman with a wrinkled face.*

2 If something is **wrinkled,** it has raised folds or ADJ QUALIT lines in it. EG *She looked to make sure her dress wasn't wrinkled.*

Would you like to get a good write-up in a newspaper?

wrist /rɪst/, **wrists.** Your **wrist** is the part of your N COUNT body between your hand and your arm which bends when you move your hand. See picture at THE HUMAN BODY.

wristwatch /rɪstwɒtʃ/, **wristwatches.** A **wrist-** N COUNT **watch** is a watch with a strap which you wear round your wrist.

writ /rɪt/, **writs.** A **writ** is a legal document that N COUNT orders a person to do a particular thing.

write /raɪt/, **writes, writing, wrote** /rəʊt/, **writ- ten** /rɪtəⁿn/. **1** When you **write** something, you use V+O OR V a pen or pencil to produce words, letters, or numbers. EG *I'm learning to read and write... Write the appropriate letter on the label.*

2 If you **write** something such as a book, a poem, V+O, V+O+O, or a piece of music, you create it and record it on OR V+O+for paper. EG *I have been asked to write a biography of Dylan Thomas.*

3 When you **write** to someone or **write** them a V OR V+O: letter, you give them information, ask them some- OFT+to OR thing, or express your feelings in a letter. EG *She* to-INF; ALSO *wrote me a letter from Singapore... She wrote a* V+O+O *note to the chief of police... I've written to invite him here.*

4 When someone **writes** something such as a V+O, V+O+O, cheque, receipt, or prescription, they put the nec- OR V+O+for essary information on it and usually sign it. EG *I remember writing a cheque for £100... I'll write you a prescription.*

5 See also **writing, written.**

write back. If you **write back** to someone who PHRASAL VB: has sent you a letter, you write them a letter in V+ADV OR reply. EG *He wrote back accepting our offer.* V+O+ADV

write down. When you **write** something **down,** PHRASAL VB: you record it on a piece of paper using a pen or V+O+ADV pencil. EG *I wrote down what the boy said.*

write in. If you **write in** to an organization, you PHRASAL VB: send them a letter. EG *People have been phoning* V+ADV *and writing in asking for advice.*

write into. If a rule or detail **is written into** a PHRASAL VB: V contract or agreement, it is included in it when the +O+PREP, USU contract or agreement is made. EG *The new ar-* PASS *rangements have been written into the agreement.*

write off. 1 If you **write off** to a company or PHRASAL VB: organization, you send them a letter, usually asking V+ADV OR for something. EG *I was writing off to various places* V+O+ADV *asking about work opportunities.* **2** If you **write off** V+O+ADV an amount of money that you have lost, you accept that you are never going to get the money back. EG *I've written off that hundred pounds.* **3** If you **write** V+O+ADV **off** a plan or project, you accept that it is not going to be successful and you do not continue with it. **4** V+O+ADV If you **write** someone **off,** you decide that they are unimportant or useless. EG *Do not shout, or you will be written off as a hysterical woman.* **5** See also **write-off.**

write out. 1 If you **write out** something such as PHRASAL VB: a report or a list, you write it on paper. EG *I always* V+O+ADV *write out a shopping list.* **2** When someone **writes** V+O+ADV **out** something such as a cheque, receipt, or pre- scription, they put the necessary information on it and usually sign it. EG *I went to write out the death certificate.*

write up. If you **write up** something that has PHRASAL VB: been done or said, you record it on paper in a neat V+O+ADV and complete form, usually using notes that you have made. EG *These are notes that you are going to write up afterwards... The results were written up into a report.* ● See also **write-up.**

write-off, write-offs. If a vehicle is a **write-off,** it N COUNT: is so badly damaged in an accident that it is not USU SING worth repairing. EG *Their car was a write-off.*

writer /raɪtə/, **writers. 1** A **writer** is a person N COUNT who writes books, stories, or articles as a job. EG *...the writer and critic, Hilary Spurling.*

2 The **writer** of a particular article, story, or other N COUNT+SUPP piece of writing is the person who wrote it. EG *I arranged an appointment with the writer of the letter.*

write-up, write-ups. A **write-up** is an article in a N COUNT: newspaper or magazine, in which someone de- USU SING scribes something such as a play or a new product and gives their opinion on it. EG *Somebody told me you got a terrific write-up in the 'Guardian'.*

writhe /raɪð/, **writhes, writhing, writhed.** If you V **writhe,** you twist and turn your body violently backwards and forwards, usually because you are in great pain. EG *He writhed in agony.*

writing /raɪtɪŋ/, **writings. 1 Writing** is **1.1** N UNCOUNT something that has been written or printed. EG *Put the papers face down on each desk so that the writing cannot be seen... You must get the offer in writing.* **1.2** a piece of written work, especially considered from the point of view of the style of language used. EG *The book contains some brilliant and very witty writing.*

2 Writing is also the activity of writing, especially N UNCOUNT of writing books for money. EG *I hate writing and I'm not very good at it.*

3 An author's **writings** are all the things that he or N PLURAL: she has written. EG *His political writings remind me* USU+SUPP *of those of Sartre.*

writing paper is paper for writing letters on. It is N MASS usually of good, smooth quality.

written /rɪtəⁿn/. **1 Written** is the past participle of **write.**

2 A **written** test or piece of work is one in which a ADJ CLASSIF student has to write something, rather than doing an experiment or giving spoken answers. EG *There are two exams. One is practical and the other is written.*

3 A **written** agreement, rule, or law has been ADJ CLASSIF: officially written down. EG *I will send written* ATTRIB *confirmation... ...a written declaration.*

wrong /rɒŋ/, **wrongs, wronging, wronged. 1** If ADJ PRED: there is something **wrong,** there is something OFT+with unsatisfactory about the situation or thing that you are talking about. EG *The front door was unlocked – something was wrong... I sat down with her and asked what was wrong... There was nothing wrong with his eyesight.*

2 Wrong means not correct or not suitable. EG *I'm* ADJ CLASSIF, OR afraid I'll make the wrong decision... They are the ADV AFTER VB wrong people for the job... Her name was spelt wrong.* ◊ **wrongly.** EG *Many of us choose wrongly.* ◊ ADV

3 If you are **wrong** about something, what you say ADJ PRED or think about it is not correct. EG *We had to admit the possibility that we might be wrong.*

◊ **wrongly.** EG *She supposed, wrongly, that the* ◊ ADV *other two agreed with her.*

4 If something that you do is **wrong,** it is bad or ADJ QUALIT immoral. EG *She never did anything wrong... You were wrong to speak to the newspapers first.*

5 Wrong is used to refer to actions that are bad or N UNCOUNT immoral. EG *Any good parent feels strongly about right and wrong.*

6 A **wrong** is an unjust action or situation. EG *In a* N COUNT *democracy wrongs should be righted by the vote and not by violence.*

7 If someone **wrongs** you, they treat you in an V+O unfair or unjust way. EG *I had wronged her terribly.*

8 The **wrong** side of a piece of cloth is the side ADJ CLASSIF: which is intended to face inwards and not be seen. ATTRIB

9 Wrong is also used in these phrases. **9.1** If you PHRASES **get** something **wrong,** you make a mistake. EG *I think she got his name wrong.* **9.2** You say **'Don't get me wrong'** when you want to make sure that someone does not misunderstand you. EG *Now don't get me wrong: we liked him.* **9.3** If you **go wrong,** you make a mistake. EG *Where did I go wrong?* **9.4** If something **goes wrong,** it stops working or progressing well. EG *Computers do go wrong... Their relationship went wrong after the birth of their child.* **9.5** If you are **in the wrong,** what you are doing is immoral or illegal. EG *We were all in the wrong then.*

wrongdoer /rɒŋduːə/, **wrongdoers.** A **wrong-** N COUNT **doer** is a person who does things that are immoral Formal or illegal. EG *Wrongdoers should be made to pay for their actions.*

wrongdoing /rɒŋduːɪŋ/, **wrongdoings. Wrongdoing** is behaviour that is illegal or immoral. EG *The bank has denied any wrongdoing.* N UNCOUNT OR N COUNT Formal

wrongful /rɒŋfʊl/. A **wrongful** act is one that is thought to be illegal, immoral, or unfair. EG *...the wrongful imprisonment of Napoleon.* ADJ CLASSIF : ATTRIB
◇ **wrongfully.** EG *The workers were wrongfully dismissed.* ◇ ADV

wrote /rəʊt/ is the past tense of **write.**

wrought /rɔːt/. 1 If something **has wrought** a change, it has caused it. EG *That moment had wrought a profound change in him.* V+O : ONLY PAST TENSES Literary
2 **Wrought** metal has been made into a particular ADJ CLASSIF : ATTRIB

shape, often in a decorative way. EG *...wrought silver... ...wrought gold.*

wrought iron is a pure type of iron that is formed into decorative shapes. EG *...a wrought-iron gate.* N UNCOUNT

wrung /rʌŋ/ is the past tense of **wring.**

wry /raɪ/. If someone has a **wry** expression, 1 it shows that they find a situation slightly amusing because they know more about it than other people. EG *He came out with a wry smile on his face... She said this with a wry glance at me.* ◇ **wryly.** EG *My friend smiled wryly when he saw me.* 2 it is rather strange or twisted, usually showing that they dislike something. EG *Over the beer she made a wry face and said 'Nasty!'* ADJ QUALIT : USU ATTRIB ◇ ADV ADJ QUALIT : USU ATTRIB

X x　Y y　Z z

X, x /ɛks/, **Xs, x's. 1 X** is the twenty-fourth letter of the English alphabet. N COUNT

2 **X** is used to represent the name of a person or place when you do not know their real name, or when you want to keep their real name a secret. EG *She was always referred to as Miss X during the trial... I was born in X, a town somewhere in the south.* N UNCOUNT

3 If you say that there are **x** number of things, you mean that the exact number is not important. EG *...a house that will cost less than x number of pounds.*

4 In algebra, **x** is used as a symbol to represent a number whose value is not known. EG $y=x^2$.

5 People sometimes write **x** on a map to mark a precise position that they want to refer to.

6 You can write **x** to represent a kiss at the end of a letter. EG *See you soon, all my love, Jenny xxx.*

xenophobia /zɛnəfəʊbɪə/ is a fear of people from other countries, or a strong dislike of them. EG *They are nationalist to the point of xenophobia.* N UNCOUNT Formal

Xerox /zɪərɒks/, **Xeroxes, Xeroxing, Xeroxed.** 1 A **Xerox** is **1.1** a machine that makes photographic copies of pieces of paper which have writing or printing on them. **1.2** a copy of what is written or printed on a piece of paper, made by using a Xerox machine. EG *I enclose a Xerox of the letter.* N COUNT Trademark

2 If you **Xerox** a document, you make a copy of it using a Xerox machine. EG *That morning, Bernstein had Xeroxed copies of notes from reporters at the scene.* V+O

Xmas /krɪsməs, ɛksməs/ is the same as Christmas. N UNCOUNT Informal

X-ray, X-rays, X-raying, X-rayed. 1 An **X-ray** is **1.1** a stream of radiation that can pass through some solid materials. X-rays are used by doctors to examine the bones or organs inside your body. EG *The X-rays are produced by this electron beam... He agreed to go for an X-ray to see if the bone was broken.* **1.2** a picture made by sending X-rays through your body. EG *The chest X-ray showed enlargement of the heart.* N COUNT

2 If a doctor **X-rays** you, he or she takes a picture of the inside of your body using an X-ray machine. EG *He should have his lungs X-rayed.* V+O

xylophone /zaɪləfəʊn/, **xylophones.** A **xylophone** is a musical instrument made of a row of wooden bars of different lengths. You play a xylophone by hitting the bars with special hammers. N COUNT

Y, y /waɪ/, **Ys, y's. 1 Y** is the twenty-fifth letter of the English alphabet. N COUNT

2 In algebra, **y** is used as a symbol to represent a number whose value is not known.

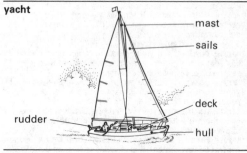

yacht

— mast

— sails

— deck

rudder —

— hull

yacht /jɒt/, **yachts.** A **yacht** is a boat with sails or a motor, used for racing or for pleasure trips. N COUNT

yachting /jɒtɪŋ/ is the sport or activity of sailing a yacht. EG *...the fun of yachting... ...yachting holidays.* N ING

yam /jæm/, **yams.** A **yam** is a root vegetable which grows in tropical regions. It is similar to a potato in appearance and texture. N COUNT

yank /jæŋk/, **yanks, yanking, yanked. 1** A **Yank** is a person from the United States of America; an offensive word. N COUNT British

2 If you **yank** something, you pull it suddenly with a lot of force. EG *Glenn yanked out the sore tooth.* V+O : USU+A

Yankee /jæŋkiː/, **Yankees.** A **Yankee** is the same as a Yank; an offensive word. N COUNT

yap /jæp/, **yaps, yapping, yapped. 1** If a dog **yaps**, it barks a lot with a high-pitched sound. EG *There was a dog running along the streets, yapping and barking.* V

2 If you say that someone **yaps,** you mean that they talk continuously in an annoying way. EG *I hate people on trains who keep yapping at you.* V Informal

yard /jɑːd/, **yards. 1** A **yard** is a unit for measuring length, equal to thirty-six inches, or approximately 91.4 centimetres. N COUNT

2 A **yard** is also a flat area of concrete or stone that is usually next to a building and often has a wall around it. EG *...a tiny cramped house without even a back yard.* N COUNT

3 You can also refer to a large area or place of work where a particular type of work is done as a **yard.** EG *...a ship repair yard.* N COUNT : USU+SUPP

yardstick /jɑːdstɪk/, **yardsticks.** If you use someone or something as a **yardstick,** you use them to compare other people or things with, when judging how good or important these other people or things are. EG *She was a yardstick against which I could* N COUNT+SUPP *measure what I had achieved... ...a situation where the yardstick for success is exam achievement.*

yarn /jɑːn/, **yarns. 1 Yarn** is thread, made for N MASS example from wool or cotton, which is used for knitting or making cloth.

2 A **yarn** is a story that someone tells, often a true N COUNT story with added details which they have invented Informal to make it more interesting.

yawn /jɔːn/, **yawns, yawning, yawned. 1** When v you **yawn**, you open your mouth wide and breathe in more air than usual. You often yawn when you are tired or bored. EG *I yawned all through the concert.* ▸ used as a noun. EG *She stifled a yawn.* ▸ N COUNT

2 If you describe something such as a book or a N SING : a+N film as a **yawn**, you mean that you think it is very Informal boring.

3 A gap or opening that **yawns** is large and wide, v : USU+A and often rather frightening. EG *A great gap* Literary *yawned between the rocks.* ◊ **yawning.** EG *They* ◊ ADJ CLASSIF : *drew back from the yawning chasm.* ATTRIB

yd, yds. yd is a written abbreviation for 'yard'. The N COUNT plural is either 'yds' or 'yd'. EG *The reel holds 400 yds of line.*

yeah /jeə/ means the same as yes. EG *'Do you* CONVENTION *understand?' – 'Yeah, I think so.'* Informal

year /jɪə/, **years. 1** A **year** is **1.1** a period of 365 or N COUNT 366 days, beginning on the first of January and ending on the thirty-first of December. EG *...at the end of next year... ...in the year 2000.* **1.2** a period of about twelve months. EG *...a hundred years ago... For seven years I was a designer... These rocks are about 650 million years old.*

2 A school **year** or a university **year** is the period N COUNT : of time in each twelve months when the school or USU+SUPP university is open and people are studying.

3 A financial or business **year** is a period of twelve N COUNT+SUPP months, beginning on a particular date, which businesses or institutions use as a basis for organizing their finances. EG *...the final account at the end of each trading year.*

4 You can use **years** to emphasize that you are N PLURAL referring to a very long time. EG *They've known each other for years and years.*

5 If you do something **all year round** or **all the** PHRASE **year round,** you do it continually throughout the year. EG *They grow crops all the year round.*

6 donkey's **years:** see donkey. ● See also leap year, New Year.

yearly /jɪəliⁱ/. You use **yearly 1** to describe ADJ CLASSIF : something that happens once a year or every year. ATTRIB OR ADV EG *...a yearly meeting... Interest is paid yearly.* **2** to describe something such as an amount that relates to a period of one year. EG *...the yearly income of the workers.*

yearn /jɜːn/, **yearns, yearning, yearned.** If you v+*for* OR **yearn** for something, you want it very much. EG *He* *to-*INF *passionately yearned for happiness... She yearned* Literary *to go back to the south.*

yearning /jɜːnɪŋ/, **yearnings.** A **yearning** is a N COUNT OR very strong desire for something. EG *...his yearning* N UNCOUNT *for power... ...to satisfy the yearnings of the workers.*

-year-old and **-year-olds** combine with numbers to describe the age of people or things. EG *...a class of 4-year-olds... ...a fifteen-year-old boy.*

yeast /jiːst/ is a kind of fungus which is used to N MASS make bread rise, and to make alcoholic drinks such as beer.

yell /jel/, **yells, yelling, yelled. 1** If you **yell,** you v : OFT+A shout loudly, usually because you are excited, OR V-SPEECH : angry, or in pain. EG *'Speed up!' he yelled to the* ONLY *that* *driver... I yelled at Richard to hang on... She came in and started yelling abuse at the cops.*

2 A **yell** is a loud shout given by someone who is N COUNT afraid or in pain. EG *I heard a yell from inside the house... He let out a terrified yell.*

yellow /jeləʊ/, **yellows, yellowing, yellowed. 1** ADJ COLOUR Something that is **yellow** is the colour of lemons or

egg yolks. EG *...a bright yellow hat... He became aware of a yellow light far across the fields.*

2 When something **yellows** or **is yellowed,** it V-ERG becomes yellow in colour, often because it is old. EG *...a photograph of her, yellowed with age.*

yellow fever is a serious infectious disease that N UNCOUNT people can catch in tropical countries.

yellowish /jeləʊɪʃ/. Something that is **yellowish** ADJ COLOUR is slightly yellow in colour. EG *He had a yellowish complexion... ...a soft yellowish glow.*

yelp /jelp/, **yelps, yelping, yelped.** When people v or animals **yelp,** they give a sudden short cry, often because they are frightened or are in pain. EG *He yelped in pain... The puppy ran indoors yelping.* ▸ used as a noun. EG *I gave a little yelp and fled* ▸ N COUNT upstairs.

yen /jen/. If you have a **yen** to do something, you N SING : have a strong desire to do it. EG *Nicholas has a yen* USU + *to-*INF *to hike through Canada.* OR *for*

yes /jes/. **1** You use **yes** to agree with someone, to CONVENTION say that something is true, or to accept something. EG *'Did you enjoy it?' – 'Yes.'... 'Do you want some coffee?' – 'Yes please.'... 'It was a beautiful day.' – 'It was nice, yes.'*

2 You also use **yes** in a conversation **2.1** to CONVENTION encourage someone to continue speaking. EG *'I miss the country very much.' – 'Yes?' – 'And yet, you see, I would hate to give up my job here.'* **2.2** to say that something that someone has denied is in fact true. EG *'Nowadays you don't learn any basic principles in maths.' – 'Oh, yes you do.'* **2.3** to introduce something that you had forgotten to say and have just remembered. EG *What was I going to mention? Ah yes, accidents.*

yesterday /jestədi³/. **1 Yesterday** means the day ADV before today. EG *It was hot yesterday... Yesterday morning there were more than 500 boats on the lake... ...an interview published in yesterday's Times.*

2 Yesterday can also mean the past, especially ADV the recent past. EG *The worker of today is different from the worker of yesterday.*

yet /jet/. **1** If you say that something has not ADV : WITH happened **yet,** you mean that it has not happened BROAD NEG up to the present time, although it probably will happen. EG *I haven't made up my mind yet... It isn't dark yet... Have you had your lunch yet?*

2 If you say that something should not be done **yet,** ADV : WITH you mean that it should not be done now, although BROAD NEG it will have to be done at a later time. EG *Loosen nuts with a spanner but don't take them off yet.*

3 You also use **yet 3.1** to say that there is still a ADV possibility that something will happen. EG *The figures may yet be revised again... There is hope for me yet.* **3.2** after an expression which refers to a period of time, when you want to say how much longer a situation will continue for. EG *He's going to be around for a long while yet... It will not be dark for half an hour yet.*

4 If you say that you have **yet** to do something or ADV+*to-*INF that something is **yet** to happen, you mean that you have not done it or that it has not happened. EG *I have yet to meet a man I can trust... A just society without a bureaucracy has yet to be established.*

5 You also use **yet** to introduce a fact which is CONJ rather surprising after the fact that you have just mentioned. EG *Everything around him was blown to pieces, yet the minister escaped without a scratch... ...a firm yet gentle hand.*

6 You can also use **yet** to emphasize a word. EG *I* ADV *am sorry to bring up the subject of money yet again.*

yield /jiːld/, **yields, yielding, yielded. 1** If you v : USU+*to* **yield** to someone or something, you stop resisting Formal them. EG *He yielded to his critics and halved the price... He was yielding to public pressure.*

2 If you **yield** something that you have control of v+O or responsibility for, you allow someone else to take control of it or have responsibility for it. EG *He* *will not yield even a limited measure of editorial control.*

3 If something **yields**, it breaks or moves its   v position because force or pressure has been put on it. EG *Any lock will yield to brute force.*

4 If an investigation or discussion **yields** some-   v+o thing, it produces a result, answer, or piece of information. EG *Talks between the two sides yielded no results.*

5 If an area of land **yields** a particular amount of   v+o food, this amount of food is produced by the land. EG *0.23 acres yields only 200 pounds of rice.*

6 A **yield** is an amount of food produced on an area   N COUNT of land. EG *They have a far better yield than any farm round here.*

7 If a tax or investment **yields** an amount of   v+o money or profit, this money or profit is obtained from it.

yippee /jɪpiː/. Some people, especially children,   EXCLAM shout **'Yippee!'** when they are very happy and excited about something.

yob /jɒb/, **yobs**. If you call a boy a **yob** or a **yobbo**,   N COUNT you mean that he behaves in a noisy, bad-   Informal mannered way in public.   British

yodel /jəʊdəˀl/, **yodels, yodelling, yodelled;**   v spelled **yodeling, yodeled** in American English. When someone **yodels**, they sing normal notes with very high quick notes in between.

yoga /jəʊgə/ is a type of exercise in which you   N UNCOUNT move your body into various positions. Yoga helps you to get fit, improves your breathing, and relaxes your mind. EG *I do two hours yoga every day.*

yoghurt /jɒgət/; also spelled **yoghourt** or **yogurt**.   N MASS Yoghurt is a slightly sour, thick liquid which is made from milk that has had bacteria added to it. You can eat it with fruit, or with meat or vegetables. EG *...a bowl of natural yoghurt.*

yoke /jəʊk/, **yokes**. **1** If people are suffering under   N SING+SUPP a **yoke** of a particular kind, they are in a difficult   Literary or unhappy state, such as having to work extremely hard or being governed by a severe leader. EG *...a war against the yoke of tyranny.*

2 A **yoke** is a long piece of wood attached to two   N COUNT collars, which is laid across the necks of two animals such as oxen, in order to make them walk close together when they are pulling a plough.

yokel /jəʊkəˀl/, **yokels**. You can refer to a person   N COUNT who lives in the countryside, especially one who   Outdated does not seem to be very intelligent, as a **yokel**.

yolk /jəʊk/, **yolks**. The **yolk** of an egg is the   N COUNT OR yellow part in the middle of the egg.   N UNCOUNT

yonder /jɒndə/ means over there. EG *They came*   ADV OR DET *galloping over that hill yonder.*   Outdated

yonks /jɒŋks/. If you say that you have not done   N UNCOUNT something for **yonks**, you mean that you have not   Informal done it for a very long time. EG *I kept spotting people I hadn't seen for yonks.*

Yorkshire pudding /jɔːkʃə pʊdɪŋ/, **Yorkshire**   N UNCOUNT **puddings**. **Yorkshire pudding** is a food which is   OR N COUNT made by baking a thick mixture of flour, milk, and eggs. It is often eaten with roast beef.

you /juː/ is used as the subject of a verb or as the object of a verb or preposition. It can refer to one or more people.
A speaker or writer uses **you** **1** to refer to the   PRON person or group of people that he or she is speaking to. EG *What do you think?* **2** to refer to people in   PRON general rather than to a particular person. EG *You*   Informal *can get freezers with security locks.*

you'd /juːd/. **1** **You'd** is the usual spoken form of 'you had', especially when 'had' is an auxiliary verb. EG *If you'd asked me that ten years ago, I'd have said yes.*
2 **You'd** is also the usual spoken form of 'you would'. EG *You'd be surprised how easy it is.*

you'll /juːl/ is the usual spoken form of 'you will'. EG *You'll have to get a job.*

young /jʌŋ/, **younger** /jʌŋgə/, **youngest** /jʌŋgəˀst/. **1** A **young** person, animal, or plant has   ADJ QUALIT

not lived or existed for very long and is not yet mature. EG *Julia has two young boys... The young seedlings grow very rapidly... She was three years younger than me.*

2 You also use **young** to describe a time when a   ADJ QUALIT: person or thing was young. EG *I was fond of dancing*   ATTRIB *in my younger days.*

3 The **young** of an animal are its babies. EG *When*   N PLURAL *the young first hatch, they are naked.*

youngish /jʌŋgɪʃ/. Someone who is **youngish** is   ADJ CLASSIF fairly young in appearance, behaviour, or age. EG *...a youngish man with blond hair.*

youngster /jʌŋkˀstə/, **youngsters**. A **youngster**   N COUNT is a young person, especially a child. EG *I don't know what the youngsters of today think.*

your /jɔː, jʊə/. **1** A speaker or writer uses **your** to   DET POSS indicate that something belongs or relates to the person or group of people that he or she is speaking to. EG *Where's your father?... ...your books.*

2 A speaker or writer also uses **your** to indicate   DET POSS that something belongs or relates to people in general rather than to a particular person. EG *You can't use your own name in a novel.*

3 A speaker or writer also uses **your** in some titles   DET POSS when he or she addresses people with that title. EG *...your Majesty.*

you're /jɔː, jʊə/ is the usual spoken form of 'you are'. EG *You're quite right.*

yours /jɔːz, jʊəz/. **1** A speaker or writer uses   PRON POSS **yours** to refer to something that belongs or relates to the person or group of people that he or she is speaking to. EG *Our swimming pool isn't as deep as yours... A student of yours came to see me.*

2 People write **yours**, **yours sincerely**, or **yours faithfully** at the end of a letter before they sign their name. EG *Yours sincerely, Richard Thomas.*

yourself /jəˀsɛlf/, **yourselves**. **1** A speaker or   PRON REFL writer uses **yourself** **1.1** as the object of a verb or preposition in a clause where 'you' is the subject or a previous object, or in a clause which consists of a command. EG *Would you call yourself a Marxist?... Help yourselves to sandwiches... Tell me about yourself.* **1.2** to emphasize the subject or object of a clause. EG *You yourself said it's only a routine check... There is always someone worse off than yourself.*

2 If you do something **yourself**, you do it without   PRON REFL any help from anyone else. EG *Did you make these cakes yourself?*

youth /juːθ/, **youths** /juːðz/. **1** Someone's **youth** is   N UNCOUNT the period of their life when they are a child, before they are a fully mature adult. EG *We change and learn from youth to old age... He had visited Calcutta in his youth.*

2 **Youth** is the quality or state of being young,   N UNCOUNT immature, and often inexperienced. EG *...the wilfulness of youth... ...marvelling at his freshness and apparent youth.*

3 A **youth** is a boy or a young man, especially a   N COUNT teenager. EG *Across the street stood two youths in leather jackets.*

4 The **youth** are young people considered as a   N PLURAL: group. EG *I think the pressures on today's youth are*   the+N *enormous... ...high unemployment among the youth of this country.*

youthful /juːθfʊl/. Someone who is **youthful** **1** is   ADJ QUALIT young, lively, and full of energy. EG *...youthful dancers... He was full of youthful curiosity and idealism.* **2** has qualities or characteristics that are thought to be typical of young people. EG *Despite her age she still had a youthful body.*

youth hostel, **youth hostels**. A **youth hostel** is a   N COUNT place where young people can stay cheaply when they are travelling around on holiday.

Is a zebra crossing a place where zebras cross?

you've /juːv/ is the usual spoken form of 'you have', especially when 'have' is an auxiliary verb. EG *You've been very lucky.*

yo-yo /ˈjəʊ jəʊ/, **yo-yos.** A **yo-yo** is a toy made of a N COUNT round piece of wood or plastic attached to a piece of string. You play with a yo-yo by making it rise and fall on the string.

yr, yrs. yr is a written abbreviation for 'year'. The N COUNT plural is either 'yrs' or 'yr'. EG *...children aged 3-11 yrs.*

yuk /jʌk/. You say **yuk** to indicate that you think EXCLAM something is very unpleasant or disgusting. EG Informal *Cornflakes, yuk!*

Yuletide /ˈjuːltaɪd/ means the time of year around N UNCOUNT Christmas. EG *...Yuletide festivities.* Outdated

yuppie /ˈjʌpiˈ/, **yuppies. Yuppies** are young N COUNT : middle-class people who earn a lot of money and USU PLURAL spend it on expensive possessions and activities.

Z, z /zed/, **Zs, z's;** pronounced /ziː/ in American N COUNT English. **Z** is the twenty-sixth letter of the English alphabet.

zany /ˈzeɪniˈ/, **zanier, zaniest.** Something or some- ADJ QUALIT one that is **zany** is strange and amusing. EG *I like* Informal *his zany wit... ...zany ideas.*

zap /zæp/, **zaps, zapping, zapped. 1** If someone V+O **zaps** someone else, they kill them, usually by Informal shooting them. EG *That guy got zapped later on the same day.*

2 If you **zap** somewhere, you go there quickly. If V+A you **zap** through something, you do it quickly. EG Informal *She's always zapping off to places.*

zeal /ziːl/ is great enthusiasm, especially in con- N UNCOUNT nection with work, religion, or politics. EG *...hate* Formal *and revolutionary zeal... He forgot about this in his zeal to damage the party.*

zealot /ˈzelət/, **zealots.** A **zealot** is a person who N COUNT acts with extreme zeal, especially in following a Formal political or religious ideal. EG *There were threats by religious zealots to prevent the excavations.*

zealous /ˈzeləs/. Someone who is **zealous** spends a ADJ QUALIT lot of time or energy in supporting something that Formal they strongly believe in, especially a political or religious ideal. EG *He was a zealous anti-racist.*

zebra /ˈzebrə, ziː-/, **zebras.** A **zebra** is an African N COUNT wild animal which looks like a horse with black and white stripes on its body.

zebra crossing, zebra crossings. In Britain, a N COUNT **zebra crossing** is a place where people can cross the road safely. The road is marked with black and white stripes and vehicles must stop to allow people to cross.

zenith /ˈzenɪθ/. The **zenith** of something such as N SING an ideal or a person's career is the time when it is Literary most successful or most powerful. EG *...Greek civilization at its zenith... He was forty-eight years old and at the zenith of his career.*

zero /ˈzɪərəʊ/, **zeros** or **zeroes, zeroing, zeroed. 1** NUMBER **Zero** is the number 0: see the entry headed NUMBER. EG *This scale goes from zero to forty.*

2 Zero is also freezing point, 0°C. EG *It was fourteen* NUMBER *below zero when they woke up.*

3 You can use **zero** to say that there is none at all ADJ CLASSIF of a particular thing. EG *We drove in zero visibility... Its running costs were zero.*

zero in on. 1 To **zero in on** a target means to PHRASAL VB : aim at it or move towards it. EG *The missile zeroed* V+ADV+PREP *in on the tank.* **2** If you **zero in on** a problem or V+ADV+PREP subject, you give your full attention to it. EG *She concentrated on the heart, zeroing in on a single cell.*

zest /zest/ is **1** a feeling of pleasure, excitement, N UNCOUNT and interest in what you are doing. EG *The children* Literary *were full of life and zest.* **2** the quality in an activity or in your life which you find exciting and enjoyable. EG *He felt that some of the zest had gone out of his life.*

zigzag /ˈzɪgzæg/, **zigzags, zigzagging, zigzagged.**
1 A **zigzag** is a line which has a series of angles in N COUNT it like a continuous series of 'W's. EG *Suddenly there was a flash and a zigzag of forked lightning.*

2 To **zigzag** means to move forward by going at an V+A angle first to the right and then to the left. EG *We zigzagged laboriously up the track.*

zinc /zɪŋk/ is a bluish-white metal which is used to N UNCOUNT make metals such as brass or to cover other metals such as iron to stop them rusting.

zip

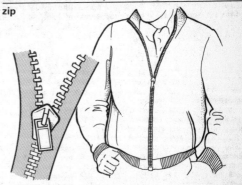

zip /zɪp/, **zips, zipping, zipped. 1** A **zip** or a **zip** N COUNT **fastener** is a fastener used on clothes and bags. It British consists of two rows of metal or plastic teeth that you pull together in order to fasten things.
2 When you **zip** something, you fasten it using a V+O : USU+A zip. EG *The sleeping bags can be zipped together.*

zip up. When you **zip up** something such as a PHRASAL VB : piece of clothing, you fasten it using a zip. EG *She* V+O+ADV *zipped up the dress with difficulty.*

zip code, zip codes. A **zip code** is a combination N COUNT of letters and numbers that are part of an address. American

zipper /ˈzɪpə/, **zippers.** A **zipper** is a zip. N COUNT

zodiac /ˈzəʊdɪæk/. The **zodiac** is a diagram used N SING : the+N by astrologers to represent the positions of the planets and stars. It is divided into 12 sections, each with a special name and symbol.

zombie /ˈzɒmbiˈ/, **zombies.** If you refer to some- N COUNT one as a **zombie**, you mean that they seem completely unaware of things around them and seem to act without thinking about what they are doing. EG *The men began to act as if they were zombies.*

zone /zəʊn/, **zones.** A **zone** is an area of land or N COUNT+SUPP sea that has particular features or characteristics. EG *...the war zone... ...a nuclear-free zone.*

zoo /zuː/, **zoos.** A **zoo** is a park where live animals N COUNT are kept so that people can look at them.

zoology /zəʊˈɒlədʒiˈ, zuː-/ is the scientific study of N UNCOUNT animals. EG *His lifelong interest was zoology.*
◊ **zoologist, zoologists.** EG *...university zoologists.* ◊ N COUNT
◊ **zoological** /zuːəˈlɒdʒəˈkəˈl/. EG *...zoological speci-* ◊ ADJ CLASSIF : *mens.* ATTRIB

zoom /zuːm/, **zooms, zooming, zoomed. 1** If you V : USU+A **zoom** somewhere, you go there very quickly. EG Informal *They zoomed down to Folkestone on their bikes.*
2 If prices or sales **zoom**, they increase very V : USU+A rapidly. EG *Sales had zoomed to 33 million.* Informal

zoom in. If a camera **zooms in** on the thing PHRASAL VB : being photographed, it gives a close-up picture of V+ADV it.

zucchini /zuˈkiːniˈ/. **Zucchini** is also the plural N COUNT : form. **Zucchini** are small vegetable marrows. USU PLURAL American

COBUILD Wordlist

Here is a list of all the words that are used ten times or more in the dictionary explanations. The actual number of times each word occurs is given so that you can see how frequently each word has been used.

How to use this list. Do you know most of these words already? Check the very common ones first - those that occur more than 1000 times. Then try those with 500 or more. If you are not sure, look the word up in the dictionary. With words like 'way', 'situation', 'form', 'keep', try to guess which uses are the common ones in the dictionary.

How many words? There are approximately 2000 words in the list. Some of them have more than one form, so that for example the form 'shape' occurs 196 times, while 'shapes' occurs 17 times, and 'shaped' occurs 45 times. All the forms and combinations that occur 10 times or more are listed. There are only 3000 different forms in the list. Where word forms conceal two quite different pronunciations (for example 'wound'), they are separated.

How the list was made. The dictionary compilers were asked to keep their explanations simple, but they were left free to choose any words they needed. During revision of the dictionary, this aspect was carefully checked. Meanwhile the computer was building up a wordlist and gathering every instance of every word for reference. The result is a natural and economical wordlist.

A

Word	Count
a	35056
an	5348
abbreviation	110
ability	139
abilities	30
able	172
about	1771
above	70
absolutely	15
abstract	11
academic	16
accept	128
accepted	50
acceptable	59
accident	36
accidentally	31
according	36
account	63
accounts	12
accurate	25
accused	10
achieve	158
achieving	31
achieved	25
achievement	26
achievements	14
across	75
act	226
acts	29
acting	18
action	408
actions	134
active	39
activity	463
activities	126
actor	23
actors	17
actual	11
actually	53
add	91
added	105
adding	28
addition	18
additional	10
address	25
addressing	12
adjective	216
adjectives	71
adjust	11
administrative	10
admiration	25
admire	34
admired	25
admit	18
adult	31
advance	13
advanced	18
advantage	60
adverb	57
adverbs	19
advice	63
aeroplane	35
affairs	25
affect	27
affects	69
affected	46
affection	38
afraid	63
after	557
afternoon	13
again	182
against	183
age	48
ages	11
aggressive	14
ago	17
agree	86
agreed	11
agreeing	10
agreement	97
aim	24
aims	19
air	256
aircraft	55
airport	11
alcohol	30
alcoholic	42
alive	31
all	545
allow	83
allowed	60
allows	36
almost	45
alone	33
along	138
aloud	13
alphabet	28
already	65
also	2097
alternatives	13
although	116
always	73
American	215
among	32
amount	631
amounts	60
amusing	48
amused	11
ancestors	12
and	8990
anger	59
angle	22
angles	14
angry	199
angrily	33
animal	353
animals	280
animal's	15
annoy	21
annoyed	55
annoys	18
annoying	17
annoyance	13
another	607
answer	52
answers	11
anxiety	13
anxious	27
any	333
anyone	76
anything	165
apart	38
appear	73
appears	56
appearance	87
applies	22
appointed	11
appreciation	10
appropriate	14
approval	39
approve	43
approved	15
approximate	16
approximately	10
area	470
areas	46
argue	20
argument	99
arguments	13
arm	33
arms	63
armed	33
army	73
around	203
arrange	53
arranged	86
arrangement	44
arrangements	11
arrive	37
arrives	16
arrived	12
art	64
article	27
articles	15
artificial	17
artist	14
artistic	10
as	4457
ashamed	21
ask	133
asking	94
asked	31
asks	15
asleep	21
aspect	39
aspects	30
associated	23
at	1526
atmosphere	24
attach	19
attached	94
attack	59
attacked	12
attacking	10
attempt	51
attention	164
attitude	94
attitudes	61
attract	32
attracted	16
attractive	117
audience	30
authority	132
automatically	10
autumn	10
auxiliary	40
available	71
average	10
avoid	76
aware	44
away	284
awkward	10

B

Word	Count
baby	61
babies	25
back	203
background	11
backwards	23
bacteria	11
bad	214
worse	44
badly	92
bad-tempered	12
bag	43
baked	11
balance	10
ball	88
balls	17
band	14
bank	41
bar	30
bars	24
barrier	10
base	15
based	73
basic	36
basis	17
bath	15
battle	26
be	1774
is	26924
are	8317
been	878
being	633
was	212
were	135
beak	10
beans	11
bear	11
beat	18
beautiful	46
beauty	13
because	1197
become	295
becomes	304
becoming	39
bed	61
beds	10
beer	26
before	415
begin	73
beginning	86
begins	51
began	11
behalf	17
behave	272
behaves	95
behaving	90
behaved	12
behaviour	397
behind	43
beings	15
belief	118
beliefs	125
believe	157
believes	41
believed	38
bell	15
belong	61
belongs	89
belonging	36
below	60
bend	31
bends	15
bent	20
benefit	20
beside	17
bet	12
between	440
beyond	13
bible	10
bicycle	23
big	44
bigger	34
bill	11
bird	101
birds	51
bird's	11
birth	18
bite	10
bits	13
bitter	15
black	71
blade	19
blame	15
blankets	12
block	13
blocked	13
blood	58
blow	30
blowing	22
blows	20
blue	19
board	32
boat	65
boats	17
body	527
bodies	22
boiling	15
bomb	20
bombs	12
bone	12
bones	32
book	223
books	64
border	10
boring	34
bored	28
born	61
both	141
bottle	20
bottom	64
boundary	10
bow /bəʊ/	17
bowl	15
box	32
boy	30
brain	14
branch	20
branches	19
brass	10
brave	18
bread	39
break	41
broken	45
breaks	32
breaking	18
breakfast	10
breasts	12
breath	12
breathe	43
breathing	23
bridge	16
brief	12
briefly	22
bright	90
brightly	21
bring	47
brought	18
British	51
broadcast	24
broadcasting	13
brother	14
brown	55

brush	17
bubbles	17
build	18
built	69
building	388
buildings	91
bullet	10
buried	12
burn	21
burning	50
burned	11
bus	41
bush	19
business	144
businesses	12
busy	33
but	357
butter	20
buttons	19
buy	124
buying	29
bought	20
buys	10
by	2388

C

cake	18
cakes	14
calculate	13
calculation	20
calendar	13
call	110
called	54
calm	62
calmly	10
camera	17
campaign	13
can	2103
cannot	421
candidate	10
capable	13
capital	23
car	136
cars	26
card	39
cards	30
cardboard	16
care	62
caring	12
career	22
careful	58
carefully	140
careless	17
carelessly	10
carpet	13
carry	79
carrying	45
carried	45
carries	33
case	164
casual	25
cat	23
catch	40
caught	11
Catholic	11
cause	249
causes	234
caused	100
causing	27
ceiling	11
cells	13
centimetres	10
central	30
centre	43
century	11
ceremony	32
certain	102
chain	16
chair	21
chalk	10

,chance	40
change	259
changes	94
changing	47
changed	45
character	75
characters	11
characteristic	43
characteristics	39
charge	67
charity	20
cheap	11
cheaply	10
check	14
cheerful	46
cheese	18
chemical	48
chemicals	16
cheque	18
chess	15
chest	21
chew	11
child	120
children	107
chin	11
choice	21
choose	57
chosen	26
Christian	38
Christians	16
Christianity	10
Christmas	17
church	67
churches	10
cigarette	18
cigarettes	13
cinema	27
circle	38
circular	39
circumstances	44
city	55
cities	15
claim	15
class	45
classes	11
.clause	66
clauses	13
claws	12
clay	19
clean	74
cleaning	19
clear	92
clearly	83
clergy	18
clever	61
cleverly	10
cliff	17
climbing	14
clock	27
close /kləus/	85
closely	40
close /kləuz/	14
closed	19
cloth	180
clothes	202
clothing	139
clouds	11
club	35
clumsy	14
coal	34
coast	15
coat	23
coffee	27
coin	21
coins	20
cold	100
collar	10
collect	21
collected	14
collecting	11
collects	10
collection	26

college	55
colleges	10
colour	179
colours	50
coloured	50
colourful	10
colourless	12
column	18
combination	12
combines	16
:come	116
comes	149
coming	27
comfort	10
comfortable	41
comment	40
commit	12
committed	19
committee	14
common	44
communicate	15
community	24
company	136
companies	13
comparative	24
compare	13
compared	13
compete	22
competition	95
competitions	11
complain	12
complaining	14
complete	74
completely	199
completed	18
complex	10
complicated	47
computer	71
concentrate	12
concern	11
concerned	87
concerning	15
concert	15
conclusion	45
concrete	12
condition	118
conditions	50
confidence	35
confident	38
confused	50
confusion	16
connection	34
connects	17
connected	115
consciousness	12
consequences	10
consider	102
considered	155
considering	36
consideration	10
consist	12
consists	187
consisting	48
contact	11
contain	20
contains	114
containing	31
container	168
contents	25
contest	32
continually	15
continue	109
continues	51
continuing	17
continuous	27
continuously	16
contract	22
contrast	22
contrasts	14
control	183
controlled	56
controls	32

controlling	15
conversation	52
cook	42
cooking	65
cooked	45
cool	12
cope	11
copy	33
copies	20
corn	11
correct	124
correctly	26
cost	22
costs	19
cotton	24
could	47
council	10
count	44
country	456
countries	116
country's	39
countryside	14
courage	23
course	86
court	87
cover	78
covered	126
covers	63
covering	55
cow	11
cows	10
crack	14
cream	34
create	27
created	27
creature	28
cricket	21
crime	100
criminal	19
criminals	16
criticism	28
criticize	38
criticized	15
criticizing	14
crops	28
cross	29
crowd	17
cruel	52
crush	11
cry	19
culture	18
cup	22
cups	11
cupboard	24
currency	10
current	19
curve	18
curved	50
curves	17
custom	18
customs	21
cut	132
cutting	28
cuts	18

D

damage	64
damaged	78
damages	12
damp	13
dance	29
dancing	17
danger	67
dangerous	107
dark	78
darker	11
darkness	10
date	47
daughter	17
day	137

days	28
dead	64
deal	163
dealing	45
dealt	43
deals	24
death	60
deceive	36
decide	116
decided	29
decides	12
deciding	10
decision	89
decisions	65
decorate	21
decorated	19
decoration	26
decorative	12
decreases	15
deep	82
deeply	36
deer	11
defeat	15
defeated	17
defend	11
definite	34
definitely	40
degree	162
degrees	10
delay	34
deliberate	14
deliberately	109
delicate	13
demand	13
department	15
departments	10
depressed	19
depressing	10
describe	834
described	53
describing	47
describes	36
description	32
deserve	15
design	55
designed	49
designs	13
desirable	21
desire	50
destroy	31
destroyed	45
destroys	15
detail	38
details	68
detailed	26
determination	21
determined	30
develop	57
develops	35
developed	32
developing	22
development	48
device	148
devices	12
diagram	11
dial	10
diamonds	10
dictionary	44
die	39
died	44
difference	35
differences	11
different	438
difficult	339
difficulty	85
difficulties	43
dinner	13
direct	26
directed	13
directly	48
direction	166
directions	25

dirt	19
dirty	42
disagree	30
disagreement	32
disappear	10
disappears	19
disappointed	17
disappointing	10
disappointment	10
disapproval	196
disapprove	32
disaster	13
discover	35
discuss	36
discussed	18
discussing	17
discussion	44
discussions	13
disease	88
disgusting	19
dish	14
dishes	13
dishonest	35
dishonestly	12
dislike	61
disorder	10
disorganized	14
display	11
displayed	15
dispute	14
distance	97
distances	10
distinct	11
disturbing	11
divide	16
divided	51
division	12
do	3273
doing	676
done	625
does	495
did	91
doctor	47
doctors	15
document	54
documents	21
dog	37
door	84
doors	23
doubt	20
doubts	10
down	237
downwards	32
draw	39
drawn	14
drawing	38
drawings	15
drawer	10
dress	28
drink	196
drinks	48
drunk	36
drinking	22
drive	24
driving	23
driver	19
drop	14
drops	26
drug	43
drugs	37
dry	37
dried	24
dull	46
during	143
dust	14
duty	37
duties	21

E

each	475

imaginary	25	involved	172	layer	62

ordered	16
orders	14
ordinary	47
organ	11
organs	18
organization	418
organizations	37
organize	28
organized	59
organizing	18
original	39
originally	13
ornament	12
ornaments	13
other	1608
others	45
ought	19
out	622
outer	17
outline	12
outside	90
outwards	10
oven	15
over	415
overcome	12
owe	16
own	167
owns	29
owned	21

P

page	25
pages	18
pain	95
painful	40
paint	36
painted	16
painting	49
paintings	13
pair	28
pale	45
paper	189
papers	15
paragraph	57
paragraphs	31
parcel	16
parcels	14
parents	47
park	11
parliament	25
part	909
parts	304
participle	211
particles	10
particular	1954
partly	33
party	68
parties	14
pass	57
passes	31
passed	27
passing	18
passage	12
passengers	31
past	517
paste	12
pastry	14
path	32
patient	11
pattern	55
patterns	10
pay	177
paid	82
paying	20
pays	14
payment	13
peaceful	14
pen	16
pencil	14
people	3603

people's	120
perfect	23
perform	39
performed	25
performs	14
performing	13
performance	43
performer	14
perhaps	11
period	387
periods	26
permission	46
person	1841
person's	166
personal	24
persuade	58
petrol	15
phone	25
photograph	30
photographs	16
phrasal	17
phrase	36
phrases	156
physical	111
physically	30
piano	10
picture	82
pictures	46
piece	854
pieces	203
pig	14
pile	19
pin	12
pink	22
pipe	40
pipes	17
pitch	18
pity	18
place	1452
places	121
placed	28
plan	129
planned	55
plans	29
planning	19
plane	40
planet	12
planets	12
plant	166
plants	138
plaster	10
plastic	103
plates	13
platform	20
play	203
played	61
playing	60
plays	53
player	36
players	44
pleasant	123
please	17
pleased	39
pleasing	13
pleasure	95
plural	160
poem	25
poetry	13
point	159
points	71
pointed	42
pointing	13
poison	12
poisonous	19
pole	20
police	67
policy	31
policies	16
polite	73
politely	21
political	156
politics	19

pool	13
poor	52
pop	16
popular	44
position	312
positions	16
possession	13
possessions	21
possibility	16
possible	172
possibly	12
post	39
pottery	12
pounds	13
powder	48
power	159
powers	15
powerful	88
practical	35
practice	43
praise	36
precious	17
precise	15
pregnant	14
prepare	40
prepared	25
preparing	11
preposition	22
present /ˈprezənt/	149
president	10
press	43
pressing	24
pressure	31
pretend	21
prevent	152
prevents	52
prevented	17
previous	50
previously	25
price	53
prices	20
principle	23
principles	38
printed	63
printing	10
prison	45
prisoner	15
private	42
prize	18
probably	31
problem	176
problems	108
process	207
processes	17
produce /prəˈdjuːs/	95
produced	89
produces	82
producing	21
product	55
products	19
profession	29
professional	15
profit	23
programme	41
programmes	27
progress	44
project	17
promise	33
pronoun	16
pronounced	187
proof	13
proper	18
properly	109
property	56
proportion	10
proposal	24
protect	92
protected	16
protects	11
protection	20
protest	16
proud	21

prove	22
proves	12
proved	14
provide	41
provides	45
provided	30
pub	19
public	145
publicly	15
publicity	12
published	20
pull	50
pulled	29
pulling	23
punish	22
punished	17
punishment	40
pupils	15
purple	17
purpose	151
purposes	14
push	58
pushing	16
pushed	12
put	425
putting	56
puts	24

Q

qualified	14
quality	443
qualities	117
quantity	83
quantities	43
quarrel	25
queen	36
question	73
questions	74
quick	73
quickly	337
quiet	60
quietly	29
quite	58

R

race	67
races	18
radio	148
railway	45
rain	51
raining	13
raise	13
raised	31
range	36
rank	59
rapidly	15
rate	33
rather	438
raw	16
reach	51
reached	31
reaches	24
react	21
reaction	41
read	50
reading	20
ready	58
real	94
realize	37
really	118
reason	89
reasons	39
reasonable	37
receive	67
receives	31
received	17
recent	14
recently	31

recognize	34
recognized	15
record	73
records	23
recorded	21
recording	16
recorder	15
recover	10
rectangular	22
red	76
reduce	27
refer	693
referring	154
referred	121
refers	73
reference	10
refusal	10
refuse	35
regard	13
regarded	34
region	36
regret	16
regular	60
regularly	89
reject	15
relate	23
relating	179
relates	67
related	35
relation	20
relationship	116
relationships	18
relative	17
relax	22
relaxed	36
released	13
relevant	22
reliable	18
religion	55
religious	85
remain	53
remains	32
remark	58
remarks	17
remember	67
remembered	13
remove	95
removed	36
removing	14
rent	17
repair	17
repairing	10
repaired	10
repeat	25
repeated	20
repeatedly	28
replace	18
replaced	13
reply	12
report	23
represent	63
represents	22
represented	12
reputation	30
request	25
requires	23
required	23
research	23
resources	16
respect	69
respected	15
responsibility	63
responsible	62
rest	68
restaurant	27
restrict	11
result	217
results	45
return	58
reveal	11
rich	29
rid	43

ride	24
riding	12
ridiculous	13
right	218
rights	25
ring	20
rise	14
rises	23
risk	11
river	84
rivers	11
road	154
roads	29
rock	41
rocks	14
rod	18
role	19
roll	12
romantic	20
roof	41
room	215
rooms	27
root	10
rope	43
ropes	13
rough	66
roughly	24
round	284
rounded	17
route	34
row /rəʊ/	30
rows	12
royal	18
rub	23
rubbing	17
rubber	47
rubbish	21
rude	66
rudely	16
rule	60
rules	79
ruler	19
run	52
running	27
runs	16
rush	12

S

sad	69
sadness	25
safe	43
safely	11
salary	11
salt	15
same	578
sand	20
satisfaction	15
satisfactory	28
satisfied	18
save	13
say	2404
saying	255
said	182
says	75
scale	34
scattered	10
scheme	12
school	129
science	23
scientific	35
score	27
screen	20
sculpture	12
sea	168
search	27
searching	12
seat	29
seats	21
second	89
secret	80

word	count	word	count	word	count	word	count	word	count	word	count
secretly	51	shout	30	soldiers	57	steam	29	Sunday	12	their	1433
section	31	show	312	solid	61	steel	17	superior	11	them	3566
sections	23	showing	238	solution	20	steep	17	superlative	15	themselves	59
see	1664	shows	203	solve	19	stem	12	supply	41	then	103
seen	88	shown	40	some	475	stems	15	supplies	11	theory	27
seeing	14	shut	10	someone	6197	step	11	support	160	theories	10
seeds	32	shy	14	someone's	534	steps	33	supports	38	there	1023
seem	104	sick	19	something	12408	stick	65	supported	28	therefore	72
seems	123	side	202	sometimes	197	sticks	42	supporting	23	they	4787
sell	52	sides	68	somewhere	417	sticking	11	supposed	27	thick	147
sold	88	sideways	10	son	18	stuck	18	sure	95	thin	233
sells	44	sight	13	song	29	sticky	29	surface	293	thing	1226
selling	34	sign	60	soon	61	stiff	37	surfaces	29	things	1929
send	68	signs	20	sore	14	still	53	surgery	12	think	571
sent	60	signing	10	sorry	23	stomach	39	surprise	46	thinking	142
sending	24	signal	21	sort	13	stone	67	surprising	59	thinks	13
sends	12	signals	21	sound	274	stones	17	surprised	55	thought	93
senior	11	significant	19	sounds	107	stop	244	surroundings	16	thoughts	52
sense	26	silk	13	sour	13	stops	86	surrounds	12	third	24
senses	11	silly	46	source	24	stopping	27	surrounded	27	this	277
sensible	47	silver	14	sources	11	stopped	23	survive	19	these	229
sentence	73	similar	136	south	27	store	24	swallow	15	thoroughly	30
sentences	11	simple	53	space	108	stored	22	swear	13	though	57
separate	59	since	11	spaces	11	storing	16	sweet	68	thread	34
separately	32	sincere	20	spacecraft	12	story	101	swim	11	threads	19
separated	18	sing	26	speak	135	stories	47	swimming	26	threatening	14
separates	10	singing	20	spoken	118	straight	54	switch	14	three	56
series	161	sung	18	speaking	83	strange	66	swollen	10	throat	25
serious	154	sings	13	speaks	22	strap	13	symbol	33	through	344
seriously	28	singer	13	speaker	31	straps	10	symbols	20	throughout	15
serve	15	single	47	special	220	stream	19	sympathetic	10	throw	46
served	23	singular	64	specially	45	street	32	sympathy	24	thrown	15
serving	18	sink	11	specific	11	streets	17	system	291	throwing	10
service	51	sinks	10	specify	11	strength	56	systems	15	thumb	17
services	47	sister	14	speech	107	stretched	24			ticket	18
set	162	sit	78	speed	42	strict	21			tickets	15
sets	14	sitting	33	spelled	476	strike	11	**T**		tidy	21
seven	13	situated	31	spend	94	string	38			tie	25
several	122	situation	906	spent	27	strings	16	table	32	tied	28
severe	46	situations	67	spends	19	strip	32	tail	26	tight	24
severely	32	six	19	spending	15	strips	15	take	368	tightly	43
sewing	13	size	101	spices	14	stripes	10	takes	116	time	1291
sewn	13	skilful	29	spirit	10	strong	376	taking	97	times	106
sex	87	skilfully	15	spirits	10	stronger	29	taken	84	tiny	25
sexual	83	skill	74	spite	18	strongly	107	talk	243	tiring	16
sexually	18	skills	27	spoil	17	structure	69	talking	197	tired	51
shake	12	skilled	16	spoils	10	struggle	14	talks	15	title	52
shallow	11	skin	182	spoon	17	student	22	tall	60	titles	11
shape	196	skirt	12	sport	65	students	30	tape	42	to	15864
shaped	45	sky	47	sports	70	study	95	target	14	tobacco	13
shapes	17	sleep	55	spots	17	studies	26	task	92	toes	11
share	36	sleeping	16	spread	54	studying	23	tasks	15	together	470
shares	20	sleeves	10	spreads	19	studied	12	taste	57	toilet	24
shared	19	slide	11	spring	13	stupid	53	tastes	14	tongue	10
sharp	115	slight	26	square	40	style	51	tax	16	too	180
she	174	slightly	128	stage	56	subject	262	tea	36	tool	60
sheep	23	slope	14	stages	14	subjects	19	teach	16	tools	12
sheet	11	sloping	15	stand	56	substance	318	teaches	21	top	153
sheets	23	slopes	11	standing	42	substances	59	teaching	18	topic	22
shelf	11	slow	24	stands	21	succeed	98	taught	18	torn	11
shell	16	slowly	99	standard	46	success	60	teacher	24	total	56
shines	23	small	1033	standards	13	successful	132	team	49	totally	13
shining	13	smaller	81	stars	19	successfully	35	teams	28	touch	49
shiny	28	smallest	11	start	157	such	1035	tears /tɪəz/	12	touching	22
ship	103	smart	18	starts	59	suck	16	teeth	51	touches	22
ships	34	smell	63	started	24	sudden	74	telephone	76	towards	243
shirt	14	smells	16	starting	10	suddenly	240	television	152	town	87
shock	25	smile	25	state	319	suffer	30	tell	194	towns	11
shocked	37	smoke	53	states	33	suffering	49	telling	91	toy	11
shocking	26	smooth	66	stating	28	suffers	15	told	49	trade	29
shocks	11	smoothly	15	stated	13	sugar	44	tells	41	traditional	20
shoes	38	snake	12	statement	196	suggest	39	temper	10	traffic	24
shoot	19	snow	30	statements	32	suggests	24	temperature	47	train	65
shot	14	so	929	station	24	suggesting	13	ten	19	training	22
shooting	10	soap	15	statue	13	suggested	36	tennis	26	trained	22
shop	92	social	104	status	36	suggestion	24	tense	277	trains	15
shops	21	socially	18	stay	82	suit	82	test	29	transport	14
shore	17	socialism	10	stays	19	suitable	72	than	893	travel	82
short	319	society	125	staying	10	sum	43	that	14687	travelling	51
shorter	15	soft	155	steady	15	summary	12	those	38	travels	21
should	235	soil	24	steadily	11	summer	13	the	15431	treat	47
shoulders	19	soldier	10	steal	25	sun	59	theatre	48	treated	41

treats	14	uncomfortable	22	up	300			well-known	12	woman	209
treating	10	unconscious	20	upper	31	**W**		west	23	women	85
treatment	48	uncontrolled	35	upright	20			western	21	woman's	44
tree	93	under	100	upset	106	wages	16	wet	45	wood	149
trees	61	underground	19	upsetting	12	waist	22	what	1060	wooden	46
trial	21	underneath	27	upwards	39	wait	24	whatever	15	wool	29
trick	22	understand	224	use /juːz/	1742	waiting	21	,wheat	16	word	223
tropical	13	understood	28	used	2754	wake	10	wheel	13	words	246
trouble	49	understanding	25	using	331	walk	92	wheels	25	work	550
trousers	29	undesirable	28	uses	107	walking	41	when	4188	working	124
true	529	unemployed	10	use /juːs/	92	wall	89	where	676	works	106
trunk	10	uneven	17	useful	97	walls	49	whether	79	workers	34
trust	21	unexpected	35	usual	149	want	498	which	3759	world	51
truth	44	unexpectedly	30	usually	613	wants	37	while	136	worry	30
try	267	unfair	33			wanted	22	whisky	13	worried	94
trying	125	unfairly	23			war	66	white	117	worrying	33
tries	51	unfavourable	12	**V**		warm	55	who	2908	worries	11
tried	10	unfortunate	16			warn	12	whole	63	worth	43
tube	42	unfriendly	30	valid	18	warning	32	whom	10	worthwhile	12
tubes	16	unhappiness	21	valley	12	wash	27	whose	175	would	126
tune	21	unhappy	68	valuable	56	washing	31	why	42	woven	10
turn	66	unhealthy	14	value	76	washed	17	wicked	10	wrapped	18
turns	33	unimportant	52	values	15	waste	26	wide	50	wrist	11
turning	20	uninteresting	17	variety	16	watch	57	wife	36	write	156
turned	13	union	16	various	22	watching	18	wild	55	written	254
twelve	14	unit	51	vegetable	41	water	385	will	563	writing	217
twenty	13	united	35	vegetables	34	wave	18	willing	41	writes	29
twist	15	university	65	vehicle	197	waves	27	win	44	writer	35
twisted	19	unjust	10	vehicles	56	way	1563	winning	18	wrong	206
two	726	unkind	24	verb	398	ways	70	wins	11	wrongly	20
type	218	unlikely	43	verbs	50	we	21	wind /wɪnd/	66		
types	27	unnatural	11	version	14	weak	69	wound /wuːnd/	18	**Y**	
typical	48	unnecessary	29	vertical	23	weaker	24	wound /waʊnd/	11		
typically	10	unpleasant	452	very	2420	weakness	11	window	61		
tyre	10	unpleasantly	22	video	14	wealth	12	windows	10	year	84
		unreasonable	25	view	32	weapon	32	wine	40	years	43
U		unsatisfactory	23	views	13	weapons	30	wings	24	yellow	44
		unsteady	17	violence	29	wear	93	winner	12	yellowish	12
		unsuccessful	28	violent	81	worn	57	winter	13	yes	14
ugly	14	untidy	49	violently	44	wearing	48	wire	47	yet	46
unable	98	until	116	violin	12	wears	20	wish	29	you	29184
unacceptable	34	untrue	30	visit	25	weather	93	wishes	18	young	112
unattractive	13	unusual	88	voice	103	week	48	with	3100	younger	10
uncertain	15	unwanted	13	volume	11	weight	47	within	59	your	3420
unclear	13	unwilling	31	vote	27	well	224	without	417	yourself	340

Key to Checkpoints

2 No, what they said would be a complete secret.
4 If you are good at studying, yes.
6 Yes, if they make mistakes they are not doing their job properly.
8 Not unless they were also an actor.
12 No, you are only doing it well enough to be acceptable.
14 A sum of money.
16 Yes, they will encounter all sorts of difficult situations.
18 Yes, if you have been given the name of somebody else.
20 No, only a ship can run aground.
22 No, you appear excited or animated.
24 You talk a little to other people.
26 Yes, otherwise you would feel immense pain.
28 Yes, a lively conversation usually includes entertaining accounts of events that have happened.
30 No, it is rude to answer back, especially a child to an adult.
32 No, you would not like something which is very bad.
34 Yes, it will increase in value year by year.
36 Yes, an archer carries arrows which are lethal weapons.
38 Artistic means to be good at art; arty means to be interested in art.
40 Not necessarily. He *may* have painted it.
42 An astrologer studies the planets and stars to predict the future; an astronomer studies the planets and stars for scientific purposes.
44 An embassy.
46 Yes, it should be a true account of a person's life.
48 No, avuncular is used to describe the friendly manner of a man.
52 No, it would be dangerous and you would be breaking the law.
54 Yes, the ironing.
56 Nothing.
58 Bathing costume and bathing suit.
62 A beaver is an animal. A bee and a beetle are insects.
64 Yes, you would say sorry because you did not give it on time.
66 A bend is the curve in an object or in a road or river. A bent is someone's natural interest in something or their ability to do something.
68 However many people you know who are engaged to be married.
70 Whatever country you were born in, or whatever nationality your parents are.
72 Yes, usually the female blackbird has brown feathers.
74 Any food mixture made up of liquid and other soft food, for example soup.
76 A blot is a stain made by spilling a drop of liquid. A blotch is an existing small area of colour.
78 Yes, because they would be upsetting the situation and causing trouble.
80 No, a bookmaker takes bets and pays out winnings on bets.
82 Plants and flowers.
84 You can wear a bowler, bowtie, bra, braces, bracelet and braid.
86 You have to be brave to show bravery; you don't need to be brave to show bravado.
88 There are six people: brethren, brewer, bricklayer, bride, bridegroom and bridesmaid.
90 You might bristle at being ignored by a friend.
92 No, you come from a family which does not live together because your parents have separated or divorced.
94 The animals are: brute, buck, budgerigar, budgie, buffalo and bug.
96 Not necessarily.
98 No, you cannot steal the contents of your own house.
100 Men: businessman, butler. Women: bust, butch, buxom.
104 Examples of callings are nursing, counselling or a religious profession.

106 Perform a particular dance.
110 No, this is a word used to describe animals, not people.
112 No, a carving has to be done with a special tool. You use a carving knife to cut cooked meat.
114 Catalogue and catalog; cauldron and caldron.
116 Cello.
118 No, she cleans and tidies the bedrooms in a hotel.
120 No, it is not something which you would normally do.
122 Three ways.
124 A chilli is a hot seed pod; chilly is a word to describe something cold.
126 Chortle, chuckle.
128 Yes, too much of any alcohol can cause this disease.
130 Clamour, clang, clank, clap, clash and clatter can refer to sounds.
132 Clientele.
134 Cloak, clobber and clog are words for clothes.
138 No, this refers to an emblem usually used by a family, town or organization.
140 You burn coke; you drink Coke.
142 No, they would be saying you were an uninteresting person.
144 Run for your life!
146 Commercial.
148 Something compact is small and takes up little space. Something commodious is large and has lots of space in it.
150 Yes, they are likely to be well suited to each other.
152 Yes, you must do it.
154 3.2: real and physical rather than abstract.
156 Yes, if you like confiding in a woman.
160 Conker and conquer.
162 A consonant.
164 Contagious.
166 Yes, it is against the law to take goods in or out of a country illegally.
168 It is easy and quick to cook.
170 Informal language.
172 Not valuable at all.
174 A countess.
176 Coup and coup-d'état.
178 No, a place crawling with people is full of people.
180 Yes, a building in which dead people are burned is likely to be frightening at night.
182 Two foods are: crisps and croissants.
184 There is one cross-reference, at **crossbar**: see picture at BICYCLE.
186 Yes, someone who has done something wrong is responsible for it.
188 Whatever system of money is used, EG peseta, yen.
190 Yes, you would be upset by an unkind remark.
192 A damp place is slightly wet, but a dank place is also cold and unpleasant.
194 No, you go quickly without wasting any time.
196 No, not necessarily. You feel that you are grateful to them because of something they have done for you.
198 No, deciduous trees lose their leaves in autumn.
200 Deer.
202 Six words: defrost, dehydrate, delectable, delicacy, delicatessen, delicious.
204 Formal, informal, technical.
206 Deputy.
208 Money.
212 No, you read it eagerly because it interests you.
214 No, you do not have the confidence to give orders in such a way.
216 No, your pupils become larger.
218 Disciplinary.
220 Disfavour and disfavor.
222 Dishevelled refers to a person's untidy appearance. Disordered refers to objects or events being untidy, badly prepared or badly organized.

224 Displace, displease, dispossess, disprove, dissatisfaction, disservice, dissimilar.
226 Dive.
228 No, this is a formal term in English.
230 A dolphin is a mammal like a large fish. A donkey and a dormouse are animals.
232 Yes, if you are not sure you would look at it again.
234 Draught and draft; draughtsman and draftsman; draughty and drafty.
236 It depends on you!
238 Your language.
240 No, just rather smelly.
244 No, you would not like anyone to listen secretly to a private conversation.
246 A graveyard could be described as eerie.
248 No, this is not a happy situation to be in.
250 Yes, people who express themselves well are able to explain things well to other people.
252 An empress.
254 No, a meeting which seems to go on forever is not pleasant.
256 Not necessarily. You are more likely to be giving them food and hospitality.
258 On a door or gate which you may not go through.
260 No. It is a moving staircase.
262 No. The important parts are correct, but some less important parts may not be correct.
264 No, he is no longer a President.
266 No, you would not punish somebody who was behaving in a way that other people should copy.
268 Yes, it can do, especially if you are not very fit!
270 No, you only think that it is true.
272 No, your face does not show what you are thinking.
274 Yes, an elaborate event costs a great deal of money.
278 No, to belong to a particular group is not painful.
280 No, a family tree is a diagram, not a physical tree.
282 A farthing.
284 No, 'fed up' means bored or annoyed.
286 Yes, if you have to look after yourself on your own.
288 Fête or fete; fiascos or fiascoes; fibre or fiber; fibreglass or fiberglass.
290 Filch.
292 Yes, because you pay great attention to details.
294 Desk, filing cabinet, shelving.
296 A flask is a small bottle for carrying alcoholic drink. A flagon is a larger bottle in which cider or wine is sold, or a jug in which it is served.
298 You may be fat, you will certainly be plump.
300 Flour and flower.
302 Yes, if you believe in spacecraft from other planets.
304 Yes, you are patient with and kind to people you like.
306 'Fore' means before or beforehand.
308 Yes, a place which is not looked after will look uncared for.
310 Yes, if you get involved in a fight you are likely to crack or break a bone.
312 No, glass doors leading onto a garden or balcony can be found in any country.
314 Yes, if you waste time on unimportant things you are being lighthearted when perhaps you should be serious.
316 No, it is a machine used for gambling.
318 No, you are insulting them.
320 Furniture is the large moveable objects in a room. Furnishings are all the objects and decorations which make up the total appearance of a room.
322 Game, gammon, garlic, garnish.
324 No, because to be gauche means to be awkward in the company of other people.
326 Yes, somebody who studies rock and soil should know something about the land formation of countries.
328 Yes, if people get together they meet.
330 No, because you will be looking at them with an angry expression on your face.
332 Gleam, glimmer, glint, glisten, glitter, glow.
334 You may not agree with it, but you accept it and you obey it.

336 No, polite people do not eat their food quickly.
338 Good-humoured, good-natured, good-tempered.
340 No, grapes grow on grapevines.
342 No, you would not feel very sad about a complaint.
344 No, a grotto is an attractive rather than an unpleasant place.
346 Grouse, growl, grudge, grumble, grumpy, grunt.
348 No, a gymnast is trained to do physical exercises, not to ride horses.
352 Not unless you have an ornament made of precious metal in your hall.
354 No, it is printed.
356 Hard luck.
358 No. A harp is a musical instrument; to 'harp on' means to keep on talking about something.
362 No, because it may not be true.
364 A hedge is made up of bushes only, whereas a hedgerow also has trees and plants growing in it.
366 Heiress, her.
368 A heroine.
370 No, you are only borrowing it.
372 No, you get very angry.
374 No, you want to go home.
376 Hooter and horn: honk and hoot.
378 No, they would be most unfriendly towards you.
380 No, it would be dirty and unpleasant.
384 Yes, if you have strong beliefs and are true to them.
388 No, it would not be clear enough for you to read it.
390 An imaginary diamond does not exist in real life. An imitation one exists, but it is not genuine, it is a copy.
392 Very soon.
394 You make a very bad impression.
396 There is no difference.
398 Yes, because you would not want to be recognized or noticed.
400 Yes, if you can't do without it.
402 Not necessarily!
404 No. Having a lot of useful information does not make you a person who tells the police about somebody else's crime.
406 They are related by marriage.
408 Insecticide.
410 No. Something that is installed is fitted in place. An instalment is a sum of money which you pay regularly over a period of time.
412 With someone else.
414 No, it happens several times. An interval is only one period of time between two dates or events.
416 Yes. All the senses of 'intrude'.
418 It may be, but it is more likely to be very useful.
420 Yes, you become annoyed very easily.
422 The examples are printed in italics.
426 No, you think that it has become annoying or worrying.
428 June and July.
432 One thousand.
434 Sir.
438 Yes, if it is surrounded by other countries and does not have its own sea coast.
440 No, Latin Americans come from South and Central America, and do not speak Latin, which is now a dead language.
442 No, they advise people about the law and represent them in court.
444 1992/1996/2000.
446 Left-luggage office.
448 Yes, it stops or becomes less.
450 Libretto. The plurals are librettos or libretti.
452 Lifebelt and lifebuoy.
454 Yes, probably.
456 Yes, a linguist can be somebody who studies or teaches linguistics.
458 Two.
460 In a part of someone else's house.
462 No, a loner is not unhappy when he or she is alone.
464 Yes, a chair with a leg cut off would be uneven.
466 Yes, what you write should always be clear and easily understood.

468 No, people who are lugubrious are sad and dull.

472 No, you give them money and anything else they need.

474 Cows, mice and pigs are examples of mammals.

476 Manner and manor are pronounced the same.

478 This depends on whether you are married, single, divorced or separated.

480 No, extremely good works of art are not produced in large quantities.

482 No, it is twisted together untidily. Matting is a floor covering.

484 Yes, it is important to you.

486 Memento. The plurals are mementos or mementoes.

488 No, it is usually women who refer to men as 'menfolk'.

490 No, they are small pieces of silicon used in modern technology.

492 No, he or she will be moderate: neither left-wing nor right-wing.

494 No, but you would quite like some mineral water.

496 Not really, they are just having fun.

498 Misfortune, misguided, misinform, misinformation, misinterpret, misjudge, misjudgement, mislay, mislead, mismanage, misprint, misread, misrepresent, misspend, mistrust, misunderstand and misuse are all examples.

500 No, you would not necessarily be confused by a mistake.

502 Yes, Britain has a Queen who reigns over it.

504 Monk, month, moo, mooch, mood, moon, mop and mope are all examples.

506 Whatever language you learnt from your parents when you were a child.

508 No, if food is mouldy it is bad.

510 Three: MP, mph and M.Sc.

512 No, mothers are not mummified, only dead bodies.

514 No, muted criticism may not be very strong, but it is not silent.

518 Navy or navy-blue.

520 No, they annoy you.

522 Happiness, loneliness, darkness, roundness, smoothness and gentleness are some examples.

524 No, a newsagent sells newspapers but a news agency collects news stories from around the world.

526 No, people wear nightdresses for sleeping in at night.

528 Yes, it does happen, but it is so uninteresting that it is not really worth talking about.

530 4: '. . . a written announcement which is put in a place where it can be read by everyone.'

536 Only if they are writing a book about unusual things.

538 No, nursery schools are for children.

540 No, if you do not dislike somebody you will not think they are unpleasant.

542 Eight.

544 Yes, if you are slightly ill, you will not work as well as usual.

546 Not necessarily. Somebody who is skilled at something because they have a lot of experience will not necessarily know everything.

548 Once upon a time.

550 No, they have strong opinions and do not accept other people's.

552 Not necessarily, you can choose whether to do it or not.

554 An ornate object has a lot of decoration on it, but may also be useful. An ornamental object is used mainly for decoration.

556 Australia.

558 No, an outsider is somebody who does not belong to a group.

560 It is likely to rain, so you should wear a raincoat, but you would probably need an overcoat in the winter.

562 No, unless they are particularly fond of music. You would be more likely to ask them out to dinner.

566 No, but it is as large and magnificent as a palace.

568 They live in a parish.

570 No, you get a parking ticket from a traffic warden.

572 No, you work only part of the day or week.

574 Pasta, paste, pastry, pasty, pâté.

576 Yes, you give someone all the money you owe them.

578 No, it means you admire them so much that you do not see their bad qualities.

580 Perfunctory.

582 Yes, it is against the law to lie in court.

584 A pharmacist prepares and sells the medicines which are produced by the pharmaceutical industry.

588 Yes, because they would look nice in a photograph.

590 No. To 'get the picture' means to understand something.

592 No, it looks thin and pale. If you are cold or ill you may look pinched.

594 No. A pitiless person shows no pity towards others. A pitiful person is someone you should feel pity towards.

596 Place and plaice.

598 Probably, but not necessarily.

600 No, he is speaking on somebody else's behalf in an unemotional way.

602 No. You decide to do something which you think is risky.

604 Yes, but not physically. They have beliefs and opinions which are very different.

606 Poly.

608 Portly.

610 At the end of an address.

612 Yes, usually people in authority do have a certain amount of power over others.

614 At the beginning of something you say or write.

616 Yes, both words have very much the same meaning in this context.

618 You give it to a chemist.

620 No, you believe something to be the case; you are not doing things that you have no right or authority to do.

622 Yes, somebody who governs a country should have high morals.

624 No, you are still doing it.

626 No, a professor is a high ranking teacher in a university. He or she does not have to claim to be able to do anything.

628 At a seaside town, next to the beach.

630 Yes, you have a tendency to do it.

632 No, it may happen.

634 There are six jobs: psychiatrist, psychoanalyst, psychologist, psychotherapist, publican, publicist.

636 Yes, if it is stopping at a bus stop.

638 No, unless he also enjoys boating!

640 Purse.

644 No, you do it without argument.

646 It depends on what sort of person you are. If you give up easily then yes, you would stop.

648 No, you are making a lot of noise.

650 Not unless you like living in poor conditions.

652 No, it is a type of lifestyle that some people have.

654 /ri̯:d/ and /red/.

656 No, you would not disagree with a sensible suggestion.

658 No, he would probably turn visitors away.

660 In a rectory.

662 Yes, either because of increasing technology, or because employers can no longer afford to pay their workers, there are fewer jobs, and workers are dismissed.

664 A record of births, marriages and deaths.

666 Reign and rein.

668 Relative clause and relative pronoun.

670 To remind somebody is to deliberately make them remember something. To remember something is to bring a past event back into your mind.

672 Because the person to whom it is directed has not understood it.

674 Yes, they will be good and reliable.

676 No, you leave it because you cannot accept it.

678 No, you are calm and unemotional.

680 On someone's birthday.

682 The word 'revolting' in this context can be either a verb (meaning 'rebelling') or an adjective (meaning 'disgusting').

684 No, a man who helps somebody most in their work does not have to use his right hand rather than his left.

686 No, you get out of bed at eight o'clock.

688 No, it is simply a very great success.

690 No, they both refer to the same thing.

692 Authors and musicians.
694 Rugby and rugger.
696 Not necessarily. He or she is the person who finishes in second place in any race or competition.
698 No, you are dismissed from your job.
700 Sail and sale.
702 No, it is an educational course of study and work experience.
704 Yes. Sausages are spicy and salty rather than sweet.
706 No, a scapegoat is somebody who is blamed for something which has happened, which may not have been their fault.
708 Yes, you mock something which you have doubts about.
710 Scotch, because it is a type of whisky.
712 Yes, an untidy child would probably have dirty and damaged shoes.
714 Yes, because you would not want to be seen.
716 Four: see if, see what you can do, see to it, let me see.
718 Yes, because there will be a large range of things to choose from.
720 No, because this is the part where the two players who will compete in the final game will be chosen.
722 Any object you have which has a special number on it to identify it, for example a camera.
724 A dinner or tea service.
726 Yes, because the tree will stop the light from falling on you.
730 Yes, they would be speaking angrily to you.
732 Eggs, nuts, peas, animals, small sea creatures, or explosives. You would find nothing inside the shell of a building.
736 Yes, you are telling them to go away in an impatient or cross way.
738 No, somebody who is nervous with other people is unlikely to try to impress people by showing them what they are good at.
740 Getting on the wrong side.
742 No, it *looks* like silver.
744 No, this word is used only for boys.
746 Skis.
748 Yes, all the informal words are slang.
750 Slender and slight.
752 No, it is a place in a city where living conditions are very bad.
754 When you smirk you smile, but in an unpleasant way.
756 Sneeze, sniff, sniffle, snigger, snivel, snore, snort, snuffle.
758 You are sociable. A socialist is a person who has left-wing political views.
760 There are six: sole, solitary, solitary confinement, solitude, solo, soloist.
762 No, they are in a bad physical or mental condition.
764 No, you are looking straight in front of you.
766 No, because the marks on your spectacles prevent you from seeing properly.
768 Either down a person's back, down the back of a book, on an animal's body or on a plant.
770 No, you spend a lot of money buying it.
772 Spotted describes a pattern of spots on something. Spotty describes a person who has a lot of pimples on their face.
774 Sputter, squabble, squawk, squeak, squeaky, squeal and squelch.
776 No, it is coloured glass.
778 No, you would not buy a meal for somebody you strongly dislike.
780 No, a stationmaster is in charge of a railway station.
782 Statue, statuette, steamer, steamroller, steel, steel wool, stem, stencil and step.
784 No, you put it down on the table.
786 Stockings.
788 Storey and story.
790 Yes, as long as you go home immediately.
792 Streets ahead, right up your street.
794 No, they are using their influence to get something done.
796 Yes, but he is more likely to work outdoors.
798 No, you need bright light to see clearly.

800 Yes, they are short and clear.
802 Yes. Suddenly, sufficiently, suffocation, suitability, suitably.
804 Sundown.
806 Sure.
808 Watt.
810 Yes, if it is the last song that a famous singer ever sings.
812 No, this item of clothing is only worn by women.
814 Syntax.
818 No, they talk to you in a patronizing way.
820 No, you get involved in a fight or quarrel with them.
822 Tea, coffee, cakes and light meals.
824 No, you have problems at the start of a new project or with something new.
826 Tennis and tenpin bowling.
828 No, you would not be frightened by something you are pleased with.
830 The phrase 'or thereabouts'.
832 Yes, because it gives you lists of words with similar meanings.
834 There are seven numbers. Third, thirteen, thirteenth, thirtieth, thirty, thousand, thousandth.
836 No, you waste money.
838 Thursday.
840 Six.
842 Any activity which makes you exhausted, for example running.
844 Not quite!
848 Toothbrush, toothpaste and toothpick.
850 Along the side of a canal or river.
852 Europe.
854 Yes, it is a bad representation of the original.
856 Treble and triple.
858 Trombone and trumpet. They are both made of brass.
860 It is rather large!
862 At the end of trouser legs.
864 No, you are persuading them to do something.
868 Uncountable noun.
870 No, he or she is fortunate to be taking a degree.
872 Yes, if you do not approve of organized crime.
874 No, just because a place has nobody living in it does not mean that it is not possible for people to live there.
876 Because they are embarrassing or unpleasant.
878 No, it has been printed and distributed.
880 Not necessarily. It has not been proved to be true.
882 Yes, it is the latest and newest information.
884 Three.
888 No. You do not cover your face to make a veiled comment.
892 Veterinarian and veterinary surgeon.
894 No.
896 Yes, there are pictures.
898 No, you make a speech thanking someone for what they have done.
902 No, they are angry and are getting ready for an argument.
904 No, you use washing powder to do the washing and washing-up liquid to do the washing up.
906 A wavelength is one radio wave used to broadcast programmes. A waveband is a group of radio waves.
908 No, you are not feeling very well.
910 Wee.
912 'Well-to-do' is an outdated word. 'Well-off' is still used.
914 Somebody who is ill or injured.
916 Not necessarily. They work in offices.
918 No, you agree with it completely.
920 A widow is a woman, a widower is a man.
922 Nothing, you only look.
924 No, it is their duty to give all the evidence.
926 Yes, they have to repeat from memory the exact words of the play.
928 The workforce.
930 No, but you want to become one.
932 Yes, it would mean that somebody had written about how good you are at something.
936 No, it is a striped section of the road where traffic will stop for you to cross safely.